Health Care Fraud and Abuse:
A Guide to Federal Sanctions

Volume 1

The West Group Health Law Library

CD-ROM

Health Law on CD-ROM
by American Health Lawyers Association

Estate and Elder Law Advisor

Treatises and Handbooks

Health Care & Antitrust Law: Principles and Practice
by John J. Miles

Health Care Financial Transactions Manual
by Thomas C. Fox, Carol Colborn Loepere, and Joseph W. Metro

Health Care Fraud and Abuse: A Guide to Federal Sanctions
by Paul P. Cacioppo

Patient Care Decision-Making: A Legal Guide for Providers
by Claire C. Obade

Health Law Handbook
edited by Alice G. Gosfield

Health Law Practice Guide
by the National Health Lawyers Association/American Academy of Healthcare Attorneys

Related Titles from West Group

Advance Medical Directives
by Alan D. Lieberson

Attorneys Medical Deskbook
by Dan J. Tennenhouse

Medical Information Systems for Lawyers
by J. Stanley McQuade

Medico-Legal Implications of Death and Dying
by David W. Meyers

The Law of Medical Practice in Illinois
by Theodore R. LeBlang, W. Eugene Basanta and Robert John Kane

The Law of Medical Practice in Ohio
by Gregory G. Binford and Janet K. Feldcamp

The Law of Medical Practice in Pennsylvania and New Jersey
by Barton L. Post, Brian M. Peters, and Stanley P. Stahl

Health Care Fraud and Abuse:

A Guide to Federal Sanctions

Paul P. Cacioppo

Volume 1

WEST GROUP
A THOMSON COMPANY

(Release #17, 12/2001)

Note: In this work, every effort has been made to use gender neutral language. Where clarity requires, however, the masculine pronoun has been used. The reader should note that it refers to persons of either gender.

Library of Congress Cataloging-in-Publication Data

Cacioppo, Paul P.
Health care fraud and abuse: a guide to federal sanctions/by Paul P. Cacioppo.
p. cm.
ISBN 0–87632–806–0
1. Medicare fraud. 2. Medicaid fraud. 3. Sanctions, Administrative–United States. I. Title. KF3608.A4C33 1991
345.73'0263—dc20
[347.305263]

90-23174
CIP

Introduction

Any person or legal entity that provides goods or services for health care may be subject to sanctions under the Medicare and Medicaid statutes, or under a variety of other federal statutes, if delivery or performance of those goods or services involves fraud or abuse. That means those who want federal or federal/state money for their health care goods or services must play by federal and state rules. [It is necessary to say federal/state because Medicaid is jointly funded by the federal government and participating states, and because there are other federal health care programs some of which involve state administration and/or state funds.]

For years, Congress has been adding to and changing those rules, struggling to fight inflationary health care costs and to improve the quality of health care services through enactment of civil and criminal sanctions. As a result, business practices that are ordinary and acceptable in other commercial endeavors, such as rebates and certain remunerative joint ventures, have been deemed illegal for health care goods or services. Billing is rigidly controlled, and numerous, costly, frequently-changing standards continuously must be met. In short, providers delivering health care goods and services have many opportunities to act at their peril.

When the Medicare and Medicaid programs were enacted in 1965, the two statutes ran about seventy pages in length. Their concepts were novel, but the rules were accessible and relatively easy to understand. Today those rules are exceedingly complex. What's more, they are buried in hundreds of pages of Titles V, XI, XVIII, XIX, and XX of the Social Security Act and thousands of pages of federal regulations. Just finding what you need to know can take an inordinate amount of time.

This book reorganizes federal statutes around the issues of health care fraud and abuse. It explains what federal sanctions apply to what acts or omissions, provides substantial extracts from relevant

* Prepared by Alice G. Gosfield, Esq., Consulting Editor.

statutes, and directs the reader to federal regulations that are on point. The aim is to provide lawyers and lay persons with basic information about health care practices of which Congress disapproves.

Immediately following this Introduction is "How to Use This Book." This section presents the most efficient, step-by-step ways to locate information. The book is then divided into three Parts. Part I contains "Guides" that are designed to function as a short-hand index to the material, and are organized around its practical usage. Each section in the Guides corresponds to the applicable chapter in Part II.

Part II contains nine text chapters. Chapter 1 describes those who may be subject to sanctions under the Medicare and Medicaid statutes and other relevant Federal laws by reference to the definition sections of Title XVIII and Title XIX of the Social Security Act, as amended, and other provisions. Chapter 2 sets forth the sanctions in Title XVIII, the Medicare statute. Chapter 3 sets forth the sanctions in Title XIX, the Medicaid statute. Chapter 4 sets forth the sanctions in Title XI of the Social Security Act, including the exclusion provisions of section 1128 of the Act, 42 U.S.C.A. §1320a-7, the Civil Monetary Penalties Law of 1981, found at section 1128A of the Act, 42 U.S.C.A. §1320a-7b, and the provisions for sanctions recommended by Peer Review Organizations in section 1156 of the Act, 42 U.S.C.A. §1320c-5. Chapter 5 sets forth the sanctions in Public Law No. 99-660, the Health Care Quality Improvement Act of 1986, 42 U.S.C.A. §11101 et seq. Chapter 6 sets forth the regulations that correspond to sanctions in Title XVIII, the Medicare statute, while Chapter 7 contains the regulations that correspond to sanctions in Title XIX, the Medicaid statute. Chapter 8 sets forth the regulations that correspond to sanctions in Title XI of the Social Security Act, and Chapter 9 contains the regulations for sanctions in the Health Care Quality Improvement Act of 1986.

For easy reference, Appendix A sets forth the False Claims Act, 31 U.S.C.A. §3729-3733. Appendix B sets forth the Program Fraud Civil Remedies Act, 31 U.S.C.A. §3801-3812. Appendix C sets forth 18 U.S.C.A. §287, the provision of the criminal code pertaining to false claims. Appendix D sets forth 18 U.S.C.A. §1001, the provision of the criminal code pertaining to false statements or entries. Appendix E sets forth the Major Fraud Act of 1988, 18 U.S.C.A. §1031, 18 U.S.C.A. §293, and 41 U.S.C.A. §256.

Appendix F sets forth Safe Harbor regulations issued or proposed by the Office of the Inspector General (OIG) of the Department of

Health and Human Services (HHS), implementing the Medicare Anti-kickback Statute, section 1128B(b) of the Social Security Act, 42 U.S.C.A. 1320a-7b(b). Included are important explanatory preambles.

Safe Harbor regulations deal with investment interests (joint ventures), space rental, equipment rental, personal services and management contracts, sale of practices, referral services, warranties, discounts, employees, group purchasing organizations, and waiver of beneficiary coinsurance and deductible amounts. They also deal with increased coverage, reduced cost-sharing amounts, and reduced premium amounts offered by certain health maintenance organizations (HMOs), competitive medical plans (CMPs), health care prepayment plans (HCPPs), prepaid health plans (PHPs), and preferred provider organizations (PPOs), and price reductions offered to such health plans.

Appendix G sets forth Fraud Alerts issued by the HHS Inspector General.

Appendix H sets forth superseded material. When Congress retained a sanction, but substantially changed the statutory provisions, the former text is in the Appendix. The main text presents the revised enactment (and minor amendments thereafter).

Parts II, III, IV, and V have the sanctions arranged in sequence as they appear in the statutes. Each chapter heading describes the kind of activity or obligation to which a sanction may apply. Then comes a summary of statutory provisions, followed by extracts of relevant statutes. Citations to relevant Federal regulations for each chapter are in Part VI, which was added in Release 5. Previously regulatory citations followed each chapter dealing with a sanction. This new format is designed to make updates and filing simpler. The author hopes the headings and summaries will help the reader quickly decide whether to study the sometimes lengthy statutory quotations.

Please note that the meaning of sanction has been expanded to include anything the author believes a health care provider might not like the government to do. That means not just civil money or criminal penalties, but such actions as adverse publicity or increased paperwork burdens as well. Not included, however, are prohibitions against reimbursement for goods or services merely because Medicare or Medicaid coverage requirements are not met. Also not included, except for the ultimate denial of Medicaid funding to a state set forth in section 1904 of the Act, 42 U.S.C.A. §1396c, are various financial penalties the federal government may impose on states for deficiencies in Medicaid programs.

Finally, statutory quotations are taken from the statutes as amended through the Medicare, Medicaid, and SCHIP Benefits Improvement and Protection Act of 2000, P.L. 106-554, enacted December 15, 2000. Regulatory citations are to the Code of Federal Regulations, or to the Federal Register, as indicated.

How to Use This Book

This book is a unique resource for attorneys and other health care professionals seeking to understand and apply federal law providing for health care related sanctions. Located in this single volume are all the relevant statutory provisions along with pertinent regulatory citations. Each section also includes relevant cross references. Each statutory section is explained in an introductory paragraph which precedes the statutory language. The statutory language itself is followed by references to relevant federal regulations.

Access to the book can be obtained through the following paths:

1. The Table of Contents presents the listing of the nine chapters and sections within each. There is a chapter dealing with persons and entities subject to sanction, a chapter on Medicare sanctions, one for Medicaid sanctions, one for Title XI of the Social Security Act, which contains combined and other Medicare and Medicaid program sanctions, a chapter on sanctions in the Health Care Quality Improvement Act, and chapters containing regulations corresponding to all of these subjects.

So, for example, the material on civil money penalties appears in Chapter 4, "Sanctions in Title XI of the Social Security Act," at §4:8 (from Section 1128A of the Social Security Act 42 U.S.C.A. §1320a-7a). It is followed by §4:9 dealing with criminal penalties for false statements, false representations, concealment, failure to disclose, and conversion with respect to benefits and payments, which comes from Section 1128B(a) of the Act. References throughout the book are to the Acts, first, followed by the parallel citation to the Code. The next section of the book at §4:10 presents material from Section 1128B(b) of the Act.

Cross references at the end of every section will point the reader to the chapter containing regulations corresponding to the material. For example, the regulations pertaining to civil money penalties are located in Chapter 8, as indicated by the cross reference at the end of that section.

2. In addition, there are "Guides" to entry into the book. These Guides are intended to function as a short-hand index to the material, and are organized around its practical usage.

a. Two guides are organized around the type of penalty that may be imposed. There is a Guide to Chapters for Civil Money Penalties and one for Exclusion Authorities, regardless of what type of entity might be affected. These Guides also summarize who is affected by the penalty and the relevant dollar amount where appropriate.

b. Additional Guides provide information that pertains generally to everyone involved in health care delivery, and then other Guides address individually the type of entity affected. There is a guide for the chapters relevant to hospitals, physicians, nursing homes, insurance companies, PROs, and risk-sharing health maintenance organizations (HMOs).

c. Within each guide the information is organized according to whether the topic presented is an action that can create liability ("Bases for Sanctions") or is the penalty one might suffer for a violation ("Penalties Imposed"), whether a fine, civil money penalty, exclusion from Medicare, or termination of the provider agreement, for example.

A practical illustration shows how one might use this book:

> An attorney evaluating a physician-client's potential exposure from problematic billing practices might want to look in the "Guide to Physicians" to identify all potentially relevant issues. If the client were a resident in training, the attorney might want to know whether he qualifies as a physician under Medicare, and so would look in the Table of Contents under Part I, Chapter 1. At the same time, the client might have already received a notice that he failed to examine or treat a patient presented to the emergency room. The attorney might look either in the "Guide for Physicians" or the "Guide for Hospitals" to find the relevant "anti-dumping" provision of the law. Finally, if the attorney knew the physician had already received notice of the potential imposition of civil money penalties for false claims, he might go directly to the "Guide to Civil Money Penalties."

In each instance he would find direction to the relevant section where he would find the summary, the statutory language itself, and citations to relevant regulations.

Finally, at the end of the book, many Appendixes are included to complete the sanction picture. The reader may find the Appendix Guide that precedes the Appendixes useful in identifying and locating material.

Comprehensive Table of Contents

Volume 1

Part I
GUIDES

Part II
TEXT

Chapter 1
PERSONS AND ENTITIES SUBJECT TO SANCTIONS

Chapter 2
SANCTIONS IN THE MEDICARE STATUTE

Chapter 3
SANCTIONS IN THE MEDICAID STATUTE

Chapter 4

SANCTIONS IN TITLE XI OF THE SOCIAL SECURITY ACT

Chapter 5

SANCTIONS IN THE HEALTH CARE QUALITY IMPROVEMENT ACT OF 1986

Volume 2

Part II
TEXT (Continued)

Chapter 6
REGULATIONS: SANCTIONS IN THE MEDICARE STATUTE

Chapter 7
REGULATIONS: SANCTIONS IN THE MEDICAID STATUTE

Chapter 8
REGULATIONS: SANCTIONS IN TITLE XI

Chapter 9

REGULATIONS: SANCTIONS IN THE HEALTH CARE QUALITY IMPROVEMENT ACT OF 1986

Part III

APPENDIXES

Volume 3

Part III
APPENDIXES (Continued)

Appendix Guide

This Guide is provided as a supplement to the Table of Contents to aid the reader in identifying and locating *Health Care Fraud and Abuse* appendix material.

Regulatory Provisions Governing Medicare Safe Harbors

Whether an outpatient radiology imaging center joint venture owned by a medical group specializing in radiology and a hospital care provider (i) generates prohibited remuneration within the meaning of the anti-kickback statute, Section 1128B of the Social Security Act; (ii) constitutes grounds for the imposition of an exclusion under Section 1128(b)(7) of the Act (as it applies to kickbacks); (iii) constitutes grounds for criminal sanctions under Section 1128B(b) of the Act; and/or (iv) satisfies the criteria set out in Section 1128B(b)(3) of the Act or associated regulations.

Advisory Opinion 97-6, October 8, 1997 Appendix F14

Whether a proposed arrangement for restocking ambulance supplies and medications (the "Proposed Arrangement") would constitute illegal remuneration as defined in the anti-kickback statute.

1998

Advisory Opinion 98-1, March 19, 1998 Appendix F17

Whether a contractual arrangement for distribution and billing services between Company A and Company B ... constitutes grounds for sanction under the anti-kickback statute.

Advisory Opinion 98-2, April 8, 1998 Appendix F17.1

Whether certain pharmaceutical discount pricing arrangements that are limited to arrangements between a manufacturer and wholesalers . . . will subject you to sanction under the anti-kickback statute.

Advisory Opinion 98-3, April 8, 1998 Appendix F17.2

Whether a hospital system's provision of an ambulance to a municipal fire department as described in your request . . .

Advisory Opinion 98-4, April 14, 1998 Appendix F17.3

Whether a proposed management services contract between a medical practice management company and a physician practice, which provides that the management company will be reimbursed for its costs and paid a percentage of net practice revenues...

Advisory Opinion 98-5, April 24, 1998 Appendix F17.4

. . .Which seeks our opinion regarding the "coordination of benefits" ("COB") provisions of a provider agreement between Nursing Home A . . . and a health care plan.

Advisory Opinion 98-6, April 24, 1998 Appendix F17.5

Whether waiving coinsurance obligations for participants in a clinical study sponsored by the Health Care Financing Administration and the National Heart, Lung, and Blood Institute...

340B of the Public Health Service Act ...would constitute grounds for sanctions under the anti-kickback statute.

Advisory Opinion 98-16, November 3, 1998 Appendix F29
Whether a proposed arrangement under which [Name redacted] would assign an employee pharmacist to work in designated hospital transplant centers for the purpose of providing pharmacy-related products and services . . . would constitute prohibited remuneration under the anti-kickback statute.

Advisory Opinion 98-17, November 6, 1998 Appendix F30
Whether donations by Company X . . . to Organization A . . . (an independent, 501(c)(3) charitable organization) for the purpose of funding a program to pay for Supplementary Medical Insurance . . . or Medicare Supplementary Health Insurance . . . premiums for financially needy Medicare beneficiaries with end-stage renal disease . . .

Advisory Opinion 98-18, November 25, 1998 Appendix F31
Whether an ophthalmologist's proposed sublease to an optometrist of certain imaging equipment . . . would meet the criteria of the equipment rental safe harbor.

Advisory Opinion 98-19, December 14, 1998 Appendix F32
Whether an arrangement whereby an independent physician association would acquire an equity interest in a managed care organization would constitute grounds for the imposition of sanctions under the anti-kickback statute.

1999

Advisory Opinion 99-1, January 20, 1999 Appendix F33
Whether the Arrangement [for the provision of back-up emergency ambulance services that involves waivers of copayments and deductible amounts] constitutes prohibited remuneration within the meaning of the anti-kickback statute.

Advisory Opinion 99-2, February 26, 1999 Appendix F34
Whether certain arrangements for discounted ambulance services provided to residents of Medicare skilled nursing facilities would result in prohibited remuneration and sanctions under the anti-kickback statute.

Advisory Opinion 99-3, March 16, 1999 Appendix F35
Whether a proposed pricing arrangement for a package of therapeutic mattresses for SNF patients to be marketed by a company, and certain commissioned agents, would result in prohibited remuneration under the anti-kickback statute.

Advisory Opinion 99-4, March 31, 1999 Appendix F36

Whether a proposed agreement . . . pursuant to which Hospital District No.1 . . . would locate a medical clinic within the geographic boundaries of Hospital District No. 2 . . . would constitute grounds for sanctions under the anti-kickback statute.

Advisory Opinion 99-5, April 1, 1999 Appendix F37

Whether an annual fee imposed by city ordinance on ambulance companies wishing to provide ambulance services in the city . . . constitutes prohibited remuneration under the anti-kickback statute, . . . and, if so, whether the Ambulance Fee assessment constitutes grounds for the imposition of sanctions.

Advisory Opinion 99-6, April 7, 1999 Appendix F38

Whether the longstanding policy of a hospital, specializing in pediatric oncology research, of not billing its patients for any amounts associated with their treatment, including copayment amounts...

Advisory Opinion 99-7, June 30, 1999 Appendix F39

Whether an across-the-board waiver of any out-of-pocket beneficiary copayments for medical services covered by the national Eye Care Project constitutes grounds for the imposition of a sanction under section 1128A(a)(5) of the Act.

Advisory Opinion 99-8, July 6, 1999 Appendix F40

Whether an arrangement to provide for personal appearances by podiatrists to certain retail stores constitutes grounds for sanctions under the anti-kickback statute.

Advisory Opinion 99-9, September 30, 1999 Appendix F41

Regarding a proposed contractual arrangement between a self-insured employer health plan and a single-specialty managed care organization to provide managed podiatry benefits for the employer's retirees.

Advisory Opinion 99-10, October 25, 1999 Appendix F42

Whether a corporate sponsorship program between Drug Company A and Charity B . . . constitutes grounds for sanctions under the anti-kickback statute.

Advisory Opinion 99-11, October 25, 1999 Appendix F43

Concerning an arrangement sponsored by Coalition A to provide psychotherapy services at free or reduced prices using residents from local teaching facilities as clinicians.

Advisory Opinion 99-12, November 23, 1999 Appendix F44

About a proposed marketing program involving the use of physician practices and health care clinics to distribute coupons redeemable by certain retailers . . . for discounts on items or services that are not reimbursable by any Federal health care program.

2000

Advisory Opinion No. 00-9, December 8, 2000 Appendix F55
Whether a proposed ambulance restocking arrangement constitutes prohibited remuneration.

Advisory Opinion No. 00-10, December 28, 2000 Appendix F56
Regarding a program designed to promote an expensive new drug used to prevent certain respiratory infections ... in pediatric patients.

Advisory Opinion No. 00-11, December 28, 2000 Appendix F57
Regarding a proposed charitable donation of up to $5,000 from Association A to EMS Service B... for the purchase of equipment and payment of paramedic training expenses.

2001

Advisory Opinion No. 01-1, January 11, 2001 Appendix F58
Concerning a proposed arrangement in which a hospital will share with a group of cardiac surgeons a percentage of the hospital's cost savings arising from the surgeons' implementation of a number of cost reduction measures in certain surgical procedures.

Advisory Opinion No. 01-2, March 17, 2001 Appendix F59
Concerning an annual charity golf tournament for which some of its vendors and suppliers pay money as sponsors and tournament participants.

Advisory Opinion No. 01-3, May —, 2001 Appendix F60
Concerning whether proposed contracts for discounted services between a Federally-recognized Indian tribe and local hospitals would constitute grounds for the imposition of exclusions under section1128(7) of the Act or civil money penalties under section 1128A(a)(7) of the Act.

Advisory Opinion No. 01-4, May 10, 2001 Appendix F61
Concerning a proposed arrangement between a hospital and a new physician whom the hospital would like to recruit to practice within its service area.

Advisory Opinion No. 01-5, May 24, 2001 Appendix F62
Concerning a proposed lease of cardiac diagnostic equipment to emergency medical services providers for a nominal charge.

Advisory Opinion No. 01-6, May 29, 2001 Appendix F63
Concerning pyments by vendors to a group purchasing organization (GPO) owned by entities affiliated with health care providers that purchase items covered by the GPO's vendor contracts.

The Office of Inspector General (OIG) was established at the Department of Health and Human Services by Congress in 1976 to identify and eliminate fraud, abuse, and waste in the Department's programs, including the Medicare and Medicaid programs, and to promote efficiency, economy, and effectiveness in departmental operations.

Office of Inspector General Advisory Opinions Under the Stark Bill—Section 1877 of the Social Security Act

Concerning whether a physician's referrals for certain services are prohibited under section 1877 of the Social Security Act

Whether the partners and physician employees of a proposed partnership may, under the "in-office ancillary services" exception defined in section 1877(b)(2) of the Social Security Act, refer Medicare and/or Medicaid patients to the partnership for eyeglass prescriptions filled subsequent to cataract surgery with the insertion of an intraocular lens.

Office of Inspector General Special Fraud Alerts

Office of Inspector General Medicare Advisory Bulletins

Office of Inspector General Special Advisory Bulletins

Office of Inspector General Compliance Program Guides

Other Civil and Criminal Statutes Pertinent to Health Care Fraud and Abuse

Recent Regulatory Provisions Applicable to Civil Money Penalties, Exclusions and Other Remedies

PART II
TEXT

Chapter 1

PERSONS AND ENTITIES SUBJECT TO SANCTIONS

One way to discover those vulnerable to sanctions is to review section 1861 of Title XVIII of the Social Security Act, as amended, 42 U.S.C.A. 1395x, the definition section of the statute. The many Medicare participants it describes are listed in sequence here as they appear there.

§ 1:1 HOSPITALS—Section 1861(e) [42 U.S.C.A. 1395x(e)]

Hospitals must be duly licensed by their State. They also must be—

> (1) . . .primarily engaged in providing, by or under the supervision of physicians, to inpatients (A) diagnostic services and therapeutic services for medical diagnosis, treatment, and care of injured, disabled, or sick persons, or (B) rehabilitation services for the rehabilitation of injured, disabled, or sick persons[.]

The term "hospital" does not include any institution which is primarily for the care and treatment of mental diseases unless it is a psychiatric hospital (as defined in subsection (f)). Nor does it include a religious nonmedical health care institution (such as a Christian Science sanitarium) or a critical access hospital. "Religious nonmedical health care institution" is defined in section 1861(ss). "Critical access hospital" is defined in section 1861(mm)(1).

◆ NOTE: The statute, and especially the regulations, contain many conditions which affect the definition of hospitals and other providers and suppliers. See, in general, Volume 42 of the Code of Federal Regulations, and the various provisions therein which set forth "conditions of participation" for the various providers. Breach of a condition of participation may be grounds for termination of a provider agreement. Termination of a provider agreement is the ultimate civil sanction because it puts a provider out of Medicare and Medicaid money altogether.

§ 1:2 PSYCHIATRIC HOSPITALS—Section 1861(f) [42 U.S.C.A. 1395x(f)]

These are institutions—

> (1) . . . primarily engaged in providing, by or under the supervision of a physician, psychiatric services for the diagnosis and treatment of mentally ill persons[.]

The definition includes the "distinct part" of an entity devoted to psychiatric care if the entity qualifies as a hospital under section 1861(e).

§ 1:3 PROVIDERS OF OUTPATIENT PHYSICAL OR OCCUPATIONAL THERAPY SERVICES—Sections 1861(g) and (p) [42 U.S.C.A. 1395x(g) and (p)]

Subsection (g) provides:

> The term "outpatient occupational therapy services" has the meaning given the term "outpatient physical therapy services" in subsection (p), except that "occupational" shall be substituted for "physical" each place it appears therein.

Subsection (p) provides in part:

> The term "outpatient physical therapy services" means physical therapy services furnished by a provider of services, a clinic, rehabilitation agency, or a public health agency, or by others under an arrangement with, and under the supervision of, such provider, clinic, rehabilitation agency, or public health agency to an individual as an outpatient[.]
>
> * * *
>
> The term "outpatient physical therapy services" also includes physical therapy services furnished an individual by a physical therapist (in his office or in such individual's home) who meets licensing and other standards prescribed by the Secretary in regulations, otherwise than under an arrangement with and under the supervision of a provider of services, clinic, rehabilitation agency, or public health agency, if the furnishing of such services meets such conditions relating to health and safety as

the Secretary may find necessary. In addition, such term includes physical therapy services which meet the requirements of the first sentence of this subsection [i.e., they are furnished by a clinic or rehabilitation agency, or by others under arrangements therewith] except that they are furnished to an individual as an inpatient of a hospital or extended care facility. The term "outpatient physical therapy services" also includes speech pathology services furnished by a provider of services, a clinic, rehabilitation agency, or by a public health agency, or by others under an arrangement with, and under the supervision of, such provider, clinic, rehabilitation agency, or public health agency to an individual as an outpatient, subject to the conditions prescribed in this subsection.

§ 1:4 SKILLED NURSING FACILITIES—Section 1861(j) [42 U.S.C.A. 1395x(j)]

This section of the Medicare statute, effective until October 1, 1990, (see section 4201(a)(1) of the Omnibus Budget Reconciliation Act of 1987 (OBRA 87), P.L. 100-203, and section 411 (l)(2)(E) of the OBRA Technical Corrections subtitle of the Medicare Catastrophic Coverage Act of 1988, P.L. 100-360) provides in part:

The term "skilled nursing facility" means (except for purposes of subsection (a)(2) [which, prior to repeal, pertains to the defini tion of a "spell of illness" for purposes of determining Medicare benefits]) an institution (or a distinct part of an institution) which has in effect a transfer agreement (meeting the requirements of subsection (1)) with one or more hospitals having agreements in effect under section 1866 [42 U.S.C.A. 1395cc] and which—

(1) is primarily engaged in providing to inpatients (A) skilled nursing care and related services for patients who require medical or nursing care, or (B) rehabilitation services for the rehabilitation of injured, disabled, or sick persons;

* * *

except that such term shall not (other than for purposes of subsection (a)(2)) include any institution which is primarily for the care and treatment of mental diseases. . .The term "skilled nursing facility" also includes an institution described in paragraph (1) of subsection (y) [which pertains to

> extended care in Christian Science skilled nursing facilities], to the extent and subject to the limitations provided in such subsection.

After October 1, 1990, by cross-reference to section 1819(a), 42 U.S.C.A. 1395i-3, a skilled nursing facility (SNF) is defined as follows:

> SKILLED NURSING FACILITY DEFINED.—In this title, the term "skilled nursing facility" means an institution (or a distinct part of an institution) which—
>
> (1) is primarily engaged in providing to residents—
>
> (A) skilled nursing care and related services for residents who require medical or nursing care, or
>
> (B) rehabilitation services for the rehabilitation of injured, disabled, or sick persons, and is not primarily for the care and treatment of mental diseases;
>
> (2) has in effect a transfer agreement (meeting the requirements of section 1861(l)) with one or more hospitals having agreements in effect under section 1866; and
>
> (3) meets the requirements for a skilled nursing facility described in subsections (b) [which pertains to provision of services], (c) [which pertains to residents' rights], and (d) [which pertains to administration of facilities] of this section.

◆ NOTE: Before and after October 1, 1990, SNF's must be duly licensed by their State and meet numerous statutory and regulatory conditions of participation. As with other providers, only defined services are covered under Medicare. Furthermore, SNF's are to be distinguished from intermediate care facilities (ICF's) and intermediate care facilities for the mentally retarded (ICF/MR's) whose services are not covered by Medicare but may be covered by Medicaid.

§ 1:5 SUPPLIERS OF DURABLE MEDICAL EQUIPMENT—Section 1861(n) [42 U.S.C.A. 1395x(n)]

Durable medical equipment suppliers furnish such items as iron lungs, oxygen tents, hospital beds, and wheelchairs, including, under certain circumstances, power-operated vehicles. Effective July 1, 1998, pursuant to section 4105 (b)(1) of the Balanced Budget

Act of 1997, P.L. 105–33, they may also furnish blood-testing strips and blood glucose monitors for persons with diabetes.

◆ NOTE: Pursuant to section 4152(a)(2) of P.L. 101-508, the Omnibus Budget Reconciliation Act of 1990 (OBRA 90), if furnished after December 1990, only the seat-lift mechanism of seat-lift chairs, and not the chair itself, is included in the definition of durable medical equipment.

§ 1:6 HOME HEALTH AGENCIES AND OTHERS ENGAGED IN PROVIDING HOME HEALTH SERVICES—Section 1861(m) and (o) [42 U.S.C.A. 1395x(m) and (o)]

Home health agencies (HHA's) are public or private organizations or subdivisions thereof (or others, such as nurses, or physical, occupational, or speech therapists, or medical social services providers, who have working arrangements with home health agencies) which are "primarily engaged in providing skilled nursing services and other therapeutic services" as defined in the statute. Not included for purposes of Part A benefits, however, is "any agency or organization which is primarily for the care and treatment of mental diseases."

§ 1:7 PHYSICIANS—Section 1861(r) [42 U.S.C.A. 1395x(r)]

The term "physician" includes M.D.'s, D.O.'s, dentists, podiatrists, optometrists, and chiropractors. How much these specialists can participate in Medicare and Medicaid varies, however, with the scope of their State licensure and the degree to which their services are covered by Titles XVIII and XIX.

§ 1:8 SUPPLIERS OF MEDICAL AND OTHER HEALTH SERVICES (NOT PREVIOUSLY MENTIONED)—Section 1861(s) [42 U.S.C.A. 1395x(s)]

Included are pharmacists and pharmacies for covered drugs and biologicals; rural health clinics; Federally qualified health clinics [applicable to services provided after September 1991, pursuant to sections 4161(a)(1) and (a)(8) of P.L. 101-508, the Omnibus Budget Reconciliation act of 1990 (OBRA 90)]; those who furnish dialysis supplies, equipment, and services; including erythropoietin furnished on or after January 1, 1994 [pursuant to section 13566(b) of P.L. 103-66, the Omnibus Budget Reconciliation Act of 1993 (OBRA 93)], and oral anti-cancer chemotherapeutic agents furnished on or after January 1, 1994 [pursuant to section 13553(a) of OBRA 93]; in limited circumstances services of physician assistants, nurse practitioners, or clinical nurse specialists, and clinical psychologists; purveyors of diagnostic X-rays and laboratory tests (like clinical diagnostic laboratories and qualified hospital laboratories); suppliers of surgical dressings, splints, casts, prosthetic devices, braces and special shoes; ambulance companies; and, effective July 1, 1990, clinical social workers; and certified nurse-midwife services, qualified psychologist services, and certified registered nurse anesthetist services.

◆ NOTE: Do not confuse "providers" and "suppliers." "Provider of services" is a term of art defined in Section 1861(u) [42 U.S.C.A. 1395x(u)]. Prior to enactment of P.L. 101-234, the Medicare Catastrophic Coverage Repeal Act of 1989 (MCCRA), and P.L. 101-239, the Omnibus Budget Reconciliation Act of 1989 (OBRA 89), section 1861(u) read as follows:

> The term "provider of services" means a hospital, critical access hospital, skilled nursing facility, comprehensive outpatient rehabilitation facility, home health agency, hospice program, or, for purposes of section 1814(g) [42 U.S.C.A. 1395f(g), which pertains to payment for services of a physician rendered in a teaching hospital] and section 1835(e) [42 U.S.C.A. 1395n(e), which pertains to inpatient hospital services provided by faculty physicians in a teaching hospital or other physicians who are part of an organized medical staff of a hospital], a fund.

Presently, section 1861(u) reads:

> The term "provider of services" means a hospital, critical access hospital, skilled nursing facility, comprehensive outpatient rehabilitation facility, home health agency, hospice program, or, for purposes of section 1814(g) [42 U.S.C.A. 1395f(g), which pertains to payment for services of a physician rendered in a teaching hospital] and section 1835(e) [42 U.S.C.A. 1395n(e), which pertains to inpatient hospital services provided by faculty physicians in a teaching hospital or other physicians who are part of an organized medical staff of a hospital], a fund.

Effective January 1, 1990, section 201(a)(1) of MCCRA removed "home intravenous drug therapy provider". Effective December 19, 1989, section 6003(g)(3)(C)(i) of OBRA 89 added "rural primary care hospital". Effective October 1, 1997, section 4201(c)(1) of the Balanced Budget Act of 1997, P.L. 105–33, replaced "rural primary care hospital" with "critical access hospital".

◆ ALSO NOTE: "Provider of services" is re-defined in the statute for special purposes. See, for example, section 1835(a), 42 U.S.C.A. 1395n(a), regarding payment procedures, which refers to clinics, rehabilitation agencies, and public health agencies. See also section 1866(e), 42 U.S.C.A. 1395cc(e), which pertains to provider agreements and their termination or non-renewal. It provides:

> For purposes of this section, the term "provider of services" shall include— (1) a clinic, rehabilitation agency, or public health agency if, in the case of a clinic or rehabilitation agency, such clinic or agency meets the requirements of section 1861(p)(4)(A) [42 U.S.C.A. 1395x(p)(4)(A), which pertains to outpatient physical therapy services] (or meets the requirements of such section through the operation of section 1861(g) [42 U.S.C.A. 1395x(g), which pertains to outpatient occupational therapy services]), or if, in the case of a public health agency, such agency meets the requirements of section 1861(p)(4)(B) (or meets the requirements of such section through the operation of section 1861(g)), but only with respect to the furnishing of outpatient physical therapy services (as therein defined) or (through the operation of section 1861(g)) with respect to the furnishing of outpatient occupational therapy services. (2) a community mental health center (as defined in section 1861(ff)(3)(B) [42 U.S.C.A. 1395x(ff)(3)(B)]), but only with respect to the furnishing of partial hospitalization services (as described in section 1861(ff)(1) [provided after September 1991, pursuant to section 4162(b)(2) of OBRA 90]).

§ 1:9 RELIGIOUS NONMEDICAL HEALTH CARE INSTITUTIONS PROVIDING EXTENDED CARE—Section 1861(y) [42 U.S.C.A. 1395x(y)]

These providers may offer limited post-hospital extended care services. The statute provides in part:

> (1) The term "skilled nursing facility" also includes religious nonmedical health care institution (as defined in subsection (ss)(1)), but only (except for purposes of subsection (a)(2)

> [which pertains to the definition of a "spell of illness"] with respect to items and services ordinarily furnished by such an institution to inpatients, and payment may be made with respect to services provided by or in such an institution only to such extent and under such conditions, limitations, and requirements (in addition to or in lieu of the conditions, limitations, and requirements otherwise applicable) as may be provided in regulations consistent with section 1821 [42 U.S.C.A 1395i-5].

◆ NOTE: Effective January 1, 1990, section 101(a)(1) of P.L. 101-234, the Medicare Catastrophic Coverage Repeal Act of 1989, restored the phrase "(except for purposes of subsection (a)(2)" to this paragraph. Effective August 5, 1997, section 4454(a)(1)(B) of the Balanced Budget Act of 1997 substituted the phrase "religious nonmedical health care institution (as defined in subsection (ss)(1)" for "Christian Science sanitorium operated, or listed and certified, by the First Church of Christ, Scientist, Boston Massachusetts" and added the phrase "consistent with section 1821".

§ 1:10 RURAL HEALTH CLINICS—Section 1861(aa) [42 U.S.C.A. 1395x(aa)]

Rural health clinics are facilities "primarily engaged in furnishing to outpatients services" of a physician, drugs and biologicals, and services of physician assistants, nurse practitioners, and clinical psychologists "as would otherwise be covered if furnished by a physician or as an incident to a physician's service[.] " In areas where a shortage of home health agencies exists, these clinics may also provide part-time or intermittent nursing care and related medical supplies furnished by a registered professional nurse or licensed practical nurse to homebound individuals under written plans of treatment established by a physician, nurse practitioner, or physician assistant, provided the plans are periodically reviewed by a physician.

These clinics help meet the needs of Medicare beneficiaries in medically underserved areas.

§ 1:11 FEDERALLY QUALIFIED HEALTH CENTERS—Sections 1861(aa)(3) and (4) [42 U.S.C.A. 1395x(aa)(3) and (4)]

Federally qualified health centers are similar to rural health clinics with respect to services provided. In addition, however, they provide preventive primary health services specified by sections 329, 330, and 340 of the Public Health Service Act.

Federally qualified health center" means an entity which —

(A)(I) is receiving a grant under section 330 (other than subsection (h)) of the Public Health Service Act; or

(ii)(I) is receiving funding from such a grant under a contract with the recipient of such a grant, and (II) meets the requirements to receive a grant under section 330 (other than subsection (h)) of such Act;

(B) based on the recommendation of the Health Resources and Services Administration within the Public Health Service, is determined by the Secretary to meet the requirements for receiving such a grant;

(C) was treated by the Secretary, for purposes of part B, as a comprehensive federally funded health center as of January 1, 1990; or

(D) is an outpatient health program or facility operated by a tribe or tribal organization under the Indian Self-Determination Act or by an urban Indian organization receiving funds under title V of the Indian Health Care Improvement Act.

§ 1:12 PHYSICIAN ASSISTANTS, NURSE PRACTITIONERS, AND CLINICAL NURSE SPECIALISTS—Section 1861(aa)(5) [42 U.S.C.A. 1395x(aa)(5)]

The term "physician assistant" and the term "nurse practitioner" mean a physician assistant or nurse practitioner who performs such services as such individual is legally authorized to perform (in the State in which the individual performs such services) in accordance with State law (or the State regulatory mechanism provided by State law), and who meets such training, education, and experience requirements (or any combination thereof) as the Secretary may prescribe in regulations.

The term "clinical nurse specialist" means an individual who is a registered nurse and is licensed to practice nursing in the State in which the clinical nurse specialist services are performed, and who holds a master's degree in a defined clinical area of nursing from an accredited education institution.

◆ NOTE: These definitions apply to services furnished and supplies provided on or after January 1, 1998, pursuant to section 4511(d) of the Balanced Budget Act of 1997, P.L. 105–33.

§ 1:13 CERTIFIED REGISTERED NURSE ANESTHETISTS—Section 1861(bb) [42 U.S.C.A. 1395x(bb)]

Certified registered nurse anesthetists (CRNA's) provide anesthesia services and such related care as is allowed by the State where they practice. According to the statute:

> (2) The term "certified registered nurse anesthetist" means a certified registered nurse anesthetist licensed by the state who meets such education, training, and other requirements relating to anesthesia services and related care as the Secretary may prescribe. In prescribing such requirements the Secretary may use the same requirements as those established by a national organization for the certification of nurse anesthetists. Such term also includes, as prescribed by the Secretary, an anesthesiologist assistant.

§ 1:14 COMPREHENSIVE OUTPATIENT REHABILITATION FACILITIES—Section 1861(cc) [42 U.S.C.A. 1395x(cc)]

Section 1861(cc)(2) provides in part:

> The term "comprehensive outpatient rehabilitation facility" means a facility which—
>
> > (A) is primarily engaged in providing (by or under the supervision of physicians) diagnostic, therapeutic, and restorative services to outpatients for the rehabilitation of injured, disabled, or sick persons[.]

Included in the definition of comprehensive outpatient rehabilitation facility services, along with services of a physician, are services of physical therapists, occupational therapists, speech-language pathologists, respiratory therapists, testers, fitters, and trainers for prosthetic and orthotic devices, social workers, psychologists, nurses; drugs, biologicals, medical supplies, and durable medical equipment; and "such other items and services as are medically necessary for the rehabilitation of the patient and are ordinarily furnished by comprehensive outpatient rehabilitation facilities," if provided pursuant to a plan established and periodically reviewed by a physician.

◆ NOTE: With respect to respiratory therapists, the Medicaid statute, section 1902(e)(9), 42 U.S.C.A. 1396a(e)(9), gives States the option to include as medical assistance respiratory care services for individuals who are dependent upon a ventilator for life support at least six hours a day, who have been so dependent for at least 30 consecutive days, or the maximum number of days authorized under the State plan, whichever is less (i.e., States can be more generous), and who meet other statutory conditions.

§ 1:15 HOSPICES—Section 1861(dd) [42 U.S.C.A. 1395x(dd)]

Hospices are public or private organizations primarily engaged in providing nursing care, physical or occupational therapy, speech-language pathology services, medical social services, services of a Medicare qualified home health aide, homemaker services, medical supplies (including drugs and biologicals and use of medical appliances), physicians' services, short-term inpatient care, including both respite care and procedures necessary for pain control and acute and chronic symptom management, and counseling, including dietary counseling, all with respect to the care of the terminally ill and their adjustment to death.

§ 1:16 CERTIFIED NURSE MIDWIVES—Section 1861(gg) [42 U.S.C.A. 1395x(gg)]

Nurse midwife services are covered only to the extent authorized by State law and only "as would otherwise be covered if furnished by a physician or as an incident to a physician's service."

Pursuant to section 1861(gg)(2), as amended by section 13554 of OBRA 93 (applicable to services furnished on or after January 1, 1994),

> The term "certified nurse-midwife" means a registered nurse who has successfully completed a program of study and clinical

experience meeting guidelines prescribed by the Secretary, or has been certified by an organization recognized by the Secretary.

Prior to that amendment, the statute read:

The term "certified nurse-midwife" means a registered nurse who has successfully completed a program of study and clinical experience meeting guidelines prescribed by the Secretary, or has been certified by an organization recognized by the Secretary, and performs services in the area of management of the care of mothers and babies throughout the maternity cycle.

§ 1:17 CLINICAL SOCIAL WORKERS—Section 1861(hh) [42 U.S.C.A. 1395x(hh)]

As amended by section 6113(b)(2)(B) of P.L. 101-239, the Omnibus Budget Reconciliation Act of 1989 (OBRA 89), effective January 1, 1990, section 1861 [42 U.S.C.A. 1395x(hh)] provides:

(1) The term "clinical social worker" means an individual who—

(A) possesses a master's or doctor's degree in social work;

(B) after obtaining such degree has performed at least 2 years of supervised clinical social work; and

(C)(i) is licensed or certified as a clinical social worker by the State in which the services are performed, or

(ii) in the case of an individual in a State which does not provide for licensure or certification—

(I) has completed at least 2 years or 3,000 hours of post-master's degree supervised clinical social work practice under the supervision of a master's level social worker in an appropriate setting (as determined by the Secretary), and

(II) meets such other criteria as the Secretary establishes.

(2) The term "clinical social worker services" means services performed by a clinical social worker (as defined in paragraph (1)) for the diagnosis and treatment of mental illnesses (other than services furnished to an inpatient of a hospital and other than services furnished to an inpatient of a skilled nursing facility which the facility is required to provide as a requirement for participation) which the clinical social worker is legally author-

ized to perform under State law (or the State regulatory mechanism provided by State law) of the State in which such services are performed as would otherwise be covered if furnished by a physician or as an incident to a physician's professional service.

◆ NOTE: Paragraph (2) above applies to services furnished on or after July 1, 1990. Prior to enactment of OBRA 89, section 1861(hh) provided:

> The term "clinical social worker" means an individual who—
>
> (1) possesses a master's or doctor's degree in social work;
>
> (2) after obtaining such degree has performed at least 2 years of supervised clinical social work; and
>
> (3)(A) is licensed or certified as a clinical social worker by the State in which the services are performed, or
>
> (B) in the case of an individual in a State which does not provide for licensure or certification—
>
> (i) has completed at least 2 years or 3,000 hours of post-master's degree supervised clinical social work practice under the supervision of a master's level social worker in an appropriate setting (as determined by the Secretary), and
>
> (ii) meets such other criteria as the Secretary establishes.

§ 1:18 PSYCHOLOGISTS—Section 1861(ii) [42 U.S.C.A. 1395x(ii)]

As amended by section 6113(a) of P.L. 101-239, the Omnibus Budget Reconciliation Act of 1989 (OBRA 89), effective January 1, 1990, section 1861(ii) [42 U.S.C.A. 1395x(ii)] provides:

> The term "qualified psychologist services" means such services and such services and supplies furnished as an incident to his service furnished by a clinical psychologist (as defined by the Secretary) which the psychologist is legally authorized to perform under State law (or the State regulatory mechanism provided by State law) as would otherwise be covered if furnished by a physician or as an incident to a physician's service.

◆ NOTE: The definition set forth above applies to services furnished on or after July 1, 1990. Prior to amendment by OBRA 89, the statute provided:

> The term "qualified psychologist services" means such services and such services and supplies furnished as an incident to his service furnished by a clinical psychologist (as defined by the Secretary) at a community mental health center (as such term is used in the Public Health Service Act [P.L. 78-410, 42 U.S.C.A. 201 et seq.]) which the psychologist is legally authorized to perform under State law (or the State regulatory mechanism provided by State law) as would otherwise be covered if furnished by a physician or as an incident to a physician's service.

So much for the definition section of the Medicare statute as an indicator of those vulnerable to Federal sanctions. Here, in the order in which they appear in the statute, are other provisions of Title XVIII which indicate additional participants in Medicare.

§ 1:18.1 SPEECH-LANGUAGE PATHOLOGISTS AND AUDIOLOGISTS—Section 1861(ll)(1) [42 U.S.C.A. 1395x(ll)(1)]

Effective, January 1, 1995, pursuant to section 146 of the Social Security Act Amendments of 1994, P.L. 103-432:

> (1) The term "speech-language pathology services" means such speech, language, and related function assessment and rehabilitation services furnished by a qualified speech-language pathologist as the speech-language pathologist is legally authorized to perform under State law (or the State regulatory mechanism provided by State law) as would otherwise be covered if furnished by a physician.

§ 1:18.2 AUDIOLOGISTS—Section 1861(ll)(2) [42 U.S.C.A. 1395x(ll)(2)]

Effective, January 1, 1995, pursuant to section 146 of the Social Security Act Amendments of 1994, P.L. 103-432:

> (2) The term "audiology services" means such hearing and balance assessment services furnished by a qualified audiologist as the audiologist is legally authorized to perform under State law

(or the State regulatory mechanism provided by state law), as would otherwise be covered if furnished by a physician.

§ 1:18.3 CRITICAL ACCESS HOSPITAL — Section 1861(mm) [42 U.S.C.A. 1395x(mm)]

Pursuant to section 1820, critical access hospital means a facility located in a State that has established a Medicare Rural Hospital Flexibility Program, that is designated by that State as a critical access hospital, and that meets other criteria established by the Secretary of Health and Human Services. The facility may be public or nonprofit, but it must be located in a rural area and distant from other more full-service hospital facilities.

◆ NOTE: Effective October 1, 1997, section 4201(a) of the Balanced Budget Act of 1997 amended section 1820 to create the Medicare Rural Hospital Flexibility Program. Prior to that, section 1820 dealt with the Essential Access Community Hospital Program (EACH). Critical access hospitals were then referred to as rural primary care hospitals.

§ 1:18.4 RELIGIOUS NONMEDICAL INSTITUTION — Section 1861(ss) [42 U.S.C.A. 1395x(ss)]

Religious nonmedical health care institution" means a facility that is tax exempt under section 501(c)(3) of the Internal Revenue Code of 1986, that is lawfully operated under all applicable Federal, State, and local laws and regulations, and that provides only non-medical nursing items and services exclusively to patients who choose to rely solely upon a religious method of healing and for whom the acceptance of medical health services would be inconsistent with their religious beliefs.

The definition of religious nonmedical health care institution was enacted by section 4454(a)(1)(C) of the Balance Budget Act of 1997, effective August 5, 1997. This broader definition supplants provisions in the Medicare statute which applied specifically and only to Christian Scientist Sanitariums. For example, previously Christian Scientist sanitariums were included in the definition of hospital in section 1861(e).

So much for the definition section of the Medicare statute as an indicator of those vulnerable to Federal sanctions. Here, in the order in which they appear in the statute, are other provisions of Title XVIII which indicate additional participants in Medicare.

§ 1:19 "NON-PROVIDERS" WHO PROVIDE EMERGENCY HOSPITAL SERVICES—Section 1814(d) [42 U.S.C.A. 1395f(d)]

Hospitals which do not have provider agreements are not "providers of service" within the meaning of the Medicare statute. They may receive payment from Medicare trust funds for certain emergency services, however, and in doing so, presumably could perpetrate some fraud or abuse.

§ 1:20 "NON-PROVIDERS" WHO PROVIDE INPATIENT HOSPITAL SERVICES OUTSIDE THE UNITED STATES—Section 1814(f) [42 U.S.C.A. 1395f(f)]

In some cases the most accessible hospital for Medicare beneficiaries may be just across a United States border. Presumably, such hospitals also could perpetrate fraud or abuse.

§ 1:21 FISCAL INTERMEDIARIES—Section 1816 [42 U.S.C.A. 1395h]

The statute provides in part:

> (a) If any group or association of providers of services wishes to have payments under this part to such providers made through a national, State, or other public or private agency or organization and nominates such agency or organization for this purpose, the Secretary is authorized to enter into an agreement with such agency or organization providing for the determination by such agency or organization (subject to the provisions of section 1878 [42 U.S.C.A. 1395oo, which pertains to the Provider Reimbursement Review Board] and to such review by the Secretary as may be provided for by the agreement) of the amount of the payments required pursuant to this part to be made to such providers (and to providers assigned to such agency or organiza tion under subsection (e) [which pertains to compulsory assignment of providers to a fiscal intermediary), and for the making of such payments by such agency or organization to such providers (and to providers assigned to such agency or organization under subsection (e)).

◆ NOTE: The term "fiscal intermediary" applies with respect to Part A benefits and providers. Blue Cross associations and such insurance companies as Mutual of Omaha and General American are examples of fiscal intermediaries.

§ 1:22 AMBULATORY SURGICAL CENTERS—Section 1832(a)(2)(F) [42 U.S.C.A. 1395k(a)(2)(F)]

These entities may participate in Medicare because their services are included within the scope of Part B benefits.

§ 1:23 CARRIERS—Section 1842 [42 U.S.C.A. 1395u]

Essentially, carriers do for Part B Medicare benefits what fiscal intermediaries do for Part A Medicare benefits. The statute provides in part:

> (a) In order to provide for the administration of the benefits under this part with maximum efficiency and convenience for individuals entitled to benefits under this part and for providers of services and other persons furnishing services to such individuals, and with a view to furthering coordination of the administration of the benefits under part A and under this part, the Secretary is authorized to enter into contracts with carriers, including carriers with which agreements under section 1816 [42 U.S.C.A. 1395h, which pertains to fiscal intermediaries] are in effect, which will perform some or all of the following functions (or, to the extent provided in such contracts, will secure performance thereof by other organizations); and, with respect to any of the following functions which involve payments for physicians' services on a reasonable charge basis, the Secretary shall to the extent possible enter into such contracts:
>
> (1)(A) make determinations of the rates and amounts of payments required pursuant to this part to be made to providers of services and other persons on a reasonable cost or reasonable charge basis (as may be applicable);
>
> (B) receive, disburse, and account for funds in making such payments; and
>
> (C) make such audits of the records of providers of services as may be necessary to assure that proper payments are made under this part;

(2)(A) determine compliance with the requirements of section 1861(k) [42 U.S.C.A. 1395x(k)] as to utilization review; and

(B) assist providers of services and other persons who furnish services for which payment may be made under this part in the development of procedures relating to utilization practices, make studies of the effectiveness of such procedures and methods for their improvement, assist in the application of safeguards against unnecessary utilization of services furnished by providers of services and other persons to individuals entitled to benefits under this part, and provide procedures for and assist in arranging, where necessary, the establishment of groups outside hospitals (meeting the requirements of section 1861(k)(2)) to make reviews of utilization;

(3) serve as a channel of communication of information relating to the administration of this part; and

(4) otherwise assist, in such manner as the contract may provide, in discharging administrative duties necessary to carry out the purposes of this part.

§ 1:23.1 MEDICARE+CHOICE ORGANIZATIONS—Section 1851–1857

A Medicare+Choice Organization is a public or private entity certified as such under section 1856. It is an alternative source for certain persons to receive health insurance benefits which Medicare provides under traditional Parts A and B, plus additional benefits. The organization may be an insurance company or a risk-bearing organization, such as an HMO. It also may be a public or private provider-sponsored organization established and operated by a health care provider or group of affiliated health care providers.

Medicare+Choice organizations may offer their benefits as a private fee-for service plan or as a plan associated with a medical savings account which must be used to meet a high deductible. All of this is subject to having a contract with the Secretary of Health and Human Services pursuant to section 1857.

§ 1:24 PEER REVIEW ORGANIZATIONS—Section 1862(g) [42 U.S.C.A. 1395y(g)]

Congress authorized and funded peer review organizations (PRO's) to help the Secretary eliminate fraud and abuse in health care and to foster high quality health care. (See Part B of Title XI of the Social Security Act, 42 U.S.C.A. 1320c et seq.) It is possible, however, that they or their officers and employees could perpetrate fraud or abuse involving Medicare and Medicaid.

§ 1:25 HEALTH MAINTENANCE ORGANIZATIONS AND COMPETITIVE MEDICAL PLANS—Section 1876 [42 U.S.C.A. 1395mm]

Congress fostered the development of health maintenance organizations (HMO's) and competitive medical plans (CMP's) in an attempt to reduce the rate of inflation in health care costs. As with any other participant, these organizations, too, might engage in fraud or abuse of Medicare and Medicaid.

According to the statute:

> (b) For purposes of this section, the term "eligible organization" means a public or private entity (which may be a health maintenance organization or a competitive medical plan), organized under the laws of any State, which—
>
> (1) is a qualified health maintenance organization (as defined in section 1310(d) of the Public Health Service Act [P.L. 78-410]), or
>
> (2) meets the following requirements:
>
> (A) The entity provides to enrolled members at least the following health care services:
>
> (i) Physicians' services performed by physicians (as defined in section 1861(r)(1) [42 U.S.C.A. 1395x(r)(1)]).
>
> (ii) Inpatient hospital services.
>
> (iii) Laboratory, X-ray, emergency, and preventive services.
>
> (iv) Out-of-area coverage.
>
> (B) The entity is compensated (except for deductibles, coinsurance, and copayments) for the provision of health care services to enrolled members by a payment which is paid on a periodic basis without regard to the date the health care services are provided and which is fixed without regard to the frequency, extent, or kind of health care service actually provided to a member.

(C) The entity provides physicians' services primarily (i) directly through physicians who are either employees or partners of such organization, or (ii) through contracts with individual physicians or one or more groups of physicians (organized on a group practice or individual practice basis).

(D) The entity assumes full financial risk on a prospective basis for the provision of the health care services listed in subparagraph (A), except that such entity may—

(i) obtain insurance or make other arrangements for the cost of providing to any enrolled member health care services listed in subparagraph (A) the aggregate value of which exceeds $5,000 in any year,

(ii) obtain insurance or make other arrangements for the cost of health care service listed in subparagraph (A) provided to its enrolled members other than through the entity because medical necessity required their provision before they could be secured through the entity,

(iii) obtain insurance or make other arrangements for not more than 90 percent of the amount by which its costs for any of its fiscal years exceed 115 percent of its income for such fiscal year, and

(iv) make arrangements with physicians or other health professionals, health care institutions, or any combination of such individuals or institutions to assume all or part of the financial risk on a prospective basis for the provision of basic health services by the physicians or other health professionals or through the institutions.

(E) The entity has made adequate provision against the risk of insolvency, which provision is satisfactory to the Secretary. Paragraph (2)(A)(ii) shall not apply to an entity which had contracted with a single State agency administering a State plan approved under title XIX for the provision of services (other than inpatient hospital services) to individuals eligible for such services under such State plan on a prepaid risk basis prior to 1970.

§ 1:26 END STAGE RENAL DISEASE NETWORK AREA ADMINISTRATIVE ORGANIZATIONS AND RENAL DIALYSIS FACILITIES—Section 1881 [42 U.S.C.A. 1395rr]

To assure effective and efficient administration of end stage renal disease (ESRD) benefits, Congress authorized the Secretary to establish at least 17 ESRD network areas and to designate for each area an administrative organization. The Secretary was then authorized to enter into agreements with these organizations pursuant to which they would perform a variety of duties, including encouraging treatment settings most compatible with successful rehabilitation, developing quality of care standards, conducting on-site reviews of facilities and providers, and preparing annual reports of goals and achievements. (See section 1881(c)(2), 42 U.S.C.A. 1395rr(c)(2)). Other business entities provide dialysis services either on their own premises or at patients' homes.

§ 1:27 SELLERS OF MEDICARE SUPPLEMENTAL HEALTH INSURANCE POLICIES—Section 1882 [42 U.S.C.A. 1395ss]

Insurance companies may sell health insurance policies to cover health care expenses not paid for by Medicare. If they meet certain standards, those of the National Association of Insurance Commissioners and/or of the Secretary, such companies may receive certification by the Secretary. Then they may use the specially designed emblem of certification in marketing their policies. Several provisions in Title XVIII deal with fraudulent and abusive actions by sellers of Medicare supplemental insurance. See the Guide to Chapters for Insurance Companies.

§ 1:27.1 PACE PROVIDERS: Section 1894 [42 U.S.C.A. 1395eee]

Section 4801 of the Balanced Budget Act of 1997, P.L. 105–33, created the Program of All-inclusive Care for the Elderly (PACE), effective August 5, 1997. "PACE Program" means a program of all-inclusive care for the elderly conducted by a public entity or a private nonprofit entity organized for a charitable purpose under section 501(c)(3) of the Internal Revenue Code of 1986. It also means a program conducted by a private, for-profit entity granted a waiver on a demonstration project basis by the Secretary of Health and

Human Services under section 1894(h). To participate as a PACE provider entities must enter into agreements with the Secretary to provide a program of comprehensive health care services to persons eligible to enroll in PACE. PACE enrollees do not receive benefits under Medicare Part A or Part B for so long as they remain enrolled in PACE.

§ 1:28 MEDICARE BENEFICIARIES

Medicare beneficiaries include persons age 65 and older, persons who meet the statutory definition of disabled (see Title II of the Social Security Act, 42 U.S.C.A. 401 et seq.), and persons with end stage renal disease. (See section 1881, 42 U.S.C.A. 1395rr).

Categories of persons and institutions vulnerable to Federal sanctions for health care fraud and abuse also may be found in Title XIX, the Medicaid statute. In some instances, that statute requires participating States to include items and services which also are covered items and services under Medicare, for example, physician services and inpatient hospital stays. In other instances, Title XIX requires participating States to include items and services not covered under Medicare, for example, care in an intermediate care facility for the mentally retarded. In addition, States may include in their Medicaid programs items and services for which there is no Federal financial participation (FFP). Thus, for a complete list of categories of the vulnerable, the Medicaid State plan for a State in question should be consulted.

§ 1:29 MEDICAID RECIPIENTS—Section 1902(a)(10) [42 U.S.C.A. 1396a(a)(10)]

Persons who receive Medicare benefits are called beneficiaries, probably because of the insurance characteristics of Medicare and because money for their care comes from trust funds. Persons entitled to Medicaid benefits, on the other hand, are called recipients, perhaps because Medicaid, although sometimes characterized as health insurance for the poor, is a welfare program funded from general revenue, not from a trust.

Federal law mandates that States which participate in Medicaid must include as recipients persons entitled to aid under the so-called categorical welfare programs: Aid to the Aged, Aid to the Blind, or Aid to the Disabled under Titles I, X, and XIV of the Social Security Act, respectively, (see 42 U.S.C.A. 301 et seq., 1201 et seq., and 1351 et seq., the latter repealed except for Puerto Rico, Guam, and the Virgin Islands); Aid to the Aged, Blind, or Disabled pursuant to the Supplemental Security Income (SSI) program established by Title XVI of the Social Security Act, 42 U.S.C.A. 1381 et seq.; and Aid to Families with Dependent Children (AFDC) under Title IV, Parts A and E, of the Social Security Act, 42 U.S.C.A. 601 et seq.

At their option, States may provide Medicaid to the so-called medically needy. Those are persons who do not qualify for payments under the categorical welfare programs, but who would meet the financial need test if they had to pay for their own medical care. In addition, States must provide Medicaid assistance for several other narrowly defined categories of persons, such as "qualified severely impaired individuals" and "qualified pregnant women." (See section 1902(a)(10), 42 U.S.C.A. 1396a(a)(10).) Pursuant to section 13603(b) of OBRA 93 (applicable to services furnished on or after January 1, 1994), States also must provide Medicaid assistance for certain individuals infected with tuberculosis. (See section 1902(z), 42 U.S.C.A. 1396a(z)).

§ 1:30 INTERMEDIATE CARE FACILITIES AND INTERMEDIATE CARE FACILITIES FOR THE MENTALLY RETARDED—Section 1902(a)(13) [42 U.S.C.A. 1396a(a)(13)]

Title XIX requires States to provide payment not only for care in nursing facilities (NF's), but also in intermediate care facilities (ICF's) and intermediate care facilities for the mentally retarded (ICF/MR's).

Starting October 1, 1990, the effective date of numerous new and more stringent nursing home standards, however, the phrase "intermediate care facilities", as it pertains to ICF's and their services, was supplanted by the more encompassing phrase "nursing facilities". That change does not apply to ICF/MR's. (See section 4211(h)(2) of P.L. 100-203, the Omnibus Budget Reconciliation Act of 1987, as amended by sections 411(l)(3)(H) and (J) of the OBRA Technical Corrections subtitle of P.L. 100-360, the Medicare Catastrophic Coverage Act of 1988, and sections 608(d)(27)(F), (G), and (H) of P.L. 100-485, the Family Support Act of 1988.)

§ 1:31 INSTITUTIONS FOR MENTAL DISEASE (PRIVATE OR PUBLIC)—Sections 1902(a)(20) and (21) and 1905(i) [42 U.S.C.A. 1396a(a)(20) and (21) and 1396d(i)]

States, at their option, may provide medical assistance for individuals 65 years of age or older who are patients in institutions for mental disease. "Institution for mental diseases" means a hospital, nursing facility, or other institution of more than 16 beds, that is primarily engaged in providing diagnosis, treatment, or care of persons with mental diseases, including medical attention, nursing care, and related services.

§ 1:32 PROVIDERS OF HOME AND COMMUNITY CARE FOR FUNCTIONALLY DISABLED ELDERLY INDIVIDUALS—Section 1929 [42 U.S.C.A. 1396u]

States, at their option, may provide home and community care services to qualified functionally disabled elderly individuals. This was authorized by section 4711(a) of P.L. 101-508, the Omnibus Budget Reconciliation Act of 1990. Authorized services include homemaker/home health aide services, chore services, personal care services, nursing care services, respite care, training for family members to manage such individuals, adult day care, day treatment or other partial hospitalization, psychosocial rehabilitation services, and clinical services.

§ 1:33 PROVIDERS OF COMMUNITY SUPPORTED LIVING ARRANGEMENTS SERVICES—Section 1930 [42 U.S.C.A. 1396v]

Pursuant to section 4712(b)(2) of OBRA 90, States may apply to add community supported living arrangements services to their Medicaid programs. That includes such assistance in activities of daily living for developmentally disabled individuals as personal assistance; training and habilitation services for increased integration, independence, and productivity; 24-hour emergency assistance; assistive technology; adaptive equipment; support services necessary to participate in community activities; and other services as approved by the Secretary of Health and Human Services.

Just as Title XVIII has a definition section, so has Title XIX: section 1905, 42 U.S.C.A. 1396d. That section is as useful as a source for categories of participants in Medicaid as the parallel section in

Title XVIII is for Medicare. The overlap of services and participants in the two programs has been pointed out, but here, by way of review, is a summary of Medicaid services derived from section 1905(a), 42 U.S.C.A. 1396d(a), which defines "medical assistance" and from which principal Medicaid participants may be deduced.

- Inpatient hospital services (other than services in an institution for mental diseases).
- Outpatient services.
- Rural health clinic services.
- Federally qualified health center services.
- Other laboratory and X-ray services.
- Nursing facility services (other than services in an institution for mental diseases).
- Family planning services and supplies.
- Physicians' services.
- Medical and surgical services furnished by a dentist to the extent such services may be performed under State law either by a doctor of medicine or by a doctor of dental surgery or dental medicine.
- Medical care, or any other type of remedial care recognized under State law, furnished by licensed practitioners within the scope of their practice as defined by State law. (In other words, if it is State licensed and relates to health care it might be part of a State Medicaid plan and constitute "medical assistance" for Federal purposes. For example, chiropractors for manual manipulation of the spine: section 1905(g), 42 U.S.C.A. 1396d(g).
- Home health care services.
- Private duty nursing services.
- Clinic services furnished by or under the direction of a physician, without regard to whether the clinic itself is administered by a physician, including such services furnished outside the clinic by clinic personnel to an eligible individual who does not reside in a permanent dwelling or does not have a fixed home or mailing address. This implies an array of unlicensed personnel who work in such clinics.
- Dental services.
- Physical therapy and related services.
- Drugs, dentures, and prosthetic devices, and eyeglasses prescribed by a physician skilled in diseases of the eye or by an optometrist, whichever the individual may select.

- Other diagnostic, screening, preventive, and rehabilitative services.
- Inpatient hospital services and nursing facility services for individuals 65 years of age or over in an institution for mental diseases.
- Services in an intermediate care facility for the mentally retarded (other than in an institution for mental diseases).
- Inpatient psychiatric hospital services.
- Services furnished by a nurse-midwife.
- Hospice care.
- Case-management services, as defined in section 1915(g)(2), 42 U.S.C.A. 1396n(g), which provides: For purposes of this subsection, the term "case management services" means services which will assist individuals eligible under the plan in gaining access to needed medical, social, educational, and other services.
- Respiratory care services.
- Services provided by a certified pediatric nurse practitioner or certified family nurse practitioner.
- Home and community care for functionally disabled elderly individuals.
- Community supported living arrangements services.
- Any other medical care, and any other type of remedial care recognized under State law, specified by the Secretary, but not care or services to inmates of a public institution (except as a patient in a medical institution), and not for care or services for persons under age 65 who are patients in an institution for mental diseases.
- Personal care services.

Chapter 2

SANCTIONS IN THE MEDICARE STATUTE

§ 2:1 VIOLATION OF REQUIREMENTS FOR PRIVATE CONTRACTS WITH MEDICARE BENEFICIARIES BY PHYSICIANS AND OTHER PRACTITIONERS — Section 1802(b) [42 U.S.C.A. 1395a(b)]

Summary

Section 1802(b) of the Social Security Act, as amended, 42 U.S.C.A. 1395a(b), permits physicians and other practitioners to enter into private contracts for any health care item or service with a Medicare beneficiary. Allowing private contracts is a major deviation from longstanding Medicare beneficiary protections against overcharging by physicians and other medical practitioners, and from longstanding Federal policy to encourage greater participation by medical professionals in Medicare. Congress made this change, effective January 1, 1998, by section 4507 of the Balanced Budget Act of 1997, P.L. 105–33. Numerous conditions apply.

In General: Private contracts are permitted if no claim for Medicare payment will be made, if no reimbursement is received from Medicare (directly or on a capitated basis), and if no amount is received by the physician or practitioner from an organization which receives reimbursement for such item or service under Medicare (directly or on a capitated basis).

Definitions: "Physician" means anyone who meets the definition of a physician for Medicare purposes under section 1861(r)(1) [42 U.S.C.A. 1395x(r)(1)] . "Practitioner", by cross-reference to section 1842(b)(18)(C) [42 U.S.C.A. 1395u(b)(18)(C)], includes:

physician assistants (as defined in section 1861(aa)(5), 42 U.S.C.A. 1395x(aa)(5))

nurse practitioners (as defined in section 1861(aa)(5))

clinical nurse specialists (as defined in section 1861(aa)(5))
certified registered nurse anesthetists (as defined in section 1861(bb)(2), 42 U.S.C.A. 1395x(bb)(2))

certified nurse-midwives (as defined in section 1861(gg)(2), 42 U.S.C.A. 1395x(gg)(2))

clinical social workers (as defined in section 1861(hh)(1), 42 U.S.C.A. 1395x(hh)(1))

clinical psychologists (as defined by the Secretary for purposes of section 1861(ii), 42 U.S.C.A. 1395x(ii)).

Requirements for Private Contracts: First, the contract must be in writing and signed by the Medicare beneficiary before any item or service is provided pursuant to the contract.

Second, the contract must not be entered into at a time when the Medicare beneficiary is facing an emergency or urgent health care situation.

Third, the contract must clearly indicate to the Medicare beneficiary that by signing his or her name the beneficiary —

agrees not to submit a claim (or request that the physician or practitioner submit a claim) for the items or services under Medicare, even if Medicare would otherwise pay for them;

agrees to be responsible, whether through insurance or otherwise, for payment for such items or services and understands that no reimbursement will be provided by Medicare for the items or services;

acknowledges that no Medicare limits, including the limits provided under section 1848(g), 42 U.S.C.A. 1395w-4(g), which pertains to the so-called "limiting charges" applicable to physicians, on what the physician or practitioner may charge apply to the amounts which the physician or practitioner will charge;

acknowledges that Medicare supplement insurers approved under section 1882, 42 U.S.C.A. 1395ss, which establishes certified Medicare supplement insurance policies, do not — and other supplemental insurance plans may

> not — make payments for such items and services because payment is not made under Medicare; and acknowledges that he or she has the right to have such items or services provided by other physicians or practitioners for whom payment would be made by Medicare.

Finally, the contract must state clearly whether the physician or practitioner is excluded from participation in Medicare under section 1128, 42 U.S.C.A. 1320a-7, which provides numerous grounds for excluding persons and entities from participation in Medicare.

Physician or Practitioner Requirements: Physicians and practitioners who wish to contract privately with Medicare beneficiaries must forego Medicare reimbursement for at least two years. To confirm that, they must sign an affidavit which —

> identifies the physician or practitioner; and
>
> provides that the physician or practitioner will not submit any claim under Medicare for any item or service provided to any Medicare beneficiary, and will not receive any reimbursement or amount for any item or service (directly or on a capitated basis) from Medicare or from an organization which receives Medicare reimbursement (directly or on a capitated basis), during the two-year period beginning on the date the affidavit is signed.

That affidavit must then be filed with the Secretary of Health and Human Services no later than 10 days after the first contract to which it applies is entered into.

Enforcement: If a physician or practitioner who signs an affidavit forgoing Medicare reimbursement knowingly and willfully submits a Medicare claim for any item or service provided during the two-year period, he or she thereafter loses the right to contract privately with respect to any items and services provided pursuant to any contract on and after the date of such a submission and before the end of the two-year period. The same applies with respect to any physician or practitioner who receives any reimbursement from Medicare for any item or service directly or on a capitated basis, or who receives any amount for such item or service from an organization which receives Medicare reimbursement (directly or on a capitated basis).

Furthermore, no payment shall be made by Medicare for any item or service furnished by the physician or practitioner during that period. Nor can any reimbursement or payment of any amount be made directly or on a capitated basis from Medicare or an organization which receives Medicare reimbursement.

No Cap on Allowable Charges: Pursuant to section 1802(b)(4), section 1848(g), 42 U.S.C. A. 1395w-4(g), which imposes limitations on charges to Medicare beneficiaries and other requirements for claims submissions, does not apply with respect to any item or service provided to a Medicare beneficiary under a private contract with a physician or practitioner.

Statutory Provisions

Section 1802(b), 42 U.S.C.A. 1395a(b) provides:

(b) USE OF PRIVATE CONTRACTS BY MEDICARE BENEFICIARIES. —

(1) IN GENERAL. — Subject to the provisions of this subsection, nothing in this title shall prohibit a physician or practitioner from entering into a private contract with a Medicare beneficiary for any item or service —

(A) for which no claim for payment is to be submitted under this title, and

(B) for which the physician or practitioner receives —

(i) no reimbursement under this title directly or on a capitated basis, and

(ii) receives no amount for such item or service from an organization which receives reimbursement for such item or service under this title directly or on a capitated basis.

(2) BENEFICIARY PROTECTIONS. —

(A) IN GENERAL. — Paragraph (1) shall not apply to any contract unless —

(i) the contract is in writing and is signed by the Medicare beneficiary before any item or service is provided pursuant to the contract;

(ii) the contract contains the items described in subparagraph (B); and

(iii) the contract is not entered into at a time when the Medicare beneficiary is facing an emergency or urgent health care situation.

(B) ITEMS REQUIRED TO BE INCLUDED IN CONTRACT.—Any contract to provide items and services to which paragraph (1) applies shall clearly indicate to the Medicare beneficiary that by signing such contract the beneficiary—

(i) agrees not to submit a claim (or to request that the physician or practitioner submit a claim) under this title for such items or services even if such items or services are otherwise covered by this title;

(ii) agrees to be responsible, whether through insurance or otherwise, for payment of such items or services and understands that no reimbursement will be provided under this title for such items or services;

(iii) acknowledges that no limits under this title (including the limits under section 1848(g) [42 U.S.C.A. 1395w-4(g)]) apply to amounts that may be charged for such items or services;

(iv) acknowledges that Medigap plans under section 1882 [42 U.S.C.A. 1395ss] do not, and other supplemental insurance plans may elect not to, make payments for such items and services because payment is not made under this title; and

(v) acknowledges that the Medicare beneficiary has the right to have such items or services provided by other physicians or practitioners for whom payment would be made under this title.

Such contract shall also clearly indicate whether the physician or practitioner is excluded from participation under the Medicare program under section 1128 [42 U.S.C.A. 1320a-7].

(3) PHYSICIAN OR PRACTITIONER REQUIREMENTS. —

(A) IN GENERAL.—Paragraph (1) shall not apply to any contract entered into by a physician or practitioner unless an affidavit described in subparagraph (B) is in effect during the period any item or service is to be provided pursuant to the contract.

(B) AFFIDAVIT. —An affidavit is described in this subparagraph if—

(i) the affidavit identifies the physician or practitioner and is in writing and is signed by the physician or practitioner;

(ii) the affidavit provides that the physician or practitioner will not submit any claim under this title for any item or service provided to any Medicare beneficiary (and will not receive any reimbursement or amount described in paragraph (1)(B) for any such item or service) during the 2year period beginning on the date the affidavit is signed; and

(iii) a copy of the affidavit is filed with the Secretary no later than 10 days after the first contract to which such affidavit applies is entered into.

(C) ENFORCEMENT. — If a physician or practitioner signing an affidavit under subparagraph (B) knowingly and willfully submits a claim under this title for any item or service provided during the 2-year period described in subparagraph (B)(ii) (or receives any reimbursement or amount described in paragraph (1)(B) for any such item or service) with respect to such affidavit —

(i) this subsection shall not apply with respect to any items and services provided by the physician or practitioner pursuant to any contract on and after the date of such submission and before the end of such period; and

(ii) no payment shall be made under this title for any item or service furnished by the physician or practitioner during the period described in clause (i) (and no reimbursement or payment of any amount described in paragraph (1)(B) shall be made for any such item or service).

(4) LIMITATION ON ACTUAL CHARGE AND CLAIM SUBMISSION REQUIREMENT NOT APPLICABLE. — Section 1848(g) shall not apply with respect to any item or service provided to a Medicare beneficiary under a contract described in paragragh (1).

(5) DEFINITIONS. — In this subsection:

(A) MEDICARE BENEFICIARY. — The term 'Medicare beneficiary' means an individual who is entitled to benefits under part A or enrolled under part B.

(B) PHYSICIAN. —The term 'physician' has the meaning given such term by section 1861(r)(1) [42 U.S.C.A. 1395x(r)(1)].

(C) PRACTITIONER. —The term 'practitioner' has the meaning given such term by section 1842(b)(18)(C) [42 U.S.C.A. 1395u(b)(18)(C)].

Section 1842(b)(18)(C) provides:

A practitioner described in this subparagraph is any of the following:

(i) A physician assistant, nurse practitioner, or clinical nurse specialist (as defined in section 1861(aa)(5) [42 U.S.C.A. 1395x(aa)(5)]).

(ii) A certified registered nurse anesthetist (as defined in section 1861(bb)(2) [42 U.S.C.A. 1395x(bb)(2)]).

(iii) A certified nurse-midwife (as defined in section 1861(gg)(2) [42 U.S.C.A. 1395x(gg)(2)]).

(iv) A clinical social worker (as defined in section 1861(hh)(1) [42 U.S.C.A. 1395x (hh)(1)]).

(v) A clinical psychologist (as defined by the Secretary for purposes of section 1861(ii) [42 U.S.C.A. 1395x (ii)]).

(vi) A registered dietition or nutrition professional. [NOTE: Subsection (vi) was added by section 105(d) of the Medicare, Medicaid, and SCHIP Benefits Improvement and Protection Act of 2000, P.L. 106-554, enacted December 15, 2000. It applies to services furnished on or after January 1, 2002.]

Section 1861(r) provides:

The term "physician", when used in connection with the performance of any function or action, means (1) a doctor of medicine or osteopathy legally authorized to practice medicine and surgery by the State in which he performs such function or action (including a physician within the meaning of section 1101(a)(7) [42 U.S.C.A. 1301(a)(7), which includes osteopathic practitioners within the scope of their practice as defined by State law]), (2) a doctor of dental surgery or of dental medicine who is legally authorized to practice dentistry by the State in which he performs such function and who is acting within the scope of his license when he performs such functions, (3) a doctor of podiatric medicine for the purposes of subsections (k), (m), (p)(1), and (s) of this section and sections 1814(a)

[42 U.S.C.A. 1395f(a)], 1832(a)(2)(F)(ii) [42 U.S.C.A. 1395k], and 1835 [42 U.S.C.A. 1395n] but only with respect to functions which he is legally authorized to perform as such by the State in which he performs them, (4) a doctor of optometry, but only with respect to the provision of items or services described in subsection (s) which he is legally authorized to perform as a doctor of optometry by the State in which he performs them, or (5) a chiropractor who is licensed as such by the State (or in a State which does not license chiropractors as such, is legally authorized to perform the services of a chiropractor in the jurisdiction in which he performs such services), and who meets uniform minimum standards promulgated by the Secretary, but only for the purpose of sections 1861(s)(1) and 1861(s)(2)(A) [42 U.S.C.A. 1395x(s)(1) and (s)(2)(A)] and only with respect to treatment by means of manual manipulation of the spine (to correct a subluxation) which he is legally authorized to perform by the State or jurisdiction in which such treatment is provided. For the purposes of section 1862(a)(4) [42 U.S.C.A. 1395y(a)(4)] and subject to the limitations and conditions provided in the previous sentence, such term includes a doctor of one of the arts, specified in such previous sentence, legally authorized to practice such art in the country in which the inpatient hospital services (referred to in such section 1862(a)(4)) are furnished.

◆ NOTE: Sec. 4513(a) of the "Balanced Budget Act of 1997," applicable to services furnished on or after January 1, 2000, amended paragraph (r)(5) by deleting the words "demonstrated by X-ray to exist" after "(to correct a subluxation". That change applies to services of chiropractors on or after January 1, 2000.

For regulatory citations, see Chapter 6

§ 2:1.1 FAILURE BY PHYSICIANS, PROVIDERS, SUPPLIERS, AND OTHERS TO FURNISH AN ITEMIZED STATEMENT OF ITEMS AND SERVICES PROVIDED TO MEDICARE BENEFICIARIES — Section 1806 [42 U.S.C.A. 1395b-7]

Summary

◆ NOTE: Section 1806 of the Social Security Act, as amended, 42 U.S.C.A. 1395b-7, was added by section 4311(b)(1) of the Balanced Budget Act of 1997, P.L. 105–33. According to section

4311(b)(3) of the latter Act, the obligation of the Secretary to furnish explanation of benefits statements became effective August 5, 1997. Obligations with respect to itemized statements were made effective not later than January 1, 1999.

Section 1806(a) of the Social Security Act, 42 U.S.C.A. 1395b-7, obligates the Secretary of Health and Human Services to furnish an explanation of Medicare benefits to each individual for whom Medicare has made a payment (or would have made a payment without regard to any deductible). The statement must list each item or service for which Medicare paid and the amount of the payment. The statement also must include a notice of the beneficiary's right under section 1806(b) to request an itemized statement from the person or entity Medicare paid.

Section 1806(b) gives a Medicare beneficiary the right to submit a written request for an itemized statement from any physician, provider, supplier, or any other person (including an organization, agency, or other entity) with respect to any item or service provided to him or her for which Medicare payment has been made. Not later than 30 days after such a written request is made, the person or entity receiving it must provide the itemized statement to the requester.

Pursuant to section 1806(b)(2)(B), whoever knowingly fails to furnish an itemized statement upon such a request is subject to a civil money penalty of not more than $100 for each such failure. The penalty shall be imposed and collected in the same manner as civil money penalties under subsection (a) of section 1128A, 42 U.S.C.A. 1320a-7a, are imposed and collected under that section.

An individual who receives an itemized statement may submit a written request for a review of the itemized statement to the Secretary of Health and Human Services. This must be done not later than 90 days after receipt of the itemized statement. The request for review must identify specific items or services the individual believes were not provided as claimed, or any other billing irregularity, such as duplicate billing. Then the Secretary must determine whether the itemized statement identifies specific items or services that were not provided as claimed, or any other billing irregularity, that resulted in unnecessary Medicare payments. Pursuant to section 1806(b)(5), the Secretary must take all appropriate measures to recover amounts unnecessarily paid by Medicare with respect to the itemized statement.

Statutory Provisions

Section 1806, 42 U.S.C.A. 1395b-7, provides:

(a) IN GENERAL. — The Secretary shall furnish to each individual for whom payment has been made under this title (or would be made without regard to any deductible) a statement which —

(1) lists the item or service for which payment has been made and the amount of such payment for each item or service; and

(2) includes a notice of the individual's right to request an itemized statement (as provided in subsection (b)).

(b) REQUEST FOR ITEMIZED STATEMENT FOR MEDICARE ITEMS AND SERVICES. —

(1) IN GENERAL. — An individual may submit a written request to any physician, provider, supplier, or any other person (including an organization, agency, or other entity) for an itemized statement for any item or service provided to such individual by such person with respect to which payment has been made under this title.

(2) 30-DAY PERIOD TO FURNISH STATEMENT. —

(A) IN GENERAL. — Not later than 30 days after the date on which a request under paragraph (1) has been made, a person described in such paragraph shall furnish an itemized statement describing each item or service provided to the individual requesting the itemized statement.

(B) PENALTY. — Whoever knowingly fails to furnish an itemized statement in accordance with subparagraph (A) shall be subject to a civil money penalty of not more than $100 for each such failure. Such penalty shall be imposed and collected in the same manner as civil money penalties under subsection (a) of section 1128A [42 U.S.C.A. 1320a-7a] are imposed and collected under that section.

(3) REVIEW OF ITEMIZED STATEMENT. —

(A) IN GENERAL. — Not later than 90 days after the receipt of an itemized statement furnished under paragraph (1), an individual may submit a written request for a review of the itemized statement to the Secretary.

(B) SPECIFIC ALLEGATIONS. — A request for a review of the itemized statement shall identify —

(I) specific items or services that the individual believes were not provided as claimed, or

(II) any other billing irregularity (including duplicate billing).

(4) FINDINGS OF SECRETARY. — The Secretary shall, with respect to each written request submitted under paragraph (3), determine whether the itemized statement identifies specific items or services that were not provided as claimed or any other billing irregularity (including duplicate billing) that has resulted in unnecessary payments under this title.

(5) RECOVERY OF AMOUNTS. — The Secretary shall take all appropriate measures to recover amounts unnecessarily paid under this title with respect to a statement described in paragraph (4).

§ 2:1.2 FALSIFYING ASSESSMENTS OF RESIDENTS OF SKILLED NURSING FACILITIES — Section 1819(b)(3)(B)(ii) [42 U.S.C.A. 1395i-3(b)(3)(B)(ii)]

Summary

Section 1819, 42 U.S.C.A. 1395i-3, sets forth comprehensive requirements for skilled nursing facilities (SNF's) participating in Medicare. These requirements pertain to provision of services (subsection (b)), to residents' rights (subsection (c)), and to administration of nursing facilities (subsection (d)). In addition, there are Federally mandated State requirements which pertain to nursing facilities (subsection (e)), such as nurse aide training and competency evaluation and State appeals processes for resident transfers and discharges.

Section 1819 also details responsibilities of the Secretary of Health and Human Services which pertain to nursing facility requirements (subsection (f)), elaborate requirements for survey and certification (subsection (g)), and specific enforcement requirements (subsection (h)). Some of these requirements come with Federal sanctions for noncompliance.

◆ NOTE: Parallel provisions regarding Medicaid obligations of nursing facilities are found in Section 1919 of the Social Security Act, 42 U.S.C.A. 1396r.

Section 1819(b)(3) requires skilled nursing facilities to make comprehensive, accurate, standardized, and reproducible assessments of each resident's functional capacity. Those assessments must describe the resident's capability to perform daily life functions and any significant impairments in functional capacity, in accordance with guidelines to be established by the Secretary and by States. They also must identify medical problems.

Assessments are to be conducted promptly upon admission (14 days thereafter) for each individual admitted on or after October 1, 1990, and by not later than January 1, 1991, for each resident of the facility on that date. They also are to be conducted promptly after a significant change in a resident's physical or mental condition, and in no case less often than once every 12 months. In addition, reviews are required for every resident no less frequently than once every three months to assure continuing accuracy of prior assessments.

Residents' assessments are to be used to develop, review, and revise plans of care. A plan of care is a written description of the scope of services and activities a resident requires which nursing facilities are obligated to prepare. As much as possible, however, residents' assessments are to be coordinated with any State-required preadmission screening program to avoid duplicate efforts.

Section 1819(b)(3) requires residents' assessments to be conducted or coordinated (with appropriate participation of health professionals) by a registered professional nurse who signs and certifies completion of the assessment. Each individual who completes a portion of such an assessment also must sign and certify the accuracy of his or her portion.

Pursuant to section 1819(b)(3)(B)(ii), any individual who willfully and knowingly certifies a material and false statement in a resident's assessment is subject to a civil money penalty not to exceed $1,000 with respect to each such assessment. Any individual who willfully and knowingly causes another individual to do that is subject to a civil money penalty not to exceed $5,000 with respect to each such assessment.

In addition, if, during a State survey of a SNF, a State determines there has been willful and knowing certification of false assessments, it may require assessments by individuals who are independent of the SNF and who are approved by the State.

◆ NOTE: These assessments apply to residents admitted to SNF's on or after October 1, 1990. See section 4201(a)(3) of the Omnibus Budget Reconciliation Act of 1987 (P.L. 100-203), as corrected by section 411(l)(1)(A)(i) and (ii), and (l)(2) of the Medicare Catastrophic Coverage Act of 1988 (P.L. 100-360) and by section 608(d)(27)(C) and (D) of the Family Support Act of 1988 (P.L. 100-485). Consult the statute for specified effective dates regarding other sanctions, too, especially with regard to obligations of nursing facilities and home health agencies.

Enforcement procedures for section 1819(b)(3)(B)(ii) are governed by section 1128A of the Act, 42 U.S.C.A. 1320a-7a, which authorizes civil money penalties for a variety of offenses.

Statutory Provisions

Section 1819(a), 42 U.S.C.A. 1395i-3, defines skilled nursing facility for Medicare purposes as follows:

> SKILLED NURSING FACILITY DEFINED. — In this title, the term "skilled nursing facility" means an institution (or a distinct part of an institution) which —
>
> (1) is primarily engaged in providing to residents —
>
> (A) skilled nursing care and related services for residents who require medical or nursing care, or
>
> (B) rehabilitation services for the rehabilitation of injured, disabled, or sick persons, and is not primarily for the care and treatment of mental diseases;
>
> (2) has in effect a transfer agreement (meeting the requirements of section 1861(l) [42 U.S.C.A. 1395x(l), which pertains to transfer agreements]) with one or more hospitals having agreements in effect under section 1866 [which pertains to provider agreements]; and
>
> (3) meets the requirements for a skilled nursing facility described in subsections (b) [which pertains to provision of services], (c) [which pertains to residents' rights], and (d) [which pertains to administration of a facility] of this section.

Section 1819(b), 42 U.S.C.A. 1395i-3(b), explains resident assessment as follows:

> (3) RESIDENTS' ASSESSMENT. —

(A) REQUIREMENT. — A skilled nursing facility must conduct a comprehensive, accurate, standardized, reproducible assessment of each resident's functional capacity, which assessment-

(i) describes the resident's capability to perform daily life functions and significant impairments in functional capacity;

(ii) is based on a uniform minimum data set specified by the Secretary under subsection (f)(6)(A) [which required the Secretary to specify a minimum data set of core elements and common definitions for use by nursing facilities not later than January 1, 1989, and to designate not later than April 1, 1990, one or more instruments for States to specify for use by nursing facilities to comply with section 1819(b)(3)(A)(iii)];

(iii) uses an instrument which is specified by the State under subsection (e)(5) [which obligates States to specify their resident assessment instrument effective July 1, 1990]; and

(iv) includes the identification of medical problems.

(B) CERTIFICATION. —

(i) IN GENERAL. — Each such assessment must be conducted or coordinated (with the appropriate participation of health professionals) by a registered professional nurse who signs and certifies the completion of the assessment. Each individual who completes a portion of such an assessment shall sign and certify as to the accuracy of that portion of the assessment.

Where certified assessments are required, opportunity for falsification may arise. Accordingly, section 1819(b)(3)(B)(ii) provides:

PENALTY FOR FALSIFICATION. —

(I) An individual who willfully and knowingly certifies under clause (i) a material and false statement in a resident assessment is subject to a civil money penalty of not more than $1,000 with respect to each assessment.

(II) An individual who willfully and knowingly causes another individual to certify under clause (i) a material and false statement in a resident assessment is subject to a civil money penalty of not more than $5,000 with respect to each assessment.

(III) The provisions of section 1128A [42 U.S.C.A. 1320a-7a] (other than subsections (a) and (b)) shall apply to a civil money penalty under this clause in the same manner as such provisions apply to a penalty or proceeding under section 1128A(a).

In addition, section 1819(b)(3)(B)(iii), 42 U.S.C.A. 1395i-3(b)(3)(B)(iii), provides:

USE OF INDEPENDENT ASSESSORS. — If a State determines, under a survey under subsection (g) [which details the nursing facility survey and certification process] or otherwise, that there has been a knowing and willful certification of false assessments under this paragraph, the State may require (for a period specified by the State) that resident assessments under this paragraph be conducted and certified by individuals who are independent of the facility and who are approved by the State.

With regard to frequency, use, and coordination of residents' assessments, section 1819(b)(3) provides in pertinent part:

(C) FREQUENCY. —

(i) IN GENERAL. — Subject to the time frames prescribed by the Secretary under section 1888(e)(6) [42 U.S.C.A. 1395yy(e)(6), which pertains to the obligations of nursing facilities to submit resident assessment data to the Secretary for purposes of establishing Medicare payment rates], such an assessment must be conducted —

(I) promptly upon (but 14 days after the date of) admission for each individual admitted on or after October 1, 1990, and by not later than January 1, 1991, for each resident of the facility on that date;

NOTE: Prior to amendment by section 110(b) of the Social Security Act Amendments of 1994, P.L. 103-432, effective October 31, 1994, the preceding parenthetical phrase read "but not later 14 days after the date of". Before that, "not later than 14 days" read "no later than 4 days". That was changed retroactive to December 22, 1987, by section 4008 (h)(2) of P.L. 101-508 , the Omnibus Budget Reconciliation Act of 1990 (OBRA 90). In addition, section 4432(b)(5)(A) of the Balanced Budget Act of 1997, P.L. 105–33, added the introductory phrase beginning "Subject to the time frames", effective for items and services furnished after July 1, 1998.;

(II) promptly after a significant change in the resident's physical or mental condition;

(III) in no case less often than once every 12 months.

(ii) RESIDENT REVIEW. — The skilled nursing facility must examine each resident no less frequently than once every 3 months and, as appropriate, revise the resident's assessment to assure the continuing accuracy of the assessment.

(D) USE. — The results of such an assessment shall be used in developing, reviewing, and revising the resident's plan of care under paragraph (2) [which obligates SNF's to describe in writing the scope of services and activities a resident requires].

(E) COORDINATION. — Such assessments shall be coordinated with any State-required preadmission screening program to the maximum extent practicable in order to avoid duplicative testing and effort.

For regulatory citations, see Chapter 6

§ 2:2 ABUSE OR NEGLECT OF SKILLED NURSING FACILITY RESIDENTS OR MISAPPROPRIATION OF THEIR PROPERTY — Section 1819(g)(1)(C) [42 U.S.C.A. 1395i-3(g)(1)(C)]

Summary

Section 1819, 42 U.S.C.A. 1395i-3, sets forth comprehensive requirements for skilled nursing facilities (SNF's) participating in Medicare. These requirements pertain to provision of services (subsection (b)), to residents' rights (subsection (c)), and to administration of nursing facilities (subsection (d)). In addition, there are Federally mandated State requirements which pertain to nursing facilities (subsection (e)), such as nurse aide training and competency evaluation and State appeals processes for resident transfers and discharges. Section 1819 also details responsibilities of the Secretary of Health and Human Services which pertain to nursing facility requirements (subsection (f)), elaborate requirements for survey and certification (subsection (g)), and specific enforcement requirements (subsection (h)). Some of these requirements come with Federal sanctions for noncompliance.

◆ NOTE: Parallel provisions regarding Medicaid obligations of nursing facilities are found in Section 1919 of the Social Security Act, 42 U.S.C.A. 1396r.

According to section 1819(g), 42 U.S.C.A. 1395i-3(g), States are responsible for surveying and certifying skilled nursing facilities for compliance with the requirements of subsections (b), (c), and (d). Most States have designated their respective health departments as the State agency for SNF survey and certification. To avoid conflicts of interest, however, the Secretary, through the Administrator of the Health Care Financing Agency, surveys State-owned SNF's.

Section 1819(g)(1)(C) requires State survey and certification agencies to provide for receipt and timely review and investigation of allegations of neglect, abuse, and misappropriation of property of a SNF resident by a nurse aide or by another individual used by a SNF to provide services to a resident. If, after notice and opportunity for a hearing, the State finds that a nurse aide has neglected or abused a resident or misappropriated a resident's property in a facility, the State must notify the nurse aide and the registry of nurse aides of such finding. (States were required to establish a registry of nurse aides by January 1, 1989.) If the State finds that any other individual has committed such offenses, the State must notify the appropriate licensure authority. But a State is not to make a finding of neglect by an individual if the individual demonstrates that the neglect was caused by factors beyond his or her control.

Furthermore, effective August 5, 1997, pursuant to section 4755(a) of the Balanced Budget Act of 1997, P.L. 105–33, States must establish a procedure to permit a nurse aide to petition for removal of his or her name from the registry. Such removal is possible if the employment and personal history of the nurse aide does not reflect a pattern of abusive behavior or neglect, and if the neglect involved in the original finding was a singular occurrence. Removal may not occur, however, prior to the expiration of a one-year period beginning the date on which the petitioner's name was placed in the registry.

◆ NOTE: According to section 1819(g)(1)(E), 42 U.S.C.A. 1395i-3(g)(1)(E), the failure of the Secretary to issue regulations to carry out subsection (g) does not relieve a State of its responsibility. Furthermore, in general, section 1819 is effective October 1, 1990. See section 4201(a)(3) of the Omnibus Budget Reconciliation Act of 1987 (P.L. 100-203), as corrected by section 411(l)(1)(A)(i) and (ii), and (l)(2) of the Medicare Catastrophic Coverage Act of 1988 (P.L. 100-360) and by section 608(d)(27)(C) and (D) of the Family Support Act of 1988 (P.L. 100-485). Consult the statute for specified effective dates regarding other sanctions, too, especially with regard to obligations of nursing facilities and home health agencies.

Statutory Provisions

Section 1819(g)(1)(C), 42 U.S.C.A. 1395i-3(g)(1)(C), provides:

> (C) INVESTIGATION OF ALLEGATIONS OF RESIDENT NEGLECT AND ABUSE AND MISAPPROPRIATION OF RESIDENT PROPERTY. — The State shall provide, through the agency responsible for surveys and certification of nursing facilities under this subsection, for a process for the receipt and timely review and investigation of allegations of neglect and abuse and misappropriation of resident property by a nurse aide of a resident in a nursing facility or by another individual used by the facility in providing services to such a resident. The State shall, after providing the individual involved with a written notice of the allegations (including a statement of the availability of a hearing for the individual to rebut the allegations) and the opportunity for a hearing on the record, make a written finding as to the accuracy of the allegations. [Prior to amendment by section 106(c)(4)(B) of the Social Security Amendments of 1994, P.L. 103-432, effective January 1, 1995, the preceding sentence read: "The State shall, after notice to the individual involved and a reasonable opportunity for a hearing for the individual to rebut allegations, make a finding as to the accuracy of the allegations."] If the State finds that a nurse aide has neglected or abused a resident or misappropriated resident property in a facility, the State shall notify the nurse aide and the registry of such finding. If the State finds that any other individual used by the facility has neglected or abused a resident or misappropriated resident property in a facility, the State shall notify the appropriate licensure authority. A State shall not make a finding that an individual has neglected a resident if the individual demonstrates that such neglect was caused by

factors beyond the control of the individual. [The last sentence was added by section 4008(h)(2)(L) of P.L. 101-508, the Omnibus Budget Reconciliation Act of 1990, effective retroactively to December 22, 1987.]

(D) REMOVAL OF NAME FROM NURSE AIDE REGISTRY.—

(I) IN GENERAL. —In the case of a finding of neglect under subparagraph (C), the State shall establish a procedure to permit a nurse aide to petition the State to have his or her name removed from the registry upon a determination by the State that—

(I) the employment and personal history of the nurse aide does not reflect a pattern of abusive behavior or neglect; and

(II) the neglect involved in the original finding was a singular occurrence.

(II) TIMING OF DETERMINATION.—In no case shall a determination on a petition submitted under clause (I) be made prior to the expiration of the 1-year period beginning on the date on which the name of the petitioner was added to the registry under subparagraph (C).

(E) CONSTRUCTION. — The failure of the Secretary to issue regulations to carry out this subsection shall not relieve a State of its responsibility under this subsection.

For regulatory citations, see Chapter 6

§ 2:3 GIVING A SKILLED NURSING FACILITY ADVANCE NOTICE OF A STATE OR FEDERAL SURVEY— Section 1819(g)(2) [42 U.S.C.A. 1395i-3(g)(2)]

Summary

Section 1819, 42 U.S.C.A. 1395i-3, sets forth comprehensive requirements for skilled nursing facilities (SNF's) participating in Medicare. These requirements pertain to provision of services (subsection (b)), to residents' rights (subsection (c)), and to administration of nursing facilities (subsection (d)). In addition, there are Federally mandated State requirements which pertain to nursing facilities (subsection (e)), such as nurse aide training and competency evaluation and State appeals processes for resident transfers and discharges. Section 1819 also details responsibilities of the Secretary of Health and Human Services which pertain to nursing facility requirements (subsection (f)), elaborate requirements for survey and certification (subsection (g)), and specific enforcement requirements (subsection (h)). Some of these requirements come with Federal sanctions for noncompliance.

◆ NOTE: Parallel provisions regarding Medicaid obligations of nursing facilities are found in Section 1919 of the Act, 42 U.S.C.A. 1396r.

According to section 1819(g), 42 U.S.C.A. 1395i-3(g), States are responsible for surveying and certifying skilled nursing facilities for compliance with the requirements of subsections (b), (c), and (d). Most States have designated their respective health departments as the State agency for survey and certification of SNF's. To avoid conflicts of interest, however, the Secretary, through the Administrator of the Health Care Financing Agency, surveys State-owned SNF's.

Pursuant to section 1819(g)(2), any individual who notifies a SNF, or causes it to be notified, of the time or date on which it will be surveyed by a State or by the Federal government is subject to a civil money penalty not to exceed $2,000.

◆ NOTE: In general, section 1819 is effective October 1, 1990. See section 4201(a)(3) of the Omnibus Budget Reconciliation Act of 1987 (P.L. 100-203), as corrected by section 411(l)(1)(A)(i) and (ii), and (l)(2) of the Medicare Catastrophic Coverage Act of 1988 (P.L. 100-360) and by section 608(d)(27)(C) and (D) of the Family Support Act of 1988 (P.L. 100-485). Consult the statute for specified effective dates regarding other sanctions, too, especially with regard to obligations of nursing facilities and home health agencies.

Enforcement procedures for section 1819(g)(2) are governed by section 1128A of the Act, 42 U.S.C.A. 1320a-7a, which authorizes civil money penalties for a variety of offenses.

Statutory Provisions

Section 1819(g)(2), 42 U.S.C.A. 1395i-3(g)(2) provides:

SURVEYS. —

(A) STANDARD SURVEY. —

(i) IN GENERAL. — Each skilled nursing facility shall be subject to a standard survey, to be conducted without any prior notice to the facility. Any individual who notifies (or causes to be notified) a skilled nursing facility of the time or date on which such a survey is scheduled to be conducted is subject to a civil money penalty of not to exceed $2,000. The provisions of section 1128A [42 U.S.C.A. 1320a-7a] (other than subsections (a) and (b)) shall apply to a civil money penalty under the previous sentence in the same manner as such provisions apply to a penalty or proceeding under Section 1128A(a). The Secretary shall review each State's procedures for the scheduling and conduct of standard surveys to assure that the State has taken all reasonable steps to avoid giving notice of such a survey through the scheduling procedures and the conduct of the surveys themselves.

For regulatory citations, see Chapter 6

§ 2:4 FAILING A SKILLED NURSING FACILITY SURVEY — Sections 1819(g) and (h) [42 U.S.C.A. 1395i-3(g) and (h)]

Summary

Section 1819, 42 U.S.C.A. 1395i-3, sets forth comprehensive requirements for skilled nursing facilities (SNF's) participating in Medicare. These requirements pertain to provision of services (subsection (b)), to residents' rights (subsection (c)), and to administration of nursing facilities (subsection (d)). In addition, there are Federally mandated State requirements which pertain to nursing facilities (subsection (e)), such as nurse aide training and competency evaluation and State appeals processes for resident transfers and discharges. Section 1819 also details responsibilities of the Secretary of Health and Human Services which pertain to nursing facility requirements (subsection (f)), elaborate requirements for survey and certification (subsection (g)), and specific enforcement requirements (subsection (h)). Some of these requirements come with Federal sanctions for noncompliance.

◆ NOTE: Parallel provisions regarding Medicaid obligations of nursing facilities are found in Section 1919 of the Act, 42 U.S.C.A. 1396r.

According to section 1819(g)(1), 42 U.S.C.A. 1395i-3(g)(1), States are responsible for surveying and certifying skilled nursing facilities (SNF's) for compliance with the requirements of subsections (b), (c), and (d). Most States have designated their respective health departments as the State agency for survey and certification of SNF's. To avoid conflicts of interest, however, the Secretary, through the Administrator of the Health Care Financing Agency, surveys State-owned SNF's. Moreover, in some situations, the Secretary may conduct his own survey of SNF's which are not State-owned.

Section 1819(g)(2)(A)(ii) requires SNF surveys to be of a case-mix stratified sample of residents and to include a quality of care assessment measured by indicators of medical, nursing, and rehabilitative care, dietary and nutrition services, activities and social participation, sanitation, infection control, and the physical environment. They also must include review of written plans of care, an audit of residents' assessments, and a review of compliance with the residents' rights provisions of the statute.

◆ NOTE: Congress obligated the Secretary to develop protocols for SNF surveys by January 1, 1990; but Congress also stated that failure to do so does not relieve a State of responsibility to conduct surveys. Nor does it relieve SNF's from meeting statutory and regulatory conditions of participation. See section 1819(g)(2)(C).

If a SNF fails to comply with applicable law and regulations, one sanction is public disclosure of the results of its survey. See section 1819(g)(5). States and the Secretary must make information respecting all surveys and certifications of SNF's, including statements of deficiencies and plans of correction, available to the public, to the State long-term care ombudsman, to physicians attending residents, to State SNF administrator licensing boards, and to State Medicaid fraud and abuse control units.

◆ NOTE: Pursuant to section 4008(h)(2)(M) of P.L. 101-508, the Omnibus Budget Reconciliation Act of 1990 (OBRA 90), this disclosure must be made within 14 days after such information is made available to those facilities. Moreover, it now applies not as before to plans of correction, but to "approved" plans of correction. These changes are effective retroactively to enactment of OBRA 87, which was December 22, 1987.

Pursuant to section 1819(h), if a State finds that a SNF no longer meets a requirement respecting the provision of services, residents' rights, or administration of the facility, and further finds that the facility's deficiencies cause immediate jeopardy to its residents, the State must recommend that the Secretary either appoint temporary management of the facility, pending closure or improvements, or terminate the facility's provider agreement.

If a State finds deficiencies but no immediate jeopardy to residents, the Secretary may deny payment with respect to all individuals admitted to the facility after the effective date of the finding. He also may impose a civil money penalty not to exceed $10,000 for each day of noncompliance, or appoint a temporary manager pending closure or improvement.

If the State survey agency finds it appropriate, the Secretary may continue payments for not longer than six months to a SNF pending remedy of the deficiencies. In cases of repeated noncompliance, however, the Secretary must deny payments to individuals admitted after the effective date of the finding and monitor the facility until the SNF demonstrates that it has come into compliance.

If the Secretary, as opposed to the State, finds noncompliance with requirements pertaining to provision of services, residents' rights, or administration of the facility, and also finds immediate jeopardy as a result thereof, the Secretary must appoint a temporary manager of the SNF or proceed to terminate the SNF's provider agreement.

Pursuant to section 4008(h)(2)(N) of OBRA 90, State long term care ombudsmen are to be informed of such adverse actions. This change, too, is effective retroactively as if it had been included in OBRA 87.

◆ NOTE: In general, section 1819 is effective October 1, 1990. See section 4201(a)(3) of the Omnibus Budget Reconciliation Act of 1987 (P.L. 100-203), as corrected by section 411(l)(1)(A)(i) and (ii), and (l)(2) of the Medicare Catastrophic Coverage Act of 1988 (P.L. 100-360) and by section 608(d)(27)(C) and (D) of the Family Support Act of 1988 (P.L. 100-485). Consult the statute for specified effective dates regarding other sanctions, too, especially with regard to obligations of nursing facilities and home health agencies.

Finally, enforcement procedures for the civil money penalty authorized by section 1819(h)(2)(B)(ii) are governed by section

1128A of the Social Security Act, 42 U.S.C.A. 1320a-7a, which authorizes civil money penalties for a variety of offenses.

Statutory Provisions

Section 1819(f), 42 U.S.C.A. 1395i-3(f), provides:

RESPONSIBILITIES OF SECRETARY RELATING TO SKILLED NURSING FACILITY REQUIREMENTS. —

(1) GENERAL RESPONSIBILITY. — It is the duty and responsibility of the Secretary to assure that requirements which govern the provision of care in skilled nursing facilities under this title, and the enforcement of such requirements, are adequate to protect the health, safety, welfare, and rights of residents and to promote the effective and efficient use of public moneys.

Section 1819(g), 42 U.S.C.A. 1395i-3(g), provides:

SURVEY AND CERTIFICATION PROCESS. —

(1) STATE AND FEDERAL RESPONSIBILITY. —

(A) IN GENERAL. — Pursuant to an agreement under section 1864 [42 U.S.C.A. 1395aa] , each State shall be responsible for certifying, in accordance with surveys conducted under paragraph (2), the compliance of skilled nursing facilities (other than facilities of the State) with the requirements of subsections (b) [which pertains to provision of services], (c) [which pertains to residents' rights], and (d) [which pertains to administration of a facility]. The Secretary shall be responsible for certifying, in accordance with surveys conducted under paragraph (2), the compliance of State skilled nursing facilities with the requirements of such subsections.

(B) EDUCATIONAL PROGRAM. — Each State shall conduct periodic educational programs for the staff and residents (and their representatives) of skilled nursing facilities in order to present current regulations, procedures, and policies under this section.

Section 1819(g)(2), 42 U.S.C.A. 1895i-3(g), provides:

SURVEYS. —

(A) STANDARD SURVEY. —

* * *

(ii) CONTENTS. — Each standard survey shall include, for a case-mix stratified sample of residents —

(I) a survey of the quality of care furnished, as measured by indicators of medical, nursing, and rehabilitative care, dietary and nutrition services, activities and social participation, and sanitation, infection control, and the physical environment.

(II) written plans of care provided under subsection (b)(2) and an audit of the residents' assessments under subsection (b)(3) to determine the accuracy of such assessments and the adequacy of such plans of care, and

(III) a review of compliance with residents' rights under subsection (c).

Regarding survey frequency, section 1819(g)(2)(A)(iii), 42 U.S.C.A. 1395i-3(g)(2)(A), provides:

(iii) FREQUENCY. —

(I) IN GENERAL. — Each skilled nursing facility shall be subject to a standard survey not later than 15 months after the date of the previous standard survey conducted under this subparagraph. The Statewide average interval between standard surveys of skilled nursing facilities under this subsection shall not exceed 12 months.

(II) SPECIAL SURVEYS. — If not otherwise conducted under subclause (I), a standard survey (or an abbreviated standard survey) may be conducted within 2 months of any change of ownership, administration, management of a skilled nursing facility, or the director of nursing in order to determine whether the change has resulted in any decline in the quality of care furnished in the facility.

Section 1819(g)(2)(B), 42 U.S.C.A. 1395i-3(g)(2)(B), provides that an extended survey must be conducted of SNF's which are found under a standard survey to have provided substandard quality of care. At the discretion of the Secretary or the State, other facilities may also be subject to an extended survey. The statute states:

EXTENDED SURVEYS. —

(i) IN GENERAL. — Each skilled nursing facility which is found, under a standard survey, to have provided substandard quality of care shall be subject to an extended survey. Any other facility may, at the Secretary's or State's discretion, be subject to such an extended survey (or a partial extended survey).

(ii) TIMING. — The extended survey shall be conducted immediately after the standard survey (or, if not practical, not later than 2 weeks after the date of completion of the standard survey).

(iii) CONTENTS. — In such an extended survey, the survey team shall review and identify the policies and procedures which produced such substandard quality of care and shall determine whether the facility has complied with all the requirements described in subsections (b), (c), and (d). Such review shall include an expansion of the size of the sample of residents' assessments reviewed and a review of the staffing, of in-service training, and, if appropriate, of contracts with consultants.

(iv) CONSTRUCTION. — Nothing in this paragraph shall be construed as requiring an extended or partial extended survey as a prerequisite to imposing a sanction against a facility under subsection (h) [which pertains to enforcement] on the basis of findings in a standard survey.

The statute goes on to provide at section 1819(g)(2)(C), 42 U.S.C.A. 1395i-3(g)(2)(C):

SURVEY PROTOCOL. — Standard and extended surveys shall be conducted —

(i) based upon a protocol which the Secretary has developed, tested, and validated by not later than January 1, 1990, and

(ii) by individuals, of a survey team, who meet such minimum qualifications as the Secretary establishes by not later than such date.

The failure of the Secretary to develop, test, or validate such protocols or to establish such minimum qualifications shall not relieve any State of its responsibility (or the Secretary of the Secretary's responsibility) to conduct surveys under this subsection.

Section 1819(g)(2)(D), 42 U.S.C.A. 1395i-3(g)(2)(D), provides:

> CONSISTENCY OF SURVEYS. — Each State and the Secretary shall implement programs to measure and reduce inconsistency in the application of survey results among surveyors.

Then, section 1819(g)(2)(E), 42 U.S.C.A. 1395i-3(g)(2)(E), provides as follows regarding survey teams:

> SURVEY TEAMS. —
>
> (i) IN GENERAL. — Surveys under this subsection shall be conducted by a multidisciplinary team of professionals (including a registered professional nurse).
>
> (ii) PROHIBITION OF CONFLICT OF INTEREST. — A State may not use as a member of a survey team under this subsection an individual who is serving (or has served within the previous 2 years) as a member of the staff of, or as a consultant to, the facility surveyed respecting compliance with the requirements of subsections (b), (c), and (d), or who has a personal or familial financial interest in the facility being surveyed.
>
> (iii) TRAINING. — The Secretary shall provide for the comprehensive training of State and Federal surveyors in the conduct of standard and extended surveys under this subsection, including the auditing of resident assessments and plans of care. No individual shall serve as a member of a survey team unless the individual has successfully completed a training and testing program in survey and certification techniques that has been approved by the Secretary.

In addition to standard annual surveys and extended surveys, the statute also provides for validation surveys. These are to be conducted by the Secretary. According to section 1819(g)(3), 42 U.S.C.A. 1395i-3(g)(3):

> (A) IN GENERAL. — The Secretary shall conduct onsite surveys of a representative sample of skilled nursing facilities in each State, within 2 months of the date of surveys conducted under paragraph (2) by the State, in a sufficient number to allow inferences about the adequacies of each State's surveys conducted under paragraph (2). In conducting such surveys, the Secretary shall use the same survey protocols as the State is

required to use under paragraph (2). If the State has determined that an individual skilled nursing facility meets the requirements of subsections (b) [which pertains to provision of services], (c) [which pertains to residents' rights], and (d) [which pertains to administration of a facility], but the Secretary determines that the facility does not meet such requirements, the Secretary's determination as to the facility's noncompliance with such requirements is binding and supersedes that of the State survey.

(B) SCOPE. — With respect to each State, the Secretary shall conduct surveys under subparagraph (A) each year with respect to at least 5 percent of the number of skilled nursing facilities surveyed by the State in the year, but in no case less than 5 skilled nursing facilities in the State.

(C) REMEDIES FOR SUBSTANDARD PERFORMANCE. — If the Secretary finds, on the basis of such surveys, that a State has failed to perform surveys as required under paragraph (2) or that a State's survey and certification performance otherwise is not adequate, the Secretary shall provide for an appropriate remedy, which may include the training of survey teams in the State.

Finally, in addition to standard annual surveys, extended surveys, and validation surveys, the statute provides for special surveys of compliance. Section 1819(g)(3)(D), 42 U.S.C.A. 1395i-3(g)(3)(D), provides:

SPECIAL SURVEYS OF COMPLIANCE. — Where the Secretary has reason to question the compliance of a skilled nursing facility with any of the requirements of subsections (b), (c), and (d), the Secretary may conduct a survey of the facility and, on the basis of that survey, make independent and binding determinations concerning the extent to which the skilled nursing facility meets such requirements.

Most of the time, investigations of SNF's and responsibility for monitoring their compliance with the law begins and ends with the States. Section 1819(g)(4), 42 U.S.C.A. 1395i-3(g)(4), spells out those State responsibilities as follows:

INVESTIGATION OF COMPLAINTS AND MONITORING COMPLIANCE. — Each State shall maintain procedures and adequate staff to —

(A) investigate complaints of violations of requirements by skilled nursing facilities, and

(B) monitor, on-site, on a regular, as needed basis, a skilled nursing facility's compliance with the requirements of subsections (b), (c), and (d), if —

(i) the facility has been found not to be in compliance with such requirements and is in the process of correcting deficiencies to achieve such compliance;

(ii) the facility was previously found not to be in compliance with such requirements, has corrected deficiencies to achieve such compliance, and verification of continued compliance is indicated; or

(iii) the State has reason to question the compliance of the facility with such requirements. A State may maintain and utilize a specialized team (including an attorney, an auditor, and appropriate health care professionals) for the purpose of identifying, surveying, gathering and preserving evidence, and carrying out appropriate enforcement actions against substandard skilled nursing facilities.

Having set forth preliminary information about the SNF survey and certification process, what sanctions apply for noncompliance by SNF's with the statutory and regulatory conditions of participation?

One sanction is public disclosure of the results of inspections and activities. Section 1819(g)(5), 42 U.S.C.A. 1395i-3(g)(5), provides as follows for notice to the public, to the State long-term care ombudsman, to physicians attending residents, to State SNF administrator licensing boards, and to State Medicaid fraud and abuse control units.

DISCLOSURE OF RESULTS OF INSPECTIONS AND ACTIVITIES. —

(A) PUBLIC INFORMATION. — Each State, and the Secretary, shall make available to the public —

(i) information respecting all surveys and certifications made respecting skilled nursing facilities, including statements of deficiencies, within 14 calendar days after such information is made available to those facilities, and approved plans of correction [the phrase beginning "within 14 days" and the adjective "approved" were added by section 4008(h)(2)(M) of OBRA 90, effective retroactively as if included in OBRA 87, which was enacted December 22, 1987],

(ii) copies of cost reports of such facilities filed under this title or title XIX,

(iii) copies of statements of ownership under section 1124 [42 U.S.C.A. 1320a-3, which pertains to requirements for disclosure of ownership details and related information by various participants in Medicare, Medicaid, and the Maternal and Child Health grant programs (for the latter, see Title V of the Social Security Act, 42 U.S.C.A. 701)], and

(iv) information disclosed under section 1126 [42 U.S.C.A. 1320a-5, which pertains to requirements for disclosure by institutions, organizations, and agencies of owners and certain other individuals who have been convicted of certain offenses].

(B) NOTICE TO OMBUDSMAN. — Each State shall notify the State long-term care ombudsman (established under section 307(a)(12) of the Older Americans Act of 1965 [42 U.S.C.A. 3027(a)(12)]) of the State's findings of noncompliance with any of the requirements of subsections (b), (c), and (d), or of any adverse action taken against a skilled nursing facility under paragraphs (1), (2), or (4) of subsection (h), with respect to a skilled nursing facility in the State. [the phrase beginning "or of any adverse action" was added by section 4008(h)(2)(N) of OBRA 90, effective retroactively to December 22, 1987]. Also, pursuant to section 106(d)(5) of the Social Security Act Amendments of 1994, P.L. 103-432, the word "paragraphs" was changed to "paragraph", effective as if included in OBRA 87, P.L. 100-203.]

(C) NOTICE TO PHYSICIANS AND SKILLED NURSING FACILITY ADMINISTRATOR LICENSING BOARD. — If a State finds that a skilled nursing facility has provided substandard quality of care, the State shall notify —

(i) the attending physician of each resident with respect to which such finding is made, and

(ii) the State board responsible for the licensing of the skilled nursing facility administrator at the facility.

(D) ACCESS TO FRAUD CONTROL UNITS. — Each State shall provide its State medicaid fraud and abuse control unit (established under section 1903(q) [42 U.S.C.A. 1396b]) with access to all information of the State agency responsible for surveys and certifications under this subsection..

In addition to public disclosure, section 1819(h), 42 U.S.C.A. 1395i-3(h), provides as follows for an enforcement process.

ENFORCEMENT PROCESS. —

(1) IN GENERAL. — If a State finds, on the basis of a standard, extended, or partial extended survey under subsection (g)(2) or otherwise, that a skilled nursing facility no longer meets a requirement of subsection (b) [which pertains to provision of services], (c) [which pertains to residents' rights], or (d) [which pertains to administration of a facility], and further finds that the facility's deficiencies-

(A) immediately jeopardize the health or safety of its residents, the State shall recommend to the Secretary that the Secretary take such action as described in paragraph (2)(A)(i); or

(B) do not immediately jeopardize the health or safety of its residents, the State may recommend to the Secretary that the Secretary take such action as described in paragraph (2)(A)(ii). If a State finds that a skilled nursing facility meets the requirements of subsections (b), (c), and (d), but, as of a previous period, did not meet such requirements, the State may recommend a civil money penalty under paragraph (2)(B)(ii) for the days in which it finds that the facility was not in compliance with such requirements.

(2) SECRETARIAL AUTHORITY. —

(A) IN GENERAL. — With respect to any skilled nursing facility in a State, if the Secretary finds, or pursuant to a recommendation of the State under paragraph (1) finds, that a skilled nursing facility no longer meets a requirement of subsection (b), (c), (d), or (e) [which pertains to Federally mandated State requirements for nurse aide training and competency evaluation, the nurse aide registry, State appeals processes for resident discharges and transfers, standards for nursing facility administrators, and the resident assessment instrument], and further finds that the facility's deficiencies —

(i) immediately jeopardize the health or safety of its residents, the Secretary shall take immediate action to remove the jeopardy and correct the deficiencies through the remedy specified in subparagraph (B)(iii), or terminate the facility's participation under this title and may provide, in addition, for one or more of the other remedies described in subparagraph (B); or

(ii) do not immediately jeopardize the health or safety of its residents, the Secretary may impose any of the remedies described in subparagraph (B). Nothing in this subparagraph shall be construed as restricting the remedies available to the Secretary to remedy a skilled nursing facility's deficiencies. If the Secretary finds, or pursuant to the recommendation of the State under paragraph (1) finds, that a skilled nursing facility meets such requirements but, as of a previous period, did not meet such requirements, the Secretary may provide for a civil money penalty under subparagraph (B)(ii) for the days on which he finds that the facility was not in compliance with such requirements.

(B) SPECIFIED REMEDIES. — The Secretary may take the following actions with respect to a finding that a facility has not met an applicable requirement:

(i) DENIAL OF PAYMENT. — The Secretary may deny any further payments under this title with respect to all individuals entitled to benefits under this title in the facility or with respect to such individuals admitted to the facility after the effective date of the finding.

(ii) AUTHORITY WITH RESPECT TO CIVIL MONEY PENALTIES. — The Secretary may impose a civil money penalty in an amount not to exceed $10,000 for each day of noncompliance. The provisions of section 1128A [42 U.S.C.A. 1320a-7a] (other than subsections (a) and (b)) shall apply to a civil money penalty under the previous sentence in the same manner as such provisions apply to a penalty or proceeding under section 1128A(a).

(iii) APPOINTMENT OF TEMPORARY MANAGEMENT. — In consultation with the State, the Secretary may appoint temporary management to oversee the operation of the facility and to assure the health and safety of the facility's residents, where there is a need for temporary management while —

(I) there is an orderly closure of the facility, or

(II) improvements are made in order to bring the facility into compliance with all the requirements of subsections (b), (c), and (d). The temporary management under this clause shall not be terminated under subclause (II) until the Secretary has determined that the facility has the management capability to ensure continued compliance with all the requirements of subsections (b), (c), and (d). The Secretary shall specify criteria, as to when and how each of such remedies is to be applied, the amounts of any fines, and the severity of each of these remedies, to be used in the imposition of such remedies. Such criteria shall be designed so as to minimize the time between the identification of violations and final imposition of the remedies and shall provide for the imposition of incrementally more severe fines for repeated or uncorrected deficiencies. In addition, the Secretary may provide for other specified remedies, such as directed plans of correction.

(C) CONTINUATION OF PAYMENTS PENDING REMEDIATION. — The Secretary may continue payments, over a period of not longer than 6 months after the date of the findings [Section 6901(d)(4)(D) of P.L. 101-239, the Omnibus Budget Reconciliation Act of 1989, enacted December 19, 1989, added "after the date of the findings", effective December 22, 1987, as though it had been part of P.L. 100-203, the Omnibus Budget Reconciliation Act of 1987], under this title with respect to a skilled nursing facility not in compliance with a requirement of subsection (b), (c), or (d), if —

(i) the State survey agency finds that it is more appropriate to take alternative action to assure compliance of the facility with the requirements than to terminate the certification of the facility,

(ii) the State has submitted a plan and timetable for corrective action to the Secretary for approval and the Secretary approves the plan of corrective action, and

(iii) the facility agrees to repay to the Federal Government payments received under this subparagraph if the corrective action is not taken in accordance with the approved plan and timetable. The Secretary shall establish guidelines for approval of corrective actions requested by States under this subparagraph.

(D) ASSURING PROMPT COMPLIANCE. — If a skilled nursing facility has not complied with any of the requirements of subsections (b), (c), and (d), within 3 months after the date the facility is found to be out of compliance with such requirements, the Secretary shall impose the remedy described in subparagraph (B)(i) [which is denial of payment] for all individuals who are admitted to the facility after such date.

(E) REPEATED NONCOMPLIANCE. — In the case of a skilled nursing facility which, on 3 consecutive standard surveys conducted under subsection (g)(2), has been found to have provided substandard quality of care, the Secretary shall (regardless of what other remedies are provided) —

(i) impose the remedy described in subparagraph (B)(i) [which is denial of payment], and

(ii) monitor the facility under subsection (g)(4)(B) [which pertains to the obligation of States to investigate complaints and monitor compliance], until the facility has demonstrated, to the satisfaction of the Secretary, that it is in compliance with the requirements of subsections (b), (c), and (d), and that it will remain in compliance with such requirements.

(3) EFFECTIVE PERIOD OF DENIAL OF PAYMENT. — A finding to deny payment under this subsection shall terminate when the Secretary finds that the facility is in substantial compliance with all the requirements of subsections (b), (c), and (d).

(4) IMMEDIATE TERMINATION OF PARTICIPATION FOR FACILITY WHERE SECRETARY FINDS NONCOMPLIANCE AND IMMEDIATE JEOPARDY. — If the Secretary

finds that a skilled nursing facility has not met a requirement of subsection (b), (c), or (d), and finds that the failure immediately jeopardizes the health or safety of its residents, the Secretary shall take immediate action to remove the jeopardy and correct the deficiencies through the remedy specified in paragraph (2)(B)(iii) [which is appointment of temporary management], or the Secretary shall terminate the facility's participation under this title. If the facility's participation under this title is terminated, the State shall provide for the safe and orderly transfer of the residents eligible under this title consistent with the requirements of subsection (c)(2) [which pertains to residents' transfer and discharge rights].

(5) CONSTRUCTION. — The remedies provided under this subsection are in addition to those otherwise available under State or Federal law and shall not be construed as limiting such other remedies, including any remedy available to an individual at common law. The remedies described in clauses (i) and (iii) of paragraph (2)(B) [which are denial of payment and appointment of temporary management] may be imposed during the pendency of any hearing.

(6) SHARING OF INFORMATION. — Notwithstanding any other provision of law, all information concerning skilled nursing facilities required by this section to be filed with the Secretary or a State agency shall be made available by such facilities to Federal or State employees for purposes consistent with the effective administration of programs established under this title and title XIX, including investigations by State medicaid fraud control units.

Finally, section 1819(i), 42 U.S.C.A. 1395i-3(i), provides:

CONSTRUCTION. — Where requirements or obligations under this section are identical to those provided under section 1919 of this Act [42 U.S.C.A. 1396r, which are the Medicaid requirements for nursing facilities], the fulfillment of those requirements or obligations under section 1919 shall be considered to be the fulfillment of the corresponding requirements or obligations under this section.

For regulatory citations, see Chapter 6

§ 2:5 IMPROPER BILLING FOR CLINICAL DIAGNOSTIC LABORATORY TESTS — Section 1833(h)(5)(D) [42 U.S.C.A. 1395l(h)(5)(D)]

Summary

Pursuant to section 1833(h)(1), 42 U.S.C.A. 1395l(h)(1), the Secretary of Health and Human Services must establish fee schedules for clinical diagnostic laboratory tests paid for by Medicare. Section 1833(h)(5)(D) provides that a person may not bill for such tests, including a test performed in a physician's office but excluding a test performed by a rural health clinic, except on an assignment-related basis. Any person who knowingly, willfully, and repeatedly bills in violation of that requirement is subject to the same sanctions which the Secretary may impose against a physician pursuant to section 1842(j)(2) and (3), 42 U.S.C.A. 1395u(j)(2) and (3). That means exclusion for a period not to exceed 5 years, in accordance with the procedures of section 1128, 42 U.S.C.A. 1329a-7(a), or imposition of a civil money penalty in accordance with the procedures of section 1128A(a), 42 U.S.C.A. 1320a-7a(a).

Statutory Provisions

Section 1833(h)(1), 42 U.S.C.A. 1395l(h)(1), provides:

> (A) Subject to section 1834(d) (1) [42 U.S.C.A. 1395m(a)(d)(1), which pertains to frequency limits and payment for fecal-occult blood tests for colorectal cancer screening] the Secretary shall establish fee schedules for clinical diagnostic laboratory tests (including prostate cancer screening tests under section 1861(oo) [42 U.S.C.A. 1395x(oo)]) for which payment is made under this part, other than such tests performed by a provider of services for an inpatient of such provider.
>
> NOTE: Section 4104(c)(2) of the Balanced Budget Act of 1997, P.L. 105–33, added the introductory phrase "Subject to section 1834(d)(1)," effective January 1, 1998. Section 4103(b) of the Balanced Budget Act added the parenthetical reference to prostate cancer screening tests. The latter applies to services furnished on or after January 1, 2000.

(B) In the case of clinical diagnostic laboratory tests performed by a physician or by a laboratory (other than tests performed by a qualified hospital laboratory (as defined in subparagraph (D)) for outpatients of such hospital), the fee schedules established under subparagraph (A) shall be established on a regional, statewide, or carrier service area basis (as the Secretary may determine to be appropriate) for tests furnished on or after July 1, 1984. [Effective December 19, 1989, section 6111(a) of P.L. 101-239, the Omnibus Budget Reconciliation Act of 1989, added "on or after July 1, 1984" and deleted "during the period beginning on July 1, 1984, and ending on December 31, 1989. For such tests furnished on or after January 1, 1990, the fee schedule shall be established on a nationwide basis."]

(C) In the case of clinical diagnostic laboratory tests performed by a qualified hospital laboratory (as defined in subparagraph (D)) for outpatients of such hospital, the fee schedules established under subparagraph (A) shall be established on a regional, statewide, or carrier service area basis (as the Secretary may determine to be appropriate) for tests furnished on or after July 1, 1984. [Effective December 19, 1989, section 6111(a) of OBRA 89, added "on or after July 1, 1984" and deleted "during the period beginning on July 1, 1984, and ending on December 31, 1989. For such tests furnished on or after January 1, 1990, the fee schedule shall be established on a nationwide basis."]

(D) In this subsection, the term "qualified hospital laboratory" means a hospital laboratory, in a sole community hospital (as defined in section 1886(d)(5)(D)(iii) [42 U.S.C.A. 1395ww(d)(5)(D)(iii); prior to amendment by section 6003(e)(2)(A) of OBRA 89, the parenthetical clause read "as defined in the last sentence of section 1886(d)(5)(C)(ii)"]), which provides some clinical diagnostic laboratory tests 24 hours a day in order to serve a hospital emergency room which is available to provide services 24 hours a day and 7 days a week.

After making numerous other provisions for adjustments in the fee schedules, section 1833(h)(5), as amended by OBRA 89, effective December 19, 1989, provides:

(A) In the case of a bill or request for payment for a clinical diagnostic laboratory test for which payment may otherwise be made under this part on an assignment-related basis, or under a provider agreement under section 1866 [42 U.S.C.A. 1395cc] , payment may be made only to the person or entity which performed or supervised the performance of such test; except that —

(i) if a physician performed or supervised the performance of such test, payment may be made to another physician with whom he shares his practice,

(ii) in the case of a test performed at the request of a laboratory by another laboratory, payment may be made to the referring laboratory but only if—

(I) the referring laboratory is located in, or is part of, a rural hospital,

(II) the referring laboratory is wholly owned by ["wholly owned by" substituted for "a wholly-owned subsidiary of" pursuant to section 4154(e)(1)(A) of P.L. 101-508, the Omnibus Budget Reconciliation Act of 1990, effective December 13, 1989, as if included in OBRA 89] the entity performing such test, the referring laboratory wholly owns the entity performing such test, or both the referring laboratory and the entity performing such test are wholly-owned by a third entity, or

(III) not more than 30 percent of the clinical diagnostic laboratory tests for which such referring laboratory (but not including a laboratory described in subclause ((II) [The parenthetical phrase was added by section 4154(e)(1)(B) of OBRA 90, effective December 13, 1989, as if included in OBRA 89.], receives requests for testing during the year in which the test is performed [This phrase replaced "submits bills or requests for payment in any year", pursuant to section 4154(e)(1)(C) of OBRA 90, effective January 1, 1991.], are performed by another laboratory, and

(iii) in the case of a clinical diagnostic laboratory test provided under an arrangement (as defined in section 1861(w)(1) [42 U.S.C.A. 1395x(w)(1), which pertains to arrangements under which receipt of payment by a hospital, skilled nursing facility, home health agency, or hospice program discharges the liability of a beneficiary or any other person to pay]) made by a hospital or critical access hospital [Section 4201(c)(1) of the Balanced Budget Act of 1997 substitute the phrase "critical access" for "rural primary care".], payment shall be made to the hospital.

(B) In the case of such a bill or request for payment for a clinical diagnostic laboratory test for which payment may otherwise be made under this part, and which is not described in subparagraph (A), payment may be made to the beneficiary only on the basis of the itemized bill of the person or entity which performed or supervised the performance of the test.

(C) Payment for a clinical diagnostic laboratory test, including a test performed in a physician's office but excluding a test performed by a rural health clinic, [The phrase within the commas was added by section 4154(c)(1)(B) of OBRA 90, effective December 22, 1987, as if included in OBRA 87, which also deleted "performed by a laboratory other than a rural health clinic".] may only be made on an assignment-related basis, or to a provider of services with an agreement in effect under section 1866 [42 U.S.C.A. 1395cc].

◆ NOTE: Prior to enactment of OBRA 89, section 1833(h)(5) read as follows:

(A) In the case of a bill or request for payment for a clinical diagnostic laboratory test for which payment may otherwise be made under this part on an assignment-related basis, or under a provider agreement under section 1866 [42 U.S.C.A. 1395cc] , payment may be made only to the person or entity which performed or supervised the performance of such test; except that —

(i) if a physician performed or supervised the performance of such test, payment may be made to another physician with whom he shares his practice,

(ii) in the case of a test performed at the request of a laboratory by another laboratory, payment may be made to the referring laboratory, and

(iii) in the case of a clinical diagnostic laboratory test provided under an arrangement (as defined in section 1861(w)(1) [42 U.S.C.A. 1395x(w)(1), which pertains to arrangements under which receipt of payment by a hospital, critical access hospital, or skilled nursing facility, home health agency, or hospice program discharges the liability of a beneficiary or any other person to pay]) made by a hospital, payment shall be made to the hospital or skilled nursing facility.

◆ NOTE: Section 321(g)(2) of the Medicare, Medicaid, and SCHIP Balanced Budget Refinement Act of 1999, as incorporated into the Omnibus Consolidated Appropriations Act, 2000, P.L. 106–113, enacted November 17, 1999, replaced "or critical access hospital" with ", critical access hospital or skilled nursing facility". It also added "or skilled nursing facility" before the period. These changes were made effective August 5, 1997.

(B) In the case of such a bill or request for payment for a clinical diagnostic laboratory test for which payment may otherwise be made under this part, and which is not described in subparagraph (A), payment may be made to the beneficiary only on the basis of the itemized bill of the person or entity which performed or supervised the performance of the test.

(C) Payment for a clinical diagnostic laboratory test performed by a laboratory other than a rural health clinic may only be made on an assignment-related basis, or to a provider of services with an agreement in effect under section 1866 [42 U.S.C.A. 1395cc].

Then section 1833(h)(5)(D) provides:

A person may not bill for a clinical diagnostic laboratory test, including a test performed in a physician's office but excluding a test performed by a rural health clinic [The phrase within the commas was added by section 4154(c)(1)(B) of OBRA 90, effective December 22, 1987, as if included in OBRA 87, which also deleted the phrase "performed by a laboratory, other than a rural health clinic], other than on an assignment-related basis. If a person knowingly and willfully and on a repeated basis bills for a clinical diagnostic laboratory test in violation of the previous sentence, the Secretary may apply sanctions against the person in the same manner as the Secretary may apply sanctions against a physician in accordance with paragraphs (2) and (3) of section 1842(j) [42 U.S.C.A. 1395u(j)] in the same manner such paragraphs apply with respect to a physician.

Section 1842(j)(2), 42 U.S.C.A. 1395u(j), provides:

Subject to paragraph (3), the sanctions which the Secretary may apply under this paragraph are —

(A) excluding a physician from participation in the programs under this Act for a period not to exceed 5 years, in accordance with the procedures of paragraphs (c) [which pertains to notice, effective date, and period of exclusion], (f) [which pertains to notice, hearing, and judicial review], and (g) [which pertains to application for termination of exclusion], of section 1128 [42 U.S.C.A. 1320a-7(c), (f), and (g)], or

(B) civil monetary penalties and assessments, in the same manner as such penalties and assessments are authorized under section 1128A(a) [42 U.S.C.A. 1320a-7a(a)], or both. The provisions of section 1128A (other than the first 2 sentences of subsection (a) and other than subsection (b)) shall apply to a civil money penalty and assessment under subparagraph (B) in the same manner as such provisions apply to a penalty, assessment, or proceeding under section 1128A(a), except to the extent such provisions are inconsistent with subparagraph (A) or paragraph (3).

Section 1842(j)(3) then provides:

(A) The Secretary may not exclude a physician pursuant to paragraph (2)(A) if such physician is a sole community physician or sole source of essential specialized services in a community.

(B) The Secretary shall take into account access of beneficiaries to physicians' services for which payment may be made under this part in determining whether to bar a physician from participation under paragraph (2)(A).

For regulatory citations, see Chapter 6

§ 2:6 IMPROPER BILLING FOR INTRAOCULAR LENSES — Section 1833(i)(6) [42 U.S.C.A. 1395l(i)(6)]

Summary

When it is safe to perform surgery in an ambulatory surgical center or in a physician's office, Congress encourages that, in lieu of surgery in a hospital. As part of that attempt to control health care costs, section 1833(i), 42 U.S.C.A. 1395l(i), required the Secretary of Health and Human Services to determine which surgical procedures meet safety criteria for performance in an ambulatory surgical center or physician's office. It also obligated him to update a list of those procedures not less often than every two years. Included on the list is cataract surgery.

With respect to eligible costs for outpatient surgery, including outpatient cataract surgery, section 1833(i)(2) required the Secretary to base Medicare payment for related facility services on 80 percent of a standard overhead amount which he must establish for each surgical procedure. The Secretary must factor that into his estimate of a fair fee, which, among other costs, in the case of insertion of an intraocular lens during or subsequent to cataract surgery, includes payment which is reasonable and related to the cost of acquiring the class of lens involved.

Also with respect to outpatient surgery, including cataract surgery, section 1833(i)(5) authorizes the Secretary, in lieu of any amounts otherwise payable, to pay a single all-inclusive fee for facility services furnished by an ambulatory surgical center and for all related services (including physicians' services, laboratory, X-ray, and diagnostic services). He can do that provided all parties furnishing all such services agree to accept that fee (divided as they may agree) as full payment for services rendered.

Section 1833(i)(6) then provides that any person who knowingly and willfully presents, or causes to be presented, a bill or request for payment, for an intraocular lens inserted during or subsequent to cataract surgery in an ambulatory surgery center is subject to a civil money penalty not to exceed $2,000. The same applies to a facility which has agreed, pursuant to section 1832(a)(2)(F)(i), 42 U.S.C.A. 1395k(a)(2)(F)(i), to accept by assignment the standard overhead amount for such service which the Secretary established.

Enforcement procedures for this civil money penalty are governed by section 1128A, 42 U.S.C.A. 1320a-7a, which authorizes civil money penalties for a variety of offenses.

Statutory Provisions

Section 1833(i), 42 U.S.C.A. 1395l(i), provides:

(1) The Secretary shall, in consultation with appropriate medical organizations —

(A) specify those surgical procedures which are appropriately (when considered in terms of the proper utilization of hospital inpatient facilities) performed on an inpatient basis in a hospital but which also can be performed safely on an ambulatory basis in an ambulatory surgical center (meeting the standards specified under section 1832(a)(2)(F)(i) [42 U.S.C.A. 1395k(a)(2)(F)(i)]), critical access hospital [the phrase "rural primary care hospital" was added, effective December 19, 1989, by section 6003(g)(D)(vii)(II) of P.L. 101–239, the Omnibus Budget Reconciliation Act of 1989. Section 4201(c)(1) of the Balanced Budget Act of 1997, P.L. 105–33, substituted the phrase "critical access" for the phrase "rural primary care", effective October 1, 1997.], or hospital outpatient department, and

(B) specify those surgical procedures which are appropriately (when considered in terms of the proper utilization of hospital inpatient facilities) performed on an inpatient basis in a hospital but which also can be performed safely on an ambulatory basis in a physician's office. The lists of procedures established under subparagraphs (A) and (B) shall be reviewed and updated not less often than every 2 years.

Section 1833(i)(2) then provides:

(A) The amount of payment to be made for facility services furnished in connection with a surgical procedure specified pursuant to paragraph (1)(A) and furnished to an individual in an ambulatory surgical center described in such paragraph shall be equal to 80 percent of a standard overhead amount established by the Secretary (with respect to each such procedure) on the basis of the Secretary's estimate of a fair fee which—

(i) takes into account the costs incurred by such centers, or classes of centers, generally in providing services furnished in connection with the performance of such procedure,

(ii) takes such costs into account in such a manner as will assure that the performance of the procedure in such a center will result in substantially less amounts paid under this title than would have been paid if the procedure had been performed on an inpatient basis in a hospital, and

(iii) in the case of insertion of an intraocular lens during or subsequent to cataract surgery includes payment which is reasonable and related to the cost of acquiring the class of lens involved. Each amount so established shall be reviewed and updated not later than July 1, 1987, and annually thereafter

> and may be adjusted by the Secretary, when appropriate, to take account of varying conditions in different areas.

After making further provisions to control costs for surgical procedures performed in ambulatory surgical centers, as well as in physicians' offices, section 1833(i)(5) states:

> (A) The Secretary is authorized to provide by regulations that in the case of a surgical procedure, specified by the Secretary pursuant to paragraph (1)(A), performed in an ambulatory surgical center described in such paragraph, there shall be paid (in lieu of any amounts otherwise payable under this part) with respect to the facility services furnished by such center and with respect to all related services (including physicians' services, laboratory, X-ray, and diagnostic services) a single all-inclusive fee established pursuant to subparagraph (B), if all parties furnishing all such services agree to accept such fee (to be divided among the parties involved in such manner as they shall have previously agreed upon) as full payment for the services furnished.
>
> (B) In implementing this paragraph, the Secretary shall establish with respect to each surgical procedure specified pursuant to paragraph (1)(A) the amount of the all-inclusive fee for such procedure, taking into account such factors as may be appropriate. The amount so established with respect to any surgical procedure shall be reviewed periodically and may be adjusted by the Secretary, when appropriate, to take account of varying conditions in different areas.

Having established those payment provisions for outpatient surgeries, section 1833(i)(6) provides with respect to the lenses used in connection with cataract surgery as follows:

> Any person, including a facility having an agreement under section 1832(a)(2)(F)(i) [42 U.S.C.A. 1395k(a)(2)(F)(i), which pertains to agreements with ambulatory surgical centers to accept by assignment the standard overhead amount which the Secretary establishes for them as payment in full for cataract surgery services, including therein the cost of intraocular lenses] who knowingly and willfully presents, or causes to be

presented, a bill or request for payment, for an intraocular lens inserted during or subsequent to cataract surgery for which payment may be made under paragraph (2)(A)(iii), is subject to a civil money penalty of not to exceed $2,000. The provisions of section 1128A [42 U.S.C.A. 1320a-7a] (other than subsections (a) and (b)) shall apply to a civil money penalty under the previous sentence in the same manner as such provisions apply to a penalty or proceeding under section 1128A(a).

For regulatory citations, see Chapter 6

§ 2:7 IMPROPER BILLING FOR SERVICES OF A CERTIFIED REGISTERED NURSE ANESTHETIST — Section 1833(l)(5)(B) [42 U.S.C.A. 1395l(l)(5)(B)]

Summary

◆ NOTE: This sanction was repealed effective January 1, 1995, by section 123(b)(2)(A)(i) of the SocialSecurity Act Amendments of 1994, P.L. 100–432.

Section 1833(l)(1), 42 U.S.C.A. 1395l(l)(1), required the Secretary of Health and Human Services to establish a fee schedule for services of certified registered nurse anesthetists (CRNA's). Such services are included in the definition of medical and other health services. See section 1861(s)(11), 42 U.S.C.A. 1395x(s)(11).

Pursuant to section 1833(l)(5)(B), 42 U.S.C.A. 1395l(l)(5)(B), payment for the services of a CRNA may be made only on an assigned claim basis. Any person who knowingly and willfully presents or causes to be presented to a beneficiary a bill or request for payment for a CRNA's services on other than an assignment basis (except for applicable deductibles and coinsurance) is subject to a civil money penalty not to exceed $2,000 for each such bill or request.

Enforcement procedures for this civil money penalty are governed by section 1128A, 42 U.S.C.A. 1320a-7a, which authorizes civil money penalties for a variety of offenses.

Statutory Provisions

Section 1833(l)(5), 42 U.S.C.A. 1395l(l)(5), provides:

(A) Payment for the services of a certified registered nurse anesthetist (for which payment may otherwise be made under this part) may be made on the basis of a claim or request for payment presented by the certified registered nurse anesthetist furnishing such services, or by a hospital, rural primary care hospital, physician, group practice, or ambulatory surgical center with which the certified registered nurse anesthetist furnishing such services has an employment or contractual relationship that provides for payment to be made under this part for such services to such hospital, rural primary care hospital, physician, group practice, or ambulatory surgical center.

(B)(i) Payment for the services of a certified registered nurse anesthetist under this part may be made only on an assignment-related basis, and any such assignment agreed to by a certified registered nurse anesthetist shall be binding upon any other person presenting a claim or request for payment for such services.

(ii) Except for deductible and coinsurance amounts applicable under this section, any person who knowingly and willfully presents or causes to be presented, to an individual enrolled under this part a bill or request for payment for services of a certified registered nurse anesthetist for which payment may be made under this part only on an assignment basis is subject to a civil money penalty of not to exceed $2,000 for each such bill or request. The provisions of section 1128A [42 U.S.C.A. 1320a-7a] (other than subsections (a) and (b)) shall apply to a civil money penalty under the previous sentence in the same manner as such provisions apply to a penalty or proceeding under section 1128A(a).

(C) No hospital or rural primary care hospital that presents a claim or request for payment for services of a certified nurse anesthetist under this part may treat any uncollected coinsurance amount imposed under this part with respect to such services as a bad debt of such hospital for purposes of this title.

◆ NOTE: Effective December 19, 1989, pursuant to sections 6003(g)(3)(D)(vii)(IV) and (V) of P.L. 101-239, the Omnibus Budget Reconciliation Act of 1989, "rural primary care hospital" was added twice to subparagraph (l)(5)(A), and "or rural primary care hospital" was added to subparagraph (l)(5)(C).

For regulatory citations, see Chapter 6

§ 2:8 OVERCHARGING BY PHYSICIANS FOR SERVICES OF A CERTIFIED REGISTERED NURSE ANESTHETIST — Section 1833(l)(6) [42 U.S.C.A. 1395l(l)(6)]

Summary

Section 1833(l)(1), 42 U.S.C.A. 1395l(l)(1), required the Secretary of Health and Human Services to establish a fee schedule for services of certified registered nurse anesthetists (CRNA's). Such services are included in the definition of medical and other health services. See section 1861(s)(11), 42 U.S.C.A. 1395x(s)(11).

◆ NOTE: Pursuant to section 4160 of P.L. 101-508, the Omnibus Budget Reconciliation Act of 1990 (OBRA 90), effective November 5, 1990, the Secretary may utilize a system of time units, a system of base and time units, or any appropriate methodology to establish this fee schedule. This process does not apply, however, to certain services furnished in certain hospitals in rural areas under the provisions of section 9320(k) of P.L. 99-509, the Omnibus Budget Reconciliation Act of 1986 (OBRA 86), as amended by section 6132 of P.L. 101-239, the Omnibus Budget Reconciliation Act of 1989 (OBRA 89).

To go along with setting such fees, Congress mandated corresponding reductions, either for the physicians who provide medical direction of CRNA's or for the CRNA fee schedule itself. That was so the estimated total amount paid for such services in 1989 and 1990 would not exceed a statutory cap. If that process requires a reduction in the reasonable charge for a physician's service, and if a nonparticipating physician furnishes the service to an individual after the effective date of the reduction, the physician's actual charge is subject to a limit under section 1842(j)(1)(D), 42 U.S.C.A. 1395u(j)(1)(D). That provision leads to section 1842(j)(2), however, which permits the Secretary to exclude such a physician for a period not to exceed 5 years in accordance with procedures set forth in section 1128 of the Act, 42 U.S.C.A. 1320a-7, and to impose a civil money penalty in accordance with section 1128A, 42 U.S.C.A. 1320a-7a, or both, for knowingly and willfully on a repeated basis charging more than the allowable amount.

Statutory Provisions

Section 1833(l)(6), 42 U.S.C.A. 1395l(l)(6), provides:

> If an adjustment under paragraph (3)(B) [of section 1833(l), which requires the Secretary to reduce the prevailing charge of physicians for medical direction of a CRNA, or the fee schedule for services of a CRNA, or both, as necessary to ensure required cost containment] results in a reduction in the reasonable charge for a physician's service and a nonparticipating physician furnishes the service to an individual entitled to benefits under this part after the effective date of the reduction, the physician's actual charge is subject to a limit under section 1842(j)(1)(D) [42 U.S.C.A. 1395u(j)(1)(D)].

Section 1842(j)(1)(D), 42 U.S.C.A. 1395u(j)(1)(D), provides:

> (i) If an action described in clause (ii) results in a reduction in a reasonable charge for a physicians' [sic physician's] service or item and a nonparticipating physician furnishes the service or item to an individual entitled to benefits under this part after the effective date of such action, the physician may not charge the individual more than 125 percent of the reduced payment allowance (as defined in clause (iii)) plus (for services or items furnished during the 12-month period (or 9-month period in the case of an action described in clause (ii)(II)) beginning on the effective date of the action) 1/2 of the amount by which the physician's maximum allowable actual charge for the service or item for the previous 12-month period exceeds such 125 percent level.
>
> (ii) The first sentence of clause (i) shall apply to —
>
> > (I) an adjustment under subsection (b)(8)(B) (relating to inherent reasonableness),
> >
> > (II) a reduction under subsection (b)(10)(A) or (b)(14)(A) (relating to certain overpriced procedures) [(b)(10)(A) pertains to reasonable charges for bronchoscopy, carpal tunnel repair, cataract surgery (including subsequent insertion of an intraocular lens), coronary artery bypass surgery, diagnostic and/or therapeutic dilation and curettage, knee arthroscopy, knee arthroplasty, pacemaker implantation surgery, total hip replacement, suprapubic prostatectomy, transurethral resection of the prostate, and upper gastrointestinal endoscopy; "or

(b)(14)(A)", added effective December 19, 1989, by section 6104(b) of P.L. 101-239, the Omnibus Budget Reconciliation Act of 1989, pertains to reduced prevailing charges for physicians' services],

(III) a reduction under subsection (b)(11)(B) (relating to certain cataract procedures) [which pertains to the reasonable charge for a cataract surgical procedure],

(IV) a prevailing charge limit established under subsection (b)(11)(C)(i) [which pertains to the prevailing charge for A-mode ophthalmic ultrasound procedures] or (b)(15)(A) ["or (b)(15)(A)", added effective December 19, 1989, by section 6108(b)(1) of OBRA 89 pertains to limitations on prevailing charges for surgery, radiology, and diagnostic physicians' services and applies to procedures performed after March 31, 1990],

(V) a reasonable charge limit established under subsection (b)(11)(C)(ii) [which pertains to the reasonable charge for an intraocular lens inserted during or subsequent to cataract surgery in a physician's office], and

(VI) an adjustment under section 1833(l)(3)(B) (relating to physician supervision of certified registered nurse anesthetists) [which pertains to the prevailing charge for physician direction of CRNA's and fee schedules for CRNA's] .

(iii) In clause (i), the term "reduced payment allowance" means, with respect to an action —

(I) under subsection (b)(8)(B), the inherently reasonable charge established under subsection (b)(8);

(II) under subsection (b)(10(A) [which pertains to reasonable charges for bronchoscopy, carpal tunnel repair, cataract surgery (including subsequent insertion of an intraocular lens), coronary artery bypass surgery, diagnostic and/or therapeutic dilation and curettage, knee arthroscopy, knee arthroplasty, pacemaker implantation surgery, total hip replacement, suprapubic prostatectomy, transurethral resection of the prostate, and upper gastrointestinal endoscopy], (b)(11)(B) [which pertains to the reasonable charge for a cataract surgical procedure], (b)(11)(C)(i) [which pertains to the prevailing charge for A-mode ophthalmic ultrasound procedures], (b)(14)(A) [added as indicated above, which pertains to reduced prevailing charges for physicians' services], or (b)(15)(A) [added as indicated above, which pertains to limitations on prevailing charges for surgery, radiology, and diagnostic physicians' services] or under section 1833(l)(3)(B) [which pertains to the prevailing charge for physician direction of CRNA's and fee schedules for CRNA's], the prevailing charge for the service after the action; or

(III) under subsection (b)(11)(C)(ii) [which pertains to the reasonable charge for an intraocular lens inserted during or subsequent to cataract surgery in a physician's office], the payment allowance established under such subsection.

(iv) If a physician knowingly and willfully bills in violation of clause (i) (whether or not such charge violates subparagraph (B)), the Secretary may apply sanctions against such physician in accordance with paragraph (2).

(v) clause (i) shall not apply to items and services furnished after December 31, 1990.

◆ NOTE: Effective December 19, 1989, section 6102(e)(9) of OBRA 89 substituted "December 31, 1990" for "the earlier of (I) December 31, 1990, or (II) one-year after the date the Secretary reports to Congress, under section 1845(e)(3) [42 U.S.C.A. 1395w-1(e)(3)] , on the development of the relative value scale under section 1845" in subparagraph (v).

Section 1842(j)(2) provides:

Subject to paragraph (3), the sanctions which the Secretary may apply under this paragraph are —

(A) excluding a physician from participation in the programs under this Act for a period not to exceed 5 years, in accordance with the procedures of paragraphs (c) [which pertains to notice, effective date, and period of exclusion], (f) [which pertains to notice, hearing, and judicial review], and (g) [which pertains to application for termination of exclusion] of section 1128 [42 U.S.C.A. 1320a-7], or

(B) civil monetary penalties and assessments, in the same manner as such penalties and assessments are authorized under section 1128A(a) [42 U.S.C.A. 1320a-7a(a)], or both. The provisions of section 1128A (other than the first 2 sentences of subsection (a) and other than subsection (b))

shall apply to a civil money penalty and assessment under subparagraph (B) in the same manner as such provisions apply to a penalty, assessment, or proceeding under section 1128A(a), except to the extent such provisions are inconsistent with subparagraph (A) or paragraph (3).

Section 1842(j)(3) then provides:

(A) The Secretary may not exclude a physician pursuant to paragraph (2)(A) if such physician is a sole community physician or sole source of essential specialized services in a community.

(B) The Secretary shall take into account access of beneficiaries to physicians' services for which payment may be made under this part in determining whether to bar a physician from participation under paragraph (2)(A).

Finally, in section 1842(j)(4), Congress gave the Secretary discretion to make restitution to Medicare beneficiaries affected by violations of this part of the law out of civil money penalties or assessments collected. That section reads as follows:

The Secretary may, out of any civil monetary penalty or assessment collected from a physician pursuant to this subsection, make a payment to a beneficiary enrolled under this part in the nature of restitution for amounts paid by such beneficiary to such physician which was determined to be an excess charge under paragraph (1).

For regulatory citations, see Chapter 6

§ 2:9 IMPROPER BILLING FOR CERTIFIED NURSE-MIDWIFE SERVICES AND SERVICES OF QUALIFIED PSYCHOLOGISTS AND CLINICAL SOCIAL WORKERS—Section 1833(p) [42 U.S.C.A. 1395l(p)]

Summary

◆ NOTE: This sanction was repealed effective January 1, 1995, by section 123(b)(2)(A)(ii) of the Social Security Act Amendments of 1994, P.L. 100-432.

Pursuant to section 1833(p), 42 U.S.C.A. 1395l(p), payment for services of a certified nurse-midwife, a qualified psychologist, or a clinical social worker may be made only on an assignment-related basis. Whoever knowingly and willfully presents, or causes to be presented, to an individual entitled to Supplementary Medical Insurance (Medicare Part B) benefits a bill or request for payment for such services, except for applicable deductible and coinsurance amounts, is subject to a civil money penalty not to exceed $2,000.

Enforcement procedures for this civil money penalty are governed by section 1128A, 42 U.S.C.A. 1320a-7a, which authorizes civil money penalties for a variety of offenses.

Statutory Provisions

Section 1833(p), 42 U.S.C.A. 1395l(p), provides:

> In the case of certified nurse-midwife services for which payment may be made under this part only pursuant to section 1861(s)(2)(L) [42 U.S.C.A. 1395x(s)(2)(L), which is the definition section that includes certified nurse-midwife services as part of medical and other health services], and in the case of qualified psychologists services for which payment may be made under this part only pursuant to section 1861(s)(2)(M) [42 U.S.C.A. 1395x(s)(2)(M), which is the definition section that includes qualified psychologist services as part of medical and other health services], and in the case of clinical social worker services for which payment may be made under this part only pursuant to section 1861(s)(2)(N) [42 U.S.C.A. 1395x(s)(2)(N), which is the definition section that includes clinical social workers as part of medical and other health services; this clause added effective December 19, 1989, for services furnished on or after July 1, 1990, by section 6113(b)(3)(B) of P.L. 101-239, the Omnibus Budget Reconciliation Act of 1989] payment may only be made under this part for such services on an assignment-related basis. Except for deductible and coinsurance amounts applicable under section 1833, whoever knowingly and willfully presents, or causes to be presented, to an individual enrolled under this part [Medicare Part B] a bill or request for payment for services described in the previous sentence, is subject to a civil money penalty of not to exceed $2,000 for each such bill or request. The provisions of section 1128A [42 U.S.C.A. 1320a-7a] (other than subsections (a) and (b)) shall apply to a civil money penalty under the previous sentence in the same manner as such provisions apply to a penalty or proceeding under section 1128A(a).

For regulatory citations, see Chapter 6

§ 2:10 FAILURE TO INCLUDE INFORMATION ABOUT REFERRING PHYSICIANS ON REQUESTS FOR PAYMENTS OR BILLS — Section 1833(q) [42 U.S.C.A. 1395l(q)]

Summary

Section 1833(q)(1), 42 U.S.C.A. 1395l(q)(1), requires any entity that submits a bill or a request for payment for an item or service covered by Medicare to include the name and provider number of a referring physician. This applies whenever the entity knows or has reason to believe there has been a referral by a referring physician within the meaning of section 1877, 42 U.S.C.A. 1395nn. In addition, the entity must indicate whether the referring physician is an interested investor within the meaning of section 1877(h).

◆ NOTE: For a discussion of section 1877, commonly known as the Stark Bill, see § 2:42.

If that information is not provided, and if the request for payment is based on a Medicare assignment of benefits, section 1833(q)(2)(A) permits the Secretary of Health and Human Services to deny payment.

If an entity knowingly and willfully fails to provide that information, and if its request for payment is not based on an assignment of Medicare benefits, section 1833(q)(2)(B) authorizes the Secretary to impose a civil money penalty not to exceed $2,000.

Enforcement procedures for this civil money penalty are governed by section 1128A, 42 U.S.C.A. 1320a-7a, which authorizes civil money penalties for a variety of offenses.

In addition, if an entity not taking a Medicare assignment knowingly and willfully and in repeated cases fails to provide the required information, after being notified by the Secretary of the obligation to do so under section 1833(q)(1), the Secretary may exclude the entity from Medicare for a period not to exceed 5 years, in accordance with the procedures of subsections (c), (f), and (g) of section 1128, 42 U.S.C.A. 1320a-7(c), (f), and (g).

◆ NOTE: For a discussion of section 1128, see § 4:6.

Statutory Provisions

Section 1833(q), 42 U.S.C.A. 1395l(q), provides:

(1) Each request for payment, or bill submitted, for an item or service furnished by an entity for which payment may be made under this part and for which the entity knows or has reason to believe there has been a referral by a referring physician (within the meaning of section 1877 [42 U.S.C.A. 1395nn]) shall include the name and provider number for the referring physician and indicate whether or not the referring physician is an interested investor (within the meaning of section 1877(h)(5)).

(2) (A) In the case of a request for payment for an item or service furnished by an entity under this part on an assignment-related basis and for which information is required to be provided under paragraph (1) but not included, payment may be denied under this part [Medicare Part B].

(B) In the case of a request for payment for an item or service furnished by an entity under this part not submitted on an assignment-related basis and for which information is required to be provided under paragraph (1) but not included —

(i) if the entity knowingly and willfully fails to provide such information promptly upon request of the Secretary or a carrier, the entity may be subject to a civil money penalty in an amount not to exceed $2,000, and

(ii) if the entity knowingly and willfully, and in repeated cases fails, after being notified by the Secretary of the obligations and requirements of this subsection to provide the information required under paragraph (1), the entity may be subject to exclusion from participation in the programs under this Act for a period not to exceed 5 years, in accordance with the procedures of subsections (c), (f), and (g) of section 1128 [42 U.S.C.A. 1320a-7(c), (f), and 1320a-7(g).] . The provisions of section 1128A [42 U.S.C.A. 1320a-7a] (other than subsections (a) and (b)) shall apply to civil money penalties under clause (i) in the same manner as they apply to a penalty or proceeding under section 1128A(a).

For regulatory citations, see Chapter 6

§ 2:11 FAILURE TO BILL ON AN ASSIGNMENT-RELATED BASIS FOR COVERED SERVICES OF A NURSE PRACTITIONER OR CLINICAL NURSE SPECIALIST —Section 1833(r)(3)(B) [42 U.S.C.A. 1395(r)(3)(B)]

Summary

◆ NOTE: This sanction was repealed effective January 1, 1995, by section 123(b)(2)(B)(iii) of the Social Security Act Amendments of 1994, P.L. 100-432.

For Medicare coverage purposes, section 1861(s)(2)(K)(iii), 42 U.S.C.A. 1395x(s)(2)(K)(iii), includes within the definition of "medical and other health services" services which would be covered physicians' services if furnished by a physician but which are performed by a nurse practitioner or clinical nurse specialist.

This applies when the nurse practitioner or clinical nurse specialist is working in collaboration with a physician in a rural area, as defined in section 1886(d)(2)(D), 42 U.S.C.A. 1395ww(d)(2)(D), but only when the nurse practitioner or clinical nurse specialist is authorized to perform such services by the State where the services are performed. Included in that definition are such services and supplies furnished as an incident to services of a nurse practitioner or clinical nurse specialist as would be covered under section 1861(s)(2)(A) if furnished as an incident to a physician's professional service.

Section 1861(s)(2)(A) speaks of services and supplies (including drugs and biologicals which cannot, as determined in accordance with regulations, be self-administered) furnished as an incident to a physician's professional service. This applies to such services and supplies commonly furnished in physicians' offices which commonly are either rendered without charge or are included in the physicians' bills.

With respect to such services by a nurse practitioner or clinical nurse specialist, section 1833(r)(1) provides that Medicare payment may be made on the basis of a claim or request for payment presented either by the nurse practitioner or clinical nurse specialist, or by a hospital, rural primary care hospital, skilled nursing facility or Medicaid nursing facility. Payment also may be made on the basis of a claim or request for payment presented by a hospital, physician, group practice, or ambulatory surgical center, provided the nurse practitioner or clinical nurse specialist has an employment or contractual relationship with the hospital, physician, group practice, or ambulatory surgical center.

Section 1833(r)(2) restricts the amount of such payments to the prevailing charge for such services capped by 75 percent in the case of services performed in a hospital, and by 85 percent in the case of services performed elsewhere. That applies for services furnished prior to January 1, 1992. For services provided thereafter, payment is determined by the fee schedule amount provided under section 1848 for such services performed by physicians who are not specialists.

Pursuant to section 1833(r)(3)(A), payment for such services must be on an assignment-related basis. Any such assignment agreed to by a nurse practitioner or clinical nurse specialist is binding on any other person presenting a claim or request for payment for such services.

Then, section 1833(r)(3)(B) provides that, except for deductible and coinsurance amounts applicable to Medicare Part B, anyone who knowingly and willfully presents, or causes to be presented, to a Medicare beneficiary a bill or request for payment for such services in violation of the compulsory Medicare assignment is subject to a civil money penalty not to exceed $2,000 for each such bill or request. Enforcement procedures for this civil money penalty are governed by section 1128A, 42 U.S.C.A. 1320a-7a, which authorizes civil money penalties for a variety of offenses.

Finally, section 1833(r)(4) provides that no hospital or rural primary care hospital that presents a claim or request for payment under Part B for such services may treat any uncollected Medicare coinsurance amount as a bad debt of such hospital for Medicare purposes.

Statutory Provisions

Section 1861(s)(2)(K)(iii), 42 U.S.C.A. 1395x(s)(2)(K)(iii), which was added by section 4155(a) of P.L. 101-508, the Omnibus Budget Reconciliation Act of 1990 (OBRA 90), applicable to services furnished after December 1990, provides:

> (s) The term "medical and other health services" means any of the following items or services:

* * *

(K)(iii) services which would be physicians' services if furnished by a physician (as defined in subsection (r)(1)) and which are performed by a nurse practitioner or clinical nurse specialist (as defined in subsection (aa)(4)) working in collaboration (as defined in subsection (aa)(5)), with a physician (as defined in subsection (r)(1)) in a rural area (as defined in section 1886(d)(2)(D) [42 U.S.C.A. 1395ww(d)(2)(D)]) which the nurse practitioner or clinical nurse specialist is authorized to perform by the State in which the services are performed, and such services and supplies furnished as an incident to such services as would be covered under subparagraph (A) if furnished as an incident to a physician's professional service. . .[.]

In that regard, section 1861(s)(2) also provides that the term "medical and other health services" means:

(A) services and supplies (including drugs and biologicals which cannot, as determined in accordance with regulations, be self-administered) furnished as an incident to a physician's professional service, of kinds which are commonly furnished in physicians' offices and are commonly either rendered without charge or included in the physicians' bills[.]

Then section 1833(r), 42 U.S.C.A. 1395l(r), added by section 4155(b)(3) of OBRA 90, provides:

(1) With respect to services described in section 1861(s)(2)(K)(iii) (relating to nurse practitioner or clinical nurse specialist services provided in a rural area), payment may be made on the basis of a claim or request for payment presented by the nurse practitioner or clinical nurse specialist furnishing such services, or by a hospital, rural primary care hospital, skilled nursing facility or nursing facility (as defined in section 1919(a) [42 U.S.C.A. 1396r(a)]), physician, group practice, ambulatory surgical center, with which the nurse practitioner or clinical nurse specialist has an employment or contractual relationship that provides for payment to be made under this part for such services to such hospital, physician, group practice, ambulatory surgical center.

(2)(A) For purposes of subsection (a)(1)(M), the prevailing charge for services described in section 1861(s)(2)(K)(iii) may not exceed the applicable percentage (as defined in subparagraph (B)) of the prevailing charge (or, for services furnished on or after January 1, 1992, the fee schedule amount provided under section 1848) determined for such services performed by physicians who are not specialists.

(B) In subparagraph (A), the term "applicable percentage" means —

(i) 75 percent in the case of services performed in a hospital, and

(ii) 85 percent in the case of other services.

(3)(A) Payment under this part for services described in section 1861(s)(2)(K)(iii) may be made only on an assignment-related basis, and any such assignment agreed to by a nurse practitioner or clinical nurse specialist shall be binding upon any other person presenting a claim or request for payment for such services.

(B) Except for deductible and coinsurance amounts applicable under this section, any person who knowingly and willfully presents, or causes to be presented, to an individual enrolled under this part a bill or request for payment for services described in section 1861(s)(2)(K)(iii) in violation of subparagraph (A) is subject to a civil money penalty of not to exceed $2,000 for each such bill or request. The provisions of section 1128A (other than subsections (a) and (B)) shall apply to a civil money penalty under the previous sentence in the same manner as such provisions apply to a penalty or proceeding under section 1128A(a).

(4) No hospital or rural primary care hospital that presents a claim or request for payment under this part for services described in section 1861(s)(2)(K)(iii) may treat any uncollected coinsurance amount imposed under this part with respect to such services as a bad debt of such hospital for purposes of this title.

Section 1833(a)(1)(O), as amended by section 4155(b)(2) of OBRA 90, applicable to services furnished after December 1990, provides:

Except as provided in section 1876, and subject to the succeeding provisions of this section, there shall be paid from the Federal Supplementary Medical Insurance Trust Fund, in the case of each individual who is covered under the insurance program established by this part and incurs expenses for services with respect to which benefits are payable under this part, amounts equal to —

* * *

(1) . . .(O) with respect to services described in section 1861(s)(2)(K)(iii), (relating to nurse practitioner or clinical nurse specialist services provided in a rural area), the amounts paid shall be 80 percent of the lesser of the actual charge or the prevailing charge that would be recognized (or, for services furnished on or after January 1, 1992, the fee schedule amount provided under section 1848) if the services had been performed by a physician (subject to the limitation described in subsection (r)(2)[.]

For regulatory citations, see Chapter 6

§ 2:12 IMPROPER BILLING FOR RENTAL ITEMS SUCH AS DURABLE MEDICAL EQUIPMENT, PROSTHETIC DEVICES, ORTHOTICS, AND PROSTHETICS — Section 1834(a)(11)(A) [42 U.S.C.A. 1395m(a)(11)(A)]

Summary

Section 1834, 42 U.S.C.A. 1395m, establishes the obligation for Medicare to pay for durable medical equipment. It deals with such matters as formulas for payment; whether reimbursement will be made as rental or purchase; how to calculate reasonable costs with respect to inexpensive and other routinely purchased durable medical equipment; payment for items requiring frequent substantial servicing; payment for certain customized items; payment for oxygen and oxygen equipment; payment for covered items other than durable medical equipment; computation of local and regional payment rates; and payment for miscellaneous devices and items.

It also deals with appropriate payment rates for transcutaneous electrical nerve stimulators (TENS units) and seat lift chairs; fee schedules for radiologist services; and limiting charges of nonparticipating physicians and suppliers.

◆ NOTE: Effective January 1, 1990, section 201(a)(1) of P.L. 101-234, the Medicare Catastrophic Coverage Repeal Act of 1989, repealed provisions of section 1834 which had authorized payment for outpatient drugs, payment for home intravenous drug therapy services, including limitations on referral fees, and payment for screening mammography.

Pursuant to section 1834(a)(11), suppliers who furnish covered items on a rental basis must continue to supply the items without charge (other than for maintenance and servicing) after rental payments may no longer be paid by Medicare. Any supplier who knowingly and willfully violates that requirement is subject to exclusion for a period not to exceed 5 years in accordance with procedures under section 1128, 42 U.S.C.A. 1320a-7, and to a civil money penalty under section 1128A, 42 U.S.C.A. 1320a-7a. See cross-reference to section 1842(j)(2), 42 U.S.C.A. 1395u(j)(2).

Statutory Provisions

Section 1834(a), 42 U.S.C.A. 1395m(a), states in part:

PAYMENT FOR DURABLE MEDICAL EQUIPMENT, PROSTHETIC DEVICES, ORTHOTICS AND PROSTHETICS. —

(1) GENERAL RULE FOR PAYMENT. —

(A) IN GENERAL. — With respect to a covered item (as defined in paragraph (13)) for which payment is determined under this subsection, payment shall be made in the frequency specified in paragraphs (2) through (7) and in an amount equal to 80 percent of the payment basis described in subparagraph (B).

(B) PAYMENT BASIS. — The payment basis described in this subparagraph is the lesser of —

(i) the actual charge for the item, or

(ii) the payment amount recognized under paragraphs (2) through (7) of this subsection for the item; except that clause (i) shall not apply if the covered item is furnished by a public home health agency (or by another home health agency which demonstrates to the satisfaction of the Secretary that a significant portion of its patients are low income) free of charge or at nominal charges to the public.

(C) EXCLUSIVE PAYMENT RULE. — This subsection shall constitute the exclusive provision of this title for payment for covered items under this part [part B] or under part A to a home health agency.

With respect to improper billing for rental items, section 1834(a)(11), 42 U.S.C.A. 1395m(a)(11), provides:

IMPROPER BILLING AND REQUIREMENT OF PHYSICIAN ORDER. —

(A) IMPROPER BILLING FOR CERTAIN RENTAL ITEMS. — Notwithstanding any other provision of this title, a supplier of a covered item for which payment is made under this subsection and which is furnished on a rental basis shall continue to supply the item without charge (other than a charge provided under this subsection for the maintenance and servicing of the item) after rental payments may no longer be made under this subsection. If a supplier knowingly and willfully violates the previous sentence, the Secretary may apply sanctions against the supplier under section 1842(j)(2) [42 U.S.C.A. 1395u(j)(2), which contains a cross reference to the exclusion and civil money penalty provisions of sections 1128 and 1128A of the Act] in the same manner such sanctions may apply with respect to a physician.

Section 1842(j)(2) provides:

Subject to paragraph (3), the sanctions which the Secretary may apply under this paragraph are —

(A) excluding a physician from participation in the programs under this Act for a period not to exceed 5 years, in accordance with the procedures of paragraphs (c) [which pertains to notice, effective date, and period of exclusion], (f) [which pertains to notice, hearing, and judicial review], and (g) [which pertains to application for termination of exclusion] of section 1128 [42 U.S.C.A. 1320a-7], or

(B) civil monetary penalties and assessments, in the same manner as such penalties and assessments are authorized under section 1128A(a) [42 U.S.C.A. 1320a-7a(a)], or both. The provisions of section 1128A (other than the first 2 sentences of subsection (a) and other than subsection (b)) shall apply to a civil money penalty and assessment under subparagraph (B) in the same manner as such provisions apply to a penalty, assessment, or proceeding under section

> 1128A(a), except to the extent such provisions are inconsistent with subparagraph (A) or paragraph (3).

Section 1842(j)(3) then provides:

> (A) The Secretary may not exclude a physician pursuant to paragraph (2)(A) if such physician is a sole community physician or sole source of essential specialized services in a community.
>
> (B) The Secretary shall take into account access of beneficiaries to physicians' services for which payment may be made under this part in determining whether to bar a physician from participation under paragraph (2)(A).

For regulatory citations, see Chapter 6

§ 2:13 IMPROPER DISTRIBUTION BY SUPPLIERS OF FORMS DOCUMENTING MEDICAL NECESSITY — Section 1834(a)(16) [42 U.S.C.A. 1395m(a)(16)]

Summary

◆ NOTE: This sanction was repealed by section 131(a)(2) of the Social Security Act Amendments of 1994, P.L. 103-432, effective after December 30, 1994.

Section 1834, 42 U.S.C.A. 1395m, authorizes Medicare payment for durable medical equipment. It deals with such matters as formulas for payment; whether reimbursement will be made as rental or purchase; how to calculate reasonable costs with respect to inexpensive and other routinely purchased durable medical equipment; payment for items requiring frequent substantial servicing; payment for certain customized items; payment for oxygen and oxygen equipment; payment for covered items other than durable medical equipment; computation of local and regional payment rates; and payment for miscellaneous devices and items.

Pursuant to section 1834(a)(16), which was added by section 4152(f) of P.L. 101-508, the Omnibus Budget Reconciliation Act of 1990 (OBRA 90), a supplier of a covered item under section 1834 may not distribute to physicians or beneficiaries any completed or partially completed forms or other documents required by the Secretary of Health and Human Services to be submitted to show that a covered item is reasonable and necessary for diagnosis or treatment of an illness or injury or to improve functioning of a malformed body member. This applies to forms and documents distributed for commercial purposes after December 1990. Any supplier who knowingly and willfully violates this prohibition is subject to a civil money penalty not to exceed $1,000 for each such form or document improperly distributed.

Enforcement procedures for this civil money penalty are governed by section 1128A, 42 U.S.C.A. 1320a-7a, which authorizes civil money penalties for a variety of offenses.

Statutory Provisions

Section 1834(a)(16), 42 U.S.C.A. 1395(a)(16), which, pursuant to section 4152(f) of P.L. 101-508, the Omnibus Budget Reconciliation Act of 1990 (OBRA 90), applies to the improper distribution of forms and documents after December 1990, provides:

> (16) PROHIBITION AGAINST DISTRIBUTION BY SUPPLIERS OF FORMS DOCUMENTING MEDICAL NECESSITY. —
>
> (A) IN GENERAL. — A supplier of a covered item under this subsection may not distribute to physicians or to individuals entitled to benefits under this part for commercial purposes any completed or partially completed forms or other documents required by the Secretary to be submitted to show that a covered item is reasonable and necessary for the diagnosis or treatment of illness or injury or to improve the functioning of a malformed body member.
>
> (B) PENALTY. — Any supplier of a covered item who knowingly and willfully distributes a form or other document in violation of subparagraph (A) is subject to a civil money penalty in an amount not to exceed $1,000 for each such form or document so distributed. The provisions of section 1128A [42 U.S.C.A. 1320a-7a] (other than subsections (a) and (b)) shall apply to civil money penalties under this subparagraph in the same manner as they apply to a penalty or proceeding under section 1128A(a).

For regulatory citations, see Chapter 6

§ 2:13.1 VIOLATION OF PROHIBITION AGAINST UNSOLICITED TELEPHONE CONTACTS BY SUPPLIERS Section 1834(a)(17) [42 U.S.C.A. 1395m(a)(17)]

Summary

Section 1834(a)(17), 42 U.S.C.A. 1395m(a)(17), of the Social Security Act, as amended by section 132(a)(1) of the Social Security Act Amendments of 1994, P.L. 100-432, prohibits suppliers from making unsolicited telephone contacts with Medicare beneficiaries to sell items covered under Medicare. This applies to items furnished after December 30, 1994.

Unsolicited contacts may be made, however, in three limited circumstances: (1) when the person contacted has given written permission to the supplier to make the unsolicited contact; (2) when the supplier has previously furnished a covered item to the person contacted and the call pertains only to the furnishing of that item; and (3) when the supplier previously furnished at least one covered item to the person within 15 months prior to making the unsolicited call.

If a supplier knowingly makes a prohibited unsolicited contact, no payment may be made to that supplier under Medicare Part B for any item subsequently furnished to the person contacted by the supplier. Furthermore, if the supplier has a pattern of making prohibited unsolicited telephone contacts, the Secretary of Health and Human Services must exclude the supplier from participation in Medicare. For that, procedures set forth in subsections (c), (f), and (g) of section 1128 of the Social Security Act, 42 U.S.C.A. 1320a-7(c), (f), and (g) apply.

Statutory Provisions

Section 1834(a)(17) of the Social Security Act, 42 U.S.C.A. 1395m(a)(17), provides:

> PROHIBITION AGAINST UNSOLICITED TELEPHONE CONTACTS BY SUPPLIERS. —
>
> (A) IN GENERAL. — A supplier of a covered item under this subsection may not contact an individual enrolled under this

part [Part B] by telephone regarding the furnishing of a covered item to the individual unless 1 of the following applies:

(i) The individual has given written permission to the supplier to make contact by telephone regarding the furnishing of a covered item.

(ii) The supplier has furnished a covered item to the individual and the supplier is contacting the individual only regarding the furnishing of such covered item.

(iii) If the contact is regarding the furnishing of a covered item other than a covered item already furnished to the individual, the supplier has furnished at least 1 covered item to the individual during the 15-month period preceding the date on which the supplier makes such contact.

(B) PROHIBITING PAYMENT FOR ITEMS FURNISHED SUBSEQUENT TO UNSOLICITED CONTACTS. — If a supplier knowingly contacts an individual in violation of subparagraph (A), no payment may be made under this part for any item subsequently furnished to the individual by the supplier.

(C) EXCLUSION FROM PROGRAM FOR SUPPLIERS ENGAGING IN PATTERN OF UNSOLICITED CONTACTS. — If a supplier knowingly contacts individuals in violation of subparagraph (A) to such an extent that the supplier's conduct establishes a pattern of contacts in violation of such subparagraph, the Secretary shall exclude the supplier from participation in the programs under this Act, in accordance with the procedures set forth in subsections (c), (f), and (g) of section 1128 [42 U.S.C.A. 1320a-7(c), (f), and (g)].

For regulatory citations, see Chapter 6

§ 2:13.2 FAILURE BY SUPPLIERS TO MAKE REQUIRED REFUNDS Section 1834(a)(18) [42 U.S.C.A. 1395m(a)(18)]

Summary

Section 1834(a)(17), 42 U.S.C.A. 1395m(a)(17), of the Social Security Act, as amended by section 132(a)(1) of the Social Security Act Amendments of 1994, P.L. 100-432, prohibits suppliers from making unsolicited telephone contacts with Medicare beneficiaries to sell items covered under Medicare. This applies to items furnished after December 30, 1994. Three limited exceptions apply. See § 2:10.2.

Section 1834(a)(18) provides that suppliers who furnish items in violation of the prohibition against unsolicited telephone contacts must make timely refunds to the Medicare beneficiary involved. This applies after December 30, 1994, pursuant to section 132(a)(2) of P.L. 100-432. "Timely basis" means within 30 days after the date the supplier receives a notice from the Medicare carrier that the item is disallowed, if the supplier does not request reconsideration or seek timely appeal, or 15 days after the date the supplier receives notice of an adverse decision after reconsideration or appeal.

If a supplier knowingly and willfully fails to make refunds in violation of section 1834(a)(18)(A), the Secretary of Health and Human Services may apply sanctions against the supplier under section 1842(j)(2), 42 U.S.C.A. 1395u(j)(2), including civil money penalties and exclusion from Medicare. This does not apply, however, if the supplier demonstrates that it did not know and could not reasonably have been expected to know Medicare payment could not be made because of a violation of the prohibition against unsolicited telephone contacts. It also does not apply if the patient was informed before the item was furnished that Medicare payment was not authorized for the item and the patient nevertheless agreed to pay for it.

Statutory Provisions

Section 1834(a)(18), 42 U.S.C.A. 1395m(a)(18), effective December 30, 1994, pursuant to section 132(a)(2) of the Social Security Act Amendments of 1994, P.L. 100-432, provides:

> REFUND OF AMOUNTS COLLECTED FOR CERTAIN DISALLOWED ITEMS. —
>
> (A) IN GENERAL. — If a nonparticipating supplier furnishes to an individual enrolled under this part [Part B] a covered item for which no payment may be made under this part by reason of paragraph (17)(B) [which pertains to items provided in violation of the prohibition against unsolicited telephone contacts (see II-10-B)], the supplier shall refund on a timely basis to the patient (and shall be liable to the patient for) any amounts collected from the patient for the item unless —

(i) the supplier establishes that the supplier did not know and could not reasonably have been expected to know that payment may not be made for the item by reason of paragraph (17)(B), or

(ii) before the item was furnished, the patient was informed that payment under this part may not be made for that item and the patient has agreed to pay for that item.

(B) SANCTIONS. —If a supplier knowingly and willfully fails to make refunds in violation of subparagraph (A), the Secretary may apply sanctions against the supplier in accordance with section 1842(j)(2) [42 U.S.C.A. 1395u(j)(2)].

(C) NOTICE. —Each carrier with a contract in effect under this part with respect to suppliers of covered items shall send any notice of denial of payment for covered items by reason of paragraph (17)(B) and for which payment is not requested on an assignment-related basis to the supplier and the patient involved.

(D) TIMELY BASIS DEFINED. —A refund under subparagraph (A) is considered to be on a timely basis only if—

(i) in the case of a supplier who does not request reconsideration or seek appeal on a timely basis, the refund is made within 30 days after the date the supplier receives a denial notice under subparagraph (C), or

(ii) in the case in which such a reconsideration or appeal is taken, the refund is made within 15 days after the date the supplier receives notice of an adverse determination on reconsideration or appeal.

Section 1842(j)(2) provides:

Subject to paragraph (3), the sanctions which the Secretary may apply under this paragraph are—

(A) excluding a physician from participation in the programs under this Act for a period not to exceed 5 years, in accordance with the procedures of paragraphs (c) [which pertains to notice, effective date, and period of exclusion], (f) [which pertains to notice, hearing, and judicial review], and (g) [which pertains to application for termination of exclusion] of section 1128 [42 U.S.C.A. 1320a-7], or

> (B) civil monetary penalties and assessments, in the same manner as such penalties and assessments are authorized under section 1128A(a) [42 U.S.C.A. 1320a-7a(a)] , or both. The provisions of section 1128A (other than the first 2 sentences of subsection (a) and other than subsection (b)) shall apply to a civil money penalty and assessment under subparagraph (B) in the same manner as such provisions apply to a penalty, assessment, or proceeding under section 1128A(a), except to the extent such provisions are inconsistent with subparagraph (A) or paragraph (3).

Section 1842(j)(3) then provides:

> (A) The Secretary may not exclude a physician pursuant to paragraph (2)(A) if such physician is a sole community physician or sole source of essential specialized services in a community.
>
> (B) The Secretary shall take into account access of beneficiaries to physicians' services for which payment may be made under this part in determining whether to bar a physician from participation under paragraph (2)(A).

For regulatory citations, see Chapter 6

§ 2:14 IMPROPER BILLING BY PHYSICIANS OR SUPPLIERS FOR RADIOLOGIST SERVICES — Section 1834(b)(5)(C) [42 U.S.C.A. 1395m(b)(5)(C)]

Summary

Section 1834(b), 42 U.S.C.A. 1395m(b), required the Secretary of Health and Human Services to establish, effective January 1, 1989, a relative value scale to determine payment for radiologist services. From that relative value scale the Secretary was to establish fee schedules for such services on a regional, statewide, locality, or carrier service area basis. He was to do that in consultation with the Physician Payment Review Commission, the American College of Radiology, and other organizations representing physicians or suppliers who furnish radiologist services.

In conjunction with that, section 1834(b)(5)(A) provides that nonparticipating physicians and suppliers may not charge more for radiologist services than a "limiting charge." Subsection (b)(5)(B) defines limiting charge as 125 percent of the fee schedule for 1989,

120 percent of the fee schedule for 1990, and 115 percent of the fee schedule after 1990.

Section 1834(b)(5)(C) provides that any physician or supplier who does not participate in Medicare and who knowingly and willfully bills in violation of the limits on charges for radiologist services is subject to exclusion for a period not to exceed 5 years in accordance with procedures under section 1128, 42 U.S.C.A. 1320a-7, and to a civil money penalty under section 1128A, 42 U.S.C.A. 1320a-7a. See cross-reference to section 1842(j)(2), 42 U.S.C.A. 1395u(j)(2).

Statutory Provisions

Section 1834(b), 42 U.S.C.A. 1395m(b), provides:

FEE SCHEDULES FOR RADIOLOGIST SERVICES. —

(1) DEVELOPMENT. — The Secretary shall develop —

(A) a relative value scale to serve as the basis for the payment for radiologist services under this part, and

(B) using such scale and appropriate conversion factors [Effective January 1, 1990, section 201(a)(1) of P.L. 101-234, the Medicare Catastrophic Coverage Repeal Act of 1989, repealed "and subject to subsection (e)(1)(A)" which had followed "conversion factors" and which referred to payment for screening mammography.] and subject to subsection (c)(1)(A) [which pertains to screening mammography subsequently re-authorized after December 1990 by section 4163(b)(2) of P.L. 101-508, the Omnibus Budget Reconciliation Act of 1990 (OBRA 90), which added a new section 1834(c)], fee schedules (on a regional, statewide, locality ["locality" added by section 4102(f) of OBRA 90, effective December 22, 1987, as if included in OBRA 87], or carrier service area basis) for payment for radiologist services under this part [Part B], to be implemented for such services furnished during 1989.

(2) CONSULTATION. — In carrying out paragraph (1), the Secretary shall regularly consult closely with the Physician Payment Review Commission, the American College of Radiology, and other organizations representing physicians or suppliers who furnish radiologist services and shall share with them the data and data analysis being used to make the determinations under paragraph (1), including data on varia-

tions in current medicare payments by geographic area, and by service and physician specialty.

(3) CONSIDERATIONS. — In developing the relative value scale and fee schedules under paragraph (1), the Secretary —

(A) shall take into consideration variations in the cost of furnishing such services among geographic areas and among different sites where services are furnished, and

(B) may also take into consideration such other factors respecting the manner in which physicians in different specialties furnish such services as may be appropriate to assure that payment amounts are equitable and designed to promote effective and efficient provision of radiologist services by physicians in the different specialties.

(4) SAVINGS. —

(A) BUDGET NEUTRAL FEE SCHEDULES. — The Secretary shall develop preliminary fee schedules for 1989, which are designed to result in the same amount of aggregate payments (net of any insurance and deductibles under section 1835(a)(1)(J) [42 U.S.C.A. 1395l(a)(1)(J), which pertains to payment for radiologist services] and 1833(b) [42 U.S.C.A. 1395l(b), which pertains to deductibles]) for radiologist services furnished in 1989 as would have been made if this subsection had not been enacted.

(B) INITIAL SAVINGS. — The fee schedules established for payment purposes under this subsection for services furnished in 1989 shall be 97 percent of the amounts permitted under these preliminary fee schedules developed under subparagraph (A).

◆ NOTE: Effective December 19, 1989, sections 6105(a), (b), and (c) of P.L. 101-239, the Omnibus Budget Reconciliation Act of 1989, added the following paragraph (C) and redesignated former paragraphs (C) and (D) respectively as (D) and (E). Subsequently, however, section 4102(a) of OBRA 90, applicable to services furnished after December 1990, redesignated subparagraphs (b)(4)(D) and E) as subparagraphs (b)(4)(E) and (F) and added a new subparagraph (B)(4)(D). In addition, section 4102(d) of OBRA 90 added an inappropriately identified second subparagraph (E). Thus what is set forth below is the statute as amended by OBRA 90.

(C) 1990 FEE SCHEDULES. — For radiologist services (other than portable X-ray services) furnished under this part during 1990, after March 31 of such year, the conversion factors used under this subsection shall be 96 percent of the conversion factors that applied under this subsection as of December 31, 1989.

(D) 1991 FEE SCHEDULES. — For radiologist services (other than portable X-ray services) furnished under this part during 1991, the conversion factors used in a locality under this subsection shall, subject to clause (vii), be reduced to the adjusted conversion factor for the locality determined as follows: [The phrase beginning "used in" and ending with the colon was changed by section 126(b)(2)(A) of the Social Security Act Amendments of 1994, P.L. 103-432, effective as if enacted by OBRA 1990 (November 5, 1990). Previously it read: "used in a locality under this subsection shall be determined as follows:".]

(i) NATIONAL WEIGHTED AVERAGE CONVERSION FACTOR. — The Secretary shall estimate the national weighted average of the conversion factors used under this subsection for services furnished during 1990 beginning on April 1, using the best available data.

(ii) REDUCED NATIONAL WEIGHTED AVERAGE. — The national weighted average estimated under clause (i) shall be reduced by 13 percent.

(iii) COMPUTATION OF 1990 LOCALITY INDEX RELATIVE TO NATIONAL AVERAGE. — The Secretary shall establish an index which reflects, for each locality, the ratio of the conversion factor used in the locality under this subsection to the national weighted average estimated under clause (i).

(iv) ADJUSTED CONVERSION FACTOR.— The adjusted conversion factor for the professional or technical component of a service in a locality is the sum of 1/2 of the locally-adjusted amount determined under clause (v) and 1/2 of the GPCI-adjusted amount determined under clause (vi). [Subsection (iv) was amended by section 126(b)(2)(B) of the Social Security Act Amendments of 1994, effective as if enacted in OBRA 90. Previously, it read: "LOCAL ADJUSTMENT.--Subject to clause (vii), the conversion factor to be applied to the professional or technical component of a service in a locality is the sum of 1/2 of the locally-adjusted amount determined under clause (v) and 1/2 of the GPCI-adjusted amount determined under clause (vi)."]

(v) LOCALLY-ADJUSTED AMOUNT. — For purposes of clause (iv), the locally adjusted amount determined under this clause is the product of (I) the national weighted average conversion factor computed under clause (ii), and (II) the index value established under clause (iii) for the locality.

(vi) GPCI-ADJUSTED AMOUNT. — For purposes of clause (iv), the GPCI-adjusted amount determined under this clause is the sum of—

(I) the product of (a) the portion of the reduced national weighted average conversion factor computed under clause (ii) which is attributable to physician work and (b) the geographic work index value for the locality (specified in Addendum C to the Model Fee Schedule for Physician Services (published on September 4, 1990, 55 Federal Register pp. 36238-36243)); and

(II) the product of (a) the remaining portion of the reduced national weighted average conversion factor computed under clause (ii), and (b) the geographic practice cost index value specified in section 1842(b)(14)(C)(iv) for the locality. In applying this clause with respect to the professional component of a service, 80 percent of the conversion factor shall be considered to be attributable to physician work and with respect to the technical component of the service, 0 percent shall be considered to be attributable to physician work.

(vii) LIMITS ON CONVERSION FACTOR. — The conversion factor to be applied to a locality under this subparagraph to the professional or technical component of a service shall not be more than 9.5 percent below the conversion factor applied in the locality under subparagraph (C) to such component, but in no case shall the conversion factor be less than 60 percent of the national weighted average of the conversion factors (computed under clause (i)).

(E) SUBSEQUENT UPDATING. — For radiologist services furnished in subsequent years, the fee schedules shall be the schedules for the previous year updated by the percentage increase in the MEI (as defined in section 1842(i)(3) [42 U.S.C.A. 1395u(i)(3), which pertains to the Medicare Economic Index]) for the year.

(F) RULE FOR CERTAIN SCANNING SERVICES. — In the case of the technical components of magnetic resonance imaging (MRI) services and computer assisted tomography (CAT) services furnished after December 31, 1990, the amount otherwise payable shall be reduced by 10 percent. [The heading "Rule for certain scanning services" was added effective as if enacted by OBRA 90 by section 126(b)(5) of the Social Security Act Amendments of 1994. section 126(b)(1) thereof corrected the former duplicate "(E)" to "(F)", and the former "(F)" was corrected to "(G)" herebelow.]

(G) NONPARTICIPATING PHYSICIANS AND SUPPLIERS. — Each fee schedule so established shall provide that the payment rate recognized for nonparticipating physicians and suppliers is equal to the appropriate percent (as defined in section 1842(b)(4)(A)(iv) [42 U.S.C.A. 1395u(b)(4)(A)(iv), which pertains to reasonable charges for physicians' services furnished on or after January 1, 1987, by nonparticipating physicians and payment limits]) of the payment rate recognized for participating physicians and suppliers.

(5) LIMITING CHARGES OF NONPARTICIPATING PHYSICIANS AND SUPPLIERS. —

(A) IN GENERAL. — In the case of radiologist services furnished after January 1, 1989, for which payment is made under a fee schedule under this subsection, if a nonparticipating physician or supplier furnishes the service to an individual entitled to benefits under this part, the physician or supplier may not charge the individual more than the limiting charge (as defined in subparagraph (B)).

(B) LIMITING CHARGE DEFINED. — In subparagraph (A), the term "limiting charge" means, with respect to a service furnished —

(i) in 1989, 125 percent of the amount specified for the service in the appropriate fee schedule established under paragraph (1),

(ii) in 1990, 120 percent of the amount specified for the service in the appropriate fee schedule established under paragraph (1), and

(iii) after 1990, 115 percent of the amount specified for the service in the appropriate fee schedule established under paragraph (1).

(C) ENFORCEMENT. — If a physician or supplier knowingly and willfully bills in violation of subparagraph (A), the Secretary may apply sanctions against such physician or supplier in accordance with section 1842(j)(2) [42 U.S.C.A. 1395u(j)(2)] in the same manner as such sanctions may apply to a physician.

(6) RADIOLOGIST SERVICES DEFINED. — For the purposes of this subsection and section 1833(a)(1)(J) [42 U.S.C.A. 1395l(a)(1)(J), which authorizes payment for expenses incurred for radiologist services (as defined in section 1834(b)(6)], the term "radiologist services" only includes radiology services performed by, or under the direction or supervision of, a physician —

(A) who is certified, or eligible to be certified, by the American Board of Radiology, or

(B) for whom radiology services account for at least 50 percent of the total amount of charges made under this part [part B].

Section 1842(j)(2) provides:

Subject to paragraph (3), the sanctions which the Secretary may apply under this paragraph are —

(A) excluding a physician from participation in the programs under this Act for a period not to exceed 5 years, in accordance with the procedures of paragraphs (c) [which pertains to notice, effective date, and period of exclusion], (f) [which pertains to notice, hearing, and judicial review], and

(g) [which pertains to application for termination of exclusion] of section 1128 [42 U.S.C.A. 1320a-7], or

(B) civil monetary penalties and assessments, in the same manner as such penalties and assessments are authorized under section 1128A(a) [42 U.S.C.A. 1320a-7a(a)], or both. The provisions of section 1128A (other than the first 2 sentences of subsection (a) and other than subsection (b)) shall apply to a civil money penalty and assessment under subparagraph (B) in the same manner as such provisions apply to a penalty, assessment, or proceeding under section 1128A(a), except to the extent such provisions are inconsistent with subparagraph (A) or paragraph (3).

Section 1842(j)(3) then provides:

(A) The Secretary may not exclude a physician pursuant to paragraph (2)(A) if such physician is a sole community physician or sole source of essential specialized services in a community.

(B) The Secretary shall take into account access of beneficiaries to physicians' services for which payment may be made under this part in determining whether to bar a physician from participation under paragraph (2)(A).

For regulatory citations, see Chapter 6

§ 2:15 OVERCHARGING FOR SERVICES OF A PHYSICIAN ASSISTANT OR NURSE PRACTITIONER — Section 1842(b)(12)(C) [42 U.S.C.A. 1395u(b)(12)(C)]

Summary

◆ NOTE: This sanction was repealed effective October 31, 1994, by section 123(b)(2)(B) of the Social Security Act Amendments of 1994, P.L. 103-432.

Sections 1842(b)(12)(A) and (B), 42 U.S.C.A. 1395u(b)(12)(A) and (B), provide that payment for services of a physician assistant or nurse practitioner may be made only on an assignment-related basis. They also provide that prevailing charges for physician assistant services at surgery may not exceed 65 percent of the amount authorized for such services when performed by a physician as an assistant at surgery. In non-surgery cases the prevailing charges for physician assistant services may not exceed 75 percent of the amount authorized for such services when performed by a non-specialist physician, if performed in a hospital, and they may not exceed 85 percent in the case of other services.

Pursuant to section 1842(b)(12)(C), any person who knowingly and willfully presents, or causes to be presented, to a beneficiary a bill or request for payment for the services of a physician assistant (except for applicable deductible and coinsurance amounts) in violation of the assignment requirement is subject to a civil money penalty not to exceed $2,000.

Enforcement procedures for this civil money penalty are governed by section 1128A, 42 U.S.C.A. 1320a-7a, which authorizes civil money penalties for a variety of offenses.

Statutory Provisions

As amended effective November 5, 1990, by sections 4118(f)(2)(C) of P.L. 101-508, the Omnibus Budget Reconciliation Act of 1990, section 1842(b)(12), 42 U.S.C.A. 1395u(b)(12), provides:

> (A) With respect to services described in clauses (i), (ii), or (iv) of section 1861(s)(2)(K) [42 U.S.C.A. 1395x(s)(2)(K), which is the definition section, as amended by the addition of "in clauses (i), (ii), or (iv) of" here and below in paragraph (C) by section 4155(c) of OBRA 90] (relating to physician assistants and nurse practitioners) [Prior to December 19, 1989, the effective date of P.L. 101-239, the Omnibus Budget Reconciliation Act of 1989 (OBRA 89 — see section 6102(e)(4)), this parenthetical clause read (relating to a physician assistant acting under the supervision of a physician)".] —
>
> (i) payment under this part may only be made on an assignment-related basis; and
>
> (ii) the prevailing charges determined under paragraph (3) shall not exceed —
>
> (I) in the case of services performed as an assistant at surgery, 65 percent of the amount that would otherwise be recognized if performed by a physician who is serving as an assistant at surgery, or
>
> (II) in other cases, the applicable percentage (as defined in subparagraph (B)) of the prevailing charge rate determined for such services (or, for services furnished on or after Janu-

ary 1, 1992, the fee schedule amount specified in section 1848 [42 U.S.C.A. 1395w-(4)(a), which establishes payment for physicians' services based on fee schedules, pursuant to section 6012(a) of OBRA 89. Note however, that this parenthetical clause became effective December 19, 1989, pursuant to section 6114(b) of OBRA 89. Also, the phrase "as the case may be" following "section 1848" was deleted by section 4118(f)(2)(C) of OBRA 90.]) performed by physicians who are not specialists.

(B) in subparagraph (A)(ii)(II), the term "applicable percentage" means —

(i) 75 percent in the case of services performed (other than as an assistant at surgery) in a hospital, and

(ii) 85 percent in the case of other services.

(C) Except for deductible and coinsurance amounts applicable under section 1833 [42 U.S.C.A. 1395l] any person who knowingly and willfully presents, or causes to be presented, to an individual enrolled under this part a bill or request for payment for services described in clauses (i), (ii), or (iv) of section 1861(s)(2)(K) [42 U.S.C.A. 1395x(s)(2)(K), which is the definition section pertaining to services of a physician assistant or nurse practitioner] in violation of (A)(i) is subject to a civil money penalty of not to exceed $2,000 for each such bill or request. The provisions of section 1128A [42 U.S.C.A. 1320a-7a] (other than subsections (a) and (b)) shall apply to a civil money penalty under the previous sentence in the same manner as such provisions apply to a penalty or proceeding under section 1128A(a).

For regulatory citations, see Chapter 6

§ 2:15.1 FAILURE BY PRACTITIONERS TO BILL ON AN ASSIGNMENT-RELATED BASIS — Section 1842(b)(18) and Sections 1834(k) and (l) [42 U.S.C.A. 1395u(b)(18)and 42 U.S.C.A. 1394m(k) and (l)]

Summary

Under Medicare Part B, certain medical practitioners are paid based on reasonable charges or in accordance with a Medicare-prescribed fee schedule. Pursuant to section 1842(b)(18)(A), 42 U.S.C.A. 1395u(b)(18)(A), such payments may only be made to those practitioners on an assignment-related basis. Section 123(b)(1) of the Social Security Act Amendments of 1994, P.L. 103–432, made this change effective for services furnished on or after January 1, 1995.

If a specified practitioner, or other person, knowingly and willfully bills or collects an amount for a service (other than applicable Medicare deductible and coinsurance amounts), section 1842(b)(18)(B) authorizes the Secretary of Health and Human Services to apply sanctions in accordance with section 1842(j), 42 U.S.C.A. 1395u(j). Those sanctions are exclusion from Medicare and imposition of civil money penalties and assessments.

According to section 1842(b)(18)(B) and (C), practitioners who must bill on an assignment-related basis include:

physician assistants (as defined in section 1861(aa)(5), 42 U.S.C.A. 1395x(aa)(5))

nurse practitioners (as defined in section 1861(aa)(5))

clinical nurse specialists (as defined in section 1861(aa)(5)) certified registered nurse anesthetists (as defined in section 1861(bb)(2), 42 U.S.C.A. 1395x(bb)(2))

certified nurse-midwives (as defined in section 1861(gg)(2), 42 U.S.C.A. 1395x(gg)(2))

clinical social workers (as defined in section 1861 (hh)(1), 42 U.S.C.A. 1395x(hh)(1))

clinical psychologists (as defined by the Secretary for purposes of section 1861(ii), 42 U.S.C.A. 1395x (ii))

By cross-reference from section 1834m(k)(6), 42 U.S.C.A. 1395m(k)(6), the requirement to bill on an assignment-related basis also applies with respect to outpatient rehabilitation services. By cross-reference from section 1834l, 42 U.S.C.A. 1395m(l), the same requirement applies to ambulance services.

◆ NOTE: Section 4541(a)(2) of the Balanced Budget Act of 1997, P.L. 105–33, made the requirement for outpatient rehabilitation services applicable to services furnished on or after January 1, 1998. That includes portions of cost reporting periods on or after that date. Section 4531(b)(2) made the requirement apply to ambulance services furnished on or after January 1, 2000.

According to section 1842(b)(18)(D), a service furnished by a practitioner described in subparagraph (C) includes any services and supplies furnished incident to the service as would otherwise be covered under Part B if furnished by a physician or as incident to a physician's service.

By cross-reference from section 1842(b)(18)(B) to section 1842(j)(2), 42 U.S.C.A. 1395u(j)(2), the penalty for violating the requirement to bill on an assignment-related basis may be exclusion of a physician from Medicare for a period not to exceed 5 years. This is to be done in accordance with procedures in subsections (c), (f), and (g) of section 1128, 42 U.S.C.A. 1320a-7. Subsection (c) pertains to notice, effective date, and period of an exclusion. Subsection (f) pertains to hearing and judicial review. Subsection (g) pertains to application for termination of exclusion,

Alternatively, the penalty for any practitioner or other person may be a civil monetary penalty and assessment in the same manner as such penalties and assessments apply under section 1128(A)(a), 42 U.S.C.A. 1320a-7a(a), which authorizes civil money penalties for various offenses.

Also by cross-reference from section 1842(b)(18)(B), section 1842(j)(4) applies to violations of the requirement to bill on an assignment-related basis. The latter section provides that the Secretary may, out of any civil money penalty or assessment collected from a physician pursuant to this subsection, make a payment to a beneficiary enrolled under Part B in the nature of restitution for amounts paid by such physician which is determined to be an excess charge.

Statutory Provisions

Section 1842(b)(18), 42 U.S.C.A. 1395u(b)(18), provides:

> (A) Payment for any service furnished by a practitioner described in subparagraph (C) and for which payment may be made under this part [Part B] on a reasonable charge or fee schedule basis may only be made under this part on an assignment-related basis.
>
> (B) A practitioner described in subparagraph (C) or other person may not bill (or collect any amount from) the individual or another person for any service described in subparagraph (A), except for deductible and coinsurance amounts applicable under this part. No person is liable for payment of any amounts billed

for such a service in violation of the previous sentence. If a practitioner or other person knowingly and willfully bills (or collects an amount) for such a service in violation of such sentence, the Secretary may apply sanctions against the practitioner or other person in the same manner as the Secretary may apply sanctions against a physician in accordance with subsection (j)(2) in the same manner as such section applies with respect to a physician. Paragraph (4) of subsection (j) shall apply in this subparagraph in the same manner as such paragraph applies to such section.

(C) A practitioner described in this subparagraph is any of the following:

(i) A physician assistant, nurse practitioner, or clinical nurse specialist (as defined in section 1861(aa)(5)).

(ii) A certified registered nurse anesthetist (as defined in section 1861(bb)(2)).

(iii) A certified nurse-midwife (as defined in section 1861(gg)(2)).

(iv) A clinical social worker (as defined in section 1861(hh)(1)).

(v) A clinical psychologist (as defined by the Secretary for purposes of section 1861(ii)).

vi (vi) A registered dietitian or nutrition professional. [NOTE: This applies to services of dietitians and nutritional professionals furnished on or after January 1, 2002. See section 105(d) of P.L. 106-544, the Medicare, Medicaid, and SCHIP Benefits Improvement and Protection Act, enacted December 15, 2000.]

(D) For purposes of this paragraph, a service furnished by a practitioner described in subparagraph (C) includes any services and supplies furnished as incident to the service as would otherwise be covered under this part if furnished by a physician or as incident to a physician's service.

Section 1834m(k)(6), 42 U.S.C.A. 1395m(k)(6), provides in pertinent part:

PAYMENT FOR OUTPATIENT THERAPY SERVICES AND COMPREHENSIVE OUTPATIENT REHABILITATION SERVICES. —

* * *

(6) RESTRAINT ON BILLING. — The provisions of subparagraphs (A) and (B) of section 1842(b)(18) shall apply to therapy services for which payment is made under this subsection in the same manner as they apply to services provided by a practitioner described in section 1842(b)(18)(C).

Section 1834l, 42 U.S.C.A. 1395m(l), provides in pertinent part:

ESTABLISHMENT OF FEE SCHEDULE FOR AMBULANCE SERVICES. —

* * *

(6) RESTRAINT ON BILLING. — The provisions of subparagraphs (A) and (B) of section 1842(b)(18) shall apply to ambulance services for which payment is made under this subsection in the same manner as they apply to services provided by a practitioner described in section 1842(b)(18)(C).

Section 1842(j)(2) provides:

Subject to paragraph (3), the sanctions which the Secretary may apply under this paragraph are —

(A) excluding a physician from participation in the programs under this Act for a period not to exceed 5 years, in accordance with the procedures of paragraphs (c) [which pertains to notice, effective date, and period of exclusion], (f) [which pertains to notice, hearing, and judicial review], and (g) [which pertains to application for termination of exclusion] of section 1128 [42 U.S.C.A. 1320a-7], or

(B) civil monetary penalties and assessments, in the same manner as such penalties and assessments are authorized under section 1128A(a) [42 U.S.C.A. 1320a-7a(a)], or both. The provisions of section 1128A (other than the first 2 sentences of subsection (a) and other than subsection (b)) shall apply to a civil money penalty and assessment under subparagraph (B) in the same manner as such provisions apply to a penalty, assessment, or proceeding under section 1128A(a), except to the extent such provisions are inconsistent with subparagraph (A) or paragraph (3).

Section 1842(j)(3) then provides:

(A) The Secretary may not exclude a physician pursuant to paragraph (2)(A) if such physician is a sole community physician or sole source of essential specialized services in a community.

(B) The Secretary shall take into account access of beneficiaries to physicians' services for which payment may be made under this part in determining whether to bar a physician from participation under paragraph (2)(A).

Finally, in section 1842(j)(4), Congress gave the Secretary discretion to make restitution to Medicare beneficiaries affected by violations of the physician fee freeze out of civil monetary penalties or assessments collected. That provision reads:

The Secretary may, out of any civil monetary penalty or assessment collected from a physician pursuant to this subsection, make a payment to a beneficiary enrolled under this part in the nature of restitution for amounts paid by such beneficiary to such physician which was determined to be an excess charge under paragraph (1).

For regulatory citations, see Chapter 6

§ 2:15.2 DENIAL, TERMINATION, AND NONRENEWAL OF PHYSICIAN AND SUPPLIER PARTICIPATION AGREEMENTS — Section 1842(h) [42 U.S.C.A. 1395u(h)]

Summary

Those who wish to participate in Medicare as a physician or supplier must enter into a participation agreement with the Secretary of Health and Human Services, in accordance with section 1842(h) of the Social Security Act, 42 U.S.C.A. 1395u(h). Among other requirements, that agreement obligates them to accept payment under Medicare Part B on an assignment-related basis for all items and services furnished to Medicare beneficiaries enrolled in Part B during the term of the agreement.

Pursuant to section 1842(h)(8), the Secretary may refuse to enter into a participation agreement with a physician or supplier, or may terminate or refuse to renew such an agreement, if the physician or supplier has been convicted of a felony under Federal or State law. The felony conviction must be for an offense which the Secretary determines is detrimental to the best interests of Medicare or Medicare beneficiaries.

This authority to deny, terminate, or not renew a participation agreement applies to the entry and renewal of agreements on or after August 5, 1997, pursuant to section 4302(b) of the Balanced Budget Act of 1997, P.L. 105–33.

Statutory Provisions

Section 1842(h)(1), 42 U.S.C.A. 1395u(h)(1), provides:

> Any physician or supplier may voluntarily enter into an agreement with the Secretary to become a participating physician or supplier. For purposes of this section, the term "participating physician or supplier" means a physician or supplier (excluding any provider of services) who, before the beginning of any year beginning with 1984, enters into an agreement with the Secretary which provides that such physician or supplier will accept payment under this part on an assignment-related basis for all items and services furnished to individuals enrolled under this part during such year. In the case of a newly licensed physician or a physician who begins a practice in a new area, or in the case of a new supplier who begins a new business, or in such similar cases as the Secretary may specify, such physician or supplier may enter into such an agreement after the beginning of a year, for items and services furnished during the remainder of the year.

Section 1842(h)(8), provides:

> The Secretary may refuse to enter into an agreement with a physician or supplier under this subsection, or may terminate or refuse to renew such agreement, in the event that such physician or supplier has been convicted of a felony under Federal or State law for an offense which the Secretary determines is detrimental to the best interests of the program or program beneficiaries.

For regulatory citations, see Chapter 6

§ 2:16 VIOLATING THE FREEZE ON PHYSICIAN FEES— Section 1842(j)(1) [42 U.S.C.A. 1395u(j)(1)]

Summary

For 30 months beginning July 1, 1984, Congress imposed a freeze on fees charged by nonparticipating physicians for items and services covered by Medicare. Congress also required the Secretary of Health and Human Services to monitor such physicians' actual charges to Medicare beneficiaries during that period. See section 1842(j), 42 U.S.C.A. 1395u(j). Then it provided that any such physician who knowingly and willfully billed beneficiaries in excess of the maximum allowed would be subject to exclusion for a period not to exceed 5 years in accordance with procedures under section 1128, 42 U.S.C.A. 1320a-7, or to imposition of a civil money penalty under section 1128A, 42 U.S.C.A. 1320a-7a.

Subsequently, Congress provided for similar monitoring during any period on or after January 1, 1987, until the earlier of either December 31, 1990, or one year after the date the Secretary reported to Congress on the development of a relative value scale for physician fees. Then it provided that such physicians who for that period of time knowingly and willfully billed on a repeated basis an excessive amount for a physician service are subject to exclusion in accordance with procedures under section 1128 and to imposition of a civil money penalty under section 1128A.

In addition, in section 1842(j)(1)(C), 42 U.S.C.A. 1395u(j)(1)(C), Congress established a formula for limiting physician fees for nonparticipating physicians. If applying that formula results in reduction in a reasonable charge for a physician's service or item and a nonparticipating physician furnished the service or item to a beneficiary thereafter, that physician may not charge the beneficiary more than 125 percent of the reduced payment allowance. Pursuant to section 1842(j)(1)(D)(iv) and section 1842(j)(2), any such physician who violates that requirement knowingly and willfully is subject to exclusion for a period not to exceed 5 years in accordance with provisions under section 1128 and to imposition of a civil money penalty under section 1128A.

◆ NOTE: Physicians who are either the "sole community physician" or who are a "sole source of essential specialized services in a community" may not be excluded under section 1842(j)(2). Furthermore, pursuant to section 1842(j)(4), the Secretary may use civil money penalties and assessments collected under this provision to make restitution to beneficiaries who paid excessive charges because of violation of the fee freeze.

Enforcement procedures for these civil money penalties are governed by section 1128A, 42 U.S.C.A. 1320a-7a, which authorizes civil money penalties for a variety of offenses.

Statutory Provisions

Section 1842(j)(1), 42 U.S.C.A. 1395u(j)(1), provides:

(A) In the case of a physician who is not a participating physician for items and services furnished during a portion of the 30-month period beginning July 1, 1984, the Secretary shall monitor the physician's actual charges to individuals enrolled under this part for physicians' services during that portion of that period. If such physician knowingly and willfully bills individuals enrolled under this part for actual charges in excess of such physician's actual charges for the calendar quarter beginning on April 1, 1984, the Secretary may apply sanctions against such physician in accordance with paragraph (2).

(B) (i) During any period (on or after January 1, 1987, and before the date specified in clause (ii)), during which a physician is a nonparticipating physician, the Secretary shall monitor the actual charges of each such physician for physicians' services furnished to individuals enrolled under this part. If such physician knowingly and willfully bills on a repeated basis for such a service an actual charge in excess of the maximum allowable actual charge determined under subparagraph (C) for that service, the Secretary may apply sanctions against such physician in accordance with paragraph (2).

(ii) Clause (i) shall not apply to services furnished after December 31, 1990.

◆ NOTE: Effective December 19, 1989, section 6102(e)(9) of P.L. 101-239, the Omnibus Budget Reconciliation Act of 1989, changed clause (ii) above to read as indicated. Previously it read: (ii) Clause (i) shall not apply to services furnished after the earlier of (I) December 31, 1990, or (II) one year after the date the Secretary reports to Congress, under section 1845(e)(3), on the development of the relative value scale under section 1845 [42 U.S.C.A. 1395w-1].

(C) (i) For a particular physicians' [sic physician's] service furnished by a nonparticipating physician to individuals enrolled under this part during a year, for purposes of subparagraph (B), the maximum allowable actual charge is determined as follows: If the physician's maximum allowable actual charge for that service in the previous year was —

(I) less than 115 percent of the applicable percent (as defined in subsection (b)(4)(A)(iv)) of the prevailing charge for the year and service involved, the maximum allowable actual charge for the year involved is the greater of the maximum allowable actual charge described in subclause (II) or the charge described in clause (ii), or

(II) equal to, or greater than, 115 percent of the applicable percent (as defined in subsection (b)(4)(A)(iv)) of the prevailing charge for the year and service involved, the maximum allowable actual charge is 101 percent of the physician's maximum allowable actual charge for the service for the previous year.

(ii) For purposes of clause (i)(I), the charge described in this clause for a particular physicians' [sic physician's] service furnished in a year is the maximum allowable actual charge for the service of the physician for the previous year plus the product of (I) the applicable fraction (as defined in clause (iii)) and (II) the amount by which 115 percent of the prevailing charge for the year involved for such service furnished by nonparticipating physicians, exceeds the physician's maximum allowable actual charge for the service for the previous year.

(iii) In clause (ii), the "applicable fraction" is —

(I) for 1987, 1/4,

(II) for 1988, 1/3,

(III) or 1989, 1/2,

(IV) for any subsequent year, 1.

(iv) For purposes of determining the maximum allowable actual charge under clauses (i) and (ii) for 1987, in the case of a physicians' [sic physician's] service for which the physician has actual charges for the calendar quarter beginning on April 1, 1984, the "maximum allowable charge" for 1986 is the physician's actual charge for such service furnished during such quarter.

(v) For purposes of determining the maximum allowable actual charge under clauses (i) and (ii) for a year after 1986, in the case of a physicians' [sic physician's] service for which the physician has no actual charges for the calendar quarter beginning on April 1, 1984, and for which a maximum allowable actual charge has not been previously established under this clause, the "maximum allowable actual charge" for the previous year shall be the 50th percentile of the customary charges for the service (weighted by frequency of the service) performed by nonparticipating physicians in the locality during the 12-month period ending June 30 of that previous year.

(vi) For purposes of this subparagraph, a "physician's actual charge" for a physicians' [sic physician's] service furnished in a year or other period is the weighted average (or, at the option of the Secretary for a service furnished in the calendar quarter beginning April 1, 1984, the median) of the physician's charges for such service furnished in the year or other period.

(vii) In the case of a nonparticipating physician who was a participating physician during a previous period, for the purpose of computing the physician's maximum allowable actual charge during the physician's period of nonparticipation, the physician shall be deemed to have had a maximum allowable actual charge during the period of participation, and such deemed maximum allowable actual charge shall be determined accordingly [sic according] to clauses (i) through (vi).

(viii) Notwithstanding any other provision of this subparagraph, the maximum allowable actual charge for a particular physician's service furnished by a nonparticipating physician to individuals enrolled under this part during the 3-month period beginning on January 1, 1988, shall be the amount determined under this subparagraph for 1987. The maximum allowable actual charge for any such service otherwise determined under this subparagraph for 1988 shall take effect on April 1, 1988.

(ix) If there is a reduction under subsection (b)(13) in the reasonable charge for medical direction furnished by a nonparticipating physician, the maximum allowable actual charge otherwise permitted under this subsection for such services shall be reduced in the same manner and in the same percentage as the reduction in such reasonable charge.

(D) (i) If an action described in clause (ii) results in a reduction in a reasonable charge for a physicians' [sic physician's] service or item and a nonparticipating physician furnishes the service or item to an individual entitled to benefits under this part after the effective date of such action, the physician may not charge the individual more than 125 percent of the reduced payment allowance (as defined in clause (iii)) plus (for services or items furnished during the 12-month period (or 9-month period in the case of an action described in clause (ii)(II)) beginning on the effective date of the action) 1/2 of the amount by which the physician's maximum allowable actual charge for the service or item for the previous 12-month period exceeds such 125 percent level.

(ii) The first sentence of clause (i) shall apply to —

(I) an adjustment under subsection (b)(8)(B) (relating to inherent reasonableness),

(II) a reduction under subsection (b)(10)(A) or (b)(14)(A) (relating to certain overpriced procedures) [(b)(10)(A) pertains to reasonable charges for bronchoscopy, carpal tunnel repair, cataract surgery (including subsequent insertion of an intraocular lens), coronary artery bypass surgery, diagnostic and/or therapeutic dilation and curettage, knee arthroscopy, knee arthroplasty, pacemaker implantation surgery, total hip replacement, suprapubic prostatectomy, transurethral resection of the prostate, and upper gastrointestinal endoscopy; "or (b)(14)(A)", added effective December 19, 1989, by section 6104(b) of P.L. 101-239, the Omnibus Budget Reconciliation of 1989, pertains to reduced prevailing charges for physicians' services],

(III) a reduction under subsection (b)(11)(B) (relating to certain cataract procedures) [which pertains to the reasonable charge for a cataract surgical procedure],

(IV) a prevailing charge limit established under subsection (b)(11)(C)(i) [which pertains to the prevailing charge for A-mode ophthalmic ultrasound procedures] or (b)(15)(A) ["or (b)(15)(A)", added effective December 19, 1989, by section 6108(b)(1) of OBRA 89 pertains to limitations on prevailing charges for surgery, radiology, and diagnostic physicians' services and applies to procedures performed after March 31, 1990],

(V) a reasonable charge limit established under subsection (b)(11)(C)(ii) [which pertains to the reasonable charge for an intraocular lens inserted during or subsequent to cataract surgery in a physician's office], and

(VI) an adjustment under section 1833(l)(3)(B) (relating to physician supervision of certified registered nurse anesthetists) [which pertains to the prevailing charge for physician direction of CRNA's and fee schedules for CRNA's].

(iii) In clause (i), the term "reduced payment allowance" means, with respect to an action —

(I) under subsection (b)(8)(B), the inherently reasonable charge established under subsection (b)(8);

(II) under subsection (b)(10)(A) [which pertains to reasonable charges for bronchoscopy, carpal tunnel repair, cataract surgery (including subsequent insertion of an intraocular lens), coronary artery bypass surgery, diagnostic and/or therapeutic dilation and curettage, knee arthroscopy, knee arthroplasty, pacemaker implantation surgery, total hip replacement, suprapubic prostatectomy, transurethral resection of the prostate, and upper gastrointestinal endoscopy], (b)(11)(B) [which pertains to the reasonable charge for a cataract surgical procedure], or (b)(11)(C)(i) [which pertains to the prevailing charge for A-mode ophthalmic ultrasound procedures], or (b)(14)(A) [added as indicated above, which pertains to reduced prevailing charges for physicians' services], or (b)(15)(A) [added as indicated above, which pertains to limitations on prevailing charges for surgery, radiology, and diagnostic physicians' services] or under section 1833(l)(3)(B) [which pertains to the prevailing charge for physician direction of CRNA's and fee schedules for CRNA's], the prevailing charge for the service after the action; or

(III) under subsection (b)(11)(C)(ii) [which pertains to the reasonable charge for an intraocular lens inserted during or subsequent to cataract surgery in a physician's office], the payment allowance established under such subsection.

* * *

(v) Clause (i) shall not apply to items and services furnished after the earlier of (I) December 31, 1990, or (II) one year after the date the Secretary reports to Congress, under section 1845(e)(3), on the development of the relative value scale under section 1845.

◆ NOTE: Effective December 19, 1989, section 6102(e)(9) of OBRA 89 substituted "December 31, 1990" for "the earlier of (I) December 31, 1990, or (II) one year after the date the Secretary reports to Congress, under section 1845(e)(3) [42 U.S.C.A. 1395w-1(e)(3)] , on the development of the relative value scale under section 1845.

Having said all that about a complicated reimbursement system, imposed during a period of perceived crisis in health care costs, Congress then imposed sanctions for physicians who violate the cost limits in sections 1842(j)(1)(D) and 1842(j)(2).

Section 1842(j)(1)(D)(iv) provides:

If a physician knowingly and willfully bills in violation of clause (i) (whether or not such charge violates subparagraph (B)), the Secretary may apply sanctions against such physician in accordance with paragraph (2).

Section 1842(j)(2) provides:

Subject to paragraph (3), the sanctions which the Secretary may apply under this paragraph are —

(A) excluding a physician from participation in the programs under this Act for a period not to exceed 5 years, in accordance with the procedures of paragraphs (c) [which pertains to notice, effective date, and period of exclusion], (f) [which pertains to notice, hearing, and judicial review], and (g) [which

> pertains to application for termination of exclusion] of section 1128 [42 U.S.C.A. 1320a-7], or
>
> (B) civil monetary penalties and assessments, in the same manner as such penalties and assessments are authorized under section 1128A(a) [42 U.S.C.A. 1320a-7a(a)], or both. The provisions of section 1128A (other than the first 2 sentences of subsection (a) and other than subsection (b)) shall apply to a civil money penalty and assessment under subparagraph (B) in the same manner as such provisions apply to a penalty, assessment, or proceeding under section 1128A(a), except to the extent such provisions are inconsistent with subparagraph (A) or paragraph (3).

Section 1842(j)(3) then provides:

> (A) The Secretary may not exclude a physician pursuant to paragraph (2)(A) if such physician is a sole community physician or sole source of essential specialized services in a community.
>
> (B) The Secretary shall take into account access of beneficiaries to physicians' services for which payment may be made under this part in determining whether to bar a physician from participation under paragraph (2)(A).

Finally, in section 1842(j)(4), Congress gave the Secretary discretion to make restitution to Medicare beneficiaries affected by violations of the physician fee freeze out of civil monetary penalties or assessments collected. That provision reads:

> The Secretary may, out of any civil monetary penalty or assessment collected from a physician pursuant to this subsection, make a payment to a beneficiary enrolled under this part in the nature of restitution for amounts paid by such beneficiary to such physician which was determined to be an excess charge under paragraph (1).

For regulatory citations, see Chapter 6

§ 2:17 IMPROPER BILLING FOR SERVICES OF ASSISTANTS AT CATARACT AND OTHER TYPES OF SURGERY — Sections 1842(k)(1) and (2) [42 U.S.C.A. 1395u(k)(1)and (2)]

Summary

Section 1862(a)(15), 42 U.S.C.A. 1395y(a)(15), excludes from coverage expenses incurred for items or services which pertain to services of an assistant at cataract surgery unless there is prior approval for use of the assistant, based on a complicating medical condition, by the appropriate utilization and quality control peer review organization or by a carrier. It also excludes from coverage expenses incurred for services of an assistant at surgery to which section 1848(i)(2)(B) [42 U.S.C.A. 1395w-4(i)(2)(B)] . The latter exclusion became effective November 5, 1990, pursuant to section 4107(b) of P.L. 101-508, the Omnibus Budget Reconciliation Act of 1990 (OBRA 90).

To back that up, sections 1842(k)(1) and (2), 42 U.S.C.A. 1395u(k)(1) and (2), provide that any physician who knowingly and willfully presents or causes to be presented a claim or who bills a beneficiary for charges either for services as or for services for an assistant at such surgery is subject to exclusion for a period not to exceed 5 years in accordance with procedures under section 1128, 42 U.S.C.A. 1320a-7, and to imposition of a civil money penalty under section 1128A, 42 U.S.C.A. 1320a-7a. See cross-reference to section 1842(j)(2), 42 U.S.C.A. 1395u(j)(2).

Enforcement procedures for this civil money penalty are governed by section 1128A, 42 U.S.C.A. 1320a-7a, which authorizes civil money penalties for a variety of offenses.

Statutory Provisions

Section 1862, 42 U.S.C.A. 1395y, provides in part:

> (a) Notwithstanding any other provision of this title, no payment may be made under part A or part B for any expenses incurred for items or services —

* * *

(15) which are for services of an assistant at surgery in a cataract operation (including subsequent insertion of an intraocular lens) unless, before the surgery is performed, the appropriate utilization and quality control peer review organization (under part B of title XI [42 U.S.C.A. 1320c]) or a carrier under section 1842 [42 U.S.C.A. 1395u] has approved of the use of such an assistant in the surgical procedure based on the existence of a complicating medical condition, or [effective November 5, 1990, pursuant to section 4107(b) of OBRA 90] (B) which are for services of an assistant at surgery to which section 1848(i)(2)(B) [42 U.S.C.A. 1395w-4(i)(2)(B)] applies.

Sections 4107(a)(1) and (2) of OBRA 90 amended section 1848(i) by adding a new paragraph (2), which pertains to assistants at surgery. It applies to services furnished after December 1991, and it provides:

(2) ASSISTANTS-AT-SURGERY. —

(A) IN GENERAL. — Subject to subparagraph (B), in the case of a surgical service furnished by a physician, if payment is made separately under this part for the services of a physician serving as an assistant-at-surgery, the fee schedule amount shall not exceed 16 percent of the fee schedule amount otherwise determined under this section for the global surgical service involved.

(B) DENIAL OF PAYMENT IN CERTAIN CASES. — If the Secretary determines, based on the most recent data available, that for a surgical procedure (or class of surgical procedures) the national average percentage of such procedure performed under this part which involve the use of a physician as an assistant at surgery is less than 5 percent, no payment may be made under this part for services of an assistant at surgery involved in the procedure.

Having said that, Congress then provided in section 1842(k), 42 U.S.C.A. 1395u(k):

(1) If a physician knowingly and willfully presents or causes to be presented a claim or bills an individual enrolled under this part for charges for services as an assistant at surgery for which payment may not be made by reason of section 1862(a)(15), the Secretary may apply sanctions against such physician in accor-

dance with subsection (j)(2) in the case of surgery performed on or after March 1, 1987.

(2) If a physician knowingly and willfully presents or causes to be presented a claim or bills an individual enrolled under this part for charges that includes [sic include] a charge for an assistant at surgery for which payment may not be made by reason of section 1862(a)(15), the Secretary may apply sanctions against such physician in accordance with subsection (j)(2) in the case of surgery performed on or after March 1, 1987.

Section 1842(j)(2), 42 U.S.C.A. 1395u(j)(2), provides:

Subject to paragraph (3), the sanctions which the Secretary may apply under this paragraph are —

(A) excluding a physician from participation in the programs under this Act for a period not to exceed 5 years, in accordance with the procedures of paragraphs (c) [which pertains to notice, effective date, and period of exclusion], (f) [which pertains to notice, hearing, and judicial review], and (g) [which pertains to application for termination of exclusion] of section 1128 [42 U.S.C.A. 1320a-7], or

(B) civil monetary penalties and assessments, in the same manner as such penalties and assessments are authorized under section 1128A(a) [42 U.S.C.A. 1320a-7a(a)], or both. The provisions of section 1128A (other than the first 2 sentences of subsection (a) and other than subsection (b)) shall apply to a civil money penalty and assessment under subparagraph (B) in the same manner as such provisions apply to a penalty, assessment, or proceeding under section 1128A(a), except to the extent such provisions are inconsistent with subparagraph (A) or paragraph (3).

Section 1842(j)(3) then provides:

(A) The Secretary may not exclude a physician pursuant to paragraph (2)(A) if such physician is a sole community physician or sole source of essential specialized services in a community.

(B) The Secretary shall take into account access of beneficiaries to physicians' services for which payment may be made under this part in determining whether to bar a physician from participation under paragraph (2)(A).

For regulatory citations, see Chapter 6

§ 2:18 WRONGFUL CHARGES BY NONPARTICIPATING PHYSICIANS — Section 1842(l) [42 U.S.C.A. 1395u(l)]

Summary

Pursuant to section 1842(l), 42 U.S.C.A. 1395u(l), if a nonparticipating physician who furnishes services to a beneficiary without taking a Medicare assignment bills for services which a carrier or peer review organization finds not reasonable and necessary (as set forth in section 1862(a)(1), 42 U.S.C.A. 1395y(a)(1)), the physician must make timely refund to the affected beneficiary. Timely means 30 days after the date the physician receives a denial notice, if the physician does not seek reconsideration or appeal timely, and 15 days after receipt of notice of an adverse determination or appeal.

This appears to a give a statutory right of action to beneficiaries who deserve timely refunds.

Furthermore, physicians who knowingly and willfully fail to make refunds are subject to exclusion for a period not to exceed 5 years in accordance with procedures under section 1128, 42 U.S.C.A. 1320a-7, and to a civil money penalty under section 1128A, 42 U.S.C.A. 1320a-7a. See cross-reference to 1842(j)(2), 42 U.S.C.A. 1395u(j)(2).

Enforcement procedures for this civil money penalty are governed by section 1128A, 42 U.S.C.A. 1320a-7a, which authorizes civil money penalties for a variety of offenses.

Statutory Provisions

Section 1842(l), 42 U.S.C.A. 1395u(l), provides:

(1)(A) Subject to subparagraph (C), if—

(i) a nonparticipating physician furnishes services to an individual enrolled for benefits under this part,

(ii) payment for such services is not accepted on an assignment-related basis,

(iii)(I) a carrier determines under this part or a peer review organization determines under part B of title XI [42 U.S.C.A. 1320c-2] that payment may not be made by reason of section 1862(a)(1) [42 U.S.C.A. 1395y(a)(1)] because a service otherwise covered under this title is not reasonable and necessary under the standards described in that section or (II) payment under this title for such services is denied under section 1154(a)(2) [42 U.S.C.A. 1320c-3(a)(2), which pertains to peer review organization utilization review] by reason of a determination under section 1154(a)(1)(B) [which pertains to quality of care determinations], and

(iv) the physician has collected any amounts for such services, the physician shall refund on a timely basis to the individual (and shall be liable to the individual for) any amounts so collected.

(B) A refund under subparagraph (A) is considered to be on a timely basis only if—

(i) in the case of a physician who does not request reconsideration or seek appeal on a timely basis, the refund is made within 30 days after the date the physician receives a denial notice under paragraph (2), or

(ii) in the case in which such a reconsideration or appeal is taken, the refund is made within 15 days after the date the physician receives notice of an adverse determination on reconsideration or appeal.

(C) Subparagraph (A) shall not apply to the furnishing of a service by a physician to an individual in the case described in subparagraph (A)(iii)(I) if—

(i) the physician establishes that the physician did not know and could not reasonably have been expected to know that payment may not be made for the service by reason of section 1862(a)(1), or

(ii) before the service was provided, the individual was informed that payment under this part may not be made for the specific service and the individual has agreed to pay for that service.

(2) Each carrier with a contract in effect under this section with respect to physicians and each peer review organization with a contract under part B of title XI shall send any notice of denial of payment for physicians' services based on section 1862(a)(1) and for which payment is not requested on an assignment-related basis to the physician and the individual involved.

(3) If a physician knowingly and willfully fails to make refunds in violation of paragraph (1)(A), the Secretary may apply sanc-

tions against such physician in accordance with subsection (j)(2).

Section 1842(j)(2), 42 U.S.C.A. 1395u(j)(2), provides:

Subject to paragraph (3), the sanctions which the Secretary may apply under this paragraph are —

(A) excluding a physician from participation in the programs under this Act for a period not to exceed 5 years, in accordance with the procedures of paragraphs (c) [which pertains to notice, effective date, and period of exclusion], (f) [which pertains to notice, hearing, and judicial review], and (g) [which pertains to application for termination of exclusion] of section 1128 [42 U.S.C.A. 1320a-7], or

(B) civil monetary penalties and assessments, in the same manner as such penalties and assessments are authorized under section 1128A(a) [42 U.S.C.A. 1320a-7a(a)], or both. The provisions of section 1128A (other than the first 2 sentences of subsection (a) and other than subsection (b)) shall apply to a civil money penalty and assessment under subparagraph (B) in the same manner as such provisions apply to a penalty, assessment, or proceeding under section 1128A(a), except to the extent such provisions are inconsistent with subparagraph (A) or paragraph (3).

Section 1842(j)(3) then provides:

(A) The Secretary may not exclude a physician pursuant to paragraph (2)(A) if such physician is a sole community physician or sole source of essential specialized services in a community.

(B) The Secretary shall take into account access of beneficiaries to physicians' services for which payment may be made under this part in determining whether to bar a physician from participation under paragraph (2)(A).

For regulatory citations, see Chapter 6

§ 2:19 WRONGFUL CHARGES BY NONPARTICIPATING PHYSICIANS FOR CERTAIN ELECTIVE SURGICAL PROCEDURES — Section 1842(m) [42 U.S.C.A. 1395u(m)]

Summary

Pursuant to section 1842(m), 42 U.S.C.A. 1395u(m), if a nonparticipating physician performs an elective surgical procedure for which the charge is at least $500, and for which the physician does not take assignment of Medicare benefits, the physician must disclose to the beneficiary in writing and in a form approved by the Secretary his estimated charge for the procedure, the approved charge under Part B, the excess of his charge over that approved, and the applicable coinsurance amount.

Any physician who does not comply with this disclosure requirement must refund the excess on a timely basis to the beneficiary and is liable to the beneficiary for the excess. This appears to give a statutory right of action to beneficiaries who deserve timely refunds.

Furthermore, any such physician who knowingly and willfully fails to comply with the disclosure and refund requirements is subject to exclusion for a period not to exceed 5 years in accordance with procedures under section 1128, 42 U.S.C.A. 1320a-7, and to a civil money penalty under section 1128A, 42 U.S.C.A. 1320a-7a. See cross-reference to section 1842(j)(2), 42 U.S.C.A. 1395u(j)(2).

Enforcement procedures for this civil money penalty are governed by section 1128A, 42 U.S.C.A. 1320a-7a, which authorizes civil money penalties for a variety of offenses.

Statutory Provisions

Section 1842(m), 42 U.S.C.A. 1395u(m), provides:

(1) In the case of a nonparticipating physician who —

(A) performs an elective surgical procedure for an individual enrolled for benefits under this part and for which the physician's actual charge is at least $500, and

(B) does not accept payment for such procedure on an assignment-related basis, the physician must disclose to the individual, in writing and in a form approved by the Secretary, the physician's estimated actual charge for the procedure, the estimated approved charge under this part [part B] for the procedure, the excess of the physician's actual charge over the approved charge, and the coinsurance amount applicable to the procedure. The written estimate may not be used as the basis for, or evidence in, a civil suit.

(2) A physician who fails to make a disclosure required under paragraph (1) with respect to a procedure shall refund on a timely basis to the individual (and shall be liable to the individual for) any amounts collected for the procedure in excess of the charges recognized and approved under this part.

(3) If a physician knowingly and willfully fails to comply with paragraph (2), the Secretary may apply sanctions against such physician in accordance with subsection (j)(2).

(4) The Secretary shall provide for such monitoring of requests for payment for physicians' services to which paragraph (1) applies as is necessary to assure compliance with paragraph (2).

Section 1842(j)(2), 42 U.S.C.A. 1395u(j)(2), provides:

Subject to paragraph (3), the sanctions which the Secretary may apply under this paragraph are —

(A) excluding a physician from participation in the programs under this Act for a period not to exceed 5 years, in accordance with the procedures of paragraphs (c) [which pertains to notice, effective date, and period of exclusion], (f) [which pertains to notice, hearing, and judicial review], and (g) [which pertains to application for termination of exclusion] of section 1128 [42 U.S.C.A. 1320a-7], or

(B) civil monetary penalties and assessments, in the same manner as such penalties and assessments are authorized under section 1128A(a) [42 U.S.C.A. 1320a-7a(a)], or both. The provisions of section 1128A (other than the first 2 sentences of subsection (a) and other than subsection (b)) shall apply to a civil money penalty and assessment under subparagraph (B) in the same manner as such provisions apply to a penalty, assessment, or proceeding under section 1128A(a), except to the extent such provisions are inconsistent with subparagraph (A) or paragraph (3).

Section 1842(j)(3) then provides:

(A) The Secretary may not exclude a physician pursuant to paragraph (2)(A) if such physician is a sole community physician or sole source of essential specialized services in a community.

(B) The Secretary shall take into account access of beneficiaries to physicians' services for which payment may be made under this part in determining whether to bar a physician from participation under paragraph (2)(A).

For regulatory citations, see Chapter 6

§ 2:20 PHYSICIAN FAILURE TO ELIMINATE THE MARK-UP FOR CERTAIN PURCHASED DIAGNOSTIC TESTS — Section 1842(n) [42 U.S.C.A. 1395u(n)]

Summary

According to section 1842(n), 42 U.S.C.A. 1395u(n), if a physician's bill or request for payment includes a charge to a patient for a diagnostic test (other than a clinical diagnostic laboratory test), it must indicate that the billing physician personally performed or supervised the performance of the test or that another physician with whom the billing physician shares a practice personally performed or supervised the test. If it does not, then the bill or request for payment must indicate that the test was performed by a supplier, it must identify the supplier, and it must indicate the amount the supplier charged the billing physician.

Payment for the test (less applicable deductible and coinsurance amounts) will be the acquisition cost (net of any discounts) or, if lesser, the supplier's reasonable charge.

If the bill or request for payment does not indicate who performed the test, or indicates that the test was performed by a supplier but does not identify the supplier or include the amount charged by the supplier, no payment will be made under Medicare.

Any physician who knowingly and willfully in repeated cases bills one or more individuals in violation of these requirements is subject to exclusion for a period not to exceed 5 years in accordance with procedures under section 1128, 42 U.S.C.A. 1320a-7, and to a civil money penalty under section 1128A, 42 U.S.C.A. 1320a-7a. See cross-reference to section 1842(j)(2), 42 U.S.C.A. 1395u(j)(2).

Enforcement procedures for this civil money penalty are governed by section 1128A, 42 U.S.C.A. 1320a-7a, which authorizes civil money penalties for a variety of offenses.

Statutory Provisions

Section 1842(n), 42 U.S.C.A. 1395u(n), provides:

(1) If a physician's bill or a request for payment for services billed by a physician includes a charge to a patient for a diagnostic test described in section 1861(s)(3) [42 U.S.C.A. 1395x(s)(3), which pertains to diagnostic X-ray tests, diagnostic laboratory tests, and other diagnostic tests] (other than a clinical diagnostic laboratory test) for which the bill or request for payment does not indicate that the billing physician personally performed or supervised the performance of the test or that another physician with whom the physician who shares a practice personally performed or supervised the performance of the test, the amount payable with respect to the test shall be determined as follows:

(A) If the bill or request for payment indicates that the test was performed by a supplier, identifies the supplier, and indicates the amount the supplier charged the billing physician, payment for the test (less the applicable deductible and coinsurance amounts) shall be the actual acquisition costs (net of any discounts) or, if lower, the supplier's reasonable charge (or other applicable limit) for the test.

(B) If the bill or request for payment (i) does not indicate who performed the test, or (ii) indicates that the test was performed by a supplier but does not identify the supplier or include the amount charged by the supplier, no payment shall be made under this part [part B].

(2) A physician may not bill an individual enrolled under this part—

(A) any amount other than the payment amount specified in paragraph (1)(A) and any applicable deductible and coinsurance for a diagnostic test for which payment is made pursuant to paragraph (1)(A), or

(B) any amount for a diagnostic test for which payment may not be made pursuant to paragraph (1)(B).

(3) If a physician knowingly and willfully in repeated cases bills one or more individuals in violation of paragraph (2), the Secre-

tary may apply sanctions against such physician in accordance with section 1842(j)(2).

Section 1842(j)(2), 42 U.S.C.A. 1395u(j)(2), provides:

Subject to paragraph (3), the sanctions which the Secretary may apply under this paragraph are —

(A) excluding a physician from participation in the programs under this Act for a period not to exceed 5 years, in accordance with the procedures of paragraphs (c) [which pertains to notice, effective date, and period of exclusion], (f) [which pertains to notice, hearing, and judicial review], and (g) [which pertains to application for termination of exclusion] of section 1128 [42 U.S.C.A. 1320a-7], or

(B) civil monetary penalties and assessments, in the same manner as such penalties and assessments are authorized under section 1128A(a) [42 U.S.C.A. 1320a-7a(a)], or both. The provisions of section 1128A (other than the first 2 sentences of subsection (a) and other than subsection (b)) shall apply to a civil money penalty and assessment under subparagraph (B) in the same manner as such provisions apply to a penalty, assessment, or proceeding under section 1128A(a), except to the extent such provisions are inconsistent with subparagraph (A) or paragraph (3).

Section 1842(j)(3) then provides:

(A) The Secretary may not exclude a physician pursuant to paragraph (2)(A) if such physician is a sole community physician or sole source of essential specialized services in a community.

(B) The Secretary shall take into account access of beneficiaries to physicians' services for which payment may be made under this part in determining whether to bar a physician from participation under paragraph (2)(A).

For regulatory citations, see Chapter 6

§ 2:21 FAILURE BY PHYSICIANS AND OTHER PRACTITIONERS TO PROVIDE APPROPRIATE DIAGNOSIS CODES ON BILLS — Section 1842(p) [42 U.S.C.A. 1395u(p)]

Summary

Section 1842(p), 42 U.S.C.A. 1395u(p), requires physicians to include appropriate diagnosis codes on bills or requests for payments. If a physician who takes Medicare assignments of benefits fails to do so, the Secretary of Health and Human Services may deny payment for the items or services furnished. Pursuant to section 4317(a) of the Balanced Budget Act of 1997, P.L. 105-33, the same applies to items and services furnished on or after January 1, 1998, by physician assistants, nurse practitioners, clinical nurse specialists, certified registered nurse anesthetics, certified nurse and mid-wives, clinical social workers, and clinical psychologists.

In addition, any physician who does not take Medicare assignments and who knowingly and willfully fails to provide the appropriate code or codes promptly upon request of the Secretary or a carrier is subject to a civil money penalty not to exceed $2,000. Furthermore, any such physician who knowingly, willfully, and in repeated cases fails to include diagnosis codes on bills or requests for payments, after being notified by the Secretary of the obligation to do so, is subject to exclusion for a period not to exceed 5 years in accordance with procedures under section 1128, 42 U.S.C.A. 1320a-7. See cross-reference to section 1842(j)(2)(A), 42 U.S.C.A. 1395u(j)(2).

Enforcement procedures for this civil money penalty are governed by section 1128A, 42 U.S.C.A. 1320a-7a, which authorizes civil money penalties for a variety of offenses.

Statutory Provisions

Section 1842(p), 42 U.S.C.A. 1395u(p), provides:

(1) Each request for payment, or bill submitted, for an item or service furnished by a physician or practitioner specified in subsection (b)(18)(C) [NOTE: The clause "or practitioner specified in subsection (b)(18)(C)" was added here and below in subsection (2) by section 4317(a) of the Balanced Budget Act of

1997, P.L. 105-33. It applies to items and services furnished on or after January 1, 1998.] for which payment may be made under this part shall include the appropriate diagnosis code (or codes) as established by the Secretary for such item or service.

(2) In the case of a request for payment for an item or service furnished by a physician or practitioner specified in subsection (b)(18)(C) on an assignment-related basis which does not include the code (or codes) required under paragraph (1), payment may be denied under this part [part B].

(3) In the case of a request for payment for an item or service furnished by a physician not submitted on an assignment-related basis and which does not include the code (or codes) required under paragraph (1)—

(A) if the physician knowingly and willfully fails to provide the code (or codes) promptly upon request of the Secretary or a carrier, the physician may be subject to a civil money penalty in an amount not to exceed $2,000, and

(B) if the physician knowingly, willfully, and in repeated cases fails, after being notified by the Secretary of the obligations and requirements of this subsection, to include the code (or codes) required under paragraph (1), the physician may be subject to the sanction described in section 1842(j)(2)(A) [42 U.S.C.A. 1395u(j)(2)(A)].

The provisions of section 1128A, [42 U.S.C.A. 1320a-7a] (other than subsections (a) and (b)) shall apply to civil money penalties under subparagraph (A) in the same manner as they apply to a penalty or proceeding under section 1128A(a).

(4) In the case of an item or service defined in paragraph (3) [diagnostic x-ray tests], (6) [durable medical equipment], (8) [prosthetic devices (other than dental) which replace all or part of an internal body organ (including colostomy bags and supplies directly related to colostomy care), including replacement of such devices, and including one pair of conventional eyeglasses or contact lenses furnshed subsequent to each cataract surgery with insertion of an intraocular lens], or (9) leg, arm, back, and neck braces, and artifical legs, arms, and eyes, including replacements if required because of change in the patient's physical condition] of subsection 1861(s) [42

U.S.C.A. x(s)] ordered by an physician or a practitioner specified in subsection (b)(18)(C), but furnished by another entity, if the Secretary (or fiscal agent of the Secretary) requires the entity furnishing the item or service to provide diagnostic or other medical information in order for payment to be made to the entity, the physician or practitioner shall provide that information to the entity at the time that the item or service is ordered by the physician or practitioner.

Section 1842(b)(18)(C) provides:

A practitioner described in the subparagraph is any of the folowing:

(i) A physician assistant, nurse practitioner, or clinical nurse specialist (as defined in section 1861(aa)(5) [42 U.S.C.A. 1395x(aa)(5)]).

(ii) A certified registered nurse anesthetist (as defined in section 1861(bb)(2) [42 U.S.C.A. 1395x(bb)(2)]).

(iii) A certified nurse-midwife (as defined in section 1861(gg)(2) [42 U.S.C.A. 1395x(gg)(2)]).

(iv) A clinical social worker (as defined in section 1861(hh)(1) [42 U.S.C.A. 1395x(hh)(2)]).

(v) A clinical psychologist (as defined by the Secretary for purposes of section 1861(ii) [42 U.S.C.A. 1395x(ii)]).

Section 1861(s) provides in pertinent part:

(3) diagnostic X-ray tests (including tests under the supervision of a physician, furnished in a place of residence used as the patient's home, if the performance of such tests meets such conditions relating to health and safety as the Secretary may find necessary and including diagnostic mammography if conducted by a facility that has a certificate (or provisional certificate) issued under section 354 of the Public Health Service Act), diagnostic laboratory tests, and other diagnostic tests;

* * *

(6) durable medical equipment;

(8) prosthetic devices (other than dental) which replace all or part of an internal body organ (including colostomy bags and supplies directly related to colostomy care), including replacement of such devices, and including one pair of conventional

eyeglasses or contact lenses furnished subsequent to each cataract surgery with insertion of an ontraocular lens;

(9) leg, arm, and neck braces, and artifical legs, arms, and eyes, inclluding replacements if required because of an change in the patient's physical condition;

Section 1842(j)(2), 42 U.S.C.A. 1395u(j)(2), provides:

Subject to paragraph (3), the sanctions which the Secretary may apply under this paragraph are —

(A) excluding a physician from participation in the programs under this Act for a period not to exceed 5 years, in accordance with the procedures of paragraphs (c) [which pertains to notice, effective date, and period of exclusion], (f) [which pertains to notice, hearing, and judicial review], and (g) [which pertains to application for termination of exclusion] of section 1128 [42 U.S.C.A. 1320a-7], or

(B) civil monetary penalties and assessments, in the same manner as such penalties and assessments are authorized under section 1128A(a) [42 U.S.C.A. 1320a-7a(a)], or both. The provisions of section 1128A (other than the first 2 sentences of subsection (a) and other than subsection (b)) shall apply to a civil money penalty and assessment under subparagraph (B) in the same manner as such provisions apply to a penalty, assessment, or proceeding under section 1128A(a), except to the extent such provisions are inconsistent with subparagraph (A) or paragraph (3).

Section 1842(j)(3) then provides:

(A) The Secretary may not exclude a physician pursuant to paragraph (2)(A) if such physician is a sole community physician or sole source of essential specialized services in a community.

(B) The Secretary shall take into account access of beneficiaries to physicians' services for which payment may be made under this part in determining whether to bar a physician from participation under paragraph (2)(A).

For regulatory citations, see Chapter 6

§ 2:22 INTERMEDIATE SANCTIONS FOR PROVIDERS OR SUPPLIERS OF CLINICAL DIAGNOSTIC LABORATORY TESTS — Section 1846 [42 U.S.C.A. 1395w-2]

Summary

If the Secretary of Health and Human Services determines that a clinical laboratory does not substantially meet Medicare conditions for coverage with respect to clinical diagnostic laboratory tests, section 1846, 42 U.S.C.A. 1395w-2, provides that the Secretary may for a period not to exceed one year impose any of the following intermediate sanctions:

- a directed plan of correction;
- a civil money penalty not to exceed $10,000 for each day of substantial noncompliance;
- payment for the costs of on-site monitoring by a survey agency;
- suspension of all or part of the payments to which a clinical laboratory would otherwise be entitled under Medicare with respect to clinical diagnostic laboratory tests furnished on or after the effective date of the intermediate sanction.

These intermediate sanctions are in lieu of immediately cancelling approval of the clinical laboratory; but they are in addition to any other sanction which may be imposed.

Enforcement procedures for the civil money penalty are governed by section 1128A, 42 U.S.C.A. 1320a-7a, which authorizes civil money penalties for a variety of offenses.

Statutory Provisions

Section 1846, 42 U.S.C.A. 1395w-2, provides:

> (a) If the Secretary determines that any provider or clinical laboratory approved for participation under this title no longer substantially meets the conditions of participation or for coverage specified under this title with respect to the provision of clinical diagnostic laboratory tests under this part [part B] , the Secretary may (for a period not to exceed one year) impose intermediate sanctions developed pursuant to subsection (b), in lieu of terminating immediately the provider agreement or cancelling immediately approval of the clinical laboratory.

◆ NOTE: Effective January 1, 1990, section 201(a)(1) of P.L. 101-234, the Medicare Catastrophic Coverage Repeal Act of 1989, repealed portions of section 1846 which applied to home intravenous drug therapy. Prior thereto, following "tests under this part" in section 1846(a) above this language appeared: or that a qualified home intravenous drug therapy provider that is certified for participation under this title no longer substantially meets the requirements of section 1861(jj)(3) [42 U.S.C.A. 1395x(jj)(3), which was the definition section pertaining to home intravenous drug therapy providers. In addition, "or home intravenous drug therapy services" previously appeared after "laboratory tests" and before "furnished" in section 1846(b)(2)(A)(iv) below.

(b)(1) The Secretary shall develop and implement—

(A) a range of intermediate sanctions to apply to providers or clinical laboratories under the conditions described in subsection (a), and

(B) appropriate procedures for appealing determinations relating to the imposition of such sanctions.

(2)(A) The intermediate sanctions developed under paragraph (1) shall include—

(i) directed plans of correction,

(ii) civil money penalties in an amount not to exceed $10,000 for each day of substantial noncompliance,

(iii) payment for the costs of onsite monitoring by an agency responsible for conducting surveys, and

(iv) suspension of all or part of the payments to which a provider or clinical laboratory would otherwise be entitled under this title with respect to clinical diagnostic laboratory tests furnished on or after the date on which the Secretary determines that intermediate sanctions should be imposed pursuant to subsection (a).

The provisions of section 1128A [42 U.S.C.A. 1320a-7a] (other than subsections (a) and (b)) shall apply to a civil money penalty under clause (ii) in the same manner as such provisions apply to a penalty or proceeding under section 1128A(a).

(C) The sanctions specified in subparagraph (A) are in addition to sanctions otherwise available under State or Federal law.

(3) The Secretary shall develop and implement specific procedures with respect to when and how each of the intermediate sanctions developed under paragraph (1) is to be applied, the amounts of any penalties, and the severity of each of these penalties. Such procedures shall be designed so as to minimize the time between identification of violations and imposition of these sanctions and shall provide for the imposition of incrementally more severe penalties for repeated or uncorrected deficiencies.

◆ NOTE: Section 4154(e)(2) of P.L. 101-508, the Omnibus Budget Reconciliation Act of 1990 (OBRA 90), added "or suppliers" after "intermediate sanctions for providers" in the heading of section 1846, effective December 13, 1989, as if included in P.L. 101-239, the Omnibus Budget Reconciliation Act of 1989 (OBRA 89).

For regulatory citations, see Chapter 6

§ 2:23 WRONGFUL CHARGES FOR INTERPRETING ELECTROCARDIOGRAMS — Section 1848(b)(3) [42 U.S.C.A. 1395w-4(b)(3)]

Summary

◆ NOTE: Pursuant to section 13514(a) of P.L. 103-66, the Omnibus Budget Reconciliation Act of 1993 (OBRA 93), the following sanction applies only for services furnished prior to January 1, 1994.

Section 1848, 42 U.S.C.A. 1395w-4(b), which was enacted by P.L 101-239, the Omnibus Budget Reconciliation Act of 1989 (OBRA 89), established the Resource Based Relative Value Scale (RBRVS) system for payment of physician services under Medicare. By its terms, fee schedules will be established for defined physicians' services, furnished on or after January 1, 1992, for which payment is otherwise made on the basis of a reasonable charge or on the basis of a fee schedule under section 1834(b), 42 U.S.C.A. 1395m-(b). (The latter applies to radiologists.) Special transition rules apply to the calculation of these fees during the period 1992 through 1995. See § 2:24.

Even before RBRVS was put into effect, however, the law was amended by section 4109(a) of P.L. 101-508, the Omnibus Budget Reconciliation Act of 1990 (OBRA 90), to add section 1848(b)(3). The amendment provides that if Medicare pays for a visit to a physician or a consultation with a physician and if in conjunction with that visit or consultation an electrocardiogram is performed or ordered to be performed, no payment may be made with respect to the interpretation of that electrocardiogram. Any physician who knowingly and willfully bills one or more individuals in violation of that prohibition is subject to sanctions under section 1842(j)(2), 42 U.S.C.A. 1395u(j)(2). The latter authorizes the Secretary of Health and Human Services to exclude a physician from Medicare for not to exceed 5 years in accordance with procedures under section 1128, 42 U.S.C.A. 1320a-7, or to impose a civil money penalty under section 1128A, 42 U.S.C.A. 1320a-7a.

Statutory Provisions

Section 1848(b)(3), 42 U.S.C.A. 1395w-4(b)(3), enacted by section 4109(a) of P.L. 101-508, the Omnibus Budget Reconciliation Act of 1990 (OBRA 90), applicable to services furnished on or after January 1, 1992, but before January 1, 1994, provides:

> (3) TREATMENT OF INTERPRETATION OF ELECTROCARDIOGRAMS. — If payment is made under this part for a visit to a physician or consultation with a physician and, as part of or in conjunction with the visit or consultation there is an electrocardiogram performed or ordered to be performed, no payment may be made under this part with respect to the interpretation of the electrocardiogram and no physician may bill an individual enrolled under this part separately for such an interpretation. if a physician knowingly and willfully bills one or more individuals in violation of the previous sentence, the Secretary may apply sanctions against the physician or entity in accordance with section 1842(j)(2).

Section 1842(j)(2) provides:

> Subject to paragraph (3), the sanctions which the Secretary may apply under this paragraph are —
>
> (A) excluding a physician from participation in the programs under this Act for a period not to exceed 5 years, in accordance

with the procedures of paragraphs (c) [which pertains to notice, effective date, and period of exclusion], (f) [which pertains to notice, hearing, and judicial review], and (g) [which pertains to application for termination of exclusion] of section 1128 [42 U.S.C.A. 1320a-7], or

(B) civil monetary penalties and assessments, in the same manner as such penalties and assessments are authorized under section 1128A(a) [42 U.S.C.A. 1320a-7a(a)], or both. The provisions of section 1128A (other than the first 2 sentences of subsection (a) and other than subsection (b)) shall apply to a civil money penalty and assessment under subparagraph (B) in the same manner as such provisions apply to a penalty, assessment, or proceeding under section 1128A(a), except to the extent such provisions are inconsistent with subparagraph (A) or paragraph (3).

Section 1842(j)(3) then provides:

(A) The Secretary may not exclude a physician pursuant to paragraph (2)(A) if such physician is a sole community physician or sole source of essential specialized services in a community.

(B) The Secretary shall take into account access of beneficiaries to physicians' services for which payment may be made under this part in determining whether to bar a physician from participation under paragraph (2)(A).

Pursuant to section 13514(a) of OBRA 93, applicable to services furnished on or after January 1, 1994, section 1848(B)(3) provides:

TREATMENT OF INTERPRETATION OF ELECTROCARDIOGRAMS. — The Secretary —

(A) shall make separate payment under this section for the interpretation of electrocardiograms performed or ordered to be performed as part of or in conjunction with a visit to or a consultation with a physician, and

(B) shall adjust the relative values established for visits and consultations under subsection (c) so as not to include relative value units for interpretations of electrocardiograms in the relative value for visits and consultations.

For regulatory citations, see Chapter 6

§ 2:24 VIOLATING LIMITATIONS ON PHYSICIAN CHARGES BY NONPARTICIPATING PHYSICIANS, SUPPLIERS, OR OTHER PERSONS AFTER 1990— Section 1848(g)(1) [42 U.S.C.A. 1395w-4(g)(1)]

Summary

For years Medicare reimbursed participating physicians on a reasonable charge basis. Simply put, that meant physicians received their actual charge, their customary charge, or the prevailing charge by physicians in the locality for a given service, whichever was least. For radiologist services furnished on or after January 1, 1989, however, section 1834(b) of the Social Security Act, 42 U.S.C.A. 1395m(b), required reimbursement to be based on a fee schedule developed by the Secretary of Health and Human Services. (Similarly, prior to amendment by section 4104(a) of P.L. 101-508, the Omnibus Budget Reconciliation Act of 1990 (OBRA 90), section 1834(f), 42 U.S.C.A. 1395m(f), required the Secretary to develop a fee schedule for physician pathology services furnished on or after January 1, 1991.)

Effective December 19, 1989, section 6102(a) of P.L. 101-239, the Omnibus Budget Reconciliation Act of 1989 (OBRA 89), amended the Social Security Act by creating section 1848, 42 U.S.C.A. 1395w-4. That enactment continued the transition from reasonable charge methodology for Medicare reimbursement of physicians' services to a fee schedule. Generally, it applies to all physicians' services furnished on or after January 1, 1992, but various provisions of section 1848 apply to services furnished at different times.

"Physicians' services" is defined in section 1848(j)(3) by cross reference to section 1861(s)(1), (2)(A), (2)(D), (2)(G) [(2)(G) added by OBRA 93], (2)(P) (with respect to services described in subparagraphs (A) and (C) of section 1861(oo)(2)), (2)(R) (with respect to services described in subparagraphs (B), (C), and (D) of section 1861(pp)(1)), (2)(S), (3), (4), (13), (14) (with respect to services described in section 1861 (nn)(2)), and (15) of section 1861(s) (other than clinical diagnostic laboratory tests and such other items and services as the Secretary may specify), 42 U.S.C.A. 1395x(s)(1), (2)(A), (2)(D), (2)(G), (2)(S), (3), (4), (13), (14), and (15).

In addition to physicians' services, the following are included: services and supplies (including drugs and biologicals which are not usually self-administered by the patient) furnished as an incident to a physician's professional service which are commonly furnished in physicians' offices and which are commonly either rendered without charge or included in physicians' bills; outpatient physical therapy services and outpatient occupational therapy services; certain antigens prepared by a physician (pursuant to OBRA 93), prostate cancer screening tests; colorectal cancer screening tests; diabetes outpatient self-management training services; diagnostic X-ray tests (including tests under the supervision of a physician, furnished in a place of residence used as the patient's home, if the performance of such tests meets such conditions relating to health and safety as the Secretary finds necessary), diagnostic laboratory tests, and other diagnostic tests; and X-ray, radium, and radioactive isotope therapy, including materials and services of technicians; screening mammography; screening pap smear and screening pelvic exam; and bone mass measurement.

NOTE: Prior to enactment of section 112(a) of the Medicare, Medicaid, and SCHIP Benefits Improvement and Protection Act of 2000, P.L. 106-554, December 15, 2000, the reference to services and supplies included "drugs and biologicals which cannot, as determined in accordance with regulations, be self-administered". This change applies to drugs and biologicals administered on or after December 21, 2000. See also section 4102(d) of the Balanced Budget Act of 1997, P.L. 105-33, enacted August 5, 1997, which added the reference to screening pap smear and screening pelvic exam (applicable to items and services furnished on or after January 1, 1998); section 4103(d), which added the reference to prostate screening tests (applicable to items and services performed on or after January 1, 2000) ; section 4104(d), which added the reference to colorectal cancer screening tests (applicable to items and services furnished on or after January 1, 2000); section 4105((a)(2), which added the reference to diabetes outpatient self-management training services (applicable to items and services furnished on or after July 1, 1998); and section 4106(b), which added the reference to bone mass measurements (effective for measurements performed on or after July 1, 1998).

Section 1848(a)(1), 42 U.S.C.A. 1395w-4(a)(1), requires payment to be based on the lesser of the actual charge for the service or the fee schedule established under section 1848(b). But section 1848(a)(2) provides limitations on reductions and increases in reimbursement for several transition years. For example, section 1848(a)(2)(A) provides that in 1992 increases and decreases in reimbursement cannot exceed 15 percent. Thus, in the case of a service in a fee schedule area for which the adjusted historical payment basis is less than 85 percent of the fee schedule amount for services furnished in 1992, instead of the fee schedule amount physicians will receive an amount equal to the adjusted historical payment basis plus 15 percent of the fee schedule amount otherwise established. Similarly, in the case of a service in a fee schedule area for which the adjusted historical payment basis exceeds 115 percent of the fee schedule amount for services furnished in 1992, instead of the fee schedule amount physicians will receive an amount equal to the adjusted historical payment basis minus 15 percent of the fee schedule amount otherwise established.

Section 1848(a)(2)(B) provides that during 1993, the formula is 75 percent of the fee schedule amount determined by applying the 15 percent limitation in section 1848(a)(2)(A), adjusted by an update based on analysis of the Medicare Economic Index, the consumer price index, and other factors required by section 1848(d)(3), and 25 percent of the fee schedule amount. For 1994 the parallel formula rates are 67 percent and 33 percent. Pursuant to section 13514(c)(1) of P.L. 103-66, the Omnibus budget Reconciliation Act of 1993 (OBRA 93), however, those rates are further adjusted (with respect to services furnished on or after January 1, 1994, by such percentage as the Secretary determines necessary to assure budget neutrality. For 1995 the parallel formula rates are 50-50. In addition, there are special transition rules for anesthesia services, special adjustments for radiologist services, and incentives for participating physicians and, applicable to services on or after January 1, 1994, for suppliers.

Section 1848(b) requires the Secretary to establish fee schedules before January 1 of each year beginning 1992 by regulation. He must do so for all physicians' services, as defined above, and for all fee schedule areas. The latter are defined in section 1848(j)(2) as the localities used by carriers for processing Part B claims.

In general, these fee schedules must be equal to the product of the relative value for the service, the conversion factor for the year, and the geographic adjustment factor for the service for the fee schedule area. Again, special provisions apply for radiology and anesthesia services. Specifically, the Secretary must take into account the fee schedules required for them by section 1834(b) and section 4048(b) of P.L. 100-203, the Omnibus Budget Reconciliation Act of 1987 (OBRA 87). He also must consult with the Physician Payment Review Commission and organizations representing physicians or suppliers who furnish radiology services and anesthesia services in developing fee schedules for such services.

Section 1848(c) describes how the relative values for physicians' services are to be determined. Section 1848(d) deals with establishment of conversion factors and updates. Section 1848(f) provides for establishment of geographic adjustment factors. Section 1848(f) deals with Medicare volume performance standard rates of increase.

Having provided for that reimbursement methodology, Congress, in section 1848(g), went on to provide limitations on physicians' charges and limitations on beneficiary liability beginning 1991.

Section 1848(g)(2) defines "limiting charges." For physicians' services furnished during 1991, the limiting charge is the same percentage (or, if less, 25 percent) above the recognized payment amount under Part B with respect to the physician (as a nonparticipating physician) as the percentage by which the maximum allowable actual charge for the service of the physician exceeds the recognized payment amount for the service of the physician (as a nonparticipating physician) as of such date. The maximum allowable actual charge is determined under section 1842(j)(1)(C), 42 U.S.C.A. 1395u(j)(1)(C), as of December 31, 1990, or, if less, the maximum actual charge otherwise permitted for the service under Part B as of that date. Note, however, that with respect to evaluation and management services authorized by section 4101(b)(1) of OBRA 90, which effective November 5, 1990, added section 1842(b)(16), 42 U.S.C.A. 1395u(b)(16), the limiting charge is 40 percent rather than 25 percent.

Section 1842(j)(1)(C) establishes maximum allowable actual charge limits for nonparticipating physicians for purposes of the freeze on physician fees, discussed in § 2:16. Section 1842(j)(1)(A) imposes sanctions, including exclusion for a period not to exceed 5 years and civil money penalties and assessments, for those who violate the freeze on fees.

As amended by section 123(a)(1) of the Social Security Act Amendments of 1994, P.L. 103-432, applicable to services furnished on or after October 31, 1994, section 1848(g)(1) provides that no physician, supplier or other person who does not accept Medicare assignment of benefits may charge more than the limiting charge. This applies to billing for and/or collecting amounts in excess of the limiting charge. Furthermore, no person is liable for payment of any amounts billed in excess of the limiting charge.

If a physician, supplier, or other person bills for but does not collect an actual charge in violation of the limiting charge, the physician, supplier, or other person must reduce the actual charge billed on "a timely basis" to an amount not exceeding the limiting charge. If the charge has been collected, the physician, supplier, or other person must refund the excess charged "on a timely basis", subject only to offset for any outstanding balance which the person billed may owe to the physician, suppler, or other person. "Timely basis" means 30 days after the physician, supplier, or other person has been notified by the Medicare carrier of the violation.

Knowingly and willfully billing for or collecting an amount in excess of the limiting charge on a repeated basis may result in civil money penalties and assessments and/or exclusion from Medicare. The same is true for failure to correct excess billing charges and failure to make refunds of excess charges collected on a timely basis. These penalties apply by cross reference to section 1842(j)(2), 42 U.S.C.A. 1395u(j)(2), and sections 1128 and 1128A of the Social Security Act, 42 U.S.C.A. 1320a-7 and 42 U.S.C.A. 1320a-7a.

◆ [NOTE: Prior to amendment by section 13517(a)(2) of OBRA 93, section 1848(g)(1) provided that if a nonparticipating physician knowingly and willfully billed on a repeated basis for physicians' services (furnished with respect to an individual enrolled under this part on or after January 1, 1991, an actual charge in excess of the limiting charge described in section 1848(g)(2) and for which payment is not made on an assignment-related basis under Part B, the Secretary could apply sanctions against such physician in accordance with section 1842(j)(2), including exclusion for a period not to exceed 5 years and civil money penalties and assessments. The latter contains a cross reference to the exclusion and civil money penalty provisions of sections 1128 and 1128A of the Act. See 42 U.S.C.A. 1320a-7 and 1320a-7a.

◆ Subsequent to that amendment by OBRA 93, section 1848(g)(1) provided: If a nonparticipating physician or nonparticipating supplier or other person (as defined in section 1842(i)(2), knowingly and willfully billed on a repeated basis for physicians' services, including services the Secretary excludes pursuant to subsection (j)(3) (which pertains to clinical diagnostic laboratory tests and such other items and services as the Secretary specifies), furnished with respect to an individual enrolled under Part B on or after January 1, 1991, an actual charge in excess of the limiting charge described in section 1848(g)(2) and for which payment is not made on an assignment-related basis under this part, the Secretary may apply sanctions against such physician supplier, or other person in accordance with section 1842(j)(2).]

Statutory Provisions

With respect to the establishment of Medicare reimbursement for all physicians' services based on a fee schedule derived from a relative value scale, section 1848, 42 U.S.C.A. 1395w-4(a), provides in part:

(a) PAYMENT BASED ON FEE SCHEDULE. —

(1) IN GENERAL. — Effective for all physicians' services (as defined in subsection (j)(3)) furnished under this part during a year (beginning with 1992) for which payment is otherwise made on the basis of a reasonable charge or on the basis of a fee schedule under section 1834(b) [42 U.S.C.A. 1395m(b), which pertains to the fee schedule for radiologist services applicable to services furnished on or after January 1, 1989. Note here, too, that section 4104(b)(2) of P.L. 101-508, the Omnibus Budget Reconciliation Act of 1990 (OBRA 90), deleted the phrase "or 1834(f)", 42 U.S.C.A. 1395m(f), which pertained to the fee schedule for physician pathology services which that provision then made applicable to services furnished on or after January 1, 1991.], payment under this part shall instead be based on the lesser of—

(A) the actual charge for the service, or

(B) subject to the succeeding provisions of this subsection, the amount determined under the fee schedule established under subsection (b) for services furnished during that year (in this subsection referred to as the "fee schedule amount").

(2) TRANSITION TO FULL FEE SCHEDULE. —

(A) LIMITING REDUCTIONS AND INCREASES TO 15 PERCENT IN 1992. —

(i) LIMIT ON INCREASE. — In the case of a service in a fee schedule area (as defined in subsection (j)(2)) for which the adjusted historical payment basis (as defined in subparagraph D)) is less than 85 percent of the fee schedule amount for services furnished in 1992, there shall be substituted for the fee schedule amount an amount equal to the adjusted historical payment basis plus 15 percent of the fee schedule amount otherwise established (without regard to this paragraph).

(ii) LIMIT IN REDUCTION. — In the case of a service in a fee schedule area for which the adjusted historical payment basis exceeds 115 percent of the fee schedule amount for services furnished in 1992, there shall be substituted for the fee schedule amount an amount equal to the adjusted historical payment basis minus 15 percent of the fee schedule amount otherwise established (without regard to this paragraph).

(B) SPECIAL RULE FOR 1993, 1994, AND 1995. — If a physicians' service in a fee schedule area is subject to the provisions of subparagraph (A) in 1992, for physicians' services furnished in the area —

(i) during 1993, there shall be substituted for the fee schedule amount an amount equal to the sum of —

(I) 75 percent of the fee schedule amount determined under subparagraph (A), adjusted by the update established under subsection (d)(3) for 1993, and

(II) 25 percent of the fee schedule amount determined under paragraph (1) for 1993 without regard to this paragraph;

(ii) during 1994, there shall be substituted for the fee schedule amount an amount equal to the sum of —

(I) 67 percent of the fee schedule amount determined under clause (i), adjusted by the update established under subsection (d)(3) for 1994 [the following clause added by section 13515(c)(1) of OBRA 93, applicable to services furnished on or after January 1, 1994] and as adjusted under subsection (c)(2)(F)(ii) and under section 13515(b) of the Omnibus budget Reconciliation Act of 1993, and

(II) 33 percent of the fee schedule amount determined under paragraph (1) for 1994 without regard to this paragraph; and

(iii) during 1995, there shall be substituted for the fee schedule amount an amount equal to the sum of—

(I) 50 percent of the fee schedule amount determined under clause (ii) adjusted by the update established under subsection (d)(3) for 1995, and

(II) 50 percent of the fee schedule amount determined under paragraph (1) for 1995 without regard to this paragraph.

(C) SPECIAL RULE FOR ANESTHESIA AND RADIOLOGY SERVICES. — With respect to physicians' services which are anesthesia services, the Secretary shall provide for a transition in the same manner as a transition is provided for other services under subparagraph (B). With respect to radiology services, "109 percent" and "9 percent" shall be substituted for "115 percent" and "15 percent", respectively, in subparagraph (A)(ii). [The last sentence and the phrase "and radiology" in the caption of paragraph (C) were added by section 4102 of OBRA 90.]

(D) ADJUSTED HISTORICAL PAYMENT BASIS DEFINED.—

(i) IN GENERAL. — In this paragraph, the term "adjusted historical payment basis" means, with respect to a physicians' service furnished in a fee schedule area, the weighted average prevailing charge applied in the area for the service in 1991 (as determined by the Secretary without regard to physician specialty and as adjusted to reflect payments for services with customary charges below the prevailing charge or other payment limitations imposed by law or regulation) adjusted by the update established under subsection (d)(3) for 1992.

(ii) APPLICATION TO RADIOLOGY SERVICES.-In applying clause (i) in the case of physicians' services which are radiology services (including radiologist services, as defined in section 1834(b)(6)), but excluding nuclear medicine services that are subject to section 6105(b) of the Omnibus Budget Reconciliation Act of 1989, there shall be substituted for the weighted average prevailing charge the amount provided under the fee schedule established for the service for the fee schedule area under section 1834(b). [The phrase "but excluding nuclear medicine services that are subject to section 6105(b) of the Omnibus Budget Reconciliation Act of 1989," was added by section 4102(g)(2) of OBRA 90, applicable to services furnished after December 1990.]

(iii) NUCLEAR MEDICINE SERVICES. — In applying clause (i) in the case of physicians' services which are nuclear medicine servicesprovided under section 6105(b) of the Omnibus Budget Reconciliation Act of 1989, there shall be substituted for the weighted average prevailing charge the amount provided under such section. [NOTE: Clause (iii) above was amended by section 126(b)(6) of the Social Security Act Amendments of 1994, P.L. 103-432, effective November 5, 1990, as if included in OBRA 1990. Previously clause (iii) read: "NUCLEAR MEDICINE SERVICES. — In applying clause (i) in the case of physicians' services that are subject to section 6105(b), there shall be substituted for the weighted average prevailing charge the amount provided under such section." That provision was added by section 4102(g)(2) of OBRA 90, applicable to services furnished after December 1990.]

(3) INCENTIVES FOR PARTICIPATING PHYSICIANS AND SUPPLIERS. — In applying paragraph (1)(B) in the case of a nonparticipating physician or a nonparticipating supplier or other person, the fee schedule amount shall be 95 percent of such amount otherwise applied under this subsection (without regard to this paragraph). In the case of physicians' services (including services which the Secretary excludes pursuant to subsection (j)(3)) of a nonparticipating physician, supplier, or other person for which payment is made under this part on a basis other than the fee schedule amount, the payment shall be based on 95 percent of the payment basis for such services furnished by a participating physician, supplier, or other person. [Section 13517(a)(1) of OBRA 93 added "and suppliers" to the caption, the phrase "or a nonparticipating supplier or other person" and the last sentence to paragraph (3), applicable to services furnished on or after January 1, 1994.]

Section 13515(a)(1) of OBRA 93 added a new paragraph 4, applicable to services furnished on or after January 1, 1994, which provides:

(4) SPECIAL RULE FOR MEDICAL DIRECTION. — .

(A) IN GENERAL. — With respect to physicians' services furnished on or after January 1, 1994, and consisting of medical direction of two, three, or four concurrent anesthesia cases, the fee schedule amount to be applied shall be equal to one-half of the amount described in subparagraph (B).

(B) AMOUNT. — The amount described in this subparagraph, for a physician's medical direction of the performance of anesthesia services, is the following percentage of the fee schedule amount otherwise applicable under this section if the anesthesia services were personally performed by the physician alone:

(i) For services furnished during 1994, 120 percent.

(ii) For services furnished during 1995, 115 percent.

(iii) For services furnished during 1996, 110 percent.

(iv) For services furnished during 1997, 105 percent.

(v) For services furnished after 1997, 100 percent.

◆ NOTE: Prior to the OBRA 93 amendment, paragraph (4) read: TREATMENT OF NEW PHYSICIANS. — In the case of physicians' services furnished by a physician before the end of the physician's first full calendar year of furnishing services for which payment may be made under this part, and during each of the 3 succeeding years, the fee schedule amount to be applied shall be 80 percent, 85 percent, 90 percent, and 95 percent, respectively, of the fee schedule amount applicable to physicians who are not subject to this paragraph. The preceding sentence shall not apply to primary care services or services furnished in a rural area (as defined in section 1886(d)(2) [42 U.S.C.A. ww(d)(2)]) that is designated under section 322(a)(1)(A) of the Public Health Service Act as a health manpower shortage area.

Section 1848(b) provides in pertinent part:

(b) ESTABLISHMENT OF FEE SCHEDULES. —

(1) IN GENERAL. — Before January 1 of each year beginning with 1992, the Secretary shall establish, by regulation, fee schedules that establish payment amounts for all physicians' services furnished in all fee schedule areas (as defined in subsection (j)(2)) for the year. Except as provided in para-

graph (2), each such payment amount for a service shall be equal to the product of—

(A) the relative value for the service (as determined in subsection (c)(2)),

(B) the conversion factor (established under subsection (d)) for the year, and

(C) the geographic adjustment factor (established under subsection (e)(2)) for the service for the fee schedule area.

(2) TREATMENT OF RADIOLOGY SERVICES AND ANESTHESIA SERVICES.—

(A) RADIOLOGY SERVICES. — With respect to radiology services (including radiologist services, as defined in section 1834(b)(6)), the Secretary shall base the relative values on the relative value scale developed under section 1834(b)(1)(A), with appropriate modifications of the relative values to assure that the relative values established for radiology services which are similar or related to other physicians' services are consistent with the relative values established for those similar or related services.

(B) ANESTHESIA SERVICES. — In establishing the fee schedule for anesthesia services for which a relative value guide has been established under section 4048(b) of the Omnibus Budget Reconciliation Act of 1987, the Secretary shall use, to the extent practicable, such relative value guide, with appropriate adjustment of the conversion factor, in a manner to assure that the fee schedule amounts for anesthesia services are consistent with the fee schedule amounts for other services determined by the Secretary to be of comparable value. In applying the previous sentence, the Secretary shall adjust the conversion factor by geographic adjustment factors in the same manner as such adjustment is made under paragraph (1)(C).

(C) CONSULTATION. — The Secretary shall consult with the Physician Payment Review Commission and organizations representing physicians or suppliers who furnish radiology services and anesthesia services in applying subparagraphs (A) and (B).

Section 1848(c) then provides for determination of relative values for physicians' services. That involves use of a "work component" that reflects physician time and intensity in furnishing service, a "practice expense component" that reflects such expenses as office rent and wages of personnel related to a physician's practice, and a "malpractice component" that gives special weight to malpractice expenses. It also involves computation of relative value units for those components.

Section 1848(d) provides for conversion factors and updates in conversion factors presumably to moderate impact of the transition to fee schedules in the near term. Section 1848(e) provides for geographic adjustment factors to reflect cost differences among physicians' services in different locales. Section 1848(f) provides for development and use of Medicare volume performance standard rates of increase to take into account such factors as inflation, changes in numbers and age composition of Medicare Part B enrollees, changes in technology, evidence of inappropriate utilization of services, and evidence of lack of access to necessary physicians' services.

As amended by section 123(a)(1) of the Social Security Act Amendments of 1994, applicable to services furnished on or after October 31, 1994, section 1848(g) reads:

> (g) LIMITATION ON BENEFICIARY LIABILITY.—
>
> (1) LIMITATION ON ACTUAL CHARGES FOR UNASSIGNED CLAIMS.—
>
> (A) IN GENERAL. —In the case of a nonparticipating physician or nonparticipating supplier or other person (as defined in section 1842(i)(2)) who does not accept payment on an assignment-related basis for a physician's service furnished with respect to an individual enrolled under this part, the following rules apply:
>
> (i) APPLICATION OF LIMITING CHARGE. —No person may bill or collect an actual charge for the service in excess of the limiting charge described in paragraph (2) for such service.
>
> (ii) NO LIABILITY FOR EXCESS CHARGES. —No person is liable for payment of any amounts billed for the service in excess of such limiting charge.

(iii) CORRECTION OF EXCESS CHARGES.— If such a physician, supplier, or other person bills, but does not collect, an actual charge for a service in violation of clause (i), the physician, supplier, or other person shall reduce on a timely basis the actual charge billed for the service to an amount not to exceed the limiting charge for the service.

(iv) REFUND OF EXCESS COLLECTIONS.— If such a physician, supplier, or other person collects an actual charge for a service in violation of clause (i), the physician, supplier, or other person shall provide on a timely basis a refund to the individual charged in the amount by which the amount collected exceeded the limiting charge for the service. The amount of such a refund shall be reduced to the extent the individual has an outstanding balance owed by the individual to the physician.

(B) SANCTIONS. —If a physician, supplier, or other person—

(i) knowingly and willfully bills or collects for services in violation of subparagraph (A)(i) on a repeated basis, or

(ii) fails to comply with clause (iii) or (iv) of subparagraph (A) on a timely basis, the Secretary may apply sanctions against the physician, supplier, or other person in accordance with paragraph (2) of section 1842(j). In applying this subparagraph, paragraph (4) of such section applies in the same manner as such paragraph applies to such section and any reference in such section to a physician is deemed also to include a reference to a supplier or other person under this subparagraph. [Section 1842(j)(2), 42 U.S.C.A. 1395u(j)(2), authorizes exclusion for a period not to exceed 5 years and civil money penalties and assessments, and makes cross reference to the exclusion and civil money penalty provisions of sections 1128 and 1128A of the Act]

(C) TIMELY BASIS. —For purposes of this paragraph, a correction of a bill for an excess charge or refund of an amount with respect to a violation of subparagraph (A)(i) in the case of a service is considered to be provided "on a timely basis", if the reduction or refund is made not later than 30 days after the date the physician, supplier, or other person is notified by the carrier under this part of such violation and of the requirements of subparagraph (A).

◆ NOTE: Prior to amendment by the Social Security Act Amendments of 1994, as amended by OBRA 93 and applicable to services furnished on or after January 1, 1994, section 1848(g) read: "(1) LIMITATION ON ACTUAL CHARGES FOR UNASSIGNED CLAIMS.— If a nonparticipating physician or nonparticipating supplier or other person (as defined in section 1842(i)(2) [which pursuant to OBRA 93 includes suppliers or other persons not providers]) knowingly and willfully bills on a repeated basis for physicians' services (including services which the Secretary excludes pursuant to subsection (j)(3), furnished with respect to an individual enrolled under this part on or after January 1, 1991) an actual charge in excess of the limiting charge described in paragraph (2) and for which payment is not made on an assignment-related basis under this part, the Secretary may apply sanctions against such physician, supplier, or other person in accordance with section 1842(j)(2). In applying this subparagraph, any reference in such section to a physician is deemed also to include a reference to a supplier or other person under this subparagraph." Prior to amendment by section 13517(a)(2) of OBRA 93, section 1848(g) read: "LIMITATION ON BENEFICIARY LIABILITY.— (1) LIMITATION ON ACTUAL CHARGES FOR UNASSIGNED CLAIMS.—If a nonparticipating physician knowingly and willfully bills on a repeated basis for physicians' services (furnished with respect to an individual enrolled under this part on or after January 1, 1991) an actual charge in excess of the limiting charge described in paragraph (2) and for which payment is not made on an assignment-related basis under this part, the Secretary may apply sanctions against such physician in accordance with section 1842(j)(2)."§ 2:10 Failure to include information about referring physicians on requests for payments or bills: Section 1833(q) [42 U.S.C.A. 1395l(q)].

(2) LIMITING CHARGE DEFINED.—

(A) FOR 1991. — For physicians' services of a physician furnished during 1991, other than radiologist services subject to section 1834(b) [this clause beginning "other than" added here and below in paragraph (B) by section

4118(f)(1)(Q) of OBRA 90], the limiting charge " shall be the same percentage (or, if less, 25 percent) above the recognized payment amount under this part with respect to the physician (as a nonparticipating physician) as the percentage by which —

(i) the maximum allowable actual charge (as determined under section 1842(j)(1)(C) as of December 31, 1990, or, if less, the maximum actual charge otherwise permitted for the service under this part as of such date) for the service of the physician, exceeds

(ii) the recognized payment amount for the service of the physician (as a nonparticipating physician) as of such date.

In the case of evaluation and management services (as specified in section 1842(b)(16)(B)(ii) [42 U.S.C.A. 1395u(b)(16)(B)(ii)], the preceding sentence shall be applied by substituting "40 percent" for "25 percent". [The last sentence was added effective November 5, 1990, by section 4116 of OBRA 90.]

(B) FOR 1992. — For physicians' services furnished during 1992, other than radiologist services subject to section 1834(b), the "limiting charge" shall be the same percentage (or, if less, 20 percent) above the recognized payment amount under this part for nonparticipating physicians as the percentage by which —

(i) the limiting charge (as determined under subparagraph (A) as of December 31, 1991) for the service, exceeds

(ii) the recognized payment amount for the service for nonparticipating physicians as of such date.

(C) AFTER 1992. — For physicians services furnished in a year after 1992, the "limiting charge" shall be 115 percent of the recognized payment amount under this part for nonparticipating physicians or for nonparticipating suppliers or other persons. [The phrase "or for nonparticipating suppliers or other persons" was added by section 13517(a)(3) of OBRA 93, applicable to services furnished on or after January 1, 1994.]

(D) RECOGNIZED PAYMENT AMOUNT. — In this section, the term "recognized payment amount" means, for services furnished on or after January 1, 1992, the fee schedule amount determined under subsection (a) (or, if payment under this part is made on a basis other than the fee schedule under this section, 95 percent of the other payment basis), and, for services furnished during 1991, the applicable percentage (as defined in section 1842(b)(4)(A)(iv) [42 U.S.C.A. 1395u(b)(4)(A)(iv), which pertains to the physician fee freeze affecting reasonable charges for physicians' services furnished on or after January 1, 1987, and before January 1, 1992: 96 percent for services furnished on or after January 1, 1987, and before April 1, 1988, 95.5 percent for services furnished on or after April 1, 1988, and before January 1, 1989, and 95 percent for services furnished on or after January 1, 1989,]) of the prevailing charge (or fee schedule amount) for nonparticipating physicians for that year. [The parenthetical reference to payment on other than a fee schedule basis was added by section 13517(a)(4) of OBRA 93, applicable to services furnished on or after January 1, 1994.]

* * *

(6) MONITORING OF CHARGES. —

(A) IN GENERAL. — The Secretary shall monitor —

(i) the actual charges of nonparticipating physicians for physicians' services furnished on or after January 1, 1991, to individuals enrolled under this part, and

(ii) changes (by specialty, type of service, and geographic area) in (I) the proportion of expenditures for physicians' services provided under this part by participating physicians, (II) the proportion of expenditures for such services for which payment is made under this part on an assignment-related basis, and (III) the amounts charged above the recognized payment amounts under this part.

(B) REPORT. — The Secretary shall, by not later than April 15 of each year (beginning in 1991), report to the Congress on the changes described in subparagraph (A)(i) and shall include in the report an examination of the factors (including factors relating to different services and specific categories and groups of services and geographic and demographic variations in utilization) which may contribute to such changes.

◆ NOTE: Prior to amendment by section 123(d) of the Social Security Act amendments of 1994, applicable to reports for years beginning with 1995, section 1848(g)(6)(B) read: "The Secretary shall, by not later than April 15, 1992, report to the Congress regarding the changes described in subparagraph (A)(ii)."

(C) PLAN. — If the Secretary finds that there has been a significant decrease in the proportions described in subclauses (I) and (II) of subparagraph (A)(ii) or an increase in the amounts described in subclause (III) of that subparagraph, the Secretary shall develop a plan to address such a problem and transmit to Congress recommendations regarding the plan. The Medicare Payment Advisory Commission [Effective not later than September 30, 1997, section 4022(b)(2)(C) of the "Balanced Budget Act of 1997", P.L. 105-33 replaced "Physician Payment Review Commission" with "Medicare Payment Advisory Commission" here and below in subsection (g)(7)(C)] shall review the Secretary's plan and recommendations and transmit to Congress its comments regarding such plan and recommendations.

(7) MONITORING OF UTILIZATION AND ACCESS. —

(A) IN GENERAL. — The Secretary shall monitor —

(i) changes in the utilization of and access to services furnished under this part within geographic, population, and service related categories,

(ii) possible sources of inappropriate utilization of services furnished under this part which contribute to the overall level of expenditures under this part, and

(iii) factors underlying these changes and their interrelationships.

(B) REPORT. — The Secretary shall by not later than April 15 of each year (beginning with 1991) report to the Congress on the changes described in subparagraph (A)(i) and shall include in the report an examination of the factors (including factors relating to different services and specific categories and groups of services and geographic and demographic variations in utilization) which may contribute to such changes.

(C) RECOMMENDATIONS. — The Secretary shall include in each annual report under subparagraph (B) recommendations —

(i) addressing any identified patterns of inappropriate utilization,

(ii) on utilization review,

(iii) on physician education or patient education,

(iv) addressing any problems of beneficiary access to care made evident by the monitoring process, and

(v) on such other matters as the Secretary deems appropriate.

The Medicare Payment Advisory Commission shall comment on the Secretary's recommendations and in developing its comments, the Commission shall convene and consult a panel of physician experts to evaluate the implications of medical utilization patterns for the quality of and access to patient care.

As amended by section 13517(a)(5) of OBRA 93, applicable to services furnished on or after January 1, 1994, section 1848(h) provides as follows for sending information to physicians and suppliers or other persons about fee schedules that apply for participants and nonparticipants and the maximum amounts that may be charged consistent with subsection (g)(2).

SENDING INFORMATION TO PHYSICIANS. — Before the beginning of each year (beginning with 1992), the Secretary shall send to each physician or nonparticipating supplier or other person furnishing physicians' services (as defined in section 1848(j)(3)) furnishing physicians' services under this part, for services commonly performed by the physician, supplier, or other person information on fee schedule amounts that apply for the year in the fee schedule area for participating and non-participating physicians, and the maximum amount that may be charged consistent with subsection (g)(2). Such information shall be transmitted in conjunction with notices to physicians, suppliers, and other persons under section 1842(h) (relating to the participating physician program) for a year.

◆ NOTE: Prior to amendment by OBRA 93, section 1848(h) read: (h) SENDING INFORMATION TO PHYSICIANS. — Before the beginning of each year (beginning with 1992), the Secretary shall send to each physician furnishing physicians' services under this part, for services commonly performed by the physician, information on fee schedule amounts that apply for the year in the fee schedule area for participating and non-participating physicians, and the maximum amount that may be charged consistent with subsection (g)(2). Such information shall be transmitted in conjunction with notices to physicians under section 1842(h) [42 U.S.C.A. 1395u(h)] (relating to the participating physician program) for a year.

With respect to restrictions on administrative and judicial review, section 1848 provides:

(i) MISCELLANEOUS PROVISIONS. —

(1) RESTRICTION ON ADMINISTRATIVE AND JUDICIAL REVIEW. — There shall be no administrative or judicial review under section 1869 [42 U.S.C.A. 1395ff, which pertains to determinations about Medicare benefits and appeal rights] or otherwise of —

(A) the determination of the adjusted historical payment basis (as defined in subsection (a)(2)(D)(i), [This subparagraph (i)(1)(A) read "historical payment basis (as defined in subsection (a)(2)(C)(i)" prior to amendment by section 4118(f)(1)(R) of OBRA 90, effective November 5, 1990.]

(B) the determination of relative values and relative value units under subsection (c) including adjustments under subsection (c)(2)(F), and section 13515(b) of the Omnibus Budget Reconciliation Act of 1993 [The phrase beginning with "including" was added by section 13514(c)(3) of OBRA 93, applicable to services furnished on or after January 1, 1994.],

(C) the determination of conversion factors under subsection (d),

(D) the establishment of geographic adjustment factors under subsection (e), and

(E) the establishment of the system for the coding of physicians' services under this section.

* * *

(3) NO COMPARABILITY ADJUSTMENT. — For physicians' services for which payment under this part is determined under this section —

(A) a carrier may not make any adjustment in the payment amount under section 1842(b)(3)(B) [42 U.S.C.A. 1395u(b)(3), which pertains to payment on reasonable cost or reasonable charge bases and customary and prevailing charges] on the basis that the payment amount is higher than the charge applicable, for a comparable services [sic services] and under comparable circumstances, to the policyholders and subscribers of the carrier,

(B) no payment adjustment may be made under section 1842(b)(8) [which pertains to inherent reasonableness adjustments], and

(C) section 1842(b)(9) [which pertains to publication of inherent reasonableness adjustments] shall not apply. [This paragraph 3 was added by section 4118(k) of OBRA 90, effective November 5, 1990.]

Finally, section 1848 provides these additional definitions:

(j) DEFINITIONS. — In this section:

(1) CATEGORY. — For services furnished after January 1, 1998, the term "category" means, with respect to physicians' services, surgical services, and all physicians' services other than surgical services (as defined by the Secretary and including anesthesia services), primary care services (as defined in section 1842(i)(4)) and all other physicians' services.

◆ [NOTE: Prior to amendment by section 4118(f)(1)(S) of OBRA, effective November 5, 1990, subparagraph (j)(1) read: "The term 'category' means, with respect to physicians' services, surgical services, and all physicians' services other than surgical services, and such other category or categories of physicians' services as the Secretary, from time to time, defines in regulation. The Secretary shall define surgical services and publish such definition in the Federal Register no later than May 1, 1990, after consultation with organizations representing physicians." Also, the introductory phrase preceding "term 'category'" was added to the amended subparagraph (j)(1), effective August

5, 1997, by section 4501 (b)(4) of the Balanced Budget Act of 1997.]

◆ [NOTE ALSO: The phrase "and including anesthesia services" and the clause "primary care services (as defined in section 1842(i)(4)" were added by section 13515(a)(2) of OBRA 93, applicable to services furnished on or after January 1, 1994.]

(2) FEE SCHEDULE AREA. — The term "fee schedule area" means a locality used under section 1842(b) [42 U.S.C.A. 1395u(b), which pertains to the use of carriers for processing Part B claims and to carrier reliance on locality data about prevailing charges for physicians' services] for purposes of computing payment amounts for physicians' services.

(3) PHYSICIANS' SERVICES. — The term "physicians' services" includes items and services described in paragraphs (1), (2)(A), (2)(D), (2)(G) ["(2)(G)" was added by section 13518(a) of OBRA 93, applicable to services furnished on or after January 1, 1995.], (2)(P) (with respect to services described in subparagraphs (A) and (C) of section 1861(oo)(2)) [42 U.S.C.A. 1395x(oo)(2)] , (2)(R) (with respect to services described in subparagraphs (B), (C), and (D) of section 1861(pp)(1)), (2)(S), (3), (4), (14) (with respect to services described in section 1861(nn)(2)), and (15) of section 1861(s) [42 U.S.C.A. 1395x(s), which defines medical and other health services reimbursable under Medicare to include physicians' services; services and supplies (including drugs and biologicals which are not usually self–administered by the patient) furnished as an incident to a physician's professional service which are commonly either rendered without charge or included in physicians' bills; outpatient physical therapy services and outpatient occupational therapy services; certain antigens prepared by a physician (per OBRA 93); diagnostic X-ray tests (including tests under the supervision of a physician, furnished in a place of residence used as the patient's home, if the performance of such tests meets such conditions relating to health and safety as the Secretary finds necessary), diagnostic laboratory tests, and other diagnostic tests; and X-ray, radium and radioactive isotope therapy, including materials and services of technicians] (other than clinical

diagnostic laboratory tests and such other items and services as the Secretary may specify).

NOTE: Section 4102(d) of the Balanced Budget Act of 1997, P.L. 105-33, enacted August 5, 1997, inserted the reference to paragraph (2)(P), applicable to items and services furnished on or after January 1, 2000. Section 4104(d) inserted the reference to (2)(R), applicable to items and services furnished on or after January 1, 1998. Section 4105(a)(2) inserted the reference to paragraph (2)(S), applicable to items and services furnished on or after July 1, 1998. Section 4106(d) substituted "(4) and (14)" and added the reference to paragraph (15), applicable to bone mass measurements performed on or after July 1, 1998. Additional minor editorial corrections were made to section 1848(j)(3) by sections 321(k)(5)(A), (B), and (C) of the Medicare, Medicaid, and SCHIP Balanced Budget Refinement Act of 1999, as incorporated into the Omnibus Consolidated Appropriations Act, 2000, P.L. 106–113, enacted November 17, 1999. These changes were made effective as of August 5, 1997. Furthermore, applicable with respect to screening mammographies furnished on or after January 1, 2002, section 104(a) of the Medicare, Medicaid, and SCHIP Benefit Improvement and Protection Act of 2000 inserted "(13)" after "(4)".

(4) PRACTICE EXPENSES. — The term "practice expenses" includes all expenses for furnishing physicians' services, excluding malpractice expenses, physician compensation, and other physician fringe benefits.

Section 1861(s), 42 U.S.C.A. 1395x(s), provides in pertinent part:

The term "medical and other health services" means any of the following items or services:

(1) physicians' services;

(2) (A) services and supplies (including drugs and biologicals which are not usually self-administered by the patient) furnished as an incident to a physician's professional service, of kinds which are commonly furnished in physicians' offices and are commonly either rendered without charge or included in the physicians' bills;

[NOTE: Prior to enactment of section 112(a) of the Medicare, Medicaid, and SCHIP Benefits Improvement and

Protection Act of 2000, P.L. 106-544, December 15, 2000, paragraph (2)(A) read "services and supplies (including drugs and biologicals which cannot, as determined in accordance with regulations, be self-administered) furnished as an incident to a physician's professional service, of kinds which are commonly furnished in physicians' offices and are commonly either rendered without charge or included in the physicians' bills[.]" The change applies to drugs and biologicals administered on or after December 21, 2000.]

* * *

(D) outpatient physical therapy services and outpatient occupational therapy services;

* * *

(G) antigens (subject to quantity limitations prescribed in regulations by the Secretary) prepared by a physician, as defined in section 1861(r)(1), for a particular patient, including antigens so prepared which are forwarded to another qualified person (including a rural health clinic) for administration to such patient, from time to time, by or under the supervision of another such physician;

* * *

(P) prostate cancer screening tests (as defined in subsection (oo); [NOTE: This provision was added by section 4103(a) of the Balanced Budget Act of 1997, P.L. 105-33, enacted August 5, 1997. It applies to items and services furnished on or after January 1, 2000.]

* * *

(R) colorectal cancer screening tests (as defined in subsection (pp);

(S) diabetes outpatient self-management training services (as defined in subsection (qq)

* * *

(3) diagnostic X-ray tests (including tests under the supervision of a physician, furnished in a place of residence used as the patient's home, if the performance of such tests meets such conditions relating to health and safety as the Secretary may find necessary and including diagnostic mammography if

conducted by a facility that has a certificate (or provisional certificate) issued under section 354 of the Public Health Service Act), diagnostic laboratory tests, and other diagnostic tests; [The phrase "and including diagnostic mammography if conducted by a facility that has a certificate (or provisional certificate) issued under section 354 of the Public Health Service Act)" was added by section 145(b) of the Social Security Act Amendments of 1994. That applies to mammography furnished by a facility on and after the first date that the certificate requirements of section 354(b) of the Public Health Service Act apply to such mammography conducted by such facility.];

(4) X-ray, radium and radioactive isotope therapy, including materials and services of technicians[.]

* * *

(13) screening mammography (as defined in subsection (jj)); and

(14) screening pap smear and screening pelvic exam; and

(15) bone mass measurement (as defined in subsection (rr)).

Finally, section 1842(j)(2), which applies by cross reference from section 1848(g)(1), provides:

Subject to paragraph (3), the sanctions which the Secretary may apply under this paragraph are —

(A) excluding a physician from participation in the programs under this Act for a period not to exceed 5 years, in accordance with the procedures of paragraphs (c) [which pertains to notice, effective date, and period of exclusion], (f) [which pertains to notice, hearing, and judicial review], and (g) [which pertains to application for termination of exclusion] of section 1128 [42 U.S.C.A. 1320a-7], or

(B) civil monetary penalties and assessments, in the same manner as such penalties and assessments are authorized under section 1128A(a) [42 U.S.C.A. 1320a-7a(a)],

or both. The provisions of section 1128A (other than the first 2 sentences of subsection (a) and other than subsection (b)) shall apply to a civil money penalty and assessment under subparagraph (B) in the same manner as such provisions apply to a penalty, assessment, or proceeding under section

1128A(a), except to the extent such provisions are inconsistent with subparagraph (A) or paragraph (3).

Section 1842(j)(3) then provides:

(A) The Secretary may not exclude a physician pursuant to paragraph (2)(A) if such physician is a sole community physician or sole source of essential specialized services in a community.

(B) The Secretary shall take into account access of beneficiaries to physicians' services for which payment may be made under this part in determining whether to bar a physician from participation under paragraph (2)(A).

For regulatory citations, see Chapter 6

§ 2:25 FAILURE TO BILL ON AN ASSIGNMENT-RELATED BASIS FOR SERVICES TO PERSONS ENROLLED UNDER MEDICARE PART B AND ELIGIBLE FOR MEDICAID —Section 1848(g)(3) [42 U.S.C.A. 1395w-4(g)(3)]

Summary

◆ NOTE: For a summary of section 1848, 42 U.S.C.A. 1395w-4, see § 2:24.

In conjunction with transition from reasonable charge reimbursement to fee schedule reimbursement, section 1848(g)(3), 42 U.S.C.A. 1395w-4(g)(3), provides that payment for physicians' services furnished on or after April 1, 1990, to an individual enrolled under Medicare Part B who is also eligible for Medicaid benefits may be made only on an assignment-related basis. Any person who knowingly and willfully bills for physicians' services in violation of that requirement is subject to exclusion for a period not to exceed 5 years and to civil money penalties in accordance with section 1842(j)(2), 42 U.S.C.A. 1395u(j)(2).

Enforcement procedures for these sanctions are governed by section 1128, 42 U.S.C.A. 1320a-7, which authorizes exclusion for a variety of offenses, and section 1128A, 42 U.S.C.A. 1320a-7a, which authorizes civil money penalties for a variety of offenses.

Statutory Provisions

Section 1848(j), 42 U.S.C.A. 1395w-4(j), which defines physicians' services for purposes of section 1848, can be found at § 2:24.

Section 1848(g)(3) provides:

> LIMITATION ON CHARGES FOR MEDICARE BENEFICIARIES ELIGIBLE FOR MEDICAID BENEFITS.—
>
> (A) IN GENERAL — Payment for physicians' services furnished on or after April 1, 1990, to an individual who is enrolled under this part and eligible for any medical assistance (including as a qualified medicare beneficiary, as defined in section 1905(p)(1) [42 U.S.C.A. 1396d(p)(1)]) with respect to such services under a State plan approved under title XIX may only be made on an assignment-related basisand the provisions of section 1902(n)(3)(A) [42 U.S.C.A. 1396a(n), which pertains to a State's payment for Medicare cost-sharing for a qualified Medicare beneficiary] apply to further limit permissible charges under this section.
>
> [NOTE: Section 4714(b)(2) of the Balanced Budget Act of 1997, P.L. 105–33, added the phrase beginning "and the provisions of" at the end of the preceding sentence. This change applies to items and services furnished on or after August 5, 1997.]
>
> (B) PENALTY — A person may not bill for physicians' services subject to subparagraph (A) other than on an assignment-related basis. No person is liable for payment of any amounts billed for such a service in violation of the previous sentence. If a person knowingly and willfully bills for physicians' services in violation of the first sentence, the Secretary may apply sanctions against the person in accordance with section 1842(j)(2) [42 U.S.C.A. 1395u(j)(2)]. Section 123(a)(2)(A)-(B) of the Social Security Act Amendments of 1994, P.L. 103-432, effective October 31, 1994, substituted the word "first" for the word "previous" in the third sentence, and added the second sentence.].

Finally, section 1842(j)(2), which applies by cross reference from section 1848(g)(3)(B), provides:

> Subject to paragraph (3), the sanctions which the Secretary may apply under this paragraph are —

(A) excluding a physician from participation in the programs under this Act for a period not to exceed 5 years, in accordance with the procedures of paragraphs (c) [which pertains to notice, effective date, and period of exclusion], (f) [which pertains to notice, hearing, and judicial review], and (g) [which pertains to application for termination of exclusion] of section 1128 [42 U.S.C.A. 1320a-7], or

(B) civil monetary penalties and assessments, in the same manner as such penalties and assessments are authorized under section 1128A(a) [42 U.S.C.A. 1320a-7a(a)],

or both. The provisions of section 1128A (other than the first 2 sentences of subsection (a) and other than subsection (b)) shall apply to a civil money penalty and assessment under subparagraph (B) in the same manner as such provisions apply to a penalty, assessment, or proceeding under section 1128A(a), except to the extent such provisions are inconsistent with subparagraph (A) or paragraph (3).

Section 1842(j)(3) then provides:

(A) The Secretary may not exclude a physician pursuant to paragraph (2)(A) if such physician is a sole community physician or sole source of essential specialized services in a community.

(B) The Secretary shall take into account access of beneficiaries to physicians' services for which payment may be made under this part in determining whether to bar a physician from participation under paragraph (2)(A).

For regulatory citations, see Chapter 6

§ 2:26 FAILURE BY PHYSICIANS, SUPPLIERS, AND OTHERS, INCLUDING THEIR EMPLOYERS AND RELATED FACILITIES, TO SUBMIT CLAIMS ON SPECIFIED CLAIM FORMS — Section 1848(g)(4) [42 U.S.C.A. 1395w-(g)(4)]

Summary

◆ NOTE: For a summary of section 1848, 42 U.S.C.A. 1395w-4, see § 2:20.

In conjunction with transition from reasonable charge reimbursement to fee schedule reimbursement, section 1848(g)(3), 42 U.S.C.A.

1395w-4(g)(3), provides that payment for physicians' services furnished on or after April 1, 1990, to an individual enrolled under Medicare Part B who is also eligible for Medicaid benefits may be made only on an assignment-related basis. Any person who knowingly and willfully bills for physicians' services in violation of that requirement is subject to exclusion for a period not to exceed 5 years and to civil money penalties in accordance with section 1842(j)(2), 42 U.S.C.A. 1395u(j)(2).

Enforcement procedures for these sanctions are governed by section 1128, 42 U.S.C.A. 1320a-7, which authorizes exclusion for a variety of offenses, and section 1128A, 42 U.S.C.A. 1320a-7a, which authorizes civil money penalties for a variety of offenses.

This also applies to an employer or a facility in two kinds of cases:

(1) where, as an exception to the prohibition against reassignment of Medicare claims, section 1842(b)(6)(A), 42 U.S.C.A. 1395u(b)(6)(A), permits payment to the employer of a physician or other person if such physician or other person is required as a condition of employment to turn over the fee for such service to the employer; and

(2) where, as an exception to the prohibition against assignment, section 1842(b)(6)(A) permits payment to a hospital, critical access hospital, clinic, or other facility if the service was provided in such a facility, and if the physician or other person has a contractual arrangement with such a facility authorizing it to submit such bills.

No charge may be imposed relating to completing and submitting the required standard claim form.

Section 1848(g)(4)(B)(i) provides that if any physician, provider, supplier, or other person (or an employer thereof or facility related thereto) fails to submit claims as required by section 1848(g)(4)(A), the Secretary must reduce by 10 percent the amount that would otherwise be paid for such claims.

In addition, section 1848(g)(4)(B)(ii) provides that any physician, supplier, or other person (or an employer thereof or facility related thereto) that fails to submit a claim as required by section 1848(g)(4)(A), or that imposes a charge for completing or submitting such a claim, is subject to a $2,000 civil money penalty and to exclusion for a period not to exceed 5 years. This applies by cross reference to section 1842(p), 42 U.S.C.A. 1395u(p), which authorizes a $2,000 civil money penalty and exclusion for failure to include appropriate diagnosis coding on claims, which, in turn, cross references section

1842(j)(2)(A), 42 U.S.C.A. 1396u(j)(2)(A), which cross references section 1128A, 42 U.S.C.A. 1320a-7a.

Statutory Provisions

Section 1848(g)(4), 42 U.S.C.A. 1395w-4(g)(4), provides:

(4) PHYSICIAN SUBMISSION OF CLAIMS. —

(A) IN GENERAL. — For services furnished on or after September 1, 1990, within 1 year after the date of providing a service for which payment is made under this part on a reasonable charge or fee schedule basis, a physician, supplier, or other person (or an employer or facility in the cases described in section 1842(b)(6)(A) [42 U.S.C.A. 1395u(b)(6)(A), which, as an exception to the prohibition against reassignment of Medicare claims, permits payment to be made to the employer of a physician or other person if such physician or other person is required as a condition of his employment to turn over his fee for such service to his employer, or, where the service was provided in a hospital, rural primary care hospital, clinic, or other facility, to the facility in which the service was provided if there is a contractual arrangement between such physician or other person and such facility under which such facility submits the bill for such service]) —

(i) shall complete and submit a claim for such service on a standard claim form specified by the Secretary to the carrier on behalf of a beneficiary, and

(ii) may not impose any charge relating to completing and submitting such a form.

(B) PENALTY. —

(i) With respect to an assigned claim wherever a physician, provider, supplier or other person (or an employer or facility in the cases described in section 1842(b)(6)(A)) fails to submit such a claim as required in subparagraph (A), the Secretary shall reduce by 10 percent the amount that would otherwise be paid for claim under this part

(ii) If a physician, supplier, or other person (or an employer or facility in the cases described in section 1842(b)(6)(A)) fails to submit a claim required to be submitted under subparagraph (A) or imposes a charge in violation of such subparagraph, the Secretary shall apply the sanction with respect to such a violation in the same manner as a sanction may be imposed under section 1842(p)(3) [42 U.S.C.A. 1395u(p)(3), which authorizes imposition of a $2,000 civil money penalty and exclusion, pursuant to section 1842(j)(2)(A) and cross reference to section 1128A, for failure to include appropriate diagnosis coding on claims for payment for a items or services furnished by physicians]) for a violation of section 1842(p)(1) [which requires use of such codes].

With respect to the exception to the prohibition against reassignment of Medicare claims, section 1842(b)(6)(A), 42 U.S.C.A. 1395u(b)(6)(A), provides in pertinent part:

No payment under this part for a service provided to any individual shall (except as provided in section 1870 [42 U.S.C.A. 1395gg, which pertains to overpayments on behalf of individuals and settlement of claims on behalf of deceased individuals) be made to anyone other than such individual or (pursuant to an assignment described in subparagraph (B)(ii) of paragraph (3) [which pertains to the requirement for carriers to make payments based on reasonable charge methodology and based on assignments which prohibit additional charges above what Medicare allows]) the physician or other person who provided the service, except that (A) payment may be made (i) to the employer of such physician or other person if such physician or other person is required as a condition of his employment to turn over his fee for such service to his employer, or (ii) (where the service was provided in a hospital, critical access hospital, clinic, or other facility) to the facility in which the service was provided if there is a contractual arrangement between such physician or other person and such facility under which such facility submits the bill for such service,... No payment which under the preceding sentence may be made directly to the physician or other person providing the service involved (pursuant to an assignment described in subparagraph (B)(ii) of paragraph (3)) shall be made to anyone else under a reassignment or power of attorney (except to an employer or facility as described in clause (A) of such sentence); but nothing in this subsection shall be construed (I) to prevent the making of such a payment in accordance with an assignment from the individual to whom the service was provided or a reassignment from the physician or other person providing such service if such assignment or reassignment is made to a governmental agency or entity or is established by or pursuant to the order of a court of competent jurisdiction, or (II) to preclude an agent of the physician or other person providing the service from receiving any such payment if (but only if) such agent does so pursuant to an agency agreement under which the compensation to be paid to the agent for his services for or in connection with the billing or collection of payments due such physician or other person under this title is unrelated (directly or indirectly) to the amount of such payments or the billings therefor, and is not dependent upon the actual collection of any such payment.

NOTE: Section 4201(c)(1) of the Balanced Budget Act of 1997, P.L. 105–33, substituted the phrase "critical access hospital" for the phrase "rural primary care hospital" in section 1842(b)(6)(A). That change applies to services furnished on or after October 1, 1997. The phrase "rural primary care hospital" had been added effective December 19, 1990, by section 6003(g)(3)(D)(ix) of P.L. 101–239, the Omnibus Budget Reconciliation Act of 1989.

Section 1842(p), 42 U.S.C.A. 1395u(p), to which section 1848(g)(4)(B)(ii) provides:

(1) Each request for payment, or bill submitted, for an item or service furnished by a physician or practitioner specified in subsection (b)(18)(C) [which includes physicians assistants, nurse practitioners, clinical nurse specialists, certified registered nurse anesthetists, certified nurse-midwives, clinical social workers, and clinical psychologists] for which payment may be made under this part shall include the appropriate diagnosis code (or codes) as established by the Secretary for such item or service.

(2) In the case of a request for payment for an item or service furnished by a physician or practitioner specified in subsection (b)(18)(C) on an assignment-related basis which does not include the code (or codes) required under paragraph (1), payment may be denied under this part.

(3) In the case of a request for payment for an item or service furnished by a physician not submitted on an assign-

ment-related basis and which does not include the code (or codes) required under paragraph (1)—

(A) if the physician knowingly and willfully fails to provide the code (or codes) promptly upon request of the Secretary or a carrier, the physician may be subject to a civil money penalty in an amount not to exceed $2,000, and

(4) (4) In the case of an item or service defined in paragraph (3) [which pertains to diagnostic X-ray tests], (6) [which pertains to durable medical equipment], (8) [which pertains to certain prosthetic devices], or (9) [which pertains to leg, arm, back, and neck braces, and artificial legs, arms, and eyes, including replacements if required because of a change in the patient's physical condition] of subsection 1861(s) ordered by a physician or a practitioner specified in subsection (b)(18)(C), but furnished by another entity, if the Secretary (or fiscal agent of the Secretary) requires the entity furnishing the item or service to provide diagnostic or other medical information in order for payment to be made to the entity, the physician or practitioner shall provide that information to the entity at the time that the item or service is ordered by the physician or practitioner.

NOTE: Section 4317(a) of the Balanced Budget Act of 1997 added the phrase "or practitioner specified in subsection (b)(18)(C)" to subsections (p)(1) and (p)(2). Section 4317(b) of the Balanced Budget Act of 1997 added paragraph (4) above. These changes apply to items and services furnished on or after January 1, 1998.

(B) if the physician knowingly, willfully, and in repeated cases fails, after being notified by the Secretary of the obligations and requirements of this subsection, to include the code (or codes) required under paragraph (1), the physician may be subject to the sanction described in section 1842(j)(2)(A).

The provisions of section 1128A [42 U.S.C.A. 1320a-7a] (other than subsections (a) and (b)) shall apply to civil money penalties under subparagraph (A) in the same manner as they apply to a penalty or proceeding under section 1128A(a).

Section 1842(j)(2) provides:

Subject to paragraph (3), the sanctions which the Secretary may apply under this paragraph are—

> (A) excluding a physician from participation in the programs under this Act for a period not to exceed 5 years, in accordance with the procedures of paragraphs (c) [which pertains to notice, effective date, and period of exclusion], (f) [which pertains to notice, hearing, and judicial review], and (g) [which pertains to application for termination of exclusion] of section 1128 [42 U.S.C.A. 1320a-7], or
>
> (B) civil monetary penalties and assessments, in the same manner as such penalties and assessments are authorized under section 1128A(a) [42 U.S.C.A. 1320a-7a(a)],
>
> or both. The provisions of section 1128A (other than the first 2 sentences of subsection (a) and other than subsection (b)) shall apply to a civil money penalty and assessment under subparagraph (B) in the same manner as such provisions apply to a penalty, assessment, or proceeding under section 1128A(a), except to the extent such provisions are inconsistent with subparagraph (A) or paragraph (3).

Section 1842(j)(3) then provides:

> (A) The Secretary may not exclude a physician pursuant to paragraph (2)(A) if such physician is a sole community physician or sole source of essential specialized services in a community.
>
> (B) The Secretary shall take into account access of beneficiaries to physicians' services for which payment may be made under this part in determining whether to bar a physician from participation under paragraph (2)(A).

Finally, for purposes of section 1848, "physicians' services" is defined in section 1848(j)(3) by cross reference to section 1861(s), 42 U.S.C.A. 1395x(s), which provides in pertinent part:

> The term "medical and other health services" means any of the following items or services:
>
> (1) physicians' services;
>
> (2) (A) services and supplies (including drugs and and biologicals which are not usually self–administered by the patient) furnished as an incident to a physician's professional service, of kinds which are commonly furnished in physicians' offices and are commonly either rendered without charge or included in the physicians' bills;

NOTE: Prior to enactment of section 112(a) of the Medicare, Medicaid, and SCHIP Benefits Improvement and Protection Act of 2000, P.L. 106-544, December 15, 2000, paragraph (2)(A) read "services and supplies (including drugs and biologicals which cannot, as determined in accordance with regulations, be self-administered) furnished as an incident to a physician's professional service, of kinds which are commonly furnished in physicians' offices and are commonly either rendered without charge or included in the physicians' bills[.]" That change applies to drugs and biologicals administered on or after December 21, 2000.

* * *

(D) outpatient physical therapy services and outpatient occupational therapy services;

* * *

(G) antigens (subject to quantity limitations prescribed in regulations by the Secretary) prepared by a physician, as defined in section 1861(r)(1), for a particular patient, including antigens so prepared which are forwarded to another qualified person (including a rural health clinic) for administration to such patient, from time to time, by or under the supervision of another such physician [Section 13518(a) of OBRA 93 added (G) to the definition of physicians' services in section 1848(j)(3).];

* * *

(P) prostate cancer screening tests (as defined in subsection (oo)); [NOTE: This provision was added by section 4103(a) of the Balanced Budget Act of 1997, P.L. 105-33, August 5, 1997. It applies to items and services furnished on or after January 1, 2000.]

* * *

(R) colorectal cancer screening tests (as defined in subsection (pp);

(S) diabetes outpatient self-management training services (as defined in subsection (qq);

* * *

(3) diagnostic X-ray tests (including tests under the supervision of a physician, furnished in a place of residence used as the patient's home, if the performance of such tests meets such conditions relating to health and safety as the Secretary may find necessary and including diagnostic mammography if conducted by a facility that has a certificate (or provisional certificate) issued under section 354 of the Public Health Service Act), diagnostic laboratory tests, and other diagnostic tests [The phrase "and including diagnostic mammography if conducted by a facility that has a certificate (or provisional certificate) issued under section 354 of the Public Health Service Act)" was added by section 145(b) of the Social Security Act Amendments of 1994. That applies to mammography furnished by a facility on and after the first date that the certificate requirements of section 354(b) of the Public Health Service Act apply to such mammography conducted by such facility.];

(4) X-ray, radium and radioactive isotope therapy, including materials and services of technicians[.]

* * *

(13) screening mammography (as defined in subsection (jj));

(14) screening pap smear and screening pelvic exam; and

(15) bone mass measurement (as defined in subsection (rr)).

NOTE: Section 4102(d) of the Balanced Budget Act of 1997, P.L. 105-33, enacted August 5, 1997, inserted the reference to paragraph (14), applicable to items and services furnished on or after January 1, 1998. Section 4103(d) inserted the reference to paragraph (2)(P), applicable to items and services furnished on or after January 1, 2000. Section 4104(d) inserted the reference to (2)(R), applicable to items and services furnished on or after January 1, 1998. Section 4105(a)(2) inserted the reference to paragraph (2)(S), applicable to items and services furnished on or after July 1, 1998. Section 4106(d) substituted "(4) and (14)" and added the reference to paragraph (15), applicable to bone mass measurements performed on or after July 1, 1998. Additional minor editorial corrections were made to section 1848(j)(3) by sections 321 (k)(5)(A), (B), and (C) of the Medicare, Medicaid, and SCHIP Balanced Budget Refinement act of 1999, as incorporated into the Omnibus Consolidated Appropriations Act, 2000, P.L. 106-113, enacted November 17, 1999. Those changes were made effective as of August 5, 1997. Furthermore, applicable with respect to screening mammographies furnished on or after January 1, 2002, section 104(a) of the Medicare, Medicaid, and SCHIP Benefit Improvement and Protection Act of 2000 inserted "(13)" after "(4)".

For regulatory citations, see Chapter 6

§ 2:26.1 TERMINATION OF MEDICARE+CHOICE CONTRACTS — Section 1857(c)(2)

Summary

◆ NOTE: Effective August 5,1997, section 4001 of the Balanced Budget Act of 1997, P.L. 105–33, authorized the use of Medicare+Choice plans to provide health care benefits to certain persons eligible for Medicare Part A and Part B. The earliest effective date for an organization to have a Medicare+Choice contract with the Secretary of Health and Human Services is January 1, 1999. See sections 1851–1859 of the Social Security Act, as amended.

Section 1851 of the Social Security Act, as amended, gives persons eligible for Medicare and enrolled under Medicare Part B the right to have their health care costs paid for by one of three types of Medicare+Choice plans, instead of by the traditional Medicare fee-for-service program.

One option is a coordinated care plan. This may be any coordinated care plan, including but not limited to a health maintenance organization (HMO) plan (with or without point of service options), a plan offered by a provider-sponsored organization, or a preferred provider organization (PPO) plan. The second option is a combination of a medical savings account plan and a contribution into a Medicare+Choice savings account (MSA). The third is a Medicare+Choice private fee-for-service plan.

Definitions: *Medicare+ Choice Organization*means a public or private entity certified under section 1856 as meeting Medicare requirements and standards for fiscal solvency and other matters.

Provider-sponsored Organization, as specified in section 1855(d)(1), means a public or private entity established or organized, and operated, by a health care provider, or group of affiliated health care providers. It must provide a substantial proportion of the health care items and services under its Medicare+Choice contract directly through the provider or affiliated group of providers. Furthermore, the affiliated providers must share, directly or indirectly, substantial financial risk with respect to the provision of such items and services. They also must have at least a majority financial interest in the entity.

Medicare+ Choice Plan means health benefits offered under a policy, contract, or plan by a Medicare+Choice organization pursuant to a contract under section 1857.

Medicare+ Choice Private Fee-for-Service Plan means a plan that:

> reimburses hospitals, physicians, and other providers at a rate determined by the plan on a fee-for-service basis without placing the provider at financial risk;
>
> does not vary such rates for such a provider based on utilization relating to such provider; and
>
> does not restrict the selection of providers among those lawfully authorized to provide the covered services who agree to accept the terms and conditions of payment established by the plan.

MSA Plan means a Medicare+Choice plan that:

> provides required basic benefits only after the enrollee incurs countable expenses equal to an annual deductible (prescribed by section 1859(b)(3)(B));
>
> counts as expenses for purposes of the deductible at least all amounts that would have been payable under Medicare Parts A and B, and that would have been payable by the enrollee as deductibles, coinsurance, or copayments if the enrollee had elected to receive benefits through Parts A and B; and
>
> provides, after the deductible is met for a year, for a level of reimbursement not less than 100% of such expenses, or 100% of the amounts that would have been paid (without regard to deductibles or coinsurance) under Medicare Parts A and B with respect to such expenses, whichever is less.

Beneficiary Eligibility: Any person who is entitled to Medicare Part A benefits and who is enrolled in Medicare Part B may elect a Medicare+Choice option, except persons who have end stage renal disease.

NOTE: Pursuant to section 1851(b)(3)(B), organizations are not obliged to accept anyone with end stage renal disease. An individual who develops end–stage renal disease while enrolled in a Medicare+Choice plan, however, may continue to be enrolled in that plan. Moreover, effective January 1, 2002, individuals who discontinued election of a Medicare+Choice plan after December 31, 1998, and before December 21, 2000, because the plan's certification was terminated, or because the plan notified the individual of impending termination of discontinuance, qualify as Medicare+Choice eligible individuals. The same applies for individuals whose plan certification was terminated or whose plan gave them notice of impending termination or discontinuance on or after December 21, 2000. This change was made by section 620(a) of the Medicare, Medicaid, and SCHIP Benefits Improvement and Protection Act of 2000, P.L. 106-554, December 15, 2000.

The following categories of people are not eligible to participate in an MSA plan: qualified Medicare beneficiaries (as defined in section 1905(p)(1), 42 U.S.C.A. 1396d(p); qualified disabled and working individuals (as described in section 1905(s), 42 U.S.C.A. 1396d(s); and individuals described in section 1902(a)(1)(E)(iii), 42 U.S.C.A. 1396a(a)(1)(E)(iii), or otherwise entitled to Medicare cost-sharing under Medicaid. Generally speaking, these are persons who are entitled to Medicare Part A who have limited income and resources.

In addition, persons may enroll in a Medicare+Choice plan only if the plan serves the geographic area where they reside. A plan may offer continued enrollment to an individual who no longer resides in the geographic area served by the plan, however, if the plan agrees to provide reasonable access within the geographic area to the full range of basic benefits, subject to reasonable cost sharing liability in obtaining such benefits.

Enrollment in a Medicare+Choice plan also is permitted under special rules for certain individuals covered under the Federal Employees Health Benefits Program and certain individuals eligible for veterans or military health benefits.

Finally, enrollment may be restricted, in the case of Medicare+Choice plans offered by religious fraternal benefit societies, to individuals who are members of the church, convention, or group with which the society is affiliated. Religious fraternal benefit society means an organization described in section 501(c)(8) of the Internal Revenue Code of 1986, which is exempt from taxes under section 501(a) of that Act, and which meets other requirements under section 1859.

Medicare+Choice Benefits: *Basic Benefits:* Section 1852 requires Medicare+Choice plans to provide all benefits available under Medicare Parts A and B plus additional benefits required under section 1854(f)(1)(A). The latter applies when an organization, other than an MSA plan, has excess funds — as defined — in a contract year available to provide additional benefits.

Supplemental Benefits: Each Medicare+Choice organization, other than an MSA plan, may provide supplemental benefits, with no option for enrollees to decline them, if the Secretary of Health and Human Services approves. A mandatory supplemental benefit must be approved, however, unless the Secretary determines that such a benefit would substantially discourage enrollment by Medicare+Choice eligible individuals with the organization. In addition, a Medicare+Choice organization may provide additional benefits which individuals may elect, at their option, to have covered.

No MSA plan may provide a supplemental benefit that covers the deductible described in section 1859(b)(3)(B). That is $6,000 per annum for 1999. For subsequent years it is that amount increased by the national per capita Medicare+Choice growth percentage under section 1853(c)(6) for year. Nothing prevents a fee-for-service plan from offering supplemental benefits that include payment for some or all of the balance billing amounts permitted by law, or coverage for additional services which the plan finds to be medically necessary.

Anti-discrimination Requirements: Pursuant to section 1852(b), a Medicare+Choice organization may not deny, limit, or condition the coverage or provision of benefits for enrollees based on any factor related to health status described in section 2702(a)(1) of the Public Health Service Act. That, however, does not require enrollment of an individual with end stage renal disease, except as indicated above.

Furthermore, a Medicare+Choice organization may not discriminate with respect to participation, reimbursement, or indemnification against any provider acting within the scope of the provider's license or certification under applicable State law, solely on the basis of such license or certification. This, however, does not prohibit a plan from limiting participation of providers to meet the needs of the plan's enrollees or to maintain quality and control costs consistent with the responsibilities of the plan.

Medicare+Choice Contracts: No individual may participate in a Medicare+Choice plan, and no payment may be made by the Secretary to a Medicare+Choice organization unless the organization enters into a contract with the Secretary which meets the requirements of section 1857. The term of a contract shall be for at least one year, as determined by the Secretary, and it may be automatically renewable from term to term, absent notice by either party of intention to terminate at the end of a term. Each contract is to specify the effective date, but the earliest effective date is January 1, 1999.

Pursuant to section 1857(c)(3), the Secretary may not enter into a contract with a Medicare+Choice organization if a previous contract with that organization was terminated at the organization's request within the preceding five-year period, unless the Secretary finds that circumstances warrant special consideration.

NOTE: Effective for years beginning 2001, the Secretary may waive or modify requirements that hinder the design of, the offering of, or the enrollment in a Medicare+Choice plan established by contract between a Medicare+Choice organization and employers, labor organizations, or the trustees of a fund established by one or more employers or labor organizations (or combination thereof). This change was made by section 617(a) of the Medicare, Medicaid, and SCHIP Benefits Improvement and Protection Act of 2000, P.L. 106-554, December 15, 2000, The aim is to facilitate offering of Medicare+Choice plans to the entity's employees, former employees (or combination thereof), or to members or former members (or combination thereof) of the labor organization.

Requirements for Medicare+Choice Organizations: *Guaranteed Issue and Renewal:* Pursuant to section 1851(g), a Medicare+Choice organization must accept without restrictions individuals who are eligible to choose a Medicare+Choice plan if they make the selection during open season. There is an exception to this requirement, however, if an organization has a capacity limit and the number of people wanting to choose a plan exceeds that capacity. In that case, the organization may limit the election of individuals as follows: first to individuals that had elected the plan at the time the plan determined it had reached its capacity; then to other individuals in a manner that does not discriminate on the basis of any health-related factor. Even so, pursuant to section 1852(b)(1)(B), organizations are not obliged to accept anyone with end stage renal disease. Furthermore, a plan is not obliged to accept applicants from its priority list if that would result in the enrollment of enrollees who are "substantially nonrepresentative". What that means is for the Secretary to determine by regulations. Presumably, the intent is to prevent overloading a plan with high risk, high cost enrollees.

Medicare+Choice organizations also are restricted in their ability to terminate the election of a plan by an individual. The only grounds for such termination are failure to pay premiums on a timely basis, complete termination of the plan in the area where the individual resides, and disruptive behavior by an individual. What constitutes disruptive behavior is to be determined by the establishment of standards, presumably by regulation.

If an individual's enrollment is terminated for nonpayment of premiums or for disruptive behavior, the individual reverts to traditional Medicare coverage. If an individual's enrollment is terminated because the plan is terminated in the area where the individual resides, the individual is entitled to a special election period in which to change to coverage under another Medicare+Choice plan.

Prior Approval of Marketing Material and Application Forms: Pursuant to section 1851(h), no marketing material or application form may be distributed by a Medicare+Choice organization to (or for the use of) Medicare+Choice eligible individuals unless the organization has submitted the material and/or forms to the Secretary for review at least 45 days before the date of distribution and the Secretary has not disapproved them. The Secretary is obligated to establish guidelines for approval of marketing material and application forms. At a minimum, however, the Secretary must require correction of any material or form which is materially inaccurate or misleading or otherwise makes a material misrepresentation.

If marketing material or application forms are not disapproved, either by the Secretary or by a regional office of the Department of Health and Human Services with respect to an area covered by a plan in the 45 day time period, the Secretary is deemed not to have disapproved the material and forms in all other areas covered by the plan.

Note: Effective for marketing material submitted on or after January 1, 2001, the 45–day prior review requirement is reduced to ten days, if the Medicare+Choice organization uses—without modification—proposed model language specified by the Secretary. See section 613(a) of the Medicare, Medicaid, and SCHIP Benefits Improvement and Protection Act.

Finally, Medicare+Choice organizations must conform to fair marketing standards. Such standards must not permit a

Medicare+Choice organization to provide for cash or other monetary rebates as an inducement for enrollment or otherwise. They also must prohibit a Medicare+Choice organization (or an agent thereof) from completing any portion of any election form used to choose a Medicare+Choice plan on behalf of any individual.

Disclosure Obligations: Section 1852(c) requires Medicare+Choice organizations to disclose in clear, accurate, and standardized form to each enrollee information about:

1 The plan's service area.
2 Benefits offered under the plan, including information about emergency services, and if it is a Medical Savings Account plan, a comparison of benefits under such a plan with benefits under other Medicare+Choice plans.
3 The number, mix, and distribution of plan providers, out-of-network coverage, if any, and any point-of-service option, including the supplemental premium for such an option.
4 Out-of-area coverage.
5 Coverage of emergency services.
6 Supplemental benefits available from the plan, including whether they are optional, what the supplemental benefits are, and the Medicare+Choice monthly supplemental beneficiary premium for the supplemental benefits.
7 Prior authorization rules.
8 Plan grievance and appeals procedures.
9 The quality assurance program.

In addition, upon request of a Medicare+Choice eligible individual, a Medicare+Choice organization must provide the following information: general coverage information and general comparative plan information about benefits under traditional Medicare Parts A and B; and a list of plans that are (or will be) available to residents of the area, presented in a comparative fashion. This must detail covered items and services beyond those provided under traditional Medicare Parts A and B; any beneficiary cost-sharing; any maximum limitations on out-of-pocket expenses; the extent to which an enrollee may obtain benefits through out-of-network health care providers; the extent to which an enrollee may select among in-network providers and the types of providers participating in the plan's network; and the organizations' coverage of emergency and urgently needed care.

In the case of MSA plan or a Medicare+Choice private fee-for-service plan, the organization must provide information about differences in cost-sharing, premiums, and balance billing, compared to other Medicare+Choice plans.

A Medicare+Choice organization also must provide information on its procedures to control utilization of services and expenditures; information on the number of grievances, redeterminations, and appeals, and on the disposition in the aggregate of such matters; and an overall summary description as to the method of compensation of participating physicians.

Access to Services: Pursuant to section 1852(d), a Medicare+Choice organization must make its benefits available and accessible to each enrollee within the plan service area with reasonable promptness and in a manner which assures continuity in the provision of benefits. When medically necessary, such benefits must be available and accessible 24 hours a day, 7 days a week.

Furthermore, the plan must provide for reimbursement with respect to covered services provided to an enrollee other than through the organization, if the services were not emergency services, but were medically necessary and immediately required because of an unforeseen illness, injury, or condition. That applies when it is not reasonable under the circumstances to obtain services through the organization. The plan also must provide for reimbursement for services provided other than through the organization if the services were renal dialysis services provided because the enrollee was temporarily out of the plan's service area, or the services are maintenance care or post-stabilization care.

In addition, a Medicare+Choice organization must provide access to appropriate providers, including credentialed specialists, for medically necessary treatment and services. The organization also must provide for emergency services without regard to prior authorization or the emergency care provider's contractual relationship with the organization.

According to section 1852(d)(3), emergency services means covered inpatient and outpatient services from Medicare qualified providers which are needed to evaluate or stabilize an emergency medical condition. Emergency medical condition means a medical condition manifesting itself by acute symptoms of such sufficient severity (including severe pain) that a prudent layperson, possessing average knowledge of health and medicine, could reasonably expect the absence of immediate medical attention to place the health of the individual (or with respect to a pregnant woman, the health of the woman or her unborn child) in serious jeopardy, or serious impairment to bodily functions, or serious dysfunction of any bodily organ or part.

In the case of a Medicare+Choice private fee-for-service plan, an organization also must demonstrate to the Secretary that it has sufficient number and range of health care professionals and providers willing to provide services under the terms of the plan. The Secretary must find this requirement met, however, if the plan has established payment rates for covered services by the provider that are not less that payment rates provided under Part A, Part B, or both for such services. The Secretary also must find the requirement met with respect to any category of health care professional or provider if the plan has contracts or agreements with a sufficient number and range of health care professionals or providers within the category to provide covered services under the terms of the plan.

Quality Assurance: Pursuant to section 1852(e), each Medicare+Choice organization must have arrangements consistent with any applicable regulation for an ongoing quality assurance program for health care services which it provides.

Quality Assurance: Plans other than a private fee-for-service plan or a non-network MSA plan: An organization's quality assurance plan must:

1. Stress health outcomes and provide for the collection, analysis, and reporting of data that will permit measurement of outcomes and other indices of the quality of Medicare+Choice plans and organizations. This must comport with a quality measurement system that the Secretary recognizes.
2. Monitor and evaluate high volume and high risk services and the care of acute and chronic conditions.
3. Evaluate the continuity and coordination of care that enrollees receive.
4. Be evaluated on an ongoing basis as to its effectiveness.
5. Include measures of consumer satisfaction.
6. Provide the Secretary with such access to information collected as may be appropriate to monitor and ensure the quality of care provided.
7. Provide review by physicians and other health care professionals of the process followed in the provision of such health care services.

8 Provide for the establishment of written protocols for utilization review, based on current standards of medical practice.
9 Have mechanisms to detect both underutilization and overutilization of services.
10 Establish or alter practice parameters, after identifying areas for improvement.
11 Take action to improve quality and assess the effectiveness of such action through systematic follow-up; and
12 Make available information on quality and outcomes measures to facilitate beneficiary comparison and choice of health coverage options, in a form and manner acceptable to the Secretary.

Quality Assurance: Private fee-for-service plans and non-network MSA plans: Organizations offering these plans must meet the first six requirements above. In addition, insofar as it provides for the establishment of written protocols for utilization review, the organization must base such protocols on current standards of medical practice. It also must have mechanisms to evaluate utilization of services and inform providers and enrollees of the results of such evaluation.

For these purposes, non-network MSA plan means a plan offered by an organization that does not provide required benefits in whole or in part through a defined set of providers under contract, or under another arrangement, with the organization.

External Review: Each Medicare+Choice organization, for each plan it operates, must have an agreement with an independent quality review and improvement organization approved by the Secretary to perform functions of the type described in sections 1154(a)(4)(B), 42 U.S.C.A. 1320c-3(a)(4)(B), which pertains to peer review for risk-sharing contracts under section 1876, and 1154(a)(14), 42 U.S.C.A. 1320c-3(a)(14), which pertains to on-site reviews. This does not apply to a Medicare+Choice private fee-for-service plan or a non-network MSA plan that does not employ utilization review.

The Secretary may waive this requirement if the Secretary determines that an organization has consistently maintained an excellent record of quality assurance and compliance with other requirements. Furthermore, except with respect to review of quality complaints, the Secretary shall ensure that the external review activities do not duplicate review activities conducted as part of an accreditation process. A Medicare+Choice organization is deemed to meet the external review requirement if it is accredited and periodically re-accredited by a private organization under a process which the Secretary has determined assures, as a condition of accreditation, application and enforcement of standards no less stringent than the standards under section 1856 to carry out the respective requirements.

Grievance Mechanisms: Pursuant to section 1852(f), each Medicare+Choice organization must provide meaningful procedures for hearing and resolving grievances between the organization and enrollees in any of the organization's Medicare+Choice plans. That also applies with respect to grievances between enrollees and any entity or individual through which the organization provides health care services.

Coverage Determinations, Reconsiderations, and Appeals: Section 1852(g) requires Medicare+Choice organizations to have a procedure for determining whether an individual enrolled in a plan is entitled to receive a health service, and the amount (if any) which the individual is required to pay for such service. The procedure must provide for such determinations to be made on a timely basis. Any determination that denies coverage in whole or in part must be in writing. It also must include a statement in understandable language of the reasons for the denial, and a description of the reconsideration and appeal process.

Reconsideration of a denial decision must be available upon request by an enrollee within a time period specified by the Secretary, but not later than 60 days after the date of receipt of a request for a reconsideration. Denials based on lack of medical necessity may only be made by a physician with appropriate expertise in the field of medicine relevant to the medical treatment denied. That physician, however, may not be the physician involved in the initial denial determination.

Section 1852(g) also requires a procedure for expedited determinations and reconsiderations, upon request, written or oral, by an enrollee or by a physician (whether or not the physician is affiliated with the Medicare+Choice organization). In general, this expedited process applies when the organization determines that application of the normal time frame for making a determination or reconsideration could seriously jeopardize the life or health of the enrollee or the enrollee's ability to regain maximum function. If the request for an expedited determination comes from a physician, however, the organization must expedite the determination or reconsideration if the physician's request indicates that application of a normal time frame could seriously jeopardize the life or health of the enrollee or the enrollee's ability to regain maximum function.

In either case, the organization must notify the enrollee, and the physician involved, of the determination or reconsideration under time limitations established by the Secretary, but not later than 72 hours from the time of receipt of the request for determination or reconsideration or 72 hours from the receipt of information necessary to make the determination or reconsideration. The Secretary may permit longer periods in specified cases.

If a reconsideration denies coverage in whole or in part, the Secretary must contract with an independent, outside entity to review and resolve the grievance in a timely manner. See section 1869 of the Social Security Act, 42 U.S.C.A. 1395ff.

Finally, pursuant to section 1852(g)(5), an enrollee with a Medicare+Choice plan of a Medicare+Choice organization who is dissatisfied by reason of the enrollee's failure to receive any health service, or who is dissatisfied by the amount the enrollee is required to pay may request a hearing before the Secretary if the amount in controversy is $100 or more. In any such hearing the Secretary shall make the Medicare+Choice organization a party. If the amount in controversy is $1,000 or more, the individual or organization, upon notice to the other party, shall be entitled to judicial review. Provisions of section 205(b) of the Social Security Act, 42 U.S.C.A. 405(b), apply to this right to an administrative hearing before the Secretary and judicial review.

Confidentiality and Accuracy of Enrollee Records: Section 1852(h) requires Medicare+Choice organizations to establish procedures:

> to safeguard the privacy of any individually identifiable enrollee information;
>
> to maintain such records and information in a manner that is accurate and timely; and
>
> to assure timely access of enrollees to such records and information.

Information on Advance Directives: Section 1852(i) requires Medicare+Choice organizations to establish and maintain policies and procedures for advanced directives with respect to enrollee decisions about terminating or withholding health care services. These policies and procedures must comply with section 1866(f), 42 U.S.C.A. 1395cc(f).

Rules Regarding Provider Participation: *Procedures*: Pursuant to section 1852(j), Medicare+Choice organizations that offer benefits through agreements with physicians must establish reasonable procedures relating to physician participation. These procedures must include notice of the rules of participation, written notice of participation decisions adverse to physicians, and a process within the organization for appealing adverse decisions. The latter process must include presentation of information and views of the physician regarding such a decision.

Consultation in Medical Policies: A Medicare+Choice organization must consult with physicians who have entered into participation agreements with the organization regarding the organization's medical policy, quality, and medical management procedures.

No Interference with Provider Advice to Enrollees: No Medicare+Choice organization may prohibit or otherwise restrict a covered health care professional from advising an enrollee who is a patient of that professional about the health status of that patient, or medical care or treatment for that patient's condition or disease. That prohibition applies regardless whether the care or treatment is provided under the Medicare+Choice plan, so long as the health care professional is acting within the lawful scope of his or her practice.

This does not require a Medicare+Choice plan to provide, reimburse for, or provide coverage of a counseling or referral service if the Medicare+Choice organization offering the plan:

> objects to the provision of such service on moral or religious grounds; and
>
> makes available information on its policies regarding such service to prospective enrollees before or during enrollment and to enrollees within 90 days after the date that the organization or plan adopts a change in policy regarding such a counseling or referral service.

This exception for moral and religious objections shall not be construed to affect disclosure requirements under State law or under the Employee Retirement Income Security Act of 1974 (ERISA).

With respect to these rules regarding provider participation, the term "health care professional" means a physician (as defined in section 1861(r), 42 U.S.C.A. 1395x(r)), or other health care professional if coverage for the professional's services is provided under the

Medicare+Choice plan for the services of the professional. The term also includes a podiatrist, optometrist, chiropractor, psychologist, dentist, physician assistant, physical or occupational therapist and therapy assistant, speech-language pathologist, audiologist, registered or licensed practical nurse (including a nurse practitioner, clinical nurse specialist, certified registered nurse anesthetist, and certified nurse midwife), licensed certified social worker, registered respiratory therapist, and certified respiratory therapy technician.

Limitations on Physician Incentive Plans: No Medicare+Choice organization may have a physician incentive plan unless it meets the following requirements:

1. No specific payment may be made, directly or indirectly, under the plan to a physician or a physician group as an inducement to reduce or limit medically necessary services provided with respect to a specific individual enrolled with the organization.

2. If the plan places a physician or physician group at substantial financial risk for services not provided by the physician or physician group, the organization must:

   a. Provide adequate stop-loss protection for the physician or group.

   b. Conduct periodic surveys of present and prior enrollees to determine the degree of access of such individuals to services provided by the organization and satisfaction with the quality of such services.

3. The organization must provide the Secretary with descriptive information regarding the plan, so that the Secretary may determine whether the plan is complying with the rules regarding limitations of physician incentive plans.

For these purposes, "physician incentive plan" means any compensation arrangement between a Medicare+Choice organization and a physician or physician group that may directly or indirectly have the effect of reducing or limiting services provided with respect to individuals enrolled with the organization.

Limitation on Provider Indemnification: A Medicare+Choice organization may not provide, directly or indirectly, for a health care professional, provider of services, or other entity providing health care services (or group of such professionals, providers, or entities) to indemnify the organization against any liability resulting from a civil action brought for any damage caused to an enrollee with a Medicare+Choice plan or organization by the organization's denial of medically necessary care.

*Special Rule for Medicare+ Choice Private Fee-for-Service Plans*A hospital or other provider of services, a physician or other health care professional, or other entity furnishing health care services shall be treated as having an agreement or contract in effect with a Medicare+Choice organization (with respect to an individual enrolled in a Medicare+Choice private fee-for-service plan it offers), if the provider, professional, or other entity furnishes service that are covered under the plan to such an enrollee, and before providing such services, the provider, professional, or other entity was informed of the individual's enrollment in the plan, and either was informed of the terms and conditions of payment for such services under the plan, or had been given a reasonable opportunity to obtain information concerning such terms and conditions, in a manner reasonably designed to effect informed agreement by a provider.

This applies only in the absence of an explicit agreement between such a provider, professional, or other entity and the Medicare+Choice organization.

*Physicians and Other Entities without Contracts with Medicare+ Choice Organizations*A physician or other entity (other than a provider of services) that does not have a contract establishing payment amounts for services to an enrollee in a Medicare+Choice plan must accept as payment in full for services covered by Medicare the same amount that the physician or other entity could collect if the individual were not enrolled in a Medicare+Choice plan. Furthermore, any penalty or other provision of law that applies to such a payment with respect to an individual entitled to Medicare benefits, but not enrolled in a Medicare+Choice plan, also applies with respect to an individual so enrolled.

For individuals enrolled in a Medicare private fee-for-service plan, balance billing limits apply. That means a physician, provider of services, or other entity must accept as full payment for covered services an amount not to exceed 115% of the plan's payment rate for services. That amount takes into account any deductibles, coinsurance, copayments, or balance billing otherwise permitted under the plan.

A Medicare+Choice organization that offers such a plan must have procedures to enforce that requirement. If it does not, it is subject to intermediate sanctions under section 1857(g).

Finally, a Medicare+Choice organization that offers a Medicare+Choice private fee-for-service plan must provide enrollees under the plan an appropriate explanation of benefits (consistent with that provided under Parts A and B, and if applicable, under Medicare supplemental policies). That explanation must include a clear statement of the amount of the enrollee's liability (including any liability for balance billing) with respect to payments for services rendered under the plan. In addition, the organization must require a hospital to provide to enrollees advance notice estimating the balance billing amount, if any, which the hospital is likely to bill an enrollee, when that amount is likely to be "substantial". That estimate must be based on the presenting condition of the enrollee.

State Licensure: Section 1855 requires a Medicare+Choice organization to be organized an licensed under State law as a risk-bearing entity eligible to offer health insurance or health benefits coverage in each State in which the organization offers a Medicare+Choice plan.

A special rule applies, however, for provider-sponsored organizations. The Secretary shall waive the State licensure requirement if such an organization applies for a waiver not later than November 1, 2002, and if the Secretary determines that State licensure was not possible because:

1 The State failed to complete action on a licensing application of the provider-sponsored organization within 90 days of the date the State received a substantially complete application. (No period before August 5, 1997, may count in calculating that 90-day period.)

2 The State denied a license based on standards or a review process which imposed material requirements, procedures, or standards (other than solvency requirements) on the provider-sponsored organization which are not generally applicable to other entities engaged in a substantially similar business.

3 The State requires the provider-sponsored organization, as a condition of licensure, to offer any product or plan other than a Medicare+Choice plan.

4 The State denied the license on the basis of solvency standards that are not the same as the solvency standards established under section 1856(a); or the State conditioned approval of a license upon documentation or information requirements relating to solvency or other material require-

> ments, procedures, or standards relating to solvency which are different that standards applied by the Secretary under section 1855(d)(2).

Any waiver granted to a provider-sponsored organization shall be conditioned upon the organization's compliance with applicable State consumer protection and quality standards which would apply to any other Medicare+Choice organization or plan in the State, and which are consistent with and not preempted by standards under Medicare, especially section 1856(b)(3)(B). This condition shall be incorporated into the Medicare+Choice contract with such an organization, and the Secretary may enter into an agreement with the State to monitor and enforce compliance with such standards.

Pursuant to section 1855(b), the provider-sponsored organization must assume full financial risk on a prospective basis for the provision of health services; however, it may protect itself with stop loss or reinsurance contracts or by passing on some of the risk to physicians and other health care professionals.

Finally, pursuant to section 1856, provider-sponsored organizations must meet strict solvency standards, and they must include provisions that protect enrollees from being held liable to any person or entity for the Medicare+Choice organization's debts in the event of the organization's insolvency.

Grounds for Termination of Medicare+Choice Contracts: Pursuant to section 1857(c)(2), the Secretary of Health and Human Services may terminate a Medicare+Choice contract at any time if the Secretary determines:

> the organization has failed substantially to carry out the contract;
>
> the organization is carrying out the contract in a manner inconsistent with the efficient and effective administration of Medicare; or
>
> the organization no longer substantially meets applicable conditions.

Section 1857(h) requires the Secretary to establish formal investigation and compliance procedures for terminating a contract with a Medicare+Choice organization. At a minimum, those procedures must include giving the organization a reasonable opportunity to develop and implement a corrective action plan to correct the deficiencies that formed the basis of the Secretary's determination should be terminated. Then the Secretary must give reasonable notice and an opportunity for a hearing to the organization, plus the right to appeal an initial decision, before terminating the contract. Those procedures need not be applied, however, if the Secretary determines that a delay in termination, caused by following the procedures, would pose an imminent and serious risk to the health of the organization's enrollees.

Statutory Provisions

Section 1851 of the Social Security Act, as amended, provides for certain persons eligible for Medicare to obtain Medicare benefits from a Medicare+Choice plan. It provides in pertinent part as follows:

> (a) CHOICE OF MEDICARE BENEFITS THROUGH MEDICARE + CHOICE PLANS. —
>
> (1) IN GENERAL. — Subject to the provisions of this section, each Medicare + Choice eligible individual (as defined in paragraph (3)) is entitled to elect to receive benefits under this title —
>
> (A) through the original Medicare fee-for-service program under parts A and B, or
>
> (B) through enrollment in a Medicare + Choice plan under this part.
>
> (2) TYPES OF MEDICARE + CHOICE PLANS THAT MAY BE AVAILABLE. — A Medicare + Choice plan may be any of the following types of plans of health insurance:
>
> (A) COORDINATED CARE PLANS. — Coordinated care plans which provide health care services, including but not limited to health maintenance organization plans (with or without point of service options), plans offered by provider-sponsored organizations (as defined in section 1855(d)), and preferred provider organization plans.
>
> (B) COMBINATION OF MSA PLAN AND CONTRIBUTIONS TO MEDICARE + CHOICE MSA. — An MSA plan, as defined in section 1859(b)(3), and a contribution into a Medicare + Choice medical savings account (MSA).

(C) PRIVATE FEE-FOR-SERVICE PLANS. — A Medicare + Choice private fee-for-service plan, as defined in section 1859(b)(2).

(3) MEDICARE + CHOICE ELIGIBLE INDIVIDUAL. —

(A) IN GENERAL. — In this title, subject to subparagraph (B), the term "Medicare + Choice eligible individual" means an individual who is entitled to benefits under part A and enrolled under part B.

(B) SPECIAL RULE FOR END-STAGE RENAL DISEASE. — Such term shall not include an individual medically determined to have end-stage renal disease, except that an individual who develops end-stage renal disease, except that—

(i) an individual who develops end–stage renal disease while enrolled in a Medicare+Choice plan may continue to be enrolled in that plan; and

(ii) in the case of such an individual enrolled in a Medicare+Choice plan under clause (i), (or subsequently under this clause), if the enrollment is discontinued under circumstances described in section 1851(e)(4)(A) [which pertains to termination of a plan's certification, and to a plan's notification to an enrollee of impending termination or discontinuance], then the individual will be treated as a "Medicare+Choice eligible individual" for purposes of electing to continue enrollment in another Medicare+Choice plan.

NOTE: Prior to amendment by section 620(a) of the Medicare, Medicaid, and SCHIP Benefits Improvement and Protection Act of 2000, P.L. 106–544, December 15, 2000, subparagraph (a)(3)(B) read: "(B) SPECIAL RULE FOR END–STAGE RENAL DISEASE.—Such term shall not include an individual medically determined to have end–stage renal disease, except that an individual who develops end–stage renal disease while enrolled in a Medicare+Choice plan may continue to be enrolled in that plan." This applies generally to terminations and discontinuations on or after December 21, 2000, and to certain persons for whom a discontinuance or termination occurred on or after December 31, 1998, and before December 21, 2000.

(b) SPECIAL RULES. —

(1) RESIDENCE REQUIREMENT. —

(A) IN GENERAL. — Except as the Secretary may otherwise provide, and except as provided in subparagraph (C), an individual is eligible to elect a Medicare + Choice plan offered by a Medicare + Choice organization only if the plan serves the geographic area in which the individual resides.

(B) CONTINUATION OF ENROLLMENT PERMITTED. — Pursuant to rules specified by the Secretary, the Secretary shall provide that a plan may offer to all individuals residing in a geographic area the option to continue enrollment in the plan, notwithstanding that the individual no longer resides in the service area of the plan, so long as the plan provides that individuals exercising this option have, as part of the basic benefits described in section 1852(a)(1)(A), reasonable access within that geographic area to the full range of basic benefits, subject to reasonable cost sharing liability in obtaining such benefits.

(C) CONTINUATION OF ENROLLMENT PERMITTED WHERE SERVICE CHANGED. — Notwithstanding subparagraph (A) and in addition to subparagraph (B), if a Medicare+Choice organization eliminates from its service area a Medicare+Choice payment area that was previously within its service area, the organization may elect to offer individuals residing in all or portions of the affected area who would otherwise be ineligible to continue enrollment the option to continue enrollment in a Medicare+Choice plan it offers so long as —

(i) the enrollee agrees to receive the full range of basic benefits (excluding emergency and urgently need care) exclusively at facilities designated by the organization with the plan service area; and

(ii) there is no other Medicare+Choice plan offered in the area in which the enrollee resides at the time of the organization's election.

◆ NOTE: Effective November 29, 1999, sections 501(c)(1) and (2) of the Medicare, Medicaid, and SCHIP Balanced Budget Refinement Act of 1999, as incorporated into the Omnibus Consolidated Appropriations Act, 2000, P.L. 106–113, added subparagraph (C) and inserted "and except as provided in subparagraph (C)" in subparagraph (b)(1)(A).

(2) SPECIAL RULE FOR CERTAIN INDIVIDUALS COVERED UNDER FEHBP OR ELIGIBLE FOR VETERANS OR MILITARY HEALTH BENEFITS, VETERANS. —

(A) FEHBP. — An individual who is enrolled in a health benefit plan under chapter 89 of title 5, United States Code, is not eligible to enroll in an MSA plan until such time as the Director of the Office of Management and Budget certifies to the Secretary that the Office of Personnel Management has adopted policies which will ensure that the enrollment of such individuals in such plans will not result in increased expenditures for the Federal Government for health benefit plans under such chapter.

(B) VA AND DOD. — The Secretary may apply rules similar to the rules described in subparagraph (A) in the case of individuals who are eligible for health care benefits under chapter 55 of title 10, United States Code, or under chapter 17 of title 38 of such Code.

(3) LIMITATION ON ELIGIBILITY OF QUALIFIED MEDICARE BENEFICIARIES AND OTHER MEDICAID BENEFICIARIES TO ENROLL IN AN MSA PLAN. — An individual who is a qualified Medicare beneficiary (as defined in section 1905(p)(1) [42 U.S.C.A. 1396d(p)(1)]), a qualified disabled and working individual (described in section 1905(s) [42 U.S.C.A. 1396d(s)]), an individual described in section 1902(a)(10)(E)(iii) [42 U.S.C.A. 1396a(a)(10)(E)(iii)], or otherwise entitled to Medicare cost-sharing under a State plan under title XIX is not eligible to enroll in an MSA plan.

(4) COVERAGE UNDER MSA PLANS ON A DEMONSTRATION BASIS. —

(A) IN GENERAL. — An individual is not eligible to enroll in an MSA plan under this part —

(i) on or after January 1, 2003, unless the enrollment is the continuation of such an enrollment in effect as of such date; or

(ii) as of any date if the number of such individuals so enrolled as of such date has reached 390,000.

Under rules established by the Secretary, an individual is not eligible to enroll (or continue enrollment) in an MSA plan for a year unless the individual provides assurances satisfactory to the Secretary that the individual will reside in the United States for at least 183 days during the year.

> (B) EVALUATION. — The Secretary shall regularly evaluate the impact of permitting enrollment in MSA plans under this part on selection (including adverse selection), use of preventive care, access to care, and the financial status of the Trust Funds under this title.
>
> (C) REPORTS. — The Secretary shall submit to Congress periodic reports on the numbers of individuals enrolled in such plans and on the evaluation being conducted under subparagraph (B). The Secretary shall submit such a report, by not later than March 1, 2002, on whether the time limitation under subparagraph (A)(I) should be extended or removed and whether to change the numerical limitation under subparagraph (A)(ii).

With respect to definitions of the types of available Medicare+Choice plans, section 1859 provides in pertinent part:

> (a) DEFINITIONS RELATING TO MEDICARE + CHOICE ORGANIZATIONS. — In this part —
>
> (1) MEDICARE + CHOICE ORGANIZATION. — The term "Medicare + Choice organization" means a public or private entity that is certified under section 1856 as meeting the requirements and standards of this part for such an organization.
>
> (2) PROVIDER-SPONSORED ORGANIZATION. — The term "provider-sponsored organization" is defined in section 1855(d)(1).

(b) DEFINITIONS RELATING TO MEDICARE + CHOICE PLANS. —

> (1) MEDICARE + CHOICE PLAN. — The term "Medicare + Choice plan" means health benefits coverage offered under a policy, contract, or plan by a Medicare + Choice organization pursuant to and in accordance with a contract under section 1857.

(2) MEDICARE + CHOICE PRIVATE FEE-FOR-SERVICE PLAN. — The term "Medicare + Choice private fee-for-service plan" means a Medicare + Choice plan that —

(A) reimburses hospitals, physicians, and other providers at a rate determined by the plan on a fee-for-service basis without placing the provider at financial risk;

(B) does not vary such rates for such a provider based on utilization relating to such provider; and

(C) does not restrict the selection of providers among those who are lawfully authorized to provide the covered services and agree to accept the terms and conditions of payment established by the plan.

(3) MSA PLAN. —

(A) IN GENERAL. — The term "MSA plan" means a Medicare + Choice plan that —

(i) provides reimbursement for at least the items and services described in section 1852(a)(1) in a year but only after the enrollee incurs countable expenses (as specified under the plan) equal to the amount of an annual deductible (described in subparagraph (B));

(ii) counts as such expenses (for purposes of such deductible) at least all amounts that would have been payable under parts A and B, and that would have been payable by the enrollee as deductibles, coinsurance, or copayments, if the enrollee had elected to receive benefits through the provisions of such parts; and

(iii) provides, after such deductible is met for a year and for all subsequent expenses for items and services referred to in clause (I) in the year, for a level of reimbursement that is not less than —

(I) 100 percent of such expenses, or

(II) 100 percent of the amounts that would have been paid (without regard to any deductibles or coinsurance) under parts A and B with respect to such expenses, whichever is less.

(B) DEDUCTIBLE. — The amount of annual deductible under an MSA plan —

(i) for contract year 1999 shall be not more than $6,000; and

(ii) for a subsequent contract year shall be not more than the maximum amount of such deductible for the previous contract year under this subparagraph increased by the national per capita Medicare + Choice growth percentage under section 1853(c)(6) for the year.

If the amount of the deductible under clause (ii) is not a multiple of $50, the amount shall be rounded to the nearest multiple of $50.

With respect to provider-sponsored organizations, section 1855(d)(1) provides in pertinent part:

IN GENERAL. — In this part, the term "provider-sponsored organization" means a public or private entity —

(A) that is established or organized, and operated, by a health care provider, or group of affiliated health care providers,

(B) that provides a substantial proportion (as defined by the Secretary in accordance with paragraph (2)) of the health care items and services under the contract under this part directly through the provider or affiliated group of providers, and

(C) with respect to which the affiliated providers share, directly or indirectly, substantial financial risk with respect to the provision of such items and services and have at least a majority financial interest in the entity.

With respect to required benefits for Medicare+Choice plans, section 1852 provides in pertinent part:

(a) BASIC BENEFITS. —

(1) IN GENERAL. — Except as provided in section 1859(b)(3) for MSA plans, each Medicare + Choice plan shall provide to members enrolled under this part, through providers and other persons that meet the applicable requirements of this title and part A of title XI —

(A) those items and services (other than hospice care) for which benefits are available under parts A and B to individuals residing in the area served by the plan, and

(B) additional benefits required under section 1854(f)(1)(A).

(2) SATISFACTION OF REQUIREMENT. —

(A) IN GENERAL. — A Medicare + Choice plan (other than an MSA plan) offered by a Medicare + Choice organization satisfies paragraph (1)(A), with respect to benefits for items and services furnished other than through a provider or other person that has a contract with the organization offering the plan, if the plan provides payment in an amount so that —

(i) the sum of such payment amount and any cost sharing provided for under the plan is equal to at least

(ii) the total dollar amount of payment for such items and services as would otherwise be authorized under parts A and B (including any balance billing permitted under such parts).

(B) REFERENCE TO RELATED PROVISIONS. — For provision relating to —

(i) limitations on balance billing against Medicare + Choice organizations for non-contract providers, see sections 1852(k) and 1866(a)(1)(O), and

(ii) limiting actuarial value of enrollee liability for covered benefits, see section 1854(e).

(C) ELECTION OF UNIFORM COVERAGE POLICY.—In the case of a Medicare+Choice organization that offers a Medicare+Choice plan in an area in which more than one local coverage policy is applied with respect to different parts of the area, the organization may elect to have the local coverage policy for the part of the area that is most beneficial to Medicare+Choice enrollees (as identified by the Secretary) apply with respect to all Medicare+Choice enrollees enrolled in the plan. [NOTE: Paragraph (C) was enacted by section 615 of the Medicare, Medicaid, and SCHIP Benefits Improvement and Protection Act of 2000, P.L. 106–554, effective December 21, 2000.]

(3) SUPPLEMENTAL BENEFITS. —

(A) BENEFITS INCLUDED SUBJECT TO SECRETARY'S APPROVAL. — Each Medicare + Choice organization may provide to individuals enrolled under this part, other than under an MSA plan (without affording those individuals an option to decline the coverage), supplemental health care benefits that the Secretary may approve. The Secretary shall approve any such supplemental benefits unless the Secretary determines that including such supplemental benefits would substantially discourage enrollment by Medicare + Choice eligible individuals with the organization.

◆ NOTE: Effective November 29, 2000, section 321(k)(6)(B) of the Medicare, Medicaid, and SCHIP Balanced Budget Refinement Act of 1999, as incorporated into the Omnibus Consolidated Appropriations Act, 2000, P.L. 106–113, struck a comma after "MSA plan" and inserted a comma after "the coverage)".

(B) AT ENROLLEES' OPTION.—

(i) IN GENERAL. —Subject to clause (ii), a Medicare + Choice organization may provide to individuals enrolled under this part supplemental health care benefits that the individuals may elect, at their option, to have covered.

(ii) SPECIAL RULE FOR MSA PLANS.—A Medicare + Choice organization may not provide, under an MSA plan, supplemental health care benefits that cover the deductible described in section 1859(b)(3)(B). In applying the previous sentence. health benefits described in section 1882(u)(2)(B) shall not be treated as covering such deductible.

(C) APPLICATION TO MEDICARE + CHOICE PRIVATE FEE-FOR-SERVICE PLANS.—Nothing in this paragraph shall be construed as preventing a Medicare + Choice private fee-for-service plan from offering supplemental benefits that include payment for some or all of the balance billing amounts permitted consistent with section 1852(k) and coverage of additional services that the plan finds to be medically necessary.

(4) ORGANIZATION AS SECONDARY PAYER.—Notwithstanding any other provision of law, a Medicare + Choice organization may (in the case of the provision of items and services to an individual under a Medicare + Choice plan under circumstances in which payment under this title is made secondary pursuant to section 1862(b)(2))

charge or authorize the provider of such services to charge, in accordance with the charges allowed under a law, plan, or policy described in such section —

(A) the insurance carrier, employer, or other entity which under such law, plan, or policy is to pay for the provision of such services, or

(B) such individual to the extent that the individual has been paid under such law, plan, or policy for such services.

Section 1852(b) prohibits discrimination by a Medicare+Choice organization against health care providers. It also prohibits discrimination against applicants for enrollment based on health status. It provides:

ANTIDISCRIMINATION. —

(1) BENEFICIARIES. —

(A) IN GENERAL. — A Medicare + Choice organization may not deny, limit, or condition the coverage or provision of benefits under this part, for individuals permitted to be enrolled with the organization under this part, based on any health status-related factor described in section 2702(a)(1) of the Public Health Service Act.

(B) CONSTRUCTION. — Subparagraph (A) shall not be construed as requiring a Medicare + Choice organization to enroll individuals who are determined to have end-stage renal disease, except as provided under section 1851(a)(3)(B).

(2) PROVIDERS. — A Medicare + Choice organization shall not discriminate with respect to participation, reimbursement, or indemnification as to any provider who is acting within the scope of the provider's license or certification under applicable State law, solely on the basis of such license or certification. This paragraph shall not be construed to prohibit a plan from including providers only to the extent necessary to meet the needs of the plan's enrollees or from establishing any measure designed to maintain quality and control costs consistent with the responsibilities of the plan.

Section 1857 requires Medicare+Choice organizations to enter into contracts with the Secretary of Health and Human Services in order to provide health care benefits to eligible individuals and receive payment therefor from the Secretary. It provides in pertinent part:

(a) IN GENERAL. — The Secretary shall not permit the election under section 1851 of a Medicare + Choice plan offered by a Medicare + Choice organization under this part, and no payment shall be made under section 1853 to an organization, unless the Secretary has entered into a contract under this section with the organization with respect to the offering of such plan. Such a contract with an organization may cover more than 1 Medicare + Choice plan. Such contract shall provide that the organization agrees to comply with the applicable requirements and standards of this part and the terms and conditions of payment as provided for in this part.

(b) MINIMUM ENROLLMENT REQUIREMENTS. —

(1) IN GENERAL. — Subject to paragraph (2), the Secretary may not enter into a contract under this section with a Medicare + Choice organization unless the organization has —

(A) at least 5,000 individuals (or 1,500 individuals in the case of an organization that is a provider-sponsored organization) who are receiving health benefits through the organization, or

(B) at least 1,500 individuals (or 500 individuals in the case of an organization that is a provider-sponsored organization) who are receiving health benefits through the organization if the organization primarily serves individuals residing outside of urbanized areas.

(2) APPLICATION TO MSA PLANS. — In applying paragraph (1) in the case of a Medicare + Choice organization that is offering an MSA plan, paragraph (1) shall be applied by substituting covered lives for individuals.

(3) ALLOWING TRANSITION. — The Secretary may waive the requirement of paragraph (1) during the first 3 contract years with respect to an organization.

(c) CONTRACT PERIOD AND EFFECTIVENESS. —

(1) PERIOD. — Each contract under this section shall be for a term of at least 1 year, as determined by the Secretary, and may be made automatically renewable from term to term in

the absence of notice by either party of intention to terminate at the end of the current term.

* * *

(3) EFFECTIVE DATE OF CONTRACTS.—The effective date of any contract executed pursuant to this section shall be specified in the contract, except that in no case shall a contract under this section which provides for coverage under an MSA plan be effective before January 1999 with respect to such coverage.

(4) PREVIOUS TERMINATIONS.—

(A) IN GENERAL.—The Secretary may not enter into a contract with a Medicare + Choice organization if a previous contract with that organization under this section was terminated at the request of the organization within the preceding 2-year period, except as provided in subparagraph (B) and except in such other circumstances which warrant special consideration, as determined by the Secretary.

(B) EARLIER RE-ENTRY PERMITTED WHERE CHANGE IN PAYMENT POLICY.—Subparagraph (A) shall not apply with respect to the offering by a Medicare+Choice plan in a Medicare+Choice payment area if during the 6-month period beginning on the date the organization notified the Secretary of the intention to terminate the most recent previous contract, there was a legislative change enacted (or a regulatory change adopted) that has the efrect of increasing payment amounts under section 1853 for that Medicare+Choice payment area.

◆ NOTE: Applicable to contract terminations occurring before, on, or after November 29, 1999, section 513 of the Medicare, Medicaid, and SCHIP Balanced Budget Refinement Act of 1999, as incorporated into the Omnibus Consolidated Appropriations Act, 2000, P.L. 106–113 (enacted November 17, 1999), struck "5-year period" and inserted "2-year period" in subparagraph (c)(4); struck "except in circumstances", and inserted "except as provided in subparagraph (B) and except in such other circumstances" in subparagraph (c)(4); redesignated the sentence following "(4)" as "(A)"; and added (c)(4)(B).

(5) CONTRACTING AUTHORITY. — The authority vested in the Secretary by this part may be performed without regard to such provisions of law or regulations relating to the making, performance, amendment, or modification of contracts of the United States as the Secretary may determine to be inconsistent with the furtherance of the purpose of this title.

Medicare+Choice organizations must comply with numerous requirements. One of these is to guarantee issuance and renewal of plans to eligible individuals. In that regard, section 1851(g) provides in pertinent part:

GUARANTEED ISSUE AND RENEWAL. —

(1) IN GENERAL. — Except as provided in this subsection, a Medicare + Choice organization shall provide that at any time during which elections are accepted under this section with respect to a Medicare + Choice plan offered by the organization, the organization will accept without restrictions individuals who are eligible to make such election.

(2) PRIORITY. — If the Secretary determines that a Medicare + Choice organization, in relation to a Medicare + Choice plan it offers, has a capacity limit and the number of Medicare + Choice eligible individuals who elect the plan under this section exceeds the capacity limit, the organization may limit the election of individuals of the plan under this section but only if priority in election is provided —

(A) first to such individuals as have elected the plan at the time of the determination, and

(B) then to other such individuals in such a manner that does not discriminate, on a basis described in section 1852(b), among the individuals (who seek to elect the plan).

The preceding sentence shall not apply if it would result in the enrollment of enrollees substantially nonrepresentative, as determined in accordance with regulations of the Secretary, of the Medicare population in the service area of the plan.

(3) LIMITATION ON TERMINATION OF ELECTION. —

(A) IN GENERAL. — Subject to subparagraph (B), a Medicare + Choice organization may not for any reason terminate the election of any individual under this section for a Medicare + Choice plan it offers.

(B) BASIS FOR TERMINATION OF ELECTION.—A Medicare + Choice organization may terminate an individual's election under this section with respect to a Medicare + Choice plan it offers if—

(i) any Medicare + Choice monthly basic and supplemental beneficiary premiums required with respect to such plan are not paid on a timely basis (consistent with standards under section 1856 that provide for a grace period for late payment of such premiums),

(ii) the individual has engaged in disruptive behavior (as specified in such standards), or

(iii) the plan is terminated with respect to all individuals under this part in the area in which the individual resides.

(C) CONSEQUENCE OF TERMINATION.—

(i) TERMINATIONS FOR CAUSE.—Any individual whose election is terminated under clause (i) or (ii) of subparagraph (B) is deemed to have elected the original Medicare fee-for-service program option described in subsection (a)(1)(A).

(ii) TERMINATION BASED ON PLAN TERMINATION OR SERVICE AREA REDUCTION.—Any individual whose election is terminated under subparagraph (B)(iii) shall have a special election period under subsection (e)(4)(A) in which to change coverage to coverage under another Medicare + Choice plan. Such an individual who fails to make an election during such period is deemed to have chosen to change coverage to the original Medicare fee-for-service program option described in subsection (a)(1)(A).

(D) ORGANIZATION OBLIGATION WITH RESPECT TO ELECTION FORMS.—Pursuant to a contract under section 1857, each Medicare + Choice organization receiving an election form under subsection (c)(2) shall transmit to the Secretary (at such time and in such manner as the Secretary may specify) a copy of such form or such other information respecting the election as the Secretary may specify.

Medicare+Choice organizations also must have prior approval by the Secretary of their marketing material and application forms. In that regard, section 1851(h) provides:

APPROVAL OF MARKETING MATERIAL AND APPLICATION FORMS. —

(1) SUBMISSION. — No marketing material or application form may be distributed by a Medicare + Choice organization to (or for the use of) Medicare + Choice eligible individuals unless —

(A) at least 45 days (or 10 days in the case described in paragraph (5)) before the date of distribution the organization has submitted the material or form to the Secretary for review, and

(B) the Secretary has not disapproved the distribution of such material or form.

(2) REVIEW. — The standards established under section 1856 shall include guidelines for the review of any material or form submitted and under such guidelines the Secretary shall disapprove (or later require the correction of) such material or form if the material or form is materially inaccurate or misleading or otherwise makes a material misrepresentation.

(3) DEEMED APPROVAL (1-STOP SHOPPING). — In the case of material or form that is submitted under paragraph (1)(A) to the Secretary or a regional office of the Department of Health and Human Services and the Secretary or the office has not disapproved the distribution of marketing material or form under paragraph (1)(B) with respect to a Medicare + Choice plan in an area, the Secretary is deemed not to have disapproved such distribution in all other areas covered by the plan and organization except with regard to that portion of such material or form that is specific only to an area involved.

(4) PROHIBITION OF CERTAIN MARKETING PRACTICES. — Each Medicare + Choice organization shall conform to fair marketing standards, in relation to Medicare + Choice plans offered under this part, included in the standards established under section 1856. Such standards —

(A) shall not permit a Medicare + Choice organization to provide for cash or other monetary rebates as an inducement for enrollment or otherwise, and

(B) may include a prohibition against a Medicare + Choice organization (or agent of such an organization) completing any portion of any election form used to carry out elections under this section on behalf of any individual.

(5) SPECIAL TREATMENT OF MARKETING MATERIAL FOLLOWING MODEL MARKETING LANGUAGE.—In the case of marketing material of an organization that uses, without modification, proposed model language specified by the Secretary, the period specified in paragraph (1)(A) shall be reduced from 45 days to 10 days. [NOTE: Paragraph (5) was added by section 613(a) of the Medicare, Medicaid, and SCHIP Benefits Improvement and Protection Act of 2000. It applies to marketing material submitted on or after January 1, 2001.]

Numerous disclosure requirements apply to Medicare+Choice organizations. In that regard, section 1852(c) provides:
DISCLOSURE REQUIREMENTS. —

(1) DETAILED DESCRIPTION OF PLAN PROVISIONS. — A Medicare + Choice organization shall disclose, in clear, accurate, and standardized form to each enrollee with a Medicare + Choice plan offered by the organization under this part at the time of enrollment and at least annually thereafter, the following information regarding such plan:

(A) SERVICE AREA. — The plan's service area.

(B) BENEFITS. — Benefits offered under the plan, including information described in section 1851(d)(3)(A) and exclusions from coverage and, if it is an MSA plan, a comparison of benefits under such a plan with benefits under other Medicare + Choice plans.

(C) ACCESS. — The number, mix, and distribution of plan providers, out-of-network coverage (if any) provided by the plan, and any point-of-service option (including the supplemental premium for such option).

(D) OUT-OF-AREA COVERAGE. — Out-of-area coverage provided by the plan.

(E) EMERGENCY COVERAGE. — Coverage of emergency services, including —

(i) the appropriate use of emergency services, including use of the 911 telephone system or its local equivalent in emergency situations and an explanation of what constitutes an emergency situation;

(ii) the process and procedures of the plan for obtaining emergency services; and

(iii) the locations of (I) emergency departments, and (II) other settings, in which plan physicians and hospitals provide emergency services and post-stabilization care.

(F) SUPPLEMENTAL BENEFITS. — Supplemental benefits available from the organization offering the plan, including —

(i) whether the supplemental benefits are optional,

(ii) the supplemental benefits covered, and

(iii) the Medicare + Choice monthly supplemental beneficiary premium for the supplemental benefits.

(G) PRIOR AUTHORIZATION RULES. — Rules regarding prior authorization or other review requirements that could result in nonpayment.

(H) PLAN GRIEVANCE AND APPEALS PROCEDURES. — All plan appeal or grievance rights and procedures.

(I) QUALITY ASSURANCE PROGRAM. — A description of the organization's quality assurance program under subsection (e).

(2) DISCLOSURE UPON REQUEST. — Upon request of a Medicare + Choice eligible individual, a Medicare + Choice organization must provide the following information to such individual:

(A) The general coverage information and general comparative plan information made available under clauses (i) and (ii) of section 1851(d)(2)(A).

(B) Information on procedures used by the organization to control utilization of services and expenditures.

(C) Information on the number of grievances, redeterminations, and appeals and on the disposition in the aggregate of such matters.

(D) An overall summary description as to the method of compensation of participating physicians.

Section 1852(d) requires Medicare+Choice organizations to assure adequate access to health care services for enrollees. It provides:

ACCESS TO SERVICES. —

(1) IN GENERAL. — A Medicare + Choice organization offering a Medicare + Choice plan may select the providers from whom the benefits under the plan are provided so long as —

(A) the organization makes such benefits available and accessible to each individual electing the plan within the plan service area with reasonable promptness and in a manner which assures continuity in the provision of benefits;

(B) when medically necessary the organization makes such benefits available and accessible 24 hours a day and 7 days a week;

(C) the plan provides for reimbursement with respect to services which are covered under subparagraphs (A) and (B) and which are provided to such an individual other than through the organization, if —

(i) the services were not emergency services (as defined in paragraph (3)), but (I) the services were medically necessary and immediately required because of an unforeseen illness, injury, or condition, and (II) it was not reasonable given the circumstances to obtain the services through the organization,

(ii) the services were renal dialysis services and were provided other than through the organization because the individual was temporarily out of the plan's service area, or

(iii) the services are maintenance care or post-stabilization care covered under the guidelines established under paragraph (2);

(D) the organization provides access to appropriate providers, including credentialed specialists, for medically necessary treatment and services; and

(E) coverage is provided for emergency services (as defined in paragraph (3)) without regard to prior authorization or the emergency care provider's contractual relationship with the organization.

(2) GUIDELINES RESPECTING CORRDINATION OF POST-STABILIZATION CARE. — A Medicare + Choice plan shall comply with such guidelines as the Secretary may prescribe relating to promoting efficient and timely coordination of appropriate maintenance and post-stabilization care of an enrollee after the enrollee has been determined to be stable under section 1867.

(3) DEFINITION OF EMERGENCY SERVICES. — In this subsection —

(A) IN GENERAL. — The term "emergency services" means, with respect to an individual enrolled with an organization, covered inpatient and outpatient services that —

(i) are furnished by a provider that is qualified to furnish such services under this title, and

(ii) are needed to evaluate or stabilize an emergency medical condition (as defined in subparagraph (B)).

(B) EMERGENCY MEDICAL CONDITION BASED ON PRUDENT LAYPERSON. — The term "emergency medical condition" means a medical condition manifesting itself by acute symptoms of sufficient severity (including severe pain) such that a prudent layperson, who possesses an average knowledge of health and medicine, could reasonably expect the absence of immediate medical attention to result in —

(i) placing the health of the individual (or, with respect to a pregnant woman, the health of the woman or her unborn child) in serious jeopardy,

(ii) serious impairment to bodily functions, or

(iii) serious dysfunction of any bodily organ or part.

(4) ASSURING ACCESS TO SERVICES IN MEDICARE + CHOICE PRIVATE FEE-FOR-SERVICE PLANS. — In addition to any other requirements under this part, in the case of a Medicare + Choice private fee-for-service plan, the organization offering the plan must demonstrate to the Secretary that the organization has sufficient number and range of health care professionals and providers willing to provide services under the terms of the plan. The Secretary shall find that an organization has met such requirement with respect to any category of health care professional or provider if. with respect to that category of provider —

(A) the plan has established payment rates for covered services furnished by that category of provider that are not less than the payment rates provided for under part A, part B, or both, for such services, or

(B) the plan has contracts or agreements with a sufficient number and range of providers within such category to provide covered services under the terms of the plan, or a combination of both.

The previous sentence shall not be construed as restricting the persons from whom enrollees under such a plan may obtain covered benefits.

Section 1852(e) requires Medicare+Choice organizations to establish quality assurance programs. It provides:

QUALITY ASSURANCE PROGRAM. —

(1) IN GENERAL. — Each Medicare + Choice organization must have arrangements, consistent with any regulation, for an ongoing quality assurance program for health care services it provides to individuals enrolled with Medicare + Choice plans of the organization.

◆ NOTE: Applicable to contract years after January 1, 2000, section 520 of the Medicare, Medicaid, and SCHIP Balanced Budget Refinement Act of 1999, as incorporated into the Omnibus Consolidated Appropriations Act, 2000, P.L. 106–113, enacted November 17, 1999, deleted "or a non-network MSA plan" and inserted ", a non-network MSA plan, or a preferred provider organization plan" in subsections (e)(2)(A) and (e)(2)(B) below. It also added subsection (e)(2)(D).

(2) ELEMENTS OF PROGRAM. —

(A) IN GENERAL. — The quality assurance program of an organization with respect to a Medicare + Choice plan (other than a Medicare + Choice private fee-for-service plan, a non-network MSA plan, or a preferred provider organization plan) that it offers shall —

(i) stress health outcomes and provide for the collection, analysis, and reporting of data (in accordance with a quality measurement system that the Secretary recognizes) that will permit measurement of outcomes and other indices of the quality of Medicare + Choice plans and organizations;

(ii) monitor and evaluate high volume and high risk services and the care of acute and chronic conditions;

(iii) evaluate the continuity and coordination of care that enrollees receive;

(iv) be evaluated on an ongoing basis as to its effectiveness;

(v) include measures of consumer satisfaction;

(vi) provide the Secretary with such access to information collected as may be appropriate to monitor and ensure the quality of care provided under this part;

(vii) provide review by physicians and other health care professionals of the process followed in the provision of such health care services;

(viii) provide for the establishment of written protocols for utilization review, based on current standards of medical practice;

(ix) have mechanisms to detect both underutilization and overutilization of services;

(x) after identifying areas for improvement, establish or alter practice parameters;

(xi) take action to improve quality and assesses the effectiveness of such action through systematic followup; and

(xii) make available information on quality and outcomes measures to facilitate beneficiary comparison and choice of health coverage options (in such form and on such quality and outcomes measures as the Secretary determines to be appropriate).

(B) ELEMENTS OF PROGRAM FOR ORGANIZATIONS OFFERING MEDICARE + CHOICE PRIVATE FEE-FOR-SERVICE PLANS AND NON-NETWORK MSA PLANS. — The quality assurance program of an organization with respect to a Medicare + Choice private fee-for-service plan, a non-network MSA plan, or a preferred provider organization plan it offers shall —

(i) meet the requirements of clauses (i) through (vi) of subparagraph (A);

(ii) insofar as it provides for the establishment of written protocols for utilization review. base such protocols on current standards of medical practice; and

(iii) have mechanisms to evaluate utilization of services and inform providers and enrollees of the results of such evaluation.

Such program shall include a separate focus (with respect to all the elements described in this subparagraph) on racial and ethnic minorities. [NOTE: The preceding sentence was added by section 616 of the Medicare, Medicaid, and SCHIP Benefits Improvement and Protection Act of 2000, effective December 15, 2000.]

(C) DEFINITION OF NON-NETWORK MSA PLAN. — In this subsection, the term "non-network MSA plan" means an MSA plan offered by a Medicare + Choice organization that does not provide benefits required to be provided by this part, in whole or in part, through a defined set of providers under contract, or under another arrangement, with the organization.

(D) DEFINITION OF PREFERRED PROVIDER ORGANIZATION PLAN. — In this paragraph, the term "preferred provider organization plan" means a Medicare + Choice plan that —

(i) has a network of providers that have agreed to a contractually specified reimbursement for covered benefits with the organization offering the plan;

(ii) provides for reimbursement for all covered benefits regardless of whether such benefits are provided within such network of providers; and

(iii) is offered by an organization that is not licensed or organized under State law as a health maintenance organization.

(3) EXTERNAL REVIEW. —

(A) IN GENERAL. — Each Medicare + Choice organization shall, for each Medicare + Choice plan it operates, have an agreement with an independent quality review and improvement organization approved by the Secretary to perform functions of the type described in sections 1154(a)(4)(B) and 1154(a)(14) with respect to services furnished by Medicare + Choice plans for which payment is made under this title. The previous sentence shall not apply to a Medicare + Choice private fee-for-service plan or a non-network MSA plan that does not employ utilization review.

(B) NONDUPLICATION OF ACCREDITATION. — Except in the case of the review of quality complaints, and consistent with subparagraph (C), the Secretary shall ensure that the external review activities conducted under subparagraph (A) are not duplicative of review activities conducted as part of the accreditation process.

(C) WAIVER AUTHORITY. — The Secretary may waive the requirement described in subparagraph (A) in the case of an organization if the Secretary determines that the organization has consistently maintained an excellent record of quality assurance and compliance with other requirements under this part.

(4) TREATMENT OF ACCREDITATION. —

(A) IN GENERAL. — The Secretary shall provide that a Medicare+Choice organization is deemed to meet all the requirements described in any specific clause of subparagraph (B) if the organization is accredited (and periodically reaccredited) by a private accrediting organization under a process that the Secretary has determined assures that the accrediting organization applies and enforces standards that meet or exceed the standards established under section 1856 to carry out the requirements in such clause.

(B) REQUIREMENTS DESCRIBED.— The provisions described in this subparagraph are the following:

(i) Paragraphs (1) and (2) of this subsection (relating to quality assurance programs).

(ii) Subsection (b) (relating to antidiscrimination).

(iii) Subsection (d) (relating to access to services).

(iv) Subsection (h) (relating to confidentiality and accuracy of enrollee records).

(v) Subsection (i) (relating to information on advance directives).

(vi) Subsection (j) (relating to provider participation rules.

(C) TIMELY ACTION ON APPLICATIONS. —The Secretary shall determine, within 210 days after the date the Secretary receives an application by a private accrediting organization and using the criteria specified in section 1865(b)(2), whether the process of the private accrediting organization meets the requirements with respect to any specific clause in subparagraph (B) with respect to which the application is made. The Secretary may not deny such an application on the basis that it seeks to meet the requirement with respect to only one, or more than one, such specific clause.

(D) CONSTRUCTION. —Nothing in this paragraph shall be construed as limiting the authority of the Secretary under section 1857, including the authority to terminate contracts with Medicare + Choice organizations under subsection (c)(2) of such section.

◆ NOTE: Effective November 29, 1999, section 518 of the Medicare, Medicaid, and SCHIP Balanced Budget Refinement Act of 1999, as incorporated into the Omnibus Consolidated Appropriations Act, 2000, P.L. 106–113, enacted November 17, 1999, amended subsection (e) (4). Prior to that amendment it read: "(4) TREATMENT OF ACCREDITATION. — The Secretary shall provide that a Medicare + Choice organization is deemed to meet requirements of paragraphs (1) and (2) of this subsection and subsection (h) (relating to confidentiality and accuracy of enrollee records) if the organization is accredited (and periodically reaccredited) by a private organization under a process that the Secretary has determined assures that the organization, as a condition of accreditation, applies and enforces standards with respect to the requirements involved that are no less stringent than the standards established under section 1856 to carry out the respective requirements."

Section 1852(f) requires Medicare + Choice organizations to have grievance procedures for dispute resolution. It provides:

GRIEVANCE MECHANISM.—Each Medicare + Choice organization must provide meaningful procedures for hearing and resolving grievances between the organization (including any entity or individual through which the organization provides health care services) and enrollees with Medicare + Choice plans of the organization under this part. Medicare+Choice organizations must provide for coverage determinations and for reconsideration and appeal rights when coverage is denied, in whole or in part, to an enrollee. In that regard, section 1852(g) provides:

COVERAGE DETERMINATIONS, RECONSIDERATIONS, AND APPEALS.—

(1) DETERMINATIONS BY ORGANIZATION.—

(A) IN GENERAL.—A Medicare + Choice organization shall have a procedure for making determinations regarding whether an individual enrolled with the plan of the organization under this part is entitled to receive a health service under this section and the amount (if any) that the individual is required to pay with respect to such service. Subject to paragraph (3), such procedures shall provide for such determination to be made on a timely basis.

(B) EXPLANATION OF DETERMINATION.—Such a determination that denies coverage, in whole in part, shall be in writing and shall include a statement in understandable language of the reasons for the denial and a description of the reconsideration and appeals processes.

(2) RECONSIDERATIONS. —

(A) IN GENERAL.—The organization shall provide for reconsideration of a determination described in paragraph (1)(B) upon request by the enrollee involved. The reconsideration shall be within a time period specified by the Secretary, but shall be made, subject to paragraph (3), not later than 60 days after the date of the receipt of the request for reconsideration.

(B) PHYSICIAN DECISION ON CERTAIN RECONSIDERATIONS. — A reconsideration relating to a determination to deny coverage based on a lack of medical necessity shall be made only by a physician with appropriate expertise in the field of medicine which necessitates treatment who is other than a physician involved in the initial determination.

(3) EXPEDITED DETERMINATIONS AND RECONSIDERATIONS. —

(A) RECEIPT OF REQUESTS. —

(i) ENROLLEE REQUESTS. — An enrollee in a Medicare + Choice plan may request, either in writing or orally, an expedited determination under paragraph (1) or an expedited reconsideration under paragraph (2) by the Medicare + Choice organization.

(ii) PHYSICIAN REQUESTS. — A physician, regardless whether the physician is affiliated with the organization or not, may request, either in writing or orally, such an expedited determination or reconsideration.

(B) ORGANIZATION PROCEDURES. —

(i) IN GENERAL. — The Medicare + Choice organization shall maintain procedures for expediting organization determinations and reconsiderations when, upon request of an enrollee, the organization determines that the application of the normal time frame for making a determination (or a reconsideration involving a determination) could seriously jeopardize the life or health of the enrollee or the enrollee's ability to regain maximum function.

(ii) EXPEDITION REQUIRED FOR PHYSICIAN REQUESTS. — In the case of a request for an expedited determination or reconsideration made under subparagraph (A)(ii), the organization shall expedite the determination or reconsideration if the request indicates that the application of the normal time frame for making a determination (or a reconsideration involving a determination) could seriously jeopardize the life or health of the enrollee or the enrollee's ability to regain maximum function.

(iii) TIMELY RESPONSE. — In cases described in clauses (i) and (ii), the organization shall notify the enrollee (and the physician involved, as appropriate) of the determination or reconsideration under time limitations established by the Secretary, but not later than 72 hours of the time of receipt of the request for the determination or reconsideration (or receipt of the information necessary to make the determination or reconsideration), or such longer period as the Secretary may permit in specified cases.

(4) INDEPENDENT REVIEW OF CERTAIN COVERAGE DENIALS. — The Secretary shall contract with an independent, outside entity to review and resolve in a timely manner reconsiderations that affirm denial of coverage, in whole or in part. The provisions of section 1869(c)(5) [42 U.S.C. 1395ff(c)(5), which deals with determinations and appeals] shall apply to independent outside entities under contract with the Secretary under this paragraph. The preceding sentence was added by section 521(b) of the Medicare, Medicaid, and SCHIP Benefits Improvement and Protection Act of 2000, applicable to initial determinations made on or after October 1, 2002.]

(5) APPEALS. — An enrollee with a Medicare + Choice plan of a Medicare + Choice organization under this part who is dissatisfied by reason of the enrollee's failure to receive any health service to which the enrollee believes the enrollee is entitled and at no greater charge than the enrollee believes the enrollee is required to pay is entitled, if the amount in controversy is $100 or more, to a hearing before the Secretary to the same extent as is provided in section 205(b), and in any such hearing the Secretary shall make the organization a party. If the amount in controversy is $1,000 or more, the individual or organization shall, upon notifying the other party, be entitled to judicial review of the Secretary's final decision as provided in section 205(g), and both the individual and the organization shall be entitled to be parties to that

judicial review. In applying subsections (b) and (g) of section 205 as provided in this paragraph, and in applying section 205(l) thereto, any reference therein to the Commissioner of Social Security or the Social Security Administration shall be considered a reference to the Secretary or the Department of Health and Human Services, respectively.

Section 1852(h) requires Medicare+Choice organizations to assure the confidentiality and accuracy of enrollee records. It provides:

CONFIDENTIALITY AND ACCURACY OF ENROLLEE RECORDS. — Insofar as a Medicare + Choice organization maintains medical records or other health information regarding enrollees under this part, the Medicare + Choice organization shall establish procedures —

(1) to safeguard the privacy of any individually identifiable enrollee information;

(2) to maintain such records and information in a manner that is accurate and timely, and

(3) to assure timely access of enrollees to such records and information.

Section 1852(i) requires Medicare+Choice organizations to provide enrollees with information about advance directives, as follows:

INFORMATION ON ADVANCE DIRECTIVES. — Each Medicare + Choice organization shall meet the requirement of section 1866(f) [42 U.S.C.A. 1395cc(f)] (relating to maintaining written policies and procedures respecting advance directives).

Section 1866(f) provides:

(1) For purposes of subsection (a)(1)(Q) and sections 1819(c)(2)(E), 1833(s), 1876(c)(8), and 1891(a)(6), the requirement of this subsection is that a provider of services, Medicare+Choice organization, or prepaid or eligible organization (as the case may be) maintain written policies and procedures with respect to all adult individuals receiving medical care by or through the provider or organization —

(A) to provide written information to each such individual concerning —

(i) an individual's rights under State law (whether statutory or as recognized by the courts of the State) to make decisions concerning such medical care, including the right to accept or refuse medical or surgical treatment and the right to formulate advance directives (as defined in paragraph (3)), and

(ii) the written policies of the provider or organization respecting the implementation of such rights;

(B) to document in a prominent part of the individual's current medical record whether or not the individual has executed an advance directive;

(C) not to condition the provision of care or otherwise discriminate against an individual based on whether or not the individual has executed an advance directive;

(D) to ensure compliance with requirements of State law (whether statutory or as recognized by the courts of the State) respecting advance directives at facilities of the provider or organization; and

(E) to provide (individually or with others) for education for staff and the community on issues concerning advance directives.

Subparagraph (C) shall not be construed as requiring the provision of care which conflicts with an advance directive.

(2) The written information described in paragraph (1)(A) shall be provided to an adult individual—

(A) in the case of a hospital, at the time of the individual's admission as an inpatient,

(B) in the case of a skilled nursing facility, at the time of the individual's admission as a resident,

(C) in the case of a home health agency, in advance of the individual coming under the care of the agency,

(D) in the case of a hospice program, at the time of initial receipt of hospice care by the individual from the program, and

(E) in the case of an eligible organization (as defined in section 1876(b)) or an organization provided payments under section 1833(a)(1)(A) or a Medicare+Choice organization, at the time of enrollment of the individual with the organization.

(3) In this subsection, the term "advance directive" means a written instruction, such as a living will or durable power of attorney for health care, recognized under State law (whether statutory or as recognized by the courts of the State) relating to the provision of such care when the individual is incapacitated.

With respect to provider participation in a Medicare+Choice plan, section 1852(j) provides:

RULES REGARDING PROVIDER PARTICIPATION. —

(1) PROCEDURES. — Insofar as a Medicare + Choice organization offers benefits under a Medicare + Choice plan through agreements with physicians, the organization shall establish reasonable procedures relating to the participation (under an agreement between a physician and the organization) of physicians under such a plan. Such procedures shall include —

(A) providing notice of the rules regarding participation,

(B) providing written notice of participation decisions that are adverse to physicians, and

(C) providing a process within the organization for appealing such adverse decisions, including the presentation of information and views of the physician regarding such decision.

(2) CONSULTATION IN MEDICAL POLICIES. — A Medicare + Choice organization shall consult with physicians who have entered into participation agreements with the organization regarding the organization's medical policy, quality, and medical management procedures.

(3) PROHIBITING INTERFERENCE WITH PROVIDER ADVICE TO ENROLLEES. —

(A) IN GENERAL. — Subject to subparagraphs (B) and (C), a Medicare + Choice organization (in relation to an individual enrolled under a Medicare + Choice plan offered by the organization under this part) shall not prohibit or otherwise restrict a covered health care professional (as defined in subparagraph (D)) from advising such an individual who is a patient of the professional about the health status of the individual or medical care or treatment for the individual's condition or disease, regardless of whether benefits for such care or treatment are provided under the plan, if the professional is acting within the lawful scope of practice.

(B) CONSCIENCE PROTECTION. — Subparagraph (A) shall not be construed as requiring a Medicare + Choice plan to provide, reimburse for, or provide coverage of a counseling or referral service if the Medicare + Choice organization offering the plan —

(i) objects to the provision of such service on moral or religious grounds; and

(ii) in the manner and through the written instrumentalities such Medicare + Choice organization deems appropriate, makes available information on its policies regarding such service to prospective enrollees before or during enrollment and to enrollees within 90 days after the date that the organization or plan adopts a change in policy regarding such a counseling or referral service.

(C) CONSTRUCTION. — Nothing in subparagraph (B) shall be construed to affect disclosure requirements under State law or under the Employee Retirement Income Security Act of 1974.

(D) HEALTH CARE PROFESSIONAL DEFINED. — For purposes of this paragraph, the term "health care professional" means a physician (as defined in section 1861(r)) or other health care professional if coverage for the professional's services is provided under the Medicare + Choice plan for the services of the professional. Such term includes a podiatrist, optometrist, chiropractor, psychologist, dentist, physician assistant, physical or occupational therapist and therapy assistant, speech-language pathologist, audiologist, registered or licensed practical nurse (including nurse practitioner, clinical nurse specialist, certified registered nurse anesthetist, and certified nurse-midwife), licensed certified social worker, registered respiratory therapist, and certified respiratory therapy technician.

(4) LIMITATIONS ON PHYSICIAN INCENTIVE PLANS. —

(A) IN GENERAL. — No Medicare + Choice organization may operate any physician incentive plan (as defined in subparagraph (B)) unless the following requirements are met:

(i) No specific payment is made directly or indirectly under the plan to a physician or physician group as an inducement to reduce or limit medically necessary services provided with respect to a specific individual enrolled with the organization.

(ii) If the plan places a physician or physician group at substantial financial risk (as determined by the Secretary) for services not provided by the physician or physician group, the organization —

(I) provides stop-loss protection for the physician or group that is adequate and appropriate, based on standards developed by the Secretary that take into account the number of physicians placed at such substantial financial risk in the group or under the plan and the number of individuals enrolled with the organization who receive services from the physician or group, and

(II) conducts periodic surveys of both individuals enrolled and individuals previously enrolled with the organization to determine the degree of access of such individuals to services provided by the organization and satisfaction with the quality of such services.

(iii) The organization provides the Secretary with descriptive information regarding the plan, sufficient to permit the Secretary to determine whether the plan is in compliance with the requirements of this subparagraph.

(B) PHYSICIAN INCENTIVE PLAN DEFINED. — In this paragraph, the term "physician incentive plan" means any compensation arrangement between a Medicare + Choice organization and a physician or physician group that may directly or indirectly have the effect of reducing or limiting services provided with respect to individuals enrolled with the organization under this part.

(5) LIMITATION ON PROVIDER INDEMNIFICATION. — A Medicare + Choice organization may not provide (directly or indirectly) for a health care professional, provider of services, or other entity providing health care services (or group of such professionals, providers, or entities) to indemnify the organization against any liability resulting from a civil action brought for any damage caused to an enrollee with a Medicare

+ Choice plan of the organization under this part by the organization's denial of medically necessary care.

(6) SPECIAL RULES FOR MEDICARE + CHOICE PRIVATE FEE-FOR-SERVICE PLANS. — For purposes of applying this part (including subsection (k)(1)) and section 1866(a)(1)(O), a hospital (or other provider of services), a physician or other health care professional, or other entity furnishing health care services is treated as having an agreement or contract in effect with a Medicare + Choice organization (with respect to an individual enrolled in a Medicare + Choice private fee-for-service plan it offers), if —

(A) the provider, professional, or other entity furnishes services that are covered under the plan to such an enrollee; and

(B) before providing such services, the provider, professional, or other entity —

(i) has been informed of the individual's enrollment under the plan, and

(ii) either —

(I) has been informed of the terms and conditions of payment for such services under the plan, or

(II) is given a reasonable opportunity to obtain information concerning such terms and conditions, in a manner reasonably designed to effect informed agreement by a provider.

The previous sentence shall only apply in the absence of an explicit agreement between such a provider, professional, or other entity and the Medicare + Choice organization.

Section 1855 prescribes the State licensure requirement obligation for Medicare+Choice organizations, as well as exceptions to the rule requiring State licensure. It provides:

(a) ORGANIZED AND LICENSED UNDER STATE LAW. —

(1) IN GENERAL. — Subject to paragraphs (2) and (3), a Medicare + Choice organization shall be organized and licensed under State law as a risk-bearing entity eligible to offer health insurance or health benefits coverage in each State in which it offers a Medicare + Choice plan.

(2) SPECIAL EXCEPTION FOR PROVIDER-SPONSORED ORGANIZATIONS.—

(A) IN GENERAL.—In the case of a provider-sponsored organization that seeks to offer a Medicare + Choice plan in a State, the Secretary shall waive the requirement of paragraph (1) that the organization be licensed in that State if—

(i) the organization files an application for such waiver with the Secretary by not later than November 1, 2002, and

(ii) the Secretary determines, based on the application and other evidence presented to the Secretary, that any of the grounds for approval of the application described in subparagraph (B), (C), or (D) has been met.

(B) FAILURE TO ACT ON LICENSURE APPLICATION ON A TIMELY BASIS.—The ground for approval of such a waiver application described in this subparagraph is that the State has failed to complete action on a licensing application of the organization within 90 days of the date of the State's receipt of a substantially complete application. No period before the date of the enactment of this section shall be included in determining such 90-day period.

(C) DENIAL OF APPLICATION BASED ON DISCRIMINATORY TREATMENT.—The ground for approval of such a waiver application described in this subparagraph is that the State has denied such a licensing application and—

(i) the standards or review process imposed by the State as a condition of approval of the license imposes any material requirements, procedures, or standards (other than solvency requirements) to such organizations that are not generally applicable to other entities engaged in a substantially similar business, or

(ii) the State requires the organization, as a condition of licensure, to offer any product or plan other than a Medicare + Choice plan.

(D) DENIAL OF APPLICATION BASED ON APPLICATION OF SOLVENCY REQUIREMENTS.—With respect to waiver applications filed on or after the date of publication of solvency standards under section 1856(a), the ground for approval of such a waiver application described in this subparagraph is that the State has denied such a licensing application based (in whole or in part) on the organization's failure to meet applicable solvency requirements and —

(i) such requirements are not the same as the solvency standards established under section 1856(a); or

(ii) the State has imposed as a condition of approval of the license documentation or information requirements relating to solvency or other material requirements, procedures, or standards relating to solvency that are different from the requirements, procedures, and standards applied by the Secretary under subsection (d)(2).

For purposes of this paragraph, the term "solvency requirements" means requirements relating to solvency and other matters covered under the standards established under section 1856(a).

(E) TREATMENT OF WAIVER. — In the case of a waiver granted under this paragraph for a provider-sponsored organization with respect to a State —

(i) LIMITATION TO STATE. — The waiver shall be effective only with respect to that State and does not apply to any other State.

(ii) LIMITATION TO 36-MONTH PERIOD. — The waiver shall be effective only for a 36-month period and may not be renewed.

(iii) CONDITIONED ON COMPLIANCE WITH CONSUMER PROTECTION AND QUALITY STANDARDS. — The continuation of the waiver is conditioned upon the organization's compliance with the requirements described in subparagraph (G).

(iv) PREEMPTION OF STATE LAW. — Any provisions of law of that State which relate to the licensing of the organization and which prohibit the organization from providing coverage pursuant to a contract under this part shall be superseded.

(F) PROMPT ACTION ON APPLICATION. — The Secretary shall grant or deny such a waiver application within 60 days after the date the Secretary determines that a substantially complete waiver application has been filed. Nothing in this section shall be construed as preventing an organization which has had such a waiver application denied from submitting a subsequent waiver application.

(G) APPLICATION AND ENFORCEMENT OF STATE CONSUMER PROTECTION AND QUALITY STANDARDS.—

(i) IN GENERAL. —A waiver granted under this paragraph to an organization with respect to licensing under State law is conditioned upon the organization's compliance with all consumer protection and quality standards insofar as such standards—

(I) would apply in the State to the organization if it were licensed under State law;

(II) are generally applicable to other Medicare + Choice organizations and plans in the State; and

(III) are consistent with the standards established under this part. Such standards shall not include any standard preempted under section 1856(b)(3)(B).

(ii) INCORPORATION INTO CONTRACT. —In the case of such a waiver granted to an organization with respect to a State, the Secretary shall incorporate the requirement that the organization (and Medicare + Choice plans it offers) comply with standards under clause (i) as part of the contract between the Secretary and the organization under section 1857.

(iii) ENFORCEMENT. —In the case of such a waiver granted to an organization with respect to a State, the Secretary may enter into an agreement with the State under which the State agrees to provide for monitoring and enforcement activities with respect to compliance of such an organization and its Medicare + Choice plans with such standards. Such monitoring and enforcement shall be conducted by the State in the same manner as the State enforces such standards with respect to other Medicare + Choice organizations and plans, without discrimination based on the type of organization to which the standards apply. Such an agreement shall specify or establish mechanisms by which compliance activities are undertaken, while not lengthening the time required to review and process applications for waivers under this paragraph.

(H) REPORT. —By not later than December 31, 2001, the Secretary shall submit to the Committee on Ways and Means and the Committee on Commerce of the House of Representatives and the Committee on Finance of the Senate a report regarding whether the waiver process under this paragraph should be continued after December 31, 2002. In making such recommendation, the Secretary shall consider, among other factors, the impact of such process on beneficiaries and on the long-term solvency of the program under this title.

(3) LICENSURE DOES NOT SUBSTITUTE FOR OR CONSTITUTE CERTIFICATION. —The fact that an organization is licensed in accordance with paragraph (1) does not deem the organization to meet other requirements imposed under this part.

(b) ASSUMPTION OF FULL FINANCIAL RISK. —The Medicare + Choice organization shall assume full financial risk on a prospective basis for the provision of the health care services for which benefits are required to be provided under section 1852(a)(1), except that the organization —

(1) may obtain insurance or make other arrangements for the cost of providing to any enrolled member such services the aggregate value of which exceeds such aggregate level as the Secretary specifies from time to time,

(2) may obtain insurance or make other arrangements for the cost of such services provided to its enrolled members other than through the organization because medical necessity required their provision before they could be secured through the organization,

(3) may obtain insurance or make other arrangements for not more than 90 percent of the amount by which its costs for any of its fiscal years exceed 115 percent of its income for such fiscal year, and

(4) may make arrangements with physicians or other health care professionals, health care institutions, or any combination of such individuals or institutions to assume all or part of the financial risk on a prospective basis for the provision of basic health services by the physicians or other health professionals or through the institutions.

(c) CERTIFICATION OF PROVISION AGAINST RISK OF INSOLVENCY FOR UNLICENSED PSOS. —

(1) IN GENERAL. — Each Medicare + Choice organization that is a provider-sponsored organization, that is not licensed by a State under subsection (a), and for which a waiver application has been approved under subsection (a)(2), shall meet standards established under section 1856(a) relating to the financial solvency and capital adequacy of the organization.

(2) CERTIFICATION PROCESS FOR SOLVENCY STANDARDS FOR PSOS. — The Secretary shall establish a process for the receipt and approval of applications of a provider-sponsored organization described in paragraph (1) for certification (and periodic recertification) of the organization as meeting such solvency standards. Under such process, the Secretary shall act upon such a certification application not later than 60 days after the date the application has been received.

(d) PROVIDER-SPONSORED ORGANIZATION DEFINED. —

(1) IN GENERAL. — In this part, the term "provider-sponsored organization" means a public or private entity —

(A) that is established or organized, and operated, by a health care provider, or group of affiliated health care providers,

(B) that provides a substantial proportion (as defined by the Secretary in accordance with paragraph (2)) of the health care items and services under the contract under this part directly through the provider or affiliated group of providers, and

(C) with respect to which the affiliated providers share, directly or indirectly, substantial financial risk with respect to the provision of such items and services and have at least a majority financial interest in the entity.

(2) SUBSTANTIAL PROPORTION. — In defining what is a "substantial proportion" for purposes of paragraph (1)(B), the Secretary —

(A) shall take into account the need for such an organization to assume responsibility for providing —

(i) significantly more than the majority of the items and services under the contract under this section through its own affiliated providers; and

(ii) most of the remainder of the items and services under the contract through providers with which the organization has an agreement to provide such items and services, in order to assure financial stability and to address the practical considerations involved in integrating the delivery of a wide range of service providers;

(B) shall take into account the need for such an organization to provide a limited proportion of the items and services under the contract through providers that are neither affiliated with nor have an agreement with the organization; and

(C) may allow for variation in the definition of substantial proportion among such organizations based on relevant differences among the organizations, such as their location in an urban or rural area.

(3) AFFILIATION. — For purposes of this subsection, a provider is "affiliated" with another provider if, through contract, ownership, or otherwise —

(A) one provider, directly or indirectly, controls, is controlled by, or is under common control with the other,

(B) both providers are part of a controlled group of corporations under section 1563 of the Internal Revenue Code of 1986,

(C) each provider is a participant in a lawful combination under which each provider shares substantial financial risk in connection with the organization's operations, or

(D) both providers are part of an affiliated service group under section 414 of such Code.

(4) CONTROL. — For purposes of paragraph (3), control is presumed to exist if one party, directly or indirectly, owns, controls, or holds the power to vote, or proxies for, not less than 51 percent of the voting rights or governance rights of another.

(5) HEALTH CARE PROVIDER DEFINED. — In this subsection, the term "health care provider" means —

(A) any individual who is engaged in the delivery of health care services in a State and who is required by State law or regulation to be licensed or certified by the State to engage in the delivery of such services in the State, and

(B) any entity that is engaged in the delivery of health care services in a State and that, if it is required by State law or regulation to be licensed or certified by the State to engage in the delivery of such services in the State, is so licensed.

(6) REGULATIONS. — The Secretary shall issue regulations to carry out this subsection.

With respect to solvency requirements for provider sponsored Medicare+Choice organizations, section 1856 provides:

(a) ESTABLISHMENT OF SOLVENCY STANDARDS FOR PROVIDER-SPONSORED ORGANIZATIONS. —

(1) ESTABLISHMENT. —

(A) IN GENERAL. — The Secretary shall establish, on an expedited basis and using a negotiated rulemaking process under subchapter III of chapter 5 of title 5, United States Code, standards described in section 1855(c)(1) (relating to the financial solvency and capital adequacy of the organization) that entities must meet to qualify as provider-sponsored organizations under this part.

(B) FACTORS TO CONSIDER FOR SOLVENCY STANDARDS. — In establishing solvency standards under subparagraph (A) for provider-sponsored organizations, the Secretary shall consult with interested parties and shall take into account —

(i) the delivery system assets of such an organization and ability of such an organization to provide services directly to enrollees through affiliated providers,

(ii) alternative means of protecting against insolvency, including reinsurance, unrestricted surplus, letters of credit, guarantees, organizational insurance coverage, partnerships with other licensed entities, and valuation attributable to the ability of such an organization to meet its service obligations through direct delivery of care, and

(iii) any standards developed by the National Association of Insurance Commissioners specifically for risk-based health care delivery organizations.

(C) ENROLLEE PROTECTION AGAINST INSOLVENCY. — Such standards shall include provisions to prevent enrollees from being held liable to any person or entity for the Medicare + Choice organization's debts in the event of the organization's insolvency.

(2) PUBLICATION OF NOTICE. — In carrying out the rulemaking process under this subsection, the Secretary, after consultation with the National Association of Insurance Commissioners, the American Academy of Actuaries, organizations representative of Medicare beneficiaries, and other interested parties, shall publish the notice provided for under section 564(a) of title 5, United States Code, by not later than 45 days after the date of the enactment of this section.

(3) TARGET DATE FOR PUBLICATION OF RULE. — As part of the notice under paragraph (2), and for purposes of this subsection, the "target date for publication" (referred to in section 564(a)(5) of such title) shall be April 1, 1998.

(4) ABBREVIATED PERIOD FOR SUBMISSION OF COMMENTS. — In applying section 564(c) of such title under this subsection, "15 days" shall be substituted for "30 days".

(5) APPOINTMENT OF NEGOTIATED RULEMAKING COMMITTEE AND FACILITATOR. — The Secretary shall provide for —

(A) the appointment of a negotiated rulemaking committee under section 565(a) of such title by not later than 30 days after the end of the comment period provided for under section 564(c) of such title (as shortened under paragraph (4)), and

(B) the nomination of a facilitator under section 566(c) of such title by not later than 10 days after the date of appointment of the committee.

(6) PRELIMINARY COMMITTEE REPORT.—The negotiated rulemaking committee appointed under paragraph (5) shall report to the Secretary, by not later than January 1, 1998, regarding the committee's progress on achieving a consensus with regard to the rulemaking proceeding and whether such consensus is likely to occur before 1 month before the target date for publication of the rule. If the committee reports that the committee has failed to make significant progress towards such consensus or is unlikely to reach such consensus by the target date, the Secretary may terminate such process and provide for the publication of a rule under this subsection through such other methods as the Secretary may provide.

(7) FINAL COMMITTEE REPORT.—If the committee is not terminated under paragraph (6), the rulemaking committee shall submit a report containing a proposed rule by not later than 1 month before the target date of publication.

(8) INTERIM, FINAL EFFECT.—The Secretary shall publish a rule under this subsection in the Federal Register by not later than the target date of publication. Such rule shall be effective and final immediately on an interim basis, but is subject to change and revision after public notice and opportunity for a period (of not less than 60 days) for public comment. In connection with such rule, the Secretary shall specify the process for the timely review and approval of applications of entities to be certified as provider-sponsored organizations pursuant to such rules and consistent with this subsection.

(9) PUBLICATION OF RULE AFTER PUBLIC COMMENT.—The Secretary shall provide for consideration of such comments and republication of such rule by not later than 1 year after the target date of publication.

(b) ESTABLISHMENT OF OTHER STANDARDS.—

(1) IN GENERAL.—The Secretary shall establish by regulation other standards (not described in subsection (a)) for Medicare + Choice organizations and plans consistent with, and to carry out, this part. The Secretary shall publish such regulations by June 1, 1998. In order to carry out this require-

ment in a timely manner, the Secretary may promulgate regulations that take effect on an interim basis, after notice and pending opportunity for public comment.

(2) USE OF CURRENT STANDARDS. — Consistent with the requirements of this part, standards established under this subsection shall be based on standards established under section 1876 to carry out analogous provisions of such section.

(3) RELATION TO STATE LAWS. —

(A) IN GENERAL. — The standards established under this subsection shall supersede any State law or regulation (including standards described in subpara-graph (B)) with respect to Medicare + Choice plans which are offered by Medicare + Choice organizations under this part to the extent such law or regulation is inconsistent with such standards.

(B) STANDARDS SPECIFICALLY SUPERSEDED. — State standards relating to the following are superseded under this paragraph:

(i) Benefit requirements (including cost–sharing requirements).

(ii) Requirements relating to inclusion or treatment of providers.

(iii) Coverage determinations (including related appeals and grievance processes).

(iv) Requirements relating to marketing materials and summaries and schedules of benefits regarding a Medicare+Choice plan.

(4) PROHIBITION OF MIDYEAR IMPLEMENTATION OF SIGNIFICANT NEW REGULATORY REQUIREMENTS.—The Secretary may not implement, other than at the beginning of a calendar year, regulations under this section that impose new, significant regulatory requirements on a Medicare+Choice organization or plan.

NOTE: Section 614(a) of the Medicare, Medicaid, and SCHIP Benefits Improvement and Protection Act of 2000 added the phrase "(including cost–sharing requirement)" to subsection (b)(3)(b)(i) and added new clause (b)(3)(iv). Section 612(a) added paragraph (4). These changes were effective December 21, 2000.

Finally, if a Medicare+Choice organization fails to comply with the foregoing statutory requirements, section 1857(c)(2) authorizes the Secretary to terminate the organization's contract as follows:

> TERMINATION AUTHORITY.—In accordance with procedures established under subsection (h), the Secretary may at any time terminate any such contract if the Secretary determines that the organization—
>
> (A) has failed substantially to carry out the contract;
>
> (B) is carrying out the contract in a manner inconsistent with the efficient and effective administration of this part; or
>
> (C) no longer substantially meets the applicable conditions of this part.

Procedures for terminating a contract with a Medicare+Choice organization are set forth in section 1857(h). It provides:

PROCEDURES FOR TERMINATION.—

> (1) IN GENERAL. —The Secretary may terminate a contract with a Medicare + Choice organization under this section in accordance with formal investigation and compliance procedures established by the Secretary under which—
>
> (A) the Secretary provides the organization with the reasonable opportunity to develop and implement a corrective action plan to correct the deficiencies that were the basis of the Secretary's determination under subsection (c)(2); and
>
> (B) the Secretary provides the organization with reasonable notice and opportunity for hearing (including the right to appeal an initial decision) before terminating the contract.
>
> (2) EXCEPTION FOR IMMINENT AND SERIOUS RISK TO HEALTH.—Paragraph (1) shall not apply if the Secretary determines that a delay in termination, resulting from compliance with the procedures specified in such paragraph prior to termination, would pose an imminent and serious risk to the health of individuals enrolled under this part with the organization.

For regulatory citations, see Chapter 6

§ 2:26.2 FAILURE BY MEDICARE + CHOICE ORGANIZATIONS TO COMPLY WITH REQUIREMENTS FOR BENEFICIARY PROTECTIONS AND PROTECTIONS AGAINST FRAUD — Section 1857(d)

Summary

◆ NOTE: Effective August 5, 1997, section 4001 of the Balanced Budget Act of 1997, P.L. 105–33, authorized the use of Medicare+Choice plans to provide health care benefits to certain persons eligible for Medicare Part A and Part B. The earliest effective date for an organization to have a Medicare+Choice contract with the Secretary of Health and Human Services is January 1, 1999. See sections 1851–1859 of the Social Security Act, as amended. For a more complete analysis of Medicare+Choice organizations, see section 2:26.1.

Section 1851 of the Social Security Act, as amended, gives persons eligible for Medicare and enrolled under Medicare Part B the right to have their health care costs paid for by one of three types of Medicare+Choice plans, instead of by the traditional Medicare fee-for-service program.

One option is a coordinated care plan. This may be any coordinated care plan, including but not limited to a health maintenance organization (HMO) plan (with or without point of service options), a plan offered by a provider-sponsored organization, or a preferred provider organization (PPO) plan. The second option is a combination of a medical savings account plan and a contribution into a Medicare+Choice savings account (MSA). The third is a Medicare+Choice private fee-for-service plan.

Definitions: *Medicare+ Choice Organization* means a public or private entity certified under section 1856 as meeting Medicare requirements and standards for fiscal solvency and other matters.

Provider-sponsored Organization, as specified in section 1855(d)(1), means a public or private entity established or organized, and operated, by a health care provider, or group of affiliated health care providers. It must provide a substantial proportion of the health care items and services under its Medicare+Choice contract directly through the provider or affiliated group of providers. Furthermore, the affiliated providers must share, directly or indirectly, substantial financial risk with respect to the provision of such items and services. They also must have at least a majority financial interest in the entity.

Medicare+ Choice Plan means health benefits offered under a policy, contract, or plan by a Medicare+Choice organization pursuant to a contract under section 1857.

Medicare+ Choice Private Fee-for-Service Plan means a plan that: reimburses hospitals, physicians, and other providers at a rate determined by the plan on a fee-for-service basis without placing the provider at financial risk; does not vary such rates for such a provider based on utilization relating to such provider; and does not restrict the selection of providers among those lawfully authorized to provide the covered services who agree to accept the terms and conditions of payment established by the plan.

MSA Plan means a Medicare+Choice plan that: provides required basic benefits only after the enrollee incurs countable expenses equal to an annual deductible (prescribed by section 1859(b)(3)(B)); counts as expenses for purposes of the deductible at least all amounts that would have been payable under Medicare Parts A and B, and that would have been payable by the enrollee as deductibles, coinsurance, or copayments if the enrollee had elected to receive benefits through Parts A and B; and provides, after the deductible is met for a year, for a level of reimbursement not less than 100% of such expenses, or 100% of the amounts that would have been paid (without regard to deductibles or coinsurance) under Medicare Parts A and B with respect to such expenses, whichever is less.

Protections Against Fraud: *Periodic Audits:* Pursuant to section 1857(d), the Secretary of Health and Human Services must provide for the annual audit of the financial records of at least one-third of the Medicare+Choice organizations offering Medicare+Choice plans. The audit is to include data relating to Medicare utilization, costs, and computation of the adjusted community rate. The Comptroller General is obliged to monitor the Secretary's audit activities.

To facilitate the audits, Medicare+Choice contracts must provide that the Secretary (or any person or entity designated by the Secretary) shall have the right to inspect or otherwise evaluate the quality, appropriateness, and timeliness of services performed under the contract. It also must provide for inspection and evaluation of the organization whenever there is reasonable evidence of some need for such inspection. Furthermore, the contract must provide that the Secretary has the right to audit and inspect any books and records of the Medicare+Choice organization that pertain to the ability of the organization to bear the risk of potential financial losses. The contract also must give the Secretary the right to review books and records that pertain to services performed or determinations of amounts payable under the contract.

Notice of Contract Termination: Each Medicare+Choice contract must require the organization to provide and pay for advance written notice of the contract's termination, as well as a description of alternatives for obtaining benefits under Medicare, to each enrollee of the organization.

Disclosures: In accordance with regulations of the Secretary, each Medicare+Choice organization must report financial information to the Secretary. That information must include:

1. Such information as the Secretary requires demonstrating that the organization is fiscally sound.

2. A copy of the report, if any, filed with the Centers for Medicare and Medicaid Services (CMS, formerly the Health Care Financing Administration) under section 1124, 42 U.S.C.A. 1320a-3, which pertains to disclosure of ownership of health care entities and related ownership and control information. [See section 4:7 for an analysis of section 1124.]

3. A description of transactions, as specified by the Secretary, between the organization and a party in interest. That includes:

   a. Any sale or exchange or leasing of any property between the organization and a party in interest.

   b. Any furnishing for consideration of goods, services (including management services), or facilities between the organization and a party in interest. That does not include salaries paid to employees for services provided in the normal course of their employment, or health services provided to members by hospitals and other providers, or by staff, medical groups, individual practice associations, or any combination thereof.

   c. Any lending of money or other extension of credit between an organization and party in interest.

The Secretary may require that information reported respecting an organization which controls, is controlled by, or is under common control with, another entity be in the form of a consolidated financial statement for the organization and such entity.

For these disclosure purposes, "party in interest" means any of the following:

1 Any director, officer, partner, or employee responsible for management or administration of a Medicare+Choice organization, any person who is directly or indirectly the beneficial owner of more than five percent of the equity of the organization, any person who is the beneficial owner of a mortgage, deed of trust, note, or other interest secured by, and valuing more than five percent of, the organization. (In the case of a non-profit corporation, "party in interest" includes an incorporator or member of such corporation under applicable State corporation law.)
2 Any entity in which a person described in 1 above is an officer or director or partner (if the entity is a partnership).
3 Any entity in which a person described in 1 above has, directly or indirectly, a beneficial interest of more than five percent of the equity.
4 Any entity in which a person described in 1 above has a mortgage, deed of trust, note, or other interest valuing more than five percent of the assets of such entity.
5 Any person directly or indirectly controlling, controlled by, or under common control with a Medicare+Choice organization.
6 Any spouse, child, or parent of a person described in 1 above.

A Medicare+Choice organization must disclose all of this information to its enrollees upon reasonable request.

With respect to loan information, a Medicare+Choice contract must require the Medicare+Choice organization to notify the Secretary of loans and other special financial arrangements made between the organization and subcontractors, affiliates, and related parties.

Additional Contract Terms: Section 1857(e) requires each Medicare+Choice contract to contain any other terms and conditions which the Secretary may find necessary and appropriate. In addition, the contract must require the organization to pay whatever fees the Secretary may establish to carry out the enrollment and dissemination of information required by section 1851, and to pay for the health insurance counseling and assistance program established by section 4360 of the Omnibus Budget Reconciliation Act of 1990.

Prompt Payment by Medicare+Choice Organizations: Section 1857(f) requires Medicare+Choice organizations to make prompt payment of claims submitted for services and supplies furnished to enrollees. This applies if the services or supplies are not furnished under a contract between the organization and the provider or supplier. It also applies if the claim is submitted to the organization by an enrollee of a private fee-for-service plan.

Prompt payment means payment consistent with the provisions of section 1816(c)(2), 42 U.S.C.A. 1395h(c)(2), and 1842(c)(2), 42 U.S.C.A. u(c)(2). Those provisions establish a prompt payment requirement for Medicare Part A and Part B benefits. In general, they require payment of 95% of all "clean claims" within 30 calendar days; otherwise interest must be paid on unpaid claim balances.

If the Secretary finds, after notice and opportunity for a hearing, that a Medicare+Choice organization has failed to make the required prompt payments, the Secretary may provide for direct payment of amounts owed to providers and suppliers, or to enrollees in private fee-for-service plans, for covered services and supplies. When that happens, the Secretary must provide for an appropriate reduction in the amount of payments otherwise made to the organization to reflect not only the amount of those direct payments, but also the Secretary's cost in making the direct payments.

Intermediate Sanctions: Pursuant to section 1857(g), if the Secretary makes any of the following determinations with respect to a Medicare+Choice organization, the Secretary may impose "intermediate sanctions":

1 The organization failed substantially to provide medically necessary items and services required to be provided to an enrollee under law or under the Medicare+Choice contract. This applies if the failure adversely affected, or has substantial likelihood of adversely affecting, the enrollee.

2 The organization imposed premiums on enrollees in excess of the amount of the Medicare+Choice monthly basic and supplemental beneficiary premiums permitted under section 1854.

3 The organization acted illegally to expel or to refuse to re-enroll an individual.

4 The organization engaged in any practice that would reasonably be expected to have the effect of denying or discouraging enrollment with the organization by eligible individuals whose medical condition or history indicates a need for substantial future medical services.

5 The organization misprepresented or falsified information furnished to the Secretary or to an individual or any other entity.

6 The organization failed to comply with section 1852(j)(3) or section 1852(k)(2)(A)(ii). Section 1852(j)(3) prohibits interference with advice from a health care professionals to enrollees. Section 1852(k)(2)(A)(ii) requires a Medicare+Choice organization to establish procedures to enforce balance billing limits for contract providers under a private fee-for-service plan.

7 The organization employed or contracted with an individual or entity excluded from participation under Medicare under section 1128, 42 U.S.C.A. 1320a-7, or section 1128A, 42 U.S.C.A. 1320a-7a, to provide health care, utilization review, medical social work, or administrative services. The same applies if the organization employed or contracted with any entity for the provision of such services (directly or indirectly) through an excluded individual or entity. [See sections 4:6 and 4:8 for analyses of section 1128 and 1128A.]

Remedies: If the Secretary makes any of the above determinations, then section 1857(g)(2) permits the Secretary to impose — in addition to any other remedy authorized by law — any of the following remedies (sanctions):

1 For any of the above determinations, a civil money penalty of not more than $25,000 for each determination.

2 For illegally acting to deny or discourage enrollment of an individual, or for making a misrepresentation of or falsifying information furnished to the Secretary, a civil money penalty of not more than $100,000 for each determination.

3 In addition, for imposing excessive premiums, a civil money penalty of double the excess charged. (That amount is to be deducted from the penalty and returned to the overcharged enrollee.)

4 In addition, for illegally acting to deny or discourage enrollment, a civil money penalty of $15,000 for each individual not enrolled as a result of the illegal act.

5 Suspension of enrollment of individuals after the date the Secretary notified the organization of a violation until the Secretary is satisfied that the basis for finding the violation has been corrected and is not likely to recur.

6 Suspension of payment to the organization for individuals enrolled after the date the Secretary notified the organization of a violation and until the Secretary is satisfied that the basis for finding the violation has been corrected and is not likely to recur.

Other Intermediate Sanctions: Pursuant to section 1857(g)(3), if the Secretary makes a determination to terminate a Medicare+Choice contract under section 1857(c)(2) [See section 2.26.1.], and if the basis for doing so is not a basis for imposing an intermediate sanction under section 1857(g)(1), then the Secretary may impose the following sanctions:

1 A civil money penalty of not more than $25,000 for each determination under section (c)(2) if the deficiency that is the basis for termination a contract has directly adversely affected an enrollee. The same applies if the basis for termination has the substantial likelihood of adversely affecting an enrollee.

2 A civil money penalty of not more than $10,000 for each week beginning after the initiation of civil money penalty procedures by the Secretary during which the deficiency exists.

3 Suspension of enrollment of individuals after the date the Secretary notifies the organization of the determination under (c)(2) and until the Secretary is satisfied that the deficiency has been corrected and is not likely to recur.

4 A civil money penalty of not more than $100,000, or such higher amount as the Secretary may establish by regulation, where the finding that an organization has failed to substantially carry out the contract is based on the organization's termination of its contract other than at a time and in a manner provided for by section 1857(a). [NOTE: Section 623(a) of the Medicare, Medicaid, and SCHIP Benefits Improvement and Protection Act of 2000, P.L. 106–554, enacted December 15, 2000, added this sanction. It applies to terminations occurring after December 21, 2000.]

Enforcement procedures in section 1128A (other than subsections (a) and (b) thereof, which pertain to other grounds for civil money penalties) apply to the civil money penalties authorized by section 1857(g)(2) and (3).

Statutory Provisions

Section 1857(d) establishes protection for beneficiaries and protection against fraud. It provides:

PROTECTIONS AGAINST FRAUD AND BENEFICIARY PROTECTIONS.—

(1) PERIODIC AUDITING.—The Secretary shall provide for the annual auditing of the financial records (including data relating to Medicare utilization, costs, and computation of the adjusted community rate) of at least one-third of the Medicare + Choice organizations offering Medicare + Choice plans under this part. The Comptroller General shall monitor auditing activities conducted under this subsection.

(2) INSPECTION AND AUDIT.—Each contract under this section shall provide that the Secretary, or any person or organization designated by the Secretary—

(A) shall have the right to inspect or otherwise evaluate (i) the quality, appropriateness, and timeliness of services performed under the contract, and (ii) the facilities of the organization when there is reasonable evidence of some need for such inspection, and

(B) shall have the right to audit and inspect any books and records of the Medicare + Choice organization that pertain (i) to the ability of the organization to bear the risk of potential financial losses, or (ii) to services performed or determinations of amounts payable under the contract.

(3) ENROLLEE NOTICE AT TIME OF TERMINATION.—Each contract under this section shall require the organization to provide (and pay for) written notice in advance of the contract's termination, as well as a description of alternatives for obtaining benefits under this title, to each individual enrolled with the organization under this part.

(4) DISCLOSURE.—

(A) IN GENERAL.—Each Medicare + Choice organization shall, in accordance with regulations of the Secretary, report to the Secretary financial information which shall include the following:

(i) Such information as the Secretary may require demonstrating that the organization has a fiscally sound operation.

(ii) A copy of the report, if any, filed with the Health Care Financing Administration containing the information required to be reported under section 1124 by disclosing entities.

(iii) A description of transactions, as specified by the Secretary, between the organization and a party in interest. Such transactions shall include —

(I) any sale or exchange, or leasing of any property between the organization and a party in interest;

(II) any furnishing for consideration of goods, services (including management services), or facilities between the organization and a party in interest, but not including salaries paid to employees for services provided in the normal course of their employment and health services provided to members by hospitals and other providers and by staff, medical group (or groups), individual practice association (or associations), or any combination thereof; and

(III) any lending of money or other extension of credit between an organization and a party in interest.

The Secretary may require that information reported respecting an organization which controls, is controlled by, or is under common control with, another entity be in the form of a consolidated financial statement for the organization and such entity.

(B) PARTY IN INTEREST DEFINED. — For the purposes of this paragraph, the term "party in interest" means —

(i) any director, officer, partner, or employee responsible for management or administration of a Medicare + Choice organization, any person who is directly or indirectly the beneficial owner of more than 5 percent of the equity of the organization, any person who is the beneficial owner of a mortgage, deed of trust, note, or other interest secured by, and valuing more than 5 percent of the organization, and, in the case of a Medicare + Choice organization organized as a nonprofit corporation, an incorporator or member of such corporation under applicable State corporation law;

(ii) any entity in which a person described in clause (i)—

(I) is an officer or director;

(II) is a partner (if such entity is organized as a partnership);

(III) has directly or indirectly a beneficial interest of more than 5 percent of the equity; or

(IV) has a mortgage, deed of trust, note, or other interest valuing more than 5 percent of the assets of such entity;

(iii) any person directly or indirectly controlling, controlled by, or under common control with an organization; and

(iv) any spouse, child, or parent of an individual described in clause (i).

(C) ACCESS TO INFORMATION.—Each Medicare + Choice organization shall make the information reported pursuant to subparagraph (A) available to its enrollees upon reasonable request.

(5) LOAN INFORMATION.—The contract shall require the organization to notify the Secretary of loans and other special financial arrangements which are made between the organization and subcontractors, affiliates, and related parties.

Additional contract requirements with respect to fees and enrollment counseling and other matters are set forth in section 1857(e). It provides:

ADDITIONAL CONTRACT TERMS.—

(1) IN GENERAL.—The contract shall contain such other terms and conditions not inconsistent with this part (including requiring the organization to provide the Secretary with such information) as the Secretary may find necessary and appropriate.

(2) COST-SHARING IN ENROLLMENT-RELATED COSTS.—

(A) IN GENERAL. — A Medicare + Choice organization shall pay the fee established by the Secretary under subparagraph (B).

(B) AUTHORIZATION. — The Secretary is authorized to charge a fee to each Medicare + Choice organization with a contract under this part that is equal to the organization's pro rata share (as determined by the Secretary) of the aggregate amount of fees which the Secretary is directed to collect in a fiscal year. Any amounts collected shall be available without further appropriation to the Secretary for the purpose of carrying out section 1851 (relating to enrollment and dissemination of information) and section 4360 of the Omnibus Budget Reconciliation Act of 1990 (relating to the health insurance counseling and assistance program).

(C) AUTHORIZATION OF APPROPRIATIONS. — There are authorized to be appropriated for the purposes described in subparagraph (B) for each fiscal year beginning with fiscal year 2001 an amount equal to $100,000,000, reduced by the amount of fees authorized to be collected under this paragraph for the fiscal year.

◆ NOTE: Section 522(a)(1) of the Medicare, Medicaid, and SCHIP Balanced Budget Refinement Act of 1999, as incorporated into the Omnibus Consolidated Appropriations Act, 2000, P.L. 106–113, enacted November 17, 1999, struck "Any amounts collected are authorized to be appropriated only for" and inserted "Any amounts collected shall be available without further appropriation to the Secretary for" in subparagraph (e)(2)(B). That applies to fees charged on or after January 1, 2001. According to section 522(b), the Secretary may not increase the fees charged for the 3-month period beginning with October 2000 above the level in effect during the previous 9-month period. Furthermore, section 522(a)(2) amended paragraph (C), which previously read: "(C) CONTINGENCY. — For any fiscal year, the fees authorized under subparagraph (B) are contingent upon enactment in an appropriations act of a provision specifying the aggregate amount of fees the Secretary is directed to collect in a fiscal year. Fees collected during any fiscal year under this paragraph shall be deposited and credited as offsetting collections." That change was effective November 29, 1999.

(D) LIMITATION. —In any fiscal year the fees collected by the Secretary under subparagraph (B) shall not exceed the lesser of—

(i) the estimated costs to be incurred by the Secretary in the fiscal year in carrying out the activities described in section 1851 and section 4360 of the Omnibus Budget Reconciliation Act of 1990; or

(ii)

(I) $200,000,000 in fiscal year 1998;

(II) $150,000,000 in fiscal year 1999;

(III) $100,000,000 in fiscal year 2000; and

(IV) the Medicare + Choice portion (as defined in subparagraph (E)) of $100,000,000 in fiscal year 2001 and each succeeding fiscal year.

◆ NOTE: Section 522(a)(3) of the Medicare, Medicaid, and SCHIP Balanced Budget Refinement Act of 1999, as incorporated into the Omnibus Consolidated Appropriations Act, 2000, P.L. 106–113, enacted November 17, 1999, struck "and" in (e)(2)(D)(ii)(II); struck "and each subsequent fiscal year.", and inserted "; and" in (III). That applies to fees charged on or after January 1, 2000. Section 522(a)(4) added subclause (IV) above and added subparagraph (e)(2)(E) below.

(E) MEDICARE+CHOICE PORTION DEFINED.—In this paragraph, the term "Medicare + Choice portion" means, for a fiscal year, the ratio, as estimated by the Secretary, of —

(i) the average number of individuals enrolled in Medicare + Choice plans during the fiscal year, to

(ii) the average number of individuals entitled to benefits under part A, and enrolled under part B, during the fiscal year.

With respect to the requirement for prompt payment of claims, section 1857(f) provides:

PROMPT PAYMENT BY MEDICARE + CHOICE ORGANIZATION.—

(1) REQUIREMENT. —A contract under this part shall require a Medicare + Choice organization to provide prompt payment (consistent with the provisions of sections 1816(c)(2)

and 1842(c)(2)) of claims submitted for services and supplies furnished to enrollees pursuant to the contract, if the services or supplies are not furnished under a contract between the organization and the provider or supplier (or in the case of a Medicare + Choice private fee-for-service plan, if a claim is submitted to such organization by an enrollee).

(2) SECRETARY'S OPTION TO BYPASS NONCOMPLYING ORGANIZATION. — In the case of a Medicare + Choice eligible organization which the Secretary determines, after notice and opportunity for a hearing, has failed to make payments of amounts in compliance with paragraph (1), the Secretary may provide for direct payment of the amounts owed to providers and suppliers (or, in the case of a Medicare + Choice private fee-for-service plan, amounts owed to the enrollees) for covered services and supplies furnished to individuals enrolled under this part under the contract. If the Secretary provides for the direct payments, the Secretary shall provide for an appropriate reduction in the amount of payments otherwise made to the organization under this part to reflect the amount of the Secretary's payments (and the Secretary's costs in making the payments).

With respect to the meaning of "prompt payment" for Medicare+Choice benefits similar to benefits under Medicare Part A, by cross-reference from section 1857(f), section 1816(c)(2), 42 U.S.C.A. 1395h(c)(2) provides:

(2)(A) Each agreement under this section shall provide that payment shall be issued, mailed, or otherwise transmitted with respect to not less than 95 percent of all claims submitted under this title —

(i) which are clean claims, and

(ii) for which payment is not made on a periodic interim payment basis, within the applicable number of calendar days after the date on which the claim is received.

(B) In this paragraph:

(i) The term "clean claim" means a claim that has no defect or impropriety (including any lack of any required substantiating documentation) or particular circumstance requiring special treatment that prevents timely payment from being made on the claim under this title.

(ii) The term "applicable number of calendar days" means—

(I) with respect to claims received in the 12-month period beginning October 1, 1986, 30 calendar days,

(II) with respect to claims received in the 12-month period beginning October 1, 1987, 26 calendar days,

(III) with respect to claims received in the 12-month period beginning October 1, 1988, 25 calendar days, and

(IV) with respect to claims received in the 12-month period beginning October 1, 1989, and claims received in any succeeding 12-month period ending on or before September 30, 1993, 24 calendar days.

(V) with respect to claims received in the 12-month period beginning October 1, 1993, and claims received in any succeeding 12-month period, 30 calendar days.

(C) If payment is not issued, mailed, or otherwise transmitted within the applicable number of calendar days (as defined in clause (ii) of subparagraph (B)) after a clean claim (as defined in clause (i) of such subparagraph) is received from a hospital, critical access hospital, skilled nursing facility, home health agency, hospice program, comprehensive outpatient rehabilitation facility, or rehabilitation agency that is not receiving payments on a periodic interim payment basis with respect to such services, interest shall be paid at the rate used for purposes of section 3902(a) of title 31, United States Code (relating to interest penalties for failure to make prompt payments) for the period beginning on the day after the required payment date and ending on the date on which payment is made.

With respect to the meaning of "prompt payment"" for Medicare+Choice benefits similar to benefits under Medicare Part B, by cross-reference from section 1857(f), section 1842(c)(2), 42 U.S.C.A. 1395u(c)(2) provides:

(2)(A) Each contract under this section which provides for the disbursement of funds, as described in subsection (a)(1)(B), shall provide that payment shall be issued, mailed, or otherwise transmitted with respect to not less than 95 percent of all claims submitted under this part —

(i) which are clean claims, and

(ii) for which payment is not made on a periodic interim payment basis, within the applicable number of calendar days after the date on which the claim is received.

(B) In this paragraph:

(i) The term "clean claim" means a claim that has no defect or impropriety (including any lack of any required substantiating documentation) or particular circumstance requiring special treatment that prevents timely payment from being made on the claim under this part.

(ii) The term "applicable number of calendar days" means —

(I) with respect to claims received in the 12-month period beginning October 1, 1986, 30 calendar days,

(II) with respect to claims received in the 12-month period beginning October 1, 1987, 26 calendar days (or 19 calendar days with respect to claims submitted by participating physicians),

(III) with respect to claims received in the 12-month period beginning October 1, 1988, 25 calendar days (or 18 calendar days with respect to claims submitted by participating physicians), and

(IV) with respect to claims received in the 12-month period beginning October 1, 1989, and claims received in any succeeding 12-month period ending on or before September 30, 1993, 24 calendar days (or 17 calendar days with respect to claims submitted by participating physicians).

(V) with respect to claims received in the 12-month period beginning October 1, 1993, and claims received in any succeeding 12-month period, 30 calendar days.

(C) If payment is not issued, mailed, or otherwise transmitted within the applicable number of calendar days (as defined in clause (ii) of subparagraph (B)) after a clean claim (as defined in clause (i) of such subparagraph) is received, interest shall be paid at the rate used for purposes of section 3902(a) of title 31, United States Code (relating to interest penalties for failure to make prompt payments) for the period beginning on the day after the required payment date and ending on the date on which payment is made.

The grounds for intermediate sanctions are set forth in section 1857(g)(1). It provides:

INTERMEDIATE SANCTIONS.—

(1) IN GENERAL. —If the Secretary determines that a Medicare + Choice organization with a contract under this section—

(A) fails substantially to provide medically necessary items and services that are required (under law or under the contract) to be provided to an individual covered under the contract, if the failure has adversely affected (or has substantial likelihood of adversely affecting) the individual;

(B) imposes premiums on individuals enrolled under this part in excess of the amount of the Medicare + Choice monthly basic and supplemental beneficiary premiums permitted under section 1854;

(C) acts to expel or to refuse to re-enroll an individual in violation of the provisions of this part;

(D) engages in any practice that would reasonably be expected to have the effect of denying or discouraging enrollment (except as permitted by this part) by eligible individuals with the organization whose medical condition or history indicates a need for substantial future medical services;

(E) misrepresents or falsifies information that is furnished—

(i) to the Secretary under this part, or

(ii) to an individual or to any other entity under this part;

(F) fails to comply with the applicable requirements of section 1852(j)(3) [which prohibits interference with advice from health care professionals to enrollees] or 1852(k)(2)(A)(ii) [which requires Medicare+Choice organizations to establish proecdures to enforce balance billing limits for contract providers under a private fee-for-service plan]; or

(G) employs or contracts with any individual or entity that is excluded from participation under this title under section 1128 or 1128A for the provision of health care, utilization review, medical social work, or administrative services or employs or contracts with any entity for the provision (directly or indirectly) through such an excluded individual or entity of such services; the Secretary may provide, in addition to any other remedies authorized by law, for any of the remedies described in paragraph (2).

Section 1857(g)(2) provides as follows with respect to those remedies:

REMEDIES. — The remedies described in this paragraph are —

(A) civil money penalties of not more than $25,000 for each determination under paragraph (1) or, with respect to a determination under subparagraph (D) or (E)(i) of such paragraph, of not more than $100,000 for each such determination, plus, with respect to a determination under paragraph (1)(B), double the excess amount charged in violation of such paragraph (and the excess amount charged shall be deducted from the penalty and returned to the individual concerned), and plus, with respect to a determination under paragraph (1)(D), $15,000 for each individual not enrolled as a result of the practice involved,

(B) suspension of enrollment of individuals under this part after the date the Secretary notifies the organization of a determination under paragraph (1) and until the Secretary is satisfied that the basis for such determination has been corrected and is not likely to recur, or

(C) suspension of payment to the organization under this part for individuals enrolled after the date the Secretary notifies the organization of a determination under paragraph (1) and until the Secretary is satisfied that the basis for such determination has been corrected and is not likely to recur.

Additional intermediate sanctions are set forth as follows in section 1857(g)(3):

OTHER INTERMEDIATE SANCTIONS. — In the case of a Medicare + Choice organization for which the Secretary makes a determination under subsection (c)(2) the basis of which is not described in paragraph (1), the Secretary may apply the following intermediate sanctions:

(A) Civil money penalties of not more than $25,000 for each determination under subsection (c)(2) if the deficiency that is the basis of the determination has directly adversely affected (or has the substantial likelihood of adversely affecting) an individual covered under the organization's contract.

(B) Civil money penalties of not more than $10,000 for each week beginning after the initiation of civil money penalty procedures by the Secretary during which the deficiency that is the basis of a determination under subsection (c)(2) exists.

(C) Suspension of enrollment of individuals under this part after the date the Secretary notifies the organization of a determination under subsection (c)(2) and until the Secretary is satisfied that the deficiency that is the basis for the determination has been corrected and is not likely to recur.

(D) Civil monetary penalties of not more than $100,000, or such higher amount as the Secretary may establish by regulation, where the finding under subsection (c)(2)(A) is based on the organization's termination of its contract under this section other than at a time and in a manner provided for under subsection (a). [NOTE: Section 623(a) of the Medicare, Medicaid, and SCHIP Benefits Improvement and Protection Act of 2000, P.L. 106–554, enacted December 15, 2000, added this sanction. It applies to terminations on or after December 21, 2000.]

Section 1857(g)(4) provides as follows with respect to procedures:

CIVIL MONEY PENALTIES. — The provisions of section 1128A (other than subsections (a) and (b)) shall apply to a civil money penalty under paragraph (2) or (3) in the same manner as they apply to a civil money penalty or proceeding under section 1128A(a).

For regulatory citations, see Chapter 6

§ 2:27 FAILURE BY PRIMARY PAYERS TO COMPLY WITH MEDICARE SECONDARY PAYER REQUIREMENTS — Section 1862(b) [42 U.S.C.A. 1395y(b)]

Summary

◆ NOTE: Effective December 19, 1989, sections 6202(a)(2), 6202(b)(1)(A), and 6202(e)(1) of P.L. 101-239, the Omnibus Budget Reconciliation Act of 1989 (OBRA 89), substantially revised the law which establishes Medicare as the secondary payer for medical expenses incurred by Medicare beneficiaries who have other resources to pay for health care. Additional changes were made by P.L. 103-66, the Omnibus Budget Reconciliation Act of 1993 (OBRA 93). See former Chapter II-23-A in Appendix H for a discussion of the law prior to OBRA 89.

Applicability of Medicare Secondary Payer Requirements Prior to OBRA 93 — Beneficiary Status Based on Age: Section 1862(b)(1)(A)(i), 42 U.S.C.A. 1395y(b)(1)(A)(i), provided that with respect to any item or service furnished to any individual 65 or older covered by a group health plan by reason of current employment of either the individual or the individual's spouse, such a plan may not take into account that individual's entitlement to Medicare benefits based upon age. (See section 226(a) of the Social Security Act, 42 U.S.C.A. 406(a), which governs Medicare entitlement based on age.) Furthermore, such plans had to provide employees, and their spouses 65 or older, the same benefits they provide to other employees and spouses.

Applicability of Medicare Secondary Payer Requirements after OBRA 93 — Regardless of Medicare Eligibility: A group health plan must provide the same benefits for any individual age 65 or over, and for the spouse age 65 or older of any individual, who has current employment status. That applies regardless of their eligibility for Medicare. Furthermore, the plan must do so under the same conditions as for any such individual or spouse with current employment status who is under age 65. See section 1862(b)(1)(A)(i), as amended by section 13561(e)(1)(A) of OBRA 93, effective August 10, 1993, and as amended by section 151(c)(1) of the Social Security Act Amendments of 1994, P.L. 103–432, effective as if included in OBRA 93.

Group Health Plans Excluded from Medicare Secondary Payer Requirements Prior to and after OBRA 93: Prior to revision by OBRA 93, section 1862(b)(1)(A)(ii) excluded from Medicare secondary payer requirements group health plans which are not sponsored by or contributed to by an employer that has 20 or more employees for each working day in each of 20 or more calendar weeks in either the current or the preceding calendar year.

Pursuant to section 13561(e)(1)(B) of OBRA 93, effective August 10, 1993, section 1862(b)(1)(A)(ii) excludes from those requirements a group health plan which is a plan of, or contributed to by, an employer or employee organization that has 20 or more individuals in current employment status for each working day in each of 20 or more calendar weeks in the current calendar year or the preceding calendar year.

Optional Exclusion of Individuals Enrolled in a Multi-employer or Multiple Employer Group Health Plan: Section 1862(b)(1)(A)(iii) excludes from Medicare secondary payer requirements individuals enrolled in a multi-employer or multiple employer group health plan. That applies if coverage of the individuals under the plan derives from current employment status (as opposed to "employment" in the pre-OBRA 93 version) with an employer that does not have 20 or more individuals in current employment status (as opposed to "employees" in the pre-OBRA 93 version) for each working day in each of 20 or more calendar weeks in either the current or the preceding calendar year. This exclusion is not mandatory; plans must elect to take advantage of it. Section 13561(e)(1)(C) of OBRA 93 made this change, effective August 10, 1993.

Applicability of Medicare Secondary Payer Requirements to Individuals with End Stage Renal Disease: Prior to OBRA 93, section 1862(b)(1)(A)(iv) excluded from Medicare secondary payer requirements items or services furnished in a month to an individual if for that month the individual is, or would upon application be, entitled to Medicare benefits based on end stage renal disease. (See section 226A of the Social Security Act, 42 U.S.C.A. 426(A), which governs Medicare entitlement based on end stage renal disease.)

As revised by OBRA 93, section 1862(b)(1)(A)(iv), in conjunction with section 1862(b)(1)(C), provides that a group health plan may not take into account that an individual is entitled to or eligible for Medicare as an individual with end stage renal disease during the

12-month period which begins with the first month the individual becomes entitled to Part A benefits, or if earlier, the first month the individual would have been entitled to Medicare because of end stage renal disease had he or she filed application for such benefits. Moreover, such a plan may not differentiate in the benefits it provides between such individuals and other individuals covered by the plan on the basis of the existence of end stage renal disease, the need for renal dialysis, or in any other manner. Presumably, after the 12-month duration requirement, the plan can take into account entitlement to Medicare on the basis of end stage renal disease. This change was made by section 13561(c)(2) of OBRA 93, effective August 10, 1993.

◆ NOTE: Prior to amendment by section 4203(c) of OBRA 90, effective November 5, 1990, the 12-month period began with the month in which a regular course of renal dialysis was initiated, or, in the case of an individual who received a kidney transplant, during the 12-month period beginning the first month in which he would be eligible for Part A benefits had he filed an application for them, whichever came earlier. With respect to items or services furnished on or after February 1, 1991, and before October 1, 1998, however, the duration is not 12 months, but 18 months. This deferral of the shorter requirement was extended from October 1, 1996, by section 13561(c)(1) of OBRA 93. The requirements for large group health plans with respect to disabled individuals apply to items and services furnished on or after January 1, 1987, and before October 1, 1998. Pursuant to section 4631(b) of the Balanced Budget Act of 1997, P.L. 105–33, however, the requirements apply to items and services furnished on or after January 1, 1987, and before August 5, 1997, the effective date of the Balanced Budget Act. In addition, section 4631(b) provided that for items and services furnished after August 5, 1997, the duration is extended to 30 months. That applies to durations beginning on or after 18 months before August 5, 1997.

◆ ***NOTE: The sunset date was changed from January 1, 1992, to January 1, 1995, by section 4203(b) of P.L. 101–508, the Omnibus Budget Reconciliation Act of 1990 (OBRA 90), effective November 5, 1990. Effective August 19, 1993, section 13561(b) of OBRA 93 extended the sunset date to 1998. Section 4631(a) of the Balanced Budget Act of 1997 repealed the sunset date, effective August 5, 1997.

Definition of Group Health Plan: For section 1862(b)(1)(A) purposes, section 1862(b)(1)(A)(v) provides that the term "group health plan" has the meaning given in section 5000(b)(1) of the Internal Revenue Code of 1986, 26 U.S.C.A. 5000(b)(1), and, pursuant to section 13561(e)(1)(D) of OBRA 93, without regard to section 5000(d) of the Code. As amended by OBRA 93, effective August 10, 1993, section 5000(b)(1) defines the term to include any plan (including a self-insured plan) of, or contributed to by, an employer (including a self-employed person), or employee organization to provide health care, directly or otherwise, to the employees, former employees, the employer, others associated or formerly associated with the employer in a business relationship, or their families. Employer does not, however, include a Federal or other governmental entity.

◆ ***NOTE: Prior to August 10, 1993 (and as amended by section 6202(b)(2) of OBRA 89), section 5000(b)(1) was less encompassing. It defined group health plan to include any plan of, or contributed to by, an employer (including a self-insured plan) to provide health care, directly or otherwise, to the employer's employees, former employees, or the families of such employees or former employees. Employer did not include a Federal or other governmental entity.

Applicability of Medicare Secondary Payer Requirement to Disabled Individuals: Prior to OBRA 93, with respect to disabled active individuals, section 1862(b)(1)(B)(i) provided that large group health plans may not take into account that an active individual is entitled to Medicare benefits based on disability. (See section 226(b) of the Social Security Act, 42 U.S.C.A. 226(b), which governs Medicare entitlement based on disability.)

As amended, large group health plans may not take into account that an individual (as opposed to an "active" individual, pre-OBRA 93), or a member of that individual's family who is covered under the plan by virtue of the individual's current employment status, is entitled to Medicare benefits under section 226(b) This change was made by section 13561(e)(1)(E) of OBRA 93, effective August 10, 1993.

Definition of Large Group Health Plan: Section 1862(b)(1)(B)(iv) provides that the term "large group health plan" has the meaning given in section 5000(b)(2) of the Internal Revenue Code of 1986, 26 U.S.C.A. 5000(b)(2), and pursuant to section 13561(e)(1)(G) of OBRA 93, without regard to section 5000(d) of the Code. As amended by OBRA 93, effective August 10, 1993, section 5000(b)(2) defines the term to include any plan of, or contributed to by, an employer or employee organization (including a self-insured plan) to provide health care, directly or otherwise, to the employees, former employees, the employer, others associated or formerly associated with the employer in a business relationship, or their families. It applies, however, only to such plans that cover employees of at least one employer that normally employed at least 100 employees on a typical business day during the previous calendar year.

That is what the law provided prior to August 10, 1993. To section 5000(b)(2), however, OBRA 93 added: (1) that employers treated as a single employer under section 52(a) or (b) of the Code would be treated as a single employer; (2) that employees of the members of an affiliated service group (as defined in section 414(m) of the Code) would be treated as employed by a single employer; and (3) that leased employees (as defined in section 414(n)(2) of the Code) would be treated as employees of the person for whom they performed services to the extent they were so treated under section 414(n).As before, employer does not include a Federal or other governmental entity.

Definition of Active Individual: Prior to amendment by section 13561(e)(1)(G) of OBRA 93, section 1862(b)(1)(B)(iv)(I) defined active individual to mean an employee (as may be defined in regulations), the employer, self-employed individual (such as the employer), an individual associated with the employer in a business relationship, or a member of the family of any of such persons. OBRA 93 deleted that definition effective August 10, 1993.

Employees of Religious Organizations: Section 1862(b)(1)(D) provides that for purposes of section 1862(b) an individual is not considered employed, or an employee, with respect to performance of services as a member of a religious order if such services are considered employment only by virtue of an election made by the religious order under section 3121(r) of the Internal Revenue Code of 1986, 26 U.S.C.A. 3121(r). The latter permits religious orders otherwise exempt from Social Security requirements to participate in the program. Pursuant to section 6202(e)(1) of OBRA 89, however, this provision applies to items and services furnished on or after October 1, 1989.

Aggregation Rules: Section 1862(b)(1)(E) provides that all employers treated as a single employer for purposes of section 52 of the Internal Revenue Code of 1986 shall be treated the same for Medicare secondary payer purposes. Moreover, all employees of the members of an affiliated service group, as defined in section 414(m) of the Code shall be treated as employed by a single employer for Medicare secondary payer purposes. Furthermore, leased employees, as defined in section 414(n) of the Code, shall be treated as employees of the person for whom they perform services to the extent they are so treated under that provision of the Code for Medicare secondary payer purposes. Section 13561(d)(1) and section 13561(e)(1)(H) of OBRA 93 made this effective 90 days after August 10, 1993, or November 8, 1993. That is consistent with the OBRA 93 changes to section 5000(b)(2) of the Code, discussed above.

Section 1862(B)(1)(E) also gives by definition current employment status with an employer to an individual who is an employee, or who is the employer, or who is an individual associated with employer in a business relationship. Moreover, by definition, the term "employer" includes a self-employed person.

Limitation on Liability: Pursuant to section 4633(b) of the Balanced Budget Act of 1997, effective August 5, 1997, a beneficiary who receives items or services for which benefits are incorrectly paid is not liable for repayment of such benefits unless the payment was made to the beneficiary.

Additional Private Health Care Coverage to Which Medicare is Secondary Payer: Having shifted some of the burden of health care coverage to the private sector in section 1862(b)(1), Congress went on to confirm Medicare as a secondary payer in even more instances in section 1862(b)(2).

Section 1862(b)(2)(A) provides that if payment has been made, or can reasonably be expected to be made promptly, for any item or service under a workmen's compensation law or plan of the United States or a State, or under an automobile or liability insurance policy or plan (including a self-insured plan), or under no-fault insurance, Medicare will not pay. The same is true with respect to items or services to the extent payment has been made for them, or can reasonably be expected to be made for them, by a group health plan or large group health plan under section 1862(b)(1). "Promptly" is left for regulations to define.

Conditional Prior Payment by Medicare: Section 1862(b)(2)(B)(i), as amended by section 151(b)(3)(B) of the Social

Security Act Amendments of 1994, effective October 31, 1994, provides for conditional prior payment by Medicare for any item or service to which subparagraph (A) applies. If a "primary plan" — that is, a group health plan or large group health plan, a workmen's compensation law or plan, an automobile or liability insurance policy or plan (including a self-insured plan), or no fault insurance — is obligated to pay for items or services furnished to a Medicare beneficiary, prior payment for such items or services by Medicare is statutorily conditioned on reimbursement to the appropriate Medicare trust fund. That applies when notice or other information is received that a primary plan either has paid or is required to pay pursuant to section 1862(b)(2)(A).

Effective October 31, 1994, if reimbursement is not made within 60 days after such notice or other information is received, the Secretary of Health and Human Services may charge interest beginning with the date the notice or other information is received. The interest rate is determined in accordance with regulations of the Secretary of the Treasury applicable to charges for late payments.

Medicare Recovery Rights/Subrogation: Pursuant to section 1862(b)(2)(B)(ii), to recover conditional Medicare payments, the United States may bring an action against any primary plan obligated to pay for an item or service.

Pursuant to section 4633(a) of the Balanced Budget Act of 1997, effective August 5, 1997, this action may be taken directly against the entity obligated to pay or against a third-party administrator(TPA). The United States may not recover from a TPA, however, if the TPA would not be able to recover the amount at issue from the employer or group health plan due to the insolvency or bankruptcy of the employer or group health plan, and if the TPA is not employed by or under contract with the employer or group health plan at the time the United States initiates recovery action.

If the United States prevails, it may recover double damages against the primary plan. Similarly, the United States may bring an action to recover conditional payments against any other entity (including any physician or provider) that has received payment from a primary plan with respect to the item or service. No mention is made of double damages in this situation.

In addition, the United States may join or intervene in any action related to events that gave rise to the need for the item or service for which a conditional Medicare payment was made. For example, the United States could join or intervene in a personal injury lawsuit.

Pursuant to section 1862(b)(2)(B)(iii), to the extent Medicare has paid for an item or service, the United States is statutorily subrogated to any right under section 1862(b) of an individual or any other entity to payment with respect to that item or service under a primary plan. Notwithstanding all those rights of the United States, the Secretary of Health and Human Services may waive in whole or in part provisions of section 1862(b)(2) on a case-by-case basis if the Secretary determines waiver is in Medicare's best interest. Furthermore, pursuant to section 151(a)(1)(C) of the Social Security Act Amendments of 1994, effective October 31, 1994, the Secretary may not fail to make a conditional payment solely on the ground that an individual failed to complete a questionnaire concerning the existence of a primary plan.

Finally, effective August 5, 1997, pursuant to section 4632(a) of the Balanced Budget Act of 1997, the United States may seek recovery of conditional payments only where the request for payment is submitted to the entity obligated to pay within the three-year period beginning on the date on which the item or service was furnished. This statute of limitations applies notwithstanding any other time limits that may exist for filing a claim under an employer group health plan.

Enforcement: Having established Medicare as the secondary payer in section 1862(b)(2), Congress enacted three provisions to enforce that status.

1. *Private Cause of Action:* Section 1862(b)(3)(A) authorizes a private cause of action for double damages when a primary plan fails to provide for primary payment or appropriate reimbursement as required by sections 1862(b)(1) and (b)(2)(A).
2. *Excise Tax:* Nonconforming group health plans are subject to an excise tax under section 5000 of the Internal Revenue Code of 1986, 26 U.S.C.A. 5000. Pursuant to section 5000(a), the tax is equal to 25 percent of the employer's or employee organization's expenses incurred during the calendar year for each group health plan to which the employer or employee organization contributes. Section 5000(c) defines a nonconforming group health plan as a group health plan or large group health plan that at any time during a calendar year does not comply with requirements of subparagraphs (A) and (C) or subparagraph (B), respectively, of section 1862(b)(1).
3. *Civil Money Penalty for Prohibited Incentives:* Section 4204(g) of OBRA 90 added a new paragraph (C) to section 1862(b)(3)

> which makes it unlawful for employers or other entities to offer financial or other incentives to Medicare beneficiaries either not to enroll in a group health plan or larger group health plan or to terminate enrollment under a group health plan or larger group health plan which would otherwise be a primary plan for purposes of section 1862(b)(2)(A). An exception applied, prior to amendment by section 147(b)(7)(A)-(C) of the Social Security Act Amendments of 1994, when the incentive was also offered to all individuals eligible under the group health plan. Effective November 5, 1990, as if included in OBRA 90, however, that exception no longer applies and the prohibition applied to group health plans and larger group health plans as well.

Any entity violating this prohibition is subject to a civil money penalty not to exceed $5,000 for each violation. This applies to incentives offered on or after November 5, 1990. Enforcement procedures are governed by section 1128A, 42 U.S.C.A. 1320a-7a, which authorizes civil money penalties for a variety of offenses.

Coordination of Benefits: To deal with situations where payment by a primary plan is legitimately less than the charge for an item or service and is not payment in full, section 1862(b)(4) provides for coordination of benefits. In such cases, Medicare will pay for the remainder of such a charge without regard to Medicare deductibles and coinsurance. Such payment is limited, however, to an amount which does not exceed what Medicare would pay if a primary plan had no obligation to pay. Furthermore, with respect to items or services paid for under Medicare on a reasonable cost (or other cost-related basis), payment by Medicare, when combined with the amount payable under the primary plan, may not exceed what Medicare would pay on such a basis. Nor may it exceed Medicare limits on costs for inpatient hospital services imposed by section 1886, 42 U.S.C.A. 1395ww, which established the Prospective Payment System based on Diagnosis Related Groups.

With respect to items or services paid for by Medicare on some other basis, such as a fee schedule, payment under section 1862(b) is limited to the amount which would be payable under the primary plan without regard to the plans deductibles and coinsurance, or the reasonable charge or other amount payable under Medicare, whichever is greater.

IRS/Medicare/Social Security Coordination for Enforcement: To help ascertain situations where Medicare should be the secondary payer, section 1862(b)(5)(A) provides for the Commissioner of Social Security to transmit to the Secretary of the Treasury a list of the names and taxpayer identifying numbers of Medicare beneficiaries, as defined in section 6103(l)(12) of the Internal Revenue Code of 1986, 26 U.S.C.A. 6103(l)(12), and to request from the Secretary of the Treasury information described in section 6103(l)(12)(A). That information includes available filing status and taxpayer identity information from individual master files of the Internal Revenue Service relating to whether any Medicare beneficiary identified by the Commissioner was a married individual for any specified year after 1986, and, if so the name of the spouse of such individual and such spouse's taxpayer identifying number. The Commissioner must make this request not less often than annually.

Then the Administrator of the Centers for Medicare and Medicaid Services (CMS, formerly the Health Care Financing Administration) must request not less often than annually that the Commissioner of the Social Security Administration disclose to him information described in section 6103(l)(12)(B). That includes:

(1) the name and taxpayer identifying number of each Medicare beneficiary identified as having received wages from a qualified employer in a previous year;
(2) for each identified married Medicare beneficiary whose spouse is identified as having receiving wages from a qualified employer in a previous year, the name and taxpayer identifying number of the Medicare beneficiary and the spouse; and
(3) with respect to each such qualified employer, the name, address, and taxpayer identifying number of the employer, and the number of individuals with respect to whom written statements were furnished under section 6051, 26 U.S.C.A. 6051 (which pertains to wages and tax withholdings), by the employer with respect to such previous year.

Once that is accomplished, section 1862(b)(5)(B) requires the Administrator to disclose that information to Medicare intermediaries and carriers (or to a single intermediary or carrier designated by the Secretary of Health and Human Services), all to further the purposes of section 1862(b) and make Medicare the secondary payer.

Statutory Provisions

Section 1862(b), 42 U.S.C.A. 1395(y)(b), provides in pertinent part:

MEDICARE AS SECONDARY PAYER. —

(1) REQUIREMENTS OF GROUP HEALTH PLANS. —

(A) WORKING AGED UNDER GROUP HEALTH PLAN. —

(i) IN GENERAL. — A group health plan —

(I) may not take into account that an individual (or the individual's spouse) who is covered under the plan by virtue of the individual's current employment status with an employer is entitled to benefits under this title under section 226(a) [42 U.S.C.A. 446(a), which provides for Medicare benefits], and

(II) shall provide that any individual age 65 or over (and the spouse age 65 or older of any individual) who has current employment status with an employer shall be entitled to the same benefits under the plan under the same conditions as any such individual (or spouse) under age 65).

◆ NOTE: Section 1862(b)(1)(A)(i)(II) was changed by section 151(c)(1) of the Social Security Act Amendments of 1994, P.L. 103-432, effective August 10, 1993, as if enacted by OBRA 93. Previously, it read: "shall provide that any individual age 65 or over (and the individual's spouse age 65 or older) who is covered under the plan by virtue of the individual's current employment status with an employer shall be entitled to the same benefits under the plan under the same conditions as any such individual (or spouse) under age 65."

Prior to amendment effective August 10, 1993, by section 13561(e)(1)(A) of P.L. 103-66, the Omnibus Budget Reconciliation Act of 1993 (OBRA 93), sections 1862(b)(1)(A)(i)(I) and (II) provided: "(I) may not take into account, for any item or service furnished to an individual 65 years of age or older at the time the individual is covered under the plan by reason of the current employment of the individual (or the individual's spouse), that the individual is entitled to benefits under this title under section 226(a), and (II) shall provide that any employee age 65 or older, and any employee's spouse age 65 or older, shall be entitled to the same benefits under the plan under the same conditions as any employee, and the spouse of such employee, under age 65."

(ii) EXCLUSION OF GROUP HEALTH PLAN OF A SMALL EMPLOYER. — Clause (i) shall not apply to a group health plan unless the plan is a plan of, or contributed to by, an employer or employee organization that has 20 or more individuals in current employment status for each working day in each of 20 or more calendar weeks in the current calendar year or the preceding calendar year.

◆ NOTE: Prior to amendment effective August 10, 1993, by section 13561(e)(1)(B) of OBRA 93, clause (ii) read: "(ii) EXCLUSION OF GROUP HEALTH PLAN OF A SMALL EMPLOYER.-Clause (i) shall not apply to a group health plan unless the plan is a plan of sponsored by or contributed to by an employer that has 20 or more employees for each working day in each of 20 or more calendar weeks in the current calendar year or the preceding calendar year."

(iii) EXCEPTION FOR SMALL EMPLOYERS IN MULTI-EMPLOYER OR MULTIPLE EMPLOYER GROUP HEALTH PLANS. — Clause (i) also shall not apply with respect to individuals enrolled in a multiemployer or multiple employer group health plan if the coverage of the individuals under the plan is by virtue of current employment status [Section 13561(e)(1)(C) of OBRA 93 substituted "current employment status" for "employment", effective August 10, 1993.] with an employer that does not have 20 or more individuals in current employment status [The same OBRA 93 section substituted "individuals in current employment status" for "employees" effective August 10, 1993.] for each working day in each of 20 or more calendar weeks in the current calendar year or the preceding calendar year; except that the exception provided in this clause shall only apply if the plan elects treatment under this clause.

(iv) EXCEPTION FOR INDIVIDUALS WITH END STAGE RENAL DISEASE. — Subparagraph C shall apply instead of clause (i) shall to an item or service furnished in a month to an individual if for the month the individual is, or (without regard to entitlement under section 226) would upon application be, entitled to benefits under section 226A. [42 U.S.C.A. 426A, which provides Medicare benefits for persons suffering end stage renal disease.]

◆ NOTE: Section 13561(c)(2) of OBRA 93, effective August 10, 1993, substituted "Subparagraph C shall apply instead of clause (i)" for "Clause (i) shall not apply" in (iv) above. It also added "(without regard to entitlement under section 226)".

(v) GROUP HEALTH PLAN DEFINED. — In this subparagraph, and subparagraph (C), the term "group health plan" has the meaning given such term in section 5000(b)(1) of the Internal Revenue Code of 1986, without regard to section 5000(d) of such Code. [The phrase "without regard to section 5000(d) of such Code" was added effective August 10, 1993, by section 13561(e)(1)(D) of OBRA 93.]

(B) DISABLED INDIVIDUALS IN LARGE GROUP HEALTH PLANS. —

(i) IN GENERAL. — A large group health plan (as defined in clause (iv) may not take into account that an individual (or a member of the individual's family) who is covered under the plan by virtue of the individual's current employment status with an employer is entitled to benefits under this title under section 226(b) [42 U.S.C.A. 426(b), which provides Medicare benefits for certain persons entitled to Social Security disability benefits].

◆ NOTE: Prior to amendment effective August 10, 1993, by section 13561(e)(1)(E) of OBRA 93, the heading of (B) above referred to disabled active individuals, and (i) read: "IN GENERAL. — A large group health plan (as defined in clause (iv)(II)) may not take into account that an active individual (as defined in clause (iv)(I)) is entitled to benefits under this title under section 226(b)."

(ii) EXCEPTION FOR INDIVIDUALS WITH END STAGE RENAL DISEASE. — Subparagraph (C) shall apply instead of clause (i) to an item or service furnished in a month to an individual if for the month the individual is, or (without regard to entitlement under section 226) would upon application be, entitled to benefits under section 226A. [Section 13561(c)(2) of OBRA 93, effective August 10, 1993, substituted "Subparagraph C shall apply instead of" for "Clause (i) shall not apply", and added "(without regard to entitlement under section 226)".]

(iii) SUNSET. — Clause (i) shall only apply to items and services furnished on or after January 1, 1987, and before October 1, 1998. [Section 4203(b) of OBRA 90 changed the latter date from January 1, 1992, to October 1, 1995, effective November 5, 1990. Section 13561(b) of OBRA 93, changed it again from October 1, 1995, to October 1, 1998, effective August 10, 1993.]

(iv) LARGE GROUP HEALTH PLAN DEFINED. — In this subparagraph, the term "large group health plan" has the meaning given such term in section 5000(b)(2) of the Internal Revenue Code of 1986 [26 U.S.C.A. 5000(b)(2)], without regard to section 5000(d) of such Code [26 U.S.C.A. 5000(d)].

◆ NOTE: Section 4631(a)(1) of the Balanced Budget Act of 1997, P.L. 105–33, replaced "clause (iv)" with "clause (iii)" in clause (1)(B)(I). It also redesignated former clause (iv) as (iii), and repealed former clause (iii). Prior to it repeal, clause (iii) read: "SUNSET. ? Clause (I) shall only apply to items and services furnished on or after January 1, 1987, and before October 1, 1998." Previously, section 4203(b) of OBRA 90 had changed the latter date from January 1, 1992, to October 1, 1995, effective November 5, 1990. Section 13561(b) of OBRA 93, changed it again from October 1, 1995, to October 1, 1998, effective August 10, 1993.

◆ NOTE: Prior to amendment by section 13561(e)(1)(G) of OBRA 93, effective August 10, 1993, (iv) above read: "(iv) DEFINITIONS. —In this subparagraph: (I) ACTIVE INDIVIDUAL. — The term 'active individual' means an employee (as may be defined in regulations), the employer, self-employed individual (such as the employer), an individual associated with the employer in a business relationship, or a member of the family of any of such persons. (II) LARGE GROUP HEALTH PLAN. —The term 'large group health plan' has the meaning given such term in section 5000(b)(2) of the Internal Revenue Code of 1986.

(C) INDIVIDUALS WITH END STAGE RENAL DISEASE. — A group health plan (as defined in subparagraph (A)(v)) —

(i) may not take into account that an individual is entitled to or eligible for benefits under this title under section 226A during the 12-month period which begins with the first month in which the individual becomes entitled to benefits under part A under the provisions of section 226A, or, if earlier, the first month in which the individual would have been entitled to benefits under such part under the provisions of section 226A if the individual had filed an application for such benefits; and

(ii) may not differentiate in the benefits it provides between individuals having end stage renal disease and other individuals covered by such plan on the basis of the existence of end stage renal disease, the need for renal dialysis, or in any other manner;

except that clause (ii) shall prohibit a plan from paying benefits secondary to this title when [NOTE: prior to amendment by section 151(c)(5) of the Social Security Act Amendments of 1994, effective December 19, 1989, as if included in OBRA 89, the preceding phrase read "shall prohibit a plan from taking into account that"] an individual is entitled to or eligible for benefits under this title under section 226A after the end of the 12 month period described in clause (i). Effective for items and services furnished on or after February 1, 1991, and before the enactment of the Balanced Budget Act of 1997, (with respect to period periods beginning on or after February 1, 1990), this subparagraph shall be applied by substituting “18-month” for “12-month” each place it appears. Effective for items and services furnished on or after the date of enactment of the Balanced Budget Act of 1997, (with respect to periods beginning on or after the date that is 18 months prior to such date), clauses (i) and (ii) shall be applied by substituting “30-month” for “12-month” each place it appears.

◆ NOTE: Section 4631(b) of the Balanced Budget Act of 1997, added the last sentence to section 1862(b)(1)(C). It also amended the next to the last sentence therein, which previously read:

"Effective for items and services furnished on or after February 1, 1991 and before October 1, 1998, (with respect to periods beginning on or after February 1, 1990), this paragraph shall be applied by substituting "18-month" for "12-month" each place it appears."

Prior to those changes, the first sentence above beginning "Effective for items and services" had been added by section 4203(c)(1)(B) of OBRA 90, effective November 5, 1990. Furthermore, section 151(c)(5) of the Social Security Act Amendments of 1994 substituted the phrase "this paragraph" for the phrase "clauses (I) and (ii)", effective as if included in OBRA 90. Prior to amendment by section 4203(c) of OBRA 90, also effective November 5, 1990, section 1862(b)(1)(C)(I) read: "may not take into account that an individual is entitled to benefits under this title solely by reason of section 226A during the 12-month period which begins with the earlier of ? (I) the month in which a regular course of renal dialysis is initiated, or (II) in the case of an individual who receives a kidney transplant, the first month in which he would be eligible for benefits under part A (if he had filed an application for such benefits) under the provisions of section 226A(b)(1)(B); and".

◆ NOTE ALSO: Section 13561(c)(1) of OBRA 93, effective August 10, 1993, inserted the phrase "or eligible for" after "entitled to" where it appears twice in (C) above; deleted the phrase "solely by reason of" after "benefits under this title" where it appeared twice in (C) above; and changed the effective dates from "February 1, 1991, and on or before January 1, 1996".

(D) TREATMENT OF CERTAIN MEMBERS OF RELIGIOUS ORDERS. — In this subsection, [applicable, pursuant to section 6202(e)(1) of OBRA 89, to items and services furnished on or after October 1, 1989] an individual shall not be considered to be employed, or an employee, with respect to the performance of services as a member of a religious order which are considered employment only by virtue of an election made by the religious order under section 3121(r) of the Internal Revenue Code of 1986 [26 U.S.C.A. 3121(r), which permits religious orders to elect to participate in Social Security].

(E) GENERAL PROVISIONS. — For purposes of this subsection:

(i) AGGREGATION RULES. —

(I) All employers treated as a single employer under subsection (a) or (b) of section 52 of the Internal Revenue Code of 1986 shall be treated as a single employer.

(II) All employees of the members of an affiliated service group (as defined in section 414(m) of such Code) shall be treated as employed by a single employer.

(III) Leased employees (as defined in section 414(n)(2) of such Code) shall be treated as employees of the person for whom they perform services to the extent they are so treated under section 414(n) of such Code.

In applying sections of the Internal Revenue Code of 1986 under this clause, the Secretary shall rely upon regulations and decisions of the Secretary of the Treasury respecting such sections.

(ii) CURRENT EMPLOYMENT STATUS DEFINED. — An individual has "current employment status" with an employer if the individual is an employee, is the employer, or is associated with the employer in a business relationship.

(iii) TREATMENT OF SELF-EMPLOYED PERSONS AS EMPLOYERS. — The term "employer" includes a self-employed person.

(F) LIMITATION ON BENEFICIARY LIABILITY. — An individual who is entitled to benefits under this title and is furnished an item or service for which such benefits are incorrectly paid is not liable for repayment of such benefits under this paragraph unless payment of such benefits was made to the individual.

◆ NOTE: Effective 90 days after August 10, 1993, sections 13561(d)(1) and 13561(e)(1)(H) of OBRA 93 added paragraph (E) above. Section 4633(b) of the Balanced Budget Act of 1997 added paragraph (F), effective August 5, 1997.

(2) MEDICARE SECONDARY PAYER. —

(A) IN GENERAL. — Payment under this title may not be made, except as provided in subparagraph (B), with respect to any item or service to the extent that —

(i) payment has been made, or can reasonably be expected to be made, with respect to the item or service as required under paragraph (1), or

(ii) payment has been made or can reasonably be expected to be made promptly (as determined in accordance with regulations) under a workmen's compensation law or plan of the United States or a State or under an automobile or liability insurance policy or plan (including a self-insured plan) or under no fault insurance.

In this subsection, the term "primary plan" means a group health plan or large group health plan, to the extent that clause (i) applies, and a workmen's compensation law or plan, an automobile or liability insurance policy or plan (including a self-insured plan) or no fault insurance, to the extent that clause (ii) applies.

(B) REPAYMENT REQUIRED.—

(i) PRIMARY PLANS.—Any payment under this title with respect to any item or service to which subparagraph (A) applies shall be conditioned on reimbursement to the appropriate Trust Fund established by this title when notice or other information is received that payment for such item or service has been or could be made under such subparagraph. If reimbursement is not made to the appropriate Trust Fund before the expiration of the 60-day period that begins on the date such notice or other information is received, the Secretary may charge interest (beginning with the date on which the notice or other information is received) on the amount of the reimbursement until reimbursement is made (at a rate determined by the Secretary in accordance with regulations of the Secretary of the Treasury applicable to charges for late payments). [NOTE: Section 151(b)(3)(B) of the Social Security Act Amendments of 1994 changed heading (B) from "Conditional Payment" Section 151(b)(3)(A) of the Social Security Act Amendments of 1994 added the last sentence regarding interest charges. Both changes were effective October 31, 1994.]

(ii) ACTION BY UNITED STATES.—In order to recover payment under this title for such an item or service, the United States may bring an action against any entity which is required or responsible directly, as a third-party administrator, or otherwise) to make payment with respect to such item or service (or any portion thereof) under a primary plan (and may, in accordance with paragraph (3)(A) collect double damages against that entity), or against any other entity (including any physician or provider) that has received payment from that entity with respect to the item or service, and may join or intervene in any action related to the events that gave rise to the need for the item or service. The United States may not recover from a third-party administrator under this clause in cases where the third-party administrator would not be able to recover the amount at issue from the employer or group health plan and is not employed by or under contract with the employer or group health plan at the time the action for recovery is initiated by the United States or for whom it provides administrative services due to the insolvency or bankruptcy of the employer or plan. [NOTE: Section 4633(a) of the Balanced Budget Act of 1997, substituted the phrase "(directly, as a third-party administrator, or otherwise) to make payment" for the phrase "under this subsection to pay". It also added the sentence beginning "The United States may not recover." These changed became effective August 5, 1997.

(iii) SUBROGATION RIGHTS. — The United States shall be subrogated (to the extent of payment made under this title for such an item or service) to any right under this subsection of an individual or any other entity to payment with respect to such item or service under a primary plan.

(iv) WAIVER OF RIGHTS. — The Secretary may waive (in whole or in part) the provisions of this subparagraph in the case of an individual claim if the Secretary determines that the waiver is in the best interests of the program established under this title.

(v) CLAIMS-FILING PERIOD. — Notwithstanding any other time limits that may exist for filing a claim under an employer group health plan, the United States may seek to recover conditional payments in accordance with this subparagraph where the request for payment is submitted to the entity required or responsible under this subsection to pay with respect to the item or service (or any portion thereof) under a primary plan within the 3-year period beginning on the date on which the item or service was furnished. [NOTE: Clause (v) was added by section 4632(a) of the Balanced Budget Act of 1997, effective August 5, 1997.]

(C) TREATMENT OF QUESTIONNAIRES. — The Secretary may not fail to make payment under subparagraph (A) solely on the ground that an individual failed to complete a questionnaire concerning the existence of a primary plan. [NOTE: Section 151(a)(1)(C) of the Social Security Act Amendments of 1994 added section 1862(b)(2)(C), effective October 31, 1994.]

(3) ENFORCEMENT. —

(A) PRIVATE CAUSE OF ACTION. — There is established a private cause of action for damages (which shall be in an amount double the amount otherwise provided) in the case of a primary plan which fails to provide for primary payment (or appropriate reimbursement) in accordance with such paragraphs (1) and (2)(A).

(B) REFERENCE TO EXCISE TAX WITH RESPECT TO NONCONFORMING GROUP HEALTH PLANS. — For provision imposing an excise tax with respect to nonconforming group health plans, see section 5000 of the Internal Revenue Code of 1986 [26 U.S.C.A. 5000].

(C) PROHIBITION OF FINANCIAL INCENTIVES NOT TO ENROLL IN A GROUP HEALTH PLAN. — It is unlawful for an employer or other entity to offer any financial or other incentive for an individual entitled to benefits under this title not to enroll (or to terminate enrollment) under a group health plan which would (in the case of such enrollment) be a primary plan (as defined in paragraph (2)(A)), unless such incentive is also offered to all individuals who are eligible for coverage under the plan. Any entity that violates the previous sentence is subject to a civil money penalty of not to exceed $5,000 for each such violation. The provisions of section 1128(A) [42 U.S.C.A. 1320a-7a] (other than the first sentence of subsection (a) and other than subsection (b)) shall apply to a civil money penalty under the previous sentence in the same manner as such provisions apply to a penalty or proceeding under section 1128A(a). [NOTE: Section 157(b)(7)(A)-(C) of the Social Security Act Amendments of 1994 added the phrase "or a larger group health plan" after "a group health plan", and deleted the phrase "unless such incentive is also offered to all individuals who are eligible for coverage under the plan", which previously followed "paragraph (2)(A)". Those changes were effective November 5, 1990, as if included in OBRA 90.]

(4) COORDINATION OF BENEFITS. — Where payment for an item or service by a primary plan is less than the amount of the charge for such item or service and is not payment in full, payment may be made under this title (without regard to deductibles and coinsurance under this title) for the remainder of such charge, but —

(A) payment under this title may not exceed an amount which would be payable under this title for such item or service if paragraph (2)(A) did not apply; and

(B) payment under this title, when combined with the amount payable under the primary plan, may not exceed —

(i) in the case of an item or service payment for which is determined under this title on the basis of reasonable cost (or other cost-related basis) or under section 1886 [42 U.S.C.A. 1395ww, which imposes limits on payment for inpatient hospital services and established the Prospect Payment System based on Diagnostic Related Groups], the amount which would be payable under this title on such basis, and

(ii) in the case of an item or service for which payment is authorized under this title on another basis —

(I) the amount which would be payable under the primary plan (without regard to deductibles and coinsurance under such plan), or

(II) the reasonable charge or other amount which would be payable under this title (without regard to deductibles and coinsurance under this title),

whichever is greater.

(5) IDENTIFICATION OF SECONDARY PAYER SITUATIONS. —

(A) REQUESTING MATCHING INFORMATION. —

(i) COMMISSIONER OF SOCIAL SECURITY. — The Commissioner of Social Security shall, not less often than annually, transmit to the Secretary of the Treasury a list of the name and TINs of medicare beneficiaries (as defined in section 6103(l)(12) of the Internal Revenue Code of 1986) and request that the Secretary disclose to the Commissioner the information described in subparagraph (A) of such section.

(ii) ADMINISTRATOR. — The Administrator of the Health Care Financing Administration [now known as the Centers for Medicare and Medicaid Services (CMS)] shall request, not less often than annually, the Commissioner of the Social Security Administration to disclose to the Administrator the information described in subparagraph (B) of section 6103(l)(12) of the Internal Revenue Code of 1986.

(B) DISCLOSURE TO FISCAL INTERMEDIARIES AND CARRIERS. — In addition to any other information provided under this title to fiscal intermediaries and carriers, the Administrator shall disclose to such intermediaries and carriers (or to such a single intermediary or carrier as the Secretary may designate) the information received under subparagraph A for purposes of carrying out this subsection. NOTE: Prior to amendment by section 1(b)(1) of the Medicare/Medicaid Data Bank Elimination Act of 1996, P.L. 104–226, effective October 2, 1996, the clause beginning "under subparagraph A" read: "under — (i) subparagraph (A), and (ii) section 1144, for purposes of carrying out this subsection." Section 1144, 42 U.S.C.A. 1320b-14, established the Medicare and Medicaid coverage data bank effective August 10, 1993. See section 13581 of OBRA 93.

Section 5000 of the Internal Revenue Code of 1986, 26 U.S.C.A. 5000, as amended by Title XII, sections 13561(d)(3) and (e)(2)(A) of P.L. 103-66, effective August 10, 1993, provides:

CERTAIN GROUP HEALTH PLANS. —

(a) IMPOSITION OF TAX. — There is hereby imposed on any employer or employee organization that contributes to a nonconforming group health plan a tax equal to 25 percent of the employer's or employee organization's expenses incurred during the calendar year for each group health plan to which the employer or employee organization contributes.

(b) GROUP HEALTH PLAN AND LARGE GROUP HEALTH PLAN. — For purposes of this section —

(1) GROUP HEALTH PLAN. — The term "group health plan" means any plan (including a self-insured plan) of, or contributed to by, an employer (including a self-insured plan) to provide health care (directly or otherwise) to the employees, former employees, others associated or formerly associated with the employer in a business relationship, or their families.

◆ NOTE: Prior to amendment by OBRA 93, subparagraph (1) provided: (1) GROUP HEALTH PLAN. — The term "group health plan" means any plan of, or contributed to by, an employer (including a self-insured plan) to provide health care (directly or otherwise) to the employer's employees, former employees, or the families of such employees or former employees. (2) LARGE GROUP HEALTH PLAN. — The term "large group health plan" means a plan of, or contributed to by, an employer or employee organization (including a self-insured plan) to provide health care (directly or otherwise) to the employees, former employees, the employer, others associated or formerly associated with the employer in a business relationship, or their families, that covers employees of at least one employer that normally employed at least 100 employees on a typical business day during the previous calendar year. For purposes of the preceding sentence — (A) all employers treated as a single employer under subsection (a) or (b) of section 52 shall be treated as a single employer, (B) all employees of the members of an affiliated service group (as defined in section 414(m)) shall be treated as employed by a single employer, and (C) leased employees (as defined in section 414(n)(2)) shall be treated as employees of the person for whom they perform services to the extent they are so treated under section 414(n).

◆ NOTE: P.L. 103-66 added the foregoing sentence beginning "For purposes of the preceding sentence". (c) NONCONFORMING GROUP HEALTH PLAN. — For purposes of this section, the term "nonconforming group health plan" means a group health plan or large group health plan that at any time during a calendar year does not comply with the requirements of subparagraphs (A) and (C) or subparagraph (B), respectively, of section 1862(b)(1) of the Social Security Act. (d) GOVERNMENT ENTITIES. — For purposes of this section, the term "employer" does not include a Federal or other governmental entity.

Section 6103(l)(12) of the Internal Revenue Code of 1986, 26 U.S.C.A. 6103(l)(12), provides:

DISCLOSURE OF CERTAIN TAXPAYER IDENTITY INFORMATION FOR VERIFICATION OF EMPLOYMENT STATUS OF MEDICARE BENEFICIARY AND SPOUSE OF MEDICARE BENEFICIARY. —

(A) RETURN INFORMATION FROM INTERNAL REVENUE SERVICE. — The Secretary shall, upon written request from the Commissioner of Social Security, disclose to the Commissioner available filing status and taxpayer identity information from the individual master files of the Internal Revenue Service relating to whether any medicare beneficiary identified by the Commissioner was a married individual (as defined in section 7703 [26 U.S.C.A. 7703]) for any specified year after 1986, and, if so, the name of the spouse of such individual and such spouse's TIN.

(B) RETURN INFORMATION FROM SOCIAL SECURITY ADMINISTRATION. — The Commissioner of Social Security shall, upon written request from the Administrator of the Health Care Financing Administration [now known as the Centers for Medicare and Medicaid Services (CMS)], disclose to the Administrator the following information:

(i) The name and TIN of each medicare beneficiary who is identified as having received wages (as defined in section 3401(a)), above an amount (if any) specified by the Secretary of Health and Human Services, [the phrase beginning "above an amount" was added here and in (ii) below by sections 13561(a)(2)(A) and (B) of P.L. 103-66, effective August 10, 1993.] from a qualified employer in a previous year.

(ii) For each medicare beneficiary who was identified as married under subparagraph (A) and whose spouse is identified as having received wages, above an amount (if any) specified by the Secretary of Health and Human Services, from a qualified employer in a previous year—

(I) the name and TIN of the medicare beneficiary, and

(II) the name and TIN of the spouse.

(iii) With respect to each such qualified employer, the name, address, and TIN of the employer and the number of individuals with respect to whom written statements were furnished under section 6051 [26 U.S.C.A. 6051, which pertains to wages and tax withholdings] by the employer with respect to such previous year.

(C) DISCLOSURE BY HEALTH CARE FINANCING ADMINISTRATION [now known as the Centers for Medicare and Medicaid Services (CMS)]. — With respect to the information disclosed under subparagraph (B), the Administrator of the Health Care Financing Administration [CMS] may disclose —

(i) to the qualified employer referred to in such subparagraph the name and TIN of each individual identified under such subparagraph as having received wages from the employer (hereinafter in this subparagraph referred to as the "employee") for purposes of determining during what period such employee or the employee's spouse may be (or have been) covered under a group health plan of the employer and what benefits are or were covered under the plan (including the name, address, and identifying number of the plan),

(ii) to any group health plan which provides or provided coverage to such an employee or spouse, the name of such employee and the employee's spouse (if the spouse is a medicare beneficiary) and the name and address of the employer, and, for the purpose of presenting a claim to the plan —

(I) the TIN of such employee if benefits were paid under title XVIII of the Social Security Act with respect to the employee during a period in which the plan was a primary plan (as defined in section 1862(b)(2)(A) of the Social Security Act), and

(II) the TIN of such spouse if benefits were paid under such title with respect to the spouse during such period, and

(iii) to any agent of such Administrator the information referred to in subparagraph (B) for purposes of carrying out clauses (i) and (ii) on behalf of such Administrator.

(D) SPECIAL RULES. —

(i) RESTRICTIONS ON DISCLOSURE. — Information may be disclosed under this paragraph only for purposes of, and to the extent necessary in, determining the extent to which any medicare beneficiary is covered under any group health plan.

(ii) TIMELY RESPONSE TO REQUESTS. — Any request made under subparagraph (A) or (B) shall be complied with as soon as possible but in no event later than 120 days after the date the request was made.

(E) DEFINITIONS. — For purposes of this paragraph —

(i) MEDICARE BENEFICIARY. — The term "medicare beneficiary" means an individual entitled to benefits under part A, or enrolled under part B, of title XVIII of the Social Security Act, but does not include such an individual enrolled in part A under section 1818 [42 U.S.C.A. 1395i-2A, which, pursuant to section 6012(a)(2) of P.L. 101-239, the Omnibus Budget Reconciliation Act of 1989, provides hospital insurance benefits starting July 1990 for disabled individuals who have exhausted other entitlement].

(ii) GROUP HEALTH PLAN. — The term "group health plan" means any group health plan (as defined in section 5000(b)(1)).

(iii) QUALIFIED EMPLOYER. — The term "qualified employer" means, for a calendar year, an employer which has furnished written statements under section 6051 with respect to at least 20 individuals for wages paid in the year.

◆ NOTE: Section 6103(l)(12) was amended by OBRA 93, effective August 10, 1993, and by P.L. 103-182, effective December 8, 1993. Prior to amendment, subparagraphs (E) and (F) read as follows: (ii) GROUP HEALTH PLAN. — The term "group health plan" means — (I) any group health plan (as defined in section 5000(b)(1)), and (II) any large group health plan (as defined in section 5000(b)(2)). (iii) QUALIFIED EMPLOYER. — The term "qualified employer" means, for a calendar year, an employer which has furnished written statements under section 6051 with respect to at least 20 individuals for wages paid in the year. (F) TERMINATION. — Subparagraphs (A) and (B) shall not apply to — (i) any request made after September 30, 1991, and

(ii) any request made before such date for information relating to—(I) 1990 or thereafter in the case of subparagraph (A), or (II) 1991 or thereafter in the case of subparagraph (B).

◆ NOTE: Effective August 5, 1997, section 4631(c)(2) of P.L. 105–33 repealed paragraph (F), which read: "(F) TERMINATION. — Subparagraphs (A) and (B) shall not apply to — (i) any request made after September 30, 1998, and (ii) any request made before such date for information relating to — (I) 1997 or thereafter in the case of subparagraph (A), or (II) 1998 or thereafter in the case of subparagraph (B)."

For regulatory citations, see Chapter 6

§ 2:28 FAILURE BY EMPLOYERS TO COMPLY WITH MEDICARE SECONDARY PAYER REQUIREMENTS —Section 1862(b)(5)(C)(ii) [42 U.S.C.A. 1395y(b)(5)(C)(ii)]

Summary

◆ NOTE: Effective December 19, 1989, sections 6202(a)(2), 6202(b)(1)(A), and 6202(e)(1) of P.L. 101-239, the Omnibus Budget Reconciliation Act of 1989 (OBRA 89), substantially revised the law which establishes Medicare as the secondary payer for medical expenses incurred by Medicare beneficiaries who have other resources to pay for health care. See former II-2-A in Appendix H for a discussion of the law prior to OBRA 89. Refer to § 2:27 for a discussion of the Medicare secondary payer provisions as amended thereafter.

In general, Medicare must be the secondary payer for medical expenses incurred by certain working aged people, certain disabled individuals, and certain persons suffering end stage renal disease when they are covered by certain employment-related group health plans or large group health plans. The same applies for individuals entitled to reimbursement for medical expenses under a workers' compensation program, an automobile or liability insurance policy or plan, including a self-insured plan, or under no-fault insurance.

Section 1862(b)(2)(A), 42 U.S.C.A. 1395y(b)(2)(A), provides that if payment has been made, or can reasonably be expected to be made promptly, for any item or service under a workmen's compensation law or plan of the United States or a State, or under an automobile or liability insurance policy or plan (including a self-insured plan), or under no fault insurance, Medicare will not pay. The same is true with respect to items or services to the extent payment has been made for them, or can reasonably be expected to be made for them, by a group health plan or large group health plan under section 1862(b)(1). "Promptly" is left for regulations to define.

Conditional Prior Payment by Medicare: Section 1862(b)(2)(B)(i), as amended by section 151(b)(3)(B) of the Social Security Act Amendments of 1994, effective October 31, 1994, provides, however, for *conditional prior* payment by Medicare for any item or service to which subparagraph (A) applies. If a "primary plan" — that is, a group health plan or large group health plan, a workmen's compensation law or plan, an automobile or liability insurance policy or plan (including a self-insured plan), or no fault insurance — is obligated to pay for items or services furnished to a Medicare beneficiary, prior payment for such items or services by Medicare is statutorily conditioned on reimbursement to the appropriate Medicare trust fund. That applies when notice or other information is received that a primary plan either has paid or is required to pay pursuant to section 1862(b)(2)(A).

Effective October 31, 1994, if reimbursement is not made within 60 days after such notice or other information is received, the Secretary of Health and Human Services may charge interest beginning with the date the notice or other information is received. The interest rate is determined in accordance with regulations of the Secretary of the Treasury applicable to charges for late payments.

Medicare Recovery Rights/Subrogation: Pursuant to section 1862(b)(2)(B)(ii), to recover conditional Medicare payments, the United States may bring an action against any primary plan obligated to pay, or against a third party administrator in certain circumstances, for an item or service. If the United States prevails, it may recover double damages against the primary plan. Similarly, the United States may bring an action to recover conditional payments against any other entity (including any physician or provider) that has received payment from a primary plan with respect to the item or service. No mention is made of double damages in this situation. See 2:27 for more details.

In addition, the United States may join or intervene in any action related to events that gave rise to the need for the item or service for which a conditional Medicare payment was made. For example, the United States could join or intervene in a personal injury lawsuit.

Pursuant to section 1862(b)(2)(B)(iii), to the extent Medicare has paid for an item or service, the United States is statutorily subrogated to any right under section 1862(b) of an individual or any other entity to payment with respect to that item or service under a primary plan.

Notwithstanding all those rights of the United States, the Secretary of Health and Human Services may waive in whole or in part provisions of section 1862(b)(2) on a case-by-case basis if the Secretary determines waiver is in Medicare's best interest. Furthermore, pursuant to section 151(a)(1)(C) of the Social Security Act Amendments of 1994, effective October 31, 1994, the Secretary may not fail to make a conditional payment solely on the ground that an individual failed to complete a questionnaire concerning the existence of a primary plan.

Enforcement: Having established Medicare as the secondary payer in section 1862(b)(2), Congress enacted three provisions to enforce that status. One is a private cause of action for double damages when a primary plan fails to provide for primary payment or appropriate reimbursement when conditional prior payment by Medicare has been made. The second is an excise tax on nonconforming group health plans equal to 25 percent of an employer's or employee organization's expenses for each group health plan to which the employer or employee organization contributes. The third is a civil money penalty for prohibited incentives by employers or other entitities to induce Medicare beneficiaries either not to enroll in a group health plan or larger group health plan or to terminate such enrollment. See § 2:27.

IRS/Medicare/Social Security Coordination for Enforcement: To help ascertain situations where Medicare should be the secondary payer, section 1862(b)(5)(A) provides for the Commissioner of Social Security to transmit to the Secretary of the Treasury a list of the names and taxpayer identifying numbers of Medicare beneficiaries, as defined in section 6103(l)(12) of the Internal Revenue Code of 1986, 26 U.S.C.A. 6103(l)(12), and to request from the Secretary of the Treasury information described in section 6103(l)(12)(A). That information includes available filing status and taxpayer identity information from individual master files of the Internal Revenue Service relating to whether any Medicare beneficiary identified by the Commissioner was a married individual for any specified year after 1986, and, if so the name of the spouse of such individual, and such spouse's taxpayer identifying number. The Commissioner must make this request not less often than annually.

Then the Administrator of the Centers for Medicare and Medicaid Services (CMS, formerly the Health Care Financing Administration) must request not less often than annually that the Commissioner of the Social Security Administration disclose to him information described in section 6103(l)(12)(B). That includes:

(1) the name and taxpayer identifying number of each Medicare beneficiary identified as having received wages from a qualified employer in a previous year;

(2) for each identified married Medicare beneficiary whose spouse is identified as having receiving wages from a qualified employer in a previous year, the name and taxpayer identifying number of the Medicare beneficiary and the spouse; and

(3) with respect to each such qualified employer, the name, address, and taxpayer identifying number of the employer, and the number of individuals with respect to whom written statements were furnished under section 6051, 26 U.S.C.A. 6051 (which pertains to wages and tax withholdings), by the employer with respect to such previous year.

Once that is accomplished, section 1862(b)(5)(B) requires the Administrator to disclose that information to Medicare intermediaries and carriers (or to a single intermediary or carrier designated by the Secretary of Health and Human Services), all to further the purposes of section 1862(b) and make Medicare the secondary payer.

Enforcement of Mandatory Cooperation by Employers: In addition to the three enforcement provisions mentioned above, section 1862(b)(5)(C)(i) requires fiscal intermediaries and carriers to contact employers to determine the period an employee or employee's spouse may be or has been covered under a group health plan of the employer, as well as the nature of the coverage that is or was provided under the plan, including the name, address, and identifying number of the plan. This applies with respect to each individual who was furnished a written statement under section 6051 of the Internal Revenue Code of 1986 by a qualified employer (as defined in section 6103(l)(12)(D)(iii) of that Code) as disclosed to the intermediary or carrier under section 1862(b)(5)(B).

Then, pursuant to section 1862(b)(5)(C)(ii), such employers must within 30 days of receiving such an inquiry from an intermediary or carrier notify the intermediary or carrier respond to that inquiry. An employer other than a Federal or other governmental entity that willfully or repeatedly fails to provide timely and accurate notice in accordance with that requirement is subject to a civil money penalty not to exceed $1,000 for each individual with respect to which such an inquiry is made.

Enforcement procedures for this civil money penalty are governed by section 1128A, 42 U.S.C.A. 1320a-7a, which authorizes civil money penalties for a variety of offenses. This obligation does not apply to inquiries by intermediaries and carriers made after September 30, 1998. (Prior to enactment of section 13561(a)(1) of P.L. 103-66, the Omnibus Budget Reconciliation Act of 1993, the sunset date on this requirement was September 30, 1995.)

To facilitate the secondary payor screening process, section 1862(b)(5)(D), which was added by section 151(c)(6) of the Social Security Act Amendments of 1994, P.L. 103-432, effective October 31, 1994, obligates the Administrator of the CMS to mail questionnaires to individuals prior to their application for Part A benefits or their enrollment for Part B benefits. The questionnaires ask whether the individual is covered under a primary plan, the nature of the coverage provided, and the name, address, and identifying number of the plan.

Statutory Provisions

◆ NOTE: See § 2:27 for other provisions of section 1862(b).

Section 1862(b)(5) provides in pertinent part:

(C) CONTACTING EMPLOYERS. —

(i) IN GENERAL. — With respect to each individual (in this subparagraph referred to as an "employee") who was furnished a written statement under section 6051 of the Internal Revenue Code of 1986 [26 U.S.C.A. 6051, which pertains to wages and tax withholdings] by a qualified employer (as defined in section 6103(l)(12)(E)(iii) of such Code), as disclosed under subparagraph (B) [Section 13581(b)(1)(B) of OBRA 93, added "(i)" after "(B)", effective January 1, 1994; but section 1(b)(2) of the Medicare/Medicaid Data Bank Elimination Act of 1996, P.L. 104–226, deleted the "(i)", effective October 2, 1996. Section 151(c)(6) of the Social Security Act Amendments of 1994 changed the citation prior to "of such Code" from "6103(l)(12)(D)(iii)", effective December 19, 1989, as if included in OBRA 89.], the appropriate fiscal intermediary or carrier shall contact the employer in order to determine during what period the employee or employee's spouse may be (or have been) covered under a group health plan of the employer and the nature of the coverage that is or was provided under the plan (including the name, address, and identifying number of the plan).

(ii) EMPLOYER RESPONSE. — Within 30 days of the date of receipt of the inquiry, the employer shall notify the intermediary or carrier making the inquiry as to the determinations described in clause (i). An employer (other than a Federal or other governmental entity) who willfully or repeatedly fails to provide timely and accurate notice in accordance with the previous sentence shall be subject to a civil money penalty of not to exceed $1,000 for each individual with respect to which such an inquiry is made. The provisions of section 1128A (other than subsections (a) and (b)) shall apply to a civil money penalty under the previous sentence in the same manner as such provisions apply to a penalty or proceeding under section 1128A(a).

(iii) SUNSET ON REQUIREMENT. — Clause (ii) shall not apply to inquiries made after September 30, 1998. [This date was changed effective November 5, 1990, from 1991 to 1995 by section 4203(a)(1) of OBRA 90. It was changed by section 13561(a)(1) of OBRA 93 to 1998, effective August 10, 1993.]

NOTE: Section 4631(c)(1) of the Balanced Budget Act of 1997, P.L. 105–33 repealed former clause (iii), which established a sunset date. Prior to repeal it read: "(iii)SUNSET ON REQUIREMENT. — Clause (ii) shall not apply to inquiries made after September 30, 1998." This sunset date had been extended twice before. It was changed effective November 5, 1990, from 1991 to 1995 by section 4203(a)(1) of OBRA 90. Then it was changed by section 13561(a)(1) of OBRA 93 to 1998, effective August 10, 1993.

(D) OBTAINING INFORMATION FROM BENEFICIARIES. — Before an individual applies for benefits under part A or enrolls under part B, the Administrator shall mail the individual a questionnaire to obtain information on whether the individual is covered under a primary plan and the nature of the coverage provided under the plan, including the name, address, and identifying number of the plan.

◆ NOTE: Provisions of section 5000 of the Internal Revenue Code of 1986 are set forth in § 2:23.

For regulatory citations, see Part VI

§ 2:28.1 VIOLATION OF MEDICARE SECONDARY PAYOR SCREENING REQUIREMENTS BY PROVIDERS AND SUPPLIERS — Section 1862(b)(6) [42 U.S.C.A. 1395y(b)(6)]

Summary

◆ NOTE: Effective December 19, 1989, sections 6202(a)(2), 6202(b)(1)(A), and 6202(e)(1) of P.L. 101-239, the Omnibus Budget Reconciliation Act of 1989 (OBRA 89), substantially revised the law which establishes Medicare as the secondary payer for medical expenses incurred by Medicare beneficiaries who have other resources to pay for health care. See former § 2:23.1in Appendix H for a discussion of the law prior to OBRA 89. Refer to § 2:27 and § 2:28 for a discussion of the Medicare secondary payer provisions as amended thereafter.

In general, Medicare must be the secondary payer for medical expenses incurred by certain working aged people, certain disabled individuals, and certain persons suffering end stage renal disease when they are covered by certain employment-related group health plans or large group health plans and when they are entitled to reimbursement for medical expenses under a workers' compensation program, an automobile or liability insurance policy or plan, including a self-insured plan, or under no-fault insurance.

Making sure Medicare does not pay first involves gathering information from beneficiaries about other health care insurance which they may have. Accordingly, section 1862(b)(6) of the Social Security Act, 42 U.S.C.A. 1395y(b)(6), provides that no payment shall be made by Medicare for any item or service furnished under Part B unless the entity furnishing such item or service completes the portion of the Medicare claim form relating to the availability of other health benefit plans. Completion must be done to the best of the entity's knowledge and on the basis of information obtained from the individual to whom the item or service is furnished.

An entity that knowingly, willfully, and repeatedly fails to complete a claim form in accordance with those requirements, or that provides inaccurate information relating to the availability of other health benefit plans on a claim form, is subject to a civil money penalty not to exceed $2,000 for each such incident. Enforcement procedures for this civil money penalty are governed by section 1128A, 42 U.S.C.A. 1320a-7a, (other than subsections (a) and (b)).

Section 1862(b)(6) was enacted by section 151(a)(2)(A) of the Social Security Act Amendments of 1994, P.L. 103-432. It applies with respect to items and services furnished on or after expiration of the 120-day period beginning October 31, 1994 (March 1, 1995).

Statutory Provisions

Section 1862(b)(6) of the Social Security Act, 42 U.S.C.A. 1395y(b)(6), effective March 1, 1995, provides:

> SCREENING REQUIREMENTS FOR PROVIDERS AND SUPPLIERS.—
>
> (A) IN GENERAL. —Notwithstanding any other provision of this title, no payment may be made for any item or service furnished under part B unless the entity furnishing such item or service completes (to the best of its knowledge and on the basis of information obtained from the individual to whom the item or service is furnished) the portion of the claim form relating to the availability of other health benefit plans.
>
> (B) PENALTIES. —An entity that knowingly, willfully, and repeatedly fails to complete a claim form in accordance with subparagraph (A) or provides inaccurate information relating to the availability of other health benefit plans on a claim form under such subparagraph shall be subject to a civil money penalty of not to exceed $2,000 for each such incident. The provisions of section 1128A [42 U.S.C.A. 1320a-7a] (other than subsections (a) and (b)) shall apply to a civil money penalty under the previous sentence in the same manner as such provisions apply to a penalty or proceeding under section 1128A(a).

For regulatory citations, see Chapter 6

§ 2:29 PROHIBITION AGAINST PAYMENT TO INDIVIDUALS AND ENTITIES SANCTIONED UNDER THE SOCIAL SECURITY ACT — Section 1862(e) [42 U.S.C.A. 1395y(e)]

Summary

Much of section 1862, 42 U.S.C.A. 1395y, pertains to exclusions from coverage for which no Medicare payment may be made. This encompasses any items or services which, as stated in section 1862(a)(1)(A), are not reasonable and necessary for diagnosis or treatment. It also includes a long list of items and services for which Congress has determined not to pay under Medicare: for example, routine physical checkups and eyeglasses, orthopedic shoes and custodial care.

Determining not to pay for non-covered items and services is not a sanction, however, and it is important to distinguish that from the nonpayment sanction in section 1862(e), 42 U.S.C.A. 1395y(e). By that section's terms, no payment may be made with respect to any item or service (other than an emergency item or service) furnished by an individual or entity during the period when such individual or entity has been excluded under:

1. section 1128, 42 U.S.C.A. 1320a-7, which pertains to mandatory and permissive exclusions based upon convictions, inappropriate charges, or other abuses;
2. section 1128A, 42 U.S.C.A. 1320a-7a, which pertains primarily to civil money penalties but also provides for exclusions;
3. section 1156, 42 U.S.C.A. 1320c-4, which pertains to sanctions, including exclusions, recommended by peer review organizations (PRO's); or
4. section 1842(j)(2), 42 U.S.C.A. 1395u(j)(2), which also pertains to exclusions and civil money penalties.

Furthermore, no payment may be made under Medicare with respect to any item or service (other than an emergency item or service) furnished at the medical direction or on the prescription of a physician during the period when he or she is excluded pursuant to sections 1128, 1128A, 1156, or 1842(j)(2).

It seems obvious that persons or entities excluded from participation in Medicare would not be entitled to payment for services to

Medicare beneficiaries during the period of exclusion. Section 1862(e)(1) makes that doubly clear.

Pursuant to section 1862(e)(2), however, beneficiaries who receive bills from excluded individuals or entities and pay them may be reimbursed by Medicare when they did not know or have reason to know that the individual or entity had been excluded from Medicare under section 1128, section 1128A, section 1156, section 1160 (as in effect on September 2, 1982, which authorized exclusions recommended by Professional Standards Review Organizations (PSRO' s), forerunners of PRO's), section 1842(j)(2), section 1862(d) (as in effect the date of enactment of the Medicare and Medicaid Patient and Program Protection Act of 1987, which was another statutory basis for excluding persons and entities from Medicare), or section 1866, 42 U.S.C.A. 1395cc, which pertains to termination of provider agreements.

Statutory Provisions

Section 1862(e), 42 U.S.C.A. 1395y(e), provides:

> (1) No payment may be made under this title with respect to any item or service (other than an emergency item or service, not including items or services furnished in an emergency room of a hospital [", not including items or services furnished in an emergency room of a hospital" was added by section 6411(d)(2) of P.L. 101-239, the Omnibus Budget Reconciliation Act of 1989, effective December 19, 1989]) furnished —
>
> > (A) by an individual or entity during the period when such individual or entity is excluded pursuant to section 1128 [42 U.S.C.A. 1320a-7 which pertains to mandatory and permissive exclusions based upon convictions, inappropriate charges, or other abuses], 1128A [42 U.S.C.A. 1320a-7a, which pertains primarily to civil money penalties but also provides for exclusions], 1156 [42 U.S.C.A. 1320c-4, which pertains to sanctions, including exclusions, recommended by PRO's], or 1842(j)(2) [42 U.S.C.A. 1395u(j)(2), which also pertains to exclusions and civil money penalties] from participation in the program under this title; or
> >
> > (B) at the medical direction or on the prescription of a physician during the period when he is excluded pursuant to section 1128, 1128A, 1156, or 1842(j)(2) from participation in the program under this title and when the person furnishing

the item or service knew or had reason to know of the exclusion (after a reasonable time period after reasonable notice has been furnished to the person).

(2) Where an individual eligible for benefits under this title submits a claim for payment for items or services furnished by an individual or entity excluded from participation in the programs under this title, pursuant to section 1128, 1128A, 1156, 1160 (as in effect on September 2, 1982) [which authorized exclusions recommended by Professional Standards Review Organizations (PSRO's), forerunners of PRO's], 1842(j)(2), 1862(d) (as in effect on the date of the enactment of the Medicare and Medicaid Patient and Program Protection Act of 1987) [which was another statutory basis for excluding persons and entities from Medicare], or 1866 [42 U.S.C.A. 1395cc, which pertains to termination of provider agreements], and such beneficiary did not know or have reason to know that such individual or entity was so excluded, then, to the extent permitted by this title, and notwithstanding such exclusion, payment shall be made for such items or services. In each such case the Secretary shall notify the beneficiary of the exclusion of the individual or entity furnishing the items or services. Payment shall not be made for items or services furnished by an excluded individual or entity to a beneficiary after a reasonable time (as determined by the Secretary in regulations) after the Secretary has notified the beneficiary of the exclusion of that individual or entity.

For regulatory citations, see Chapter 6

§ 2:30 SPECIAL OBLIGATIONS REGARDING PACEMAKERS — Section 1862(h) [42 U.S.C.A. 1395y(h)]

NOTE: This sanction was repealed effective October 2, 1996 by section 1 of P.L. 104–224.

Summary

To help determine when Medicare payments properly may be made for cardiac pacemaker devices and leads, Congress required the Secretary of Health and Human Services to establish, via the Commissioner of the Food and Drug Administration, a registry of all cardiac pacemaker devices and pacemaker leads for which payment was made by Medicare. See section 1862(h)(1), 42 U.S.C.A. 1395y(h)(1).

The registry must include the manufacturer, the model, and serial number of each such device or lead, the name of the recipient thereof, the date and location of the implantation or removal of the device or lead, the name of the physician implanting or removing either, the name of the hospital or other provider billing for the procedure, any express or implied warranties covering the device or lead, whether under contract or by State law, as well as any amount paid to a provider under any such warranty, and such other information as the Secretary deems appropriate.

This information must be provided by the physician or provider performing the implantation or replacement.

◆ NOTE: In addition, any person or organization may provide information to the registry about cardiac pacemaker devices and leads which are not paid for by Medicare.

The stated purpose for the registry is to assist the Secretary in determining when payments may properly be made under Medicare, in tracing the performance of cardiac pacemaker devices and leads, in determining when inspection by the manufacturer thereof may be necessary, in determining the amount subject to repayment when devices have been replaced, and in carrying out studies with respect to the use of such devices and leads.

Pursuant to section 1862(h)(2), the Secretary may require a provider to return to the manufacturer for testing any pacemaker device or lead which is removed from a patient if Medicare paid for implantation or replacement of the device or lead. Providers failing to do so may not charge an affected beneficiary for a replacement and must make repayment to the Secretary for amounts previously paid by Medicare. The Secretary also may require manufacturers of pacemaker devices and leads to test them when they have been returned and to report to providers involved in the return about the results of the test.

In addition, with respect to the implantation or replacement of a pacemaker device or lead of a manufacturer by a physician and provider of services, the Secretary may deny payment in whole or in part and for such period of time as he deems appropriate if he determines that the physician or provider failed to submit required information to the Food and Drug Administration's pacemaker registry, or that the provider failed to return devices and leads to the manufacturer as required, violated the prohibition against charging beneficiaries, or failed to make repayment to the Secretary as required.

The Secretary also may deny payment in whole or in part and for such period of time as he deems appropriate if he determines that a manufacturer has failed to perform and to report on the testing of returned devices and leads as required.

Statutory Provisions

Section 1862(h)(1), 42 U.S.C.A. 1396y(h)(1), provides as follows with regard to the required central registry of cardiac pacemaker devices and pacemaker leads paid for by Medicare:

> (A) The Secretary shall, through the Commissioner of the Food and Drug Administration, provide for a registry of all cardiac pacemaker devices and pacemaker leads for which payment was made under this title.
>
> (B) Such registry shall include the manufacturer, model, and serial number of each such device or lead, the name of the recipient of such device or lead, the date and location of the implantation or removal of the device or lead, the name of the physician implanting or removing such device or lead, the name of the hospital or other provider billing for such procedure, any express or implied warranties associated with such device or lead under contract or State law (and any amount paid to a provider under any such warranty), and such other information as the Secretary deems to be appropriate.
>
> (C) Each physician and provider of services performing the implantation or replacement of pacemaker devices and leads for which payment is made or requested to be made under this title shall, in accordance with regulations of the Secretary, submit information respecting such implantation or replacement for the registry.
>
> (D) Such registry shall be for the purposes of assisting the Secretary in determining when payments may properly be made under this title, in tracing the performance of cardiac pacemaker devices and leads, in determining when inspection by the manufacturer of such a device or lead may be necessary under paragraph (3), in determining the amount subject to repayment under paragraph (2)(C), and in carrying out studies with respect

to the use of such devices and leads. In carrying out any such study, the Secretary may not reveal any specific information which identifies any pacemaker device or lead recipient by name (or which would otherwise identify a specific recipient).

(E) Any person or organization may provide information to the registry with respect to cardiac pacemaker devices and leads other than those for which payment is made under this title.

Then, for quality and cost controls, section 1862(h)(2) provides:

The Secretary may, by regulation, require each provider of services —

(A) to return, to the manufacturer of the device or lead for testing under paragraph (3), any cardiac pacemaker device or lead which is removed from a patient and payment for the implantation or replacement of which was made or requested by such provider under this title, and

(B) not to charge any beneficiary for replacement of such a device or lead if the device or lead has not been returned in accordance with subparagraph (A), and

(C) to make repayment to the Secretary of amounts paid under this title to the provider with respect to any cardiac pacemaker device which has been replaced by the manufacturer, or for which the manufacturer has made payment to the provider, under an express or implied warranty.

Subsection (3), which permits the Secretary to require the manufacturer to test and report on such products, states:

The Secretary may, by regulation, require the manufacturer of a cardiac pacemaker device or lead (A) to test or analyze each pacemaker device or lead for which payment is made or requested under this title and which is returned to the manufacturer by a provider of services under paragraph (2), and (B) to provide the results of such test or analysis to that provider, together with information and documentation with respect to any warranties covering such device or lead. In any case where the Secretary has reason to believe, based upon information in the pacemaker registry or otherwise available to him, that replacement of a cardiac pacemaker device or lead for which payment is or may be requested under this title is related to the malfunction of a device or lead, the Secretary may require that

> personnel of the Food and Drug Administration be present at the testing of such device by the manufacturer, to determine whether such device was functioning properly.

Then subsection (4) provides:

> The Secretary may deny payment under this title, in whole or in part and for such period of time as the Secretary determines to be appropriate, with respect to the implantation or replacement of a pacemaker device or lead of a manufacturer performed by a physician and provider of services after the Secretary determines (in accordance with the procedures established under subsections (c) [which pertains to notice, effective date, and period of exclusion], (f) [which pertains to notice, hearing, and judicial review], and (g) [which pertains to application for termination of exclusion] of section 1128 that —
>
> (A) the physician or provider of services has failed to submit information to the registry as required under paragraph (1)(C),
>
> (B) the provider of services has failed to return devices and leads as required under paragraph (2)(A), has improperly charged beneficiaries as prohibited under paragraph (2)(B), or has failed to make repayment to the Secretary as required under paragraph (2)(C), or
>
> (C) the manufacturer of the device or lead has failed to perform and to report on the testing of devices and leads returned to it as required under paragraph (3).

For regulatory citations, see Chapter 6

§ 2:31 PUBLICIZING PROVIDER SURVEY RESULTS — Section 1864 [42 U.S.C.A. 1395aa]

Summary

The Medicare statute, Medicare regulations, and provider agreements establish numerous conditions providers must meet to participate in Medicare. Perhaps because establishing those conditions and keeping them up-to-date is difficult and politically sensitive work, Congress, in section 1863, 42 U.S.C.A. 1395z, required the Secretary of Health and Human Services to do so in consultation with appropriate State agencies and recognized national listing or accrediting bodies. It authorized the Secretary to consult with appropriate local agencies, too.

Section 1864, 42 U.S.C.A. 1395aa, requires the Secretary to enter into agreements with able and willing States authorizing them to use their respective State health agency, or some other appropriate State or local agency, to determine whether various providers meet Medicare conditions of participation. The agency designated thus becomes the State survey agency for Medicare purposes.

Among other duties, State survey agencies are obligated to determine whether an institution is a hospital or skilled nursing facility; whether an agency is a home health agency; whether an agency is a hospice program or whether a facility is a rural health clinic, a critical access hospital as defined in section 1861 (mm)(1) [42 U.S.C.A 1395x(mm)(1). NOTE: Prior to amendment by section 4201(c)(1) of the Balanced Budget Act of 1997, critical access hospitals were known as rural primary care hospitals.], or a comprehensive outpatient rehabilitation facility; whether a laboratory meets statutory requirements; whether a clinic, rehabilitation agency, or public health agency meets statutory requirements for outpatient physical therapy services; and whether an ambulatory surgical center meets statutory requirements.

◆ NOTE: Pursuant to section 4154 of P.L. 101-508, the Omnibus Budget Reconciliation Act of 1990 (OBRA 90), State survey agencies were also obligated to determine whether clinical laboratories that do not participate or seek to participate in Medicare met the requirements of section 353 of the Public Health Service Act. That obligation was repealed by section 160(a)(1)(B) of the Social Security Act Amendments of 1994, P.L. 103-432, effective October 31, 1994. Pursuant to section 4163(c)(2) of OBRA 90, State survey agencies also were obligated to determine whether screening mammography performed after December 1990 met statutory requirements. That obligation was repealed by section 145(c)(3) of the Social Security Act Amendments of 1994. Repeal applies to mammography furnished by a facility on and after the first date that the certificate requirements of section 354(b) of the Public Service Health Act apply to such mammography conducted by such facility.

Generally, when a State survey agency certifies compliance, the Secretary accepts the State finding. For exceptions regarding skilled nursing facilities (SNF's) in particular, see § 2:4. With regard to terminating provider agreements in general, see § 2:32.

Within 90 days following completion of each survey of a health care facility, ambulatory surgical center, rural health clinic, comprehensive outpatient rehabilitation facility, laboratory, clinic, agency, or organization by the appropriate State survey agency, the Secretary must make public, in readily available form and place, each survey's pertinent findings regarding compliance with conditions of participation imposed by the statute and major additional conditions which the Secretary finds necessary for the health and safety of individuals furnished care or services by any such entity. In the case of SNF's, effective October 1, 1990, the Secretary must require the posting of such survey findings in a place readily accessible to SNF patients and their representatives.

In addition, the State survey agency (or local agency, as the case may be) must establish a toll-free hotline to collect, maintain, and continually update information on home health agencies participating in Medicare in the State or locality. That information must include any significant deficiencies found with respect to patient care in the most recent certification survey (whether conducted by the State agency or by an accreditation agency under section 1865, 42 U.S.C.A. 1395bb); when that survey was completed; whether corrective actions have been taken or are planned; and the sanctions, if any, imposed by Medicare. The hotline also must be available to receive complaints and answer questions regarding home health agencies in the State or locality.

Finally, the State survey agency (or local agency, as the case may be) must maintain a unit for investigating such complaints that has enforcement authority and access to survey and certification reports, to information gathered by any private accreditation agency used by the Secretary under section 1865, and to consumer medical records — the latter only with consent of the consumer or his or her legal representative.

Pursuant to section 1865, if hospitals are accredited by the Joint Commission on Accreditation of Hospitals (JCAH) — more recently known as the Joint Commission on Accreditation of Health Care Organizations (JCAHO) — and if they give the Secretary access to copies of the Commission's most recent survey, they are deemed to meet the statutory requirements of the definition of a hospital in section 1861(e), 42 U.S.C.A. 1395x(e), except for utilization review and discharge planning processes and any standards promulgated by the Secretary which are higher than JCAH standards. The statute provides similar deemed compliance for hospitals accredited by the American Osteopathic Association or by any other national accreditation body which provides reasonable assurance that relevant statutory requirements have been met.

In addition, section 1865 permits deemed compliance with certain conditions of participation for a "provider entity." Section 1865(b)(4), enacted by section 516(b) of the Omnibus Consolidated Rescissions and Appropriations Act of 1996, P.L. 104–134, defined provider entity to mean a provider of services, supplier, facility, clinic, agency, or laboratory. The change was effective as if enacted in the regular appropriations act.

◆ NOTE: Prior to that amendment, section 1865 specified deemed compliance for ambulatory surgical centers, psychiatric hospitals, skilled nursing facilities, home health agencies, clinics and rehabilitation agencies performing outpatient physical therapy and those doing so under arrangements with such clinics and rehabilitation agencies and public agencies performing outpatient physical therapy, clinical diagnostic laboratories, rural health clinics, outpatient rehabilitation facilities, and hospices. These entities still fit within the phrase "provider entity."

Formerly, the statute prohibited the Secretary from disclosing any survey report prepared by JCAH, AOA, or other accrediting entities, other than a survey with respect to a home health agency. Subsequent to amendment by section 6019(b) of P.L. 101-239, the Omnibus Budget Reconciliation Act of 1989, effective December 19, 1989, however, the Secretary may disclose accreditation surveys and information related to such surveys by JCAH, AOA, or other accred[HD] iting agencies, to the extent such disclosure relates to an enforcement action taken by the Secretary.

On a selective sample basis or when substantial allegations of a significant deficiency which could adversely affect the health and safety of patients has been made, however, the Secretary can direct a State agency to survey that hospital even though it has been accredited by JCAH or AOA or another accrediting agency. See section 1864(c), 42 U.S.C.A. 1395aa(c). Then, if the State survey confirms the significant deficiency, the facility loses its deemed status.

◆ NOTE: Pursuant to section 4207(g) of OBRA 90, the Secretary may not impose or require a State to impose any fee on any facility or entity subject to a compliance survey under section

1864, nor on any renal dialysis facility subject to a compliance survey under section 1881(b)(1).

Statutory Provisions

Section 1864(a), 42 U.S.C.A. 1395aa(a), provides:

> The Secretary shall make an agreement with any State which is able and willing to do so under which the services of the State health agency or other appropriate State agency (or the appropriate local agencies) will be utilized by him for the purpose of determining whether an institution therein is a hospital or skilled nursing facility, or whether an agency therein is a home health agency, or whether an agency is a hospice program, or whether a facility therein is a rural health clinic as defined in section 1861(aa)(2) [42 U.S.C.A. 1395x(aa)(2)] , a critical access hospital, as defined in section 1861(mm)(1) [42 U.S.C.A. 1395x(mm)(1). NOTE: Effective December 19, 1989, section 6003(g)(3)(C)(iii) of P.L. 101–239, the Omnibus Budget Reconciliation Act of 1989, added "rural primary care hospital". Section 4201(c) (1) of the Balanced Budget Act of 1997, P.L. 105–33, substituted the phrase "critical access hospital" for "rural primary care hospital", effective October 1, 1997.], or a comprehensive outpatient rehabilitation facility as defined in section 1861(cc)(2) [42 U.S.C.A. 1395x(cc)(2)], or whether a laboratory meets the requirements of paragraphs (16) and (17) of section 1861(s) [42 U.S.C.A. 1395x(s), which pertain to State licensure and other conditions regarding health and safety established by the Secretary. Section 4106(c) of the Balanced Budget Act replaced "paragraphs (15) and (16)" with "paragraphs (16) and (17)". This change is applicable to bone mass measurements performed on or after July 1, 1998.], or whether a clinic, rehabilitation agency or public health agency meets the requirements of subparagraph (A) or (B), as the case may be, of section 1861(p)(4) [42 U.S.C.A. 1395x(p)(4), which pertain to standards of practice], or whether an ambulatory surgical center meets the standards specified under section 1832(a)(2)(F)(i) (42 U.S.C.A. 1395k(a)(2)(F)(i)]. To the extent the Secretary finds it appropriate, an institution or agency which such a State (or local) agency certifies is a hospital, skilled nursing facility, rural health clinic, comprehensive outpatient rehabilitation facility, home health agency, or hospice program,

(as those terms are defined in section 1861 [42 U.S.C.A. 1395x]) may be treated as such by the Secretary. Any State agency which has such an agreement may (subject to approval of the Secretary) furnish to a skilled nursing facility, after proper request by such facility, such specialized consultative services (which such agency is able and willing to furnish in a manner satisfactory to the Secretary) as such facility may need to meet one or more of the conditions specified in section 1819(a) [42 U.S.C.A. 1395i-3(a), generally effective October 1, 1990]. Any such services furnished by a State agency shall be deemed to have been furnished pursuant to such agreement. Within 90 days following the completion of each survey of any health care facility, ambulatory surgical center, rural health clinic, comprehensive outpatient rehabilitation facility, laboratory, clinic, agency, or organization by the appropriate State or local agency described in the first sentence of this subsection, the Secretary shall make public in readily available form and place, and [effective October 1, 1990,] require (in the case of skilled nursing facilities) the posting in a place readily accessible to patients (and patients' representatives), the pertinent findings of each such survey relating to the compliance of each such health care facility, ambulatory surgical center, rural health clinic, comprehensive outpatient rehabilitation facility, laboratory, clinic, agency or organization with (1) the statutory conditions of participation imposed under this title and (2) the major additional conditions which the Secretary finds necessary in the interest of health and safety of individuals who are furnished care or services by any such health care facility, ambulatory surgical center, rural health clinic, comprehensive outpatient rehabilitation facility, laboratory, clinic, agency, or organization. Any agreement under this subsection shall provide for the appropriate State or local agency to maintain a toll-free hotline (1) to collect, maintain, and continually update information on home health agencies located in the State or locality that are certified to participate in the program established under this title (which information shall include any significant deficiencies found with respect to patient care in the most recent certification survey conducted by a State agency or accreditation survey conducted by a private accreditation agency under section 1865 [42 U.S.C.A. 1395bb] with respect to the home health agency, when that survey was completed, whether corrective actions have been taken or are planned, and the sanctions, if any, imposed under this title with respect to the agency) and (2) to receive complaints (and answer questions) with respect to home health agencies in the State or locality. Any such agreement shall provide for such State or local agency to maintain a unit for investigating such complaints that possesses enforcement authority and has access to survey and certification reports, information gathered by any private accreditation agency utilized by the Secretary under section 1865, and consumer medical records (but only with the consent of the consumer or his or her legal representative).

◆ NOTE: The phrase "or (in the case of a laboratory that does not participate or seek to participate in the medicare program) the requirements of section 353 of the Public Health Service Act", was deleted by section 160(a)(1)(B) of the Social Security Act Amendments of 1994, P.L. 103-432, effective October 31, 1994. Previously, it followed "or whether a laboratory meets the requirements of paragraphs (15) and (16) of section 1861(s)" in section 1862(a) above. The deleted phrase pertained to laboratories not participating in Medicare. It had been added by section 4154(d) of P.L. 101-508, the Omnibus Budget Reconciliation Act of 1990 (OBRA 90), effective as if included in the Clinical Laboratory Improvement Amendments of 1988. The phrase ", or whether screening mammography meets the standards established under section 1834(c)(3) [42 U.S.C.A. 1395m(c)(3)]" was deleted by section 145(c)(3) of the Social Security Act Amendments of 1994. The deletion applies to mammography furnished by a facility on and after the first date that the certificate requirements of section 354(b) of the Public Service Health Act apply to such mammography conducted by such facility. Previously, the deleted phrase followed "or whether an ambulatory surgical center meets the standards specified under section 1832(a)(2)(F)(i) [42 U.S.C.A. 1395k(a)(2)(F)(i)]" . It had been added by section 4163(c)(2) of OBRA 90, applicable to screening mammography performed after December 1990.

(b) The Secretary shall pay any such State, in advance or by way of reimbursement, as may be provided in the agreement with it (and may make adjustments in such payments on account of overpayments or underpayments previously made), for the reasonable cost of performing the functions specified in subsection (a), and for the Federal Hospital Insurance Trust Fund's fair share of the costs attributable to the planning and other efforts directed toward coordination of activities in carrying out its agreement and other activities related to the provision of services similar to those for which payment may be made under part A, or related to the facilities and personnel required for the provision of such services, or related to improving the quality of such services.

(c) The Secretary is authorized to enter int o an agreement with any State under which the appropriate State or local agency which performs the certification function described in subsection (a) will survey, on a selective sample basis (or where the Secretary finds that a survey is appropriate because of substantial allegations of the existence of a significant deficiency or deficiencies which would, if found to be present, adversely affect health and safety of patients), hospitals which have an agreement with the Secretary under section 1866 and which are accredited by the Joint Commission on Accreditation of Hospitals. The Secretary shall pay for such services in the manner prescribed in subsection (b).

Pursuant to sections 4202(a)(1), 4202(a)(2), and 4203(a)(1) of P.L. 100-203, the Omnibus Budget Reconciliation Act of 1987, subsection (d), below, became effective October 1, 1990.

(d) The Secretary may not enter an agreement under this section with a State with respect to determining whether an institution therein is a skilled nursing facility unless the State meets the requirements specified in section 1819(e) and 1819(g) [42 U.S.C.A. 1395i-3(e), which pertains to nurse aide training and competency evaluation, and 1395i-3(g), which pertains to survey and certification process] and the establishment of remedies under sections 1819(h)(2)(B) and 1819(h)(2)(C) [42 U.S.C.A. 1395i-3(h)(2)(B), which pertains to denial of payment, civil money penalties, and appointment of temporary management, and 1395i-3(h)(2)(C), which pertains to continuation of payments pending remediation] (relating to establishment and application of remedies).

Furthermore, pursuant to section 4207(g) of OBRA 90, effective November 5, 1990, the following provision protecting providers from being charged fees for compliance surveys was added to section 1864:

> (e) Notwithstanding any other provision of law, the Secretary may not impose, or require a State to impose, any fee on any facility or entity subject to a determination under subsection (a), or any renal dialysis facility subject to the requirements of section 1881(b)(1) [42 U.S.C.A. 1395rr, which pertains to Medicare coverage for end stage renal disease], for any such determination or any survey relating to determining the compliance of such facility or entity with any requirement of this title.

With regard to accreditation by private agencies, section 1865, 42 U.S.C.A. 1395bb, as amended by section 201(a)(1) of P.L. 101-234, the Medicare Catastrophic Coverage Repeal Act of 1989, effective January 1, 1989, and sections 6003(g)(3)(C)(iv), 6019(a), (b), and (c), and 6115(c) of P.L. 101-239, the Omnibus Budget Reconciliation Act of 1989, effective December 19, 1989, provides:

> (a) Except as provided in subsection (b) and the second sentence of section 1863 [42 U.S.C.A.1395z, which requires the Secretary to consult with State agencies and other organizations to develop conditions of participation for providers of services], if —
>
> (1) an institution is accredited as a hospital by the Joint Commission on Accreditation of Hospitals, and
>
> (2) (A) such institution authorizes the Commission to release to the Secretary upon his request (or such State agency as the Secretary may designate) a copy of the most current accreditation survey of such institution made by such Commission, together with any other information directly related to the survey as the Secretary may require (including corrective action plans) [this clause effective as amended six months after December 19, 1989],
>
> (B) such Commission releases such a copy and any such information to the Secretary [this clause effective as amended six months after December 19, 1989], then, such institution shall be deemed to meet the requirements of the numbered paragraphs of section 1861(e) [42 U.S.C.A.

1395x(e), which pertains to the definition of a hospital]; except —

(3) paragraph (6) thereof [which pertains to utilization review and discharge planning], and

(4) any standard, promulgated by the Secretary pursuant to paragraph (9) thereof [which pertains to any other requirements which the Secretary may find necessary for the health and safety of individuals furnished services in the institution], which is higher than the requirements prescribed for accreditation by such Commission.

If such Commission, as a condition for accreditation of a hospital, requires a utilization review plan (or imposes another requirement which serves substantially the same purpose), requires a discharge planning process (or imposes another requirement which serves substantially the same purpose), or imposes a standard which the Secretary determines is a least equivalent to the standard promulgated by the Secretary as described in paragraph (4) of this subsection, the Secretary is authorized to find that all institutions so accredited by such Commission comply also with clause (A) or (B) of section 1861(e)(6) [which pertains to utilization review and discharge planning] or the standard described in such paragraph (4), as the case may be.

◆ NOTE: Prior to amendment by section 516(b) of the Omnibus Consolidated Rescissions and Appropriations Act of 1996, P.L. 104–134 (effective as if enacted into law as the regular appropriations act), the following sentence followed the phrase "as the case may be" above: "In addition, if the Secretary finds that accreditation of an entity by the American Osteopathic Association or any other national accreditation body provides reasonable assurance that any or all of the conditions of section 1832(a)(2)(F)(i) [42 U.S.C.A. 1395k(a)(2)(F)(i), which pertains to ambulatory surgery centers], 1834(c)(3) [42 U.S.C.A. 1395m(c)(3), which applies to screening mammography performed after December 1990, pursuant to section 4163(c)(3) of OBRA 90], 1861(e) [42 U.S.C.A. 1395x(e), which pertains to the definition of a hospital], 1861(f) [42 U.S.C.A. 1395x(f), which pertains to the definition of a psychiatric hospital], 1861(j) [42 U.S.C.A. 1395x(j), which pertains to the definition of a skilled nursing facility (by cross-reference to section 1819(a))], 1861(o)

[42 U.S.C.A. 1395x(o), which pertains to the definition of a home health agency], 1861(p)(4)(A) or (B) [42 U.S.C.A. 1395x(p)(4)(A) or (B), which pertain to the definition of outpatient physical therapy as provided by a clinic or rehabilitation agency, or by others under arrangements with such a clinic or agency, or by a public health agency], paragraphs (15) and (16) of section 1861(s) [42 U.S.C.A. 1395x(s)(15) or (16), which pertain to requirements for clinical diagnostic laboratories], section 1861(aa)(2) [42 U.S.C.A. 1395x(aa)(2), which pertains to the definition of rural health clinics], 1861(cc)(2) [42 U.S.C.A. 1395x(cc)(2), which pertains to the definition of comprehensive outpatient rehabilitation facilities], or 1861(dd)(2) [42 U.S.C.A. 1395x(dd)(2), which pertains to the definition of hospice program], or 1861(mm)(1) [42 U.S.C.A. 1395x(mm)(1), which pertains to the definition of rural primary care hospital and rural primary care hospital services], as the case may be, are met, he may, to the extent he deems it appropriate, treat such entity as meeting the condition or conditions with respect to which he made such finding."

In place of that deleted sentence, section 516(b) added the following subsection (b), effective as if enacted into law as the regular appropriations Act. It also redesignated former subsection (b) as subsection (d), which appears below.

◆ FURTHER NOTE: With respect to the foregoing deleted sentence, section 145(c)(3) of the Social Security Act Amendments of 1994 deleted "1834(c)(3)" [42 U.S.C.A. 1395m(c)(3)], which, pursuant to section 4163(c)(3) of OBRA 90 applied to screening mammography performed after December 1990. Repeal applies to mammography furnished by a facility on and after the first date that the certificate requirements of section 354(b) of the Public Service Health Act apply to such mammography conducted by such facility.

(b) (1) In addition, if the Secretary finds that accreditation of a provider entity (as defined in paragraph (4) by the American Osteopathic Association or any other national accreditation body demonstrates that all of the applicable conditions or requirements of this title (other than the requirements of section 1834(j) [which pertains to requirements for suppliers of medical equipment and supplies] or the conditions or requirements under section 1881(b) [which pertains to coverage for end stage renal disease] are met or exceeded —

(A) in the case of a provider entity described in paragraph (3)(B), the Secretary may treat such entity as meeting those conditions or requirements with respect to which the Secretary made such finding.

(B) in the case of a provider entity described in paragraph (3)(B), the Secretary may treat such entity as meeting those conditions or requirements with respect to which the Secretary made such finding.

(2) In making such a finding, the Secretary shall consider, among other factors with respect to a national accreditation body, its requirements for accreditation, its survey procedures, its ability to provide adequate resources for conducting required surveys and supplying information for use in enforcement activities, its monitoring procedures for provider entities found out of compliance with the conditions or requirements, and its ability to provide the Secretary with necessary data for validation.

(3) (A) Except as provided in subparagraph (B), not later than 60 days after the date of receipt of a written request for finding under paragraph (1) (with any documentation necessary to make a determination on the request), the Secretary shall publish a notice identifying the national accreditation body making the request, describing the nature of the request, and providing a period of at least 30 days for the public to comment on the request. The Secretary shall approve or deny a request for such a finding, and shall publish notice of such approval or denial, not later than 210 days after the date of receipt of the request (with such documentation). Such an approval shall be effective with respect to accreditation determinations made on or after such effective date (which may not be later than the date of publication of the approval) as the Secretary specifies in the publication notice.

(B) The 210-day and 60-day deadlines specified in subparagraph (A) shall not apply in the case of any request for a finding with respect to accreditation of a provider entity to which the conditions and requirements of section 1819 [which pertains to conditions of participation for skilled nursing facilities] and 1861(j) [which defines skilled nursing facility] apply.

(4) For the purpose of this section the term "provider entity" means a provider of services, supplier, facility, a clinic, agency, or laboratory.

(c) The Secretary may not disclose any accreditation survey (other than a survey with respect to a home health agency) made and released to him by the Joint Commission on Accreditation of Hospitals, the American Osteopathic Association, or any other national accreditation body, of an entity accredited by such body, except that the Secretary may disclose such a survey and information related to such a survey to the extent such survey and information relate to an enforcement action taken by the Secretary. [NOTE: Section 516(b) of the Omnibus Consolidated Rescissions and Appropriations Act of 1996 removed this sentence from subsection (a) and redesignated it as subsection (c).]

(d) Notwithstanding any other provision of this title, if the Secretary finds that a hospital has significant deficiencies (as defined in regulations pertaining to health and safety), the hospital shall, after the date of notice of such finding to the hospital and for such period as may be prescribed in regulations, be deemed not to meet the requirements of the numbered paragraphs of section 1861(e).

◆ NOTE: Prior to amendment by section 516(c)(2)(A) of the Omnibus Consolidated Rescissions and Appropriations Act of 1996, the clause after "deemed not to meet" read: "the requirements of the numbered paragraphs of section 1861(e). The same amendment substituted "provider entity" and "entity" for "hospital" where they appear prior to the phrase "deemed not to meet". Section 516(c)(2)(B) added the following subsection (e).

(e) For provisions relating to validation surveys of entities that are treated as meeting applicable conditions or requirements of this title pursuant to subsection (a) or (b)(1), see section 1864(c).

◆ NOTE: Prior to amendment by the Medicare Catastrophic Coverage Repeal Act of 1989 and OBRA 89, section 1865 provided as follows:

(a) Except as provided in subsection (b) and the second sentence of section 1863 [42 U.S.C.A. 1395z] , which requires the Secretary to consult with State agencies and other organizations to develop conditions of participation for providers of services], if —

(1) an institution is accredited as a hospital by the Joint Commission on Accreditation of Hospitals, and

(2) such institution (if it is included within a survey described in section 1864(c) [42 U.S.C.A. 1395aa, which authorizes the Secretary to enter into agreements with appropriate State and local agencies which certify providers to survey hospital providers) authorizes the Commission to release to the Secretary upon his request (or such State agency as the Secretary may designate) a copy of the most current accreditation survey of such institution made by such Commission, then, such institution shall be deemed to meet the requirements of the numbered paragraphs of section 1861(e) [42 U.S.C.A. 1395x(e), which pertains to the definition of a hospital]; except —

(3) paragraph (6) thereof [which pertains to utilization review and discharge planning], and

(4) any standard, promulgated by the Secretary pursuant to paragraph (9) thereof [which pertains to any other requirements which the Secretary may find necessary for the health and safety of individuals furnished services in the institution], which is higher than the requirements prescribed for accreditation by such Commission.

If such Commission, as a condition for accreditation of a hospital requires a utilization review plan (or imposes another requirement which serves substantially the same purpose), requires a discharge planning process (or imposes another requirement which serves substantially the same purpose), or imposes a standard which the Secretary determines is a least equivalent to the standard promulgated by the Secretary as described in paragraph (4) of this subsection, the Secretary is authorized to find that all institutions so accredited by such Commission comply also with clause (A) or (B) of section 1861(e)(6) [which pertains to utilization review and discharge planning] or the standard described in such paragraph (4), as the case may be. In addition, if the Secretary finds that accreditation of an entity by the American Osteopathic Association or any other national accreditation body provides reasonable assurance that any or all of the conditions of section 1832(a)(2)(F)(i) [42 U.S.C.A. 1395k(a)(2)(F)(i), which pertains to ambulatory surgery centers], 1834(e)(3) [42 U.S.C.A. 1395m(e)(3), which pertains to screening mammography], 1861(e) [42 U.S.C.A. 1395x(e), which pertains to the definition of a hospital], 1861(f) [42 U.S.C.A. 1395x(f), which pertains to the definition of a psychiatric hospital], 1861(j) [42 U.S.C.A. 1395x(j), which pertains to the definition of a skilled nursing facility (by cross-reference to section 1819(a))], 1861(o) [42 U.S.C.A. 1395x(o), which pertains to the definition of a home health agency], 1861(p)(4)(A) or (B) [42 U.S.C.A. 1395x(p)(4)(A) or (B), which pertain to the definition of outpatient physical therapy as provided by a clinic or reha[HD] bilitation agency, or by others under arrangements with such a clinic or agency, or by a public health agency], paragraphs (14) and (15) of section 1861(s) [42 U.S.C.A. 1395x(s)(14)or (15), which pertain to requirements for clinical diagnostic laboratories], section 1861(aa)(2) [42 U.S.C.A. 1395x(aa)(2), which pertains to the definition of rural health clinics], 1861(cc)(2) [42 U.S.C.A. 1395x(cc)(2), which pertains to the definition of comprehensive outpatient rehabilitation facilities], or 1861(dd)(2) [42 U.S.C.A. 1395x(dd)(2), which pertains to the definition of hospice program], as the case may be, are met, he may, to the extent he deems it appropriate, treat such entity as meeting the condition or conditions with respect to which he made such finding. The Secretary may not disclose any accreditation survey (other than a survey with respect to a home health agency) made and released to him by the Joint Commission on Accreditation of Hospitals, the American Osteopathic Association, or any other national accreditation body, of an entity accredited by such body.

(b) Notwithstanding any other provision of this title, if the Secretary finds following a survey made pursuant to section 1864(c) that a hospital has significant deficiencies (as defined in regulations pertaining to health and safety), the hospital shall, after the date of notice of such finding to the hospital and for such period as may be prescribed in regulations, be deemed not to meet the requirements of the numbered paragraphs of section 1861(e).

For regulatory citations, see Chapter 6

§ 2:32 TERMINATING PROVIDER AGREEMENTS— Section 1866(b) [42 U.S.C.A. 1395cc]

Summary

Termination of a provider agreement is the ultimate Medicare sanction because it removes a provider from the Medicare program, and usually from Medicaid, the Maternal and Child Health programs (Title V of the Social Security Act, 42 U.S.C.A. 701), and the program of Block Grants to States for Social Services (Title XX of the Act, 42 U.S.C.A. 1397). The process is complicated, however, because the statute, the regulations, and provider agreements contain numerous conditions which providers must meet.

In general, pursuant to section 1866(b), 42 U.S.C.A. 1395cc, the Secretary of Health and Human Services may refuse to enter into an agreement or may refuse to renew an agreement or may terminate an agreement with a provider if he determines, after notice and opportunity for hearing, that a provider failed to comply either with provisions of its provider agreement, with provisions of the statute or regulations, or, with respect to hospitals, with a corrective action plan required under section 1886(f)(2)(B), 42 U.S.C.A. 1395ww(f)(2)(B), because of prior inappropriate hospital admissions. The same is true if a provider fails substantially to meet the definition requirements of section 1861, 42 U.S.C.A. 1395x, or if a provider has been excluded under section 1128, 42 U.S.C.A. 1320a-7, or section 1128A, 42 U.S.C.A. 1320a-7a.

Section 1864, 42 U.S.C.A. 1395aa, requires the Secretary to enter into agreements with able and willing States authorizing them to use their respective State health agency, or some other appropriate State or local agency, to determine whether various providers meet Medicare conditions of participation. The agency designated thus becomes the State survey agency for Medicare purposes.

Among other duties, State survey agencies are obligated to determine whether an institution is a hospital or skilled nursing facility; whether an agency is a home health agency; whether an agency is a hospice program or whether a facility is a rural health clinic, a critical access hospital [NOTE: Section 4201(c)(1) of the Balanced Budget Act of 1997, P.L. 105–33, substituted the phrase "critical access hospital" for the phrase "rural primary care hospital", effective October 1, 1997.], or a comprehensive outpatient rehabilitation facility; whether a laboratory meets statutory requirements; whether a clinic, rehabilitation agency, or public health agency meets statutory requirements for outpatient physical therapy services; and whether an ambulatory surgical center meets statutory requirements.

◆ NOTE: Pursuant to section 4154 of P.L. 101-508, the Omnibus Budget Reconciliation Act of 1990 (OBRA 90), State survey agencies were also obligated to determine whether clinical laboratories that do not participate or seek to participate in Medicare met the requirements of section 353 of the Public Health Service Act. That obligation was repealed by section 160(a)(1)(B) of the Social Security Act Amendments of 1994, P.L. 103-432, effective October 31, 1994. Pursuant to section 4163(c)(2) of OBRA 90, State survey agencies also were obligated to determine whether screening mammography performed after December 1990 met statutory requirements. That obligation was repealed by section 145(c)(3) of the Social Security Act Amendments of 1994. Repeal applies to mammography furnished by a facility on and after the first date that the certificate requirements of section 354(b) of the Public Service Health Act apply to such mammography conducted by such facility.

Generally, when a State survey agency certifies compliance, the Secretary accepts the State finding. (For exceptions regarding skilled nursing facilities (SNF's) in particular, see § 2:4.)

Within 90 days following completion of each survey of a health care facility, ambulatory surgical center, rural health clinic, comprehensive outpatient rehabilitation facility, laboratory, clinic, agency, or organization by the appropriate State survey agency, the Secretary must make public, in readily available form and place each survey's pertinent findings regarding compliance with conditions of participation imposed by the statute and major additional conditions which the Secretary finds necessary for the health and safety of individuals furnished care or services by any such entity. In the case of SNF's, effective October 1, 1990, the Secretary must require the posting of such survey findings in a place readily accessible to SNF patients and their representatives.

In addition, the State survey agency (or local agency, as the case may be) must establish a toll-free hotline to collect, maintain, and continually update information on home health agencies participating in Medicare in the State or locality. That information must include any significant deficiencies found with respect to patient care in the most recent certification survey (whether conducted by the State agency or by an accreditation agency under section 1865, 42 U.S.C.A. 1395bb); when that survey was completed; whether corrective actions have been taken or are planned; and the sanctions, if any, imposed by Medicare. The hotline also must be available to receive complaints and answer questions regarding home health agencies in the State or locality.

Finally, the State survey agency (or local agency, as the case may be) must maintain a unit for investigating such complaints that has enforcement authority and access to survey and certification reports, to information gathered by any private accreditation agency used by the Secretary under section 1865, and to consumer medical records — the latter only with consent of the consumer or his or her legal representative.

Section 1865 provides that if hospitals are accredited by the Joint Commission on Accreditation of Hospitals (JCAH) — more recently known as the Joint Commission on Accreditation of Health Care Organizations (JCAHO) — and if they give the Secretary access to copies of the Commission's most recent survey, they are deemed to meet the statutory requirements of the definition of a hospital in section 1861(e), 42 U.S.C.A. 1395x(e), except for utilization review and discharge planning processes and any standards promulgated by the Secretary which are higher than JCAH standards. The statute provides similar deemed compliance for hospitals accredited by the American Osteopathic Association or any other national accreditation body which provides reasonable assurance that relevant statutory requirements have been met.

In addition, section 1865 permits deemed compliance with certain conditions of participation for a "provider entity." Section 1865(b)(4), enacted by section 516(b) of the Omnibus Consolidated Rescissions and Appropriations Act of 1996, P.L. 104–134, defined provider entity to mean a provider of services, supplier, facility, clinic, agency, or laboratory. The change was effective as if enacted in the regular appropriations act.

◆ NOTE: Prior to that amendment, section 1865 specified deemed compliance for ambulatory surgical centers, psychiatric hospitals, skilled nursing facilities, home health agencies, clinics and rehabilitation agencies performing outpatient physical therapy and those doing so under arrangements with such clinics and rehabilitation agencies and public agencies performing outpatient physical therapy, clinical diagnostic laboratories, rural health clinics, outpatient rehabilitation facilities, and hospices. These entities still fit within the phrase "provider entity."

Formerly, the statute prohibited the Secretary from disclosing any survey report prepared by JCAH, AOA, or other accrediting entities, other than a survey with respect to a home health agency. Subsequent to amendment by section 6019(b) of P.L. 101-239, the Omnibus Budget Reconciliation Act of 1989, effective December 19, 1989, however, the Secretary may disclose accreditation surveys and information related to such surveys by JCAH, AOA, or other accrediting agencies, to the extent such disclosure relates to an enforcement action taken by the Secretary.

On a selective sample basis or when substantial allegations of a significant deficiency which could adversely affect the health and safety of patients has been made, however, the Secretary can direct a State agency to survey that hospital even though it has been accredited by JCAH or AOA or another accrediting agency. See section 1864(c), 42 U.S.C.A. 1395aa(c). Then, if the State survey confirms the significant deficiency, the facility loses its deemed status.

◆ NOTE: Pursuant to section 4207(g) of OBRA 90, the Secretary may not impose or require a State to impose any fee on any facility or entity subject to a compliance survey under section 1864, nor on any renal dialysis facility subject to a compliance survey under section 1881(b)(1).

Having established in sections 1864 and 1865 various conditions of participation for providers, Congress then required in section 1866, 42 U.S.C.A. 1395cc, for them to sign "provider agreements." These agreements require providers not to charge any person for items more than what Medicare pays (plus applicable deductibles and coinsurance); to return any monies incorrectly collected; to notify the Secretary about employment of any individual who at any time during the previous year preceding such employment was employed in a managerial, auditing, or similar capacity by a fiscal intermediary or carrier with respect to the provider; to furnish to fiscal intermediaries and PRO's information they find necessary to determine the appropriateness of reimbursement and to otherwise perform their duties.

In addition, hospitals are obliged to maintain agreements with PRO's under which the PRO will review the validity of diagnostic information provided by the hospital, the completeness, adequacy and quality of care provided, the appropriateness of admissions and discharges, and the appropriateness of care provided; to accept other charge limitations peculiar to certain situations; to give inpatients upon admission notice of certain rights, including appeal rights; to make available to patients the directory or directories of participating physicians published for the area, and if hospital personnel refer a patient to a nonparticipating physician for further medical care on an outpatient basis, to inform the patient that the physician is nonparticipating, and, whenever practicable, identify at least one qualified participating physician listed in the directory.

All providers are also obliged to comply with the nondiscrimination requirements of Title VI of the Civil Rights Act of 1964, P.L. 88-352, 42 U.S.C.A. 2000d, and Section 504 of the Rehabilitation Act of 1973, P.L. 93-112, 42 U.S.C.A. 794.

Finally, provider agreements stipulate that they are binding when signed and that they are automatically assigned to a buyer when there is a transfer of ownership. Providers may terminate their agreements voluntarily, however, upon proper notice to the Secretary and the public, and the Secretary cannot require more than six months' notice. The Secretary, on the other hand, may refuse to enter into an agreement with a provider or refuse to renew a provider agreement or terminate a provider agreement.

Statutory Provisions

Section 1864(a), 42 U.S.C.A. 1395aa(a), provides:

> The Secretary shall make an agreement with any State which is able and willing to do so under which the services of the State health agency or other appropriate State agency (or the appropriate local agencies) will be utilized by him for the purpose of determining whether an institution therein is a hospital or skilled nursing facility, or whether an agency therein is a home health agency, or whether an agency is a hospice program, or whether a facility therein is a rural health clinic as defined in section 1861(aa)(2) [42 U.S.C.A. 1395x(aa)(2)] , a critical access hospital, as defined in section 1861(mm)(1) [42 U.S.C.A. 1395x(mm)(1). NOTE: Effective December 19, 1989, section 6003(g)(3)(C)(iii) of P.L. 101–239, the Omnibus Budget Reconcil-

iation Act of 1989 added rural primary care hospital. Section 4201(c)(1) of the Balanced Budget Act of 1997, P.L. 105–33, substituted the phrase "critical access hospital" for the phrase "rural primary care hospital", effective October 1, 1997.], or a comprehensive outpatient rehabilitation facility as defined in section 1861(cc)(2) [42 U.S.C.A. 1395x(cc)(2)], or whether a laboratory meets the requirements of paragraphs (15) and (16) of section 1861(s) [42 U.S.C.A. 1395x(s), which pertain to State licensure and other conditions regarding health and safety established by the Secretary], or whether a clinic, rehabilitation agency or public health agency meets the requirements of subparagraph (A) or (B), as the case may be, of section 1861(p)(4) [42 U.S.C.A. 1395x(p)(4), which pertain to standards of practice], or whether an ambulatory surgical center meets the standards specified under section 1832(a)(2)(F)(i) [42 U.S.C.A. 13395k(a)(2)(F)(i)] . To the extent the Secretary finds it appropriate, an institution or agency which such a State (or local) agency certifies is a hospital, skilled nursing facility, rural health clinic, comprehensive outpatient rehabilitation facility, home health agency, or hospice program, (as those terms are defined in section 1861 [42 U.S.C.A. 1395x]) may be treated as such by the Secretary. Any State agency which has such an agreement may (subject to approval of the Secretary) furnish to a skilled nursing facility, after proper request by such facility, such specialized consultative services (which such agency is able and willing to furnish in a manner satisfactory to the Secretary) as such facility may need to meet one or more of the conditions specified in section 1819(a) [42 U.S.C.A. 1395i-3(a), generally effective October 1, 1990]. Any such services furnished by a State agency shall be deemed to have been furnished pursuant to such agreement. Within 90 days following the completion of each survey of any health care facility, ambulatory surgical center, rural health clinic, comprehensive outpatient rehabilitation facility, laboratory, clinic, agency, or organization by the appropriate State or local agency described in the first sentence of this subsection, the Secretary shall make public in readily available form and place, and [effective October 1, 1990,] require (in the case of skilled nursing facilities) the posting in a place readily accessible to patients (and patients' representatives), the pertinent findings of each such survey relating to the compliance of each such health care facility, ambulatory surgical center, rural health clinic, comprehensive outpatient rehabilitation facility, laboratory, clinic, agency or organization with (1) the statutory conditions of participation imposed under this title and (2) the major additional conditions which the Secretary finds necessary in the interest of health and safety of individuals who are furnished care or services by any such health care facility, ambulatory surgical center, rural health clinic, comprehensive outpatient rehabilitation facility, laboratory, clinic, agency, or organization. Any agreement under this subsection shall provide for the appropriate State or local agency to maintain a toll-free hotline (1) to collect, maintain, and continually update information on home health agencies located in the State or locality that are certified to participate in the program established under this title (which information shall include any significant deficiencies found with respect to patient care in the most recent certification survey conducted by a State agency or accreditation survey conducted by a private accreditation agency under section 1865 [42 U.S.C.A. 1395bb] with respect to the home health agency, when that survey was completed, whether corrective actions have been taken or are planned, and the sanctions, if any, imposed under this title with respect to the agency) and (2) to receive complaints (and answer questions) with respect to home health agencies in the State or locality. Any such agreement shall provide for such State or local agency to maintain a unit for investigating such complaints that possesses enforcement authority and has access to survey and certification reports, information gathered by any private accreditation agency utilized by the Secretary under section 1865, and consumer medical records (but only with the consent of the consumer or his or her legal representative).

◆ NOTE: The phrase "or (in the case of a laboratory that does not participate or seek to participate in the medicare program) the requirements of section 353 of the Public Health Service Act", was deleted by section 160(a)(1)(B) of the Social Security Act Amendments of 1994, P.L. 103-432, effective October 31, 1994. Previously, it followed "or whether a laboratory meets the requirements of paragraphs (15) and (16) of section 1861(s)" in section 1862(a) above. The deleted phrase pertained to laboratories not participating in Medicare. It had been added by section 4154(d) of P.L. 101-508, the Omnibus Budget Reconciliation Act of 1990 (OBRA 90), effective as if included in the Clinical Laboratory Improvement Amendments of 1988. The phrase, "or whether screening mammography meets the standards established under section 1834(c)(3) [42 U.S.C.A. 1395m(c)(3)]" was deleted by section 145(c)(3) of the Social Security Act Amendments of 1994. The deletion applies to mammography furnished by a facility on and after the first date that the certificate requirements of section 354(b) of the Public Service Health Act apply to such mammography conducted by such facility. Previously, the deleted phrase followed "or whether an ambulatory surgical center meets the standards specified under section 1832(a)(2)(F)(i) [42 U.S.C.A. 1395k(a)(2)(F)(i)]" . It had been added by section 4163(c)(2) of OBRA 90, applicable to screening mammography performed after December 1990.

(b) The Secretary shall pay any such State, in advance or by way of reimbursement, as may be provided in the agreement with it (and may make adjustments in such payments on account of overpayments or underpayments previously made), for the reasonable cost of performing the functions specified in subsection (a), and for the Federal Hospital Insurance Trust Fund's fair share of the costs attributable to the planning and other efforts directed toward coordination of activities in carrying out its agreement and other activities related to the provision of services similar to those for which payment may be made under part A, or related to the facilities and personnel required for the provision of such services, or related to improving the quality of such services.

(c) The Secretary is authorized to enter into an agreement with any State under which the appropriate State or local agency which performs the certification function described in subsection (a) will survey, on a selective sample basis (or where the Secretary finds that a survey is appropriate because of substantial allegations of the existence of a significant deficiency or deficiencies which would, if found to be present, adversely affect health and safety of patients), hospitals which have an agreement with the Secretary under section 1866 and which are accredited by the Joint Commission on Accreditation of Hospitals. The Secretary shall pay for such services in the manner prescribed in subsection (b).

Pursuant to sections 4202(a)(1), 4202(a)(2), and 4203(a)(1) of P.L. 100-203, the Omnibus Budget Reconciliation Act of 1987, subsection (d), below, became effective October 1, 1990.

> (d) The Secretary may not enter an agreement under this section with a State with respect to determining whether an institution therein is a skilled nursing facility unless the State meets the requirements specified in section 1819(e) and 1819(g) [42 U.S.C.A. 1395i-3(e), which pertains to nurse aide training and competency evaluation, and 1395i-3(g), which pertains to survey and certification process] and the establishment of remedies under sections 1819(h)(2)(B) and 1819(h)(2)(C) [42 U.S.C.A. 1395i-3(h)(2)(B), which pertains to denial of payment, civil money penalties, and appointment of temporary management, and 1395i-3(h)(2)(C), which pertains to continuation of payments pending remediation] (relating to establishment and application of remedies).

Furthermore, pursuant to section 4207(g) of OBRA 90, effective November 5, 1990, the following provision protecting providers from being charged fees for compliance surveys was added to section 1864:

> (e) Notwithstanding any other provision of law, the Secretary may not impose, or require a State to impose, any fee on any facility or entity subject to a determination under subsection (a), or any renal dialysis facility subject to the requirements of section 1881(b)(1) [42 U.S.C.A. 1395rr, which pertains to Medicare coverage for end stage renal disease], for any such determination or any survey relating to determining the compliance of such facility or entity with any requirement of this title.

With regard to accreditation by private agencies, section 1865, 42 U.S.C.A. 1395bb, as amended by section 201(a)(1) of P.L. 101-234, the Medicare Catastrophic Coverage Repeal Act of 1989, effective January 1, 1989, and sections 6003(g)(3)(C)(iv), 6019(a), (b), and (c), and 6115(c) of P.L. 101-239, the Omnibus Budget Reconciliation Act of 1989, effective December 19, 1989, provides:

> (a) Except as provided in subsection (b) and the second sentence of section 1863 [42 U.S.C.A.1395z] , which requires the Secretary to consult with State agencies and other organizations to develop conditions of participation for providers of services], if —

(1) an institution is accredited as a hospital by the Joint Commission on Accreditation of Hospitals, and

(2) (A) such institution authorizes the Commission to release to the Secretary upon his request (or such State agency as the Secretary may designate) a copy of the most current accreditation survey of such institution made by such Commission, together with any other information directly related to the survey as the Secretary may require (including corrective action plans) [this clause effective as amended six months after December 19, 1989],

(B) such Commission releases such a copy and any such information to the Secretary [this clause effective as amended six months after December 19, 1989],

then, such institution shall be deemed to meet the requirements of the numbered paragraphs of section 1861(e) [42 U.S.C.A. 1395x(e), which pertains to the definition of a hospital]; except —

(3) paragraph (6) thereof [which pertains to utilization review and discharge planning], and

(4) any standard, promulgated by the Secretary pursuant to paragraph (9) thereof [which pertains to any other requirements which the Secretary may find necessary for the health and safety of individuals furnished services in the institution], which is higher than the requirements prescribed for accreditation by such Commission.

If such Commission, as a condition for accreditation of a hospital, requires a utilization review plan (or imposes another requirement which serves substantially the same purpose), requires a discharge planning process (or imposes another requirement which serves substantially the same purpose), or imposes a standard which the Secretary determines is a least equivalent to the standard promulgated by the Secretary as described in paragraph (4) of this subsection, the Secretary is authorized to find that all institutions so accredited by such Commission comply also with clause (A) or (B) of section 1861(e)(6) [which pertains to utilization review and discharge planning] or the standard described in such paragraph (4), as the case may be.

◆ NOTE: Prior to amendment by section 516(b) of the Omnibus Consolidated Rescissions and Appropriations Act of 1996, P.L. 104–134 (effective as if enacted into law as the regular appropriations act), the following sentence followed the phrase "as the case may be" above: "In addition, if the Secretary finds that accreditation of an entity by the American Osteopathic Association or any other national accreditation body provides reasonable assurance that any or all of the conditions of section 1832(a)(2)(F)(i) [42 U.S.C.A. 1395k(a)(2)(F)(i), which pertains to ambulatory surgery centers], 1834(c)(3) [42 U.S.C.A. 1395m(c)(3), which applies to screening mammography performed after December 1990, pursuant to section 4163(c)(3) of OBRA 90], 1861(e) [42 U.S.C.A. 1395x(e), which pertains to the definition of a hospital], 1861(f) [42 U.S.C.A. 1395x(f), which pertains to the definition of a psychiatric hospital], 1861(j) [42 U.S.C.A. 1395x(j), which pertains to the definition of a skilled nursing facility (by cross-reference to section 1819(a))], 1861(o) [42 U.S.C.A. 1395x(o), which pertains to the definition of a home health agency], 1861(p)(4)(A) or (B) [42 U.S.C.A. 1395x(p)(4)(A) or (B), which pertain to the definition of outpatient physical therapy as provided by a clinic or rehabilitation agency, or by others under arrangements with such a clinic or agency, or by a public health agency], paragraphs (15) and (16) of section 1861(s) [42 U.S.C.A. 1395x(s)(15) or (16), which pertain to requirements for clinical diagnostic laboratories], section 1861(aa)(2) [42 U.S.C.A. 1395x(aa)(2), which pertains to the definition of rural health clinics], 1861(cc)(2) [42 U.S.C.A. 1395x(cc)(2), which pertains to the definition of comprehensive outpatient rehabilitation facilities], or 1861(dd)(2) [42 U.S.C.A. 1395x(dd)(2), which pertains to the definition of hospice program], or 1861(mm)(1) [42 U.S.C.A. 1395x(mm)(1), which pertains to the definition of rural primary care hospital and rural primary care hospital services], as the case may be, are met, he may, to the extent he deems it appropriate, treat such entity as meeting the condition or conditions with respect to which he made such finding.

In place of that deleted sentence, section 516(b) added the following subsection (b), effective as if enacted into law as the regular appropriations Act. It also redesignated former subsection (b) as subsection (d), which appears below.

◆ FURTHER NOTE: With respect to the foregoing deleted sentence, section 145(c)(3) of the Social Security Act Amendments of 1994 deleted "1834(c)(3)" [42 U.S.C.A. 1395m(c)(3)], which, pursuant to section 4163(c)(3) of OBRA 90 applied to screening mammography performed after December 1990. Repeal applies to mammography furnished by a facility on and after the first date that the certificate requirements of section 354(b) of the Public Service Health Act apply to such mammography conducted by such facility.

(b) (1) In addition, if the Secretary finds that accreditation of a provider entity (as defined in paragraph (4) by the American Osteopathic Association or any other national accreditation body demonstrates that all of the applicable conditions or requirements of this title (other than the requirements of section 1834(j) [which pertains to requirements for suppliers of medical equipment and supplies] or the conditions or requirements under section 1881(b) [which pertains to coverage for end stage renal disease] are met or exceeded —

(A) in the case of a provider entity described in paragraph (3)(B), the Secretary may treat such entity as meeting those conditions or requirements with respect to which the Secretary made such finding.

(B) in the case of a provider entity described in paragraph (3)(B), the Secretary may treat such entity as meeting those conditions or requirements with respect to which the Secretary made such finding.

(2) In making such a finding, the Secretary shall consider, among other factors with respect to a national accreditation body, its requirements for accreditation, its survey procedures, its ability to provide adequate resources for conducting required surveys and supplying information for use in enforcement activities, its monitoring procedures for provider entities found out of compliance with the conditions or requirements, and its ability to provide the Secretary with necessary data for validation.

(3) (A) Except as provided in subparagraph (B), not later than 60 days after the date of receipt of a written request for finding under paragraph (1) (with any documentation necessary to make a determination on the request), the

Secretary shall publish a notice identifying the national accreditation body making the request, describing the nature of the request, and providing a period of at least 30 days for the public to comment on the request. The Secretary shall approve or deny a request for such a finding, and shall publish notice of such approval or denial, not later than 210 days after the date of receipt of the request (with such documentation). Such an approval shall be effective with respect to accredition determinations made on or after such effective date (which may not be later than the date of publication of the approval) as the Secretary specifies in the publication notice.

(B) The 210-day and 60-day deadlines specified in subparagraph (A) shall not apply in the case of any request for a finding with respect to accreditation of a provider entity to which the conditions and requirements of section 1819 [which pertains to conditions of participation for skilled nursing facilities] and 1861(j) [which defines skilled nursing facility] apply.

(4) For the purpose of this section the term "provider entity" means a provider of services, supplier, facility, a clinic, agency, or laboratory.

(c) The Secretary may not disclose any accreditation survey (other than a survey with respect to a home health agency) made and released to him by the Joint Commission on Accreditation of Hospitals, the American Osteopathic Association, or any other national accreditation body, of an entity accredited by such body, except that the Secretary may disclose such a survey and information related to such a survey to the extent such survey and information relate to an enforcement action taken by the Secretary. [NOTE: Section 516(b) of the Omnibus Consolidated Rescissions and Appropriations Act of 1996 removed this sentence from subsection (a) and redesignated it as subsection (c).]

(d) Notwithstanding any other provision of this title, if the Secretary finds that a hospital has significant deficiencies (as defined in regulations pertaining to health and safety), the hospital shall, after the date of notice of such finding to the hospital and for such period as may be prescribed in regulations, be deemed not to meet the requirements of the numbered paragraphs of section 1861(e).

◆ NOTE: Prior to amendment by section 516(c)(2)(A) of the Omnibus Consolidated Rescissions and Appropriations Act of 1996, the clause after "deemed not to meet" read: "the requirements of the numbered paragraphs of section 1861(e). The same amendment substituted "provider entity" and "entity" for "hospital" where they appear prior to the phrase "deemed not to meet". Section 516(c)(2)(B) added the following subsection (e).

(e) For provisions relating to validation surveys of entities that are treated as meeting applicable conditions or requirements of this title pursuant to subsection (a) or (b)(1), see section 1864(c).

◆ NOTE: Prior to amendment by the Medicare Catastrophic Coverage Repeal Act of 1989 and OBRA 89, section 1865 provided as follows:

(a) Except as provided in subsection (b) and the second sentence of section 1863 [42 U.S.C.A. 1395z] , which requires the Secretary to consult with State agencies and other organizations to develop conditions of participation for providers of services], if —

(1) an institution is accredited as a hospital by the Joint Commission on Accreditation of Hospitals, and

(2) such institution (if it is included within a survey described in section 1864(c) [42 U.S.C.A. 1395aa, which authorizes the Secretary to enter into agreements with appropriate State and local agencies which certify providers to survey hospital providers) authorizes the Commission to release to the Secretary upon his request (or such State agency as the Secretary may designate) a copy of the most current accreditation survey of such institution made by such Commission,

then, such institution shall be deemed to meet the requirements of the numbered paragraphs of section 1861(e) [42 U.S.C.A. 1395x(e), which pertains to the definition of a hospital]; except —

(3) paragraph (6) thereof [which pertains to utilization review and discharge planning], and

(4) any standard, promulgated by the Secretary pursuant to paragraph (9) thereof [which pertains to any other requirements which the Secretary may find necessary for the health and safety of individuals furnished services in the institu-

tion], which is higher than the requirements prescribed for accreditation by such Commission.

If such Commission, as a condition for accreditation of a hospital requires a utilization review plan (or imposes another requirement which serves substantially the same purpose), requires a discharge planning process (or imposes another requirement which serves substantially the same purpose), or imposes a standard which the Secretary determines is a least equivalent to the standard promulgated by the Secretary as described in paragraph (4) of this subsection, the Secretary is authorized to find that all institutions so accredited by such Commission comply also with clause (A) or (B) of section 1861(e)(6) [which pertains to utilization review and discharge planning] or the standard described in such paragraph (4), as the case may be. In addition, if the Secretary finds that accreditation of an entity by the American Osteopathic Association or any other national accreditation body provides reasonable assurance that any or all of the conditions of section 1832(a)(2)(F)(i) [42 U.S.C.A. 1395k(a)(2)(F)(i), which pertains to ambulatory surgery centers], 1834(e)(3) [42 U.S.C.A. 1395m(e)(3), which pertains to screening mammography], 1861(e) [42 U.S.C.A. 1395x(e), which pertains to the definition of a hospital], 1861(f) [42 U.S.C.A. 1395x(f), which pertains to the definition of a psychiatric hospital], 1861(j) [42 U.S.C.A. 1395x(j), which pertains to the definition of a skilled nursing facility (by cross-reference to section 1819(a))], 1861(o) [42 U.S.C.A. 1395x(o), which pertains to the definition of a home health agency], 1861(p)(4)(A) or (B) [42 U.S.C.A. 1395x(p)(4)(A) or (B), which pertain to the definition of outpatient physical therapy as provided by a clinic or rehabilitation agency, or by others under arrangements with such a clinic or agency, or by a public health agency], paragraphs (14) and (15) of section 1861(s) [42 U.S.C.A. 1395x(s)(14) or (15), which pertain to requirements for clinical diagnostic laboratories], section 1861(aa)(2) [42 U.S.C.A. 1395x(aa)(2), which pertains to the definition of rural health clinics], 1861(cc)(2) [42 U.S.C.A. 1395x(cc)(2), which pertains to the definition of comprehensive outpatient rehabilitation facilities], or 1861(dd)(2) [42 U.S.C.A. 1395x(dd)(2), which pertains to the definition of hospice program], as the case may be, are met, he may, to the extent he deems it appropriate, treat such entity as meeting the condition or conditions with respect to which he made such finding. The Secretary may not disclose any accreditation survey (other than a survey with respect to a home health agency) made and released to him by the Joint Commission on Accreditation of Hospitals, the American Osteopathic Association, or any other national accreditation body, of an entity accredited by such body.

(b) Notwithstanding any other provision of this title, if the Secretary finds following a survey made pursuant to section 1864(c) that a hospital has significant deficiencies (as defined in regulations pertaining to health and safety), the hospital shall, after the date of notice of such finding to the hospital and for such period as may be prescribed in regulations, be deemed not to meet the requirements of the numbered paragraphs of section 1861(e).

With regard to termination of provider agreements, section 1866(b), 42 U.S.C.A. 1395cc(b), states:

(1) A provider of services may terminate an agreement with the Secretary under this section at such time and upon such notice to the Secretary and the public as may be provided in regulations, except that notice of more than six months shall not be required.

(2) The Secretary may refuse to enter into an agreement under this section or, upon such reasonable notice to the provider and the public as may be specified in regulations, may refuse to renew or may terminate such an agreement after the Secretary—

(A) has determined that the provider fails to comply with the provisions of the agreement, with the provisions of this title and regulations thereunder, or with a corrective action required under section 1886(f)(2)(B) [42 U.S.C.A. 1395ww(f)(2)(B), which pertains to inappropriate hospital admissions],

(B) has determined that the provider fails substantially to meet the applicable provisions of section 1861 [42 U.S.C.A. 1395x, which pertains to definitions], or

(C) has excluded the provider from participation in a program under this title pursuant to section 1128 [42 U.S.C.A. 1320a-7] or section 1128A [42 U.S.C.A. 1320a-7a].

(D) has ascertained that the provider has been convicted of a felony under Federal or State law for an offense which the Secretary determines is detrimental to the best interests of the program or program beneficiaries. [NOTE: Section 4302(a) of the Balanced Budget Act of 1997 deleted "or" from the end of (b)(2)(B); removed the period at the end of (b)(2)(C) and added ", or"; and added subparagraph (D). This change applies to the entry into and renewal of contracts on or after August 5, 1997.]

(3) A termination of an agreement or a refusal to renew an agreement under this subsection shall become effective on the same date and in the same manner as an exclusion from participation under the programs under this title becomes effective under section 1128(c).

Section 1128(c), 42 U.S.C.A. 1320a-7(c), provides in pertinent part:

NOTICE, EFFECTIVE DATE, AND PERIOD OF EXCLUSION. —

(1) An exclusion under this section or under section 1128A shall be effective at such time and upon such reasonable notice to the public and to the individual or entity excluded as may be specified in regulations consistent with paragraph (2).

(2) (A) Except as provided in subparagraph (B), such an exclusion shall be effective with respect to services furnished to an individual on or after the effective date of the exclusion.

(B) Unless the Secretary determines that the health and safety of individuals receiving services warrants the exclusion taking effect earlier, an exclusion shall not apply to payments made under title XVIII or under a State health care program for —

(i) inpatient institutional services furnished to an individual who was admitted to such institution before the date of the exclusion, or

(ii) home health services and hospice care furnished to an individual under a plan of care established before the date of the exclusion, until the passage of 30 days after the effective date of the exclusion.

With regard to readmission to the Medicare program, section 1866(c), 42 U.S.C.A. 1395cc(c), provides:

(1) Where the Secretary has terminated or has refused to renew an agreement under this title with a provider of services, such provider may not file another agreement under this title unless the Secretary finds that the reason for the termination or nonrenewal has been removed and that there is reasonable assurance that it will not recur.

That section goes on to provide:

(2) Where the Secretary has terminated or has refused to renew an agreement under this title with a provider of services, the Secretary shall promptly notify each State agency which administers or supervises the administration of a State plan approved under title XIX of such termination or nonrenewal.

◆ NOTE: Pursuant to section 4212(e)(4) of P.L. 100-203, the Omnibus Budget Reconciliation Act of 1987, for the period prior to October 1, 1990, paragraph (2) above is designated paragraph (3), and the following paragraph (2) applies:

(2) In the case of a skilled nursing facility participating in the programs established by this title and title XIX [Medicaid], the Secretary may enter into an agreement under this section only if such facility has been approved pursuant to section 1910(a) [42 U.S.C.A. 1396i(a), which pertains to certification of SNF's, and which does not apply after October 1, 1990], and the term of any such agreement shall be in accordance with the period of approval of eligibility specified by the Secretary pursuant to such section.

As amended by section 4162(a) of P.L. 101-508, the Omnibus Budget Reconciliation Act of 1990 (OBRA 90), effective November 5, 1990, and applicable with respect to partial hospitalization services provided after September 1991, for section 1866 purposes, provider of services is redefined as follows:

(e) For purposes of this section, the term "provider of services" shall include —

(1) a clinic, rehabilitation agency, or public health agency if, in the case of a clinic or rehabilitation agency, such clinic or agency meets the requirements of section 1861(p)(4)(A) [42 U.S.C.A. 1395x(p)(4)(A), which pertains to outpatient physical therapy services] (or meets the requirements of such section through the operation of section 1861(g) [42 U.S.C.A. 1395x(g), which pertains to outpatient occupational therapy services]), or if, in the case of a public health agency, such agency meets the requirements of section 1861(p)(4)(B) [which pertains to outpatient rehabilitation therapy services] (or meets the requirements of such section through the operation of section 1861(g)), but only with respect to the furnishing of outpatient physical therapy services (as therein defined) or (through the operation of section 1861(g)) with respect to the furnishing of outpatient occupational therapy services; and

(2) a community mental health center (as defined in section 1861(ff)(3)(B) [42 U.S.C.A. 1395x(ff)(3)(B), which defines partial hospitalization services]), but only with respect to the furnishing of partial hospitalization services (as described in section 1861(ff)(1)).

◆ NOTE: Prior to enactment of section 4162(b)(2) of OBRA 90, subsection (e) read as follows:

(e) For purposes of this section, the term "provider of services" shall include a clinic, rehabilitation agency, or public health agency if, in the case of a clinic or rehabilitation agency, such clinic or agency meets the requirements of section 1861(p)(4)(A) [42 U.S.C.A. 1395x(p)(4)(A), which pertains to outpatient physical therapy services] (or meets the requirements of such section through the operation of section 1861(g) [42 U.S.C.A. 1395x(g), which pertains to outpatient occupational therapy services]), or if, in the case of a public health agency, such agency meets the requirements of section 1861(p)(4)(B) [which pertains to outpatient rehabilitation therapy services] (or meets the requirements of such section through the operation of section 1861(g)), but only with respect to the furnishing of outpatient physical therapy services (as therein defined) or (through the operation of section 1861(g)) with respect to the furnishing of outpatient occupational therapy services.

Pursuant to section 6020 of OBRA 89, effective December 19, 1989, a new section 1866(i) provides as follows with respect to termination of provider agreements with psychiatric hospitals:

> (1) If the Secretary determines that a psychiatric hospital which has an agreement in effect under this section no longer meets the requirements for a psychiatric hospital under this title and further finds that the hospital's deficiencies —
>
> (A) immediately jeopardize the health and safety of its patients, the Secretary shall terminate such agreement; or
>
> (B) do not immediately jeopardize the health and safety of its patients, the Secretary may terminate such agreement, or provide that no payment will be made under this title with respect to any individual admitted to such hospital after the effective date of the finding, or both.
>
> (2) If a psychiatric hospital, found to have deficiencies described in paragraph (1)(B), has not complied with the requirements of this title —
>
> (A) within 3 months after the date the hospital is found to be out of compliance with such requirements, the Secretary shall provide that no payment will be made under this title with respect to any individual admitted to such hospital after the end of such 3-month period, or
>
> (B) within 6 months after the date the hospital is found to be out of compliance with such requirements, no payment may be made under this title with respect to any individual in the hospital until the Secretary finds that the hospital is in compliance with the requirements of this title.

Having provided for termination of provider agreements, Congress, in section 1866(h), 42 U.S.C.A. 1395cc(h), provided as follows for due process hearings on the issue of termination:

> (1) Except as provided in paragraph (2), an institution or agency dissatisfied with a determination by the Secretary that it is not a provider of services or with a determination described in subsection (b)(2) shall be entitled to a hearing thereon by the Secretary (after reasonable notice) to the same extent as is provided in section 205(b) [42 U.S.C.A. 405(b), which pertains to the due process hearings provided for social security benefit claims], and to judicial review of the Secretary's final decision

after such hearing as is provided in section 205(g) [which pertains to judicial review], except that, in so applying such sections and in applying section 205(l) thereto, any reference therein to the Commissioner of Social Security or the Social Security Administration shall be considered a reference to the Secretary or the Department of Health and Human Services, respectively. [NOTE: The clause beginning "except that" was added, effective March 31, 1995, by section 108(c)(5) of the Social Security Independence and Program Improvements Act of 1994, P.L. 103-296] .

(2) An institution or agency is not entitled to separate notice and opportunity for a hearing under both section 1128 and this section with respect to a determination or determinations based on the same underlying facts and issues.

Finally, section 205 provides as follows regarding administrative hearings and judicial review:

(b) (1) The Secretary is directed to make findings of fact, and decisions as to the rights of any individual applying for a payment under this title. Any such decision by the Secretary which involves a determination of disability and which is in whole or in part unfavorable to such individual shall contain a statement of the case, in understandable language, setting forth a discussion of the evidence, and stating the Secretary's determination and the reason or reasons upon which it is based. Upon request by any such individual or upon request by a wife, divorced wife, widow, surviving divorced wife, surviving divorced mother, surviving divorced father, husband, divorced husband, widower, surviving divorced husband, child or parent who makes a showing in writing that his or her rights may be prejudiced by any decision the Secretary has rendered, he shall give such applicant and such other individual reasonable notice and opportunity for a hearing with respect to such decision, and, if a hearing is held, shall, on the basis of evidence adduced at the hearing, affirm, modify, or reverse his findings of fact and such decision. Any such request with respect to such a decision must be filed within sixty days after notice of such decision is received by the individual making such request. The Commissioner of Social Security is further authorized, on the Commissioner's own motion, to hold such hearings and to conduct such investigations and other proceedings as the Commissioner may deem necessary or proper for the administration of this title. In the course of any hearing, investigation, or other proceeding, the Commissioner may administer oaths and affirmations, examine witnesses, and receive evidence. Evidence may be received at any hearing before the Commissioner of Social Security even though inadmissible under rules of evidence applicable to court procedure.

* * *

(g) Any individual, after any final decision of the Commissioner of Social Security made after a hearing to which he was a party, irrespective of the amount in controversy, may obtain a review of such decision by a civil action commenced within sixty days after the mailing to him of notice of such decision or within such further time as the Commissioner of Social Security may allow. Such action shall be brought in the district court of the United States for the judicial district in which the plaintiff resides, or has his principal place of business, or, if he does not reside or have his principal place of business within any such judicial district, in the District Court of the United States for the District of Columbia [United States District Court for the District of Columbia]. As part of the Commissioner's answer the Commissioner of Social Security shall file a certified copy of the transcript of the record including the evidence upon which the findings and decision complained of are based. The court shall have power to enter, upon the pleadings and transcript of the record, a judgment affirming, modifying, or reversing the decision of the Commissioner of Social Security, with or without remanding the cause for a rehearing. The findings of the Commissioner of Social Security as to any fact, if supported by substantial evidence, shall be conclusive, and where a claim has been denied by the Commissioner or a decision is rendered under subsection (b) hereof which is adverse to an individual who was a party to the hearing before the Commissioner of Social Security, because of failure of the claimant or such individual to submit proof in conformity with any regulation prescribed under subsection (a) hereof, the court shall review only the question of conformity with such regulations and the validity of such regulations. The court may, on motion of the Commissioner of Social Security made for good cause shown before the Commissioner files his answer, remand the case to the Commissioner of Social Security for further action by the Commissioner of Social Security, and it may at any time order additional evidence to be taken before the Commissioner of Social Security, but only upon a showing that there is new evidence which is material and that there is good cause for the failure to incorporate such evidence into the record in a prior proceeding; and the Commissioner of Social Security shall, after the case is remanded, and after hearing such additional evidence if so ordered, modify or affirm the Commissioner's findings of fact or the Commissioner's decision, or both, and shall file with the court any such additional and modified findings of fact and decision and a transcript of the additional record and testimony upon which the Commissioner's action in modifying or affirming was based. Such additional or modified findings of fact and decision shall be reviewable only to the extent provided for review of the original findings of fact and decision. The judgment of the court shall be final except that it shall be subject to review in the same manner as a judgment in other civil actions. Any action instituted in accordance with this subsection shall survive notwithstanding any change in the person occupying the office of Commissioner of Social Security or any vacancy in such office.

Subsection (a) of section 205, to which subsection (g) refers back, provides:

(a) The Commissioner of Social Security shall have full power and authority to make rules and regulations and to establish procedures, not inconsistent with the provisions of this title, which are necessary or appropriate to carry out such provisions, and shall adopt reasonable and proper rules and regulations to regulate and provide for the nature and extent of the proofs and evidence and the method of taking and furnishing the same in order to establish the right to benefits hereunder.

◆ NOTE: Effective March 31, 1995, section 110(a) of P.L. 203-296, the Social Security Program Independence and Program Improvement Act of 1994, changed references to the Department of Health and Human Services to the Social Security Administration, and references to the Secretary of Health and Human Services to the Commissioner of Social Security, and references to the pronouns "she", "her", "he", "him", and "his" to "the Commissioner" or "the Commissioner's", as appropriate, throughout section 205 of the Social Security Act.

For regulatory citations, see Chapter 6

§ 2:33 FAILURE BY HOSPITALS TO MAKE TIMELY REVIEW OF LONG-STAY CASES — Section 1866(d) [42 U.S.C.A. 1395cc(d)]

Summary

If there is a substantial failure by a hospital to make timely review of long-stay cases, section 1866(d), 42 U.S.C.A. 1395cc(d), provides that, in lieu of terminating the provider agreement of the hospital, the Secretary of Health and Human Services may deny payment for inpatient hospital services after the twentieth day of a continuous period of such service. The Secretary must give public notice of this sanction, as may be prescribed by regulations, to the hospital, the public, and the facility with which the hospital has a transfer agreement prior to imposing it. The Secretary may not impose it until he has given notice and opportunity for a hearing to the affected hospital. Denied payment may continue until there is reasonable assurance that failure to make timely review will not recur.

◆ NOTE: Prior to amendment of section 1866(d) by section 106(b)(1)(B)(i)-(iv) of the Social Security Act Amendments of 1994, P.L. 103-432, effective December 22, 1987, as if included in the Omnibus Budget Reconciliation Act of 1987, P.L. 100-203 (OBRA 87), this sanction also applied with respect to substantial failure by a skilled nursing facility to make timely review of long stay cases. See also section 101(a)(1) of the Medicare Catastrophic Coverage Repeal Act of 1989, P.L. 101-234, effective January 1, 1990, and section 104(d)(5) of the Medicare Catastrophic Coverage Act of 1988, P.L. 100-360, as corrected by section 608(d)(3)(F) of the Family Support Act of 1988, P.L. 100-485, effective January 1, 1989.

This implements the utilization review process described in section 1861(k), 42 U.S.C.A. 1395x(k). Pursuant to that process, hospitals and SNF's must review, on a sample or other basis, their admissions, the duration of patient stays, and the professional services (including drugs and biologicals) furnished — all with respect to medical necessity and to promote the most efficient use of available health facilities and services.

Utilization review committees (URC's) must be composed of two or more staff physicians. That means physicians as defined in section 1861(r)(1), 42 U.S.C.A. 1395x(r)(1)). URC's may include other professional personnel, as well. Moreover, a group similarly composed but from outside the institution may conduct utilization reviews for an institution if the group is established by the local medical society and some or all of the hospitals and skilled nursing facilities in the locality. (The latter is required in the case of a hospital or SNF where, because of the small size of the institution, or in the case of a SNF, because of the lack of an organized medical staff, or for any other reason established by regulation, it is impracticable for the institution to have its own committee.) If, and for so long as no outside group has been established, however, the review may be conducted by a group established in such other manner as the Secretary approves.

Utilization review committees must perform their reviews according to timetables established appropriately for different types of cases, but no later than one week following the scheduled day. They also must notify the institution, the individual, and the attending physician of their findings promptly, and they must provide an opportunity for consultation with the attending physician before making their findings.

If the Secretary finds that a utilization review process established under Medicaid is superior to the process required by Medicare, he may require hospitals and SNF's to use the Medicaid process instead. Presumably, this would avoid dual processes.

Finally, transfer agreements, as described in section 1861(l), 42 U.S.C.A. 1395x(l), are required of hospitals and SNF's in order to effect the transfer of patients from one such institution to the other to provide the most appropriate care at the least cost, which is the goal of utilization review.

Transfer agreements must be in writing, whether between related or unrelated organizations. They must provide that transfer will be effected whenever an attending physician determines that to be appropriate. And they must provide that the institutions will transmit medical and other information necessary or useful to the care or treatment of the individual transferred. The only exception is for SNF's which have attempted without success but in good faith to enter into such an agreement with a hospital sufficiently close to make a transfer feasible. In such cases, the Secretary will deem them to have in effect a transfer agreement if he finds doing so is in the public interest and essential to assuring extended care services for Medicare eligibles in the community.

Statutory Provisions

Section 1866(d), 42 U.S.C.A. 1395cc(d), provides:

> If the Secretary finds that there is a substantial failure to make timely review in accordance with section 1861(k) [42 U.S.C.A. 1395x(k), which pertains to utilization review requirements] of long-stay cases in a hospital, he may, in lieu of terminating his agreement with such hospital, decide that, with respect to any individual admitted to such hospital or facility after a subsequent date specified by him, no payment shall be made under this title for inpatient hospital services (including inpatient psychiatric hospital services) after the 20th day of a continuous period of such services. Such decision may be made effective only after such notice to the hospital, or (in the case of a skilled nursing facility) to the facility and the hospital or hospitals with which it has a transfer agreement, and to the public, as may be prescribed by regulations, and its effectiveness shall terminate when the Secretary finds that the reason therefor has been removed and that there is reasonable assurance that it will not recur. The Secretary shall not make any such decision except after reasonable notice and opportunity for hearing to the institution or agency affected thereby.

◆ NOTE: Prior to amendment by section 106(b)(1)(B)(i)-(iv) of the Social Security Act Amendments of 1994, P.L. 103-432, effective December 22, 1987, as if included in OBRA 87, section 1866(d) read: "If the Secretary finds that there is a substantial failure to make timely review in accordance with section 1861(k) [42 U.S.C.A. 1395x(k), which pertains to utilization review requirements] of long-stay cases in a hospital or skilled nursing facility, he may, in lieu of terminating his agreement with such hospital or facility, decide that, with respect to any individual admitted to such hospital or facility after a subsequent date specified by him, no payment shall be made under this title for inpatient hospital services (including inpatient psychiatric hospital services) after the 20th day of a continuous period of such services or for post-hospital extended care services after such day of a continuous period of such care as is prescribed in or pursuant to regulations, as the case may be. Such decision may be made effective only after such notice to the hospital, or (in the case of a skilled nursing facility) to the facility and the hospital or hospitals with which it has a transfer agreement, and to the public, as may be prescribed by regulations, and its effectiveness shall terminate when the Secretary finds that the reason therefor has been removed and that there is reasonable assurance that it will not recur. The Secretary shall not make any such decision except after reasonable notice and opportunity for hearing to the institution or agency affected thereby."

With regard to utilization review, section 1861(k), 42 U.S.C.A. 1395x(k), provides:

A utilization review plan of a hospital or skilled nursing facility shall be considered sufficient if it is applicable to services furnished by the institution to individuals entitled to insurance benefits under this title and if it provides —

(1) for the review, on a sample or other basis, of admissions to the institution, the duration of stays therein, and the professional services (including drugs and biologicals) furnished, (A) with respect to the medical necessity of the services, and (b) for the purpose of promoting the most efficient use of available health facilities and services;

(2) for the review to be made by either (A) a staff committee of the institution composed of two or more physicians (of which at least two must be physicians described in subsection (r)(1) of this section [which defines "physician" to include the various kinds of practitioners who may participate in Medicare]), with or without participation of other professional personnel, or (B) a group outside the institution which is similarly composed and (i) which is established by the local medical society and some or all of the hospitals and skilled nursing facilities in the locality, or (ii) if (and for as long as) there has not been established such a group which serves such institution, which is established in such other manner as may be approved by the Secretary;

(3) for such review, in each case of inpatient hospital services or extended care services furnished to such an individual dur-

ing a continuous period of extended duration, as of such days of such period (which may differ for different classes of cases) as may be specified in regulations, with such review to be made as promptly as possible, after each day so specified, and in no event later than one week following such day; and

(4) for prompt notification to the institution, the individual, and his attending physician of any finding (made after opportunity for consultation to such attending physician) by the physician members of such committee or group that any further stay in the institution is not medically necessary.

The review committee must be composed as provided in clause (B) of paragraph (2) rather than as provided in clause (A) of such paragraph in the case of any hospital or skilled nursing facility where, because of the small size of the institution, or (in the case of a skilled nursing facility) because of lack of an organized medical staff, or for such other reason or reasons as may be included in regulations, it is impracticable for the institution to have a properly functioning staff committee for the purposes of this subsection. If the Secretary determines that the utilization review procedures established pursuant to title XIX are superior in their effectiveness to the procedures required under this section, he may, to the extent that he deems it appropriate, require for purposes of this title that the procedures established pursuant to title XIX be utilized instead of the procedures required by this section.

With regard to agreements for transfers of patients between hospitals and skilled nursing facilities, section 1861(l), 42 U.S.C.A. 1395x(l), provides:

A hospital and a skilled nursing facility shall be considered to have a transfer agreement in effect if, by reason of a written agreement between them or (in case the two institutions are under common control) by reason of a written undertaking by the person or body which controls them, there is reasonable assurance that—

(1) transfer of patients will be effected between the hospital and the skilled nursing facility whenever such transfer is medically appropriate as determined by the attending physician; and

(2) there will be interchange of medical and other information necessary or useful in the care and treatment of individuals transferred between the institutions, or in determining whether such individuals can be adequately cared for otherwise than in either of such institutions.

Any skilled nursing facility which does not have such an agreement in effect, but which is found by a State agency (of the State in which such facility is situated) with which an agreement under section 1864 is in effect (or, in the case of a State in which no such agency has an agreement under section 1864, by the Secretary) to have attempted in good faith to enter into such an agreement with a hospital sufficiently close to the facility to make feasible the transfer between them of patients and the information referred to in paragraph (2), shall be considered to have such an agreement in effect if and for so long as such agency (or the Secretary, as the case may be) finds that to do so is in the public interest and essential to assuring extended care services for persons in the community who are eligible for payments with respect to such services under this title.

For regulatory citations, see Chapter 6

§ 2:34 FAILURE BY HOSPITALS TO HAVE ARRANGEMENTS WHICH PRECLUDE CERTAIN PRACTITIONERS AND SUPPLIERS FROM SEEKING FURTHER PAYMENT FROM BENEFICIARIES — Section 1866(g) [42 U.S.C.A. 1395cc(g)]

Summary

Section 1866(g), 42 U.S.C.A. 1395cc(g), requires hospital providers to have "arrangements" with health care practitioners and suppliers which preclude liability for Medicare beneficiaries to make additional payments to such practioners and suppliers. Pursuant to section 1861(w)(1), 42 U.S.C.A. 1395x(w)(1), "arrangements" means arrangements under which receipt of payment by a hospital, skilled nursing facility, home health agency, or hospice program with respect to services for which an individual is entitled to have Medicare pay discharges the liability of the individual or any other person.

Except as permitted under the statutory authorization for provider agreements, any person who knowingly and willfully presents, or causes to be presented, a bill or request for payment inconsistent with such arrangements is subject to a civil money penalty not to exceed $2,000. Enforcement procedures for this civil money penalty are governed by section 1128A, 42 U.S.C.A. 1320a-7a, which authorizes civil money penalties for a variety of offenses.

This requirement for arrangements does not apply with respect to physicians' services and services of a certified registered nurse anesthetist (CRNA). Pursuant to section 4147(c)(2) of P.L. 101-508, the Omnibus Budget Reconciliation Act of 1990 (OBRA 90), applicable to services furnished after December 1990, it does not apply to certain services furnished by physician assistants, certified nurse-midwives, and qualified psychologists. Pursuant to section 147(e)(7) of the Social Security Act Amendments of 1994, P.L. 103-432, effective November 5, 1990, as if included in OBRA 90, it also does not apply to certain services furnished by a nurse practitioner or clinical nurse specialist working in collaboration with a physician in a rural area.

Statutory Provisions

Section 1866(g), 42 U.S.C.A. 1395cc(g), provides:

> Except as permitted under subsection (a)(2) [42 U.S.C.A. 1395cc(a)(2), the basic provider agreement provision], any person who knowingly and willfully presents, or causes to be presented, a bill or request for payment inconsistent with an arrangement under subsection (a)(1)(H) [42 U.S.C.A. 1395cc(a)(1)(H), which requires hospital providers to have all items and services covered under Medicare (other than physicians' services and services of a certified registered nurse anesthetist, and, with respect to services furnished after December 1990, other than certain services furnished by physician assistants, and services of certified nurse-midwives and qualified psychologists, and certain services furnished by a nurse practioner or clinical nurse specialist working in collaboration with a physician in a rural area) furnished to an inpatient provided by the hospital under "arrangements" that preclude further liability for payment by the patient] or in violation of the requirement [of section 1861(w)(1)] for such an arrangement, is subject to a civil money penalty of not to exceed $2,000. The

provisions of section 1128A [42 U.S.C.A. 1320a-7a] (other than subsections (a) and (b)) shall apply to a civil money penalty under the previous sentence in the same manner as such provisions apply to a penalty or proceeding under section 1128A(a).

Section 1866(a)(1)(H) provides:

(a) (1) Any provider of services (except a fund designated for purposes of section 1814(g) [42 U.S.C.A. 1395f(g), which pertains to payment for services of a physician in a teaching hospital] and section 1835(e) [42 U.S.C.A. 1395n(e), which pertains to procedure for payment of claims for inpatient hospital services to funds designated by organized medical staff of the hospital where services are furnished or by faculty of a medical school where services are furnished]) shall be qualified to participate under this title and shall be eligible for payments under this title if it files with the Secretary an agreement—

* * *

(H) in the case of hospitals which provide services for which payment may be made under this title, and in the case of rural primary care hospitals which provide rural primary care hospital services [this clause pertaining to rural primary care hospitals added effective December 19, 1989, by section 6003(g)(3)(D)(xii) and (xiii) of P.L. 101-239, the Omnibus Budget Reconciliation Act of 1989] to have all items and services (other than physicians' services as defined in regulations for purposes of section 1862(a)(14) [42 U.S.C.A. 1395y(a)(14), which excludes from coverage expenses incurred for items or services other than physicians' services furnished to a patient in a hospital by an entity other than the hospital unless the services are furnished under "arrangements" which preclude further liability for the patient] and other than services described by section 1861(s)(2)(K)(i) [42 U.S.C.A. 1395x(s)(2)(K)(i), which pertains to certain services furnished by physician assistants], or 1861(s)(2)(K)(iii) [42 U.S.C.A. 1395x(s)(2)(K)(iii), which pertains to certain services performed by a nurse practioner or clinical nurse specialist working in collaboration with a physician in a rural area], certified nurse-midwife services, qualified psychologist ser-

> vices, and services of a certified registered nurse anesthetist) (i) that are furnished to an individual who is a patient of the hospital, and (ii) for which the individual is entitled to have payment made under this title, furnished by the hospital or otherwise under arrangements (as defined in section 1861(w)(1) [42 U.S.C.A. 1395x(w)(1)]) made by the hospital,. . .

◆ NOTE: The reference above to section 1861(s)(2)(K)(i), to certified nurse-midwife services, and to qualified psychologist services applies to such services furnished after December 1990, pursuant to section 4157(c)(2) of OBRA 90. The reference to section 1861(s)(2)(K)(iii), regarding certain services performed by a nurse practitioner or clinical nurse specialist, applies effective November 5, 1990, as if included in OBRA 90, pursuant to section 147(e)(7) of the Social Security Act Amendments of 1994, P.L. 103-432.

Those references had been, respectively, to 1861(s)(2)(K)(i) and 1861(s)(2)(K)(iii). Section 4302(a) of the Balanced Budget Act of 1997 replaced the references to section 1861(s)(2)(K)(i) or 1861(s)(2)(K)(iii) with references to section 1861(s)(2)(K). That change applies with respect to services furnished and supplies provided on and after January 1, 1998.]

Section 1861(s)(2)(K), as amended by section 4512(a) of the Balanced Budget Act of 1997, P.L. 105–33, applicable to services furnished and supplies provided on or after January 1, 1998, defines medical services to include:

> (K)(i) services which would be physicians' services if furnished by a physician (as defined in subsection (r)(1)) and which are performed by a physician assistant (as defined in subsection (aa)(5)) under the supervision of a physician (as so defined) but only if no facility or other provider charges or is paid any amounts with respect to the furnishing of such services, and which the physician assistant is legally authorized to perform by the State in which the services are performed and such services and supplies furnished as incident to such services as would be covered under subparagraph (A) if furnished incident to a physician's professional service; and

(ii) services which would be physicians' services if furnished by a physician (as defined in subsection (r)(1)) and which are performed by a nurse practitioner or clinical nurse specialist (as defined in subsection (aa)(5)) working in collaboration (as defined in subsection (aa)(6)) with a physician (as defined in subsection (r)(1)) which the nurse practitioner or clinical nurse specialist is legally authorized to perform by the State in which the services are performed, and such services and supplies furnished as an incident to such services as would be covered under subparagraph (A) if furnished incident to a physician's professional service, but only if no facility or other provider charges or is paid any amounts with respect to the furnishing of such services;

◆ NOTE: Prior to amendment by section 4512 of the Balanced Budget Act of 1997, section 1861(s)(2)(K)(i) and, as amended by section 147(e)(1)(a)-(b) of the Social Security Act Amendments of 1994, effective November 5, 1990, as if included in OBRA 90, section 1861(s)(2)(K)(iii) define medical services to include:

◆ (i) services which would be physicians' services if furnished by a physician (as defined in subsection (r)(1)) and which are performed by a physician assistant (as defined in subsection (aa)(5)) under the supervision of a physician (as so defined) (I) in a hospital, skilled nursing facility, or nursing facility (as defined in section 1919(a) [42 U.S.C.A. 1396r(a)]), (II) as an assistant at surgery, or (III) in a rural area (as defined in section 1886(d)(2)(D) [42 U.S.C.A. 1395ww(d)(2)(D)]) that is designated, under section 332(a)(1)(a) of the Public Service Act [sic Public Health Service Act], as a health manpower shortage area, and which the physician assistant is legally authorized to perform by the State in which the services are performed,

* * *

◆ (iii) services which would be physicians' services if furnished by a physician (as defined in subsection (r)(1)) and which are performed by a nurse practitioner or clinical nurse specialist (as defined in subsection (aa)(3)) working in collaboration (as defined in subsection (aa)(6)), with a physician (as defined in subsection (r)(1)) in a rural area (as defined in 1886(d)(2)(D)) which the nurse practitioner or clinical nurse specialist is authorized to perform by the State in which the services are performed, and such services and supplies furnished as an incident to such services as would be covered under subparagraph (A) if furnished as an incident to a physician's professional service[.]

Section 1861(w) provides:

> (1) The term "arrangements" is limited to arrangements under which receipt of payment by the hospital, critical care access hospital, skilled nursing facility, home health agency, or hospice program (whether in its own right or as agent), with respect to services for which an individual is entitled to have payment made under this title, discharges the liability of such individual or any other person to pay for the services.

◆ [NOTE: Effective with repsect to items and services furnished on or after October 1, 1997, section 4201(c)(1) of the Balanced Budget Act of 1997 substituted the phrase "critical accesss hospital" for "rural primary care hospital".]

For regulatory citations, see Chapter 6

§ 2:35 FAILURE BY HOSPITALS AND CERTAIN PHYSICIANS TO EXAMINE AND TREAT PERSONS FOR EMERGENCY MEDICAL CONDITIONS AND WOMEN IN LABOR—Section 1867 [42 U.S.C.A. 1395(dd)]

Summary

Section 1867, 42 U.S.C.A. 1395(dd), as amended by P.L. 101-508, the Omnibus Budget Reconciliation Act of 1990 (OBRA 90), requires any hospital that has an emergency department to provide for an appropriate medical screening examination of any person, whether or not a Medicare beneficiary, who appears at the emergency department and requests treatment for a medical condition. The purpose of that screening examination is to determine whether an emergency medical condition exists.

According to section 1867(b), such a hospital then must, within staff and facilities available at the hospital, provide for such medical examination and treatment as may be required to stabilize any emergency medical condition of the individual that is found. Alternatively, it must provide for transfer of the individual to another medical facility. If an individual, or a person acting on the individual's behalf, refuses to accept examination or treatment or refuses to accept transfer to another facility, the hospital must "take all reasonable steps" to obtain written informed consent documenting such refusal.

Pursuant to section 1867(c)(1), no hospital may transfer an individual with an emergency medical condition if the medical condition has not been stabilized unless —

1. the individual, or a legally responsible person acting on the individual's behalf, has been informed of the hospital's obligations under section 1867 and of the risk of transfer, and the individual or legally responsible person then requests transfer to another facility in writing;
2. a physician certifies in writing that, based on information available at the time of transfer, medical benefits reasonably expected from appropriate medical treatment at another medical facility outweigh increased risks to the individual, and, in the case of a woman in labor, to the unborn child from effecting the transfer; and
3. the transfer is an appropriate transfer to the receiving facility.

According to section 1867(c)(2), an appropriate transfer is one —

1. in which the transferring hospital provides medical treatment within its capacity which minimizes risks to the individual's health, and, in the case of a woman in labor, to the health of the unborn child;
2. in which the receiving hospital has available space and qualified personnel to treat the individual and has agreed to accept transfer and to provide appropriate medical treatment;
3. in which the transferring hospital sends to the receiving facility all medical records, or copies thereof, related to the emergency condition of the individual which are available at the time of the transfer, along with the individual's informed written consent to transfer, the required physician certification authorizing transfer to the receiving hospital, and the name and address of any on-call physician who refused or failed to appear within a reasonable time to provide necessary stabilizing treatment;
4. in which the transfer is effected through qualified personnel and transportation equipment, as required, including use of

necessary and appropriate life support measures during the transfer; and

5. which meet such other requirements as the Secretary of Health and Human Services finds necessary for the health and safety of individuals transferred.

Pursuant to section 1867(d)(1)(A), a participating hospital that negligently violates this requirement is subject to a civil money penalty not to exceed $50,000 for each violation (or, in the case of a hospital with fewer than 100 beds, not to exceed $25,000). Enforcement procedures for this civil money penalty are governed by section 1128A, 42 U.S.C.A. 1320a-7a, which authorizes civil money penalties for a variety of offenses.

Pursuant to section 1867(d)(1)(B), any physician responsible for examination, treatment, or transfer of an individual in a participating hospital, including a physician on-call for the care of such an individual, who negligently violates a requirement of section 1867, is subject to a civil money penalty under section 1128A. As with the hospital, the civil money penalty for the physician's violation may not exceed $50,000. If the violation is gross and flagrant or is repeated, the physician is subject also to exclusion from Medicare and "State health care programs".

The same applies to a physician who certifies that medical benefits reasonably to be expected from transfer outweigh risks associated with transfer, if the physician knew or should have known benefits did not outweigh risks, or if the physician misrepresents an individual's condition or other information, including a hospital's obligations under section 1867.

If, after an initial examination, a physician determines an individual requires services of a physician on the hospital's required list of on-call physicians, and if that physician notifies the on-call physician, and if the on-call physician fails or refuses to appear within a reasonable time, and if the physician orders transfer of the individual because the physician determines that without the services of the on-call physician benefits of transfer outweigh risks of transfer, the physician authorizing the transfer is not subject to a penalty. That exemption does not apply, however, to the hospital or to the on-call physician.

◆ NOTE: Pursuant to section 1867(d)(1), prior to amendment by section 4008(b)(3)(A)(i) of OBRA 90, which applies to actions occurring on or after the first day of the sixth month beginning after November 5, 1990, any hospital that knowingly and willfully, or negligently, failed to comply is subject to termination of its Medicare provider agreement pursuant to section 1866(b), 42 U.S.C.A. 1395cc(b), or, at the option of the Secretary of Health and Human Services, upon reasonable notice to the hospital and the public, to suspension of its provider agreement for such period as the Secretary deems appropriate.

Thus OBRA 90 broadened the scope of the statute, effective with respect to acts occurring on or after May 1, 1991, by applying it to negligent violations, as opposed to knowing violations. In addition, OBRA 90 reduced the civil money penalty maximum for hospitals with fewer than 100 beds to $25,000, and it made the exclusion penalty for physicians applicable in cases where the violation is gross and flagrant or repeated, instead of where it is knowing and willful or negligent.

Section 1867(d)(2)(A) gives an individual who suffers personal harm as a direct result of a participating hospital's violation of section 1867 a private cause of action against that hospital. In such a case, the individual may recover whatever damages are available under the law of the State where the hospital is located and such equitable relief as is appropriate.

Section 1867(d)(2)(B) gives a private cause of action to any medical facility that suffers financial loss as a direct result of a participating hospital's violation.

Pursuant to section 1867(d)(2)(C), these private rights expire two years after the date of the violation.

◆ NOTE: Section 4207(a)(1)(A) of OBRA 90 added a new section 1867(d)(3) which applies to actions occurring on or after May 1, 1991. It requires the Secretary to request the appropriate PRO with a contract under Title XI to assess whether a transferred individual had an emergency medical condition which had not been stabilized and to provide a report on its findings. Except when delay will jeopardize health or safety of individuals, the Secretary must request this review and provide at least 60 days to obtain it before imposing a sanction under section 1867.

For section 1867 purposes, subsection (e) defines "emergency medical condition" as a medical condition manifested by acute symptoms, including severe pain, of such severity that absence of immediate medical attention could reasonably be expected to result in —

1. serious jeopardy to an individual's health, or, with respect to a pregnant woman, to the health of the woman or her unborn child;
2. serious impairment to bodily functions; or
3. serious dysfunction of any bodily organ or part.

With respect to a pregnant woman having contractions, an emergency medical condition is one where there is inadequate time to effect a safe transfer to another hospital before delivery, or where transfer may pose a threat to the health or safety of the woman or the unborn child.

With respect to emergency medical condition, "to stabilize" means to provide such medical treatment as may be necessary to assure, within reasonable medical probability, that no material deterioration of the condition is likely to result from or occur during transfer of the individual. In the case of a pregnant woman having contractions, it means to assure that the woman is not likely to deliver (including the placenta).

"Stabilized" means that no material deterioration of the condition is likely, within reasonable medical probability, to result from or occur during transfer of the individual. In the case of a pregnant woman having contractions, it means that the woman has delivered (including the placenta).

"Transfer" means movement, including discharge, of an individual outside a hospital's facilities at the direction of any person employed by, or affiliated or associated, directly or indirectly, with the hospital. It does not include such movement of an individual who has been declared dead, or who leaves the facility without permission of such a person.

"Hospital" includes a critical access hospital. [NOTE: These were formerly known as rural primary care hospitals. Section 4201(c)(1) of the Balanced Budget Act of 1997 changed the designation to critical access hospital, effective October 1, 1997.

These sanctions are designed to prevent "patient dumping." The statute specifies in section 1867(f), however, that its provisions do not preempt any State or local law except to the extent they directly conflict. Furthermore, section 1867(g) provides that a participating hospital with specialized capabilities or facilities, such as a burn unit, a shock trauma unit, a neonatal intensive care unit, or (with respect to rural areas) a regional referral center identified by the Secretary in regulation, may not refuse to accept an appropriate transfer of an individual who requires such specialized capabilities or facilities if the hospital has the capacity to treat the individual.

Finally, section 1867(h) provides that a participating hospital may not delay provision of an appropriate medical screening examination or further medical examination and treatment to inquire about the individual's method of payment or insurance status. And section 1867(i) provides that a participating hospital may not penalize or take adverse action against any qualified medical person (as defined by the Secretary) or any physician because the physician refuses to authorize transfer of an individual with an emergency medical condition that has not been stabilized. It also prohibits a participating hospital from penalizing or taking any adverse action against any hospital employee because the employee reports a violation of a requirement of section 1867. Prior to amendment by section 4207(k)(3) of OBRA 90, effective November 5, 1990, this whistleblower protection applied only to physicians.

◆ NOTE: Effective December 19, 1989, section 6003(g)(3)(D)(xiv) of OBRA 89 added a new paragraph (e)(6) to section 1876. This was subsequently redesignated (e)(5). Section 6211 of OBRA 89 made even more substantial changes in section 1867. These were effective July 1, 1990. Compare the two versions of the statute set forth below.

Statutory Provisions

Subsequent to amendment by sections 6003(g)(3)(D)(xiv) and 6211 of P.L. 101-239, the Omnibus Budget Reconciliation Act of 1989, section 1867, 42 U.S.C.A. 1395dd, provides:

(a) MEDICAL SCREENING REQUIREMENT. — In the case of a hospital that has a hospital emergency department, if any individual (whether or not eligible for benefits under this title) comes to the emergency department and a request is made on the individual's behalf for examination or treatment for a medical condition, the hospital must provide for an appropriate medical screening examination within the capability of the hospital's emergency department, including ancillary services routinely available to the emergency department, to determine whether or not an emergency medical condition (within the meaning of subsection (e)(1)) exists.

The statute goes on, as follows, to prescribe the scope of required treatment and, under certain circumstances, to permit hospitals to transfer such persons to other facilities:

(b) NECESSARY STABILIZING TREATMENT FOR EMERGENCY MEDICAL CONDITIONS AND LABOR.—

(1) IN GENERAL.—If any individual (whether or not eligible for benefits under this title) comes to a hospital and the hospital determines that the individual has an emergency medical condition, the hospital must provide either—

(A) within the staff and facilities available at the hospital, for such further medical examination and such treatment as may be required to stabilize the medical condition, or

(B) for transfer of the individual to another medical facility in accordance with subsection (c).

(2) REFUSAL TO CONSENT TO TREATMENT.—A hospital is deemed to meet the requirement of paragraph (1)(A) with respect to an individual if the hospital offers the individual the further medical examination and treatment described in that paragraph and informs the individual or a person acting on the individual's behalf) of the risks and benefits to the individual of such examination and treatment, but the individual (or a person acting on the individual's behalf) refuses to consent to the examination or treatment. The hospital shall take all reasonable steps to secure the individual's (or person's) written informed consent to refuse such examination and treatment.

(3) REFUSAL TO CONSENT TO TRANSFER.—A hospital is deemed to meet the requirement of paragraph (1) with respect to an individual if the hospital offers to transfer the individual to another medical facility in accordance with subsection (c) and informs the individual (or a person acting on the individual's behalf) of the risks and benefits to the individual of such transfer, but the individual (or a person acting on the individual's behalf) refuses to consent to the transfer. The hospital shall take all reasonable steps to secure the individual's (or person's) written informed consent to refuse such transfer.

(c) RESTRICTING TRANSFERS UNTIL INDIVIDUAL STABILIZED.—

(1) RULE. — If an individual at a hospital has an emergency medical condition which has not been stabilized (within the meaning of subsection (e)(3)(B)), the hospital may not transfer the patient unless —

(A) (i) the individual (or a legally responsible person acting on the individual's behalf) after being informed of the hospital's obligations under this section and of the risk of transfer, in writing requests transfer to another medical facility,

(ii) a physician (within the meaning of section 1861(r)(1) [42 U.S.C.A. 1395x(r)(1), which describes the various practitioners who may participate in Medicare]) has signed a certification that, based upon the information available at the time of transfer, the medical benefits reasonably expected from the provision of appropriate medical treatment at another medical facility outweigh the increased risks to the individual and, in the case of labor, to the unborn child from effecting the transfer, or

(iii) if a physician is not physically present in the emergency department at the time an individual is transferred, a qualified medical person (as defined by the Secretary in regulations) has signed a certification described in clause (ii) after a physician (as defined in section 1861(r)), in consultation with the person, has made the determination described in such clause, and subsequently countersigns the certification; and

(B) the transfer is an appropriate transfer (within the meaning of paragraph (2)) to that facility.

A certification described in clause (ii) or (iii) of subparagraph (A) shall include a summary of the risks and benefits upon which the certification is based.

(2) APPROPRIATE TRANSFER. — An appropriate transfer to a medical facility is a transfer —

(A) in which the transferring hospital provides the medical treatment within its capacity which minimizes the risks to the individual's health and, in the case of a woman in labor, the health of the unborn child;

(B) in which the receiving facility —

(i) has available space and qualified personnel for the treatment of the individual, and

(ii) has agreed to accept transfer of the individual and to provide appropriate medical treatment;

(C) in which the transferring hospital sends to the receiving facility all medical records (or copies thereof), related to the emergency condition for which the individual has presented, available at the time of the transfer, including records related to the individual's emergency medical condition, observations of signs or symptoms, preliminary diagnosis, treatment provided, results of any tests and the informed written consent or certification (or copy thereof) provided under paragraph (1)(A), and the name and address of any on-call physician (described in subsection (d)(1)(C) [Prior to amendment by section 4008(b)(3)(A)(iii) of P.L. 101-508, the Omnibus Budget Reconciliation Act of 1990 (OBRA 90), which applies to actions occurring on or after the first day of the sixth month beginning after November 5, 1990, i.e., May 1, 1991, the reference was to "(d)(2)(C)".]) who has refused or failed to appear within a reasonable time to provide necessary stabilizing treatment;

(D) in which the transfer is effected through qualified personnel and transportation equipment, as required including the use of necessary and medically appropriate life support measures during the transfer; and

(E) which meets such other requirements as the Secretary may find necessary in the interest of the health and safety of individuals transferred.

The statute then provides the following sanctions for hospitals which fail to comply:

(d) ENFORCEMENT. —

(1) CIVIL MONETARY PENALTIES. — (A) A participating hospital that negligently [Pursuant to sections 4008(b)(1) and 4207(a)(2) of OBRA 90, respectively, "negligently" was substituted for "knowingly" here and below in paragraph (B). These changes apply to actions occurring on or after the first day of the sixth month beginning after November 5, 1990.] violates a requirement of this section is subject to a civil money penalty of not more than $50,000 (or not more than $25,000 in the case

of a hospital with less than 100 beds) [Section 4008(b)(2) of OBRA 90 added this parenthetical clause which applies to actions occurring on or after the first day of the sixth month beginning after November 5, 1990.] for each such violation. The provisions of section 1128A [42 U.S.C.A. 1320a-7a] (other than subsections (a) and (b)) shall apply to a civil money penalty under this subparagraph in the same manner as such provisions apply with respect to a penalty or proceeding under section 1128A(a).

(B) Subject to subparagraph (C), any physician who is responsible for the examination, treatment, or transfer of an individual in a participating hospital, including a physician on-call for the care of such an individual, and who negligently violates a requirement of this section, including a physician who—

(i) signs a certification under subsection (c)(1)(A) that the medical benefits reasonably to be expected from a transfer to another facility outweigh the risks associated with the transfer, if the physician knew or should have known that the benefits did not outweigh the risks, or

(ii) misrepresents an individual's condition or other information, including a hospital's obligations under this section,

is subject to a civil money penalty of not more than $50,000 for each such violation and, if the violation is gross and flagrant or is repeated [Pursuant to section 4207(a)(3) of OBRA 90, the phrase "gross and flagrant or is repeated" was substituted for "knowing and willful or negligent". This change applies to actions occurring on or after the first day of the sixth month beginning after November 5, 1990.], to exclusion from participation in this title and State health care programs. The provisions of section 1128A (other than the first and second sentences of subsection (a) and subsection (b)) shall apply to a civil money penalty and exclusion under this subparagraph in the same manner as such provisions apply with respect to a penalty, exclusion, or proceeding under section 1128A(a).

(C) If, after an initial examination, a physician determines that the individual requires the services of a physician listed by the hospital on its list of on-call physicians (required to be maintained under section 1866(a)(1)(I)) and notifies the on-call physician and the on-call physician fails or refuses to appear within a reasonable period of time, and the physician orders the transfer of the individual because the physician determines that without the services of the on-call physician the benefits of transfer outweigh the risks of transfer, the physician authorizing the transfer shall not be subject to a penalty under subparagraph (B). However, the previous sentence shall not apply to the hospital or to the on-call physician who failed or refused to appear.

In the following terms, section 1867(d) grants a private cause of action to patients when personal harm results from violation of the duty to examine and treat, and to a receiving facility when a wrongful transfer results in financial loss:

(2) CIVIL ENFORCEMENT. —

(A) PERSONAL HARM. — Any individual who suffers personal harm as a direct result of a participating hospital's violation of a requirement of this section may, in a civil action against the participating hospital, obtain those damages available for personal injury under the law of the State in which the hospital is located, and such equitable relief as is appropriate.

(B) FINANCIAL LOSS TO OTHER MEDICAL FACILITY. — Any medical facility that suffers a financial loss as a direct result of a participating hospital's violation of a requirement of this section may, in a civil action against the participating hospital, obtain those damages available for financial loss, under the law of the State in which the hospital is located, and such equitable relief as is appropriate.

(C) LIMITATIONS ON ACTIONS. — No action may be brought under this paragraph more than two years after the date of the violation with respect to which the action is brought.

◆ NOTE: Section 4008(b)(3)(A)(i) of OBRA 90, applicable to actions occurring on or after the first day of the sixth month beginning after November 5, 1990, deleted former section 1867(d)(1) which read as follows:

ENFORCEMENT. —

(1) AS REQUIREMENT OF MEDICARE PROVIDER AGREEMENT. — If a hospital knowingly and willfully, or negligently, fails to meet the requirements of this section, such hospital is subject to —

(A) termination of its provider agreement under this title in accordance with section 1866(b) [42 U.S.C.A. 1395cc(b)], or

(B) at the option of the Secretary, suspension of such agreement for such period of time as the Secretary determines to be appropriate, upon reasonable notice to the hospital and to the public.

Effective the same time, section 4008(b)(3)(A)(ii) of OBRA 90 renumbered former paragraphs (2) and (3) as (1) and (2), presented above, respectively. In addition, also effective the same time, section 4207(a)(1)(A) of OBRA 90 added the following paragraph.

(3) CONSULTATION WITH PEER REVIEW ORGANIZATIONS. — In considering allegations of violations of the requirements of this section in imposing sanctions under paragraph (1), the Secretary shall request the appropriate utilization and quality control peer review organization (with a contract under part B of title XI) to assess whether the individual involved had an emergency medical condition which had not been stabilized, and provide a report on its findings. Except in the case in which a delay would jeopardize the health or safety of individuals, the Secretary shall request such a review before effecting a sanction under paragraph (1) and shall provide a period of at least 60 days for such review.

Subsection (e) then provides:

DEFINITIONS. — In this section:

(1) The term "emergency medical condition" means —

(A) a medical condition manifesting itself by acute symptoms of sufficient severity (including severe pain) such that the absence of immediate medical attention could reasonably be expected to result in —

(i) placing the health of the individual (or, with respect to a pregnant woman, the health of the woman or her unborn child) in serious jeopardy,

(ii) serious impairment to bodily functions, or

(iii) serious dysfunction of any bodily organ or part.

(B) with respect to a pregnant woman who is having contractions —

(i) that there is inadequate time to effect a safe transfer to another hospital before delivery, or

(ii) that transfer may pose a threat to the health or safety of the woman or unborn child.

(2) The term "participating hospital" means [a] hospital that has entered into a provider agreement under section 1866 [42 U.S.C.A. 1395cc].

(3) (A) The term "to stabilize" means, with respect to an emergency medical condition described in paragraph (1)(A), to provide such medical treatment of the condition as may be necessary to assure, within reasonable medical probability, that no material deterioration of the condition is likely to result from or occur during the transfer of the individual from a facility, or with respect to an emergency medical condition described in paragraph (1)(B), to deliver (including the placenta).

(B) The term "stabilized" means, with respect to an emergency medical condition described in paragraph (1)(A), that no material deterioration of the condition is likely, within reasonable medical probability, to result from or occur during the transfer of the individual from a facility, or, with respect to an emergency medical condition described in paragraph (1)(B), that the woman has delivered (including the placenta).

(4) The term "transfer" means the movement (including the discharge) of an individual outside a hospital's facilities at the direction of any person employed by (or affiliated or associated, directly or indirectly, with) the hospital, but does not include such a movement of an individual who (A) has been declared dead, or (B) leaves the facility without the permission of any such person.

(5) The term "hospital" includes a critical access hospital hospital (as defined in section 1861(mm)(1) [42 U.S.C.A. 1395x(mm)(1). NOTE: Effective October 1, 1997, section 4201(c)(1) of the Balanced Budget Act of 1997, P.L. 105–33,

substituted the phrase "critical access hospital" for "rural primary care hospital".].

Section 1867 goes on to provide:

(f) PREEMPTION. — The provisions of this section do not preempt any State or local law requirement, except to the extent that the requirement directly conflicts with a requirement of this section.

(g) NONDISCRIMINATION. — A participating hospital that has specialized capabilities or facilities (such as burn units, shock-trauma units, neonatal intensive care units, or (with respect to rural areas) regional referral centers as identified by the Secretary in regulation) shall not refuse to accept an appropriate transfer of an individual who requires such specialized capabilities or facilities if the hospital has the capacity to treat the individual.

(h) NO DELAY IN EXAMINATION OR TREATMENT. — A participating hospital may not delay provision of an appropriate medical screening examination required under subsection (a) or further medical examination and treatment required under subsection (b) in order to inquire about the individual's method of payment or insurance status.

Effective November 5, 1990, pursuant to section 4207(k)(3) of OBRA 90, section 1867(i) provides:

(i) WHISTLEBLOWER PROTECTIONS. — A participating hospital may not penalize or take adverse action against a qualified medical person described in subsection (c)(1)(A)(iii) or a physician because the person or physician refuses to authorize the transfer of an individual with an emergency medical condition that has not been stabilized or against any hospital employee because the employee reports a violation of a requirement of this section.

Previously, section 1867(i) read as follows:

(i) WHISTLEBLOWER PROTECTIONS. — A participating hospital may not penalize or take adverse action against a physician because the physician refuses to authorize the transfer of an individual with an emergency medical condition that has not been stabilized.

◆ NOTE: Effective December 19, 1989, section 6003(g)(3)(D)(xiv) of P.L. 101-239, the Omnibus Budget Reconciliation Act of 1989 added a new paragraph (e)(6) to section 1876. This was subsequently redesignated (e)(5). In addition, effective the first day of the first month that begins more than 180 days after December 19, 1989 (July 1, 1990), section 6211 of P.L. 101-239, the Omnibus Budget Reconciliation Act of 1989, made substantial changes in section 1867 of the Social Security Act.

Prior to those changes, section 1867, 42 U.S.C.A. 1395dd, provided:

> (a) MEDICAL SCREENING REQUIREMENT. — In the case of a hospital that has a hospital emergency department, if any individual (whether or not eligible for benefits under this title) comes to the emergency department and a request is made on the individual's behalf for examination or treatment for a medical condition, the hospital must provide for an appropriate medical screening examination within the capability of the hospital's emergency department to determine whether or not an emergency medical condition (within the meaning of subsection (e)(1)) exists or to determine if the individual is in active labor (within the meaning of subsection (e)(2)).

The statute prescribed the scope of required treatment and, under certain circumstances, permitted hospitals to transfer such persons to other facilities as follows:

> (b) NECESSARY STABILIZING TREATMENT FOR EMERGENCY MEDICAL CONDITIONS AND ACTIVE LABOR. —
>
> (1) IN GENERAL. — If any individual (whether or not eligible for benefits under this title) comes to a hospital and the hospital determines that the individual has an emergency medical condition or is in active labor, the hospital must provide either —
>
> (A) within the staff and facilities available at the hospital, for such further medical examination and such treatment as may be required to stabilize the medical condition or to provide for treatment of the labor, or
>
> (B) for transfer of the individual to another medical facility in accordance with subsection (c).

(2) REFUSAL TO CONSENT TO TREATMENT.—A hospital is deemed to meet the requirement of paragraph (1)(A) with respect to an individual if the hospital offers the individual the further medical examination and treatment described in that paragraph but the individual (or a person acting on the individual's behalf) refuses to consent to the examination or treatment.

(3) REFUSAL TO CONSENT TO TRANSFER.—A hospital is deemed to meet the requirement of paragraph (1) with respect to an individual if the hospital offers to transfer the individual to another medical facility in accordance with subsection (c) but the individual (or a person acting on the individual's behalf) refuses to consent to the transfer.

(c) RESTRICTING TRANSFERS UNTIL PATIENT STABILIZED.—

(1) RULE. — If a patient at a hospital has an emergency medical condition which has not been stabilized (within the meaning of subsection (e)(4)(B)) or is in active labor, the hospital may not transfer the patient unless—

(A) (i) the patient (or a legally responsible person acting on the patient's behalf) requests that the transfer be effected, or

(ii) a physician (within the meaning of section 1861(r)(1) [42 U.S.C.A. 1395x(r)(1), which describes the various practitioners who may participate in Medicare]) or other qualified medical personnel when a physician is not readily available in the emergency department, has signed a certification that, based upon the reasonable risks and benefits to the patient, and based upon the information available at the time, the medical benefits reasonably expected from the provision of appropriate medical treatment at another medical facility outweigh the increased risks to the individual's medical condition from effecting the transfer; and

(B) the transfer is an appropriate transfer (within the meaning of paragraph (2)) to that facility.

(2) APPROPRIATE TRANSFER. — An appropriate transfer to a medical facility is a transfer—

(A) in which the receiving facility—

(i) has available space and qualified personnel for the treatment of the patient, and

(ii) has agreed to accept transfer of the patient and to provide appropriate medical treatment;

(B) in which the transferring hospital provides the receiving facility with appropriate medical records (or copies thereof) of the examination and treatment effected at the transferring hospital;

(C) in which the transfer is effected through qualified personnel and transportation equipment, as required including the use of necessary and medically appropriate life support measures during the transfer; and

(D) which meets such other requirements as the Secretary may find necessary in the interest of the health and safety of patients transferred.

The statute then provided sanctions as follows for hospitals which failed to comply:

(d) ENFORCEMENT. —

(1) AS REQUIREMENT OF MEDICARE PROVIDER AGREEMENT. — If a hospital knowingly and willfully, or negligently, fails to meet the requirements of this section, such hospital is subject to —

(A) termination of its provider agreement under this title in accordance with section 1866(b) [42 U.S.C.A. 1395cc(b)], or

(B) at the option of the Secretary, suspension of such agreement for such period of time as the Secretary determines to be appropriate, upon reasonable notice to the hospital and to the public.

(2) CIVIL MONETARY PENALTIES. — (A) A participating hospital that knowingly violates a requirement of this section is subject to a civil money penalty of not more than $50,000 for each such violation. The provisions of section 1128A [42 U.S.C.A. 1320a-7a] (other than subsections (a) and (b)) shall apply to a civil money penalty under this subparagraph in the same manner as such provisions apply with respect to a penalty or proceeding under section 1128A(a).

(B) The responsible physician in a participating hospital with respect to the hospital's violation of a requirement of this subsection is subject to the sanctions described in section 1842(j)(2) [42 U.S.C.A. 1395u(j)(2), which authorizes exclusion from Medicare for a period not to exceed 5 years], except that, for purposes of this subparagraph, the civil money penalty with respect to each violation may not exceed $50,000, rather than $2,000.

(C) As used in this paragraph, the term "responsible physician" means, with respect to a hospital's violation of a requirement of this section, a physician who —

(i) is employed by, or under contract with, the participating hospital, and

(ii) acting as such an employee or under such a contract, has professional responsibility for the provision of examinations or treatments for the individual, or transfers of the individual, with respect to which the violation occurred.

Section 1842(j)(2), 42 U.S.C.A. 1395u(j)(2), provides and provided then:

Subject to paragraph (3), the sanctions which the Secretary may apply under this paragraph are —

(A) excluding a physician from participation in the programs under this Act for a period not to exceed 5 years, in accordance with the procedures of paragraphs (c) [which pertains to notice, effective date, and period of exclusion], (f) [which pertains to notice, hearing, and judicial review], and (g) [which pertains to application for termination of exclusion] of section 1128 [42 U.S.C.A. 1320a-7], or

(B) civil monetary penalties and assessments, in the same manner as such penalties and assessments are authorized under section 1128A(a) [42 U.S.C.A. 1320a-7a(a)],

or both. The provisions of section 1128A (other than the first 2 sentences of subsection (a) and other than subsection (b)) shall apply to a civil money penalty and assessment under subparagraph (B) in the same manner as such provisions apply to a penalty, assessment, or proceeding under section 1128A(a), except to the extent such provisions are inconsistent with subparagraph (A) or paragraph (3).

Section 1842(j)(3) provides and then provided:

(A) The Secretary may not exclude a physician pursuant to paragraph (2)(A) if such physician is a sole community physician or sole source of essential specialized services in a community.

(B) The Secretary shall take into account access of beneficiaries to physicians' services for which payment may be made under this part in determining whether to bar a physician from participation under paragraph (2)(A).

Section 1867(d) provided as follows for enforcement:

(3) CIVIL ENFORCEMENT. —

(A) PERSONAL HARM. — Any individual who suffers personal harm as a direct result of a participating hospital's violation of a requirement of this section may, in a civil action against the participating hospital, obtain those damages available for personal injury under the law of the State in which the hospital is located, and such equitable relief as is appropriate.

(B) FINANCIAL LOSS TO OTHER MEDICAL FACILITY. — Any medical facility that suffers a financial loss as a direct result of a participating hospital's violation of a requirement of this section may, in a civil action against the participating hospital, obtain those damages available for financial loss, under the law of the State in which the hospital is located, and such equitable relief as is appropriate.

(C) LIMITATIONS ON ACTIONS. — No action may be brought under this paragraph more than two years after the date of the violation with respect to which the action is brought.

Subsection (e) provided:

DEFINITIONS. — In this section:

(1) The term "emergency medical condition" means a medical condition manifesting itself by acute symptoms of sufficient severity (including severe pain) such that the absence of immediate medical attention could reasonably be expected to result in —

(A) placing the patient's health in serious jeopardy,

(B) serious impairment to bodily functions, or

(C) serious dysfunction of any bodily organ or part.

(2) The term "active labor" means labor at a time at which —

(A) delivery is imminent,

(B) there is inadequate time to effect safe transfer to another hospital prior to delivery, or

(C) a transfer may pose a threat to the health and safety of the patient or the unborn child.

(3) The term "participating hospital" means [a] hospital that has entered into a provider agreement under section 1866 [42 U.S.C.A. 1395cc].

(4) (A) The term "to stabilize" means, with respect to an emergency medical condition, to provide such medical treatment of the condition as may be necessary to assure, within reasonable medical probability, that no material deterioration of the condition is likely to result from the transfer of the individual from a facility.

(B) The term "stabilized" means, with respect to an emergency medical condition, that no material deterioration of the condition is likely, within reasonable medical probability, to result from the transfer of the individual from a facility.

(5) The term "transfer" means the movement (including the discharge) of a patient outside a hospital's facilities at the direction of any person employed by (or affiliated or associated, directly or indirectly, with) the hospital, but does not include such a movement of a patient who (A) has been declared dead, or (B) leaves the facility without the permission of any such person.

Finally, subsection (f) provided:

PREEMPTION. — The provisions of this section do not preempt any State or local law requirement, except to the extent that the requirement directly conflicts with a requirement of this section.

For regulatory citations, see Chapter 6

§ 2:36 FAILURE BY ORGANIZATIONS WITH RISK-SHARING CONTRACTS UNDER MEDICARE (SUCH AS HEALTH MAINTENANCE ORGANIZATIONS AND COMPETITIVE MEDICAL PLANS) TO PROVIDE REQUIRED INFORMATION ABOUT THEIR SERVICES — Section 1876(c)(3)(C) [42 U.S.C.A. 1395mm(c)(3)(C)]

Summary

Organizations with risk-sharing contracts under Medicare, such as health maintenance organizations (HMO's) and competitive medical plans (CMP's), must inform the public about their services to market them. That presents opportunity for misrepresentation. Congress therefore authorized the Secretary of Health and Human Services to prescribe procedures and conditions for such entities to meet before they can distribute brochures, application forms, or other promotional or informational material. In accord with that, section 1876(c)(3)(C), 42 U.S.C.A. 1395mm(c)(3)(C), permits the Secretary to review all such material and to disapprove any which is materially inaccurate or misleading or otherwise makes a material misrepresentation.

Statutory Provisions

Section 1876(c)(3)(C), 42 U.S.C.A. 1395mm(c)(3)(C), provides:

> The Secretary may prescribe the procedures and conditions under which an eligible organization [i.e., an organization with a risk-sharing contract under Medicare, such as an HMO or CMP] that has entered into a contract with the Secretary under this subsection may inform individuals eligible to enroll under this section with the organization about the organization, or may enroll such individuals with the organization. No brochures, application forms, or other promotional or informational material may be distributed by an organization to (or for the use of) individuals eligible to enroll with the organization under this section unless (i) at least 45 days before its distribution, the organization has submitted the material to the Secretary for review and (ii) the Secretary has not disapproved the distribution of the material. The Secretary shall review all

such material submitted and shall disapprove such material if the Secretary determines, in the Secretary's discretion, that the material is materially inaccurate or misleading or otherwise makes a material misrepresentation.

For regulatory citations, see Chapter 6

§ 2:37 FAILURE BY ORGANIZATIONS WITH RISK-SHARING CONTRACTS UNDER MEDICARE (SUCH AS HEALTH MAINTENANCE ORGANIZATIONS AND COMPETITIVE MEDICAL PLANS) TO HAVE AT LEAST ONE-HALF OF THEIR ENROLLED MEMBERS BE PERSONS NOT ELIGIBLE FOR MEDICARE OR MEDICAID— Section 1876(f) [42 U.S.C.A. 1395mm(f)]

Summary

Congress fostered development of health maintenance organizations (HMO's) and competitive medical plans (CMP's) to help contain health care costs. As with traditional insurance, they would not be able to do that if they did not practice prudent management. But having membership exclusively or predominantly consist of Medicare beneficiaries and Medicaid recipients would create a relatively high probability of financial failure. That's because such persons are relatively high users of medical care compared to a membership more reflective of the general population, and because there is no assurance premiums could match the increased risk.

Accordingly, Congress provided in section 1876(f), 42 U.S.C.A. 1395mm(f), that, if an HMO or CMP wanted to be "qualified" under Title XVIII, it would have to comply with numerous conditions. One condition is that at least one-half of its enrolled members be persons not eligible for Medicare. If such an entity fails to comply, the Secretary may provide for suspension of enrollment of individuals in the plan, or for suspension of payment for individuals newly enrolled after the date the Secretary notified the entity of its noncompliance.

◆ NOTE: Prior to amendment by sections 4002(a)(1), (2), and (3) of the Balanced Budget Act of 1997, effective August 5, 1997, an HMO or CMP had to have at least one-half of its enrolled members not be persons eligible for Medicare or Medicaid. That applied to all contracts. The amended condition applies only to contract periods beginning before January 1, 1999. Furthermore, for contract periods beginning after December 31, 1996, the Secretary of Health and Human Services may waive the fifty percent requirement when the Secretary finds waiver in the public interest.

◆ NOTE ALSO: Different requirements with respect to enrollment and residency apply to risk-sharing organizations with contracts in effect on November 10, 1988, or with extensions (not exceeding 90 days) thereof. See section 8412(a)(1) of the Medicare and Medicaid subtitle of the Technical and Miscellaneous Revenue Act of 1988, P.L. 100-647.

Statutory Provisions

Section 1876(f), 42 U.S.C.A. 1395mm(f), provides:

> (1) For contract periods beginning before January 1, 1999, each eligible organization with which the Secretary enters into a contract under this section shall have, for the duration of such contract, an enrolled membership at least one-half of which consists of individuals who are not entitled to benefits under this title or under a State plan approved under title XIX.

◆ NOTE: Section 4002(a)(1) of the Balanced Budget Act of 1997, P.L. 105–33, inserted the introductory clause beginning "For contract periods". It also deleted after "under this title" the phrase "or under a State plan approved under title XIX." Section 4002(a)(2) of the Balance Budget Act inserted in paragraph (2) below the introductory phrase "Subject to paragraph (4). Section 4002(a)(3) added paragraph (4) below. These changes became effective August 5, 1997.

> (2) Subject to paragraph 4, the Secretary may modify or waive the requirement imposed by paragraph (1) —
>
> > (A) to the extent that more than 50 percent of the population of the area served by the organization consists of individuals who are entitled to benefits under this title or under a State plan approved under title XIX, or
> >
> > (B) in the case of an eligible organization that is owned and operated by a governmental entity, only with respect to a period of three years beginning on the date the organization first enters into a contract under this section, and only if the organization has taken and is making reasonable efforts to

enroll individuals who are not entitled to benefits under this title or under a State plan approved under title XIX.

(3) If the Secretary determines that an eligible organization has failed to comply with the requirements of this subsection, the Secretary may provide for the suspension of enrollment of individuals under this section or of payment to the organization under this section for individuals newly enrolled with the organization, after the date the Secretary notifies the organization of such noncompliance.

(4) Effective for contract periods beginning after December 31, 1996, the Secretary may waive or modify the requirement imposed by paragraph (1) to the extent the Secretary finds that it is in the public interest.

For regulatory citations, see Chapter 6

§ 2:38 FAILURE BY ORGANIZATIONS WITH RISK-SHARING CONTRACTS (SUCH AS HEALTH MAINTENANCE ORGANIZATIONS AND COMPETITIVE MEDICAL PLANS) TO MAKE PROMPT PAYMENT OF CLAIMS — Section 1876(g) [42 U.S.C.A. 1395mm(g)]

Summary

Section 1876(g), 42 U.S.C.A. 1395mm(g), requires health maintenance organizations (HMO's) and competitive medical plans (CMP's) participating in Medicare to make prompt payment of claims submitted for services and supplies furnished to individuals pursuant to their risk-sharing contracts if those services and supplies are not furnished under a contract between the organization and the provider or supplier. If an HMO or CMP does not pay such claims promptly, the Secretary of Health and Human Services, after notice and opportunity for a hearing, may provide for direct payment of the amounts owed to providers and suppliers. If he does, he must reduce payments otherwise due the HMO or CMP to reflect not only the amount of the direct payment but costs incurred in making it as well.

This offset provision may protect providers and suppliers who have suffered financially at the hands of an HMO or CMP.

Statutory Provisions

Section 1876(g)(1), 42 U.S.C.A. 1395mm(g)(1), provides:

> The Secretary may enter a risk-sharing contract with any eligible organization, as defined in subsection (b), which has at least 5,000 members, except that the Secretary may enter into such a contract with an eligible organization that has fewer members if the organization primarily serves members residing outside of urbanized areas.

Then section 1876(g)(6) provides:

> (A) A risk-sharing contract under this section shall require the eligible organization to provide prompt payment (consistent with the provisions of sections 1816(c)(2) [42 U.S.C.A. 1395h(c)(2), which pertains to the requirements for fiscal intermediaries to make prompt payments] and 1842(c)(2) [42 U.S.C.A. 1395u(c)(2), which pertains to the requirements of carriers to make prompt payments]) of claims submitted for services and supplies furnished to individuals pursuant to such contract, if the services or supplies are not furnished under a contract between the organization and the provider or supplier.
>
> (B) In the case of an eligible organization which the Secretary determines, after notice and opportunity for a hearing, has failed to make payments of amounts in compliance with subparagraph (A), the Secretary may provide for direct payment of the amounts owed to providers and suppliers for such covered services furnished to individuals enrolled under this section under the contract. If the Secretary provides for such direct payments, the Secretary shall provide for an appropriate reduction in the amount of payments otherwise made to the organization under this section to reflect the amount of the Secretary's payments (and costs incurred by the Secretary in making such payments).

For regulatory citations, see Chapter 6

§ 2:39 LIMITING COST REIMBURSEMENT TO RISK-SHARING ORGANIZATIONS (SUCH AS HEALTH MAINTENANCE ORGANIZATIONS AND COMPETITIVE MEDICAL PLANS) NOT ELIGIBLE TO PARTICIPATE IN MEDICARE — Section 1876(h) [42 U.S.C.A. 1395mm(h)]

Summary

Section 1876(h), 42 U.S.C.A. 1395mm(h), permits the Secretary of Health and Human Services to deal with risk-sharing organizations, such as health maintenance organizations (HMO's) and competitive medical plans (CMP's), not eligible to participate in Medicare on a cost-reimbursement basis. If he does, however, they must provide him with costs certified in independent financial statements as in accord with prescribed accounting procedures. Failure to do so may be deemed evidence of likely overpayment. That, in turn, may be the basis for appropriate collection action.

In addition, in any case in which such an organization is related to another organization by common ownership or control, a consolidated financial statement must be filed. Furthermore, the allowable costs for such organization may not include costs for the types of expense otherwise reimbursable under Medicare in excess of those which would be reasonable according to regulations which limit reimbursement to costs rather than charges to an eligible organization by related organizations and owners. This seems to prohibit sweetheart arrangements whereby one affiliate's inflated charges become the other's costs.

Furthermore, in any case in which compensation is paid by such an organization substantially in excess of what is normally paid for similar services by similar practitioners (regardless of method of compensation), such compensation may, as appropriate, be considered a distribution of profits. Presumably, this prohibits excessive portions of salaries from becoming costs, which would abuse the cost reimbursement system.

Pursuant to section 4002(b)(2)(A) of the Balanced Budget Act of 1997, P.L. 105–33, which was enacted August 5, 1997, the Secretary may not enter into a reasonable cost reimbursement contract under section 1876(h) if the contract is not in effect on August 5, 1997. This restriction does not apply to prepaid health plans sponsored by a union or employer. Furthermore, the Secretary may not extend or renew a reasonable cost reimbursement contract under section 1876(h) for any period beyond December 31, 2002.

Statutory Provisions

Section 1876(h)(1), 42 U.S.C.A. 1395mm(h)(1)), provides:

> If—
>
> (A) the Secretary is not satisfied that an eligible organization has the capacity to bear the risk of potential losses under a risk-sharing contract under this section, or
>
> (B) the eligible organization so elects or has an insufficient number of members to be eligible to enter into a risk-sharing contract under subsection (g)(1),
>
> the Secretary may, if he is otherwise satisfied that the eligible organization is able to perform its contractual obligations effectively and efficiently, enter into a contract with such organization pursuant to which such organization is reimbursed on the basis of its reasonable cost (as defined in section 1861(v) [42 U.S.C.A. 1395x(v)]) in the manner prescribed in paragraph (3) [which permits "appropriate retroactive corrective adjustment" of payments at the end of each contract year].

Subparagraph 4 then provides:

> Any reasonable cost reimbursement contract with an eligible organization under this subsection shall provide that the Secretary shall require, at such time following the expiration of each accounting period of the eligible organization (and in such form and in such detail) as he may prescribe —
>
> (A) that the organization report to him in an independently certified financial statement its per capita incurred cost based on the types of components of expenses otherwise reimbursable under this title for providing services described in subsection (a)(1), including therein, in accordance with accounting procedures prescribed by the Secretary, its methods of allocating costs between individuals enrolled under this section and other individuals enrolled with such organization;

(B) that failure to report such information as may be required may be deemed to constitute evidence of likely overpayment on the basis of which appropriate collection action may be taken;

(C) that in any case in which an eligible organization is related to another organization by common ownership or control, a consolidated financial statement shall be filed and that the allowable costs for such organization may not include costs for the types of expense otherwise reimbursable under this title, in excess of those which would be determined to be reasonable in accordance with regulations (providing for limiting reimbursement to costs rather than charges to the eligible organization by related organizations and owners) issued by the Secretary; and

(D) that in any case in which compensation is paid by an eligible organization substantially in excess of what is normally paid for similar services by similar practitioners (regardless of method of compensation), such compensation may as appropriate be considered to constitute a distribution of profits.

Section 4002(b)(2)(A) of the Balanced Budget Act of 1997, P.L. 105–33, enacted Section 1876(h)(5) which provides:

(A) After the date of the enactment of this paragraph [August 5, 1997], the Secretary may not enter into a reasonable cost reimbursement contract under this subsection (if the contract is not in effect as of such date), except for a contract with an eligible organization which, immediately previous to entering into such contract had an agreement in effect under section 1833(a)(1)(A) [42 U.S.C.A.1395l(a)(1)(A), which pertains to prepaid health care plans sponsored by a union or employer].

(B) Subject to subparagraph (C), the Secretary shall approve an application for a modification to a reasonable cost contract under this section in order to expand the service area of such contract if (i) such application is submitted to the Secretary on or before September 1, 2003; and (ii) the Secretary determines that the organization with the contract continues to meet the requirements applicable to such organizatiions and contracts under this section.

(C) The Secretary may not extend or renew a reasonable cost reimbursement contract under this subsection for any period beyond December 31, 2004.

NOTE: Effective November 29, 1999, section 503 of the Medicare, Medicaid, and SCHIP Balanced Budget Refinement Act of 1999, as incorporated into the Omnibus Consolidated Appropriations Act, 2000, P.L. 106–113, enacted November 17, 1999, replace "2002" with "2004". Furthermore, section 634 of the Medicare, Medicaid, and SCHIP Benefits Improvement and Protection Act of 2000, P.L. 106–544, enacted December 15, 2000, added paragraph (B) above and made former paragraph (B) paragraph (C). That change was effective, December 21, 2000.

For regulatory citations, see Chapter 6

§ 2:40 TERMINATING CONTRACTS OF RISK-SHARING ORGANIZATIONS (SUCH AS HEALTH MAINTENANCE ORGANIZATIONS AND COMPETITIVE MEDICAL PLANS) —Section 1876(i)(1) [42 U.S.C.A. 1395mm(i)(1)]

Summary

Medicare contracts with risk-sharing organizations, such as HMO's and CMP's, may be for one year or longer, and may be automatically renewable. Section 1876(i)(1), 42 U.S.C.A. 1395mm(i)(1), permits the Secretary of Health and Human Services to terminate any such contract, however, at any time, after reasonable notice and opportunity for hearing, if he finds the organization has failed substantially to carry out the contract, or if it is carrying out the contract in a manner inconsistent with the efficient and effective administration of the statute, or if it no longer meets substantive requirements for participation.

Effective January 1, 1997, pursuant to sections 215 and 231(g) of the Health Insurance Portability and Accountability Act of 1996, the Secretary may impose one or more of the following intermediate sanctions, in lieu of termination, if the basis for action is not failure substantially to carry out the contract (section 1876(i)(1)(A)).

1 If the deficiency that is the basis for a determination under section 1876(i)(1) has directly adversely affected an individual

covered under the organization's contract, the Secretary may impose a civil money penalty of not more than $25,000 for each such determination. The same applies if the deficiency has the substantial likelihood of adversely affecting a covered individual.

2 If a deficiency that is the basis for a determination under section 1876(i) continues after initiation of the notice and hearing procedures governing termination or imposition of an intermediate sanction, the Secretary may impose a civil money penalty of not more than $10,000 for each week the deficiency exists.

3 The Secretary may suspend enrollment of individuals pursuant to the contract after giving notice of the deficiency to the organization and until the Secretary is satisfied that the deficiency has been corrected and is not likely to recur.

Before taking action to terminate a contract or impose an intermediate sanction, section 1876(i)(9) requires the Secretary to provide the organization an opportunity to develop and implement a corrective action plan to correct the deficiencies. If the organization fails to develop or implement such a plan, the Secretary may proceed with enforcement.

As part of that process, the Secretary must take into account aggravating factors, such as whether the organization has a history of deficiencies or has not taken action to correct deficiencies the Secretary brought to its attention. There must be no unreasonable or unnecessary delay between the finding of a deficiency and the imposition of a sanction. Finally, there must be reasonable notice and opportunity for a hearing, including the right to appeal an initial decision, before imposing a sanction or terminating the contract.

Enforcement procedures for a civil money penalty under section 1876(i)(6)(C)(i) are governed by section 1128A, (other than subsections (a) and (b)) 42 U.S.C.A. 1320a-7a, which authorizes civil money penalties for a variety of offenses.

Statutory Provisions

Section 1876(i), 42 U.S.C.A. 1395mm(i), provides:

(1) Each contract under this section shall be for a term of at least one year, as determined by the Secretary, and may be made automatically renewable from term to term in the absence of notice by either party of intention to terminate at the end of the

current term; except that in accordance with procedures established under paragraph (9), the Secretary may at any time terminate any such contract or may impose the intermediate sanctions described in paragraph (6)(B) or (6)(C) (whichever is applicable) on the eligible organization if the Secretary determines that the organization —

(A) has failed substantially to carry out the contract,

(B) is carrying out the contract in a manner substantially inconsistent with the efficient and effective administration of this section, or

(C no longer substantially meets the applicable conditions of subsections (b), (c), (e), and (f) [which are substantive requirements for participation as a risk-sharing organization].

◆ NOTE: Prior to amendment by section 215(a)(1) of the Health Insurance Portability and Accountability Act of 1996, P.L. 104–191, effective January 1, 1997, the phrase beginning "except that" and extending to paragraph (A) read: "except that the Secretary may terminate any such contract at any time (after such reasonable notice and opportunity for hearing to the eligible organization involved as he may provide in regulations), if he finds that the organization (A) . . .." It also added the word "substantially" before "inconsistent" in paragraph (B).

Then section 1876(i) goes on to provide:

(2) The effective date of any contract executed pursuant to this section shall be specified in the contract.

(3) Each contract under this section —

(A) shall provide that the Secretary, or any person or organization designated by him —

(i) shall have the right to inspect or otherwise evaluate (I) the quality, appropriateness, and timeliness of services performed under the contract and (II) the facilities of the organization when there is reasonable evidence of some need for such inspection, and

(ii) shall have the right to audit and inspect any books and records of the eligible organization that pertain (I) to the ability of the organization to bear the risk of potential financial losses, or (II) to services performed or determinations of amounts payable under the contract;

(B) shall require the organization with a risk-sharing contract to provide (and pay for) written notice in advance of the contract's termination, as well as a description of alternatives for obtaining benefits under this title, to each individual enrolled under this section with the organization; and

(C) (i) shall require the organization to comply with subsections (a) and (c) of section 1318 of the Public Health Service Act (relating to disclosure of certain financial information) and with the requirement of section 1301(c)(8) of such Act (relating to liability arrangements to protect members);

(ii) (shall require the organization to provide and supply information (described in section 1866(b)(2)(C)(ii)) to in the manner such information is required to be provided or supplied under that section;

(iii) shall require the organization to notify the Secretary of loans and other special financial arrangements which are made between the organization and subcontractors, affiliates and related parties; and

(D) shall contain such other terms and conditions not inconsistent with this section (including requiring the organization to provide the Secretary with such information) as the Secretary may find necessary and appropriate.

(4) The Secretary may not enter into a risk-sharing contract with an eligible organization if a previous risk-sharing contract with that organization under this section was terminated at the request of the organization within the preceding five-year period, except in circumstances which warrant special consideration, as determined by the Secretary.

(5) The authority vested in the Secretary by this section may be performed without regard to such provisions of law or regulations relating to the making, performance, amendment, or modification of contracts of the United States as the Secretary may determine to be inconsistent with the furtherance of the purpose of this title.

Then, pursuant to sections 215(a)(2) and 231(g) of the Health Insurance Portability and Accountability Act of 1996, section 1876(i)(6) goes on to provide:

(C) In the case of an eligible organization for which the Secretary makes a determination under paragraph (1), the basis of which is not described in subparagraph (A), the Secretary may apply the following intermediate sanctions.

(i) Civil money penalties of not more than $25,000 for each determination under paragraph (1), if the deficiency that is the basis of the determination has directly adversely affected (or has the substantial likelihood of adversely affecting) an individual covered under the organization's contract

(ii) Civil money penalties of not more than $10,000 for each week beginning after the initiation of procedures by the Secretary under paragraph (9) during which the deficiency that is the basis of a determination under paragraph (1) exists.

(iii) Suspension of enrollment of individuals under this section after the date the Secretary notifies the organization of a determination under paragraph (1) and until the Secretary is satisfied that the deficiency that is the basis for the determination has been corrected and is not likely to recur.

(D) The provisions of section 1128A (other than subsections (a) and (b)) shall apply to a civil money penalty under subparagraph (B)(i) or (C)(i) in the same manner as such provisions apply to a civil money penalty or proceeding under section 1128(A)(a).

Pursuant to section 215(3) of the Health Insurance Portability and Accountability Act of 1996, procedures for contract termination or imposition of intermediate sanctions are governed by section 1876(i)(9), which provides:

The Secretary may terminate a contract with an eligible organization under this section or may impose the intermediate sanctions described in paragraph (6) on the organization in accordance with formal investigation and compliance procedures established by the Secretary under which—

(A) the Secretary first provides the organization with the reasonable opportunity to develop and implement a corrective action plan to correct the deficiencies that were the basis of the Secretary's determination under paragraph (1) and the organization fails to develop or implement such a plan;

(B) in deciding whether to impose sanctions, the Secretary considers aggravating factors such as whether an organization has a history of deficiencies or has not taken action to correct deficiencies the Secretary has brought to the organization's attention;

(C) there are no unreasonable or unnecessary delays between the finding of a deficiency and the imposition of sanctions; and

(D) the Secretary provides the organization with reasonable notice and opportunity for hearing (including the right to appeal an initial decision) before imposing any sanction or terminating the contract.

For regulatory citations, see Chapter 6

§ 2:41 FAILURE BY RISK-SHARING ORGANIZATIONS (SUCH AS HEALTH MAINTENANCE ORGANIZATIONS AND COMPETITIVE MEDICAL PLANS) TO COMPLY WITH REQUIREMENTS FOR PROVISION OF SERVICES, PREMIUMS, TREATMENT OF APPLICANTS AND MEMBERS, TRUTHFULNESS, PROMPT PAYMENT, AND AVOIDING BUSINESS RELATIONSHIPS WITH EXCLUDED INDIVIDUALS AND ENTITIES— Section 1876(i)(6) [42 U.S.C.A. 1395mm(i)(6)]

Summary

Section 1876(i)(6), 42 U.S.C.A. 1395mm(i)(6), authorizes the Secretary of Health and Human Services to impose a civil money penalty upon any organization with a risk-sharing contract under Medicare, such as a health maintenance organization (HMO) or a competitive medical plan (CMP), if it fails substantially to provide to an individual covered under its contract medically necessary items and services required either under law or by its contract when such failure has adversely affected or has substantial likelihood of adversely affecting the individual.

The same is true if such an organization imposes premiums on individuals in excess of the amount permitted; or if it acts wrongfully to expel or to refuse to re-enroll an individual; or if it engages in any practice that would reasonably be expected to have the effect of denying or discouraging enrollment (except as permitted) by individuals whose medical condition or history indicates a need for substantial future medical services; or if it misrepresents or falsifies information furnished to the Secretary or to an individual or to any other entity; or if it fails to meet prompt payment requirements.

The same is also true, in the case of a risk-sharing contract, if an organization employs or contracts with any individual or entity for provision of health care, utilization review, medical social work, or administrative services, and that individual or entity has been excluded from participation in Medicare under section 1128, 42 U.S.C.A. 1320a-7, or section 1128A, 42 U.S.C.A. 1320a-7a. So also it is if an organization employs or contracts with any entity to provide such services directly or indirectly through an individual or entity excluded under section 1128 or section 1128A.

In any such case, the civil money penalty may not exceed $25,000 for each violation.

Alternatively, for discouraging potential high users of medical services from enrolling, the Secretary may impose a civil money penalty not to exceed $100,000 for each violation, plus $15,000 for each individual not enrolled as a result of such wrongful practice.

For misrepresentations made or falsified information given him, the Secretary alternatively may impose a civil money penalty not to exceed $100,000 for each violation.

In addition, for overcharging of premiums, the Secretary may impose a penalty of double the excess amount charged. From the penalty collected, however, he must deduct and return the excess amount charged to affected individuals.

Finally, the Secretary may suspend enrollment of individuals in the organization after the date notice of the violations is given until the Secretary is satisfied that the basis for the finding has been corrected and is not likely to recur. As an alternative, the Secretary may suspend payment to the organization for individuals enrolled after the date notice of the violations is given until the Secretary is satisfied that the basis for the finding has been corrected and is not likely to recur.

These civil money penalties are in addition to any other remedies authorized by law. Enforcement procedures for them are governed by section 1128A, 42 U.S.C.A. 1320a-7a, which authorizes civil money penalties for a variety of offenses.

Statutory Provisions

Section 1876(i)(6), 42 U.S.C.A. 1395mm(i)(6), provides:

(A) If the Secretary determines that an eligible organization with a contract under this section —

(i) fails substantially to provide medically necessary items and services that are required (under law or under the contract) to be provided to an individual covered under the contract, if the failure has adversely affected (or has substantial likelihood of adversely affecting) the individual;

(ii) imposes premiums on individuals enrolled under this section in excess of the premiums permitted;

(iii) acts to expel or to refuse to re-enroll an individual in violation of the provisions of this section;

(iv) engages in any practice that would reasonably be expected to have the effect of denying or discouraging enrollment (except as permitted by this section) by eligible individuals with the organization whose medical condition or history indicates a need for substantial future medical services;

(v) misrepresents or falsifies information that is furnished —

(I) to the Secretary under this section, or

(II) to an individual or to any other entity under this section; or

(vi) fails to comply with the requirements of subsection (g)(6)(A) [which pertains to prompt payment of claims] or paragraph (8) [which prohibits organizations from having physician incentive plans that do not meet certain requirements, notably a prohibition against incentives to physicians to reduce or limit medically necessary services to a specific enrollee; this provision applies to contract years beginning on or after January 1, 1992, pursuant to section 4204(a) of P.L. 101-508]; the Omnibus Budget Reconciliation Act of 1990 (OBRA 90)]; or

(vii) in the case of a risk-sharing contract, employs or contracts with any individual or entity that is excluded from participation under this title under section 1128 [42 U.S.C.A. 1320a-7] or 1128A [42 U.S.C.A. 1320a-7a] for the provision of health care, utilization review, medical social work, or administrative services or employs or contracts with any entity for the provision (directly or indirectly) through such an excluded individual or entity of such services;

the Secretary may provide, in addition to any other remedies authorized by law, for any of the remedies described in subparagraph (B).

(B) The remedies described in this subparagraph are —

(i) civil money penalties of not more than $25,000 for each determination under subparagraph (A) or, with respect to a determination under clause (iv) or (v)(I), of not more than $100,000 for each such determination, plus, with respect to a determination under subparagraph (A)(ii), double the excess amount charged in violation of such subparagraph (and the excess amount charged shall be deducted from the penalty and returned to the individual concerned), and plus, with respect to a determination under subparagraph (A)(iv), $15,000 for each individual not enrolled as a result of the practice involved,

(ii) suspension of enrollment of individuals under this section after the date the Secretary notifies the organization of a determination under subparagraph (A) and until the Secretary is satisfied that the basis for such determination has been corrected and is not likely to recur, or

(iii) suspension of payment to the organization under this section for individuals enrolled after the date the Secretary notifies the organization of a determination under subparagraph (A) and until the Secretary is satisfied that the basis for such determination has been corrected and is not likely to recur.

The provisions of section 1128A [42 U.S.C.A. 1320a-7a] (other than subsections (a) and (b)) shall apply to a civil money penalty under clause (i) in the same manner as they apply to a civil money penalty or proceeding under section 1128A(a).

For regulatory citations, see Chapter 6

§ 2:42 VIOLATING LIMITATIONS ON PHYSICIAN REFERRALS AND RELATED REPORTING REQUIREMENTS — Section 1877 [42 U.S.C.A. 1395nn]

Summary

◆ NOTE: Section 1877, 42 U.S.C.A. 1396nn, commonly known as the Stark Bill, after its champion, Congressman Fortney Stark of California, was substantially revised by section 13562 of P.L. 103-66, the Omnibus Budget Reconciliation Act of 1993. Previously, the aim was to prohibit referrals to clinical laboratories. As amended, the aim is to prohibit physician referrals for a much wider array of "designated health services". For a discussion of Stark Bill provisions prior to OBRA 93, see II-38-A in Appendix H.

In addition, pursuant to section 13624 of OBRA 93, effective for referrals on or after December 31, 1994, States will not receive Federal matching funds for Medicaid payments made for such designated health services which violate section 1877. See section 1903(s), 42 U.S.C.A. 1396b(s). Accordingly, provisions of a given State's Medicaid plan regarding physician referrals should be reviewed.

Section 1877(a)(1) prohibits a physician from making a referral to an entity which delivers designated health services if the physician, or an immediate family member of the physician, has a financial interest in the entity and if Medicare would pay for those services. It also prohibits the entity to which the physician referral is made from presenting or causing to be presented a claim under Medicare. In addition, it prohibits the entity from billing any individual, third party payor or other entity for any designated health services for which the physician made a referral.

Prior to amendment by sections 152(b)(1) and (2) of the Social Security Act Amendments of 1994, P.L. 103-432, section 1877(h)(6) defined designated health services to include: clinical laboratory services; physical therapy services; occupational therapy services; radiology or other diagnostic services; radiation therapy services; durable medical equipment; parenteral and enteral nutrients, equipment, and supplies; prosthetics, orthotics, and prosthetic devices; home health services; outpatient prescription drugs; and inpatient and outpatient hospital services. The amendments expanded the prohibition regarding radiology or other diagnostic services to specify radiology, including magnetic resonance imaging, computerized axial tomography scans, and ultrasound services. The prohibitions with respect to radiation therapy services, durable medical equipment, and home health services were expanded to include related supplies.

The prohibition applies to referrals for clinical laboratory services furnished on or after January 1, 1992, and to referrals for other services furnished after December 31, 1994.

Section 1877(h)(5) defines "referral" and "referring physician". In the case of an item or service payable under Medicare Part B, the request by a physician for the item or service, including the request by a physician for a consultation with another physician — and any test or procedure ordered by, or to be performed by or under supervision of that other physician — constitutes a referral by a referring physician. Furthermore, the request or establishment of a plan of care by a physician which includes provision of a designated health services also constitutes a referral by a referring physician.

With respect to both of those situations, however, a request by a pathologist for clinical diagnostic laboratory tests and pathological examination services, a request by a radiologist for diagnostic radiology services, and a request by a radiation oncologist for radiation therapy do not constitute a referral by a referring physician for Stark Bill purposes. There is, however, a proviso: the services must be furnished by (or under supervision of) such pathologist, radiologist, or radiation oncologist pursuant to a consultation requested by another physician.

Pursuant to section 1877(g), violators risk several sanctions: (1) denial of payment; (2) mandatory refunds "on a timely basis" to individuals who were billed; and (3) a civil money penalty. The civil money penalty, which may be not more than $15,000 for each bill or claim, applies if the person who bills or presents the claim "knows or should know" the bill or claim violates the statute. The same penalty applies if a mandatory refund is not made.

In addition, a civil money penalty of not more than $100,000 applies to circumvention schemes, such as cross-referral arrangements, when a physical or entity "knows or should know" the arrangement has a principal purpose of assuring referrals by the physician to the entity. If the referral by a physician directly would violate the statute, the circumvention also violates the statute.

Enforcement procedures for these civil money penalties are governed by section 1128A, 42 U.S.C.A. 1320a-7a (which authorizes civil money penalties for a variety of offenses), other than the first sentence of subsection (a) and other than subsection (b) (which pertain to certain offenses). Section 1128A also permits the Secretary of Health and Human Services to exclude a person from Medicare and to direct the appropriate State agency to exclude the person from Medicaid or any other State health care program. (Presumably, that accounts for the reference in the captions of sections 1877(g)(3) and (4) to both civil money penalty and exclusion, when those subparagraphs do not independently provide for exclusion.)

Section 1877(a)(2) defines what constitutes a financial relationship between a physician or an immediate family member of a physician and entity to include an ownership or investment interest in the entity or a compensation arrangement with the entity. Ownership or investment interest may be through equity, debt, or other means. A financial relationship also includes interests in an entity that holds an ownership or investment interest in the entity providing the designated health service, thus reaching indirect ownership and investment interests.

Section 1877(f) requires each entity that provides covered items or services to inform the Secretary about its ownership, investment and compensation arrangements. Specifically, the entity must report the covered items or services it has provided. It also must report the names and unique physician identification numbers of all physicians who have an ownership or investment interest or compensation arrangement in the entity and all physicians whose immediate relatives have an ownership or investment interest or compensation relationship in the entity. This information must be provided in such form, manner, and at such times as the Secretary specifies.

◆ NOTE: Prior to enactment of section 152(a)(5) of the Social Security Act Amendments of 1994, this information first had to be reported October 1, 1991, with respect to referrals to clinical laboratories pre-OBRA 93. That requirement was repealed. Furthermore, the above requirements with respect to investment and compensation arrangements apply to referrals on or after January 1, 1995, pursuant to sections 152(a)(1) and (3) of the Social Security Act Amendments of 1994.

The ownership reporting obligation does not apply to covered items and services provided outside the United States, nor to entities which the Secretary determines provide services under Medicare very infrequently.

◆ NOTE: Prior to enactment of section 152(a)(5) of the Social Security Act Amendments of 1994, applicable to referrals made on or after January 1, 1995, the Secretary was authorized to waive the reporting requirements with respect to entities in a State, if such reporting was required in at least 10 States. The Secretary could not, however, waive such requirements in a State with similar reporting requirements with respect to parenteral and enteral suppliers, end stage renal disease facilities, suppliers of ambulance services, hospitals, entities providing physical therapy services, and entities providing diagnostic imaging services of any type.

Pursuant to section 1877(g)(4), any person who is required, but fails, to meet a reporting requirement is subject to a civil money penalty of not more than $10,000 for each day for which reporting is required to have been made. There is no mention about exclusion in the caption of this subsection, but (g)(4) contains the same cross-reference to section 1128A, discussed above.

Having set forth the general prohibition on referrals in 1877(a), Congress then authorized exemptions in section 1877(b). These focus on both ownership and compensation arrangements.

Pursuant to section 1877(b)(1), a referral by a physician and billing by an entity providing a designated health service are not prohibited in the case of physician services provided personally by (or under personal supervision of) another physician in the same group practice as the referring physician. By cross reference to section 1861(a), 42 U.S.C.A. 1395x(q), this applies with respect to referrals for surgery, consultation, and home, office and institutional calls; but it does not apply to services of interns or residents.

Pursuant to section 1877(b)(2), the prohibitions do not apply to in-office ancillary services — other than durable medical equipment (except referral and billing for infusion pumps are not prohibited) and parenteral and enteral nutrients, equipment, and supplies).

This exemption applies only when the permitted in-office ancillary services are personally furnished by the referring physician, or by a physician member of the same group practice, or by individuals directly supervised by the referring physician or physician member of the same group practice. Moreover, the in-office ancillary services must be furnished in a building where the referring physician or physician member of the group practice furnishes services unrelated to the furnishing of designated health services. Alternatively, the in-office ancillary services may be furnished in another building, in the case of a referring physician who is a member of a group practice, if that building is used by the group practice for provision of some or all of the group's clinical laboratory services, or for the centralized provision of the group's designated health services other than clinical laboratory services. (A proviso permits the Secretary to determine other terms and conditions under which provision of such services will not risk program or patient abuse.)

Furthermore, the in-office ancillary services must be billed by the physician performing or supervising the services, or by the group practice of which such physician is a member under a billing number assigned to the group practice, or by an entity wholly owned by such physician or group practice.

Pursuant to section 1877(b)(3), a referral by a physician and billing by an entity providing a designated health service are not prohibited in the case of services furnished by a health maintenance organization (HMO) or competitive medical plan (CMP) to an enrollee of the HMO or CMP, if the HMO or CMP has a contract under section 1876, 42 U.S.C.A. 1395mm.

The same applies with respect to Part B services provided by a prepaid health plan to a member of the plan, if the plan meets requirements of section 1833(a)(1)(A), 42 U.S.C.A. 13951. It also applies with respect to organizations receiving payments for services to enrollees on a prepaid basis under a demonstration project under section 402(a) of the Social Security Amendments of 1967, or under section 222(a) of the Social Security Amendments of 1972; and with respect to a qualified health maintenance organization (within the meaning of section 1310(d) of the Public Health Service Act) for services to an enrollee.

Furthermore, the exemption applies to services furnished on or after November 29, 1999, by a Medicare + Choice organization under Part C that is offering a coordinated care program (as described in section 1851(a)(2)(A), 42 U.S.C.A. 1395w-21,) to an individual enrolled with that organization. This exemption was added by section 524 of the Medicare, Medicaid, and SCHIP Balanced Budget Refinement Act of 1999, as incorporated into the Omnibus Consolidated Appropriations Act, 2000, P.L. 106–113, enacted November 17, 1999.

The Stark Bill limitations on referrals was effective with respect to referrals for clinical laboratory services on or after January 1, 1992, and generally for referrals for other designated services after December 31, 1994.

Pursuant to section 1877(b)(4), the Secretary is authorized to make determinations of other physician financial relationships with entities providing designated health services which pose no risk of program or patient abuse.

Pursuant to section 1877(c), referral and billing are not prohibited in a case where the ownership or investment interest of a physician (or an immediate family member of a physician) is in certain publicly traded securities and mutual funds.

Specifically, "ownership" and "investment interest" within the meaning of section 1877(a)(2)(A) does not include ownership of shares or bonds, debentures, notes, or other debt instruments, provided: (1) those securities may be purchased on terms generally available to the public, and they are either securities listed on the New York Stock Exchange, the American Stock Exchange, or any regional exchange in which quotations are published on a daily basis, or they are foreign securities listed on a recognized foreign, national, or regional exchange in which quotations are published on a daily basis, or they are traded under an automated interdealer quotation system operated by the National Association of Securities Dealers; and (2) they are securities in a corporation that had, either at the end of its most recent fiscal year or on average during its previous 3 fiscal years, stockholder equity exceeding $75,000,000.

Ownership and investment interest also does not include ownership of shares in a regulated investment company, as defined in section 851(a) of the Internal Revenue Code of 1986, if the company's total assets exceeded $75,000,000 either at the end of its most recent fiscal year or on average during the previous 3 fiscal years.

This applies to referrals for clinical laboratory services on or after January 1, 1992, and generally for referrals made after December 31, 1994, for other designated health services.

Pursuant to section 1877(d), the following, if not otherwise exempted under subsection (b) are also deemed not to be an ownership or investment interest within the meaning of section 1877(a)(2)(A): hospitals in Puerto Rico for designated health services provided by such a hospital; rural providers, if substantially all of the designated health services are furnished to individuals residing in the rural area (as defined by section 1886(d)(2)(D), 42 U.S.C.A.

1395ww(d)(2)(D) (which defines rural area for purposes of the prospective payment system for inpatient hospital services); and hospitals not in Puerto Rico which provide designated health services, provided the ownership or investment interest is in the hospital itself and not merely in a subdivision of the hospital, and provided the referring physician is authorized to perform services at the hospital.

This applies to referrals for clinical laboratory services on or after January 1, 1992, and generally for referrals made after December 31, 1994, for other designated health services.

The following exceptions to the referral and billing prohibitions pertain to compensation arrangements, specifically: rental of office space and equipment; bona fide employment relationships; personal service arrangements; physician incentive plans; remuneration unrelated to provision of designated health services; physician recruitment; isolated transactions; certain group practice arrangements with a hospital; and payments by a physician for items and services.

Section 1877(h)(1)(B) defines remuneration to include remuneration in cash or in kind, whether paid directly or indirectly, overtly or covertly. Section 1877(h)(1)(A) defines compensation arrangement as any arrangement involving any remuneration between a physician (or an immediate family member of such physician) and an entity which provides a designated health service.

The definition excludes: (1) any arrangement involving only remuneration which is merely the forgiveness of amounts owed for inaccurate tests or procedures, mistakenly performed tests or procedures, or the correction of minor billing errors; (2) remuneration for the provision of items, devices, or supplies used solely to collect, transport, process, or store specimens for the entity providing the item, device, or supply, or to order or communicate the results of tests or procedures for such entity; and (3) payment by an insurer or a self-insured plan to a physician to satisfy a claim, submitted on a fee for service basis, for the furnishing of health services by that physician to an individual covered by a policy with the insurer or by the self-insured plan.

With respect to (3), however, the health services must not be furnished and payment must not be made pursuant to a contract or other arrangement between the insurer or the plan and the physician; the payment must be made to the physician on behalf of the covered individual where it otherwise would be made directly to such individual; the amount must be set in advance, must not exceed fair market value, and must not be based, directly or indirectly, on the volume or value of any referrals; and the payment must meet any other requirements the Secretary imposes by regulation to protect against program or patient abuse.

Pursuant to section 1877(e)(1)(A), a referral by a physician and billing by an entity providing a designated health service are not prohibited merely because of a compensation arrangement between the physician and the entity to rent space.

These provisos apply: The lease must be in writing, signed by the parties, and specify the premises it affects. The space must not exceed that reasonable and necessary for the legitimate business purposes of the lease or rental, and it must be used exclusively by the lessee when being used by the lessee (except that the lessee may make payments for use of common areas on a pro rata basis based on the ratio of space used exclusively by the lessee to the total space — other than common areas occupied by all who use such common areas). The lease must be for a term of at least one year. The rent over the term of the lease must be set in advance, must be consistent with fair market value, and must not be based on the volume or value of any referrals or other business generated between the parties. The lease must be commercially reasonable even if no referrals were made between the parties. Finally, the lease must meet such other requirements as the Secretary imposes by regulation to protect against program or patient abuse.

Similarly, pursuant to section 1877(e)(1)(B), a referral by a physician and billing by an entity providing a designated health service are not prohibited merely because of a compensation arrangement between the physician and the entity to rent equipment.

As with space rental, similar provisos apply: The lease must in writing, signed by the parties, and specify the equipment it affects. The equipment must not exceed that reasonable and necessary for the legitimate business purposes of the lease or rental, and it must be used exclusively by the lessee when being used by the lessee. The lease must be for a term of at least one year. The rent over the term of the lease must be set in advance, must be consistent with fair market value, and must not be based on the volume or value of any referrals or other business generated between the parties. The lease must be commercially reasonable even if no referrals were made between the parties. Finally, the lease must meet such other requirements as the

Secretary imposes by regulation to protect against program or patient abuse.

Section 1877(e)(2) pertains to bona fide employment relationships. Employee is defined by section 1877(h)(2) by reference to the common law rules applicable in determining employer/employee relationships, as applied for Internal Revenue Service purposes. See section 3121(d)(2) of the Internal Revenue Code of 1986, 26 U.S.C.A. 3121(d)(2).

A referral by a physician and billing by an entity providing a designated health service are not prohibited merely because of an employment relationship between the two if the employment is for identifiable services; if the amount of the remuneration under the employment is consistent with fair market value for the services; if the amount is not based, directly or indirectly, on the volume or value of any referrals by the referring physician; if the remuneration would be commercially reasonable even if no referrals were made to the employer; and if the employment meets such other requirements as the Secretary imposes by regulation to protect against program or patient abuse.

This does not prohibit payment of a productivity bonus based on services personally performed by the physician (or by an immediate family member of such physician). In that regard, section 1877(h)(4)(B)(i) provides that a physician in a group practice may be paid a share of overall profits of the group, or a productivity bonus based on services personally performed or services incident to such personally performed services. That applies, however, only if the share or bonus is not determined in any manner directly related to the volume or value of referrals by such physician.

Section 1877(h)(4)(A) defines "group practice" as a group of two or more physicians legally organized as a partnership, professional corporation, foundation, not-for-profit corporation, faculty practice, or similar association.

Several provisos apply. Each physician in the group must provide substantially the full range of services which the physician routinely provides. That includes medical consultation, diagnosis, or treatment, through joint use of shared office space, facilities, equipment and personnel. Substantially all services of physician members must be provided through the group and billed under a billing number assigned to the group, and amounts so received must be treated as receipts of the group. Overhead expenses of and income from the practice must be allocated in accordance with methods previously determined. Except for authorized productivity bonus and profit sharing, no physician member must receive directly or indirectly compensation based on the volume or value of his or her referrals. Members of the group must personally conduct no less than 75 percent of the physician/patient encounters of the group. Finally, the group must meet such other standards as the Secretary imposes by regulation.

According to section 1877(h)(4)(B)(ii) provisos applicable to a group practice apply only with respect to services within a faculty practice plan in the case of a plan associated with a hospital, an institution of higher education, or a medical school with an approved medical residency training program where physician members may provide a variety of different specialty services, and where they provide professional services both within and outside their group, and perform other tasks as well, such as research.

Section 1877(e)(3) pertains to personal service arrangements. A referral by a physician and billing by an entity providing a designated health service are not prohibited merely because the physician and the entity have a compensation arrangement to provide one or more personal services.

Provisos similar to those for space and equipment rental apply: The arrangement must be set out in writing, signed by the parties, and specify the services it covers. It must cover all services to be provided by the physician (or an immediate family member of the physician) to the entity. The aggregate services contracted for must not exceed those reasonable and necessary for the legitimate business purposes of the arrangement. The term must be for at least one year. The compensation over the term must be set in advance, must not exceed fair market value, and (except for a physician incentive plan, discussed below) must not be based on volume or value of business generated between the parties. In addition, the services to be performed under the arrangement must not involve counseling or promotion of a business arrangement or other activity that violates any State or Federal law. Finally, the arrangement must meet such other requirements as the Secretary imposes by regulation to protect against program or patient abuse.

Special rules apply with respect to physician incentive plans. These are defined by section 1877(e)(3)(B)(ii) as any compensation arrangement between an entity and a physician or physician group that may directly or indirectly have the effect of reducing or limiting services provided with respect to an individual enrolled with the entity.

Pursuant to section 1877(e)(3)(B)(i), compensation may be determined in a manner, whether through a withhold, capitation, bonus, or otherwise, that takes into account directly or indirectly the volume or value of any referrals or other business generated between the parties. The following provisos apply: No specific payment may be made directly or indirectly under the plan to a physician or a physician group as an inducement to reduce or limit medically necessary services provided with respect to a specific individual enrolled in the plan. Plans which place a physician or physician group at substantial risk must comply with all requirements of section 1876(i)(8)(A)(ii), 42 U.S.C.A. 1395mm(i)(8)(A)(ii), which pertains to HMO's and CMP's. Finally, the entity must provide the Secretary access upon request to descriptive information regarding the plan to permit the Secretary to determine whether the plan complies with these requirements.

Section 1877(e)(4) exempts remuneration provided by a hospital to a physician if the remuneration does not relate to the provision of designated health services.

Section 1877(e)(5) exempts remuneration provided by a hospital to a physician to induce the physician to relocate to the geographic area served by the hospital to become a member of the medical staff of the hospital. This applies provided the physician is not required to refer patients to the hospital; the remuneration under the recruitment arrangement is not based on the volume or value of any referrals by the referring physician; and the arrangement meets any requirements the Secretary imposes by regulation to protect against program or patient abuse.

Section 1877(e)(6) exempts remuneration in the case of an isolated financial transaction, such as a one-time sale of property or a practice, provided: The remuneration is consistent with fair market value; is not based on the volume or value of referrals; would be commercially reasonable even if no referrals were made; and the transaction meets such requirements as the Secretary imposes by regulation to protect against program or patient abuse.

By grandfathering, section 1877(e)(7) exempts compensation arrangements between a hospital and a group under which designated health services are provided by the group but are billed by the hospital. That applies: if, with respect to services to inpatients, the arrangement is pursuant to the provision of inpatient hospital services under section 1861(b)(3), 42 U.S.C.A. 1395x(b)(3) (which includes certain diagnostic or therapeutic items or services ordinarily furnished to inpatients by a hospital or by others under arrangement with the hospital); if the arrangement began before December 19, 1989, and has continued without interruption since then; if with respect to services covered under the arrangement substantially all such services furnished to patients of the hospital are furnished by the group under the arrangement; if the arrangement is pursuant to a written agreement which specifies the services to be provided by the parties and the compensation for services provided under the agreement; if the compensation paid over the term of the agreement is consistent with fair market value and the compensation per unit of services is fixed in advance and is not based on the volume or value of any referrals or other business generated between the parties; if the compensation is provided pursuant to an agreement which would be commercially reasonable even if no referrals were made to the entity; and if the arrangement meets such requirements as the Secretary imposes by regulation to protect against program or patient abuse.

Section 1877(e)(8) exempts payments made by a physician to a laboratory in exchange for the provision of clinical laboratory services, or to an entity as compensation for other items or services provided the items or services are furnished at a price consistent with fair market value. This applies to referrals on or after January 1, 1992.

Section 1877(h)(3) defines fair market value as the value in an arms length transaction which is consistent with general market value, and (with respect to rentals or leases) consistent with the value of rental property for general commercial purposes (not taking into account intended use), and, in the case of a lease of space, not taking into account additional value the prospective lessee or lessor would attribute to the proximity or convenience to the lessor where the lessor is a potential source of patient referrals to the lessee.

Generally, effective dates for referral prohibitions are January 1, 1992, with respect to clinical laboratory services, and after December 31, 1994, for other designated health services. Specifically, however, provisions applicable to physician incentive plans and group practices apply to referrals after December 31, 1994. The same is true for section 1877(a)(2) with respect to indirect financial relationships; for section 1877(b)(2)(B) with respect to billing numbers; for section 1877(c) with respect to publicly traded securities; for section 1877(d)(2) with respect to rural providers; and for section 1877(e)(1)(A) with respect to office rental.

ADVISORY OPINIONS: Section 4314 of the Balanced Budge Act of 1997, P.L. 105–33, obligates the Secretary of Health and Human Services to provide written advisory opinions on whether a referral relating to designated health services (other than clinical laboratory services) is prohibited under section 1877. These advisory opinions are binding only on the Secretary and the party or parties requesting the opinion. See also section 1128D [42 U.S.C.A. 1329a-7d] , which pertains to guidance regarding application of health care fraud and abuse sanctions in the form of safe harbor regulations, fraud alerts, and advisory opinions.

Statutory Provisions

Section 1877(a), 42 U.S.C.A. 1395nn(a), provides:

PROHIBITION OF CERTAIN REFERRALS. —

(1) IN GENERAL. — Except as provided in subsection (b), if a physician (or immediate family member of such physician) has a financial relationship with an entity specified in paragraph (2), then —

(A) the physician may not make a referral to the entity for the furnishing of designated health services for which payment otherwise may be made under this title, and

(B) the entity may not present or cause to be presented a claim under this title or bill to any individual, third party payor, or other entity for designated health services furnished pursuant to a referral prohibited under subparagraph (A).

(2) FINANCIAL RELATIONSHIP SPECIFIED. — For purposes of this section, a financial relationship of a physician (or an immediate family member of such physician) with an entity specified in this paragraph is —

(A) except as provided in subsections (c) and (d), an ownership or investment interest in the entity, or

(B) except as provided in subsection (e), a compensation arrangement (as defined in subsection (h)(1)) between the physician (or an immediate family member of such physician) and the entity.

An ownership or investment interest described in subparagraph (A) may be through equity, debt, or other means and includes an interest in an entity that holds an ownership or investment interest in any entity providing the designated health service.

Section 1877(b) provides as follows with respect to exceptions to the ownership and compensation prohibitions:

GENERAL EXCEPTIONS TO BOTH OWNERSHIP AND COMPENSATION ARRANGEMENT PROHIBITIONS. — Subsection (a)(1) shall not apply in the following cases:

(1) PHYSICIANS' SERVICES. — In the case of physicians' services (as defined in section 1861(q) [42 U.S.C.A. 1395x(q), which defines physicians' services as professional services performed by a physician, including surgery, consultation, and home, office, and institutional calls, but not services of interns or residents]) provided personally by (or under the personal supervision of) another physician in the same group practice (as defined in subsection (h)(4)) as the referring physician.

(2) IN-OFFICE ANCILLARY SERVICES. — In the case of services (other than durable medical equipment (excluding infusion pumps) and parenteral and enteral nutrients, equipment, and supplies) —

(A) that are furnished —

(i) personally by the referring physician, personally by a physician who is a member of the same group practice as the referring physician, or personally by individuals who are directly supervised by the physician or by another physician in the group practice, and

(ii) (I) in a building in which the referring physician (or another physician who is a member of the same group practice) furnishes physicians' services unrelated to the furnishing of designated health services, or

(II) in the case of a referring physician who is a member of a group practice, in another building which is used by the group practice —

(aa) for the provision of some or all of the group's clinical laboratory services, or (bb) for the centralized provision of the group's designated health services (other than clinical laboratory services), unless the Secretary determines other terms and conditions under which the provision of such services does not present a risk of program or patient abuse, and

(B) that are billed by the physician performing or supervising the services, by a group practice of which such physician is a member under a billing number assigned to the group practice, or by an entity that is wholly owned by such physician or such group practice, if the ownership or investment interest in such services meets such other requirements as the Secretary may impose by regulation as needed to protect against program or patient abuse.

(3) PREPAID PLANS. — In the case of services furnished by an organization —

(A) with a contract under section 1876 [42 U.S.C.A. 1395mm, which pertains to payments to health maintenance organizations (HMO's) and competitive medical plans (CMP's)] to an individual enrolled with the organization,

(B) described in section 1833(a)(1)(A) [42 U.S.C.A. 1395l, which pertains to Part B payments to prepaid health plans] to an individual enrolled with the organization,

(C) receiving payments on a prepaid basis, under a demonstration project under section 402(a) of the Social Security Amendments of 1967 or under section 222(a) of the Social Security Amendments of 1972, to an individual enrolled with the organization,

(D) that is a qualified health maintenance organization (within the meaning of section 1310(d) of the Public Health Service Act) to an individual enrolled with the organization, or

(E) that is a Medicare + Choice organization under part C that is offering a coordinated care plan described in section 1851(a)(2)(A) [42 U.S.C.A. 1395w-21] to an individual enrolled with the organization.

◆ NOTE: Section 524 of the Medicare, Medicaid, and SCHIP Balanced Budget Refinement Act of 1999, as incorporated into the Omnibus Consolidated Appropriations Act, 2000, P.L. 106–113, enacted November 17, 1999, struck "or" from subparagraph (b)(3)(C), inserted ", or" in subparagraph (b)(3)(D), and added subparagraph (E). This applies to services furnished on or after November 29, 1999.

(4) OTHER PERMISSIBLE EXCEPTIONS. — In the case of any other financial relationship which the Secretary determines, and specified in regulations, does not pose a risk of program or patient abuse.

Section 1877(c) provides the following exception to the referral restrictions applicable to ownership or investment in publicly traded securities and mutual funds:

GENERAL EXCEPTION RELATED ONLY TO OWNERSHIP OR INVESTMENT PROHIBITION FOR OWNERSHIP IN PUBLICLY TRADED SECURITIES AND MUTUAL FUNDS. — Ownership of the following shall not be considered to be an ownership or investment interest described in subsection (a)(2)(A):

(1) Ownership of investment securities (including shares or bonds, debentures, notes, or other debt instruments) which may be purchased on terms generally available to the public and which are —

(A) (i) securities listed on the New York Stock Exchange, the American Stock Exchange, or any regional exchange in which quotations are published on a daily basis or foreign securities listed on a recognized foreign, national, or regional exchange in which quotations are published on a daily basis, or

(ii) traded under an automated interdealer quotation system operated by the National Association of Securities Dealers, and

(B) in a corporation that had, at the end of the corporations' most recent fiscal year, or on average during the previous 3 fiscal years, stockholder equity exceeding $75,000,000.

(2) Ownership of shares in a regulated investment company as defined in section 851(a) of the Internal Revenue Code of 1986 [26 U.S.C.A. 851(a)], if such company had, at the end of the company's most recent fiscal year, or on average during

the previous 3, fiscal years, total assets exceeding $75,000,000.

Section 1877(d) sets forth the following additional exceptions applicable to ownership or investment interests:

ADDITIONAL EXCEPTIONS RELATED ONLY TO OWNERSHIP OR INVESTMENT PROHIBITION. — The following, if not otherwise excepted under subsection (b), shall not be considered to be an ownership or investment interest described in subsection (a)(2)(A):

(1) HOSPITALS IN PUERTO RICO. — In the case of designated health services provided by a hospital located in Puerto Rico.

(2) RURAL PROVIDER. — In the case of designated health services furnished in a rural area (as defined in section 1886(d)(2)(D) [42 U.S.C.A. 1395ww(d)(2)(D), which for purposes of the prospective payment system for inpatient hospital services defines rural areas]) by an entity, if substantially all of the designated health services furnished by such entity are furnished to individuals residing in such a rural area.

(3) HOSPITAL OWNERSHIP. — In the case of designated health services provided by a hospital (other than a hospital described in paragraph (1)) if—

(A) the referring physician is authorized to perform services at the hospital, and

(B) the ownership or investment interest is in the hospital itself (and not merely in a subdivision of the hospital).

Section 1877(e) provides as follows with respect to exceptions relating to other compensation arrangements:

EXCEPTION RELATING TO OTHER COMPENSATION ARRANGEMENTS. — The following shall not be considered to be a compensation arrangement described in subsection (a)(2)(B):

(1) RENTAL OF OFFICE SPACE; RENTAL OF EQUIPMENT. —

(A) OFFICE SPACE. — Payment made by a lessee to a lessor for the use of premises if—

(i) the lease is set out in writing, signed by the parties, and specifies the premises covered by the lease,

(ii) the space rented or leased does not exceed that which is reasonable and necessary for the legitimate business purposes of the lease or rental and is used exclusively by the lessee when being used by the lessee, except that the lessee may make payments for the use of space consisting of common areas if such payments do not exceed the lessee's pro rata share of expenses for such space based upon the ratio of the space used exclusively by the lessee to the total amount of space (other than common areas) occupied by all persons using such common areas,

(iii) the lease provides for a term of rental or lease for at least 1 year,

(iv) the rental charges over the term of the lease are set in advance, are consistent with fair market value, and are not determined in a manner that takes into account the volume or value of any referrals or other business generated between the parties,

(v) the lease would be commercially reasonable even if no referrals were made between the parties, and

(vi) the lease meets such other requirements as the Secretary may impose by regulation as needed to protect against program or patient abuse.

(B) EQUIPMENT. — Payments made by a lessee of equipment to the lessor of the equipment for the use of the equipment if —

(i) the lease is set out in writing, signed by the parties, and specifies the equipment covered by the lease,

(ii) the equipment rented or leased does not exceed that which is reasonable and necessary for the legitimate business purposes of the lease or rental and is used exclusively by the lessee when being used by the lessee,

(iii) the lease provides for a term of rental or lease of at least 1 year,

(iv) the rental charges over the term of the lease are set in advance, are consistent with fair market value, and are not determined in a manner that takes into account the volume or value of any referrals or other business generated between the parties,

(v) the lease would be commercially reasonable even if no referrals were made between the parties, and

(vi) the lease meets such other requirements as the Secretary may impose by regulation as needed to protect against program or patient abuse.

(2) BONA FIDE EMPLOYMENT RELATIONSHIPS. — Any amount paid by an employer to a physician (or an immediate family member of such physician) who has a bona fide employment relationship with the employer for the provision of services if—

(A) the employment is for identifiable services,

(B) the amount of the remuneration under the employment —

(i) is consistent with the fair market value of the services, and

(ii) is not determined in a manner that takes into account (directly or indirectly) the volume or value of any referrals by the referring physician,

(C) the remuneration is provided pursuant to an agreement which would be commercially reasonable even if no referrals were made to the employer, and

(D) the employment meets such other requirements as the Secretary may impose by regulation as needed to protect against program or patient abuse.

Subparagraph (B)(ii) shall not prohibit the payment of remuneration in the form of a productivity bonus based on services performed personally by the physician (or an immediate family member of such physician).

(3) PERSONAL SERVICE ARRANGEMENTS. —

(A) IN GENERAL. — Remuneration from an entity under an arrangement (including remuneration for specific physicians' services furnished to a nonprofit blood center) if—

(i) the arrangement is set out in writing, signed by the parties, and specifies the services covered by the arrangement,

(ii) the arrangement covers all of the services to be provided by the physician (or an immediate family member of such physician) to the entity,

(iii) the aggregate services contracted for do not exceed those that are reasonable and necessary for the legitimate business purposes of the arrangement,

(iv) the term of the arrangement is for at least 1 year,

(v) the compensation to be paid over the term of the arrangement is set in advance, does not exceed fair market value, and except in the case of a physician incentive plan described in subparagraph (b), is not determined in a manner that takes into account the volume or value of any referrals or other business generated between the parties,

(vi) the services to be performed under the arrangement do not involve the counseling or promotion of a business arrangement or other activity that violates any State or Federal law, and

(vii) the arrangement meets such other requirements as the Secretary may impose by regulation as needed to protect against program or patient abuse.

(B) PHYSICIAN INCENTIVE PLAN EXCEPTION. —

(i) IN GENERAL. — In the case of a physician incentive plan (as defined in clause (ii)) between a physician and an entity, the compensation may be determined in a manner (through a withhold, capitation, bonus, or otherwise) that takes into account directly or indirectly the volume or value of any referrals or other business generated between the parties, if the plan meets the following requirements:

(I) No specific payment is made directly or indirectly under the plan to a physician or a physician group as an inducement to reduce or limit medically necessary services provided with respect to a specific individual enrolled with the entity.

(II) In the case of a plan that places a physician or a physician group at substantial financial risk as determined by the Secretary pursuant to section

1876(i)(8)(A)(ii) [42 U.S.C.A. 1395mm(i)(8)(A)(ii), which pertains to risk requirements for HMO's and CMP's with physician incentive plans which put a physician or physician group at risk for services the physician or physician group do not provide], the plan complies with any requirements the Secretary may impose pursuant to such section.

(III) Upon request by the Secretary, the entity provides the Secretary with access to descriptive information regarding the plan, in order to permit the Secretary to determine whether the plan is in compliance with the requirements of this clause.

(ii) PHYSICIAN INCENTIVE PLAN DEFINED. — For purposes of this subparagraph, the term "physician incentive plan" means any compensation arrangement between an entity and a physician or physician group that may directly or indirectly have the effect of reducing or limiting services provided with respect to individuals enrolled with the entity.

(4) REMUNERATION UNRELATED TO THE PROVISION OF DESIGNATED HEALTH SERVICES. — In the case of remuneration which is provided by a hospital to a physician if such remuneration does not relate to the provision of designated health services.

(5) PHYSICIAN RECRUITMENT. — In the case of remuneration which is provided by a hospital to a physician to induce the physician to relocate to the geographic area served by the hospital in order to be a member of the medical staff of the hospital, if —

(A) the physician is not required to refer patients to the hospital,

(B) the amount of the remuneration under the arrangement is not determined in a manner that takes into account (directly or indirectly) the volume or value of any referrals by the referring physician, and

(C) the arrangement meets such other requirements as the Secretary may impose by regulation as needed to protect against program or patient abuse.

(6) ISOLATED TRANSACTIONS. — In the case of an isolated financial transaction, such as a one-time sale of property or practice, if —

(A) the requirements described in subparagraphs (B) and (C) of paragraph (2) are met with respect to the entity in the same manner as they apply to an employer, and

(B) the transaction meets such other requirements as the Secretary may impose by regulation as needed to protect against program or patient abuse.

(7) CERTAIN GROUP PRACTICE ARRANGEMENTS WITH A HOSPITAL. —

(A) IN GENERAL. — An arrangement between a hospital and a group under which designated health services are provided by the group but are billed by the hospital if —

(i) with respect to services provided to an inpatient of the hospital, the arrangement is pursuant to the provision of inpatient hospital services under section 1861(b)(3) [42 U.S.C.A. 1395x(b)(3), which includes certain diagnostic or therapeutic items or services ordinarily furnished to inpatients by a hospital or by others under arrangements with the hospital],

(ii) the arrangement began before December 19, 1989, and has continued in effect without interruption since such date,

(iii) with respect to the designated health services covered under the arrangement, substantially all of such services furnished to patients of the hospital are furnished by the group under the arrangement,

(iv) the arrangement is pursuant to an agreement that is set out in writing and that specifies the services to be provided by the parties and the compensation for services provided under the agreement,

(v) the compensation paid over the term of the agreement is consistent with fair market value and the compensation per unit of services is fixed in advance and is not determined in a manner that takes into account the volume or value of any referrals or other business generated between the parties,

(vi) he compensation is provided pursuant to an agreement which would be commercially reasonable even if no referrals were made to the entity, and

(vii) the arrangement between the parties meets such other requirements as the Secretary may impose by regulation as needed to protect against program or patient abuse.

(8) PAYMENTS BY A PHYSICIAN FOR ITEMS AND SERVICES. — Payments made by a physician —

(A) to a laboratory in exchange for the provision of clinical laboratory services, or

(B) to an entity as compensation for other items or services if the items or services are furnished at a price that is consistent with fair market value.

Section 1877(f), which deals with reporting requirements, was substantially the same pre- and post-OBRA 93. The difference is the substitution of "designated health services" for "clinical laboratory services". Refer to the statutory provisions under II-38-A in Appendix H for effective dates of changes made by prior amendments. As amended by OBRA 93, and the Social Security Act Amendments of 1994, P.L. 103-432, subsection (f) provides:

REPORTING REQUIREMENTS. — Each entity providing covered items or services for which payment may be made under this title shall provide the Secretary with the information concerning the entity's ownership, investment and compensation arrangements, including —

(1) the covered items and services provided by the entity, and

(2) the names and unique physician identification numbers of all physicians with an ownership or investment interest (as described in subsection (a)(2)(A)), or with a compensation arrangement (as described in subsection (a)(2)(B), in the entity, or whose immediate relatives have such an ownership or investment interest or who have such a compensation relationship with the entity.

◆ NOTE: Sections 152(a)(1)-(3) of the Social Security Act Amendments of 1994, added the phrase "investment and compensation" following "ownership" in the introductory clause above. They also added the phrase ", or with a compensation arrangement (as described in subsection (a)(2)(B)" after "investment interest (as described in subsection (a)(2)(A))" in (2). These changes apply to referrals made on or after January 1, 1995.

> Such information shall be provided in such form, manner, and at such times as the Secretary shall specify. The requirement of this subsection shall not apply to designated health services provided outside the United States or to entities which the Secretary determines provides [sic provide] services for which payment may be made under this title very infrequently.

◆ NOTE: Section 152(a)(4) of the Social Security Act Amendments of 1994, substituted the phrase "designated health services" just above for the phrase "covered items and services". Section 152(1)(5) deleted the sentence: "Such information shall first be provided not later than October 1, 1991.", which previously followed "Such information shall be provided in such form, manner, and at such times as the Secretary shall specify." The following sentence, which previously followed the phrase "under this title very infrequently" was deleted by Section 152(a)(5) of the Social Security Act Amendments of 1994: "The Secretary may waive the requirements of this subsection (and the requirements of chapter 35 of title 44, United States Code, with respect to information provided under this subsection) with respect to reporting by entities in a State (except for entities providing designated health services) so long as such reporting occurs in at least 10 States, and the Secretary may waive such requirements with respect to the providers in a State required to report so long as such requirements are not waived with respect to parenteral and enteral suppliers, end stage renal disease facilities, suppliers of ambulance services, hospitals, entities providing physical therapy services, and entities providing diagnostic imaging services of any type." All of these changes apply to referrals made on or after January 1, 1995.

Section 1877(g), which sets for sanctions for violating restriction of physician referrals, is substantially the same pre- and post-OBRA 93. The difference is the substitution of "designated health service" for "clinical laboratory service" in (g)(1). Refer to the statutory provisions under former II-38-A in Appendix H for effective dates of changes made by prior amendments. As amended by OBRA 93, subsection (g) provides:

SANCTIONS. —

(1) DENIAL OF PAYMENT. — No payment may be made under this title for a designated health service which is provided in violation of subsection (a)(1).

(2) REQUIRING REFUNDS FOR CERTAIN CLAIMS. — If a person collects any amounts that were billed in violation of subsection (a) (1), the person shall be liable to the individual for, and shall refund on a timely basis to the individual, any amounts so collected.

(3) CIVIL MONEY PENALTY AND EXCLUSION FOR IMPROPER CLAIMS. — Any person that presents or causes to be presented a bill or a claim for a service that such person knows or should know is for a service for which payment may not be made under paragraph (1) or for which a refund has not been made under paragraph (2) shall be subject to a civil money penalty of not more than $15,000 for each such service. The provisions of section 1128A [42 U.S.C.A. 1320a-7a, which authorizes civil money penalties for a variety of offenses] (other than the first sentence of subsection (a) and other than subsection (b) [which pertain to certain offenses]) shall apply to a civil money penalty under the previous sentence in the same manner as such provisions apply to a penalty or proceeding under section 1128A(a).

(4) CIVIL MONEY PENALTY AND EXCLUSION FOR CIRCUMVENTION SCHEMES. — Any physician or other entity that enters into an arrangement or scheme (such as a cross-referral arrangement) which the physician or entity knows or should know has a principal purpose of assuring referrals by the physician to a particular entity which, if the physician directly made referrals to such entity, would be in violation of this section, shall be subject to a civil money penalty of not more than $100,000 for each such arrangement or scheme. The provisions of section 1128A (other than the first sentence of subsection (a) and other than subsection (b)) shall apply to a civil money penalty under the previous sentence in the same manner as such provisions apply to a penalty or proceeding under section 1128A(a).

(5) FAILURE TO REPORT INFORMATION. — Any person who is required, but fails, to meet a reporting requirement of subsection (f) is subject to a civil money penalty of not more

than $10,000 for each day for which reporting is required to have been made. The provisions of section 1128A [42 U.S.C.A. 1320a-7a] (other than the first sentence of subsection (a) and other than subsection (b)) shall apply to a civil money penalty under the previous sentence in the same manner as such provisions apply to a penalty or proceeding under section 1128A(a).

(6) ADVISORY OPINIONS. —

(A) IN GENERAL. — The Secretary shall issue written advisory opinions concerning whether a referral relating to designated health services (other than clinical laboratory services) is prohibited under this section. Each advisory opinion issued by the Secretary shall be binding as to the Secretary and the party or parties requesting the opinion.

(B) APPLICATION OF CERTAIN RULES. — The Secretary shall, to the extent practicable, apply the rules under subsections (b)(3) and (b)(4) and take into account the regulations promulgated under subsection (b)(5) of section 1128D [42 U.S.C.A 1320a-7d] in the issuance of advisory opinions under this paragraph.

(C) REGULATIONS. — In order to implement this paragraph in a timely manner, the Secretary may promulgate regulations that take effect on an interim basis, after notice and pending opportunity for public comment.

(D) APPLICABILITY. — This paragraph shall apply to requests for advisory opinions made after the date which is 90 days after the date of the enactment of this paragraph and before the close of the period described in section 1128D(b)(6).

Finally, section 1877(h) provides the following definitions and special rules:

DEFINITIONS AND SPECIAL RULES. — For purposes of this section:

(1) COMPENSATION ARRANGEMENT; REMUNERATION. — (A) The term "compensation arrangement" means any arrangement involving any remuneration between a physician (or an immediate family member of such physician) and

an entity other than an arrangement involving only remuneration described in subparagraph (C).

(B) The term "remuneration" includes any remuneration, directly or indirectly, overtly or covertly, in cash or in kind.

(C) Remuneration described in this subparagraph is any remuneration consisting of any of the following:

(i) The forgiveness of amounts owed for inaccurate tests or procedures, mistakenly performed tests or procedures, or the correction of minor billing errors.

(ii) The provision of items, devices, or supplies that are used solely to—

(I) collect, transport, process, or store specimens for the entity providing the item, device, or supply, or

(II) order or communicate the results of tests or procedures for such entity.

(iii) A payment made by an insurer or a self-insured plan to a physician to satisfy a claim, submitted on a fee for service basis, for the furnishing of health services by that physician to an individual who is covered by a policy with the insurer or by the self-insured plan, if—

(I) the health services are not furnished, and the payment is not made, pursuant to a contract or other arrangement between the insurer or the plan and the physician,

(II) the payment is made to the physician on behalf of the covered individual and would otherwise be made directly to such individual,

(III) the amount of the payment is set in advance, does not exceed fair market value, and is not determined in a manner that takes into account directly or indirectly the volume or value of any referrals, and

(IV) the payment meets such other requirements as the Secretary may impose by regulation as needed to protect against program or patient abuse.

(2) EMPLOYEE. — An individual is considered to be "employed by" or and "employee" of an entity if the individual would be considered to be an employee of the entity under the usual common law rules applicable in determining the

employer-employee relationship (as applied for purposes of section 3121(d)(2) of the Internal Revenue Code of 1986).

(3) FAIR MARKET VALUE. — The term "fair market value" means the value in arms length transactions, consistent with the general market value, and, with respect to rentals or leases, the value of rental property for general commercial purposes (not taking into account its intended use) and, in the case of a lease of space, not adjusted to reflect the additional value the prospective lessee or lessor would attribute to the proximity or convenience to the lessor where the lessor is a potential source of patient referrals to the lessee.

(4) GROUP PRACTICE. —

(A) DEFINITION OF GROUP PRACTICE. — The term "group practice" means a group of 2 or more physicians legally organized as a partnership, professional corporation, foundation, not-for-profit corporation, faculty practice plan, or similar association —

(i) in which each physician who is a member of the group provides substantially the full range of services which the physician routinely provides, including medical consultation, diagnosis, or treatment, through the joint use of shared office space, facilities, equipment and personnel,

(ii) for which substantially all of the services of the physicians who are member of the group are provided through the group and are billed under a billing number assigned to the group and amounts so received are treated as receipts of the group,

(iii) in which the overhead expenses of and the income from the practice are distributed in accordance with methods previously determined,

(iv) except as provided in subparagraph (B)(i), in which no physician who is a member of the group directly or indirectly receives compensation based on the volume or value of referrals by the physician,

(v) in which members of the group personally conduct no less than 75 percent of the physician-patient encounters of the group practice, and

(vi) which meets such other standards as the Secretary may impose by regulation.

(B) SPECIAL RULES. —

(i) PROFITS AND PRODUCTIVITY BONUSES. — A physician in a group practice may be paid a share of overall profits of the group, or a productivity bonus based on services personally performed or services incident to such personally performed services, so long as the share or bonus is not determined in any manner which is directly related to the volume or value of referrals by such physician.

(ii) FACULTY PRACTICE PLANS. — In the case of a faculty practice plan associated with a hospital, institution of higher education, or medical school with an approved medical residency training program in which physician members may provide a variety of different specialty services and provide professional services both within and outside the group, as well as perform other tasks such as research, subparagraph (A) shall be applied only with respect to the services provided within the faculty practice plan.

(5) REFERRAL; REFERRING PHYSICIAN. —

(A) PHYSICIANS' SERVICES. — Except as provided in subparagraph C, in the case of an item or service for which payment may be made under part B, the request by a physician for the item or service, including the request by a physician for a consultation with another physician (and any test or procedure ordered by, or to be performed by (or under the supervision of) that other physician), constitutes a "referral" by a "referring physician".

(B) OTHER ITEMS. — Except as provided in subparagraph (C), the request or establishment of a plan of care by a physician which includes the provision of the designated health service constitutes a "referral" by a "referring physician".

(C) CLARIFICATION RESPECTING CERTAIN SERVICES INTEGRAL TO A CONSULTATION BY CERTAIN SPECIALISTS. — A request by a pathologist for clinical diagnostic laboratory tests and pathological examination services, a request by a radiologist for diagnostic radiology services, and a request by a radiation oncologist for radiation therapy, if such services are furnished by (or under the supervision of) such pathologist, radiologist, or radiation oncologist pursuant to a consultation requested by another physician does not constitute a "referral" by a "referring physician".

(6) DESIGNATED HEALTH SERVICES. — The term "designated health services" means any of the following items or services:

(A) Clinical laboratory services.

(B) Physical therapy services.

(C) Occupational therapy services.

(D) Radiology, including magnetic resonance imaging, computerized axial tomography scans, and ultrasound services.

◆ NOTE: Prior to amendment by section 152(b)(1) of the Social Security Act Amendments of 1994, section 1877(h)(6)(D) read: "Radiology or other diagnostic services." The phrase "and supplies" was added by section 152(b)(2) in sections 1877(h)(6)(E), (F), and (I) below. These changes apply to referrals made on or after January 1, 1995.

(E) Radiation therapy services and supplies.

(F) Durable medical equipment and supplies.

(G) Parenteral and enteral nutrients, equipment, and supplies.

(H) Prosthetics, orthotics, and prosthetic devices.

(I) Home health services and supplies.

(J) Outpatient prescription drugs.

(K) Inpatient and outpatient hospital services.

For regulatory citations, see Chapter 6

§ 2:43 TERMINATING AGREEMENTS WITH END STAGE RENAL DISEASE NETWORK AREA ORGANIZATIONS — Section 1881(c)(1) [42 U.S.C.A. 1395rr(c)(1)]

Summary

To assure effective and efficient administration of end stage renal disease (ESRD) benefits under Medicare, Congress authorized the Secretary of Health and Human Services to establish at least 17 ESRD network areas and to designate an administrative organization for each area. Each administrative organization was obliged to establish a network council and a medical review board. The medical review board must include physicians, nurses, and social workers engaged in treatment relating to end stage renal disease, and at least one patient representative. See section 1881(c)(1), 42 U.S.C.A. 1395rr(c)(1).

Applicants had to compete to get an agreement with the Secretary to become an ESRD network administrative organization. (Competition is required when new ones are to be selected, too.) The Secretary, in turn, had to establish standards, criteria, and procedures to evaluate applicants and to measure their performance once selected. In that evaluation, the Secretary must consider the quality and scope of services proposed and must not accord more than 20 percent of the weight to the element of price.

In accordance with section 1881(c)(1), 42 U.S.C.A. 1395rr(c)(1), the Secretary may terminate an agreement with an ESRD network administrative organization only if he finds, after applying his published criteria, that it has failed to perform its prescribed responsibilities effectively and efficiently.

The statute does not mention appeal rights for such a termination.

Statutory Provisions

Section 1881(c)(1), 42 U.S.C.A. 1395rr(c)(1), provides:

> (A) (i) For the purpose of assuring effective and efficient administration of the benefits provided under this section, the Secretary shall, in accordance with such criteria as he finds necessary to assure the performance of the

responsibilities and functions specified in paragraph (2) —

(I) establish at least 17 end stage renal disease network areas, and

(II) for each such area, designate a network administrative organization which, in accordance with regulations of the Secretary, shall establish (aa) a network council of renal dialysis and transplant facilities located in the area and (bb) a medical review board, which has a membership including at least one patient representative and physicians, nurses, and social workers engaged in treatment relating to end stage renal disease.

The Secretary shall publish in the Federal Register a description of the geographic area that he determines, after consultation with appropriate professional and patient organizations, constitutes each network area and the criteria on the basis of which such determination is made.

(ii) (I) In order to determine whether the Secretary should enter into, continue, or terminate an agreement with a network administrative organization designated for an area established under clause (i), the Secretary shall develop and publish in the Federal Register standards, criteria, and procedures to evaluate an applicant organization's capabilities to perform (and, in the case of an organization with which such an agreement is in effect, actual performance of) the responsibilities described in paragraph (2). The Secretary shall evaluate each applicant based on quality and scope of services and may not accord more than 20 percent of the weight of the evaluation to the element of price.

(II) An agreement with a network administrative organization may be terminated by the Secretary only if he finds, after applying such standards and criteria, that the organization has failed to perform its prescribed responsibilities effectively and efficiently. If such an agreement is to be terminated, the Secretary shall select a successor to the agreement on the basis of

> competitive bidding and in a manner that provides an orderly transition.

No mention is made in this section of appeal rights if the Secretary decides to terminate a network administrative organization's agreement.

Section 1881(c)(1) goes on to provide:

> (B) At least one patient representative shall serve as a member of each network council and each medical review board.
>
> (C) The Secretary shall, in regulations, prescribe requirements with respect to membership in network organizations by individuals (and the relatives of such individuals) (i) who have an ownership or control interest in a facility or provider which furnishes services referred to in section 1861(s)(2)(F) [42 U.S.C.A. 1395x(s)(2)(F), which is the definition section pertaining to home dialysis supplies and equipment, self-care home dialysis support services, and institutional dialysis services and supplies], or (ii) who have received remuneration from any such facility or provider in excess of such amounts as constitute reasonable compensation for services (including time and effort relative to the provision of professional medical services) or goods supplied to such facility or provider; and such requirements shall provide for the definition, disclosure, and, to the maximum extent consistent with effective administration, prevention of potential or actual financial or professional conflicts of interest with respect to decisions concerning the appropriateness, nature, or site of patient care.

Effective December 19, 1989, section 6219(b) of P.L. 101-239, the Omnibus Budget Reconciliation Act of 1989, added subparagraph (8) to section 1881(c). It provides:

> (8) The provisions of sections 1157 [42 U.S.C.A. 1320c-6, which limits civil and criminal liability of Peer Review Organizations and persons assisting them in the course of their contractual duties and which authorizes reimbursement for their legal expenses when because of such actions they are sued] and 1160 [42 U.S.C.A. 1320c-9, which restricts disclosure of information obtained by PRO's notwithstanding

provisions of the Freedom of Information Act] shall apply with respect to network administrative organizations (including such organizations as medical review boards) with which the Secretary has entered into agreements under this subsection.

For regulatory citations, see Chapter 6

§ 2:44 FAILURE BY END STAGE RENAL DISEASE FACILITIES AND PROVIDERS OF END STAGE RENAL DISEASE CARE TO COOPERATE WITH END STAGE RENAL DISEASE NETWORK PLANS AND GOALS AND FAILURE TO FOLLOW END STAGE RENAL DISEASE MEDICAL REVIEW BOARD RECOMMENDATIONS — Section 1881(c)(3) and (g) [42 U.S.C.A. 1395rr(c)(3) and (g)]

Summary

To assure effective and efficient administration of end stage renal disease (ESRD) benefits under Medicare, Congress authorized the Secretary of Health and Human Services to establish at least 17 ESRD network areas and to designate an administrative organization for each area. Each administrative organization then had to establish a network council and a medical review board. The medical review board must include physicians, nurses, and social workers engaged in treatment relating to end stage renal disease, and at least one patient representative. See section 1881(c)(1), 42 U.S.C.A. 1395rr(c)(1).

If the Secretary finds that an ESRD facility or provider has consistently failed to cooperate with ESRD network plans and goals or to follow the recommendations of the ESRD medical review board, section 1881(c)(3), 42 U.S.C.A. 1395rr(c)(3), permits him to terminate or withhold certification of such facility or provider for purposes of payment for services furnished to individuals with end stage renal disease until he determines that it is making reasonable and appropriate efforts to cooperate with the network's plans and goals.

If the Secretary determines failure to cooperate does not jeopardize patient health or safety or justify termination of certification, then, alternatively, after reasonable notice to the provider or facility and to the public, he may impose such other sanctions as denial of reimbursement with respect to some or all patients admitted to the facility after the date of notice to the facility or provider, and graduated reduction in reimbursement for all patients.

In addition, if the Secretary finds that a renal dialysis facility is not in substantial compliance with requirements pertaining to the scope of renal dialysis services and supplies and the criteria for payment therefor, and if he finds that the facility's deficiencies do not immediately jeopardize the health and safety of patients, and if he has given the facility reasonable opportunity to correct its deficiencies, then, according to section 1881(g), 42 U.S.C.A. 1395rr(g), in lieu of terminating approval of the facility, he may determine that payment shall be made to the facility only for services furnished to individuals who were patients of the facility before the effective date of the notice.

The latter determination requires notice and opportunity for a hearing, followed by a right to judicial review, in accordance with the hearing and judicial review rights found in Title II of the Social Security Act, 42 U.S.C.A. 405(b) and (g).

A decision to restrict payments becomes effective after notice to the facility and the public. It remains in effect until the Secretary either finds substantial compliance or terminates the agreement.

Statutory Provisions

Section 1881(c)(3), 42 U.S.C.A. 1395rr(c)(3), provides:

> Where the Secretary determines, on the basis of the data contained in the [end stage renal disease] network's annual report and such other relevant data as may be available to him, that a facility or provider has consistently failed to cooperate with network plans and goals or to follow the recommendations of the medical review board, he may terminate or withhold certification of such facility or provider (for purposes of payment for services furnished to individuals with end stage renal disease) until he determines that such provider or facility is making reasonable and appropriate efforts to cooperate with the network's plans and goals. If the Secretary determines that the facility's or provider's failure to cooperate with network plans and goals does not jeopardize patient health or safety or justify termination of certification, he may instead, after reasonable notice to the provider or facility and to the public, impose such other sanctions as he determines to be appropriate, which sanctions may include denial of reimbursement with respect to some

or all patients admitted to the facility after the date of notice to the facility or provider, and graduated reduction in reimbursement for all patients.

Section 1881(g), 42 U.S.C.A. 1395rr(g), provides:

(1) In any case where the Secretary —

(A) finds that a renal dialysis facility is not in substantial compliance with requirements for such facilities prescribed under subsection (b)(1)(A) [which pertains to the scope of renal dialysis services and supplies and the criteria for payment therefor which the Secretary was obligated to establish by regulations],

(B) finds that the facility's deficiencies do not immediately jeopardize the health and safety of patients, and

(C) has given the facility a reasonable opportunity to correct its deficiencies,

the Secretary may, in lieu of terminating approval of the facility, determine that payment under this title shall be made to the facility only for services furnished to individuals who were patients of the facility before the effective date of the notice.

(2) The Secretary's decision to restrict payments under this subsection shall be made effective only after such notice to the public and to the facility as may be prescribed in regulations, and shall remain in effect until (A) the Secretary finds that the facility is in substantial compliance with the requirements under subsection (b)(1)(A), or (B) the Secretary terminates the agreement under this title with the facility.

(3) A facility dissatisfied with a determination by the Secretary under paragraph (1) shall be entitled to a hearing thereon by the Secretary (after reasonable notice) to the same extent as is provided in section 205(b) [42 U.S.C.A. 405(b)] , and to judicial review of the Secretary's final decision after such hearing as is provided in section 205(g) [42 U.S.C.A. 405(g)], except that, in so applying such sections and in applying section 205(l) thereto, any reference therein to the Commissioner of Social Security or the Social Security Administration shall be considered a reference to the Secretary or the Department of Health and Human Services, respectively. [NOTE: The phrase beginning "except that" was added by

section 108(c)(5) of the Social Security Independence and Program Improvements Act of 1994, P.L. 1-3-296, effective March 31, 1995.].

Section 205 provides as follows regarding administrative hearings and judicial review:

(b) (1) The Commissioner of Social Security is directed to make findings of fact, and decisions as to the rights of any individual applying for a payment under this title. Any such decision by the Commissioner of Social Security which involves a determination of disability and which is in whole or in part unfavorable to such individual shall contain a statement of the case, in understandable language, setting forth a discussion of the evidence, and stating the Commissioner's determination and the reason or reasons upon which it is based. Upon request by any such individual or upon request by a wife, divorced wife, widow, surviving divorced wife, surviving divorced mother, surviving divorced father, husband, divorced husband, widower, surviving divorced husband, child or parent who makes a showing in writing that his or her rights may be prejudiced by any decision the Commissioner of Social Security has rendered, the Commissioner shall give such applicant and such other individual reasonable notice and opportunity for a hearing with respect to such decision, and, if a hearing is held, shall, on the basis of evidence adduced at the hearing, affirm, modify, or reverse his findings of fact and such decision. Any such request with respect to such a decision must be filed within sixty days after notice of such decision is received by the individual making such request. The Commissioner of Social Security is further authorized, on the Commissioner's own motion, to hold such hearings and to conduct such investigations and other proceedings as the Commissioner may deem necessary or proper for the administration of this title. In the course of any hearing, investigation, or other proceeding, the Commissioner may administer oaths and affirmations, examine witnesses, and receive evidence. Evidence may be received at any hearing before the Commissioner of Social Security even though inadmissible under rules of evidence applicable to court procedure.

* * *

(g) Any individual, after any final decision of the Commissioner of Social Security made after a hearing to which he was a party, irrespective of the amount in controversy, may obtain a review of such decision by a civil action commenced within sixty days after the mailing to him of notice of such decision or within such further time as the Commissioner of Social Security may allow. Such action shall be brought in the district court of the United States for the judicial district in which the plaintiff resides, or has his principal place of business, or, if he does not reside or have his principal place of business within any such judicial district, in the District Court of the United States for the District of Columbia [United States District Court for the District of Columbia]. As part of the Commissioner's answer the Commissioner of Social Security shall file a certified copy of the transcript of the record including the evidence upon which the findings and decision complained of are based. The court shall have power to enter, upon the pleadings and transcript of the record, a judgment affirming, modifying, or reversing the decision of the Commissioner of Social Security, with or without remanding the cause for a rehearing. The findings of the Commissioner of Social Security as to any fact, if supported by substantial evidence, shall be conclusive, and where a claim has been denied by the Commissioner or a decision is rendered under subsection (b) hereof which is adverse to an individual who was a party to the hearing before the Commissioner of Social Security, because of failure of the claimant or such individual to submit proof in conformity with any regulation prescribed under subsection (a) hereof, the court shall review only the question of conformity with such regulations and the validity of such regulations. The court may, on motion of the Commissioner of Social Security made for good cause shown before the Commissioner files his answer, remand the case to the Commissioner of Social Security for further action by the Commissioner of Social Security, and it may at any time order additional evidence to be taken before the Commissioner of Social Security, but only upon a showing that there is new evidence which is material and that there is good cause for the failure to incorporate such evidence into the record in a prior proceeding; and the Commissioner of Social Security shall, after the case is remanded, and after hearing such additional evidence if so ordered, modify or affirm the Commissioner's

> findings of fact or the Commissioner's decision, or both, and shall file with the court any such additional and modified findings of fact and decision and a transcript of the additional record and testimony upon which the Commissioner's action in modifying or affirming was based. Such additional or modified findings of fact and decision shall be reviewable only to the extent provided for review of the original findings of fact and decision. The judgment of the court shall be final except that it shall be subject to review in the same manner as a judgment in other civil actions. Any action instituted in accordance with this subsection shall survive notwithstanding any change in the person occupying the office of Commissioner of Social Security or any vacancy in such office.

Subsection (a) of section 205, to which subsection (g) refers, provides:

> (a) The Commissioner of Social Security shall have full power and authority to make rules and regulations and to establish procedures, not inconsistent with the provisions of this title, which are necessary or appropriate to carry out such provisions, and shall adopt reasonable and proper rules and regulations to regulate and provide for the nature and extent of the proofs and evidence and the method of taking and furnishing the same in order to establish the right to benefits hereunder.

◆ NOTE: Effective March 31, 1995, section 110(a) of P.L. 203-296, the Social Security Program Independence and Program Improvement Act of 1994, changed references to the Department of Health and Human Services to the Social Security Administration, and references to the Secretary of Health and Human Services to the Commissioner of Social Security, and references to the pronouns "she", "her", "he", "him", and "his" to "the Commissioner" or "the Commissioner's", as appropriate, throughout section 205 of the Social Security Act.

For regulatory citations, see Chapter 6

§ 2:45 ISSUING MEDICARE SUPPLEMENTAL HEALTH INSURANCE POLICIES IN VIOLATION OF STATE OR FEDERAL STANDARDS — Section 1882(a)(2) [42 U.S.C.A. 1395ss(a)(2)]

Summary

◆ NOTE: P.L. 101-508, the Omnibus Budget Reconciliation Act of 1990 (OBRA 90), effective November 5, 1990, made substantial changes in the law applicable to Medicare supplemental health insurance policies. For a summary of the law and statutory provisions pre-OBRA 90, see former § 2:40.1 in Appendix H.

The Sanction: Any person who issues a Medicare supplemental policy after the effective date of the 1991 NAIC Model Regulation or 1991 Federal Regulation with respect to the policy, in violation of section 1882 is subject to a civil money penalty not to exceed $25,000 for each such violation. Enforcement procedures for this civil money penalty are governed by section 1128A, 42 U.S.C.A. 1320a-7a, which authorizes civil money penalties for a variety of offenses.

To educate consumers and help with enforcement, section 1882(e) obligates the Secretary to provide to all Medicare beneficiaries, and, as much as possible, to those about to become beneficiaries, information to help them evaluate not only Medicare supplemental policies but also their relationship to Medicare benefits. That information must include a listing of addresses and telephone numbers of State and Federal agencies and offices that can provide assistance with respect to selection of Medicare supplemental policies. The Secretary also must inform them about sanctionable actions under section 1882, including the manner in which they may report improper actions and the availability of a toll-free telephone number for making such reports.

Establishing the Standards: Pursuant to section 171(c)(1)(B) of the Social Security Act Amendments of 1994, the effective date of this requirement is the date the State adopts the 1991 NAIC Model Regulation or the date the 1991 Federal Regulation applies, as the case may be, or one year after the date the NAIC or the Secretary first adopts such standards, whichever is earlier. This applies effective November 5, 1990, as if included in OBRA 90.

The effective date depended on whether and when the NAIC produced "NAIC standards" for such policies. Section 1882(p)(1)(A) required NAIC to do so within nine months after enactment of OBRA 90, which ended August 5, 1991. Had the NAIC not met that requirement, the Secretary was obligated to produce "Federal standards" within a subsequent period of nine months, which ended May 5, 1992. Depending on which of those outcomes occurred, the effective date of this requirement was either the date the State adopted the NAIC or Federal standards or one year after the date NAIC or the Secretary first adopted such standards, whichever is earlier. The NAIC Model Regulation was timely adopted.

◆ NOTE: Where States required legislation (other than legislation appropriating funds) to meet NAIC or Federal standards, the effective date was the first day of the first calendar quarter beginning after the close of the first State legislative session that begins on or after January 1, 1992. For a State with a two-year legislative session, each year was deemed a separate regular session.

The standards provide limitations on the groups or packages of benefits that may be offered under a Medicare supplemental policy, uniform language and definitions to be used with respect to such benefits, and a uniform format for the policy. They also reflect other requirements imposed by OBRA 90. In establishing them, the NAIC (or the Secretary) had to consult with representatives of issuers of Medicare supplemental policies, consumer groups, Medicare beneficiaries, and other qualified individuals, a working group selected in a manner to assure balanced representation.

Definition: A Medicare supplemental policy, according to section 1882(g)(1), is a health insurance policy or other health benefit plan offered by a private entity to Medicare beneficiaries which provides reimbursement for items not payable by Medicare because of deductibles, coinsurance amounts, or other limitations on payment.

Specifically excluded from the definition are:

(1) Any such policy or plan of one or more employers or labor organizations, or of trustees of a fund established by one or more employers or labor organizations (or combination thereof) which is for employees or former employees (or combination thereof) or for members or former members (or combination thereof) of the labor organizations.

(2) Policies or plans of health maintenance organizations or competitive medical plans which provide health insurance to Medicare beneficiaries under contract with Medicare or which are an approved demonstration project under section 603(c) of the Social Security Act Amendments of 1983 or under section 2355 of the Deficit Reduction Act of 1984.

(3) During the period between the time the State adopted the 1991 NAIC Model Regulation or 1991 Federal Regulation and December 31, 1995, policies or plans of an organization which provides benefits pursuant to an agreement under section 1833, 42 U.S.C.A. 1395l (pre-paid health plans).

(4) A Medicare + Choice plan. [Section 4002(j)(2) of the Balanced Budget Act of 1997, P.L. 105–33, added this exemption for Medicare + Choice plans effective January 1, 1999.

Form and Content Requirements: Pursuant to section 1882(p)(2), policies under the 1991 NAIC Model Regulation or 1991 Federal Regulation must provide for such groups or packages of benefits that enable consumers to purchase benefits available in the market as of November 5, 1990. They also must balance the objectives of simplifying comparison among policies, avoiding adverse selection, providing consumer choice, providing market stability, and promoting competition. This does not preclude offering new or innovative benefits, provided they are approved by the State or the Secretary, as the case may be. Nor does it preclude a State from restricting the groups of benefits that may be offered in a Medicare supplemental policy, but the restriction may not reduce the statutory core group of benefits which must be common to all policies.

Maximum Number of Plans: Pursuant to section 1882(p)(2)(C), the total number of different benefit packages (including the core group and each other combination of benefits offered separately) that may be established in all the States and by all issuers may not exceed 10, plus the two plans described in section 1882(p)(11)(A).

Section 4032(a) of the Balanced Budget Act of 1997, P.L. 105–33, added the two plans described in (p)(11)(A), effective August 5, 1997. These are the same as Standard Plans F and J, except that they have high deductible features. A high deductible feature is one which requires the beneficiary to pay annual out-of-pocket expenses (other than premiums) which are higher than the deductibles for the 10 standard plans. For 1998 and 1999, the high deductible amount is $1,500. For subsequent years, the high deductible amount is the amount for the previous year increased by the percentage increase in the Consumer Price Index for all urban consumers (all items, U.S. city average) for the 12-month period ending with August of the preceding year. Any amount determined by that formula which is not a multiple of $10 shall be rounded to the nearest multiple of $10.

Mandatory Core Benefits Policy: Pursuant to section 1882(o)(2), if a Medicare supplemental policy provides coverage for a group of benefits other than the core group described in section 1882(p)(2)(B), the issuer must make a policy available consisting only of that core group of benefits. Furthermore, pursuant to section 1882(q), each Medicare supplemental policy must be guaranteed renewable; the issuer may not cancel or decline to renew the policy solely because of the insured's health status; and the issuer may not cancel and may not decline to renew for any reason other than nonpayment of premium or material misrepresentation.

Option for New or Innovative Benefits: Pursuant to section 1882(p)(4)(B), an issuer of a Medicare supplement policy or plan may offer benefits which are not otherwise available and which are cost-effective if the benefits are new and innovative and they are offered in a manner consistent with the statutory goal of simplification of Medicare supplement policies. Such benefits must be approved first, however, by the State or the Secretary.

Mandatory Standard Outlines of Coverage: Pursuant to section 1882(o)(3) and section 1882(p)(9)(B), sellers of Medicare supplement policies or plans must provide individuals with a standard outline of coverage approved by the State regulatory program or the Secretary (as the case may be) consistent with the 1991 NAIC Model Regulation or 1991 Federal Regulation before the sale so individuals may compare various benefit packages.

Guaranteed Renewability: Pursuant to section 1882(q)(1), each Medicare supplemental policy or plan must be guaranteed renewable.

Continuation of Benefits: Pursuant to section 1882(q)(2), if a group policy is terminated and not replaced, the issuer must make an individual policy available, and it must provide for continuation of the group policy's benefits or such other benefits as meets the requirements of section 1882. If an individual terminates membership in a group, the issuer similarly must offer the individual an individual policy or offer continuation of coverage in the group.

Replacement of Group Policies: Pursuant to section 1882(q)(4), if a group Medicare supplemental policy is replaced by another group Medicare supplemental policy purchased by the same policyholder, effective October 31, 1994, section 171(b)(2) of the Social Security Act Amendments of 1994 requires the issuer of the replacement policy to make an individual policy available. (Prior to that amendment the obligation fell to the "succeeding issuer".) Furthermore, the issuer of the replacement policy must offer coverage to all persons covered under the old group policy on its termination date, with no exclusion for preexisting conditions that would have been covered under the former group policy.

Suspension and Re-instatement Rights for Medicaid Recipients: Pursuant to section 1882(q)(5), with respect to policies issued or sold after November 5, 1991, provision must be made to reinstate a policy which may be suspended at policyholder request where the policyholder becomes entitled to Medicaid benefits, but only if the policyholder notifies the issuer within 90 days after becoming entitled to Medicaid.

Loss Ratio Requirements: Pursuant to section 1882(r), no Medicare supplemental policy may be issued or renewed or otherwise provide coverage in any State unless the policy can be expected to return to policyholders in the form of aggregate benefits at least 75 percent of the aggregate amount of premiums collected in the case of group policies, and at least 65 percent in the case of individual policies. Prior to amendment by section 171(e)(1) of the Social Security Act Amendments of 1994, effective October 31, 1994, this requirement applied only to policies "issued or sold" in any State.

States are nevertheless free to require higher percentages, and NAIC and the Comptroller General are to study, report to, and recommend to Congress about adjustment of these percentages. Furthermore, the issuer must issue a proportional refund or credit against future premiums (with interest) to assure that these ratios are met. Prior to amendment by section 171(e)(1) of the Social Security Act Amendments of 1994, the latter, however, did not apply to a policy with respect to the first two years in which it is in effect. Effective October 31, 1994, it applies after the first year following issue. For ratio purposes, policies issued as a result of solicitations of individuals through the mails or by mass media advertising, including print and broadcast advertising, are deemed to be individual policies.

Credit for Meeting Preexisting Condition, Waiting Period, Elimination Period and Probationary Period Requirements Under Prior Policy: Pursuant to section 1882(s), if one Medicare supplemental policy replaces another, the issuer of the replacement must waive any time periods applicable to preexisting conditions, waiting period, elimination periods, and probationary periods for similar benefits to the extent such time was spent under the original policy.

Open Enrollment: Pursuant to section 1882(s)(2), the issuer of a Medicare supplemental policy may not deny or condition issuance or effectiveness of a policy, or discriminate in the pricing of the policy, because of health status, claims experience, receipt of health care, or medical condition for which an application is submitted during the six-month period beginning the first month. This does not prevent exclusion of benefits under a policy during that six-month period based on a pre-existing condition for which the policyholder received treatment or was otherwise diagnosed during the six months before it became effective. Nevertheless, if a policy or certificate replaced another such policy or certificate that had been in effect for six months or longer, the replacing policy may not provide any time period applicable to pre-existing conditions, waiting periods, elimination periods, and probationary periods in the new policy or certificate for similar benefits.

◆ NOTE: Prior to amendment by section 171(g)(1)-(3) of the Social Security Act Amendments of 1994, effective October 31, 1994, this requirement applied to applications submitted during the 6-month period beginning with the first month in which an individual who is 65 years or older first enrolled for benefits under Part B.

Furthermore, in the case of a policy issued during the first six months of open enrollment based on attaining age 65, insurers must credit applicants for periods of creditable coverage, as defined in section 2701(c) of the Public Health Service Act.

Claims Processing: Pursuant to section 1882(c), the Secretary may certify a Medicare supplemental policy only if (1) the issuer accepts a Medicare notice of benefits as a claim form for benefits under the policy in lieu of any other claim form and agrees to make a payment determination on the basis of information in that Medicare notice; (2) where such a notice is received, the issuer provides notice to such physician or supplier and the beneficiary of the payment determination under the policy, and provides any payment covered by such policy directly to the participating physician or supplier involved; (3) the issuer provides each enrollee upon enrollment a card listing the policy name and number and a single mailing address to which to send claim notices under the policy; (4) the issuer agrees to pay any user fees established under Medicare with respect to information transmitted to the issuer; (5) the issuer provides to the Secretary at least annually, for transmittal to Medicare carriers, a single mailing address to which Medicare notices of payment are to be sent; and (6) where the issuer will make full refund of any premiums paid when a policyholder decides to cancel the policy within 30 days after issuance.

No Restriction on Vendor Discounts: Pursuant to section 1882(p)(7), nothing in this statute prevents an issuer of a Medicare supplement policy that otherwise meets requirements of section 1882 from providing, through an arrangement with a vendor, for discounts from that vendor to policyholders or certificateholders for the purchase of items or services not covered under its Medicare supplement policy.

Preferred Provider Plans: Special provisions apply for Medicare supplement policies or plans which restrict benefits to items and services furnished by preferred providers or which reduce benefits when items or services are not provided by such sources. These are commonly referred to as Medicare SELECT plans.

Pursuant to section 1882(t), an issuer of a Medicare SELECT policy or plan must provide full benefits through a network of providers with whom it has contracts or agreements. It must provide for items and services furnished by non-network providers in emergencies and when network providers cannot deliver medically necessary services. It must assure sufficient access to an appropriate array of health care providers. It must have arrangements for an ongoing quality assurance program for items and services furnished through the network. It must explain the restrictions on payment for services furnished by non-network providers, the availability of out-of-area coverage under the policy, and coverage for medical emergencies, and it must obtain a written acknowledgement prior to enrollment from the enrollee that it has received such an explanation. Finally, the issuer must offer a standard non-preferred provider plan as an alternative.

Additional Rules Relating to Individuals Enrolled in MSA Plans and Private Fee-for -Service Plans: Pursuant to section 4003(b) of the Balanced Budget Act of 1997, it is unlawful to sell or issue a Medicare supplement policy to an individual with knowledge that the individual has in effect under section 1851 [42 U.S.C.A. 1395 —] an election of an MSA (Medical Savings Account) plan or a

Medicare + Choice private fee-for service plan. This prohibition does not apply, however, with respect to the following:

> Policies which provide coverage for accidents, disability, dental care, vision care, or long-term care.
>
> Policies to which substantially all of the coverage relates to liabilities incurred under workers' compensation laws, tort liabilities, liabilities relating to ownership or use of property, or such other similar liabilities as the Secretary may specify by regulations.
>
> Policies which provide coverage for a specified disease or illness.
>
> Policies which pay a fixed amount per day (or other period) of hospitalization.

Statutory Provisions

Section 1882(a), 42 U.S.C.A. 1395ss(a), provides:

> The Secretary shall establish a procedure whereby medicare supplemental policies (as defined in subsection (g)(1)) may be certified by the Secretary as meeting minimum standards and requirements set forth in subsection (c). Such procedure shall provide an opportunity for any insurer to submit any such policy, and such additional data as the Secretary finds necessary, to the Secretary for his examination and for his certification thereof as meeting the standards and requirements set forth in subsection (c). Subject to subsections (k)(3) [which prohibits Secretarial certification from being made, being continued, or being deemed unless the Medicare supplemental insurance policy meets or exceeds standards set forth in the NAIC Model Regulation, if amended to comply with P.L. 100-360, the Medicare Catastrophic Coverage Act of 1988, or, if not so amended, meets or exceeds Federal model standards — effective either one year after the date the Association first adopts such amended Model Regulation or one year after the date the Secretary first promulgates such standards, as the case may be], (m), and (n) [(m), and (n) added, effective January 1, 1990, by section 203 of P.L. 101-234, the Medicare Catastrophic Coverage Repeal Act of 1989, to permit insurers to comply with changes required by enactment and repeal of P.L. 100-360, the Medicare Catastrophic Coverage Act of 1988], such certification shall remain in effect if the insurer files a notarized statement with the Secre-

tary no later than June 30 of each year stating that the policy continues to meet such standards and requirements and if the insurer submits such additional data as the Secretary finds necessary to independently verify the accuracy of such notarized statement. Where the Secretary determines such a policy meets (or continues to meet) such standards and requirements, he shall authorize the insurer to have printed on such policy (but only in accordance with such requirements and conditions as the Secretary may prescribe) an emblem which the Secretary shall cause to be designed for use as an indication that a policy has received the Secretary's certification. The Secretary shall provide each State commissioner or superintendent of insurance with a list of all the policies which have received his certification.

(2) No Medicare supplemental policy may be issued in a State on or after the date specified in subsection (p)(1)(C) unless —

(A) the State's regulatory program under subsection (b)(1) provides for the application and enforcement of the standards and requirements set forth in such subsection (including the 1991 NAIC Model Regulation or 1991 Federal Regulation (as the case may be)) by the date specified in subsection (p)(1)(C); or

◆ NOTE: Prior to amendment by section 171(c)(1)(a) of the Social Security Act Amendments of 1994, P.L. 103-432, the preceding paragraph (A) read: "the State's regulatory program under subsection (b)(1) provides for the application and enforcement of the standards and requirements set forth in such subsection (including the NAIC standards or the Federal standards (as the case may be)) by the date specified in subsection (p)(1)(C); or[.]" The change was effective November 5, 1990, as if included in OBRA 90.

(B) if the State's program does not provide for the application and enforcement of such standards and requirements, the policy has been certified by the Secretary under paragraph (a) as meeting the standards and requirements set forth in subsection (c) (including such applicable standards) by such date.

Any person who issues a medicare supplemental policy, after the effective date specified in subsection (p)(1)(C) [Prior to amendment by section 171(c)(1)(B) of the Social Security Act Amendments of 1994, effective November 5, 1990, as if included in OBRA 90, the phrase "after the effective date of the NAIC or Federal standards with respect to the policy," appeared in place of "after the effective date specified in subsection (p)(1)(C)".] in violation of this paragraph is subject to a civil money penalty of not to exceed $25,000 for each such violation. The provisions of section 1128A [42 U.S.C.A. 1320a-7a] (other than the first sentence of subsection (a) and other than subsection (b)) shall apply to a civil money penalty under the previous sentence in the same manner as such provisions apply to a penalty or proceeding under section 1128A(a).

Section 1882(g) provides:

(1) For purposes of this section, a medicare supplemental policy is a health insurance policy or other health benefit plan offered by a private entity to individuals who are entitled to have payment made under this title, which provides reimbursement for expenses incurred for services and items for which payment may be made under this title but which are not reimbursable by reason of the applicability of deductibles, coinsurance amounts, or other limitations imposed pursuant to this title; but does not include a Medicare + Choice plan or any such policy or plan of one or more employers or labor organizations, or of the trustees of a fund established by one or more employers or labor organizations (or combination thereof), for employees or former employees (or combination thereof) or for members or former members (or combination thereof) of the labor organizations and does not include a policy or plan of an eligible organization (as defined in section 1876(b) [42 U.S.C.A. 1395mm(b), which pertains to HMO's and CMP's paid by Medicare to provide health insurance benefits to Medicare beneficiaries]) if the policy or plan provides benefits pursuant to a contract under section 1876 or an approved demonstration project described in section 603(c) of the Social Security Amendments of 1983, section 2355 of the Deficit Reduction Act of 1984, of 1986 [sic], or during the period beginning on the date specified in subsection (p)(1)(C) and ending on December 31, 1995, a policy or plan of an organization if the policy or plan provides benefits pursuant to

an agreement under section 1833(a)(1)(A) [42.U.S.C.A. 1395l(a), which pertains to pre-paid plans]. For purposes of this section, the term "policy" includes a certificate issued under such policy.

◆ NOTE: The reference to Medicare + Choice plan in section 1882(g)(1) above was added by section 4002(j)(2) of P.L. 105–33, the Balanced Budget Act of 1997, effective January 1, 1999.

◆ NOTE: Prior to amendment by section 171(f)(1) of the Social Security Act Amendments of 1994, effective October 31, 1994, section 1882(g)(1) read: "For purposes of this section, a medicare supplemental policy is a health insurance policy or other health benefit plan offered by a private entity to individuals who are entitled to have payment made under this title, which provides reimbursement for expenses incurred for services and items for which payment may be made under this title but which are not reimbursable by reason of the applicability of deductibles, coinsurance amounts, or other limitations imposed pursuant to this title; but does not include any such policy or plan of one or more employers or labor organizations, or of the trustees of a fund established by one or more employers or labor organizations (or combination thereof), for employees or former employees (or combination thereof) or for members or former members (or combination thereof) of the labor organizations and does not include a policy or plan of a health maintenance organization or other direct service organization which offers benefits under this title, including such services under a contract under section 1876 [42 U.S.C.A. 1395mm] or an agreement under section 1833 [42 U.S.C.A. 1395l(a)] . For purposes of this section, the term "policy" includes a certificate issued under such policy."

(2) For purposes of this section:

(A) The term "NAIC Model Standards" means the "NAIC Model Regulation to Implement the Individual Accident and Sickness Insurance Minimum Standards Act", adopted by the National Association of Insurance Commissioners on June 6, 1979, as it applies to medicare supplemental policies.

(B) The term "State with an approved regulatory program" means a State for which the Secretary has made a determination under subsection (b)(1). [NOTE: Prior to amendment by section 171(c)(3) of the Social Security Act Amendments of 1994, effective October 31,1994, the word "Panel" appeared (see summary of pre-OBRA 90 law in Appendix H) in place of the word "Secretary".]

(C) The State in which a policy is issued means—

(i) in the case of an individual policy, the State in which the policyholder resides; and

(ii) in the case of a group policy, the State in which the holder of the master policy resides.

Section 1882(b) provides:

(1) Any medicare supplemental policy issued in any State which the Secretary determines has established under State law a regulatory program that —

(A) provides for the application and enforcement of standards with respect to such policies equal to or more stringent than the NAIC Model Standards (as defined in subsection (g)(2)(A)), except as otherwise provided by subparagraph (H);

(B) includes requirements equal to or more stringent than the requirements described in paragraphs (2) through (5) of subsection (c);

(C) provides that —

(i) information with respect to the actual ratio of benefits provided to premiums collected under such policies will be reported to the State on forms conforming to those developed by the National Association of Insurance Commissioners for such purpose, or

(ii) such ratios will be monitored under the program in an alternative manner approved by the Secretary and [effective with respect to policies issued or sold more than one year after November 5, 1990] that a copy of each such policy, the most recent premium for each such policy, and a listing of the ratio of benefits provided to premiums collected for the most recent 3-year period for each such policy issued or sold in the State is maintained and made available to interested persons;

(D) provides for application of the standards and requirements described in subparagraphs (A), (B), and (C) to all medicare supplemental policies (as defined in subsection (g)(1)) issued in such State, and

(E) provides the Secretary periodically (but at least annually) with a list containing the name and address of the issuer of each such policy and the name and number of each such policy (including an indication of policies that have been previously approved, newly approved, or withdrawn from approval since the previous list was provided),

(F) reports to the Secretary on the implementation and enforcement of standards and requirements of this paragraph at intervals established by the Secretary,

(G) [with respect to policies sold or issued more than one year after November 5, 1990, according to section 4355(c) of OBRA 90] provides for a process for approving or disapproving proposed premium increases with respect to such policies, and establishes a policy for the holding of public hearings prior to approval of a premium increase, and

(H) [applicable, pursuant to section 4358(b)(2) of OBRA 90, in 15 States determined by the Secretary and only for a 3-year period beginning 1992] in the case of a policy that meets the standards under subparagraph (A) except that benefits under the policy are limited to items and services furnished by certain entities (or reduced benefits are provided when items or services are furnished by other entities), provides for the application of requirements equal to or more stringent than the requirements under subsection (t), shall be deemed (subject to subsection (k)(3), (m), and (n) [(m), and (n) added effective January 1, 1990] for so long as the Secretary finds that such State regulatory program continues to meet the standards and requirements of this paragraph) to meet the standards and requirements set forth in subsection (c). The report required under subsection (F) shall include information on loss ratios of policies sold in the State, frequency and types of instances in which policies approved by the State fail to meet the standards and requirements of this paragraph, actions taken by the State to bring such policies into compliance, and information regarding State programs implementing consumer protection provisions, and such further information as the Secretary in consultation with the National Association of Insurance Commissioners, may specify.

◆ NOTE: Section 171(c)(2)(A)-(D) of the Social Security Act Amendments of 1994, substituted "Each" for "The" at the beginning of the preceding sentence, inserted "and requirements" after "standards", removed "and" following "compliance", and removed a comma after "Commissioners". In addition, section 171(c)(4) removed a redundant "the" preceding "the Secretary"; and section 171(e)(2) substituted "subparagraph (F)" for "subsection (F)". These changes were effective November 5, 1990, as if included in OBRA 90.]

(2) The Secretary periodically shall review State regulatory programs to determine if they continue to meet the standards and requirements specified in paragraph (1). If the Secretary finds that a State regulatory program no longer meets the standards and requirements, before making a final determination, the Secretary shall provide the State an opportunity to adopt such a plan of correction as would permit the State regulatory program to continue to meet such standards and requirements. If the Secretary makes a final determination that the State regulatory program, after such an opportunity, fails to meet such standards and requirements, the program shall no longer be considered to have in operation a program meeting such standards and requirements.

(3) Notwithstanding paragraph (1), a medicare supplemental policy offered in a State shall not be deemed to meet the standards and requirements set forth in subsection (c), with respect to an advertisement (whether through written, radio, or television medium) used (or, at a State's option, to be used) for the policy in the State, unless the entity issuing the policy provides a copy of each advertisement to the Commissioner of Insurance (or comparable officer identified by the Secretary) of that State for review or approval to the extent it may be required under State law.

Then section 1882(c) spells out the standards as follows:

The Secretary shall certify under this section any medicare supplemental policy, or continue certification of such a policy, only if he finds that such policy (or, with respect to paragraph (3) or the requirement described in subsection (s), the issuer of the policy) —

(1) meets or exceeds (either in a single policy or, in the case of nonprofit hospital and medical service associations, in one or more policies issued in conjunction with one another) the NAIC Model Standards (except as otherwise provided by subsection (t));

(2) [applicable with respect to policies sold or issued more than one year after November 5, 1990, according to section 4355(a)(1) of OBRA 90] meets the requirements of subsection (r);

(3) (A) accepts a notice under section 1842(h)(3)(B) [42 U.S.C.A. 1395u(h)(3)(B), which pertains to assignment of Medicare claims and the form of notice of payment determination prepared by the Medicare carrier in assignment cases] as a claim form for benefits under such policy in lieu of any claim form otherwise required and agrees to make a payment determination on the basis of the information contained in such notice;

(B) where such a notice is received —

(i) provides notice to such physician or supplier and the beneficiary of the payment determination under the policy, and

(ii) provides any payment covered by such policy directly to the participating physician or supplier involved;

(C) provides each enrollee at the time of enrollment a card listing the policy name and number and a single mailing address to which notices under section 1842(h)(3)(B) respecting the policy are to be sent;

(D) agrees to pay any user fees established under section 1842(h)(3)(B) with respect to information transmitted to the issuer of the policy; and

(E) provides to the Secretary at least annually, for transmittal to carriers, a single mailing address to which notices under section 1842(h)(3)(B) respecting the policy are to be sent; and

(4) may, during a period of not less than 30 days after the policy is issued, be returned for a full refund of any premiums

paid (without regard to the manner in which the purchase of the policy was solicited);

(5) meets the applicable requirements of subsections (o) through (t).

Regarding the notice of Medicare benefits sent by carriers to issuers of Medicare supplemental policies or plans, section 1842(h)(3)(B), 42 U.S.C.A. 1395u(h)(3)(B), provides:

The Secretary shall establish a procedure whereby an individual enrolled under this part may assign, in an appropriate manner on the form claiming a benefit under this part for an item or service furnished by a participating physician or supplier, the individual's rights of payment under a medicare supplemental policy (described in section 1882(g)(1)) in which the individual is enrolled. In the case such an assignment is properly executed and a payment determination is made by a carrier with a contract under this section, the carrier shall transmit to the private entity issuing the medicare supplemental policy notice of such fact and shall include an explanation of benefits and any additional information that the Secretary may determine to be appropriate in order to enable the entity to decide whether (and the amount of) any payment is due under the policy. The Secretary may enter into agreements for the transmittal of such information to entities electronically. The Secretary shall impose user fees for the transmittal of information under this subparagraph by a carrier, whether electronically or otherwise, and such user fees shall be collected and retained by the carrier.

Section 1882(e), 42 U.S.C.A. 1395ss(e), provides:

(1) The Secretary shall provide to all individuals entitled to benefits under this title (and, to the extent feasible, to individuals about to become so entitled) such information as will permit such individuals to evaluate the value of medicare supplemental policies to them and the relationship of any such policies to benefits provided under this title.

(2) The Secretary shall—

(A) inform all individuals entitled to benefits under this title (and, to the extent feasible, individuals about to become so entitled) of—

(i) the actions and practices that are subject to sanctions under subsection (d), and

(ii) the manner in which they may report any such action or practice to an appropriate official of the Department of Health and Human Services (or to an appropriate State official), and

(B) publish the toll-free telephone number for individuals to report suspected violations of the provisions of such subsection.

(3) The Secretary shall provide individuals entitled to benefits under this title (and, to the extent feasible, individuals about to become so entitled) with a listing of the addresses and telephone numbers of State and Federal agencies and offices that provide information and assistance to individuals with respect to the selection of medicare supplemental policies.

Section 1882(f), 42 U.S.C.A. 1395ss(f), provides:

(1) (A) The Secretary shall, in consultation with Federal and State regulatory agencies, the National Association of Insurance Commissioners, private insurers, and organizations representing consumers and the aged, conduct a comprehensive study and evaluation of the comparative effectiveness of various State approaches to the regulation of medicare supplemental policies in (i) limiting marketing and agent abuse, (ii) assuring the dissemination of such information to individuals entitled to benefits under this title (and to other consumers) as is necessary to permit informed choice, (iii) promoting policies which provide reasonable economic benefits for such individuals, (iv) reducing the purchase of unnecessary duplicative coverage, (v) improving price competition, and (vi) establishing effective approved State regulatory programs described in subsection (b).

(B) Such study shall also address the need for standards or certification of health insurance policies, other than medicare supplemental policies, sold to individuals eligible for benefits under this title.

(C) The Secretary shall, no later than January 1, 1982, submit a report to the Congress on the results of such study and evaluation, accompanied by such recommendations as the Secretary finds warranted by such results with respect to the need for legislative or administrative changes to accomplish the objectives set forth in subparagraphs (A) and (B), including the need for a mandatory Federal regulatory program to assure the marketing of appropriate types of medicare supplemental policies, and such other means as he finds may be appropriate to enhance effective State regulations of such policies.

(2) The Secretary shall submit to the Congress no later than July 1, 1982, and periodically as may be appropriate thereafter (but not less often than once every 2 years), a report evaluating the effectiveness of the certification procedure and the criminal penalties established under this section, and shall include in such reports an analysis of—

(A) the impact of such procedure and penalties on the types, market share, value, and cost to individuals entitled to benefits under this title of medicare supplemental policies which have been certified by the Secretary;

(B) the need for any change in the certification procedure to improve its administration or effectiveness; and

(C) whether the certification program and criminal penalties should be continued.

(3) The Secretary shall provide information via a toll-free telephone number on medicare supplemental policies (including the relationship of State programs under title XIX to such policies). [NOTE: Paragraph (3) was added by section 171(j)(2) of the Social Security Act Amendments of 1994, effective October 31, 1994.]

With regard to regulations, section 1882(h), 42 U.S.C.A. 1395ss(h), provides:

The Secretary shall prescribe such regulations as may be necessary for the effective, efficient, and equitable administration of the certification procedure established under this section. The Secretary shall first issue final regulations to implement the certification procedure established under subsection (a) not later than March 1, 1981.

Section 1882(i), 42 U.S.C.A. 1395ss(i), provides:

(1) No medicare supplemental policy shall be certified and no such policy may be issued bearing the emblem authorized by the Secretary under subsection (1) until July 1, 1982. On and after such date policies certified by the Secretary may bear such emblem, including policies which were issued prior to such date and were subsequently certified, and insurers may notify holders of such certified policies issued prior to such date using such emblem in the notification.

(2) (A) The Secretary shall not implement the certification program established under subsection (a) with respect to policies issued in a State unless the Panel [see statute pre-OBRA 90] makes a finding that such State cannot be expected to have established, by July 1, 1982, an approved State regulatory program meeting the standards and requirements of subsection (b)(1). If the Panel makes such a finding, the Secretary shall implement such program under subsection (a) with respect to medicare supplemental policies issued in such State, until such time as the Panel determines that such State has a program that meets the standards and requirements of subsection (b)(1).

(B) Any finding by the Panel under subparagraph (A) shall be transmitted in writing, not later than January 1, 1982, to the Committee on Finance of the Senate and to the Committee on Interstate and Foreign Commerce and the Committee on Ways and Means of the House of Representatives and shall not become effective until 60 days after the date of its transmittal to the Committees of the Congress under this subparagraph. In counting such days, days on which either House is not in session because of an adjournment sine die or an adjournment of more than three days to a day certain are excluded in the computation.

To preserve State regulatory rights (see section 1882(g)(2) above), section 1882(j), 42 U.S.C.A. 1395ss(j), provides:

> Nothing in this section shall be construed so as to affect the right of any State to regulate medicare supplemental policies which, under the provisions of this section, are considered to be issued in another State.

Section 1882(k), 42 U.S.C.A. 1395ss(k), provides:

(1) (A) If, within the 90-day period beginning on the date of the enactment of this subsection, the National Association of Insurance Commissioners (in this subsection referred to as the "Association") amends the NAIC Model Regulation adopted on June 6, 1979 (as it relates to medicare supplemental policies), with respect to matters such as minimum benefit standards, loss ratios, disclosure requirements, and replacement requirements and provisions otherwise necessary to reflect the changes in law made by the Medicare Catastrophic Coverage Act of 1988, except as provided in subsection (m) ["except as provided in subsection (m)" added effective January 1, 1990], subsection (g)(2)(A) shall be applied in a State, effective on and after the date specified in subparagraph (B), as if the reference to the Model Regulation adopted on June 6, 1979, were a reference to the Model Regulation as amended by the Association in accordance with this paragraph (in this subsection and subsection (l) referred to as the "amended NAIC Model Regulation").

(B) The date specified in this subparagraph for a State is the earlier of the date the State adopts standards equal to or more stringent than the amended NAIC Model Regulation or 1 year after the date the Association first adopts such amended Regulation.

(2) (A) If the Association does not amend the NAIC Model Regulation within the 90-day period specified in paragraph (1)(A), the Secretary shall promulgate, not later than 60 days after the end of such period, Federal model standards (in this subsection and subsection (l) referred to as "Federal model standards") for medicare supplemental policies to reflect the changes in law made by the Medicare Catastrophic Coverage Act of 1988, and subsection (g)(2)(A) shall be applied in a State, effective on and after the date specified in subparagraph (B), as if the reference to the Model Regulation adopted on June 6, 1979, were a reference to Federal model standards.

(B) The date specified in this subparagraph for a State is the earlier of the date the State adopts standards equal to or more stringent than the Federal model standards or 1 year after the date the Secretary first promulgates such standards.

(3) Notwithstanding any other provision of this section (except as provided in subsections (l), (m), and (n) [changed from "subsection (l)" to "subsections (l), (m), and (n)" effective January 1, 1990] —

(A) no medicare supplemental policy may be certified by the Secretary pursuant to subsection (a),

(B) no certification made pursuant to subsection (a) shall remain in effect, and

(C) no State regulatory program shall be found to meet (or to continue to meet) the requirements of subsection (b)(1)(A), unless such policy meets (or such program provides for the application of standards equal to or more stringent than) the standards set forth in the amended NAIC Model Regulation or the Federal model standards (as the case may be) by the date specified in paragraph (1)(B) or (2)(B) (as the case may be).

Section 1882(l), 42 U.S.C.A. 1395ss(l), provides:

(1) Until the date specified in paragraph (3), in the case of a qualifying medicare supplemental policy described in paragraph (2) issued —

(A) before January 1, 1989, the policy is deemed to remain in compliance with this section if the insurer issuing the policy complies with the NAIC Model Transition Regulation (including giving notices to subscribers and filing for premium adjustments with the State as described in section 5.B. of such Regulation) by January 1, 1989; or

(B) on or after January 1, 1989, the policy is deemed to be in compliance with this section if the insurer issuing the policy complies with the NAIC Model Transition Regulation before the date of the sale of the policy.

(2) In paragraph (1), the term "qualifying medicare supplemental policy" means a medicare supplemental policy —

(A) issued in a State which —

(i) has not adopted standards equal to or more stringent than the NAIC Model Transition Regulation by January 1, 1989, and

(ii) has not adopted standards equal to or more stringent than the amended NAIC Model Regulation (or Federal model standards) by January 1, 1989; and

(B) which has been issued in compliance with this section (as in effect on June 1, 1988).

(3) (A) The date specified in this paragraph is the earlier of—

(i) the first date a State adopts, after January 1, 1989, standards equal to or more stringent than the NAIC Model Transition Regulation or equal to or more stringent than the amended NAIC Model Regulation (or Federal model standards), as the case may be, or

(ii) the later of (I) the date specified in subsection (k)(1)(B) or (k)(2)(B) (as the case may be), or (II) the date specified in subparagraph (B).

(B) In the case of a State which the Secretary identifies as—

(i) requiring State legislation (other than legislation appropriating funds) in order for medicare supplemental policies to meet standards described in subparagraph (A)(i), but

(ii) having a legislature which is not scheduled to meet in 1989 in a legislative session in which such legislation may be considered, the date specified in this subparagraph is the first day of the first calendar quarter beginning after the close of the first legislative session of the State legislature that begins on or after January 1, 1989, and in which legislation described in clause (i) may be considered. For purposes of the previous sentence, in the case of a State that has a 2-year legislative session, each year of such session shall be deemed to be a separate regular session of the State legislature.

(4) In the case of a medicare supplemental policy in effect on January 1, 1989, and offered in a State which, as of such date —

(A) has adopted standards equal to or more stringent than the amended NAIC Model Regulation (or Federal model standards), but

(B) does not have in effect standards equal to or more stringent than the NAIC Model Transition Regulation (or otherwise requiring notice substantially the same as the notice required in section 5.B. of such Regulation), the policy shall not be deemed to meet the standards in subsection (c) unless each individual who is entitled to benefits under this title and is a policyholder under such policy on January 1, 1989, is sent such a notice in any appropriate form by not later than January 31, 1989, that explains —

(A) the improved benefits under this title contained in the Medicare Catastrophic Coverage Act of 1988, and

(B) how these improvements affect the benefits contained in the policies and the premium for the policy.

(5) In this subsection, the term "NAIC Model Transition Regulation" refers to the standards contained in the "Model Regulation to Implement Transitional Requirements for the Conversion of Medicare Supplement Insurance Benefits and Premiums to conform to Medicare Program Revision" (as adopted by the National Association of Insurance Commissioners in September 1987).

(6) The Secretary shall report to the Congress in March 1989 and in July 1990 on actions States have taken in adopting standards equal to or more stringent than the NAIC Model Transition Regulation or the amended NAIC Model Regulation (or Federal model standards).

Section 1882(m), added effective January 1, 1990, by section 203(b) of the Medicare Catastrophic Coverage Repeal Act of 1989, provides:

(1) (A) If, within the 90-day period beginning on the date of the enactment of this subsection, the National Association of Insurance Commissioners (in this subsection and subsection (n) referred to as the "Association") revises the amended NAIC Model Regulation referred to in subsection (k)(1)(A) and adopted on September 20, 1988) to improve such regulation and otherwise to reflect the changes in law made by the Medicare Catastrophic Coverage Repeal Act of 1989, subsection (g)(2)(A) shall be applied in a State, effective on and after the date specified in subparagraph (B), as if the reference to the Model Regulation adopted on June 6, 1979, were a reference to the amended NAIC Model Regulation (referred to in subsection (k)(1)(A)) as revised by the Association in accordance

with this paragraph (in this subsection and subsection (n) referred to as the revised NAIC Model Regulation ").

(B) The date specified in this subparagraph for a State is the earlier of the date the State adopts standards equal to or more stringent than the revised NAIC Model Regulation or 1 year after the date the Association first adopts such revised Regulation.

(2) (A) If the Association does not revise the amended NAIC Model Regulation, within the 90-day period specified in paragraph (1)(A), the Secretary shall promulgate, not later than 60 days after the end of such period, revised Federal model standards (in this subsection and subsection (n) referred to as revised Federal model standards ") for medicare supplemental policies to improve such standards and otherwise to reflect the changes in law made by the Medicare Catastrophic Coverage Repeal Act of 1989, subsection (g)(2)(A) shall be applied in a State, effective on and after the date specified in subparagraph (B), as if the reference to the Model Regulation adopted on June 6, 1979, were a reference to the revised Federal model standards.

(B) The date specified in this subparagraph for a State is the earlier of the date the State adopts standards equal to or more stringent than the revised Federal model standards or 1 year after the date the Secretary first promulgates such standards.

(3) Notwithstanding any other provision of this section (except as provided in subsection (n)) —

(A) no medicare supplemental policy may be certified by the Secretary pursuant to subsection (a),

(B) no certification made pursuant to subsection (a) shall remain in effect, and

(C) no State regulatory program shall be found to meet (or to continue to meet) the requirements of subsection (b))1)(A), unless such policy meets (or such program provides for the application of standards equal to or more stringent than) the standards set forth in the revised NAIC Model Regulation or the revised Federal model standards (as the case may be) by the date specified in paragraph (1)(B) or (2)(B) (as the case may be).

Section 1882(n), added effective January 1, 1990, by section 203(b) of the Medicare Catastrophic Coverage Repeal Act of 1989, provides:

(1) Until the date specified in paragraph (4), in the case of a qualifying medicare supplemental policy described in paragraph (3) issued in a State —

(A) before the transition deadline, the policy is deemed to remain in compliance with the standards described in subsection (b)(1)(A) only if the insurer issuing the policy complies with the transition provision described in paragraph (2), or

(B) on or after the transition deadline, the policy is deemed to be in compliance with the standards described in subsection (b)(1)(A) only if the insurer issuing the policy complies with the revised NAIC Model Regulation or the revised Federal model standards (as the case may be) before the date of the sale of the policy.

In this paragraph, the term "transition deadline" means 1 year after the date the Association adopts the revised NAIC Model Regulation or 1 year after the date the Secretary promulgates revised Federal model standards (as the case may be).

(2) The transition provision described in this paragraph is —

(A) such transition provision as the Association provides, by not later than December 15, 1989, so as to provide for an appropriate transition (i) to restore benefit provisions which are no longer duplicative as a result of the changes in benefits under this title made by the Medicare Catastrophic Coverage Repeal Act of 1989 and (ii) to eliminate the requirement of payment for the first 8 days of coinsurance for extended care services, or

(B) if the Association does not provide for a transition provision by the date described in subparagraph (A), such transition provision as the Secretary shall provide, by January 1, 1990, so as to provide for an appropriate transition described in subparagraph (A).

(3) In paragraph (1), the term "qualifying medicare supplemental policy" means a medicare supplemental policy " which

has been issued in compliance with this section as in effect on the date before the date of the enactment of this subsection.

(4) (A) the date specified in this paragraph for a policy issued in a State is—

(i) the first date a State adopts, after the date of the enactment of this subsection, standards equal to or more stringent than the revised NAIC Model Regulation (or revised Federal model standards), as the case may be, or

(ii) the date specified in subparagraph (B), whichever is earlier.

(B) In the case of a State which the Secretary identifies, in consultation with the Association, as—

(i) requiring State legislation (other than legislation appropriating funds) in order for medicare supplemental policies to meet standards described in subparagraph (A)(i), but

(ii) having a legislature which is not scheduled to meet in 1990 in a legislative session in which such legislation may be considered, the date specified in this subparagraph is the first day of the first calendar quarter beginning after the close of the first legislative session of the State legislature that begins on or after January 1, 1990. For purposes of the previous sentence, in the case of a State that has a 2-year legislative session, each year of such session shall be deemed to be a separate regular session of the State legislature.

(5) In the case of a medicare supplemental policy in effect on January 1, 1990, the policy shall not be deemed to meet the standards in subsection (c) unless each individual who is entitled to benefits under this title and is a policyholder or certificate holder under such policy on such date is sent a notice in an appropriate form by not later than January 31, 1990, that explains—

(A) the changes in benefits under this title effected by the Medicare Catastrophic Coverage Repeal Act of 1989, and

(B) how these changes may affect the benefits contained in such policy and the premium for the policy.

(6) (A) Except as provided in subparagraph (B), in the case of an individual who had in effect, as of December 31, 1988, a

medicare supplemental policy with an insurer (as a policyholder or, in the case of a group policy, as a certificate holder) and the individual terminated coverage under such policy before the date of the enactment of this subsection, no medicare supplemental policy of the insurer shall be deemed to meet the standards in subsection (c) unless the insurer —

(i) provides written notice, no earlier than December 15, 1989, and no later than January 30, 1990, to the policyholder or certificate holder (at the most recent available address) of the offer described in clause (ii), and

(ii) offers the individual, during a period of at least 60 days beginning not later than February 1, 1990, reinstitution of coverage (with coverage effective as of January 1, 1990), under the terms which (I) do not provide for any waiting period with respect to treatment of pre-existing conditions, (II) provides for coverage which is substantially equivalent to coverage in effect before the date of such termination, and (III) provides for classification of premiums on which terms are at least as favorable to the policyholder or certificate holder as the premium classification terms that would have applied to the policyholder or certificate holder had the coverage never terminated.

(B) An insurer is not required to make the offer under subparagraph (A)(ii) in the case of an individual who is a policyholder or certificate holder in another medicare supplemental policy as of the date of the enactment of this subsection, if (as of January 1, 1990) the individual is not subject to a waiting period with respect to treatment of a pre-existing condition under such other policy.

Section 4351 of OBRA 90 added subsections (o) and (p) to section 1882. Subsection (o) provides in pertinent part:

(o) The requirements of this subsection are as follows:

(1) Each medicare supplemental policy shall provide for coverage of a group of benefits consistent with subsection (p).

(2) If the medicare supplemental policy provides for coverage of a group of benefits other than the core group of basic benefits described in subsection (p)(2)(B), the issuer of the policy

must make available to the individual a medicare supplemental policy with only such core group of basic benefits.

(3) The issuer of the policy has provided, before the sale of the policy, an outline of coverage that uses uniform language and format (including layout and print size) that facilitates comparison among medicare supplemental policies and comparison with medicare benefits.

As amended by section 171(a)(2)(A)-(L) of the Social Security Act Amendments of 1994, effective October 31, 1994, section 1882(p) provides in pertinent part:

(p)(1) (A) If, within 9 months after the date of the enactment of this subsection, the National Association of Insurance Commissioners (in this subsection referred to as the "association" changes the revised NAIC Model Regulation (described in subsection (m)) to incorporate—

(i) limitations on the groups or packages of benefits that may be offered under a medicare supplemental policy consistent with paragraphs (2) and (3) of this subsection,

(ii) uniform language and definitions to be used with respect to such benefits,

(iii) uniform format to be used in the policy with respect to such benefits, and

(iv) other standards to meet the additional requirements imposed by the amendments made by the Omnibus Budget Reconciliation Act of 1990, subsection (g)(2)(A) shall be applied in each State, effective for policies issued to policyholders on and after the date specified in subparagraph (C), as if the reference to the Model Regulation adopted on June 6, 1979, were a reference to the revised NAIC Model Regulation as changed by the Secretary under this subparagraph (such changed regulation referred to in this section as the "1991 NAIC Model Regulation").

(B) If the Association does not make the changes in the revised NAIC Model Regulation within the 9-month period specified in subparagraph (A), the Secretary shall promulgate, not later than 9 months after the end of such period, a regulation and subsection (g)(2)(A) shall be applied in each State, effective for policies issued to policyholders on and after the date specified in subparagraph (C), as if the reference to the Model Regulation adopted on June 6, 1979, were a reference to the revised NAIC Model Regulation as changed by the Secretary under this subparagraph (such changed regulation referred to in this section as the "1991 Federal Regulation").

(C) (i) Subject to clause (ii), the date specified in this subparagraph for a State is the date the State adopts the 1991 NAIC Model Regulation or 1991 Federal Regulation or 1 year after the date the Association or the Secretary first adopts such standards, whichever is earlier.

(ii) In the case of a State which the Secretary identifies, in consultation with the Association, as

(I) requiring State legislation (other than legislation appropriating funds) in order for medicare supplemental policies to meet the 1991 NAIC Model Regulation or 1991 Federal Regulation, but

(II) having a legislature which is not scheduled to meet in 1992 in a legislative session in which such legislation may be considered, the date specified in this subparagraph is the first day of the first calendar quarter beginning after the close of the first legislative session of the State legislature that begins on or after January 1, 1992. For purposes of the previous sentence, in the case of a State that has a 2-year legislative session, each year of such session shall be deemed to be a separate regular session of the State legislature.

(D) In promulgating standards under this paragraph, the Association or Secretary shall consult with a working group composed of representatives of issuers of medicare supplemental policies, consumer groups, medicare beneficiaries, and other qualified individuals. Such representatives shall be selected in a manner so as to assure balanced representation among the interested groups.

(E) If benefits (including deductibles and coinsurance) under this title are changed and the Secretary determines, in consultation with the Association, that changes in the 1991 NAIC Model Regulation or 1991 Federal Regulation are needed to reflect such changes, the preceding provisions of this paragraph shall apply to the modification of standards previously established in the same manner as they applied to the original establishment of such standards.

(2) The benefits under the 1991 NAIC Model Regulation or 1991 Federal Regulation shall provide—

(A) for such groups or packages of benefits as may be appropriate taking into account the considerations specified in paragraph (3) and the requirements of the succeeding subparagraphs;

(B) for identification of a core group of basic benefits common to all policies, and

(C) that, subject to paragraph (4)(B), the total number of different benefit packages (counting the core group of basic benefits described in subparagraph (B) and each other combination of benefits that may be offered as a separate benefit package) that may be established in all the States and by all issuers shall not exceed 10 plus the 2 plans described in paragraph 11(A). [NOTE: Section 4032(a) of the Balanced Budget Act of 1997, P.L. 105–33, added the phrase "plus the 2 plans described in paragraph (11)(A). It also added paragraph (11)(A) below. These changes became effective August 5, 1997, subject to the transition provisions in section 4031 of that Act.].

(3) The benefits under paragraph (2) shall, to the extent possible—

(A) provide for benefits that offer consumer [sic consumers] the ability to purchase the benefits that are available in the market as of the date of the enactment of this subsection; and

(B) balance the objectives of (i) simplifying the market to facilitate comparisons among policies, (ii) avoiding adverse selection, (iii) providing consumer choice, (iv) providing market stability, and (v) promoting competition.

(4)(A) (i) Except as provided in subparagraph (B) or paragraph (6), no State with a regulatory program approved under subsection (b)(1) may provide for or permit the grouping of benefits (or language or format with respect to such benefits) under a medicare supplemental policy unless such grouping meets the applicable 1991 NAIC Model Regulation or 1991 Federal Regulation.

(ii) Except as provided in subparagraph (B), the Secretary may not provide for or permit the grouping of benefits (or language or format with respect to such benefits) under a medicare supplemental policy seeking approval by the Secretary unless such grouping meets the applicable 1991 NAIC Model Regulation or 1991 Federal Regulation.

(B) With the approval of the State (in the case of a policy issued in a State with an approved regulatory program) or the Secretary (in the case of any other policy), the issuer of a medicare supplemental policy may offer new or innovative benefits in addition to the benefits provided in a policy that otherwise complies with the applicable standards. Any such new or innovative benefits may include benefits that are not otherwise available and are cost-effective and shall be offered in a manner which is consistent with the goal of simplification of medicare supplemental policies.

(5) (A) Except as provided in subparagraph (B), this subsection shall not be construed as preventing a State from restricting the groups of benefits that may be offered in medicare supplemental policies in the State.

(B) A State with a regulatory program approved under subsection (b)(1) may not restrict under subparagraph (A) the offering of a medicare supplemental policy consisting only of the core group of benefits described in paragraph (2)(B).

(6) The Secretary may waive the application of standards in regard to the limitation of benefits described in clauses (i) through (iii) of paragraph (1)(A) in those States that on the date of enactment of this subsection had in place an alternative simplification program.

(7) This subsection shall not be construed as preventing an issuer of a medicare supplemental policy who otherwise meets the requirements of this section from providing, through an arrangement with a vendor, for discounts from that vendor to policyholders or certificateholders for the purchase of items or services not covered under its medicare supplemental policies.

* * *

(9) (A) Anyone who sells a medicare supplemental policy to an individual shall make available for sale to the individual a medicare supplemental policy with only the core group of basic benefits (described in paragraph (2) (B)).

(B) Anyone who sells a medicare supplemental policy to an individual shall provide the individual, before the sale of the policy, an outline of coverage which describes the benefits under the policy. Such outline shall be on a standard form approved by the State regulatory program or the Secretary (as the case may be) consistent with the 1991 NAIC Model Regulation or 1991 Federal Regulation under this subsection.

* * *

(11)(A) For purposes of paragraph (2), the benefit packages described in this subparagraph are as follows:

(i) The benefit package classified as 'F' under the standards established by such paragraph, except that it has a high deductible feature.

(ii) The benefit package classified as 'J' under the standards established by such paragraph, except that it has a high deductible feature.

(B) For purposes of subparagraph (A), a high deductible feature is one which—

(i) requires the beneficiary of the policy to pay annual out-of-pocket expenses (other than premiums) in the amount specified in subparagraph (c) before the policy begins payment of benefits, and

(ii) covers 100 percent of covered out-of-pocket expenses once such deductible has been satisfied in a year.

(C) The amount specified in this subparagraph—

(i) for 1998 and 1999 is $1,500, and

(ii) for a subsequent year, is the amount specified in this subparagraph for the previous year increased by the percentage increase in the Consumer Price Index for all urban consumers (all items; U.S. city average) for the 12-month period ending with August of the preceding year.

If any amount determined under clause (ii) is not a multiple of $10, it shall be rounded to the nearest multiple of $10.

◆ NOTE: Prior to amendment by section 171(a)(2)(A)-(L) of the Social Security Act Amendments of 1994, effective October 31 1994, section 1882(p) read in pertinent part:

(p)(1) (A) If, within 9 months after the date of the enactment of this subsection, the National Association of Insurance Commissioners (in this subsection referred to as the "association" promulgates —

(i) limitations on the groups or packages of benefits that may be offered under a medicare supplemental policy consistent with paragraphs (2) and (3) of this subsection,

(ii) uniform language and definitions to be used with respect to such benefits,

(iii) uniform format to be used in the policy with respect to such benefits, and

(iv) other standards to meet the additional requirements imposed by the amendments made by the Omnibus Budget Reconciliation Act of 1990, (such limitations, language, definitions, format, and standards referred to collectively in this subsection as "NAIC standards"), subsection (g)(2)(A) shall be applied in each State, effective for policies issued to policyholders on and after the date specified in subparagraph (C), as if the reference to the Model Regulation adopted on June 6, 1979, included a reference to the NAIC standards.

(B) If the Association does not promulgate NAIC standards within the 9-month period specified in subparagraph (A), the Secretary shall promulgate, not later than 9 months after the end of such period, limitations, language, definitions, format, and standards described in clauses (i) through (iv) of such subparagraph (in this subsection referred to collectively as "Federal standards") and subsection (g)(2)(A) shall be applied in each State, effective for policies issued to policyholders on and after the date specified in subparagraph (C), as if the reference to the Model Regulation adopted on June 6, 1979, included a reference to the Federal standards.

(C) (i) Subject to clause (ii), the date specified in this subparagraph for a State is the date the State adopts the NAIC standards or the Federal standards or 1 year after the date the Association or the Secretary first adopts such standards, whichever is earlier.

(ii) In the case of a State which the Secretary identifies, in consultation with the Association, as

(I) requiring State legislation (other than legislation appropriating funds) in order for medicare supplemental policies to meet the NAIC or Federal standards, but

(II) having a legislature which is not scheduled to meet in 1992 in a legislative session in which such legislation may be considered, the date specified in this subparagraph is the first day of the first calendar quarter beginning after the close of the first legislative session of the State legislature that begins on or after January 1, 1992. For purposes of the previous sentence, in the case of a State that has a 2-year legislative session, each year of such session shall be deemed to be a separate regular session of the State legislature.

(D) In promulgating standards under this paragraph, the Association or Secretary shall consult with a working group composed of representatives of issuers of medicare supplemental policies, consumer groups, medicare beneficiaries, and other qualified individuals. Such representatives shall be selected in a manner so as to assure balanced representation among the interested groups.

(E) If benefits (including deductibles and coinsurance) under this title are changed and the Secretary determines, in consultation with the Association, that changes in the NAIC or Federal standards are needed to reflect such changes, the preceding provisions of this paragraph shall apply to the modification of standards previously established in the same manner as they applied to the original establishment of such standards.

(2) The benefits under the NAIC or Federal standards shall provide —

(A) for such groups or packages of benefits as may be appropriate taking into account the considerations specified in paragraph (3) and the requirements of the succeeding subparagraphs;

(B) for identification of a core group of basic benefits common to all policies, and

(C) that, subject to paragraph (5)(B), the total number of different benefit packages (counting the core group of basic benefits described in subparagraph (B) and each other combination of benefits that may be offered as a separate benefit package) that may be established in all the States and by all issuers shall not exceed 10.

(3) The benefits under paragraph (2) shall, to the extent possible —

(A) provide for benefits that offer consumer [sic consumers] the ability to purchase the benefits that are available in the market as of the date of the enactment of this subsection; and

(B) balance the objectives of (i) simplifying the market to facilitate comparisons among policies, (ii) avoiding adverse selection, (iii) providing consumer choice, (iv) providing market stability, and (v) promoting competition.

(4)(A) (i) Except as provided in subparagraph (B), no State with a regulatory program approved under subsection (b)(1) may provide for or permit the grouping of benefits (or language or format with respect to such benefits) under a medicare supplemental policy unless such grouping meets the applicable standards.

(ii) Except as provided in subparagraph (B), the Secretary may not provide for or permit the grouping of benefits (or language or format with respect to such benefits) under a medicare supplemental policy seeking approval by the Secretary unless such grouping meets the applicable standards.

(B) With the approval of the State (in the case of a policy issued in a State with an approved regulatory program) or the Secretary (in the case of any other policy), the issuer of a medicare supplemental policy may offer new or innovative benefits in addition to the benefits provided in a policy that otherwise complies with the applicable standards. Any such new or innovative benefits may include benefits that are not otherwise available and are cost-effective and shall be offered in a manner which is consistent with the goal of simplification of medicare supplemental policies.

(5) (A) Except as provided in subparagraph (B), this subsection shall not be construed as preventing a State from restricting the groups of benefits that may be offered in medicare supplemental policies in the State.

(B) A State with a regulatory program approved under subsection (b)(1) may not restrict under subparagraph (A) the offering of a medicare supplemental policy consisting only of the core group of benefits described in paragraph (2)(B).

(6) The Secretary may waive the application of standards in regard to the limitation of benefits described in paragraph (4) in those States that on the date of enactment of this subsection had in place an alternative simplification program.

(7) This subsection shall not be construed as preventing an issuer of a medicare supplemental policy who otherwise meets the requirements of this section from providing, through an arrangement with a vendor, for discounts from that vendor to policyholder or certificateholders for the purchase of items or services not covered under its medicare supplemental policies.

* * *

(9) (A) Anyone who sells a medicare supplemental policy to an individual shall make available for sale to the individual a medicare supplemental policy with only the core group of basic benefits (described in paragraph (2) (B)).

(B) Anyone who sells a medicare supplemental policy to an individual shall provide the individual, before the sale of the policy, an outline of coverage which describes the benefits under the policy. Such outline shall be on a standard form approved by the State regulatory program or the Secretary (as the case may be) consistent with the NAIC or Federal standards under this subsection.

* * *

Section 4532 of OBRA 90 added subsection (q) to section 1882. It provides in pertinent part:

The requirements of this subsection are as follows:

(1) Each medicare supplemental policy shall be guaranteed renewable and—

(A) the issuer may not cancel or nonrenew the policy solely on the ground of health status of the individual; and

(B) the issuer shall not cancel or nonrenew the policy for any reason other than nonpayment of premium or material misrepresentation.

(2) If the medicare supplemental policy is terminated by the group policyholder and is not replaced as provided under paragraph (4) [Section 171(b)(1) of the Social Security Act Amendments of 1994 substituted "paragraph (4)" for "paragraph (2)", effective October 31, 1994.], the issuer shall offer certificateholders an individual medicare supplemental policy which (at the option of the certificateholder)—

(A) provides for continuation of the benefits contained in the group policy, or

(B) provides for such benefits as otherwise meets the requirements of this section.

(3) If an individual is a certificateholder in a group medicare supplemental policy and the individual terminates membership in the group, the issuer shall—

(A) offer the certificateholder the conversion opportunity described in paragraph (2), or

(B) at the option of the group policyholder, offer the certificateholder continuation of coverage under the group policy.

(4) If a group medicare supplemental policy is replaced by another group medicare supplemental policy purchased by the same policyholder, the succeeding issuer shall offer coverage to all persons covered under the old group policy on its date of termination. [Section 171(b)(2) of the Social Security Act Amendments of 1994 substituted "issuer of the replacement policy" for "succeeding issuer" in the preceding sentence, effective October 31, 1994.] Coverage under the new group policy shall not result in any exclusion for preexisting conditions that would have been covered under the group policy being replaced.

(5) [With respect to policies issued or sold more than one year after November 5, 1990] (A) Each medicare supplemental pol-

icy shall provide that benefits and premiums under the policy shall be suspended at the request of the policyholder for the period (not to exceed 24 months) in which the policyholder has applied for and is determined to be entitled to medical assistance under title XIX of the Social Security Act, but only if the policyholder notifies the issuer of such policy within 90 days after the date the individual becomes entitled to such assistance. [Section 171(d)(4) of the Social Security Act Amendments of 1994 deleted "of the Social Security Act" following "title XIX", here and in (B) below, effective October 31, 1994.] If such suspension occurs and if the policyholder or certificate holder loses entitlement to such medical assistance, such policy shall be automatically reinstituted (effective as of the date of termination of such entitlement) under terms described in subsection (n)(6)(A)(ii) as of the termination of such entitlement if the policyholder provides notice of loss of such entitlement within 90 days after the date of such loss.

(B) Nothing in this section shall be construed as affecting the authority of a State under title XIX, to purchase a medicare supplemental policy for an individual otherwise entitled to assistance under such title.

* * *

Section 4355(a)(3) of OBRA 90 added subsection (r) to section 1882. With respect to policies sold or issued more than one year after November 5, 1990, it provides in pertinent part:

(1) A medicare supplemental policy may not be issued or renewed (or otherwise provide coverage after the date described in subsection (p)(1)(C) in any State unless —

(A) the policy can be expected for periods after the effective date these provisions (as estimated for the entire period for which rates are computed) to provide coverage, on the basis of incurred claims experience and earned premiums for such periods and in accordance with a uniform methodology, including uniform reporting standards, developed by the National Association of Insurance Commissioners, to return to policyholders in the form of aggregate benefits provided under the policy, at least 75 percent of the aggregate amount of premiums collected in the case of group policies and at least 65 percent in the case of individual policies; and

(B) the issuer of the policy provides for the issuance of a proportional refund, or a credit against future premiums of a proportional amount, based on the premium paid and in accordance with paragraph (2), of the amount of premiums received necessary to assure that the ratio of aggregate benefits provided to the aggregate premiums collected (net of such refunds or credits) complies with the expectation required under subparagraph (A), treating policies of the same type as a single policy for each standard package.

For purposes of applying subparagraph (A) only, policies issued as a result of solicitations of individuals through the mails or by mass media advertising (including both print and broadcast advertising) shall be deemed to be individual policies. For the purpose of calculating the refund or credit required under paragraph (1)(B) for a policy issued before the date specified in subsection (p)(1)(C), the refund or credit calculation shall be based on the aggregate benefits provided and premiums collected under all such policies issued by an insurer in a State (separated as to individual and group policies) and shall be based only on aggregate benefits provided and premiums collected under such policies after the date specified in section 171(m)(4) of the Social Security Act Amendments of 1994.

◆ NOTE: Sections 171(e)(1)(A)-(M) of the Social Security Act Amendments of 1994, effective October 31, 1994, substituted "or renewed (or otherwise provide coverage after the date described in subsection (p)(1)(C))" for "or sold"; inserted "for periods after the effective date of these provisions" after "the policy can be expected"; substituted "Commissioners)" for "Commissioners"; added ", treating policies of the same type as a single policy for each standard package" before the period; and added the last sentence in section 1882(r)(1). In section 1882(r)(2)(A) below, the phrase "by standard package" was substituted for "by policy number".

(2) (A) Paragraph (1)(B) shall be applied with respect to each type of policy by policy number. Paragraph (1)(B) shall not apply to a policy until 12 months following issue. The Comp-

troller General, in consultation with the National Association of Insurance Commissioners, shall submit to Congress a report containing recommendations on adjustments in the percentages under paragraph (1)(A) that may be appropriate. In the case of a policy issued before the date specified in subsection (P)(1)(C), paragraph (1)(B) shall not apply until 1 year after the date specified in section 171(m)(4) of the Social Security Act Amendments of 1994.

◆ NOTE: Prior to amendment by sections 171(e)(1)(G) and (H) of the Social Security Act Amendments of 1994, effective October 31, 1994, the second and third sentences of paragraph (2)(A) above read: "Paragraph (1)(B) shall not apply to a policy with respect to the first 2 years in which it is in effect. The Comptroller General, in consultation with the National Association of Insurance Commissioners, shall submit to Congress a report containing recommendations on adjustments in the percentages under paragraph (1)(A) that may be appropriate in order to apply paragraph (1)(B) to the first 2 years in which policies are effective." Section 171(e)(1)(I) added the last sentence, also effective October 31, 1994.

(B) A refund or credit required under paragraph (1)(B) shall be made to each policyholder insured under the applicable policy as of the last day of the year involved.

(C) Such a refund or credit shall include interest from the end of the policy year involved until the date of the refund or credit at a rate as specified by the Secretary for this purpose from time to time which is not less than the average rate of interest for 13-week Treasury notes.

(D) For purposes of this paragraph and paragraph (1)(B), refunds or credits against premiums due shall be made, with respect to a policy year, not later than the third quarter of the succeeding policy year.

(3) The provisions of this subsection do not preempt a State from requiring a higher percentage than that specified in paragraph (1)(A).

(4) The Secretary shall submit in October of each year (beginning with 1993) a report to the Committees on Energy and Commerce and Ways and Means of the House of Representatives and the Committee on Finance of the Senate on

> loss-ratios under medicare supplemental policies and the use of sanctions, such as a required rebate or credit or the disallowance of premium increases, for policies that fail to meet the requirements of this subsection (relating to loss ratios). Such report shall include a list of the policies that failed to comply with such loss-ratio requirements or other requirements of this section. [NOTE: Section 171(e)(1)(K) of the Social Security Act Amendments of 1994, effective October 31, 1994, substituted "October" for "February", "loss ratios" for "loss-ratios", and "disallowance" for "disllowance".]
>
> (5) (A) The Comptroller General shall periodically, not less often than once every 3 years, perform audits with respect to the compliance of medicare supplemental policies with the loss ratio requirements of this subsection and shall report the results of such audits to the State involved and to the Secretary.
>
> (B) The Secretary may independently perform such compliance audits.

* * *

Section 4357 of OBRA 90 added subsection (s) to section 1882. Effective one year after November 5, 1990, it provides in pertinent part:

> (1) If a medicare supplemental policy replaces another medicare supplemental policy, the issuer of the replacing policy shall waive any time periods applicable to preexisting conditions, waiting period, elimination periods and probationary periods in the new medicare supplemental policy for similar benefits to the extent such time was spent under the original policy.
>
> (2) (A) The issuer of a medicare supplemental policy may not deny or condition the issuance or effectiveness of a medicare supplemental policy, or discriminate in the pricing of the policy, because of health status, claims experience, receipt of health care, or medical condition in the case of an individual for whom an application is submitted prior to or during the 6 month period beginning with the first month.
>
> (B) Subject to subparagraphs (C) and (D), subparagraph (A) shall not be construed as preventing the exclusion of bene-

fits under a policy, during its first 6 months, based on a pre-existing condition for which the policyholder received treatment or was otherwise diagnosed during the 6 months before the policy became effective.

(C) If a medicare supplemental policy or certificate replaces another such policy or certificate which has been in effect for 6 months or longer, the replacing policy may not provide any time period applicable to pre-existing conditions, waiting periods, elimination periods, and probationary periods in the new policy or certificate for similar benefits.

(D) In the case of a policy issued during the 6-month period described in subparagraph (A) to an individual who is 65 years of age or older as of the date of issuance and who as of the date of the application for enrollment has a continuous period of creditable coverage (as defined in section 2701(c) of the Public Health Service Act) of—

(i) at least 6 months, the policy may not exclude benefits based on a pre-existing condition; or

(ii) less than 6 months, if the policy excludes benefits based on a preexisting condition, the policy shall reduce the period of any preexisting condition exclusion by the aggregate of the periods of creditable coverage (if any, as so defined) applicable to the individual as of the enrollment date.

The Secretary shall specify the manner of the reduction under clause (ii), based upon the rules used by the Secretary in carrying out section 27091(a)(3) of such Act.

◆ NOTE: Prior to amendment by section 171(g)(1), (2), and (3) of the Social Security Act Amendments of 1994, effective October 31, 1994, section 1882(s)(2)(A) and (B) read: "(A) The issuer of a medicare supplemental policy may not deny or condition the issuance or effectiveness of a medicare supplemental policy, or discriminate in the pricing of the policy, because of health status, claims experience, receipt of health care, or medical condition for which an application is submitted during the 6 month period beginning with the first month in which the individual (who is 65 years of age or older) first enrolled for benefits under part B. (B) Subject to subparagraph (C), subparagraph (A) shall not be construed as preventing the exclusion of benefits under a policy, during its first 6 months, based on a pre-existing condition for which the policyholder received treatment or was otherwise diagnosed during the 6 months before it became effective."

◆ NOTE ALSO: Section 4031(b) of the Balanced Budget Act of 1997 substituted "subparagraphs (C) and (D)" for "subparagraph (C)" after "Subject to" in subparagraph (s)(2)(B) and added subparagraph (s)(2)(D). This applies to policies issued on or after July 1, 1998, and subject to the transition provisions in section 4031(e) of the Balanced Budget Act of 1997.

Section 4031(a) of the Balanced Budget Act of 1997, effective July 1, 1998, added new paragraph (s)(3), which further restricts insurers from excluding coverage of pre-existing conditions and otherwise discriminating against applicants. For more information about that, see section 2:53.

Section 4358(a) of OBRA 90 added subsection (t) to section 1882, applicable only in 15 States, as determined by the Secretary, and only during the 3-year period beginning 1992. Those limits were removed, however, by section 1719(h)(1) of the Social Security Act Amendments of 1994. Effective October 31, 1994, section 1882(t) now provides in pertinent part:

> (1) If a medicare supplemental policy meets the 1991 NAIC Model Regulation or 1991 Federal Regulation and otherwise complies with the requirements of this section except that benefits under the policy are restricted to items and services furnished by certain entities (or reduced benefits are provided when items or services are furnished by other entities), the policy shall nevertheless be treated as meeting those standards if—
>
> (A) full benefits are provided for items and services furnished through a network of entities which have entered into contracts or agreements with the issuer of the policy;
>
> (B) full benefits are provided for items and services furnished by other entities if the services are medically necessary and immediately required because of an unforeseen illness, injury, or condition and it is not reasonable given the circumstances to obtain the services through the network;

(C) the network offers sufficient access;

(D) the issuer of the policy has arrangements for an ongoing quality assurance program for items and services furnished through the network;

(E) (i) the issuer of the policy provides to each enrollee at the time of enrollment an explanation of (I) the restrictions on payment under the policy for services furnished other than by or through the network, (II) out of area coverage under the policy, (III) the policy's coverage of emergency services and urgently needed care, and (IV) the availability of a policy through the entity that meets the standards in the 1991 NAIC Model Regulation or 1991 Federal Regulation or other requirements of this section without reference to this subsection and the premium charged for such policy, and

(ii) each enrollee prior to enrollment acknowledges receipt of the explanation provided under clause (i); and

(F) the issuer of the policy makes available to individuals, in addition to the policy described in this subsection, any policy (otherwise offered by the issuer to individuals in the State) that meets the NAIC standards and other requirements of this section without reference to this subsection.

* * *

◆ NOTE: Section 171(h)(1) of the Social Security Act Amendments of 1994, added "medicare supplemental" before "policy", added "or agreements" after "contracts" and substituted "standards in the 1991 NAIC Model Regulation or 1991 Federal Regulation" in section 1882(t)(1) where that phrase appears in (E) and (F) for "NAIC standards".

(3) The Secretary may enter into a contract with an entity whose policy has been certified under paragraph (1) or has been approved by a State under subsection (b)(1)(H) to determine whether items and services (furnished to individuals entitled to benefits under this title and under that policy) are not allowable under section 1862(a)(1) [42 U.S.C.A. 1395y(a)(1), which pertains to exclusions from coverage]. Payments to the entity shall be in such amounts as the Secretary may determine, taking into account estimated savings under contracts with carriers and fiscal intermediaries and other

factors that the Secretary finds appropriate. Paragraph 1 [which pertains to carrier contracts], the first sentence of paragraph (2)(A) [which pertains to carrier performance requirements], paragraph (2)(B) [which pertains to standards for evaluating carriers' performance], paragraph (3)(C) [which pertains to carrier obligations for fair hearings], paragraph (3)(D) [which pertains to carrier obligations to furnish timely information and reports to the Secretary], and paragraph (3)(E) [which pertains to carrier recordkeeping and access to records by the Secretary] of section 1842(b) [42 U.S.C.A. 1395u(b)] shall apply to the entity.

(1) It is unlawful for a person to sell or issue a policy described in paragraph (2) to an individual with knowledge that the individual has in effect under section 1851 an election of an MSA plan or a Medicare + Choice private fee-for-service plan.

(2)(A) A policy described in this subparagraph is a health insurance policy (other than a policy described in subparagraph (B)) that provides for coverage of expenses that are otherwise required to be counted toward meeting the annual deductible amount provided under the MSA plan.

(B) A policy described in this subparagraph is any of the following:

(i) A policy that provides coverage (whether through insurance or otherwise) for accidents, disability, dental care, vision care, or long-term care.

(ii) A policy of insurance to which substantially all of the coverage relates to —

(I) liabilities incurred under workers' compensation laws,

(II) tort liabilities,

(III) liabilities relating to ownership or use of property, or

(IV) such other similar liabilities as the Secretary may specify by regulations.

(iii) A policy of insurance that provides coverage for a specified disease or illness.

(iv) A policy of insurance that pays a fixed amount per day (or other period) of hospitalization.

For regulatory citations, see Chapter 6

§ 2:46 MISREPRESENTATION AND FRAUD IN OBTAINING AND USING SECRETARIAL CERTIFICATION OF MEDICARE SUPPLEMENTAL HEALTH INSURANCE POLICIES—Section 1882(d)(1) [42 U.S.C.A. 1395ss(d)(1)]

Summary

◆ NOTE: P.L. 101-508, the Omnibus Budget Reconciliation Act of 1990 (OBRA 90), effective November 5, 1990, made substantial changes in the law applicable to Medicare supplemental health insurance policies. For a summary of the law and statutory provisions pre-OBRA 90, see former § 2:40.1 in Appendix H. For a more complete summary of the law and statutory provisions after OBRA 90, see § 2:45.

In section 1882(a), 42 U.S.C.A. 1395ss(a), Congress authorized the Secretary of Health and Human Services to certify that Medicare supplemental health insurance policies meet established standards for coverage and benefits. It also authorized the Secretary to permit approved entities to use a Secretarial emblem of certification in their marketing.

A Medicare supplemental policy, according to section 1882(g)(1), is a health insurance policy or other health benefit plan offered by a private entity to Medicare beneficiaries which provides reimbursement for items not payable by Medicare because of deductibles, coinsurance amounts, or other limitations on payment.

Specifically excluded from the definition are:

1. Any such policy or plan of one or more employers or labor organizations, or of trustees of a fund established by one or more employers or labor organizations (or combination thereof) which is for employees or former employees (or combination thereof) or for members or former members (or combination thereof) of the labor organizations.
2. Policies or plans of health maintenance organizations or competitive medical plans which provide health insurance to Medicare beneficiaries under contract with Medicare or which are an approved demonstration project under section 603(c) of

the Social Security Act Amendments of 1983 or under section 2355 of the Deficit Reduction Act of 1984.

3. During the period between the time the State adopted the 1991 NAIC Model Regulation or 1991 Federal Regulation and December 31, 1995, policies or plans of an organization which provides benefits pursuant to an agreement under section 1833, 42 U.S.C.A. 1395l (pre-paid health plans).
4. A Medicare + Choice plan.

◆ NOTE: Section 4002(j)(2) of the Balanced Budget Act of 1997, P.L. 105–33, added this exemption for Medicare + Choice plans effective January 1, 1999.

No Medicare supplemental policy may be issued in a State unless the State has a regulatory program which provides for application and enforcement of standards and requirements set forth in section 1882. Those must be standards of the National Association of Insurance Commissioners (NAIC) or Federal standards. If a State does not adopt such a program, Medicare supplemental policies may not be issued in that State unless the Secretary certifies the policy as meeting Federal standards. Pursuant to section 171(c)(1)(A) of the Social Security Act Amendments of 1994, P.L. 103-432, effective November 5, 1990, as if included in OBRA 90, the relevant standards are the 1991 NAIC Model Regulation or the 1991 Federal Regulation.

Pursuant to section 171(c)(1)(B) of the Social Security Act Amendments of 1994, the effective date of this requirement is the date the State adopts the 1991 NAIC Model Regulation or the date the 1991 Federal Regulation applies, as the case may be, or one year after the date the NAIC or the Secretary first adopts such standards, whichever is earlier. This applies effective November 5, 1990, as if included in OBRA 90.

The effective date depended on whether and when the NAIC produced "NAIC standards" for such policies. Section 1882(p)(1)(A) required NAIC to do so within nine months after enactment of OBRA 90, which would be August 5, 1991. Had the NAIC not met that requirement, the Secretary was obligated to produce "Federal standards" within a subsequent period of nine months, which ended May 5, 1992. Depending on which of those outcomes occurred, the effective date of this requirement was either the date the State adopted the NAIC or Federal standards or one year after the date NAIC or the Secretary first adopted such standards, whichever is earlier. The NAIC Model Regulation was timely adopted.

The standards provide limitations on the groups or packages of benefits that may be offered under a Medicare supplemental policy, uniform language and definitions to be used with respect to such benefits, and a uniform format for the policy. They also reflect other requirements imposed by OBRA 90. In establishing them, the NAIC (or the Secretary) had to consult with representatives of issuers of Medicare supplemental policies, consumer groups, Medicare beneficiaries, and other qualified individuals, a working group selected in a manner to assure balanced representation.

Pursuant to section 1882(d)(1), anyone who knowingly and willfully makes or causes to be made or induces or seeks to induce the making of any false statement or representation of a material fact with respect to compliance of any such insurance policy with the statutory standards and requirements or with respect to use of the emblem shall be fined under Title 18 of the U.S. Code, or imprisoned not more than 5 years, or both. In addition to or in lieu of those criminal penalties, such persons are subject to a civil money penalty not to exceed $5,000 for each prohibited act.

Enforcement procedures for this civil money penalty are governed by section 1128A, 42 U.S.C.A. 1320a-7a, which authorizes civil money penalties for a variety of offenses.

To educate consumers and help with enforcement, section 1882(e) obligates the Secretary to provide to all Medicare beneficiaries, and, as much as possible, to those about to become beneficiaries, information to help them evaluate not only Medicare supplemental policies but also their relationship to Medicare benefits. That information must include a listing of addresses and telephone numbers of State and Federal agencies and offices that can provide assistance with respect to selection of Medicare supplemental policies. The Secretary also must inform them about sanctionable actions under section 1882, including the manner in which they may report improper actions and the availability of a toll-free telephone number for making such reports.

Statutory Provisions

Section 1882(d)(1), 42 U.S.C.A. 1395ss(d)(1), provides:

> Whoever knowingly and willfully makes or causes to be made or induces or seeks to induce the making of any false statement or

representation of a material fact with respect to the compliance of any policy with the standards and requirements set forth in subsection (c) or in regulations promulgated pursuant to such subsection, or with respect to the use of the emblem designed by the Secretary under subsection (a), shall be fined under title 18, United States Code, or imprisoned not more than 5 years, or both, and in addition to or in lieu of such a criminal penalty, is subject to a civil money penalty of not to exceed $5,000 for each such prohibited act.

Pursuant to section 1882(d)(5):

The provisions of section 1128A [42 U.S.C.A. 1320a-7a] (other than subsections (a) and (b)) shall apply to civil money penalties under paragraphs (1), (2), (3A), and (4A) in the same manner as such provisions apply to penalties and proceedings under section 1128A(a).

Section 1882(e), 42 U.S.C.A. 1395ss(e), provides:

(1) The Secretary shall provide to all individuals entitled to benefits under this title (and, to the extent feasible, to individuals about to become so entitled) such information as will permit such individuals to evaluate the value of medicare supplemental policies to them and the relationship of any such policies to benefits provided under this title.

(2) The Secretary shall —

(A) inform all individuals entitled to benefits under this title (and, to the extent feasible, individuals about to become so entitled) of —

(i) the actions and practices that are subject to sanctions under subsection (d), and

(ii) the manner in which they may report any such action or practice to an appropriate official of the Department of Health and Human Services (or to an appropriate state official), and

(B) publish the toll-free telephone number for individuals to report suspected violations of the provisions of such subsection.

(3) The Secretary shall provide individuals entitled to benefits under this title (and, to the extent feasible, individuals about

to become so entitled) with a listing of the addresses and telephone numbers of State and Federal agencies and offices that provide information and assistance to individuals with respect to the selection of medicare supplemental policies.

For regulatory citations, see Chapter 6

§ 2:47 MISREPRESENTATION BY SELLERS OF MEDICARE SUPPLEMENTAL HEALTH INSURANCE POLICIES THAT THEY ACT BY AUTHORITY OF OR IN ASSOCIATION WITH MEDICARE OR ANY FEDERAL AGENCY — Section 1882(d)(2) [42 U.S.C.A. 1395ss(d)(2)]

Summary

◆ NOTE: P.L. 101-508, the Omnibus Budget Reconciliation Act of 1990 (OBRA 90), effective November 5, 1990, made substantial changes in the law applicable to Medicare supplemental health insurance policies. For a summary of the law and statutory provisions pre-OBRA 90, see former § 2:40.1 in Appendix H. For a more complete summary of the law and statutory provisions after OBRA 90, see § 2:45.

Section 1882(d)(2), 42 U.S.C.A. 1395ss(d)(2), provides that anyone who falsely assumes or pretends to be acting or misrepresents in any way that he is acting under the authority of or in association with Medicare or any Federal agency to sell or attempt to sell insurance, or anyone who in such pretended character demands, or obtains money, paper, documents, or anything of value is guilty of a felony and upon conviction thereof shall be fined under Title 18 of the U.S. Code or imprisoned not more than 5 years, or both. In addition to or in lieu of those criminal penalties, such persons are subject to a civil money penalty not to exceed $5,000 for each prohibited act.

Enforcement procedures for this civil money penalty are governed by section 1128A, 42 U.S.C.A. 1320a-7a, which authorizes civil money penalties for a variety of offenses.

To educate consumers and help with enforcement, section 1882(e) obligates the Secretary to provide to all Medicare beneficiaries, and, as much as possible, to those about to become beneficiaries, information to help them evaluate not only Medicare supplemental policies but also their relationship to Medicare benefits. That information must include a listing of addresses and telephone numbers of State and Federal agencies and offices that can provide assistance with respect to selection of Medicare supplemental policies. The Secretary also must inform them about sanctionable actions under section 1882, including the manner in which they may report improper actions and the availability of a toll-free telephone number for making such reports.

Statutory Provisions

Section 1882(d)(2), 42 U.S.C.A. 1395ss(d)(2), provides:

> Whoever falsely assumes or pretends to be acting, or misrepresents in any way that he is acting, under the authority of or in association with, the program of health insurance established by this title, or any Federal agency, for the purpose of selling or attempting to sell insurance, or in such pretended character demands, or obtains money, paper, documents, or anything of value, shall be guilty of a felony and upon conviction thereof shall be fined under title 18, United States Code, or imprisoned not more than 5 years, or both, and in addition to or in lieu of such a criminal penalty, is subject to a civil money penalty of not to exceed $5,000 for each such prohibited act.

Pursuant to section 1882(d)(5):

> The provisions of section 1128A [42 U.S.C.A. 1320a-7a] (other than subsections (a) and (b)) shall apply to civil money penalties under paragraphs (1), (2), (3A), and (4A) in the same manner as such provisions apply to penalties and proceedings under section 1128A(a).

Section 1882(e), 42 U.S.C.A. 1395ss(e), provides:

> (1) The Secretary shall provide to all individuals entitled to benefits under this title (and, to the extent feasible, to individuals about to become so entitled) such information as will permit such individuals to evaluate the value of medicare supplemental policies to them and the relationship of any such policies to benefits provided under this title.
>
> (2) The Secretary shall—
>
> (A) inform all individuals entitled to benefits under this title (and, to the extent feasible, individuals about to become so entitled) of—

(i) the actions and practices that are subject to sanctions under subsection (d), and

(ii) the manner in which they may report any such action or practice to an appropriate official of the Department of Health and Human Services (or to an appropriate state official), and

(B) publish the toll-free telephone number for individuals to report suspected violations of the provisions of such subsection.

(3) The Secretary shall provide individuals entitled to benefits under this title (and, to the extent feasible, individuals about to become so entitled) with a listing of the addresses and telephone numbers of State and Federal agencies and offices that provide information and assistance to individuals with respect to the selection of medicare supplemental policies.

For regulatory citations, see Chapter 6

§ 2:48 SELLING MEDICARE BENEFICIARIES SUPPLEMENTAL HEALTH INSURANCE POLICIES THAT DUPLICATE MEDICARE BENEFITS/NOT OBTAINING A VALID BUYER'S STATEMENT/NOT PREPARING SELLER'S ACKNOWLEDGMENT/FAILING TO COMPLY WITH DISCLOSURE REQUIREMENTS Section 1882(d)(3) [42 U.S.C.A. 1395ss(d)(3)]

Summary

◆ ***NOTE: The Health Insurance Portability and Accountability Act of 1996, P.L. 104–191, generally effective January 1, 1997, made substantial changes affecting the issuance of Medicare supplement insurance policies that duplicate Medicare benefits. For a discussion of the law and statutory provisions pertaining to that, and to not obtaining a valid buyer's statement and not preparing a seller's acknowledgment, prior to that amendment, see former § 2:48 in Appendix H.

P.L. 101–508, the Omnibus Budget Reconciliation Act of 1990 (OBRA 90), effective November 5, 1990, made substantial changes in the general law applicable to Medicare supplemental health insurance policies. For a summary of the law and the statutory provisions pre-OBRA 90, see former § 2:40.1 in Appendix H. For a more complete summary of the law and statutory provisions after OBRA 90, see § 2:45.

The Sanction for Selling or Issuing Duplicate Coverage: Section 1882(d)(3), 42 U.S.C.A. 1395ss(d)(3) makes it unlawful to sell or issue to an individual entitled to benefits under Medicare Part A or enrolled under Medicare Part B (including an individual electing a Medicare + Choice plan):

1. a health insurance policy with knowledge that the policy duplicates health benefits to which the individual is otherwise entitled under Medicare or Medicaid;
2. in the case of an individual not electing a Medicare + Choice plan a Medicare supplemental policy with knowledge that the individual is entitled to benefits under another Medicare supplemental policy; or in the case of an individual electing a Medicare + Choice plan, a Medicare supplemental policy with knowledge that the policy duplicates health benefits to which the individual is otherwise entitled under the Medicare + Choice plan or under another Medicare supplemental policy; or
3. a health insurance policy (other than a Medicare supplemental policy) with knowledge that the policy duplicates health benefits to which the individual is otherwise entitled, other than benefits to which the individual is entitled under a requirement of State or Federal law.

Whoever violates these prohibitions may be fined under Title 18 of the United States Code, or imprisoned not more than five years, or both. In addition to or in lieu of such a criminal penalty, a violator is subject to a civil money penalty not to exceed $25,000 (or $15,000 in the case of a person other than the issuer of the policy) for each such prohibited act.

Exceptions: Pursuant to section 1882(d)(3)(C), these sanctions do not apply with respect to the sale or issuance of a group policy or plan of one or more employers or labor organizations. They also do not apply with respect to the trustees of a fund established by one or more employers or labor organizations (or combination thereof), for employees or former employees (or combination thereof), or for members or former members (or combination thereof) of the labor organizations.

Defenses: *Proper Documentation:* Pursuant to section 1882(d)(3)(A)(iii) and section 1882(d)(3)(B), a seller who is not the issuer of a health insurance policy (*e.g.*, an insurance agent) shall not be considered to have violated the prohibition against selling with knowledge of duplicate coverage if the seller fulfills the following requirements.

1. *The Buyer's Statement:* The seller must obtain a buyer's written statement, signed by the buyer, stating to the best of the buyer's knowledge: (a) the health insurance policies the buyer has (including any Medicare + Choice Plan); (b) their source; and (c) whether the buyer is entitled to Medicaid as a qualified Medicare beneficiary or otherwise.
2. *The Seller's Acknowledgment:* Second, that written statement must be accompanied by a written acknowledgment, signed by the seller of the policy, of the request for and receipt of such a statement from the buyer.
3. *The Required Form for Those Statements:* The buyer's statement must be made on a form that states: (a) that a Medicare-eligible individual does not need more than one Medicare supplemental policy; (b) that individuals may be eligible for Medicaid benefits, and, if so, such persons usually do not need a Medicare supplemental policy; (c) that benefits and premiums under any such policy shall be suspended upon request of the policyholder during a period (not longer than 24 months) of entitlement to Medicaid benefits; (d) that the policy may be reinstated upon loss of Medicaid entitlement; (e) that counseling services, with a telephone number to call, may be available in the State to provide advice concerning the purchase of Medicare supplemental policies and enrollment under Medicaid.

Replacement Coverage: A buyer's statement which indicates that an individual has a Medicare supplemental policy or is entitled to Medicaid will not indicate a violation if the buyer states in writing, as part of the application for purchase, that the policy being purchased replaces such other policy and the buyer intends to terminate the policy being replaced when the new policy becomes effective. The issuer or seller also must certify in writing, however, that such policy will not, to the best of the issuer or seller's knowledge, duplicate coverage (taking into account any such replacement).

Medicaid Involvement: If a buyer's statement indicates the buyer is entitled to Medicaid, sale of a policy is not a violation of the buyer's statement and seller's acknowledgment requirements if the State Medicaid plan pays the premium for the policy; or if, in the case of a qualified Medicare beneficiary, the policy provides for coverage of outpatient prescription drugs; or if the only medical assistance to which the buyer is entitled under the State plan is Medicare cost sharing.

The Meaning of Duplicate Coverage: Pursuant to section 1882(d)(3)(A)(iv), a health insurance policy (other than a Medicare supplemental policy) providing for benefits payable to or on behalf of an individual without regard to other health benefit coverage of such individual is not considered to "duplicate" Medicare benefits, or Medicaid benefits, or benefits under a health insurance policy. This permits sale of certain cash payment hospital indemnity policies to persons with a Medicare supplemental policy, for example.

Similarly, a health insurance policy, or a rider to an insurance contract which is not a health insurance policy, is not considered to "duplicate" Medicare benefits or benefits under another health insurance policy if that policy or rider: (a) provides health care benefits only for long-term care, nursing home care, home health care, or community-based care, or any combination thereof; (b) coordinates against or excludes items and services available or paid for under Medicare or under another health insurance policy; and (c) contains a disclosure of the coordination or exclusion in the policy's outline of coverage.

Coordination means that the policy under its terms is secondary to, or excludes from payment, items and services to the extent available or paid for under Medicare or under another health insurance policy.

This disclosure requirement applies to policies sold or issued on or after the end of the 90-day period beginning on the date of enactment of the Health Insurance Portability and Accountability Act of 1996. There is an exception from the disclosure requirement, however, for policies identified as exempt in 60 Federal Register 30880, June 12, 1995.

Disclosure Statement Requirements: Pursuant to section 1882(d)(3)(A)(vi) mandates inclusion of form disclosures as part of or together with the application for a permitted additional health insurance policy. The form for those disclosures is set forth in section 1882(d)(3)(A)(vii) below. That subsection requires reference, however, to the disclosure forms required prior to enactment of the Health Insurance Portability and Accountability Act of 1996. Those forms are available from the National Association of Insurance Commissioners (NAIC).

The Sanction for Violating the Requirement for a Disclosure Statement: Whoever issues or sells a health insurance policy (other than one listed as exempt in 60 Federal Register 30880, June 12, 1995) to a Medicare beneficiary without furnishing the required disclosure statement shall be fined under Title 18 of the United States Code, or imprisoned not more than 5 years, or both. In addition to or in lieu of such a criminal penalty, a violator also is subject to a civil money penalty not to exceed $25,000 (or $15,000 in the case of a person other than the issuer of the policy) for each such violation.

Federal Pre-emption: Pursuant to section 1882(d)(3)(A)(viii), States remain generally free to regulate health insurance policies. A State may not declare or specify in statute, regulation, or otherwise, however, that a health insurance policy (other than a Medicare supplemental policy) or rider to an insurance policy that is not a health insurance policy that is sold, issued, or renewed to a Medicare beneficiary or Part B enrollee "duplicates" health benefits under Medicare or under a Medicare supplemental policy. This applies to health insurance policies that provide benefits payable to or on behalf of an individual without regard to other health benefit coverage (such as a hospital indemnity or dread disease policy); to policies which provide benefits only for long-term care, nursing home care, home health care, or community-based care, or any combination thereof; and to policies listed as exempt in 60 Federal Register 30880, June 12, 1995.

Statutory Provisions

◆ NOTE: Section 271 of the Health Insurance Portability and Accountability of 1996, P.L. 104–191, amended section 1882(d)(3)(A) by inserting "clause (I)(II)" in lieu of "clause (I)" in clause (iii), and by adding new clauses (iv) through (viii)(II). Those changes were made effective as if included in the enactment of section 4354 of the Omnibus Budget Reconciliation Act of 1990, P.L. 101–508. Amendment of subparagraph C and deletion of former subparagraph (D) were made effective August 21, 1996.

Section 1882(d)(3), 42 U.S.C.A. 1395ss(d)(3), provides:

(A) (i) It is unlawful for a person to sell or issue to an individual entitled to benefits under part A or enrolled under part B of this title (including an individual electing a Medicare + Choice plan under section 1851 [42 U.S.C.A. — —])—

(I) a health insurance policy with knowledge that the policy duplicates health benefits to which the individual is otherwise entitled under this Title or Title XIX,

(II) in the case of an individual not electing a Medicare + Choice plan, a Medicare supplemental policy with knowledge that the individual is entitled to benefits under another Medicare supplemental policy or in the case of an individual electing a Medicare + Choice plan, a Medicare supplemental policy with knowledge that the policy duplicates health benefits to which the individual is otherwise entitled under the Medicare + Choice plan or under another Medicare supplemental policy, or

(III) a health insurance policy (other than a Medicare supplemental policy) with knowledge that the policy duplicates health benefits to which the individual is otherwise entitled, other than benefits to which the individual is entitled under a requirement of State or Federal law.

◆ NOTE: Effective August 5, 1997, section 4003(a)(1) of the Balanced Budget Act of 1997, P.L. 105–33, inserted the phrase "(including an individual electing a Medicare + Choice plan under section 1851)" after "of this title" in the sentence preceding "(I)". It also inserted "in the case of an individual electing a Medicare + Choice plan" after "(II)", and inserted the phrase beginning "or in the case of an individual electing a Medicare + Choice plan" in "II".

(ii) Whoever violates clause (I) shall be fined under Title 18 or imprisoned not more than 5 years, or both, and, in addition to or in lieu of such a criminal penalty, is subject to a civil money penalty of not to exceed $25,000 (or $15,000 in the case of a person other than the issuer of the policy) for each such prohibited act.

(iii) A seller (who is not the issuer of a health insurance policy) shall not be considered to violate clause (I)(II) with respect to the sale of a Medicare supplemental policy if the policy is sold in compliance with subparagraph (B).

(iv) For purposes of this subparagraph, a health insurance policy (other than a Medicare supplemental policy) providing for benefits which are payable to or on behalf of an individual without regard to other health benefit coverage of such individual is not considered to "duplicate" any health benefits under this title, under title XIX, or under a health insurance policy, and subclauses (I) and (III) of clause (I) do not apply to such a policy.

(v) For purposes of this subparagraph, a health insurance policy (or a rider to an insurance contract which is not a health insurance policy) is not considered to "duplicate" health benefits under this title or under another health insurance policy if it—

(I) provides health care benefits only for long-term care, nursing home care, home health care, or community-based care, or any combination thereof,

(II) coordinates against or excludes items and services available or paid for under this title or under another health insurance policy, and

(III) for policies sold or issued on or after the end of the 90-day period beginning on the date of enactment of the Health Insurance Portability and Accountability Act of 1996 discloses such coordination or exclusion in the policy's outline of coverage.

For purposes of this clause, the terms "coordinates" and "coordination" mean, with respect to a policy in relation to health benefits under this title or under another health insurance policy, that the policy under its terms is secondary to, or excludes from payment, items and services to the extent available or paid for under this title or under another health insurance policy.

(vi) (I) An individual entitled to benefits under part A or enrolled under part B of this title who is applying for a health insurance policy (other than a policy described in subclause (III)) shall be furnished a disclosure statement described in clause (vii) for the type of policy being applied for. Such statement shall be furnished as a part of (or together with) the application for such policy.

(II) Whoever issues or sells a health insurance policy (other than a policy described in subclause (III)) to an individual described in subclause (I) and fails to furnish the appropriate disclosure statement as required under such subclause shall be fined under Title 18, United States Code, or imprisoned not more than 5 years, or both, and, in addition to or in lieu of such a criminal penalty, is subject to a civil money penalty of not to exceed $25,000 (or $15,000 in the case of a person other than the issuer of the policy) for each such violation.

(III) A policy described in this subclause (to which subclauses (I) and (II) do not apply) is a Medicare supplemental policy, a policy described in clause (v) [This clause added by section 4031(c) of the Balanced Budget Act of 1997, applicable to policies issued or sold more than one year after November 5, 1990, and subject to the transition provisions of section 4031(e) of that Act], or a health insurance policy identified under 60 Federal Register 30880 (June 12, 1995) as a policy not required to have a disclosure statement.

(IV) Any reference in this section to the revised NAIC model regulation (referred to in subsection (m)(1)(A)) is deemed a reference to such regulation as revised by section 171(m)(2) of the Social Security Act Amendments of 1994 (Public Law 103–432) and as modified by substituting, for the disclosure required under section 16D(2), disclosure under subclause (I) of an appropriate disclosure statement under clause (vii).

(vii) The disclosure statement described in this clause for a type of policy is the statement specified under subparagraph (D) of this paragraph (as in effect before the date of the enactment of the Health Insurance Portability and Accountability Act of 1996) for that type of policy, as revised as follows:

(I) In each statement, amend the second line to read as follows:

" THIS IS NOT MEDICARE SUPPLEMENT INSURANCE."

(II) In each statement, strike the third line and insert the following: "**Some health care services paid for by Medicare may also trigger the payment of benefits under this policy.**"

(III) In each statement not described in subclause (V), strike the boldface matter that begins "**This insurance**" and all that follows up to the next paragraph that begins "**Medicare**".

(IV) In each statement not described in subclause (V), insert before the boxed matter (that states "**Before You Buy This Insurance**") the following: "**This policy must pay benefits without regard to other health benefit coverage to which you may be entitled under Medicare or other insurance.**"

(V) In a statement relating to policies providing both nursing home and non-institutional coverage, to policies providing nursing home benefits only, or policies providing home care benefits only, amend the sentence that begins "Federal law" to read as follows: "Federal law requires us to inform you that in certain situations this insurance may pay for some care also covered by Medicare."

(viii) (I) Subject to subclause (II), nothing in this subparagraph shall restrict or preclude a State's ability to regulate health insurance policies, including any health insurance policy that is described in clause (iv), (v), or (vi)(III).

(II) A State may not declare or specify, in statute, regulation, or otherwise, that a health insurance policy (other than a Medicare supplemental policy) or rider to an insurance contract which is not a health insurance policy, that is described in clause (iv), (v), or (vi)(III) and that is sold, issued, or renewed to an individual entitled to benefits under part A or enrolled under part

B "duplicates" health benefits under this title or under a Medicare supplemental policy.

(B) (i) It is unlawful for a person to issue or sell a Medicare supplemental policy to an individual entitled to benefits under part A or enrolled under part B, whether directly, through the mail, or otherwise, unless —

(I) the person obtains from the individual, as part of the application for the issuance or purchase and on a form described in clause (ii), a written statement signed by the individual stating, to the best of the individual's knowledge, what health insurance policies (including any Medicare + Choice plan) the individual has, [NOTE: The reference to Medicare + Choice plan was added by section 4003(a)(2) of the Balanced Budget Act of 1997, effective August 5, 1997.] from what source, and whether the individual is entitled to any medical assistance under Title XIX, whether as a qualified Medicare beneficiary or otherwise, and

(II) the written statement is accompanied by a written acknowledgment, signed by the seller of the policy, of the request for and receipt of such statement.

(ii) The statement required by clause (i) shall be made on a form that —

(I) states in substance that a Medicare-eligible individual does not need more than one Medicare supplemental policy,

(II) states in substance that individuals may be eligible for benefits under the State Medicaid program under Title XIX and that such individuals who are entitled to benefits under that program usually do not need a Medicare supplemental policy and that benefits and premiums under any such policy shall be suspended upon request of the policyholder during the period (of not longer than 24 months) of entitlement to benefits under such title and may be reinstated upon loss of such entitlement, and

(III) states that counseling services may be available in the State to provide advice concerning the purchase of Medicare supplemental policies and enrollment under the Medicaid program and may provide the telephone number for such services.

(iii) (I) Except as provided in subclauses (II) and (III), if the statement required by clause (i) is not obtained or indicates that the individual has a Medicare supplemental policy or indicates that the individual is entitled to any medical assistance under Title XIX, the sale of a Medicare supplemental policy shall be considered to be a violation of subparagraph (A).

(II) Subclause (I) shall not apply in the case of an individual who has another policy, if the individual indicates in writing, as part of the application for purchase, that the policy being purchased replaces such other policy and indicates an intent to terminate the policy being replaced when the new policy becomes effective and the issuer or seller certifies in writing that such policy will not, to the best of the issuer or seller's knowledge, duplicate coverage (taking into account any such replacement).

(III) If the statement required by clause (i) is obtained and indicates that the individual is entitled to any medical assistance under Title XIX, the sale of the policy is not in violation of clause (i) (insofar as such clause relates to such medical assistance), if (aa) a State Medicaid plan under such title pays the premiums for the policy, (bb) in the case of a qualified Medicare beneficiary described in section 1905(p)(1) [42 U.S.C.A. 1396d(p)(1), which defines qualified Medicare beneficiary], the policy provides for coverage of outpatient prescription drugs, or (cc) the only medical assistance to which the individual is entitled under the State plan is Medicare cost sharing described in section 1905(p)(3)(A)(ii).

(IV) Whoever issues or sells a Medicare supplemental policy in violation of this subparagraph shall be fined under Title 18, United States Code, or imprisoned not more than 5 years, or both, and, in addition to or in lieu of such a criminal penalty, is subject to a civil money penalty of not to exceed $25,000 (or $15,000 in the case of a seller who is not the issuer of a policy) for each such violation.

(C) Subparagraph (A) shall not apply with respect to the sale or issuance of a group policy or plan of one or more employers or labor organizations, or of the trustees of a fund established by one or more employers or labor organizations (or combination thereof), for employees or former employees (or combination thereof) or for members or former members (or combination thereof) of the labor organizations.

For regulatory citations, see Chapter 6

§ 2:49 USING THE MAIL TO MARKET MEDICARE SUPPLEMENTAL HEALTH INSURANCE POLICIES WHICH HAVE NOT BEEN STATE-APPROVED — Section 1882(d)(4) [42 U.S.C.A. 1395ss(d)(4)]

Summary

◆ NOTE: P.L. 101-508, the Omnibus Budget Reconciliation Act of 1990 (OBRA 90), effective November 5, 1990, made substantial changes in the law applicable to Medicare supplemental health insurance policies. For a summary of the law and statutory provisions pre-OBRA 90, see former § 2:40.1 in Appendix H. For a more complete summary of the law and statutory provisions after OBRA 90, see § 2:45.

Pursuant to section 1882(d)(4), 42 U.S.C.A. 1395ss(d)(4), anyone who knowingly, directly or through his agent, mails or causes to be mailed an advertisement, solicitation, or offer for the sale of a Medicare supplemental policy, or who delivers such a policy in or into any State in which such policy has not been approved by the State commissioner or superintendent of insurance shall be fined under Title 18 of the U.S. Code, or imprisoned not more than 5 years, or both. In addition to or in lieu of those criminal penalties, such persons are subject to a civil money penalty not to exceed $5,000 for each prohibited act.

This prohibition does not apply: (1) where the person who does or who causes the mailing ascertains that the insured recipient is located in that State on a temporary basis; (2) to mailing a duplicate copy of a Medicare supplement policy previously issued; and (3) to policies, certificates, and other matters mailed solely to comply with Section 1882(q).

Section 1882(q) provides: (1) that Medicare supplement policies must be guaranteed renewable; (2) that individual Medicare supplemental policies must be offered to members of a group when the group policy is terminated and not replaced; (3) that a conversion policy, or continuation in the group coverage, must be offered to an individual who terminates membership in a group which previously made a Medicare supplemental policy available to the individual; (4) that a replacement group policy must be offered to all persons covered under a prior group policy; and (5) that a policy suspended because the insured became eligible for Medicaid must be reinstated if the insured's Medicaid eligibility ends.

Enforcement procedures for this civil money penalty are governed by section 1128A, 42 U.S.C.A. 1320a-7a, which authorizes civil money penalties for a variety of offenses.

To educate consumers and help with enforcement, section 1882(e) obligates the Secretary to provide to all Medicare beneficiaries, and, as much as possible, to those about to become beneficiaries, information to help them evaluate not only Medicare supplemental policies but also their relationship to Medicare benefits. That information must include a listing of addresses and telephone numbers of State and Federal agencies and offices that can provide assistance with respect to selection of Medicare supplemental policies. The Secretary also must inform them about sanctionable actions under section 1882, including the manner in which they may report improper actions and the availability of a toll-free telephone number for making such reports.

Statutory Provisions

Section 1882(d)(4), 42 U.S.C.A. 1396d(d)(4), provides:

> (A) Whoever knowingly, directly or through his agent, mails or causes to be mailed any matter for a prohibited purpose (as determined under subparagraph (B)) shall be fined under Title 18, United States Code, or imprisoned not more than 5 years, or both, and, in addition to or in lieu of such a criminal penalty, is subject to a civil money penalty of not to exceed $5,000 for each such prohibited act.
>
> (B) For purposes of subparagraph (A), a prohibited purpose means the advertising, solicitation, or offer for sale of a

medicare supplemental policy, or the delivery of such a policy, in or into any State in which such policy has not been approved by the State commissioner or superintendent of insurance.

(C) Subparagraph (A) shall not apply in the case of a person who mails or causes to be mailed a medicare supplemental policy into a State if such person has ascertained that the party insured under such policy to whom (or on whose behalf) such policy is mailed is located in such State on a temporary basis.

(D) Subparagraph (A) shall not apply in the case of an issuer who mails or causes to be mailed a duplicate copy of a medicare supplemental policy previously issued to the party to whom (or on whose behalf) such duplicate copy is mailed.

◆ NOTE: Prior to amendment by section 171(i)(1) of the Social Security Act Amendments of 1994, P.L. 103-432, effective October 31, 1994, paragraph (D) read: "Subparagraph (A) shall not apply in the case of a person who mails or causes to be mailed a duplicate copy of a medicare supplemental policy previously issued to the party to whom (or on whose behalf) such duplicate copy is mailed, if such policy expires not more than 12 months after the date on which the duplicate copy is mailed."

In addition, section 171(k)(2) of the Social Security Act Amendments of 1994 added paragraph (E) below, also effective October 31, 1994.

(E) Subparagraph (A) shall not apply in the case of an issuer who mails or causes to be mailed a policy, certificate, or other matter solely to comply with the requirements of subsection (q).

Section 4532 of OBRA 90 added subsection (q) to section 1882. It provides in pertinent part:

The requirements of this subsection are as follows:

(1) Each medicare supplemental policy shall be guaranteed renewable and —

(A) the issuer may not cancel or nonrenew the policy solely on the ground of health status of the individual; and

(B) the issuer shall not cancel or nonrenew the policy for any reason other than nonpayment of premium or material misrepresentation.

(2) If the medicare supplemental policy is terminated by the group policyholder and is not replaced as provided under paragraph (4) [Section 171(b)(1) of the Social Security Act Amendments of 1994 substituted "paragraph (4)" for "paragraph (2)", effective October 31, 1994.], the issuer shall offer certificateholders an individual medicare supplemental policy which (at the option of the certificateholder)—

(A) provides for continuation of the benefits contained in the group policy, or

(B) provides for such benefits as otherwise meets the requirements of this section.

(3) If an individual is a certificateholder in a group medicare supplemental policy and the individual terminates membership in the group, the issuer shall—

(A) offer the certificateholder the conversion opportunity described in paragraph (2), or

(B) at the option of the group policyholder, offer the certificateholder continuation of coverage under the group policy.

(4) If a group medicare supplemental policy is replaced by another group medicare supplemental policy purchased by the same policyholder, the issuer of the replacement policy shall offer coverage to all persons covered under the old group policy on its date of termination. [Section 171(b)(2) of the Social Security Act Amendments of 1994 substituted "issuer of the replacement policy" for "succeeding issuer" in the preceding sentence, effective October 31, 1994.] Coverage under the new group policy shall not result in any exclusion for preexisting conditions that would have been covered under the group policy being replaced.

(5) [With respect to policies issued or sold more than one year after November 5, 1990]

(A) Each medicare supplemental policy shall provide that benefits and premiums under the policy shall be suspended at the request of the policyholder for the period (not to exceed 24 months) in which the policyholder has applied for and is determined to be entitled to medical assistance under title XIX, but only if the policyholder notifies the issuer of such policy within 90 days after the date the individual becomes entitled to such assistance. [Section 171(d)(4) of the Social Security Act Amendments of 1994 deleted "of the Social Security Act" following "title XIX", here and in (B) below, effective October 31, 1994.] If such suspension occurs and if the policyholder or certificate holder loses entitlement to such medical assistance, such policy shall be automatically reinstituted [sic reinstated] (effective as of the date of termination of such entitlement) under terms described in subsection (n)(6)(A)(ii) as of the termination of such entitlement if the policyholder provides notice of loss of such entitlement within 90 days after the date of such loss.

(B) Nothing in this section shall be construed as affecting the authority of a State under title XIX, to purchase a medicare supplemental policy for an individual otherwise entitled to assistance under such title.

* * *

◆ NOTE: Prior to amendment by section 4353(d) of OBRA 90, applicable to policies mailed, or caused to be mailed, after June 1991, subparagraph (d)(4)(B) read as follows:

For purposes of this paragraph, a medicare supplemental policy shall be deemed to be approved by the commissioner or superintendent of insurance of a State if—

(i) the policy has been certified by the Secretary pursuant to subsection (c) or was issued in a State with an approved regulatory program (as defined in subsection (g)(2)(B));

(ii) the policy has been approved by the commissioners or superintendents of insurance in States in which more than 30 percent of such policies are sold; or

(iii) the State has in effect a law which the commissioner or superintendent of insurance of the State has determined gives him the authority to review, and to approve, or effectively bar from sale in the State, such policy; except that such a policy shall not be deemed to be approved by a State commissioner or superintendent of insurance if the State notifies the Secretary that such policy has been submitted for approval to the State and has been specifically disapproved by such State after providing appropriate notice and opportunity for hearing pursuant to the procedures (if any) of the State.

Pursuant to section 1882(d)(5):

The provisions of section 1128A [42 U.S.C.A. 1320a-7a] (other than subsections (a) and (b)) shall apply to civil money penalties under paragraphs (1) [which pertains to misrepresentation and fraud in connection with obtaining and using Secretarial certification of Medicare supplemental health insurance policies (see § 2:46)], (2) [which pertains to misrepresentation by sellers of Medicare supplemental policies that they are acting by authority of or in association with the Medicare program (see § 2:47)], (3)(A) [which pertains to selling Medicare beneficiaries supplemental health insurance policies that duplicate Medicare benefits, not obtaining a valid buyer's statement, and not preparing a seller's acknowledgement (see § 2:48)], and (4)(A) in the same manner as such provisions apply to penalties and proceedings under section 1128A(a).

Section 1882(e), 42 U.S.C.A. 1395ss(e), provides:

(1) The Secretary shall provide to all individuals entitled to benefits under this title (and, to the extent feasible, to individuals about to become so entitled) such information as will permit such individuals to evaluate the value of medicare supplemental policies to them and the relationship of any such policies to benefits provided under this title.

(2) The Secretary shall—

(A) inform all individuals entitled to benefits under this title (and, to the extent feasible, individuals about to become so entitled) of—

(i) the actions and practices that are subject to sanctions under subsection (d), and

(ii) the manner in which they may report any such action or practice to an appropriate official of the Department of Health and Human Services (or to an appropriate state official), and

(B) publish the toll-free telephone number for individuals to report suspected violations of the provisions of such subsection.

(3) The Secretary shall provide individuals entitled to benefits under this title (and, to the extent feasible, individuals about to become so entitled) with a listing of the addresses and telephone numbers of State and Federal agencies and offices that provide information and assistance to individuals with respect to the selection of medicare supplemental policies.

For regulatory citations, see Chapter 6

§ 2:50 ISSUING OR SELLING MEDICARE SUPPLEMENTAL HEALTH INSURANCE POLICIES THAT DO NOT COMPLY WITH FORM AND CONTENT REQUIREMENTS —Section 1882(p)(8) [42 U.S.C.A. 1395ss(p)(8)]

Summary

◆ NOTE: P.L. 101-508, the Omnibus Budget Reconciliation Act of 1990 (OBRA 90), effective November 5, 1990, made substantial changes in the law applicable to Medicare supplemental health insurance policies. For a summary of the law and statutory provisions pre-OBRA-90, see former § 2:40.1 in Appendix H. For a more complete summary of the law and statutory provisions after OBRA 90, see § 2:45.

In section 1882(a), 42 U.S.C.A. 1395ss(a), Congress authorized the Secretary of Health and Human Services to certify that Medicare supplemental health insurance policies meet established standards for coverage and benefits. It also authorized him to permit approved entities to use a Secretarial emblem of certification in their marketing.

Definition: A Medicare supplemental policy, according to section 1882(g)(1), is a health insurance policy or other health benefit plan offered by a private entity to Medicare beneficiaries which provides reimbursement for items not payable by Medicare because of deductibles, coinsurance amounts, or other limitations on payment.

Specifically excluded from the definition are:

1. Any such policy or plan of one or more employers or labor organizations, or of trustees of a fund established by one or more employers or labor organizations (or combination thereof) which is for employees or former employees (or combi-

nation thereof) or for members or former members (or combination thereof) of the labor organizations.

2. Policies or plans of health maintenance organizations or competitive medical plans which provide health insurance to Medicare beneficiaries under contract with Medicare or which are an approved demonstration project under section 603(c) of the Social Security Act Amendments of 1983 or under section 2355 of the Deficit Reduction Act of 1984.
3. During the period between the time the State adopted the 1991 NAIC Model Regulation or 1991 Federal Regulation and December 31, 1995, policies or plans of an organization which provides benefits pursuant to an agreement under section 1833, 42 U.S.C.A. 1395l (pre-paid health plans).
4. A Medicare + Choice plan.

◆ NOTE: Section 4002(j)(2) of the Balanced Budget Act of 1997, P.L. 105–33, added this exemption for Medicare + Choice plans effective January 1, 1999.

Establishing the Standards: No Medicare supplemental policy may be issued in a State unless the State has a regulatory program which provides for application and enforcement of standards and requirements set forth in section 1882. Those must be standards of the National Association of Insurance Commissioners (NAIC) or Federal standards. If a State does not adopt such a program, Medicare supplemental policies may not be issued in that State unless the Secretary certifies the policy as meeting Federal standards. Pursuant to section 171(c)(1)(A) of the Social Security Act Amendments of 1994, P.L. 103-432, effective November 5, 1990, as if included in OBRA 90, the relevant standards are the 1991 NAIC Model Regulation or the 1991 Federal Regulation.

Pursuant to section 171(c)(1)(B) of the Social Security Act Amendments of 1994, the effective date of this requirement is the date the State adopts the 1991 NAIC Model Regulation or the date the 1991 Federal Regulation applies, as the case may be, or one year after the date the NAIC or the Secretary first adopts such standards, whichever is earlier. This applies effective November 5, 1990, as if included in OBRA 90.

The effective date depended on whether and when the NAIC produced "NAIC standards" for such policies. Section 1882(p)(1)(A) required NAIC to do so within nine months after enactment of OBRA 90, which ended August 5, 1991. Had the NAIC not met that requirement, the Secretary was obligated to produce "Federal standards" within a subsequent period of nine months, which ended May 5, 1992. Depending on which of those outcomes occurred, the effective date of this requirement was either the date the State adopted the NAIC or Federal standards or one year after the date NAIC or the Secretary first adopted such standards, whichever is earlier. The NAIC Model Regulation was timely adopted.

Form and Content Requirements: Pursuant to section 1882(p)(2), policies under the 1991 NAIC Model Regulation or 1991 Federal Regulation must provide for such groups or packages of benefits that enable consumers to purchase benefits available in the market as of November 5, 1990. They also must balance the objectives of simplifying comparison among policies, avoiding adverse selection, providing consumer choice, providing market stability, and promoting competition. This does not preclude offering new or innovative benefits, provided they are approved by the State or the Secretary, as the case may be. Nor does it preclude a State from restricting the groups of benefits that may be offered in a Medicare supplemental policy, but the restriction may not reduce the statutory core group of benefits which must be common to all policies.

Maximum Number of Plans: Pursuant to section 1882(p)(2)(C), the total number of different benefit packages (including the core group and each other combination of benefits offered separately) that may be established in all the States and by all issuers may not exceed 10, plus the two plans described in section 1882(p)(11)(A) [42 U.S.C.A. 1395ss(p)(11)(a)].

The latter plans are Standard Plans F and J, except that they have high deductible features. For 1998 and 1999, the high deductible amount is $1,500 per year. For subsequent years the high deductible is the amount for the previous year increased by the percentage increase in the Consumer Price Index for all urban consumers (all items, U.S. city average) for the 12-month period ending with August of the preceding year. Any amount determined by that formula which is not a multiple of $10 must be rounded to the nearest multiple of $10. The high deductible plans were added by section 4032(a) of the Balanced Budget Act of 1997, P.L. 105–33, effective August 5, 1997.

Mandatory Core Benefits Policy: Pursuant to section 1882(o)(2), if a Medicare supplemental policy provides coverage for a group of benefits other than the core group described in section 1882(p)(2)(B), the issuer must make a policy available consisting only of that core group of benefits. Furthermore, pursuant to section 1882(q), each Medicare supplemental policy must be guaranteed renewable; the issuer may not cancel or decline to renew the policy solely because of the insured's health status; and the issuer may not cancel and may not decline to renew for any reason other than nonpayment of premium or material misrepresentation.

Option for New or Innovative Benefits: Pursuant to section 1882(p)(4)(B), an issuer of a Medicare supplement policy or plan may offer benefits which are not otherwise available and which are cost-effective if the benefits are new and innovative and they are offered in a manner consistent with the statutory goal of simplification of Medicare supplement policies. Such benefits must be approved first, however, by the State or the Secretary.

Mandatory Standard Outlines of Coverage: Pursuant to section 1882(o)(3) and section 1882(p)(9)(B), sellers of Medicare supplement policies or plans must provide individuals with a standard outline of coverage approved by the State regulatory program or the Secretary (as the case may be) consistent with the 1991 NAIC Model Regulation or 1991 Federal Regulation before the sale so individuals may compare various benefit packages.

Guaranteed Renewability: Pursuant to section 1882(q)(1), each Medicare supplemental policy or plan must be guaranteed renewable.

Continuation of Benefits: Pursuant to section 1882(q)(2), if a group policy is terminated and not replaced, the issuer must make an individual policy available, and it must provide for continuation of the group policy's benefits or such other benefits as meets the requirements of section 1882. If an individual terminates membership in a group, the issuer similarly must offer the individual an individual policy or offer continuation of coverage in the group.

Replacement of Group Policies: Pursuant to section 1882(q)(4), if a group Medicare supplemental policy is replaced by another group Medicare supplemental policy purchased by the same policyholder, effective October 31, 1994, section 171(b)(2) of the Social Security Act Amendments of 1994 requires the issuer of the replacement policy to make an individual policy available. (Prior to that amendment the obligation fell to the "succeeding issuer".) Furthermore, the issuer of the replacement policy must offer coverage to all persons covered under the old group policy on its termination date, with no exclusion for preexisting conditions that would have been covered under the former group policy.

Suspension and Re-instatement Rights for Medicaid Recipients: Pursuant to section 1882(q)(5), with respect to policies issued or sold after November 5, 1991, provision must be made to reinstate a policy which may be suspended at policyholder request where the policyholder becomes entitled to Medicaid benefits, but only if the policyholder notifies the issuer within 90 days after becoming entitled to Medicaid.

Loss Ratio Requirements: Pursuant to section 1882(r), no Medicare supplemental policy may be issued or renewed or otherwise provide coverage in any State unless the policy can be expected to return to policyholders in the form of aggregate benefits at least 75 percent of the aggregate amount of premiums collected in the case of group policies, and at least 65 percent in the case of individual policies. Prior to amendment by section 171(e)(1) of the Social Security Act Amendments of 1994, effective October 31, 1994, this requirement applied only to policies "issued or sold" in any State.

States are nevertheless free to require higher percentages, and NAIC and the Comptroller General are to study, report to, and recommend to Congress about adjustment of these percentages. Furthermore, the issuer must issue a proportional refund or credit against future premiums (with interest) to assure that these ratios are met. Prior to amendment by section 171(e)(1) of the Social Security Act Amendments of 1994, the latter, however, did not apply to a policy with respect to the first two years in which it is in effect. Effective October 31, 1994, it applies after the first year following issue. For ratio purposes, policies issued as a result of solicitations of individuals through the mails or by mass media advertising, including print and broadcast advertising, are deemed to be individual policies.

Credit for Meeting Preexisting Condition, Waiting Period, Elimination Period and Probationary Period Requirements Under Prior Policy: Pursuant to section 1882(s), if one Medicare supplemental policy replaces another, the issuer of the replacement must waive any time periods applicable to preexisting conditions, waiting period, elimination periods, and probationary periods for similar benefits to the extent such time was spent under the original policy.

Open Enrollment: Generally, pursuant to section 1882(s)(2), the issuer of a Medicare supplemental policy may not deny or condition issuance or effectiveness of a policy, or discriminate in the pricing of the policy, because of health status, claims experience, receipt of health care, or medical condition for which an application is submitted during the six-month period beginning the first month. This does not prevent exclusion of benefits under a policy during that six-month period based on a pre-existing condition for which the policyholder received treatment or was otherwise diagnosed during the six months before it became effective. Nevertheless, if a policy or certificate replaced another such policy or certificate that had been in effect for six months or longer, the replacing policy may not provide any time period applicable to pre-existing conditions, waiting periods, elimination periods, and probationary periods in the new policy or certificate for similar benefits. For more information about open enrollment requirements, see II–53.

◆ NOTE: Prior to amendment by section 171(g)(1)-(3) of the Social Security Act Amendments of 1994, effective October 31, 1994, this requirement applied to applications submitted during the 6-month period beginning with the first month in which an individual who is 65 years or older first enrolled for benefits under Part B.

Furthermore, in the case of a policy issued during the first six months of open enrollment based on attaining age 65, insurers must credit applicants for periods of creditable coverage, as defined in section 2701(c) of the Public Health Service Act.

Claims Processing: Pursuant to section 1882(c), the Secretary may certify a Medicare supplemental policy only if (1) the issuer accepts a Medicare notice of benefits as a claim form for benefits under the policy in lieu of any other claim form and agrees to make a payment determination on the basis of information in that Medicare notice; (2) where such a notice is received, the issuer provides notice to such physician or supplier and the beneficiary of the payment determination under the policy, and provides any payment covered by such policy directly to the participating physician or supplier involved; (3) the issuer provides each enrollee upon enrollment a card listing the policy name and number and a single mailing address to which to send claim notices under the policy; (4) the issuer agrees to pay any user fees established under Medicare with respect to information transmitted to the issuer; (5) the issuer provides to the Secretary at least annually, for transmittal to Medicare carriers, a single mailing address to which Medicare notices of payment are to be sent; and (6) where the issuer will make full refund of any premiums paid when a policyholder decides to cancel the policy within 30 days after issuance.

No Restriction on Vendor Discounts: Pursuant to section 1882(p)(7), nothing in this statute prevents an issuer of a Medicare supplement policy that otherwise meets requirements of section 1882 from providing, through an arrangement with a vendor, for discounts from that vendor to policyholders or certificateholders for the purchase of items or services not covered under its Medicare supplement policy.

Preferred Provider Plans: Special provisions apply for Medicare supplement policies or plans which restrict benefits to items and services furnished by preferred providers or which reduce benefits when items or services are not provided by such sources. These are commonly referred to as Medicare SELECT plans.

Pursuant to section 1882(t), an issuer of a Medicare SELECT policy or plan must provide full benefits through a network of providers with whom it has contracts or agreements. It must provide for items and services furnished by non-network providers in emergencies and when network providers cannot deliver medically necessary services. It must assure sufficient access to an appropriate array of health care providers. It must have arrangements for an ongoing quality assurance program for items and services furnished through the network. It must explain the restrictions on payment for services furnished by non-network providers, the availability of out-of-area coverage under the policy, and coverage for medical emergencies, and it must obtain a written acknowledgement prior to enrollment from the enrollee that it has received such an explanation. Finally, the issuer must offer a standard non-preferred provider plan as an alternative.

Additional Rules Relating to Individuals Enrolled in MSA Plans and Private Fee-for -Service Plans: Pursuant to section 4003(b) of the Balanced Budget Act of 1997, it is unlawful to sell or issue a Medicare supplement policy to an individual with knowledge that the individual has in effect under section 1851 [42 U.S.C.A. 1395 —] an election of an MSA (Medical Savings Account) plan or a Medicare + Choice private fee-for service plan. This prohibition does not apply, however, with respect to the following:

> Policies which provide coverage for accidents, disability, dental care, vision care, or long-term care.
>
> Policies to which substantially all of the coverage relates to liabilities incurred under workers' compensation laws, tort liabilities, liabilities relating to ownership or use of property, or

such other similar liabilities as the Secretary may specify by regulations.

Policies which provide coverage for a specified disease or illness. Policies which pay a fixed amount per day (or other period) of hospitalization.

Pursuant to section 1882(p)(8), as added by section 4351 of OBRA 90, effective November 5, 1990, any person who sells or issues a Medicare supplemental policy, after the effective date of the 1991 NAIC Model Regulation or the date the 1991 Federal Regulation with respect to the policy, in violation of requirements of subsection (p)(1)-(7) is subject to a civil money penalty not to exceed $25,000 (or $15,000 in the case of a seller who is not an issuer of a policy) for each such violation.

Enforcement procedures for this civil money penalty are governed by section 1128A, 42 U.S.C.A. 1320a-7a, which authorizes civil money penalties for a variety of offenses.

Statutory Provisions

As amended by section 171(a)(2)(A)-(L) of the Social Security Act Amendments of 1994, P.L. 103-432, effective October 31, 1994, section 1882(p) provides in pertinent part:

(1) (A) If, within 9 months after the date of the enactment of this subsection, the National Association of Insurance Commissioners (in this subsection referred to as the "association" changes the revised NAIC Model Regulation (described in subsection (m)) to incorporate —

(i) limitations on the groups or packages of benefits that may be offered under a medicare supplemental policy consistent with paragraphs (2) and (3) of this subsection,

(ii) uniform language and definitions to be used with respect to such benefits,

(iii) uniform format to be used in the policy with respect to such benefits, and

(iv) other standards to meet the additional requirements imposed by the amendments made by the Omnibus Budget Reconciliation Act of 1990,

subsection (g)(2)(A) shall be applied in each State, effective for policies issued to policyholders on and after the date specified in subparagraph (C), as if the reference to the Model Regulation adopted on June 6, 1979, were a reference to the revised NAIC Model Regulation as changed by the Secretary under this subparagraph (such changed regulation referred to in this section as the "1991 NAIC Model Regulation").

(B) If the Association does not make the changes in the revised NAIC Model Regulation within the 9-month period specified in subparagraph (A), the Secretary shall promulgate, not later than 9 months after the end of such period, a regulation and subsection (g)(2)(A) shall be applied in each State, effective for policies issued to policyholders on and after the date specified in subparagraph (C), as if the reference to the Model Regulation adopted on June 6, 1979, were a reference to the revised NAIC Model Regulation as changed by the Secretary under this subparagraph (such changed regulation referred to in this section as the "1991 Federal Regulation").

(C) (i) Subject to clause (ii), the date specified in this subparagraph for a State is the date the State adopts the 1991 NAIC Model Regulation or 1991 Federal Regulation or 1 year after the date the Association or the Secretary first adopts such standards, whichever is earlier.

(ii) In the case of a State which the Secretary identifies, in consultation with the Association, as

(I) requiring State legislation (other than legislation appropriating funds) in order for medicare supplemental policies to meet the 1991 NAIC Model Regulation or 1991 Federal Regulation, but

(II) having a legislature which is not scheduled to meet in 1992 in a legislative session in which such legislation may be considered,

the date specified in this subparagraph is the first day of the first calendar quarter beginning after the close of the first legislative session of the State legislature that begins on or after January 1, 1992. For purposes of the previous sentence, in the case of a State that has a 2-year legislative session, each year of such session shall be deemed to be a separate regular session of the State legislature.

(D) In promulgating standards under this paragraph, the Association or Secretary shall consult with a working group composed of representatives of issuers of medicare supplemental policies, consumer groups, medicare beneficiaries, and other qualified individuals. Such representatives shall be selected in a manner so as to assure balanced representation among the interested groups.

(E) If benefits (including deductibles and coinsurance) under this title are changed and the Secretary determines, in consultation with the Association, that changes in the 1991 NAIC Model Regulation or 1991 Federal Regulation are needed to reflect such changes, the preceding provisions of this paragraph shall apply to the modification of standards previously established in the same manner as they applied to the original establishment of such standards.

(2) The benefits under the 1991 NAIC Model Regulation or 1991 Federal Regulation shall provide —

(A) for such groups or packages of benefits as may be appropriate taking into account the considerations specified in paragraph (3) and the requirements of the succeeding subparagraphs;

(B) for identification of a core group of basic benefits common to all policies, and

(C) that, subject to paragraph (4)(B), the total number of different benefit packages (counting the core group of basic benefits described in subparagraph (B) and each other combination of benefits that may be offered as a separate benefit package) that may be established in all the States and by all issuers shall not exceed 10 plus the 2 plans described in paragraph 11(A). [NOTE: Section 4032(a) of the Balanced Budget Act of 1997, P.L. 105–33, added the phrase "plus the 2 plans described in paragraph (11)(A). It also added paragraph (11)(A) below. These changes became effective August 5, 1997, subject to the transition provisions in section 4031 of that Act.].

(3) The benefits under paragraph (2) shall, to the extent possible —

(A) provide for benefits that offer consumer [sic consumers] the ability to purchase the benefits that are available in the market as of the date of the enactment of this subsection; and

(B) balance the objectives of (i) simplifying the market to facilitate comparisons among policies, (ii) avoiding adverse selection, (iii) providing consumer choice, (iv) providing market stability, and (v) promoting competition.

(4)(A) (i) Except as provided in subparagraph (B) or paragraph (6), no State with a regulatory program approved under subsection (b)(1) may provide for or permit the grouping of benefits (or language or format with respect to such benefits) under a medicare supplemental policy unless such grouping meets the applicable 1991 NAIC Model Regulation or 1991 Federal Regulation.

(ii) Except as provided in subparagraph (B), the Secretary may not provide for or permit the grouping of benefits (or language or format with respect to such benefits) under a medicare supplemental policy seeking approval by the Secretary unless such grouping meets the applicable 1991 NAIC Model Regulation or 1991 Federal Regulation.

(B) With the approval of the State (in the case of a policy issued in a State with an approved regulatory program) or the Secretary (in the case of any other policy), the issuer of a medicare supplemental policy may offer new or innovative benefits in addition to the benefits provided in a policy that otherwise complies with the applicable standards. Any such new or innovative benefits may include benefits that are not otherwise available and are cost-effective and shall be offered in a manner which is consistent with the goal of simplification of medicare supplemental policies.

(5) (A) Except as provided in subparagraph (B), this subsection shall not be construed as preventing a State from restricting the groups of benefits that may be offered in medicare supplemental policies in the State.

(B) A State with a regulatory program approved under subsection (b)(1) may not restrict under subparagraph (A) the offering of a medicare supplemental policy consisting only of the core group of benefits described in paragraph (2)(B).

(6) The Secretary may waive the application of standards in regard to the limitation of benefits described in clauses (i) through (iii) of paragraph (1)(A) in those States that on the date of enactment of this subsection had in place an alternative simplification program.

(7) This subsection shall not be construed as preventing an issuer of a medicare supplemental policy who otherwise meets the requirements of this section from providing, through an arrangement with a vendor, for discounts from that vendor to policyholders or certificateholders for the purchase of items or services not covered under its medicare supplemental policies.

(8) Any person who sells or issues a medicare supplemental policy, after the effective date specified in paragraph (1)(C) (but subject to paragraph (10)), in violation of the applicable 1991 NAIC Model Regulation or 1991 Federal Regulation insofar as such regulation relates to the requirements of subsection (o) or (q) or clause (i), (ii), or (iii) of paragraph (1)(A) is subject to a civil money penalty of not to exceed $25,000 (or $15,000 in the case of a seller who is not an issuer of a policy) for each such violation. The provisions of section 1128A [42 U.S.C.A. 1320a-7a] (other than the first sentence of subsection (a) and other than subsection (b)) shall apply to a civil money penalty under the previous sentence in the same manner as such provisions apply to a penalty or proceeding under section 1128A(a).

* * *

(9) (A) Anyone who sells a medicare supplemental policy to an individual shall make available for sale to the individual a medicare supplemental policy with only the core group of basic benefits (described in paragraph (2) (B)).

(B) Anyone who sells a medicare supplemental policy to an individual shall provide the individual, before the sale of the policy, an outline of coverage which describes the benefits under the policy. Such outline shall be on a standard form approved by the State regulatory program or the Secretary (as the case may be) consistent with the 1991 NAIC Model Regulation or 1991 Federal Regulation under this subsection.

* * *

(10) No penalty may be imposed under paragraph (8) or (9) in the case of a seller who is not the issuer of a policy until the Secretary has published a list of the groups of benefit packages that may be sold or issued consistent with this subsection.

(11) (A) For purposes of paragraph (2), the benefit packages described in this subparagraph are as follows:

(i) The benefit package classified as 'F' under the standards established by such paragraph, except that it has a high deductible feature.

(ii) The benefit package classified as 'J' under the standards established by such paragraph, except that it has a high deductible feature.

(B) For purposes of subparagraph (A), a high deductible feature is one which—

(i) requires the beneficiary of the policy to pay annual out-of-pocket expenses (other than premiums) in the amount specified in subparagraph (c) before the policy begins payment of benefits, and

(ii) covers 100 percent of covered out-of-pocket expenses once such deductible has been satisfied in a year.

(C) The amount specified in this subparagraph—

(i) for 1998 and 1999 is $1,500, and

(ii) for a subsequent year, is the amount specified in this subparagraph for the previous year increased by the percentage increase in the Consumer Price Index for all urban consumers (all items; U.S. city average) for the 12-month period ending with August of the preceding year.

If any amount determined under clause (ii) is not a multiple of $10, it shall be rounded to the nearest multiple of $10.

◆ NOTE: Prior to amendment by section 171(a)(2)(A)-(L) of the Social Security Act Amendments of 1994, effective October 31, 1994, section 1882(p) read in pertinent part:

(1) (A) If, within 9 months after the date of the enactment of this subsection, the National Association of Insurance Com-

missioners (in this subsection referred to as the "association" promulgates—

(i) limitations on the groups or packages of benefits that may be offered under a medicare supplemental policy consistent with paragraphs (2) and (3) of this subsection,

(ii) uniform language and definitions to be used with respect to such benefits,

(iii) uniform format to be used in the policy with respect to such benefits, and

(iv) other standards to meet the additional requirements imposed by the amendments made by the Omnibus Budget Reconciliation Act of 1990,

(such limitations, language, definitions, format, and standards referred to collectively in this subsection as "NAIC standards"), subsection (g)(2)(A) shall be applied in each State, effective for policies issued to policyholders on and after the date specified in subparagraph (C), as if the reference to the Model Regulation adopted on June 6, 1979, included a reference to the NAIC standards.

(B) If the Association does not promulgate NAIC standards within the 9-month period specified in subparagraph (A), the Secretary shall promulgate, not later than 9 months after the end of such period, limitations, language, definitions, format, and standards described in clauses (i) through (iv) of such subparagraph (in this subsection referred to collectively as "Federal standards") and subsection (g)(2)(A) shall be applied in each State, effective for policies issued to policyholders on and after the date specified in subparagraph (C), as if the reference to the Model Regulation adopted on June 6, 1979, included a reference to the Federal standards.

(C) (i) Subject to clause (ii), the date specified in this subparagraph for a State is the date the State adopts the NAIC standards or the Federal standards or 1 year after the date the Association or the Secretary first adopts such standards, whichever is earlier.

(ii) In the case of a State which the Secretary identifies, in consultation with the Association, as

(I) requiring State legislation (other than legislation appropriating funds) in order for medicare supplemental policies to meet the NAIC or Federal standards, but

(II) having a legislature which is not scheduled to meet in 1992 in a legislative session in which such legislation may be considered,

the date specified in this subparagraph is the first day of the first calendar quarter beginning after the close of the first legislative session of the State legislature that begins on or after January 1, 1992. For purposes of the previous sentence, in the case of a State that has a 2-year legislative session, each year of such session shall be deemed to be a separate regular session of the State legislature.

(D) In promulgating standards under this paragraph, the Association or Secretary shall consult with a working group composed of representatives of issuers of medicare supplemental policies, consumer groups, medicare beneficiaries, and other qualified individuals. Such representatives shall be selected in a manner so as to assure balanced representation among the interested groups.

(E) If benefits (including deductibles and coinsurance) under this title are changed and the Secretary determines, in consultation with the Association, that changes in the NAIC or Federal standards are needed to reflect such changes, the preceding provisions of this paragraph shall apply to the modification of standards previously established in the same manner as they applied to the original establishment of such standards.

(2) The benefits under the NAIC or Federal standards shall provide—

(A) for such groups or packages of benefits as may be appropriate taking into account the considerations specified in paragraph (3) and the requirements of the succeeding subparagraphs;

(B) for identification of a core group of basic benefits common to all policies, and

(C) that, subject to paragraph (5)(B), the total number of different benefit packages (counting the core group of basic benefits described in subparagraph (B) and each other combination of benefits that may be offered as a separate benefit package) that may be established in all the States and by all issuers shall not exceed 10.

(3) The benefits under paragraph (2) shall, to the extent possible —

(A) provide for benefits that offer consumer [sic consumers] the ability to purchase the benefits that are available in the market as of the date of the enactment of this subsection; and

(B) balance the objectives of (i) simplifying the market to facilitate comparisons among policies, (ii) avoiding adverse selection, (iii) providing consumer choice, (iv) providing market stability, and (v) promoting competition.

(4)(A) (i) Except as provided in subparagraph (B), no State with a regulatory program approved under subsection (b)(1) may provide for or permit the grouping of benefits (or language or format with respect to such benefits) under a medicare supplemental policy unless such grouping meets the applicable standards.

(ii) Except as provided in subparagraph (B), the Secretary may not provide for or permit the grouping of benefits (or language or format with respect to such benefits) under a medicare supplemental policy seeking approval by the Secretary unless such grouping meets the applicable standards.

(B) With the approval of the State (in the case of a policy issued in a State with an approved regulatory program) or the Secretary (in the case of any other policy), the issuer of a medicare supplemental policy may offer new or innovative benefits in addition to the benefits provided in a policy that otherwise complies with the applicable standards. Any such new or innovative benefits may include benefits that are not otherwise available and are cost-effective and shall be offered in a manner which is consistent with the goal of simplification of medicare supplemental policies.

(5) (A) Except as provided in subparagraph (B), this subsection shall not be construed as preventing a State from

restricting the groups of benefits that may be offered in medicare supplemental policies in the State.

(B) A State with a regulatory program approved under subsection (b)(1) may not restrict under subparagraph (A) the offering of a medicare supplemental policy consisting only of the core group of benefits described in paragraph (2)(B).

(6) The Secretary may waive the application of standards in regard to the limitation of benefits described in paragraph (4) in those States that on the date of enactment of this subsection had in place an alternative simplification program.

(7) This subsection shall not be construed as preventing an issuer of a medicare supplemental policy who otherwise meets the requirements of this section from providing, through an arrangement with a vendor, for discounts from that vendor to policyholder or certificateholders for the purchase of items or services not covered under its medicare supplemental policies.

* * *

(9) (A) Anyone who sells a medicare supplemental policy to an individual shall make available for sale to the individual a medicare supplemental policy with only the core group of basic benefits (described in paragraph (2) (B)).

(B) Anyone who sells a medicare supplemental policy to an individual shall provide the individual, before the sale of the policy, an outline of coverage which describes the benefits under the policy. Such outline shall be on a standard form approved by the State regulatory program or the Secretary (as the case may be) consistent with the NAIC or Federal standards under this subsection.

* * *

For regulatory citations, see Chapter 6

§ 2:51 FAILURE TO OFFER A MEDICARE SUPPLEMENTAL HEALTH INSURANCE POLICY THAT PROVIDES ONLY THE CORE GROUP OF BASIC BENEFITS — Section 1882(p)(9)(C) [42 U.S.C.A. 1395ss(p)(9)(C)]

Summary

◆ NOTE: P.L. 101-508, the Omnibus Budget Reconciliation Act of 1990 (OBRA 90), effective November 5, 1990, made substantial changes in the law applicable to Medicare supplemental health insurance policies. For a summary of the law and statutory provisions pre-OBRA 90, see former § 2:40.1 in Appendix H. For a more complete summary of the law and statutory provisions after OBRA 90, see § 2:45.

In section 1882(a), 42 U.S.C.A. 1395ss(a), Congress authorized the Secretary of Health and Human Services to certify that Medicare supplemental health insurance policies meet established standards for coverage and benefits. It also authorized the Secretary to permit approved entities to use a Secretarial emblem of certification in their marketing.

Establishing the Standards: No Medicare supplemental policy may be issued in a State unless the State has a regulatory program which provides for application and enforcement of standards and requirements set forth in section 1882. Those must be standards of the National Association of Insurance Commissioners (NAIC) or Federal standards. If a State does not adopt such a program, Medicare supplemental policies may not be issued in that State unless the Secretary certifies the policy as meeting Federal standards. Pursuant to section 171(c)(1)(A) of the Social Security Act Amendments of 1994, P.L. 103-432, effective November 5, 1990, as if included in OBRA 90, the relevant standards are the 1991 NAIC Model Regulation or the 1991 Federal Regulation.

Pursuant to section 171(c)(1)(B) of the Social Security Act Amendments of 1994, the effective date of this requirement is the date the State adopts the 1991 NAIC Model Regulation or the date the 1991 Federal Regulation applies, as the case may be, or one year after the date the NAIC or the Secretary first adopts such standards, whichever is earlier. This applies effective November 5, 1990, as if included in OBRA 90.

The effective date depended on whether and when the NAIC produced "NAIC standards" for such policies. Section 1882(p)(1)(A) required NAIC to do so within nine months after enactment of OBRA 90, which ended August 5, 1991. Had the NAIC not met that requirement, the Secretary was obligated to produce "Federal standards" within a subsequent period of nine months, which ended May 5, 1992. Depending on which of those outcomes occurred, the effective date of this requirement was either the date the State adopted the NAIC or Federal standards or one year after the date NAIC or the Secretary first adopted such standards, whichever is earlier. The NAIC Model Regulation was timely adopted.

Form and Content Requirements: Pursuant to section 1882(p)(2), policies under the 1991 NAIC Model Regulation or 1991 Federal Regulation must provide for such groups or packages of benefits that enable consumers to purchase benefits available in the market as of November 5, 1990. They also must balance the objectives of simplifying comparison among policies, avoiding adverse selection, providing consumer choice, providing market stability, and promoting competition. This does not preclude offering new or innovative benefits, provided they are approved by the State or the Secretary, as the case may be. Nor does it preclude a State from restricting the groups of benefits that may be offered in a Medicare supplemental policy, but the restriction may not reduce the statutory core group of benefits which must be common to all policies.

Under the 1991 NAIC Model Regulation or the 1991 Federal Regulation issuers must identify a core group of basic benefits common to all policies. Moreover, the total number of different benefit packages (including the core group and each other combination of benefits offered separately) that may be established in all the States and by all issuers may not exceed 10.

Pursuant to section 1882(p)(9)(C), added by section 4351 of OBRA 90, effective November 5, 1990, anyone who sells a Medicare supplemental health insurance policy to an individual must make available for sale to that individual a Medicare supplemental policy with only the core group of basic benefits. Whoever violates that requirement is subject to a civil money penalty of not to exceed $25,000 (or $15,000 in the case of a seller who is not also the issuer of the policy) for each violation.

Enforcement procedures for this civil money penalty are governed by section 1128A, 42 U.S.C.A. 1320a-7a, which authorizes civil money penalties for a variety of offenses.

Statutory Provisions

As amended by section 171(a)(2)(A)-(L) of the Social Security Act Amendments of 1994, P.L. 103-432, effective October 31, 1994, section 1882(p) provides in pertinent part:

(1) (A) If, within 9 months after the date of the enactment of this subsection, the National Association of Insurance Commissioners (in this subsection referred to as the "association" changes the revised NAIC Model Regulation (described in subsection (m)) to incorporate —

(i) limitations on the groups or packages of benefits that may be offered under a medicare supplemental policy consistent with paragraphs (2) and (3) of this subsection,

(ii) uniform language and definitions to be used with respect to such benefits,

(iii) uniform format to be used in the policy with respect to such benefits, and

(iv) other standards to meet the additional requirements imposed by the amendments made by the Omnibus Budget Reconciliation Act of 1990,

subsection (g)(2)(A) shall be applied in each State, effective for policies issued to policyholders on and after the date specified in subparagraph (C), as if the reference to the Model Regulation adopted on June 6, 1979, were a reference to the revised NAIC Model Regulation as changed by the Secretary under this subparagraph (such changed regulation referred to in this section as the "1991 NAIC Model Regulation").

(B) If the Association does not make the changes in the revised NAIC Model Regulation within the 9-month period specified in subparagraph (A), the Secretary shall promulgate, not later than 9 months after the end of such period, a regulation and subsection (g)(2)(A) shall be applied in each State, effective for policies issued to policyholders on and after the date specified in subparagraph (C), as if the reference to the Model Regulation adopted on June 6, 1979, were a reference to the revised NAIC Model Regulation as changed by the Secretary under this subparagraph (such changed regulation referred to in this section as the "1991 Federal Regulation").

(C) (i) Subject to clause (ii), the date specified in this subparagraph for a State is the date the State adopts the 1991 NAIC Model Regulation or 1991 Federal Regulation or 1 year after the date the Association or the Secretary first adopts such standards, whichever is earlier.

(ii) In the case of a State which the Secretary identifies, in consultation with the Association, as

(I) requiring State legislation (other than legislation appropriating funds) in order for medicare supplemental policies to meet the 1991 NAIC Model Regulation or 1991 Federal Regulation, but

(II) having a legislature which is not scheduled to meet in 1992 in a legislative session in which such legislation may be considered,

the date specified in this subparagraph is the first day of the first calendar quarter beginning after the close of the first legislative session of the State legislature that begins on or after January 1, 1992. For purposes of the previous sentence, in the case of a State that has a 2-year legislative session, each year of such session shall be deemed to be a separate regular session of the State legislature.

(D) In promulgating standards under this paragraph, the Association or Secretary shall consult with a working group composed of representatives of issuers of medicare supplemental policies, consumer groups, medicare beneficiaries, and other qualified individuals. Such representatives shall be selected in a manner so as to assure balanced representation among the interested groups.

(E) If benefits (including deductibles and coinsurance) under this title are changed and the Secretary determines, in consultation with the Association, that changes in the 1991 NAIC Model Regulation or 1991 Federal Regulation are needed to reflect such changes, the preceding provisions of this paragraph shall apply to the modification of standards previously established in the same manner as they applied to the original establishment of such standards.

(2) The benefits under the 1991 NAIC Model Regulation or 1991 Federal Regulation shall provide —

(A) for such groups or packages of benefits as may be appropriate taking into account the considerations specified in paragraph (3) and the requirements of the succeeding subparagraphs;

(B) for identification of a core group of basic benefits common to all policies, and

(C) that, subject to paragraph (4)(B), the total number of different benefit packages (counting the core group of basic benefits described in subparagraph (B) and each other combination of benefits that may be offered as a separate benefit package) that may be established in all the States and by all issuers shall not exceed 10.

(3) The benefits under paragraph (2) shall, to the extent possible—

(A) provide for benefits that offer consumer [sic consumers] the ability to purchase the benefits that are available in the market as of the date of the enactment of this subsection; and

(B) balance the objectives of (i) simplifying the market to facilitate comparisons among policies, (ii) avoiding adverse selection, (iii) providing consumer choice, (iv) providing market stability, and (v) promoting competition.

(4)(A) (i) Except as provided in subparagraph (B) or paragraph (6), no State with a regulatory program approved under subsection (b)(1) may provide for or permit the grouping of benefits (or language or format with respect to such benefits) under a medicare supplemental policy unless such grouping meets the applicable 1991 NAIC Model Regulation or 1991 Federal Regulation.

(ii) Except as provided in subparagraph (B), the Secretary may not provide for or permit the grouping of benefits (or language or format with respect to such benefits) under a medicare supplemental policy seeking approval by the Secretary unless such grouping meets the applicable 1991 NAIC Model Regulation or 1991 Federal Regulation.

(B) With the approval of the State (in the case of a policy issued in a State with an approved regulatory program) or the Secretary (in the case of any other policy), the issuer of a medicare supplemental policy may offer new or innovative benefits in addition to the benefits provided in a policy that otherwise complies with the applicable standards. Any such new or innovative benefits may include benefits that are not otherwise available and are cost-effective and shall be offered in a manner which is consistent with the goal of simplification of medicare supplemental policies.

(5) (A) Except as provided in subparagraph (B), this subsection shall not be construed as preventing a State from restricting the groups of benefits that may be offered in medicare supplemental policies in the State.

(B) A State with a regulatory program approved under subsection (b)(1) may not restrict under subparagraph (A) the offering of a medicare supplemental policy consisting only of the core group of benefits described in paragraph (2)(B).

(6) The Secretary may waive the application of standards in regard to the limitation of benefits described in clauses (i) through (iii) of paragraph (1)(A) in those States that on the date of enactment of this subsection had in place an alternative simplification program.

(7) This subsection shall not be construed as preventing an issuer of a medicare supplemental policy who otherwise meets the requirements of this section from providing, through an arrangement with a vendor, for discounts from that vendor to policyholders or certificateholders for the purchase of items or services not covered under its medicare supplemental policies.

* * *

(9) (A) Anyone who sells a medicare supplemental policy to an individual shall make available for sale to the individual a medicare supplemental policy with only the core group of basic benefits (described in paragraph (2) (B)).

* * *

(C) Whoever sells a medicare supplemental policy in violation of this paragraph is subject to a civil money penalty of not to exceed $25,000 (or $15,000 in the case of a seller who is not the issuer of the policy) for each such violation. The provisions of section 1128A [42 U.S.C.A. 1320a-7A] (other than the first sentence of subsection (a) and other than subsection (b)) shall apply to a civil money penalty under the previous sentence in the same manner as such provisions apply to a penalty or proceeding under section 1128A(a).

* * *

(10) No penalty may be imposed under paragraph (8) or (9) in the case of a seller who is not the issuer of a policy until the Secretary has published a list of the groups of benefit packages that may be sold or issued consistent with this subsection.

◆ NOTE: Prior to amendment by section 171(a)(2)(A)-(L) of the Social Security Act Amendments of 1994, effective October 31, 1994, section 1882(p) read in pertinent part:

(1) (A) If, within 9 months after the date of the enactment of this subsection, the National Association of Insurance Commissioners (in this subsection referred to as the "association" promulgates —

(i) limitations on the groups or packages of benefits that may be offered under a medicare supplemental policy consistent with paragraphs (2) and (3) of this subsection,

(ii) uniform language and definitions to be used with respect to such benefits,

(iii) uniform format to be used in the policy with respect to such benefits, and

(iv) other standards to meet the additional requirements imposed by the amendments made by the Omnibus Budget Reconciliation Act of 1990,

(such limitations, language, definitions, format, and standards referred to collectively in this subsection as "NAIC standards"), subsection (g)(2)(A) shall be applied in each State, effective for policies issued to policyholders on and after the date specified in subparagraph (C), as if the reference to the Model Regulation adopted on June 6, 1979, included a reference to the NAIC standards.

(B) If the Association does not promulgate NAIC standards within the 9-month period specified in subparagraph (A), the Secretary shall promulgate, not later than 9 months after the end of such period, limitations, language, definitions, format, and standards described in clauses (i) through (iv) of such subparagraph (in this subsection referred to collectively as "Federal standards") and subsection (g)(2)(A) shall be applied in each State, effective for policies issued to policyholders on and after the date specified in subparagraph (C), as if the reference to the Model Regulation adopted on June 6, 1979, included a reference to the Federal standards.

(C) (i) Subject to clause (ii), the date specified in this subparagraph for a State is the date the State adopts the NAIC standards or the Federal standards or 1 year after the date the Association or the Secretary first adopts such standards, whichever is earlier.

(ii) In the case of a State which the Secretary identifies, in consultation with the Association, as

(I) requiring State legislation (other than legislation appropriating funds) in order for medicare supplemental policies to meet the NAIC or Federal standards, but

(II) having a legislature which is not scheduled to meet in 1992 in a legislative session in which such legislation may be considered,

the date specified in this subparagraph is the first day of the first calendar quarter beginning after the close of the first legislative session of the State legislature that begins on or after January 1, 1992. For purposes of the previous sentence, in the case of a State that has a 2-year legislative session, each year of such session shall be deemed to be a separate regular session of the State legislature.

(D) In promulgating standards under this paragraph, the Association or Secretary shall consult with a working group composed of representatives of issuers of medicare supplemental policies, consumer groups, medicare beneficiaries, and other qualified individuals. Such representatives shall be selected in a manner so as to assure balanced representation among the interested groups.

(E) If benefits (including deductibles and coinsurance) under this title are changed and the Secretary determines, in consultation with the Association, that changes in the

NAIC or Federal standards are needed to reflect such changes, the preceding provisions of this paragraph shall apply to the modification of standards previously established in the same manner as they applied to the original establishment of such standards.

(2) The benefits under the NAIC or Federal standards shall provide —

(A) for such groups or packages of benefits as may be appropriate taking into account the considerations specified in paragraph (3) and the requirements of the succeeding subparagraphs;

(B) for identification of a core group of basic benefits common to all policies, and

(C) that, subject to paragraph (5)(B), the total number of different benefit packages (counting the core group of basic benefits described in subparagraph (B) and each other combination of benefits that may be offered as a separate benefit package) that may be established in all the States and by all issuers shall not exceed 10.

(3) The benefits under paragraph (2) shall, to the extent possible —

(A) provide for benefits that offer consumer [sic consumers] the ability to purchase the benefits that are available in the market as of the date of the enactment of this subsection; and

(B) balance the objectives of (i) simplifying the market to facilitate comparisons among policies, (ii) avoiding adverse selection, (iii) providing consumer choice, (iv) providing market stability, and (v) promoting competition.

(4)(A) (i) Except as provided in subparagraph (B), no State with a regulatory program approved under subsection (b)(1) may provide for or permit the grouping of benefits (or language or format with respect to such benefits) under a medicare supplemental policy unless such grouping meets the applicable standards.

(ii) Except as provided in subparagraph (B), the Secretary may not provide for or permit the grouping of benefits (or language or format with respect to such benefits) under a medicare supplemental policy seeking approval by the

Secretary unless such grouping meets the applicable standards.

(B) With the approval of the State (in the case of a policy issued in a State with an approved regulatory program) or the Secretary (in the case of any other policy), the issuer of a medicare supplemental policy may offer new or innovative benefits in addition to the benefits provided in a policy that otherwise complies with the applicable standards. Any such new or innovative benefits may include benefits that are not otherwise available and are cost-effective and shall be offered in a manner which is consistent with the goal of simplification of medicare supplemental policies.

(5) (A) Except as provided in subparagraph (B), this subsection shall not be construed as preventing a State from restricting the groups of benefits that may be offered in medicare supplemental policies in the State.

(B) A State with a regulatory program approved under subsection (b)(1) may not restrict under subparagraph (A) the offering of a medicare supplemental policy consisting only of the core group of benefits described in paragraph (2)(B).

(6) The Secretary may waive the application of standards in regard to the limitation of benefits described in paragraph (4) in those States that on the date of enactment of this subsection had in place an alternative simplification program.

(7) This subsection shall not be construed as preventing an issuer of a medicare supplemental policy who otherwise meets the requirements of this section from providing, through an arrangement with a vendor, for discounts from that vendor to policyholder or certificateholders for the purchase of items or services not covered under its medicare supplemental policies.

* * *

(9) (A) Anyone who sells a medicare supplemental policy to an individual shall make available for sale to the individual a medicare supplemental policy with only the core group of basic benefits (described in paragraph (2) (B)).

* * *

(C) Whoever sells a medicare supplemental policy in violation of this paragraph is subject to a civil money penalty of not to exceed $25,000 (or $15,000 in the case of a seller who is not the issuer of the policy) for each such violation. The provisions of section 1128A [42 U.S.C.A. 1320a-7A] (other than the first sentence of subsection (a) and other than subsection (b)) shall apply to a civil money penalty under the previous sentence in the same manner as such provisions apply to a penalty or proceeding under section 1128A(a).

For regulatory citations, see Chapter 6

§ 2:52 FAILURE TO PROVIDE REINSTATEMENT RIGHTS TO PURCHASERS OF MEDICARE SUPPLEMENTAL HEALTH INSURANCE POLICIES WHO BECOME ELIGIBLE FOR MEDICAID — Section 1882(q)(5) [42 U.S.C.A. 1395ss(q)(5)]

Summary

◆ NOTE: P.L. 101-508, the Omnibus Budget Reconciliation Act of 1990 (OBRA 90), effective November 5, 1990, made substantial changes in the law applicable to Medicare supplemental health insurance policies. For a summary of the law and statutory provisions pre-OBRA 90, see former § 2:40.1 in Appendix H. For a more complete summary of the law and statutory provisions after OBRA 90 see § 2:45.

In section 1882(a), 42 U.S.C.A. 1395ss(a), Congress authorized the Secretary of Health and Human Services to certify that Medicare supplemental health insurance policies meet established standards for coverage and benefits. It also authorized the Secretary to permit approved entities to use a Secretarial emblem of certification in their marketing.

No Medicare supplemental policy may be issued in a State unless the State has a regulatory program which provides for application and enforcement of standards and requirements set forth in section 1882. Those must be standards of the National Association of Insurance Commissioners (NAIC) or Federal standards. If a State does not adopt such a program, Medicare supplemental policies may not be issued in that State unless the Secretary certifies the policy as meeting Federal standards. Pursuant to section 171(c)(1)(A) of the Social Security Act Amendments of 1994, P.L. 103-432, effective November 5, 1990, as if included in OBRA 90, the relevant standards are the 1991 NAIC Model Regulation or the 1991 Federal Regulation.

Pursuant to section 171(c)(1)(B) of the Social Security Act Amendments of 1994, the effective date of this requirement was the date the State adopted the 1991 NAIC Model Regulation or the date the 1991 Federal Regulation applies, as the case may be, or one year after the date the NAIC or the Secretary first adopted such standards, whichever is earlier. This applies effective November 5, 1990, as if included in OBRA 90.

The effective date depended on whether and when the NAIC produced "NAIC standards" for such policies. Section 1882(p)(1)(A) required NAIC to do so within nine months after enactment of OBRA 90, which ended August 5, 1991. Had the NAIC not met that requirement, the Secretary was obligated to produce "Federal standards" within a subsequent period of nine months, which ended May 5, 1992. Depending on which of those outcomes occurred, the effective date of this requirement would have been either the date the State adopted the NAIC or Federal standards or one year after the date NAIC or the Secretary first adopted such standards, whichever was earlier. The NAIC Model Regulation was timely adopted.

Section 1882(q)(5) requires issuers of Medicare supplemental policies to suspend benefits and premiums for a period not to exceed 24 months, at the request of a policyholder or certificateholder, if the insured has applied for and is determined to be entitled to Medicaid and if the insured notifies the issuer of the policy of the request within 90 days after becoming entitled to Medicaid. This applies to policies issued or sold after November 5, 1991.

If suspension occurs and if the policyholder or certificateholder loses entitlement to Medicaid, the issuer of the policy must reinstitute coverage, under terms described in subsection (n)(6)(A)(ii), effective as of the termination of Medicaid. Reinstitution applies if the policyholder provides notice of loss of Medicaid entitlement within 90 days after the date of such loss.

Section 1882(n)(6)(A)(ii) requires reinstitution under terms which do not provide for any waiting period with respect to treatment of pre-existing conditions; which provide for coverage substantially equivalent to coverage in effect before the date of the suspension; and which provides for classification of premiums on which terms are at least as favorable to the policyholder or certificateholder as the premium classification terms that would have applied to the policyholder or certificateholder had the coverage never been suspended.

Any person who issues a Medicare supplemental policy and fails to comply with this suspension and reinstatement requirement is subject to a civil money penalty not to exceed $25,000 for each such violation. Enforcement procedures for this civil money penalty are governed by section 1128A, 42 U.S.C.A. 1320a-7a, which authorizes civil money penalties for a variety of offenses.

Statutory Provisions

Section 4532 of OBRA 90 added subsection (q) to section 1882. As amended by the Social Security Act Amendments of 1994, P.L. 103-432, it provides in pertinent part:

> The requirements of this subsection are as follows:
>
> * * *
>
> (5) [With respect to policies issued or sold more than one year after November 5, 1990]
>
> (A) Each medicare supplemental policy shall provide that benefits and premiums under the policy shall be suspended at the request of the policyholder for the period (not to exceed 24 months) in which the policyholder has applied for and is determined to be entitled to medical assistance under title XIX, but only if the policyholder notifies the issuer of such policy within 90 days after the date the individual becomes entitled to such assistance. [Section 171(d)(4) of the Social Security Act Amendments of 1994 deleted "of the Social Security Act" following "title XIX", here and in (B) below, effective October 31, 1994.] If such suspension occurs and if the policyholder or certificate holder loses entitlement to such medical assistance, such policy shall be automatically reinstituted (effective as of the date of termination of such entitlement) under terms described in subsection (n)(6)(A)(ii) as of the termination of such entitlement if the policyholder provides notice of loss of such entitlement within 90 days after the date of such loss.
>
> (B) Nothing in this section shall be construed as affecting the authority of a State under title XIX, to purchase a medicare supplemental policy for an individual otherwise entitled to assistance under such title.

(C) Any person who issues a medicare supplemental policy and fails to comply with the requirements of this paragraph is subject to a civil money penalty of not to exceed $25,000 for each such violation. The provisions of section 1128A [42 U.S.C.A. 1320a-7a] (other than the first sentence of subsection (a) and other than subsection (b)) shall apply to a civil money penalty under the previous sentence in the same manner as such provisions apply to a penalty or proceeding under section 1128A(a).

Section 1882(n)(6)(A)(ii) provides in pertinent part:

Except as provided in subparagraph (B), in the case of an individual who had in effect, as of December 31, 1988, a medicare supplemental policy with an insurer (as a policyholder or, in the case of a group policy, as a certificate holder) and the individual terminated coverage under such policy before the date of the enactment of this subsection, no medicare supplemental policy of the insurer shall be deemed to meet the standards in subsection (c) unless the insurer—

* * *

(ii) offers the individual, during the period of at least 60 days beginning not later than February 1, 1990, reinstitution of coverage (with coverage effective as of January 1, 1990), under the terms which (I) do not provide for any waiting period with respect to treatment of pre-existing conditions, (II) provides for coverage which is substantially equivalent to coverage in effect before the date of such termination, and (III) provides for classification of premiums on which terms are at least as favorable to the policyholder or certificate holder as the premium classification terms that would have applied to the policyholder or certificate holder had the coverage never terminated.

For regulatory citations, see Chapter 6

§ 2:53 FAILURE BY ISSUERS OF MEDICARE SUPPLEMENTAL HEALTH INSURANCE POLICIES TO MEET REQUIREMENTS FOR PREEXISTING CONDITIONS, WAITING PERIODS, ELIMINATION PERIODS, PROBATIONARY PERIODS, AND PRICE AND COVERAGE NONDISCRIMINATION—Section 1882(s)(3) [42 U.S.C.A. 1395ss(s)(3)]

Summary

◆ NOTE: P.L. 101-508, the Omnibus Budget Reconciliation Act of 1990 (OBRA 90), effective November 5, 1990, made substantial changes in the law applicable to Medicare supplemental health insurance policies. For a summary of the law and statutory provisions pre-OBRA 90, see former § 2:40.1 in Appendix H. For a more complete summary of the law and statutory provisions after OBRA 90, see § 2:45.

In section 1882(a), 42 U.S.C.A. 1395ss(a), Congress authorized the Secretary of Health and Human Services to certify that Medicare supplemental health insurance policies meet established standards for coverage and benefits. It also authorized the Secretary to permit approved entities to use a Secretarial emblem of certification in their marketing.

No Medicare supplemental policy may be issued in a State unless the State has a regulatory program which provides for application and enforcement of standards and requirements set forth in section 1882. Those must be standards of the National Association of Insurance Commissioners (NAIC) or Federal standards. If a State does not adopt such a program, Medicare supplemental policies may not be issued in that State unless the Secretary certifies the policy as meeting Federal standards. Pursuant to section 171(c)(1)(A) of the Social Security Act Amendments of 1994, P.L. 103-432, effective November 5, 1990, as if included in OBRA 90, the relevant standards are the 1991 NAIC Model Regulation or the 1991 Federal Regulation.

Pursuant to section 171(c)(1)(B) of the Social Security Act Amendments of 1994, the effective date of this requirement was the date the State adopted the 1991 NAIC Model Regulation or the date the 1991 Federal Regulation applies, as the case may be, or one year after the date the NAIC or the Secretary first adopted such standards, whichever is earlier. This applies effective November 5, 1990, as if included in OBRA 90.

The effective date depended on whether and when the NAIC produced "NAIC standards" for such policies. Section 1882(p)(1)(A) required NAIC to do so within nine months after enactment of OBRA 90, which ended August 5, 1991. Had the NAIC not met that requirement, the Secretary was obligated to produce "Federal standards" within a subsequent period of nine months, which ended May 5, 1992. Depending on which of those outcomes occurred, the effective date of this requirement would have been either the date the State adopted the NAIC or Federal standards or one year after the date NAIC or the Secretary first adopted such standards, whichever was earlier. The NAIC Model Regulation was timely adopted.

OBRA 90 Requirements: Pursuant to section 1882(s), which was added by section 4357 of OBRA 90 effective November 5, 1991, if one Medicare supplemental policy replaces another, the issuer of the replacement must waive any time periods applicable to preexisting conditions, waiting period, elimination periods, and probationary periods for similar benefits to the extent such time was spent under the original policy.

Furthermore, the issuer of a Medicare supplemental policy may not deny or condition issuance or effectiveness of a policy, or discriminate in the pricing of the policy, because of health status, claims experience, receipt of health care, or medical condition for which an application is submitted prior to or during the six-month period beginning with the first month. This does not prevent exclusion of benefits under a policy, however, during that 6-month period based on a pre-existing condition for which the policyholder received treatment or was otherwise diagnosed during the six months before the policy became effective. But if a policy or certificate replaced another such policy or certificate that had been in effect for six months or longer, the replacing policy may not provide any time period applicable to pre-existing conditions, waiting periods, elimination periods, and probationary periods in the new policy or certificate for similar benefits.

Requirements Imposed by the Balanced Budget Act of 1997: Effective July 1, 1998, but subject to the transition provisions of section 4031 of the Balanced Budget Act of 1997, P.L. 105–33, section 4031(a) of that Act imposed additional restrictions on the imposition of pre-existing conditions on individuals applying for a

Medicare supplement policy. It also created new opportunities for certain individuals to obtain Medicare supplement policies.

Pre-existing Conditions: In the case of a policy issued during the 6-month period when an individual becomes age 65 and is enrolled in Medicare Part B, if the individual as of the date of application has a continuous period of creditable coverage (as defined in section 2701(c) of the Public Health Service Act) of at least 6 months, a Medicare supplement policy may not exclude benefits based on a pre-existing condition.

If such an individual has less than 6 months of creditable coverage, any Medicare supplement policy which excludes benefits based on a pre-existing condition must reduce the period of any exclusion by the aggregate of the periods of creditable coverage applicable to the individual as of the enrollment date.

New Coverage Opportunities: As amended by the Balanced Budget Act of 1997, section 1882(s)(3) provides additional opportunities to obtain a Medicare supplement policy for the following:

> Individuals enrolled under an employee welfare benefit plan that provides health benefits that supplement Medicare benefits whose plan terminates or ceases to provide all such supplemental health benefits to the individual.
>
> Individuals enrolled with a Medicare + Choice organization or with a PACE provider (Program of All-inclusive Care for the Elderly) under section 1894, 42 U.S.C. 13953eee, who discontinue their election to participate in a Medicare + Choice plan or PACE provider program.

◆ NOTE: The reference to PACE providers was added by section 536 of the Medicare, Medicaid, and SCHIP Balanced Budget Refinement Act of 1999, as incorporated into the Omnibus Consolidated Appropriations Act, 2000, P.L. 106–113, enacted November 17, 1999. This change applies to terminations or discontinuances on or after November 29, 1999.

> Individuals enrolled with HMOs or CMPs or similar organizations operating under demonstration project authority for periods before April 1, 1999, or having a Medicare SELECT plan whose enrollment ceases becauses the plan terminates or the individual's eligibility to continue ends (for example, by change of residence), or because there is no provision under applicable

State law for continuation or conversion of a Medicare SELECT policy.

Individuals whose enrollment in a Medicare supplement policy ceases because of the bankruptcy or insolvency of the issuer, or because of other involuntary termination of coverage or enrollment under such policy, when applicable State law does not provide for continuation or conversion of such coverage; or because the issuer of the policy substantially violated a material provision of the policy; or because the issuer (or an agent or other entity acting on its behalf) materially misrepresented the policy's provisions in marketing the policy to the individual.

Individuals with a Medicare supplement policy who terminated their enrollment and who for the first time enroll with any Medicare + Choice organization under a Medicare + Choice plan, or any HMO or CMP, or any similar organization operating under demonstration project authority, or with a PACE provider, or who obtain a Medicare SELECT policy, and that enrollment is terminated during the first 12 months when termination is permitted.

Individuals who, upon first eligibility for Medicare, enroll in a Medicare + Choice plan or with a PACE provider and disenroll within the first 12 months.

For any individual meeting any of the above conditions, an issuer of a Medicare supplemental policy may not deny or condition the issuance or effectiveness of Medicare supplement standard plans A, B, C, or F offered and available to new enrollees.

For an individual who had a Medicare supplement policy and who enrolled for the first time in a Medicare + Choice plan, or an HMO or CMP or demonstration project authority, or a Medicare SELECT plan, who then disenrolls as permitted during the first 12 months of such enrollment, an issuer must offer the Medicare supplement policy in which the individual was enrolled prior to enrolling in Medicare + Choice or any of the other plans. That applies if the prior Medicare supplement policy is still available; otherwise, the issuer must offer standard plans A, B, C, or F.

For an individual who enrolled in Medicare + Choice when first eligible for Medicare benefits, who subsequently disenrolls, as permitted during the first 12 months of such an enrollment, an issuer must offer any of the standard plans available.

In the case of a State that provides for offering of benefit packages other than under the classification referred to as standard plans A, B, C, or F, references to those standard plans are deemed references to comparable benefit packages offered in that State.

Furthermore, issuers of Medicare supplement policies may not discriminate in the pricing of such a policy because of the health status, claims experience, receipt of health care, or medical condition of such an individual. Nor may an issuer impose an exclusion based on a pre-existing condition.

Under the Balanced budget Act of 1997, the foregoing coverage opportunities were available only to individuals who seek to enroll under a Medicare supplement policy not later than 63 days after the date of the termination of enrollment in any of the qualifying prior health benefit plans or policies and who submit evidence of the date of termination or disenrollment along with their applications for a Medicare supplement policy. This was changed, effective December 21, 2000. See below.

Requirements Imposed by the Medicare, Medicaid, and SCHIP Benefits Improvement and Protection Act of 2000: Section 618 (a)(1) of the Medicare, Medicaid, and SCHIP Benefits Improvement and Protection Act of 2000, P.L. 106–554, effective December 21, 2000, broadened open enrollment opportunities as follows:

> *For individuals enrolled under an employee welfare benefit plan which provides Medicare supplement benefits:* If the plan terminates or ceases to provide all such supplemental health benefits, open enrollment extends for 63 days from the date the individual receives a notice of termination or cessation of such benefits. If no such notice is received, then open enrollment extends for 63 days after notice that a claim has been denied because of such a termination or cessation;
>
> *For individuals enrolled with a Medicare+ Choice organization, For individuals age 65 or older enrolled with a PACE provider, For individuals enrolled with an HMO or competitive medical plan under section 1876 of the Social Security Act, 42 U.S.C. 1395mm, (or a similar organization under demonstration authority—effective for periods after April 1, 1999);*
>
> *For individuals enrolled with an employee benefit health plan under section 1833(a)(1) of the Social Security Act, 42 U.S.C. 1395l(a)(1):* If the individual enrollment is terminated *involuntarily*, open enrollment begins the date the individual receives notice of termination and ends 63 days after the date

the applicable coverage is terminated. This applies when circumstances permit discontinuance of the individual's election to enroll;

For individuals enrolled in a Medicare SELECT plan: If the indivdual enrollment is terminated *involuntarily*, open enrollment begins the date the individual receives notice of termination and ends 63 days after the date the applicable coverage is terminated. This applies if there is no provision under applicable State law for continuation or conversion of coverage under such a policy;

For individuals enrolled under a Medicare supplement policy who terminate such enrollment and enroll—for the first time—with a Medicare+ Choice organization, a section 1876 health plan (or similar organization operating under demonstration authority), a PACE provider, or under a Medicare SELECT plan: If the individual enrollment is *involuntarily* terminated, open enrollment begins the date the individual receives notice of termination and ends 63 days after the date the applicable coverage is terminated. This applies when the subsequent enrollment is terminated by the enrollee during any period within the first 12 months of such enrollment (during which the enrollee is permitted to terminate such subsequent enrollment under section 1851(e), 42 U.S.C. 1395w-21(e);

For individuals first becoming eligible for benefits under Part A at age 65 who enroll in a Medicare+ Choice plan, or in a PACE program, and who disenroll from such plan or program not later than 12 months after the effective date of such enrollment: If the individual's enrollment is involuntarily terminated, open enrollment begins the date the individual receives notice of termination and ends 63 days after the date the applicable coverage is terminated;

For individuals enrolled under a Medicare supplement policy whose enrollment ceases because of the bankruptcy or insolvency of the issuer or because of other involuntary termination of coverage or enrollment under such policy: Open enrollment begins on the date the individual receives notice of termination, or notice of the issuer's bankruptcy or insolvency, or other similar notice, if any, and the date the applicable coverage is terminated (whichever is earlier) and ends 63 days after the date coverage is terminated;

For individuals who voluntarily disenroll from a Medicare+ Choice organization, a PACE provider, a health plan under section 1876 (or similar organization operating under demonstration authority), an employee benefit health plan under section 1833, or from a Medicare SELECT policy;
For individuals who voluntarily disenroll because the issuer of their policy substantially violated a material provision of the policy, or the issuer or its agent or other entity acting on its behalf materially misrepresented the policy's provisions in marketing the policy to the indivual;
For individuals who had a Medicare supplement policy, then terminated such enrollment and enrolled for the first time with a Medicare+ Choice organization, or a PACE provider, or a section 1876 health plan (or similar organization operating under demonstration authority), or who had a Medicare SELECT policy, then terminated such enrollment, as permitted within the first 12 months of enrollment;
For individuals who upon first becoming eligible for Part A benefits at age 65 enroll in a Medicare+ Choice program, or with a PACE provider, then disenroll not more than 12 months later: Open enrollment begins on the date that is 60 days before the effective date of the disenrollment and ends on the date that is 63 days after such effective date; and
For all other individuals, open enrollment begins on the effective date of the disenrollment and ends 63 days after that date.

Finally, whenever an individual ceases enrollment or loses coverage or benefits under a contract or agreement, policy, or plan, the organization that offers the contract or agreement, the insurer offering the policy, or the administrator of the plan, respectively, must notify the individual of his or her rights under section 1882(s). They also must notify the individual of the obligations of issuers of Medicare supplement policies under section 1882(s)(3)(A) with respect to mandatory offers of policies, restrictions of imposition of pre-existing conditions, and non-discrimination in pricing based on health status, claims experience, receipt of health care, or medical condition.

◆ NOTE: Prior to amendment by section 171(g)(1)-(2) of the Social Security Act Amendments of 1994, the prohibition with respect to health status, claims experience, receipt of health care, or medical condition applied during the 6-month period beginning the first month an individual who is 65 years or older first enrolled for benefits under part B.

Any issuer of a Medicare supplemental policy that fails to meet these requirements is subject to a civil money penalty not to exceed $5,000 for each such failure. Enforcement procedures for this civil money penalty are governed by section 1128A, 42 U.S.C.A. 1320a-7a, which authorizes civil money penalties for a variety of offenses.

Statutory Provisions

Section 4357 of OBRA 90 added subsection (s) to section 1882, effective one year after November 5, 1990. As amended by section 171(g)(1), (2), and (3) of the Social Security Act Amendments of 1994, effective October 31, 1994, it provides in pertinent part:

> (1) If a medicare supplemental policy replaces another medicare supplemental policy, the issuer of the replacing policy shall waive any time periods applicable to preexisting conditions, waiting period, elimination periods and probationary periods in the new medicare supplemental policy for similar benefits to the extent such time was spent under the original policy.
>
> (2) (A) The issuer of a medicare supplemental policy may not deny or condition the issuance or effectiveness of a medicare supplemental policy, or discriminate in the pricing of the policy, because of health status, claims experience, receipt of health care, or medical condition in the case of an individual for whom an application is submitted prior to or during the 6 month period beginning with the first month as of the first day on which the individual is 65 years of age or oldwer and is enrolled for benefits under part B of this subchapter.
>
> (B) Subject to subparagraphs (C) and (D), subparagraph (A) shall not be construed as preventing the exclusion of benefits under a policy, during its first 6 months, based on a pre-existing condition for which the policyholder received treatment or was otherwise diagnosed during the 6 months before the policy became effective.

◆ NOTE: Prior to amendment by section 171(g)(1), (2), and (3) of the Social Security Act Amendments of 1994, effective October 31, 1994, section 1882(s)(2)(A) and (B) read:

(A) The issuer of a medicare supplemental policy may not deny or condition the issuance or effectiveness of a medicare supplemental policy, or discriminate in the pricing of the policy, because of health status, claims experience, receipt of health care, or medical condition for which an application is submitted during the 6 month period beginning with the first month in which the individual (who is 65 years of age or older) first enrolled for benefits under part B.

(B) Subject to subparagraph (C), subparagraph (A) shall not be construed as preventing the exclusion of benefits under a policy, during its first 6 months, based on a pre-existing condition for which the policyholder received treatment or was otherwise diagnosed during the 6 months before it became effective.

The Balanced Budget Act of 1997, P.L. 105–33, made substantial changes to section 1882(s). Specifically, section 4031(b) of that Act substituted "subparagraphs (C) and (D)" for "subparagraph (C)" in subparagraph (B) above. It also added subparagraph (D) below. In addition, section 4031(a) of the Balanced Budget Act of 1997 redesignated former paragraph (s)(3) as (s)(4) and added new paragraph (s)(3) below. It also substituted "this subsection" for "paragraphs (1) and (2)" after "the requirements of" in paragraph (s)(4). These changes became effective July 1, 1998, subject to the transition provisions in section 4031(e) of the Balanced Budget Act. Additional changes were made by the Medicare, Medicaid, and SCHIP Benefits Improvement and Protection Act of 2000. See below.

(C) If a medicare supplemental policy or certificate replaces another such policy or certificate which has been in effect for 6 months or longer, the replacing policy may not provide any time period applicable to pre-existing conditions, waiting periods, elimination periods, and probationary periods in the new policy or certificate for similar benefits.

(D) In the case of a policy issued during the 6-month period described in subparagraph (A) to an individual who is 65 years of age or older as of the date of issuance and who as of the date of the application for enrollment has a continuous period of creditable coverage (as defined in section 2701(c) of the Public Health Service Act) of— *(i) at least 6 months, the policy may not exclude benefits based on a pre-existing condition; or (ii) less than 6 months, if the policy excludes benefits based on a preexisting condition, the policy shall reduce the period of any preexisting condition exclusion by the aggregate of the periods of creditable coverage (if any, as so defined) applicable to the individual as of the enrollment date.*

The Secretary shall specify the manner of the reduction under clause (ii), based upon the rules used by the Secretary in carrying out section 2701(a)(3) of such Act.

Section 1882(s)(3) provides:

(3)(A) The issuer of a Medicare supplemental policy —

(i) may not deny or condition the issuance or effectiveness of a Medicare supplemental policy described in subparagraph (C) that is offered and is available for issuance to new enrollees by such issuer;

(ii) may not discriminate in the pricing of such policy, because of health status, claims experience, receipt of health care, or medical condition; and

(iii) may not impose an exclusion of benefits based on a pre-existing condition under such policy,

in the case of an individual described in subparagraph (B) who seeks to enroll under the policy during the period specified in subparagraph (E) and who submits evidence of the date of termination or disenrollment along with the application for such Medicare supplemental policy.

NOTE: Previously, the preceding clause read: "in the case of an individual described in subparagraph (B) who, subject to subparagraph (E), seeks to enroll under the policy not later than 63 days after the date of the termination of enrollment described in such subparagraph and who submits evidence of the date of termination or disenrollment along with the application for such Medicare supplemental policy." This change was made effective December 21, 2000, by section 618(a)(1) of the Medicare, Medicaid, and SCHIP Benefits Improvement and Protection Act of 2000, P.L. 106–544.

(B) An individual described in this subparagraph is an individual described in any of the following clauses:

(i) The individual is enrolled under an employee welfare benefit plan that provides health benefits that supplement the benefits under this title and the plan terminates or ceases to provide all such supplemental health benefits to the individual.

(ii) The individual is enrolled with a Medicare + Choice organization under a Medicare + Choice plan under part C. and there are circumstances permitting discontinuance of the individual's election of the plan under the first sentence of section 1851(e)(4) or the individual is 65 years of age or older and is enrolled with a PACE provider under section 1894 and there are circumstances that would permit the discontinuance of the individual's enrollment with such provider under circumstances that are similar to the circumstances that would permit discontinuance of the individual's election under the first sentence of such section if the individual were enrolled in a Medicare + Choice plan.

(iii) The individual is enrolled with an eligible organization under a contract under section 1876, a similar organization operating under demonstration project authority, effective for periods before April 1, 1999, with an organization under an agreement under section 1833(a)(1)(A), or with an organization under a policy described in subsection (t), and such enrollment ceases under the same circumstances that would permit discontinuance of an individual's election of coverage under the first sentence of section 1851(e)(4) and, in the case of a policy described in subsection (t), there is no provision under applicable State law for the continuation or conversion of coverage under such policy.

(iv) The individual is enrolled under a Medicare supplemental policy under this section and such enrollment ceases because —

(I) of the bankruptcy or insolvency of the issuer or because of other involuntary termination of coverage or enrollment under such policy and there is no provision under applicable State law for the continuation or conversion of such coverage;

(II) the issuer of the policy substantially violated a material provision of the policy; or

(III) the issuer (or an agent or other entity acting on the issuer's behalf) materially misrepresented the policy's provisions in marketing the policy to the individual.

(v) The individual —

(I) was enrolled under a Medicare supplemental policy under this section.

(II) subsequently terminates such enrollment and enrolls, for the first time, with any Medicare + Choice organization under a Medicare + Choice plan under part C, any eligible organization under a contract under section 1876, any similar organization operating under demonstration project authority, any PACE provider under section 1894, or any policy described in subsection (t), and

(III) the subsequent enrollment under subclause (II) is terminated by the enrollee during any period within the first 12 months of such enrollment (during which the enrollee is permitted to terminate such subsequent enrollment under section 1851(e)).

(vi) The individual, upon first becoming eligible for benefits under part A at age 65, enrolls in a Medicare + Choice plan under part C, or in a PACE program under section 1894, and disenrolls from such plan by not later than 12 months after the effective date of such enrollment.

(C)(i) Subject to clauses (ii) and (iii), a Medicare supplemental policy described in this subparagraph is a Medicare supplemental policy which has a benefit package classified as 'A' , 'B' , 'C' , or 'F' under the standards established under subsection (p)(2).

(ii) Only for purposes of an individual described in subparagraph (B)(v), a Medicare supplemental policy described in this subparagraph is the same Medicare supplemental policy referred to in such subparagraph in which the individual was most recently previously enrolled, if available from the same issuer, or, if not so available, a policy described in clause (i).

(iii) Only for purposes of an individual described in subparagraph (B)(vi), a Medicare supplemental policy described in this subparagraph shall include any Medicare supplemental policy.

(iv) For purposes of applying this paragraph in the case of a State that provides for offering of benefit packages other than under the classification referred to in clause (i), the references to benefit packages in such clause are deemed references to comparable benefit packages offered in such State.

(D) At the time of an event described in subparagraph (B) because of which an individual ceases enrollment or loses coverage or benefits under a contract or agreement, policy, or plan, the organization that offers the contract or agreement, the insurer offering the policy, or the administrator of the plan, respectively, shall notify the individual of the rights of the individual under this paragraph, and obligations of issuers of Medicare supplemental policies, under subparagraph (A).

(E) For purposes of subparagraph (A), the time period specified in this subparagraph is—

(i) in the case of an individual described in subparagraph (B)(i), the period beginning on the date the individual receives a notice of termination or cessation of all supplemental health benefits (or, if no such notice is received, notice that a claim has been denied because of such a termination or cessation) and ending on the date that is 63 days after the applicable notice;

(ii) in the case of an individual described in clause (ii), (iii), (v), or (vi) of subparagraph (B) whose enrollment is terminated involuntarily, the period beginning on the date that the individual receives a notice of termination and ending on the date that is 63 days after the date the applicable coverage is terminated;

(iii) in the case of an individual described in subparagraph (B)(iv)(I), the period beginning on the earlier of (I) the date that the individual receives a notice of termination, a notice of the issuer's bankruptcy or insolvency, or other such similar notice, if any, and (II) the date that the applicable coverage is terminated, and ending on the date that is 63 days after the date the coverage is terminated;

(iv) in the case of an individual described in clause (ii), (iii), (iv)(II), (v), or (vi) of subparagraph (B) who disenrolls voluntarily, the period beginning on the date that is 60 days before the effective date of the disenrollment and ending on the date that is 63 days afer such effective date; and

(v) in the case of an individual described in subparagraph (B) but not described in the preceding provisions of this subparagraph, the period beginning on the effective date of the disenrollment and ending on the date that is 63 days after such effective date.

◆ NOTE: Prior to amendment by section 618(a)(2) of the Medicare, Medicaid, and SCHIP Benefits Improvement and Protection Act of 2000, effective December 21, 2000, subparagraph (s)(3)(E) read:

(i) An individual described in subparagraph (B)(ii) may elect to apply subparagraph (A) by substituting, for the date of termination of enrollment, the date on which the individual was notified by the Medicare + Choice organization of the impending termination or discontinuance of the Medicare + Choice plan it offers in the area in which the individual resides, but only if the individual disenrolls from the plan as a result of such notification.

(ii) In the case of an individual making such an election, the issuer involved shall accept the application of the individual submitted before the date of termination of enrollment, but the coverage under subparagraph (a) shall only become effective upon termination of coverage under the Medicare + Choice plan involved.

Section 618(b) of the Medicare, Medicaid, and SCHIP Benefits Improvement and Protection Act of 2000 also added new paragraph (F), which, effective December 21, 2000, reads:

(F)(i) Subject to clause (ii), for purposes of this paragraph—

(I) in the case of an individual described in subparagraph (B)(v) (or deemed to be so described, pursuant to this subparagraph) whose enrollment with an organization or provider described in subclause (II) of such subparagraph is involuntarily terminated within the first 12 months of such enrollment, and who, without an intervening enrollment, enrolls with another such organization or provider, such subsequent enrollment shall be deemed to be an initial enrollment described in such subparagraph; and

(II) in the case of an individual described in clause (vi) of subparagraph (B) (or deemed to be so described, pursuant to this subparagraph) whose enrollment with a plan or in a program described in such clause is involuntarily terminated within the first 12 months of such enrollment, and who, without an intervening enrollment, enrolls in another such plan or program, such subsequent enrollment shall be deemed to be an initial enrollment described in such clause.

(ii) For purposes of clauses (v) and (vi) of subparagraph (B), no enrollment of an individual with an organization or provider described in clause (v)(II), or with a plan or in a program described in clause (vi), may be deemed to be an initial enrollment under this clause after the 2– year period beginning on the date on which the individual first enrolled with such an organization, provider, plan or program.

(4) Any issuer of a medicare supplemental policy that fails to meet the requirements of this subsection is subject to a civil money penalty of not to exceed $5,000 for each such failure. The provision of section 1128A [42 U.S.C.A. 1320a-7a] other than the first sentence of subsection (a) and other than subsection (b) shall apply to a civil money penalty under the previous sentence in the same manner as such provisions apply to a penalty or proceeding under section 1128A(a).

◆ NOTE: Section 501(a)(2) of the Medicare, Medicaid, and SCHIP Balanced Budget Refinement Act of 1999, as incorporated into the Omnibus Consolidated Appropriations Act, 2000, P.L. 106–113, enacted November 17, 1999, inserted the language ", subject to subparagraph (E)" in the paragraph following (A)(iii) and added subparagraph (E). This change applies to terminations or discontinuances made on or after November 29, 1999. Section 536 of the same Act inserted "or the individual is 65 years of age or older and is enrolled with a PACE provider under section 1894, and there are circumstances that would permit the discontinuance of the individual's enrollment with such provider under circumstances that are similar to the circumstances that would permit discontinuance of the individual's election under the first sentence of such section if such individual were enrolled in a Medicare + Choice plan" in (3)(B)(ii); inserted "any PACE provider under section 1894" in (3)(B)(v)(II); inserted "or in a Pace program under section 1894" in (3)(B)(vi); and deleted "such plan" and inserted "such plan or such program" in (3)(B)(vi). These changes apply to terminations or discontinuances made on or after November 29, 1999. Finally, effective November 29, 1999, section 321(k)(14) of the Act inserted "section" after "as defined in" in subparagraph (s)(2)(D).

For regulatory citations, see Chapter 6

§ 2:54 SPECIAL OBLIGATIONS FOR ISSUERS OF MEDICARE SUPPLEMENTAL HEALTH INSURANCE POLICIES WHO PROVIDE BENEFITS THROUGH CONTRACTS WITH NETWORKS OF PROVIDERS (MEDICARE SELECT) — Section 1882(t)(2) [42 U.S.C.A. 1395ss(t)(2)]

Summary

◆ NOTE: P.L. 101-508, the Omnibus Budget Reconciliation Act of 1990 (OBRA 90), effective November 5, 1990, made substantial changes in the law applicable to Medicare supplemental health insurance policies. For a summary of the law and statutory provisions pre-OBRA 90, see former § 2:40.1 in Appendix H. For a more complete summary of the law and statutory provisions after OBRA 90, see § 2:45.

In section 1882(a), 42 U.S.C.A. 1395ss(a), Congress authorized the Secretary of Health and Human Services to certify that Medicare supplemental health insurance policies meet established standards for coverage and benefits. It also authorized the Secretary to permit approved entities to use a Secretarial emblem of certification in their marketing.

No Medicare supplemental policy may be issued in a State unless the State has a regulatory program which provides for application and enforcement of standards and requirements set forth in section 1882. Those must be standards of the National Association of Insurance Commissioners (NAIC) or Federal standards. If a State does not adopt such a program, Medicare supplemental policies may not be issued in that State unless the Secretary certifies the policy as meeting Federal standards. Pursuant to section 171(c)(1)(A) of the Social Security Act Amendments of 1994, P.L. 103-432, effective November 5, 1990, as if included in OBRA 90, the relevant standards are the 1991 NAIC Model Regulation or the 1991 Federal Regulation.

Pursuant to section 171(c)(1)(B) of the Social Security Act Amendments of 1994, the effective date of this requirement was the date the State adopted the 1991 NAIC Model Regulation or the date the 1991 Federal Regulation applies, as the case may be, or one year after the date the NAIC or the Secretary first adopted such standards, whichever is earlier. This applies effective November 5, 1990, as if included in OBRA 90.

The effective date depended on whether and when the NAIC produced "NAIC standards" for such policies. Section 1882(p)(1)(A) required NAIC to do so within nine months after enactment of OBRA 90, which ended August 5, 1991. Had the NAIC not met that requirement, the Secretary was obligated to produce "Federal standards" within a subsequent period of nine months, which ended May 5, 1992. Depending on which of those outcomes occurred, the effective date of this requirement would have been either the date the State adopted the NAIC or Federal standards or one year after the date NAIC or the Secretary first adopted such standards, whichever was earlier. The NAIC Model Regulation was timely adopted.

As enacted by section 4358(a) of OBRA 90, and amended by section 171(h)(1) of the Social Security Act Amendments of 1994, P.L. 103-432, effective October 31, 1994, section 1882(t) authorizes issuers of Medicare supplemental health insurance policies to issue a policy which restricts benefits to items and services furnished by certain entities or networks of entities, commonly referred to as preferred provider organizations (PPO's), or to reduce benefits when items or services are not obtained from those entities. This type of Medicare supplemental policy is known as Medicare SELECT. This authorization applied in 15 States, as determined by the Secretary, and only during a three-year period beginning 1992.

◆ NOTE: Originally, this authorization applied in 15 States, as determined by the Secretary, and only during a three-year period beginning 1992. The program was extended indefinitely and expanded to all states by P. L. 104–8, effective July 7, 1995.

Pursuant to section 1882(t), an issuer of a Medicare SELECT policy or plan must:

1. Provide full benefits through a network of providers with whom it has contracts or agreements.
2. Provide for items and services furnished by non-network providers in emergencies and when network providers cannot deliver medically necessary services.

3. Assure sufficient access to an appropriate array of health care providers.
4. Have arrangements for an ongoing quality assurance program for items and services furnished through the network.
5. Explain the restrictions on payment for services furnished by non-network providers, the availability of out-of-area coverage under the policy, and coverage for medical emergencies.
6. Obtain a written acknowledgement prior to enrollment from the enrollee that it has received such an explanation.
7. Offer a standard non-preferred provider plan as an alternative.

If the Secretary finds that an issuer of a policy approved under section 1882(t), fails substantially to provide medically necessary items and services to enrollees seeking such items and services through the issuer's network and the failure adversely affected or has substantial likelihood of adversely affecting an enrollee, or that the issuer imposes premiums on enrollees in excess of those approved by the State, or that an issuer acted to expel an enrollee for reasons other than nonpayment of premiums, or that an issuer does not provide the required explanation of benefits to enrollees or does not obtain their required acknowledgment of that explanation, the issuer is subject to a civil money penalty not to exceed $25,000 for each such violation. Enforcement proceedings for this civil money penalty are governed by section 1128A, 42 U.S.C.A. 1320a-7a, which authorizes civil money penalties for a variety of offenses.

Statutory Provisions

Section 4358(a) of P.L. 101-508, the Omnibus Budget Reconciliation Act of 1990 (OBRA 90) added subsection (t) to section 1882, applicable only in 15 States, as determined by the Secretary, and only during the 3-year period beginning 1992. As amended by section 171(h)(1) of the Social Security Act Amendments of 1994, effective October 31, 1994, section 1882(t) provides in pertinent part:

(1) If a medicare supplemental policy meets the 1991 NAIC Model Regulation or 1991 Federal Regulation and otherwise complies with the requirements of this section except that benefits under the policy are restricted to items and services furnished by certain entities (or reduced benefits are provided when items or services are furnished by other entities), the

policy shall nevertheless be treated as meeting those standards if—

(A) full benefits are provided for items and services furnished through a network of entities which have entered into contracts or agreements with the issuer of the policy;

(B) full benefits are provided for items and services furnished by other entities if the services are medically necessary and immediately required because of an unforeseen illness, injury, or condition and it is not reasonable given the circumstances to obtain the services through the network;

(C) the network offers sufficient access;

(D) the issuer of the policy has arrangements for an ongoing quality assurance program for items and services furnished through the network;

(E) (i) the issuer of the policy provides to each enrollee at the time of enrollment an explanation of (I) the restrictions on payment under the policy for services furnished other than by or through the network, (II) out of area coverage under the policy, (III) the policy's coverage of emergency services and urgently needed care, and (IV) the availability of a policy through the entity that meets the standards in the 1991 NAIC Model Regulation or 1991 Federal Regulation or other requirements of this section without reference to this subsection and the premium charged for such policy, and

(ii) each enrollee prior to enrollment acknowledges receipt of the explanation provided under clause (i); and

(F) the issuer of the policy makes available to individuals, in addition to the policy described in this subsection, any policy (otherwise offered by the issuer to individuals in the State) that meets the standards in the 1991 NAIC Model Regulation or 1991 Federal Regulation and other requirements of this section without reference to this subsection.

◆ NOTE: Section 171(h)(1) of the Social Security Act Amendments of 1994, added "medicare supplemental" before "policy", added "or agreements" after "contracts" and substituted "standards in the 1991 NAIC Model Regulation or 1991 Federal

Regulation" in section 1882(t)(1) where that phrase appears in (E) and (F) for "NAIC standards".

(2) If the Secretary determines that an issuer of a policy approved under paragraph (1)—

(A) fails substantially to provide medically necessary items and services to enrollees seeking such items and services through the issuer's network, if the failure has adversely affected (or has substantial likelihood of adversely affecting) the individual,

(B) imposes premiums on enrollees in excess of the premiums approved by the State,

(C) acts to expel an enrollee for reasons other than nonpayment of premiums, or

(D) does not provide the explanation required under paragraph (1)(E)(i) or does not obtain the acknowledgment required under paragraph (1)(E)(ii),

the issuer is subject to a civil money penalty in an amount not to exceed $25,000 for each such violation. The provisions of section 1128A [42 U.S.C.A. 1320a-7a] (other than the first sentence of subsection (a) and other than subsection (b)) shall apply to a civil money penalty under the previous sentence in the same manner as such provisions apply to a penalty or proceeding under section 1128A(a).

(3) The Secretary may enter into a contract with an entity whose policy has been certified under paragraph (1) or has been approved by a State under subsection (b)(1)(H) to determine whether items and services (furnished to individuals entitled to benefits under this title and under that policy) are not allowable under section 1862(a)(1) [42 U.S.C.A. 1395y(a)(1), which pertains to exclusions from coverage]. Payments to the entity shall be in such amounts as the Secretary may determine, taking into account estimated savings under contracts with carriers and fiscal intermediaries and other factors that the Secretary finds appropriate. Paragraph 1 [which pertains to carrier contracts], the first sentence of paragraph (2)(A) [which pertains to carrier performance requirements], paragraph (2)(B) [which pertains to standards for evaluating carriers' performance], paragraph (3)(C) [which pertains to carrier obligations for fair hearings], paragraph

(3)(D) [which pertains to carrier obligations to furnish timely information and reports to the Secretary], and paragraph (3)(E) [which pertains to carrier recordkeeping and access to records by the Secretary] of section 1842(b) [42 U.S.C.A. 1395u(b)] shall apply to the entity.

For regulatory citations, see Chapter 6

§ 2:55 TERMINATING PROVIDER AGREEMENTS OF HOSPITAL PROVIDERS OF EXTENDED CARE SERVICES — Section 1883 [42 U.S.C.A. 1395tt]

Summary

Section 1883, 42 U.S.C.A. 1395tt, permits rural hospitals which have less than 100 beds and certificates of need from their State health planning agency to provide long-term care services to obtain Medicare provider agreements to use their inpatient hospital facilities for skilled nursing care. Other hospitals, designated by the Secretary of Health and Human Services on a demonstration basis, can do so also. For those services they are paid on a cost-reimbursement basis, however, not on the basis of the diagnostic related group (DRG) prospective payment system (PPS) which applies to hospital services. These agreements for hospital-based skilled nursing facilities (SNF's) are governed, as are other SNF agreements, by section 1866, 42 U.S.C.A. 1395cc, and they are subject to the same termination provisions that apply to SNF's which are not hospital-based.

Statutory Provisions

Section 1883(a), 42 U.S.C.A. 1395tt(a), provides:

> (1) Any hospital which has an agreement under section 1866 [42 U.S.C.A. 1395cc, which pertains to provider agreements in general] may (subject to subsection (b)) enter into an agreement with the Secretary under which its inpatient hospital facilities may be used for the furnishing of services of the type which, if furnished by a skilled nursing facility, would constitute extended care services.

◆ NOTE: Section 403(f)(1) of the Medicare, Medicaid, and SCHIP Balanced Budget Refinement Act of 1999, as incorporated into the Omnibus Consolidated Appropriations Act, 2000,

P.L. 106–113, enacted November 17, 1999, struck from section 1883(a)(1) the phrase "(other than a hospital which has in effect a waiver under subparagraph (A) of the last sentence of section 1861(e) [42 U.S.C.A.1395x(e)(A), which, within the definition of hospital, permits waiver of the requirement for 24-hour registered professional nurse services for certain rural hospitals] ". This change was made effective August 5, 1997.

(2) (A) Notwithstanding any other provision of this title, payment to any hospital (other than a critical access hospital) for services furnished under an agreement entered into under this section shall be based upon the reasonable cost of the services as determined under subparagraph (B).

◆ [NOTE: The exception for critical access hospitals in paragraph (2)(A) was added by section 203(b)of the Medicare, Medicaid, and SCHIP Benefits Improvement Act of 2000, P.L. 106–554. It is applicable to cost reporting periods beginning on or after December 21, 2000. The same enactment added paragraph (3) below.]

(B) (i) The reasonable cost of the services consists of the reasonable cost of routine services (determined under clause (ii)) and the reasonable cost of ancillary services (determined under clause (iii)).

(ii) The reasonable cost of routine services furnished during any calendar year by a hospital under an agreement under this section is equal to the product of—

(I) the number of patient-days during the year for which the services were furnished, and

(II) the average reasonable cost per patient-day, such average reasonable cost per patient-day being the average rate per patient-day paid for routine services during the most recent year for which cost reporting data are available with respect to such services (increased in a compounded manner by the applicable increase for payments for routine service costs of skilled nursing facilities undersubsections (a) through (d) of section 1888 [42 U.S.C.A. 1395yy] for subsequent cost reporting periods and up to and including such calendar year) under this title to freestanding nursing facilities in the region (as defined in section 1866(d)(2)(D) [42 U.S.C.A. 1395cc(d)(2)(D)] in which the facility is located.

(iii) the reasonable cost of ancillary services shall be determined in the same manner as the reasonable cost of ancillary services provided for inpatient hospital services.

3 Notwithstanding any other provision of this title, a critical access hospital shall be paid for covered skilled nursing facility services furnished under an agreement entered into under this section on the basis of the reasonable costs of such services (as determined under section 1861(v) [42 U.S.C. 1395x(v), which defines reasonable cost)].

◆ NOTE: The phrase above beginning "during the most recent year" was added by sections 4008(j)(1), (2), and (3) of P.L. 101-508, the Omnibus Budget Reconciliation Act of 1990 (OBRA 90), applicable to services furnished after September 1990. Prior to amendment, the phrase read "during the previous calendar year under the State plan (of the State in which the hospital is located) under title XIX [Medicaid] to skilled nursing facilities located in the State and which meet the requirements specified in section 1902(a)(28) [42 U.S.C.A. 1396a(a)(28), which pertains to the State Medicaid plan requirements for standards of and payment for nursing facility services], or, in the case of a hospital located in a State which does not have such a State plan, the average rate per patient-day paid for routine services during the previous calendar year under this title to skilled nursing facilities in such State." Section 4432(b)(5)(G) of the Balanced Budget Act of 1997 inserted "subsections (a) through (d) of" before "section 1888" in subclause (a)(2)(B)(ii)(II). That change applies to items and services furnished on or after July 1, 1998.

(iii) The reasonable cost of ancillary services shall be determined in the same manner as the reasonable cost of ancillary services provided for inpatient hospital services.

Section 1883(b) provides:

The Secretary may not enter into an agreement under this section with any hospital, except as provided under subsection (g), unless the hospital is located in a rural area and has less than 100 beds.

◆ NOTE: Prior to amendment by section 408(a) of the Medicare, Medicaid, and SCHIP Balanced Budget Refinement Act of 1999, as incorporated into the Omnibus Consolidated Appropriations Act, 2000, subsection (b) read: "The Secretary may not enter into an agreement with any hospital unless — (1) except as provided under subsection (g), the hospital is located in a rural area and has less than 100 beds, and (2) the hospital has been granted a certificate of need for the provision of long-term care services from the State health planning and development agency (designated under section 1521 of the Public Health Service Act) for the State in which the hospital is located." This change was made effective on the date that is the first day after the expiration of the transition period under section 1888(e)(2)(E) of the Social Security Act, 42 U.S.C.A. 1395yy(e)(2)(E)) for payments for covered skilled nursing facility services under the Medicare program.

Section 1883(c) provides:

> An agreement with a hospital under this section shall, except as otherwise provided under regulations of the Secretary, be of the same duration and subject to termination on the same conditions as are agreements with skilled nursing facilities under section 1866 and shall, where not inconsistent with any provision of this section, impose the same duties, responsibilities, conditions, and limitations, as those imposed under such agreements entered into under section 1866; except that no such agreement with any hospital shall be in effect for any period during which the hospital does not have in effect an agreement under section 1866, and shall, where not inconsistent with any provision of this section, impose the same duties, responsibilities, conditions, and limitations, as those imposed under such agreements entered into under section 1866; except that no such agreement with any hospital shall be in effect for any period during which the hospital does not have in effect an agreement under section 1866. A hospital with respect to which an agreement under this section has been terminated shall not be eligible to enter into a new agreement until a two-year period has elapsed from the termination date.

◆ NOTE: Section 408(a) of the Medicare, Medicaid, and SCHIP Balanced Budget Refinement Act of 1999 deleted after "agreement under section 1866" the phrase "or during which there is in effect for the hospital a waiver under subparagraph (A) of the last sentence of section 1861(e)". That change was made effective August 5, 1997.

The remainder of section 1883 provides as follows:

(d) Any agreement with a hospital under this section shall provide that payment for services will be made only for services for which payment would be made as post-hospital extended care services if those services had been furnished by a skilled nursing facility under an agreement entered into under section 1866; and any individual who is furnished services, for which payment may be made under an agreement under this section, shall, for purposes of this title (other than this section), be deemed to have received post-hospital extended care services in like manner and to the same extent as if the services furnished to him had been post-hospital extended care services furnished by a skilled nursing facility under an agreement under section 1866.

◆ NOTE: Section 408(b)(2) of the Medicare, Medicaid, and SCHIP Balanced Budget Refinement Act of 1999, amended subsection (d) by removing "(d)(1)" and inserting "(d)". Also, section 408(b)(1) of that Act removed former paragraphs (2) and (3), which read:

(2)(A) Any agreement under this section with a hospital with more than 49 beds shall provide that no payment may be made for extended care services which are furnished to an extended care patient after the end of the 5-day period (excluding weekends and holidays) beginning on an availability date for a skilled nursing facility, unless the patient' s physician certifies, within such 5-day period, that the transfer of that patient to that facility is not medically appropriate on the availability date. The Secretary shall prescribe regulations to provide for notice by skilled nursing facilities of availability dates to hospitals which have agreements under this section and which are located within the same geographic region (as defined by the Secretary).

(B) In this paragraph:

(i) The term "availability date" means, with respect to an extended care patient at a hospital, any date on which a bed is available for the patient in a skilled nursing facility located within the geographic region in which the hospital is located.

(ii) The term "extended care patient" means an individual being furnished extended care services at a hospital pursuant to an agreement with the Secretary under this section.

(3) In the case of an agreement for a cost reporting period under this section with a hospital that has more than 49 beds, payment may not be made in the period for patient-days of extended care services that exceed 15 percent of the product of the number of days in the period and the average number of licensed beds in the hospital in the period, except that such payment shall continue to be made in the period for those patients who are receiving extended care services at the time the hospital reaches the limit specified in this paragraph.

(e) During a period for which a hospital has in effect an agreement under this section, in order to allocate routine costs between hospital and long-term care services for purposes of determining payment for inpatient hospital services, the total reimbursement due for routine services from all classes of long-term care patients (including title XVIII, title XIX, and private pay patients) shall be subtracted from the hospital's total routine costs before calculations are made to determine title XVIII reimbursement for routine hospital services.

(f) A hospital which enters into an agreement with the Secretary under this section shall be required to meet those conditions applicable to skilled nursing facilities relating to discharge planning and the social services function (and staffing requirements to satisfy it) which are promulgated by the Secretary under section 1819 [42 U.S.C.A. 1395i-3] . Services furnished by such a hospital which would otherwise constitute post-hospital extended care services if furnished by a skilled nursing facility shall be subject to the same requirements applicable to such services when furnished by a skilled nursing facility except for those requirements the Secretary determines are inappropriate in the case of these services being furnished by a hospital under this section.

(g) The Secretary may enter into an agreement under this section on a demonstration basis with any hospital which does not meet the requirement of subsection (b)(1), if the hospital otherwise meets the requirements of this section.

◆ NOTE: Effective January 1, 1990, section 101(a)(1) of P.L. 101-234, the Medicare Catastrophic Coverage Repeal Act of 1989, added "post-hospital" in section 1883(f) and each place it appears in section 1883(d)(1).

For regulatory citations, see Chapter 6

§ 2:56 WITHHOLDING MEDICARE PAYMENTS FROM OVERPAID MEDICAID PROVIDERS — Section 1885 [42 U.S.C.A. 1395vv]

Summary

If a Medicaid provider has been overpaid and the Medicaid State agency has been unable to recover the overpayment, or if the Medicaid State agency has been unable to collect information necessary to determine the amount (if any) of the overpayment, the Secretary of Health and Human Services, pursuant to section 1885, 42 U.S.C.A. 1395vv, may adjust payments under Part A and Part B of Medicare to any institution with a provider agreement under section 1866, 42 U.S.C.A.1395ww. He may do the same with any person that has accepted Medicare payment on the basis of assigned claims as authorized by section 1842(b)(3)(B)(ii) [42 U.S.C.A. 1395u(b)(3)(B)(ii)].

Congress thus provided a Medicare offset against actual or suspected Medicaid overpayments.

Statutory Provisions

Section 1885, 42 U.S.C.A. 1395vv, provides:

(a) The Secretary may adjust, in accordance with this section, payments under parts A and B to any institution which has in effect an agreement with the Secretary under section 1866 [42 U.S.C.A. 1395ww], and any person who has accepted payment on the basis of an assignment under section 1842(b)(3)(B)(ii) [42 U.S.C.A. 1395u(b)(3)(B)(ii), which pertains to carriers making payments to those who furnish items or services covered by Medicare on the basis of assigned claims], where such institution or person —

(1) has (or previously had) in effect an agreement with a State agency to furnish medical care and services under a State plan approved under title XIX [Medicaid], and

(2) from which (or from whom) such State agency (A) has been unable to recover overpayments made under the State plan, or (B) has been unable to collect the information necessary to enable it to determine the amount (if any) of the overpay-

ments made to such institution or person under the State plan.

(b) The Secretary shall by regulation provide procedures for implementation of this section, which procedures shall —

(1) assure that the authority under this section is exercised only on behalf of a state agency which demonstrates to the Secretary's satisfaction that it has provided adequate notice of a determination or of a need for information, and an opportunity to appeal such determination or to provide such information,

(2) determine the amount of the payment to which the institution or person would otherwise be entitled under this title which shall be treated as a setoff against overpayments under title XIX, and

(3) assure the restoration to the institution or person of amounts withheld under this section which are ultimately determined to be in excess of overpayments under title XIX and to which the institution or person would otherwise be entitled under this title.

(c) Notwithstanding any other provision of this Act, from the trust funds established under sections 1817 and 1841 [42 U.S.C.A. 1395i and 42 U.S.C.A. 1395t], as appropriate, the Secretary shall pay to the appropriate State agency amounts recovered under this section to offset the State agency's overpayment under title XIX. Such payments shall be accounted for by the State agency as recoveries of overpayments under the State plan.

For regulatory citations, see Chapter 6

§ 2:57 DISCONTINUING AND REDUCING PAYMENTS TO HOSPITALS FOR INPATIENT HOSPITAL SERVICES IN STATES WHICH HAVE ALTERNATIVE (NON-FEDERAL DRG) HOSPITAL REIMBURSEMENT SYSTEMS — Section 1886(c) [42 U.S.C.A. 1395ww(c)]

Summary

After many years of cost reimbursement with retrospective adjustments, Congress established, via section 1886(d), 42 U.S.C.A.

1395ww(d), the prospective payment system (PPS) based upon diagnosis-related groups (DRG's) to determine Medicare reimbursement for inpatient hospital services. Most hospitals are governed by that system.

Pursuant to section 1886(c), however, States may establish alternative reimbursement systems — even ones which do not rely on diagnosis-related groups. If a State applies to establish an alternative system which meets statutory requirements, the Secretary of Health and Human Services must approve the application. But if the State system subsequently fails to meet statutory requirements, the Secretary may discontinue payments under that system.

Furthermore, if the required State assurances (that under the State system over 36 months the amount of payments made will not exceed what would otherwise have been paid under Medicare) have not been met, the Secretary may reduce payments to hospitals to what Medicare would have been paid for that period.

Statutory Provisions

Section 1866(c), 42 U.S.C.A. 1395ww(c), provides:

> (1) The Secretary may provide, in his discretion, that payment with respect to services provided by a hospital in a State may be made in accordance with a hospital reimbursement control system in a State, rather than in accordance with the other provisions of this title, if the chief executive officer of the State requests such treatment and if—
>
> (A) the Secretary determines that the system, if approved under this subsection, will apply (i) to substantially all non-Federal acute care hospitals (as defined by the Secretary) in the State and (ii) to the review of at least 75 percent of all revenues or expenses in the State for inpatient hospital services and of revenues or expenses for inpatient hospital services provided under the State's plan approved under title XIX;
>
> (B) the Secretary has been provided satisfactory assurances as to the equitable treatment under the system of all entities (including Federal and State programs) that pay hospitals for inpatient hospital services, of hospital employees, and of hospital patients;
>
> (C) the Secretary has been provided satisfactory assurances that under the system, over 36-month periods (the first

such period beginning with the first month in which this subsection applies to that system in the State), the amount of payments made under this title under such system will not exceed the amount of payments which would otherwise have been made under this title not using such system;

(D) the Secretary determines that the system will not preclude an eligible organization (as defined in section 1876(b) [42 U.S.C.A. 1395mm(b), which pertains to health maintenance organizations (HMO's) and competitive medical plans (CMP's)]) from negotiating directly with hospitals with respect to the organization's rate of payment for inpatient hospital services; and

(E) the Secretary determines that the system requires hospitals to meet the requirement of section 1866(a)(1)(G) [42 U.S.C.A. 1395cc(a)(1)(G), which pertains to the provider agreement requirement not to charge beneficiaries more than what Medicare pays (except for applicable deductibles and co-insurance)] and the system provides for the exclusion of certain costs in accordance with section 1862(a)(14) [42 U.S.C.A. 1395y(a)(14), which pertains to excluding from coverage charges by a hospital for items or services which are furnished by entities other than the hospital and other than physician services or services of a certified registered nurse anesthetist (CRNA)] (except for such waivers thereof as the Secretary provides by regulation).

The Secretary cannot deny the application of a State under this subsection on the ground that the State's hospital reimbursement control system is based on a payment methodology other than on the basis of a diagnosis-related group or on the ground that the amount of payments made under this title under such system must be less than the amount of payments which would otherwise have been made under this title not using such system. If the Secretary determines that the conditions described in subparagraph (C) are based on maintaining payment amounts at no more than a specified percentage increase above the payment amounts in a base period, the State has the option of applying such test (for inpatient hospital services under part A) on an aggregate payment basis or on the basis of the amount of payment per inpatient discharge or admission. If the Secretary determines that the conditions described in subparagraph (C) are based on maintaining aggregate payment amounts below a national average percentage increase in total payments under part A for inpatient hospital services, the Secretary cannot deny the application of a State under this subsection on the ground that the State's rate of increase in such payments for such services must be less than such national average rate of increase.

(2) In determining under paragraph (1)(C) the amount of payment which would otherwise have been made under this title for a State, the Secretary may provide for appropriate adjustment of such amount to take into account previous reductions effected in the amount of payments made under this title in the State due to the operation of the hospital reimbursement control system in the State if the system has resulted in an aggregate rate of increase in operating costs of inpatient hospital services (as defined in subsection (a)(4)) under this title for hospitals in the State which is less than the aggregate rate of increase in such costs under this title for hospitals in the United States.

(3) The Secretary shall discontinue payments under a system described in paragraph (1) if the Secretary—

(A) determines that the system no longer meets the requirements of subparagraphs (A), (D), and (E) of paragraph (1) and, if applicable, the requirements of paragraph (5), or

(B) has reason to believe that the assurances described in subparagraph (B) or (C) of paragraph (1) (or, if applicable, in paragraph (5)) are not being (or will not be) met.

(4) The Secretary shall approve the request of a State under paragraph (1) with respect to a hospital reimbursement control system if—

(A) the requirements of subparagraphs (A), (B), (C), (D), and (E) of paragraph (1) have been met with respect to the system, and (B) with respect to that system a waiver of certain requirements of title XVIII of the Social Security Act has been approved on or before (and which is in effect as of) the date of the enactment of the Social Security Amendments of 1983, pursuant to section 402(a) of the Social Security Amendments of 1967 [P.L. 90-248] or section

222(a) of the Social Security Amendments of 1972 [P.L. 92-603].

With respect to a State system described in this paragraph, the Secretary shall judge the effectiveness of such system on the basis of its rate of increase or inflation in inpatient hospital payments for individuals under this title, as compared to the national rate of increase or inflation for such payments, with the State retaining the option to have the test applied on the basis of the aggregate payments under the State system as compared to aggregate payments which would have been made under the national system since October 1, 1984, to the most recent date for which annual data are available.

◆ NOTE: Prior to amendment by section 4008(f) of P.L. 101-508, the Omnibus Budget Reconciliation Act of 1990 (OBRA 90), effective December 19, 1989, as if included in P. L. 101-239, the Omnibus Budget Reconciliation Act of 1989 (OBRA 89), the phrase beginning "on the basis of the aggregate" previously read "on the basis of the aggregate rate of increase from October 1, 1984, to the most recent date for which annual data are available." Prior to amendment by section 6022 of OBRA 89, the preceding paragraph read:

With respect to a State system described in this paragraph, the Secretary shall judge the effectiveness of such system on the basis of its rate of increase or inflation in inpatient hospital payments for individuals under this title, as compared to the national rate of increase or inflation for such payments, with the State retaining the option to have the test applied on the basis of the aggregate payment or payments per inpatient admission or discharge during the three cost reporting periods beginning on or after October 1, 1983, after which such test, at the option of the Secretary, shall no longer apply, and such State systems shall be treated in the same manner as under other waivers.

(5) The Secretary shall approve the request of a State under paragraph (1) with respect to a hospital reimbursement control system if—

(A) the requirements of subparagraphs (A), (B), (C), (D), and (E) of paragraph (1) have been met with respect to the system;

(B) the Secretary determines that the system—

(i) is operated directly by the State or by an entity designated pursuant to State law,

(ii) provides for payment of hospitals covered under the system under a methodology (which sets forth exceptions and adjustments, as well as any method for changes in the methodology) by which rates or amounts to be paid for hospital services during a specified period are established under the system prior to the defined rate period, and

(iii) hospitals covered under the system will make such reports (in lieu of cost and other reports, identified by the Secretary, otherwise required under this title) as the Secretary may require in order to properly monitor assurances provided under this subsection;

(C) the State has provided the Secretary with satisfactory assurances that operation of the system will not result in any change in hospital admission practices which result in —

(i) a significant reduction in the proportion of patients (receiving hospital services covered under the system) who have no third-party coverage and who are unable to pay for hospital services,

(ii) a significant reduction in the proportion of individuals admitted to hospitals for inpatient hospital services for which payment is (or is likely to be) less than the anticipated charges for or costs of such services,

(iii) the refusal to admit patients who would be expected to require unusually costly or prolonged treatment for reasons other than those related to the appropriateness of the care available at the hospital, or

(iv) the refusal to provide emergency services to any person who is in need of emergency services if the hospital provides such services;

(D) any change by the State in the system which has the effect of materially reducing payments to hospitals can only take effect upon 60 days notice to the Secretary and to the hospitals the payment to which is likely to be materially affected by the change; and

(E) the State has provided the Secretary with satisfactory assurances that in the development of the system the State has consulted with local governmental officials concerning the impact of the system on public hospitals.

The Secretary shall respond to requests of States under this paragraph within 60 days of the date the request is submitted to the Secretary.

(6) If the Secretary determines that the assurances described in paragraph (1)(C) have not been met with respect to any 36-month period, the Secretary may reduce payments under this title to hospitals under the system in an amount equal to the amount by which the payment under this title under such system for such period exceeded the amount of payments which would otherwise have been made under this title not using such system.

(7) In the case of a State which made a request under paragraph (5) before December 31, 1984, for the approval of a State hospital reimbursement control system and which request was approved —

(A) in applying paragraphs (1)(C) and (6), a reference to a "36-month period" is deemed a reference to a "48-month period", and

(B) in order to allow the State the opportunity to provide the assurances described in paragraph (1)(C) for a 48-month period, the Secretary may not discontinue payments under the system, under the authority of paragraph (3)(A) because the Secretary has reason to believe that such assurances are not being (or will not be) met, before July 1, 1986.

For regulatory citations, see Chapter 6

§ 2:58 UNNECESSARY HOSPITAL ADMISSIONS AND OTHER INAPPROPRIATE PRACTICES BY HOSPITALS TO CIRCUMVENT REIMBURSEMENT REQUIREMENTS — Section 1886(f) [42 U.S.C.A. 1395ww(f)]

Summary

After many years of cost reimbursement with retrospective adjustments, Congress established, via section 1886(d), 42 U.S.C.A.

1395ww(d), the prospective payment system (PPS) based upon diagnosis-related groups (DRG's) to determine Medicare reimbursement for inpatient hospital services. Most hospitals are governed by that system.

One way to subvert DRG methodology would be to have as many hospital admissions as a hospital might obtain, whether or not patients required hospitalization. Another way would be for a hospital to repeatedly admit and discharge the same patient inappropriately. Other practices also might be devised.

To preclude such abuse, section 1886(f), 42 U.S.C.A. 1395ww(f), provides that if the Secretary of Health and Human Services determines, based upon information supplied by a utilization and quality control peer review organization (PRO) under part B of Title XI, 42 U.S.C.A. 1320c—

1. that a hospital has admitted beneficiaries unnecessarily, or
2. has made unnecessary multiple admissions, or
3. has engaged in any other inappropriate medical or other practice with respect to such individuals to circumvent the payment method established under section 1886(b), which pertains to reimbursement based on target amounts for operating costs vis-a-vis the defined market basket percentage increase for hospitals not subject to PPS and DRG's, or under section 1886(d), which pertains to reimbursing hospitals subject to PPS and DRG's, the Secretary may deny payment in whole or in part under Part A with respect to inpatient hospital services related to an unnecessary admission or subsequent admission of the same individual. Alternatively, he may require the hospital to take other corrective action to prevent or correct the inappropriate practice.

Procedural matters for these sanctions are governed by subsections (c) through (g) of section 1128, 42 U.S.C.A. 1320a-7(c) through (g), which pertain to requirements for notice, effective date, and period of an exclusion from Medicare and Medicaid, notice to State agencies and exclusion under State health care programs, notice to State licensing agencies, notice and opportunity for hearings and judicial review, and the application process for termination of an exclusion.

In addition, pursuant to section 1128(b)(13), 42 U.S.C.A. 1320a-7(b)(13), hospitals which fail to comply or fail to take required corrective actions are subject to exclusion from Medicare, Medicaid, and any State health care programs funded under the Maternal and Child Health Services Block Grant program (see Title V of the Social Security Act, 42 U.S.C.A. 701 et seq.), or under the program of Block Grants to States for Social Services (see Title XX of the Act, 42 U.S.C.A. 1397 et seq.).

Statutory Provisions

Section 1886(f), 42 U.S.C.A. 1395ww(f), provides:

(1) (A) The Secretary shall maintain a system for the reporting of costs of hospitals receiving payments computed under subsection (d) [which pertains to reimbursing hospitals under PPS and DRG's].

(B) (i) Subject to clause (ii), the Secretary shall place into effect a standardized electronic cost reporting format for hospitals under this title.

(ii) The Secretary may delay or waive the implementation of such format in particular instances where such implementation would result in financial hardship (in particular with respect to hospitals with a small percentage of inpatients entitled to benefits under this title.)

(2) If the Secretary determines, based upon information supplied by a utilization and quality control peer review organization under part B of title XI [42 U.S.C.A. 1320c], that a hospital, in order to circumvent the payment method established under subsection (b) [42 U.S.C.A. 1395ww(b), which pertains to reimbursement based on target amounts for operating costs vis-a-vis the defined market basket percentage increase for hospitals not subject to PPS and DRG's] or (d) of this section, has taken an action that results in the admission of individuals entitled to benefits under part A unnecessarily, unnecessary multiple admissions of the same such individuals, or other inappropriate medical or other practices with respect to such individuals, the Secretary may —

(A) deny payment (in whole or in part) under part A with respect to inpatient hospital services provided with respect to such an unnecessary admission (or subsequent admission of the same individual), or

(B) require the hospital to take other corrective action necessary to prevent or correct the inappropriate practice.

(3) The provisions of subsection (c) through (g) of section 1128 [42 U.S.C.A. 1320a-7, which pertain to requirements for notice, effective date, and period of an exclusion from Medicare and Medicaid, notice to State agencies and exclusion under State health care programs, notice to State licensing agencies, notice and opportunity for hearings and judicial review, and the application process for termination of an exclusion] shall apply to determinations made under paragraph (2) in the same manner as they apply to exclusions effected under section 1128(b)(13) [which authorizes excluding hospitals from Medicare and Medicaid if they fail to comply with required a corrective action under section 1886(f)(2)(B)].

Finally, section 1128(b) provides in pertinent part:

PERMISSIVE EXCLUSION. — The Secretary may exclude the following individuals and entities from participation in any program under title XVIII and may direct that the following individuals and entities be excluded from participation in any State health care program:

* * *

(13) FAILURE TO TAKE CORRECTIVE ACTION. — Any hospital that fails to comply substantially with a corrective action required under section 1886(f)(2)(B).

For regulatory citations, see Chapter 6

§ 2:59 GIVING A HOME HEALTH AGENCY ADVANCE NOTICE OF A STANDARD SURVEY — Section 1891(c)(1) [42 U.S.C.A. 1395bbb(c)(1)]

Summary

Section 1891(a), 42 U.S.C.A. 1395bbb(a), sets forth conditions for home health agencies (HHA's) to participate in Medicare. Section 1861(o), 42 U.S.C.A. 1395x(o), establishes their definition requirements. Some conditions and requirements became applicable June 1, 1989. Others apply thereafter, as specified. See, for example, a new requirement to maintain written policies and procedures with regard to advance directives, applicable to services furnished after December 1, 1991, pursuant to section 4206(d)(2) of P.L. 101-508, the

Omnibus Budget Reconciliation Act of 1990 (OBRA 90): section 1866(f), 42 U.S.C.A. 1395cc(f).

In general, HHA conditions and requirements pertain to patient's rights; ownership and control issues; standards for home health aides (including training and competency evaluation by January 1, 1990, for aides used by an HHA as of July 1, 1989); and quality of care standards, such as plans of care for patients and compliance with professional standards and applicable laws.

Section 1891(b) declares the duty and responsibility of the Secretary of Health and Human Services to assure that the conditions specified in section 1891(a) and the requirements of section 1861(o) are met.

Section 1891(c) provides that agreements which the Secretary enters into with State agencies pursuant to section 1864, 42 U.S.C.A. 1395aa, authorizing them to determine compliance by providers of services with Medicare conditions of participation, must permit appropriate State or local agencies to conduct, without any prior notice, standard surveys of home health agencies. Those surveys are to be based on a protocol the Secretary was obliged to develop, test, and validate not later than January 1, 1989. Moreover, they must be conducted by individuals who meet minimum qualifications which the Secretary was obliged to establish not later than July 1, 1989. Those individuals must have no financial or familial conflict of interests with the HHA, and they must not be serving as a member of the HHA staff or as a consultant to the HHA. Nor may they have served as either within two years prior to the survey.

To protect the integrity of surprise standard surveys, section 1891(c)(1) provides that any individual who notifies or causes to be notified a home health agency of the time or date on which such a survey is scheduled to be conducted is subject to a civil money penalty not to exceed $2,000.

Enforcement procedures for this civil money penalty are governed by section 1128A, 42 U.S.C.A. 1320a-7a, which authorizes civil money penalties for a variety of offenses.

Statutory Provisions

Section 1861(o), 42 U.S.C.A. 1395x(o), provides:

> The term "home health agency" means a public agency or private organization, or a subdivision of such an agency or organization, which —

(1) is primarily engaged in providing skilled nursing services and other therapeutic services;

(2) has policies, established by a group of professional personnel (associated with the agency or organization), including one or more physicians and one or more registered professional nurses, to govern the services (referred to in paragraph (1)) which it provides, and provides for supervision of such services by a physician or registered professional nurse;

(3) maintains clinical records on all patients;

(4) in the case of an agency or organization in any State in which State or applicable local law provides for the licensing of agencies or organizations of this nature, (A) is licensed pursuant to such law, or (B) is approved, by the agency of such State or locality responsible for licensing agencies or organizations of this nature, as meeting the standards established for such licensing;

(5) has in effect an overall plan and budget that meets the requirements of subsection (z) [which pertains to institutional planning requirements for hospitals, skilled nursing facilities, comprehensive outpatient rehabilitation facilities, and home health agencies];

(6) meets the conditions of participation specified in section 1891(a) and such other conditions of participation as the Secretary may find necessary in the interest of the health and safety of individuals who are furnished services by such agency or organization;

(7) provides the Secretary on a continuing basis with a surety bond in a form specified by the Secretary and in an amount that is not less than $50,000; and

(8) meets such additional requirements (including conditions relating to bonding or establishing of escrow accounts as the Secretary finds necessary for the financial security of the program) as the Secretary finds necessary for the effective and efficient operation of the program; except that for purposes of part A such term shall not include any agency or organization which is primarily for the care and treatment of mental diseases. The Secretary may waive the requirement of a surety bond under paragraph (7) in the case of an agency or organization that provides a comparable surety bond under State law.

◆ NOTE: Section 4312(b)(1) of the Balanced Budget Act of 1997, P.L. 105–33, deleted "and" from the end of paragraph (6), redesignated former paragraph (7) as paragraph (8), and added new paragraph (7) pertaining to the surety bond requirement. It also added the last sentence of paragraph (8). These changes apply to services furnished on or after January 1, 1998.

Section 1891(a) provides:

The conditions of participation that a home health agency is required to meet under this subsection are as follows:

(1) The agency protects and promotes the rights of each individual under its care, including each of the following rights:

(A) The right to be fully informed in advance about the care and treatment to be provided by the agency, to be fully informed in advance of any changes in the care or treatment to be provided by the agency that may affect the individual's well-being, and (except with respect to an individual adjudged incompetent) to participate in planning care and treatment or changes in care or treatment.

(B) The right to voice grievances with respect to treatment or care that is (or fails to be) furnished without discrimination or reprisal for voicing grievances.

(C) The right to confidentiality of the clinical records described in section 1861(o)(3).

(D) The right to have one's property treated with respect.

(E) The right to be fully informed orally and in writing (in advance of coming under the care of the agency) of—

(i) all items and services furnished by (or under arrangements with) the agency for which payment may be made under this title,

(ii) the coverage available for such items and services under this title, title XIX, and any other Federal program of which the agency is reasonably aware,

(iii) any charges for items and services not covered under this title and any charges the individual may have to pay with respect to items and services furnished by (or under arrangements with) the agency, and

(iv) any changes in the charges or items and services described in clause (i), (ii), or (iii).

(F) The right to be fully informed in writing (in advance of coming under the care of the agency) of the individual's rights and obligations under this title.

(G) The right to be informed of the availability of the State home health agency hot-line established under section 1864(a) [42 U.S.C.A. 1395aa(a)].

(2) The agency notifies the State entity responsible for the licensing or certification of the agency of a change in—

(A) the persons with an ownership or control interest (as defined in section 1124(a)(3) [42 U.S.C.A. 1320a-3(a)(3), which pertains to disclosure of ownership and related information pertaining to entities participating in Medicare, Medicare, or the Federally-funded Maternal and Child Health programs authorized by Title V of the Social Security Act, 42 U.S.C.A. 701et seq.]) in the agency,

(B) the persons who are officers, directors, agents, or managing employees (as defined in section 1126(b) [42 U.S.C.A. 1320a-5(b), which pertains to disclosure by institutions, organizations, and agencies of owners and certain other individuals who have been convicted of various crimes or who have committed other offenses punishable under section 1128, 42 U.S.C.A. 1320a-7]) of the agency, and

(C) the corporation, association, or other company responsible for the management of the agency.

Such notice shall be given at the time of the change and shall include the identity of each new person or company described in the previous sentence.

(3) (A) The agency must not use as a home health aide (on a full-time, temporary, per diem, or other basis), any individual to provide items or services described in section 1861(m) [42 U.S.C.A. 1395x(m), which defines home health services] on or after January 1, 1990, unless the individual—

(i) has completed a training and competency evaluation program, or a competency evaluation program, that meets the minimum standards established by the Secretary under subparagraph (D), and

(ii) is competent to provide such items and services.

For purposes of clause (i), an individual is not considered to have completed a training and competency evaluation program, or a competency evaluation program if, since the individual's most recent completion of such a program, there has been a continuous period of 24 consecutive months during none of which the individual provided items and services described in section 1861(m) for compensation.

(B) (i) The agency must provide, with respect to individuals used as a home health aide by the agency as of July 1, 1989, for a competency evaluation program (as described in subparagraph (A)(i)) and such preparation as may be necessary for the individual to complete such a program by January 1, 1990.

(ii) The agency must provide such regular performance review and regular in-service education as assures that individuals used to provide items and services described in section 1861(m) are competent to provide those items and services.

(C) The agency must not permit an individual, other than in a training and competency evaluation program that meets the minimum standards established by the Secretary under subparagraph (D), to provide items or services of a type for which the individual has not demonstrated competency.

(B) (i) The Secretary shall establish minimum standards for the programs described in subparagraph (A) by not later than October 1, 1988.

(ii) Such standards shall include the content of the curriculum, minimum hours of training, qualification of instructors, and procedures for determination of competency.

(iii) Such standards may permit approval of programs offered by or in home health agencies, as well as outside agencies (including employee organizations), and of programs in effect on the date of the enactment of this section [December 22, 1987; P.L. 100-203] , except that they may not provide for the approval of a program offered by or in a home health agency which, within the previous 2 years —

(I) has been determined to be out of compliance with subparagraph (A), (B), or (C);

(II) has been subject to an extended (or partial extended) survey under subsection (c)(2)(D);

(III) has been assessed a civil money penalty described in subsection (f)(2)(A)(i) of not less than $5,000; or

(IV) has been subject to the remedies described in subsection (e)(1) or in clauses (ii) or (iii) of subsection (f)(2)(A).

◆ NOTE: Previously, the phrase beginning "home health agency which, within the previous 2 years" read "home health agency which has been determined to be out of compliance with the requirements specified in or pursuant to section 1861(o) or subsection (a) within the previous 2 years." The language above was added by section 4207(i)(1) of P.L. 101-508, the Omnibus Budget Reconciliation Act of 1990 (OBRA 90), effective December 22, 1987, as if included in OBRA 87.

(iv) Such standards shall permit a determination that an individual who has completed (before July 1, 1989) a training and competency evaluation program or a competency evaluation program shall be deemed for purposes of subparagraph (A) to have completed a program that is approved by the Secretary under the standards established under this subparagraph if the Secretary determines that, at the time the program was offered, the program met such standards.

(E) In this paragraph, the term "home health aide" means any individual who provides the items and services described in section 1861(m), but does not include an individual —

(i) who is a licensed health professional (as defined in subparagraph (F)), or

(ii) who volunteers to provide such services without monetary compensation.

(F) In this paragraph, the term "licensed health professional" means a physician, physician assistant, nurse practitioner, physical, speech, or occupational therapist, physical or occupational therapy assistant, registered professional nurse, licensed practical nurse, or licensed or certified social worker.

(4) The agency includes an individual's plan of care required under section 1861(m) as part of the clinical records described in section 1861(o)(3).

(5) The agency operates and provides services in compliance with all applicable Federal, State, and local laws and regulation (including the requirements of section 1124) and with accepted professional standards and principles which apply to professionals providing items and services in such an agency.

(6) [Applicable to services furnished on or after December 1, 1991, pursuant to section 4206(d)(2) of OBRA 90] The agency complies with the requirement of section 1866(f) [42 U.S.C.A. 1395cc(f)] (relating to maintaining written policies and procedures respecting advance directives).

Section 1891(b) provides:

It is the duty and responsibility of the Secretary to assure that the conditions of participation and requirements specified in or pursuant to section 1861(o) and subsection (a) of this section and the enforcement of such conditions and requirements are adequate to protect the health and safety of individuals under the care of a home health agency and to promote the effective and efficient use of public moneys.

Section 1891(c), 42 U.S.C.A. 1395bbb(c), provides:

(1) Any agreement entered into or renewed by the Secretary pursuant to section 1864 [42 U.S.C.A. 1395aa, which provides for the use of State agencies to determine compliance by providers of services with Medicare conditions of participation] relating to home health agencies shall provide that the appropriate State or local agency shall conduct, without any prior notice, a standard survey of each home health agency. Any individual who notifies (or causes to be notified) a home health agency of the time or date on which such a survey is scheduled to be conducted is subject to a civil money penalty of not to exceed $2,000. The provisions of section 1128A [42 U.S.C.A. 1320a-7a] (other than subsections (a) and (b)) shall

apply to a civil money penalty under this paragraph in the same manner as such provisions apply to a penalty or proceeding under section 1128A. The Secretary shall review each State's or local agency's procedures for scheduling and conduct of standard surveys to assure that the State or agency has taken all reasonable steps to avoid giving notice of such a survey through the scheduling procedures and the conduct of the surveys themselves.

(2) Except as provided in subparagraph (B), each home health agency shall be subject to a standard survey not later than 36 months after the date of the previous standard survey conducted under this paragraph. The Secretary shall establish a frequency for surveys of home health agencies within this 36-month interval commensurate with the need to assure the delivery of quality home health services. [NOTE: Prior to amendment by section 516(a) of the Omnibus Consolidated Rescissions and Appropriations Act of 1996, P.L. 104–134, standard surveys were to be conducted not later than 15 months after a previous standard survey. Furthermore, the second sentence in this paragraph (2)(A) read: "The statewide averrage interval between standard surveys of any home health agency shall not exceed 12 months."]

If not otherwise conducted under subparagraph (A), a standard survey (or an abbreviated standard survey) of an agency — may be conducted within 2 months of any change of ownership, administration, or management of the agency to determine whether the change has resulted in any decline in the quality of care furnished by the agency, and shall be conducted within 2 months of when a significant number of complaints have been reported with respect to the agency to the Secretary, the State, the entity responsible for the licensing of the agency, the State or local agency responsible for maintaining a toll-free hotline and investigative unit (under section (1864(a) [42 U.S.C.A. 1395aa(a)]), or any other appropriate Federal, State, or local agency.

(C) A standard survey conducted under this paragraph with respect to a home health agency —

(i) shall include (to the extent practicable), for a case-mix stratified sample of individuals furnished items or services by the agency —

(I) visits to the homes of such individuals, but only with the consent of such individuals, for the purpose of evaluating (in accordance with a standardized reproducible assessment instrument (or instruments) approved by the Secretary under subsection (d)) the extent to which the quality and scope of items and services furnished by the agency attained and maintained the highest practicable functional capacity of each such individual as reflected in such individual's written plan of care required under section 1861(m) and clinical records required under section 1861(o)(3); and

(II) a survey of the quality of care and services furnished by the agency as measured by indicators of medical, nursing, and rehabilitative care;

(ii) shall be based upon a protocol that is developed, tested, and validated by the Secretary not later than January 1, 1989; and

(iii) shall be conducted by an individual —

(I) who meets minimum qualifications established by the Secretary not later than July 1, 1989,

(II) who is not serving (or has not served within the previous 2 years) as a member of the staff of, or as a consultant to, the home health agency surveyed respecting compliance with the conditions of participation specified in or pursuant to section 1861(o) or subsection (a) of this section, and

(III) who has no personal or familial financial interest in the home health agency surveyed.

Section 1891(d) provides as follows with respect to the required assessment instrument or instruments to be used in standard surveys:

(1) Not later than January 1, 1989, the Secretary shall designate an assessment instrument (or instruments) for use by an agency complying with subsection (c)(2)(C)(I) [sic, probably should read (c)(2)(C)(i)(I)]

(2) (A) Not later than January 1, 1992, the Secretary shall—

(i) evaluate the assessment process,

(ii) report to Congress on the results of such evaluation, and

(iii) based on such evaluation, make such modifications in the assessment process as the Secretary determines are appropriate.

(B) The Secretary shall periodically update the evaluation conducted under subparagraph (A), report the results of such update to Congress, and, based on such update, make such modifications in the assessment process as the Secretary determines are appropriate.

(3) The Secretary shall provide for the comprehensive training of State and Federal surveyors in matters relating to the performance of standard and extended surveys under this section, including the use of any assessment instrument (or instruments) designated under paragraph (1).

For regulatory citations, see Chapter 6

§ 2:60 FAILURE BY A HOME HEALTH AGENCY TO COMPLY WITH MEDICARE CONDITIONS OF PARTICIPATION—Sections 1891(e) and (f) [42 U.S.C.A. 1395bbb(e) and (f)]

Summary

Section 1891(a), 42 U.S.C.A. 1395bbb(a), sets forth conditions for home health agencies (HHA's) to participate in Medicare. Section 1861(o), 42 U.S.C.A. 1395x(o), establishes their definition requirements. Some conditions and requirements became applicable June 1, 1989. Others apply thereafter, as specified.

In general, HHA conditions and requirements pertain to patient's rights; ownership and control issues; standards for home health aides (including training and competency evaluation by January 1, 1990, for aides used by an HHA as of July 1, 1989); and quality of care standards, such as plans of care for patients and compliance with professional standards and applicable laws.

Section 1891(b) declares the duty and responsibility of the Secretary of Health and Human Services to assure that the conditions specified in section 1891(a) and the requirements of section 1861(o) are met.

Section 1891(c) provides that agreements which the Secretary enters into with State agencies pursuant to section 1864, 42 U.S.C.A. 1395aa, authorizing them to determine compliance by providers of services with Medicare conditions of participation, must permit appropriate State or local agencies to conduct, without any prior notice, standard surveys of home health agencies. Those surveys are to be based on a protocol the Secretary was obliged to develop, test, and validate not later than January 1, 1989. Moreover, the surveys must be conducted by individuals who meet minimum qualifications which the Secretary was obliged to establish not later than July 1, 1989. Those individuals must have no financial or familial conflict of interests with the HHA, and they must not be serving as a member of the HHA staff or as a consultant to the HHA. Nor may they have served as either within two years prior to the survey.

Pursuant to section 1891(d), the Secretary was obliged to designate an assessment instrument not later than January 1, 1989. Not later than January 1, 1992, and periodically thereafter, he must evaluate the assessment process and report to Congress on results of that evaluation, and he must make such modifications as he deems appropriate in the instrument. The Secretary also must provide for comprehensive training of State and Federal surveyors in matters relating to the performance of standard and extended surveys, including use of any assessment instrument or instruments developed.

If an HHA is found under a standard survey to have provided substandard care, an extended survey must be made to determine whether it has complied with the conditions of participation. The extended survey must be conducted immediately after the standard survey, or, if not practical, then not later than two weeks after the date the standard survey was completed.

◆ NOTE: Any HHA, whether or not having undergone a standard survey, also may be subject to an extended or partial extended survey. Moreover, there is no requirement for an extended or partial extended survey to be conducted prior to imposing a sanction against an HHA. A standard survey may suffice for that.

If the Secretary determines on the basis of a survey, or otherwise, that an HHA no longer complies with statutory requirements, and if he determines that its deficiencies immediately jeopardize the health and safety of individuals to whom the HHA furnishes items and services, section 1891(e)(1) requires him to take immediate action to remove the jeopardy and correct the deficiencies. He can do that either by appointing a temporary manager to oversee operation of the HHA while improvements are being made to achieve compliance, or by terminating the HHA's certification. In addition, the Secretary may impose a civil money penalty not to exceed $10,000 for each day of noncompliance, or he may suspend all or part of payments due with respect to items and services furnished by the HHA after a specified date, or both.

Enforcement procedures for this civil money penalty are governed by section 1128A, 42 U.S.C.A. 1320a-7a, which authorizes civil money penalties for a variety of offenses.

Pursuant to section 1891(e)(4), the Secretary may continue Medicare payments to an HHA that is not in compliance for not longer than six months if the State or local survey agency finds that appropriate, if that survey agency submits a plan and timetable for corrective action which the Secretary approves, and if that agency agrees to repay Medicare payments received by the HHA for that period should corrective actions not be made in accordance with the plan and timetable. The Secretary was obligated to establish guidelines for approval of such corrective action proposals.

Pursuant to section 1891(f)(1), the Secretary was obliged to develop and implement by April 1, 1989, a range of intermediate sanctions to apply to home health agencies, along with appropriate procedures for appealing sanction determinations. In addition, the Secretary was required to develop and implement specific procedures with respect to conditions under which intermediate sanctions will be applied, including the amount of any fines and the severity of each sanction.

Pursuant to section 1891(g), home health agencies must submit claims for payment for home health services only on the basis of the geographic location at which the service is furnished, as determined by the Secretary. This requirement was added by section 4601(a) of the Balanced Budget Act of 1997, P.L. 105–33. It applies to cost reporting services beginning on or after October 1, 1997.

If the Secretary determines on the basis of a survey, or otherwise, that an HHA no longer complies with the statutory requirements, and if he determines that its deficiencies do not immediately jeopardize the health and safety of individuals to whom the agency furnishes items and services, section 1891(e)(2) provides that the Secretary may for a period not to exceed six months impose intermediate sanctions in lieu of terminating the HHA's certification. These include an intermediate sanction from among the range the Secretary was charged with developing; a civil money penalty not to exceed $10,000 for each day of noncompliance; suspension of all or part of payments with respect to items and services furnished by the HHA after a specified date; or appointment of a temporary manager to oversee operation of the HHA while improvements are made to come into compliance. Again, procedures for assessment of the civil money penalty are governed by section 1128A.

◆ NOTE: Pursuant to section 1891(f)(2)(B), the civil money penalty, the suspension of payments, and the appointment of a temporary manager sanctions (sometimes referred to as remedies in the statute) are in addition to those otherwise available under State or Federal law. Moreover, the statute specifies that they shall not be construed as limiting other remedies, including any remedy available to an individual at common law.

If the Secretary determines that an HHA complies with applicable conditions and requirements, but did not do so for a previous period, section 1891(e)(3) permits him to impose a civil money penalty not to exceed $10,000 for each day in which the HHA was not in compliance, subject to procedural requirements under section 1128A.

Finally, according to section 1891(f)(2)(C), a decision by the Secretary to suspend payments to an HHA terminates when the Secretary finds that the HHA is in substantial compliance with the conditions of section 1891(a) and the requirements of section 1861(o).

Statutory Provisions

Section 1861(o), 42 U.S.C.A. 1395x(o), provides:

> The term "home health agency" means a public agency or private organization, or a subdivision of such an agency or organization, which—
>
> (1) is primarily engaged in providing skilled nursing services and other therapeutic services;
>
> (2) has policies, established by a group of professional personnel (associated with the agency or organization), including one or more physicians and one or more registered profes-

sional nurses, to govern the services (referred to in paragraph (1)) which it provides, and provides for supervision of such services by a physician or registered professional nurse;

(3) maintains clinical records on all patients;

(4) in the case of an agency or organization in any State in which State or applicable local law provides for the licensing of agencies or organizations of this nature, (A) is licensed pursuant to such law, or (B) is approved, by the agency of such State or locality responsible for licensing agencies or organizations of this nature, as meeting the standards established for such licensing;

(5) has in effect an overall plan and budget that meets the requirements of subsection (z) [which pertains to institutional planning requirements for hospitals, skilled nursing facilities, comprehensive outpatient rehabilitation facilities, and home health agencies];

(6) meets the conditions of participation specified in section 1891(a) and such other conditions of participation as the Secretary may find necessary in the interest of the health and safety of individuals who are furnished services by such agency or organization;

(7) provides the Secretary on a continuing basis with a surety bond in a form specified by the Secretary and in an amount that is not less than $50,000; and

◆ NOTE: Section 1128F of the Social Security Act [42 U.S.C.A. 1320a-7f] , provides: "In the case of a home health agency that is subject to a surety bond requirement under title XVIII and title XIX, the surety bond provided to satisfy the requirement under one such title shall satisfy the requirement under the other such title so long as the bond applies to guarantee return of overpayments under both such titles." This provision became effective November 29, 1999, pursuant to section 304(b) of the Medicare, Medicaid, and SCHIP Balanced Budget Refinement Act of 1999, as incorporated into the Omnibus Consolidated Appropriations Act, 2000, P.L. 106–113, enacted November 17, 1999.

(8) meets such additional requirements (including conditions relating to bonding or establishing of escrow accounts as the Secretary finds necessary for the financial security of the program) as the Secretary finds necessary for the effective and

efficient operation of the program; except that for purposes of part A such term shall not include any agency or organization which is primarily for the care and treatment of mental diseases. The Secretary may waive the requirement of a surety bond under paragraph (7) in the case of an agency or organization that provides a comparable surety bond under State law.

◆ NOTE: Section 4312(b)(1) of the Balanced Budget Act of 1997, P.L. 105–33, deleted "and" from the end of paragraph (6), redesignated former paragraph (7) as paragraph (8), and added new paragraph (7) pertaining to the surety bond requirement. It also added the last sentence of paragraph (8). These changes apply to services furnished on or after January 1, 1998.

Section 1891(a) provides:

The conditions of participation that a home health agency is required to meet under this subsection are as follows:

(1) The agency protects and promotes the rights of each individual under its care, including each of the following rights:

(A) The right to be fully informed in advance about the care and treatment to be provided by the agency, to be fully informed in advance of any changes in the care or treatment to be provided by the agency that may affect the individual's well-being, and (except with respect to an individual adjudged incompetent) to participate in planning care and treatment or changes in care or treatment.

(B) The right to voice grievances with respect to treatment or care that is (or fails to be) furnished without discrimination or reprisal for voicing grievances.

(C) The right to confidentiality of the clinical records described in section 1861(o)(3).

(D) The right to have one's property treated with respect.

(E) The right to be fully informed orally and in writing (in advance of coming under the care of the agency) of—

(i) all items and services furnished by (or under arrangements with) the agency for which payment may be made under this title,

(ii) the coverage available for such items and services under this title, title XIX, and any other Federal program of which the agency is reasonably aware,

(iii) any charges for items and services not covered under this title and any charges the individual may have to pay with respect to items and services furnished by (or under arrangements with) the agency, and

(iv) any changes in the charges or items and services described in clause (i), (ii), or (iii).

(F) The right to be fully informed in writing (in advance of coming under the care of the agency) of the individual's rights and obligations under this title.

(G) The right to be informed of the availability of the State home health agency hot-line established under section 1864(a) [42 U.S.C.A. 1395aa(a)]

(2) The agency notifies the State entity responsible for the licensing or certification of the agency of a change in —

(A) the persons with an ownership or control interest (as defined in section 1124(a)(3) [42 U.S.C.A. 1320a-3(a)(3), which pertains to disclosure of ownership and related information pertaining to entities participating in Medicare, Medicare, or the Federally-funded Maternal and Child Health programs authorized by Title V of the Social Security Act, 42 U.S.C.A. 701et seq.]) in the agency,

(B) the persons who are officers, directors, agents, or managing employees (as defined in section 1126(b) [42 U.S.C.A. 1320a-5(b), which pertains to disclosure by institutions, organizations, and agencies of owners and certain other individuals who have been convicted of various crimes or who have committed other offenses punishable under section 1128, 42 U.S.C.A. 1320a-7]) of the agency, and

(C) the corporation, association, or other company responsible for the management of the agency.

Such notice shall be given at the time of the change and shall include the identity of each new person or company described in the previous sentence.

(3) (A) The agency must not use as a home health aide (on a full-time, temporary, per diem, or other basis), any individual to provide items or services described in section 1861(m)

[42 U.S.C.A. 1395x(m), which defines home health services] on or after January 1, 1990, unless the individual—

(i) has completed a training and competency evaluation program, or a competency evaluation program, that meets the minimum standards established by the Secretary under subparagraph (D), and

(ii) is competent to provide such items and services.

For purposes of clause (i), an individual is not considered to have completed a training and competency evaluation program, or a competency evaluation program if, since the individual's most recent completion of such a program, there has been a continuous period of 24 consecutive months during none of which the individual provided items and services described in section 1861(m) for compensation.

(B) (i) The agency must provide, with respect to individuals used as a home health aide by the agency as of July 1, 1989, for a competency evaluation program (as described in subparagraph (A)(i)) and such preparation as may be necessary for the individual to complete such a program by January 1, 1990.

(ii) The agency must provide such regular performance review and regular in-service education as assures that individuals used to provide items and services described in section 1861(m) are competent to provide those items and services.

(C) The agency must not permit an individual, other than in a training and competency evaluation program that meets the minimum standards established by the Secretary under subparagraph (D), to provide items or services of a type for which the individual has not demonstrated competency.

(D) (i) The Secretary shall establish minimum standards for the programs described in subparagraph (A) by not later than October 1, 1988.

(ii) Such standards shall include the content of the curriculum, minimum hours of training, qualification of instructors, and procedures for determination of competency.

(iii) Such standards may permit approval of programs offered by or in home health agencies, as well as outside agencies (including employee organizations), and of programs in effect on the date of the enactment of this section [December 22, 1987; P.L. 100-203] , except that they may not provide for the approval of a program offered by or in a home health agency which has been determined to be out of compliance with the requirements specified in or pursuant to section 1861(o) or subsection (a) within the previous 2 years.

(iv) Such standards shall permit a determination that an individual who has completed (before July 1, 1989) a training and competency evaluation program or a competency evaluation program shall be deemed for purposes of subparagraph (A) to have completed a program that is approved by the Secretary under the standards established under this subparagraph if the Secretary determines that, at the time the program was offered, the program met such standards.

(E) In this paragraph, the term "home health aide" means any individual who provides the items and services described in section 1861(m), but does not include an individual —

(i) who is a licensed health professional (as defined in subparagraph (F)), or

(ii) who volunteers to provide such services without monetary compensation.

(F) In this paragraph, the term "licensed health professional" means a physician, physician assistant, nurse practitioner, physical, speech, or occupational therapist, physical or occupational therapy assistant, registered professional nurse, licensed practical nurse, or licensed or certified social worker.

(4) The agency includes an individual's plan of care required under section 1861(m) as part of the clinical records described in section 1861(o)(3).

(5) The agency operates and provides services in compliance with all applicable Federal, State, and local laws and regulation (including the requirements of section 1124) and with

> accepted professional standards and principles which apply to professionals providing items and services in such an agency.

Section 1891(b) provides:

> It is the duty and responsibility of the Secretary to assure that the conditions of participation and requirements specified in or pursuant to section 1861(o) and subsection (a) of this section and the enforcement of such conditions and requirements are adequate to protect the health and safety of individuals under the care of a home health agency and to promote the effective and efficient use of public moneys.

Section 1891(c)(2) provides:

> (A) Except as provided in subparagraph (B), each home health agency shall be subject to a standard survey not later than 15 months after the date of the previous standard survey conducted under this paragraph. The statewide average interval between standard surveys of any home health agency shall not exceed 12 months.
>
> (B) If not otherwise conducted under subparagraph (A), a standard survey (or an abbreviated standard survey) of an agency—
>
> (i) may be conducted within 2 months of any change of ownership, administration, or management of the agency to determine whether the change has resulted in any decline in the quality of care furnished by the agency, and
>
> (ii) shall be conducted within 2 months of when a significant number of complaints have been reported with respect to the agency to the Secretary, the State, the entity responsible for the licensing of the agency, the State or local agency responsible for maintaining a toll-free hotline and investigative unit (under section 1864(a)), or any other appropriate Federal, State, or local agency.
>
> (C) A standard survey conducted under this paragraph with respect to a home health agency—
>
> (i) shall include (to the extent practicable), for a case-mix stratified sample of individuals furnished items or services by the agency—

(I) visits to the homes of such individuals, but only with the consent of such individuals, for the purpose of evaluating (in accordance with a standardized reproducible assessment instrument (or instruments) approved by the Secretary under subsection (d)) the extent to which the quality and scope of items and services furnished by the agency attained and maintained the highest practicable functional capacity of each such individual as reflected in such individual's written plan of care required under section 1861(m) and clinical records required under section 1861(o)(3); and

(II) a survey of the quality of care and services furnished by the agency as measured by indicators of medical, nursing, and rehabilitative care;

(ii) shall be based upon a protocol that is developed, tested, and validated by the Secretary not later than January 1, 1989; and

(iii) shall be conducted by an individual—

(I) who meets minimum qualifications established by the Secretary not later than July 1, 1989,

(II) who is not serving (or has not served within the previous 2 years) as a member of the staff of, or as a consultant to, the home health agency surveyed respecting compliance with the conditions of participation specified in or pursuant to section 1861(o) or subsection (a) of this section, and

(III) who has no personal or familial financial interest in the home health agency surveyed.

(D) Each home health agency that is found, under a standard survey, to have provided substandard care shall be subject to an extended survey to review and identify the policies and procedures which produced such substandard care and to determine whether the agency has complied with the conditions of participation specified in or pursuant to section 1861(o) or subsection (a) of this section. Any other agency may, at the Secretary's or State's discretion, be subject to such an extended survey (or a partial extended survey). The extended survey shall be conducted immediately after the standard survey (or, if not practical, not later than 2 weeks after the date of completion of the standard survey).

(E) Nothing in this paragraph shall be construed as requiring an extended (or partial extended) survey as a prerequisite to imposing a sanction against an agency under subsection (e) on the basis of the findings of a standard survey.

Section 1891(d) provides as follows with respect to the required assessment instrument or instruments to be used in standard surveys:

(1) Not later than January 1, 1989, the Secretary shall designate an assessment instrument (or instruments) for use by an agency complying with subsection (c)(2)(C)(I) [sic, probably should read (c)(2)(C)(i)(I)]

(2) (A) Not later than January 1, 1992, the Secretary shall —

(i) evaluate the assessment process,

(ii) report to Congress on the results of such evaluation, and

(iii) based on such evaluation, make such modifications in the assessment process as the Secretary determines are appropriate.

(B) The Secretary shall periodically update the evaluation conducted under subparagraph (A), report the results of such update to Congress, and, based on such update, make such modifications in the assessment process as the Secretary determines are appropriate.

(3) The Secretary shall provide for the comprehensive training of State and Federal surveyors in matters relating to the performance of standard and extended surveys under this section, including the use of any assessment instrument (or instruments) designated under paragraph (1).

Having said all that about HHA standards and surveys, Congress then provided in section 1891(e):

(1) If the Secretary determines on the basis of a standard, extended, or partial extended survey or otherwise, that a home health agency that is certified for participation under this title is no longer in compliance with the requirements

specified in section 1861(o) or subsection (a) and determines that the deficiencies involved immediately jeopardize the health and safety of the individuals to whom the agency furnishes items and services, the Secretary shall take immediate action to remove the jeopardy and correct the deficiencies through the remedy specified in subsection (f)(2)(A)(iii) or terminate the certification of the agency, and may provide, in addition, for 1 or more of the other remedies described in subsection (f)(2)(A).

(2) If the Secretary determines on the basis of a standard, extended, or partial extended survey or otherwise, that a home health agency that is certified for participation under this title is no longer in compliance with the requirements specified in or pursuant to section 1861(o) or subsection (a) and determines that the deficiencies involved do not immediately jeopardize the health and safety of the individuals to whom the agency furnishes items and services, the Secretary may (for a period not to exceed 6 months) impose intermediate sanctions developed pursuant to subsection (f), in lieu of terminating the certification of the agency. If, after such a period of intermediate sanctions, the agency is still no longer in compliance with the requirements specified in or pursuant to section 1861(o) or subsection (a), the Secretary shall terminate the certification of the agency.

(3) If the Secretary determines that a home health agency that is certified for participation under this title is in compliance with the requirements specified in or pursuant to section 1861(o) or subsection (a) but, as of a previous period, did not meet such requirements, the Secretary may provide for a civil money penalty under subsection (f)(2)(A)(i) for the days in which it finds that the agency was not in compliance with such requirements.

(4) The Secretary may continue payments under this title with respect to a home health agency not in compliance with the requirements specified in or pursuant to section 1861(o) or subsection (a) over a period of not longer than 6 months if—

(A) the State or local survey agency finds that it is more appropriate to take alternative action to assure compliance of the agency with the requirements than to terminate the certification of the agency,

(B) the agency has submitted a plan and timetable for corrective action to the Secretary for approval and the Secretary approves the plan of corrective action, and

(C) the agency agrees to repay to the Federal Government payments received under this subparagraph if the corrective action is not taken in accordance with the approved plan and timetable.

The Secretary shall establish guidelines for approval of corrective actions requested by home health agencies under this subparagraph.

Section 1891(f) provides:

(1) The Secretary shall develop and implement, by not later than April 1, 1989—

(A) a range of intermediate sanctions to apply to home health agencies under the conditions described in subsection (e), and

(B) appropriate procedures for appealing determinations relating to the imposition of such sanctions.

(2) (A) The intermediate sanctions developed under paragraph (1) shall include—

(i) civil money penalties in an amount not to exceed $10,000 for each day of noncompliance,

(ii) suspension of all or part of the payments to which a home health agency would otherwise be entitled under this title with respect to items and services furnished by a home health agency on or after the date on which the Secretary determines that intermediate sanctions should be imposed pursuant to subsection (e)(2), and

(iii) the appointment of temporary management to oversee the operation of the home health agency and to protect and assure the health and safety of the individuals under the care of the agency while improvements are made in order to bring the agency into compliance with all the requirements specified in or pursuant to section 1861(o) or subsection (a).

The provisions of section 1128A [42 U.S.C.A. 1320a-7a] (other than subsections (a) and (b)) shall apply to a civil money penalty under clause (i) in the same manner as such provisions apply to a penalty or proceeding under section 1128A(a). The temporary management under clause (iii) shall not be terminated until the Secretary has determined that the agency has the management capability to ensure continued compliance with all the requirements referred to in that clause.

(B) The sanctions specified in subparagraph (A) are in addition to sanctions otherwise available under State or Federal law and shall not be construed as limiting other remedies, including any remedy available to an individual at common law.

(C) A finding to suspend payment under subparagraph (A)(ii) shall terminate when the Secretary finds that the home health agency is in substantial compliance with all the requirements specified in or pursuant to section 1861(o) and subsection (a).

(3) The Secretary shall develop and implement, by not later than April 1, 1989, specific procedures with respect to the conditions under which each of the intermediate sanctions developed under paragraph (1) is to be applied, including the amount of any fines and the severity of each of these sanctions. Such procedures shall be designed so as to minimize the time between identification of deficiencies and imposition of these sanctions and shall provide for the imposition of incrementally more severe fines for repeated or uncorrected deficiencies.

Finally, section 1891(g), provides:

PAYMENT ON BASIS OF LOCATION OF SERVICE. —A home health agency shall submit claims for payment for home health services under this title only on the basis of the geographic location at which the service is furnished, as determined by the Secretary.

◆ NOTE: Subsection (g) was added by section 4604(a) of the Balanced Budget Act of 1997, P.L. 105–33. It applies to cost reporting periods beginning on or after October 1, 1997.

For regulatory citations, see Chapter 6

§ 2:61 OFFSETTING MEDICARE PAYMENTS TO INDIVIDUALS TO COLLECT PAST-DUE OBLIGATIONS ARISING FROM BREACH OF SCHOLARSHIP AND LOAN CONTRACTS — Section 1892 [42 U.S.C.A. 1395ccc]

Summary

The Federal government provides scholarships and loans to physicians and other health care professionals pursuant to the National Health Service Corps Scholarship Program, the Physician Shortage Area Scholarship Program, and the Health Education Assistance Loan Program. Not all of those who received such financial assistance have repaid their debts or lived up to other obligations, such as to provide medical services in designated medically underserved areas. Accordingly, Congress provided in section 1892, 42 U.S.C.A. 1395ccc, that any recipient of a scholarship or loan under any of those programs who wants to participate in Medicare, who has breached his or her contract, who has past-due obligations, and whose obligations have not been canceled, waived, or suspended by the Secretary of Health and Human Services must enter into an agreement with the Secretary providing for deductions from amounts otherwise payable to them on an assignment basis under Medicare until the obligation and any accrued interest have been repaid.

If such an individual does not provide services under Medicare of sufficient quantity to maintain the offset collection according to the agreed formula and schedule, the Secretary must inform the Attorney General, and the Attorney General must immediately commence a recovery action. In addition, unless the individual is a sole community practitioner or sole source of essential specialized services in a community and unless the State requests otherwise, the Secretary must immediately exclude the individual from Medicare until the entire past-due obligation has been repaid.

If such an individual refuses to enter into an agreement or breaches any provision of the required agreement, the Secretary must immediately inform the Attorney General, and the Attorney General must immediately commence an action to recover the full amount of the past-due obligation. The Secretary also must immediately exclude the individual from Medicare until the entire past-due obligation has been repaid, unless the individual is a sole community practitioner or sole source of essential specialized services in a community and unless the State requests otherwise.

◆ NOTE: Unlike most provisions in title XVIII which authorize exclusion from Medicare, section 1892 does not cross-reference section 1128, 42 U.S.C.A. 1320a-7, for procedural matters. This seems to give the Secretary more procedural discretion. Furthermore, nothing in this provision of the law precludes the United States from applying any other law to recover these past-due obligations.

Finally, pursuant to section 1892(d), if a delinquent individual works for an entity with a provider agreement under section 1866, 42 U.S.C.A. 1395cc, or for a health maintenance organization (HMO) or competitive medical plan (CMP), or is part of a group of physicians that submits Medicare claims as a group rather than as individuals, the statute provides for deductions against payments otherwise due to the employer or group to effect the offset. There is a 6-month notice period, however, within which the parties may negotiate a settlement before offset begins. In addition, the statute calls for agreements with the individual and the other affected party or parties, and gives the latter a private right of action against the individual to collect the amount deducted plus interest.

Statutory Provisions

Section 1892, 42 U.S.C.A. 1395ccc, provides:

(a) IN GENERAL.—

(1) (A) Subject to subparagraph (B), the Secretary shall enter into an agreement under this section with any individual who, by reason of a breach of a contract entered into by such individual pursuant to the National Health Service Corps Scholarship Program, the Physician Shortage Area Scholarship Program, or the Health Education Assistance Loan Program, owes a past-due obligation to the United States (as defined in subsection (b)).

(B) The Secretary shall not enter into an agreement with an individual under this section to the extent—

(i) (I) the individual has entered into a contract with the Secretary pursuant to section 204(a)(1) of the Public

Health Service Amendments of 1987 [P.L. 100-177], and

(II) the individual has fulfilled or (as determined by the Secretary) is fulfilling the terms of such contract; or

(ii) the liability of the individual under such section 204(a)(1) has otherwise been relieved under such section; or

(iii) the individual is performing such physician's service obligation under a forbearance agreement entered into with the Secretary under subpart II of part D of title III of the Public Health Service Act [P.L.78-410].

(2) The agreement under this section shall provide that —

(A) deductions shall be made from the amounts otherwise payable to the individual under this title, in accordance with a formula and schedule agreed to by the Secretary and the individual, until such past-due obligation (and accrued interest) have been repaid;

(B) payment under this title for services provided by such individual shall be made only on an assignment-related basis;

(C) if the individual does not provide services, for which payment would otherwise by made under this title, of a sufficient quantity to maintain the offset collection according to the agreed formula and schedule —

(i) the Secretary shall immediately inform the Attorney General, and the Attorney General shall immediately commence an action to recover the full amount of the past-due obligation, and

(ii) subject to paragraph (4), the Secretary shall immediately exclude the individual from the program under this title, until such time as the entire past-due obligation has been repaid.

(3) If the individual refuses to enter into an agreement or breaches any provision of the agreement —

(A) the Secretary shall immediately inform the Attorney General, and the Attorney General shall immediately commence an action to recover the full amount of the past-due obligation, and

(B) subject to paragraph (4), the Secretary shall immediately exclude the individual from the program under this title, until such time as the entire past-due obligation has been repaid.

(4) The Secretary shall not exclude an individual pursuant to paragraph (2)(C)(ii) or paragraph (3)(B) if such individual is a sole community practitioner or sole source of essential specialized services in a community if a State requests that the physician not be excluded.

Section 1892(b) provides:

PAST-DUE OBLIGATION. — For purposes of this section, a past-due obligation is any amount —

(1) owed by an individual to the United States by reason of a breach of a scholarship contract under section 338E of the Public Health Service Act [P.L. 78-410] or under subpart III of part F of title VII of such Act (as in effect before October 1, 1976) and which has not been paid by the deadline established by the Secretary pursuant to such respective section, and has not been canceled, waived, or suspended by the Secretary pursuant to such section; or

(2) owed by an individual to the United States by reason of a loan covered by Federal loan insurance under subpart I of part C of title VII of the Public Health Service Act and payment for which has not been canceled, waived, or suspended by the Secretary under such subpart.

Section 1892(c) provides:

COLLECTION UNDER THIS SECTION SHALL NOT BE EXCLUSIVE. —

This section shall not preclude the United States from applying other provisions of law otherwise applicable to the collection of obligations owed to the United States, including (but not limited to) the use of tax refund offsets pursuant to section 3720A of title 31, United States Code, and the application of other procedures provided under chapter 37 of title 31, United States Code.

Section 1892(d) provides:

COLLECTION FROM PROVIDERS AND HEALTH MAINTENANCE ORGANIZATIONS. —

(1) In the case of an individual who owes a past-due obligation, and who is an employee of, or affiliated by a medical services agreement with, a provider having an agreement under section 1866 [42 U.S.C.A. 1395cc] or a health maintenance organization or competitive medical plan having a contract under section 1833 [42 U.S.C.A. 1395l] or section 1876 [42 U.S.C.A. 1395mm] , the Secretary shall deduct the amounts of such past-due obligation from amounts otherwise payable under this title to such provider, organization, or plan.

(2) Deductions shall be in accordance with a formula and schedule agreed to by the Secretary, the individual and the provider, organization, or plan. The deductions shall be made from the amounts otherwise payable to the individual under this title as long as the individual continues to be employed or affiliated by a medical services agreement.

(3) Such deduction shall not be made until 6 months after the Secretary notifies the provider, organization, or plan of the amount to be deducted and the particular physicians to whom the deductions are attributable.

(4) A deduction made under this subsection shall relieve the individual of the obligation (to the extent of the amount collected) to the United States, but the provider, organization, or plan shall have a right of action to collect from such individual the amount deducted pursuant to this subsection (including accumulated interest).

(5) No deduction shall be made under this subsection if, within the 6-month period after notice is given to the provider, organization, or plan, the individual pays the past-due obligation, or ceases to be employed by the provider, organization, or plan.

(6) The Secretary shall also apply the provisions of this subsection in the case of an individual who is a member of a group practice, if such group practice submits bills under this program as a group, rather than by individual physicians.

Finally, section 1892(e) provides:

TRANSFER FROM TRUST FUNDS. — Amounts equal to the amounts deducted pursuant to this section shall be transferred from the Trust Fund from which the payment to the individual, provider, or other entity would otherwise have been made, to the general fund in the Treasury, and shall be credited as payment of the pastdue obligation of the individual from whom (or with respect to whom) the deduction was made.

For regulatory citations, see Chapter 6

§ 2:62 TERMINATION OF PACE PROVIDER AGREEMENTS — Section 1894 [42 U.S.C.A. 1395eee]

Summary

◆ NOTE: Section 4801 of the Balanced Budget Act of 1997, P.L. 105–33, created the Program of All-inclusive Care for the Elderly (PACE), effective August 5, 1997.

In General: According to section 1894 of the Social Security Act, as amended, 42 U.S.C.A. 1395eee, the term "PACE Program" means a program of all-inclusive care for the elderly conducted by a public entity or a private nonprofit entity organized for a charitable purpose under section 501(c)(3) of the Internal Revenue Code of 1986. It also means a program conducted by a private, for-profit entity granted a waiver on a demonstration project basis by the Secretary of Health and Human Services under section 1894(h).

To participate as a PACE provider entities must enter into agreements with the Secretary to provide a program of comprehensive health care services to persons eligible to enroll in PACE. PACE enrollees do not receive benefits under Medicare Part A or Part B for so long as they remain enrolled in PACE.

Basically, according to section 1894(a)(5), a PACE-eligible person is an individual age 55 or older who is determined to require the level of care required under a State Medicaid plan for coverage of nursing facility services, and who meets such other eligibility conditions as may be imposed under a PACE agreement.

Pursuant to section 1894(b), the comprehensive benefits to be provided under PACE must, at a minimum, include all items and services covered under Medicare or Medicaid, but without any limitation or condition as to amount, duration, or scope, and without application of deductibles, copayments, coinsurance, or other cost-sharing that would otherwise apply under Medicare or Medicaid. They also must provide all additional items and services specified in regulations, based on the PACE protocol.

Section 1894(a)(6) defines PACE protocol as the Protocol for the Program of All-inclusive Care for the Elderly (PACE), as published by On Lok, Inc., as of April 14, 1995, or any successor protocol agreed upon by the Secretary and On Lok, Inc.

Pursuant to section 1894(c), enrollment in PACE is voluntary and enrolled persons may disenroll without cause at any time. PACE providers may not disenroll an eligible individual, however, except for nonpayment of premiums (if applicable) on a timely basis, or for engaging in disruptive or threatening behavior. Nevertheless, there can be no involuntary disenrollment if the bad behavior is related to a mental or physical condition of the individual.

A proposed involuntary disenrollment is subject to timely review and final determination by the Secretary or by the State administering agency (as applicable) before disenrollment becomes effective.

PACE providers are paid monthly on a capitated basis in the same manner and from the same sources as payments are made to a Medicare + Choice organization under section 1853 (or, for periods prior to January 1, 1999, to an eligible organization under a risk-sharing agreement pursuant to section 1876, 42 U.S.C.A. 1395mm).

Cause for Termination of a PACE Agreement: Pursuant to section 1894(e)(5), the Secretary or a State administering agency may terminate a PACE program agreement for cause. Among other things, cause for termination exists if the Secretary or State administering agency finds: significant deficiencies in the quality of care provided to enrollees; or the provider failed to comply substantially with conditions for a program or provider under section 1894 or section 1934, 42 U.S.C.A. 1396, which pertains to use of the PACE option for Medicaid recipients; and the provider has failed to develop and successfully initiate a plan to correct deficiencies within 30 days of the date of the receipt of written notice thereof, or has failed to continue implementation of a plan of correction.

Enforcement Actions: Pursuant to section 1894(e)(6)(A), if the Secretary, after consultation with the State administering agency, determines that a PACE provider is failing substantially to comply with applicable requirements and regulations, the Secretary (and the State administering agency) may take any or all of the following actions:

1 Condition continuation of the PACE program agreement upon timely execution of a corrective action plan.
2 Withhold some or all further payments under the PACE program agreement under section 1894 or section 1934 with respect to PACE program services furnished by the provider until the deficiencies have been corrected.
3 Terminate the agreement.

Intermediate Sanctions: *Sanctions on or after January 1, 1999:* Pursuant to section 1894(e)(6)(B), under regulations, the Secretary may provide for the application of remedies described in section 1857(g)(2), in the case of violations by the provider of the type described in section 1857(g)(1), or section 1903(m)(5)(A), 42 U.S.C.A. 1396b(m)(5)(A), respectively (in relation to agreements, enrollees, and requirements under this section or section 1934, respectively).

Violations described in section 1857(g)(1) include:

1 Failure substantially to provide medically necessary items and services that are required under law or contract to an enrollee, if the failure has adversely affected (or has substantial likelihood of adversely affecting) the individual.
2 Imposing a premium on an enrollee in excess of the amount of the Medicare + Choice monthly basic and supplemental beneficiary premiums permitted under section 1854.
3 Acting illegally to expel or to refuse to re-enroll an individual.
4 Engaging in any practice that would reasonably be expected to have the effect of denying or discouraging enrollment by eligible individuals whose medical condition or history indicates a need for substantial future medical services.
5 Misrepresenting or falsifying information furnished to the Secretary or to an individual or any other entity under Part C.
6 Failure to comply with applicable requirements of section 1852(j)(3), which prohibits interference with medical advice by healtcare practitioners to enrollees, or section 1852(k)(2)(A)(ii), which requires procedures to enforce limits on balance billing under Medicare + Choice by physicians, providers, and suppliers in fee-for-service plans.
7 Employing or contracting with any individual or entity that is excluded from Medicare under section 1128, 42 U.S.C.A. 1320a-7, or 1128A, 42 U.S.C.A. 1320a-7a, for the provision of health care, utilization review, medical social work, or administrative services; or employing or contracting with any entity

for the provision of such services (directly or indirectly) through an excluded individual or entity.

Violations described in section 1903(m)(5)(A) are similar to those in section 1847(g)(1) and 1876(i)(6)(A), but they apply to PACE under the Medicaid program.

Sanctions described in section 1857(g)(2) include:

1 A civil money penalty not to exceed $25,000 for each violation.
2 A civil money penalty not to exceed $100,000 for each finding of illegally denying or discouraging enrollment.
3 A civil money penalty not to exceed $100,000 for misrepresenting or falsifying information to the Secretary.
4 Double the excess charge for imposing a premium in excess of the amount of the Medicare + Choice monthly basic and supplemental beneficiary premiums permitted. (In this event, the excess premium shall be deducted from the penalty and paid to the enrollee who overpaid.)
5 A civil money penalty of $15,000 for each individual not enrolled as a result of illegally denying or discouraging enrollment.
6 Suspension of enrollment of individuals after the date the Secretary notifies the organization of a violation until the Secretary is satisfied that the basis for finding the violation has been corrected and is not likely to recur.
7 Suspension of payment to the provider for individuals enrolled after the date the Secretary notified the provider of the violation until the Secretary is satisfied that the basis for finding the violation has been corrected and is not likely to recur.

Enforcement Procedures on or after January 1, 1999: Pursuant to section 1894(e)(7), the provisions of section 1857(h) apply to termination and sanctions with respect to a PACE program agreement and PACE provider in the same manner as they apply to termination and sanctions with respect to a contract and a Medicare + Choice organization under Medicare Part C.

Section 1857(h) provides for reasonable opportunity to develop and implement a corrective action plan to correct the deficiencies which led to the Secretary to impose a sanction. It also provides for reasonable notice and opportunity for hearing, and subsequent appeal of an initial decision, before terminating a PACE agreement.

Sanctions Prior to January 1, 1999: For periods prior to January 1, 1999, the Secretary may provide for remedies described in section 1876(i)(6)(B), 42 U.S.C.A. 1395mm(i)(6)(B), or section 1903(m)(5)(B), in the case of violations described in section 1876(i)(6)(A).

Violations described in section 1876(i)(6)(A) include:

1 Failure to substantially provide medically necessary items and services required under law or contract to an enrollee, if the failure has adversely affected (or has substantial likelihood to adversely affect) the enrollee.
2 Imposition of a premium in excess of the permitted amount.
3 Acting illegally to expel or to refuse to re-enroll an individual.
4 Engaging in any practice that reasonably would be expected to have the effect of denying or discouraging enrollment by eligible individuals whose medical condition or history indicates a need for future medical services.
5 Misrepresenting or falsifying information furnished to the Secretary, or to an individual or any other entity.
6 Failure to comply with requirements of section 1876(g)(A) (which pertains to community rating for premiums) or paragraph 8 (which pertains to prohibited physician incentive plans which directly or indirectly might induce a physician or physician group to reduce or limit medically necessary services to an enrollee).
7 In the case of a risk-sharing contract, employing or contracting with any individual that is excluded from participation under section 1128 or 1128A for the provision of health care, utilization review, medical social work, or administrative services; or employing or contracting with any entity for the provision of such services directly or indirectly through an excluded individual or entity.

Sanctions described in section 1876(i)(6)(B) include:

1 A civil money penalty of not more than $25,000 for each determination that a provider failed to provide medically necessary items and services required by law or contract, if the failure has adversely affected (or has substantial likelihood of adversely affecting an enrollee).
2 A civil money penalty of not more than $100,000 for each determination that a provider engaged in any practice that would reasonably be expected to have the effect of denying or discouraging enrollment by eligible individual whose medical

condition or history indicates a need for substantial future medical services.

3 A civil money penalty of $15,000 for each individual not enrolled as a result of engaging in such a practice to discourage enrollment.

4 A civil money penalty of not more than $100,000 for each determination that a provider misrepresented or falsified information furnished to the Secretary.

5 Double damages if a provider imposes a premium on an enrollee in excess of the permitted premium amount. (In this event, the excess premium shall be deducted from the civil money penalty and paid to the enrollee who overpaid.)

6 Suspension of enrollment of individuals until the Secretary is satisfied that the basis for a prohibited action has been corrected and is not likely to recur.

7 Suspension of payment to the provider for individuals enrolled after the Secretary notifies the provider of findings of a violation.

Sanctions described in section 1903(m)(5)(B) are similar, but they apply to PACE under the Medicaid program.

Enforcement Procedures Prior to January 1, 1999: For periods, prior to January 1, 1999, however, provisions of section 1876(i)(9) apply.

Section 1876(i)(9) provides for notice and reasonable opportunity to develop and implement a corrective action plan; no unreasonable or unnecessary delays between the finding of a deficiency and the imposition of a sanction; and reasonable notice an opportunity for hearing, and subsequent appeal of an initial decision, before imposing a sanction or terminating an agreement. It also provides for the Secretary to consider aggravating factors, such as whether an organization has a history of deficiencies, or has not taken action to correct deficiencies brought to its attention by the Secretary.

Statutory Provisions

Section 1894(a), 42 U.S.C.A. 1395eee(a) provides in pertinent part:

(a) RECEIPT OF BENEFITS THROUGH ENROLLMENT IN PACE PROGRAM; DEFINITIONS FOR PACE PROGRAM RELATED TERMS. —

(1) BENEFITS THROUGH ENROLLMENT IN A PACE PROGRAM. — In accordance with this section, in the case of an individual who is entitled to benefits under part A or enrolled under part B and who is a PACE program eligible individual (as defined in paragraph (5)) with respect to a PACE program offered by a PACE provider under a PACE program agreement —

(A) the individual may enroll in the program under this section; and

(B) so long as the individual is so enrolled and in accordance with regulations —

(i) the individual shall receive benefits under this title solely through such program; and

(ii) the PACE provider is entitled to payment under and in accordance with this section and such agreement for provision of such benefits.

(2) PACE PROGRAM DEFINED. — For purposes of this section, the term 'PACE program' means a program of all-inclusive care for the elderly that meets the following requirements:

(A) OPERATION. — The entity operating the program is a PACE provider (as defined in paragraph (3)).

(B) COMPREHENSIVE BENEFITS. — The program provides comprehensive health care services to PACE program eligible individuals in accordance with the PACE program agreement and regulations under this section.

(C) TRANSITION. — In the case of an individual who is enrolled under the program under this section and whose enrollment ceases for any reason (including that the individual no longer qualifies as a PACE program eligible individual, the termination of a PACE program agreement, or otherwise), the program provides assistance to the individual in obtaining necessary transitional care through appropriate referrals and making the individual's medical records available to new providers.

(3) PACE PROVIDER DEFINED. —

(A) IN GENERAL. — For purposes of this section, the term 'PACE provider' means an entity that —

(i) subject to subparagraph (B), is (or is a distinct part of) a public entity or a private, nonprofit entity organized for charitable purposes under section 501(c)(3) of the Internal Revenue Code of 1986; and

(ii) has entered into a PACE program agreement with respect to its operation of a PACE program.

(B) TREATMENT OF PRIVATE, FOR-PROFIT PROVIDERS. — Clause (i) of subparagraph (A) shall not apply —

(i) to entities subject to a demonstration project waiver under subsection (h); and

(ii) after the date the report under section 4804(b) of the Balanced Budget Act of 1997 is submitted, unless the Secretary determines that any of the findings described in subparagraph (A), (B), (C), or (D) of paragraph (2) of such section are true.

(4) PACE PROGRAM AGREEMENT DEFINED. — For purposes of this section, the term 'PACE program agreement' means, with respect to a PACE provider, an agreement, consistent with this section, section 1934, 42 U.S.C.A. 1396u-4, which pertains to PACE under Medicaid, (if applicable), and regulations promulgated to carry out such sections, between the PACE provider and the Secretary, or an agreement between the PACE provider and a State administering agency for the operation of a PACE program by the provider under such sections.

(5) PACE PROGRAM ELIGIBLE INDIVIDUAL DEFINED. — For purposes of this section, the term 'PACE program eligible individual' means, with respect to a PACE program, an individual who —

(A) is 55 years of age or older;

(B) subject to subsection (c)(4), is determined under subsection (c) to require the level of care required under the State Medicaid plan for coverage of nursing facility services;

(C) resides in the service area of the PACE program; and

(D) meets such other eligibility conditions as may be imposed under the PACE program agreement for the program under subsection (e)(2)(A)(ii).

(6) PACE PROTOCOL. — For purposes of this section, the term 'PACE protocol' means the Protocol for the Program of All-inclusive Care for the Elderly (PACE), as published by On Lok, Inc., as of April 14, 1995, or any successor protocol that may be agreed upon between the Secretary and On Lok, Inc.

With regard to required PACE benefits, section 1894(b) provides:
SCOPE OF BENEFITS; BENEFICIARY SAFEGUARDS. —

(1) IN GENERAL. — Under a PACE program agreement, a PACE provider shall —

(A) provide to PACE program eligible individuals enrolled with the provider, regardless of source of payment and directly or under contracts with other entities, at a minimum —

(i) all items and services covered under this title (for individuals enrolled under this section) and all items and services covered under title XIX, but without any limitation or condition as to amount, duration, or scope and without application of deductibles, copayments, coinsurance, or other cost-sharing that would otherwise apply under this title or such title, respectively; and

(ii) all additional items and services specified in regulations, based upon those required under the PACE protocol;

(B) provide such enrollees access to necessary covered items and services 24 hours per day, every day of the year;

(C) provide services to such enrollees through a comprehensive, multidisciplinary health and social services delivery system which integrates acute and long-term care services pursuant to regulations; and

(D) specify the covered items and services that will not be provided directly by the entity, and to arrange for delivery of those items and services through contracts meeting the requirements of regulations.

(2) QUALITY ASSURANCE; PATIENT SAFEGUARDS. — The PACE program agreement shall require the PACE provider to have in effect at a minimum —

(A) a written plan of quality assurance and improvement, and procedures implementing such plan, in accordance with regulations; and

(B) written safeguards of the rights of enrolled participants (including a patient bill of rights and procedures for grievances and appeals) in accordance with regulations and with other requirements of this title and Federal and State law that are designed for the protection of patients.

With regard to voluntary and involuntary disenrollment in PACE, section 1894(c) provides in pertinent part:
(5) ENROLLMENT; DISENROLLMENT.—

(A) VOLUNTARY DISENROLLMENT AT ANY TIME.—The enrollment and disenrollment of PACE program eligible individuals in a PACE program shall be pursuant to regulations and the PACE program agreement and shall permit enrollees to voluntarily disenroll without cause at any time.

(B) LIMITATIONS ON DISENROLLMENT.—

(i) IN GENERAL. —Regulations promulgated by the Secretary under this section and section 1934, and the PACE program agreement, shall provide that the PACE program may not disenroll a PACE program eligible individual except—

(I) for nonpayment of premiums (if applicable) on a timely basis; or

(II) for engaging in disruptive or threatening behavior, as defined in such regulations (developed in close consultation with State administering agencies).

(ii) NO DISENROLLMENT FOR NONCOMPLIANT BEHAVIOR.—Except as allowed under regulations promulgated to carry out clause (i)(II), a PACE program may not disenroll a PACE program eligible individual on the ground that the individual has engaged in noncompliant behavior if such behavior is related to a mental or physical condition of the individual. For purposes of the preceding sentence, the term 'noncompliant behavior' includes repeated noncompliance with medical advice and repeated failure to appear for appointments.

(iii) TIMELY REVIEW OF PROPOSED NONVOLUNTARY DISENROLLMENT. — A proposed disenrollment, other than a voluntary disenrollment, shall be subject to timely review and final determination by the Secretary or by the State administering agency (as applicable), prior to the proposed disenrollment becoming effective.

With respect to termination of a PACE agreement, Section 1894(e)(5) provides:

TERMINATION OF PACE PROVIDER AGREEMENTS. —

(A) IN GENERAL. — Under regulations —

(i) the Secretary or a State administering agency may terminate a PACE program agreement for cause; and

(ii) a PACE provider may terminate an agreement after appropriate notice to the Secretary, the State agency, and enrollees.

(B) CAUSES FOR TERMINATION. — In accordance with regulations establishing procedures for termination of PACE program agreements, the Secretary or a State administering agency may terminate a PACE program agreement with a PACE provider for, among other reasons, the fact that —

(i) the Secretary or State administering agency determines that —

(I) there are significant deficiencies in the quality of care provided to enrolled participants; or

(II) the provider has failed to comply substantially with conditions for a program or provider under this section or section 1934, which pertains to PACE under Medicaid; and

(ii) the entity has failed to develop and successfully initiate, within 30 days of the date of the receipt of written notice of such a determination, a plan to correct the deficiencies, or has failed to continue implementation of such a plan.

With respect to enforcement, sections 1894(e)(6) and (7) provide:

(6) SECRETARY'S OVERSIGHT; ENFORCEMENT AUTHORITY. —

(A) IN GENERAL. — Under regulations, if the Secretary determines (after consultation with the State administering agency) that a PACE provider is failing substantially to comply with the requirements of this section and regulations, the Secretary (and the State administering agency) may take any or all of the following actions:

(i) Condition the continuation of the PACE program agreement upon timely execution of a corrective action plan.

(ii) Withhold some or all further payments under the PACE program agreement under this section or section 1934 with respect to PACE program services furnished by such provider until the deficiencies have been corrected.

(iii) Terminate such agreement.

(B) APPLICATION OF INTERMEDIATE SANCTIONS. — Under regulations, the Secretary may provide for the application against a PACE provider of remedies described in section 1857(g)(2) (or, for periods before January 1, 1999, section 1876(i)(6)(B) [42 U.S.C.A. 1395mm(i)(6)(B), which pertains to HMOs and CMPs]) or 1903(m)(5)(B), [42 U.S.C.A. 1396b(m)(5)(B)] in the case of violations by the provider of the type described in section 1857(g)(1) (or section 1876(i)(6)(A) for such periods) or 1903(m)(5)(A), respectively (in relation to agreements, enrollees, and requirements under this section or section 1934, respectively).

(7) PROCEDURES FOR TERMINATION OR IMPOSITION OF SANCTIONS. — Under regulations, the provisions of section 1857(h) (or for periods before January 1, 1999, section 1876(i)(9)) shall apply to termination and sanctions respecting a PACE program agreement and PACE provider under this subsection in the same manner as they apply to a termination and sanctions with respect to a contract and a Medicare + Choice organization under part C (or for such periods an eligible organization under section 1876).

With respect to violations on or after January 1, 1999, section 1857(g)(1) provides:

(g) INTERMEDIATE SANCTIONS.—

(1) IN GENERAL.—If the Secretary determines that a Medicare + Choice organization with a contract under this section—

(A) fails substantially to provide medically necessary items and services that are required (under law or under the contract) to be provided to an individual covered under the contract, if the failure has adversely affected (or has substantial likelihood of adversely affecting) the individual;

(B) imposes premiums on individuals enrolled under this part in excess of the amount of the Medicare + Choice monthly basic and supplemental beneficiary premiums permitted under section 1854;

(C) acts to expel or to refuse to re-enroll an individual in violation of the provisions of this part;

(D) engages in any practice that would reasonably be expected to have the effect of denying or discouraging enrollment (except as permitted by this part) by eligible individuals with the organization whose medical condition or history indicates a need for substantial future medical services;

(E) misrepresents or falsifies information that is furnished—

(i) to the Secretary under this part, or

(ii) to an individual or to any other entity under this part;

(F) fails to comply with the applicable requirements of section 1852(j)(3) or 1852(k)(2)(A)(ii); or

(G) employs or contracts with any individual or entity that is excluded from participation under this title under section 1128, 42 U.S.C.A. 1320a-7, or 1128A, 42 U.S.C.A. 1320a-7a, for the provision of health care, utilization review, medical social work, or administrative services or employs or contracts with any entity for the provision (directly or indirectly) through such an excluded individual or entity of such services; the Secretary may provide, in addition to any other remedies authorized by law, for any of the remedies described in paragraph (2).

With respect to sanctions (remedies) on or after January 1, 1999, section 1857(g)(2) provides:

REMEDIES. — The remedies described in this paragraph are —

> (A) civil money penalties of not more than $25,000 for each determination under paragraph (1) or, with respect to a determination under subparagraph (D) or (E)(i) of such paragraph, of not more than $100,000 for each such determination, plus, with respect to a determination under paragraph (1)(B), double the excess amount charged in violation of such paragraph (and the excess amount charged shall be deducted from the penalty and returned to the individual concerned), and plus, with respect to a determination under paragraph (1)(D), $15,000 for each individual not enrolled as a result of the practice involved,
>
> (B) suspension of enrollment of individuals under this part after the date the Secretary notifies the organization of a determination under paragraph (1) and until the Secretary is satisfied that the basis for such determination has been corrected and is not likely to recur, or
>
> (C) suspension of payment to the organization under this part for individuals enrolled after the date the Secretary notifies the organization of a determination under paragraph (1) and until the Secretary is satisfied that the basis for such determination has been corrected and is not likely to recur.

(3) OTHER INTERMEDIATE SANCTIONS. — In the case of a Medicare + Choice organization for which the Secretary makes a determination under subsection (c)(2) the basis of which is not described in paragraph (1), the Secretary may apply the following intermediate sanctions:

> (A) Civil money penalties of not more than $25,000 for each determination under subsection (c)(2) if the deficiency that is the basis of the determination has directly adversely affected (or has the substantial likelihood of adversely affecting) an individual covered under the organization's contract.
>
> (B) Civil money penalties of not more than $10,000 for each week beginning after the initiation of civil money penalty procedures by the Secretary during which the deficiency

that is the basis of a determination under subsection (c)(2) exists.

(C) Suspension of enrollment of individuals under this part after the date the Secretary notifies the organization of a determination under subsection (c)(2) and until the Secretary is satisfied that the deficiency that is the basis for the determination has been corrected and is not likely to recur.

(4) CIVIL MONEY PENALTIES. — The provisions of section 1128A (other than subsections (a) and (b)) shall apply to a civil money penalty under paragraph (2) or (3) in the same manner as they apply to a civil money penalty or proceeding under section 1128A(a).

(h) PROCEDURES FOR TERMINATION. —

(1) IN GENERAL. — The Secretary may terminate a contract with a Medicare + Choice organization under this section in accordance with formal investigation and compliance procedures established by the Secretary under which —

(A) the Secretary provides the organization with the reasonable opportunity to develop and implement a corrective action plan to correct the deficiencies that were the basis of the Secretary's determination under subsection (c)(2); and

(B) the Secretary provides the organization with reasonable notice and opportunity for hearing (including the right to appeal an initial decision) before terminating the contract.

(2) EXCEPTION FOR IMMINENT AND SERIOUS RISK TO HEALTH. — Paragraph (1) shall not apply if the Secretary determines that a delay in termination, resulting from compliance with the procedures specified in such paragraph prior to termination, would pose an imminent and serious risk to the health of individuals enrolled under this part with the organization.

With respect to violations and sanctions prior to January 1, 1999, section 1876(i)(6)(A) and (B) provide:

(A) If the Secretary determines that an eligible organization with a contract under this section —

(i) fails substantially to provide medically necessary items and services that are required (under law or under the contract) to be provided to an individual covered under the contract, if the failure has adversely affected (or has substantial likelihood of adversely affecting) the individual;

(ii) imposes premiums on individuals enrolled under this section in excess of the premiums permitted;

(iii) acts to expel or to refuse to re-enroll an individual in violation of the provisions of this section;

(iv) engages in any practice that would reasonably be expected to have the effect of denying or discouraging enrollment (except as permitted by this section) by eligible individuals with the organization whose medical condition or history indicates a need for substantial future medical services;

(v) misrepresents or falsifies information that is furnished —

(I) to the Secretary under this section, or

(II) to an individual or to any other entity under this section;

(vi) fails to comply with the requirements of subsection (g)(6)(A) or paragraph (8); or

(vii) in the case of a risk-sharing contract, employs or contracts with any individual or entity that is excluded from participation under this title under section 1128 or 1128A for the provision of health care, utilization review, medical social work, or administrative services or employs or contracts with any entity for the provision (directly or indirectly) through such an excluded individual or entity of such services; the Secretary may provide, in addition to any other remedies authorized by law, for any of the remedies described in subparagraph (B).

(B) The remedies described in this subparagraph are —

(i) civil money penalties of not more than $25,000 for each determination under subparagraph (A) or, with respect to a determination under clause (iv) or (v)(I), of not more than $100,000 for each such determination, plus, with respect to a determinationunder subparagraph (A)(ii), double the excess amount charged in violation of such subparagraph (and the excess amount charged shall be deducted from the penalty and returned to the individual concerned), and plus, with respect to a determination under subparagraph (A)(iv), $15,000 for each individual not enrolled as a result of the practice involved,

(ii) suspension of enrollment of individuals under this section after the date the Secretary notifies the organization of a determination under subparagraph (A) and until the Secretary is satisfied that the basis for such determination has been corrected and is not likely to recur, or

(iii) suspension of payment to the organization under this section for individuals enrolled after the date the Secretary notifies the organization of a determination under subparagraph (A) and until the Secretary is satisfied that the basis for such determination has been corrected and is not likely to recur.

With respect to enforcement procedures prior to January 1, 1999, section 1876(i)(9) provides:

> The Secretary may terminate a contract with an eligible organization under this section or may impose the intermediate sanctions described in paragraph (6) on the organization in accordance with formal investigation and compliance procedures established by the Secretary under which —
>
> (A) the Secretary first provides the organization with the reasonable opportunity to develop and implement a corrective action plan to correct the deficiencies that were the basis of the Secretary's determination under paragraph (1) and the organization fails to develop or implement such a plan;
>
> (B) in deciding whether to impose sanctions, the Secretary considers aggravating factors such as whether an organization has a history of deficiencies or has not taken action to correct deficiencies the Secretary has brought to the organization's attention;
>
> (C) there are no unreasonable or unnecessary delays between the finding of a deficiency and the imposition of sanctions; and
>
> (D) the Secretary provides the organization with reasonable notice and opportunity for hearing (including the right to

appeal an initial decision) before imposing any sanction or terminating the contract.

For regulatory citations, see Chapter 6

Chapter 3

SANCTIONS IN THE MEDICAID STATUTE

§ 3:1 PUBLICIZING FINDINGS OF STATE SURVEYS OF HEALTH CARE FACILITIES — Section 1902(a)(36) [42 U.S.C.A. 1396a(a)(36)]

Summary

States may receive Federal matching funds for their Medicaid programs if they submit to the Secretary of Health and Human Services a Medicaid State plan which meets Federal requirements. See section 1902(b), 42 U.S.C.A. 1396a(b), and section 1903, 42 U.S.C.A. 1396b. States which do not meet the requirements do not get, or, having once participated, subsequently lose, Federal matching funds. See section 1904, 42 U.S.C.A. 1396c.

Pursuant to section 1902(a)(9), 42 U.S.C.A. 1396a(a)(9), State Medicaid plans must provide for the State health agency, or some other appropriate State medical agency (whichever has an agreement with the Secretary under Medicare to survey and certify compliance by providers with conditions of participation) to establish and maintain health standards for private or public institutions in which Medicaid recipients may receive care or services. They also must provide for establishment or designation of a State authority or authorities to establish and maintain standards other than those relating to health for such institutions. In addition, they must assure that any laboratory services paid for by Medicaid are provided by labs that meet Medicare requirements.

Then, pursuant to section 1902(a)(36), 42 U.S.C.A. 1396a(a)(36), a State plan must provide that, within 90 days following completion of a State survey of any health care facility, laboratory, agency, clinic, or organization, the State agency will make public in a readily available form and place pertinent survey findings. That applies to findings regarding compliance with statutory conditions of participation imposed under Medicaid and any major additional conditions which the Secretary finds necessary for health and safety of individuals furnished care or services therein. Presumably, with this information consumers will be better equipped to choose sources for their medical care.

Statutory Provisions

Section 1902(a)(9), 42 U.S.C.A. 1396a(a)(9), provides:

A State plan for medical assistance must —

* * *

(9) provide —

(A) that the State health agency, or other appropriate State medical agency (whichever is utilized by the Secretary for the purpose specified in the first sentence of section 1864(a) [42 U.S.C.A. 1395aa, which pertains to use of State agencies to determine compliance by providers of services with Medicare conditions of participation]), shall be responsible for establishing and maintaining health standards for private or public institutions in which recipients of medical assistance under the plan may receive care or services,

(B) for the establishment or designation of a State authority or authorities which shall be responsible for establishing and maintaining standards, other than those relating to health, for such institutions, and

(C) that any laboratory services paid for under such plan must be provided by a laboratory which meets the applicable requirements of section 1861(e)(9) [42 U.S.C.A. 1395x(e)(9), which pertains to the definition of "hospital" and the requirement that hospitals meet such other requirements as the Secretary finds necessary for the health and safety of patients] or paragraphs (16) and (17) of section 1861(s) [42 U.S.C.A. 1395x(s)(16) and (17), which pertain to the definition of "medical and other health services" and the obligation of laboratories to meet State licensing requirements and such other requirements as the Secretary finds necessary for the health and safety of individuals for whom laboratory tests are performed], or, in the case of a laboratory which is in a rural health clinic, of section 1861(aa)(2)(G) [42 U.S.C.A. 1395x(aa)(2)(G), which pertains to the definition of "rural health clinic" and the ability of such clinics to provide clinical laboratory services in accordance with regulations of the Secretary.]

◆ NOTE: Effective December 19, 1989, section 6115(c) of P.L. 101-239, the Omnibus Budget Reconciliation Act of 1989, substituted "paragraphs (15) and (16)" for "paragraphs (14) and (15)" in subparagraph (C) above. This applies to screening pap smears performed after June 30, 1990. Subsequently, section 4106(a)(1) of the Balanced Budget Act of 1997, P.L. 105–33, redesignated former paragraphs (15) and (16) as (16) and (17), respectively, effective July 1, 1998.

Section 1902(a)(36), 42 U.S.C.A. 1396a(a)(36), provides:

A State plan for medical assistance must—

(36) provide that within 90 days following the completion of each survey of any health care facility, laboratory, agency, clinic, or organization, by the appropriate State agency described in paragraph (9), such agency shall (in accordance with regulations of the Secretary) make public in readily

available form and place the pertinent findings of each such survey relating to the compliance of each such health care facility, laboratory, clinic agency, or organization with (A) the statutory conditions of participation imposed under this title, and (B) the major additional conditions which the Secretary finds necessary in the interest of health and safety of individuals who are furnished care or services by any such facility, laboratory, clinic, agency, or organization[.]

For regulatory citations, see Chapter 7

§ 3:2 ADDITIONAL PENALTIES FOR PERSONS OR ENTITIES SANCTIONED BY EXCLUSION UNDER SECTION 1128 OR UNDER SECTION 1128A — Section 1902(a)(39) [42 U.S.C.A. 1396a(a)(39)]

Summary

States may receive Federal matching funds for their Medicaid programs if they submit to the Secretary of Health and Human Services a Medicaid State plan which meets Federal requirements. See section 1902(b), 42 U.S.C.A. 1396a(b), and section 1903, 42 U.S.C.A. 1396b. States which do not meet the requirements do not get, or, having once participated, subsequently lose, Federal matching funds. See section 1904, 42 U.S.C.A. 1396c.

According to section 1902(a)(39), 42 U.S.C.A. 1396a(a)(39), a Medicaid State plan must provide for the State Medicaid agency to exclude any specified individual or entity from participation in the State's Medicaid program for the period stipulated by the Secretary when required by the Secretary to do so pursuant to section 1128, 42 U.S.C.A. 1320a-7, or section 1128A, 42 U.S.C.A. 1320a-7a.

Section 1128 pertains to exclusion of certain persons and entities convicted of Medicare or Medicaid related crimes and perpetrators of other abuses. For some offenses exclusion is mandatory; for others the Secretary has discretion to exclude. Section 1128A pertains to civil money penalties, but also permits exclusions based on evidence received in a civil money penalty proceeding. See Chapter 4, § 4:6 for analysis of section 1128 and § 4:8 for analysis of section 1128A.

In addition, a State plan must provide that no payment may be made with respect to any item or service furnished by such individual or entity during the specified period. Thus, no Medicare money, no Medicaid money — the point being if you are disqualified from receiving Federal funds from one program, you should not receive them from the other. States are free, however, to impose longer periods of exclusion than the Secretary requires.

Conversely, section 1902(a)(41), 42 U.S.C.A. 1396a(a)(41), requires States to notify the Secretary promptly whenever a Medicaid provider of services or any other person is terminated, suspended, or otherwise sanctioned or prohibited from participating in a State Medicaid program. And, pursuant to section 4754(a) of P.L. 101-508, the Omnibus Budget Reconciliation Act of 1990, (OBRA 90), in the case of a physician, States also must notify the State medical licensing board. This applies to sanctions effected on or after January 4, 1991.

Statutory Provisions

Section 1902(a)(39), 42 U.S.C.A. 1396a(a)(39), provides:

> A State plan for medical assistance must—
>
> * * *
>
> (39) provide that the State agency shall exclude any specified individual or entity from participation in the program under the State plan for the period specified by the Secretary, when required by him to do so pursuant to section 1128 or section 1128A, and provide that no payment may be made under the plan with respect to any item or service furnished by such individual or entity during such period[.]

Section 1902(a)(41), 42 U.S.C.A. 1396a(a)(41), provides:

> A State plan for medical assistance must—
>
> * * *
>
> (41) provide that whenever a provider of services or any other person is terminated, suspended, or otherwise sanctioned or prohibited from participating under the State plan, the State agency shall promptly notify the Secretary and, in the case of a physician and notwithstanding paragraph (7) [which pertains to required restrictions on use or disclosure of information concerning applicants and recipients], the State medical licensing board [this clause about reporting physicians added by section 4754(a) of P.L. 101-508, the Omnibus Budget Reconciliation Act of 1990 (OBRA 90) applies to sanc-

tions effected 60 days after OBRA 90's enactment, or January 4, 1991] of such action[.]

◆ NOTE: For statutory provisions and analysis of section 1128, see Chapter 4, § 4:6. For statutory provisions and analysis of section 1128A, see Chapter 4, § 4:8.

◆ NOTE: Refer to Table of Contents for specific providers or offenses subject to sanction by exclusion or civil money penalty.

For regulatory citations, see Chapter 7

§ 3:3 DISCLOSING INFORMATION ABOUT SANCTIONS AGAINST HEALTH CARE PRACTITIONERS AND PROVIDERS — Section 1902(a)(49) and Section 1921 [42 U.S.C.A. 1396a(a)(49) and 42 U.S.C.A. 1396r-2]

Summary

States may receive Federal matching funds for their Medicaid programs if they submit to the Secretary of Health and Human Services a Medicaid State plan which meets Federal requirements. See section 1902(b), 42 U.S.C.A. 1396a(b), and section 1903, 42 U.S.C.A. 1396b. States which do not meet the requirements do not get, or, having once participated, subsequently lose, Federal matching funds. See section 1904, 42 U.S.C.A. 1396c.

Pursuant to section 1902(a)(49), 42 U.S.C.A. 1396a(a)(49), a State plan must require the State Medicaid agency to provide information and access to information about sanctions taken against health care practitioners and providers by State licensing authorities, all in accordance with section 1921, 42 U.S.C.A. 1396r-2.

According to section 1921, information about formal proceedings concluded against a health care practitioner or entity by any authority of a State, or of a political subdivision thereof, or (effective January 1, 1992) by a peer review organization or private accreditation entity which licenses health care practitioners or entities must be made available. That includes any adverse action taken, such as revocation or suspension of a license (and the duration thereof), reprimand, censure, or probation; any dismissal or closure of the proceedings by reason of the practitioner or entity surrendering a license or leaving the State or jurisdiction; and any other loss of the license, whether by operation of law, voluntary surrender, or otherwise.

The State also must provide the Secretary, or appropriate private or public agencies with whom he has suitable arrangements for receipt, storage, protection of confidentiality and dissemination, access to such documents as may be necessary to determine the facts and circumstances concerning the State's actions and determinations. Furthermore, that information must be provided, in an appropriate form and manner, as determined by the Secretary.

The Secretary may then, directly or through suitable arrangements with others, disseminate that information to:

1. agencies administering Federal health care programs, including private entities administering such programs under contract;
2. State and local licensing authorities;
3. State agencies administering or supervising the administration of State health care programs (as defined in section 1128(h), 42 U.S.C.A. 1320a-7(h), which includes Medicaid, the Maternal and Child Health Services Block Grant program authorized by Title V of the Social Security Act, as amended, 42 U.S.C.A. 701 et seq., and the program of Block Grants to States for Social Services authorized by Title XX of the Act, 42 U.S.C.A. 1397);
4. utilization and quality control peer review organizations (PRO's) working under Part B of Title XI and their subcontractors;
5. State Medicaid fraud control units;
6. hospitals and other health care entities, with respect to physicians or other licensed health care practitioners that have entered or may be entering into an employment or affiliation relationship with, or that have applied for clinical privileges or appointments to the medical staff of, such hospitals or other health care entities, in accordance with provisions of the Health Care Quality Improvement Act of 1986, 42 U.S.C.A. 11111et seq.;
7. the Attorney General and such other law enforcement officials as the Secretary deems appropriate; and
8. upon request, to the Comptroller General.

Presumably, given the knowledge this disclosure permits, individuals and other entities will impose additional sanctions.

Statutory Provisions

Section 1902(a)(49), 42 U.S.C.A. 1396a(a)(49), provides:

A State plan for medical assistance must —

* * *

(49) provide that the State will provide information and access to certain information respecting sanctions taken against health care practitioners and providers by State licensing authorities in accordance with section 1921[.]

Section 1921, 42 U.S.C.A. 1396r-2, provides:

(a) INFORMATION REPORTING REQUIREMENT. — The requirement referred to in section 1902(a)(49) is that the State must provide for the following:

(1) INFORMATION REPORTING SYSTEM. — The State must have in effect a system of reporting the following information with respect to formal proceedings (as defined by the Secretary in regulations) concluded against a health care practitioner or entity by any authority of the State (or of a political subdivision thereof) responsible for the licensing of health care practitioners (or any peer review organization or private accreditation entity reviewing the services provided by health care practitioners) [parenthetical clause added by section 4752(f)(1)(a) of P.L. 101-508, the Omnibus Budget Reconciliation Act of 1990 (OBRA 90), effective January 1, 1992] or entities:

(A) Any adverse action taken by such licensing authority as a result of the proceeding, including any revocation or suspension of a license (and the length of any such suspension), reprimand, censure, or probation.

(B) Any dismissal or closure of the proceedings by reason of the practitioner or entity surrendering the license or leaving the State or jurisdiction.

(C) Any other loss of the license of the practitioner or entity, whether by operation of law, voluntary surrender, or otherwise.

(D) [Effective January 1, 1992, pursuant to section 4752(f)(1)(B) of OBRA 90, regardless whether the Secretary has promulgated regulations] [a]ny negative action or finding by such authority, organization, or entity regarding the practitioner or entity.

(2) ACCESS TO DOCUMENTS. — The State must provide the Secretary (or an entity designated by the Secretary) with access to such documents of the authority described in paragraph (1) as may be necessary for the Secretary to determine the facts and circumstances concerning the actions and determinations described in such paragraph for the purpose of carrying out this Act.

(b) FORM OF INFORMATION. — The information described in subsection (a)(1) shall be provided to the Secretary (or to an appropriate private or public agency, under suitable arrangements made by the Secretary with respect to receipt, storage, protection of confidentiality, and dissemination of information) in such a form and manner as the Secretary determines to be appropriate in order to provide for activities of the Secretary under this Act and in order to provide, directly or through suitable arrangements made by the Secretary, information —

(1) to agencies administering Federal health care programs, including private entities administering such programs under contract,

(2) to licensing authorities described in subsection (a)(1),

(3) to State agencies administering or supervising the administration of State health care programs (as defined in section 1128(h) [which includes Medicaid, the Maternal and Child Health Services Block Grant program authorized by Title V of the Social Security Act, as amended, 42 U.S.C.A. 701 et seq., and the program of Block Grants to States for Social Services authorized by Title XX of the Act, 42 U.S.C.A. 1397]),

(4) to utilization and quality control peer review organizations described in part B of title XI and to appropriate entities with contracts under section 1154(a)(4)(C) [42 U.S.C.A. 1320c-3(a)(4)(C), which pertains to contracting for quality of care reviews of inpatient and outpatient services provided by eligible organizations, such as health maintenance organizations and competitive medical plans, pursuant to a risk-sharing contract under section 1876, 42 U.S.C.A. 1395mm] with respect to eligible organizations reviewed under the contracts,

(5) to State Medicaid fraud control units (as defined in section 1903(q) [42 U.S.C.A. 1396b(q)]),

(6) to hospitals and other health care entities (as defined in section 431 of the Health Care Quality Improvement Act of 1986 [42 U.S.C.A. 11151]), with respect to physicians or other licensed health care practitioners that have entered (or may be entering) into an employment or affiliation relationship with, or have applied for clinical privileges or appointments to the medical staff of, such hospitals or other health care entities (and such information shall be deemed to be disclosed pursuant to section 427 of, and be subject to the provisions of, that Act [42 U.S.C.A. 11137]),

(7) to the Attorney General and such other law enforcement officials as the Secretary deems appropriate, and,

(8) upon request, to the Comptroller General, in order for such authorities to determine the fitness of individuals to provide health care services, to protect the health and safety of individuals receiving health care through such programs, and to protect the fiscal integrity of such programs.

(c) CONFIDENTIALITY OF INFORMATION PROVIDED. — The Secretary shall provide for suitable safeguards for the confidentiality of the information furnished under subsection (a). Nothing in this subsection shall prevent the disclosure of such information by a party which is otherwise authorized, under applicable State law, to make such disclosure.

(d) APPROPRIATE COORDINATION. — The Secretary shall provide for the maximum appropriate coordination in the implementation of subsection (a) of this section and section 422 of the Health Care Quality Improvement Act of 1986 [42 U.S.C.A. 11132].

◆ NOTE: Refer to Table of Contents for specific providers or offenses subject to sanction by exclusion or civil money penalty or termination of provider agreement.

For regulatory citations, see Chapter 7

§ 3:4 BILLING MEDICAID ELIGIBLES OR FINANCIALLY RESPONSIBLE RELATIVES OR REPRESENTATIVES FOR MEDICAL EXPENSES WHEN THIRD PARTIES ARE LIABLE TO PAY — Sections 1902(g) and 1902(a)(25) [42 U.S.C.A. 1396a(g) and 1396a(a)(25)]

Summary

States may receive Federal matching funds for their Medicaid programs if they submit to the Secretary of Health and Human Services a Medicaid State plan which meets Federal requirements. See section 1902(b), 42 U.S.C.A. 1396a(b), and section 1903, 42 U.S.C.A. 1396b. States which do not meet the requirements do not get, or, having once participated, subsequently lose, Federal matching funds. See section 1904, 42 U.S.C.A. 1396c.

According to section 1902(a)(25)(A), 42 U.S.C.A. 1396a(a)(25)(A), a State Medicaid plan must provide for the State or local agency administering the plan to ascertain the liability of third parties, including health insurers, to pay for care and services available under the plan.

Prior to P.L. 103-66, the Omnibus Budget Reconciliation Act of 1993 (OBRA 93), health insurers were private insurers as defined by the Secretary by regulation. Pursuant to section 13622(a)(1) of OBRA 93, however, the definition was expanded to include not only private health insurers as defined by regulation of the Secretary of HHS, but also: a group health plan as defined in section 607(l) of the Employee Retirement Income Security Act of 1974 (ERISA), a service benefit plan, and a health maintenance organization (HMO).

Section 1902(a)(25)(B) provides that if a State finds that a third party is liable for medical expenses paid under the plan, and if the amount of reimbursement the State reasonably can expect to recover exceeds the costs of such recovery, the State (or local agency) must seek that reimbursement.

If the liability of third parties to pay for service to a Medicaid eligible equals or exceeds the amount payable under the State plan (disregarding section 1916, 42 U.S.C.A. 1396o, which regulates use of enrollment fees, premiums, deductions, cost sharing, and similar charges), section 1902(a)(25)(C) requires that the plan prohibit any person furnishing the service from seeking to collect from either the Medicaid eligible or from any financially responsible relative or representative. The same is true if the liability of third parties exceeds the lesser of either the amount which may be collected under section 1916, or the amount by which what is payable under the plan, disregarding section 1916, exceeds total liabilities of third parties for the service.

In short, if Medicaid pays and a third party is liable for payment, the State must seek reimbursement from the third party, provided the cost of doing so will not exceed the amount the State reasonably can expect to recover. Moreover, anyone furnishing care and services who charges more than what Medicaid pays must look to those third parties for additional compensation, and not to the Medicaid eligible or any financially responsible relative or representative.

According to section 1902(a)(25)(D), the plan must provide that a person who furnishes services and participates in Medicaid may not refuse to furnish services to a Medicaid eligible because of a third party's potential liability for payment.

With respect to prenatal or preventive pediatric care, including early and periodic screening and diagnosis services covered under the plan, section 1902(a)(25)(E) provides that the State must pay for such services according to its payment schedule and without regard to the liability of a third party for such services. Then the State must seek reimbursement from the third party.

Similarly, with respect to services covered under a State plan which are provided to an individual on whose behalf child support enforcement is being carried out by the State agency pursuant to Title IV-D of the Social Security Act, 42 U.S.C.A. 651 et seq., section 1902(a)(25)(F) provides that the State must pay for such services according to its payment schedule and without regard to the liability of a third party for such services, if that third-party liability derives, through insurance or otherwise, from the parent whose obligation to pay support is being enforced by the State, and if payment has not been made by such third party within 30 days after the services were furnished. Then the State must seek reimbursement from the third party.

Section 1902(a)(25)(G), which was added by section 13622(b) of OBRA 93, requires a State to prohibit any of the defined health insurers from taking into account that an individual is eligible for or is provided Medicaid assistance by it or any other State when it enrolls an individual or when it make any payments to an individual or on an individual's behalf.

Section 1902(a)(25)(I), which was added by section 13622(c) of OBRA 93, requires a State to have a law granting it subrogation rights against a liable third party to the extent payment has been made under Medicaid for health care items or services.

To deal with those who violate the requirements of section 1902(a)(25)(C) by improperly billing a Medicaid eligible or any financially responsible relative or representative of a Medicaid eligible, section 1902(g), 42 U.S.C.A. 1396a(g), permits States, at their option and in addition to any other sanction, to provide for a reduction of Medicaid payments otherwise due the person furnishing the items or services in an amount up to three times the amount improperly sought. To ascertain whether a State has exercised this option, consult the State's plan.

◆ NOTE: Pursuant to section 1903(o), 42 U.S.C.A. 1396b(o), a State will not receive Federal financial participation (FFP) for its Medicaid program to the extent that a private health insurer would have been obligated to provide such assistance but for a provision of its insurance contract which limits or excludes such an obligation because the person is eligible for or is provided assistance under Medicaid. Furthermore, section 13622(a)(2) of OBRA 93 expanded the definition of private health insurer for section 1903(o) purposes, too. As amended, the latter included group health plans under ERISA, service benefit plans, and HMO's, as well as private insurers as defined by the Secretary by regulation. Presumably, if States want to avoid this loss of FFP, they can preclude such provisions in health insurance policies, ERISA group health plans, service benefit plans, and HMO's.

Statutory Provisions

Section 1902(a)(25), 42 U.S.C.A. 1396a(a)(25), provides:

A State plan for medical assistance must—

* * *

(25) provide—

(A) that the State or local agency administering such plan will take all reasonable measures to ascertain the legal liability of third parties (including health insurers, group health plans (as defined in section 607(1) of the Employee Retirement Income Security Act of 1974), service benefit plans, and health maintenance organizations [the phrase beginning ", group health plans" through "organizations" was added by section 13622(a)(1) of P.L. 103-66, the Omnibus Budget Reconciliation Act of 1993 (OBRA 93)]) to pay for care and services available under the plan, including—

(i) the collection of sufficient information (including the use of information collected by the Medicare and Medicaid Coverage Data Bank under section 1144 and any additional measures [the phrase beginning "including the use" through "additional measures" was added by section 13581(b)(2) of OBRA 93] as specified by the Secretary in regulations) to enable the State to pursue claims against such third parties, with such information being collected at the time of any determination or redetermination of eligibility for medical assistance, and

(ii) the submission to the Secretary of a plan (subject to approval by the Secretary) for pursuing claims against such third parties, which plan shall be integrated with, and be monitored as a part of the Secretary's review of, the State's mechanized claims processing and information retrieval system under section 1903(r) [42 U.S.C.A. 1396b(r)] , and be subject to the provisions of section 1903(r)(4) [42 U.S.C.A. 1396b(r)(4)];

◆ NOTE: Prior to amendment by section 4753(b) of the Balanced Budget Act of 1997, P.L. 105–33, the clause after "such third parties" read: "which plan shall? be integrated with, and be monitored as a part of the Secretary's review of, the State's mechanized claims processing and information retrieval system under section 1903(r) [42 U.S.C.A. 1396b(r)], and be subject to the provisions of section 1903(r)(4) [42 U.S.C.A. 1396b(r)(4)] relating to reductions in Federal payments for failure to meet conditions of approval, but shall not be subject to any other financial penalty as a result of any other monitoring, quality control, or auditing requirements."

(B) that in any case where such a legal liability is found to exist after medical assistance has been made available on behalf of the individual and where the amount of reimbursement the State can reasonably expect to recover exceeds the costs of such recovery, the State or local agency will seek reimbursement for such assistance to the extent of such legal liability;

(C) that in the case of an individual who is entitled to medical assistance under the State plan with respect to a service for which a third party is liable for payment, the person furnishing the service may not seek to collect from the individual (or any financially responsible relative or representative of that individual) payment of an amount for that service (i) if the total of the amount of the liabilities of third parties for that service is at least equal to the amount payable for that service under the plan (disregarding section 1916) [42 U.S.C.A. 1396o, which pertains to use of enrollment fees, premiums, deductions, cost sharing, and similar charges], or (ii) in an amount which exceeds the lesser of (I) the amount which may be collected under section 1916, or (II) the amount by which the amount payable for that service under the plan (disregarding section 1916) exceeds the total of the amount of the liabilities of third parties for that service;

(D) that a person who furnishes services and is participating under the plan may not refuse to furnish services to an individual (who is entitled to have payment made under the plan for the services the person furnishes) because of a third party's potential liability for payment for the service;

(E) that in the case of prenatal or preventive pediatric care (including early and periodic screening and diagnosis services under section 1905(a)(4)(B) [42 U.S.C.A. 1396d(a)(4)(B)] covered under the State plan, the State shall—

(i) make payment for such service in accordance with the usual payment schedule under such plan for such services without regard to the liability of a third party for payment for such services; and

(ii) seek reimbursement from such third party in accordance with subparagraph (B);

(F) that in the case of any services covered under such plan which are provided to an individual on whose behalf child support enforcement is being carried out by the State agency under part D of title IV of this Act, the State shall—

(i) make payment for such service in accordance with the usual payment schedule under such plan for such services without regard to any third-party liability for payment for such services, if such third-party liability is derived (through insurance or otherwise) from the parent whose obligation to pay support is being enforced by such agency, if payment has not been made by such third party within 30 days after such services are furnished;

(ii) seek reimbursement from such third party in accordance with subparagraph (B);

◆ NOTE: Prior to repeal by section 4741(a)(1) of the Balanced Budget Act of 1997, former paragraph (G), which had been added by section 4402(a)(2) of P.L. 101–508, the Omnibus Budget Reconciliation Act of 1990 (OBRA 90), read: "(G) that the State shall meet the requirements of section 1906 [42 U.S.C.A. 1396(e)(a)] (relating to enrollment of individuals under group health plans in certain cases)[.]" Section 4741(a)(1) also redesignated former paragraphs (H) and (I) as (G) and (H), respectively. These changes were effective August 5, 1997.

(G) that the State prohibits any health insurer (including a group health plan, as defined in section 607(l) of the Employee Retirement Income Security Act of 1974, a service benefit plan, and a health maintenance organization), in enrolling an individual or in making any payments for benefits to the individual or on the individual's behalf from taking into account that the individual is eligible for or is provided medical assistance under a plan under this title for such State, or any other State, and

(H) that to the extent that payment has been made under the State plan for medical assistance in any case where a third party has a legal liability to make payment for such assistance, the State has in effect laws under which, to the extent that payment has been made under the State plan for medical assistance for health care items or services furnished to an individual, the State is considered to have acquired the rights of such individual to payment by any other party for such health care items or services.

◆ NOTE: Section 13622(b) of OBRA 93 deleted "and" from the end of subparagraph (F)(i) and from the end of subparagraph (g) and added subparagraph (H). Section 13622(d) deleted "and" from the end of subparagraph (G), added "and" to the end of subparagraph (H), and added subparagraph (I).

With respect to the prohibition against improper billing of a Medicaid eligible or the financially responsible relative or representative thereof, section 1902(g), 42 U.S.C.A. 1396a(g), provides:

> In addition to any other sanction available to a State, a State may provide for a reduction of any payment amount otherwise due with respect to a person who furnishes services under the plan in an amount equal to up to three times the amount of any payment sought to be collected by that person in violation of subsection (a)(25)(C).

Finally, with respect to withholding Federal financial participation from States, section 1903(o), 42 U.S.C.A. 1396b(o), as amended by section 13622(a)(2) of OBRA 93, provides:

> Notwithstanding the preceding provisions of this section, no payment shall be made to a State under the preceding provisions of this section for expenditures for medical assistance provided for an individual under its State plan approved under this title to the extent that a private insurer (as defined by the Secretary by regulation and including a group health plan (as defined in section 607(l) of the Employee Retirement Income Security Act of 1974), a service benefit plan, and a health maintenance organization [OBRA 93 added the phrase beginning "and including" through "organization"]) would have been obligated to provide such assistance but for a provision of its insurance contract which has the effect of limiting or excluding such obligation because the individual is eligible for or is provided medical assistance under the plan.

For regulatory citations, see Chapter 7

§ 3:5 FAILURE BY AN INTERMEDIATE CARE FACILITY FOR THE MENTALLY RETARDED TO COMPLY WITH MEDICAID CONDITIONS FOR PARTICIPATION — Section 1902(i) [42 U.S.C.A. 1396a(i)]

Summary

According to section 1902(i), 42 U.S.C.A. 1396a(i), if a State determines that an intermediate care facility for the mentally retarded (ICF/MR) no longer substantially complies with Medicaid requirements, and also determines that the facility's deficiencies immediately jeopardize the health and safety of its patients, the State must terminate the facility's certification for participation in Medicaid.

If a State determines that an ICF/MR no longer substantially complies with Medicaid requirements, but finds that the facility's deficiencies do not immediately jeopardize the health and safety of its patients, then, in lieu of terminating the facility's certification for participation in Medicaid, the State may provide that no Medicaid payment will be made with respect to any individual admitted to the facility after a specified date. In addition, effective August 5, 1997, pursuant to section 4752(a) of the Balanced Budget Act of 1997, P.L. 105–33, a State may establish alternative remedies if the State establishes to the satisfaction of the Secretary of Health and Human Services that such alternatives are effective in deterring noncompliance and correcting deficiencies.

In any case, the State must provide notice and opportunity for a hearing to the facility before effecting its decision. Even so, it cannot effect its decision until it has given the facility reasonable opportunity, following the initial determination, to correct its deficiencies. Furthermore, the State's decision to deny payment may be made effective only after notice to the public and to the facility. Payment denial terminates when the State finds the facility is in substantial compliance (or is making good faith efforts to achieve substantial compliance) with its requirements, or, with respect to cases where immediate jeopardy to the health and safety of residents is not involved, with the end of the eleventh month following the month the decision is made effective, whichever occurs first.

With respect to a facility where immediate jeopardy is not involved, however, if noncompliance continues, the State must terminate certification effective the first day of the first month following the month specified in the initial denial decision.

◆ NOTE: For obligations of the Secretary of Health and Human Services vis-a-vis ICF/MR's and the concept of correction and reduction plans for bringing them into compliance with Medicaid requirements, see section 1922, 42 U.S.C.A. 1396r-3, discussed at § 3:18.

Statutory Provisions

Section 1902(i), 42 U.S.C.A. 1396a(i), provides:

(1) In addition to any other authority under State law, where a State determines that a[n] intermediate care facility for the mentally retarded which is certified for participation under its plan no longer substantially meets the requirements for such a facility under this title and further determines that the facility's deficiencies —

(A) immediately jeopardize the health and safety of its patients, the State shall provide for the termination of the facility's certification for participation under the plan and may provide, or

(B) do not immediately jeopardize the health and safety of its patients, the State may, in lieu of providing for terminating the facility's certification for participation under the plan, establish alternative remedies if the State demonstrates to the Secretary's satisfaction that the alternative remedies are effective in deterring noncompliance and correcting deficiencies, and may provide that no payment will be made under the State plan with respect to any individual admitted to such facility after a date specified by the State.

◆ NOTE: Effective August 5, 1997, section 4752(a) of the Balanced Budget Act of 1997, P.L. 105–33, added to section 1902(i)(1)(B), the phrase: "establish alternative remedies if the State demonstrates to the Secretary's satisfaction that the alternative remedies are effective in deterring noncompliance and correcting deficiencies, and may."

(2) The State shall not make such a decision with respect to a facility until the facility has had a reasonable opportunity, following the initial determination that it no longer substantially meets the requirements for such a facility under this title, to correct its deficiencies, and, following this period, has been given reasonable notice and opportunity for a hearing.

(3) The State's decision to deny payment may be made effective only after such notice to the public and to the facility as may be provided for by the State, and its effectiveness shall terminate (A) when the State finds that the facility is in substantial compliance (or is making good faith efforts to achieve substantial compliance) with the requirements for such a facility under this title, or (B) in the case described in paragraph (1)(B), with the end of the eleventh month following the month such decision is made effective, whichever occurs first. If a facility to which clause (B) of the previous sentence applies still fails to substantially meet the provisions of the respective section on the date specified in such clause, the State shall terminate such facility's certification for participation under the plan effective with the first day of the first month following the month specified in such clause.

For regulatory citations, see Chapter 7

§ 3:5.1 OVERCHARGING MEDICAID ELIGIBLES WHO ARE QUALIFIED MEDICARE BENEFICIARIES—Section 1902(n)(3) [42 U.S.C.A. 1396a(n)(3)]

Summary

A State Medicaid plan may provide payment for Medicare cost-sharing amounts for an item or service furnished to a Qualified Medicare Beneficiary (QMB). QMB's are persons whose incomes are at or below the poverty level, but not low enough for them to qualify for Medicaid. They are entitled to have their Medicare premiums, deductibles, and co-insurance paid for by Medicaid. See section 1905(p), 42 U.S.C.A. 1396d(p).

Pursuant to section 1902(n)(1) of the Social Security Act, as amended, 42 U.S.C.A. 1396a(n)(1), a State payment for Medicare cost-sharing amounts, combined with payment under Medicare for the same item or service, may exceed the amount otherwise payable under Medicaid for Medicaid recipients who are not QMB's.

If a State makes such a cost-sharing payment, however, pursuant to section 1902(n)(2), it is not required to pay for any expenses incurred related to deductible, coinsurance, or copayments for Medicare cost-sharing to the extent that a Medicare payment would exceed the amount which otherwise would be paid under Medicaid if the service were provided to an eligible recipient who is not a Medicare beneficiary.

If a State's Medicare cost-sharing for a QMB is reduced or eliminated through application of section 1902(n)(2), then pursuant to section 1902(n)(3), three rules apply:

1. For purposes of applying any payment limitation under Medicare on the amount a beneficiary may be billed or charged for the service, the amount of the Medicare payment plus the amount of the Medicaid payment shall be considered payment in full.
2. The Medicare beneficiary shall have no liability to pay any Medicaid managed care organization for the service.
3. Any sanction that may be imposed upon a provider or Medicaid managed care organization for excess charges under Medicaid or Medicare applies to imposition of such a charge to a QMB. [NOTE: Refer to Chapter Guides for other sanctions applicable to excessive charges.]

Pursuant to section 1903(m)(1)(A), "Medicaid managed care organization" means a health maintenance organization, a risk-sharing organization with a contract under section 1876, 42 U.S.C.A. 1395mm, a Medicare+Choice organization with a contract under Medicare Part C, a provider-sponsored organization, or any other qualifying public or private organization.

Section 1902(n)(3) may not be construed to prevent payment of any Medicare cost-sharing by a Medicare supplemental policy or by an employer retiree health plan on behalf of an individual.

◆ NOTE: This sanction was added by sections 4714(a)(1)(A) and (B) of the Balanced Budget Act of 1997, P.L.105–33. In general, it applies to items and services furnished on or after August 5, 1997. In the case of a payment that is subject to a lawsuit pending as of, or initiated after, August 5, 1997, however, it applies to items and services furnished before August 5, 1997.

Statutory Provisions

Section 1902(n), 42 U.S.C.A. 1396a(n), provides as follows:

> (1) In the case of medical assistance furnished under this title for Medicare cost-sharing respecting the furnishing of a service or item to a qualified Medicare beneficiary, the State plan may provide payment in an amount with respect to the service or item that results in the sum of such payment amount and any amount of payment made under title XVIII with respect to the service or item exceeding the amount that is otherwise payable under the State plan for the item or service for eligible individuals who are not qualified Medicare beneficiaries.
>
> (2) In carrying out paragraph (1), a State is not required to provide any payment for any expenses incurred relating to payment for deductibles, coinsurance, or copayments for Medicare cost-sharing to the extent that payment under title XVIII for the service would exceed the payment amount that otherwise would be made under the State plan under this title for such service if provided to an eligible recipient other than a Medicare beneficiary.
>
> (3) In the case in which a State's payment for Medicare cost-sharing for a qualified Medicare beneficiary with respect to an item or service is reduced or eliminated through the application of paragraph (2) —
>
> > (A) for purposes of applying any limitation under title XVIII on the amount that the beneficiary may be billed or charged for the service, the amount of payment made under title XVIII plus the amount of payment (if any) under the State plan shall be considered to be payment in full for the service;
> >
> > (B) the beneficiary shall not have any legal liability to make payment to a provider or to an organization described in section 1903(m)(1)(A) for the service; and
> >
> > (C) any lawful sanction that may be imposed upon a provider or such an organization for excess charges under this title or title XVIII shall apply to the imposition of any charge imposed upon the individual in such case.

This paragraph shall not be construed as preventing payment of any Medicare cost-sharing by a Medicare supplemental policy or an employer retiree health plan on behalf of an individual.

Section 1903(m)(1)(A) defines "Medicaid managed care organization." It provides:

> The term "Medicaid managed care organization" means a health maintenance organization, an eligible organization with a contract under section 1876 [42 U.S.C.A. 1395mm] or a Medicare+Choice organization with a contract under part C of title XVIII, a provider sponsored organization, or any other public or private organization, which meets the requirement of section 1902(w) [42 U.S.C.A. 1396b(w), which pertains to policies and procedures for advance directives] and—
>
> (i) makes services it provides to individuals eligible for benefits under this title accessible to such individuals, within the area served by the organization, to the same extent as such services are made accessible to individuals (eligible for medical assistance under the State plan) not enrolled with the organization, and
>
> (ii) has made adequate provision against the risk of insolvency, which provision is satisfactory to the State, meets the requirements of subparagraph (C)(i) (if applicable), and which assures that individuals eligible for benefits under this title are in no case held liable for debts of the organization in case of the organization's insolvency.

An organization that is a qualified health maintenance organization (as defined in section 1310(d) of the Public Health Service Act) is deemed to meet the requirements of clauses (i) and (ii).

For regulatory citations, see Chapter 7

§ 3:6 PROVIDING MEDICAID EXCLUSIONS FOR THE SAME GROUNDS AS MEDICARE EXCLUSIONS— Section 1902(p)(1) [42 U.S.C.A. 1396a(p)(1)]

Summary

Pursuant to section 1902(p)(1), 42 U.S.C.A. 1396a(p)(1), a State may exclude any individual or entity from its Medicaid program for any reason for which the Secretary could exclude the individual or entity from participation in Medicare under section 1128, 42 U.S.C.A. 1320a-7, which pertains to exclusions for crimes related to Medicare or Medicaid or to a State health care program funded by a Maternal and Child Health Services Block Grant authorized by Title V of the Social Security Act, 42 U.S.C.A. 701 et seq., or to a State health care program funded under the program of Block Grants to States for Social Services established by Title XX of the Social Security Act, 42 U.S.C.A. 1397 et seq.; under section 1128A, 42 U.S.C.A. 1320a-7a, which pertains to civil money penalties but which also provides for exclusion; or under section 1866(b)(2), 42 U.S.C.A. 1395cc(b)(2), which pertains to failure to comply with terms of a Medicare provider agreement. This exclusion authority is in addition to any other authority which the State may have.

Statutory Provisions

Section 1902(p)(1), 42 U.S.C.A. 1396a(p)(1), provides:

> In addition to any other authority, a State may exclude any individual or entity for purposes of participating under the State plan under this title for any reason for which the Secretary could exclude the individual or entity from participation in a program under title XVIII under section 1128 [42 U.S.C.A. 1320a-7, which pertains to exclusion of certain individuals convicted of crimes related to Medicare or Medicaid or to a State health care program funded by a Maternal and Child Health Services Block Grant authorized by Title V of the Social Security Act, 42 U.S.C.A. 701 et seq., or to a State health care program funded under the program of Block Grants to States for Social Services established by Title XX of the Social Security Act, 42 U.S.C.A. 1397 et seq.], 1128A [42 U.S.C.A. 1320a-7a, which pertains to civil money penalties but which also provides for exclusion], or 1866(b)(2) [42 U.S.C.A. 1395cc(b)(2), which pertains to failure to comply with the terms of a Medicare provider agreement].

For regulatory citations, see Chapter 7

§ 3:7 EXCLUDING MANAGED CARE ORGANIZATIONS AND OTHER ENTITIES AUTHORIZED TO IMPLEMENT PRIMARY CARE CASE MANAGEMENT OR SPECIALTY PHYSICIAN SERVICES — Section 1902(p)(2) [42 U.S.C.A. 1396a(p)(2)]

Summary

Section 1902(p)(2), 42 U.S.C.A. 1396a(p)(2), requires States to exclude a managed care organization from Medicaid if the organization could be excluded from Medicare under section 1128(b)(8), 42 U.S.C.A. 1320a-7(b)(8). The same goes for any entity furnishing services pursuant to a waiver authorized by section 1915(b)(1), 42 U.S.C.A. 1396n(b)(1), which pertains to implementing a primary care case-management system or a specialty physician services arrangement.

◆ NOTE: Prior to amendment by section 4701(b)(2)(A)(iii) of the Balanced Budget Act of 1997, P.L. 105–33, effective August 5, 1997, section 1902(p)(2) referred not to managed care organizations but to health maintenance organizations.

Section 1128(b)(8) pertains to owners and managing employees who have been convicted of Medicare-related crimes or offenses related to patient abuse, fraud, obstruction of a Medicare investigation, or controlled substances, or who have suffered a civil money penalty under section 1128A, 42 U.S.C.A. 1320a-7a, or who have been excluded from Medicare or from a State health care program.

Medicaid exclusion is also required if such an organization or entity has, directly or indirectly, a substantial contractual relationship with individuals or entities described in section 1128(b)(8)(B).

Statutory Provisions

Section 1902(p)(2), 42 U.S.C.A. 1396a(p)(2), provides:

> In order for a State to receive payments for medical assistance under section 1903(a) [42 U.S.C.A. 1396b(a), which authorizes Federal financial participation in State Medicaid programs], with respect to payments the State makes to a managed care organization (as defined in section 1903(m) [42 U.S.C.A. 1396b(m)]) or to an entity furnishing services under a waiver approved under section 1915(b)(1) [42 U.S.C.A. 1396n(b),

which pertains to implementing a primary care case-management system or a specialty physician services arrangement], the State must provide that it will exclude from participation, as such an organization or entity, any organization or entity that —

(A) could be excluded under section 1128(b)(8) [42 U.S.C.A. 1320a-7(b)(8)] (relating to owners and managing employees who have been convicted of certain crimes or received other sanctions),

(B) has, directly or indirectly, a substantial contractual relationship (as defined by the Secretary) with an individual or entity that is described in section 1128(b)(8)(B) [42 U.S.C.A. 1320a-7(b)(8)(B)], or

(C) employs or contracts with any individual or entity that is excluded from participation under this title under section 1128 or 1128A for the provision of health care, utilization review, medical social work, or administrative services or employs or contracts with any entity for the provision (directly or indirectly) through such an excluded individual or entity of such services.

◆ NOTE: Section 6411(d)(3)(B) of P.L. 101-239, the Omnibus Budget Reconciliation Act of 1989, added subparagraph (C) above. It applies to employment and contracts as of 90 days after December 19, 1989. Furthermore, section 4701(b)(2)(A)(iii) of the Balanced Budget Act of 1997, P.L. 105–33, changed a reference in section 1902(p)(2) from "health maintenance organization" to "managed care organization." That change was effective August 5, 1997.

Section 1902(p)(3), 42 U.S.C.A. 1396a(p)(2), provides:

(3) As used in this subsection, the term 'exclude' includes the refusal to enter into or renew a participation agreement or the termination of such an agreement.

Section 1128(b)(8), 42 U.S.C.A. 1320a-7(b)(8), provides:

(b) PERMISSIVE EXCLUSION. — The Secretary may exclude the following individuals and entities from participation in any Federal health care program (as defined in section 1128B(f) [42 U.S.C.S 1320a-7b(f)]:

◆ NOTE: Effective August 5, 1997, section 4331(c)(1) of the Balanced Budget Act of 1997, P.L. 105–33, substituted "any Federal health care program as defined in section 1128B(f)" for "any program under title XVIII and may direct that the following individuals and entities be excluded from participation in any State health care program."

* * *

(8) ENTITIES CONTROLLED BY A SANCTIONED INDIVIDUAL.-Any entity with respect to which the Secretary determines that a person —

(A) (i) who has a direct or indirect ownership or control interest of 5 percent or more in the entity or with an ownership or control interest (as defined in section 1124(a)(3) [42 U.S.C.A. 1320a-3(a)(3), which requires certain entities participating in Medicare, Medicaid, and Maternal and Child Health grant programs to disclose ownership and related information]) in that entity;

(ii) who is an officer, director, agent, or managing employee (as defined in section 1126(b) [42 U.S.C.A. 1320a-5(b), which, in the course of requiring disclosure by institutions, organizations, and agencies of owners and certain other individuals who have been convicted of certain offenses, defines managing employee to include a general manager, business manager, administrator, and director, who exercises operational or managerial control over the entity, or who directly or indirectly conducts day-to-day operations]) of that entity; or

(iii) who was described in clause (i) but is no longer so described because of a transfer of ownership or control interest, in anticipation of (or following) a conviction, assessment, or exclusion described in subparagraph (B) against the person, to an immediate family member (as defined in subsection (j)(1)) or a member of the household of the person (as defined in subsection (j)(2)) who continues to maintain an interest described in such clause —

is a person —

(B) (i) who has been convicted of any offense described in subsection (a) [which pertains to mandatory exclusion of individuals and entities convicted of crimes related to Medicare or any State health care program or crimes related to patient abuse] or in paragraph (1) [which permits exclusion of individuals and entities convicted of fraud, theft, embezzlement, breach of fiduciary responsibility, or other financial misconduct], (2) [which permits exclusion of individuals and entities convicted for obstruction of an investigation of Medicare fraud], or (3) [which permits exclusion of individuals and entities convicted of an offense related to the unlawful manufacture, distribution, prescription, or dispensing of a controlled substance] of this subsection;

(ii) against whom a civil monetary penalty has been assessed under section 1128A [42 U.S.C.A. 1320a-7a]; or 1129 [42 U.S.C.A. 1320a-8, which pertains to civil monetary penalties and assessments for violations under Title II (Social Security) and Title XVI (welfare benefits) of the Social Security Act. NOTE: Section 206(b)(2) of the Social Security Independence and Program Improvements Act of 1994, P.L. 103-296, added the phrase "or 1129".]; or

(iii) who has been excluded from participation under a program under title XVIII or under a State health care program.

Section 1128(h) provides:

(h) DEFINITION OF STATE HEALTH CARE PROGRAM. — For purposes of this section and sections 1128A and 1128B, the term "State health care program" means —

(1) a State plan approved under title XIX,any program receiving funds under title V or from an allotment to a State under such title,

(2) any program receiving funds under title XX or from an allotment to a State under such title, orSection 1128(h) provides:

(3) any program receiving funds under title XX or from an allotment to a State under such title, or

(4) a State child health plan approved under title XXI.

Section 1128(j) provides:

(j) DEFINITION OF IMMEDIATE FAMILY MEMBER AND MEMBER OF THE HOUSEHOLD. — For purposes of subsection (b)(8)(A)(iii):

(1) The term 'immediate family member' means, with respect to a person —

(A) the husband or wife of the person;

(B) the natural or adoptive parent, child, or sibling of the person;

(C) the stepparent, stepchild, stepbrother, or stepsister of the person;

(D) the father-, mother-, daughter-, son-, brother-, or sister-in-law of the person;

(E) the grandparent or grandchild of the person; and

(F) the spouse of a grandparent or grandchild of the person.

(2) The term 'member of the household' means, with respect to any person, any individual sharing a common abode as part of a single family unit with the person, including domestic employees and others who live together as a family unit, but not including a roomer or boarder.

◆ NOTE: Section 4303(a)(1) of the Balanced Budget Act of 1997, removed "or" at the end of clause (b)(8)(A)(i); substituted "; or" for a dash at the end of clause (ii); and added clause (iii). That change was effective September 19, 1997. Section 4303(a)(2) added subsection (j). Section 4901(b)(2) deleted "or" from the end of paragraph (h)(2); substituted " , or" for a period at the end of paragraph (h)(3); and added paragraph (h)(4). Those changes were effective August 5, 1997.

With respect to the definition of Federal health care program, section 1128B(f), 42 U.S.C.A. 1320a-7b(f), provides:

(f) For purposes of this section, the term "Federal health care program" means —

(1) any plan or program that provides health benefits, whether directly, through insurance, or otherwise, which is funded directly, in whole or in part, by the United States Government (other than the health insurance program under chapter 89 of title 5, United States Code); or

(2) any State health care program, as defined in section 1128(h).

For regulatory citations, see Chapter 7

§ 3:8 TERMINATION OF MEDICAID CERTIFICATION OF AND INTERMEDIATE SANCTIONS FOR PSYCHIATRIC HOSPITALS — Section 1902(y) [42 U.S.C.A. 1396a(y)]

Summary

A State may find a psychiatric hospital certified to participate in its Medicaid program no longer meets statutory requirements in two sets of circumstances: one where the noncompliance results in immediate jeopardy to the health and safety of patients, and one where it does not.

Statutory requirements include those set forth in section 1905(h), 42 U.S.C.A. 1396d(h), which defines "inpatient psychiatric hospital services for individuals under age 21," and, by cross reference from section 1905(h), requirements in the Medicare definition of psychiatric hospital set forth at section 1861(f), 42 U.S.C.A. 1395x(f).

Pursuant to section 1902(y), 42 U.S.C.A. 1396a(y), which was added to the Medicaid statute by section 4755(a)(2) of P.L. 101-508, the Omnibus Budget Reconciliation Act of 1990 (OBRA 90), effective November 5, 1990, if a State finds noncompliance which immediately jeopardizes the health and safety of a psychiatric hospital' s patients, the State must terminate the hospital's participation in Medicaid.

Even if the State finds deficiencies which do not immediately jeopardize the health and safety of the hospital's patients, it may terminate the hospital's participation in Medicaid. Alternatively, however, it may provide that no Medicaid payments will be made to the hospital with respect to any individual admitted after the effective date of the finding. But it could do both, and it may impose any other sanction authorized by State law, as well, such as license revocation or a ban on admissions.

A sanction less than termination, such as payment denial, is considered "intermediate."

According to the statute, if a psychiatric hospital does not comply with requirements within three months after being found out of compliance, the State must deny Medicaid payments with respect to patients admitted thereafter. Furthermore, after six months of non-compliance, no Federal financial participation will be provided to the State with respect to further services provided in the hospital until the State finds the hospital has come back into compliance.

This provision, however, is subject to some amelioration. If the State finds it more appropriate to take alternative action (short of termination of certification to participate in Medicaid), and if the State submits a plan and timetable for corrective action to the Secretary of Health and Human Services which the Secretary approves, and if the State agrees to repay Federal payments received in the interim if corrective action is not taken in accordance with the approved plan and timetable, the Secretary may continue Federal financial participation for not more than six months from the date the hospital is found out of compliance.

Statutory Provisions

Section 1902(y), 42 U.S.C.A. 1396a(y), effective November 5, 1992, pursuant to section 4755(a)(2) of P.L. 101-508, the Omnibus Budget Reconciliation Act of 1990 (OBRA 90), provides:

> (1) In addition to any other authority under State law, where a State determines that a psychiatric hospital which is certified for participation under its plan no longer meets the requirements for a psychiatric hospital (referred to in section 1905(h) [42 U.S.C.A. 1396d(h), which pertains to inpatient psychiatric hospital services for persons under 21]) and further finds that the hospital's deficiencies —
>
> (A) immediately jeopardize the health and safety of its patients, the State shall terminate the hospital's participation under the State plan; or
>
> (B) do not immediately jeopardize the health and safety of its patients, the State may terminate the hospital's participation under the State plan, or provide that no payment will be made under the State plan with respect to any individual admitted to such hospital after the effective date of the finding, or both.
>
> (2) Except as provided in paragraph (3), if a psychiatric hospital described in paragraph (1)(B) has not complied with the requirements for a psychiatric hospital under this title —
>
> (A) within 3 months after the date the hospital is found to be out of compliance with such requirements the State shall pro-

vide that no payment will be made under the State plan with respect to any individual admitted to such hospital after the end of such 3-month period, or

(B) within 6 months after the date the hospital is found to be out of compliance with such requirements, no Federal financial participation shall be provided under section 1903(a) [42 U.S.C.A. 1396b(a)] with respect to further services provided in the hospital until the State finds that the hospital is in compliance with the requirements of this title.

(3) The Secretary may continue payments, over a period of not longer than 6 months from the date the hospital is found to be out of compliance with such requirements, if—

(A) the State finds that it is more appropriate to take alternative action to assure compliance of the hospital with the requirements than to terminate the certification of the hospital,

(B) the State has submitted a plan and timetable for corrective action to the Secretary for approval and the Secretary approves the plan of corrective action, and

(C) the State agrees to repay to the Federal Government payments received under this paragraph if the corrective action is not taken in accordance with the approved plan and timetable.

Section 1905(h) provides:

(1) For purposes of paragraph (16) of subsection (a), the term "inpatient psychiatric hospital services for individuals under age 21" includes only—

(A) inpatient services which are provided in an institution (or distinct part thereof) which is a psychiatric hospital as defined in section 1861(f) or in another inpatient setting that the Secretary has specified in regulations;

(B) inpatient services which, in the case of any individual (i) involve active treatment which meets such standards as may be prescribed in regulations by the Secretary, and (ii) a team, consisting of physicians and other personnel qualified to make determinations with respect to mental health conditions and the treatment thereof, has determined are necessary on an inpatient basis and can reasonably be expected to improve the condition, by reason of which such services are necessary, to the extent that eventually such services will no longer be necessary; and

(C) inpatient services which, in the case of any individual, are provided prior to (i) the date such individual attains age 21, or (ii) in the case of an individual who was receiving such services in the period immediately preceding the date on which he attained age 21, (I) the date such individual no longer requires such services, or (II) if earlier, the date such individual attains age 22;

(2) Such term does not include services provided during any calendar quarter under the State plan of any State if the total amount of the funds expended, during such quarter, by the State (and the political subdivisions thereof) from non-Federal funds for inpatient services included under paragraph (1), and for active psychiatric care and treatment provided on an outpatient basis for eligible mentally ill children, is less than the average quarterly amount of the funds expended, during the 4-quarter period ending December 31, 1971, by the State (and the political subdivisions thereof) from non-Federal funds for such services.

Section 1861(f) provides:

The term "psychiatric hospital" means an institution which—

(1) is primarily engaged in providing, by or under the supervision of a physician, psychiatric services for the diagnosis and treatment of mentally ill persons;

(2) satisfies the requirements of paragraphs (3) through (9) of subsection (e) [which pertain to bylaws for staff physicians, patient supervision by a physician, 24-hour nursing service rendered or supervised by an R.N. plus a licensed practical nurse or R.N. 24-hours a day, utilization review and discharge planning, appropriate licensure, appropriate planning and budgeting, and such other requirements as the Secretary may find necessary for the health and safety of patients;

(3) maintains clinical records on all patients and maintains such records as the Secretary finds to be necessary to determine the degree and intensity of the treatment provided to individuals entitled to hospital insurance benefits under part A; and

(4) meets such staffing requirements as the Secretary finds necessary for the institution to carry out an active program of treatment for individuals who are furnished services in the institution.

In the case of an institution which satisfies paragraphs (1) and (2) of the preceding sentence and which contains a distinct part which also satisfies paragraphs (3) and (4) of such sentence, such distinct part shall be considered to be a "psychiatric hospital."

For regulatory citations, see Chapter 7

§ 3:9 FAILURE BY MANAGED CARE ORGANIZATIONS TO COMPLY WITH MEDICAID REQUIREMENTS — Section 1903(m)(5) [42 U.S.C.A. 1396b(m)(5)]

Summary

◆ NOTE: Section 1903, 42 U.S.C.A. 1396b, sets forth a complex methodology for determining the amount of Federal payments to participating States for their Medicaid programs. As a cost-cutting measure, and to further development of health maintenance organizations (HMO's), Congress encouraged States to include HMO's as reimbursable sources for health care under Medicaid State plans. See section 1903(k), 42 U.S.C.A. 1396b(k). Gradually, other forms of managed care organizations came into being, such as Medicare+Choice organizations, which may or may not be an HMO. Congress took steps to allow their participation in Medicaid as well, and, effective August 5, 1997, sections 4701(b)(1)(A) and (b)(2)(A)(v) of the Balanced Budget Act of 1997, P.L. 105–33, substituted the more encompassing term "managed care organization" for the more specific term "health maintenance organization" in section 1903(k). As a result sanctions which previously applied only to HMO's participating in Medicaid, then became applicable to all types of managed care organizations participating in Medicaid. That amendment applies to contracts entered into or renewed on or after October 1, 1997.

Pursuant to section 1903(m)(5)(A)(i), 42 U.S.C.A. 1396b(m)(5)(A)(i), if the Secretary of Health and Human Services determines that a managed care organization with a Medicaid contract fails substantially to provide medically necessary items and services required under law or by its contract to covered individuals, and if the failure has adversely affected, or has substantial likelihood of adversely affecting, the individual, the Secretary, in addition to any other available remedy (sanction), may impose a civil money penalty not to exceed $25,000 for each such determination.

Pursuant to section 1903(m)(5)(A)(ii), if the Secretary determines that a managed care organization with a Medicaid contract imposes premiums on individuals in excess of what Title XIX permits, the Secretary, in addition to any other available remedy (sanction), may impose a civil money penalty not to exceed $25,000 for each such determination.

Pursuant to section 1903(m)(5)(A)(iii), if the Secretary determines that a managed care organization with a Medicaid contract discriminates among individuals on the basis of their health status or requirements for health care services, including expulsion or refusal to re-enroll an individual, or engaging in any practice that would reasonably be expected to have the effect of denying or discouraging enrollment by eligible individuals with the organization whose medical condition or history indicates a need for substantial future medical services, the Secretary, in addition to any other available remedy (sanction), may impose a civil money penalty not to exceed $25,000 for each such determination.

Pursuant to section 1903(m)(5)(A)(iv), if the Secretary determines that a managed care organization with a Medicaid contract misrepresents or falsifies information furnished to the Secretary or to the State or to an individual or to any other entity, the Secretary, in addition to any other available remedy (sanction), may impose a civil money penalty not to exceed $25,000 for each such determination.

Pursuant to section 1903m(5)(A)(v), as added by section 4731(b)(2) of P.L. 101-508, the Omnibus Budget Reconciliation Act of 1990 (OBRA 90), applicable to contract years beginning January 1, 1992, or later, if the Secretary determines that an HMO or Competitive Medical Plan (CMP) with a Medicaid contract fails to comply with requirements of section 1876(i)(8), 42 U.S.C.A. 1395mm(i)(8), the Secretary may impose a civil money penalty not to exceed $25,000 for each such determination. According to section 1876(i)(8), such an organization may impose "physician incentive plans" which directly or indirectly have the effect by means of compensation of reducing or limiting services to enrollees; but such plans may not permit any payment directly or indirectly as an inducement for a physician or physician group to reduce or limit medically necessary services to any specific individual enrollee. Furthermore, if the plan places a physician or physician group at substantial financial risk, as determined by the Secretary, for services not provided by the physician or physician group, the organization must provide stop-loss protection satisfactory to the Secretary; it must conduct period surveys of enrollees and former enrollees to determine the degree of access they had to services provided by the organization their satisfaction with the quality of those services; and the organization must provide the Secretary with sufficient information to permit him to determine whether the plan is complying with these requirements.

With respect to discrimination among eligible persons and misrepresentation made to and false information furnished to the Secretary or to the State, the Secretary may impose a civil money penalty not to exceed $100,000 for each such determination; plus, with respect to a determination under (A)(ii) that excessive premiums were charged, double the excess amount (which sum will be deducted from the penalty and returned to the overcharged individual); plus, with respect to a determination of discrimination under (A)(iii), $15,000 for each individual not enrolled as a result of the prohibited practice.

Alternatively, the Secretary may deny Federal financial participation to the State for medical assistance furnished under a Medicaid contract for individuals enrolled after the date the Secretary notifies the organization of his determination that it has violated section 1903(m)(5)(A) and until the Secretary is satisfied that the basis for such determination has been corrected and is not likely to recur.

Enforcement procedures for these civil money penalty provisions are governed by section 1128A of the Social Security Act, 42 U.S.C.A. 1320a-7a, which authorizes civil money penalties for a variety of offenses.

Statutory Provisions

Section 1903(m)(5), 42 U.S.C.A. 1396b(m)(5), provides:

(A) If the Secretary determines that an entity with a contract under this subsection —

(i) fails substantially to provide medically necessary items and services that are required (under law or under the contract) to be provided to an individual covered under the contract, if the failure has adversely affected (or has substantial likelihood of adversely affecting) the individual;

(ii) imposes premiums on individuals enrolled under this subsection in excess of the premiums permitted under this title;

(iii) acts to discriminate among individuals in violation of the provision of paragraph (2)(A)(v), [which pertains to discrimination based on health status or need for health care services] including expulsion or refusal to re-enroll an individual or engaging in any practice that would reasonably be expected to have the effect of denying or discouraging enrollment (except as permitted by this subsection) by eligible individuals with the organization whose medical condition or history indicates a need for substantial future medical services;

(iv) misrepresents or falsifies information that is furnished —

(I) to the Secretary or the State under this subsection, or

(II) to an individual or to any other entity under this subsection, or

(v) [applicable with respect to contract years beginning January 1, 1992, or later, pursuant to section 4731(b)(2) of P.L. 101-508, the Omnibus Budget Reconciliation Act of 1990 (OBRA 90),] fails to comply with the requirements of section 1876(i)(8) [42 U.S.C.A. 1395mm(i)(8), which pertains to restrictions on physician incentive plans offered by health maintenance organizations, added by section 4202(a) of OBRA 90],

the Secretary may provide, in addition to any other remedies available under law, for any of the remedies described in subparagraph (B).

(B) The remedies described in this subparagraph are —

(i) civil money penalties of not more than $25,000 for each determination under subparagraph (A), or, with respect to a determination under clause (iii) or (iv)(I) of such subparagraph, of not more than $100,000 for each such determination, plus, with respect to a determination under subparagraph (A)(ii), double the excess amount charged in violation of such subparagraph (and the excess amount charged shall be deducted from the penalty and returned to the individual concerned), and plus, with respect to a determination under subparagraph (A)(iii), $15,000 for each individual not enrolled as a result of a practice described in such subparagraph, or

(ii) denial of payment to the State for medical assistance furnished under the contract under this subsection for individuals enrolled after the date the Secretary notifies the organization of a determination under subparagraph (A) and until the Secretary is satisfied that the basis for such determination has been corrected and is not likely to recur.

The provisions of section 1128A (other than subsections (a) and (b) [42 U.S.C.A. 1329a-7a(a) and (b), which independently authorize civil money penalties]) shall apply to a civil money penalty under clause (i) in the same manner as such provisions apply to a penalty or proceeding under section 1128A(a).

Section 1876(i)(8) provides:

(A) Each contract with an eligible organization under this section shall provide that the organization may not operate any physician incentive plan (as defined in subparagraph (B)) unless the following requirements are met:

(i) No specific payment is made directly or indirectly under the plan to a physician or physician group as an inducement to reduce or limit medically necessary services provided with respect to a specific individual enrolled with the organization.

(ii) If the plan places a physician or physician group at substantial financial risk (as determined by the Secretary) for services not provided by the physician or physician group, the organization —

(I) provides stop-loss protection for the physician or group that is adequate and appropriate, based on standards developed by the Secretary that take into account the number of physicians placed at such substantial financial risk in the group or under the plan and the number of individuals enrolled with the organization who receive services from the physician or the physician group, and

(II) conducts periodic surveys of both individuals enrolled and individuals previously enrolled with the organization to determine the degree of access of such individuals to services provided by the organization and satisfaction with the quality of such services.

(iii) The organization provides the Secretary with descriptive information regarding the plan, sufficient to permit the Secretary to determine whether the plan is in compliance with the requirements of this subparagraph.

(B) In this paragraph, the term "physician incentive plan" means any compensation arrangement between an eligible organization and a physician or physician group that may directly or indirectly have the effect of reducing or limiting services provided with respect to individuals enrolled with the organization.

For regulatory citations, see Chapter 7

§ 3:10 FAILURE BY STATES TO MEET MEDICAID PLAN REQUIREMENTS — Section 1904 [42 U.S.C.A. 1396c]

Summary

Pursuant to section 1902(b), 42 U.S.C.A. 1396a(b), and section 1903, 42 U.S.C.A. 1396b, States may receive Federal matching funds for their Medicaid programs if they submit to the Secretary of Health and Human Services a Medicaid State plan which meets Federal requirements. Pursuant to section 1904, 42 U.S.C.A. 1396c, States which do not meet the requirements do not get, or, having once participated, subsequently lose, Federal matching funds.

According to section 1904, a State may lose Federal financial participation if its Medicaid plan is changed that it no longer complies with section 1902, which in subsection (a) details extraordinarily complex plan requirements. The same is true if in the administration of its plan a State fails to comply substantially with any provision of section 1902. If, after reasonable notice and opportunity for a hearing, the Secretary makes either determination, he must either withhold all further Federal financial participation from the State, or, in his discretion, permit such payments only for categories under or parts of the State plan not affected by the State's failure. In either case, withholding must continue until the Secretary is satisfied that there will no longer be any such failure to comply.

Statutory Provisions

Section 1904, 42 U.S.C.A. 1396c, provides:

If the Secretary, after reasonable notice and opportunity for hearing to the State agency administering or supervising the administration of the State plan approved under this title, finds —

(1) that the plan has been so changed that it no longer complies with the provisions of section 1902; or

(2) that in the administration of the plan there is a failure to comply substantially with any such provision; the Secretary shall notify such State agency that further payments will not be made to the State (or, in his discretion, that payments will be limited to categories under or parts of the State plan not affected by such failure), until the Secretary is satisfied that there will no longer be any such failure to comply. Until he is so satisfied he shall make no further payments to such State (or shall limit payments to categories under or parts of the State plan not affected by such failure).

For regulatory citations, see Chapter 7

§ 3:11 CANCELLING CERTIFICATION AND APPROVAL OF SKILLED NURSING FACILITIES, INTERMEDIATE CARE FACILITIES, AND INTERMEDIATE CARE FACILITIES FOR THE MENTALLY RETARDED — Section 1910 [42 U.S.C.A. 1396i]

Summary

Section 1910(a)(1), 42 U.S.C.A. 1396i(a)(1), provides that whenever the Secretary of Health and Human Services certifies an institution as a skilled nursing facility (SNF) for Medicare purposes, it is deemed to meet standards for Medicaid certification. Section 1910(a)(2) provides that the Secretary must notify the State Medicaid agency of his approval or disapproval of any institution which has applied for certification by him as a qualified skilled nursing facility. There is no comparable provision for intermediate care facilities (ICF's) because they do not participate in Medicare.

Effective October 1, 1990, section 1910(a) is deleted.

Prior to amendment by P.L. 101-239, the Omnibus Budget Reconciliation Act of 1989, enacted December 19, 1989, section 1910(c) authorized the Secretary to cancel approval of a SNF or ICF at any time if he found, on the basis of a State agency determination —

1. that a facility failed to meet State Medicaid plan requirements, or
2. that a facility failed to meet the Medicaid definition of a nursing facility. He was also authorized to cancel approval of a SNF if he found grounds for termination of its Medicare provider agreement.

Approval of a SNF or ICF to participate in Medicare and Medicaid could not be reinstated unless the Secretary found the reason for termination had been removed and there was reasonable assurance it would not recur. Notice and opportunity for a hearing had to be given to the affected SNF or ICF, and judicial review was available for adverse hearing decisions. Moreover, the agreement between the facility and the State remained in effect until time for filing a request for a hearing had expired or, if a request were filed, until a decision was made by the Secretary. Nevertheless, the agreement could not be extended—

1. if the Secretary made a written determination, specifying the reasons therefor, that continuation of provider status constituted an immediate and serious threat to the health and safety of patients, and
2. if the Secretary certified that the facility had been notified of its deficiencies and had failed to correct them.

Effective October 1, 1990, section 1910(c) is redesignated as section 1910(b) and the reference to skilled nursing facilities is deleted.

Furthermore, pursuant to section 6901(d)(5)(A) of OBRA 89, "intermediate care facilities for the mentally retarded" was added to the title of section 1910. Section 6901(d)(5)(B) of OBRA 89 substituted "intermediate care facility for the mentally retarded" for "skilled nursing or intermediate care facility" in redesignated section 1910(b)(1). Section 6901(d)(5)(C) substituted "1902(a)(31) or section 1905(d)" for "1902(a)(28) or section 1919 or section 1905(c)" in redesignated section 1910(b)(1). And section 6901(d)(5)(D) substituted "intermediate care facility for the mentally retarded" for "skilled nursing facility or intermediate care facility" wherever the latter appeared in redesignated sections 1910(b)(1) and (b)(2).

These OBRA 89 changes are effective as if enacted by P.L. 100-203, the Omnibus Budget Reconciliation Act of 1987. Thus they make section 1910 applicable to intermediate care facilities for the mentally retarded (ICF/MR's) retroactively. And they take into account recent statutory and regulatory changes which make nursing facilities, whether skilled or intermediate care, subject to similar Medicare and Medicaid requirements.

Consequently, as amended by OBRA 89, the Secretary may cancel approval of an ICF/MR at any time if, on the basis of a State agency determination, he finds —

1. that it fails to meet requirements for services to residents as determined by professional review teams and inspections in accordance with section 1902(a)(31), 42 U.S.C.A. 1396a(a)(31), which pertains to pre-admission written plans of care and periodic assessment of resident needs, or
2. that, if a public institution, it fails to meet Medicaid plan requirements, including active treatment for residents, required by section 1905(d), 42 U.S.C.A. 1396d.

In addition, the Secretary may cancel approval of an ICF/MR if he finds grounds for termination of its Medicare provider agreement.

As before with respect to SNF's or ICF's, approval of an ICF/MR to participate in Medicare and Medicaid can not be reinstated unless the Secretary finds the reason for termination has been removed and there is reasonable assurance it will not recur. In addition, notice and opportunity for a hearing must be given to the ICF/MR, and judicial review is available for adverse hearing decisions.

Also, as before with SNF's and ICF's, the agreement between an ICF/MR and the State remains in effect until time for filing a request for a hearing expires or, if a request is filed, until a decision is made by the Secretary. Nevertheless, the agreement can not be extended —

1. if the Secretary makes a written determination, specifying the reasons therefor, that continuation of provider status constitutes an immediate and serious threat to the health and safety of patients, and
2. if the Secretary certifies that the facility has been notified of its deficiencies and has failed to correct them.

Statutory Provisions

Section 1910(a), 42 U.S.C.A. 1396i(a), until October 1, 1990, provided:

> (1) Whenever the Secretary certifies an institution in a State to be qualified as a skilled nursing facility under title XVIII, such institution shall be deemed to meet the standards for certifica-

tion as a skilled nursing facility for purposes of section 1902(a)(28) [42 U.S.C.A. 1396a(a)(28)].

(2) The Secretary shall notify the State agency administering the medical assistance plan of his approval or disapproval of any institution which has applied for certification by him as a qualified skilled nursing facility.

Section 1910(c), 42 U.S.C.A. 1396i(c), which, effective October 1, 1990, is redesignated as section 1910(b), provides:

(1) The Secretary may cancel approval of any intermediate care facility for the mentally retarded at any time if he finds on the basis of a determination made by him as provided in section 1902(a)(33)(B) [42 U.S.C.A. 1396a(a)(33)(B), which pertains to having State licensure agencies determine whether institutions meet requirements for participation in Medicaid] that a facility fails to meet the requirements contained in section 1902(a)(31) [42 U.S.C.A. 1396a(a)(31), which pertains to professional review and inspections of intermediate care facilities for the mentally retarded] or section 1905(d) [42 U.S.C.A. 1396d, which pertains to intermediate care facility services in public institutions for the mentally retarded], or if he finds grounds for termination of his agreement with the facility pursuant to section 1866(b) [42 U.S.C.A. 1395cc, which pertains to termination of Medicare provider agreements]. In that event the Secretary shall notify the State agency and the intermediate care facility for the mentally retarded that approval of eligibility of the facility to participate in the programs established by this title and title XVIII shall be terminated at a time specified by the Secretary. The approval of eligibility of any such facility to participate in such programs may not be reinstated unless the Secretary finds that the reason for termination has been removed and there is reasonable assurance that it will not recur.

(2) Any intermediate care facility for the mentally retarded which is dissatisfied with a determination by the Secretary that it no longer qualifies as an intermediate care facility for the mentally retarded for purposes of this title, shall be entitled to a hearing by the Secretary to the same extent as is provided in section 205(b) [42 U.S.C.A. 405(b)] and to judicial review of the Secretary's final decision after such hearing as is provided in section 205(g) [42 U.S.C.A. 405(g)] . Any agreement between such facility and the State agency shall remain in effect until the

period for filing a request for a hearing has expired or, if a request has been filed, until a decision has been made by the Secretary; except that the agreement shall not be extended if the Secretary makes a written determination, specifying the reasons therefor, that the continuation of provider status constitutes an immediate and serious threat to the health and safety of patients, and the Secretary certifies that the facility has been notified of its deficiencies and has failed to correct them.

Section 1902(a)(31), 42 U.S.C.A. 1396a(a)(31), provides:

A state plan for medical assistance must —

* * *

(31) with respect to services in an intermediate care facility for the mentally retarded (where the State plan includes medical assistance for such services) [preceding phrase changed, effective October 1, 1990, from "with respect to skilled nursing facility services (and with respect to intermediate care facility services, where the State plan includes medical assistance for such services)"] provide with respect to each patient receiving such services, for a written plan of care, prior to admission to or authorization of benefits in such facility, in accordance with regulations of the Secretary, and for a regular program of independent professional review (including medical evaluation) which shall periodically review his need for such services;

◆ NOTE: Effective August 5, 1997, sections 4751(b)(1) and (2) of the Balanced Budget Act of 1997, P.L. 105–33, deleted "—(A)" after "provide" above, and deleted former subparagraphs (B) and (C), which read: "(B) with respect to each intermediate care facility for the mentally retarded within the State, for periodic onsite inspections of the care being provided to each person receiving medical assistance, by one or more independent professional review teams (composed of a physician or registered nurse and other appropriate health and social service personnel), including with respect to each such person (i) the adequacy of the services available to meet his current health needs and promote his maximum physical well-being, (ii) the necessity and desirability of his continued placement in the facility, and (iii) the feasibility of meeting his health care needs through alternative institutional or noninstitutional services; and (C) for full reports to the State agency by each independent professional review team of the findings of each inspection under subparagraph (B), together with any recommendations[.]"

Section 1905(d), 42 U.S.C.A. 1396d, provides:

> The term "intermediate care facility for the mentally retarded" means an ["intermediate care facility for the mentally retarded means an" changed from "'intermediate care facility services' may include services in a public" effective October 1, 1990] institution (or distinct part thereof) for the mentally retarded or persons with related conditions if—
>
> (1) the primary purpose of such institution (or distinct part thereof) is to provide health or rehabilitative services for mentally retarded individuals and the institution meets such standards as may be prescribed by the Secretary;
>
> (2) the mentally retarded individual with respect to whom a request for payment is made under a plan approved under this title is receiving active treatment under such a program; and
>
> (3) in the case of a public institution ["in the case of a public institution" added effective October 1, 1990] the State or political subdivision responsible for the operation of such institution has agreed that the non-Federal expenditures in any calendar quarter prior to January 1, 1975, with respect to services furnished to patients in such institution (or distinct part thereof) in the State will not, because of payments made under this title, be reduced below the average amount expended for such services in such institution in the four quarters immediately preceding the quarter in which the State in which such institution is located elected to make such services available under its plan approved under this title.

◆ NOTE: Prior to amendment by sections 6901(d)(5)(A), (B), (C), and (D) of P.L. 101-239, the Omnibus Budget Reconciliation Act of 1989, section 1910(c), redesignated section 1910(b) effective October 1, 1990, read as follows:

(1) The Secretary may cancel approval of any skilled nursing or intermediate care facility at any time if he finds on the basis of a determination made by him as provided in section 1902(a)(33)(B) [42 U.S.C.A. 1396a(a)(33)(B), which pertains to having State licensure agencies determine whether institutions meet the requirements for participation in Medicaid] that a facility fails to meet the requirements contained in section 1902(a)(28) [42 U.S.C.A. 1396a(a)(28), which pertains to State plan requirements for nursing facilities] or section 1919 [42 U.S.C.A. 1396r, which details requirements for nursing facilities and which is generally applicable effective October 1, 1990,] or section 1905(c) [42 U.S.C.A. 1396d(c), which, applicable for services on or after October 1, 1990, pertains to meeting the definition of a nursing facility], or if he finds grounds for termination of his agreement with the facility pursuant to section 1866(b) [42 U.S.C.A. 1395cc, which pertains to termination of Medicare provider agreements]. In that event the Secretary shall notify the State agency and the skilled nursing facility or intermediate care facility that approval of eligibility of the facility to participate in the programs established by this title and title XVIII shall be terminated at a time specified by the Secretary. The approval of eligibility of any such facility to participate in such programs may not be reinstated unless the Secretary finds that the reason for termination has been removed and there is reasonable assurance that it will not recur.

(2) Any skilled nursing facility or intermediate care facility which is dissatisfied with a determination by the Secretary that it no longer qualifies as a skilled nursing facility or intermediate care facility for purposes of this title, shall be entitled to a hearing by the Secretary to the same extent as is provided in section 205(b) [42 U.S.C.A. 405(b)] and to judicial review of the Secretary's final decision after such hearing as is provided in section 205(g) [42 U.S.C.A. 405(g)] . Any agreement between such facility and the State agency shall remain in effect until the period for filing a request for a hearing has expired or, if a request has been filed, until a decision has been made by the Secretary; except that the agreement shall not be extended if the Secretary makes a written determination, specifying the reasons therefor, that the continuation of provider status constitutes an immediate and serious threat to the health and

safety of patients, and the Secretary certifies that the facility has been notified of its deficiencies and has failed to correct them.

For regulatory citations, see Chapter 7

§ 3:12 DISAPPROVING RURAL HEALTH CLINIC APPLICATIONS FOR CERTIFICATION — Section 1910(a) [42 U.S.C.A. 1396i(a)]

Summary

Rural health clinics may be reimbursed under Medicare for services of physicians, nurse practitioners, and physician assistants, and for supplies incidental to services of those practitioners. They also may be reimbursed for visiting nurse services. For Medicaid reimbursement, check the State Medicaid plan.

When the Secretary of Health and Human Services certifies a facility as a rural health clinic for Medicare purposes, section 1910(a), 42 U.S.C.A. 1396i(a), designated as section 1910(b) prior to October 1, 1990, provides that the facility shall be deemed to meet Medicaid standards for certification as a rural health clinic.

The statute requires the Secretary to notify the relevant State Medicaid agency of his approval or disapproval of any facility which has applied for certification by him as a qualified rural health clinic. Prior to October 1, 1990, section 1910(a), discussed in § 3:11, provided for deemed Medicaid certification of skilled nursing facilities (SNF's) when the Secretary has given Medicare certification. Then section 1910(c), redesignated section 1910(b) effective October 1, 1990, provided for cancellation of approval of SNF and intermediate care facility (ICF) certifications. Although nothing is said in section 1910(c), or redesignated (b), about canceling approval of rural health clinic certifications, the Medicare regulation, 42 CFR Section 405.2404(b), provides for termination by the Secretary.

Statutory Provisions

Section 1910(a), 42 U.S.C.A. 1396i(a), designated as section 1910(a) prior to October 1, 1990, provides:

(1) Whenever the Secretary certifies a facility in a State to be qualified as a rural health clinic under title XVIII, such facility shall be deemed to meet the standards for certification as a rural

health clinic for purposes of providing rural health clinic services under this title.

(2) The Secretary shall notify the State agency administering the medical assistance plan of his approval or disapproval of any facility in the State which has applied for certification by him as a qualified rural health clinic.

For regulatory citations, see Chapter 7

§ 3:13 REQUIRING STATES TO WITHHOLD MEDICAID UNDERPAYMENTS TO OFFSET MEDICARE OVERPAYMENTS — Section 1914 [42 U.S.C.A. 1396m]

Summary

If a Medicare provider has been overpaid and the Secretary of Health and Human Services has been unable to recover the overpayment from Medicare payments subsequently due, or if the Secretary has been unable to collect information necessary to determine the amount of a Medicare overpayment, or if any person who had been accepting Medicare assignments either stopped doing so or submitted subsequent claims inadequate to recoup an overpayment, and the Secretary has been unable to recover the overpayment or has been unable to collect information necessary to determine the amount, if any, of the overpayment, section 1914, 42 U.S.C.A. 1396m, permits the Secretary to adjust the Federal matching payment to a State with respect to expenditures for medical assistance in any quarter. In addition, the Secretary may require the State to reduce its payment to such institution or person by such amount.

This means the Secretary may recoup Medicare overpayments from a State if the overpaid institution or person is entitled to Medicaid payments. Moreover, the Secretary may or may not require the State to recoup from the overpaid institution or person. The Secretary may not make any adjustment in the payment to a State, however, nor require any adjustment in payment to an institution or person until he provides adequate notice (not less than 60 days) to the State agency and the institution or person overpaid. Once the State has effected the offset, however, an institution or person affected may not recover the amount from the State. Recourse may be had, if at all, only against the Secretary.

Statutory Provisions

Section 1914, 42 U.S.C.A. 1396m, provides:

(a) The Secretary may adjust, in accordance with this section, the Federal matching payment to a State with respect to expenditures for medical assistance for care or services furnished in any quarter by —

(1) an institution (A) which has or previously had in effect an agreement with the Secretary under section 1866 [42 U.S.C.A. 1395cc, which pertains to provider agreements]; and (B)(i) from which the Secretary has been unable to recover overpayments made under title XVIII, or (ii) from which the Secretary has been unable to collect the information necessary to enable him to determine the amount (if any) of the overpayments made to such institution under title XVIII; and

(2) any person (A) who (i) has previously accepted payment on the basis of an assignment under section 1842(b)(3)(B)(ii) [42 U.S.C.A. 1395u(b)(3)(B)(ii), which requires carriers to make payments on the basis of assignment agreements], and (ii) during the annual period immediately preceding such quarter submitted no claims for payment under title XVIII, or submitted claims for payment under title XVIII which aggregated less than the amount of overpayments made to him, and (B)(i) from whom the Secretary has been unable to recover overpayments received in violation of the terms of such assignment, or (ii) from whom the Secretary has been unable to collect the information necessary to enable him to determine the amount (if any) of the overpayments made to such person under title XVIII.

(b) The Secretary may (subject to the remaining provisions of this section reduce payment to a State under this title for any quarter by an amount equal to the lesser of the Federal matching share of payments to any institution or person specified in subsection (a), or the total overpayments to such institution or person specified in subsection (a), or the total overpayments to such institution or person under title XVIII, and may require the State to reduce its payment to such institution or person by such amount.

(c) The Secretary shall not make any adjustment in the payment to a State, nor require any adjustment in the payment to an institution or person, pursuant to subsection (b) until after he has provided adequate notice (which shall be not less than 60 days) to the State agency and the institution or person.

(d) The Secretary shall by regulation provide procedures for implementation of this section, which procedures shall (1) determine the amount of the Federal payment to which the institution or person would otherwise be entitled under this section which shall be treated as a setoff against overpayments under title XVIII, and (2) assure the restoration to the institution or person of amounts withheld under this section which are ultimately determined to be in excess of overpayments under title XVIII and to which the institution or person would otherwise be entitled under this title.

(e) The Secretary shall restore to the trust funds established under sections 1817 [42 U.S.C.A. 1395i, which is the Federal Hospital Insurance Trust Fund] and 1841 [42 U.S.C.A. 1395t, which is the Federal Supplementary Medical Insurance Trust Fund], as appropriate, amounts recovered under this section as setoffs against overpayments under title XVIII.

(f) Notwithstanding any other provision of this title, an institution or person shall not be entitled to recover from any State any amount in payment for medical care and services under this title which is withheld by the State agency pursuant to an order by the Secretary under subsection (b).

For regulatory citations, see Chapter 7

§ 3:14 FAILURE BY NURSING FACILITIES TO COMPLY WITH MEDICAID REQUIREMENTS FOR RESIDENT ASSESSMENTS — Section 1919(b) [42 U.S.C.A. 1396r(b)]

Summary

Medicaid, like Medicare, prescribes numerous requirements for nursing facilities. Medicaid's requirements extend beyond skilled nursing facilities (SNF's), however, to intermediate care facilities (ICF's). They also apply to intermediate care facilities for the mentally retarded (ICF/MR's), many of which are State-owned and State-operated.

These requirements pertain to provision of services, section 1919(b), 42 U.S.C.A. 1396r(b); to residents' rights, section 1919(c), 42 U.S.C.A. 1396r(c); to administration of the facilities, section 1919(d), 42 U.S.C.A. 1396r(d); and to Federally-mandated State requirements, section 1919(e), 42 U.S.C.A. 1396r(e), such as for training nurses' aides and for State appeals processes for transfer and discharge of residents. In addition, there are responsibilities of the Secretary of Health and Human Services relating to nursing facility requirements, section 1919(f), 42 U.S.C.A. 1396r(f); elaborate requirements for survey and certification of nursing facilities, section 1919(g), 42 U.S.C.A. 1396r(g); and detailed enforcement requirements, section 1919(h), 42 U.S.C.A. 1396r(h).

Section 1919(b), 42 U.S.C.A. 1396r(b), requires nursing facilities to make assessments of residents. These must be comprehensive, accurate, standardized, and reproducible assessments of each resident' s functional capacity. They must be conducted or coordinated (with appropriate participation of health professionals) by a registered professional nurse who signs and certifies completion of the assessment. Furthermore, each individual who completes a portion of such an assessment must sign and certify as to accuracy of that portion of the assessment.

Pursuant to section 1919(b)(3)(B)(I), any individual who willfully and knowingly certifies a material and false statement in a resident assessment is subject to a civil money penalty not to exceed $1,000 with respect to each assessment. Pursuant to section 1919(b)(3)(B)(II), any individual who willfully and knowingly causes another individual to certify a material and false statement in a resident assessment is subject to a civil money penalty not to exceed $5,000 with respect to each assessment. Furthermore, if a State finds knowing and willful certification of false assessments, section 1919(b)(3)(B)(iii) permits it to require (for a period which it specifies) that resident assessments be conducted and certified by individuals who are independent of the facility and who are approved by the State.

Enforcement procedures for these civil money penalties are governed by section 1128A of the Act, 42 U.S.C.A. 1320a-7a, which authorizes civil money penalties for a variety of offenses.

◆ NOTE: Generally, section 1919 became effective October 1, 1990. See the Omnibus Budget Reconciliation Act of 1987, P.L. 100-203, as amended by the Medicare Catastrophic Coverage Act of 1988, P.L. 100-360. Moreover, effective October 1, 1990,

SNF's and ICF's were collectively referred to as nursing facilities.

Statutory Provisions

For Medicaid purposes, section 1919(a), 42 U.S.C.A. 1396r(a), defines nursing facility as follows:

NURSING FACILITY DEFINED. — In this title, the term "nursing facility" means an institution (or a distinct part of an institution) which —

(1) is primarily engaged in providing to residents —

(A) skilled nursing care and related services for residents who require medical or nursing care,

(B) rehabilitation services for the rehabilitation of injured, disabled, or sick persons, or

(C) on a regular basis, health-related care and services to individuals who because of their mental or physical condition require care and services (above the level of room and board) which can be made available to them only through institutional facilities,

and is not primarily for the care and treatment of mental diseases;

(2) has in effect a transfer agreement (meeting the requirements of section 1861(l) [42 U.S.C.A. 1395x(l)], which pertains to agreements for the transfer of patients from hospitals to skilled nursing facilities and vice versa, as medically appropriate) with one or more hospitals having agreements in effect under section 1866 [42 U.S.C.A. 1395cc, which pertains to Medicare provider agreements]; and

(3) meets the requirements for a nursing facility described in subsections (b) [which pertains to provision of services], (c) [which pertains to residents' rights], and (d) of this section [which pertains to administration of nursing facilities].

Such term also includes any facility which is located in a State on an Indian reservation and is certified by the Secretary as meeting the requirements of paragraph (1) and subsections (b), (c), and (d).

Pursuant to section 1919(b), 42 U.S.C.A. 1396r(b), one requirement relating to the provision of nursing facility services is to make assessments of residents. The statute provides:

REQUIREMENTS RELATING TO PROVISION OF SERVICES. —

(1) QUALITY OF LIFE. —

(A) IN GENERAL. — A nursing facility must care for its residents in such a manner and in such an environment as will promote maintenance or enhancement of the quality of life of each resident.

(B) QUALITY ASSESSMENT AND ASSURANCE. — A nursing facility must maintain a quality assessment and assurance committee, consisting of the director of nursing services, a physician designated by the facility, and at least 3 other members of the facility's staff, which (i) meets at least quarterly to identify issues with respect to which quality assessment and assurance activities are necessary and (ii) develops and implements appropriate plans of action to correct identified quality deficiencies. A State or the Secretary may not require disclosure of the records of such committee except insofar as such disclosure is related to the compliance of such committee with the requirements of this subparagraph. [The last sentence was added by section 4801(e)(2) of P.L. 101-508, the Omnibus Budget Reconciliation Act of 1990 (OBRA 90), effective as if included in OBRA 87.]

(2) SCOPE OF SERVICES AND ACTIVITIES UNDER PLAN OF CARE. — A nursing facility must provide services and activities to attain or maintain the highest practicable physical, mental, and psychosocial well-being of each resident in accordance with a written plan of care which-

(A) describes the medical, nursing, and psychosocial needs of the resident and how such needs will be met;

(B) is initially prepared, with the participation to the extent practicable of the resident or the resident's family or legal representative, by a team which includes the resident's attending physician and a registered professional nurse with responsibility for the resident; and

(C)) is periodically reviewed and revised by such team after each assessment under paragraph (3).

(3) RESIDENTS' ASSESSMENT. —

(A) REQUIREMENT. — A nursing facility must conduct a comprehensive, accurate, standardized, reproducible assessment of each resident's functional capacity, which assessment —

(i) describes the resident's capability to perform daily life functions and significant impairments in functional capacity;

(ii) is based on a uniform minimum data set specified by the Secretary under subsection (f)(6)(A) [which requires the Secretary to establish such a data set of core elements and common definitions for use by nursing facilities in conducting the assessments, and to establish guidelines for utilization of the data set not later than January 1, 1989];

(iii) uses an instrument which is specified by the State under subsection (e)(5) [which, as a condition of approval of State Medicaid plans, effective July 1, 1990, requires States to specify the instrument to be used by nursing facilities in the State to comply with the resident assessment requirement and the subsection (f)(6)(B) requirement for the Secretary, not later than April 1, 1990, to designate one or more instruments for making resident assessments]; and

(iv) includes the identification of medical problems.

(B) CERTIFICATION. —

(i) IN GENERAL. — Each such assessment must be conducted or coordinated (with the appropriate participation of health professionals) by a registered professional nurse who signs and certifies the completion of the assessment. Each individual who completes a portion of such an assessment shall sign and certify as to the accuracy of that portion of the assessment.

Where there must be certified assessments, there may be opportunity for falsification. Accordingly, section 1919(b)(3)(B)(ii) provides:

PENALTY FOR FALSIFICATION. —

(I) An individual who willfully and knowingly certifies under clause (i) a material and false statement in a resident assessment is subject to a civil money penalty of not more than $1,000 with respect to each assessment.

(II) An individual who willfully and knowingly causes another individual to certify under clause (i) a material and false statement in a resident assessment is subject to a civil money penalty of not more than $5,000 with respect to each assessment.

(III) The provisions of section 1128A [42 U.S.C.A. 1320a-7a] (other than subsections (a) and (b) shall apply to a civil money penalty under this clause in the same manner as such provisions apply to a penalty or proceeding under section 1128A(a).

Then subsection (B)(iii) provides:

USE OF INDEPENDENT ASSESSORS. — If a State determines, under a survey under subsection (g) or otherwise, that there has been a knowing and willful certification of false assessments under this paragraph, the State may require (for a period specified by the State) that resident assessments under this paragraph be conducted and certified by individuals who are independent of the facility and who are approved by the State.

With regard to how often resident assessments must be made, what use is to be made of resident assessments, how they are to be coordinated with State pre-admission screening programs, and requirements for pre-admission screening for mentally ill and mentally retarded individuals, section 1919(b)(3) further provides:

(C) FREQUENCY:

(i) IN GENERAL. — Such an assessment must be conducted —

(I) promptly upon (but no later than 14 days after the date of [changed from 4 days pursuant to section 4801(e)(3) of OBRA 90, effective as if enacted by OBRA 87]) admission for each individual admitted on or after October 1, 1990, and by October 1, 1991, for each resident of the facility on that date [NOTE: Effective November 29,1999, section 608(p)(1) of the Medicare, Medicaid, and SCHIP Balanced Budget Refinement Act of 1999, as incorporated into the

Omnibus Consolidated Appropriations Act, 2000, P.L. 106–113, enacted November 17, 1999, removed "not later than" after 1990, and "by and before "October 1, 1991,"];

(II) promptly after a significant change in the resident's physical or mental condition; and

(III) in no case less often than once every 12 months.

(ii) RESIDENT REVIEW. — The nursing facility must examine each resident no less frequently than once every 3 months and, as appropriate, revise the resident's assessment to assure the continuing accuracy of the assessment.

(D) USE. — The results of such an assessment shall be used in developing, reviewing, and revising the resident's plan of care under paragraph (2).

(E) COORDINATION. — Such assessments shall be coordinated with any State-required preadmission screening program to the maximum extent practicable in order to avoid duplicative testing and effort. In addition, a nursing facility shall notify the State mental health authority or State mental retardation or developmental disability authority, as applicable, promptly after a significant change in the physical or mental condition of a resident who is mentally ill or mentally retarded. [NOTE: The preceding sentence was added by section 2(a) of the Medicaid Nursing Homes Annual Resident Review Act of 1996, effective October 19, 1996.]

(F) REQUIREMENTS RELATING TO PREADMISSION SCREENING FOR MENTALLY ILL AND MENTALLY RETARDED INDIVIDUALS. — Except as provided in clauses (ii) and (iii) of subsection (e)(7)(A) [which pertains to preadmission screening, (this introductory clause added by section 4801(b)(2)(A) of OBRA 90, effective as if enacted by OBRA 87)] , a nursing facility must not admit, on or after January 1, 1989, any new resident who —

(i) is mentally ill (as defined in subsection (e)(7)(G)(i)) unless the State mental health authority has determined (based on an independent physical and mental evaluation performed by a person or entity other than the State mental health authority) prior to admission that, because of the physical and mental condition of the individual, the individual requires the level of services provided by a nursing facility, and, if the individual requires such level of services, whether the individual requires specialized services ["specialized services substituted for "active treatment" here and in (ii) below pursuant to section 4801(b)(8) of OBRA 90, effective November 5, 1990 whether or not regulations have been promulgated] for mental illness, or

(ii) is mentally retarded (as defined in subsection (e)(7)(G)(ii) unless the State mental retardation or developmental disability authority has determined prior to admission that, because of the physical and mental condition of the individual, the individual requires the level of services provided by a nursing facility, and, if the individual requires such level of services, whether the individual requires specialized services for mental retardation.

A State mental health authority and a State mental retardation or developmental disability authority may not delegate (by subcontract or otherwise) their responsibilities under this subparagraph to a nursing facility (or to an entity that has a direct or indirect affiliation or relationship with such a facility). [This sentence was added by section 4801(b)(4)(A) of OBRA 90, effective November 5, 1990, whether or not regulations have been promulgated.]

For regulatory citations, see Chapter 7

§ 3:15 ABUSE OR NEGLECT OF NURSING FACILITY RESIDENTS OR MISAPPROPRIATION OF THEIR PROPERTY — Section 1919(g)(1)(C) [42 U.S.C.A. 1396r(g)(1)(C)]

Summary

Pursuant to section 1919(g)(1), 42 U.S.C.A. 1396r(g)(1)(C), nursing facilities not owned by a State undergo State Medicaid survey and certification, a process which includes review of the requirements relating to provision of services, residents' rights, and administration of the facilities. State-owned nursing facilities undergo similar survey and certification by the Secretary. Part of this process requires States to investigate allegations of resident neglect and abuse and of misappropriation of resident property by a nurse aide or any other individual used by a facility to provide services to a resident.

Section 1919(g)(1)(C), 42 U.S.C.A. 1396r(g)(1)(C), provides that if, after notice to an accused individual and reasonable opportunity for a hearing to rebut allegations, a State finds that a nurse aide has neglected or abused a resident or misappropriated resident property in a facility, it must notify the nurse aide and the nurse aide registry (which section 1919(e)(2), 42 U.S.C.A. 1396r(e)(2), requires each State to establish). If, after notice and opportunity for a hearing, a State finds that any other individual has neglected or abused a resident or misappropriated resident property in a facility, the State must notify the appropriate licensure authority.

Section 1919(g)(1)(D), which was added by section 4755(b) of the Balanced Budget Act of 1997, P.L. 105–33, effective August 5, 1997, requires States to establish a procedure to permit a nurse aide to petition to have his or her name removed from the nurse aide registry. That procedure may apply only in the case of a finding of neglect, and only if the employment and personal history of the nurse aide does not reflect a pattern of abusive behavior or neglect, and if the neglect involved in the original finding was a single occurrence. There can be no determination on such a petition, however, prior to the expiration of a one-year period commencing the date on which the petitioner's name was placed on the registry.

◆ NOTE: Generally, section 1919 became effective October 1, 1990. See the Omnibus Budget Reconciliation Act of 1987, P.L. 100-203, as amended by the Medicare Catastrophic Coverage Act of 1988, P.L. 100-360. Furthermore, with respect to the survey and certification process for nursing facilities set forth in section 1919(g), section 1919(g)(1)(D) provides that the failure of the Secretary to issue regulations to carry out this subsection shall not relieve a State of its responsibility under this subsection.

Statutory Provisions

Section 1919(g)(1)(C), 42 U.S.C.A. 1396r(g)(1)(C), provides:

> INVESTIGATION OF ALLEGATIONS OF RESIDENT NEGLECT AND ABUSE AND MISAPPROPRIATION OF RESIDENT PROPERTY. — The State shall provide, through the agency responsible for surveys and certification of nursing facilities under this subsection, for a process for the receipt and timely review and investigation of allegations of neglect and

abuse and misappropriation of resident property by a nurse aide of a resident in a nursing facility or by another individual used by the facility in providing services to such a resident. The State shall, after notice to the individual involved and a reasonable opportunity for a hearing for the individual to rebut allegations, make a finding as to the accuracy of the allegations. If the State finds that a nurse aide has neglected or abused a resident or misappropriated resident property in a facility, the State shall notify the nurse aide and the registry of such finding. If the State finds that any other individual used by the facility has neglected or abused a resident or misappropriated resident property in a facility, the State shall notify the appropriate licensure authority. A State shall not make a finding that an individual has neglected a resident if the individual demonstrates that such neglect was caused by factors beyond the control of the individual. [The last sentence was added by section 4801(e)(13) of P.L. 101-508, the Omnibus Budget Reconciliation Act of 1990 (OBRA 90), effective as if included in OBRA 87.]

With regard to the nurse aide registry, section 1919(e)(2), 42 U.S.C.A. 1396r(e)(2), provides:

NURSE AIDE REGISTRY. —

(A) IN GENERAL. — By not later than January 1, 1989, the State shall establish and maintain a registry of all individuals who have satisfactorily completed a nurse aide training and competency evaluation program, or a nurse aide competency evaluation program, approved under paragraph 1 in the State, or any individual described in subsection (f)(2)(B)(ii) or in subparagraph (B), (C), or (D) of section 6901 of the Omnibus Budget Reconciliation Act of 1989. [The clause beginning "or any individual" was added by section 4801(e)(12)(A) of OBRA 90, effective as if enacted by OBRA 87.]

(B) INFORMATION IN REGISTRY. — The registry under subparagraph (A) shall provide (in accordance with regulations of the Secretary) for the inclusion of specific documented findings by a State under subsection (g)(1)(C) of resident neglect or abuse or misappropriation of resident property involving an individual listed in the registry, as well as any brief statement of the individual disputing the findings. The State shall make available to the public information in the registry. In the case of inquiries to the registry concerning an individual listed in the registry, any information disclosed concerning such a finding shall also include disclosure of any such statement in the registry relating to the finding or a clear and accurate summary of such a statement.

(C) [Effective as if enacted by OBRA 87, pursuant to section 4801(e)(12)(B) of OBRA 90] PROHIBITION AGAINST CHARGES. — A state may not impose any charges on a nurse aide relating to the registry established under subparagraph (A).

With regard to removal of a name from the nurse aide registry, section 1919(g)(1)(D), which was added, effective August 5, 1997, by section 4755(b) of the Balanced Budget Act of 1997, P.L. 105–33, provides:

REMOVAL OF NAME FROM NURSE AIDE REGISTRY. —

(i) IN GENERAL. — In the case of a finding of neglect under subparagraph (C), the State shall establish a procedure to permit a nurse aide to petition the State to have his or her name removed from the registry upon a determination by the State that —

(I) the employment and personal history of the nurse aide does not reflect a pattern of abusive behavior or neglect; and

(II) the neglect involved in the original finding was a singular occurrence.

(ii) TIMING OF DETERMINATION. — In no case shall a determination on a petition submitted under clause (i) be made prior to the expiration of the 1-year period beginning on the date on which the name of the petitioner was added to the registry under subparagraph (C).

For regulatory citations, see Chapter 7

§ 3:16 GIVING NURSING FACILITIES ADVANCE NOTICE OF A SURVEY — Section 1919(g)(2)(A)(i) [42 U.S.C.A. 1396r(g)(2)(A)(i)]

Summary

Pursuant to section 1919(g)(1) and section 1919(g)(2), 42 U.S.C.A. 1396r(g)(1) and 1396r(g)(2), nursing facilities participating in Medicaid are subject to surveys to determine whether they meet State and Federal requirements. The law provides for standard surveys, extended surveys (full or partial), validation surveys, and special surveys. These are distinguished by their timing, their scope, and whether they are conducted by State or Federal surveyors.

Most nursing facilities will be subject only to standard surveys. These are the initial and, hence, most common type. According to section 1902(g)(2)(A), standard surveys must be of a case-mix stratified sample of residents. They must include a quality of care assessment, as measured by indicators of medical, nursing, and rehabilitative care, dietary and nutrition services, activities and social participation, sanitation, infection control, and the physical environment. Standard surveys also must include review of required written plans of care, an audit of required residents' assessments to determine their accuracy and adequacy, and a review of compliance with residents' rights provisions of the statute.

Section 1902(g)(2)(C) required the Secretary of Health and Human Services to develop, test, and validate a protocol for standard and extended surveys not later than January 1, 1990. It also required such surveys to be conducted by individuals who meet minimum qualifications to be established by the Secretary by that date. The Secretary's failure to develop, test, or validate such protocols or to establish minimum qualifications for surveyors, however, does not relieve a State or the Secretary of their responsibility to conduct surveys.

According to section 1919(g)(2)(E), surveys must be conducted by a multi-disciplinary team of professionals, including a registered professional nurse. Moreover, a State may not use as a survey team member any individual who is serving, or who within the previous two years has served, as a member of the staff of, or as a consultant to, the facility to be surveyed. Nor may a State use any person who has a personal or familial financial interest in the facility being surveyed. Furthermore, no individual may serve as a member of a survey team unless the individual has successfully completed a training and testing program in survey and certification techniques that has been approved by the Secretary.

Because failing a survey can put a nursing facility out of the Medicaid program and subject the facility and its owners, operators, and employees to other onerous sanctions as well, knowing when a facility will be surveyed would be advantageous. Congress, however, wanted standard surveys to come as a surprise. Accordingly, section 1919(g)(2)(A)(i) provides that any individual who notifies, or causes to be notified, a nursing facility of the time or date on which a Medicaid standard survey is scheduled to be conducted is subject to a civil money penalty not to exceed $2,000. Furthermore, the Secretary must review each State's procedures for scheduling and conducting standard surveys to ensure that the State has taken all reasonable steps to avoid giving notice through the scheduling procedures and the conduct of the surveys themselves.

Enforcement procedures for this civil money penalty are governed by section 1128A of the Social Security Act, 42 U.S.C.A. 1320a-7a, which authorizes civil money penalties for a variety of offenses.

◆ NOTE: Generally, section 1919 became effective October 1, 1990. See the Omnibus Budget Reconciliation Act of 1987, P.L. 100-203, as amended by the Medicare Catastrophic Coverage Act of 1988, P.L. 100-360. Furthermore, with respect to the survey and certification process for nursing facilities set forth in section 1919(g), section 1919(g)(1)(D) provides that the failure of the Secretary to issue regulations to carry out this subsection shall not relieve a State of its responsibility under this subsection.

Statutory Provisions

Section 1919(g)(1), 42 U.S.C.A. 1396r(g)(1), provides in pertinent part:

SURVEY AND CERTIFICATION PROCESS. —

(1) STATE AND FEDERAL RESPONSIBILITY. —

(A) IN GENERAL. — Under each State plan under this title, the State shall be responsible for certifying, in accordance with surveys conducted under paragraph (2), the compliance of nursing facilities (other than facilities of the

State) with the requirements of subsections (b) [which pertains to provisions of services], (c) [which pertains to residents' rights], and (d) [which pertains to administration of a facility]. The Secretary shall be responsible for certifying, in accordance with surveys conducted under paragraph (2), the compliance of State nursing facilities with the requirements of such subsections.

(B) EDUCATIONAL PROGRAM. — Each State shall conduct periodic educational programs for the staff and residents (and their representatives) of nursing facilities in order to present current regulations, procedures, and policies under this section.

* * *

(E) CONSTRUCTION. — The failure of the Secretary to issue regulations to carry out this subsection shall not relieve a State of its responsibility under this subsection.

Section 1919(g)(2), 42 U.S.C.A. 1396r(g)(2), provides:

SURVEYS. —

(A) ANNUAL STANDARD SURVEY. —

(i) IN GENERAL. — Each nursing facility shall be subject to a standard survey, to be conducted without any prior notice to the facility. Any individual who notifies (or causes to be notified) a nursing facility of the time or date on which such a survey is scheduled to be conducted is subject to a civil money penalty of not to exceed $2,000. The provisions of section 1128A [42 U.S.C.A. 1320a-7a] (other than subsections (a) and (b)) shall apply to a civil money penalty under the previous sentence in the same manner as such provisions apply to a penalty or proceeding under section 1128A(a) [42 U.S.C.A. 1320a-7a(a)]. The Secretary shall review each State's procedures for scheduling and conduct of standard surveys to assure that the State has taken all reasonable steps to avoid giving notice of such a survey through the scheduling procedures and the conduct of the surveys themselves.

(ii) CONTENTS. — Each standard survey shall include, for a case-mix stratified sample of residents —

(I) a survey of the quality of care furnished, as measured by indicators of medical, nursing, and rehabilitative care, dietary and nutrition services, activities and social participation, and sanitation, infection control, and the physical environment,

(II) written plans of care provided under subsection (b)(2) and an audit of the residents' assessments under subsection (b)(3) to determine the accuracy of such assessments and the adequacy of such plans of care, and

(III) a review of compliance with residents' rights under subsection (c).

(iii) FREQUENCY. —

(I) IN GENERAL. — Each nursing facility shall be subject to a standard survey not later than 15 months after the date of the previous standard survey conducted under this subparagraph. The statewide average interval between standard surveys of a nursing facility shall not exceed 12 months.

(II) SPECIAL SURVEYS. — If not otherwise conducted under subclause (I), a standard survey (or an abbreviated standard survey) may be conducted within 2 months of any change of ownership, administration, management of a nursing facility, or director of nursing in order to determine whether the change has resulted in any decline in the quality of care furnished in the facility.

(B) EXTENDED SURVEYS. —

(i) IN GENERAL. — Each nursing facility which is found, under a standard survey, to have provided substandard quality of care shall be subject to an extended survey. Any other facility may, at the Secretary's or State's discretion, be subject to such an extended survey (or a partial extended survey).

(ii) TIMING. — The extended survey shall be conducted immediately after the standard survey (or, if not practical, not later than 2 weeks after the date of completion of the standard survey).

(iii) CONTENTS. — In such an extended survey, the survey team shall review and identify the policies and procedures which produced such substandard quality of care and shall determine whether the facility has complied with all the requirements described in subsections (b), (c), and (d). Such review shall include an expansion of the size of the sample of residents' assessments reviewed and a review of the staffing, of in-service training, and, if appropriate, of contracts with consultants.

(iv) CONSTRUCTION. — Nothing in this paragraph shall be construed as requiring an extended or partial extended survey as a prerequisite to imposing a sanction against a facility under subsection (h) on the basis of findings in a standard survey.

(C) SURVEY PROTOCOL. — Standard and extended surveys shall be conducted —

(i) based upon a protocol which the Secretary has developed, tested, and validated by not later than January 1, 1990, and

(ii) by individuals, of a survey team, who meet such minimum qualifications as the Secretary establishes by not later than such date. The failure of the Secretary to develop, test, or validate such protocols or to establish such minimum qualifications shall not relieve any State of its responsibility (or the Secretary of the Secretary's responsibility) to conduct surveys under this subsection.

(D) CONSISTENCY OF SURVEYS. — Each State shall implement programs to measure and reduce inconsistency in the application of survey results among surveyors.

(E) SURVEY TEAMS. —

(i) IN GENERAL. — Surveys under this subsection shall be conducted by a multidisciplinary team of professionals (including a registered professional nurse),

(ii) PROHIBITION OF CONFLICTS OF INTEREST. — A State may not use as a member of a survey team under this subsection an individual who is serving (or has served within the previous 2 years) as a member of the staff of, or as a consultant to, the facility surveyed respecting compliance with the requirements of subsections (b), (c), and (d), or who has a personal or familial financial interest in the facility being surveyed, or who has a personal or familial financial interest in the facility being surveyed.

(iii) TRAINING. — The Secretary shall provide for the comprehensive training of State and Federal surveyors in the conduct of standard and extended surveys under this subsection, including the auditing of resident assessments and plans of care. No individual shall serve as a member of a survey team unless the individual has successfully completed a training and testing program in survey and certification techniques that has been approved by the Secretary.

With respect to validation and special surveys, section 1919(g)(3) provides in pertinent part:

(3) VALIDATION SURVEYS. —

(A) IN GENERAL. — The Secretary shall conduct onsite surveys of a representative sample of nursing facilities in each State, within 2 months of the date of surveys conducted under paragraph (2) by the State, in a sufficient number to allow inferences about the adequacies of each State's surveys conducted under paragraph (2). In conducting such surveys, the Secretary shall use the same survey protocols as the State is required to use under paragraph (2). If the State has determined that an individual nursing facility meets the requirements of subsections (b), (c), and (d), but the Secretary determines that the facility does not meet such requirements, the Secretary's determination as to the facility's noncompliance with such requirements is binding and supersedes that of the State survey.

(B) SCOPE. — With respect to each State, the Secretary shall conduct surveys under subparagraph (A) each year with respect to at least 5 percent of the number of nursing facilities surveyed by the State in the year, but in no case less than 5 nursing facilities in the State.

* * *

(D) SPECIAL SURVEYS OF COMPLIANCE. — Where the Secretary has reason to question the compliance of a nursing facility with any of the requirements of subsections (b) [which pertains to provision of services], (c) [which pertains to residents' rights], and (d) [which pertains to administration of a facility], the Secretary may conduct a survey of the facility and, on the basis of that survey, make independent and binding determinations concerning the extent to which the nursing facility meets such requirements.

For regulatory citations, see Chapter 7

§ 3:17 FAILING A NURSING FACILITY SURVEY — Section 1919(g)(5), 1919(h), and 1919(i) [42 U.S.C.A. 1396r(g)(5), 1396r(h), and 1396r(i)]

Summary

Pursuant to section 1919(g)(1) and section 1919(g)(2), 42 U.S.C.A. 1396r(g)(1) and 1396r(g)(2), nursing facilities participating in Medicaid are subject to surveys to determine whether they meet State and Federal requirements. The law provides for standard surveys, extended surveys (full or partial), validation surveys, and special surveys. These are distinguished by their timing, their scope, and whether they are conducted by State or Federal surveyors.

According to section 1902(g)(2)(A), standard surveys must be of a case-mix stratified sample of residents. They must include a quality of care assessment, as measured by indicators of medical, nursing, and rehabilitative care, dietary and nutrition services, activities and social participation, sanitation, infection control, and the physical environment. Standard surveys also must include review of required written plans of care, an audit of required residents' assessments to determine their accuracy and adequacy, and a review of compliance with residents' rights provisions of the statute.

Section 1902(g)(2)(C) required the Secretary of Health and Human Services to develop, test, and validate a protocol for standard and extended surveys not later than January 1, 1990. It also required such surveys to be conducted by individuals who meet minimum qualifications to be established by the Secretary by that date. The Secretary's failure to develop, test, or validate such protocols or to establish such minimum qualifications, however, does not relieve a State or the Secretary of their responsibility to conduct surveys.

According to section 1919(g)(2)(E), surveys must be conducted by a multi-disciplinary team of professionals, including a registered professional nurse. Moreover, a State may not use as a survey team member any individual who is serving, or who within the previous two years has served, as a member of the staff of, or as a consultant to, the facility to be surveyed. Nor may it use any person who has a personal or familial financial interest in the facility being surveyed.

Furthermore, no individual may serve as a member of a survey team unless the individual has successfully completed a training and testing program in survey and certification techniques that has been approved by the Secretary.

Section 1919(g)(2)(A)(iii) requires each Medicaid nursing facility to be surveyed not later than 15 months after the date of a previous standard survey. The statewide average interval between standard surveys, however, must not exceed 12 months. Furthermore, a standard survey (or an abbreviated standard survey) may be conducted within two months of any change of ownership, administration, or management of a nursing facility, or of a director of nursing. That is to determine whether the change has resulted in decline in the quality of care furnished in the facility.

Pursuant to section 1919(g)(2)(B), extended surveys must be conducted of nursing facilities found under a standard survey to have provided substandard care. At the discretion of the Secretary or the State, however, other facilities also may be subjected to extended surveys. Moreover, when an extended survey is required, it must be conducted immediately after a standard survey or, if not practical, not later than two weeks after completion of the standard survey.

According to section 1919(g)(2)(B)(iii), the purpose of an extended survey is to review and identify policies and procedures which produced substandard care and to determine whether the facility has complied with legal requirements. Therefore, an extended survey must include an expansion of the sample of residents' assessments reviewed and a review of staffing, of in-service training, and, if appropriate, of contracts with consultants. Pursuant to section 1919(g)(2)(B)(iv), however, an extended or partial extended survey is not a prerequisite to imposing a sanction against a facility on the basis of findings in a standard survey.

In addition to standard and extended surveys, the Secretary is obliged by section 1919(g)(3) to conduct validation surveys. These are to be on site, they must include a representative sample of nursing facilities in each State, they are to be conducted within two months of the date of standard surveys conducted by the State, and they must be in sufficient number to allow inferences about the adequacies of each State's surveys. Furthermore, when he conducts a validation survey, the Secretary must use the same survey protocols the State must use.

Given surveys of the same facility by State and Federal authorities, the possibility arises for conflicting assessments even though the same protocol is used by both. Accordingly, section 1919(g)(3)(A) provides that if the State has determined a nursing facility meets Medicaid requirements, but the Secretary determines it does not, the Secretary's determination of noncompliance is binding and supersedes the State's determination.

In addition to standard, extended, and validation surveys, section 1919(g)(3)(D) provides that whenever the Secretary has reason to question the compliance of a nursing facility with any of the requirements pertaining to provision of services, residents' rights, or administration of the facility, the Secretary may conduct a special survey of the facility, and, on the basis of that survey, make independent and binding determinations concerning the extent to which the nursing facility complies.

Section 1919(g)(5) requires States and the Secretary to make information respecting all surveys and certifications of nursing facilities, including statements of deficiencies and approved plans of correction, cost reports, copies of statements of ownership, and information pertaining to entities and individuals convicted of offenses related to Medicare and Medicaid publicly available. Pursuant to section 4801(e)(14) of P.L. 101-508, the Omnibus Budget Reconciliation Act of 1990 (OBRA 90), effective as if enacted by OBRA 87, statements of deficiencies are to be made available within 14 calendar days after they are made available to the facilities. Furthermore, only approved plans of correction must be made available.

In addition, States must notify the State long-term care ombudsman of State findings of noncompliance with respect to any nursing facility. Furthermore, if a State finds that a nursing facility has provided substandard quality of care, the State must notify the attending physician of each resident with respect to whom such finding is made, as well as any State board responsible for the licensing of the administrator of the nursing facility. States also must provide their Medicaid fraud and abuse control units with access to all information of the agency responsible for Medicaid surveys and certifications.

If a State finds, on the basis of a standard, extended, or partial extended survey, or otherwise, that a nursing facility no longer meets statutory requirements with respect to provision of services, residents' rights, or facility administration, and if the State further finds that the facility's deficiencies immediately jeopardize the health or safety of its residents, section 1919(h)(1)(A) requires the State to take immediate action to remove the jeopardy and correct the deficiencies. The State may do that by appointing temporary management to oversee the operation of the facility and to assure the health and safety of the residents pending orderly closure of the facility or pending improvements to come into compliance. Alternatively, the State must terminate the facility's participation in Medicaid.

In addition, the State may provide for denial of payment with respect to any individual admitted to the nursing facility after giving notice to the facility and the public. Or it may assess a civil money penalty to be collected with interest for each day of noncompliance. Or it may appoint temporary management. In case of an emergency, it may close the facility and/or transfer the residents to other facilities.

If a State finds, on the basis of a standard, extended, or partial extended survey, or otherwise, that a nursing facility no longer meets statutory requirements with respect to provision of services, residents' rights, or facility administration, but does not find immediate jeopardy to the health or safety of the facility's residents as a result of those deficiencies, section 1919(h)(1)(B) authorizes the State to terminate the facility's participation under the State plan, or to deny payments, or to impose a civil money penalty, or to appoint temporary management, or, in case of an emergency, to close the facility and/or transfer the residents to other facilities.

◆ NOTE: Imposition of these sanctions (referred to as remedies in section 1919) does not preclude or restrict States from imposing any other available remedies (sanctions).

In addition, pursuant to section 1919(h)(1)(A), if a State finds that a nursing facility meets statutory requirements, but, as of a previous period did not meet them, it may impose a civil money penalty for the days of noncompliance. Pursuant to section 1919(h)(2(A)(ii), funds collected as a result of such a penalty must be applied to protection of the health or property of residents of deficient nursing facilities, including payment for costs of relocating such residents, maintenance of operation of a facility pending corrections or closure, and reimbursement of residents for personal funds lost.

In cases where temporary management is imposed to bring about compliance, section 1919(h)(2)(iii) requires that remedy (sanction) to be continued until the State determines the nursing facility has the management capability to ensure continued compliance.

Pursuant to section 1919(h)(2), states are obliged to specify criteria as to when and how the various remedies (sanctions) are to be applied, the amounts of any fines, and the severity of each remedy (sanction) to be used in their imposition. The criteria must be designed to minimize the time between identification of violations and final imposition of the remedies (sanctions) and must provide for imposition of incrementally more severe fines for repeated or uncorrected deficiencies. In addition, the State may provide for other specified remedies (sanctions), such as directed plans of correction.

◆ NOTE: States were obliged to establish the denial of payment, civil money penalty, temporary management, and emergency closure remedies (sanctions) not later than October 1, 1989.

If a nursing facility has not complied with requirements within three months after the date it has been found out of compliance, section 1919(h)(2)(C) requires the State to deny payment with respect to any individual admitted to the facility after that date. If a nursing facility has been found to have provided substandard care on three consecutive standard surveys, then, regardless what other remedies (sanctions) are available, section 1919(h)(2)(D) requires the State to deny payment with respect to individuals subsequently admitted to the facility and to monitor the facility until it demonstrates to the State's satisfaction that it is in compliance and will remain in compliance.

With respect to State nursing facilities, section 1919(h)(3) provides that the Secretary may impose the denial of payment, the civil money penalty, and the temporary management remedies (sanctions).

In addition to what the State can or must do, if the Secretary finds noncompliance with requirements pertaining to provision of services, residents' rights, facility administration, or such matters as nurse aide training and competency evaluation, the nurse aide registry, State appeals processes for transfers and discharges of residents, nursing facility administrator standards, specification of resident assessment instruments, and pre-admission screening and resident review, and if he further finds that the facility's deficiencies immediately jeopardize the health or safety of its residents, section 1919(h)(3) requires the Secretary to take immediate action to remove the jeopardy and correct the deficiencies. One way he can do that is by appointing temporary management, in consultation with the State, pending closure of the facility or correction of the deficiencies, or by terminating the facility's participation in Medicaid. In addition, however, the Secretary may deny payment to the State for medical assistance furnished by the facility to all individuals in the facility, or to individuals admitted to the facility after the effective date of the finding. Or he can impose a civil money penalty not to exceed $10,000 for each day of noncompliance.

If the Secretary finds such noncompliance, but does not find immediate jeopardy to the health or safety of the residents, he may impose denial of payment to the State, the $10,000 per day civil money penalty, or temporary management.

If the Secretary finds that a nursing facility met the requirements, but did not meet them during a previous period, he may impose a $10,000 civil money penalty for each day of noncompliance.

Enforcement procedures for these Secretarially-imposed civil money penalties are governed by section 1128A of the Social Security Act, 42 U.S.C.A. 1320a-7a, which authorizes civil money penalties for a variety of offenses.

◆ NOTE: Imposition of these remedies (sanctions) does not preclude or restrict the Secretary from imposing others that are available.

Pursuant to section 1919(h)(3)(C) the Secretary was obligated to specify criteria as to when and how each of these remedies (sanctions) is to be applied, the amounts of any fines, and the severity of each. As with the States, those criteria must be designed to minimize the time between the identification of violations and final imposition of the remedies and to provide for incrementally more severe fines for repeated or uncorrected deficiencies.

Pursuant to section 1919(h)(3)(D), the Secretary may continue payments, over a period not to exceed six months, with respect to facilities not complying with the provision of services, residents' rights, and facility administration requirements, if the State survey agency finds alternative action more appropriate, if the State submits a plan and timetable for corrective action which the Secretary approves, and if the State agrees to repay payments received as Federal financial participation to the facility in the event corrective action is not taken in accordance with the approved plan and timetable.

According to section 1919(h)(4), when a State or the Secretary imposes the denial of payment remedy (sanction), it must continue until the facility comes into compliance.

Pursuant to section 1919(h)(5), if the State or the Secretary finds noncompliance by a nursing facility with the provision of services, residents' rights, or facility administration requirements, and also finds immediate jeopardy to the health and safety of the residents as a result thereof, the State or the Secretary, respectively, must notify the other of such finding. Then the State or the Secretary, respectively, must take immediate action to remove the jeopardy and correct the deficiencies either by appointing temporary management or by terminating the facility's participation in Medicaid. If participation is terminated by either the State or the Secretary, the State must provide for safe and orderly transfer of residents entitled to Medicaid.

To deal with the possibility of conflicting determinations by a State and the Secretary, section 1919(h)(6) provides as follows: If the Secretary finds compliance but a State finds noncompliance which does not cause immediate jeopardy to the health or safety of residents, the State's findings control and the remedies (sanctions) imposed by the State apply. If the Secretary finds noncompliance which does not cause immediate jeopardy to the health or safety of the residents, but the State has not made such a finding, the Secretary may impose denial of payment, the $10,000 per day civil money penalty, or temporary management. Pending any termination action by him, the Secretary must allow the State to continue Medicaid payments for not to exceed six months if the State guarantees a corrective action plan and timetable which the Secretary approves.

With regard to timing termination of participation, section 1919(h)(7) provides that if both the Secretary and the State find noncompliance and both find no immediate jeopardy to residents' health or safety, and if both find termination of the facility's participation in Medicaid appropriate, then the State's timing for the termination controls, provided it is not more than six months after the decision to terminate.

If the Secretary, but not the State, finds termination appropriate, the Secretary shall, pending any termination action by him, permit up to six months continued Medicaid payments, provided the State guarantees a Secretarially-approved corrective action plan and timetable.

If the State, but not the Secretary, finds termination appropriate, the State's decision and timing control.

If either the Secretary or the State, but not both, establishes one or more remedies (sanctions) which are additional or alternative to termination, section 1919(h)(7)(B)(i) provides that such additional or alternative remedies (sanctions) must also be applied. If both the Secretary and the State establish one or more remedies (sanctions) which are additional or alternative to termination, section 1919(h)(7)(B)(ii) provides that only the additional or alternative remedies (sanctions) of the Secretary apply.

Pursuant to section 1919(h)(8), these remedies (sanctions) are in addition to those otherwise available under State or Federal law and may not be construed to limit such other remedies (sanctions), including any available to an individual at common law.

Furthermore, where requirements or obligations under section 1919 are identical to those provided under section 1819 of the Medicare statute, fulfillment of the Medicare requirements is considered fulfillment of the Medicaid requirements.

◆ NOTE: Generally, section 1919 became effective October 1, 1990. See the Omnibus Budget Reconciliation Act of 1987, P.L. 100-203, as amended by the Medicare Catastrophic Coverage Act of 1988, P.L. 100-360. Moreover, with respect to the survey and certification process for nursing facilities set forth in section 1919(g), section 1919(g)(1)(D) provides that the failure of the Secretary to issue regulations to carry out this subsection shall not relieve a State of its responsibility under this subsection.

Statutory Provisions

Section 1919(g), 42 U.S.C.A. 1396r(g), provides in pertinent part:

SURVEY AND CERTIFICATION PROCESS. —

(1) STATE AND FEDERAL RESPONSIBILITY. —

(A) IN GENERAL. — Under each State plan under this title, the State shall be responsible for certifying, in accordance with surveys conducted under paragraph (2), the compliance of nursing facilities (other than facilities of the State) with the requirements of subsections (b) [which pertains to provisions of services], (c) [which pertains to residents' rights], and (d) [which pertains to administration of a facility]. The Secretary shall be responsible for certifying, in accordance with surveys conducted under paragraph (2), the compliance of State nursing facilities with the requirements of such subsections.

(B) EDUCATIONAL PROGRAM. — Each State shall conduct periodic educational programs for the staff and residents (and their representatives) of nursing facilities in order to present current regulations, procedures, and policies under this section.

* * *

(E) CONSTRUCTION. — The failure of the Secretary to issue regulations to carry out this subsection shall not relieve a State of its responsibility under this subsection.

(2) SURVEYS. —

(A) ANNUAL STANDARD SURVEY. —

(i) IN GENERAL. — Each nursing facility shall be subject to a standard survey, to be conducted without any prior notice to the facility. . ..

(ii) CONTENTS. — Each standard survey shall include, for a case-mix stratified sample of residents —

(I) a survey of the quality of care furnished, as measured by indicators of medical, nursing, and rehabilitative care, dietary and nutrition services, activities and social participation, and sanitation, infection control, and the physical environment,

(II) written plans of care provided under subsection (b)(2) and an audit of the residents' assessments under subsection (b)(3) to determine the accuracy of such assessments and the adequacy of such plans of care, and

(III) a review of compliance with residents' rights under subsection (c).

(iii) FREQUENCY. —

(I) IN GENERAL. — Each nursing facility shall be subject to a standard survey not later than 15 months after the date of the previous standard survey conducted under this subparagraph. The statewide average interval between standard surveys of a nursing facility shall not exceed 12 months.

(II) SPECIAL SURVEYS. — If not otherwise conducted under subclause (I), a standard survey (or an abbreviated standard survey) may be conducted within 2 months of any change of ownership, administration, management of a nursing facility, or director of nursing in order to determine whether the change has resulted in any decline in the quality of care furnished in the facility.

(B) EXTENDED SURVEYS. —

(i) IN GENERAL. — Each nursing facility which is found, under a standard survey, to have provided substandard quality of care shall be subject to an extended survey. Any other facility may, at the Secretary's or State's discretion, be subject to such an extended survey (or a partial extended survey).

(ii) TIMING. — The extended survey shall be conducted immediately after the standard survey (or, if not practical, not later than 2 weeks after the date of completion of the standard survey).

(iii) CONTENTS. — In such an extended survey, the survey team shall review and identify the policies and procedures which produced such substandard quality of care and shall determine whether the facility has complied with all the requirements described in subsections (b), (c), and (d). Such review shall include an expansion of the size of the sample of residents' assessments reviewed and a review of the staffing, of in-service training, and, if appropriate, of contracts with consultants.

(iv) CONSTRUCTION. — Nothing in this paragraph shall be construed as requiring an extended or partial extended survey as a prerequisite to imposing a sanction against a facility under subsection (h) on the basis of findings in a standard survey.

(C) SURVEY PROTOCOL. — Standard and extended surveys shall be conducted —

(i) based upon a protocol which the Secretary has developed, tested, and validated by not later than January 1, 1990, and

(ii) by individuals, of a survey team, who meet such minimum qualifications as the Secretary establishes by not later than such date. The failure of the Secretary to develop, test, or validate such protocols or to establish such minimum qualifications shall not relieve any State of its responsibility (or the Secretary of the Secretary's responsibility) to conduct surveys under this subsection.

(D) CONSISTENCY OF SURVEYS. — Each State shall implement programs to measure and reduce inconsistency in the application of survey results among surveyors.

(E) SURVEY TEAMS. —

(i) IN GENERAL. — Surveys under this subsection shall be conducted by a multidisciplinary team of professionals (including a registered professional nurse),

(ii) PROHIBITION OF CONFLICTS OF INTEREST. — A State may not use as a member of a survey team under this subsection an individual who is serving (or has served within the previous 2 years) as a member of the staff of, or as a consultant to, the facility surveyed respecting compliance with the requirements of subsections (b), (c), and (d), or who has a personal or familial financial interest in the facility being surveyed, or who has a personal or familial financial interest in the facility being surveyed.

(iii) TRAINING. — The Secretary shall provide for the comprehensive training of State and Federal surveyors in the conduct of standard and extended surveys under this subsection, including the auditing of resident assessments and plans of care. No individual shall serve as a member of a survey team unless the individual has successfully completed a training and testing program in survey and certification techniques that has been approved by the Secretary.

(3) VALIDATION SURVEYS. —

(A) IN GENERAL. — The Secretary shall conduct onsite surveys of a representative sample of nursing facilities in each State, within 2 months of the date of surveys conducted under paragraph (2) by the State, in a sufficient number to allow inferences about the adequacies of each

State's surveys conducted under paragraph (2). In conducting such surveys, the Secretary shall use the same survey protocols as the State is required to use under paragraph (2). If the State has determined that an individual nursing facility meets the requirements of subsections (b), (c), and (d), but the Secretary determines that the facility does not meet such requirements, the Secretary's determination as to the facility's noncompliance with such requirements is binding and supersedes that of the State survey.

(B) SCOPE. — With respect to each State, the Secretary shall conduct surveys under subparagraph (A) each year with respect to at least 5 percent of the number of nursing facilities surveyed by the State in the year, but in no case less than 5 nursing facilities in the State.

◆ NOTE: States which fail to perform the required surveys or which perform inadequate surveys and certifications are subject to financial penalties via reduction in the Federal financial participation in their Medicaid programs (subject, however, to procedural rights to reconsideration and review under section 1116 of the Social Security Act, 42 U.S.C.A. 1316] . See section 1919(g)(3)(C), 42 U.S.C.A. 1396r(g)(3)(C). That, however, involves a failure of a State to meet State plan requirements, rather than fraud or abuse. Accordingly, it is not dealt with in this treatise.

(D) SPECIAL SURVEYS OF COMPLIANCE. — Where the Secretary has reason to question the compliance of a nursing facility with any of the requirements of subsections (b) [which pertains to provision of services], (c) [which pertains to residents' rights], and (d) [which pertains to administration of a facility], the Secretary may conduct a survey of the facility and, on the basis of that survey, make independent and binding determinations concerning the extent to which the nursing facility meets such requirements.

(4) INVESTIGATION OF COMPLAINTS AND MONITORING NURSING FACILITY COMPLIANCE. — Each State shall maintain procedures and adequate staff to —

(A) investigate complaints of violations of requirements by nursing facilities, and

(B) monitor, on-site, on a regular, as needed basis, a nursing facility's compliance with the requirements of subsections (b), (c), and (d), if—

(i) the facility has been found not to be in compliance with such requirements and is in the process of correcting deficiencies to achieve such compliance;

(ii) the facility was previously found not to be in compliance with such requirements, has corrected deficiencies to achieve such compliance, and verification of continued compliance is indicated; or

(iii) the State has reason to question the compliance of the facility with such requirements.

A State may maintain and utilize a specialized team (including an attorney, an auditor, and appropriate health care professionals) for the purpose of identifying, surveying, gathering and preserving evidence, and carrying out appropriate enforcement actions against substandard nursing facilities.

Given that statutory process for nursing facility survey and certification, what are the sanctions for noncompliance?

One is public disclosure of the results of inspections and activities. Section 1919(g), 42 U.S.C.A. 1396r(g), provides for notice to the public, to the State long-term care ombudsman, to physicians and nursing facility administrator licensing boards, and to State Medicaid fraud and abuse control units as follows:

(5) DISCLOSURE OF RESULTS OF INSPECTIONS AND ACTIVITIES.—

(A) PUBLIC INFORMATION.—Each State, and the Secretary, shall make available to the public-

(i) information respecting all surveys and certifications made respecting nursing facilities, including statements of deficiencies, within 14 calendar days after such information is made available to those facilities, and approved plans of correction, [Section 4801(e)(14) of P.L. 101-508, the Omnibus Budget Reconciliation Act of 1990 (OBRA 90) added the clause beginning "within 14 calendar days" and inserted "approved" before "plans of corrections, effective as if enacted by OBRA 87.]

(ii) copies of cost reports of such facilities filed under this title or under title XVIII,

(iii) copies of statements of ownership under section 1124 [42 U.S.C.A. 1320a-3, which pertains to disclosure of ownership and related information],

(iv) information disclosed under section 1126 [42 U.S.C.A. 1329a-5, which pertains to disclosure by institutions, organizations, and agencies of owners and certain other individuals who have been convicted of offenses related to Titles XVIII and XIX].

(B) NOTICE TO OMBUDSMAN. — Each State shall notify the State long-term care ombudsman (established under section 307(a)(12) of the Older Americans Act of 1965) of the State's findings of noncompliance with any of the requirements of subsections (b), (c), and (d), or of any adverse action taken against a nursing facility under paragraphs (1), (2), or (3) of subsection (h) [The clause beginning "or of any adverse action" was added by section 4801(e)(15) of OBRA 90, effective as if enacted by OBRA 87], with respect to a nursing facility in the State.

(C) NOTICE TO PHYSICIANS AND NURSING FACILITY ADMINISTRATOR LICENSING BOARD. — If a State finds that a nursing facility has provided substandard quality of care, the State shall notify —

(i) the attending physician of each resident with respect to which such finding is made, and

(ii) any State board responsible for the licensing of the nursing facility administrator of the facility.

(D) ACCESS TO FRAUD CONTROL UNITS. — Each State shall provide its State medicaid fraud and abuse control unit (established under section 1903 (q) [42 U.S.C.A. 1396b(q)]) with access to all information of the State agency responsible for surveys and certifications under this subsection.

In addition to public disclosure, section 1919(h), 42 U.S.C.A. 1396r(h), provides as follows for enforcement:

ENFORCEMENT PROCESS. —

(1) IN GENERAL. — If a State finds, on the basis of a standard, extended, or partial extended survey under subsection (g)(2) or otherwise, that a nursing facility no longer meets a requirement of subsection (b) [which pertains to provision of services], (c) [which pertains to residents' rights], or (d) [which pertains to administration of a facility], and further finds that the facility's deficiencies —

(A) immediately jeopardize the health or safety of its residents, the State shall take immediate action to remove the jeopardy and correct the deficiencies through the remedy specified in paragraph (2)(A)(iii), or terminate the facility's participation under the State plan and may provide, in addition, for one or more of the other remedies described in paragraph (2); or

(B) do not immediately jeopardize the health or safety of its residents, the State may —

(i) terminate the facility's participation under the State plan,

(ii) provide for one or more of the remedies described in paragraph (2), or

(iii) do both.

Nothing in this paragraph shall be construed as restricting the remedies available to a State to remedy a nursing facility's deficiencies. If a State finds that a nursing facility meets the requirements of subsections (b), (c), and (d), but, as of a previous period, did not meet such requirements, the State may provide for a civil money penalty under paragraph (2)(A)(ii) for the days in which it finds that the facility was not in compliance with such requirements.

(2) SPECIFIED REMEDIES. —

(A) LISTING. — Except as provided in subparagraph (B)(ii), each State shall establish by law (whether statute or regulation) at least the following remedies:

(i) Denial of payment under the State plan with respect to any individual admitted to the nursing facility involved after such notice to the public and to the facility as may be provided for by the State.

(ii) A civil money penalty assessed and collected, with interest, for each day in which the facility is or was out of compliance with a requirement of subsection (b), (c), or (d). Funds collected by a State as a result of imposition of such a penalty (or as a result of the imposition by the State of a civil money penalty for activities described in subsections (b)(3)(B)(ii)(I) [which pertains to falsification of resident assessments], (b)(3)(B)(ii)(II) [which pertains to causing others to falsify resident assessments], or (g)(2)(A)(i) [which pertains to warning nursing facilities of surprise surveys] shall be applied to the protection of the health or property of residents of nursing facilities that the State or the Secretary finds deficient, including payment for the costs of relocation of residents to other facilities, maintenance of operation of a facility pending correction of deficiencies or closure, and reimbursement of residents for personal funds lost.

(iii) The appointment of temporary management to oversee the operation of the facility and to assure the health and safety of the facility's residents, where there is a need for temporary management while —

(I) there is an orderly closure of the facility, or

(II) improvements are made in order to bring the facility into compliance with all the requirements of subsection (b), (c), and (d).

The temporary management under this clause shall not be terminated under subclause (II) until the State has determined that the facility has the management capability to ensure continued compliance with all the requirements of subsections (b), (c), and (d).

(iv) The authority, in the case of an emergency, to close the facility, to transfer residents in that facility to other facilities, or both.

The State also shall specify criteria, as to when and how each of such remedies is to be applied, the amounts of any fines, and the severity of each of these remedies, to be used in the imposition of such remedies. Such criteria shall be designed so as to minimize the time between identification of violations and final imposition of the remedies and shall provide for the imposition of incrementally more severe fines for repeated or uncorrected deficiencies. In addition, the State may provide for other specified remedies, such as directed plans of correction.

(B) DEADLINE AND GUIDANCE. — (i) Except as provided in clause (ii), as a condition for approval of a State plan for calendar quarters beginning on or after October 1, 1989, each State shall establish the remedies described in clauses (i) through (iv) of subparagraph (A) by not later than October 1, 1989. The Secretary shall provide, through regulations by not later than October 1, 1988, guidance to States in establishing such remedies; but the failure of the Secretary to provide such guidance shall not relieve a State of the responsibility for establishing such remedies.

(ii) a State may establish alternative remedies other than termination of participation) other than those described in clauses (i) through (iv) of subparagraph (A), if the State demonstrates to the Secretary's satisfaction that the alternative remedies are as effective in deterring noncompliance and correcting deficiencies as those described in subparagraph (A).

(C) ASSURING PROMPT COMPLIANCE. — If a nursing facility has not complied with any of the requirements of subsections (b), (c), and (d), within 3 months after the date the facility is found to be out of compliance with such requirements, the State shall impose the remedy described in subparagraph (A)(i) for all individuals who are admitted to the facility after such date.

(D) REPEATED NONCOMPLIANCE. — In the case of a nursing facility which, on 3 consecutive standard surveys conducted under subsection (g)(2), has been found to have provided substandard quality of care, the State shall (regardless of what other remedies are provided) —

(i) impose the remedy described in subparagraph (A)(i) [i.e., deny payment for individuals subsequently admitted to the facility], and

(ii) monitor the facility under subsection (g)(4)(B) [which pertains to investigating complaints and monitoring compliance] until the facility has demonstrated, to the satisfaction of the State, that it is in compliance with the requirements of subsections (b), (c), and (d), and that it will remain in compliance with such requirements.

Having said that about sanctions, Congress then provided financial incentives for States to live up to their survey and certification obligations. Specifically, section 1919(h)(2) goes on to provide:

> (E) FUNDING. — The reasonable expenditures of a State to provide for temporary management and other expenses associated with implementing the remedies described in clauses (iii) and (iv) of subparagraph (A) shall be considered, for purposes of section 1903(a)(7) [42 U.S.C.A. 1396b(a)(7), which pertains to Federal payments to States for Medicaid expenditures], to be necessary for the proper and efficient administration of the State plan [which means Federal financial participation is available for those costs].
>
> (F) INCENTIVES FOR HIGH QUALITY CARE. — In addition to the remedies specified in this paragraph, a State may establish a program to reward, through public recognition, incentive payments, or both, nursing facilities that provide the highest quality care to residents who are entitled to medical assistance under this title. For purposes of section 1903(a)(7), proper expenses incurred by a State in carrying out such a program shall be considered to be expenses necessary for the proper and efficient administration of the State plan under this title, [which means States can pay extra to high quality nursing facilities, and if they do, Federal financial participation is available for such payments].

With respect to State nursing facilities and other nursing facilities, section 1919(h)(3) provides:

> SECRETARIAL AUTHORITY. —
>
> (A) FOR STATE NURSING FACILITIES. — With respect to a State nursing facility, the Secretary shall have the authority and duties of a State under this subsection, including the authority to impose remedies described in clauses (i), (ii), and (iii) of paragraph (2)(A).
>
> (B) OTHER NURSING FACILITIES. — With respect to any other nursing facility in a State, if the Secretary finds that a nursing facility no longer meets a requirement of subsection (b) [which pertains to provision of services], (c) [which pertains to residents' rights], (d) [which pertains to

administration of a facility], or (e) [which pertains to such State requirements as nurse aide training and competency evaluation, processes for resident transfers and discharges, and preadmission screening and resident review], and further finds that the facility's deficiencies —

(i) immediately jeopardize the health or safety of its residents, the Secretary shall take immediate action to remove the jeopardy and correct the deficiencies through the remedy specified in subparagraph (C)(iii), or terminate the facility's participation under the State plan and may provide, in addition, for one or more of the other remedies described in subparagraph (C); or

(ii) do not immediately jeopardize the health or safety of its residents, the Secretary may impose any of the remedies described in subparagraph (C).

Nothing in this subparagraph shall be construed as restricting the remedies available to the Secretary to remedy a nursing facility's deficiencies. If the Secretary finds that a nursing facility meets such requirements but, as of a previous period, did not meet such requirements, the Secretary may provide for a civil money penalty under subparagraph (C)(ii) for the days on which he finds that the facility was not in compliance with such requirements.

Section 1919(h)(3) then authorizes the following sanctions (remedies) for the Secretary to take action against nursing facilities:

(C) SPECIFIED REMEDIES. — The Secretary may take the following actions with respect to a finding that a facility has not met an applicable requirement:

(i) DENIAL OF PAYMENT. — The Secretary may deny any further payments to the State for medical assistance furnished by the facility to all individuals in the facility or to individuals admitted to the facility after the effective date of the finding.

(ii) AUTHORITY WITH RESPECT TO CIVIL MONEY PENALTIES. — The Secretary may impose a civil money penalty in an amount not to exceed $10,000 for each day of noncompliance. The provisions of section 1128A [42 U.S.C.A. 1320a-7a] (other than subsections (a) and (b)) shall apply to a civil money penalty under the previous sentence in the same manner as such provisions apply to a penalty or proceeding under section 1128A(a).

(iii) APPOINTMENT OF TEMPORARY MANAGEMENT. — In consultation with the State, the Secretary may appoint temporary management to oversee the operation of the facility and to assure the health and safety of the facility's residents, where there is a need for temporary management while —

(I) there is an orderly closure of the facility, or

(II) improvements are made in order to bring the facility into compliance with all the requirements of subsections (b), (c), and (d). The temporary management under this clause shall not be terminated under subclause (II) until the Secretary has determined that the facility has the management capability to ensure continued compliance with all the requirements of subsections (b), (c), and (d). The Secretary shall specify criteria, as to when and how each of such remedies is to be applied, the amounts of any fines, and the severity of each of these remedies, to be used in the imposition of such remedies. Such criteria shall be designed so as to minimize the time between the identification of violations and final imposition of the remedies and shall provide for the imposition of incrementally more severe fines for repeated or uncorrected deficiencies. In addition, the Secretary may provide for other specified remedies, such as directed plans of correction.

Section 1919(h)(3) softens the blow of the Secretary's sanctions (remedies), however, by providing:

(D) CONTINUATION OF PAYMENTS PENDING REMEDIATION. — The Secretary may continue payments, over a period of not longer than 6 months after the effective date of the findings ["after the effective date of the findings" added December 19, 1989, by section 6901(d)(4)(D) of P.L. 101-239, the Omnibus Budget Reconciliation Act of 1989, effective as if included in P.L. 100-203, the Omnibus Budget Reconciliation Act of 1987], under this title with respect to a nursing facility not in compliance with a requirement of subsection (b), (c), or (d), if —

(i) the State survey agency finds that it is more appropriate to take alternative action to assure compliance of the facility with the requirements than to terminate the certification of the facility, and

(ii) the State has submitted a plan and timetable for corrective action to the Secretary for approval and the Secretary approves the plan of corrective action.

◆ NOTE: Section 4754(a)(1) of the Balanced Budget Act of 1997, P.L. 105–33, inserted "and" at the end of clause (i). Section 4754(a)(2) struck ", and" at the end of clause (ii) and added a period; and section 4754(a)(3) deleted former clause (iii), which read: "(iii) the State agrees to repay to the Federal Government payments received under this subparagraph if the corrective action is not taken in accordance with the approved plan and timetable." Those changes were effective August 5, 1997.

The Secretary shall establish guidelines for approval of corrective actions requested by States under this subparagraph.

With respect to the duration of denial of payment, section 1919(h)(4) provides:

EFFECTIVE PERIOD OF DENIAL OF PAYMENT. — A finding to deny payment under this subsection shall terminate when the State or Secretary (or both, as the case may be) finds that the facility is in substantial compliance with all the requirements of subsections (b), (c), and (d).

Section 1919(h)(5) augments the Secretary's termination authority in cases where a facility's noncompliance causes immediate jeopardy to residents by providing:

IMMEDIATE TERMINATION OF PARTICIPATION FOR FACILITY WHERE STATE OR SECRETARY FINDS NONCOMPLIANCE AND IMMEDIATE JEOPARDY. — If either the State or the Secretary finds that a nursing facility has not met a requirement of subsection (b), (c), or (d), and finds that the failure immediately jeopardizes the health or safety of its residents, the State or the Secretary, respectively shall notify the other of such finding, and the State or the Secretary, respectively, shall take immediate action to remove the jeopardy and correct the deficiencies through the remedy specified in paragraph (2)(A)(iii) [which is temporary management

> appointed by the State] or (3)(C)(iii) [which is temporary management appointed by the Secretary], or terminate the facility's participation under the State plan. If the facility's participation in the State plan is terminated by either the State or the Secretary, the State shall provide for the safe and orderly transfer of the residents eligible under the State plan consistent with the requirements of subsection (c)(2) [which pertains to transfer and discharge rights of residents].

Given overlapping State and Federal powers with respect to nursing facilities, Congress established in section 1916(h)(6) the following rules in the event conflicts arose between the findings of the Secretary and the findings of a State:

> SPECIAL RULES WHERE STATE AND SECRETARY DO NOT AGREE ON FINDING OF NONCOMPLIANCE.—
>
> (A) STATE FINDING OF NONCOMPLIANCE AND NO SECRETARIAL FINDING OF NONCOMPLIANCE. — If the Secretary finds that a nursing facility has met all the requirements of subsections (b), (c), and (d), but a State finds that the facility has not met such requirements and the failure does not immediately jeopardize the health or safety of its residents, the State's findings shall control and the remedies imposed by the State shall be applied.
>
> (B) SECRETARIAL FINDING OF NONCOMPLIANCE AND NO STATE FINDING OF NONCOMPLIANCE. — If the Secretary finds that a nursing facility has not met all the requirements of subsections (b), (c), and (d), and that the failure does not immediately jeopardize the health or safety of its residents, but the State has not made such a finding, the Secretary—
>
> (i) may impose any remedies specified in paragraph (3)(C) with respect to the facility [i.e., denial of payment, civil monetary penalty, or appointment of temporary management], and
>
> (ii) shall (pending any termination by the Secretary) permit continuation of payments in accordance with paragraph (3)(D).

Section 1919(h)(7) then provides as follows for the timing of overlapping sanctions (remedies):

SPECIAL RULES FOR TIMING OF TERMINATION OF PARTICIPATION WHERE REMEDIES OVERLAP. — If both the Secretary and the State find that a nursing facility has not met all the requirements of subsections (b), (c), and (d), and neither finds that the failure immediately jeopardizes the health or safety of its residents —

(A) (i) if both find that the facility's participation under the State plan should be terminated, the State's timing of any termination shall control so long as the termination date does not occur later than 6 months after the date of the finding to terminate;

(ii) if the Secretary, but not the State, finds that the facility's participation under the State plan should be terminated, the Secretary shall (pending any termination by the Secretary) permit continuation of payments in accordance with paragraph (3)(D); or

(iii) if the State, but not the Secretary, finds that the facility's participation under the State plan should be terminated, the State's decision to terminate, and timing of such termination, shall control; and

(B) (i) if the Secretary or the State, but not both, establishes one or more remedies which are additional or alternative to the remedy of terminating the facility's participation under the State plan, such additional or alternative remedies shall also be applied, or

(ii) if both the Secretary and the State establish one or more remedies which are additional or alternative to the remedy of terminating the facility's participation under the State plan, only the additional or alternative remedies of the Secretary shall apply.

Congress then provided in section 1919(h) the following provisions, presumably to tidy up procedural matters:

(8) CONSTRUCTION. — The remedies provided under this subsection are in addition to those otherwise available under State or Federal law and shall not be construed as limiting such other remedies, including any remedy available to an individual at common law. The remedies described in clauses (i), (iii), and (iv) of paragraph (2)(A) [State denial of payment, appointment of temporary management, and closure of a facil-

ity and transfer of its residents] may be imposed during the pendency of any hearing. The provisions of this subsection shall apply to a nursing facility (or portion thereof) notwithstanding that the facility (or portion thereof) also is a skilled nursing facility for purposes of title XVIII.

◆ NOTE: The last sentence of paragraph (8) was added by section 6901(d)(1) of P.L. 101-239, the Omnibus Budget Reconciliation Act of 1989, effective December 19, 1989.

(9) SHARING OF INFORMATION. — Notwithstanding any other provision of law, all information concerning nursing facilities required by this section to be filed with the Secretary or a State agency shall be made available by such facilities to Federal or State employees for purposes consistent with the effective administration of programs established under this title and title XVIII, including investigation by State medicaid fraud control units.

Finally, section 1919(i), 42 U.S.C.A. 1396r(i), provides:

CONSTRUCTION. — Where requirements or obligations under this section are identical to those provided under section 1819 of this Act, the fulfillment of those requirements or obligations under section 1819 shall be considered to be the fulfillment of the corresponding requirements or obligations under this section.

For regulatory citations, see Chapter 7

§ 3:18 FAILURE BY INTERMEDIATE CARE FACILITIES FOR THE MENTALLY RETARDED TO MEET FEDERAL STANDARDS — Section 1922 [42 U.S.C.S. 1396r-3]

Summary

Intermediate care facilities for the mentally retarded (ICF/MR's) must meet Federal standards to participate in Medicaid, as must other types of nursing facilities. Those that fail may have their provider agreements terminated pursuant to section 1910(b), 42 U.S.C.A. 1396i(b).

Unfortunately, these institutions are the only places many mentally retarded persons have to live. Consequently, even when a facility is not up to standards, cutting off its access to Federal funds by terminating its provider agreement may not the best way to get that facility improved. Such a sanction seems especially draconian when deficiencies do not constitute an immediate and serious threat to the health and safety of residents. Perhaps Congress had that dilemma in mind when it authorized plans of correction and plans of reduction of certified beds in lieu of provider agreement termination for such facilities.

If the Secretary of Health and Human Services finds that an ICF/MR has substantial deficiencies which do not pose an immediate threat to the health and safety of residents (including failure to provide active treatment), section 1922(a)(1) permits the State to submit a written plan of correction. The plan must detail the extent of the facility's current compliance with Federal standards, including all deficiencies identified during a validation survey. It must provide a timetable for completion of necessary steps to correct all staffing deficiencies within six months, and it must include a timetable for rectifying all physical plant deficiencies within six months.

Pursuant to section 1922(e)(1), if the Secretary, after the conclusion of a six-month plan of correction, determines that the State has substantially failed to correct an ICF/MR's deficiencies, he may terminate the facility's provider agreement pursuant to section 1910(b).

In lieu of a plan of correction, section 1922(a)(2) permits a State to submit a written plan for permanently reducing the number of certified beds in an ICF/MR within a maximum of 36 months. That is to allow time for any noncomplying buildings (or distinct parts thereof) to be vacated and any staffing deficiencies to be corrected.

A State must provide for a hearing to be held on a reduction plan at the affected facility at least 35 days prior to submission of the plan to the Secretary, with reasonable notice of the hearing to the staff and residents of the facility, to responsible members of the residents' families, and to the general public. Furthermore, a reduction plan must demonstrate that the State has successfully provided home and community services similar to the services proposed to be provided under the plan for similar individuals eligible for Medicaid. It must identify the number and the service needs of existing residents to be provided home or community services and the timetable for providing such services in six-month intervals within the 36 months. It must describe methods to select residents for home and community services and to develop alternative home and community services to meet their needs. It must describe necessary safeguards to protect the health and welfare of former residents who will receive home or community services, including adequate standards for consumer and provider participation, and it must include assurances that applicable State licensure and State and Federal certification requirements will be met in providing such home or community services.

In addition, a reduction plan must provide placement for residents eligible for Medicaid that will permit Medicaid eligibility to continue if the residents so desire. It must specify actions which will be taken to protect the health and safety of residents and to provide active treatment for those that remain in the facility while the reduction plan is in effect. It must provide a ratio of qualified staff to residents at the facility or part thereof subject to the reduction plan that will be the higher of the ratio at the time the deficiencies were found or the ratio the Secretary determines is necessary for health and safety of the residents. Finally, it must protect the interests of employees affected by the reduction plan by preserving employee rights and benefits, by offering training and retraining, where necessary, by providing for redeployment of employees to community settings under the plan, and by making "maximum efforts" to guarantee employment; however, the plan need not, in fact, guarantee employment.

Pursuant to section 1922(d)(1), the Secretary must provide not less than 30 days after the submission of a reduction plan for submission of public comment before he approves or disapproves it. Pursuant to section 1922(d)(2), if the Secretary approves more than 15 reduction plans in a fiscal year, the next plan may be approved only if the State demonstrates that costs for correcting deficiencies will exceed $2,000,000.

Pursuant to section 1922(e)(2), if the Secretary determines at the conclusion of the initial six-month period of a reduction plan, or any six-month interval thereafter, that the State has substantially failed to meet the requirements of the plan, the Secretary must either terminate the facility's provider agreement pursuant to section 1910(b), or, if the State has failed to meet plan requirements despite good faith efforts, the Secretary must disallow Federal financial participation to the State in an amount equal to five percent of the cost of care for all Medicaid eligibles in the facility for each month for which the State fails to meet the requirements.

◆ NOTE: Section 1922 used to be section 1919. See P.L. 100-203, the Omnibus Budget Reconciliation Act of 1987, section 4214. These current provisions apply only to plans of correction and reduction plans approved by the Secretary by January 1, 1990. Regulations implementing section 1922 were published in Volume 53, No. 15 of the Federal Register, at page 1984, on January 25, 1988. Pursuant to OBRA of 1987, however, they were deemed effective as of April 7, 1986. See 42 CFR, Part 442. Changes with respect to active treatment requirements, and the extended January 1, 1990, sunset date were passed by Congress October 22, 1988, (effective with the President's signature November 10, 1988,) as section 8433 of P.L. 100-647, the Technical and Miscellaneous Revenue Act.

For obligations of States regarding ICF/MR's which do not comply with Medicaid requirements, see section 1902(i), 42 U.S.C.A. 1396a(i), discussed at § 3:5.

Statutory Provisions

Section 1922, 42 U.S.C.A. 1396r-3, provides:

(a) If the Secretary finds that an intermediate care facility for the mentally retarded has substantial deficiencies which do not pose an immediate threat to the health and safety of residents (including failure to provide active treatment), the State may elect, subject to the limitations in this section, to —

(1) submit, within the number of days specified by the Secretary in regulations which apply to submission of compliance plans with respect to deficiencies of such type, a written plan of correction which details the extent of the facility's current compliance with the standards promulgated by the Secretary, including all deficiencies identified during a validation survey, and which provides for a timetable for completion of necessary steps to correct all staffing deficiencies within 6 months, and a timetable for rectifying all physical plant deficiencies within 6 months; or

(2) submit, within a time period consisting of the number of days specified for submissions under paragraph (1) plus 35 days, a written plan for permanently reducing the number of certified beds, within a maximum of 36 months, in order to permit any noncomplying buildings (or distinct parts thereof)

to be vacated and any staffing deficiencies to be corrected (hereinafter in this section referred to as a "reduction plan").

(b) As conditions of approval of any reduction plan submitted pursuant to subsection (a)(2), the State must —

(1) provide for a hearing to be held at the affected facility at least 35 days prior to submission of the reduction plan, with reasonable notice thereof to the staff and residents of the facility, responsible members of the residents' families, and the general public;

(2) demonstrate that the State has successfully provided home and community services similar to the services proposed to be provided under the reduction plan for similar individuals eligible for medical assistance; and

(3) provide assurances that the requirements of subsection (c) shall be met with respect to the reduction plan.

(c) The reduction plan must —

(1) identify the number and service needs of existing facility residents to be provided home or community services and the timetable for providing such services, in 6 month intervals, within the 36-month period;

(2) describe the methods to be used to select such residents for home and community services and to develop the alternative home and community services to meet their needs effectively;

(3) describe the necessary safeguards that will be applied to protect the health and welfare of the former residents of the facility who are to receive home or community services, including adequate standards for consumer and provider participation and assurances that applicable State licensure and applicable State and Federal certification requirements will be met in providing such home or community services;

(4) provide that residents of the affected facility who are eligible for medical assistance while in the facility shall, at their option, be placed in another setting (or another part of the affected facility) so as to retain their eligibility for medical assistance;

(5) specify the actions which will be taken to protect the health and safety of and to provide active treatment for the residents

who remain in the affected facility while the reduction plan is in effect;

(6) provide that the ratio of qualified staff to residents at the affected facility (or the part thereof) which is subject to the reduction plan will be the higher of—

(A) the ratio which the Secretary determines is necessary in order to assure the health and safety of the residents of such facility (or part thereof); or

(B) the ratio which was in effect at the time that the finding of substantial deficiencies (referred to in subsection (a)) was made; and

(7) provide for the protection of the interests of employees affected by actions under the reduction plan, including—

(A) arrangements to preserve employee rights and benefits;

(B) training and retraining of such employees where necessary;

(C) redeployment of such employees to community settings under the reduction plan;

(D) making maximum efforts to guarantee the employment of such employees (but this requirement shall not be construed to guarantee the employment of any employee).

(d) (1) The Secretary must provide for a period of not less than 30 days after the submission of a reduction plan by a State, during which comments on such reduction plan may be submitted to the Secretary, before the Secretary approves or disapproves such reduction plan.

(2) If the Secretary approves more than 15 reduction plans under this section in a fiscal year, any reduction plans approved in addition to the first 15 such plans approved, must be for a facility (or part thereof) for which the costs of correcting the substantial deficiencies (referred to in subsection (a)) are $2,000,000 or greater (as demonstrated by the State to the satisfaction of the Secretary).

(e) (1) If the Secretary, at the conclusion of the 6-month plan of correction described in subsection (a)(1), determines that the State has substantially failed to correct the deficiencies described in subsection (a), the Secretary may terminate the facility's provider agreement in accordance with the provisions of section 1910(b).

(2) In the case of a reduction plan described in subsection (a)(2), if the Secretary determines, at the conclusion of the initial 6-month period or any 6-month interval thereafter, that the State has substantially failed to meet the requirements of subsection (c), the Secretary shall —

(A) terminate the facility's provider agreement in accordance with the provisions of section 1910(b); or

(B) if the State has failed to meet such requirements despite good faith efforts, disallow, for purposes of Federal financial participation, an amount equal to 5 percent of the cost of care for all eligible individuals in the facility for each month for which the State fails to meet such requirements.

(f) The provisions of this section shall apply only to plans of correction and reduction plans approved by the Secretary by January 1, 1990.

For regulatory citations, see Chapter 7

§ 3:19 FAILURE BY DRUG MANUFACTURERS AND WHOLESALERS TO COMPLY WITH MEDICAID DRUG REBATE REQUIREMENTS — Section 1927 [42 U.S.C.S. 1396s]

Summary

Section 4401(a)(3) of P.L. 101-508, the Omnibus Budget Reconciliation Act of 1990 (OBRA 90), effective November 5, 1990, established a new Medicaid drug rebate program. It is intended to assure that Medicaid receives purchase price advantages available to other purchasers. It applies to drugs dispensed under Medicaid on or after January 1, 1991.

Pursuant to section 1927(a), 42 U.S.C.A. 1396s(a), State Medicaid programs may not pay for covered outpatient drugs of a manufacturer unless the manufacturer has entered into and has in effect a rebate agreement. This agreement may be with the Secretary of Health and Human Services, or the Secretary may authorize a State to enter such an agreement with a manufacturer.

If a State and a manufacturer had a rebate agreement in effect when section 4401 (a)(3) of OBRA 90 was enacted, then for the initial period of such agreement it shall be deemed to comply with section 1927, provided the State reports to the Secretary any rebates paid pursuant thereto, and provided the agreement specifies a minimum aggregate rebate of 10 percent of the State's total expenditures under the State plan for coverage of the manufacturer's drugs. Such a "deemed" complying agreement may be continued by a State after the initial period if the State establishes to the Secretary' s satisfaction that rebates it provides are at least as large as rebates required under section 1927.

Each manufacturer with a rebate agreement in effect must report to the Secretary, not later than 30 days after the last day of each quarter beginning on or after January 1, 1991, the average manufacturer price and for single source drugs and innovator multiple source drugs the manufacturer's best price for covered outpatient drugs for the quarter. Each such manufacturer also must report not later than 30 days after the date of entering into a rebate agreement the average manufacturer price as of October 1, 1990, for each of its covered outpatient drugs.

Pursuant to section 1927(b)(3)(D), neither the Secretary nor a State agency nor any of its contractors may disclose information provided by manufacturers or wholesalers in compliance with section 1927 in a form that discloses the identity of a specific manufacturer or wholesaler or prices charged for drugs by such manufacturer or wholesaler. Two exceptions apply: one is if the Secretary determines disclosure is necessary to carry out section 1927; the other is to permit the Comptroller General to review the information provided.

To verify "average manufacturer price," the Secretary is authorized to survey, when necessary, wholesalers and manufacturers that directly distribute their covered outpatient drugs. Pursuant to section 1927(b)(3)(B), if a wholesaler, manufacturer, or direct seller refuses a request for information about charges or prices by the Secretary in connection with such a survey, or knowingly provides false information in response, the Secretary may impose a civil money penalty not to exceed $100,000.

Furthermore, pursuant to section 1927(b)(3)(C)(i), if a manufacturer with a rebate agreement fails to provide required information on prices on a timely basis, the Secretary may impose a civil money penalty not to exceed $10,000 for each day the information has not been provided. If the required information is not provided with 90 days of the deadline imposed, the rebate agreement must be suspended for services furnished after the end of such 90-day period and until the date the required information is reported. In no case, however, may such a suspension be less than 30 days.

Pursuant to section 1927(b)(3)(C)(ii), any manufacturer with a rebate agreement that knowingly provides false information to the Secretary is subject to a civil money penalty not to exceed $100,000 for each item of false information.

Enforcement procedures for these civil money penalty provisions are governed by section 1128A of the Social Security Act, 42 U.S.C.A. 1320a-7a, which authorizes civil money penalties for a variety of offenses.

Rebate agreements are to be for an initial period of not less than one year and are to be automatically renewable for not less than one year, unless terminated in accordance with section 1927(b)(4).

Pursuant to section 1927(b)(4)(ii), a rebate agreement may be terminated by a manufacturer for any reason, but the termination may not be effective until such period after the date of the notice as the Secretary may provide, though not beyond the stated term. On the other hand, pursuant to section 1927(b)(4)(i), the Secretary may provide for termination of a rebate agreement for violation of its requirements or "other good cause shown." Such termination shall not be effective, however, earlier than 60 days after the date of notice. Furthermore, the Secretary must provide a manufacturer with a hearing on the issue of termination upon request. Nevertheless, that hearing may not delay the effective date of the termination.

Finally, when a rebate agreement with a manufacturer is terminated, a new one with that manufacturer or its successor may not be entered into until one calendar quarter has elapsed since the termination date. Earlier reentry is permitted only if the Secretary finds good cause for reinstatement of such an agreement.

Statutory Provisions

Section 1927, 42 U.S.C.A. 1396s, which was added by section 4401(a)(3) of P.L. 101-508, the Omnibus Budget Reconciliation Act of 1990 (OBRA 90), effective November 5, 1990, provides in pertinent part:

> (a) REQUIREMENT FOR REBATE AGREEMENT. —
>
> (1) IN GENERAL. — In order for payment to be available under section 1903(a) for covered outpatient drugs of a manu-

facturer, the manufacturer must have entered into and have in effect a rebate agreement described in subsection (b) with the Secretary, on behalf of States (except that the Secretary may authorize a State to enter directly into agreements with a manufacturer). Any agreement between a State and a manufacturer prior to April 1, 1991, shall be deemed to have been entered into on January 1, 1991, and payment to such manufacturer shall be retroactively calculated as if the agreement between the manufacturer and the State had been entered into on January 1, 1991. If a manufacturer has not entered into such an agreement before March 1, 1991, such an agreement, subsequently entered into, shall become effective as of the date on which the agreement is entered into or, at State option, on any date thereafter on or before the first day of the calendar quarter that begins more than 60 days after the date the agreement is entered into.

◆ NOTE: Section 606(a) of the Medicare, Medicaid, and SCHIP Balanced Budget Refinement Act of 1999, as incorporated into the Omnibus Consolidated Appropriations Act, 2000, P.L. 106-113, enacted November 17, 1999, removed "shall not be effective until" after "subsequently entered into" and before "the first day of" and inserted "shall become effective as of the date on which the agreement is entered into or, at State option, on any date thereafter on or before". That change applies to agreements entered into on or after November 29, 1999.

(2) EFFECTIVE DATE. — Paragraph (1) shall first apply to drugs dispensed under this title on or after January 1, 1991.

(3) AUTHORIZING PAYMENT FOR DRUGS NOT COVERED UNDER REBATE AGREEMENTS. — Paragraph (1), and section 1903(i)(10)(A), shall not apply to the dispensing of a single source drug or innovator multiple source drug if (A)(i) the State has made a determination that the availability of the drug is essential to the health of beneficiaries under the State plan for medical assistance; (ii) such drug has been given a rating of 1-A by the Food and Drug Administration; and (iii)(I) the physician has obtained approval for use of the drug in advance of its dispensing in accordance with a prior authorization program described in subsection (d), or (II) the Secretary has reviewed and approved the State's determination under subparagraph (A); or (B) the Secretary determines

that in the first calendar quarter of 1991, there were extenuating circumstances.

(4) EFFECT ON EXISTING AGREEMENTS. — In the case of a rebate agreement in effect between a State and a manufacturer on the date of the enactment of this section, such agreement, for the initial agreement period specified therein, shall be considered to be a rebate agreement in compliance with this section with respect to that State, if the State agrees to report to the Secretary any rebates paid pursuant to the agreement and such agreement provides for a minimum aggregate rebate of 10 percent of the State's total expenditures under the State plan for coverage of the manufacturer's drugs under this title. If, after the initial agreement period, the State establishes to the satisfaction of the Secretary that an agreement in effect on the date of the enactment of this section provides for rebates that are at least as large as the rebates otherwise required under this section, and the State agrees to report any rebates under the agreement to the Secretary, the agreement shall be considered to be a rebate agreement in compliance with the section for the renewal periods of such agreement.

(b) TERMS OF REBATE AGREEMENT. —

(1) PERIODIC REBATES. —

(A) IN GENERAL. — A rebate agreement under this subsection shall require the manufacturer to provide, to each State plan approved under this title, a rebate each calendar quarter (or periodically in accordance with a schedule specified by the Secretary) in an amount specified in subsection (c) for covered outpatient drugs of the manufacturer dispensed under the plan during the quarter (or such other period as the Secretary may specify). Such rebate shall be paid by the manufacturer not later than 30 days after the date of receipt of the information described in paragraph (2) for the period involved.

(B) OFFSET AGAINST MEDICAL ASSISTANCE. — Amounts received by a State under this section (or under an agreement authorized by the Secretary under subsection (a)(1) or an agreement described in subsection (a)(4) in any quarter shall be considered to be a reduction in the amount expended under the State plan in the quarter for medical assistance for purposes of section 1903(a)(1).

(2) STATE PROVISION OF INFORMATION.—

(A) STATE RESPONSIBILITY.—Each State agency under this title shall report to each manufacturer not later than 60 days after the end of each calendar quarter and in a form consistent with a standard reporting format established by the Secretary, information on the total number of dosage units of each covered outpatient drug dispensed under the plan during the quarter, and shall promptly transmit a copy of such report to the Secretary.

(B) AUDITS.—A manufacturer may audit the information provided (or required to be provided) under subparagraph (A). Adjustments to rebates shall be made to the extent that information indicates that utilization was greater or less than the amount previously specified.

(3) MANUFACTURER PROVISION OF PRICE INFORMATION.—

(A) IN GENERAL.— Each manufacturer with an agreement in effect under this section shall report to the Secretary—

(i) not later than 30 days after the last day of each quarter (beginning on or after January 1, 1991), on the average manufacturer price (as defined in subsection (k)(1) and, (for single source drugs and innovator multiple source drugs), the manufacturer's best price (as defined in subsection (c)(2)(B)) for covered outpatient drugs for the quarter, and

(ii) not later than 30 days after the date of entering into an agreement under this section on the average manufacturer price (as defined in subsection (k)(1)) as of October 1, 1990 for each of the manufacturer's covered outpatient drugs.

(B) VERIFICATION SURVEYS OF AVERAGE MANUFACTURER PRICE. — The Secretary may survey wholesalers and manufacturers that directly distribute their covered outpatient drugs, when necessary, to verify manufacturer prices reported under subparagraph (A). The Secretary may impose a civil monetary penalty in an amount not to exceed $100,000 on a wholesaler, manufacturer, or direct seller, if the wholesaler, manufacturer, or direct seller of a covered outpatient drug refuses a request for information about charges or prices by the Secretary in connection with a survey under this subparagraph or knowingly provides false information. The provisions of section 1128A (other than subsections (a) (with respect to amounts of penalties or additional assessments) and (b)) shall apply to a civil money penalty under this subparagraph in the same manner as such provisions apply to a penalty or proceeding under section 1128A(a).

(C) PENALTIES. —

(i) FAILURE TO PROVIDE TIMELY INFORMATION. — In the case of a manufacturer with an agreement under this section that fails to provide information required under subparagraph (A) on a timely basis, the amount of the penalty shall be increased by $10,000 for each day in which such information has not been provided and such amount shall be paid to the Treasury, and, if such information is not reported within 90 days of the deadline imposed, the agreement shall be suspended for services furnished after the end of such 90-day period and until the date such information is reported (but in no case shall such suspension be for a period of less than 30 days).

(ii) FALSE INFORMATION. — Any manufacturer with an agreement under this section that knowingly provides false information is subject to a civil money penalty in an amount not to exceed $100,000 for each item of false information. Such civil money penalties are in addition to other penalties as may be prescribed by law. The provisions of section 1128A (other than subsections (a) and (b)) shall apply to a civil money penalty under this subparagraph in the same manner as such provisions apply to a penalty or proceeding under section 1128A(a).

(D) CONFIDENTIALITY OF INFORMATION. — Notwithstanding any other provision of law, information disclosed by manufacturers or wholesalers under this paragraph is confidential and shall not be disclosed by the Secretary or a State agency (or contractor therewith) in a form which discloses the identity of a specific manufacturer or wholesaler, prices charged for drugs by such manufacturer or wholesaler, except as the Secretary determines to be necessary to carry out this section and to permit the Comptroller General to review the information provided.

(4) LENGTH OF AGREEMENT. —

(A) IN GENERAL. — A rebate agreement shall be effective for an initial period of not less than 1 year and shall be automatically renewed for a period of not less than one year unless terminated under subparagraph (B).

(B) TERMINATION. —

(i) BY THE SECRETARY. — The Secretary may provide for termination of a rebate agreement for violation of the requirements of the agreement or other good cause shown. Such termination shall not be effective earlier than 60 days after the date of notice of such termination. The Secretary shall provide, upon request, a manufacturer with a hearing concerning such a termination, but such hearing shall not delay the effective date of the termination.

(ii) BY A MANUFACTURER. — A manufacturer may terminate a rebate agreement under this section for any reason. Any such termination shall not be effective until such period after the date of the notice as the Secretary may provide (but not beyond the term of the agreement).

(iii) EFFECTIVENESS OF TERMINATION. — Any termination under this subparagraph shall not affect rebates due under the agreement before the effective date of its termination.

(C) DELAY BEFORE REENTRY. — In the case of any rebate agreement with a manufacturer under this section which is terminated, another such agreement with the manufacturer (or a successor manufacturer) may not be entered into until a period of 1 calendar quarter has elapsed since the date of the termination, unless the Secretary finds good cause for an earlier reinstatement of such an agreement.

Section 1927(k) defines "average manufacture price" for purposes of the Medicaid drug rebate program as follows:

(1) The term "average manufacturer price" means, with respect to a covered outpatient drug of a manufacturer for a calendar quarter, the average price paid to the manufacturer for the drug in the United States by wholesalers for drugs distributed to the retail pharmacy class of trade.

Section 1927(k) defines "manufacturer" for purposes of the Medicaid drug rebate requirement as follows:

(5) The term "manufacturer" means any entity which is engaged in —

(A) the production, preparation, propagation, compounding, conversion, or processing of prescription drug products, either directly or indirectly by extraction from substances of natural origin, or independently by means of chemical synthesis, or by a combination of extraction and chemical synthesis, or

(B) in the packaging, repackaging, labeling, relabeling, or distribution of prescription drug products.

Such term does not include a wholesale distributor of drugs or a retail pharmacy licensed under State law.

For regulatory citations, see Chapter 7

§ 3:20 GIVING ADVANCE NOTICE OF A SURVEY TO A COMMUNITY CARE SETTING FOR FUNCTIONALLY DISABLED ELDERLY INDIVIDUALS — Section 1929(i)(3)(A) [42 U.S.C.S. 1396u(i)(3)(A)]

Summary

Section 4711(a) of P.L. 101-508, the Omnibus Budget Reconciliation Act of 1990 (OBRA 90), authorizes States to include home and community care for functionally disabled elderly individuals within the definition of medical assistance. This applies to the extent allowed and as defined in section 1929 of the Social Security Act, 42 U.S.C.A. 1396u. See also section 1905(a)(22) of the Act, 42 U.S.C.A. 1396d.

Section 4711(b)(2) of OBRA 90 sets forth requirements for Medicaid programs of home and community care for functionally disabled individuals. These provisions apply to such care furnished on or after

July 1, 1991, whether or not final regulations to carry out the program have been promulgated by then. For details, see § 3:23.

Section 1929(i) spells out an elaborate process for survey and certification by States and, in certain circumstances, by the Secretary of Health and Human Service to determine whether home and community care settings comply with Medicaid requirements. Surveys must be conducted without prior notice to the setting. Pursuant to section 1919(i)(3)(B), any individual who notifies, or causes to be notified, a community care setting of the time or date on which a survey is scheduled to be conducted is subject to a civil money penalty not to exceed $2,000.

Enforcement provisions for this civil money penalty are governed by section 1128A, 42 U.S.C.A. 1320a-7a, which authorizes civil money penalties for a variety of offenses.

Statutory Provisions

Section 1929(i)(3)(A), 42 U.S.C.A. 1396u(i)(3)(A), as enacted by section 4711(b)(2) of P.L. 101-508, the Omnibus Budget Reconciliation Act of 1990 (OBRA 90), applicable to home and community care furnished on or after July 1, 1991, whether or not final regulations to carry out the program have been promulgated by then, provides as follows:

> (3) SURVEYS OF COMMUNITY CARE SETTINGS. —
>
> (A) IN GENERAL. — The certification under this subsection with respect to community care settings must be based on a survey. Such survey for such a setting must be conducted without prior notice to the setting. Any individual who notifies (or causes to be notified) a community care setting of the time or date on which such a survey is scheduled to be conducted is subject to a civil money penalty of not to exceed $2,000. The provisions of section 1128A [42 U.S.C.S. 1320a-7a] (other than subsections (a) and (b) shall apply to a civil money penalty under the previous sentence in the same manner as such provisions apply to a penalty or proceeding under section 1128A(a). The Secretary shall review each State's procedures for scheduling and conducting such surveys to assure that the State has taken all reasonable steps to avoid giving notice of such a survey through the scheduling procedures and the conduct of the surveys themselves.

For regulatory citations, see Chapter 7

§ 3:21 NEGLECT AND ABUSE AND MISAPPROPRIATION OF PROPERTY OF INDIVIDUALS IN HOME AND COMMUNITY CARE SETTINGS FOR FUNCTIONALLY DISABLED ELDERLY INDIVIDUALS — Section 1929(i)(5) [42 U.S.C.S. 1396u(i)(5)]

Summary

Section 4711(a) of P.L. 101-508, the Omnibus Budget Reconciliation Act of 1990 (OBRA 90), authorizes States to include home and community care for functionally disabled elderly individuals within the definition of medical assistance. This applies to the extent allowed and as defined in section 1929 of the Social Security Act, 42 U.S.C.A. 1396u. See also section 1905(a)(22) of the Act, 42 U.S.C.A. 1396d.

Section 4711(b)(2) of OBRA 90 sets forth requirements for Medicaid programs of home and community care for functionally disabled individuals. These provisions apply to such care furnished on or after July 1, 1991, whether or not final regulations to carry out the program have been promulgated by then. For details, see § 3:23.

Section 1929(i)(5) requires State agencies responsible for survey and certification of providers of home and community care and community care settings to establish a process for receipt, review, and investigation of allegations of individual neglect and abuse, including injuries of unknown source, by individuals providing such care or in a community care setting. The same is true with respect to allegations of misappropriation of individual property by such individuals.

After notice to the individual involved and a reasonable opportunity for hearing for the individual to rebut allegations, the State must make a finding about the accuracy of the allegations. If the State finds the allegations are accurate, it must notify the individual against whom the finding or findings are made. Then the State must provide for public disclosure of the findings upon request. When it does, it also must include any brief statement, or a clear and accurate summary thereof, of the individual disputing such findings.

A State may not make a finding that a person has neglected an individual receiving community care if the person charged demonstrates that the neglect was caused by factors beyond his or her control.

Statutory Provisions

Section 1929(i)(5), 42 U.S.C.A. 1396u(i)(5), as enacted by section 4711(b)(2) of P.L. 101-508, the Omnibus Budget Reconciliation Act of 1990 (OBRA 90), applicable to home and community care furnished on or after July 1, 1991, whether or not final regulations to carry out the program have been promulgated by then, provides as follows:

> (5) INVESTIGATION OF ALLEGATIONS OF INDIVIDUAL NEGLECT AND ABUSE AND MISAPPROPRIATION OF INDIVIDUAL PROPERTY. — The State shall provide, through the agency responsible for surveys and certification of providers of home or community care and community care settings under this subsection, for a process for the receipt, review, and investigation of allegations of individual neglect and abuse (including injuries of unknown source) by individuals providing such care or in such setting and of misappropriation of individual property by such individuals. The State shall, after notice to the individual involved and a reasonable opportunity for hearing for the individual to rebut allegations, make a finding as to the accuracy of the allegations. If the State finds that an individual has neglected or abused an individual receiving community care or misappropriated such individual's property, the State shall notify the individual against whom the finding is made. A State shall not make a finding that a person has neglected an individual receiving community care if the person demonstrates that such neglect was caused by factors beyond the control of the person. The State shall provide for public disclosure of findings under this paragraph upon request and for inclusion, in any such disclosure of such findings, of any brief statement (or of a clear and accurate summary thereof) of the individual disputing such findings.

For regulatory citations, see Chapter 7

§ 3:22 DISCLOSURE OF INSPECTION REPORTS AND ACTIVITIES RELATED TO HOME AND COMMUNITY CARE SETTINGS FOR FUNCTIONALLY DISABLED ELDERLY INDIVIDUALS — Section 1929(i)(6) [42 U.S.C.S. 1396u(i)(6)]

Summary

Section 4711(a) of P.L. 101-508, the Omnibus Budget Reconciliation Act of 1990 (OBRA 90), authorizes States to include home and community care for functionally disabled elderly individuals within the definition of medical assistance. This applies to the extent allowed and as defined in section 1929 of the Social Security Act, 42 U.S.C.A. 1396u. See also section 1905(a)(22) of the Act, 42 U.S.C.A. 1396d.

Section 4711(b)(2) of OBRA 90 sets forth requirements for Medicaid programs of home and community care for functionally disabled individuals. These provisions apply to such care furnished on or after July 1, 1991, whether or not final regulations to carry out the program have been promulgated by then. For details, see § 3:23.

Section 1929(i)(6) requires States and the Secretary of Health and Human Services to make the following information available to the public:

1. information about surveys, reviews, and certifications made under this provision of the Medicaid statute respecting providers of home or community care and community care settings, including statements of deficiencies;
2. copies of cost reports (if any) of such providers and settings filed under Title XIX;
3. copies of statements of ownership under section 1124, 42 U.S.C.A. 1320a-3, which pertains to disclosure requirements for certain Medicare Part B providers; and
4. information about institutions, organizations, and agencies of owners and certain other individuals who have been convicted of certain offenses required to be disclosed under section 1126, 42 U.S.C.A. 1320a-5.

In addition, if a State finds a provider of home or community care has provided substandard care with respect to an individual, the

State must make a reasonable effort to notify promptly an immediate family member of the individual and other individuals receiving home or community care from that provider under Medicaid. Furthermore, if a State finds that a community care setting is substandard, it must make a reasonable effort to notify individuals receiving community care in that setting, as well as immediate family members of such individuals. Finally, each State must provide access to all information of the State agency responsible for surveys, reviews, and certifications under section 1929 to the State Medicaid fraud and abuse control unit established under section 1903(q), 42 U.S.C.A. 1396b(q).

Statutory Provisions

Section 1929(i)(6), 42 U.S.C.A. 1396u(i)(6), as enacted by section 4711(b)(2) of P.L. 101-508, the Omnibus Budget Reconciliation Act of 1990 (OBRA 90), applicable to home and community care furnished on or after July 1, 1991, whether or not final regulations to carry out the program have been promulgated by then, provides as follows:

(6) DISCLOSURE OF RESULTS OF INSPECTIONS AND ACTIVITIES. —

(A) PUBLIC INFORMATION. — Each State, and the Secretary, shall make available to the public —

(i) information respecting all surveys, reviews, and certifications made under this subsection respecting providers of home or community care and community care settings, including statements of deficiencies,

(ii) copies of cost reports (if any) of such providers and settings filed under this title,

(iii) copies of statements of ownership under section 1124 [42 U.S.C.S. 1320a-3, which pertains to disclosure requirements for certain Medicare Part B providers], and

(iv) information disclosed under section 1126 [42 U.S.C.S. 1320a-5, which pertains to disclosure by institutions, organizations, and agencies of owners and certain other individuals who have been convicted of certain offenses].

(B) NOTICES OF SUBSTANDARD CARE. — If a State finds that —

(i) a provider of home or community care has provided care of substandard quality with respect to an individual, the State shall make a reasonable effort to notify promptly (I) an immediate family member of each such individual and (II) individuals receiving home or community care from that provider under this title, or

(ii) a community care setting is substandard, the State shall make a reasonable effort to notify promptly (I) individuals receiving community care in that setting, and (II) immediate family members of such individuals.

(C) ACCESS TO FRAUD CONTROL UNITS. — Each State shall provide its state medicaid fraud and abuse control unit (established under section 1903(q) [42 U.S.C.S. 1396b(q)]) with access to all information of the State agency responsible for surveys, reviews, and certifications under this subsection.

For regulatory citations, see Chapter 7

§ 3:23 FAILURE BY HOME AND COMMUNITY CARE SETTINGS FOR FUNCTIONALLY DISABLED ELDERLY INDIVIDUALS TO COMPLY WITH MEDICAID REQUIREMENTS —Section 1929(j) [42 U.S.C.S. 1396u(j)]

Summary

Section 4711(a) of P.L. 101-508, the Omnibus Budget Reconciliation Act of 1990 (OBRA 90), authorizes States to include home and community care for functionally disabled elderly individuals within the definition of medical assistance. This applies to the extent allowed and as defined in section 1929 of the Social Security Act, 42 U.S.C.A. 1396u. See also section 1905(a)(22) of the Act, 42 U.S.C.A. 1396d.

Section 4711(b)(2) of OBRA 90 sets forth requirements for Medicaid programs of home and community care for functionally disabled individuals. These provisions apply to such care furnished on or after July 1, 1991, whether or not final regulations to carry out the program have been promulgated by then.

Pursuant to section 1929(a), "home and community care" means one or more of the following services when provided to a person who qualifies as a functionally disabled elderly individual: homemaker/home health aide services; chore services; personal care services; nursing care services provided by, or under supervision of, a registered nurse; respite care; training for family members to manage the individual; adult day care; day treatment or other partial hospitalization, psychosocial rehabilitation services, and clinical services (whether or not furnished in a facility) to individuals with chronic mental illness; and such other services, but not room and board, as the Secretary of Health and Human Services may approve.

These services must be provided in accordance with an individual community care plan (ICCP) which is established and periodically reviewed and revised by a qualified community care case manager.

Section 1929(b) defines functionally disabled elderly individual as a person 65 or older who is determined to be functionally disabled and who either receives supplemental security income benefits (SSI) under Title XVI of the Social Security Act, or, at the option of the State, meets other qualifying requirements for medical assistance. The definition also includes certain individuals previously covered under Federally approved waivers granted to States authorized by sections 1915(c) or (d), 42 U.S.C.A. 1396n(c) and (d), which was intended in part to expand coverage of this type of care as a cost containment effort. It also includes certain individuals who had been covered under a Medicaid health insuring organization mechanism between January 1, 1986, and December 31, 1990. The latter two categories are grandfathered into coverage.

According to section 1929(c)(1), a functionally disabled individual is someone who is unable to perform without substantial assistance from someone else at least two of the following three activities of daily living: toileting, transferring, and eating.

The definition also includes anyone with a primary or secondary diagnosis of Alzheimer's disease who is unable to perform without substantial human assistance, including verbal reminding or physical cueing, or supervision at least two of the following five activities of daily living: bathing, dressing, toileting, transferring, and eating. Alternatively, it includes anyone with such a diagnosis who is so cognitively impaired as to require substantial supervision because he or she engages in inappropriate behaviors which pose serious health or safety to himself or herself or to others.

To determine whether someone meets the definition of a functionally disabled individual, pursuant to section 1929(c)(2)(A), (B), (C) and (D), a State must, upon request of an elderly person or someone on the elderly person's behalf, provide for a comprehensive functional assessment. This assessment must be conducted using a uniform minimum data set specified by the Secretary and an instrument specified by the State in accordance with the statute. The data set and the State instrument were to be established not later than July 1, 1991.

No fee may be charged for such assessments. Furthermore, once an assessment establishes an individual as functionally disabled, a State must review and revise, presumably as appropriate, that assessment not less often than once every 12 months.

Pursuant to section 1929(c)(2)(E), assessments and their periodic reviews are to conducted by an interdisciplinary team; however, the Secretary may authorize a State to contract for their provision with public organizations, or with nonpublic organizations that do not provide home and community care or nursing facility services and which do not have direct or indirect ownership or control interests in, or direct or indirect affiliations or relationship with, entities that provide community care or nursing facility services.

Section 1929(c)(2)(F) requires these interdisciplinary teams to identify in each assessment or review of an assessment each individual's functional disabilities and need for home and community care. That includes information about the individual's health status, home and community environment, and informal support system. Then assessments and their reviews must result in an initial or revised ICCP. According to section 1929(c)(2)(G), a State must provide an appeal mechanism to anyone adversely affected by an assessment or review of an assessment.

Section 1929(d)(1) defines an ICCP as a written plan established by a qualified case manager after a face-to-face interview with the individual or the primary caregiver which is based on the most recent comprehensive functional assessment of the individual. Furthermore, the ICCP must specify the home and community care to be provided to the individual (subject to the amount, duration, and scope authorized under the State Medicaid plan), and it must indicate the individual's preferences for types and providers of services. In addition, an ICCP may specify other services required by the individual, and it may designate specific qualified providers to provide the home and community care. With respect to the latter, however, nothing in this section may be construed to restrict the specific persons or individuals who will provide the home and community care if they are competent to provide such care under the State plan.

Section 1929(d)(2) defines qualified community care case manager as a nonprofit or public agency or organization —

(a) experienced or trained to establish and periodically review and revise ICCP's;

(b) responsible for assuring that care specified in the ICCP is provided, for visiting the place where the care is being provided not less often than every 90 days, and for informing the individual or primary caregiver how to contact the case manager if providers fail to provide services properly or if other similar problems occur;

(c) which, in the case of a nonpublic agency, has no conflict of interest via ownership, control, affiliation, or relationship with an entity that provides home and community care or nursing facility services;

(d) with procedures, including a peer review process, to assure the quality of case management;

(e) which completes the ICCP in a timely manner and reviews and discusses new and revised ICCP's with individuals or their primary caregivers; and

(f) which meets such other standards established by the Secretary to assure that a manager is competent, that individuals whose home and community care the manager manage are not at risk of financial exploitation by the manager, and that meet such other standards as a State may establish.

An exception is that the Secretary may waive the conflict of interest requirement with respect to a nonpublic agency if it is located in a rural area.

Pursuant to section 1929(d)(3), if a State elects to provide home and community care it must provide an appeals process for individuals who disagree with the ICCP established.

Section 1929(f) establishes minimum requirements for home and community care. These include requirements for individuals' rights and quality of care as established by the Secretary, including a requirement that individuals providing care be competent. They also include the following specific rights:

1. to be fully informed in advance, orally and in writing, of the care to be provided, and if competent, to participate in planning care and changes in care;
2. to voice grievances with respect to services or the lack thereof without discrimination or reprisal, and to be told how to complain to State and local authorities;
3. to confidentiality of personal and clinical records;

4. to privacy and to have property treated with respect;
5. to refuse all or part of any care and to be informed of likely consequences of such refusal;
6. to education or training, either of the individual or the individual's family or household member, on the management of care;
7. to be free from physical or mental abuse, corporal punishment, and any physical or chemical restraints imposed for purposes of discipline or convenience and not included in the ICCP;
8. to be fully informed orally and in writing of the individual's rights;
9. to guidelines for minimum compensation for individuals providing care to assure availability and continuity of competent individuals, taking into account the degree of disability; and
10. to any other rights established by the Secretary.

In addition, pursuant to section 1929(g), there are minimum requirements for small community care settings. "Small community care setting" means a nonresidential setting serving more than two but less than eight individual, or a residential setting where more than two but less than eight unrelated adults reside and in which personal services other than merely board are provided in conjunction with residence. These small settings must —

1. meet requirements established by the Secretary under section 1929(k);
2. meet requirements numbered 1, 3, 4, above, and, as applicable to such a setting, requirements in section 1919(c)(3) and section 1919(c)(6), 42 U.S.C.A. 1396r(c)(3) and (6), which pertain to rights of residents in nursing facilities;
3. inform each recipient of care under this section in the setting, orally and in writing at the time the individual first receives such care in the setting, of his or her legal rights with respect to such a setting and to the care provided in the setting; and
4. meet any applicable State or local requirements regarding certification or licensure;
5. meet any applicable State and local zoning, building, and housing codes, and State and local fire and safety regulations; and
6. be designed, constructed, equipped, and maintained in a manner to protect the health and safety of residents.

Similarly, section 1919(h) specifies minimum requirements for "large community care settings." These are defined as either a non-residential setting where more than eight individuals are served, or a residential setting where more than eight unrelated adults reside and where personal services are provided in conjunction with residence in the setting. In addition, large community care settings must —

1. meet requirements established by the Secretary under section 1929(k);
2. meet the requirements numbered 1, 3, and 4 above in the discussion of section 1929(f), and, as applicable to such a setting, requirements in section 1919(c)(3) and section 1919(c)(6), 42 U.S.C.A. 1396r(c)(3) and (6), which pertain to rights of residents in nursing facilities;
3. inform each recipient of care under this section in the setting, orally and in writing at the time the individual first receives such care in the setting, of his or her legal rights with respect to such a setting and to the care provided in the setting; and
4. meet, as applicable, requirements of paragraphs (2) and (3) of section 1919(d), which relate to administration of nursing facilities, except that the Secretary may modify life safety code requirement of section 1919(d)(2) as appropriate to the setting.

In addition, pursuant to section 1929(h)(3), a community care setting must disclose persons with ownership or control interests in the setting, including such persons as defined in the more general ownership and control provisions of section 1124(a)(3), 42 U.S.C.A. 1320a-3(a)(3). Moreover, a community care setting may not have as a person with an ownership or control interest in the setting anyone who has been excluded from Medicaid, nor anyone who has had an ownership or control interest in one or more community care settings that have been found repeatedly to be substandard or to have failed to meet requirements set forth above.

Having set forth all those definitions and requirements, Congress than went on in section 1929(i) to spell out an elaborate process for survey and certification of home and community care providers and settings for functionally disabled elderly individuals by States and, in certain circumstances, by the Secretary of Health and Human Service to determine whether they comply with Medicaid requirements.

According to section 1929(i)(1)(A), States are responsible for certification of compliance with requirements of subsections (f), (g), and (h), and they must do so even if the Secretary does not issue regulations to carry out section 1929. According to section 1929(i)(1)(B), the Secretary is responsible for certification of State providers of home and community care and of State community care settings. Subparagraph (C) specifies that certification of providers and settings must occur no less often than annually.

Section 1929(i)(2) requires certification to be based on periodic review of the provider's performance in providing the care required under ICCP's. Furthermore, if the Secretary has reason to question compliance of a provider with any of the requirements of subsection (f), he may conduct a review of the provider and, on that basis thereof, make independent and binding determinations concerning compliance.

In general, pursuant to section 1929(i)(3)(A), certification with respect to community care settings must be based on a survey conducted with out prior notice. See § 3:20. Moreover, pursuant to section 1929(i)(3)(B), such surveys must be based on a protocol established by the Secretary. Furthermore, pursuant to section 1929(i)(3)(C), neither a State nor the Secretary may use as a member of a survey team any individual who serves, or who within the prior two years served, as a staff member of or consultant either to the setting being surveyed or to the person responsible for the setting, with respect to compliance with subsections (g) or (h). Nor may a State or the Secretary have a survey team member who has a personal or familial financial interest in the setting being surveyed.

According to section 1929(i)(3)(D) and (E), there are two kinds of surveys other than a standard survey discussed above. One is a validation survey. These must be conducted onsite by the Secretary, and they must include a representative sample of community care settings in each State, within two months of the date of surveys conducted by the State. The sample must be sufficient in number to allow inferences about the adequacies of the State surveys. Moreover, these validation surveys must use the same survey protocols required for State surveys.

If a conflict arises between a State survey and the Secretary's validation survey of a setting, a finding of noncompliance by the Secretary is binding and supersedes a contrary finding by the State.

The other type of survey is a so-called special survey by the Secretary. If he has reason to question compliance of a community care setting, he may survey it and on the basis of his survey make independent and binding determinations about compliance with subsections (g) and (h).

Section 1929(i)(4) requires States and the Secretary to maintain procedures and adequate staff to investigate complaints of violations of subsections (f), (g), and (h). Section 1929(i)(5) provides for investigation of allegations of individual neglect and abuse and misappropriation of property. See § 3:21. Furthermore, section 1929(i)(6) obligates States and the Secretary to disclose results of inspections and related activities. See § 3:22.

Then, having set forth as indicated above a process for survey and certification of providers of home and community care and community care settings for functionally disabled elderly individuals, Congress spelled out enforcement procedures and sanctions in section 1929(j).

According to section 1929(j)(1)(A), if a State finds, whether by survey or otherwise, that a provider of home or community care no longer meets requirements of section 1929, it may terminate the provider's participation in Medicaid. It also may provide for a civil money penalty for any period of noncompliance which the State establishes.

In addition, according to section 1929(j)(1)(B), each State by statute or regulation at least must provide for a civil money penalty to be assessed and collected with interest for each day of noncompliance by a provider. Any such funds collected may be applied to reimburse individuals personal funds lost due to failure of a provider of home or community care to meet requirements of section 1929. The statute further requires that States specify criteria regarding when and how this remedy is to be applied and the amounts of any penalties. In so doing, each State must minimize the time between identification of violations and final imposition of penalties. Each also must provide for incrementally more severe penalties for repeated or uncorrected deficiencies. States must comply with this minimal sanction obligation even if the Secretary fails to meet his obligation to provide regulatory guidelines for doing so by July 1, 1990.

For State providers of home and community care, pursuant to section 1929(j)(2), the Secretary is obliged to establish a civil money penalty. With respect to any other such provider in a State, the Secretary may terminate participation in Medicaid and also provide for a civil money penalty. Moreover, if the Secretary finds that a provider meets statutory requirement, but didn't during a prior period, he may provide for a civil money penalty pursuant to section 1929(j)(2)(C).

According to that subparagraph, if the Secretary finds by survey or otherwise that a home or community care provider no longer complies with section 1929, he must impose a civil money penalty not exceeding $10,000 for each day of noncompliance. Furthermore, as with States, the Secretary must specify criteria regarding when and how this remedy (sanction) is to be applied and the amounts of any penalties. Similarly, in so doing he must minimize the time between identification of violations and final imposition of penalties, and provide for incrementally more severe penalties for repeated or uncorrected deficiencies.

Enforcement provisions for this civil money penalty are governed by section 1128A, 42 U.S.C.A. 1320a-7a, which authorizes civil money penalties for a variety of offenses.

Finally, section 1929(k) obligated the Secretary to publish by December 1, 1991, a proposed regulation setting forth interim requirements for provision of home and community care and for community care settings. These must include requirements related to comprehensive functional assessments, including use of assessment instruments; to qualifications for qualified case managers; to minimum requirements for home and community care; to minimum requirements for small care settings; to minimum requirements for large community care settings; and to survey protocols. These must assure through methods other than reliance on State licensure processes that individuals receiving home and community care are protected from neglect, physical and sexual abuse, financial exploitation, inappropriate involuntary restraint, and provision of health care services by unqualified personnel in community care settings. None of these obligations of the Secretary may be delegated to States, and nothing in section 1929 precludes a State from establishing requirements more stringent than requirements published or developed by the Secretary pursuant to subsection (k).

Statutory Provisions

Section 1929, 42 U.S.C.A. 1396u, provides in pertinent part:

> (a) HOME AND COMMUNITY CARE DEFINED. — In this title, the term "home and community care" means one or more of the following services furnished to an individual who has been determined, after an assessment under subsection (c), to be a

functionally disabled elderly individual, furnished in accordance with an individual community care plan (established and periodically reviewed and revised by a qualified community care case manager under subsection (d)):

(1) Homemaker/home health aide services.

(2) Chore services.

(3) Personal care services.

(4) Nursing care services provided by, or under the supervision of, a registered nurse.

(5) Respite care.

(6) Training for family members in managing the individual.

(7) Adult day care.

(8) In the case of an individual with chronic mental illness, day treatment or other partial hospitalization, psychosocial rehabilitation services, and clinic services (whether or not furnished in a facility).

(9) Such other home and community-based services (other than room and board) as the Secretary may approve.

(b) FUNCTIONALLY DISABLED ELDERLY INDIVIDUAL DEFINED. —

(1) IN GENERAL. — In this title, the term "functionally disabled elderly individual" means an individual who —

(A) is 65 years of age or older,

(B) is determined to be a functionally disabled individual under subsection (c), and

(C) subject to section 1902(f) (as applied consistent with section 1902(r)(2)), is receiving supplemental security income benefits under title XVI (or under a State plan approved under title XVI) or, at the option of the State, is described in section 1902(a)(10)(C).

(2) TREATMENT OF CERTAIN INDIVIDUALS PREVIOUSLY COVERED UNDER A WAIVER. —

(A) In the case of a State which —

(i) at the time of its election to provide coverage for home and community care under this section has a waiver approved under section 1915(c) or 1915(d) with respect to individuals 65 years of age or older, and

(ii) subsequently discontinues such waiver, individuals who were eligible for benefits under the waiver as of the date of its discontinuance and who would, but for income or resources, be eligible for medical assistance for home and community care under the plan shall, notwithstanding any other provision of this title, be deemed a functionally disabled elderly individual for so long as the individual would have remained eligible for medical assistance under such waiver.

(B) In the case of a State which used a health insuring organization before January 1, 1986, and which, as of December 31, 1990, had in effect a waiver under section 1115 that provides under the State plan under this title for personal care services for functionally disabled individuals, the term "functionally disabled elderly individual" may include, at the option of the State, an individual who —

(i) is 65 years of age or older or is disabled (as determined under the supplemental security income program under title XVI);

(ii) is determined to meet the test of functional disability applied under the waiver as of such date; and

(iii) meets the resource requirement and income standard that apply in the State to individuals described in section 1902(a)(10)(A)(ii)(V).

(3) USE OF PROJECTED INCOME. — In applying section 1903(f)(1) in determining the eligibility of an individual (described in section 1902(a)(10)(C)) for medical assistance for home and community care, a State may, at its option, provide for the determination of the individual's anticipated medical expenses (to be deducted from income) over a period of up to 6 months.

(c) DETERMINATIONS OF FUNCTIONAL DISABILITY. —

(1) IN GENERAL. — In this section, an individual is "functionally disabled" if the individual —

(A) is unable to perform without substantial assistance from another individual at least 2 of the following 3 activities of daily living: toileting, transferring, and eating; or

(B) has a primary or secondary diagnosis of Alzheimer's disease and is (i) unable to perform without substantial human assistance (including verbal reminding or physical cueing) or supervision of at least 2 of the following 5 activities of daily living: bathing, dressing, toileting, transferring, and eating; or (ii) cognitively impaired so as to require substantial supervision from another individual because he or she engages in inappropriate behaviors that pose serious health or safety hazards to himself or herself or others.

(2) ASSESSMENTS OF FUNCTIONAL DISABILITY. —

(A) REQUESTS FOR ASSESSMENTS. — If a State has elected to provide home and community care under this section, upon the request of an individual who is 65 years of age or older and who meets the requirements of subsection (b)(10)(C) (or another person on such individual's behalf), the State shall provide for a comprehensive functional assessment under this subparagraph which —

(i) is used to determine whether or not the individual is functionally disabled,

(ii) is based on a uniform minimum data set specified by the Secretary under subparagraph (C)(i), and

(iii) uses an instrument which has been specified by the State under subparagraph (B).

No fee may be charged for such an assessment.

(B) SPECIFICATION OF ASSESSMENT INSTRUMENT. — The State shall specify the instrument to be used in the State in complying with the requirement of subparagraph (A)(iii) which instrument shall be —

(i) one of the instruments designated under subparagraph (C)(ii); or

(ii) an instrument which the Secretary has approved as being consistent with the minimum data set of core elements, common definitions, and utilization guidelines specified by the Secretary in subparagraph (C)(i).

(C) SPECIFICATION OF ASSESSMENT DATA SET AND INSTRUMENTS. — The Secretary shall —

(i) not later than July 1, 1991 —

(I) specify a minimum data set of core elements and common definitions for use in conducting the assessments required under subparagraph (A); and

(II) establish guidelines for use of the data set; and

(ii) by not later than July 1, 1991, designate one or more instruments which are consistent with the specification made under subparagraph (A) and which a State may specify under subparagraph (B) for use in complying with the requirements of subparagraph (A).

(D) PERIODIC REVIEW. — Each individual who qualifies as a functionally disabled elderly individual shall have the individual's assessment periodically reviewed and revised not less often than once every 12 months.

(E) CONDUCT OF ASSESSMENT BY INTERDISCIPLINARY TEAMS. — An assessment under subparagraph (A) and a review under subparagraph (D) must be conducted by an interdisciplinary team designated by the State. The Secretary shall permit a State to provide for assessments and reviews through teams under contracts —

(i) with public organizations; or

(ii) with nonpublic organizations which do not provide home and community care or nursing facility services and do not have a direct or indirect ownership or control interest in, or direct or indirect affiliation or relationship with, an entity that provides, community care or nursing facility services.

(F) CONTENTS OF ASSESSMENT. — The interdisciplinary team must —

(i) identify in each such assessment or review each individual's functional disabilities and need for home and community care, including information about the individual's health status, home and community environment, and informal support system; and

(ii) based on such assessment or review, determine whether the individual is (or continues to be) functionally disabled. The results of such an assessment or review shall be used in establishing, reviewing, and revising the individual's ICCP under subsection (d)(1).

(G) APPEAL PROCEDURES. — Each State which elects to provide home and community care under this section must have in effect an appeals process for individuals adversely affected by determinations under subparagraph (F).

(d) INDIVIDUAL COMMUNITY CARE PLAN (ICCP). —

(1) INDIVIDUAL COMMUNITY CARE PLAN DEFINED. — In this section, the terms "individual community care plan" and "ICCP" mean, with respect to a functionally disabled elderly individual, a written plan which —

(A) is established, and is periodically reviewed and revised, by a qualified case manager after a face-to-face interview with the individual or primary caregiver and based upon the most recent comprehensive functional assessment of such individual conducted under subsection (c)(2);

(B) specifies, within any amount, duration, and scope limitations imposed on home and community care provided under the State plan, the home and community care to be provided to such individual under the plan, and indicates the individual's preferences for the types and providers of services; and

(C) may specify other services required by such individual. An ICCP may also designate the specific providers (qualified to provide home and community care under the State plan) which will provide the home and community care described in subparagraph (B). Nothing in this section shall be construed as authorizing an ICCP or the State to restrict the specific persons or individuals (who are competent to provide home and community care under the State plan) who will provide the home and community care described in subparagraph (B).

(2) QUALIFIED COMMUNITY CARE CASE MANAGER DEFINED. — In this section, the term "qualified community care case manager" means a nonprofit or public agency or organization which —

(A) has experience or has been trained in establishing, and in periodically reviewing and revising, individual community care plans and in the provision of case management services to the elderly;

(B) is responsible for (i) assuring that home and community care covered under the State plan and specified in the ICCP is being provided, (ii) visiting each individual's home or community setting where care is being provided not less often than once every 90 days, and (iii) informing the elderly individual or primary caregiver on how to contact the case manager if service providers fail to properly provide services or other similar problems occur;

(C) in the case of a nonpublic agency, does not provide home and community care or nursing facility services and does not have a direct or indirect ownership or control interest in, or direct or indirect affiliation or relationship with, an entity that provides home and community care or nursing facility services;

(D) has procedures for assuring the quality of case management services that includes a peer review process;

(E) completes the ICCP in a timely manner and reviews and discusses new and revised ICCPs with elderly individuals or primary caregivers; and

(F) meets such other standards, established by the Secretary, as to assure that —

(i) such a manager is competent to perform case management functions;

(ii) individuals whose home and community care they manage are not at risk of financial exploitation due to such a manager; and

(iii) meets such other standards as the State may establish.

The Secretary may waive the requirement of subparagraph (C) in the case of a nonprofit agency located in a rural area.

(3) APPEALS PROCESS. — Each State which elects to provide home and community care under this section must have in effect an appeals process for individuals who disagree with the ICCP established.

* * *

(f) MINIMUM REQUIREMENTS FOR HOME AND COMMUNITY CARE. —

(1) REQUIREMENTS.—Home and community care provided under this section must meet such requirements for individuals' rights and quality as are published or developed by the Secretary under subsection (k). Such requirements shall include—

(A) the requirement that individuals providing care are competent to provide such care; and

(B) the rights specified in paragraph (2).

(2) SPECIFIED RIGHTS.—The rights specified in this paragraph are as follows:

(A) The right to be fully informed in advance, orally and in writing, of the care to be provided, to be fully informed in advance of any changes in care to be provided, and (except with respect to an individual determined incompetent) to participate in planning care or changes in care.

(B) The right to voice grievances with respect to services that are (or fail to be) furnished without discrimination or reprisal for voicing grievances, and to be told how to complain to State and local authorities.

(C) The right to confidentiality of personal and clinical records.

(D) The right to privacy and to have one's property treated with respect.

(E) The right to refuse all or part of any care and to be informed of the likely consequences of such refusal.

(F) The right to education or training for oneself and for members of one's family or household on the management of care.

(G) The right to be free from physical or mental abuse, corporal punishment, and any physical or chemical restraints imposed for purposes of discipline or convenience and not included in an individual's ICCP.

(H) The right to be fully informed orally and in writing of the individual's rights.

(I) Guidelines for such minimum compensation for individuals providing such care as will assure the availability and continuity of competent individuals to provide such care for functionally disabled individuals who have functional disabilities of varying levels of severity

(J) Any other rights established by the Secretary.

(g) MINIMUM REQUIREMENTS FOR SMALL COMMUNITY CARE SETTINGS. —

(1) SMALL COMMUNITY SETTINGS DEFINED. — In this section, the term "small community care setting" means —

(A) a nonresidential setting that serves more than 2 and less than 8 individuals; or

(B) a residential setting in which more than 2 and less than 8 unrelated adults reside and in which personal services (other than merely board) are provided in conjunction with residing in the setting.

(2) MINIMUM REQUIREMENTS. — A small community care setting in which community care is provided under this section must —

(A) meet such requirements as are published or developed by the Secretary under subsection (k);

(B) meet the requirements of paragraphs (1)(A), (1)(C), (1)(D), (3), and (6) of section 1919(c) [42 U.S.C.S. 1396r(c)(3) and (6), which pertain to rights of residents in nursing facilities], to the extent applicable to such a setting;

(C) inform each individual receiving community care under this section in the setting, orally and in writing at the time the individual first receives community care in the setting, of the individual's legal rights with respect to such a setting and the care provided in the setting;

(D) meet any applicable State or local requirements regarding certification or licensure

(E) meet any applicable State and local zoning, building, and housing codes, and State and local fire and safety regulations; and

(F) be designed, constructed, equipped, and maintained in a manner to protect the health and safety of residents.

(h) MINIMUM REQUIREMENTS FOR LARGE COMMUNITY CARE SETTINGS. —

(1) LARGE COMMUNITY CARE SETTING DEFINED. — In this section, the term "large community care setting" means —

(A) a nonresidential setting in which more than 8 individuals are served; or

(B) a residential setting in which more than 8 unrelated adults reside and in which personal services are provided in conjunction with residing in the setting in which home and community care under this section is provided.

(2) MINIMUM REQUIREMENTS. — A large community care setting in which community care is provided under this section must —

(A) meet such requirements as are published or developed by the Secretary under subsection (k);

(B) meet the requirements of paragraphs (1)(A), (1)(C), (1)(D), (3), and (6) of section 1919(c), to the extent applicable to such a setting;

(C) inform each individual receiving community care under this section in the setting, orally and in writing at the time the individual first receives home and community care in the setting, of the individual's legal rights with respect to such a setting and the care provided in the setting; and

(D) meet the requirements of paragraphs (2) and (3) of section 1919(d) (relating to administration [of nursing facilities] and other matters) in the same manner as such requirements apply to nursing facilities under such section; except that, in applying the requirement of section 1919(d)(2) (relating to life safety code), the Secretary shall provide for the application of such life safety requirements (if any) that are appropriate to the setting.

(3) DISCLOSURE OF OWNERSHIP AND CONTROL INTERESTS AND EXCLUSION OF REPEATED VIOLATORS. — A community care setting —

(A) must disclose persons with an ownership or control interest (including such persons as defined in section 1124(a)(3) [42 U.S.C.S. 1320a-3(a)(3)]) in the setting; and

(B) may not have, as a person with an ownership or control interest in the setting, any individual or person who has been excluded from participation in the program under this title or who has had such an ownership or control interest in one or more community care settings which have been found repeatedly to be substandard or to have failed to meet the requirements of paragraph (2).

Then with respect to survey and certification, section 1929(i) provides:

(i) SURVEY AND CERTIFICATION PROCESS.—

(1) CERTIFICATIONS.—

(A) RESPONSIBILITIES OF THE STATE. — Under each State plan under this title, the State shall be responsible for certifying the compliance of providers of home and community care and community care settings with the applicable requirements of subsections (f), (g) and (h). The failure of the Secretary to issue regulations to carry out this subsection shall not relieve a State of its responsibility under this subsection.

(B) RESPONSIBILITIES OF THE SECRETARY. — The Secretary shall be responsible for certifying the compliance of State providers of home and community care, and of State community care settings in which such care is provided, with the requirements of subsections (f), (g) and (h).

(C) FREQUENCY OF CERTIFICATIONS. — Certification of providers and settings under this subsection shall occur no less frequently than once every 12 months.

(2) REVIEWS OF PROVIDERS.

(A) IN GENERAL. — The certification under this subsection with respect to a provider of home or community care must be based on a periodic review of the provider's performance in providing the care required under ICCP's in accordance with the requirements of subsection (f).

(B) SPECIAL REVIEW OF COMPLIANCE. — Where the Secretary has reason to question the compliance of a provider of home or community care with any of the requirements of subsection (f), the Secretary may conduct a review of the provider and, on the basis of that review, make independent and binding determinations concerning the extent to which the provider meets such requirements.

(3) SURVEYS OF COMMUNITY CARE SETTINGS.—

(A) IN GENERAL. — The certification under this subsection with respect to community care settings must be based on a survey. Such survey for such a setting must be conducted without prior notice to the setting. Any individual who notifies (or causes to be notified) a community care setting of the time or date on which such a survey is scheduled to be conducted is subject to a civil money penalty of not to exceed $2,000. The provisions of section 1128A [42 U.S.C.S. 1320a-7a] (other than subsections (a) and (b) shall apply to a civil money penalty under the previous sentence in the same manner as such provisions apply to a penalty or proceeding under section 1128A(a). The Secretary shall review each State's procedures for scheduling and conducting such surveys to assure that the State has taken all reasonable steps to avoid giving notice of such a survey through the scheduling procedures and the conduct of the surveys themselves.

(B) SURVEY PROTOCOL. — Surveys under this paragraph shall be conducted based upon a protocol which the Secretary has provided for under subsection (k).

(C) PROHIBITION OF CONFLICT OF INTEREST IN SURVEY TEAM MEMBERSHIP. — A State and the Secretary may not use as a member of a survey team under this paragraph an individual who is serving (or has served within the previous 2 years) as a member of the staff of, or as a consultant to, the community care setting being surveyed (or the person responsible for such setting) respecting compliance with the requirements of subsection (g) or (h) or who has a personal or familial financial interest in the setting being surveyed.

(D) VALIDATION SURVEYS OF COMMUNITY CARE SETTINGS. — The Secretary shall conduct onsite surveys of a representative sample of community care settings in each State, within 2 months of the date of surveys conducted under subparagraph (A) by the State, in a sufficient number to allow inferences about the adequacies of each State's surveys conducted under subparagraph (A). In conducting such surveys, the Secretary shall use the same survey protocols as the State is required to use under subparagraph (B). If the State has determined that an individual setting meets the requirements of subsection (g), but the Secretary determines that the setting does not meet such requirements, the Secretary's determination as to the setting's noncompliance with such requirements is binding and supersedes that of the State survey.

(E) SPECIAL SURVEYS OF COMPLIANCE. — Where the Secretary has reason to question the compliance of a community care setting with any of the requirements of subsection (g) or (h), the Secretary may conduct a survey of the setting and, on the basis of that survey, make independent and binding determinations concerning the extent to which the setting meets such requirements.

(4) INVESTIGATION OF COMPLAINTS AND MONITORING OF PROVIDERS AND SETTINGS. — Each State and the Secretary shall maintain procedures and adequate staff to investigate complaints of violations of applicable requirements imposed on providers of community care or on community care settings under subsections (f), (g) and (h).

(5) INVESTIGATION OF ALLEGATIONS OF INDIVIDUAL NEGLECT AND ABUSE AND MISAPPROPRIATION OF INDIVIDUAL PROPERTY. — The State shall provide, through the agency responsible for surveys and certification of providers of home or community care and community care settings under this subsection, for a process for the receipt, review, and investigation of allegations of individual neglect and abuse (including injuries of unknown source) by individuals providing such care or in such setting and of misappropriation of individual property by such individuals. The State shall, after notice to the individual involved and a reasonable opportunity for hearing for the individual to rebut allegations, make a finding as to the accuracy of the allegations. If the State finds that an individual has neglected or abused an individual receiving community care or misappropriated such individual's property, the State shall notify the individual against whom the finding is made. A State shall not make a finding that a person has neglected an individual receiving community care if the person demonstrates that such neglect was caused by factors beyond the control of the person. The State shall provide for public disclosure of findings under this paragraph upon request and for inclusion, in

any such disclosure of such findings, of any brief statement (or of a clear and accurate summary thereof) of the individual disputing such findings.

(6) DISCLOSURE OF RESULTS OF INSPECTIONS AND ACTIVITIES. —

(A) PUBLIC INFORMATION. — Each State, and the Secretary, shall make available to the public —

(i) information respecting all surveys, reviews, and certifications made under this subsection respecting providers of home or community care and community care settings, including statements of deficiencies,

(ii) copies of cost reports (if any) of such providers and settings filed under this title,

(iii) copies of statements of ownership under section 1124 [42 U.S.C.S. 1320a-3, which pertains to disclosure requirements for certain Medicare Part B providers], and

(iv) information disclosed under section 1126 [42 U.S.C.S. 1320a-5, which pertains to disclosure by institutions, organizations, and agencies of owners and certain other individuals who have been convicted of certain offenses].

(B) NOTICES OF SUBSTANDARD CARE. — If a State finds that —

(i) a provider of home or community care has provided care of substandard quality with respect to an individual, the State shall make a reasonable effort to notify promptly (I) an immediate family member of each such individual and (II) individuals receiving home or community care from that provider under this title, or

(ii) a community care setting is substandard, the State shall make a reasonable effort to notify promptly (I) individuals receiving community care in that setting, and (II) immediate family members of such individuals.

(C) ACCESS TO FRAUD CONTROL UNITS. — Each State shall provide its state medicaid fraud and abuse control unit (established under section 1903(q) [42 U.S.C.S. 1396b(q)]) with access to all information of the State agency responsible for surveys, reviews, and certifications under this subsection.

With regard to enforcement, section 1929(j) provides:

(j) ENFORCEMENT PROCESS FOR PROVIDERS OF COMMUNITY CARE.

(1) STATE AUTHORITY. —

(A) IN GENERAL. — If a State finds, on the basis of a review under subsection (i)(2) or otherwise, that a provider of home or community care no longer meets the requirements of this section, the State may terminate the provider's participation under the State plan and may provide in addition for a civil money penalty. Nothing in this subparagraph shall be construed as restricting the remedies available to a State to remedy a provider's deficiencies. If the State finds that a provider meets such requirements but, as of a previous period, did not meet such requirements, the State may provide for a civil money penalty under paragraph (2)(A) for the period during which it finds that the provider was not in compliance with such requirements.

(B) CIVIL MONEY PENALTY. —

(i) IN GENERAL. — Each State shall establish by law (whether statute or regulation) at least the following remedy: A civil money penalty assessed and collected, with interest, for each day in which the provider is or was out of compliance with a requirement of this section. Funds collected by a State as a result of imposition of such a penalty (or as a result of the imposition by the State of a civil money penalty under subsection (i)(3)(A)) may be applied to reimbursement of individuals for personal funds lost due to a failure of home or community care providers to meet the requirements of this section. The State also shall specify criteria, as to when and how this remedy is to be applied and the amounts of any penalties. Such criteria shall be designed so as to minimize the time between the identification of violations and final imposition of the penalties and shall provide for the imposition of incrementally more severe penalties for repeated or uncorrected deficiencies.

(ii) DEADLINE AND GUIDANCE. — Each State which elects to provide home and community care under this section must establish the civil money penalty remedy described in clause (i) applicable to all providers of community care covered under this section. The Secretary shall provide, through regulations or otherwise by not later than July 1, 1990, guidance to States in establishing such remedy; but the failure of the Secretary to provide such guidance shall not relieve a State of the responsibility for establishing such remedy.

(2) SECRETARIAL AUTHORITY. —

(A) FOR STATE PROVIDERS. — With respect to a State provider of home or community care, the Secretary shall have the authority and duties of a State under this subsection, except that the civil money penalty remedy described in subparagraph (C) shall be substituted for the civil money remedy described in paragraph (1)(B)(i).

(B) OTHER PROVIDERS. — With respect to any other provider of home or community care in a State, if the Secretary finds that a provider no longer meets a requirement of this section, the Secretary may terminate the provider's participation under the State plan and may provide, in addition, for a civil money penalty under subparagraph (C). If the Secretary finds that a provider meets such requirements but, as of a previous period did not meet such requirements, the Secretary may provide for a civil money penalty under subparagraph (C) for the period during which the Secretary finds that the provider was not in compliance with such requirements.

(C) CIVIL MONEY PENALTY. — If the Secretary finds on the basis of a review under subsection (i)(2) or otherwise that a home or community care provider no longer meets the requirements of this section, the Secretary shall impose a civil money penalty in an amount not to exceed $10,000 for each day of noncompliance. The provisions of section 1128A (other than subsections (a) and (b)) shall apply to a civil money penalty under the previous sentence in the same manner as such provisions apply to a penalty or proceeding under section 1128A(a). The Secretary shall specify criteria, as to when and how this remedy is to be applied and the amounts of any penalties. Such criteria shall be designed so as to minimize the time between the identification of violations and final imposition of the penalties and shall provide for the imposition of incrementally more severe penalties for repeated or uncorrected deficiencies.

Section 1929(k) provides:

(k) SECRETARIAL RESPONSIBILITIES. —

(1) PUBLICATION OF INTERIM REQUIREMENTS. —

(A) IN GENERAL. — The Secretary shall publish, by December 1, 1991, a proposed regulation that sets forth interim requirements, consistent with subparagraph (B), for the provision of home and community care and for community care settings, including —

(i) the requirements of subsection (c)(2) (relating to comprehensive functional assessments, including the use of assessment instruments), of subsection (d)(2)(E) (relating to qualifications for qualified case managers), of subsection (f) (relating to minimum requirements for home and community care), of subsection (g) (relating to minimum requirements for small community care settings), and of subsection (h) (relating to minimum requirements for large community care settings), and

(ii) survey protocols (for use under subsection (i)(3)(A)) which relate to such requirements.

(B) MINIMUM PROTECTIONS. — Interim requirements under subparagraph (A) and final requirements under paragraph (2) shall assure, through methods other than reliance on State licensure processes, that individuals receiving home and community care are protected from neglect, physical and sexual abuse, financial exploitation, inappropriate involuntary restraint, and the provision of health care services by unqualified personnel in community care settings.

(2) DEVELOPMENT OF FINAL REQUIREMENTS. — The Secretary shall develop, by not later than October 1, 1992 —

(A) final requirements, consistent with paragraph (1)(B), respecting the provision of appropriate, quality home and community care and respecting community care settings under this section, and including at least the requirements referred to in paragraph (1)(A)(i), and

(B) survey protocols and methods for evaluating and assuring the quality of community care settings.

The Secretary may, from time to time, revise such requirements, protocols, and methods.

(3) NO DELEGATION TO STATES. — The Secretary's authority under this subsection shall not be delegated to States.

(4) NO PREVENTION OF MORE STRINGENT REQUIREMENTS BY STATES. — Nothing in this section shall be construed as preventing States from imposing requirements that are more stringent than the requirements published or developed by the Secretary under this subsection.

For regulatory citations, see Chapter 7

§ 3:24 FAILURE BY PROVIDERS OF COMMUNITY SUPPORTED LIVING ARRANGEMENTS SERVICES TO COMPLY WITH STATUTORY REQUIREMENTS — Section 1930(h)(2) [42 U.S.C.S. 1396v(h)(2)]

Summary

Section 1930, 42 U.S.C.A. 1396v, which was added by section 4712(b)(2) of P.L. 101-508, the Omnibus Budget Reconciliation Act of 1990 (OBRA 90), authorizes States to add community supported living arrangements services to their Medicaid programs.

Section 1930(a) defines "community supported living arrangements services" to mean one or more of the following services provided in eligible States to assist developmentally disabled individuals in activities of daily living: personal assistance; training and habilitation services necessary to achieve increased integration, independence, and productivity; 24-hour emergency assistance; assistive technology; adaptive equipment; support services necessary to aid in participation in community activities; and other services as approved by the Secretary of Health and Human Services.

Each such service must be necessary to permit a developmentally disabled individual to live in his or her own home, apartment, family home, or rental unit furnished in a community supported living arrangement setting.

Section 1930(b) defines a developmentally disabled individual as one who, as defined by the Secretary is described within the term "mental retardation and related conditions" as defined in regulations in effect July 1, 1990, and who resides with his or her family or legal guardian in his or her own home. This applies, however, only if no more than three other recipients of services under section 1930 also reside there and without regard to whether the individual is at risk of institutionalization.

Pursuant to section 1930(c), no less than two and no more than eight States may receive Federal financial participation (FFP) for providing community supported living arrangements services during the first five years this section is effective. States are to apply for FFP in accordance with criteria the Secretary must establish for reviewing State applications.

Pursuant to section 1930(d), States approved to provide such services must establish and maintain a quality assurance program in order to continue to receive FFP. The quality assurance program must provide for the State to certify and survey providers of community supported living arrangements services. Furthermore, those surveys must be unannounced and must occur on average at least once a year.

In addition, the State must adopt standards for survey and certification that include minimum qualifications and training requirements for provider staff, financial operating standards, and a consumer grievance process. The State also must provide a system that allows for monitoring boards consisting of providers, family members, consumers, and neighbors. It must establish reporting procedures to make information available to the public. It must provide ongoing monitoring of the health and well-being of each recipient of such services; and it must provide the services authorized in section 1930(a) in accordance with an individual support plan. The statute requires the Secretary to define "individual support plan" in regulations.

State Medicaid plan amendments to allow for community supported living arrangements services must be reviewed by the State Planning Council established under section 124 of the Developmental Disabilities Assistance and Bill of Rights Act, and the Protection and Advocacy System established under section 142 of that Act. Furthermore, the Secretary may not approve a State's quality assurance program under section 1930 nor allow a State to continue to receive FFP under section 1930 unless the State provides for public hearings on the plan prior to adoption and implementation of its plan amendment.

Pursuant to section 1930(f), FFP is not available to States for the provision of room and board or for the cost of pre-vocational, vocational, and supported employment.

Pursuant to section 1930(h), the Secretary was obliged to publish interim regulations by July 1, 1991, and to publish by October 1, 1992, a final regulation setting forth interim and final requirements to protect the health, safety, and welfare of individuals receiving community supported living arrangements services.

Those regulations at a minimum must assure:

1. that individuals receiving community supported living arrangements services are protected from neglect, physical and sexual abuse, and financial exploitation;
2. that service providers may not use anyone convicted of child or client abuse, neglect, or mistreatment, or of a felony involving physical harm to an individual;
3. that providers must take all reasonable steps to determine whether applicants for employment have histories indicating such behavior;
4. that individuals or entities delivering such services are not unjustly enriched as a result of abusive financial arrangements, such as owner lease-backs; and
5. that individuals or entities delivering such services to clients, or relatives of such individuals, are prohibited from being named beneficiaries of life insurance policies purchased by (or on behalf of) such clients.

Furthermore, these "minimum protections" must be assured through methods other than reliance on State licensure processes or the State quality assurance programs under subsection (d).

Finally, pursuant to section 1930(h)(2), if the Secretary finds that a provider has not met a requirement under section 1930(h), he must impose a civil money penalty not to exceed $10,000 for each day of noncompliance. Enforcement provisions for this civil money penalty are governed by section 1128A, 42 U.S.C.A. 1320a-7a, which authorizes civil money penalties for a variety of offenses.

Statutory Provisions

Section 1930, as enacted by section 4712(b(2) of P.L. 101-508, the Omnibus Budget Reconciliation Act of 1990 (OBRA 90), provides:

(a) COMMUNITY SUPPORTED LIVING ARRANGEMENTS SERVICES. — In this title, the term "community supported living arrangements services" means one or more of the following services meeting the requirements of subsection (h) provided in a State eligible to provide services under this section (as defined in subsection (d)) to assist a developmentally disabled individual (as defined in subsection (b)) in activities of daily living necessary to permit such individual to live in the individual's own home, apartment, family home, or rental unit furnished in a community supported living arrangement setting:

(1) Personal assistance.

(2) Training and habilitation services (necessary to assist the individual in achieving increased integration, independence and productivity).

(3) 24-hour emergency assistance (as defined by the Secretary).

(4) Assistive technology.

(5) Adaptive equipment.

(6) Other services (as approved by the Secretary, except those services described in subsection (g)).

(7) Support services necessary to aid an individual to participate in community activities.

(b) DEVELOPMENTALLY DISABLED INDIVIDUAL DEFINED. — In this title the term, "developmentally disabled individual" means an individual who as defined by the Secretary is described within the term "mental retardation and related conditions" as defined in regulations as in effect on July 1, 1990, and who is residing with the individual's family or legal guardian in such individual's own home in which no more than 3 other recipients of services under this section are residing and without regard to whether or not such individual is at risk of institutionalization (as defined by the Secretary).

(c) CRITERIA FOR SELECTION OF PARTICIPATING STATES. — The Secretary shall develop criteria to review the applications of States submitted under this section to provide community supported living arrangement services. The Secretary shall provide in such criteria that during the first 5 years of the provision of services under this section that no less than 2 and no more than 8 States shall be allowed to receive Federal financial participation for providing the services described in this section.

(d) QUALITY ASSURANCE. — A State selected by the Secretary to provide services under this section shall in order to continue to receive Federal financial participation for providing services under this section be required to establish and maintain a quality assurance program, that provides that —

(1) the State will certify and survey providers of services under this section (such surveys to be unannounced and average at least 1 a year);

(2) the State will adopt standards for survey and certification that include —

(A) minimum qualifications and training requirements for provider staff;

(B) financial operating standards; and

(C) a consumer grievance process;

(3) the State will provide a system that allows for monitoring boards consisting of providers, family members, consumers, and neighbors;

(4) the State will establish reporting procedures to make available information to the public;

(5) the State will provide ongoing monitoring of the health and well-being of each recipient;

(6) the State will provide the services defined in subsection (a) in accordance with an individual support plan (as defined by the Secretary in regulations); and

(7) the State plan amendment under this section shall be reviewed by the State Planning Council established under section 124 of the Developmental Disabilities Assistance and Bill of Rights Act, and the Protection and Advocacy System established under section 142 of such Act.

The Secretary shall not approve a quality assurance plan under this subsection and allow a State to continue to receive Federal financial participation under this section unless the State provides for public hearings on the plan prior to adoption and implementation of its plan under this subsection.

* * *

(f) EXCLUDED SERVICES. — No Federal financial participation shall be allowed for the provision of the following services under this section:

(1) Room and board.

(2) Cost of prevocational, vocational and supported employment.

* * *

(h) MINIMUM PROTECTIONS. —

(1) PUBLICATION OF INTERIM AND FINAL REQUIREMENTS. —

(A) IN GENERAL. — The Secretary shall publish, by July 1, 1991, a regulation (that shall be effective on an interim basis pending the promulgation of final regulations), and by October 1, 1992, a final regulation, that sets forth interim and final requirements, respectively, consistent with subparagraph (B), to protect the health, safety, and welfare of individuals receiving community supported living arrangements services.

(B) MINIMUM PROTECTIONS. — Interim and final requirements under subparagraph (A) shall assure, through methods other than reliance on State licensure processes or the State quality assurance programs under subsection (d), that —

(i) individuals receiving community supported living arrangements services are protected from neglect, physical and sexual abuse, and financial exploitation;

(ii) a provider of community supported living arrangements services may not use individuals who have been convicted of child or client abuse, neglect, or mistreatment or of a felony involving physical harm to an individual and shall take all reasonable steps to determine whether applicants for employment by the provider have histories indicating involvement in child or client abuse, neglect, or mistreatment or a criminal record involving physical harm to an individual;

(iii) individuals or entities delivering such services to clients, or relatives of such individuals, are prohibited from being named beneficiaries of life insurance policies purchased by (or on behalf of) such clients.

Finally, with respect to violation of the foregoing requirements, section 1930(h) provides:

> (2) SPECIFIED REMEDIES. — If the Secretary finds that a provider has not met an applicable requirement under subsection (h), the Secretary shall impose a civil money penalty in an amount not to exceed $10,000 for each day of noncompliance. The provisions of section 1128A, [42 U.S.C.A. 1320a-7a] (other than subsections (a) and (b)) shall apply to a civil money penalty under the previous sentence in the same manner as such provisions apply to a penalty or proceeding under section 1128A(a).

For regulatory citations, see Chapter 7

§ 3:25 FAILURE BY MEDICAID MANAGED CARE ORGANIZATIONS TO COMPLY WITH FRAUD AND ABUSE PROTECTION REQUIREMENTS — Sections 1932(d) and (e) [42 U.S.C.A. 1396u-2(e)]

◆ NOTE: Section 4701(a) of the Balanced Budget Act of 1997, P.L. 105–33, enacted a new section 1932 of the Social Security Act, 42 U.S.C.A. 1396u-2. The amendment was effective August 5, 1997. It applies to contracts entered into or renewed on or after October 1, 1997. For additional information about Medicare managed care organizations and primary care case managers, see § 3:26.

Summary

Section 1932(a) gives a State the option to require certain Medicaid recipients to enroll with a managed care entity as a condition of receiving medical assistance. "Managed care entity" means a Medicaid managed care organization, as defined in section 1903(m)(1)(A), 42 U.S.C.A. 1396b(m)(1)(A), that provides or arranges for services for enrollees under a contract pursuant to section 1903(m). It also means a primary care case manager, as defined in section 1905(t)(2), 42 U.S.C.A. 1396d(t)(2).

Definitions: Section 1903(m)(1)(A) defines "Medicaid managed care organization" to include:

1. A health maintenance organization (HMO).

2. An eligible organization with a contract under section 1876, 42 U.S.C.A. 1395mm, which pertains to Medicare payments to HMO's and competitive medical plans (CMP's).
3. A Medicare+Choice organization with a contract under Medicare Part C. (See section 1851 *et seq*. of the Social Security Act and sections 2:26.1 and 2:26.2.)
4. A provider-sponsored organization.
5. Any other public or private organization.

To qualify as a Medicaid managed care organization under the statutory definition, these entities must comply with requirements for advance directives under section 1902(w), 42 U.S.C.A. 1396a(w). They also must make the services they provide accessible to enrollees, within the area they serve, to the same extent as such services are made accessible to individuals eligible for Medicaid who are not enrolled with them. Furthermore, these entities must have adequate provisions against the risk of their insolvency. In that regard, they must provide that no enrollee shall be held liable for their debts if insolvency occurs.

A qualified HMO as defined in section 1310(d) of the Public Health Service Act is deemed to meet the above requirements.

Section 1905(t)(2) defines "primary care case manager" as any of the following who have a primary care case management contract:

1. A physician, a physician group practice, or an entity employing or having other arrangements with physicians to provide such services.
2. A nurse practitioner, as described in section 1905(a)(21), 42 U.S.C.A. 1396d(a)(21).
3. A certified nurse-midwife, as defined in section 1861(gg), 42 U.S.C.A. 1395xx(gg).
4. A physician assistant, as defined in section 1861(aa)(5), 42 U.S.C.A. 1395xx(aa)(5).

Protections Against Fraud and Abuse: *Prohibiting Affiliations with Individuals Debarred by Federal Agencies:* Section 1932(d)(1) prohibits a managed care entity from knowingly affiliating with persons or entities, or their affiliates, that have been debarred, suspended, or otherwise excluded:

- from participating in procurement activities under the Federal Acquisition Regulation, or

- from participating in nonprocurement activities under regulations issued pursuant to Executive Order No. 12549, or under guidelines implementing such order.

If a State finds that a managed care entity is not in compliance, it must notify the Secretary of the noncompliance. The State may continue an existing agreement with the entity, unless the Secretary, in consultation with the Inspector General, directs otherwise; but it may not renew or otherwise extend the duration of an existing agreement unless the Secretary, in consultation with the Inspector General, provides to the State and to Congress a written statement describing compelling reasons for renewing or extending the agreement.

For these purposes, affiliation encompasses having a debarred, suspended, or excluded person as a director, officer, or partner. It also encompasses having such a person possess beneficial ownership of more than five percent of the entity's equity, or having an employment, consulting, or other agreement with such a person for the provision of items and services that are significant and material to the entity's obligations under its contract with the State.

Restrictions on Marketing: Section 1932(d)(2)(A) prohibits a managed care entity from distributing marketing materials, either directly or through any agent or independent contractor, without prior approval of the State. That prohibition takes effect when the Secretary specifies (but after consulting on a start time with the State). Section 1932(d)(2)(A) also prohibits marketing materials that contain false or materially misleading information. In reviewing and approving marketing materials, however, the State must provide for consultation with a medical care advisory committee.

Section 1932(d)(2)(B) requires managed care entities to distribute marketing materials to the entire service area covered under their contract. Sections 1932(d)(2)(C), (D), and (E) prohibit, respectively, tie-ins, marketing fraud, and "cold-call" marketing. "Tie-in" refers to attempting to influence an individual's enrollment in conjunction with the sale of any other insurance. The prohibition against cold calls reaches uninvited efforts made directly or indirectly, whether door-to-door or by telephone or other means.

State Conflict of Interest Safeguards: Section 1932(d)(3) prohibits a Medicaid managed care organization from entering into a contract with a State under section 1903(m), unless the State has in effect conflict of interest safeguards with respect to officers and employees of the State with responsibilities relating to contracts with such organizations or to the default enrollment process described in subsection (a)(4)(C)(ii). Those safeguards must be at least as effective as the Federal safeguards provided under section 27 of the Office of Federal Procurement Policy Act, 41 U.S.C.A. 423, against conflicts of interest that apply with respect to Federal procurement officials with comparable responsibilities with respect to such contracts.

Unique Physician Identifiers: Pursuant to section 1932(d)(4), each Medicaid managed care organization must require each physician providing services to enrollees to have a unique identifier in accordance with the system established under section 1173(b), 42 U.S.C.A. 1320d-2(b).

Sanctions for Noncompliance: *Grounds for Intermediate Sanctions:* Before a State can enter into or renew a contract under section 1903(m) with a managed care organization, the State must establish intermediate sanctions for such organizations. Pursuant to section 1932(e), grounds for imposing intermediate sanctions must include:

1. Substantial failure to provide medically necessary items and services required under law or under the contract with the State to enrollees. This does not apply to provision of abortion services, except that a State may impose a sanction on any Medicaid managed care organization that has a contract to provide abortion services if the organization does not provide such services as provided for in its contract.
2. Imposing premiums or charges on enrollees in excess of permitted amounts.
3. Discriminating among enrollees on the basis of health status or requirements for health care services. That includes expelling or refusing to re-enroll an individual. It also includes any practice which would reasonably be expected to have the effect of denying or discouraging enrollment with the organization by individuals whose medical condition or history indicates a need for substantial future medical services.
4. Misrepresenting or falsifying information furnished to the Secretary or the State, or to an enrollee, a potential enrollee, or a health care provider.
5. Failing to comply with applicable requirements of section 1903(m)(2)(A)(x), 42 U.S.C.A. 1396b(m)(2)(A)(x), which pertains to requirements for physician incentive plans under section 1876(i)(8).

6. Violating, directly or through any agent or independent contractor, the prohibition in section 1902(d)(2)(A)(I)(II) against distributing false or misleading marketing materials.

Intermediate Sanctions: A State must have the following intermediate sanctions available:

1. Civil Money Penalties:
   a. For discrimination based on health status of requirements for health care services, a civil money penalty not to exceed $100,000, plus $15,000 for each individual affected by the discrimination.
   b. For imposing an illegal premium, a civil money penalty which is double the excess amount charged. (That excess amount charged shall be deducted from the penalty and returned to the individual who was overcharged.)
   c. For any other violation, a civil money penalty of not more than $25,000.
2. Appointment of Temporary Management:
   a. Temporary management must be available so a State may oversee the operation of a Medicaid managed care organization if there has been continued egregious behavior or substantial risk to the health of enrollees.
   b. Temporary management also must be available to assure the health of the organization's enrollees while there is an orderly termination or reorganization of the organization, or while improvements are made to remedy violations involving egregious behavior or substantial risk to the health of enrollees.

   Temporary management may not be terminated until the State determines that the managed care organization has the capability to ensure that the violations will not recur.
3. Permitting enrollees to terminate enrollment without cause, and notifying them of their right to do so.
4. Suspension or default of all enrollment of individuals after the date the Secretary or the State notifies the entity of a determination of a violation of any requirement of section 1903(m) or section 1932.
5. Suspension of payment to the entity for individuals enrolled after the date the Secretary or state notifies the entity of such a

determination and until the Secretary or State is satisfied that the basis for such determination has been corrected and is not likely to recur.

In the case of an organization which has repeatedly failed to meet requirements of section 1903(m) and section 1932, then, regardless what other sanctions are provided, the State must appoint a temporary manager and permit enrollees to disenroll without cause.

Procedural Matters: Pursuant to section 1932(e)(5), before imposing any sanction against a managed care entity other than termination of the entity's contract, the State must give the entity notice and such other due process protections as it wishes to provide. A State may not provide an entity with a pre-termination hearing, however, if appointment of temporary management is called for.

Statutory Provisions

Section 1903(m)(1)(A), 42 U.S.C.A. 1396b(m)(1)(A), defines Medicaid managed care organization as follows:

> The term "Medicaid managed care organization" means a health maintenance organization, an eligible organization with a contract under section 1876 [42 U.S.C.A. 1395mm] or a Medicare+Choice organization with a contract under part C of title XVIII, a provider sponsored organization, or any other public or private organization, which meets the requirement of section 1902(w) [42 U.S.C.A. 1396a(w)] and—
>
> (i) makes services it provides to individuals eligible for benefits under this title accessible to such individuals, within the area served by the organization, to the same extent as such services are made accessible to individuals (eligible for medical assistance under the State plan) not enrolled with the organization, and
>
> (ii) has made adequate provision against the risk of insolvency, which provision is satisfactory to the State, meets the requirements of subparagraph (C)(i) (if applicable), and which assures that individuals eligible for benefits under this title are in no case held liable for debts of the organization in case of the organization's insolvency.
>
> An organization that is a qualified health maintenance organization (as defined in section 1310(d) of the Public

Health Service Act) is deemed to meet the requirements of clauses (i) and (ii).

Section 1905(t)(2), 42 U.S.C.A. 1396d(t)(2), defines primary care case manager as follows:

The term "primary care case manager" means any of the following that provides services of the type described in paragraph (1) under a contract referred to in such paragraph:

(A) A physician, a physician group practice, or an entity employing or having other arrangements with physicians to provide such services.

(B) At State option —

(i) a nurse practitioner (as described in section 1905(a)(21));

(ii) a certified nurse-midwife (as defined in section 1861(gg)); or

(iii) a physician assistant (as defined in section 1861(aa)(5)).

Protections against fraud and abuse are set forth in section 1932(d), which provides:

PROTECTIONS AGAINST FRAUD AND ABUSE. —

(1) PROHIBITING AFFILIATIONS WITH INDIVIDUALS DEBARRED BY FEDERAL AGENCIES. —

(A) IN GENERAL. — A managed care entity may not knowingly —

(i) have a person described in subparagraph (C) as a director, officer, partner, or person with beneficial ownership of more than 5 percent of the entity's equity, or

(ii) have an employment, consulting, or other agreement with a person described in such subparagraph for the provision of items and services that are significant and material to the entity's obligations under its contract with the State.

(B) EFFECT OF NONCOMPLIANCE. — If a State finds that a managed care entity is not in compliance with clause (i) or (ii) of subparagraph (A), the State —

(i) shall notify the Secretary of such noncompliance;

(ii) may continue an existing agreement with the entity unless the Secretary (in consultation with the Inspector General of the Department of Health and Human Services) directs otherwise; and

(iii) may not renew or otherwise extend the duration of an existing agreement with the entity unless the Secretary (in consultation with the Inspector General of the Department of Health and Human Services) provides to the State and to Congress a written statement describing compelling reasons that exist for renewing or extending the agreement.

(C) PERSONS DESCRIBED. — A person is described in this subparagraph if such person —

(i) is debarred, suspended, or otherwise excluded from participating in procurement activities under the Federal Acquisition Regulation or from participating in nonprocurement activities under regulations issued pursuant to Executive Order No. 12549 or under guidelines implementing such order; or

(ii) is an affiliate (as defined in such Act) of a person described in clause (i).

(2) RESTRICTIONS ON MARKETING. —

(A) DISTRIBUTION OF MATERIALS. —

(i) IN GENERAL — A managed care entity, with respect to activities under this title, may not distribute directly or through any agent or independent contractor marketing materials with any State —

(I) without the prior approval of the State, and

(II) that contain false or materially misleading information.

The requirement of subclause (I) shall not apply with respect to a State until such date as the Secretary specifies in consultation with such State.

(ii) CONSULTATION IN REVIEW OF MARKET MATERIALS. — In the process of reviewing and approving such materials, the State shall provide for consultation with a medical care advisory committee.

(B) SERVICE MARKET.—A managed care entity shall distribute marketing materials to the entire service area of such entity covered under the contract under section 1903(m) or section 1903(t)(3).

(C) PROHIBITION OF TIE-INS.—A managed care entity, or any agency of such entity, may not seek to influence an individual's enrollment with the entity in conjunction with the sale of any other insurance.

(D) PROHIBITING MARKETING FRAUD.—Each managed care entity shall comply with such procedures and conditions as the Secretary prescribes in order to ensure that, before an individual is enrolled with the entity, the individual is provided accurate oral and written information sufficient to make an informed decision whether or not to enroll.

(E) PROHIBITION OF "COLD-CALL" MARKETING.—Each managed care entity shall not, directly or indirectly, conduct door-to-door, telephonic, or other "cold-call" marketing of enrollment under this title.

(3) STATE CONFLICT OF INTEREST SAFEGUARDS IN MEDICAID RISK CONTRACTING.—A Medicaid managed care organization may not enter into a contract with any State under section 1903(m) unless the State has in effect conflict-of-interest safeguards with respect to officers and employees of the State with responsibilities relating to contracts with such organizations or to the default enrollment process described in subsection (a)(4)(C)(ii) that are at least as effective as the Federal safeguards provided under section 27 of the Office of Federal Procurement Policy Act (41 U.S.C.A. 423), against conflicts of interest that apply with respect to Federal procurement officials with comparable responsibilities with respect to such contracts.

(4) USE OF UNIQUE PHYSICIAN IDENTIFIER FOR PARTICIPATING PHYSICIANS.—Each Medicaid managed care organization shall require each physician providing services to enrollees eligible for medical assistance under the State plan under this title to have a unique identifier in accordance with the system established under section 1173(b) [42 U.S.C.A. 320d-2(b)]

Grounds for sanctions for violation of the statutory protections against fraud and abuse are set forth in section 1903(e)(1) [42 U.S.C.A. 1396b(e)(1)], which provides:

SANCTIONS FOR NONCOMPLIANCE.—

(1) USE OF INTERMEDIATE SANCTIONS BY THE STATE TO ENFORCE REQUIREMENTS.—

(A) IN GENERAL.—A State may not enter into or renew a contract under section 1903(m) unless the State has established intermediate sanctions, which may include any of the types described in paragraph (2), other than the termination of a contract with a Medicaid managed care organization, which the State may impose against a Medicaid managed care organization with such a contract, if the organization—

(i) fails substantially to provide medically necessary items and services that are required (under law or under such organization's contract with the State) to be provided to an enrollee covered under the contract;

(ii) imposes premiums or charges on enrollees in excess of the premiums or charges permitted under this title;

(iii) acts to discriminate among enrollees on the basis of their health status or requirements for health care services, including expulsion or refusal to reenroll an individual, except as permitted by this title, or engaging in any practice that would reasonably be expected to have the effect of denying or discouraging enrollment with the organization by eligible individuals whose medical condition or history indicates a need for substantial future medical services;

(iv) misrepresents or falsifies information that is furnished—

(I) to the Secretary or the State under this title; or

(II) to an enrollee, potential enrollee, or a health care provider under such title; or

(v) fails to comply with the applicable requirements of section 1903(m)(2)(A)(x).

The State may also impose such intermediate sanction against a managed care entity if the State determines that the entity distributed directly or through any agent or independent contractor marketing materials in violation of subsection (d)(2)(A)(i)(II).

(B) RULE OF CONSTRUCTION. — Clause (i) of subparagraph (A) shall not apply to the provision of abortion services, except that a State may impose a sanction on any Medicaid managed care organization that has a contract to provide abortion services if the organization does not provide such services as provided for under the contract.

Section 1932(e)(2) sets forth the types of intermediate sanctions that must be available to the State. It provides in pertinent part as follows:

INTERMEDIATE SANCTIONS. — The sanctions described in this paragraph are as follows:

(A) Civil money penalties as follows:

(i) Except as provided in clause (ii), (iii), or (iv), not more than $25,000 for each determination under paragraph (1)(A).

(ii) With respect to a determination under clause (iii) or (iv)(I) of paragraph (1)(A), not more than $100,000 for each such determination.

(iii) With respect to a determination under paragraph (1)(A)(ii), double the excess amount charged in violation of such subsection (and the excess amount charged shall be deducted from the penalty and returned to the individual concerned).

(iv) Subject to clause (ii), with respect to a determination under paragraph (1)(A)(iii), $15,000 for each individual not enrolled as a result of a practice described in such subsection.

(B) The appointment of temporary management —

(i) to oversee the operation of the Medicaid managed care organization upon a finding by the State that there is continued egregious behavior by the organization or there is a substantial risk to the health of enrollees; or

(ii) to assure the health of the organization's enrollees, if there is a need for temporary management while —

(I) there is an orderly termination or reorganization of the organization; or

(II) improvements are made to remedy the violations found under paragraph (1), except that temporary management under this subparagraph may not be terminated until the State has determined that the Medicaid managed care organization has the capability to ensure that the violations shall not recur.

(C) Permitting individuals enrolled with the managed care entity to terminate enrollment without cause, and notifying such individuals of such right to terminate enrollment.

(D) Suspension or default of all enrollment of individuals under this title after the date the Secretary or the State notifies the entity of a determination of a violation of any requirement of section 1903(m) or this section.

(E) Suspension of payment to the entity under this title for individuals enrolled after the date the Secretary or State notifies the entity of such a determination and until the Secretary or State is satisfied that the basis for such determination has been corrected and is not likely to recur.

(3) TREATMENT OF CHRONIC SUBSTANDARD ENTITIES. — In the case of a Medicaid managed care organization which has repeatedly failed to meet the requirements of section 1903(m) and this section, the State shall (regardless of what other sanctions are provided) impose the sanctions described in subparagraphs (B) and (C) of paragraph (2).

Section 1932(e)(5) deals with procedural requirements for imposing sanctions against a Medicaid managed care entity. It provides:

OTHER PROTECTIONS FOR MANAGED CARE ENTITIES AGAINST SANCTIONS IMPOSED BY STATE. — Before imposing any sanction against a managed care entity other than termination of the entity's contract, the State shall provide the entity with notice and such other due process protections as the State may provide, except that a State may not provide a managed care entity with a pre-termination hearing before imposing the sanction described in paragraph (2)(B).

For regulatory citations, see Chapter 7

§ 3:26 TERMINATION OF MEDICAID CONTRACTS WITH MANAGED CARE ENTITIES — Section 1932(e)(4) [42 U.S.C.A. 1396u-2(e)(4)]

◆ NOTE: Section 4701(a) of the Balanced Budget Act of 1997, P.L. 105–33, enacted a new section 1932 of the Social Security Act, 42 U.S.C.A. 1396u-2. The amendment was effective August 5, 1997. It applies to contracts entered into or renewed on or after October 1, 1997. For analysis of obligations of managed care entities to comply with Medicaid fraud and abuse protection requirements, see section 3:25.

Summary

Section 1932(a) gives a State the option to require certain Medicaid recipients to enroll with a managed care entity as a condition of receiving medical assistance. "Managed care entity" means a Medicaid managed care organization, as defined in section 1903(m)(1)(A), 42 U.S.C.A. 1396b(m)(1)(A), that provides or arranges for services for enrollees under a contract pursuant to section 1903(m). It also means a primary care case manager, as defined in section 1905(t)(2), 42 U.S.C.A. 1396d(t)(2).

Definitions: Section 1903(m)(1)(A) defines "Medicaid managed care organization" to include:

1. A health maintenance organization (HMO).
2. An eligible organization with a contract under section 1876, 42 U.S.C.A. 1395mm, which pertains to Medicare payments to HMO's and competitive medical plans (CMP's).
3. A Medicare+Choice organization with a contract under Medicare Part C. (See section 1851 *et seq.* of the Social Security Act, and sections 2: 26.1 and 2:26.2.)
4. A provider-sponsored organization.
5. Any other public or private organization.

To qualify as a Medicaid managed care organization under the statutory definition, these entities must comply with requirements for advance directives under section 1902(w), 42 U.S.C.A. 1396a(w). They also must make the services they provide accessible to enrollees, within the area they serve, to the same extent as such services are made accessible to individuals eligible for Medicaid who are not enrolled with them. Furthermore, these entities must have adequate provisions against the risk of their insolvency. In that regard, they must provide that no enrollee shall be held liable for their debts if insolvency occurs.

A qualified HMO as defined in section 1310(d) of the Public Health Service Act is deemed to meet the above requirements.

Section 1905(t)(2) defines "primary care case manager" as any of the following who have a primary care case management contract:

1. A physician, a physician group practice, or an entity employing or having other arrangements with physicians to provide such services.
2. A nurse practitioner, as described in section 1905(a)(21), 42 U.S.C.A. 1396d(a)(21).
3. A certified nurse-midwife, as defined in section 1861(gg), 42 U.S.C.A. 1395xx(gg).
4. A physician assistant, as defined in section 1861(aa)(5), 42 U.S.C.A. 1395xx(aa)(5).

Enrollment Information Requirements: Pursuant to section 1932(a)(5), States, enrollment brokers, and managed care entities must provide all enrollment notices and informational and instructional materials to enrollees and potential enrollees in a manner and form which may be easily understood by them. Upon request, Medicaid managed care organizations must make available to enrollees and potential enrollees in their respective service area information about:

- the identity, locations, qualifications, and availability of participating health care providers;
- enrollee rights and responsibilities;
- grievance and appeal procedures; and
- covered items and services.

Primary care case managers, too, must provide, upon request, information about their grievance and appeal procedures to enrollees and potential enrollees in their service area.

Furthermore, States must provide, directly or through managed care entities, a list identifying the managed care entities that are or will be available to Medicaid recipients. The list must be presented in a comparative, chart-like form, which includes information about:

- benefits covered;
- cost-sharing imposed;
- the entity's service area; and
- to the extent available, quality and performance indicators for benefits covered.

States also must provide, directly or through the managed care entity, information about the benefits to which enrollees may be entitled under Medicaid, but which are not available through the managed care entity. In addition, States must explain where and how enrollees may have access to benefits not provided by the managed care entity. This information must be made available annually and upon request.

Contract Requirements: *Beneficiary Protections — Specification of benefits:* Pursuant to section 1932(b)(1), each contract with a managed care entity must specify the benefits for which it is responsible, and whether the benefits are provided directly or by arrangement with others.

Assuring coverage for emergency services: Pursuant to section 1932(b)(2), the contract also must assure coverage for emergency services without regard to prior authorization or the emergency care provider's contractual relationship with the managed care organization or primary care case manager. Furthermore, the contract must require the managed care organization or primary care case manager to comply with guidelines for coordination of post-stabilization established by section 1852(d)(2), to the same extent as such guidelines apply to Medicare+Choice plans. (This requirement applies 30 days after the date of promulgation of the guidelines.)

Emergency services means covered inpatient and outpatient services furnished by a Medicaid qualified provider which are needed to evaluate or stabilize an emergency medical condition. Emergency medical condition means a condition manifesting itself by acute symptoms of sufficient severity (including severe pain) such that a prudent layperson, who possesses an average knowledge of health and medicine, could reasonably expect the absence of immediate medical attention to result in:

- serious jeopardy of the health of the individual (or, in the case of a pregnant woman, to the health of the woman or her unborn child);
- serious impairment to bodily functions; or
- serious dysfunction of any bodily organ or part.

Protection of enrollee-provider communications: Pursuant to section 1932(b)(3), a Medicaid managed care organization must not prohibit or otherwise restrict a covered health care professional from advising an enrollee patient about his or her health status, or about medical care or treatment for his or her condition or disease. This applies regardless whether benefits for such care or treatment are provided under the contract, so long as the health care professional is acting within the lawful scope of his or her practice.

For these purposes, "health care professional" means a physician (as defined in section 1861(r), 42 U.S.C.A. 1395x(r)), or other health care profession if coverage for the professional's services is provided under the contract with a primary care case manager. The term also includes a podiatrist, optometrist, chiropractor, psychologist, dentist, physician assistant, physical or occupational therapist and therapy assistant, speech-language pathologist, audiologist, registered or licensed practical nurse (including nurse practitioner, clinical nurse specialist, certified registered nurse anesthetist, and certified nurse-midwife), licensed certified social worker, registered respiratory therapist, and certified respiratory therapy technician.

This requirement does not obligate a Medicaid managed care organization to provide, reimburse for, or provide coverage of, a counseling or referral service if the organization objects to the provision of such service on moral or religious grounds. The organization must make available information on its policies regarding such service to prospective enrollees before or during enrollment, however, in such a manner and through such writings as the organization deems appropriate. The organization also must make that information available within 90 days after the date it adopts a change in policy regarding such a counseling or referral service.

This requirement shall not be construed to affect disclosure requirements under State law or under the Employee Retirement Income Security Act of 1974 (ERISA).

Grievance procedures: Pursuant to section 1932(b)(4), each Medicaid managed care organization must establish an internal grievance procedure under which an enrollee, or a provider on behalf of an enrollee, may challenge the denial of coverage of or payment for medical assistance.

Proof of adequate capacity and services: Pursuant to section 1932(b)(5), each Medicaid managed care organization must provide the State and the Secretary of Health and Human Services adequate assurances that the organization has, within its service area, the capacity to serve the expected enrollment in that service area. These assurances must be made in a form and manner determined by the Secretary. They must demonstrate an appropriate range of services and access to preventive and primary care services for the population expected to be enrolled in the service area. They also must demonstrate that the organization maintains a sufficient number, mix, and geographic distribution of providers of services.

No enrollee liability for payment: Pursuant to section 1932(b)(6), each Medicaid managed care organization must provide:

1. No enrollee will be held liable for debts of the organization in the event of the organization's insolvency.
2. No enrollee will be held liable for services provided in the event the organization fails to receive payment for such services from the State, or in the event a health care provider with a contractual, referral, or other arrangement with the organization fails to receive payment from the State or the organization for such services.
3. No enrollee will be held liable for payments to a provider that furnishes covered services under a contractual, referral, or other arrangement with the organization in excess of the amount that would be owed by the individual if the organization had directly provided the services.

Antidiscrimination: Pursuant to section 1932(b)(7), a Medicaid managed care organization may not discriminate with respect to participation, reimbursement, or indemnification as to any provider who is acting within the scope of his or her license or certification under applicable State law solely on the basis of such licensure or certification. This, however, does not prohibit an organization from including providers only to the extent necessary to meet the needs of the organization's enrollees or from establishing any measure designed to maintain quality and control costs consistent with the responsibilities of the organization.

Compliance with maternity and mental health requirements: Pursuant to section 1932(b)(8), Medicaid managed care organizations must comply with provisions of Subpart 2 of Part A of Title XXVII of the Public Health Service Act applicable to insurers offering group health insurance.

Quality Assurance Standards: *Quality Assessment and Improvement Strategy:* Section 1932(c)(1) requires States to develop and implement a quality assessment and improvement strategy for

Medicaid managed care organizations. That strategy must include standards for access to care so that covered services are available within reasonable time frames and in a manner that ensures continuity of care and adequate capacity to provide primary care and specialized services.

The strategy must provide for examination of other aspects of care and service directly related to improvement of quality of care, including grievance procedures and marketing and information standards.

Procedures for monitoring and evaluating the quality and appropriateness of care and services must reflect the full spectrum of populations enrolled under the contract with the State. They also must include requirements for provision of quality assurance data to the State using the data and information set which the Secretary has specified for use under Medicare Part C, or such alternative data as the Secretary approves, in consultation with the State. Furthermore, the strategy itself must be subject to regular, periodic examinations of its scope and content.

One year after enactment of section 1932 (which was August 5, 1997), the Secretary must establish standards for quality assurance. Prior thereto, guidelines relating to quality assurance which are applied under section 1915(b)(1), 42 U.S.C.A. 1396b(b)(1), which also permits Medicaid primary care case management, apply.

External Independent Review of Managed Care Activities: Pursuant to section 1932(c)(2), each contract with a Medicaid managed care organization must provide for an annual external independent review, conducted by a qualified independent entity. The review must assess the quality outcomes, and timeliness of, and access to the items and services for which the organization is responsible under its contract. This requirement becomes effective only upon establishment of methods to identify entities qualified to conduct such reviews and development of review protocols. Results of each external independent review must be available to participating health care providers, enrollees, and potential enrollees or the organization; however, the identity of patients must not be disclosed.

If a Medicaid managed care organization is accredited by a private independent entity such as those prescribed in section 1852(e)(4) for Medicare+Choice organizations, or if it has an external review conducted under section 1852(e)(3), a State need not provide for a review that would duplicate that. Furthermore, at State option, the independent review requirement need not apply with respect to a Medicaid managed care organization if the organization is an eligible organization with a contract under section 1876 or a Medicare+Choice organization with a contract under Medicare Part C and the organization had a contract in effect under section 1903 at least during the previous two-year period.

Protections Against Fraud and Abuse: *Prohibiting Affiliations with Individuals Debarred by Federal Agencies:* Section 1932(d)(1) prohibits a managed care entity from knowingly affiliating with persons or entities, or their affiliates, that have been debarred, suspended, or otherwise excluded:

- from participating in procurement activities under the Federal Acquisition Regulation, or
- from participating in nonprocurement activities under regulations issued pursuant to Executive Order No. 12549, or under guidelines implementing such order.

If a State finds that a managed care entity is not in compliance, it must notify the Secretary of the noncompliance. The State may continue an existing agreement with the entity, unless the Secretary, in consultation with the Inspector General, directs otherwise; but it may not renew or otherwise extend the duration of an existing agreement unless the Secretary, in consultation with the Inspector General, provides to the State and to Congress a written statement describing compelling reasons for renewing or extending the agreement.

For these purposes, affiliation encompasses having a debarred, suspended, or excluded person as a director, officer, or partner. It also encompasses having such a person possess beneficial ownership of more than five percent of the entity's equity, or having an employment, consulting, or other agreement with such a person for the provision of items and services that are significant and material to the entity's obligations under its contract with the State.

Restrictions on Marketing: Section 1932(d)(2)(A) prohibits a managed care entity from distributing marketing materials, either directly or through any agent or independent contractor, without prior approval of the State. That prohibition takes effect when the Secretary specifies (but after consulting on a start time with the State). Section 1932(d)(2)(A) also prohibits marketing materials that contain false or materially misleading information. In reviewing and approving marketing materials, however, the State must provide for consultation with a medical care advisory committee.

Section 1932(d)(2)(B) requires managed care entities to distribute marketing materials to the entire service area covered under their contract. Sections 1932(d)(2)(C), (D), and (E) prohibit, respectively, tie-ins, marketing fraud, and "cold-call" marketing. "Tie-in" refers to attempting to influence an individual's enrollment in conjunction with the sale of any other insurance. The prohibition against cold calls reaches uninvited efforts made directly or indirectly, whether door-to-door or by telephone or other means.

State Conflict of Interest Safeguards: Section 1932(d)(3) prohibits a Medicaid managed care organization from entering into a contract with a State under section 1903(m), unless the State has in effect conflict of interest safeguards with respect to officers and employees of the State with responsibilities relating to contracts with such organizations or to the default enrollment process described in subsection (a)(4)(C)(ii). Those safeguards must be at least as effective as the Federal safeguards provided under section 27 of the Office of Federal Procurement Policy Act, 41 U.S.C.A. 423, against conflicts of interest that apply with respect to Federal procurement officials with comparable responsibilities with respect to such contracts.

Unique Physician Identifiers: Pursuant to section 1932(d)(4), each Medicaid managed care organization must require each physician providing services to enrollees to have a unique identifier in accordance with the system established under section 1173(b), 42 U.S.C.A. 1320d-2(b).

Timeliness of Payment: Pursuant to section 1932(f), a contract under section 1903(m) with a Medicaid managed care organization must provide for timely payment to health care providers for items and services subject to the contract which are furnished to enrollees. This must be consistent with the claims payment procedures described in section 1902(a)(37)(a), 42 U.S.C.A. 1395a(a)(37), unless the health care provider and the organization agree to an alternate payment schedule. Section 1902(a)(37)(a) applies to Medicaid claims processing. It calls for payment of 90% of all "clean" claims within 30 days of receipt, and payment of 99% of all claims within 90 days of receipt.

Contract Termination: Section 1932(e)(4) authorizes termination of a contract with a managed care entity or primary care case manager for failure to comply with requirements of the contract or the statute. A State may establish its own procedures for terminating a contract but it may not take final action without a pre-termination hearing. If a State decides to terminate a contract with a managed care organization, however, it may notify enrollees about the intended termination. The State also may allow enrollees to disenroll immediately with the entity without cause.

Statutory Provisions

Section 1903(m)(1)(A), 42 U.S.C.A. 1396b(m)(1)(A), defines Medicaid managed care organization as follows:

> The term "Medicaid managed care organization" means a health maintenance organization, an eligible organization with a contract under section 1876 or a Medicare+Choice organization with a contract under part C of title XVIII, a provider sponsored organization, or any other public or private organization, which meets the requirement of section 1902(w) and —
>
> (i) makes services it provides to individuals eligible for benefits under this title accessible to such individuals, within the area served by the organization, to the same extent as such services are made accessible to individuals (eligible for medical assistance under the State plan) not enrolled with the organization, and
>
> (ii) has made adequate provision against the risk of insolvency, which provision is satisfactory to the State, meets the requirements of subparagraph (C)(i) (if applicable), and which assures that individuals eligible for benefits under this title are in no case held liable for debts of the organization in case of the organization's insolvency.
>
> An organization that is a qualified health maintenance organization (as defined in section 1310(d) of the Public Health Service Act) is deemed to meet the requirements of clauses (i) and (ii).

Section 1905(t)(2), 42 U.S.C.A. 1396d(t)(2), defines primary care case manager as follows:

> The term "primary care case manager" means any of the following that provides services of the type described in paragraph (1) under a contract referred to in such paragraph:
>
> (A) A physician, a physician group practice, or an entity employing or having other arrangements with physicians to provide such services.

(B) At State option —

(i) a nurse practitioner (as described in section 1905(a)(21));

(ii) a certified nurse-midwife (as defined in section 1861(gg)); or

(iii) a physician assistant (as defined in section 1861(aa)(5)).

Section 1932(a)(5) sets forth enrollment information requirements for Medicaid managed care organizations. It provides:

PROVISION OF INFORMATION. —

(A) INFORMATION IN EASILY UNDERSTOOD FORM. — Each State, enrollment broker, or managed care entity shall provide all enrollment notices and informational and instructional materials relating to such an entity under this title in a manner and form which may be easily understood by enrollees and potential enrollees of the entity who are eligible for medical assistance under the State plan under this title.

(B) INFORMATION TO ENROLLEES AND POTENTIAL ENROLLEES. — Each managed care entity that is a Medicaid managed care organization shall, upon request, make available to enrollees and potential enrollees in the organization's service area information concerning the following:

(i) PROVIDERS. — The identity, locations, qualifications, and availability of health care providers that participate with the organization.

(ii) ENROLLEE RIGHTS AND RESPONSIBILITIES. — The rights and responsibilities of enrollees.

(iii) GRIEVANCE AND APPEAL PROCEDURES. — The procedures available to an enrollee and a health care provider to challenge or appeal the failure of the organization to cover a service.

(iv) INFORMATION ON COVERED ITEMS AND SERVICES. — All items and services that are available to enrollees under the contract between the State and the organization that are covered either directly or through a method of referral and prior authorization. Each managed care entity that is a primary care case manager shall, upon request, make available to enrollees and potential enrollees in the organization's service area the information described in clause (iii).

(C) COMPARATIVE INFORMATION. — A State that requires individuals to enroll with managed care entities under paragraph (1)(A) shall annually (and upon request) provide, directly or through the managed care entity, to such individuals a list identifying the managed care entities that are (or will be) available and information (presented in a comparative, chart-like form) relating to the following for each such entity offered:

(i) BENEFITS AND COST-SHARING. — The benefits covered and cost-sharing imposed by the entity.

(ii) SERVICE AREA. — The service area of the entity.

(iii) QUALITY AND PERFORMANCE. — To the extent available, quality and performance indicators for the benefits under the entity.

(D) INFORMATION ON BENEFITS NOT COVERED UNDER MANAGED CARE ARRANGEMENT. — A State, directly or through managed care entities, shall, on or before an individual enrolls with such an entity under this title, inform the enrollee in a written and prominent manner of any benefits to which the enrollee may be entitled to under this title but which are not made available to the enrollee through the entity. Such information shall include information on where and how such enrollees may access benefits not made available to the enrollee through the entity.

Section 1932(b) sets forth Medicaid managed care contract requirements for beneficiary protections. It provides:

BENEFICIARY PROTECTIONS. —

(1) SPECIFICATION OF BENEFITS. — Each contract with a managed care entity under section 1903(m) or under section 1905(t)(3) shall specify the benefits the provision (or arrangement) for which the entity is responsible.

(2) ASSURING COVERAGE TO EMERGENCY SERVICES. —

(A) IN GENERAL. — Each contract with a Medicaid managed care organization under section 1903(m) and each contract with a primary care case manager under section 1905(t)(3) shall require the organization or manager —

(i) to provide coverage for emergency services (as defined in subparagraph (B)) without regard to prior authorization or the emergency care provider's contractual relationship with the organization or manager, and

(ii) to comply with guidelines established under section 1852(d)(2) (respecting coordination of post-stabilization care) in the same manner as such guidelines apply to Medicare+Choice plans offered under part C of title XVIII.

The requirement under clause (ii) shall first apply 30 days after the date of promulgation of the guidelines referred to in such clause.

(B) EMERGENCY SERVICES DEFINED. — In subparagraph (A)(i), the term "emergency services" means, with respect to an individual enrolled with an organization, covered inpatient and outpatient services that —

(i) are furnished by a provider that is qualified to furnish such services under this title, and

(ii) are needed to evaluate or stabilize an emergency medical condition (as defined in subparagraph (C)).

(C) EMERGENCY MEDICAL CONDITION DEFINED. — In subparagraph (B)(ii), the term "emergency medical condition" means a medical condition manifesting itself by acute symptoms of sufficient severity (including severe pain) such that a prudent layperson, who possesses an average knowledge of health and medicine, could reasonably expect the absence of immediate medical attention to result in —

(i) placing the health of the individual (or, with respect to a pregnant woman, the health of the woman or her unborn child) in serious jeopardy,

(ii) serious impairment to bodily functions, or

(iii) serious dysfunction of any bodily organ or part.

(3) PROTECTION OF ENROLLEE-PROVIDER COMMUNICATIONS.—

(A) IN GENERAL.—Subject to subparagraphs (B) and (C), under a contract under section 1903(m) a Medicaid managed care organization (in relation to an individual enrolled under the contract) shall not prohibit or otherwise restrict a covered health care professional (as defined in subparagraph (D)) from advising such an individual who is a patient of the professional about the health status of the individual or medical care or treatment for the individual's condition or disease, regardless of whether benefits for such care or treatment are provided under the contract, if the professional is acting within the lawful scope of practice.

(B) CONSTRUCTION. —Subparagraph (A) shall not be construed as requiring a Medicaid managed care organization to provide, reimburse for, or provide coverage of, a counseling or referral service if the organization—

(i) objects to the provision of such service on moral or religious grounds; and

(ii) in the manner and through the written instrumentalities such organization deems appropriate, makes available information on its policies regarding such service to prospective enrollees before or during enrollment and to enrollees within 90 days after the date that the organization adopts a change in policy regarding such a counseling or referral service.

Nothing in this subparagraph shall be construed to affect disclosure requirements under State law or under the Employee Retirement Income Security Act of 1974.

(C) HEALTH CARE PROFESSIONAL DEFINED.—For purposes of this paragraph, the term "health care professional" means a physician (as defined in section 1861(r)) or other health care professional if coverage for the professional's services is provided under the contract referred to in subparagraph (A) for the services of the professional. Such term includes a podiatrist, optometrist, chiropractor, psychologist, dentist, physician assistant, physical or occupational therapist and therapy assistant, speech-language pathologist, audiologist, registered or licensed practical nurse (including nurse practitioner, clinical nurse specialist, certified registered nurse anesthetist, and certified nurse-midwife), licensed certified social worker, registered respiratory therapist, and certified respiratory therapy technician.

(4) GRIEVANCE PROCEDURES. — Each Medicaid managed care organization shall establish an internal grievance procedure under which an enrollee who is eligible for medical assistance under the State plan under this title, or a provider on behalf of such an enrollee, may challenge the denial of coverage of or payment for such assistance.

(5) DEMONSTRATION OF ADEQUATE CAPACITY AND SERVICES. — Each Medicaid managed care organization shall provide the State and the Secretary with adequate assurances (in a time and manner determined by the Secretary) that the organization, with respect to a service area, has the capacity to serve the expected enrollment in such service area, including assurances that the organization —

(A) offers an appropriate range of services and access to preventive and primary care services for the population expected to be enrolled in such service area, and

(B) maintains a sufficient number, mix, and geographic distribution of providers of services.

(6) PROTECTING ENROLLEES AGAINST LIABILITY FOR PAYMENT. — Each Medicaid managed care organization shall provide that an individual eligible for medical assistance under the State plan under this title who is enrolled with the organization may not be held liable —

(A) for the debts of the organization, in the event of the organization's insolvency,

(B) for services provided to the individual —

(i) in the event of the organization failing to receive payment from the State for such services; or

(ii) in the event of a health care provider with a contractual, referral, or other arrangement with the organization failing to receive payment from the State or the organization for such services, or

(C) for payments to a provider that furnishes covered services under a contractual, referral, or other arrangement with the organization in excess of the amount that would be owed by the individual if the organization had directly provided the services.

(7) ANTIDISCRIMINATION. —A Medicaid managed care organization shall not discriminate with respect to participation, reimbursement, or indemnification as to any provider who is acting within the scope of the provider's license or certification under applicable State law, solely on the basis of such license or certification. This paragraph shall not be construed to prohibit an organization from including providers only to the extent necessary to meet the needs of the organization's enrollees or from establishing any measure designed to maintain quality and control costs consistent with the responsibilities of the organization.

(8) COMPLIANCE WITH CERTAIN MATERNITY AND MENTAL HEALTH REQUIREMENTS. — Each Medicaid managed care organization shall comply with the requirements of subpart 2 of part A of title XXVII of the Public Health Service Act insofar as such requirements apply and are effective with respect to a health insurance issuer that offers group health insurance coverage.

With respect to requirements for quality assurance, section 1932(c) provides:

QUALITY ASSURANCE STANDARDS. —

(1) QUALITY ASSESSMENT AND IMPROVEMENT STRATEGY. —

(A) IN GENERAL. — If a State provides for contracts with Medicaid managed care organizations under section 1903(m), the State shall develop and implement a quality assessment and improvement strategy consistent with this paragraph. Such strategy shall include the following:

(i) ACCESS STANDARDS. — Standards for access to care so that covered services are available within reasonable timeframes and in a manner that ensures continuity of care and adequate primary care and specialized services capacity.

(ii) OTHER MEASURES. — Examination of other aspects of care and service directly related to the improvement of quality of care (including grievance procedures and marketing and information standards).

(iii) MONITORING PROCEDURES. — Procedures for monitoring and evaluating the quality and appropriateness of care and services to enrollees that reflect the full spectrum of populations enrolled under the contract and that includes requirements for provision of quality assurance data to the State using the data and information set that the Secretary has specified for use under part C of title XVIII or such alternative data as the Secretary approves, in consultation with the State.

(iv) PERIODIC REVIEW. — Regular, periodic examinations of the scope and content of the strategy.

(B) STANDARDS. — The strategy developed under subparagraph (A) shall be consistent with standards that the Secretary first establishes within 1 year after the date of the enactment of this section. Such standards shall not preempt any State standards that are more stringent than such standards. Guidelines relating to quality assurance that are applied under section 1915(b)(1) shall apply under this subsection until the effective date of standards for quality assurance established under this subparagraph.

(C) MONITORING. — The Secretary shall monitor the development and implementation of strategies under subparagraph (A).

(D) CONSULTATION. — The Secretary shall conduct activities under subparagraphs (B) and (C) in consultation with the States.

(2) EXTERNAL INDEPENDENT REVIEW OF MANAGED CARE ACTIVITIES. —

(A) REVIEW OF CONTRACTS. —

(i) IN GENERAL. — Each contract under section 1903(m) with a Medicaid managed care organization shall provide for an annual (as appropriate) external independent review conducted by a qualified independent entity of the quality outcomes and timeliness of, and access to, the items and services for which the organization is responsible under the contract. The requirement for such a review shall not apply until after the date that the Secretary establishes the identification method described in clause (ii).

(ii) QUALIFICATIONS OF REVIEWER.—The Secretary, in consultation with the States, shall establish a method for the identification of entities that are qualified to conduct reviews under clause (i).

(iii) USE OF PROTOCOLS.—The Secretary, in coordination with the National Governors' Association, shall contract with an independent quality review organization (such as the National Committee for Quality Assurance) to develop the protocols to be used in external independent reviews conducted under this paragraph on and after January 1, 1999.

(iv) AVAILABILITY OF RESULTS.—The results of each external independent review conducted under this subparagraph shall be available to participating health care providers, enrollees, and potential enrollees of the organization, except that the results may not be made available in a manner that discloses the identity of any individual patient.

(B) NONDUPLICATION OF ACCREDITATION.—A State may provide that, in the case of a Medicaid managed care organization that is accredited by a private independent entity (such as those described in section 1852(e)(4)) or that has an external review conducted under section 1852(e)(3), the external review activities conducted under subparagraph (A) with respect to the organization shall not be duplicative of review activities conducted as part of the accreditation process or the external review conducted under such section.

(C) DEEMED COMPLIANCE FOR MEDICARE MANAGED CARE ORGANIZATIONS.—At the option of a State, the requirements of subparagraph (A) shall not apply with respect to a Medicaid managed care organization if the organization is an eligible organization with a contract in effect under section 1876 or a Medicare+Choice organization with a contract in effect under part C of title XVIII and the organization has had a contract in effect under section 1903(m) at least during the previous 2-year period.

◆ NOTE: Section 608(w)(1) of the Medicare, Medicaid, and SCHIP Balanced Budget Refinement Act of 1999, as incorporated into the Omnibus Consolidated Appropriations Act, 2000, P.L. 106-113, enacted November 17, 1999, inserted "part" before "C". Section 608(w)(2)(A) and (B) of that Act also amended clause (d)(1)(C)(ii) by removing "Act" after "defined in such" and before ") of a person" and inserting "Regulation", and by replacing "1903(t)(3)" with "1905(t)(3)". These changes were made effective November 29, 1999.

Section 1932(d) sets forth protections against fraud and abuse which apply to Medicaid managed care entities. It provides:

PROTECTIONS AGAINST FRAUD AND ABUSE.—

(1) PROHIBITING AFFILIATIONS WITH INDIVIDUALS DEBARRED BY FEDERAL AGENCIES.—

(A) IN GENERAL.—A managed care entity may not knowingly—

(i) have a person described in subparagraph (C) as a director, officer, partner, or person with beneficial ownership of more than 5 percent of the entity's equity, or

(ii) have an employment, consulting, or other agreement with a person described in such subparagraph for the provision of items and services that are significant and material to the entity's obligations under its contract with the State.

(B) EFFECT OF NONCOMPLIANCE.—If a State finds that a managed care entity is not in compliance with clause (i) or (ii) of subparagraph (A), the State—

(i) shall notify the Secretary of such noncompliance;

(ii) may continue an existing agreement with the entity unless the Secretary (in consultation with the Inspector General of the Department of Health and Human Services) directs otherwise; and

(iii) may not renew or otherwise extend the duration of an existing agreement with the entity unless the Secretary (in consultation with the Inspector General of the Department of Health and Human Services) provides to the State and to Congress a written statement describing compelling reasons that exist for renewing or extending the agreement.

(C) PERSONS DESCRIBED. — A person is described in this subparagraph if such person —

(i) is debarred, suspended, or otherwise excluded from participating in procurement activities under the Federal Acquisition Regulation or from participating in non-procurement activities under regulations issued pursuant to Executive Order No. 12549 or under guidelines implementing such order; or

(ii) is an affiliate (as defined in such Regulation) of a person described in clause (i).

(2) RESTRICTIONS ON MARKETING. —

(A) DISTRIBUTION OF MATERIALS. —

(i) IN GENERAL. — A managed care entity, with respect to activities under this title, may not distribute directly or through any agent or independent contractor marketing materials within any State —

(I) without the prior approval of the State, and

(II) that contain false or materially misleading information.

The requirement of subclause (I) shall not apply with respect to a State until such date as the Secretary specifies in consultation with such State.

(ii) CONSULTATION IN REVIEW OF MARKET MATERIALS. — In the process of reviewing and approving such materials, the State shall provide for consultation with a medical care advisory committee.

(B) SERVICE MARKET. — A managed care entity shall distribute marketing materials to the entire service area of such entity covered under the contract under section 1903(m) or section 1905(t)(3).

(C) PROHIBITION OF TIE-INS. — A managed care entity, or any agency of such entity, may not seek to influence an individual's enrollment with the entity in conjunction with the sale of any other insurance.

(D) PROHIBITING MARKETING FRAUD. — Each managed care entity shall comply with such procedures and conditions as the Secretary prescribes in order to ensure that, before an individual is enrolled with the entity, the individual is provided accurate oral and written information sufficient to make an informed decision whether or not to enroll.

(E) PROHIBITION OF "COLD-CALL" MARKETING. — Each managed care entity shall not, directly or indirectly, conduct door-to-door, telephonic, or other "cold-call" marketing of enrollment under this title.

(3) STATE CONFLICT-OF-INTEREST SAFEGUARDS IN MEDICAID RISK CONTRACTING. — A Medicaid managed care organization may not enter into a contract with any State under section 1903(m) unless the State has in effect conflict-of-interest safeguards with respect to officers and employees of the State with responsibilities relating to contracts with such organizations or to the default enrollment process described in subsection (a)(4)(C)(ii) that are at least as effective as the Federal safeguards provided under section 27 of the Office of Federal Procurement Policy Act (41 U.S.C.A. 423), against conflicts of interest that apply with respect to Federal procurement officials with comparable responsibilities with respect to such contracts.

(4) USE OF UNIQUE PHYSICIAN IDENTIFIER FOR PARTICIPATING PHYSICIANS. — Each Medicaid managed care organization shall require each physician providing services to enrollees eligible for medical assistance under the State plan under this title to have a unique identifier in accordance with the system established under section 1173(b).

With respect to requirements for timely payment to health care providers by Medicaid manage care organizations, section 1932(f) provides:

TIMELINESS OF PAYMENT. — A contract under section 1903(m) with a Medicaid managed care organization shall provide that the organization shall make payment to health care providers for items and services which are subject to the contract and that are furnished to individuals eligible for medical assistance under the State plan under this title who are enrolled with the organization on a timely basis consistent with the claims payment procedures described in section 1902(a)(37)(A), unless the health care provider and the organization agree to an alternate payment schedule.

Section 1902(a)(37) provides timeliness standards for Medicaid claims in pertinent part as follows:

(a) A State plan for Medicaid must —

* * *

(37) provide for claims payment procedures which (A) ensure that 90 per centum of claims for payment (for which no further written information or substantiation is required in order to make payment) made for services covered under the plan and furnished by health care practitioners through individual or group practices or through shared health facilities are paid within 30 days of the date of receipt of such claims and that 99 per centum of such claims are paid within 90 days of the date of receipt of such claims, . . .

Finally, section 1932(e)(4) authorizes States to terminate contracts with a managed care organization or primary care case manager. It provides:

(A) IN GENERAL. — In the case of a managed care entity which has failed to meet the requirements of this part or a contract under section 1903(m) or 1905(t)(3), the State shall have the authority to terminate such contract with the entity and to enroll such entity's enrollees with other managed care entities (or to permit such enrollees to receive medical assistance under the State plan under this title other than through a managed care entity).

(B) AVAILABILITY OF HEARING PRIOR TO TERMINATION OF CONTRACT. — A State may not terminate a contract with a managed care entity under subparagraph (A) unless the entity is provided with a hearing prior to the termination.

(C) NOTICE AND RIGHT TO DISENROLL IN CASES OF TERMINATION HEARING. — A State may —

(i) notify individuals enrolled with a managed care entity which is the subject of a hearing to terminate the entity's contract with the State of the hearing, and

(ii) in the case of such an entity, permit such enrollees to disenroll immediately with the entity without cause.

For regulatory citations, see Chapter 7

§ 3:27 TERMINATION OF MEDICAID PACE PROVIDER AGREEMENTS — Section 1934(e)(5) [42 U.C.S.A. 1396u-4(e)(5)]

◆ NOTE: Section 4802(a)(3) of the Balanced Budget Act of 1997, P.L. 105–33, created the Program of All-inclusive Care for the Elderly (PACE), effective August 5, 1997. For a discussion of PACE and Medicare, see section 2:62. For a discussion of intermediate sanctions applicable to Medicaid PACE providers, see section 2:28.

Summary

Pursuant to section 1934 of the Social Security Act, as amended, 42 U.S.C.A. 1396u-4, a State may elect to provide medical assistance under a Program of All-inclusive Care for the Elderly (PACE). This is in lieu of regular Medicaid benefits. Individuals need not be eligible for Medicare Part A or B to be eligible to enroll with a Medicaid PACE program; however, a State may limit the number of individuals who may enroll. PACE providers receive payment for the provision of benefits to PACE enrollees based on capitation, in accordance with a mandatory PACE program agreement.

Definitions — Section 1934(a): *"PACE Program"* means a program operated by a PACE provider that provides comprehensive health care services to eligible individuals in accordance with a PACE program agreement with a State.

PACE Program also means continued assistance to an enrollee during his or her transition from status as a PACE enrollee to other care providers. This continued assistance includes making appropriate referrals to other providers and making the individual's medical records available to those providers. Continued assistance applies when an individual no longer qualifies for PACE, or when a PACE program agreement terminates, or for any other reason transition may be necessary.

"PACE Provider" means a public entity, or a private, non-profit entity organized for charitable purposes under section 501(c)(3) of the Internal Revenue Code of 1986, that has a PACE program agree-

ment in effect with a State. It also means a private, for-profit provider eligible by reason of a demonstration project waiver under section 1934(h). The Secretary of Health and Human Services, in consultation with States, may grant as many as ten such waivers.

"PACE Program Agreement" means a provider agreement that is consistent with section 1934 (and, if applicable, with section 1894, 42 U.S.C.A. 1395eee, which authorizes PACE for Medicare purposes), and with applicable regulations. Parties to the agreement are the Secretary, the State Medicaid agency, and the PACE provider.

"PACE Program Eligible Individual" means an individual 55 years of age or older who requires the level of care required under the State Medicaid plan for coverage of nursing facility services. The individual must reside in the service area of the PACE program, and he or she must meet such other eligibility conditions as may be imposed under the PACE program agreement.

"PACE Protocol" means the protocol for the Program of All-inclusive Care for the Elderly (PACE, as published by On Lok, Inc., as of April 14, 1995, or any successor protocol that may be agreed upon between the Secretary and On Lok, Inc.

"PACE Demonstration Waiver Program" means a demonstration program under either of the following sections (as in effect prior to the date of their repeal): section 603(c) of the Social Security Amendments of 1983, P.L. 98–21, as extended by section 9220 of the Consolidated Omnibus Budget Reconciliation Act of 1985, P.L. 99–272; or section 9412(b) of the Omnibus Budget Reconciliation Act of 1986, P.L. 99–509.

"State Administering Agency" means the State agency responsible for administering PACE program agreements under section 1934 (Medicaid PACE) and section 1894 (Medicare PACE). That may or may not be the State Medicaid agency.

"Trial Period" means, with respect to PACE, the first three contract years under a PACE agreement. For entities that had a PACE demonstration waiver program in effect, each contract year of that demonstration-waivered contract counts as a contract year for trial period purposes under a section 1934 PACE agreement.

Scope of Benefits: Pursuant to section 1934(b)(1), PACE providers must provide at a minimum all items and services covered under Medicare for individuals enrolled under a Medicare PACE program. They also must provide all items and services covered under Medicaid, but without any limitation or condition as to amount, duration, or scope, and without application of deductibles, copayments, coinsurance, or other cost-sharing that otherwise would apply under Medicare or Medicaid. A PACE provider also must provide all additional items and service specified in regulations, based upon what is required under the PACE protocol. All necessary items and services must be accessible to enrollees twenty-four hours per day, every day.

Services must be provided through a comprehensive, multi-disciplinary health and social services delivery system which integrates acute and long-term care services, pursuant to regulations. Furthermore, the PACE provider must specify covered items and services that it will not provide directly, and it must arrange for delivery of those items and services through contracts that meet regulatory requirements.

Quality Assurance: Pursuant to section 1934(b)(2), a PACE program agreement must require a PACE provider to have a written plan of quality assurance and improvement, and procedures for implementing such a plan. The agreement also must require written safeguards of the rights of enrollees, including a patient bill of rights and procedures for grievances and appeals.

Eligibility: Pursuant to section 1934(c), determining who is eligible for medical assistance remains a responsibility of the State administering agency. Determining whether someone eligible for Medicaid is eligible for PACE, however, is to be made in accordance with a given PACE program agreement. Nevertheless, an individual is not eligible for PACE unless the individual's health status has been determined by the Secretary or by the State administering agency, in accordance with regulations, to be comparable to the health status of individuals who have participated in PACE demonstration waiver programs. Such determinations are to be based on health status and related indicators, such as medical diagnoses and measures of activities of daily living, instrumental activities of daily living, and cognitive impairment that are part of a uniform minimum data set collected by PACE providers on potential eligible individuals.

Eligibility is to be redetermined at least annually, unless there is no reasonable expectation of improvement or significant change in an individual's condition (because of a severe chronic condition or the degree of impairment of his or her functional capacity). Even if there has been improvement, an individual can continue as an enrollee under deemed status if, in accordance with regulations, in the absence of continued coverage under PACE the individual reasonably would be expected to need nursing facility services within the succeeding six-month period.

PACE enrollment and disenrollment must be made pursuant to regulations and the PACE agreement; however, any enrollee must be allowed to disenroll without cause at any time. Regulations must not allow involuntary disenrollment except for nonpayment of premiums, if applicable, on a timely basis, or for engaging in disruptive or threatening behavior. The phrase "disruptive and threatening behavior" is to be defined by regulations developed in close consultation with State administering agencies.

Nevertheless, involuntary disenrollment may not be allowed on the grounds of noncompliant behavior if the behavior is related to a mental or physical condition of the individual. "Noncompliant behavior" includes repeated noncompliance with medical advice and repeated failure to appear for medical appointments.

All involuntary disenrollments must be subject to timely review and final determination by the State administering agency or by the Secretary before disenrollment becomes effective.

Capitation Payments: Section 1934(d) provides for PACE providers to be paid prospectively, monthly, based on capitation. The capitation amount must be an amount which is less than the amount that would otherwise have been made under the State Medicaid plan if the individuals were not enrolled in PACE. The capitation amount shall be adjusted, however, to take into account the comparative frailty of PACE enrollees and such other factors as the Secretary finds appropriate. The payment under Medicaid PACE is in addition, however, to any payment under Medicare PACE (for individuals who are enrolled in both programs).

Contract Requirements: Section 1934(e) specifies PACE program agreement requirements. These are to be established in close cooperation with the State administering agency, and they are to deal with procedures for entering into, extending, and terminating PACE agreements. Section 1934(e) also specifies limits on the number of PACE providers.

Service Area and Eligibility: The program agreement must designate the service area of the program. It also may provide additional requirements for individuals to qualify as PACE program eligible individuals with respect to the program. The agreement is to be effective for one year, but it may be extended for additional years absent notice by a party to terminate. All agreements are subject, however, to termination at any time for cause by the Secretary and the State administering agency.

The agreement must require PACE providers to comply with all applicable State and local laws and requirements. Additional mutually agreed to terms and conditions are allowable so long as they are consistent with section 1934 and regulations.

Data Collection and Outcome Measures: With respect to data collection, the program agreement must require the PACE provider to:

- collect data;
- maintain records relating to the program, including pertinent financial, medical, and personnel records;
- afford access to those records to the Secretary and the State administering agency;
- submit such reports as the Secretary, in consultation with the State administering agency, finds necessary to monitor the operation, cost, and effectiveness of the PACE program; and
- provide such additional data as the Secretary specifies in regulations in order to perform the Secretary's oversight duties. (This applies during the first three years of operation of a PACE program — which period includes operation either under section 1934 or under a PACE demonstration waiver program.)

With respect to outcome measures, the program agreement must require the PACE provider, the Secretary, and the State administering agency to jointly cooperate in developing and implementing health status and quality of life outcome measures with respect to PACE program eligible individuals.

Oversight: During the trial period for a PACE program, the Secretary, in cooperation with the State administering agency, shall conduct a comprehensive annual review of the operation of the PACE program by each provider. This is to assure compliance with section 1934 and related regulatory requirements. The review must include:

- a visit to the program site;
- comprehensive assessment of a provider's fiscal soundness;
- comprehensive assessment of the provider's capacity to provide all PACE services to all enrollees;
- detailed analysis of the entity's substantial compliance with all significant requirements of section 1934 and related regulations;

- and any other elements the Secretary or the State administering agency considers necessary or appropriate.

After the trial period, the Secretary, in cooperation with the State administering agency, shall continue to review the operation of PACE providers and PACE programs as appropriate. This continuing review process may take into account the performance level of provider and compliance of a provider with all significant requirements of section 1934 and related regulations.

Pursuant to section 1934(e)(4)(C), the results of these reviews must be reported promptly to the PACE provider, along with any recommendations for changes to the provider's program. They are also to be available upon request to the public.

Termination of PACE Provider Agreements: Pursuant to section 1934(e)(5), a PACE provider may terminate an agreement after appropriate notice to the Secretary, the State administering agency, and enrollees.

Under regulations, the Secretary or a State administering agency may terminate a PACE program agreement for cause. "Cause" means, among other reasons, a finding by the Secretary or the State administering agency that there are significant deficiencies in the quality of care provided to enrollees. It also means failure to comply substantially with conditions for a program or provider under either section 1934 or section 1894. Termination for cause applies if, within thirty days of receipt of written notice of a cause determination, the entity has failed to develop and successfully initiate a plan to correct the deficiencies, or has failed to continue implementation of such a plan.

An entity whose PACE provider agreement has been terminated must implement the transition procedures required under section 1934(a)(2)(C).

Additional Oversight and Enforcement Authority: After determining that a PACE provider is failing substantially to comply with section 1934 and related regulations, the Secretary and the State administering agency may take any or all of the following actions:

- condition the continuation of the PACE program agreement upon timely execution of a corrective action plan;
- withhold some or all further payments under the PACE program agreement under section 1934 or section 1894, with

respect to PACE program services furnished by such provider until the deficiencies have been corrected; or

- terminate the PACE program agreement.

Termination Procedures: Pursuant to section 1934(e)(7), and by regulations, procedural provisions of section 1857(h) apply for termination of a PACE program agreement for periods on or after January 1, 1999, in the same manner as they apply to Medicare+Choice organization under Medicare Part C. For periods prior to January 1, 1999, procedural provisions in section 1876(i)(9) apply in the same manner as they apply to a risk-bearing organization, such as a health maintenance organization of competitive medical plan, eligible under section 1876.

On or after January 1, 1999: Section 1857(h) calls for notice and a reasonable opportunity for the PACE provider to develop and implement a corrective action plan to correct deficiencies that formed the basis for a termination decision. It also calls for a hearing, and a right to appeal an initial decision, prior to termination of an agreement. No pre-termination hearing or opportunity for implementing a corrective action plan is required, however, if delay in termination would pose an imminent and serious risk to the health of enrollees.

Prior to January 1, 1999: Section 1876(i)(9) calls for reasonable opportunity to develop and implement a corrective action plan to correct deficiencies that formed the basis for a termination decision. If a corrective action plan is not developed or implemented, then the PACE provider must be given notice and opportunity for a hearing, and the right to appeal an initial decision, prior to termination.

Statutory Provisions

Section 1934(a) of the Social Security Act, as amended, 42 U.S.C.A. 1396u-4(a), provides as follows with respect to the nature of the PACE program and defined terms:

STATE OPTION.—

(1) IN GENERAL. —A State may elect to provide medical assistance under this section with respect to PACE program services to PACE program eligible individuals who are eligible for medical assistance under the State plan and who are enrolled in a PACE program under a PACE program agreement. Such individuals need not be eligible for benefits under part A, or enrolled under part B, of title XVIII to be eligible to

enroll under this section. In the case of an individual enrolled with a PACE program pursuant to such an election —

(A) the individual shall receive benefits under the plan solely through such program, and

(B) the PACE provider shall receive payment in accordance with the PACE program agreement for provision of such benefits.

A State may establish a numerical limit on the number of individuals who may be enrolled in a PACE program under a PACE program agreement.

(2) PACE PROGRAM DEFINED. — For purposes of this section, the term "PACE program" means a program of all-inclusive care for the elderly that meets the following requirements:

(A) OPERATION. — The entity operating the program is a PACE provider (as defined in paragraph (3)).

(B) COMPREHENSIVE BENEFITS. — The program provides comprehensive health care services to PACE program eligible individuals in accordance with the PACE program agreement and regulations under this section.

(C) TRANSITION. — In the case of an individual who is enrolled under the program under this section and whose enrollment ceases for any reason (including that the individual no longer qualifies as a PACE program eligible individual, the termination of a PACE program agreement, or otherwise), the program provides assistance to the individual in obtaining necessary transitional care through appropriate referrals and making the individual's medical records available to new providers.

(3) PACE PROVIDER DEFINED. —

(A) IN GENERAL. — For purposes of this section, the term "PACE provider" means an entity that —

(i) subject to subparagraph (B), is (or is a distinct part of) a public entity or a private, nonprofit entity organized for charitable purposes under section 501(c)(3) of the Internal Revenue Code of 1986, and

(ii) has entered into a PACE program agreement with respect to its operation of a PACE program.

(B) TREATMENT OF PRIVATE, FOR-PROFIT PROVIDERS. — Clause (i) of subparagraph (A) shall not apply —

(i) to entities subject to a demonstration project waiver under subsection (h); and

(ii) after the date the report under section 4804(b) of the Balanced Budget Act of 1997 is submitted, unless the Secretary determines that any of the findings described in subparagraph (A), (B), (C), or (D) of paragraph (2) of such section are true.

(4) PACE PROGRAM AGREEMENT DEFINED. — For purposes of this section, the term "PACE program agreement" means, with respect to a PACE provider, an agreement, consistent with this section, section 1894 [42 U.S.C.A. 1395eee] (if applicable), and regulations promulgated to carry out such sections, among the PACE provider, the Secretary, and a State administering agency for the operation of a PACE program by the provider under such sections.

(5) PACE PROGRAM ELIGIBLE INDIVIDUAL DEFINED. — For purposes of this section, the term "PACE program eligible individual" means, with respect to a PACE program, an individual who —

(A) is 55 years of age or older;

(B) subject to subsection (c)(4), is determined under subsection (c) to require the level of care required under the State Medicaid plan for coverage of nursing facility services;

(C) resides in the service area of the PACE program; and

(D) meets such other eligibility conditions as may be imposed under the PACE program agreement for the program under subsection (e)(2)(A)(ii).

(6) PACE PROTOCOL. — For purposes of this section, the term "PACE protocol" means the Protocol for the Program of All-inclusive Care for the Elderly (PACE), as published by On Lok, Inc., as of April 14, 1995, or any successor protocol that may be agreed upon between the Secretary and On Lok, Inc.

(7) PACE DEMONSTRATION WAIVER PROGRAM DEFINED. — For purposes of this section, the term "PACE demonstration waiver program" means a demonstration pro-

gram under either of the following sections (as in effect before the date of their repeal):

(A) Section 603(c) of the Social Security Amendments of 1983 (Public Law 98–21), as extended by section 9220 of the Consolidated Omnibus Budget Reconciliation Act of 1985 (Public Law 99–272).

(B) Section 9412(b) of the Omnibus Budget Reconciliation Act of 1986 (Public Law 99–509).

(8) STATE ADMINISTERING AGENCY DEFINED. — For purposes of this section, the term "State administering agency" means, with respect to the operation of a PACE program in a State, the agency of that State (which may be the single agency responsible for administration of the State plan under this title in the State) responsible for administering PACE program agreements under this section and section 1894 in the State.

(9) TRIAL PERIOD DEFINED. —

(A) IN GENERAL. — For purposes of this section, the term "trial period" means, with respect to a PACE program operated by a PACE provider under a PACE program agreement, the first 3 contract years under such agreement with respect to such program.

(B) TREATMENT OF ENTITIES PREVIOUSLY OPERATING PACE DEMONSTRATION WAIVER PROGRAMS. — Each contract year (including a year occurring before the effective date of this section) during which an entity has operated a PACE demonstration waiver program shall be counted under subparagraph (A) as a contract year during which the entity operated a PACE program as a PACE provider under a PACE program agreement.

(10) REGULATIONS. — For purposes of this section, the term "regulations" refers to interim final or final regulations promulgated under subsection (f) to carry out this section and section 1894.

Section 1934(b)(1) establishes the scope of benefits for a PACE program. It provides:

SCOPE OF BENEFITS; BENEFICIARY SAFEGUARDS. —

(1) IN GENERAL. — Under a PACE program agreement, a PACE provider shall —

(A) provide to PACE program eligible individuals, regardless of source of payment and directly or under contracts with other entities, at a minimum —

(i) all items and services covered under title XVIII (for individuals enrolled under section 1894), and all items and services covered under this title, but without any limitation or condition as to amount, duration, or scope and without application of deductibles, copayments, coinsurance, or other cost-sharing that would otherwise apply under such title or this title, respectively; and

(ii) all additional items and services specified in regulations, based upon those required under the PACE protocol;

(B) provide such enrollees access to necessary covered items and services 24 hours per day, every day of the year;

(C) provide services to such enrollees through a comprehensive, multidisciplinary health and social services delivery system which integrates acute and long-term care services pursuant to regulations; and

(D) specify the covered items and services that will not be provided directly by the entity, and to arrange for delivery of those items and services through contracts meeting the requirements of regulations.

Section 1934(b)(2) establishes quality assurance requirements for PACE programs. It provides:

QUALITY ASSURANCE; PATIENT SAFEGUARDS. — The PACE program agreement shall require the PACE provider to have in effect at a minimum —

(A) a written plan of quality assurance and improvement, and procedures implementing such plan, in accordance with regulations, and

(B) written safeguards of the rights of enrolled participants (including a patient bill of rights and procedures for grievances and appeals) in accordance with regulations and with other requirements of this title and Federal and State law designed for the protection of patients.

With regard to eligibility to enroll in a PACE program, section 1934(c) provides:

ELIGIBILITY DETERMINATIONS.—

(1) IN GENERAL. —The determination of—

(A) whether an individual is a PACE program eligible individual shall be made under and in accordance with the PACE program agreement, and

(B) who is entitled to medical assistance under this title shall be made (or who is not so entitled, may be made) by the State administering agency.

(2) CONDITION. —An individual is not a PACE program eligible individual (with respect to payment under this section) unless the individual's health status has been determined by the Secretary or the State administering agency, in accordance with regulations, to be comparable to the health status of individuals who have participated in the PACE demonstration waiver programs. Such determination shall be based upon information on health status and related indicators (such as medical diagnoses and measures of activities of daily living, instrumental activities of daily living, and cognitive impairment) that are part of a uniform minimum data set collected by PACE providers on potential eligible individuals.

(3) ANNUAL ELIGIBILITY RECERTIFICATIONS.—

(A) IN GENERAL.—Subject to subparagraph (B), the determination described in subsection (a)(5)(B) for an individual shall be reevaluated at least annually.

(B) EXCEPTION. —The requirement of annual reevaluation under subparagraph (A) may be waived during a period in accordance with regulations in those cases in which the State administering agency determines that there is no reasonable expectation of improvement or significant change in an individual's condition during the period because of the severity of chronic condition, or degree of impairment of functional capacity of the individual involved.

(4) CONTINUATION OF ELIGIBILITY.—An individual who is a PACE program eligible individual may be deemed to continue to be such an individual notwithstanding a determination that the individual no longer meets the requirement of

subsection (a)(5)(B) if, in accordance with regulations, in the absence of continued coverage under a PACE program the individual reasonably would be expected to meet such requirement within the succeeding 6-month period.

(5) ENROLLMENT; DISENROLLMENT. —

(A) VOLUNTARY DISENROLLMENT AT ANY TIME. — The enrollment and disenrollment of PACE program eligible individuals in a PACE program shall be pursuant to regulations and the PACE program agreement and shall permit enrollees to voluntarily disenroll without cause at any time.

(B) LIMITATIONS ON DISENROLLMENT. —

(i) IN GENERAL. — Regulations promulgated by the Secretary under this section and section 1894, and the PACE program agreement, shall provide that the PACE program may not disenroll a PACE program eligible individual except —

(I) for nonpayment of premiums (if applicable) on a timely basis; or

(II) for engaging in disruptive or threatening behavior, as defined in such regulations (developed in close consultation with State administering agencies).

(ii) NO DISENROLLMENT FOR NONCOMPLIANT BEHAVIOR. — Except as allowed under regulations promulgated to carry out clause (i)(II), a PACE program may not disenroll a PACE program eligible individual on the ground that the individual has engaged in noncompliant behavior if such behavior is related to a mental or physical condition of the individual. For purposes of the preceding sentence, the term "noncompliant behavior" includes repeated noncompliance with medical advice and repeated failure to appear for appointments.

(iii) TIMELY REVIEW OF PROPOSED NONVOLUNTARY DISENROLLMENT. — A proposed disenrollment, other than a voluntary disenrollment, shall be subject to timely review and final determination by the Secretary or by the State administering agency (as applicable), prior to the proposed disenrollment becoming effective.

The capitation basis for payment of PACE providers is set forth in section 1934(d),which provides:

PAYMENTS TO PACE PROVIDERS ON A CAPITATED BASIS. —

(1) IN GENERAL. — In the case of a PACE provider with a PACE program agreement under this section, except as provided in this subsection or by regulations, the State shall make prospective monthly payments of a capitation amount for each PACE program eligible individual enrolled under the agreement under this section.

(2) CAPITATION AMOUNT. — The capitation amount to be applied under this subsection for a provider for a contract year shall be an amount specified in the PACE program agreement for the year. Such amount shall be an amount, specified under the PACE agreement, which is less than the amount that would otherwise have been made under the State plan if the individuals were not so enrolled and shall be adjusted to take into account the comparative frailty of PACE enrollees and such other factors as the Secretary determines to be appropriate. The payment under this section shall be in addition to any payment made under section 1894 for individuals who are enrolled in a PACE program under such section.

Basic requirements for a PACE program agreement are set forth in section 1934(e). That section provides:

PACE PROGRAM AGREEMENT. —

(1) REQUIREMENT. —

(A) IN GENERAL. — The Secretary, in close cooperation with the State administering agency, shall establish procedures for entering into, extending, and terminating PACE program agreements for the operation of PACE programs by entities that meet the requirements for a PACE provider under this section, section 1894, and regulations.

(B) NUMERICAL LIMITATION. —

(i) IN GENERAL. — The Secretary shall not permit the number of PACE providers with which agreements are in effect under this section or under section 9412(b) of the Omnibus Budget Reconciliation Act of 1986 to exceed —

(I) 40 as of the date of the enactment of this section, or

(II) as of each succeeding anniversary of such date, the numerical limitation under this subparagraph for the preceding year plus 20.

Subclause (II) shall apply without regard to the actual number of agreements in effect as of a previous anniversary date.

(ii) TREATMENT OF CERTAIN PRIVATE, FOR-PROFIT PROVIDERS. — The numerical limitation in clause (i) shall not apply to a PACE provider that —

(I) is operating under a demonstration project waiver under subsection (h), or

(II) was operating under such a waiver and subsequently qualifies for PACE provider status pursuant to subsection (a)(3)(B)(ii).

(2) SERVICE AREA AND ELIGIBILITY. —

(A) IN GENERAL. — A PACE program agreement for a PACE program —

(i) shall designate the service area of the program;

(ii) may provide additional requirements for individuals to qualify as PACE program eligible individuals with respect to the program;

(iii) shall be effective for a contract year, but may be extended for additional contract years in the absence of a notice by a party to terminate, and is subject to termination by the Secretary and the State administering agency at any time for cause (as provided under the agreement);

(iv) shall require a PACE provider to meet all applicable State and local laws and requirements; and

(v) shall contain such additional terms and conditions as the parties may agree to, so long as such terms and conditions are consistent with this section and regulations.

(B) SERVICE AREA OVERLAP. — In designating a service area under a PACE program agreement under subparagraph (A)(i), the Secretary (in consultation with the State administering agency) may exclude from designation an area that is already covered under another PACE program agreement, in order to avoid unnecessary duplication of services and avoid impairing the financial and service viability of an existing program.

(3) DATA COLLECTION; DEVELOPMENT OF OUTCOME MEASURES. —

(A) DATA COLLECTION. —

(i) IN GENERAL. — Under a PACE program agreement, the PACE provider shall —

(I) collect data;

(II) maintain, and afford the Secretary and the State administering agency access to, the records relating to the program, including pertinent financial, medical, and personnel records; and

(III) submit to the Secretary and the State administering agency such reports as the Secretary finds (in consultation with State administering agencies) necessary to monitor the operation, cost, and effectiveness of the PACE program.

(ii) REQUIREMENTS DURING TRIAL PERIOD. — During the first 3 years of operation of a PACE program (either under this section or under a PACE demonstration waiver program), the PACE provider shall provide such additional data as the Secretary specifies in regulations in order to perform the oversight required under paragraph (4)(A).

(B) DEVELOPMENT OF OUTCOME MEASURES. — Under a PACE program agreement, the PACE provider, the Secretary, and the State administering agency shall jointly cooperate in the development and implementation of health status and quality of life outcome measures with respect to PACE program eligible individuals.

(4) OVERSIGHT. —

(A) ANNUAL, CLOSE OVERSIGHT DURING TRIAL PERIOD. — During the trial period (as defined in subsection (a)(9)) with respect to a PACE program operated by a PACE provider, the Secretary (in cooperation with the State administering agency) shall conduct a comprehensive annual review of the operation of the PACE program by the provider in order to assure compliance with the requirements of this section and regulations. Such a review shall include —

(i) an onsite visit to the program site;

(ii) comprehensive assessment of a provider's fiscal soundness;

(iii) comprehensive assessment of the provider's capacity to provide all PACE services to all enrolled participants;

(iv) detailed analysis of the entity's substantial compliance with all significant requirements of this section and regulations; and

(v) any other elements the Secretary or the State administering agency considers necessary or appropriate.

(B) CONTINUING OVERSIGHT. — After the trial period, the Secretary (in cooperation with the State administering agency) shall continue to conduct such review of the operation of PACE providers and PACE programs as may be appropriate, taking into account the performance level of a provider and compliance of a provider with all significant requirements of this section and regulations.

(C) DISCLOSURE. — The results of reviews under this paragraph shall be reported promptly to the PACE provider, along with any recommendations for changes to the provider's program, and shall be made available to the public upon request.

Authority to terminate a PACE provider agreement is in section 1934(e)(5), which provides:

TERMINATION OF PACE PROVIDER AGREEMENTS. —

(A) IN GENERAL. — Under regulations —

(i) the Secretary or a State administering agency may terminate a PACE program agreement for cause, and

(ii) a PACE provider may terminate such an agreement after appropriate notice to the Secretary, the State administering agency, and enrollees.

(B) CAUSES FOR TERMINATION. — In accordance with regulations establishing procedures for termination of PACE program agreements, the Secretary or a State administering agency may terminate a PACE program agreement with a PACE provider for, among other reasons, the fact that—

(i) the Secretary or State administering agency determines that—

(I) there are significant deficiencies in the quality of care provided to enrolled participants; or

(II) the provider has failed to comply substantially with conditions for a program or provider under this section or section 1894; and

(ii) the entity has failed to develop and successfully initiate, within 30 days of the date of the receipt of written notice of such a determination, a plan to correct the deficiencies, or has failed to continue implementation of such a plan.

(C) TERMINATION AND TRANSITION PROCEDURES.—An entity whose PACE provider agreement is terminated under this paragraph shall implement the transition procedures required under subsection (a)(2)(C).

Additional oversight and enforcement authority for the Secretary of Health and Human Services and the State administering agency is set forth in section 1934(e)(6), which provides in pertinent part:

SECRETARY'S OVERSIGHT; ENFORCEMENT AUTHORITY.—

(A) IN GENERAL.—Under regulations, if the Secretary determines (after consultation with the State administering agency) that a PACE provider is failing substantially to comply with the requirements of this section and regulations, the Secretary (and the State administering agency) may take any or all of the following actions:

(i) Condition the continuation of the PACE program agreement upon timely execution of a corrective action plan.

(ii) Withhold some or all further payments under the PACE program agreement under this section or section 1894 with respect to PACE program services furnished by such provider until the deficiencies have been corrected.

(iii) Terminate such agreement.

Finally, procedures for taking action to terminate a PACE provider agreement are found in section 1934(e)(7), which provides:

> PROCEDURES FOR TERMINATION OR IMPOSITION OF SANCTIONS. — Under regulations, the provisions of section 1857(h) (or for periods before January 1, 1999, section 1876(i)(9) [42 U.S.C.A. 1395mm]) shall apply to termination and sanctions respecting a PACE program agreement and PACE provider under this subsection in the same manner as they apply to a termination and sanctions with respect to a contract and a Medicare+Choice organization under part C of title XVIII (or for such periods an eligible organization under section 1876).

For periods on or after January 1, 1999, section 1857(h) provides:

> PROCEDURES FOR TERMINATION. —
>
> (1) IN GENERAL. — The Secretary may terminate a contract with a Medicare+Choice organization under this section in accordance with formal investigation and compliance procedures established by the Secretary under which —
>
> (A) the Secretary provides the organization with the reasonable opportunity to develop and implement a corrective action plan to correct the deficiencies that were the basis of the Secretary's determination under subsection (c)(2); and
> (B) the Secretary provides the organization with reasonable notice and opportunity for hearing (including the right to appeal an initial decision) before terminating the contract.
>
> (2) EXCEPTION FOR IMMINENT AND SERIOUS RISK TO HEALTH. — Paragraph (1) shall not apply if the Secretary determines that a delay in termination, resulting from compliance with the procedures specified in such paragraph prior to termination, would pose an imminent and serious risk to the health of individuals enrolled under this part with the organization.

For periods prior to January 1, 1999, section 1876(i)(9) provides:

> The Secretary may terminate a contract with an eligible organization under this section or may impose the intermediate sanctions described in paragraph (6) on the organization

in accordance with formal investigation and compliance procedures established by the Secretary under which —

(A) the Secretary first provides the organization with the reasonable opportunity to develop and implement a corrective action plan to correct the deficiencies that were the basis of the Secretary's determination under paragraph (1) and the organization fails to develop or implement such a plan;

(B) in deciding whether to impose sanctions, the Secretary considers aggravating factors such as whether an organization has a history of deficiencies or has not taken action to correct deficiencies the Secretary has brought to the organization's attention;

(C) there are no unreasonable or unnecessary delays between the finding of a deficiency and the imposition of sanctions; and

(D) the Secretary provides the organization with reasonable notice and opportunity for hearing (including the right to appeal an initial decision) before imposing any sanction or terminating the contract.

For regulatory citations, see Chapter 7

§ 3:28 INTERMEDIATE SANCTIONS FOR MEDICAID PACE PROVIDERS — Section 1934(e)(6)(B) [42 U.S.C.A. 1396u-4(e)(6)(B)]

◆ NOTE: Section 4802(a)(3) of the Balanced Budget Act of 1997, P.L. 105–33, created the Program of All-inclusive Care for the Elderly (PACE), effective August 5, 1997. For a discussion of PACE and Medicare, see section 2:62. For a more complete discussion of requirements applicable to Medicaid PACE providers, including grounds and authority for terminating a PACE provider agreement, see section 2:27.

Summary

Pursuant to section 1934 of the Social Security Act, as amended, 42 U.S.C.A. 1396u-4, a State may elect to provide medical assistance under a Program of All-inclusive Care for the Elderly (PACE). This is in lieu of regular Medicaid benefits. Individuals need not be eligible for Medicare Part A or B to be eligible to enroll with a Medicaid

PACE program; however, a State may limit the number of individuals who may enroll. PACE providers receive payment for the provision of benefits to PACE enrollees based on capitation, in accordance with a mandatory PACE program agreement.

Application of Intermediate Sanctions: Pursuant to section 1934(e)(6)(B), the Secretary of Health and Human Services may provide by regulation for application of intermediate sanctions against a PACE provider.

For periods on or after January 1, 1999, the Secretary may provide for the remedies specified in section 1857(g)(2), or section 1903(m)(5)(B), 42 U.S.C.A. 1396b(m)(5)(B), in the case of violations described in section 1857(g)(1), or section 1903(m)(5)(A), respectively in relation to agreements, enrollees, and requirements under section 1934.

For periods prior to January 1, 1999, the Secretary may provide for remedies described in section 1876(i)(6)(B), 42 U.S.C.A. 1395mm(i)(6)(B), in the case of violations by the provider of the type described in section 1876(i)(6)(A), in relation to agreements, enrollees, and requirements under section 1934.

Remedies in Section 1857(g)(2) for PACE Provider Violations on or after January 1, 1999: By cross-reference from section 1934(e)(6)(B), the Secretary may provide for the application of remedies described in section 1857(g)(2), in the case of violations by the provider of the type described in section 1857(g)(1), or section 1903(m)(5)(A), 42 U.S.C.A. 1396b(m)(5)(A), respectively, in relation to agreements, enrollees, and requirements under section 1934.

Violations described in section 1857(g)(1) include:

1. Failure substantially to provide medically necessary items and services that are required under law or contract to an enrollee, if the failure has adversely affected (or has substantial likelihood of adversely affecting) the individual.
2. Imposing a premium on an enrollee in excess of the amount of the Medicare+Choice monthly basic and supplemental beneficiary premiums permitted under section 1854.
3. Acting illegally to expel or to refuse to re-enroll an individual.
4. Engaging in any practice that would reasonably be expected to have the effect of denying or discouraging enrollment by eligible individuals whose medical condition or history indicates a need for substantial future medical services.

5. Misrepresenting or falsifying information furnished to the Secretary or to an individual or any other entity under Part C.
6. Failure to comply with applicable requirements of section 1852(j)(3), which prohibits interference with medical advice by healthcare practitioners to enrollees, or section 1852(k)(2)(A)(ii), which requires procedures to enforce limits on balance billing under Medicare+Choice by physicians, providers, and suppliers in fee-for-service plans.
7. Employing or contracting with any individual or entity that is excluded from Medicare under section 1128, 42 U.S.C.A. 1320a-7, or section 1128A, 42 U.S.C.A. 1320a-7a, for the provision of health care, utilization review, medical social work, or administrative services; or employing or contracting with any entity for the provision of such services (directly or indirectly) through an excluded individual or entity.

Violations described in section 1903(m)(5)(A) are similar to those in section 1857(g)(1) and 1876(i)(6)(A). See statutory provisions below.

Sanctions described in section 1857(g)(2) include:

1. A civil money penalty not to exceed $25,000 for each violation.
2. A civil money penalty not to exceed $100,000 for each finding of illegally denying or discouraging enrollment.
3. A civil money penalty not to exceed $100,000 for misrepresenting or falsifying information to the Secretary.
4. Double the excess charge for imposing a premium in excess of the amount of the Medicare+Choice monthly basic and supplemental beneficiary premiums permitted. (In this event, the excess premium shall be deducted from the penalty and paid to the enrollee who overpaid.)
5. A civil money penalty of $15,000 for each individual not enrolled as a result of illegally denying or discouraging enrollment.
6. Suspension of enrollment of individuals after the date the Secretary notifies the organization of a violation until the Secretary is satisfied that the basis for finding the violation has been corrected and is not likely to recur.
7. Suspension of payment to the provider for individuals enrolled after the date the Secretary notified the provider of the violation until the Secretary is satisfied that the basis for

finding the violation has been corrected and is not likely to recur.

Remedies in Section 1876(i)(6)(B) for PACE Provider Violations Prior to January 1, 1999: By cross reference from section 1934(e)(6)(B), the Secretary may provide for remedies described in section 1876(i)(6)(B), 42 U.S.C.A. 1395mm(i)(6)(B), in the case of violations described in section 1876(i)(6)(A).

Violations described in section 1876(i)(6)(A) include:

1. Failure to substantially provide medically necessary items and services required under law or contract to an enrollee, if the failure has adversely affected (or has substantial likelihood to adversely affect) the enrollee.
2. Imposition of a premium in excess of the permitted amount.
3. Acting illegally to expel or to refuse to re-enroll an individual.
4. Engaging in any practice that reasonably would be expected to have the effect of denying or discouraging enrollment by eligible individuals whose medical condition or history indicates a need for future medical services.
5. Misrepresenting or falsifying information furnished to the Secretary, or to an individual or any other entity.
6. Failure to comply with requirements of section 1876(g)(A) (which pertains to community rating for premiums) or paragraph 8 (which pertains to prohibited physician incentive plans which directly or indirectly might induce a physician or physician group to reduce or limit medically necessary services to an enrollee).
7. In the case of a risk-sharing contract, employing or contracting with any individual that is excluded from participation under section 1128 or 1128A for the provision of health care, utilization review, medical social work, or administrative services; or employing or contracting with any entity for the provision of such services directly or indirectly through an excluded individual or entity.

Sanctions described in section 1876(i)(6)(B) include:

1. A civil money penalty of not more than $25,000 for each determination that a provider failed to provide medically necessary items and services required by law or contract, if the failure has adversely affected (or has substantial likelihood of adversely affecting an enrollee).

2. A civil money penalty of not more than $100,000 for each determination that a provider engaged in any practice that would reasonably be expected to have the effect of denying or discouraging enrollment by eligible individual whose medical condition or history indicates a need for substantial future medical services.
3. A civil money penalty of $15,000 for each individual not enrolled as a result of engaging in such a practice to discourage enrollment.
4. A civil money penalty of not more than $100,000 for each determination that a provider misrepresented or falsified information furnished to the Secretary.
5. Double damages if a provider imposes a premium on an enrollee in excess of the permitted premium amount. (In this event, the excess premium shall be deducted from the civil money penalty and paid to the enrollee who overpaid.)
6. Suspension of enrollment of individuals until the Secretary is satisfied that the basis for a prohibited action has been corrected and is not likely to recur.
7. Suspension of payment to the provider for individuals enrolled after the Secretary notifies the provider of findings of a violation.

Procedures for Imposition of Intermediate Sanctions: Pursuant to section 1934(e)(7), by regulations, procedural provisions of section 1857(h) are to apply for imposition of intermediate sanctions against a PACE provider for periods on or after January 1, 1999, in the same manner as they apply to Medicare+Choice organization under Medicare Part C. For periods prior to January 1, 1999, procedural provisions in section 1876(i)(9) are to apply in the same manner as they apply to a risk-bearing organization, such as a health maintenance organization of competitive medical plan, eligible under section 1876.

Procedures on or after January 1, 1999: Section 1857(h) calls for notice and a reasonable opportunity for the PACE provider to develop and implement a corrective action plan to correct deficiencies that formed the basis for a termination decision. It also calls for a hearing, and a right to appeal an initial decision, prior to termination of an agreement. No pre-termination hearing or opportunity for implementing a corrective action plan is required, however, if delay in termination would pose an imminent and serious risk to the health of enrollees.

Procedures Prior to January 1, 1999: Section 1876(i)(9) calls for reasonable opportunity to develop and implement a corrective action plan to correct deficiencies that formed the basis for a termination decision. If a corrective action plan is not developed or implemented, then the PACE provider must be given notice and opportunity for a hearing, and the right to appeal an initial decision, prior to termination.

Statutory Provisions

Section 1934(e)(6)(B) of the Social Security Act, as amended, 42 U.S.C.A. 1396u-4(e)(6)(B) authorizes the Secretary of Health and Human Services to provide by regulation for intermediate sanctions for Medicaid PACE providers. That section reads:

> APPLICATION OF INTERMEDIATE SANCTIONS. — Under regulations, the Secretary may provide for the application against a PACE provider of remedies described in section 1857(g)(2) (or, for periods before January 1, 1999, section 1876(i)(6)(B) [42 U.S.C.A. 1395 mm(i)(6)(B)]) or 1903(m)(5)(B) [42 U.S.C.A. 1396b(m)(5)(B)] , in the case of violations by the provider of the type described in section 1857(g)(1) (or 1876(i)(6)(A) for such periods) or 1903(m)(5)(A), respectively (in relation to agreements, enrollees, and requirements under section 1894 [42 U.S.C.A. 1395eee] or this section, respectively).
>
> By cross reference, for violations on or after January 1, 1999, the Secretary may provide remedies specified in section 1857(g)(2), or section 1903(m)(5)(B) in the case of violations described in sections 1857(g)(1) and 1903(m)(5)(A), respectively.

Sections 1857(g)(1) and (2) provide as follows:

> INTERMEDIATE SANCTIONS. —
>
> (1) IN GENERAL. — If the Secretary determines that a Medicare + Choice organization with a contract under this section —
>
> (A) fails substantially to provide medically necessary items and services that are required (under law or under the contract) to be provided to an individual covered under the

contract, if the failure has adversely affected (or has substantial likelihood of adversely affecting) the individual;

(B) imposes premiums on individuals enrolled under this part in excess of the amount of the Medicare+Choice monthly basic and supplemental beneficiary premiums permitted under section 1854;

(C) acts to expel or to refuse to re-enroll an individual in violation of the provisions of this part;

(D) engages in any practice that would reasonably be expected to have the effect of denying or discouraging enrollment (except as permitted by this part) by eligible individuals with the organization whose medical condition or history indicates a need for substantial future medical services;

(E) misrepresents or falsifies information that is furnished—

(i) to the Secretary under this part, or

(ii) to an individual or to any other entity under this part;

(F) fails to comply with the applicable requirements of section 1852(j)(3) [which prohibits interference with medical advice by health care practitioners to enrollees] or 1852(k)(2)(A)(ii) [which requires procedures to enforce limits on balance billing under Medicare+Choice by physicians, providers, and suppliers in fee-for-service plans]; or

(G) employs or contracts with any individual or entity that is excluded from participation under this title under section 1128 [42 U.S.C.A. 1320a-7] or 1128A [42 U.S.C.A. 1320a-7a] for the provision of health care, utilization review, medical social work, or administrative services or employs or contracts with any entity for the provision (directly or indirectly) through such an excluded individual or entity of such services;

the Secretary may provide, in addition to any other remedies authorized by law, for any of the remedies described in paragraph (2).

(2) REMEDIES. —The remedies described in this paragraph are—

(A) civil money penalties of not more than $25,000 for each determination under paragraph (1) or, with respect to a determination under subparagraph (D) or (E)(i) of such paragraph, of not more than $100,000 for each such determination, plus, with respect to a determination under paragraph (1)(B), double the excess amount charged in violation of such paragraph (and the excess amount charged shall be deducted from the penalty and returned to the individual concerned), and plus, with respect to a determination under paragraph (1)(D), $15,000 for each individual not enrolled as a result of the practice involved,

(B) suspension of enrollment of individuals under this part after the date the Secretary notifies the organization of a determination under paragraph (1) and until the Secretary is satisfied that the basis for such determination has been corrected and is not likely to recur, or

(C) suspension of payment to the organization under this part for individuals enrolled after the date the Secretary notifies the organization of a determination under paragraph (1) and until the Secretary is satisfied that the basis for such determination has been corrected and is not likely to recur.

Sections 1903(m)(5)(A) and (B) provide:

(A) If the Secretary determines that an entity with a contract under this subsection —

(i) fails substantially to provide medically necessary items and services that are required (under law or under the contract) to be provided to an individual covered under the contract, if the failure has adversely affected (or has substantial likelihood of adversely affecting) the individual;

(ii) imposes premiums on individuals enrolled under this subsection in excess of the premiums permitted under this title;

(iii) acts to discriminate among individuals in violation of the provision of paragraph (2)(A)(v), including expulsion or refusal to re-enroll an individual or engaging in any practice that would reasonably be expected to have the effect of denying or discouraging enrollment (except as permitted by this subsection) by eligible individuals with the organization whose medical condition or history indicates a need for substantial future medical services;

(iv) misrepresents or falsifies information that is furnished —

(I) to the Secretary or the State under this subsection, or

(II) to an individual or to any other entity under this subsection, or

(v) [applicable to contract years on or after January 1, 1992] fails to comply with the requirements of section 1876(i)(8),

the Secretary may provide, in addition to any other remedies available under law, for any of the remedies described in subparagraph (B).

(B) The remedies described in this subparagraph are —

(i) civil money penalties of not more than $25,000 for each determination under subparagraph (A), or, with respect to a determination under clause (iii) or (iv)(I) of such subparagraph, of not more than $100,000 for each such determination, plus, with respect to a determination under subparagraph (A)(ii), double the excess amount charged in violation of such subparagraph (and the excess amount charged shall be deducted from the penalty and returned to the individual concerned), and plus, with respect to a determination under subparagraph (A)(iii), $15,000 for each individual not enrolled as a result of a practice described in such subparagraph, or

(ii) denial of payment to the State for medical assistance furnished under the contract under this subsection for individuals enrolled after the date the Secretary notifies the organization of a determination under subparagraph (A) and until the Secretary is satisfied that the basis for such determination has been corrected and is not likely to recur.

The provisions of section 1128A (other than subsections (a) and (b)) shall apply to a civil money penalty under clause (i)

> in the same manner as such provisions apply to a penalty or proceeding under section 1128A(a).

By cross-reference, intermediate sanctions for violations prior to January 1, 1999, are governed by sections 1876(i)(6)(A) and (B), which provide:

> (A) If the Secretary determines that an eligible organization with a contract under this section —
>
> (i) fails substantially to provide medically necessary items and services that are required (under law or under the contract) to be provided to an individual covered under the contract, if the failure has adversely affected (or has substantial likelihood of adversely affecting) the individual;
>
> (ii) imposes premiums on individuals enrolled under this section in excess of the premiums permitted;
>
> (iii) acts to expel or to refuse to re-enroll an individual in violation of the provisions of this section;
>
> (iv) engages in any practice that would reasonably be expected to have the effect of denying or discouraging enrollment (except as permitted by this section) by eligible individuals with the organization whose medical condition or history indicates a need for substantial future medical services;
>
> (v) misrepresents or falsifies information that is furnished —
>
> (I) to the Secretary under this section, or
>
> (II) to an individual or to any other entity under this section;
>
> (vi) fails to comply with the requirements of subsection (g)(6)(A) or paragraph (8); or
>
> (vii) in the case of a risk-sharing contract, employs or contracts with any individual or entity that is excluded from participation under this title under section 1128 or 1128A for the provision of health care, utilization review, medical social work, or administrative services or employs or contracts with any entity for the provision

(directly or indirectly) through such an excluded individual or entity of such services;

the Secretary may provide, in addition to any other remedies authorized by law, for any of the remedies described in subparagraph (B).

(B) The remedies described in this subparagraph are —

(i) civil money penalties of not more than $25,000 for each determination under subparagraph (A) or, with respect to a determination under clause (iv) or (v)(I), of not more than $100,000 for each such determination, plus, with respect to a determinationunder subparagraph (A)(ii), double the excess amount charged in violation of such subparagraph (and the excess amount charged shall be deducted from the penalty and returned to the individual concerned), and plus, with respect to a determination under subparagraph (A)(iv), $15,000 for each individual not enrolled as a result of the practice involved,

(ii) suspension of enrollment of individuals under this section after the date the Secretary notifies the organization of a determination under subparagraph (A) and until the Secretary is satisfied that the basis for such determination has been corrected and is not likely to recur, or

(iii) suspension of payment to the organization under this section for individuals enrolled after the date the Secretary notifies the organization of a determination under subparagraph (A) and until the Secretary is satisfied that the basis for such determination has been corrected and is not likely to recur.

Procedures for imposing intermediate sanctions are governed by section 1934(e)(7), which provides:

PROCEDURES FOR TERMINATION OR IMPOSITION OF SANCTIONS. — Under regulations, the provisions of section 1857(h) (or for periods before January 1, 1999, section 1876(i)(9)) shall apply to termination and sanctions respecting a PACE program agreement and PACE provider under this subsection in the same manner as they apply to a termination and sanctions with respect to a contract and a Medicare+Choice organization under part C of title XVIII (or for such periods an eligible organization under section 1876).

For violations on or after January 1, 1999, section 1857(h), applicable by cross-reference, provides:

> (1) IN GENERAL. — The Secretary may terminate a contract with a Medicare+Choice organization under this section in accordance with formal investigation and compliance procedures established by the Secretary under which —
>
> (A) the Secretary provides the organization with the reasonable opportunity to develop and implement a corrective action plan to correct the deficiencies that were the basis of the Secretary's determination under subsection (c)(2); and
>
> (B) the Secretary provides the organization with reasonable notice and opportunity for hearing (including the right to appeal an initial decision) before terminating the contract.
>
> (2) EXCEPTION FOR IMMINENT AND SERIOUS RISK TO HEALTH. — Paragraph (1) shall not apply if the Secretary determines that a delay in termination, resulting from compliance with the procedures specified in such paragraph prior to termination, would pose an imminent and serious risk to the health of individuals enrolled under this part with the organization.

For violations prior to January 1, 1999, section 1876(i)(9), applicable by cross-reference, provides:

> The Secretary may terminate a contract with an eligible organization under this section or may impose the intermediate sanctions described in paragraph (6) on the organization in accordance with formal investigation and compliance procedures established by the Secretary under which —
>
> (A) the Secretary first provides the organization with the reasonable opportunity to develop and implement a corrective action plan to correct the deficiencies that were the basis of the Secretary's determination under paragraph (1) and the organization fails to develop or implement such a plan;
>
> (B) in deciding whether to impose sanctions, the Secretary considers aggravating factors such as whether an organization has a history of deficiencies or has not taken action to correct deficiencies the Secretary has brought to the organization's attention;

(C) there are no unreasonable or unnecessary delays between the finding of a deficiency and the imposition of sanctions; and

(D) the Secretary provides the organization with reasonable notice and opportunity for hearing (including the right to appeal an initial decision) before imposing any sanction or terminating the contract.

For regulatory citations, see Chapter 7

Chapter 4

SANCTIONS IN TITLE XI OF THE SOCIAL SECURITY ACT

§ 4:1 DISCLOSURE OF INFORMATION IN THE POSSESSION OF THE SECRETARY OF HEALTH AND HUMAN SERVICES — Section 1106 [42 U.S.C.A. 1306]

Summary

Section 1106, 42 U.S.C.A. 1306, details the obligations and authority of the Secretary of Health and Human Services for disclosure and nondisclosure of information obtained in the course of administering the Social Security Act. These provisions apply to the Secretary and to all officers and employees of the Department of Health and Human Services. Hence, they apply to the subsidiary Health Care Financing Administration, which administers the Medicare and Medicaid programs. They also apply to fiscal intermediaries (see section 1816, 42 U.S.C.A. 1395h) and carriers (see section 1842, 42 U.S.C.A. 1395u), the independent contractors which process Medicare claims under Part A (hospital insurance benefits) and Part B (supplementary medical insurance benefits).

◆ NOTE: Section 1106 was amended by the Social Security Independence and Program Improvements Act of 1994, P.L. 103-296, generally effective March 31, 1995. That law established the Social Security Administration as an independent agency, removing it from its former subsidiary status as part of the Department of Health and Human Services. Only duties of the Secretary under section 1106 are dealt with here.

Pursuant to section 1106(a), no disclosure of any return filed with the Commissioner of Internal Revenue, or of any file, record, report, or other paper, or any information obtained by the Secretary, or by any officer or employee of the Department of Health and Human Services in the course of discharging duties of the Secretary under the Social Security Act shall be made except as the Secretary may by regulations prescribe and except as otherwise provided by Federal law. The same applies to any file, record, report, or other paper, or information obtained at any time by any person from the Secretary or from any officer or employee of the Department. Any person who violates any provision of section 1106 is guilty of a felony, and upon conviction thereof is subject to a fine not to exceed $10,000, or to imprisonment not exceeding 5 years, or both.

Prior to amendment by section 313(a)(2) of the Social Security Independence and Program Improvements Act, such violations were misdemeanors punishable by a fine not to exceed $1,000, or by imprisonment not exceeding one year, or both. This change was effective August 15, 1994.

◆ NOTE: Section 1106 should be read in conjunction with the Freedom of Information Act, 5 U.S.C.A. 552(b), and the Privacy Act of 1974, as amended, 5 U.S.C.A. 552a(a), and other statutes pertaining to access to public information and privacy rights of citizens. See 42 CFR Part 401.

Section 1106(b) authorizes the Secretary to charge for the release of accessible information and related services, either in advance of release or by reimbursement. But such charges may not exceed the cost of furnishing the information or services. Those provisions do not apply, however, to requests for the use of Federal records to locate parents which are made pursuant to title IV-D of the Social Security Act, 42 U.S.C.A. 451 et seq., which pertains to child support enforcement and related efforts to establish paternity. Such requests are governed by provisions of that title instead.

In addition, notwithstanding the Freedom of Information Act and the Privacy Act, section 1106(c) authorizes the Secretary to charge the full cost for providing information requested with respect to administration of employee benefit plans as defined under section 3 of the Employee Retirement Income Security Act of 1974 (ERISA), 29 U.S.C.A. 1002, and for providing information requested for any other purpose not directly related to administration of the program or programs for which the Secretary is responsible under the Social Security Act.

Section 1106(d) obliges the Secretary to make available for public inspection and to make available to State Medicaid agencies, in readily accessible form and fashion, the following official reports dealing with the operation of Medicare and Medicaid:

1. contractor performance reviews and other formal evaluations of the performance of carriers, intermediaries, and State agencies, including reports of follow-up reviews;
2. comparative evaluations of the performance of such contractors; and
3. program validation survey reports and other formal evaluations of the performance of providers of services.

Thus, if a health care provider's performance has been evaluated by the Secretary, the public and State Medicaid agencies can obtain copies of the evaluation. Nevertheless, such reports must not identify individual patients, individual health care practitioners, or other individuals.

Section 1106(e) restricts section 1106(d), however, by providing that such reports may not be made public by the Secretary or by a State Medicaid agency until the contractor or provider of services whose performance has been evaluated has had a reasonable opportunity (not exceeding 60 days) to review such report and to offer comments, pertinent parts of which may be incorporated in the public report. Moreover, the Secretary may not be required to include in such reports information with respect to any deficiency or improper practice or procedures which the Secretary knows had been corrected within 60 days of the date first brought to the attention of the contractor or provider of services.

Statutory Provisions

Section 1106, as amended by the Social Security Independence and Program Improvements Act of 1994, P.L. 103-296, 42 U.S.C.A. 1306, provides:

> (a) (1) No disclosure of any return or portion of a return (including information returns and other written statements) filed with the Commissioner of Internal Revenue under title VIII of the Social Security Act or under subchapter E of chapter 1 or subchapter A of chapter 9 of the Internal Revenue Code [P.L. 76-1. Should refer, instead, to P.L. 83-591, the Internal Revenue Code of 1954, Subtitles A and C.], or under regulations made under authority thereof, which has been transmitted to the head of the applicable agency by the Commissioner of Internal Revenue, or of any file, record, report, or other paper, or any information, obtained at any time by the head of the applicable agency or by any officer or employee of the applicable agency in the course of discharging the duties of the head of the applicable agency under this Act, and no disclosure of any such file, record, report, or other paper, or information, obtained at any time by any person from the head of the applicable agency or from any officer or employee of the applicable agency, shall be made except as the head of the applicable agency may by regulations prescribe and except as

otherwise provided by Federal law. Any person who shall violate any provision of this section shall be deemed guilty of a felony and, upon conviction thereof, shall be punished by a fine not exceeding $10,000 for each occurrence of a violation, or by imprisonment not exceeding 5 years, or both.

(2) For purposes of this subsection and subsection (b), the term "applicable agency" means —

(A) the Social Security Administration, with respect to matter transmitted to or obtained by such Administration or matter disclosed by such Administration, or

(B) the Department of Health and Human Services, with respect to matter transmitted to or obtained by such Department or matter disclosed by such Department.

(b) Requests for information, disclosure of which is authorized by regulations prescribed pursuant to subsection (a) of this section, and requests for services, may, subject to such limitations as may be prescribed by the head of the applicable agency to avoid undue interference with his functions under this Act, be complied with if the agency, person, or organization making the request agrees to pay for the information or services requested in such amount, if any (not exceeding the cost of furnishing the information or services), as may be determined by the head of the applicable agency. Payments for information or services furnished pursuant to this section shall be made in advance or by way of reimbursement, as may be requested by the head of the applicable agency, and shall be deposited in the Treasury as a special deposit to be used to reimburse the appropriations (including authorizations to make expenditures from the Federal Old–Age and Survivors Insurance Trust Fund, the Federal Disability Insurance Trust Fund, the Federal Hospital Insurance Trust Fund, and the Federal Supplementary Medical Insurance Trust Fund) for the unit or units of the applicable agency which furnished the information or services. Notwithstanding the preceding provisions of this subsection, requests for information made pursuant to the provisions of part D of title IV of this Act for the purpose of using Federal records for locating parents shall be complied with and the cost incurred in providing such information shall be paid for as provided in such part D of title IV.

(c) Notwithstanding sections 552 and 552a of title 5, United States Code, [the Freedom of Information Act and the Privacy Act of 1974, as amended, respectively], or any other provision of law, whenever the Commissioner of Social Security or the Secretary determines that a request for information is made in order to assist a party in interest (as defined in section 3 of the Employee Retirement Income Security Act of 1974 (29 U.S.C.A. 1002)) with respect to the administration of an employee benefit plan (as so defined), or is made for any other purpose not directly related to the administration of the program or programs under this act to which such information relates, such Commissioner or Secretary may require the requester to pay the full cost, as determined by such Commissioner or Secretary, of providing such information.

(d) Notwithstanding any other provision of this section, in any case in which—

(1) information regarding whether an individual is shown on the records of the Commissioner of Social Security as being alive or deceased is requested from the Commissioner for purposes of epidemiological or similar research which the Commissioner in consultation with the Secretary of Health and Human Services finds may reasonably be expected to contribute to a national health interest, and

(2) the requester agrees to reimburse the Commissioner for providing such information and to comply with limitations on safeguarding and rerelease or redisclosure of such information as may be specified by the Commissioner,

the Commissioner shall comply with such request, except to the extent that compliance with such request would constitute a violation of the terms of any contract entered into under section 205(r).

(e) Notwithstanding any other provision of this section the Commissioner of Social Security [sic Secretary?] shall make available to each State agency operating a program under title XIX and shall, subject to the limitations contained in subsection (e), make available for public inspection in readily accessible form and fashion, the following official reports (not including, however, references to any internal tolerance rules and practices that may be contained therein, internal working papers or other informal memoranda) dealing with the operation of the health programs established by titles XVIII and XIX —

(1) individual contractor performance reviews and other formal evaluations of the performance of carriers, intermediaries, and State agencies, including the reports of follow-up reviews;

(2) comparative evaluations of the performance of such contractors, including comparisons of either overall performance or of any particular aspect of contractor operation; and

(3) program validation survey reports and other formal evaluations of the performance of providers of services, including the reports of follow-up review, except that such reports shall not identify individual patients, individual health care practitioners, or other individuals.

(f) No report described in subsection (e) shall be made public by the Secretary or the State title XIX agency until the contractor or provider of services whose performance is being evaluated has had a reasonable opportunity (not exceeding 60 days) to review such report and to offer comments pertinent parts of which may be incorporated in the public report; nor shall the Secretary be required to include in any such report information with respect to any deficiency (or improper practice or procedures) which is known by the Secretary to have been fully corrected, within 60 days of the date such deficiency was first brought to the attention of such contractor or provider of services, as the case may be.

NOTE: Sections 108(b)(2) of the Social Security Independence and Program Improvements Act of 1994, P.L. 103-296, inserted "(1)" after "(a)"; removed "Department of Health and Human Services" each place it appeared and substituted "applicable agency"; removed "Secretary" each place it appeared and substituted "head of the applicable agency"; and added new paragraph (2) in subsection (a).

Section 108(b)(3) removed "Secretary" each place it appeared and substituted "head of the applicable agency"; removed "Department of Health and Human Services", and substituted "applicable agency" in subsection (b).

Section 108(b)(4) removed "Secretary" the first place it appeared and substituted "the Commissioner of Social Security or the Secretary"; and removed "the Secretary" each subsequent place it appeared and substituted "such Commissioner or Secretary" in subsection (c).

Section 108(b)(5) removed "Secretary" the first place it appeared and substituted "Commissioner of Social Security"; removed "Secretary" the second place it appeared and substituted "Commissioner"; removed "Secretary" the third place it appeared and substituted "Commissioner in consultation with the Secretary of Health Human Services"; and removed "Secretary" each subsequent place it appeared and substituted "Commissioner" in subsection (d), which was added by section 311 of the Act.

The foregoing changes were effective March 31, 1995. They accommodate establishment of the Social Security Administration as an agency independent from the Department of Health and Human Services.

Section 311(a) of the Social Security Independence and Program Improvements Act of 1994 redesignated subsections (d) and (e) as subsections (e) and (f) respectively; substituted "subsection (e)" for "subsection (d)" in redesignated subsection (f); and added new subsection (d).

Section 313(a)(2) substituted "felony" for "misdemeanor"; substituted $10,000 for each occurrence of a violation" for "$1,000"; and substituted "5 years" for "one year" in subsection (a).

These changes were effective August 15, 1994. Prior to the foregoing changes section 1106 read:

> (a) No disclosure of any return or portion of a return (including information returns and other written statements) filed with the Commissioner of Internal Revenue under title VIII of the Social Security Act or under subchapter E of chapter 1 or subchapter A of chapter 9 of the Internal Revenue Code [P.L. 76-1. Should refer, instead, to P.L. 83-591, the Internal Revenue Code of 1954, Subtitles A and C.], or under regulations made under authority thereof, which has been transmitted to the Secretary by the Commissioner of Internal Revenue, or of any file, record, report, or other paper, or any information, obtained at any time by the Secretary or by any officer or employee of the Department of Health and Human Services in the course of discharging the duties of the Secretary under this Act, and no disclosure of any such file, record, report, or other paper, or information, obtained at any time by any person from the Secretary or from any officer or employee of the Department of Health and Human Services, shall be made except as the Secretary may by regulations pre-

scribe and except as otherwise provided by Federal law. Any person who shall violate any provision of this section shall be deemed guilty of a misdemeanor and, upon conviction thereof, shall be punished by a fine not exceeding $1,000, or by imprisonment not exceeding one year, or both.

(b) Requests for information, disclosure of which is authorized by regulations prescribed pursuant to subsection (a) of this section, and requests for services, may, subject to such limitations as may be prescribed by the Secretary to avoid undue interference with his functions under this Act, be complied with if the agency, person, or organization making the request agrees to pay for the information or services requested in such amount, if any (not exceeding the cost of furnishing the information or services), as may be determined by the Secretary. Payments for information or services furnished pursuant to this section shall be made in advance or by way of reimbursement, as may be requested by the Secretary, and shall be deposited in the Treasury as a special deposit to be used to reimburse the appropriations (including authorizations to make expenditures from the Federal Old-Age and Survivors Insurance Trust Fund, the Federal Disability Insurance Trust Fund, the Federal Hospital Insurance Trust Fund, and the Federal Supplementary Medical Insurance Trust Fund) for the unit or units of the Department of Health and Human Services which furnished the information or services. Notwithstanding the preceding provisions of this subsection, requests for information made pursuant to the provisions of part D of title IV of this Act for the purpose of using Federal records for locating parents shall be complied with and the cost incurred in providing such information shall be paid for as provided in such part D of title IV.

(c) Notwithstanding sections 552 and 552a of title 5, United States Code, [the Freedom of Information Act and the Privacy Act of 1974, as amended, respectively], or any other provision of law, whenever the Secretary determines that a request for information is made in order to assist a party in interest (as defined in section 3 of the Employee Retirement Income Security Act of 1974 (29 U.S.C.A. 1002)) with respect to the administration of an employee benefit plan (as so defined), or is made for any other purpose not directly related to the administration of the program or programs under this act to which such information relates, the Secretary may require the requester to pay the full cost, as determined by the Secretary, of providing such information.

(d) Notwithstanding any other provision of this section the Secretary shall make available to each State agency operating a program under title XIX and shall, subject to the limitations contained in subsection (e), make available for public inspection in readily accessible form and fashion, the following official reports (not including, however, references to any internal tolerance rules and practices that may be contained therein, internal working papers or other informal memoranda) dealing with the operation of the health programs established by titles XVIII and XIX—

(1) individual contractor performance reviews and other formal evaluations of the performance of carriers, intermediaries, and State agencies, including the reports of follow-up reviews;

(2) comparative evaluations of the performance of such contractors, including comparisons of either overall performance or of any particular aspect of contractor operation; and

(3) program validation survey reports and other formal evaluations of the performance of providers of services, including the reports of follow-up review, except that such reports shall not identify individual patients, individual health care practitioners, or other individuals.

(e) No report described in subsection (d) shall be made public by the Secretary or the State title XIX agency until the contractor or provider of services whose performance is being evaluated has had a reasonable opportunity (not exceeding 60 days) to review such report and to offer comments pertinent parts of which may be incorporated in the public report; nor shall the Secretary be required to include in any such report information with respect to any deficiency (or improper practice or procedures) which is known by the Secretary to have been fully corrected, within 60 days of the date such deficiency was first brought to the attention of such contractor or provider of services, as the case may be.

For regulatory citations, see Chapter 8

§ 4:2 FALSE REPRESENTATIONS ABOUT REQUIREMENTS OF THE SOCIAL SECURITY ACT — Section 1107(a) [42 U.S.C.A. 1307]

Summary

Pursuant to section 1107(a), 42 U.S.C.A. 1307(a), anyone who, intending to defraud, makes or causes to be made any false representation concerning the requirements of the Social Security Act, or related provisions of the Internal Revenue Code, or of rules and regulations promulgated thereunder, knowing the representation is false, is guilty of a misdemeanor.

By definition, this sanction applies to the Medicare and Medicaid programs, which are Titles XVIII and XIX of the Social Security Act. By way of example, it might apply to someone who tries to sell a health insurance policy to cover expenses not covered by Medicare, like the Medicare deductible or Medicare co-insurance amounts, if that person made a false representation about the requirements of Title XVIII, knowing the representation to be false and intending to defraud the prospective purchaser.

Anyone convicted under section 1107(a) is subject to a fine not to exceed $1,000, or by imprisonment not to exceed one year, or both.

Statutory Provisions

Section 1107(a), 42 U.S.C.A. 1307(a), provides:

> Whoever, with the intent to defraud any person, shall make or cause to be made any false representation concerning the requirements of this Act, of chapter 2, 21, or 23 of the Internal Revenue Code of 1954 [P.L. 83-591], or of any provision of subtitle F of such Code which corresponds (within the meaning of section 7852(b) of such Code) to a provision contained in subchapter E of chapter 9 of the Internal Revenue Code of 1939 [P.L. 76-1] , or of any rules or regulations issued thereunder, knowing such representations to be false, shall be deemed guilty of a misdemeanor, and, upon conviction thereof, shall be punished by a fine not exceeding $1,000, or by imprisonment not exceeding one year, or both.

For regulatory citations, see Chapter 8

§ 4:3 FALSE REPRESENTATIONS TO ELICIT INFORMATION FROM THE SECRETARY OF HEALTH AND HUMAN SERVICES — Section 1107(b) [42 U.S.C.A. 1307(b)]

Summary

Section 1107(b)(1) of the Social Security Act, as amended by the Social Security Independence and Program Improvements Act of 1994, P.L. 103-296, 42 U.S.C.A. 1307(b)(1), provides that anyone who tries to elicit information about the Social Security account number, date of birth, employment, wages, or benefits of any individual from the Commissioner of Social Security or the Secretary of Health and Human Services by falsely representing to be that individual, or the individual's wife, husband, widow, widower, divorced wife, divorced husband, surviving divorced wife, surviving divorced husband, surviving divorced mother, surviving divorced father, child, or parent of such individual, or to be the duly authorized agent of such individual, or of the wife, husband, widow, widower, divorced wife, divorced husband, surviving divorced wife, surviving divorced husband, surviving divorced mother, surviving divorced father, child, or parent of such individual is guilty of a felony. Punishment may be a fine not to exceed $10,000 for each violation that occurs, or imprisonment not to exceed five years, or both.

Pursuant to section 1107(b)(2), the same applies to anyone who tries to elicit such information by falsely representing to any person that he is an employee or agent of the United States.

Section 313(b) of the Social Security Independence and Program Improvements Act of 1994 expanded section 1107(b) to cover attempts to elicit a person's Social Security account number. It also made violation a felony instead of a misdemeanor, increased the fine from $1,000, and increased the period of imprisonment from not to exceed one year. These changes apply to violations on or after August 15, 1994.

For the most part such fraudulent efforts have occurred with respect to social security retirement, survivor, and disability benefits, for example, by one person trying to discover the financial resources of another during contested divorce proceedings. Conceivably, however, health care providers or suppliers might make similar fraudulent efforts to discover an individual's entitlement to Medicare or Medicaid benefits.

Statutory Provisions

Section 1107(b)(1), as amended by the Social Security Independence and Program Improvements Act of 1994, P.L. 103-296, 42 U.S.C.A. 1307(b)(1), provides in pertinent part:

> Whoever, with the intent to elicit information as to the social security account number, date of birth, employment, wages, or benefits of any individual (1) falsely represents to the Commissioner of Social Security or the Secretary of Health and Human Services that he is such individual, or the wife, husband, widow, widower, divorced wife, divorced husband, surviving divorced wife, surviving divorced husband, surviving divorced mother, surviving divorced father, child, or parent of such individual, or the duly authorized agent of such individual, or of the wife, husband, widow, widower, divorced wife, divorced husband, surviving divorced wife, surviving divorced husband, surviving divorced mother, surviving divorced father, child, or parent of such individual, or (2) falsely represents to any person that he is an employee or agent of the United States, shall be deemed guilty of a felony, and, upon conviction thereof, shall be punished by a fine not exceeding $10,000 for each occurrence of a violation, or by imprisonment not exceeding five years, or both.

◆ NOTE: Effective March 31, 1995, section 108(b)(6) of the Social Security Independence and Program Improvements Act of 1994 substituted "the Commissioner of Social Security or the Secretary" for "the Secretary of Health and Human Services". Effective August 15, 1994, section 313(b) of that Act inserted "social security account number" prior to "date of birth"; substituted "felony" for "misdemeanor"; deleted "$1,000" and substituted "$10,000 for each occurrence of a violation"; and substituted "5 years" for "one year".

For regulatory citations, see Chapter 8

§ 4:4 FAILURE TO COMPLY WITH STATE HEALTH PLANNING REQUIREMENTS — Section 1122 [42 U.S.C.A. 1320a-1]

Summary

Pursuant to section 1122(a), 42 U.S.C.A. 1320a-1(a), Medicare and Medicaid funds are not to be used to support certain unnecessary capital expenditures made by or on behalf of health care facilities which are reimbursed under either program. On the other hand, "to the extent possible" Medicare and Medicaid funds are to be used to support planning activities with respect to health services and facilities in the various States.

Section 1122(b) provides that the Secretary of Health and Human Services, after consultation with the Governor (or other chief executive officer) of a State, and with appropriate local public officials, shall make a health planning agreement with any State able and willing to do so. Pursuant thereto, a designated State planning agency will make findings and recommendations, within the scope of its responsibilities, with respect to capital expenditures proposed by or on behalf of any health care facility in such State. Then it must submit those findings and recommendations to the Secretary, together with any supporting materials the Secretary finds necessary. That State planning agency must be one established pursuant to sections 314(a) and 604(a) of the Public Health Service Act, P.L. 78-410, and it must have a governing body or advisory board at least half of whose members represent consumer interests. (Regarding grants and services to States for comprehensive health planning, see 42 U.S.C.A. 246.)

In addition, the State planning agency must receive findings and recommendations with respect to capital expenditures proposed by or on behalf of health care facilities from other agencies in such State within the scope of their respective responsibilities. That includes any agency involved in health planning which is established pursuant to sections 314(a) and 604(a) of the Public Health Service Act, any public or nonprofit private agency or organization responsible for the comprehensive regional, metropolitan area, or other local area plan or plans referred to in section 314(b) of the Public Health Service Act which covers the area where the health care facility proposing the capital expenditure is located, or if there is no such agency, such other public or nonprofit private agency or organization, if any, which performs similar functions. Then the State planning agency must submit those findings and recommendations to the Secretary, together with any supporting materials the Secretary finds necessary.

Finally, the State planning agency must establish and maintain procedures under which a person proposing any affected capital expenditure may appeal a recommendation by the designated agency. That appeal right must include an opportunity for a fair hearing by such agency or person other than the designated agency as the Governor (or other chief executive officer) may designate.

All that is to be done under the State/Federal agreement whenever and to the extent that the findings of the designated State agency or any other such agency indicate that any health care facility's proposed capital expenditure is not consistent with the standards, criteria, or plans developed pursuant to the Public Health Service Act to meet the need for adequate health care facilities in the area covered by the plan or plans so developed.

Pursuant to section 1122(c), States having such an agreement with the Secretary will be reimbursed from the Treasury for the reasonable cost of performing those functions.

Having set up that procedure, involving interrelationships with the Public Health Service's health planning initiatives and the multiple, varying initiatives for health planning among the States, Congress then provided as follows in section 1122(d).

If the Secretary determines that neither the State planning agency designated in the agreement nor any regional, metropolitan, or local agency alluded to above had been given notice of any proposed capital expenditure, in accordance with established procedures, at least 60 days prior to obligation for such expenditure, then for such period as the Secretary finds necessary to effect the purpose of section 1122, the Secretary must not include in any Medicare or Medicaid reimbursement any amount which is attributable to depreciation, interest on borrowed funds, a return on equity capital (in the case of proprietary facilities), or other expenses related to such capital expenditure. With respect to any organization reimbursed on a per capita or fixed fee or negotiated rate basis, the Secretary must exclude an amount which in his judgment is a reasonable equivalent to the amount which would otherwise be excluded if payment were to be made on other than a per capita or fixed fee or negotiated rate basis.

Furthermore, if the Secretary determines that the designated State planning agency, or an agency so described, received timely notice of the intention to make an affected capital expenditure and had, within a reasonable period after receiving such notice and prior to obligation for such expenditure, notified the person proposing such expenditure that it would not conform to the standards, criteria, or plans developed by that agency or by a relevant regional, metropolitan, or local planning agency, for adequate health care facilities in such State or in the area under the jurisdiction of a regional, metropolitan, or local agency, and if the designated planning agency had, prior to submitting to the Secretary its required findings, consulted with and taken into consideration the findings and recommendations of the relevant regional, metropolitan, or local planning agency, and if the required opportunity for a fair hearing had been granted, then for such period as the Secretary finds necessary to effect the purpose of section 1122, the Secretary must not include in any Medicare or Medicaid reimbursement any amount attributable to depreciation, interest on borrowed funds, return on equity capital (in the case of proprietary facilities), or other expenses related to such capital expenditure.

With respect to any organization reimbursed on a per capita or fixed fee or negotiated rate basis, the Secretary must exclude an amount which in his judgment is a reasonable equivalent to the amount which would otherwise be excluded if payment were to be made on other than a per capita or fixed fee or negotiated rate basis.

Pursuant to section 1122(d)(2), however, there is an exception to this limitation on Medicare and Medicaid reimbursement. Section 1122(i) required the Secretary to establish and/or designate a national advisory council to help him prepare regulations to implement section 1122 and to advise him on related policy matters, including coordination of section 1122 activities with activities under other parts of the Social Security Act or under other Federal or federally assisted health programs. That council is also obliged to consult with the Federal Hospital Council, the National Advisory Health Council, the Health Insurance Benefits Advisory Council, and other appropriate national advisory councils about matters bearing on the purposes of section 1122. If, after submitting the issue to the section 1122 national advisory council, the Secretary determines that exclusion of expenses related to any capital expenditure would discourage operation or expansion of an affected health care facility which has demonstrated its ability to provide comprehensive health care services (including institutional services) efficiently, effectively, and economically, or would otherwise be inconsistent with effective organization and delivery of health services or the effective administration of Medicare or Medicaid, he must not exclude those expenses from reimbursement.

To avoid circumvention of section 1122, which on the surface seems to apply to capital expenditures which are purchases, subsection (e) provides that where a person obtains under lease or comparable arrangement any facility or part thereof, or equipment for a facility, which would have been subject to exclusion from Medicare and Medicaid reimbursement had the acquisition been a purchase, the Secretary must deduct an amount which in his judgment is reasonably equivalent to what would have been excluded if the acquisition had been a purchase. Moreover, in computing the person's return on equity capital, the Secretary must deduct any amount deposited under the terms of the lease or comparable arrangement.

Any person dissatisfied with a determination by the Secretary to restrict Medicare and Medicaid reimbursement may, pursuant to section 1122(f), request reconsideration by the Secretary within six months following notification. Further administrative review is not available, however, and judicial review is specifically denied.

For section 1122 purposes, subsection (g) defines capital expenditure as an expenditure which, under generally accepted accounting principles, is not properly chargeable as an expense of operation and maintenance and which exceeds $600,000, or such lesser amount as a State may establish, which changes the bed capacity of a facility with respect to which the expenditure is made, or which substantially changes the services of the facility with respect to which the expenditure is made. To determine whether the $600,000 threshold, or such lesser amount a State establishes, has been met, the Secretary will include in his calculation the cost of studies, surveys, designs, plans, working drawings, specifications, and other activities essential to the acquisition, improvement, expansion, or replacement of the plant and equipment with respect to which such expenditure is made.

Pursuant to section 1122(h), the reimbursement restrictions of section 1122 do not apply to a religious nonmedical institution (as defined in section 1861(ss)(1)), 42 U.S.C.A. 1395x(ss)(1).

◆ NOTE: Prior to amendment by section 4454 of the Balanced Budget Act of 1997, P.L. 105-33, effective August 5, 1997, the exemption in section 1122(h) only applied to Christian Science sanatoriums operated, or listed and certified, by the First Church of Christ, Scientist, Boston, Massachusetts.

Finally, pursuant to section 1122(j), no capital expenditure made by or on behalf of a health care facility is subject to review under section 1122 if 75 percent of the patients who can reasonably be expected to use the service with respect to which the capital expenditure is made will be individuals enrolled in an eligible health maintenance organization (HMO) or competitive medical plan (CMP), as defined in section 1876(b), 42 U.S.C.A. 1395mm(b). That is so, however, only if the Secretary finds that the expenditure is for services and facilities needed by the HMO or CMP to operate efficiently and economically and if the services and facilities are not otherwise readily accessible to such organization because the facilities do not provide common services at the same site (as usually provided by the organization), or because the facilities are not available under a contract of reasonable duration, or because full and equal medical staff privileges in the facilities are not available, or because arrangements with such facilities are not administratively feasible, or because the purchase of such services is more costly than if the organization provided the services directly.

Statutory Provisions

Section 1122, 42 U.S.C.A. 1320a-1, provides as follows:

(a) The purpose of this section is to assure that Federal funds appropriated under titles XVIII and XIX are not used to support unnecessary capital expenditures made by or on behalf of health care facilities which are reimbursed under any of such titles and that, to the extent possible, reimbursement under such titles shall support planning activities with respect to health services and facilities in the various States.

(b) The Secretary, after consultation with the Governor (or other chief executive officer) and with appropriate local public officials, shall make an agreement with any State which is able and willing to do so under which a designated planning agency (which shall be an agency described in clause (ii) of subsection (d)(1)(B) that has a governing body or advisory board at least half of whose members represent consumer interests) will —

(1) make, and submit to the Secretary together with such supporting materials as he may find necessary, findings and recommendations with respect to capital expenditures proposed by or on behalf of any health care facility in such State within the field of its responsibilities,

(2) receive from other agencies described in clause (ii) of subsection (d)(1)(B), and submit to the Secretary together with such supporting material as he may find necessary, the findings and recommendations of such other agencies with respect to capital expenditures proposed by or on behalf of health care facilities in such State within the fields of their respective responsibilities, and

(3) establish and maintain procedures pursuant to which a person proposing any such capital expenditure may appeal a recommendation by the designated agency and will be granted an opportunity for a fair hearing by such agency or person other than the designated agency as the Governor (or other chief executive officer) may designate to hold such hearings,

whenever and to the extent that the findings of such designated agency or any such other agency indicate that any such expenditure is not consistent with the standards, criteria, or plans developed pursuant to the Public Health Service Act [P.L. 78-410, 42 U.S.C.A. 201 et seq.] to meet the need for adequate health care facilities in the area covered by the plan or plans so developed.

(c) The Secretary shall pay any such State from the general fund in the Treasury, in advance or by way of reimbursement as may be provided in the agreement with it (and may make adjustments in such payments on account of overpayments or underpayments previously made), for the reasonable cost of performing the functions specified in subsection (b).

(d) (1) Except as provided in paragraph (2), if the Secretary determines that—

(A) neither the planning agency designated in the agreement described in subsection (b) nor an agency described in clause (ii) of subparagraph (B) of this paragraph had been given notice of any proposed capital expenditure (in accordance with such procedure or in such detail as may be required by such agency) at least 60 days prior to obligation for such expenditure; or

(B) (i) the planning agency so designated or an agency so described had received such timely notice of the intention to make such capital expenditure and had, within a reasonable period after receiving such notice and prior to obligation for such expenditure, notified the person proposing such expenditure that the expenditure would not be in conformity with the standards, criteria, or plans developed by such agency or any other agency described in clause (ii) for adequate health care facilities in such State or in the area for which such other agency has responsibility, and

(ii) the planning agency so designated had, prior to submitting to the Secretary the findings referred to in subsection (b)—

(I) consulted with, and taken into consideration the findings and recommendations of, the State planning agencies established pursuant to sections 314(a) and 604(a) of the Public Health Service Act [See generally 42 U.S.C.A. 246 regarding grants and services to States for comprehensive health planning, and 42 U.S.C.A. 300k et seq. regarding the National Health Planning and Development Act.] (to the extent that either such agency is not the agency so designated) as well as the public or nonprofit private agency or organization responsible for the comprehensive regional, metropolitan area, or other local area plan or plans referred to in section 314(b) of the Public Health Service Act and covering the area in which the health care facility or health maintenance organization proposing such capital expenditure is located (where such agency is not the agency designated in the agreement), or, if there is no such agency, such other public or nonprofit private agency or organization (if any) as performs, as determined in accordance with criteria included in regulations, similar functions, and

(II) granted to the person proposing such capital expenditure an opportunity for a fair hearing with respect to such findings; then, for such period as he finds necessary in any case to effectuate the purpose of this section, he shall, in determining the Federal payments to be made under titles XVIII and XIX with respect to services furnished in the health care facility for which such capital expenditure is made, not include any amount which is attributable to depreciation, interest on borrowed funds, a return on equity capital (in the case of proprietary facilities), or other expenses related to such capital expenditure. With respect to any organization which is reimbursed on a per capita or a fixed fee or negotiated rate basis, in determining the Federal payments to be made under titles XVIII and XIX, the Secretary shall exclude an amount which in his judgment is a reasonable equivalent to the amount which would otherwise be excluded under this subsection if payment were to be made on other than a per capita or a fixed fee or negotiated rate basis.

(2) If the Secretary, after submitting the matters involved to the advisory council established or designated under subsection (i), determines that an exclusion of expenses related to any capital expenditure of any health care facility would discourage the operation or expansion of such facility which has demonstrated to his satisfaction proof of capability to provide comprehensive health care services (including institutional services) efficiently, effectively, and economically, or would otherwise be inconsistent with the effective organization and delivery of health services or the effective administration of title XVIII or XIX, he shall not exclude such expenses pursuant to paragraph (1).

(e) Where a person obtains under lease or comparable arrangement any facility or part thereof, or equipment for a facility, which would have been subject to an exclusion under subsection (d) if the person had acquired it by purchase, the Secretary shall (1) in computing such person's rental expense in determining the Federal payments to be made under titles XVIII and XIX with respect to services furnished in such facility, deduct the amount which in his judgment is a reasonable equivalent of the amount that would have been excluded if the person had acquired such facility or such equipment by purchase, and (2) in computing such person's return on equity capital deduct any amount deposited under the terms of the lease or comparable arrangement.

(f) Any person dissatisfied with a determination by the Secretary under this section may within six months following notification of such determination request the Secretary to reconsider such determination. A determination by the Secretary under this section shall not be subject to administrative or judicial review.

(g) For purposes of this section, a "capital expenditure" is an expenditure which, under generally accepted accounting principles, is not properly chargeable as an expense of operation and maintenance and which (1) exceeds $600,000 (or such lesser amount as the State may establish), (2) changes the bed capacity of the facility with respect to which such expenditure is made, or (3) substantially changes the services of the facility with respect to which such expenditure is made. For purposes of clause (1) of the preceding sentence, the cost of the studies, surveys, designs, plans, working drawings, specifications, and other activities essential to the acquisition, improvement, expansion, or replacement of the plant and equipment with respect to which such expenditure is made shall be included in determining whether such expenditure exceeds the dollar amount specified in clause (1).

(h) The provisions of this section shall not apply to a religious nonmedical health care institution (as defined in section 1861(ss)(1) [42 U.S.C.A. 1395x(ss)(a)].

◆ NOTE: Prior to amendment by section 4454 of the Balanced Budget Act of 1997, P.L. 105-33, effective August 5, 1997, the exemption in section 1122(h) applied only to Christian Science sanatoriums operated, or listed and certified, by the First Church of Christ, Scientist, Boston, Massachusetts.

(i) (1) The Secretary shall establish a national advisory council, or designate an appropriate existing national advisory council, to advise and assist him in the preparation of general regulations to carry out the purposes of this section and on policy matters arising in the administration of this section, including the coordination of activities under this section with those under other parts of this Act or under other Federal or federally assisted health programs.

(2) The Secretary shall make appropriate provision for consultation between and coordination of the work of the advisory council established or designated under paragraph (1) and the Federal Hospital Council, the National Advisory Health Council, the Health Insurance Benefits Advisory Council, and other appropriate national advisory councils with respect to matters bearing on the purposes and administration of this section and the coordination of activities under this section with related Federal health programs.

(3) If an advisory council is established by the Secretary under paragraph (1), it shall be composed of members who are not otherwise in the regular full-time employ of the United States, and who shall be appointed by the Secretary without regard to the civil service laws from among leaders in the fields of the fundamental sciences, the medical sciences, and the organization, delivery, and financing of health care, and persons who are State or local officials or are active in community affairs or public or civic affairs or who are representative of minority groups. Members of such advisory council, while attending meetings of the council or otherwise serving on business of the council, shall be entitled to receive compensation at rates fixed by the Secretary, but not exceeding the maximum rate specified at the time of such service for grade GS-18 in section 5332 of title 5, United States Code, including traveltime, and while away from their homes or regular places of business they may also be allowed travel expenses, including per diem in lieu of subsistence, as authorized by section 5703 of title 5 for persons in the Government service employed intermittently.

(j) A capital expenditure made by or on behalf of a health care facility shall not be subject to review pursuant to this section if 75 percent of the patients who can reasonably be expected to use the service with respect to which the capital expenditure is made will be individuals enrolled in an eligible organization as defined in section 1876(b), and if the Secretary determines that such capital expenditure is for services and facilities which are needed by such organization in order to operate efficiently and economically and which are not otherwise readily accessible to such organization because —

(1) the facilities do not provide common services at the same site (as usually provided by the organization),

(2) the facilities are not available under a contract of reasonable duration,

(3) full and equal medical staff privileges in the facilities are not available,

(4) arrangements with such facilities are not administratively feasible, or

(5) the purchase of such services is more costly than if the organization provided the services directly.

For regulatory citations, see Chapter 8

§ 4:5 FAILURE TO COMPLY WITH SUBPOENAS ISSUED BY THE COMPTROLLER GENERAL — Section 1125(b) [42 U.S.C.A. 1320a-4(b)]

Summary

Section 1125(a), 42 U.S.C.A. 1320a-4(a), provides that the Comptroller General of the United States may sign and issue subpoenas to any person requiring production of books, records, documents, or other information relevant to any audit, investigation, examination, analysis, review, evaluation, or any other authorized function with respect to any program under the Social Security Act. That includes Medicare (Title XVIII), Medicaid (Title XIX), the Maternal and Child Health Services Block Grant program (Title V, 42 U.S.C.A. 701 et seq.), and the program of Block Grants to States for Social Services (Title XX, 42 U.S.C.A. 1397 et seq.)

Subpoenas issued by the Comptroller General may be served by anyone authorized by him by delivering them to the person named therein, or by registered mail or certified mail addressed to such person at his last dwelling place or principal place of business. Verified returns constitute proof of service.

Pursuant to section 1125(b), any failure to comply with a subpoena duly served by the Comptroller General may be brought by the Comptroller General before the Federal District Court of the United States for the judicial district in which the person failing to comply is found, resides, or transacts business. The District Court then has jurisdiction to issue an order requiring production of the books, records, documents, or other information sought by the subpoena.

Any person then failing to comply with the District Court's order may be punished by that court for contempt of court.

Section 1125(c) provides that no personal medical record in the possession of the General Accounting Office is subject to subpoena or discovery proceedings in a civil action. This protects the privacy of persons whose medical records may be acquired by the Comptroller General in the course of his audits, investigations, reviews, evaluations, or other examinations of the records and books of health care providers and suppliers.

Statutory Provisions

Section 1125, 42 U.S.C.A. 1320a-4, provides:

> (a) For the purpose of any audit, investigation, examination, analysis, review, evaluation, or other function authorized by law with respect to any program authorized under this Act, the Comptroller General of the United States shall have power to sign and issue subpoenas to any person requiring the production of any pertinent books, records, documents, or other information. Subpoenas so issued by the Comptroller General shall be served by anyone authorized by him (1) by delivering a copy thereof to the person named therein, or (2) by registered mail or by certified mail addressed to such person at his last dwelling place or principal place of business. A verified return by the person so serving the subpoena setting forth the manner of service, or, in the case of service by registered mail or by certified mail, the return post office receipt therefor signed by the person so served, shall be proof of service.
>
> (b) In case of contumacy by, or refusal to obey a subpoena issued pursuant to subsection (a) of this section and duly served upon, any person, any district court of the United States for the judicial district in which such person charged with contumacy or refusal to obey is found or resides or transacts business, upon application by the Comptroller General, shall have jurisdiction to issue an order requiring such person to produce the books, records, documents, or other information sought by the subpoena; and any failure to obey such order of the court may be punished by the court as a contempt thereof. In proceedings brought under this subsection, the Comptroller General shall be represented by attorneys employed in the General Accounting Office or by counsel whom he may employ without regard to the

provisions of title 5, United States Code, governing appointments in the competitive service, and the provisions of chapter 51 and subchapters III and VI of chapter 53 of such title, relating to classification and General Schedule pay rates.

(c) No personal medical record in the possession of the General Accounting Office shall be subject to subpoena or discovery proceedings in a civil action.

For regulatory citations, see Chapter 8

§ 4:6 EXCLUSION FROM MEDICARE AND STATE HEALTH CARE PROGRAMS — Section 1128 [42 U.S.C.A. 1320a-6]

Summary

Section 1128 of the Social Security Act, 42 U.S.C.A. 1320a-6, is the statutory authority generally used by the Secretary of Health and Human Services to exclude individuals and entities from Federal health care programs for fraud or other abuses in the delivery of health care. It specifies mandatory exclusions and permissive exclusions and the grounds therefor. It also sets forth requirements with respect to the duration of an exclusion order, and spells out hearing rights and readmission procedures.

Formerly, section 1128 applied to Medicare. Pursuant to amendment by section 4331(a) of the Balanced Budget Act of 1997, P.L. 105-33, effective August 5, 1997, however, by cross-reference to section 1128B(f), 42 U.S.C.A. 1320a-7b(f), section 1128 exclusion authority applies more broadly to "Federal health care programs". That term is defined to include any plan or program that provides health benefits, whether directly, through insurance, or otherwise, which is funded directly, in whole or in part, by the United States. (The one statutory exception is the Federal employees health insurance program established by chapter 89 of Title 5 of the United States Code.)

The term "Federal health care programs" also includes any State health care program as defined by section 1128(h). That means Medicaid; any program receiving funds under Title V of the Social Security Act (42 U.S.C.A. 701, et seq., which funds Maternal and Child Health Services through block grants); any program receiving funds under Title XX (42 U.S.C.A. 1397 et seq., which authorizes Block Grants to States for Social Services); and any State Child

Health Plan approved under Title XXI. Consequently, when an exclusion is based on section 1128, exclusion from Federally-funded State health care programs usually follows.

Mandatory Exclusions: Section 1128(a) describes four bases for mandatory exclusion.

1. Program-related Crimes: The Secretary must exclude from Medicare any individual or entity convicted of a criminal offense related to the delivery of an item or service under Medicare or under any State health care program. This applies to felonies or misdemeanors.

2. Patient Neglect or Abuse: The Secretary must exclude any individual or entity convicted under Federal or State law of a criminal offense (felony or misdemeanor) relating to neglect or abuse of patients in connection with delivery of a health care item or service. For these offenses the Secretary also must order exclusion from the defined State health care programs.

3. Felonious Health Care Fraud: The Secretary must exclude from Medicare any individual or entity convicted of a felony under Federal or State law related to the delivery of a health care item or service, or with respect to any act or omission in a health care program operated by or financed in whole or in part by any Federal, State, or local government. This applies to convictions relating to fraud, theft, embezzlement, breach of fiduciary responsibility, or other financial misconduct involving offenses which occurred after enactment of the Health Insurance Portability and Accountability Act of 1996, P.L. 104–191 (August 21, 1996). This amendment reaches offenses not falling under paragraph 1 above.

4. Felonious Involvement with Controlled Substances: The Secretary must exclude from Medicare any individual or entity convicted of a felony relating to the unlawful manufacture, distribution, prescription, or dispensing of a controlled substance. This also applies to offenses which occurred after enactment of the Health Insurance Portability and Accountability Act of 1996.

Permissive Exclusions: Section 1128(b) authorizes the Secretary to exclude individuals and entities from Medicare and to order their exclusion from State health care programs in 15 situations.

1. Convictions Related to Fraud: Exclusion may be ordered for any individual or entity convicted under Federal or State law for offenses in connection with delivery of a health care item or service. It also may be ordered with respect to any offensive act or omission in a health care program operated by or financed in whole or in part by

any Federal, State, or local government agency. The latter reaches acts or omissions not described in section 1128(a)(1).

This applies to felony or misdemeanor convictions for offenses relating to fraud, theft, embezzlement, breach of fiduciary responsibility, or other financial misconduct which occurred after enactment of the Health Insurance Portability and Accountability Act of 1996. It also applies to criminal offenses after that date related to programs (other than a health care program) which are operated by or financed in whole or in part by any Federal, State, or local government agency.

2. Conviction Relating to Obstruction of an Investigation: Exclusion may be ordered when an individual or entity has been convicted under Federal or State law in connection with interference with or obstruction of any investigation into any criminal offense described in paragraph 1 above, or described in section 1128(a) as a basis for mandatory exclusion.

3. Misdemeanor Conviction Involving Controlled Substances: Exclusion may be ordered when an individual or entity has been convicted under Federal or State law of a misdemeanor relating to the unlawful manufacture, distribution, prescription, or dispensing of a controlled substance.

4. License Revocation or Suspension: Exclusion may be ordered when an individual or entity has had his or its license to provide health care revoked or suspended by any State licensing authority. Exclusion also may be ordered when the individual or entity has otherwise lost such a license, or, effective December 19, 1989 (pursuant to section 6411(d) of P.L. 101-239, the Omnibus Budget Reconciliation Act of 1989), lost the right to apply for or renew such a license, for reasons bearing on professional competence, professional performance, or financial integrity. Similarly, exclusion may be ordered when the individual or entity has surrendered such a license while a formal disciplinary proceeding was pending before such an authority and the proceeding concerned professional competence, professional performance, or financial integrity.

5. Exclusion or Suspension under a Federal or State Health Care Program: Exclusion may be ordered when an individual or entity has been suspended or excluded from participation, or otherwise sanctioned, under any Federal program, including programs of the Department of Defense or the Veterans' Administration, involving provision of health care, or under any State health care program, for

reasons bearing on professional competence, professional performance, or financial integrity.

6. Claims for Excess Charges or for Unnecessary Services: Exclusion may be ordered when the Secretary determines an individual or entity —

(a) has submitted or caused to be submitted bills or requests for payment (where such bills or requests are based on charges or cost) under Medicare or a State health care program containing charges (or, in applicable cases, requests for payment of costs) for items or services furnished substantially in excess of the individual's or entity's usual charges (or, in applicable cases, substantially in excess of costs) for such items or services, unless the Secretary finds good cause for having done so;

(b) has furnished or caused to be furnished items or services to patients (whether or not eligible for benefits under Medicare or under a State health care program) substantially in excess of the needs of such patients or of a quality which fails to meet professionally recognized standards of health care;

(c) is a health maintenance organization providing items and services under an approved Medicaid plan, or is an entity furnishing services under a Medicaid waiver under section 1915(b)(1), 42 U.S.C.A. 1396n(b)(1), which aims to foster primary care case-management systems or specialty physician services arrangements, and the entity has failed substantially to provide medically necessary items and services required under law or by its Medicaid contract to be provided to individuals covered under that plan or waiver, if the failure has adversely affected, or has a substantial likelihood of adversely affecting those individuals; or

(d) is an entity providing items and services as an eligible organization under a risk-sharing contract under section 1876, 42 U.S.C.A. 1395mm, i.e., a health maintenance organization (HMO) or a competitive medical plan (CMP), and it has failed substantially to provide medically necessary items and services required under law or by contract to be provided to individuals covered under their contracts, if the failure has adversely affected or has a substantial likelihood of adversely affecting) these individuals.

7. Fraud, Kickbacks, and Other Prohibited Activities: Exclusion may be ordered when the Secretary determines that an individual or entity has committed an act described in section 1128A, 42 U.S.C.A. 1320a-7a, which authorizes civil money penalties for a variety of abuses. It also may be ordered for an act described in section 1128B,

42 U.S.C.A. 1320a-7b, which provides criminal penalties for fraud, illegal kickbacks, and the like. In addition, effective October 31, 1994, pursuant to section 206(b)(2) of the Social Security Independence and Program Improvements Act of 1994, P.L. 103-296, exclusion may be ordered for committing an act described in section 1129, 42 U.S.C.A. 1320a-8, which pertains to civil money penalties and assessments for violations of Titles II and XVI of the Social Security Act. (Title II provides Social Security benefits. Title XVI provides welfare benefits for the aged, blind, and disabled.)

8. Entities Controlled by a Sanctioned Individual: Exclusion may be ordered when the Secretary determines an entity is controlled, within the meaning of section 1128(b)(8)(A), by an individual convicted of an offense described in paragraphs 1, 2, and 3, above, or which is the basis for mandatory exclusion under section 1128(a).

This applies to anyone who has a direct or indirect ownership or control interest of five percent or more in an entity.

Pursuant to section 4303(a)(1) of the Balanced Budget Act of 1997, effective September 19, 1997, it also applies to anyone with an ownership or control interest in an entity who is an officer, director, agent, or managing employee of the entity.

Furthermore, it applies to anyone with a five percent interest who no longer has that status because of a transfer of an ownership or control interest, either in anticipation of or following a conviction, assessment, or exclusion against the person to an immediate family member, or to a member of the household of that person who continues then to maintain that interest. For these purposes, pursuant to amendment by section 4303(a)(2) of the Balanced Budget Act of 1997, effective September 19, 1997, section 1128(j) defines immediate family member to include the husband or wife of the person; the natural or adoptive parent, child, or sibling of the person; the stepparent, stepchild, stepbrother, or stepsister of the person; the father-in-law, mother-in-law, daughter-in-law, son-in-law, brother-in-law, or sister-in-law of the person; the grandparent or grandchild of the person; and the spouse of a grandparent or grandchild of a person.

Section 1128(j) defines member of the household to include, with respect to any person, any individual sharing a common abod as part of a single family unit with the person, including domestic employees and others who live together as a family unit (but not including a roomer or boarder).

Exclusion also may be ordered for an individual against whom a civil money penalty has been assessed under section 1128A, or for an individual who has been excluded from participation in Medicare or a State health care program. Effective October 31, 1994, exclusion may be ordered for an individual against whom a civil money penalty had been assessed under section 1129, 42 U.S.C.A. 1320a-8, which pertains to civil money penalties for violations of Titles II and XVI of the Social Security Act.

9. Failure to Disclose Required Information: Exclusion may be ordered when an entity did not fully and accurately make any disclosure about ownership and control required by section 1124, 42 U.S.C.A. 1320a-3, or section 1126, 42 U.S.C.A. 1320a-5, or, applicable to items and services furnished on or after January 1, 1992, pursuant to section 4164(b)(1) and (3) of P.L. 101-508, the Omnibus Budget Reconciliation Act of 1990 (OBRA 90), section 1124A, 42 U.S.C.A. 1320a-3a.

10. Failure to Supply Payment Information: Exclusion may be ordered when an entity is a disclosing entity, as defined in section 1124(a)(2), and it failed to supply timely upon request by the Secretary or by a State agency administering or supervising the administration of a State health care program full and complete information about the ownership of a subcontractor with whom the entity had, during the previous 12 months, business transactions in an aggregate amount in excess of $25,000. Exclusion also may be ordered when the entity failed to supply timely upon request by the Secretary or such a State agency full and complete information as to any significant business transactions occurring during the five-year period ending on the date of such request, between the entity and any wholly owned supplier or between the entity and any subcontractor.

◆ NOTE: With respect to items 9 and 10 above, section 1124(a) obligates each disclosing entity to supply the Secretary or the appropriate State agency with full and complete information as to the identity of each person with an ownership or control interest in the entity, or in any subcontractor in which the entity directly or indirectly has a five per cent or more ownership interest. Furthermore, pursuant to section 4313(a) of the Balanced Budget Act of 1997, each disclosing entity must supply the Secretary with both the employer identification number assigned pursuant to section 6109 of the Internal Revenue Code of 1986, and with the Social Security account number assigned under section 205(c)(2)(B) of the Social Security Act, for the disclosing entity and each person with an ownership or control interest, and any subcontractor in which the disclosing entity has a five percent ownership interest. The latter requirement for IRS and Social Security numbers applies to conditions of participation and to the entering into or renewal of contracts and agreements occurring more than 90 days after submission of a report required by section 4313(d) of the Balanced Budget Act of 1997. That report is to be made to the Congress by the Secretary on the steps the Secretary has taken to assure the confidentiality of Social Security account numbers used for these purposes.

"Disclosing entity" is defined by section 1124(a)(2). "Person with an ownership or control interest" is defined in section 1124(a)(3). See statutory provisions below.

11. Failure to Supply Payment Information: Exclusion may be ordered when an individual or entity failed to provide such information as the Secretary or the appropriate State agency finds necessary to determine whether payments under Medicare or a State health care program are or were due and the amounts thereof. It also may be ordered when an individual or entity refused to permit such examination of his or its records by or on behalf of the Secretary or the State agency as may be necessary to verify such information.

12. Failure to Grant Immediate Access for Investigative Purposes: Exclusion may be ordered when an individual or entity failed to grant immediate access upon reasonable request —

(a) to the Secretary, or to the State agency used by the Secretary, to determine whether as providers of services the individual or entity is meeting Medicare conditions of participation or payment, as required by section 1864, 42 U.S.C.A. 1395aa;

(b) to the Secretary or the State agency to perform reviews and surveys required under State Medicaid plans pursuant to section 1902(a)(26), 42 U.S.C.A. 1396a(a)(26), which pertains to mental institutions and inpatient mental hospital services; pursuant to section 1902(a)(31), which pertains to services in intermediate care facilities for the mentally retarded; pursuant to section 1902(a)(33), which pertains to State agency surveys, and Federal validation of such surveys, of the appropriateness and quality of care and services furnished to Medicaid recipients; and pursuant to section 1903(g), 42 U.S.C.A. 1396b(g), which pertains to determining appropriate Federal financial participation in Medicaid payments for care in intermediate care facilities for the mentally retarded and for inpatient mental hospital services and to required State programs to review the effectiveness of such care;

(c) to the Inspector General of the Department of Health and Human Services so he can review records, documents, and other data necessary to perform his statutory duties;

(d) to a State Medicaid fraud control unit, as defined in section 1903(q), 42 U.S.C.A. 1396b(q), so it can investigate allegations of criminal activities and complaints of patient abuse or neglect and attempt to collect overpayments.

13. Failure by a Hospital to Take Corrective Action: Exclusion may be ordered when a hospital fails to comply substantially with a corrective action required under section 1886(f)(2)(B), 42 U.S.C.A. 1395ww(f)(2)(B), which pertains to DRG reimbursement methodology and eliminating unnecessary hospital admissions which circumvent that methodology.

14. Default on a Health Education Loan or Scholarship Obligation: Exclusion may be authorized when an individual is determined by the Secretary to be in default on repayment of scholarship obligations or loans in connection with health professions education made or secured, in whole or in part, by the Secretary. Nevertheless, the Secretary may not exclude for this reason a physician who is the sole community physician or sole source of essential specialized services in a community if a State requests that the physician not be excluded. Furthermore, the Secretary must take into account, in determining whether to exclude any other physician for this reason, the access of beneficiaries to physician services for which payment may be made under Medicare or Medicaid.

15. Individuals Controlling a Sanctioned Entity: Exclusion may be ordered for any individual who has a direct or indirect ownership or control interest in a sanctioned entity if that individual knows or should know of the action constituting the basis for the conviction or exclusion. Exclusion also may be ordered for an officer or managing employee of such an entity. For this purpose, sanctioned entity means an entity convicted of an offense described in paragraph 1, 2, or 3 above, or of an offense which is the basis for mandatory exclusion under section 1128(a). Sanctioned entity also means an entity excluded from participation in Medicare or a State health care program. This basis for a permissive exclusion was added by section 213

of the Health Insurance Portability Act of 1996, effective January 1, 1997.

Public Notice and Effective Date of an Exclusion Order: Pursuant to section 1128(c), exclusions under section 1128, (and under section 1128A, which permits exclusion in conjunction with imposition of a civil money penalty,) become effective at such time and upon such reasonable notice to the public and to the individual or entity excluded as the Secretary may determine by regulation. Ordinarily, they must become effective with respect to services furnished to an individual on or after the specified effective date. An exclusion shall not apply, however, to payments made under Medicare or under a State health care program for inpatient institutional services furnished to an individual admitted to such an institution before the date of the exclusion, or for home health services and hospice care furnished to an individual under a plan of care established before the date of the exclusion, until 30 days after the effective date. But this deferral does not apply if the Secretary determines that the health and safety of individuals receiving services warrants an earlier effective date.

Duration of Exclusion: Section 1128(c)(3) requires the Secretary to specify in the notice of exclusion the minimum duration of the exclusion. In the case of an exclusion for failure to grant immediate access under section 1128(b)(12), he must specify the exact duration.

Generally, exclusions mandatory under section 1128(a) must be for not less than five years. Pursuant to section 4301 of the Balanced Budget Act of 1997, however, if a person has been convicted of an offense for which exclusion is authorized on or after August 5, 1997, and that individual previously had been convicted of such an offense, the period of exclusion must be a minimum of 10 years. If that person had two or more prior convictions for an offense justifying exclusion, the exclusion must be permanent.

At the request of a State, however, the Secretary may waive an exclusion under section 1128(a)(1), which pertains to convictions based on program-related offenses, in the case of an individual or entity that is the sole community physician or sole source of essential specialized services in a community. The Secretary's decision whether to waive the exclusion is not reviewable.

The Secretary has broad discretion to determine the length of exclusions which are permissive under section 1128(b) and no minimum required durations. With respect to exclusions based on section 1128(b)(12), however, for failure to grant immediate access to the

Secretary, to an appropriate State agency, to the Inspector General of the Department of Health and Human Services, or to a State Medicaid fraud control unit, the period of exclusion must equal the length of the period in which the individual failed to grant the required immediate access plus an additional period not to exceed 90 days, as set by the Secretary.

Prior to enactment of the Health Insurance Portability and Accountability Act of 1996, the Secretary had broad latitude to determine the period of other permissive exclusions. Effective January 1, 1997, however, that discretion was restrained as follows:

For permissive exclusions under section 1128(b)(1), (2), and (3) the period of exclusion must be three years, unless the Secretary determines a shorter period is appropriate because of mitigating circumstances, or a longer period is appropriate because of aggravating circumstances.

For permissive exclusions under section 1128(b)(4) or (5), the period of exclusion must not be less than the period during which the individual's or the entity's license to provide health care is revoked, suspended, or surrendered, nor less than the period the individual or entity is excluded or suspended from a Federal or State health care program.

For a permissive exclusion under section 1128(b)(6)(B) — furnishing excessive services or providing substandard quality of care — the period of exclusion must not be less than one year.

Coordination of Exclusions with State Health Care Programs: Pursuant to section 1128(d), the Secretary must exercise his authority to exclude under section 1128 (and under section 1128A) in a manner which results in complete exclusion from Medicare and all the defined State health care programs in which the individual or entity otherwise may participate. To that end, the Secretary must promptly notify each appropriate State agency administering or supervising administration of each State health care program of the fact and circumstances of each exclusion and of the duration for which the State agency must exclude the individual or entity from participation in the State health care program or programs. At the least, the State's exclusion must equal the duration of the Medicare exclusion; however, it may be longer, if the State so desires. On the other hand, upon State request, the Secretary may waive an individual's or entity's exclusion under a State health care program. Such waivers presumably would be rare and likely to apply only when the public interest would be better served, as when the individual or entity provides health care items or services not otherwise readily available in a community.

Notice to the U.S. Attorney General about Certain Controlled Substance Violations: With respect to a mandatory exclusion under section 1128(a), to which section 304(a)(5) of the Controlled Substances Act, P.L. 91-513, Title II, may apply, section 1128(d) also requires the Secretary to notify the United States Attorney General promptly of the fact, the circumstances, and the duration of the exclusion.

Notice to State and Local Licensing Agencies: Pursuant to section 1128(e), the Secretary also must notify promptly the State or local agency or authority responsible for licensing or certification of an individual or entity excluded or directed to be excluded from participation under section 1128 (or section 1128A) of the fact and circumstances of exclusions. Furthermore, the Secretary must request such agencies to make their own investigations and impose whatever sanctions State law and policy may require. And the Secretary must request the State or local agency or authority to keep him and the Inspector General of the Department of Health and Human Services fully and currently informed about actions taken in response to that request.

Notice and Hearing Rights: Any individual or entity excluded or directed to be excluded under section 1128, shall, pursuant to section 1128(f), receive reasonable notice and opportunity for a hearing thereon by the Secretary to the same extent provided for persons claiming Social Security benefits under Title II of the Social Security Act. Moreover, such individuals and entities are entitled to judicial review of the Secretary's final decision after such a hearing. See sections 205(b) and 205(g) of the Act, 42 U.S.C.A. 405(b) and 405(g), respectively.

Effective Date of Exclusions: Exclusions often take effect prior to the hearing required by section 1128(f). Indeed, that is what most formal notices of exclusion provide and what most grounds for exclusion permit. Pursuant to section 1128(f)(2), however, unless the Secretary determines that the health or safety of individuals receiving services from an individual or entity warrants immediate exclusion, exclusion will not take place until after a hearing and decision by an administrative law judge, as provided by section 205(b), in the case of any individual or entity whose exclusion is based on section 1128(b)(7). That is the permissive exclusion authorized for individuals and entities who have committed fraud, kickbacks, or other prohibited acts described in section 1128A or section 1128B.

Effect of a Hearing Decision: Pursuant to section 1128(f)(3), the findings and decision of the Secretary after an exclusion hearing are binding upon all parties, and they are subject only to such further review as the statute may allow, as specified in section 205(h), 42 U.S.C.A. 405(h). The same is true for exclusions authorized under section 1128A and under section 1156, 42 U.S.C.A. 1320c-5, which pertains to exclusions based on recommendations by Peer Review Organizations.

Readmission Rights for Excluded Individuals and Entities: An individual or entity excluded or directed to be excluded under section 1128 (or 1128A) may want to be readmitted to participation in Medicare or State health care programs. Accordingly, section 1128(g) provides for the Secretary to establish a readmission process. Once the minimum exclusion period has elapsed, the individual or entity may apply to the Secretary for termination of his exclusion. If the Secretary determines, on the basis of the applicant's conduct after the date of the notice of exclusion, or of conduct unknown to the Secretary at the time of the exclusion, that there is no basis under section 1128(a), 1128(b) (or 1128A) to continue the exclusion, and that there are reasonable assurances that actions like those which formed the basis for the original exclusion have not recurred and will not recur, the Secretary may terminate the exclusion. When he does so, he must notify promptly the State agency administering or supervising administration of relevant State health care programs of the fact and circumstances of each termination of an exclusion made under section 1128(g). With respect to a section 1128(a) exclusion to which section 304(a)(5) of the Controlled Substances Act may apply, the Secretary must give similar notice to the United States Attorney General.

The Meaning of "Conviction": For section 1128 purposes, subsection (i) defines conviction in broadly inclusive terms. An individual or entity is considered "convicted" of a criminal offense when a judgment of conviction has been entered by a Federal, State, or local court, regardless whether an appeal is pending or whether that judgment or other record relating to criminal conduct has been expunged; when a Federal, State, or local court has made a finding of guilt; when a plea of guilty or nolo contendere has been accepted by a Federal, State, or local court; and when the individual or entity has entered into a first offender, deferred adjudication, or other arrangement or program where judgment of conviction has been withheld.

Statutory Provisions

Section 1128(a), 42 U.S.C.A. 1320a-7(a), provides:

MANDATORY EXCLUSION. — The Secretary shall exclude the following individuals and entities from participation in any Federal health care program (as defined in section 1128B(f)):

◆ NOTE: Section 4331(a) of the Balanced Budget Act of 1997, P.L. 105-33, substituted the phrase "any Federal health care program (as defined in section 1128(B)(f))" for "any program under title XVIII and shall direct that the following individuals and entities be excluded from participation in any State health care program (as defined in subsection (h))". A similar change was made in section 1128(b) by section 4331(c)(2) of the Balanced Budget Act of 1997:

(1) CONVICTION OF PROGRAM-RELATED CRIMES. —Any individual or entity that has been convicted of a criminal offense related to the delivery of an item or service under title XVIII or under any State health care program.

(2) CONVICTION RELATING TO PATIENT ABUSE. — Any individual or entity that has been convicted, under Federal or State law, of a criminal offense relating to neglect or abuse of patients in connection with the delivery of a health care item or service.

(3) FELONY CONVICTION RELATING TO HEALTH CARE FRAUD. — Any individual or entity that has been convicted for an offense which occurred after the date of the enactment of the Health Insurance Portability and Accountability Act of 1996 [August 21, 1996] under Federal or State law, in connection with the delivery of a health care item or service or with respect to any act or omission in a health care program (other than those specifically described in paragraph (1)) operated by or financed in whole or in part by any Federal, State, or local government agency, of a criminal offense consisting of a felony relating to fraud, theft, embezzlement, breach of fiduciary responsibility, or other financial misconduct.

(4) FELONY CONVICTION RELATING TO CONTROLLED SUBSTANCE. — Any individual or entity that has been convicted for an offense which occurred after the enactment of the Health Insurance Portability and Accountability Act of 1996, under Federal or State Law, of a criminal offense consisting of a felony relating to the unlawful manufacture, distribution, prescription, or dispensing of a controlled substance.

◆ NOTE: Sections 211(a)(1) and 211(b)(4) of the Health Insurance Portability and Accountability Act of 1996, P.L. 104–191, effective January 1, 1997, added paragraphs (3) and (4) respectively to section 1128(a).

Section 1128(b) provides:

PERMISSIVE EXCLUSION. — The Secretary may exclude the following individuals and entities from participation in any Federal health care program (as defined in section 1128(B)(f)):

(1) CONVICTION RELATING TO FRAUD. — Any individual or entity that has been convicted for an offense which occurred after the date of the enactment of the Health Insurance Portability and Accountability Act of 1996, under Federal or State law —

(A) of a criminal offense consisting of a misdemeanor relating to fraud, theft, embezzlement, breach of fiduciary responsibility, or other financial misconduct —

(i) in connection with the delivery of a health care item or service; or

(ii) with respect to any act or omission in a health care program (other than those specifically described in subsection (a)(1)) operated by or financed in whole or in part by any Federal, State, or local government agency; or

(B) of a criminal offense relating to fraud, theft, embezzlement, breach of fiduciary responsibility, or other financial misconduct with respect to any act or omission in a program other than a health care program) operated by or financed in whole or in part by any Federal, State or local government agency.

◆ NOTE: Prior to amendment by section 211(a)(2) of the Health Insurance Portability and Accountability Act of 1996, section

1128(b)(1) read: "(1)CONVICTION RELATING TO FRAUD. — Any individual or entity that has been convicted, under Federal or State law, in connection with the delivery of a health care item or service or with respect to any act or omission in a program operated by or financed in whole or in part by any Federal, State, or local government agency, of a criminal offense relating to fraud, theft, embezzlement, breach of fiduciary responsibility, or other financial misconduct;"

(2) CONVICTION RELATING TO OBSTRUCTION OF AN INVESTIGATION. — Any individual or entity that has been convicted, under Federal or State law, in connection with the interference with or obstruction of any investigation into any criminal offense described in paragraph (1) or in subsection (a).

(3) MISDEMEANOR CONVICTION RELATING TO CONTROLLED SUBSTANCE. — Any individual or entity that has been convicted, under Federal or State law, of a criminal offense relating to the unlawful manufacture, distribution, prescription, or dispensing of a controlled substance.

◆ NOTE: Prior to amendment by section 211(a)(2) of the Health Insurance Portability and Accountability Act of 1996, effective January 1, 1997, paragraph (3) read: "(3)CONVICTION RELATING TO CONTROLLED SUBSTANCE. — Any individual or entity that has been convicted, under Federal or State law, of a criminal offense relating to the unlawful manufacture, distribution, prescription, or dispensing of a controlled substance."

(4) LICENSE REVOCATION OR SUSPENSION. — Any individual or entity —

(A) whose license to provide health care has been revoked or suspended by any State licensing authority, or who otherwise lost such a license or the right to apply for or renew such a license ["or the right to apply for or renew such a license" added, effective December 19, 1989, pursuant to section 6411(d) of P.L. 101-239, the Omnibus Budget Reconciliation Act of 1989], for reasons bearing on the individual's or entity's professional competence, professional performance, or financial integrity, or

(B) who surrendered such a license while a formal disciplinary proceeding was pending before such an authority and the proceeding concerned the individual's or entity's professional competence, professional performance, or financial integrity.

(5) EXCLUSION OR SUSPENSION UNDER FEDERAL OR STATE HEALTH CARE PROGRAM. — Any individual or entity which has been suspended or excluded from participation, or otherwise sanctioned, under —

(A) any Federal program, including programs of the Department of Defense or the Veterans' Administration, involving the provision of health care, or

(B) a State health care program, for reasons bearing on the individual's or entity's professional competence, professional performance, or financial integrity.

(6) CLAIMS FOR EXCESSIVE CHARGES OR UNNECESSARY SERVICES AND FAILURE OF CERTAIN ORGANIZATIONS TO FURNISH MEDICALLY NECESSARY SERVICES. — Any individual or entity that the Secretary determines —

(A) has submitted or caused to be submitted bills or requests for payment (where such bills or requests are based on charges or cost) under title XVIII or a State health care program containing charges (or, in applicable cases, requests for payment of costs) for items or services furnished substantially in excess of such individual's or entity's usual charges (or, in applicable cases, substantially in excess of such individual's or entity's costs) for such items or services, unless the Secretary finds there is good cause for such bills or requests containing such charges or costs;

(B) has furnished or caused to be furnished items or services to patients (whether or not eligible for benefits under title XVIII or under a State health care program) substantially in excess of the needs of such patients or of a quality which fails to meet professionally recognized standards of health care;

(C) is —

(i) a health maintenance organization (as defined in section 1903(m) [42 U.S.C.A. 1396b(m)]) providing items and services under a State plan approved under title XIX, or

(ii) an entity furnishing services under a waiver approved under section 1915(b)(1) [42 U.S.C.A. 1396n(b)(1), which aims to foster primary care case-management systems or specialty physician services arrangements],

and has failed substantially to provide medically necessary items and services that are required (under law or the contract with the State under title XIX) to be provided to individuals covered under that plan or waiver, if the failure has adversely affected (or has a substantial likelihood of adversely affecting) these individuals; or

(D) is an entity providing items and services as an eligible organization under a risk-sharing contract under section 1876 [42 U.S.C.A. 1395mm, i.e., a health maintenance organization or a competitive medical plan] and has failed substantially to provide medically necessary items and services that are required (under law or such contract) to be provided to individuals covered under the risk-sharing contract, if the failure has adversely affected (or has a substantial likelihood of adversely affecting) these individuals.

(7) FRAUD, KICKBACKS, AND OTHER PROHIBITED ACTIVITIES. — Any individual or entity that the Secretary determines has committed an act which is described in section 1128A [42 U.S.C.A. 1320a-7a, which authorizes civil money penalties for a variety of offenses], section 1128B [42 U.S.C.A. 1320a-7b, which provides criminal penalties for acts involving Medicare or State health care programs], or 1129 [42 U.S.C.A. 1320a-8, which pertains to civil money penalties and assessments for violations of Title II (Social Security benefits) or Title XVI (welfare benefits)].

◆ NOTE: Effective October 31, 1994, section 206(b)(2) of the Social Security Independence and Program Improvements Act of 1994, P.L. 103-296, substituted "1128B, or 1129" for "or section 1128B" in subsection (b)(7) above; and inserted "or 1129" after "section 1128A" in subsection (b)(8)(B)(ii) below. Effective September 19, 1997, section 4303(a)(1) of the Balanced Budget Act of 1997, removed "or" at the end of clause (i) below; substituted "; or" for a dash at the end of clause (ii); and added clause (iii).

(8) ENTITIES CONTROLLED BY A SANCTIONED INDIVIDUAL — Any entity with respect to which the Secretary determines that a person —

(A) (i) who has a direct or indirect ownership or control interest of 5 percent or more in the entity or with an ownership or control interest (as defined in section 1124(a)(3) [42 U.S.C.A. 1320a-3(a)(3)]) in that entity,

(ii) who is an officer, director, agent, or managing employee (as defined in section 1126(b) [42 U.S.C.A. 1320a-5(b)]) of that entity; or

(iii) who was described in clause (i) but is no longer so described because of a transfer of ownership or control interest, in anticipation of (or following) a conviction, assessment, or exclusion described in subparagraph (B) against the person, to an immediate family member (as defined in subsection (j)(1) or a member of the household of the person (as defined in subsection (j)(2)) who continues to maintain an interest described in such clause —

is a person —

(B) (i) who has been convicted of any offense described in subsection (a) or in paragraph (1), (2), or (3) of this subsection;

(ii) against whom a civil monetary penalty has been assessed under section 1128A or 1129; or

(iii) who has been excluded from participation under a program under title XVIII or under a State health care program.

(9) FAILURE TO DISCLOSE REQUIRED INFORMATION. — Any entity that did not fully and accurately make any disclosure required by section 1124, section 1124A ["section 1124A", added by section 4164(b)(3) of OBRA 90 (applicable with respect to items and services furnished on or after January 1, 1992), requires certain Part B providers to disclose certain ownership and control interests and information about penalties, assessments, or exclusions imposed under section 1128, 1128A, or 1128B.], or section 1126.

(10) FAILURE TO SUPPLY REQUESTED INFORMATION ON SUBCONTRACTORS AND SUPPLIERS. — Any disclosing entity (as defined in section 1124(a)(2)) that fails to supply (within such period as may be specified by the Secretary in regulations) upon request specifically addressed to the entity by the Secretary or by the State agency administering or supervising the administration of a State health care program —

(A) full and complete information as to the ownership of a subcontractor (as defined by the Secretary in regulations) with whom the entity has had, during the previous 12 months, business transactions in an aggregate amount in excess of $25,000, or

(B) full and complete information as to any significant business transactions (as defined by the Secretary in regulations), occurring during the five-year period ending on the date of such request, between the entity and any wholly owned supplier or between the entity and any subcontractor.

(11) FAILURE TO SUPPLY PAYMENT INFORMATION. —Any individual or entity furnishing items or services for which payment may be made under title XVIII or a State health care program that fails to provide such information as the Secretary or the appropriate State agency finds necessary to determine whether such payments are or were due and the amounts thereof, or has refused to permit such examination of its records by or on behalf of the Secretary or that agency as may be necessary to verify such information.

(12) FAILURE TO GRANT IMMEDIATE ACCESS. — Any individual or entity that fails to grant immediate access, upon reasonable request (as defined by the Secretary in regulations) to any of the following:

(A) To the Secretary, or to the agency used by the Secretary, for the purpose specified in the first sentence of section 1864(a) [42 U.S.C.A. 1395aa] (relating to compliance with conditions of participation or payment).

(B) To the Secretary or the State agency, to perform the reviews and surveys required under State plans under paragraphs (26), (31), and (33) of section 1902(a) [42 U.S.C.A. 1396a(a)(26), (31), and (33), which respectively pertain to mental institutions and inpatient mental hospital services, to services in intermediate care facilities for the mentally retarded, and to State agency surveys and Federal validation of such surveys of the appropriateness and quality of care and services furnished to Medicaid recipients] and under section 1903(g) [42 U.S.C.A. 1396b(g), which pertains to determining the appropriate Federal financial participation in Medicaid payments for care in intermediate care facilities for the mentally retarded and for inpatient mental hospital services and to required State programs to review the effectiveness of such care].

(C) To the Inspector General of the Department of Health and Human Services, for the purpose of reviewing records, documents, and other data necessary to the performance of the statutory functions of the Inspector General.

(D) To a State medicaid fraud control unit (as defined in section 1903(q) [42 U.S.C.A. 1396b(q)]), for the purpose of conducting activities described in that section [i.e., investigation of allegations of criminal activities and complaints of patient abuse or neglect, and collection of overpayments].

(13) FAILURE TO TAKE CORRECTIVE ACTION. — Any hospital that fails to comply substantially with a corrective action required under section 1886(f)(2)(B) [42 U.S.C.A. 1395ww(f)(2)(b), which pertains to DRG reimbursement methodology and eliminating unnecessary hospital admissions which circumvent that methodology].

(14) DEFAULT ON HEALTH EDUCATION LOAN OR SCHOLARSHIP OBLIGATIONS. — Any individual who the Secretary determines is in default on repayments of scholarship obligations or loans in connection with health professions education made or secured, in whole or in part, by the Secretary and with respect to whom the Secretary has taken all reasonable steps available to the Secretary to secure repayment of such obligations or loans, except that (A) the Secretary shall not exclude pursuant to this paragraph a physician who is the sole community physician or sole source of essential specialized services in a community if a State requests that the physician not be excluded, and (B) the Secretary shall take into account, in determining whether to exclude any other physician pursuant to this paragraph,

access of beneficiaries to physician services for which payment may be made under title XVIII or XIX.

(15) INDIVIDUALS CONTROLLING A SANCTIONED ENTITY.—

(A) Any individual—

(i) who has a direct or indirect ownership or control interest in a sanctioned entity and who knows or should know (as defined in section 1128A(I)(6)) of the action constituting the basis for the conviction or exclusion described in subparagraph (B); or

(ii) who is an officer or managing employee (as defined in section 1126(b)) of such an entity.

(B) For purposes of subparagraph (A), the term "sanctioned entity" means an entity—

(i) that has been convicted of any offense described in subsection (a) or in paragraph (1), (2), or (3) of this subsection; or

(ii) that has been excluded from participation under a program under title XVIII or under a State health care program.

◆ NOTE: Section 213 of the Health Insurance Portability and Accountability Act of 1996 added paragraph (15) to section 1128(b), effective January 1, 1997.

Section 1128(c) provides:

NOTICE, EFFECTIVE DATE, AND PERIOD OF EXCLUSION.—(1) An exclusion under this section or under section 1128A [which permits exclusion in conjunction with imposition of a civil money penalty] shall be effective at such time and upon such reasonable notice to the public and to the individual or entity excluded as may be specified in regulations consistent with paragraph (2).

(2) (A) Except as provided in subparagraph (B), such an exclusion shall be effective with respect to services furnished to an individual on or after the effective date of the exclusion.

(B) Unless the Secretary determines that the health and safety of individuals receiving services warrants the exclusion taking effect earlier, an exclusion shall not apply to payments made under title XVIII or under a State health care program for —

(i) inpatient institutional services furnished to an individual who was admitted to such institution before the date of the exclusion, or

(ii) home health services and hospice care furnished to an individual under a plan of care established before the date of the exclusion,

until the passage of 30 days after the effective date of the exclusion.

◆ NOTE: Section 4301 of the Balanced Budget Act of 1997, added the phrase "or in the case described in subparagraph (G)" in (3)(A) below; inserted "Subject to subparagraph (G), in the case" in lieu of "In the case" in (3)(B) and (3)(D) below; and added paragraph (G). These changes were effective August 5, 1997.

(3) (A) The Secretary shall specify, in the notice of exclusion under paragraph (1) and the written notice under section 1128A, the minimum period (or, in the case of an exclusion of an individual under subsection (b)(12) [which pertains to failure by individuals and entities to grant immediate access to the Secretary, the Inspector General, certain State agencies, and State medicaid fraud control units], or in the case described in subparagraph (G), the period) of the exclusion.

(B) Subject to subparagraph (G), in the case of an exclusion under subsection (a), the minimum period of exclusion shall be not less than five years, except that, upon the request of a State, the Secretary may waive the exclusion under subsection (a)(1) [which pertains to program-related crimes] in the case of an individual or entity that is the sole community physician or sole source of essential specialized services in a community. The Secretary's decision whether to waive the exclusion shall not be reviewable. Subject to subparagraph (G), in the case of an exclusion of an individual under subsection (b)(12) [which pertains to failure to grant immediate access], the period of the exclusion shall be equal to the sum of —

(i) the length of the period in which the individual failed to grant the immediate access described in that subsection, and

(ii) an additional period, not to exceed 90 days, set by the Secretary.

(D) In the case of an exclusion of an individual or entity under paragraph (1), (2), or (3) of subsection (b), the period of the exclusion shall be 3 years, unless the Secretary determines in accordance with published regulations that a shorter period is appropriate because of mitigating circumstances or that a longer period is appropriate because of aggravating circumstances.

(E) In the case of an exclusion of an individual or entity under subsection (b)(4) or (b)(5), the period of the exclusion shall not be less than the period during which the individual's or entity's license to provide health care is revoked, suspended, or surrendered, or the individual or the entity is excluded or suspended from a Federal or State health care program.

(F) In the case of an exclusion of an individual or entity under subsection (b)(6)(B), the period of the exclusion shall be not less than 1 year.

(G) In the case of an exclusion of an individual under subsection (a) based on a conviction occurring on or after the date of the enactment of this subparagraph, if the individual has (before, on, or after such date) been convicted —

(i) on one previous occasion of one or more offenses for which an exclusion may be effected under such subsection, the period of the exclusion shall be not less than 10 years, or

(ii) on 2 or more previous occasions of one or more offenses for which an exclusion may be effected under such subsection, the period of the exclusion shall be permanent.

◆ NOTE: Section 212 of the Health Insurance Portability and Accountability Act of 1996 added subparagraphs (D), (E), and (F) to section 1128(c)3), effective January 1, 1997.

Section 1128(d) provides:

NOTICE TO STATE AGENCIES AND EXCLUSION UNDER STATE HEALTH CARE PROGRAMS. — (1) Subject to paragraph (3), the Secretary shall exercise the authority under this section and section 1128A in a manner that results in an individual's or entity's exclusion from all the programs under title XVIII and all the State health care programs in which the individual or entity may otherwise participate.

(2) The Secretary shall promptly notify each appropriate State agency administering or supervising the administration of each State health care program (and, in the case of an exclusion effected pursuant to subsection (a) [which pertains to mandatory exclusions for program-related crimes and convictions relating to patient abuse] and to which section 304(a)(5) of the Controlled Substances Act [P.L. 91-513; Title II] may apply, the Attorney General —

(A) of the fact and circumstances of each exclusion effected against an individual or entity under this section or section 1128A, and

(B) of the period (described in paragraph (3)) for which the State agency is directed to exclude the individual or entity from participation in the State health care program.

(3) (A) Except as provided in subparagraph (B), the period of the exclusion under a State health care program under paragraph (2) shall be the same as any period of exclusion under title XVIII.

(B) (i) The Secretary may waive an individual's or entity's exclusion under a State health care program under paragraph (2) if the Secretary receives and approves a request for the waiver with respect to the individual or entity from the State agency administering or supervising the administration of the program.

(ii) A State health care program may provide for a period of exclusion which is longer than the period of exclusion under title XVIII.

Section 1128(e) provides:

NOTICE TO STATE LICENSING AGENCIES. — The Secretary shall —

(1) promptly notify the appropriate State or local agency or authority having responsibility for the licensing or certification of an individual or entity excluded (or directed to be

excluded) from participation under this section or section 1128A, of the fact and circumstances of the exclusion,

(2) request that appropriate investigations be made and sanctions invoked in accordance with applicable State law and policy, and

(3) request that the State or local agency or authority keep the Secretary and the Inspector General of the Department of Health and Human Services fully and currently informed with respect to any actions taken in response to the request.

Section 1128(f) provides:

NOTICE, HEARING, AND JUDICIAL REVIEW. — (1) Subject to paragraph (2), any individual or entity that is excluded (or directed to be excluded) from participation under this section is entitled to reasonable notice and opportunity for a hearing thereon by the Secretary to the same extent as is provided in section 205(b) [42 U.S.C.A. 405(b)] , and to judicial review of the Secretary's final decision after such hearing as is provided in section 205(g) [42 U.S.C.A. 405(g)] except that, in so applying such sections and section 205(l), any reference therein to the Commissioner of Social Security or the Social Security Administration shall be considered a reference to the Secretary or the Department of Health and Human Services, respectively.

(2) Unless the Secretary determines that the health or safety of individuals receiving services warrants the exclusion taking effect earlier, any individual or entity that is the subject of an adverse determination under subsection (b)(7) [which pertains to fraud, kickbacks, and other prohibited activities described in section 1128A and section 1128B] shall be entitled to a hearing by an administrative law judge (as provided under section 205(b)) on the determination under subsection (b)(7) before any exclusion based upon the determination takes effect.

(3) The provisions of section 205(h) [42 U.S.C.A. 405(h)] shall apply with respect to this section and sections 1128A, 1129, and 1156 [which pertains to exclusions based on recommendations by Peer Review Organizations] to the same extent as it is applicable with respect to title II, except that, in so applying such section and section 205(l), any reference therein to the

Commissioner of Social Security shall be considered a reference to the Secretary.

With respect to the meaning of "any Federal health care program", sections 1128(a)(1) and (b)(1) make cross reference to section 1128B(f), which provides:

(f) For purposes of this section, the term "Federal health care program" means —

(1) any plan or program that provides health benefits, whether directly, through insurance, or otherwise, which is funded directly, in whole or in part, by the United States Government (other than the health insurance program under chapter 89 of title 5, United States Code [which provides health insurance for Federal employees]; or

(2) any State health care program, as defined in section 1128(h).

◆ NOTE: Section 108(b)(9) of the Social Security Independence and Program Improvements Act of 1994 added the phrases beginning "except that" at the end of subsections (f)(1) and (f)(3) above, effective March 31, 1995. Section 206(b)(2) of that Act inserted ", 1129" after "sections 1128A" in subsection (f)(3), effective October 1, 1994.

With respect to hearing rights and judicial review, sections 205, 42 U.S.C.A. 405, as amended by the Social Security Independence and Program Improvements Act of 1994, provides in pertinent part:

(b) (1) The Commissioner of Social Security is directed to make findings of fact, and decisions as to the rights of any individual applying for a payment under this title. Any such decision by the Commissioner of Social Security which involves a determination of disability and which is in whole or in part unfavorable to such individual shall contain a statement of the case, in understandable language, setting forth a discussion of the evidence, and stating the Commissioner's determination and the reason or reasons upon which it is based. Upon request by any such individual or upon request by a wife, divorced wife, widow, surviving divorced wife, surviving divorced mother, surviving divorced father, husband, divorced husband, widower, surviving divorced husband, child or parent who makes a showing in writing that his or her rights may be prejudiced by any decision the Commissioner of Social Security has rendered, the Commissioner shall give such applicant and such other individual reasonable notice and opportunity for a hearing with respect to such decision, and, if a hearing is held, shall, on the basis of evidence adduced at the hearing, affirm, modify, or reverse his findings of fact and such decision. Any such request with respect to such a decision must be filed within sixty days after notice of such decision is received by the individual making such request. The Commissioner of Social Security is further authorized, on the Commissioner's own motion, to hold such hearings and to conduct such investigations and other proceedings as the Commissioner may deem necessary or proper for the administration of this title. In the course of any hearing, investigation, or other proceeding, the Commissioner may administer oaths and affirmations, examine witnesses, and receive evidence. Evidence may be received at any hearing before the Commissioner of Social Security even though inadmissible under rules of evidence applicable to court procedure.

* * *

(g) Any individual, after any final decision of the Commissioner of Social Security made after a hearing to which he was a party, irrespective of the amount in controversy, may obtain a review of such decision by a civil action commenced within sixty days after the mailing to him of notice of such decision or within such further time as the Commissioner of Social Security may allow. Such action shall be brought in the district court of the United States for the judicial district in which the plaintiff resides, or has his principal place of business, or, if he does not reside or have his principal place of business within any such judicial district, in the District Court of the United States for the District of Columbia [United States District Court for the District of Columbia]. As part of the Commissioner's answer the Commissioner of Social Security shall file a certified copy of the transcript of the record including the evidence upon which the findings and decision complained of are based. The court shall have power to enter, upon the pleadings and transcript of the record, a judgment affirming, modifying, or reversing the deci-

> sion of the Commissioner of Social Security, with or without remanding the cause for a rehearing. The findings of the Commissioner of Social Security as to any fact, if supported by substantial evidence, shall be conclusive, and where a claim has been denied by the Commissioner or a decision is rendered under subsection (b) hereof which is adverse to an individual who was a party to the hearing before the Commissioner of Social Security, because of failure of the claimant or such individual to submit proof in conformity with any regulation prescribed under subsection (a) hereof, the court shall review only the question of conformity with such regulations and the validity of such regulations. The court may, on motion of the Commissioner of Social Security made for good cause shown before the Commissioner files his answer, remand the case to the Commissioner of Social Security for further action by the Commissioner of Social Security, and it may at any time order additional evidence to be taken before the Commissioner of Social Security, but only upon a showing that there is new evidence which is material and that there is good cause for the failure to incorporate such evidence into the record in a prior proceeding; and the Commissioner of Social Security shall, after the case is remanded, and after hearing such additional evidence if so ordered, modify or affirm the Commissioner's findings of fact or the Commissioner's decision, or both, and shall file with the court any such additional and modified findings of fact and decision and a transcript of the additional record and testimony upon which the Commissioner's action in modifying or affirming was based. Such additional or modified findings of fact and decision shall be reviewable only to the extent provided for review of the original findings of fact and decision. The judgment of the court shall be final except that it shall be subject to review in the same manner as a judgment in other civil actions. Any action instituted in accordance with this subsection shall survive notwithstanding any change in the person occupying the office of Commissioner of Social Security or any vacancy in such office.

Subsection (a) of section 205, to which subsection (g) refers back, provides:

> (a) The Commissioner of Social Security shall have full power and authority to make rules and regulations and to establish

> procedures, not inconsistent with the provisions of this title, which are necessary or appropriate to carry out such provisions, and shall adopt reasonable and proper rules and regulations to regulate and provide for the nature and extent of the proofs and evidence and the method of taking and furnishing the same in order to establish the right to benefits hereunder.

Section 205(h), 42 U.S.C.A. 405(h), provides:

> The findings and decision of the Commissioner after a hearing shall be binding upon all individuals who were parties to such hearing. No findings of fact or decision of the Commissioner shall be reviewed by any person, tribunal, or governmental agency except as herein provided. No action against the United States, the Secretary, or any officer or employee thereof shall be brought under section 1331 or 1346 of title 28, United States Code, to recover on any claim arising under this title.

◆ NOTE: Effective March 31, 1995, section 110(a) of P.L. 203-296, the Social Security Program Independence and Program Improvement Act of 1994, changed references to the Department of Health and Human Services to the Social Security Administration, and references to the Secretary of Health and Human Services to the Commissioner of Social Security, and references to the pronouns "she", "her", "he", "him", and "his" to "the Commissioner" or "the Commissioner's", as appropriate, throughout section 205 of the Social Security Act.

Section 1128(g) provides:

> APPLICATION FOR TERMINATION OF EXCLUSION. — (1) An individual or entity excluded (or directed to be excluded) from participation under this section or section 1128A may apply to the Secretary, in the manner specified by the Secretary in regulations and at the end of the minimum period of exclusion provided under subsection (c)(3) and at such other times as the Secretary may provide, for termination of the exclusion effected under this section or section 1128A.
>
> (2) The Secretary may terminate the exclusion if the Secretary determines, on the basis of the conduct of the applicant which occurred after the date of the notice of exclusion or which was unknown to the Secretary at the time of the exclusion, that —

(A) there is no basis under subsection (a) or (b) or section 1128A(a) for a continuation of the exclusion, and

(B) there are reasonable assurances that the types of actions which formed the basis for the original exclusion have not recurred and will not recur.

(3) The Secretary shall promptly notify each appropriate State agency administering or supervising the administration of each State health care program (and, in the case of an exclusion effected pursuant to subsection (a) and to which section 304(a)(5) of the Controlled Substances Act [P.L. 91-513; Title II] may apply, the Attorney General) of the fact and circumstances of each termination of exclusion made under this subsection.

Section 1128(h) provides:

DEFINITION OF STATE HEALTH CARE PROGRAM. — For purposes of this section and sections 1128A and 1128(B) [42 U.S.C.A. 1320a-7b, which pertains to criminal penalties for acts involving Medicare or State health care programs] the term "State health care program" means —

(1) a State plan approved under title XIX [Medicaid, 42 U.S.C.A. 1396 et seq.],

(2) any program receiving funds under title V [Maternal and Child Health Services Block Grants, 42 U.S.C.A. 701 et seq.] or from an allotment to a State under such title,

(3) any program receiving funds under title XX [Block Grants to States for Social Services, 42 U.S.C.A. 1397 et seq.] or from an allotment to a State under such title; or

(4) a State child health plan approved under title XXI.

◆ NOTE: Effective August 5, 1997, section 4901(b)(2) of the Balanced Budget Act of 1997 deleted "or" from the end of paragraph (h)(2); substituted ", or" for the period at the end of paragraph (h)(3); and added paragraph (h)(4).

Section 1128(i) provides:

CONVICTED DEFINED. — For purposes of subsections (a) and (b), an individual or entity is considered to have been "convicted" of a criminal offense —

(1) when a judgment of conviction has been entered against the individual or entity by a Federal, State, or local court, regardless of whether there is an appeal pending or whether the judgment of conviction or other record relating to criminal conduct has been expunged;

(2) when there has been a finding of guilt against the individual or entity by a Federal, State, or local court;

(3) when a plea of guilty or nolo contendere by the individual or entity has been accepted by a Federal, State, or local court; or

(4) when the individual or entity has entered into participation in a first offender, deferred adjudication, or other arrangement or program where judgment of conviction has been withheld.

With respect to the definition of immediate family member for purposes of section 1128(b)(8)(A)(iii), section 4303(a)(2) of the Balanced Budget Act of 1997 added new section 1128(j), effective September 19, 1997. Section 1128(j) provides:

> DEFINITION OF IMMEDIATE FAMILY MEMBER AND MEMBER OF THE HOUSEHOLD.— For purposes of subsection (b)(8)(A)(iii):
>
> (1) The term 'immediate family member' means, with respect to a person—
>
> (A) the husband or wife of the person;
>
> (B) the natural or adoptive parent, child, or sibling of the person;
>
> (C) the stepparent, stepchild, stepbrother, or stepsister of the person;
>
> (D) the father-, mother-, daughter-, son-, brother-, or sister-in-law of the person;
>
> (E) the grandparent or grandchild of the person; and
>
> (F) the spouse of a grandparent or grandchild of the person.
>
> (2) The term 'member of the household' means, with respect to any person, any individual sharing a common abode as part of a single family unit with the person, including domestic employees and others who live together as a family unit, but not including a roomer or boarder.

With respect to disclosure of ownership and control of entities and their subcontractors, to which sections 1128(b)(8), (9), and (10) apply, section 1124, 42 U.S.C.A. 1320a-3, provides:

> (a) (1) The Secretary shall by regulation or by contract provision provide that each disclosing entity (as defined in paragraph (2)) shall —
>
> (A) as a condition of the disclosing entity's participation in, or certification or recertification under, any of the programs established by titles V, XVIII, and XIX, or
>
> (B) as a condition for the approval or renewal of a contract or agreement between the disclosing entity and the Secretary or the appropriate State agency under any of the programs established under titles V, XVIII, and XIX,
>
> supply the Secretary or the appropriate State agency with full and complete information as to the identity of each person with an ownership or control interest (as defined in paragraph (3)) in the entity or in any subcontractor (as defined by the Secretary in regulations) in which the entity directly or indirectly has a 5 per centum or more ownership interest and supply the Secretary with both the employer identification number (assigned pursuant to section 6109 of the Internal Revenue Code of 1986) and social security account number (assigned under section 205(c)(2)(B)) of the disclosing entity, each person with an ownership or control interest (as defined in subsection (a)(3)), and any subcontractor in which the entity directly or indirectly has a 5 percent or more ownership interest.

◆ NOTE: Section 4313(a) of the Balanced Budget Act of 1997 added the phrase beginning "and supply the Secretary". This change pertains to the application of conditions of participation, and to the entering into or renewal of contracts and agreements, occurring more than 90 days after the submission of a report required by section 4313(d). The latter section reads: "(d) REPORT. — Before the amendments made by this subsection may become effective, the Secretary of Health and Human Services shall submit to Congress a report on steps the Secretary has taken to assure the confidentiality of social security account numbers that will be provided to the Secretary under such amendments."

(2) As used in this section, the term "disclosing entity" means an entity which is —

(A) a provider of services (as defined in section 1861(u) [42 U.S.C.A. 1395x(u), which means a hospital, skilled nursing facility, comprehensive outpatient rehabilitation facility, home health agency, hospice program, or home intravenous drug therapy provider], other than a fund), an independent clinical laboratory, a renal disease facility, a managed care entity, as defined in section 1932(a)(1)(B) [42 U.S.C.A. 1396u-2(a)(1)(B), which pertains to the use of managed care in the Medicaid program. This reference to a managed care entity was added by section 4707(c) of the Balanced Budget Act of 1997, effective August 5, 1997], or a health maintenance organization (as defined in section 1301(a) of the Public Health Service Act [P.L. 78-410];

(B) an entity (other than an individual practitioner or group of practitioners) that furnishes, or arranges for the furnishing of items or services with respect to which payment may be claimed by the entity under any plan or program established pursuant to title V or under a State plan approved under title XIX; or

(C) a carrier or other agency or organization that is acting as a fiscal intermediary or agent with respect to one or more providers of services (for purposes of part A or part B of title XVIII, or both, or for purposes of a State plan approved under title XIX) pursuant to (i) an agreement under section 1816 [42 U.S.C.A. 1395h, which pertains to fiscal intermediaries], (ii) a contract under section 1842 [42 U.S.C.A. 1395u, which pertains to carriers], or (iii) an agreement with a single State agency administering or supervising the administration of a State plan approved under title XIX.

(3) As used in this section, the term "person with an ownership or control interest" means, with respect to an entity, a person who —

A) (i) has directly or indirectly (as determined by the Secretary in regulations) an ownership interest of 5 per centum or more in the entity; or

(ii) is the owner of a whole or part interest in any mortgage, deed of trust, note, or other obligation secured (in whole or in part) by the entity or any of the property or assets thereof, which whole or part interest is equal to or exceeds 5 per centum of the total property and assets of the entity; or

(B) is an officer or director of the entity, if the entity is organized as a corporation; or

(C) is a partner in the entity, if the entity is organized as a partnership.

(b) To the extent determined to be feasible under regulations of the Secretary, a disclosing entity shall also include in the information supplied under subsection (a)(1), with respect to each person with an ownership or control interest in the entity, the name of any other disclosing entity with respect to which the person is a person with an ownership or control interest.

And section 1124A, which applies to items and services furnished on or after January 1, 1992, pursuant to section 4164(b)(1) of OBRA 90, provides:

(a) DISCLOSURE REQUIRED TO RECEIVE PAYMENT.—No payment may be made under part B of title XVIII for items or services furnished by any disclosing part B provider unless such provider has provided the Secretary with full and complete information—

(1) on the identity of each person with an ownership or control interest in the provider or in any subcontractor (as defined by the Secretary in regulations) in which the provider directly or indirectly has a 5 percent or more ownership interest;

◆ NOTE: Section 4313(b)(1) of the Balanced Budget Act of 1997 removed "and" from the end of paragraph (a)(1); substituted "; and" for the period at the end of paragraph (a)(2); and added paragraph (a)(3). Those changes apply to payment for items and services furnished more than 90 days after the submission of the report required by section 4313(d), which is quoted in a NOTE above.

(2) with respect to any person identified under paragraph (1) or any managing employee of the provider—

(A) on the identity of any other entities providing items or services for which payment may be made under title XVIII with respect to which such person or managing employee is a person with an ownership or control interest at the time such information is supplied or at any time during the 3-year period ending on the date such information is supplied, and

◆ NOTE: Section 147(f)(7)(a)(i) of the Social Security Act Amendments of 1994, P.L. 103-432, deleted the phrase "of the Social Security Act" which previously followed "title XVIII" in (2)(A) above, effective November 5, 1990, as if enacted by the Omnibus Budget Reconciliation Act of 1990, P.L. 101-508.

(B) as to whether any penalties, assessments, or exclusions have been assessed against such person or managing employee under section 1128, 1128A, or 1128B; and

(3) including the employer identification number (assigned pursuant to section 6109 of the Internal Revenue Code of 1986) and social security account number (assigned under section 205(c)(2)(B)) of the disclosing part B provider and any person, managing employee, or other entity identified or described under paragraph (1) or (2).

(b) UPDATES TO INFORMATION SUPPLIED. — A disclosing part B provider shall notify the Secretary of any changes or updates to the information supplied under subsection (a) not later than 180 days after such changes or updates take effect.

◆ NOTE: Section 147(f)(7)(a)(i) of the Social Security Act Amendments of 1994, P.L. 103-432, deleted the phrase "of the Social Security Act" which previously followed "title XVIII" in (2)(A) above, effective November 5, 1990, as if enacted by the Omnibus Budget Reconciliation Act of 1990, P.L. 101-508. Also, section 4313(b)(1) of the Balanced Budget Act of 1997 removed "and" from the end of paragraph (a)(1); substituted "; and" for the period at the end of paragraph (a)(2); and added paragraph (a)(3). Section 4313(b)(2) inserted "(or, for purposes of subsection (a)(3), any entity receiving payment)" after "on an assignment-related basis" in paragraph (c)(1), now (d)(1). Changes made by section 4313(b) apply to payment for items and services furnished more than 90 days after the submission of the report required by section 4313(d), which is quoted in a NOTE above. Effective August 5, 1997, section 4313(c) redesignated subsection (c) as subsection (d), and added new subsection (c).

(c) VERIFICATION. —

(1) TRANSMITTAL BY HHS. — The Secretary shall transmit —

(A) to the Commissioner of Social Security information concerning each social security account number (assigned under section 205(c)(2)(B)), and

(B) to the Secretary of the Treasury information concerning each employer identification number (assigned pursuant to section 6109 of the Internal Revenue Code of 1986), supplied to the Secretary pursuant to subsection (a)(3) or section 1124(c) to the extent necessary for verification of such information in accordance with paragraph (2).

(2) VERIFICATION. — The Commissioner of Social Security and the Secretary of the Treasury shall verify the accuracy of, or correct, the information supplied by the Secretary to such official pursuant to paragraph (1), and shall report such verifications or corrections to the Secretary.

(3) FEES FOR VERIFICATION. — The Secretary shall reimburse the Commissioner and Secretary of the Treasury, at a rate negotiated between the Secretary and such official, for the costs incurred by such official in performing the verification and correction services described in this subsection.

(d) DEFINITIONS. — For purposes of this section —

(1) the term "disclosing part B provider" means any entity receiving payment on an assignment-related basis (or, for purposes of subsection (a)(3), any entity receiving payment)[This phrase beginning "or, for purposes of" was added by section 4313(b)(2) of the Balanced Budget Act, effective as indicated in the NOTE above.] for furnishing items or services for which payment may be made under part B of title XVIII, except that such term does not include an entity described in section 1124(a)(2);

(2) the term "managing employee" means, with respect to a provider, a person described in section 1126(b); and

(3) the term person with an ownership or control interest " means, with respect to a provider —

(A) a person described in section 1124(a)(3), or

(B) a person who has one of the 5 largest direct or indirect ownership or control interests in the provider.

Finally, section 1126, 42 U.S.C.A. 1320a-5, provides:

(a) As a condition of participation in or certification or recertification under the programs established by titles XVIII and XIX, any hospital, nursing facility, or other entity (other than an individual practitioner or group of practitioners) shall be required to disclose to the Secretary or to the appropriate State agency the name of any person that is a person described in subparagraphs (A) and (B) of section 1128(b)(8). The Secretary or the appropriate State agency shall promptly notify the Inspector General in the Department of Health and Human Services of the receipt from any entity of any application or request for such participation, certification, or recertification which discloses the name of any such person, and shall notify the Inspector General of the action taken with respect to such application or request.

(b) For the purposes of this section, the term "managing employee" means, with respect to an entity, an individual, including a general manager, business manager, administrator, and director, who exercises operational or managerial control over the entity, or who directly or indirectly conducts the day-to-day operations of the entity.

For regulatory citations, see Chapter 8

§ 4:7 DISCLOSURE BY INSTITUTIONS, ORGANIZATIONS, AND AGENCIES OF OWNERS AND OTHER INDIVIDUALS SANCTIONED OR CONVICTED AND OF CERTAIN BUSINESS RELATIONSHIPS — Sections 1128(b)(9) and (10), 1124, 1124A, and 1126 [42 U.S.C.A. 1320a-7(b)(9) and (10), 1320a-3, 1320a-3a, and 1320a-5]

Summary

Pursuant to section 1128(b)(8), 42 U.S.C.A. 1320a-7(b)(8), the Secretary of Health and Human Services may exclude any entity from participation in any Federal health care program (as defined in section 1128B(f), 42 U.S.C.A. 1320a-7b(f), if a person who has a direct or indirect ownership or control interest in, or who is an officer, director, agent, or managing employee of, that entity is a person who —

(1) has been convicted of a criminal offense (felony or misdemeanor) related to the delivery of an item or service under Medicare or Medicaid or any State health care program;

(2) has been convicted under Federal or State law of a criminal offense (felony or misdemeanor) relating to neglect or abuse of patients in connection with the delivery of a health care item or service;

(3) has been convicted under Federal or State law of a felony or misdemeanor in connection with the delivery of a health care item or service or with respect to any act or omission in a program operated by or financed in whole or in part by any Federal, State, or local government agency, of a criminal offense relating to fraud, theft, embezzlement, breach of fiduciary responsibility, or other financial misconduct;

(4) has been convicted under Federal or State law of a felony relating to the unlawful manufacture, distribution, prescription, or dispensing of a controlled substance;

◆ NOTE: Paragraphs (3) and (4) above apply to convictions involving offenses which occurred after enactment of the Health Insurance Portability and Accountability Act of 1996, P.L. 104-191 (August 21, 1996).

(5) has been convicted under Federal or State law in connection with interference with or obstruction of any investigation into any criminal offense described in paragraphs (1)-(4) above;

(6) has been convicted under Federal or State law of a misdemeanor relating to the unlawful manufacture, distribution, prescription, or dispensing of a controlled substance;

(7) has had a civil money penalty assessed against him under section 1128A, 42 U.S.C.A. 1320a-7a, or effective October 31, 1994, pursuant to section 206(b)(2) of the Social Security Independence and Program Improvements Act of 1994, P.L. 103-296, under section 1129, 42 U.S.C.A. 1320a-8, which pertains to violations under Title II (Social Security benefits) or Title XVI (welfare benefits) of the Social Security Act;

(8) has been excluded from participation under any Federal or State health care program.

Pursuant to section 4303(a)(1) of the Balanced Budget Act of 1997, P.L. 105-33, effective September 19,1997, section 1128(b)(8) also applies to persons who had an ownership or control interest but transferred it in anticipation of, or following, a conviction, assessment, or exclusion to an immediate family member or to a member of his or her household.

Pursuant to section 1128B(f), which applies by cross-reference, "Federal health care program" means any plan or program that provides health benefits, whether directly, through insurance, or otherwise, which is funded directly, in whole or in part by the United States Government. (The only statutory exception is the health insurance program for Federal employees authorized by Chapter 89 of Title 5 of the United States Code.)

"Federal health care program" also means any State health care program, as defined in section 1128(h). Thus the Secretary also may direct the exclusion of such entities from participation in Medicaid; the Maternal and Child Health Services Block Grant programs authorized under Title V, 42 U.S.C.A. 701 et seq.; programs under Title XX, which authorizes Block Grants to States for Social Services, 42 U.S.C.A. 1397 et seq.; and a State child health plan approved under Title XXI.

Section 1124(a)(3), 42 U.S.C.A. 1320a-3(a)(3), defines a person with an ownership or control interest with respect to an entity as one who directly or indirectly owns 5 percent of the entity; or who is the owner of a whole or part interest in any mortgage, deed of trust, note, or other obligation secured in whole or in part by the entity or any of the property or assets thereof if that whole or part interest equals or exceeds 5 percent of the total property and assets of the entity; or who is an officer or director of the entity and the entity is a corporation; or who is a partner in the entity.

Section 1128(j)(1) defines "immediate family member" for purposes of subsection (b)(8)(A)(iii) to include the husband or wife of the person; the natural or adoptive parent, child, or sibling of the person; the stepparent, stepchild, stepbrother, or stepsister of the person; the father-in-law, mother-in-law, daughter-in-law, son-in-law, brother-in-law, or sister-in-law of the person; the grandparent or grandchild of the person; and the spouse of a grandparent or grandchild of the person. Section 1128(j)(2) defines "member of the household", with respect to any person, as any individual sharing a common abode as part of a single family unit with the person, including domestic employees and others who live together as a family unit (but not including a roomer or boarder).

◆ NOTE: The definitions in section 1128(j) were added, effective September 19, 1997, by section 4303(a)(2) of the Balanced Budget Act of 1997.

In that context, section 1126(a), 42 U.S.C.A. 1320a-5(a), then provides that, as a condition of participation in or certification or recertification under Medicare and Medicaid, any hospital, nursing facility, or other entity (other than an individual practitioner or group of practitioners) must disclose to the Secretary or to the appropriate State agency the name of any person who meets the description set forth in section 1128(b)(8). The Secretary or the appropriate State agency then must promptly notify the Inspector General of the Department of Health and Human Services of the receipt from any entity of any application or request for such participation, certification, or recertification which discloses the name of any such person, and must notify the Inspector General of the action taken with respect to such application or request.

For purposes of section 1126 and 1128(b)(8), section 1126(b) defines managing employee with respect to an entity as an individual, including a general manager, business manager, administrator, and director, who exercises operational or managerial control over the entity, or who directly or indirectly conducts the day-to-day operations of the entity.

Section 1126 should be read in conjunction with section 1124, 42 U.S.C.A. 1320a-3, which obligates the Secretary to require by regulation or by contract more disclosure of ownership and related information. By its terms, as a condition of participation in, or certification or recertification under, Titles V, XVIII, or XIX, or as a condition for the approval or renewal of a contract or agreement with the Secretary or the appropriate State agency under those titles, disclosing entities must disclose to the Secretary and to the appropriate State agency full and complete information as to the identity of each person with an ownership or control interest in the entity or in any subcontractor in which the entity directly or indirectly has a 5 percent or more ownership.

"Disclosing entity" is defined by section 1124(a)(2) as: providers (meaning hospitals, skilled nursing facilities, comprehensive outpatient rehabilitation facilities, home health agencies, hospices, and home intravenous drug therapy providers); independent clinical laboratories; renal disease facilities; effective August 5, 1997, a managed care entity, as defined in section 1932(a)(1)(B); health maintenance organizations; suppliers; carriers; and fiscal intermediaries. To the extent feasible, the Secretary also by regulation must require disclosing entities to include with information about persons with ownership or control interests in them the name of any other disclosing entity with respect to which that person is a person with an ownership or control interest.

In addition, disclosing entities must supply the Secretary with both the employer identification number (assigned pursuant to section 6109 of the Internal Revenue Code of 1986), and the Social Security account number (assigned under section 205(c)(2)(B)) of the disclosing entity, each person with an ownership or control interest, and any subcontractor in which the entity directly or indirectly has a five percent or more ownerhip interest. This requirement was added by section 4313(a) of the Balanced Budget Act of 1997. It pertains to application of conditions of participation, and to the entering into or renewal of contracts and agreements, occurring more than 90 days after submission of a report required by Section 4313(d). That reference is to a report to Congress which the Secretary must make on steps the Secretary has taken to assure the confidentiality of Social Security account numbers to be provided to the Secretary under this provision.

Presumably, armed with this data, the Secretary, through the Health Care Financing Administration, and the Inspector General can ferret out sweetheart deals and punish nefarious activities which unduly increase the cost of health care.

Indeed, to further that cause, section 1128(b)(9) permits the Secretary to exclude an entity from Medicare and to direct its exclusion from State health care programs if it does not fully and accurately make any disclosure about ownership and control required by section 1124 or section 1126. In addition, pursuant to section 4601(b)(1) and (3) of P.L. 101-508, the Omnibus Budget Reconciliation Act of 1990 (OBRA 90), applicable to items and services furnished on or after January 1, 1992, exclusion is authorized for certain Part B providers who do not comply with ownership and disclosure requirements.

Furthermore, section 1128(b)(10) permits the Secretary to exclude from Medicare any disclosing entity, as defined in section 1124(a)(2), and to direct its exclusion from State health care programs, if the entity failed to supply timely upon his or a relevant State agency's request full and complete information about the ownership of a subcontractor with whom the entity had, during the previous 12 months, business transactions in an aggregate amount exceeding $25,000. The same is true if the entity failed to supply timely upon request by the Secretary or the relevant State agency full and complete information about any significant business transactions occurring during the five-year period ending on the date of such request between the entity and any wholly owned supplier or between the entity and any subcontractor.

Statutory Provisions

Section 1126, 42 U.S.C.A. 1320a-5, provides:

(a) As a condition of participation in or certification or recertification under the programs established by titles XVIII and XIX, any hospital, nursing facility, or other entity (other than an individual practitioner or group of practitioners) shall be required to disclose to the Secretary or to the appropriate State agency the name of any person that is a person described in subparagraphs (A) and (B) of section 1128(b)(8). The Secretary or the appropriate State agency shall promptly notify the Inspector General in the Department of Health and Human Services of the receipt from any entity of any application or request for such participation, certification, or recertification which discloses the name of any such person, and shall notify the Inspector General of the action taken with respect to such application or request.

(b) For the purposes of this section, the term "managing employee" means, with respect to an entity, an individual, including a general manager, business manager, administrator, and director, who exercises operational or managerial control over the entity, or who directly or indirectly conducts the day-to-day operations of the entity.

Section 1128(b), 42 U.S.C.A. 1320a-7(b), provides in pertinent part:

(b) PERMISSIVE EXCLUSION. — The Secretary may exclude the following individuals and entities from participation in any Federal health care program (as defined in section 1128B(f) [42 U.S.C.A. 1320a-7b(f)]:

◆ NOTE: Section 4331(c) of the Balanced Budget Act of 1997, P.L. 105-33, substituted "any Federal health care program (as defined in section 1128B(f)" for "any program under title XVIII and may direct that the following individuals and entities be excluded from partitipation in any State health care program". That change was effective August 5, 1997.

* * *

(8) ENTITIES CONTROLLED BY A SANCTIONED INDIVIDUAL — Any entity with respect to which the Secretary determines that a person —

(A) (i) who has a direct or indirect ownership or control interest of 5 percent or more in the entity or with an ownership or control interest (as defined in section 1124(a)(3)) in that entity, or

(ii) who is an officer, director, agent, or managing employee (as defined in section 1126(b)) of that entity; or

(iii) who was described in clause (i) but is no longer so described because of a transfer of ownership or control interest, in anticipation of (or following) a conviction, assessment, or exclusion described in subparagraph (B) against the person, to an immediate family member (as defined in subsection (j)(1)) or a member of the household of the person (as defined in subsection (j)(2)) who continues to maintain an interest described in such clause —

is a person —

(B) (i) who has been convicted of any offense described in subsection (a) or in paragraph (1), (2), or (3) of this subsection;

(ii) against whom a civil monetary penalty has been assessed under section 1128A [42 U.S.C.A. 1320a-7a] or 1129 [42 U.S.C.A. 1320a-8, which pertains to civil monetary penalties and assessments for violations under Title II (Social Security) and Title XVI (welfare benefits) of the Social Security Act]; or

◆ NOTE: Section 206(b)(2) of the Social Security Independence and Program Improvements Act of 1994, P.L. 103-296, added the phrase "or 1129", effective October 31, 1994.

(iii) who has been excluded from participation under a program under title XVIII or under a State health care program.

◆ NOTE: Effective October 31, 1994, section 206(b)(2) of the Social Security Independence and Program Improvements Act of 1994, P.L. 103-296, inserted "or 1129" after "section 1128A" in subsection (b)(8)(B)(ii) below. Effective September 19, 1997, section 4303(a)(1) of the Balanced Budget Act of 1997, removed "or" at the end of clause (A)(i) above; substituted "; or" for a dash at the end of clause (A)(ii); and added clause (A)(iii).

For purposes of section 1128(b)(8)(A)(iii), section 4303(a)(2) of the Balanced Budget Act of 1997 added new section 1128(j), effective September 19, 1997. Section 1128(j) defines immediate family member and member of the household, as follows:

DEFINITION OF IMMEDIATE FAMILY MEMBER AND MEMBER OF THE HOUSEHOLD. — For purposes of subsection (b)(8)(A)(iii):

(1) The term 'immediate family member' means, with respect to a person —

(A) the husband or wife of the person;

(B) the natural or adoptive parent, child, or sibling of the person;

(C) the stepparent, stepchild, stepbrother, or stepsister of the person;

(D) the father-, mother-, daughter-, son-, brother-, or sister-in-law of the person;

(E) the grandparent or grandchild of the person; and

(F) the spouse of a grandparent or grandchild of the person.

(2) The term 'member of the household' means, with respect to any person, any individual sharing a common abode as part of a single family unit with the person, including domestic employees and others who live together as a family unit, but not including a roomer or boarder.

Section 1128(a) provides in pertinent part:

MANDATORY EXCLUSION. — The Secretary shall exclude the following individuals and entities from participation in any Federal health care program (as defined in section 1128B(f)):

◆ NOTE: Effective August 5, 1997, section 4331(c)(1) of the Balanced Budget Act of 1997, P.L. 105-33, substituted the phrase "any Federal health care program (as defined in section 1128(B)(f))" for "any program under title XVIII and shall direct that the following individuals and entities be excluded from participation in any State health care program (as defined in subsection (h))".

(1) CONVICTION OF PROGRAM-RELATED CRIMES. — Any individual or entity that has been convicted of a criminal offense related to the delivery of an item or service under title XVIII or under any State health care program.

(2) CONVICTION RELATING TO PATIENT ABUSE. — Any individual or entity that has been convicted, under Federal or State law, of a criminal offense relating to neglect or abuse of patients in connection with the delivery of a health care item or service.

(3) FELONY CONVICTION RELATING TO HEALTH CARE FRAUD. — Any individual or entity that has been convicted for an offense which occurred after the date of the enactment of the Health Insurance Portability and Accountability Act of 1996 [August 21, 1996] under Federal or State law, in connection with the delivery of a health care item or service or with respect to any act or omission in a health care program (other than those specifically described in paragraph (1)) operated by or financed in whole or in part by any Federal, State, or local government agency, of a criminal offense consisting of a felony relating to fraud, theft, embezzlement, breach of fiduciary responsibility, or other financial misconduct.

(4) FELONY CONVICTION RELATING TO CONTROLLED SUBSTANCE. — Any individual or entity that has been convicted for an offense which occurred after the enactment of the Health Insurance Portability and Accountability Act of 1996, under Federal or State Law, of a criminal offense consisting of a felony relating to the unlawful manufacture, distribution, prescription, or dispensing of a controlled substance.

◆ NOTE: Sections 211(a)(1) and 211(b)(4) of the Health Insurance Portability and Accountability Act of 1996, P.L. 104–191, effective January 1, 1997, added paragraphs (3) and (4) respectively to section 1128(a).

Section 1128(b) also provides in pertinent part:

PERMISSIVE EXCLUSION. — The Secretary may exclude the following individuals and entities from participation in any Federal helaht care program (as defined in section 1128(B)(f):

(1) CONVICTION RELATING TO FRAUD. — Any individual or entity that has been convicted for an offense which occurred after the date of the enactment of the Health Insurance Portability and Accountability Act of 1996, under Federal or State law —

(A) of a criminal offense consisting of a misdemeanor relating to fraud, theft, embezzlement, breach of fiduciary responsibility, or other financial misconduct —

(i) in connection with the delivery of a health care item or service; or

(ii) with respect to any act or omission in a health care program (other than those specifically described in subsection (a)(1)) operated by or financed in whole or in part by any Federal, State, or local government agency; or

(B) of a criminal offense relating to fraud, theft, embezzlement, breach of fiduciary responsibility, or other financial misconduct with respect to any act or omission in a program other than a health care program) operated by or financed in whole or in part by any Federal, State or local government agency.

◆ NOTE: Prior to amendment by section 211(a)(2) of the Health Insurance Portability and Accountability Act of 1996, section 1128(b)(1) read: "(1)CONVICTION RELATING TO FRAUD. — Any individual or entity that has been convicted, under Federal or State law, in connection with the delivery of a health care item or service or with respect to any act or omission in a program operated by or financed in whole or in part by any Federal, State, or local government agency, of a criminal offense relating to fraud, theft, embezzlement, breach of fiduciary responsibility, or other financial misconduct;"

(2) CONVICTION RELATING TO OBSTRUCTION OF AN INVESTIGATION. — Any individual or entity that has been convicted, under Federal or State law, in connection with the interference with or obstruction of any investigation into any criminal offense described in paragraph (1) or in subsection (a).

(3) MISDEMEANOR CONVICTION RELATING TO CONTROLLED SUBSTANCE. —Any individual or entity that has been convicted, under Federal or State law, of a criminal offense consisting of a misdemeanor relating to the unlawful manufacture, distribution, prescription, or dispensing of a controlled substance.

◆ NOTE: Prior to amendment by section 211(a)(2) of the Health Insurance Portability and Accountability Act of 1996, effective January 1, 1997,, paragraph (3) read: "(3)CONVICTION RELATING TO CONTROLLED SUBSTANCE. — Any individual or entity that has been convicted, under Federal or State law, of a criminal offense relating to the unlawful manufacture, distribution, prescription, or dispensing of a controlled substance."

* * *

(9) FAILURE TO DISCLOSE REQUIRED INFORMATION.-Any entity that did not fully and accurately make any disclosure required by section 1124, section 1124A ["section 1124A", added by section 4164(b)(3) of OBRA 90 (applicable with respect to items and services furnished on or after January 1, 1992), requires certain Part B providers to disclose certain ownership and control interests and information about penalties, assessments, or exclusions imposed under section 1128, 1128A, or 1128B.], or section 1126.

(10) FAILURE TO SUPPLY REQUESTED INFORMATION ON SUBCONTRACTORS AND SUPPLIERS. — Any disclosing entity (as defined in section 1124(a)(2)) that fails to supply (within such period as may be specified by the Secretary in regulations) upon request specifically addressed to the entity by the Secretary or by the State agency administering or supervising the administration of a State health care program —

(A) full and complete information as to the ownership of a subcontractor (as defined by the Secretary in regulations) with whom the entity has had, during the previous 12 months, business transactions in an aggregate amount in excess of $25,000, or

(B) full and complete information as to any significant business transactions (as defined by the Secretary in regulations), occurring during the five-year period ending on the date of such request, between the entity and any wholly owned supplier or between the entity and any subcontractor.

Section 1128B(f) defines "Federal health care program" as:

(1) any plan or program that provides health benefits, whether directly, through insurance, or otherwise, which is funded directly, in whole or in part, by the United States Government (other than the health insurance program under chapter 89 of title 5, United States code [which is the health insurance program for Federal employees]; or

(2) any State health care program, as defined in section 1128(h)

Section 1128(h) provides:

DEFINITION OF STATE HEALTH CARE PROGRAM. — For purposes of this section and sections 1128A and 1128(B) [42 U.S.C.A. 1320a-7b, which pertains to criminal penalties for acts involving Medicare or State health care programs] the term "State health care program" means —

(1) a State plan approved under title XIX [Medicaid, 42 U.S.C.A. 1396 et seq.],

(2) any program receiving funds under title V [Maternal and Child Health Services Block Grants, 42 U.S.C.A. 701 et seq.] or from an allotment to a State under such title

(3) any program receiving funds under title XX [Block Grants to States for Social Services, 42 U.S.C.A. 1397 et seq.] or from an allotment to a State under such title; or

(4) a State child health plan approved under title XXI.

◆ NOTE: Effective August 5, 1997 section 4901(b)(2) of the Balanced Budget Act of 1997 deleted "or" from the end of paragraph (h)(2); substituted ", or" for the period at the end of paragraph (h)(3); and added parapgraph (h)(4).

Section 1128(i) provides:

> CONVICTED DEFINED. — For purposes of subsections (a) and (b), an individual or entity is considered to have been "convicted" of a criminal offense —
>
> (1) when a judgment of conviction has been entered against the individual or entity by a Federal, State, or local court, regardless of whether there is an appeal pending or whether the judgment of conviction or other record relating to criminal conduct has been expunged;
>
> (2) when there has been a finding of guilt against the individual or entity by a Federal, State, or local court;
>
> (3) when a plea of guilty or nolo contendere by the individual or entity has been accepted by a Federal, State, or local court; or
>
> (4) when the individual or entity has entered into participation in a first offender, deferred adjudication, or other arrangement or program where judgment of conviction has been withheld.

Section 1128A, which authorizes civil money penalties for a variety of offenses, provides in pertinent part:

> (a) Any person (including an organization, agency, or other entity, but excluding a beneficiary, as defined in subsection (i)(5) [which means persons eligible to receive items or services for which payment may be made under Titles V, XVIII, XIX, or XX, but does not mean a provider, supplier, or practitioner]) that —
>
> (1) knowingly presents or causes to be presented to an officer, employee, or agent of the United States, or of any department or agency thereof, or of any State agency (as defined in subsection (i)(1) [which means the State Medicaid agency or the State agency for programs under Titles V or XX]), a claim (as defined in subsection (i)(2) [which means an application for payment for items or services under Titles V, XVIII, XIX, or XX]) that the Secretary determines —

(A) is for a medical or other item or service that the person knows or should know was not provided as claimed, including any person who engages in a pattern or practice of presenting or causing to be presented a claim for an item or service that is based on a code that the person knows or should know will result in a greater payment to the person than the code the person knows or should know is applicable to the item or service actually provided,

(B) is for a medical or other item or service and the person knows or should know the claim is false or fraudulent,

(C) is presented for a physician's service (or an item or service incident to a physician's service) by a person who knows or should know that the individual who furnished (or supervised the furnishing of) the service —

(i) was not licensed as a physician,

(ii) was licensed as a physician, but such license had been obtained through a misrepresentation of material fact (including cheating on an examination required for licensing), or

(iii) represented to the patient at the time the service was furnished that the physician was certified in a medical specialty by a medical specialty board when the individual was not so certified,

(D) is for a medical or other item or service furnished during a period in which the person was excluded from the program under which the claim was made pursuant to a determination by the Secretary under this section or under section 1128 [42 U.S.C.A. 1320a-7, which pertains to exclusions from Medicare and State health care programs, as indicated above], 1156 [42 U.S.C.A. 1320c-5, which pertains to exclusions from Medicare and State health care programs based on recommendations from Peer Review Organizations], 1160(b) (as in effect on September 2, 1982) [which pertained to exclusions from Medicare and State health care programs based on recommendations of Professional Standards Review Organizations], 1862(d) (as in effect on the date of the enactment of the Medicare and Medicaid Patient and Program Protection Act of 1987 [P.L. 100-93]) [which was an alternative basis for exclusion of individuals from Medicare], or 1866(b) [42 U.S.C.A. 1395cc(b), which pertains to termination of or refusal to renew provider agreements] or as a result of the application of the provisions of section 1842(j)(2) [42 U.S.C.A. 1395u(j)(2), which provides alternative grounds for excluding individuals and entities from Medicare and State health care programs and for imposing civil money penalties], or

(E) is for a pattern of medical or other items or services that a person knows or should know are not medically necessary.

◆ NOTE: Prior to amendment by section 231(e) of the Health Insurance Portability and Accountability Act of 1996, section 1128A(a)(1)(A) read: "is for a medical or other item or service that the person knows or should know was not provided as claimed. The same section struck "or" and substituted ", or" for a semicolon in subparagraph (D); and inserted new subparagraph (E). Section 231(a)(3) inserted "knowingly" before "presents" each place it appears in paragraph (1) above and paragraph (2) below, and inserted "knowingly gives or causes to be given" in lieu of "gives" in paragraph (3) below.

(2) knowingly presents or causes to be presented to any person a request for payment which is in violation of the terms of (A) an assignment under section 1842(b)(3)(B)(ii) [42 U.S.C.A. 1395u(b)(3)(B)(ii), which pertains to assignment of claims for benefits], or (B) an agreement with a State agency (or other requirement of a State plan under title XIX) not to charge a person for an item or service in excess of the amount permitted to be charged, or (C) an agreement to be a participating physician or supplier under section 1842(h)(1) [42 U.S.C.A. 1395u(h)(1)] or [with respect to items dispensed on or after January 1, 1990,] to be a participating pharmacy under section 1842(o) [42 U.S.C.A. 1395u(o), which pertains to payment agreements for pharmacies], or (D) an agreement pursuant to section 1866(a)(1)(G) [42 U.S.C.A. 1395cc(a)(1)(G), which pertains to hospital provider agreements not to charge for inpatient hospital services for which an individual would be entitled to have payment made under Part A but for a denial or reduction of payments under section 1886(f)(2), 42 U.S.C.A. 1395ww(f)(2), which, in turn, pertains to the DRG reimbursement methodology];

(3) knowingly gives or causes to be given to any person, with respect to coverage under title XVIII of inpatient hospital services subject to the provisions of section 1886 [42 U.S.C.A. 1395ww, which pertains to DRG reimbursement methodology for hospitals], information that he knows or should know is false or misleading, and that could reasonably be expected to influence the decision when to discharge such person or another individual from the hospital; or

(4) in the case of a person who is not an organization, agency, or other entity, is excluded from participating in a program under title XVIII or a State health care program in accordance with this subsection or under section 1128 and who, at the time of a violation of this subsection —

(A) retains a direct or indirect ownership or control interest in any entity that is participating in a program under title XVIII or a State health care program, and who knows or shoudl know of the action constituting the basis for the exclusion;

(B) is an officer or managing employee (as defined in section 1126(b)) of such an entity;

(5) offers to or transfers remuneration to any individual eligible for benefits under title XVIII of this Act, or under a State health care program (as defined in section 1128(h)) that such person knows or should know is likely to influence such individual to order to receive from a particular provider, practitioner, or supplier any item or service for which payment may be made, in whole or in part under title XVIII, or a State health care program (as so defined);

(6) arranges or contracts (by employment or otherwise) with an individual or entity that the person knows or should know is excluded from participation in a Federal health care program (as defined in section 1128B(f) [42 U.S.C.A. 1320a-7b(f)]), for the provision of items or services for which payment may be made under such a program; or

(7) commits an act described in paragraph (1) or (2) of section 1128B(b) [which pertains to illegal remuneration for referrals, such as kickbacks, bribes or rebates]

shall be subject, in addition to any other penalties that may be prescribed by law, to a civil money penalty of not more than

$15,000 for each item or service (or in cases under paragraph (3), $15,000 for each individual with respect to whom false or misleading information was given; in cases under paragraph (5), $10,000 for each day the prohibited relationship occurs; or in cases under paragraph (7), $50,000 for each such act). In addition, such a person shall be subject to an assessment of not more than three times the amount claimed for each such item or service in lieu of damages sustained by the United States or a State agency because of such claim (or, in cases under paragraph (7), damaged of not more than 3 times the total amount of remuneration offered, paid, solicited, or received, without regard to whether a portion of such remuneration was offered, paid, solicited, or received for a lawful purpose). In addition the Secretary may make a determination in the same proceeding to exclude the person from participation in the Federal health care programs (as defined in section 1128B(f)(1)) and to direct the appropriate State agency to exclude the person from participation in any State health care program.

◆ NOTE: Effective January 1, 1997, section 231(a)(2) of the Health Insurance Portability and Accountability Act of 1996 amended section 1128A(a) by substituting a semicolon for "or" at the end of paragraph (2) and substituting "or" for a semicolon at the end of paragraph (3). Then it inserted a new paragraph (4). It also substituted "$10,000" for "$2,000" in the phrase beginning "shall be subject" immediately hereafter; inserted the phrase, "; in cases under paragraph (4), $10,000 for each day the prohibited relationship occurs" after "false or misleading information was given"; and inserted "three times the amount" in lieu of twice the amount". In the sentence below beginning "In addition the Secretary", it substituted "Federal health care programs (as defined in section 1128(f)(1))" for "programs under title XVIII".

◆ ALSO NOTE: Effective August 5, 1997, section 4304(a) of the Balanced Budget Act of 1997, removed "or" from the end of paragraph (a)(4); added "or" to the end of paragraph (a)(5); and added paragraph (a)(6). Then section 4304(b)(1) removed "or" from the end of paragraph (a)(5); added "or" to the end of paragraph (a)(6); and added paragraph (a)(7). In the matter following (a)(7), section 4304(b)(2) substituted "occurs; or in cases under paragraph (7), $50,000 for each such act)." for "occurs" after "the prohibited relationship". It also inserted "or, in cases under paragraph (7), damages of not more than 3 times the total amount of remuneration offered, paid, solicited, or received, without regard to whether a portion of such remuneration was offered, paid, solicited, or received for a lawful purpose)" after "of such claim". These changes are applicable to arrangements and contracts entered into on or after August 5, 1997.

(b) (1) If a hospital, an eligible organization with a risk-sharing contract under section 1876 [42 U.S.C.A. 1395mm, which pertains to health maintenance organizations and competitive medical plans], or an entity with a contract under section 1903(m) [42 U.S.C.A. 1396b(m), which pertains to health maintenance organizations] knowingly makes a payment, directly or indirectly, to a physician as an inducement to reduce or limit services provided with respect to individuals who—

(A) are entitled to benefits under part A or part B of title XVIII or to medical assistance under a State plan approved under title XIX,

(B) in the case of an eligible organization or an entity, are enrolled with the organization or entity, and

(C) are under the direct care of the physician,

the hospital or organization shall be subject, in addition to any other penalties that may be prescribed by law, to a civil money penalty of not more than $2,000 for each such individual with respect to whom the payment is made.

(2) Any physician who knowingly accepts receipt of a payment described in paragraph (1) shall be subject, in addition to any other penalties that may be prescribed by law, to a civil money penalty of not more than $2,000 for each individual described in such paragraph with respect to whom the payment is made.

(3)(A) Any physician who executes a document described in subparagraph (B) with respect to an individual knowing that all of the requirements referred to in such subparagraph are not met with respect to the individual shall be subject to a civil monetary penalty of not more than the greater of—

(i) $5,000, or

(ii) three times the amount of payments under title XVIII for home health services which are made pursuant to such certification

(B) A document described in this subparagraph is any document that certifies, for purposes of title XVIII, that an individual meets the requirements of section 1814(a)(2)(C) [42 U.S.C.A. 1395f(a)(2)(C), which pertains to limitations on payments for home health services under Medicare Part A] or 1835(a)(2)(A) [42 U.S.C.A. 1395n(a)(2)(A), which pertains to limitations on payments for home health services under Medicare Part B] in the case of home health services furnished to the individual.

◆ [NOTE: Section 232 of the Health Insurance Portability and Accountability Act of 1996 added paragraph (3)(A) above, effective for certifications made on or after August 21, 1996.]

Finally, additional disclosure of ownership and control is required by section 1124, 42 U.S.C.A. 1320a-3, and section 1124A, 42 U.S.C.A. 13201-3a. Section 1124 provides:

(a) (1) The Secretary shall by regulation or by contract provision provide that each disclosing entity (as defined in paragraph (2)) shall—

(A) as a condition of the disclosing entity's participation in, or certification or recertification under, any of the programs established by titles V, XVIII, and XIX, or

(B) as a condition for the approval or renewal of a contract or agreement between the disclosing entity and the Secretary or the appropriate State agency under any of the programs established under titles V, XVIII, and XIX,

supply the Secretary or the appropriate State agency with full and complete information as to the identity of each person with an ownership or control interest (as defined in paragraph (3)) in the entity or in any subcontractor (as defined by the Secretary in regulations) in which the entity directly or indirectly has a 5 per centum or more ownership interest and supply the Secretary with both the employer identification number (assigned pursuant to section 6109 of the Internal Revenue Code of 1986) and social security account number (assigned under section 205(c)(2)(B)) of the disclosing entity, each person with an ownership or control interest (as defined in subsection (a)(3)), and any subcontractor in which the entity directly or indirectly has a 5 percent or more ownership interest.

◆ NOTE: Section 4313(a) of the Balanced Budget Act of 1997 added the phrase beginning "and supply the Secretary with". This change pertains to the application of conditions of participation, and to the entering into or renewal of contracts and agreements, occurring more than 90 days after the submission of a report required by section 4313(d). The latter section reads: "(d) REPORT. — Before the amendments made by this subsection may become effective, the Secretary of Health and Human Services shall submit to Congress a report on steps the Secretary has taken to assure the confidentiality of social security account numbers that will be provided to the Secretary under such amendments."

(2) As used in this section, the term "disclosing entity" means an entity which is —

(A) a provider of services (as defined in section 1861(u) [42 U.S.C.A. 1395x(u), which means a hospital, skilled nursing facility, comprehensive outpatient rehabilitation facility, home health agency, hospice program, or home intravenous drug therapy provider], other than a fund), an independent clinical laboratory, a renal disease facility, a managed care entity, as defined in section 1932(a)(1)(B) [42 U.S.C.A. 1396u-2(a)(1)(B), which pertains to the use of managed care in the Medicaid program. This reference to a managed care entity was added by section 4707(c) of the Balanced Budget Act of 1997, effective August 5, 1997], or a health maintenance organization (as defined in section 1301(a) of the Public Health Service Act [P.L. 78-410];

(B) an entity (other than an individual practitioner or group of practitioners) that furnishes, or arranges for the furnishing of items or services with respect to which payment may be claimed by the entity under any plan or program established pursuant to title V or under a State plan approved under title XIX; or

(C) a carrier or other agency or organization that is acting as a fiscal intermediary or agent with respect to one or more providers of services (for purposes of part A or part B of title XVIII, or both, or for purposes of a State plan approved under title XIX) pursuant to (i) an agreement under section 1816 [42 U.S.C.A. 1395h, which pertains to fiscal intermediaries], (ii) a contract under section 1842 [42 U.S.C.A. 1395u, which pertains to carriers], or (iii) an agreement with a single State agency administering or supervising the administration of a State plan approved under title XIX.

(3) As used in this section, the term "person with an ownership or control interest" means, with respect to an entity, a person who—

(A) (i) has directly or indirectly (as determined by the Secretary in regulations) an ownership interest of 5 per centum or more in the entity; or

(ii) is the owner of a whole or part interest in any mortgage, deed of trust, note, or other obligation secured (in whole or in part) by the entity or any of the property or assets thereof, which whole or part interest is equal to or exceeds 5 per centum of the total property and assets of the entity; or

(B) is an officer or director of the entity, if the entity is organized as a corporation; or

(C) is a partner in the entity, if the entity is organized as a partnership.

(b) To the extent determined to be feasible under regulations of the Secretary, a disclosing entity shall also include in the information supplied under subsection (a)(1), with respect to each person with an ownership or control interest in the entity, the name of any other disclosing entity with respect to which the person is a person with an ownership or control interest.

Section 1124A, applicable to items and services furnished on or after January 1, 1992, pursuant to section 4164(b)(1) and (3) of OBRA 90, provides:

(a) DISCLOSURE REQUIRED TO RECEIVE PAYMENT.—No payment may be made under part B of title XVIII for items or services furnished by any disclosing part B provider unless such provider has provided the Secretary with full and complete information —

(1) on the identity of each person with an ownership or control interest in the provider or in any subcontractor (as defined by the Secretary in regulations) in which the provider directly or indirectly has a 5 percent or more ownership interest;

(2) with respect to any person identified under paragraph (1) or any managing employee of the provider —

(A) on the identity of any other entities providing items or services for which payment may be made under title XVIII of the Social Security Act with respect to which such person or managing employee is a person with an ownership or control interest at the time such information is supplied or at any time during the 3-year period ending on the date such information is supplied; and

(B) as to whether any penalties, assessments, or exclusions have been assessed against such person or managing employee under section 1128, 1128A, or 1128B; and

(3) including the employer identification number (assigned pursuant to section 6109 of the Internal Revenue Code of 1986) and social security account number (assigned under section 205(c)(2)(B)) of the disclosing part B provider and any person, managing employee, or other entity identified or described under paragraph (1) or (2).

(b) UPDATES TO INFORMATION SUPPLIED. — A disclosing part B provider shall notify the Secretary of any changes or updates to the information supplied under subsection (a) not later than 180 days after such changes or updates take effect.

◆ NOTE: Section 4313(b)(1) of the Balanced Budget Act of 1997 removed "and" from the end of paragraph (a)(1); substituted "; and" for the period at the end of paragraph (a)(2); and added paragraph (a)(3). Section 4313(b)(2) inserted "(or, for purposes of subsection (a)(3), any entity receiving payment)" after "on an assignment-related basis" in paragraph (c)(1), now (d)(1). Changes made by section 4313(b) apply to payment for items and services furnished more than 90 days after the submission of the report required by section 4313(d), which is quoted in a NOTE above. Effective August 5, 1997, section 4313(c) redesignated subsection (c) as subsection (d), and added new subsection (c).

(c) VERIFICATION. —

(1) TRANSMITTAL BY HHS. — The Secretary shall transmit —

(A) to the Commissioner of Social Security information concerning each social security account number (assigned under section 205(c)(2)(B)), and

(B) to the Secretary of the Treasury information concerning each employer identification number (assigned pursuant to section 6109 of the Internal Revenue Code of 1986), supplied to the Secretary pursuant to subsection (a)(3) or section 1124(c) to the extent necessary for verification of such information in accordance with paragraph (2).

(2) VERIFICATION. — The Commissioner of Social Security and the Secretary of the Treasury shall verify the accuracy of, or correct, the information supplied by the Secretary to such official pursuant to paragraph (1), and shall report such verifications or corrections to the Secretary.

(3) FEES FOR VERIFICATION. — The Secretary shall reimburse the Commissioner and Secretary of the Treasury, at a rate negotiated between the Secretary and such official, for the costs incurred by such official in performing the verification and correction services described in this subsection.

(d) DEFINITIONS. — For purposes of this section —

(1) the term "disclosing part B provider" means any entity receiving payment on an assignment-related basis (or, for purposes of subsection (a)(3), any entity receiving payment) for furnishing items or services for which payment may be made under part B of title XVIII, except that such term does not include an entity described in section 1124(a)(2);

(2) the term "managing employee" means, with respect to a provider, a person described in section 1126(b); and

(3) the term person with an ownership or control interest " means, with respect to a provider —

(A) a person described in section 1124(a)(3), or

(B) a person who has one of the 5 largest direct or indirect ownership or control interests in the provider.

For regulatory citations, see Chapter 8

§ 4:8 CIVIL MONEY PENALTIES — Section 1128A [42 U.S.C.A. 1320a-7a]

Summary

Section 1128A, 42 U.S.C.A. 1320a-7a, is the primary statutory authority for the Secretary of Health and Human Services to impose civil money penalties for fraud and abuse against a Federal health care program. It applies to individuals and entities, but not to beneficiaries.

"Federal health care program" includes any plan or program that provides health benefits, whether directly, through insurance, or otherwise, which is funded directly, in whole or in part by the United States Government (other than the health insurance program for Federal employees authorized by Chapter 89 of title 5 of the United States Code). See section 1128B(f), 42 U.S.C.A. 1320a-7b(f).

"Federal health care program" also includes any State health care program, as defined in section 1128(h), 42 U.S.C.A. 1320a-7(h). That means Medicaid, any program receiving funds under Title V of the Social Security Act (the Maternal and Child Health Services Block Grant program, 42 U.S.C.A. 701 et seq.), or from an allotment to a State under such title, and any program receiving funds under Title XX of the Social Security Act (the program of Block Grants to States for Social Services, 42 U.S.C.A. 1397 et seq.), or from an allotment to a State under such title. State health care program also means a State child health plan approved under title XXI.

◆ NOTE: This reference to "Federal health care program" greatly broadens the scope of section 1128A. It was enacted by the Health Insurance Portability and Accountability Act of 1996, P.L. 104-191, effective January 1, 1997. Prior to amendment by section 231(a)(2) of that Act, section 1128A applied only to offenses against Medicare, Medicaid, and programs funded by Titles V and XX of the Social Security Act. Section 4901(b)(2) of the Balanced Budget Act of 1997, P.L. 105-33 added the reference to State child health plans approved under title XXI, effective August 5, 1997.

Definitions: The following terms (along with "Federal health care program") are defined in section 1128A(i).

Beneficiary means an individual who is eligible to receive items or services for which payment may be made under a Federal health care program. The term does not, however, include a provider, supplier, or practitioner, who also may be entitled to payments under those programs.

State agency means an agency established or designated to administer or supervise the administration of a State Medicaid program or a State program funded by Titles V or XX of the Social Security Act.

Claim means an application for payments for items and services under a Federal health care program.

◆ NOTE: Prior to amendment by section 231(a)(2) of the Health Insurance Portability and Accountability Act of 1996, "claim" referred only to a claim under Medicare, Medicaid, or programs funded under Titles V and XX.

Item or service includes any particular item, device, medical supply, or service claimed to have been provided to a patient and listed in an itemized claim for payment. With respect to a claim based on costs, it also includes an entry in a cost report, books of account, or other documents supporting such a claim.

Agency of the United States includes any contractor acting as a fiscal intermediary, carrier, or fiscal agent or any other claims processing agent for a Federal health care program.

◆ NOTE: Prior to amendment by section 231(a)(2) of the Health Insurance Portability and Accountability Act of 1996, "agency of the United States" referred only to contractors acting as fiscal intermediaries for Medicare and Medicaid.

Remuneration includes the waiver of coinsurance and deductible amounts (or any part thereof). It also includes transfers of items or services for free or for other than fair market value.

Remuneration does not include the waiver of coinsurance and deductible amounts by a person if the waiver is not offered as part of any advertisement or solicitation, and if the person does not routinely waive coinsurance or deductible amounts. This exception is further restricted to cases when the waiver is made: (1) after determining in good faith that the individual granted the waiver is in financial need; (2) after making reasonable collection efforts; or (3) when permitted by section 1128B(b)(3), which authorizes waivers of coinsurance under Medicare Part B by Federally qualified health care centers, or when permitted by regulations issued by the Secretary.

Remuneration also does not include differentials in coinsurance and deductible amounts as part of a benefit plan design. This exception applies, however, only when those differentials have been disclosed in writing to all beneficiaries, third party payers, and providers, to whom claims are presented. Furthermore, the exception applies only as long as the differentials meet standards as defined in regulations. Those regulations were to be promulgated by the Secretary not later than 180 days after the date of the enactment of the Health Insurance Portability and Accountability Act of 1996 (August 21, 1996).

In addition, remuneration does not include incentives given to individuals to promote the delivery of preventive care. What that means is to be determined by regulations.

Finally, remuneration does not include a reduction in copayment amount for covered hospital outpatient department services under section 1833(t)(5)(B), 42 U.S.C.A. 1395l(t)(5)(B).

Should know means that a person, with respect to information, acts in deliberate ignorance of the truth or falsity of the information, or acts in reckless disregard of the truth or falsity of the information. No proof of specific intent to defraud is required to impose a civil monetary penalty under section 1128A.

◆ NOTE: Definitions of "should know" and "remuneration" were enacted by section 231(a)(2) of the Health Insurance Portability and Accountability Act of 1996, effective January 1, 1997. Section 4523(c) of the Balanced Budget Act of 1997 added the exclusion from the definition of remuneration pertaining to reduction in copayment for outpatient department services, effective August 5, 1997.

Grounds for Penalties under Section 1128A(a): Pursuant to section 1128A(a)(1), the Secretary may impose a civil money penalty on any person, organization, agency, or other entity (other than a beneficiary) that knowingly presents a prohibited claim or causes a prohibited claim to be presented to an officer, employee, or agent of the United States, or of any department or agency thereof. The same applies to prohibited claims presented to any State agency which administers or supervises administration of Medicaid or State programs funded by Title V or Title XX.

◆ NOTE: The requirement that a claim be "knowingly" presented or "knowingly" given was added to sections 1128A(a)(1), (2), and (3) by section 231(a)(2) of the Health Insurance Portability and Accountability Act of 1996, effective January 1, 1997.

This applies to any claim, as defined in section 1128A(i)(2), which the Secretary determines —

(1) is for a medical or other item or service that the person knows or should know was not provided as claimed, including any person who engages in a pattern or practice of presenting a claim for an item or service that is based on a code that the person knows or should know will result in a greater payment to the person than the code the person knows or should know is applicable to the item or service actually provided;

◆ NOTE: Section 231(e) of the Health Insurance Portability and Accountability Act of 1996 made miscoding a claim a basis for a civil money penalty, effective January 1, 1997.

(2) is for a medical or other item or service and the person knows or should know the claim is false or fraudulent;

(3) is presented for a physician's service, or for an item or service incident to a physician's service, by a person who knows or should know that the individual who furnished or supervised the furnishing of the service —

(a) was not licensed as a physician,

(b) was licensed as a physician, but the license was obtained through misrepresentation of material fact, including cheating on an examination required for licensing, or

(c) represented to the patient at the time the service was furnished that the physician was certified in a medical specialty by a medical specialty board when the individual was not so certified; or

(4) is for a medical or other item or service furnished during a period when the person was excluded from the program under which the claim was made pursuant to a determination by the Secretary —

(a) under section 1128A, which authorizes the Secretary to exclude individuals and entities from Medicare and to direct States to exclude them from Medicaid and State health care programs funded under Title V and Title XX in conjunction with imposition of a civil money penalty,

(b) or under section 1128, 42 U.S.C.A. 1320a-7, which authorizes the Secretary to exclude individuals and entities from Medicare and to direct States to exclude them from Medicaid and State health care programs funded under Title V and Title XX,

(c) section 1156, 42 U.S.C.A. 1320c-5, which pertains to exclusions from Medicare and State health care programs based on recommendations of Peer Review Organizations,

(d) section 1160(b) as in effect on September 2, 1982, which pertained to exclusions from Medicare and State health care programs based on recommendations of Professional Standards Review Organizations,

(e) section 1862(d), as in effect on the date of the enactment of the Medicare and Medicaid Patient and Program Protection Act of 1987 (P.L. 100-93), which was an alternative basis for exclusion of individuals from Medicare,

(f) section 1866(b), 42 U.S.C.A. 1395cc(b), which pertains to termination of or refusal to renew provider agreements;

(g) by application of section 1842(j)(2), 42 U.S.C.A. 1395u(j)(2), which provides alternative grounds for excluding individuals and entities from Medicare and the State health care programs indicated above and for imposing civil money penalties; or

(h) is for a pattern of medical or other items or services that the person know or should know are not medically necessary.

◆ NOTE: Making a claim for medically unnecessary items or services a basis for penalty was added by section 231(e) of the Health Insurance Portability and Accountability Act of 1996, effective January 1, 1997.

Pursuant to section 1128A(a)(2), the Secretary may impose a civil money penalty on any person, organization, agency, or other entity that knowingly presents or causes to be presented to any person a request for payment that violates —

(a) the terms of an assignment under section 1842(b)(3)(B)(ii), 42 U.S.C.A. 1395u(b)(3)(B)(ii), which pertains to assignment of claims for benefits,

(b) an agreement with a State agency, or a requirement under a Medicaid plan, not to charge a person for an item or service in excess of the agreed or allowed charge,

(c) an agreement to be a participating physician or supplier under section 1842(h)(1), 42 U.S.C.A. 1395u(h)(1), or

(d) an agreement pursuant to section 1866(a)(1)(G), which pertains to hospital provider agreements not to charge for inpatient hospital services for which an individual would be entitled to have payment made under Part A but for a denial or reduction of payments under section 1886(f)(2), 42 U.S.C.A. 1395ww(f)(2), which, in turn, pertains to the DRG reimbursement methodology.

Pursuant to section 1128A(a)(3), the Secretary may impose a civil money penalty on any person, organization, agency, or other entity that knowingly gives or causes to be given to any person, with respect to Medicare coverage of inpatient hospital services subject to DRG reimbursement methodology, information that he knows or should know is false or misleading, and which could reasonably be expected to influence the decision when to discharge such person or another individual from the hospital.

Pursuant to section 1128A(a)(4), the Secretary may impose a civil money penalty on any person excluded from participating in Medicare or a State health care program under section 1128 or section 1128A who retains a direct or indirect ownership or control interest in any entity participating in Medicare or a State health care program, and who knows or should know of the action which is the basis for such exclusion. The same applies to a person who is an officer or managing employee (as defined in section 1126(b), 42 U.S.C.A. 1320a-5(b)) of such an entity. This basis for a civil money penalty does not apply to "an organization, agency, or other entity", only to a person. It was added to section 1128A by section 231(a)(3) of the Health Insurance Portability and Accountability Act of 1996, effective January 1, 1997.

Pursuant to section 1128A(a)(5), the Secretary may impose a civil money penalty on any person or entity that offers to transfer or transfers remuneration to anyone eligible for benefits under Medicare or a State health care program which that person or entity knows or should know is likely to influence the eligible person to receive any item or service from a particular provider, practitioner or supplier. This applies when payment for the item or service may be made in whole or in part by Medicare or a State health care program.

Pursuant to section 1128A(a)(6), the Secretary may impose a civil money penalty on any person or entity that arranges or contracts (by employment or otherwise) with an individual or entity that the person knows or should know is excluded from participation in a Federal health care program for the provision of items or services for which payment may be made under such a program.

Pursuant to section 1128A(a)(7), the Secretary may impose a civil money penalty on any person or entity that commits an act which constitutes an illegal kickback, bribe, rebate, or other illegal remuneration within the meaning of sections 1128B(b)(1) and (2).

◆ NOTE: The provisions of sections 1128(A)(6) and (7) were added by section 4304(a) and section 4304(b)(1) of the Balanced Budget Act of 1997, effective August 5, 1997.

Penalty Amounts under Section 1128A(a): The civil money penalty authorized for offenses described in sections 1128A(a)(1) through (a)(6) is in addition to any other penalties that may be prescribed by law. For the offenses described in subsections (a)(1), (a)(2), and (a)(5), the penalty may not exceed $10,000. For the offense described in subsection (a)(3), however, which typically involves efforts to get patients who need expensive care prematurely discharged from a hospital so the hospital will not have to absorb costs not reimbursable under DRG methodology, the penalty may not exceed $15,000 for each individual with respect to whom false or misleading information was given. For the prohibited relationship described in subsection (a)(4), the penalty is $10,000 for each day the relationship occurs. Pursuant to section 4304(b)(2), for cases involving illegal remuneration, the penalty may not exceed $50,000 for each such act. That penalty applies to arrangements and contracts entered into on or after August 5, 1997).

In addition, for any of the offenses described in sections 1128A(a)(1) through (a)(6), an offender may be assessed not more than three times the amount claimed for each such item or service in lieu of damages sustained by the United States or by a State agency because of the claim. For illegal remuneration cases, the offender may be subject to damages of not more than three times the total amount of remuneration offered, paid, solicited, or received. That applies to arrangements or contracts entered into on or after August 5, 1997, pursuant to section 4304(b)(2) of the Balanced Budget Act of 1997. It also applies without regard to whether a portion of such remuneration was offered, paid, solicited, or received for a lawful purpose. Furthermore, with respect to those offenses, the Secretary may determine in the same civil money penalty proceeding to exclude an offender from Medicare and to direct the appropriate State agency to exclude the offender from State health care programs.

◆ NOTE: Section 231(a)(2) of the Health Insurance Portability and Accountability Act of 1996 increased the general penalty from $2,000 to $10,000 and added the $10,000 penalty for prohibited relationships. It also increased the assessments from two to three times the amount claimed. These changes were effective January 1, 1997.

Grounds for Penalties under Section 1128A(b): Prior to November 5, 1990, pursuant to section 1128A(b)(1), the Secretary could, in addition to any other penalties prescribed by law, impose a civil money penalty on any health maintenance organization (HMO) or competitive medical plan (CMP) participating in Medicare or Medicaid, or on any hospital, or, effective December 19, 1989, pursuant to section 6003(g)(D)(i), any critical access hospital, that knowingly makes a payment, directly or indirectly, to a physician as an inducement to reduce or limit services provided to individuals who are under the direct care of a physician and who are entitled to Medicare or Medicaid, or who are enrolled with the HMO or CMP. The penalty may not exceed $2,000 for each individual with respect to whom such a payment is made. Pursuant to sections 4204(a)(3) and 4731(b) of P.L. 101-508 of the Omnibus Budget Reconciliation Act of 1990 (OBRA 90), however, this provision does not apply to such HMO's and CMP's on or after November 5, 1990. It continues to apply to hospitals and critical access hospitals.

◆ NOTE: Section 4201(c) of the Balanced Budget Act of 1997 substituted the phrase "critical access hospital" wherever the phrase "rural primary care hospital" had appeared in section 1128A. That change was effective October 1, 1997.

Section 1128A(b)(2) provides a similar penalty for any physician who knowingly receives a payment under such circumstances, that is, $2,000 for each individual with respect to whom such a payment is received. That penalty, too, is in addition to any other penalty which may be prescribed by law.

Pursuant to section 1128A(b)(3), the Secretary may impose a civil money penalty on any physician who executes a document which certifies that an individual is entitled to home health benefits under Medicare Part A or Part B if the physician knows that all of the requirements for entitlement are not met. The penalty amount is not more than $5,000, or three times the amount of payments under Medicare for the home health services made pursuant to such a certification, whichever is greater. This basis for a penalty was added by section 232 of the Health Insurance Portability and Accountability Act of 1996, effective January 1, 1997.

Coordination with the U.S. Department of Justice: Pursuant to section 1128A(c)(1), the Secretary may institute a civil money penalty, assessment, and exclusion proceeding under sections 1128A(a) and a civil money penalty under section 1128A(b) only as authorized by the Attorney General pursuant to procedures which they establish. Presumably that will help the Department of Justice and the Department of Health and Human Services coordinate civil money penalty actions with criminal proceedings that arise from the same set of facts or affect the same individuals or entities.

Statute of Limitations: Section 1128A(c)(1) establishes a statute of limitations for bringing civil money penalty or exclusion proceedings under section 1128A. By its terms, the Secretary may not initiate such proceedings with respect to any claim, request for payment, or other punishable occurrence later than six years after the date the unlawful claim was presented, the date the request for payment was made, or the date the occurrence took place. That subsection further provides for the Secretary to initiate such actions by serving notice in the manner prescribed by Rule 4 of the Federal Rules of Civil Procedure.

Hearing Rights: Pursuant to section 1128A(c)(2), the Secretary may not make an adverse determination against any individual or entity under section 1128A(a) or (b) until he has given the individual or entity written notice and an opportunity for the determination to be made on the record after a hearing. Furthermore, at that hearing the individual or entity may be represented by counsel, may present witnesses, and may cross-examine adverse witnesses. If a person or entity has been convicted, however, whether upon verdict after trial or upon a plea of guilty or nolo contendere, of a Federal crime charging fraud or false statements, and if the criminal action involved the same transaction, section 1128A(c)(3) precludes the convicted individual or entity from denying the essential elements of the criminal offense. Thus, the individual prosecuting the civil money penalty proceeding need not re-litigate the facts in the criminal proceeding.

Authority of the Administrative Law Judge: Section 1128A(c)(4) spells out the authority of the presiding officer at a section 1128A civil money penalty or exclusion proceeding. Specifically, that individual may sanction a person, including any party or attorney, for failing to comply with an order or procedure, for failing to defend an action, or for other misconduct which would interfere with the speedy, orderly, or fair conduct of the hearing. The sanction must reasonably relate to the severity and nature of the failure or misconduct, but it may include drawing negative inferences about the facts when there is a refusal to provide or permit discovery, or treating such a refusal as an admission by deeming the matter, or certain facts, to be established; prohibiting a party from introducing certain evidence or otherwise supporting a particular claim or defense; striking pleadings, in whole or in part; staying the proceedings; dismissing the action; entering a default judgment; ordering the party or attorney to pay attorneys' fees and other costs caused by the failure or misconduct; and refusing to consider any motion or other action which is not filed in a timely manner.

Criteria for Determining Punishment: In determining the amount or scope of any penalty, assessment, or exclusion imposed pursuant to section 1128A(a) or (b), section 1128A(d) requires the Secretary to take into account the nature of the claims and the circumstances under which they were presented, the degree of culpability, history of prior offenses, and financial condition of the person presenting the claims, and any other matters which justice may require.

Judicial Review: Pursuant to section 1128A(e), any person adversely affected by a determination of the Secretary to impose a civil money penalty or exclusion under section 1128A may obtain judicial review of the determination in the United States Court of Appeals for the circuit in which the person resides, or in which the claim was presented. To do that, he must file a written petition with the court within 60 days after the date he was notified of the Secretary's determination. The Clerk of the Court will transmit the petition to the Secretary, and the Secretary will then file in the Court the record of his proceeding, as provided in 28 U.S.C.A. 2112. Upon that filing, the Court has jurisdiction of the proceeding and of the question determined therein, and it has the power to make and enter upon the pleadings, testimony, and proceedings set forth in the Secretary's record a decree affirming, modifying, remanding for further consideration, or setting aside, in whole or in part the Secretary's determination, and to enforce its order as entered.

The Court of Appeals may not consider any objection not raised before the Secretary unless the failure or neglect to do so should be excused because of "extraordinary circumstances." Furthermore, the findings of the Secretary with respect to questions of fact are conclusive if they are supported by substantial evidence. On the other hand, upon the request of a party for permission to adduce additional evidence, and a showing that such evidence is material and that there were reasonable grounds for failure to have presented it before the Secretary, the Court may order such additional evidence to be taken before the Secretary and to be made a part of the record. This, in effect, is a good cause test for remanding a case to the Secretary for a supplemental hearing. At that point, the Secretary may modify his findings of fact, or make new ones, and then refile the modified or new findings with the Court. Thereafter, the Court may undertake anew its substantial evidence review of the Secretary's determination. Upon filing of the record with it, however, the Court's jurisdiction is exclusive, and its judgment and decree is final, subject only to review by the United States Supreme Court, as provided in 28 U.S.C.A. 1254.

Furthermore, with respect to judicial review, section 1128A(j) provides that the provisions of subsections (d) and (e) of section 205, 42 U.S.C.A. 405(d) and (e), apply to the same extent they apply to Social Security benefits under Title II of the Social Security Act. Significantly, however, the Secretary may delegate the authority granted by section 205(d), which pertains to hearings, investigations, and issuance of subpoenas, to the Inspector General of the Department of Health and Human Services for purposes of any investigation under section 1128A. Subsection (e) authorizes the Secretary to seek judicial enforcement of subpoenas and permits Federal District Courts to punish contumacy or refusal to obey such subpoenas as contempt of court.

Compromise and Collection: Once civil money penalties and assessments have been imposed under section 1128A, section 1128A(f) provides that the Secretary may compromise them or seek recovery of them by civil action in the Federal District Court where the claim was presented or where the claimant resides. Amounts recovered which arose from Medicaid claims must be paid to the relevant State, in proportion to the State's share of Medicaid expenditures. Three-sevenths of amounts recovered which arose from Title V grants must be paid to the relevant State. Amounts recovered which arose from the Medicare Part A and Medicare Part B trust funds must be deposited in those trust accounts. The remainder of amounts recovered go to miscellaneous receipts of the United States Treasury.

Section 1128A(f) also provides that the amount of any civil money penalty or assessment under section 1128A, when finally determined or agreed to by compromise, may be deducted from any sum then or later owing by the United States or a State agency to the person against whom the penalty or assessment was imposed.

Finality of a Decision: Pursuant to section 1128A(g), a determination by the Secretary to impose a penalty, assessment, or exclusion under section 1128A(a) or to impose a penalty under section 1128A(b) becomes final upon expiration of the 60 days allowed by section 1128A(e) to appeal a determination by the Secretary to the Court of Appeals. Moreover, matters raised or which could have been raised in a hearing before the Secretary or in an appeal to the Court of Appeals may not be raised as a defense to a civil action by the United States to collect a penalty or assessment or to impose an exclusion under section 1128A.

Notification to the Public and Other Government Agencies: Pursuant to section 1128A(h), the Secretary must notify the appropriate State or local medical or professional organization, the appropriate State agency or agencies administering or supervising the administration of State health care programs (i.e., Medicaid, and programs funded under Title V and Title XX), the appropriate utilization and quality control peer review organization, and the appropriate State or local licensing agency or organization (including State agencies involved in Medicare and Medicaid provider survey and certification) whenever a penalty, assessment, or exclusion has become final. He also must inform them of the reasons for such actions.

In addition to defining "State agency" and "beneficiary", as indicated above, section 1128A(i) defines "claim" as an application for payments for items and services under Titles V, XVIII, XIX, or XX. It defines "item or service" to include any particular item, device, medical supply, or service claimed to have been provided to a patient and listed in an itemized claim for payment. And, in the case of a claim based on costs, it includes any entry in the cost report, books of account, or other documents supporting the claim. Section 1128A(i) also defines "agency of the United States" to include any contractor acting as a fiscal intermediary, carrier, or fiscal agent or any other claims processing agent for a health insurance or medical services program under Title XVIII or Title XIX.

With respect to judicial review, section 1128A(j) provides that the provisions of subsections (d) and (e) of section 205, 42 U.S.C.A. 405(d) and (e), apply to the same extent they apply to Social Security benefits under Title II of the Social Security Act. Significantly, however, the Secretary may delegate the authority granted by section

205(d), which pertains to hearings, investigations, and issuance of subpoenas, to the Inspector General of the Department of Health and Human Services for purposes of any investigation under section 1128A. Subsection (e) authorizes the Secretary to seek judicial enforcement of subpoenas and permits Federal District Courts to punish contumacy or refusal to obey such subpoenas as contempt of court.

Injunctive Relief: Pursuant to section 1128A(k), whenever the Secretary has reason to believe any person has engaged in, is engaging in, or is about to engage in any activity for which a civil money penalty may be imposed under section 1128A, he may bring an action in an appropriate Federal District Court to enjoin that activity. He also may seek to enjoin that person from concealing, removing, encumbering, or disposing of assets which may be required in order to pay a civil money penalty, as well as any other appropriate relief.

Vicarious Liability: Section 1128A(l) provides that for purposes of section 1128A a principal is liable for penalties and assessments and is subject to exclusion for the actions of an agent acting within the scope of the agency.

Effective Date and Duration of Exclusion: Pursuant to section 1128(c), 42 U.S.C.A. 1320a-7(c), which independently authorizes exclusion of individuals and entities from Medicare for a variety of offenses, an exclusion pursuant to section 1128A becomes effective at such time and upon such reasonable notice to the public and to the individual or entity excluded as the Secretary may determine by regulation. Ordinarily, it will become effective with respect to services furnished to an individual on or after the specified effective date. An exclusion shall not apply, however, to payments made under Medicare or under a State health care program for inpatient institutional services furnished to an individual admitted to such an institution before the date of the exclusion, or for home health services and hospice care furnished to an individual under a plan of care established before the date of the exclusion, until 30 days after the effective date. But this deferral does not apply if the Secretary determines that the health and safety of individuals receiving services warrants an earlier effective date.

Section 1128(c)(3) requires the Secretary to specify in the notice of exclusion pursuant to section 1128A the minimum duration of the exclusion.

Requirement for Exclusion from State Health Programs: Section 1128(d) requires the Secretary to exercise his authority to exclude under section 1128A in a manner which results in complete exclusion from Medicare and all the defined State health care programs in which the individual or entity otherwise may participate. Accordingly, it, as well as section 1128A(h), requires the Secretary to notify promptly each appropriate State agency administering or supervising the administration of each State health care program of the fact and circumstances of each exclusion and of the duration for which the State agency must exclude the individual or entity from participation in the State health care program or programs. At the least, the State's exclusion must equal the duration of the Medicare exclusion; however, it may be longer, if the State so desires. On the other hand, upon State request, the Secretary may waive an individual's or entity's exclusion under a State health care program. Such waivers presumably would be rare and likely to apply only when the public interest would be better served, as when the individual or entity provides health care items or services not otherwise readily available in a community.

Notice to Licensing Authorities: Section 1128(e), as well as section 1128A(h), provides that the Secretary also must notify promptly the State or local agency or authority responsible for licensing or certification of an individual or entity excluded or directed to be excluded from participation under section 1128A of the fact and circumstances of exclusions. Furthermore, the Secretary must request such agencies to make their own investigations and impose whatever sanctions State law and policy may require. In addition, the Secretary must request the State or local agency or authority to keep him and the Inspector General of the Department of Health and Human Services fully and currently informed about actions taken in response to that request.

Finalty of an Exclusion Decision: Section 1128(f)(3) provides that the findings and decision of the Secretary after an exclusion hearing pursuant to section 1128A are binding upon all parties, and they are subject only to such further review as the statute may allow, as specified in section 205(h), 42 U.S.C.A. 405(h).

Procedure for Readmission after Exclusion: Because an individual or entity excluded or directed to be excluded under section 1128A may want to be readmitted to participation in Medicare or State health care programs, section 1128(g) provides for the Secretary to establish a readmission process. By its terms, once the minimum exclusion period has elapsed, the individual or entity may apply to the Secretary for termination of his exclusion. If the Secretary determines, on the basis of the applicant's conduct after the date of the notice of exclusion, or of conduct unknown to the Secretary at the time of the exclusion, that there is no basis under section 1128A to continue the exclusion, and that there are reasonable assurances that actions like those which formed the basis for the original exclusion have not recurred and will not recur, the Secretary may terminate the exclusion. When he does so, he must notify promptly the State agency administering or supervising the administration of relevant State health care programs of the fact and circumstances of each termination of an exclusion made under section 1128(g).

Statutory Provisions

Section 1128A, 42 U.S.C.A. 1320a-7a, provides:

(a) Any person (including an organization, agency, or other entity, but excluding a beneficiary, as defined in subsection (i)(5) [which means persons eligible to receive items or services for which payment may be made under Titles V, XVIII, XIX, or XX, but does not mean a provider, supplier, or practitioner]) that—

(1) knowingly presents or causes to be presented to an officer, employee, or agent of the United States, or of any department or agency thereof, or of any State agency (as defined in subsection (i)(1) [which means the State Medicaid agency or the State agency for programs under Titles V or XX]), a claim (as defined in subsection (i)(2) [which means an application for payment for items or services under Titles V, XVIII, XIX, or XX]) that the Secretary determines—

(A) is for a medical or other item or service that the person knows or should know was not provided as claimed, including any person who engages in a pattern or practice of presenting or causing to be presented a claim for an item or service that is based on a code that the person knows or should know will result in a greater payment to the person than the code the person knows or should know is applicable to the item or service actually provided.

(B) is for a medical or other item or service and the person knows or should know the claim is false or fraudulent,

(C) is presented for a physician's service (or an item or service incident to a physician's service) by a person who knows or should know that the individual who furnished (or supervised the furnishing of) the service —

(i) was not licensed as a physician

(ii) was licensed as a physician, but such license had been obtained through a misrepresentation of material fact (including cheating on an examination required for licensing), or

(iii) represented to the patient at the time the service was furnished that the physician was certified in a medical specialty by a medical specialty board when the individual was not so certified,

(D) is for a medical or other item or service furnished during a period in which the person was excluded from the program under which the claim was made pursuant to a determination by the Secretary under this section or under section 1128 [42 U.S.C.A. 1320a-7, which pertains to exclusions from Medicare and State health care programs, as indicated above], 1156 [42 U.S.C.A. 1320c-5, which pertains to exclusions from Medicare and State health care programs based on recommendations from Peer Review Organizations], 1160(b) (as in effect on September 2, 1982) [which pertained to exclusions from Medicare and State health care programs based on recommendations of Professional Standards Review Organizations], 1862(d) (as in effect on the date of the enactment of the Medicare and Medicaid Patient and Program Protection Act of 1987 [P.L. 100-93]) [which was an alternative basis for exclusion of individuals from Medicare], or 1866(b) [42 U.S.C.A. 1395cc(b), which pertains to termination of or refusal to renew provider agreements] or as a result of the application of the provisions of section 1842(j)(2) [42 U.S.C.A. 1395u(j)(2), which provides alternative grounds for excluding individuals and entities from Medicare and State health care programs and for imposing civil money penalties], or

(E) is for a pattern of medical or other items or services that a person knows or should know are not medically necessary.

◆ NOTE: Prior to amendment by section 231(e) of the Health Insurance Portability and Accountability Act of 1996, P.L. 104-191, section 1128A(a)(1)(A)read: "is for a medical or other item or service that the person knows or should know was not provided as claimed". The same section struck "or" and substituted ", or" for a semicolon in subparagraph (D); and inserted new subparagraph (E). Section 231(a)(3) inserted "knowingly" before "presents" each place it appears in paragraph (1) above and paragraph (2) below, and inserted "knowingly gives or causes to be given" in lieu of "gives" in paragraph (3) below.

(2) knowingly presents or causes to be presented to any person a request for payment which is in violation of the terms of (A) an assignment under section 1842(b)(3)(B)(ii) [42 U.S.C.A. 1395u(b)(3)(B)(ii), which pertains to assignment of claims for benefits], or (B) an agreement with a State agency (or other requirement of a State plan under title XIX) not to charge a person for an item or service in excess of the amount permitted to be charged, or (C) an agreement to be a participating physician or supplier under section 1842(h)(1) [42 U.S.C.A. 1395u(h)(1)], or (D) an agreement pursuant to section 1866(a)(1)(G) [42 U.S.C.A. 1395cc(a)(1)(G), which pertains to hospital provider agreements not to charge for inpatient hospital services for which an individual would be entitled to have payment made under Part A but for a denial or reduction of payments under section 1886(f)(2), 42 U.S.C.A. 1395ww(f)(2), which, in turn, pertains to the DRG reimbursement methodology];

(3) knowingly gives or causes to be given to any person, with respect to coverage under title XVIII of inpatient hospital services subject to the provisions of section 1886 [42 U.S.C.A. 1395ww, which pertains to DRG reimbursement methodology for hospitals], information that he knows or should know is false or misleading, and that could reasonably be expected to influence the decision when to discharge such person or another individual from the hospital;

(4) in the case of a person who is not an organization, agency, or other entity, is excluded from participating in a program under title XVIII or a State health care program in accordance

with this subsection or under section 1128 and who, at the time of a violation of this subsection —

(A) retains a direct or indirect ownership or control interest in any entity that is participating in a program under title XVIII or a State health care program, and who knows or should know of the action constituting the basis for the exclusion;

(B) is an officer or managing employee (as defined in section 1126(b)) of such an entity; or

(5) offers to or transfers remuneration to any individual eligible for benefits under title XVIII of this Act, or under a State health care program (as defined in section 1128(h)) that such person knows or should know is likely to influence such individual in order to receive from a particular provider, practitioner, or supplier any item or service for which payment may be made, in whole or in part under title XVIII, or a State health care program (as so defined);

(6) arranges or contracts (by employment or otherwise) with an individual or entity that the person knows or should know is excluded from participation in a Federal health care program (as defined in section 1128B(f) [42 U.S.C.A. 1320a-7b(f)] , for the provision of items or services for which payment may be made under such a program; or

(7) commits an act described in paragraph (1) or (2) of section 1128B(b) [which pertains to illegal remuneration for referrals];

◆ NOTE: Effective January 1, 1997, section 231(a)(2) of the Health Insurance Portability and Accountability Act of 1996 amended section 1128A(a) by substituting a semicolon for "or" at the end of paragraph (2) and substituting "or" for a semicolon at the end of paragraph (3). Then it inserted a new paragraph (4). It also substituted "$10,000" for "$2,000" in the phrase beginning "shall be subject" immediately hereafter; inserted the phrase, "; in cases under paragraph (4), $10,000 for each day the prohibited relationship occurs" after "false or misleading information was given;" and inserted "three times the amount" in lieu of "twice the amount". In the sentence below beginning "In addition the Secretary", it substituted "Federal health care programs (as defined in section 1128(f)(1))" for "programs under title XVIII".

◆ Effective August 5, 1997, section 4304(a) of the Balanced Budget Act of 1997, P.L. 105-33, removed "or" from the end of paragraph (a)(4) above; added "or" to the end of paragraph (a)(5); and added paragraph (a)(6). Section 4304(b)(1) removed "or" from the end of paragraph (a)(5); added "or" to the end of paragraph (a)(6); and added paragraph (a)(7). Then, applicable to arrangements and contracts entered into on or after August 5, 1997, section 4304(b)(2) substituted "occurs; or in cases under paragraph (7), $50,000 for each such act)" for "occurs)." after "the prohibited relationship;" and inserted "(or, in cases under paragraph (7), damages of not more than 3 times the total amount of remuneration offered, paid, solicited, or received, without regard to whether a portion of such remuneration was offered, paid, solicited, or received for a lawful purpose)" after "of such claim".

shall be subject, in addition to any other penalties that may be prescribed by law, to a civil money penalty of not more than $10,000 for each item or service (or, in cases under paragraph (3), $15,000 for each individual with respect to whom false or misleading information was given; in cases under paragraph (4), $10,000 for each day the prohibited relationship occurs; or in cases under paragraph (7), $50,000 for each such act). In addition, such a person shall be subject to an assessment of not more than three times the amount claimed for each such item or service in lieu of damages sustained by the United States or a State agency because of such claim (or, in cases under paragraph (7), damages of not more than 3 times the total amount of remuneration offered, paid, solicited, or received, without regard to whether a portion of such remuneration was offered, paid, solicited, or received for a lawful purpose). In addition, the Secretary may make a determination in the same proceeding to exclude the person from participation in the Federal health care programs (as defined in section 1128B(f)(1)) and to direct the appropriate State agency to exclude the person from participation in any State health care program.

(1) If a hospital or critical access hospital knowingly makes a payment, directly or indirectly, to a physician as an induce-

ment to reduce or limit services provided with respect to individuals who—

(A) are entitled to benefits under part A or part B of title XVIII or to medical assistance under a State plan approved under title XIX, and

(B) are under the direct care of the physician,

the hospital or critical access hospital shall be subject, in addition to any other penalties that may be prescribed by law, to a civil money penalty of not more than $2,000 for each such individual with respect to whom the payment is made.

◆ NOTE: The phrase "critical access" was substituted for "or rural primary care" everywhere the latter appeared in section 1128A, effective October 1, 1997, by section 4201(c) of the Balanced Budget Act of 1997. Previously, "or rural primary care hospital" had been added to this subsection effective December 19, 1989, pursuant to section 6003(g)(D)(i) of P.L. 101-239, the Omnibus Budget Reconciliation Act of 1989.

Pursuant to section 4204(a)(3) of P.L. 101-508, the Omnibus Budget Reconciliation Act of 1990 (OBRA 90), prior to November 5, 1990, subsection (b)(1) applied to "an eligible organization with a risk-sharing contract under section 1876", 42 U.S.C.A. 1395mm, which pertains to health maintenance organizations and competitive medical plans, as well, and the present subparagraph (B) was designated (C). The same provision of OBRA 90 also deleted former subparagraph (B), which read "in the case of an eligible organization or an entity, are enrolled with the organization or entity, and" and the phrase "or organization" which had followed "the hospital or rural primary care hospital" where the latter appears after subparagraph (B). Also effective November 5, 1990, section 4731(b) of OBRA 90 deleted "or an entity with a contract under section 1903(m)", 42 U.S.C.A. 1396b(m), which pertains to health maintenance organizations.

(2) Any physician who knowingly accepts receipt of a payment described in paragraph (1) shall be subject, in addition to any other penalties that may be prescribed by law, to a civil money penalty of not more than $2,000 for each individual described in such paragraph with respect to whom the payment is made.

(3)(A) Any physician who executes a document described in subparagraph (B) with respect to an individual knowing that all of the requirements referred to in such subparagraph are not met with respect to the individual shall be subject to a civil monetary penalty of not more than the greater of—

(i) $5,000, or

(ii) three times the amount of payments under title XVIII for home health services which are made pursuant to such certification.

(B) A document described in this subparagraph is any document that certifies, for purposes of title XVIII, that an individual meets the requirements of section 1814(a)(2)(C) [42 U.S.C.A. 1395f(a)(2)(C), which pertains to limitations on payments for home health services under Medicare Part A] or 1835(a)(2)(A) [42 U.S.C.A. 1395n(a)(2)(A), which pertains to limitations on payments for home health services under Medicare Part B] in the case of home health services furnished to the individual.

◆ [NOTE: Section 232 of the Health Insurance Portability and Accountability Act of 1996 added paragraph (3)(A) above, effective for certifications made on or after August 21, 1996.]

(1) The Secretary may initiate a proceeding to determine whether to impose a civil money penalty, assessment, or exclusion under subsection (a) or (b) only as authorized by the Attorney General pursuant to procedures agreed upon by them. The Secretary may not initiate an action under this section with respect to any claim, request for payment, or other occurrence described in this section later than six years after the date the claim was presented, the request for payment was made, or the occurrence took place. The Secretary may initiate an action under this section by serving notice of the action in any manner authorized by rule 4 of the Federal Rules of Civil Procedure.

(2) The Secretary shall not make a determination adverse to any person under subsection (a) or (b) until the person has been given written notice and an opportunity for the determination to be made on the record after a hearing at which the person is entitled to be represented by counsel, to present witnesses, and to cross-examine witnesses against the person.

(3) In a proceeding under subsection (a) or (b) which—

(A) is against a person who has been convicted (whether upon a verdict after trial or upon a plea of guilty or nolo contendere) of a Federal crime charging fraud or false statements, and

(B) involves the same transaction as in the criminal action,

the person is estopped from denying the essential elements of the criminal offense.

(4) The official conducting a hearing under this section may sanction a person, including any party or attorney, for failing to comply with an order or procedure, failing to defend an action, or other misconduct as would interfere with the speedy, orderly, or fair conduct of the hearing. Such sanction shall reasonably relate to the severity and nature of the failure or misconduct. Such sanction may include—

(A) in the case of refusal to provide or permit discovery, drawing negative factual inferences or treating such refusal as an admission by deeming the matter, or certain facts, to be established,

(B) prohibiting a party from introducing certain evidence or otherwise supporting a particular claim or defense,

(C) striking pleadings, in whole or in part,

(D) staying the proceedings,

(E) dismissal of the action,

(F) entering a default judgment,

(G) ordering the party or attorney to pay attorneys' fees and other costs caused by the failure or misconduct, and

(H) refusing to consider any motion or other action which is not filed in a timely manner.

In determining the amount or scope of any penalty, assessment, or exclusion imposed pursuant to subsection (a) or (b), the Secretary shall take into account—

(1) the nature of claims and the circumstances under which they were presented,

(2) the degree of culpability, history of prior offenses, and financial condition of the person presenting the claims, and

(3) such other matters as justice may require.

Any person adversely affected by a determination of the Secretary under this section may obtain a review of such determination in the United States Court of Appeals for the circuit in which the person resides, or in which the claim was presented, by filing in such court (within sixty days following the date the person is notified of the Secretary's determination) a written petition requesting that the determination be modified or set aside. A copy of the petition shall be forthwith transmitted by the clerk of the court to the Secretary, and thereupon the Secretary shall file in the Court the record in the proceeding as provided in section 2112 of title 28, United States Code. Upon such filing, the court shall have jurisdiction of the proceeding and of the question determined therein, and shall have the power to make and enter upon the pleadings, testimony, and proceedings set forth in such record a decree affirming, modifying, remanding for further consideration, or setting aside, in whole or in part, the determination of the Secretary and enforcing the same to the extent that such order is affirmed or modified. No objection that has not been urged before the Secretary shall be considered by the court, unless the failure or neglect to urge such objection shall be excused because of extraordinary circumstances. The findings of the Secretary with respect to questions of fact, if supported by substantial evidence on the record considered as a whole, shall be conclusive. If any party shall apply to the court for leave to adduce additional evidence and shall show to the satisfaction of the court that such additional evidence is material and that there were reasonable grounds for the failure to adduce such evidence in the hearing before the Secretary, the court may order such additional evidence to be taken before the Secretary and to be made a part of the record. The Secretary may modify his findings as to the facts, or make new findings, by reason of additional evidence so taken and filed, and he shall file with the court such modified or new findings, which findings with respect to questions of fact, if supported by substantial evidence on the record considered as a whole, shall be conclusive, and his recommendations, if any, for the modification or setting aside of his original order. Upon the filing of the record with it, the jurisdiction of the court shall be exclusive and its judgment and decree shall be final, except that the same shall be subject to review by the Supreme Court of the

United States, as provided in section 1254 of title 28, United States Code.

Civil money penalties and assessments imposed under this section may be compromised by the Secretary and may be recovered in a civil action in the name of the United States brought in United States district court for the district where the claim was presented, or where the claimant resides, as determined by the Secretary. Amounts recovered under this section shall be paid to the Secretary and disposed of as follows:

(1) (A) In the case of amounts recovered arising out of a claim under title XIX, there shall be paid to the State agency an amount bearing the same proportion to the total amount recovered as the State's share of the amount paid by the State agency for such claim bears to the total amount paid for such claim.

(B) In the case of amounts recovered arising out of a claim under an allotment to a State under title V, there shall be paid to the State agency an amount equal to three-sevenths of the amount recovered.

(2) Such portion of the amounts recovered as is determined to have been paid out of the trust funds under sections 1817 [42 U.S.C.A. 1395i, the hospital insurance trust fund for Part A benefits] and 1841 [42 U.S.C.A. 1395t, the supplementary medical insurance trust fund for Part B benefits] shall be repaid to such trust funds.

(3) With respect to amounts recovered arising out of a claim under a Federal health program (as defined in section 1128B(f) [42 U.S.C.A. 1320a-7b(f)]), the portion of such amounts as is determined to have been paid by the program shall be repaid to the program, and the portion of such amounts attributable to the amounts recovered under this section by reason of the amendments made by the Health Insurance Portability and Accountability Act of 1996 (as estimated by the Secretary) shall be deposited into the Federal Hospital Insurance Trust Fund pursuant to section 1817(k)(2)(C) [42 U.S.C.A. 1395i(k)(2)(C), which established the Health Care Fraud and Abuse Control Account to hold funds obtained from fines and penalties related to fraud and abuse and to use them to pay for the costs of health care fraud and abuse investigations and prosecutions].

◆ NOTE: Section 231(a)(2) of the Health Insurance Portability and Accountability Act of 1996 redesignated former paragraph (3) in section 1128A(f) as paragraph (4), now just below, and inserted new paragraph (3) just above, effective January 1, 1997.

(4) The remainder of the amounts recovered shall be deposited as miscellaneous receipts of the Treasury of the United States.

The amount of such penalty or assessment, when finally determined, or the amount agreed upon in compromise, may be deducted from any sum then or later owing by the United States or a State agency to the person against whom the penalty or assessment has been assessed.

A determination by the Secretary to impose a penalty, assessment, or exclusion under subsection (a) or (b) shall be final upon the expiration of the sixty-day period referred to in subsection (e). Matters that were raised or that could have been raised in a hearing before the Secretary or in an appeal pursuant to subsection (e) may not be raised as a defense to a civil action by the United States to collect a penalty, assessment, or exclusion assessed under this section.

Whenever the Secretary's determination to impose a penalty, assessment, or exclusion under subsection (a) or (b) becomes final, he shall notify the appropriate State or local medical or professional organization, the appropriate State agency or agencies administering or supervising the administration of State health care programs (as defined in section 1128(h) [42 U.S.C.A. 1320a-7(h), which means Medicaid and programs funded under Title V (Maternal and Child Health Services Block Grants) and Title XX (Block Grants to States for Social Services)]), and the appropriate utilization and quality control peer review organization, and the appropriate State or local licensing agency or organization (including the agency specified in section[s] 1864(a) and 1902(a)(33) [42 U.S.C.A. 1395aa(a) and 42 U.S.C.A. 1396a(a)(33), respectively, which pertain to State agencies involved in Medicare and Medicaid provider survey and certification]) that such a penalty, assessment, or exclusion has become final and the reasons therefor.

For purposes of this section:

(1) The term "State agency" means the agency established or designated to administer or supervise the administration of the State plan under title XIX of this Act or designated to administer the State's program under title V or title XX of this Act.

(2) The term "claim" means an application for payments for items and services under a Federal health care program (as defined in section 1128B(f)).

(3) The term "item or service" includes (A) any particular item, device, medical supply, or service claimed to have been provided to a patient and listed in an itemized claim for payment, and (B) in the case of a claim based on costs, any entry in the cost report, books of account or other documents supporting such claim.

(4) The term "agency of the United States" includes any contractor acting as a fiscal intermediary, carrier, or fiscal agent or any other claims processing agent for a Federal health care program (as so defined).

(5) The term "beneficiary" means an individual who is eligible to receive items or services for which payment may be made under a Federal health care program (as so defined) but does not include a provider, supplier, or practitioner.

(6) The term "remuneration" includes the waiver of coinsurance and deductible amounts (or any part thereof), and transfers of items or services for free or for other than fair market value. The term "remuneration" does not include —

(A) the waiver of coinsurance and deductible amounts by a person, if—

(i) the waiver is not offered as part of any advertisement or solicitation;

(ii) the person does not routinely waive coinsurance or deductible amounts; and

(iii) the person —

(I) waives the coinsurance and deductible amounts after determining in good faith that the individual is in financial need; or

(II) fails to collect coinsurance or deductible amounts after making reasonable collection efforts;

(B) subject to subsection (n), any permissible waiver as specified in section 1128B(b)(3) or in regulations issued by the Secretary [NOTE: The phrase beginning "subject to subsection (n)," was added effective October 21, 1998, by section 5201(a) of the Tax and Trade Relief Extension Act of 1998, which is in "Omnibus Consolidated Emergency and Supplemental Appropriations for Fiscal Year 1999", P.L. 105–277.];

(C) differentials in coinsurance and deductible amounts as part of a benefit plan design as long as the differentials have been disclosed in writing to all beneficiaries, third party payers, and providers, to whom claims are presented and as long as the differentials meet the standards as defined in regulations promulgated by the Secretary not later than 180 days after the date of the enactment of the Health Insurance Portability and Accountability Act of 1996;

(D) incentives given to individuals to promote the delivery of preventive care as determined by the Secretary in regulations so promulgated.

(D) [sic] a reduction in the copayment amount for covered OPD services under section 1833(t)(5)(B) [42 U.S.C.A. 1395l(t)m, which pertains to prospective payment for hospital outpatient department services].

◆ NOTE: Section 4331(e)(1) of the Balanced Budget Act of 1997 added "or" at the end of subclause (i)(6)(A)(ii)(I); removed "or" from the end of subclause (i)(6)(A)(ii)(II); and removed subclause (i)(6)(A)(ii)(III), which had read "provides for any permissible waiver as specified in section 1128B(b)(3) or in regulations issued by the Secretary." Section 4331(e)(2) redesignated subparagraphs (i)(6)(B) and (C) as subparagraphs (i)(6)(C) and (D); and added subparagraph (i)(6)(B). Those changes were effective August 21, 1996, as if included in the Health Insurance Portability and Accountability Act of 1996. Then, effective August 5, 1997, section 4523(c) of the Balanced Budget Act of 1997 removed "or" from the end of subparagraph (i)(6)(B); substituted "; or" for the period at the end of subparagraph (i)(6)(C); and added subparagraph (i)(6)(D), which made (erroneously) two subparagraphs (D).

(7) The term "should know" means that a person, with respect to information —

(A) acts in deliberate ignorance of the truth or falsity of the information; or

(B) acts in reckless disregard of the truth or falsity of the information, and no proof of specific intent to defraud is required.

◆ NOTE: Section 231(a)(3) of the Health Insurance Portability and Accountability Act of 1996 added paragraphs (6) and (7) above to section 1128A(i). It also substituted "a Federal health care program (as defined in section 1128B(f))" for "title V, XVIII, XIX, or XX of this Act" in paragraph (2); substituted "a Federal health care program (as so defined)" for "a health insurance or medical services program under title XVIII or XIX of this Act in paragraph (4) and" for "title V, XVIII, XIX, or XX" in paragraph (5). These changes were effective January 1, 1997.

(1) The provisions of subsections (d) and (e) of section 205 [42 U.S.C.A. 405(d) and (e), which pertain, respectively, to issuance of subpoenas and punishment for failure to comply with them] shall apply with respect to this section to the same extent as they are applicable with respect to title II [which pertains to retirement, survivor, and disability benefits under the Social Security Act]. The Secretary may delegate the authority granted by section 205(d) (as made applicable to this section) to the Inspector General of the Department of Health and Human Services for purposes of any investigation under this section.

(2) The Secretary may delegate authority granted under this section and under section 1128 to the Inspector General of the Department of Health and Human Services. [This subparagraph (2) was added by sections 4207(h) and 4753 of OBRA 90, effective November 5, 1990.]

(k) Whenever the Secretary has reason to believe that any person has engaged, is engaging, or is about to engage in any activity which makes the person subject to a civil monetary penalty under this section, the Secretary may bring an action in an appropriate district court of the United States (or, if applicable, a United States court of any territory) to enjoin such activity, or to enjoin the person from concealing, removing, encumbering, or disposing of assets which may be required in order to pay a civil monetary penalty if any such penalty were to be imposed or to seek other appropriate relief.

(l) A principal is liable for penalties, assessments, and an exclusion under this section for the actions of the principal's agent acting within the scope of the agency.

(m)(1) For purposes of this section, with respect to Federal health care programs not contained in this Act, references to the Secretary in this section shall be deemed to be references to the Secretary or Administrator of the department or agency with jurisdiction over such program and references to the Inspector General of the Department of Health and Human Services in this section shall be deemed to be references to the Inspector General of the applicable department or agency.

(2)(A) The Secretary and Administrator of the departments and agencies referred to in paragraph (1) may include in any action pursuant to this section, claims within the jurisdiction of other Federal departments or agencies as long as the following conditions are satisfied:

(i) The case involves primarily claims submitted to the Federal health care programs of the department or agency initiating the action.

(ii) The Secretary or Administrator of the department or agency initiating the action gives notice and an opportunity to participate in the investigation to the Inspector General of the department or agency with primary jurisdiction over the Federal health care programs to which the claims were submitted.

(B) If the conditions specified in subparagraph (A) are fulfilled, the Inspector General of the department or agency initiating the action is authorized to exercise all powers granted under the Inspector General Act of 1978 (5 U.S.C.A. App.) with respect to the claims submitted to the other departments or agencies to the same manner and extent as provided in that Act with respect to claims submitted to such departments or agencies.

◆ NOTE: Section 231(a)(3) of the Health Insurance Portability and Accountability Act of 1996 added subsection (m), January 1, 1997.

(n)(1) Subparagraph (B) of subsection (i)(6) shall not apply to a practice described in paragraph (2) unless —

(A) the Secretary, through the Inspector General of the Department of Health and Human Services, promulgates a rule authorizing such a practice as an exception to remuneration; and

(B) the remuneration is offered or transferred by a person under such rule during the 2-year period beginning on the date the rule is first promulgated.

(2) A practice described in this paragraph is a practice under which a health care provider or facility pays, in whole or in part, premiums for Medicare supplemental policies for individual entitled to benefits under part A of title XVIII pursuant to section 226A [42 U.S.C.A. 426A.]

◆ NOTE: Subsection (n) was added by section 5201(b)(1) of the Tax and Trade Relief Extension Act of 1998, which is in "Omnibus Consolidated Emergency and Supplemental Appropriations for Fiscal Year 1999, effective October 21, 1998.

With respect to issuance of subpoenas and their enforcement, section 205 of the Social Security Act, 42 U.S.C.A. 405, made applicable to section 1128A civil money penalty and exclusion actions by section 1128A(j), provides in pertinent part as follows:

For the purpose of any hearing, investigation, or other proceeding authorized or directed under this title, or relative to any other matter within his jurisdiction hereunder, the Secretary shall have power to issue subpoenas requiring the attendance and testimony of witnesses and the production of any evidence that relates to any matter under investigation or in question before the Secretary. Such attendance of witnesses and production of evidence at the designated place of such hearing, investigation, or other proceeding may be required from any place in the United States or in any Territory or possession thereof. Subpoenas of the Secretary shall be served by anyone authorized by him (1) by delivering a copy thereof to the individual named therein, or (2) by registered mail or by certified mail addressed to such individual at his last dwelling place or principal place of business. A verified return by the individual so serving the subpoena setting forth the manner of service, or, in the case of service by registered mail or by certified mail, the return post-office receipt therefor signed by the individual so served, shall be proof of service. Witnesses so subpoenaed shall be paid the same fees and mileage as are paid witnesses in the district courts of the United States.

In case of contumacy by, or refusal to obey a subpoena duly served upon, any person, any district court of the United States for the judicial district in which said person charged with contumacy or refusal to obey is found or resides or transacts business, upon application by the Secretary, shall have jurisdiction to issue an order requiring such person to appear and give testimony, or to appear and produce evidence, or both; any failure to obey such order of the court may be punished by said court as contempt thereof.

The following provisions of section 1128, 42 U.S.C.A. 1320a-7, which provides alternative grounds for excluding individuals and entities from Medicare, Medicaid, and programs funded by Title V and Title XX, also apply to exclusions which the Secretary may authorize and/or direct in conjunction with a civil money penalty action under section 1128A.

Section 1128(c) provides in pertinent part:

NOTICE, EFFECTIVE DATE, AND PERIOD OF EXCLUSION.—

(1) An exclusion under. . .1128A shall be effective at such time and upon such reasonable notice to the public and to the individual or entity excluded as may be specified in regulations consistent with paragraph (2).

(2) (A) Except as provided in subparagraph (B), such an exclusion shall be effective with respect to services furnished to an individual on or after the effective date of the exclusion.

(B) Unless the Secretary determines that the health and safety of individuals receiving services warrants the exclusion taking effect earlier, an exclusion shall not apply to payments made under title XVIII or under a State health care program for—

(i) inpatient institutional services furnished to an individual who was admitted to such institution before the date of the exclusion, or

(ii) home health services and hospice care furnished to an individual under a plan of care established before the date of the exclusion,

until the passage of 30 days after the effective date of the exclusion.

(3) (A) The Secretary shall specify, in the. . .written notice under section 1128A, the minimum period. . .of the exclusion.

Section 1128(d) provides in pertinent part:

NOTICE TO STATE AGENCIES AND EXCLUSION UNDER STATE HEALTH CARE PROGRAMS. —

(1) Subject to paragraph (3), the Secretary shall exercise the authority under. . .section 1128A in a manner that results in an individual's or entity's exclusion from all the programs under title XVIII and all the State health care programs in which the individual or entity may otherwise participate.

(2) The Secretary shall promptly notify each appropriate State agency administering or supervising the administration of each State health care program. . .

(A) of the fact and circumstances of each exclusion effected against an individual or entity under. . .section 1128A, and

(B) of the period (described in paragraph (3)) for which the State agency is directed to exclude the individual or entity from participation in the State health care program.

(3) (A) Except as provided in subparagraph (B), the period of the exclusion under a State health care program under paragraph (2) shall be the same as any period of exclusion under title XVIII.

(B) (i) The Secretary may waive an individual's or entity's exclusion under a State health care program under paragraph (2) if the Secretary receives and approves a request for the waiver with respect to the individual or entity from the State agency administering or supervising the administration of the program.

(ii) A State health care program may provide for a period of exclusion which is longer than the period of exclusion under title XVIII.

Section 1128(e) provides in pertinent part:

NOTICE TO STATE LICENSING AGENCIES. —The Secretary shall—

(1) promptly notify the appropriate State or local agency or authority having responsibility for the licensing or certification of an individual or entity excluded (or directed to be excluded) from participation under. . .section 1128A, of the fact and circumstances of the exclusion,

(2) request that appropriate investigations be made and sanctions invoked in accordance with applicable State law and policy, and

(3) request that the State or local agency or authority keep the Secretary and the Inspector General of the Department of Health and Human Services fully and currently informed with respect to any actions taken in response to the request.

Section 1128(f) provides in pertinent part:

NOTICE, HEARING, AND JUDICIAL REVIEW. —

* * *

(2) Unless the Secretary determines that the health or safety of individuals receiving services warrants the exclusion taking effect earlier, any individual or entity that is the subject of an adverse determination under subsection (b)(7) [of section 1128, which pertains to exclusions based on fraud, kickbacks, and other prohibited activities described in section 1128A and section 1128B] shall be entitled to a hearing by an administrative law judge (as provided under section 205(b)) on the determination under subsection (b)(7) before any exclusion based upon the determination takes effect.

(3) The provisions of section 205(h) [42 U.S.C.A. 405(h)] shall apply with respect to. . .sections 1128A and 1156 [which pertains to exclusions based on recommendations by Peer Review Organizations] to the same extent as it is applicable with respect to title II.

Finally, section 205(h), 42 U.S.C.A. 405(h), provides:

> The findings and decision of the Secretary after a hearing shall be binding upon all individuals who were parties to such hearing. No findings of fact or decision of the Secretary shall be reviewed by any person, tribunal, or governmental agency except as herein provided. No action against the United States, the Secretary, or any officer or employee thereof shall be brought under section 1331 or 1346 of title 28, United States Code, to recover on any claim arising under this title.

With respect to the definition of Federal health care program, section 1128B(f) provides:

For purposes of this section, the term "Federal health care program" means —

> (1) any plan or program that provides health benefits, whether directly, through insurance, or otherwise, which is funded directly, in whole or in part, by the United States Government (other than the health insurance program under chapter 89 of title 5, United States Code [which is the health insurance program for Federal employees]); or
>
> (2) any State health care program, as defined in section 1128(h).

Finally, section 1128(h) provides:

> DEFINITION OF STATE HEALTH CARE PROGRAM. — For purposes of this section and sections 1128A and 1128B, the term "State health care program" means —
>
> (1) a State plan approved under title XIX,
>
> (2) any program receiving funds under title V or from an allotment to a State under such title,
>
> (3) any program receiving funds under title XX or from an allotment to a State under such title, or
>
> (4) a State child health plan approved under title XXI.

◆ NOTE: Section 4901(b)(2) of the Balanced Budget Act of 1997 deleted "or" from the end of paragraph (2); substituted ", or" for the period at the end of paragraph (3); and added paragraph (4), effective August 5, 1997.

◆ NOTE: See IV-6 for provisions of section 205 of the Social Security Act applicable to administrative hearings and judicial review.

For regulatory citations, see Chapter 8

§ 4:9 CRIMINAL PENALTIES: FALSE STATEMENTS, FALSE REPRESENTATIONS, CONCEALMENT, FAILURE TO DISCLOSE, WRONGFUL CONVERSION OF BENEFITS AND PAYMENTS, CLAIMS FOR PHYSICIANS' SERVICES BY PERSONS NOT LICENSED AS A PHYSICIAN, AND DISPOSAL OF ASSETS TO OBTAIN MEDICAID ELIGIBILITY — Section 1128B(a) [42 U.S.C.A. 1320a-7b(a)]

Summary

Section 1128B(a), 42 U.S.C.A. 1320a-7b(a), makes it a felony for any person to commit any of the following acts in connection with respect to a Federal health care program.

1. Knowingly and willfully making or causing to be made any false statement or representation of a material fact in any application for any benefit or payment under a Federal health care program (as defined in section 1128B(f).

2. Knowingly and willfully making or causing to be made any false statement or representation of a material fact for use in determining rights to such a benefit or payment.

3. Having knowledge of the occurrence of any event affecting either his initial or continued right to any such benefit or payment, or the initial or continued right to any such benefit or payment of any other individual in whose behalf he has applied for or is receiving such a benefit or payment, and concealing or failing to disclose such event with the intent to fraudulently secure the benefit or payment when none is authorized, or to secure a benefit or payment in a greater amount or quantity than is due.

4. Having made application for such a benefit or payment for the use and benefit of another, and having received it, and then knowingly and willfully converting it, or any part thereof, to a use other than for the use and benefit of the entitled person.

5. Presenting or causing to be presented a claim for a physician's service for which payment may be paid under a Federal health care

program while knowing that the individual who furnished the service was not licensed as a physician.

6. For a fee knowingly and willfully counseling or assisting an individual to dispose of assets (including by any transfer in trust) in order for an individual to become eligible for medical assistance under a State Medicaid program. This applies if disposing of the assets results in the imposition of a period of ineligibility for such assistance under section 1917(c), 42 U.S.C.A. 1396p. Section 1917 requires States to establish a 36-month look-back for Medicaid ineligibility based on disposal of the assets of an individual seeking Medicaid assistance for institutional care (nursing home) or noninstitutional care (home health services). If the assets disposed of are payments from a trust or portions of a trust, the look-back period is 60 months. This look-back period commences the first day of the first month during or after which assets have been transferred for less than fair market value and which does not occur in any other periods of ineligibility.

◆ NOTE: Prior to amendment by section 4734(1) of the Balanced Budget Act of 1997, P.L. 105-33, item 6 above made no reference to a fee, or to counseling and assisting. Instead it applied more broadly to the knowing and willful disposal of assets by anyone. This change was effective August 5, 1997.

Section 1128(B)(f) defines "Federal health care program" to include any plan that provides benefits funded directly in whole or in part by the United States Government. The only exception is the health benefits program for Federal employees authorized by Title V, Chapter 89, of the U.S. Code.

"Federal health care program" also includes State Medicaid programs, State health care programs funded by a Maternal and Child Health Services Block Grant (Title V of the Social Security Act, 42 U.S.C.A. 701 et seq.), or by a Block Grant to States for Social Services (Title XX of the Act, 42 U.S.C.A. 1397 et seq.), and a State child health plan approved under title XXI.

◆ NOTE: Section 204 of the Health Insurance Portability and Accountability Act of 1996, P.L. 104-191, added this definition of Federal health care program to section 1128B, effective January 1, 1997. This dramatically broadens the statute's reach. Prior to that amendment the statute applied only to acts committed with respect to Medicare, Medicaid, and State health care programs funded by Titles V and XX of the Social Security Act. Section

4901(b)(2) of the Balanced Budget Act of 1997, P.L. 105-33 added the reference to State child health plans approved under title XXI, effective August 5, 1997.

Anyone convicted of any of these offenses may be punished by a fine not exceeding $25,000, by imprisonment for not more than five years, or both.

Anyone other than a person furnishing the items of services who commits any of these offenses is guilty of a misdemeanor, and, upon conviction, may be punished by a fine not exceeding $10,000, by imprisonment for not more than one year, or both.

In addition, with respect to anyone who commits any of the foregoing offenses who is otherwise eligible for assistance under a Federal health care program, the Administrator of that program may, at his or her option, limit, restrict, or suspend that person's eligibility for up to one year. This optional punishment applies notwithstanding any other provision of such a Federal health care program. Such punishment may not be applied, however, to others, such as a child or spouse, whose eligibility is based on their relationship to the guilty party.

◆ NOTE: The reach of this optional punishment also was broadened by section 204 of the Health Insurance Portabllity and Accountability Act of 1996. Previously, it applied only to Medicaid eligibility. The change was effective January 1, 1997.

Statutory Provisions

Section 1128B(a), 42 U.S.C.A. 1320a-7b(a), provides:

Whoever —

(1) knowingly and willfully makes or causes to be made any false statement or representation of a material fact in any application for any benefit or payment under a program under a Federal health care program (as defined in subsection (f)),

(2) at any time knowingly and willfully makes or causes to be made any false statement or representation of a material fact for use in determining rights to such benefit or payment,

(3) having knowledge of the occurrence of any event affecting (A) his initial or continued right to any such benefit or payment, or (B) the initial or continued right to any such benefit or payment of any other individual in whose behalf he has

applied for or is receiving such benefit or payment, conceals or fails to disclose such event with an intent fraudulently to secure such benefit or payment either in a greater amount or quantity than is due or when no such benefit or payment is authorized,

(4) having made application to receive any such benefit or payment for the use and benefit of another and having received it, knowingly and willfully converts such benefit or payment or any part thereof to a use other than for the use and benefit of such other person,

(5) presents or causes to be presented a claim for a physician's service for which payment may be made under a program under a Federal health care program and knows that the individual who furnished the service was not licensed as a physician, or

(6) for a fee knowingly and willfully counsels or assists an individual to dispose of assets (including by any transfer in trust) in order for the individual to become eligible for medical assistance under a State plan under title XIX, if disposing of the assets results in the imposition of a period of ineligibility for such assistance under section 1917(c) [42 U.S.C.A. 1396p(c)].

shall (i) in the case of such a statement, representation, concealment, failure, or conversion by any person in connection with the furnishing (by that person) of items or services for which payment is or may be made under the program, be guilty of a felony and upon conviction thereof fined not more than $25,000 or imprisoned for not more than five years or both, or (ii) in the case of such a statement, representation, concealment, failure, conversion, or provision of counsel or assistance by any other person, be guilty of a misdemeanor and upon conviction thereof fined not more than $10,000 or imprisoned for not more than one year, or both. In addition, in any case where an individual who is otherwise eligible for assistance under a Federal health care program is convicted of an offense under the preceding provisions of this subsection, the administrator of such program may at its option (notwithstanding any other provision of such program) limit, restrict, or suspend the eligibility of that individual for such period (not exceeding one year) as it deems appropriate; but the imposition of a limitation, restriction, or suspension with respect to the eligibility of any individual under this sentence shall not affect the eligibility of any other person for assistance under the plan, regardless of the relationship between that individual and such other person.

◆ NOTE: Section 204 of the Health Insurance Portability and Accountability Act of 1996, P.L. 104-191, substituted "a Federal health care program (as defined in subsection (f)" for "a program under title XVIII or a State health care program (as defined in section 1128(h))" in subsection (a)(1). It substituted "a Federal health care program" for "a program under title XVIII or a State health care program" in subsection (a)(5). In the second sentence of subsection (a), it substituted "a Federal health care program" for "a State plan approved under title XIX"; and it substituted "the administrator of such program may at its option (notwithstanding any other provision of such program)" for "the State may at its option (notwithstanding any other provision of that title or of such plan)." These changes were effective January 1, 1997.

◆ ALSO NOTE: Prior to amendment by section 4734(1) of the Balanced Budget Act of 1997, P.L. 105-33, section 1128B(a)(6) read: "knowingly and willfully disposes of assets (including by any transfer in trust) in order for an individual to become eligible for medical assistance under a State plan under title XIX [Medicaid], if disposing of the assets results in the imposition of a period of ineligibility for such assistance under section 1917(c)." Furthermore, section 4734(2) of the Balanced Budget Act of 1997, substituted "failure, conversion, or provision of counsel or assistance by any other person" for "failure, or conversion by any other person" to the clause following paragraph (6). These changes were effective August 5, 1997.

Section 1128B(f) provides:

For purposes of this section, the term "Federal health care program" means —

(1) any plan or program that provides health benefits, whether directly, through insurance, or otherwise, which is funded directly, in whole or in part, by the United States Government (other than the health insurance program under chapter 89 of title 5, United States Code [which pertains to Federal employees]); or

(2) any State health care program, as defined in section 1128(h).

Section 1128(h), 42 U.S.C.A. 1320a-7(h), provides:

DEFINITION OF STATE HEALTH CARE PROGRAM. — For purposes of this section [section 1128] and sections 1128A [42 U.S.C.A. 1320a-7a, which provides civil money penalties and an alternative basis for exclusion from Medicare and State health care programs for a variety of offenses] and 1128(B) the term "State health care program" means —

(1) a State plan approved under title XIX [Medicaid, 42 U.S.C.A. 1396 et seq.],

(2) any program receiving funds under title V or from an allotment to a State under such title, or

(3) any program receiving funds under title XX or from an allotment to a State under such title; or

(4) a State child health plan approved under title XXI.

◆ NOTE: Section 4901(b)(2) of the Balanced Budget Act of 1997 deleted "or" from the end of paragraph (h)(2); substituted ", or" for the period at the end of paragraph (h)(3); and added paragraph (h)(4), effective August 5, 1997.

Section 1917(c), 42 U.S.C.A. 1396p, provides in pertinent part:

TAKING INTO ACCOUNT CERTAIN TRANSFERS OF ASSETS. —

(1)(A) In order to meet the requirements of this subsection for purposes of section 1902(a)(18) [42 U.S.C.A. 1396a(a)(18)], the State plan must provide that if an institutionalized individual or the spouse of such an individual (or, at the option of a State, a noninstitutionalized individual or the spouse of such an individual) disposes of assets for less than fair market value on or after the look-back date specified in subparagraph (B)(i), the individual is ineligible for medical assistance for services described in subparagraph (C)(i) (or, in the case of a noninstitutionalized individual, for the services described in subparagraph (C)(ii)) during the period beginning on the date specified in subparagraph (D) and equal to the number of months specified in subparagraph (E).

(B)(1) The look-back date specified in this subparagraph is a date that is 36 months (or, in the case of payments from a trust or portions of a trust that are treated as assets disposed of by the individual pursuant to paragraph (3)(A)(iii) or (3)(B)(ii) of subsection (d), 60 months) before the date specified in clause (ii).

(ii) The date specified in this clause, with respect to —

(I) an institutionalized individual is the first date as of which the individual both is an institutionalized individual and has applied for medical assistance under the State plan, or

(II) a noninstitutionalized individual is the date on which the individual applies for medical assistance under the State plan or, if later, the date on which the individual disposes of assets for less than fair market value.

(C)(i) The services described in this subparagraph with respect to an institutionalized individual are the following:

(I) Nursing facility services.

(II) A level of care in any institution equivalent to that of nursing facility services.

(III) Home or community-based services furnished under a waiver granted under subsection (c) or (d) of section 1915 [42 U.S.C.A. 1396n(c) or (d)] .

(ii) The services described in this subparagraph with respect to a noninstitutionalized individual are services (not including any services described in clause (I)) that are described in paragraph (7), (22), or (24) of section 1905(a) [42 U.S.C.A. 1396d(a)] , and, at the option of a State, other long-term care services for which medical assistance is otherwise available under the State plan to individuals requiring long-term care.

(D) The date specified in this subparagraph is the first day of the first month during or after which assets have been transferred for less than fair market value and which does not occur in any other periods of ineligibility under this subsection.

(E)(i) With respect to an institutionalized individual, the number of months of ineligibility under this subparagraph for an individual shall be equal to —

(I) the total, cumulative uncompensated value of all assets transferred by the individual (or individual's spouse) on or after the look-back date specified in subparagraph (B)(I), divided by

(II) the average monthly cost to a private patient of nursing facility services in the State (or, at the option of the State, in the community in which the individual is institutionalized) at the time of application.

(ii) With respect to a noninstitutionalized individual, the number of months of ineligibility under this subparagraph for an individual shall not be greater than a number equal to —

(I) the total, cumulative uncompensated value of all assets transferred by the individual (or individual's spouse) on or after the look-back date specified in subparagraph (B)(i), divided by

(II) the average monthly cost to a private patient of nursing facility services in the State (or, at the option of the State, in the community in which the individual is institutionalized) at the time of application.

(iii) The number of months of ineligibility otherwise determined under clause (I) or (ii) with respect to the disposal of an asset shall be reduced —

(I) in the case of periods of ineligibility determined under clause (I), by the number of months of ineligibility applicable to the individual under clause (ii) as a result of such disposal, and

(II) in the case of periods of ineligibility determined under clause (ii), by the number of months of ineligibility applicable to the individual under clause (I) as a result of such disposal.

(2) An individual shall not be ineligible for medical assistance by reason of paragraph (1) to the extent that —

(A) the assets transferred were a home and title to the home was transferred to —

(i) the spouse of such individual;

(ii) a child of such individual who (I) is under age 21, or (II) (with respect to States eligible to participate in the State program established under title XVI) is blind or permanently and totally disabled, or (with respect to States which are not eligible to participate in such program) is blind or disabled as defined in section 1614;

(iii) a sibling of such individual who has an equity interest in such home and who was residing in such individual's home for a period of at least one year immediately before the date the individual becomes an institutionalized individual, or

(iv) a son or daughter of such individual (other than a child described in clause (ii)) who was residing in such individual's home for a period of at least two years immediately before the date the individual becomes an institutionalized individual, and who (as determined by the State) provided care to such individual which permitted such individual to reside at home rather than in such an institution or facility;

(B) the assets —

(i) were transferred to the individual's spouse or to another for the sole benefit of the individual's spouse,

(ii) were transferred from the individual's spouse to another for the sole benefit of the individual's spouse,

(iii) were transferred to, or to a trust (including a trust described in subsection (d)(4)) established solely for the benefit of, the individual's child described in subparagraph (A)(ii)(II), or

(iv) were transferred to a trust (including a trust described in subsection (d)(4)) established solely for the benefit of an individual under 65 years of age who is disabled (as defined in section 1614(a)(3));

(C) a satisfactory showing is made to the State (in accordance with regulations promulgated by the Secretary) that (i) the individual intended to dispose of the assets either at fair market value, or for other valuable consideration, (ii) the assets were transferred exclusively for a purpose other than to qualify for medical assistance, or (iii) all assets transferred for less than fair market value have been returned to the individual; or

(D) the State determines, under procedures established by the State (in accordance with standards specified by the Secretary), that the denial of eligibility would work an undue hardship as determined on the basis of criteria established by the Secretary.

(3) For purposes of this subsection, in the case of an asset held by an individual in common with another person or persons in a joint tenancy, tenancy in common, or similar arrangement, the asset (or the affected portion of such asset) shall be considered to be transferred by such individual when any action is taken, either by such individual or by any other person, that reduces or eliminates such individual's ownership or control of such asset.

(4) A State (including a State which has elected treatment under section 1902(f)) may not provide for any period of ineligibility for an individual due to transfer of resources for less than fair market value except in accordance with this subsection. In the case of a transfer by the spouse of an individual which results in a period of ineligibility for medical assistance under a State plan for such individual, a State shall, using a reasonable methodology (as specified by the Secretary), apportion such period of ineligibility (or any portion of such period) among the individual and the individual's spouse if the spouse otherwise becomes eligible for medical assistance under the State plan.

(5) In this subsection, the term "resources" has the meaning given such term in section 1613, without regard to the exclusion described in subsection (a)(1) thereof.

For regulatory citations, see Chapter 8

§ 4:10 CRIMINAL PENALTIES: KICKBACKS, BRIBES, AND REBATES — Section 1128B(b) [42 U.S.C.A. 1320a-7b(b)]

Summary

Grounds for Sanction: *Solicitation or Receipt of Remuneration for Referrals:* Section 1128B(b)(1), 42 U.S.C.A. 1320a-7b(b)(1), makes it a felony for anyone to knowingly and willfully solicit or receive any remuneration, including any kickback, bribe, or rebate, directly or indirectly, overtly or covertly, in cash or in kind, in return for referring an individual to a person for furnishing, or for arranging for furnishing, any item or service for which payment may be made, in whole or in part, under a Federal health care program.

Solicitation or Receipt of Remuneration for Purchases, Leases, or Orders: Section 1128B(b)(1) also makes it a felony to solicit or receive such remuneration in return for purchasing, leasing, ordering, or arranging for or recommending purchasing, leasing, or ordering any good, facility, service, or item for which payment may be made in whole or in part under a Federal health care program.

Anyone who commits these offenses may, upon conviction, be fined not more than $25,000, or imprisoned for not more than five years, or both.

Offers and Payments for Referrals: Section 1128B(b)(2) makes it a felony for anyone to knowingly and willfully offer or pay any remuneration, including any kickback, bribe, or rebate, directly or indirectly, overtly or covertly, in cash or in kind to any person to induce such person to refer an individual to a person for furnishing, or for arranging for furnishing, any item or service for which payment may be made in whole or in part under a Federal health care program.

Offers and Payments for Purchases, Leases, and Orders: Section 1128B(b)(2) also makes it a felony for anyone to knowingly and willfully offer or pay such remuneration in return for purchasing, leasing, ordering, or arranging for or recommending purchasing, leasing, or ordering any good, facility, service, or item for which payment may be made in whole or in part under a Federal health care program.

Anyone who commits these offenses may, upon conviction, be fined not more than $25,000, or imprisoned for not more than five years, or both.

Thus, section 1128B(b)(1) provides punishment for those who solicit or receive kickbacks, bribes, rebates, or other unlawful remuneration, and section 1128B(b)(2) provides punishment for those who offer or pay them. On either side of the unlawful transaction, the offenses are felonies, and the punishment parameters are the same.

Definition of Federal Health Care Program: Section 1128(B)(f) defines "Federal health care program" to include any plan that provides benefits funded directly in whole or in part by the

United States Government. The only exception is the health insurance program for Federal employees authorized by Title V, Chapter 89, of the U.S. Code.

"Federal health care program" also includes State Medicaid programs and State health care programs funded by a Maternal and Child Health Services Block Grant (Title V of the Social Security Act, 42 U.S.C.A. 701 et seq.), by a Block Grant to States for Social Services (Title XX of the Act, 42 U.S.C.A. 1397 et seq.), or a State child health plan approved under title XXI.

◆ NOTE: Section 204 of the Health Insurance Portability and Accountability Act of 1996, P.L. 104-191, added this definition of Federal health care program to section 1128B, effective January 1, 1997. This dramatically broadens the statute's reach. Prior to that amendment the statute applied only to acts committed with respect to Medicare, Medicaid, and State health care programs funded by Titles V and XX of the Social Security Act. Section 4901(b)(2) of the Balanced Budget Act of 1997, P.L. 105-33 added the reference to State child health plans approved under title XXI, effective August 5, 1997.

Statutory Exemptions: Perhaps no other language in the Social Security Act is more troublesome than the language of sections 1128B(b)(1) and (2). On its face, it seems to prohibit not just what most people think of as patently illegal in commerce, such as kickbacks and bribes, but also an array of practices commonly accepted in businesses and professions unrelated to health care. For example, rebates, common marketing devices for everything from household appliances to automobiles, are felonious when applied to pacemakers or durable medical equipment. Equally felonious are the common you scratch my back/I'll scratch yours deals, or the volume-based graduated incentives for business development upon which much commerce thrives.

In an attempt to clarify the confusion Congress provided the following statutory exemptions from subsections (b)(1) and (b)(2).

Discounts and Other Price Reductions: Section 1128B(b)(3) provides that subsections (b)(1) and (b)(2) do not apply to discounts or other price reductions obtained by health care providers or other entities reimbursed under a Federal health care program if the reduction is properly disclosed and appropriately reflected in costs claimed or charges made by such providers and entities. Nor do they apply to any amount paid by an employer to an employee, in a bona fide employment relationship, for employment in the provision of covered items or services.

Purchasing Agents: Subsections (b)(1) and (b)(2) do not apply with respect to any amount paid by a vendor to an authorized purchasing agent for a group of individuals or entities who furnish services reimbursed under a Federal health care program. This applies if the purchasing agent has a written contract with each such individual or entity in the group which specifies the amount to be paid the purchasing agent. That amount may be fixed or a fixed percentage of the value of the purchases made by each such individual or entity under the contract.

The same is true in the case of an entity that is a provider of services, as defined in section 1861(u), 42 U.S.C.A. 1395x(u), if the purchasing agent discloses, in such form and manner as the Secretary of Health and Human Services requires, to the entity and, upon request, to the Secretary the amount received from each such vendor with respect to purchases made by or on behalf of the entity. Provider of services, in this context, means a hospital, skilled nursing facility, comprehensive outpatient rehabilitation facility, home health agency, hospice program, home intravenous drug therapy provider, or a fund eligible to participate in Medicare pursuant to section 1814(g), 42 U.S.C.A. 1395f(g), and section 1835(e), 42 U.S.C.A. 1395n(e), which pertain to payment for services of physicians rendered in teaching hospitals.

Waiver of Coinsurance and Deductibles: Pursuant to section 4161(a)(4) of P.L. 101-508, the Omnibus Budget Reconciliation Act of 1990 (OBRA 90), subsections (b)(1) and (b)(2) also do not apply to a waiver of any coinsurance under part B of title XVIII by a Federally qualified health care center with respect to an individual who qualifies for subsidized services under a provision of the Public Health Service Act. That change was effective November 5, 1990.

Regulatory Safe Harbors: Subsections (b)(1) and (b)(2) do not apply with respect to any payment practice specified by the Secretary in regulations promulgated pursuant to section 14(a) of the Medicare and Medicaid Patient and Program Protection Act of 1987, P.L. 100-93. The latter are commonly referred to as the Safe Harbor regulations.

◆ NOTE: The Safe Harbor Regulations are in Appendix F.

Risk-sharing Arrangements: Subsections (b)(1) and (b)(2) do not apply to any remuneration between an organization and an individual or entity providing items or services, or a combination thereof, pursuant to a written agreement. This applies if the organization is a Health Maintenance Organization or Competitive Medical Plan qualified under section 1876, 42 U.S.C.A. 1395mm, or if the written agreement, through a risk-sharing arrangement, places the individual or entity at substantial financial risk for the cost or utilization of the items or services, or a combination thereof, which the individual or entity is obliged to provide. This exemption was added to section 1128B by section 216 of the Health Insurance Portability and Accountability Act of 1996, effective January 1, 1997.

Legislative History and the Problems of Interpretation: At U.S. Congressional and Administrative News, pp. 707-708, the legislative history of P.L. 100-93 provides in pertinent part:

Standards for Anti-Kickback Provisions (Section 14)

Current law provides criminal penalties for individuals or entities participating in Medicare or Medicaid that knowingly and willfully offer, pay, solicit, or receive bribes, kickbacks, or rebates under certain circumstances. These actions are defined as felonies and are subject, upon conviction, to fines of up to $25,000 and imprisonment for up to 5 years. Sections 4(c), (d), and (e) of the Committee bill recodify these authorities, now found at sections 1877(d) and 1909 of the Social Security Act, in a new section 1128B(b).

It is the understanding of the Committee that the breadth of this statutory language has created uncertainty among health care providers as to which commercial arrangements are legitimate, and which are proscribed. The Committee bill therefore directs the Secretary, in consultation with the Attorney General, to promulgate regulations specifying payment practices that will not be subject to criminal prosecution under the new section 1128B(b) and that will not provide a basis for exclusion from participation in Medicare or the State health care programs under the new section 1128(b)(7). These regulations must be published in final form within two years after enactment of this Act [September 1, 1987]. In order to assure adequate time for public comment and agency consideration of those comments, the Committee bill requires the Secretary to publish a proposed rule within one year after enactment.

Those comments about uncertainty proved to be an extraordinary understatement. Furthermore, few Safe Harbors were written as a consequence, and the first few that were didn't seem to help much. For years, the industry complained about them and lobbied for advisory opinions. The Secretary of Health and Human Services and the

Department of Justice, which has ultimate authority over criminal sanctions, resisted. To mollify criticism, the Inspector General of the Department of Health and Human Services responded with Fraud Alerts.

◆ NOTE: Fraud Alerts are in Appendix G.

Finally, Congress intervened. Section 205 of the Health Insurance Portability and Accountability Act of 1996 created section 1128(D) of the Social Security Act, 42 U.S.C.A. 1320a-7d, effective August 21, 1996. This statute directs the Secretary to solicit proposals for modifications to existing Safe Harbors and for new Safe Harbors. It also directs the Secretary to provide advisory opinions and special fraud alerts.

The Safe Harbors are to be modified or written in consultation with the U.S. Attorney General, with opportunity for public comments when changes are proposed by the Department. The Attorney General also must be consulted about advisory opinions.

Advisory Opinions: Section 1128D(b)(2) specifies matters which advisory opinions may address and section 1128D(b)(3) specifies matters which advisory opinions may not address.

Matters Subject to Advisory Opinions

Advisory opinions may address the following:

1 What constitutes prohibited remuneration within the meaning of section 1128B(b).

2 Whether an arrangement or proposed arrangement satisfies the criteria set forth in section 1128B(b)(3) for activities which do not result in prohibited remuneration.

3 Whether an arrangement or proposed arrangement satisfies the criteria which the Secretary has established, or shall establish by regulation for activities which do not result in prohibited remuneration.

4 What constitutes an inducement to reduce or limit services to individuals entitled to Medicare or Medicaid, within the meaning of section 1128B(b).

5 Whether any activity or proposed activity constitutes grounds for imposition of a sanction under section 1128, 1128(A), or 1128B.

Matters Not Subject to Advisory Opinions

Advisory opinions may not address:

1 Whether the fair market value shall be or was paid or received for any goods, services or property.

2 Whether an individual is a bona fide employee within the requirements of section 3121(d)(2) of the Internal Revenue Code of 1986.

Effect of Advisory Opinions: An advisory opinion is binding on the Secretary and the parties requesting the opinion. No one else. In addition, the failure of a party to seek an advisory opinion may not be introduced into evidence to prove that the party intended to violate the provisions of section 1128, 42 U.S.C.S 1320a7, which authorizes exclusion from Medicare and Medicaid for a variety of offenses, section 1128A, 42 U.S.C.A. 1320a-7a, which authorizes civil money penalties for a variety of offenses, or section 1128B.

Statutory Provisions

Section 1128B(b), 42 U.S.C.A. 1320a-7b(b), provides:

> (1) Whoever knowingly and willfully solicits or receives any remuneration (including any kickback, bribe, or rebate) directly or indirectly, overtly or covertly, in cash or in kind —
>
> (A) in return for referring an individual to a person for the furnishing or arranging for the furnishing of any item or service for which payment may be made in whole or in part under a Federal health care program, or
>
> (B) in return for purchasing, leasing, ordering, or arranging for or recommending purchasing, leasing, or ordering any good, facility, service, or item for which payment may be made in whole or in part under a Federal health care program, shall be guilty of a felony and upon conviction thereof, shall be fined not more than $25,000 or imprisoned for not more than five years, or both.
>
> (2) Whoever knowingly and willfully offers or pays any remuneration (including any kickback, bribe, or rebate) directly or indirectly, overtly or covertly, in cash or in kind to any person to induce such person —
>
> (A) to refer an individual to a person for the furnishing or arranging for the furnishing of any item or service for which

payment may be made in whole or in part under a Federal health care program, or

(B) to purchase, lease, order, or arrange for or recommend purchasing, leasing, or ordering any good, facility, service, or item for which payment may be made in whole or in part under a Federal health care program,

shall be guilty of a felony and upon conviction thereof, shall be fined not more than $25,000 or imprisoned for not more than five years, or both.

(3) Paragraphs (1) and (2) shall not apply to —

(A) a discount or other reduction in price obtained by a provider of services or other entity under title XVIII or a State health care program if the reduction in price is properly disclosed and appropriately reflected in the costs claimed or charges made by the provider or entity under a Federal health care program,

(B) any amount paid by an employer to an employee (who has a bona fide employment relationship with such employer) for employment in the provision of covered items or services;

(C) any amount paid by a vendor of goods or services to a person authorized to act as a purchasing agent for a group of individuals or entities who are furnishing services reimbursed under title XVIII or a state health care program if —

(i) the person has a written contract, with each such individual or entity, which specifies the amount to be paid the person, which amount may be a fixed amount or a fixed percentage of the value of the purchases made by each such individual or entity under the contract, and

(ii) in the case of an entity that is a provider of services (as defined in section 1861(u) [42 U.S.C.A. 1395x(u), which means a hospital, skilled nursing facility, comprehensive outpatient rehabilitation facility, home health agency, hospice program, home intravenous drug therapy provider, or a fund eligible to participate in Medicare pursuant to section 1814(g), 42 U.S.C.A. 1395f(g), and section 1835(e), 42 U.S.C.A. 1395n(e), which pertain to payment for services of physicians rendered in teaching hospitals.]), the person disclosed (in such form and manner as the Secretary requires) to the entity and upon request, to the Secretary the amount received from each such vendor with respect to purchases made by or on behalf of the entity;

(D) a waiver of any coinsurance under part B of title XVIII by a Federally qualified health care center with respect to an individual who qualifies for subsidized services under a provision of the Public Health Service Act [Pursuant to section 4161(a)(4) of P.L. 101-508, the Omnibus Budget Reconciliation Act of 1990 (OBRA 90), former subparagraph (D) was redesignated (E) and this subparagraph (D) was added, effective November 5, 1990.]; and

(E) any payment practice specified by the Secretary in regulations promulgated pursuant to section 14(a) of the Medicare and Medicaid Patient and Program Protection Act of 1987 [P.L. 100-93] .

(F) any remuneration between an organization and an individual or entity providing items or services, or a combination thereof, pursuant to a written agreement between the organization and the individual or entity if the organization is an eligible organization under section 1876 [42 U.S.C.A. 1395mm, which pertains to Health Maintenance Organizations and Competitive Medical Plans] or if the written agreement, through a risk-sharing arrangement, places the individual or entity at substantial financial risk for the cost or utilization of the items or services, or a combination thereof, which the individual is obliged to provide.

Section 1128(B)(f), 42 U.S.C.A. 1320a-7b(f), defines "Federal health care program" as follows:

For purposes of this section, the term "Federal health care program" means —

(1) any plan or program that provides health benefits, whether directly, through insurance, or otherwise, which is funded directly, in whole or in part, by the United States Government (other than the health insurance program under chapter 89 of title 5, United States Code [which pertains to health insurance for Federal employees]); or

(2) any State health care program, as defined in section 1128(h).

Section 1128(h), 42 U.S.C.A. 1320a-7(h), provides:

DEFINITION OF STATE HEALTH CARE PROGRAM. — For purposes of this section [section 1128] and sections 1128A [42 U.S.C.A. 1320a-7a, which provides civil money penalties and an alternative basis for exclusion from Medicare and State health care programs for a variety of offenses] and 1128(B) the term "State health care program" means —

(1) a State plan approved under title XIX [Medicaid, 42 U.S.C.A. 1396 et seq.],

(2) any program receiving funds under title V or from an allotment to a State under such title, or

(3) any program receiving funds under title XX or from an allotment to a State under such title; or

(4) a State child health plan approved under title XXI.

◆ NOTE: Section 4901(b)(2) of the Balanced Budget Act of 1997 deleted "or" from the end of paragraph (h)(2); substituted ", or" for the period at the end of paragraph (h)(3); and added paragraph (h)(4), effective August 5, 1997.

Section 14(a) of the Medicare and Medicaid Patient and Program Protection Act of 1987 provides as follows:

REGULATIONS. — The Secretary of Health and Human Services, in consultation with the Attorney General, not later than 1 year after the date of the enactment of this Act [September 1, 1987] shall publish proposed regulations, and not later than 2 years after the date of the enactment of this Act shall promulgate final regulations, specifying payment practices that shall not be treated as a criminal offense under section 1128B(b) of the Social Security Act and shall not serve as the basis for an exclusion under section 1128(b)(7) of such Act. Any practices specified in regulations pursuant to the preceding sentence shall be in addition to the practices described in subparagraphs (A) through (C) of section 1128B(b)(3).

Section 1128D, 42 U.S.C.A. 1320a-7d, which was enacted August 21, 1996, via section 205 of the Health Insurance Portability and Accountability Act of 1996, provides:

(a) SOLICITATION AND PUBLICATION OF MODIFICATIONS TO EXISTING SAFE HARBORS AND NEW SAFE HARBORS.—

(1) IN GENERAL. —

(A) SOLICITATION OF PROPOSALS FOR SAFE HARBORS.—Not later than January 1, 1997, and not less than annually thereafter, the Secretary shall publish a notice in the Federal Register soliciting proposals, which will be accepted during a 60-day period, for—

(i) modifications to existing safe harbors issued pursuant to section 14(a) of the Medicare and Medicaid Patient and Program Protection Act of 1987 (42 U.S.C.A. 1320a-7b note);

(ii) additional safe harbors specifying payment practices that shall not be treated as a criminal offense under section 1128B(b) and shall not serve as the basis for an exclusion under section 1128(b)(7);

(iii) advisory opinions to be issued pursuant to subsection (b); and

(iv) special fraud alerts to be issued pursuant to subsection (c).

(B) PUBLICATION OF PROPOSED MODIFICATIONS AND PROPOSED ADDITIONAL SAFE HARBORS.—After considering the proposals described in clauses (i) and (ii) of subparagraph (A), the Secretary, in consultation with the Attorney General, shall publish in the Federal Register proposed modifications to existing safe harbors and proposed additional safe harbors, if appropriate, with a 60-day comment period. After considering any public comments received during this period, the Secretary shall issue final rules modifying the existing safe harbors and establishing new safe harbors, as appropriate.

(C) REPORT. —The Inspector General of the Department of Health and Human Services (in this section referred to as the "Inspector General") shall, in an annual report to Congress or as part of the year-end semiannual report required by section 5 of the Inspector General Act of 1978 (5 U.S.C.A. App.), describe the proposals received under clauses (i) and (ii) of subparagraph (A) and explain which proposals were included in the publication described in subparagraph (B), which proposals were not included in that publication, and the reasons for the rejection of the proposals that were not included.

(2) CRITERIA FOR MODIFYING AND ESTABLISHING SAFE HARBORS. — In modifying and establishing safe harbors under paragraph (1)(B), the Secretary may consider the extent to which providing a safe harbor for the specified payment practice may result in any of the following:

(A) An increase or decrease in access to health care services.

(B) An increase or decrease in the quality of health care services.

(C) An increase or decrease in patient freedom of choice among health care providers.

(D) An increase or decrease in competition among health care providers.

(E) An increase or decrease in the ability of health care facilities to provide services in medically underserved areas or to medically underserved populations.

(F) An increase or decrease in the cost to Federal health care programs (as defined in section 1128B(f)).

(G) An increase or decrease in the potential overutilization of health care services.

(H) The existence or nonexistence of any potential financial benefit to a health care professional or provider which may vary based on their decisions of —

(i) whether to order a health care item or service; or

(ii) whether to arrange for a referral of health care items or services to a particular practitioner or provider.

(I) Any other factors the Secretary deems appropriate in the interest of preventing fraud and abuse in Federal health care programs (as so defined).

(b) ADVISORY OPINIONS. —

(1) ISSUANCE OF ADVISORY OPINIONS. — The Secretary, in consultation with the Attorney General, shall issue written advisory opinions as provided in this subsection.

(2) MATTERS SUBJECT TO ADVISORY OPINIONS. — The Secretary shall issue advisory opinions as to the following matters:

(A) What constitutes prohibited remuneration within the meaning of section 1128B(b) or section 1128A(i)(6), 42 U.S.C.A. 1320a-7a(i)(6) [which defines remuneration for purposes of civil money penalties authorized by section 1128A].
[NOTE: The clause beginning "or section 1128A(i)(6) " was added by section 5201(c) of the Tax and Trade Relief Extension Act of 1998, which is in "Omnibus Consolidated Emergency and Supplemental Appropriations for Fiscal Year 1999", effective October 21, 1998].

(B) Whether an arrangement or proposed arrangement satisfies the criteria set forth in section 1128B(b)(3) for activities which do not result in prohibited remuneration.

(C) Whether an arrangement or proposed arrangement satisfies the criteria which the Secretary has established, or shall establish by regulation for activities which do not result in prohibited remuneration.

(D) What constitutes an inducement to reduce or limit services to individuals entitled to benefits under title XVIII or title XIX within the meaning of section 1128A(b). [NOTE: Section 4331(a)(1) of the Balanced Budget Act of 1997 substituted "1128A(b)" for "1128B(b)", effective August 21, 1996, as if included in the Health Insurance Portability and Accountability Act of 1996.]

(E) Whether any activity or proposed activity constitutes grounds for the imposition of a sanction under section 1128 [42 U.S.C.A. 1320a-7, which authorizes exclusion from Medicare or Medicaid for a variety of offenses], 1128A [42 U.S.C.A. 1320a-7a, which authorizes civil money penalties for a variety of offenses], or 1128B.

(3) MATTERS NOT SUBJECT TO ADVISORY OPINIONS. — Such advisory opinions shall not address the following matters:

(A) Whether the fair market value shall be, or was paid or received for any goods, services or property.

(B) Whether an individual is a bona fide employee within the requirements of section 3121(d)(2) of the Internal Revenue Code of 1986.

(4) EFFECT OF ADVISORY OPINIONS. —

(A) Binding as to secretary and parties involved. — Each advisory opinion issued by the Secretary shall be binding as to the Secretary and the party or parties requesting the opinion.

(B) Failure to seek opinion. — The failure of a party to seek an advisory opinion may not be introduced into evidence to prove that the party intended to violate the provisions of sections 1128, 1128A, or 1128B.

(5) REGULATIONS. —

(A) IN GENERAL. — Not later than 180 days after the date of the enactment of this section, the Secretary shall issue regulations to carry out this section. Such regulations shall provide for —

(i) the procedure to be followed by a party applying for an advisory opinion;

(ii) the procedure to be followed by the Secretary in responding to a request for an advisory opinion;

(iii) the interval in which the Secretary shall respond;

(iv) the reasonable fee to be charged to the party requesting an advisory opinion; and

(v) the manner in which advisory opinions will be made available to the public.

(B) SPECIFIC CONTENTS. — Under the regulations promulgated pursuant to subparagraph (A) —

(i) the Secretary shall be required to issue to a party requesting an advisory opinion by not later than 60 days after the request is received; and

(ii) the fee charged to the party requesting an advisory opinion shall be equal to the costs incurred by the Secretary in responding to the request.

(6) APPLICATION OF SUBSECTION. — This subsection shall apply to requests for advisory opinions made on or after the date which is 6 months after the date of enactment of this

section. [NOTE: Section 543 of the Medicare, Medicaid, and SCHIP Benefits Improvement and Protection Act of 2000, P.L. 106–554, deleted the phrase "and before the date which is 4 years after such date of enactment", which previously followed "this section". This change was effective December 21, 2000.]

(C) SPECIAL FRAUD ALERTS.—

(1) IN GENERAL. —

(A) REQUEST FOR SPECIAL FRAUD ALERTS.—Any person may present, at any time, a request to the Inspector General for a notice which informs the public of practices which the Inspector General considers to be suspect or of particular concern under the Medicare program under title XVIII or a State health care program, as defined in section 1128(h) (in this subsection referred to as a "special fraud alert").

(B) ISSUANCE AND PUBLICATION OF SPECIAL FRAUD ALERTS.—Upon receipt of a request described in subparagraph (A), the Inspector General shall investigate the subject matter of the request to determine whether a special fraud alert should be issued. If appropriate, the Inspector General shall issue a special fraud alert in response to the request. All special fraud alerts issued pursuant to this subparagraph shall be published in the Federal Register.

(2) CRITERIA FOR SPECIAL FRAUD ALERTS.—In determining whether to issue a special fraud alert upon a request described in paragraph (1), the Inspector General may consider—

(A) whether and to what extent the practices that would be identified in the special fraud alert may result in any of the consequences described in subsection (a)(2); and

(B) the volume and frequency of the conduct that would be identified in the special fraud alert.

For regulatory citations, see Chapter 8

§ 4:11 CRIMINAL PENALTIES: FALSE STATEMENTS AND FALSE REPRESENTATIONS TO QUALIFY FOR PROVIDER STATUS — Section 1128B(c) [42 U.S.C.A. 1320a-7b(c)]

Summary

Section 1128B(c), 42 U.S.C.A. 1320a-7b(c), makes it a felony for anyone to knowingly and willfully make or cause to be made any false statement or representation of a material fact about the conditions or about the operation of any institution, facility, or entity in order to qualify that institution, facility, or entity for participation in Medicare or in a State health care program as a hospital, critical access hospital, skilled nursing facility, nursing facility, intermediate care facility for the mentally retarded (ICF/MR), intermediate care facility, home health agency, or other entity, including eligible health maintenance organizations (HMO's) and competitive medical plans (CMP's). This applies to statements and representations made either upon initial certification or upon recertification.

◆ NOTE: Critical access hospitals previously were referred to as rural primary care hospitals. The designation was changed effective October 1, 1997, by section 4201(c)(1) of the Balanced Budget Act of 1997, P.L. 105-33.

Pursuant to section 4164(b)(2) of P.L. 101-508, the Omnibus Budget Reconciliation Act of 1990 (OBRA 90), the same applies with respect to false statements or representations about ownership and control information which section 1124A, 42 U.S.C.A. 1320a-3a requires certain Medicare Part B providers to disclose. This pertains to items or services furnished after January 1, 1992.

"State health program" means Medicaid, any program funded under the Maternal and Child Health grant program established by Title V of the Social Security Act, 42 U.S.C.A. 701 et seq., any program funded under the program of Block Grants for Social Services authorized by Title XX of the Social Security Act, 42 U.S.C.A. 1397 et seq., and a State child health plan approved under Title XXI. [NOTE: State child health plans were added to the definition by section 4901(b)(2) of the Balanced Budget Act of 1997, effective August 5, 1997.]

Anyone who commits such an offense may, upon conviction, be fined not more than $25,000, or imprisoned for not more than five years, or both. The same is true for anyone who knowingly and willfully induces or seeks to induce the making of such false statements or representations.

◆ NOTE: This sanction applies with respect to critical access facilities effective December 19, 1990, pursuant to section 6003(g)(3)(D)(ii) of P.L. 101-239, the Omnibus Budget Reconciliation Act of 1989. Pursuant to section 4211(h)(7) of P.L. 100-203, the Omnibus Budget Reconciliation Act of 1987, it applies with respect to "intermediate care facilities" until October 1, 1990; thereafter, "nursing facilities" encompasses the intermediate level of care. It also applies with respect to intermediate care facilities for the mentally retarded effective October 1, 1990.

Statutory Provisions

Section 1128B(c), 42 U.S.C.A. 1320a-7b(c), provides:

> Whoever knowingly and willfully makes or causes to be made, or induces or seeks to induce the making of, any false statement or representation of a material fact with respect to the conditions or operation of any institution, facility, or entity in order that such institution, facility, or entity may qualify (either upon initial certification or upon recertification) as a hospital, critical asccess hospital, skilled nursing facility, nursing facility, intermediate care facility for the mentally retarded, home health agency, or other entity (including an eligible organization under section 1876(b) [42 U.S.C.A. 1395mm(b), which pertains to health maintenance organizations (HMO's) and competitive medical plans (CMP's]) for which certification is required under title XVIII or a State health care program (as defined in section 1128(h)), or with respect to information required to be provided under section 1124A [This clause referring to section 1124A, 42 U.S.C.A. 1320a-3a, which pertains to certain disclosure requirements for certain Part B providers, applicable to items or services furnished after January 1, 1992, was added by section 4164(b)(2) of P.L. 101-508, the Omnibus Budget Reconciliation Act of 1990 (OBRA 90).], shall be guilty of a felony and upon conviction thereof shall be fined not more than $25,000 or imprisoned for not more than five years, or both.

◆ NOTE: The phrase "rural primary care hospital" was added by section 6003(g)(3)(D)(ii) of the Omnibus Budget Reconciliation Act of 1989, P.L. 101-239, effective December 19, 1989. Effective October 1, 1997, however, section 4201(c)(1) of the Balanced Budget Act of 1997 substituted "critical access" for "rural primary care" in section 1128B. Section 4211(h)(7) of the Omnibus Budget Reconciliation Act of 1987, P.L. 100-203, substituted "nursing facility, intermediate care facility for the mentally retarded" for "intermediate care facility" after "skilled nursing facility", effective October 1, 1990.

Section 1128(h), 42 U.S.C.A. 1320a-7(h), provides:

> DEFINITION OF STATE HEALTH CARE PROGRAM. — For purposes of this section [section 1128, which authorizes exclusion from Medicare for a variety of offenses] and sections 1128A [42 U.S.C.A. 1320a-7a, which provides civil money penalties and an alternative basis for exclusion from Medicare and State health care programs for a variety of offenses] and 1128(B) the term "State health care program" means —
>
> (1) a State plan approved under title XIX [Medicaid, 42 U.S.C.A. 1396 et seq.],
>
> (2) any program receiving funds under title V or from an allotment to a State under such title [Title V of the Social Security Act, 42 U.S.C.A. 701 et seq., established the maternal and Child Health Services Block Grant program.],
>
> (3) any program receiving funds under title XX or from an allotment to a State under such title [Title XX of the Social Security Act, 42 U.S.C.A. 1397 et seq., established program of Block Grants for Social Services.], or
>
> (4) a State child health plan approved under title XXI.

◆ NOTE: Section 4901(b)(2) of the Balanced Budget Act of 1997 deleted "or" from the end of paragraph (h)(2); substituted ", or" for the period at the end of paragraph (h)(3); and added paragraph (h)(4), effective August 5, 1997.

For regulatory citations, see Chapter 8

§ 4:12 CRIMINAL PENALTIES: EXCESSIVE MEDICAID CHARGES AND UNLAWFUL FINANCIAL PRECONDITIONS FOR CARE IN HOSPITALS AND NURSING FACILITIES—Section 1128B(d) [42 U.S.C.A. 1320a-7b(d)]

Summary

Section 1128B(d)(1), 42 U.S.C.A. 1320a-7b(d)(1), makes it a felony to knowingly and willfully charge for any service to a patient under a State Medicaid plan more than rates established by the State. This covers excess charges whether they are in cash or in kind. Section 1128B(d)(1) also makes it a felony to charge more than the rate permitted under a Medicaid managed care contract. This applies with respect to individuals enrolled with a Medicaid managed care organization under a contract pursuant to section 1903(m), 42 U.S.C.A. 1396b(m), or under a contractual, referral, or other arrangement under such a contract. This provision with respect to managed care was added effective August 5, 1997, by section 4704(b) of the Balanced Budget Act of 1997, P.L. 105-33.

Anyone who commits this offense may, upon conviction, be fined not more than $25,000, or imprisoned for not more than five years, or both.

Section 1128B(d)(2) makes it a felony to charge, solicit, accept, or receive any gift, money, donation, or other consideration, in addition to any amount otherwise required to be paid under Medicaid, as a precondition to admit a patient to a hospital, or (after October 1, 1990), to a nursing facility or intermediate care facility for the mentally retarded (ICF/MR), or (prior to October 1, 1990), to a skilled nursing facility or intermediate care facility, as a precondition to remain in such a facility. This applies whenever the cost of the services provided in the hospital or other facility are paid for in whole or in part by Medicaid. It does not apply, however, to a charitable, religious, or philanthropic contribution from an organization or from a person unrelated to the patient.

Anyone who commits this offense may, upon conviction, be fined not more than $25,000, or imprisoned for not more than five years, or both.

Statutory Provisions

Section 1128B(d), 42 U.S.C.A. 1320a-7b(d), provides:

Whoever knowingly and willfully—

(1) charges, for any service provided to a patient under a State plan approved under title XIX, money or other consideration at a rate in excess of the rates established by the State, (or, in the case of services provided to an individual enrolled with a Medicaid managed care organization under title XIX under a contract under section 1903(m), 42 U.S.C.A. 1396b(m), or under a contractual, referral, or other arrangement under such contract, at a rate in excess of the rate permitted under such contract) [preceding parenthetical clause added effective August 5, 1997, by section 4704(b) of the Balanced Budget Act of 1997, P.L. 105-33] , or

(2) charges, solicits, accepts, or receives, in addition to any amount otherwise required to be paid under a State plan approved under title XIX, any gift, money, donation, or other consideration (other than a charitable, religious, or philanthropic contribution from an organization or from a person unrelated to the patient)—

(A) as a precondition of admitting a patient to a hospital, nursing facility, or intermediate care facility for the mentally retarded [pursuant to section 4211(h)(7) of P.L. 100-203, the Omnibus Budget Reconciliation Act of 1987, effective October 1, 1990, changed from "skilled nursing facility, or intermediate care facility" to "nursing facility, or intermediate care facility for the mentally retarded"], or

(B) as a requirement for the patient's continued stay in such a facility,

when the cost of the services provided therein to the patient is paid for (in whole or in part) under the State plan,shall be guilty of a felony and upon conviction thereof shall be fined not more than $25,000 or imprisoned for not more than five years, or both.

For regulatory citations, see Chapter 8

§ 4:13 CRIMINAL PENALTIES: VIOLATING A PHYSICIAN OR SUPPLIER PARTICIPATION AGREEMENT OR A MEDICARE ASSIGNMENT OF BENEFITS AGREEMENT—Section 1128B(e) [42 U.S.C.A. 1320a-7b(e)]

Summary

Section 1842(b)(3)(B)(ii), 42 U.S.C.A. 1395u(b)(3)(B)(ii), provides that certain Medicare Part B benefits can be paid on the basis of an assignment to persons furnishing the service. When there is an assignment, the reasonable charge must be the full charge for the service. Furthermore, the physician or other person furnishing the service must agree not to charge for services for which payment is denied for reasons of poor quality as determined by a Peer Review Organization under sections 1154(a)(2) and 1154(a)(1)(B), 42 U.S.C.A. 1320c-3(a)(2) and (1)(B). He also must agree to refund such amounts already collected. In addition, the physician or other person furnishing such service must agree not to charge (and to refund amounts already collected) for such service if payment is not allowed by section 1862(a)(1), 42 U.S.C.A. 1395y(a)(1), which specifies items and services not covered by Medicare.

Section 1128B(e), 42 U.S.C.A. 1320a-7b(e), makes it a misdemeanor to knowingly, willfully, and repeatedly violate a term of a Medicare assignment agreement. Anyone who commits this offense may, upon conviction, be fined not more than $2,000, or imprisoned for not more than six months, or both.

Section 1842(h)(1), 42 U.S.C.A. 1395u(h)(1), provides that any physician or supplier may enter into an agreement with the Secretary of Health and Human Services to become a participating physician or supplier. A participating physician or supplier is one who, before the start of any year (beginning 1984), enters into an agreement with the Secretary to accept payment under Part B on an assignment-related basis for all items and services furnished to individuals enrolled under Part B during such year. Newly licensed physicians, physicians beginning a practice in a new area, and suppliers beginning a new business may enter into participation agreements after the start of a year with respect to items and services furnished during the remainder of the year.

Section 1128B(e) makes it a misdemeanor to knowingly, willfully, and repeatedly violate a term of an agreement to be a participating physician or supplier. Anyone who commits this offense may, upon conviction, be fined not more than $2,000, or imprisoned for not more than six months, or both.

Statutory Provisions

Section 1128B(e), 42 U.S.C.A. 1320a-7b(e), provides:

> Whoever accepts assignments described in section 1842(b)(3)(B)(ii) or agrees to be a participating physician or supplier under section 1842(h)(1) and knowingly, willfully, and repeatedly violates the term of such assignments or agreement, shall be guilty of a misdemeanor and upon conviction thereof shall be fined not more than $2,000 or imprisoned for not more than six months, or both.

Section 1842(b)(3)(B), 42 U.S.C.A. 1395u(b)(3)(B), provides as follows with respect to carriers who process Medicare payments under Part B:

> (3) Each such contract [between the Secretary and a carrier] shall provide that the carrier —
>
> * * *
>
> (B) will take such action as may be necessary to assure that, where payment under this part for a service is on a charge basis, such charge will be reasonable and not higher than the charge applicable, for a comparable service and under comparable circumstances, to the policyholders and subscribers of the carrier, and such payment will (except as otherwise provided in section 1870(f) [42 U.S.C.A. 1395gg(f), which permits payment in certain cases as though there had been an assignment of benefits when Part B beneficiaries die without executing an assignment]) be made —
>
> (i) on the basis of an itemized bill; or
>
> (ii) on the basis of an assignment under the terms of which (I) the reasonable charge is the full charge for the service, (II) the physician or other person furnishing such service agrees not to charge (and to refund amounts

already collected) for services for which payment under this title is denied under section 1154(a)(2) by reason of a determination under section 1154(a)(1)(B) [42 U.S.C.A. 1320c-3(a)(2) and 3(a)(1)(B), which pertain to denial of payment because a service was determined by a Peer Review Organization to be of poor quality], and (III) the physician or other person furnishing such service agrees not to charge (and to refund amounts already collected) for such service if payment may not be made therefor by reason of the provisions of paragraph (1) of section 1862(a) [42 U.S.C.A. 1395y(a)(1), which specifies items and services not covered by Medicare], and if the individual to whom such service was furnished was without fault in incurring the expenses of such service, and if the Secretary's determination that payment (pursuant to such assignment) was incorrect and was made subsequent to the third year following the year in which notice of such payment was sent to such individual; except that the Secretary may reduce such three-year period to not less than one year if he finds such reduction is consistent with the objectives of this title (except in the case of physicians' services and ambulance service furnished as described in section 1862(a)(4) [42 U.S.C.A. 1395y(a)(4), which pertains to services not provided in the United States], other than for purposes of section 1870(f));

but (in the case of bills submitted, or requests for payment made, after March 1968) only if the bill is submitted, or a written request for payment is made in such other form as may be permitted under regulations, no later than the close of the calendar year following the year in with such service is furnished (deeming any service furnished in the last 3 months of any calendar year to have been furnished in the succeeding calendar year)[.]

Section 1842(h)(1), 42 U.S.C.A. 1395u(h)(1), provides:

Any physician or supplier may voluntarily enter into an agreement with the Secretary to become a participating physician or supplier. For purposes of this section, the term "participating physician or supplier" means a physician or supplier (excluding any provider of services) who, before the beginning of any year beginning with 1984, enters into an agreement with the Secretary which provides that such physician or supplier will accept payment under this part on an assignment-related basis for all items and services furnished to individuals enrolled under this part during such year. In the case of a newly licensed physician or a physician who begins a practice in a new area, or in the case of a new supplier who begins a new business, or in such similar cases as the Secretary may specify, such physician or supplier may enter into such an agreement after the beginning of a year, for items and services furnished during the remainder of the year.

For regulatory citations, see Chapter 8

§ 4:13.1 FAILURE TO REPORT INFORMATION ABOUT FINAL ADVERSE ACTIONS AGAINST HEALTH CARE PROVIDERS, SUPPLIERS, AND PRACTITIONERS TO THE NATIONAL HEALTH CARE FRAUD AND ABUSE DATA COLLECTION PROGRAM — Section 1128E(b)(6) [42 U.S.C.A. 1320a-7e(b)(6)]

Summary

Section 1128E(a) of the Social Security Act, as amended, 42 U.S.C.A. 1320a-7e(a), required the Secretary of Health and Human Services to establish, no later than January 1, 1997, a national health care fraud and abuse data collection program. This provision was enacted by section 221(a) of the Health Insurance Portability and Accountability Act of 1996, P.L. 104–191, effective August 21, 1996.

The purpose of this program is to collect reports from government agencies and health plans of final adverse actions against health care providers, suppliers, or practitioners.

Definitions — Section 1128E(g)(1): *"Final adverse action"* includes:

1. A civil judgment related to the delivery of a health care item or service against a health care provider, supplier, or practitioner in Federal or State court.
2. A Federal or State criminal conviction related to the delivery of a health care item or service.
3. Actions by Federal or State agencies responsible for licensing and certification of health care providers, suppliers, and

licensed health care practitioners. That includes formal or official actions, such as revocation or suspension of a license, reprimand, censure, or probation; any other loss of license or the right to apply for or renew a license, whether by operation of law, voluntary surrender, non-renewability, or otherwise; and any other negative action or finding by such Federal or State agency that is publicly available information.

4. Any other adjudicated action or decision that the Secretary provides for by regulation.

A final adverse action does not include a settlement in which no findings of liability have been made. It also does not include any action with respect to a malpractice claim.

"Practitioner" includes the terms "licensed health care practitioner", "licensed practitioner", and "practitioner" with respect to a State. As such, the term means an individual who is licensed or otherwise authorized by the State to provide health care services. It also means any individual who, without authority holds himself or herself out to be so licensed or authorized.

"Government agency" means the Department of Justice; the Department of Health and Human Services; any other Federal agency that either administers or provides payment for delivery of health care services, including but not limited to the Department of Defense and the Department of Veterans Affairs; State law enforcement agencies; State Medicaid fraud control units; and Federal or State agencies responsible for licensing and certification of health care providers and licensed health care practitioners.

"Health plan" means (by cross-reference to section 1128C(c), 42 U.S.C.A. 1320a-7c(c)), a plan or program that provides health benefits, whether directly, through insurance, or otherwise. That includes a policy of health insurance, a contract of a service benefit organization, and a membership agreement with a health maintenance organization or other prepaid health plan.

"Determination of conviction" means a determination in accordance with sections 1128(i)(1)-(4), 42 U.S.C.A. 1320a-7(i)(1)-(4). That includes:

1. When a judgment of conviction has been entered against the individual or entity by a Federal, State, or local court, regardless of whether there is an appeal pending or whether the judgment of conviction or other record relating to criminal conduct has been expunged.

2. When there has been a finding of guilt against the individual or entity by a Federal, State, or local court.
3. When a plea of guilty or nolo contendere by the individual or entity has been accepted by a Federal, State, or local court.
4. When the individual or entity has entered into participation in a first offender, deferred adjudication, or other arrangement or program where judgment of conviction has been withheld.

Information to Be Reported: According to section 1128E(b)(2), government agencies and health plans must report the following information about health care providers, suppliers, and practitioners who have been the subject of a final adverse action:

1. The name and taxpayer identification number (TIN), as defined in section 7701(a)(41) of the Internal Revenue Code of 1986, of the health care provider, supplier, or practitioner.
2. The name (if known) of any health care entity with which the health care provider, supplier, or practitioner is affiliated or associated.
3. The nature of the final adverse action and whether such action is on appeal.
4. A description of the acts or omissions and injuries upon which the final adverse action was based.
5. Such other information as the Secretary determines by regulation is required for appropriate interpretation of information reported under section 1128E.

These reports are to be filed regularly with the Secretary, but not less than monthly, and they must be filed in a form and manner prescribed by the Secretary.

In determining what information must be reported, section 1128E(b)(3) requires the Secretary to assure that the privacy of individuals receiving health care services is kept confidential.

Disclosure of Information: Section 1128E(c)(1) obligates the Secretary to provide by regulation for the disclosure of the information reported to the program to the health care provider, supplier, or licensed practitioner to whom the information pertains, and to establish procedures for cases where the accuracy of the reported information is disputed. Section 1128E(c)(2) obligates health care plans and government agencies to report corrections of information already reported about any final adverse action against a health care provider, supplier, or practitioner.

Availability of Information and Fees: Section 1128E(d)(1) provides that information in the database of the program shall be available to Federal and State government agencies and health plans pursuant to procedures established by the Secretary by regulation. Section 1128E(d)(2) authorizes the Secretary to establish or approve reasonable fees for the disclosure of information in the program database. The amount of the fees is intended to be sufficient to cover the full costs of operating the database. Fees do not apply, however, to requests by other Federal agencies.

Immunity from Civil Litigation: Section 1128E(e) provides that no person or entity, and no designee of the Secretary responsible for administering the program, shall be liable in any civil action with respect to any report made as required by section 1128E, if the report was made without knowledge of the falsity of information contained in it.

Coordination with the National Practitioner Data Bank: Section 1128E(f) obligates the Secretary to implement the health care fraud and abuse data collection program in a manner that will avoid duplication of the reporting requirements established for the National Practitioner Data Bank under the Health Care Quality Improvement Act of 1986, 42 U.S.C.A. 11101 *et seq*. See Chapter 5.

Sanctions: When section 1128E was first enacted, it contained no sanction for non-compliance with its requirements. Section 4331(d) of the Balanced Budget Act of 1997 changed that, effective August 5, 1997. As a result, section 1128E(b)(6) provides a sanction for health plans and a sanction for governmental agencies.

Sanction for Health Plans: Any health plan that fails to report information on an adverse action required to be reported is subject to a civil money penalty of not more than $25,000 for each such adverse action not reported. The penalty is to be imposed and collected just as civil money penalties are imposed and collected under section 1128A, 42 U.S.C.A. 1128a-7a. See § 4:8.

Sanction for Governmental Agencies: The Secretary must publish a report that identifies those government agencies that have failed to report information on adverse actions.

◆ NOTE: Effective August 21, 1996 (as if included in the Health Insurance Portability and Accountability Act of 1996), section 4331(a)(2) of the Balanced Budget Act of 1997 substituted "Department of Veterans Affairs" for "Veterans Administration" after "Department of Defense and the" in subparagraph (g)(3)(C). Section 4331(b) of the Balanced Budget Act of 1997 substituted "paragraphs (1) and (4)" for "paragraph (4)" after "shall be determined under" in paragraph (g)(5).

Statutory Provisions

Section 1128E of the Social Security Act, as amended, established the national health care fraud and abuse data collection program. It provides in part:

(a) GENERAL PURPOSE. — Not later than January 1, 1997, the Secretary shall establish a national health care fraud and abuse data collection program for the reporting of final adverse actions (not including settlements in which no findings of liability have been made) against health care providers, suppliers, or practitioners as required by subsection (b), with access as set forth in subsection (c), and shall maintain a database of the information collected under this section.

(b) REPORTING OF INFORMATION. —

(1) IN GENERAL. — Each Government agency and health plan shall report any final adverse action (not including settlements in which no findings of liability have been made) taken against a health care provider, supplier, or practitioner.

(2) INFORMATION TO BE REPORTED. — The information to be reported under paragraph (1) includes:

(A) The name and TIN (as defined in section 7701(a)(41) of the Internal Revenue Code of 1986) of any health care provider, supplier, or practitioner who is the subject of a final adverse action.

(B) The name (if known) of any health care entity with which a health care provider, supplier, or practitioner, who is the subject of a final adverse action, is affiliated or associated.

(C) The nature of the final adverse action and whether such action is on appeal.

(D) A description of the acts or omissions and injuries upon which the final adverse action was based, and such other information as the Secretary determines by regulation is required for appropriate interpretation of information reported under this section.

(3) CONFIDENTIALITY. — In determining what information is required, the Secretary shall include procedures to assure that the privacy of individuals receiving health care services is appropriately protected.

(4) TIMING AND FORM OF REPORTING. — The information required to be reported under this subsection shall be reported regularly (but not less often than monthly) and in such form and manner as the Secretary prescribes. Such information shall first be required to be reported on a date specified by the Secretary.

(5) TO WHOM REPORTED. — The information required to be reported under this subsection shall be reported to the Secretary.

The meaning of crucial terms in the statute is set forth in section 1128E(g) as follows:

(g) DEFINITIONS AND SPECIAL RULES. — For purposes of this section:

(1) FINAL ADVERSE ACTION. —

(A) IN GENERAL. — The term 'final adverse action' includes:

(i) Civil judgments against a health care provider, supplier, or practitioner in Federal or State court related to the delivery of a health care item or service.

(ii) Federal or State criminal convictions related to the delivery of a health care item or service.

(iii) Actions by Federal or State agencies responsible for the licensing and certification of health care providers, suppliers, and licensed health care practitioners, including —

(I) formal or official actions, such as revocation or suspension of a license (and the length of any such suspension), reprimand, censure or probation,

(II) any other loss of license or the right to apply for, or renew, a license of the provider, supplier, or practitioner, whether by operation of law, voluntary surrender, non-renewability, or otherwise, or

(III) any other negative action or finding by such Federal or State agency that is publicly available information.

(iv) Exclusion from participation in Federal or State health care programs (as defined in sections 1128B(f) [42 U.S.C.A. 1128a-7b(f)] and 1128(h) [42 U.S.C.A. 1128(h)], respectively).

(v) Any other adjudicated actions or decisions that the Secretary shall establish by regulation.

(B) EXCEPTION. —The term does not include any action with respect to a malpractice claim.

(2) PRACTITIONER. —The terms 'licensed health care practitioner', 'licensed practitioner', and 'practitioner' mean, with respect to a State, an individual who is licensed or otherwise authorized by the State to provide health care services (or any individual who, without authority holds himself or herself out to be so licensed or authorized).

(3) GOVERNMENT AGENCY. —The term 'Government agency' shall include:

(A) The Department of Justice.

(B) The Department of Health and Human Services.

(C) Any other Federal agency that either administers or provides payment for the delivery of health care services, including, but not limited to the Department of Defense and the Department of Veterans Affairs.

(D) State law enforcement agencies.

(E) State medicaid fraud control units.

(F) Federal or State agencies responsible for the licensing and certification of health care providers and licensed health care practitioners.

(4) HEALTH PLAN. —The term 'health plan' has the meaning given such term by section 1128C(c).

(5) DETERMINATION OF CONVICTION. —For purposes of paragraph (1), the existence of a conviction shall be determined under paragraphs (1) through (4) of section 1128(i).

With respect to disclosure of the information collected, and opportunities to correct errors, section 1128E(c) provides:

(c) DISCLOSURE AND CORRECTION OF INFORMATION. —

(1) DISCLOSURE. — With respect to the information about final adverse actions (not including settlements in which no findings of liability have been made) reported to the Secretary under this section with respect to a health care provider, supplier, or practitioner, the Secretary shall, by regulation, provide for —

(A) disclosure of the information, upon request, to the health care provider, supplier, or licensed practitioner, and

(B) procedures in the case of disputed accuracy of the information.

(2) CORRECTIONS. — Each Government agency and health plan shall report corrections of information already reported about any final adverse action taken against a health care provider, supplier, or practitioner, in such form and manner that the Secretary prescribes by regulation.

Section 1128E(d) specifies who can have access to the information collected. It states:

(d) ACCESS TO REPORTED INFORMATION. —

(1) AVAILABILITY. — The information in the database maintained under this section shall be available to Federal and State government agencies and health plans pursuant to procedures that the Secretary shall provide by regulation.

(2) FEES FOR DISCLOSURE. — The Secretary may establish or approve reasonable fees for the disclosure of information in such database (other than with respect to requests by Federal agencies). The amount of such a fee shall be sufficient to recover the full costs of operating the database. Such fees shall be available to the Secretary or, in the Secretary's discretion to the agency designated under this section to cover such costs.

Section 1128E(e) provides immunity from civil actions with respect to making reports required by the statute. It states:

(e) PROTECTION FROM LIABILITY FOR REPORTING. — No person or entity, including the agency designated by the Secretary in subsection (b)(5) shall be held liable in any civil action with respect to any report made as required by this section, without knowledge of the falsity of the information contained in the report.

Section 1128E(f) deals as follows with the apparent overlapping of reporting requirements with requirements of the National Practitioner Data Bank:

(f) COORDINATION WITH NATIONAL PRACTITIONER DATA BANK.—The Secretary shall implement this section in such a manner as to avoid duplication with the reporting requirements established for the National Practitioner Data Bank under the Health Care Quality Improvement Act of 1986 (42 U.S.C.A. 11101 *et seq.*).

With respect to sanctions, section 1128(b)(6) provides:

(6) SANCTIONS FOR FAILURE TO REPORT.—

(A) HEALTH PLANS.—Any health plan that fails to report information on an adverse action required to be reported under this subsection shall be subject to a civil money penalty of not more than $25,000 for each such adverse action not reported. Such penalty shall be imposed and collected in the same manner as civil money penalties under subsection (a) of section 1128A are imposed and collected under that section.

(B) GOVERNMENTAL AGENCIES.—The Secretary shall provide for a publication of a public report that identifies those Government agencies that have failed to report information on adverse actions as required to be reported under this subsection.

Section 1128(i), which applies by cross-reference from section 1128E(b)(5) deals with the meaning of a "conviction". It provides:

(i) CONVICTED DEFINED.—For purposes of subsections (a) and (b), an individual or entity is considered to have been "convicted" of a criminal offense—

(1) when a judgment of conviction has been entered against the individual or entity by a Federal, State, or local court, regardless of whether there is an appeal pending or whether the judgment of conviction or other record relating to criminal conduct has been expunged;

(2) when there has been a finding of guilt against the individual or entity by a Federal, State, or local court;

(3) when a plea of guilty or nolo contendere by the individual or entity has been accepted by a Federal, State, or local court; or

(4) when the individual or entity has entered into participation in a first offender, deferred adjudication, or other arrangement or program where judgment of conviction has been withheld.

Section 1128C(c), which applies by cross-reference from section 1128E(b)(4) defines health plan as follows:

(c) HEALTH PLAN DEFINED. — For purposes of this section, the term 'health plan' means a plan or program that provides health benefits, whether directly, through insurance, or otherwise, and includes —

(1) a policy of health insurance;

(2) a contract of a service benefit organization; and

(3) a membership agreement with a health maintenance organization or other prepaid health plan.

For regulatory citations, see Chapter 8

§ 4:14 MISUSE OF FEDERAL GOVERNMENT NAMES, SYMBOLS, AND EMBLEMS — Section 1140 [42 U.S.C.A. 1320b-10]

Summary

◆ NOTE: Effective March 31, 1995, the Social Security Independence and Program Improvements Act of 1994, P.L. 103-296, established the Social Security Administration as an independent agency, removing it from its former subsidiary status as part of the Department of Health and Human Services. This necessitated numerous technical amendments to the Social Security Act, including substantial changes in section 1140. For a discussion of section 1140 prior to this amendment, see H-4: Former Chapter IV-14 in Appendix H.

Section 1140(a)(1) of the Social Security Act, 42 U.S.C.A. 1320b-10(a), restricts use of the words "Social Security", "Social Security Account", "Social Security System", "Social Security

Administration", "Medicare", "Health Care Financing Administration", "Department of Health and Human Services", "Health and Human Services", "Supplemental Security Income Programs", or "Medicaid", the letters "SSA", "HCFA", "DHHS", "HHS", or "SSI". Specifically, those words and letters may not be used in any manner which a person knows, or should know, would convey the false impression that an item is approved, endorsed, or authorized by the Social Security Administration (SSA), the Health Care Financing Administration (HCFA), or the Department of Health and Human Services (HHS), or that such person has some connection with, or authorization from, SSA, HCFA, or HHS. The same applies if the act is done in a manner which reasonably could be interpreted or construed as conveying such a false impression.

The statute also prohibits such misuse of a symbol or emblem of SSA, HCFA, and HHS, including the design of, or a reasonable facsimile of the design of, the Social Security card, or the Medicare care, or the check used for payment of Social Security benefits, and envelopes or other stationery used by SSA, HCFA, or HHS.

These prohibitions reach misuse in connection with any item constituting an advertisement, solicitation, circular, book, pamphlet, or other communication, or a play, motion picture, broadcast, telecast, or other production; and they apply whether the names, acronyms, symbols, or emblems are used alone or with other words, letters, symbols, or emblems in any combination or variation. They do not apply to agencies or instrumentalities of a State or political subdivisions of a State.

Section 1140(a)(2) prohibits reproduction, reprinting, or distributing for a fee any form, application, or other publication of SSA or HHS without specific, written authorization for such activity by the Commissioner or Secretary, as applicable.

Pursuant to section 1140(a)(3), including a disclaimer of affiliation with the United States Government or any agency or instrumentality thereof on offensive material is not a defense to a determination that subsections (a)(1) or (a)(2) have been violated.

Section 1140(b) authorizes the Commissioner of Social Security or the Secretary of Health and Human Services, as applicable, to impose a civil money penalty on anyone who violates section 1140(a). The amount of the penalty may not to exceed $5,000 for each violation, unless the violation consists of a broadcast or telecast. For such cases, the Secretary may impose a civil money penalty not to exceed $25,000.

For purposes of subsection (a)(1), each piece of mail which contains one or more misused words, letters, symbol, or emblems represents a separate violation. For purposes of subsection (a)(2), each copy reproduced, reprinted, or distributed represents a separate violation.

Section 1140(c)(1) provides that subsections (c),(d), (e), (g), (j), (k), and (l) of section 1128A, 42 U.S.C.A. 1320a-7a, which authorizes civil money penalties for a variety of offenses, apply to this civil money penalty provision as well. For a discussion of section 1128A, see § 4:8.

Section 1140(c)(2) permits the Commissioner or the Secretary, as applicable, to compromise a civil money penalty imposed under section 1140, or to seek recovery of the penalty by civil action in the Federal District Court for the district where the violation occurred, or where the violator resides, has a principal office, or may be found — as determined by the Commissioner or the Secretary. Amounts recovered go to the Federal Old-Age and Survivors Insurance Trust Fund to the extent that the penalties reflect misuse of words, letters, symbols, or emblems relating to the Social Security Administration. To the extent that the penalties reflect misuse of words, letters, symbols, or emblems relating to the Department of Health and Human Services, amounts recovered go to the Federal Hospital Insurance Trust Fund or the Federal Supplementary Medical Insurance Trust Fund, as appropriate.

Finally, section 1140(d) authorizes the Offices of the Inspector General for the Social Security Administration or the Department of Health and Human Services, as appropriate, to enforce section 1140.

Statutory Provisions

Section 1140(a), 42 U.S.C.A. 1320b-10(a), provides:

> (1) No person may use, in connection with any item constituting an advertisement, solicitation, circular, book, pamphlet, or other communication, or a play, motion picture, broadcast, telecast, or other production, alone or with other words, letters, symbols, or emblems —
>
> (A) the words "Social Security", "Social Security Account", "Social Security System", "Social Security Administration", "Medicare", "Health Care Financing Administration", the letters "SSA" or "HCFA", "DHHS", "HHS", or "SSI", or any other combination or variation of such words or letters, or

(B) a symbol or emblem of the Social Security Administration, Health Care Financing Administration, or Department of Health and Human Services (including the design of, or a reasonable facsimile of the design of, the social security card issued pursuant to section 205(c)(2)(F), [42 U.S.C.A. 405(c)(2)(F)] , or the Medicare card, the check used for payment of benefits under title II, or envelopes or other stationery used by the Social Security Administration, Health Care Financing Administration, or Department of Health and Human Services), or any other combination or variation of such symbols or emblems,

in a manner which such person knows or should know would convey, or in a manner which reasonably could be interpreted or construed as conveying, the false impression that such item is approved, endorsed, or authorized by the Social Security Administration, the Health Care Financing Administration, or the Department of Health and Human Services or that such person has some connection with, or authorization from, the Social Security Administration, the Health Care Financing Administration, or the Department of Health and Human Services. The preceding provisions of this subsection shall not apply with respect to the use by any agency or instrumentality of a State or political subdivision of a State of any words or letters which identify an agency or instrumentality of such State or of a political subdivision of such State or the use by any such agency or instrumentality of any symbol or emblem of an agency or instrumentality of such State or a political subdivision of such State.

(2) (A) No person may for a fee, reproduce, reprint, or distribute any item consisting of a form, application, or other publication of the Social Security Administration unless such person has obtained specific, written authorization for such activity in accordance with regulations.

(B) No person may, for a fee, reproduce, reprint, or distribute any item consisting of a form, application, or other publication of the Department of Health and Human Services unless such person has obtained specific, written authorization for such activity in accordance with regulations which the Secretary shall prescribe.

(3) Any determination of whether the use of one or more words, letters, symbols, or emblems (or any combination or variation

thereof) in connection with an item described in paragraph (1) or the reproduction, reprinting, or distribution of an item described in paragraph (2) is a violation of this subsection shall be made without regard to any inclusion in such item (or any so reproduced, reprinted, or distributed copy thereof) of a disclaimer of affiliation with the United States Government or any particular agency or instrumentality thereof.

Section 1140(b) provides:

> The Commissioner or the Secretary (as applicable) may, pursuant to regulations, impose a civil money penalty not to exceed —
>
> (1) except as provided in subparagraph (2), $5,000, or
>
> (2) in the case of a violation consisting of a broadcast or telecast, $25,000,
>
> against any person for each violation by such person of subsection (a). In the case of any items referred to in subsection (a)(1) consisting of pieces of mail, each such piece of mail which contains one or more words, letters, symbols, or emblems in violation of subsection (a) shall represent a separate violation. In the case of any item referred to in subsection (a)(2), the reproduction, reprinting, or distribution of such item shall be treated as a separate violation with respect to each copy thereof so reproduced, reprinted, or distributed.

Section 1140(c) provides:

> (1) The provisions of section 1128A [42 U.S.C.A. 1320a-7a, which authorizes civil money penalties for a variety of offenses] (other than subsections (a), (b), (f), (h), and (i) and the first sentence of subsection (c)) shall apply to civil money penalties under subsection (b) in the same manner as such provisions apply to a penalty or proceeding under section 1128A(a).
>
> (2) Penalties imposed against a person under subsection (b) may be compromised by the Commissioner or the Secretary (as applicable) and may be recovered in a civil action in the name of the United States brought in the district court of the United States for the district in which the violation occurred or where the person resides, has its principal office, or may be

found, as determined by the Commissioner or the Secretary. Amounts recovered under this section shall be paid to the Commissioner or the Secretary (as applicable) and shall be deposited as miscellaneous receipts of the Treasury of the United States, except that (A) to the extent that such amounts are recovered under this section as penalties imposed for misuse of words, letters, symbols, or emblems relating to the Social Security Administration, such amounts shall be deposited into the Federal Old-Age and Survivors Insurance Trust Fund, and (B) to the extent that such amounts are recovered under this section as penalties imposed for misuse of words, letters, symbols, or emblems relating to the Department of Health and Human Services, such amounts shall be deposited into the Federal Hospital Insurance Trust Fund or the Federal Supplementary Medical Insurance Trust Fund, as appropriate. The amount of such penalty when finally determined, or the amount agreed upon in compromise, may be deducted from any sum then or later owing by the United States to the person against whom the penalty has been imposed.

(d) The preceding provisions of this section may be enforced through the Office of the Inspector General of the Social Security Administration or the Office of the Inspector General of the Department of Health and Human Services (as appropriate).

NOTE: Section 108(b)(12) of the Social Security Independence and Program Improvements Act amended subsection (a)(2), as amended by section 312 of that same Act, by inserting "(A)" after "(2)"; by removing "or of the Department of Health and Human Services"; by removing "which the Secretary shall prescribe" and inserting "which the commissioner of Social Security shall prescribe"; and by adding new subparagraph (B).

In subsection (b), section 108(b)(12) substituted "the Commissioner or the Secretary (as applicable)" for "the Secretary".

In subsection (c)(2), section 108(b)(12) substituted "the Commissioner or the Secretary (as applicable)" for "the Secretary" each place the latter had appeared.

In subsection (d), section 108(b)(12) substituted "the Office of the Inspector General of the Social Security Administration or the Office of the Inspector General of the Department of Health and Human Services (as appropriate)" for "the Office of Inspector General of the

Department of Health and Human Services". The foregoing changes were effective March 31, 1995.

Section 312(a)(1)-(3) of the Act redesignated paragraphs (1) and (2) as subparagraphs (A) and (B) respectively in subsection (a); and inserted "(1)" after "(a)"; and inserted new paragraph (2).

Section 312(b) removed " 'Administration', the letters 'SSA' or 'HCFA'" and substituted " 'Administration', 'department of Health and Human Services', 'Health and Human Services', 'supplemental Security Income Program', or 'Medicaid', the letters 'SSA', 'HCFA', 'DHHS', 'HHS', or 'SSI'." It also removed from subparagraph (b), as amended by section 304 and as redesignated, "Social Security Administration" each place it appeared, and substituted "Social Security Administration, Health Care Financing Administration, or Department of Health and Human Services"; and it removed "or of the Health Care Financing Administration" and inserted "or the Medicare card" after "205(c)(2)(F)".

Section 312(c) added a new sentence at the end of subsection (a)(1). Section 312(d) substituted "convey, or in a manner which reasonably could be interpreted or construed as conveying," for "convey in subsection (a)(1)(B).

Section 312(e) added new paragraph (3) to the end of subsection (a). Section 312(f) added a new sentence at the end of subsection (b)(1). Section 312(g) repealed former paragraph (2) of subsection (b). Section 312(h) inserted "and the first sentence of subsection (c)" after "and (i)" in subsection (c)(1). Section 312(i) removed "United States" and replaced it with a new sentence, which begins "United States, except" and ends with "Fund, as appropriate." Section 312(j) added new subsection (d).

The foregoing changes made by section 312 were effective August 15, 1994.

For regulatory citations, see Chapter 8

§ 4:15 [RESERVED]

§ 4:16 VIOLATING REPORTING AND DISCLOSURE OBLIGATIONS REGARDING THE MEDICARE AND MEDICAID COVERAGE DATA BANK — Section 1144 [42 U.S.C.A. 1320b-14]

Summary

◆ NOTE: This sanction was repealed effective October 2, 1996, by section 1(a) of the Medicare/Medicaid Data Bank Elimination Act of 1996, P.L. 104–226.

Section 1144 of the Social Security Act, enacted by section 13581 of P.L. 103-66, the Omnibus Budget Reconciliation Act of 1993 (OBRA 93), created the Medicare and Medicaid Coverage Data Bank.

The purpose of the Data Bank is to support the Medicare secondary payer requirements established by section 1862(b), 42 U.S.C.A. 1395y(b), and similar secondary payer initiatives established by States for their respective Medicaid programs.

◆ NOTE: For a discussion of the Medicare secondary payer requirements, see §§ 2:27 and 2:28.

Section 1144(a) obligated the Secretary of Health and Human Services (HHS) to establish the Data Bank to identify and collect information from third parties responsible for payment for health care goods and services furnished to Medicare beneficiaries and from third parties responsible to reimburse costs incurred by State Medicaid programs on behalf of Medicaid recipients. Although section 1862(b) makes Medicare secondary payer to a variety of sources which provide health care benefits, such as workers compensation programs, automobile and other liability insurance, and no-fault insurance, the focus of section 1144 is on health insurance provided by defined employment-related group health plans.

◆ NOTE: Section 1144(d) authorizes the Secretary to establish fees for services provided under section 1144, and to use such fees to cover administrative costs to the Data Bank of providing such services. The statute does not indicate, however, who would be charged for what services. Presumably, the Secretary will promulgate regulations to deal with that.

According to section 1144(b), the Data Bank shall contain information obtained pursuant to section 6103(l)(12) of the Internal Revenue Code of 1986, 26 U.S.C.A. 6103(l)(12). The latter statute authorizes the Internal Revenue Service (IRS) to disclose to the Commissioner of Social Security, upon written request, from its individual master files available filing status and taxpayer identity information relating to whether any Medicare beneficiary was married for any year after 1986 and, if so, the name of the spouse of such individual and such spouse's taxpayer identification number (TIN). Then the Commissioner of Social Security may disclose to the Administrator of the Health Care Financing Administration (HCFA), upon written request:

1. the name and TIN of each Medicare beneficiary identified as having received wages from a qualified employer in a previous year;
2. the name and TIN of each Medicare beneficiary, identified by the IRS as having been married, whose spouse received wages from a qualified employer in a previous year;
3. the name and TIN of such spouse; and
4. the name, address, and TIN of the employer and the number of individuals with respect to whom the employer furnished tax withholding statements under 26 U.S.C.A. 6051 the previous year.

Then the HCFA Administrator may disclose to the identified qualified employer the name and TIN of the identified individuals to determine whether the employee or the employee's spouse was covered under the employer's group health plan, and, if so, the period of coverage, the benefits provided under the plan, and the name and address and identifying number of the plan. Having that information, the Administrator then may disclose names and TINs to any group health plan which provides or provided coverage to an identified employee or employee's spouse in order to present a claim to the plan. That applies, however, only if Medicare had paid for health care goods and services during a period when the plan was to be the primary payer.

For these purposes, a qualified employer is one that furnished written statements under 26 U.S.C.A. 6051 to at least 20 individuals for wages paid in a calendar year.

For section 1144 purposes, a group health plan is a plan that meets the definition in 26 U.S.C.A. 5000(b)(1). That includes any plan (including a self-insured plan) of, or contributed to by, an employer (including a self-employed person) or employee organization to provide health care (directly or otherwise) to employees, former employees, the employer, others associated or formerly associated with the employer in a business relationship, or their families.

◆ NOTE: Prior to amendment by OBRA 93, group health plan, as defined in 26 U.S.C.A. 5000(b)(1), meant any plan of, or contributed to by, an employer (including a self-insured plan) to provide health care, directly or otherwise, to employees, former employees, or the families thereof.

The Data Bank also will contain the following information which employers and group health plans must provide pursuant to section 1144(c).

For each calendar year beginning on or after January 1, 1994, and before January 1, 1998, an employer that has, or contributes to, a group health plan with at least one employee electing to participate in the plan must report to the Secretary of HHS:

1. the name and TIN of the electing individual;
2. the type of group health plan coverage (single or family) elected by the individual;
3. the name, address, and identifying number of the group health plan elected by such electing individual;
4. the name and TIN of each other individual covered under the group health plan pursuant to such election;
5. the period during which such coverage was elected; and
6. the name, address, and TIN of the employer.

Employers must report this information the same time they report withholding statements under 26 U.S.C.A. 6051(d) — generally January 31 of the year following the calendar year for which wages were reported. Furthermore, the report must be in a form and manner determined by the Secretary of HHS to minimize the reporting burden.

Section 1144(c)(1)(B) provides a special rule, however, with respect to this reporting obligation. To the extent a group health plan provides the above information in a form and manner specified by the Secretary (in consultation with the Secretary of Labor) on behalf of an employer in accordance with section 101(f) of the Employee Retirement Income Security Act of 1974 (ERISA), the employer is deemed to have complied with this reporting requirement.

For section 1144 purposes, an electing individual is an individual associated or formerly associated with the employer in a business relationship who elects coverage under the employer's group health plan. Excluded from that definition, however, are those who provide domestic service in a private home of the employer and who receive less than $50 per calendar quarter.

◆ NOTE: "Domestic service in a private home of the employer" does not include such service on a farm operated for profit. See 26 U.S.C.A. 3121(a)(7)(B)and 3121(g)(5).

Until September 30, 1998, the Secretary is authorized to disclose any information in the Data Bank obtained pursuant to section 6103(l)(12), but solely for the purposes of that section, and only to the extent necessary to determine whether a beneficiary is covered under a group health plan. Similarly, the Secretary may disclose any other information in the Data Bank to any State agency administering a State's Medicaid program, and to any employer, or group health plan, but solely for purposes of section 1144(a).

Having established the Data Bank and the disclosure and reporting requirements described above, section 1144(c)(7)(B) provides a sanction for unauthorized willful disclosure of information reported under (c)(1), and section 1144(c)(8) [erroneously labeled (9) in the statute] provides a sanction for failure to report as required under(c)(1)(A).

With respect to the unauthorized willful disclosure of information, section 1144(c)(7)(B) provides for the same penalties found in section 7213(a)(1), (2), (3), and (4) of the Internal Revenue Code of 1986, 26 U.S.C.A. 7213(a)(1)-(4).

In the case of Federal officers or employees, or former officers or employees, and certain other persons (or an officer or employer of same) who obtain such information from the IRS in connection with processing, storage, transmission, and reproduction of returns and return information, or in connection with the programming, maintenance, repair, testing, and procurement of equipment, and providing of other services for purposes of tax administration, whoever makes an unauthorized willful disclosure is guilty of a felony. Upon conviction, the punishment may be a fine not exceeding $5,000, or imprisonment of not more than 5 years, or both, plus costs of prosecution. In addition, a violator who is a Federal officer or employee must, upon conviction, be dismissed from office or discharged from employment.

In the case of State and other employees, the violation is also a felony punishable by a fine not exceeding $5,000, or imprisonment not more than 5 years, or both, plus costs of prosecution.

Furthermore, any person who willfully prints or publishes in any manner not provided by law any information obtained by an unauthorized disclosure is guilty of a felony. Punishment upon conviction may be a fine not exceeding $5,000, or imprisonment not more than 5 years, or both, plus costs of prosecution.

Finally, any person who willfully offers any item of material value in exchange for the unauthorized disclosure of information who receives such information as a result of that solicitation is guilty of a felony. Punishment upon conviction may be a fine not exceeding $5,000, imprisonment not more than 5 years, or both, plus costs of prosecution.

With respect to failure by an employer (other than a Federal or other governmental entity) to report information required by section 1144(c)(1)(A), section 1144(c)(8) requires the Secretary of HHS to impose a penalty "as described in part II of subchapter B of chapter 68 of the Internal Revenue Code of 1986", 26 U.S.C.A. 6721-6724. A variety of penalties are imposed for a variety of offenses in that part of the Internal Revenue Code, but a plausible interpretation is that the Secretary of HHS should apply 26 U.S.C.A. 6723. It provides that "in the case of a failure by any person to comply with a specified information requirement on or before the time prescribed", the penalty shall be $50 for each such failure. The total penalty, however, may not exceed $100,000 for all such failures in any calendar year.

Statutory Provisions

Section 1144, 42 U.S.C.A. 1320b-14, required the Secretary of Health and Human Services to establish a Medicare and Medicaid Coverage Data Bank. It provides:

> (a) ESTABLISHMENT OF DATA BANK. — The Secretary shall establish a Medicare and Medicaid Coverage Data Bank (hereafter in this section referred to as the "Data Bank") to —
>
> (1) further the purposes of section 1862(b) [42 U.S.C.A. 1395y(b), which establishes Medicare as the secondary payer when payment for health care is available from certain third party payers] in the identification of, and collection from,

third parties responsible for payment for health care items and services furnished to medicare beneficiaries, and

(2) assist in the identification of, and the collection from, third parties responsible for the reimbursement of costs incurred by any State plan under title XIX with respect to medicaid beneficiaries, upon request by the State agency described in section 1902(a)(5) [42 U.S.C.A. 1396a(a)(5), which requires a State to have its Medicaid program administered by a single State agency] administering such plan.

(b) INFORMATION IN DATA BANK. —

(1) IN GENERAL. — The Data Bank shall contain information obtained pursuant to section 6103(l)(12) of the Internal Revenue Code of 1986 [26 U.S.C.A. 6301(l)(12), which pertains to disclosure of certain taxpayer identity information for verification of employment status of medicare beneficiaries and their spouses] and subsection (c).

(2) DISCLOSURE OF INFORMATION IN DATA BANK. —The Secretary is authorized until September 30, 1998 —

(A) (subject to restriction in subparagraph (D)(i) of section 6103(l)(12) of the Internal Revenue Code of 1986 [which restricts disclosure solely for purposes of and to the extent necessary to determine whether a Medicare beneficiary is covered under a group health plan]) to disclose any information in the Data Bank obtained pursuant to such section solely for the purposes of such section, and

(B) (subject to the restriction in subsection (c)(7)) to disclose any other information in the Data Bank to any State agency described in section 1902(a)(5), employer, or group health plan solely for the purposes described in subsection (a).

(c) REQUIREMENT THAT EMPLOYERS REPORT INFORMATION. —

(1) REPORTING REQUIREMENT. —

(A) IN GENERAL. — Any employer described in paragraph (2) shall report to the Secretary (in such form and manner as the Secretary determines will minimize the burden of such reporting) with respect to each electing individual the information required under paragraph (5) for each calendar year beginning on or after January 1, 1994, and before January 1, 1998.

(B) SPECIAL RULE. — To the extent a group health plan provides information required under paragraph (5) in a form and manner specified by the Secretary (in consultation with the Secretary of Labor on behalf of an employer in accordance with section 101(f) of the Employee Retirement Income Security Act of 1974, the employer has complied with the reporting requirement under subparagraph (A) with respect to the reporting of such information.

(2) EMPLOYER DESCRIBED. — An employer is described in this paragraph if such employer has, or contributes to, a group health plan, with respect to which at least 1 employee of such employer is an electing individual.

(3) ELECTING INDIVIDUAL. — For purposes of this subsection, the term "electing individual" means an individual associated or formerly associated with the employer in a business relationship who elects coverage under the employer's group health plan.

(4) CERTAIN INDIVIDUALS EXCLUDED. — For purposes of this subsection, an individual providing service referred to in section 3121(a)(7)(B) of the Internal Revenue Code of 1986 [26 U.S.C.A. 3121(a)(7)(B), which pertains to certain domestic workers in private homes of employers] shall not be considered an employee or electing individual with respect to an employer.

(5) INFORMATION REQUIRED. — For purposes of paragraph (1), each employer shall provide the following information:

(A) The name and TIN of the electing individual.

(B) The type of group health plan coverage (single or family) elected by the electing individual.

(C) The name, address, and identifying number of the group health plan elected by such electing individual.

(D) The name and TIN of each other individual covered under the group health plan pursuant to such election.

(E) The period during which such coverage is elected.

(F) The name, address, and TIN of the employer.

(6) TIME OF FILING. — For purposes of determining the date for filing the report under paragraph (1), such report

shall be treated as a statement described in section 6051(d) of the Internal Revenue Code of 1986 [26 U.S.C.A. 6051(d), which pertains to duplicate FICA statements].

(7) LIMITS ON DISCLOSURE OF INFORMATION REPORTED. —

(A) IN GENERAL. — The disclosure of the information reported under rules similar to the rules of subsections (a) and (p) of section 6103 of the Internal Revenue Code of 1986 [26 U.S.C.A. 6103(a) and (p), which respectively pertain to confidentiality and disclosure rules in general and procedure and recordkeeping requirements].

(B) PENALTY FOR UNAUTHORIZED WILLFUL DISCLOSURE OF INFORMATION. — The unauthorized disclosure of any information reported under paragraph (1) shall be subject to the penalty described in paragraph (1), (2), (3), or (4) of section 7213(a) of such Code [26 U.S.C.A. 7213(a), which is set forth below].

(9) [sic (8)] PENALTY FOR FAILURE TO REPORT. — In the case of the failure of an employer (other than a Federal or other governmental entity) to report under paragraph (1)(A) with respect to each electing individual, the Secretary shall impose a penalty as described in part II of subchapter B of chapter 68 of the Internal Revenue Code of 1986 [26 U.S.C.A. 6721-6724].

(d) FEES FOR DATA BANK SERVICES. — The Secretary shall establish fees for services provided under this section which shall remain available, without fiscal year limitation, to the Secretary to cover the administrative costs to the Data Bank of providing such services.

(f) [sic (e)] DEFINITIONS. — In this section:

(1) MEDICARE BENEFICIARY. — The term "medicare beneficiary" means an individual entitled to benefits under part A, or enrolled under part B, of title XVIII, but does not include such an individual enrolled in part A under section 1818 [42 U.S.C.A. 1395i-2, which authorizes hospital insurance benefits for individuals 65 or older who enroll under Part B, who are residents of the United States and who are citizens or who are aliens lawfully admitted for permanent residence who have resided in the U.S. for five years continuously prior to

the month application is made under this section, and who are not otherwise eligible to enroll under Part A].

(2) MEDICAID BENEFICIARY. — The term "medicaid beneficiary" means an individual entitled to benefits under a State plan for medical assistance under title XIX (including a State plan operating under a Statewide waiver under section 1115 [42 U.S.C.A. 1315, which authorizes experimental, pilot, or demonstration projects which the Secretary determines may promote the objectives of the various Federally funded welfare programs or Medicaid]).

(3) GROUP HEALTH PLAN. — The term "group health plan" shall have the meaning given to such term by section 5000(b)(1) of the Internal Revenue Code of 1986 [26 U.S.C.A. 5000(b)(1), which is set forth below].

(4) TIN. — The term "TIN" shall have the meaning given to such term by section 7701(a)(41) of such Code [26 U.S.C.A. 7701(a)(41), which is set forth below].

Section 6103(l)(12) of the Internal Revenue Code of 1986 provides:

DISCLOSURE OF CERTAIN TAXPAYER IDENTITY INFORMATION FOR VERIFICATION OF EMPLOYMENT STATUS OF MEDICARE BENEFICIARY AND SPOUSE OF MEDICARE BENEFICIARY. —

(A) IN GENERAL. — The Secretary shall, upon written request from the Commissioner of Social Security, disclose to the Commissioner available filing status and taxpayer identity information from the individual master files of the Internal Revenue Service relating to whether any medicare beneficiary identified by the Commissioner was a married individual (as defined in section 7703) for any specified year after 1986, and, if so, the name of the spouse of such individual and such spouse's TIN.

(B) RETURN INFORMATION FROM SOCIAL SECURITY ADMINISTRATION. — The Commissioner of Social Security shall, upon written request from the Administrator of the Health Care Financing Administration, disclose to the Administrator the following information:

(i) The name and TIN of each medicare beneficiary who is identified as having received wages (as defined in section

3401(a)), above an amount (if any) specified by the Secretary of Health and Human Services, from a qualified employer in a previous year.

(ii) For each medicare beneficiary who was identified as married under subparagraph (A) and whose spouse is identified as having received wages, above an amount (if any) specified by the Secretary of Health and Human Services, from a qualified employer in a previous year —

(I) the name and TIN of the medicare beneficiary, and

(II) the name and TIN of the spouse.

(iii) With respect to each such qualified employer, the name, address, and TIN of the employer and the number of individuals with respect to whom written statements were furnished under section 6051 by the employer with respect to such previous year.

(C) DISCLOSURE BY HEALTH CARE FINANCING ADMINISTRATION. — With respect to the information disclosed under subparagraph (B), the Administrator of the Health Care Financing Administration may disclose —

(i) to the qualified employer referred to in such subparagraph the name and TIN of each individual identified under such subparagraph as having received wages from the employer (hereinafter in this subparagraph referred to as the "employee") for purposes of determining during what period such employee or the employee's spouse may be (or have been) covered under a group health plan of the employer and what benefits are or were covered under the plan (including the name, address, and identifying number of the plan),

(ii) to any group health plan which provides or provided coverage to such an employee or spouse, the name of such employee and the employee's spouse (if the spouse is a medicare beneficiary) and the name and address of the employer, and, for the purpose of presenting a claim to the plan —

(I) the TIN of such employee if benefits were paid under title XVIII of the Social Security Act with respect to the employee during a period in which the plan was a primary plan (as defined in section 1862(b)(2)(A) of the Social Security Act), and

(II) the TIN of such spouse if benefits were paid under such title with respect to the spouse during such period, and

(iii) to any agent of such Administrator the information referred to in subparagraph (B) for purposes of carrying out clauses (i) and (ii) on behalf of such Administrator.

(D) SPECIAL RULES. —

(i) RESTRICTION ON DISCLOSURE. — Information may be disclosed under this paragraph only for purposes of, and to the extent necessary in, determining the extent to which any medicare beneficiary is covered under any group health plan.

(ii) TIMELY RESPONSE TO REQUESTS. — Any request made under subparagraph (A) or (B) shall be complied with as soon as possible but in no event later than 120 days after the date the request was made.

(E) DEFINITIONS. — For purposes of this paragraph —

(i) MEDICARE BENEFICIARY. — The term "medicare beneficiary" means an individual entitled to benefits under part A, or enrolled under part B, of title XVIII of the Social Security Act, but does not include such an individual enrolled in part A under section 1818.

(ii) GROUP HEALTH PLAN. — The term group health plan means any group health plan (as defined in section 5000(b)(1).

◆ NOTE: Prior to amendment by OBRA 93, subparagraph (ii) read as follows:

(ii) GROUP HEALTH PLAN. — The term "group health plan" means —

(I) any group health plan (as defined in section 5000(b)(1)), and

(II) any large group health plan (as defined in section 5000(b)(2))

(iii) QUALIFIED EMPLOYER. — The term "qualified employer" means, for a calendar year, an employer which has furnished written statements under section 6051 with respect to at least 20 individuals for wages paid in the year.

(F) TERMINATION. — Subparagraphs (A) and (B) shall not apply to —

(i) any request made after September 30, 1998, and

(ii) any request made before such date for information relating to —

(I) 1997 or thereafter in the case of subparagraph (A), or

(II) 1998 or thereafter in the case of subparagraph (B).

◆ NOTE: Prior to amendment by OBRA 93 and P.L. 103-182, the sunset dates listed above in (F) were September 30, 1995, 1994, and 1995 respectively.

With respect to the exclusion of certain domestic workers, section 3121(a)(7)(B) of the Internal Revenue Code provides that wages does not include:

cash remuneration paid by an employer in any calendar quarter to an employee for domestic service in a private home of the employer, if the cash remuneration paid in such quarter by the employer to the employee for such service is less than $50. As used in this subparagraph, the term "domestic services in a private home of the employer" does not include service described in subsection (g)(5)[.]

Section 3121(g)(5) provides:

AGRICULTURAL LABOR. — For purposes of this chapter, the term "agricultural labor" includes all service performed —

* * *

(5) on a farm operated for profit if such service is not in the course of the employer's trade or business or is domestic service in a private home of the employer.

With respect to the definition of a group health plan, section 5000(b) of the Internal Revenue Code provides in pertinent part:

GROUP HEALTH PLAN AND LARGE GROUP HEALTH PLAN. — For purposes of this section. —

> (1) GROUP HEALTH PLAN. — The term "group health plan" means a plan (including a self-insured plan) of, or contributed to by, an employer (including a self-employed person) or employee organization to provide health care (directly or otherwise) to the employees, former employees, the employer, others associated or formerly associated with the employer in a business relationship, or their families.

◆ NOTE: Prior to amendment by OBRA 93, section 5000(b)(1) read as follows:

> (1) GROUP HEALTH PLAN. — The term "group health plan" means any plan of, or contributed to by, an employer (including a self-insured plan) to provide health care (directly or otherwise) to the employer's employees, former employees, or the families of such employees or former employees.

Section 7701(a)(41) of the Internal Revenue Code of 1986 defines TIN as follows:

> The term "TIN" means the identifying number assigned to a person under section 6109.

Section 6109 provides that for individuals and their estates an individual's social security number is his or her TIN.

The penalty for unauthorized willful disclosure of information in the Data Bank is set forth in section 7213(a)(1), (2), (3), and (4) of the Internal Revenue Code of 1986 (by cross-reference from section 1144(c)(7)(B)) as follows:

> UNAUTHORIZED DISCLOSURE OF INFORMATION
>
> (a) RETURNS AND RETURN INFORMATION. —
>
> (1) FEDERAL EMPLOYEES AND OTHER PERSONS. — It shall be unlawful for any officer or employee of the United States or any person described in section 6103(n) (or an officer or employee of any such person), or any former officer or employee, willfully to disclose to any person, except as authorized in this title, any return or return information (as defined in section 6103(b)). Any violation of this paragraph shall be a felony punishable upon conviction by a fine in any amount not exceeding $5,000, or imprisonment of not more than 5 years, or both, together with the costs of prosecution, and if such offense is committed by any officer or employee of the United

States, he shall, in addition to any other punishment, be dismissed from office or discharged from employment upon conviction for such offense.

(2) STATE AND OTHER EMPLOYEES. — It shall be unlawful for any person (not described in paragraph (1)) willfully to disclose to any person, except as authorized in this title, any return or return information (as defined in section 6103(b)) acquired by him or another person under subsection . . . (l)(12) . . . of section 6103. Any violation of this paragraph shall be a felony punishable by a fine in any amount not exceeding $5,000, or imprisonment of not more than 5 years, or both, together with the costs of prosecution.

(3) OTHER PERSONS. — It shall be unlawful for any person to whom any return or return information (as defined in section 6103(b)) is disclosed in a manner unauthorized by this title thereafter willfully to print or publish in any manner not provided by law any such return or return information. Any violation of this paragraph shall be a felony punishable by a fine in any amount not exceeding $5,000, or imprisonment of not more than 5 years, or both, together with the costs of prosecution.

(4) SOLICITATION. — It shall be unlawful for any person willfully to offer any item of material value in exchange for any return or return information (as defined in section 6103(b)) and to receive as a result of such solicitation any such return or return information. Any violation of this paragraph shall be a felony punishable by a fine in any amount not exceeding $5,000, or imprisonment of not more than 5 years, or both, together with the costs of prosecution.

For purposes of application of section 7213's penalties, section 6103(b) of the Internal Revenue Code provides definitions as follows:

For purposes of this section —

* * *

(2) RETURN INFORMATION. — The term "return information" means —

(A) a taxpayer's identity, the nature, source, or amount of his income, payments, receipts, deductions, exemptions, credits, assets, liabilities, net worth, tax liability, tax withheld, deficiencies, overassessments, or tax payments, whether the taxpayer's return was, is being, or will be examined or subject to other investigation or processing, or any other data, received by, recorded by, prepared by, furnished to, or collected by the Secretary with respect to a return or with respect to the determination of the existence, or possible existence, of liability (or the amount thereof) of any person under this title for any tax, penalty, interest, fine, forfeiture, or other imposition, or offense, and

(B) any part of any written determination or any background file document relating to such written determination (as such terms are defined in section 6110(b)) which is not open to public inspection under section 6110,

but such term does not include data in a form which cannot be associated with, or otherwise identify, directly or indirectly, a particular taxpayer. Nothing in the preceding sentence, or in any other provision of law, shall be construed to require the disclosure of standards used or to be used for the selection of returns for examination, or data used or to be used for determining such standards, if the Secretary determines that such disclosure will seriously impair assessment, collection, or enforcement under the internal revenue laws.

(3) TAXPAYER RETURN INFORMATION. — The term "taxpayer return information" means return information as defined in paragraph (2) which is filed, with, or furnished to, the Secretary by or on behalf of the taxpayer to whom such return information relates.

* * *

(6) TAXPAYER IDENTITY. — The term "taxpayer identity" means the name of a person with respect to whom a return is filed, his mailing address, his taxpayer identifying number (as described in section 6109), or a combination thereof.

* * *

(8) DISCLOSURE. — The term "disclosure" means the making known to any person in any manner whatever a return or return information. . . .

With respect to penalties for failure to report by an employer (other than a Federal or other governmental entity, section

1144(c)(9) [sic (8)] requires the Secretary of Health and Human Services to impose a penalty "as described in part II of subchapter B of chapter 68 of the Internal Revenue Code of 1986," 26 U.S.C.A. 6721-6724. Section 6723 thereof provides as follows:

> FAILURE TO COMPLY WITH OTHER INFORMATION REPORTING REQUIREMENTS
>
> In the case of a failure by any person to comply with a specified information reporting requirement on or before the time prescribed therefor, such person shall pay a penalty of $50 for each such failure, but the total amount imposed on such person for all such failures during any calendar year shall not exceed $100,000.

Section 6724 provides:

> WAIVER; DEFINITIONS AND SPECIAL RULES
>
> (a) REASONABLE CAUSE WAIVER. — No penalty shall be imposed under this part with respect to any failure if it is shown that such failure is due to reasonable cause and not to willful neglect.
>
> (b) PAYMENT OF PENALTY. — Any penalty imposed by this part shall be paid on notice and demand by the Secretary and in the same manner as tax.
>
> * * *
>
> (d) DEFINITIONS. — For purposes of this part —
>
> * * *
>
> (3) SPECIFIED INFORMATION REPORTING REQUIREMENT. — The term "specified information reporting requirement" means —
>
> * * *
>
> (B) any requirement contained in the regulations prescribed under section 6109 that a person —
>
> (i) include his TIN on any return, statement, or other document (other than an information return or payee statement),
>
> (ii) furnish his TIN to another person, or
>
> (iii) include on any return, statement, or other document (other than an information return or payee statement)

made with respect to another person the TIN of such person[.]

For regulatory citations, see Chapter 8

§ 4:16.1 PUBLIC ACCESS TO INFORMATION ABOUT HOSPITAL FINANCIAL INTERESTS IN ENTITIES TO WHICH REFERRALS OF PATIENTS ARE MADE — Sections 1146 and 1866(a)(1)(S) [42 U.S.C.A. 1320b-16 and 1395cc(a)(1)(S)]

Summary

Section 1866(a)(1) of the Social Security Act, as amended, 42 U.S.C.A. 1395cc, requires those who wish to become Medicare providers to file provider agreements with the Secretary of Health and Human Services. Provider agreements have been part of Medicare since the program was enacted in 1965. They obligate providers who accept Medicare assignments of benefits to limit their charges to beneficiaries and to comply with numerous other requirements as well.

Section 1866(a)(1)(S) provides that if a hospital provider has a financial interest in an entity to which individuals are referred for post-hospital care (as part of the hospital discharge planning process described in section 1861(ee)(2)(H)(ii), 42 U.S.C.A. 1395x(ee)(2)(H)(ii)), the hospital must maintain and disclose to the Secretary information on:

- the nature of the financial interest,
- the number of individuals who were discharged from the hospital and who were identified as requiring home health services, and
- the percentage of such individuals who received such services from such provider (or another such provider).

This also applies if the hospital has a financial interest in an entity and the hospital makes a referral to an entity in which the intermediate entity has a financial interest. It applies when the hospital provider makes a referral to another entity which has a financial interest (directly or indirectly) with such hospital and such an entity; and it applies when the entity to which the referral has been made has a financial interest in the hospital making the referral.

This provision, which was added by section 4321(b) of the Balanced Budget Act of 1997, P.L. 105–33, obligates the Secretary to specify in regulations the nature of the financial interest which brings section 1866(a)(1)(S) into play.

The point of this reporting requirement is to identify situations where hospitals may profit, perhaps inappropriately, through referrals to providers of post-hospital care as part of the discharge planning process mandated by section 1861(ee). That statute required the Secretary to develop guidelines and standards for hospital discharge planning processes to ensure timely and smooth transition to the most appropriate type of and setting for post-hospital or rehabilitative care.

Section 1861(ee)(2)(H), which was added by section 4321(a)(2) of the Balanced Budget Act of 1997, specifies that a discharge plan:

- may not specify or otherwise limit the qualified provider which may provide post-hospital home health services,
- must identify (in a form and manner specified by the Secretary) any entity to whom the individual is referred in which the hospital has a disclosable financial interest, or which has such an interest in the hospital.

This applies to discharges occurring on or after November 3, 1997.

Finally, with that reporting system in place, section 1146, 42 U.S.C.A. 1320b(16), specifies that the Secretary shall make available to the public, in a form and manner specified by the Secretary, the information which the Secretary receives pursuant to section 1866(a)(1)(S). This became effective August 5, 1997, pursuant to section 4312(c) of the Balanced Budget Act.

Statutory Provisions

With respect to the reporting of financial interests required for hospital providers as part of the Medicare provider agreement, section 1866(a)(1)(S), 42 U.S.C.A. 1395cc(a)(1)(S), provides:

> (a)(1) Any provider of services (except a fund designated for purposes of section 1814(g) [42 U.S.C.A. 1395f(a)] and section 1835(e) [42 U.S.C.A. 1395n(e)]) shall be qualified to participate under this title and shall be eligible for payments under this title if it files with the Secretary an agreement —

* * *

(S) in the case of a hospital that has a financial interest (as specified by the Secretary in regulations) in an entity to which individuals are referred as described in section1861(ee)(2)(H)(ii) [42 U.S.C.A. 1395x(ee)(2)(H)(ii)] , or in which such an entity has such a financial interest, or in which another entity has such a financial interest (directly or indirectly) with such hospital and such an entity, to maintain and disclose to the Secretary (in a form and manner specified by the Secretary) information on —

(i) the nature of such financial interest,

(ii) the number of individuals who were discharged from the hospital and who were identified as requiring home health services, and

(iii) the percentage of such individuals who received such services from such provider (or another such provider).

With respect to the discharge planning process required of hospitals, section 1861ee, 42 U.S.C.A. 1395x(ee), provides:

(1) A discharge planning process of a hospital shall be considered sufficient if it is applicable to services furnished by the hospital to individuals entitled to benefits under this title and if it meets the guidelines and standards established by the Secretary under paragraph (2).

(2) The Secretary shall develop guidelines and standards for the discharge planning process in order to ensure a timely and smooth transition to the most appropriate type of and setting for post-hospital or rehabilitative care. The guidelines and standards shall include the following:

(A) The hospital must identify, at an early stage of hospitalization, those patients who are likely to suffer adverse health consequences upon discharge in the absence of adequate discharge planning.

(B) Hospitals must provide a discharge planning evaluation for patients identified under subparagraph (A) and for other patients upon the request of the patient, patient's representative, or patient's physician.

(C) Any discharge planning evaluation must be made on a timely basis to ensure that appropriate arrangements for post-hospital care will be made before discharge and to avoid unnecessary delays in discharge.

(D) A discharge planning evaluation must include an evaluation of a patient's likely need for appropriate post-hospital services, including hospice services, and the availability of those services including the availability of home health services through individuals and entities that participate in the program under this title and that serve the area in which the patient resides and that request to be listed by the hospital as available.

(E) The discharge planning evaluation must be included in the patient's medical record for use in establishing an appropriate discharge plan and the results of the evaluation must be discussed with the patient (or the patient's representative).

(F) Upon the request of a patient's physician, the hospital must arrange for the development and initial implementation of a discharge plan for the patient.

(G) Any discharge planning evaluation or discharge plan required under this paragraph must be developed by, or under the supervision of, a registered professional nurse, social worker, or other appropriately qualified personnel.

(H) Consistent with section 1802 [42 U.S.C.A. 1395a, which guarantees beneficiaries the freedom to choose persons and entities to provide health care goods and services for them], the discharge plan shall—

(i) not specify or otherwise limit the qualified provider which may provide post-hospital home health services, and

(ii) identify (in a form and manner specified by the Secretary) any entity to whom the individual is referred in which the hospital has a disclosable financial interest (as specified by the Secretary consistent with section 1866(a)(1)(S)) or which has such an interest in the hospital.

With regard to public access to hospital referrals for post-hospital care, section 1146, 42 U.S.C.A. 1320b-16, provides:

The Secretary shall make available to the public, in a form and manner specified by the Secretary, information disclosed to the Secretary pursuant to section 1866(a)(1)(S).

For regulatory citations, see Chapter 8

§ 4:17 TERMINATING CONTRACTS WITH PEER REVIEW ORGANIZATIONS — Section 1153 [42 U.S.C.A. 1320c-2]

Summary

When Medicare was enacted, one way to control costs was to exclude from coverage items and services not reasonable and necessary for health care. That meant someone with medical expertise had to make judgments about "reasonableness" and "necessity." In time, that gave rise to Peer Review Organizations (PRO's), not only to help control the seemingly endless rise in health care costs, but also to help improve the quality of health care in the nation.

Cost Control — Exclusions from Coverage under Medicare: With respect to cost control, section 1862(a)(1), 42 U.S.C.A. 1395y(a)(1), excludes the following from coverage under Medicare:

1. items or services which are not reasonable and necessary for diagnosis or treatment of illness or injury or to improve functioning of a malformed body member;

2. items or services pertaining to pneumococcal and influenza vaccines, and to their administration, and to hepatitis B vaccine and its administration when furnished to an individual at high or intermediate risk of contracting hepatitis B, if they are not reasonable and necessary for prevention of illness;

3. items or services pertaining to hospice care which are not reasonable and necessary for palliation or management of terminal illness;

4. clinical care items or services provided with respect to research and experimentation conducted by, or under contract with, the Prospective Payment Assessment Commission (ProPAC) or the Secretary, which are not reasonable and necessary to carry out the purposes of section 1886(e)(6), 42 U.S.C.A. 1395ww(e)(6), which pertains to ProPAC's obligation to assess safety, efficacy, and cost-effectiveness of new and existing medical and surgical procedures;

5. items or services with respect to research conducted pursuant to section 1142, 42 U.S.C.A. 1320b-12, which pertains to the obligation of the Secretary of Health and Human Services to conduct and support research regarding the outcomes, effectiveness, and appropriateness of health care services and to evaluate alternative services and procedures, which are not reasonable and necessary to carry out such purposes;

◆ NOTE: Section 1142 was added by section 6103(b) of P.L. 101-239, the Omnibus Budget Reconciliation Act of 1989, effective December 19, 1989. Prior thereto, the reference in section 1862(a) was to section 1875(c), 42 U.S.C.A. 1395ll(c), which pertained to ongoing obligations of the Secretary of Health and Human Services, via the National Center for Health Services Research and Health Care Technology, to study appropriateness, necessity, and effectiveness of selected medical treatments and surgical procedures, and only items and services not reasonable and necessary to carry out such research purposes were excluded from Medicare coverage;

6. screening mammography performed after December 1990, pursuant to section 4163(b)(2) of P.L. 101-508, the Omnibus Budget Reconciliation Act of 1990 (OBRA 90), more frequently than is provided under section 1834(c)(2), 42 U.S.C.A. 1395m(c)(2), which is once for a woman over 34 but under 40, which requires 11-month intervals for women over 39 but under 50 if at high risk of developing breast cancer, or 23-month intervals if not at high risk, which requires 11-month intervals for a woman over 49 but under 65, and which requires 23-month intervals for a woman over 64; and screening pap smears performed more frequently than is provided under section 1861(nn), 42 U.S.C.A. 1395x(nn), which is once every three years, except when the Secretary specifies otherwise with regard to women at high risk of developing cervical cancer; and

7. items or services with respect to in-home care for chronically dependent individuals which are not reasonable and necessary to assure that the health and condition of the individual is maintained in the individual's noninstitutional residence.

In addition, among other exclusions not here relevant, section 1862(a)(9) excludes expenses for custodial care other than authorized hospice care.

Purpose of PRO's: Section 1862(g), 42 U.S.C.A. 1395(g), provides that to determine whether these exclusions should be applied to a given Medicare beneficiary, to promote the effective, efficient, and economical delivery of health care services, and to promote high quality of such services under Medicare, the Secretary must enter into contracts with utilization and quality control peer review organizations pursuant to part B of title XI, 42 U.S.C.A. 1151 et seq.

Definition/Composition: Section 1152, 42 U.S.C.A. 1320c-1, defines "utilization and quality control peer review organization" as an entity —

1. which is comprised of a substantial number of the licensed doctors of medicine and osteopathy engaged in the practice of medicine or surgery in the area who are representative of practicing physicians in the area;

2. which has available to it the services of a sufficient number of licensed doctors of medicine or osteopathy engaged in the practice of medicine or surgery in such area to assure adequate peer review of services provided by the various medical specialties and subspecialties;

3. which is able, in the judgment of the Secretary, to perform peer review functions effectively and efficiently, and to perform review of the pattern of quality of care in an area of medical practice where performance is measured against objective criteria which define acceptable and adequate practice; and

4. which has at least one individual who is a representative of consumers on its governing body.

Regional Scope: Section 1153(a)(1), 42 U.S.C.A. 1320c-2(a)(1), required the Secretary to establish geographic areas throughout the United States with respect to which PRO contracts were to be made. But it also provided for him to use PRO areas established under section 1152 of the Social Security Act as in effect immediately prior to enactment of the Peer Review Improvement Act of 1982, within the Tax Equity and Fiscal Responsibility Act of 1982, P.L. 97-248, Title I, subtitle C, September 2, 1982. (The predecessor of a PRO was called a Professional Standards Review Organization, or PSRO.) That requirement, however, is subject to provisions of section 1153(a)(2).

Pursuant to section 1153(a)(2), in general, PRO areas must be Statewide. Where warranted by the volume of review activity or other factors determined by the Secretary to be relevant, however, Congress authorized the Secretary to establish local or regional areas, provided he takes into account the volume of hospital admissions within each State for which Medicare or Medicaid payments may be made. Any State having fewer than 180,000 admissions annually must have a Statewide PRO. Moreover, no local or regional area may be established which has fewer than 60,000 hospital admissions, including public and private pay patients, under review annually. Furthermore, no local or regional PRO area may be established which is not a self-contained medical service area with a full spectrum of services, including medical specialists' services. These limitations do not apply, however, if the Secretary finds other relevant factors warrant a different decision.

Requirement to Contract/Preference to Prior Contractors: Once the Secretary established PRO areas, section 1153(b) required him to enter into a contract with a PRO for each area if a qualified organization was available in the area and if he and the organization negotiated a contract which the Secretary determined would be carried out in a manner consistent with efficient and effective administration of Title XI, Part B. If more than one organization were qualified for such a contract, however, priority had to be given to the organization with a contract under the prior law.

◆ NOTE: In addition, section 1153(i) prohibits the Secretary from renewing a contract with any organization that is not an in-State organization unless the Secretary, not later than six months before expiration of the contract, published in the Federal Register the date on which the contract expires and the period of time in which an in-State organization could submit a proposal for the contract about to end. Then, if one or more qualified in-State organizations submits a timely proposal, the Secretary may not automatically renew the current contract, but instead must provide for competition as if a new contract were being solicited. For this purpose, an in-State organization is one which has its primary place of business in the State where review will be conducted, or which is owned by a parent corporation with headquarters in that State.

Review Authority: According to section 1154(a)(1), 42 U.S.C.A. 1320c-3(a)(1), a PRO must review, within its jurisdiction and according to its contract, some or all of the professional activities of physicians and other health care practitioners and institutional and noninstitutional providers of health care services with respect to provision of health care services and items for which payment may be made, in whole or in part, by Medicare. That includes health maintenance organizations (HMO's) and competitive medical plans (CMP's).

Review Purposes: One purpose of that review is to determine whether the services and items are or were reasonable and medically necessary and whether they are not allowable under section 1862, as indicated above. Another purpose is to determine whether the quality of such services meets professionally recognized standards of health care. A third purpose is to determine whether services and items proposed to be provided in a hospital or health care facility on an inpatient basis could be provided effectively but more economically on an outpatient basis or in an inpatient health care facility of a different type (for example, in a nursing facility instead of a hospital.)

Payment Determinations: Section 1154(a)(2) provides that, when a PRO makes such a review, it will then determine whether payment shall be made for the services under Medicare. It also provides that the PRO payment determination is conclusive, with exceptions not here relevant.

Contract Requirements: *Types of Cases:* Section 1154(a)(4)(A) requires a PRO, after consultation with the Secretary, to determine types and kinds of cases over which it will exercise review authority. This may by done by type of health care or by diagnosis. Then the PRO must notify the Secretary periodically with respect to such determinations.

Quality of Care: A PRO contract must provide that a reasonable proportion of PRO activities will involve reviewing quality of services. Also, a reasonable allocation of that activity must be made among different cases and settings, including post-acute care settings, ambulatory settings, and health maintenance organizations. In establishing such allocations, a PRO must consider whether there is need to review particular cases or settings because of previous problems with quality of care. It also must consider the cost of such reviews and the likely yield in terms of number and seriousness of quality of care problems likely to discovered. In addition, it must consider the availability and adequacy of alternative quality review and assurance methods.

Review of HMO's and CMP's/Access to Care and Quality of Care: Section 1154(a)(4)(B) requires a PRO to review inpatient and outpatient services provided by health maintenance organizations and competitive medical plans. Such reviews are to determine whether the quality of services meets professionally recognized standards of health care, including appropriateness of the settings where the care was rendered, and to determine whether individuals enrolled in the HMO or CMP have adequate access to health care services provided by the HMO or CMP. The latter determination must be based in part on a survey of individuals enrolled with the HMO or CMP who have not yet used the organization to obtain health care. In relation to this, HMO's and CMP's must maintain a beneficiary outreach program designed to apprise their enrollees about the peer review system, of their rights under that system, and of the method by and purposes for which they may contact the PRO.

Quality of Care Case Selection: With respect to PRO quality of care reviews under section 1154(a)(4), section 1154(f) requires the Secretary, in consultation with appropriate experts, to identify methods that would be available to assist PRO's to identify cases which are more likely than others to be associated with a quality of services that does not meet professionally recognized standards of health care.

◆ NOTE: Pursuant to section 1154(a)(4)(C), the Secretary may provide, by contract under competitive procurement procedures on a State-by-State basis in up to 25 States, for review of HMO' s and CMP's by an appropriate entity, which may be a peer review organization. Nevertheless, the entity selected must meet the requirements of section 1152 to be a PRO, other than the ability to perform review functions not described in section 1154(a)(4)(B), must meet the requirement of section 1153(b)(3) not to be affiliated with, through management, ownership, or common control, a health care facility or association of such facilities within the area it is to service, and must commit to an appropriate level of effort that would not be less than what would be required absent this alternative.

PRO Obligation to Consult with Health Care Professionals: Section 1154(a)(5) requires a PRO to consult with nurses and other professional health care practitioners, other than physicians, and with representatives of institutional and noninstitutional providers of health care services, with respect to the PRO's responsibility to review professional activities of such practitioners and providers.

Application of Professional Standards/National Norms: Section 1154(a)(6)(A) requires a PRO to apply professionally developed norms of care, diagnosis, and treatment, based on typical patterns of practice within the PRO area, as principal points of evaluation and review. Nevertheless, a PRO must take national norms into consideration, where appropriate. Such norms must include types and extent of health care services which are considered within the range of appropriate diagnosis and treatment of such illness or health condition, taking into account, however, differing but acceptable modes of treatment and methods of organizing and delivering care. Moreover, those norms must include the type of health care facility in which health care services which are medically appropriate for such illness or condition can most economically be provided.

Special Consideration for Remote Rural Areas: When applying professional standards, a PRO must take into account, within its established norms, the special problems associated with delivering care in remote rural areas, the availability of service alternatives to inpatient hospitalization, and other appropriate factors that could adversely affect the safety or effectiveness of treatment provided on an outpatient basis. The latter include the distance from a patient' s residence to the site of care, family support, availability of alternative sites of care nearby, and the patient's ability to carry out necessary or prescribed self-care regimens.

Meetings with Hospital Medical and Administrative Personnel: Section 1154(a)(6)(B) requires a PRO, several times a year, to offer one of its physicians to meet at a hospital, or at a regional meeting with medical and administrative staff of each hospital, subject to its review and to discuss the PRO's review of the hospital's or hospitals' services for which Medicare may pay. It also requires a PRO to publish, not less often than once a year, and to distribute to providers and practitioners whose services are subject to its review, a report describing its findings about types of cases in which the PRO has frequently determined that inappropriate or unnecessary care has been provided, that services were rendered in an inappropriate setting, or that services did not meet professionally recognized standards of health care.

Involvement of Health Care Professionals: Section 1154(a)(7) requires a PRO, as necessary and appropriate under its contract, to use services of persons who are practitioners of, or specialists in, the various areas of medicine, including dentistry, or other types of health care. With respect to contracts entered into or renewed after November 5, 1990, pursuant to section 4205(b)(1)(A) of OBRA 90, optometrists and podiatrists also must be included. To the maximum extent practicable, such persons must be engaged in the practice of their respective professions within the area served by the PRO. In addition, with respect to psychiatric and physical rehabilitation services, the PRO must ensure to the extent possible that initial review of such services will be made by a physician trained in psychiatry or physical rehabilitation, as appropriate. Furthermore, the PRO must make such professional inquiries, before or after (or both before and after) provision of services subject to its review, as will facilitate its activities; it must examine pertinent records of any practitioner or provider of health care services providing services under its jurisdiction; and it must inspect the facilities in which care is rendered or services are provided of any practitioner or provider of health care services subject to its jurisdiction.

Cooperation with the Secretary / Special Assistance with Respect to Cataract Surgery: Section 1154(a)(8) requires a PRO to comply with its statutory and contractual obligations and with the Secretary's regulations to carry out provisions of Title XI, Part B, and to comply with requirements of section 1862(a)(15), 42 U.S.C.A. 1395y(a)(15), which pertains to exclusion of claims for services of an assistant at surgery in a cataract operation which did not have prior approval of a PRO or a carrier.

Data Collection and Disclosure Obligations: Section 1154(a)(9) requires a PRO to collect information relevant to its functions and to keep and maintain them in such form as the Secretary may require for purposes of Title XI, Part B. It also requires a PRO to permit access to and use of any such information and records as the Secretary may require for such purposes. The latter is subject, however, to provisions of section 1160, 42 U.S.C.A. 1320c-9, which restricts disclosure of information by PRO's, including any entity which obtains a contract to review HMO's and CMP's under section 1154(a)(4)(C), notwithstanding provisions of the Freedom of Information Act, 5 U.S.C.A. 552. Pursuant to section 4205(d)(1)(A) of OBRA 90, a PRO, after notice and hearing, also must notify the State board or boards responsible for licensing or disciplining a physician when it finds that a physician has furnished services in violation of section 1154(a). This applies to notices of proposed sanctions issued January 4, 1991, or later.

Coordination with Fiscal Intermediaries and Other Organizations: Section 1154(a)(10) requires a PRO to coordinate its activities, including information exchanges, with fiscal intermediaries, carriers, other PRO's, and such other public or private review organizations as may be appropriate. In that regard, see also section 1156(c), 42 U.S.C.A. 1320c-5(c), which requires a PRO to use its influence and authority, and to enlist support of other professional and governmental organizations and agencies to assure compliance with section 1156(a). The latter requires practitioners and other persons, including hospitals and other health care facilities, organizations, and agencies, to provide goods and services economically, only when medically necessary, and of a quality that meets professionally recognized standards. It also requires them to document that they did so as required by a PRO.

Assisting Other Entities with Peer Review: Section 1154(a)(11) requires a PRO, to the extent feasible and appropriate, to make its facilities and resources available for contracting with private and public entities paying for health care in its area for similar review purposes. Section 1154(a)(12) requires a PRO to perform the review, referral, and other functions pertinent to the 100 percent peer review of certain surgical procedures required by section 1164, 42 U.S.C.A. 1320c-13.

Review of Early Hospital Readmission Cases: Section 1154(a)(12) requires a PRO to review early readmission cases to determine if the previous inpatient hospital services and post-hospital services met professionally recognized standards of health care. An early readmission case is defined as one where an individual after discharge from a hospital is readmitted less than 31 days later. Such reviews may, however, be done on a sample basis if the PRO and the Secretary find that appropriate.

Review of Written Complaints about Substandard Medical Care: Section 1154(a)(13) requires a PRO to review all written complaints about substandard quality of health care which are filed with it by a Medicare beneficiary or by a person acting on the beneficiary's behalf. It also must inform the complainant or his representative of the PRO's disposition of the complaint. Furthermore, before concluding that the quality of care complained about does not meet professionally recognized standards of health care, the PRO must provide the practitioner or person concerned reasonable notice and opportunity to discuss the matter.

On-site Reviews: Section 1154(a)(14) requires a PRO to perform "significant" on-site review activities each contract year. That must include on-site review in at least 20 percent of the rural hospitals in the PRO's jurisdiction.

Patient Dumping Allegations: Section 1154(a)(15), which was added by section 4207(a)(1)(B) of OBRA 90, applicable to contracts under Part B January 4, 1991, requires a PRO to provide for a review and report to the Secretary on allegations of "patient dumping" , which is prohibited by section 1867, 42 U.S.C.A. 1395dd. In so doing, the PRO must provide a reasonable opportunity for discussion with the physician and hospital involved, and an opportunity for the physician and hospital to submit additional information before issuing the PRO report to the Secretary.

Conflict of Interest Requirements: To guard against conflicts of interest, section 1154(b) provides that no physician can review health care services provided to a patient if he or she was directly responsible for providing those services. Nor can a physician review health care services provided in or by an institution, organization, or agency, if the physician, or any member of his or her family has, directly or indirectly, a significant financial interest therein. For these purposes, family is defined to include a spouse (unless legally separated under a decree of divorce or separate maintenance), children, whether natural or adopted, grandchildren, parents, and grandparents.

License Requirements for Reviewers: Pursuant to section 1154(c), no PRO may use services of any individual not a duly licensed doctor of medicine, osteopathy, or dentistry to make final denial decisions with respect to professional conduct of any other duly licensed doctor of medicine, osteopathy, or dentistry, or with respect to any act performed by any duly licensed doctor of medicine, osteopathy, or dentistry in the exercise of his or her profession. Effective with respect to PRO contracts entered into or renewed on or after November 5, 1990, PRO's must also include the services of licensed optometrists and podiatrists, as appropriate, in making final denial decisions. This puts the "peer" into peer review.

Review of Ambulatory Surgical Procedures: Section 1154(d) requires a PRO to review all ambulatory surgical procedures specified in section 1833(i)(1)(A), 42 U.S.C.A. 1395l(i)(1)(A), which are performed in the PRO's area. The latter statute requires the Secretary, in consultation with appropriate medical organizations, to specify surgical procedures appropriately performed on an inpatient basis in a hospital which also can be performed safely on an ambulatory basis in an ambulatory surgical center or hospital outpatient department. At the Secretary's discretion, however, this review may be done on a sample basis.

Determinations that Hospital Care is Not Required/Notice to Medicare Beneficiaries: Section 1154(e) provides that if a hospital has determined that a patient no longer requires inpatient hospital care, and if the attending physician agrees, the hospital may notify the patient or the patient's representative of that determination. If it does, the notice must meet conditions prescribed by the Secretary pursuant to section 1879, 42 U.S.C.A. 1395pp. Section 1879 pertains to continuation of payment for hospital care when beneficiaries and providers or other practitioners did not know, and could not have been expected reasonably to know, that payment would be denied.

◆ NOTE: Prior to enactment of section 421(c) of the Medicare, Medicaid, and SCHIP Benefits Improvement and Protection Act of 2000, P.L. 106–544, December 21, 2000, there were three additional situations where Medicare beneficiaries or their representatives may or must be given notice that further hospital care is not required:

1. If a hospital has determined that a patient no longer requires inpatient hospital care, but the attending physician does not agree, the hospital may request a PRO to review its decision. If it does, the hospital must notify the patient of that request.

2. If a patient, or a patient's representative, receives a notice that a hospital and the attending physician agree that further hospital care is not required, the patient or the patient's representative may request the appropriate PRO to review that decision. The PRO must make that review, then provide notice, by telephone and in writing, to the patient or representative and to the hospital and attending physician of its finding. Such reviews must be conducted regardless whether the hospital will charge for continued hospital care or whether the patient will be liable to pay for such continued care. If the request comes to the PRO while the patient is still an inpatient in a hospital, and not later than noon of the first working day after receiving notice that the hospital and attending physician have agreed further hospital care is not required, the hospital must provide the PRO the records necessary to make the review by close of business on that first working day. Then the PRO must provide notice of its finding not later than one full working day after it received the request and the records.

3. If a patient or a patient's representative makes a request, as indicated in 2 above, not later than noon of the first working day after the patient or the patient's representative receives notice that the hospital and the attending physician agree that further hospital care is not required, and if the patient or the patient's representative

did not know, and could not have been expected reasonably to know that payment for continued hospital care would not be made by Medicare, as required by section 1879(a)(2), then the hospital may not charge the patient for inpatient hospital services furnished before noon of the day after the patient or patient's representative received notice of the PRO decision.

In any case described in 1 or 2 above, the PRO must solicit the views of the patient involved or that patient's representative.

That change became effective with respect to initial determinations made on or after October 1, 2002.

◆ NOTE: Pursuant to section 1158, 42 U.S.C.A. 1320c-7, States with approved Medicaid plans may provide for functions specified in section 1154 to be performed in an area by contract with a PRO having a contract with the Secretary. If they do, they will receive Federal matching funds at the rate of 75 percent for expenditures related thereto.

◆ NOTE ALSO: In addition to the foregoing obligations, section 1164 obligated PRO's to perform 100 percent reviews of certain surgical procedures. That obligation ended when section 1164 was repealed, effective October 31, 1994, by section 146(a)(1) of the Social Security Act Amendments of 1994, P.L. 103-432. For a discussion of section 1164 as it applied prior to repeal, see § 4:21.

PRO Sanction Authority: With respect to PRO duties, section 1156, 42 U.S.C.A. 1320c-5, sets forth the role of a PRO in sanctioning health care practitioners and other persons, including hospitals and health care facilities, organizations, and agencies participating in programs funded under the Social Security Act.

Contract Duration and Renewal Criteria: Generally, PRO contracts are for three years and renewable on a triennial basis. Nevertheless, section 1153(c)(2) gives the Secretary authority to evaluate the quality and effectiveness of the organization in carrying out its obligations under the contract. In doing so, he must place emphasis on performance of the PRO in educating providers and practitioners, particularly those in rural areas, concerning the PRO review process and PRO criteria.

Notice of Intent Not to Renew A Contract: According to section 1153(c)(4), if the Secretary does not intend to renew a PRO contract, he must give the PRO notice 90 days prior to expiration of its contract. He also must provide the organization an opportunity to present data, interpretations of data, and other information pertinent to its performance under the contract. Then the Secretary must review what the PRO submits in a timely manner.

Review Rights/Review Panels: If the Secretary determines that a PRO does not meet the definition requirements of section 1152, or if the Secretary determines that a PRO has failed substantially to carry out its contract, or is carrying out the contract in a manner inconsistent with efficient and effective administration of Title XI, Part B, section 1153(c)(6) authorizes the Secretary to terminate the contract upon 90 days notice. This may be done, however, only after the PRO has had an opportunity to submit data and have it reviewed by a panel appointed by the Secretary.

Composition of Review Panels: Pursuant to section 1153(d)(3), such panels must consist of not more than five individuals, each of whom is a member of a utilization and quality control peer review organization with a contract under Title XI, Part B. Section 1153(d)(1) requires them to conduct their review, then report their findings in a timely manner to the Secretary. A copy of such a report must be given to a PRO under review.

Secretarial Review: Pursuant to section 1153(d)(2), the Secretary may accept or not accept a review panel's findings. After receiving its report, he may, with concurrence of the PRO, amend the contract to modify the scope of functions to be carried out by the organization, or he may amend the contract in any other manner. In the case of a substantial failure to comply with contract requirements, however, the Secretary may terminate a contract upon 90 days notice after the panel has submitted its report; earlier, if the PRO agrees.

Interim Transfer of Peer Review Responsibilities: After the Secretary has given notice of intent to terminate a PRO contract and prior to the time he enters into a contract with another PRO, the Secretary may transfer review responsibilities of the organization under the contract being terminated to another PRO or to a fiscal intermediary with an agreement under section 1816, 42 U.S.C.A. 1395h, which pertains to processing claims for benefits under Part A of Title XVIII, or to a carrier with a contract under section 1842, 42 U.S.C.A. 1395u, which pertains to processing claims for benefits under Part B of Title XVIII.

Applicable Law: Pursuant to section 1153(e)(1), the Secretary's contracting authority under Title XI, Part B, may be carried out without regard to any law relating to making, performance, amendment, or modification of contracts of the United States which the

Secretary finds inconsistent with the purposes of Title XI, Part B. Moreover, he may use different contracting methods with respect to different geographical areas. The sole exception to this applies when a PRO is being required to carry out functions in addition to those required when the Secretary entered into or renewed his contract with the organization. In that case, the Secretary must negotiate necessary contractual modifications, including appropriate adjustment of reimbursement, before requiring the PRO to carry out the additional functions.

Judicial Review: Pursuant to section 1153(f), any determination by the Secretary to terminate or not to renew a contract under section 1153 is not subject to judicial review.

Criteria for Evaluating PRO Performance/Publication of New Policies or Procedures: Section 1153(h) requires the Secretary to publish in the Federal Register any new policy or procedure which he adopts which affects substantially the performance of contract obligations of PRO's not less than 30 days before they take effect, subject only to any other statutory deadlines. It also requires the Secretary to publish in the Federal Register the general criteria and standards used to evaluate the efficient and effective performance of PRO obligations, with opportunity for public comment thereon. Finally, it provides that the Secretary must regularly furnish each PRO with a report documenting its performance in relation to the performance of other PRO's with contracts under Title XI, Part B.

Statutory Provisions

With respect to exclusions from coverage under Medicare relevant to PRO's, section 1862(a), 42 U.S.C.A. 1395y(a), as amended by section 201(a)(1) of P.L. 101-234, the Medicare Catastrophic Coverage Repeal Act of 1989, and sections 6103(b)(3)(B) and 6115(b) of P.L. 101-239, the Omnibus Budget Reconciliation Act of 1989, provides in pertinent part:

> Notwithstanding any other provision of this title, no payment may be made under part A or part B for any expenses incurred for items or services —
>
> (1) (A) which, except for items and services described in a succeeding subparagraph [Pursuant to section 4163(d)(2)(A) of P.L. 101-508, the Omnibus Budget Reconciliation Act of 1990 (OBRA 90), applicable to screening

mammography performed after December 1990, "a succeeding subparagraph" replaced "subparagraph (B), (C), (D), or (E)"; "and" was deleted at the end of subparagraph (1)(D); ", and" was substituted for the period at the end of subparagraph (1)(E); subparagraph (1)(F) was added. Also, section 4163(d)(2)(B) of OBRA 90 added "or under paragraph (1)(F)" after "(1)(B)" in paragraph (a)(7).], are not reasonable and necessary for the diagnosis or treatment of illness or injury or to improve the functioning of a malformed body member,

(B) in the case of items and services described in section 1861(s)(10) [42 U.S.C.A. 1395x(s)(10), which pertains to pneumococcal, influenza, and hepatitis B vaccines and their administration], which are not reasonable and necessary for the prevention of illness,

(C) in the case of hospice care, which are not reasonable and necessary for the palliation or management of terminal illness,

(D) in the case of clinical care items and services provided with the concurrence of the Secretary and with respect to research and experimentation conducted by, or under contract with, the Prospective Payment Assessment Commission or the Secretary, which are not reasonable and necessary to carry out the purposes of section 1886(e)(6) [42 U.S.C.A. 1395ww(e)(6), which pertains to ProPAC's obligation to assess safety, efficacy, and cost-effectiveness of new and existing medical and surgical procedures],

(E) in the case of research conducted pursuant to section 1142, [42 U.S.C.A. 1320b-12, which pertains to the obligation of the Secretary of Health and Human Services to conduct and support research regarding the outcomes, effectiveness, and appropriateness of health care services and to evaluate alternative services and procedures], which is not reasonable and necessary to carry out the purposes of that section, and

(F) in the case of screening mammography, which is performed more frequently than is provided under 1834(c)(2) [42 U.S.C.A. 1395m(c)(2); 1834(c) was added by section 4163(b)(2) of OBRA 90, applicable to screening mammography performed after December 1990. Frequency varies by age: once for a woman over 34 but under 40; 11-month intervals for women over 39 but under 50, if at high risk of developing breast cancer, but 23-month intervals for those not at high risk; 11-month intervals for a woman over 49 but under 65; and 23-month intervals for a woman over 64.] or which is not conducted by a facility described in section 1834(c)(1)(B), and in the case of a screening pap smear, which is performed more frequently than is provided under 1861(nn) [42 U.S.C.A. 1395x(nn), which is once every three years, except when the Secretary specifies otherwise with regard to women at high risk of developing cervical cancer;

◆ NOTE: Section 145(c)(1) of the Social Security Act Amendments of 1994, P.L. 103-432, substituted "or which is not conducted by a facility described in section 1834(c)(1)(B)", for "or which does not meet the standards established under 1834(c)(3)." That change applies to mammography furnished by a facility on and after the first date that the certificate requirements of section 354(b) of the Public Health Service Act apply to such mammography conducted by such facility.

* * *

(9) where such expenses are for custodial care (except, in the case of hospice care, as is otherwise permitted under paragraph (1)(C))[.]

◆ NOTE: Prior to amendment by section 201(a)(1) of P.L. 101-234, the Medicare Catastrophic Coverage Repeal Act of 1989, and sections 6103(b)(3)(B) and 6115(b) of P.L. 101-239, the Omnibus Budget Reconciliation Act of 1989, the relevant portions of section 1862(a), as indicated above, read as follows:

Notwithstanding any other provision of this title, no payment may be made under part A or part B for any expenses incurred for items or services —

(1) (A) which, except for items and services described in a succeeding subparagraph, are not reasonable and necessary for the diagnosis or treatment of illness or injury or to improve the functioning of a malformed body member,

(B) in the case of items and services described in section 1861(s)(10) [42 U.S.C.A. 1395x(s)(10), which pertains to pneumococcal, influenza, and hepatitis B vaccines and their administration], which are not reasonable and necessary for the prevention of illness,

(C) in the case of hospice care, which are not reasonable and necessary for the palliation or management of terminal illness,

(D) in the case of clinical care items and services provided with the concurrence of the Secretary and with respect to research and experimentation conducted by, or under contract with, the Prospective Payment Assessment Commission or the Secretary, which are not reasonable and necessary to carry out the purposes of section 1886(e)(6) [42 U.S.C.A. 1395ww(e)(6), which pertains to ProPAC's obligation to assess safety, efficacy, and cost-effectiveness of new and existing medical and surgical procedures],

(E) in the case of research conducted pursuant to section 1875(c) [42 U.S.C.A. 1395ll(c), which pertained to ongoing obligations of the Secretary of Health and Human Services, via the National Center for Health Services Research and Health Care Technology, to study appropriateness, necessity, and effectiveness of selected medical treatments and surgical procedures], which is not reasonable and necessary to carry out the purposes of that section,

(F) in the case of screening mammography, which is performed more frequently than is covered under section 1834(e)(2) [42 U.S.C.A. 1395m(e)(2), which was once for a woman over 34 but under 40 years of age, once every 11 months after a previous screening for every woman over 39 but under 50 years of age who is at high risk of developing breast cancer, once every 23 months after a previous screening for every woman over 39 but under 50 who is not at high risk of developing breast cancer, and once every 11 months after a previous screening for a woman over 49 but under 65] or which does not meet the standards established under section 1834(e)(3) [42 U.S.C.A. 1395m(e)(3), which pertained to safety and accuracy]; and

(G) in the case of in-home care for chronically dependent individuals, which is not reasonable and necessary to assure the health and condition of the individual is maintained in the individual's noninstitutional residence;

* * *

(9) where such expenses are for custodial care (except, in the case of hospice care, as is otherwise permitted under paragraph (1)(C))[.]

Section 1862(g), 42 U.S.C.A. 1395y(g), then relates review of these exclusions to PRO's by providing:

The Secretary shall, in making the determinations under paragraphs (1) and (9) of subsection (a), and for the purposes of promoting the effective, efficient, and economical delivery of health care services, and of promoting the quality of services of the type for which payment may be made under this title, enter into contracts with utilization and quality control peer review organizations pursuant to part B of title XI of this Act.

Section 1152, 42 U.S.C.A. 1320c-1, defines utilization and quality control peer review organization as follows:

The term "utilization and quality control peer review organization" means an entity which—

(1) (A) is composed of a substantial number of the licensed doctors of medicine and osteopathy engaged in the practice of medicine or surgery in the area and who are representative of the practicing physicians in the area, designated by the Secretary under section 1153 [42 U.S.C.A. 1320c-2] , with respect to which the entity shall perform services under this part, or (B) has available to it, by arrangement or otherwise, the services of a sufficient number of licensed doctors of medicine or osteopathy engaged in the practice of medicine or surgery in such area to assure that adequate peer review of the services provided by the various medical specialties and subspecialties can be assured;

(2) is able, in the judgment of the Secretary, to perform review functions required under section 1154 [42 U.S.C.A. 1320c-3] in a manner consistent with the efficient and effective administration of this part and to perform reviews of the pattern of quality of care in an area of medical practice where actual

performance is measured against objective criteria which define acceptable and adequate practice; and

(3) has at least one individual who is a representative of consumers on its governing body.

Section 1153, 42 U.S.C.A. 13951320c-2, provides:

(a) (1) The Secretary shall establish throughout the United States geographic areas with respect to which contracts under this part will be made. In establishing such areas, the Secretary shall use the same areas as established under section 1152 of this Act as in effect immediately prior to the date of the enactment of the Peer Review Improvement Act of 1982, but subject to the provisions of paragraph (2) [September 2, 1982. See section 143 of the Peer Review Improvement Act of 1982 of the Tax Equity and Fiscal Responsibility Act of 1982, P.L. 97-248].

(2) As soon as practicable after the date of the enactment of the Peer Review Improvement Act of 1982, the Secretary shall consolidate such geographic areas, taking into account the following criteria:

(A) Each State shall generally be designated as a geographic area for purposes of paragraph (1).

(B) The Secretary shall establish local or regional areas rather than State areas only where the volume of review activity or other relevant factors (as determined by the Secretary) warrant such an establishment, and the Secretary determines that review activity can be carried out with equal or greater efficiency by establishing such local or regional areas. In applying this subparagraph the Secretary shall take into account the number of hospital admissions within each State for which payment may be made under title XVIII or a State plan approved under title XIX, with any State having fewer than 180,000 such admissions annually being established as a single statewide area, and no local or regional area being established which has fewer than 60,000 total hospital admissions (including public and private pay patients) under review annually, unless the Secretary determines that other relevant factors warrant otherwise.

(C) No local or regional area shall be designated which is not a self-contained medical service area, having a full spectrum of services, including medical specialists' services.

(b) (1) The Secretary shall enter into a contract with a utilization and quality control peer review organization for each area established under subsection (a) if a qualified organization is available in such area and such organization and the Secretary have negotiated a proposed contract which the Secretary determines will be carried out by such organization in a manner consistent with the efficient and effective administration of this part. If more than one such qualified organization meets the requirements of the preceding sentence, priority shall be given to any such organization which is described in section 1152(1)(A).

(2) (A) Prior to November 15, 1984, the Secretary shall not enter into a contract under this part with any entity which is, or is affiliated with (through management, ownership, or common control), an entity (other than a self-insured employer) which directly or indirectly makes payments to any practitioner or provider whose health care services are reviewed by such entity or would be reviewed by such entity if it entered into a contract with the Secretary under this part. For purposes of this paragraph, an entity shall not be considered to be affiliated with another entity which makes payments (directly or indirectly) to any practitioner or provider, by reason of management, ownership, or common control, if the management, ownership or common control consists only of members of the governing board being affiliated (through management, ownership, or common control) with a health maintenance organization or competitive medical plan which is an "eligible organization" as defined in section 1876(b) [42 U.S.C.A. 1395mm(b)].

(B) If, after November 14, 1984, the Secretary determines that there is no other entity available for an area with which the Secretary can enter into a contract under this part, the Secretary may then enter into a contract under this part with an entity described in subparagraph (A) for such area if such entity otherwise meets the requirements of this part.

(3) (A) The Secretary shall not enter into a contract under this part with any entity which is, or is affiliated with (through management, ownership, or common control), a health care facility, or association of such facilities, within the area served by such entity or which would be served by such entity if it entered into a contract with the Secretary under this part.

(B) For purposes of subparagraph (A), an entity shall not be considered to be affiliated with a health care facility or association of facilities by reason of management, ownership, or common control if the management, ownership, or common control consists only of not more than 20 percent of the members of the governing board of the entity being affiliated (through management, ownership, or common control) with one or more of such facilities or associations.

(c) Each contract with an organization under this section shall provide that —

(1) the organization shall perform the functions set forth in section 1154(a), or may subcontract for the performance of all or some of such functions (and for purposes of paragraphs (2) and (3) of subsection (b), a subcontract under this paragraph shall not constitute an affiliation with the subcontractor);

(2) the Secretary shall have the right to evaluate the quality and effectiveness of the organization in carrying out the functions specified in the contract;

(3) the contract shall be for an initial term of three years and shall be renewable on a triennial basis thereafter;

(4) if the Secretary intends not to renew a contract, he shall notify the organization of his decision at least 90 days prior to the expiration of the contract term, and shall provide the organization an opportunity to present data, interpretations of data, and other information pertinent to its performance under the contract, which shall be reviewed in a timely manner by the Secretary;

(5) the organization may terminate the contract upon 90 days notice to the Secretary;

(6) the Secretary may terminate the contract prior to the expiration of the contract term upon 90 days notice to the organization if the Secretary determines that —

(A) the organization does not substantially meet the requirements of section 1152; or

(B) the organization has failed substantially to carry out the contract or is carrying out the contract in a manner inconsistent with the efficient and effective administration of this part, but only after such organization has had an opportunity to submit data and have such data reviewed by the panel established under subsection (d);

(7) the Secretary shall include in the contract negotiated objectives against which the organization's performance will be judged, and negotiated specifications for use of regional norms, or modifications thereof based on national norms, for performing review functions under the contract; and

(8) reimbursement shall be made to the organization on a monthly basis, with payments for any month being made not later than 14 days after the close of such month.

In evaluating the performance of utilization and quality control peer review organization under contracts under this part, the Secretary shall place emphasis on the performance of such organization in educating providers and practitioners (particularly those in rural areas) concerning the review process and criteria being applied by the organization.

(d) (1) Prior to making any termination under subsection (c)(6)(B), the Secretary must provide the organization with an opportunity to provide data, interpretations of data, and other information pertinent to its performance under the contract. Such data and other information shall be reviewed in a timely manner by a panel appointed by the Secretary, and the panel shall submit a report of its findings to the Secretary in a timely manner. The Secretary shall make a copy of the report available to the organization.

(2) The Secretary may accept or not accept the findings of the panel. After the panel has submitted a report with respect to an organization, the Secretary may, with the concurrence of the organization, amend the contract to modify the scope of the functions to be carried out by the organization, or in any other manner. The Secretary may terminate a contract under the authority of subsection (c)(6)(B) upon 90 days notice after the panel has submitted a report, or earlier if the organization so agrees.

(3) A panel appointed by the Secretary under this subsection shall consist of not more than five individuals, each of whom shall be a member of a utilization and quality control peer review organization having a contract with the Secretary under this part. While serving on such panel individuals shall be paid at a per diem rate not to exceed the current per diem equivalent at the time that service on the panel is rendered for grade GS-18 under section 5332 of title 5, United States Code. Appointments shall be made without regard to title 5, United States Code.

(4) During the period after the Secretary has given notice of intent to terminate a contract, and prior to the time that the Secretary enters into a contract with another utilization and quality control peer review organization the Secretary may transfer review responsibilities of the organization under the contract being terminated to another utilization and quality control peer review organization, or to an intermediary or carrier having an agreement under section 1816 or a contract under section 1842.

(e) (1) Except as provided in paragraph (2), contracting authority of the Secretary under this section may be carried out without regard to any provision of law relating to the making, performance, amendment, or modification of contracts of the United States as the Secretary may determine to be inconsistent with the purposes of this part. The Secretary may use different contracting methods with respect to different geographical areas.

(2) If a peer review organization with a contract under this section is required to carry out a review function in addition to any function required to be carried out at the time the Secretary entered into or renewed the contract with the organization, the Secretary shall, before requiring such organization to carry out such additional function, negotiate the necessary contractual modifications, including modifications that provide for an appropriate adjustment (in light of the cost of such additional function) to the amount of reimbursement made to the organization.

(f) Any determination by the Secretary to terminate or not to renew a contract under this section shall not be subject to judicial review.

(g) The Secretary shall provide that fiscal intermediaries furnish to peer review organizations, each month on a timely basis, data necessary to initiate the review process under section 1154(a) on a timely basis. If the Secretary determines that a fiscal intermediary is unable to furnish such data on a timely basis, the Secretary shall require the hospital to do so.

(h) (1) The Secretary shall publish in the Federal Register any new policy or procedure adopted by the Secretary that affects substantially the performance of contract obligations under this section not less than 30 days before the date on which such policy or procedure is to take effect. This paragraph shall not apply to the extent it is inconsistent with a statutory deadline.

(2) The Secretary shall publish in the Federal Register the general criteria and standards used for evaluating the efficient and effective performance of contract obligations under this section and shall provide opportunity for public comment with respect to such criteria and standards.

(3) The Secretary shall regularly furnish each peer review organization with a contract under this section with a report that documents the performance of the organization in relation to the performance of other such organizations.

Pursuant to section 4092(a) of the Omnibus Budget Reconciliation Act of 1987 (OBRA), P.L. 100-203, with respect to PRO contracts scheduled to be renewed on or after the first day of the eighth month to begin after December 22, 1987, i.e., August, 1988, section 1153(i) provides:

(1) Notwithstanding any other provision of this section, the Secretary shall not renew a contract with any organization that is not an in-state organization (as defined in paragraph (3)) unless the Secretary has first complied with the requirements of paragraph (2).

(2) (A) Not later than six months before the date on which a contract period ends with respect to an organization that is not an in-State organization, the Secretary shall publish in the Federal Register —

(i) the date on which such period ends; and

(ii) the period of time in which an in-state organization may submit a proposal for the contract ending on such date.

(B) If one or more qualified in-State organizations submits a proposal within the period of time specified under subparagraph (A)(ii), the Secretary shall not automatically renew the current contract on a noncompetitive basis, but shall provide for competition for the contract in the same manner as a new contract under subsection (b).

(3) For purposes of this subsection, an in-State organization is an organization that has its primary place of business in the State in which review will be conducted (or, which is owned by a parent corporation the headquarters of which is located in such State).

With respect to functions of Peer Review Organizations, section 1154(a), 42 U.S.C.A. 1320c-3(a), provides in pertinent part:

(a) Any utilization and quality control peer review organization entering into a contract with the Secretary under this part must perform the following functions:

(1) The organization shall review some or all of the professional activities in the area, subject to the terms of the contract and subject to the requirements of subsection (d), of physicians and other health care practitioners and institutional and noninstitutional providers of health care services in the provision of health care services and items for which payment may be made (in whole or in part) under title XVIII (including where payment is made for such services to eligible organizations pursuant to contracts under section 1876 [42 U.S.C.A. 1395mm, which pertains to health maintenance organizations and competitive medical plans]) for the purpose of determining whether—

(A) such services and items are or were reasonable and medically necessary and whether such services and items are not allowable under subsection (a)(1) or (a)(9) of section 1862 [42 U.S.C.A. 1395y(a)(1) and (9);

(B) the quality of such services meets professionally recognized standards of health care; and

(C) in case such services and items are proposed to be provided in a hospital or other health care facility on an inpatient basis, such services and items could, consistent with the provision of appropriate medical care, be effectively provided more economically on an outpatient basis or in an inpatient health care facility of a different type.

If the organization performs such reviews with respect to a type of health care practitioner other than medical doctors, the organization shall establish procedures for the involvement of health care practitioners of that type in such reviews.

◆ NOTE: Pursuant to section 6224(a) of P.L. 101-239, the Omnibus Budget Reconciliation Act of 1989, the preceding sentence applies to PRO contracts entered into after December 19, 1989.

(2) The organization shall determine, on the basis of the review carried out under subparagraphs (A), (B), and (C) of paragraph (1), whether payment shall be made for services under title XVIII. Such determination shall constitute the conclusive determination on those issues for purposes of payment under title XVIII, except that payment may be made if —

(A) such payment is allowed by reason of section 1879 [42 U.S.C.A. 1395pp, which permits payment of Medicare benefits otherwise to be disallowed under section 1862(a)(1) and (a)(9) in cases where providers and beneficiaries did not know, and could not reasonably have been expected to know, that disallowance was required];

(B) in the case of inpatient hospital services or extended care services, the peer review organization determines that additional time is required in order to arrange for postdischarge care, but payment may be continued under this subparagraph for not more than two days, but only in the case where the provider of such services did not know and could not reasonably have been expected to know (as determined under section 1879) that payment would not otherwise be made for such services under title XVIII prior to notification by the organization under paragraph (3);

(C) such determination is changed as the result of any hearing or review of the determination under section 1155 [42 U.S.C.A. 1320c-4]; or

(D) such payment is authorized under section 1861(v)(1)(G) [42 U.S.C.A. 1395x(v)(1)(G), which in certain cases permits payment of Medicare benefits equivalent to those for skilled nursing care in any case in which a hospital provides inpatient services to an individual which are determined by a PRO or the Secretary or his designee to have been not medically necessary but which would constitute medically necessary extended care services if provided by a skilled nursing facility].

The organization shall identify cases for which payment should not be made by reason of paragraph (1)(B) only through the use of criteria developed pursuant to guidelines established by the Secretary. [Pursuant to section 4205(g)(2) of OBRA 90, effective as if enacted by the Consolidated Omnibus Budget Reconciliation Act of 1985, the previous sentence replaced "Determinations that payment should not be made by reason of subparagraph (B) of paragraph (1) shall be made only on the basis of criteria which are consistent with guidelines established by the Secretary."

(3) (A) Subject to subparagraphs (B) and (D), whenever the organization makes a determination that any health care services or items furnished or to be furnished to a patient by any practitioner or provider are disapproved, the organization shall promptly notify such patient and the agency or organization responsible for the payment of claims under title XVIII of this Act of such determination.

(B) The notification under subparagraph (A) with respect to services and items disapproved by reason of subparagraph (A) or (C) of paragraph (1) shall not occur until 20 days after the date that the organization has —

(i) made a preliminary notification to such practitioner or provider of such proposed determination, and

(ii) provided such practitioner or provider an opportunity for discussion and review of the proposed determination.

(C) The discussion and review conducted under subparagraph (B)(ii) shall not affect the rights of a practitioner or provider to a formal reconsideration of a determination under this part (as provided under section 1155 [42 U.S.C.A. 1320c-4, which provides for administrative hearing and judicial review of denied claims]).

(D) The notification under subparagraph (A) with respect to services or items disapproved by reason of paragraph (1)(B) shall not occur until after—

(i) the organization has notified the practitioner or provider involved of the determination and of the practitioner's or provider's right to a formal reconsideration of the determination under section 1155, and

(ii) if the provider or practitioner requests such a reconsideration, the organization has made such a reconsideration.

If a provider or practitioner is provided a reconsideration, such reconsideration shall be in lieu of any subsequent reconsideration to which the provider or practitioner may be otherwise entitled under section 1155, but shall not affect the right of a beneficiary from seeking reconsideration under such section of the organization's determination (after any reconsideration requested by the provider or physician under clause (ii)).

(E) (i) In the case of services and items provided by a physician that were disapproved by reason of paragraph (1)(b), the notice to the patient shall state the following: "In the judgment of the peer review organization, the medical care received was not acceptable under the medicare program. The reasons for the denial have been discussed with your physician."

(ii) In the case of services or items provided by an entity or practitioner other than a physician, the Secretary may substitute the entity or practitioner which provided the services or items for the term "physician" in the notice described in clause (i). [This clause (ii) and redesignation of the prior clause as (i) was added by section 4205(g)(1) of OBRA 90, effective as if enacted by the Consolidated Omnibus Budget Reconciliation Act of 1985. Similarly, the phrase "provided by a physician that were" was added to clause (i), and the phrase "and hospital" was deleted after "discussed with your physician."]

◆ NOTE: Section 6224(b)(1) of P.L. 101-239, the Omnibus Budget Reconciliation Act of 1989, effective December 19, 1989, substituted "subparagraphs (B) and (D)" for "subparagraph (B)" in subsection (a)(3)(A). It also added "with respect to services or items disapproved by reason of subparagraph (A) or (C) of paragraph (1)" after "under subparagraph (A)" in subsection (a)(3)(B). And it added new subparagraphs (D) and (E) to subsection (a)(3).

(4) (A) The organization shall, after consultation with the Secretary, determine the types and kinds of cases (whether by type of health care or diagnosis involved, or whether in terms of other relevant criteria relating to the provision of health care services) with respect to which such organization will, in order to most effectively carry out the purposes of this part, exercise review authority under the contract. The organization shall notify the Secretary periodically with respect to such determinations. Each peer review organization shall provide that a reasonable proportion of its activities are involved with reviewing, under paragraph (1)(B), the quality of services and that a reasonable allocation of such activities is made among the different cases and settings (including post-acute-care settings, ambulatory settings, and health maintenance organizations). In establishing such allocation the organization shall consider (i) whether there is reason to believe that there is a particular need for reviews of particular cases or settings because of previous problems regarding quality of care, (ii) the cost of such reviews and the likely yield of such reviews in terms of number and seriousness of quality of care problems likely to be discovered as a result of such reviews, and (iii) the availability and adequacy of alternative quality review and assurance mechanisms.

(B) The contract of each organization shall provide for the review of services (including both inpatient and outpatient services) provided by eligible organizations pursuant to a risk-sharing contract under section 1876 [42 U.S.C.A. 1395mm, which pertains to HMO's and CMP's] (or subject to review under section 1882(t)(3) [42 U.S.C.A. 1395ss(t)(3), which pertains to certain Medicare supplemental health insurance policies, commonly known as Medicare SELECT policies. Available since 1992 in some States, those policies channel insureds to preferred providers under contract with insurers to deliver health care goods and services at negotiated rates. See section 4358(b)(3) of OBRA 90 as amended by section 171(h)(2)(A)–(B) of the Social Security Act Amendments of 1994. For a more complete discussion, see § 2:54.]) for the purpose of determining whether the quality of such services meets professionally recognized standards of health care, including whether appropriate health care services have not been provided or have been provided in inappropriate settings and whether individuals enrolled with an eligible organization have adequate access to health care services provided by or through such organization (as determined, in part, by a survey of individuals enrolled with the organization who have not yet used the organization to receive such services). The contract of each organization shall also provide that with respect to health care provided by a health maintenance organization or competitive medical plan under section 1876, the organization shall maintain a beneficiary outreach program designed to apprise individuals receiving care under such section of the role of the peer review system, of the rights of the individual under such system, and of the method and purposes for contacting the organization. The previous two sentences shall not apply with respect to a contract year if another entity has been awarded a contract under subparagraph (C). Under the contract the level of effort expended by the organization on reviews under this subparagraph shall be equivalent, on a per enrollee basis, to the level of effort expended by the organization on utilization and quality reviews performed with respect to individuals not enrolled with an eligible organization.

(C) The Secretary may provide, by contract under competitive procurement procedures on a State-by-State basis in up to 25 States, for the review described in subparagraph (B) by an appropriate entity (which may be a peer review organization described in that subparagraph). In selecting among States in which to conduct such competitive procurement procedures, the Secretary may not select States which, as a group, have more than 50 percent of the total number of individuals enrolled with eligible organizations under section 1876. Under a contract with an entity under this subparagraph—

(i) the entity must be, or must meet all the requirements under section 1152 to be, a utilization and quality control peer review organization (other than the ability to perform review functions under this section that are not described in subparagraph (B)),

(ii) the contract must meet the requirement of section 1153(b)(3) [42 U.S.C.A. 1320c-2(b)(3), i.e., the PRO must not be affiliated with, through management, ownership, or common control (defined as having more than 20 percent of the members of the governing board of the affiliate), a health care facility or association of such facilities within the area serviced by the PRO], and

(iii) the level of effort expended under the contract shall be, to the extent practicable, not less than the level of effort that would otherwise be required under the third sentence of subparagraph (B) if this subparagraph did not apply.

(5) The organization shall consult with nurses and other professional health care practitioners (other than physicians described in section 1861(r)(1) [42 U.S.C.A. 1395x(r)(1), which defines physician to include M.D.'s and D.O.'s legally authorized to practice in their respective States]) and with representatives of institutional and noninstitutional providers of health care services, with respect to the organization's responsibility for the review under paragraph (1) of the professional activities of such practitioners and providers.

(6) (A) The organization shall, consistent with the provisions of its contract under this part, apply professionally developed norms of care, diagnosis, and treatment based upon typical patterns of practice within the geographic area served by the organization as principal points of evaluation and review, taking into consideration national norms where appropriate. Such norms with respect to treatment for particular illnesses or health conditions shall include—

(i) the types and extent of the health care services which, taking into account differing, but acceptable, modes of treatment and methods of organizing and delivering care,

are considered within the range of appropriate diagnosis and treatment of such illness or health condition, consistent with professionally recognized and accepted patterns of care; and

(ii) the type of health care facility which is considered, consistent with such standards, to be the type in which health care services which are medically appropriate for such illness or condition can most economically be provided.

As a component of the norms described in clause (i) or (ii), the organization shall take into account the special problems associated with delivering care in remote rural areas, the availability of service alternatives to inpatient hospitalization, and other appropriate factors (such as the distance from a patient's residence to the site of care, family support, availability of proximate alternative sites of care, and the patient's ability to carry out necessary or prescribed self-care regimens) that could adversely affect the safety or effectiveness of treatment provided on an outpatient basis.

(B) The organization shall—

(i) offer to provide, several times each year, for a physician representing the organization to meet (at a hospital or at a regional meeting) with medical and administrative staff of each hospital (the services of which are reviewed by the organization) respecting the organization's review of the hospital's services for which payment may be made under title XVIII, and

(ii) publish (not less often than annually) and distribute to providers and practitioners whose services are subject to review a report that describes the organization's findings with respect to the types of cases in which the organization has frequently determined that (I) inappropriate or unnecessary care has been provided, (II) services were rendered in an inappropriate setting, or (III) services did not meet professionally recognized standards of health care.

(7) The organization, to the extent necessary and appropriate to the performance of the contract, shall—

(A) (i) make arrangements to utilize the services of persons who are practitioners of, or specialists in, the various areas of medicine (including dentistry, optometry, and podiatry [Section 4205(b)(1)(A) of OBRA 90 added optometry and podiatry, applicable to contracts entered into or renewed on or after November 5, 1990.]), or other types of health care, which persons shall, to the maximum extent practicable, be individuals engaged in the practice of their profession within the area served by such organization; and

(ii) in the case of psychiatric and physical rehabilitation services, make arrangements to ensure that (to the extent possible) initial review of such services be made by a physician who is trained in psychiatry or physical rehabilitation (as appropriate).

(B) undertake such professional inquiries either before or after, or both before and after, the provision of services with respect to which such organization has a responsibility for review which in the judgment of such organization will facilitate its activities;

(C) examine the pertinent records of any practitioner or provider of health care services providing services with respect to which such organization has a responsibility for review under paragraph (1); and

(D) inspect the facilities in which care is rendered or services are provided (which are located in such area) of any practitioner or provider of health care services providing services with respect to which such organization has a responsibility for review under paragraph (1).

(8) The organization shall perform such duties and functions and assume such responsibilities and comply with such other requirements as may be required by this part or under regulations of the Secretary promulgated to carry out the provisions of this part or as may be required to carry out section 1862(a)(15) [42 U.S.C.A. 1395y(a)(15), which pertains to exclusion of claims for services of an assistant at surgery in a cataract operation which did not have prior approval of a PRO or a carrier].

(9) (A) The organization shall collect such information relevant to its functions, and keep and maintain such records, in such form as the Secretary may require to carry out the purposes of this part, and shall permit access to and use of any such information and records as the Secretary may require for such purposes, subject to the provisions of section 1160 [42 U.S.C.A. 1320c-9, which restricts disclosure of information by PRO's, notwithstanding provisions of the Freedom of Information Act, 5 U.S.C.A. 552] .

(B) If the organization finds, after reasonable notice to and opportunity for discussion with the physician or practitioner concerned, that the physician or practitioner has furnished services in violation of section 1156(a) and the organization determines that the physician or practitioner should enter into corrective action plan under section 1156(b)(1), the organization shall notify the state board or boards responsible for the licensing or disciplining of the physician or practitioner of its finding and of any action taken as a result of the finding.

◆ NOTE: Prior to amendment by section 156(b)(2)(A) of the Social Security Act Amendments of 1994, effective October 31, 1994, subparagraph (B) read: "If the organization finds, after notice and hearing, that a physician has furnished services in violation of this subsection, the organization shall notify the State board or boards responsible for the licensing or disciplining of the physician of its finding and decision. [Section 4205(d)(1)(A) of OBRA 90 added "A" and this subparagraph (B), applicable to notices of proposed sanctions issued more than 60 days after November 5, 1990.]

(10) The organization shall coordinate activities, including information exchanges, which are consistent with economical and efficient operation of programs among appropriate public and private agencies or organizations including—

(A) agencies under contract pursuant to sections 1816 and 1842 of this Act [42 U.S.C.A. 1395h and 42 U.S.C.A. 1395u, which pertain, respectively, to use of fiscal intermediaries to process Medicare Part A claims and use of carriers to process Medicare Part B claims];

(B) other peer review organizations having contracts under this part; and

(C) other public or private review organizations as may be appropriate.

(11) The organization shall make available its facilities and resources for contracting with private and public entities paying for health care in its area for review, as feasible and appropriate, of services reimbursed by such entities.

◆ NOTE: Former paragraph (12) which obligated PRO's to perform the review, referral, and oter functions required under former section 1164, 42 U.S.C.A. 1320c13, was repealed, effective October 31, 1994, by section 156(a)(2)(A) of the Social Security Act Amendments of 1994.

(12) Notwithstanding paragraph (4), the organization shall perform the review described in paragraph (1) with respect to early readmission cases to determine if the previous inpatient hospital services and the post-hospital services met professionally recognized standards of health care. Such reviews may be performed on a sample basis if the organization and the Secretary determine it to be appropriate. In this paragraph, an "early readmission case" is a case in which an individual, after discharge from a hospital, is readmitted to a hospital less than 31 days after the date of the most recent previous discharge.

(13) The organization shall conduct an appropriate review of all written complaints about the quality of services (for which payment may otherwise be made under title XVIII) not meeting professionally recognized standards of health care, if the complaint is filed with the organization by an individual entitled to benefits for such services under such title (or a person acting on the individual's behalf). The organization shall inform the individual (or representative) of the organization's final disposition of the complaint. Before the organization concludes that the quality of services does not meet professionally recognized standards of health care, the organization must provide the practitioner or person concerned with reasonable notice and opportunity for discussion.

(14) During each year of the contract entered into under section 1153(b), the organization shall perform significant on-site review activities, including on-site review in at least 20 percent of the rural hospitals in the organization's area.

(15) The organization shall provide for a review and report to the Secretary when requested by the Secretary under section 1867(d)(3) [42 U.S.C.A. 1395dd(d)(3), which prohibits "patient dumping" in certain emergency situations]. The organization shall provide reasonable notice of the review to the physician and hospital involved. Within the time period permitted by the Secretary, the organization shall provide a reasonable opportunity for discussion with the physician and hospital involved, and an opportunity for the physician and hospital to submit additional information, before issuing its report to the Secretary under such section. [Paragraph (15) was added by section 4207(a)(1)(B) of OBRA 90, applicable to contracts under Part B 60 days after November 5, 1990.]

(b) (1) No physician shall be permitted to review —

(A) health care services provided to a patient if he was directly responsible for providing such services; or

(B) health care services provided in or by an institution, organization, or agency, if he or any member of his family has, directly or indirectly, a significant financial interest in such institution, organization, or agency.

(2) For purposes of this subsection, a physician's family includes only his spouse (other than a spouse who is legally separated from him under a decree of divorce or separate maintenance), children (including legally adopted children), grandchildren, parents, and grandparents.

(c) No utilization and quality control peer review organization shall utilize the services of any individual who is not a duly licensed doctor of medicine, osteopathy, dentistry, optometry, or podiatry to make final determinations of denial decisions in accordance with its duties and functions under this part with respect to the professional conduct of any other duly licensed doctor of medicine, osteopathy, dentistry, optometry, or podiatry, or any act performed by any duly licensed doctor of medicine, osteopathy, dentistry, optometry, or podiatry in the exercise of his profession. [Section 4205(b)(1)(B) of OBRA 90 added "dentistry, optometry, or podiatry" in lieu of "or dentistry" each place the phrase appears, applicable to contracts entered into or renewed on or after November 5, 1990.]

(d) Each contract under this part shall require that the utilization and quality control peer review organization's review responsibility pursuant to subsection (a)(1) will include review of all ambulatory surgical procedures specified pursuant to section 1833(i)(1)(A) [42 U.S.C.A. 1395l(i)(1)(A), which requires the Secretary to establish, in consultation with appropriate medical organizations, lists of surgical procedures appropriately performed on an inpatient hospital basis which also could be performed in a qualified ambulatory surgical center] which are performed in the area, or, at the discretion of the Secretary (and except as provided in section 1164) a sample of such procedures.

◆ [NOTE: Effective October 31, 1994, section 156(a)(2)(A) of the Social Security Act Amendments of 1994 deleted the phrase "(and except as provided in section 1164)", which preceded "a sample of such procedures."]

(e) (1) If—

(A) a hospital has determined that a patient no longer requires inpatient hospital care, and

(B) the attending physician has agreed with the hospital's determination,

the hospital may provide the patient (or the patient's representative) with a notice (meeting conditions prescribed by the Secretary under section 1879 [42 U.S.C.A. 1395pp, which pertains to limitation on liability of Medicare beneficiaries where their Medicare claims are disallowed] of the determination.

◆ NOTE: Prior to amendment by section 521(c) of the Medicare, Medicaid, and SCHIP Benefits and Improvement Act of 2000, P.L. 106–544, December 21, 2000, subsection (e) had the following additional provisions:

(2) If—

(A) a hospital has determined that a patient no longer requires inpatient hospital care, but

(B) the attending physician has not agreed with the hospital's determination, the hospital may request the appropriate peer review organization to review under subsection (a) the validity of the hospital's determination. If the hospital requests such a review, it shall also notify the patient that the review has been requested.

(3) (A) If a patient (or a patient's representative)—

(i) has received a notice under paragraph (1), and

(ii) requests the appropriate peer review organization to review the determination,

then, the organization shall conduct a review under subsection (a) of the validity of the hospital's determination and shall provide notice (by telephone and in writing) to the patient or representative and the hospital and attending physician involved of the results of the review. Such review shall be conducted regardless of whether or not the hospital will charge for continued hospital care or whether or not the patient will be liable for payment for such continued care.

(B) If a patient (or a patient's representative) requests a review under subparagraph (A) while the patient is still an inpatient in the hospital and not later than noon of the first working day after the date the patient receives the notice under paragraph (1), then—

(i) the hospital shall provide to the appropriate peer review organization the records required to review the determination by the close of business of such first working day, and

(ii) the peer review organization must provide the notice under subparagraph (A) by not later than one full working day after the date the organization has received the request and such records.

(4) If—

(A) a request is made under paragraph (3)(A) not later than noon of the first working day after the date the patient (or patient's representative receives the notice under paragraph (1), and

(B) the conditions described in section 1879(a)(2) [42 U.S.C.A. 1395pp(a)(2), which refers to situations where neither the beneficiary nor the provider knew, or could have reasonably been expected to have known, that a claim for

Medicare payment would be disallowed] with respect to the patient or representative are met,

the hospital may not charge the patient for inpatient hospital services furnished before noon of the day after the date the patient or representative receives notice of the peer review organization's decision.

(5) In any review conducted under paragraph (2) or (3), the organization shall solicit the views of the patient involved (or the patient's representative).

(f) The Secretary, in consultation with appropriate experts, shall identify methods that would be available to assist peer review organizations (under subsection (a)(4)) in identifying those cases which are more likely than others to be associated with a quality of services which does not meet professionally recognized standards of health care.

Finally, with respect to Medicaid programs contracting with PRO's, section 1158, 42 U.S.C.A. 1320c-7, provides:

(a) A State plan approved under title XIX of this Act may provide that the functions specified in section 1154 may be performed in an area by contract with a utilization and quality control peer review organization that has entered into a contract with the Secretary in accordance with the provisions of section 1862(g).

(b) In the event a State enters into a contract in accordance with subsection (a), the Federal share of the expenditures made to the contracting organization for its costs in the performance of its functions under the State plan shall be 75 percent (as provided in section 1903(a)(3)(C) [42 U.S.C.A. 1396b(a)(3)(C), which pertains to Federal matching funds for administrative costs]).

With respect to Christian Science sanatoriums, section 1162, 42 U.S.C.A. 1320c-11, provides:

The provisions of this part [B of Title XI] shall not apply with respect to a Christian Science sanatorium operated, or listed and certified, by the First Church of Christ, Scientist, Boston, Massachusetts.

And, with respect to medical officers in American Samoa, the Northern Mariana Islands, and the Trust Territory of the Pacific Islands, section 1163, 42 U.S.C.A. 1320c-12, provides:

For purposes of applying this part [B of Title XI] to American Samoa, the Northern Mariana Islands, and the Trust Territory of the Pacific Islands, individuals licensed to practice medicine in those places shall be considered to be physicians and doctors of medicine.

For regulatory citations, see Chapter 8

§ 4:18 DISALLOWANCE OF MEDICARE CLAIMS BY PEER REVIEW ORGANIZATIONS — Section 1154 [42 U.S.C.A. 1320c-3]

Summary

When Medicare was enacted, one way to control costs was to exclude from coverage items and services not reasonable and necessary for health care. That meant someone with medical expertise had to make judgments about "reasonableness" and "necessity." In time, that gave rise to Peer Review Organizations (PRO's), not only to help control the seemingly endless rise in health care costs, but also to help improve the quality of health care in the nation.

Cost Control — Exclusions from Coverage under Medicare: With respect to cost control, section 1862(a)(1), 42 U.S.C.A. 1395y(a)(1), now excludes the following from coverage under Medicare:

1. items or services which are not reasonable and necessary for the diagnosis or treatment of illness or injury or to improve the functioning of a malformed body member;

2. items or services pertaining to pneumococcal and influenza vaccines, and to their administration, and to hepatitis B vaccine and its administration when furnished to an individual at high or intermediate risk of contracting hepatitis B, if they are not reasonable and necessary for prevention of illness;

3. items or services pertaining to hospice care which are not reasonable and necessary for palliation or management of terminal illness;

4. clinical care items or services provided with respect to research and experimentation conducted by, or under contract with, the Prospective Payment Assessment Commission (ProPAC) or the Secretary, which are not reasonable and necessary to carry out the purposes of section 1886(e)(6), 42 U.S.C.A. 1395ww(e)(6), which pertains to ProPAC's obligation to assess safety, efficacy, and

cost-effectiveness of new and existing medical and surgical procedures;

5. items or services with respect to research conducted pursuant to section 1142, 42 U.S.C.A. 1320b-12, which pertains to the obligation of the Secretary of Health and Human Services to conduct and support research regarding the outcomes, effectiveness, and appropriateness of health care services and to evaluate alternative services and procedures, which are not reasonable and necessary to carry out such purposes;

◆ NOTE: Section 1142 was added by section 6103(b) of P.L. 101-239, the Omnibus Budget Reconciliation Act of 1989, effective December 19, 1989. Prior thereto, the reference in section 1862(a) was to section 1875(c), 42 U.S.C.A. 1395ll(c), which pertained to ongoing obligations of the Secretary of Health and Human Services, via the National Center for Health Services Research and Health Care Technology, to study appropriateness, necessity, and effectiveness of selected medical treatments and surgical procedures, and only items and services not reasonable and necessary to carry out such research purposes were excluded from Medicare coverage.

6. screening mammography performed after December 1990, pursuant to section 4163(b)(2) of P.L. 101-508, the Omnibus Budget Reconciliation Act of 1990 (OBRA 90), more frequently than is provided under section 1834(c)(2), 42 U.S.C.A. 1395m(c)(2), which is once for a woman over 34 but under 40, which requires 11-month intervals for women over 39 but under 50 if at high risk of developing breast cancer, or 23-month intervals if not at high risk, which requires 11-month intervals for a woman over 49 but under 65, and which requires 23-month intervals for a woman over 64; and screening pap smears performed more frequently than is provided under section 1861(nn), 42 U.S.C.A. 1395x(nn), which is once every three years, except when the Secretary specifies otherwise with regard to women at high risk of developing cervical cancer; and

7. items or services with respect to in-home care for chronically dependent individuals which are not reasonable and necessary to assure that the health and condition of the individual is maintained in the individual's noninstitutional residence;

In addition, among other exclusions not here relevant, section 1862(a)(9) excludes expenses for custodial care other than authorized hospice care.

Purpose of PRO's: Section 1862(g), 42 U.S.C.A. 1395(g), then provides that to determine whether these exclusions should be applied to a given Medicare beneficiary, to promote effective, efficient, and economical delivery of health care services, and to promote high quality of such services under Medicare, the Secretary must enter into contracts with utilization and quality control peer review organizations pursuant to part B of title XI, 42 U.S.C.A. 1151 et seq.

Definition/Composition: Section 1152, 42 U.S.C.A. 1320c-1, defines "utilization and quality control peer review organization" as an entity —

1. which is comprised of a substantial number of the licensed doctors of medicine and osteopathy engaged in the practice of medicine or surgery in the area who are representative of practicing physicians in the area;
2. which has available to it services of a sufficient number of licensed doctors of medicine or osteopathy engaged in the practice of medicine or surgery in such area to assure adequate peer review of services provided by the various medical specialties and subspecialties;
3. which is able, in the judgment of the Secretary, to perform peer review functions effectively and efficiently, and to perform review of the pattern of quality of care in an area of medical practice where performance is measured against objective criteria which define acceptable and adequate practice; and
4. which has at least one individual who is a representative of consumers on its governing body.

Regional Scope: Section 1153(a)(1), 42 U.S.C.A. 1320c-2(a)(1), required the Secretary to establish geographic areas throughout the United States with respect to which PRO contracts were to be made. But it also provided for him to use PRO areas established under section 1152 of the Social Security Act as in effect immediately prior to enactment of the Peer Review Improvement Act of 1982, within the Tax Equity and Fiscal Responsibility Act of 1982, P.L. 97-248, Title I, subtitle C, September 2, 1982. (The predecessor of a PRO was called a Professional Standards Review Organization, or PSRO.) That requirement, however, is subject to provisions of section 1153(a)(2).

Pursuant to section 1153(a)(2), in general, PRO areas must be Statewide. Where warranted by the volume of review activity or other factors determined by the Secretary to be relevant, however, Congress authorized the Secretary to establish local or regional areas, provided he takes into account the volume of hospital admissions within each State for which Medicare or Medicaid payments may be made. Any State having fewer than 180,000 admissions annually must have a Statewide PRO. Moreover, no local or regional area may be established which has fewer than 60,000 hospital admissions, including public and private pay patients, under review annually. Furthermore, no local or regional PRO area may be established which is not a self-contained medical service area with a full spectrum of services, including medical specialists' services. These limitations do not apply, however, if the Secretary finds other relevant factors warrant a different decision.

Requirements to Contract/Preference to Prior Contractors: Once the Secretary established PRO areas, section 1153(b) required him to enter into a contract with a PRO for each area if a qualified organization was available in the area and if he and the organization negotiated a contract which the Secretary determined would be carried out in a manner consistent with efficient and effective administration of Title XI, Part B. If more than one organization were qualified for such a contract, however, priority had to be given to the organization with a contract under the prior law.

◆ NOTE: In addition, section 1153(i) prohibits the Secretary from renewing a contract with any organization that is not an in-State organization unless the Secretary, not later than six months before expiration of the contract, published in the Federal Register the date on which the contract expires and the period of time in which an in-State organization could submit a proposal for the contract about to end. Then, if one or more qualified in-State organizations submits a timely proposal, the Secretary may not automatically renew the current contract, but instead must provide for competition as if a new contract were being solicited. For this purpose, an in-State organization is one which has its primary place of business in the State where review will be conducted, or which is owned by a parent corporation with headquarters in that State.

Review Authority: Section 1154(a)(1), 42 U.S.C.A. 1320c-3(a)(1), requires a PRO to review, within its jurisdiction and according to its contract, some or all of the professional activities of physicians and other health care practitioners and institutional and noninstitutional providers of health care services with respect to health care services and items for which payment may be made, in whole or in part, by Medicare. That includes health maintenance organizations and competitive medical plans.

Review Purposes: One purpose of that review is to determine whether the services and items are or were reasonable and medically necessary and whether they are not allowable under section 1862, as indicated above. Another purpose is to determine whether the quality of such services meets professionally recognized standards of health care. A third purpose is to determine whether services and items proposed to be provided in a hospital or health care facility on an inpatient basis could be provided effectively but more economically on an outpatient basis or in an inpatient health care facility of a different type (for example, in a nursing facility instead of a hospital.)

Payment Determinations: Section 1154(a)(2) provides that, when a PRO makes such a review, it will then determine whether payment shall be made for the services under Medicare. It also provides that the PRO payment determination is conclusive; however, there are exceptions:

1. when payment is allowed pursuant to section 1879, 42 U.S.C.A. 1395pp, which permits payment otherwise to be disallowed under section 1862(a)(1) and (a)(9) in cases where providers and beneficiaries did not know, and could not reasonably have been expected to know disallowance was required;
2. when, with respect to inpatient hospital services or extended care services, the PRO determines additional time is required to arrange for postdischarge care, but no more than two days' payment may be allowed in such cases, and only when the provider did not know, and could not reasonably have been expected to know, payment would not otherwise be made by Medicare, and only prior to notification thereof by the PRO;
3. when an adverse determination by a PRO is changed as a result of a hearing or review thereof pursuant to section 1155, 42 U.S.C.A. 1320c-4, which gives beneficiaries, providers, and practitioners, rights to reconsideration of such matters, to administrative hearings where more than $200 is involved,

and to judicial review where more than $2,000 is involved; and

4. where payment is authorized under section 1861(v)(1)(G), 42 U.S.C.A. 1395x(v)(1)(G), which in certain cases permits payment of benefits equivalent to those for skilled nursing care in any case in which a hospital provides inpatient services to an individual which are determined by the PRO or the Secretary or his designee to have been not medically necessary, but which would constitute medically necessary extended care services if provided by a skilled nursing facility.

Section 1154(a)(2) further provides that PRO determinations not to pay based on substandard quality shall be made only on the basis of criteria which are consistent with guidelines established by the Secretary.

Contract Requirements: *Types of Cases:* Section 1154(a)(4)(A) requires a PRO, after consultation with the Secretary, to determine types and kinds of cases over which it will exercise review authority. This may by done by type of health care or by diagnosis. Then the PRO must notify the Secretary periodically with respect to such determinations.

Quality of Care: A PRO contract must provide that a reasonable proportion of PRO activities will involve reviewing quality of services. Also, a reasonable allocation of that activity must be made among different cases and settings, including post-acute care settings, ambulatory settings, and health maintenance organizations. In establishing such allocations, a PRO must consider whether there is need to review particular cases or settings because of previous problems with quality of care. It also must consider cost of such reviews and likely yield in terms of number and seriousness of quality of care problems likely to discovered. In addition, it must consider the availability and adequacy of alternative quality review and assurance methods.

Review of HMO's and CMP's/Access to Care and Quality of Care: Section 1154(a)(4)(B) requires a PRO to review inpatient and outpatient services provided by health maintenance organizations and competitive medical plans. Such reviews are to determine whether the quality of services meets professionally recognized standards of health care, including appropriateness of the settings where the care was rendered, and to determine whether individuals enrolled in the HMO or CMP have adequate access to health care services provided by the HMO or CMP. The latter determination must be based in part on a survey of individuals enrolled with the HMO or CMP who have not yet used the organization to obtain health care. In relation to this, HMO's and CMP's must maintain a beneficiary outreach program designed to apprise their enrollees about the peer review system, of their rights under that system, and of the method by and purposes for which they may contact the PRO.

Quality of Care Case Selection: With respect to PRO quality of care reviews under section 1154(a)(4), section 1154(f) requires the Secretary, in consultation with appropriate experts, to identify methods that would be available to assist PRO's to identify cases which are more likely than others to be associated with a quality of services which does not meet professionally recognized standards of health care.

◆ NOTE: Pursuant to section 1154(a)(4)(C), the Secretary may provide, by contract under competitive procurement procedures on a State-by-State basis in up to 25 States, for review of HMO' s and CMP's by an appropriate entity, which may be a peer review organization. Nevertheless, the entity selected must meet the requirements of section 1152 to be a PRO, other than the ability to perform review functions not described in section 1154(a)(4)(B), must meet the requirement of section 1153(b)(3) not to be affiliated with, through management, ownership, or common control, a health care facility or association of such facilities within the area it is to service, and must commit to an appropriate level of effort that would not be less than what would be required absent this alternative.

PRO Obligations to Consult with Health Care Professionals: Section 1154(a)(5) requires a PRO to consult with nurses and other professional health care practitioners, other than physicians, and with representatives of institutional and noninstitutional providers of health care services, with respect to the PRO's responsibility to review the professional activities of such practitioners and providers.

Application of Professional Standards/National Norms: Section 1154(a)(6)(A) requires a PRO to apply professionally developed norms of care, diagnosis, and treatment, based on typical patterns of practice within their area, as principal points of evaluation and review. Yet they must take national norms into consideration, where appropriate. Such norms must include types and extent of health care services which are considered within the range of appropriate diagnosis and treatment of such illness or health condition, taking into account, however, differing but acceptable modes of treatment and methods of organizing and delivering care. Moreover, those norms must include the type of health care facility in which health care services medically appropriate for such illness or condition can most economically be provided.

Special Consideration for Remote Rural Areas: When applying professional standards, a PRO must take into account, within its established norms, the special problems associated with delivering care in remote rural areas, the availability of service alternatives to inpatient hospitalization, and other appropriate factors that could adversely affect the safety or effectiveness of treatment provided on an outpatient basis. The latter include the distance from a patient' s residence to the site of care, family support, availability of alternative sites of care nearby, and the patient's ability to carry out necessary or prescribed self-care regimens.

Meetings with Hospital Medical and Administrative Personnel: Section 1154(a)(6)(B) requires a PRO, several times a year, to offer one of its physicians to meet at a hospital, or at a regional meeting with medical and administrative staff of each hospital, subject to its review and to discuss the PRO's review of the hospital's or hospitals' services for which Medicare may pay. It also requires a PRO to publish, not less often than once a year, and to distribute to providers and practitioners whose services are subject to its review, a report describing its findings about types of cases in which the PRO has frequently determined that inappropriate or unnecessary care has been provided, that services were rendered in an inappropriate setting, or that services did not meet professionally recognized standards of health care.

Involvement of Health Care Professionals: Section 1154(a)(7) requires a PRO, as necessary and appropriate under its contract, to use the services of persons who are practitioners of, or specialists in, the various areas of medicine, including dentistry, or other types of health care. With respect to contracts entered into or renewed after November 5, 1990, pursuant to section 4205(b)(1)(A) of OBRA 90, optometrists and podiatrists also must be included. To the maximum extent practicable, such persons must be engaged in the practice of their respective professions within the area served by the PRO. In addition, with respect to psychiatric and physical rehabilitation services, the PRO must ensure to the extent possible that initial review of such services will be made by a physician trained in psychiatry or physical rehabilitation, as appropriate. Furthermore, the PRO must make such professional inquiries, before or after (or both before and after) provision of services subject to its review, as will facilitate its activities; it must examine pertinent records of any practitioner or provider of health care services providing services under its jurisdiction; and it must inspect the facilities in which care is rendered or services are provided of any practitioner or provider of health care services subject to its jurisdiction.

Cooperation with the Secretary / Special Assistance with Respect to Cataract Surgery: Section 1154(a)(8) requires a PRO to comply with its statutory and contractual obligations and with the Secretary's regulations to carry out provisions of Title XI, Part B, and to comply with requirements of section 1862(a)(15), 42 U.S.C.A. 1395y(a)(15), which pertains to exclusion of claims for services of an assistant at surgery in a cataract operation which did not have prior approval of a PRO or a carrier.

Data Collection and Disclosure Obligations: Section 1154(a)(9) requires a PRO to collect information relevant to its functions and to keep and maintain them in such form as the Secretary may require for purposes of Title XI, Part B. It also requires a PRO to permit access to and use of any such information and records as the Secretary may require for such purposes. The latter is subject, however, to provisions of section 1160, 42 U.S.C.A. 1320c-9, which restricts disclosure of information by PRO's, including any entity which obtains a contract to review HMO's and CMP's under section 1154(a)(4)(C), notwithstanding provisions of the Freedom of Information Act, 5 U.S.C.A. 552. Pursuant to section 4205(d)(1)(A) of OBRA 90, a PRO, after notice and hearing, also must notify the State board or boards responsible for licensing or disciplining a physician when it finds that a physician has furnished services in violation of section 1154(a). This applies to notices of proposed sanctions issued January 4, 1991, or later.

Coordination with Fiscal Intermediaries and Other Organizations: Section 1154(a)(10) requires a PRO to coordinate its activities, including information exchanges, with fiscal intermediaries, carriers, other PRO's, and such other public or private review organizations as may be appropriate. In that regard, see also section 1156(c), 42 U.S.C.A. 1320c-5(c), which requires a PRO to use its influence and authority, and to enlist support of other professional and governmental organizations and agencies to assure compliance with section 1156(a). The latter requires practitioners and other persons, including hospitals and other health care facilities, organizations, and agencies, to provide goods and services economically, only when medically necessary, and of a quality that meets professionally recognized standards. It also requires them to document that they did so as required by a PRO.

Assisting Other Entities with Peer Review: Section 1154(a)(11) requires a PRO, to the extent feasible and appropriate, to make its facilities and resources available for contracting with private and public entities paying for health care in its area for similar review purposes. Section 1154(a)(12) requires a PRO to perform review, referral, and other functions pertinent to the 100 percent peer review of certain surgical procedures required by section 1164, 42 U.S.C.A. 1320c-13.

Review of Early Hospital Readmission Cases: Section 1154(a)(12) requires a PRO to review early readmission cases to determine if the previous inpatient hospital services and post-hospital services met professionally recognized standards of health care. An early readmission case is defined as one where an individual after discharge from a hospital is readmitted less than 31 days later. Such reviews may, however, be done on a sample basis if the PRO and the Secretary find that appropriate.

Review of Written Complaints about Substandard Medical Care: Section 1154(a)(13) requires a PRO to review all written complaints about substandard quality of health care filed with it by a Medicare beneficiary or by a person acting on the beneficiary's behalf. It also must inform the complainant or his representative of the PRO' s disposition of the complaint. Furthermore, before concluding that the quality of care complained about does not meet professionally recognized standards of health care, the PRO must provide the practitioner or person concerned reasonable notice and opportunity to discuss the matter.

On-site Reviews: Section 1154(a)(14) requires a PRO to perform "significant" on-site review activities each contract year. That must include on-site review in at least 20 percent of the rural hospitals in the PRO's jurisdiction.

Patient Dumping Allegations: Section 1154(a)(15), which was added by section 4207(a)(1)(B) of OBRA 90, applicable to contracts under Part B January 4, 1991, requires a PRO to provide for a review and report to the Secretary on allegations of "patient dumping" , which is prohibited by section 1867, 42 U.S.C.A. 1395dd. In so doing, the PRO must provide a reasonable opportunity for discussion with the physician and hospital involved, and an opportunity for the physician and hospital to submit additional information before issuing the PRO report to the Secretary.

Conflict of Interest Requirements: To guard against conflicts of interest, section 1154(b) provides that no physician can review health care services provided to a patient if he or she was directly responsible for providing those services. Nor can a physician review health care services provided in or by an institution, organization, or agency, if the physician, or any member of his or her family has, directly or indirectly, a significant financial interest therein. For these purposes, family is defined to include a spouse (unless legally separated under a decree of divorce or separate maintenance), children, whether natural or adopted, grandchildren, parents, and grandparents.

License Requirements for Reviewers: Pursuant to section 1154(c), no PRO may use services of any individual not a duly licensed doctor of medicine, osteopathy, or dentistry to make final denial decisions with respect to professional conduct of any other duly licensed doctor of medicine, osteopathy, or dentistry, or with respect to any act performed by any duly licensed doctor of medicine, osteopathy, or dentistry in the exercise of his or her profession. This, of course, puts the "peer" into peer review.

Review of Ambulatory Surgical Procedures: Section 1154(d) requires a PRO to review all ambulatory surgical procedures specified in section 1833(i)(1)(A), 42 U.S.C.A. 1395l(i)(1)(A), which are performed in the PRO's area. The latter statute requires the Secretary, in consultation with appropriate medical organizations, to specify surgical procedures appropriately performed on an inpatient basis in a hospital which also can be performed safely on an ambulatory basis in an ambulatory surgical center or hospital outpatient department. At the Secretary's discretion, however, this review may be done on a sample basis.

Determination that Hospital Care is Not Required/Notice to Medicare Beneficiaries: Section 1154(e) provides that if a hospital has determined that a patient no longer requires inpatient hospital care, and if the attending physician agrees, the hospital may notify the patient or the patient's representative of that determination. If it does, the notice must meet conditions prescribed by the Secretary pursuant to section 1879, 42 U.S.C.A. 1395pp. Section 1879 pertains to continuation of payment for hospital care when beneficiaries and providers or other practitioners did not know, and could not have been expected reasonably to know, that payment would be denied.

◆ NOTE: Prior to enactment of section 421(c) of the Medicare, Medicaid, and SCHIP Benefits Improvement and Protection Act of 2000, P.L. 106–544, December 21, 2000, there were three additional situations where Medicare beneficiaries or their representatives may or must be given notice that further hospital care is not required:

1. If a hospital has determined that a patient no longer requires inpatient hospital care, but the attending physician does not agree, the hospital may request a PRO to review its decision. If it does, the hospital must notify the patient of that request.
2. If a patient, or a patient's representative, receives a notice that a hospital and the attending physician agree that further hospital care is not required, the patient or the patient's representative may request the appropriate PRO to review that decision. The PRO must make that review, then provide notice, by telephone and in writing, to the patient or representative and to the hospital and attending physician of its finding. Such reviews must be conducted regardless whether the hospital will charge for continued hospital care or whether the patient will be liable to pay for such continued care. If the request comes to the PRO while the patient is still an inpatient in a hospital, and not later than noon of the first working day after receiving notice that the hospital and attending physician have agreed further hospital care is not required, the hospital must provide the PRO the records necessary to make the review by close of business on that first working day. Then the PRO must provide notice of its finding not later than one full working day after it received the request and the records.
3. If a patient or a patient's representative makes a request, as indicated in 2 above, not later than noon of the first working day after the patient or the patient's representative receives notice that the hospital and the attending physician agree that further hospital care is not required, and if the patient or the patient's representative did not know, and could not have been expected reasonably to know that payment for continued hospital care would not be made by Medicare, as required by

section 1879(a)(2), then the hospital may not charge the patient for inpatient hospital services furnished before noon of the day after the patient or patient's representative received notice of the PRO decision.

In any case described in 1 or 2 above, the PRO must solicit the views of the patient involved or that patient's representative.

That change became effective with respect to initial determinations made on or after October 1, 2002.

◆ NOTE: Pursuant to section 1158, 42 U.S.C.A. 1320c-7, States with approved Medicaid plans may provide for functions specified in section 1154 to be performed in an area by contract with a PRO having a contract with the Secretary. If they do, they will receive Federal matching funds at the rate of 75 percent for expenditures related thereto.

◆ NOTE ALSO: In addition to the foregoing obligations, section 1164 obligated PRO's to perform 100 percent reviews of certain surgical procedures. That obligation ended when section 1164 was repealed, effective October 31, 1994, by section 146(a)(1) of the Social Security Act Amendments of 1994, P.L. 103-432. For a discussion of section 1164 as it applied prior to repeal, see § 4:21.

PRO Sanction Authority: With respect to PRO duties, section 1156, 42 U.S.C.A. 1320c-5, sets forth the role of a PRO in sanctioning health care practitioners and other persons, including hospitals and health care facilities, organizations, and agencies participating in programs funded under the Social Security Act.

Notice to the Patient and the Intermediary or Carrier: Whenever a PRO determines that items or services furnished or to be furnished to a patient must be disapproved for Medicare payment, section 1154(a)(3) requires the PRO to promptly notify the patient and the intermediary or carrier responsible for paying the Medicare claim. This may not occur, however, until 20 days after the PRO has made a preliminary notification to the affected practitioner or provider of the proposed determination and has given the practitioner or provider an opportunity to discuss and review the matter.

Hearing Rights: Preliminary notice is only the first step in resolution of disputes arising from adverse PRO determinations. Section 1155, 42 U.S.C.A. 1320c-4, provides that any beneficiary and any practitioner or provider dissatisfied with an initial PRO determination is entitled to reconsideration by the PRO. Then, if the reconsideration determination is adverse to a beneficiary, and if the amount in controversy is $200 or more, the beneficiary is entitled to a hearing by the Secretary, in accordance with section 205(b) of the Social Security Act, 42 U.S.C.A. 405(b). If the administrative hearing is also adverse to a beneficiary, and if the amount in controversy is $2,000 or more, the beneficiary may seek judicial review.

Statutory Provisions

Section 1152, 42 U.S.C.A. 1320c-1, defines utilization and quality control peer review organization as follows:

> The term "utilization and quality control peer review organization" means an entity which —
>
> (1) (A) is composed of a substantial number of the licensed doctors of medicine and osteopathy engaged in the practice of medicine or surgery in the area and who are representative of the practicing physicians in the area, designated by the Secretary under section 1153 [42 U.S.C.A. 1320c-2] , with respect to which the entity shall perform services under this part, or (B) has available to it, by arrangement or otherwise, the services of a sufficient number of licensed doctors of medicine or osteopathy engaged in the practice of medicine or surgery in such area to assure that adequate peer review of the services provided by the various medical specialties and subspecialties can be assured;
>
> (2) is able, in the judgment of the Secretary, to perform review functions required under section 1154 [42 U.S.C.A. 1320c-3] in a manner consistent with the efficient and effective administration of this part and to perform reviews of the pattern of quality of care in an area of medical practice where actual performance is measured against objective criteria which define acceptable and adequate practice; and
>
> (3) has at least one individual who is a representative of consumers on its governing body.

With respect to exclusions from coverage under Medicare relevant to PRO's, section 1862(a), 42 U.S.C.A. 1395y(a), as amended by section 201(a)(1) of P.L. 101-234, the Medicare Catastrophic Coverage Repeal Act of 1989, and sections 6103(b)(3)(B) and 6115(b) of P.L. 101-239, the Omnibus Budget Reconciliation Act of 1989, provides in pertinent part:

Notwithstanding any other provision of this title, no payment may be made under part A or part B for any expenses incurred for items or services —

(1) (A) which, except for items and services described in a succeeding subparagraph [Pursuant to section 4163(d)(2)(A) of P.L. 101-508, the Omnibus Budget Reconciliation Act of 1990 (OBRA 90), applicable to screening mammography performed after December 1990, "a succeeding subparagraph" replaced "subparagraph (B), (C), (D), or (E)"; "and" was deleted at the end of subparagraph (1)(D); ", and" was substituted for the period at the end of subparagraph (1)(E); subparagraph (1)(F) was added. Also, section 4163(d)(2)(B) of OBRA 90 added "or under paragraph (1)(F)" after "(1)(B)" in paragraph (a)(7).], are not reasonable and necessary for the diagnosis or treatment of illness or injury or to improve the functioning of a malformed body member,

(B) in the case of items and services described in section 1861(s)(10) [42 U.S.C.A. 1395x(s)(10), which pertains to pneumococcal, influenza, and hepatitis B vaccines and their administration], which are not reasonable and necessary for the prevention of illness,

(C) in the case of hospice care, which are not reasonable and necessary for the palliation or management of terminal illness,

(D) in the case of clinical care items and services provided with the concurrence of the Secretary and with respect to research and experimentation conducted by, or under contract with, the Prospective Payment Assessment Commission or the Secretary, which are not reasonable and necessary to carry out the purposes of section 1886(e)(6) [42 U.S.C.A. 1395ww(e)(6), which pertains to ProPAC's obligation to assess safety, efficacy, and cost-effectiveness of new and existing medical and surgical procedures],

(E) in the case of research conducted pursuant to section 1142, [42 U.S.C.A. 1320b-12, which pertains to the obligation of the Secretary of Health and Human Services to conduct and support research regarding the outcomes, effectiveness, and appropriateness of health care services and to evaluate alternative services and procedures], which is not reasonable and necessary to carry out the purposes of that section, and

(F) in the case of screening mammography, which is performed more frequently than is provided under 1834(c)(2) [42 U.S.C.A. 1395m(c)(2); 1834(c) was added by section 4163(b)(2) of OBRA 90, applicable to screening mammography performed after December 1990. Frequency varies by age: once for a woman over 34 but under 40; 11-month intervals for women over 39 but under 50, if at high risk of developing breast cancer, but 23-month intervals for those not at high risk; 11-month intervals for a woman over 49 but under 65; and 23-month intervals for a woman over 64.] or which is not conducted by a facility described in section 1834(c)(1)(B), and in the case of screening pap smear, which is performed more frequently than is provided under 1861(nn) [42 U.S.C.A. 1395x(nn), which is once every three years, except when the Secretary specifies otherwise with regard to women at high risk of developing cervical cancer];

◆ NOTE: Section 145(c)(1) of the Social Security Act Amendments of 1994, P.L. 103-432, substituted "or which is not conducted by a facility described in section 1834(c)(1)(B)", for "or which does not meet the standards established under 1834(c)(3)." That change applies to mammography furnished by a facility on and after the first date that the certificate requirements of section 354(b) of the Public Health Service Act apply to such mammography conducted by such facility.

* * *

(9) where such expenses are for custodial care (except, in the case of hospice care, as is otherwise permitted under paragraph (1)(C))[.]

◆ NOTE: Prior to amendment by section 201(a)(1) of P.L. 101-234, the Medicare Catastrophic Coverage Repeal Act of 1989, and sections 6103(b)(3)(B) and 6115(b) of P.L. 101-239, the Omnibus Budget Reconciliation Act of 1989, the relevant portions of section 1862(a), as indicated above, read as follows:

Notwithstanding any other provision of this title, no payment may be made under part A or part B for any expenses incurred for items or services —

(1) (A) which, except for items and services described in a succeeding subparagraph, are not reasonable and necessary for the diagnosis or treatment of illness or injury or to improve the functioning of a malformed body member,

(B) in the case of items and services described in section 1861(s)(10) [42 U.S.C.A. 1395x(s)(10), which pertains to pneumococcal, influenza, and hepatitis B vaccines and their administration], which are not reasonable and necessary for the prevention of illness,

(C) in the case of hospice care, which are not reasonable and necessary for the palliation or management of terminal illness,

(D) in the case of clinical care items and services provided with the concurrence of the Secretary and with respect to research and experimentation conducted by, or under contract with, the Prospective Payment Assessment Commission or the Secretary, which are not reasonable and necessary to carry out the purposes of section 1886(e)(6) [42 U.S.C.A. 1395ww(e)(6), which pertains to ProPAC's obligation to assess safety, efficacy, and cost-effectiveness of new and existing medical and surgical procedures],

(E) in the case of research conducted pursuant to section 1875(c) [42 U.S.C.A. 1395ll(c), which pertained to ongoing obligations of the Secretary of Health and Human Services, via the National Center for Health Services Research and Health Care Technology, to study appropriateness, necessity, and effectiveness of selected medical treatments and surgical procedures], which is not reasonable and necessary to carry out the purposes of that section,

(F) in the case of screening mammography, which is performed more frequently than is covered under section 1834(e)(2) [42 U.S.C.A. 1395m(e)(2), which was once for a woman over 34 but under 40 years of age, once every 11 months after a previous screening for every woman over 39 but under 50 years of age who is at high risk of developing breast cancer, once every 23 months after a previous screening for every woman over 39 but under 50 who is not at high risk of developing breast cancer, and once every 11 months after a previous screening for a woman over 49 but under 65] or which does not meet the standards established under section 1834(e)(3) [42 U.S.C.A. 1395m(e)(3), which pertained to safety and accuracy]; and

(G) in the case of in-home care for chronically dependent individuals, which is not reasonable and necessary to assure the health and condition of the individual is maintained in the individual's noninstitutional residence;

* * *

(9) where such expenses are for custodial care (except, in the case of hospice care, as is otherwise permitted under paragraph (1)(C))[.]

Section 1862(g), 42 U.S.C.A. 1395y(g), then relates review of these exclusions to PRO's by providing:

> The Secretary shall, in making the determinations under paragraphs (1) and (9) of subsection (a), and for the purposes of promoting the effective, efficient, and economical delivery of health care services, and of promoting the quality of services of the type for which payment may be made under this title, enter into contracts with utilization and quality control peer review organizations pursuant to part B of title XI of this Act.

Section 1153, 42 U.S.C.A. 13951320c-2, provides in pertinent part:

(a) (1) The Secretary shall establish throughout the United States geographic areas with respect to which contracts under this part will be made. In establishing such areas, the Secretary shall use the same areas as established under section 1152 of this Act as in effect immediately prior to the date of the enactment of the Peer Review Improvement Act of 1982, but subject to the provisions of paragraph (2) [September 2, 1982. See section 143 of the Peer Review Improvement Act of 1982 of the Tax Equity and Fiscal Responsibility Act of 1982, P.L. 97-248].

(2) As soon as practicable after the date of the enactment of the Peer Review Improvement Act of 1982, the Secretary shall consolidate such geographic areas, taking into account the following criteria:

(A) Each State shall generally be designated as a geographic area for purposes of paragraph (1).

(B) The Secretary shall establish local or regional areas rather than State areas only where the volume of review activity or other relevant factors (as determined by the Secretary) warrant such an establishment, and the Secretary determines that review activity can be carried out with equal or greater efficiency by establishing such local or regional areas. In applying this subparagraph the Secretary shall take into account the number of hospital admissions within each State for which payment may be made under title XVIII or a State plan approved under title XIX, with any State having fewer than 180,000 such admissions annually being established as a single statewide area, and no local or regional area being established which has fewer than 60,000 total hospital admissions (including public and private pay patients) under review annually, unless the Secretary determines that other relevant factors warrant otherwise.

(C) No local or regional area shall be designated which is not a self-contained medical service area, having a full spectrum of services, including medical specialists' services.

(b) (1) The Secretary shall enter into a contract with a utilization and quality control peer review organization for each area established under subsection (a) if a qualified organization is available in such area and such organization and the Secretary have negotiated a proposed contract which the Secretary determines will be carried out by such organization in a manner consistent with the efficient and effective administration of this part. If more than one such qualified organization meets the requirements of the preceding sentence, priority shall be given to any such organization which is described in section 1152(1)(A).

(2) (A) Prior to November 15, 1984, the Secretary shall not enter into a contract under this part with any entity which is, or is affiliated with (through management, ownership, or common control), an entity (other than a self-insured employer) which directly or indirectly makes payments to any practitioner or provider whose health care services are reviewed by such entity or would be reviewed by such entity

if it entered into a contract with the Secretary under this part. For purposes of this paragraph, an entity shall not be considered to be affiliated with another entity which makes payments (directly or indirectly) to any practitioner or provider, by reason of management, ownership, or common control, if the management, ownership or common control consists only of members of the governing board being affiliated (through management, ownership, or common control) with a health maintenance organization or competitive medical plan which is an "eligible organization" as defined in section 1876(b) [42 U.S.C.A. 1395mm(b)].

(B) If, after November 14, 1984, the Secretary determines that there is no other entity available for an area with which the Secretary can enter into a contract under this part, the Secretary may then enter into a contract under this part with an entity described in subparagraph (A) for such area if such entity otherwise meets the requirements of this part.

(3) (A) The Secretary shall not enter into a contract under this part with any entity which is, or is affiliated with (through management, ownership, or common control), a health care facility, or association of such facilities, within the area served by such entity or which would be served by such entity if it entered into a contract with the Secretary under this part.

(B) For purposes of subparagraph (A), an entity shall not be considered to be affiliated with a health care facility or association of facilities by reason of management, ownership, or common control if the management, ownership, or common control consists only of not more than 20 percent of the members of the governing board of the entity being affiliated (through management, ownership, or common control) with one or more of such facilities or associations.

(c) Each contract with an organization under this section shall provide that —

(1) the organization shall perform the functions set forth in section 1154(a), or may subcontract for the performance of all or some of such functions (and for purposes of paragraphs (2)

and (3) of subsection (b), a subcontract under this paragraph shall not constitute an affiliation with the subcontractor)[.]

* * *

(g) The Secretary shall provide that fiscal intermediaries furnish to peer review organizations, each month on a timely basis, data necessary to initiate the review process under section 1154(a) on a timely basis. If the Secretary determines that a fiscal intermediary is unable to furnish such data on a timely basis, the Secretary shall require the hospital to do so.

With respect to the functions of Peer Review Organizations, section 1154, 42 U.S.C.A. 1320c-3, provides:

(a) Any utilization and quality control peer review organization entering into a contract with the Secretary under this part must perform the following functions:

(1) The organization shall review some or all of the professional activities in the area, subject to the terms of the contract and subject to the requirements of subsection (d), of physicians and other health care practitioners and institutional and noninstitutional providers of health care services in the provision of health care services and items for which payment may be made (in whole or in part) under title XVIII (including where payment is made for such services to eligible organizations pursuant to contracts under section 1876 [42 U.S.C.A. 1395mm, which pertains to health maintenance organizations and competitive medical plans]) for the purpose of determining whether—

(A) such services and items are or were reasonable and medically necessary and whether such services and items are not allowable under subsection (a)(1) or (a)(9) of section 1862 [42 U.S.C.A. 1395y(a)(1) and (9);

(B) the quality of such services meets professionally recognized standards of health care; and

(C) in case such services and items are proposed to be provided in a hospital or other health care facility on an inpatient basis, such services and items could, consistent with the provision of appropriate medical care, be effectively provided more economically on an outpatient basis or in an inpatient health care facility of a different type.

If the organization performs such reviews with respect to a type of health care practitioner other than medical doctors, the organization shall establish procedures for the involvement of health care practitioners of that type in such reviews.

◆ NOTE: Pursuant to section 6224(a) of P.L. 101-239, the Omnibus Budget Reconciliation Act of 1989, the preceding sentence applies to PRO contracts entered into after December 19, 1989.

(2) The organization shall determine, on the basis of the review carried out under subparagraphs (A), (B), and (C) of paragraph (1), whether payment shall be made for services under title XVIII. Such determination shall constitute the conclusive determination on those issues for purposes of payment under title XVIII, except that payment may be made if —

(A) such payment is allowed by reason of section 1879 [42 U.S.C.A. 1395pp, which permits payment of Medicare benefits otherwise to be disallowed under section 1862(a)(1) and (a)(9) in cases where providers and beneficiaries did not know, and could not reasonably have been expected to know, disallowance was required];

(B) in the case of inpatient hospital services or extended care services, the peer review organization determines that additional time is required in order to arrange for postdischarge care, but payment may be continued under this subparagraph for not more than two days, but only in the case where the provider of such services did not know and could not reasonably have been expected to know (as determined under section 1879) that payment would not otherwise be made for such services under title XVIII prior to notification by the organization under paragraph (3);

(C) such determination is changed as the result of any hearing or review of the determination under section 1155 [42 U.S.C.A. 1320c-4]; or

(D) such payment is authorized under section 1861(v)(1)(G) [42 U.S.C.A. 1395x(v)(1)(G), which in certain cases permits payment of Medicare benefits equivalent to those for skilled nursing care in any case in which a hospital provides inpatient services to an individual which are determined by a PRO or the Secretary or his designee to have been not medically necessary but which would constitute medically necessary extended care services if provided by a skilled nursing facility].

The organization shall identify cases for which payment should not be made by reason of paragraph (1)(B) only through the use of criteria developed pursuant to guidelines established by the Secretary. [Pursuant to section 4205(g)(2) of OBRA 90, effective as if enacted by the Consolidated Omnibus Budget Reconciliation Act of 1985, the previous sentence replaced "Determinations that payment should not be made by reason of subparagraph (B) of paragraph (1) shall be made only on the basis of criteria which are consistent with guidelines established by the Secretary."

(3) (A) Subject to subparagraphs (B) and (D), whenever the organization makes a determination that any health care services or items furnished or to be furnished to a patient by any practitioner or provider are disapproved, the organization shall promptly notify such patient and the agency or organization responsible for the payment of claims under title XVIII of this Act of such determination.

(B) The notification under subparagraph (A) with respect to services and items disapproved by reason of subparagraph (A) or (C) of paragraph (1) shall not occur until 20 days after the date that the organization has—

(i) made a preliminary notification to such practitioner or provider of such proposed determination, and

(ii) provided such practitioner or provider an opportunity for discussion and review of the proposed determination.

(C) The discussion and review conducted under subparagraph (B)(ii) shall not affect the rights of a practitioner or provider to a formal reconsideration of a determination under this part (as provided under section 1155 [42 U.S.C.A. 1320c-4, which provides for administrative hearing and judicial review of denied claims]).

(D) The notification under subparagraph (A) with respect to services or items disapproved by reason of paragraph (1)(B) shall not occur until after—

(i) the organization has notified the practitioner or provider involved of the determination and of the practitioner's or provider's right to a formal reconsideration of the determination under section 1155, and

(ii) if the provider or practitioner requests such a reconsideration, the organization has made such a reconsideration.

If a provider or practitioner is provided a reconsideration, such reconsideration shall be in lieu of any subsequent reconsideration to which the provider or practitioner may be otherwise entitled under section 1155, but shall not affect the right of a beneficiary from seeking reconsideration under such section of the organization's determination (after any reconsideration requested by the provider or physician under clause (ii)).

(E) (i) In the case of services and items provided by a physician that were disapproved by reason of paragraph (1)(b), the notice to the patient shall state the following: "In the judgment of the peer review organization, the medical care received was not acceptable under the medicare program. The reasons for the denial have been discussed with your physician."

(ii) In the case of services or items provided by an entity or practitioner other than a physician, the Secretary may substitute the entity or practitioner which provided the services or items for the term "physician" in the notice described in clause (i). [This clause (ii) and redesignation of the prior clause as (i) was added by section 4205(g)(1) of OBRA 90, effective as if enacted by the Consolidated Omnibus Budget Reconciliation Act of 1985. Similarly, the phrase "provided by a physician that were" was added to clause (i), and the phrase "and hospital" was deleted after "discussed with your physician."]

◆ NOTE: Section 6224(b)(1) of P.L. 101-239, the Omnibus Budget Reconciliation Act of 1989, effective December 19, 1989, substituted "subparagraphs (B) and (D)" for "subparagraph (B)" in subsection (a)(3)(A). It also added "with respect to services or items disapproved by reason of subparagraph (A) or (C) of paragraph (1)" after "under subparagraph (A)" in subsection (a)(3)(B). And it added new subparagraphs (D) and (E) to subsection (a)(3).

(4) (A) The organization shall, after consultation with the Secretary, determine the types and kinds of cases (whether by type of health care or diagnosis involved, or whether in terms of other relevant criteria relating to the provision of health care services) with respect to which such organization will, in order to most effectively carry out the purposes of this part, exercise review authority under the contract. The organization shall notify the Secretary periodically with respect to such determinations. Each peer review organization shall provide that a reasonable proportion of its activities are involved with reviewing, under paragraph (1)(B), the quality of services and that a reasonable allocation of such activities is made among the different cases and settings (including post-acute-care settings, ambulatory settings, and health maintenance organizations). In establishing such allocation the organization shall consider (i) whether there is reason to believe that there is a particular need for reviews of particular cases or settings because of previous problems regarding quality of care, (ii) the cost of such reviews and the likely yield of such reviews in terms of number and seriousness of quality of care problems likely to be discovered as a result of such reviews, and (iii) the availability and adequacy of alternative quality review and assurance mechanisms.

(B) The contract of each organization shall provide for the review of services (including both inpatient and outpatient services) provided by eligible organizations pursuant to a risk-sharing contract under section 1876 [42 U.S.C.A. 1395mm, which pertains to health maintenance organizations and competitive medical plans] (or that is subject to review under section 1882(t)(3) [42 U.S.C.A. 1395ss(t)(3), which pertains to Medicare supplemental health insurance policies commonly commonly known as Medicare SELECT policies. Available since 1992 in some States, those policies channel insureds to preferred providers under contract with insurers to deliver health care goods and services at negotiated rates. See section 4358(b)(3) of OBRA 90, as amended by section 171(h)(2)(A)-(B) of the Social Security Act

Amendments of 1994. For a more complete discussion, see § 2:54.]) for the purpose of determining whether the quality of such services meets professionally recognized standards of health care, including whether appropriate health care services have not been provided or have been provided in inappropriate settings and whether individuals enrolled with an eligible organization have adequate access to health care services provided by or through such organization (as determined, in part, by a survey of individuals enrolled with the organization who have not yet used the organization to receive such services). The contract of each organization shall also provide that with respect to health care provided by a health maintenance organization or competitive medical plan under section 1876, the organization shall maintain a beneficiary outreach program designed to apprise individuals receiving care under such section of the role of the peer review system, of the rights of the individual under such system, and of the method and purposes for contacting the organization. The previous two sentences shall not apply with respect to a contract year if another entity has been awarded a contract under subparagraph (C). Under the contract the level of effort expended by the organization on reviews under this subparagraph shall be equivalent, on a per enrollee basis, to the level of effort expended by the organization on utilization and quality reviews performed with respect to individuals not enrolled with an eligible organization.

(C) The Secretary may provide, by contract under competitive procurement procedures on a State-by-State basis in up to 25 States, for the review described in subparagraph (B) by an appropriate entity (which may be a peer review organization described in that subparagraph). In selecting among States in which to conduct such competitive procurement procedures, the Secretary may not select States which, as a group, have more than 50 percent of the total number of individuals enrolled with eligible organizations under section 1876. Under a contract with an entity under this subparagraph—

(i) the entity must be, or must meet all the requirements under section 1152 to be, a utilization and quality control peer review organization (other than the ability to perform review functions under this section that are not described in subparagraph (B)),

(ii) the contract must meet the requirement of section 1153(b)(3) [42 U.S.C.A. 1320c-2(b)(3), i.e., the PRO must not be affiliated with, through management, ownership, or common control (defined as having more than 20 percent of the members of the governing board of the affiliate), a health care facility or association of such facilities within the area serviced by the PRO], and

(iii) the level of effort expended under the contract shall be, to the extent practicable, not less than the level of effort that would otherwise be required under the third sentence of subparagraph (B) if this subparagraph did not apply.

(5) The organization shall consult with nurses and other professional health care practitioners (other than physicians described in section 1861(r)(1) [42 U.S.C.A. 1395x(r)(1), which defines physician to include M.D.'s and D.O.'s legally authorized to practice in their respective States]) and with representatives of institutional and noninstitutional providers of health care services, with respect to the organization's responsibility for the review under paragraph (1) of the professional activities of such practitioners and providers.

(6) (A) The organization shall, consistent with the provisions of its contract under this part, apply professionally developed norms of care, diagnosis, and treatment based upon typical patterns of practice within the geographic area served by the organization as principal points of evaluation and review, taking into consideration national norms where appropriate. Such norms with respect to treatment for particular illnesses or health conditions shall include—

(i) the types and extent of the health care services which, taking into account differing, but acceptable, modes of treatment and methods of organizing and delivering care, are considered within the range of appropriate diagnosis and treatment of such illness or health condition, consistent with professionally recognized and accepted patterns of care; and

(ii) the type of health care facility which is considered, consistent with such standards, to be the type in which health care services which are medically appropriate for such illness or condition can most economically be provided.

As a component of the norms described in clause (i) or (ii), the organization shall take into account the special problems associated with delivering care in remote rural areas, the availability of service alternatives to inpatient hospitalization, and other appropriate factors (such as the distance from a patient's residence to the site of care, family support, availability of proximate alternative sites of care, and the patient's ability to carry out necessary or prescribed self-care regimens) that could adversely affect the safety or effectiveness of treatment provided on an outpatient basis.

(B) The organization shall —

(i) offer to provide, several times each year, for a physician representing the organization to meet (at a hospital or at a regional meeting) with medical and administrative staff of each hospital (the services of which are reviewed by the organization) respecting the organization's review of the hospital's services for which payment may be made under title XVIII, and

(ii) publish (not less often than annually) and distribute to providers and practitioners whose services are subject to review a report that describes the organization's findings with respect to the types of cases in which the organization has frequently determined that (I) inappropriate or unnecessary care has been provided, (II) services were rendered in an inappropriate setting, or (III) services did not meet professionally recognized standards of health care.

(7) The organization, to the extent necessary and appropriate to the performance of the contract, shall —

(A) (i) make arrangements to utilize the services of persons who are practitioners of, or specialists in, the various areas of medicine (including dentistry, optometry, and podiatry [Section 4205(b)(1)(A) of OBRA 90 added optometry and podiatry, applicable to contracts entered into or renewed on or after November 5, 1990.]), or other types of health care, which persons shall, to the maximum extent practicable, be individuals engaged in the practice of their profession within the area served by such organization; and

(ii) in the case of psychiatric and physical rehabilitation services, make arrangements to ensure that (to the extent possible) initial review of such services be made by a physician who is trained in psychiatry or physical rehabilitation (as appropriate).

(B) undertake such professional inquiries either before or after, or both before and after, the provision of services with respect to which such organization has a responsibility for review which in the judgment of such organization will facilitate its activities;

(C) examine the pertinent records of any practitioner or provider of health care services providing services with respect to which such organization has a responsibility for review under paragraph (1); and

(D) inspect the facilities in which care is rendered or services are provided (which are located in such area) of any practitioner or provider of health care services providing services with respect to which such organization has a responsibility for review under paragraph (1).

(8) The organization shall perform such duties and functions and assume such responsibilities and comply with such other requirements as may be required by this part or under regulations of the Secretary promulgated to carry out the provisions of this part or as may be required to carry out section 1862(a)(15) [42 U.S.C.A. 1395y(a)(15), which pertains to exclusion of claims for services of an assistant at surgery in a cataract operation which did not have prior approval of a PRO or a carrier].

(9) (A) The organization shall collect such information relevant to its functions, and keep and maintain such records, in such form as the Secretary may require to carry out the purposes of this part, and shall permit access to and use of any such information and records as the Secretary may require for such purposes, subject to the provisions of section 1160 [42 U.S.C.A. 1320c-9, which restricts disclosure of

information by PRO's, notwithstanding provisions of the Freedom of Information Act, 5 U.S.C.A. 552] .

(B) If the organization finds, after reasonable notice to and opportunity for discussion with the physician or practitioner concerned, that the physician or practitioner has furnished services in violation of section 1156(a) and theorganization determines that the physician or practitioner should enter into a corrective action plan under section 1156(b)(1), the organization shall notify the state board or boards responsible for the licensing or disciplining of the physician or practitioner of its finding and of any action taken as a result of the finding.

◆ NOTE: Prior to amendment by section 156(b)(2)(A) of the Social Security Act Amendments of 1994, effective October 31, 1994, subparagraph (B) read: "If the organization finds, after notice and hearing, that a physician has furnished services in violation of this subsection, the organization shall notify the State board or boards responsible for the licensing or disciplining of the physician of its finding and decision. [Section 4205(d)(1)(A) of OBRA 90 added "A" and this subparagraph (B), applicable to notices of proposed sanctions issued more than 60 days after November 5, 1990.]

(10) The organization shall coordinate activities, including information exchanges, which are consistent with economical and efficient operation of programs among appropriate public and private agencies or organizations including—

(A) agencies under contract pursuant to sections 1816 and 1842 of this Act [42 U.S.C.A. 1395h and 42 U.S.C.A. 1395u, which pertain, respectively, to use of fiscal intermediaries to process Medicare Part A claims and use of carriers to process Medicare Part B claims];

(B) other peer review organizations having contracts under this part; and

(C) other public or private review organizations as may be appropriate.

(11) The organization shall make available its facilities and resources for contracting with private and public entities pay-

ing for health care in its area for review, as feasible and appropriate, of services reimbursed by such entities.

◆ NOTE: Former paragraph (12) whic h obligated PRO's to perform the review, referral, and other functions required under former section 1164, 42 U.S.C. 1320c-13, was repealed, effective October 31, 1994, by section 156(a)(2)(A) of the Social Security Act Amendments of 1994.

[(12)] Notwithstanding paragraph (4), the organization shall perform the review described in paragraph (1) with respect to early readmission cases to determine if the previous inpatient hospital services and the post-hospital services met professionally recognized standards of health care. Such reviews may be performed on a sample basis if the organization and the Secretary determine it to be appropriate. In this paragraph, an "early readmission case" is a case in which an individual, after discharge from a hospital, is readmitted to a hospital less than 31 days after the date of the most recent previous discharge.

[(13)] The organization shall conduct an appropriate review of all written complaints about the quality of services (for which payment may otherwise be made under title XVIII) not meeting professionally recognized standards of health care, if the complaint is filed with the organization by an individual entitled to benefits for such services under such title (or a person acting on the individual's behalf). The organization shall inform the individual (or representative) of the organization's final disposition of the complaint. Before the organization concludes that the quality of services does not meet professionally recognized standards of health care, the organization must provide the practitioner or person concerned with reasonable notice and opportunity for discussion.

[(14)] During each year of the contract entered into under section 1153(b), the organization shall perform significant on-site review activities, including on-site review in at least 20 percent of the rural hospitals in the organization's area.

[(15)] The organization shall provide for a review and report to the Secretary when requested by the Secretary under section 1867(d)(3) [42 U.S.C.A. 1395dd(d)(3), which prohibits "patient dumping" in certain emergency situations]. The organization shall provide reasonable notice of the review to the physician and hospital involved. Within the time period permitted by the Secretary, the organization shall provide a reasonable opportunity for discussion with the physician and hospital involved, and an opportunity for the physician and hospital to submit additional information, before issuing its report to the Secretary under such section. [Paragraph (15) was added by section 4207(a)(1)(B) of OBRA 90, applicable to contracts under Part B 60 days after November 5, 1990.]

(b) (1) No physician shall be permitted to review —

(A) health care services provided to a patient if he was directly responsible for providing such services; or

(B) health care services provided in or by an institution, organization, or agency, if he or any member of his family has, directly or indirectly, a significant financial interest in such institution, organization, or agency.

(2) For purposes of this subsection, a physician's family includes only his spouse (other than a spouse who is legally separated from him under a decree of divorce or separate maintenance), children (including legally adopted children), grandchildren, parents, and grandparents.

(c) No utilization and quality control peer review organization shall utilize the services of any individual who is not a duly licensed doctor of medicine, osteopathy, dentistry, optometry, or podiatry to make final determinations of denial decisions in accordance with its duties and functions under this part with respect to the professional conduct of any other duly licensed doctor of medicine, osteopathy, dentistry, optometry, or podiatry, or any act performed by any duly licensed doctor of medicine, osteopathy, dentistry, optometry, or podiatry in the exercise of his profession. [Section 4205(b)(1)(B) of OBRA 90 added "dentistry, optometry, or podiatry" in lieu of "or dentistry" each place the phrase appears, applicable to contracts entered into or renewed on or after November 5, 1990.]

(d) Each contract under this part shall require that the utilization and quality control peer review organization's review responsibility pursuant to subsection (a)(1) will include review of all ambulatory surgical procedures specified pursuant to section 1833(i)(1)(A) [42 U.S.C.A. 1395l(i)(1)(A), which requires the

Secretary to establish, in consultation with appropriate medical organizations, lists of surgical procedures appropriately performed on an inpatient hospital basis which also could be performed in a qualified ambulatory surgical center] which are performed in the area, or, at the discretion of the Secretary) a sample of such procedures. [NOTE: Effective October 31, 1994, section 156(a)(2)(A) of the Social Security Act amendments of 1994 deleted the phrase "(and except as provided in section 1164)", which preceded "a sample of such procedures."]

(e) (1) If—

(A) a hospital has determined that a patient no longer requires inpatient hospital care, and

(B) the attending physician has agreed with the hospital's determination,

the hospital may provide the patient (or the patient's representative) with a notice (meeting conditions prescribed by the Secretary under section 1879 [42 U.S.C.A. 1395pp, which pertains to limitation on liability of Medicare beneficiaries where their Medicare claims are disallowed] of the determination.

◆ NOTE: Prior to amendment by section 521(c) of the Medicare, Medicaid, and SCHIP Benefits and Improvement Act of 2000, P.L. 106–544, December 21, 2000, subsection (e) had the following additional provisions:

(2) If—

(A) a hospital has determined that a patient no longer requires inpatient hospital care, but

(B) the attending physician has not agreed with the hospital's determination, the hospital may request the appropriate peer review organization to review under subsection (a) the validity of the hospital's determination. If the hospital requests such a review, it shall also notify the patient that the review has been requested.

(3) (A) If a patient (or a patient's representative)—

(i) has received a notice under paragraph (1), and

(ii) requests the appropriate peer review organization to review the determination,

then, the organization shall conduct a review under subsection (a) of the validity of the hospital's determination and shall provide notice (by telephone and in writing) to the patient or representative and the hospital and attending physician involved of the results of the review. Such review shall be conducted regardless of whether or not the hospital will charge for continued hospital care or whether or not the patient will be liable for payment for such continued care.

(B) If a patient (or a patient's representative) requests a review under subparagraph (A) while the patient is still an inpatient in the hospital and not later than noon of the first working day after the date the patient receives the notice under paragraph (1), then

(i) the hospital shall provide to the appropriate peer review organization the records required to review the determination by the close of business of such first working day, and

(ii) the peer review organization must provide the notice under subparagraph (A) by not later than one full working day after the date the organization has received the request and such records.

(4) If—

(A) a request is made under paragraph (3)(A) not later than noon of the first working day after the date the patient (or patient's representative receives the notice under paragraph (1), and

(B) the conditions described in section 1879(a)(2) [42 U.S.C.A. 1395pp(a)(2), which refers to situations where neither the beneficiary nor the provider knew, or could have reasonably been expected to have known, that a claim for Medicare payment would be disallowed] with respect to the patient or representative are met,

the hospital may not charge the patient for inpatient hospital services furnished before noon of the day after the date the patient or representative receives notice of the peer review organization's decision.

(5) In any review conducted under paragraph (2) or (3), the organization shall solicit the views of the patient involved (or the patient's representative).

(f) The Secretary, in consultation with appropriate experts, shall identify methods that would be available to assist peer review organizations (under subsection (a)(4)) in identifying those cases which are more likely than others to be associated with a quality of services which does not meet professionally recognized standards of health care.

◆ NOTE: Previously, section 1164, 42 U.S.C.A. 1320c-13, obligated PRO's to perform 100 percent peer review for certain surgical procedures. Section 146(a)(1) of the Social Security Act Amendments of 1994, repealed that requirement effective October 31, 1994. For a discussion of section 1164 prior to repeal, see § 4:21.

With respect to reconsideration of adverse PRO determinations and the right to an administrative hearing and subsequent judicial review, section 1155, 42 U.S.C.A. 1320c-4, provides:

> Any beneficiary who is entitled to benefits under title XVIII, and, subject to section 1154(a)(3)(D) [42 U.S.C.A. 1320c-3(a)(3)(D), which also pertains to rights of providers and practitioners to obtain reconsideration of PRO decisions disapproving claims for Medicare payment], any practitioner or provider, who is dissatisfied with a determination made by a contracting peer review organization in conducting its review responsibilities under this part, shall be entitled to a reconsideration of such determination by the reviewing organization. Where the reconsideration is adverse to the beneficiary and where the matter in controversy is $200 or more, such beneficiary shall be entitled to a hearing by the Secretary (to the same extent as is provided in section 205(b) [42 U.S.C.A. 405(b)]), and, where the amount in controversy is $2,000 or more, to judicial review of the Secretary's final decision.

◆ NOTE: Section 6224(b)(2) of P.L. 101-239, the Omnibus Budget Reconciliation Act of 1989 added "subject to section 1154(a)(3)(D)" to the preceding paragraph. It applies to determinations by PRO's with respect to which preliminary notifications were made under section 1154(a)(3)(B) after January 19, 1990.

With respect to hearing rights and judicial review, section 205, 42 U.S.C.A. 405, provides in pertinent part:

(b) (1) The Commissioner of Social Security is directed to make findings of fact, and decisions as to the rights of any individual applying for a payment under this title. Any such decision by the Commissioner of Social Security which involves a determination of disability and which is in whole or in part unfavorable to such individual shall contain a statement of the case, in understandable language, setting forth a discussion of the evidence, and stating the Commissioner's determination and the reason or reasons upon which it is based. Upon request by any such individual or upon request by a wife, divorced wife, widow, surviving divorced wife, surviving divorced mother, surviving divorced father, husband, divorced husband, widower, surviving divorced husband, child or parent who makes a showing in writing that his or her rights may be prejudiced by any decision the Commissioner of Social Security has rendered, he shall give such applicant and such other individual reasonable notice and opportunity for a hearing with respect to such decision, and, if a hearing is held, shall, on the basis of evidence adduced at the hearing, affirm, modify, or reverse his findings of fact and such decision. Any such request with respect to such a decision must be filed within sixty days after notice of such decision is received by the individual making such request. The Commissioner of Social Security is further authorized, on the Commissioner's own motion, to hold such hearings and to conduct such investigations and other proceedings as the Commissioner may deem necessary or proper for the administration of this title. In the course of any hearing, investigation, or other proceeding, the Commissioner of may administer oaths and affirmations, examine witnesses, and receive evidence. Evidence may be received at any hearing before the Commissioner of Social Security even though inadmissible under rules of evidence applicable to court procedure.

* * *

(g) Any individual, after any final decision of the Commissioner of Social Security made after a hearing to which he was a party, irrespective of the amount in controversy, may obtain a review of such decision by a civil action commenced within sixty days after the mailing to him of notice of such decision or within such further time as the Commissioner of Social Security may allow.

Such action shall be brought in the district court of the United States for the judicial district in which the plaintiff resides, or has his principal place of business, or, if he does not reside or have his principal place of business within any such judicial district, in the District Court of the United States for the District of Columbia [United States District Court for the District of Columbia]. As part of the Commissioner's answer the Commissioner of Social Security shall file a certified copy of the transcript of the record including the evidence upon which the findings and decision complained of are based. The court shall have power to enter, upon the pleadings and transcript of the record, a judgment affirming, modifying, or reversing the decision of the Commissioner of Social Security, with or without remanding the cause for a rehearing. The findings of the Commissioner of Social Security as to any fact, if supported by substantial evidence, shall be conclusive, and where a claim has been denied by the Commissioner or a decision is rendered under subsection (b) hereof which is adverse to an individual who was a party to the hearing before the Commissioner of Social Security, because of failure of the claimant or such individual to submit proof in conformity with any regulation prescribed under subsection (a) hereof, the court shall review only the question of conformity with such regulations and the validity of such regulations. The court may, on motion of the Commissioner of Social Security made for good cause shown before the Commissioner files his answer, remand the case to the Commissioner of Social Security for further action by the Commissioner of Social Security, and it may at any time order additional evidence to be taken before the Commissioner of Social Security, but only upon a showing that there is new evidence which is material and that there is good cause for the failure to incorporate such evidence into the record in a prior proceeding; and the Commissioner of Social Security shall, after the case is remanded, and after hearing such additional evidence if so ordered, modify or affirm the Commissioner's findings of fact or the Commissioner's decision, or both, and shall file with the court any such additional and modified findings of fact and decision and a transcript of the additional record and testimony upon which the Commissioner's action in modifying or affirming was based. Such additional or modified findings of fact and decision shall be reviewable only to the extent pro-

> vided for review of the original findings of fact and decision. The judgment of the court shall be final except that it shall be subject to review in the same manner as a judgment in other civil actions. Any action instituted in accordance with this subsection shall survive notwithstanding any change in the person occupying the office of Commissioner of Social Security or any vacancy in such office.

Subsection (a) of section 205, to which subsection (g) refers, provides:

> (a) The Commissioner of Social Security shall have full power and authority to make rules and regulations and to establish procedures, not inconsistent with the provisions of this title, which are necessary or appropriate to carry out such provisions, and shall adopt reasonable and proper rules and regulations to regulate and provide for the nature and extent of the proofs and evidence and the method of taking and furnishing the same in order to establish the right to benefits hereunder.

Section 205(h), 42 U.S.C.A. 405(h), provides:

> The findings and decision of the Commissioner of Social Security after a hearing shall be binding upon all individuals who were parties to such hearing. No findings of fact or decision of the Commissioner of Social Security shall be reviewed by any person, tribunal, or governmental agency except as herein provided. No action against the United States, the Commissioner of Social Security, or any officer or employee thereof shall be brought under section 1331 or 1346 of title 28, United States Code, to recover on any claim arising under this title.

◆ Note: Effective March 31, 1995, section 110(a) of P.L. 203-296, the Social Security Program Independence and Program Improvement Act of 1994, changed references to the Department of Health and Human Services to the Social Security Administration, and references to the Secretary of Health and Human Services to the Commissioner of Social Security, and references to the pronouns "she", "her", "he", "him", and "his" to "the Commissioner" or "the Commissioner's", as appropriate, throughout section 205 of the Social Security Act.

Finally, with respect to Medicaid programs contracting with PRO's, section 1158, 42 U.S.C.A. 1320c-7, provides:

(a) A State plan approved under title XIX of this Act may provide that the functions specified in section 1154 may be performed in an area by contract with a utilization and quality control peer review organization that has entered into a contract with the Secretary in accordance with the provisions of section 1862(g).

(b) In the event a State enters into a contract in accordance with subsection (a), the Federal share of the expenditures made to the contracting organization for its costs in the performance of its functions under the State plan shall be 75 percent (as provided in section 1903(a)(3)(C) [42 U.S.C.A. 1396b(a)(3)(C), which pertains to Federal matching funds for administrative costs]).

With respect to Christian Science sanatoriums, section 1162, 42 U.S.C.A. 1320c-11, provides:

The provisions of this part [B of Title XI] shall not apply with respect to a Christian Science sanatorium operated, or listed and certified, by the First Church of Christ, Scientist, Boston, Massachusetts.

And, with respect to medical officers in American Samoa, the Northern Mariana Islands, and the Trust Territory of the Pacific Islands, section 1163, 42 U.S.C.A. 1320c-12, provides:

For purposes of applying this part [B of Title XI] to American Samoa, the Northern Mariana Islands, and the Trust Territory of the Pacific Islands, individuals licensed to practice medicine in those places shall be considered to be physicians and doctors of medicine.

For regulatory citations, see Chapter 8

§ 4:19 SANCTIONS RECOMMENDED BY PEER REVIEW ORGANIZATIONS — Section 1156 [42 U.S.C.A. 1320c-5]

Summary

In General: Section 1156(a) of the Social Security Act, 42 U.S.C.A. 1320c-5(b), requires every health care practitioner, and any other person (including a hospital or other health care facility, organization, or agency) that provides health care services to assure, to the extent of their authority, that services or items which they order or provide to beneficiaries or recipients will be —

1. provided economically and only when, and to the extent, medically necessary;
2. of a quality which meets professionally recognized standards of health care; and
3. supported by evidence of medical necessity and quality in such form and fashion as may reasonably be required by a peer review organization (PRO) in the exercise of its duties.

This applies to any health care services for which payment may be made, in whole or in part, under Medicare or Medicaid, or under a Maternal and Child Health Services Block Grant (Title V of the Social Security Act, 42 U.S.C.A. 701 *et seq.*), or under a Block Grant to States for Social Services (Title XX of the Act, 42 U.S.C.A. 1397 *et seq.*).

PRO Sanction Recommendations: If a PRO determines that a practitioner or other person has failed in a substantial number of cases substantially to comply with any of those obligations, or has grossly and flagrantly violated any such obligation in one or more instances, section 1156(b)(1) requires the PRO to submit a report and recommendations on the violation to the Secretary of Health and Human Services. That is to be done, however, only after reasonable notice and opportunity for discussion of the matter by the PRO with the party involved. Furthermore, with respect to initial determinations by a PRO made on or after November 5, 1990, section 4205(a) of P.L. 101-508, the Omnibus Budget Reconciliation Act of 1990 (OBRA 90) provides that "if appropriate" a practitioner or other person may be given a reasonable opportunity to enter into and complete a corrective action plan agreed to by the PRO. Such a plan may include remedial education.

The Secretary's Exclusion Authority: If the Secretary agrees with the PRO report and finds a practitioner or other person has demonstrated an unwillingness or lack of ability substantially to comply with such obligations, then, in addition to any other sanction provided under law, the Secretary may exclude such practitioner or person from eligibility to provide services under the Act on a reimbursable basis. The exclusion may be permanent or for such period as the Secretary prescribes, but it must be for at least one year. That minimum duration requirement became effective January 1, 1997, pursuant to section 214 of the Health Insurance Portability and Accountability Act of 1996, P.L. 104–191.

Corrective Action Plans: With respect to a PRO initial determination made on or after November 5, 1990, section 4205(a) of OBRA 90 requires the Secretary, in determining whether a practitioner or person has demonstrated an unwillingness or lack of ability to comply with such obligations to consider the practitioner's or person's willingness or lack of ability to successfully complete a corrective action plan during the period before the PRO submits its recommendation to the Secretary.

Exclusion without Secretarial Review: If the Secretary fails to act upon a PRO recommendation within 120 days after submission, section 1156(b)(1) requires the practitioner or other person to be excluded until such time as the Secretary determines otherwise. In other words, if the Secretary takes too long to adopt an adverse PRO recommendation against a practitioner or person, Congress deemed the adverse recommendation sufficient basis for exclusion. That puts the burden to move the wheels of bureaucracy along on the practitioner or other person involved.

Effective Date of an Exclusion Order: Section 1156(b)(2) provides that a decision by the Secretary to exclude a practitioner or other person under section 1156(b) becomes effective on the same date and in the same manner as a section 1128 exclusion becomes effective under section 1128(c), 42 U.S.C.A. 1320a-6(c). The latter statute makes exclusions effective at such time and upon such reasonable notice to the public and to the individual or entity excluded as the Secretary may determine by regulation. Ordinarily, that means with respect to services furnished to an individual on or after a specified date. An exclusion does not apply, however, to payments made under Medicare or under a State health care program for inpatient institutional services furnished to an individual admitted to such an institution before the date of the exclusion, or for home health services and hospice care furnished to an individual under a plan of care established before the date of the exclusion, until 30 days after the effective date. Then the exclusion remains in effect, subject to the one year minimum period, until the Secretary finds and gives reasonable notice to the public that the basis for such determination has been removed and that there is reasonable assurance that it will not recur.

Assessing Costs in Lieu of Exclusion: Section 1156(b)(3) provides that, in cases where the offensive conduct involved providing or ordering health care services which were medically improper or unnecessary, the Secretary, in lieu of exclusion, may require a practitioner or other person to pay an amount not in excess of $10,000 for each instance of medically improper or unnecessary services provided. That amount may be deducted from any sums owing by the United States, or any instrumentality thereof, to the practitioner or person involved.

◆ NOTE: Prior to amendment by section 231(f) of the Health Insurance Portability and Accountability Act of 1996, effective January 1, 1997, the assessment was not to exceed the actual or estimated cost of the medically improper or unnecessary services.

Hearing Rights/Judicial Review: Pursuant to section 1156(b)(4), any practitioner or other person dissatisfied with a determination made by the Secretary under section 1156(b) is entitled to reasonable notice and opportunity for a hearing thereon by the Secretary to the same extent as provided in section 205(b), 42 U.S.C.A. 405(b), and to judicial review of the Secretary's final decision after such hearing as provided in section 205(g), 42 U.S.C.A. 405(g).

Special Hearing Rights for Practitioners in Medically Underserved Areas: Section 1156(b)(5) establishes special rights, however, for practitioners and other persons from rural health manpower shortage areas and counties with less than 70,000 population. Before a section 1156(b)(2) exclusion may be effected against them, they must be offered a hearing before an administrative law judge, as described in section 205(b). The purpose of that hearing is to determine whether the practitioner or other person should be able to continue furnishing services to individuals eligible for benefits under the Act pending completion of the administrative review procedure under section 1156(b)(4). If an administrative law judge does not determine, by a preponderance of the evidence, that the practitioner or other person will pose a serious risk to such individuals if permitted to continue furnishing services, the Secretary may not effect the exclusion until completion of the hearing authorized by section 1156(b)(4).

In other words, these practitioners and other persons can have a mini-hearing about the danger, if any, they impose by continuing to be reimbursed before their full hearing on exclusion.

PRO Coordination with Other Organizations: Section 1156(c) requires a PRO to use whatever authority or influence it has to enlist support of other professional or governmental organizations with influence or authority over health care practitioners and other persons providing health care services within the jurisdiction of the PRO to assure compliance with section 1156(a). This implies, for example, coordination of PRO efforts with State health care licensure boards.

Qualified Immunity for PRO's and PRO Reviewers: Making judgments about medical necessity of health care items and services, and about whether they meet professionally recognized standards, and about whether their provision is supported with appropriate documentation is not easy. In fact, it has been highly controversial, and fear of litigation was thought to inhibit PRO's from obtaining cooperation of health care professionals to make those judgments. Accordingly, pursuant to section 1157(a), no person who provides information to a PRO may be held, by reason thereof, to have violated any criminal law, or to be civilly liable under any law of the United States, or of any State or political subdivision thereof. This applies unless the information is unrelated to performance of the PRO contract with the Secretary, or unless the information is false and the person who provided it knew, or had reason to believe, it was false.

Prior to OBRA 90, section 1157(b) provided that no person employed by or having a fiduciary relationship with a PRO, and no person who furnishes professional services to a PRO, may be held by reason of performance of any duty, function, or activity required or authorized under Part B of Title XI, or by a valid contract entered into thereunder, to have violated any criminal law, or to be civilly liable under any law of the United States, or of any State or political subdivision thereof, if that person exercised due care.

Pursuant to section 4205(f) of OBRA 90, effective November 5, 1990, this protection also applies to an organization having a contract with the Secretary, that is, the PRO itself. Moreover, the required "due care" thereafter applies to the performance of an authorized or required PRO duty, function, or activity.

Apparently, some health care professionals and providers feared litigation if they followed PRO directives in the delivery of health care items and services where they disputed PRO judgments. Perhaps for that and other reasons, section 1157(c) provides that no M.D. or D.O. and no provider of health care services (including directors, trustees, employees, or officials thereof) may be held civilly liable to any person under any law of the United States, or of any State or political subdivision thereof, because of any action taken by such person in compliance with or reliance upon professionally developed norms of care and treatment applied by a PRO under a contract with the Secretary and operating in the area where the action was taken.

That is so, however, only if the M.D. or D.O. takes such action in the exercise of his or her profession, or if the provider takes such action in the exercise of his or her functions as a provider of health care services. Furthermore, that is so only if the M.D., D.O., or provider exercised due care in all professional conduct taken or directed and reasonably related to and resulting from the actions taken in compliance with or reliance upon PRO norms of care and treatment.

Reimbursement of Legal Expenses for PRO's and PRO Reviewers: Given the prospect of litigation against a PRO in the exercise of its judgments about medical necessity, professional standards of quality, and appropriate documentation of the delivery of health care goods and services, section 1157(d) provides for the Secretary to pay a PRO with whom he has a contract, or a member or employee thereof, or any person who furnishes legal counsel or services to a PRO, an amount equal to reasonable expenses incurred to defend any suit, action, or proceeding brought against a PRO, or a member or employee thereof. That is so, however, only if the suit, action, or proceeding is related to performance of a duty or function under the PRO contract by the PRO, its member or employee. Moreover, the reasonableness of the amount paid or reimbursed will be determined by the Secretary.

◆ NOTE: Section 1160(e) provides that for purposes of section 1157, "an organization with a contract with the Secretary under this part" includes an entity which competes for a utilization and quality control peer review contract under section 1154(a)(4)(C), 42 U.S.C.A. 1320c-5(a)(4)(C), which pertains to review of health maintenance organizations and competitive medical plans.

◆ NOTE ALSO: Pursuant to section 1162, the provisions of Part B of Title XI do not apply to sanatoriums operated, or listed and certified, by the First Church of Christ, Scientist, Boston, Massachusetts. Pursuant to section 1163, however, individuals licensed to practice medicine in American Samoa, the Northern Mariana Islands, and the Trust Territory of the Pacific Islands are considered to be physicians and doctors of medicine for purposes of Part B of Title XI and they are subject to its provisions.

Statutory Provisions

With respect to the obligations of health care practitioners and providers of health care goods and services, and to sanctions and penalties recommended by PRO's, section 1156, 42 U.S.C.A. 1320c-5, provides:

(a) It shall be the obligation of any health care practitioner and any other person (including a hospital or other health care facility, organization, or agency) who provides health care services for which payment may be made (in whole or in part) under this Act, to assure, to the extent of his authority that services or items ordered or provided by such practitioner or person to beneficiaries and recipients under this Act —

(1) will be provided economically and only when, and to the extent, medically necessary;

(2) will be of a quality which meets professionally recognized standards of health care; and

(3) will be supported by evidence of medical necessity and quality in such form and fashion and at such time as may reasonably be required by a reviewing peer review organization in the exercise of its duties and responsibilities.

(b) (1) If after reasonable notice and opportunity for discussion with the practitioner or person concerned, and, if appropriate, after the practitioner or person has been given a reasonable opportunity to enter into and complete a corrective action plan (which may include remedial education) agreed to by the organization, and has failed successfully to complete such plan, [This phrase beginning "and, if appropriate" and ending "to complete such plan" and the next to last sentence below were added by section 4205(a) of P.L. 101-508, the Omnibus Budget Reconciliation Act of 1990 (OBRA 90), applicable to initial determinations made by a PRO on or after November 5, 1990.] any organization having a contract with the Secretary under this part determines that such practitioner or person has —

(A) failed in a substantial number of cases substantially to comply with any obligation imposed on him under subsection (a), or

(B) grossly and flagrantly violated any such obligation in one or more instances, such organization shall submit a report and recommendations to the Secretary. If the Secretary agrees with such determination, the Secretary (in addition to any other sanction provided under law) may exclude (permanently or for such period as the Secretary may prescribe, except that such period may not be less than one year) such practitioner or person from eligibility to provide services under this Act on a reimbursable basis. If the Secretary fails to act upon the recommendations submitted to him by such organization within 120 days after such submission, such practitioner or person shall be excluded from eligibility to provide services on a reimbursable basis until such time as the Secretary determines otherwise.

◆ NOTE: Prior to amendment by section 214 of the Health Insurance Portability and Accountability Act of 1996 P.L. 104–191, effective January 1, 1997, section 1156(b)(1)(B) read: "grossly and flagrantly violated any such obligation in one or more instances, such organization shall submit a report and recommendations to the Secretary. If the Secretary agrees with such determination, and determines that such practitioner or person, in providing health care services over which such organization has review responsibility and for which payment (in whole or in part) may be made under this Act, has demonstrated an unwillingness or a lack of ability substantially to comply with such obligations, the Secretary (in addition to any other sanction provided under law) may exclude (permanently or for such period as the Secretary may prescribe) such practitioner or person from eligibility to provide services under this Act on a reimbursable basis. In determining whether a practitioner or person has demonstrated an unwillingness or lack of ability substantially to comply with such obligations, the Secretary shall consider the practitioner's or person's willingness or lack of ability, during the period before the organization submits its report and recommendations, to enter into and successfully complete a corrective action plan. If the Secretary fails to act upon the recommendations submitted to him by such organization within 120 days after such submission, such practitioner or person shall be excluded from eligibility to provide services on a reimbursable basis until such time as the Secretary determines otherwise."

(2) A determination made by the Secretary under this subsection to exclude a practitioner or person shall be effective on the same date and in the same manner as an exclusion from participation under the programs under this Act becomes effective under section 1128(c) [42 U.S.C.A. 1320a-6(c)] , and shall (subject to the minimum period specified in the second sentence of paragraph (1)) remain in effect until the Secretary finds and gives reasonable notice to the public that the basis for such determination has been removed and that there is reasonable assurance that it will not recur.

◆ NOTE: Section 214 of the Health Insurance Portability and Accountability Act of 1996, substituted "shall (subject to the minimum period specified in the second sentence of paragraph (1)) remain" for "shall remain", effective January 1, 1997.

(3) In lieu of the sanction authorized by paragraph (1), the Secretary may require that (as a condition to the continued eligibility of such practitioner or person to provide such health care services on a reimbursable basis) such practitioner or person pays to the United States, in case such acts or conduct involved the provision or ordering by such practitioner or person of health care services which were medically improper or unnecessary, an amount not in excess of up to $10,000 for each instance of the medically improper or unnecessary services so provided. Such amount may be deducted from any sums owing by the United States (or any instrumentality thereof) to the practitioner or person from whom such amount is claimed.

◆ NOTE: Section 231(f) of the Health Insurance Portability and Accountability Act of 1996 substituted "up to $10,000 for each instance" for "the actual or estimated cost", effective January 1, 1997.

(4) Any practitioner or person furnishing services described in paragraph (1) who is dissatisfied with a determination made by the Secretary under this subsection shall be entitled to reasonable notice and opportunity for a hearing thereon by the Secretary to the same extent as is provided in section 205(b) [42 U.S.C.A. 405(b)] , and to judicial review of the Secretary's final decision after such hearing as is provided in section 205(g) [42 U.S.C.A. 405(g)].

(5) Before the Secretary may effect an exclusion under paragraph (2) in the case of a provider or practitioner located in a rural health manpower shortage area (HMSA) or in a county with a population of less than 70,000, the provider or practitioner adversely affected by the determination is entitled to a hearing before an administrative law judge (described in section 205(b)) respecting whether the provider or practitioner should be able to continue furnishing services to individuals entitled to benefits under this Act, pending completion of the administrative review procedure under paragraph (4). If the judge does not determine, by a preponderance of the evidence, that the provider or practitioner will pose a serious risk to such individuals if permitted to continue furnishing such services, the Secretary shall not effect the exclusion under paragraph (2) until the provider or practitioner has been provided reasonable notice and opportunity for an administrative hearing thereon under paragraph (4).

(6) [Applicable to sanctions effected more than 60 days after November 5, 1990, pursuant to section 4205(d)(2) of OBRA 90] When the Secretary effects an exclusion of a physician under paragraph (2), the Secretary shall notify the State board responsible for the licensing of the physician of the exclusion.

(c) It shall be the duty of each utilization and quality control peer review organization to use such authority or influence it may possess as a professional organization, and to enlist the support of any other professional or governmental organization having influence or authority over health care practitioners and any other person (including a hospital or other health care facility, organization, or agency) providing health care services in the area served by such review organization, in assuring that each practitioner or person (referred to in subsection (a)) providing health care services in such area shall comply with all obligations imposed on him under subsection (a).

With respect to limiting liability of PRO's, their members, employees, and contractors, and of those who comply with PRO norms in rendering care and treatment, section 1157, 42 U.S.C.A. 1320c-6, provides:

(a) Notwithstanding any other provision of law, no person providing information to any organization having a contract with the Secretary under this part shall be held, by reason of having provided such information, to have violated any criminal law, or to be civilly liable under any law of the United States or of any State (or political subdivision thereof) unless —

(1) such information is unrelated to the performance of the contract of such organization; or

(2) such information is false and the person providing it knew, or had reason to believe, that such information was false.

(b) No organization having a contract with the Secretary under this part, and no [The phrase "organization having a contract with the Secretary under this part, and no" was added by section 4205(f) of OBRA 90, effective November 5, 1990.] person who is employed by, or who has a fiduciary relationship with, any such organization or who furnishes professional services to such organization, shall be held by reason of the performance [The same OBRA provision deleted "by him" which previously appeared here.] of any duty, function, or activity required or authorized pursuant to this part or to a valid contract entered into under this part, to have violated any criminal law, or to be civilly liable under any law of the United States or of any State (or political subdivision thereof) provided due care was exercised in the performance of such duty, function, or activity. [The same OBRA provision substituted "due care was exercised in the performance of such duty, function, or activity" for "he has exercised due care.]

(c) No doctor of medicine or osteopathy and no provider (including directors, trustees, employees, or officials thereof) of health care services shall be civilly liable to any person under any law of the United States or of any State (or political subdivision thereof) on account of any action taken by him in compliance with or reliance upon professionally developed norms of care and treatment applied by an organization under contract pursuant to section 1153 [42 U.S.C.A. 1320c-2] operating in the area where such doctor of medicine or osteopathy or provider took such action; but only if—

(1) he takes such action in the exercise of his profession as a doctor of medicine or osteopathy or in the exercise of his functions as a provider of health care services; and

(2) he exercised due care in all professional conduct taken or directed by him and reasonably related to, and resulting from,

the actions taken in compliance with or reliance upon such professionally accepted norms of care and treatment.

(d) The Secretary shall make payment to an organization under contract with him pursuant to this part, or to any member or employee thereof, or to any person who furnishes legal counsel or services to such organization, in an amount equal to the reasonable amount of the expenses incurred, as determined by the Secretary, in connection with the defense of any suit, action, or proceeding brought against such organization, member, or employee related to the performance of any duty or function under such contract by such organization, member, or employee.

With respect to the effective date of an exclusion under section 1156, section 1128(c), 42 U.S.C.A. 1320a-6(c), which applies by cross-reference, provides in pertinent part:

NOTICE, EFFECTIVE DATE, AND PERIOD OF EXCLUSION. —

(1) An exclusion under this section [which pertains to mandatory and permissive exclusions for a variety of criminal and civil offenses] or under section 1128A [which permits exclusion in conjunction with imposition of a civil money penalty] shall be effective at such time and upon such reasonable notice to the public and to the individual or entity excluded as may be specified in regulations consistent with paragraph (2).

(2) (A) Except as provided in subparagraph (B), such an exclusion shall be effective with respect to services furnished to an individual on or after the effective date of the exclusion.

(B) Unless the Secretary determines that the health and safety of individuals receiving services warrants the exclusion taking effect earlier, an exclusion shall not apply to payments made under title XVIII or under a State health care program for —

(i) inpatient institutional services furnished to an individual who was admitted to such institution before the date of the exclusion, or

(ii) home health services and hospice care furnished to an individual under a plan of care established before the date of the exclusion, until the passage of 30 days after the effective date of the exclusion.

(3) (A) The Secretary shall specify, in the notice of exclusion under paragraph (1) and the written notice under section 1128A, the minimum period (or, in the case of an exclusion of an individual under subsection (b)(12) [which pertains to failure by individuals and entities to grant immediate access to the Secretary, the Inspector General, certain State agencies, and State medicaid fraud control units], the period) of the exclusion.

With respect to hearing rights and judicial review, section 205, 42 U.S.C.A. 405, provides in pertinent part:

(b) (1) The Commissioner of Social Security is directed to make findings of fact, and decisions as to the rights of any individual applying for a payment under this title. Any such decision by the Commissioner of Social Security which involves a determination of disability and which is in whole or in part unfavorable to such individual shall contain a statement of the case, in understandable language, setting forth a discussion of the evidence, and stating the Commissoner's determination and the reason or reasons upon which it is based. Upon request by any such individual or upon request by a wife, divorced wife, widow, surviving divorced wife, surviving divorced mother, surviving divorced father, husband, divorced husband, widower, surviving divorced husband, child or parent who makes a showing in writing that his or her rights may be prejudiced by any decision the Commissioner of Social Security has rendered, the Commissioner shall give such applicant and such other individual reasonable notice and opportunity for a hearing with respect to such decision, and, if a hearing is held, shall, on the basis of evidence adduced at the hearing, affirm, modify, or reverse his findings of fact and such decision. Any such request with respect to such a decision must be filed within sixty days after notice of such decision is received by the individual making such request. The Commissioner of Social Security is further authorized, on the Commissioner's own motion, to hold such hearings and to conduct such investigations and other proceedings as the Commissioner may deem necessary or proper for the administration of this title. In the course of any hearing, investigation, or other proceeding, the Commissioner may administer oaths and affirmations, examine witnesses, and receive evidence. Evidence may be received at any hearing before the Commissioner of Social Security even though inadmissible under rules of evidence applicable to court procedure.

* * *

(g) Any individual, after any final decision of the Commissioner of Social Security made after a hearing to which he was a party, irrespective of the amount in controversy, may obtain a review of such decision by a civil action commenced within sixty days after the mailing to him of notice of such decision or within such further time as the Commissioner of Social Security may allow. Such action shall be brought in the district court of the United States for the judicial district in which the plaintiff resides, or has his principal place of business, or, if he does not reside or have his principal place of business within any such judicial district, in the District of Court of the United States for the District of Columbia [United States District Court for the District of Columbia]. As part of the Commissioner's answer the Commissioner of Social Security shall file a certified copy of the transcript of the record including the evidence upon which the findings and decision complained of are based. The court shall have power to enter, upon the pleadings and transcript of the record, a judgment affirming, modifying, or reversing the decision of the Commissioner of Social Security, with or without remanding the cause for a rehearing. The findings of the Commissioner of Social Security as to any fact, if supported by substantial evidence, shall be conclusive, and where a claim has been denied by the Commissioner or a decision is rendered under subsection (b) hereof which is adverse to an individual who was a party to the hearing before the Commissioner of Social Security, because of failure of the claimant or such individual to submit proof in conformity with any regulation prescribed under subsection (a) hereof, the court shall review only the question of conformity with such regulations and the validity of such regulations. The court may, on motion of the Commissioner of Social Security made for good cause shown before he files his answer, remand the case to the Commissioner of Social Security for further action by the Commissioner of

> Social Security, and it may at any time order additional evidence to be taken before the Commissioner of Social Security, but only upon a showing that there is new evidence which is material and that there is good cause for the failure to incorporate such evidence into the record in a prior proceeding; and the Commissioner of Social Security shall, after the case is remanded, and after hearing such additional evidence if so ordered, modify or affirm his findings of fact or the Commissioner's decision, or both, and shall file with the court any such additional and modified findings of fact and decision and a transcript of the additional record and testimony upon which the Commissioner's action in modifying or affirming was based. Such additional or modified findings of fact and decision shall be reviewable only to the extent provided for review of the original findings of fact and decision. The judgment of the court shall be final except that it shall be subject to review in the same manner as a judgment in other civil actions. Any action instituted in accordance with this subsection shall survive notwithstanding any change in the person occupying the office of Commissioner of Social Security or any vacancy in such office.

Subsection (a) of section 205, to which subsection (g) refers, provides:

> (a) The Commissioner of Social Security shall have full power and authority to make rules and regulations and to establish procedures, not inconsistent with the provisions of this title, which are necessary or appropriate to carry out such provisions, and shall adopt reasonable and proper rules and regulations to regulate and provide for the nature and extent of the proofs and evidence and the method of taking and furnishing the same in order to establish the right to benefits hereunder.

Section 205(h), 42 U.S.C.A. 405(h), provides:

> The findings and decision of the Commissioner of Social Security after a hearing shall be binding upon all individuals who were parties to such hearing. No findings of fact or decision of the Commissioner of Social Security shall be reviewed by any person, tribunal, or governmental agency except as herein provided. No action against the United States, the Commissioner of Social Security, or any officer or employee thereof shall be

> brought under section 1331 or 1346 of title 28, United States Code, to recover on any claim arising under this title.

◆ NOTE: Effective March 31, 1995, section 110(a) of P.L. 203-296, the Social Security Program Independence and Program Improvement Act of 1994, changed references to the Department of Health and Human Services to the Social Security Administration, and references to the Secretary of Health and Human Services to the Commissioner of Social Security, and references to the pronouns "she", "her", "he", "him", and "his" to "the Commissioner" or "the Commissioner's", as appropriate, throughout section 205 of the Social Security Act.

Finally, with respect to Christian Science sanatoriums, section 1162, 42 U.S.C.A. 1320c-11, provides:

> The provisions of this part [B of Title XI] shall not apply with respect to a Christian Science sanatorium operated, or listed and certified, by the First Church of Christ, Scientist, Boston, Massachusetts.

And, with respect to medical officers in American Samoa, the Northern Mariana Islands, and the Trust Territory of the Pacific Islands, section 1163, 42 U.S.C.A. 1320c-12, provides:

> For purposes of applying this part [B of Title XI] to American Samoa, the Northern Mariana Islands, and the Trust Territory of the Pacific Islands, individuals licensed to practice medicine in those places shall be considered to be physicians and doctors of medicine.

For regulatory citations, see Chapter 8

§ 4:20 UNLAWFUL DISCLOSURE OF INFORMATION OBTAINED BY PEER REVIEW ORGANIZATIONS — Section 1160 [42 U.S.C.A. 1320c-9]

Summary

The Freedom of Information Act, 5 U.S.C.A. 552, gives the public access to much information in the hands of the Federal government. The rights it grants apply to information held by Federal agencies and instrumentalities as well. Hence, absent section 1160, 42 U.S.C.A. 1320c-9, the public would seem to have broad rights to information in the hands of Peer Review Organizations (PRO's). In fact, however, those rights are limited.

Section 1160(a) declares that a PRO with a contract with the Secretary of Health and Human Services shall not be a Federal agency for Freedom of Information Act purposes. Furthermore, any data or information acquired by a PRO in the exercise of its duties and functions must be held in confidence and may not be disclosed to any person. That is the general rule.

There are three exceptions: One, PRO data and information may be disclosed to the extent necessary to carry out the purposes of Part B of Title XI of the Social Security Act. Two, PRO data and information may be disclosed in such cases and under such circumstances as the Secretary by regulation provides to assure adequate protection of the rights and interests of patients, health care practitioners, or providers of health care. Three, PRO data and information may be disclosed in accordance with section 1160(b).

Section 1160(b) provides that, in accordance with procedures and safeguards established by the Secretary, a PRO must disclose such data and information as may be necessary to assist Federal and State agencies which the Secretary finds have responsibility for identifying and investigating cases or patterns of fraud or abuse. For that purpose, data and information relating to a specific case or pattern, including that which may identify specific providers or practitioners, is to be provided to such agencies upon request.

In addition, a PRO can provide such data and information to assist appropriate Federal and State agencies which the Secretary finds have responsibility for identifying cases or patterns involving risks to public health. In such cases disclosure may be made, at the discretion of a PRO, upon request relating to a specific case or pattern with respect to which such an agency has made a finding, or has a reasonable belief, that there may be a substantial risk to public health. Such data and information must be provided, however, if the PRO, rather than the requesting agency, has made a finding or has a reasonable belief that a substantial public health risk exists.

Similarly, such data and information must be disclosed by a PRO to assist appropriate State agencies which the Secretary finds have responsibility for licensing or certification of providers or practitioners. It also must be disclosed to assist national accreditation bodies acting pursuant to section 1865, 42 U.S.C.A. 1395bb, to accredit providers for purposes of meeting Medicare conditions. In such cases, disclosure is to be made by the PRO upon request of the agency or body relating to a specific case or to a possible pattern of substandard care, but only to the extent required by the agency or body to carry out its function under State law or under section 1865.

Finally, such data and information must be disclosed to assist the Secretary, and such Federal and State agencies which the Secretary finds have health planning or related responsibilities under Federal or State law, to carry out appropriate health care planning and related activities. That includes health systems agencies and State health planning and development agencies. In such cases, the data and information must be provided in such format and manner as may be prescribed by the Secretary or agreed upon by the responsible Federal and State agencies and the PRO. Nevertheless, for this purpose, disclosure must be in the form of aggregate statistical data, without identifying any individual, on a geographic, institutional, or other basis reflecting the volume and frequency of services furnished, as well as demographic characteristics of the population subject to the PRO's review.

For any of these authorized disclosures, a PRO may charge a reasonable fee.

Section 1160(c) makes it a misdemeanor for any person to disclose PRO data and information acquired in the exercise of PRO duties and functions, other than for the purposes described above. Any person who does so is, upon conviction, subject to a fine of not more than $1,000 or to imprisonment for not more than six months, or both, and, in addition will have to pay the costs of prosecution.

This penalty does not apply to disclosure of any information received under section 1160(b), but it does apply to disclosure by an entity that receives such information for fraud and abuse investigation, public health risk assessment, and licensure and accreditation purposes. Even those agencies are exempt from punishment, however, if their disclosure is made in a judicial, administrative, or other formal legal proceeding resulting from an investigation which they conduct.

Section 1160(d) provides that no patient record in the possession of a PRO shall be subject to subpoena or discovery proceedings in a civil action. Furthermore, pursuant to section 4205(e) of P.L. 101-508, the Omnibus Budget Reconciliation Act of 1990 (OBRA 90), applicable to all proceedings as of November 5, 1990, no document or other information produced by a PRO in connection with its deliberations in making determinations under section 1154(a)(1)(B), 42 U.S.C.A. 1320c-3(a)(1)(B), or section 1156(a)(2), 42 U.S.C.A. 1320c-5(a)(2), shall be subject to subpoena or discovery in a civil proceeding. The only exception is for a summary of the PRO's findings and conclusions. That, however, may be made available only to a practitioner or other person adversely affected by a PRO determination.

Finally, section 1160(e) defines a PRO to include an entity which successfully competed for utilization review and quality control contracts with the Secretary pursuant to section 1154(a)(4)(C). The latter pertains to review of health maintenance organizations and competitive medical plans.

Statutory Provisions

With respect to the prohibition against disclosure of data and information in the possession of a PRO, section 1160, 42 U.S.C.A. 1320c-9, provides:

> (a) An organization, in carrying out its functions under a contract entered into under this part, shall not be a Federal agency for purposes of the provisions of section 553 of title 5, United States Code (commonly referred to as the Freedom of Information Act). Any data or information acquired by any such organization in the exercise of its duties and functions shall be held in confidence and shall not be disclosed to any person except—
>
> (1) to the extent that may be necessary to carry out the purposes of this part,
>
> (2) in such cases and under such circumstances as the Secretary shall by regulations provide to assure adequate protection of the rights and interests of patients, health care practitioners, or providers of health care, or
>
> (3) in accordance with subsection (b).
>
> (b) An organization having a contract with the Secretary under this part shall provide in accordance with procedures and safeguards established by the Secretary, data and information—
>
> (1) which may identify specific providers or practitioners as may be necessary—
>
> (A) to assist Federal and State agencies recognized by the Secretary as having responsibility for identifying and investigating cases or patterns of fraud or abuse, which data and information shall be provided by the peer review organiza-

tion to any such agency at the request of such agency relating to a specific case or pattern;

(B) to assist appropriate Federal and State agencies recognized by the Secretary as having responsibility for identifying cases or patterns involving risks to the public health, which data and information shall be provided by the peer review organization to any such agency —

(i) at the discretion of the peer review organization, at the request of such agency relating to a specific case or pattern with respect to which such agency has made a finding, or has a reasonable belief, that there may be a substantial risk to the public health, or

(ii) upon a finding by, or the reasonable belief of, the peer review organization that there may be a substantial risk to the public health;

(C) to assist appropriate State agencies recognized by the Secretary as having responsibility for licensing or certification of providers or practitioners or to assist national accreditation bodies acting pursuant to section 1865 [42 U.S.C.A. 1395bb] in accrediting providers for purposes of meeting the conditions described in title XVIII, which data and information shall be provided by the peer review organization to any such agency or body at the request of such agency or body relating to a specific case or to a possible pattern of substandard care, but only to the extent that such data and information are required by the agency or body to carry out its respective function which is within the jurisdiction of the agency or body under State law or under section 1865; and

(D) to provide notice in accordance with section 1154(a)(9)(B);

◆ NOTE: Section 156(b)(2)(B) of the Social Security Act Amendments of 1994, P.L. 103-432, amended paragraph (D), effective October 31, 1994. Previously, it read: "to provide notice to the State medical board in accordance with section 1154(a)(9)(B) when the organization submits a report and recommendations to the Secretary under section 1156(b)(1) with respect to a physician whom the board is responsible for licensing." Paragraph (D) was added by section 4205(d)(1)(B) of P.L.

101-508, the Omnibus Budget Reconciliation Act of 1990 (OBRA 90), applicable to notices of proposed sanctions issued more than 60 days after November 5, 1990.

(2) to assist the Secretary, and such Federal and State agencies recognized by the Secretary as having health planning or related responsibilities under Federal or State law (including health systems agencies and State health planning and development agencies), in carrying out appropriate health care planning and related activities, which data and information shall be provided in such format and manner as may be prescribed by the Secretary or agreed upon by the responsible Federal and State agencies and such organization, and shall be in the form of aggregate statistical data (without explicitly identifying any individual) on a geographic, institutional, or other basis reflecting the volume and frequency of services furnished, as well as the demographic characteristics of the population subject to review by such organization.

The penalty provided in subsection (c) shall not apply to the disclosure of any information received under this subsection, except that such penalty shall apply to the disclosure (by the agency receiving such information) of any such information described in paragraph (1) unless such disclosure is made in a judicial, administrative, or other formal legal proceeding resulting from an investigation conducted by the agency receiving the information. An organization may require payment of a reasonable fee for providing information under this subsection in response to a request for such information.

(c) It shall be unlawful for any person to disclose any such information described in subsection (a) other than for the purposes provided in subsections (a) and (b), and any person violating the provisions of this section shall, upon conviction, be fined not more than $1,000, and imprisoned for not more than 6 months, or both, and shall be required to pay the costs of prosecution.

(d) No patient record in the possession of an organization having a contract with the Secretary under this part shall be subject to subpoena or discovery proceedings in a civil action. No document or other information produced by such an organization in connection with its deliberations in making determinations under section 1154(a)(1)(B) [42 U.S.C.A. 1320c-3(a)(1)(B)] or

1156(a)(2) [42 U.S.C.A. 1320c-5(a)(2)] shall be subject to subpoena or discovery in any administrative or civil proceeding; except that such an organization shall provide, upon request of a practitioner or other person adversely affected by such a determination, a summary of the organization's findings and conclusions in making the determination. [The preceding sentence was added by section 4205(e) of OBRA 90, applicable to all proceedings as of November 5, 1990.]

(e) For purposes of this section and section 1157, the term "organization with a contract with the Secretary under this part" includes an entity with a contract with the Secretary under section 1154(a)(4)(C) [42 U.S.C.A. 1320c-3(a)(4)(C)].

For regulatory citations, see Chapter 8

§ 4:21 DISQUALIFICATION OF PHYSICIANS FROM GIVING SECOND OPINIONS ABOUT SURGERY — Section 1164(b)(4)(D) [42 U.S.C.A. 1320c-13(b)(4)(D)]

Summary

◆ NOTE: This sanction was repealed effective October 31, 1994, by section 156(a)(1) of the Social Security Act Amendments of 1994, P.L. 103-432

When Medicare was enacted, one way to control costs was to exclude from coverage items and services not reasonable and necessary for health care. That meant someone with medical expertise had to make judgments about "reasonableness" and "necessity." In time, that gave rise to Peer Review Organizations (PRO's), not only to help control the seemingly endless rise in health care costs, but also to help improve the quality of health care in the nation.

While section 1164 was law, section 1152, 42 U.S.C.A. 1320c-1, defines "utilization and quality control peer review organization" as an entity —

1. which is comprised of a substantial number of the licensed doctors of medicine and osteopathy engaged in the practice of medicine or surgery in the area who are representative of practicing physicians in the area;
2. which has available to it services of a sufficient number of licensed doctors of medicine or osteopathy engaged in the practice of medicine or surgery in such area to assure ade-

quate peer review of services provided by the various medical specialties and subspecialties;

3. which is able, in the judgment of the Secretary, to perform peer review functions effectively and efficiently, and to perform review of the pattern of quality of care in an area of medical practice where performance is measured against objective criteria which define acceptable and adequate practice; and
4. which has at least one individual who is a representative of consumers on its governing body.

Section 1153(a)(1), 42 U.S.C.A. 1320c-2(a)(1), required the Secretary of Health and Human Services to establish geographic areas throughout the United States with respect to which PRO contracts were to be made. In general, pursuant to section 1153(a)(2), PRO areas had to be Statewide. Where warranted by the volume of review activity or other factors determined by the Secretary to be relevant, however, Congress authorized the Secretary to establish local or regional areas, provided he took into account the volume of hospital admissions within each State for which Medicare or Medicaid payments may be made. Any State having fewer than 180,000 admissions annually must have a Statewide PRO. Moreover, no local or regional area could be established which had fewer than 60,000 hospital admissions, including public and private pay patients, under review annually. Furthermore, no local or regional PRO area could be established which is not a self-contained medical service area with a full spectrum of services, including medical specialists' services. These limitations do not apply, however, if the Secretary found other relevant factors warrant a different decision.

Once the Secretary established PRO areas, section 1153(b) required him to enter into a contract with a PRO for each area if a qualified organization was available in the area and if he and the organization negotiated a contract which the Secretary determined would be carried out in a manner consistent with efficient and effective administration of Title XI, Part B.

Section 1154(a)(1), 42 U.S.C.A. 1320c-3(a)(1), requires a PRO to review, within its jurisdiction and according to its contract, some or all of the professional activities of physicians and other health care practitioners and institutional and noninstitutional providers of health care services with respect to provision of health care services and items for which payment may be made, in whole or in part, by

Medicare. That includes health maintenance organizations and competitive medical plans.

One purpose of that review was to determine whether the services and items are or were reasonable and medically necessary and whether they are excluded from coverage for a variety of reasons specified in the law. Another purpose was to determine whether the quality of the such services meets professionally recognized standards of health care. A third purpose was to determine whether services and items proposed to be provided in a hospital or health care facility on an inpatient basis could be provided effectively but more economically on an outpatient basis or in an inpatient health care facility of a different type (for example, in a nursing facility instead of a hospital.)

Section 1154(a)(2) provided that, when a PRO makes such a review, it will then determine whether payment should be made for the services under Medicare. It also provided that the PRO payment determination is conclusive, with exceptions not relevant here.

Section 1154(a)(2) further provided that PRO determinations not to pay based on substandard quality would be made only on the basis of criteria which are consistent with guidelines established by the Secretary.

PRO's had many obligations, one of which was to specify at least 10 surgical procedures which it will always review. That was to be done in accordance with guidelines of the Secretary. Generally, procedures specified were to be ones which usually can be postponed without undue risk to a patient, procedures which are high volume for Medicare patients, or which are high cost, and procedures which have a comparatively high rate of nonconfirmation upon examination by another qualified physician, or for which there is substantial geographic variation in rates of performance. Other reasons also might be found to place a procedure on the 100 percent review list.

For procedures on the list which are done on an outpatient basis, PRO review had to be done prior to performance. For procedures on the list which are done on a hospital inpatient basis, PRO review had to be done prior to admission to the hospital. Exceptions to these requirements were for medical emergency or such other circumstances as the Secretary may specify.

In conducting 100 percent review, a PRO had to rely on second opinions from a cadre of board certified or board eligible specialists appropriate to the procedure under review. In most cases, however, a patient may choose any physician of the proper specialty to render the second opinion. Patients could not choose such a physician, however, who is affiliated with, or has a common financial interest with, the physician who rendered the first opinion that the procedure was necessary. Furthermore, section 1164(b)(4)(D), 42 U.S.C.A. 1320c-13(b)(4)(D), provided that patients cannot choose a physician that a PRO has disqualified from providing a second opinion because of the "gross unreliability" of second opinions such physician has provided.

According to section 1164(c), one purpose of requiring a second opinion for a 100 percent review surgical procedure was to determine whether the procedure is reasonable and medically necessary or not. Another purpose was to determine whether the procedure, though reasonable and medically necessary, nonetheless raises questions of medical appropriateness. Again, the latter would be determined by a second opinion. When a decision is made that a surgical procedure on the 100 percent review list is not reasonable and medically necessary, or that it is, but nevertheless is found medically inappropriate, a PRO must give notice thereof to the physician, the patient, and hospital or other entity furnishing the service.

If such a procedure was performed, despite a PRO decision that it is reasonable and medically necessary, but nonetheless medically inappropriate, section 1164(c)(2) prohibits Medicare payment for it unless the patient obtains a second opinion. That is known as an elective second opinion. Pursuant to section 1164(c)(3), however, an elective second opinion was not required if a delay in performing the procedure would result in a risk to the patient, or if no physician was available who was qualified to provide the second opinion and who accepts payment by Medicare assignment for rendering second opinions, or if the procedure will be performed on a patient who belongs to a health maintenance organization (HMO) or competitive medical plan (CMP).

Pursuant to section 1164(d), a PRO was to function as a referral center for second opinions required by the statute. To do that, a list had to be maintained of physicians qualified to provide second opinions, and patients were to be advised which physicians are Medicare participating physicians who have agreed to accept Medicare assignments to obtain payment for their services.

In addition, under section 1164(d), a PRO must, upon request of a patient seeking a second opinion, was to obtain the relevant medical records from the physician who rendered the first opinion that the surgical procedure was necessary and provide it to the physician selected by the patient to render the second opinion.

Finally, section 1164(e) required the Secretary to assure that notice is provided to physicians, hospitals, ambulatory surgical centers, and beneficiaries about the 100 percent review process, including the list of surgical procedures for which such review is required.

Statutory Provisions

Section 1152, 42 U.S.C.A. 1320c-1, as it was while section 1164 was law, defined utilization and quality control peer review organization as follows:

> The term "utilization and quality control peer review organization" means an entity which —
>
> (1) (A) is composed of a substantial number of the licensed doctors of medicine and osteopathy engaged in the practice of medicine or surgery in the area and who are representative of the practicing physicians in the area, designated by the Secretary under section 1153 [42 U.S.C.A. 1320c-2] , with respect to which the entity shall perform services under this part, or (B) has available to it, by arrangement or otherwise, the services of a sufficient number of licensed doctors of medicine or osteopathy engaged in the practice of medicine or surgery in such area to assure that adequate peer review of the services provided by the various medical specialties and subspecialties can be assured;
>
> (2) is able, in the judgment of the Secretary, to perform review functions required under section 1154 [42 U.S.C.A. 1320c-3] in a manner consistent with the efficient and effective administration of this part and to perform reviews of the pattern of quality of care in an area of medical practice where actual performance is measured against objective criteria which define acceptable and adequate practice; and
>
> (3) has at least one individual who is a representative of consumers on its governing body.

Section 1153, 42 U.S.C.A. 13951320c-2, then provided in pertinent part:

> (a) (1) The Secretary shall establish throughout the United States geographic areas with respect to which contracts under this part will be made. In establishing such areas, the Secre-

tary shall use the same areas as established under section 1152 of this Act as in effect immediately prior to the date of the enactment of the Peer Review Improvement Act of 1982, but subject to the provisions of paragraph (2) [September 2, 1982. See section 143 of the Peer Review Improvement Act of 1982 of the Tax Equity and Fiscal Responsibility Act of 1982, P.L. 97-248].

(2) As soon as practicable after the date of the enactment of the Peer Review Improvement Act of 1982, the Secretary shall consolidate such geographic areas, taking into account the following criteria:

(A) Each State shall generally be designated as a geographic area for purposes of paragraph (1).

(B) The Secretary shall establish local or regional areas rather than State areas only where the volume of review activity or other relevant factors (as determined by the Secretary) warrant such an establishment, and the Secretary determines that review activity can be carried out with equal or greater efficiency by establishing such local or regional areas. In applying this subparagraph the Secretary shall take into account the number of hospital admissions within each State for which payment may be made under title XVIII or a State plan approved under title XIX, with any State having fewer than 180,000 such admissions annually being established as a single statewide area, and no local or regional area being established which has fewer than 60,000 total hospital admissions (including public and private pay patients) under review annually, unless the Secretary determines that other relevant factors warrant otherwise.

(C) No local or regional area shall be designated which is not a self-contained medical service area, having a full spectrum of services, including medical specialists' services.

(b) (1) The Secretary shall enter into a contract with a utilization and quality control peer review organization for each area established under subsection (a) if a qualified organization is available in such area and such organization and the Secretary have negotiated a proposed contract which the Secretary determines will be carried out by such organization in a manner consistent with the efficient and effective administration of this part. If more than one such qualified organization meets the requirements of the preceding sentence, priority shall be given to any such organization which is described in section 1152(1)(A).

(2) (A) Prior to November 15, 1984, the Secretary shall not enter into a contract under this part with any entity which is, or is affiliated with (through management, ownership, or common control), an entity (other than a self-insured employer) which directly or indirectly makes payments to any practitioner or provider whose health care services are reviewed by such entity or would be reviewed by such entity if it entered into a contract with the Secretary under this part. For purposes of this paragraph, an entity shall not be considered to be affiliated with another entity which makes payments (directly or indirectly) to any practitioner or provider, by reason of management, ownership, or common control, if the management, ownership or common control consists only of members of the governing board being affiliated (through management, ownership, or common control) with a health maintenance organization or competitive medical plan which is an "eligible organization" as defined in section 1876(b) [42 U.S.C.A. 1395mm(b)].

(B) If, after November 14, 1984, the Secretary determines that there is no other entity available for an area with which the Secretary can enter into a contract under this part, the Secretary may then enter into a contract under this part with an entity described in subparagraph (A) for such area if such entity otherwise meets the requirements of this part.

(3) (A) The Secretary shall not enter into a contract under this part with any entity which is, or is affiliated with (through management, ownership, or common control), a health care facility, or association of such facilities, within the area served by such entity or which would be served by such entity if it entered into a contract with the Secretary under this part.

(B) For purposes of subparagraph (A), an entity shall not be considered to be affiliated with a health care facility or association of facilities by reason of management, ownership, or common control if the management, ownership, or common control consists only of not more than 20 percent of the members of the governing board of the entity being affiliated (through management, ownership, or common control) with one or more of such facilities or associations.

(c) Each contract with an organization under this section shall provide that—

(1) the organization shall perform the functions set forth in section 1154(a), or may subcontract for the performance of all or some of such functions (and for purposes of paragraphs (2) and (3) of subsection (b), a subcontract under this paragraph shall not constitute an affiliation with the subcontractor);...[.]

* * *

(g) The Secretary shall provide that fiscal intermediaries furnish to peer review organizations, each month on a timely basis, data necessary to initiate the review process under section 1154(a) on a timely basis. If the Secretary determines that a fiscal intermediary is unable to furnish such data on a timely basis, the Secretary shall require the hospital to do so.

With respect to the functions of Peer Review Organizations, section 1154, 42 U.S.C.A. 1320c-3, then provided in pertinent part:

(a) Any utilization and quality control peer review organization entering into a contract with the Secretary under this part must perform the following functions:

(1) The organization shall review some or all of the professional activities in the area, subject to the terms of the contract and subject to the requirements of subsection (d), of physicians and other health care practitioners and institutional and noninstitutional providers of health care services in the provision of health care services and items for which payment may be made (in whole or in part) under title XVIII (including where payment is made for such services to eligible organizations pursuant to contracts under section 1876 [42 U.S.C.A. 1395mm, which pertains to health maintenance organizations and competitive medical plans]) for the purpose of determining whether—

(A) such services and items are or were reasonable and medically necessary and whether such services and items are not allowable under subsection (a)(1) or (a)(9) of section 1862 [42 U.S.C.A. 1395y(a)(1) and (9);

(B) the quality of such services meets professionally recognized standards of health care; and

(C) in case such services and items are proposed to be provided in a hospital or other health care facility on an inpatient basis, such services and items could, consistent with the provision of appropriate medical care, be effectively provided more economically on an outpatient basis or in an inpatient health care facility of a different type.

If the organization performs such reviews with respect to a type of health care practitioner other than medical doctors, the organization shall establish procedures for the involvement of health care practitioners of that type in such reviews.

◆ NOTE: Pursuant to section 6224(a) of P.L. 101-239, the Omnibus Budget Reconciliation Act of 1989, the preceding sentence applied to PRO contracts entered into after December 19, 1989.

(2) The organization shall determine, on the basis of the review carried out under subparagraphs (A), (B), and (C) of paragraph (1), whether payment shall be made for services under title XVIII. Such determination shall constitute the conclusive determination on those issues for purposes of payment under title XVIII, except that payment may be made if —

(A) such payment is allowed by reason of section 1879 [42 U.S.C.A. 1395pp, which permitted payment of Medicare benefits otherwise to be disallowed under section 1862(a)(1) and (a)(9) in cases where providers and beneficiaries did not know, and could not reasonably have been expected to know, disallowance was required];

(B) in the case of inpatient hospital services or extended care services, the peer review organization determines that additional time is required in order to arrange for postdischarge care, but payment may be continued under this subparagraph for not more than two days, but only in the case where the provider of such services did not know and could not reasonably have been expected to know (as determined under section 1879) that payment would not otherwise be made for such services under title XVIII prior to notification by the organization under paragraph (3);

(C) such determination is changed as the result of any hearing or review of the determination under section 1155 [42 U.S.C.A. 1320c-4]; or

(D) such payment is authorized under section 1861(v)(1)(G) [42 U.S.C.A. 1395x(v)(1)(G), which in certain cases permitted payment of Medicare benefits equivalent to those for skilled nursing care in any case in which a hospital provides inpatient services to an individual which are determined by a PRO or the Secretary or his designee to have been not medically necessary but which have constituted medically necessary extended care services if provided by a skilled nursing facility].

Determinations that payment should not be made by reason of subparagraph (B) of paragraph (1) shall be made only on the basis of criteria which are consistent with guidelines established by the Secretary.

(3) (A) Subject to subparagraphs (B) and (D), whenever the organization makes a determination that any health care services or items furnished or to be furnished to a patient by any practitioner or provider are disapproved, the organization shall promptly notify such patient and the agency or organization responsible for the payment of claims under title XVIII of this Act of such determination.

(B) The notification under subparagraph (A) with respect to services and items disapproved by reason of subparagraph (A) or (C) of paragraph (1) shall not occur until 20 days after the date that the organization has —

(i) made a preliminary notification to such practitioner or provider of such proposed determination, and

(ii) provided such practitioner or provider an opportunity for discussion and review of the proposed determination.

(C) The discussion and review conducted under subparagraph (B)(ii) shall not affect the rights of a practitioner or provider to a formal reconsideration of a determination under this part (as provided under section 1155 [42

U.S.C.A. 1320c-4, which provided for administrative hearing and judicial review of denied claims]).

(D) The notification under subparagraph (A) with respect to services or items disapproved by reason of paragraph (1)(B) shall not occur until after —

(i) the organization has notified the practitioner or provider involved of the determination and of the practitioner's or provider's right to a formal reconsideration of the determination under section 1155, and

(ii) if the provider or practitioner requests such a reconsideration, the organization has made such a reconsideration.

If a provider or practitioner is provided a reconsideration, such reconsideration shall be in lieu of any subsequent reconsideration to which the provider or practitioner may be otherwise entitled under section 1155, but shall not affect the right of a beneficiary from seeking reconsideration under such section of the organization's determination (after any reconsideration requested by the provider or physician under clause (ii)).

(E) In the case of services and items disapproved by reason of paragraph (1)(b), the notice to the patient shall state the following: "In the judgment of the peer review organization, the medical care received was not acceptable under the medicare program. The reasons for the denial have been discussed with your physician and hospital."

◆ NOTE: Section 6224(b)(1) of P.L. 101-239, the Omnibus Budget Reconciliation Act of 1989, effective December 19, 1989, substituted "subparagraphs (B) and (D)" for "subparagraph (B)" in subsection (a)(3)(A). It also added "with respect to services or items disapproved by reason of subparagraph (A) or (C) of paragraph (1)" after "under subparagraph (A)" in subsection (a)(3)(B). And it added new subparagraphs (D) and (E) to subsection (a)(3).

* * *

(5) The organization shall consult with nurses and other professional health care practitioners (other than physicians described in section 1861(r)(1) [42 U.S.C.A. 1395x(r)(1), which

defined physician to include M.D.'s and D.O.'s legally authorized to practice in their respective States]) and with representatives of institutional and noninstitutional providers of health care services, with respect to the organization's responsibility for the review under paragraph (1) of the professional activities of such practitioners and providers.

(6) (A) The organization shall, consistent with the provisions of its contract under this part, apply professionally developed norms of care, diagnosis, and treatment based upon typical patterns of practice within the geographic area served by the organization as principal points of evaluation and review, taking into consideration national norms where appropriate. Such norms with respect to treatment for particular illnesses or health conditions shall include—

(i) the types and extent of the health care services which, taking into account differing, but acceptable, modes of treatment and methods of organizing and delivering care, are considered within the range of appropriate diagnosis and treatment of such illness or health condition, consistent with professionally recognized and accepted patterns of care; and

(ii) the type of health care facility which is considered, consistent with such standards, to be the type in which health care services which are medically appropriate for such illness or condition can most economically be provided.

As a component of the norms described in clause (i) or (ii), the organization shall take into account the special problems associated with delivering care in remote rural areas, the availability of service alternatives to inpatient hospitalization, and other appropriate factors (such as the distance from a patient's residence to the site of care, family support, availability of proximate alternative sites of care, and the patient's ability to carry out necessary or prescribed self-care regimens) that could adversely affect the safety or effectiveness of treatment provided on an outpatient basis.

* * *

(7) The organization, to the extent necessary and appropriate to the performance of the contract, shall—

(A) (i) make arrangements to utilize the services of persons who are practitioners of, or specialists in, the various areas of medicine (including dentistry), or other types of health care, which persons shall, to the maximum extent practicable, be individuals engaged in the practice of their profession within the area served by such organization; and

(ii) in the case of psychiatric and physical rehabilitation services, make arrangements to ensure that (to the extent possible) initial review of such services be made by a physician who is trained in psychiatry or physical rehabilitation (as appropriate).

(B) undertake such professional inquiries either before or after, or both before and after, the provision of services with respect to which such organization has a responsibility for review which in the judgment of such organization will facilitate its activities;

(C) examine the pertinent records of any practitioner or provider of health care services providing services with respect to which such organization has a responsibility for review under paragraph (1); and

(D) inspect the facilities in which care is rendered or services are provided (which are located in such area) of any practitioner or provider of health care services providing services with respect to which such organization has a responsibility for review under paragraph (1).

* * *

(12) The organization shall perform the review, referral, and other functions required under section 1164 [42 U.S.C.A. 1320c-13, which pertained to 100 percent peer review of certain surgical procedures].

* * *

(14) The organization shall conduct an appropriate review of all written complaints about the quality of services (for which payment may otherwise be made under title XVIII) not meeting professionally recognized standards of health care, if the complaint is filed with the organization by an individual entitled to benefits for such services under such title (or a person

acting on the individual's behalf). The organization shall inform the individual (or representative) of the organization's final disposition of the complaint. Before the organization concludes that the quality of services does not meet professionally recognized standards of health care, the organization must provide the practitioner or person concerned with reasonable notice and opportunity for discussion.

* * *

(b) (1) No physician shall be permitted to review —

(A) health care services provided to a patient if he was directly responsible for providing such services; or

(B) health care services provided in or by an institution, organization, or agency, if he or any member of his family has, directly or indirectly, a significant financial interest in such institution, organization, or agency.

(2) For purposes of this subsection, a physician's family includes only his spouse (other than a spouse who is legally separated from him under a decree of divorce or separate maintenance), children (including legally adopted children), grandchildren, parents, and grandparents.

(c) No utilization and quality control peer review organization shall utilize the services of any individual who is not a duly licensed doctor of medicine, osteopathy, or dentistry to make final determinations of denial decisions in accordance with its duties and functions under this part with respect to the professional conduct of any other duly licensed doctor of medicine, osteopathy, or dentistry, or any act performed by any duly licensed doctor of medicine, osteopathy, or dentistry in the exercise of his profession.

(d) Each contract under this part shall require that the utilization and quality control peer review organization's review responsibility pursuant to subsection (a)(1) will include review of all ambulatory surgical procedures specified pursuant to section 1833(i)(1)(A) [42 U.S.C.A. 1395l(i)(1)(A), which required the Secretary to establish, in consultation with appropriate medical organizations, lists of surgical procedures appropriately performed on an inpatient hospital basis which also could be performed in a qualified ambulatory surgical center] which are performed in the area, or, at the discretion of the Secretary (and except as provided in section 1164 [42 U.S.C.A. 1320c-13, which pertained to 100 percent peer review for certain surgical procedures]) a sample of such procedures.

* * *

(f) The Secretary, in consultation with appropriate experts, shall identify methods that would be available to assist peer review organizations (under subsection (a)(4)) in identifying those cases which are more likely than others to be associated with a quality of services which does not meet professionally recognized standards of health care.

With respect to the obligation of PRO's to perform 100 percent peer review for certain surgical procedures, section 1164, 42 U.S.C.A. 1320c-13, provided:

(a) 100 PERCENT REVIEW FUNCTION. —

(1) IN GENERAL. — Each utilization and quality control peer review organization shall perform the review described in section 1154(a)(1) for 100 percent of the surgical procedures specified pursuant to subsection (b).

(2) TIMING OF REVIEW. —

(A) IN GENERAL. — Except as provided in subparagraph (B), the review required under paragraph (1) shall be performed —

(i) before the performance of the procedure, in the case of an outpatient procedure, or

(ii) before admission to the hospital for the provision of services in connection with the procedure, in the case of a procedure performed on an inpatient basis.

(B) EXCEPTION. — The review with respect to a procedure need not be performed by the time specified in subparagraph (A) in cases of a medical emergency and under such other circumstances as the Secretary may specify.

(b) SPECIFICATION OF SURGICAL PROCEDURES AND QUALIFIED REVIEWERS. —

(1) IN CONTRACT. — The contract with each organization under this part shall specify at least 10 surgical procedures to be covered under this section.

(2) SELECTION GUIDELINES. —

(A) IN GENERAL. — The specification of procedures shall be consistent with selection guidelines established by the Secretary under paragraph (3). The procedures specified shall be included among the surgical procedures which the Secretary has identified as reasonably being able to meet such guidelines.

(B) EXCEPTION. — The Secretary may permit an organization to include among the procedures specified under paragraph (1) procedures not identified by the Secretary under paragraph (2)(A) if to do so would be cost effective and consistent with the criteria described in paragraph (3).

(3) CRITERIA. — The Secretary shall establish such guidelines and identify such surgical procedures consistent with the following criteria:

(A) The procedure is one which generally can be postponed without undue risk to the patient.

(B) The procedure is a high volume procedure among patients who are covered under the programs established under title XVIII or is a high cost procedure.

(C) The procedure has a comparatively high rate of nonconfirmation upon examination by another qualified physician, there is substantial geographic variation in the rates of performance of the procedure, or there are other reasons why pre-procedure review for 100 percent of the procedures would be cost effective.

(4) QUALIFICATIONS FOR PHYSICIANS PROVIDING SECOND OPINIONS.—

(A) IN GENERAL. — The Secretary shall specify, for each procedure identified under paragraphs (2) and (3), the type or types of board certified or board eligible specialists who may conduct a second opinion, required under subsection (c), based upon the nature of the procedure.

(B) FREEDOM OF CHOICE OF PATIENT TO CHOOSE PHYSICIAN. — Subject to subparagraphs (C) and (D), the patient may choose any physician of the proper specialty under subparagraph (A) to provide the second opinion.

(C) PHYSICIANS PROHIBITED FROM PROVIDING SECOND OPINIONS. — For purposes of this section, a second opinion may not be provided by a physician who is affiliated with, or has a common financial interest with, the physician who rendered the first opinion that the procedure was necessary.

(D) RESTRICTED LIST. — In accordance with guidelines of the Secretary, an organization may disqualify a physician from providing a second opinion under this section because of the gross unreliability of the second opinions provided.

(c) REQUIRING A SECOND OPINION IN CERTAIN CASES. —

(1) DETERMINATIONS BY ORGANIZATION. — In the case of a review performed pursuant to subsection (a), the organization shall determine, based on such review, that the surgical procedure —

(A) is reasonable and medically necessary,

(B) is not reasonable and medically necessary, or

(C) may be considered reasonable and necessary, but, because of questions as to the medical appropriateness of performing the procedure, it is appropriate to require the patient to seek a second opinion as to the necessity and appropriateness of performing the procedure before the performance of the procedure.

The Secretary shall develop appropriate measures to ensure that second opinions are only required in situations where a second opinion is needed to resolve outstanding uncertainties as to the medical necessity of the procedure. The organization shall notify, in accordance with section 1154(a)(3), the physician, patient, and hospital or other entity furnishing the service, in the event of a determination under subparagraph (B) or (C) of this paragraph.

(2) PROHIBITION OF PAYMENT IF REQUIRED SECOND OPINION NOT PROVIDED. — No payment may be made under part A or part B of title XVIII with respect to items or services furnished in connection with a surgical procedure for which there is a determination described in paragraph (1)(C), unless the individual undergoing the procedure obtains the second opinion required under that paragraph. The second opinion need not necessarily agree with the first opinion in order for payment to be made.

(3) EXCEPTIONS FOR ELECTIVE SECOND OPINIONS.- Paragraphs (1)(C) and (2) shall not apply to a surgical procedure if—

(A) a delay in providing the procedure would result in a risk to the patient;

(B) no physician is available (within such reasonable limits as the Secretary shall specify) who is (i) qualified to provide the second opinion, and (ii) a participating physician or a physician who has agreed to accept assignment for the second opinion; or

(C) the procedure is to be performed on a patient who is a member of a health maintenance organization or competitive medical plan having a risk-sharing contract with the Secretary under section 1876.

(d) REFERRAL MECHANISM FOR SECOND OPINIONS. —

(1) ACTING AS A REFERRAL CENTER. — Each organization shall serve as a referral center for second opinions required under this section.

(2) REFERRAL OF PATIENT. — The organization shall maintain a list of physicians qualified to provide a second opinion and shall advise the patient as to which physicians are participating physicians (within the meaning of section 1842(h) [42 U.S.C.A. 1395u(h), which pertains to agreements with the Secretary to become participating physicians in Medicare and to accept payment on an assignment-related basis]) and which physicians have agreed to accept assignment to perform second opinions. The organization shall assist patients in referral to a qualified physician of the appropriate specialty for purposes of providing the opinion.

(3) FORWARDING OF RELEVANT MEDICAL RECORDS. — Each peer review organization shall, if the patient seeking the second opinion so requests, obtain the relevant medical records from the physician who rendered the first opinion that the procedure was necessary, and provide the relevant information to the physician selected by the patient to render the second opinion.

(e) NOTICE TO PHYSICIANS, HOSPITALS, AND BENEFICIARIES. — The Secretary shall assure that notice is provided to physicians, hospitals, rural primary care hospitals ["rural primary care hospitals" added, effective December 19, 1989, by section 6003(g)(3)(D) of P.L. 101-239, the Omnibus Budget Reconciliation Act of 1989], ambulatory surgical centers, and beneficiaries respecting the activities under this section, including the applicable list of surgical procedures specified under this section.

Finally, with respect to medical officers in American Samoa, the Northern Mariana Islands, and the Trust Territory of the Pacific Islands, section 1163, 42 U.S.C.A. 1320c-12, provides:

> For purposes of applying this part [B of Title XI] to American Samoa, the Northern Mariana Islands, and the Trust Territ ory of the Pacific Islands, individuals licensed to practice medicine in those places shall be considered to be physicians and doctors of medicine.

For regulatory citations, see Chapter 8

Chapter 5

SANCTIONS IN THE HEALTH CARE QUALITY IMPROVEMENT ACT OF 1986

§ 5:1 FAILURE BY HEALTH CARE ENTITIES TO REPORT ADVERSE ACTIONS AGAINST PHYSICIANS — Section 411(b) and Section 423(c)(1) [42 U.S.C.A. 11111(b) and 11133(c)(1)]

Summary

In 1986 Congress concluded that too much medical malpractice was going on in the United States. One way to deal with that was to restrict the ability of incompetent physicians to move from State to

State without disclosure or discovery of their previous damaging or incompetent performance. And one way to accomplish that was by more use of peer review. The legislative result was the Health Care Quality Improvement Act of 1986, P.L. 99-660, 42 U.S.C.A. 11101 et seq.

Congress also concluded the threat of private money damages under Federal laws, including treble damages liability under Federal antitrust law, discouraged physicians from participating in peer review. Thus, it found a "need to improve the quality of medical care", and "an overriding national need to provide incentive and protection for physicians engaging in effective professional peer review." See section 402 of the Act, 42 U.S.C.A. 11101.

Accordingly, section 411(a), 42 U.S.C.A. 11111(a), prohibits the award of damages with respect to any action, as defined in section 431(9), 42 U.S.C.A. 11151(9), of a professional review body which meets statutory standards. This protects the professional review body, any person acting as a member or staff to the body, any person under a contract or other formal agreement with the body, and any person who participates with or assists the body with respect to the action. That protection does not apply, however, to damages under Federal or State law relating to the civil rights of any person. Nor does it prohibit the United States or any State Attorney General from bringing an antitrust action under section 4C of the Clayton Act, 15 U.S.C.A. 15C, where such an action is otherwise authorized.

The tort and antitrust liability protection of section 411(a) also extends to persons providing information to a professional review body regarding competence or professional conduct of a physician, unless the information is false and the person providing it knew it was false. See section 427(c), 42 U.S.C.A. 11137(c).

Pursuant to section 431(9), the term "professional review action" means an action or recommendation of a professional review body taken or made in the conduct of a professional review of competence or professional conduct of a physician. The term applies when the physician's competence or professional conduct affects or could affect adversely the health or welfare of a patient and when it affects or may affect adversely either the clinical privileges or the membership in a professional society of the physician. The term also includes a formal decision of a professional review body not to take or recommend an adverse action, and it includes professional review activities relating to a professional review action.

A professional review action is not considered based on a physician's competence or professional conduct, however, if it is primarily based on the physician's association or lack thereof with a professional society or association; fees or advertising or other competitive acts of the physician intended to solicit or retain business; the physician's participation in prepaid group health plans, salaried employment, or any other manner of delivering health services; or the physician's association with, supervision of, delegation of authority to, support for, training of, or participation in a private group practice with, a member or members of a particular class of health care practitioner or profession.

Pursuant to section 431(10), the term "professional review activity" means an activity of a health care entity with respect to a physician to determine whether the physician may have clinical privileges with respect to, or membership in, the entity; to determine the scope or conditions of such privileges or membership; or to change or modify such privileges or membership.

Pursuant to section 431(11), the term "professional review body" means a health care entity and the governing body or any committee of a health care entity which conducts professional review activity, and it includes any committee of the medical staff of such an entity when assisting the governing body in a professional review activity.

Pursuant to section 431(8), the term "physician" means doctor of medicine, doctor of osteopathy, and doctor of dental surgery or medical dentistry legally authorized to practice medicine and surgery or dentistry by a State (or any individual who, without authority holds himself or herself out to be so authorized). Pursuant to section 431(6), the terms "licensed health care practitioner" and "practitioner" mean, with respect to a State, an individual other than a physician who is licensed to provide health care services.

Pursuant to section 431(4), the term "health care entity" means a hospital licensed to provide health care services by the State in which it is located; an entity (including a health maintenance organization or group medical practice) that provides health care services and that follows a formal peer review process to improve the quality of health care; and a professional society or committee thereof of physicians or other licensed health care practitioners that follows a formal peer review process to further quality health care. But it does not include a professional society or committee thereof if, within the prior 5 years it had been found by the Federal Trade Commission or any court to have engaged in any anti-competitive practice which had the effect of restricting the practice of licensed health care practitioners.

Section 412, 42 U.S.C.A. 11112, sets standards for these professional review actions. In order to obtain the protection against damages provided by section 411(a), the action must be taken in the reasonable belief that it would further quality health care; it must be taken only after a reasonable effort to obtain the relevant facts; it must be taken only after adequate notice and hearing procedures are afforded to the physician involved; and it must be taken in the reasonable belief that action was warranted by the facts known after the required investigation and hearing. Such review actions are presumed to have met these standards, but that presumption is rebuttable by a preponderance of the evidence.

Pursuant to section 412(b), a health care entity is deemed to have met adequate notice and hearing requirements if the following conditions are met or are waived voluntarily by the physician:

1. The physician has been given notice stating that review action has been proposed.
2. The notice gives the physician the reasons for the proposed action.
3. The physician is informed of the right to a hearing on the matter and is given at least 30 days to request such a hearing.
4. The notice provides a summary of the physician's hearing rights.
5. The notice states the place, time, and date of the hearing and the hearing is not less than 30 days after the date of the notice.
6. The hearing notice lists the witnesses, if any, expected to testify at the hearing on behalf of the review body.
7. The hearing is conducted, as determined by the health care entity, by an arbitrator mutually acceptable to the physician and the health care entity, by a hearing officer appointed by the entity who is not in direct economic competition with the physician involved, or by a panel of individuals appointed by the entity who are not in direct economic competition with the physician.
8. Failure by a physician to appear at a hearing without good cause may justify forfeiture of the hearing right.
9. The physician is allowed to be represented by an attorney or other person of his or her choice.

10. A record is made of the proceedings, with copies available to the physician upon payment of reasonable charges therefor.
11. The physician is allowed to call, examine, and cross-examine witnesses, to present evidence determined relevant by the presiding officer (regardless of its admissibility in a court of law), and to submit a written statement at the close of the hearing.
12. Upon completion of the hearing, the physician receives the written recommendation of the presiding officer, including a statement of the basis for the recommendation, and a written decision of the health care entity, including a statement of the basis for the decision.

Those are merely "deemed compliance" conditions, however, because the statute states that a professional review body's failure to meet the conditions described in section 412(b) does not, in itself, constitute failure to meet the requirement for notice and hearing set forth in section 412(a)(3).

Section 412(c) goes on to provide that nothing in section 412 shall be construed as requiring those procedures where no adverse professional review action is taken. Nor are they required in the case of a suspension or restriction of clinical privileges, for a period of not longer than 14 days, during which an investigation is being conducted to determine the need for a professional review action. Furthermore, section 412 is not to be construed to preclude immediate suspension or restriction of clinical privileges, subject to subsequent notice and hearing or other adequate procedures, where failure to take such an action may result in imminent danger to anyone's health.

According to section 413, 42 U.S.C.A. 11113, in the event of litigation arising from professional review activity, to the extent the defendant has met the standards set forth under section 412(a) and to the extent the defendant substantially prevails, the court must award him, her, or it the cost of the suit attributable to the claim, including a reasonable attorney's fee. That is so, however, only if the claim or the claimant's conduct during litigation was frivolous, unreasonable, without foundation, or in bad faith. Furthermore, a defendant will not be considered to have substantially prevailed when the plaintiff obtains an award for damages or permanent injunctive or declaratory relief.

This is a strong incentive for professional review bodies and health care entities to assure that the standards of section 412(a) are met.

In connection with that, section 414, 42 U.S.C.A. 11114, authorizes the Secretary to adopt voluntary guidelines to assist professional review bodies to meet the standards described in section 412(a).

Having made all those provisions for promoting and protecting professional review activities, section 423(a), 42 U.S.C.A. 11133, goes on to provide that a health care entity must report to its State Board of Medical Examiners, or any comparable board dealing with physician licensure, any action it takes which adversely affects clinical privileges of a physician for a period longer than 30 days. It also must report if it accepts surrender of clinical privileges of a physician under investigation for incompetence or improper professional conduct or in return for not conducting such an investigation. In addition, if the health care entity is a professional society, it must report if it takes action which adversely affects membership of a physician in the society.

Pursuant to section 431(3), the term "clinical privileges" includes privileges, membership on the medical staff, and other circumstances pertaining to furnishing medical care under which a physician or other licensed health care practitioner is permitted to furnish such care by a health care entity.

Section 423(a)(2) specifies that the information to be reported by a health care entity is the name of the physician or practitioner involved, a description of the acts or omissions or other reasons for the action or, if known, for the surrender of privileges or membership, and such other information respecting the circumstances of the action or surrender as the Secretary of Health and Human Services deems appropriate. Section 424, 42 U.S.C.A. 11134, requires such information to be reported not less often than monthly and in such form and manner as the Secretary prescribes. Furthermore, it must be reported to the Secretary, or, in the Secretary's discretion, to an appropriate private or public agency which has made suitable arrangements with the Secretary with respect to receipt, storage, protection of confidentiality, and dissemination. The information also must be reported to the appropriate State licensing board in the State in which the health care entity is located.

Section 427(a), 42 U.S.C.A. 11137(a), requires the Secretary or his designee to provide upon request the information reported with respect to a physician or other licensed health care practitioner to State licensing boards, to hospitals, and to other health care entities (including health maintenance organizations) that have entered or may be entering into an employment or affiliation relationship with the physician or practitioner or to which the physician or practitioner has applied for clinical privileges or appointment to the medical staff.

If the Secretary has reason to believe that a health care entity has failed to report such information, section 411(b) requires him to investigate the matter. If, after providing notice of noncompliance, an opportunity to correct the noncompliance, and an opportunity for a hearing, the Secretary determines the health care entity has failed substantially to report information as required, the Secretary must publish the entity's name in the Federal Register. In addition, the entity loses the protection against damage awards provided by section 411(a) with respect to professional review actions commenced during the 3-year period beginning 30 days after publication of its name. See section 411(b) and section 423(c)(1).

Finally, Congress initially declared that provisions of section 411(a) limiting damages to protect professional review bodies and those providing information to them did not have to apply in a given State if a State's legislature so declared. With respect to actions commenced on or after October 14, 1989, States could opt out. Pursuant to section 6103(e)(6)(A) of P.L. 101-239, the Omnibus Budget Reconciliation Act of 1989, the opt-out provision was repealed.

Statutory Provisions

Section 402, 42 U.S.C.A. 11101, provides:

Findings.

The Congress finds the following:

(1) The increasing occurrence of medical malpractice and the need to improve the quality of medical care have become nationwide problems that warrant greater efforts than those that can be undertaken by any individual State.

(2) There is a national need to restrict the ability of incompetent physicians to move from State to State without disclosure or discovery of the physician's previous damaging or incompetent performance.

(3) This nationwide problem can be remedied through effective professional peer review.

(4) The threat of private money damage liability under Federal laws, including treble damage liability under Federal

antitrust law, unreasonably discourages physicians from participating in effective professional peer review.

(5) There is an overriding national need to provide incentive and protection for physicians engaging in effective professional peer review.

Section 411, 42 U.S.C.A. 11111, provides in pertinent part:

PROFESSIONAL REVIEW.

(a) IN GENERAL. —

(1) LIMITATION ON DAMAGES FOR PROFESSIONAL REVIEW ACTIONS. —If a professional review action (as defined in section 431(9) [42 U.S.C.S. 11151(9)]) of a professional review body meets all the standards specified in section 412(a) [42 U.S.C.S. 1112(a)] , except as provided in subsection (b) —

(A) the professional review body,

(B) any person acting as a member or staff to the body,

(C) any person under a contract or other formal agreement with the body, and

(D) any person who participates with or assists the body with respect to the action, shall not be liable in damages under any law of the United States or of any State (or political subdivision thereof) with respect to the action. The preceding sentence shall not apply to damages under any law of the United States or any State relating to the civil rights of any person or persons, including the Civil Rights Act of 1964, 42 U.S.C.S. 2000e, et seq. and the Civil Rights Acts, 42 U.S.C.S. 1981, et seq. Nothing in this paragraph shall prevent the United States or any Attorney General of a State from bringing an action, including an action under section 4C of the Clayton Act, 15 U.S.C.S. 15C, where such an action is otherwise authorized.

(2) PROTECTION FOR THOSE PROVIDING INFORMATION TO PROFESSIONAL REVIEW BODIES. —Notwithstanding any other provision of law, no person (whether as a witness or otherwise) providing information to a professional review body regarding the competence or professional conduct of a physician shall be held, by reason of having provided such information, to be liable in damages under any

law of the United States or of any State (or political subdivision thereof) unless such information is false and the person providing it knew that such information was false.

(b) EXCEPTION. —If the Secretary has reason to believe that a health care entity has failed to report information in accordance with section 423(a) [42 U.S.C.S. 11133(a)] , the Secretary shall conduct an investigation. If, after providing notice of noncompliance, an opportunity to correct the noncompliance, and an opportunity for a hearing, the Secretary determines that a health care entity has failed substantially to report information in accordance with section 423(a), the Secretary shall publish the name of the entity in the Federal Register. The protections of subsection (a)(1) shall not apply to an entity the name of which is published in the Federal Register under the previous sentence with respect to professional review actions of the entity commenced during the 3-year period beginning 30 days after the date of publication of the name.

(c) TREATMENT UNDER STATE LAWS. —

(1) PROFESSIONAL REVIEW ACTIONS TAKEN ON OR AFTER OCTOBER 14, 1989. —Except as provided in paragraph (2), subsection (a) shall apply to State laws in a State only for professional review actions commenced on or after October 14, 1989.

(2) EXCEPTIONS. —

(A) STATE EARLY OPT-IN. —Subsection (a) shall apply to State laws in a State for actions commenced before October 14, 1989, if the State by legislation elects such treatment.

(B) EFFECTIVE DATE OF ELECTION. —An election under State law is not effective, for purposes of subparagraphs (A) and (B), [so in the original] for actions commenced before the effective date of the State law, which may not be earlier than the date of the enactment of that law.

◆ NOTE: Prior to amendment by section 6103(e)(6)(A) of P.L. 101-239, the Omnibus Budget Reconciliation Act of 1989, effective December 19, 1989, section 411(c)(2) had subparagraphs (B) and (C), which read as follows: (B) STATE OPT- OUT. —Subsection (a) shall not apply to State laws in a State for actions commenced on or after October 14, 1989, if the State by legislation elects such treatment. (C) EFFECTIVE DATE OF ELECTION. —An election under State law is not effective, for purposes of subparagraphs (A) and (B), for actions commenced before the effective date of the State law, which may not be earlier than the date of the enactment of that law.

Section 423, 42 U.S.C.A. 11133, provides:

REPORTING OF CERTAIN PROFESSIONAL REVIEW ACTIONS TAKEN BY HEALTH CARE ENTITIES.

(a) REPORTING BY HEALTH CARE ENTITIES. —

(1) ON PHYSICIANS. —Each health care entity which—

(A) takes a professional review action that adversely affects the clinical privileges of a physician for a period longer than 30 days;

(B) accepts the surrender of clinical privileges of a physician —

(i) while the physician is under an investigation by the entity relating to possible incompetence or improper professional conduct, or

(ii) in return for not conducting such an investigation or proceeding; or

(C) in the case of such an entity which is a professional society, takes a professional review action which adversely affects the membership of a physician in the society,

shall report to the Board of Medical Examiners, in accordance with section 424(a) [42 U.S.C.S. 1134(a)], the information described in paragraph (3).

(2) PERMISSIVE REPORTING ON OTHER LICENSED HEALTH CARE PRACTITIONERS. —A health care entity may report to the Board of Medical Examiners, in accordance with section 424(a), the information described in paragraph (3) in the case of a licensed health care practitioner who is not a physician, if the entity would be required to report such information under paragraph (1) with respect to the practitioner if the practitioner were a physician.

(3) INFORMATION TO BE REPORTED. —The information to be reported under this subsection is —

(A) the name of the physician or practitioner involved,

(B) a description of the acts or omissions or other reasons for the action or, if known, for the surrender, and

(C) such other information respecting the circumstances of the action or surrender as the Secretary deems appropriate.

* * *

(c) SANCTIONS.—

(1) HEALTH CARE ENTITIES.—A health care entity that fails substantially to meet the requirement of subsection (a)(1) shall lose the protections of section 411(a)(1) if the Secretary publishes the name of the entity under section 411(b).

Section 424, 42 U.S.C.A. 1134, provides:

FORM OF REPORTING.

(a) TIMING AND FORM.—The information required to be reported under sections 421 [which pertains to reporting medical malpractice payments], 422(a) [which pertains to reporting sanctions taken by boards of medical examiners], and 423 [which pertains to reporting adverse actions against physicians by health care entities and boards of medical examiners] shall be reported regularly (but not less often than monthly) and in such form and manner as the Secretary prescribes. Such information shall first be required to be reported on a date (not later than one year after the date of the enactment of this Act) specified by the Secretary.

(b) TO WHOM REPORTED.—The information required to be reported under sections 421, 422(a), and 423(b) [which pertains to reports required by boards of medical examiners] shall be reported to the Secretary, or, in the Secretary's discretion, to an appropriate private or public agency which has made suitable arrangements with the Secretary with respect to receipt, storage, protection of confidentiality, and dissemination of the information under this part.

(c) REPORTING TO STATE LICENSING BOARDS.—

(1) MALPRACTICE PAYMENTS.—Information required to be reported under section 421 shall also be reported to the appropriate State licensing board (or boards) in the State in which the medical malpractice claim arose.

(2) REPORTING TO OTHER LICENSING BOARDS.-Information required to be reported under section

423(b) shall also be reported to the appropriate State licensing board in the State in which the health care entity is located if it is not otherwise reported to such board under subsection (b).

In addition, section 427, 42 U.S.C.A. 11137, provides:

MISCELLANEOUS PROVISIONS.

(a) PROVIDING LICENSING BOARDS AND OTHER HEALTH CARE ENTITIES WITH ACCESS TO INFORMATION. —The Secretary (or the agency designated under section 424(b) [42 U.S.C.S. 11134]) shall, upon request, provide information reported under this part with respect to a physician or other licensed health care practitioner to State licensing boards, to hospitals, and to other health care entities (including health maintenance organizations) that have entered (or may be entering) into an employment or affiliation relationship with the physician or practitioner or to which the physician or practitioner has applied for clinical privileges or appointment to the medical staff.

(b) CONFIDENTIALITY OF INFORMATION. —

(1) IN GENERAL. —Information reported under this part is considered confidential and shall not be disclosed (other than to the physician or practitioner involved) except with respect to professional review activity, with respect to medical malpractice actions, or in accordance with regulations of the Secretary promulgated pursuant to subsection (a). Nothing in this subsection shall prevent the disclosure of such information by a party which is otherwise authorized, under applicable State law, to make such disclosure.

(2) PENALTY FOR VIOLATIONS. —Any person who violates paragraph (1) shall be subject to a civil money penalty of not more than $10,000 for each such violation involved. Such penalty shall be imposed and collected in the same manner as civil money penalties under subsection (a) of section 1128A of the Social Security Act [42 U.S.C.S. 1320a-7a(a)] are imposed and collected under that section.

(3) USE OF INFORMATION. —Subject to paragraph (1), information provided under section 425 and subsection (a) is intended to be used solely with respect to activities in the furtherance of the quality of health care.

(c) RELIEF FROM LIABILITY FOR REPORTING.—No person or entity shall be held liable in any civil action with respect to any report made under this part without knowledge of the falsity of the information contained in the report.

(d) INTERPRETATION OF INFORMATION.—In interpreting information reported under this part, a payment in settlement of a medical malpractice action or claim shall not be construed as creating a presumption that medical malpractice has occurred.

With respect to standards for professional review actions, section 412, 42 U.S.C.A. 1112, provides:

STANDARDS FOR PROFESSIONAL REVIEW ACTIONS.

(a) IN GENERAL.—For purposes of the protection set forth in section 411(a), a professional review action must be taken—

(1) in the reasonable belief that the action was in the furtherance of quality health care,

(2) after a reasonable effort to obtain the facts of the matter,

(3) after adequate notice and hearing procedures are afforded to the physician involved or after such other procedures as are fair to the physician under the circumstances, and

(4) in the reasonable belief that the action was warranted by the facts known after such reasonable effort to obtain facts and after meeting the requirement of paragraph (3).

A professional review action shall be presumed to have met the preceding standards necessary for the protection set out in section 411(a) unless the presumption is rebutted by a preponderance of the evidence.

(b) ADEQUATE NOTICE AND HEARING.—A health care entity is deemed to have met the adequate notice and hearing requirement of subsection (a)(3) with respect to a physician if the following conditions are met (or are waived voluntarily by the physician):

(1) NOTICE OF PROPOSED ACTION.—The physician has been given notice stating—

(A) (i) that a professional review action has been proposed to be taken against the physician,

(ii) reasons for the proposed action,

(B) (i) that the physician has the right to request a hearing on the proposed action,

(ii) any time limit (of not less than 30 days) within which to request such a hearing, and

(C) a summary of the rights in the hearing under paragraph (3).

(2) NOTICE OF HEARING. —If a hearing is requested on a timely basis under paragraph (1)(B), the physician involved must be given notice stating —

(A) the place, time, and date, of the hearing, which date shall not be less than 30 days after the date of the notice, and

(B) a list of the witnesses (if any) expected to testify at the hearing on behalf of the professional review body.

(3) CONDUCT OF HEARING AND NOTICE. —If a hearing is requested on a timely basis under paragraph (1)(B) —

(A) subject to subparagraph (b), the hearing shall be held (as determined by the health care entity) —

(i) before an arbitrator mutually acceptable to the physician and the health care entity,

(ii) before a hearing officer who is appointed by the entity and who is not in direct economic competition with the physician involved, or

(iii) before a panel of individuals who are appointed by the entity and are not in direct economic competition with the physician involved;

(B) the right to the hearing may be forfeited if the physician fails, without good cause, to appear;

(C) in the hearing the physician involved has the right —

(i) to representation by an attorney or other person of the physician's choice,

(ii) to have a record made of the proceedings, copies of which may be obtained by the physician upon payment of any reasonable charges associated with the preparation thereof,

(iii) to call, examine, and cross-examine witnesses,

(iv) to present evidence determined to be relevant by the hearing officer, regardless of its admissibility in a court of law, and

(v) to submit a written statement at the close of the hearing; and

(D) upon completion of the hearing, the physician involved has the right—

(i) to receive the written recommendation of the arbitrator, officer, or panel, including a statement of the basis for the recommendations, and

(ii) to receive a written decision of the health care entity, including a statement of the basis for the decision.

A professional review body's failure to meet the conditions described in this subsection shall not, in itself, constitute failure to meet the standards of subsection (a)(3).

(c) ADEQUATE PROCEDURES IN INVESTIGATIONS OR HEALTH EMERGENCIES. —For purposes of section 411(a), nothing in this section shall be construed as—

(1) requiring the procedures referred to in subsection (a)(3)—

(A) where there is no adverse professional review action taken, or

(B) in the case of a suspension or restriction of clinical privileges, for a period of not longer than 14 days, during which an investigation is being conducted to determine the need for a professional review action; or

(2) precluding an immediate suspension or restriction of clinical privileges, subject to subsequent notice and hearing or other adequate procedures, where the failure to take such an action may result in an imminent danger to the health of any individual.

Section 413, 42 U.S.C.A. 11113, provides:

PAYMENT OF REASONABLE ATTORNEYS' FEES AND COSTS IN DEFENSE OF SUIT.

In any suit brought against a defendant, to the extent that a defendant has met the standards set forth under section 412(a) and the defendant substantially prevails, the court shall, at the conclusion of the action, award to a substantially prevailing party defending against any such claim the cost of the suit attributable to such claim, including a reasonable attorney's fee, if the claim, or the claimant's conduct during the litigation of the claim, was frivolous, unreasonable, without foundation, or in bad faith. For the purposes of this section, a defendant shall not be considered to have substantially prevailed when the plaintiff obtains an award for damages or permanent injunctive or declaratory relief.

Section 414, 42 U.S.C.A. 11114, provides:

GUIDELINES OF THE SECRETARY.

The Secretary may establish, after notice and opportunity for comment, such voluntary guidelines as may assist the professional review bodies in meeting the standards described in section 412(a).

Section 415, 42 U.S.C.A. 11115, provides:

CONSTRUCTION.

(a) IN GENERAL. —Except as specifically provided in this part, nothing in this part shall be construed as changing the liabilities or immunities under law or as preempting or overriding any State law which provides incentives, immunities, or protection for those engaged in a professional review action that is in addition to or greater than that provided by this part [phrase beginning "or as preempting" added by section 6103(e)(6)(A) of P.L. 101-239, the Omnibus Budget Reconciliation Act of 1989, effective December 19, 1989].

(b) SCOPE OF CLINICAL PRIVILEGES. —Nothing in this part shall be construed as requiring health care entities to provide clinical privileges to any or all classes or types of physicians or other licensed health care practitioners.

(c) TREATMENT OF NURSES AND OTHER PRACTITIONERS. —Nothing in this part shall be construed as affecting, or modifying any provision of Federal or State law, with respect to activities of professional review bodies regarding nurses, other licensed health care practitioners, or other health professionals who are not physicians.

(d) TREATMENT OF PATIENT MALPRACTICE CLAIMS.- Nothing in this title shall be construed as affecting in any manner the rights and remedies afforded patients under any provision of Federal or State law to seek redress for any harm or injury suffered as a result of negligent treatment or care by any physician, health care practitioner, or health care entity, or as limiting any defenses or immunities available to any physician, health care practitioner, or health care entity.

Finally, section 431, 42 U.S.C.A. 11151, provides the following definitions:

DEFINITIONS.

In this title:

(1) The term "adversely affecting" includes reducing, restricting, suspending, revoking, denying, or failing to renew clinical privileges or membership in a health care entity.

(2) The term "Board of Medical Examiners" includes a body comparable to such a Board (as determined by the State) with responsibility for the licensing of physicians and also includes a subdivision of such a Board or body.

(3) The term "clinical privileges" includes privileges, membership on the medical staff, and the other circumstances pertaining to the furnishing of medical care under which a physician or other licensed health care practitioner is permitted to furnish such care by a health care entity.

(4) (A) The term "health care entity" means —

(i) a hospital that is licensed to provide health care services by the State in which it is located,

(ii) an entity (including a health maintenance organization or group medical practice) that provides health care services and that follows a formal peer review process for the purpose of furthering quality health care (as determined under regulations of the Secretary), and

(iii) subject to subparagraph (B), a professional society (or committee thereof) of physicians or other licensed health care practitioners that follows a formal peer review process for the purpose of furthering quality health care (as determined under regulations of the Secretary).

(B) The term "health care entity" does not include a professional society (or committee thereof) if, within the previous 5 years, the society has been found by the Federal Trade

Commission or any court to have engaged in any anti-competitive practice which had the effect of restricting the practice of licensed health care practitioners.

(5) The term "hospital" means an entity described in paragraphs (1) and (7) of section 1861(e) [42 U.S.C.S. 1395x(e)(1) and (7), which defines hospital for Medicare purposes] of the Social Security Act.

(6) The terms "licensed health care practitioner" and "practitioner" mean, with respect to a State, an individual (other than a physician) who is licensed or otherwise authorized by the State to provide health care services.

(7) The term "medical malpractice action or claim" means a written claim or demand for payment based on a health care provider's furnishing or failure to furnish) health care services, and includes the filing of a cause of action, based on the law of tort, brought in any court of any State or the United States seeking monetary damages.

(8) The term "physician" means a doctor of medicine or osteopathy or a doctor of dental surgery or medical dentistry legally authorized to practice medicine and surgery or dentistry by a State (or any individual who, without authority holds himself or herself out to be so authorized.)

(9) The term "professional review action" means an action or recommendation of a professional review body which is taken or made in the conduct of professional review activity, which is based on the competence or professional conduct of an individual physician (which conduct affects or could affect adversely the health or welfare of a patient or patients), and which affects (or may affect) adversely the clinical privileges, or membership in a professional society, of the physician. Such term includes a formal decision of a professional review body not to take an action or make a recommendation described in the previous sentence and also includes professional review activities relating to a professional review action. In this title, an action is not considered to be based on the competence or professional conduct of a physician if the action is primarily based on —

(A) the physician's association, or lack of association, with a professional society or association,

(B) the physician's fees or the physician's advertising or engaging in other competitive acts intended to solicit or retain business,

(C) the physician's participation in prepaid group health plans, salaried employment, or any other manner of delivering health services whether on a fee-for-service or other basis,

(D) a physician's association with, supervision of, delegation of authority to, support for, training of, or participation in a private group practice with, a member or members of a particular class of health care practitioner or professional, or

(E) any other matter that does not relate to the competence or professional conduct of a physician.

(10) The term "professional review activity" means an activity of a health care entity with respect to an individual physician —

(A) to determine whether the physician may have clinical privileges with respect to, or membership in, the entity,

(B) to determine the scope or conditions of such privileges or membership, or

(C) to change or modify such privileges or membership.

(11) The term "professional review body" means a health care entity and the governing body or any committee of a health care entity which conducts professional review activity, and includes any committee of the medical staff of such an entity when assisting the governing body in a professional review activity.

(12) The term "Secretary" means the Secretary of Health and Human Services.

(13) The term "State" means the 50 States, the District of Columbia, Puerto Rico, the Virgin Islands, Guam, American Samoa, and the Northern Mariana Islands.

(14) The term "State licensing board" means, with respect to a physician or health care provider in a State, the agency of the State which is primarily responsible for the licensing of the physician or provider to furnish health care services.

For regulatory citations, see Chapter 9

§ 5:2 FAILURE TO REPORT MEDICAL MALPRACTICE PAYMENTS — Section 421 [42 U.S.C.S. 11131]

Summary

Section 421(a), 42 U.S.C.A. 11131(a), requires each entity, including an insurance company, which makes a payment under a policy of insurance, self-insurance, or otherwise in settlement, or partial settlement of, or in satisfaction of a judgment in, a medical malpractice action or claim to report information about the payment, and the circumstances which led to the payment, to the Secretary of Health and Human Services or his designee.

"Medical malpractice action or claim" means a written claim or demand for payment based on a health care provider's furnishing, or failure to furnish, health care services. It also includes the filing of a tort action in any court of any State or the United States seeking monetary damages.

Section 421(b) requires such reports to include the name of the physician or licensed health care practitioner for whose benefit the payment was made, the amount of the payment, the name, if known, of any hospital with which the physician or practitioner is affiliated or associated, a description of the acts or omissions and injuries or illnesses upon which the action or claim was based, and any other information which the Secretary deems necessary. Furthermore, section 424, 42 U.S.C.A. 11134, requires such reports to be made regularly, but not less often than monthly, and in the form and manner prescribed by the Secretary. They also must be made to the appropriate State licensing board or boards in the State where the malpractice claim arose.

Pursuant to section 421(c), any entity that fails to report such information is subject to a civil money penalty of not more than $10,000 for each such payment involved. Enforcement procedures for this civil money penalty provision are governed by section 1128A of the Social Security Act, 42 U.S.C.A. 1320a-7a, which authorizes civil money penalties for a variety of offenses.

Pursuant to section 427(c), 42 U.S.C.A. 11137(c), however, no person or entity may be held liable in any civil action with respect to any report made under section 421 unless they had knowledge that information in the report was false.

Statutory Provisions

Section 421, 42 U.S.C.A. 11131, provides:

REQUIRING REPORTS ON MEDICAL MALPRACTICE PAYMENTS.

(a) IN GENERAL. —Each entity (including an insurance company) which makes payment under a policy of insurance, self-insurance, or otherwise in settlement (or partial settlement) of, or in satisfaction of a judgment in, a medical malpractice action or claim shall report, in accordance with section 424 [42 U.S.C.S. 11134] , information respecting the payment and circumstances thereof.

(b) INFORMATION TO BE REPORTED. —The information to be reported under subsection (a) includes-

(1) the name of any physician or licensed health care practitioner for whose benefit the payment is made,

(2) the amount of the payment,

(3) the name (if known) of any hospital with which the physician or practitioner is affiliated or associated,

(4) a description of the acts or omissions and injuries or illnesses upon which the action or claim was based, and

(5) such other information as the Secretary determines is required for appropriate interpretation of information reported under this section.

(c) SANCTIONS FOR FAILURE TO REPORT. —Any entity that fails to report information on a payment required to be reported under this section shall be subject to a civil money penalty of not more than $10,000 for each such payment involved. Such penalty shall be imposed and collected in the same manner as civil money penalties under subsection (a) of section 1128A of the Social Security Act [42 U.S.C.S. 1320a-7a(a)] are imposed and collected under that section.

(d) REPORT ON TREATMENT OF SMALL PAYMENTS. —The Secretary shall study and report to Congress, not later than two years after the date of the enactment of this Act, on whether information respecting small payments should continue to be required to be reported under subsection (a) and whether information respecting all claims made concerning a medical malpractice action should be required to be reported under such subsection.

Section 424, 42 U.S.C.A. 1134, provides in pertinent part:

FORM OF REPORTING.

(a) TIMING AND FORM. —The information required to be reported under sections 421 [which pertains to reporting medical malpractice payments], 422(a) [which pertains to reporting sanctions taken by boards of medical examiners], and 423 [which pertains to reporting adverse actions against physicians by health care entities and boards of medical examiners] shall be reported regularly (but not less often than monthly) and in such form and manner as the Secretary prescribes. Such information shall first be required to be reported on a date (not later than one year after the date of the enactment of this Act) specified by the Secretary.

(b) TO WHOM REPORTED. —The information required to be reported under sections 421, 422(a), and 423(b) [which pertains to reports required by boards of medical examiners] shall be reported to the Secretary, or, in the Secretary's discretion, to an appropriate private or public agency which has made suitable arrangements with the Secretary with respect to receipt, storage, protection of confidentiality, and dissemination of the information under this part.

(c) REPORTING TO STATE LICENSING BOARDS. —

(1) MALPRACTICE PAYMENTS. —Information required to be reported under section 421 shall also be reported to the appropriate State licensing board (or boards) in the State in which the medical malpractice claim arose.

Section 427, 42 U.S.C.A. 11137, provides:

MISCELLANEOUS PROVISIONS.

(a) PROVIDING LICENSING BOARDS AND OTHER HEALTH CARE ENTITIES WITH ACCESS TO INFORMATION. —The Secretary (or the agency designated under section 424(b) [42 U.S.C.S. 11134]) shall, upon request, provide information reported under this part with respect to a physician or other licensed health care practitioner to State licensing boards, to hospitals, and to other health care entities (including health maintenance organizations) that have entered (or may be entering) into an employment or affiliation relationship with the physician or practitioner or to which the physician or practitioner has applied for clinical privileges or appointment to the medical staff.

(b) CONFIDENTIALITY OF INFORMATION.—

(1) IN GENERAL.—Information reported under this part is considered confidential and shall not be disclosed (other than to the physician or practitioner involved) except with respect to professional review activity, with respect to medical malpractice actions, or in accordance with regulations of the Secretary promulgated pursuant to subsection (a). Nothing in this subsection shall prevent the disclosure of such information by a party which is otherwise authorized, under applicable State law, to make such disclosure.

(2) PENALTY FOR VIOLATIONS.—Any person who violates paragraph (1) shall be subject to a civil money penalty of not more than $10,000 for each such violation involved. Such penalty shall be imposed and collected in the same manner as civil money penalties under subsection (a) of section 1128A of the Social Security Act [42 U.S.C.S. 1320a-7a(a)] are imposed and collected under that section.

(3) USE OF INFORMATION.—Subject to paragraph (1), information provided under section 425 and subsection (a) is intended to be used solely with respect to activities in the furtherance of the quality of health care.

(c) RELIEF FROM LIABILITY FOR REPORTING.—No person or entity shall be held liable in any civil action with respect to any report made under this part without knowledge of the falsity of the information contained in the report.

(d) INTERPRETATION OF INFORMATION.—In interpreting information reported under this part, a payment in settlement of a medical malpractice action or claim shall not be construed as creating a presumption that medical malpractice has occurred.

With respect to definitions, section 431, 42 U.S.C.A. 11151, provides in pertinent part:

(7) The term "medical malpractice action or claim" means a written claim or demand for payment based on a health care

provider's furnishing (or failure to furnish) health care services, and includes the filing of a cause of action, based on the law of tort, brought in any court of any State or the United States seeking monetary damages.

(8) The term "physician" means a doctor of medicine or osteopathy or a doctor of dental surgery or medical dentistry legally authorized to practice medicine and surgery or dentistry by a State (or any individual who, without authority holds himself or herself out to be so authorized.)

For regulatory citations, see Chapter 9

§ 5:3 FAILURE BY MEDICAL EXAMINER BOARDS TO REPORT INFORMATION ABOUT ADVERSE ACTIONS TAKEN BY HEALTH CARE ENTITIES AGAINST PHYSICIANS AND ABOUT HEALTH CARE ENTITIES THAT FAIL TO MAKE SUCH REPORTS — Sections 422 and 423(c)(2) [42 U.S.C.S. 11132 and 11133(c)(2)]

Summary

In 1986 Congress concluded that too much medical malpractice was going on in the United States. One way to deal with that was to restrict the ability of incompetent physicians to move from State to State without disclosure or discovery of their previous damaging or incompetent performance. One way to accomplish that was by more use of peer review. Another way was to require State boards of medical examiners to report to the Secretary of Health and Human Services about sanctions which they impose on physicians subject to their jurisdiction.

Section 422 of the Health Care Quality Improvement Act of 1986, 42 U.S.C.A. 11132, requires State boards of medical examiners to report to the Secretary or his designee every instance in which they revoke or suspend or otherwise restrict a physician's license. They also must report instances when a physician is censured, reprimanded, or placed on probation. This applies when such action relates to a physician's professional competence or professional conduct. Furthermore, medical examiner boards must report instances when a physician surrenders his or her license.

In addition, section 423(b), 42 U.S.C.A. 11133(b), provides that such boards must report to the Secretary or his designee information which health care entities are required to send them regarding professional review actions those entities have taken that adversely affect either clinical privileges of a physician or membership of a physician in such an entity. Medical examiner boards also must report known instances of a health care entity's failure to report required information.

If, after notice of noncompliance and providing an opportunity to correct noncompliance, the Secretary finds that a State board of medical examiners has failed to report that information, sections 422(b) and 423(c) require the Secretary to designate another qualified entity to do so. Pursuant to section 423(d), the obligation to report and the potential for disqualification by the Secretary then apply to the substitute.

Pursuant to section 424, 42 U.S.C.A. 11134, reports by boards of medical examiners must be made regularly, but not less often than monthly, and in such form and manner as the Secretary prescribes.

Pursuant to section 431(9), 42 U.S.C.A. 11151(9) the term "professional review action" means an action or recommendation of a professional review body taken or made in the conduct of a professional review of the competence or professional conduct of a physician. The term applies when the physician's competence or professional conduct affects or could affect adversely the health or welfare of a patient and when it affects or may affect adversely either the clinical privileges or the membership in a professional society of the physician. The term also includes a formal decision of a professional review body not to take or recommend an adverse action, and it includes professional review activities relating to a professional review action.

A professional review action is not considered based on a physician's competence or professional conduct, however, if it is primarily based on the physician's association or lack thereof with a professional society or association; fees or advertising or other competitive acts of the physician intended to solicit or retain business; the physician's participation in prepaid group health plans, salaried employment, or any other manner of delivering health services; or the physician's association with, supervision of, delegation of authority to, support for, training of, or participation in a private group practice with, a member or members of a particular class of health care practitioner or profession.

Pursuant to section 431(10), the term "professional review activity" means an activity of a health care entity with respect to a physician to determine whether the physician may have clinical privileges with respect to, or membership in, the entity; to determine the scope or conditions of such privileges or membership; or to change or modify such privileges or membership.

Pursuant to section 431(11), the term "professional review body" means a health care entity and the governing body or any committee of a health care entity which conducts professional review activity, and it includes any committee of the medical staff of such an entity when assisting the governing body in a professional review activity.

Pursuant to section 431(8), the term "physician" means doctor of medicine, doctor of osteopathy, and doctor of dental surgery or medical dentistry legally authorized to practice medicine and surgery or dentistry by a State (or any individual who, without authority holds himself or herself out to be so authorized). Pursuant to section 431(6), the terms "licensed health care practitioner" and "practitioner" mean, with respect to a State, an individual other than a physician who is licensed to provide health care services.

Pursuant to section 431(4), the term "health care entity" means a hospital licensed to provide health care services by the State in which it is located; an entity (including a health maintenance organization or group medical practice) that provides health care services and that follows a formal peer review process to improve the quality of health care; and a professional society or committee thereof of physicians or other licensed health care practitioners that follows a formal peer review process to further quality health care. But it does not include a professional society or committee thereof if, within the prior 5 years it had been found by the Federal Trade Commission or any court to have engaged in any anti-competitive practice which had the effect of restricting the practice of licensed health care practitioners.

Section 423(a) goes on to provide that a health care entity must report to its State board of medical examiners, or any comparable board dealing with physician licensure, any action it takes which adversely affects clinical privileges of a physician for a period longer than 30 days. It also must report if it accepts surrender of clinical privileges of a physician under investigation for incompetence or improper professional conduct or in return for not conducting such an investigation. In addition, if the health care entity is a professional society, it must report if it takes action which adversely affects membership of a physician in the society.

Pursuant to section 431(3), the term "clinical privileges" includes privileges, membership on the medical staff, and other circumstances pertaining to the furnishing of medical care under which a physician or other licensed health care practitioner is permitted to furnish such care by a health care entity.

Section 423(a)(2) specifies that the information to be reported by a health care entity is the name of the physician or practitioner involved, a description of the acts or omissions or other reasons for the action or, if known, for the surrender of privileges or membership, and such other information respecting the circumstances of the action or surrender as the Secretary of Health and Human Services deems appropriate. Section 424, 42 U.S.C.A. 11134, requires such information to be reported not less often than monthly and in such form and manner as the Secretary prescribes. Furthermore, it must be reported to the Secretary, or, in the Secretary's discretion, to an appropriate private or public agency which has made suitable arrangements with the Secretary with respect to receipt, storage, protection of confidentiality, and dissemination. The information also must be reported to the appropriate State licensing board in the State in which the health care entity is located.

Section 427(a), 42 U.S.C.A. 11137(a), then requires the Secretary or his designee to provide upon request the information reported with respect to a physician or other licensed health care practitioner to State licensing boards, to hospitals, and to other health care entities (including health maintenance organizations) that have entered or may be entering into an employment or affiliation relationship with the physician or practitioner or to which the physician or practitioner has applied for clinical privileges or appointment to the medical staff. Section 427(c) provides, however, that no person or entity may be held liable in any civil action with respect to any report made under this part unless they knew information in the report was false.

Statutory Provisions

Section 422, 42 U.S.C.A. 11132, provides:

REPORTING OF SANCTIONS TAKEN BY BOARDS OF MEDICAL EXAMINERS.

(a) IN GENERAL.—

(1) ACTIONS SUBJECT TO REPORTING.—Each Board of Medical Examiners—

(A) which revokes or suspends (or otherwise restricts) a physician's license or censures, reprimands, or places on probation a physician, for reasons relating to the physician's professional competence or professional conduct, or

(B) to which a physician's license is surrendered,

shall report, in accordance with section 424 [42 U.S.C.S. 11134] , the information described in paragraph (2).

(2) INFORMATION TO BE REPORTED. —The information to be reported under paragraph (1) is —

(A) the name of the physician involved,

(B) a description of the acts or omissions or other reasons (if known) for the revocation, suspension, or surrender of license, and

(C) such other information respecting the circumstances of the action or surrender as the Secretary deems appropriate.

(b) FAILURE TO REPORT. —If, after notice of noncompliance and providing opportunity to correct noncompliance, the Secretary determines that a Board of Medical Examiners has failed to report information in accordance with subsection (a), the Secretary shall designate another qualified entity for the reporting of information under section 423.

Section 423, 42 U.S.C.A. 11133, provides in pertinent part:

REPORTING OF CERTAIN PROFESSIONAL REVIEW ACTIONS TAKEN BY HEALTH CARE ENTITIES.

(a) REPORTING BY HEALTH CARE ENTITIES. —

(1) ON PHYSICIANS. —Each health care entity which —

(A) takes a professional review action that adversely affects the clinical privileges of a physician for a period longer than 30 days;

(B) accepts the surrender of clinical privileges of a physician —

(i) while the physician is under an investigation by the entity relating to possible incompetence or improper professional conduct, or

(ii) in return for not conducting such an investigation or proceeding; or

(C) in the case of such an entity which is a professional society, takes a professional review action which adversely affects the membership of a physician in the society,

shall report to the Board of Medical Examiners, in accordance with section 424(a) [42 U.S.C.S. 1134(a)], the information described in paragraph (3).

(2) PERMISSIVE REPORTING ON OTHER LICENSED HEALTH CARE PRACTITIONERS. —A health care entity may report to the Board of Medical Examiners, in accordance with section 424(a), the information described in paragraph (3) in the case of a licensed health care practitioner who is not a physician, if the entity would be required to report such information under paragraph (1) with respect to the practitioner if the practitioner were a physician.

(3) INFORMATION TO BE REPORTED. —The information to be reported under this subsection is —

(A) the name of the physician or practitioner involved,

(B) a description of the acts or omissions or other reasons for the action or, if known, for the surrender, and

(C) such other information respecting the circumstances of the action or surrender as the Secretary deems appropriate.

(b) REPORTING BY BOARD OF MEDICAL EXAMINERS. —Each Board of Medical Examiners shall report, in accordance with section 424, the information reported to it under subsection (a) and known instances of a health care entity's failure to report information under subsection (a)(1).

(c) SANCTIONS. —

(1) HEALTH CARE ENTITIES. —A health care entity that fails substantially to meet the requirement of subsection (a)(1) shall lose the protections of section 411(a)(1) if the Secretary publishes the name of the entity under section 411(b).

Section 424, 42 U.S.C.A. 1134, provides:

FORM OF REPORTING.

(a) TIMING AND FORM. —The information required to be reported under sections 421 [which pertains to reporting medical malpractice payments], 422(a) [which pertains to reporting sanctions taken by boards of medical examiners], and 423 [which pertains to reporting adverse actions against physicians by health care entities and boards of medical examiners] shall be reported regularly (but not less often than monthly) and in such form and manner as the Secretary prescribes. Such information shall first be required to be reported on a date (not later than one year after the date of the enactment of this Act) specified by the Secretary.

(b) TO WHOM REPORTED. —The information required to be reported under sections 421, 422(a), and 423(b) [which pertains to reports required by boards of medical examiners] shall be reported to the Secretary, or, in the Secretary's discretion, to an appropriate private or public agency which has made suitable arrangements with the Secretary with respect to receipt, storage, protection of confidentiality, and dissemination of the information under this part.

(c) REPORTING TO STATE LICENSING BOARDS. —

(1) MALPRACTICE PAYMENTS. —Information required to be reported under section 421 shall also be reported to the appropriate State licensing board (or boards) in the State in which the medical malpractice claim arose.

(2) REPORTING TO OTHER LICENSING BOARDS.-Information required to be reported under section 423(b) shall also be reported to the appropriate State licensing board in the State in which the health care entity is located if it is not otherwise reported to such board under subsection (b).

In addition section 427, 42 U.S.C.A. 11137, provides:

MISCELLANEOUS PROVISIONS.

(a) PROVIDING LICENSING BOARDS AND OTHER HEALTH CARE ENTITIES WITH ACCESS TO INFORMATION. —The Secretary (or the agency designated under section 424(b)) shall, upon request, provide information reported under this part with respect to a physician or other licensed health care practitioner to State licensing boards, to hospitals, and to other health care entities (including health maintenance organizations) that have entered (or may be entering) into an employment or affiliation relationship with the physician or practitioner or to which the physician or practitioner has applied for clinical privileges or appointment to the medical staff.

(b) CONFIDENTIALITY OF INFORMATION. —

(1) IN GENERAL. —Information reported under this part is considered confidential and shall not be disclosed (other than to the physician or practitioner involved) except with respect to professional review activity, with respect to medical malpractice actions, or in accordance with regulations of the Secretary promulgated pursuant to subsection (a). Nothing in this subsection shall prevent the disclosure of such information by a party which is otherwise authorized, under applicable State law, to make such disclosure.

(2) PENALTY FOR VIOLATIONS. —Any person who violates paragraph (1) shall be subject to a civil money penalty of not more than $10,000 for each such violation involved. Such penalty shall be imposed and collected in the same manner as civil money penalties under subsection (a) of section 1128A of the Social Security Act [42 U.S.C.S. 1320a-7a(a)] are imposed and collected under that section.

(3) USE OF INFORMATION. —Subject to paragraph (1), information provided under section 425 and subsection (a) is intended to be used solely with respect to activities in the furtherance of the quality of health care.

(c) RELIEF FROM LIABILITY FOR REPORTING. —No person or entity shall be held liable in any civil action with respect to any report made under this part without knowledge of the falsity of the information contained in the report.

(d) INTERPRETATION OF INFORMATION. —In interpreting information reported under this part, a payment in settlement of a medical malpractice action or claim shall not be construed as creating a presumption that medical malpractice has occurred.

Finally, section 431, 42 U.S.C.A. 11151, provides in pertinent part:

DEFINITIONS.

In this title:

(1) The term "adversely affecting" includes reducing, restricting, suspending, revoking, denying, or failing to renew clinical privileges or membership in a health care entity.

(2) The term "Board of Medical Examiners" includes a body comparable to such a Board (as determined by the State) with

responsibility for the licensing of physicians and also includes a subdivision of such a Board or body.

(3) The term "clinical privileges" includes privileges, membership on the medical staff, and the other circumstances pertaining to the furnishing of medical care under which a physician or other licensed health care practitioner is permitted to furnish such care by a health care entity.

(4) (A) The term "health care entity" means —

(i) a hospital that is licensed to provide health care services by the State in which it is located,

(ii) an entity (including a health maintenance organization or group medical practice) that provides health care services and that follows a formal peer review process for the purpose of furthering quality health care (as determined under regulations of the Secretary), and

(iii) subject to subparagraph (B), a professional society (or committee thereof) of physicians or other licensed health care practitioners that follows a formal peer review process for the purpose of furthering quality health care (as determined under regulations of the Secretary).

(B) The term "health care entity" does not include a professional society (or committee thereof) if, within the previous 5 years, the society has been found by the Federal Trade Commission or any court to have engaged in any anti-competitive practice which had the effect of restricting the practice of licensed health care practitioners.

(5) The term "hospital" means an entity described in paragraphs (1) and (7) of section 1861(e) [42 U.S.C.S. 1395x(e)(1) and (7), which defines hospital for Medicare purposes] of the Social Security Act.

(6) The terms "licensed health care practitioner" and "practitioner" mean, with respect to a State, an individual (other than a physician) who is licensed or otherwise authorized by the State to provide health care services.

* * *

(8) The term "physician" means a doctor of medicine or osteopathy or a doctor of dental surgery or medical dentistry legally authorized to practice medicine and surgery or dentistry by a

State (or any individual who, without authority holds himself or herself out to be so authorized.)

(9) The term "professional review action" means an action or recommendation of a professional review body which is taken or made in the conduct of professional review activity, which is based on the competence or professional conduct of an individual physician (which conduct affects or could affect adversely the health or welfare of a patient or patients), and which affects (or may affect) adversely the clinical privileges, or membership in a professional society, of the physician. Such term includes a formal decision of a professional review body not to take an action or make a recommendation described in the previous sentence and also includes professional review activities relating to a professional review action. In this title, an action is not considered to be based on the competence or professional conduct of a physician if the action is primarily based on —

(A) the physician's association, or lack of association, with a professional society or association,

(B) the physician's fees or the physician's advertising or engaging in other competitive acts intended to solicit or retain business,

(C) the physician's participation in prepaid group health plans, salaried employment, or any other manner of delivering health services whether on a fee-for-service or other basis,

(D) a physician's association with, supervision of, delegation of authority to, support for, training of, or participation in a private group practice with, a member or members of a particular class of health care practitioner or professional, or

(E) any other matter that does not relate to the competence or professional conduct of a physician.

(10) The term "professional review activity" means an activity of a health care entity with respect to an individual physician —

(A) to determine whether the physician may have clinical privileges with respect to, or membership in, the entity,

(B) to determine the scope or conditions of such privileges or membership, or

(C) to change or modify such privileges or membership.

(11) The term "professional review body" means a health care entity and the governing body or any committee of a health care entity which conducts professional review activity, and includes any committee of the medical staff of such an entity when assisting the governing body in a professional review activity.

(12) The term "Secretary" means the Secretary of Health and Human Services.

(13) The term "State" means the 50 States, the District of Columbia, Puerto Rico, the Virgin Islands, Guam, American Samoa, and the Northern Mariana Islands.

(14) The term "State licensing board" means, with respect to a physician or health care provider in a State, the agency of the State which is primarily responsible for the licensing of the physician or provider to furnish health care services.

For regulatory citations, see Chapter 9

§ 5:4 FAILURE BY HOSPITALS TO OBTAIN ADVERSE INFORMATION ABOUT PHYSICIANS FROM THE SECRETARY OF HEALTH AND HUMAN SERVICES AND FROM STATE MEDICAL EXAMINER BOARDS — Section 425 [42 U.S.C.S. 11135]

Summary

In 1986 Congress concluded that too much medical malpractice was going on in the United States. One way to deal with that was to restrict the ability of incompetent physicians to move from State to State without disclosure or discovery of their previous damaging or incompetent performance. One way to accomplish that was to require State boards of medical examiners to report to the Secretary of Health and Human Services about sanctions which they impose on physicians subject to their jurisdiction. Another way was to have professional review bodies report adverse professional review actions against physicians.

Section 422 of the Health Care Quality Improvement Act of 1986, 42 U.S.C.A. 11132, requires State boards of medical examiners to report to the Secretary or his designee every instance in which they revoke or suspend or otherwise restrict a physician's license. They also must report instances when a physician is censured, reprimanded, or placed on probation. This applies when such action relates to a physician's professional competence or professional conduct. Furthermore, medical examiner boards must report instances when a physician surrenders his or her license.

In addition, section 423(b) provides that such boards must report to the Secretary or his designee information which health care entities are required to send them regarding professional review actions those entities have taken that adversely affect either clinical privileges of a physician or membership of a physician in such an entity. Medical examiner boards also must report known instances of a health care entity's failure to report required information.

Section 423(a), 42 U.S.C.A. 11133, requires health care entities to report, either to their State medical examiner board or to any comparable board dealing with physician licensure, any action they take which adversely affects clinical privileges of a physician for a period longer than 30 days. They also must report when they accept surrender of clinical privileges of a physician under investigation for incompetence or improper professional conduct or in return for not conducting such an investigation. In addition, if the health care entity is a professional society, it must report if it takes action which adversely affects membership of a physician in the society.

Pursuant to section 431(3), the term "clinical privileges" includes privileges, membership on the medical staff, and other circumstances pertaining to the furnishing of medical care under which a physician or other licensed health care practitioner is permitted to furnish such care by a health care entity.

Section 423(a)(2) specifies that the information to be reported by a health care entity is the name of the physician or practitioner involved, a description of the acts or omissions or other reasons for the action or, if known, for the surrender of privileges or membership, and such other information respecting the circumstances of the action or surrender as the Secretary of Health and Human Services deems appropriate. Section 424, 42 U.S.C.A. 11134, requires such information to be reported not less often than monthly and in such form and manner as the Secretary prescribes. Furthermore, it must be reported to the Secretary, or, in the Secretary's discretion, to an appropriate private or public agency which has made suitable arrangements with the Secretary with respect to receipt, storage, protection of confidentiality, and dissemination. The information also must be reported to the appropriate State licensing board in the State in which the health care entity is located.

Section 427(a), 42 U.S.C.A. 11137(a), requires the Secretary or his designee to provide upon request the information reported with respect to a physician or other licensed health care practitioner to State licensing boards, to hospitals, and to other health care entities (including health maintenance organizations) that have entered or may be entering into an employment or affiliation relationship with the physician or practitioner or to which the physician or practitioner has applied for clinical privileges or appointment to the medical staff. Section 427(c), however, provides that no person or entity may be held liable in any civil action with respect to any report made under this part unless they knew information in the report was false.

Those provisions having provided for reports to publicize adverse actions against physicians, section 425, 42 U.S.C.A. 11135, then obligates hospitals to request from the Secretary, or from the agency designated by him as a State medical examiner board, information which health care entities must report pursuant to section 423(a). This must be done at the time a physician or licensed health care practitioner applies to be on a hospital's medical staff (courtesy or otherwise). It also must be done when a physician or licensed health care practitioner applies for clinical privileges at a hospital. For any physician or licensed health care practitioner who is on a hospital' s medical staff (courtesy or otherwise) or who has clinical privileges at a hospital, it must be done once every 2 years. Hospitals may request this information at any other time, too.

If a hospital fails to comply with this requirement, section 425(b) provides that it will be presumed to have knowledge of any information reported to the Secretary or to his designated State medical examiner board with respect to the physician or practitioner in any medical malpractice action to which they are party. This could severely impede a hospital's ability to defend itself in such a case.

On the other hand, section 425(c) provides that a hospital may rely upon information provided to it under the Health Care Quality Improvement Act, and may not be held liable for that reliance absent knowledge that the information provided was false.

Section 426, 42 U.S.C.A. 11136, provides that the Secretary must disclose information reported to him, or to his designated State medical examiner board, with respect to a physician or other licensed health care practitioner, to that physician or practitioner. He also must provide for them to dispute the accuracy of information which he obtains about them.

Statutory Provisions

Section 422, 42 U.S.C.A. 11132, provides:

REPORTING OF SANCTIONS TAKEN BY BOARDS OF MEDICAL EXAMINERS.

(a) IN GENERAL.—

(1) ACTIONS SUBJECT TO REPORTING.—Each Board of Medical Examiners—

(A) which revokes or suspends (or otherwise restricts) a physician's license or censures, reprimands, or places on probation a physician, for reasons relating to the physician's professional competence or professional conduct, or

(B) to which a physician's license is surrendered,

shall report, in accordance with section 424 [42 U.S.C.S. 11134], the information described in paragraph (2).

(2) INFORMATION TO BE REPORTED.—The information to be reported under paragraph (1) is—

(A) the name of the physician involved,

(B) a description of the acts or omissions or other reasons (if known) for the revocation, suspension, or surrender of license, and

(C) such other information respecting the circumstances of the action or surrender as the Secretary deems appropriate.

(b) FAILURE TO REPORT.—If, after notice of noncompliance and providing opportunity to correct noncompliance, the Secretary determines that a Board of Medical Examiners has failed to report information in accordance with subsection (a), the Secretary shall designate another qualified entity for the reporting of information under section 423.

Section 423, 42 U.S.C.A. 11133, provides in pertinent part:

REPORTING OF CERTAIN PROFESSIONAL REVIEW ACTIONS TAKEN BY HEALTH CARE ENTITIES.

(a) REPORTING BY HEALTH CARE ENTITIES.—

(1) ON PHYSICIANS. —Each health care entity which —

(A) takes a professional review action that adversely affects the clinical privileges of a physician for a period longer than 30 days;

(B) accepts the surrender of clinical privileges of a physician —

(i) while the physician is under an investigation by the entity relating to possible incompetence or improper professional conduct, or

(ii) in return for not conducting such an investigation or proceeding; or

(C) in the case of such an entity which is a professional society, takes a professional review action which adversely affects the membership of a physician in the society,

shall report to the Board of Medical Examiners, in accordance with section 424(a) [42 U.S.C.S. 1134(a)], the information described in paragraph (3).

(2) PERMISSIVE REPORTING ON OTHER LICENSED HEALTH CARE PRACTITIONERS. —A health care entity may report to the Board of Medical Examiners, in accordance with section 424(a), the information described in paragraph (3) in the case of a licensed health care practitioner who is not a physician, if the entity would be required to report such information under paragraph (1) with respect to the practitioner if the practitioner were a physician.

(3) INFORMATION TO BE REPORTED. —The information to be reported under this subsection is —

(A) the name of the physician or practitioner involved,

(B) a description of the acts or omissions or other reasons for the action or, if known, for the surrender, and

(C) such other information respecting the circumstances of the action or surrender as the Secretary deems appropriate.

(b) REPORTING BY BOARD OF MEDICAL EXAMINERS. —Each Board of Medical Examiners shall report, in accordance with section 424, the information reported to it under subsection (a) and known instances of a health care entity's failure to report information under subsection (a)(1).

Section 424, 42 U.S.C.A. 1134, provides:

FORM OF REPORTING.

(a) TIMING AND FORM. —The information required to be reported under sections 421 [which pertains to payors reporting medical malpractice payments], 422(a) [which pertains to reporting sanctions taken by boards of medical examiners], and 423 [which pertains to reporting adverse actions against physicians by health care entities and boards of medical examiners] shall be reported regularly (but not less often than monthly) and in such form and manner as the Secretary prescribes. Such information shall first be required to be reported on a date (not later than one year after the date of the enactment of this Act) specified by the Secretary.

(b) TO WHOM REPORTED. —The information required to be reported under sections 421, 422(a), and 423(b) [which pertains to reports required by boards of medical examiners] shall be reported to the Secretary, or, in the Secretary's discretion, to an appropriate private or public agency which has made suitable arrangements with the Secretary with respect to receipt, storage, protection of confidentiality, and dissemination of the information under this part.

(c) REPORTING TO STATE LICENSING BOARDS. —

(1) MALPRACTICE PAYMENTS. —Information required to be reported under section 421 shall also be reported to the appropriate State licensing board (or boards) in the State in which the medical malpractice claim arose.

(2) REPORTING TO OTHER LICENSING BOARDS. —Information required to be reported under section 423(b) shall also be reported to the appropriate State licensing board in the State in which the health care entity is located if it is not otherwise reported to such board under subsection (b).

Section 426, 42 U.S.C.A. 11136, provides:

With respect to the information reported to the Secretary (or the agency designated under section 424(b)) under this part respecting a physician or other licensed health care practitioner, the Secretary shall by regulation, provide for —

(1) disclosure of the information, upon request, to the physician or practitioner, and

(2) procedures in the case of disputed accuracy of the information.

In addition section 427, 42 U.S.C.A. 11137, provides in pertinent part:

MISCELLANEOUS PROVISIONS.

(a) PROVIDING LICENSING BOARDS AND OTHER HEALTH CARE ENTITIES WITH ACCESS TO INFORMATION. —The Secretary (or the agency designated under section 424(b)) shall, upon request, provide information reported under this part with respect to a physician or other licensed health care practitioner to State licensing boards, to hospitals, and to other health care entities (including health maintenance organizations) that have entered (or may be entering) into an employment or affiliation relationship with the physician or practitioner or to which the physician or practitioner has applied for clinical privileges or appointment to the medical staff.

(b) CONFIDENTIALITY OF INFORMATION. —

(1) IN GENERAL. —Information reported under this part is considered confidential and shall not be disclosed (other than to the physician or practitioner involved) except with respect to professional review activity, with respect to medical malpractice actions, or in accordance with regulations of the Secretary promulgated pursuant to subsection (a). Nothing in this subsection shall prevent the disclosure of such information by a party which is otherwise authorized, under applicable State law, to make such disclosure.

(2) PENALTY FOR VIOLATIONS. —Any person who violates paragraph (1) shall be subject to a civil money penalty of not more than $10,000 for each such violation involved. Such penalty shall be imposed and collected in the same manner as civil money penalties under subsection (a) of section 1128A of the Social Security Act [42 U.S.C.S. 1320a-7a(a)] are imposed and collected under that section.

(3) USE OF INFORMATION. —Subject to paragraph (1), information provided under section 425 and subsection (a) is intended to be used solely with respect to activities in the furtherance of the quality of health care.

(c) RELIEF FROM LIABILITY FOR REPORTING.—No person or entity shall be held liable in any civil action with respect to any report made under this part without knowledge of the falsity of the information contained in the report.

(d) INTERPRETATION OF INFORMATION.—In interpreting information reported under this part, a payment in settlement of a medical malpractice action or claim shall not be construed as creating a presumption that medical malpractice has occurred.

Finally, section 431, 42 U.S.C.A. 11151, provides in pertinent part:

DEFINITIONS.

In this title:

(1) The term "adversely affecting" includes reducing, restricting, suspending, revoking, denying, or failing to renew clinical privileges or membership in a health care entity.

(2) The term "Board of Medical Examiners" includes a body comparable to such a Board (as determined by the State) with responsibility for the licensing of physicians and also includes a subdivision of such a Board or body.

(3) The term "clinical privileges" includes privileges, membership on the medical staff, and the other circumstances pertaining to the furnishing of medical care under which a physician or other licensed health care practitioner is permitted to furnish such care by a health care entity.

(4) (A) The term "health care entity" means —

(i) a hospital that is licensed to provide health care services by the State in which it is located,

(ii) an entity (including a health maintenance organization or group medical practice) that provides health care services and that follows a formal peer review process for the purpose of furthering quality health care (as determined under regulations of the Secretary), and

(iii) subject to subparagraph (B), a professional society (or committee thereof) of physicians or other licensed health care practitioners that follows a formal peer review process for the purpose of furthering quality health care (as determined under regulations of the Secretary).

(B) The term "health care entity" does not include a professional society (or committee thereof) if, within the previous 5 years, the society has been found by the Federal Trade Commission or any court to have engaged in any anti-competitive practice which had the effect of restricting the practice of licensed health care practitioners.

(5) The term "hospital" means an entity described in paragraphs (1) and (7) of section 1861(e) [42 U.S.C.S. 1395x(e)(1) and (7), which defines hospital for Medicare purposes] of the Social Security Act.

(6) The terms "licensed health care practitioner" and "practitioner" mean, with respect to a State, an individual (other than a physician) who is licensed or otherwise authorized by the State to provide health care services.

(7) The term "medical malpractice action or claim" means a written claim or demand for payment based on a health care provider's furnishing (or failure to furnish) health care services, and includes the filing of a cause of action, based on the law of tort, brought in any court of any State or the United States seeking monetary damages.

(8) The term "physician" means a doctor of medicine or osteopathy or a doctor of dental surgery or medical dentistry legally authorized to practice medicine and surgery or dentistry by a State (or any individual who, without authority holds himself or herself out to be so authorized.)

(9) The term "professional review action" means an action or recommendation of a professional review body which is taken or made in the conduct of professional review activity, which is based on the competence or professional conduct of an individual physician (which conduct affects or could affect adversely the health or welfare of a patient or patients), and which affects (or may affect) adversely the clinical privileges, or membership in a professional society, of the physician. Such term includes a formal decision of a professional review body not to take an action or make a recommendation described in the previous sentence and also includes professional review activities relating to a professional review action. In this title, an action is not considered to be based on

the competence or professional conduct of a physician if the action is primarily based on —

(A) the physician's association, or lack of association, with a professional society or association,

(B) the physician's fees or the physician's advertising or engaging in other competitive acts intended to solicit or retain business,

(C) the physician's participation in prepaid group health plans, salaried employment, or any other manner of delivering health services whether on a fee-for-service or other basis,

(D) a physician's association with, supervision of, delegation of authority to, support for, training of, or participation in a private group practice with, a member or members of a particular class of health care practitioner or professional, or

(E) any other matter that does not relate to the competence or professional conduct of a physician.

(10) The term "professional review activity" means an activity of a health care entity with respect to an individual physician —

(A) to determine whether the physician may have clinical privileges with respect to, or membership in, the entity,

(B) to determine the scope or conditions of such privileges or membership, or

(C) to change or modify such privileges or membership.

(11) The term "professional review body" means a health care entity and the governing body or any committee of a health care entity which conducts professional review activity, and includes any committee of the medical staff of such an entity when assisting the governing body in a professional review activity.

(12) The term "Secretary" means the Secretary of Health and Human Services.

(13) The term "State" means the 50 States, the District of Columbia, Puerto Rico, the Virgin Islands, Guam, American Samoa, and the Northern Mariana Islands.

(14) The term "State licensing board" means, with respect to a physician or health care provider in a State, the agency of the State which is primarily responsible for the licensing of the physician or provider to furnish health care services.

For regulatory citations, see Chapter 9

§ 5:5 UNLAWFUL DISCLOSURE OF INFORMATION COLLECTED PURSUANT TO THE HEALTH CARE QUALITY IMPROVEMENT ACT — Section 427 [42 U.S.C.S. 11137]

Summary

In 1986 Congress concluded that too much medical malpractice was going on in the United States. One way to deal with that was to restrict the ability of incompetent physicians to move from State to State without disclosure or discovery of their previous damaging or incompetent performance. One way to accomplish that was to require those who make payments to settle medical malpractice claims to report such matters. Another way was to require State boards of medical examiners to report sanctions which they impose on physicians subject to their jurisdiction. Still another way was to have professional review bodies report adverse professional review actions against physicians.

Section 421(a), 42 U.S.C.A. 11131(a), requires each entity, including an insurance company, which makes a payment under a policy of insurance, self-insurance, or otherwise in settlement, or partial settlement of, or in satisfaction of a judgment in, a medical malpractice action or claim to report information about the payment, and the circumstances which led to the payment, to the Secretary of Health and Human Services or his designee.

"Medical malpractice action or claim" means a written claim or demand for payment based on a health care provider's furnishing, or failure to furnish, health care services. It also includes the filing of a tort action in any court of any State or the United States seeking monetary damages.

Section 421(b) requires such reports to include the name of the physician or licensed health care practitioner for whose benefit the payment was made, the amount of the payment, the name, if known, of any hospital with which the physician or practitioner is affiliated or associated, a description of the acts or omissions and injuries or illnesses upon which the action or claim was based, and any other information which the Secretary deems necessary. Furthermore, section 424, 42 U.S.C.A. 11134, requires such reports to be made regularly, but not less often than monthly, and in the form and manner prescribed by the Secretary. They also must be made to the appropriate State licensing board or boards in the State where the malpractice claim arose.

Section 422, 42 U.S.C.A. 11132, requires State boards of medical examiners to report to the Secretary or his designee every instance in which they revoke or suspend or otherwise restrict a physician's license. They also must report instances when a physician is censured, reprimanded, or placed on probation. This applies when such action relates to a physician's professional competence or professional conduct. Furthermore, medical examiner boards must report instances when a physician surrenders his or her license.

In addition, section 423(b) provides that such boards must report to the Secretary or his designee information which health care entities are obliged to send them regarding professional review actions those entities have taken that adversely affect either clinical privileges of a physician or membership of a physician in such an entity. Medical examiner boards also must report known instances of a health care entity's failure to report required information.

Section 423(a), 42 U.S.C.A. 11133, requires health care entities to report, either to their State medical examiner board or to any comparable board dealing with physician licensure, any action they take which adversely affects clinical privileges of a physician for a period longer than 30 days. They also must report when they accept surrender of clinical privileges of a physician under investigation for incompetence or improper professional conduct or in return for not conducting such an investigation. In addition, if the health care entity is a professional society, it must report if it takes action which adversely affects membership of a physician in the society.

Pursuant to section 431(3), the term "clinical privileges" includes privileges, membership on the medical staff, and other circumstances pertaining to the furnishing of medical care under which a physician or other licensed health care practitioner is permitted to furnish such care by a health care entity.

Section 423(a)(2) specifies that the information to be reported by a health care entity is the name of the physician or practitioner involved, a description of the acts or omissions or other reasons for the action or, if known, for the surrender of privileges or membership, and such other information respecting the circumstances of the action or surrender as the Secretary of Health and Human Services deems appropriate. Again, section 424, 42 U.S.C.A. 11134, requires such information to be reported not less often than monthly and in such form and manner as the Secretary prescribes. Furthermore, it must be reported to the Secretary, or, in the Secretary's discretion, to an appropriate private or public agency which has made suitable arrangements with the Secretary with respect to receipt, storage, protection of confidentiality, and dissemination. The information also must be reported to the appropriate State licensing board in the State in which the health care entity is located.

Section 427(a), 42 U.S.C.A. 11137(a), requires the Secretary or his designee to provide upon request the information reported with respect to a physician or other licensed health care practitioner to State licensing boards, to hospitals, and to other health care entities (including health maintenance organizations) that have entered or may be entering into an employment or affiliation relationship with the physician or practitioner or to which the physician or practitioner has applied for clinical privileges or appointment to the medical staff. Section 427(c) provides, however, that no person or entity may be held liable in any civil action with respect to any report made unless they knew information in the report was false.

Section 427(b) provides that information reported under Part B of the Act, that is, reports of medical malpractice payments required by section 421, reports of sanctions by boards of medical examiners required by section 422, and reports of professional review actions required by section 423, must be kept confidential. It may not be disclosed, other than to the physician or practitioner involved, except with respect to professional review activity, with respect to medical malpractice actions, or in accordance with regulations promulgated by the Secretary. That prohibition, however, does not prevent disclosure by an otherwise authorized party under applicable State law.

Any person who makes unlawful disclosure is subject to a civil money penalty not to exceed $10,000 for each violation. Enforcement procedures for this civil money penalty provision are governed by section 1128A of the Social Security Act, 42 U.S.C.A. 1320a-7a, which authorizes civil money penalties for a variety of offenses.

Statutory Provisions

Section 421, 42 U.S.C.A. 11131, provides:

REQUIRING REPORTS ON MEDICAL MALPRACTICE PAYMENTS.

(a) IN GENERAL. —Each entity (including an insurance company) which makes payment under a policy of insurance, self-insurance, or otherwise in settlement (or partial settlement) of, or in satisfaction of a judgment in, a medical malpractice action or claim shall report, in accordance with section 424 [42 U.S.C.S. 11134] , information respecting the payment and circumstances thereof.

(b) INFORMATION TO BE REPORTED. —The information to be reported under subsection (a) includes-

(1) the name of any physician or licensed health care practitioner for whose benefit the payment is made,

(2) the amount of the payment,

(3) the name (if known) of any hospital with which the physician or practitioner is affiliated or associated,

(4) a description of the acts or omissions and injuries or illnesses upon which the action or claim was based, and

(5) such other information as the Secretary determines is required for appropriate interpretation of information reported under this section.

(c) SANCTIONS FOR FAILURE TO REPORT. —Any entity that fails to report information on a payment required to be reported under this section shall be subject to a civil money penalty of not more than $10,000 for each such payment involved. Such penalty shall be imposed and collected in the same manner as civil money penalties under subsection (a) of section 1128A of the Social Security Act [42 U.S.C.S. 1320a-7a(a)] are imposed and collected under that section.

(d) REPORT ON TREATMENT OF SMALL PAYMENTS. —The Secretary shall study and report to Congress, not later than two years after the date of the enactment of this Act, on whether information respecting small payments should continue to be required to be reported under subsection (a) and whether information respecting all claims made concerning a medical malpractice action should be required to be reported under such subsection.

Section 422, 42 U.S.C.A. 11132, provides:

REPORTING OF SANCTIONS TAKEN BY BOARDS OF MEDICAL EXAMINERS.

(a) IN GENERAL. —

(1) ACTIONS SUBJECT TO REPORTING. —Each Board of Medical Examiners —

(A) which revokes or suspends (or otherwise restricts) a physician's license or censures, reprimands, or places on probation a physician, for reasons relating to the physician's professional competence or professional conduct, or

(B) to which a physician's license is surrendered,

shall report, in accordance with section 424 [42 U.S.C.S. 11134] , the information described in paragraph (2).

(2) INFORMATION TO BE REPORTED. —The information to be reported under paragraph (1) is —

(A) the name of the physician involved,

(B) a description of the acts or omissions or other reasons (if known) for the revocation, suspension, or surrender of license, and

(C) such other information respecting the circumstances of the action or surrender as the Secretary deems appropriate.

(b) FAILURE TO REPORT. —If, after notice of noncompliance and providing opportunity to correct noncompliance, the Secretary determines that a Board of Medical Examiners has failed to report information in accordance with subsection (a), the Secretary shall designate another qualified entity for the reporting of information under section 423.

Section 423, 42 U.S.C.A. 11133, provides in pertinent part:

REPORTING OF CERTAIN PROFESSIONAL REVIEW ACTIONS TAKEN BY HEALTH CARE ENTITIES.

(a) REPORTING BY HEALTH CARE ENTITIES. —

(1) ON PHYSICIANS. —Each health care entity which —

(A) takes a professional review action that adversely affects the clinical privileges of a physician for a period longer than 30 days;

(B) accepts the surrender of clinical privileges of a physician —

(i) while the physician is under an investigation by the entity relating to possible incompetence or improper professional conduct, or

(ii) in return for not conducting such an investigation or proceeding; or

(C) in the case of such an entity which is a professional society, takes a professional review action which adversely affects the membership of a physician in the society,

shall report to the Board of Medical Examiners, in accordance with section 424(a) [42 U.S.C.S. 1134(a)], the information described in paragraph (3).

(2) PERMISSIVE REPORTING ON OTHER LICENSED HEALTH CARE PRACTITIONERS. —A health care entity may report to the Board of Medical Examiners, in accordance with section 424(a), the information described in paragraph (3) in the case of a licensed health care practitioner who is not a physician, if the entity would be required to report such information under paragraph (1) with respect to the practitioner if the practitioner were a physician.

(3) INFORMATION TO BE REPORTED. —The information to be reported under this subsection is —

(A) the name of the physician or practitioner involved,

(B) a description of the acts or omissions or other reasons for the action or, if known, for the surrender, and

(C) such other information respecting the circumstances of the action or surrender as the Secretary deems appropriate.

(b) REPORTING BY BOARD OF MEDICAL EXAMINERS. —Each Board of Medical Examiners shall report, in accordance with section 424, the information reported to it under subsection (a) and known instances of a health care entity's failure to report information under subsection (a)(1).

(c) SANCTIONS. —

(1) HEALTH CARE ENTITIES. —A health care entity that fails substantially to meet the requirement of subsection (a)(1) shall lose the protections of section 411(a)(1) if the Secretary publishes the name of the entity under section 411(b).

Section 424, 42 U.S.C.A. 1134, provides:

FORM OF REPORTING.

(a) TIMING AND FORM. —The information required to be reported under sections 421 [which pertains to reporting medical malpractice payments], 422(a) [which pertains to reporting sanctions taken by boards of medical examiners], and 423 [which pertains to reporting adverse actions against physicians by health care entities and boards of medical examiners] shall be reported regularly (but not less often than monthly) and in such form and manner as the Secretary prescribes. Such information shall first be required to be reported on a date (not later than one year after the date of the enactment of this Act) specified by the Secretary.

(b) TO WHOM REPORTED. —The information required to be reported under sections 421, 422(a), and 423(b) [which pertains to reports required by boards of medical examiners] shall be reported to the Secretary, or, in the Secretary's discretion, to an appropriate private or public agency which has made suitable arrangements with the Secretary with respect to receipt, storage, protection of confidentiality, and dissemination of the information under this part.

(c) REPORTING TO STATE LICENSING BOARDS. —

(1) MALPRACTICE PAYMENTS. —Information required to be reported under section 421 shall also be reported to the appropriate State licensing board (or boards) in the State in which the medical malpractice claim arose.

(2) REPORTING TO OTHER LICENSING BOARDS.-Information required to be reported under section 423(b) shall also be reported to the appropriate State licensing board in the State in which the health care entity is located if it is not otherwise reported to such board under subsection (b).

Section 427, 42 U.S.C.A. 11137, provides:

MISCELLANEOUS PROVISIONS.

(a) PROVIDING LICENSING BOARDS AND OTHER HEALTH CARE ENTITIES WITH ACCESS TO INFORMATION. —The Secretary (or the agency designated under section 424(b) [42 U.S.C.S. 11134]) shall, upon request, provide information reported under this part with respect to a physician or other licensed health care practitioner to State licensing boards, to hospitals, and to other health care entities (including health maintenance organizations) that have entered (or may be entering) into an employment or affiliation relationship with the physician or practitioner or to which the physician or practitioner has applied for clinical privileges or appointment to the medical staff.

(b) CONFIDENTIALITY OF INFORMATION.—

(1) IN GENERAL.—Information reported under this part is considered confidential and shall not be disclosed (other than to the physician or practitioner involved) except with respect to professional review activity, with respect to medical malpractice actions, or in accordance with regulations of the Secretary promulgated pursuant to subsection (a). Nothing in this subsection shall prevent the disclosure of such information by a party which is otherwise authorized, under applicable State law, to make such disclosure.

(2) PENALTY FOR VIOLATIONS.—Any person who violates paragraph (1) shall be subject to a civil money penalty of not more than $10,000 for each such violation involved. Such penalty shall be imposed and collected in the same manner as civil money penalties under subsection (a) of section 1128A of the Social Security Act [42 U.S.C.S. 1320a-7a(a)] are imposed and collected under that section.

(3) USE OF INFORMATION.—Subject to paragraph (1), information provided under section 425 and subsection (a) is intended to be used solely with respect to activities in the furtherance of the quality of health care.

(c) RELIEF FROM LIABILITY FOR REPORTING.—No person or entity shall be held liable in any civil action with respect to any report made under this part without knowledge of the falsity of the information contained in the report.

(d) INTERPRETATION OF INFORMATION.—In interpreting information reported under this part, a payment in settlement of a medical malpractice action or claim shall not be construed as creating a presumption that medical malpractice has occurred.

Finally, section 431, 42 U.S.C.A. 11151, provides in pertinent part:

DEFINITIONS.

In this title:

(1) The term "adversely affecting" includes reducing, restricting, suspending, revoking, denying, or failing to renew clinical privileges or membership in a health care entity.

(2) The term "Board of Medical Examiners" includes a body comparable to such a Board (as determined by the State) with responsibility for the licensing of physicians and also includes a subdivision of such a Board or body.

(3) The term "clinical privileges" includes privileges, membership on the medical staff, and the other circumstances pertaining to the furnishing of medical care under which a physician or other licensed health care practitioner is permitted to furnish such care by a health care entity.

(4) (A) The term "health care entity" means —

(i) a hospital that is licensed to provide health care services by the State in which it is located,

(ii) an entity (including a health maintenance organization or group medical practice) that provides health care services and that follows a formal peer review process for the purpose of furthering quality health care (as determined under regulations of the Secretary), and

(iii) subject to subparagraph (B), a professional society (or committee thereof) of physicians or other licensed health care practitioners that follows a formal peer review process for the purpose of furthering quality health care (as determined under regulations of the Secretary).

(B) The term "health care entity" does not include a professional society (or committee thereof) if, within the previous 5 years, the society has been found by the Federal Trade Commission or any court to have engaged in any anti-competitive practice which had the effect of restricting the practice of licensed health care practitioners.

(5) The term "hospital" means an entity described in paragraphs (1) and (7) of section 1861(e) [42 U.S.C.S. 1395x(e)(1) and (7), which defines hospital for Medicare purposes] of the Social Security Act.

(6) The terms "licensed health care practitioner" and "practitioner" mean, with respect to a State, an individual (other

than a physician) who is licensed or otherwise authorized by the State to provide health care services.

(7) The term "medical malpractice action or claim" means a written claim or demand for payment based on a health care provider's furnishing (or failure to furnish) health care services, and includes the filing of a cause of action, based on the law of tort, brought in any court of any State or the United States seeking monetary damages.

(8) The term "physician" means a doctor of medicine or osteopathy or a doctor of dental surgery or medical dentistry legally authorized to practice medicine and surgery or dentistry by a State (or any individual who, without authority holds himself or herself out to be so authorized.)

(9) The term "professional review action" means an action or recommendation of a professional review body which is taken or made in the conduct of professional review activity, which is based on the competence or professional conduct of an individual physician (which conduct affects or could affect adversely the health or welfare of a patient or patients), and which affects (or may affect) adversely the clinical privileges, or membership in a professional society, of the physician. Such term includes a formal decision of a professional review body not to take an action or make a recommendation described in the previous sentence and also includes professional review activities relating to a professional review action. In this title, an action is not considered to be based on the competence or professional conduct of a physician if the action is primarily based on —

(A) the physician's association, or lack of association, with a professional society or association,

(B) the physician's fees or the physician's advertising or engaging in other competitive acts intended to solicit or retain business,

(C) the physician's participation in prepaid group health plans, salaried employment, or any other manner of delivering health services whether on a fee-for-service or other basis,

(D) a physician's association with, supervision of, delegation of authority to, support for, training of, or participation in a private group practice with, a member or members of a particular class of health care practitioner or professional, or

(E) any other matter that does not relate to the competence or professional conduct of a physician.

(10) The term "professional review activity" means an activity of a health care entity with respect to an individual physician —

(A) to determine whether the physician may have clinical privileges with respect to, or membership in, the entity,

(B) to determine the scope or conditions of such privileges or membership, or

(C) to change or modify such privileges or membership.

(11) The term "professional review body" means a health care entity and the governing body or any committee of a health care entity which conducts professional review activity, and includes any committee of the medical staff of such an entity when assisting the governing body in a professional review activity.

(12) The term "Secretary" means the Secretary of Health and Human Services.

(13) The term "State" means the 50 States, the District of Columbia, Puerto Rico, the Virgin Islands, Guam, American Samoa, and the Northern Mariana Islands.

(14) The term "State licensing board" means, with respect to a physician or health care provider in a State, the agency of the State which is primarily responsible for the licensing of the physician or provider to furnish health care services.

For regulatory citations, see Chapter 9

Health Care Fraud and Abuse: A Guide to Federal Sanctions

Volume 2

Health Care Fraud and Abuse:

A Guide to Federal Sanctions

Paul P. Cacioppo

Volume 2

WEST GROUP
A THOMSON COMPANY

(Release #17, 12/2001)

Note: In this work, every effort has been made to use gender neutral language. Where clarity requires, however, the masculine pronoun has been used. The reader should note that it refers to persons of either gender.

Library of Congress Cataloging-in-Publication Data

Cacioppo, Paul P.
Health care fraud and abuse: a guide to federal sanctions/by Paul P. Cacioppo.
p. cm.
ISBN 0–87632–806–0
1. Medicare fraud. 2. Medicaid fraud. 3. Sanctions, Administrative–United States. I. Title. KF3608.A4C33 1991
345.73'0263—dc20
[347.305263]

90-23174
CIP

Table of Contents

Volume 2

Part II TEXT (Continued)

Chapter 6 REGULATIONS: SANCTIONS IN THE MEDICARE STATUTE

Chapter 8 REGULATIONS: SANCTIONS IN TITLE XI

Appendix Guide

This Guide is provided as a supplement to the Table of Contents to aid the reader in identifying and locating *Health Care Fraud and Abuse* appendix material.

Regulatory Provisions Governing Medicare Safe Harbors

Office of Inspector General Advisory Opinions—Section 1128D Of the Social Security Act, 42 U.S.C. 1320a-7(d)

1997

Whether an outpatient radiology imaging center joint venture owned by a medical group specializing in radiology and a hospital care provider (i) generates prohibited remuneration within the meaning of the anti-kickback statute, Section 1128B of the Social Security Act; (ii) constitutes grounds for the imposition of an exclusion under Section 1128(b)(7) of the Act (as it applies to kickbacks); (iii) constitutes grounds for criminal sanctions under Section 1128B(b) of the Act; and/or (iv) satisfies the criteria set out in Section 1128B(b)(3) of the Act or associated regulations.

Advisory Opinion 97-6, October 8, 1997 Appendix F14
Whether a proposed arrangement for restocking ambulance supplies and medications (the "Proposed Arrangement") would constitute illegal remuneration as defined in the anti-kickback statute.

1998

Advisory Opinion 98-1, March 19, 1998 Appendix F17
Whether a contractual arrangement for distribution and billing services between Company A and Company B ... constitutes grounds for sanction under the anti-kickback statute.

Advisory Opinion 98-2, April 8, 1998 Appendix F17.1
Whether certain pharmaceutical discount pricing arrangements that are limited to arrangements between a manufacturer and wholesalers . . . will subject you to sanction under the anti-kickback statute.

Advisory Opinion 98-3, April 8, 1998 Appendix F17.2
Whether a hospital system's provision of an ambulance to a municipal fire department as described in your request . . .

Advisory Opinion 98-4, April 14, 1998 Appendix F17.3
Whether a proposed management services contract between a medical practice management company and a physician practice, which provides that the management company will be reimbursed for its costs and paid a percentage of net practice revenues...

Advisory Opinion 98-5, April 24, 1998 Appendix F17.4
. . .Which seeks our opinion regarding the "coordination of benefits" ("COB") provisions of a provider agreement between Nursing Home A . . . and a health care plan.

Advisory Opinion 98-6, April 24, 1998 Appendix F17.5
Whether waiving coinsurance obligations for participants in a clinical study sponsored by the Health Care Financing Administration and the National Heart, Lung, and Blood Institute...

Advisory Opinion 98-7, June 11, 1998 Appendix F17.6

Whether an ambulance restocking and continuing education arrangement . . . constitutes prohibited remuneration under the anti-kickback statute.

Advisory Opinion 98-8, July 6, 1998 Appendix F18

Whether Company A . . ., a wholly-owned subsidiary of Company B . . . would be subject to exclusion from Federal health care programs pursuant to 42 U.S.C. § 1320a-7(b) . . .

Advisory Opinion 98-9, July 13, 1998 Appendix F19

Whether a compensation arrangement for registered nurses and certain other employees pursuant to a collective bargaining agreement with the nurses' union...

Advisory Opinion 98-10, August 31, 1998 Appendix F23

Whether the payment of a sales commission to an independent manufacturers' representative . . . constitutes grounds for sanctions under the anti-kickback statute.

Advisory Opinion 98-11, September 14, 1998 Appendix F24

Whether a proposed purchasing arrangement involving a trade association, its nursing home members, and an electrical utility consultant . . . constitutes prohibited remuneration under the anti-kickback statute.

Advisory Opinion 98-12, September 16, 1998 Appendix F25

Whether a proposed joint venture among several orthopedic surgeons and anesthesiologists specializing in pain management to establish an ambulatory surgical center, as described in your request letter and supplemental submissions . . ., would generate prohibited remuneration . . .

Advisory Opinion 98-13, September 23, 1998 Appendix F26

Whether an ambulance restocking program, coordinated through a local emergency medical services council ..., constitutes prohibited remuneration under the anti-kickback statute...and, if so, whether the Program constitutes grounds for the imposition of sanctions under the anti-kickback statute.

Advisory Opinion 98-14, October 21, 1998 Appendix F27

Whether an existing pharmaceutical restocking program ... and a proposed medical supplies restocking program . . . constitute prohibited remuneration under the anti-kickback statute.

Advisory Opinion 98-15, November 2, 1998 Appendix F28

Whether an arrangement for contracted pharmacy services between University A and Pharmacy Company B to facilitate an outpatient pharmacy program for the University's hemophilia center pursuant to section

340B of the Public Health Service Act ...would constitute grounds for sanctions under the anti-kickback statute.

Advisory Opinion 98-16, November 3, 1998 Appendix F29

Whether a proposed arrangement under which [Name redacted] would assign an employee pharmacist to work in designated hospital transplant centers for the purpose of providing pharmacy-related products and services . . . would constitute prohibited remuneration under the anti-kickback statute.

Advisory Opinion 98-17, November 6, 1998 Appendix F30

Whether donations by Company X . . . to Organization A . . . (an independent, 501(c)(3) charitable organization) for the purpose of funding a program to pay for Supplementary Medical Insurance . . . or Medicare Supplementary Health Insurance . . . premiums for financially needy Medicare beneficiaries with end-stage renal disease . . .

Advisory Opinion 98-18, November 25, 1998 Appendix F31

Whether an ophthalmologist's proposed sublease to an optometrist of certain imaging equipment . . . would meet the criteria of the equipment rental safe harbor.

Advisory Opinion 98-19, December 14, 1998 Appendix F32

Whether an arrangement whereby an independent physician association would acquire an equity interest in a managed care organization would constitute grounds for the imposition of sanctions under the anti-kickback statute.

1999

Advisory Opinion 99-1, January 20, 1999 Appendix F33

Whether the Arrangement [for the provision of back-up emergency ambulance services that involves waivers of copayments and deductible amounts] constitutes prohibited remuneration within the meaning of the anti-kickback statute.

Advisory Opinion 99-2, February 26, 1999 Appendix F34

Whether certain arrangements for discounted ambulance services provided to residents of Medicare skilled nursing facilities would result in prohibited remuneration and sanctions under the anti-kickback statute.

Advisory Opinion 99-3, March 16, 1999 Appendix F35

Whether a proposed pricing arrangement for a package of therapeutic mattresses for SNF patients to be marketed by a company, and certain commissioned agents, would result in prohibited remuneration under the anti-kickback statute.

Advisory Opinion 99-4, March 31, 1999 Appendix F36

Whether a proposed agreement . . . pursuant to which Hospital District No.1 . . . would locate a medical clinic within the geographic boundaries of Hospital District No. 2 . . . would constitute grounds for sanctions under the anti-kickback statute.

Advisory Opinion 99-5, April 1, 1999 Appendix F37

Whether an annual fee imposed by city ordinance on ambulance companies wishing to provide ambulance services in the city . . . constitutes prohibited remuneration under the anti-kickback statute, . . . and, if so, whether the Ambulance Fee assessment constitutes grounds for the imposition of sanctions.

Advisory Opinion 99-6, April 7, 1999 Appendix F38

Whether the longstanding policy of a hospital, specializing in pediatric oncology research, of not billing its patients for any amounts associated with their treatment, including copayment amounts...

Advisory Opinion 99-7, June 30, 1999 Appendix F39

Whether an across-the-board waiver of any out-of-pocket beneficiary copayments for medical services covered by the national Eye Care Project constitutes grounds for the imposition of a sanction under section 1128A(a)(5) of the Act.

Advisory Opinion 99-8, July 6, 1999 Appendix F40

Whether an arrangement to provide for personal appearances by podiatrists to certain retail stores constitutes grounds for sanctions under the anti-kickback statute.

Advisory Opinion 99-9, September 30, 1999 Appendix F41

Regarding a proposed contractual arrangement between a self-insured employer health plan and a single-specialty managed care organization to provide managed podiatry benefits for the employer's retirees.

Advisory Opinion 99-10, October 25, 1999 Appendix F42

Whether a corporate sponsorship program between Drug Company A and Charity B . . . constitutes grounds for sanctions under the anti-kickback statute.

Advisory Opinion 99-11, October 25, 1999 Appendix F43

Concerning an arrangement sponsored by Coalition A to provide psychotherapy services at free or reduced prices using residents from local teaching facilities as clinicians.

Advisory Opinion 99-12, November 23, 1999 Appendix F44

About a proposed marketing program involving the use of physician practices and health care clinics to distribute coupons redeemable by certain retailers . . . for discounts on items or services that are not reimbursable by any Federal health care program.

2000

2001

The Office of Inspector General (OIG) was established at the Department of Health and Human Services by Congress in 1976 to identify and eliminate fraud, abuse, and waste in the Department's programs, including the Medicare and Medicaid programs, and to promote efficiency, economy, and effectiveness in departmental operations.

Office of Inspector General Advisory Opinions Under the Stark Bill—Section 1877 of the Social Security Act

Concerning whether a physician's referrals for certain services are prohibited under section 1877 of the Social Security Act

Whether the partners and physician employees of a proposed partnership may, under the "in-office ancillary services" exception defined in section 1877(b)(2) of the Social Security Act, refer Medicare and/or Medicaid patients to the partnership for eyeglass prescriptions filled subsequent to cataract surgery with the insertion of an intraocular lens.

Office of Inspector General Special Fraud Alerts

Office of Inspector General Medicare Advisory Bulletins

Office of Inspector General Special Advisory Bulletins

Office of Inspector General Compliance Program Guides

Other Civil and Criminal Statutes Pertinent to Health Care Fraud and Abuse

Recent Regulatory Provisions Applicable to Civil Money Penalties, Exclusions and Other Remedies

PART II

TEXT (Continued)

Chapter 6

REGULATIONS: SANCTIONS IN THE MEDICARE STATUTE

§ 6:1 FALSIFYING ASSESSMENTS OF RESIDENTS OF SKILLED NURSING FACILITIES — Section 1819(b)(3)(B)(ii) [42 U.S.C.A. 1395i-3(b)(3)(B)(ii)]

Regulations

42 CFR Part 402 — Civil Money Penalties, Assessments, and Exclusions

42 CFR Part 420 — Program Integrity: Medicare

42 CFR Part 431 — State Organization and General Administration, especially Subpart C — Administrative Requirements: Provider Relations; Subpart D — Appeals Process for NF's and ICF's/MR; and Subpart M — Relations with Other Agencies [Medicaid]

42 CFR Part 442 — Standards for Payment for Nursing Facilities and Intermediate Care Facilities for the Mentally Retarded

42 CFR Part 455 — Program Integrity: Medicaid

42 CFR Part 456 — Utilization Control [Medicaid]

42 CFR Part 483 — Requirements for States and Long Term Care Facilities

42 CFR Part 488 — Survey, Certification, and Enforcement Procedures

42 CFR Part 489 — Provider Agreements and Supplier Approval

42 CFR Part 498 — Appeals Procedures for Determinations that Affect Participation in the Medicare Program and for Determinations that Affect the Participation of ICF's/MR and Certain NF's in the Medicaid Program

42 CFR Chapter V — Office of Inspector General — Health Care, Department of Health and Human Services

Subchapter A — General Provisions

Part 1000 — Introduction; General Definitions

Subchapter B — OIG Authorities

Part 1001 — Program Integrity: Medicare and State Health Care Programs

Part 1002 — Program Integrity: State-initiated Exclusion from Medicaid

Part 1003 — Civil Money Penalties, Assessments and Exclusions

Part 1004 — Imposition of Sanctions on Health Care Practitioners and Providers of Health Care Services by a Peer Review Organization

Part 1005 — Appeals of Exclusions, Civil Money Penalties and Assessments

Part 1006 — Investigational Inquiries

Part 1007 — State Medicaid Fraud Control Units

Part 1008 — Advisory Opinions by the OIG

54 FR 5316, February 2, 1989: Medicare and Medicaid; Requirements for Long Term Care Facilities — Final rule with comment period, amending 42 CFR Parts 405, 442, 447, 483, 488, 489, and 498. See also delay in effective date at 54 FR 29717, July 14, 1989; corrections at 54 FR 8361, February 27, 1989, and 54 FR 37466, September 11, 1989; and final rule delaying effective date from January 1, 1990, to October 1, 1990, at 54 FR 53611, December 29, 1989.

55 FR 10938, March 23, 1990: Medicare and Medicaid Programs; Nurse Aide Training and Competency Evaluation Programs — Proposed rule to amend 42 CFR Parts 431, 433, and 483.

55 FR 10951, March 23, 1990: Medicare and Medicaid Programs; Preadmission Screening and Annual Resident Review — Proposed rule to amend 42 CFR Parts 405, 431, and 483.

56 FR 48826, September 26, 1991: Medicare and Medicaid; Requirements for Long Term Care Facilities — Final rule affecting 42 CFR Parts 422 , 447, 483, 488, 489, and 498. See also correction at 57 FR 43922, September 23, 1992.

56 FR 48880, September 26, 1991: Medicare and Medicaid Programs; Nurse Aide Training and Competency Evaluation Programs — Final rule affecting 42 CFR Parts 431, 433, and 483. See also correction at 56 FR 59331, November 25, 1991.

57 FR 4516, February 5, 1992: Medicare and Medicaid Programs; Omnibus Nursing Home Requirements — Proposed rule affecting

42 CFR Parts 418, 440, 441, 482, 483, and 488. See also correction at 57 FR 8961, March 13, 1992.

57 FR 39278, August 28, 1992: Medicare and Medicaid Programs; Survey, Certification and Enforcement of Skilled Nursing Facilities and Nursing Facilities — Proposed rule affecting 42 CFR Parts 431, 442, 488, and 489.

57 FR 53572, November 12, 1992: Medicare and Medicaid; Charges to Residents' Funds in Nursing Homes — Final rule affecting 42 CFR Part 483.

57 FR 54710, November 20, 1992: Medicaid Program; Elimination of Certain Written Documentation Pertaining to Medicaid Long-Term Care Facilities — Final rule affecting 42 CFR Part 442.

57 FR 56450, November 30, 1992: Medicare and Medicaid Programs; Preadmission Screening and Annual Resident Review — Final rule with comment period, affecting 42 CFR Parts 405, 431, 433, and 483. See also correction published at 58 FR 25784, April 28, 1993.

57 FR 61614, December 28, 1992: Medicare and Medicaid; Resident Assessment in Long Term Care Facilities — Proposed rule affecting 42 CFR Parts 456 and 483.

59 FR 56116, November 10, 1994: Medicare and Medicaid Programs; Survey, Certification and Enforcement of Skilled Nursing Facilities and Nursing Facilities — Final rule affecting 42 CFR Parts 401, 431, 435, 440, 441, 442, 447, 483, 488, 489, and 498. See also corrective amendment, effective July 1, 1995, at 62 FR 44221, August 20, 1997.

59 FR 66969, December 28, 1994: HCFA Public Information Collection Requirements Submitted to the Office of Management and Budget (OMB) for Clearance (pertaining to physician certification in skilled nursing facilities, and criteria for Medicare coverage of adult liver transplants).

60 FR 21525, May 2, 1995: HCFA Public Information Collection Requirements Submitted to the Office of Management and Budget (OMB) for Clearance (pertaining to intermediary requests for information from skilled nursing facilities, reimbursement for CLIA compliance surveys, patient outcome data in home health agencies, common claim forms for Medicare/Medicaid reimbursement, and a study of childhood immunization costs).

60 FR 37590, July 21, 1995: Medicare Program; Optional Payment System for Low Medicare Volume Skilled Nursing Facilities — Final rule affecting 42 CFR Part 413.

60 FR 50115, September 28, 1995: Medicare and Medicaid Programs; Survey, Certification and Enforcement of Skilled Nursing Facilities and Nursing Facilities — Final rule and correction to final regulations, affecting 42 CFR Parts 431, 440, 442, 488, 489, and 498. See also corrections at 60 FR 52731, October 10, 1995, and at 60 FR 534456, October 13, 1995.

61 FR 30623, June 17, 1996: Office of Inspector General Publication of OIG Special Fraud Alert: Fraud and Abuse in the Provision of Services in Nursing Homes — Notice.

61 FR 35231, July 5, 1996: HCFA Agency Information Collection Activities: Proposed Collection; Comment Request (pertaining to Medicaid payment standards for inpatient hospital or long-term care services).

61 FR 38395, July 24, 1996: Medicaid Program; Medicaid Eligibility Quality Control, Progressive Reductions in Federal Financial Participation for FYs 1982–1984, Payment for Physician Billing for Clinical Laboratory Services, and Utilization Control of Skilled Nursing Facility Services: Removal of Obsolete Requirements — Final rule.

61 FR 46466, September 3, 1996: Medicare Program; Schedule of Prospectively Determined Payment Rates for Skilled Nursing Facility Inpatient Routine Service Costs — Final rule with comment period.

61 FR 51295, October 1, 1996: HCFA Public Information Requirements Submitted for Collection of Public Comment: Submission for OMB Review (pertaining to approval of Medicaid payment rates for inpatient hospital or long term care services).

61 FR 64913, December 9, 1996: HCFA Agency Information Collection Activities: Proposed Collection; Comment request (pertaining to survey report forms for ICF/MRs; and current Medicare beneficiary surveys).

61 FR 68270, December 27, 1996: HCFA Agency Information Collection Activities: Submission for OMB Review; Comment request (pertaining to a facility identification and screening form for hospital providers of extended care services (swing-beds) in the the Medicare and Medicaid programs).

62 FR 26, January 2, 1997: Medicare Program; Electronic Cost Reporting for Skilled Nursing Facilities and Home Health Agencies — Final Rule. See also correction at 62 FR 27210, May 19, 1997.

62 FR 11214, March 11, 1997: HCFA Agency Information Collection Activities: Submission for OMB Review; Comment request

(pertaining to intermediate care facility for the mentally retarded or persons with related conditions survey report forms).

62 FR 11458, March 12, 1997: HCFA Agency Information Collection Activities: Proposed Collection; Comment request (pertaining to skilled nursing facility and skilled nursing facility health care complex cost report form).

62 FR 30603, June 4, 1997: HCFA Agency Information Collection Activities: Submission for OMB Review; Comment request (pertaining to skilled nursing facility and skilled nursing facility health care complex cost reports; and hospital conditions of participation).

62 FR 33095, June 18, 1997: HCFA Agency Information Collection Activities: Proposed Collection; Comment request (pertaining to skilled nursing facility prospective payment system cost report form).

62 FR 23140, April 29, 1997: Office of Inspector General: Health Care Programs: Fraud and Abuse; Revised PRO Sanctions for Failing to Meet Statutory Obligations — Final rule.

62 FR 43931, August 18, 1997: Medicare and Medicaid Programs: Effective Dates of Provider Agreements and Supplier Approvals — Final rule affecting 42 CFR Parts 431, 442, 488, 489, and 498.

62 FR 51536, October 1, 1997: Medicare Program; Schedules of Limits and Prospectively Determined Payment Rates for Skilled Nursing Facility Inpatient Routine Service Costs — Final notice with comment period.

62 FR 48736, October 30, 1997: HCFA Agency Information Collection Activities: Submission for OMB Review; Comment request (pertaining to prospective payment for skilled nursing facilities).

62 FR 67174, December 23, 1997: Medicare and Medicaid; Resident Assessment in Long Term Care Facilities — Final rule affecting 42 CFR Part 483.

63 FR 14719, March 26, 1998: HCFA Agency Information Collection Activities: Proposed Collection; Comment request (pertaining to physician certification and re-certification in skilled nursing facilities).

63 FR 20415, April 24, 1998: Office of Inspector General: Publication of OIG Special Fraud Alert: Fraud and Abuse in Nursing Home Arrangements with Hospices — Notice.

63 FR 26252, May 12, 1998: Medicare Program: Prospective Payment System and Consolidated Billing for Skilled Nursing Facilities — Final rule, affecting 42 CFR Parts 409, 410, 411, 413,

424, 483, and 489. See also correction at 63 FR 53301, October 5, 1998.

63 FR 28395, May 22, 1998: HCFA Agency Information Collection Activities: Submission for OMB Review; Comment request (pertaining to physician certifications and recertifications in skilled nursing facilities).

63 FR 28396, May 22, 1998: HCFA Privacy Act of 1974 — Notice of New System of Records (pertaining to the long term care minimum data set).

63 FR 37498, July 13, 1998: Medicare Program; Prospective Payment System and Consolidated Billing for Skilled Nursing Facilities — Notice of extension of comment period for interim final rule, affecting 42 CFR 409, 410, 411,413, 424, 483, and 489.

63 FR 42797, August 11, 1998: Medicare Program; Revision of the Procedures for Requesting Exceptions to Cost Limits for Skilled Nursing Facilities and Elimination of Reclassifications — Proposed rule affecting 42 CFR Part 413.

63 FR 58399, October 30, 1998: Office of Inspector General: Publication of the OIG's Provider Self-Disclosure Protocol — Notice.

63 FR 60356, November 9, 1998: HCFA Agency Information Collection activities: Proposed Collection; Comment request (pertaining to skilled nursing facility resident assessment MDS data).

63 FR 65561, November 27, 1998: Medicare Program; Prospective Payment System and Consolidated Billing for Skilled Nursing Facilities — Notice of re-opening of comment period for interim final rule, affecting 42 CFR 409, 410, 411, 413, 424, 483, and 489.

63 FR 66551, December 2, 1998: HCFA Agency Information Collection Activities: Submission for OMB review; Comment request (pertaining to EverCare coverage for nursing home residents under Medicare).

63 FR 68290, December 10, 1998: HCFA Agency Information Collection Activities: Submission for OMB Review; Comment request (pertaining to outpatient rehabilitation cost reports; SNF and SNF health care complex cost reports).

63 FR 70137, December 18, 1998: Office of Inspector General: Solicitation of Information and Recommendations for Developing OIG Compliance Program Guidance for the Nursing Home Industry — Notice.

63 FR 72317, December 31, 1998: HCFA Agency Information Collection Activities: Proposed Collection; Comment request (pertaining

to advanced directives under Medicare and Medicaid; and Medicare/Medicaid disclosure of ownership and control interests).

63 FR 72318, December 31, 1998: HCFA Agency Information Collection Activities: Proposed Collection; Comment request (pertaining to fire safety survey report forms for health care facilities).

1999

64 FR 6664, February 10, 1999: HCFA Agency Information Collection Activities: Submission for OMB Review; Comment request (pertaining to skilled nursing facility (SNF) resident assessment MDS data).

64 FR 13354, March 18, 1999: Medicare and Medicaid Programs; Civil Money Penalties for Nursing Homes (SNF/NF), Change in Notice Requirements, and Expansion of Discretionary Remedy Delegation — Final rule with comment period, affecting 42 CFR Part 488.

64 FR 13997, March 23, 1999: HCFA Agency Information Collection Activities: Submission for OMB Review; Comment request (pertaining to Medicare and Medicaid requirements for advanced directives, and disclosure of ownership and financial control interest).

64 FR 17184, April 8, 1999: HCFA Medicare Program; April 23, 1999 Open Town Hall Meeting to Discuss the Skilled Nursing Facility Prospective Payment System (SNF/PPS) and Quality of Care in Nursing Facilities — Notice of meeting.

64 FR 39934, July 23, 1999: Medicare and Medicaid Program; Appeal of the Loss of Nurse Aide Training Programs — Interim final rule with comment period, affecting 42 CFR Parts 431 and 498. See also correction at 64 FR 43295, August 10, 1999.

64 FR 41644, July 30, 1999: Medicare Program; Prospective Payment System and Consolidated Billing for Skilled Nursing Facilities — Final rule affecting 42 CFR Parts 409, 411, 413, and 489. See also correction at 64 FR 60122, November 4, 1999.

64 FR 41684, July 30, 1999: Medicare Program; Prospective Payment System and Consolidated Billing for Skilled Nursing Facilities — Update — Notice. See also correction at 64 FR 54030, October 5, 1999

64 FR 42610, August 5, 1999: Medicare Program; Revision of the Procedures for Requesting Exceptions to Cost Limits for Skilled Nursing Facilities and Elimination of Reclassifications — Final rule. See also correction at 65 FR 60104, October 10, 2000.

64 FR 54263, October 6, 1999: Medicaid Program; Flexibility in Payment Methods for Services of Hospitals, Nursing Facilities, and Intermediate Care Facilities for the Mentally Retarded — Proposed rule affecting 42 CFR Part 447.

64 FR 55949, October 15, 1999: HCFA Agency Information Collection Activities: Proposed Collection; Comment request (pertaining to physician certifications and re-certifications about the necessity for skilled nursing facility care).

64 FR 66482, November 26, 1999: HCFA Agency Information Collection Activities: Proposed Collection; Comment request (pertaining to resident assessment in skilled nursing facilities).

64 FR 67028, November 30, 1999: Medicare and Medicaid Programs; Religious Nonmedical Health Care Institutions and Advance Directives — Interim final rule with comment period, affecting 42 CFR Parts 403, 412, 431, 440, 442, 446, 456, 488, and 489.

64 FR 69271, December 10, 1999: HCFA Agency Information Collection Activities: Proposed Collection; Comment request (pertaining to hospital providers of extender care (swing bed) services in Medicare and Medicaid).

2000

65 FR 2186, January 13, 2000HCFA Agency Information Collection Activities; Submission for OMB Review; Comment request (pertaining to physician certifications/re-certifications in skilled nursing facilities).

65 FR 12560, March 9, 2000: HCFA Agency Information Collection Activities: Submission for OMB Review; Comment request (pertaining to hospital provider of extended care services (swing beds) in the Medicare and Medicaid programs).

65 FR 14289, March 16, 2000: Office of Inspector General: Publication of the OIG Compliance Program Guidance for Nursing Facilities — Notice.

65 FR 14986, March 20, 2000: HCFA Agency Information Collection Activities: Submission for OMB Review; Comment request (pertaining to skilled nursing facility resident assessment MDS data).

65 FR 19187, April 10, 2000: Medicare Program; Prospective Payment System and Consolidated Billing for Skilled Nursing Facilities; Update — Proposed rule affecting 42 CFR Parts 411 and 489.

65 FR 54856, September 11, 2000: HCFA Agency Information Collection Activities: Submission for OMB Review; Comment request (pertaining to skilled nursing facility cost reports).

65 FR 54857, September 11, 2000: HCFA Agency Information Collection Activities: Submission for OMB Review; Comment request (pertaining to ICF/MR survey report forms).

65 FR 60151, October 10, 2000: Medicaid Program; Revision to Medicaid Upper Payment Limit Requirements for Hospital Services, Nursing Facility Services, Intermediate Care Facility Services for the Mentally Retarded, and Clinic Services — Proposed rule affection 42 CFR Part 447.

65 FR 64227, October 26, 2000: HCFA Agency Information Collection Activities: Proposed Collection; Comment request (pertaining to home health agency cost reports; skilled nursing facility cost reports; and hospital cost reports).

2001

66 FR 3148, January 12, 2001: Medicaid Program; Revision to Medicaid Upper Payment Limit Requirements for Hospital Services, Nursing Facility Services, Intermediate Care Facility Services for the Mentally Retarded, and Clinic Services—Final rule affecting 42 CFR Part 447.

66 FR 3497, January 16, 2001: Medicare Program; Prospective Payment System and Consolidated Billing for Skilled Nursing Facilities—Update; Correction notice affecting 42 FR Parts 411, 313, and 489. See FR Doc. 00–19004, July 31, 2000.

66 FR 16062, March 23, 2001: HCFA Agency Information Collection Activities: Submission for OMB Review; Comment request (pertaining to SNF cost report forms).

66 FR 17657, April 3, 2001: Medicaid Program; Modification of the Medicaid Upper Payment Limit Transition Period for Inpatient Hospital Services, Outpatient Hospital Services, Nursing Facility Services, Intermediate Care Facility Services for the Mentally Retarded and Clinic Services—Proposed rule affecting 42 CFR Part 447.

66 FR 27151, May 16, 2001: HCFA Agency Information Collection Activities: Proposed Collection; Comment request (pertaining to the Long Term Care Awareness Project).

See § 2:1.

§ 6:1.1 VIOLATION OF REQUIREMENTS FOR PRIVATE CONTRACTS WITH MEDICARE BENEFICIARIES BY PHYSICIANS AND OTHER PRACTITIONERS — Section 1802(b) [42 U.S.C.A. 1395a(b)]

Regulations

42 CFR Part 402 — Civil Money Penalties, Assessments, and Exclusions

42 CFR Part 405, Subpart D — Private Contracts

42 CFR Part 405, Subpart X — Rural Health Clinic and Federally Qualified Health Center Services, especially Section 405.2414: Nurse practitioner and physician assistant services, and Section 405.2415: Services and supplies incident to nurse practitioner and physician assistant services

42 CFR Part 410 — Supplementary Medical Insurance (SMI) Benefits

42 CFR Part 414 — Payment for Part B Medical and Other Health Services

42 CFR Part 420 — Program Integrity: Medicare

42 CFR Part 455 — Program Integrity: Medicaid

42 CFR Part 489 — Provider Agreements and Supplier Approval

42 CFR Chapter V — Office of Inspector General — Health Care, Department of Health and Human Services

Subchapter A — General Provisions

Part 1000 — Introduction; General Definitions

Subchapter B — OIG Authorities

Part 1001 — Program Integrity: Medicare and State Health Care Programs

Part 1002 — Program Integrity: State-initiated Exclusion from Medicaid

Part 1003 — Civil Money Penalties, Assessments and Exclusions

Part 1004 — Imposition of Sanctions on Health Care Practitioners and Providers of Health Care Services by a Peer Review Organization

Part 1005 — Appeals of Exclusions, Civil Money Penalties and Assessments

Part 1006 — Investigational Inquiries

Part 1007 — State Medicaid Fraud Control Units

Part 1008 — Advisory Opinions by the OIG

1999

64 FR 10478, March 4, 1999: HCFA Agency Information Collection Activities: Proposed Collection; Comment request (pertaining to refunds to patients from physicians when Medicare does not provide coverage for the physician services provided).

64 FR 32239, June 16, 1999: HCFA Agency Information Collection Activities: Submission for OMB Review; Comment request (pertaining to the requirement that physicians must notify beneficiaries that Medicare is likely to deny payment for a specified service).

2000

65 FR 42021, July 7, 2000: HCFA Agency Information Collection Activities: Proposed Collection; Comment request (pertaining to notice to providers, suppliers, and practitioners about non-covered services to beneficiaries).

65 FR 57821, September 26, 2000: HCFA Emergency Clearance: Public Information Collection Requirements Submitted to the Office of Management and Budget (OMB) (pertaining to home health advanced beneficiary notices of liability).

65 FR 59858, October 6, 2000: HCFA Notice of Extension of Emergency Office of Management and Budget Clearance of Agency Information Collection Activities (pertaining to notices and demand bills from home health agencies).

65 FR 64227, October 26, 2000: HCFA Agency Information Collection Activities: Proposed Collection; Comment Request; Public Information Collection Meeting to Discuss Proposed Revisions (pertaining to notice requirements from suppliers, physicians, and practitioners to beneficiaries when Medicare Part B payment may be denied).

2001

66 FR 1997, January 10, 2001: HCFA Notice of OMB Approval (pertaining to uniform home health advance beneficiary notice).

66 FR 16061, March 22, 2001: HCFA Agency Information Collection Activities: Proposed Collection; Comment request (pertaining to private contracts of physicians who opt out of Medicare).

66 FR 20316, April 20, 2001: HCFA Agency Information Collection Activities: Submission for OMB Review; Comment request (pertaining to advance beneficiary notice by physicians, practitioners,

suppliers, and providers about items and services denied by Medicare as not reasonable and necessary).

66 FR 32630, June 15, 2001: HCFA Agency Information Collection Activities; Submission for OMB Review; Comment request (pertaining to contracts by practitioners and physicians who opt–out of Medicare).

See § 2:1.1.

§ 6:1.2 FAILURE BY PHYSICIANS, PROVIDERS, SUPPLIERS, AND OTHERS TO FURNISH AN ITEMIZED STATEMENT OF ITEMS AND SERVICES PROVIDED TO MEDICARE BENEFICIARIES — Section 1806 [42 U.S.C.A. 1395b-7]

Regulations

42 CFR Part 402 — Civil Money Penalties, Assessments, and Exclusions

42 CFR Part 405, Subpart X — Rural Health Clinic and Federally Qualified Health Center Services, especially Section 405.2414: Nurse practitioner and physician assistant services, and Section 405.2415: Services and supplies incident to nurse practitioner and physician assistant services

42 CFR Part 410 — Supplementary Medical Insurance (SMI) Benefits

42 CFR Part 414 — Payment for Part B Medical and Other Health Services

42 CFR Part 420 — Program Integrity: Medicare

42 CFR Part 455 — Program Integrity: Medicaid

42 CFR Part 489 — Provider Agreements and Supplier Approval

42 CFR Chapter V — Office of Inspector General — Health Care, Department of Health and Human Services

Subchapter A — General Provisions

Part 1000 — Introduction; General Definitions

Subchapter B — OIG Authorities

Part 1001 — Program Integrity: Medicare and State Health Care Programs

Part 1002 — Program Integrity: State-initiated Exclusion from Medicaid

Part 1003 — Civil Money Penalties, Assessments and Exclusions

Part 1004 — Imposition of Sanctions on Health Care Practitioners and Providers of Health Care Services by a Peer Review Organization

Part 1005 — Appeals of Exclusions, Civil Money Penalties and Assessments

Part 1006 — Investigational Inquiries

Part 1007 — State Medicaid Fraud Control Units

Part 1008 — Advisory Opinions by the OIG

1999

64 FR 10478, March 4, 1999: HCFA Agency Information Collection Activities: Proposed Collection; Comment request (pertaining to refunds to patients from physicians when Medicare does not provide coverage for the physician services provided).

64 FR 11922, March 10, 1999: HCFA Agency Information Collection Activities: Proposed Collection; Comment request (pertaining to attending physician's statement and documentation regarding medical emergency care).

64 FR 17673, April 12, 1999: HCFA Agency Information Collection Activities: Proposed Collection; Comment request (pertaining to Medicare participating physician or supplier agreements).

64 FR 24956, May 10, 1999: Medicare and Medicaid Programs; Effective Dates of Provider Agreements and Supplier Approvals-Correction restoring regulations inadvertently removed when a final rule concerning effective dates for provider agreements and supplier approvals was published at 62 FR 43931, August 18, 1997.

64 FR 32239, June 16, 1999: HCFA Agency Information Collection Activities: Submission for OMB Review; Comment request (pertaining to the requirement that physicians must notify beneficiaries that Medicare is likely to deny payment for a specified service).

64 FR 39517, July 22, 1999: HCFA Agency Information Collection Activities: Submission for OMB Review; Comment request (pertaining to Medicare participating physician or supplier agreement form HCFA-460).

64 FR 55949, October 15, 1999: HCFA Agency Information Collection Activities: Proposed Collection; Comment request (pertaining to physician certifications and re-certifications about the necessity for skilled nursing facility care).

65 FR 2186, January 13, 2000: HCFA Agency Information Collection Activities; Submission for OMB Review; Comment request

(pertaining to physician certifications/re-certifications in skilled nursing facilities).

65 FR 42021, July 7, 2000: HCFA Agency Information Collection Activities: Proposed Collection; Comment request (pertaining to notice to providers, suppliers, and practitioners about non-covered services to beneficiaries).

65 FR 53727, September 5, 2000: HCFA Agency Information Collection Activities: Proposed Collection; Comment request (pertaining to ambulance services reimbursement request form for physicians, suppliers, and beneficiaries).

65 FR 53963, September 6, 2000: Medicare Program: Appeals of Carrier Determinations that a Physician or Other Supplier Fails to Meet the Requirements for Medicare Billing Privileges; Reopening of Comment Period — Notice of reopening of comment period for proposed rule affecting 42 CFR Part 405.

65 FR 57821, September 26, 2000: HCFA Emergency Clearance: Public Information Collection Requirements Submitted to the Office of Management and Budget (OMB) (pertaining to home health advanced beneficiary notices of liability).

65 FR 59858, October 6, 2000: HCFA Notice of Extension of Emergency Office of Management and Budget Clearance of Agency Information Collection Activities (pertaining to notices and demand bills from home health agencies).

65 FR 60366, October 11, 2000: Medicare Program; Additional Supplier Standards — Final rule with comment period, affecting 42 CFR Part 424.

2001

66 FR 1996, January 10, 2001: HCFA Agency Information Collection Activities; Comment request (pertaining to Medicare uniform institutional provider bill for reimbursement of covered services by all providers that accept assignment of claims.

66 FR 1997, January 10, 2001: HCFA Notice of OMB Approval (pertaining to uniform home health advance beneficiary notice).

66 FR 2912, January 12, 2001: HCFA Agency Information Collection Activities: Proposed Collection; Comment request (pertaining to Medicare/Medicaid health insurance common claim form).

66 FR 6628, January 22, 2001: HCFA Agency Information Collection Activities: Proposed Collection; Comment request (pertaining to ambulance supplier claim forms).

66 FR 8807, February 2, 2001: HCFA Agency Information Collection Activities: Proposed Collection; Comment request (pertaining to Medicare Federal Health Care Programs Provider/ Supplier enrollment Application).

66 FR 18646, April 10, 2001: HCFA Agency Information Collection Activities: Submission for OMB Review; Comment request (pertaining to Medicare/Medicaid health insurance common claim form).

66 FR 20316, April 20, 2001: HCFA Agency Information Collection Activities: Submission for OMB Review; Comment request (pertaining to advance beneficiary notice by physicians, practitioners, suppliers, and providers about items and services denied by Medicare as not reasonable and necessary).

66 FR 20997, April 26, 2001: HCFA Agency Information Collection Activities: Submission for OMB Review; Comment request (pertaining to health insurance provider agreement form).

66 FR 21770, May 1, 2001: HCFA Agency Information Collection Activities: Submission for OMB Review; Comment request (pertaining to Medicare uniform institutional provider bill form).

66 FR 33102, June 20, 2001: HCFA Agency Information Collection Activities; Submission for OMB Review; Comment request (pertaining to provider/supplier enrollment application form).

See § 2:1.2.

§ 6:2 ABUSE OR NEGLECT OF SKILLED NURSING FACILITY RESIDENTS OR MISAPPROPRIATION OF THEIR PROPERTY —Section 1819(g)(1)(C) [42 U.S.C.A. 1395i-3(g)(1)(C)]

Regulations

42 CFR Part 402 — Civil Money Penalties, Assessments, and Exclusions

42 CFR Part 420 — Program Integrity: Medicare

42 CFR Part 431 — State Organization and General Administration, especially Subpart C — Administrative Requirements: Provider Relations; Subpart D — Appeals Process for SNF's and ICF's/MR; and Subpart M — Relations with Other Agencies [Medicaid]

42 CFR Part 442 — Standards for Payment for Skilled Nursing and Intermediate Care Facilities for the Mentally Retarded

42 CFR Part 455 — Program Integrity: Medicaid

42 CFR Part 456 — Utilization Control [Medicaid]

42 CFR Part 483 — Requirements for States and Long Term Care Facilities

42 CFR Part 488 — Survey, Certification, and Enforcement Procedures

42 CFR Part 489 — Provider Agreements and Supplier Approval

42 CFR Part 498 — Appeals Procedures for Determinations that Affect Participation in the Medicare Program and for Determinations that Affect the Participation of ICF's/MR and Certain NF's in the Medicaid Program

42 CFR Chapter V — Office of Inspector General — Health Care, Department of Health and Human Services

Subchapter A — General Provisions

Part 1000 — Introduction; General Definitions

Subchapter B — OIG Authorities

Part 1001 — Program Integrity: Medicare and State Health Care Programs

Part 1002 — Program Integrity: State-initiated Exclusion from Medicaid

Part 1003 — Civil Money Penalties, Assessments and Exclusions

Part 1004 — Imposition of Sanctions on Health Care Practitioners and Providers of Health Care Services by a Peer Review Organization

Part 1005 — Appeals of Exclusions, Civil Money Penalties and Assessments

Part 1006 — Investigational Inquiries

Part 1007 — State Medicaid Fraud Control Units

Part 1008 — Advisory Opinions by the OIG

54 FR 5316, February 2, 1989: Medicare and Medicaid; Requirements for Long Term Care Facilities — Final rule with comment period, amending 42 CFR Parts 405, 442, 447, 483, 488, 489, and 498. See also delay in effective date at 54 FR 29717, July 14, 1989; corrections at 54 FR 8361, February 27, 1989, and 54 FR 37466, September 11, 1989; and final rule delaying effective date from January 1, 1990, to October 1, 1990, at 54 FR 53611, December 29, 1989.

55 FR 10938, March 23, 1990: Medicare and Medicaid Programs; Nurse Aide Training and Competency Evaluation Programs — Proposed rule to amend 42 CFR Parts 431 , 433, and 483.

55 FR 10951, March 23, 1990: Medicare and Medicaid Programs; Preadmission Screening and Annual Resident Review — Proposed rule to amend 42 CFR Parts 405, 431, and 483.

56 FR 48826, September 26, 1991: Medicare and Medicaid; Requirements for Long Term Care Facilities — Final rule affecting 42 CFR Parts 422, 447, 483, 488, 489, and 498. See also correction at 57 FR 43922, September 23, 1992.

56 FR 48880, September 26, 1991: Medicare and Medicaid Programs; Nurse Aide Training and Competency Evaluation Programs — Final rule affecting 42 CFR Parts 431, 433, and 483. See also correction at 56 FR 59331, November 25, 1991.

57 FR 4516, February 5, 1992: Medicare and Medicaid Programs; Omnibus Nursing Home Requirements — Proposed rule affecting 42 CFR Parts 418, 440, 441, 482, 483, and 488. See also correction at 57 FR 8961, March 13, 1992.

57 FR 39278, August 28, 1992: Medicare and Medicaid Programs; Survey, Certification and Enforcement of Skilled Nursing Facilities and Nursing Facilities — Proposed rule affecting 42 CFR Parts 431, 442, 488, and 489.

57 FR 53572, November 12, 1992: Medicare and Medicaid; Charges to Residents' Funds in Nursing Homes — Final rule affecting 42 CFR Part 483.

57 FR 54710, November 20, 1992: Medicaid Program; Elimination of Certain Written Documentation Pertaining to Medicaid Long-Term Care Facilities — Final rule affecting 42 CFR Part 442.

57 FR 56450, November 30, 1992: Medicare and Medicaid Programs; Preadmission Screening and Annual Resident Review — Final rule with comment period, affecting 42 CFR Parts 405, 431, 433, and 483. See also correction published at 58 FR 25784, April 28, 1993.

57 FR 61614, December 28, 1992: Medicare and Medicaid; Resident Assessment in Long Term Care Facilities — Proposed rule affecting 42 CFR Parts 456 and 483.

59 FR 56116, November 10, 1994: Medicare and Medicaid Programs; Survey, Certification and Enforcement of Skilled Nursing Facilities and Nursing Facilities — Final rule affecting 42 CFR Parts 401, 431, 435, 440, 441, 442, 447, 483, 488, 489, and 498. See also correcting amendment, effective July 1, 1995, at 62 FR 44221, August 20, 1997.

59 FR 66969, December 28, 1994: HCFA Public Information Collection Requirements Submitted to the Office of Management and Budget (OMB) for Clearance (pertaining to physician certification in skilled nursing facilities, and criteria for Medicare coverage of adult liver transplants).

60 FR 21525, May 2, 1995: HCFA Public Information Collection Requirements Submitted to the Office of Management and Budget (OMB) for Clearance (pertaining to intermediary requests for information from skilled nursing facilities, reimbursement for CLIA compliance surveys, patient outcome data in home health agencies, common claim forms for Medicare/Medicaid reimbursement, and a study of childhood immunization costs).

60 FR 37590, July 21, 1995: Medicare Program; Optional Payment System for Low Medicare Volume Skilled Nursing Facilities — Final rule affecting 42 CFR Part 413.

60 FR 50115, September 28, 1995: Medicare and Medicaid Programs; Survey, Certification and Enforcement of Skilled Nursing Facilities and Nursing Facilities — Final rule and correction to final regulations, affecting 42 CFR Parts 431, 440, 442, 488, 489, and 498. See also corrections at 60 FR 52731, October 10, 1995, and at 60 FR 534456, October 13, 1995.

61 FR 30623, June 17, 1996: Office of Inspector General Publication of OIG Special Fraud Alert: Fraud and Abuse in the Provision of Services in Nursing Homes — Notice.

61 FR 35231, July 5, 1996: HCFA Agency Information Collection Activities: Proposed Collection; Comment Request (pertaining to Medicaid payment standards for inpatient hospital or long-term care services).

61 FR 38395, July 24, 1996: Medicaid Program; Medicaid Eligibility Quality Control, Progressive Reductions in Federal Financial Participation for FYs 1982–1984, Payment for Physician Billing for Clinical Laboratory Services, and Utilization Control of Skilled Nursing Facility Services: Removal of Obsolete Requirements — Final rule.

61 FR 46466, September 3, 1996: Medicare Program; Schedule of Prospectively Determined Payment Rates for Skilled Nursing Facility Inpatient Routine Service Costs — Final rule with comment period.

61 FR 51295, October 1, 1996: HCFA Public Information Requirements Submitted for Collection of Public Comment: Submission for OMB Review (pertaining to approval of Medicaid payment rates for inpatient hospital or long term care services).

61 FR 64913, December 9, 1996: HCFA Agency Information Collection Activities: Proposed Collection; Comment request (pertaining to survey report forms for ICF/MRs; and current Medicare beneficiary surveys).

61 FR 68270, December 27, 1996: HCFA Agency Information Collection Activities: Submission for OMB Review; Comment request (pertaining to a facility identification and screening form for hospital providers of extended care services (swing-beds) in the the Medicare and Medicaid programs).

62 FR 26, January 2, 1997: Medicare Program; Electronic Cost Reporting for Skilled Nursing Facilities and Home Health Agencies — Final Rule. See also correction at 62 FR 27210, May 19, 1997.

62 FR 11214, March 11, 1997: HCFA Agency Information Collection Activities: Submission for OMB Review; Comment request (pertaining to intermediate care facility for the mentally retarded or persons with related conditions survey report forms).

62 FR 11458, March 12, 1997: HCFA Agency Information Collection Activities: Proposed Collection; Comment request (pertaining to skilled nursing facility and skilled nursing facility health care complex cost report form).

62 FR 30603, June 4, 1997: HCFA Agency Information Collection Activities: Submission for OMB Review; Comment request (pertaining to skilled nursing facility and skilled nursing facility health care complex cost reports; and hospital conditions of participation).

62 FR 33095, June 18, 1997: HCFA Agency Information Collection Activities: Proposed Collection; Comment request (pertaining to skilled nursing facility prospective payment system cost report form).

62 FR 23140, April 29, 1997: Office of Inspector General: Health Care Programs: Fraud and Abuse; Revised PRO Sanctions for Failing to Meet Statutory Obligations — Final rule.

62 FR 43931, August 18, 1997: Medicare and Medicaid Programs: Effective Dates of Provider Agreements and Supplier Approvals — Final rule affecting 42 CFR Parts 431, 442, 488, 489, and 498.

62 FR 51536, October 1, 1997: Medicare Program; Schedules of Limits and Prospectively Determined Payment Rates for Skilled Nursing Facility Inpatient Routine Service Costs — Final notice with comment period.

62 FR 55410, October 24, 1997: HCFA Agency Information Collection Activities: Submission for OMB Review; Comment request (pertaining to Medicare/Medicaid disclosure of ownership and control forms).

62 FR 48736, October 30, 1997: HCFA Agency Information Collection Activities: Submission for OMB Review; Comment request (pertaining to prospective payment for skilled nursing facilities).

62 FR 66726, December 19, 1997: Medicare and Medicaid Programs; Hospital Conditions of Participation; Provider Agreements and Supplier Approval — Proposed rule affecting 42 CFR Parts 416, 482, 485, and 489.

62 FR 67174, December 23, 1997: Medicare and Medicaid; Resident Assessment in Long Term Care Facilities — Final rule affecting 42 CFR Part 483.

63 FR 14719, March 26, 1998: HCFA Agency Information Collection Activities: Proposed Collection; Comment request (pertaining to physician certification and re-certification in skilled nursing facilities).

63 FR 20415, April 24, 1998: Office of Inspector General: Publication of OIG Special Fraud Alert: Fraud and Abuse in Nursing Home Arrangements with Hospices — Notice.

63 FR 26252, May 12, 1998: Medicare Program: Prospective Payment System and Consolidated Billing for Skilled Nursing Facilities — Final rule, affecting 42 CFR Parts 409, 410, 411, 413, 424, 483, and 489. See also correction at 63 FR 53301, October 5, 1998.

63 FR 28395, May 22, 1998: HCFA Agency Information Collection Activities: Submission for OMB Review; Comment request (pertaining to physician certifications and recertifications in skilled nursing facilities).

63 FR 28396, May 22, 1998: HCFA Privacy Act of 1974 — Notice of New System of Records (pertaining to the long term care minimum data set).

63 FR 37498, July 13, 1998: Medicare Program; Prospective Payment System and Consolidated Billing for Skilled Nursing Facilities — Notice of extension of comment period for interim final rule, affecting 42 CFR 409, 410, 411,413, 424, 483, and 489.

63 FR 42797, August 11, 1998: Medicare Program; Revision of the Procedures for Requesting Exceptions to Cost Limits for Skilled Nursing Facilities and Elimination of Reclassifications — Proposed rule affecting 42 CFR Part 413.

63 FR 58399, October 30, 1998: Office of Inspector General: Publication of the OIG's Provider Self-Disclosure Protocol — Notice.

63 FR 60356, November 9, 1998: HCFA Agency Information Collection activities: Proposed Collection; Comment request (pertaining to skilled nursing facility resident assessment MDS data).

63 FR 65561, November 27, 1998: Medicare Program; Prospective Payment System and Consolidated Billing for Skilled Nursing Facil-

ities — Notice of re-opening of comment period for interim final rule, affecting 42 CFR 409, 410, 411, 413, 424, 483, and 489.

63 FR 66551, December 2, 1998: HCFA Agency Information Collection Activities: Submission for OMB review; Comment request (pertaining to EverCare coverage for nursing home residents under Medicare).

63 FR 68290, December 10, 1998: HCFA Agency Information Collection Activities: Submission for OMB Review; Comment request (pertaining to outpatient rehabilitation cost reports; SNF and SNF health care complex cost reports).

63 FR 70137, December 18, 1998: Office of Inspector General: Solicitation of Information and Recommendations for Developing OIG Compliance Program Guidance for the Nursing Home Industry — Notice.

63 FR 72317, December 31, 1998: HCFA Agency Information Collection Activities: Proposed Collection; Comment request (pertaining to advanced directives under Medicare and Medicaid; and Medicare/Medicaid disclosure of ownership and control interests).

63 FR 72318, December 31, 1998: HCFA Agency Information Collection Activities: Proposed Collection; Comment request (pertaining to fire safety survey report forms for health care facilities).

1999

64 FR 6664, February 10, 1999: HCFA Agency Information Collection Activities: Submission for OMB Review; Comment request (pertaining to skilled nursing facility (SNF) resident assessment MDS data).

64 FR 13354, March 18, 1999: Medicare and Medicaid Programs; Civil Money Penalties for Nursing Homes (SNF/NF), Change in Notice Requirements, and Expansion of Discretionary Remedy Delegation — Final rule with comment period, affecting 42 CFR Part 488.

64 FR 13997, March 23, 1999: HCFA Agency Information Collection Activities: Submission for OMB Review; Comment request (pertaining to Medicare and Medicaid requirements for advanced directives, and disclosure of ownership and financial control interest).

64 FR 17184, April 8, 1999: HCFA Medicare Program; April 23, 1999 Open Town Hall Meeting to Discuss the Skilled Nursing Facility Prospective Payment System (SNF/PPS) and Quality of Care in Nursing Facilities — Notice of meeting.

64 FR 39934, July 23, 1999: Medicare and Medicaid Program; Appeal of the Loss of Nurse Aide Training Programs — Interim final rule with comment period, affecting 42 CFR Parts 431 and 498. See also correction at 64 FR 43295, August 10, 1999.

64 FR 41644, July 30, 1999: Medicare Program; Prospective Payment System and Consolidated Billing for Skilled Nursing Facilities — Final rule affecting 42 CFR Parts 409, 411, 413, and 489. See also correction at 64 FR 60122, November 4, 1999.

64 FR 41684, July 30, 1999: Medicare Program; Prospective Payment System and Consolidated Billing for Skilled Nursing Facilities — Update — Notice. See also correction at 64 FR 54030, October 5, 1999

64 FR 42610, August 5, 1999: Medicare Program; Revision of the Procedures for Requesting Exceptions to Cost Limits for Skilled Nursing Facilities and Elimination of Reclassifications — Final rule.

64 FR 54263, October 6, 1999: Medicaid Program; Flexibility in Payment Methods for Services of Hospitals, Nursing Facilities, and Intermediate Care Facilities for the Mentally Retarded — Proposed rule affecting 42 CFR Part 447.

64 FR 55949, October 15, 1999: HCFA Agency Information Collection Activities: Proposed Collection; Comment request (pertaining to physician certifications and re-certifications about the necessity for skilled nursing facility care).

64 FR 66482, November 26, 1999: HCFA Agency Information Collection Activities: Proposed Collection; Comment request (pertaining to resident assessment in skilled nursing facilities).

64 FR 67028, November 30, 1999: Medicare and Medicaid Programs; Religious Nonmedical Health Care Institutions and Advance Directives — Interim final rule with comment period, affecting 42 CFR Parts 403, 412, 431, 440, 442, 446, 456, 488, and 489.

64 FR 69271, December 10, 1999: HCFA Agency Information Collection Activities: Proposed Collection; Comment request (pertaining to hospital providers of extender care (swing bed) services in Medicare and Medicaid).

2000

65 FR 2186, January 13, 2000: HCFA Agency Information Collection Activities; Submission for OMB Review; Comment request

(pertaining to physician certifications/re-certifications in skilled nursing facilities).

65 FR 12560, March 9, 2000: HCFA Agency Information Collection Activities: Submission for OMB Review; Comment request (pertaining to hospital provider of extended care services (swing beds) in the Medicare and Medicaid programs).

65 FR 14289, March 16, 2000: Office of Inspector General: Publication of the OIG Compliance Program Guidance for Nursing Facilities — Notice.

65 FR 14986, March 20, 2000: HCFA Agency Information Collection Activities: Submission for OMB Review; Comment request (pertaining to skilled nursing facility resident assessment MDS data).

65 FR 19187, April 10, 2000: Medicare Program; Prospective Payment System and Consolidated Billing for Skilled Nursing Facilities; Update — Proposed rule affecting 42 CFR Parts 411 and 489.

65 FR 54856, September 11, 2000: HCFA Agency Information Collection Activities: Submission for OMB Review; Comment request (pertaining to skilled nursing facility cost reports).

65 FR 54857, September 11, 2000: HCFA Agency Information Collection Activities: Submission for OMB Review; Comment request (pertaining to ICF/MR survey report forms).

65 FR 60151, October 10, 2000: Medicaid Program; Revision to Medicaid Upper Payment Limit Requirements for Hospital Services, Nursing Facility Services, Intermediate Care Facility Services for the Mentally Retarded, and Clinic Services — Proposed rule affection 42 CFR Part 447.

65 FR 64227, October 26, 2000: HCFA Agency Information Collection Activities: Proposed Collection; Comment request (pertaining to home health agency cost reports; skilled nursing facility cost reports; and hospital cost reports).

2001

66 FR 3148, January 12, 2001: Medicaid Program; Revision to Medicaid Upper Payment Limit Requirements for Hospital Services, Nursing Facility Services, Intermediate Care Facility Services for the Mentally Retarded, and Clinic Services—Final rule affecting 42 CFR Part 447.

66 FR 3497, January 16, 2001: Medicare Program; Prospective Payment System and Consolidated Billing for Skilled Nursing Facil-

ities—Update; Correction notice affecting 42 FR Parts 411, 313, and 489. See FR Doc. 00–19004, July 31, 2000.

66 FR 16062, March 23, 2001: HCFA Agency Information Collection Activities: Submission for OMB Review; Comment request (pertaining to SNF cost report forms).

66 FR 17657, April 3, 2001: Medicaid Program; Modification of the Medicaid Upper Payment Limit Transition Period for Inpatient Hospital Services, Outpatient Hospital Services, Nursing Facility Services, Intermediate Care Facility Services for the Mentally Retarded and Clinic Services—Proposed rule affecting 42 CFR Part 447.

66 FR 19507, April 16, 2001: HCFA Agency Information Collection Activities: Proposed Collection; Comment request (pertaining to conflict of interest and ownership and control information form).

66 FR 27151, May 16, 2001: HCFA Agency Information Collection Activities: Proposed Collection; Comment request (pertaining to the Long Term Care Awareness Project).

See § 2:2.

§ 6:3 GIVING A SKILLED NURSING FACILITY ADVANCE NOTICE OF A STATE OR FEDERAL SURVEY — Section 1819(g)(2) [42 U.S.C.A. 1395i-3(g)(2)]

Regulations

42 CFR Part 402 — Civil Money Penalties, Assessments, and Exclusions

42 CFR Part 420 — Program Integrity: Medicare

42 CFR Part 431 — State Organization and General Administration, especially Subpart C — Administrative Requirements: Provider Relations; Subpart D — Appeals Process for NF's and ICF's/MR; and Subpart M — Relations with Other Agencies [Medicaid]

42 CFR Part 442 — Standards for Payment for Skilled Nursing and Intermediate Care Facilites for the Mentally Retarded

42 CFR Part 455 — Program Integrity: Medicaid

42 CFR Part 456 — Utilization Control [Medicaid]

42 CFR Part 483 — Requirements for States and Long Term Care Facilities

42 CFR Part 488 — Survey, Certification, and Enforcement Procedures

42 CFR Part 489 — Provider Agreements and Supplier Approval

42 CFR Part 498 — Appeals Procedures for Determinations that Affect Participation in the Medicare Program and for Determinations that Affect the Participation of ICF's/MR and Certain NF's in the Medicaid Program

42 CFR Chapter V — Office of Inspector General — Health Care, Department of Health and Human Services

Subchapter A — General Provisions

Part 1000 — Introduction; General Definitions

Subchapter B — OIG Authorities

Part 1001 — Program Integrity: Medicare and State Health Care Programs

Part 1002 — Program Integrity: State-initiated Exclusion from Medicaid

Part 1003 — Civil Money Penalties, Assessments and Exclusions

Part 1004 — Imposition of Sanctions on Health Care Practitioners and Providers of Health Care Services by a Peer Review Organization

Part 1005 — Appeals of Exclusions, Civil Money Penalties and Assessments

Part 1006 — Investigational Inquiries

Part 1007 — State Medicaid Fraud Control Units

Part 1008 — Advisory Opinions by the OIG

54 FR 5316, February 2, 1989: Medicare and Medicaid; Requirements for Long Term Care Facilities — Final rule with comment period, amending 42 CFR Parts 405, 442, 447, 483, 488, 489, and 498. See also delay in effective date at 54 FR 29717, July 14, 1989; corrections at 54 FR 8361, February 27, 1989, and 54 FR 37466, September 11, 1989; and final rule delaying effective date from January 1, 1990, to October 1, 1990, at 54 FR 53611, December 29, 1989.

55 FR 10938, March 23, 1990: Medicare and Medicaid Programs; Nurse Aide Training and Competency Evaluation Programs — Proposed rule to amend 42 CFR Parts 431, 433, and 483.

55 FR 10951, March 23, 1990: Medicare and Medicaid Programs; Preadmission Screening and Annual Resident Review — Proposed rule to amend 42 CFR Parts 405, 431, and 483.

56 FR 48826, September 26, 1991: Medicare and Medicaid; Requirements for Long Term Care Facilities — Final rule affecting 42 CFR Parts 422, 447, 483, 488, 489, and 498. See also correction at 57 FR 43922, September 23, 1992.

56 FR 48880, September 26, 1991: Medicare and Medicaid Programs; Nurse Aide Training and Competency Evaluation Programs

—Final rule affecting 42 CFR Parts 431, 433, and 483. See also correction at 56 FR 59331, November 25, 1991.

57 FR 4516, February 5, 1992: Medicare and Medicaid Programs; Omnibus Nursing Home Requirements —Proposed rule affecting 42 CFR Parts 418, 440, 441, 482, 483, and 488. See also correction at 57 FR 8961, March 13, 1992.

57 FR 39278, August 28, 1992: Medicare and Medicaid Programs; Survey, Certification and Enforcement of Skilled Nursing Facilities and Nursing Facilities — Proposed rule affecting 42 CFR Parts 431, 442, 488, and 489.

57 FR 53572, November 12, 1992: Medicare and Medicaid; Charges to Residents' Funds in Nursing Homes — Final rule affecting 42 CFR Part 483.

57 FR 54710, November 20, 1992: Medicaid Program; Elimination of Certain Written Documentation Pertaining to Medicaid Long-Term Care Facilities —Final rule affecting 42 CFR Part 442.

57 FR 56450, November 30, 1992: Medicare and Medicaid Programs; Preadmission Screening and Annual Resident Review — Final rule with comment period, affecting 42 CFR Parts 405, 431, 433, and 483. See also correction published at 58 FR 25784, April 28, 1993.

57 FR 61614, December 28, 1992: Medicare and Medicaid; Resident Assessment in Long Term Care Facilities —Proposed rule affecting 42 CFR Parts 456 and 483.

59 FR 56116, November 10, 1994: Medicare and Medicaid Programs; Survey, Certification and Enforcement of Skilled Nursing Facilities and Nursing Facilities — Final rule affecting 42 CFR Parts 401, 431, 435, 440, 441, 442, 447, 483, 488, 489, and 498. See also correcting amendment, effective July 1, 1995, at 62 FR 44221, August 20, 1997.

59 FR 66969, December 28, 1994: HCFA Public Information Collection Requirements Submitted to the Office of Management and Budget (OMB) for Clearance (pertaining to physician certification in skilled nursing facilities, and criteria for Medicare coverage of adult liver transplants).

60 FR 21525, May 2, 1995: HCFA Public Information Collection Requirements Submitted to the Office of Management and Budget (OMB) for Clearance (pertaining to intermediary requests for information from skilled nursing facilities, reimbursement for CLIA compliance surveys, patient outcome data in home health agencies,

common claim forms for Medicare/Medicaid reimbursement, and a study of childhood immunization costs).

60 FR 37590, July 21, 1995: Medicare Program; Optional Payment System for Low Medicare Volume Skilled Nursing Facilities — Final rule affecting 42 CFR Part 413.

60 FR 50115, September 28, 1995: Medicare and Medicaid Programs; Survey, Certification and Enforcement of Skilled Nursing Facilities and Nursing Facilities — Final rule and correction to final regulations, affecting 42 CFR Parts 431, 440, 442, 488, 489, and 498. See also corrections at 60 FR 52731, October 10, 1995, and at 60 FR 534456, October 13, 1995.

61 FR 30623, June 17, 1996: Office of Inspector General Publication of OIG Special Fraud Alert: Fraud and Abuse in the Provision of Services in Nursing Homes — Notice.

61 FR 35231, July 5, 1996: HCFA Agency Information Collection Activities: Proposed Collection; Comment Request (pertaining to Medicaid payment standards for inpatient hospital or long-term care services).

61 FR 38395, July 24, 1996: Medicaid Program; Medicaid Eligibility Quality Control, Progressive Reductions in Federal Financial Participation for FYs 1982–1984, Payment for Physician Billing for Clinical Laboratory Services, and Utilization Control of Skilled Nursing Facility Services: Removal of Obsolete Requirements — Final rule.

61 FR 46466, September 3, 1996: Medicare Program; Schedule of Prospectively Determined Payment Rates for Skilled Nursing Facility Inpatient Routine Service Costs — Final rule with comment period.

61 FR 51295, October 1, 1996: HCFA Public Information Requirements Submitted for Collection of Public Comment: Submission for OMB Review (pertaining to approval of Medicaid payment rates for inpatient hospital or long term care services).

61 FR 64913, December 9, 1996: HCFA Agency Information Collection Activities: Proposed Collection; Comment request (pertaining to survey report forms for ICF/MRs; and current Medicare beneficiary surveys).

61 FR 68270, December 27, 1996: HCFA Agency Information Collection Activities: Submission for OMB Review; Comment request (pertaining to a facility identification and screening form for hospital providers of extended care services (swing-beds) in the the Medicare and Medicaid programs).

62 FR 26, January 2, 1997: Medicare Program; Electronic Cost Reporting for Skilled Nursing Facilities and Home Health Agencies — Final Rule. See also correction at 62 FR 27210, May 19, 1997.

62 FR 11214, March 11, 1997: HCFA Agency Information Collection Activities: Submission for OMB Review; Comment request (pertaining to intermediate care facility for the mentally retarded or persons with related conditions survey report forms).

62 FR 11458, March 12, 1997: HCFA Agency Information Collection Activities: Proposed Collection; Comment request (pertaining to skilled nursing facility and skilled nursing facility health care complex cost report form).

62 FR 30603, June 4, 1997: HCFA Agency Information Collection Activities: Submission for OMB Review; Comment request (pertaining to skilled nursing facility and skilled nursing facility health care complex cost reports; and hospital conditions of participation).

62 FR 33095, June 18, 1997: HCFA Agency Information Collection Activities: Proposed Collection; Comment request (pertaining to skilled nursing facility prospective payment system cost report form).

62 FR 23140, April 29, 1997: Office of Inspector General: Health Care Programs: Fraud and Abuse; Revised PRO Sanctions for Failing to Meet Statutory Obligations — Final rule.

62 FR 43931, August 18, 1997: Medicare and Medicaid Programs: Effective Dates of Provider Agreements and Supplier Approvals — Final rule affecting 42 CFR Parts 431, 442, 488, 489, and 498.

62 FR 51536, October 1, 1997: Medicare Program; Schedules of Limits and Prospectively Determined Payment Rates for Skilled Nursing Facility Inpatient Routine Service Costs — Final notice with comment period.

62 FR 55410, October 24, 1997: HCFA Agency Information Collection Activities: Submission for OMB Review; Comment request (pertaining to Medicare/Medicaid disclosure of ownership and control forms).

62 FR 48736, October 30, 1997: HCFA Agency Information Collection Activities: Submission for OMB Review; Comment request (pertaining to prospective payment for skilled nursing facilities).

62 FR 66726, December 19, 1997: Medicare and Medicaid Programs; Hospital Conditions of Participation; Provider Agreements and Supplier Approval — Proposed rule affecting 42 CFR Parts 416, 482, 485, and 489.

62 FR 67174, December 23, 1997: Medicare and Medicaid; Resident Assessment in Long Term Care Facilities — Final rule affecting 42 CFR Part 483.

63 FR 14719, March 26, 1998: HCFA Agency Information Collection Activities: Proposed Collection; Comment request (pertaining to physician certification and re-certification in skilled nursing facilities).

63 FR 20415, April 24, 1998: Office of Inspector General: Publication of OIG Special Fraud Alert: Fraud and Abuse in Nursing Home Arrangements with Hospices — Notice.

63 FR 26252, May 12, 1998: Medicare Program: Prospective Payment System and Consolidated Billing for Skilled Nursing Facilities — Final rule, affecting 42 CFR Parts 409, 410, 411, 413, 424, 483, and 489. See also correction at 63 FR 53301, October 5, 1998.

63 FR 28395, May 22, 1998: HCFA Agency Information Collection Activities: Submission for OMB Review; Comment request (pertaining to physician certifications and recertifications in skilled nursing facilities).

63 FR 28396, May 22, 1998: HCFA Privacy Act of 1974 — Notice of New System of Records (pertaining to the long term care minimum data set).

63 FR 37498, July 13, 1998: Medicare Program; Prospective Payment System and Consolidated Billing for Skilled Nursing Facilities — Notice of extension of comment period for interim final rule, affecting 42 CFR 409, 410, 411,413, 424, 483, and 489.

63 FR 42797, August 11, 1998: Medicare Program; Revision of the Procedures for Requesting Exceptions to Cost Limits for Skilled Nursing Facilities and Elimination of Reclassifications — Proposed rule affecting 42 CFR Part 413.

63 FR 58399, October 30, 1998: Office of Inspector General: Publication of the OIG's Provider Self-Disclosure Protocol — Notice.

63 FR 60356, November 9, 1998: HCFA Agency Information Collection activities: Proposed Collection; Comment request (pertaining to skilled nursing facility resident assessment MDS data).

63 FR 65561, November 27, 1998: Medicare Program; Prospective Payment System and Consolidated Billing for Skilled Nursing Facilities — Notice of re-opening of comment period for interim final rule, affecting 42 CFR 409, 410, 411, 413, 424, 483, and 489.

63 FR 66551, December 2, 1998: HCFA Agency Information Collection Activities: Submission for OMB review; Comment request

(pertaining to EverCare coverage for nursing home residents under Medicare).

63 FR 68290, December 10, 1998: HCFA Agency Information Collection Activities: Submission for OMB Review; Comment request (pertaining to outpatient rehabilitation cost reports; SNF and SNF health care complex cost reports).

63 FR 70137, December 18, 1998: Office of Inspector General: Solicitation of Information and Recommendations for Developing OIG Compliance Program Guidance for the Nursing Home Industry — Notice.

63 FR 72317, December 31, 1998: HCFA Agency Information Collection Activities: Proposed Collection; Comment request (pertaining to advanced directives under Medicare and Medicaid; and Medicare/Medicaid disclosure of ownership and control interests).

63 FR 72318, December 31, 1998: HCFA Agency Information Collection Activities: Proposed Collection; Comment request (pertaining to fire safety survey report forms for health care facilities).

1999

64 FR 6664, February 10, 1999: HCFA Agency Information Collection Activities: Submission for OMB Review; Comment request (pertaining to skilled nursing facility (SNF) resident assessment MDS data).

64 FR 13354, March 18, 1999: Medicare and Medicaid Programs; Civil Money Penalties for Nursing Homes (SNF/NF), Change in Notice Requirements, and Expansion of Discretionary Remedy Delegation — Final rule with comment period, affecting 42 CFR Part 488.

64 FR 13997, March 23, 1999: HCFA Agency Information Collection Activities: Submission for OMB Review; Comment request (pertaining to Medicare and Medicaid requirements for advanced directives, and disclosure of ownership and financial control interest).

64 FR 17184, April 8, 1999: HCFA Medicare Program; April 23, 1999 Open Town Hall Meeting to Discuss the Skilled Nursing Facility Prospective Payment System (SNF/PPS) and Quality of Care in Nursing Facilities — Notice of meeting.

64 FR 39934, July 23, 1999: Medicare and Medicaid Program; Appeal of the Loss of Nurse Aide Training Programs — Interim

final rule with comment period, affecting 42 CFR Parts 431 and 498. See also correction at 64 FR 43295, August 10, 1999.

64 FR 41644, July 30, 1999: Medicare Program; Prospective Payment System and Consolidated Billing for Skilled Nursing Facilities — Final rule affecting 42 CFR Parts 409, 411, 413, and 489. See also correction at 64 FR 60122, November 4, 1999.

64 FR 41684, July 30, 1999: Medicare Program; Prospective Payment System and Consolidated Billing for Skilled Nursing Facilities — Update — Notice. See also correction at 64 FR 54030, October 5, 1999

64 FR 42610, August 5, 1999: Medicare Program; Revision of the Procedures for Requesting Exceptions to Cost Limits for Skilled Nursing Facilities and Elimination of Reclassifications — Final rule.

64 FR 54263, October 6, 1999: Medicaid Program; Flexibility in Payment Methods for Services of Hospitals, Nursing Facilities, and Intermediate Care Facilities for the Mentally Retarded — Proposed rule affecting 42 CFR Part 447.

64 FR 55949, October 15, 1999: HCFA Agency Information Collection Activities: Proposed Collection; Comment request (pertaining to physician certifications and re-certifications about the necessity for skilled nursing facility care).

64 FR 66482, November 26, 1999: HCFA Agency Information Collection Activities: Proposed Collection; Comment request (pertaining to resident assessment in skilled nursing facilities).

64 FR 67028, November 30, 1999: Medicare and Medicaid Programs; Religious Nonmedical Health Care Institutions and Advance Directives — Interim final rule with comment period, affecting 42 CFR Parts 403, 412, 431, 440, 442, 446, 456, 488, and 489.

64 FR 69271, December 10, 1999: HCFA Agency Information Collection Activities: Proposed Collection; Comment request (pertaining to hospital providers of extender care (swing bed) services in Medicare and Medicaid).

2000

65 FR 2186, January 13, 2000: HCFA Agency Information Collection Activities; Submission for OMB Review; Comment request (pertaining to physician certifications/re-certifications in skilled nursing facilities).

65 FR 12560, March 9, 2000: HCFA Agency Information Collection Activities: Submission for OMB Review; Comment request (pertain-

ing to hospital provider of extended care services (swing beds) in the Medicare and Medicaid programs).

65 FR 14289, March 16, 2000: Office of Inspector General: Publication of the OIG Compliance Program Guidance for Nursing Facilities — Notice.

65 FR 14986, March 20, 2000: HCFA Agency Information Collection Activities: Submission for OMB Review; Comment request (pertaining to skilled nursing facility resident assessment MDS data).

65 FR 19187, April 10, 2000: Medicare Program; Prospective Payment System and Consolidated Billing for Skilled Nursing Facilities; Update — Proposed rule affecting 42 CFR Parts 411 and 489.

65 FR 54856, September 11, 2000: HCFA Agency Information Collection Activities: Submission for OMB Review; Comment request (pertaining to skilled nursing facility cost reports).

65 FR 54857, September 11, 2000: HCFA Agency Information Collection Activities: Submission for OMB Review; Comment request (pertaining to ICF/MR survey report forms).

65 FR 60151, October 10, 2000: Medicaid Program; Revision to Medicaid Upper Payment Limit Requirements for Hospital Services, Nursing Facility Services, Intermediate Care Facility Services for the Mentally Retarded, and Clinic Services — Proposed rule affection 42 CFR Part 447.

65 FR 64227, October 26, 2000: HCFA Agency Information Collection Activities: Proposed Collection; Comment request (pertaining to home health agency cost reports; skilled nursing facility cost reports; and hospital cost reports).

2001

66 FR 3148, January 12, 2001: Medicaid Program; Revision to Medicaid Upper Payment Limit Requirements for Hospital Services, Nursing Facility Services, Intermediate Care Facility Services for the Mentally Retarded, and Clinic Services—Final rule affecting 42 CFR Part 447.

66 FR 3497, January 16, 2001: Medicare Program; Prospective Payment System and Consolidated Billing for Skilled Nursing Facilities—Update; Correction notice affecting 42 FR Parts 411, 313, and 489. See FR Doc. 00-19004, July 31, 2000.

66 FR 16062, March 23, 2001: HCFA Agency Information Collection Activities: Submission for OMB Review; Comment request (pertaining to SNF cost report forms).

66 FR 17657, April 3, 2001: Medicaid Program; Modification of the Medicaid Upper Payment Limit Transition Period for Inpatient Hospital Services, Outpatient Hospital Services, Nursing Facility Services, Intermediate Care Facility Services for the Mentally Retarded and Clinic Services—Proposed rule affecting 42 CFR Part 447.

66 FR 19507, April 16, 2001: HCFA Agency Information Collection Activities: Proposed Collection; Comment request (pertaining to conflict of interest and ownership and control information form).

66 FR 27151, May 16, 2001: HCFA Agency Information Collection Activities: Proposed Collection; Comment request (pertaining to the Long Term Care Awareness Project).

See § 2:3.

§ 6:4 FAILING A SKILLED NURSING FACILITY SURVEY — Sections 1819(g) and (h) [42 U.S.C.A. 1395i-3(g)and (h)]

Regulations

42 CFR Part 402 — Civil Money Penalties, Assessments, and Exclusions

42 CFR Part 420 — Program Integrity: Medicare

42 CFR Part 431 — State Organization and General Administration, especially Subpart C — Administrative Requirements: Provider Relations; Subpart D — Appeals Process for NF's and ICF's; and Subpart M — Relations with Other Agencies [Medicaid]

42 CFR Part 442 — Standards for Payment for Skilled Nursing and Intermediate Care Facility Services [Medicaid]

42 CFR Part 455 — Program Integrity: Medicaid

42 CFR Part 456 — Utilization Control [Medicaid]

42 CFR Part 483 — Requirements for States and Long Term Care Facilities

42 CFR Part 488 — Survey and Certification Procedures

42 CFR Part 489 — Provider Agreements under Medicare

42 CFR Part 498 — Appeals Procedures for Determinations that Affect Participation in the Medicare Program

42 CFR Chapter V — Office of Inspector General — Health Care, Department of Health and Human Services

Subchapter A — General Provisions
Part 1000 — Introduction; General Definitions
Subchapter B — OIG Authorities
Part 1001 — Program Integrity: Medicare
Part 1002 — Program Integrity: Medicaid
Part 1003 — Civil Money Penalties and Assessments
Part 1004 — Imposition of Sanctions on Health Care Practitioners and Providers of Health Care Services by a Peer Review Organization
Part 1005 — Appeals of Exclusions, Civil Money Penalties and Assessments
Part 1006 — Investigational Inquiries
Part 1007 — State Medicaid Fraud Control Units
Part 1008 — Advisory Opinions by the OIG

54 FR 5316, February 2, 1989: Medicare and Medicaid; Requirements for Long Term Care Facilities — Final rule with comment period, amending 42 CFR Parts 405, 442, 447, 483, 488, 489, and 498. See also delay in effective date at 54 FR 29717, July 14, 1989; corrections at 54 FR 8361, February 27, 1989, and 54 FR 37466, September 11, 1989; and final rule delaying effective date from January 1, 1990, to October 1, 1990, at 54 FR 53611, December 29, 1989.

55 FR 10938, March 23, 1990: Medicare and Medicaid Programs; Nurse Aide Training and Competency Evaluation Programs — Proposed rule to amend 42 CFR Parts 431, 433, and 483.

55 FR 10951, March 23, 1990: Medicare and Medicaid Programs; Preadmission Screening and Annual Resident Review — Proposed rule to amend 42 CFR Parts 405, 431, and 483.

56 FR 48826, September 26, 1991: Medicare and Medicaid; Requirements for Long Term Care Facilities — Final rule affecting 42 CFR Parts 422, 447, 483, 488, 489, and 498. See also correction at 57 FR 43922, September 23, 1992.

56 FR 48880, September 26, 1991: Medicare and Medicaid Programs; Nurse Aide Training and Competency Evaluation Programs — Final rule affecting 42 CFR Parts 431, 433, and 483. See also correction at 56 FR 59331, November 25, 1991.

57 FR 4516, February 5, 1992: Medicare and Medicaid Programs; Omnibus Nursing Home Requirements — Proposed rule affecting 42 CFR Parts 418, 440, 441, 482, 483, and 488. See also correction at 57 FR 8961, March 13, 1992.

57 FR 39278, August 28, 1992: Medicare and Medicaid Programs; Survey, Certification and Enforcement of Skilled Nursing Facilities

and Nursing Facilities — Proposed rule affecting 42 CFR Parts 431, 442, 488, and 489.

57 FR 53572, November 12, 1992: Medicare and Medicaid; Charges to Residents' Funds in Nursing Homes — Final rule affecting 42 CFR Part 483.

57 FR 54710, November 20, 1992: Medicaid Program; Elimination of Certain Written Documentation Pertaining to Medicaid Long-Term Care Facilities — Final rule affecting 42 CFR Part 442.

57 FR 56450, November 30, 1992: Medicare and Medicaid Programs; Preadmission Screening and Annual Resident Review — Final rule with comment period, affecting 42 CFR Parts 405, 431, 433, and 483. See also correction published at 58 FR 25784, April 28, 1993.

57 FR 61614, December 28, 1992: Medicare and Medicaid; Resident Assessment in Long Term Care Facilities — Proposed rule affecting 42 CFR Parts 456 and 483.

59 FR 52178, October 14, 1994: HCFA Public Information Collection Requirements Submitted to the Office of Management and Budget (OMB) for Clearance (pertaining to Medicare reimbursement for outpatient services, cost reports for free-standing skilled nursing facilities; Medicare coverage criteria for adult heart transplants, drug rebates for Medicaid, optional prospective payment cost report for certain skilled nursing facilities, reimbursable costs for organ procurement agencies, distribution and use of end stage renal disease treatment sources, conditions of coverage for ambulatory surgical centers, and waivers for home and community based services).

59 FR 56116, November 10, 1994: Medicare and Medicaid Programs; Survey, Certification and Enforcement of Skilled Nursing Facilities and Nursing Facilities — Final rule affecting 42 CFR Parts 401, 431, 435, 440, 441, 442, 447, 483, 488, 489, and 498. See also correcting amendment, effective July 1, 1995, at 62 FR 44221, August 20, 1997.

59 FR 66969, December 28, 1994: HCFA Public Information Collection Requirements Submitted to the Office of Management and Budget (OMB) for Clearance (pertaining to physician certification in skilled nursing facilities, and criteria for Medicare coverage of adult liver transplants).

60 FR 21525, May 2, 1995: HCFA Public Information Collection Requirements Submitted to the Office of Management and Budget (OMB) for Clearance (pertaining to intermediary requests for infor-

mation from skilled nursing facilities, reimbursement for CLIA compliance surveys, patient outcome data in home health agencies, common claim forms for Medicare/Medicaid reimbursement, and a study of childhood immunization costs).

60 FR 37590, July 21, 1995: Medicare Program; Optional Payment System for Low Medicare Volume Skilled Nursing Facilities — Final rule affecting 42 CFR Part 413.

60 FR 50115, September 28, 1995: Medicare and Medicaid Programs; Survey, Certification and Enforcement of Skilled Nursing Facilities and Nursing Facilities — Final rule and correction to final regulations, affecting 42 CFR Parts 431, 440, 442, 488, 489, and 498. See also corrections at 60 FR 52731, October 10, 1995, and at 60 FR 534456, October 13, 1995.

61 FR 35231, July 5, 1996: HCFA Agency Information Collection Activities: Proposed Collection; Comment Request (pertaining to Medicaid payment standards for inpatient hospital or long-term care services).

61 FR 38395, July 24, 1996: Medicaid Program; Medicaid Eligibility Quality Control, Progressive Reductions in Federal Financial Participation for FYs 1982–1984, Payment for Physician Billing for Clinical Laboratory Services, and Utilization Control of Skilled Nursing Facility Services: Removal of Obsolete Requirements — Final rule.

61 FR 46466, September 3, 1996: Medicare Program; Schedule of Prospectively Determined Payment Rates for Skilled Nursing Facility Inpatient Routine Service Costs — Final rule with comment period.

61 FR 51295, October 1, 1996: HCFA Public Information Requirements Submitted for Collection of Public Comment: Submission for OMB Review (pertaining to approval of Medicaid payment rates for inpatient hospital or long term care services).

61 FR 64913, December 9, 1996: HCFA Agency Information Collection Activities: Proposed Collection; Comment request (pertaining to survey report forms for ICF/MRs; and current Medicare beneficiary surveys).

61 FR 68270, December 27, 1996: HCFA Agency Information Collection Activities: Submission for OMB Review; Comment request (pertaining to a facility identification and screening form for hospital providers of extended care services (swing-beds) in the the Medicare and Medicaid programs).

62 FR 26, January 2, 1997: Medicare Program; Electronic Cost Reporting for Skilled Nursing Facilities and Home Health Agencies — Final Rule. See also correction at 62 FR 27210, May 19, 1997.

62 FR 11214, March 11, 1997: HCFA Agency Information Collection Activities: Submission for OMB Review; Comment request (pertaining to intermediate care facility for the mentally retarded or persons with related conditions survey report forms).

62 FR 11458, March 12, 1997: HCFA Agency Information Collection Activities: Proposed Collection; Comment request (pertaining to skilled nursing facility and skilled nursing facility health care complex cost report form).

62 FR 30603, June 4, 1997: HCFA Agency Information Collection Activities: Submission for OMB Review; Comment request (pertaining to skilled nursing facility and skilled nursing facility health care complex cost reports; and hospital conditions of participation).

62 FR 33095, June 18, 1997: HCFA Agency Information Collection Activities: Proposed Collection; Comment request (pertaining to skilled nursing facility prospective payment system cost report form).

62 FR 23140, April 29, 1997: Office of Inspector General: Health Care Programs: Fraud and Abuse; Revised PRO Sanctions for Failing to Meet Statutory Obligations — Final rule.

62 FR 43931, August 18, 1997: Medicare and Medicaid Programs: Effective Dates of Provider Agreements and Supplier Approvals — Final rule affecting 42 CFR Parts 431, 442, 488, 489, and 498.

62 FR 51536, October 1, 1997: Medicare Program; Schedules of Limits and Prospectively Determined Payment Rates for Skilled Nursing Facility Inpatient Routine Service Costs — Final notice with comment period.

62 FR 55410, October 24, 1997: HCFA Agency Information Collection Activities: Submission for OMB Review; Comment request (pertaining to Medicare/Medicaid disclosure of ownership and control forms).

62 FR 48736, October 30, 1997: HCFA Agency Information Collection Activities: Submission for OMB Review; Comment request (pertaining to prospective payment for skilled nursing facilities).

62 FR 66726, December 19, 1997: Medicare and Medicaid Programs; Hospital Conditions of Participation; Provider Agreements and Supplier Approval — Proposed rule affecting 42 CFR Parts 416, 482, 485, and 489.

62 FR 67174, December 23, 1997: Medicare and Medicaid; Resident Assessment in Long Term Care Facilities — Final rule affecting 42 CFR Part 483.

63 FR 14719, March 26, 1998: HCFA Agency Information Collection Activities: Proposed Collection; Comment request (pertaining to physician certification and re-certification in skilled nursing facilities).

63 FR 20415, April 24, 1998: Office of Inspector General: Publication of OIG Special Fraud Alert: Fraud and Abuse in Nursing Home Arrangements with Hospices — Notice.

63 FR 26252, May 12, 1998: Medicare Program: Prospective Payment System and Consolidated Billing for Skilled Nursing Facilities — Final rule, affecting 42 CFR Parts 409, 410, 411, 413, 424, 483, and 489. See also correction at 63 FR 53301, October 5, 1998.

63 FR 28395, May 22, 1998: HCFA Agency Information Collection Activities: Submission for OMB Review; Comment request (pertaining to physician certifications and recertifications in skilled nursing facilities).

63 FR 28396, May 22, 1998: HCFA Privacy Act of 1974 — Notice of New System of Records (pertaining to the long term care minimum data set).

63 FR 37498, July 13, 1998: Medicare Program; Prospective Payment System and Consolidated Billing for Skilled Nursing Facilities — Notice of extension of comment period for interim final rule, affecting 42 CFR 409, 410, 411,413, 424, 483, and 489.

63 FR 42797, August 11, 1998: Medicare Program; Revision of the Procedures for Requesting Exceptions to Cost Limits for Skilled Nursing Facilities and Elimination of Reclassifications — Proposed rule affecting 42 CFR Part 413.

63 FR 58399, October 30, 1998: Office of Inspector General: Publication of the OIG's Provider Self-Disclosure Protocol — Notice.

63 FR 60356, November 9, 1998: HCFA Agency Information Collection activities: Proposed Collection; Comment request (pertaining to skilled nursing facility resident assessment MDS data).

63 FR 65561, November 27, 1998: Medicare Program; Prospective Payment System and Consolidated Billing for Skilled Nursing Facilities — Notice of re-opening of comment period for interim final rule, affecting 42 CFR 409, 410, 411, 413, 424, 483, and 489.

63 FR 66551, December 2, 1998: HCFA Agency Information Collection Activities: Submission for OMB review; Comment request

(pertaining to EverCare coverage for nursing home residents under Medicare).

63 FR 68290, December 10, 1998: HCFA Agency Information Collection Activities: Submission for OMB Review; Comment request (pertaining to outpatient rehabilitation cost reports; SNF and SNF health care complex cost reports).

63 FR 70137, December 18, 1998: Office of Inspector General: Solicitation of Information and Recommendations for Developing OIG Compliance Program Guidance for the Nursing Home Industry — Notice.

63 FR 72317, December 31, 1998: HCFA Agency Information Collection Activities: Proposed Collection; Comment request (pertaining to advanced directives under Medicare and Medicaid; and Medicare/Medicaid disclosure of ownership and control interests).

63 FR 72318, December 31, 1998: HCFA Agency Information Collection Activities: Proposed Collection; Comment request (pertaining to fire safety survey report forms for health care facilities).

1999

64 FR 6664, February 10, 1999: HCFA Agency Information Collection Activities: Submission for OMB Review; Comment request (pertaining to skilled nursing facility (SNF) resident assessment MDS data).

64 FR 13354, March 18, 1999: Medicare and Medicaid Programs; Civil Money Penalties for Nursing Homes (SNF/NF), Change in Notice Requirements, and Expansion of Discretionary Remedy Delegation — Final rule with comment period, affecting 42 CFR Part 488.

64 FR 13997, March 23, 1999: HCFA Agency Information Collection Activities: Submission for OMB Review; Comment request (pertaining to Medicare and Medicaid requirements for advanced directives, and disclosure of ownership and financial control interest).

64 FR 17184, April 8, 1999: HCFA Medicare Program; April 23, 1999 Open Town Hall Meeting to Discuss the Skilled Nursing Facility Prospective Payment System (SNF/PPS) and Quality of Care in Nursing Facilities — Notice of meeting.

64 FR 39934, July 23, 1999: Medicare and Medicaid Program; Appeal of the Loss of Nurse Aide Training Programs — Interim final rule with comment period, affecting 42 CFR Parts 431 and 498. See also correction at 64 FR 43295, August 10, 1999.

64 FR 41644, July 30, 1999: Medicare Program; Prospective Payment System and Consolidated Billing for Skilled Nursing Facilities — Final rule affecting 42 CFR Parts 409, 411, 413, and 489. See also correction at 64 FR 60122, November 4, 1999.

64 FR 41684, July 30, 1999: Medicare Program; Prospective Payment System and Consolidated Billing for Skilled Nursing Facilities — Update — Notice. See also correction at 64 FR 54030, October 5, 1999

64 FR 42610, August 5, 1999: Medicare Program; Revision of the Procedures for Requesting Exceptions to Cost Limits for Skilled Nursing Facilities and Elimination of Reclassifications — Final rule.

64 FR 54263, October 6, 1999: Medicaid Program; Flexibility in Payment Methods for Services of Hospitals, Nursing Facilities, and Intermediate Care Facilities for the Mentally Retarded — Proposed rule affecting 42 CFR Part 447.

64 FR 55949, October 15, 1999: HCFA Agency Information Collection Activities: Proposed Collection; Comment request (pertaining to physician certifications and re-certifications about the necessity for skilled nursing facility care).

64 FR 66482, November 26, 1999: HCFA Agency Information Collection Activities: Proposed Collection; Comment request (pertaining to resident assessment in skilled nursing facilities).

64 FR 67028, November 30, 1999: Medicare and Medicaid Programs; Religious Nonmedical Health Care Institutions and Advance Directives — Interim final rule with comment period, affecting 42 CFR Parts 403, 412, 431, 440, 442, 446, 456, 488, and 489.

64 FR 69271, December 10, 1999: HCFA Agency Information Collection Activities: Proposed Collection; Comment request (pertaining to hospital providers of extender care (swing bed) services in Medicare and Medicaid).

2000

65 FR 2186, January 13, 2000: HCFA Agency Information Collection Activities; Submission for OMB Review; Comment request (pertaining to physician certifications/re-certifications in skilled nursing facilities).

65 FR 12560, March 9, 2000: HCFA Agency Information Collection Activities: Submission for OMB Review; Comment request (pertain-

ing to hospital provider of extended care services (swing beds) in the Medicare and Medicaid programs).

65 FR 14289, March 16, 2000: Office of Inspector General: Publication of the OIG Compliance Program Guidance for Nursing Facilities — Notice.

65 FR 14986, March 20, 2000: HCFA Agency Information Collection Activities: Submission for OMB Review; Comment request (pertaining to skilled nursing facility resident assessment MDS data).

65 FR 19187, April 10, 2000: Medicare Program; Prospective Payment System and Consolidated Billing for Skilled Nursing Facilities; Update — Proposed rule affecting 42 CFR Parts 411 and 489.

65 FR 54856, September 11, 2000: HCFA Agency Information Collection Activities: Submission for OMB Review; Comment request (pertaining to skilled nursing facility cost reports).

65 FR 54857, September 11, 2000: HCFA Agency Information Collection Activities: Submission for OMB Review; Comment request (pertaining to ICF/MR survey report forms).

65 FR 60151, October 10, 2000: Medicaid Program; Revision to Medicaid Upper Payment Limit Requirements for Hospital Services, Nursing Facility Services, Intermediate Care Facility Services for the Mentally Retarded, and Clinic Services — Proposed rule affection 42 CFR Part 447.

65 FR 64227, October 26, 2000: HCFA Agency Information Collection Activities: Proposed Collection; Comment request (pertaining to home health agency cost reports; skilled nursing facility cost reports; and hospital cost reports).

2001

66 FR 3148, January 12, 2001: Medicaid Program; Revision to Medicaid Upper Payment Limit Requirements for Hospital Services, Nursing Facility Services, Intermediate Care Facility Services for the Mentally Retarded, and Clinic Services—Final rule affecting 42 CFR Part 447.

66 FR 3497, January 16, 2001: Medicare Program; Prospective Payment System and Consolidated Billing for Skilled Nursing Facilities—Update; Correction notice affecting 42 FR Parts 411, 313, and 489. See FR Doc. 00–19004, July 31, 2000.

66 FR 16062, March 23, 2001: HCFA Agency Information Collection Activities: Submission for OMB Review; Comment request (pertaining to SNF cost report forms).

66 FR 17657, April 3, 2001: Medicaid Program; Modification of the Medicaid Upper Payment Limit Transition Period for Inpatient Hospital Services, Outpatient Hospital Services, Nursing Facility Services, Intermediate Care Facility Services for the Mentally Retarded and Clinic Services—Proposed rule affecting 42 CFR Part 447.

66 FR 19507, April 16, 2001: HCFA Agency Information Collection Activities: Proposed Collection; Comment request (pertaining to conflict of interest and ownership and control information form).

66 FR 27151, May 16, 2001: HCFA Agency Information Collection Activities: Proposed Collection; Comment request (pertaining to the Long Term Care Awareness Project).

See § 2:4.

§ 6:5 IMPROPER BILLING FOR CLINICAL DIAGNOSTIC LABORATORY TESTS — Section 1833(h)(5)(D) [42 U.S.C.A. 1395l(h)(5)(D)]

Regulations

42 CFR Part 402 — Civil Money Penalties, Assessments, and Exclusions

42 CFR Part 405, Subpart E — Criteria for Determination of Reasonable Charges; Payment for Services of Hospital Interns, Residents, and Supervising Physicians, especially Section 405.515: Reimbursement for clinical laboratory services billed by physicians

42 CFR Part 410 — Supplementary Medical Insurance (SMI) Benefits, especially section 410.32: Diagnostic X-ray tests, diagnostic laboratory tests, and other diagnostic tests: Conditions

42 CFR Part 411, Subpart J — Physician Ownership of, and Referral of Patients or Laboratory Specimens to, Entities Furnishing Clinical Laboratory or Other Health Services

42 CFR Part 414 — Payment for Part B Medical and Other Health Services

42 CFR Part 415 — Services Furnished by Physicians in Providers, Supervising Physicians in Teaching Settings, and Residents in Certain Settings

42 CFR Part 420 — Program Integrity: Medicare

42 CFR Part 440 — Services: General Provisions [Medicaid], Subpart A — Definitions, especially Section 440.30: Other laboratory and X-ray services

42 CFR Part 447 — Payments for Services [Medicaid], Subpart D — Payment Methods for Other Institutional and Noninstitutional Services, especially Section 447.342: Physician billing for clinical laboratory services

42 CFR Part 455 — Program Integrity: Medicaid

42 CFR 493 — Laboratory Requirements

42 CFR Part 498 — Appeals Procedures for Determinations that Affect Participation in the Medicare Program and for Determinations that Affect the Participation of ICF's/MR and Certain NF's in the Medicaid Program

42 CFR Chapter V — Office of Inspector General — Health Care, Department of Health and Human Services

Subchapter A — General Provisions

Part 1000 — Introduction; General Definitions

Subchapter B — OIG Authorities

Part 1001 — Program Integrity: Medicare and State Health Care Programs

Part 1002 — Program Integrity: State-initiated Exclusion from Medicaid

Part 1003 — Civil Money Penalties, Assessments and Exclusions

Part 1005 — Appeals of Exclusions, Civil Money Penalties and Assessments

Part 1006 — Investigational Inquiries

Part 1007 — State Medicaid Fraud Control Units

Part 1008 — Advisory Opinions by the OIG

53 FR 48645, December 2, 1988: Medicare and Medicaid Programs; Medicare, Medicaid, and Clinical Laboratories Improvement Act (CLIA) Patient Confidentiality Rules — Final rule [Amends 42 CFR Parts 74, 405, and 441]

55 FR 9538, March 14, 1990: Medicare, Medicaid and CLIA Programs; Revision of the Laboratory Regulations for the Medicare, Medicaid, and Clinical Laboratories Improvement Act of 1967 Programs — Final rule with comment period, amending 42 CFR Parts 74, 405, 416, 440, 482, 483, 488, and 493.

55 FR 20896, May 21, 1990: Medicare, Medicaid and CLIA Programs; Regulations Implementing the Clinical Laboratory Improvement Amendments of 1988 (CLIA '88) — Proposed rule. See also extension of time for public comment to September 21, 1990, published at 55 FR 34289on August 22, 1990.

55 FR 31758, August 3, 1990: Clinical Laboratory Improvement Act Programs; Fee Collection —Proposed rule affecting 42 CFR Part 493.

56 FR 13430, April 2, 1991: Medicare and Laboratory Certification Programs; Enforcement Procedures for Laboratories — Proposed rule.

57 FR 7002, February 28, 1992: Medicare, Medicaid and CLIA Programs; Regulations Implementing the Clinical Laboratory Improvement Amendments of 1988 (CLIA) — Final rule with comment period, affecting 42 CFR Parts 405, 410, 416, 417, 418, 440, 482, 483, 484, 485, 488, 491, 493, and 494. See also correction at 57 FR 35760, August 11, 1992, and correction amendments at 58 FR 5212, January 19, 1993.

57 FR 7188, February 28, 1992: Clinical Laboratory Improvement Act Program Fee Collection — Final rule with comment affecting 42 CFR Part 493. See also correction at 57 FR 31664, July 17, 1992, and correction amendments at 58 FR 5212, January 19, 1993.

57 FR 7218, February 28, 1992: Medicare Program; Medicare and Laboratory Certification Program; Enforcement Procedures for Laboratories —Final rule affecting 42 CFR Part 493. See also correction amendments at 58 FR 5212, January 19, 1993.

57 FR 8588, March 11, 1992: Medicare Program; Physician Ownership of, and Referrals to, Health Care Entities that Furnish Clinical Laboratory Services — Proposed rule affecting 42 CFR Part 411.

57 FR 33992, July 31, 1992: Clinical Laboratories Improvement Act Program; Granting and Withdrawal of Deeming Authority to Private Nonprofit Accreditation Organizations and of CLIA Exemption under State Laboratory Programs —Final rule.

58 FR 5212, January 19, 1993: Medicare, Medicaid and CLIA Programs; CLIA Program Fee Collection; Correction Amendments —Correcting 57 FR 7002-7186 and 57 FR 7188-7218 and 57 FR 7218-7243, published February 28, 1992, affecting 42 CFR Part 493. See also correction at 58 FR 48323, September 15, 1993.

58 FR 5215, January 19, 1993: Medicare, Medicaid and CLIA Programs; Regulations Implementing the Clinical Laboratory Improvement Amendments of 1988 (CLIA) and Clinical Laboratory Improvement Act Program Fee Collection —Final rule with comment period, affecting 42 CFR Part 493. See also correction published at 58 FR 39154, July 22, 1993.

58 FR 38579, July 19, 1993: HCFA Public Information Collection Requirements Submitted to the Office of Management and Budget (OMB) for Clearance re survey of home health agencies; CLIA survey report form; validation of state surveys; Medicaid listing of participating home health agencies; financial information regarding Medicare benefits from Medicare contractors; and third-party liability under Medicaid.

58 FR 43832, August 18, 1993: Medicare and Medicaid Programs; Payment for Clinical Diagnostic Laboratory Tests — Proposed rule affecting 42 CFR Parts 405, 413, 414, 424, 431, and 447.

58 FR 52112, October 6, 1993: Medicare, Medicaid, and CLIA Programs; Clinical Laboratory Improvement Amendments of 1988 Exemption of Laboratories Licensed by the State of Washington — Notice.

58 FR 54096, October 20, 1993: Office of Inspector General: Civil Money Penalties for Prohibited Referrals to Entities Providing Clinical Laboratory Services and for Prohibited Arrangements and Schemes — Proposed rule affecting 42 CFR Part 1003.

58 FR 67795, December 22, 1993: HCFA Public Information Collection Requirements Submitted to the Office of Management and Budget (OMB) for Clearance (pertaining to clinical laboratory improvement amendments; third party premium billing request form; ambulatory surgical center payment rate survey; online survey, certification and reporting system (OSCAR); conditions of participation for rehabilitation agencies and conditions for coverage for physical therapists in independent practice) — Notice.

58 FR 68148, December 23, 1993: HCFA Approval of the Commission on Office Laboratory Accreditation — Notice.

59 FR 23069, May 4, 1994: HCFA Public Information Collection Requirements Submitted to the Office of Management and Budget (OMB) for Clearance (pertaining to clinical laboratory improvement amendments (CLIA) flexible survey protocol form; application for health insurance benefits under Medicare for individual with chronic renal disease form; Medicare Qualification Statement for Federal employees form; attending physician's statement and documentation of Medicare emergency form; request for Part B Medicare hearing by an Administrative Law Judge forms; CLIA adverse action extract; and medicare and Medicaid coverage data bank reports form.)

59 FR 27023, May 25, 1994: HCFA Public Information Collection Requirements Submitted to the Office of Management and Budget

(OMB) for Clearance (pertaining to Medicare beneficiary survey of influenza vaccination form; Medicaid integrated quality control review worksheet; post laboratory survey questionnaire form; and post laboratory survey questionnaire — surveyor form).

59 FR 52968, October 20, 1994: HCFA; CLIA Program; Approval of the American Society for Histocompatibility and Immunogenetics for the Specialty of Histocompatibility — Notice.

59 FR 56500, November 14, 1994: HCFA Public Information Collection Requirements Submitted to the Office of Management and Budget (OMB) for Clearance (pertaining to monitoring and evaluation of Medicare cataract surgery alternate payment demonstration, form for listing deficiencies for laboratory surveys, form for personnel requirements for laboratory CLIA certification, and CLIA reinstatement form).

59 FR 62606, December 6, 1994: Medicare, Medicaid, and CLIA Programs; Extension of Certain Effective Dates for Clinical Laboratory Requirements and Personnel Requirements for Cytologists — Final rule with comment period, affecting 42 CFR Part 493.

59 FR 65372, December 19, 1994: Office of Inspector General — Notice of Publication of Special Fraud Alerts (pertaining to joint venture arrangements, routine waiver of Medicare Part B copayments and deductibles, hospital incentives to referring physicians, prescription drug marketing practices, and arrangements for provision of clinical laboratory services).

59 FR 66314, December 23, 1994: Medicare, Medicaid, and CLIA Programs; Clinical Laboratory Improvement Amendments of 1988 Continuance of Exemption of Laboratories Licensed by the State of Washington — Notice.

60 FR 7774, February 9, 1995: HCFA, CLIA Program; Approval of the College of American Pathologists as an Accrediting Organization for Clinical Laboratories — Notice.

60 FR 12770, March 8, 1995: HCFA Public Information Collection Requirements Submitted to the Office of Management and Budget (OMB) for Clearance (pertaining to survey forms for compliance with CLIA; CLIA application forms for testing on human specimens, and forms for outcome-based quality assurance programs for home health agencies).

60 FR 16580, March 31, 1995: Office of Inspector General: Civil Money Penalties for Referrals to Entities and for Prohibited

Arrangements and Schemes — Final rule with comment period, affecting 42 CFR Part 1003.

60 FR 21525, May 2, 1995: HCFA Public Information Collection Requirements Submitted to the Office of Management and Budget (OMB) for Clearance (pertaining to intermediary requests for information from skilled nursing facilities, reimbursement for CLIA compliance surveys, patient outcome data in home health agencies, common claim forms for Medicare/Medicaid reimbursement, and a study of childhood immunization costs).

60 FR 37657, July 21, 1995: CLIA Program; Approval of the American Osteopathic Association as an Accrediting Organization — Notice.

60 FR 37660, July 21, 1995: CLIA Program; Approval of the American Association of blood Banks as an Accrediting Organization — Notice.

60 FR 39403, August 2, 1995: HCFA Public Information Collection Requirements Submitted for Public Comment and Recommendations (pertaining to PRO reporting forms; Oregon Medicaid reform demonstration; review functions of PRO's; medical records review under PPS; evaluation of Medicare cataract surgery alternate payment demonstration; home health agency survey and deficiencies report; CLIA survey forms; field testing of uniform needs assessment instrument for hospital discharge planning).

60 FR 40184, August 7, 1995: HCFA Public Information Collection Requirements Submitted for Public Comment and Recommendations (pertaining to CLIA alternative quality assessment survey forms; and data collection and analysis for generating procedure specific physician cost estimates).

60 FR 41914, August 14, 1995: Medicare Program; Physician Financial Relationships with, and Referrals to, Health Care Entities that Furnish Clinical Laboratory Services; Financial Relationship Reporting Requirements — Final rule affecting 42 CFR Part 411.

60 FR 44503, August 28, 1995: Medicare, Medicaid, and CLIA Programs; Clinical Laboratory Improvement Amendments of 1988 Exemption of Permit-holding Laboratories in the State of New York — Notice.

60 FR 47534, September 13, 1995: HCFA; Public Health Service; CLIA Program; Categorization of Waived Tests — Proposed rule affecting 42 CFR Part 493.

60 FR 47982, September 15, 1995: CLIA Program; Categorization and Certification Requirements for a New Subcategory of Moderate Complexity Testing — Proposed rule affecting 42 CFR Part 493.

60 FR 55719, November 2, 1995: HCFA Public Information Collection Requirements Submitted for Public Comment and Recommendations (pertaining to evaluation of the Oregon Medicaid reform demonstration; field testing of the uniform needs assessment instrument for hospital discharge planning; survey of physician practice costs; evaluation of the Medicare cataract surgery alternate payment demonstration; and alternative CLIA quality assessment surveys).

60 FR 58088, November 24, 1995: HCFA Public Information Collection Requirements Submitted for Public Comment and Recommendations (pertaining to granting and withdrawal of deeming authority to private nonprofit accreditation organizations and the CLIA exemption under State laboratory programs).

60 FR 61509, November 30, 1995: CLIA Program; Cytology Proficiency Testing — Proposed rule affecting 42 CFR Part 493.

61 FR 7012, February 23, 1996: HCFA Notice Submitted for Collection of Public Comment: Submission for OMB Review (pertaining to granting and withdrawing of deeming authority to private non-profit Accreditation organizations and the Clinical Laboratory Improvement Act Exemption under State laboratory programs; and the rules for participation of home health agencies to participate as sole community home health agencies).

61 FR 7522, February 28, 1996: HCFA Public Information Collection Requirements Submitted for Public Comment and Recommendations (pertaining to Medicare and Medicaid disclosure of ownership and control interest statements).

61 FR 11646, March 21, 1996: HCFA Agency Information Collection Activities: Proposed Collection; Comment Request (pertaining to advance directives; video display terminal (VDT) operators eye care program; peer review organization sanction regulations; and deficiency correction status information under CLIA).

61 FR 29406, June 10, 1996: HCFA Agency Information Collection Activities: proposed Collection; Comment Request (pertaining to end stage renal disease application and survey and certification report forms; withholding Medicare payments to recover Medicaid overpayments; acquisition, protection, and disclosure of PRO information; clinical laboratory certification and recertification survey forms; CLIA laboratory personnel report forms; prepaid health plan cost

reports; Medicare credit balance reporting requirements; statement of deficiencies and plan of correction requirements for organ procurement organizations; Medicare/Medicaid hospital survey report forms; advance directive requirements for Medicare and Medicaid; payment adjustments for sole community hospitals; survey reports for physical therapists in independent practice; HMO and CMP national data reporting requirements; identification of extension units of outpatient physical therapy and outpatient speech pathology providers; and fire safety survey reports).

61 FR 30072, June 13, 1996: Medicare, Medicaid, and CLIA Programs; Clinical Laboratory Improvement Amendments of 1988 Exemption of Laboratories in the State of Oregon — Notice.

61 FR 31141, June 19, 1996: HCFA Agency Information Collection Activities: Proposed Collection; Comment Request (pertaining to authorization agreements for electronic funds transfer; applications for health insurance under Medicare for individuals with chronic renal disease; CLIA application forms; forms for surveyors to evaluate laboratory survey processes; post laboratory survey questionnaires for laboratories to evaluate the survey process).

61 FR 38395, July 24, 1996: Medicaid Program; Medicaid Eligibility Quality Control, Progressive Reductions in Federal Financial Participation for FYs 1982–1984, Payment for Physician Billing for Clinical Laboratory Services, and Utilization Control of Skilled Nursing Facility Services: Removal of Obsolete Requirements — Final rule.

61 FR 46814, September 5, 1996: HCFA Agency Information Collection Activities: Submission for OMB Review; Comment request (pertaining to authorization agreements for electronic funds transfers; entitlement to Medicare for individuals with chronic renal disease; application forms for clinical laboratories; and clinical laboratory survey questionnaires).

61 FR 48157, September 12, 1996: HCFA Agency Information Collection Activities: Submission for OMB Review; Comment request (pertaining to authorization agreement for electronic funds transfer; entitlement to Medicare for individuals with chronic renal disease; application forms for clinical laboratories; and clinical laboratory survey forms).

61 FR 57688, November 7, 1996: HCFA Agency Information Collection Activities: Comment request (pertaining toclinical laboratory surveys; clinical laboratory personnel qualifications; Medicare/Medicaid hospital survey report forms; beneficiary

disenrollment from HMOs and CMPs; survey reports for ambulatory surgical centers; the Medigap complaint database; and survey forms for Comprehensive Outpatient Rehabilitation Facilities).

62 FR 5433, February 5, 1997: CLIA Program; Clinical Laboratory Improvement Amendments of 1988 — Denial of Exemption of Laboratories in the Commonwealth of Puerto Rico — Notice.

62 FR 8026, February 21, 1997: HCFA Agency Information Collection Activities: Proposed Collection; Comment request (pertaining to Clinical Laboratory Improvement Act adverse action extract).

62 FR 9435, March 3, 1997: Office of Inspector General: Publication of the OIG Model Compliance Plan for Clinical Laboratories — Notice.

62 FR 11213, March 11, 1997: HCFA Agency Information Collection Activities: Proposed Collection; Comment request (pertaining to post-laboratory survey questionnaire).

62 FR 25855, May 12, 1997: Medicare, Medicaid, and CLIA Programs; Clinical Laboratory Requirements — Extension of Certain Effective Dates for Clinical Laboratory Requirements under CLIA — Final rule with comment period, affecting 42 CFR Part 493.

62 FR 27262, May 19, 1997: HCFA Approval of the Commission on Office Laboratory Accreditation for Immunohematology — Notice.

62 FR 35214, June 30, 1997: HCFA Agency Information Collection Activities: Submission for OMB Review; Comment request (pertaining to CLIA adverse actions).

62 FR 35513, July 1, 1997: Medicare, Medicaid, and CLIA Programs; Clinical Laboratory Improvement Amendments of 1988 — Continuance of Exemption of Laboratories Licensed by the State of Washington — Notice.

62 FR 43931, August 18, 1997: Medicare and Medicaid Programs: Effective Dates of Provider Agreements and Supplier Approvals — Final rule affecting 42 CFR Parts 431, 442, 488, 489, and 498.

62 FR 45815, August 29, 1997: HCFA CLIA Program; Fee Schedule Revision — Notice with comment period.

62 FR 66119, December 17, 1997: HCFA Agency Information Collection Activities: Proposed Collection; Comment request (pertaining to clinical laboratory compliance inspections).

62 FR 67881, December 30, 1997: HCFA Agency Information Collection activities: Proposed Collection; Comment request (pertaining to clinical laboratory survey forms).

63 FR 9845, February 26, 1998: HCFA Agency Information Collection Activities: Proposed Collection; Comment request (pertaining to CLIA budget workload reports).

63 FR 12474, March 13, 1998: HCFA Agency Information Collection Activities: Submission for OMB Review; Comment request (pertaining to requirements for clinical laboratory testing on human specimens).

63 FR 12476, March 13, 1998: HCFA Agency Information Collection Activities: Submission for OMB Review; Comment request (pertaining to alternate quality assessment form for clinical laboratories with good performance records).

63 FR 17429, April 9, 1998: Medicare, Medicaid, and CLIA Programs; Clinical Laboratory Improvement Amendments of 1988 Continuance of Approval as an Accrediting Organization; the Joint Commission on Accreditation of Healthcare Organizations, the American Association of Blood Banks, and the American Osteopathic Association — Notice.

63 FR 26722, May 14, 1998: HCFA CLIA Program; Simplifying CLIA Regulations Relating to Accreditation, Exemption of Laboratories under a State Licensure Program, Proficiency Testing, and Inspection — Final rule affecting 42 CFR Part 493. See also correction at 63 FR 32699, June 15, 1998.

63 FR 28394, May 22, 1998: HCFA Agency Information Collection Activities: Submission for OMB Review; Comment request (pertaining to CLIA budget workload reports).

63 FR 30166, June 3, 1998: Medicare Program; Coverage and Administrative Policies for Clinical Diagnostic Laboratory Tests — Notice of intent to form negotiated rulemaking committee and notice of meeting.

63 FR 38413, July 16, 1998: HCFA Agency Information Collection Activities: Submission for OMB Review; Comment request (pertaining to Clinical Laboratory Improvement Act certification requirements; EPSDT participation reports; limitations on provider-related donations and health care-related taxes, and limitations on payments to disproportionate share hospitals; and Medicare+Choice provider sponsored organization waiver requests forms).

63 FR 42054, August 6, 1998: HCFA Agency Information Collection Activities: Submission for OMB Review; Comment Request (pertaining to Medicare/Medicaid/CLIA conditions of participation).

63 FR 42796, August 11, 1998: Medicare Program; Negotiated Rulemaking; Coverage and Administrative Policies for Clinical Diagnostic Laboratory Tests; Change in Meeting Time — Notice of meetings.

63 FR 45076, August 24, 1998: Office of Inspector General-Publication of OIG Compliance Program Guidance for Clinical Laboratories.

63 FR 55031, October 14, 1998: Medicare, Medicaid, and CLIA Programs; Extension of Certain Effective Dates for Clinical Laboratory Requirements under CLIA — Final rule with comment period, affecting 42 CFR 493.

63 FR 60356, November 9, 1998: HCFA Agency Information Collection Activities: Proposed Collection; Comment request (pertaining to collection of information on resource utilization by Medicare providers, suppliers, and CLIA laboratories).

1999

64 FR 69, January 4, 1999: Medicare Program; Negotiated Rulemaking; Coverage and Administrative Policies for Clinical Diagnostic Laboratory Tests — Notice of meetings.

64 FR 1813, January 12, 1999: Office of Inspector General Publication of OIG Special Fraud Alert on Physician Liability for Certifications in the Provision of Medical Equipment and Supplies and Home Health Services — Notice.

64 FR 13997, March 23, 1999: HCFA Agency Information Collection Activities: Submission for OMB Review; Comment request (pertaining to Medicare and Medicaid requirements for advanced directives, and disclosure of ownership and financial control interest).

64 FR 14454, March 25, 1999: HCFA Agency Information Collection Activities: Proposed Collection; Comment request (pertaining to blood bank inspection checklist under CLIA).

64 FR 38202, July 15, 1999: HCFA Agency Information Collection Activities: Proposed Collection; Comment request (pertaining to CLIA personnel reports; and CLIA certification for tests on human specimens).

64 FR 43295, August 10, 1999: Medicare Program; Negotiated Rulemaking; Coverage and Administrative Policies for Clinical Diagnostic Laboratory Tests; Announcement of Additional Public Meetings — Notice of meetings.

64 FR 55738, October 14, 1999: Medicare Program; Meeting of the Laboratory and Diagnostic Services Panel of the Medicare Coverage Advisory Committee — November 15 and 16, 1999 — Notice of meeting.

64 FR 73561, December 31, 1999: HCFA CLIA Program; Transfer of Clinical Laboratory Complexity Categorization Responsibility from the Center for Disease Control and Prevention to the Food and Drug Administration — Notice.

2000

65 FR 4824, February 1, 2000: HCFA Agency Information Collection Activities: Submission for OMB Review; Comment request (pertaining to clinical laboratory personnel reports).

65 FR 9274, February 24, 2000: Office of Inspector General: Publication of OIG Special Fraud Alert on Rental of Space in Physician Offices by Persons or Entities to Which Physicians Refer — Notice.

65 FR 13082, March 10, 2000: Medicare Program; Negotiated Rulemaking: Coverage and Administrative Policies for Clinical Diagnostic Laboratory Services — Proposed rule affecting 42 CFR Part 410.

65 FR 14510, March 17, 2000: HCFA and Centers for Disease Control and Prevention: CLIA Program; Cytology Proficiency Testing-Withdrawal of proposed rule published November 30, 1995, at 60 FR 61509, affecting 42 CFR Part 493.

65 FR 25492, May 2, 2000: Medicare, Medicaid and CLIA Programs; Clinical Laboratory Improvement Amendments of 1988 Removal of Exemption of Laboratories in the State of Oregon — Notice.

65 FR 26218, May 5, 2000: HCFA Agency Information Collection Activities: Proposed Collection; Comment request (pertaining to CLIA amendments adverse action extract).

65 FR 30415, May 11, 2000: HCFA Agency Information Collection Activities: Submission for OMB Review; Comment request (pertaining to conflict of interest and ownership and control information).

65 FR 37566, June 15, 2000: HCFA Agency Information Collection Activities: Submission for OMB Review; Comment request (pertaining to post-laboratory survey questionnaire under CLIA).

65 FR 47739, August 3, 2000: HCFA Agency Information Collection Activities: Submission for OMB Review; Comment request (pertaining to CLIA adverse action extract).

65 FR 64966, October 31, 2000: Medicare, Medicaid, and CLIA Programs; Continuance of the Approval of COLA as a CLIA Accreditation Organization — Notice. See also correction at 65 FR 70575, November 24, 2000.

65 FR 76647, December 7, 2000: HCFA Agency Information Collection Activities: Proposed Collection; Comment request (pertaining to alternate quality assessment survey in lieu of onsite survey for CLIA labs with good performance).

65 FR 82941, December 29, 2000: Medicare, Medicaid, and CLIA Programs; Extension of Certain Effective Dates for Clinical Laboratory Requirements under CLIA — Final rule with comment period, affecing 42 CFR Part 493.

See § 2:5.

§ 6:6 IMPROPER BILLING FOR INTRAOCULAR LENSES — Section 1833(i)(6) [42 U.S.C.A. 1395l(i)(6)]

Regulations

42 CFR Part 402 — Civil Money Penalties, Assessments, and Exclusions

42 CFR Part 405, Subpart E — Criteria for Determination of Reasonable Charges

42 CFR Part 410 — Supplementary Medical Insurance (SMI) Benefits, especially Section 410.165: Payment for rural health clinic services and ambulatory surgical center services: Conditions

42 CFR Part 411, Subpart K — Payment for Certain Excluded Services

42 CFR Part 415 — Services Furnished by Physicians in Providers, Supervising Physicians in Teaching Settings, and Residents in Certain Settings

42 CFR Part 416 — Ambulatory Surgical Services

42 CFR Part 420 — Program Integrity: Medicare

42 CFR Part 455 — Program Integrity: Medicaid

42 CFR Part 498 — Appeals Procedures for Determinations that Affect Participation in the Medicare Program and for Determinations that Affect the Participation of ICF's/MR and Certain NF's in the Medicaid Program

42 CFR Chapter V — Office of Inspector General — Health Care, Department of Health and Human Services

Subchapter A — General Provisions

Part 1000 — Introduction; General Definitions

Subchapter B — OIG Authorities

Part 1001 — Program Integrity: Medicare and State Health Care Programs

Part 1002 — Program Integrity: State-initiated Exclusion from Medicaid

Part 1003 — Civil Money Penalties, Assessments and Exclusions

Part 1004 — Imposition of Sanctions on Health Care Practitioners and Providers of Health Care Services by a Peer Review Organization

Part 1005 — Appeals of Exclusions, Civil Money Penalties and Assessments

Part 1006 — Investigational Inquiries

Part 1007 — State Medicaid Fraud Control Units

Part 1008 — Advisory Opinions by the OIG

55 FR 4526, February 8, 1990: Medicare Program; Revision of Ambulatory Surgical Center Payment Rate Methodology — Final notice of payment rates. See also correction published at 55 FR 32150 on August 7, 1990.

55 FR 4577, February 8, 1990: Medicare Program; Update of Ambulatory Surgical Center Payment Rates — Notice with comment period. See also correction published at 55 FR 32150 on August 7, 1990.

55 FR 18668, May 3, 1990: Medicare Program; Definition of Surgical Services — Notice of definition of surgical services for physician volume performance standard rates for increase with comment.

55 FR 21250, May 23, 1990: Medicare Program; Withdrawal of Coverage for Certain Investigational Intraocular Lenses — Proposed notice.

55 FR 24561, June 18, 1990: Medicare Program; Physician Liability on Non-Assigned Claims — Final rule affecting 42 CFR Parts 400 and 411. See also correction published at 55 FR 35142, August 28, 1990.

55 FR 33697, August 17, 1990: Medicare Program; Payment for Outpatient Surgery at Eye Specialty Hospitals and Eye and Ear Specialty Hospitals — Final rule affecting 42 CFR Part 413. See also correction published at 55 FR 34797, August 24, 1990.

55 FR 36178, September 4, 1990: Medicare Program; Model Fee Schedule for Physicians' Services — Notice with comment period.

55 FR 46689, November 6, 1990: Medicare Program; Limit on Payment for the Cost of Intraocular Lens Furnished by a Hospital on Outpatient Basis — Proposed rule.

55 FR 50590, December 7, 1990: Medicare Program; Proposed Additions to and Deletions from the Current List of Covered Surgical Procedures for Ambulatory Surgical Centers — Proposed notice. See also correction published at 55 FR 53100, December 26, 1990.

56 FR 19874, April 30, 1991: Medicare Program; Withdrawal of Coverage of Certain Investigational Intraocular Lenses — Final notice.

56 FR 25458, June 4, 1991: Medicare Program; Medicare Geographic Classification Review Board — Procedures and Criteria — Final rule with comment period affecting 42 CFR Part 412.

56 FR 25792, June 5, 1991: Medicare Program; Fee Schedule for Physicians' Services — Proposed rule affecting 42 CFR Parts 405 and 415.

56 FR 59502, November 25, 1991: Medicare Program; Fee Schedule for Physicians' Services, Fee Schedule Update for Calendar Year 1992 and Physician Performance Standard Rates of Increase for Federal FY 1992 — Final rules and notice affecting 42 CFR Parts 405, 413, 414, and 415. See also correction at 57 FR 42491, September 15, 1992.

56 FR 67666, December 31, 1991: Medicare Program; Update of Ambulatory Surgical Center Payment Rates and Additions to and Deletions from the Current List of Covered Surgical Procedures — Notice with comment period. See also correction at 57 FR 35836, August 11, 1992.

57 FR 23420, June 3, 1992: HCFA Privacy Act of 1974; System of Records (pertaining to Medicare supplier identification file for suppliers of durable medical equipment, prosthetics, orthotics, and supplies) — Notice.

57 FR 23618, June 4, 1992: Medicare Program; Changes to the Hospital Inpatient Prospective Payment Systems and Fiscal Year 1993 Rates — Proposed rule affecting 42 CFR Parts 412 and 413. See also correction at 57 FR 30301, July 8, 1992.

57 FR 27309, June 18, 1992: Medicare Program; Criteria and Standards for Evaluating Regional Durable Medical Equipment, Prosthetics, Orthotics and Suppliers (DMEPOS) Carriers; Request for comments.

57 FR 27290, June 18, 1992: Medicare Program; Carrier Jurisdiction for Claims for Durable Medical Equipment, Prosthetics, Orthotics and Supplies (DMEPOS) and Other Issues Involving Suppliers, and Criteria and Standards for Evaluating Regional DMEPOS Carriers —Final rule with comment period, affecting 42 CFR Parts 405, 420, 421, and 424. See also correction at 57 FR 35760, August 11, 1992.

57 FR 36006, August 12, 1992: Medicare Program; Self-implementing Coverage and Payments Provisions: 1990 Legislation —Final rule with comment period, affecting 42 CFR Parts 405, 406, 409, 420, 411, 412, 413, 418, and 489. Pertains to capital-related inpatient hospital costs; capital-related outpatient hospital costs; non-capital related outpatient hospital costs; payment for physician pathology services; payment for services of physicians as assistants-at-surgery; payments for ambulatory surgical procedures in hospital outpatient departments; payments for radiology services performed in hospital outpatient departments; hospice benefit extension; enrollment of HMO members in Medicare Part A; coverage of ostomy supplies; application of pre-entitlement stay in psychiatric hospital to limit on payment for inpatient hospital services; payments to dialysis facilities; payment rates for erythropoietin (EPO); and Medicare secondary payer provision for individuals with ESRD. See also confirmation of final rule at 58 FR 58502, November 2, 1993.

57 FR 45544, October 1, 1992: Medicare Program; Update of Ambulatory Surgical Center Payment Rates —Notice with comment period.

57 FR 55914, November 25, 1992: Medicare Program; Fee Schedule for Physicians' Services for Calendar Year 1993 —Final notice with comment period. See also corrections published at 57 FR 59379, December 15, 1992, and at 58 FR 31964, June 7, 1993.

57 FR 57675, December 7, 1992: Medicare Program; Payment for Durable Medicaid Equipment and Orthotic, and Prosthetic Devices —Interim final rule with comment period.

58 FR 29416, May 20, 1993: HCFA Public Information Collection Requirements Submitted to the Office of Management and Budget (OMB) for Clearance re cataract surgery; Medicaid utilization management initiatives; Medicare coverage of screening mammography; psychiatric unit criteria worksheet and rehabilitation unit criteria worksheet; Medicare secondary payor forms; ambulatory surgical center survey forms; ambulance service compliance with State and

local requirements; and early and periodic screening, diagnostic and treatment reports.

58 FR 33826, June 21, 1993: HCFA, Privacy Act of 1974; Report of New System of Records re Cataract Surgery Alternate Payment Demonstration —Notice.

58 FR 60789, November 18, 1993: Medicare Program; Carrier Jurisdiction for Claims for Durable Medical Equipment, Prosthetics, Orthotics, and Supplies (DMEPOS)—Final rule affecting 42 CFR Part 421.

58 FR 63626, December 2, 1993: Medicare Program; Revisions to Payment Policies and Adjustments to the Relative Value Units under the Physician Fee Schedule for Calendar Year 1994 —Final rule with comment period, affecting 42 CFR Parts 405 and 414. See also correction at 59 FR 36069, July 15, 1994.

58 FR 63856, December 2, 1993: Medicare Program; Physician Performance Standard Rates of Increase for Federal Fiscal Year 1994 and Physician Fee Schedule Update for Calendar Year 1994—Final notice with comment period. See also correction at 59 FR 26410, June 1, 1994.

58 FR 65357, December 14, 1993: Medicare Program; Proposed Additions to and Deletions from the Current List of Covered Procedures for Ambulatory Surgical Centers—Proposed notice.

59 FR 26955, May 25, 1994: Medicare Program; Self-implementing Coverage and Payment Provisions: 1993 Legislation —Final rule with comment period (pertaining to reductions in payments for skilled nursing facility services —return on equity; reductions in payments for hospice services; reduction in Part A premium for certain individuals with 30 or more quarters of Social Security coverage; extension of 10 percent reduction in payments for capital-related costs of outpatient hospital services; extension of reduction in payments for other costs for outpatient hospital services; reduction in payments for intraocular lenses; payment for parenteral and enteral nutrients, supplies and equipment during 1994 and 1995; increase in annual cap on amount of Medicare payment for outpatient physical therapy and occupational therapy services; rural health clinics and Federally qualified health centers; reduction in payments for Epoetin; and changes in Part B premium.)

59 FR 32754, June 24, 1994: Medicare Program; Refinements to Geographic Adjustment Factor Values and Other Policies under the Physician Fee Schedule—Proposed rule affection 42 CFR parts 410 and 414

60 FR 35492, July 10, 1995: Medicare Program; Payment for Durable Medical Equipment and Orthotic and Prosthetic Devices — Final rule affecting 42 CFR Part 414.

60 FR 42888, August 17, 1995: HCFA Public Information Collection Requirements Submitted for Public Comment and Recommendations (pertaining to evaluation of the Medicare cataract surgery alternate payment demonstration and Medicaid eligibility quality control).

60 FR 49619, September 26, 1995: Medicare Program; Update of Ambulatory Surgical Center (ASC) Payment Rates Effective for Services on or after October 1, 1995 — Notice.

60 FR 52396, October 6, 1995: Medicare Program; Limitations on Medicare Coverage of Cataract Surgery — Proposed notice.

60 FR 63124, December 8, 1995: Medicare Program; Revisions to Payment Policies and Adjustments to the Relative Value Units under the Physician Fee Schedule for Calendar Year 1996 — Final rule with comment period, affecting 42 CFR Parts 400, 405, 410, 411, 412, 413, 414, 415, 417, and 489. See also correction at 61 FR 42385, August 15, 1996.

60 FR 63440, December 11, 1995: Medicare Program; Additional Supplier Standards — Final rule with comment period, affecting 42 CFR Parts 411 and 424.

61 FR 2516, January 26, 1996: Medicare Program; Revised Criteria and Standards for Evaluating Durable Medical Equipment, Prosthetics, Orthotics, and Supplies Regional Carriers' Performance Beginning February 1, 1996 — Notice with comment period.

61 FR 19992, May 3, 1996: Medicare Program; Five-year Review of Work Relative Value Units under the Physician Fee Schedule — Proposed notice.

61 FR 34614, July 2, 1996: Medicare Program: Revisions to Payment Policies under the Physician Fee Schedule for Calendar year 1997: Proposed rule.

61 FR 37278, July 17, 1996: HCFA Agency Information Collection Activities: Proposed Collection; Comment request (pertaining to Medicare provider/supplier enrollment forms).

61 FR 38207, July 23, 1996: Medicare Program; Recognition of the Ambulatory Surgical Center Standards of the Joint Commission on the Accreditation of Healthcare Organizations and the Accreditation Association for Ambulatory Health Care — Proposed notice.

61 FR 40422, August 2, 1996: HCFA Agency Information Collection Activities: Proposed Collection; Comment request (pertaining to

survey and certification of ambulatory surgical centers; the Medigap complaint database; fiscal intermediaries' provider overpayment actions; and hospital standards for potentially HIV infectious blood and blood products).

61 FR 49271, September 19, 1996: Medicare Program; Part B Advance Payments to Suppliers Furnishing Items or Services under Medicare Part B — Final rule affecting 42 CFR Part 421.

61 FR 51295, October 1, 1996: Medicare Program; Update of Ambulatory Surgical Center Payment Rates Effective for Services on or after October 1, 1996 — Notice.

61 FR 56963, November 5, 1996: HCFA Agency Information Collection Activities: Proposed Collection; Comment request (pertaining to geographic adjustment factors for existing payment localities used in calculating the Medicare fee schedule; demonstration project to test capitated payments for home health services, medical devices, durable medical equipment, and certain ambulatory care under Medicare; and certification of medical necessity forms for durable medical equipment and supplies).

61 FR 59490, November 22, 1996: Medicare Program; Revisions to Payment Policies and Five-year Review of and Adjustments to the Relative Value Units under the Physician Fee Schedule for Calendar year 1997 — Final rule with comment period, affecting 42 CFR Parts 410 and 415. See also correction at 62 FR 7945, February 21, 1997.

61 FR 59717, November 22, 1996: Medicare Program; Physician Fee Schedule Update for Calendar year 1997 and Physician Volume Performance Standard Rates of Increase for Federal Fiscal Year 1997 — Final notice.

61 FR 67041, December 19, 1996: Medicare Program; Recognition of the Ambulatory Surgical Center Standards of the Joint Commission on the Accreditation of Healthcare Organizations and the Accreditation Association for Ambulatory Health Care — Final notice.

62 FR 46698, September 4, 1997: Medicare Program; Adjustment in Payment Amounts for New Technology Intraocular Lenses — Proposed rule affecting 42 CFR Part 416.

63 FR 2926, January 20, 1998: Medicare Program; Additional Supplier Standards — Proposed rule affecting 42 CFR Part 424.

63 FR 8462, February 19, 1998: Medicare Program; Update of Ambulatory Surgical Center Payment Rates Effective for Services on or after October 1, 1997 — Notice

63 FR 30818, June 5, 1998: Medicare Program; Revisions to Payment Policies under the Physician Fee Schedule for Calendar Year 1999 — Proposed rule, affecting 42 CFR Parts 405, 410, 413, 414, 415, 424, and 485. See also correction at 63 FR 50545, September 22, 1998.

63 FR 36250, July 2, 1998: HCFA Agency Information Collection Activities; Submission for OMB review; Comment request (pertaining to provider/supplier enrollment applications).

63 FR 43655, August 14, 1998: Medicare Program; Update of Rate-setting Methodology, Payment Rates, Payment Policies, and the List of Covered Procedures for Ambulatory Surgical Centers Effective October 1, 1998 — Notice of extension of comment period for proposed rule affecting 42 CFR 416and 488.

63 FR 52663, October 1, 1998: Medicare Program; Update of Rate-setting Methodology, Payment Rates, Payment Policies, and the List of Covered Procedures for Ambulatory Surgical Centers Effective October 1, 1998; Re-opening of Comment Period and Delay in Adoption of the Proposed Rule as Final — Notice.

63 FR 58814, November 2, 1998: Medicare Program; Revisions to Payment Policies and Adjustments to the Relative Value Units under the Physician Fee Schedule for Calendar Year 1999 — Final rule with comment period, affecting 42 CFR 405, 410, 413, 414, 415, 424, and 485. See also correction at 64 FR 25456, May 12, 1999.

63 FR 63430, November 13, 1998: Medicare Program; Update of Rate-setting Methodology, Payment Rates, Payment Policies, and the List of Covered Procedures for Ambulatory Surgical Centers Effective October 1, 1998 — Notice of extension of comment period for proposed rule affecting 42 CFR 416and 488.

63 FR 66554, December 2, 1998: Medicare Program; Recognition of the American Association for Accreditation of Ambulatory Surgery Facilities, Inc., for Ambulatory Surgical Centers Program — Final notice.

63 FR 71654, December 29, 1998: HCFA Emergency Clearance: Public Information Collection Requirements Submitted to the Office of Management and Budget (OMB) (pertaining to evaluation of competitive bidding demonstration for durable medical equipment and prosthetics, orthotics, and supplies).

1999

64 FR 1785, January 12, 1999: Medicare Program; Update of Ratesetting Methodology, Payment Rates, Payment Policies, and the

List of Covered Procedures for Ambulatory Surgical Centers Effective October 1, 1998 — Notice of extension of comment period for proposed rule, affecting 42 CFR Parts 416 and 488.

64 FR 1813, January 12, 1999: Office of Inspector General Publication of OIG Special Fraud Alert on Physician Liability for Certifications in the Provision of Medical Equipment and Supplies and Home Health Services — Notice.

64 FR 4435, January 28, 1999: Office of Inspector General: Draft Compliance Guidance for the Durable Medical Equipment, Prosthetics, Orthotics and Supply Industry — Notice and comment period.

64 FR 9160, February 24, 1999: HCFA Agency Information Collection Activities: Proposed Collection; Comment request (pertaining to Medicare DMEPOS competitive bidding demonstration).

64 FR 9161, February 24, 1999: HCFA Agency Information Collection Activities: Proposed Collection; Comment request (pertaining Medicare DMEPOS competitive bidding demonstration).

64 FR 10478, March 4, 1999: HCFA Agency Information Collection Activities: Proposed Collection; Comment request (pertaining to refunds to patients from physicians when Medicare does not provide coverage for the physician services provided).

64 FR 12278, March 12, 1999: Medicare Program; Update of Ratesetting Methodology, Payment Rates, Payment Policies, and the List of Covered Procedures for Ambulatory Surgical Centers Effective October 1, 1999 — Notice of extension of comment period for proposed rule.

64 FR 13997, March 23, 1999: HCFA Agency Information Collection Activities: Submission for OMB Review; Comment request (pertaining to Medicare and Medicaid requirements for advanced directives, and disclosure of ownership and financial control interest).

64 FR 17673, April 12, 1999: HCFA Agency Information Collection Activities: Proposed Collection; Comment request (pertaining to Medicare participating physician or supplier agreements).

64 FR 24956, May 10, 1999: Medicare and Medicaid Programs; Effective Dates of Provider Agreements and Supplier Approvals-Correction restoring regulations inadvertently removed when a final rule concerning effective dates for provider agreements and supplier approvals was published at 62 FR 43931, August 18, 1997.

64 FR 25891, May 13, 1999: HCFA Agency Information Collection Activities: Submission for OMB Review; Comment request (pertaining to Medicare DMEPOS competitive bidding demonstration).

64 FR 28826, May 27, 1999: HCFA Agency Information Collection Activities: Submission for OMB Review; Comment request (pertaining to evaluation of competitive bidding demonstration for durable medical equipment and prosthetics, orthotics, and supplies (DMEPOS)).

64 FR 32198, June 16, 1999: Medicare Program; Adjustment in Payment Amounts for New Technology Intraocular Lenses Furnished by Ambulatory Surgical Centers — Final rule affection 42 CFR Part 416.

64 FR 32239, June 16, 1999: HCFA Agency Information Collection Activities: Submission for OMB Review; Comment request (pertaining to the requirement that physicians must notify beneficiaries that Medicare is likely to deny payment for a specified service).

64 FR 36321, July 6, 1999: Medicare Program; Update of Ratesetting Methodology, Payment Rates, Payment Policies, and the List of Covered Procedures for Ambulatory Surgical Centers Effective October 1, 1998 — Notice of extension of comment period for proposed rule affecting 42 CFR Parts 416 and 488.

64 FR 36368, July 6, 1999: Office of Inspector General Publication of OIG Compliance Program Guidance for the Durable Medical Equipment, Prosthetics, Orthotics and Supply Industry — Notice.

64 FR 39517, July 22, 1999: HCFA Agency Information Collection Activities: Submission for OMB Review; Comment request (pertaining to Medicare participating physician or supplier agreement form HCFA-460).

64 FR 40534, July 27, 1999: Medicare Program; Replacement of Reasonable Charge Methodology by Fee Schedules — Proposed action affecting 42 CFR 414.

64 FR 44227, August 13, 1999: Medicare Program; Special Payment Limits for Certain Durable Medical Equipment and Prosthetic Devices — Proposed notice.

64 FR 49020, September 9, 1999: Medicare Program; Open Public Meeting to Discuss the Conduct of a Second Competitive Bidding Demonstration for durable medical equipment, prosthetics, orthotics, and supplies (DMEPOS) — Notice of meeting.

64 FR 57431, October 25, 1999: Medicare Program; Appeals of Carrier Determinations that a Supplier Fails to Meet the Requirements for Medicare Billing Privileges — Proposed rule affecting 42 CFR Part 405.

64 FR 59380, November 2, 1999: Medicare Program; Revisions to Payment Policies under the Physician Fee Schedule for Calendar

Year 2000 — Final rule with comment period, affecting 42 CFR Parts 410, 411, 414, 415, and 485. See also correction at 65 FR 19329, April 11, 2000.

64 FR 69273, December 10, 1999: HCFA Agency Information Collection Activities: Submission for OMB Review; Comment request (pertaining to HCFA-377 ambulatory surgical center survey report form).

64 FR 71148, December 20, 1999: Medicare Program; Adjustment in Payment Amounts for New Technology Intraocular Lenses Furnished by Ambulatory Surgical Centers — Notice with comment period.

2000

65 FR 6380, February 9, 2000: Medicare Program; Update of Ambulatory Surgical Center Payment Rates Effective for Services on or after October 1, 1999 — Notice.

65 FR 25738, May 3, 2000: Medicare Program; Lenses Eligible for an Adjustment in Payment Amount for New Technology Intraocular Lenses Furnished by Ambulatory Surgical Centers.

65 FR 25939, May 4, 2000: HCFA Agency Information Collection Activities: Proposed Collection; Comment request (pertaining to ambulatory surgical center payment rate survey).

65 FR 42021, July 7, 2000: HCFA Agency Information Collection Activities: Proposed Collection; Comment request (pertaining to notice to providers, suppliers, and practitioners about non-covered services to beneficiaries).

65 FR 42022, July 7, 2000: Medicare Program; Question and Answer Session on July 24, 2000, to Discuss Remaining Concerns about the Implementation of the Hospital Outpatient Prospective Payment System (PPS) — Notice of meeting.

65 FR 44176, July 17, 2000: Medicare Program; Revisions to Payment Policies under the Physician Fee Schedule for Calendar Year 2001 — Proposed rule affection 42 CFR Parts 410 and 414.

65 FR 44798, HCFA Agency Information Collection Activities: Submission for OMB Review; Comment request (pertaining to Medicare DMEPOS competitive bidding demonstrations follow-up to original survey).

65 FR 45090, July 20, 2000: HCFA Agency Information Collection Activities: Proposed Collection; Comment request (pertaining to Medicare DMEPOS competitive bidding demonstration).

65 FR 47670, August 3, 2000: Medicare Program; Prospective Payment System for Hospital Outpatient Services: Revisions to Criteria to Define New or Innovative Medical Devices, Drugs, and Biologicals Eligible for Pass-Through Payments and Corrections to the Criteria for the Grandfather Provision for Certain Federally Qualified Health Centers-Interim final rule with comment period, affecting 42 CFR Parts 413 and 419.

65 FR 47706, August 3, 2000: Medicare Program; Prospective Payment System for Hospital Outpatient Services: Revision of the Provider-based Location Criteria for Certain PPS-exempt Facilities — Proposed rule affecting 42 CFR Part 413.

65 FR 53963, September 6, 2000: Medicare Program: Appeals of Carrier Determinations that a Physician or Other Supplier Fails to Meet the Requirements for Medicare Billing Privileges; Reopening of Comment Period — Notice of reopening of comment period for proposed rule affecting 42 CFR Part 405.

65 FR 60366, October 11, 2000: Medicare Program; Additional Supplier Standards — Final rule with comment period, affecting 42 CFR Part 424.

65 FR 64229, October 26, 2000: HCFA Emergency Clearance: Public Information Collection Requirements Submitted to the Office of Management and Budget (OMB) (pertaining to DMEPOS supplier survey).

65 FR 65376, November 1, 2000: Medicare Program; Revisions to Payment Policies under the Physician Fee Schedule for Calendar Year 2001—Final rule with comment period. See also correction at 66 FR 16607, March 27, 2001.

65 FR 69944, November 21, 2000: HCFA Agency Information Collection Activities: Proposed Collection; Comment request (pertaining to additional DMEPOS supplier standards).

65 FR 77035, December 8, 2000: HCFA Agency Information Collection Activities: Proposed Collection; Comment request (pertaining to DMEPOS supplier survey).

2001

66 FR 8807, February 2, 2001: HCFA Agency Information Collection Activities: Proposed Collection; Comment request (pertaining to Medicare Federal Health Care Programs Provider/ Supplier enrollment Application).

66 FR 18959, April 12, 2001: Medicare Program; Annual Review of the Appropriateness of Payment Amounts for New Technology

Intraocular Lenses (NTIOLs) Furnished by Ambulatory Surgical Centers (ASCs)—Notice.

66 FR 19508, April 16, 2001: HCFA Agency Information Collection Activities: Proposed Collection; Comment request (pertaining to on site inspection for durable medical equipment (DME) suppliers).

66 FR 20316, April 20, 2001: HCFA Agency Information Collection Activities: Submission for OMB Review; Comment request (pertaining to DMEPOS supplier survey).

66 FR 20316, April 20, 2001: HCFA Agency Information Collection Activities: Submission for OMB Review; Comment request (pertaining to advance beneficiary notice by physicians, practitioners, suppliers, and providers about items and services denied by Medicare as not reasonable and necessary).

66 FR 31038, June 8, 2001: Medicare Program; Five–year Review of Work Relative Value Units under the Physician Fee Schedule—Proposed notice.

66 FR 33102, June 20, 2001: HCFA Agency Information Collection Activities; Submission for OMB Review; Comment request (pertaining to provider/supplier enrollment application form).

66 FR 34457, June 28, 2001: HCRA Agency Information Collection Activities: Proposed Collection; Comment request (pertaining to durable medical equipment and prosthetics, orthotics, and supplies supplier survey).

See § 2:6.

§ 6:7 IMPROPER BILLING FOR SERVICES OF A CERTIFIED REGISTERED NURSE ANESTHETIST — Section 1833(l)(5)(B) [42 U.S.C.A. 1395l(l)(5)(B)]

Regulations

42 CFR Part 402 — Civil Money Penalties, Assessments, and Exclusions

42 CFR Part 405, Subpart E — Criteria for Determination of Reasonable Charges

42 CFR Part 410 — Supplementary Medical Insurance (SMI) Benefits, especially Section 410.69: Services of a certified registered nurse anesthetist or an anesthesiologist's assistant: Basic rule and definitions

42 CFR Part 414 — Payment for Part B Medical and Other Health Services

42 CFR Part 415 — Services Furnished by Physicians in Providers, Supervising Physicians in Teaching Settings, and Residents in Certain Settings

42 CFR Part 420 — Program Integrity: Medicare

42 CFR Part 455 — Program Integrity: Medicaid

42 CFR Part 482 — Conditions of Participation for Hospitals, Subpart D — Optional Hospital Services, especially Section 482.52: Condition of participation: Anesthesia services

42 CFR Part 498 — Appeals Procedures for Determinations that Affect Participation in the Medicare Program and for Determinations that Affect the Participation of ICF's/MR and Certain NF's in the Medicaid Program

42 CFR Chapter V — Office of Inspector General — Health Care, Department of Health and Human Services

Subchapter A — General Provisions

Part 1000 — Introduction; General Definitions

Subchapter B — OIG Authorities

Part 1001 — Program Integrity: Medicare and State Health Care Programs

Part 1002 — Program Integrity: State-initiated Exclusion from Medicaid

Part 1003 — Civil Money Penalties, Assessments and Exclusions

Part 1005 — Appeals of Exclusions, Civil Money Penalties and Assessments

Part 1006 — Investigational Inquiries

Part 1007 — State Medicaid Fraud Control Units

Part 1008 — Advisory Opinions by the OIG

54 FR 3794, January 26, 1989: Medicare Program; Uniform Relative Value Guide for Anesthesia Services Furnished by Physicians — Proposed rule to amend 42 CFR Part 405.

54 FR 3803, January 26, 1989: Medicare Program; Fee Schedules for the Services of Certified Registered Nurse Anesthetists — Proposed rule to amend 42 CFR Parts 405, 410, 412, 413, and 482.

57 FR 33878, July 31, 1992: Medicare Program; Fee Schedules for the Services of Certified Registered Nurse Anesthetists — Final rule affecting 42 CFR Parts 405, 410, 412, 413, and 482. See also correction at 57 CFR 39743, September 1, 1992.

See § 2:7.

§ 6:8 OVERCHARGING BY PHYSICIANS FOR SERVICES OF A CERTIFIED REGISTERED NURSE ANESTHETIST — Section 1833(l)(6) [42 U.S.C.A. 1395l(l)(6)]

Regulations

42 CFR Part 402 — Civil Money Penalties, Assessments, and Exclusions

42 CFR Part 405, Subpart E — Criteria for Determination of Reasonable Charges

42 CFR Part 410 — Supplementary Medical Insurance (SMI) Benefits, especially Section 410.69: Services of a certified registered nurse anesthetist or an anesthesiologist's assistant: Basic rule and definitions

42 CFR Part 414 — Payment for Part B Medical and Other Health Services

42 CFR Part 415 — Services Furnished by Physicians in Providers, Supervising Physicians in Teaching Settings, and Residents in Certain Settings

42 CFR Part 420 — Program Integrity: Medicare

42 CFR Part 455 — Program Integrity: Medicaid

42 CFR Part 482 — Conditions of Participation for Hospitals, Subpart D — Optional Hospital Services, especially Section 482.52: Condition of participation: Anesthesia services

42 CFR Part 498 — Appeals Procedures for Determinations that Affect Participation in the Medicare Program and for Determinations that Affect the Participation of ICF's/MR and Certain NF's in the Medicaid Program

42 CFR Chapter V — Office of Inspector General — Health Care, Department of Health and Human Services

Subchapter A — General Provisions

Part 1000 — Introduction; General Definitions

Subchapter B — OIG Authorities

Part 1001 — Program Integrity: Medicare and State Health Care Programs

Part 1002 — Program Integrity: State-initiated Exclusion from Medicaid

Part 1003 — Civil Money Penalties, Assessments and Exclusions

Part 1004 — Imposition of Sanctions on Health Care Practitioners and Providers of Health Care Services by a Peer Review Organization

Part 1005 — Appeals of Exclusions, Civil Money Penalties and Assessments

Part 1006 — Investigational Inquiries

Part 1007 — State Medicaid Fraud Control Units

Part 1008 — Advisory Opinions by the OIG

54 FR 3794, January 26, 1989: Medicare Program; Uniform Relative Value Guide for Anesthesia Services Furnished by Physicians — Proposed rule to amend 42 CFR Part 405.

54 FR 3803, January 26, 1989: Medicare Program; Fee Schedules for the Services of Certified Registered Nurse Anesthetists — Proposed rule to amend 42 CFR Parts 405, 410, 412, 413, and 482.

57 FR 33878, July 31, 1992: Medicare Program; Fee Schedules for the Services of Certified Registered Nurse Anesthetists — Final rule affecting 42 CFR Parts 405, 410, 412, 413, and 482.

See § 2:8.

§ 6:9 IMPROPER BILLING FOR CERTIFIED NURSE-MIDWIFE SERVICES AND SERVICES OF QUALIFIED PSYCHOLOGISTS AND CLINICAL SOCIAL WORKERS — Section 1833(p) [42 U.S.C.A. 1395l(p)]

◆ NOTE: Repealed effective January 1, 1995, by section 123(b)(2)(A)(ii) of the Social Security Act Amendments of 1994, P.L. 103-432.

Regulations

42 CFR Part 410 — Supplementary Medical Insurance (SMI) Benefits

42 CFR Part 414 — Payment for Part B Medical and Other Health Services

42 CFR Part 420 — Program Integrity: Medicare

42 CFR Part 424 — Conditions for Medicare Payment

42 CFR Part 440 — Services: General Provisions [Medicaid]

42 CFR Part 441 — Services: Requirements and Limits Applicable to Specific Services [Medicaid]

42 CFR Part 447 — Payments for Services [Medicaid]

42 CFR Part 455 — Program Integrity: Medicaid

42 CFR Part 498 — Appeals Procedures for Determinations that Affect Participation in the Medicare Program and for Determinations that Affect the Participation of ICF's/MR and Certain NF's in the Medicaid Program

42 CFR Chapter V — Office of Inspector General — Health Care, Department of Health and Human Services

Subchapter A — General Provisions

Part 1000 — Introduction; General Definitions

Subchapter B — OIG Authorities

Part 1001 — Program Integrity: Medicare and State Health Care Programs

Part 1002 — Program Integrity: State-initiated Exclusion from Medicaid

Part 1003 — Civil Money Penalties, Assessments and Exclusions

Part 1004 — Imposition of Sanctions on Health Care Practitioners and Providers of Health Care Services by a Peer Review Organization

Part 1005 — Appeals of Exclusions, Civil Money Penalties and Assessments

Part 1006 — Investigational Inquiries

Part 1007 — State Medicaid Fraud Control Units

Part 1008 — Advisory Opinions by the OIG

58 FR 68829, December 29, 1993: Medicare Program; Medicare Coverage and Payment of Clinical Psychologist, Other Psychologist, and Clinical Social Worker Services — Proposed rule affecting 42 CFR Parts 410, 417, and 424.

59 FR 36419, July 18, 1994: Medicaid Program: Nurse-Midwife Services — Proposed rule affecting 42 CFR Part 440.

60 FR 61483, November 30, 1995: Medicaid Program: Nurse-midwife Services — Final rule affecting 42 CFR Part 440.

See § 2:9.

§ 6:10 FAILURE TO INCLUDE INFORMATION ABOUT REFERRING PHYSICIANS ON REQUESTS FOR PAYMENTS OR BILLS — Section 1833(q) [42 U.S.C.A. 1395l(q)]

Regulations

42 CFR Part 402 — Civil Money Penalties, Assessments, and Exclusions

42 CFR Part 411, Subpart J — Physician Ownership of, and Referral of Patients or Laboratory Specimens to, Entities Furnishing Clinical Laboratory or Other Health Services

42 CFR Part 414 — Payment for Part B Medical and Other Health Services

42 CFR Part 420 — Program Integrity: Medicare

42 CFR Part 440 — Services: General Provisions [Medicaid], Subpart A — Definitions, especially Section 440.30: Other laboratory and X-ray services

42 CFR Part 447 — Payments for Services [Medicaid], Subpart D — Payment Methods for Other Institutional and Noninstitutional Services, especially Section 447.342: Physician billing for clinical laboratory services

42 CFR Part 455 — Program Integrity: Medicaid

42 CFR Part 498 — Appeals Procedures for Determinations that Affect Participation in the Medicare Program and for Determinations that Affect the Participation of ICF's/MR and Certain NF's in the Medicaid Program

42 CFR Chapter V — Office of Inspector General — Health Care, Department of Health and Human Services

Subchapter A — General Provisions

Part 1000 — Introduction; General Definitions

Subchapter B — OIG Authorities

Part 1001 — Program Integrity: Medicare and State Health Care Programs

Part 1002 — Program Integrity: State-initiated Exclusion from Medicaid

Part 1003 — Civil Money Penalties, Assessments and Exclusions

Part 1005 — Appeals of Exclusions, Civil Money Penalties and Assessments

Part 1006 — Investigational Inquiries

Part 1007 — State Medicaid Fraud Control Units

Part 1008 — Advisory Opinions by the OIG

55 FR 12205, April 2, 1990: Health Care Programs: Fraud and Abuse; Amendments to OIG Exclusion and CMP Authorities Resulting from Public Law 100-93, the Medicare and Medicaid Patient and Program Protection Act of 1987, Public Law 99-272, the Consolidated Omnibus Budget Reconciliation Act of 1985, and Public Law 100-360, the Medicare Catastrophic Coverage Act of 1988 — Proposed rule to amend 42 CFR Parts 1000, 1001, 1002, 1003, 1004,

1005, 1006, and 1007. See also correction published at 55 FR 17461, April 25, 1990.

57 FR 3298, January 29, 1992: Health Care Programs: Fraud and Abuse; Amendments to OIG Exclusion and CMP Authorities Resulting From Public Law 100-93 —Final rule affecting 42 CFR Parts 1001, 1002, 1003, 1004, 1005, 1006, and 1007. See also final rule and correction at 57 FR 9669, March 20, 1992; final rule affecting 42 CFR Parts 1001and 1005, with clarification at 58 FR 5617, January 22, 1993; and final rule affecting 42 CFR Part 1001, with correction, at 58 FR 40752, July 30, 1993.

57 FR 8588, March 11, 1992: Medicare Program; Physician Ownership of, and Referrals to, Health Care Entities that Furnish Clinical Laboratory Services — Proposed rule affecting 42 CFR Part 411.

58 FR 54096, October 20, 1993: Office of Inspector General: Civil Money Penalties for Prohibited Referrals to Entities Providing Clinical Laboratory Services and for Prohibited Arrangements and Schemes —Proposed rule affecting 42 CFR Part 1003.

59 FR 50762, October 5, 1994: HCFA Public Information Collection Requirements Submitted to the Office of Management and Budget (OMB) for Clearance (pertaining to reimbursement of hospital costs for residents and interns, criteria for psychiatric and rehabilitation hospital units' reimbursement under the prospective payment system, disclosure of owners and managers of suppliers for fraud and abuse detection purposes, reimbursement of municipal health services clinics, survey form for hospital compliance with anti-dumping requirements, and evaluation of patient and physician satisfaction with the Medicare participating heart bypass center demonstration).

59 FR 65372, December 19, 1994: Office of Inspector General — Notice of Publication of Special Fraud Alerts (pertaining to joint venture arrangements, routine waiver of Medicare Part B copayments and deductibles, hospital incentives to referring physicians, prescription drug marketing practices, and arrangements for provision of clinical laboratory services).

60 FR 2325, January 9, 1995: Medicare Program; Providers and Suppliers of Specialized Services: Technical Amendments —Final rule with comment period, affecting 42 CFR Parts 400, 405, 410, 484, 485, 486, and 498. See also correction at 60 FR 11632, March 2, 1995and correction at 60 FR 45086, August 30, 1995. 60 FR 16580, March 31, 1995: Office of Inspector General: Civil Money Penalties

for Referrals to Entities and for Prohibited Arrangements and Schemes — Final rule with comment period, affecting 42 CFR Part 1003.

60 FR 32916, June 26, 1995: Office of Inspector General; Health Care Programs; Fraud and Abuse; Technical Revision to the Scope and Effect of the OIG Exclusion Regulations — Final rule affecting 42 CFR Part 1001.

60 FR 41914, August 14, 1995: Medicare Program; Physician Financial Relationships with, and Referrals to, Health Care Entities that Furnish Clinical Laboratory Services; Financial Relationship Reporting Requirements — Final rule affecting 42 CFR Part 411.

61 FR 7522, February 28, 1996: HCFA Public Information Collection Requirements Submitted for Public Comment and Recommendations (pertaining to Medicare and Medicaid disclosure of ownership and control interest statements).

62 FR 7350, February 19, 1997: Office of Inspector General: Medicare and State Health Care Programs: Fraud and Abuse; Issuance of Advisory Opinions by the OIG — Interim final rule with comment period, affecting 42 CFR Part 1008.

63 FR 9844, February 26, 1998: HCFA Agency Information Collection Activities: Proposed Collection; Comment request (pertaining to procedures for advisory opinions concerning physician referrals and supporting regulations in 42 CFR Sections 411.370ndash;411.389).

63 FR 14393, March 25, 1998: Office of Inspector General: Health Care Programs: Fraud and Abuse; Revised OIG Civil Money Penalties Resulting from the Health Insurance Portability and Accountability Act of 1996 — Notice of proposed rulemaking, affecting 42 CFR Parts 1003, 1005, and 1006.

63 FR 28395, May 22, 1998: HCFA Agency Information Collection Activities: Submission for OMB Review; Comment request (pertaining to procedures for advisory opinions concerning physician referrals and supporting regulations in 42 CFR 411.370 through 411.389).

63 FR 36250, July 2, 1998: HCFA Agency Information Collection Activities; Submission for OMB review; Comment request (pertaining to provider/supplier enrollment applications).

63 FR 38311, July 16, 1998: Office of Inspector General: Medicare and State Health Care Programs: Fraud and Abuse; Issuance of Advisory Opinions by the OIG — Final rule affecting 42 CFR 1008. See also correction at 63 FR 43449, August 13, 1998.

63 FR 38414, July 16, 1998: HCFA Privacy Act of 1974; Report of Altered System (pertaining to disclosure of individual-specific information to combat fraud or abuse in health benefit programs).

63 FR 40297, July 28, 1998: HCFA Privacy Act of 1974; Report of New System (pertaining to establishment of the National Provider System (NPS) database).

63 FR 46676, September 2, 1998: Office of Inspector General: Health Care Programs; Fraud and Abuse; Revised OIG Exclusion Authorities Resulting from Public Law 104-191 — Final rule affecting 42 CFR Parts 1000, 1001, 1002, and 1005. See also correction at 63 FR 57918, October 29, 1998.

63 FR 46736, September 2, 1998: Office of Inspector General: Health Care Programs; Fraud and Abuse; Revised OIG Sanction Authorities Resulting from Public Law 105-33 — Notice of proposed rulemaking affecting 42 CFR 1001, 1002, and 1003.

63 FR 58341, October 30, 1998: Office of Inspector General: Health Care Fraud and Abuse Data Collection Program: Reporting of Final Adverse Actions — Notice of proposed rulemaking under section 1128E of the Social Security Act, affecting 45 CFR 61.

63 FR 58399, October 30, 1998: Office of Inspector General: Publication of the OIG's Provider Self-Disclosure Protocol — Notice.

63 FR 72317, December 31, 1998: HCFA Agency Information Collection Activities: Proposed Collection; Comment request (pertaining to advanced directives under Medicare and Medicaid; and Medicare/Medicaid disclosure of ownership and control interests).

1999

64 FR 5666, February 4, 1999: HCFA Emergency Clearance: Public Information Collection Requirements Submitted to the Office of Management and Budget (OMB) (pertaining to the Medicare/Medicaid health insurance common claim form).

64 FR 10478, March 4, 1999: HCFA Agency Information Collection Activities: Proposed Collection; Comment request (pertaining to refunds to patients from physicians when Medicare does not provide coverage for the physician services provided).

64 FR 13997, March 23, 1999: HCFA Agency Information Collection Activities: Submission for OMB Review; Comment request (pertaining to Medicare and Medicaid requirements for advanced directives, and disclosure of ownership and financial control interest).

64 FR 17673, April 12, 1999: HCFA Agency Information Collection Activities: Proposed Collection; Comment request (pertaining to Medicare participating physician or supplier agreements).

64 FR 24956, May 10, 1999: Medicare and Medicaid Programs; Effective Dates of Provider Agreements and Supplier Approvals-Correction restoring regulations inadvertently removed when a final rule concerning effective dates for provider agreements and supplier approvals was published at 62 FR 43931, August 18, 1997.

64 FR 32239, June 16, 1999: HCFA Agency Information Collection Activities: Submission for OMB Review; Comment request (pertaining to the requirement that physicians must notify beneficiaries that Medicare is likely to deny payment for a specified service).

64 FR 39420, July 22, 1999: Office of Inspector General; Health Care Programs; Fraud and Abuse; Revised OIG Sanction Authorities Resulting from P.L. 105–33, the Balanced Budget Act of 1997 — Final rule affecting 42 CFR Parts 1001, 1002, and 1003. See also correction at 64 FR 42174, August 3, 1999.

64 FR 48846, September 8, 1999: Office of Inspector General: Solicitation of Information and Recommendations for Developing OIG Compliance Program Guidance for Individual Physicians and Small Group Practices — Notice.

64 FR 42791, September 30, 1999: Office of Inspector General; Publication of the OIG Special Advisory Bulletin on the Effect of Exclusion from Participation in Federal Health Care Programs — Notice. See also correction at 64 FR 55484, October 13, 1999.

64 FR 57740, October 26, 1999: Office of Inspector General; Healthcare Fraud and Abuse Data Collection Program: Reporting of Final Adverse Actions Final rule affecting 45 CFR Part 61. See also correction at 65 FR 70506, November 24, 2000.

64 FR 63518, November 19, 1999: Office of Inspector General; Fraud and Abuse; Clarification of the Initial OIG Safe Harbor Provisions and Establishment of Additional Safe Harbor Provisions under the Anti-kickback Statute — Final rule affecting 42 CFR Part 1001.

64 FR 69217, December 10, 1999: Office of Inspector General; Solicitation of New Safe Harbors and Special Fraud Alerts — Intent to develop regulations affecting 42 CFR Part 1001.

64 FR 73563, December 30, 1999: HCFA Agency Information Collection Activities: Submission for OMB Review; Comment request pertaining to Medicare program integrity organizational conflict of interest disclosure certificates).

2000

65 FR 9274, February 24, 2000: Office of Inspector General: Publication of OIG Special Fraud Alert on Rental of Space in Physician Offices by Persons or Entities to Which Physicians Refer — Notice.

65 FR 24400, April 26, 2000: Office of Inspector General; Health Care Programs: Fraud and Abuse; Revised OIG Civil Money Penalties Resulting from Public Law 104-191 (HIPAA) — Final rule affecting 42 CFR Parts 1001, 1003, 1005, and 1006. See also correction at 65 FR 35583, June 5, 2000.

65 FR 30415, May 11, 2000: HCFA Agency Information Collection Activities: Submission for OMB Review; Comment request (pertaining to conflict of interest and ownership and control information).

65 FR 36818, June 12, 2000: Office of Inspector General: Draft OIG Compliance Program for Individual and Small Group Physician Practices — Notice and comment period.

65 FR 42021, July 7, 2000: HCFA Agency Information Collection Activities: Proposed Collection; Comment request (pertaining to notice to providers, suppliers, and practitioners about non-covered services to beneficiaries).

65 FR 50552, August 18, 2000: HCFA Privacy Act of 1974; Report of Modified or Altered System (pertaining to revision of language in global fraud and abuse routine uses).

65 FR 53319, September 1, 2000: HCFA Agency Information Collection Activities: Proposed Collection; Comment request (pertaining to incentive arrangement disclosure form for managed care organizations and their related medical groups and physicians).

65 FR 53963, September 6, 2000: Medicare Program: Appeals of Carrier Determinations that a Physician or Other Supplier Fails to Meet the Requirements for Medicare Billing Privileges; Reopening of Comment Period — Notice of reopening of comment period for proposed rule affecting 42 CFR Part 405.

65 FR 59434, October 5, 2000: Office of Inspector General Compliance Program for Individual and Small Group Physician Practices — Notice.

65 FR 60366, October 11, 2000: Medicare Program; Additional Supplier Standards — Final rule with comment period, affecting 42 CFR Part 424.

65 FR 63035, October 20, 2000: Office of Inspector General: Medicare and State Health Care Programs: Fraud and Abuse; Revisions

and Technical Corrections—Proposed rule affecting 42 CFR Parts 1001, 1003, 1005, and 1008.

65 FR 64227, October 26, 2000: HCFA Agency Information Collection Activities: Proposed Collection; Comment Request; Public Information Collection Meeting to Discuss Proposed Revisions (pertaining to notice requirements from suppliers, physicians, and practitioners to beneficiaries when Medicare Part B payment may be denied).

65 FR 65861, November 2, 2000: HCFA Agency Information Collection Activities: Proposed Collection; Comment request (pertaining to conflict of interest disclosure requirements for Medicare program integrity).

65 FR 78124, December 14, 2000: Office of Inspector General: Solicitation of New Safe Harbors and Special Fraud Alerts —Notice of intent to develop regulations.

2001

66 FR 856, January 4, 2001: Medicare and Medicaid Programs; Physicians Referrals to Health Care Entities with which They Have Financial Relationships—Final rule with comment period, affecting 42 CFR Parts 411 and 424.

66 FR 8771, February 2, 2001: Medicare and Medicaid Programs; Physicians' Referrals to Health Care Entities with which They Have Financial Relationships: Delay of Effective Date of Final Rule and Technical Amendment, affecting 42 CFR Parts 411 and 424.

66 FR 17813, April 4, 2001: Medicare and Medicaid Programs; Physicians' Referrals to Health Care Entities with which They Have Financial Relationships; Extension of Comment period—Notice, affecting 42 CFR Parts 411 and 424.

66 FR 19507, April 16, 2001: HCFA Agency Information Collection Activities: Proposed Collection; Comment request (pertaining to conflict of interest and ownership and control information form).

66 FR 28916, May 25, 2001: HCFA Agency Information Collection Activities; Proposed Collection; Comment request (pertaining to procedures for advisory opinions concerning physician referrals under section 1877 of the Social Security Act).

66 FR 31245, June 11, 2001: Office of Inspector General; Healthcare Integrity and Protection Data Bank: Change in User Fees—Notice.

See § 2:10.

§ 6:11 FAILURE TO BILL ON AN ASSIGNMENT-RELATED BASIS FOR COVERED SERVICES OF A NURSE PRACTITIONER OR CLINICAL NURSE SPECIALIST — Section 1833(r)(3)(B) [42 U.S.C.A. 1395(r)(3)(B)]

◆ NOTE: Repealed effective January 18, 1995, by section 123(b)(2)(B)(iii) of the Social Security Act Amendments of 1994, P.L. 103-432.

Regulations

42 CFR Part 405, Subpart E — Criteria for Determination of Reasonable Charges

42 CFR Part 410 — Supplementary Medical Insurance (SMI) benefits

42 CFR Part 414 — Payment for Part B Medical and Other Health Services

42 CFR Part 415 — Services Furnished by Physicians in Providers, Supervising Physicians in Teaching Settings, and Residents in Certain Settings

42 CFR Part 420 — Program Integrity: Medicare

42 CFR Part 424 — Conditions for Medicare Payment

42 CFR Chapter V — Office of Inspector General — Health Care, Department of Health and Human Services

Subchapter A — General Provisions

Part 1000 — Introduction; General Definitions

Subchapter B — OIG Authorities

Part 1001 — Program Integrity: Medicare and State Health Care Programs

Part 1002 — Program Integrity:State-initiated Exclusion from Medicaid

Part 1003 — Civil Money Penalties, Assessments and Exclusions

Part 1004 — Imposition of Sanctions on Health Care Practitioners and Providers of Health Care Services by a Peer Review Organization

Part 1005 — Appeals of Exclusions, Civil Money Penalties and Assessments

Part 1006 — Investigational Inquiries

Part 1007 — State Medicaid Fraud Control Units

Part 1008 — Advisory Opinions by the OIG

55 FR 36178, September 4, 1990: Medicare Program; Model Fee Schedule for Physicians' Services — Notice with comment period.

56 FR 25792, June 5, 1991: Medicare Program; Fee Schedule for Physicians' Services —Proposed rule affecting 42 CFR Parts 405 and 415.

56 FR 31666, July 11, 1991: Medicare Program; Revised Procedures for Paying Claims from Providers of Services (re direct deposits) —Notice with comment period.

56 FR 59502, November 25, 1991: Medicare Program; Fee Schedule for Physicians' Services, Fee Schedule Update for Calendar Year 1992 and Physician Performance Standard Rates of Increase for Federal FY 1992 —Final rules and notice affecting 42 CFR Parts 405, 413, 414, and 415. See also correction at 57 FR 42491, September 15, 1992.

56 FR 61023, November 29, 1991: Medicare Program; Standard Claim Forms for Part B Claims Completed and Submitted by Physicians, Suppliers and Other Persons —General notice with comment period.

56 FR 66392, December 23, 1991: Medicaid Program; Required Coverage of Nurse Practitioner Services —Proposed rule affecting 42 CFR Parts 440 and 441. See also correction at 57 FR 4085, February 3, 1992.

58 FR 63626, December 2, 1993: Medicare Program; Revisions to Payment Policies and Adjustments to the Relative Value Units under the Physician Fee Schedule for Calendar Year 1994 —Final rule with comment period, affecting 42 CFR Parts 405 and 414. See also correction at 59 FR 36069, July 15, 1994.

58 FR 63856, December 2, 1993: Medicare Program; Physician Performance Standard Rates of Increase for Federal Fiscal Year 1994 and Physician Fee Schedule Update for Calendar Year 1994—Final notice with comment period. See also correction at 59 FR 26410, June 1, 1994.

59 FR 10290, March 4, 1994: Medicare Program; Diagnosis Codes on Physician Bills —Final rule affecting 42 CFR Parts 405 and 424. See also correction at 59 FR 26739, May 24, 1994.

59 FR 11000, March 9, 1994: Medicare Program; Changes to the Requirement for Annual Physician Acknowledgment of Physician Attestation Responsibilities—Final rule with comment period, affecting 42 CFR Part 412. See also correction at 59 FR 30389, June 13, 1994.

59 FR 32754, June 24, 1994: Medicare Program; Refinements to Geographic Adjustment Factor Values and Other Policies under the

Physician Fee Schedule — Proposed rule affection 42 CFR parts 410 and 414.

59 FR 39828, August 4, 1994: Medicare Program; Payment Policies and Adjustments to the Relative Value Units Under the Physician Fee Schedule for Calendar Year 1994, affecting 42 CFR Parts 405 and 414.

59 FR 63410, December 8, 1994: Medicare Program; Refinements to Geographic Adjustment Factor Values, Revisions to Payment Policies, Adjustments to the Relative Value Units (RVUs) under the Physician Fee Schedule for Calendar Year 1995, and the 5-Year Refinement of RVUs — Final rule with comment period, affecting 42 CFR parts 410 and 414. See also correction at 60 FR 46, January 3, 1995.

59 FR 63638, December 8, 1994: Medicare Program; Physician Fee Schedule Update for Calendar Year 1995 and Physician Volume Performance Standard Rates of Increase for Federal Fiscal Year 1995 — Final notice.

60 FR 2325, January 9, 1995: Medicare Program; Providers and Suppliers of Specialized Services: Technical Amendments — Final rule with comment period, affecting 42 CFR Parts 400, 405, 410, 484, 485, 486, and 498. See also correction at 60 FR 11632, March 2, 1995 and correction at 60 FR 45086, August 30, 1995.

60 FR 19856, April 21, 1995: Medicaid Program; Required Coverage of Nurse Practitioner Services — Final rule affecting 42 CFR Parts 440 and 441.

60 FR 38266, July 26, 1995: Medicare Program; Allowing Certifications and Recertification by Nurse Practitioners and Clinical Nurse Specialists for Certain Services — Final rule with comment period, affecting 42 CFR Part 424.

See § 2:11.

§ 6:12 IMPROPER BILLING FOR RENTAL ITEMS SUCH AS DURABLE MEDICAL EQUIPMENT, PROSTHETIC DEVICES, ORTHOTICS, AND PROSTHETICS — Section 1834(a)(11)(A) [42 U.S.C.A. 1395m(a)(11)(A)]

Regulations

42 CFR Part 402 — Civil Money Penalties, Assessments, and Exclusions

42 CFR Part 409 — Hospital Insurance Benefits

42 CFR Part 410 — Supplementary Medical Insurance (SMI) Benefits

42 CFR Part 411, Subpart J — Physician Ownership of, and Referral of Patients or Laboratory Specimens to, Entities Furnishing Clinical Laboratory or Other Health Services

42 CFR Part 414 — Payment for Part B Medical and Other Health Services

42 CFR Part 420 — Program Integrity: Medicare

42 CFR Part 424 — Conditions for Medicare Payment

42 CFR Part 440 — Services: General Provisions [Medicaid]

42 CFR Part 455 — Program Integrity: Medicaid

42 CFR Part 498 — Appeals Procedures for Determinations that Affect Participation in the Medicare Program

42 CFR Chapter V — Office of Inspector General — Health Care, Department of Health and Human Services

Subchapter A — General Provisions

Part 1000 — Introduction; General Definitions

Subchapter B — OIG Authorities

Part 1001 — Program Integrity: Medicare and State Health Care Programs

Part 1002 — Program Integrity: State-initiated Exclusion from Medicaid

Part 1003 — Civil Money Penalties, Assessments and Exclusions

Part 1004 — Imposition of Sanctions on Health Care Practitioners and Providers of Health Care Services by a Peer Review Organization

Part 1005 — Appeals of Exclusions, Civil Money Penalties and Assessments

Part 1006 — Investigational Inquiries

Part 1007 — State Medicaid Fraud Control Units

Part 1008 — Advisory Opinions by the OIG

56 FR 50821, October 9, 1991: Medicare Program; Continuous Use of Durable Medical Equipment — Interim final rule with comment period affecting 42 CFR Part 414.

56 FR 56612, November 6, 1991: Medicare Program; Carrier Jurisdiction for Claims for Durable Medical Equipment, Prosthetics, Orthotics and Supplies, and Other Issues Involving Suppliers — Proposed rule affecting 42 CFR Parts 400, 420, and 421.

56 FR 61023, November 29, 1991: Medicare Program; Standard Claim Forms for Part B Claims Completed and Submitted by Physi-

cians, Suppliers and Other Persons — General notice with comment period.

56 FR 65995, December 20, 1991: Medicare Program; Payment for Customized Wheelchairs — Interim final rule with comment period, affecting 42 CFR Part 414.

57 FR 23420, June 3, 1992: HCFA Privacy Act of 1974; System of Records (pertaining to Medicare supplier identification file for suppliers of durable medical equipment, prosthetics, orthotics, and supplies) — Notice.

57 FR 27290, June 18, 1992: Medicare Program; Carrier Jurisdiction for Claims for Durable Medical Equipment, Prosthetics, Orthotics and Supplies (DMEPOS) and Other Issues Involving Suppliers, and Criteria and Standards for Evaluating Regional DMEPOS Carriers — Final rule with comment period, affecting 42 CFR Parts 405, 420, 421, and 424. See also correction at 57 FR 35760, August 11, 1992.

57 FR 27309, June 18, 1992: Medicare Program; Criteria and Standards for Evaluating Regional Durable Medical Equipment, Prosthetics, Orthotics and Suppliers (DMEPOS) Carriers; Request for comments.

57 FR 46362, October 8, 1992: Medicare and Medicaid Programs; Revised Effective Date of Medicare/Medicaid Provider Agreement and Supplier Participation — Proposed rule affecting 42 CFR Parts 431, 440 , 442, 488, 489, and 498.

57 FR 57109, December 3, 1992: Medicare Program; Continuous Use of Durable Medical Equipment — Final rule affecting 42 CFR Part 414.

57 FR 57675, December 7, 1992: Medicare Program; Payment for Durable Medicaid Equipment and Orthotic, and Prosthetic Devices — Interim final rule with comment period.

58 FR 34916, June 30, 1993: Medicare Program; Payment for Customized Wheelchairs — Final rule.

58 FR 60789, November 18, 1993: Medicare Program; Carrier Jurisdiction for Claims for Durable Medical Equipment, Prosthetics, Orthotics, and Supplies (DMEPOS) — Final rule affecting 42 CFR Part 421.

59 FR 54197, October 28, 1994: HCFA Public Information Collection Requirements Submitted to the Office of Management and Budget (OMB) for Clearance (pertaining to Medicare beneficiary surveys, estimated acquisition costs of injectable drugs, reconsideration of adverse determinations made on Part A claims, beneficiary

and supplier or physician hearing requests, and compliance with hospital anti-dumping requirements.

60 FR 2325, January 9, 1995: Medicare Program; Providers and Suppliers of Specialized Services: Technical Amendments — Final rule with comment period, affecting 42 CFR Parts 400, 405, 410, 484, 485, 486, and 498. See also correction at 60 FR 11632, March 2, 1995 and correction at 60 FR 45086, August 30, 1995.

60 FR 3405, January 17, 1995: Medicare Program; Special Payment Limits for Home Blood Glucose Monitors — Final notice.

60 FR 35492, July 10, 1995: Medicare Program; Payment for Durable Medical Equipment and Orthotic and Prosthetic Devices — Final rule affecting 42 CFR Part 414.

60 FR 40847, August 10, 1995: Office of Inspector General: Publication of OIG Special Fraud Alerts: Home Health Fraud, and Fraud and Abuse in the Provision of Medical Supplies to Nursing Facilities — Notice.

60 FR 52530, October 6, 1995: HCFA Public Information Collection Requirements Submitted to the Office of Management and Budget (OMB) for Clearance (pertaining to durable medical equipment regional carriers and certificates of medical necessity).

60 FR 53383, October 13, 1995: HCFA Public Information Collection Requirements Submitted for Public Comment and Recommendations (pertaining to durable medical equipment regional carriers and certificates of medical necessity).

61 FR 2516, January 26, 1996: Medicare Program; Revised Criteria and Standards for Evaluating Durable Medical Equipment, Prosthetics, Orthotics, and Supplies Regional Carriers' Performance Beginning February 1, 1996 — Notice with comment period.

62 FR 7350, February 19, 1997: Office of Inspector General: Medicare and State Health Care Programs: Fraud and Abuse; Issuance of Advisory Opinions by the OIG — Interim final rule with comment period, affecting 42 CFR Part 1008.

62 FR 8026, February 21, 1997: HCFA Agency Information Collection Activities: Submission for OMB Review; Comment request (pertaining to durable medical equipment regional carrier certificate of medical necessity).

62 FR 43931, August 18, 1997: Medicare and Medicaid Programs: Effective Dates of Provider Agreements and Supplier Approvals — Final rule affecting 42 CFR Parts 431, 442, 488, 489, and 498.

62 FR 65049, December 10, 1997: Office of Inspector General: Solicitation of New Safe Harbors and Special Fraud Alerts — Notice of intent to develop regulations, affecting 42 CFR Part 1001.

62 FR 66726, December 19, 1997: Medicare and Medicaid Programs; Hospital Conditions of Participation; Provider Agreements and Supplier Approval — Proposed rule affecting 42 CFR Parts 416, 482, 485, and 489.

63 FR 687, January 7, 1998: Medicare Program; Application of Inherent Reasonableness to All Medicare Part B Services (Other than Physician Services) — Interim final rule with comment period, affecting 42 CFR Part 405.

63 FR 1646, January 9, 1998: Medicare Program; Physicians' Referrals; Issuance of Advisory Opinions — Final rule with comment period, affecting 42 CFR Part 411.

63 FR 1659, January 9, 1998: Medicare and Medicaid Programs; Physicians' Referrals to Health Care Entities with Which They Have Financial Relationships — Proposed rule affecting 42 CFR Parts 411, 424, 435, and 455.

63 FR 9844, February 26, 1998: HCFA Agency Information Collection Activities: Proposed Collection; Comment request (pertaining to procedures for advisory opinions concerning physician referrals and supporting regulations in 42 CFR Sections 411.370ndash;411.389).

63 FR 11649, March 10, 1998: Medicare and Medicaid Programs; Physicians' Referrals to Health Care Entities with Which They Have Financial Relationships — Notice of extension of comment period for proposed rule.

63 FR 28395, May 22, 1998: HCFA Agency Information Collection Activities: Submission for OMB Review; Comment request (pertaining to procedures for advisory opinions concerning physician referrals).

63 FR 20415, April 24, 1998: Office of Inspector General: Publication of OIG Special Fraud Alert: Fraud and Abuse in Nursing Home Arrangements with Hospices — Notice.

63 FR 28395, May 22, 1998: HCFA Agency Information Collection Activities: Submission for OMB Review; Comment request (pertaining to procedures for advisory opinions concerning physician referrals and supporting regulations in 42 CFR 411.370 through 411.389).

63 FR 36250, July 2, 1998: HCFA Agency Information Collection Activities; Submission for OMB review; Comment request (pertaining to provider/supplier enrollment applications).

63 FR 38311, July 16, 1998: Office of Inspector General: Medicare and State Health Care Programs: Fraud and Abuse; Issuance of Advisory Opinions by the OIG — Final rule affecting 42 CFR 1008. See also correction at 63 FR 43449, August 13, 1998.

63 FR 38414, July 16, 1998: HCFA Privacy Act of 1974; Report of Altered System (pertaining to disclosure of individual-specific information to combat fraud or abuse in health benefit programs).

63 FR 42409, August 7, 1998: Office of Inspector General: Solicitation of Information and Recommendations for Developing OIG Compliance Program Guidance for the Durable Medical Equipment Industry — Notice.

63 FR 55631, October 16, 1998: HCFA Emergency Clearance: Public Information Collection Requirements Submitted to the Office of Management and Budget (OMB) (pertaining to DMEPOS supplier competitive bidding demonstration).

63 FR 58058, October 29, 1998: HCFA Emergency Clearance: Public Information Collection Requirements Submitted to the Office of Management and Budget (OMB) (pertaining to on-site inspection for durable medical equipment (DME) suppliers).

63 FR 58399, October 30, 1998: Office of Inspector General: Publication of the OIG's Provider Self-Disclosure Protocol — Notice.

63 FR 60356, November 9, 1998: HCFA Agency Information Collection Activities: Proposed Collection; Comment request (pertaining to collection of information on resource utilization by Medicare providers, suppliers, and CLIA laboratories).

63 FR 63936, November 17, 1998: HCFA Emergency Clearance: Public Information Collection Requirements Submitted to the Office of Management and Budget (OMB) (pertaining to collection of DMEPOS supplier data in support of the Medicare DMEPOS competitive bidding demonstration).

63 FR 68223, December 10, 1998: Office of Inspector General; Solicitation of New Safe Harbors and Special Fraud Alerts — Notice of intent to develop regulations, affecting 42 CFR 1001.

63 FR 71654, December 29, 1998: HCFA Emergency Clearance: Public Information Collection Requirements Submitted to the Office of Management and Budget (OMB) (pertaining to evaluation of competitive bidding demonstration for durable medical equipment and prosthetics, orthotics, and supplies).

63 FR 72317, December 31, 1998: HCFA Agency Information Collection Activities: Proposed Collection; Comment request (pertaining

to advanced directives under Medicare and Medicaid; and Medicare/Medicaid disclosure of ownership and control interests).

1999

64 FR 1813, January 12, 1999: Office of Inspector General Publication of OIG Special Fraud Alert on Physician Liability for Certifications in the Provision of Medical Equipment and Supplies and Home Health Services — Notice.

64 FR 3303, January 21, 1999: HCFA Agency Information Collection Activities: Proposed Collection; Comment request (pertaining to on-site inspection for durable medical equipment suppliers).

64 FR 4435, January 28, 1999: Office of Inspector General: Draft Compliance Guidance for the Durable Medical Equipment, Prosthetics, Orthotics and Supply Industry — Notice and comment period.

64 FR 5666, February 4, 1999: HCFA Emergency Clearance: Public Information Collection Requirements Submitted to the Office of Management and Budget (OMB) (pertaining to the Medicare/Medicaid health insurance common claim form).

64 FR 9160, February 24, 1999: HCFA Agency Information Collection Activities: Proposed Collection; Comment request (pertaining to Medicare DMEPOS competitive bidding demonstration).

64 FR 9161, February 24, 1999: HCFA Agency Information Collection Activities: Proposed Collection; Comment request (pertaining Medicare DMEPOS competitive bidding demonstration).

64 FR 9335, February 25, 1999: HCFA Agency Information Collection Activities: Proposed Collection; Comment request (pertaining to evaluation of competitive bidding demonstration for DMEPOS).

64 FR 10305, March 3, 1999: HCFA Agency Information Collection Activities: Proposed Collection; Comment request (pertaining to attending physician's certification of medical necessity for home oxygen therapy).

64 FR 10478, March 4, 1999: HCFA Agency Information Collection Activities: Proposed Collection; Comment request (pertaining to refunds to patients from physicians when Medicare does not provide coverage for the physician services provided).

64 FR 13997, March 23, 1999: HCFA Agency Information Collection Activities: Submission for OMB Review; Comment request (pertaining to Medicare and Medicaid requirements for advanced directives, and disclosure of ownership and financial control interest).

64 FR 24956, May 10, 1999: Medicare and Medicaid Programs; Effective Dates of Provider Agreements and Supplier Approvals-Correction restoring regulations inadvertently removed when a final rule concerning effective dates for provider agreements and supplier approvals was published at 62 FR 43931, August 18, 1997.

64 FR 25891, May 13, 1999: HCFA Agency Information Collection Activities: Submission for OMB Review; Comment request (pertaining to Medicare DMEPOS competitive bidding demonstration).

64 FR 28826, May 27, 1999: HCFA Agency Information Collection Activities: Submission for OMB Review; Comment request (pertaining to evaluation of competitive bidding demonstration for durable medical equipment and prosthetics, orthotics, and supplies (DMEPOS)).

64 FR 29049, May 28, 1999: HCFA Agency Information Collection Activities: Proposed Collection; Comment request (pertaining to Medicare credit balance reporting requirements for Medicare providers who have been overpaid).

64 FR 32239, June 16, 1999: HCFA Agency Information Collection Activities: Submission for OMB Review; Comment request (pertaining to the requirement that physicians must notify beneficiaries that Medicare is likely to deny payment for a specified service).

64 FR 36368, July 6, 1999: Office of Inspector General Publication of OIG Compliance Program Guidance for the Durable Medical Equipment, Prosthetics, Orthotics and Supply Industry — Notice.

64 FR 38203, July 15, 1999: HCFA Agency Information Collection Activities: Submission for OMB Review; Comment request (pertaining to attending physician's certification of medical necessity for home oxygen therapy).

64 FR 39517, July 22, 1999: HCFA Agency Information Collection Activities: Submission for OMB Review; Comment request (pertaining to Medicare participating physician or supplier agreement form HCFA-460).

64 FR 49020, September 9, 1999: Medicare Program; Open Public Meeting to Discuss the Conduct of a Second Competitive Bidding Demonstration for durable medical equipment, prosthetics, orthotics, and supplies (DMEPOS) — Notice of meeting.

64 FR 57431, October 25, 1999: Medicare Program; Appeals of Carrier Determinations that a Supplier Fails to Meet the Requirements for Medicare Billing Privileges — Proposed rule affecting 42 CFR Part 405.

64 FR 57619, October 26, 1999: Office of Inspector General; Privacy Act; Exempt Record System, Pertaining to the Healthcare Integrity and Protection Data Bank (HIPDB) — Notice of proposed rulemaking affecting 45 CFR Part 5b.

64 FR 73563, December 30, 1999: HCFA Agency Information Collection Activities: Submission for OMB Review; Comment request pertaining to Medicare program integrity organizational conflict of interest disclosure certificates).

2000

65 FR 4437, January 27, 2000: HCFA Agency Information Collection Activities:Proposed Collection; Comment request (pertaining to durable medical equipment regional carrier certificate of medical necessity).

65 FR 5354, February 3, 2000: HCFA Agency Information Collection Activities: Proposed Collection; Comment request (pertaining to standardized Medicare/Medicaid claim form for reimbursement of covered services).

65 FR 24666, April 27, 2000: Medicare Program; Payment for Upgraded Durable Medical Equipment — Proposed rule affecting 42 CFR Part 414.

65 FR 25736, May 3, 2000: HCFA Agency Information Collection Activities: Proposed Collection; Comment request (pertaining to Medicare DMEPOS competitive bidding demonstration; follow-up to original survey).

65 FR 30414, May 11, 2000: HCFA Agency Information Collection Activities: Submission for OMB Review; Comment request (pertaining to health insurance common claims form).

65 FR 30415, May 11, 2000: HCFA Agency Information Collection Activities: Submission for OMB Review; Comment request (pertaining to conflict of interest and ownership and control information).

65 FR 42021, July 7, 2000: HCFA Agency Information Collection Activities: Proposed Collection; Comment request (pertaining to notice to providers, suppliers, and practitioners about non-covered services to beneficiaries).

65 FR 44798, July 19, 2000: HCFA Agency Information Collection Activities: Submission for OMB Review; Comment request (pertaining to Medicare DMEPOS competitive bidding demonstrations follow-up to original survey).

65 FR 45090, July 20, 2000: HCFA Agency Information Collection Activities: Proposed Collection; Comment request (pertaining to Medicare DMEPOS competitive bidding demonstration).

65 FR 49002, August 10, 2000: HCFA Emergency Clearance: Public Information Collection Requirements Submitted to the Office of Management and Budget (OMB) (pertaining to oxygen consumer survey for medical equipment and supplies).

65 FR 60366, October 11, 2000: Medicare Program; Additional Supplier Standards — Final rule with comment period, affecting 42 CFR Part 424.

65 FR 63035, October 20, 2000: Office of Inspector General: Medicare and State Health Care Programs: Fraud and Abuse; Revisions and Technical Corrections — Proposed rule affecting 42 CFR Parts 1001, 1003, 1005, and 1008.

65 FR 64227, October 26, 2000: HCFA Agency Information Collection Activities: Proposed Collection; Comment Request; Public Information Collection Meeting to Discuss Proposed Revisions (pertaining to notice requirements from suppliers, physicians, and practitioners to beneficiaries when Medicare Part B payment may be denied).

65 FR 64229, October 26, 2000: HCFA Emergency Clearance: Public Information Collection Requirements Submitted to the Office of Management and Budget (OMB) (pertaining to DMEPOS supplier survey).

65 FR 69944, November 21, 2000: HCFA Agency Information Collection Activities: Proposed Collection; Comment request (pertaining to additional DMEPOS supplier standards).

65 FR 77035, December 8, 2000: HCFA Agency Information Collection Activities: Proposed Collection; Comment request (pertaining to DMEPOS supplier survey).

2001

66 FR 1996, January 10, 2001: HCFA Agency Information Collection Activities; Comment request (pertaining to Medicare uniform institutional provider bill for reimbursement of covered services by all providers that accept assignment of claims.

66 FR 1997, January 10, 2001: HCFA Notice of OMB Approval (pertaining to uniform home health advance beneficiary notice).

66 FR 2912, January 12, 2001: HCFA Agency Information Collection Activities: Proposed Collection; Comment request (pertaining to Medicare/Medicaid health insurance common claim form).

66 FR 7919, January 26, 2001: HCFA Agency Information Collection Activities: Proposed Collection; Comment request (pertaining to provider Medicare agreements).

66 FR 8807, February 2, 2001: HCFA Agency Information Collection Activities: Proposed Collection; Comment request (pertaining to Medicare Federal health care programs provider/supplier enrollment application).

66 FR 18646, April 10, 2001: HCFA Agency Information Collection Activities: Submission for OMB Review; Comment request (pertaining to Medicare/Medicaid health insurance common claim form).

66 FR 19508, April 16, 2001: HCFA Agency Information Collection Activities: Proposed Collection; Comment request (pertaining to on site inspection for durable medical equipment (DME) suppliers).

66 FR 20315, April 20, 2001: HCFA Agency Information Collection Activities: Submission for OMB Review; Comment request (pertaining to DMEPOS supplier standards).

66 FR 20316, April 20, 2001: HCFA Agency Information Collection Activities: Submission for OMB Review; Comment request (pertaining to DMEPOS supplier survey).

66 FR 20316, April 20, 2001: HCFA Agency Information Collection Activities: Submission for OMB Review; Comment request (pertaining to advance beneficiary notice by physicians, practitioners, suppliers, and providers about items and services denied by Medicare as not reasonable and necessary).

66 FR 20997, April 26, 2001: HCFA Agency Information Collection Activities: Submission for OMB Review; Comment request (pertaining to health insurance provider agreement form).

66 FR 21770, May 1, 2001: HCFA Agency Information Collection Activities: Submission for OMB Review; Comment request (pertaining to Medicare uniform institutional provider bill form).

66 FR 33102, June 20, 2001: HCFA Agency Information Collection Activities; Submission for OMB Review; Comment request (pertaining to provider/supplier enrollment application form).

66 FR 34457, June 28, 2001: HCFA Agency Information Collection Activities: Proposed Collection; Comment request (pertaining to durable medical equipment and prosthetics, orthotics, and supplies supplier survey).

See § 2:12.

§ 6:13 IMPROPER DISTRIBUTION BY SUPPLIERS OF FORMS DOCUMENTING MEDICAL NECESSITY — Section 1834(a)(16) [42 U.S.C.A. 1395m(a)(16)]

◆ NOTE: Repealed effective after December 30, 1994, by section 131(a)(2) of the Social Security Act Amendments of 1994, P.L. 103-432.

Regulations

42 CFR Part 410 — Supplementary Medical Insurance (SMI) benefits, especially section 410.36: Medical supplies, appliances, and devices: Scope; and section 410.38: Durable medical equipment: Scope and conditions

42 CFR Part 414 — Payment for Part B Medical and Other Health Services

42 CFR Part 420 — Program Integrity: Medicare

42 CFR Part 424 — Conditions for Medicare Payment

42 CFR Part 440 — Services: General Provisions [Medicaid]

42 CFR Part 447 — Payments for Services [Medicaid]

42 CFR Part 455 — Program Integrity: Medicaid

42 CFR Chapter V — Office of Inspector General — Health Care, Department of Health and Human Services

Subchapter A — General Provisions

Part 1000 — Introduction; General Definitions

Subchapter B — OIG Authorities

Part 1001 — Program Integrity: Medicare and State Health Care Programs

Part 1002 — Program Integrity: State-initiated Exclusion from Medicaid

Part 1003 — Civil Money Penalties, Assessments and Exclusions

Part 1004 — Imposition of Sanctions on Health Care Practitioners and Providers of Health Care Services by a Peer Review Organization

Part 1005 — Appeals of Exclusions, Civil Money Penalties and Assessments

Part 1006 — Investigational Inquiries

Part 1007 — State Medicaid Fraud Control Units

Part 1008 — Advisory Opinions by the OIG

56 FR 50821, October 9, 1991: Medicare Program; Continuous Use of Durable Medical Equipment — Interim final rule with comment period affecting 42 CFR Part 414.

56 FR 56612, November 6, 1991: Medicare Program; Carrier Jurisdiction for Claims for Durable Medical Equipment, Prosthetics, Orthotics and Supplies, and Other Issues Involving Suppliers — Proposed rule affecting 42 CFR Parts 400, 420, and 421.

56 FR 61023, November 29, 1991: Medicare Program; Standard Claim Forms for Part B Claims Completed and Submitted by Physicians, Suppliers and Other Persons — General notice with comment period.

56 FR 65995, December 20, 1991: Medicare Program; Payment for Customized Wheelchairs — Interim final rule with comment period, affecting 42 CFR Part 414.

57 FR 3298, January 29, 1992: Health Care Programs: Fraud and Abuse; Amendments to OIG Exclusion and CMP Authorities Resulting From Public Law 100-93 — Final rule affecting 42 CFR Parts 1001, 1002, 1003, 1004, 1005, 1006, and 1007. See also final rule and correction at 57 FR 9669, March 20, 1992; final rule affecting 42 CFR Parts 1001and 1005, with clarification at 58 FR 5617, January 22, 1993; and final rule affecting 42 CFR Part 1001, with correction, at 58 FR 40752, July 30, 1993.

57 FR 23420, June 3, 1992: HCFA Privacy Act of 1974; System of Records (pertaining to Medicare supplier identification file for suppliers of durable medical equipment, prosthetics, orthotics, and supplies) — Notice.

57 FR 27290, June 18, 1992: Medicare Program; Carrier Jurisdiction for Claims for Durable Medical Equipment, Prosthetics, Orthotics and Supplies (DMEPOS) and Other Issues Involving Suppliers, and Criteria and Standards for Evaluating Regional DMEPOS Carriers — Final rule with comment period, affecting 42 CFR Parts 405, 420, 421, and 424. See also correction at 57 FR 35760, August 11, 1992.

57 FR 27309, June 18, 1992: Medicare Program; Criteria and Standards for Evaluating Regional Durable Medical Equipment, Prosthetics, Orthotics and Suppliers (DMEPOS) Carriers; Request for comments.

57 FR 47587, October 19, 1992: Medicare and Medicaid Programs; Use of Standardized Federal Claims Processing Forms and Procedures — Advance notice of proposed rulemaking.

57 FR 57109, December 3, 1992: Medicare Program; Continuous Use of Durable Medical Equipment — Final rule affecting 42 CFR Part 414.

58 FR 34916, June 30, 1993: Medicare Program; Payment for Customized Wheelchairs — Final rule.

58 FR 60789, November 18, 1993: Medicare Program; Carrier Jurisdiction for Claims for Durable Medical Equipment, Prosthetics, Orthotics, and Supplies (DMEPOS) — Final rule affecting 42 CFR Part 421.

See § 2:13.

§ 6:13.1 VIOLATION OF PROHIBITION AGAINST UNSOLICITED TELEPHONE CONTACTS BY SUPPLIERS Section 1834(a)(17) [42 U.S.C.A. 1395m(a)(17)]

Regulations

42 CFR Part 402 — Civil Money Penalties, Assessments, and Exclusions

42 CFR Part 410 — Supplementary Medical Insurance (SMI) benefits, especially section 410.36: Medical supplies, appliances, and devices: Scope; and section 410.38: Durable medical equipment: Scope and conditions

42 CFR Part 414 — Payment for Part B Medical and Other Health Services

42 CFR Part 420 — Program Integrity: Medicare

42 CFR Part 424 — Conditions for Medicare Payment

42 CFR Part 440 — Services: General Provisions [Medicaid]

42 CFR Part 447 — Payments for Services [Medicaid]

42 CFR Part 455 — Program Integrity: Medicaid

42 CFR Chapter V — Office of Inspector General — Health Care, Department of Health and Human Services

Subchapter A — General Provisions

Part 1000 — Introduction; General Definitions

Subchapter B — OIG Authorities

Part 1001 — Program Integrity: Medicare and State Health Care Programs

Part 1002 — Program Integrity: State-initiated Exclusion from Medicaid

Part 1003 — Civil Money Penalties, Assessments and Exclusions

Part 1004 — Imposition of Sanctions on Health Care Practitioners and Providers of Health Care Services by a Peer Review Organization

Part 1005 — Appeals of Exclusions, Civil Money Penalties and Assessments

Part 1006 — Investigational Inquiries

Part 1007 — State Medicaid Fraud Control Units

Part 1008 — Advisory Opinions by the OIG

56 FR 50821, October 9, 1991: Medicare Program; Continuous Use of Durable Medical Equipment — Interim final rule with comment period affecting 42 CFR Part 414.

56 FR 56612, November 6, 1991: Medicare Program; Carrier Jurisdiction for Claims for Durable Medical Equipment, Prosthetics, Orthotics and Supplies, and Other Issues Involving Suppliers — Proposed rule affecting 42 CFR Parts 400, 420, and 421.

56 FR 61023, November 29, 1991: Medicare Program; Standard Claim Forms for Part B Claims Completed and Submitted by Physicians, Suppliers and Other Persons — General notice with comment period.

56 FR 65995, December 20, 1991: Medicare Program; Payment for Customized Wheelchairs — Interim final rule with comment period, affecting 42 CFR Part 414.

57 FR 23420, June 3, 1992: HCFA Privacy Act of 1974; System of Records (pertaining to Medicare supplier identification file for suppliers of durable medical equipment, prosthetics, orthotics, and supplies) — Notice.

57 FR 27290, June 18, 1992: Medicare Program; Carrier Jurisdiction for Claims for Durable Medical Equipment, Prosthetics, Orthotics and Supplies (DMEPOS) and Other Issues Involving Suppliers, and Criteria and Standards for Evaluating Regional DMEPOS Carriers — Final rule with comment period, affecting 42 CFR Parts 405, 420, 421, and 424. See also correction at 57 FR 35760, August 11, 1992.

57 FR 27309, June 18, 1992: Medicare Program; Criteria and Standards for Evaluating Regional Durable Medical Equipment, Prosthetics, Orthotics and Suppliers (DMEPOS) Carriers; Request for comments.

57 FR 47587, October 19, 1992: Medicare and Medicaid Programs; Use of Standardized Federal Claims Processing Forms and Procedures — Advance notice of proposed rulemaking.

57 FR 57109, December 3, 1992: Medicare Program; Continuous Use of Durable Medical Equipment — Final rule affecting 42 CFR Part 414.

58 FR 34916, June 30, 1993: Medicare Program; Payment for Customized Wheelchairs — Final rule.

58 FR 60789, November 18, 1993: Medicare Program; Carrier Jurisdiction for Claims for Durable Medical Equipment, Prosthetics, Orthotics, and Supplies (DMEPOS) — Final rule affecting 42 CFR Part 421.

60 FR 2325, January 9, 1995: Medicare Program; Providers and Suppliers of Specialized Services: Technical Amendments — Final rule with comment period, affecting 42 CFR Parts 400, 405, 410, 484, 485, 486, and 498. See also correction at 60 FR 11632, March 2, 1995. See also correction at 60 FR 11632, March 2, 1995 and correction at 60 FR 45086, August 30, 1995.

60 FR 40847, August 10, 1995: Office of Inspector General: Publication of OIG Special Fraud Alerts: Home Health Fraud, and Fraud and Abuse in the Provision of Medical Supplies to Nursing Facilities — Notice.

60 FR 42887, August 17, 1995: HCFA Public Information Collection Requirements Submitted for Public Comment and Recommendations (pertaining to national provider identifier and Medicare payment of ambulance service charges).

60 FR 48417, September 19, 1995: Medicare Program; Criteria and Procedures for Extending Coverage to Certain Devices and Related Services — Final rule with comment period, affecting 42 CFR Parts 405and 411.

60 FR 50466, September 29, 1995: Medicare Program — Providers and Suppliers of Specialized Services: Technical Amendments — Final rule with comment period, affecting 42 CFR Parts 485and 486. See also correction at 60 FR 53877, October 18, 1995.

60 FR 52530, October 6, 1995: HCFA Public Information Collection Requirements Submitted to the Office of Management and Budget (OMB) for Clearance (pertaining to durable medical equipment regional carriers and certificates of medical necessity).

60 FR 53383, October 13, 1995: HCFA Public Information Collection Requirements Submitted for Public Comment and Recommendations (pertaining to durable medical equipment regional carriers and certificates of medical necessity).

60 FR 64167, December 14, 1995: HCFA Public Information Collection Requirements Submitted for Public Comment and Recommendations (pertaining to home health care; Medicare/Medicaid certification of physical therapy and speech pathology

services; certification as suppliers of Portable X-ray Services; certification of organ procurement organizations; certification for physical therapists in independent practice; and approval as a hospital provider of extended care services (swing bed)).

61 FR 2516, January 26, 1996: Medicare Program; Revised Criteria and Standards for Evaluating Durable Medical Equipment, Prosthetics, Orthotics, and Supplies Regional Carriers' Performance Beginning February 1, 1996 — Notice with comment period.

61 FR 30623, June 17, 1996: Office of Inspector General Publication of OIG Special Fraud Alert: Fraud and Abuse in the Provision of Services in Nursing Homes — Notice.

61 FR 37278, July 17, 1996: HCFA Agency Information Collection Activities: Proposed Collection; Comment request (pertaining to Medicare provider/supplier enrollment forms).

61 FR 56963, November 5, 1996: HCFA Agency Information Collection Activities: Proposed Collection; Comment request (pertaining to geographic adjustment factors for existing payment localities used in calculating the Medicare fee schedule; demonstration project to test capitated payments for home health services, medical devices, durable medical equipment, and certain ambulatory care under Medicare; and certification of medical necessity forms for durable medical equipment and supplies).

62 FR 7350, February 19, 1997: Office of Inspector General: Medicare and State Health Care Programs: Fraud and Abuse; Issuance of Advisory Opinions by the OIG — Interim final rule with comment period, affecting 42 CFR Part 1008.

62 FR 8026, February 21, 1997: HCFA Agency Information Collection Activities: Submission for OMB Review; Comment request (pertaining to durable medical equipment regional carrier certificate of medical necessity).

62 FR 8744, February 26, 1997: HCFA Agency Information Collection Activities: Submission for OMB Review; Comment request (pertaining to Medicare provider/supplier enrollment application).

62 FR 43931, August 18, 1997: Medicare and Medicaid Programs: Effective Dates of Provider Agreements and Supplier Approvals — Final rule affecting 42 CFR Parts 431, 442, 488, 489, and 498.

62 FR 65049, December 10, 1997: Office of Inspector General: Solicitation of New Safe Harbors and Special Fraud Alerts — Notice of intent to develop regulations, affecting 42 CFR Part 1001.

62 FR 66726, December 19, 1997: Medicare and Medicaid Programs; Hospital Conditions of Participation; Provider Agreements

and Supplier Approval — Proposed rule affecting 42 CFR Parts 416, 482, 485, and 489.

63 FR 2926, January 20, 1998: Medicare Program; Additional Supplier Standards — Proposed rule affecting 42 CFR Part 424.

63 FR 7743, February 17, 1998: Medicare and Medicaid Programs; Hospital Conditions of Participation; Provider Agreements and Supplier Approval — Notice of extension of comment period, affecting 42 CFR Parts 416, 482, 485, and 489.

63 FR 10920, March 5, 1998: HCFA Emergency Clearance: Public Information Collection Requirements Submitted to the Office of Management and Budget (OMB) (pertaining to Medicare and other Federal health care program provider and supplier application forms).

63 FR 19502, April 20, 1998: HCFA Agency Information Collection Activities: Proposed Collection; Comment request (pertaining to annual early and periodic screening, diagnostic, and treatment services (EPSDT) participation report; Medicare and other health care programs provider/supplier enrollment application; and research and analytic support for implementing performance measurement in Medicare fee for service).

63 FR 36250, July 2, 1998: HCFA Agency Information Collection Activities; Submission for OMB review; Comment request (pertaining to provider/supplier enrollment applications).

63 FR 38311, July 16, 1998: Office of Inspector General: Medicare and State Health Care Programs: Fraud and Abuse; Issuance of Advisory Opinions by the OIG — Final rule affecting 42 CFR 1008. See also correction at 63 FR 43449, August 13, 1998.

63 FR 38414, July 16, 1998: HCFA Privacy Act of 1974; Report of Altered System (pertaining to disclosure of individual-specific information to combat fraud or abuse in health benefit programs).

63 FR 42409, August 7, 1998: Office of Inspector General: Solicitation of Information and Recommendations for Developing OIG Compliance Program Guidance for the Durable Medical Equipment Industry — Notice.

63 FR 55631, October 16, 1998: HCFA Emergency Clearance: Public Information Collection Requirements Submitted to the Office of Management and Budget (OMB) (pertaining to DMEPOS supplier competitive bidding demonstration).

63 FR 58058, October 29, 1998: HCFA Emergency Clearance: Public Information Collection Requirements Submitted to the Office of

Management and Budget (OMB) (pertaining to on-site inspection for durable medical equipment (DME) suppliers).

63 FR 58399, October 30, 1998: Office of Inspector General: Publication of the OIG's Provider Self-Disclosure Protocol — Notice.

63 FR 60356, November 9, 1998: HCFA Agency Information Collection Activities: Proposed Collection; Comment request (pertaining to collection of information on resource utilization by Medicare providers, suppliers, and CLIA laboratories).

63 FR 63936, November 17, 1998: HCFA Emergency Clearance: Public Information Collection Requirements Submitted to the Office of Management and Budget (OMB) (pertaining to collection of DMEPOS supplier data in support of the Medicare DMEPOS competitive bidding demonstration).

63 FR 71654, December 29, 1998: HCFA Emergency Clearance: Public Information Collection Requirements Submitted to the Office of Management and Budget (OMB) (pertaining to evaluation of competitive bidding demonstration for durable medical equipment and prosthetics, orthotics, and supplies).

1999

64 FR 1810, January 12, 1999: HCFA Agency Information Collection Activities: Proposed Collection; Comment request (pertaining to Medicaid eligibility quality control MEQC) samples; identification of extension units of outpatient physical therapy (OPT) and outpatient speech pathology (OSP) providers; request for certification in the Medicare and/or Medicaid program(s) to provide OPT or OSP services; and request for certification as a supplier of portable X-ray services under Medicare and/or Medicaid).

64 FR 1813, January 12, 1999: Office of Inspector General Publication of OIG Special Fraud Alert on Physician Liability for Certifications in the Provision of Medical Equipment and Supplies and Home Health Services — Notice.

64 FR 3303, January 21, 1999: HCFA Agency Information Collection Activities: Proposed Collection; Comment request (pertaining to on-site inspection for durable medical equipment suppliers).

64 FR 4435, January 28, 1999: Office of Inspector General: Draft Compliance Guidance for the Durable Medical Equipment, Prosthetics, Orthotics and Supply Industry — Notice and comment period.

64 FR 9160, February 24, 1999: HCFA Agency Information Collection Activities: Proposed Collection; Comment request (pertaining to Medicare DMEPOS competitive bidding demonstration).

64 FR 9161, February 24, 1999: HCFA Agency Information Collection Activities: Proposed Collection; Comment request (pertaining Medicare DMEPOS competitive bidding demonstration).

64 FR 9335, February 25, 1999: HCFA Agency Information Collection Activities: Proposed Collection; Comment request (pertaining to evaluation of competitive bidding demonstration for DMEPOS).

64 FR 10479, March 4, 1999: HCFA Agency Information Collection Activities: Proposed Collection; Comment request (pertaining to conditions of participation for portable X-ray suppliers).

64 FR 17673, April 12, 1999: HCFA Agency Information Collection Activities: Proposed Collection; Comment request (pertaining to Medicare participating physician or supplier agreements).

64 FR 24956, May 10, 1999: Medicare and Medicaid Programs; Effective Dates of Provider Agreements and Supplier Approvals-Correction restoring regulations inadvertently removed when a final rule concerning effective dates for provider agreements and supplier approvals was published at 62 FR 43931, August 18, 1997.

64 FR 25891, May 13, 1999: HCFA Agency Information Collection Activities: Submission for OMB Review; Comment request (pertaining to Medicare DMEPOS competitive bidding demonstration).

64 FR 28826, May 27, 1999: HCFA Agency Information Collection Activities: Submission for OMB Review; Comment request (pertaining to evaluation of competitive bidding demonstration for durable medical equipment and prosthetics, orthotics, and supplies (DMEPOS)).

64 FR 32239, June 16, 1999: HCFA Agency Information Collection Activities: Submission for OMB Review; Comment request (pertaining to the requirement that physicians must notify beneficiaries that Medicare is likely to deny payment for a specified service).

64 FR 32240, June 16, 1999: HCFA Agency Information Collection Activities: Submission for OMB Review; Comment request (pertaining to conditions of participation for portable x-ray suppliers).

64 FR 36368, July 6, 1999: Office of Inspector General Publication of OIG Compliance Program Guidance for the Durable Medical Equipment, Prosthetics, Orthotics and Supply Industry — Notice.

64 FR 38203, July 15, 1999: HCFA Agency Information Collection Activities: Submission for OMB Review; Comment request (pertain-

ing to attending physician's certification of medical necessity for home oxygen therapy).

64 FR 39517, July 22, 1999: HCFA Agency Information Collection Activities: Submission for OMB Review; Comment request (pertaining to Medicare participating physician or supplier agreement form HCFA-460).

64 FR 49020, September 9, 1999: Medicare Program; Open Public Meeting to Discuss the Conduct of a Second Competitive Bidding Demonstration for durable medical equipment, prosthetics, orthotics, and supplies (DMEPOS) — Notice of meeting.

64 FR 57431, October 25, 1999: Medicare Program; Appeals of Carrier Determinations that a Supplier Fails to Meet the Requirements for Medicare Billing Privileges — Proposed rule affecting 42 CFR Part 405.

64 FR 57619, October 26, 1999: Office of Inspector General; Privacy Act; Exempt Record System, Pertaining to the Healthcare Integrity and Protection Data Bank (HIPDB) — Notice of proposed rulemaking affecting 45 CFR Part 5b.

64 FR 73563, December 30, 1999: HCFA Agency Information Collection Activities: Submission for OMB Review; Comment request pertaining to Medicare program integrity organizational conflict of interest disclosure certificates).

2000

65 FR 4437, January 27, 2000: HCFA Agency Information Collection Activities: Proposed Collection; Comment request (pertaining to durable medical equipment regional carrier certificate of medical necessity).

65 FR 5354, February 3, 2000: HCFA Agency Information Collection Activities: Proposed Collection; Comment request (pertaining to standardized Medicare/Medicaid claim form for reimbursement of covered services).

65 FR 24666, April 27, 2000: Medicare Program; Payment for Upgraded Durable Medical Equipment — Proposed rule affecting 42 CFR Part 414.

65 FR 25736, May 3, 2000: HCFA Agency Information Collection Activities: Proposed Collection; Comment request (pertaining to Medicare DMEPOS competitive bidding demonstration; follow-up to original survey).

65 FR 30414, May 11, 2000: HCFA Agency Information Collection Activities: Submission for OMB Review; Comment request (pertaining to health insurance common claims form).

65 FR 30415, May 11, 2000: HCFA Agency Information Collection Activities: Submission for OMB Review; Comment request (pertaining to conflict of interest and ownership and control information).

65 FR 42021, July 7, 2000: HCFA Agency Information Collection Activities: Proposed Collection; Comment request (pertaining to notice to providers, suppliers, and practitioners about non-covered services to beneficiaries).

65 FR 45090, July 20, 2000: HCFA Agency Information Collection Activities: Proposed Collection; Comment request (pertaining to Medicare DMEPOS competitive bidding demonstration).

65 FR 49002, August 10, 2000: HCFA Emergency Clearance: Public Information Collection Requirements Submitted to the Office of Management and Budget (OMB) (pertaining to oxygen consumer survey for medical equipment and supplies).

65 FR 50312, August 17, 2000: HCFA; Health Insurance Reform: Standards for Electronic Transactions — Final rule affecting 45 CFR Parts 160 and 162.

65 FR 53727, September 5, 2000: HCFA Agency Information Collection Activities: Proposed Collection; Comment request (pertaining to ambulance services reimbursement request form for physicians, suppliers, and beneficiaries).

65 FR 53963, September 6, 2000: Medicare Program: Appeals of Carrier Determinations that a Physician or Other Supplier Fails to Meet the Requirements for Medicare Billing Privileges; Reopening of Comment Period — Notice of reopening of comment period for proposed rule affecting 42 CFR Part 405.

65 FR 59432, October 5, 2000: HCFA Agency Information Collection Activities: Submission for OMB Review; Comment request (pertaining to Medicare DMEPOS competitive bidding demonstration).

65 FR 65861, November 2, 2000: HCFA Agency Information Collection Activities: Proposed Collection; Comment request (pertaining to conflict of interest disclosure requirements for Medicare program integrity).

65 FR 69944, November 21, 2000: HCFA Agency Information Collection Activities: Proposed Collection; Comment request (pertaining to additional DMEPOS supplier standards).

2001

66 FR 1996, January 10, 2001: HCFA Agency Information Collection Activities; Comment request (pertaining to Medicare uniform institutional provider bill for reimbursement of covered services by all providers that accept assignment of claims.

66 FR 1997, January 10, 2001: HCFA Notice of OMB Approval (pertaining to uniform home health advance beneficiary notice).

66 FR 2912, January 12, 2001: HCFA Agency Information Collection Activities: Proposed Collection; Comment request (pertaining to Medicare/Medicaid health insurance common claim form).

66 FR 7919, January 26, 2001: HCFA Agency Information Collection Activities: Proposed Collection; Comment request (pertaining to provider Medicare agreements).

66 FR 8807, February 2, 2001: HCFA Agency Information Collection Activities: Proposed Collection; Comment request (pertaining to Medicare Federal health care programs provider/supplier enrollment application).

66 FR 18646, April 10, 2001: HCFA Agency Information Collection Activities: Submission for OMB Review; Comment request (pertaining to Medicare/Medicaid health insurance common claim form).

66 FR 19508, April 16, 2001: HCFA Agency Information Collection Activities: Proposed Collection; Comment request (pertaining to on site inspection for durable medical equipment (DME) suppliers).

66 FR 20315, April 20, 2001: HCFA Agency Information Collection Activities: Submission for OMB Review; Comment request (pertaining to DMEPOS supplier standards).

66 FR 20316, April 20, 2001: HCFA Agency Information Collection Activities: Submission for OMB Review; Comment request (pertaining to DMEPOS supplier survey).

66 FR 20316, April 20, 2001: HCFA Agency Information Collection Activities: Submission for OMB Review; Comment request (pertaining to advance beneficiary notice by physicians, practitioners, suppliers, and providers about items and services denied by Medicare as not reasonable and necessary).

66 FR 20997, April 26, 2001: HCFA Agency Information Collection Activities: Submission for OMB Review; Comment request (pertaining to health insurance provider agreement form).

66 FR 21770, May 1, 2001: HCFA Agency Information Collection Activities: Submission for OMB Review; Comment request (pertaining to Medicare uniform institutional provider bill form).

66 FR 33102, June 20, 2001: HCFA Agency Information Collection Activities; Submission for OMB Review; Comment request (pertaining to provider/supplier enrollment application form).

66 FR 34457, June 28, 2001: HCFA Agency Information Collection Activities: Proposed Collection; Comment request (pertaining to durable medical equipment and prosthetics, orthotics, and supplies supplier survey).

See § 2:13.1.

§ 6:13.2 FAILURE BY SUPPLIERS TO MAKE REQUIRED REFUNDS Section 1834(a)(18) [42 U.S.C.A. 1395m(a)(18)]

Regulations

42 CFR Part 402 — Civil Money Penalties, Assessments, and Exclusions

42 CFR Part 410 — Supplementary Medical Insurance (SMI) benefits, especially section 410.36: Medical supplies, appliances, and devices: Scope; and section 410.38: Durable medical equipment: Scope and conditions

42 CFR Part 414 — Payment for Part B Medical and Other Health Services

42 CFR Part 420 — Program Integrity: Medicare

42 CFR Part 424 — Conditions for Medicare Payment

42 CFR Part 440 — Services: General Provisions [Medicaid]

42 CFR Part 447 — Payments for Services [Medicaid]

42 CFR Part 455 — Program Integrity: Medicaid

42 CFR Chapter V — Office of Inspector General — Health Care, Department of Health and Human Services

Subchapter A — General Provisions

Part 1000 — Introduction; General Definitions

Subchapter B — OIG Authorities

Part 1001 — Program Integrity: Medicare and State Health Care Programs

Part 1002 — Program Integrity: State-initiated Exclusion from Medicaid

Part 1003 — Civil Money Penalties, Assessments and Exclusions

Part 1004 — Imposition of Sanctions on Health Care Practitioners and Providers of Health Care Services by a Peer Review Organization

Part 1005 — Appeals of Exclusions, Civil Money Penalties and Assessments

Part 1006 — Investigational Inquiries

Part 1007 — State Medicaid Fraud Control Units

Part 1008 — Advisory Opinions by the OIG

56 FR 50821, October 9, 1991: Medicare Program; Continuous Use of Durable Medical Equipment — Interim final rule with comment period affecting 42 CFR Part 414.

56 FR 56612, November 6, 1991: Medicare Program; Carrier Jurisdiction for Claims for Durable Medical Equipment, Prosthetics, Orthotics and Supplies, and Other Issues Involving Suppliers — Proposed rule affecting 42 CFR Parts 400, 420, and 421.

56 FR 61023, November 29, 1991: Medicare Program; Standard Claim Forms for Part B Claims Completed and Submitted by Physicians, Suppliers and Other Persons — General notice with comment period.

56 FR 65995, December 20, 1991: Medicare Program; Payment for Customized Wheelchairs — Interim final rule with comment period, affecting 42 CFR Part 414.

57 FR 23420, June 3, 1992: HCFA Privacy Act of 1974; System of Records (pertaining to Medicare supplier identification file for suppliers of durable medical equipment, prosthetics, orthotics, and supplies) — Notice.

57 FR 27290, June 18, 1992: Medicare Program; Carrier Jurisdiction for Claims for Durable Medical Equipment, Prosthetics, Orthotics and Supplies (DMEPOS) and Other Issues Involving Suppliers, and Criteria and Standards for Evaluating Regional DMEPOS Carriers — Final rule with comment period, affecting 42 CFR Parts 405, 420, 421, and 424. See also correction at 57 FR 35760, August 11, 1992.

57 FR 27309, June 18, 1992: Medicare Program; Criteria and Standards for Evaluating Regional Durable Medical Equipment, Prosthetics, Orthotics and Suppliers (DMEPOS) Carriers; Request for comments.

57 FR 47587, October 19, 1992: Medicare and Medicaid Programs; Use of Standardized Federal Claims Processing Forms and Procedures — Advance notice of proposed rulemaking.

57 FR 57109, December 3, 1992: Medicare Program; Continuous Use of Durable Medical Equipment — Final rule affecting 42 CFR Part 414.

58 FR 34916, June 30, 1993: Medicare Program; Payment for Customized Wheelchairs — Final rule.

58 FR 60789, November 18, 1993: Medicare Program; Carrier Jurisdiction for Claims for Durable Medical Equipment, Prosthetics, Orthotics, and Supplies (DMEPOS) — Final rule affecting 42 CFR Part 421.

60 FR 2325, January 9, 1995: Medicare Program; Providers and Suppliers of Specialized Services: Technical Amendments — Final rule with comment period, affecting 42 CFR Parts 400, 405, 410, 484, 485, 486, and 498. See also correction at 60 FR 11632, March 2, 1995. See also correction at 60 FR 11632, March 2, 1995 and correction at 60 FR 45086, August 30, 1995.

60 FR 40847, August 10, 1995: Office of Inspector General: Publication of OIG Special Fraud Alerts: Home Health Fraud, and Fraud and Abuse in the Provision of Medical Supplies to Nursing Facilities — Notice.

60 FR 42887, August 17, 1995: HCFA Public Information Collection Requirements Submitted for Public Comment and Recommendations (pertaining to national provider identifier and Medicare payment of ambulance service charges).

60 FR 48417, September 19, 1995: Medicare Program; Criteria and Procedures for Extending Coverage to Certain Devices and Related Services — Final rule with comment period, affecting 42 CFR Parts 405and 411.

60 FR 50466, September 29, 1995: Medicare Program — Providers and Suppliers of Specialized Services: Technical Amendments — Final rule with comment period, affecting 42 CFR Parts 485and 486. See also correction at 60 FR 53877, October 18, 1995.

60 FR 52530, October 6, 1995: HCFA Public Information Collection Requirements Submitted to the Office of Management and Budget (OMB) for Clearance (pertaining to durable medical equipment regional carriers and certificates of medical necessity).

60 FR 53383, October 13, 1995: HCFA Public Information Collection Requirements Submitted for Public Comment and Recommendations (pertaining to durable medical equipment regional carriers and certificates of medical necessity).

60 FR 64167, December 14, 1995: HCFA Public Information Collection Requirements Submitted for Public Comment and Recommendations (pertaining to home health care; Medicare/Medicaid certification of physical therapy and speech pathology

services; certification as suppliers of Portable X-ray Services; certification of organ procurement organizations; certification for physical therapists in independent practice; and approval as a hospital provider of extended care services (swing bed)).

61 FR 2516, January 26, 1996: Medicare Program; Revised Criteria and Standards for Evaluating Durable Medical Equipment, Prosthetics, Orthotics, and Supplies Regional Carriers' Performance Beginning February 1, 1996 — Notice with comment period.

61 FR 30623, June 17, 1996: Office of Inspector General Publication of OIG Special Fraud Alert: Fraud and Abuse in the Provision of Services in Nursing Homes — Notice.

61 FR 37278, July 17, 1996: HCFA Agency Information Collection Activities: Proposed Collection; Comment request (pertaining to Medicare provider/supplier enrollment forms).

61 FR 56963, November 5, 1996: HCFA Agency Information Collection Activities: Proposed Collection; Comment request (pertaining to geographic adjustment factors for existing payment localities used in calculating the Medicare fee schedule; demonstration project to test capitated payments for home health services, medical devices, durable medical equipment, and certain ambulatory care under Medicare; and certification of medical necessity forms for durable medical equipment and supplies).

62 FR 8026, February 21, 1997: HCFA Agency Information Collection Activities: Submission for OMB Review; Comment request (pertaining to durable medical equipment regional carrier certificate of medical necessity).

62 FR 8744, February 26, 1997: HCFA Agency Information Collection Activities: Submission for OMB Review; Comment request (pertaining to Medicare provider/supplier enrollment application).

62 FR 42258, August 6, 1997: HCFA Agency Information Collection Activities: Proposed Collection; Comment request (pertaining to provider and supplier liability for certain noncovered services; and data about interns and residents for medical education reimbursement to hospitals).

62 FR 43931, August 18, 1997: Medicare and Medicaid Programs: Effective Dates of Provider Agreements and Supplier Approvals — Final rule affecting 42 CFR Parts 431, 442, 488, 489, and 498.

62 FR 52566, October 8, 1997: HCFA Agency Information Collection Activities: Submission for OMB Review; Comment request (pertaining to reimbursement for psychiatric units; and procedures

for determining liability of providers, practitioners, and suppliers for noncovered services).

62 FR 66376, December 18, 1997: HCFA Emergency Clearance: Public Information Collection Requirements Submitted to the Office of Management and Budget (OMB) (pertaining to Medicare and other Federal health care program enrollment forms for providers and suppliers).

62 FR 66726, December 19, 1997: Medicare and Medicaid Programs; Hospital Conditions of Participation; Provider Agreements and Supplier Approval — Proposed rule affecting 42 CFR Parts 416, 482, 485, and 489.

63 FR 687, January 7, 1998: Medicare Program; Application of Inherent Reasonableness to All Medicare Part B Services (Other than Physician Services) — Interim final rule with comment period, affecting 42 CFR Part 405.

63 FR 2926, January 20, 1998: Medicare Program; Additional Supplier Standards — Proposed rule affecting 42 CFR Part 424.

63 FR 7743, February 17, 1998: Medicare and Medicaid Programs; Hospital Conditions of Participation; Provider Agreements and Supplier Approval — Notice of extension of comment period, affecting 42 CFR Parts 416, 482, 485, and 489.

63 FR 14719, March 26, 1998: HCFA Agency Information Collection Activities: Proposed Collection; Comment request (pertaining to physician certification and re-certification in skilled nursing facilities).

63 FR 19502, April 20, 1998: HCFA Agency Information Collection Activities: Proposed collection; Comment request (pertaining to annual early and periodic screening, diagnostic, and treatment services (EPSDT) participation report; Medicare and other health care programs provider/supplier enrollment application; and research and analytic support for implementing performance measurement in Medicare fee for service).

63 FR 20415, April 24, 1998: Office of Inspector General: Publication of OIG Special Fraud Alert: Fraud and Abuse in Nursing Home Arrangements with Hospices — Notice.

63 FR 20639, April 27, 1998: HCFA Agency Information Collection Activities: Proposed Collection; Comment request (pertaining to financial reports to evaluate requests from physicians or suppliers to pay debts under extended repayment schedule or to compromise a debt for less than the full amount).

63 FR 28395, May 22, 1998: HCFA Agency Information Collection Activities: Submission for OMB Review; Comment request (pertaining to physician certifications and recertifications in skilled nursing facilities).

63 FR 36250, July 2, 1998: HCFA Agency Information Collection Activities; Submission for OMB review; Comment request (pertaining to provider/supplier enrollment applications).

63 FR 38311, July 16, 1998: Office of Inspector General: Medicare and State Health Care Programs: Fraud and Abuse; Issuance of Advisory Opinions by the OIG — Final rule affecting 42 CFR 1008. See also correction at 63 FR 43449, August 13, 1998.

63 FR 38414, July 16, 1998: HCFA Privacy Act of 1974; Report of Altered System (pertaining to disclosure of individual-specific information to combat fraud or abuse in health benefit programs).

63 FR 42409, August 7, 1998: Office of Inspector General: Solicitation of Information and Recommendations for Developing OIG Compliance Program Guidance for the Durable Medical Equipment Industry — Notice.

63 FR 58058, October 29, 1998: HCFA Emergency Clearance: Public Information Collection Requirements Submitted to the Office of Management and Budget (OMB) (pertaining to on-site inspection for durable medical equipment (DME) suppliers).

63 FR 60356, November 9, 1998: HCFA Agency Information Collection Activities: Proposed Collection; Comment request (pertaining to collection of information on resource utilization by Medicare providers, suppliers, and CLIA laboratories).

1999

64 FR 1810, January 12, 1999: HCFA Agency Information Collection Activities: Proposed Collection; Comment request (pertaining to Medicaid eligibility quality control MEQC) samples; identification of extension units of outpatient physical therapy (OPT) and outpatient speech pathology (OSP) providers; request for certification in the Medicare and/or Medicaid program(s) to provide OPT or OSP services; and request for certification as a supplier of portable X-ray services under Medicare and/or Medicaid).

64 FR 1813, January 12, 1999: Office of Inspector General Publication of OIG Special Fraud Alert on Physician Liability for Certifications in the Provision of Medical Equipment and Supplies and Home Health Services — Notice.

64 FR 4435, January 28, 1999: Office of Inspector General: Draft Compliance Guidance for the Durable Medical Equipment, Prosthetics, Orthotics and Supply Industry — Notice and comment period.

64 FR 9160, February 24, 1999: HCFA Agency Information Collection Activities: Proposed Collection; Comment request (pertaining to Medicare DMEPOS competitive bidding demonstration).

64 FR 9161, February 24, 1999: HCFA Agency Information Collection Activities: Proposed Collection; Comment request (pertaining Medicare DMEPOS competitive bidding demonstration).

64 FR 9335, February 25, 1999: HCFA Agency Information Collection Activities: Proposed Collection; Comment request (pertaining to evaluation of competitive bidding demonstration for DMEPOS).

64 FR 10478, March 4, 1999: HCFA Agency Information Collection Activities: Proposed Collection; Comment request (pertaining to refunds to patients from physicians when Medicare does not provide coverage for the physician services provided).

64 FR 10479, March 4, 1999: HCFA Agency Information Collection Activities: Proposed Collection; Comment request (pertaining to conditions of participation for portable X-ray suppliers).

64 FR 17673, April 12, 1999: HCFA Agency Information Collection Activities: Proposed Collection; Comment request (pertaining to Medicare participating physician or supplier agreements).

64 FR 24956, May 10, 1999: Medicare and Medicaid Programs; Effective Dates of Provider Agreements and Supplier Approvals-Correction restoring regulations inadvertently removed when a final rule concerning effective dates for provider agreements and supplier approvals was published at 62 FR 43931, August 18, 1997.

64 FR 25891, May 13, 1999: HCFA Agency Information Collection Activities: Submission for OMB Review; Comment request (pertaining to Medicare DMEPOS competitive bidding demonstration).

64 FR 28826, May 27, 1999: HCFA Agency Information Collection Activities: Submission for OMB Review; Comment request (pertaining to evaluation of competitive bidding demonstration for durable medical equipment and prosthetics, orthotics, and supplies (DMEPOS)).

64 FR 32239, June 16, 1999: HCFA Agency Information Collection Activities: Submission for OMB Review; Comment request (pertaining to the requirement that physicians must notify beneficiaries that Medicare is likely to deny payment for a specified service).

64 FR 32240, June 16, 1999: HCFA Agency Information Collection Activities: Submission for OMB Review; Comment request (pertaining to conditions of participation for portable x-ray suppliers).

64 FR 36368, July 6, 1999: Office of Inspector General Publication of OIG Compliance Program Guidance for the Durable Medical Equipment, Prosthetics, Orthotics and Supply Industry — Notice.

64 FR 38203, July 15, 1999: HCFA Agency Information Collection Activities: Submission for OMB Review; Comment request (pertaining to attending physician's certification of medical necessity for home oxygen therapy).

64 FR 39517, July 22, 1999: HCFA Agency Information Collection Activities: Submission for OMB Review; Comment request (pertaining to Medicare participating physician or supplier agreement form HCFA-460).

64 FR 49020, September 9, 1999: Medicare Program; Open Public Meeting to Discuss the Conduct of a Second Competitive Bidding Demonstration for durable medical equipment, prosthetics, orthotics, and supplies (DMEPOS) — Notice of meeting.

64 FR 57431, October 25, 1999: Medicare Program; Appeals of Carrier Determinations that a Supplier Fails to Meet the Requirements for Medicare Billing Privileges — Proposed rule affecting 42 CFR Part 405.

64 FR 57619, October 26, 1999: Office of Inspector General; Privacy Act; Exempt Record System, Pertaining to the Healthcare Integrity and Protection Data Bank (HIPDB) — Notice of proposed rulemaking affecting 45 CFR Part 5b.

64 FR 73563, December 30, 1999: HCFA Agency Information Collection Activities: Submission for OMB Review; Comment request pertaining to Medicare program integrity organizational conflict of interest disclosure certificates).

2000

65 FR 4437, January 27, 2000: HCFA Agency Information Collection Activities: Proposed Collection; Comment request (pertaining to durable medical equipment regional carrier certificate of medical necessity).

65 FR 5354, February 3, 2000: HCFA Agency Information Collection Activities: Proposed Collection; Comment request (pertaining to standardized Medicare/Medicaid claim form for reimbursement of covered services).

65 FR 24666, April 27, 2000: Medicare Program; Payment for Upgraded Durable Medical Equipment — Proposed rule affecting 42 CFR Part 414.

65 FR 25736, May 3, 2000: HCFA Agency Information Collection Activities: Proposed Collection; Comment request (pertaining to Medicare DMEPOS competitive bidding demonstration; follow-up to original survey).

65 FR 30414, May 11, 2000: HCFA Agency Information Collection Activities: Submission for OMB Review; Comment request (pertaining to health insurance common claims form).

65 FR 30415, May 11, 2000: HCFA Agency Information Collection Activities: Submission for OMB Review; Comment request (pertaining to conflict of interest and ownership and control information).

65 FR 42021, July 7, 2000: HCFA Agency Information Collection Activities: Proposed Collection; Comment request (pertaining to notice to providers, suppliers, and practitioners about non-covered services to beneficiaries).

65 FR 45090, July 20, 2000: HCFA Agency Information Collection Activities: Proposed Collection; Comment request (pertaining to Medicare DMEPOS competitive bidding demonstration).

65 FR 49002, August 10, 2000: HCFA Emergency Clearance: Public Information Collection Requirements Submitted to the Office of Management and Budget (OMB) (pertaining to oxygen consumer survey for medical equipment and supplies).

65 FR 50312, August 17, 2000: HCFA; Health Insurance Reform: Standards for Electronic Transactions — Final rule affecting 45 CFR Parts 160 and 162.

65 FR 53727, September 5, 2000: HCFA Agency Information Collection Activities: Proposed Collection; Comment request (pertaining to ambulance services reimbursement request form for physicians, suppliers, and beneficiaries).

65 FR 53963, September 6, 2000: Medicare Program: Appeals of Carrier Determinations that a Physician or Other Supplier Fails to Meet the Requirements for Medicare Billing Privileges; Reopening of Comment Period — Notice of reopening of comment period for proposed rule affecting 42 CFR Part 405.

65 FR 59432, October 5, 2000: HCFA Agency Information Collection Activities: Submission for OMB Review; Comment request (pertaining to Medicare DMEPOS competitive bidding demonstration).

65 FR 65861, November 2, 2000: HCFA Agency Information Collection Activities: Proposed Collection; Comment request (pertaining to conflict of interest disclosure requirements for Medicare program integrity).

65 FR 69944, November 21, 2000: HCFA Agency Information Collection Activities: Proposed Collection; Comment request (pertaining to additional DMEPOS supplier standards).

2001

66 FR 1996, January 10, 2001: HCFA Agency Information Collection Activities; Comment request (pertaining to Medicare uniform institutional provider bill for reimbursement of covered services by all providers that accept assignment of claims.

66 FR 1997, January 10, 2001: HCFA Notice of OMB Approval (pertaining to uniform home health advance beneficiary notice).

66 FR 2912, January 12, 2001: HCFA Agency Information Collection Activities: Proposed Collection; Comment request (pertaining to Medicare/Medicaid health insurance common claim form).

66 FR 7919, January 26, 2001: HCFA Agency Information Collection Activities: Proposed Collection; Comment request (pertaining to provider Medicare agreements).

66 FR 8807, February 2, 2001: HCFA Agency Information Collection Activities: Proposed Collection; Comment request (pertaining to Medicare Federal health care programs provider/supplier enrollment application).

66 FR 18646, April 10, 2001: HCFA Agency Information Collection Activities: Submission for OMB Review; Comment request (pertaining to Medicare/Medicaid health insurance common claim form).

66 FR 19508, April 16, 2001: HCFA Agency Information Collection Activities: Proposed Collection; Comment request (pertaining to on site inspection for durable medical equipment (DME) suppliers).

66 FR 20315, April 20, 2001: HCFA Agency Information Collection Activities: Submission for OMB Review; Comment request (pertaining to DMEPOS supplier standards).

66 FR 20316, April 20, 2001: HCFA Agency Information Collection Activities: Submission for OMB Review; Comment request (pertaining to DMEPOS supplier survey).

66 FR 20316, April 20, 2001: HCFA Agency Information Collection Activities: Submission for OMB Review; Comment request (pertaining to advance beneficiary notice by physicians, practitioners,

suppliers, and providers about items and services denied by Medicare as not reasonable and necessary).

66 FR 20997, April 26, 2001: HCFA Agency Information Collection Activities: Submission for OMB Review; Comment request (pertaining to health insurance provider agreement form).

66 FR 21770, May 1, 2001: HCFA Agency Information Collection Activities: Submission for OMB Review; Comment request (pertaining to Medicare uniform institutional provider bill form).

66 FR 33102, June 20, 2001: HCFA Agency Information Collection Activities; Submission for OMB Review; Comment request (pertaining to provider/supplier enrollment application form).

66 FR 34457, June 28, 2001: HCFA Agency Information Collection Activities: Proposed Collection; Comment request (pertaining to durable medical equipment and prosthetics, orthotics, and supplies supplier survey).

See § 2:13.2.

§ 6:14 IMPROPER BILLING BY PHYSICIANS OR SUPPLIERS FOR RADIOLOGIST SERVICES — Section 1834(b)(5)(C) [42 U.S.C.A. 1395m(b)(5)(C)]

Regulations

42 CFR Part 402 — Civil Money Penalties, Assessments, and Exclusions

42 CFR Part 405, Subpart E — Criteria for Determination of Reasonable Charges

42 CFR Part 409 — Hospital Insurance Benefits

42 CFR Part 410 — Supplementary Medical Insurance (SMI) Benefits, especially Section 410.32: Diagnostic X-ray tests, diagnostic laboratory tests, and other diagnostic tests: Conditions; Section 410.34: Conditions for coverage for and limitations on screening mammography services; and Section 410.35: X-ray therapy and other radiation therapy services: Scope

42 CFR Part 414 — Payment for Part B Medical and Other Health Services

42 CFR Part 415 — Services Furnished by Physicians in Providers, Supervising Physicians in Teaching Settings, and Residents in Certain Settings

42 CFR Part 416 — Ambulatory Surgical Services, especially Section 416.49: Condition for coverage — Laboratory and radiologic services

42 CFR Part 419 — Prospective Payment System for Hospital Outpatient Department Services

42 CFR Part 420 — Program Integrity: Medicare

42 CFR Part 424 — Conditions for Medicare Payment

42 CFR Part 440 — Services: General Provisions [Medicaid], especially Section 440.30: Other laboratory and X-ray services

42 CFR Part 447 — Payments for Services [Medicaid]

42 CFR Part 455 — Program Integrity: Medicaid

42 CFR Part 498 — Appeals Procedures for Determinations that Affect Participation in the Medicare Program and for Determinations that Affect the Participation of ICF's/MR and Certain NF's in the Medicaid Program

42 CFR Chapter V — Office of Inspector General — Health Care, Department of Health and Human Services

Subchapter A — General Provisions

Part 1000 — Introduction; General Definitions

Subchapter B — OIG Authorities

Part 1001 — Program Integrity: Medicare and State Health Care Programs

Part 1002 — Program Integrity: State-initiated Exclusion from Medicaid

Part 1003 — Civil Money Penalties, Assessments and Exclusions

Part 1004 — Imposition of Sanctions on Health Care Practitioners and Providers of Health Care Services by a Peer Review Organization

Part 1005 — Appeals of Exclusions, Civil Money Penalties and Assessments

Part 1006 — Investigational Inquiries

Part 1007 — State Medicaid Fraud Control Units

Part 1008 — Advisory Opinions by the OIG

55 FR 3487, February 1, 1990: Medicare Program; Establishment of Medicare Economic Index Effective April 1, 1990 — Notice.

55 FR 36178, September 4, 1990: Medicare Program; Model Fee Schedule for Physicians' Services — Notice with comment period.

55 FR 42907, October 24, 1990: Medicare Program; Standards Applied by Utilization and Quality Control Peer Review Organizations: Consideration of Remote Rural Location and Other Relevant Factors — Notice of policy and request for comments.

55 FR 53510, December 31, 1990: Medicare Program; Medicare Coverage of Screening Mammography — Interim final rule with

comment. See also correction published at 55 FR 4675, February 5, 1991.

56 FR 279, January 3, 1991: Medicare Program; Medicare Economic Index Update for 1991.

56 FR 25792, June 5, 1991: Medicare Program; Fee Schedule for Physicians' Services — Proposed rule affecting 42 CFR Parts 405 and 415.

56 FR 45926, September 9, 1991: Medicare Program; Revision of the Medicare Economic Index — Proposed rule affecting 42 CFR Part 405.

56 FR 59502, November 25, 1991: Medicare Program; Fee Schedule for Physicians' Services, Fee Schedule Update for Calendar Year 1992 and Physician Performance Standard Rates of Increase for Federal FY 1992 — Final rules and notice affecting 42 CFR Parts 405, 413, 414, and 415. See also correction at 57 FR 42491, September 15, 1992.

57 FR 36006, August 12, 1992: Medicare Program; Self-implementing Coverage and Payments Provisions: 1990 Legislation — Final rule with comment period, affecting 42 CFR Parts 405, 406, 409, 420, 411, 412, 413, 418, and 489. Pertains to capital-related inpatient hospital costs; capital-related outpatient hospital costs; non-capital related outpatient hospital costs; payment for physician pathology services; payment for services of physicians as assistants-at-surgery; payments for ambulatory surgical procedures in hospital outpatient departments; payments for radiology services performed in hospital outpatient departments; hospice benefit extension; enrollment of HMO members in Medicare Part A; coverage of ostomy supplies; application of pre-entitlement stay in psychiatric hospital to limit on payment for inpatient hospital services; payments to dialysis facilities; payment rates for erythropoietin (EPO); and Medicare secondary payer provision for individuals with ESRD. See also confirmation of final rule at 58 FR 58502, November 2, 1993.

57 FR 55896, November 25, 1992: Medicare Program; Revision of the Medicare Economic Index — Final rule affecting 42 CFR Parts 400 and 405.

57 FR 55914, November 25, 1992: Medicare Program; Fee Schedule for Physicians' Services for Calendar Year 1993 — Final notice with comment period. See also corrections published at 57 FR 59379, December 15, 1992, and at 58 FR 31964, June 7, 1993.

58 FR 29416, May 20, 1993: HCFA Public Information Collection Requirements Submitted to the Office of Management and Budget (OMB) for Clearance re cataract surgery; Medicaid utilization management initiatives; Medicare coverage of screening mammography; psychiatric unit criteria worksheet and rehabilitation unit criteria worksheet; Medicare secondary payor forms; ambulatory surgical center survey forms; ambulance service compliance with State and local requirements; and early and periodic screening, diagnostic and treatment reports.

58 FR 54159, October 20, 1993: HCFA Public Information Collection Requirements Submitted to the Office of Management and Budget (OMB) for Clearance (pertaining to CLIA certification recommendation; CLIA laboratory personnel report; Medigap complaint data base; certification as a rural health clinic (RHC) and RHC survey report form; screening mammography services data report; ambulatory surgical center request for certification and survey report form; blood bank inspection checklist and report; Medicaid program budget report form; supplier of ESRD services form; and grantee data collection instrument) — Notice.

58 FR 63626, December 2, 1993: Medicare Program; Revisions to Payment Policies and Adjustments to the Relative Value Units under the Physician Fee Schedule for Calendar Year 1994 — Final rule with comment period, affecting 42 CFR Parts 405 and 414. See also correction at 59 FR 36069, July 15, 1994.

58 FR 63856, December 2, 1993: Medicare Program; Physician Performance Standard Rates of Increase for Federal Fiscal Year 1994 and Physician Fee Schedule Update for Calendar Year 1994 — Final notice with comment period. See also correction at 59 FR 26410, June 1, 1994.

59 FR 32754, June 24, 1994: Medicare Program; Refinements to Geographic Adjustment Factor Values and Other Policies under the Physician Fee Schedule — Proposed rule affection 42 CFR parts 410 and 414.

59 FR 39828, August 4, 1994: Medicare Program; Payment Policies and Adjustments to the Relative Value Units Under the Physician Fee Schedule for Calendar Year 1994, affecting 42 CFR Parts 405 and 414.

59 FR 49826, September 30, 1994: Medicare Program; Medicare Coverage of Screening Mammography — Final rule affecting 42 CFR Parts 405, 410, 411, 413, and 494. See also correction at 60 FR 14223, March 16, 1995.

59 FR 61571, December 1, 1994: Office of Inspector General; Fraud and Abuse; Civil Money Penalties for Hospital Physician Incentive Plans — Proposed rule affecting 42 CFR Part 1003.

59 FR 63410, December 8, 1994: Medicare Program; Refinements to Geographic Adjustment Factor Values, Revisions to Payment Policies, Adjustments to the Relative Value Units (RVUs) under the Physician Fee Schedule for Calendar Year 1995, and the 5-Year Refinement of RVUs — Final rule with comment period, affecting 42 CFR parts 410 and 414. See also correction at 60 FR 46, January 3, 1995. See also correction at 60 FR 36733, July 18, 1995.

59 FR 63638, December 8, 1994: Medicare Program; Physician Fee Schedule Update for Calendar Year 1995 and Physician Volume Performance Standard Rates of Increase for Federal Fiscal Year 1995 — Final notice.

60 FR 16580, March 31, 1995: Office of Inspector General: Civil Money Penalties for Referrals to Entities and for Prohibited Arrangements and Schemes — Final rule with comment period, affecting 42 CFR Part 1003.

60 FR 37066, July 19, 1995: HCFA Public Information Collection Requirements Submitted to the Office of Management and Budget (OMB) for Clearance (pertaining to actuarial forecasts for Medicaid utilization and cost, employers identified through a match of IRS, SSA, and Medicare records for purposes of the Medicare Secondary Payer provision, health and safety requirements for portable X-ray suppliers, and evaluation of Intermediate Care Facilities for Persons with Mental Retardation — establishing psychoactive drug use baselines).

60 FR 38400, July 26, 1995: Medicare Program; Revisions to Payment Policies under the Physician Fee Schedule for Calendar Year 1996 — Proposed rule affecting 42 CFR Parts 400, 405, 410, 411, 412, 413, 414, 415, 417, and 489.

60 FR 63124, December 8, 1995: Medicare Program; Revisions to Payment Policies and Adjustments to the Relative Value Units under the Physician Fee Schedule for Calendar Year 1996 — Final rule with comment period, affecting 42 CFR Parts 400, 405, 410, 411, 412, 413, 414, 415, 417, and 489. See also correction at 61 FR 42385, August 15, 1996.

60 FR 64167, December 14, 1995: HCFA Public Information Collection Requirements Submitted for Public Comment and Recommendations (pertaining to home health care; Medicare/Medicaid certification of physical therapy and speech pathology

services; certification as suppliers of Portable X-ray Services; certification of organ procurement organizations; certification for physical therapists in independent practice; and approval as a hospital provider of extended care services (swing bed)).

61 FR 17710, April 22, 1996: HCFA Agency Information Collection Activities: Proposed Collection; Comment Request (pertaining to payment adjustments for sole community hospitals; conditions of participation for portable x-ray suppliers; and cost reports for independent rural health centers and freestanding Federally qualified health centers).

61 FR 19992, May 3, 1996: Medicare Program; Five-year Review of Work Relative Value Units under the Physician Fee Schedule — Proposed notice.

61 FR 37487, July 18, 1996: HCFA Agency Information Collection Activities: Submission for OMB Review; Comment request (pertaining to cost reports for independent rural health centers and freestanding federally qualified health centers; and conditions of participation for portable x-ray suppliers).

61 FR 59490, November 22, 1996: Medicare Program; Revisions to Payment Policies and Five-year Review of and Adjustments to the Relative value Units under the Physician Fee Schedule for Calendar yeat 1997 — Final rule with comment period, affecting 42 CFR Parts 410and 415. See also correction at 62 FR 7945, February 21, 1997.

61 FR 59717, November 22, 1996: Medicare Program; Physician Fee Schedule Update for Calendar year 1997 and Physician Volume Performance Standard Rates of Increase for Federal Fiscal Year 1997 — Final notice.

62 FR 8744, February 26, 1997: HCFA Agency Information Collection Activities: Submission for OMB Review; Comment request (pertaining to Medicare provider/supplier enrollment application).

62 FR 33158, June 18, 1997: Medicare Program; Revisions to Payment Policies Under the Physician fee Schedule, Other Part B Payment Policies, and Establishment of the Clinical Psychologist Fee Schedule for Calendar year 1998, Proposed rule affecting 42 CFR Parts 400, 405, 410, and 414.

62 FR 49048, October 31, 1997: Medicare Program; Revisions to Payment Policies and Adjustments to the Relative Value Units Under the Physician Fee Schedule, Other Part B Payment Policies, and Establishment of the Clinical Psychologist Fee Schedule for Calendar Year 1998; Correction of final rule with comment period. See also correction at 63 FR 4595, January 30, 1998.

62 FR 59261, October 31, 1997: Medicare Program; Physician Fee Schedule Conversion Factor for Calendar Year 1998 and Sustainable Growth Rate for Fiscal Year 1998 — Final notice.

62 FR 59267, October 31, 1997: Medicare Program; Delay in Implementing the Adjustments to the Practice Expense Relative Value Units under the Physician Fee Schedule for Calendar Year 1998 — Notice of intent to regulate.

63 FR 1659, January 9, 1998: Medicare and Medicaid Programs; Physicians' Referrals to Health Care Entities with Which They Have Financial Relationships — Proposed rule affecting 42 CFR Parts 411, 424, 435, and 455.

63 FR 2926, January 20, 1998: Medicare Program; Additional Supplier Standards — Proposed rule affecting 42 CFR Part 424.

63 FR 7743, February 17, 1998: Medicare and Medicaid Programs; Hospital Conditions of Participation; Provider Agreements and Supplier Approval — Notice of extension of comment period, affecting 42 CFR Parts 416, 482, 485, and 489.

63 FR 9844, February 26, 1998: HCFA Agency Information Collection Activities: Proposed Collection; Comment request (pertaining to procedures for advisory opinions concerning physician referrals and supporting regulations in 42 CFR Sections 411.370- 411.389).

63 FR 10920, March 5, 1998: HCFA Emergency Clearance: Public Information Collection Requirements Submitted to the Office of Management and Budget (OMB) (pertaining to Medicare and other Federal health care program provider and supplier application forms).

63 FR 11649, March 10, 1998: Medicare and Medicaid Programs; Physicians' Referrals to Health Care Entities with Which They Have Financial Relationships — Notice of extension of comment period for proposed rule.

63 FR 20639, April 27, 1998: HCFA Agency Information Collection Activities: Proposed Collection; Comment request (pertaining to financial reports to evaluate requests from physicians or suppliers to pay debts under extended repayment schedule or to compromise a debt for less than the full amount).

63 FR 30818, June 5, 1998: Medicare Program; Revisions to Payment Policies under the Physician Fee Schedule for Calendar Year 1999 — Proposed rule, affecting 42 CFR Parts 405, 410, 413, 414, 415, 424, and 485. See also correction at 63 FR 50545, September 22, 1998.

63 FR 58814, November 2, 1998: Medicare Program; Revisions to Payment Policies and Adjustments to the Relative Value Units under the Physician Fee Schedule for Calendar Year 1999 — Final rule with comment period, affecting 42 CFR 405, 410, 413, 414, 415, 424, and 485. See also correction at 64 FR 25456, May 12, 1999.

1999

64 FR 1813, January 12, 1999: Office of Inspector General Publication of OIG Special Fraud Alert on Physician Liability for Certifications in the Provision of Medical Equipment and Supplies and Home Health Services — Notice.

64 FR 10478, March 4, 1999: HCFA Agency Information Collection Activities: Proposed Collection; Comment request (pertaining to refunds to patients from physicians when Medicare does not provide coverage for the physician services provided).

64 FR 17673, April 12, 1999: HCFA Agency Information Collection Activities: Proposed Collection; Comment request (pertaining to Medicare participating physician or supplier agreements).

64 FR 24956, May 10, 1999: Medicare and Medicaid Programs; Effective Dates of Provider Agreements and Supplier Approvals-Correction restoring regulations inadvertently removed when a final rule concerning effective dates for provider agreements and supplier approvals was published at 62 FR 43931, August 18, 1997.

64 FR 37142, July 9, 1999: HCFA Agency Information Collection Activities: Submission for OMB Review; Comment request (pertaining to request for certification in the Medicare/Medicaid program to provide outpatient physical therapy and/or speech-language pathology and the outpatient physcal therapy and/or speech-language pathology survey report form; request for certification as a supplier of portable X-ray services); and procedures for making national coverage decisions).

64 FR 40017, July 23, 1999: HCFA Agency Information Collection Activities: Submission for OMB Review; Comment request (pertaining to Medicare geographical classification review board procedures and criteria).

64 FR 40534, July 27, 1999: Medicare Program; Replacement of Reasonable Charge Methodology by Fee Schedules — Proposed action affecting 42 CFR 414.

64 FR 57431, October 25, 1999: Medicare Program; Appeals of Carrier Determinations that a Supplier Fails to Meet the Require-

ments for Medicare Billing Privileges — Proposed rule affecting 42 CFR Part 405.

64 FR 59380, November 2, 1999: Medicare Program; Revisions to Payment Policies under the Physician Fee Schedule for Calendar Year 2000 — Final rule with comment period, affecting 42 CFR Parts 410, 411, 414, 415, and 485. See also correction at 65 FR 19329, April 11, 2000.

64 FR 69021, December 9, 1999: HCFA Agency Information Collection Activities: Proposed Collection; Comment request (pertaining to analysis of malpractice premium data to compute the physician fee schedule).

2000

65 FR 5354, February 3, 2000: HCFA Agency Information Collection Activities: Proposed Collection; Comment request (pertaining to standardized Medicare/Medicaid claim form for reimbursement of covered services).

65 FR 25939, May 4, 2000: HCFA Agency Information Collection Activities: Proposed Collection; Comment request (pertaining to ambulatory surgical center payment rate survey).

65 FR 42022, July 7, 2000: Medicare Program; Question and Answer Session on July 24, 2000, to Discuss Remaining Concerns about the Implementation of the Hospital Outpatient Prospective Payment System (PPS) — Notice of meeting.

65 FR 44176, July 17, 2000: Medicare Program; Revisions to Payment Policies under the Physician Fee Schedule for Calendar Year 2001 — Proposed rule affection 42 CFR Parts 410 and 414.

65 FR 53319, September 1, 2000: HCFA Agency Information Collection Activities: Proposed Collection; Comment request (pertaining to incentive arrangement disclosure form for managed care organizations and their related medical groups and physicians).

65 FR 50312, August 17, 2000: Office of the Secretary; Health Insurance Reform: Standards for Electronic Transactions — Final rule affecting 45 CFR Parts 160 and 162.

65 FR 65376, November 1, 2000: Medicare Program; Revisions to Payment Policies under the Physician Fee Schedule for Calendar Year 2001—Final rule with comment period. See also correction at 66 FR 16607, March 27, 2001.

2001

66 FR 1996, January 10, 2001: HCFA Agency Information Collection Activities; Comment request (pertaining to Medicare uniform institutional provider bill for reimbursement of covered services by all providers that accept assignment of claims.

66 FR 2912, January 12, 2001: HCFA Agency Information Collection Activities: Proposed Collection; Comment request (pertaining to Medicare/Medicaid health insurance common claim form).

66 FR 7919, January 26, 2001: HCFA Agency Information Collection Activities: Proposed Collection; Comment request (pertaining to provider Medicare agreements).

66 FR 8807, February 2, 2001: HCFA Agency Information Collection Activities: Proposed Collection; Comment request (pertaining to Medicare Federal health care programs provider/supplier enrollment application).

66 FR 18646, April 10, 2001: HCFA Agency Information Collection Activities: Submission for OMB Review; Comment request (pertaining to Medicare/Medicaid health insurance common claim form).

66 FR 20316, April 20, 2001: HCFA Agency Information Collection Activities: Submission for OMB Review; Comment request (pertaining to advance beneficiary notice by physicians, practitioners, suppliers, and providers about items and services denied by Medicare as not reasonable and necessary).

66 FR 20997, April 26, 2001: HCFA Agency Information Collection Activities: Submission for OMB Review; Comment request (pertaining to health insurance provider agreement form).

66 FR 31038, June 8, 2001: Medicare Program; Five–year Review of Work Relative Value Units under the Physician Fee Schedule—Proposed notice.

66 FR 33102, June 20, 2001: HCFA Agency Information Collection Activities; Submission for OMB Review; Comment request (pertaining to provider/supplier enrollment application form).

See § 2:14.

§ 6:15 OVERCHARGING FOR SERVICES OF A PHYSICIAN ASSISTANT OR NURSE PRACTITIONER — Section 1842(b)(12)(C) [42 U.S.C.A. 1395u(b)(12)(C)]

◆ NOTE: Repealed effective October 31, 1994, by section 123(b)(2)(B) of the Social Security Act Amendments of 1994, P.L. 103-432.

Regulations

42 CFR Part 405, Subpart X — Rural Health Clinic and Federally Qualified Health Center Services, especially Section 405.2414: Nurse practitioner and physician assistant services, and Section 405.2415: Services and supplies incident to nurse practitioner and physician assistant services

42 CFR Part 414 — Payment for Part B Medical and Other Health Services

42 CFR Part 420 — Program Integrity: Medicare

42 CFR Part 440 — Services: General Provisions [Medicaid], especially Section 440.20: Outpatient hospital services and rural health clinic services

42 CFR Part 455 — Program Integrity: Medicaid

42 CFR Chapter V — Office of Inspector General — Health Care, Department of Health and Human Services

Subchapter A — General Provisions

Part 1000 — Introduction; General Definitions

Subchapter B — OIG Authorities

Part 1001 — Program Integrity: Medicare

Part 1002 — Program Integrity: Medicaid

Part 1003 — Civil Money Penalties and Assessments

Part 1004 — Imposition of Sanctions on Health Care Practitioners and Providers of Health Care Services by a Peer Review Organization

Part 1005 — Appeals of Exclusions, Civil Money Penalties and Assessments

Part 1006 — Investigational Inquiries

Part 1007 — State Medicaid Fraud Control Units

Part 1008 — Advisory Opinions by the OIG

56 FR 29609 June 28, 1991: Medicare Program; Allowing Certifications and Recertifications by Nurse Practitioners and Clinical Nurse Specialists for Certain Services — Proposed rule.

56 FR 66392, December 23, 1991: Medicaid Program; Required Coverage of Nurse Practitioner Services — Proposed rule affecting 42 CFR Parts 440 and 441. See also correction at 57 FR 4085, February 3, 1992.

57 FR 36006, August 12, 1992: Medicare Program; Self-implementing Coverage and Payments Provisions: 1990 Legislation — Final rule with comment period, affecting 42 CFR Parts 405, 406, 409, 420, 411, 412, 413, 418, and 489. Pertains to capital-related inpatient hospital costs; capital-related outpatient

hospital costs; non-capital related outpatient hospital costs; payment for physician pathology services; payment for services of physicians as assistants-at-surgery; payments for ambulatory surgical procedures in hospital outpatient departments; payments for radiology services performed in hospital outpatient departments; hospice benefit extension; enrollment of HMO members in Medicare Part A; coverage of ostomy supplies; application of pre-entitlement stay in psychiatric hospital to limit on payment for inpatient hospital services; payments to dialysis facilities; payment rates for erythropoietin (EPO); and Medicare secondary payer provision for individuals with ESRD. See also confirmation of final rule at 58 FR 58502, November 2, 1993.

57 FR 43462, September 21, 1992: Health Care Financing Administration Public Information Collection Requirements Submitted to the Office of Management and Budget for Clearance (pertaining to sole community home health agencies; physician/supplier overpayment reports; physician or supplier Medicare agreements; conditions of participation for rural health clinics; Medicare provider refunds; conditions of participation for comprehensive outpatient rehabilitation facilities; Medicaid income and eligibility verification system; Medicaid integrated review schedule; provider overpayment report; financial statement of Medicare provider debtors; negative case action review schedule for Medicaid quality control; outpatient resource costing study; Medicaid intermediate care facility for the mentally retarded or persons with related conditions survey report form; installment agreement of beneficiary refund of overpayment; PRO assumption of responsibilities; Medicare contractor administrative budget and cost reporting system forms; fire safety survey report forms; medical records review under prospective payment system; and Qualified Medicare Beneficiary supplement to the Medicare current beneficiary survey).

See § 2:15.

§ 6:15.1 FAILURE BY PRACTITIONERS TO BILL ON AN ASSIGNMENT-RELATED BASIS — Section 1842(b)(18) and Sections 1834(k) and (l) [42 U.S.C.A. 1395u(b)(18) and 42 U.S.C.A. 1394m(k) and (l)]

Regulations

42 CFR Part 402 — Civil Money Penalties, Assessments, and Exclusions

42 CFR Part 405, Subpart X — Rural Health Clinic and Federally Qualified Health Center Services, especially Section 405.2414: Nurse practitioner and physician assistant services, and Section 405.2415: Services and supplies incident to nurse practitioner and physician assistant services

42 CFR Part 414 — Payment for Part B Medical and Other Health Services

42 CFR Part 420 — Program Integrity: Medicare

42 CFR Part 440 — Services: General Provisions [Medicaid], especially Section 440.20: Outpatient hospital services and rural health clinic services

42 CFR Part 455 — Program Integrity: Medicaid

42 CFR Chapter V — Office of Inspector General — Health Care, Department of Health and Human Services

Subchapter A — General Provisions

Part 1000 — Introduction; General Definitions

Subchapter B — OIG Authorities

Part 1001 — Program Integrity: Medicare

Part 1002 — Program Integrity: Medicaid

Part 1003 — Civil Money Penalties and Assessments

Part 1004 — Imposition of Sanctions on Health Care Practitioners and Providers of Health Care Services by a Peer Review Organization

Part 1005 — Appeals of Exclusions, Civil Money Penalties and Assessments

Part 1006 — Investigational Inquiries

Part 1007 — State Medicaid Fraud Control Units

Part 1008 — Advisory Opinions by the OIG

63 FR 4459, January 29, 1998: HCFA Emergency Clearance: Public Information Collection Requirements Submitted to the Office of Management and Budget (OMB) (pertaining to Medicare/Medicaid health insurance common claim form and instructions).

63 FR 36250, July 2, 1998: HCFA Agency Information Collection Activities; Submission for OMB review; Comment request (pertaining to provider/supplier enrollment applications).

1999

64 FR 5666, February 4, 1999: HCFA Emergency Clearance: Public Information Collection Requirements Submitted to the Office of Management and Budget (OMB) (pertaining to the Medicare/Medicaid health insurance common claim form).

64 FR 10478, March 4, 1999: HCFA Agency Information Collection Activities: Proposed Collection; Comment request (pertaining to refunds to patients from physicians when Medicare does not provide coverage for the physician services provided).

64 FR 17673, April 12, 1999: HCFA Agency Information Collection Activities: Proposed Collection; Comment request (pertaining to Medicare participating physician or supplier agreements).

64 FR 24956, May 10, 1999: Medicare and Medicaid Programs; Effective Dates of Provider Agreements and Supplier Approvals-Correction restoring regulations inadvertently removed when a final rule concerning effective dates for provider agreements and supplier approvals was published at 62 FR 43931, August 18, 1997.

64 FR 29049, May 28, 1999: HCFA Agency Information Collection Activities: Proposed Collection; Comment request (pertaining to Medicare credit balance reporting requirements for Medicare providers who have been overpaid).

64 FR 32239, June 16, 1999: HCFA Agency Information Collection Activities: Submission for OMB Review; Comment request (pertaining to the requirement that physicians must notify beneficiaries that Medicare is likely to deny payment for a specified service).

64 FR 39517, July 22, 1999: HCFA Agency Information Collection Activities: Submission for OMB Review; Comment request (pertaining to Medicare participating physician or supplier agreement form HCFA-460).

64 FR 48846, September 8, 1999: Office of Inspector General: Solicitation of Information and Recommendations for Developing OIG Compliance Program Guidance for Individual Physicians and Small Group Practices — Notice.

64 FR 57431, October 25, 1999: Medicare Program; Appeals of Carrier Determinations that a Supplier Fails to Meet the Requirements for Medicare Billing Privileges — Proposed rule affecting 42 CFR Part 405.

2000

65 FR 5354, February 3, 2000: HCFA Agency Information Collection Activities: Proposed Collection; Comment request (pertaining to standardized Medicare/Medicaid claim form for reimbursement of covered services).

65 FR 30414, May 11, 2000: HCFA Agency Information Collection Activities: Submission for OMB Review; Comment request (pertaining to health insurance common claims form).

65 FR 36818, June 12, 2000: Office of Inspector General: Draft OIG Compliance Program for Individual and Small Group Physician Practices — Notice and comment period.

65 FR 42021, July 7, 2000: HCFA Agency Information Collection Activities: Proposed Collection; Comment request (pertaining to notice to providers, suppliers, and practitioners about non-covered services to beneficiaries).

65 FR 50204, August 17, 2000: Office of Inspector General: Solicitation of Information and Recommendations for Developing a Compliance Risk Guidance for the Ambulance Industry — Notice.

65 FR 50312, August 17, 2000: HCFA; Health Insurance Reform: Standards for Electronic Transactions — Final rule affecting 45 CFR Parts 160 and 162.

65 FR 53727, September 5, 2000: HCFA Agency Information Collection Activities: Proposed Collection; Comment request (pertaining to ambulance services reimbursement request form for physicians, suppliers, and beneficiaries).

65 FR 53963, September 6, 2000: Medicare Program: Appeals of Carrier Determinations that a Physician or Other Supplier Fails to Meet the Requirements for Medicare Billing Privileges; Reopening of Comment Period — Notice of reopening of comment period for proposed rule affecting 42 CFR Part 405.

65 FR 57821, September 26, 2000: HCFA Emergency Clearance: Public Information Collection Requirements Submitted to the Office of Management and Budget (OMB) (pertaining to home health advanced beneficiary notices of liability).

65 FR 59858, October 6, 2000: HCFA Notice of Extension of Emergency Office of Management and Budget Clearance of Agency Information Collection Activities (pertaining to notices and demand bills from home health agencies).

65 FR 64227, October 26, 2000: HCFA Agency Information Collection Activities: Proposed Collection; Comment Request; Public Information Collection Meeting to Discuss Proposed Revisions (pertaining to notice requirements from suppliers, physicians, and practitioners to beneficiaries when Medicare Part B payment may be denied).

2001

66 FR 1996, January 10, 2001: HCFA Agency Information Collection Activities; Comment request (pertaining to Medicare uniform institutional provider bill for reimbursement of covered services by all providers that accept assignment of claims).

66 FR 1997, January 10, 2001: HCFA Notice of OMB Approval (pertaining to uniform home health advance beneficiary notice).

66 FR 2912, January 12, 2001: HCFA Agency Information Collection Activities: Proposed Collection; Comment request (pertaining to Medicare/Medicaid health insurance common claim form).

66 FR 7919, January 26, 2001: HCFA Agency Information Collection Activities: Proposed Collection; Comment request (pertaining to provider Medicare agreements).

66 FR 8807, February 2, 2001: HCFA Agency Information Collection Activities: Proposed Collection; Comment request (pertaining to Medicare Federal health care programs provider/supplier enrollment application).

66 FR 18646, April 10, 2001: HCFA Agency Information Collection Activities: Submission for OMB Review; Comment request (pertaining to Medicare/Medicaid health insurance common claim form).

66 FR 20316, April 20, 2001: HCFA Agency Information Collection Activities: Submission for OMB Review; Comment request (pertaining to advance beneficiary notice by physicians, practitioners, suppliers, and providers about items and services denied by Medicare as not reasonable and necessary).

66 FR 20997, April 26, 2001: HCFA Agency Information Collection Activities: Submission for OMB Review; Comment request (pertaining to health insurance provider agreement form).

66 FR 21770, May 1, 2001: HCFA Agency Information Collection Activities: Submission for OMB Review; Comment request (pertaining to Medicare uniform institutional provider bill form).

66 FR 33102, June 20, 2001: HCFA Agency Information Collection Activities; Submission for OMB Review; Comment request (pertaining to provider/supplier enrollment application form).

See § 2:15.1.

§ 6:15.2 DENIAL, TERMINATION, AND NONRENEWAL OF PHYSICIAN AND SUPPLIER PARTICIPATION AGREEMENTS — Section 1842(h) [42 U.S.C.A. 1395u(h)]

Regulations

42 CFR Part 402 — Civil Money Penalties, Assessments, and Exclusions

42 CFR Part 405, Subpart X — Rural Health Clinic and Federally Qualified Health Center Services, especially Section 405.2414: Nurse practitioner and physician assistant services, and Section 405.2415: Services and supplies incident to nurse practitioner and physician assistant services

42 CFR Part 414 — Payment for Part B Medical and Other Health Services

42 CFR Part 420 — Program Integrity: Medicare

42 CFR Part 440 — Services: General Provisions [Medicaid], especially Section 440.20: Outpatient hospital services and rural health clinic services

42 CFR Part 455 — Program Integrity: Medicaid

42 CFR Chapter V — Office of Inspector General — Health Care, Department of Health and Human Services

Subchapter A — General Provisions

Part 1000 — Introduction; General Definitions

Subchapter B — OIG Authorities

Part 1001 — Program Integrity: Medicare

Part 1002 — Program Integrity: Medicaid

Part 1003 — Civil Money Penalties and Assessments

Part 1004 — Imposition of Sanctions on Health Care Practitioners and Providers of Health Care Services by a Peer Review Organization

Part 1005 — Appeals of Exclusions, Civil Money Penalties and Assessments

Part 1006 — Investigational Inquiries

Part 1007 — State Medicaid Fraud Control Units

Part 1008 — Advisory Opinions by the OIG

63 FR 2926, January 20, 1998: Medicare Program; Additional Supplier Standards — Proposed rule affecting 42 CFR Part 424.

63 FR 7743, February 17, 1998: Medicare and Medicaid Programs; Hospital Conditions of Participation; Provider Agreements and Sup-

plier Approval — Notice of extension of comment period, affecting 42 CFR Parts 416, 482, 485, and 489.

63 FR 10920, March 5, 1998: HCFA Emergency Clearance: Public Information Collection Requirements Submitted to the Office of Management and Budget (OMB) (pertaining to Medicare and other Federal health care program provider and supplier application forms).

63 FR 19502, April 20, 1998: HCFA Agency Information Collection Activities: Proposed Collection; Comment request (pertaining to annual early and periodic screening, diagnostic, and treatment services (EPSDT) participation report; Medicare and other health care programs provider/supplier enrollment application; and research and analytic support for implementing performance measurement in Medicare fee for service).

63 FR 36250, July 2, 1998: HCFA Agency Information Collection Activities; Submission for OMB review; Comment request (pertaining to provider/supplier enrollment applications).

1999

64 FR 5666, February 4, 1999: HCFA Emergency Clearance: Public Information Collection Requirements Submitted to the Office of Management and Budget (OMB) (pertaining to the Medicare/Medicaid health insurance common claim form).

64 FR 10478, March 4, 1999: HCFA Agency Information Collection Activities: Proposed Collection; Comment request (pertaining to refunds to patients from physicians when Medicare does not provide coverage for the physician services provided).

64 FR 17673, April 12, 1999: HCFA Agency Information Collection Activities: Proposed Collection; Comment request (pertaining to Medicare participating physician or supplier agreements).

64 FR 24956, May 10, 1999: Medicare and Medicaid Programs; Effective Dates of Provider Agreements and Supplier Approvals-Correction restoring regulations inadvertently removed when a final rule concerning effective dates for provider agreements and supplier approvals was published at 62 FR 43931, August 18, 1997.

64 FR 29049, May 28, 1999: HCFA Agency Information Collection Activities: Proposed Collection; Comment request (pertaining to Medicare credit balance reporting requirements for Medicare providers who have been overpaid).

64 FR 32239, June 16, 1999: HCFA Agency Information Collection Activities: Submission for OMB Review; Comment request (pertaining to the requirement that physicians must notify beneficiaries that Medicare is likely to deny payment for a specified service).

64 FR 39517, July 22, 1999: HCFA Agency Information Collection Activities: Submission for OMB Review; Comment request (pertaining to Medicare participating physician or supplier agreement form HCFA-460).

64 FR 48846, September 8, 1999: Office of Inspector General: Solicitation of Information and Recommendations for Developing OIG Compliance Program Guidance for Individual Physicians and Small Group Practices — Notice.

64 FR 57431, October 25, 1999: Medicare Program; Appeals of Carrier Determinations that a Supplier Fails to Meet the Requirements for Medicare Billing Privileges — Proposed rule affecting 42 CFR Part 405.

2000

65 FR 5354, February 3, 2000: HCFA Agency Information Collection Activities: Proposed Collection; Comment request (pertaining to standardized Medicare/Medicaid claim form for reimbursement of covered services).

65 FR 30414, May 11, 2000: HCFA Agency Information Collection Activities: Submission for OMB Review; Comment request (pertaining to health insurance common claims form).

65 FR 36818, June 12, 2000: Office of Inspector General: Draft OIG Compliance Program for Individual and Small Group Physician Practices — Notice and comment period.

65 FR 42021, July 7, 2000: HCFA Agency Information Collection Activities: Proposed Collection; Comment request (pertaining to notice to providers, suppliers, and practitioners about non-covered services to beneficiaries).

65 FR 50312, August 17, 2000: HCFA; Health Insurance Reform: Standards for Electronic Transactions — Final rule affecting 45 CFR Parts 160 and 162.

65 FR 53727, September 5, 2000: HCFA Agency Information Collection Activities: Proposed Collection; Comment request (pertaining to ambulance services reimbursement request form for physicians, suppliers, and beneficiaries).

65 FR 53963, September 6, 2000: Medicare Program: Appeals of Carrier Determinations that a Physician or Other Supplier Fails to

Meet the Requirements for Medicare Billing Privileges; Reopening of Comment Period — Notice of reopening of comment period for proposed rule affecting 42 CFR Part 405.

65 FR 59434, October 5, 2000: Office of Inspector General Compliance Program for Individual and Small Group Physician Practices — Notice.

65 FR 64227, October 26, 2000: HCFA Agency Information Collection Activities: Proposed Collection; Comment Request; Public Information Collection Meeting to Discuss Proposed Revisions (pertaining to notice requirements from suppliers, physicians, and practitioners to beneficiaries when Medicare Part B payment may be denied).

2001

66 FR 1996, January 10, 2001: HCFA Agency Information Collection Activities; Comment request (pertaining to Medicare uniform institutional provider bill for reimbursement of covered services by all providers that accept assignment of claims).

66 FR 1997, January 10, 2001: HCFA Notice of OMB Approval (pertaining to uniform home health advance beneficiary notice).

66 FR 2912, January 12, 2001: HCFA Agency Information Collection Activities: Proposed Collection; Comment request (pertaining to Medicare/Medicaid health insurance common claim form).

66 FR 7919, January 26, 2001: HCFA Agency Information Collection Activities: Proposed Collection; Comment request (pertaining to provider Medicare agreements).

66 FR 8807, February 2, 2001: HCFA Agency Information Collection Activities: Proposed Collection; Comment request (pertaining to Medicare Federal health care programs provider/supplier enrollment application).

66 FR 18646, April 10, 2001: HCFA Agency Information Collection Activities: Submission for OMB Review; Comment request (pertaining to Medicare/Medicaid health insurance common claim form).

66 FR 20316, April 20, 2001: HCFA Agency Information Collection Activities: Submission for OMB Review; Comment request (pertaining to advance beneficiary notice by physicians, practitioners, suppliers, and providers about items and services denied by Medicare as not reasonable and necessary).

66 FR 20997, April 26, 2001: HCFA Agency Information Collection Activities: Submission for OMB Review; Comment request (pertaining to health insurance provider agreement form).

66 FR 21770, May 1, 2001: HCFA Agency Information Collection Activities: Submission for OMB Review; Comment request (pertaining to Medicare uniform institutional provider bill form).

66 FR 23944, May 10, 2001: HCFA Agency Information Collection Activities: Proposed Collection; Comment request (pertaining to financial reports for providers indebted to Medicare who want to repay over time).

66 FR 33102, June 20, 2001: HCFA Agency Information Collection Activities; Submission for OMB Review; Comment request (pertaining to provider/supplier enrollment application form).

See § 2:15.2.

§ 6:16 VIOLATING THE FREEZE ON PHYSICIAN FEES — Section 1842(j)(1) [42 U.S.C.A. 1395u(j)(1)]

Regulations

42 CFR Part 402 — Civil Money Penalties, Assessments, and Exclusions

42 CFR Part 405, Subpart C — Suspension of Payment, Recovery of Overpayments, and Repayment of Scholarships and Loans; and Subpart E — Criteria for Determination of Reasonable Charges

42 CFR Part 410 — Supplementary Medical Insurance (SMI) Benefits

42 CFR Part 414 — Payment for Part B Medical and Other Health Services

42 CFR Part 415 — Services Furnished by Physicians in Providers, Supervising Physicians in Teaching Settings, and Residents in Certain Settings

42 CFR Part 420 — Program Integrity: Medicare

42 CFR Part 424 — Conditions for Medicare Payment

42 CFR Part 498 — Appeals Procedures for Determinations that Affect Participation in the Medicare Program

42 CFR Chapter V — Office of Inspector General — Health Care, Department of Health and Human Services

Subchapter A — General Provisions

Part 1000 — Introduction; General Definitions

Subchapter B — OIG Authorities

Part 1001 — Program Integrity: Medicare and State Health Care Programs

Part 1002 — Program Integrity: State–initiated Exclusion from Medicaid

Part 1003 — Civil Money Penalties, Assessments and Exclusions

Part 1004 — Imposition of Sanctions on Health Care Practitioners and Providers of Health Care Services by a Peer Review Organization

Part 1005 — Appeals of Exclusions, Civil Money Penalties and Assessments

Part 1006 — Investigational Inquiries

Part 1007 — State Medicaid Fraud Control Units

Part 1008 — Advisory Opinions by the OIG

53 FR 53025, December 30, 1988: Medicare Program; Physician Liability on Non-assigned Claims — Proposed rule [To amend 42 CFR Part 405]

55 FR 18668, May 3, 1990: Medicare Program; Definition of Surgical Services — Notice of definition of surgical services for physician volume performance standard rates for increase with comment.

55 FR 24561, June 18, 1990: Medicare Program; Physician Liability on Non-Assigned Claims — Final rule affecting 42 CFR Parts 400 and 411. See also correction published at 55 FR 35142, August 28, 1990.

55 FR 36178, September 4, 1990: Medicare Program; Model Fee Schedule for Physicians' Services — Notice with comment period.

55 FR 53356, December 28, 1990: Medicare Program; Physician Performance Standard Rates of Increase for Federal Fiscal Year 1991 — Notice.

56 FR 699, January 8, 1991: Medicare Program; National Standardization of "Global Surgery" Policy — Proposed notice.

56 FR 61023, November 29, 1991: Medicare Program; Standard Claim Forms for Part B Claims Completed and Submitted by Physicians, Suppliers and Other Persons — General notice with comment period.

57 FR 36006, August 12, 1992: Medicare Program; Self-implementing Coverage and Payments Provisions: 1990 Legislation — Final rule with comment period, affecting 42 CFR Parts 405, 406, 409, 420, 411, 412, 413, 418, and 489. Pertains to capital-related inpatient hospital costs; capital-related outpatient hospital costs; non-capital related outpatient hospital costs; pay-

ment for physician pathology services; payment for services of physicians as assistants-at-surgery; payments for ambulatory surgical procedures in hospital outpatient departments; payments for radiology services performed in hospital outpatient departments; hospice benefit extension; enrollment of HMO members in Medicare Part A; coverage of ostomy supplies; application of pre-entitlement stay in psychiatric hospital to limit on payment for inpatient hospital services; payments to dialysis facilities; payment rates for erythropoietin (EPO); and Medicare secondary payer provision for individuals with ESRD. See also confirmation of final rule at 58 FR 58502, November 2, 1993.

57 FR 43462, September 21, 1992: Health Care Financing Administration Public Information Collection Requirements Submitted to the Office of Management and Budget for Clearance (pertaining to sole community home health agencies; physician/supplier overpayment reports; physician or supplier Medicare agreements; conditions of participation for rural health clinics; Medicare provider refunds; conditions of participation for comprehensive outpatient rehabilitation facilities; Medicaid income and eligibility verification system; Medicaid integrated review schedule; provider overpayment report; financial statement of Medicare provider debtors; negative case action review schedule for Medicaid quality control; outpatient resource costing study; Medicaid intermediate care facility for the mentally retarded or persons with related conditions survey report form; installment agreement of beneficiary refund of overpayment; PRO assumption of responsibilities; Medicare contractor administrative budget and cost reporting system forms; fire safety survey report forms; medical records review under prospective payment system; and Qualified Medicare Beneficiary supplement to the Medicare current beneficiary survey).

57 FR 46362, October 8, 1992: Medicare and Medicaid Programs; Revised Effective Date of Medicare/Medicaid Provider Agreement and Supplier Participation — Proposed rule affecting 42 CFR Parts 431, 440, 442, 488, 489, and 498.

See § 2:16.

§ 6:17 IMPROPER BILLING FOR SERVICES OF ASSISTANTS AT CATARACT AND OTHER TYPES OF SURGERY — Sections 1842(k)(1) and (2) [42 U.S.C.A. 1395u(k)(1) and (2)]

Regulations

42 CFR Part 402 — Civil Money Penalties, Assessments, and Exclusions

42 CFR Part 405, Subpart C — Suspension of Payment, Recovery of Overpayments, and Repayment of Scholarships and Loans; and Subpart E — Criteria for Determination of Reasonable Charges

42 CFR Part 410 — Supplementary Medical Insurance (SMI) Benefits

42 CFR Part 411 — Exclusions from Medicare and Limitations on Medicare Payment

42 CFR Part 414 — Payment for Part B Medical and Other Health Services

42 CFR Part 415 — Services Furnished by Physicians in Providers, Supervising Physicians in Teaching Settings, and Residents in Certain Settings

42 CFR Part 419 — Prospective Payment System for Hospital Outpatient Department Services

42 CFR Part 420 — Program Integrity: Medicare

42 CFR Part 424 — Conditions for Medicare Payment

42 CFR Part 466 — Utilization and Quality Control Review

42 CFR Part 476 — Acquisition, Protection, and Disclosure of Peer Review Information

42 CFR Part 498 — Appeals Procedures for Determinations that Affect Participation in the Medicare Program and for Determinations that Affect the Participation of ICF's/MR and Certain NF's in the Medicaid Program

42 CFR Chapter V — Office of Inspector General — Health Care, Department of Health and Human Services

Subchapter A — General Provisions

Part 1000 — Introduction; General Definitions

Subchapter B — OIG Authorities

Part 1001 — Program Integrity: Medicare

Part 1003 — Civil Money Penalties and Assessments

Part 1004 — Imposition of Sanctions on Health Care Practitioners and Providers of Health Care Services by a Peer Review Organization

Part 1005 — Appeals of Exclusions, Civil Money Penalties and Assessments

Part 1006 — Investigational Inquiries

Part 1007 — State Medicaid Fraud Control Units

Part 1008 — Advisory Opinions by the OIG

55 FR 18668, May 3, 1990: Medicare Program; Definition of Surgical Services — Notice of definition of surgical services for physician volume performance standard rates for increase with comment.

55 FR 33697, August 17, 1990: Medicare Program; Payment for Outpatient Surgery at Eye Specialty Hospitals and Eye and Ear Specialty Hospitals — Final rule affecting 42 CFR Part 413. See also correction published at 55 FR 34797, August 24, 1990.

55 FR 36178, September 4, 1990: Medicare Program; Model Fee Schedule for Physicians' Services — Notice with comment period.

55 FR 46689, November 6, 1990: Medicare Program; Limit on Payment for the Cost of Intraocular Lens Furnished by a Hospital on Outpatient Basis — Proposed rule.

56 FR 699, January 8, 1991: Medicare Program; National Standardization of "Global Surgery" Policy — Proposed notice.

56 FR 19874, April 30, 1991: Medicare Program; Withdrawal of Coverage of Certain Investigational Intraocular Lenses — Final notice.

56 FR 25792, June 5, 1991: Medicare Program; Fee Schedule for Physicians' Services — Proposed rule affecting 42 CFR Parts 405 and 415.

56 FR 59502, November 25, 1991: Medicare Program; Fee Schedule for Physicians' Services, Fee Schedule Update for Calendar Year 1992 and Physician Performance Standard Rates of Increase for Federal FY 1992 — Final rules and notice affecting 42 CFR Parts 405, 413, 414, and 415. See also correction at 57 FR 42491, September 15, 1992.

56 FR 61023, November 29, 1991: Medicare Program; Standard Claim Forms for Part B Claims Completed and Submitted by Physicians, Suppliers and Other Persons — General notice with comment period.

57 FR 46362, October 8, 1992: Medicare and Medicaid Programs; Revised Effective Date of Medicare/Medicaid Provider Agreement

and Supplier Participation — Proposed rule affecting 42 CFR Parts 431, 440, 442, 488, 489, and 498.

57 FR 55914, November 25, 1992: Medicare Program; Fee Schedule for Physicians' Services for Calendar Year 1993 — Final notice with comment period. See also corrections published at 57 FR 59379, December 15, 1992, and at 58 FR 31964, June 7, 1993.

58 FR 63626, December 2, 1993: Medicare Program; Revisions to Payment Policies and Adjustments to the Relative Value Units under the Physician Fee Schedule for Calendar Year 1994 — Final rule with comment period, affecting 42 CFR Parts 405 and 414. See also correction at 59 FR 36069, July 15, 1994.

58 FR 63856, December 2, 1993: Medicare Program; Physician Performance Standard Rates of Increase for Federal Fiscal Year 1994 and Physician Fee Schedule Update for Calendar Year 1994 — Final notice with comment period. See also correction at 59 FR 26410, June 1, 1994.

59 FR 26955, May 25, 1994: Medicare Program; Self-implementing Coverage and Payment Provisions: 1993 Legislation — Final rule with comment period (pertaining to reductions in payments for skilled nursing facility services — return on equity; reductions in payments for hospice services; reduction in Part A premium for certain individuals with 30 or more quarters of Social Security coverage; extension of 10 percent reduction in payments for capital-related costs of outpatient hospital services; extension of reduction in payments for other costs for outpatient hospital services; reduction in payments for intraocular lenses; payment for parenteral and enteral nutrients, supplies and equipment during 1994 and 1995; increase in annual cap on amount of Medicare payment for outpatient physical therapy and occupational therapy services; rural health clinics and Federally qualified health centers; reduction in payments for Epoetin; and changes in Part B premium.)

59 FR 32754, June 24, 1994: Medicare Program; Refinements to Geographic Adjustment Factor Values and Other Policies under the Physician Fee Schedule — Proposed rule affection 42 CFR parts 410 and 414.

59 FR 39828, August 4, 1994: Medicare Program; Payment Policies and Adjustments to the Relative Value Units Under the Physician Fee Schedule for Calendar Year 1994, affecting 42 CFR Parts 405 and 414.

59 FR 56500, November 14, 1994: HCFA Public Information Collection Requirements Submitted to the Office of Management

and Budget (OMB) for Clearance (pertaining to monitoring and evaluation of Medicare cataract surgery alternate payment demonstration, form for listing deficiencies for laboratory surveys, form for personnel requirements for laboratory CLIA certification, and CLIA reinstatement form).

59 FR 63410, December 8, 1994: Medicare Program; Refinements to Geographic Adjustment Factor Values, Revisions to Payment Policies, Adjustments to the Relative Value Units (RVUs) under the Physician Fee Schedule for Calendar Year 1995, and the 5-Year Refinement of RVUs — Final rule with comment period, affecting 42 CFR parts 410 and 414. See also correction at 60 FR 46, January 3, 1995. See also correction at 60 FR 36733, July 18, 1995.

59 FR 63638, December 8, 1994: Medicare Program; Physician Fee Schedule Update for Calendar Year 1995 and Physician Volume Performance Standard Rates of Increase for Federal Fiscal Year 1995 — Final notice.

60 FR 38400, July 26, 1995: Medicare Program; Revisions to Payment Policies under the Physician Fee Schedule for Calendar Year 1996 — Proposed rule affecting 42 CFR Parts 400, 405, 410, 411, 412, 413, 414, 415, 417, and 489.

60 FR 39403, August 2, 1995: HCFA Public Information Collection Requirements Submitted for Public Comment and Recommendations (pertaining to PRO reporting forms; Oregon Medicaid reform demonstration; review functions of PRO's; medical records review under PPS; evaluation of Medicare cataract surgery alternate payment demonstration; home health agency survey and deficiencies report; CLIA survey forms; field testing of uniform needs assessment instrument for hospital discharge planning).

60 FR 45778, September 1, 1995: Medicare Program; Changes to the Hospital Inpatient Prospective Payment Systems and Fiscal Year 1996 Rates — Final rule affecting 42 CFR Part 412, 413, 424, 485, and 489.

60 FR 52396, October 6, 1995: Medicare Program; Limitations on Medicare Coverage of Cataract Surgery — Proposed notice.

61 FR 16925, April 18, 1996: HCFA Agency Information Collection Activities: Proposed Collection; Comment Request (pertaining to Medicare participating physician or supplier agreements; and hospital conditions of participation).

61 FR 19992, May 3, 1996: Medicare Program; Five-year Review of Work Relative Value Units under the Physician Fee Schedule — Proposed notice.

61 FR 37487, July 18, 1996: HCFA Agency Information Collection Activities: Submission for OMB Review; Comment request (pertaining to cost reports for independent rural health centers and freestanding federally qualified health centers; and conditions of participation for portable x-ray suppliers).

61 FR 59490, November 22, 1996: Medicare Program; Revisions to Payment Policies and Five-year Review of and Adjustments to the Relative Value Units under the Physician Fee Schedule for Calendar Year 1997 — Final rule with comment period, affecting 42 CFR Parts 410and 415. See also correction at 62 FR 7945, February 21, 1997.

61 FR 59717, November 22, 1996: Medicare Program; Physician Fee Schedule Update for Calendar year 1997 and Physician Volume Performance Standard Rates of Increase for Federal Fiscal Year 1997 — Final notice.

62 FR 7350, February 19, 1997: Office of Inspector General: Medicare and State Health Care Programs: Fraud and Abuse; Issuance of Advisory Opinions by the OIG — Interim final rule with comment period, affecting 42 CFR Part 1008.

62 FR 33158, June 18, 1997: Medicare Program; Revisions to Payment Policies Under the Physician Fee Schedule, Other Part B Payment Policies, and Establishment of the Clinical Psychologist Fee Schedule for Calendar year 1998, Proposed rule affecting 42 CFR Parts 400, 405, 410, and 414.

62 FR 46698, September 4, 1997: Medicare Program; Adjustment in Payment Amounts for New Technology Intraocular Lenses — Proposed rule affecting 42 CFR Part 416.

62 FR 49048, October 31, 1997: Medicare Program; Revisions to Payment Policies and Adjustments to the Relative Value Units Under the Physician Fee Schedule, Other Part B Payment Policies, and Establishment of the Clinical Psychologist Fee Schedule for Calendar Year 1998. See also correction of final rule with comment period at 63 FR 4595, January 30, 1998

63 FR 7743, February 17, 1998: Medicare and Medicaid Programs; Hospital Conditions of Participation; Provider Agreements and Supplier Approval — Notice of extension of comment period, affecting 42 CFR Parts 416, 482, 485, and 489.

63 FR 8462, February 19, 1998: Medicare Program; Update of Ambulatory Surgical Center Payment Rates Effective for Services on or after October 1, 1997 — Notice

63 FR 10920, March 5, 1998: HCFA Emergency Clearance: Public Information Collection Requirements Submitted to the Office of Management and Budget (OMB) (pertaining to Medicare and other Federal health care program provider and supplier application forms).

63 FR 19502, April 20, 1998: HCFA Agency Information Collection Activities: Proposed collection; Comment request (pertaining to annual early and periodic screening, diagnostic, and treatment services (EPSDT) participation report; Medicare and other health care programs provider/supplier enrollment application; and research and analytic support for implementing performance measurement in Medicare fee for service).

63 FR 25320, May 7, 1998: HCFA National Standard Health Care Provider Identifier — Proposed Rule affecting 45 CFR Part 142.

63 FR 30818, June 5, 1998: Medicare Program; Revisions to Payment Policies under the Physician Fee Schedule for Calendar Year 1999 — Proposed rule, affecting 42 CFR Parts 405, 410, 413, 414, 415, 424, and 485. See also correction at 63 FR 50545, September 22, 1998.

63 FR 32290, June 12, 1998: Medicare Program; Update of Rate-setting Methodology, Payment Rates, Payment Policies, and the List of Covered Surgical Procedures for Ambulatory Surgical Centers Effective October 1, 1998 — Proposed rule affecting 42 CFR Parts 416 and 488.

63 FR 36250, July 2, 1998: HCFA Agency Information Collection Activities; Submission for OMB review; Comment request (pertaining to provider/supplier enrollment applications).

63 FR 58814, November 2, 1998: Medicare Program; Revisions to Payment Policies and Adjustments to the Relative Value Units under the Physician Fee Schedule for Calendar Year 1999 — Final rule with comment period, affecting 42 CFR 405, 410, 413, 414, 415, 424, and 485. See also correction at 64 FR 25456, May 12, 1999.

1999

64 FR 1813, January 12, 1999: Office of Inspector General Publication of OIG Special Fraud Alert on Physician Liability for Certifications in the Provision of Medical Equipment and Supplies and Home Health Services — Notice.

64 FR 5666, February 4, 1999: HCFA Emergency Clearance: Public Information Collection Requirements Submitted to the Office of

Management and Budget (OMB) (pertaining to the Medicare/Medicaid health insurance common claim form).

64 FR 10478, March 4, 1999: HCFA Agency Information Collection Activities: Proposed Collection; Comment request (pertaining to refunds to patients from physicians when Medicare does not provide coverage for the physician services provided).

64 FR 17673, April 12, 1999: HCFA Agency Information Collection Activities: Proposed Collection; Comment request (pertaining to Medicare participating physician or supplier agreements).

64 FR 23845, May 4, 1999: HCFA Agency Information Collection Activities: Proposed Collection; Comment request (pertaining to Medicare geographical classification review board procedures).

64 FR 24956, May 10, 1999: Medicare and Medicaid Programs; Effective Dates of Provider Agreements and Supplier Approvals — Correction restoring regulations inadvertently removed when a final rule concerning effective dates for provider agreements and supplier approvals was published at 62 FR 43931, August 18, 1997.

64 FR 29049, May 28, 1999: HCFA Agency Information Collection Activities: Proposed Collection; Comment request (pertaining to Medicare credit balance reporting requirements for Medicare providers who have been overpaid).

64 FR 32239, June 16, 1999: HCFA Agency Information Collection Activities: Submission for OMB Review; Comment request (pertaining to the requirement that physicians must notify beneficiaries that Medicare is likely to deny payment for a specified service).

64 FR 36321, July 6, 1999: Medicare Program; Update of Ratesetting Methodology, Payment Rates, Payment Policies, and the List of Covered Procedures for Ambulatory Surgical Centers Effective October 1, 1998 — Notice of extension of comment period for proposed rule affecting 42 CFR Parts 416 and 488.

64 FR 39517, July 22, 1999: HCFA Agency Information Collection Activities: Submission for OM B Review; Comment request (pertaining to Medicare participating physician or supplier agreement form HCFA-460).

64 FR 40017, July 23, 1999: HCFA Agency Information Collection Activities: Submission for OMB Review; Comment request (pertaining to Medicare geographical classification review board procedures and criteria).

64 FR 40534, July 27, 1999: Medicare Program; Replacement of Reasonable Charge Methodology by Fee Schedules — Proposed action affecting 42 CFR 414.

64 FR 48846, September 8, 1999: Office of Inspector General: Solicitation of Information and Recommendations for Developing OIG Compliance Program Guidance for Individual Physicians and Small Group Practices — Notice.

64 FR 57431, October 25, 1999: Medicare Program; Appeals of Carrier Determinations that a Supplier Fails to Meet the Requirements for Medicare Billing Privileges — Proposed rule affecting 42 CFR Part 405.

64 FR 59380, November 2, 1999: Medicare Program; Revisions to Payment Policies under the Physician Fee Schedule for Calendar Year 2000 — Final rule with comment period, affecting 42 CFR Parts 410, 411, 414, 415, and 485. See also correction at 65 FR 19329, April 11, 2000.

64 FR 71148, December 20, 1999: Medicare Program; Adjustment in Payment Amounts for New Technology Intraocular Lenses Furnished by Ambulatory Surgical Centers — Notice with comment period.

2000

65 FR 5354, February 3, 2000: HCFA Agency Information Collection Activities: Proposed Collection; Comment request (pertaining to standardized Medicare/Medicaid claim form for reimbursement of covered services).

65 FR 25738, May 3, 2000: Medicare Program; Lenses Eligible for an Adjustment in Payment Amount for New Technology Intraocular Lenses Furnished by Ambulatory Surgical Centers.

65 FR 25939, May 4, 2000: HCFA Agency Information Collection Activities: Proposed Collection; Comment request (pertaining to ambulatory surgical center payment rate survey).

65 FR 36818, June 12, 2000: Office of Inspector General: Draft OIG Compliance Program for Individual and Small Group Physician Practices — Notice and comment period.

65 FR 42021, July 7, 2000: HCFA Agency Information Collection Activities: Proposed Collection; Comment request (pertaining to notice to providers, suppliers, and practitioners about non-covered services to beneficiaries).

65 FR 42022, July 7, 2000: Medicare Program; Question and Answer Session on July 24, 2000, to Discuss Remaining Concerns about the Implementation of the Hospital Outpatient Prospective Payment System (PPS) — Notice of meeting.

65 FR 44176, July 17, 2000: Medicare Program; Revisions to Payment Policies under the Physician Fee Schedule for Calendar Year 2001 — Proposed rule affection 42 CFR Parts 410 and 414.

65 FR 47670, August 3, 2000: Medicare Program; Prospective Payment System for Hospital Outpatient Services: Revisions to Criteria to Define New or Innovative Medical Devices, Drugs, and Biologicals Eligible for Pass-Through Payments and Corrections to the Criteria for the Grandfather Provision for Certain Federally Qualified Health Centers-Interim final rule with comment period, affecting 42 CFR Parts 413 and 419.

65 FR 47706, August 3, 2000: Medicare Program; Prospective Payment System for Hospital Outpatient Services: Revision of the Provider-based Location Criteria for Certain PPS-exempt Facilities — Proposed rule affecting 42 CFR Part 413.

65 FR 50312, August 17, 2000: Office of the Secretary; Health Insurance Reform: Standards for Electronic Transactions — Final rule affecting 45 CFR Parts 160 and 162.

65 FR 53963, September 6, 2000: Medicare Program: Appeals of Carrier Determinations that a Physician or Other Supplier Fails to Meet the Requirements for Medicare Billing Privileges; Reopening of Comment Period — Notice of reopening of comment period for proposed rule affecting 42 CFR Part 405.

65 FR 59434, October 5, 2000: Office of Inspector General Compliance Program for Individual and Small Group Physician Practices — Notice.

65 FR 64227, October 26, 2000: HCFA Agency Information Collection Activities: Proposed Collection; Comment Request; Public Information Collection Meeting to Discuss Proposed Revisions (pertaining to notice requirements from suppliers, physicians, and practitioners to beneficiaries when Medicare Part B payment may be denied).

65 FR 65376, November 1, 2000: Medicare Program; Revisions to Payment Policies under the Physician Fee Schedule for Calendar Year 2001—Final rule with comment period. See also correction at 66 FR 16607, March 27, 2001.

65 FR 65603, November 1, 2000: Medicare Program; Revisions to Payment Policies under the Physician Fee Schedule for Calendar Year 2001 — Final rule with comment period.

2001

66 FR 1996, January 10, 2001: HCFA Agency Information Collection Activities; Comment request (pertaining to Medicare uniform institutional provider bill for reimbursement of covered services by all providers that accept assignment of claims).

66 FR 2912, January 12, 2001: HCFA Agency Information Collection Activities: Proposed Collection; Comment request (pertaining to Medicare/Medicaid health insurance common claim form).

66 FR 8807, February 2, 2001: HCFA Agency Information Collection Activities: Proposed Collection; Comment request (pertaining to Medicare Federal health care programs provider/supplier enrollment application).

66 FR 18646, April 10, 2001: HCFA Agency Information Collection Activities: Submission for OMB Review; Comment request (pertaining to Medicare/Medicaid health insurance common claim form).

66 FR 18959, April 12, 2001: Medicare Program; Annual Review of the Appropriateness of Payment Amounts for New Technology Intraocular Lenses (NTIOLs) Furnished by Ambulatory Surgical Centers (ASCs)—Notice.

66 FR 20316, April 20, 2001: HCFA Agency Information Collection Activities: Submission for OMB Review; Comment request (pertaining to advance beneficiary notice by physicians, practitioners, suppliers, and providers about items and services denied by Medicare as not reasonable and necessary).

66 FR 20997, April 26, 2001: HCFA Agency Information Collection Activities: Submission for OMB Review; Comment request (pertaining to health insurance provider agreement form).

66 FR 21770, May 1, 2001: HCFA Agency Information Collection Activities: Submission for OMB Review; Comment request (pertaining to Medicare uniform institutional provider bill form).

66 FR 31038, June 8, 2001: Medicare Program; Five–year Review of Work Relative Value Units under the Physician Fee Schedule—Proposed notice.

66 FR 33102, June 20, 2001: HCFA Agency Information Collection Activities; Submission for OMB Review; Comment request (pertaining to provider/supplier enrollment application form).

See § 2:17.

§ 6:18 WRONGFUL CHARGES BY NONPARTICIPATING PHYSICIANS — Section 1842(l) [42 U.S.C.A. 1395u(l)]

Regulations

42 CFR Part 402 — Civil Money Penalties, Assessments, and Exclusions

42 CFR Part 405, Subpart C — Suspension of Payment, Recovery of Overpayments, and Repayment of Scholarships and Loans; Subpart D — Private Contracts; and Subpart E — Criteria for Determination of Reasonable Charges

42 CFR Part 410 — Supplementary Medical Insurance (SMI) Benefits

42 CFR Part 411 — Exclusions from Medicare and Limitations on Medicare Payment

42 CFR Part 414 — Payment for Part B Medical and Other Health Services

42 CFR Part 415 — Services Furnished by Physicians in Providers, Supervising Physicians in Teaching Settings, and Residents in Certain Settings

42 CFR Part 420 — Program Integrity: Medicare

42 CFR Part 424 — Conditions for Medicare Payment

42 CFR Part 498 — Appeals Procedures for Determinations that Affect Participation in the Medicare Program and for Determinations that Affect the Participation of ICF's/MR and Certain NF's in the Medicaid Program

42 CFR Chapter V — Office of Inspector General — Health Care, Department of Health and Human Services

Subchapter A — General Provisions

Part 1000 — Introduction; General Definitions

Subchapter B — OIG Authorities

Part 1001 — Program Integrity: Medicare and State Health Care Programs

Part 1002 — Program Integrity: State– initiated Exclusion from Medicaid

Part 1003 — Civil Money Penalties, Assessments and Exclusions

Part 1004 — Imposition of Sanctions on Health Care Practitioners and Providers of Health Care Services by a Peer Review Organization

Part 1005 — Appeals of Exclusions, Civil Money Penalties and Assessments

Part 1006 — Investigational Inquiries
Part 1007 — State Medicaid Fraud Control Units
Part 1008 — Advisory Opinions by the OIG

53 FR 53025, December 30, 1988: Medicare Program; Physician Liability on Non-assigned Claims — Proposed rule to amend 42 CFR Part 405.

55 FR 24561, June 18, 1990: Medicare Program; Physician Liability on Non-assigned Claims — Final rule affecting 42 CFR Parts 400 and 411. See also correction published at 55 FR 35142, August 28, 1990.

55 FR 36178, September 4, 1990: Medicare Program; Model Fee Schedule for Physicians' Services — Notice with comment period.

55 FR 42907, October 24, 1990: Medicare Program; Standards Applied by Utilization and Quality Control Peer Review Organizations: Consideration of Remote Rural Location and Other Relevant Factors — Notice of policy and request for comments.

56 FR 699, January 8, 1991: Medicare Program; National Standardization of "Global Surgery" Policy — Proposed notice.

56 FR 25792, June 5, 1991: Medicare Program; Fee Schedule for Physicians' Services — Proposed rule affecting 42 CFR Parts 405 and 415.

56 FR 59502, November 25, 1991: Medicare Program; Fee Schedule for Physicians' Services, Fee Schedule Update for Calendar Year 1992 and Physician Performance Standard Rates of Increase for Federal FY 1992 — Final rules and notice affecting 42 CFR Parts 405, 413, 414, and 415. See also correction at 57 FR 42491, September 15, 1992.

56 FR 61023, November 29, 1991: Medicare Program; Standard Claim Forms for Part B Claims Completed and Submitted by Physicians, Suppliers and Other Persons — General notice with comment period.

57 FR 46362, October 8, 1992: Medicare and Medicaid Programs; Revised Effective Date of Medicare/Medicaid Provider Agreement and Supplier Participation — Proposed rule affecting 42 CFR Parts 431, 440, 442, 488, 489, and 498.

57 FR 55914, November 25, 1992: Medicare Program; Fee Schedule for Physicians' Services for Calendar Year 1993 — Final notice with comment period. See also corrections published at 57 FR 59379, December 15, 1992, and at 58 FR 31964, June 7, 1993.

58 FR 63626, December 2, 1993: Medicare Program; Revisions to Payment Policies and Adjustments to the Relative Value Units

under the Physician Fee Schedule for Calendar Year 1994 — Final rule with comment period, affecting 42 CFR Parts 405 and 414. See also correction at 59 FR 36069, July 15, 1994.

58 FR 63856, December 2, 1993: Medicare Program; Physician Performance Standard Rates of Increase for Federal Fiscal Year 1994 and Physician Fee Schedule Update for Calendar Year 1994 — Final notice with comment period. See also correction at 59 FR 26410, June 1, 1994.

59 FR 32754, June 24, 1994: Medicare Program; Refinements to Geographic Adjustment Factor Values and Other Policies under the Physician Fee Schedule — Proposed rule affection 42 CFR parts 410 and 414.

59 FR 39828, August 4, 1994: Medicare Program; Payment Policies and Adjustments to the Relative Value Units Under the Physician Fee Schedule for Calendar Year 1994, affecting 42 CFR Parts 405 and 414.

59 FR 63410, December 8, 1994: Medicare Program; Refinements to Geographic Adjustment Factor Values, Revisions to Payment Policies, Adjustments to the Relative Value Units (RVUs) under the Physician Fee Schedule for Calendar Year 1995, and the 5-Year Refinement of RVUs — Final rule with comment period, affecting 42 CFR parts 410 and 414. See also correction at 60 FR 46, January 3, 1995. See also correction at 60 FR 36733, July 18, 1995.

59 FR 63638, December 8, 1994: Medicare Program; Physician Fee Schedule Update for Calendar Year 1995 and Physician Volume Performance Standard Rates of Increase for Federal Fiscal Year 1995 — Final notice.

60 FR 38400, July 26, 1995: Medicare Program; Revisions to Payment Policies under the Physician Fee Schedule for Calendar Year 1996 — Proposed rule affecting 42 CFR Parts 400, 405, 410, 411, 412, 413, 414, 415, 417, and 489.

60 FR 63124, December 8, 1995: Medicare Program; Revisions to Payment Policies and Adjustments to the Relative Value Units under the Physician Fee Schedule for Calendar Year 1996 — Final rule with comment period, affecting 42 CFR Parts 400, 405, 410, 411, 412, 413, 414, 415, 417, and 489.

61 FR 6645, February 21, 1996: HCFA Agency Information Collection Activities: Proposed Collection; Comment Request (pertaining to survey forms to evaluate Federally qualified health centers; and the Medicare Carrier provider/supplier application form).

61 FR 13205, March 26, 1996: HCFA Agency Information Collection Activities: Submission for OMB Review; Comment Request (pertaining to Medicare standardized forms for reimbursement of covered services by all providers that accept Medicare assignment).

61 FR 16925, April 18, 1996: HCFA Agency Information Collection Activities: Proposed Collection; Comment Request (pertaining to Medicare participating physician or supplier agreements; and hospital conditions of participation).

61 FR 19628, May 2, 1996: HCFA Agency Information Collection Activities: Proposed Collection; Comment Request (pertaining to permissible billing for physicians that do not accept Medicare assignments).

61 FR 19992, May 3, 1996: Medicare Program; Five-year Review of Work Relative Value Units under the Physician Fee Schedule — Proposed notice.

61 FR 20528, May 7, 1996: HCFA Privacy Act of 1974; System of Records (pertaining to the Medicare physician identification and eligibility system).

61 FR 37487, July 18, 1996: HCFA Agency Information Collection Activities: Submission for OMB Review; Comment request (pertaining to cost reports for independent rural health centers and freestanding federally qualified health centers; and conditions of participation for portable x-ray suppliers).

61 FR 38454, July 24, 1996: HCFA Agency Information Collection Activities: Submission for OMB Review; Comment request (pertaining to physicians who do not accept Medicare assignment).

61 FR 59490, November 22, 1996: Medicare Program; Revisions to Payment Policies and Five-year Review of and Adjustments to the Relative value Units under the Physician Fee Schedule for Calendar yeat 1997 — Final rule with comment period, affecting 42 CFR Parts 410and 415. See also correction at 62 FR 7945, February 21, 1997.

61 FR 59717, November 22, 1996: Medicare Program; Physician Fee Schedule Update for Calendar year 1997 and Physician Volume Performance Standard Rates of Increase for Federal Fiscal Year 1997 — Final notice.

62 FR 8744, February 26, 1997: HCFA Agency Information Collection Activities: Submission for OMB Review; Comment request (pertaining to Medicare provider/supplier enrollment application).

62 FR 24483, May 5, 1997: Medicare Program; Update of the Reasonable Compensation Equivalent Limits for Services Furnished by Physicians — Notice.

62 FR 33158, June 18, 1997: Medicare Program; Revisions to Payment Policies Under the Physician fee Schedule, Other Part B Payment Policies, and Establishment of the Clinical Psychologist Fee Schedule for Calendar year 1998, Proposed rule affecting 42 CFR Parts 400, 405, 410, and 414. Psychologist Fee Schedule for Calendar year 1998, Proposed rule affecting 42 CFR Parts 400, 405, 410, and 414. See also correction at 62 FR 43962, August 18, 1997.

62 FR 59261, October 31, 1997: Medicare Program; Physician Fee Schedule Conversion Factor for Calendar Year 1998 and Sustainable Growth Rate for Fiscal Year 1998 — Final notice.

62 FR 59267, October 31, 1997: Medicare Program; Delay in Implementing the Adjustments to the Practice Expense Relative Value Units under the Physician Fee Schedule for Calendar Year 1998 — Notice of intent to regulate.

63 FR 10920, March 5, 1998: HCFA Emergency Clearance: Public Information Collection Requirements Submitted to the Office of Management and Budget (OMB) (pertaining to Medicare and other Federal health care program provider and supplier application forms).

63 FR 19502, April 20, 1998: HCFA Agency Information Collection Activities: Proposed collection; Comment request (pertaining to annual early and periodic screening, diagnostic, and treatment services (EPSDT) participation report; Medicare and other health care programs provider/supplier enrollment application; and research and analytic support for implementing performance measurement in Medicare fee for service).

63 FR 25320, May 7, 1998: HCFA National Standard Health Care Provider Identifier — Proposed Rule affecting 45 CFR Part 142.

63 FR 28394, May 22, 1998: HCFA Agency Information Collection Activities: Proposed Collection; Comment request (pertaining to application for health insurance forms).

63 FR 30818, June 5, 1998: Medicare Program; Revisions to Payment Policies under the Physician Fee Schedule for Calendar Year 1999 — Proposed rule, affecting 42 CFR Parts 405, 410, 413, 414, 415, 424, and 485. See also correction at 63 FR 50545, September 22, 1998.

63 FR 36250, July 2, 1998: HCFA Agency Information Collection Activities; Submission for OMB review; Comment request (pertaining to provider/supplier enrollment applications).

63 FR 58814, November 2, 1998: Medicare Program; Revisions to Payment Policies and Adjustments to the Relative Value Units

under the Physician Fee Schedule for Calendar Year 1999— Final rule with comment period, affecting 42 CFR 405, 410, 413, 414, 415, 424, and 485. See also correction at 64 FR 25456, May 12, 1999.

1999

64 FR 1813, January 12, 1999: Office of Inspector General Publication of OIG Special Fraud Alert on Physician Liability for Certifications in the Provision of Medical Equipment and Supplies and Home Health Services — Notice.

64 FR 5666, February 4, 1999: HCFA Emergency Clearance: Public Information Collection Requirements Submitted to the Office of Management and Budget (OMB) (pertaining to the Medicare/Medicaid health insurance common claim form).

64 FR 10478, March 4, 1999: HCFA Agency Information Collection Activities: Proposed Collection; Comment request (pertaining to refunds to patients from physicians when Medicare does not provide coverage for the physician services provided).

64 FR 17673, April 12, 1999: HCFA Agency Information Collection Activities: Proposed Collection; Comment request (pertaining to Medicare participating physician or supplier agreements).

64 FR 23845, May 4, 1999: HCFA Agency Information Collection Activities: Proposed Collection; Comment request (pertaining to Medicare geographical classification review board procedures).

64 FR 24956, May 10, 1999: Medicare and Medicaid Programs; Effective Dates of Provider Agreements and Supplier Approvals-Correction restoring regulations inadvertently removed when a final rule concerning effective dates for provider agreements and supplier approvals was published at 62 FR 43931, August 18, 1997.

64 FR 29049, May 28, 1999: HCFA Agency Information Collection Activities: Proposed Collection; Comment request (pertaining to Medicare credit balance reporting requirements for Medicare providers who have been overpaid).

64 FR 32239, June 16, 1999: HCFA Agency Information Collection Activities: Submission for OMB Review; Comment request (pertaining to the requirement that physicians must notify beneficiaries that Medicare is likely to deny payment for a specified service).

64 FR 36321, July 6, 1999: Medicare Program; Update of Ratesetting Methodology, Payment Rates, Payment Policies, and the List of Covered Procedures for Ambulatory Surgical Centers Effective October 1, 1998 — Notice of extension of comment period for proposed rule affecting 42 CFR Parts 416 and 488.

64 FR 39517, July 22, 1999: HCFA Agency Information Collection Activities: Submission for OM B Review; Comment request (pertaining to Medicare participating physician or supplier agreement form HCFA-460).

64 FR 40017, July 23, 1999: HCFA Agency Information Collection Activities: Submission for OMB Review; Comment request (pertaining to Medicare geographical classification review board procedures and criteria).

64 FR 40534, July 27, 1999: Medicare Program; Replacement of Reasonable Charge Methodology by Fee Schedules — Proposed action affecting 42 CFR 414.

64 FR 48846, September 8, 1999: Office of Inspector General: Solicitation of Information and Recommendations for Developing OIG Compliance Program Guidance for Individual Physicians and Small Group Practices — Notice.

64 FR 57431, October 25, 1999: Medicare Program; Appeals of Carrier Determinations that a Supplier Fails to Meet the Requirements for Medicare Billing Privileges — Proposed rule affecting 42 CFR Part 405.

64 FR 59380, November 2, 1999: Medicare Program; Revisions to Payment Policies under the Physician Fee Schedule for Calendar Year 2000 — Final rule with comment period, affecting 42 CFR Parts 410, 411, 414, 415, and 485.

64 FR 71148, December 20, 1999: Medicare Program; Adjustment in Payment Amounts for New Technology Intraocular Lenses Furnished by Ambulatory Surgical Centers — Notice with comment period.

2000

65 FR 5354, February 3, 2000: HCFA Agency Information Collection Activities: Proposed Collection; Comment request (pertaining to standardized Medicare/Medicaid claim form for reimbursement of covered services).

65 FR 30414, May 11, 2000: HCFA Agency Information Collection Activities: Submission for OMB Review; Comment request (pertaining to health insurance common claims form).

65 FR 36818, June 12, 2000: Office of Inspector General: Draft OIG Compliance Program for Individual and Small Group Physician Practices — Notice and comment period.

65 FR 42021, July 7, 2000: HCFA Agency Information Collection Activities: Proposed Collection; Comment request (pertaining to notice to providers, suppliers, and practitioners about non-covered services to beneficiaries).

65 FR 42022, July 7, 2000: Medicare Program; Question and Answer Session on July 24, 2000, to Discuss Remaining Concerns about the Implementation of the Hospital Outpatient Prospective Payment System (PPS) — Notice of meeting.

65 FR 44176, July 17, 2000: Medicare Program; Revisions to Payment Policies under the Physician Fee Schedule for Calendar Year 2001 — Proposed rule affection 42 CFR Parts 410 and 414.

65 FR 47670, August 3, 2000: Medicare Program; Prospective Payment System for Hospital Outpatient Services: Revisions to Criteria to Define New or Innovative Medical Devices, Drugs, and Biologicals Eligible for Pass-Through Payments and Corrections to the Criteria for the Grandfather Provision for Certain Federally Qualified Health Centers-Interim final rule with comment period, affecting 42 CFR Parts 413 and 419.

65 FR 47706, August 3, 2000: Medicare Program; Prospective Payment System for Hospital Outpatient Services: Revision of the Provider-based Location Criteria for Certain PPS-exempt Facilities — Proposed rule affecting 42 CFR Part 413.

65 FR 50312, August 17, 2000: Office of the Secretary; Health Insurance Reform: Standards for Electronic Transactions — Final rule affecting 45 CFR Parts 160 and 162.

65 FR 53963, September 6, 2000: Medicare Program: Appeals of Carrier Determinations that a Physician or Other Supplier Fails to Meet the Requirements for Medicare Billing Privileges; Reopening of Comment Period — Notice of reopening of comment period for proposed rule affecting 42 CFR Part 405.

65 FR 59434, October 5, 2000: Office of Inspector General Compliance Program for Individual and Small Group Physician Practices — Notice.

65 FR 64227, October 26, 2000: HCFA Agency Information Collection Activities: Proposed Collection; Comment Request; Public Information Collection Meeting to Discuss Proposed Revisions (pertaining to notice requirements from suppliers, physicians, and practitioners to beneficiaries when Medicare Part B payment may be denied).

65 FR 65376, November 1, 2000: Medicare Program; Revisions to Payment Policies under the Physician Fee Schedule for Calendar

Year 2001—Final rule with comment period. See also correction at 66 FR 16607, March 27, 2001.

65 FR 65603, November 1, 2000: Medicare Program; Revisions to Payment Policies under the Physician Fee Schedule for Calendar Year 2001 — Final rule with comment period.

2001

66 FR 1996, January 10, 2001: HCFA Agency Information Collection Activities; Comment request (pertaining to Medicare uniform institutional provider bill for reimbursement of covered services by all providers that accept assignment of claims).

66 FR 1997, January 10, 2001: HCFA Notice of OMB Approval (pertaining to uniform home health advance beneficiary notice).

66 FR 2912, January 12, 2001: HCFA Agency Information Collection Activities: Proposed Collection; Comment request (pertaining to Medicare/Medicaid health insurance common claim form).

66 FR 8807, February 2, 2001: HCFA Agency Information Collection Activities: Proposed Collection; Comment request (pertaining to Medicare Federal health care programs provider/supplier enrollment application).

66 FR 16061, March 22, 2001: HCFA Agency Information Collection Activities: Proposed Collection; Comment request (pertaining to private contracts of physicians who opt out of Medicare).

66 FR 18646, April 10, 2001: HCFA Agency Information Collection Activities: Submission for OMB Review; Comment request (pertaining to Medicare/Medicaid health insurance common claim form).

66 FR 20316, April 20, 2001: HCFA Agency Information Collection Activities: Submission for OMB Review; Comment request (pertaining to advance beneficiary notice by physicians, practitioners, suppliers, and providers about items and services denied by Medicare as not reasonable and necessary).

66 FR 20997, April 26, 2001: HCFA Agency Information Collection Activities: Submission for OMB Review; Comment request (pertaining to health insurance provider agreement form).

66 FR 21770, May 1, 2001: HCFA Agency Information Collection Activities: Submission for OMB Review; Comment request (pertaining to Medicare uniform institutional provider bill form).

66 FR 31038, June 8, 2001: Medicare Program; Five–year Review of Work Relative Value Units under the Physician Fee Schedule—Proposed notice.

66 FR 32630, June 15, 2001: HCFA Agency Information Collection Activities; Submission for OMB Review; Comment request (pertaining to contracts by practitioners and physicians who opt–out of Medicare).

66 FR 33102, June 20, 2001: HCFA Agency Information Collection Activities; Submission for OMB Review; Comment request (pertaining to provider/supplier enrollment application form).

See § 2:18.

§ 6:19 WRONGFUL CHARGES BY NONPARTICIPATING PHYSICIANS FOR CERTAIN ELECTIVE SURGICAL PROCEDURES — Section 1842(m) [42 U.S.C.A. 1395u(m)]

Regulations

42 CFR Part 402 — Civil Money Penalties, Assessments, and Exclusions

42 CFR Part 405, Subpart C — Suspension of Payment, Recovery of Overpayments, and Repayment of Scholarships and Loans; Subpart D — Private Contracts; and Subpart E — Criteria for Determination of Reasonable Charges; Payment for Services of Hospital Interns, Residents, and Supervising Physicians

42 CFR Part 410 — Supplementary Medical Insurance (SMI) Benefits

42 CFR Part 411 — Exclusions from Medicare and Limitations on Medicare Payment

42 CFR Part 414 — Payment for Part B Medical and Other Health Services

42 CFR Part 420 — Program Integrity: Medicare

42 CFR Part 424 — Conditions for Medicare Payment

42 CFR Part 498 — Appeals Procedures for Determinations that Affect Participation in the Medicare Program and for Determinations that Affect the Participation of ICF's/MR and Certain NF's in the Medicaid Program

42 CFR Chapter V — Office of Inspector General — Health Care, Department of Health and Human Services

Subchapter A — General Provisions

Part 1000 — Introduction; General Definitions

Subchapter B — OIG Authorities

Part 1001 — Program Integrity: Medicare and State Health Care Programs

Part 1003 — Civil Money Penalties, Assessments and Exclusions

Part 1004 — Imposition of Sanctions on Health Care Practitioners and Providers of Health Care Services by a Peer Review Organization

Part 1005 — Appeals of Exclusions, Civil Money Penalties and Assessments

Part 1006 — Investigational Inquiries

Part 1007 — State Medicaid Fraud Control Units

53 FR 53025, December 30, 1988: Medicare Program; Physician Liability on Non-assigned Claims — Proposed rule to amend 42 CFR Part 405.

55 FR 24561, June 18, 1990: Medicare Program; Physician Liability on Non-Assigned Claims — Final rule affecting 42 CFR Parts 400 and 411. See also correction published at 55 FR 35142, August 28, 1990.

55 FR 36178, September 4, 1990: Medicare Program; Model Fee Schedule for Physicians' Services — Notice with comment period.

55 FR 42907, October 24, 1990: Medicare Program; Standards Applied by Utilization and Quality Control Peer Review Organizations: Consideration of Remote Rural Location and Other Relevant Factors — Notice of policy and request for comments.

56 FR 699, January 8, 1991: Medicare Program; National Standardization of "Global Surgery" Policy — Proposed notice.

56 FR 25792, June 5, 1991: Medicare Program; Fee Schedule for Physicians' Services — Proposed rule affecting 42 CFR Parts 405 and 415.

56 FR 59502, November 25, 1991: Medicare Program; Fee Schedule for Physicians' Services, Fee Schedule Update for Calendar Year 1992 and Physician Performance Standard Rates of Increase for Federal FY 1992 — Final rules and notice affecting 42 CFR Parts 405, 413, 414, and 415. See also correction at 57 FR 42491, September 15, 1992.

56 FR 61023, November 29, 1991: Medicare Program; Standard Claim Forms for Part B Claims Completed and Submitted by Physicians, Suppliers and Other Persons — General notice with comment period.

57 FR 46362, October 8, 1992: Medicare and Medicaid Programs; Revised Effective Date of Medicare/Medicaid Provider Agreement and Supplier Participation — Proposed rule affecting 42 CFR Parts 431, 440, 442, 488, 489, and 498.

57 FR 55914, November 25, 1992: Medicare Program; Fee Schedule for Physicians' Services for Calendar Year 1993 — Final notice with comment period. See also corrections published at 57 FR 59379, December 15, 1992, and at 58 FR 31964, June 7, 1993.

58 FR 63626, December 2, 1993: Medicare Program; Revisions to Payment Policies and Adjustments to the Relative Value Units under the Physician Fee Schedule for Calendar Year 1994 — Final rule with comment period, affecting 42 CFR Parts 405 and 414. See also correction at 59 FR 36069, July 15, 1994.

58 FR 63856, December 2, 1993: Medicare Program; Physician Performance Standard Rates of Increase for Federal Fiscal Year 1994 and Physician Fee Schedule Update for Calendar Year 1994 — Final notice with comment period. See also correction at 59 FR 26410, June 1, 1994.

59 FR 32754, June 24, 1994: Medicare Program; Refinements to Geographic Adjustment Factor Values and Other Policies under the Physician Fee Schedule — Proposed rule affection 42 CFR parts 410 and 414.

59 FR 39828, August 4, 1994: Medicare Program; Payment Policies and Adjustments to the Relative Value Units Under the Physician Fee Schedule for Calendar Year 1994, affecting 42 CFR Parts 405 and 414.

59 FR 63410, December 8, 1994: Medicare Program; Refinements to Geographic Adjustment Factor Values, Revisions to Payment Policies, Adjustments to the Relative Value Units (RVUs) under the Physician Fee Schedule for Calendar Year 1995, and the 5-Year Refinement of RVUs — Final rule with comment period, affecting 42 CFR parts 410 and 414. See also correction at 60 FR 46, January 3, 1995.

59 FR 63638, December 8, 1994: Medicare Program; Physician Fee Schedule Update for Calendar Year 1995 and Physician Volume Performance Standard Rates of Increase for Federal Fiscal Year 1995 — Final notice.

60 FR 38400, July 26, 1995: Medicare Program; Revisions to Payment Policies under the Physician Fee Schedule for Calendar Year 1996 — Proposed rule affecting 42 CFR Parts 400, 405, 410, 411, 412, 413, 414, 415, 417, and 489.

60 FR 63124, December 8, 1995: Medicare Program; Revisions to Payment Policies and Adjustments to the Relative Value Units under the Physician Fee Schedule for Calendar Year 1996 — Final

rule with comment period, affecting 42 CFR Parts 400, 405, 410, 411, 412, 413, 414, 415, 417, and 489.

61 FR 6645, February 21, 1996: HCFA Agency Information Collection Activities: Proposed Collection; Comment Request (pertaining to survey forms to evaluate Federally qualified health centers; and the Medicare Carrier provider/supplier application form).

61 FR 13205, March 26, 1996: HCFA Agency Information Collection Activities: Submission for OMB Review; Comment Request (pertaining to Medicare standardized forms for reimbursement of covered services by all providers that accept Medicare assignment).

61 FR 16925, April 18, 1996: HCFA Agency Information Collection Activities: Proposed Collection; Comment Request (pertaining to Medicare participating physician or supplier agreements; and hospital conditions of participation).

61 FR 19628, May 2, 1996: HCFA Agency Information Collection Activities: Proposed Collection; Comment Request (pertaining to permissible billing for physicians that do not accept Medicare assignments).

61 FR 19992, May 3, 1996: Medicare Program; Five-year Review of Work Relative Value Units under the Physician Fee Schedule — Proposed notice.

61 FR 20528, May 7, 1996: HCFA Privacy Act of 1974; System of Records (pertaining to the Medicare physician identification and eligibility system).

61 FR 38454, July 24, 1996: HCFA Agency Information Collection Activities: Submission for OMB Review; Comment request (pertaining to physicians who do not accept Medicare assignment).

62 FR 59261, October 31, 1997: Medicare Program; Physician Fee Schedule Conversion Factor for Calendar Year 1998 and Sustainable Growth Rate for Fiscal Year 1998 — Final notice.

62 FR 59267, October 31, 1997: Medicare Program; Delay in Implementing the Adjustments to the Practice Expense Relative Value Units under the Physician Fee Schedule for Calendar Year 1998 — Notice of intent to regulate.

63 FR 7743, February 17, 1998: Medicare and Medicaid Programs; Hospital Conditions of Participation; Provider Agreements and Supplier Approval — Notice of extension of comment period, affecting 42 CFR Parts 416, 482, 485, and 489.

63 FR 8462, February 19, 1998: Medicare Program; Update of Ambulatory Surgical Center Payment Rates Effective for Services on or after October 1, 1997 — Notice

63 FR 10920, March 5, 1998: HCFA Emergency Clearance: Public Information Collection Requirements Submitted to the Office of Management and Budget (OMB) (pertaining to Medicare and other Federal health care program provider and supplier application forms).

63 FR 19502, April 20, 1998: HCFA Agency Information Collection Activities: Proposed collection; Comment request (pertaining to annual early and periodic screening, diagnostic, and treatment services (EPSDT) participation report; Medicare and other health care programs provider/supplier enrollment application; and research and analytic support for implementing performance measurement in Medicare fee for service).

63 FR 25320, May 7, 1998: HCFA National Standard Health Care Provider Identifier — Proposed Rule affecting 45 CFR Part 142.

63 FR 28394, May 22, 1998: HCFA Agency Information Collection Activities: Proposed Collection; Comment request (pertaining to application for health insurance forms).

63 FR 30818, June 5, 1998: Medicare Program; Revisions to Payment Policies under the Physician Fee Schedule for Calendar Year 1999 — Proposed rule, affecting 42 CFR Parts 405, 410, 413, 414, 415, 424, and 485. See also correction at 63 FR 50545, September 22, 1998.

63 FR 36250, July 2, 1998: HCFA Agency Information Collection Activities; Submission for OMB review; Comment request (pertaining to provider/supplier enrollment applications).

63 FR 58814, November 2, 1998: Medicare Program; Revisions to Payment Policies and Adjustments to the Relative Value Units under the Physician Fee Schedule for Calendar Year 1999 — Final rule with comment period, affecting 42 CFR 405, 410, 413, 414, 415, 424, and 485. See also correction at 64 FR 25456, May 12, 1999.

1999

64 FR 5666, February 4, 1999: HCFA Emergency Clearance: Public Information Collection Requirements Submitted to the Office of Management and Budget (OMB) (pertaining to the Medicare/Medicaid health insurance common claim form).

64 FR 10478, March 4, 1999: HCFA Agency Information Collection Activities: Proposed Collection; Comment request (pertaining to refunds to patients from physicians when Medicare does not provide coverage for the physician services provided).

64 FR 17673, April 12, 1999: HCFA Agency Information Collection Activities: Proposed Collection; Comment request (pertaining to Medicare participating physician or supplier agreements).

64 FR 23845, May 4, 1999: HCFA Agency Information Collection Activities: Proposed Collection; Comment request (pertaining to Medicare geographical classification review board procedures).

64 FR 24956, May 10, 1999: Medicare and Medicaid Programs; Effective Dates of Provider Agreements and Supplier Approvals-Correction restoring regulations inadvertently removed when a final rule concerning effective dates for provider agreements and supplier approvals was published at 62 FR 43931, August 18, 1997.

64 FR 29049, May 28, 1999: HCFA Agency Information Collection Activities: Proposed Collection; Comment request (pertaining to Medicare credit balance reporting requirements for Medicare providers who have been overpaid).

64 FR 32239, June 16, 1999: HCFA Agency Information Collection Activities: Submission for OMB Review; Comment request (pertaining to the requirement that physicians must notify beneficiaries that Medicare is likely to deny payment for a specified service).

64 FR 36321, July 6, 1999: Medicare Program; Update of Ratesetting Methodology, Payment Rates, Payment Policies, and the List of Covered Procedures for Ambulatory Surgical Centers Effective October 1, 1998 — Notice of extension of comment period for proposed rule affecting 42 CFR Parts 416 and 488.

64 FR 39517, July 22, 1999: HCFA Agency Information Collection Activities: Submission for OM B Review; Comment request (pertaining to Medicare participating physician or supplier agreement form HCFA-460).

64 FR 40017, July 23, 1999: HCFA Agency Information Collection Activities: Submission for OMB Review; Comment request (pertaining to Medicare geographical classification review board procedures and criteria).

64 FR 40534, July 27, 1999: Medicare Program; Replacement of Reasonable Charge Methodology by Fee Schedules — Proposed action affecting 42 CFR 414.

64 FR 48846, September 8, 1999: Office of Inspector General: Solicitation of Information and Recommendations for Developing OIG Compliance Program Guidance for Individual Physicians and Small Group Practices — Notice.

64 FR 57431, October 25, 1999: Medicare Program; Appeals of Carrier Determinations that a Supplier Fails to Meet the Require-

ments for Medicare Billing Privileges — Proposed rule affecting 42 CFR Part 405.

64 FR 59380, November 2, 1999: Medicare Program; Revisions to Payment Policies under the Physician Fee Schedule for Calendar Year 2000 — Final rule with comment period, affecting 42 CFR Parts 410, 411, 414, 415, and 485. See also correction at 65 FR 19329, April 11, 2000.

64 FR 71148, December 20, 1999: Medicare Program; Adjustment in Payment Amounts for New Technology Intraocular Lenses Furnished by Ambulatory Surgical Centers — Notice with comment period.

2000

65 FR 5354, February 3, 2000: HCFA Agency Information Collection Activities: Proposed Collection; Comment request (pertaining to standardized Medicare/Medicaid claim form for reimbursement of covered services).

65 FR 25738, May 3, 2000: Medicare Program; Lenses Eligible for an Adjustment in Payment Amount for New Technology Intraocular Lenses Furnished by Ambulatory Surgical Centers.

65 FR 25939, May 4, 2000: HCFA Agency Information Collection Activities: Proposed Collection; Comment request (pertaining to ambulatory surgical center payment rate survey).

65 FR 36818, June 12, 2000: Office of Inspector General: Draft OIG Compliance Program for Individual and Small Group Physician Practices — Notice and comment period.

65 FR 42021, July 7, 2000: HCFA Agency Information Collection Activities: Proposed Collection; Comment request (pertaining to notice to providers, suppliers, and practitioners about non-covered services to beneficiaries).

65 FR 42022, July 7, 2000: Medicare Program; Question and Answer Session on July 24, 2000, to Discuss Remaining Concerns about the Implementation of the Hospital Outpatient Prospective Payment System (PPS) — Notice of meeting.

65 FR 44176, July 17, 2000: Medicare Program; Revisions to Payment Policies under the Physician Fee Schedule for Calendar Year 2001 — Proposed rule affection 42 CFR Parts 410 and 414.

65 FR 47670, August 3, 2000: Medicare Program; Prospective Payment System for Hospital Outpatient Services: Revisions to Criteria to Define New or Innovative Medical Devices, Drugs, and Biologicals Eligible for Pass-Through Payments and Corrections to the Criteria

for the Grandfather Provision for Certain Federally Qualified Health Centers-Interim final rule with comment period, affecting 42 CFR Parts 413 and 419.

65 FR 47706, August 3, 2000: Medicare Program; Prospective Payment System for Hospital Outpatient Services: Revision of the Provider-based Location Criteria for Certain PPS-exempt Facilities — Proposed rule affecting 42 CFR Part 413.

65 FR 50312, August 17, 2000: Office of the Secretary; Health Insurance Reform: Standards for Electronic Transactions — Final rule affecting 45 CFR Parts 160 and 162.

65 FR 53963, September 6, 2000: Medicare Program: Appeals of Carrier Determinations that a Physician or Other Supplier Fails to Meet the Requirements for Medicare Billing Privileges; Reopening of Comment Period — Notice of reopening of comment period for proposed rule affecting 42 CFR Part 405.

65 FR 59434, October 5, 2000: Office of Inspector General Compliance Program for Individual and Small Group Physician Practices — Notice.

65 FR 64227, October 26, 2000: HCFA Agency Information Collection Activities: Proposed Collection; Comment Request; Public Information Collection Meeting to Discuss Proposed Revisions (pertaining to notice requirements from suppliers, physicians, and practitioners to beneficiaries when Medicare Part B payment may be denied).

65 FR 65376, November 1, 2000: Medicare Program; Revisions to Payment Policies under the Physician Fee Schedule for Calendar Year 2001—Final rule with comment period. See also correction at 66 FR 16607, March 27, 2001.

65 FR 65603, November 1, 2000: Medicare Program; Revisions to Payment Policies under the Physician Fee Schedule for Calendar Year 2001 — Final rule with comment period.

2001

66 FR 1996, January 10, 2001: HCFA Agency Information Collection Activities; Comment request (pertaining to Medicare uniform institutional provider bill for reimbursement of covered services by all providers that accept assignment of claims).

66 FR 1997, January 10, 2001: HCFA Notice of OMB Approval (pertaining to uniform home health advance beneficiary notice).

66 FR 2912, January 12, 2001: HCFA Agency Information Collection Activities: Proposed Collection; Comment request (pertaining to Medicare/Medicaid health insurance common claim form).

66 FR 8807, February 2, 2001: HCFA Agency Information Collection Activities: Proposed Collection; Comment request (pertaining to Medicare Federal health care programs provider/supplier enrollment application).

66 FR 16061, March 22, 2001: HCFA Agency Information Collection Activities: Proposed Collection; Comment request (pertaining to private contracts of physicians who opt out of Medicare).

66 FR 18646, April 10, 2001: HCFA Agency Information Collection Activities: Submission for OMB Review; Comment request (pertaining to Medicare/Medicaid health insurance common claim form).

66 FR 20316, April 20, 2001: HCFA Agency Information Collection Activities: Submission for OMB Review; Comment request (pertaining to advance beneficiary notice by physicians, practitioners, suppliers, and providers about items and services denied by Medicare as not reasonable and necessary).

66 FR 20997, April 26, 2001: HCFA Agency Information Collection Activities: Submission for OMB Review; Comment request (pertaining to health insurance provider agreement form).

66 FR 21770, May 1, 2001: HCFA Agency Information Collection Activities: Submission for OMB Review; Comment request (pertaining to Medicare uniform institutional provider bill form).

66 FR 31038, June 8, 2001: Medicare Program; Five–year Review of Work Relative Value Units under the Physician Fee Schedule—Proposed notice.

66 FR 32630, June 15, 2001: HCFA Agency Information Collection Activities; Submission for OMB Review; Comment request (pertaining to contracts by practitioners and physicians who opt–out of Medicare).

66 FR 33102, June 20, 2001: HCFA Agency Information Collection Activities; Submission for OMB Review; Comment request (pertaining to provider/supplier enrollment application form).

See § 2:19.

§ 6:20 PHYSICIAN FAILURE TO ELIMINATE THE MARK-UP FOR CERTAIN PURCHASED DIAGNOSTIC TESTS — Section 1842(n) [42 U.S.C.A. 1395u(n)]

Regulations

42 CFR Part 402 — Civil Money Penalties, Assessments, and Exclusions

42 CFR Part 405, Subpart C — Suspension of Payment, Recovery of Overpayments, and Repayment of Scholarships and Loans; and Subpart E — Criteria for Determination of Reasonable Charges; Payment for Services of Hospital Interns, Residents, and Supervising Physicians

42 CFR Part 410 — Supplementary Medical Insurance (SMI) Benefits

42 CFR Part 411 — Exclusions from Medicare and Limitations on Medicare Payment

42 CFR Part 414 — Payment for Part B Medical and Other Health Services

42 CFR Part 420 — Program Integrity: Medicare

42 CFR Part 424 — Conditions for Medicare Payment

42 CFR Part 498 — Appeals Procedures for Determinations that Affect Participation in the Medicare Program and for Determinations that Affect the Participation of ICF's/MR and Certain NF's in the Medicaid Program

42 CFR Chapter V — Office of Inspector General — Health Care, Department of Health and Human Services

Subchapter A — General Provisions

Part 1000 — Introduction; General Definitions

Subchapter B — OIG Authorities

Part 1001 — Program Integrity: Medicare and State Health Care Programs

Part 1002 — Program Integrity: State-initiated Exclusion from Medicaid

Part 1003 — Civil Money Penalties, Assessments and Exclusions

Part 1004 — Imposition of Sanctions on Health Care Practitioners and Providers of Health Care Services by a Peer Review Organization

Part 1005 — Appeals of Exclusions, Civil Money Penalties and Assessments

Part 1006 — Investigational Inquiries
Part 1007 — State Medicaid Fraud Control Units

56 FR 61023, November 29, 1991: Medicare Program; Standard Claim Forms for Part B Claims Completed and Submitted by Physicians, Suppliers and Other Persons — General notice with comment period.

57 FR 46362, October 8, 1992: Medicare and Medicaid Programs; Revised Effective Date of Medicare/Medicaid Provider Agreement and Supplier Participation — Proposed rule affecting 42 CFR Parts 431, 440, 442, 488, 489, and 498.

58 FR 43832, August 18, 1993: Medicare and Medicaid Programs; Payment for Clinical Diagnostic Laboratory Tests — Proposed rule affecting 42 CFR Parts 405, 413, 414, 424, 431, and 447.

58 FR 54096, October 20, 1993: Office of Inspector General: Civil Money Penalties for Prohibited Referrals to Entities Providing Clinical Laboratory Services and for Prohibited Arrangements and Schemes — Proposed rule affecting 42 CFR Part 1003.

59 FR 65372, December 19, 1994: Office of Inspector General — Notice of Publication of Special Fraud Alerts (pertaining to joint venture arrangements, routine waiver of Medicare Part B copayments and deductibles, hospital incentives to referring physicians, prescription drug marketing practices, and arrangements for provision of clinical laboratory services).

60 FR 2325, January 9, 1995: Medicare Program; Providers and Suppliers of Specialized Services: Technical Amendments — Final rule with comment period, affecting 42 CFR Parts 400, 405, 410, 484, 485, 486, and 498. See also correction at 60 FR 11632, March 2, 1995 and correction at 60 FR 45086, August 30, 1995.

60 FR 16580, March 31, 1995: Office of Inspector General: Civil Money Penalties for Referrals to Entities and for Prohibited Arrangements and Schemes — Final rule with comment period, affecting 42 CFR Part 1003.

60 FR 41914, August 14, 1995: Medicare Program; Physician Financial Relationships with, and Referrals to, Health Care Entities that Furnish Clinical Laboratory Services; Financial Relationship Reporting Requirements — Final rule affecting 42 CFR Part 411.

61 FR 7522, February 28, 1996: HCFA Public Information Collection Requirements Submitted for Public Comment and Recommendations (pertaining to Medicare and Medicaid disclosure of ownership and control interest statements).

61 FR 16925, April 18, 1996: HCFA Agency Information Collection Activities: Proposed Collection; Comment Request (pertaining to Medicare participating physician or supplier agreements; and hospital conditions of participation).

62 FR 65049, December 10, 1997: Office of Inspector General: Solicitation of New Safe Harbors and Special Fraud Alerts — Notice of intent to develop regulations, affecting 42 CFR Part 1001.

63 FR 7743, February 17, 1998: Medicare and Medicaid Programs; Hospital Conditions of Participation; Provider Agreements and Supplier Approval — Notice of extension of comment period, affecting 42 CFR Parts 416, 482, 485, and 489.

63 FR 8462, February 19, 1998: Medicare Program; Update of Ambulatory Surgical Center Payment Rates Effective for Services on or after October 1, 1997 — Notice

63 FR 9844, February 26, 1998: HCFA Agency Information Collection Activities: Proposed Collection; Comment request (pertaining to procedures for advisory opinions concerning physician referrals and supporting regulations in 42 CFR Sections 411.370- 411.389).

63 FR 10920, March 5, 1998: HCFA Emergency Clearance: Public Information Collection Requirements Submitted to the Office of Management and Budget (OMB) (pertaining to Medicare and other Federal health care program provider and supplier application forms).

63 FR 19502, April 20, 1998: HCFA Agency Information Collection Activities: Proposed collection; Comment request (pertaining to annual early and periodic screening, diagnostic, and treatment services (EPSDT) participation report; Medicare and other health care programs provider/supplier enrollment application; and research and analytic support for implementing performance measurement in Medicare fee for service).

63 FR 20415, April 24, 1998: Office of Inspector General: Publication of OIG Special Fraud Alert: Fraud and Abuse in Nursing Home Arrangements with Hospices — Notice.

63 FR 25320, May 7, 1998: HCFA National Standard Health Care Provider Identifier — Proposed Rule affecting 45 CFR Part 142.

63 FR 28394, May 22, 1998: HCFA Agency Information Collection Activities: Proposed Collection; Comment request (pertaining to application for health insurance forms).

63 FR 28395, May 22, 1998: HCFA Agency Information Collection Activities: Submission for OMB Review; Comment request (pertaining to procedures for advisory opinions concerning physician

referrals and supporting regulations in 42 CFR 411.370 through 411.389).

63 FR 36250, July 2, 1998: HCFA Agency Information Collection Activities; Submission for OMB review; Comment request (pertaining to provider/supplier enrollment applications).

63 FR 38311, July 16, 1998: Office of Inspector General: Medicare and State Health Care Programs: Fraud and Abuse; Issuance of Advisory Opinions by the OIG — Final rule affecting 42 CFR 1008. See also correction at 63 FR 43449, August 13, 1998.

63 FR 38414, July 16, 1998: HCFA Privacy Act of 1974; Report of Altered System (pertaining to disclosure of individual-specific information to combat fraud or abuse in health benefit programs).

63 FR 58399, October 30, 1998: Office of Inspector General: Publication of the OIG's Provider Self-Disclosure Protocol — Notice.

63 FR 58814, November 2, 1998: Medicare Program; Revisions to Payment Policies and Adjustments to the Relative Value Units under the Physician Fee Schedule for Calendar Year 1999 — Final rule with comment period, affecting 42 CFR 405, 410, 413, 414, 415, 424, and 485. See also correction at 64 FR 25456, May 12, 1999.

63 FR 68223, December 10, 1998: Office of Inspector General; Solicitation of New Safe Harbors and Special Fraud Alerts — Notice of intent to develop regulations, affecting 42 CFR 1001.

1999

64 FR 1813, January 12, 1999: Office of Inspector General Publication of OIG Special Fraud Alert on Physician Liability for Certifications in the Provision of Medical Equipment and Supplies and Home Health Services — Notice.

64 FR 13997, March 23, 1999: HCFA Agency Information Collection Activities: Submission for OMB Review; Comment request (pertaining to Medicare and Medicaid requirements for advanced directives, and disclosure of ownership and financial control interest).

64 FR 17673, April 12, 1999: HCFA Agency Information Collection Activities: Proposed Collection; Comment request (pertaining to Medicare participating physician or supplier agreements).

64 FR 24956, May 10, 1999: Medicare and Medicaid Programs; Effective Dates of Provider Agreements and Supplier Approvals-Correction restoring regulations inadvertently removed when a final rule concerning effective dates for provider agreements and supplier approvals was published at 62 FR 43931, August 18, 1997.

64 FR 32239, June 16, 1999: HCFA Agency Information Collection Activities: Submission for OMB Review; Comment request (pertaining to the requirement that physicians must notify beneficiaries that Medicare is likely to deny payment for a specified service).

64 FR 36368, July 6, 1999: Office of Inspector General Publication of OIG Compliance Program Guidance for the Durable Medical Equipment, Prosthetics, Orthotics and Supply Industry — Notice.

64 FR 39517, July 22, 1999: HCFA Agency Information Collection Activities: Submission for OMB Review; Comment request (pertaining to Medicare participating physician or supplier agreement form HCFA-460).

64 FR 43295, August 10, 1999: Medicare Program; Negotiated Rulemaking; Coverage and Administrative Policies for Clinical Diagnostic Laboratory Tests; Announcement of Additional Public Meetings — Notice of meetings.

64 FR 48846, September 8, 1999: Office of Inspector General: Solicitation of Information and Recommendations for Developing OIG Compliance Program Guidance for Individual Physicians and Small Group Practices — Notice.

2000

65 FR 5354, February 3, 2000: HCFA Agency Information Collection Activities: Proposed Collection; Comment request (pertaining to standardized Medicare/Medicaid claim form for reimbursement of covered services).

65 FR 30414, May 11, 2000: HCFA Agency Information Collection Activities: Submission for OMB Review; Comment request (pertaining to health insurance common claims form).

65 FR 36818, June 12, 2000: Office of Inspector General: Draft OIG Compliance Program for Individual and Small Group Physician Practices — Notice and comment period.

65 FR 42021, July 7, 2000: HCFA Agency Information Collection Activities: Proposed Collection; Comment request (pertaining to notice to providers, suppliers, and practitioners about non-covered services to beneficiaries).

65 FR 42022, July 7, 2000: Medicare Program; Question and Answer Session on July 24, 2000, to Discuss Remaining Concerns about the Implementation of the Hospital Outpatient Prospective Payment System (PPS) — Notice of meeting.

65 FR 44176, July 17, 2000: Medicare Program; Revisions to Payment Policies under the Physician Fee Schedule for Calendar Year 2001 — Proposed rule affection 42 CFR Parts 410 and 414.

65 FR 47670, August 3, 2000: Medicare Program; Prospective Payment System for Hospital Outpatient Services: Revisions to Criteria to Define New or Innovative Medical Devices, Drugs, and Biologicals Eligible for Pass-Through Payments and Corrections to the Criteria for the Grandfather Provision for Certain Federally Qualified Health Centers-Interim final rule with comment period, affecting 42 CFR Parts 413 and 419.

65 FR 47706, August 3, 2000: Medicare Program; Prospective Payment System for Hospital Outpatient Services: Revision of the Provider-based Location Criteria for Certain PPS-exempt Facilities — Proposed rule affecting 42 CFR Part 413.

65 FR 50312, August 17, 2000: Office of the Secretary; Health Insurance Reform: Standards for Electronic Transactions — Final rule affecting 45 CFR Parts 160 and 162.

65 FR 53963, September 6, 2000: Medicare Program: Appeals of Carrier Determinations that a Physician or Other Supplier Fails to Meet the Requirements for Medicare Billing Privileges; Reopening of Comment Period — Notice of reopening of comment period for proposed rule affecting 42 CFR Part 405.

65 FR 59434, October 5, 2000: Office of Inspector General Compliance Program for Individual and Small Group Physician Practices — Notice.

65 FR 64227, October 26, 2000: HCFA Agency Information Collection Activities: Proposed Collection; Comment Request; Public Information Collection Meeting to Discuss Proposed Revisions (pertaining to notice requirements from suppliers, physicians, and practitioners to beneficiaries when Medicare Part B payment may be denied).

65 FR 65376, November 1, 2000: Medicare Program; Revisions to Payment Policies under the Physician Fee Schedule for Calendar Year 2001—Final rule with comment period. See also correction at 66 FR 16607, March 27, 2001.

65 FR 65603, November 1, 2000: Medicare Program; Revisions to Payment Policies under the Physician Fee Schedule for Calendar Year 2001 — Final rule with comment period.

2001

66 FR 856, January 4, 2001: Medicare and Medicaid Programs; Physicians Referrals to Health Care Entities with which They Have Financial Relationships—Final rule with comment period, affecting 42 CFR Parts 411 and 424.

66 FR 1996, January 10, 2001: HCFA Agency Information Collection Activities; Comment request (pertaining to Medicare uniform institutional provider bill for reimbursement of covered services by all providers that accept assignment of claims).

66 FR 2912, January 12, 2001: HCFA Agency Information Collection Activities: Proposed Collection; Comment request (pertaining to Medicare/Medicaid health insurance common claim form).

66 FR 6629, January 22, 2001: HCFA Agency Information Collection Activities: Submission for OMB Review; Comment request (pertaining to Medicare Integrity Program Organizational Conflict of Interest Disclosure Certificate).

66 FR 7919, January 26, 2001: HCFA Agency Information Collection Activities: Proposed Collection; Comment request (pertaining to provider Medicare agreements).

66 FR 8771, February 2, 2001: Medicare and Medicaid Programs; Physicians' Referrals to Health Care Entities with which They Have Financial Relationships: Delay of Effective Date of Final Rule and Technical Amendment, affecting 42 CFR Parts 411 and 424.

66 FR 8807, February 2, 2001: HCFA Agency Information Collection Activities: Proposed Collection; Comment request (pertaining to Medicare Federal health care programs provider/supplier enrollment application).

66 FR 17813, April 4, 2001: Medicare and Medicaid Programs; Physicians' Referrals to Health Care Entities with which They Have Financial Relationships; Extension of Comment period—Notice, affecting 42 CFR Parts 411 and 424.

66 FR 18646, April 10, 2001: HCFA Agency Information Collection Activities: Submission for OMB Review; Comment request (pertaining to Medicare/Medicaid health insurance common claim form).

66 FR 19507, April 16, 2001: HCFA Agency Information Collection Activities: Proposed Collection; Comment request (pertaining to conflict of interest and ownership and control information form).

66 FR 20316, April 20, 2001: HCFA Agency Information Collection Activities: Submission for OMB Review; Comment request (pertaining to advance beneficiary notice by physicians, practitioners,

suppliers, and providers about items and services denied by Medicare as not reasonable and necessary).

66 FR 20997, April 26, 2001: HCFA Agency Information Collection Activities: Submission for OMB Review; Comment request (pertaining to health insurance provider agreement form).

66 FR 31038, June 8, 2001: Medicare Program; Five–year Review of Work Relative Value Units under the Physician Fee Schedule—Proposed notice.

66 FR 33102, June 20, 2001: HCFA Agency Information Collection Activities; Submission for OMB Review; Comment request (pertaining to provider/supplier enrollment application form).

See § 2:20.

§ 6:21 PHYSICIAN FAILURE TO PROVIDE APPROPRIATE DIAGNOSIS CODES ON BILLS — Section 1842(p) [42 U.S.C.A. 1395u(p)]

Regulations

42 CFR Part 402 — Civil Money Penalties, Assessments, and Exclusions

42 CFR Part 405, Subpart C — Suspension of Payment, Recovery of Overpayments, and Repayment of Scholarships and Loans; and Subpart E — Criteria for Determination of Reasonable Charges

42 CFR Part 412 — Prospective Payment System for Inpatient Hospital Services, especially Section 412.46: Medical review requirements; DRG validation

42 CFR Part 414 — Payment for Part B Medical and Other Health Services

42 CFR Part 415 — Services Furnished by Physicians in Providers, Supervising Physicians in Teaching Settings, and Residents in Certain Settings

42 CFR Part 420 — Program Integrity: Medicare

42 CFR Part 424 — Conditions for Medicare Payment

42 CFR Part 498 — Appeals Procedures for Determinations that Affect Participation in the Medicare Program and for Determinations that Affect the Participation of ICF's/MR and Certain NF's in the Medicaid Program

42 CFR Chapter V — Office of Inspector General — Health Care, Department of Health and Human Services

Subchapter A — General Provisions

Part 1000 — Introduction; General Definitions

Subchapter B — OIG Authorities

Part 1001 — Program Integrity: Medicare and State Health Care Programs

Part 1002 — Program Integrity: State-initiated Exclusion from Medicaid

Part 1003 — Civil Money Penalties, Assessments and Exclusions

Part 1004 — Imposition of Sanctions on Health Care Practitioners and Providers of Health Care Services by a Peer Review Organization

Part 1005 — Appeals of Exclusions, Civil Money Penalties and Assessments

Part 1006 — Investigational Inquiries

Part 1007 — State Medicaid Fraud Control Units

Part 1008 — Advisory Opinions by the OIG

54 FR 30558, July 21, 1989: Medicare Program; Diagnosis Codes on Physician Bills — Proposed rule to amend 42 CFR Part 424.

56 FR 61023, November 29, 1991: Medicare Program; Standard Claim Forms for Part B Claims Completed and Submitted by Physicians, Suppliers and Other Persons — General notice with comment period.

57 FR 46362, October 8, 1992: Medicare and Medicaid Programs; Revised Effective Date of Medicare/Medicaid Provider Agreement and Supplier Participation — Proposed rule affecting 42 CFR Parts 431, 440, 442, 488, 489, and 498.

59 FR 10290, March 4, 1994: Medicare Program; Diagnosis Codes on Physician Bills — Final rule affecting 42 CFR Parts 405 and 424. See also correction at 59 FR 26739, May 24, 1994.

1999

64 FR 5666, February 4, 1999: HCFA Emergency Clearance: Public Information Collection Requirements Submitted to the Office of Management and Budget (OMB) (pertaining to the Medicare/Medicaid health insurance common claim form).

64 FR 17673, April 12, 1999: HCFA Agency Information Collection Activities: Proposed Collection; Comment request (pertaining to Medicare participating physician or supplier agreements).

64 FR 24956, May 10, 1999: Medicare and Medicaid Programs; Effective Dates of Provider Agreements and Supplier Approvals-Correction restoring regulations inadvertently removed when a

final rule concerning effective dates for provider agreements and supplier approvals was published at 62 FR 43931, August 18, 1997.

64 FR 36368, July 6, 1999: Office of Inspector General Publication of OIG Compliance Program Guidance for the Durable Medical Equipment, Prosthetics, Orthotics and Supply Industry — Notice.

64 FR 39517, July 22, 1999: HCFA Agency Information Collection Activities: Submission for OMB Review; Comment request (pertaining to Medicare participating physician or supplier agreement form HCFA-460).

64 FR 43295, August 10, 1999: Medicare Program; Negotiated Rulemaking; Coverage and Administrative Policies for Clinical Diagnostic Laboratory Tests; Announcement of Additional Public Meetings — Notice of meetings.

64 FR 48846, September 8, 1999: Office of Inspector General: Solicitation of Information and Recommendations for Developing OIG Compliance Program Guidance for Individual Physicians and Small Group Practices — Notice.

2000

65 FR 5354, February 3, 2000: HCFA Agency Information Collection Activities: Proposed Collection; Comment request (pertaining to standardized Medicare/Medicaid claim form for reimbursement of covered services).

65 FR 30414, May 11, 2000: HCFA Agency Information Collection Activities: Submission for OMB Review; Comment request (pertaining to health insurance common claims form).

65 FR 36818, June 12, 2000: Office of Inspector General: Draft OIG Compliance Program for Individual and Small Group Physician Practices — Notice and comment period.

65 FR 42021, July 7, 2000: HCFA Agency Information Collection Activities: Proposed Collection; Comment request (pertaining to notice to providers, suppliers, and practitioners about non-covered services to beneficiaries).

65 FR 44176, July 17, 2000: Medicare Program; Revisions to Payment Policies under the Physician Fee Schedule for Calendar Year 2001 — Proposed rule affection 42 CFR Parts 410 and 414.

65 FR 47670, August 3, 2000: Medicare Program; Prospective Payment System for Hospital Outpatient Services: Revisions to Criteria to Define New or Innovative Medical Devices, Drugs, and Biologicals Eligible for Pass-Through Payments and Corrections to the Criteria for the Grandfather Provision for Certain Federally Qualified

Health Centers-Interim final rule with comment period, affecting 42 CFR Parts 413 and 419.

65 FR 47706, August 3, 2000: Medicare Program; Prospective Payment System for Hospital Outpatient Services: Revision of the Provider-based Location Criteria for Certain PPS-exempt Facilities — Proposed rule affecting 42 CFR Part 413.

65 FR 50312, August 17, 2000: Office of the Secretary; Health Insurance Reform: Standards for Electronic Transactions — Final rule affecting 45 CFR Parts 160 and 162.

65 FR 53963, September 6, 2000: Medicare Program: Appeals of Carrier Determinations that a Physician or Other Supplier Fails to Meet the Requirements for Medicare Billing Privileges; Reopening of Comment Period — Notice of reopening of comment period for proposed rule affecting 42 CFR Part 405.

65 FR 59434, October 5, 2000: Office of Inspector General Compliance Program for Individual and Small Group Physician Practices — Notice.

65 FR 64227, October 26, 2000: HCFA Agency Information Collection Activities: Proposed Collection; Comment Request; Public Information Collection Meeting to Discuss Proposed Revisions (pertaining to notice requirements from suppliers, physicians, and practitioners to beneficiaries when Medicare Part B payment may be denied).

65 FR 65376, November 1, 2000: Medicare Program; Revisions to Payment Policies under the Physician Fee Schedule for Calendar Year 2001—Final rule with comment period. See also correction at 66 FR 16607, March 27, 2001.

65 FR 65603, November 1, 2000: Medicare Program; Revisions to Payment Policies under the Physician Fee Schedule for Calendar Year 2001 — Final rule with comment period.

2001

66 FR 1996, January 10, 2001: HCFA Agency Information Collection Activities; Comment request (pertaining to Medicare uniform institutional provider bill for reimbursement of covered services by all providers that accept assignment of claims).

66 FR 2912, January 12, 2001: HCFA Agency Information Collection Activities: Proposed Collection; Comment request (pertaining to Medicare/Medicaid health insurance common claim form).

66 FR 7919, January 26, 2001: HCFA Agency Information Collection Activities: Proposed Collection; Comment request (pertaining to provider Medicare agreements).

66 FR 8807, February 2, 2001: HCFA Agency Information Collection Activities: Proposed Collection; Comment request (pertaining to Medicare Federal health care programs provider/supplier enrollment application).

66 FR 18646, April 10, 2001: HCFA Agency Information Collection Activities: Submission for OMB Review; Comment request (pertaining to Medicare/Medicaid health insurance common claim form).

66 FR 20316, April 20, 2001: HCFA Agency Information Collection Activities: Submission for OMB Review; Comment request (pertaining to advance beneficiary notice by physicians, practitioners, suppliers, and providers about items and services denied by Medicare as not reasonable and necessary).

66 FR 20997, April 26, 2001: HCFA Agency Information Collection Activities: Submission for OMB Review; Comment request (pertaining to health insurance provider agreement form).

66 FR 31038, June 8, 2001: Medicare Program; Five–year Review of Work Relative Value Units under the Physician Fee Schedule—Proposed notice.

66 FR 33102, June 20, 2001: HCFA Agency Information Collection Activities; Submission for OMB Review; Comment request (pertaining to provider/supplier enrollment application form).

See § 2:21.

§ 6:22 INTERMEDIATE SANCTIONS FOR PROVIDERS OR SUPPLIERS OF CLINICAL DIAGNOSTIC LABORATORY TESTS — Section 1846 [42 U.S.C.A. 1395w-2]

Regulations

42 CFR Part 402 — Civil Money Penalties, Assessments, and Exclusions

42 CFR Part 405, Subpart E — Criteria for Determination of Reasonable Charges

42 CFR Part 410 — Supplementary Medical Insurance (SMI) Benefits, especially section 410.32: Diagnostic X-ray tests, diagnostic laboratory tests, and other diagnostic tests: Conditions

42 CFR Part 411, Subpart J — Physician Ownership of, and Referral of Patients or Laboratory Specimens to, Entities Furnishing Clinical Laboratory or Other Health Services

42 CFR Part 414 — Payment for Part B Medical and Other Health Services

42 CFR Part 415 — Services Furnished by Physicians in Providers, Supervising Physicians in Teaching Settings, and Residents in Certain Settings

42 CFR Part 420 — Program Integrity: Medicare

42 CFR Part 440 — Services: General Provisions [Medicaid], Subpart A — Definitions, especially Section 440.30: Other laboratory and X-ray services

42 CFR Part 447 — Payments for Services [Medicaid], Subpart D — Payment Methods for Other Institutional and Noninstitutional Services, especially Section 447.342: Physician billing for clinical laboratory services

42 CFR Part 455 — Program Integrity: Medicaid

42 CFR 493 — Laboratory Requirements

42 CFR Part 498 — Appeals Procedures for Determinations that Affect Participation in the Medicare Program and for Determinations that Affect the Participation of ICF's/MR and Certain NF's in the Medicaid Program

42 CFR Chapter V — Office of Inspector General — Health Care, Department of Health and Human Services

Subchapter A — General Provisions

Part 1000 — Introduction; General Definitions

Subchapter B — OIG Authorities

Part 1001 — Program Integrity: Medicare and State Health Care Programs

Part 1002 — Program Integrity: State-initiated Exclusion from Medicaid

Part 1003 — Civil Money Penalties, Assessments and Exclusions

Part 1005 — Appeals of Exclusions, Civil Money Penalties and Assessments

Part 1006 — Investigational Inquiries

Part 1007 — State Medicaid Fraud Control Units

Part 1008 — Advisory Opinions by the OIG

53 FR 48645, December 2, 1988: Medicare and Medicaid Programs; Medicare, Medicaid, and Clinical Laboratories Improvement Act (CLIA) Patient Confidentiality Rules — Final rule [Amends 42 CFR Parts 74, 405, and 441]

55 FR 9538, March 14, 1990: Medicare, Medicaid and CLIA Programs; Revision of the Laboratory Regulations for the Medicare, Medicaid, and Clinical Laboratories Improvement Act of 1967 Programs — Final rule with comment period, amending 42 CFR Parts 74, 405, 416, 440, 482, 483, 488, and 493.

55 FR 20896, May 21, 1990: Medicare, Medicaid and CLIA Programs; Regulations Implementing the Clinical Laboratory Improvement Amendments of 1988 (CLIA '88) — Proposed rule. See also extension of time for public comment to September 21, 1990, published at 55 FR 34289, August 22, 1990.

55 FR 31758, August 3, 1990: Clinical Laboratory Improvement Act Programs; Fee Collection — Proposed rule affecting 42 CFR Part 493.

56 FR 13430, April 2, 1991: Medicare and Laboratory Certification Programs; Enforcement Procedures for Laboratories — Proposed rule.

57 FR 7002, February 28, 1992: Medicare, Medicaid and CLIA Programs; Regulations Implementing the Clinical Laboratory Improvement Amendments of 1988 (CLIA) — Final rule with comment period, affecting 42 CFR Parts 405, 410, 416, 417, 418, 440, 482, 483, 484, 485, 488, 491, 493, and 494. See also correction at 57 FR 35760, August 11, 1992, and correction amendments at 58 FR 5212, January 19, 1993.

57 FR 7188, February 28, 1992: Clinical Laboratory Improvement Act Program Fee Collection — Final rule with comment affecting 42 CFR Part 493. See also correction at 57 FR 31664, July 17, 1992, and correction amendments at 58 FR 5212, January 19, 1993.

57 FR 7218, February 28, 1992: Medicare Program; Medicare and Laboratory Certification Program; Enforcement Procedures for Laboratories — Final rule affecting 42 CFR Part 493. See also correction amendments at 58 FR 5212, January 19, 1993.

57 FR 8588, March 11, 1992: Medicare Program; Physician Ownership of, and Referrals to, Health Care Entities that Furnish Clinical Laboratory Services — Proposed rule affecting 42 CFR Part 411.

57 FR 25041, June 12, 1992: HCFA Public Information Collection Requirements Submitted to the Office of Management and Budget for clearance (pertaining to CLIA application forms) — Notice.

57 FR 33992, July 31, 1992: Clinical Laboratories Improvement Act Program; Granting and Withdrawal of Deeming Authority to

Private Nonprofit Accreditation Organizations and of CLIA Exemption under State Laboratory Programs — Final rule.

58 FR 5215, January 19, 1993: Medicare, Medicaid and CLIA Programs; Regulations Implementing the Clinical Laboratory Improvement Amendments of 1988 (CLIA) and Clinical Laboratory Improvement Act Program Fee Collection — Final rule with comment period, affecting 42 CFR Part 493. See also correction published at 58 FR 39154, July 22, 1993.

58 FR 38579, July 19, 1993: HCFA Public Information Collection Requirements Submitted to the Office of Management and Budget (OMB) for Clearance re survey of home health agencies; CLIA survey report form; validation of state surveys; Medicaid listing of participating home health agencies; financial information regarding Medicare benefits from Medicare contractors; and third-party liability under Medicaid.

58 FR 43832, August 18, 1993: Medicare and Medicaid Programs; Payment for Clinical Diagnostic Laboratory Tests — Proposed rule affecting 42 CFR Parts 405, 413, 414, 424, 431, and 447.

58 FR 52112, October 6, 1993: Medicare, Medicaid, and CLIA Programs; Clinical Laboratory Improvement Amendments of 1988 Exemption of Laboratories Licensed by the State of Washington — Notice.

58 FR 54096, October 20, 1993: Office of Inspector General: Civil Money Penalties for Prohibited Referrals to Entities Providing Clinical Laboratory Services and for Prohibited Arrangements and Schemes — Proposed rule affecting 42 CFR Part 1003.

58 FR 67795, December 22, 1993: HCFA Public Information Collection Requirements Submitted to the Office of Management and Budget (OMB) for Clearance (pertaining to clinical laboratory improvement amendments; third party premium billing request form; ambulatory surgical center payment rate survey; online survey, certification and reporting system (OSCAR); conditions of participation for rehabilitation agencies and conditions for coverage for physical therapists in independent practice) — Notice.

58 FR 68148, December 23, 1993: HCFA Approval of the Commission on Office Laboratory Accreditation — Notice.

59 FR 23069, May 4, 1994: HCFA Public Information Collection Requirements Submitted to the Office of Management and Budget (OMB) for Clearance (pertaining to clinical laboratory improvement amendments (CLIA) flexible survey protocol form; application for health insurance benefits under Medicare for individual with

chronic renal disease form; Medicare Qualification Statement for Federal employees form; attending physician's statement and documentation of Medicare emergency form; request for Part B Medicare hearing by an Administrative Law Judge forms; CLIA adverse action extract; and Medicare and Medicaid coverage data bank reports form).

59 FR 27023, May 25, 1994: HCFA Public Information Collection Requirements Submitted to the Office of Management and Budget (OMB) for Clearance (pertaining to Medicare beneficiary survey of influenza vaccination form; Medicaid integrated quality control review worksheet; post laboratory survey questionnaire form; and post laboratory survey questionnaire — surveyor form).

59 FR 52968, October 20, 1994: HCFA; CLIA Program; Approval of the American Society for Histocompatibility and Immunogenetics for the Specialty of Histocompatibility — Notice.

59 FR 56500, November 14, 1994: HCFA Public Information Collection Requirements Submitted to the Office of Management and Budget (OMB) for Clearance (pertaining to monitoring and evaluation of Medicare cataract surgery alternate payment demonstration, form for listing deficiencies for laboratory surveys, form for personnel requirements for laboratory CLIA certification, and CLIA reinstatement form).

59 FR 62606, December 6, 1994: Medicare, Medicaid, and CLIA Programs; Extension of Certain Effective Dates for Clinical Laboratory Requirements and Personnel Requirements for Cytologists-Final rule with comment period, affecting 42 CFR Part 493.

59 FR 65372, December 19, 1994: Office of Inspector General — Notice of Publication of Special Fraud Alerts (pertaining to joint venture arrangements, routine waiver of Medicare Part B copayments and deductibles, hospital incentives to referring physicians, prescription drug marketing practices, and arrangements for provision of clinical laboratory services).

59 FR 66314, December 23, 1994: Medicare, Medicaid, and CLIA Programs; Clinical Laboratory Improvement Amendments of 1988 Continuance of Exemption of Laboratories Licensed by the State of Washington — Notice.

60 FR 7774, February 9, 1995: HCFA, CLIA Program; Approval of the College of American Pathologists as an Accrediting Organization for Clinical Laboratories — Notice.

60 FR 12770, March 8, 1995: HCFA Public Information Collection Requirements Submitted to the Office of Management and Budget

(OMB) for Clearance (pertaining to survey forms for compliance with CLIA; CLIA application forms for testing on human specimens, and forms for outcome-based quality assurance programs for home health agencies).

60 FR 21525, May 2, 1995: HCFA Public Information Collection Requirements Submitted to the Office of Management and Budget (OMB) for Clearance (pertaining to intermediary requests for information from skilled nursing facilities, reimbursement for CLIA compliance surveys, patient outcome data in home health agencies, common claim forms for Medicare/Medicaid reimbursement, and a study of childhood immunization costs).

60 FR 37657, July 21, 1995: CLIA Program; Approval of the American Osteopathic Association as an Accrediting Organization — Notice.

60 FR 37660, July 21, 1995: CLIA Program; Approval of the American Association of blood Banks as an Accrediting Organization — Notice.

60 FR 39403, August 2, 1995: HCFA Public Information Collection Requirements Submitted for Public Comment and Recommendations (pertaining to PRO reporting forms; Oregon Medicaid reform demonstration; review functions of PRO's; medical records review under PPS; evaluation of Medicare cataract surgery alternate payment demonstration; home health agency survey and deficiencies report; CLIA survey forms; field testing of uniform needs assessment instrument for hospital discharge planning).

60 FR 40184, August 7, 1995: HCFA Public Information Collection Requirements Submitted for Public Comment and Recommendations (pertaining to CLIA alternative quality assessment survey forms; and data collection and analysis for generating procedure specific physician cost estimates).

60 FR 41914, August 14, 1995: Medicare Program; Physician Financial Relationships with, and Referrals to, Health Care Entities that Furnish Clinical Laboratory Services; Financial Relationship Reporting Requirements — Final rule affecting 42 CFR Part 411.

60 FR 44503, August 28, 1995: Medicare, Medicaid, and CLIA Programs; Clinical Laboratory Improvement Amendments of 1988 Exemption of Permit-holding Laboratories in the State of New York — Notice.

60 FR 47534, September 13, 1995: HCFA; Public Health Service; CLIA Program; Categorization of Waived Tests — Proposed rule affecting 42 CFR Part 493.

60 FR 47982, September 15, 1995: CLIA Program; Categorization and Certification Requirements for a New Subcategory of Moderate Complexity Testing — Proposed rule affecting 42 CFR Part 493.

60 FR 55719, November 2, 1995: HCFA Public Information Collection Requirements Submitted for Public Comment and Recommendations (pertaining to evaluation of the Oregon Medicaid reform demonstration; field testing of the uniform needs assessment instrument for hospital discharge planning; survey of physician practice costs; evaluation of the Medicare cataract surgery alternate payment demonstration; and alternative CLIA quality assessment surveys).

60 FR 58088, November 24, 1995: HCFA Public Information Collection Requirements Submitted for Public Comment and Recommendations (pertaining to granting and withdrawal of deeming authority to private nonprofit accreditation organizations and the CLIA exemption under State laboratory programs).

60 FR 61509, November 30, 1995: CLIA Program; Cytology Proficiency Testing — Proposed rule affecting 42 CFR Part 493.

61 FR 4278, February 5, 1996: HCFA Public Information Collection Requirements Submitted for Public Comment and Recommendations (pertaining to national provider system numbers to replace the enumeration functions of the Medicare Online Survey, Certification and Reporting system, Clinical Laboratories Improvement Amendments of 1988, and National Supplier Clearing House provider numbering systems).

61 FR 7012, February 23, 1996: HCFA Notice Submitted for Collection of Public Comment: Submission for OMB Review (pertaining to granting and withdrawing of deeming authority to private non-profit Accreditation organizations and the Clinical Laboratory Improvement Act Exemption under State laboratory programs; and the rules for participation of home health agencies to participate as sole community home health agencies).

61 FR 7522, February 28, 1996: HCFA Public Information Collection Requirements Submitted for Public Comment and Recommendations (pertaining to Medicare and Medicaid disclosure of ownership and control interest statements).

61 FR 11646, March 21, 1996: HCFA Agency Information Collection Activities: Proposed Collection; Comment Request (pertaining to advance directives; video display terminal (VDT) operators eye care program; peer review organization sanction regulations; and deficiency correction status information under CLIA).

61 FR 25229, May 20, 1996: HCFA Agency Information Collection Activities: Proposed Collection; Comment Request (pertaining to evaluation of the Oregon reform demonstration; evaluation of the per-episode home health prospective payment demonstration; and the blood bank inspection checklist instrument used by State agencies to determine compliance with CLIA).

61 FR 29406, June 10, 1996: HCFA Agency Information Collection Activities: proposed Collection; Comment Request (pertaining to end stage renal disease application and survey and certification report forms; withholding Medicare payments to recover Medicaid overpayments; acquisition, protection, and disclosure of PRO information; clinical laboratory certification and recertification survey forms; CLIA laboratory personnel report forms; prepaid health plan cost reports; Medicare credit balance reporting requirements; statement of deficiencies and plan of correction requirements for organ procurement organizations; Medicare/Medicaid hospital survey report forms; advance directive requirements for Medicare and Medicaid; payment adjustments for sole community hospitals; survey reports for physical therapists in independent practice; HMO and CMP national data reporting requirements; identification of extension units of outpatient physical therapy and outpatient speech pathology providers; and fire safety survey reports).

61 FR 30072, June 13, 1996: Medicare, Medicaid, and CLIA Programs; Clinical Laboratory Improvement Amendments of 1988 Exemption of Laboratories in the State of Oregon — Notice.

61 FR 31141, June 19, 1996: HCFA Agency Information Collection Activities: Proposed Collection; Comment Request (pertaining to authorization agreements for electronic funds transfer; applications for health insurance under Medicare for individuals with chronic renal disease; CLIA application forms; forms for surveyors to evaluate laboratory survey processes; post laboratory survey questionnaires for laboratories to evaluate the survey process).

61 FR 38395, July 24, 1996: Medicaid Program; Medicaid Eligibility Quality Control, Progressive Reductions in Federal Financial Participation for FYs 1982–1984, Payment for Physician Billing for Clinical Laboratory Services, and Utilization Control of Skilled Nursing Facility Services: Removal of Obsolete Requirements — Final rule.

61 FR 46814, September 5, 1996: HCFA Agency Information Collection Activities: Submission for OMB Review; Comment request (pertaining to authorization agreements for electronic funds trans-

fers; entitlement to Medicare for individuals with chronic renal disease; application forms for clinical laboratories; and clinical laboratory survey questionnaires).

61 FR 48157, September 12, 1996: HCFA Agency Information Collection Activities: Submission for OMB Review; Comment request (pertaining to authorization agreement for electronic funds transfer; entitlement to Medicare for individuals with chronic renal disease; application forms for clinical laboratories; and clinical laboratory survey forms).

61 FR 57688, November 7, 1996: HCFA Agency Information Collection Activities: Comment request (pertaining toclinical laboratory surveys; clinical laboratory personnel qualifications; Medicare/Medicaid hospital survey report forms; beneficiary disenrollment from HMOs and CMPs; survey reports for ambulatory surgical centers; the Medigap complaint database; and survey forms for Comprehensive Outpatient Rehabilitation Facilities).

62 FR 5433, February 5, 1997: CLIA Program; Clinical Laboratory Improvement Amendments of 1988 — Denial of Exemption of Laboratories in the Commonwealth of Puerto Rico — Notice.

62 FR 7350, February 19, 1997: Office of Inspector General: Medicare and State Health Care Programs: Fraud and Abuse; Issuance of Advisory Opinions by the OIG — Interim final rule with comment period, affecting 42 CFR Part 1008.

62 FR 8026, February 21, 1997: HCFA Agency Information Collection Activities: Proposed Collection; Comment request (pertaining to Clinical Laboratory Improvement Act adverse action extract).

62 FR 9435, March 3, 1997: Office of Inspector General: Publication of the OIG Model Compliance Plan for Clinical Laboratories — Notice.

62 FR 11213, March 11, 1997: HCFA Agency Information Collection Activities: Proposed Collection; Comment request (pertaining to post-laboratory survey questionnaire).

62 FR 25855, May 12, 1997: Medicare, Medicaid, and CLIA Programs; Clinical Laboratory Requirements — Extension of Certain Effective Dates for Clinical Laboratory Requirements under CLIA — Final rule with comment period, affecting 42 CFR Part 493.

62 FR 27262, May 19, 1997: HCFA Approval of the Commission on Office Laboratory Accreditation for Immunohematology — Notice.

62 FR 35214, June 30, 1997: HCFA Agency Information Collection Activities: Submission for OMB Review; Comment request (pertaining to CLIA adverse actions).

62 FR 35513, July 1, 1997: Medicare, Medicaid, and CLIA Programs; Clinical Laboratory Improvement Amendments of 1988 — Continuance of Exemption of Laboratories Licensed by the State of Washington — Notice.

62 FR 43931, August 18, 1997: Medicare and Medicaid Programs: Effective Dates of Provider Agreements and Supplier Approvals — Final rule affecting 42 CFR Parts 431, 442, 488, 489, and 498.

62 FR 45815, August 29, 1997: HCFA CLIA Program; Fee Schedule Revision — Notice with comment period.

62 FR 65049, December 10, 1997: Office of Inspector General: Solicitation of New Safe Harbors and Special Fraud Alerts — Notice of intent to develop regulations, affecting 42 CFR Part 1001.

62 FR 66119, December 17, 1997: HCFA Agency Information Collection Activities: Proposed Collection; Comment request (pertaining to clinical laboratory compliance inspections).

62 FR 67881, December 30, 1997: HCFA Agency Information Collection activities: Proposed Collection; Comment request (pertaining to clinical laboratory survey forms).

63 FR 9845, February 26, 1998: HCFA Agency Information Collection Activities: Proposed Collection; Comment request (pertaining to CLIA budget workload reports).

63 FR 9844, February 26, 1998: HCFA Agency Information Collection Activities: Proposed Collection; Comment request (pertaining to procedures for advisory opinions concerning physician referrals and supporting regulations in 42 CFR Sections 411.370- 411.389).

63 FR 12474, March 13, 1998: HCFA Agency Information Collection Activities: Submission for OMB Review; Comment request (pertaining to requirements for clinical laboratory testing on human specimens).

63 FR 12476, March 13, 1998: HCFA Agency Information Collection Activities: Submission for OMB Review; Comment request (pertaining to alternate quality assessment form for clinical laboratories with good performance records).

63 FR 17429, April 9, 1998: Medicare, Medicaid, and CLIA Programs; Clinical Laboratory Improvement Amendments of 1988 Continuance of Approval as an Accrediting Organization; the Joint Commission on Accreditation of Healthcare Organizations, the American Association of Blood Banks, and the American Osteopathic Association — Notice.

63 FR 26722, May 14, 1998: HCFA CLIA Program; Simplifying CLIA Regulations Relating to Accreditation, Exemption of Laborato-

ries under a State Licensure Program, Proficiency Testing, and Inspection — Final rule affecting 42 CFR Part 493. See also correction at 63 FR 32699, June 15, 1998.

63 FR 28394, May 22, 1998: HCFA Agency Information Collection Activities: Submission for OMB Review; Comment request (pertaining to CLIA budget workload reports).

63 FR 28395, May 22, 1998: HCFA Agency Information Collection Activities: Submission for OMB Review; Comment request (pertaining to procedures for advisory opinions concerning physician referrals and supporting regulations in 42 CFR 411.370 through 411.389).

63 FR 30166, June 3, 1998: Medicare Program; Coverage and Administrative Policies for Clinical Diagnostic Laboratory Tests — Notice of intent to form negotiated rulemaking committee and notice of meeting.

63 FR 38413, July 16, 1998: HCFA Agency Information Collection Activities: Submission for OMB Review; Comment request (pertaining to Clinical Laboratory Improvement Act certification requirements; EPSDT participation reports; limitations on provider-related donations and health care-related taxes, and limitations on payments to disproportionate share hospitals; and Medicare+Choice provider sponsored organization waiver requests forms).

63 FR 42054, August 6, 1998: HCFA Agency Information Collection Activities: Submission for OMB Review; Comment Request (pertaining to Medicare/Medicaid/CLIA conditions of participation).

63 FR 42796, August 11, 1998: Medicare Program; Negotiated Rulemaking; Coverage and Administrative Policies for Clinical Diagnostic Laboratory Tests; Change in Meeting Time — Notice of meetings.

63 FR 45076, August 24, 1998: Office of Inspector General-Publication of OIG Compliance Program Guidance for Clinical Laboratories.

63 FR 55031, October 14, 1998: Medicare, Medicaid, and CLIA Programs; Extension of Certain Effective Dates for Clinical Laboratory Requirements under CLIA — Final rule with comment period, affecting 42 CFR 493.

63 FR 60356, November 9, 1998: HCFA Agency Information Collection Activities: Proposed Collection; Comment request (pertaining to collection of information on resource utilization by Medicare providers, suppliers, and CLIA laboratories).

1999

64 FR 69, January 4, 1999: Medicare Program; Negotiated Rulemaking; Coverage and Administrative Policies for Clinical Diagnostic Laboratory Tests — Notice of meetings.

64 FR 14454, March 25, 1999: HCFA Agency Information Collection Activities: Proposed Collection; Comment request (pertaining to blood bank inspection checklist under CLIA).

64 FR 38202, July 15, 1999: HCFA Agency Information Collection Activities: Proposed Collection; Comment request (pertaining to CLIA personnel reports; and CLIA certification for tests on human specimens).

64 FR 43295, August 10, 1999: Medicare Program; Negotiated Rulemaking; Coverage and Administrative Policies for Clinical Diagnostic Laboratory Tests; Announcement of Additional Public Meetings — Notice of meetings.

64 FR 55738, October 14, 1999: Medicare Program; Meeting of the Laboratory and Diagnostic Services Panel of the Medicare Coverage Advisory Committee — November 15 and 16, 1999 — Notice of meeting.

64 FR 73561, December 31, 1999: HCFA CLIA Program; Transfer of Clinical Laboratory Complexity Categorization Responsibility from the Center for Disease Control and Prevention to the Food and Drug Administration — Notice.

2000

65 FR 4824, February 1, 2000: HCFA Agency Information Collection Activities: Submission for OMB Review; Comment request (pertaining to clinical laboratory personnel reports).

65 FR 9274, February 24, 2000: Office of Inspector General: Publication of OIG Special Fraud Alert on Rental of Space in Physician Offices by Persons or Entities to Which Physicians Refer — Notice.

65 FR 13082, March 10, 2000: Medicare Program; Negotiated Rulemaking: Coverage and Administrative Policies for Clinical Diagnostic Laboratory Services — Proposed rule affecting 42 CFR Part 410.

65 FR 14510, March 17, 2000: HCFA and Centers for Disease Control and Prevention: CLIA Program; Cytology Proficiency Testing-Withdrawal of proposed rule published November 30, 1995, at 60 FR 61509, affecting 42 CFR Part 493.

65 FR 25492, May 2, 2000: Medicare, Medicaid and CLIA Programs; Clinical Laboratory Improvement Amendments of 1988 Removal of Exemption of Laboratories in the State of Oregon — Notice.

65 FR 26218, May 5, 2000: HCFA Agency Information Collection Activities: Proposed Collection; Comment request (pertaining to CLIA amendments adverse action extract).

65 FR 30415, May 11, 2000: HCFA Agency Information Collection Activities: Submission for OMB Review; Comment request (pertaining to conflict of interest and ownership and control information).

65 FR 37566, June 15, 2000: HCFA Agency Information Collection Activities: Submission for OMB Review; Comment request (pertaining to post-laboratory survey questionnaire under CLIA).

65 FR 47739, August 3, 2000: HCFA Agency Information Collection Activities: Submission for OMB Review; Comment request (pertaining to CLIA adverse action extract).

65 FR 64966, October 31, 2000: Medicare, Medicaid, and CLIA Programs; Continuance of the Approval of COLA as a CLIA Accreditation Organization — Notice. See also correction at 65 FR 70575, November 24, 2000.

65 FR 69416, November 16, 2000: Medicare and Medicaid Programs; Hospital Conditions of Participation: Laboratory Services — Proposed rule affecting 42 CFR Part 482.

65 FR 76647, December 7, 2000: HCFA Agency Information Collection Activities: Proposed Collection; Comment request (pertaining to alternate quality assessment survey in lieu of onsite survey for CLIA labs with good performance).

65 FR 82941, December 29, 2000: Medicare, Medicaid, and CLIA Programs; Extension of Certain Effective Dates for Clinical Laboratory Requirements under CLIA — Final rule with comment period, affecing 42 CFR Part 493.

2001

66 FR 856, January 4, 2001: Medicare and Medicaid Programs; Physicians Referrals to Health Care Entities with which They Have Financial Relationships—Final rule with comment period, affecting 42 CFR Parts 411 and 424.

66 FR 6629, January 22, 2001: HCFA Agency Information Collection Activities: Submission for OMB Review; Comment request (pertaining to Medicare Integrity Program Organizational Conflict of Interest Disclosure Certificate).

66 FR 8771, February 2, 2001: Medicare and Medicaid Programs; Physicians' Referrals to Health Care Entities with which They Have Financial Relationships: Delay of Effective Date of Final Rule and Technical Amendment, affecting 42 CFR Parts 411 and 424.

66 FR 17813, April 4, 2001: Medicare and Medicaid Programs; Physicians' Referrals to Health Care Entities with which They Have Financial Relationships; Extension of Comment period—Notice, affecting 42 CFR Parts 411 and 424.

66 FR 18647, April 10, 2001: HCFA Agency Information Collection Activities: Submission for OMB Review; Comment request (pertaining to CLIA compliance).

66 FR 19507, April 16, 2001: HCFA Agency Information Collection Activities: Proposed Collection; Comment request (pertaining to conflict of interest and ownership and control information form).

66 FR 22242, May 3, 2001: HCFA Agency Information Collection Activities: Proposed Collection; Comment request (pertaining to CLIA certification requirements).

66 FR 28916, May 25, 2001: HCFA Agency Information Collection Activities; Proposed Collection; Comment request (pertaining to procedures for advisory opinions concerning physician referrals under section 1877 of the Social Security Act).

66 FR 34222, June 27, 2001: HCFA Agency Information Collection Activities: Proposed Collection; Comment request (pertaining to CLIA budget workload reports).

See § 2:22.

§ 6:23 WRONGFUL CHARGES FOR INTERPRETING ELECTROCARDIOGRAMS — Section 1848(b)(3) [42 U.S.C.A. 1395w-4(b)(3)]

◆ NOTE: Repealed for services performed after January 1, 1994, by section 13514(a) of the Omnibus Budget Reconciliation Act of 1993.

Regulations

42 CFR Part 405, Subpart C — Recovery of Overpayments and Suspension of Payment; and Subpart E — Criteria for Determination of Reasonable Charges

42 CFR Part 410 — Supplementary Medical Insurance (SMI) Benefits

42 CFR Part 414 — Payment for Part B Medical and Other Health Services

42 CFR Part 415 — Services Furnished by Physicians in Providers, Supervising Physicians in Teaching Settings, and Residents in Certain Settings

42 CFR Part 420 — Program Integrity: Medicare

42 CFR Part 424 — Conditions for Medicare Payment

42 CFR Part 498 — Appeals Procedures for Determinations that Affect Participation in the Medicare Program and for Determinations that Affect the Participation of ICF's/MR and Certain NF's in the Medicaid Program

42 CFR Chapter V — Office of Inspector General — Health Care, Department of Health and Human Services

Subchapter A — General Provisions

Part 1000 — Introduction; General Definitions

Subchapter B — OIG Authorities

Part 1001 — Program Integrity: Medicare and State Health Care Programs

Part 1002 — Program Integrity: State-initiated Exclusion from Medicaid

Part 1003 — Civil Money Penalties, Assessments and Exclusions

Part 1004 — Imposition of Sanctions on Health Care Practitioners and Providers of Health Care Services by a Peer Review Organization

Part 1005 — Appeals of Exclusions, Civil Money Penalties and Assessments

Part 1006 — Investigational Inquiries

Part 1007 — State Medicaid Fraud Control Units

Part 1008 — Advisory Opinions by the OIG

53 FR 53025, December 30, 1988: Medicare Program; Physician Liability on Non-assigned Claims — Proposed rule to amend 42 CFR Part 405

54 FR 30558, July 21, 1989: Medicare Program; Diagnosis Codes on Physician Bills — Proposed rule to amend 42 CFR 424

54 FR 53818, December 29, 1989: Medicare Program; Physician Performance Standard Rate of Increase for Federal Fiscal Year 1990-Announcement of physician performance standard rate of increase.

55 FR 24561, June 18, 1990: Medicare Program; Physician Liability on Non-Assigned Claims — Final rule affecting 42 CFR Parts 400

and 411. See also correction published at 55 FR 35142, August 28, 1990.

55 FR 36178, September 4, 1990: Medicare Program; Model Fee Schedule for Physicians' Services — Notice with comment period.

55 FR 53356, December 28, 1990: Medicare Program; Physician Performance Standard Rates of Increase for Federal Fiscal Year 1991 — Notice.

56 FR 25792, June 5, 1991: Medicare Program; Fee Schedule for Physicians' Services — Proposed rule affecting 42 CFR Parts 405 and 415.

56 FR 59502, November 25, 1991: Medicare Program; Fee Schedule for Physicians' Services, Fee Schedule Update for Calendar Year 1992 and Physician Performance Standard Rates of Increase for Federal FY 1992 — Final rules and notice affecting 42 CFR Parts 405, 413, 414, and 415. See also correction at 57 FR 42491, September 15, 1992.

56 FR 61023, November 29, 1991: Medicare Program; Standard Claim Forms for Part B Claims Completed and Submitted by Physicians, Suppliers and Other Persons — General notice with comment period.

57 FR 36006, August 12, 1992: Medicare Program; Self-implementing Coverage and Payments Provisions: 1990 Legislation — Final rule with comment period, affecting 42 CFR Parts 405, 406, 409, 420, 411, 412, 413, 418, and 489. Pertains to capital-related inpatient hospital costs; capital-related outpatient hospital costs; non-capital related outpatient hospital costs; payment for physician pathology services; payment for services of physicians as assistants-at-surgery; payments for ambulatory surgical procedures in hospital outpatient departments; payments for radiology services performed in hospital outpatient departments; hospice benefit extension; enrollment of HMO members in Medicare Part A; coverage of ostomy supplies; application of pre-entitlement stay in psychiatric hospital to limit on payment for inpatient hospital services; payments to dialysis facilities; payment rates for erythropoietin (EPO); and Medicare secondary payer provision for individuals with ESRD. See also confirmation of final rule at 58 FR 58502, November 2, 1993.

57 FR 43462, September 21, 1992: Health Care Financing Administration Public Information Collection Requirements Submitted to the Office of Management and Budget for Clearance (pertaining to sole community home health agencies; physician/supplier overpay-

ment reports; physician or supplier Medicare agreements; conditions of participation for rural health clinics; Medicare provider refunds; conditions of participation for comprehensive outpatient rehabilitation facilities; Medicaid income and eligibility verification system; Medicaid integrated review schedule; provider overpayment report; financial statement of Medicare provider debtors; negative case action review schedule for Medicaid quality control; outpatient resource costing study; Medicaid intermediate care facility for the mentally retarded or persons with related conditions survey report form; installment agreement of beneficiary refund of overpayment; PRO assumption of responsibilities; Medicare contractor administrative budget and cost reporting system forms; fire safety survey report forms; medical records review under prospective payment system; and Qualified Medicare Beneficiary supplement to the Medicare current beneficiary survey).

57 FR 46362, October 8, 1992: Medicare and Medicaid Programs; Revised Effective Date of Medicare/Medicaid Provider Agreement and Supplier Participation — Proposed rule affecting 42 CFR Parts 431, 440, 442, 488, 489, and 498.

57 FR 47587, October 19, 1992: Medicare and Medicaid Programs; Use of Standardized Federal Claims Processing Forms and Procedures — Advance notice of proposed rulemaking.

57 FR 48033, October 21, 1992: Medicare Program; Revised Procedures for Paying Claims From Providers of Services — Final notice.

57 FR 55914, November 25, 1992: Medicare Program; Fee Schedule for Physicians' Services for Calendar Year 1993 — Final notice with comment period. See also corrections published at 57 FR 59379, December 15, 1992, and at 58 FR 31964, June 7, 1993.

58 FR 63626, December 2, 1993: Medicare Program; Revisions to Payment Policies and Adjustments to the Relative Value Units under the Physician Fee Schedule for Calendar Year 1994 — Final rule with comment period, affecting 42 CFR Parts 405 and 414. See also correction at 59 FR 36069, July 15, 1994.

See § 2:23.

§ 6:24 VIOLATING LIMITATIONS ON PHYSICIAN CHARGES BY NONPARTICIPATING PHYSICIANS, SUPPLIERS, OR OTHER PERSONS AFTER 1990 — Section 1848(g)(1) [42 U.S.C.A. 1395w-4(g)(1)]

Regulations

42 CFR Part 402 — Civil Money Penalties, Assessments, and Exclusions

42 CFR Part 405, Subpart C — Recovery of Overpayments and Suspension of Payment; Subpart D — Private Contracts; and Subpart E — Criteria for Determination of Reasonable Charges

42 CFR Part 410 — Supplementary Medical Insurance (SMI) Benefits

42 CFR Part 414 — Payment for Part B Medical and Other Health Services

42 CFR Part 415 — Services Furnished by Physicians in Providers, Supervising Physicians in Teaching Settings, and Residents in Certain Settings

42 CFR Part 420 — Program Integrity: Medicare

42 CFR Part 424 — Conditions for Medicare Payment

42 CFR Part 498 — Appeals Procedures for Determinations that Affect Participation in the Medicare Program and for Determinations that Affect the Participation of ICF's/MR and Certain NF's in the Medicaid Program

42 CFR Chapter V — Office of Inspector General — Health Care, Department of Health and Human Services

Subchapter A — General Provisions

Part 1000 — Introduction; General Definitions

Subchapter B — OIG Authorities

Part 1001 — Program Integrity: Medicare and State Health Care Programs

Part 1003 — Civil Money Penalties, Assessments and Exclusions

Part 1004 — Imposition of Sanctions on Health Care Practitioners and Providers of Health Care Services by a Peer Review Organization

Part 1005 — Appeals of Exclusions, Civil Money Penalties and Assessments

Part 1006 — Investigational Inquiries

Part 1007 — State Medicaid Fraud Control Units

Part 1008 — Advisory Opinions by the OIG

53 FR 53025, December 30, 1988: Medicare Program; Physician Liability on Non-assigned Claims — Proposed rule to amend 42 CFR Part 405

54 FR 3794, January 26, 1989: Medicare Program; Uniform Relative Value Guide for Anesthesia Services Furnished by Physicians — Proposed rule to amend 42 CFR part 405

54 FR 3803, January 26, 1989: Medicare Program; Fee Schedules for the Services of Certified Registered Nurse Anesthetists — Proposed rule to amend 42 CFR Parts 405, 410, 412, 413, and 482.

54 FR 8994, March 2, 1989: Medicare Program; Fee Schedules for Radiologist Services — Interim rule with comment period to amend 42 CFR Part 405.

54 FR 13294, March 31, 1989: Medicare Program; Fee Schedules for Radiologist Services — Correction of notice published at 54 FR 8994, March 2, 1989.

54 FR 30558, July 21, 1989: Medicare Program; Diagnosis Codes on Physician Bills — Proposed rule to amend 42 CFR 424.

54 FR 53818, December 29, 1989: Medicare Program; Physician Performance Standard Rate of Increase for Federal Fiscal Year 1990-Announcement of physician performance standard rate of increase.

55 FR 18668, May 3, 1990: Medicare Program; Definition of Surgical Services — Notice of definition of surgical services for physician volume performance standard rates for increase with comment.

55 FR 24561, June 18, 1990: Medicare Program; Physician Liability on Non-Assigned Claims — Final rule affecting 42 CFR Parts 400 and 411. See also correction published at 55 FR 35142, August 28, 1990.

55 FR 32078, August 7, 1990: Medicare Program; Uniform Relative Value Guide for Anesthesia Services Furnished by Physicians — Final rule affecting 42 CFR Part 405.

55 FR 36178, September 4, 1990: Medicare Program; Model Fee Schedule for Physicians' Services — Notice with comment period.

55 FR 42907, October 24, 1990: Medicare Program; Standards Applied by Utilization and Quality Control Peer Review Organizations: Consideration of Remote Rural Location and Other Relevant Factors — Notice of policy and request for comments.

55 FR 53356, December 28, 1990: Medicare Program; Physician Performance Standard Rates of Increase for Federal Fiscal Year 1991 — Notice.

56 FR 699, January 8, 1991: Medicare Program; National Standardization of "Global Surgery" Policy — Proposed notice.

56 FR 25792, June 5, 1991: Medicare Program; Fee Schedule for Physicians' Services — Proposed rule affecting 42 CFR Parts 405 and 415.

56 FR 59502, November 25, 1991: Medicare Program; Fee Schedule for Physicians' Services, Fee Schedule Update for Calendar Year 1992 and Physician Performance Standard Rates of Increase for Federal FY 1992 — Final rules and notice affecting 42 CFR Parts 405, 413, 414, and 415. See also correction at 57 FR 42491, September 15, 1992.

56 FR 61023, November 29, 1991: Medicare Program; Standard Claim Forms for Part B Claims Completed and Submitted by Physicians, Suppliers and Other Persons — General notice with comment period.

57 FR 36006, August 12, 1992: Medicare Program; Self-implementing Coverage and Payments Provisions: 1990 Legislation — Final rule with comment period, affecting 42 CFR Parts 405, 406, 409, 420, 411, 412, 413, 418, and 489. Pertains to capital-related inpatient hospital costs; capital-related outpatient hospital costs; non-capital related outpatient hospital costs; payment for physician pathology services; payment for services of physicians as assistants-at-surgery; payments for ambulatory surgical procedures in hospital outpatient departments; payments for radiology services performed in hospital outpatient departments; hospice benefit extension; enrollment of HMO members in Medicare Part A; coverage of ostomy supplies; application of pre-entitlement stay in psychiatric hospital to limit on payment for inpatient hospital services; payments to dialysis facilities; payment rates for erythropoietin (EPO); and Medicare secondary payer provision for individuals with ESRD. See also confirmation of final rule at 58 FR 58502, November 2, 1993.

57 FR 43462, September 21, 1992: Health Care Financing Administration Public Information Collection Requirements Submitted to the Office of Management and Budget for Clearance (pertaining to sole community home health agencies; physician/supplier overpayment reports; physician or supplier Medicare agreements; conditions of participation for rural health clinics; Medicare provider

refunds; conditions of participation for comprehensive outpatient rehabilitation facilities; Medicaid income and eligibility verification system; Medicaid integrated review schedule; provider overpayment report; financial statement of Medicare provider debtors; negative case action review schedule for Medicaid quality control; outpatient resource costing study; Medicaid intermediate care facility for the mentally retarded or persons with related conditions survey report form; installment agreement of beneficiary refund of overpayment; PRO assumption of responsibilities; Medicare contractor administrative budget and cost reporting system forms; fire safety survey report forms; medical records review under prospective payment system; and Qualified Medicare Beneficiary supplement to the Medicare current beneficiary survey).

57 FR 46362, October 8, 1992: Medicare and Medicaid Programs; Revised Effective Date of Medicare/Medicaid Provider Agreement and Supplier Participation — Proposed rule affecting 42 CFR Parts 431, 440, 442, 488, 489, and 498.

57 FR 47587, October 19, 1992: Medicare and Medicaid Programs; Use of Standardized Federal Claims Processing Forms and Procedures — Advance notice of proposed rulemaking.

57 FR 55914, November 25, 1992: Medicare Program; Fee Schedule for Physicians' Services for Calendar Year 1993 — Final notice with comment period. See also corrections published at 57 FR 59379, December 15, 1992, and at 58 FR 31964, June 7, 1993.

58 FR 54096, October 20, 1993: Office of Inspector General: Civil Money Penalties for Prohibited Referrals to Entities Providing Clinical Laboratory Services and for Prohibited Arrangements and Schemes — Proposed rule affecting 42 CFR Part 1003.

58 FR 63626, December 2, 1993: Medicare Program; Revisions to Payment Policies and Adjustments to the Relative Value Units under the Physician Fee Schedule for Calendar Year 1994 — Final rule with comment period, affecting 42 CFR Parts 405 and 414. See also correction at 59 FR 36069, July 15, 1994.

59 FR 10290, March 4, 1994: Medicare Program; Diagnosis Codes on Physician Bills — Final rule affecting 42 CFR Parts 405 and 424. See also correction at 59 FR 26739, May 24, 1994.

59 FR 32754, June 24, 1994: Medicare Program; Refinements to Geographic Adjustment Factor Values and Other Policies under the Physician Fee Schedule — Proposed rule affection 42 CFR parts 410 and 414.

59 FR 39828, August 4, 1994: Medicare Program; Payment Policies and Adjustments to the Relative Value Units Under the Physician Fee Schedule for Calendar Year 1994, affecting 42 CFR Parts 405 and 414.

59 FR 63410, December 8, 1994: Medicare Program; Refinements to Geographic Adjustment Factor Values, Revisions to Payment Policies, Adjustments to the Relative Value Units (RVUs) under the Physician Fee Schedule for Calendar Year 1995, and the 5-Year Refinement of RVUs — Final rule with comment period, affecting 42 CFR parts 410 and 414. See also correction at 60 FR 46, January 3, 1995 and at 60 FR 36733, July 18, 1995.

59 FR 63638, December 8, 1994: Medicare Program; Physician Fee Schedule Update for Calendar Year 1995 and Physician Volume Performance Standard Rates of Increase for Federal Fiscal Year 1995 — Final notice.

59 FR 65372, December 19, 1994: Office of Inspector General — Notice of Publication of Special Fraud Alerts (pertaining to joint venture arrangements, routine waiver of Medicare Part B copayments and deductibles, hospital incentives to referring physicians, prescription drug marketing practices, and arrangements for provision of clinical laboratory services).

60 FR 2325, January 9, 1995: Medicare Program; Providers and Suppliers of Specialized Services: Technical Amendments — Final rule with comment period, affecting 42 CFR Parts 400, 405, 410, 484, 485, 486, and 498. See also correction at 60 FR 11632, March 2, 1995.

60 FR 16580, March 31, 1995: Office of Inspector General: Civil Money Penalties for Referrals to Entities and for Prohibited Arrangements and Schemes — Final rule with comment period, affecting 42 CFR Part 1003.

60 FR 38400, July 26, 1995: Medicare Program; Revisions to Payment Policies under the Physician Fee Schedule for Calendar Year 1996 — Proposed rule affecting 42 CFR Parts 400, 405, 410, 411, 412, 413, 414, 415, 417, and 489.

60 FR 63124, December 8, 1995: Medicare Program; Revisions to Payment Policies and Adjustments to the Relative Value Units under the Physician Fee Schedule for Calendar Year 1996 — Final rule with comment period, affecting 42 CFR Parts 400, 405, 410, 411, 412, 413, 414, 415, 417, and 489. See also correction at 61 FR 42385, August 15, 1996.

61 FR 13205, March 26, 1996: HCFA Agency Information Collection Activities: Submission for OMB Review; Comment Request

(pertaining to Medicare standardized forms for reimbursement of covered services by all providers that accept Medicare assignment).

61 FR 16925, April 18, 1996: HCFA Agency Information Collection Activities: Proposed Collection; Comment Request (pertaining to Medicare participating physician or supplier agreements; and hospital conditions of participation).

61 FR 19992, May 3, 1996: Medicare Program; Five-year Review of Work Relative Value Units under the Physician Fee Schedule — Proposed notice.

61 FR 38454, July 24, 1996: HCFA Agency Information Collection Activities: Submission for OMB Review; Comment request (pertaining to physicians who do not accept Medicare assignment).

61 FR 59490, November 22, 1996: Medicare Program; Revisions to Payment Policies and Five-year Review of and Adjustments to the Relative value Units under the Physician Fee Schedule for Calendar yeat 1997 — Final rule with comment period, affecting 42 CFR Parts 410and 415. See also correction at 62 FR 7945, February 21, 1997.

61 FR 59717, November 22, 1996: Medicare Program; Physician Fee Schedule Update for Calendar year 1997 and Physician Volume Performance Standard Rates of Increase for Federal Fiscal Year 1997 — Final notice.

62 FR 7945, February 21, 1997: Medicare Program; Revisions to Payment Policies and Five-year Review of and Adjustments to the Relative Value Units Under the Physician Fee Schedule for Calendar Year 1997; Correction of final rule with comment period.

62 FR 24483, May 5, 1997: Medicare Program; Update of the Reasonable Compensation Equivalent Limits for Services Furnished by Physicians — Notice.

62 FR 33158, June 18, 1997: Medicare Program; Revisions to Payment Policies Under the Physician Fee Schedule, Other Part B Payment Policies, and Establishment of the Clinical Psychologist Fee Schedule for Calendar year 1998, Proposed rule affecting 42 CFR Parts 400, 405, 410, and 414. See also correction at 62 FR 43962, August 18, 1997.

62 FR 59261, October 31, 1997: Medicare Program; Physician Fee Schedule Conversion Factor for Calendar Year 1998 and Sustainable Growth Rate for Fiscal Year 1998 — Final notice.

62 FR 59267, October 31, 1997: Medicare Program; Delay in Implementing the Adjustments to the Practice Expense Relative Value Units under the Physician Fee Schedule for Calendar Year 1998 — Notice of intent to regulate.

62 FR 65049, December 10, 1997: Office of Inspector General: Solicitation of New Safe Harbors and Special Fraud Alerts — Notice of intent to develop regulations, affecting 42 CFR Part 1001.

62 FR 66376, December 18, 1997: HCFA Emergency Clearance: Public Information Collection Requirements Submitted to the Office of Management and Budget (OMB) (pertaining to Medicare and other Federal health care program enrollment forms for providers and suppliers).

62 FR 66726, December 19, 1997: Medicare and Medicaid Programs; Hospital Conditions of Participation; Provider Agreements and Supplier Approval — Proposed rule affecting 42 CFR Parts 416, 482, 485, and 489.

63 FR 687, January 7, 1998: Medicare Program; Application of Inherent Reasonableness to All Medicare Part B Services (Other than Physician Services) — Interim final rule with comment period, affecting 42 CFR Part 405.

63 FR 2926, January 20, 1998: Medicare Program; Additional Supplier Standards — Proposed rule affecting 42 CFR Part 424.

63 FR 4459, January 29, 1998: HCFA Emergency Clearance: Public Information Collection Requirements Submitted to the Office of Management and Budget (OMB) (pertaining to Medicare/Medicaid health insurance common claim form and instructions).

63 FR 5106, January 30, 1998: Medicare and Medicaid Programs; Salary Equivalency Guidelines for Physical Therapy, Respiratory Therapy, Speech Language Pathology, and Occupational Therapy Services — Final rule affecting 42 CFR Part 413. See also revised effective date and technical correction at 63 FR 15315, March 31, 1998.

63 FR 7175, February 12, 1998: HCFA Emergency Clearance: Public Information Collection Requirements Submitted to the Office of Management and Budget (OMB) (pertaining to research and analytic support for implementing performance measurement in fee for service Medicare and group practices).

63 FR 7743, February 17, 1998: Medicare and Medicaid Programs; Hospital Conditions of Participation; Provider Agreements and Supplier Approval — Notice of extension of comment period, affecting 42 CFR Parts 416, 482, 485, and 489.

63 FR 10920, March 5, 1998: HCFA Emergency Clearance: Public Information Collection Requirements Submitted to the Office of Management and Budget (OMB) (pertaining to Medicare and other

Federal health care program provider and supplier application forms).

63 FR 25320, May 7, 1998: HCFA National Standard Health Care Provider Identifier — Proposed Rule affecting 45 CFR Part 142.

63 FR 30818, June 5, 1998: Medicare Program; Revisions to Payment Policies under the Physician Fee Schedule for Calendar Year 1999 — Proposed rule, affecting 42 CFR Parts 405, 410, 413, 414, 415, 424, and 485. See also correction at 63 FR 50545, September 22, 1998.

63 FR 36250, July 2, 1998: HCFA Agency Information Collection Activities; Submission for OMB review; Comment request (pertaining to provider/supplier enrollment applications).

63 FR 38311, July 16, 1998: Office of Inspector General: Medicare and State Health Care Programs: Fraud and Abuse; Issuance of Advisory Opinions by the OIG — Final rule affecting 42 CFR 1008. See also correction at 63 FR 43449, August 13, 1998.

63 FR 38414, July 16, 1998: HCFA Privacy Act of 1974; Report of Altered System (pertaining to disclosure of individual-specific information to combat fraud or abuse in health benefit programs).

63 FR 58399, October 30, 1998: Office of Inspector General: Publication of the OIG's Provider Self-Disclosure Protocol — Notice.

63 FR 58814, November 2, 1998: Medicare Program; Revisions to Payment Policies and Adjustments to the Relative Value Units under the Physician Fee Schedule for Calendar Year 1999 — Final rule with comment period, affecting 42 CFR 405, 410, 413, 414, 415, 424, and 485. See also correction at 64 FR 35258, June 30, 1999

63 FR 68223, December 10, 1998: Office of Inspector General; Solicitation of New Safe Harbors and Special Fraud Alerts — Notice of intent to develop regulations, affecting 42 CFR 1001.

1999

64 FR 1813, January 12, 1999: Office of Inspector General Publication of OIG Special Fraud Alert on Physician Liability for Certifications in the Provision of Medical Equipment and Supplies and Home Health Services — Notice.

64 FR 17673, April 12, 1999: HCFA Agency Information Collection Activities: Proposed Collection; Comment request (pertaining to Medicare participating physician or supplier agreements).

64 FR 23845, May 4, 1999: HCFA Agency Information Collection Activities: Proposed Collection; Comment request (pertaining to Medicare geographical classification review board procedures).

64 FR 24956, May 10, 1999: Medicare and Medicaid Programs; Effective Dates of Provider Agreements and Supplier Approvals-Correction restoring regulations inadvertently removed when a final rule concerning effective dates for provider agreements and supplier approvals was published at 62 FR 43931, August 18, 1997.

64 FR 32239, June 16, 1999: HCFA Agency Information Collection Activities: Submission for OMB Review; Comment request (pertaining to the requirement that physicians must notify beneficiaries that Medicare is likely to deny payment for a specified service).

64 FR 39517, July 22, 1999: HCFA Agency Information Collection Activities: Submission for OMB Review; Comment request (pertaining to Medicare participating physician or supplier agreement form HCFA-460).

64 FR 40017, July 23, 1999: HCFA Agency Information Collection Activities: Submission for OMB Review; Comment request (pertaining to Medicare geographical classification review board procedures and criteria).

64 FR 40534, July 27, 1999: Medicare Program; Replacement of Reasonable Charge Methodology by Fee Schedules — Proposed action affecting 42 CFR 414.

64 FR 48846, September 8, 1999: Office of Inspector General: Solicitation of Information and Recommendations for Developing OIG Compliance Program Guidance for Individual Physicians and Small Group Practices — Notice.

64 FR 57431, October 25, 1999: Medicare Program; Appeals of Carrier Determinations that a Supplier Fails to Meet the Requirements for Medicare Billing Privileges — Proposed rule affecting 42 CFR Part 405.

64 FR 59380, November 2, 1999: Medicare Program; Revisions to Payment Policies under the Physician Fee Schedule for Calendar Year 2000 — Final rule with comment period, affecting 42 CFR Parts 410, 411, 414, 415, and 485. See also correction at 65 FR 19329, April 11, 2000.

64 FR 69021, December 9, 1999: HCFA Agency Information Collection Activities: Proposed Collection; Comment request (pertaining to analysis of malpractice premium data to compute the physician fee schedule).

2000

65 FR 5354, February 3, 2000: HCFA Agency Information Collection Activities: Proposed Collection; Comment request (pertaining to standardized Medicare/Medicaid claim form for reimbursement of covered services).

65 FR 15912, March 24, 2000: HCFA Agency Information Collection Activities: Submission for OMB Review; Comment request (pertaining to Medicare uniform institutional provider claim forms).

65 FR 30414, May 11, 2000: HCFA Agency Information Collection Activities: Submission for OMB Review; Comment request (pertaining to health insurance common claims form).

65 FR 36818, June 12, 2000: Office of Inspector General: Draft OIG Compliance Program for Individual and Small Group Physician Practices — Notice and comment period.

65 FR 42021, July 7, 2000: HCFA Agency Information Collection Activities: Proposed Collection; Comment request (pertaining to notice to providers, suppliers, and practitioners about non-covered services to beneficiaries).

65 FR 44176, July 17, 2000: Medicare Program; Revisions to Payment Policies under the Physician Fee Schedule for Calendar Year 2001 — Proposed rule affection 42 CFR Parts 410 and 414.

65 FR 50312, August 17, 2000: Office of the Secretary; Health Insurance Reform: Standards for Electronic Transactions — Final rule affecting 45 CFR Parts 160 and 162.

65 FR 53319, September 1, 2000: HCFA Agency Information Collection Activities: Proposed Collection; Comment request (pertaining to incentive arrangement disclosure form for managed care organizations and their related medical groups and physicians).

65 FR 59434, October 5, 2000: Office of Inspector General Compliance Program for Individual and Small Group Physician Practices — Notice.

65 FR 64227, October 26, 2000: HCFA Agency Information Collection Activities: Proposed Collection; Comment Request; Public Information Collection Meeting to Discuss Proposed Revisions (pertaining to notice requirements from suppliers, physicians, and practitioners to beneficiaries when Medicare Part B payment may be denied).

65 FR 65376, November 1, 2000: Medicare Program; Revisions to Payment Policies under the Physician Fee Schedule for Calendar Year 2001—Final rule with comment period. See also correction at 66 FR 16607, March 27, 2001.

65 FR 65603, November 1, 2000: Medicare Program; Revisions to Payment Policies under the Physician Fee Schedule for Calendar Year 2001 — Final rule with comment period.

65 FR 65861, November 2, 2000: HCFA Agency Information Collection Activities: Proposed Collection; Comment request (pertaining to conflict of interest disclosure requirements for Medicare program integrity).

2001

66 FR 1996, January 10, 2001: HCFA Agency Information Collection Activities; Comment request (pertaining to Medicare uniform institutional provider bill for reimbursement of covered services by all providers that accept assignment of claims).

66 FR 1997, January 10, 2001: HCFA Notice of OMB Approval (pertaining to uniform home health advance beneficiary notice).

66 FR 2912, January 12, 2001: HCFA Agency Information Collection Activities: Proposed Collection; Comment request (pertaining to Medicare/Medicaid health insurance common claim form).

66 FR 8807, February 2, 2001: HCFA Agency Information Collection Activities: Proposed Collection; Comment request (pertaining to Medicare Federal health care programs provider/supplier enrollment application).

66 FR 16061, March 22, 2001: HCFA Agency Information Collection Activities: Proposed Collection; Comment request (pertaining to private contracts of physicians who opt out of Medicare).

66 FR 18646, April 10, 2001: HCFA Agency Information Collection Activities: Submission for OMB Review; Comment request (pertaining to Medicare/Medicaid health insurance common claim form).

66 FR 20316, April 20, 2001: HCFA Agency Information Collection Activities: Submission for OMB Review; Comment request (pertaining to advance beneficiary notice by physicians, practitioners, suppliers, and providers about items and services denied by Medicare as not reasonable and necessary).

66 FR 20997, April 26, 2001: HCFA Agency Information Collection Activities: Submission for OMB Review; Comment request (pertaining to health insurance provider agreement form).

66 FR 21770, May 1, 2001: HCFA Agency Information Collection Activities: Submission for OMB Review; Comment request (pertaining to Medicare uniform institutional provider bill form).

66 FR 31038, June 8, 2001: Medicare Program; Five–year Review of Work Relative Value Units under the Physician Fee Schedule—Proposed notice.

66 FR 32630, June 15, 2001: HCFA Agency Information Collection Activities; Submission for OMB Review; Comment request (pertaining to contracts by practitioners and physicians who opt–out of Medicare).

66 FR 33102, June 20, 2001: HCFA Agency Information Collection Activities; Submission for OMB Review; Comment request (pertaining to provider/supplier enrollment application form).

See § 2:24.

§ 6:25 FAILURE TO BILL ON AN ASSIGNMENT-RELATED BASIS FOR SERVICES TO PERSONS ENROLLED UNDER MEDICARE PART B AND ELIGIBLE FOR MEDICAID — Section 1848(g)(3) [42 U.S.C.A. 1395w-4(g)(3)]

Regulations

42 CFR Part 402 — Civil Money Penalties, Assessments, and Exclusions

42 CFR Part 405, Subpart C — Recovery of Overpayments and Suspension of Payment; and Subpart E — Criteria for Determination of Reasonable Charges

42 CFR Part 410 — Supplementary Medical Insurance (SMI) Benefits

42 CFR Part 414 — Payment for Part B Medical and Other Health Services

42 CFR Part 415 — Services Furnished by Physicians in Providers, Supervising Physicians in Teaching Settings, and Residents in Certain Settings

42 CFR Part 420 — Program Integrity: Medicare

42 CFR Part 424 — Conditions for Medicare Payment

42 CFR Part 498 — Appeals Procedures for Determinations that Affect Participation in the Medicare Program and for Determinations that Affect the Participation of ICF's/MR and Certain NF's in the Medicaid Program

42 CFR Chapter V — Office of Inspector General — Health Care, Department of Health and Human Services

Subchapter A — General Provisions

Part 1000 — Introduction; General Definitions

Subchapter B — OIG Authorities

Part 1001 — Program Integrity: Medicare and State Health Care Programs

Part 1003 — Civil Money Penalties, Assessments and Exclusions

Part 1004 — Imposition of Sanctions on Health Care Practitioners and Providers of Health Care Services by a Peer Review Organization

Part 1005 — Appeals of Exclusions, Civil Money Penalties and Assessments

Part 1006 — Investigational Inquiries

Part 1007 — State Medicaid Fraud Control Units

Part 1008 — Advisory Opinions by the OIG

53 FR 53025, December 30, 1988: Medicare Program; Physician Liability on Non-assigned Claims — Proposed rule to amend 42 CFR Part 405.

54 FR 3794, January 26, 1989: Medicare Program; Uniform Relative Value Guide for Anesthesia Services Furnished by Physicians — Proposed rule to amend 42 CFR part 405.

54 FR 3803, January 26, 1989: Medicare Program; Fee Schedules for the Services of Certified Registered Nurse Anesthetists — Proposed rule to amend 42 CFR Parts 405, 410, 412, 413, and 482.

54 FR 8994, March 2, 1989: Medicare Program; Fee Schedules for Radiologist Services — Interim rule with comment period to amend 42 CFR Part 405. See also correction at 54 FR 13294, March 31, 1989.

54 FR 30558, July 21, 1989: Medicare Program; Diagnosis Codes on Physician Bills — Proposed rule to amend 42 CFR 424.

54 FR 53818, December 29, 1989: Medicare Program; Physician Performance Standard Rate of Increase for Federal Fiscal Year 1990-Announcement of physician performance standard rate of increase.

55 FR 18668, May 3, 1990: Medicare Program; Definition of Surgical Services — Notice of definition of surgical services for physician volume performance standard rates for increase with comment.

55 FR 24561, June 18, 1990: Medicare Program; Physician Liability on Non-Assigned Claims — Final rule affecting 42 CFR Parts 400 and 411. See also correction published at 55 FR 35142, August 28, 1990.

55 FR 36178, September 4, 1990: Medicare Program; Model Fee Schedule for Physicians' Services — Notice with comment period.

56 FR 25792, June 5, 1991: Medicare Program; Fee Schedule for Physicians' Services — Proposed rule affecting 42 CFR Parts 405 and 415.

56 FR 59502, November 25, 1991: Medicare Program; Fee Schedule for Physicians' Services, Fee Schedule Update for Calendar Year 1992 and Physician Performance Standard Rates of Increase for Federal FY 1992 — Final rules and notice affecting 42 CFR Parts 405, 413, 414, and 415. See also correction at 57 FR 42491, September 15, 1992.

56 FR 61023, November 29, 1991: Medicare Program; Standard Claim Forms for Part B Claims Completed and Submitted by Physicians, Suppliers and Other Persons — General notice with comment period.

57 FR 36006, August 12, 1992: Medicare Program; Self-implementing Coverage and Payments Provisions: 1990 Legislation — Final rule with comment period, affecting 42 CFR Parts 405, 406, 409, 420, 411, 412, 413, 418, and 489. Pertains to capital-related inpatient hospital costs; capital-related outpatient hospital costs; non-capital related outpatient hospital costs; payment for physician pathology services; payment for services of physicians as assistants-at-surgery; payments for ambulatory surgical procedures in hospital outpatient departments; payments for radiology services performed in hospital outpatient departments; hospice benefit extension; enrollment of HMO members in Medicare Part A; coverage of ostomy supplies; application of pre-entitlement stay in psychiatric hospital to limit on payment for inpatient hospital services; payments to dialysis facilities; payment rates for erythropoietin (EPO); and Medicare secondary payer provision for individuals with ESRD. See also confirmation of final rule at 58 FR 58502, November 2, 1993.

57 FR 43462, September 21, 1992: Health Care Financing Administration Public Information Collection Requirements Submitted to the Office of Management and Budget for Clearance (pertaining to sole community home health agencies; physician/supplier overpayment reports; physician or supplier Medicare agreements; conditions of participation for rural health clinics; Medicare provider refunds; conditions of participation for comprehensive outpatient rehabilitation facilities; Medicaid income and eligibility verification system; Medicaid integrated review schedule; provider overpayment

report; financial statement of Medicare provider debtors; negative case action review schedule for Medicaid quality control; outpatient resource costing study; Medicaid intermediate care facility for the mentally retarded or persons with related conditions survey report form; installment agreement of beneficiary refund of overpayment; PRO assumption of responsibilities; Medicare contractor administrative budget and cost reporting system forms; fire safety survey report forms; medical records review under prospective payment system; and Qualified Medicare Beneficiary supplement to the Medicare current beneficiary survey).

57 FR 46362, October 8, 1992: Medicare and Medicaid Programs; Revised Effective Date of Medicare/Medicaid Provider Agreement and Supplier Participation — Proposed rule affecting 42 CFR Parts 431, 440, 442, 488, 489, and 498.

57 FR 47587, October 19, 1992: Medicare and Medicaid Programs; Use of Standardized Federal Claims Processing Forms and Procedures — Advance notice of proposed rulemaking.

57 FR 55914, November 25, 1992: Medicare Program; Fee Schedule for Physicians' Services for Calendar Year 1993 — Final notice with comment period. See also corrections published at 57 FR 59379, December 15, 1992, and at 58 FR 31964, June 7, 1993.

58 FR 63626, December 2, 1993: Medicare Program; Revisions to Payment Policies and Adjustments to the Relative Value Units under the Physician Fee Schedule for Calendar Year 1994 — Final rule with comment period, affecting 42 CFR Parts 405 and 414. See also correction at 59 FR 36069, July 15, 1994.

59 FR 10290, March 4, 1994: Medicare Program; Diagnosis Codes on Physician Bills — Final rule affecting 42 CFR Parts 405 and 424. See also correction at 59 FR 26739, May 24, 1994.

59 FR 32754, June 24, 1994: Medicare Program; Refinements to Geographic Adjustment Factor Values and Other Policies under the Physician Fee Schedule — Proposed rule affection 42 CFR parts 410 and 414.

59 FR 39828, August 4, 1994: Medicare Program; Payment Policies and Adjustments to the Relative Value Units Under the Physician Fee Schedule for Calendar Year 1994, affecting 42 CFR Parts 405 and 414.

59 FR 63410, December 8, 1994: Medicare Program; Refinements to Geographic Adjustment Factor Values, Revisions to Payment Policies, Adjustments to the Relative Value Units (RVUs) under the Physician Fee Schedule for Calendar Year 1995, and the 5-Year

Refinement of RVUs — Final rule with comment period, affecting 42 CFR parts 410 and 414. See also correction at 60 FR 46, January 3, 1995 and at 60 FR 36733, July 18, 1995.

59 FR 63638, December 8, 1994: Medicare Program; Physician Fee Schedule Update for Calendar Year 1995 and Physician Volume Performance Standard Rates of Increase for Federal Fiscal Year 1995 — Final notice.

60 FR 2325, January 9, 1995: Medicare Program; Providers and Suppliers of Specialized Services: Technical Amendments — Final rule with comment period, affecting 42 CFR Parts 400, 405, 410, 484, 485, 486, and 498. See also correction at 60 FR 11632, March 2, 1995.

60 FR 38400, July 26, 1995: Medicare Program; Revisions to Payment Policies under the Physician Fee Schedule for Calendar Year 1996 — Proposed rule affecting 42 CFR Parts 400, 405, 410, 411, 412, 413, 414, 415, 417, and 489.

60 FR 63124, December 8, 1995: Medicare Program; Revisions to Payment Policies and Adjustments to the Relative Value Units under the Physician Fee Schedule for Calendar Year 1996 — Final rule with comment period, affecting 42 CFR Parts 400, 405, 410, 411, 412, 413, 414, 415, 417, and 489. See also correction at 61 FR 42385, August 15, 1996.

61 FR 13205, March 26, 1996: HCFA Agency Information Collection Activities: Submission for OMB Review; Comment Request (pertaining to Medicare standardized forms for reimbursement of covered services by all providers that accept Medicare assignment).

61 FR 16925, April 18, 1996: HCFA Agency Information Collection Activities: Proposed Collection; Comment Request (pertaining to Medicare participating physician or supplier agreements; and hospital conditions of participation).

61 FR 19992, May 3, 1996: Medicare Program; Five-year Review of Work Relative Value Units under the Physician Fee Schedule — Proposed notice.

61 FR 59490, November 22, 1996: Medicare Program; Revisions to Payment Policies and Five-year Review of and Adjustments to the Relative value Units under the Physician Fee Schedule for Calendar yeat 1997 — Final rule with comment period, affecting 42 CFR Parts 410and 415. See also correction at 62 FR 7945, February 21, 1997.

61 FR 59717, November 22, 1996: Medicare Program; Physician Fee Schedule Update for Calendar year 1997 and Physician Volume Performance Standard Rates of Increase for Federal Fiscal Year 1997 — Final notice.

62 FR 7945, February 21, 1997: Medicare Program; Revisions to Payment Policies and Five-year Review of and Adjustments to the Relative Value Units Under the Physician Fee Schedule for Calendar Year 1997; Correction of final rule with comment period.

62 FR 24483, May 5, 1997: Medicare Program; Update of the Reasonable Compensation Equivalent Limits for Services Furnished by Physicians — Notice.

62 FR 33158, June 18, 1997: Medicare Program; Revisions to Payment Policies Under the Physician Fee Schedule, Other Part B Payment Policies, and Establishment of the Clinical Psychologist Fee Schedule for Calendar year 1998, Proposed rule affecting 42 CFR Parts 400, 405, 410, and 414.

62 FR 59261, October 31, 1997: Medicare Program; Physician Fee Schedule Conversion Factor for Calendar Year 1998 and Sustainable Growth Rate for Fiscal Year 1998 — Final notice.

62 FR 59267, October 31, 1997: Medicare Program; Delay in Implementing the Adjustments to the Practice Expense Relative Value Units under the Physician Fee Schedule for Calendar Year 1998 — Notice of intent to regulate.

62 FR 66376, December 18, 1997: HCFA Emergency Clearance: Public Information Collection Requirements Submitted to the Office of Management and Budget (OMB) (pertaining to Medicare and other Federal health care program enrollment forms for providers and suppliers).

62 FR 66726, December 19, 1997: Medicare and Medicaid Programs; Hospital Conditions of Participation; Provider Agreements and Supplier Approval — Proposed rule affecting 42 CFR Parts 416, 482, 485, and 489.

63 FR 687, January 7, 1998: Medicare Program; Application of Inherent Reasonableness to All Medicare Part B Services (Other than Physician Services) — Interim final rule with comment period, affecting 42 CFR Part 405.

63 FR 2926, January 20, 1998: Medicare Program; Additional Supplier Standards — Proposed rule affecting 42 CFR Part 424.

63 FR 4459, January 29, 1998: HCFA Emergency Clearance: Public Information Collection Requirements Submitted to the Office of Management and Budget (OMB) (pertaining to Medicare/Medicaid health insurance common claim form and instructions).

63 FR 5106, January 30, 1998: Medicare and Medicaid Programs; Salary Equivalency Guidelines for Physical Therapy, Respiratory Therapy, Speech Language Pathology, and Occupational Therapy

Services — Final rule affecting 42 CFR Part 413. See also revised effective date and technical correction at 63 FR 15315, March 31, 1998.

63 FR 7175, February 12, 1998: HCFA Emergency Clearance: Public Information Collection Requirements Submitted to the Office of Management and Budget (OMB) (pertaining to research and analytic support for implementing performance measurement in fee for service Medicare and group practices).

63 FR 7743, February 17, 1998: Medicare and Medicaid Programs; Hospital Conditions of Participation; Provider Agreements and Supplier Approval — Notice of extension of comment period, affecting 42 CFR Parts 416, 482, 485, and 489.

63 FR 10920, March 5, 1998: HCFA Emergency Clearance: Public Information Collection Requirements Submitted to the Office of Management and Budget (OMB) (pertaining to Medicare and other Federal health care program provider and supplier application forms).

63 FR 25320, May 7, 1998: HCFA National Standard Health Care Provider Identifier — Proposed Rule affecting 45 CFR Part 142.

63 FR 30818, June 5, 1998: Medicare Program; Revisions to Payment Policies under the Physician Fee Schedule for Calendar Year 1999 — Proposed rule, affecting 42 CFR Parts 405, 410, 413, 414, 415, 424, and 485. See also correction at 63 FR 50545, September 22, 1998.

63 FR 36250, July 2, 1998: HCFA Agency Information Collection Activities; Submission for OMB review; Comment request (pertaining to provider/supplier enrollment applications).

63 FR 38311, July 16, 1998: Office of Inspector General: Medicare and State Health Care Programs: Fraud and Abuse; Issuance of Advisory Opinions by the OIG — Final rule affecting 42 CFR 1008. See also correction at 63 FR 43449, August 13, 1998.

63 FR 38414, July 16, 1998: HCFA Privacy Act of 1974; Report of Altered System (pertaining to disclosure of individual-specific information to combat fraud or abuse in health benefit programs).

63 FR 58399, October 30, 1998: Office of Inspector General: Publication of the OIG's Provider Self-Disclosure Protocol — Notice.

63 FR 58814, November 2, 1998: Medicare Program; Revisions to Payment Policies and Adjustments to the Relative Value Units under the Physician Fee Schedule for Calendar Year 1999 — Final rule with comment period, affecting 42 CFR 405, 410, 413, 414, 415, 424, and 485. See also correction at 64 FR 35258, June 30, 1999

June 1999

64 FR 1813, January 12, 1999: Office of Inspector General Publication of OIG Special Fraud Alert on Physician Liability for Certifications in the Provision of Medical Equipment and Supplies and Home Health Services — Notice.

64 FR 17673, April 12, 1999: HCFA Agency Information Collection Activities: Proposed Collection; Comment request (pertaining to Medicare participating physician or supplier agreements).

64 FR 23845, May 4, 1999: HCFA Agency Information Collection Activities: Proposed Collection; Comment request (pertaining to Medicare geographical classification review board procedures).

64 FR 24956, May 10, 1999: Medicare and Medicaid Programs; Effective Dates of Provider Agreements and Supplier Approvals-Correction restoring regulations inadvertently removed when a final rule concerning effective dates for provider agreements and supplier approvals was published at 62 FR 43931, August 18, 1997.

64 FR 32239, June 16, 1999: HCFA Agency Information Collection Activities: Submission for OMB Review; Comment request (pertaining to the requirement that physicians must notify beneficiaries that Medicare is likely to deny payment for a specified service).

64 FR 39517, July 22, 1999: HCFA Agency Information Collection Activities: Submission for OMB Review; Comment request (pertaining to Medicare participating physician or supplier agreement form HCFA-460).

64 FR 40017, July 23, 1999: HCFA Agency Information Collection Activities: Submission for OMB Review; Comment request (pertaining to Medicare geographical classification review board procedures and criteria).

64 FR 40534, July 27, 1999: Medicare Program; Replacement of Reasonable Charge Methodology by Fee Schedules — Proposed action affecting 42 CFR 414.

64 FR 48846, September 8, 1999: Office of Inspector General: Solicitation of Information and Recommendations for Developing OIG Compliance Program Guidance for Individual Physicians and Small Group Practices — Notice.

64 FR 57431, October 25, 1999: Medicare Program; Appeals of Carrier Determinations that a Supplier Fails to Meet the Requirements for Medicare Billing Privileges — Proposed rule affecting 42 CFR Part 405.

64 FR 59380, November 2, 1999: Medicare Program; Revisions to Payment Policies under the Physician Fee Schedule for Calendar Year 2000 — Final rule with comment period, affecting 42 CFR Parts 410, 411, 414, 415, and 485. See also correction at 65 FR 19329, April 11, 2000.

64 FR 69021, December 9, 1999: HCFA Agency Information Collection Activities: Proposed Collection; Comment request (pertaining to analysis of malpractice premium data to compute the physician fee schedule).

2000

65 FR 5354, February 3, 2000: HCFA Agency Information Collection Activities: Proposed Collection; Comment request (pertaining to standardized Medicare/Medicaid claim form for reimbursement of covered services).

65 FR 15912, March 24, 2000: HCFA Agency Information Collection Activities: Submission for OMB Review; Comment request (pertaining to Medicare uniform institutional provider claim forms).

65 FR 30414, May 11, 2000: HCFA Agency Information Collection Activities: Submission for OMB Review; Comment request (pertaining to health insurance common claims form).

65 FR 36818, June 12, 2000: Office of Inspector General: Draft OIG Compliance Program for Individual and Small Group Physician Practices — Notice and comment period.

65 FR 42021, July 7, 2000: HCFA Agency Information Collection Activities: Proposed Collection; Comment request (pertaining to notice to providers, suppliers, and practitioners about non-covered services to beneficiaries).

65 FR 44176, July 17, 2000: Medicare Program; Revisions to Payment Policies under the Physician Fee Schedule for Calendar Year 2001 — Proposed rule affection 42 CFR Parts 410 and 414.

65 FR 50312, August 17, 2000: Office of the Secretary; Health Insurance Reform: Standards for Electronic Transactions — Final rule affecting 45 CFR Parts 160 and 162.

65 FR 53319, September 1, 2000: HCFA Agency Information Collection Activities: Proposed Collection; Comment request (pertaining to incentive arrangement disclosure form for managed care organizations and their related medical groups and physicians).

65 FR 59434, October 5, 2000: Office of Inspector General Compliance Program for Individual and Small Group Physician Practices — Notice.

65 FR 64227, October 26, 2000: HCFA Agency Information Collection Activities: Proposed Collection; Comment Request; Public Information Collection Meeting to Discuss Proposed Revisions (pertaining to notice requirements from suppliers, physicians, and practitioners to beneficiaries when Medicare Part B payment may be denied).

65 FR 65376, November 1, 2000: Medicare Program; Revisions to Payment Policies under the Physician Fee Schedule for Calendar Year 2001—Final rule with comment period. See also correction at 66 FR 16607, March 27, 2001.

65 FR 65603, November 1, 2000: Medicare Program; Revisions to Payment Policies under the Physician Fee Schedule for Calendar Year 2001 — Final rule with comment period.

65 FR 65861, November 2, 2000: HCFA Agency Information Collection Activities: Proposed Collection; Comment request (pertaining to conflict of interest disclosure requirements for Medicare program integrity).

2001

66 FR 1996, January 10, 2001: HCFA Agency Information Collection Activities; Comment request (pertaining to Medicare uniform institutional provider bill for reimbursement of covered services by all providers that accept assignment of claims).

66 FR 1997, January 10, 2001: HCFA Notice of OMB Approval (pertaining to uniform home health advance beneficiary notice).

66 FR 2912, January 12, 2001: HCFA Agency Information Collection Activities: Proposed Collection; Comment request (pertaining to Medicare/Medicaid health insurance common claim form).

66 FR 8807, February 2, 2001: HCFA Agency Information Collection Activities: Proposed Collection; Comment request (pertaining to Medicare Federal health care programs provider/supplier enrollment application).

66 FR 16061, March 22, 2001: HCFA Agency Information Collection Activities: Proposed Collection; Comment request (pertaining to private contracts of physicians who opt out of Medicare).

66 FR 18646, April 10, 2001: HCFA Agency Information Collection Activities: Submission for OMB Review; Comment request (pertaining to Medicare/Medicaid health insurance common claim form).

66 FR 20316, April 20, 2001: HCFA Agency Information Collection Activities: Submission for OMB Review; Comment request (pertain-

ing to advance beneficiary notice by physicians, practitioners, suppliers, and providers about items and services denied by Medicare as not reasonable and necessary).

66 FR 20997, April 26, 2001: HCFA Agency Information Collection Activities: Submission for OMB Review; Comment request (pertaining to health insurance provider agreement form).

66 FR 21770, May 1, 2001: HCFA Agency Information Collection Activities: Submission for OMB Review; Comment request (pertaining to Medicare uniform institutional provider bill form).

66 FR 31038, June 8, 2001: Medicare Program; Five–year Review of Work Relative Value Units under the Physician Fee Schedule—Proposed notice.

66 FR 32630, June 15, 2001: HCFA Agency Information Collection Activities; Submission for OMB Review; Comment request (pertaining to contracts by practitioners and physicians who opt–out of Medicare).

66 FR 33102, June 20, 2001: HCFA Agency Information Collection Activities; Submission for OMB Review; Comment request (pertaining to provider/supplier enrollment application form).

See § 2:25.

§ 6:26 FAILURE BY PHYSICIANS, SUPPLIERS, AND OTHERS, INCLUDING THEIR EMPLOYERS AND RELATED FACILITIES, TO SUBMIT CLAIMS ON SPECIFIED CLAIM FORMS — Section 1848(g)(4) [42 U.S.C.A. 1395w-(g)(4)]

Regulations

42 CFR Part 402 — Civil Money Penalties, Assessments, and Exclusions

42 CFR Part 405, Subpart C — Recovery of Overpayments and Suspension of Payment; and Subpart E — Criteria for Determination of Reasonable Charges

42 CFR Part 410 — Supplementary Medical Insurance (SMI) Benefits

42 CFR Part 414 — Payment for Part B Medical and Other Health Services

42 CFR Part 415 — Services Furnished by Physicians in Providers, Supervising Physicians in Teaching Settings, and Residents in Certain Settings

42 CFR Part 420 — Program Integrity: Medicare

42 CFR Part 424 — Conditions for Medicare Payment

42 CFR Part 498 — Appeals Procedures for Determinations that Affect Participation in the Medicare Program and for Determinations that Affect the Participation of ICF's/MR and Certain NF's in the Medicaid Program

42 CFR Chapter V — Office of Inspector General — Health Care, Department of Health and Human Services

Subchapter A — General Provisions

Part 1000 — Introduction; General Definitions

Subchapter B — OIG Authorities

Part 1001 — Program Integrity: Medicare and State Health Care Programs

Part 1003 — Civil Money Penalties, Assessments and Exclusions

Part 1004 — Imposition of Sanctions on Health Care Practitioners and Providers of Health Care Services by a Peer Review Organization

Part 1005 — Appeals of Exclusions, Civil Money Penalties and Assessments

Part 1006 — Investigational Inquiries

Part 1007 — State Medicaid Fraud Control Units

Part 1008 — Advisory Opinions by the OIG

53 FR 53025, December 30, 1988: Medicare Program; Physician Liability on Non-assigned Claims — Proposed rule to amend 42 CFR Part 405.

54 FR 30558, July 21, 1989: Medicare Program; Diagnosis Codes on Physician Bills — Proposed rule to amend 42 CFR 424.

55 FR 24561, June 18, 1990: Medicare Program; Physician Liability on Non-Assigned Claims — Final rule affecting 42 CFR Parts 400 and 411. See also correction published at 55 FR 35142, August 28, 1990.

56 FR 56612, November 6, 1991: Medicare Program; Carrier Jurisdiction for Claims for Durable Medical Equipment, Prosthetics, Orthotics and Supplies, and Other Issues Involving Suppliers — Proposed rule affecting 42 CFR Parts 400, 420, and 421.

56 FR 61023, November 29, 1991: Medicare Program; Standard Claim Forms for Part B Claims Completed and Submitted by Physicians, Suppliers and Other Persons — General notice with comment period.

57 FR 27290, June 18, 1992: Medicare Program; Carrier Jurisdiction for Claims for Durable Medical Equipment, Prosthetics, Orthotics and Supplies (DMEPOS) and Other Issues Involving Sup-

pliers, and Criteria and Standards for Evaluating Regional DMEPOS Carriers — Final rule with comment period, affecting 42 CFR Parts 405, 420, 421, and 424. See also correction at 57 FR 35760, August 11, 1992.

57 FR 27309, June 18, 1992: Medicare Program; Criteria and Standards for Evaluating Regional Durable Medical Equipment, Prosthetics, Orthotics and Suppliers (DMEPOS) Carriers; Request for comments.

57 FR 46362, October 8, 1992: Medicare and Medicaid Programs; Revised Effective Date of Medicare/Medicaid Provider Agreement and Supplier Participation — Proposed rule affecting 42 CFR Parts 431, 440, 442, 488, 489, and 498.

57 FR 47587, October 19, 1992: Medicare and Medicaid Programs; Use of Standardized Federal Claims Processing Forms and Procedures — Advance notice of proposed rulemaking.

57 FR 48033, October 21, 1992: Medicare Program; Revised Procedures for Paying Claims From Providers of Services — Final notice.

58 FR 60789, November 18, 1993: Medicare Program; Carrier Jurisdiction for Claims for Durable Medical Equipment, Prosthetics, Orthotics, and Supplies (DMEPOS) — Final rule affecting 42 CFR Part 421.

59 FR 10290, March 4, 1994: Medicare Program; Diagnosis Codes on Physician Bills — Final rule affecting 42 CFR Parts 405 and 424. See also correction at 59 FR 26739, May 24, 1994.

59 FR 11000, March 9, 1994: Medicare Program; Changes to the Requirement for Annual Physician Acknowledgment of Physician Attestation Responsibilities — Final rule with comment period, affecting 42 CFR Part 412. See also correction at 59 FR 30389, June 13, 1994.

59 FR 36415, July 18, 1994: Medicare Program; Part B Advance Payments to Suppliers Furnishing Items or Services under Medicare Part B — Proposed rule affecting 42 CFR Part 421.

60 FR 2325, January 9, 1995: Medicare Program; Providers and Suppliers of Specialized Services: Technical Amendments — Final rule with comment period, affecting 42 CFR Parts 400, 405, 410, 484, 485, 486, and 498. See also correction at 60 FR 11632, March 2, 1995 and correction at 60 FR 45086, August 30, 1995.

60 FR 35492, July 10, 1995: Medicare Program; Payment for Durable Medical Equipment and Orthotic and Prosthetic Devices — Final rule affecting 42 CFR Part 414.

60 FR 45487, August 31, 1995: HCFA Public Information Collection Requirements Submitted for Public Comment and Recommendations (pertaining to the standardized form for applying for Medicare reimbursement by providers).

60 FR 50466, September 29, 1995: Medicare Program — Providers and Suppliers of Specialized Services: Technical Amendments — Final rule with comment period, affecting 42 CFR Parts 485and 486. See also correction at 60 FR 53877, October 18, 1995.

60 FR 53383, October 13, 1995: HCFA Public Information Collection Requirements Submitted for Public Comment and Recommendations (pertaining to durable medical equipment regional carriers and certificates of medical necessity).

60 FR 63440, December 11, 1995: Medicare Program; Additional Supplier Standards — Final rule with comment period, affecting 42 CFR Parts 411 and 424.

61 FR 13205, March 26, 1996: HCFA Agency Information Collection Activities: Submission for OMB Review; Comment Request (pertaining to Medicare standardized forms for reimbursement of covered services by all providers that accept Medicare assignment).

61 FR 19628, May 2, 1996: HCFA Agency Information Collection Activities: Proposed Collection; Comment Request (pertaining to permissible billing for physicians that do not accept Medicare assignments).

61 FR 38454, July 24, 1996: HCFA Agency Information Collection Activities: Submission for OMB Review; Comment request (pertaining to physicians who do not accept Medicare assignment).

61 FR 49271, September 19, 1996: Medicare Program; Part B Advance Payments to Suppliers Furnishing Items or Services under Medicare Part B — Final rule affecting 42 CFR Part 421.

61 FR 58199, November 13, 1996: HCFA Agency Information Collection Activities: Proposed Collection; Comment request (pertaining to Medicare uniform institutional provider bill Form 1450 (UB-92) and instructions).

62 FR 4304, January 29, 1997: HCFA Emergency Clearance: Public Information Collection Requirements Submitted to the Office of Management and Budget (OMB) (pertaining to Medicare/Medicaid health insurance common claim form).

62 FR 8026, February 21, 1997: HCFA Agency Information Collection Activities: Submission for OMB Review; Comment request

(pertaining to durable medical equipment regional carrier certificate of medical necessity).

62 FR 8744, February 26, 1997: HCFA Agency Information Collection Activities: Submission for OMB Review; Comment request (pertaining to Medicare provider/supplier enrollment application).

62 FR 66376, December 18, 1997: HCFA Emergency Clearance: Public Information Collection Requirements Submitted to the Office of Management and Budget (OMB) (pertaining to Medicare and other Federal health care program enrollment forms for providers and suppliers).

62 FR 66726, December 19, 1997: Medicare and Medicaid Programs; Hospital Conditions of Participation; Provider Agreements and Supplier Approval — Proposed rule affecting 42 CFR Parts 416, 482, 485, and 489.

63 FR 2926, January 20, 1998: Medicare Program; Additional Supplier Standards — Proposed rule affecting 42 CFR Part 424.

63 FR 4459, January 29, 1998: HCFA Emergency Clearance: Public Information Collection Requirements Submitted to the Office of Management and Budget (OMB) (pertaining to Medicare/Medicaid health insurance common claim form and instructions).

63 FR 7743, February 17, 1998: Medicare and Medicaid Programs; Hospital Conditions of Participation; Provider Agreements and Supplier Approval — Notice of extension of comment period, affecting 42 CFR Parts 416, 482, 485, and 489.

63 FR 10920, March 5, 1998: HCFA Emergency Clearance: Public Information Collection Requirements Submitted to the Office of Management and Budget (OMB) (pertaining to Medicare and other Federal health care program provider and supplier application forms).

63 FR 25320, May 7, 1998: HCFA National Standard Health Care Provider Identifier — Proposed Rule affecting 45 CFR Part 142.

63 FR 36250, July 2, 1998: HCFA Agency Information Collection Activities; Submission for OMB review; Comment request (pertaining to provider/supplier enrollment applications).

63 FR 70138, December 18, 1998: Office of Inspector General: Publication of the OIG Compliance Program Guidance for Third-party Medical Billing Companies — Notice.

June 1999

64 FR 1813, January 12, 1999: Office of Inspector General Publication of OIG Special Fraud Alert on Physician Liability for

Certifications in the Provision of Medical Equipment and Supplies and Home Health Services — Notice.

64 FR 17673, April 12, 1999: HCFA Agency Information Collection Activities: Proposed Collection; Comment request (pertaining to Medicare participating physician or supplier agreements).

64 FR 23845, May 4, 1999: HCFA Agency Information Collection Activities: Proposed Collection; Comment request (pertaining to Medicare geographical classification review board procedures).

64 FR 24956, May 10, 1999: Medicare and Medicaid Programs; Effective Dates of Provider Agreements and Supplier Approvals-Correction restoring regulations inadvertently removed when a final rule concerning effective dates for provider agreements and supplier approvals was published at 62 FR 43931, August 18, 1997.

64 FR 32239, June 16, 1999: HCFA Agency Information Collection Activities: Submission for OMB Review; Comment request (pertaining to the requirement that physicians must notify beneficiaries that Medicare is likely to deny payment for a specified service).

64 FR 39517, July 22, 1999: HCFA Agency Information Collection Activities: Submission for OMB Review; Comment request (pertaining to Medicare participating physician or supplier agreement form HCFA-460).

64 FR 40017, July 23, 1999: HCFA Agency Information Collection Activities: Submission for OMB Review; Comment request (pertaining to Medicare geographical classification review board procedures and criteria).

64 FR 40534, July 27, 1999: Medicare Program; Replacement of Reasonable Charge Methodology by Fee Schedules — Proposed action affecting 42 CFR 414.

64 FR 48846, September 8, 1999: Office of Inspector General: Solicitation of Information and Recommendations for Developing OIG Compliance Program Guidance for Individual Physicians and Small Group Practices — Notice.

64 FR 57431, October 25, 1999: Medicare Program; Appeals of Carrier Determinations that a Supplier Fails to Meet the Requirements for Medicare Billing Privileges — Proposed rule affecting 42 CFR Part 405.

64 FR 59380, November 2, 1999: Medicare Program; Revisions to Payment Policies under the Physician Fee Schedule for Calendar Year 2000 — Final rule with comment period, affecting 42 CFR Parts 410, 411, 414, 415, and 485. See also correction at 65 FR 19329, April 11, 2000.

64 FR 69021, December 9, 1999: HCFA Agency Information Collection Activities: Proposed Collection; Comment request (pertaining to analysis of malpractice premium data to compute the physician fee schedule).

2000

65 FR 5354, February 3, 2000: HCFA Agency Information Collection Activities: Proposed Collection; Comment request (pertaining to standardized Medicare/Medicaid claim form for reimbursement of covered services).

65 FR 15912, March 24, 2000: HCFA Agency Information Collection Activities: Submission for OMB Review; Comment request (pertaining to Medicare uniform institutional provider claim forms).

65 FR 30414, May 11, 2000: HCFA Agency Information Collection Activities: Submission for OMB Review; Comment request (pertaining to health insurance common claims form).

65 FR 36818, June 12, 2000: Office of Inspector General: Draft OIG Compliance Program for Individual and Small Group Physician Practices — Notice and comment period.

65 FR 42021, July 7, 2000: HCFA Agency Information Collection Activities: Proposed Collection; Comment request (pertaining to notice to providers, suppliers, and practitioners about non-covered services to beneficiaries).

65 FR 44176, July 17, 2000: Medicare Program; Revisions to Payment Policies under the Physician Fee Schedule for Calendar Year 2001 — Proposed rule affection 42 CFR Parts 410 and 414.

65 FR 50312, August 17, 2000: Office of the Secretary; Health Insurance Reform: Standards for Electronic Transactions — Final rule affecting 45 CFR Parts 160 and 162.

65 FR 53319, September 1, 2000: HCFA Agency Information Collection Activities: Proposed Collection; Comment request (pertaining to incentive arrangement disclosure form for managed care organizations and their related medical groups and physicians).

65 FR 59434, October 5, 2000: Office of Inspector General Compliance Program for Individual and Small Group Physician Practices — Notice.

65 FR 64227, October 26, 2000: HCFA Agency Information Collection Activities: Proposed Collection; Comment Request; Public Information Collection Meeting to Discuss Proposed Revisions (pertaining to notice requirements from suppliers, physicians, and

practitioners to beneficiaries when Medicare Part B payment may be denied).

65 FR 65376, November 1, 2000: Medicare Program; Revisions to Payment Policies under the Physician Fee Schedule for Calendar Year 2001—Final rule with comment period. See also correction at 66 FR 16607, March 27, 2001.

65 FR 65603, November 1, 2000: Medicare Program; Revisions to Payment Policies under the Physician Fee Schedule for Calendar Year 2001 — Final rule with comment period.

65 FR 65861, November 2, 2000: HCFA Agency Information Collection Activities: Proposed Collection; Comment request (pertaining to conflict of interest disclosure requirements for Medicare program integrity).

2001

66 FR 1996, January 10, 2001: HCFA Agency Information Collection Activities; Comment request (pertaining to Medicare uniform institutional provider bill for reimbursement of covered services by all providers that accept assignment of claims).

66 FR 1997, January 10, 2001: HCFA Notice of OMB Approval (pertaining to uniform home health advance beneficiary notice).

66 FR 2912, January 12, 2001: HCFA Agency Information Collection Activities: Proposed Collection; Comment request (pertaining to Medicare/Medicaid health insurance common claim form).

66 FR 8807, February 2, 2001: HCFA Agency Information Collection Activities: Proposed Collection; Comment request (pertaining to Medicare Federal health care programs provider/supplier enrollment application).

66 FR 16061, March 22, 2001: HCFA Agency Information Collection Activities: Proposed Collection; Comment request (pertaining to private contracts of physicians who opt out of Medicare).

66 FR 18646, April 10, 2001: HCFA Agency Information Collection Activities: Submission for OMB Review; Comment request (pertaining to Medicare/Medicaid health insurance common claim form).

66 FR 20316, April 20, 2001: HCFA Agency Information Collection Activities: Submission for OMB Review; Comment request (pertaining to advance beneficiary notice by physicians, practitioners, suppliers, and providers about items and services denied by Medicare as not reasonable and necessary).

66 FR 20997, April 26, 2001: HCFA Agency Information Collection Activities: Submission for OMB Review; Comment request (pertaining to health insurance provider agreement form).

66 FR 21770, May 1, 2001: HCFA Agency Information Collection Activities: Submission for OMB Review; Comment request (pertaining to Medicare uniform institutional provider bill form).

66 FR 31038, June 8, 2001: Medicare Program; Five–year Review of Work Relative Value Units under the Physician Fee Schedule—Proposed notice.

66 FR 32630, June 15, 2001: HCFA Agency Information Collection Activities; Submission for OMB Review; Comment request (pertaining to contracts by practitioners and physicians who opt–out of Medicare).

66 FR 33102, June 20, 2001: HCFA Agency Information Collection Activities; Submission for OMB Review; Comment request (pertaining to provider/supplier enrollment application form).

See § 2:26.

§ 6:26.1 TERMINATION OF MEDICARE+CHOICE CONTRACTS — Section 1857(c)(2)

Regulations

42 CFR Part 417 — Health Maintenance Organizations, Competitive Medical Plans, and Health Care Prepayment Plans

42 CFR Part 420 — Program Integrity: Medicare

42 CFR Part 422-Medicare+Choice Program

42 CFR Chapter V — Office of Inspector General — Health Care, Department of Health and Human Services

Subchapter A — General Provisions

Part 1000 — Introduction; General Definitions

Subchapter B — OIG Authorities

Part 1001 — Program Integrity: Medicare and State Health Care Programs

Part 1003 — Civil Money Penalties, Assessments and Exclusions

Part 1004 — Imposition of Sanctions on Health Care Practitioners and Providers of Health Care Services by a Peer Review Organization

Part 1005 — Appeals of Exclusions, Civil Money Penalties and Assessments

Part 1006 — Investigational Inquiries

Part 1007 — State Medicaid Fraud Control Units

Part 1008 — Advisory Opinions by the OIG

62 FR 63669, December 2, 1997: Medicare+Choice Program; Collection of User Fees from Medicare+Choice Plans and Risk-sharing Contractors — Interim final rule with request for comments, affecting 42 CFR part 417.

62 FR 67388, December 24, 1997: HCFA Emergency Clearance: Public Information Collection Requirements Submitted to the Office of Management and Budget (OMB) (pertaining to collection of inpatient data for Medicare+Choice organizations).

63 FR 2920, January 20, 1998: Medicare Program: Request for Public Comments on Implementation of the Medicare+Choice Program, and Notice of Timeframes for Submission of Applications for Contracts — Notice of intent to regulate and solicitation of comments.

63 FR 7175, February 12, 1998: HCFA Emergency Clearance: Public Information Collection Requirements Submitted to the Office of Managment and Budget (OMB) (pertaining to managed care adjusted community rate (ACR) proposal).

63 FR 7359, February 13, 1998: Medicare Program; Meeting of the Negotiated Rulemaking Committee on the Provider-Sponsored Organization Solvency Standards — Notice of meeting.

63 FR 11263, March 6, 1998: HCFA Agency Information Collection Activities: Submission for OMB Review; Comment request (pertaining to end stage renal disease managed care demonstration.

63 FR 12475, March 13, 1998: HCFA Agency Information Collection Activities; Submission for OMB Review; Comment request (pertaining to HMO and CMP national data reporting requirements).

63 FR 12476, March 13, 1998: HCFA Emergency Clearance: Public Information Collection Requirements Submitted to the Office of Management and Budget (OMB) (pertaining to Medicare+Choice Provider Sponsored Organization (PSO) waiver request forms).

63 FR 16563, April 3, 1998: HCFA Agency Information Collection Activities: Submission for OMB Review; Comment request (pertaining to evaluation of Medicare Choices demonstration).

63 FR 18124, April 14, 1998: Medicare Program; Definition of Provider-Sponsored Organization and Related Requirements — Interim final rule with comment period, affecting 42 CFR 422.

63 FR 18924, April 16, 1998: HCFA Emergency Clearance: Public Information Collection Requirements Submitted to the Office of

Management and Budget (OMB) (pertaining to collection of managed care data using the uniform institutional providers form).

63 FR 25215, May 7, 1998: HCFA Agency Information Collection Activities: Proposed Collection; Comment request (pertaining to clinical laboratory improvement amendments application forms; limits on provider-related donations and health care-related taxes and payments to disproportionate share hospitals; and Medicare+Choice provider sponsored organization waiver request forms).

63 FR 25360, May 7, 1998: Medicare Program; Waiver Requirements and Solvency Standards for Provider Sponsored Organizations — Interim final rule with comment period, affecting 42 CFR 422.

63 FR 26811, May 14, 1998: Medicare and Medicaid Programs: Request for Public Comments on the Quality Improvement System for Managed Care — Solicitation of comments; notice of public meeting.

63 FR 34968, June 26, 1998: Medicare Program; Establishment of the Medicare+Choice Program — Interim final rule with comment period, affecting 42 CFR Parts 400, 403, 410, 411, 417, and 422. See also corrections at 63 FR 36488, July 6, 1998, 63 FR 52610, October 1, 1998, and 63 FR 54526, October 9, 1998.

63 FR 38413, July 16, 1998: HCFA Agency Information Collection Activities: Submission for OMB Review; Comment request (pertaining to Clinical Laboratory Improvement Act certification requirements; EPSDT participation reports; limitations on provider-related donations and health care-related taxes, and limitations on payments to disproportionate share hospitals; and Medicare+Choice provider sponsored organization waiver requests forms).

63 FR 43403, August 13, 1998: HCFA Emergency Clearance: Public Information Collection Requirements Submitted to the Office of Management and Budget (OMB) (pertaining to the Medicare and You survey form to collect information from internet users accessing the Medicare+Choice Handbook on the Medicare.gov web site).

63 FR 45828, August 27, 1998: HCFA Emergency Clearance: Public Information Collection Requirements Submitted to the Office of Management and Budget (OMB) (pertaining to surveys of the effectiveness of the Medicare+Choice education campaign).

63 FR 45829, August 27, 1998: HCFA Emergency Clearance: Public Information Collection Requirements Submitted to the Office of Management and Budget (OMB) (pertaining to a survey of callers to

determine consumer satisfaction with the Medicare+Choice toll-free information line).

63 FR 47506, September 8, 1998: Medicare Program: Request for Public Comments on Implementation of Risk Adjusted Payment for the Medicare+Choice Program and Announcement of Public Meeting-Solicitation of comments.

63 FR 50577, September 22, 1998: Office of Inspector General: Solicitation of Information and Recommendations for Developing OIG Compliance Program Guidance for Certain Medicare+Choice Organizations — Notice.

63 FR 53923, October 7, 1998: HCFA Emergency Clearance: Public Information Collection Requirements Submitted to the Office of Management and Budget (OMB) (pertaining to Medicare+Choice requirements for quality assurance and enrollee services).

63 FR 63478, November 13, 1998: HCFA Agency Information Collection Activities: Proposed Collection; Comment request (pertaining to processing Medicare+Choice disenrollment requests from beneficiaries; creation of the Utilization and Quality Control Peer Review Organization; and rules for participation of HHA's in Medicare and review of plans of care for home health services).

63 FR 69079, December 15, 1998: HCFA Agency Information Collection Activities: Proposed Collection; Comment request (pertaining to Managed care adjusted community rate for Medicare+Choice organizations).

1999

64 FR 2907, January 19, 1999: HCFA Agency Information Collection Activities: Submission for OMB Review; Comment request (pertaining to call-back survey of callers to Medicare+Choice toll-free line).

64 FR 5665, February 4, 1999: HCFA Agency Information Collection Activities: Proposed Collection; Comment request (pertaining to Medicare+Choice disenrollment forms, and utilization and quality control peer review organizations (PROs)).

64 FR 7968, February 17, 1999: Medicare Program; Changes to the Medicare+Choice Program — Final rule affecting 42 CFR Part 422.

64 FR 10156, March 2, 1999: HCFA Agency Information Collection Activities: Submission for OMB Review; Comment request (pertaining to Medicare+Choice adjusted community rate proposal).

64 FR 13432, March 18, 1999: HCFA Emergency Clearance: Public Information Collection requirements submitted to the Office of Management and Budget (OMB) (pertaining to Medicare+Choice managed care plan benefit package and adjusted community rate proposal).

64 FR 32508, June 17, 1999: HCFA Agency Information Collection Activities: Submission for OMB Review; Comment Request (pertaining to the quality improvement system for managed care (QISMC)).

64 FR 38204, July 15, 1999: HCFA Agency Information Collection Activities: Submission for OMB Review; Comment request (pertaining to the national Medicare education program survey about Medicare+Choice awareness).

64 FR 41445, July 30, 1999: HCFA Emergency Clearance: Public Information Collection Requirements Submitted to the Office of Management and Budget (OMB) (pertaining to Medicare+Choice organization appeals and grievance data collection and reporting requirements).

64 FR 46919, August 27, 1999: HCFA Emergency Clearance: Public Information Collection Requirements Submitted to the Office of Management and Budget (OMB) (pertaining to survey of disenrollment by Medicare beneficiaries from alternative health plans).

64 FR 55737, October 14, 1999: HCFA Agency Information Collection Activities: Proposed Collection; Comment request (pertaining to the adjusted community rate proposal for Medicare+Choice plans).

64 FR 55949, October 15, 1999: Medicare Program; Open Public Meeting November 1, 1999, to Discuss Activities Related to the Collection of Encounter Data from Medicare+Choice Organizations for Risk Adjustment.

64 FR 57902, October 27, 1999: HCFA Agency Information Collection Activites: Proposed Collection; Comment request (pertaining to evaluation of new Medicare+Choice plans).

64 FR 61893, November 15, 1999: Office of Inspector General; Publication of the OIG's Compliance Program Guidance for Medicare+Choice Organizations Offering Coordinated Care Plans — Notice.

64 FR 71673, December 22, 1999: Medicare Program; Solvency Standards for Provider-sponsored organizations (Medicare+Choice) — Final rule affecting 42 CFR Part 422.

2000

65 FR 3724, January 24, 2000: HCFA Agency Information Collection Activities: Submission for OMB Review; Comment request (pertaining to evaluation by new Medicare members of Medicare+Choice plans).

65 FR 3725, January 24, 2000: HCFA Agency Information Collection Activities: submission for OMB Review; Comment request (pertaining to the adjusted community rate proposal for Medicare+Choice plan benefit packages).

65 FR 10812, February 29, 2000: Medicare Program; Open Public Meeting on March 15, 2000, to Provide an Overview of Data Requirements for Collection of Physician and Hospital Outpatient Encounter Data from Medicare+Choice Organizations for Risk Adjustment — Notice of meeting.

65 FR 19382, April 11, 2000: HCFA Emergency Clearance: Public Information Collection Requirements Submitted to the Office of Management and Budget (OMB) (pertaining to adjusted community rate for Medicare+Choice organizations.

65 FR 19782, April 12, 2000: HCFA Agency Information Collection Activities: Proposed Collection; Comment request (pertaining to Medicare+Choice beneficiary notices).

65 FR 19783, April 12, 2000: HCFA Emergency Clearance: Public Information Collection Requirements Submitted to the Office of Management and Budget (OMB) (pertaining to Medicare+Choice beneficiary notices).

65 FR 24707, April 27, 2000: HCFA Agency Information Collection Activities: Proposed Collection; Comment request (pertaining to collection of data on physician encounters from Medicare+Choice organizations).

65 FR 25737, May 3, 2000: HCFA Agency Information Collection Activities: Proposed Collection; Comment request (pertaining to managed care disenrollment form).

65 FR 25738, May 3, 2000: HCFA Emergency Clearance: Public Informatiion Collection Requirements Submitted to the Office of Management and Budget (OMB) (pertaining to the Medicare managed care CAHPS Survey).

65 FR 26618, May 5, 2000: HCFA Emergency Clearance: Public Information Collection Requirements Submitted to the Office of Management and Budget (OMB) (pertaining to Medicare consumer assessment survey of health plans).

65 FR 39416, June 26, 2000: HCFA Agency Information Collection Activities: Proposed Collection; Comment request (pertaining to Medicare+Choice organization appeals and grievance data disclosure requirements).

65 FR 40111, June 29, 2000: HCFA Agency Information Collection Activities: Proposed Collection; comment request (pertaining to qualification applications for prepaid health plans (HMOs).

65 FR 40112, June 29, 2000: Medicare Program: Medicare+Choice Deeming Authority — Notice regarding accrediting organizations.

65 FR 40170, June 29, 2000: Medicare Program; Medicare+Choice Program — Final rule with comment period, affecting 42 CFR parts 417 and 422. See also correction at 65 FR 59748, October 6, 2000.

65 FR 40668, June 30, 2000: HCFA Agency Information Collection Activities: Submission for OMB Review; Comment request (pertaining to Medicare comprehensive health plan disenrollment).

65 FR 43026, July 12, 2000: HCFA Agency Information Collection Activities: Submission for OMB Review; Comment request (pertaining to collection of data on physician encounters from Medicare+Choice organizations).

65 FR 46473, July 28, 2000: Medicare Program; Announcement of a Series of Regional Training Sessions to Provide Training to Medicare+Choice Organization Physicians, Medicare+Choice Organization Non-physician Practitioners, and Medicare+Choice Organization Medicare Directors, As Well As Physician Organizations and Billing Associations Involved in the Timely and Accurate Submission of Physician Encounter Data to Support a Comprehensive Risk Adjustment Model — Notice of training sessions.

65 FR 50713, August 21, 2000: HCFA Agency Information Collection Activities: Proposed Collection; Comment request (pertaining to social HMO demonstration payment methodology)

65 FR 53319, September 1, 2000: HCFA Agency Information Collection Activities: Proposed Collection; Comment request (pertaining to incentive arrangement disclosure form for managed care organizations and their related medical groups and physicians).

65 FR 57195, September 21, 2000: HCFA Agency Information Collection Activities; Proposed Collection; Comment request (pertaining to Medicare managed care CAHPS survey for quality of care purposes).

65 FR 60674, October 12, 2000: HCFA Agency Information Collection Activities: Submission for OMB Review; Comment request

(pertaining to Medicare+Choice organization appeals and grievance data disclosure requirements).

65 FR 64228, October 26, 2000: HCFA Agency Information Collection Activities: Proposed Collection; Comment request (pertaining to collection of data on physician encounters from Medicare+Choice organizations).

65 FR 65860, November 2, 2000: HCFA Agency Information Collection Activities: Proposed Collection; Comment request (pertaining to follow-up of Medicare+Choice disenrollees receiving fee-for service inpatient hospital care).

65 FR 79867, December 20, 2000: HCFA Agency Information Collection Activities: Proposed Collection; Comment request (pertaining to quality improvement system for managed care).

65 FR 79868, December 20, 2000: HCFA Agency Information Collection Activities: Proposed Collection; Comment request (pertaining to Medicare consumer assessment survey of health plans).

65 FR 79868, December 20, 2000: HCFA Emergency Clearance: Public Information Collection Requirements Submitted to the Office of Management and Budget (OMB) (pertaining to survey of beneficiaries who involuntarily disenroll from their managed care plan).

65 FR 81813, December 27, 2000: Medicare Program; Requirements for the Re-credentialing of Medicare+Choice Organization Providers — Proposed rule affecting 42 CFR Part 422.

2001

66 FR 1995, January 10, 2001: HCFA Agency Information Collection Activities: Proposed Collection; Comment request (pertaining to hospital outpatient encounters from Medicare+Choice programs).

66 FR 2913, January 12, 2001: HCFA Agency Information Collection Activities: Submission for OMB Review; Comment request (pertaining to collection of data about physician encounters from Medicare+Choice organizations).

66 FR 6228, January 19, 2001: Medicaid Program; Medicaid Managed Care—Final rule with comment period, affecting 42 CFR Part 400, 430, 431, 435, 438, 440, and 447.

66 FR 7593, January 24, 2001: Medicare Program; Improvements to the Medicare+Choice Appeal and Grievance Procedures—Proposed rule affecting 42 CFR Parts 422 and 489.

66 FR 8807, February 2, 2001: HCFA Agency Information Collection Activities: Submission for OMB Review; Comment request

(pertaining to follow–up of Medicare+Choice disenrollees receiving fee–for–service inpatient hospital care).

66 FR 9858, February 12, 2001: HCFA Privacy Act of 1974; Report of New System (pertaining to complaints against health insurance issuers and health plans).

66 FR 11546, February 26, 2001: Medicaid Program; Medicaid Managed Care: Delay of Effective Date—Final rule delay, affecting 42 CFR Parts 400, 430, 431, 434, 435, 438, 440, and 447.

66 FR 11591, February 26, 2001: HCFA Agency Information Collection Activities: Proposed Collection; Comment request (pertaining to Medicare+Choice program requirements).

66 FR 13854, March 8, 2001: Medicare+Choice Program—CFR correction.

66 FR 15122, March 15, 2001: HCFA Agency Information Collection Activities: Submission for OMB Review; Comment request (pertaining to quality improvement system for managed care).

66 FR 16062, March 23, 2001: HCFA Agency Information Collection Activities: Submission for OMB Review; Comment request (pertaining to Medicare+Choice beneficiary appeal notices).

66 FR 16268, March 23, 2001: HCFA Agency Information Collection Activities; Proposed Collection; Comment request (pertaining to data collection to support policy analysis of choices offered to Medicare+Choice enrollees and choices made by enrollees).

66 FR 16481, March 26, 2001: HCFA Agency Information Collection Activities: Submission for OMB Review; Comment request (pertaining to managed care adjusted community rate proposal for Medicare+Choice organizations).

66 FR 16678, March 27, 2001: HCFA Agency Information Collection Activities: Submission for OMB Review; Comment request (pertaining to Medicare managed care CAHPS survey).

66 FR 17431, March 30, 2001: HCFA Agency Information Collection Activities: Proposed Collection; Comment request (pertaining to data collection of quality indicators for congestive heart failure submitted by Medicare+Choice organizations requesting extra payments in CY 2002 and CY 2003).

66 FR 21770, May 1, 2001: Medicare Program; Revision of Payment Rates for End–Stage Renal Disease (ESRD) Patients Enrolled in Medicare+Choice Plans—Proposed notice.

66 FR 21987, May 2, 2001: HCFA Agency Information Collection Activities: Proposed Collection; Comment request (pertaining to

Medicare+Choice provider sponsored organization (PSO) waiver request form).

66 FR 24391, May 14, 2001: HCFA Agency Information Collection Activities: Submission for OMB Review; Comment request (pertaining to Medicare+Choice program requirements).

66 FR 28916, May 25, 2001: HCFA Agency Information Collection Activities: Proposed Collection; Comment request (pertaining to collection of managed care data using the uniform institutional providers form).

66 FR 29823, June 1, 2001: HCFA Agency Information Collection Activities: Proposed Collection; Comment request (pertaining to data reporting requirements for managed care organizations in the Medicare+Choice program).

66 FR 32776, June 18, 2001: Medicaid Program; Medicaid Managed Care: Further Delay of Effective Date for Final Rule affecting 42 CFR Parts 400, 430, 431, 434, 435, 438, 440, and 447.

See § 2:26.1.

§ 6:26.2 FAILURE BY MEDICARE+CHOICE ORGANIZATIONS TO COMPLY WITH REQUIREMENTS FOR BENEFICIARY PROTECTIONS AND PROTECTIONS AGAINST FRAUD — Section 1857(d)

Regulations

42 CFR Part 417 — Health Maintenance Organizations, Competitive Medical Plans, and Health Care Prepayment Plans

42 CFR Part 420 — Program Integrity: Medicare

42 CFR Chapter V — Office of Inspector General — Health Care, Department of Health and Human Services

Subchapter A — General Provisions

Part 1000 — Introduction; General Definitions

Subchapter B — OIG Authorities

Part 1001 — Program Integrity: Medicare and State Health Care Programs

Part 1003 — Civil Money Penalties, Assessments and Exclusions

Part 1004 — Imposition of Sanctions on Health Care Practitioners and Providers of Health Care Services by a Peer Review Organization

Part 1005 — Appeals of Exclusions, Civil Money Penalties and Assessments

Part 1006 — Investigational Inquiries
Part 1007 — State Medicaid Fraud Control Units
Part 1008 — Advisory Opinions by the OIG

62 FR 63669, December 2, 1997: Medicare+Choice Program; Collection of User Fees from Medicare+Choice Plans and Risk-sharing Contractors — Interim final rule with request for comments, affecting 42 CFR part 417.

62 FR 67388, December 24, 1997: HCFA Emergency Clearance: Public Information Collection Requirements Submitted to the Office of Management and Budget (OMB) (pertaining to collection of inpatient data for Medicare+Choice organizations).

63 FR 2920, January 20, 1998: Medicare Program: Request for Public Comments on Implementation of the Medicare+Choice Program, and Notice of Timeframes for Submission of Applications for Contracts — Notice of intent to regulate and solicitation of comments.

63 FR 7175, February 12, 1998: HCFA Emergency Clearance: Public Information Collection Requirements Submitted to the Office of Managment and Budget (OMB) (pertaining to managed care adjusted community rate (ACR) proposal).

63 FR 7359, February 13, 1998: Medicare Program; Meeting of the Negotiated Rulemaking Committee on the Provider-Sponsored Organization Solvency Standards — Notice of meeting.

63 FR 11263, March 6, 1998: HCFA Agency Information Collection Activities: Submission for OMB Review; Comment request (pertaining to end stage renal disease managed care demonstration.

63 FR 12475, March 13, 1998: HCFA Agency Information Collection Activities; Submission for OMB Review; Comment request (pertaining to HMO and CMP national data reporting requirements).

63 FR 12476, March 13, 1998: HCFA Emergency Clearance: Public Information Collection Requirements Submitted to the Office of Management and Budget (OMB) (pertaining to Medicare+Choice Provider Sponsored Organization (PSO) waiver request forms).

63 FR 16563, April 3, 1998: HCFA Agency Information Collection Activities: Submission for OMB Review; Comment request (pertaining to evaluation of Medicare Choices demonstration).

63 FR 18124, April 14, 1998: Medicare Program; Definition of Provider-Sponsored Organization and Related Requirements — Interim final rule with comment period, affecting 42 CFR 422.

63 FR 18924, April 16, 1998: HCFA Emergency Clearance: Public Information Collection Requirements Submitted to the Office of Management and Budget (OMB) (pertaining to collection of managed care data using the uniform institutional providers form).

63 FR 25215, May 7, 1998: HCFA Agency Information Collection Activities: Proposed Collection; Comment request (pertaining to clinical laboratory improvement amendments application forms; limits on provider-related donations and health care-related taxes and payments to disproportionate share hospitals; and Medicare+Choice provider sponsored organization waiver request forms).

63 FR 25360, May 7, 1998: Medicare Program; Waiver Requirements and Solvency Standards for Provider Sponsored Organizations — Interim final rule with comment period, affecting 42 CFR 422.

63 FR 26811, May 14, 1998: Medicare and Medicaid Programs: Request for Public Comments on the Quality Improvement System for Managed Care — Solicitation of comments; notice of public meeting.

63 FR 34968, June 26, 1998: Medicare Program; Establishment of the Medicare+Choice Program — Interim final rule with comment period, affecting 42 CFR Parts 400, 403, 410, 411, 417, and 422. See also corrections at 63 FR 36488, July 6, 1998, 63 FR 52610, October 1, 1998, and 63 FR 54526, October 9, 1998.

63 FR 38413, July 16, 1998: HCFA Agency Information Collection Activities: Submission for OMB Review; Comment request (pertaining to Clinical Laboratory Improvement Act certification requirements; EPSDT participation reports; limitations on provider-related donations and health care-related taxes, and limitations on payments to disproportionate share hospitals; and Medicare+Choice provider sponsored organization waiver requests forms).

63 FR 43403, August 13, 1998: HCFA Emergency Clearance: Public Information Collection Requirements Submitted to the Office of Management and Budget (OMB) (pertaining to the Medicare and You survey form to collect information from internet users accessing the Medicare+Choice Handbook on the Medicare.gov web site).

63 FR 45828, August 27, 1998: HCFA Emergency Clearance: Public Information Collection Requirements Submitted to the Office of Management and Budget (OMB) (pertaining to surveys of the effectiveness of the Medicare+Choice education campaign).

63 FR 45829, August 27, 1998: HCFA Emergency Clearance: Public Information Collection Requirements Submitted to the Office of Management and Budget (OMB) (pertaining to a survey of callers to determine consumer satisfaction with the Medicare+Choice toll-free information line).

63 FR 47506, September 8, 1998: Medicare Program: Request for Public Comments on Implementation of Risk Adjusted Payment for the Medicare+Choice Program and Announcement of Public Meeting-Solicitation of comments.

63 FR 50577, September 22, 1998: Office of Inspector General: Solicitation of Information and Recommendations for Developing OIG Compliance Program Guidance for Certain Medicare+Choice Organizations — Notice.

63 FR 53923, October 7, 1998: HCFA Emergency Clearance: Public Information Collection Requirements Submitted to the Office of Management and Budget (OMB) (pertaining to Medicare+Choice requirements for quality assurance and enrollee services).

63 FR 63478, November 13, 1998: HCFA Agency Information Collection Activities: Proposed Collection; Comment request (pertaining to processing Medicare+Choice disenrollment requests from beneficiaries; creation of the Utilization and Quality Control Peer Review Organization; and rules for participation of HHA's in Medicare and review of plans of care for home health services).

63 FR 69079, December 15, 1998: HCFA Agency Information Collection Activities: Proposed Collection; Comment request (pertaining to Managed care adjusted community rate for Medicare+Choice organizations).

1999

64 FR 2907, January 19, 1999: HCFA Agency Information Collection Activities: Submission for OMB Review; Comment request (pertaining to call-back survey of callers to Medicare+Choice toll-free line).

64 FR 5665, February 4, 1999: HCFA Agency Information Collection Activities: Proposed Collection; Comment request (pertaining to Medicare+Choice disenrollment forms, and utilization and quality control peer review organizations (PROs)).

64 FR 7968, February 17, 1999: Medicare Program; Changes to the Medicare+Choice Program — Final rule affecting 42 CFR Part 422.

64 FR 10156, March 2, 1999: HCFA Agency Information Collection Activities: Submission for OMB Review; Comment request (pertaining to Medicare+Choice adjusted community rate proposal).

64 FR 13432, March 18, 1999: HCFA Emergency Clearance: Public Information Collection requirements submitted to the Office of Management and Budget (OMB) (pertaining to Medicare+Choice managed care plan benefit package and adjusted community rate proposal).

64 FR 32508, June 17, 1999: HCFA Agency Information Collection Activities: Submission for OMB Review; Comment Request (pertaining to the quality improvement system for managed care (QISMC)).

64 FR 38204, July 15, 1999: HCFA Agency Information Collection Activities: Submission for OMB Review; Comment request (pertaining to the national Medicare education program survey about Medicare+Choice awareness).

64 FR 41445, July 30, 1999: HCFA Emergency Clearance: Public Information Collection Requirements Submitted to the Office of Management and Budget (OMB) (pertaining to Medicare+Choice organization appeals and grievance data collection and reporting requirements).

64 FR 46919, August 27, 1999: HCFA Emergency Clearance: Public Information Collection Requirements Submitted to the Office of Management and Budget (OMB) (pertaining to survey of disenrollment by Medicare beneficiaries from alternative health plans).

64 FR 55737, October 14, 1999: HCFA Agency Information Collection Activities: Proposed Collection; Comment request (pertaining to the adjusted community rate proposal for Medicare+Choice plans).

64 FR 55949, October 15, 1999: Medicare Program; Open Public Meeting November 1, 1999, to Discuss Activities Related to the Collection of Encounter Data from Medicare+Choice Organizations for Risk Adjustment.

64 FR 57902, October 27, 1999: HCFA Agency Information Collection Activites: Proposed Collection; Comment request (pertaining to evaluation of new Medicare+Choice plans).

64 FR 61893, November 15, 1999: Office of Inspector General; Publication of the OIG's Compliance Program Guidance for Medicare+Choice Organizations Offering Coordinated Care Plans — Notice.

64 FR 71673, December 22, 1999: Medicare Program; Solvency Standards for Provider-sponsored organizations (Medicare+Choice) — Final rule affecting 42 CFR Part 422.

2000

65 FR 3724, January 24, 2000: HCFA Agency Information Collection Activities: Submission for OMB Review; Comment request (pertaining to evaluation by new Medicare members of Medicare+Choice plans).

65 FR 3725, January 24, 2000: HCFA Agency Information Collection Activities: submission for OMB Review; Comment request (pertaining to the adjusted community rate proposal for Medicare+Choice plan benefit packages).

65 FR 10812, February 29, 2000: Medicare Program; Open Public Meeting on March 15, 2000, to Provide an Overview of Data Requirements for Collection of Physician and Hospital Outpatient Encounter Data from Medicare+Choice Organizations for Risk Adjustment — Notice of meeting.

65 FR 19382, April 11, 2000: HCFA Emergency Clearance: Public Information Collection Requirements Submitted to the Office of Management and Budget (OMB) (pertaining to adjusted community rate for Medicare+Choice organizations.

65 FR 19782, April 12, 2000: HCFA Agency Information Collection Activities: Proposed Collection; Comment request (pertaining to Medicare+Choice beneficiary notices).

65 FR 19783, April 12, 2000: HCFA Emergency Clearance: Public Information Collection Requirements Submitted to the Office of Management and Budget (OMB) (pertaining to Medicare+Choice beneficiary notices).

65 FR 24707, April 27, 2000: HCFA Agency Information Collection Activities: Proposed Collection; Comment request (pertaining to collection of data on physician encounters from Medicare+Choice organizations).

65 FR 25737, May 3, 2000: HCFA Agency Information Collection Activities: Proposed Collection; Comment request (pertaining to managed care disenrollment form).

65 FR 25738, May 3, 2000: HCFA Emergency Clearance: Public Informatiion Collection Requirements Submitted to the Office of Management and Budget (OMB) (pertaining to the Medicare managed care CAHPS Survey).

65 FR 26618, May 5, 2000: HCFA Emergency Clearance: Public Information Collection Requirements Submitted to the Office of Management and Budget (OMB) (pertaining to Medicare consumer assessment survey of health plans).

65 FR 39416, June 26, 2000: HCFA Agency Information Collection Activities: Proposed Collection; Comment request (pertaining to Medicare+Choice organization appeals and grievance data disclosure requirements).

65 FR 40111, June 29, 2000: HCFA Agency Information Collection Activities: Proposed Collection; comment request (pertaining to qualification applications for prepaid health plans (HMOs).

65 FR 40112, June 29, 2000: Medicare Program: Medicare+Choice Deeming Authority — Notice regarding accrediting organizations.

65 FR 40170, June 29, 2000: Medicare Program; Medicare+Choice Program — Final rule with comment period, affecting 42 CFR parts 417 and 422.

65 FR 40668, June 30, 2000: HCFA Agency Information Collection Activities: Submission for OMB Review; Comment request (pertaining to Medicare comprehensive health plan disenrollment).

65 FR 43026, July 12, 2000: HCFA Agency Information Collection Activities: Submission for OMB Review; Comment request (pertaining to collection of data on physician encounters from Medicare+Choice organizations).

65 FR 46473, July 28, 2000: Medicare Program; Announcement of a Series of Regional Training Sessions to Provide Training to Medicare+Choice Organization Physicians, Medicare+Choice Organization Non-physician Practitioners, and Medicare+Choice Organization Medicare Directors, As Well As Physician Organizations and Billing Associations Involved in the Timely and Accurate Submission of Physician Encounter Data to Support a Comprehensive Risk Adjustment Model — Notice of training sessions.

65 FR 50713, August 21, 2000: HCFA Agency Information Collection Activities: Proposed Collection; Comment request (pertaining to social HMO demonstration payment methodology)

65 FR 53319, September 1, 2000: HCFA Agency Information Collection Activities: Proposed Collection; Comment request (pertaining to incentive arrangement disclosure form for managed care organizations and their related medical groups and physicians).

65 FR 57195, September 21, 2000: HCFA Agency Information Collection Activities; Proposed Collection; Comment request (pertaining to Medicare managed care CAHPS survey for quality of care purposes).

65 FR 60674, October 12, 2000: HCFA Agency Information Collection Activities: Submission for OMB Review; Comment request

(pertaining to Medicare+Choice organization appeals and grievance data disclosure requirements).

65 FR 64228, October 26, 2000: HCFA Agency Information Collection Activities: Proposed Collection; Comment request (pertaining to collection of data on physician encounters from Medicare+Choice organizations).

65 FR 65860, November 2, 2000: HCFA Agency Information Collection Activities: Proposed Collection; Comment request (pertaining to follow-up of Medicare+Choice disenrollees receiving fee-for service inpatient hospital care).

65 FR 79867, December 20, 2000: HCFA Agency Information Collection Activities: Proposed Collection; Comment request (pertaining to quality improvement system for managed care).

65 FR 79868, December 20, 2000: HCFA Agency Information Collection Activities: Proposed Collection; Comment request (pertaining to Medicare consumer assessment survey of health plans).

65 FR 79868, December 20, 2000: HCFA Emergency Clearance: Public Information Collection Requirements Submitted to the Office of Management and Budget (OMB) (pertaining to survey of beneficiaries who involuntarily disenroll from their managed care plan).

65 FR 81813, December 27, 2000: Medicare Program; Requirements for the Re-credentialing of Medicare+Choice Organization Providers — Proposed rule affecting 42 CFR Part 422.

2001

66 FR 1995, January 10, 2001: HCFA Agency Information Collection Activities: Proposed Collection; Comment request (pertaining to hospital outpatient encounters from Medicare+Choice programs).

66 FR 2913, January 12, 2001: HCFA Agency Information Collection Activities: Submission for OMB Review; Comment request (pertaining to collection of data about physician encounters from Medicare+Choice organizations).

66 FR 6228, January 19, 2001: Medicaid Program; Medicaid Managed Care—Final rule with comment period, affecting 42 CFR Part 400, 430, 431, 435, 438, 440, and 447.

66 FR 7593, January 24, 2001: Medicare Program; Improvements to the Medicare+Choice Appeal and Grievance Procedures—Proposed rule affecting 42 CFR Parts 422 and 489.

66 FR 8807, February 2, 2001: HCFA Agency Information Collection Activities: Submission for OMB Review; Comment request

(pertaining to follow–up of Medicare+Choice disenrollees receiving fee–for–service inpatient hospital care).

66 FR 9858, February 12, 2001: HCFA Privacy Act of 1974; Report of New System (pertaining to complaints against health insurance issuers and health plans).

66 FR 11546, February 26, 2001: Medicaid Program; Medicaid Managed Care: Delay of Effective Date—Final rule delay, affecting 42 CFR Parts 400, 430, 431, 434, 435, 438, 440, and 447.

66 FR 11591, February 26, 2001: HCFA Agency Information Collection Activities: Proposed Collection; Comment request (pertaining to Medicare+Choice program requirements).

66 FR 13854, March 8, 2001: Medicare+Choice Program—CFR correction.

66 FR 15122, March 15, 2001: HCFA Agency Information Collection Activities: Submission for OMB Review; Comment request (pertaining to quality improvement system for managed care).

66 FR 16062, March 23, 2001: HCFA Agency Information Collection Activities: Submission for OMB Review; Comment request (pertaining to Medicare+Choice beneficiary appeal notices).

66 FR 16268, March 23, 2001: HCFA Agency Information Collection Activities; Proposed Collection; Comment request (pertaining to data collection to support policy analysis of choices offered to Medicare+Choice enrollees and choices made by enrollees).

66 FR 16481, March 26, 2001: HCFA Agency Information Collection Activities: Submission for OMB Review; Comment request (pertaining to managed care adjusted community rate proposal for Medicare+Choice organizations).

66 FR 16678, March 27, 2001: HCFA Agency Information Collection Activities: Submission for OMB Review; Comment request (pertaining to Medicare managed care CAHPS survey).

66 FR 17431, March 30, 2001: HCFA Agency Information Collection Activities: Proposed Collection; Comment request (pertaining to data collection of quality indicators for congestive heart failure submitted by Medicare+Choice organizations requesting extra payments in CY 2002 and CY 2003).

66 FR 21770, May 1, 2001: Medicare Program; Revision of Payment Rates for End–Stage Renal Disease (ESRD) Patients Enrolled in Medicare+Choice Plans—Proposed notice.

66 FR 21987, May 2, 2001: HCFA Agency Information Collection Activities: Proposed Collection; Comment request (pertaining to

Medicare+Choice provider sponsored organization (PSO) waiver request form).

66 FR 24391, May 14, 2001: HCFA Agency Information Collection Activities: Submission for OMB Review; Comment request (pertaining to Medicare+Choice program requirements).

66 FR 28916, May 25, 2001: HCFA Agency Information Collection Activities: Proposed Collection; Comment request (pertaining to collection of managed care data using the uniform institutional providers form).

66 FR 29823, June 1, 2001: HCFA Agency Information Collection Activities: Proposed Collection; Comment request (pertaining to data reporting requirements for managed care organizations in the Medicare+Choice program).

66 FR 32776, June 18, 2001: Medicaid Program; Medicaid Managed Care: Further Delay of Effective Date for Final Rule affecting 42 CFR Parts 400, 430, 431, 434, 435, 438, 440, and 447.

See § 2:26.2.

§ 6:27 FAILURE BY PRIMARY PAYERS TO COMPLY WITH MEDICARE SECONDARY PAYER REQUIREMENTS — Section 1862(b) [42 U.S.C.A. 1395y(b)]

Regulations

42 CFR Part 402 — Civil Money Penalties, Assessments, and Exclusions

42 CFR Part 411 — Exclusions from Medicare and Limitations on Medicare Payment

42 CFR Part 433, Subpart D — Third Party Liability [Medicaid]

42 CFR Chapter V — Office of Inspector General — Health Care, Department of Health and Human Services

Subchapter A — General Provisions

Part 1000 — Introduction; General Definitions

Subchapter B — OIG Authorities

Part 1001 — Program Integrity: Medicare and State Health Care Programs

Part 1003 — Civil Money Penalties, Assessments and Exclusions

Part 1005 — Appeals of Exclusions, Civil Money Penalties and Assessments

Part 1006 — Investigational Inquiries

Part 1007 — State Medicaid Fraud Control Units

Part 1008 — Advisory Opinions by the OIG

54 FR 41716, October 11, 1989: Medicare as Secondary Payer and Medicare Recovery Against Third Parties — Final rule.

54 FR 47678, November 16, 1989: Medicare Program; Medicare as Secondary Payer and Medicare Recovery Against Third Parties; Publication of Court Orders — Publication of court orders.

55 FR 1432, January 16, 1990: Medicaid Program; State Plan Requirements and Other Provisions Relating to State Third Party Liability Programs — Final rule. See also correction published at 55 FR 5118, February 13, 1990.

55 FR 1819, January 19, 1990: Medicare as Secondary Payer and Medicare Recovery Against Third Parties — Correction of final rule published at 54 FR 41716, October 11, 1989.

55 FR 8491, March 8, 1990: Medicare Program; Medicare Secondary Payer for Disabled Active Individuals — Proposed rule to amend 42 CFR Part 411.

55 FR 11019, March 26, 1990: Medicare Program; Medicare as Secondary Payer and Medicare Recovery Against Third Parties — Final rule and reinstatement of regulations published at 54 FR 41716 on October 11, 1989.

56 FR 1200, January 11, 1991: Changes to Medicare Secondary Payer (MSP) Provisions — Notice.

56 FR 31952, July 12, 1991: Medicare Program; Medicare Secondary Payer Data Match — Notice.

57 FR 36006, August 12, 1992: Medicare Program; Self-implementing Coverage and Payments Provisions: 1990 Legislation — Final rule with comment period, affecting 42 CFR Parts 405, 406, 409, 420, 411, 412, 413, 418, and 489. Pertains to capital-related inpatient hospital costs; capital-related outpatient hospital costs; non-capital related outpatient hospital costs; payment for physician pathology services; payment for services of physicians as assistants-at-surgery; payments for ambulatory surgical procedures in hospital outpatient departments; payments for radiology services performed in hospital outpatient departments; hospice benefit extension; enrollment of HMO members in Medicare Part A; coverage of ostomy supplies; application of pre-entitlement stay in psychiatric hospital to limit on payment for inpatient hospital services; payments to dialysis facilities; payment rates for erythropoietin (EPO); and Medicare secondary payer provision for individuals with ESRD. See also confirmation of final rule at 58 FR 58502, November 2, 1993.

58 FR 29416, May 20, 1993: HCFA Public Information Collection Requirements Submitted to the Office of Management and Budget (OMB) for Clearance re cataract surgery; Medicaid utilization management initiatives; Medicare coverage of screening mammography; psychiatric unit criteria worksheet and rehabilitation unit criteria worksheet; Medicare secondary payor forms; ambulatory surgical center survey forms; ambulance service compliance with State and local requirements; and early and periodic screening, diagnostic and treatment reports.

58 FR 38579, July 19, 1993: HCFA Public Information Collection Requirements Submitted to the Office of Management and Budget (OMB) for Clearance re survey of home health agencies; CLIA survey report form; validation of state surveys; Medicaid listing of participating home health agencies; financial information regarding Medicare benefits from Medicare contractors; and third-party liability under Medicaid.

59 FR 4285, January 31, 1994: Medicare Program; Medicare Secondary Payment — General notice.

59 FR 31569, June 20, 1994: Medicaid Program; Requirements for Enrollment in or Payment for Certain Employer Group Health Plans — Proposed rule affecting 42 CFR Parts 435 and 436.

60 FR 35498, July 10, 1995: Medicaid Program; Third Party Liability (TPL) Cost-effectiveness Waivers — Final rule affecting 42 CFR Part 433. See also correction at 62 FR 23140, April 29, 1997.

60 FR 37066, July 19, 1995: HCFA Public Information Collection Requirements Submitted to the Office of Management and Budget (OMB) for Clearance (pertaining to actuarial forecasts for Medicaid utilization and cost, employers identified through a match of IRS, SSA, and Medicare records for purposes of the Medicare Secondary Payer provision, health and safety requirements for portable X-ray suppliers, and evaluation of Intermediate Care Facilities for Persons with Mental Retardation — establishing psychoactive drug use baselines).

61 FR 55155, October 24, 1996: HCFA Emergency Clearance: Agency Public Information Collection Requirements Submitted to OMB (pertaining to employer identifiers to ensure compliance with Medicare secondary payor requirements).

61 FR 56689, November 4, 1996: HCFA Agency Information Collection Activities: Proposed Collection; Comment request (pertaining to employer identifiers to ensure compliance with Medicare secondary payor requirements).

63 FR 32888, June 16, 1998: HCFA Agency Information Collection Activities: Proposed Collection; Comment request (pertaining to Medicare secondary payer reports; and drug utilization review for Medicaid patients).

63 FR 39880, July 24, 1998: HCFA Agency Information Collection Activities: Proposed Collection; Comment request (pertaining to Medicare secondary payer information collection).

1999

64 FR 1025, January 7, 1999: HCFA Emergency Clearance: Public Information Collection Requirements Submitted to the Office of Management and Budget (OMB) (pertaining to group health plans and Medicare secondary payor requirements).

64 FR 27798, May 21, 1999: HCFA Agency Information Collection Activities: Proposed collection; Comment request (pertaining to determining third party liability (TPL) by State Medicaid agencies).

64 FR 30042, June 4, 1999: HCFA Agency Information Activities: Proposed Collection; Comment request (pertaining to IRS/SSA/HCFA Medicare secondary payor data match).

64 FR 44031, August 12, 1999: HCFA Agency Information Collection Activites: Submission for OMB Review; Comment request (pertaining to survey and certification of rural health clinics; and determining third party liability in Medicaid programs).

64 FR 46401, August 25, 1999: HCFA Agency Information Collection Activities: Submission for OMB Review; Comment request (pertaining to SSA/IRS/HCFA data match to implement the Medicare secondary payer provisions).

64 FR 55483, October 13, 1999: HCFA Agency Information Collection Activities: Proposed Collection; Comment request (pertaining to forms used to determine whether Medicare beneficiaries have coverage under an employer group health plan based on current employment).

2000

65 FR 2186, January 13, 2000: HCFA Agency Information Collection Activities; Submission for OMB Review; Comment request (pertaining to request for employment information from employers to determine whether a Medicare beneficiary's coverage under a group health plan is based on current employment.

65 FR 62724, October 19, 2000: HCFA Notice of Emergency Clearance and Public Meeting: Public Information Collection Requirements Submitted to the Office of Management and Budget (OMB) (pertaining to Medicare secondary payment requirements).

See § 2:27.

§ 6:28 FAILURE BY EMPLOYERS TO COMPLY WITH MEDICARE SECONDARY PAYER REQUIREMENTS — Section 1862(b)(5)(C)(ii) [42 U.S.C.A. 1395y(b)(5)(C)(ii)]

Regulations

42 CFR Part 402 — Civil Money Penalties, Assessments, and Exclusions

42 CFR Part 411 — Exclusions from Medicare and Limitations on Medicare Payment

42 CFR Part 433, Subpart D — Third Party Liability [Medicaid]

42 CFR Chapter V — Office of Inspector General — Health Care, Department of Health and Human Services

Subchapter A — General Provisions

Part 1000 — Introduction; General Definitions

Subchapter B — OIG Authorities

Part 1001 — Program Integrity: Medicare and State Health Care Programs

Part 1003 — Civil Money Penalties, Assessments and Exclusions

Part 1005 — Appeals of Exclusions, Civil Money Penalties and Assessments

Part 1006 — Investigational Inquiries

Part 1007 — State Medicaid Fraud Control Units

Part 1008 — Advisory Opinions by the OIG

54 FR 41716, October 11, 1989: Medicare as Secondary Payer and Medicare Recovery Against Third Parties — Final rule.

54 FR 47678, November 16, 1989: Medicare Program; Medicare as Secondary Payer and Medicare Recovery Against Third Parties; Publication of Court Orders — Publication of court orders.

55 FR 1432, January 16, 1990: Medicaid Program; State plan Requirements and Other Provisions Relating to State Third Party Liability Programs — Final rule. See also correction published at 55 FR 5118, February 13, 1990.

55 FR 1819, January 19, 1990: Medicare as Secondary Payer and Medicare Recovery Against Third Parties — Correction of final rule published at 54 FR 41716, October 11, 1989.

55 FR 8491, March 8, 1990: Medicare Program; Medicare Secondary Payer for Disabled Active Individuals — Proposed rule to amend 42 CFR Part 411.

55 FR 11019, March 26, 1990: Medicare Program; Medicare as Secondary Payer and Medicare Recovery Against Third Parties — Final rule and reinstatement of regulations published at 54 FR 41716 on October 11, 1989.

56 FR 1200, January 11, 1991: Changes to Medicare Secondary Payer (MSP) Provisions — Notice.

56 FR 31952, July 12, 1991: Medicare Program; Medicare Secondary Payer Data Match — Notice.

57 FR 36006, August 12, 1992: Medicare Program; Self-implementing Coverage and Payments Provisions: 1990 Legislation — Final rule with comment period, affecting 42 CFR Parts 405, 406, 409, 420, 411, 412, 413, 418, and 489. Pertains to capital-related inpatient hospital costs; capital-related outpatient hospital costs; non-capital related outpatient hospital costs; payment for physician pathology services; payment for services of physicians as assistants-at-surgery; payments for ambulatory surgical procedures in hospital outpatient departments; payments for radiology services performed in hospital outpatient departments; hospice benefit extension; enrollment of HMO members in Medicare Part A; coverage of ostomy supplies; application of pre-entitlement stay in psychiatric hospital to limit on payment for inpatient hospital services; payments to dialysis facilities; payment rates for erythropoietin (EPO); and Medicare secondary payer provision for individuals with ESRD. See also confirmation of final rule at 58 FR 58502, November 2, 1993.

58 FR 29416, May 20, 1993: HCFA Public Information Collection Requirements Submitted to the Office of Management and Budget (OMB) for Clearance re cataract surgery; Medicaid utilization management initiatives; Medicare coverage of screening mammography; psychiatric unit criteria worksheet and rehabilitation unit criteria worksheet; Medicare secondary payor forms; ambulatory surgical center survey forms; ambulance service compliance with State and local requirements; and early and periodic screening, diagnostic and treatment reports.

58 FR 38579, July 19, 1993: HCFA Public Information Collection Requirements Submitted to the Office of Management and Budget (OMB) for Clearance re survey of home health agencies; CLIA survey report form; validation of state surveys; Medicaid listing of participating home health agencies; financial information regarding Medicare benefits from Medicare contractors; and third-party liability under Medicaid.

59 FR 4285, January 31, 1994: Medicare Program; Medicare Secondary Payment — General notice.

59 FR 31569, June 20, 1994: Medicaid Program; Requirements for Enrollment in or Payment for Certain Employer Group Health Plans — Proposed rule affecting 42 CFR Parts 435 and 436.

60 FR 35498, July 10, 1995: Medicaid Program; Third Party Liability (TPL) Cost-effectiveness Waivers — Final rule affecting 42 CFR Part 433. See also correction at 62 FR 23140, April 29, 1997.

60 FR 37066, July 19, 1995: HCFA Public Information Collection Requirements Submitted to the Office of Management and Budget (OMB) for Clearance (pertaining to actuarial forecasts for Medicaid utilization and cost, employers identified through a match of IRS, SSA, and Medicare records for purposes of the Medicare Secondary Payer provision, health and safety requirements for portable X-ray suppliers, and evaluation of Intermediate Care Facilities for Persons with Mental Retardation — establishing psychoactive drug use baselines).

61 FR 55155, October 24, 1996: HCFA Emergency Clearance: Agency Public Information Collection Requirements Submitted to OMB (pertaining to employer identifiers to ensure compliance with Medicare secondary payor requirements).

61 FR 56689, November 4, 1996: HCFA Agency Information Collection Activities: Proposed Collection; Comment request (pertaining to employer identifiers to ensure compliance with Medicare secondary payor requirements).

63 FR 32888, June 16, 1998: HCFA Agency Information Collection Activities: Proposed Collection; Comment request (pertaining to Medicare secondary payer reports; and drug utilization review for Medicaid patients).

63 FR 39880, July 24, 1998: HCFA Agency Information Collection Activities: Proposed Collection; Comment request (pertaining to Medicare secondary payer information collection).

1999

64 FR 1025, January 7, 1999: HCFA Emergency Clearance: Public Information Collection Requirements Submitted to the Office of Management and Budget (OMB) (pertaining to group health plans and Medicare secondary payor requirements).

64 FR 27798, May 21, 1999: HCFA Agency Information Collection Activities: Proposed collection; Comment request (pertaining to determining third party liability (TPL) by State Medicaid agencies).

64 FR 30042, June 4, 1999: HCFA Agency Information Activities: Proposed Collection; Comment request (pertaining to IRS/SSA/HCFA Medicare secondary payor data match).

64 FR 44031, August 12, 1999: HCFA Agency Information Collection Activites: Submission for OMB Review; Comment request (pertaining to survey and certification of rural health clinics; and determining third party liability in Medicaid programs).

64 FR 46401, August 25, 1999: HCFA Agency Information Collection Activities: Submission for OMB Review; Comment request (pertaining to SSA/IRS/HCFA data match to implement the Medicare secondary payer provisions).

64 FR 55483, October 13, 1999: HCFA Agency Information Collection Activities: Proposed Collection; Comment request (pertaining to forms used to determine whether Medicare beneficiaries have coverage under an employer group health plan based on current employment).

2000

65 FR 2186, January 13, 2000: HCFA Agency Information Collection Activities; Submission for OMB Review; Comment request (pertaining to request for employment information from employers to determine whether a Medicare beneficiary's coverage under a group health plan is based on current employment.

65 FR 62724, October 19, 2000: HCFA Notice of Emergency Clearance and Public Meeting: Public Information Collection Requirements Submitted to the Office of Management and Budget (OMB) (pertaining to Medicare secondary payment requirements).

See § 2:28.

§ 6:28.1 VIOLATION OF MEDICARE SECONDARY PAYER REQUIREMENTS BY PROVIDERS AND SUPPLIERS — Section 1862(b)(6) [42 U.S.C.A. 1395y(b)(6)]

Regulations

42 CFR Part 402 — Civil Money Penalties, Assessments, and Exclusions

42 CFR Part 411 — Exclusions from Medicare and Limitations on Medicare Payment

42 CFR Part 433, Subpart D — Third Party Liability [Medicaid]

42 CFR Chapter V — Office of Inspector General — Health Care, Department of Health and Human Services

Subchapter A — General Provisions

Part 1000 — Introduction; General Definitions

Subchapter B — OIG Authorities

Part 1001 — Program Integrity: Medicare and State Health Care Programs

Part 1003 — Civil Money Penalties, Assessments and Exclusions

Part 1005 — Appeals of Exclusions, Civil Money Penalties and Assessments

Part 1006 — Investigational Inquiries

Part 1007 — State Medicaid Fraud Control Units

Part 1008 — Advisory Opinions by the OIG

54 FR 41716, October 11, 1989: Medicare as Secondary Payer and Medicare Recovery Against Third Parties — Final rule.

54 FR 47678, November 16, 1989: Medicare Program; Medicare as Secondary Payer and Medicare Recovery Against Third Parties; Publication of Court Orders — Publication of court orders.

55 FR 1432, January 16, 1990: Medicaid Program; State Plan Requirements and Other Provisions Relating to State Third Party Liability Programs — Final rule. See also correction published at 55 FR 5118, February 13, 1990.

55 FR 1819, January 19, 1990: Medicare as Secondary Payer and Medicare Recovery Against Third Parties — Correction of final rule published at 54 FR 41716, October 11, 1989.

55 FR 8491, March 8, 1990: Medicare Program; Medicare Secondary Payer for Disabled Active Individuals — Proposed rule to amend 42 CFR Part 411.

55 FR 11019, March 26, 1990: Medicare Program; Medicare as Secondary Payer and Medicare Recovery Against Third Par-

ties — Final rule and reinstatement of regulations published at 54 FR 41716 on October 11, 1989.

56 FR 1200, January 11, 1991: Changes to Medicare Secondary Payer (MSP) Provisions — Notice.

56 FR 31952, July 12, 1991: Medicare Program; Medicare Secondary Payer Data Match — Notice.

57 FR 36006, August 12, 1992: Medicare Program; Self-implementing Coverage and Payments Provisions: 1990 Legislation — Final rule with comment period, affecting 42 CFR Parts 405, 406, 409, 420, 411, 412, 413, 418, and 489. Pertains to capital-related inpatient hospital costs; capital-related outpatient hospital costs; non-capital related outpatient hospital costs; payment for physician pathology services; payment for services of physicians as assistants-at-surgery; payments for ambulatory surgical procedures in hospital outpatient departments; payments for radiology services performed in hospital outpatient departments; hospice benefit extension; enrollment of HMO members in Medicare Part A; coverage of ostomy supplies; application of pre-entitlement stay in psychiatric hospital to limit on payment for inpatient hospital services; payments to dialysis facilities; payment rates for erythropoietin (EPO); and Medicare secondary payer provision for individuals with ESRD. See also confirmation of final rule at 58 FR 58502, November 2, 1993.

58 FR 29416, May 20, 1993: HCFA Public Information Collection Requirements Submitted to the Office of Management and Budget (OMB) for Clearance re cataract surgery; Medicaid utilization management initiatives; Medicare coverage of screening mammography; psychiatric unit criteria worksheet and rehabilitation unit criteria worksheet; Medicare secondary payor forms; ambulatory surgical center survey forms; ambulance service compliance with State and local requirements; and early and periodic screening, diagnostic and treatment reports.

58 FR 38579, July 19, 1993: HCFA Public Information Collection Requirements Submitted to the Office of Management and Budget (OMB) for Clearance re survey of home health agencies; CLIA survey report form; validation of state surveys; Medicaid listing of participating home health agencies; financial information regarding Medicare benefits from Medicare contractors; and third-party liability under Medicaid.

59 FR 4285, January 31, 1994: Medicare Program; Medicare Secondary Payment — General notice.

59 FR 31569, June 20, 1994: Medicaid Program; Requirements for Enrollment in or Payment for Certain Employer Group Health Plans — Proposed rule affecting 42 CFR Parts 435 and 436.

60 FR 35498, July 10, 1995: Medicaid Program; Third Party Liability (TPL) Cost-effectiveness Waivers — Final rule affecting 42 CFR Part 433. See also correction at 62 FR 23140, April 29, 1997.

60 FR 37066, July 19, 1995: HCFA Public Information Collection Requirements Submitted to the Office of Management and Budget (OMB) for Clearance (pertaining to actuarial forecasts for Medicaid utilization and cost, employers identified through a match of IRS, SSA, and Medicare records for purposes of the Medicare Secondary Payer provision, health and safety requirements for portable X-ray suppliers, and evaluation of Intermediate Care Facilities for Persons with Mental Retardation — establishing psychoactive drug use baselines).

61 FR 55155, October 24, 1996: HCFA Emergency Clearance: Agency Public Information Collection Requirements Submitted to OMB (pertaining to employer identifiers to ensure compliance with Medicare secondary payor requirements).

61 FR 56689, November 4, 1996: HCFA Agency Information Collection Activities: Proposed Collection; Comment request (pertaining to employer identifiers to ensure compliance with Medicare secondary payor requirements).

63 FR 32888, June 16, 1998: HCFA Agency Information Collection Activities: Proposed Collection; Comment request (pertaining to Medicare secondary payer reports; and drug utilization review for Medicaid patients).

63 FR 39880, July 24, 1998: HCFA Agency Information Collection Activities: Proposed Collection; Comment request (pertaining to Medicare secondary payer information collection).

1999

64 FR 1025, January 7, 1999: HCFA Emergency Clearance: Public Information Collection Requirements Submitted to the Office of Management and Budget (OMB) (pertaining to group health plans and Medicare secondary payor requirements).

64 FR 27798, May 21, 1999: HCFA Agency Information Collection Activities: Proposed collection; Comment request (pertaining to determining third party liability (TPL) by State Medicaid agencies).

64 FR 30042, June 4, 1999: HCFA Agency Information Activities: Proposed Collection; Comment request (pertaining to IRS/SSA/HCFA Medicare secondary payor data match).

64 FR 44031, August 12, 1999: HCFA Agency Information Collection Activites: Submission for OMB Review; Comment request (pertaining to survey and certification of rural health clinics; and determining third party liability in Medicaid programs).

64 FR 46401, August 25, 1999: HCFA Agency Information Collection Activities: Submission for OMB Review; Comment request (pertaining to SSA/IRS/HCFA data match to implement the Medicare secondary payer provisions).

64 FR 55483, October 13, 1999: HCFA Agency Information Collection Activities: Proposed Collection; Comment request (pertaining to forms used to determine whether Medicare beneficiaries have coverage under an employer group health plan based on current employment).

2000

65 FR 2186, January 13, 2000: HCFA Agency Information Collection Activities; Submission for OMB Review; Comment request (pertaining to request for employment information from employers to determine whether a Medicare beneficiary's coverage under a group health plan is based on current employment.

65 FR 62724, October 19, 2000: HCFA Notice of Emergency Clearance and Public Meeting: Public Information Collection Requirements Submitted to the Office of Management and Budget (OMB) (pertaining to Medicare secondary payment requirements).

See § 2:28.1.

§ 6:29 PROHIBITION AGAINST PAYMENT TO INDIVIDUALS AND ENTITIES SANCTIONED UNDER THE SOCIAL SECURITY ACT — Section 1862(e) [42 U.S.C.A. 1395y(e)]

Regulations

42 CFR Part 402 — Civil Money Penalties, Assessments, and Exclusions

42 CFR Part 405, Subpart C — Recovery of Overpayments and Suspension of Payment

42 CFR Part 411 — Exclusions from Medicare and Limitations on Medicare Payment

42 CFR Part 420 — Program Integrity: Medicare
42 CFR Part 455 — Program Integrity: Medicaid
42 CFR Part 475 — Peer Review Organizations
42 CFR Part 476 — Utilization and Quality Control Review
42 CFR Part 480 — Acquisition, Protection, and Disclosure of Peer Review Information.

42 CFR Part 498 — Appeals Procedures for Determinations that Affect Participation in the Medicare Program and for Determinations that Affect the Participation of ICF's/MR and Certain NF's in the Medicaid Program

42 CFR Chapter V — Office of Inspector General — Health Care, Department of Health and Human Services

Subchapter A — General Provisions
Part 1000 — Introduction; General Definitions
Subchapter B — OIG Authorities
Part 1001 — Program Integrity: Medicare and State Health Care Programs
Part 1002 — Program Integrity: State–initiated Exclusion from Medicaid
Part 1003 — Civil Money Penalties, Assessments and Exclusions
Part 1004 — Imposition of Sanctions on Health Care Practitioners and Providers of Health Care Services by a Peer Review Organization
Part 1005 — Appeals of Exclusions, Civil Money Penalties and Assessments
Part 1006 — Investigational Inquiries
Part 1007 — State Medicaid Fraud Control Units
Part 1008 — Advisory Opinions by the OIG

55 FR 12205, April 2, 1990: Health Care Programs: Fraud and Abuse; Amendments to OIG Exclusion and CMP Authorities Resulting from Public Law 100-93, the Medicare and Medicaid Patient and Program Protection Act of 1987, Public Law 99-272, the Consolidated Omnibus Budget Reconciliation Act of 1985, and Public Law 100-360, the Medicare Catastrophic Coverage Act of 1988 — Proposed rule to amend 42 CFR Parts 1000, 1001, 1002, 1003, 1004, 1005, 1006, and 1007. See also correction published at 55 FR 17461, April 25, 1990.

55 FR 42907, October 24, 1990: Medicare Program; Standards Applied by Utilization and Quality Control Peer Review Organizations: Consideration of Remote Rural Location and Other Relevant Factors — Notice of policy and request for comments.

57 FR 3298, January 29, 1992: Health Care Programs: Fraud and Abuse; Amendments to OIG Exclusion and CMP Authorities Resulting From Public Law 100-93 — Final rule affecting 42 CFR Parts 1001, 1002, 1003, 1004, 1005, 1006, and 1007. See also final rule and correction at 57 FR 9669, March 20, 1992; final rule affecting 42 CFR Parts 1001and 1005, with clarification at 58 FR 5617, January 22, 1993; and final rule affecting 42 CFR Part 1001, with correction, at 58 FR 40752, July 30, 1993.

57 FR 26871, June 16, 1992: Medicare Program; Peer Review Organizations: Revised Scopes of Work for the District of Columbia, Puerto Rico, the Virgin Islands, and All States Except Delaware, Florida, Missouri, Montana, Nebraska, Nevada, Oklahoma, Rhode Island, South Carolina, Washington, and Wyoming — Final notice. See also correction at 57 FR 35837, August 11, 1992.

57 FR 46362, October 8, 1992: Medicare and Medicaid Programs; Revised Effective Date of Medicare/Medicaid Provider Agreement and Supplier Participation — Proposed rule affecting 42 CFR Parts 431, 440, 442, 488, 489, and 498.

57 FR 46865, October 13, 1992: HCFA Public Information Collection Requirements Submitted to the Office of Management and Budget for Clearance (pertaining to impact of home health care plan management and evaluation; end-stage renal disease medical case review; Medicare/Medicaid hospital swing-bed survey report form; quarterly Medicaid statement of expenditures; Medicaid program budget report; information collection requirements in final peer review organization sanction regulations; appeals procedures for determinations that affect participation in Medicare; request for medical review information for Part B intermediary outpatient therapy bills and other Part B outpatient bills; and Medicaid limitations on provider-related donations and health care-related taxes, and limitations on payment to disproportionate share hospitals).

57 FR 48033, October 21, 1992: Medicare Program; Revised Procedures for Paying Claims From Providers of Services — Final notice.

58 FR 12042, March 2, 1993: Medicare Program; Peer Review Organizations: New PRO Contracts for All States and Territories and the District of Columbia — Notice.

58 FR 46198, September 1, 1993: HCFA Public Information Collection Requirements (ICR) Submitted to the Office of Management and Budget (OMB) for Clearance (pertaining to prenatal services and assistance screening; home health agency treatment

forms; conditions of participation for intermediate care facilities for the mentally retarded; State Medicaid eligibility quality control sample selection lists; prepaid health plan cost report; hospital survey report form; procedures for determining whether providers, practitioners, or other suppliers of services are liable for certain noncovered services; Medicare credit balance reporting requirements; Medicare provider cost report questionnaire form; Medicare current beneficiary survey rounds 7-10; sterilization regulation/consent form; PRO reconsideration and appeals information requirements; information collection requirements in HSQ-110, acquisition, protection and disclosure of PRO information; Medicare/Medicaid organ procurement organization's (OPO) request for certification) — Notice.

58 FR 47904, September 13, 1993: HCFA, Public Information Collection Requirements (ICR) Submitted to the Office of Management and Budget (OMB) for Clearance (pertaining to chronic renal disease medical evidence report; Medicare common claims form; Social Security Office report of State buy-in problem; Medicare physician survey form; beneficiary survey form; Medicaid payment rate changes for inpatient hospital or long term care services; home and community-based services: waiver requirements; Medicare peer review organizations reporting forms; uniform institutional provider claim form) — Notice.

58 FR 54096, October 20, 1993: Office of Inspector General: Civil Money Penalties for Prohibited Referrals to Entities Providing Clinical Laboratory Services and for Prohibited Arrangements and Schemes — Proposed rule affecting 42 CFR Part 1003.

59 FR 9452, February 28, 1994: Office of Inspector General: Health Care Programs; Fraud and Abuse; Revisions to the PRO Sanctions Process — Proposed rule affecting 42 CFR Part 1004. 59 FR 36072, July 15, 1994: Medicare and State Health Care Programs: Fraud and Abuse, Civil Money Penalties and Intermediate Sanctions for Certain Violations by Health Maintenance Organizations and Competitive Medical Plans — Final rule affecting 42 CFR Parts 417, 431, 434, and 1003. See also correction at 59 FR 48566, September 22, 1994.

59 FR 50762, October 5, 1994: HCFA Public Information Collection Requirements Submitted to the Office of Management and Budget (OMB) for Clearance (pertaining to reimbursement of hospital costs for residents and interns, criteria for psychiatric and rehabilitation hospital units' reimbursement under the prospective

payment system, disclosure of owners and managers of suppliers for fraud and abuse detection purposes, reimbursement of municipal health services clinics, survey form for hospital compliance with anti-dumping requirements, and evaluation of patient and physician satisfaction with the Medicare participating heart bypass center demonstration).

59 FR 65372, December 19, 1994: Office of Inspector General — Notice of Publication of Special Fraud Alerts (pertaining to joint venture arrangements, routine waiver of Medicare Part B copayments and deductibles, hospital incentives to referring physicians, prescription drug marketing practices, and arrangements for provision of clinical laboratory services).

60 FR 32916, June 26, 1995: Office of Inspector General; Health Care Programs; Fraud and Abuse; Technical Revision to the Scope and Effect of the OIG Exclusion Regulations — Final rule affecting 42 CFR Part 1001.

60 FR 40847, August 10, 1995: Office of Inspector General: Publication of OIG Special Fraud Alerts: Home Health Fraud, and Fraud and Abuse in the Provision of Medical Supplies to Nursing Facilities — Notice.

60 FR 58239, November 27, 1995: Office of Inspector General; Health Care Programs: Fraud and Abuse; Revisions to the Civil Money Penalty Provisions Relating to the Misuse of Certain Names, Symbols and Emblems — Final rule affecting 42 CFR Part 1003.

60 FR 63634, December 12, 1995: Office of Inspector General; Health Care Programs: Fraud and Abuse; Revisions to the PRO Sanctions Process — Final rule. See also correction at 61 FR 1841, January 24, 1996.

61 FR 2122, January 25, 1996: Medicare and State Health Care Programs; Fraud and Abuse; Safe Harbors for Protecting Health Plans — Final rule.

61 FR 30623, June 17, 1996: Office of Inspector General Publication of OIG Special Fraud Alert: Fraud and Abuse in the Provision of Services in Nursing Homes — Notice.

62 FR 7350, February 19, 1997: Office of Inspector General: Medicare and State Health Care Programs: Fraud and Abuse; Issuance of Advisory Opinions by the OIG — Interim final rule with comment period, affecting 42 CFR Part 1008.

62 FR 28410, May 23, 1997: Office of Inspector General: Health Care Programs: Fraud and Abuse — Notice of Intent to Form the Negotiated Rulemaking Committee for the Shared Risk Exception

(statutory exceptions to the anti-kickback statute)— affecting 42 CFR Part 1001.

62 FR 9435, March 3, 1997: Office of Inspector General: Publication of the OIG Model Compliance Plan for Clinical Laboratories — Notice.

62 FR 23140, April 29, 1997: Office of Inspector General: Health Care Programs: Fraud and Abuse; Revised PRO Sanctions for Failing to Meet Statutory Obligations — Final rule.

62 FR 47182, September 8, 1997: Office of Inspector General: Health Care Programs: Fraud and Abuse; Revised OIG Exclusion Authorities Resulting from Public Law 104–191 — Notice of Proposed rulemaking, affecting 42 CFR Parts 1000, 1001, 1002, and 1005.

62 FR 55410, October 24, 1997: Office of Inspector General: Criteria for Implementing Permissive Exclusion Authority under Section 1128(b)(7) of the Social Security Act — Notice.

62 FR 65049, December 10, 1997: Office of Inspector General: Solicitation of New Safe Harbors and Special Fraud Alerts — Notice of intent to develop regulations, affecting 42 CFR Part 1001.

62 FR 67392, December 24, 1997: Office of Inspector General: Criteria for Implementing Permissive Exclusion Authority under Section 1128(b)(7) of the Social Security Act — Notice.

63 FR 187, January 5, 1998: Office of Inspector General; Negotiated Rulemaking Committee on the Shared Risk Exception — Notice of meeting.

63 FR 8987, February 23, 1998: Office of Inspector General: Publication of the OIG Compliance Program for Hospitals — Notice.

63 FR 9844, February 26, 1998: HCFA Agency Information Collection Activities: Proposed Collection; Comment request (pertaining to procedures for advisory opinions concerning physician referrals and supporting regulations in 42 CFR Sections 411.370- 411.389).

63 FR 14393, March 25, 1998: Office of Inspector General: Health Care Programs: Fraud and Abuse; Revised OIG Civil Money Penalties Resulting from the Health Insurance Portability and Accountability Act of 1996 — Notice of proposed rulemaking, affecting 42 CFR Parts 1003, 1005, and 1006.

63 FR 20415, April 24, 1998: Office of Inspector General: Publication of OIG Special Fraud Alert: Fraud and Abuse in Nursing Home Arrangements with Hospices — Notice.

63 FR 28395, May 22, 1998: HCFA Agency Information Collection Activities: Submission for OMB Review; Comment request (pertain-

ing to procedures for advisory opinions concerning physician referrals and supporting regulations in 42 CFR 411.370 through 411.389).

63 FR 31123, June 8, 1998: Medicare Program; Incentive Programs — Fraud and Abuse — Final rule affecting 42 CFR Part 420.

63 FR 38311, July 16, 1998: Office of Inspector General: Medicare and State Health Care Programs: Fraud and Abuse; Issuance of Advisory Opinions by the OIG — Final rule affecting 42 CFR 1008. See also correction at 63 FR 43449, August 13, 1998.

63 FR 38414, July 16, 1998: HCFA Privacy Act of 1974; Report of Altered System (pertaining to disclosure of individual-specific information to combat fraud or abuse in health benefit programs).

63 FR 42409, August 7, 1998: Office of Inspector General: Solicitation of Information and Recommendations for Developing OIG Compliance Program Guidance for the Durable Medical Equipment Industry — Notice.

FR 42410, August 7, 1998: Office of Inspector General: Publication of the OIG Compliance Program Guidance for Home Health Agencies — Notice.

63 FR 45076, August 24, 1998: Office of Inspector General-Publication of OIG Compliance Program Guidance for Clinical Laboratories.

63 FR 46676, September 2, 1998: Office of Inspector General: Health Care Programs; Fraud and Abuse; Revised OIG Exclusion Authorities Resulting from Public Law 104-191 — Final rule affecting 42 CFR Parts 1000, 1001, 1002, and 1005. See also correction at 63 FR 57918, October 29, 1998.

63 FR 46736, September 2, 1998: Office of Inspector General: Health Care Programs; Fraud and Abuse; Revised OIG Sanction Authorities Resulting from Public Law 105-33 — Notice of proposed rulemaking affecting 42 CFR 1001, 1002, and 1003.

63 FR 50577, September 22, 1998: Office of Inspector General: Solicitation of Information and Recommendations for Developing OIG Compliance Program Guidance for Certain Medicare+Choice Organizations — Notice.

63 FR 53059, October 2, 1998: Office of Inspector General; Statement of Organization, Functions and Delegations of Authority.

63 FR 58341, October 30, 1998: Office of Inspector General: Health Care Fraud and Abuse Data Collection Program: Reporting of Final Adverse Actions — Notice of proposed rulemaking under section 1128E of the Social Security Act, affecting 45 CFR 61.

63 FR 58399, October 30, 1998: Office of Inspector General: Publication of the OIG's Provider Self-Disclosure Protocol — Notice.

63 FR 67486, December 7, 1998: Office of Inspector General and HCFA; Solicitation of Comments on the OIG/HCFA Special Advisory Bulletin on the Patient Anti-Dumping Statute — Notice.

63 FR 68223, December 10, 1998: Office of Inspector General; Solicitation of New Safe Harbors and Special Fraud Alerts — Notice of intent to develop regulations, affecting 42 CFR 1001.

63 FR 70137, December 18, 1998: Office of Inspector General: Solicitation of Information and Recommendations for Developing OIG Compliance Program Guidance for the Nursing Home Industry — Notice.

63 FR 70138, December 18, 1998: Office of Inspector General: Publication of the OIG Compliance Program Guidance for Third-party Medical Billing Companies — Notice.

63 FR 71819, December 30, 1998: Office of Inspector General; Health Care Fraud and Abuse Data Collection Program; Reporting under section 1128E of the Social Security Act of Final Adverse Actions — Notice of proposed rule-making; extension of comment period, affecting 45 CFR 61.

64 FR 1813, January 12, 1999: Office of Inspector General Publication of OIG Special Fraud Alert on Physician Liability for Certifications in the Provision of Medical Equipment and Supplies and Home Health Services — Notice.

64 FR 2228, January 13, 1999: Office of Inspector General: Solicitation of Information and Recommendations for Developing OIG Compliance Program Guidance for the Hospice Industry — Notice.

64 FR 6753, February 16, 1999: Office of Inspector General: Privacy Act; Notification of New System of Records in Conjunction with the Healthcare Integrity and Protection Data Bank — Notice of a new system of records.

64 FR 10478, March 4, 1999: HCFA Agency Information Collection Activities: Proposed Collection; Comment request (pertaining to information collection requirements in final peer review organization (PRO) sanction regulations).

64 FR 19375, April 20, 1999: HCFA Agency Information Collection Activities: Proposed Collection; Comment request (pertaining to acquisition, protection, and disclosure of peer review organization (PRO) information).

64 FR 24956, May 10, 1999: Medicare and Medicaid Programs; Effective Dates of Provider Agreements and Supplier Approv-

als-Correction restoring regulations inadvertently removed when a final rule concerning effective dates for provider agreements and supplier approvals was published at 62 FR 43931, August 18, 1997.

64 FR 30340, June 7, 1999: HCFA Agency Information Collection Activities: Submission for OMB Review; Comment request (pertaining to information collection requirements in the final peer review organization (PRO) sanction regulations).

64 FR 36368, July 6, 1999: Office of Inspector General Publication of OIG Compliance Program Guidance for the Durable Medical Equipment, Prosthetics, Orthotics and Supply Industry — Notice.

64 FR 37985, July 14, 1999: Office of Inspector General; Publication of the OIG Special Advisory Bulletin on Gainsharing Arrangements and CMPs for Hospital Payments to Physicians to Reduce or Limit Services to Beneficiaries — Notice.

64 FR 39150, July 21, 1999: Office of Inspector General; Draft OIG Compliance Program Guidance for Hospices — Notice and comment period.

64 FR 39420, July 22, 1999: Office of Inspector General; Health Care Programs; Fraud and Abuse; Revised OIG Sanction Authorities Resulting from P.L. 105–33, the Balanced Budget Act of 1997 — Final rule affecting 42 CFR Parts 1001, 1002, and 1003. See also correction at 64 FR 42174, August 3, 1999.

64 FR 48846, September 8, 1999: Office of Inspector General: Solicitation of Information and Recommendations for Developing OIG Compliance Program Guidance for Individual Physicians and Small Group Practices — Notice.

64 FR 42791, September 30, 1999: Office of Inspector General; Publication of the OIG Special Advisory Bulletin on the Effect of Exclusion from Participation in Federal Health Care Programs — Notice. See also correction at 64 FR 55484, October 13, 1999.

64 FR 57619, October 26, 1999: Office of Inspector General; Privacy Act; Exempt Record System, Pertaining to the Healthcare Integrity and Protection Data Bank (HIPDB) — Notice of proposed rulemaking affecting 45 CFR Part 5b.

64 FR 57740, October 26, 1999: Office of Inspector General; Healthcare Fraud and Abuse Data Collection Program: Reporting of Final Adverse Actions - Final rule affecting 45 CFR Part 61. See also correction at 65 FR 70506, November 24, 2000.

64 FR 58419, October 29, 1999: Office of Inspector General; Draft OIG Compliance Program Guidance for Nursing Facilities — Notice and comment period.

64 FR 58851, November 1, 1999: Office of Inspector General; Healthcare Integrity and Protection Data Bank: Announcement of Opening Date for Reporting and Self-query Fee — Notice.

64 FR 61353, November 10, 1999: Office of Inspector General/HCFA; OIG/HCFA Special Advisory Bulletin on the Patient Anti-dumping Statute.

64 FR 61893, November 15, 1999: Office of Inspector General; Publication of the OIG's Compliance Program Guidance for Medicare+Choice Organizations Offering Coordinated Care Plans — Notice.

64 FR 63504, November 19, 1999: Office of Inspector General; Fraud and Abuse; Statutory Exception to the Anti-kickback Statute for Shared Risk Arrangements — Interim final rule with request for comment, affection 42 CFR Part 1001. See also correction at 64 FR 71317, December 21, 1999.

64 FR 63518, November 19, 1999: Office of Inspector General; Fraud and Abuse; Clarification of the Initial OIG Safe Harbor Provisions and Establishment of Additional Safe Harbor Provisions under the Anti-kickback Statute — Final rule affecting 42 CFR Part 1001.

64 FR 69217, December 10, 1999: Office of Inspector General; Solicitation of New Safe Harbors and Special Fraud Alerts — Intent to develop regulations affecting 42 CFR Part 1001.

2000

65 FR 9274, February 24, 2000: Office of Inspector General: Publication of OIG Special Fraud Alert on Rental of Space in Physician Offices by Persons or Entities to Which Physicians Refer — Notice.

65 FR 11589, March 3, 2000: Office of Inspector General: Health Care Integrity and Protection Data Bank under Section 1128E of the Social Security Act: Announcement of Opening Date for Querying and User Fees — Notice.

65 FR 14289, March 16, 2000: Office of Inspector General: Publication of the OIG Compliance Program Guidance for Nursing Facilities — Notice.

65 FR 24400, April 26, 2000: Office of Inspector General; Health Care Programs: Fraud and Abuse; Revised OIG Civil Money Penalties Resulting from Public Law 104-191 (HIPAA) — Final rule

affecting 42 CFR Parts 1001, 1003, 1005, and 1006. See also correction at 65 FR 35583, June 5, 2000.

65 FR 32060, May 22, 2000: Office of Inspector General Medicare and State Health Care Programs: Fraud and Abuse: Ambulance Restocking Safe Harbor under the Anti-kickback Statute — Notice of proposed rulemaking affecting 42 CFR 1001.

65 FR 34986, June 1, 2000: Office of Inspector General; Privacy Act; Implementation (exempting the Healthcare Integrity and Protection Data Bank under Section 1128C of the Social Security Act from certain provisions of the Privacy Act (5 U.S.C.A. 552a) — Final rule.

65 FR 36818, June 12, 2000: Office of Inspector General: Draft OIG Compliance Program for Individual and Small Group Physician Practices — Notice and comment period.

65 FR 47739, August 3, 2000: HCFA Agency Information Collection Activities: Submission for OMB Review; Comment request (pertaining to CLIA adverse action extract).

65 FR 50204, August 17, 2000: Office of Inspector General: Solicitation of Information and Recommendations for Developing a Compliance Risk Guidance for the Ambulance Industry — Notice.

65 FR 50552, August 18, 2000: HCFA Privacy Act of 1974; Report of Modified or Altered System (pertaining to revision of language in global fraud and abuse routine uses).

65 FR 53319, September 1, 2000: HCFA Agency Information Collection Activities: Proposed Collection; Comment request (pertaining to incentive arrangement disclosure form for managed care organizations and their related medical groups and physicians).

65 FR 59434, October 5, 2000: Office of Inspector General Compliance Program for Individual and Small Group Physician Practices — Notice.

65 FR 63035, October 20, 2000: Office of Inspector General: Medicare and State Health Care Programs: Fraud and Abuse; Revisions and Technical Corrections — Proposed rule affecting 42 CFR Parts 1001, 1003, 1005, and 1008.

65 FR 78124, December 14, 2000: Office of Inspector General: Solicitation of New Safe Harbors and Special Fraud Alerts — Notice of intent to develop regulations.

2001

66 FR 856, January 4, 2001: Medicare and Medicaid Programs; Physicians Referrals to Health Care Entities with which They Have Financial Relationships—Final rule with comment period, affecting 42 CFR Parts 411 and 424.

66 FR 6629, January 22, 2001: HCFA Agency Information Collection Activities: Submission for OMB Review; Comment request (pertaining to Medicare Integrity Program Organizational Conflict of Interest Disclosure Certificate).

66 FR 8771, February 2, 2001: Medicare and Medicaid Programs; Physicians' Referrals to Health Care Entities with which They Have Financial Relationships: Delay of Effective Date of Final Rule and Technical Amendment, affecting 42 CFR Parts 411 and 424.

66 FR 9858, February 12, 2001: HCFA Privacy Act of 1974; Report of New System (pertaining to complaints against health insurance issuers and health plans).

66 FR 9865, February 12, 2001: Office of Inspector General: Privacy Act of 1974; Amendment to the Health Care Program Violations System of Records—Notice and comment period (pertaining to including Social Security numbers of sanctioned individual in the Health Care Program Violations record).

66 FR 17813, April 4, 2001: Medicare and Medicaid Programs; Physicians' Referrals to Health Care Entities with which They Have Financial Relationships; Extension of Comment period—Notice, affecting 42 CFR Parts 411 and 424.

66 FR 19507, April 16, 2001: HCFA Agency Information Collection Activities: Proposed Collection; Comment request (pertaining to conflict of interest and ownership and control information form).

66 FR 23944, May 10, 2001: HCFA Agency Information Collection Activities: Proposed Collection; Comment request (pertaining to financial reports for providers indebted to Medicare who want to repay over time).

66 FR 28916, May 25, 2001: HCFA Agency Information Collection Activities; Proposed Collection; Comment request (pertaining to procedures for advisory opinions concerning physician referrals under section 1877 of the Social Security Act).

66 FR 31245, June 11, 2001: Office of Inspector General; Healthcare Integrity and Protection Data Bank: Change in User Fees—Notice.

66 FR 31246, June 11, 2001: Office of Inspector General; Solicitation of Information and Recommendations for Developing a

Compliance Program Guidance for the Pharmaceutical Industry—Notice.

Office of Inspector General Notices of Program Exclusions

58 FR 41794, August 5, 1993: For March through June 1993.
58 FR 44686, August 24, 1993: For July 1993.
58 FR 48073, September 14, 1993: For August 1993.
58 FR 53519, October 15, 1993: For September 1993.
58 FR 60205, November 15, 1993: For October 1993.
58 FR 66007, December 17, 1993: For November 1993.
58 FR 3862, January 27, 1994: For December 1993.
59 FR 6285, February 10, 1994: For January 1994.
59 FR 15919, April 5, 1994: For February 1994.
59 FR 21769, April 26, 1994: For March 1994.
59 FR 25951, May 18, 1994: For April 1994.
59 FR 31255, June 17, 1994: For May 1994.
59 FR 35941, July 14, 1994: For June 1994.
59 FR 41776, August 15, 1994: For July 1994.
59 FR 47341, September 15, 1994: For August 1994.
59 FR 52973, October 20, 1994: For September 1994.
59 FR 60155, November 22, 1994: For October 1994.
59 FR 65371, December 19, 1994: For November 1994.
60 FR 4179, January 20, 1995: For December 1994.
60 FR 7780, February 9, 1995: For January 1995.
60 FR 14763, March 20, 1995: For February 1995.
60 FR 19072, April 14, 1995: For March 1995.
60 FR 27532, May 24, 1995: For April 1995.
60 FR 32016, June 19, 1995: For May 1995.
60 FR 37459, July 20, 1995: For June 1995.
60 FR 46296, September 6, 1995: For July 1995.
60 FR 48999, September 21, 1995: For August 1995.
60 FR 54880, October 26, 1995: For September 1995.
60 FR 57448, November 15, 1995: For October 1995.
60 FR 64174, December 14, 1995: For November 1995.
61 FR 6017, February 15, 1996: For December 1995 and January 1996.
61 FR 11055, March 18, 1996: For February 1996.
61 FR 17711, April 22, 1996: For March 1996.
61 FR 24502, May 15, 1996: For April 1996.
61 FR 30243, June 14, 1996: For May 1996.

61 FR 38455, July 24, 1996: For June 1996.
61 FR 42258, August 14, 1996: For July 1996.
61 FR 48710, September 16, 1996: For August 1996.
61 FR 53231, October 10, 1996: For September 1996.
61 FR 59102, November 20, 1996: For October 1996.
61 FR 66285, December 17, 1996: For November 1996.
62 FR 4315, January 29, 1997: For December 1996.
62 FR 8028, February 21, 1997: For January 1997.
62 FR 13888, March 24, 1997: For February 1997.
62 FR 19340, April 21, 1997: For March, 1997.
62 FR 26807, May 15, 1997: For April, 1997.
62 FR 33663, June 20, 1997: For May, 1997.
62 FR 41064, July 31, 1997: For June 1997.
62 FR 43177, August 12, 1997: For July 1997.
62 FR 48873, September 17, 1997: For August 1997.
62 FR 53642, October 15, 1997: For September 1997.
62 FR 60903, November 13, 1997: For October 1997.
62 FR 66377, December 18, 1997: For November 1997.
63 FR 2989, January 20, 1998: For December 1997.
63 FR 8998, February 23, 1998: For January 1998.
63 FR 12477, March 13, 1998: For February 1998.
63 FR 17431, April 9, 1998: For March 1998.
63 FR 26812, May 14, 1998: For April 1998.
63 FR 32109, June 11, 1998: For May 1998.
63 FR 37891, July 14, 1998: For June 1998.
63 FR 43404, August 13, 1998: For July 1998.
63 FR 49703, September 17, 1998: For August 1998.
63 FR 55133, October 14, 1998: For September 1998.
63 FR 60357, November 9, 1998: For October 1998.
63 FR 69638, December 17, 1998: For November 1998.
64 FR 3525, January 22, 1999: For December 1998.
64 FR 8390, February 19, 1999: For January 1999.
64 FR 14456, March 25, 1999: For February 1999.
64 FR 17185, April 8, 1999: For March 1999.
64 FR 25509, May 12, 1999: For April 1999.
64 FR 31007, June 9, 1999: For May 1999.
64 FR 38205, July 15, 1999: For June 1999.
64 FR 43708, August 11, 1999: For July 1999.
64 FR 51128, September 21, 1999: For August 1999.
64 FR 55740, October 14, 1999: For September 1999.
64 FR 62682, November 17, 1999: For October 1999.

64 FR 69539, December 13, 1999: For November 1999.
65 FR 8376, February 18, 2000: For January 2000.
65 FR 14986, March 20, 2000: For February 2000.
65 FR 19006, April 10, 2000: For March 2000.
65 FR 30415, May 11, 2000: For April 2000.
65 FR 37156, June 13, 2000: For May 2000.
65 FR 45093, July 20, 2000: For June 2000.
65 FR 53321, September 1, 2000: For July 2000.
65 FR 57358, September 22, 2000: For August 2000.
65 FR 61172, October 16, 2000: For September 2000.
65 FR 68153, November 14, 2000: For October 2000.
65 FR 77884, December 13, 2000: For November 2000.
66 FR 6634, January 22, 2001: For December 2000.
66 FR 10305, February 14, 2001: For January 2001.
66 FR 14591, March 13, 2001: For February 2001.
66 FR 18962, April 12, 2001: For March 2001.
66 FR 27520, May 17, 2001: For April 2001.
66 FR 31941, June 13, 2001: For May, 2001.
See § 2:29.

§ 6:30 SPECIAL OBLIGATIONS REGARDING PACEMAKERS — Section 1862(h) [42 U.S.C.A. 1395y(h)]

◆ NOTE: This sanction was repealed effective October 2, 1996, by section 1 of P.L. 104–224.

Regulations

21 CFR Part 805 — Pacemaker Registry
42 CFR Part 409 — Hospital Insurance Benefits
42 CFR Part 410 — Supplementary Medical Insurance (SMI) Benefits
42 CFR Part 498 — Appeals Procedures for Determinations that Affect Participation in the Medicare Program and for Determinations that Affect the Participation of ICF's/MR and Certain NF's in the Medicaid Program
42 CFR Chapter V — Office of Inspector General — Health Care, Department of Health and Human Services
Subchapter A — General Provisions
Part 1000 — Introduction; General Definitions
Subchapter B — OIG Authorities

Part 1001 — Program Integrity: Medicare and State Health Care Programs

Part 1003 — Civil Money Penalties, Assessments, and Exclusions

Part 1004 — Imposition of Sanctions on Health Care Practitioners and Providers of Health Care Services by a Peer Review Organization

Part 1005 — Appeals of Exclusions, Civil Money Penalties and Assessments

Part 1006 — Investigational Inquiries

Part 1007 — State Medicaid Fraud Control Units

Part 1008 — Advisory Opinions by the OIG

See § 2:30.

§ 6:31 PUBLICIZING PROVIDER SURVEY RESULTS — Section 1864 [42 U.S.C.A. 1395aa]

Regulations

42 CFR Part 402 — Civil Money Penalties, Assessments, and Exclusions

42 CFR Part 405, Subpart U — Conditions for Coverage of Suppliers of End-Stage Renal Disease (ESRD) Services; and Subpart X — Rural Health Clinic and Federally Qualified Health Center Services

42 CFR Part 416 — Ambulatory Surgical Services

42 CFR Part 418 — Hospice Care

42 CFR Part 424 — Conditions for Medicare Payment

42 CFR Part 440 — Services: General Provisions [Medicaid]

42 CFR Part 441 — Services: Requirements and Limits Applicable to Specific Services [Medicaid]

42 CFR Part 442 — Standards for Payment for Nursing Facilities and Intermediate Care Facilities for the Mentally Retarded

42 CFR Part 475 — Peer Review Organizations

42 CFR Part 476 — Utilization and Quality Control Review

42 CFR Part 478 — Reconsiderations and Appeals

42 CFR Part 480 — Acquisition, Protection, and Disclosure of Peer Review Information

42 CFR Part 482 — Conditions of Participation for Hospitals

42 CFR Part 483 — Requirements for States and Long Term Care Facilities

42 CFR Part 484 — Conditions of Participation: Home Health Agencies

42 CFR Part 485 — Conditions of Participation: Specialized Providers

42 CFR Part 486 — Conditions for Coverage of Specialized Services Furnished by Suppliers

42 CFR Part 488 — Survey and Certification Procedures

42 CFR Part 489 — Provider Agreements and SupplierApproval

42 CFR Part 491 — Certification of Certain Health Facilities

42 CFR Part 493 — Laboratory Requirements

42 CFR Part 498 — Appeals Procedures for Determinations that Affect Participation in the Medicare Program and for Determinations that Affect the Participation of ICF's/MR and Certain NF's in the Medicaid Program

53 FR 48645, December 2, 1988: Medicare and Medicaid Programs; Medicare, Medicaid, and Clinical Laboratories Improvement Act (CLIA) Patient Confidentiality Rules — Final rule amending 42 CFR Parts 74, 405, and 441.

54 FR 5316, February 2, 1989: Medicare and Medicaid; Requirements for Long Term Care Facilities — Final rule with comment period, amending 42 CFR Parts 405, 442, 447, 483, 488, 489, and 498. See also delay in effective date at 54 FR 29717, July 14, 1989; corrections at 54 FR 8361, February 27, 1989, and 54 FR 37466, September 11, 1989; and final rule delaying effective date from January 1, 1990, to October 1, 1990, at 54 FR 53611, December 29, 1989.

54 FR 1956, January 18, 1989: Medicare and Medicaid Programs; Denial of Payment for Substandard Quality Care and Review of Beneficiary Complaints — Proposed rule to amend 42 CFR Parts 405, 424, 462, 466, 473, 476, and 489.

54 FR 33354, August 14, 1989: Medicare Program; Home Health Agencies: Conditions of Participation and Reduction in Recordkeeping Requirements — Interim final rule with comment period, amending 42 CFR Part 405by redesignating Subpart L as 42 CFR Part 484. See also correction at 54 FR 35131, August 23, 1989.

55 FR 9538, March 14, 1990: Medicare, Medicaid and CLIA Programs; Revision of the Laboratory Regulations for the Medicare, Medicaid, and Clinical Laboratories Improvement Act of 1967 Programs — Final rule with comment period, amending 42 CFR Parts 74, 405, 416, 440, 482, 483, 488, and 493.

55 FR 9740, March 15, 1990: Medicare Program; Catastrophic Outpatient Drug Benefit, Home Intravenous Drug Therapy Benefit, and Screening Mammography Services — Withdrawal of proposed rules.

55 FR 10256, March 20, 1990: Medicare and Medicaid; Charges to Residents' Funds in Nursing Homes — Proposed rule to amend 42 CFR Part 483.

55 FR 10938, March 23, 1990: Medicare and Medicaid Programs; Nurse Aide Training and Competency Evaluation Programs — Proposed rule to amend 42 CFR Parts 431, 433, and 483.

55 FR 10951, March 23, 1990: Medicare and Medicaid Programs; Preadmission Screening and Annual Resident Review — Proposed rule to amend 42 CFR Parts 405, 431, and 483.

55 FR 20896, May 21, 1990: Medicare, Medicaid and CLIA Programs; Regulations Implementing the Clinical Laboratory Improvement Amendments of 1988 (CLIA '88) — Proposed rule. See also extension of time for public comment to September 21, 1990, published at 55 FR 34289on August 22, 1990.

55 FR 23435, June 8, 1990: Medicare Program; Payment for Physician Outpatient Maintenance Dialysis Services and Other Physician Services for ESRD Patients — Final rule affecting 42 CFR Parts 405, 413, and 414. See also correction published at 55 FR 31185, August 1, 1990.

55 FR 42907, October 24, 1990: Medicare Program; Standards Applied by Utilization and Quality Control Peer Review Organizations: Consideration of Remote Rural Location and Other Relevant Factors — Notice of policy and request for comments.

55 FR 50831, December 11, 1990: Medicare Program; Hospice Care Amendments: Medicare — Final rule with comment period, amends 42 CFR Part 418.

55 FR 51434, December 14, 1990: Medicare Program; Granting and Withdrawal of Deeming Authority to National Accreditation Organizations — Proposed rule.

55 FR 53510, December 31, 1990: Medicare Program; Medicare Coverage of Screening Mammography — Interim final rule with comment. See also correction published at 55 FR 4675, February 5, 1991.

56 FR 13430, April 2, 1991: Medicare and Laboratory Certification Programs; Enforcement Procedures for Laboratories — Proposed rule.

56 FR 26916, June 12, 1991: Medicare Program; Payment for Hospice Care — Final rule with comment period affecting 42 CFR Part 418.

56 FR 30696, July 5, 1991: Medicaid Program; Correction and Reduction Plans for Intermediate Care Facilities for the Mentally

Retarded — Final rule affecting 42 CFR Part 442. See also correction at 56 FR 49147, September 27, 1991.

56 FR 32967, July 18, 1991: Medicare Program; Home Health Agencies: Conditions of Participation — Final rule. See also correction at 56 FR 51334, October 11, 1991, affecting 42 CFR Part 484.

56 FR 37054, August 2, 1991: Medicare and Medicaid Programs; Survey and Enforcement Requirements and Alternative Sanctions for Home Health Agencies — Proposed rule affecting 42 CFR Parts 441, 488, and 489.

56 FR 43929, September 5, 1991: Medicare and Medicaid Programs; Recognition of the Community Health Accreditation Program Standards for Home Care Organizations — Proposed notice.

56 FR 48112, September 24, 1991: Medicaid Program; Community Supported Living Arrangements Services — Interim final rule with comment period, affecting 42 CFR Part 441.

56 FR 48826, September 26, 1991: Medicare and Medicaid; Requirements for Long Term Care Facilities — Final rule affecting 42 CFR Parts 422, 447, 483, 488, 489, and 498. See also correction at 57 FR 43922, September 23, 1992.

56 FR 48880, September 26, 1991: Medicare and Medicaid Programs; Nurse Aide Training and Competency Evaluation Programs — Final rule affecting 42 CFR Parts 431, 433, and 483. See also correction at 56 FR 59331, November 25, 1991.

56 FR 49154, September 27, 1991: Medicare Program; Medicare Coverage of Home Health Services, Medicare Conditions of Participation, and Home Health Aide Supervision — Proposed rule affecting 42 CFR Parts 409, 418, and 484.

57 FR 4044, February 3, 1992: Medicare Program; Recognition of the Joint Commission of the Accreditation of Healthcare Organizations' Standards for Home Care Organizations — Proposed notice.

57 FR 4516, February 5, 1992: Medicare and Medicaid Programs; Omnibus Nursing Home Requirements — Proposed rule affecting 42 CFR Parts 418, 440, 441, 482, 483, and 488. See also correction at 57 FR 8961, March 13, 1992.

57 FR 7002, February 28, 1992: Medicare, Medicaid and CLIA Programs; Regulations Implementing the Clinical Laboratory Improvement Amendments of 1988 (CLIA) — Final rule with comment period, affecting 42 CFR Parts 405, 410, 416, 417, 418, 440, 482, 483, 484, 485, 488, 491, 493, and 494. See also correction at 57

FR 35760, August 11, 1992, and correction amendments at 58 FR 5212, January 19, 1993.

57 FR 7218, February 28, 1992: Medicare Program; Medicare and Laboratory Certification Program; Enforcement Procedures for Laboratories — Final rule affecting 42 CFR Part 493. See also correction amendments at 58 FR 5212, January 19, 1993.

57 FR 22773, May 29, 1992: Medicare Program; Recognition of Community Health Accreditation Program Standards for Home Care Organizations — Final notice.

57 FR 33992, July 31, 1992: Clinical Laboratories Improvement Act Program; Granting and Withdrawal of Deeming Authority to Private Nonprofit Accreditation Organizations and of CLIA Exemption under State Laboratory Programs — Final rule.

57 FR 39278, August 28, 1992: Medicare and Medicaid Programs; Survey, Certification and Enforcement of Skilled Nursing Facilities and Nursing Facilities — Proposed rule affecting 42 CFR Parts 431, 442, 488, and 489.

57 FR 43462, September 21, 1992: Health Care Financing Administration Public Information Collection Requirements Submitted to the Office of Management and Budget for Clearance (pertaining to sole community home health agencies; physician/supplier overpayment reports; physician or supplier Medicare agreements; conditions of participation for rural health clinics; Medicare provider refunds; conditions of participation for comprehensive outpatient rehabilitation facilities; Medicaid income and eligibility verification system; Medicaid integrated review schedule; provider overpayment report; financial statement of Medicare provider debtors; negative case action review schedule for Medicaid quality control; outpatient resource costing study; Medicaid intermediate care facility for the mentally retarded or persons with related conditions survey report form; installment agreement of beneficiary refund of overpayment; PRO assumption of responsibilities; Medicare contractor administrative budget and cost reporting system forms; fire safety survey report forms; medical records review under prospective payment system; and Qualified Medicare Beneficiary supplement to the Medicare current beneficiary survey).

57 FR 46362, October 8, 1992: Medicare and Medicaid Programs; Revised Effective Date of Medicare/Medicaid Provider Agreement and Supplier Participation — Proposed rule affecting 42 CFR Parts 431, 440, 442, 488, 489, and 498.

57 FR 46865, October 13, 1992: HCFA Public Information Collection Requirements Submitted to the Office of Management and Budget for Clearance (pertaining to impact of home health care plan management and evaluation; end-stage renal disease medical case review; Medicare/Medicaid hospital swing-bed survey report form; quarterly Medicaid statement of expenditures; Medicaid program budget report; information collection requirements in final peer review organization sanction regulations; appeals procedures for determinations that affect participation in Medicare; request for medical review information for Part B intermediary outpatient therapy bills and other Part B outpatient bills; and Medicaid limitations on provider-related donations and health care-related taxes, and limitations on payment to disproportionate share hospitals).

57 FR 53572, November 12, 1992: Medicare and Medicaid; Charges to Residents' Funds in Nursing Homes — Final rule affecting 42 CFR Part 483.

57 FR 54710, November 20, 1992: Medicaid Program; Elimination of Certain Written Documentation Pertaining to Medicaid Long-Term Care Facilities — Final rule affecting 42 CFR Part 442.

57 FR 56450, November 30, 1992: Medicare and Medicaid Programs; Preadmission Screening and Annual Resident Review — Final rule with comment period, affecting 42 CFR Parts 405, 431, 433, and 483. See also correction published at 58 FR 25784, April 28, 1993.

57 FR 61614, December 28, 1992: Medicare and Medicaid; Resident Assessment in Long Term Care Facilities — Proposed rule affecting 42 CFR Parts 456 and 483.

58 FR 5215, January 19, 1993: Medicare, Medicaid and CLIA Programs; Regulations Implementing the Clinical Laboratory Improvement Amendments of 1988 (CLIA) and Clinical Laboratory Improvement Act Program Fee Collection — Final rule with comment period, affecting 42 CFR Part 493. See also correction published at 58 FR 39154, July 22, 1993.

58 FR 21174, April 19, 1993: HCFA Public Information Collection Requirements Submitted to the Office of Management and Budget for Clearance re end stage renal disease survey forms; municipal health services cost reports forms; advance directives; withholding Medicare payments to recover Medicaid overpayments; home office cost statements; and statistical report on medical care.

58 FR 29416, May 20, 1993: HCFA Public Information Collection Requirements Submitted to the Office of Management and Budget

(OMB) for Clearance re cataract surgery; Medicaid utilization management initiatives; Medicare coverage of screening mammography; psychiatric unit criteria worksheet and rehabilitation unit criteria worksheet; Medicare secondary payor forms; ambulatory surgical center survey forms; ambulance service compliance with State and local requirements; and early and periodic screening, diagnostic and treatment reports.

58 FR 30630, May 26, 1993: Medicare Program; Essential Access Community Hospitals (EACHs) and Rural Primary Care Hospitals (RPCHs)—Final rule affecting 42 CFR Parts 400, 409, 410, 411, 412, 413, 424, 440, 485, 488, 489, and 498.

58 FR 38579, July 19, 1993: HCFA Public Information Collection Requirements Submitted to the Office of Management and Budget (OMB) for Clearance re survey of home health agencies; CLIA survey report form; validation of state surveys; Medicaid listing of participating home health agencies; financial information regarding Medicare benefits from Medicare contractors; and third-party liability under Medicaid.

58 FR 46198, September 1, 1993: HCFA Public Information Collection Requirements (ICR) Submitted to the Office of Management and Budget (OMB) for Clearance (pertaining to prenatal services and assistance screening; home health agency treatment forms; conditions of participation for intermediate care facilities for the mentally retarded; State Medicaid eligibility quality control sample selection lists; prepaid health plan cost report; hospital survey report form; procedures for determining whether providers, practitioners, or other suppliers of services are liable for certain noncovered services; Medicare credit balance reporting requirements; Medicare provider cost report questionnaire form; Medicare current beneficiary survey rounds 7-10; sterilization regulation/consent form; PRO reconsideration and appeals information requirements; information collection requirements in HSQ-110, acquisition, protection and disclosure of PRO information; Medicare/Medicaid organ procurement organization's (OPO) request for certification)—Notice.

58 FR 52112, October 6, 1993: Medicare, Medicaid, and CLIA Programs; Clinical Laboratory Improvement Amendments of 1988 Exemption of Laboratories Licensed by the State of Washington—Notice.

58 FR 54159, October 20, 1993: HCFA Public Information Collection Requirements Submitted to the Office of Management and

Budget (OMB) for Clearance (pertaining to CLIA certification recommendation; CLIA laboratory personnel report; Medigap complaint data base; certification as a rural health clinic (RHC) and RHC survey report form; screening mammography services data report; ambulatory surgical center request for certification and survey report form; blood bank inspection checklist and report; Medicaid program budget report form; supplier of ESRD services form; and grantee data collection instrument) — Notice.

58 FR 59270, November 8, 1993: HCFA Public Information Collection Requirements Submitted to the Office of Management and Budget (OMB) for Clearance (pertaining to formats for utilization and quality control peer review organizations (PROs); home health agency plan of treatment forms; State survey agency budget expenditure report and certification workload report; home health agency cost report; recordkeeping requirements in provider reimbursement manual; quarterly Medicaid statement of expenditures; Medicare contract application for Federally qualified health maintenance organizations; hospice survey and deficiencies report form; organ procurement agency/histocompatibility laboratory statement of reimbursable costs) — Notice.

58 FR 60204, November 15, 1993: HCFA Public Information Collection Requirements Submitted to the Office of Management and Budget (OMB) for Clearance (pertaining to procedures for transmitting information between Medicare carriers and Medicare supplemental insurers; Medicare physician or supplier agreement; patient intake data form for the National Home Health Agency; agency characteristics form for the National Home Health Agency prospective payment demonstration; intake and assessment survey package for the community nursing organization demonstration; comprehensive outpatient rehabilitation facility (CORF eligibility and survey forms and information collection requirements) — Notice.

58 FR 63533, December 2, 1993: Medicare Program; Required Laboratory Procedures for Rural Health Clinics — Final rule with comment period, affecting 42 CFR Part 491.

59 FR 5201, February 3, 1994: HCFA Public Information Collection Requirements Submitted to the Office of Management and Budget (OMB) for Clearance (pertaining to evaluation of the Medicare case management demonstration; evaluation of the Medicaid uninsured demonstrations; Internal Revenue Service, Social Security Administration, and HCFA data match; survey of physician

owned medical liability insurers for use in computing the input component of the physician liability component of the Geographic Practice Cost Index and the Medicare Economic Index; emergency and foreign hospital services for Canadian travel claims; CLIA survey report form; Medicaid management information system (MMIS) data form) — Notice.

59 FR 6228, February 10, 1994: Medicare Program; Change in Provider Agreement Regulations Related to Federal Employee Health Benefits — Proposed rule affecting 42 CFR Part 489.

59 FR 14865, March 30, 1994: HCFA Public Information Collection Requirements Submitted to the Office of Management and Budget (OMB) for Clearance (pertaining to home health agency Medicare and Medicaid survey report forms for conditions of participation; conditions of participation for rural health clinics; Medicaid re-evaluation of assets for determining payment rates to hospitals and nursing homes; statistical report on medical care, eligible, recipients, payments, and services.)

59 FR 23069, May 4, 1994: HCFA Public Information Collection Requirements Submitted to the Office of Management and Budget (OMB) for Clearance (pertaining to clinical laboratory improvement amendments (CLIA) flexible survey protocol form; application for health insurance benefits under Medicare for individual with chronic renal disease form; Medicare Qualification Statement for Federal employees form; attending physician's statement and documentation of Medicare emergency form; request for Part B Medicare hearing by an Administrative Law Judge forms; CLIA adverse action extract; and medicare and Medicaid coverage data bank reports form.)

59 FR 25460, May 16, 1994: HCFA Public Information Collection Requirements Submitted to the Office of Management and Budget (OMB) for Clearance (pertaining to Medicare uniform institutional provider bill; hospice survey and deficiencies report form; HMO financial information reports to members; hospital request for certification in Medicare and Medicaid form.)

59 FR 27023, May 25, 1994: HCFA Public Information Collection Requirements Submitted to the Office of Management and Budget (OMB) for Clearance (pertaining to Medicare beneficiary survey of influenza vaccination form; Medicaid integrated quality control review worksheet; post laboratory survey questionnaire form; and post laboratory survey questionnaire — surveyor form).

59 FR 46500, September 8, 1994: Medicare and Medicaid Programs; Conditions of Coverage for Organ Procurement Organizations — Interim final rule with comment, affecting 42 CFR Parts 405, 482, and 485.

59 FR 50762, October 5, 1994: HCFA Public Information Collection Requirements Submitted to the Office of Management and Budget (OMB) for Clearance (pertaining to reimbursement of hospital costs for residents and interns, criteria for psychiatric and rehabilitation hospital units' reimbursement under the prospective payment system, disclosure of owners and managers of suppliers for fraud and abuse detection purposes, reimbursement of municipal health services clinics, survey form for hospital compliance with anti-dumping requirements, and evaluation of patient and physician satisfaction with the Medicare participating heart bypass center demonstration).

59 FR 52178, October 14, 1994: HCFA Public Information Collection Requirements Submitted to the Office of Management and Budget (OMB) for Clearance (pertaining to Medicare reimbursement for outpatient services, cost reports for free-standing skilled nursing facilities; Medicare coverage criteria for adult heart transplants, drug rebates for Medicaid, optional prospective payment cost report for certain skilled nursing facilities, reimbursable costs for organ procurement agencies, distribution and use of end stage renal disease treatment sources, conditions of coverage for ambulatory surgical centers, and waivers for home and community based services).

59 FR 56116, November 10, 1994: Medicare and Medicaid Programs; Survey, Certification and Enforcement of Skilled Nursing Facilities and Nursing Facilities — Final rule affecting 42 CFR Parts 401, 431, 435, 440, 441, 442, 447, 483, 488, 489, and 498. See also correcting amendment, effective July 1, 1995, at 62 FR 44221, August 20, 1997.

59 FR 56500, November 14, 1994: HCFA Public Information Collection Requirements Submitted to the Office of Management and Budget (OMB) for Clearance (pertaining to monitoring and evaluation of Medicare cataract surgery alternate payment demonstration, form for listing deficiencies for laboratory surveys, form for personnel requirements for laboratory CLIA certification, and CLIA reinstatement form).

59 FR 62606, December 6, 1994: Medicare, Medicaid, and CLIA Programs; Extension of Certain Effective Dates for Clinical Labora-

tory Requirements and Personnel Requirements for Cytologists-Final rule with comment period, affecting 42 CFR Part 493.

59 FR 64141, December 13, 1994: Medicare and Medicaid Programs; Revisions to Conditions of Participation for Hospitals — Final rule affecting 42 CFR Parts 405 and 482.

59 FR 65482, December 20, 1994: Medicare Program; Medicare Coverage of Home Health Services, Medicare Conditions of Participation, and Home Health Aide Supervision — Final rule affecting 42 CFR Parts 409, 413, 418, and 484. See also correction at 60 FR 39122, August 1, 1995.

60 FR 7774, February 9, 1995: HCFA Public Information Collection Requirements Submitted to the Office of Management and Budget (OMB) for Clearance (pertaining to justification for ESRD composite rates for outpatient dialysis services, and home health agency compliance with health and safety requirements).

60 FR 12770, March 8, 1995: HCFA Public Information Collection Requirements Submitted to the Office of Management and Budget (OMB) for Clearance (pertaining to survey forms for compliance with CLIA; CLIA application forms for testing on human specimens, and forms for outcome-based quality assurance programs for home health agencies).

60 FR 21525, May 2, 1995: HCFA Public Information Collection Requirements Submitted to the Office of Management and Budget (OMB) for Clearance (pertaining to intermediary requests for information from skilled nursing facilities, reimbursement for CLIA compliance surveys, patient outcome data in home health agencies, common claim forms for Medicare/Medicaid reimbursement, and a study of childhood immunization costs).

60 FR 26445, May 17, 1995: HCFA Public Information Collection Requirements Submitted to the Office of Management and Budget (OMB) for Clearance (pertaining to Medicare/Medicaid psychiatric hospital survey data, and hospice requests for Medicare certification).

60 FR 37066, July 19, 1995: HCFA Public Information Collection Requirements Submitted to the Office of Management and Budget (OMB) for Clearance (pertaining to actuarial forecasts for Medicaid utilization and cost, employers identified through a match of IRS, SSA, and Medicare records for purposes of the Medicare Secondary Payer provision, health and safety requirements for portable X-ray suppliers, and evaluation of Intermediate Care Facilities for Persons

with Mental Retardation — establishing psychoactive drug use baselines).

60 FR 39403, August 2, 1995: HCFA Public Information Collection Requirements Submitted for Public Comment and Recommendations (pertaining to PRO reporting forms; Oregon Medicaid reform demonstration; review functions of PRO's; medical records review under PPS; evaluation of Medicare cataract surgery alternate payment demonstration; home health agency survey and deficiencies report; CLIA survey forms; field testing of uniform needs assessment instrument for hospital discharge planning).

60 FR 50115, September 28, 1995: Medicare and Medicaid Programs; Survey, Certification and Enforcement of Skilled Nursing Facilities and Nursing Facilities — Final rule and correction to final regulations, affecting 42 CFR Parts 431, 440, 442, 488, 489, and 498. See also corrections at 60 FR 52731, October 10, 1995, and at 60 FR 534456, October 13, 1995.

60 FR 50466, September 29, 1995: Medicare Program — Providers and Suppliers of Specialized Services: Technical Amendments — Final rule with comment period, affecting 42 CFR Parts 485and 486. See also correction at 60 FR 53877, October 18, 1995.

60 FR 50630, September 29, 1995: HCFA Public Information Collection Requirements Submitted for Public Comment and Recommendations (pertaining to sole community home health agencies).

60 FR 55719, November 2, 1995: HCFA Public Information Collection Requirements Submitted for Public Comment and Recommendations (pertaining to evaluation of the Oregon Medicaid reform demonstration; field testing of the uniform needs assessment instrument for hospital discharge planning; survey of physician practice costs; evaluation of the Medicare cataract surgery alternate payment demonstration; and alternative CLIA quality assessment surveys).

60 FR 64167, December 14, 1995: HCFA Public Information Collection Requirements Submitted for Public Comment and Recommendations (pertaining to home health care; Medicare/Medicaid certification of physical therapy and speech pathology services; certification as suppliers of Portable X-ray Services; certification of organ procurement organizations; certification for physical therapists in independent practice; and approval as a hospital provider of extended care services (swing bed)).

61 FR 2255, January 25, 1996: HCFA Public Information Collection Requirements Submitted for Public Comment and Recommendations (pertaining to survey forms about health and safety requirements for physical therapists in independent practice; and national data reporting requirements for HMOs and CMPs).

61 FR 6645, February 21, 1996: HCFA Agency Information Collection Activities: Proposed Collection; Comment Request (pertaining to survey forms to evaluate Federally qualified health centers; and the Medicare Carrier provider/supplier application form).

61 FR 7012, February 23, 1996: HCFA Notice Submitted for Collection of Public Comment: Submission for OMB Review (pertaining to granting and withdrawing of deeming authority to private non-profit accreditation organizations and the Clinical Laboratory Improvement Act Exemption under State laboratory programs; and the rules for participation of home health agencies to participate as sole community home health agencies).

61 FR 14798, April 3, 1996: HCFA Agency Information Collection Activities: Proposed Collection; Comment Request (pertaining to statistical reports on medical care eligibility, payments and services under Medicaid; State survey agency lists of positions and schedule of equipment purchases; granting and withdrawing of deeming authority to national accreditation organizations; maximizing the effectiveness of home health care; requests for certification in the Medicare or Medicaid program to provide outpatient physical therapy and/or speech pathology services; physical therapists in independent practice; requests for provider approval as a hospital provider of extended care services (swing bed) under Medicare and Medicaid; and requests for designation as an organ procurement organization).

61 FR 16925, April 18, 1996: HCFA Agency Information Collection Activities: Proposed Collection; Comment Request (pertaining to Medicare participating physician or supplier agreements; and hospital conditions of participation).

61 FR 17710, April 22, 1996: HCFA Agency Information Collection Activities: Proposed Collection; Comment Request (pertaining to payment adjustments for sole community hospitals; conditions of participation for portable x-ray suppliers; and cost reports for independent rural health centers and freestanding Federally qualified health centers).

61 FR 25229, May 20, 1996: HCFA Agency Information Collection Activities: Proposed Collection; Comment Request (pertaining to

evaluation of the Oregon reform demonstration; evaluation of the per-episode home health prospective payment demonstration; and the blood bank inspection checklist instrument used by State agencies to determine compliance with CLIA).

61 FR 26914, May 29, 1996: HCFA Emergency Clearance: Public Information Collection Requirements Submitted to the Office of Management and Budget (OMB) (pertaining to re-designation, certification and recertification of organ procurement organizations).

61 FR 29406, June 10, 1996: HCFA Agency Information Collection Activities: proposed Collection; Comment Request (pertaining to end stage renal disease application and survey and certification report forms; withholding Medicare payments to recover Medicaid overpayments; acquisition, protection, and disclosure of PRO information; clinical laboratory certification and recertification survey forms; CLIA laboratory personnel report forms; prepaid health plan cost reports; Medicare credit balance reporting requirements; statement of deficiencies and plan of correction requirements for organ procurement organizations; Medicare/Medicaid hospital survey report forms; advance directive requirements for Medicare and Medicaid; payment adjustments for sole community hospitals; survey reports for physical therapists in independent practice; HMO and CMP national data reporting requirements; identification of extension units of outpatient physical therapy and outpatient speech pathology providers; and fire safety survey reports).

61 FR 30072, June 13, 1996: HCFA Agency Information Collection Activities: Proposed Collection; Comment Request (pertaining to conditions of coverage for organ procurement organizations).

61 FR 31141, June 19, 1996: HCFA Agency Information Collection Activities: Proposed Collection; Comment Request (pertaining to authorization agreements for electronic funds transfer; applications for health insurance under Medicare for individuals with chronic renal disease; CLIA application forms; forms for surveyors to evaluate laboratory survey processes; post laboratory survey questionnaires for laboratories to evaluate the survey process).

61 FR 34437, July 2, 1996: HCFA Agency Information Collection Activities: Submission for OMB Review; Comment Request (pertaining to Peer Review Organization procedures for reconsideration of initial decisions; Part B enrollment forms; certification of rural health clinics for Medicare participation; Medicaid utilization review requirements for home health agencies; State listings of Medicaid recipients in institutions and procedures for State inspection of care

review; procedures for disenrollment of beneficiaries from HMOs or CMPs; effectiveness of telemedicine services; formats for PROs to submit data to HCFA; and request for accelerated payments forms for providers).

61 FR 34855, July 3, 1996: HCFA Agency Information Collection Activities: Submission for OMB Review; Comment Request (pertaining to information collection requirements for hospital conditions of participation in Medicare).

61 FR 37487, July 18, 1996: HCFA Agency Information Collection Activities: Submission for OMB Review; Comment request (pertaining to cost reports for independent rural health centers and freestanding federally qualified health centers; and conditions of participation for portable x-ray suppliers).

61 FR 40847, August 6, 1996: HCFA Agency Information Collection Activities: Proposed Collection; Comment request (pertaining to survey and certification of comprehensive outpatient rehabilitation facilities (CORFs)).

61 FR 41417, August 8, 1996: HCFA Agency Information Collection Activities: Submission for OMB Review; Comment request (pertaining to prospective payment for home health care; and Medicare standards for hospices).

61 FR 42257, August 14, 1996: HCFA Proposals Submitted for Collection of Public Comment: Submission for OMB Review (pertaining to third-party liability in Medicaid programs; surveys of federally qualified health centers (FQHCs); distribution of Medicare information by hospitals; Medicare reimbursement for hospitals with a disproportionate share of Medicare inpatients; Medicaid quality control; and the National Payer Identifier).

61 FR 43373, August 22, 1996: HCFA Agency Information Collection Activities: Proposed Collection; Comment request (pertaining to hospital claims for inpatient care for statutorily excluded services; and hospice standards for Medicare participation).

61 FR 43374, August 22, 1996: HCFA Agency Information Collection Activities: Submission for OMB Review; Comment request (pertaining to conditions of participation for rehabilitation agencies and conditions for coverage for physical therapist in independent practice).

61 FR 46814, September 5, 1996: HCFA Agency Information Collection Activities: Submission for OMB Review; Comment request (pertaining to authorization agreements for electronic funds transfers; entitlement to Medicare for individuals with chronic renal

disease; application forms for clinical laboratories; and clinical laboratory survey questionnaires).

61 FR 47131, September 6, 1996: HCFA Agency Information Collection Activities: Submission for OMB Review; Comment request (pertaining to conditions of coverage for organ procurement organizations; and statements of deficiencies and plan of correction forms for organ procurement organizations).

61 FR 48157, September 12, 1996: HCFA Agency Information Collection Activities: Submission for OMB Review; Comment request (pertaining to authorization agreement for electronic funds transfer; entitlement to Medicare for individuals with chronic renal disease; application forms for clinical laboratories; and clinical laboratory survey forms).

61 FR 57688, November 7, 1996: HCFA Agency Information Collection Activities: Comment request (pertaining to clinical laboratory surveys; clinical laboratory personnel qualifications; Medicare/Medicaid hospital survey report forms; beneficiary disenrollment from HMOs and CMPs; survey reports for ambulatory surgical centers; the Medigap complaint database; and survey forms for comprehensive outpatient rehabilitation facilities).

61 FR 64913, December 9, 1996: HCFA Agency Information Collection Activities: Proposed Collection; Comment request (pertaining to survey report forms for ICF/MRs; and current Medicare beneficiary surveys).

61 FR 67041, December 19, 1996: Medicare Program; Recognition of the Ambulatory Surgical Center Standards of the Joint Commission on the Accreditation of Healthcare Organizations and the Accreditation Association for Ambulatory Health Care— Final notice.

62 FR 3902, January 27, 1997: HCFA Agency Information Collection Activities: Proposed Collection; Comment request (pertaining to hospice survey and deficiencies report form).

62 FR 7467, February 19, 1997: HCFA Agency Information Collection Activities: Proposed Collection; Comment request (pertaining to form for a hospital request for certification in the Medicare and Medicaid programs).

62 FR 8252, February 24, 1997: HCFA Agency Information Collection Activities: Submission for OMB Review; Comment request (pertaining to conditions of participation for rural health clinics).

62 FR 8744, February 26, 1997: HCFA Agency Information Collection Activities: Submission for OMB Review; Comment request (pertaining to Medicare provider/supplier enrollment application).

62 FR 9435, March 3, 1997: Office of Inspector General: Publication of the OIG Model Compliance Plan for Clinical Laboratories — Notice.

62 FR 10285, March 6, 1997: HCFA Agency Information collection Activities: Submission for OMB Review; Comment request (pertaining to end stage renal disease (ESRD) application and survey and certification report form).

62 FR 11004, March 10, 1997: Medicare and Medicaid Programs; Revision of the Conditions of Participation for Home Health Agencies and Use of the Outcome and Assessment Information Set (OASIS) as Part of the Revised Conditions of Participation for Home Health Agencies — Introduction to proposed rules, affecting 42 CFR Part 484.

62 FR 11005, March 10, 1997: Medicare and Medicaid Programs; Conditions of Participation for Home Health Agencies — Proposed rule affecting 42 CFR Part 484. See also correction at 62 FR 11953, March 13, 1997.

62 FR 11035, March 10, 1997: Medicare and Medicaid Programs; Use of the OASIS as Part of the Conditions of Participation for Home Health Agencies — Proposed rule.

62 FR 11213, March 11, 1997: HCFA Agency Information Collection Activities: Proposed Collection; Comment request (pertaining to post-laboratory survey questionnaire).

62 FR 11214, March 11, 1997: HCFA Agency Information Collection Activities: Submission for OMB Review; Comment request (pertaining to intermediate care facility for the mentally retarded or persons with related conditions survey report forms).

62 FR 16863, April 8, 1997: HCFA Agency Information Collection Activities: Submission for OMB Review; Comment request (pertaining to hospice survey and deficiencies report form).

62 FR 18639, April 16, 1997: HCFA Agency Information Collection Activities: Proposed Collection; Comment request (pertaining to the hospital request for certification in the Medicare and Medicaid programs form).

62 FR 25636, May 9, 1997: HCFA Agency Information Collection Activities: Proposed Collection; Comment request (pertaining to information collection requirements about examination and treatment for emergency medical conditions and women in labor).

62 FR 27262, May 19, 1997: HCFA Approval of the Commission on Office Laboratory Accreditation for Immunohematology — Notice.

62 FR 28057, May 22, 1997: HCFA Agency Information Collection Activities: Submission for OMB Review; Comment request (pertaining to post laboratory survey questionnaire).

62 FR 35214, June 30, 1997: HCFA Agency Information Collection Activities: Submission for OMB Review; Comment request (pertaining to CLIA adverse actions).

63 FR 291, January 5, 1998: Medicare and Medicaid Programs; Surety Bond and Capitalization Requirements for Home Health Agencies; Final rule affecting 42 CFR Parts 413, 440, 441, and 489.

63 FR 2926, January 20, 1998: Medicare Program; Additional Supplier Standards — Proposed rule affecting 42 CFR Part 424.

63 FR 7743, February 17, 1998: Medicare and Medicaid Programs; Hospital Conditions of Participation; Provider Agreements and Supplier Approval — Notice of extension of comment period, affecting 42 CFR Parts 416, 482, 485, and 489.

63 FR 8987, February 23, 1998: Office of Inspector General: Publication of the OIG Compliance Program for Hospitals — Notice.

63 FR 9844, February 26, 1998: HCFA Emergency Clearance: Public Information Collection Requirements Submitted to the Office of Management and Budget (OMB) (pertaining to development of an assessment system for post acute care).

63 FR 10730, March 4, 1998: Medicare and Medicaid Programs; Surety Bond Requirements for Home Health Agencies — Final rule affecting 42 CFR Parts 441 and 489.

63 FR 10732, March 4, 1998: Medicare and Medicaid Programs; Surety Bond Requirements for Home Health Agencies — Notice of Intent to Amend Regulations.

63 FR 10920, March 5, 1998: HCFA Emergency Clearance: Public Information Collection Requirements Submitted to the Office of Management and Budget (OMB) (pertaining to Medicare and other Federal health care program provider and supplier application forms).

63 FR 12474, March 13, 1998: HCFA Agency Information Collection Activities: Proposed Collection; Comment request (pertaining to hospice request for certification in the Medicare program and Medicare/Medicaid psychiatric hospital survey data).

63 FR 12474, March 13, 1998: HCFA Agency Information Collection Activities: Submission for OMB Review; Comment request

(pertaining to requirements for clinical laboratory testing on human specimens).

63 FR 12475, March 13, 1998: HCFA Agency Information Collection Activities; Submission for OMB Review; Comment request (pertaining to HMO and CMP national data reporting requirements).

63 FR 12476, March 13, 1998: HCFA Agency Information Collection Activities: Submission for OMB Review; Comment request (pertaining to alternate quality assessment form for clinical laboratories with good performance records).

63 FR 14719, March 26, 1998: HCFA Agency Information Collection Activities: Proposed Collection; Comment request (pertaining to physician certification and re-certification in skilled nursing facilities).

63 FR 17429, April 9, 1998: Medicare, Medicaid, and CLIA Programs; Clinical Laboratory Improvement Amendments of 1988 Continuance of Approval as an Accrediting Organization; the Joint Commission on Accreditation of Healthcare Organizations, the American Association of Blood Banks, and the American Osteopathic Association — Notice.

63 FR 19502, April 20, 1998: HCFA Agency Information Collection Activities: Proposed collection; Comment request (pertaining to annual early and periodic screening, diagnostic, and treatment services (EPSDT) participation report; Medicare and other health care programs provider/supplier enrollment application; and research and analytic support for implementing performance measurement in Medicare fee for service).

63 FR 20415, April 24, 1998: Office of Inspector General: Publication of OIG Special Fraud Alert: Fraud and Abuse in Nursing Home Arrangements with Hospices — Notice.

63 FR 20652, April 27, 1998: HCFA Agency Information Collection Activities: Proposed Collection; Comment request (pertaining information collection requirements applicable to the obligation of hospitals to examine and treat emergency medical conditions and women in labor).

63 FR 23790, April 30, 1998: Medicare and Medicaid Programs; Recognition of the American Association for Accreditation of Ambulatory Surgery Facilities, Inc., for Ambulatory Surgical Centers — Proposed notice.

63 FR 25214, May 7, 1998: HCFA Agency Information Collection Activities: Proposed Collection; Comment request (pertaining to

organ procurement organization statement of deficiencies and plan of correction forms).

63 FR 26722, May 14, 1998: HCFA CLIA Program; Simplifying CLIA Regulations Relating to Accreditation, Exemption of Laboratories under a State Licensure Program, Proficiency Testing, and Inspection — Final rule affecting 42 CFR Part 493. See also correction at 63 FR 32699, June 15, 1998.

63 FR 26810, May 14, 1998: HCFA Agency Information Collection Activities: Proposed Collection; Comment request (pertaining to development of an assessment system for post-acute care).

63 FR 28396, May 22, 1998: HCFA Privacy Act of 1974 — Notice of New System of Records (pertaining to the long term care minimum data set).

63 FR 29415, May 29, 1998: HCFA Agency Information Collection Activities: Submission for OMB Review; Comment request (pertaining to hospice request for certification in the Medicare program).

63 FR 29648, June 1, 1998: Medicare and Medicaid Programs; Surety Bond Requirements for Home Health Agencies — Final rule affecting 42 CFR Parts 441 and 489.

63 FR 31123, June 8, 1998: Medicare Program; Incentive Programs — Fraud and Abuse — Final rule affecting 42 CFR Part 420.

63 FR 32234, June 12, 1998: HCFA Agency Information Collection Activities: Submission for OMB Review; Comment request (pertaining to Medicare/Medicaid psychiatric hospital survey data).

63 FR 36250, July 2, 1998: HCFA Agency Information Collection Activities; Submission for OMB review; Comment request (pertaining to provider/supplier enrollment applications).

63 FR 37129, July 9, 1998: HCFA Agency Information Collection Activities; Submission for OMB Review; Comment request (pertaining to organ procurement organization requests for participation in Medicare and Medicaid).

63 FR 38413, July 16, 1998: HCFA Agency Information Collection Activities: Submission for OMB Review; Comment request (pertaining to Clinical Laboratory Improvement Act certification requirements; EPSDT participation reports; limitations on provider-related donations and health care-related taxes, and limitations on payments to disproportionate share hospitals; and Medicare+Choice provider sponsored organization waiver requests forms).

63 FR 42409, August 7, 1998: Office of Inspector General: Solicitation of Information and Recommendations for Developing OIG

Compliance Program Guidance for the Durable Medical Equipment Industry — Notice.

63 FR 42410, August 7, 1998: Office of Inspector General: Publication of the OIG Compliance Program Guidance for Home Health Agencies — Notice.

63 FR 45076, August 24, 1998: Office of Inspector General-Publication of OIG Compliance Program Guidance for Clinical Laboratories.

63 FR 48734, September 11, 1998: HCFA Agency Information Collection Activities: Proposed Collection; Comment request (pertaining to medical review activities under PPS by Peer Review Organizations; and survey and deficiency reports for home health agencies).

63 FR 50577, September 22, 1998: Office of Inspector General: Solicitation of Information and Recommendations for Developing OIG Compliance Program Guidance for Certain Medicare+Choice Organizations — Notice.

63 FR 58341, October 30, 1998: Office of Inspector General: Health Care Fraud and Abuse Data Collection Program: Reporting of Final Adverse Actions — Notice of proposed rulemaking under section 1128E of the Social Security Act, affecting 45 CFR 61.

63 FR 58399, October 30, 1998: Office of Inspector General: Publication of the OIG's Provider Self-Disclosure Protocol — Notice.

63 FR 63478, November 13, 1998: HCFA Agency Information Collection Activities: Proposed Collection; Comment request (pertaining to processing Medicare+Choice disenrollment requests from beneficiaries; creation of the Utilization and Quality Control Peer Review Organization; and rules for participation of HHA's in Medicare and review of plans of care for home health services).

63 FR 65601, November 27, 1998: HCFA Agency Information Collection Activities: Submission for OMB Review; Comment request (pertaining to medical records review under PPS; and home health agency survey and deficiencies reports, and home health functional assessment instruments).

63 FR 70137, December 18, 1998: Office of Inspector General: Solicitation of Information and Recommendations for Developing OIG Compliance Program Guidance for the Nursing Home Industry — Notice.

63 FR 71819, December 30, 1998: Office of Inspector General; Health Care Fraud and Abuse Data Collection Program; Reporting under section 1128E of the Social Security Act of Final Adverse

Actions — Notice of proposed rule-making; extension of comment period, affecting 45 CFR 61.

63 FR 72318, December 31, 1998: HCFA Agency Information Collection Activities: Proposed Collection; Comment request (pertaining to fire safety survey report forms for health care facilities). Health Care Fraud and Abuse-Chapter 6: Release # 12

1999

64 FR 1024, January 7, 1999: HCFA Agency Information Collection Activities: Proposed Collection; Comment request (pertaining to granting and withdrawal of deeming authority to national accreditation organizations).

64 FR 1810, January 12, 1999: HCFA Agency Information Collection Activities: Proposed Collection; Comment request (pertaining to Medicaid eligibility quality control MEQC) samples; identification of extension units of outpatient physical therapy (OPT) and outpatient speech pathology (OSP) providers; request for certification in the Medicare and/or Medicaid program(s) to provide OPT or OSP services; and request for certification as a supplier of portable X-ray services under Medicare and/or Medicaid).

64 FR 1813, January 12, 1999: Office of Inspector General Publication of OIG Special Fraud Alert on Physician Liability for Certifications in the Provision of Medical Equipment and Supplies and Home Health Services — Notice.

64 FR 2228, January 13, 1999: Office of Inspector General: Solicitation of Information and Recommendations for Developing OIG Compliance Program Guidance for the Hospice Industry — Notice.

64 FR 3303, January 21, 1999: HCFA Agency Information Collection Activities: Proposed Collection; Comment request (pertaining to on-site inspection for durable medical equipment suppliers).

64 FR 3748, January 25, 1999: Medicare and Medicaid Programs: Reporting Outcome and Assessment Information Set (OASIS) Data as Part of the Conditions of Participation for Home Health Agencies-Interim final rule with comment period, affecting 42 CFR Parts 484 and 488.

64 FR 3637, January 25, 1999: Medicare Program; Coverage of Ambulance Services and Vehicle and Staff Requirements — Final rule with comment period, affecting 42 CFR Parts 499, 410, and 424.

64 FR 3764, January 25, 1999: Medicare and Medicaid Programs: Comprehensive Assessment and Use of the OASIS as Part of the

Conditions of Participation for Home Health Agencies — Final rule affecting 42 CFR Part 484.

64 FR 4435, January 28, 1999: HCFA Agency Information Collection Activities: Submission for OMB Review; Comment request (pertaining to hospice cost reports).

64 FR 4435, January 28, 1999: HCFA Agency Information Collection Activities; Submission for OMB Review; Comment request (pertaining to home and community-based services waiver requests).

64 FR 4435, January 28, 1999: Office of Inspector General: Draft Compliance Guidance for the Durable Medical Equipment, Prosthetics, Orthotics and Supply Industry — Notice and comment period.

64 FR 6664, February 10, 1999: HCFA Agency Information Collection Activities: Submission for OMB Review; Comment request (pertaining to skilled nursing facility (SNF) resident assessment MDS data).

64 FR 6665, February 10, 1999: HCFA Agency Information Collection Activities: Proposed Collection; Comment request (pertaining to sole community home health agencies (HHS)).

64 FR 9336, February 25, 1999: HCFA Agency Information Collection Activities: Submission for OMB Review; Comment request (pertaining to home office cost reports for chain organizations; ambulance requests for Medicare payment; a supplement to the Medicare current beneficiary survey; and the Medicaid program budget report prepared by State Medicaid agencies).

64 FR 10478, March 4, 1999: HCFA Agency Information Collection Activities: Proposed Collection; Comment request (pertaining to information collection requirements in final peer review organization (PRO) sanction regulations).

64 FR 13354, March 18, 1999: Medicare and Medicaid Programs; Civil Money Penalties for Nursing Homes (SNF/NF), Change in Notice Requirements, and Expansion of Discretionary Remedy Delegation — Final rule with comment period, affecting 42 CFR Part 488.

64 FR 13997, March 23, 1999: HCFA Agency Information Collection Activities: Submission for OMB Review; Comment request (pertaining to Medicare and Medicaid requirements for advanced directives, and disclosure of ownership and financial control interest).

64 FR 14454, March 25, 1999: HCFA Agency Information Collection Activities: Proposed Collection; Comment request (pertaining to blood bank inspection checklist under CLIA).

64 FR 14454, March 25, 1999: HCFA Agency Information Collection Activities: Submission for OMB Review; Comment request (pertaining to Medicaid eligibility quality control sampling; fire safety survey report forms; and income and eligibility verification systems under Medicaid).

64 FR 17184, April 8, 1999: HCFA Medicare Program; April 23, 1999 Open Town Hall Meeting to Discuss the Skilled Nursing Facility Prospective Payment System (SNF/PPS) and Quality of Care in Nursing Facilities — Notice of meeting.

64 FR 17673, April 12, 1999: HCFA Agency Information Collection Activities: Proposed Collection; Comment request (pertaining to Medicare participating physician or supplier agreements).

64 FR 18624, April 15, 1999: HCFA Agency Information Collection Activities: Proposed Collection; Comment request (pertaining to classification system for patients in inpatient rehabilitation hospitals and exempt rehabilitation units).

64 FR 19375, April 20, 1999: HCFA Agency Information Collection Activities: Proposed Collection; Comment request (pertaining to acquisition, protection, and disclosure of peer review organization (PRO) information).

64 FR 19376, April 20, 1999: Medicare Program; Recognition of the Community Health Accreditation Program, Inc. (CHAP) for Hospices).

64 FR 23846, May 4, 1999: HCFA Emergency Clearance: Public Information Collection Requirements Submitted to the Office of Management and Budget (OMB) (pertaining to the outcome and assessment information set (OASIS) for home health care agencies).

64 FR 23847, May 4, 1999: HCFA Agency Information Collection Activities: Submission for OMB Review; Comment request (pertaining to uniform needs assessment instrument (UNIA) for patients being discharged from Medicare-certified hospitals).

64 FR 25891, May 13, 1999: HCFA Agency Information Collection Activities: Submission for OMB Review; Comment request (pertaining to Medicare agreement application for health care prepayment plans under section 1833).

64 FR 25892, May 13, 1999: HCFA Agency Information Collection Activities: Submission for OMB Review; Comment request (pertain-

ing to granting and withdrawal of deeming authority to national accreditation organizations).

64 FR 25893, May 13, 1999: HCFA Agency Information Collection Activities: Submission for OMB Review; Comment request (pertaining to identification of extension units of outpatient physical therapy (OPT) and outpatient speech pathology (OSP) providers).

64 FR 29048, May 28, 1999: HCFA Agency Information Collection Activities: Proposed Collection; Comment request (pertaining to certification as a rural health clinic).

64 FR 29050, May 28, 1999: HCFA Emergency Clearance: Public Information Collection Requirements Submitted to the Office of Management and Budget (OMB) (pertaining to the community mental health center site visit assessment tool).

64 FR 30340, June 7, 1999: HCFA Agency Information Collection Activities: Submission for OMB Review; Comment request (pertaining to information collection requirements in the final peer review organization (PRO) sanction regulations).

64 FR 32239, June 16, 1999: HCFA Agency Information Collection Activities: Proposed Collection; Comment request (pertaining to conditions of coverage for organ procurement organizations).

64 FR 32240, June 16, 1999: HCFA Agency Information Collection Activities: Submission for OMB Review; Comment request (pertaining to conditions of participation for portable x-ray suppliers).

64 FR 32881, June 18, 1999: Medicare Program; Recognition of the Joint Commission for Accreditation of Healthcare Organizations (JCAHO) for Hospices — Final notice.

64 FR 32984, June 18, 1999: Medicare and Medicaid Programs; Mandatory Use, Collection, Encoding, and Transmission of Outcome and Assessment Information Set (OASIS) for Home Health Agencies — Notice.

64 FR 32992, June 18, 1999: HCFA Privacy Act of 1974; Report of New System (pertaining to a new system of records containing data on the physical, mental, functional, and psychosocial status of all patients receiving the services of home health agencies (HHAs) approved to participate in Medicare or Medicaid).

64 FR 36070, July 2, 1999: Medicare and Medicaid Programs; Hospital Conditions of Participation: Patient Rights — Interim final rule with comment, affecting 42 CFR 482.

64 FR 36368, July 6, 1999: Office of Inspector General Publication of OIG Compliance Program Guidance for the Durable Medical Equipment, Prosthetics, Orthotics and Supply Industry — Notice.

64 FR 36887, July 8, 1999: HCFA Agency Information Collection Activities: Proposed Collection; Comment request (pertaining to reporting outcome and assessment information data set (OASIS) as part of the conditions of participation for home health agencies).

64 FR 37142, July 9, 1999: HCFA Agency Information Collection Activities: Submission for OMB Review; Comment request (pertaining to request for certification in the Medicare/Medicaid program to provide outpatient physical therapy and/or speech-language pathology and the outpatient physcal therapy and/or speech-language pathology survey report form; request for certification as a supplier of portable X-ray services); and procedures for making national coverage decisions).

64 FR 38910, July 20, 1999: HCFA Agency Information Collection Activities: Proposed Collection; Comment request (pertaining to comprehensive outpatient rehabilitation facility (CORF) eligibility requirements).

64 FR 39150, July 21, 1999: Office of Inspector General; Draft OIG Compliance Program Guidance for Hospices — Notice and comment period.

64 FR 39517, July 22, 1999: HCFA Agency Information Collection Activities: Submission for OMB Review; Comment request (pertaining to Medicare participating physician or supplier agreement form HCFA-460).

64 FR 40888, July 28, 1999: HCFA Agency Information Collection Activities: Proposed Collection; Comment request (pertaining to community mental health center site visit assessment tool).

64 FR 41444, July 30, 1999: HCFA Agency Information Collection Activities: Proposed Collection; Comment request (pertaining to ambulatory surgical center survey report form).

64 FR 44030, August 12, 1999: HCFA Agency Information Collection Activites: Submission for OMB Review; Comment request (pertaining to blood bank inspection checklists and reports under CLIA; and Medicaid eligibility quality control).

64 FR 44031, August 12, 1999: HCFA Agency Information Collection Activites: Submission for OMB Review; Comment request (pertaining to survey and certification of rural health clinics; and determining third party liability in Medicaid programs).

64 FR 45267, August 19, 1999: HCFA Agency Information Collection Activities: Submission for OMB Review; Comment request (pertaining to Medicare credit balance reporting requirements).

64 FR 46400, August 25, 1999: HCFA Agency Information Collection Activities: Proposed Collection; Comment request (pertaining to hospice information collection requirements).

64 FR 48846, September 8, 1999: Office of Inspector General: Solicitation of Information and Recommendations for Developing OIG Compliance Program Guidance for Individual Physicians and Small Group Practices — Notice.

64 FR 49196, September 10, 1999: HCFA Agency Information Collection Activities; Submission for OMB Review; Comment request (pertaining to conditions of coverage for organ procurement organizations).

64 FR 49197, September 10, 1999: Medicare and Medicaid Programs; Application of the Joint Commission for Accreditaton of Healthcare Organizations (JCAHO) for Continued Approval of Deeming Authority for Home Health Agencies — Proposed notice.

64 FR 49198, September 10, 1999: Medicare and Medicaid Programs; Application of the Community Health Accreditation Program, Incorporated, CHAP) for Continued Approval of Deeming Authority for Home Health Agencies — Proposed notice.

64 FR 49199, September 10, 1999: Medicare and Medicaid Programs; Reapplication of the American Osteopathic Association (AOA) for Continued Approval of Deeming Authority for Hospitals — Proposed notice.

64 FR 42791, September 30, 1999: Office of Inspector General; Publication of the OIG Special Advisory Bulletin on the Effect of Exclusion from Participation in Federal Health Care Programs — Notice. See also correction at 64 FR 55484, October 13, 1999.

64 FR 54031, October 5, 1999: Office of Inspector General; Publication of the OIG Compliance Program, Guidance for Hospices — Notice.

64 FR 57431, October 25, 1999: Medicare Program; Appeals of Carrier Determinations that a Supplier Fails to Meet the Requirements for Medicare Billing Privileges — Proposed rule affecting 42 CFR Part 405.

64 FR 57619, October 26, 1999: Office of Inspector General; Privacy Act; Exempt Record System, Pertaining to the Healthcare Integrity and Protection Data Bank (HIPDB) — Notice of proposed rulemaking affecting 45 CFR Part 5b.

64 FR 57740, October 26, 1999: Office of Inspector General; Healthcare Fraud and Abuse Data Collection Program: Reporting of Final Adverse Actions — Final rule affecting 45 CFR Part 61.

64 FR 58851, November 1, 1999: Office of Inspector General; Healthcare Integrity and Protection Data Bank: Announcement of Opening Date for Reporting and Self-query Fee — Notice.

64 FR 61353, November 10, 1999: Office of Inspector General/HCFA; OIG/HCFA Special Advisory Bulletin on the Patient Anti-dumping Statute.

64 FR 61893, November 15, 1999: Office of Inspector General; Publication of the OIG's Compliance Program Guidance for Medicare+Choice Organizations Offering Coordinated Care Plans — Notice.

64 FR 62679, November 17, 1999: HCFA Agency Information Collection Activities: Proposed Collection; Comment request (pertaining to hospital conditions of participation).

64 FR 62679, November 17, 1999: HCFA Agency Information Collection Activities: Proposed Collection; Comment request (pertaining to surveys of end stage renal disease facilities).

64 FR 62680, November 17, 1999: HCFA Agency Information Collection Activities: Submission for OMB Review; Comment request (pertaining to hospice care eligibility standards, reimbursement procedures, and conditions of participation).

64 FR 66482, November 26, 1999: HCFA Agency Information Collection Activities: Proposed Collection; Comment request (pertaining to resident assessment in skilled nursing facilities).

64 FR 67028, November 30, 1999: Medicare and Medicaid Programs; Religious Nonmedical Health Care Institutions and Advance Directives — Interim final rule with comment period, affecting 42 CFR Parts 403, 412, 431, 440, 442, 446, 456, 488, and 489.

64 FR 67223, December 1, 1999: Medicaid Program; External Quality Review of Medicaid Managed Care Organizations — Proposed rule affecting 42 CFR Parts 433 and 438.

64 FR 67918, December 3, 1999: HCFA Agency Information Collection Activities: Proposed Collection; Comment request (pertaining to conditions of participation for rural health clinics).

64 FR 69217, December 10, 1999: Office of Inspector General; Solicitation of New Safe Harbors and Special Fraud Alerts — Intent to develop regulations affecting 42 CFR Part 1001.

64 FR 69271, December 10, 1999: HCFA Agency Information Collection Activities: Proposed Collection; Comment request (pertaining

to hospital providers of extender care (swing bed) services in Medicare and Medicaid).

64 FR 69272, December 10, 1999: HCFA Agency Information Collection Activities: Submission for OMB Review; Comment request (pertaining to community mental health center site visit assessment tools).

64 FR 69272, December 10, 1999: HCFA Agency Information Collection Activities: Submission for OMB Review; Comment request (pertaining to comprehensive outpatient rehabilitation facility (CORF) eligibility and survey forms).

64 FR 69273, December 10, 1999: HCFA Agency Information Collection Activities: Submission for OMB Review; Comment request (pertaining to Medicare/Medicaid hospital survey reports).

64 FR 69273, December 10, 1999: HCFA Agency Information Collection Activities: Submission for OMB Review; Comment request (pertaining to HCFA-377 ambulatory surgical center survey report form).

2000

65 FR 1400, January 10, 2000: HCFA Agency Information Collection Activities: Submission for OMB Review; Comment request (pertaining to reporting outcome and assessment information set (OASIS) data set as a condition of participation for HHAs).

65 FR 8722, February 22, 2000: Medicare and Medicaid Programs; Re-approval of the Deeming Authority of the Joint Commission on Accreditation of Healthcare Organizations (JCAHO) for Home Health Agencies (HHAs) — Final notice.

65 FR 8725, February 22, 2000: Medicare and Medicaid Programs; Reapproval of the Deeming Authority of the Community Health Accreditation Program, Incorporated (CHAP) for Home Health Agencies (HHAs) — Final notice.

65 FR 8727, February 22, 2000: Medicare and Medicaid Programs; Recognition of the American Osteopathic Association (AOA) for Continued Approval of Deeming Authority for Hospitals — Final notice.

65 FR 8983, February 23, 2000: HCFA Agency Information collection Activities: Submission for OMB Review; Comment request (pertaining to conditions of participation for rural health clinics).

65 FR 10450, February 28, 2000: Medicare Program; Rural Health Clinics: Amendments to Participation Requirements and Payment Provisions; and Establishment of a Quality Assessment and Per-

formance Improvement Program — Proposed rule affecting 42 CFR Parts 405 and 491.

65 FR 12556, March 9, 2000: HCFA Agency Information Collection Activities: Proposed Collection; Comment request (pertaining to hospital request for certification in the Medicare/Medicaid program).

65 FR 12560, March 9, 2000: HCFA Agency Information Collection Activities: Submission for OMB Review; Comment request (pertaining to hospital provider of extended care services (swing beds) in the Medicare and Medicaid programs).

65 FR 13082, March 10, 2000: Medicare Program; Negotiated Rulemaking: Coverage and Administrative Policies for Clinical Diagnostic Laboratory Services — Proposed rule affecting 42 CFR Part 410.

65 FR 14288, March 16, 2000: HCFA Agency Information Collection Activities: Proposed Collection; Comment request (pertaining to end stage renal disease application and survey and certification).

65 FR 14289, March 16, 2000: Office of Inspector General: Publication of the OIG Compliance Program Guidance for Nursing Facilities — Notice.

65 FR 14986, March 20, 2000: HCFA Agency Information Collection Activities: Submission for OMB Review; Comment request (pertaining to skilled nursing facility resident assessment MDS data).

65 FR 25738, May 3, 2000: HCFA Emergency Clearance: Public Informatiion Collection Requirements Submitted to the Office of Management and Budget (OMB) (pertaining to the Medicare managed care CAHPS Survey).

65 FR 37566, June 15, 2000: HCFA Agency Information Collection Activities: Submission for OMB Review; Comment request (pertaining to hospice survey and deficiencies report form).

65 FR 37566, June 15, 2000: HCFA Agency Information Collection Activities: Submission for OMB Review; Comment request (pertaining to post-laboratory survey questionnaire under CLIA).

65 FR 40111, June 29, 2000: HCFA Agency Information Collection Activities: Proposed Collection; comment request (pertaining to qualification applications for prepaid health plans (HMOs).

65 FR 47739, August 3, 2000: HCFA Agency Information Collection Activities: Submission for OMB Review; Comment request (pertaining to CLIA adverse action extract).

65 FR 50204, August 17, 2000: Office of Inspector General: Solicitation of Information and Recommendations for Developing a Compliance Risk Guidance for the Ambulance Industry — Notice.

65 FR 53319, September 1, 2000: HCFA Agency Information Collection Activities: Proposed Collection; Comment request (pertaining to incentive arrangement disclosure form for managed care organizations and their related medical groups and physicians).

65 FR 53320, September 1, 2000: Medicare Program; September 21, 2000, Meeting of the Advisory Panel on Medicare Education — Notice of meeting.

65 FR 53963, September 6, 2000: Medicare Program: Appeals of Carrier Determinations that a Physician or Other Supplier Fails to Meet the Requirements for Medicare Billing Privileges; Reopening of Comment Period — Notice of reopening of comment period for proposed rule affecting 42 CFR Part 405.

65 FR 54857, September 11, 2000: HCFA Agency Information Collection Activities: Submission for OMB Review; Comment request (pertaining to ICF/MR survey report forms).

65 FR 54857, September 11, 2000: HCFA Agency Information Collection Activities: Submission for OMB Review; Comment request (pertaining to hospital conditions of participation-identification of potential organ, tissue, and eye donors, and transplant hospitals' provision of transplant-related data).

65 FR 57195, September 21, 2000: HCFA Agency Information Collection Activities; Proposed Collection; Comment request (pertaining to Medicare managed care CAHPS survey for quality of care purposes).

65 FR 58092, September 27, 2000: Medicare and Medicaid Programs; Announcement of Additional Applications from Hospitals Requesting Waivers for Organ Procurement Service Areas — Notice with comment period.

65 FR 58279, September 28, 2000: HCFA Agency Information Collection Activities: Proposed Collection; Comment request (pertaining to Medicare consumer assessment survey of health plans-CAHPS).

65 FR 59431, October 5, 2000: HCFA Agency Information Collection Activities: Proposed Collection; Comment request (pertaining to conditions for coverage of suppliers of end stage renal disease services).

65 FR 59432, October 5, 2000: HCFA Agency Information Collection Activities: Submission for OMB Review; Comment request

(pertaining to end stage renal disease application and survey and certification report).

65 FR 60366, October 11, 2000: Medicare Program; Additional Supplier Standards — Final rule with comment period, affecting 42 CFR Part 424.

65 FR 63035, October 20, 2000: Office of Inspector General: Medicare and State Health Care Programs: Fraud and Abuse; Revisions and Technical Corrections — Proposed rule affecting 42 CFR Parts 1001, 1003, 1005, and 1008.

65 FR 64966, October 31, 2000: Medicare, Medicaid, and CLIA Programs; Continuance of the Approval of COLA as a CLIA Accreditation Organization — Notice. See also correction at 65 FR 70575, November 24, 2000.

65 FR 65860, November 2, 2000: HCFA Agency Information Collection Activities: Proposed Collection; Comment request (pertaining to reporting outcome and assessment (OASIS) data as part of conditions of participation for home health agencies).

65 FR 65861, November 2, 2000: HCFA Agency Information Collection Activities: Proposed Collection; Comment request (pertaining to conflict of interest disclosure requirements for Medicare program integrity).

65 FR 76647, December 7, 2000: HCFA Agency Information Collection Activities: Proposed Collection; Comment request (pertaining to alternate quality assessment survey in lieu of onsite survey for CLIA labs with good performance).

65 FR 78124, December 14, 2000: Office of Inspector General: Solicitation of New Safe Harbors and Special Fraud Alerts — Notice of intent to develop regulations.

65 FR 79867, December 20, 2000: HCFA Agency Information Collection Activities: Proposed Collection; Comment request (pertaining to home health Medicare conditions of participation information collection requirements).

65 FR 79867, December 20, 2000: HCFA Agency Information Collection Activities: Proposed Collection; Comment request (pertaining to quality improvement system for managed care).

65 FR 79868, December 20, 2000: HCFA Agency Information Collection Activities: Proposed Collection; Comment request (pertaining to Medicare consumer assessment survey of health plans).

65 FR 82941, December 29, 2000: Medicare, Medicaid, and CLIA Programs; Extension of Certain Effective Dates for Clinical Labora-

tory Requirements under CLIA — Final rule with comment period, affecting 42 CFR Part 493.

2001

66 FR 856, January 4, 2001: Medicare and Medicaid Programs; Physicians Referrals to Health Care Entities with which They Have Financial Relationships—Final rule with comment period, affecting 42 CFR Parts 411 and 424.

66 FR 2912, January 12, 2001: HCFA Agency Information Collection Activities: Proposed Collection; Comment request (pertaining to clinical laboratory ICRs contained in supporting regulations at 42 CFR section 493.1–.2001).

66 FR 4674, January 18, 2001: Medicare and Medicaid Programs; Hospital Conditions of Participation: Anesthesia—Final rule affecting 42 CFR Parts 416, 482, and 485.

66 FR 6629, January 22, 2001: HCFA Agency Information Collection Activities: Submission for OMB Review; Comment request (pertaining to Medicare Integrity Program Organizational Conflict of Interest Disclosure Certificate).

66 FR 7147, January 22, 2001: Medicaid Program; Use of Restraint and Seclusion in Psychiatric Residential Treatment Facilities Providing Psychiatric Services to Individuals Under Age 21—Final rule affecting 42 CFR Parts 441 and 483.

66 FR 9586, February 8, 2001: HCFA Agency Information Collection Activities: Proposed Collection; Comment request (pertaining to a project to develop an outcome–based continuous quality improvement system for PACE).

66 FR 9587, February 8, 2001: HCFA Agency Information Collection Activities: Proposed Collection; Comment request (pertaining to a project to develop an outcome–reporting of restraints and seclusion deaths by hospitals).

66 FR 11591, February 26, 2001: HCFA Agency Information Collection Activities: Proposed Collection; Comment request (pertaining to Medicare+Choice program requirements).

66 FR 13546, March 6, 2001: HCFA Agency Information Collection Activities: Proposed Collection; Comment request (pertaining to independent diagnostic testing facility documentation of proficiency of medical personnel and resources).

66 FR 13547, March 6, 2001: HCFA Agency Information Collection Activities: Proposed Collection; Comment request (pertaining to Medicare/Medicaid psychiatric hospital survey data).

66 FR 13547, March 6, 2001: HCFA Agency Information Collection Activities: Proposed Collection; Comment request (pertaining to hospice request for certification as a provider).

66 FR 14157, March 9, 2001: HCFA Agency Information Collection Activities: Submission for OMB review; Comment request (pertaining to home health Medicare conditions of participation information collection requirements).

66 FR 14157, March 9, 2001: HCFA Agency Information Collection Activities: Submission for OMB review; Comment request (pertaining to alternate quality assessment form for CLIA compliance).

66 FR 14906, March 14, 2001: Medicare and Medicaid Programs; Recognition of the American Osteopathic Association for Ambulatory Surgical Centers Program—Proposed notice.

66 FR 15122, March 15, 2001: HCFA Agency Information Collection Activities: Submission for OMB Review; Comment request (pertaining to quality improvement system for managed care).

66 FR 15800, March 21, 2001: Medicare Program; Use of Restraint and Seclusion in Residential Treatment Facilities Providing Inpatient Psychiatric Services to Individuals under Age 21: Delay of effective date, affecting 42 CFR Parts 441 and 483.

66 FR 16480, March 26, 2001: HCFA Agency Information Collection Activities; Proposed Collection; Comment request (pertaining to conditions of coverage of suppliers of end stage renal disease services). See also correction at 66 FR 18096, April 5, 2001.

66 FR 18645, April 10, 2001: HCFA Agency Information Collection Activities: Submission for OMB Review; Comment request (pertaining to Medicare and Medicaid outcome and assessment information set (OASIS) as part of the conditions of participation for home health agencies).

66 FR 18647, April 10, 2001: HCFA Agency Information Collection Activities: Submission for OMB Review; Comment request (pertaining to CLIA compliance).

66 FR 18959, April 12, 2001: HCFA Agency Information Collection Activities: Submission for OMB Review; Comment request (pertaining to home health services under Part A).

66 FR 19507, April 16, 2001: HCFA Agency Information Collection Activities: Proposed Collection; Comment request (pertaining to conflict of interest and ownership and control information form).

66 FR 19508, April 16, 2001: HCFA Agency Information Collection Activities: Proposed Collection; Comment request (pertaining to on site inspection for durable medical equipment (DME) suppliers).

66 FR 19509, April 16, 2001: Medicare and Medicaid Programs; Application by the American Osteopathic Association (AOF) for Approval of Deeming Authority for Critical Access Hospitals—Proposed notice.

66 FR 20997, April 26, 2001: HCFA Agency Information Collection Activities: Submission for OMB Review; Comment request (pertaining to health insurance provider agreement form).

66 FR 22242, May 3, 2001: HCFA Agency Information Collection Activities: Proposed Collection; Comment request (pertaining to CLIA certification requirements).

66 FR 23944, May 10, 2001: HCFA Agency Information Collection Activities: Proposed Collection; Comment request (pertaining to examination and treatment for emergency conditions and women in labor).

66 FR 23945, May 10, 2001: HCFA Agency Information Collection Activities: Submission for OMB Review; Comment request (pertaining to development of an outcome–based continuous quality improvement system for PACE).

66 FR 27598, May 18, 2001: Medicare and Medicaid Programs; Hospital Conditions of Participation; Anesthesia Services: Delay of Effective Date—Notice of final rule affecting 42 CFR Parts 416, 482, and 485.

66 FR 34457, June 28, 2001: HCFA Agency Information Collection Activities: Proposed Collection; Comment request (pertaining to durable medical equipment and prosthetics, orthotics, and supplies supplier survey).

See § 2:31.

§ 6:32 TERMINATING PROVIDER AGREEMENTS — Section 1866(b) [42 U.S.C.A. 1395cc]

Regulations

42 CFR Part 402 — Civil Money Penalties, Assessments, and Exclusions

42 CFR Part 405, Subpart U — Conditions for Coverage of Suppliers of End-Stage Renal Disease (ESRD) Services; Subpart X — Rural Health Clinic Services

42 CFR Part 416 — Ambulatory Surgical Services

42 CFR Part 418 — Hospice Care

42 CFR Part 422 — Medicare+Choice Program

42 CFR Part 424 — Conditions for Medicare Payment

42 CFR Part 440 — Services: General Provisions [Medicaid]

42 CFR Part 441 — Services: Requirements and Limits Applicable to Specific Services [Medicaid]

42 CFR Part 442 — Standards for Payment for Nursing Facilities and Intermediate Care Facilities for the Mentally Retarded

42 CFR Part 475 — Peer Review organizations

42 CFR Part 476 — Utilization and Quality Control Review

42 CFR Part 478 — Reconsiderations and Appeals

42 CFR Part 480 — Acquisition, Protection, and Disclosure of Peer Review Information

42 CFR Part 482 — Conditions of Participation for Hospitals

42 CFR Part 483 — Requirements for States and Long Term Care Facilities

42 CFR Part 484 — Conditions of Participation: Home Health Agencies

42 CFR Part 485 — Conditions of Participation: Specialized Providers

42 CFR Part 486 — Conditions for Coverage of Specialized Services Furnished by Suppliers

42 CFR Part 488 — Survey and Certification Procedures

42 CFR Part 489 — Provider Agreements and Supplier Approval

42 CFR Part 491 — Certification of Certain Health Facilities

42 CFR Part 493 — Laboratory Requirements

42 CFR Part 498 — Appeals Procedures for Determinations that Affect Participation in the Medicare Program and for Determinations that Affect the Participation of ICF's/MR and Certain NF's in the Medicaid Program

53 FR 48645, December 2, 1988: Medicare and Medicaid Programs; Medicare, Medicaid, and Clinical Laboratories Improvement Act (CLIA) Patient Confidentiality Rules — Final rule amending 42 CFR Parts 74, 405, and 441.

54 FR 5316, February 2, 1989: Medicare and Medicaid; Requirements for Long Term Care Facilities — Final rule with comment period, amending 42 CFR Parts 405, 442, 447, 483, 488, 489, and 498. See also delay in effective date at 54 FR 29717, July 14, 1989; corrections at 54 FR 8361, February 27, 1989, and 54 FR 37466, September 11, 1989; and final rule delaying effective date from January 1, 1990, to October 1, 1990, at 54 FR 53611, December 29, 1989.

54 FR 1956, January 18, 1989: Medicare and Medicaid Programs; Denial of Payment for Substandard Quality Care and Review of

Beneficiary Complaints — Proposed rule to amend 42 CFR Parts 405, 424, 462, 466, 473, 476, and 489.

54 FR 33354, August 14, 1989: Medicare Program; Home Health Agencies: Conditions of Participation and Reduction in Recordkeeping Requirements — Interim final rule with comment period, amending 42 CFR Part 405by redesignating Subpart L as 42 CFR Part 484. See also correction at 54 FR 35131, August 23, 1989.

55 FR 9538, March 14, 1990: Medicare, Medicaid and CLIA Programs; Revision of the Laboratory Regulations for the Medicare, Medicaid, and Clinical Laboratories Improvement Act of 1967 Programs — Final rule with comment period, amending 42 CFR Parts 74, 405, 416, 440, 482, 483, 488, and 493.

55 FR 10256, March 20, 1990: Medicare and Medicaid; Charges to Residents' Funds in Nursing Homes — Proposed rule to amend 42 CFR Part 483.

55 FR 10938, March 23, 1990: Medicare and Medicaid Programs; Nurse Aide Training and Competency Evaluation Programs — Proposed rule to amend 42 CFR Parts 431, 433, and 483.

55 FR 10951, March 23, 1990: Medicare and Medicaid Programs; Preadmission Screening and Annual Resident Review — Proposed rule to amend 42 CFR Parts 405, 431, and 483.

55 FR 20896, May 21, 1990: Medicare, Medicaid and CLIA Programs; Regulations Implementing the Clinical Laboratory Improvement Amendments of 1988 (CLIA '88) — Proposed rule. See also extension of time for public comment to September 21, 1990, published at 55 FR 34289 on August 22, 1990.

55 FR 23435, June 8, 1990: Medicare Program; Payment for Physician Outpatient Maintenance Dialysis Services and Other Physician Services for ESRD Patients — Final rule affecting 42 CFR Parts 405, 413, and 414. See also correction published at 55 FR 31185, August 1, 1990.

55 FR 42907, October 24, 1990: Medicare Program; Standards Applied by Utilization and Quality Control Peer Review Organizations: Consideration of Remote Rural Location and Other Relevant Factors — Notice of policy and request for comments.

55 FR 50831, December 11, 1990: Medicare Program; Hospice Care Amendments: Medicare — Final rule with comment period, amends 42 CFR Part 418.

55 FR 51434, December 14, 1990: Medicare Program; Granting and Withdrawal of Deeming Authority to National Accreditation Organizations — Proposed rule.

56 FR 13430, April 2, 1991: Medicare and Laboratory Certification Programs; Enforcement Procedures for Laboratories — Proposed rule.

56 FR 26916, June 12, 1991: Medicare Program; Payment for Hospice Care — Final rule with comment period affecting 42 CFR Part 418.

56 FR 30696, July 5, 1991: Medicaid Program; Correction and Reduction Plans for Intermediate Care Facilities for the Mentally Retarded — Final rule affecting 42 CFR Part 442. See also correction at 56 FR 49147, September 27, 1991.

56 FR 32967, July 18, 1991: Medicare Program; Home Health Agencies: Conditions of Participation — Final rule.

56 FR 37054, August 2, 1991: Medicare and Medicaid Programs; Survey and Enforcement Requirements and Alternative Sanctions for Home Health Agencies — Proposed rule affecting 42 CFR Parts 441, 488, and 489.

56 FR 43929, September 5, 1991: Medicare and Medicaid Programs; Recognition of the Community Health Accreditation Program Standards for Home Care Organizations — Proposed notice.

56 FR 48112, September 24, 1991: Medicaid Program; Community Supported Living Arrangements Services — Interim final rule with comment period, affecting 42 CFR Part 441.

56 FR 48826, September 26, 1991: Medicare and Medicaid; Requirements for Long Term Care Facilities — Final rule affecting 42 CFR Parts 422, 447, 483, 488, 489, and 498. See also correction at 57 FR 43922, September 23, 1992.

56 FR 48880, September 26, 1991: Medicare and Medicaid Programs; Nurse Aide Training and Competency Evaluation Programs — Final rule affecting 42 CFR Parts 431, 433, and 483. See also correction at 56 FR 59331, November 25, 1991.

56 FR 49154, September 27, 1991: Medicare Program; Medicare Coverage of Home Health Services, Medicare Conditions of Participation, and Home Health Aide Supervision — Proposed rule affecting 42 CFR Parts 409, 418, and 484.

57 FR 3298, January 29, 1992: Health Care Programs: Fraud and Abuse; Amendments to OIG Exclusion and CMP Authorities Resulting From Public Law 100-93 — Final rule affecting 42 CFR Parts 1001, 1002, 1003, 1004, 1005, 1006, and 1007. See also final rule and correction at 57 FR 9669, March 20, 1992; final rule affecting 42 CFR Parts 1001 and 1005, with clarification at 58 FR 5617, January 22,

1993; and final rule affecting 42 CFR Part 1001, with correction, at 58 FR 40752, July 30, 1993.

57 FR 4044, February 3, 1992: Medicare Program; Recognition of the Joint Commission of the Accreditation of Healthcare Organizations' Standards for Home Care Organizations — Proposed notice.

57 FR 4516, February 5, 1992: Medicare and Medicaid Programs; Omnibus Nursing Home Requirements — Proposed rule affecting 42 CFR Parts 418, 440, 441, 482, 483, and 488. See also correction at 57 FR 8961, March 13, 1992.

57 FR 7002, February 28, 1992: Medicare, Medicaid and CLIA Programs; Regulations Implementing the Clinical Laboratory Improvement Amendments of 1988 (CLIA) — Final rule with comment period, affecting 42 CFR Parts 405, 410, 416, 417, 418, 440, 482, 483, 484, 485, 488, 491, 493, and 494. See also correction at 57 FR 35760, August 11, 1992, and correction amendments at 58 FR 5212, January 19, 1993.

57 FR 7218, February 28, 1992: Medicare Program; Medicare and Laboratory Certification Program; Enforcement Procedures for Laboratories — Final rule affecting 42 CFR Part 493. See also correction amendments at 58 FR 5212, January 19, 1993.

57 FR 22773, May 29, 1992: Medicare Program; Recognition of Community Health Accreditation Program Standards for Home Care Organizations — Final notice.

57 FR 33992, July 31, 1992: Clinical Laboratories Improvement Act Program; Granting and Withdrawal of Deeming Authority to Private Nonprofit Accreditation Organizations and of CLIA Exemption under State Laboratory Programs — Final rule.

57 FR 39278, August 28, 1992: Medicare and Medicaid Programs; Survey, Certification and Enforcement of Skilled Nursing Facilities and Nursing Facilities — Proposed rule affecting 42 CFR Parts 431, 442, 488, and 489.

57 FR 43462, September 21, 1992: Health Care Financing Administration Public Information Collection Requirements Submitted to the Office of Management and Budget for Clearance (pertaining to sole community home health agencies; physician/supplier overpayment reports; physician or supplier Medicare agreements; conditions of participation for rural health clinics; Medicare provider refunds; conditions of participation for comprehensive outpatient rehabilitation facilities; Medicaid income and eligibility verification system; Medicaid integrated review schedule; provider overpayment report; financial statement of Medicare provider debtors; negative

case action review schedule for Medicaid quality control; outpatient resource costing study; Medicaid intermediate care facility for the mentally retarded or persons with related conditions survey report form; installment agreement of beneficiary refund of overpayment; PRO assumption of responsibilities; Medicare contractor administrative budget and cost reporting system forms; fire safety survey report forms; medical records review under prospective payment system; and Qualified Medicare Beneficiary supplement to the Medicare current beneficiary survey).

57 FR 46362, October 8, 1992: Medicare and Medicaid Programs; Revised Effective Date of Medicare/Medicaid Provider Agreement and Supplier Participation — Proposed rule affecting 42 CFR Parts 431, 440, 442, 488, 489, and 498.

57 FR 46865, October 13, 1992: HCFA Public Information Collection Requirements Submitted to the Office of Management and Budget for Clearance (pertaining to impact of home health care plan management and evaluation; end-stage renal disease medical case review; Medicare/Medicaid hospital swing-bed survey report form; quarterly Medicaid statement of expenditures; Medicaid program budget report; information collection requirements in final peer review organization sanction regulations; appeals procedures for determinations that affect participation in Medicare; request for medical review information for Part B intermediary outpatient therapy bills and other Part B outpatient bills; and Medicaid limitations on provider-related donations and health care-related taxes, and limitations on payment to disproportionate share hospitals).

57 FR 53572, November 12, 1992: Medicare and Medicaid; Charges to Residents' Funds in Nursing Homes — Final rule affecting 42 CFR Part 483.

57 FR 54710, November 20, 1992: Medicaid Program; Elimination of Certain Written Documentation Pertaining to Medicaid Long-Term Care Facilities — Final rule affecting 42 CFR Part 442.

57 FR 56450, November 30, 1992: Medicare and Medicaid Programs; Preadmission Screening and Annual Resident Review — Final rule with comment period, affecting 42 CFR Parts 405, 431, 433, and 483. See also correction published at 58 FR 25784, April 28, 1993.

57 FR 61614, December 28, 1992: Medicare and Medicaid; Resident Assessment in Long Term Care Facilities — Proposed rule affecting 42 CFR Parts 456 and 483.

58 FR 5215, January 19, 1993: Medicare, Medicaid and CLIA Programs; Regulations Implementing the Clinical Laboratory Improvement Amendments of 1988 (CLIA) and Clinical Laboratory Improvement Act Program Fee Collection — Final rule with comment period, affecting 42 CFR Part 493. See also correction published at 58 FR 39154, July 22, 1993.

58 FR 21174, April 19, 1993: HCFA Public Information Collection Requirements Submitted to the Office of Management and Budget for Clearance re end stage renal disease survey forms; municipal health services cost reports forms; advance directives; withholding Medicare payments to recover Medicaid overpayments; home office cost statements; and statistical report on medical care.

58 FR 29416, May 20, 1993: HCFA Public Information Collection Requirements Submitted to the Office of Management and Budget (OMB) for Clearance re cataract surgery; Medicaid utilization management initiatives; Medicare coverage of screening mammography; psychiatric unit criteria worksheet and rehabilitation unit criteria worksheet; Medicare secondary payor forms; ambulatory surgical center survey forms; ambulance service compliance with State and local requirements; and early and periodic screening, diagnostic and treatment reports.

58 FR 30630, May 26, 1993: Medicare Program; Essential Access Community Hospitals (EACHs) and Rural Primary Care Hospitals (RPCHs) — Final rule affecting 42 CFR Parts 400, 409, 410, 411, 412, 413, 424, 440, 485, 488, 489, and 498.

58 FR 38579, July 19, 1993: HCFA Public Information Collection Requirements Submitted to the Office of Management and Budget (OMB) for Clearance re survey of home health agencies; CLIA survey report form; validation of state surveys; Medicaid listing of participating home health agencies; financial information regarding Medicare benefits from Medicare contractors; and third-party liability under Medicaid.

58 FR 46198, September 1, 1993: HCFA Public Information Collection Requirements (ICR) Submitted to the Office of Management and Budget (OMB) for Clearance (pertaining to prenatal services and assistance screening; home health agency treatment forms; conditions of participation for intermediate care facilities for the mentally retarded; State Medicaid eligibility quality control sample selection lists; prepaid health plan cost report; hospital survey report form; procedures for determining whether providers, practitioners, or other suppliers of services are liable for certain

noncovered services; Medicare credit balance reporting requirements; Medicare provider cost report questionnaire form; Medicare current beneficiary survey rounds 7-10; sterilization regulation/consent form; PRO reconsideration and appeals information requirements; information collection requirements in HSQ-110, acquisition, protection and disclosure of PRO information; Medicare/Medicaid organ procurement organization's (OPO) request for certification) — Notice.

58 FR 52112, October 6, 1993: Medicare, Medicaid, and CLIA Programs; Clinical Laboratory Improvement Amendments of 1988 Exemption of Laboratories Licensed by the State of Washington — Notice.

58 FR 54159, October 20, 1993: HCFA Public Information Collection Requirements Submitted to the Office of Management and Budget (OMB) for Clearance (pertaining to CLIA certification recommendation; CLIA laboratory personnel report; Medigap complaint data base; certification as a rural health clinic (RHC) and RHC survey report form; screening mammography services data report; ambulatory surgical center request for certification and survey report form; blood bank inspection checklist and report; Medicaid program budget report form; supplier of ESRD services form; and grantee data collection instrument) — Notice.

58 FR 59270, November 8, 1993: HCFA Public Information Collection Requirements Submitted to the Office of Management and Budget (OMB) for Clearance (pertaining to formats for utilization and quality control peer review organizations (PROs); home health agency plan of treatment forms; State survey agency budget expenditure report and certification workload report; home health agency cost report; recordkeeping requirements in provider reimbursement manual; quarterly Medicaid statement of expenditures; Medicare contract application for Federally qualified health maintenance organizations; hospice survey and deficiencies report form; organ procurement agency/histocompatibility laboratory statement of reimbursable costs) — Notice.

58 FR 60204, November 15, 1993: HCFA Public Information Collection Requirements Submitted to the Office of Management and Budget (OMB) for Clearance (pertaining to procedures for transmitting information between Medicare carriers and Medicare supplemental insurers; Medicare physician or supplier agreement; patient intake data form for the National Home Health Agency; agency characteristics form for the National Home Health Agency

prospective payment demonstration; intake and assessment survey package for the community nursing organization demonstration; comprehensive outpatient rehabilitation facility (CORF eligibility and survey forms and information collection requirements) — Notice.

58 FR 63533, December 2, 1993: Medicare Program; Required Laboratory Procedures for Rural Health Clinics — Final rule with comment period, affecting 42 CFR Part 491.

59 FR 5201, February 3, 1994: HCFA Public Information Collection Requirements Submitted to the Office of Management and Budget (OMB) for Clearance (pertaining to evaluation of the Medicare case management demonstration; evaluation of the Medicaid uninsured demonstrations; Internal Revenue Service, Social Security Administration, and HCFA data match; survey of physician owned medical liability insurers for use in computing the input component of the physician liability component of the Geographic Practice Cost Index and the Medicare Economic Index; emergency and foreign hospital services for Canadian travel claims; CLIA survey report form; Medicaid management information system (MMIS) data form) — Notice.

59 FR 6228, February 10, 1994: Medicare Program; Change in Provider Agreement Regulations Related to Federal Employee Health Benefits — Proposed rule affecting 42 CFR Part 489.

59 FR 14865, March 30, 1994: HCFA Public Information Collection Requirements Submitted to the Office of Management and Budget (OMB) for Clearance (pertaining to home health agency Medicare and Medicaid survey report forms for conditions of participation; conditions of participation for rural health clinics; Medicaid re-evaluation of assets for determining payment rates to hospitals and nursing homes; statistical report on medical care, eligible, recipients, payments, and services.)

59 FR 23069, May 4, 1994: HCFA Public Information Collection Requirements Submitted to the Office of Management and Budget (OMB) for Clearance (pertaining to clinical laboratory improvement amendments (CLIA) flexible survey protocol form; application for health insurance benefits under Medicare for individual with chronic renal disease form; Medicare Qualification Statement for Federal employees form; attending physician's statement and documentation of Medicare emergency form; request for Part B Medicare hearing by an Administrative Law Judge forms; CLIA adverse

action extract; and medicare and Medicaid coverage data bank reports form.)

59 FR 25460, May 16, 1994: HCFA Public Information Collection Requirements Submitted to the Office of Management and Budget (OMB) for Clearance (pertaining to Medicare uniform institutional provider bill; hospice survey and deficiencies report form; HMO financial information reports to members; hospital request for certification in Medicare and Medicaid form.)

59 FR 27023, May 25, 1994: HCFA Public Information Collection Requirements Submitted to the Office of Management and Budget (OMB) for Clearance (pertaining to Medicare beneficiary survey of influenza vaccination form; Medicaid integrated quality control review worksheet; post laboratory survey questionnaire form; and post laboratory survey questionnaire — surveyor form).

59 FR 50762, October 5, 1994: HCFA Public Information Collection Requirements Submitted to the Office of Management and Budget (OMB) for Clearance (pertaining to reimbursement of hospital costs for residents and interns, criteria for psychiatric and rehabilitation hospital units' reimbursement under the prospective payment system, disclosure of owners and managers of suppliers for fraud and abuse detection purposes, reimbursement of municipal health services clinics, survey form for hospital compliance with anti-dumping requirements, and evaluation of patient and physician satisfaction with the Medicare participating heart bypass center demonstration).

59 FR 54197, October 28, 1994: HCFA Public Information Collection Requirements Submitted to the Office of Management and Budget (OMB) for Clearance (pertaining to Medicare beneficiary surveys, estimated acquisition costs of injectable drugs, reconsideration of adverse determinations made on Part a claims, beneficiary and supplier or physician hearing requests, and compliance with hospital anti-dumping requirements).

59 FR 56116, November 10, 1994: Medicare and Medicaid Programs; Survey, Certification and Enforcement of Skilled Nursing Facilities and Nursing Facilities — Final rule affecting 42 CFR Parts 401, 431, 435, 440, 441, 442, 447, 483, 488, 489, and 498.

59 FR 62606, December 6, 1994: Medicare, Medicaid, and CLIA Programs; Extension of Certain Effective Dates for Clinical Laboratory Requirements and Personnel Requirements for Cytologists — Final rule with comment period, affecting 42 CFR Part 493.

59 FR 64141, December 13, 1994: Medicare and Medicaid Programs; Revisions to Conditions of Participation for Hospitals — Final rule affecting 42 CFR Parts 405 and 482.

59 FR 65482, December 20, 1994: Medicare Program; Medicare Coverage of Home Health Services, Medicare Conditions of Participation, and Home Health Aide Supervision — Final rule affecting 42 CFR Parts 409, 413, 418, and 484. See also correction at 60 FR 39122, August 1, 1995.

60 FR 130, January 3, 1995: HCFA; CLIA Program: Approval of the Joint Commission on Accreditation of Healthcare Organizations as an Accrediting Organization — Notice.

60 FR 7774, February 9, 1995: HCFA Public Information Collection Requirements Submitted to the Office of Management and Budget (OMB) for Clearance (pertaining to justification for ESRD composite rates for outpatient dialysis services, and home health agency compliance with health and safety requirements).

60 FR 12770, March 8, 1995: HCFA Public Information Collection Requirements Submitted to the Office of Management and Budget (OMB) for Clearance (pertaining to survey forms for compliance with CLIA; CLIA application forms for testing on human specimens, and forms for outcome-based quality assurance programs for home health agencies).

60 FR 21525, May 2, 1995: HCFA Public Information Collection Requirements Submitted to the Office of Management and Budget (OMB) for Clearance (pertaining to intermediary requests for information from skilled nursing facilities, reimbursement for CLIA compliance surveys, patient outcome data in home health agencies, common claim forms for Medicare/Medicaid reimbursement, and a study of childhood immunization costs).

60 FR 26445, May 17, 1995: HCFA Public Information Collection Requirements Submitted to the Office of Management and Budget (OMB) for Clearance (pertaining to Medicare/Medicaid psychiatric hospital survey data, and hospice requests for Medicare certification).

60 FR 37066, July 19, 1995: HCFA Public Information Collection Requirements Submitted to the Office of Management and Budget (OMB) for Clearance (pertaining to actuarial forecasts for Medicaid utilization and cost, employers identified through a match of IRS, SSA, and Medicare records for purposes of the Medicare Secondary Payer provision, health and safety requirements for portable X-ray suppliers, and evaluation of Intermediate Care Facilities for Persons

with Mental Retardation — establishing psychoactive drug use baselines).

60 FR 39403, August 2, 1995: HCFA Public Information Collection Requirements Submitted for Public Comment and Recommendations (pertaining to PRO reporting forms; Oregon Medicaid reform demonstration; review functions of PRO's; medical records review under PPS; evaluation of Medicare cataract surgery alternate payment demonstration; home health agency survey and deficiencies report; CLIA survey forms; field testing of uniform needs assessment instrument for hospital discharge planning).

60 FR 50115, September 28, 1995: Medicare and Medicaid Programs; Survey, Certification and Enforcement of Skilled Nursing Facilities and Nursing Facilities — Final rule and correction to final regulations, affecting 42 CFR Parts 431, 440, 442, 488, 489, and 498. See also corrections at 60 FR 52731, October 10, 1995, and at 60 FR 534456, October 13, 1995.

60 FR 50466, September 29, 1995: Medicare Program — Providers and Suppliers of Specialized Services: Technical Amendments — Final rule with comment period, affecting 42 CFR Parts 485 and 486. See also correction at 60 FR 53877, October 18, 1995.

60 FR 50630, September 29, 1995: HCFA Public Information Collection Requirements Submitted for Public Comment and Recommendations (pertaining to sole community home health agencies).

60 FR 55719, November 2, 1995: HCFA Public Information Collection Requirements Submitted for Public Comment and Recommendations (pertaining to evaluation of the Oregon Medicaid reform demonstration; field testing of the uniform needs assessment instrument for hospital discharge planning; survey of physician practice costs; evaluation of the Medicare cataract surgery alternate payment demonstration; and alternative CLIA quality assessment surveys).

60 FR 64167, December 14, 1995: HCFA Public Information Collection Requirements Submitted for Public Comment and Recommendations (pertaining to home health care; Medicare/Medicaid certification of physical therapy and speech pathology services; certification as suppliers of Portable X-ray Services; certification of organ procurement organizations; certification for physical therapists in independent practice; and approval as a hospital provider of extended care services (swing bed)).

61 FR 2255, January 25, 1996: HCFA Public Information Collection Requirements Submitted for Public Comment and Recommendations (pertaining to survey forms about health and safety requirements for physical therapists in independent practice; and national data reporting requirements for HMOs and CMPs).

61 FR 6645, February 21, 1996: HCFA Agency Information Collection Activities: Proposed Collection; Comment Request (pertaining to survey forms to evaluate Federally qualified health centers; and the Medicare Carrier provider/supplier application form).

61 FR 7012, February 23, 1996: HCFA Notice Submitted for Collection of Public Comment: Submission for OMB Review (pertaining to granting and withdrawing of deeming authority to private non-profit accreditation organizations and the Clinical Laboratory Improvement Act Exemption under State laboratory programs; and the rules for participation of home health agencies to participate as sole community home health agencies).

61 FR 14798, April 3, 1996: HCFA Agency Information Collection Activities: Proposed Collection; Comment Request (pertaining to statistical reports on medical care eligibility, payments and services under Medicaid; State survey agency lists of positions and schedule of equipment purchases; granting and withdrawing of deeming authority to national accreditation organizations; maximizing the effectiveness of home health care; requests for certification in the Medicare or Medicaid program to provide outpatient physical therapy and/or speech pathology services; physical therapists in independent practice; requests for provider approval as a hospital provider of extended care services (swing bed) under Medicare and Medicaid; and requests for designation as an organ procurement organization).

61 FR 16925, April 18, 1996: HCFA Agency Information Collection Activities: Proposed Collection; Comment Request (pertaining to Medicare participating physician or supplier agreements; and hospital conditions of participation).

61 FR 17710, April 22, 1996: HCFA Agency Information Collection Activities: Proposed Collection; Comment Request (pertaining to payment adjustments for sole community hospitals; conditions of participation for portable x-ray suppliers; and cost reports for independent rural health centers and freestanding Federally qualified health centers).

61 FR 25229, May 20, 1996: HCFA Agency Information Collection Activities: Proposed Collection; Comment Request (pertaining to

evaluation of the Oregon reform demonstration; evaluation of the per-episode home health prospective payment demonstration; and the blood bank inspection checklist instrument used by State agencies to determine compliance with CLIA).

61 FR 26914, May 29, 1996: HCFA Emergency Clearance: Public Information Collection Requirements Submitted to the Office of Management and Budget (OMB) (pertaining to re-designation, certification and recertification of organ procurement organizations).

61 FR 29406, June 10, 1996: HCFA Agency Information Collection Activities: proposed Collection; Comment Request (pertaining to end stage renal disease application and survey and certification report forms; withholding Medicare payments to recover Medicaid overpayments; acquisition, protection, and disclosure of PRO information; clinical laboratory certification and recertification survey forms; CLIA laboratory personnel report forms; prepaid health plan cost reports; Medicare credit balance reporting requirements; statement of deficiencies and plan of correction requirements for organ procurement organizations; Medicare/Medicaid hospital survey report forms; advance directive requirements for Medicare and Medicaid; payment adjustments for sole community hospitals; survey reports for physical therapists in independent practice; HMO and CMP national data reporting requirements; identification of extension units of outpatient physical therapy and outpatient speech pathology providers; and fire safety survey reports).

61 FR 30072, June 13, 1996: HCFA Agency Information Collection Activities: Proposed Collection; Comment Request (pertaining to conditions of coverage for organ procurement organizations).

61 FR 31141, June 19, 1996: HCFA Agency Information Collection Activities: Proposed Collection; Comment Request (pertaining to authorization agreements for electronic funds transfer; applications for health insurance under Medicare for individuals with chronic renal disease; CLIA application forms; forms for surveyors to evaluate laboratory survey processes; post laboratory survey questionnaires for laboratories to evaluate the survey process).

61 FR 34437, July 2, 1996: HCFA Agency Information Collection Activities: Submission for OMB Review; Comment Request (pertaining to Peer Review Organization procedures for reconsideration of initial decisions; Part B enrollment forms; certification of rural health clinics for Medicare participation; Medicaid utilization review requirements for home health agencies; State listings of Medicaid recipients in institutions and procedures for State inspection of care

review; procedures for disenrollment of beneficiaries from HMOs or CMPs; effectiveness of telemedicine services; formats for PROs to submit data to HCFA; and request for accelerated payments forms for providers).

61 FR 34855, July 3, 1996: HCFA Agency Information Collection Activities: Submission for OMB Review; Comment Request (pertaining to information collection requirements for hospital conditions of participation in Medicare).

61 FR 37487, July 18, 1996: HCFA Agency Information Collection Activities: Submission for OMB Review; Comment request (pertaining to cost reports for independent rural health centers and freestanding federally qualified health centers; and conditions of participation for portable x-ray suppliers).

61 FR 40847, August 6, 1996: HCFA Agency Information Collection Activities: Proposed Collection; Comment request (pertaining to survey and certification of comprehensive outpatient rehabilitation facilities (CORFs)).

61 FR 41417, August 8, 1996: HCFA Agency Information Collection Activities: Submission for OMB Review; Comment request (pertaining to prospective payment for home health care; and Medicare standards for hospices).

61 FR 42257, August 14, 1996: HCFA Proposals Submitted for Collection of Public Comment: Submission for OMB Review (pertaining to third-party liability in Medicaid programs; surveys of federally qualified health centers (FQHCs); distribution of Medicare information by hospitals; Medicare reimbursement for hospitals with a disproportionate share of Medicare inpatients; Medicaid quality control; and the National Payer Identifier).

61 FR 43373, August 22, 1996: HCFA Agency Information Collection Activities: Proposed Collection; Comment request (pertaining to hospital claims for inpatient care for statutorily excluded services; and hospice standards for Medicare participation).

61 FR 43374, August 22, 1996: HCFA Agency Information Collection Activities: Submission for OMB Review; Comment request (pertaining to conditions of participation for rehabilitation agencies and conditions for coverage for physical therapist in independent practice).

61 FR 46814, September 5, 1996: HCFA Agency Information Collection Activities: Submission for OMB Review; Comment request (pertaining to authorization agreements for electronic funds transfers; entitlement to Medicare for individuals with chronic renal

disease; application forms for clinical laboratories; and clinical laboratory survey questionnaires).

61 FR 47131, September 6, 1996: HCFA Agency Information Collection Activities: Submission for OMB Review; Comment request (pertaining to conditions of coverage for organ procurement organizations; and statements of deficiencies and plan of correction forms for organ procurement organizations).

61 FR 48157, September 12, 1996: HCFA Agency Information Collection Activities: Submission for OMB Review; Comment request (pertaining to authorization agreement for electronic funds transfer; entitlement to Medicare for individuals with chronic renal disease; application forms for clinical laboratories; and clinical laboratory survey forms).

61 FR 57688, November 7, 1996: HCFA Agency Information Collection Activities: Comment request (pertaining to clinical laboratory surveys; clinical laboratory personnel qualifications; Medicare/Medicaid hospital survey report forms; beneficiary disenrollment from HMOs and CMPs; survey reports for ambulatory surgical centers; the Medigap complaint database; and survey forms for comprehensive outpatient rehabilitation facilities).

61 FR 64913, December 9, 1996: HCFA Agency Information Collection Activities: Proposed Collection; Comment request (pertaining to survey report forms for ICF/MRs; and current Medicare beneficiary surveys).

61 FR 67041, December 19, 1996: Medicare Program; Recognition of the Ambulatory Surgical Center Standards of the Joint Commission on the Accreditation of Healthcare Organizations and the Accreditation Association for Ambulatory Health Care — Final notice.

62 FR 3902, January 27, 1997: HCFA Agency Information Collection Activities: Proposed Collection; Comment request (pertaining to hospice survey and deficiencies report form).

62 FR 7467, February 19, 1997: HCFA Agency Information Collection Activities: Proposed Collection; Comment request (pertaining to form for a hospital request for certification in the Medicare and Medicaid programs).

62 FR 8026, February 21, 1997: HCFA Agency Information Collection Activities: Proposed Collection; Comment request (pertaining to Clinical Laboratory Improvement Act adverse action extract).

62 FR 8252, February 24, 1997: HCFA Agency Information Collection Activities: Submission for OMB Review; Comment request (pertaining to conditions of participation for rural health clinics).

62 FR 8744, February 26, 1997: HCFA Agency Information Collection Activities: Submission for OMB Review; Comment request (pertaining to Medicare provider/supplier enrollment application).

62 FR 9435, March 3, 1997: Office of Inspector General: Publication of the OIG Model Compliance Plan for Clinical Laboratories — Notice.

62 FR 10285, March 6, 1997: HCFA Agency Information collection Activities: Submission for OMB Review; Comment request (pertaining to end stage renal disease (ESRD) application and survey and certification report form).

62 FR 11004, March 10, 1997: Medicare and Medicaid Programs; Revision of the Conditions of Participation for Home Health Agencies and Use of the Outcome and Assessment Information Set (OASIS) as Part of the Revised Conditions of Participation for Home Health Agencies — Introduction to proposed rules, affecting 42 CFR Part 484.

62 FR 11005, March 10, 1997: Medicare and Medicaid Programs; Conditions of Participation for Home Health Agencies — Proposed rule affecting 42 CFR Part 484. See also correction at 62 FR 11953, March 13, 1997.

62 FR 11035, March 10, 1997: Medicare and Medicaid Programs; Use of the OASIS as Part of the Conditions of Participation for Home Health Agencies — Proposed rule.

62 FR 11213, March 11, 1997: HCFA Agency Information Collection Activities: Proposed Collection; Comment request (pertaining to post-laboratory survey questionnaire).

62 FR 11214, March 11, 1997: HCFA Agency Information Collection Activities: Submission for OMB Review; Comment request (pertaining to intermediate care facility for the mentally retarded or persons with related conditions survey report forms).

62 FR 16863, April 8, 1997: HCFA Agency Information Collection Activities: Submission for OMB Review; Comment request (pertaining to hospice survey and deficiencies report form).

62 FR 23140, April 29, 1997: Office of Inspector General: Health Care Programs: Fraud and Abuse; Revised PRO Sanctions for Failing to Meet Statutory Obligations — Final rule.

62 FR 23251, April 29, 1997: Medicare Program: Initiative Involving Facilities that Furnish Hemodialysis Treatments — Notice.

62 FR 25855, May 12, 1997: Medicare, Medicaid, and CLIA Programs; Clinical Laboratory Requirements — Extension of Certain Effective Dates for Clinical Laboratory Requirements under CLIA — Final rule with comment period, affecting 42 CFR Part 493.

62 FR 31613, June 10, 1997: HCFA Agency Information Collection Activities: Submission for OMB Review; Comment request (pertaining to requests for hearing for Part B claims; requests for hearings for Part A benefits; requests for a Part A Medicare hearing by an administrative law judge; requests for a Part B Medicare hearing by an administrative law judge; and information about provider refunds when claims are denied by Medicare).

62 FR 32615, June 17, 1997: Medicare Program; Ambulance Services — Proposed rule affecting 42 CFR Parts 410 and 424.

62 FR 43931, August 18, 1997: Medicare and Medicaid Programs: Effective Dates of Provider Agreements and Supplier Approvals — Final rule affecting 42 CFR Parts 431, 442, 488, 489, and 498.

62 FR 45672, August 28, 1997: HCFA Agency Information Collection Activities: Proposed Collection; Comment request (pertaining to conditions of participation for home health agencies; and negative case action review process annual reports for States).

62 FR 48871, September 17, 1997: HCFA Agency Information Collection Activities: Proposed Collection; Comment request (pertaining to conditions of coverage of supplier of ESRD services).

62 FR 63551, December 1, 1997: HCFA Agency Information Collection Activities: Proposed Collection; Comment request (pertaining to conditions of coverage of suppliers of ESRD services).

62 FR 66119, December 17, 1997: HCFA Agency Information Collection Activities: Proposed Collection; Comment request (pertaining to clinical laboratory compliance inspections).

63 FR 291, January 5, 1998: Medicare and Medicaid Programs; Surety Bond and Capitalization Requirements for Home Health Agencies; Final rule affecting 42 CFR Parts 413, 440, 441, and 489.

63 FR 2926, January 20, 1998: Medicare Program; Additional Supplier Standards — Proposed rule affecting 42 CFR Part 424.

63 FR 7743, February 17, 1998: Medicare and Medicaid Programs; Hospital Conditions of Participation; Provider Agreements and Supplier Approval — Notice of extension of comment period, affecting 42 CFR Parts 416, 482, 485, and 489.

63 FR 8987, February 23, 1998: Office of Inspector General: Publication of the OIG Compliance Program for Hospitals — Notice.

63 FR 9844, February 26, 1998: HCFA Emergency Clearance: Public Information Collection Requirements Submitted to the Office of Management and Budget (OMB) (pertaining to development of an assessment system for post acute care).

63 FR 10730, March 4, 1998: Medicare and Medicaid Programs; Surety Bond Requirements for Home Health Agencies — Final rule affecting 42 CFR Parts 441 and 489.

63 FR 10732, March 4, 1998: Medicare and Medicaid Programs; Surety Bond Requirements for Home Health Agencies — Notice of Intent to Amend Regulations.

63 FR 10920, March 5, 1998: HCFA Emergency Clearance: Public Information Collection Requirements Submitted to the Office of Management and Budget (OMB) (pertaining to Medicare and other Federal health care program provider and supplier application forms).

63 FR 12474, March 13, 1998: HCFA Agency Information Collection Activities: Proposed Collection; Comment request (pertaining to hospice request for certification in the Medicare program and Medicare/Medicaid psychiatric hospital survey data).

63 FR 12474, March 13, 1998: HCFA Agency Information Collection Activities: Submission for OMB Review; Comment request (pertaining to requirements for clinical laboratory testing on human specimens).

63 FR 12475, March 13, 1998: HCFA Agency Information Collection Activities; Submission for OMB Review; Comment request (pertaining to HMO and CMP national data reporting requirements).

63 FR 12476, March 13, 1998: HCFA Agency Information Collection Activities: Submission for OMB Review; Comment request (pertaining to alternate quality assessment form for clinical laboratories with good performance records).

63 FR 14719, March 26, 1998: HCFA Agency Information Collection Activities: Proposed Collection; Comment request (pertaining to physician certification and re-certification in skilled nursing facilities).

63 FR 17429, April 9, 1998: Medicare, Medicaid, and CLIA Programs; Clinical Laboratory Improvement Amendments of 1988 Continuance of Approval as an Accrediting Organization; the Joint Commission on Accreditation of Healthcare Organizations, the American Association of Blood Banks, and the American Osteopathic Association — Notice.

63 FR 19502, April 20, 1998: HCFA Agency Information Collection Activities: Proposed collection; Comment request (pertaining to annual early and periodic screening, diagnostic, and treatment services (EPSDT) participation report; Medicare and other health care programs provider/supplier enrollment application; and research and analytic support for implementing performance measurement in Medicare fee for service).

63 FR 20415, April 24, 1998: Office of Inspector General: Publication of OIG Special Fraud Alert: Fraud and Abuse in Nursing Home Arrangements with Hospices — Notice.

63 FR 20652, April 27, 1998: HCFA Agency Information Collection Activities: Proposed Collection; Comment request (pertaining information collection requirements applicable to the obligation of hospitals to examine and treat emergency medical conditions and women in labor).

63 FR 23790, April 30, 1998: Medicare and Medicaid Programs; Recognition of the American Association for Accreditation of Ambulatory Surgery Facilities, Inc., for Ambulatory Surgical Centers — Proposed notice.

63 FR 25214, May 7, 1998: HCFA Agency Information Collection Activities: Proposed Collection; Comment request (pertaining to organ procurement organization statement of deficiencies and plan of correction forms).

63 FR 26722, May 14, 1998: HCFA CLIA Program; Simplifying CLIA Regulations Relating to Accreditation, Exemption of Laboratories under a State Licensure Program, Proficiency Testing, and Inspection — Final rule affecting 42 CFR Part 493. See also correction at 63 FR 32699, June 15, 1998.

63 FR 26810, May 14, 1998: HCFA Agency Information Collection Activities: Proposed Collection; Comment request (pertaining to development of an assessment system for post-acute care).

63 FR 28396, May 22, 1998: HCFA Privacy Act of 1974 — Notice of New System of Records (pertaining to the long term care minimum data set).

63 FR 29415, May 29, 1998: HCFA Agency Information Collection Activities: Submission for OMB Review; Comment request (pertaining to hospice request for certification in the Medicare program).

63 FR 29648, June 1, 1998: Medicare and Medicaid Programs; Surety Bond Requirements for Home Health Agencies — Final rule affecting 42 CFR Parts 441 and 489.

63 FR 31123, June 8, 1998: Medicare Program; Incentive Programs — Fraud and Abuse — Final rule affecting 42 CFR Part 420.

63 FR 32234, June 12, 1998: HCFA Agency Information Collection Activities: Submission for OMB Review; Comment request (pertaining to Medicare/Medicaid psychiatric hospital survey data).

63 FR 36250, July 2, 1998: HCFA Agency Information Collection Activities; Submission for OMB review; Comment request (pertaining to provider/supplier enrollment applications).

63 FR 37129, July 9, 1998: HCFA Agency Information Collection Activities; Submission for OMB Review; Comment request (pertaining to organ procurement organization requests for participation in Medicare and Medicaid).

63 FR 38413, July 16, 1998: HCFA Agency Information Collection Activities: Submission for OMB Review; Comment request (pertaining to Clinical Laboratory Improvement Act certification requirements; EPSDT participation reports; limitations on provider-related donations and health care-related taxes, and limitations on payments to disproportionate share hospitals; and Medicare+Choice provider sponsored organization waiver requests forms).

63 FR 42409, August 7, 1998: Office of Inspector General: Solicitation of Information and Recommendations for Developing OIG Compliance Program Guidance for the Durable Medical Equipment Industry — Notice.

63 FR 42410, August 7, 1998: Office of Inspector General: Publication of the OIG Compliance Program Guidance for Home Health Agencies — Notice.

63 FR 45076, August 24, 1998: Office of Inspector General-Publication of OIG Compliance Program Guidance for Clinical Laboratories.

63 FR 46676, September 2, 1998: Office of Inspector General: Health Care Programs; Fraud and Abuse; Revised OIG Exclusion Authorities Resulting from Public Law 104–191 — Final rule affecting 42 CFR Parts 1000, 1001, 1002, and 1005. See also correction at 63 FR 57918, October 29, 1998.

63 FR 46736, September 2, 1998: Office of Inspector General: Health Care Programs; Fraud and Abuse; Revised OIG Sanction Authorities Resulting from Public Law 105–33 — Notice of proposed rulemaking affecting 42 CFR 1001, 1002, and 1003.

63 FR 48734, September 11, 1998: HCFA Agency Information Collection Activities: Proposed Collection; Comment request (per-

taining to medical review activities under PPS by Peer Review Organizations; and survey and deficiency reports for home health agencies).

63 FR 50577, September 22, 1998: Office of Inspector General: Solicitation of Information and Recommendations for Developing OIG Compliance Program Guidance for Certain Medicare+Choice Organizations — Notice.

63 FR 58341, October 30, 1998: Office of Inspector General: Health Care Fraud and Abuse Data Collection Program: Reporting of Final Adverse Actions — Notice of proposed rulemaking under section 1128E of the Social Security Act, affecting 45 CFR 61.

63 FR 58399, October 30, 1998: Office of Inspector General: Publication of the OIG's Provider Self-Disclosure Protocol — Notice.

63 FR 63478, November 13, 1998: HCFA Agency Information Collection Activities: Proposed Collection; Comment request (pertaining to processing Medicare+Choice disenrollment requests from beneficiaries; creation of the Utilization and Quality Control Peer Review Organization; and rules for participation of HHA's in Medicare and review of plans of care for home health services).

63 FR 65601, November 27, 1998: HCFA Agency Information Collection Activities: Submission for OMB Review; Comment request (pertaining to medical records review under PPS; and home health agency survey and deficiencies reports, and home health functional assessment instruments).

63 FR 68687, December 14, 1998: Medicare and Medicaid Program; Civil Money Penalties, Assessments, Exclusions, and Related Appeals Procedures — Final rule with comment period, affecting 42 CFR 400 and 402.

63 FR 70137, December 18, 1998: Office of Inspector General: Solicitation of Information and Recommendations for Developing OIG Compliance Program Guidance for the Nursing Home Industry — Notice.

63 FR 72318, December 31, 1998: HCFA Agency Information Collection Activities: Proposed Collection; Comment request (pertaining to fire safety survey report forms for health care facilities).

1999

64 FR 69, January 4, 1999: Medicare Program; Negotiated Rulemaking; Coverage and Administrative Policies for Clinical Diagnostic Laboratory Tests — Notice of meetings.

64 FR 1024, January 7, 1999: HCFA Agency Information Collection Activities: Proposed Collection; Comment request (pertaining to granting and withdrawal of deeming authority to national accreditation organizations).

64 FR 1810, January 12, 1999: HCFA Agency Information Collection Activities: Proposed Collection; Comment request (pertaining to Medicaid eligibility quality control MEQC) samples; identification of extension units of outpatient physical therapy (OPT) and outpatient speech pathology (OSP) providers; request for certification in the Medicare and/or Medicaid program(s) to provide OPT or OSP services; and request for certification as a supplier of portable X-ray services under Medicare and/or Medicaid).

64 FR 2228, January 13, 1999: Office of Inspector General: Solicitation of Information and Recommendations for Developing OIG Compliance Program Guidance for the Hospice Industry— Notice.

64 FR 3303, January 21, 1999: HCFA Agency Information Collection Activities: Proposed Collection; Comment request (pertaining to on-site inspection for durable medical equipment suppliers).

64 FR 3748, January 25, 1999: Medicare and Medicaid Programs: Reporting Outcome and Assessment Information Set (OASIS) Data as Part of the Conditions of Participation for Home Health Agencies-Interim final rule with comment period, affecting 42 CFR Parts 484 and 488.

64 FR 3764, January 25, 1999: Medicare and Medicaid Programs: Comprehensive Assessment and Use of the OASIS as Part of the Conditions of Participation for Home Health Agencies— Final rule affecting 42 CFR Part 484.

64 FR 4435, January 28, 1999: Office of Inspector General: Draft Compliance Guidance for the Durable Medical Equipment, Prosthetics, Orthotics and Supply Industry—Notice and comment period.

64 FR 6664, February 10, 1999: HCFA Agency Information Collection Activities: Proposed Collection; Comment request (pertaining to Medicare agreement applications for health care prepayment plans).

64 FR 6664, February 10, 1999: HCFA Agency Information Collection Activities: Submission for OMB Review; Comment request (pertaining to skilled nursing facility (SNF) resident assessment MDS data).

64 FR 6665, February 10, 1999: HCFA Agency Information Collection Activities: Proposed Collection; Comment request (pertaining to sole community home health agencies (HHS)).

64 FR 10478, March 4, 1999: HCFA Agency Information Collection Activities: Proposed Collection; Comment request (pertaining to information collection requirements in final peer review organization (PRO) sanction regulations).

64 FR 10479, March 4, 1999: HCFA Agency Information Collection Activities: Proposed Collection; Comment request (pertaining to conditions of participation for portable X-ray suppliers).

64 FR 13354, March 18, 1999: Medicare and Medicaid Programs; Civil Money Penalties for Nursing Homes (SNF/NF), Change in Notice Requirements, and Expansion of Discretionary Remedy Delegation — Final rule with comment period, affecting 42 CFR Part 488.

64 FR 13997, March 23, 1999: HCFA Agency Information Collection Activities: Submission for OMB Review; Comment request (pertaining to Medicare and Medicaid requirements for advanced directives, and disclosure of ownership and financial control interest).

64 FR 14454, March 25, 1999: HCFA Agency Information Collection Activities: Submission for OMB Review; Comment request (pertaining to Medicaid eligibility quality control sampling; fire safety survey report forms; and income and eligibility verification systems under Medicaid).

64 FR 17673, April 12, 1999: HCFA Agency Information Collection Activities: Proposed Collection; Comment request (pertaining to Medicare participating physician or supplier agreements).

64 FR 19375, April 20, 1999: HCFA Agency Information Collection Activities: Proposed Collection; Comment request (pertaining to acquisition, protection, and disclosure of peer review organization (PRO) information).

64 FR 19376, April 20, 1999: Medicare Program; Recognition of the Community Health Accreditation Program, Inc. (CHAP) for Hospices).

64 FR 23846, May 4, 1999: HCFA Emergency Clearance: Public Information Collection Requirements Submitted to the Office of Management and Budget (OMB) (pertaining to the outcome and assessment information set (OASIS) for home health care agencies).

64 FR 23847, May 4, 1999: HCFA Agency Information Collection Activities: Submission for OMB Review; Comment request (pertaining to uniform needs assessment instrument (UNIA) for patients being discharged from Medicare-certified hospitals).

64 FR 24956, May 10, 1999: Medicare and Medicaid Programs; Effective Dates of Provider Agreements and Supplier Approvals-Correction restoring regulations inadvertently removed when a final rule concerning effective dates for provider agreements and supplier approvals was published at 62 FR 43931, August 18, 1997.

64 FR 25891, May 13, 1999: HCFA Agency Information Collection Activities: Submission for OMB Review; Comment request (pertaining to Medicare agreement application for health care prepayment plans under section 1833).

64 FR 25892, May 13, 1999: HCFA Agency Information Collection Activities: Submission for OMB Review; Comment request (pertaining to granting and withdrawal of deeming authority to national accreditation organizations).

64 FR 29048, May 28, 1999: HCFA Agency Information Collection Activities: Proposed Collection; Comment request (pertaining to certification as a rural health clinic).

64 FR 29050, May 28, 1999: HCFA Emergency Clearance: Public Information Collection Requirements Submitted to the Office of Management and Budget (OMB) (pertaining to the community mental health center site visit assessment tool).

64 FR 32239, June 16, 1999: HCFA Agency Information Collection Activities: Proposed Collection; Comment request (pertaining to conditions of coverage for organ procurement organizations).

64 FR 32240, June 16, 1999: HCFA Agency Information Collection Activities: Submission for OMB Review; Comment request (pertaining to conditions of participation for portable x-ray suppliers).

64 FR 32508, June 17, 1999: HCFA Agency Information Collection Activities: Submission for OMB Review; Comment Request (pertaining to the quality improvement system for managed care (QISMC)).

64 FR 32881, June 18, 1999: Medicare Program; Recognition of the Joint Commission for Accreditation of Healthcare Organizations (JCAHO) for Hospices — Final notice.

64 FR 32984, June 18, 1999: Medicare and Medicaid Programs; Mandatory Use, Collection, Encoding, and Transmission of Outcome and Assessment Information Set (OASIS) for Home Health Agencies — Notice.

64 FR 32992, June 18, 1999: HCFA Privacy Act of 1974; Report of New System (pertaining to a new system of records containing data on the physical, mental, functional, and psychosocial status of all patients receiving the services of home health agencies (HHAs) approved to participate in Medicare or Medicaid).

64 FR 36070, July 2, 1999: Medicare and Medicaid Programs; Hospital Conditions of Participation: Patient Rights — Interim final rule with comment, affecting 42 CFR 482.

64 FR 36368, July 6, 1999: Office of Inspector General Publication of OIG Compliance Program Guidance for the Durable Medical Equipment, Prosthetics, Orthotics and Supply Industry — Notice.

64 FR 36887, July 8, 1999: HCFA Agency Information Collection Activities: Proposed Collection; Comment request (pertaining to reporting outcome and assessment information data set (OASIS) as part of the conditions of participation for home health agencies).

64 FR 37142, July 9, 1999: HCFA Agency Information Collection Activities: Submission for OMB Review; Comment request (pertaining to request for certification in the Medicare/Medicaid program to provide outpatient physical therapy and/or speech-language pathology and the outpatient physcal therapy and/or speech-language pathology survey report form; request for certification as a supplier of portable X-ray services); and procedures for making national coverage decisions).

64 FR 38910, July 20, 1999: HCFA Agency Information Collection Activities: Proposed Collection; Comment request (pertaining to comprehensive outpatient rehabilitation facility (CORF) eligibility requirements).

64 FR 39150, July 21, 1999: Office of Inspector General; Draft OIG Compliance Program Guidance for Hospices — Notice and comment period.

64 FR 39517, July 22, 1999: HCFA Agency Information Collection Activities: Submission for OMB Review; Comment request (pertaining to Medicare participating physician or supplier agreement form HCFA-460).

64 FR 40888, July 28, 1999: HCFA Agency Information Collection Activities: Proposed Collection; Comment request (pertaining to community mental health center site visit assessment tool).

64 FR 41444, July 30, 1999: HCFA Agency Information Collection Activities: Proposed Collection; Comment request (pertaining to ambulatory surgical center survey report form).

64 FR 44030, August 12, 1999: HCFA Agency Information Collection Activites: Submission for OMB Review; Comment request (pertaining to blood bank inspection checklists and reports under CLIA; and Medicaid eligibility quality control).

64 FR 44031, August 12, 1999: HCFA Agency Information Collection Activites: Submission for OMB Review; Comment request

(pertaining to survey and certification of rural health clinics; and determining third party liability in Medicaid programs).

64 FR 45267, August 19, 1999: HCFA Agency Information Collection Activities: Submission for OMB Review; Comment request (pertaining to Medicare credit balance reporting requirements).

64 FR 46400, August 25, 1999: HCFA Agency Information Collection Activities: Proposed Collection; Comment request (pertaining to hospice information collection requirements).

64 FR 48846, September 8, 1999: Office of Inspector General: Solicitation of Information and Recommendations for Developing OIG Compliance Program Guidance for Individual Physicians and Small Group Practices — Notice.

64 FR 49196, September 10, 1999: HCFA Agency Information Collection Activities; Submission for OMB Review; Comment request (pertaining to conditions of coverage for organ procurement organizations).

64 FR 49197, September 10, 1999: Medicare and Medicaid Programs; Application of the Joint Commission for Accreditaton of Healthcare Organizations (JCAHO) for Continued Approval of Deeming Authority for Home Health Agencies — Proposed notice.

64 FR 49198, September 10, 1999: Medicare and Medicaid Programs; Application of the Community Health Accreditation Program, Incorporated, CHAP) for Continued Approval of Deeming Authority for Home Health Agencies — Proposed notice.

64 FR 49199, September 10, 1999: Medicare and Medicaid Programs; Reapplication of the American Osteopathic Association (AOA) for Continued Approval of Deeming Authority for Hospitals — Proposed notice.

64 FR 42791, September 30, 1999: Office of Inspector General; Publication of the OIG Special Advisory Bulletin on the Effect of Exclusion from Participation in Federal Health Care Programs — Notice. See also correction at 64 FR 55484, October 13, 1999.

64 FR 54031, October 5, 1999: Office of Inspector General; Publication of the OIG Compliance Program, Guidance for Hospices — Notice.

64 FR 57431, October 25, 1999: Medicare Program; Appeals of Carrier Determinations that a Supplier Fails to Meet the Requirements for Medicare Billing Privileges — Proposed rule affecting 42 CFR Part 405.

64 FR 57619, October 26, 1999: Office of Inspector General; Privacy Act; Exempt Record System, Pertaining to the Healthcare Integrity and Protection Data Bank (HIPDB) — Notice of proposed rulemaking affecting 45 CFR Part 5b.

64 FR 57740, October 26, 1999: Office of Inspector General; Healthcare Fraud and Abuse Data Collection Program: Reporting of Final Adverse Actions - Final rule affecting 45 CFR Part 61. See also correction at 65 FR 70506, November 24, 2000.

64 FR 58851, November 1, 1999: Office of Inspector General; Healthcare Integrity and Protection Data Bank: Announcement of Opening Date for Reporting and Self-query Fee — Notice.

64 FR 61353, November 10, 1999: Office of Inspector General/HCFA; OIG/HCFA Special Advisory Bulletin on the Patient Anti-dumping Statute.

64 FR 61893, November 15, 1999: Office of Inspector General; Publication of the OIG's Compliance Program Guidance for Medicare+Choice Organizations Offering Coordinated Care Plans — Notice.

64 FR 62679, November 17, 1999: HCFA Agency Information Collection Activities: Proposed Collection; Comment request (pertaining to hospital conditions of participation).

64 FR 62679, November 17, 1999: HCFA Agency Information Collection Activities: Proposed Collection; Comment request (pertaining to surveys of end stage renal disease facilities).

64 FR 62680, November 17, 1999: HCFA Agency Information Collection Activities: Submission for OMB Review; Comment request (pertaining to hospice care eligibility standards, reimbursement procedures, and conditions of participation).

64 FR 66482, November 26, 1999: HCFA Agency Information Collection Activities: Proposed Collection; Comment request (pertaining to resident assessment in skilled nursing facilities).

64 FR 67028, November 30, 1999: Medicare and Medicaid Programs; Religious Nonmedical Health Care Institutions and Advance Directives — Interim final rule with comment period, affecting 42 CFR Parts 403, 412, 431, 440, 442, 446, 456, 488, and 489.

64 FR 67223, December 1, 1999: Medicaid Program; External Quality Review of Medicaid Managed Care Organizations — Proposed rule affecting 42 CFR Parts 433 and 438.

64 FR 67918, December 3, 1999: HCFA Agency Information Collection Activities: Proposed Collection; Comment request (pertaining to conditions of participation for rural health clinics).

64 FR 69217, December 10, 1999: Office of Inspector General; Solicitation of New Safe Harbors and Special Fraud Alerts — Intent to develop regulations affecting 42 CFR Part 1001.

64 FR 69271, December 10, 1999: HCFA Agency Information Collection Activities: Proposed Collection; Comment request (pertaining to hospital providers of extender care (swing bed) services in Medicare and Medicaid).

64 FR 69272, December 10, 1999: HCFA Agency Information Collection Activities: Submission for OMB Review; Comment request (pertaining to community mental health center site visit assessment tools).

64 FR 69272, December 10, 1999: HCFA Agency Information Collection Activities: Submission for OMB Review; Comment request (pertaining to comprehensive outpatient rehabilitation facility (CORF) eligibility and survey forms).

64 FR 69273, December 10, 1999: HCFA Agency Information Collection Activities: Submission for OMB Review; Comment request (pertaining to Medicare/Medicaid hospital survey reports).

64 FR 69273, December 10, 1999: HCFA Agency Information Collection Activities: Submission for OMB Review; Comment request (pertaining to HCFA-377 ambulatory surgical center survey report form).

2000

65 FR 1400, January 10, 2000: HCFA Agency Information Collection Activities: Submission for OMB Review; Comment request (pertaining to reporting outcome and assessment information set (OASIS) data set as a condition of participation for HHAs).

65 FR 8722, February 22, 2000: Medicare and Medicaid Programs; Re-approval of the Deeming Authority of the Joint Commission on Accreditation of Healthcare Organizations (JCAHO) for Home Health Agencies (HHAs) — Final notice.

65 FR 8725, February 22, 2000: Medicare and Medicaid Programs; Reapproval of the Deeming Authority of the Community Health Accreditation Program, Incorporated (CHAP) for Home Health Agencies (HHAs) — Final notice.

65 FR 8727, February 22, 2000: Medicare and Medicaid Programs; Recognition of the American Osteopathic Association (AOA) for Continued Approval of Deeming Authority for Hospitals — Final notice.

65 FR 8983, February 23, 2000: HCFA Agency Information collection Activities: Submission for OMB Review; Comment request (pertaining to conditions of participation for rural health clinics).

65 FR 10450, February 28, 2000: Medicare Program; Rural Health Clinics: Amendments to Participation Requirements and Payment Provisions; and Establishment of a Quality Assessment and Performance Improvement Program — Proposed rule affecting 42 CFR Parts 405 and 491.

65 FR 11589, March 3, 2000: HCFA Agency Information Collection Activities: Submission for OMB Review: Comment request (pertaining to end stage renal disease medical information system/ESRD facility survey).

65 FR 12556, March 9, 2000: HCFA Agency Information Collection Activities: Proposed Collection; Comment request (pertaining to hospital request for certification in the Medicare/Medicaid program).

65 FR 14288, March 16, 2000: HCFA Agency Information Collection Activities: Proposed Collection; Comment request (pertaining to end stage renal disease application and survey and certification).

65 FR 14289, March 16, 2000: Office of Inspector General: Publication of the OIG Compliance Program Guidance for Nursing Facilities — Notice.

65 FR 25738, May 3, 2000: HCFA Emergency Clearance: Public Informatiion Collection Requirements Submitted to the Office of Management and Budget (OMB) (pertaining to the Medicare managed care CAHPS Survey).

65 FR 35652, June 5, 2000: HCFA Agency Information Collection Activities: Proposed Collection; Comment request (pertaining to hospital conditions of participation; identification of potential organ, tissue, and eye donors and transplant hospitals' provision of transplant-related data).

65 FR 35653, June 5, 2000: HCFA Agency Information Collection Activities: Proposed Collection; Comment request (pertaining to ICF/MR survey forms).

65 FR 35654, June 5, 2000: HCFA Agency Information Collection Activities: Submission for OMB Review; Comment request (pertaining to hospital request for certification in Medicare and Medicaid).

65 FR 36818, June 12, 2000: Office of Inspector General: Draft OIG Compliance Program for Individual and Small Group Physician Practices — Notice and comment period.

65 FR 37566, June 15, 2000: HCFA Agency Information Collection Activities: Submission for OMB Review; Comment request (pertaining to hospice survey and deficiencies report form).

65 FR 40111, June 29, 2000: HCFA Agency Information Collection Activities: Proposed Collection; comment request (pertaining to qualification applications for prepaid health plans (HMOs).

65 FR 40112, June 29, 2000: Medicare Program: Medicare+Choice Deeming Authority — Notice regarding accrediting organizations.

65 FR 40170, June 29, 2000: Medicare Program; Medicare+Choice Program - Final rule with comment period, affecting 42 CFR parts 417 and 422. See also correction at 65 FR 59748, October 6, 2000.

65 FR 45992, July 26, 2000: HCFA Agency Information Collection Activities: Proposed Collection; Comment request (pertaining to psychiatric unit, rehabilitation unit, and rehabilitation hospital criteria worksheets).

65 FR 47739, August 3, 2000: HCFA Agency Information Collection Activities: Submission for OMB Review; Comment request (pertaining to CLIA adverse action extract).

65 FR 50204, August 17, 2000: Office of Inspector General: Solicitation of Information and Recommendations for Developing a Compliance Risk Guidance for the Ambulance Industry — Notice.

65 FR 50312, August 17, 2000: HCFA; Health Insurance Reform: Standards for Electronic Transactions — Final rule affecting 45 CFR Parts 160 and 162.

65 FR 53319, September 1, 2000: HCFA Agency Information Collection Activities: Proposed Collection; Comment request (pertaining to incentive arrangement disclosure form for managed care organizations and their related medical groups and physicians).

65 FR 53727, September 5, 2000: HCFA Agency Information Collection Activities: Proposed Collection; Comment request (pertaining to ambulance services reimbursement request form for physicians, suppliers, and beneficiaries).

65 FR 53963, September 6, 2000: Medicare Program: Appeals of Carrier Determinations that a Physician or Other Supplier Fails to Meet the Requirements for Medicare Billing Privileges; Reopening of Comment Period — Notice of reopening of comment period for proposed rule affecting 42 CFR Part 405.

65 FR 54857, September 11, 2000: HCFA Agency Information Collection Activities: Submission for OMB Review; Comment request (pertaining to ICF/MR survey report forms).

65 FR 54857, September 11, 2000: HCFA Agency Information Collection Activities: Submission for OMB Review; Comment request (pertaining to hospital conditions of participation-identification of potential organ, tissue, and eye donors, and transplant hospitals' provision of transplant-related data).

65 FR 57195, September 21, 2000: HCFA Agency Information Collection Activities; Proposed Collection; Comment request (pertaining to Medicare managed care CAHPS survey for quality of care purposes).

65 FR 58279, September 28, 2000: HCFA Agency Information Collection Activities: Proposed Collection; Comment request (pertaining to Medicare consumer assessment survey of health plans-CAHPS).

65 FR 59431, October 5, 2000: HCFA Agency Information Collection Activities: Proposed Collection; Comment request (pertaining to conditions for coverage of suppliers of end stage renal disease services).

65 FR 59432, October 5, 2000: HCFA Agency Information Collection Activities: Submission for OMB Review; Comment request (pertaining to end stage renal disease application and survey and certification report).

65 FR 59434, October 5, 2000: Office of Inspector General Compliance Program for Individual and Small Group Physician Practices — Notice.

65 FR 60105, October 10, 2000: Medicaid Program; Home and Community-based Services — Final rule with comment period, affecting 42 CFR Parts 440 and 441.

65 FR 60366, October 11, 2000: Medicare Program; Additional Supplier Standards — Final rule with comment period, affecting 42 CFR Part 424.

65 FR 61171, October 16, 2000: HCFA Agency Information Collection Activities: Submission for OMB Review; Comment request (pertaining to psychiatric unit, rehabilitation unit, and rehabilitation hospital criteria worksheets).

65 FR 63035, October 20, 2000: Office of Inspector General: Medicare and State Health Care Programs: Fraud and Abuse; Revisions and Technical Corrections — Proposed rule affecting 42 CFR Parts 1001, 1003, 1005, and 1008.

65 FR 65860, November 2, 2000: HCFA Agency Information Collection Activities: Proposed Collection; Comment request (pertaining

to reporting outcome and assessment (OASIS) data as part of conditions of participation for home health agencies).

65 FR 65861, November 2, 2000: HCFA Agency Information Collection Activities: Proposed Collection; Comment request (pertaining to conflict of interest disclosure requirements for Medicare program integrity).

65 FR 69416, November 16, 2000: Medicare and Medicaid Programs; Hospital Conditions of Participation: Laboratory Services — Proposed rule affecting 42 CFR Part 482.

65 FR 69942, November 21, 2000: HCFA Agency Information Collection Activities: Proposed Collection; Comment request (pertaining to restraints/seclusion death reporting by hospitals).

65 FR 76647, December 7, 2000: HCFA Agency Information Collection Activities: Proposed Collection; Comment request (pertaining to alternate quality assessment survey in lieu of onsite survey for CLIA labs with good performance).

65 FR 78124, December 14, 2000: Office of Inspector General: Solicitation of New Safe Harbors and Special Fraud Alerts — Notice of intent to develop regulations.

65 FR 79867, December 20, 2000: HCFA Agency Information Collection Activities: Proposed Collection; Comment request (pertaining to home health Medicare conditions of participation information collection requirements).

65 FR 79867, December 20, 2000: HCFA Agency Information Collection Activities: Proposed Collection; Comment request (pertaining to quality improvement system for managed care).

65 FR 79868, December 20, 2000: HCFA Agency Information Collection Activities: Proposed Collection; Comment request (pertaining to Medicare consumer assessment survey of health plans).

65 FR 81813, December 27, 2000: Medicare Program; Requirements for the Re-credentialing of Medicare+Choice Organization Providers — Proposed rule affecting 42 CFR Part 422.

65 FR 82941, December 29, 2000: Medicare, Medicaid, and CLIA Programs; Extension of Certain Effective Dates for Clinical Laboratory Requirements under CLIA — Final rule with comment period, affecting 42 CFR Part 493.

2001

66 FR 2912, January 12, 2001: HCFA Agency Information Collection Activities: Proposed Collection; Comment request (pertaining to

clinical laboratory ICRs contained in supporting regulations at 42 CFR section 493.1–.2001).

66 FR 4674, January 18, 2001: Medicare and Medicaid Programs; Hospital Conditions of Participation: Anesthesia—Final rule affecting 42 CFR Parts 416, 482, and 485.

66 FR 6629, January 22, 2001: HCFA Agency Information Collection Activities: Submission for OMB Review; Comment request (pertaining to Medicare Integrity Program Organizational Conflict of Interest Disclosure Certificate).

66 FR 7147, January 22, 2001: Medicaid Program; Use of Restraint and Seclusion in Psychiatric Residential Treatment Facilities Providing Psychiatric Services to Individuals Under Age 21—Final rule affecting 42 CFR Parts 441 and 483.

66 FR 7919, January 26, 2001: HCFA Agency Information Collection Activities: Proposed Collection; Comment request (pertaining to provider Medicare agreements).

66 FR 8807, February 2, 2001: HCFA Agency Information Collection Activities: Proposed Collection; Comment request (pertaining to Medicare Federal health care programs provider/supplier enrollment application).

66 FR 9587, February 8, 2001: HCFA Agency Information Collection Activities: Proposed Collection; Comment request (pertaining to a project to develop an outcome–reporting of restraints and seclusion deaths by hospitals).

66 FR 13546, March 6, 2001: HCFA Agency Information Collection Activities: Proposed Collection; Comment request (pertaining to independent diagnostic testing facility documentation of proficiency of medical personnel and resources).

66 FR 13547, March 6, 2001: HCFA Agency Information Collection Activities: Proposed Collection; Comment request (pertaining to Medicare/Medicaid psychiatric hospital survey data).

66 FR 13547, March 6, 2001: HCFA Agency Information Collection Activities: Proposed Collection; Comment request (pertaining to hospice request for certification as a provider).

66 FR 14157, March 9, 2001: HCFA Agency Information Collection Activities: Submission for OMB review; Comment request (pertaining to home health Medicare conditions of participation information collection requirements).

66 FR 14157, March 9, 2001: HCFA Agency Information Collection Activities: Submission for OMB review; Comment request (pertaining to alternate quality assessment form for CLIA compliance).

66 FR 14906, March 14, 2001: Medicare and Medicaid Programs; Recognition of the American Osteopathic Association for Ambulatory Surgical Centers Program—Proposed notice.

66 FR 15800, March 21, 2001: Medicare Program; Use of Restraint and Seclusion in Residential Treatment Facilities Providing Inpatient Psychiatric Services to Individuals under Age 21: Delay of effective date, affecting 42 CFR Parts 441 and 483.

66 FR 16480, March 26, 2001: HCFA Agency Information Collection Activities; Proposed Collection; Comment request (pertaining to conditions of coverage of suppliers of end stage renal disease services). See also correction at 66 FR 18096, April 5, 2001.

66 FR 18645, April 10, 2001: HCFA Agency Information Collection Activities: Submission for OMB Review; Comment request (pertaining to Medicare and Medicaid outcome and assessment information set (OASIS) as part of the conditions of participation for home health agencies).

66 FR 18647, April 10, 2001: HCFA Agency Information Collection Activities: Submission for OMB Review; Comment request (pertaining to CLIA compliance).

66 FR 18958, April 12, 2001: HCFA Agency Information Collection Activities: Submission for OMB Review; Comment request (pertaining to information collection requirements for ambulance services).

66 FR 18959, April 12, 2001: HCFA Agency Information Collection Activities: Submission for OMB Review; Comment request (pertaining to organ procurement organization requests for designation).

66 FR 19507, April 16, 2001: HCFA Agency Information Collection Activities: Proposed Collection; Comment request (pertaining to conflict of interest and ownership and control information form).

66 FR 19508, April 16, 2001: HCFA Agency Information Collection Activities: Proposed Collection; Comment request (pertaining to on site inspection for durable medical equipment (DME) suppliers).

66 FR 19509, April 16, 2001: Medicare and Medicaid Programs; Application by the American Osteopathic Association (AOF) for Approval of Deeming Authority for Critical Access Hospitals—Proposed notice.

66 FR 20315, April 20, 2001: HCFA Agency Information Collection Activities: Proposed Collection; Comment request (pertaining to inpatient rehabilitation assessment instrument).

66 FR 20315, April 20, 2001: HCFA Agency Information Collection Activities: Submission for OMB Review; Comment request (pertaining to DMEPOS supplier standards).

66 FR 20316, April 20, 2001: HCFA Agency Information Collection Activities: Submission for OMB Review; Comment request (pertaining to DMEPOS supplier survey).

66 FR 20997, April 26, 2001: HCFA Agency Information Collection Activities: Submission for OMB Review; Comment request (pertaining to health insurance provider agreement form).

66 FR 22242, May 3, 2001: HCFA Agency Information Collection Activities: Proposed Collection; Comment request (pertaining to CLIA certification requirements).

66 FR 23944, May 10, 2001: HCFA Agency Information Collection Activities: Proposed Collection; Comment request (pertaining to examination and treatment for emergency conditions and women in labor).

66 FR 27598, May 18, 2001: Medicare and Medicaid Programs; Hospital Conditions of Participation; Anesthesia Services: Delay of Effective Date—Notice of final rule affecting 42 CFR Parts 416, 482, and 485.

66 FR 28110, May 22, 2001: Medicaid Program; Use of Restraint and Seclusion in Psychiatric Residential Treatment Facilities Providing Inpatient Psychiatric Services to Individuals under Age 21—Interim final rule, amendment and clarification with request for comment, affecting 42 CFR Parts 441 and 483.

66 FR 33102, June 20, 2001: HCFA Agency Information Collection Activities; Submission for OMB Review; Comment request (pertaining to provider/supplier enrollment application form).

66 FR 34223, June 27, 2001: Medicare Program; Application by the American Diabetes Association (ADA) for Recognition as a National Accreditation Program for Accrediting Entities that Furnish Outpatient Diabetes Self–management Training—Proposed notice.

See § 2:32.

§ 6:33 FAILURE BY HOSPITALS TO MAKE TIMELY REVIEW OF LONG-STAY CASES — Section 1866(d) [42 U.S.C.A. 1395cc(d)]

◆ NOTE: Nursing facilities formerly had review obligations. See § 2:33.

Regulations

42 CFR Part 402 — Civil Money Penalties, Assessments, and Exclusions

42 CFR Part 409 — Hospital Insurance Benefits

42 CFR Part 424 — Conditions for Medicare Payment

42 CFR Part 440 — Services: General Provisions [Medicaid]

42 CFR Part 442 — Standards for Payment for Nursing Facilities and Intermediate Care Facilities for the Mentally Retarded

42 CFR Part 447 — Payment for Services [Medicaid]

42 CFR Part 456 — Utilization Control

42 CFR Part 476 — Utilization and Quality Control Review

42 CFR Part 482 — Conditions of Participation for Hospitals

42 CFR Part 483 — Requirements for States and Long Term Care Facilities

42 CFR Part 488 — Survey, Certification, and Enforcement Procedures

42 CFR Part 489 — Provider Agreements and Supplier Approval

42 CFR Part 498 — Appeals Procedures for Determinations that Affect Participation in the Medicare Program and for Determinations that Affect the Participation of ICF's/MR and Certain NF's in the Medicaid Program

54 FR 5316, February 2, 1989: Medicare and Medicaid; Requirements for Long Term Care Facilities — Final rule with comment period, amending 42 CFR Parts 405, 442, 447, 483, 488, 489, and 498. See also delay in effective date at 54 FR 29717, July 14, 1989; corrections at 54 FR 8361, February 27, 1989, and 54 FR 37466, September 11, 1989; and final rule delaying effective date from January 1, 1990, to October 1, 1990, at 54 FR 53611, December 29, 1989.

55 FR 10951, March 23, 1990: Medicare and Medicaid Programs; Preadmission Screening and Annual Resident Review — Proposed rule to amend 42 CFR Parts 405, 431, and 483.

55 FR 42907, October 24, 1990: Medicare Program; Standards Applied by Utilization and Quality Control Peer Review Organizations: Consideration of Remote Rural Location and Other Relevant Factors — Notice of policy and request for comments.

56 FR 48826, September 26, 1991: Medicare and Medicaid; Requirements for Long Term Care Facilities — Final rule affecting 42 CFR Parts 422, 447, 483, 488, 489, and 498. See also correction at 57 FR 43922, September 23, 1992.

56 FR 54539, October 22, 1991: Medicare Program; Swing-Bed Program Changes — Final rule affecting 42 CFR Parts 413, 482, 483.

56 FR 55382, October 25, 1991: Medicare Program; Essential Access Community Hospitals (EACHs) and Rural Primary Care Hospitals (RPCHs) — Proposed rule affecting 42 CFR Parts 400, 409, 410, 411, 412, 413, 424, 440, 485, 488, 489. See also final rule affecting those parts and Part 498 at 58 FR 30630, May 26, 1993.

57 FR 4516, February 5, 1992: Medicare and Medicaid Programs; Omnibus Nursing Home Requirements — Proposed rule affecting 42 CFR Parts 418, 440, 441, 482, 483, and 488. See also correction at 57 FR 8961, March 13, 1992.

57 FR 46865, October 13, 1992: HCFA Public Information Collection Requirements Submitted to the Office of Management and Budget for Clearance (pertaining to impact of home health care plan management and evaluation; end-stage renal disease medical case review; Medicare/Medicaid hospital swing-bed survey report form; quarterly Medicaid statement of expenditures; Medicaid program budget report; information collection requirements in final peer review organization sanction regulations; appeals procedures for determinations that affect participation in Medicare; request for medical review information for Part B intermediary outpatient therapy bills and other Part B outpatient bills; and Medicaid limitations on provider-related donations and health care-related taxes, and limitations on payment to disproportionate share hospitals).

57 FR 53572, November 12, 1992: Medicare and Medicaid; Charges to Residents' Funds in Nursing Homes — Final rule affecting 42 CFR Part 483.

57 FR 54710, November 20, 1992: Medicaid Program; Elimination of Certain Written Documentation Pertaining to Medicaid Long-Term Care Facilities — Final rule affecting 42 CFR Part 442.

57 FR 56450, November 30, 1992: Medicare and Medicaid Programs; Preadmission Screening and Annual Resident Review — Final rule with comment period, affecting 42 CFR Parts 405, 431, 433, and 483. See also correction published at 58 FR 25784, April 28, 1993.

57 FR 61614, December 28, 1992: Medicare and Medicaid; Resident Assessment in Long Term Care Facilities — Proposed rule affecting 42 CFR Parts 456 and 483.

58 FR 30630, May 26, 1993: Medicare Program; Essential Access Community Hospitals (EACHs) and Rural Primary Care Hospitals

(RPCHs)—Final rule affecting 42 CFR Parts 400, 409, 410, 411, 412, 413, 424, 440, 485, 488, 489, and 498. See also correction at 58 FR 49934, September 24, 1993.

58 FR 59270, November 8, 1993: HCFA Public Information Collection Requirements Submitted to the Office of Management and Budget (OMB) for Clearance (pertaining to formats for utilization and quality control peer review organizations (PROs); home health agency plan of treatment forms; State survey agency budget expenditure report and certification workload report; home health agency cost report; recordkeeping requirements in provider reimbursement manual; quarterly Medicaid statement of expenditures; Medicare contract application for Federally qualified health maintenance organizations; hospice survey and deficiencies report form; organ procurement agency/histocompatibility laboratory statement of reimbursable costs)—Notice.

60 FR 39403, August 2, 1995: HCFA Public Information Collection Requirements Submitted for Public Comment and Recommendations (pertaining to PRO reporting forms; Oregon Medicaid reform demonstration; review functions of PRO's; medical records review under PPS; evaluation of Medicare cataract surgery alternate payment demonstration; home health agency survey and deficiencies report; CLIA survey forms; field testing of uniform needs assessment instrument for hospital discharge planning).

60 FR 55719, November 2, 1995: HCFA Public Information Collection Requirements Submitted for Public Comment and Recommendations (pertaining to evaluation of the Oregon Medicaid reform demonstration; field testing of the uniform needs assessment instrument for hospital discharge planning; survey of physician practice costs; evaluation of the Medicare cataract surgery alternate payment demonstration; and alternative CLIA quality assessment surveys).

61 FR 14798, April 3, 1996: HCFA Agency Information Collection Activities: Proposed Collection; Comment Request (pertaining to statistical reports on medical care eligibility, payments and services under Medicaid; State survey agency lists of positions and schedule of equipment purchases; granting and withdrawing of deeming authority to national accreditation organizations; maximizing the effectiveness of home health care; requests for certification in the Medicare or Medicaid program to provide outpatient physical therapy and/or speech pathology services; physical therapists in independent practice; requests for provider approval as a hospital

provider of extended care services (swing bed) under Medicare and Medicaid; and requests for designation as an organ procurement organization).

61 FR 16925, April 18, 1996: HCFA Agency Information Collection Activities: Proposed Collection; Comment Request (pertaining to Medicare participating physician or supplier agreements; and hospital conditions of participation).

61 FR 17677, April 22, 1996: Medicare and Medicaid Programs; New Payment Methodology for Routine Extended Care Services Provided in a Swing-bed Hospital — Proposed rule affecting 42 CFR Part 413.

61 FR 35231, July 5, 1996: HCFA Agency Information Collection Activities: Proposed Collection; Comment Request (pertaining to Medicaid payment standards for inpatient hospital or long-term care services).

61 FR 38395, July 24, 1996: Medicaid Program; Medicaid Eligibility Quality Control, Progressive Reductions in Federal Financial Participation for FYs 1982–1984, Payment for Physician Billing for Clinical Laboratory Services, and Utilization Control of Skilled Nursing Facility Services: Removal of Obsolete Requirements — Final rule.

61 FR 46466, September 3, 1996: Medicare Program; Schedule of Prospectively Determined Payment Rates for Skilled Nursing Facility Inpatient Routine Service Costs — Final rule with comment period.

61 FR 51295, October 1, 1996: HCFA Public Information Requirements Submitted for Collection of Public Comment: Submission for OMB Review (pertaining to approval of Medicaid payment rates for inpatient hospital or long term care services).

61 FR 51611, October 3, 1996: Medicare and Medicaid Programs; New Payment Methodology for Routine Extended Care Services Provided in a Swing-bed Hospital — Final Rule affecting 42 CFR Part 413. See also correction at 61 FR 58631, November 18, 1996.

61 FR 54209, October 17, 1996: HCFA Agency Information Collection Activities: Proposed Collection; Comment request (pertaining to hospital eligibility for swing-bed status).

63 FR 8987, February 23, 1998: Office of Inspector General: Publication of the OIG Compliance Program for Hospitals — Notice.

63 FR 9844, February 26, 1998: HCFA Emergency Clearance: Public Information Collection Requirements Submitted to the Office

of Management and Budget (OMB) (pertaining to development of an assessment system for post acute care).

63 FR 14719, March 26, 1998: HCFA Agency Information Collection Activities: Proposed Collection; Comment request (pertaining to physician certification and re-certification in skilled nursing facilities).

63 FR 20415, April 24, 1998: Office of Inspector General: Publication of OIG Special Fraud Alert: Fraud and Abuse in Nursing Home Arrangements with Hospices — Notice.

63 FR 26810, May 14, 1998: HCFA Agency Information Collection Activities: Proposed Collection; Comment request (pertaining to development of an assessment system for post-acute care).

63 FR 28395, May 22, 1998: HCFA Agency Information Collection Activities: Submission for OMB Review; Comment request (pertaining to physician certifications and recertifications in skilled nursing facilities).

63 FR 28396, May 22, 1998: HCFA Privacy Act of 1974 — Notice of New System of Records (pertaining to the long term care minimum data set).

1999

64 FR 3304, January 21, 1999: HCFA Agency Information Collection Activities: Proposed Collection; Comment request (pertaining to field testing of the uniform needs assessment instrument for patients discharged from hospitals).

64 FR 13998, March 23, 1999: Medicare Program; Medicare Coordinated Care Demonstration Project and Request for Information on Potential Best Practices of Coordinated Care-Solicitation of comments.

64 FR 18624, April 15, 1999: HCFA Agency Information Collection Activities: Proposed Collection; Comment request (pertaining to classification system for patients in inpatient rehabilitation hospitals and exempt rehabilitation units).

64 FR 23847, May 4, 1999: HCFA Agency Information Collection Activities: Submission for OMB Review; Comment request (pertaining to uniform needs assessment instrument (UNIA) for patients being discharged from Medicare-certified hospitals).

64 FR 42610, August 5, 1999: Medicare Program; Revision of the Procedures for Requesting Exceptions to Cost Limits for Skilled Nursing Facilities and Elimination of Reclassifications — Final rule. See also correction at 65 FR 60104, October 10, 2000.

64 FR 55949, October 15, 1999: HCFA Agency Information Collection Activities: Proposed Collection; Comment request (pertaining to physician certifications and re-certifications about the necessity for skilled nursing facility care).

2000

65 FR 2186, January 13, 2000: HCFA Agency Information Collection Activities; Submission for OMB Review; Comment request (pertaining to physician certifications/re-certifications in skilled nursing facilities).

65 FR 35652, June 5, 2000: HCFA Agency Information Collection Activities: Proposed Collection; Comment request (pertaining to hospital conditions of participation; identification of potential organ, tissue, and eye donors and transplant hospitals' provision of transplant-related data).

65 FR 35654, June 5, 2000: HCFA Agency Information Collection Activities: Submission for OMB Review; Comment request (pertaining to hospital request for certification in Medicare and Medicaid).

65 FR 50548, August 18, 2000: HCFA Privacy Act of 1974; Report of New System (pertaining to Medicare Provider Analysis and Review (MEDPAR) of all services rendered to a beneficiary from admission to discharge for hospital inpatient and SNF stays).

65 FR 54857, September 11, 2000: HCFA Agency Information Collection Activities: Submission for OMB Review; Comment request (pertaining to ICF/MR survey report forms).

65 FR 60151, October 10, 2000: Medicaid Program; Revision to Medicaid Upper Payment Limit Requirements for Hospital Services, Nursing Facility Services, Intermediate Care Facility Services for the Mentally Retarded, and Clinic Services — Proposed rule affecting 42 CFR Part 447.

65 FR 64227, October 26, 2000: HCFA Agency Information Collection Activities: Proposed Collection; Comment Request; Public Information Collection Meeting to Discuss Proposed Revisions (pertaining to notice requirements from suppliers, physicians, and practitioners to beneficiaries when Medicare Part B payment may be denied).

2001

66 FR 7919, January 26, 2001: HCFA Agency Information Collection Activities: Proposed Collection; Comment request (pertaining to provider Medicare agreements).

66 FR 20316, April 20, 2001: HCFA Agency Information Collection Activities: Submission for OMB Review; Comment request (pertaining to advance beneficiary notice by physicians, practitioners, suppliers, and providers about items and services denied by Medicare as not reasonable and necessary).

66 FR 33102, June 20, 2001: HCFA Agency Information Collection Activities; Submission for OMB Review; Comment request (pertaining to provider/supplier enrollment application form).

See § 2:33.

§ 6:34 FAILURE BY HOSPITALS TO HAVE ARRANGEMENTS WHICH PRECLUDE CERTAIN PRACTITIONERS AND SUPPLIERS FROM SEEKING FURTHER PAYMENT FROM BENEFICIARIES — Section 1866(g) [42 U.S.C.A. 1395cc(g)]

Regulations

42 CFR Part 402 — Civil Money Penalties, Assessments, and Exclusions

42 CFR Part 405, Subpart D — Principles of Reimbursement for Services by Hospital-Based Physicians; and Subpart E — Criteria for Determination of Reasonable Charges

42 CFR Part 415 — Services Furnished by Physicians in Providers, Supervising Physicians in Teaching Settings, and Residents in Certain Settings

42 CFR Part 420 — Program Integrity: Medicare

42 CFR Part 482 — Conditions of Participation for Hospitals

42 CFR Part 488 — Survey, Certification, and Enforcement Procedures

42 CFR Part 489 — Provider Agreements and Supplier Approval

42 CFR Part 498 — Appeals Procedures for Determinations that Affect Participation in the Medicare Program and for Determinations that Affect the Participation of ICF's/MR and Certain NF's in the Medicaid Program

42 CFR Chapter V — Office of Inspector General — Health Care, Department of Health and Human Services

Subchapter A — General Provisions
Part 1000 — Introduction; General Definitions
Subchapter B — OIG Authorities
Part 1001 — Program Integrity: Medicare and State Health Care Programs
Part 1003 — Civil Money Penalties, Assessments and Exclusions
Part 1004 — Imposition of Sanctions on Health Care Practitioners and Providers of Health Care Services by a Peer Review Organization
Part 1005 — Appeals of Exclusions, Civil Money Penalties and Assessments
Part 1006 — Investigational Inquiries
Part 1007 — State Medicaid Fraud Control Units
Part 1008 — Advisory Opinions by the OIG
See § 2:34.

§ 6:35 FAILURE BY HOSPITALS AND CERTAIN PHYSICIANS TO EXAMINE AND TREAT PERSONS FOR EMERGENCY MEDICAL CONDITIONS AND WOMEN IN LABOR — Section 1867 [42 U.S.C.A. 1395(dd)]

Regulations

42 CFR Part 482 — Conditions of Participation for Hospitals
42 CFR Part 488 — Survey, Certification, and Enforcement Procedures
42 CFR Part 489 — Provider Agreementsand Supplier Approval
42 CFR Part 498 — Appeals Procedures for Determinations that Affect Participation in the Medicare Program and for Determinations that Affect the Participation of ICF's/MR and Certain NF's in the Medicaid Program
42 CFR Chapter V — Office of Inspector General — Health Care, Department of Health and Human Services
Subchapter A — General Provisions
Part 1000 — Introduction; General Definitions
Subchapter B — OIG Authorities
Part 1001 — Program Integrity: Medicare and State Health Care Programs
Part 1003 — Civil Money Penalties, Assessments and Exclusions

Part 1004 — Imposition of Sanctions on Health Care Practitioners and Providers of Health Care Services by a Peer Review Organization

Part 1005 — Appeals of Exclusions, Civil Money Penalties and Assessments

Part 1006 — Investigational Inquiries

Part 1007 — State Medicaid Fraud Control Units

42 CFR Part 415 — Services Furnished by Physicians in Providers, Supervising Physicians in Teaching Settings, and Residents in Certain Settings

55 FR 42907, October 24, 1990: Medicare Program; Standards Applied by Utilization and Quality Control Peer Review Organizations: Consideration of Remote Rural Location and Other Relevant Factors — Notice of policy and request for comments.

57 FR 3298, January 29, 1992: Health Care Programs: Fraud and Abuse; Amendments to OIG Exclusion and CMP Authorities Resulting From Public Law 100-93 — Final rule affecting 42 CFR Parts 1001, 1002, 1003, 1004, 1005, 1006, and 1007. See also final rule and correction at 57 FR 9669, March 20, 1992; final rule affecting 42 CFR Parts 1001and 1005, with clarification at 58 FR 5617, January 22, 1993; and final rule affecting 42 CFR Part 1001, with correction, at 58 FR 40752, July 30, 1993. 59 FR 50762, October 5, 1994: HCFA Public Information Collection Requirements Submitted to the Office of Management and Budget (OMB) for Clearance (pertaining to reimbursement of hospital costs for residents and interns, criteria for psychiatric and rehabilitation hospital units' reimbursement under the prospective payment system, disclosure of owners and managers of suppliers for fraud and abuse detection purposes, reimbursement of municipal health services clinics, survey form for hospital compliance with anti-dumping requirements, and evaluation of patient and physician satisfaction with the Medicare participating heart bypass center demonstration).

59 FR 54197, October 28, 1994: HCFA Public Information Collection Requirements Submitted to the Office of Management and Budget (OMB) for Clearance (pertaining to Medicare beneficiary surveys, estimated acquisition costs of injectable drugs, reconsideration of adverse determinations made on Part A claims, beneficiary and supplier or physician hearing requests, and compliance with hospital anti-dumping requirements.

61 FR 3715, February 1, 1996: HCFA Emergency Clearance: Public Information Collection Requirements Submitted to the Office of

Management and Budget (OMB) (pertaining to requirements for examination and treatment for emergency medical conditions and women in labor).

61 FR 28882, June 6, 1996: HCFA Agency Information Collection Activities: Submission for OMB Review; Comment Request (pertaining to end stage renal disease medical evidence reports to determine Medicare eligibility; and examination and treatment for emergency medical conditions and women in labor).

62 FR 25636, May 9, 1997: HCFA Agency Information Collection Activities: Proposed Collection; Comment request (pertaining to information collection requirements about examination and treatment for emergency medical conditions and women in labor).

62 FR 38313, July 17, 1997: HCFA Agency Information Collection Activities: Proposed Collection; Comment request (pertaining to examination and treatment for emergency medical conditions and women in labor).

62 FR 44976, August 25, 1997: HCFA Agency Information Collection Activities: Submission for OMB Review; Comment request (pertaining to beneficiary termination from hospital and/or supplementary medical insurance; outpatient rehabilitation cost report forms; and data collection regarding examination and treatment for emergency medical conditions and women in labor).

63 FR 20652, April 27, 1998: HCFA Agency Information Collection Activities: Proposed Collection; Comment request (pertaining information collection requirements applicable to the obligation of hospitals to examine and treat emergency medical conditions and women in labor).

63 FR 37129, July 9, 1998: HCFA Agency Information Collection Activities: Submission for OMB Review; Comment request (pertaining to examination and treatment for emergency medical conditions and women in labor).

63 FR 67486, December 7, 1998: Office of Inspector General and HCFA; Solicitation of Comments on the OIG/HCFA Special Advisory Bulletin on the Patient Anti-Dumping Statute — Notice.

1999

64 FR 11922, March 10, 1999: HCFA Agency Information Collection Activities: Proposed Collection; Comment request (pertaining to attending physician's statement and documentation regarding medical emergency care).

64 FR 30340, June 7, 1999: HCFA Agency Information Collection Activities: Submission for OMB Review; Comment request (pertaining to attending physicians statement and documentation of medical emergencies).

64 FR 61353, November 10, 1999: Office of Inspector General/HCFA; OIG/HCFA Special Advisory Bulletin on the Patient Anti-dumping Statute.

2001

66 FR 23944, May 10, 2001: HCFA Agency Information Collection Activities: Proposed Collection; Comment request (pertaining to examination and treatment for emergency conditions and women in labor).

See § 2:35.

§ 6:36 FAILURE BY ORGANIZATIONS WITH RISK-SHARING CONTRACTS UNDER MEDICARE (SUCH AS HEALTH MAINTENANCE ORGANIZATIONS AND COMPETITIVE MEDICAL PLANS) TO PROVIDE REQUIRED INFORMATION ABOUT THEIR SERVICES — Section 1876(c)(3)(C) [42 U.S.C.A. 1395mm(c)(3)(C)]

Regulations

42 CFR Part 417 — Health Maintenance Organizations, Competitive Medical Plans, and Health Care Prepayment Plans

42 CFR Part 420 — Program Integrity: Medicare

42 CFR Part 434 — Contracts [Medicaid]

42 CFR Part 455 — Program Integrity: Medicaid

55 FR 12738, June 12, 1990: Waiver of Certain Membership Requirements for Certain Health Maintenance Organizations, (HMOs), and State Option for Disenrollment Restrictions for Certain HMOs under Medicaid — Final rule affecting 42 CFR Parts 434 and 435. See also corrections published at 55 FR 25774, June 22, 1990, and 55 FR 33407, August 15, 1990.

56 FR 29248, June 26, 1991: Medicare Program; HMO Qualification Determinations and Compliance Actions — Notice. 56 FR 30723, July 5, 1991: Health Maintenance Organizations; Conforming Health Maintenance Organization Rules to Statutory Requirements — Proposed rule.

56 FR 31597, July 11, 1991: Health Maintenance Organizations; Group Specific Ratings — Notice of proposed rulemaking.

56 FR 33403, July 22, 1991: Medicare and State Health Care Programs: Fraud and Abuse; Civil Monetary Penalties and Intermediate Sanctions for Certain Violations by Health Maintenance Organizations and Competitive Medical Plans — Proposed rule.

56 FR 46562, September 13, 1991: Medicare Program; Explanation of Enrollee Rights and Other Provisions Applicable to Health Maintenance Organizations and Competitive Medical Plans — Final rule affecting 42 CFR Part 417.

57 FR 33202, July 27, 1992: Health Maintenance Organizations; HMO Qualification Determinations and Compliance Actions — Notice. See also correction at 57 FR 41810, September 11, 1992.

57 FR 36006, August 12, 1992: Medicare Program; Self-implementing Coverage and Payments Provisions: 1990 Legislation — Final rule with comment period, affecting 42 CFR Parts 405, 406, 409, 420, 411, 412, 413, 418, and 489. Pertains to capital-related inpatient hospital costs; capital-related outpatient hospital costs; non-capital related outpatient hospital costs; payment for physician pathology services; payment for services of physicians as assistants-at-surgery; payments for ambulatory surgical procedures in hospital outpatient departments; payments for radiology services performed in hospital outpatient departments; hospice benefit extension; enrollment of HMO members in Medicare Part A; coverage of ostomy supplies; application of pre-entitlement stay in psychiatric hospital to limit on payment for inpatient hospital services; payments to dialysis facilities; payment rates for erythropoietin (EPO); and Medicare secondary payer provision for individuals with ESRD. See also confirmation of final rule at 58 FR 58502, November 2, 1993.

57 FR 46119, October 7, 1992: Medicare Program; Appeal Rights and Procedures for Beneficiaries Enrolled in Prepaid Health Care Plans — Notice of proposed rulemaking affecting 42 CFR Part 417.

57 FR 52723, November 5, 1992: Medicare and State Health Care Programs: Fraud and Abuse; Safe Harbors for Protecting Health Plans — Interim final rule with request for comment. See also extension of comment period at 58 FR 2989, January 7, 1993, affecting 42 CFR 1001.

57 FR 59024, December 14, 1992: Medicare and Medicaid Programs; Requirements for Physician Incentive Plans in Prepaid

Health Care Organizations — Proposed rule affecting 42 CFR Parts 417 and 434 (HCFA) and 42 CFR Part 1003 (Office of Inspector General). See also extension of comment period at 58 FR 8568, February 16, 1993.

58 FR 5402, January 21, 1993: Health Maintenance Organizations; HMO Qualification Determinations and Compliance Actions — Notice.

58 FR 31407, June 2, 1993: Health Maintenance Organizations: Qualification Determinations and Compliance Actions for Calendar Year 1992, Fourth Quarter — Notice.

58 FR 38062, July 15, 1993: Medicare Program, Health Maintenance Organizations: Technical Amendments — Final rule with comment period, affecting 42 CFR Part 417.

58 FR 38170, July 15, 1993: Health Maintenance Organizations: Organizational Structure and Services — Notice of proposed rulemaking, affecting 42 CFR Part 417. See also correction at 58 FR 46925, September 3, 1993.

58 FR 39820, July 26, 1993: Health Maintenance Organizations: Qualification Determinations and Compliance Actions During the Period January 1, 1993, through March 31, 1993 — Notice.

58 FR 68366, December 27, 1993: Medicare Program; Retroactive Enrollment and Disenrollment in Risk Health Maintenance Organizations and Competitive Medical Plans — Proposed rule affecting 42 CFR Part 417.

59 FR 8429, February 22, 1994: Medicare Program; Health Maintenance Organization and Competitive Medical Plan National Coverage Decisions — Proposed rule affecting 42 CFR Part 417.

59 FR 8435, February 22, 1994: Medicare Program; Limits on Payment to Health Maintenance Organizations (HMOs), Competitive Medical Plans (CMPs), and Health Care Prepayment Plans (HCPPs) — Proposed rule affecting 42 CFR Part 417.

59 FR 11230, March 10, 1994: Medicare Program; Post Contract Protections and Other Coordinated Care Issues (involving HMOs and CMPs that cease to furnish services under Medicare risk or cost contracts) — Proposed rule affecting 42 CFR Part 417.

59 FR 18820, April 20, 1994: HCFA: Health Maintenance Organizations: Qualification Determinations and Compliance Actions During the Period October 1, 1993, through December 31, 1993.

59 FR 23820, May 9, 1994: Medicaid Program; Requirements for Certain Health Insuring Organizations and OBRA '90 Technical Amendments, affecting 42 CFR Parts 434 and 435.

59 FR 25460, May 16, 1994: HCFA Public Information Collection Requirements Submitted to the Office of Management and Budget (OMB) for Clearance (pertaining to Medicare uniform institutional provider bill; hospice survey and deficiencies report form; HMO financial information reports to members; hospital request for certification in Medicare and Medicaid form).

59 FR 36072, July 15, 1994: Medicare and State Health Care Programs: Fraud and Abuse, Civil Money Penalties and Intermediate Sanctions for Certain Violations by Health Maintenance Organizations and Competitive Medical Plans — Final rule affecting 42 CFR Parts 417, 431, 434, and 1003. See also correction at 59 FR 48566, September 22, 1994.

59 FR 49834, September 30, 1994: Medicare Program; Qualified Health Maintenance Organizations; Technical Amendments — Final rule with comment period, affecting 42 CFR Part 417.

59 FR 59933, November 21, 1994: Medicare Program; Appeal Rights and Procedures for Beneficiaries Enrolled in Prepaid Health Care Plans — Final rule affecting 42 CFR Part 417.

60 FR 14435, March 17, 1995: HCFA Public Information Collection Requirements Submitted to the Office of Management and Budget (OMB) for Clearance (pertaining to Medicaid drug rebates, termination of enrollment in Federally Qualified HMOs, imposition of cost-sharing charges in Medicaid, Medicare current beneficiary surveys, and forms for establishing entitlement to hospital insurance).

60 FR 34885, July 5, 1995: HCFA Full Reporting by Health Maintenance Organizations (HMOs) and Competitive Medical Plans (CMP's) Paid on a Cost Basis — Final rule affecting 42 CFR Part 417. See also correction at 60 FR 45372, August 31, 1995.

60 FR 45673, September 1, 1995: Medicare Program; Contracts with Health Maintenance Organizations (HMOs) and Competitive Medical Plans (CMP's) — Final rule with comment period, affecting 42 CFR Part 417.

60 FR 46228, September 6, 1995: Medicare Program; Payments of HMO's and CMP's and Appeals: Technical Amendments — Final rule with comment period, affecting 42 CFR Part 417.

61 FR 2122, January 25, 1996: Medicare and State Health Care Programs; Fraud and Abuse; Safe Harbors for Protecting Health Plans — Final rule.

61 FR 2255, January 25, 1996: HCFA Public Information Collection Requirements Submitted for Public Comment and Recommendations (pertaining to survey forms about health and safety requirements for physical therapists in independent practice; and national data reporting requirements for HMOs and CMPs).

61 FR 13430, March 27, 1996: Medicare and Medicaid Programs; Requirements for Physician Incentive Plans in Prepaid Health Care Organizations — Final rule with comment period, affecting 42 CFR Parts 417, 434, and 1003. See also correction at 61 FR 46384, September 3, 1996.

61 FR 29406, June 10, 1996: HCFA Agency Information Collection Activities: proposed Collection; Comment Request (pertaining to end stage renal disease application and survey and certification report forms; withholding Medicare payments to recover Medicaid overpayments; acquisition, protection, and disclosure of PRO information; clinical laboratory certification and recertification survey forms; CLIA laboratory personnel report forms; prepaid health plan cost reports; Medicare credit balance reporting requirements; statement of deficiencies and plan of correction requirements for organ procurement organizations; Medicare/Medicaid hospital survey report forms; advance directive requirements for Medicare and Medicaid; payment adjustments for sole community hospitals; survey reports for physical therapists in independent practice; HMO and CMP national data reporting requirements; identification of extension units of outpatient physical therapy and outpatient speech pathology providers; and fire safety survey reports).

61 FR 34437, July 2, 1996: HCFA Agency Information Collection Activities: Submission for OMB Review; Comment Request (pertaining to Peer Review Organization procedures for reconsideration of initial decisions; Part B enrollment forms; certification of rural health clinics for Medicare participation; Medicaid utilization review requirements for home health agencies; State listings of Medicaid recipients in institutions and procedures for State inspection of care review; procedures for disenrollment of beneficiaries from HMOs or CMPs; effectiveness of telemedicine services; formats for PROs to submit data to HCFA; and request for accelerated payments forms for providers).

61 FR 58568, November 15, 1996: Office of Inspector General; Publication of the Medicare Beneficiary Advisory Bulletin on HMO Arrangements — Notice.

61 FR 67566, December 23, 1996: HCFA Emergency Clearance: Public Information Collection Requirements Submitted to OMB (pertaining to assessment of health plans).

61 FR 69034, December 30, 1996: Medicare and Medicaid Programs; Requirements for Physician Incentive Plans in Prepaid Health Care Organizations — Final rule affecting 42 CFR Parts 417 and 434.

62 FR 12834, March 18, 1997: HCFA Correction Notice: Agency Information Collection Activities: Submission for Emergency OMB Review; Comment request (pertaining to managed care organization incentive arrangement disclosure form).

62 FR 23368, April 30, 1997: Medicare Program; Establishment of an Expedited Review process for Medicare Beneficiaries Enrolled in Health Maintenance Organizations, Competitive Medical Plans, and Health Care Prepayment Plans — Final rule with comment period, affecting 42 CFR Part 417.

62 FR 23781, May 1, 1997: HCFA Agency Information Collection Activities: Proposed Collection; Comment request (pertaining to requirement to disclose HMO financial information to members).

62 FR 28410, May 23, 1997: Office of Inspector General: Health Care Programs: Fraud and Abuse — Notice of Intent to Form the Negotiated Rulemaking Committee for the Shared Risk Exception (statutory exceptions to the anti-kickback statute) — affecting 42 CFR Part 1001.

62 FR 34761, June 27, 1997: HCFA Agency Information Collection activities: Proposed Collection; Comment request (pertaining to managed care organization, incentive arrangement disclosure forms; and qualification application form for competitive medical plans, and Medicare contract application for Federally qualified HMO's.

62 FR 45426, August 27, 1997: HCFA Agency Information Collection Activities: Submission for OMB Review; Comment request (pertaining to qualification applications for competitive medical plans and Federally qualified HMOs).

62 FR 61825, November 19, 1997: HCFA Agency Information Collection Activities; Submission for OMB Review; Comment request (pertaining to survey forms for consumer assessment of health plans).

63 FR 187, January 5, 1998: Office of Inspector General; Negotiated Rulemaking Committee on the Shared Risk Exception — Notice of meeting.

63 FR 7175, February 12, 1998: HCFA Emergency Clearance: Public Information Collection Requirements Submitted to the Office of Managment and Budget (OMB) (pertaining to managed care adjusted community rate (ACR) proposal).

63 FR 11263, March 6, 1998: HCFA Agency Information Collection Activities: Submission for OMB Review; Comment request (pertaining to end stage renal disease managed care demonstration.

63 FR 12475, March 13, 1998: HCFA Agency Information Collection Activities; Submission for OMB Review; Comment request (pertaining to HMO and CMP national data reporting requirements).

63 FR 18924, April 16, 1998: HCFA Emergency Clearance: Public Information Collection Requirements Submitted to the Office of Management and Budget (OMB) (pertaining to collection of managed care data using the uniform institutional providers form).

63 FR 26811, May 14, 1998: Medicare and Medicaid Programs: Request for Public Comments on the Quality Improvement System for Managed Care — Solicitation of comments; notice of public meeting.

63 FR 38311, July 16, 1998: Office of Inspector General: Medicare and State Health Care Programs: Fraud and Abuse; Issuance of Advisory Opinions by the OIG — Final rule affecting 42 CFR 1008. See also correction at 63 FR 43449, August 13, 1998.

63 FR 38414, July 16, 1998: HCFA Privacy Act of 1974; Report of Altered System (pertaining to disclosure of individual-specific information to combat fraud or abuse in health benefit programs).

63 FR 40723, July 30, 1998: HCFA Agency Information Collection Activities: Proposed Collection; Comment request (pertaining to requirements for health care prepayment plan (HCPP) eligibility under Section 1833 of the Social Security Act).

63 FR 42409, August 7, 1998: HCFA Agency Information Collection Activities: Proposed Collection; Comment request (pertaining to health plan data and information consumer assessment survey).

63 FR 43187, August 12, 1998: HCFA Privacy Act of 1974; System of Records — Notice of new system of records pertaining to indicators of the performance of health plans.

63 FR 58059, October 29, 1998: HCFA Agency Information Collection Activities: Submission for OMB Review; Comment request (pertaining to consumer assessment of managed care plans).

63 FR 58341, October 30, 1998: Office of Inspector General: Health Care Fraud and Abuse Data Collection Program: Reporting of Final

Adverse Actions — Notice of proposed rulemaking under section 1128E of the Social Security Act, affecting 45 CFR 61.

63 FR 58399, October 30, 1998: Office of Inspector General: Publication of the OIG's Provider Self-Disclosure Protocol — Notice.

63 FR 63478, November 13, 1998: HCFA Agency Information Collection Activities: Proposed Collection; Comment request (pertaining to processing Medicare+Choice disenrollment requests from beneficiaries; creation of the Utilization and Quality Control Peer Review Organization; and rules for participation of HHA's in Medicare and review of plans of care for home health services).

63 FR 68223, December 10, 1998: Office of Inspector General; Solicitation of New Safe Harbors and Special Fraud Alerts — Notice of intent to develop regulations, affecting 42 CFR 1001.

1999

64 FR 2907, January 19, 1999: HCFA Agency Information Collection Activities: Submission for OMB Review; Comment request (pertaining to call-back survey of callers to Medicare+Choice toll-free line).

64 FR 6664, February 10, 1999: HCFA Agency Information Collection Activities: Proposed Collection; Comment request (pertaining to Medicare agreement applications for health care prepayment plans).

64 FR 25891, May 13, 1999: HCFA Agency Information Collection Activities: Submission for OMB Review; Comment request (pertaining to Medicare agreement application for health care prepayment plans under section 1833).

64 FR 32508, June 17, 1999: HCFA Agency Information Collection Activities: Submission for OMB Review; Comment Request (pertaining to the quality improvement system for managed care (QISMC)).

64 FR 38204, July 15, 1999: HCFA Agency Information Collection Activities: Submission for OMB Review; Comment request (pertaining to the national Medicare education program survey about Medicare+Choice awareness).

64 FR 43707, August 11, 1999: HCFA Agency Information Collection Activities: Proposed Collection; Comment request (pertaining to cost reports for prepaid health plans (HMOs and CMPs)).

64 FR 46919, August 27, 1999: HCFA Emergency Clearance: Public Information Collection Requirements Submitted to the Office of Management and Budget (OMB) (pertaining to survey of disenrollment by Medicare beneficiaries from alternative health plans).

64 FR 67223, December 1, 1999: Medicaid Program; External Quality Review of Medicaid Managed Care Organizations — Proposed rule affecting 42 CFR Parts 433 and 438.

2000

65 FR 25737, May 3, 2000: HCFA Agency Information Collection Activities: Proposed Collection; Comment request (pertaining to managed care disenrollment form).

65 FR 25738, May 3, 2000: HCFA Emergency Clearance: Public Informatiion Collection Requirements Submitted to the Office of Management and Budget (OMB) (pertaining to the Medicare managed care CAHPS Survey).

65 FR 26618, May 5, 2000: HCFA Emergency Clearance: Public Information Collection Requirements Submitted to the Office of Management and Budget (OMB) (pertaining to Medicare consumer assessment survey of health plans).

65 FR 40111, June 29, 2000: HCFA Agency Information Collection Activities: Proposed Collection; comment request (pertaining to qualification applications for prepaid health plans (HMOs).

65 FR 40668, June 30, 2000: HCFA Agency Information Collection Activities: Submission for OMB Review; Comment request (pertaining to Medicare comprehensive health plan disenrollment).

65 FR 43026, July 12, 2000: HCFA Agency Information Collection Activities: Submission for OMB Review; Comment request (pertaining to collection of data on physician encounters from Medicare+Choice organizations).

65 FR 46473, July 28, 2000: Medicare Program; Announcement of a Series of Regional Training Sessions to Provide Training to Medicare+Choice Organization Physicians, Medicare+Choice Organization Non-physician Practitioners, and Medicare+Choice Organization Medicare Directors, As Well As Physician Organizations and Billing Associations Involved in the Timely and Accurate Submission of Physician Encounter Data to Support a Comprehensive Risk Adjustment Model — Notice of training sessions.

65 FR 50713, August 21, 2000: HCFA Agency Information Collection Activities: Proposed Collection; Comment request (pertaining to social HMO demonstration payment methodology)

65 FR 53319, September 1, 2000: HCFA Agency Information Collection Activities: Proposed Collection; Comment request (pertaining to incentive arrangement disclosure form for managed care organizations and their related medical groups and physicians).

65 FR 57195, September 21, 2000: HCFA Agency Information Collection Activities; Proposed Collection; Comment request (pertaining to Medicare managed care CAHPS survey for quality of care purposes).

65 FR 60674, October 12, 2000: HCFA Agency Information Collection Activities: Submission for OMB Review; Comment request (pertaining to Medicare+Choice organization appeals and grievance data disclosure requirements).

65 FR 64228, October 26, 2000: HCFA Agency Information Collection Activities: Proposed Collection; Comment request (pertaining to collection of data on physician encounters from Medicare+Choice organizations).

65 FR 65860, November 2, 2000: HCFA Agency Information Collection Activities: Proposed Collection; Comment request (pertaining to follow-up of Medicare+Choice disenrollees receiving fee-for service inpatient hospital care).

65 FR 79867, December 20, 2000: HCFA Agency Information Collection Activities: Proposed Collection; Comment request (pertaining to quality improvement system for managed care).

65 FR 79868, December 20, 2000: HCFA Agency Information Collection Activities: Proposed Collection; Comment request (pertaining to Medicare consumer assessment survey of health plans).

65 FR 79868, December 20, 2000: HCFA Emergency Clearance: Public Information Collection Requirements Submitted to the Office of Management and Budget (OMB) (pertaining to survey of beneficiaries who involuntarily disenroll from their managed care plan).

65 FR 81813, December 27, 2000: Medicare Program; Requirements for the Re-credentialing of Medicare+Choice Organization Providers — Proposed rule affecting 42 CFR Part 422.

2001

66 FR 1995, January 10, 2001: HCFA Agency Information Collection Activities: Proposed Collection; Comment request (pertaining to hospital outpatient encounters from Medicare+Choice programs).

66 FR 2913, January 12, 2001: HCFA Agency Information Collection Activities: Submission for OMB Review; Comment request (pertaining to collection of data about physician encounters from Medicare+Choice organizations).

66 FR 6228, January 19, 2001: Medicaid Program; Medicaid Managed Care—Final rule with comment period, affecting 42 CFR Part 400, 430, 431, 435, 438, 440, and 447.

66 FR 7593, January 24, 2001: Medicare Program; Improvements to the Medicare+Choice Appeal and Grievance Procedures—Proposed rule affecting 42 CFR Parts 422 and 489.

66 FR 8807, February 2, 2001: HCFA Agency Information Collection Activities: Submission for OMB Review; Comment request (pertaining to follow–up of Medicare+Choice disenrollees receiving fee–for–service inpatient hospital care).

66 FR 9858, February 12, 2001: HCFA Privacy Act of 1974; Report of New System (pertaining to complaints against health insurance issuers and health plans).

66 FR 11546, February 26, 2001: Medicaid Program; Medicaid Managed Care: Delay of Effective Date—Final rule delay, affecting 42 CFR Parts 400, 430, 431, 434, 435, 438, 440, and 447.

66 FR 11591, February 26, 2001: HCFA Agency Information Collection Activities: Proposed Collection; Comment request (pertaining to Medicare+Choice program requirements).

66 FR 13854, March 8, 2001: Medicare+Choice Program—CFR correction.

66 FR 15122, March 15, 2001: HCFA Agency Information Collection Activities: Submission for OMB Review; Comment request (pertaining to quality improvement system for managed care).

66 FR 16062, March 23, 2001: HCFA Agency Information Collection Activities: Submission for OMB Review; Comment request (pertaining to Medicare+Choice beneficiary appeal notices).

66 FR 16268, March 23, 2001: HCFA Agency Information Collection Activities; Proposed Collection; Comment request (pertaining to data collection to support policy analysis of choices offered to Medicare+Choice enrollees and choices made by enrollees).

66 FR 16481, March 26, 2001: HCFA Agency Information Collection Activities: Submission for OMB Review; Comment request (pertaining to managed care adjusted community rate proposal for Medicare+Choice organizations).

66 FR 16678, March 27, 2001: HCFA Agency Information Collection Activities: Submission for OMB Review; Comment request (pertaining to Medicare managed care CAHPS survey).

66 FR 17431, March 30, 2001: HCFA Agency Information Collection Activities: Proposed Collection; Comment request (pertaining to data collection of quality indicators for congestive heart failure sub-

mitted by Medicare+Choice organizations requesting extra payments in CY 2002 and CY 2003).

66 FR 21770, May 1, 2001: Medicare Program; Revision of Payment Rates for End–Stage Renal Disease (ESRD) Patients Enrolled in Medicare+Choice Plans—Proposed notice.

66 FR 21987, May 2, 2001: HCFA Agency Information Collection Activities: Proposed Collection; Comment request (pertaining to Medicare+Choice provider sponsored organization (PSO) waiver request form).

66 FR 24391, May 14, 2001: HCFA Agency Information Collection Activities: Submission for OMB Review; Comment request (pertaining to Medicare+Choice program requirements).

66 FR 28916, May 25, 2001: HCFA Agency Information Collection Activities: Proposed Collection; Comment request (pertaining to collection of managed care data using the uniform institutional providers form).

66 FR 29823, June 1, 2001: HCFA Agency Information Collection Activities: Proposed Collection; Comment request (pertaining to data reporting requirements for managed care organizations in the Medicare+Choice program).

66 FR 32776, June 18, 2001: Medicaid Program; Medicaid Managed Care: Further Delay of Effective Date for Final Rule affecting 42 CFR Parts 400, 430, 431, 434, 435, 438, 440, and 447.

See § 2:36.

§ 6:37 FAILURE BY ORGANIZATIONS WITH RISK-SHARING CONTRACTS UNDER MEDICARE (SUCH AS HEALTH MAINTENANCE ORGANIZATIONS AND COMPETITIVE MEDICAL PLANS) TO HAVE AT LEAST ONE-HALF OF THEIR ENROLLED MEMBERS BE PERSONS NOT ELIGIBLE FOR MEDICARE OR MEDICAID — Section 1876(f) [42 U.S.C.A. 1395mm(f)]

Regulations

42 CFR Part 417 — Health Maintenance Organizations, Competitive Medical Plans, and Health Care Prepayment Plans

42 CFR Part 420 — Program Integrity: Medicare

42 CFR Part 434 — Contracts [Medicaid]

42 CFR Part 455 — Program Integrity: Medicaid

55 FR 12738, June 12, 1990: Waiver of Certain Membership Requirements for Certain Health Maintenance Organizations, (HMOs), and State Option for Disenrollment Restrictions for Certain HMOs under Medicaid — Final rule affecting 42 CFR Parts 434 and 435. See also corrections published at 55 FR 25774, June 22, 1990, and 55 FR 33407, August 15, 1990.

56 FR 29248, June 26, 1991: Medicare Program; HMO Qualification Determinations and Compliance Actions — Notice.

56 FR 30723, July 5, 1991: Health Maintenance Organizations; Conforming Health Maintenance Organization Rules to Statutory Requirements — Proposed rule.

56 FR 31597, July 11, 1991: Health Maintenance Organizations; Group Specific Ratings — Notice of proposed rulemaking.

56 FR 33403, July 22, 1991: Medicare and State Health Care Programs: Fraud and Abuse; Civil Monetary Penalties and Intermediate Sanctions for Certain Violations by Health Maintenance Organizations and Competitive Medical Plans — Proposed rule.

56 FR 46562, September 13, 1991: Medicare Program; Explanation of Enrollee Rights and Other Provisions Applicable to Health Maintenance Organizations and Competitive Medical Plans — Final rule affecting 42 CFR Part 417.

57 FR 33202, July 27, 1992: Health Maintenance Organizations; HMO Qualification Determinations and Compliance Actions — Notice. See also correction at 57 FR 41810, September 11, 1992.

57 FR 36006, August 12, 1992: Medicare Program; Self-implementing Coverage and Payments Provisions: 1990 Legislation — Final rule with comment period, affecting 42 CFR Parts 405, 406, 409, 420, 411, 412, 413, 418, and 489. Pertains to capital-related inpatient hospital costs; capital-related outpatient hospital costs; non-capital related outpatient hospital costs; payment for physician pathology services; payment for services of physicians as assistants-at-surgery; payments for ambulatory surgical procedures in hospital outpatient departments; payments for radiology services performed in hospital outpatient departments; hospice benefit extension; enrollment of HMO members in Medicare Part A; coverage of ostomy supplies; application of pre-entitlement stay in psychiatric hospital to limit on payment for inpatient hospital services; payments to dialysis facilities; payment rates for erythropoietin (EPO); and Medicare secondary payer provision for

individuals with ESRD. See also confirmation of final rule at 58 FR 58502, November 2, 1993.

57 FR 46119, October 7, 1992: Medicare Program; Appeal Rights and Procedures for Beneficiaries Enrolled in Prepaid Health Care Plans — Notice of proposed rulemaking affecting 42 CFR Part 417.

57 FR 52723, November 5, 1992: Medicare and State Health Care Programs: Fraud and Abuse; Safe Harbors for Protecting Health Plans — Interim final rule with request for comment. See also extension of comment period at 58 FR 2989, January 7, 1993, affecting 42 CFR 1001.

57 FR 59024, December 14, 1992: Medicare and Medicaid Programs; Requirements for Physician Incentive Plans in Prepaid Health Care Organizations — Proposed rule affecting 42 CFR Parts 417 and 434 (HCFA) and 42 CFR Part 1003 (Office of Inspector General). See also extension of comment period at 58 FR 8568, February 16, 1993.

58 FR 5402, January 21, 1993: Health Maintenance Organizations; HMO Qualification Determinations and Compliance Actions — Notice.

58 FR 31407, June 2, 1993: Health Maintenance Organizations: Qualification Determinations and Compliance Actions for Calendar Year 1992, Fourth Quarter — Notice.

58 FR 38062, July 15, 1993: Medicare Program, Health Maintenance Organizations: Technical Amendments — Final rule with comment period, affecting 42 CFR Part 417.

58 FR 38170, July 15, 1993: Health Maintenance Organizations: Organizational Structure and Services — Notice of proposed rulemaking, affecting 42 CFR Part 417. See also correction at 58 FR 46925, September 3, 1993.

58 FR 39820, July 26, 1993: Health Maintenance Organizations: Qualification Determinations and Compliance Actions During the Period January 1, 1993, through March 31, 1993 — Notice.

58 FR 68366, December 27, 1993: Medicare Program; Retroactive Enrollment and Disenrollment in Risk Health Maintenance Organizations and Competitive Medical Plans — Proposed rule affecting 42 CFR Part 417.

59 FR 8429, February 22, 1994: Medicare Program; Health Maintenance Organization and Competitive Medical Plan National Coverage Decisions — Proposed rule affecting 42 CFR Part 417.

59 FR 8435, February 22, 1994: Medicare Program; Limits on Payment to Health Maintenance Organizations (HMOs), Competi-

tive Medical Plans (CMPs), and Health Care Prepayment Plans (HCPPs) — Proposed rule affecting 42 CFR Part 417.

59 FR 11230, March 10, 1994: Medicare Program; Post Contract Protections and Other Coordinated Care Issues (involving HMOs and CMPs that cease to furnish services under Medicare risk or cost contracts) — Proposed rule affecting 42 CFR Part 417.

59 FR 18820, April 20, 1994: HCFA: Health Maintenance Organizations: Qualification Determinations and Compliance Actions During the Period October 1, 1993, through December 31, 1993.

59 FR 23820, May 9, 1994: Medicaid Program; Requirements for Certain Health Insuring Organizations and OBRA '90 Technical Amendments, affecting 42 CFR Parts 434 and 435.

59 FR 25460, May 16, 1994: HCFA Public Information Collection Requirements Submitted to the Office of Management and Budget (OMB) for Clearance (pertaining to Medicare uniform institutional provider bill; hospice survey and deficiencies report form; HMO financial information reports to members; hospital request for certification in Medicare and Medicaid form.

59 FR 36072, July 15, 1994: Medicare and State Health Care Programs: Fraud and Abuse, Civil Money Penalties and Intermediate Sanctions for Certain Violations by Health Maintenance Organizations and Competitive Medical Plans — Final rule affecting 42 CFR Parts 417, 431, 434, and 1003. See also correction at 59 FR 48566, September 22, 1994.

59 FR 49834, September 30, 1994: Medicare Program; Qualified Health Maintenance Organizations; Technical Amendments — Final rule with comment period, affecting 42 CFR Part 417.

59 FR 59933, November 21, 1994: Medicare Program; Appeal Rights and Procedures for Beneficiaries Enrolled in Prepaid Health Care Plans — Final rule affecting 42 CFR Part 417.

60 FR 14435, March 17, 1995: HCFA Public Information Collection Requirements Submitted to the Office of Management and Budget (OMB) for Clearance (pertaining to Medicaid drug rebates, termination of enrollment in Federally Qualified HMOs, imposition of cost-sharing charges in Medicaid, Medicare current beneficiary surveys, and forms for establishing entitlement to hospital insurance).

60 FR 34885, July 5, 1995: HCFA Full Reporting by Health Maintenance Organizations (HMO's) and Competitive Medical Plans

(CMP's) Paid on a Cost Basis — Final rule affecting 42 CFR Part 417. See also correction at 60 FR 45372, August 31, 1995.

60 FR 45673, September 1, 1995: Medicare Program; Contracts with Health Maintenance Organizations (HMO's) and Competitive Medical Plans (CMP's) — Final rule with comment period, affecting 42 CFR Part 417.

60 FR 46228, September 6, 1995: Medicare Program; Payments of HMO's and CMP's and Appeals: Technical Amendments — Final rule with comment period, affecting 42 CFR Part 417.

61 FR 2122, January 25, 1996: Medicare and State Health Care Programs; Fraud and Abuse; Safe Harbors for Protecting Health Plans — Final rule.

61 FR 2255, January 25, 1996: HCFA Public Information Collection Requirements Submitted for Public Comment and Recommendations (pertaining to survey forms about health and safety requirements for physical therapists in independent practice; and national data reporting requirements for HMOs and CMPs).

61 FR 13430, March 27, 1996: Medicare and Medicaid Programs; Requirements for Physician Incentive Plans in Prepaid Health Care Organizations — Final rule with comment period, affecting 42 CFR Parts 417, 434, and 1003.

61 FR 29406, June 10, 1996: HCFA Agency Information Collection Activities: proposed Collection; Comment Request (pertaining to end stage renal disease application and survey and certification report forms; withholding Medicare payments to recover Medicaid overpayments; acquisition, protection, and disclosure of PRO information; clinical laboratory certification and recertification survey forms; CLIA laboratory personnel report forms; prepaid health plan cost reports; Medicare credit balance reporting requirements; statement of deficiencies and plan of correction requirements for organ procurement organizations; Medicare/Medicaid hospital survey report forms; advance directive requirements for Medicare and Medicaid; payment adjustments for sole community hospitals; survey reports for physical therapists in independent practice; HMO and CMP national data reporting requirements; identification of extension units of outpatient physical therapy and outpatient speech pathology providers; and fire safety survey reports).

61 FR 34437, July 2, 1996: HCFA Agency Information Collection Activities: Submission for OMB Review; Comment Request (pertaining to Peer Review Organization procedures for reconsideration of initial decisions; Part B enrollment forms; certification of rural

health clinics for Medicare participation; Medicaid utilization review requirements for home health agencies; State listings of Medicaid recipients in institutions and procedures for State inspection of care review; procedures for disenrollment of beneficiaries from HMOs or CMPs; effectiveness of telemedicine services; formats for PROs to submit data to HCFA; and request for accelerated payments forms for providers).

61 FR 58568, November 15, 1996: Office of Inspector General; Publication of the Medicare Beneficiary Advisory Bulletin on HMO Arrangements — Notice.

61 FR 67566, December 23, 1996: HCFA Emergency Clearance: Public Information Collection Requirements Submitted to OMB (pertaining to assessment of health plans).

61 FR 69034, December 30, 1996: Medicare and Medicaid Programs; Requirements for Physician Incentive Plans in Prepaid Health Care Organizations — Final rule affecting 42 CFR Parts 417 and 434.

62 FR 12834, March 18, 1997: HCFA Correction Notice: Agency Information Collection Activities: Submission for Emergency OMB Review; Comment request (pertaining to managed care organization incentive arrangement disclosure form).

62 FR 23368, April 30, 1997: Medicare Program; Establishment of an Expedited Review process for Medicare Beneficiaries Enrolled in Health Maintenance Organizations, Competitive Medical Plans, and Health Care Prepayment Plans — Final rule with comment period, affecting 42 CFR Part 417.

62 FR 23781, May 1, 1997: HCFA Agency Information Collection Activities: Proposed Collection; Comment request (pertaining to requirement to disclose HMO financial information to members).

62 FR 28410, May 23, 1997: Office of Inspector General: Health Care Programs: Fraud and Abuse — Notice of Intent to Form the Negotiated Rulemaking Committee for the Shared Risk Exception (statutory exceptions to the anti-kickback statute) — affecting 42 CFR Part 1001.

62 FR 34761, June 27, 1997: HCFA Agency Information Collection activities: Proposed Collection; Comment request (pertaining to managed care organization, incentive arrangement disclosure forms; and qualification application form for competitive medical plans, and Medicare contract application for Federally qualified HMO's.

62 FR 45426, August 27, 1997: HCFA Agency Information Collection Activities: Submission for OMB Review; Comment request (pertaining to qualification applications for competitive medical plans and Federally qualified HMOs).

62 FR 61825, November 19, 1997: HCFA Agency Information Collection Activities; Submission for OMB Review; Comment request (pertaining to survey forms for consumer assessment of health plans).

63 FR 187, January 5, 1998: Office of Inspector General; Negotiated Rulemaking Committee on the Shared Risk Exception — Notice of meeting.

63 FR 7175, February 12, 1998: HCFA Emergency Clearance: Public Information Collection Requirements Submitted to the Office of Managment and Budget (OMB) (pertaining to managed care adjusted community rate (ACR) proposal).

63 FR 11263, March 6, 1998: HCFA Agency Information Collection Activities: Submission for OMB Review; Comment request (pertaining to end stage renal disease managed care demonstration.

63 FR 12475, March 13, 1998: HCFA Agency Information Collection Activities; Submission for OMB Review; Comment request (pertaining to HMO and CMP national data reporting requirements).

63 FR 18924, April 16, 1998: HCFA Emergency Clearance: Public Information Collection Requirements Submitted to the Office of Management and Budget (OMB) (pertaining to collection of managed care data using the uniform institutional providers form).

63 FR 26811, May 14, 1998: Medicare and Medicaid Programs: Request for Public Comments on the Quality Improvement System for Managed Care — Solicitation of comments; notice of public meeting.

63 FR 38414, July 16, 1998: HCFA Privacy Act of 1974; Report of Altered System (pertaining to disclosure of individual-specific information to combat fraud or abuse in health benefit programs).

63 FR 40723, July 30, 1998: HCFA Agency Information Collection Activities: Proposed Collection; Comment request (pertaining to requirements for health care prepayment plan (HCPP) eligibility under Section 1833 of the Social Security Act).

63 FR 42409, August 7, 1998: HCFA Agency Information Collection Activities: Proposed Collection; Comment request (pertaining to health plan data and information consumer assessment survey).

63 FR 43187, August 12, 1998: HCFA Privacy Act of 1974; System of Records — Notice of new system of records pertaining to indicators of the performance of health plans.

63 FR 58059, October 29, 1998: HCFA Agency Information Collection Activities: Submission for OMB Review; Comment request (pertaining to consumer assessment of managed care plans).

63 FR 58341, October 30, 1998: Office of Inspector General: Health Care Fraud and Abuse Data Collection Program: Reporting of Final Adverse Actions — Notice of proposed rulemaking under section 1128E of the Social Security Act, affecting 45 CFR 61.

63 FR 58399, October 30, 1998: Office of Inspector General: Publication of the OIG's Provider Self-Disclosure Protocol — Notice.

63 FR 68223, December 10, 1998: Office of Inspector General; Solicitation of New Safe Harbors and Special Fraud Alerts — Notice of intent to develop regulations, affecting 42 CFR 1001.

1999

64 FR 6664, February 10, 1999: HCFA Agency Information Collection Activities: Proposed Collection; Comment request (pertaining to Medicare agreement applications for health care prepayment plans).

64 FR 25891, May 13, 1999: HCFA Agency Information Collection Activities: Submission for OMB Review; Comment request (pertaining to Medicare agreement application for health care prepayment plans under section 1833).

64 FR 32508, June 17, 1999: HCFA Agency Information Collection Activities: Submission for OMB Review; Comment Request (pertaining to the quality improvement system for managed care (QISMC)).

64 FR 43707, August 11, 1999: HCFA Agency Information Collection Activities: Proposed Collection; Comment request (pertaining to cost reports for prepaid health plans (HMOs and CMPs)).

64 FR 46919, August 27, 1999: HCFA Emergency Clearance: Public Information Collection Requirements Submitted to the Office of Management and Budget (OMB) (pertaining to survey of disenrollment by Medicare beneficiaries from alternative health plans).

64 FR 67223, December 1, 1999: Medicaid Program; External Quality Review of Medicaid Managed Care Organizations — Proposed rule affecting 42 CFR Parts 433 and 438.

2000

65 FR 25737, May 3, 2000: HCFA Agency Information Collection Activities: Proposed Collection; Comment request (pertaining to managed care disenrollment form).

65 FR 25738, May 3, 2000: HCFA Emergency Clearance: Public Informatiion Collection Requirements Submitted to the Office of Management and Budget (OMB) (pertaining to the Medicare managed care CAHPS Survey).

65 FR 26618, May 5, 2000: HCFA Emergency Clearance: Public Information Collection Requirements Submitted to the Office of Management and Budget (OMB) (pertaining to Medicare consumer assessment survey of health plans).

65 FR 40111, June 29, 2000: HCFA Agency Information Collection Activities: Proposed Collection; comment request (pertaining to qualification applications for prepaid health plans (HMOs).

65 FR 40668, June 30, 2000: HCFA Agency Information Collection Activities: Submission for OMB Review; Comment request (pertaining to Medicare comprehensive health plan disenrollment).

65 FR 43026, July 12, 2000: HCFA Agency Information Collection Activities: Submission for OMB Review; Comment request (pertaining to collection of data on physician encounters from Medicare+Choice organizations).

65 FR 46473, July 28, 2000: Medicare Program; Announcement of a Series of Regional Training Sessions to Provide Training to Medicare+Choice Organization Physicians, Medicare+Choice Organization Non-physician Practitioners, and Medicare+Choice Organization Medicare Directors, As Well As Physician Organizations and Billing Associations Involved in the Timely and Accurate Submission of Physician Encounter Data to Support a Comprehensive Risk Adjustment Model — Notice of training sessions.

65 FR 50713, August 21, 2000: HCFA Agency Information Collection Activities: Proposed Collection; Comment request (pertaining to social HMO demonstration payment methodology)

65 FR 53319, September 1, 2000: HCFA Agency Information Collection Activities: Proposed Collection; Comment request (pertaining to incentive arrangement disclosure form for managed care organizations and their related medical groups and physicians).

65 FR 57195, September 21, 2000: HCFA Agency Information Collection Activities; Proposed Collection; Comment request (per-

taining to Medicare managed care CAHPS survey for quality of care purposes).

65 FR 60674, October 12, 2000: HCFA Agency Information Collection Activities: Submission for OMB Review; Comment request (pertaining to Medicare+Choice organization appeals and grievance data disclosure requirements).

65 FR 64228, October 26, 2000: HCFA Agency Information Collection Activities: Proposed Collection; Comment request (pertaining to collection of data on physician encounters from Medicare+Choice organizations).

65 FR 65860, November 2, 2000: HCFA Agency Information Collection Activities: Proposed Collection; Comment request (pertaining to follow-up of Medicare+Choice disenrollees receiving fee-for service inpatient hospital care).

65 FR 79867, December 20, 2000: HCFA Agency Information Collection Activities: Proposed Collection; Comment request (pertaining to quality improvement system for managed care).

65 FR 79868, December 20, 2000: HCFA Agency Information Collection Activities: Proposed Collection; Comment request (pertaining to Medicare consumer assessment survey of health plans).

65 FR 79868, December 20, 2000: HCFA Emergency Clearance: Public Information Collection Requirements Submitted to the Office of Management and Budget (OMB) (pertaining to survey of beneficiaries who involuntarily disenroll from their managed care plan).

65 FR 81813, December 27, 2000: Medicare Program; Requirements for the Re-credentialing of Medicare+Choice Organization Providers — Proposed rule affecting 42 CFR Part 422.

2001

66 FR 1995, January 10, 2001: HCFA Agency Information Collection Activities: Proposed Collection; Comment request (pertaining to hospital outpatient encounters from Medicare+Choice programs).

66 FR 2913, January 12, 2001: HCFA Agency Information Collection Activities: Submission for OMB Review; Comment request (pertaining to collection of data about physician encounters from Medicare+Choice organizations).

66 FR 6228, January 19, 2001: Medicaid Program; Medicaid Managed Care—Final rule with comment period, affecting 42 CFR Part 400, 430, 431, 435, 438, 440, and 447.

66 FR 7593, January 24, 2001: Medicare Program; Improvements to the Medicare+Choice Appeal and Grievance Procedures—Proposed rule affecting 42 CFR Parts 422 and 489.

66 FR 8807, February 2, 2001: HCFA Agency Information Collection Activities: Submission for OMB Review; Comment request (pertaining to follow–up of Medicare+Choice disenrollees receiving fee–for–service inpatient hospital care).

66 FR 9858, February 12, 2001: HCFA Privacy Act of 1974; Report of New System (pertaining to complaints against health insurance issuers and health plans).

66 FR 11546, February 26, 2001: Medicaid Program; Medicaid Managed Care: Delay of Effective Date—Final rule delay, affecting 42 CFR Parts 400, 430, 431, 434, 435, 438, 440, and 447.

66 FR 11591, February 26, 2001: HCFA Agency Information Collection Activities: Proposed Collection; Comment request (pertaining to Medicare+Choice program requirements).

66 FR 13854, March 8, 2001: Medicare+Choice Program—CFR correction.

66 FR 15122, March 15, 2001: HCFA Agency Information Collection Activities: Submission for OMB Review; Comment request (pertaining to quality improvement system for managed care).

66 FR 16062, March 23, 2001: HCFA Agency Information Collection Activities: Submission for OMB Review; Comment request (pertaining to Medicare+Choice beneficiary appeal notices).

66 FR 16268, March 23, 2001: HCFA Agency Information Collection Activities; Proposed Collection; Comment request (pertaining to data collection to support policy analysis of choices offered to Medicare+Choice enrollees and choices made by enrollees).

66 FR 16481, March 26, 2001: HCFA Agency Information Collection Activities: Submission for OMB Review; Comment request (pertaining to managed care adjusted community rate proposal for Medicare+Choice organizations).

66 FR 16678, March 27, 2001: HCFA Agency Information Collection Activities: Submission for OMB Review; Comment request (pertaining to Medicare managed care CAHPS survey).

66 FR 17431, March 30, 2001: HCFA Agency Information Collection Activities: Proposed Collection; Comment request (pertaining to data collection of quality indicators for congestive heart failure submitted by Medicare+Choice organizations requesting extra payments in CY 2002 and CY 2003).

66 FR 21770, May 1, 2001: Medicare Program; Revision of Payment Rates for End–Stage Renal Disease (ESRD) Patients Enrolled in Medicare+Choice Plans—Proposed notice.

66 FR 21987, May 2, 2001: HCFA Agency Information Collection Activities: Proposed Collection; Comment request (pertaining to Medicare+Choice provider sponsored organization (PSO) waiver request form).

66 FR 24391, May 14, 2001: HCFA Agency Information Collection Activities: Submission for OMB Review; Comment request (pertaining to Medicare+Choice program requirements).

66 FR 28916, May 25, 2001: HCFA Agency Information Collection Activities: Proposed Collection; Comment request (pertaining to collection of managed care data using the uniform institutional providers form).

66 FR 29823, June 1, 2001: HCFA Agency Information Collection Activities: Proposed Collection; Comment request (pertaining to data reporting requirements for managed care organizations in the Medicare+Choice program).

66 FR 32776, June 18, 2001: Medicaid Program; Medicaid Managed Care: Further Delay of Effective Date for Final Rule affecting 42 CFR Parts 400, 430, 431, 434, 435, 438, 440, and 447.

See § 2:37.

§ 6:38 FAILURE BY ORGANIZATIONS WITH RISK-SHARING CONTRACTS (SUCH AS HEALTH MAINTENANCE ORGANIZATIONS AND COMPETITIVE MEDICAL PLANS) TO MAKE PROMPT PAYMENT OF CLAIMS — Section 1876(g) [42 U.S.C.A. 1395mm(g)]

Regulations

42 CFR Part 417 — Health Maintenance Organizations, Competitive Medical Plans, and Health Care Prepayment Plans

42 CFR Part 420 — Program Integrity: Medicare

42 CFR Part 434 — Contracts [Medicaid]

42 CFR Part 455 — Program Integrity: Medicaid

55 FR 12738, June 12, 1990: Waiver of Certain Membership Requirements for Certain Health Maintenance Organizations, (HMOs), and State Option for Disenrollment Restrictions for Certain HMOs under Medicaid — Final rule affecting 42 CFR Parts 434

and 435. See also corrections published at 55 FR 25774, June 22, 1990, and 55 FR 33407, August 15, 1990.

56 FR 29248, June 26, 1991: Medicare Program; HMO Qualification Determinations and Compliance Actions — Notice.

56 FR 30723, July 5, 1991: Health Maintenance Organizations; Conforming Health Maintenance Organization Rules to Statutory Requirements — Proposed rule.

56 FR 31597, July 11, 1991: Health Maintenance Organizations; Group Specific Ratings — Notice of proposed rulemaking.

56 FR 33403, July 22, 1991: Medicare and State Health Care Programs: Fraud and Abuse; Civil Monetary Penalties and Intermediate Sanctions for Certain Violations by Health Maintenance Organizations and Competitive Medical Plans — Proposed rule.

56 FR 46562, September 13, 1991: Medicare Program; Explanation of Enrollee Rights and Other Provisions Applicable to Health Maintenance Organizations and Competitive Medical Plans — Final rule affecting 42 CFR Part 417.

57 FR 33202, July 27, 1992: Health Maintenance Organizations; HMO Qualification Determinations and Compliance Actions — Notice. See also correction at 57 FR 41810, September 11, 1992.

57 FR 36006, August 12, 1992: Medicare Program; Self-implementing Coverage and Payments Provisions: 1990 Legislation — Final rule with comment period, affecting 42 CFR Parts 405, 406, 409, 420, 411, 412, 413, 418, and 489. Pertains to capital-related inpatient hospital costs; capital-related outpatient hospital costs; non-capital related outpatient hospital costs; payment for physician pathology services; payment for services of physicians as assistants-at-surgery; payments for ambulatory surgical procedures in hospital outpatient departments; payments for radiology services performed in hospital outpatient departments; hospice benefit extension; enrollment of HMO members in Medicare Part A; coverage of ostomy supplies; application of pre-entitlement stay in psychiatric hospital to limit on payment for inpatient hospital services; payments to dialysis facilities; payment rates for erythropoietin (EPO); and Medicare secondary payer provision for individuals with ESRD. See also confirmation of final rule at 58 FR 58502, November 2, 1993.

57 FR 46119, October 7, 1992: Medicare Program; Appeal Rights and Procedures for Beneficiaries Enrolled in Prepaid Health Care Plans — Notice of proposed rulemaking affecting 42 CFR Part 417.

57 FR 52723, November 5, 1992: Medicare and State Health Care Programs: Fraud and Abuse; Safe Harbors for Protecting Health Plans — Interim final rule with request for comment. See also extension of comment period at 58 FR 2989, January 7, 1993, affecting 42 CFR 1001.

57 FR 59024, December 14, 1992: Medicare and Medicaid Programs; Requirements for Physician Incentive Plans in Prepaid Health Care Organizations — Proposed rule affecting 42 CFR Parts 417 and 434 (HCFA) and 42 CFR Part 1003 (Office of Inspector General). See also extension of comment period at 58 FR 8568, February 16, 1993.

58 FR 5402, January 21, 1993: Health Maintenance Organizations; HMO Qualification Determinations and Compliance Actions — Notice.

58 FR 31407, June 2, 1993: Health Maintenance Organizations: Qualification Determinations and Compliance Actions for Calendar Year 1992, Fourth Quarter — Notice.

58 FR 38062, July 15, 1993: Medicare Program, Health Maintenance Organizations: Technical Amendments — Final rule with comment period, affecting 42 CFR Part 417.

58 FR 38170, July 15, 1993: Health Maintenance Organizations: Organizational Structure and Services — Notice of proposed rulemaking, affecting 42 CFR Part 417. See also correction at 58 FR 46925, September 3, 1993.

58 FR 39820, July 26, 1993: Health Maintenance Organizations: Qualification Determinations and Compliance Actions During the Period January 1, 1993, through March 31, 1993 — Notice.

58 FR 68366, December 27, 1993: Medicare Program; Retroactive Enrollment and Disenrollment in Risk Health Maintenance Organizations and Competitive Medical Plans — Proposed rule affecting 42 CFR Part 417.

59 FR 8429, February 22, 1994: Medicare Program; Health Maintenance Organization and Competitive Medical Plan National Coverage Decisions — Proposed rule affecting 42 CFR Part 417.

59 FR 8435, February 22, 1994: Medicare Program; Limits on Payment to Health Maintenance Organizations (HMOs), Competitive Medical Plans (CMPs), and Health Care Prepayment Plans (HCPPs) — Proposed rule affecting 42 CFR Part 417.

59 FR 11230, March 10, 1994: Medicare Program; Post Contract Protections and Other Coordinated Care Issues (involving HMOs

and CMPs that cease to furnish services under Medicare risk or cost contracts) — Proposed rule affecting 42 CFR Part 417.

59 FR 18820, April 20, 1994: HCFA: Health Maintenance Organizations: Qualification Determinations and Compliance Actions During the Period October 1, 1993, through December 31, 1993.

59 FR 23820, May 9, 1994: Medicaid Program; Requirements for Certain Health Insuring Organizations and OBRA '90 Technical Amendments, affecting 42 CFR Parts 434 and 435.

59 FR 25460, May 16, 1994: HCFA Public Information Collection Requirements Submitted to the Office of Management and Budget (OMB) for Clearance (pertaining to Medicare uniform institutional provider bill; hospice survey and deficiencies report form; HMO financial information reports to members; hospital request for certification in Medicare and Medicaid form).

59 FR 36072, July 15, 1994: Medicare and State Health Care Programs: Fraud and Abuse, Civil Money Penalties and Intermediate Sanctions for Certain Violations by Health Maintenance Organizations and Competitive Medical Plans — Final rule affecting 42 CFR Parts 417, 431, 434, and 1003. See also correction at 59 FR 48566, September 22, 1994.

59 FR 49834, September 30, 1994: Medicare Program; Qualified Health Maintenance Organizations; Technical Amendments — Final rule with comment period, affecting 42 CFR Part 417.

59 FR 59933, November 21, 1994: Medicare Program; Appeal Rights and Procedures for Beneficiaries Enrolled in Prepaid Health Care Plans — Final rule affecting 42 CFR Part 417.

60 FR 14435, March 17, 1995: HCFA Public Information Collection Requirements Submitted to the Office of Management and Budget (OMB) for Clearance (pertaining to Medicaid drug rebates, termination of enrollment in Federally Qualified HMOs, imposition of cost-sharing charges in Medicaid, Medicare current beneficiary surveys, and forms for establishing entitlement to hospital insurance).

60 FR 34885, July 5, 1995: HCFA Full Reporting by Health Maintenance Organizations (HMO's) and Competitive Medical Plans (CMP's) Paid on a Cost Basis — Final rule affecting 42 CFR Part 417. See also correction at 60 FR 45372, August 31, 1995.

60 FR 45673, September 1, 1995: Medicare Program; Contracts with Health Maintenance Organizations (HMO's) and Competitive

Medical Plans (CMP's) — Final rule with comment period, affecting 42 CFR Part 417.

60 FR 46228, September 6, 1995: Medicare Program; Payments of HMO's and CMP's and Appeals: Technical Amendments — Final rule with comment period, affecting 42 CFR Part 417.

61 FR 2122, January 25, 1996: Medicare and State Health Care Programs; Fraud and Abuse; Safe Harbors for Protecting Health Plans — Final rule.

61 FR 2255, January 25, 1996: HCFA Public Information Collection Requirements Submitted for Public Comment and Recommendations (pertaining to survey forms about health and safety requirements for physical therapists in independent practice; and national data reporting requirements for HMOs and CMPs).

61 FR 13430, March 27, 1996: Medicare and Medicaid Programs; Requirements for Physician Incentive Plans in Prepaid Health Care Organizations — Final rule with comment period, affecting 42 CFR Parts 417, 434, and 1003.

61 FR 29406, June 10, 1996: HCFA Agency Information Collection Activities: proposed Collection; Comment Request (pertaining to end stage renal disease application and survey and certification report forms; withholding Medicare payments to recover Medicaid overpayments; acquisition, protection, and disclosure of PRO information; clinical laboratory certification and recertification survey forms; CLIA laboratory personnel report forms; prepaid health plan cost reports; Medicare credit balance reporting requirements; statement of deficiencies and plan of correction requirements for organ procurement organizations; Medicare/Medicaid hospital survey report forms; advance directive requirements for Medicare and Medicaid; payment adjustments for sole community hospitals; survey reports for physical therapists in independent practice; HMO and CMP national data reporting requirements; identification of extension units of outpatient physical therapy and outpatient speech pathology providers; and fire safety survey reports).

61 FR 34437, July 2, 1996: HCFA Agency Information Collection Activities: Submission for OMB Review; Comment Request (pertaining to Peer Review Organization procedures for reconsideration of initial decisions; Part B enrollment forms; certification of rural health clinics for Medicare participation; Medicaid utilization review requirements for home health agencies; State listings of Medicaid recipients in institutions and procedures for State inspection of care review; procedures for disenrollment of beneficiaries from HMOs or

CMPs; effectiveness of telemedicine services; formats for PROs to submit data to HCFA; and request for accelerated payments forms for providers).

61 FR 58568, November 15, 1996: Office of Inspector General; Publication of the Medicare Beneficiary Advisory Bulletin on HMO Arrangements — Notice.

61 FR 67566, December 23, 1996: HCFA Emergency Clearance: Public Information Collection Requirements Submitted to OMB (pertaining to assessment of health plans).

61 FR 69034, December 30, 1996: Medicare and Medicaid Programs; Requirements for Physician Incentive Plans in Prepaid Health Care Organizations — Final rule affecting 42 CFR Parts 417 and 434.

62 FR 12834, March 18, 1997: HCFA Correction Notice: Agency Information Collection Activities: Submission for Emergency OMB Review; Comment request (pertaining to managed care organization incentive arrangement disclosure form).

62 FR 23368, April 30, 1997: Medicare Program; Establishment of an Expedited Review process for Medicare Beneficiaries Enrolled in Health Maintenance Organizations, Competitive Medical Plans, and Health Care Prepayment Plans — Final rule with comment period, affecting 42 CFR Part 417.

62 FR 23781, May 1, 1997: HCFA Agency Information Collection Activities: Proposed Collection; Comment request (pertaining to requirement to disclose HMO financial information to members).

62 FR 28410, May 23, 1997: Office of Inspector General: Health Care Programs: Fraud and Abuse — Notice of Intent to Form the Negotiated Rulemaking Committee for the Shared Risk Exception (statutory exceptions to the anti-kickback statute) — affecting 42 CFR Part 1001.

62 FR 34761, June 27, 1997: HCFA Agency Information Collection activities: Proposed Collection; Comment request (pertaining to managed care organization, incentive arrangement disclosure forms; and qualification application form for competitive medical plans, and Medicare contract application for Federally qualified HMO's).

62 FR 45426, August 27, 1997: HCFA Agency Information Collection Activities: Submission for OMB Review; Comment request (pertaining to qualification applications for competitive medical plans and Federally qualified HMOs).

62 FR 61825, November 19, 1997: HCFA Agency Information Collection Activities; Submission for OMB Review; Comment request (pertaining to survey forms for consumer assessment of health plans).

63 FR 187, January 5, 1998: Office of Inspector General; Negotiated Rulemaking Committee on the Shared Risk Exception — Notice of meeting.

63 FR 7175, February 12, 1998: HCFA Emergency Clearance: Public Information Collection Requirements Submitted to the Office of Managment and Budget (OMB) (pertaining to managed care adjusted community rate (ACR) proposal).

63 FR 11263, March 6, 1998: HCFA Agency Information Collection Activities: Submission for OMB Review; Comment request (pertaining to end stage renal disease managed care demonstration.

63 FR 12475, March 13, 1998: HCFA Agency Information Collection Activities; Submission for OMB Review; Comment request (pertaining to HMO and CMP national data reporting requirements).

63 FR 18124, April 14, 1998: Medicare Program; Definition of Provider-Sponsored Organization and Related Requirements — Interim final rule with comment period, affecting 42 CFR 422.

63 FR 18924, April 16, 1998: HCFA Emergency Clearance: Public Information Collection Requirements Submitted to the Office of Management and Budget (OMB) (pertaining to collection of managed care data using the uniform institutional providers form).

63 FR 26811, May 14, 1998: Medicare and Medicaid Programs: Request for Public Comments on the Quality Improvement System for Managed Care — Solicitation of comments; notice of public meeting.

63 FR 38311, July 16, 1998: Office of Inspector General: Medicare and State Health Care Programs: Fraud and Abuse; Issuance of Advisory Opinions by the OIG — Final rule affecting 42 CFR 1008. See also correction at 63 FR 43449, August 13, 1998.

63 FR 38414, July 16, 1998: HCFA Privacy Act of 1974; Report of Altered System (pertaining to disclosure of individual-specific information to combat fraud or abuse in health benefit programs).

63 FR 40723, July 30, 1998: HCFA Agency Information Collection Activities: Proposed Collection; Comment request (pertaining to requirements for health care prepayment plan (HCPP) eligibility under Section 1833 of the Social Security Act).

63 FR 42409, August 7, 1998: HCFA Agency Information Collection Activities: Proposed Collection; Comment request (pertaining to health plan data and information consumer assessment survey).

63 FR 43187, August 12, 1998: HCFA Privacy Act of 1974; System of Records — Notice of new system of records pertaining to indicators of the performance of health plans.

63 FR 43403, August 13, 1998: HCFA Emergency Clearance: Public Information Collection Requirements Submitted to the Office of Management and Budget (OMB) (pertaining to the Medicare and You survey form to collect information from internet users accessing the Medicare+Choice Handbook on the Medicare.gov web site).

63 FR 45828, August 27, 1998: HCFA Emergency Clearance: Public Information Collection Requirements Submitted to the Office of Management and Budget (OMB) (pertaining to surveys of the effectiveness of the Medicare+Choice education campaign).

63 FR 58059, October 29, 1998: HCFA Agency Information Collection Activities: Submission for OMB Review; Comment request (pertaining to consumer assessment of managed care plans).

63 FR 58399, October 30, 1998: Office of Inspector General: Publication of the OIG's Provider Self-Disclosure Protocol — Notice.

63 FR 68223, December 10, 1998: Office of Inspector General; Solicitation of New Safe Harbors and Special Fraud Alerts — Notice of intent to develop regulations, affecting 42 CFR 1001.

1999

64 FR 6664, February 10, 1999: HCFA Agency Information Collection Activities: Proposed Collection; Comment request (pertaining to Medicare agreement applications for health care prepayment plans).

64 FR 25891, May 13, 1999: HCFA Agency Information Collection Activities: Submission for OMB Review; Comment request (pertaining to Medicare agreement application for health care prepayment plans under section 1833).

64 FR 32508, June 17, 1999: HCFA Agency Information Collection Activities: Submission for OMB Review; Comment Request (pertaining to the quality improvement system for managed care (QISMC)).

64 FR 43707, August 11, 1999: HCFA Agency Information Collection Activities: Proposed Collection; Comment request (pertaining to cost reports for prepaid health plans (HMOs and CMPs)).

64 FR 46919, August 27, 1999: HCFA Emergency Clearance: Public Information Collection Requirements Submitted to the Office of

Management and Budget (OMB) (pertaining to survey of disenrollment by Medicare beneficiaries from alternative health plans).

64 FR 67223, December 1, 1999: Medicaid Program; External Quality Review of Medicaid Managed Care Organizations — Proposed rule affecting 42 CFR Parts 433 and 438.

2000

65 FR 25737, May 3, 2000: HCFA Agency Information Collection Activities: Proposed Collection; Comment request (pertaining to managed care disenrollment form).

65 FR 25738, May 3, 2000: HCFA Emergency Clearance: Public Informatiion Collection Requirements Submitted to the Office of Management and Budget (OMB) (pertaining to the Medicare managed care CAHPS Survey).

65 FR 26618, May 5, 2000: HCFA Emergency Clearance: Public Information Collection Requirements Submitted to the Office of Management and Budget (OMB) (pertaining to Medicare consumer assessment survey of health plans).

65 FR 40111, June 29, 2000: HCFA Agency Information Collection Activities: Proposed Collection; comment request (pertaining to qualification applications for prepaid health plans (HMOs).

65 FR 40668, June 30, 2000: HCFA Agency Information Collection Activities: Submission for OMB Review; Comment request (pertaining to Medicare comprehensive health plan disenrollment).

65 FR 43026, July 12, 2000: HCFA Agency Information Collection Activities: Submission for OMB Review; Comment request (pertaining to collection of data on physician encounters from Medicare+Choice organizations).

65 FR 46473, July 28, 2000: Medicare Program; Announcement of a Series of Regional Training Sessions to Provide Training to Medicare+Choice Organization Physicians, Medicare+Choice Organization Non-physician Practitioners, and Medicare+Choice Organization Medicare Directors, As Well As Physician Organizations and Billing Associations Involved in the Timely and Accurate Submission of Physician Encounter Data to Support a Comprehensive Risk Adjustment Model — Notice of training sessions.

65 FR 50713, August 21, 2000: HCFA Agency Information Collection Activities: Proposed Collection; Comment request (pertaining to social HMO demonstration payment methodology)

65 FR 53319, September 1, 2000: HCFA Agency Information Collection Activities: Proposed Collection; Comment request (pertaining

to incentive arrangement disclosure form for managed care organizations and their related medical groups and physicians).

65 FR 57195, September 21, 2000: HCFA Agency Information Collection Activities; Proposed Collection; Comment request (pertaining to Medicare managed care CAHPS survey for quality of care purposes).

65 FR 60674, October 12, 2000: HCFA Agency Information Collection Activities: Submission for OMB Review; Comment request (pertaining to Medicare+Choice organization appeals and grievance data disclosure requirements).

65 FR 64228, October 26, 2000: HCFA Agency Information Collection Activities: Proposed Collection; Comment request (pertaining to collection of data on physician encounters from Medicare+Choice organizations).

65 FR 65860, November 2, 2000: HCFA Agency Information Collection Activities: Proposed Collection; Comment request (pertaining to follow-up of Medicare+Choice disenrollees receiving fee-for service inpatient hospital care).

65 FR 79867, December 20, 2000: HCFA Agency Information Collection Activities: Proposed Collection; Comment request (pertaining to quality improvement system for managed care).

65 FR 79868, December 20, 2000: HCFA Agency Information Collection Activities: Proposed Collection; Comment request (pertaining to Medicare consumer assessment survey of health plans).

65 FR 79868, December 20, 2000: HCFA Emergency Clearance: Public Information Collection Requirements Submitted to the Office of Management and Budget (OMB) (pertaining to survey of beneficiaries who involuntarily disenroll from their managed care plan).

65 FR 81813, December 27, 2000: Medicare Program; Requirements for the Re-credentialing of Medicare+Choice Organization Providers — Proposed rule affecting 42 CFR Part 422.

2001

66 FR 1995, January 10, 2001: HCFA Agency Information Collection Activities: Proposed Collection; Comment request (pertaining to hospital outpatient encounters from Medicare+Choice programs).

66 FR 2913, January 12, 2001: HCFA Agency Information Collection Activities: Submission for OMB Review; Comment request (pertaining to collection of data about physician encounters from Medicare+Choice organizations).

66 FR 6228, January 19, 2001: Medicaid Program; Medicaid Managed Care—Final rule with comment period, affecting 42 CFR Part 400, 430, 431, 435, 438, 440, and 447.

66 FR 7593, January 24, 2001: Medicare Program; Improvements to the Medicare+Choice Appeal and Grievance Procedures—Proposed rule affecting 42 CFR Parts 422 and 489.

66 FR 8807, February 2, 2001: HCFA Agency Information Collection Activities: Submission for OMB Review; Comment request (pertaining to follow–up of Medicare+Choice disenrollees receiving fee–for–service inpatient hospital care).

66 FR 9858, February 12, 2001: HCFA Privacy Act of 1974; Report of New System (pertaining to complaints against health insurance issuers and health plans).

66 FR 11546, February 26, 2001: Medicaid Program; Medicaid Managed Care: Delay of Effective Date—Final rule delay, affecting 42 CFR Parts 400, 430, 431, 434, 435, 438, 440, and 447.

66 FR 11591, February 26, 2001: HCFA Agency Information Collection Activities: Proposed Collection; Comment request (pertaining to Medicare+Choice program requirements).

66 FR 13854, March 8, 2001: Medicare+Choice Program—CFR correction.

66 FR 15122, March 15, 2001: HCFA Agency Information Collection Activities: Submission for OMB Review; Comment request (pertaining to quality improvement system for managed care).

66 FR 16062, March 23, 2001: HCFA Agency Information Collection Activities: Submission for OMB Review; Comment request (pertaining to Medicare+Choice beneficiary appeal notices).

66 FR 16268, March 23, 2001: HCFA Agency Information Collection Activities; Proposed Collection; Comment request (pertaining to data collection to support policy analysis of choices offered to Medicare+Choice enrollees and choices made by enrollees).

66 FR 16481, March 26, 2001: HCFA Agency Information Collection Activities: Submission for OMB Review; Comment request (pertaining to managed care adjusted community rate proposal for Medicare+Choice organizations).

66 FR 16678, March 27, 2001: HCFA Agency Information Collection Activities: Submission for OMB Review; Comment request (pertaining to Medicare managed care CAHPS survey).

66 FR 17431, March 30, 2001: HCFA Agency Information Collection Activities: Proposed Collection; Comment request (pertaining to data collection of quality indicators for congestive heart failure sub-

mitted by Medicare+Choice organizations requesting extra payments in CY 2002 and CY 2003).

66 FR 21770, May 1, 2001: Medicare Program; Revision of Payment Rates for End–Stage Renal Disease (ESRD) Patients Enrolled in Medicare+Choice Plans—Proposed notice.

66 FR 21987, May 2, 2001: HCFA Agency Information Collection Activities: Proposed Collection; Comment request (pertaining to Medicare+Choice provider sponsored organization (PSO) waiver request form).

66 FR 24391, May 14, 2001: HCFA Agency Information Collection Activities: Submission for OMB Review; Comment request (pertaining to Medicare+Choice program requirements).

66 FR 28916, May 25, 2001: HCFA Agency Information Collection Activities: Proposed Collection; Comment request (pertaining to collection of managed care data using the uniform institutional providers form).

66 FR 29823, June 1, 2001: HCFA Agency Information Collection Activities: Proposed Collection; Comment request (pertaining to data reporting requirements for managed care organizations in the Medicare+Choice program).

66 FR 32776, June 18, 2001: Medicaid Program; Medicaid Managed Care: Further Delay of Effective Date for Final Rule affecting 42 CFR Parts 400, 430, 431, 434, 435, 438, 440, and 447.

See § 2:38.

§ 6:39 LIMITING COST REIMBURSEMENT TO RISK-SHARING ORGANIZATIONS (SUCH AS HEALTH MAINTENANCE ORGANIZATIONS AND COMPETITIVE MEDICAL PLANS) NOT ELIGIBLE TO PARTICIPATE IN MEDICARE — Section 1876(h) [42 U.S.C.A. 1395mm(h)]

Regulations

42 CFR Part 401, Subpart F — Claims Collection and Compromise

42 CFR Part 417 — Health Maintenance Organizations, Competitive Medical Plans, and Health Care Prepayment Plans

42 CFR Part 420 — Program Integrity: Medicare

42 CFR Part 434 — Contracts [Medicaid]

42 CFR Part 455 — Program Integrity: Medicaid

56 FR 29248, June 26, 1991: Medicare Program; HMO Qualification Determinations and Compliance Actions — Notice.

56 FR 30723, July 5, 1991: Health Maintenance Organizations; Conforming Health Maintenance Organization Rules to Statutory Requirements — Proposed rule.

56 FR 31597, July 11, 1991: Health Maintenance Organizations; Group Specific Ratings — Notice of proposed rulemaking.

56 FR 33403, July 22, 1991: Medicare and State Health Care Programs: Fraud and Abuse; Civil Monetary Penalties and Intermediate Sanctions for Certain Violations by Health Maintenance Organizations and Competitive Medical Plans — Proposed rule.

56 FR 46562, September 13, 1991: Medicare Program; Explanation of Enrollee Rights and Other Provisions Applicable to Health Maintenance Organizations and Competitive Medical Plans — Final rule affecting 42 CFR Part 417.

57 FR 33202, July 27, 1992: Health Maintenance Organizations; HMO Qualification Determinations and Compliance Actions — Notice. See also correction at 57 FR 41810, September 11, 1992.

57 FR 36006, August 12, 1992: Medicare Program; Self-implementing Coverage and Payments Provisions: 1990 Legislation — Final rule with comment period, affecting 42 CFR Parts 405, 406, 409, 420, 411, 412, 413, 418, and 489. Pertains to capital-related inpatient hospital costs; capital-related outpatient hospital costs; non-capital related outpatient hospital costs; payment for physician pathology services; payment for services of physicians as assistants-at-surgery; payments for ambulatory surgical procedures in hospital outpatient departments; payments for radiology services performed in hospital outpatient departments; hospice benefit extension; enrollment of HMO members in Medicare Part A; coverage of ostomy supplies; application of pre-entitlement stay in psychiatric hospital to limit on payment for inpatient hospital services; payments to dialysis facilities; payment rates for erythropoietin (EPO); and Medicare secondary payer provision for individuals with ESRD. See also confirmation of final rule at 58 FR 58502, November 2, 1993.

57 FR 46119, October 7, 1992: Medicare Program; Appeal Rights and Procedures for Beneficiaries Enrolled in Prepaid Health Care Plans — Notice of proposed rulemaking affecting 42 CFR Part 417.

57 FR 52723, November 5, 1992: Medicare and State Health Care Programs: Fraud and Abuse; Safe Harbors for Protecting Health Plans — Interim final rule with request for comment. See also exten-

sion of comment period at 58 FR 2989, January 7, 1993, affecting 42 CFR 1001.

57 FR 59024, December 14, 1992: Medicare and Medicaid Programs; Requirements for Physician Incentive Plans in Prepaid Health Care Organizations — Proposed rule affecting 42 CFR Parts 417 and 434 (HCFA) and 42 CFR Part 1003 (Office of Inspector General). See also extension of comment period at 58 FR 8568, February 16, 1993.

58 FR 5402, January 21, 1993: Health Maintenance Organizations; HMO Qualification Determinations and Compliance Actions — Notice.

58 FR 31407, June 2, 1993: Health Maintenance Organizations: Qualification Determinations and Compliance Actions for Calendar Year 1992, Fourth Quarter — Notice.

58 FR 38062, July 15, 1993: Medicare Program, Health Maintenance Organizations: Technical Amendments — Final rule with comment period, affecting 42 CFR Part 417.

58 FR 38170, July 15, 1993: Health Maintenance Organizations: Organizational Structure and Services — Notice of proposed rulemaking, affecting 42 CFR Part 417. See also correction at 58 FR 46925, September 3, 1993.

58 FR 39820, July 26, 1993: Health Maintenance Organizations: Qualification Determinations and Compliance Actions During the Period January 1, 1993, through March 31, 1993 — Notice.

58 FR 68366, December 27, 1993: Medicare Program; Retroactive Enrollment and Disenrollment in Risk Health Maintenance Organizations and Competitive Medical Plans — Proposed rule affecting 42 CFR Part 417.

59 FR 8429, February 22, 1994: Medicare Program; Health Maintenance Organization and Competitive Medical Plan National Coverage Decisions — Proposed rule affecting 42 CFR Part 417.

59 FR 8435, February 22, 1994: Medicare Program; Limits on Payment to Health Maintenance Organizations (HMOs), Competitive Medical Plans (CMPs), and Health Care Prepayment Plans (HCPPs) — Proposed rule affecting 42 CFR Part 417.

59 FR 11230, March 10, 1994: Medicare Program; Post Contract Protections and Other Coordinated Care Issues (involving HMOs and CMPs that cease to furnish services under Medicare risk or cost contracts) — Proposed rule affecting 42 CFR Part 417.

59 FR 18820, April 20, 1994: HCFA: Health Maintenance Organizations: Qualification Determinations and Compliance Actions During the Period October 1, 1993, through December 31, 1993.

59 FR 23820, May 9, 1994: Medicaid Program; Requirements for Certain Health Insuring Organizations and OBRA '90 Technical Amendments, affecting 42 CFR Parts 434 and 435.

59 FR 25460, May 16, 1994: HCFA Public Information Collection Requirements Submitted to the Office of Management and Budget (OMB) for Clearance (pertaining to Medicare uniform institutional provider bill; hospice survey and deficiencies report form; HMO financial information reports to members; hospital request for certification in Medicare and Medicaid form).

59 FR 36072, July 15, 1994: Medicare and State Health Care Programs: Fraud and Abuse, Civil Money Penalties and Intermediate Sanctions for Certain Violations by Health Maintenance Organizations and Competitive Medical Plans — Final rule affecting 42 CFR Parts 417, 431, 434, and 1003. See also correction at 59 FR 48566, September 22, 1994.

59 FR 49834, September 30, 1994: Medicare Program; Qualified Health Maintenance Organizations; Technical Amendments — Final rule with comment period, affecting 42 CFR Part 417.

59 FR 59933, November 21, 1994: Medicare Program; Appeal Rights and Procedures for Beneficiaries Enrolled in Prepaid Health Care Plans — Final rule affecting 42 CFR Part 417.

60 FR 14435, March 17, 1995: HCFA Public Information Collection Requirements Submitted to the Office of Management and Budget (OMB) for Clearance (pertaining to Medicaid drug rebates, termination of enrollment in Federally Qualified HMOs, imposition of cost-sharing charges in Medicaid, Medicare current beneficiary surveys, and forms for establishing entitlement to hospital insurance).

60 FR 34885, July 5, 1995: HCFA Full Reporting by Health Maintenance Organizations (HMO's) and Competitive Medical Plans (CMP's) Paid on a Cost Basis — Final rule affecting 42 CFR Part 417. See also correction at 60 FR 45372, August 31, 1995.

60 FR 45673, September 1, 1995: Medicare Program; Contracts with Health Maintenance Organizations (HMO's) and Competitive Medical Plans (CMP's) — Final rule with comment period, affecting 42 CFR Part 417.

60 FR 46228, September 6, 1995: Medicare Program; Payments of HMO's and CMP's and Appeals: Technical Amendments — Final rule with comment period, affecting 42 CFR Part 417.

61 FR 2122, January 25, 1996: Medicare and State Health Care Programs; Fraud and Abuse; Safe Harbors for Protecting Health Plans — Final rule.

61 FR 2255, January 25, 1996: HCFA Public Information Collection Requirements Submitted for Public Comment and Recommendations (pertaining to survey forms about health and safety requirements for physical therapists in independent practice; and national data reporting requirements for HMOs and CMPs).

61 FR 13430, March 27, 1996: Medicare and Medicaid Programs; Requirements for Physician Incentive Plans in Prepaid Health Care Organizations — Final rule with comment period, affecting 42 CFR Parts 417, 434, and 1003.

61 FR 29406, June 10, 1996: HCFA Agency Information Collection Activities: proposed Collection; Comment Request (pertaining to end stage renal disease application and survey and certification report forms; withholding Medicare payments to recover Medicaid overpayments; acquisition, protection, and disclosure of PRO information; clinical laboratory certification and recertification survey forms; CLIA laboratory personnel report forms; prepaid health plan cost reports; Medicare credit balance reporting requirements; statement of deficiencies and plan of correction requirements for organ procurement organizations; Medicare/Medicaid hospital survey report forms; advance directive requirements for Medicare and Medicaid; payment adjustments for sole community hospitals; survey reports for physical therapists in independent practice; HMO and CMP national data reporting requirements; identification of extension units of outpatient physical therapy and outpatient speech pathology providers; and fire safety survey reports).

61 FR 34437, July 2, 1996: HCFA Agency Information Collection Activities: Submission for OMB Review; Comment Request (pertaining to Peer Review Organization procedures for reconsideration of initial decisions; Part B enrollment forms; certification of rural health clinics for Medicare participation; Medicaid utilization review requirements for home health agencies; State listings of Medicaid recipients in institutions and procedures for State inspection of care review; procedures for disenrollment of beneficiaries from HMOs or CMPs; effectiveness of telemedicine services; formats for PROs to

submit data to HCFA; and request for accelerated payments forms for providers).

61 FR 58568, November 15, 1996: Office of Inspector General; Publication of the Medicare Beneficiary Advisory Bulletin on HMO Arrangements — Notice.

61 FR 67566, December 23, 1996: HCFA Emergency Clearance: Public Information Collection Requirements Submitted to OMB (pertaining to assessment of health plans).

61 FR 69034, December 30, 1996: Medicare and Medicaid Programs; Requirements for Physician Incentive Plans in Prepaid Health Care Organizations — Final rule affecting 42 CFR Parts 417 and 434.

62 FR 12834, March 18, 1997: HCFA Correction Notice: Agency Information Collection Activities: Submission for Emergency OMB Review; Comment request (pertaining to managed care organization incentive arrangement disclosure form).

62 FR 23368, April 30, 1997: Medicare Program; Establishment of an Expedited Review process for Medicare Beneficiaries Enrolled in Health Maintenance Organizations, Competitive Medical Plans, and Health Care Prepayment Plans — Final rule with comment period, affecting 42 CFR Part 417.

62 FR 23781, May 1, 1997: HCFA Agency Information Collection Activities: Proposed Collection; Comment request (pertaining to requirement to disclose HMO financial information to members).

62 FR 28410, May 23, 1997: Office of Inspector General: Health Care Programs: Fraud and Abuse — Notice of Intent to Form the Negotiated Rulemaking Committee for the Shared Risk Exception (statutory exceptions to the anti-kickback statute) — affecting 42 CFR Part 1001.

62 FR 34761, June 27, 1997: HCFA Agency Information Collection activities: Proposed Collection; Comment request (pertaining to managed care organization, incentive arrangement disclosure forms; and qualification application form for competitive medical plans, and Medicare contract application for Federally qualified HMO's).

62 FR 45426, August 27, 1997: HCFA Agency Information Collection Activities: Submission for OMB Review; Comment request (pertaining to qualification applications for competitive medical plans and Federally qualified HMOs).

62 FR 61825, November 19, 1997: HCFA Agency Information Collection Activities; Submission for OMB Review; Comment request

(pertaining to survey forms for consumer assessment of health plans).

63 FR 187, January 5, 1998: Office of Inspector General; Negotiated Rulemaking Committee on the Shared Risk Exception — Notice of meeting.

63 FR 7175, February 12, 1998: HCFA Emergency Clearance: Public Information Collection Requirements Submitted to the Office of Managment and Budget (OMB) (pertaining to managed care adjusted community rate (ACR) proposal).

63 FR 7359, February 13, 1998: Medicare Program; Meeting of the Negotiated Rulemaking Committee on the Provider-Sponsored Organization Solvency Standards — Notice of Meeting

63 FR 11263, March 6, 1998: HCFA Agency Information Collection Activities: Submission for OMB Review; Comment request (pertaining to end stage renal disease managed care demonstration.

63 FR 12475, March 13, 1998: HCFA Agency Information Collection Activities; Submission for OMB Review; Comment request (pertaining to HMO and CMP national data reporting requirements).

63 FR 18924, April 16, 1998: HCFA Emergency Clearance: Public Information Collection Requirements Submitted to the Office of Management and Budget (OMB) (pertaining to collection of managed care data using the uniform institutional providers form).

63 FR 26811, May 14, 1998: Medicare and Medicaid Programs: Request for Public Comments on the Quality Improvement System for Managed Care — Solicitation of comments; notice of public meeting.

63 FR 38311, July 16, 1998: Office of Inspector General: Medicare and State Health Care Programs: Fraud and Abuse; Issuance of Advisory Opinions by the OIG — Final rule affecting 42 CFR 1008. See also correction at 63 FR 43449, August 13, 1998.

63 FR 38414, July 16, 1998: HCFA Privacy Act of 1974; Report of Altered System (pertaining to disclosure of individual-specific information to combat fraud or abuse in health benefit programs).

63 FR 40723, July 30, 1998: HCFA Agency Information Collection Activities: Proposed Collection; Comment request (pertaining to requirements for health care prepayment plan (HCPP) eligibility under Section 1833 of the Social Security Act).

63 FR 42409, August 7, 1998: HCFA Agency Information Collection Activities: Proposed Collection; Comment request (pertaining to health plan data and information consumer assessment survey).

63 FR 43187, August 12, 1998: HCFA Privacy Act of 1974; System of Records — Notice of new system of records pertaining to indicators of the performance of health plans.

63 FR 58059, October 29, 1998: HCFA Agency Information Collection Activities: Submission for OMB Review; Comment request (pertaining to consumer assessment of managed care plans).

63 FR 58399, October 30, 1998: Office of Inspector General: Publication of the OIG's Provider.

63 FR 68223, December 10, 1998: Office of Inspector General; Solicitation of New Safe Harbors and Special Fraud Alerts — Notice of intent to develop regulations, affecting 42 CFR 1001.

1999

64 FR 6664, February 10, 1999: HCFA Agency Information Collection Activities: Proposed Collection; Comment request (pertaining to Medicare agreement applications for health care prepayment plans).

64 FR 25891, May 13, 1999: HCFA Agency Information Collection Activities: Submission for OMB Review; Comment request (pertaining to Medicare agreement application for health care prepayment plans under section 1833).

64 FR 32508, June 17, 1999: HCFA Agency Information Collection Activities: Submission for OMB Review; Comment Request (pertaining to the quality improvement system for managed care (QISMC)).

64 FR 43707, August 11, 1999: HCFA Agency Information Collection Activities: Proposed Collection; Comment request (pertaining to cost reports for prepaid health plans (HMOs and CMPs)).

64 FR 46919, August 27, 1999: HCFA Emergency Clearance: Public Information Collection Requirements Submitted to the Office of Management and Budget (OMB) (pertaining to survey of disenrollment by Medicare beneficiaries from alternative health plans).

64 FR 67223, December 1, 1999: Medicaid Program; External Quality Review of Medicaid Managed Care Organizations — Proposed rule affecting 42 CFR Parts 433 and 438.

2000

65 FR 25737, May 3, 2000: HCFA Agency Information Collection Activities: Proposed Collection; Comment request (pertaining to managed care disenrollment form).

65 FR 25738, May 3, 2000: HCFA Emergency Clearance: Public Informatiion Collection Requirements Submitted to the Office of

Management and Budget (OMB) (pertaining to the Medicare managed care CAHPS Survey).

65 FR 26618, May 5, 2000: HCFA Emergency Clearance: Public Information Collection Requirements Submitted to the Office of Management and Budget (OMB) (pertaining to Medicare consumer assessment survey of health plans).

65 FR 40111, June 29, 2000: HCFA Agency Information Collection Activities: Proposed Collection; comment request (pertaining to qualification applications for prepaid health plans (HMOs).

65 FR 40668, June 30, 2000: HCFA Agency Information Collection Activities: Submission for OMB Review; Comment request (pertaining to Medicare comprehensive health plan disenrollment).

65 FR 43026, July 12, 2000: HCFA Agency Information Collection Activities: Submission for OMB Review; Comment request (pertaining to collection of data on physician encounters from Medicare+Choice organizations).

65 FR 46473, July 28, 2000: Medicare Program; Announcement of a Series of Regional Training Sessions to Provide Training to Medicare+Choice Organization Physicians, Medicare+Choice Organization Non-physician Practitioners, and Medicare+Choice Organization Medicare Directors, As Well As Physician Organizations and Billing Associations Involved in the Timely and Accurate Submission of Physician Encounter Data to Support a Comprehensive Risk Adjustment Model — Notice of training sessions.

65 FR 50713, August 21, 2000: HCFA Agency Information Collection Activities: Proposed Collection; Comment request (pertaining to social HMO demonstration payment methodology)

65 FR 53319, September 1, 2000: HCFA Agency Information Collection Activities: Proposed Collection; Comment request (pertaining to incentive arrangement disclosure form for managed care organizations and their related medical groups and physicians).

65 FR 57195, September 21, 2000: HCFA Agency Information Collection Activities; Proposed Collection; Comment request (pertaining to Medicare managed care CAHPS survey for quality of care purposes).

65 FR 60674, October 12, 2000: HCFA Agency Information Collection Activities: Submission for OMB Review; Comment request (pertaining to Medicare+Choice organization appeals and grievance data disclosure requirements).

65 FR 64228, October 26, 2000: HCFA Agency Information Collection Activities: Proposed Collection; Comment request (pertaining to

collection of data on physician encounters from Medicare+Choice organizations).

65 FR 65860, November 2, 2000: HCFA Agency Information Collection Activities: Proposed Collection; Comment request (pertaining to follow-up of Medicare+Choice disenrollees receiving fee-for service inpatient hospital care).

65 FR 79867, December 20, 2000: HCFA Agency Information Collection Activities: Proposed Collection; Comment request (pertaining to quality improvement system for managed care).

65 FR 79868, December 20, 2000: HCFA Agency Information Collection Activities: Proposed Collection; Comment request (pertaining to Medicare consumer assessment survey of health plans).

65 FR 79868, December 20, 2000: HCFA Emergency Clearance: Public Information Collection Requirements Submitted to the Office of Management and Budget (OMB) (pertaining to survey of beneficiaries who involuntarily disenroll from their managed care plan).

65 FR 81813, December 27, 2000: Medicare Program; Requirements for the Re-credentialing of Medicare+Choice Organization Providers — Proposed rule affecting 42 CFR Part 422.

2001

66 FR 1995, January 10, 2001: HCFA Agency Information Collection Activities: Proposed Collection; Comment request (pertaining to hospital outpatient encounters from Medicare+Choice programs).

66 FR 2913, January 12, 2001: HCFA Agency Information Collection Activities: Submission for OMB Review; Comment request (pertaining to collection of data about physician encounters from Medicare+Choice organizations).

66 FR 6228, January 19, 2001: Medicaid Program; Medicaid Managed Care—Final rule with comment period, affecting 42 CFR Part 400, 430, 431, 435, 438, 440, and 447.

66 FR 7593, January 24, 2001: Medicare Program; Improvements to the Medicare+Choice Appeal and Grievance Procedures—Proposed rule affecting 42 CFR Parts 422 and 489.

66 FR 8807, February 2, 2001: HCFA Agency Information Collection Activities: Submission for OMB Review; Comment request (pertaining to follow–up of Medicare+Choice disenrollees receiving fee–for–service inpatient hospital care).

66 FR 9858, February 12, 2001: HCFA Privacy Act of 1974; Report of New System (pertaining to complaints against health insurance issuers and health plans).

66 FR 11546, February 26, 2001: Medicaid Program; Medicaid Managed Care: Delay of Effective Date—Final rule delay, affecting 42 CFR Parts 400, 430, 431, 434, 435, 438, 440, and 447.

66 FR 11591, February 26, 2001: HCFA Agency Information Collection Activities: Proposed Collection; Comment request (pertaining to Medicare+Choice program requirements).

66 FR 13854, March 8, 2001: Medicare+Choice Program—CFR correction.

66 FR 15122, March 15, 2001: HCFA Agency Information Collection Activities: Submission for OMB Review; Comment request (pertaining to quality improvement system for managed care).

66 FR 16062, March 23, 2001: HCFA Agency Information Collection Activities: Submission for OMB Review; Comment request (pertaining to Medicare+Choice beneficiary appeal notices).

66 FR 16268, March 23, 2001: HCFA Agency Information Collection Activities; Proposed Collection; Comment request (pertaining to data collection to support policy analysis of choices offered to Medicare+Choice enrollees and choices made by enrollees).

66 FR 16481, March 26, 2001: HCFA Agency Information Collection Activities: Submission for OMB Review; Comment request (pertaining to managed care adjusted community rate proposal for Medicare+Choice organizations).

66 FR 16678, March 27, 2001: HCFA Agency Information Collection Activities: Submission for OMB Review; Comment request (pertaining to Medicare managed care CAHPS survey).

66 FR 17431, March 30, 2001: HCFA Agency Information Collection Activities: Proposed Collection; Comment request (pertaining to data collection of quality indicators for congestive heart failure submitted by Medicare+Choice organizations requesting extra payments in CY 2002 and CY 2003).

66 FR 21770, May 1, 2001: Medicare Program; Revision of Payment Rates for End–Stage Renal Disease (ESRD) Patients Enrolled in Medicare+Choice Plans—Proposed notice.

66 FR 21987, May 2, 2001: HCFA Agency Information Collection Activities: Proposed Collection; Comment request (pertaining to Medicare+Choice provider sponsored organization (PSO) waiver request form).

66 FR 24391, May 14, 2001: HCFA Agency Information Collection Activities: Submission for OMB Review; Comment request (pertaining to Medicare+Choice program requirements).

66 FR 28916, May 25, 2001: HCFA Agency Information Collection Activities: Proposed Collection; Comment request (pertaining to collection of managed care data using the uniform institutional providers form).

66 FR 29823, June 1, 2001: HCFA Agency Information Collection Activities: Proposed Collection; Comment request (pertaining to data reporting requirements for managed care organizations in the Medicare+Choice program).

66 FR 32776, June 18, 2001: Medicaid Program; Medicaid Managed Care: Further Delay of Effective Date for Final Rule affecting 42 CFR Parts 400, 430, 431, 434, 435, 438, 440, and 447.

See § 2:39.

§ 6:40 TERMINATING CONTRACTS OF RISK-SHARING ORGANIZATIONS (SUCH AS HEALTH MAINTENANCE ORGANIZATIONS AND COMPETITIVE MEDICAL PLANS) — Section 1876(i)(1) [42 U.S.C.A. 1395mm(i)(1)]

Regulations

42 CFR Part 417 — Health Maintenance Organizations, Competitive Medical Plans, and Health Care Prepayment Plans

42 CFR Part 420 — Program Integrity: Medicare

42 CFR Part 434 — Contracts [Medicaid]

42 CFR Part 455 — Program Integrity: Medicaid

55 FR 12738, June 12, 1990: Waiver of Certain Membership Requirements for Certain Health Maintenance Organizations, (HMOs), and State Option for Disenrollment Restrictions for Certain HMOs under Medicaid — Final rule affecting 42 CFR Parts 434 and 435. See also corrections published at 55 FR 25774, June 22, 1990, and 55 FR 33407, August 15, 1990.

56 FR 29248, June 26, 1991: Medicare Program; HMO Qualification Determinations and Compliance Actions — Notice.

56 FR 30723, July 5, 1991: Health Maintenance Organizations; Conforming Health Maintenance Organization Rules to Statutory Requirements — Proposed rule.

56 FR 31597, July 11, 1991: Health Maintenance Organizations; Group Specific Ratings — Notice of proposed rulemaking.

56 FR 33403, July 22, 1991: Medicare and State Health Care Programs: Fraud and Abuse; Civil Monetary Penalties and Interme-

diate Sanctions for Certain Violations by Health Maintenance Organizations and Competitive Medical Plans — Proposed rule.

56 FR 46562, September 13, 1991: Medicare Program; Explanation of Enrollee Rights and Other Provisions Applicable to Health Maintenance Organizations and Competitive Medical Plans — Final rule affecting 42 CFR Part 417.

57 FR 33202, July 27, 1992: Health Maintenance Organizations; HMO Qualification Determinations and Compliance Actions — Notice. See also correction at 57 FR 41810, September 11, 1992.

57 FR 36006, August 12, 1992: Medicare Program; Self-implementing Coverage and Payments Provisions: 1990 Legislation — Final rule with comment period, affecting 42 CFR Parts 405, 406, 409, 420, 411, 412, 413, 418, and 489. Pertains to capital-related inpatient hospital costs; capital-related outpatient hospital costs; non-capital related outpatient hospital costs; payment for physician pathology services; payment for services of physicians as assistants-at-surgery; payments for ambulatory surgical procedures in hospital outpatient departments; payments for radiology services performed in hospital outpatient departments; hospice benefit extension; enrollment of HMO members in Medicare Part A; coverage of ostomy supplies; application of pre-entitlement stay in psychiatric hospital to limit on payment for inpatient hospital services; payments to dialysis facilities; payment rates for erythropoietin (EPO); and Medicare secondary payer provision for individuals with ESRD. See also confirmation of final rule at 58 FR 58502, November 2, 1993.

57 FR 46119, October 7, 1992: Medicare Program; Appeal Rights and Procedures for Beneficiaries Enrolled in Prepaid Health Care Plans — Notice of proposed rulemaking affecting 42 CFR Part 417.

57 FR 52723, November 5, 1992: Medicare and State Health Care Programs: Fraud and Abuse; Safe Harbors for Protecting Health Plans — Interim final rule with request for comment. See also extension of comment period at 58 FR 2989, January 7, 1993, affecting 42 CFR 1001.

57 FR 59024, December 14, 1992: Medicare and Medicaid Programs; Requirements for Physician Incentive Plans in Prepaid Health Care Organizations — Proposed rule affecting 42 CFR Parts 417 and 434 (HCFA) and 42 CFR Part 1003 (Office of Inspector General). See also extension of comment period at 58 FR 8568, February 16, 1993.

58 FR 5402, January 21, 1993: Health Maintenance Organizations; HMO Qualification Determinations and Compliance Actions — Notice.

58 FR 31407, June 2, 1993: Health Maintenance Organizations: Qualification Determinations and Compliance Actions for Calendar Year 1992, Fourth Quarter — Notice.

58 FR 38062, July 15, 1993: Medicare Program, Health Maintenance Organizations: Technical Amendments — Final rule with comment period, affecting 42 CFR Part 417.

58 FR 38170, July 15, 1993: Health Maintenance Organizations: Organizational Structure and Services — Notice of proposed rulemaking, affecting 42 CFR Part 417. See also correction at 58 FR 46925, September 3, 1993.

58 FR 39820, July 26, 1993: Health Maintenance Organizations: Qualification Determinations and Compliance Actions During the Period January 1, 1993, through March 31, 1993 — Notice.

58 FR 68366, December 27, 1993: Medicare Program; Retroactive Enrollment and Disenrollment in Risk Health Maintenance Organizations and Competitive Medical Plans — Proposed rule affecting 42 CFR Part 417.

59 FR 8429, February 22, 1994: Medicare Program; Health Maintenance Organization and Competitive Medical Plan National Coverage Decisions — Proposed rule affecting 42 CFR Part 417.

59 FR 8435, February 22, 1994: Medicare Program; Limits on Payment to Health Maintenance Organizations (HMOs), Competitive Medical Plans (CMPs), and Health Care Prepayment Plans (HCPPs) — Proposed rule affecting 42 CFR Part 417.

59 FR 11230, March 10, 1994: Medicare Program; Post Contract Protections and Other Coordinated Care Issues (involving HMOs and CMPs that cease to furnish services under Medicare risk or cost contracts) — Proposed rule affecting 42 CFR Part 417.

59 FR 18820, April 20, 1994: HCFA: Health Maintenance Organizations: Qualification Determinations and Compliance Actions During the Period October 1, 1993, through December 31, 1993.

59 FR 23820, May 9, 1994: Medicaid Program; Requirements for Certain Health Insuring Organizations and OBRA '90 Technical Amendments, affecting 42 CFR Parts 434 and 435.

59 FR 25460, May 16, 1994: HCFA Public Information Collection Requirements Submitted to the Office of Management and Budget (OMB) for Clearance (pertaining to Medicare uniform institutional provider bill; hospice survey and deficiencies report form; HMO

financial information reports to members; hospital request for certification in Medicare and Medicaid form).

59 FR 36072, July 15, 1994: Medicare and State Health Care Programs: Fraud and Abuse, Civil Money Penalties and Intermediate Sanctions for Certain Violations by Health Maintenance Organizations and Competitive Medical Plans — Final rule affecting 42 CFR Parts 417, 431, 434, and 1003. See also correction at 59 FR 48566, September 22, 1994.

59 FR 49834, September 30, 1994: Medicare Program; Qualified Health Maintenance Organizations; Technical Amendments — Final rule with comment period, affecting 42 CFR Part 417.

59 FR 59933, November 21, 1994: Medicare Program; Appeal Rights and Procedures for Beneficiaries Enrolled in Prepaid Health Care Plans — Final rule affecting 42 CFR Part 417.

60 FR 14435, March 17, 1995: HCFA Public Information Collection Requirements Submitted to the Office of Management and Budget (OMB) for Clearance (pertaining to Medicaid drug rebates, termination of enrollment in Federally Qualified HMOs, imposition of cost-sharing charges in Medicaid, Medicare current beneficiary surveys, and forms for establishing entitlement to hospital insurance).

60 FR 34885, July 5, 1995: HCFA Full Reporting by Health Maintenance Organizations (HMO's) and Competitive Medical Plans (CMP's) Paid on a Cost Basis — Final rule affecting 42 CFR Part 417. See also correction at 60 FR 45372, August 31, 1995.

60 FR 45673, September 1, 1995: Medicare Program; Contracts with Health Maintenance Organizations (HMO's) and Competitive Medical Plans (CMP's) — Final rule with comment period, affecting 42 CFR Part 417.

60 FR 46228, September 6, 1995: Medicare Program; Payments of HMO's and CMP's and Appeals: Technical Amendments — Final rule with comment period, affecting 42 CFR Part 417.

61 FR 2122, January 25, 1996: Medicare and State Health Care Programs; Fraud and Abuse; Safe Harbors for Protecting Health Plans — Final rule.

61 FR 2255, January 25, 1996: HCFA Public Information Collection Requirements Submitted for Public Comment and Recommendations (pertaining to survey forms about health and safety requirements for physical therapists in independent practice; and national data reporting requirements for HMOs and CMPs).

61 FR 13430, March 27, 1996: Medicare and Medicaid Programs; Requirements for Physician Incentive Plans in Prepaid Health Care Organizations — Final rule with comment period, affecting 42 CFR Parts 417, 434, and 1003.

61 FR 29406, June 10, 1996: HCFA Agency Information Collection Activities: proposed Collection; Comment Request (pertaining to end stage renal disease application and survey and certification report forms; withholding Medicare payments to recover Medicaid overpayments; acquisition, protection, and disclosure of PRO information; clinical laboratory certification and recertification survey forms; CLIA laboratory personnel report forms; prepaid health plan cost reports; Medicare credit balance reporting requirements; statement of deficiencies and plan of correction requirements for organ procurement organizations; Medicare/Medicaid hospital survey report forms; advance directive requirements for Medicare and Medicaid; payment adjustments for sole community hospitals; survey reports for physical therapists in independent practice; HMO and CMP national data reporting requirements; identification of extension units of outpatient physical therapy and outpatient speech pathology providers; and fire safety survey reports).

61 FR 34437, July 2, 1996: HCFA Agency Information Collection Activities: Submission for OMB Review; Comment Request (pertaining to Peer Review Organization procedures for reconsideration of initial decisions; Part B enrollment forms; certification of rural health clinics for Medicare participation; Medicaid utilization review requirements for home health agencies; State listings of Medicaid recipients in institutions and procedures for State inspection of care review; procedures for disenrollment of beneficiaries from HMOs or CMPs; effectiveness of telemedicine services; formats for PROs to submit data to HCFA; and request for accelerated payments forms for providers).

61 FR 58568, November 15, 1996: Office of Inspector General; Publication of the Medicare Beneficiary Advisory Bulletin on HMO Arrangements — Notice.

61 FR 67566, December 23, 1996: HCFA Emergency Clearance: Public Information Collection Requirements Submitted to OMB (pertaining to assessment of health plans).

61 FR 69034, December 30, 1996: Medicare and Medicaid Programs; Requirements for Physician Incentive Plans in Prepaid Health Care Organizations — Final rule affecting 42 CFR Parts 417 and 434.

62 FR 12834, March 18, 1997: HCFA Correction Notice: Agency Information Collection Activities: Submission for Emergency OMB Review; Comment request (pertaining to managed care organization incentive arrangement disclosure form).

62 FR 23368, April 30, 1997: Medicare Program; Establishment of an Expedited Review process for Medicare Beneficiaries Enrolled in Health Maintenance Organizations, Competitive Medical Plans, and Health Care Prepayment Plans — Final rule with comment period, affecting 42 CFR Part 417.

62 FR 23781, May 1, 1997: HCFA Agency Information Collection Activities: Proposed Collection; Comment request (pertaining to requirement to disclose HMO financial information to members).

62 FR 28410, May 23, 1997: Office of Inspector General: Health Care Programs: Fraud and Abuse — Notice of Intent to Form the Negotiated Rulemaking Committee for the Shared Risk Exception (statutory exceptions to the anti-kickback statute) — affecting 42 CFR Part 1001.

62 FR 34761, June 27, 1997: HCFA Agency Information Collection activities: Proposed Collection; Comment request (pertaining to managed care organization, incentive arrangement disclosure forms; and qualification application form for competitive medical plans, and Medicare contract application for Federally qualified HMO's).

62 FR 45426, August 27, 1997: HCFA Agency Information Collection Activities: Submission for OMB Review; Comment request (pertaining to qualification applications for competitive medical plans and Federally qualified HMOs).

62 FR 61825, November 19, 1997: HCFA Agency Information Collection Activities; Submission for OMB Review; Comment request (pertaining to survey forms for consumer assessment of health plans).

63 FR 187, January 5, 1998: Office of Inspector General; Negotiated Rulemaking Committee on the Shared Risk Exception — Notice of meeting.

63 FR 7175, February 12, 1998: HCFA Emergency Clearance: Public Information Collection Requirements Submitted to the Office of Managment and Budget (OMB) (pertaining to managed care adjusted community rate (ACR) proposal).

63 FR 11263, March 6, 1998: HCFA Agency Information Collection Activities: Submission for OMB Review; Comment request (pertaining to end stage renal disease managed care demonstration.

63 FR 12475, March 13, 1998: HCFA Agency Information Collection Activities; Submission for OMB Review; Comment request (pertaining to HMO and CMP national data reporting requirements).

63 FR 18924, April 16, 1998: HCFA Emergency Clearance: Public Information Collection Requirements Submitted to the Office of Management and Budget (OMB) (pertaining to collection of managed care data using the uniform institutional providers form).

63 FR 26811, May 14, 1998: Medicare and Medicaid Programs: Request for Public Comments on the Quality Improvement System for Managed Care — Solicitation of comments; notice of public meeting.

63 FR 38311, July 16, 1998: Office of Inspector General: Medicare and State Health Care Programs: Fraud and Abuse; Issuance of Advisory Opinions by the OIG — Final rule affecting 42 CFR 1008. See also correction at 63 FR 43449, August 13, 1998.

63 FR 38414, July 16, 1998: HCFA Privacy Act of 1974; Report of Altered System (pertaining to disclosure of individual-specific information to combat fraud or abuse in health benefit programs).

63 FR 40723, July 30, 1998: HCFA Agency Information Collection Activities: Proposed Collection; Comment request (pertaining to requirements for health care prepayment plan (HCPP) eligibility under Section 1833 of the Social Security Act).

63 FR 42409, August 7, 1998: HCFA Agency Information Collection Activities: Proposed Collection; Comment request (pertaining to health plan data and information consumer assessment survey).

63 FR 43187, August 12, 1998: HCFA Privacy Act of 1974; System of Records — Notice of new system of records pertaining to indicators of the performance of health plans.

63 FR 58059, October 29, 1998: HCFA Agency Information Collection Activities: Submission for OMB Review; Comment request (pertaining to consumer assessment of managed care plans).

63 FR 58399, October 30, 1998: Office of Inspector General: Publication of the OIG's Provider Self-Disclosure Protocol — Notice.

63 FR 68223, December 10, 1998: Office of Inspector General; Solicitation of New Safe Harbors and Special Fraud Alerts — Notice of intent to develop regulations, affecting 42 CFR 1001.

1999

64 FR 6664, February 10, 1999: HCFA Agency Information Collection Activities: Proposed Collection; Comment request (pertaining to Medicare agreement applications for health care prepayment plans).

64 FR 7968, February 17, 1999: Medicare Program; Changes to the Medicare+Choice Program — Final rule affecting 42 CFR Part 422.

64 FR 25891, May 13, 1999: HCFA Agency Information Collection Activities: Submission for OMB Review; Comment request (pertaining to Medicare agreement application for health care prepayment plans under section 1833).

64 FR 32508, June 17, 1999: HCFA Agency Information Collection Activities: Submission for OMB Review; Comment Request (pertaining to the quality improvement system for managed care (QISMC)).

64 FR 43707, August 11, 1999: HCFA Agency Information Collection Activities: Proposed Collection; Comment request (pertaining to cost reports for prepaid health plans (HMOs and CMPs)).

64 FR 46919, August 27, 1999: HCFA Emergency Clearance: Public Information Collection Requirements Submitted to the Office of Management and Budget (OMB) (pertaining to survey of disenrollment by Medicare beneficiaries from alternative health plans).

64 FR 42791, September 30, 1999: Office of Inspector General; Publication of the OIG Special Advisory Bulletin on the Effect of Exclusion from Participation in Federal Health Care Programs — Notice. See also correction at 64 FR 55484, October 13, 1999.

64 FR 67223, December 1, 1999: Medicaid Program; External Quality Review of Medicaid Managed Care Organizations — Proposed rule affecting 42 CFR Parts 433 and 438.

64 FR 69217, December 10, 1999: Office of Inspector General; Solicitation of New Safe Harbors and Special Fraud Alerts — Intent to develop regulations affecting 42 CFR Part 1001.

2000

65 FR 25737, May 3, 2000: HCFA Agency Information Collection Activities: Proposed Collection; Comment request (pertaining to managed care disenrollment form).

65 FR 25738, May 3, 2000: HCFA Emergency Clearance: Public Informatiion Collection Requirements Submitted to the Office of Management and Budget (OMB) (pertaining to the Medicare managed care CAHPS Survey).

65 FR 26618, May 5, 2000: HCFA Emergency Clearance: Public Information Collection Requirements Submitted to the Office of Management and Budget (OMB) (pertaining to Medicare consumer assessment survey of health plans).

65 FR 40111, June 29, 2000: HCFA Agency Information Collection Activities: Proposed Collection; comment request (pertaining to qualification applications for prepaid health plans (HMOs).

65 FR 40668, June 30, 2000: HCFA Agency Information Collection Activities: Submission for OMB Review; Comment request (pertaining to Medicare comprehensive health plan disenrollment).

65 FR 43026, July 12, 2000: HCFA Agency Information Collection Activities: Submission for OMB Review; Comment request (pertaining to collection of data on physician encounters from Medicare+Choice organizations).

65 FR 46473, July 28, 2000: Medicare Program; Announcement of a Series of Regional Training Sessions to Provide Training to Medicare+Choice Organization Physicians, Medicare+Choice Organization Non-physician Practitioners, and Medicare+Choice Organization Medicare Directors, As Well As Physician Organizations and Billing Associations Involved in the Timely and Accurate Submission of Physician Encounter Data to Support a Comprehensive Risk Adjustment Model — Notice of training sessions.

65 FR 50713, August 21, 2000: HCFA Agency Information Collection Activities: Proposed Collection; Comment request (pertaining to social HMO demonstration payment methodology)

65 FR 53319, September 1, 2000: HCFA Agency Information Collection Activities: Proposed Collection; Comment request (pertaining to incentive arrangement disclosure form for managed care organizations and their related medical groups and physicians).

65 FR 57195, September 21, 2000: HCFA Agency Information Collection Activities; Proposed Collection; Comment request (pertaining to Medicare managed care CAHPS survey for quality of care purposes).

65 FR 60674, October 12, 2000: HCFA Agency Information Collection Activities: Submission for OMB Review; Comment request (pertaining to Medicare+Choice organization appeals and grievance data disclosure requirements).

65 FR 64228, October 26, 2000: HCFA Agency Information Collection Activities: Proposed Collection; Comment request (pertaining to collection of data on physician encounters from Medicare+Choice organizations).

65 FR 65860, November 2, 2000: HCFA Agency Information Collection Activities: Proposed Collection; Comment request (pertaining to follow-up of Medicare+Choice disenrollees receiving fee-for service inpatient hospital care).

65 FR 79867, December 20, 2000: HCFA Agency Information Collection Activities: Proposed Collection; Comment request (pertaining to quality improvement system for managed care).

65 FR 79868, December 20, 2000: HCFA Agency Information Collection Activities: Proposed Collection; Comment request (pertaining to Medicare consumer assessment survey of health plans).

65 FR 79868, December 20, 2000: HCFA Emergency Clearance: Public Information Collection Requirements Submitted to the Office of Management and Budget (OMB) (pertaining to survey of beneficiaries who involuntarily disenroll from their managed care plan).

65 FR 81813, December 27, 2000: Medicare Program; Requirements for the Re-credentialing of Medicare+Choice Organization Providers — Proposed rule affecting 42 CFR Part 422.

2001

66 FR 1995, January 10, 2001: HCFA Agency Information Collection Activities: Proposed Collection; Comment request (pertaining to hospital outpatient encounters from Medicare+Choice programs).

66 FR 2913, January 12, 2001: HCFA Agency Information Collection Activities: Submission for OMB Review; Comment request (pertaining to collection of data about physician encounters from Medicare+Choice organizations).

66 FR 6228, January 19, 2001: Medicaid Program; Medicaid Managed Care—Final rule with comment period, affecting 42 CFR Part 400, 430, 431, 435, 438, 440, and 447.

66 FR 7593, January 24, 2001: Medicare Program; Improvements to the Medicare+Choice Appeal and Grievance Procedures—Proposed rule affecting 42 CFR Parts 422 and 489.

66 FR 8807, February 2, 2001: HCFA Agency Information Collection Activities: Submission for OMB Review; Comment request (pertaining to follow–up of Medicare+Choice disenrollees receiving fee–for–service inpatient hospital care).

66 FR 9858, February 12, 2001: HCFA Privacy Act of 1974; Report of New System (pertaining to complaints against health insurance issuers and health plans).

66 FR 11546, February 26, 2001: Medicaid Program; Medicaid Managed Care: Delay of Effective Date—Final rule delay, affecting 42 CFR Parts 400, 430, 431, 434, 435, 438, 440, and 447.

66 FR 11591, February 26, 2001: HCFA Agency Information Collection Activities: Proposed Collection; Comment request (pertaining to Medicare+Choice program requirements).

66 FR 13854, March 8, 2001: Medicare+Choice Program—CFR correction.

66 FR 15122, March 15, 2001: HCFA Agency Information Collection Activities: Submission for OMB Review; Comment request (pertaining to quality improvement system for managed care).

66 FR 16062, March 23, 2001: HCFA Agency Information Collection Activities: Submission for OMB Review; Comment request (pertaining to Medicare+Choice beneficiary appeal notices).

66 FR 16268, March 23, 2001: HCFA Agency Information Collection Activities; Proposed Collection; Comment request (pertaining to data collection to support policy analysis of choices offered to Medicare+Choice enrollees and choices made by enrollees).

66 FR 16481, March 26, 2001: HCFA Agency Information Collection Activities: Submission for OMB Review; Comment request (pertaining to managed care adjusted community rate proposal for Medicare+Choice organizations).

66 FR 16678, March 27, 2001: HCFA Agency Information Collection Activities: Submission for OMB Review; Comment request (pertaining to Medicare managed care CAHPS survey).

66 FR 17431, March 30, 2001: HCFA Agency Information Collection Activities: Proposed Collection; Comment request (pertaining to data collection of quality indicators for congestive heart failure submitted by Medicare+Choice organizations requesting extra payments in CY 2002 and CY 2003).

66 FR 21770, May 1, 2001: Medicare Program; Revision of Payment Rates for End–Stage Renal Disease (ESRD) Patients Enrolled in Medicare+Choice Plans—Proposed notice.

66 FR 21987, May 2, 2001: HCFA Agency Information Collection Activities: Proposed Collection; Comment request (pertaining to Medicare+Choice provider sponsored organization (PSO) waiver request form).

66 FR 24391, May 14, 2001: HCFA Agency Information Collection Activities: Submission for OMB Review; Comment request (pertaining to Medicare+Choice program requirements).

66 FR 28916, May 25, 2001: HCFA Agency Information Collection Activities: Proposed Collection; Comment request (pertaining to collection of managed care data using the uniform institutional providers form).

66 FR 29823, June 1, 2001: HCFA Agency Information Collection Activities: Proposed Collection; Comment request (pertaining to data reporting requirements for managed care organizations in the Medicare+Choice program).

66 FR 32776, June 18, 2001: Medicaid Program; Medicaid Managed Care: Further Delay of Effective Date for Final Rule affecting 42 CFR Parts 400, 430, 431, 434, 435, 438, 440, and 447.

See § 2:40.

§ 6:41 FAILURE BY RISK-SHARING ORGANIZATIONS (SUCH AS HEALTH MAINTENANCE ORGANIZATIONS AND COMPETITIVE MEDICAL PLANS) TO COMPLY WITH REQUIREMENTS FOR PROVISION OF SERVICES, PREMIUMS, TREATMENT OF APPLICANTS AND MEMBERS, TRUTHFULNESS, PROMPT PAYMENT, AND AVOIDING BUSINESS RELATIONSHIPS WITH EXCLUDED INDIVIDUALS AND ENTITIES — Section 1876(i)(6) [42 U.S.C.A. 1395mm(i)(6)]

Regulations

42 CFR Part 417 — Health Maintenance Organizations, Competitive Medical Plans, and Health Care Prepayment Plans

42 CFR Part 420 — Program Integrity: Medicare

42 CFR Part 434 — Contracts [Medicaid]

42 CFR Part 455 — Program Integrity: Medicaid

42 CFR Chapter V — Office of Inspector General — Health Care, Department of Health and Human Services

Subchapter A — General Provisions

Part 1000 — Introduction; General Definitions

Subchapter B — OIG Authorities

Part 1001 — Program Integrity: Medicare and State Health Care Programs

Part 1002 — Program Integrity: State–initiated Exclusions from Medicaid

Part 1003 — Civil Money Penalties, Assessments and Exclusions

Part 1004 — Imposition of Sanctions on Health Care Practitioners and Providers of Health Care Services by a Peer Review Organization

Part 1005 — Appeals of Exclusions, Civil Money Penalties and Assessments

Part 1006 — Investigational Inquiries

Part 1007 — State Medicaid Fraud Control Units

Part 1008 — Advisory Opinions by the OIG

55 FR 12738, June 12, 1990: Waiver of Certain Membership Requirements for Certain Health Maintenance Organizations, (HMOs), and State Option for Disenrollment Restrictions for Certain HMOs under Medicaid — Final rule affecting 42 CFR Parts 434 and 435. See also corrections published at 55 FR 25774, June 22, 1990, and 55 FR 33407, August 15, 1990.

56 FR 29248, June 26, 1991: Medicare Program; HMO Qualification Determinations and Compliance Actions — Notice.

56 FR 30723, July 5, 1991: Health Maintenance Organizations; Conforming Health Maintenance Organization Rules to Statutory Requirements — Proposed rule.

56 FR 31597, July 11, 1991: Health Maintenance Organizations; Group Specific Ratings — Notice of proposed rulemaking.

56 FR 33403, July 22, 1991: Medicare and State Health Care Programs: Fraud and Abuse; Civil Monetary Penalties and Intermediate Sanctions for Certain Violations by Health Maintenance Organizations and Competitive Medical Plans — Proposed rule.

56 FR 46562, September 13, 1991: Medicare Program; Explanation of Enrollee Rights and Other Provisions Applicable to Health Maintenance Organizations and Competitive Medical Plans — Final rule affecting 42 CFR Part 417.

57 FR 33202, July 27, 1992: Health Maintenance Organizations; HMO Qualification Determinations and Compliance Actions — Notice. See also correction at 57 FR 41810, September 11, 1992.

57 FR 36006, August 12, 1992: Medicare Program; Self-implementing Coverage and Payments Provisions: 1990 Legislation — Final rule with comment period, affecting 42 CFR Parts 405, 406, 409, 420, 411, 412, 413, 418, and 489. Pertains to capital-related inpatient hospital costs; capital-related outpatient hospital costs; non-capital related outpatient hospital costs; payment for physician pathology services; payment for services of physicians as assistants-at-surgery; payments for ambulatory surgi-

cal procedures in hospital outpatient departments; payments for radiology services performed in hospital outpatient departments; hospice benefit extension; enrollment of HMO members in Medicare Part A; coverage of ostomy supplies; application of pre-entitlement stay in psychiatric hospital to limit on payment for inpatient hospital services; payments to dialysis facilities; payment rates for erythropoietin (EPO); and Medicare secondary payer provision for individuals with ESRD. See also confirmation of final rule at 58 FR 58502, November 2, 1993.

57 FR 46119, October 7, 1992: Medicare Program; Appeal Rights and Procedures for Beneficiaries Enrolled in Prepaid Health Care Plans — Notice of proposed rulemaking affecting 42 CFR Part 417.

57 FR 52723, November 5, 1992: Medicare and State Health Care Programs: Fraud and Abuse; Safe Harbors for Protecting Health Plans — Interim final rule with request for comment. See also extension of comment period at 58 FR 2989, January 7, 1993, affecting 42 CFR 1001.

57 FR 59024, December 14, 1992: Medicare and Medicaid Programs; Requirements for Physician Incentive Plans in Prepaid Health Care Organizations — Proposed rule affecting 42 CFR Parts 417 and 434 (HCFA) and 42 CFR Part 1003 (Office of Inspector General). See also extension of comment period at 58 FR 8568, February 16, 1993.

58 FR 5402, January 21, 1993: Health Maintenance Organizations; HMO Qualification Determinations and Compliance Actions — Notice.

58 FR 31407, June 2, 1993: Health Maintenance Organizations: Qualification Determinations and Compliance Actions for Calendar Year 1992, Fourth Quarter — Notice.

58 FR 38062, July 15, 1993: Medicare Program, Health Maintenance Organizations: Technical Amendments — Final rule with comment period, affecting 42 CFR Part 417.

58 FR 38170, July 15, 1993: Health Maintenance Organizations: Organizational Structure and Services — Notice of proposed rulemaking, affecting 42 CFR Part 417. See also correction at 58 FR 46925, September 3, 1993.

58 FR 39820, July 26, 1993: Health Maintenance Organizations: Qualification Determinations and Compliance Actions During the Period January 1, 1993, through March 31, 1993 — Notice.

58 FR 68366, December 27, 1993: Medicare Program; Retroactive Enrollment and Disenrollment in Risk Health Maintenance Organi-

zations and Competitive Medical Plans — Proposed rule affecting 42 CFR Part 417.

59 FR 8429, February 22, 1994: Medicare Program; Health Maintenance Organization and Competitive Medical Plan National Coverage Decisions — Proposed rule affecting 42 CFR Part 417.

59 FR 8435, February 22, 1994: Medicare Program; Limits on Payment to Health Maintenance Organizations (HMOs), Competitive Medical Plans (CMPs), and Health Care Prepayment Plans (HCPPs) — Proposed rule affecting 42 CFR Part 417.

59 FR 11230, March 10, 1994: Medicare Program; Post Contract Protections and Other Coordinated Care Issues (involving HMOs and CMPs that cease to furnish services under Medicare risk or cost contracts) — Proposed rule affecting 42 CFR Part 417.

59 FR 18820, April 20, 1994: HCFA: Health Maintenance Organizations: Qualification Determinations and Compliance Actions During the Period October 1, 1993, through December 31, 1993.

59 FR 23820, May 9, 1994: Medicaid Program; Requirements for Certain Health Insuring Organizations and OBRA '90 Technical Amendments, affecting 42 CFR Parts 434 and 435.

59 FR 25460, May 16, 1994: HCFA Public Information Collection Requirements Submitted to the Office of Management and Budget (OMB) for Clearance (pertaining to Medicare uniform institutional provider bill; hospice survey and deficiencies report form; HMO financial information reports to members; hospital request for certification in Medicare and Medicaid form).

59 FR 36072, July 15, 1994: Medicare and State Health Care Programs: Fraud and Abuse, Civil Money Penalties and Intermediate Sanctions for Certain Violations by Health Maintenance Organizations and Competitive Medical Plans — Final rule affecting 42 CFR Parts 417, 431, 434, and 1003. See also correction at 59 FR 48566, September 22, 1994.

59 FR 49834, September 30, 1994: Medicare Program; Qualified Health Maintenance Organizations; Technical Amendments — Final rule with comment period, affecting 42 CFR Part 417.

59 FR 59933, November 21, 1994: Medicare Program; Appeal Rights and Procedures for Beneficiaries Enrolled in Prepaid Health Care Plans — Final rule affecting 42 CFR Part 417.

60 FR 14435, March 17, 1995: HCFA Public Information Collection Requirements Submitted to the Office of Management and Budget (OMB) for Clearance (pertaining to Medicaid drug rebates,

termination of enrollment in Federally Qualified HMOs, imposition of cost-sharing charges in Medicaid, Medicare current beneficiary surveys, and forms for establishing entitlement to hospital insurance).

60 FR 34885, July 5, 1995: HCFA Full Reporting by Health Maintenance Organizations (HMO's) and Competitive Medical Plans (CMP's) Paid on a Cost Basis — Final rule affecting 42 CFR Part 417. See also correction at 60 FR 45372, August 31, 1995.

60 FR 45673, September 1, 1995: Medicare Program; Contracts with Health Maintenance Organizations (HMO's) and Competitive Medical Plans (CMP's) — Final rule with comment period, affecting 42 CFR Part 417.

60 FR 46228, September 6, 1995: Medicare Program; Payments of HMO's and CMP's and Appeals: Technical Amendments — Final rule with comment period, affecting 42 CFR Part 417.

61 FR 2122, January 25, 1996: Medicare and State Health Care Programs; Fraud and Abuse; Safe Harbors for Protecting Health Plans — Final rule.

61 FR 2255, January 25, 1996: HCFA Public Information Collection Requirements Submitted for Public Comment and Recommendations (pertaining to survey forms about health and safety requirements for physical therapists in independent practice; and national data reporting requirements for HMOs and CMPs).

61 FR 13430, March 27, 1996: Medicare and Medicaid Programs; Requirements for Physician Incentive Plans in Prepaid Health Care Organizations — Final rule with comment period, affecting 42 CFR Parts 417, 434, and 1003.

61 FR 29406, June 10, 1996: HCFA Agency Information Collection Activities: proposed Collection; Comment Request (pertaining to end stage renal disease application and survey and certification report forms; withholding Medicare payments to recover Medicaid overpayments; acquisition, protection, and disclosure of PRO information; clinical laboratory certification and recertification survey forms; CLIA laboratory personnel report forms; prepaid health plan cost reports; Medicare credit balance reporting requirements; statement of deficiencies and plan of correction requirements for organ procurement organizations; Medicare/Medicaid hospital survey report forms; advance directive requirements for Medicare and Medicaid; payment adjustments for sole community hospitals; survey reports for physical therapists in independent practice; HMO and CMP national data reporting requirements; identification of extension

units of outpatient physical therapy and outpatient speech pathology providers; and fire safety survey reports).

61 FR 34437, July 2, 1996: HCFA Agency Information Collection Activities: Submission for OMB Review; Comment Request (pertaining to Peer Review Organization procedures for reconsideration of initial decisions; Part B enrollment forms; certification of rural health clinics for Medicare participation; Medicaid utilization review requirements for home health agencies; State listings of Medicaid recipients in institutions and procedures for State inspection of care review; procedures for disenrollment of beneficiaries from HMOs or CMPs; effectiveness of telemedicine services; formats for PROs to submit data to HCFA; and request for accelerated payments forms for providers).

61 FR 58568, November 15, 1996: Office of Inspector General; Publication of the Medicare Beneficiary Advisory Bulletin on HMO Arrangements — Notice.

61 FR 67566, December 23, 1996: HCFA Emergency Clearance: Public Information Collection Requirements Submitted to OMB (pertaining to assessment of health plans).

61 FR 69034, December 30, 1996: Medicare and Medicaid Programs; Requirements for Physician Incentive Plans in Prepaid Health Care Organizations — Final rule affecting 42 CFR Parts 417 and 434.

62 FR 12834, March 18, 1997: HCFA Correction Notice: Agency Information Collection Activities: Submission for Emergency OMB Review; Comment request (pertaining to managed care organization incentive arrangement disclosure form).

62 FR 23368, April 30, 1997: Medicare Program; Establishment of an Expedited Review process for Medicare Beneficiaries Enrolled in Health Maintenance Organizations, Competitive Medical Plans, and Health Care Prepayment Plans — Final rule with comment period, affecting 42 CFR Part 417.

62 FR 23781, May 1, 1997: HCFA Agency Information Collection Activities: Proposed Collection; Comment request (pertaining to requirement to disclose HMO financial information to members).

62 FR 28410, May 23, 1997: Office of Inspector General: Health Care Programs: Fraud and Abuse — Notice of Intent to Form the Negotiated Rulemaking Committee for the Shared Risk Exception (statutory exceptions to the anti-kickback statute) — affecting 42 CFR Part 1001.

62 FR 34761, June 27, 1997: HCFA Agency Information Collection activities: Proposed Collection; Comment request (pertaining to managed care organization, incentive arrangement disclosure forms; and qualification application form for competitive medical plans, and Medicare contract application for Federally qualified HMO's).

62 FR 45426, August 27, 1997: HCFA Agency Information Collection Activities: Submission for OMB Review; Comment request (pertaining to qualification applications for competitive medical plans and Federally qualified HMOs).

62 FR 61825, November 19, 1997: HCFA Agency Information Collection Activities; Submission for OMB Review; Comment request (pertaining to survey forms for consumer assessment of health plans).

63 FR 187, January 5, 1998: Office of Inspector General; Negotiated Rulemaking Committee on the Shared Risk Exception — Notice of meeting.

63 FR 7175, February 12, 1998: HCFA Emergency Clearance: Public Information Collection Requirements Submitted to the Office of Managment and Budget (OMB) (pertaining to managed care adjusted community rate (ACR) proposal).

63 FR 11263, March 6, 1998: HCFA Agency Information Collection Activities: Submission for OMB Review; Comment request (pertaining to end stage renal disease managed care demonstration.

63 FR 12475, March 13, 1998: HCFA Agency Information Collection Activities; Submission for OMB Review; Comment request (pertaining to HMO and CMP national data reporting requirements).

63 FR 18124, April 14, 1998: Medicare Program; Definition of Provider-Sponsored Organization and Related Requirements — Interim final rule with comment period, affecting 42 CFR 422.

63 FR 18924, April 16, 1998: HCFA Emergency Clearance: Public Information Collection Requirements Submitted to the Office of Management and Budget (OMB) (pertaining to collection of managed care data using the uniform institutional providers form).

63 FR 26811, May 14, 1998: Medicare and Medicaid Programs: Request for Public Comments on the Quality Improvement System for Managed Care — Solicitation of comments; notice of public meeting.

63 FR 38311, July 16, 1998: Office of Inspector General: Medicare and State Health Care Programs: Fraud and Abuse; Issuance of Advisory Opinions by the OIG — Final rule affecting 42 CFR 1008. See also correction at 63 FR 43449, August 13, 1998.

63 FR 38414, July 16, 1998: HCFA Privacy Act of 1974; Report of Altered System (pertaining to disclosure of individual-specific information to combat fraud or abuse in health benefit programs).

63 FR 40723, July 30, 1998: HCFA Agency Information Collection Activities: Proposed Collection; Comment request (pertaining to requirements for health care prepayment plan (HCPP) eligibility under Section 1833 of the Social Security Act).

63 FR 42409, August 7, 1998: HCFA Agency Information Collection Activities: Proposed Collection; Comment request (pertaining to health plan data and information consumer assessment survey).

63 FR 43187, August 12, 1998: HCFA Privacy Act of 1974; System of Records — Notice of new system of records pertaining to indicators of the performance of health plans.

63 FR 58059, October 29, 1998: HCFA Agency Information Collection Activities: Submission for OMB Review; Comment request (pertaining to consumer assessment of managed care plans).

63 FR 58399, October 30, 1998: Office of Inspector General: Publication of the OIG's Provider Self-Disclosure Protocol — Notice.

63 FR 68223, December 10, 1998: Office of Inspector General; Solicitation of New Safe Harbors and Special Fraud Alerts — Notice of intent to develop regulations, affecting 42 CFR 1001.

1999

64 FR 6664, February 10, 1999: HCFA Agency Information Collection Activities: Proposed Collection; Comment request (pertaining to Medicare agreement applications for health care prepayment plans).

64 FR 25891, May 13, 1999: HCFA Agency Information Collection Activities: Submission for OMB Review; Comment request (pertaining to Medicare agreement application for health care prepayment plans under section 1833).

64 FR 32508, June 17, 1999: HCFA Agency Information Collection Activities: Submission for OMB Review; Comment Request (pertaining to the quality improvement system for managed care (QISMC)).

64 FR 43707, August 11, 1999: HCFA Agency Information Collection Activities: Proposed Collection; Comment request (pertaining to cost reports for prepaid health plans (HMOs and CMPs)).

64 FR 46919, August 27, 1999: HCFA Emergency Clearance: Public Information Collection Requirements Submitted to the Office of Management and Budget (OMB) (pertaining to survey of disenrollment by Medicare beneficiaries from alternative health plans).

64 FR 42791, September 30, 1999: Office of Inspector General; Publication of the OIG Special Advisory Bulletin on the Effect of Exclusion from Participation in Federal Health Care Programs — Notice. See also correction at 64 FR 55484, October 13, 1999.

64 FR 67223, December 1, 1999: Medicaid Program; External Quality Review of Medicaid Managed Care Organizations — Proposed rule affecting 42 CFR Parts 433 and 438.

64 FR 69217, December 10, 1999: Office of Inspector General; Solicitation of New Safe Harbors and Special Fraud Alerts — Intent to develop regulations affecting 42 CFR Part 1001.

2000

65 FR 25737, May 3, 2000: HCFA Agency Information Collection Activities: Proposed Collection; Comment request (pertaining to managed care disenrollment form).

65 FR 25737, May 3, 2000: HCFA Agency Information Collection Activities: Proposed Collection; Comment request (pertaining to managed care disenrollment form).

65 FR 25738, May 3, 2000: HCFA Emergency Clearance: Public Informatiion Collection Requirements Submitted to the Office of Management and Budget (OMB) (pertaining to the Medicare managed care CAHPS Survey).

65 FR 26618, May 5, 2000: HCFA Emergency Clearance: Public Information Collection Requirements Submitted to the Office of Management and Budget (OMB) (pertaining to Medicare consumer assessment survey of health plans).

65 FR 40111, June 29, 2000: HCFA Agency Information Collection Activities: Proposed Collection; comment request (pertaining to qualification applications for prepaid health plans (HMOs).

65 FR 40668, June 30, 2000: HCFA Agency Information Collection Activities: Submission for OMB Review; Comment request (pertaining to Medicare comprehensive health plan disenrollment).

65 FR 43026, July 12, 2000: HCFA Agency Information Collection Activities: Submission for OMB Review; Comment request (pertaining to collection of data on physician encounters from Medicare+Choice organizations).

65 FR 46473, July 28, 2000: Medicare Program; Announcement of a Series of Regional Training Sessions to Provide Training to Medicare+Choice Organization Physicians, Medicare+Choice Organization Non-physician Practitioners, and Medicare+Choice Organization Medicare Directors, As Well As Physician Organizations and Billing Associations Involved in the Timely and Accurate Submission of Physician Encounter Data to Support a Comprehensive Risk Adjustment Model — Notice of training sessions.

65 FR 50713, August 21, 2000: HCFA Agency Information Collection Activities: Proposed Collection; Comment request (pertaining to social HMO demonstration payment methodology)

65 FR 53319, September 1, 2000: HCFA Agency Information Collection Activities: Proposed Collection; Comment request (pertaining to incentive arrangement disclosure form for managed care organizations and their related medical groups and physicians).

65 FR 57195, September 21, 2000: HCFA Agency Information Collection Activities; Proposed Collection; Comment request (pertaining to Medicare managed care CAHPS survey for quality of care purposes).

65 FR 60674, October 12, 2000: HCFA Agency Information Collection Activities: Submission for OMB Review; Comment request (pertaining to Medicare+Choice organization appeals and grievance data disclosure requirements).

65 FR 64228, October 26, 2000: HCFA Agency Information Collection Activities: Proposed Collection; Comment request (pertaining to collection of data on physician encounters from Medicare+Choice organizations).

65 FR 65860, November 2, 2000: HCFA Agency Information Collection Activities: Proposed Collection; Comment request (pertaining to follow-up of Medicare+Choice disenrollees receiving fee-for service inpatient hospital care).

65 FR 79867, December 20, 2000: HCFA Agency Information Collection Activities: Proposed Collection; Comment request (pertaining to quality improvement system for managed care).

65 FR 79868, December 20, 2000: HCFA Agency Information Collection Activities: Proposed Collection; Comment request (pertaining to Medicare consumer assessment survey of health plans).

65 FR 79868, December 20, 2000: HCFA Emergency Clearance: Public Information Collection Requirements Submitted to the Office of Management and Budget (OMB) (pertaining to survey of beneficiaries who involuntarily disenroll from their managed care plan).

65 FR 81813, December 27, 2000: Medicare Program; Requirements for the Re-credentialing of Medicare+Choice Organization Providers — Proposed rule affecting 42 CFR Part 422.

2001

66 FR 1995, January 10, 2001: HCFA Agency Information Collection Activities: Proposed Collection; Comment request (pertaining to hospital outpatient encounters from Medicare+Choice programs).

66 FR 2913, January 12, 2001: HCFA Agency Information Collection Activities: Submission for OMB Review; Comment request (pertaining to collection of data about physician encounters from Medicare+Choice organizations).

66 FR 6228, January 19, 2001: Medicaid Program; Medicaid Managed Care—Final rule with comment period, affecting 42 CFR Part 400, 430, 431, 435, 438, 440, and 447.

66 FR 7593, January 24, 2001: Medicare Program; Improvements to the Medicare+Choice Appeal and Grievance Procedures—Proposed rule affecting 42 CFR Parts 422 and 489.

66 FR 8807, February 2, 2001: HCFA Agency Information Collection Activities: Submission for OMB Review; Comment request (pertaining to follow–up of Medicare+Choice disenrollees receiving fee–for–service inpatient hospital care).

66 FR 9858, February 12, 2001: HCFA Privacy Act of 1974; Report of New System (pertaining to complaints against health insurance issuers and health plans).

66 FR 11546, February 26, 2001: Medicaid Program; Medicaid Managed Care: Delay of Effective Date—Final rule delay, affecting 42 CFR Parts 400, 430, 431, 434, 435, 438, 440, and 447.

66 FR 11591, February 26, 2001: HCFA Agency Information Collection Activities: Proposed Collection; Comment request (pertaining to Medicare+Choice program requirements).

66 FR 13854, March 8, 2001: Medicare+Choice Program—CFR correction.

66 FR 15122, March 15, 2001: HCFA Agency Information Collection Activities: Submission for OMB Review; Comment request (pertaining to quality improvement system for managed care).

66 FR 16062, March 23, 2001: HCFA Agency Information Collection Activities: Submission for OMB Review; Comment request (pertaining to Medicare+Choice beneficiary appeal notices).

66 FR 16268, March 23, 2001: HCFA Agency Information Collection Activities; Proposed Collection; Comment request (pertaining to data collection to support policy analysis of choices offered to Medicare+Choice enrollees and choices made by enrollees).

66 FR 16481, March 26, 2001: HCFA Agency Information Collection Activities: Submission for OMB Review; Comment request (pertaining to managed care adjusted community rate proposal for Medicare+Choice organizations).

66 FR 16678, March 27, 2001: HCFA Agency Information Collection Activities: Submission for OMB Review; Comment request (pertaining to Medicare managed care CAHPS survey).

66 FR 17431, March 30, 2001: HCFA Agency Information Collection Activities: Proposed Collection; Comment request (pertaining to data collection of quality indicators for congestive heart failure submitted by Medicare+Choice organizations requesting extra payments in CY 2002 and CY 2003).

66 FR 21770, May 1, 2001: Medicare Program; Revision of Payment Rates for End–Stage Renal Disease (ESRD) Patients Enrolled in Medicare+Choice Plans—Proposed notice.

66 FR 21987, May 2, 2001: HCFA Agency Information Collection Activities: Proposed Collection; Comment request (pertaining to Medicare+Choice provider sponsored organization (PSO) waiver request form).

66 FR 24391, May 14, 2001: HCFA Agency Information Collection Activities: Submission for OMB Review; Comment request (pertaining to Medicare+Choice program requirements).

66 FR 28916, May 25, 2001: HCFA Agency Information Collection Activities: Proposed Collection; Comment request (pertaining to collection of managed care data using the uniform institutional providers form).

66 FR 29823, June 1, 2001: HCFA Agency Information Collection Activities: Proposed Collection; Comment request (pertaining to data reporting requirements for managed care organizations in the Medicare+Choice program).

66 FR 32776, June 18, 2001: Medicaid Program; Medicaid Managed Care: Further Delay of Effective Date for Final Rule affecting 42 CFR Parts 400, 430, 431, 434, 435, 438, 440, and 447.

See § 2:41.

§ 6:42 VIOLATING LIMITATIONS ON PHYSICIAN REFERRALS AND RELATED REPORTING REQUIREMENTS — Section 1877 [42 U.S.C.A. 1395nn]

Regulations

42 CFR Part 402 — Civil Money Penalties, Assessments, and Exclusions

42 CFR Part 405, Subpart E — Criteria for Determination of Reasonable Charges, especially Section 405.515: Payment for clinical laboratory services billed by physicians

42 CFR Part 410 — Supplementary Medical Insurance (SMI) Benefits, especially section 410.32: Diagnostic X-ray tests, diagnostic laboratory tests, and other diagnostic tests: Conditions

42 CFR Part 411, Subpart J — Physician Ownership of, and Referral of Patients or Laboratory Specimens to, Entities Furnishing Clinical Laboratory or Other Health Services

42 CFR Part 415 — Services Furnished by Physicians in Providers, Supervising Physicians in Teaching Settings, and Residents in Certain Settings

42 CFR Part 417 — Health Maintenance Organizations, Competitive Medical Plans, and Health Care Prepayment Plans

42 CFR Part 418 — Hospice Care

42 CFR Part 420 — Program Integrity: Medicare

42 CFR Part 424 — Conditions for Medicare Payment

42 CFR Part 440 — Services: General Provisions [Medicaid], Subpart A — Definitions, especially Section 440.30: Other laboratory and X-ray services

42 CFR Part 447 — Payments for Services [Medicaid], Subpart D — Payment Methods for Other Institutional and Noninstitutional Services, especially Section 447.342: Physician billing for clinical laboratory services

42 CFR 493 — Laboratory Requirements

42 CFR Part 498 — Appeals Procedures for Determinations that Affect Participation in the Medicare Program and for Determinations that Affect the Participation of ICF's/MR and Certain NF's in the Medicaid Program

42 CFR Chapter V — Office of Inspector General — Health Care, Department of Health and Human Services

Subchapter A — General Provisions

Part 1000 — Introduction; General Definitions

Subchapter B — OIG Authorities

Part 1001 — Program Integrity: Medicare and State Health Care Programs

Part 1002 — Program Integrity: State–initiated Exclusion from Medicaid

Part 1003 — Civil Money Penalties, Assessments and Exclusions

Part 1005 — Appeals of Exclusions, Civil Money Penalties and Assessments

Part 1006 — Investigational Inquiries

Part 1007 — State Medicaid Fraud Control Units

Part 1008 — Advisory Opinions by the OIG

55 FR 12205, April 2, 1990: Health Care Programs: Fraud and Abuse; Amendments to OIG Exclusion and CMP Authorities Resulting from Public Law 100–93, the Medicare and Medicaid Patient and Program Protection Act of 1987, Public Law 99–272, the Consolidated Omnibus Budget Reconciliation Act of 1985, and Public Law 100–360, the Medicare Catastrophic Coverage Act of 1988 — Proposed rule to amend 42 CFR Parts 1000, 1001, 1002, 1003, 1004, 1005, 1006, and 1007. See also correction published at 55 FR 17461, April 25, 1990.

56 FR 31647, July 11, 1991: Public Information Collection Requirements Submitted to the Office of Management and Budget for Clearance (re community supported living arrangements and physician financial interest in clinical laboratories survey — Notice.

56 FR 35952, July 29, 1991: Medicare and State Health Care Programs: Fraud and Abuse; OIG Anti-Kickback Provisions — Final rule.

56 FR 61374, December 3, 1991: Medicare Program; Reporting Requirements for Financial Relationships Between Physicians and Health Care Entities That Furnish Selected items and Services — Interim final rule with comment period, affecting 42 CFR Part 411.

57 FR 3298, January 29, 1992: Health Care Programs: Fraud and Abuse; Amendments to OIG Exclusion and CMP Authorities Resulting From Public Law 100–93 — Final rule affecting 42 CFR Parts 1001, 1002, 1003, 1004, 1005, 1006, and 1007. See also final rule and correction at 57 FR 9669, March 20, 1992; final rule affecting 42 CFR Parts 1001 and 1005, with clarification at 58 FR 5617, January 22, 1993; and final rule affecting 42 CFR Part 1001, with correction, at 58 FR 40752, July 30, 1993.

57 FR 8588, March 11, 1992: Medicare Program; Physician Ownership of, and Referrals to, Health Care Entities that Furnish Clinical Laboratory Services — Proposed rule affecting 42 CFR Part 411.

58 FR 49008, September 21, 1993: Office of Inspector General: Additional Safe Harbor Provisions under the OIG Anti-Kickback Statute — Proposed rule pertaining to investment interests in rural areas, in ambulatory surgical centers, and in group practices composed exclusively of active investors; practitioner recruitment; obstetrical malpractice insurance subsidies; referral agreements for specialty services; and cooperative hospital service organizations.

58 FR 54096, October 20, 1993: Office of Inspector General: Civil Money Penalties for Prohibited Referrals to Entities Providing Clinical Laboratory Services and for Prohibited Arrangements and Schemes — Proposed rule affecting 42 CFR Part 1003.

59 FR 9452, February 28, 1994: Office of Inspector General: Health Care Programs; Fraud and Abuse; Revisions to the PRO Sanctions Process — Proposed rule affecting 42 CFR Part 1004.

59 FR 37202, July 21, 1994: Medicare and State Health Care Programs; Fraud and Abuse; Clarification of the OIG Safe Harbor Anti-kickback Provisions — Proposed rule affecting 42 CFR Part 1001.

59 FR 50762, October 5, 1994: HCFA Public Information Collection Requirements Submitted to the Office of Management and Budget (OMB) for Clearance (pertaining to reimbursement of hospital costs for residents and interns, criteria for psychiatric and rehabilitation hospital units' reimbursement under the prospective payment system, disclosure of owners and managers of suppliers for fraud and abuse detection purposes, reimbursement of municipal health services clinics, survey form for hospital compliance with anti-dumping requirements, and evaluation of patient and physician satisfaction with the Medicare participating heart bypass center demonstration).

59 FR 65372, December 19, 1994: Office of Inspector General — Notice of Publication of Special Fraud Alerts (pertaining to joint venture arrangements, routine waiver of Medicare Part B copayments and deductibles, hospital incentives to referring physicians, prescription drug marketing practices, and arrangements for provision of clinical laboratory services).

60 FR 16580, March 31, 1995: Office of Inspector General: Civil Money Penalties for Referrals to Entities and for Prohibited

Arrangements and Schemes — Final rule with comment period, affecting 42 CFR Part 1003.

60 FR 41914, August 14, 1995: Medicare Program; Physician Financial Relationships with, and Referrals to, Health Care Entities that Furnish Clinical Laboratory Services; Financial Relationship Reporting Requirements — Final rule affecting 42 CFR Part 411.

60 FR 32916, June 26, 1995: Office of Inspector General; Health Care Programs; Fraud and Abuse; Technical Revision to the Scope and Effect of the OIG Exclusion Regulations — Final rule affecting 42 CFR Part 1001.

60 FR 63634, December 12, 1995: Office of Inspector General; Health Care Programs: Fraud and Abuse; Revisions to the PRO Sanctions Process — Final rule. See also correction at 61 FR 1841, January 24, 1996.

61 FR 7522, February 28, 1996: HCFA Public Information Collection Requirements Submitted for Public Comment and Recommendations (pertaining to Medicare and Medicaid disclosure of ownership and control interest statements).

61 FR 11646, March 21, 1996: HCFA Agency Information Collection Activities: Proposed Collection; Comment Request (pertaining to advance directives; video display terminal (VDT) operators eye care program; peer review organization sanction regulations; and deficiency correction status information under CLIA).

61 FR 52299, October 7, 1996: Office of Inspector General; Medicare and State Health Care Programs and Program Fraud Civil Remedies: Fraud and Abuse; Civil Money Penalties Inflation Adjustments — Final rule affecting 42 CFR Part 1003.

61 FR 69060, December 31, 1996: Office of Inspector General: Solicitation of New Safe Harbors and Modifications to Existing Safe Harbors — Notice of intent to develop regulations, affecting 42 CFR Part 1001.

62 FR 7350, February 19, 1997: Office of Inspector General: Medicare and State Health Care Programs: Fraud and Abuse; Issuance of Advisory Opinions by the OIG — Interim final rule with comment period, affecting 42 CFR Part 1008.

62 FR 28410, May 23, 1997: Office of Inspector General: Health Care Programs: Fraud and Abuse — Notice of Intent to Form the Negotiated Rulemaking Committee for the Shared Risk Exception (statutory exceptions to the anti-kickback statute) — affecting 42 CFR Part 1001.

62 FR 47182, September 8, 1997: Office of Inspector General: Health Care Programs: Fraud and Abuse; Revised OIG Exclusion Authorities Resulting from Public Law 104–191 — Notice of Proposed rulemaking, affecting 42 CFR Parts 1000, 1001, 1002, and 1005.

62 FR 55410, October 24, 1997: Office of Inspector General: Criteria for Implementing Permissive Exclusion Authority under Section 1128(b)(7) of the Social Security Act — Notice.

62 FR 65049, December 10, 1997: Office of Inspector General: Solicitation of New Safe Harbors and Special Fraud Alerts — Notice of intent to develop regulations, affecting 42 CFR Part 1001.

62 FR 67392, December 24, 1997: Office of Inspector General: Criteria for Implementing Permissive Exclusion Authority under Section 1128(b)(7) of the Social Security Act — Notice.

63 FR 187, January 5, 1998: Office of Inspector General; Negotiated Rulemaking Committee on the Shared Risk Exception — Notice of meeting.

63 FR 8987, February 23, 1998: Office of Inspector General: Publication of the OIG Compliance Program for Hospitals — Notice.

63 FR 9844, February 26, 1998: HCFA Agency Information Collection Activities: Proposed Collection; Comment request (pertaining to procedures for advisory opinions concerning physician referrals and supporting regulations in 42 CFR Sections 411.370- 411.389).

63 FR 14393, March 25, 1998: Office of Inspector General: Health Care Programs: Fraud and Abuse; Revised OIG Civil Money Penalties Resulting from the Health Insurance Portability and Accountability Act of 1996 — Notice of proposed rulemaking, affecting 42 CFR Parts 1003, 1005, and 1006.

63 FR 20415, April 24, 1998: Office of Inspector General: Publication of OIG Special Fraud Alert: Fraud and Abuse in Nursing Home Arrangements with Hospices — Notice.

63 FR 28395, May 22, 1998: HCFA Agency Information Collection Activities: Submission for OMB Review; Comment request (pertaining to procedures for advisory opinions concerning physician referrals and supporting regulations in 42 CFR 411.370 through 411.389).

63 FR 31123, June 8, 1998: Medicare Program; Incentive Programs — Fraud and Abuse — Final rule affecting 42 CFR Part 420.

63 FR 38311, July 16, 1998: Office of Inspector General: Medicare and State Health Care Programs: Fraud and Abuse; Issuance of

Advisory Opinions by the OIG — Final rule affecting 42 CFR 1008. See also correction at 63 FR 43449, August 13, 1998.

63 FR 38414, July 16, 1998: HCFA Privacy Act of 1974; Report of Altered System (pertaining to disclosure of individual-specific information to combat fraud or abuse in health benefit programs).

63 FR 42409, August 7, 1998: Office of Inspector General: Solicitation of Information and Recommendations for Developing OIG Compliance Program Guidance for the Durable Medical Equipment Industry — Notice.

63 FR 42410, August 7, 1998: Office of Inspector General: Publication of the OIG Compliance Program Guidance for Home Health Agencies — Notice.

63 FR 45076, August 24, 1998: Office of Inspector General-Publication of OIG Compliance Program Guidance for Clinical Laboratories.

63 FR 46676, September 2, 1998: Office of Inspector General: Health Care Programs; Fraud and Abuse; Revised OIG Exclusion Authorities Resulting from Public Law 104–191 — Final rule affecting 42 CFR Parts 1000, 1001, 1002, and 1005. See also correction at 63 FR 57918, October 29, 1998.

63 FR 46736, September 2, 1998: Office of Inspector General: Health Care Programs; Fraud and Abuse; Revised OIG Sanction Authorities Resulting from Public Law 105–33 — Notice of proposed rulemaking affecting 42 CFR 1001, 1002, and 1003.

63 FR 58341, October 30, 1998: Office of Inspector General: Health Care Fraud and Abuse Data Collection Program: Reporting of Final Adverse Actions — Notice of proposed rulemaking under section 1128E of the Social Security Act, affecting 45 CFR 61.

63 FR 58399, October 30, 1998: Office of Inspector General: Publication of the OIG's Provider Self-Disclosure Protocol — Notice.

63 FR 68223, December 10, 1998: Office of Inspector General; Solicitation of New Safe Harbors and Special Fraud Alerts — Notice of intent to develop regulations, affecting 42 CFR 1001.

63 FR 70137, December 18, 1998: Office of Inspector General: Solicitation of Information and Recommendations for Developing OIG Compliance Program Guidance for the Nursing Home Industry — Notice.

63 FR 71819, December 30, 1998: Office of Inspector General; Health Care Fraud and Abuse Data Collection Program; Reporting under Section 1128E of the Social Security Act of Final Adverse

Actions — Notice of proposed rule-making; extension of comment period, affecting 45 CFR 61.

1999

64 FR 1813, January 12, 1999: Office of Inspector General Publication of OIG Special Fraud Alert on Physician Liability for Certifications in the Provision of Medical Equipment and Supplies and Home Health Services — Notice.

64 FR 2228, January 13, 1999: Office of Inspector General: Solicitation of Information and Recommendations for Developing OIG Compliance Program Guidance for the Hospice Industry — Notice.

64 FR 6753, February 16, 1999: Office of Inspector General: Privacy Act; Notification of New System of Records in Conjunction with the Healthcare Integrity and Protection Data Bank — Notice of a new system of records.

64 FR 13997, March 23, 1999: HCFA Agency Information Collection Activities: Submission for OMB Review; Comment request (pertaining to Medicare and Medicaid requirements for advanced directives, and disclosure of ownership and financial control interest).

64 FR 36368, July 6, 1999: Office of Inspector General Publication of OIG Compliance Program Guidance for the Durable Medical Equipment, Prosthetics, Orthotics and Supply Industry — Notice.

64 FR 37985, July 14, 1999: Office of Inspector General; Publication of the OIG Special Advisory Bulletin on Gainsharing Arrangements and CMPs for Hospital Payments to Physicians to Reduce or Limit Services to Beneficiaries — Notice.

64 FR 39150, July 21, 1999: Office of Inspector General; Draft OIG Compliance Program Guidance for Hospices — Notice and comment period.

64 FR 39420, July 22, 1999: Office of Inspector General; Health Care Programs; Fraud and Abuse; Revised OIG Sanction Authorities Resulting from P.L. 105–33, the Balanced Budget Act of 1997 — Final rule affecting 42 CFR Parts 1001, 1002, and 1003. See also correction at 64 FR 42174, August 3, 1999.

64 FR 48846, September 8, 1999: Office of Inspector General: Solicitation of Information and Recommendations for Developing OIG Compliance Program Guidance for Individual Physicians and Small Group Practices — Notice.

64 FR 42791, September 30, 1999: Office of Inspector General; Publication of the OIG Special Advisory Bulletin on the Effect of Exclusion from Participation in Federal Health Care Programs — Notice. See also correction at 64 FR 55484, October 13, 1999.

64 FR 57619, October 26, 1999: Office of Inspector General; Privacy Act; Exempt Record System, Pertaining to the Healthcare Integrity and Protection Data Bank (HIPDB) — Notice of proposed rulemaking affecting 45 CFR Part 5b.

64 FR 57740, October 26, 1999: Office of Inspector General; Healthcare Fraud and Abuse Data Collection Program: Reporting of Final Adverse Actions - Final rule affecting 45 CFR Part 61. See also correction at 65 FR 70506, November 24, 2000.

64 FR 58419, October 29, 1999: Office of Inspector General; Draft OIG Compliance Program Guidance for Nursing Facilities — Notice and comment period.

64 FR 58851, November 1, 1999: Office of Inspector General; Healthcare Integrity and Protection Data Bank: Announcement of Opening Date for Reporting and Self-query Fee — Notice.

64 FR 61893, November 15, 1999: Office of Inspector General; Publication of the OIG's Compliance Program Guidance for Medicare+Choice Organizations Offering Coordinated Care Plans — Notice.

64 FR 63504, November 19, 1999: Office of Inspector General; Fraud and Abuse; Statutory Exception to the Anti-kickback Statute for Shared Risk Arrangements — Interim final rule with request for comment, affection 42 CFR Part 1001. See also correction at 64 FR 71317, December 21, 1999.

64 FR 63518, November 19, 1999: Office of Inspector General; Fraud and Abuse; Clarification of the Initial OIG Safe Harbor Provisions and Establishment of Additional Safe Harbor Provisions under the Anti-kickback Statute — Final rule affecting 42 CFR Part 1001.

64 FR 69217, December 10, 1999: Office of Inspector General; Solicitation of New Safe Harbors and Special Fraud Alerts — Intent to develop regulations affecting 42 CFR Part 1001.

2000

65 FR 9274, February 24, 2000: Office of Inspector General: Publication of OIG Special Fraud Alert on Rental of Space in Physician Offices by Persons or Entities to Which Physicians Refer — Notice.

65 FR 11589, March 3, 2000: Office of Inspector General: Health Care Integrity and Protection Data Bank under Section 1128E of the Social Security Act: Announcement of Opening Date for Querying and User Fees — Notice.

65 FR 14289, March 16, 2000: Office of Inspector General: Publication of the OIG Compliance Program Guidance for Nursing Facilities — Notice.

65 FR 24400, April 26, 2000: Office of Inspector General; Health Care Programs: Fraud and Abuse; Revised OIG Civil Money Penalties Resulting from Public Law 104-191 (HIPAA) — Final rule affecting 42 CFR Parts 1001, 1003, 1005, and 1006. See also correction at 65 FR 35583, June 5, 2000.

65 FR 32060, May 22, 2000: Office of Inspector General Medicare and State Health Care Programs: Fraud and Abuse: Ambulance Restocking Safe Harbor under the Anti-kickback Statute — Notice of proposed rulemaking affecting 42 CFR 1001.

65 FR 34986, June 1, 2000: Office of Inspector General; Privacy Act; Implementation (exempting the Healthcare Integrity and Protection Data Bank under Section 1128C of the Social Security Act from certain provisions of the Privacy Act (5 U.S.C.A. 552a) — Final rule.

65 FR 36818, June 12, 2000: Office of Inspector General: Draft OIG Compliance Program for Individual and Small Group Physician Practices — Notice and comment period.

65 FR 50204, August 17, 2000: Office of Inspector General: Solicitation of Information and Recommendations for Developing a Compliance Risk Guidance for the Ambulance Industry — Notice.

65 FR 50552, August 18, 2000: HCFA Privacy Act of 1974; Report of Modified or Altered System (pertaining to revision of language in global fraud and abuse routine uses).

65 FR 53319, September 1, 2000: HCFA Agency Information Collection Activities: Proposed Collection; Comment request (pertaining to incentive arrangement disclosure form for managed care organizations and their related medical groups and physicians).

65 FR 59434, October 5, 2000: Office of Inspector General Compliance Program for Individual and Small Group Physician Practices — Notice.

65 FR 63035, October 20, 2000: Office of Inspector General: Medicare and State Health Care Programs: Fraud and Abuse; Revisions and Technical Corrections — Proposed rule affecting 42 CFR Parts 1001, 1003, 1005, and 1008.

65 FR 65861, November 2, 2000: HCFA Agency Information Collection Activities: Proposed Collection; Comment request (pertaining to conflict of interest disclosure requirements for Medicare program integrity).

65 FR 78124, December 14, 2000: Office of Inspector General: Solicitation of New Safe Harbors and Special Fraud Alerts — Notice of intent to develop regulations.

See § 2:42.

§ 6:43 TERMINATING AGREEMENTS WITH END STAGE RENAL DISEASE NETWORK AREA ORGANIZATIONS — Section 1881(c)(1) [42 U.S.C.A. 1395rr(c)(1)]

Regulations

42 CFR Part 402 — Civil Money Penalties, Assessments, and Exclusions

42 CFR Part 405, Subpart C — Recovery of Overpayments and Suspension of Payment; and Subpart U — Conditions for Coverage of Suppliers of End-Stage Renal Disease (ESRD) Services

42 CFR Part 409 — Hospital Insurance Benefits

42 CFR Part 410 — Supplementary Medical Insurance (SMI) Benefits

42 CFR Part 413 — Principles of Reasonable Cost Reimbursement; Payment for End-Stage Renal Disease Services; Prospectively Determined Payment Rates for Skilled Nursing Facilities

42 CFR Part 414, Subpart E — Determination of Reasonable Charges Under the ESRD Program

42 CFR Part 441 — Services: Requirements and Limits Applicable to Specific Services [Medicaid]

42 CFR Part 488 — Survey, Certification, and Enforcement Procedures

55 FR 23435, June 8, 1990: Medicare Program; Payment for Physician Outpatient Maintenance Dialysis Services and Other Physician Services for ESRD Patients — Final rule affecting 42 CFR Parts 405, 413, and 414. See also correction published at 55 FR 31185, August 1, 1990.

55 FR 53007, December 26, 1990: Medicare Program; Payment Change for Home Dialysis — Proposed rule to amend 42 CFR Parts 405 and 414.

56 FR 43706, September 4, 1991: Medicare Program; Coverage of Erythropoietin (EPO) Used by Competent Home Dialysis Patients — Interim final rule with comment period, affecting 42 CFR Parts 405, 410, 413, and 414.

57 FR 36006, August 12, 1992: Medicare Program; Self-implementing Coverage and Payments Provisions: 1990 Legislation — Final rule with comment period, affecting 42 CFR Parts 405, 406, 409, 420, 411, 412, 413, 418, and 489. Pertains to capital-related inpatient hospital costs; capital-related outpatient hospital costs; non-capital related outpatient hospital costs; payment for physician pathology services; payment for services of physicians as assistants-at-surgery; payments for ambulatory surgical procedures in hospital outpatient departments; payments for radiology services performed in hospital outpatient departments; hospice benefit extension; enrollment of HMO members in Medicare Part A; coverage of ostomy supplies; application of pre-entitlement stay in psychiatric hospital to limit on payment for inpatient hospital services; payments to dialysis facilities; payment rates for erythropoietin (EPO); and Medicare secondary payer provision for individuals with ESRD. See also confirmation of final rule at 58 FR 58502, November 2, 1993.

57 FR 46865, October 13, 1992: HCFA Public Information Collection Requirements Submitted to the Office of Management and Budget for Clearance (pertaining to impact of home health care plan management and evaluation; end-stage renal disease medical case review; Medicare/Medicaid hospital swing-bed survey report form; quarterly Medicaid statement of expenditures; Medicaid program budget report; information collection requirements in final peer review organization sanction regulations; appeals procedures for determinations that affect participation in Medicare; request for medical review information for Part B intermediary outpatient therapy bills and other Part B outpatient bills; and Medicaid limitations on provider-related donations and health care-related taxes, and limitations on payment to disproportionate share hospitals).

57 FR 54179, November 17, 1992: Medicare Program; Payment Change for Home Dialysis — Final rule.

58 FR 21174, April 19, 1993: HCFA Public Information Collection Requirements Submitted to the Office of Management and Budget for Clearance re end stage renal disease survey forms; municipal health services cost reports forms; advance directives; withholding

Medicare payments to recover Medicaid overpayments; home office cost statements; and statistical report on medical care.

58 FR 46198, September 1, 1993: HCFA Public Information Collection Requirements (ICR) Submitted to the Office of Management and Budget (OMB) for Clearance (pertaining to prenatal services and assistance screening; home health agency treatment forms; conditions of participation for intermediate care facilities for the mentally retarded; State Medicaid eligibility quality control sample selection lists; prepaid health plan cost report; hospital survey report form; procedures for determining whether providers, practitioners, or other suppliers of services are liable for certain noncovered services; Medicare credit balance reporting requirements; Medicare provider cost report questionnaire form; Medicare current beneficiary survey rounds 7-10; sterilization regulation/consent form; PRO reconsideration and appeals information requirements; information collection requirements in HSQ-110, acquisition, protection and disclosure of PRO information; Medicare/Medicaid organ procurement organization's (OPO) request for certification) — Notice.

58 FR 47904, September 13, 1993: HCFA, Public Information Collection Requirements (ICR) Submitted to the Office of Management and Budget (OMB) for Clearance (pertaining to chronic renal disease medical evidence report; Medicare common claims form; Social Security Office report of State buy-in problem; Medicare physician survey form; beneficiary survey form; Medicaid payment rate changes for inpatient hospital or long term care services; home and community-based services: waiver requirements; Medicare peer review organizations reporting forms; uniform institutional provider claim form) — Notice.

58 FR 54159, October 20, 1993: HCFA Public Information Collection Requirements Submitted to the Office of Management and Budget (OMB) for Clearance (pertaining to CLIA certification recommendation; CLIA laboratory personnel report; Medigap complaint data base; certification as a rural health clinic (RHC) and RHC survey report form; screening mammography services data report; ambulatory surgical center request for certification and survey report form; blood bank inspection checklist and report; Medicaid program budget report form; supplier of ESRD services form; and grantee data collection instrument) — Notice.

59 FR 714, January 6, 1994: Medicare Program; Revisions to the Definition of End-Stage Renal Disease and Resumption of Entitlement — Proposed rule affecting 42 CFR Part 406.

59 FR 1278, January 10, 1994: Medicare Program; Coverage of Epoetin (EPO) Used by Competent Home Dialysis Patients — Final rule affecting 42 CFR Parts 405, 410, 413, and 414.

59 FR 6937, February 14, 1994: Medicare Program; Standards for Quality of Water Used in Dialysis and Revised Guidelines on Reuse of Hemodialysis Filters for End-Stage Renal Disease Patients — Proposed rule affecting 42 CFR Part 405.

59 FR 26955, May 25, 1994: Medicare Program; Self-implementing Coverage and Payment Provisions: 1993 Legislation — Final rule with comment period (pertaining to reductions in payments for skilled nursing facility services — return on equity; reductions in payments for hospice services; reduction in Part A premium for certain individuals with 30 or more quarters of Social Security coverage; extension of 10 percent reduction in payments for capital-related costs of outpatient hospital services; extension of reduction in payments for other costs for outpatient hospital services; reduction in payments for intraocular lenses; payment for parenteral and enteral nutrients, supplies and equipment during 1994 and 1995; increase in annual cap on amount of Medicare payment for outpatient physical therapy and occupational therapy services; rural health clinics and Federally qualified health centers; reduction in payments for Epoetin; and changes in Part B premium.)

59 FR 35739, July 13, 1994: HCFA Public Information Collection Requirements Submitted to the Office of Management and Budget (OMB) for Clearance (pertaining to current beneficiary survey forms; and Medicare independent renal dialysis facility cost report forms).

59 FR 37046, July 20, 1994: HCFA Public Information Collection Requirements Submitted to the Office of Management and Budget (OMB) for Clearance (pertaining to notification to providers, practitioners, and suppliers that they are liable for certain noncovered services; medical review of Part B intermediary outpatient therapy claims; end stage renal disease network cost report forms; hospital request for certification in the Medicare/Medicaid programs form; and end stage renal disease network business proposal forms).

59 FR 44097, August 26, 1994: Medicare Program; End Stage Renal Disease (ESRD) Payment Exception Requests and Organ Pro-

curement Costs — Proposed rule affecting 42 CFR Parts 412, 413, and 414.

59 FR 52178, October 14, 1994: HCFA Public Information Collection Requirements Submitted to the Office of Management and Budget (OMB) for Clearance (pertaining to Medicare reimbursement for outpatient services, cost reports for free-standing skilled nursing facilities; Medicare coverage criteria for adult heart transplants, drug rebates for Medicaid, optional prospective payment cost report for certain skilled nursing facilities, reimbursable costs for organ procurement agencies, distribution and use of end stage renal disease treatment sources, conditions of coverage for ambulatory surgical centers, and waivers for home and community based services).

60 FR 7774, February 9, 1995: HCFA Public Information Collection Requirements Submitted to the Office of Management and Budget (OMB) for Clearance (pertaining to justification for ESRD composite rates for outpatient dialysis services, and home health agency compliance with health and safety requirements).

60 FR 22533, May 8, 1995: Medicare Program; Clarification of Resumption of Entitlement Rules for Medicare Patients with End-stage Renal Disease (ESRD) — Final rule affecting 42 CFR Part 406.

60 FR 48039, September 18, 1995: Medicare Program; Standards for Quality of Water Used in Dialysis and Revised Guidelines on Reuse of Hemodialysis Filters for End-stage Renal Disease (ESRD) Patients — Final rule affecting 42 CFR Part 405.

60 FR 61263, November 29, 1995: HCFA Public Information Collection Requirements Submitted for Public Comment and Recommendations (pertaining to Medicare uniform institutional provider bills, and end stage renal disease medical evidence reports for Medicare entitlement and patient registration).

61 FR 2516, January 26, 1996: Medicare Program; Announcement of Funding Availability for a Cooperative Agreement for an End-stage Renal Disease (ESRD) Managed Care Demonstration — Notice.

61 FR 28882, June 6, 1996: HCFA Agency Information Collection Activities: Submission for OMB Review; Comment Request (pertaining to end stage renal disease medical evidence reports to determine Medicare eligibility; and examination and treatment for emergency medical conditions and women in labor).

61 FR 29406, June 10, 1996: HCFA Agency Information Collection Activities: proposed Collection; Comment Request (pertaining to end stage renal disease application and survey and certification report forms; withholding Medicare payments to recover Medicaid overpayments; acquisition, protection, and disclosure of PRO information; clinical laboratory certification and recertification survey forms; CLIA laboratory personnel report forms; prepaid health plan cost reports; Medicare credit balance reporting requirements; statement of deficiencies and plan of correction requirements for organ procurement organizations; Medicare/Medicaid hospital survey report forms; advance directive requirements for Medicare and Medicaid; payment adjustments for sole community hospitals; survey reports for physical therapists in independent practice; HMO and CMP national data reporting requirements; identification of extension units of outpatient physical therapy and outpatient speech pathology providers; and fire safety survey reports).

61 FR 31141, June 19, 1996: HCFA Agency Information Collection Activities: Proposed Collection; Comment Request (pertaining to authorization agreements for electronic funds transfer; applications for health insurance under Medicare for individuals with chronic renal disease; CLIA application forms; forms for surveyors to evaluate laboratory survey processes; post laboratory survey questionnaires for laboratories to evaluate the survey process).

61 FR 33752, June 28, 1996: HCFA Agency Information Collection Activities: Submission for OMB Review; Comment Request (pertaining to end stage renal disease medical information systems; and end stage renal disease death notifications).

61 FR 46814, September 5, 1996: HCFA Agency Information Collection Activities: Submission for OMB Review; Comment request (pertaining to authorization agreements for electronic funds transfers; entitlement to Medicare for individuals with chronic renal disease; application forms for clinical laboratories; and clinical laboratory survey questionnaires).

62 FR 10285, March 6, 1997: HCFA Agency Information collection Activities: Submission for OMB Review; Comment request (pertaining to end stage renal disease (ESRD) application and survey and certification report form).

62 FR 28884, May 28, 1997: HCFA Agency Information Collection Activities: Proposed Collection; Comment request (pertaining to end stage renal disease beneficiary selection).

62 FR 36068, July 3, 1997: HCFA Agency Information Collection Activities; Proposed Collection; Comment request (pertaining to ESRD Network semi-annual cost report forms, and ESRD Network contract proposals).

62 FR 48871, September 17, 1997: HCFA Agency Information Collection Activities: Proposed Collection; Comment request (pertaining to conditions of coverage of supplier of ESRD services).

62 FR 49017, September 18, 1997: HCFA Agency Information Collection Activities: Submission for OMB Review; Comment request (pertaining to ESRD network semi-annual cost reports; and ESRD business proposal forms).

62 FR 51669, October 2, 1997: HCFA Agency Information Collection Activities: Submission for OMB Review; Comment request (pertaining to Medicare reimbursement options for ESRD patients).

62 FR 62063, November 20, 1997: HCFA Agency Information Collection Activities: Proposed Collection; Comment request (pertaining to managed care of ESRD).

62 FR 63551, December 1, 1997: HCFA Agency Information Collection Activities: Proposed Collection; Comment request (pertaining to conditions of coverage of suppliers of ESRD services).

63 FR 5958, February 5, 1998: HCFA Agency Information Collection Activities: Proposed Collection; Comment request (pertaining to end stage renal disease medical evidence report Medicare entitlement and patient registration).

63 FR 11263, March 6, 1998: HCFA Agency Information Collection Activities: Submission for OMB Review; Comment request (pertaining to end stage renal disease managed care demonstration).

63 FR 12475, March 13, 1998: HCFA Agency Information Collection Activities: Submission for OMB Review; Comment request (pertaining to independent renal dialysis facility cost report forms).

63 FR 16563, April 3, 1998: HCFA Agency Information Collection Activities: Submission for OMB Review; Comment request (pertaining to end stage renal disease medical evidence report Medicare entitlement and/or patient registration).

63 FR 39101, July 21, 1998: HCFA Privacy Act of 1974; Report of New System (pertaining to end stage renal disease managed care demonstration).

1999

64 FR 1811, January 12, 1999: Medicare and Medicaid Programs; Announcement of Additional Applications from Hospitals Request-

ing Waivers for Organ Procurement Service Area Assignments — Notice with comment period.

64 FR 32239, June 16, 1999: HCFA Agency Information Collection Activities: Proposed Collection; Comment request (pertaining to conditions of coverage for organ procurement organizations).

64 FR 42139, August 3, 1999: Medicare Program; August 31, 1999, Open Town Hall Meeting to Discuss the End Stage Renal Disease Network Organizations (SRD Networks) Activities — Notice of meeting.

64 FR 43198, August 9, 1999: Medicare and Medicaid Programs; Announcement of Additional Applications from Hospitals Requesting Waivers for Organ Procurement Service Areas — Notice with comment period.

64 FR 49196, September 10, 1999: HCFA Agency Information Collection Activities; Submission for OMB Review; Comment request (pertaining to conditions of coverage for organ procurement organizations).

64 FR 62679, November 17, 1999: HCFA Agency Information Collection Activities: Proposed Collection; Comment request (pertaining to surveys of end stage renal disease facilities).

64 FR 62680, November 17, 1999: HCFA Agency Information Collection Activities: Proposed Collection; Comment request (pertaining to applications for Medicare benefits for chronic renal disease).

64 FR 63680, November 17, 1999: HCFA Agency Information Collection Activities: Proposed Collection; Comment request (pertaining to end stage renal disease death notices).

2000

65 FR 11588, March 3, 2000: HCFA Agency Information Collection Activities: Submission for OMB Review; Comment request (pertaining to application for health insurance benefits under Medicare for individuals with chronic renal disease).

65 FR 11589, March 3, 2000: HCFA Agency Information Collection Activities: Submission for OMB Review; Comment request (pertaining to end stage renal disease medical information system/ESRD facility survey).

65 FR 12559, March 9, 2000: HCFA Agency Information Collection Activities: Submission for OMB Review; Comment request (pertaining to end stage renal disease death notification).

65 FR 14288, March 16, 2000: HCFA Agency Information Collection Activities: Proposed Collection; Comment request (pertaining to end stage renal disease application and survey and certification).

65 FR 25460, May 2, 2000: Medicare and State Health Care Programs: Fraud and Abuse; Civil Money Penalty Safe Harbor to Protect Payment of Medicare Supplemental Insurance and Medigap Premiums for ESRD Beneficiaries — Notice of proposed rulemaking affecting 42 CFR Part 1003.

65 FR 35652, June 5, 2000: HCFA Agency Information Collection Activities: Proposed Collection; Comment request (pertaining to hospital conditions of participation; identification of potential organ, tissue, and eye donors and transplant hospitals' provision of transplant-related data).

65 FR 36454, June 8, 2000: HCFA Agency Information Collection Activities: Proposed Collection; Comment request (pertaining to organ procurement organization histocompatibility laboratory statement of reimbursable costs).

65 FR 45090, July 20, 2000: HCFA Agency Information Collection Activities; Proposed Collection; Comment request (pertaining to end stage renal disease (ESRD) network business proposal forms).

65 FR 54536, September 8, 2000: HCFA Agency Information Collection Activities: Submission for OMB Review; Comment request (pertaining to reasonable costs incurred to furnish treatment to end stage renal disease patients by organ procurement organizations and histocompatibility laboratories; and third party premium billing request forms).

65 FR 54857, September 11, 2000: HCFA Agency Information Collection Activities: Submission for OMB Review; Comment request (pertaining to hospital conditions of participation-identification of potential organ, tissue, and eye donors, and transplant hospitals' provision of transplant-related data).

65 FR 59431, October 5, 2000: HCFA Agency Information Collection Activities: Proposed Collection; Comment request (pertaining to conditions for coverage of suppliers of end stage renal disease services).

65 FR 59432, October 5, 2000: HCFA Agency Information Collection Activities: Submission for OMB Review; Comment request (pertaining to end stage renal disease application and survey and certification report).

65 FR 5957, October 6, 2000: HCFA Agency Information Collection Activities: Proposed Collection; Comment request (pertaining to

end stage renal disease provisions in provider reimbursement manual).

65 FR 75943, December 5, 2000: HCFA Agency Information Collection Activities: Submission for OMB Review; Comment Request (pertaining to Medicare payment for ambulance services); end stage renal disease reimbursement; and evaluation of the State Medicaid reform demonstrations).

2001

66 FR 11035, February 21, 2001: HCFA Agency Information Collection Activities: Submission for OMB Review; Comment request (pertaining to reimbursement for ESRD providers).

66 FR 12940, March 1, 2001: HCFA Agency Information Collection Activities: Proposed Collection, Comment request (pertaining to independent renal dialysis facility cost report form).

66 FR 14155, March 9, 2001: HCFA Agency Information Collection Activities: Proposed Collection; Comment request (pertaining to end stage renal disease medical evidence report for Medicare entitlement and/or patient registration).

66 FR 16480, March 26, 2001: HCFA Agency Information Collection Activities; Proposed Collection; Comment request (pertaining to conditions of coverage of suppliers of end stage renal disease services). See also correction at 66 FR 18096, April 5, 2001.

66 FR 21770, May 1, 2001: Medicare Program; Revision of Payment Rates for End–Stage Renal Disease (ESRD) Patients Enrolled in Medicare+Choice Plans—Proposed notice.

66 FR 29824, June 1, 2001: HCFA Agency Information Collection Activities: Submission for OMB review; Comment request (pertaining to end stage renal disease medical evidence report for Medicare entitlement and patient registration).

66 FR 32360, June 14, 2001: HCFA Agency Information Collection Activities: Proposed Collection; Comment request (pertaining to end stage renal disease death notification).

66 FR 33030, June 20, 2001: Medicare and Medicaid Program; End Stage Renal Disease—Waiver of Conditions for Coverage under a State of Emergency in Houston, TX Area—Final rule, affecting 42 CFR Part 405.

See § 2:43.

§ 6:44 FAILURE BY END STAGE RENAL DISEASE FACILITIES AND PROVIDERS OF END STAGE RENAL DISEASE CARE TO COOPERATE WITH END STAGE RENAL DISEASE NETWORK PLANS AND GOALS AND FAILURE TO FOLLOW END STAGE RENAL DISEASE MEDICAL REVIEW BOARD RECOMMENDATIONS — Section 1881(c)(3) and (g) [42 U.S.C.A. 1395rr(c)(3) and (g)]

Regulations

42 CFR Part 402 — Civil Money Penalties, Assessments, and Exclusions

42 CFR Part 405, Subpart C — Recovery of Overpayments and Suspension of Payment; and Subpart U — Conditions for Coverage of Suppliers of End-Stage Renal Disease (ESRD) Services

42 CFR Part 409 — Hospital Insurance Benefits

42 CFR Part 410 — Supplementary Medical Insurance (SMI) Benefits

42 CFR Part 413 — Principles of Reasonable Cost Reimbursement; Payment for End-Stage Renal Disease Services; Prospectively Determined Payment Rates for Skilled Nursing Facilities

42 CFR Part 414, Subpart E — Determination of Reasonable Charges Under the ESRD Program

42 CFR Part 441 — Services: Requirements and Limits Applicable to Specific Services [Medicaid]

42 CFR Part 488 — Survey, Certification, and Enforcement Procedures

42 CFR Part 498 — Appeals Procedures for Determinations that Affect Participation in the Medicare Program and for Determinations that Affect the Participation of ICF's/MR and Certain NF's in the Medicaid Program

55 FR 23435, June 8, 1990: Medicare Program; Payment for Physician Outpatient Maintenance Dialysis Services and Other Physician Services for ESRD Patients — Final rule affecting 42 CFR Parts 405, 413, and 414. See also correction published at 55 FR 31185, August 1, 1990.

55 FR 53007, December 26, 1990: Medicare Program; Payment Change for Home Dialysis — Proposed rule to amend 42 CFR Parts 405 and 414.

56 FR 43706, September 4, 1991: Medicare Program; Coverage of Erythropoietin (EPO) Used by Competent Home Dialysis

Patients — Interim final rule with comment period, affecting 42 CFR Parts 405, 410, 413, and 414.

57 FR 36006, August 12, 1992: Medicare Program; Self-implementing Coverage and Payments Provisions: 1990 Legislation — Final rule with comment period, affecting 42 CFR Parts 405, 406, 409, 420, 411, 412, 413, 418, and 489. Pertains to capital-related inpatient hospital costs; capital-related outpatient hospital costs; non-capital related outpatient hospital costs; payment for physician pathology services; payment for services of physicians as assistants-at-surgery; payments for ambulatory surgical procedures in hospital outpatient departments; payments for radiology services performed in hospital outpatient departments; hospice benefit extension; enrollment of HMO members in Medicare Part A; coverage of ostomy supplies; application of pre-entitlement stay in psychiatric hospital to limit on payment for inpatient hospital services; payments to dialysis facilities; payment rates for erythropoietin (EPO); and Medicare secondary payer provision for individuals with ESRD. See also confirmation of final rule at 58 FR 58502, November 2, 1993.

57 FR 46865, October 13, 1992: HCFA Public Information Collection Requirements Submitted to the Office of Management and Budget for Clearance (pertaining to impact of home health care plan management and evaluation; end-stage renal disease medical case review; Medicare/Medicaid hospital swing-bed survey report form; quarterly Medicaid statement of expenditures; Medicaid program budget report; information collection requirements in final peer review organization sanction regulations; appeals procedures for determinations that affect participation in Medicare; request for medical review information for Part B intermediary outpatient therapy bills and other Part B outpatient bills; and Medicaid limitations on provider-related donations and health care-related taxes, and limitations on payment to disproportionate share hospitals).

57 FR 54179, November 17, 1992: Medicare Program; Payment Change for Home Dialysis — Final rule.

58 FR 21174, April 19, 1993: HCFA Public Information Collection Requirements Submitted to the Office of Management and Budget for Clearance re end stage renal disease survey forms; municipal health services cost reports forms; advance directives; withholding Medicare payments to recover Medicaid overpayments; home office cost statements; and statistical report on medical care.

58 FR 46198, September 1, 1993: HCFA Public Information Collection Requirements (ICR) Submitted to the Office of Management and Budget (OMB) for Clearance (pertaining to prenatal services and assistance screening; home health agency treatment forms; conditions of participation for intermediate care facilities for the mentally retarded; State Medicaid eligibility quality control sample selection lists; prepaid health plan cost report; hospital survey report form; procedures for determining whether providers, practitioners, or other suppliers of services are liable for certain noncovered services; Medicare credit balance reporting requirements; Medicare provider cost report questionnaire form; Medicare current beneficiary survey rounds 7-10; sterilization regulation/consent form; PRO reconsideration and appeals information requirements; information collection requirements in HSQ-110, acquisition, protection and disclosure of PRO information; Medicare/Medicaid organ procurement organization's (OPO) request for certification) — Notice.

58 FR 47904, September 13, 1993: HCFA, Public Information Collection Requirements (ICR) Submitted to the Office of Management and Budget (OMB) for Clearance (pertaining to chronic renal disease medical evidence report; Medicare common claims form; Social Security Office report of State buy-in problem; Medicare physician survey form; beneficiary survey form; Medicaid payment rate changes for inpatient hospital or long term care services; home and community-based services: waiver requirements; Medicare peer review organizations reporting forms; uniform institutional provider claim form) — Notice.

58 FR 54159, October 20, 1993: HCFA Public Information Collection Requirements Submitted to the Office of Management and Budget (OMB) for Clearance (pertaining to CLIA certification recommendation; CLIA laboratory personnel report; Medigap complaint data base; certification as a rural health clinic (RHC) and RHC survey report form; screening mammography services data report; ambulatory surgical center request for certification and survey report form; blood bank inspection checklist and report; Medicaid program budget report form; supplier of ESRD services form; and grantee data collection instrument) — Notice.

59 FR 714, January 6, 1994: Medicare Program; Revisions to the Definition of End-Stage Renal Disease and Resumption of Entitlement — Proposed rule affecting 42 CFR Part 406.

59 FR 1278, January 10, 1994: Medicare Program; Coverage of Epoetin (EPO) Used by Competent Home Dialysis Patients — Final rule affecting 42 CFR Parts 405, 410, 413, and 414.

59 FR 6937, February 14, 1994: Medicare Program; Standards for Quality of Water Used in Dialysis and Revised Guidelines on Reuse of Hemodialysis Filters for End-Stage Renal Disease Patients — Proposed rule affecting 42 CFR Part 405.

59 FR 26955, May 25, 1994: Medicare Program; Self-implementing Coverage and Payment Provisions: 1993 Legislation — Final rule with comment period (pertaining to reductions in payments for skilled nursing facility services — return on equity; reductions in payments for hospice services; reduction in Part A premium for certain individuals with 30 or more quarters of Social Security coverage; extension of 10 percent reduction in payments for capital-related costs of outpatient hospital services; extension of reduction in payments for other costs for outpatient hospital services; reduction in payments for intraocular lenses; payment for parenteral and enteral nutrients, supplies and equipment during 1994 and 1995; increase in annual cap on amount of Medicare payment for outpatient physical therapy and occupational therapy services; rural health clinics and Federally qualified health centers; reduction in payments for Epoetin; and changes in Part B premium.)

59 FR 35739, July 13, 1994: HCFA Public Information Collection Requirements Submitted to the Office of Management and Budget (OMB) for Clearance (pertaining to current beneficiary survey forms; and Medicare independent renal dialysis facility cost report forms).

59 FR 37046, July 20, 1994: HCFA Public Information Collection Requirements Submitted to the Office of Management and Budget (OMB) for Clearance (pertaining to notification to providers, practitioners, and suppliers that they are liable for certain noncovered services; medical review of Part B intermediary outpatient therapy claims; end stage renal disease network cost report forms; hospital request for certification in the Medicare/Medicaid programs form; and end stage renal disease network business proposal forms).

59 FR 44097, August 26, 1994: Medicare Program; End Stage Renal Disease (ESRD) Payment Exception Requests and Organ Procurement Costs — Proposed rule affecting 42 CFR Parts 412, 413, and 414.

59 FR 52178, October 14, 1994: HCFA Public Information Collection Requirements Submitted to the Office of Management and

Budget (OMB) for Clearance (pertaining to Medicare reimbursement for outpatient services, cost reports for free-standing skilled nursing facilities; Medicare coverage criteria for adult heart transplants, drug rebates for Medicaid, optional prospective payment cost report for certain skilled nursing facilities, reimbursable costs for organ procurement agencies, distribution and use of end stage renal disease treatment sources, conditions of coverage for ambulatory surgical centers, and waivers for home and community based services).

60 FR 7774, February 9, 1995: HCFA Public Information Collection Requirements Submitted to the Office of Management and Budget (OMB) for Clearance (pertaining to justification for ESRD composite rates for outpatient dialysis services, and home health agency compliance with health and safety requirements).

60 FR 22533, May 8, 1995: Medicare Program; Clarification of Resumption of Entitlement Rules for Medicare Patients with End-stage Renal Disease (ESRD) — Final rule affecting 42 CFR Part 406.

60 FR 48039, September 18, 1995: Medicare Program; Standards for Quality of Water Used in Dialysis and Revised Guidelines on Reuse of Hemodialysis Filters for End-stage Renal Disease (ESRD) Patients — Final rule affecting 42 CFR Part 405.

60 FR 61263, November 29, 1995: HCFA Public Information Collection Requirements Submitted for Public Comment and Recommendations (pertaining to Medicare uniform institutional provider bills, and end stage renal disease medical evidence reports for Medicare entitlement and patient registration).

61 FR 2516, January 26, 1996: Medicare Program; Announcement of Funding Availability for a Cooperative Agreement for an End-stage Renal Disease (ESRD) Managed Care Demonstration — Notice.

61 FR 28882, June 6, 1996: HCFA Agency Information Collection Activities: Submission for OMB Review; Comment Request (pertaining to end stage renal disease medical evidence reports to determine Medicare eligibility; and examination and treatment for emergency medical conditions and women in labor).

61 FR 29406, June 10, 1996: HCFA Agency Information Collection Activities: proposed Collection; Comment Request (pertaining to end stage renal disease application and survey and certification report forms; withholding Medicare payments to recover Medicaid overpayments; acquisition, protection, and disclosure of PRO information;

clinical laboratory certification and recertification survey forms; CLIA laboratory personnel report forms; prepaid health plan cost reports; Medicare credit balance reporting requirements; statement of deficiencies and plan of correction requirements for organ procurement organizations; Medicare/Medicaid hospital survey report forms; advance directive requirements for Medicare and Medicaid; payment adjustments for sole community hospitals; survey reports for physical therapists in independent practice; HMO and CMP national data reporting requirements; identification of extension units of outpatient physical therapy and outpatient speech pathology providers; and fire safety survey reports).

61 FR 31141, June 19, 1996: HCFA Agency Information Collection Activities: Proposed Collection; Comment Request (pertaining to authorization agreements for electronic funds transfer; applications for health insurance under Medicare for individuals with chronic renal disease; CLIA application forms; forms for surveyors to evaluate laboratory survey processes; post laboratory survey questionnaires for laboratories to evaluate the survey process).

61 FR 33752, June 28, 1996: HCFA Agency Information Collection Activities: Submission for OMB Review; Comment Request (pertaining to end stage renal disease medical information systems; and end stage renal disease death notifications).

61 FR 46814, September 5, 1996: HCFA Agency Information Collection Activities: Submission for OMB Review; Comment request (pertaining to authorization agreements for electronic funds transfers; entitlement to Medicare for individuals with chronic renal disease; application forms for clinical laboratories; and clinical laboratory survey questionnaires).

62 FR 10285, March 6, 1997: HCFA Agency Information collection Activities: Submission for OMB Review; Comment request (pertaining to end stage renal disease (ESRD) application and survey and certification report form).

62 FR 28884, May 28, 1997: HCFA Agency Information Collection Activities: Proposed Collection; Comment request (pertaining to end stage renal disease beneficiary selection).

62 FR 36068, July 3, 1997: HCFA Agency Information Collection Activities; Proposed Collection; Comment request (pertaining to ESRD Network semi-annual cost report forms, and ESRD Network contract proposals).

62 FR 48871, September 17, 1997: HCFA Agency Information Collection Activities: Proposed Collection; Comment request (pertaining to conditions of coverage of supplier of ESRD services).

62 FR 49017, September 18, 1997: HCFA Agency Information Collection Activities: Submission for OMB Review; Comment request (pertaining to ESRD network semi-annual cost reports; and ESRD business proposal forms).

62 FR 51669, October 2, 1997: HCFA Agency Information Collection Activities: Submission for OMB Review; Comment request (pertaining to Medicare reimbursement options for ESRD patients).

62 FR 62063, November 20, 1997: HCFA Agency Information Collection Activities: Proposed Collection; Comment request (pertaining to managed care of ESRD).

62 FR 63551, December 1, 1997: HCFA Agency Information Collection Activities: Proposed Collection; Comment request (pertaining to conditions of coverage of suppliers of ESRD services).

63 FR 5958, February 5, 1998: HCFA Agency Information Collection Activities: Proposed Collection; Comment request (pertaining to end stage renal disease medical evidence report Medicare entitlement and patient registration).

63 FR 11263, March 6, 1998: HCFA Agency Information Collection Activities: Submission for OMB Review; Comment request (pertaining to end stage renal disease managed care demonstration).

63 FR 12475, March 13, 1998: HCFA Agency Information Collection Activities: Submission for OMB Review; Comment request (pertaining to independent renal dialysis facility cost report forms).

63 FR 16563, April 3, 1998: HCFA Agency Information Collection Activities: Submission for OMB Review; Comment request (pertaining to end stage renal disease medical evidence report Medicare entitlement and/or patient registration).

63 FR 39101, July 21, 1998: HCFA Privacy Act of 1974; Report of New System (pertaining to end stage renal disease managed care demonstration).

1999

64 FR 1811, January 12, 1999: Medicare and Medicaid Programs; Announcement of Additional Applications from Hospitals Requesting Waivers for Organ Procurement Service Area Assignments — Notice with comment period.

64 FR 32239, June 16, 1999: HCFA Agency Information Collection Activities: Proposed Collection; Comment request (pertaining to conditions of coverage for organ procurement organizations).

64 FR 42139, August 3, 1999: Medicare Program; August 31, 1999, Open Town Hall Meeting to Discuss the End Stage Renal Disease Network Organizations (SRD Networks) Activities — Notice of meeting.

64 FR 43198, August 9, 1999: Medicare and Medicaid Programs; Announcement of Additional Applications from Hospitals Requesting Waivers for Organ Procurement Service Areas — Notice with comment period.

64 FR 49196, September 10, 1999: HCFA Agency Information Collection Activities; Submission for OMB Review; Comment request (pertaining to conditions of coverage for organ procurement organizations).

64 FR 62679, November 17, 1999: HCFA Agency Information Collection Activities: Proposed Collection; Comment request (pertaining to surveys of end stage renal disease facilities).

64 FR 62680, November 17, 1999: HCFA Agency Information Collection Activities: Proposed Collection; Comment request (pertaining to applications for Medicare benefits for chronic renal disease).

64 FR 63680, November 17, 1999: HCFA Agency Information Collection Activities: Proposed Collection; Comment request (pertaining to end stage renal disease death notices).

2000

65 FR 11588, March 3, 2000: HCFA Agency Information Collection Activities: Submission for OMB Review; Comment request (pertaining to application for health insurance benefits under Medicare for individuals with chronic renal disease).

65 FR 11589, March 3, 2000: HCFA Agency Information Collection Activities: Submission for OMB Review; Comment request (pertaining to end stage renal disease medical information system/ESRD facility survey).

65 FR 12559, March 9, 2000: HCFA Agency Information Collection Activities: Submission for OMB Review; Comment request (pertaining to end stage renal disease death notification).

65 FR 14288, March 16, 2000: HCFA Agency Information Collection Activities: Proposed Collection; Comment request (pertaining to end stage renal disease application and survey and certification).

65 FR 25460, May 2, 2000: Medicare and State Health Care Programs: Fraud and Abuse; Civil Money Penalty Safe Harbor to Protect Payment of Medicare Supplemental Insurance and Medigap Premiums for ESRD Beneficiaries — Notice of proposed rulemaking affecting 42 CFR Part 1003.

65 FR 35652, June 5, 2000: HCFA Agency Information Collection Activities: Proposed Collection; Comment request (pertaining to hospital conditions of participation; identification of potential organ, tissue, and eye donors and transplant hospitals' provision of transplant-related data).

65 FR 36454, June 8, 2000: HCFA Agency Information Collection Activities: Proposed Collection; Comment request (pertaining to organ procurement organization histocompatibility laboratory statement of reimbursable costs).

65 FR 45090, July 20, 2000: HCFA Agency Information Collection Activities; Proposed Collection; Comment request (pertaining to end stage renal disease (ESRD) network business proposal forms).

65 FR 54536, September 8, 2000: HCFA Agency Information Collection Activities: Submission for OMB Review; Comment request (pertaining to reasonable costs incurred to furnish treatment to end stage renal disease patients by organ procurement organizations and histocompatibility laboratories; and third party premium billing request forms).

65 FR 54857, September 11, 2000: HCFA Agency Information Collection Activities: Submission for OMB Review; Comment request (pertaining to hospital conditions of participation-identification of potential organ, tissue, and eye donors, and transplant hospitals' provision of transplant-related data).

65 FR 59431, October 5, 2000: HCFA Agency Information Collection Activities: Proposed Collection; Comment request (pertaining to conditions for coverage of suppliers of end stage renal disease services).

65 FR 59432, October 5, 2000: HCFA Agency Information Collection Activities: Submission for OMB Review; Comment request (pertaining to end stage renal disease application and survey and certification report).

65 FR 5957, October 6, 2000: HCFA Agency Information Collection Activities: Proposed Collection; Comment request (pertaining to end stage renal disease provisions in provider reimbursement manual).

65 FR 75943, December 5, 2000: HCFA Agency Information Collection Activities: Submission for OMB Review; Comment Request (pertaining to Medicare payment for ambulance services); end stage renal disease reimbursement; and evaluation of the State Medicaid reform demonstrations).

2001

66 FR 11035, February 21, 2001: HCFA Agency Information Collection Activities: Submission for OMB Review; Comment request (pertaining to reimbursement for ESRD providers).

66 FR 12940, March 1, 2001: HCFA Agency Information Collection Activities: Proposed Collection, Comment request (pertaining to independent renal dialysis facility cost report form).

66 FR 14155, March 9, 2001: HCFA Agency Information Collection Activities: Proposed Collection; Comment request (pertaining to end stage renal disease medical evidence report for Medicare entitlement and/or patient registration).

66 FR 16480, March 26, 2001: HCFA Agency Information Collection Activities; Proposed Collection; Comment request (pertaining to conditions of coverage of suppliers of end stage renal disease services). See also correction at 66 FR 18096, April 5, 2001.

66 FR 21770, May 1, 2001: Medicare Program; Revision of Payment Rates for End–Stage Renal Disease (ESRD) Patients Enrolled in Medicare+Choice Plans—Proposed notice.

66 FR 29824, June 1, 2001: HCFA Agency Information Collection Activities: Submission for OMB review; Comment request (pertaining to end stage renal disease medical evidence report for Medicare entitlement and patient registration).

66 FR 32360, June 14, 2001: HCFA Agency Information Collection Activities: Proposed Collection; Comment request (pertaining to end stage renal disease death notification).

66 FR 33030, June 20, 2001: Medicare and Medicaid Program; End Stage Renal Disease—Waiver of Conditions for Coverage under a State of Emergency in Houston, TX Area—Final rule, affecting 42 CFR Part 405.

See § 2:44.

§ 6:45 ISSUING MEDICARE SUPPLEMENTAL HEALTH INSURANCE POLICIES IN VIOLATION OF STATE OR FEDERAL STANDARDS — Section 1882(a)(2) [42 U.S.C.A. 1395ss(a)(2)]

Regulations

42 CFR Part 402 — Civil Money Penalties, Assessments, and Exclusions

42 CFR Part 403, Subpart B — Medicare Supplemental Policies

42 CFR Part 409 — Hospital Insurance Benefits

42 CFR Part 410 — Supplementary Medical Insurance (SMI) Benefits

42 CFR Part 420 — Program Integrity: Medicare

42 CFR Chapter V — Office of Inspector General — Health Care, Department of Health and Human Services

Subchapter A — General Provisions

Part 1000 — Introduction; General Definitions

Subchapter B — OIG Authorities

Part 1001 — Program Integrity: Medicare and State Health Care Programs

Part 1003 — Civil Money Penalties, Assessments and Exclusions

Part 1005 — Appeals of Exclusions, Civil Money Penalties and Assessments

Part 1006 — Investigational Inquiries

56 FR 47763, September 20, 1991: Medicare Program; Conditional Designation of States in Which Medicare SELECT Insurance Policies May be Issued — General notice with comment period. See also correction at 56 FR 65269, December 16, 1991.

57 FR 37980, August 21, 1992: Medicare Program; HHS' Recognition of NAIC Model Standards for Regulation of Medigap Policies — Notice. 57 FR 58507, December 10, 1992: Privacy Act of 1974; Report of New System — Notice of new system of records (pertaining to data necessary to evaluate the Medicare SELECT program).

58 FR 35017, June 30, 1993: Medicare Program; Revised Designation of States In Which Medicare SELECT Insurance Policies May Be Issued — Notice.

58 FR 54159, October 20, 1993: HCFA Public Information Collection Requirements Submitted to the Office of Management and Budget (OMB) for Clearance (pertaining to CLIA certification recommendation; CLIA laboratory personnel report; Medigap

complaint data base; certification as a rural health clinic (RHC) and RHC survey report form; screening mammography services data report; ambulatory surgical center request for certification and survey report form; blood bank inspection checklist and report; Medicaid program budget report form; supplier of ESRD services form; and grantee data collection instrument) — Notice.

58 FR 60204, November 15, 1993: HCFA Public Information Collection Requirements Submitted to the Office of Management and Budget (OMB) for Clearance (pertaining to procedures for transmitting information between Medicare carriers and Medicare supplemental insurers; Medicare physician or supplier agreement; patient intake data form for the National Home Health Agency; agency characteristics form for the National Home Health Agency prospective payment demonstration; intake and assessment survey package for the community nursing organization demonstration; comprehensive outpatient rehabilitation facility (CORF eligibility and survey forms and information collection requirements) — Notice.

59 FR 30941, June 16, 1994: HCFA Public Information Collection Requirements Submitted to the Office of Management and Budget (OMB) for Clearance (pertaining to evaluation of Medicare SELECT amendments; and hospital and hospital health care complex cost report forms).

60 FR 30877, June 12, 1995: Medicare Program; HHS' Approval of NAIC Statements Relating to Duplication of Medicare Benefits — Notice.

61 FR 40422, August 2, 1996: HCFA Agency Information Collection Activities: Proposed Collection; Comment request (pertaining to survey and certification of ambulatory surgical centers; the Medigap complaint database; fiscal intermediaries' provider overpayment actions; and hospital standards for potentially HIV infectious blood and blood products).

61 FR 57688, November 7, 1996: HCFA Agency Information Collection Activities: Comment request (pertaining to clinical laboratory surveys; clinical laboratory personnel qualifications; Medicare/Medicaid hospital survey report forms; beneficiary disenrollment from HMOs and CMPs; survey reports for ambulatory surgical centers; the Medigap complaint database; and survey forms for comprehensive outpatient rehabilitation facilities).

62 FR 31612, June 10, 1997: HCFA Agency Information Collection Activities; Proposed Collection; Comment request (pertaining to

request for termination of premium hospital and/or supplementary medical insurance).

63 FR 67078, December 4, 1998: Medicare Program; Recognition of NAIC Model Standards for Regulation of Medicare Supplemental Insurance — Notice.

1999

64 FR 23087, April 29, 1999: HCFA Emergency Clearance: Public Information Collection Requirements Submitted to the Office of Management and Budget (OMB) (pertaining to Medigap comparison data available of the Medicare web site medicare.gov).

2000

65 FR 11588, March 3, 2000: HCFA Agency Information Collection Activities: Proposed Collection; Comment request (pertaining to Medigap compare).

65 FR 18999, April 10, 2000: Medicare Program; Deductible Amount for Medigap High Deductible Options for Calendar Year 2000 — Notice.

65 FR 25460, May 2, 2000: Medicare and State Health Care Programs: Fraud and Abuse; Civil Money Penalty Safe Harbor to Protect Payment of Medicare Supplemental Insurance and Medigap Premiums for ESRD Beneficiaries — Notice of proposed rulemaking affecting 42 CFR Part 1003.

65 FR 35946, June 6, 2000: HCFA Agency Information Collection Activities: Submission for OMB Review; Comment request (pertaining to Medigap compare).

2001

66 FR 9858, February 12, 2001: HCFA Privacy Act of 1974; Report of New System (pertaining to complaints against health insurance issuers and health plans).

66 FR 15122, March 15, 2001: HCFA Agency Information Collection Activities: Proposed Collection; Comment request (pertaining to Medigap Compare data form).

66 FR 33102, June 20, 2001: HCFA Agency Information Collection Activities; Submission for OMB Review; Comment request (pertaining to Medigap Compare data).

See § 2:45.

§ 6:46 MISREPRESENTATION AND FRAUD IN OBTAINING AND USING SECRETARIAL CERTIFICATION OF MEDICARE SUPPLEMENTAL HEALTH INSURANCE POLICIES — Section 1882(d)(1) [42 U.S.C.A. 1395ss(d)(1)]

Regulations

42 CFR Part 402 — Civil Money Penalties, Assessments, and Exclusions

42 CFR Part 403, Subpart B — Medicare Supplemental Policies

42 CFR Part 409 — Hospital Insurance Benefits

42 CFR Part 410 — Supplementary Medical Insurance (SMI) Benefits

42 CFR Part 420 — Program Integrity: Medicare

42 CFR Chapter V — Office of Inspector General — Health Care, Department of Health and Human Services

Subchapter A — General Provisions

Part 1000 — Introduction; General Definitions

Subchapter B — OIG Authorities

Part 1001 — Program Integrity: Medicare and State Health Care Programs

Part 1003 — Civil Money Penalties, Assessments and Exclusions

Part 1005 — Appeals of Exclusions, Civil Money Penalties and Assessments

Part 1006 — Investigational Inquiries

56 FR 47763, September 20, 1991: Medicare Program; Conditional Designation of States in Which Medicare SELECT Insurance Policies May be Issued — General notice with comment period. See also correction at 56 FR 65269, December 16, 1991.

57 FR 37980, August 21, 1992: Medicare Program; HHS' Recognition of NAIC Model Standards for Regulation of Medigap Policies — Notice. 57 FR 58507, December 10, 1992: Privacy Act of 1974; Report of New System — Notice of new system of records (pertaining to data necessary to evaluate the Medicare SELECT program).

58 FR 35017, June 30, 1993: Medicare Program; Revised Designation of States In Which Medicare SELECT Insurance Policies May Be Issued — Notice.

58 FR 54159, October 20, 1993: HCFA Public Information Collection Requirements Submitted to the Office of Management and

Budget (OMB) for Clearance (pertaining to CLIA certification recommendation; CLIA laboratory personnel report; Medigap complaint data base; certification as a rural health clinic (RHC) and RHC survey report form; screening mammography services data report; ambulatory surgical center request for certification and survey report form; blood bank inspection checklist and report; Medicaid program budget report form; supplier of ESRD services form; and grantee data collection instrument) — Notice.

58 FR 60204, November 15, 1993: HCFA Public Information Collection Requirements Submitted to the Office of Management and Budget (OMB) for Clearance (pertaining to procedures for transmitting information between Medicare carriers and Medicare supplemental insurers; Medicare physician or supplier agreement; patient intake data form for the National Home Health Agency; agency characteristics form for the National Home Health Agency prospective payment demonstration; intake and assessment survey package for the community nursing organization demonstration; comprehensive outpatient rehabilitation facility (CORF eligibility and survey forms and information collection requirements) — Notice.

59 FR 30941, June 16, 1994: HCFA Public Information Collection Requirements Submitted to the Office of Management and Budget (OMB) for Clearance (pertaining to evaluation of Medicare SELECT amendments; and hospital and hospital health care complex cost report forms).

60 FR 30877, June 12, 1995: Medicare Program; HHS' Approval of NAIC Statements Relating to Duplication of Medicare Benefits — Notice.

61 FR 40422, August 2, 1996: HCFA Agency Information Collection Activities: Proposed Collection; Comment request (pertaining to survey and certification of ambulatory surgical centers; the Medigap complaint database; fiscal intermediaries' provider overpayment actions; and hospital standards for potentially HIV infectious blood and blood products).

61 FR 57688, November 7, 1996: HCFA Agency Information Collection Activities: Comment request (pertaining to clinical laboratory surveys; clinical laboratory personnel qualifications; Medicare/Medicaid hospital survey report forms; beneficiary disenrollment from HMOs and CMPs; survey reports for ambulatory surgical centers; the Medigap complaint database; and survey forms for comprehensive outpatient rehabilitation facilities).

62 FR 31612, June 10, 1997: HCFA Agency Information Collection Activities; Proposed Collection; Comment request (pertaining to request for termination of premium hospital and/or supplementary medical insurance).

63 FR 67078, December 4, 1998: Medicare Program; Recognition of NAIC Model Standards for Regulation of Medicare Supplemental Insurance — Notice.

1999

64 FR 23087, April 29, 1999: HCFA Emergency Clearance: Public Information Collection Requirements Submitted to the Office of Management and Budget (OMB) (pertaining to Medigap comparison data available of the Medicare web site medicare.gov).

2000

65 FR 11588, March 3, 2000: HCFA Agency Information Collection Activities: Proposed Collection; Comment request (pertaining to Medigap compare).

65 FR 18999, April 10, 2000: Medicare Program; Deductible Amount for Medigap High Deductible Options for Calendar Year 2000 — Notice.

65 FR 25460, May 2, 2000: Medicare and State Health Care Programs: Fraud and Abuse; Civil Money Penalty Safe Harbor to Protect Payment of Medicare Supplemental Insurance and Medigap Premiums for ESRD Beneficiaries — Notice of proposed rulemaking affecting 42 CFR Part 1003.

65 FR 35946, June 6, 2000: HCFA Agency Information Collection Activities: Submission for OMB Review; Comment request (pertaining to Medigap compare).

2001

66 FR 9858, February 12, 2001: HCFA Privacy Act of 1974; Report of New System (pertaining to complaints against health insurance issuers and health plans).

66 FR 15122, March 15, 2001: HCFA Agency Information Collection Activities: Proposed Collection; Comment request (pertaining to Medigap compare data form).

66 FR 33102, June 20, 2001: HCFA Agency Information Collection Activities; Submission for OMB Review; Comment request (pertaining to "Medigap Compare" data).

See § 2:46.

§ 6:47 MISREPRESENTATION BY SELLERS OF MEDICARE SUPPLEMENTAL HEALTH INSURANCE POLICIES THAT THEY ACT BY AUTHORITY OF OR IN ASSOCIATION WITH MEDICARE OR ANY FEDERAL AGENCY — Section 1882(d)(2) [42 U.S.C.A. 1395ss(d)(2)]

Regulations

42 CFR Part 402 — Civil Money Penalties, Assessments, and Exclusions

42 CFR Part 403, Subpart B — Medicare Supplemental Policies

42 CFR Part 409 — Hospital Insurance Benefits

42 CFR Part 410 — Supplementary Medical Insurance (SMI) Benefits

42 CFR Part 420 — Program Integrity: Medicare

42 CFR Chapter V — Office of Inspector General — Health Care, Department of Health and Human Services

Subchapter A — General Provisions

Part 1000 — Introduction; General Definitions

Subchapter B — OIG Authorities

Part 1001 — Program Integrity: Medicare and State Health Care Programs

Part 1003 — Civil Money Penalties, Assessments and Exclusions

Part 1005 — Appeals of Exclusions, Civil Money Penalties and Assessments

Part 1006 — Investigational Inquiries

56 FR 47763, September 20, 1991: Medicare Program; Conditional Designation of States in Which Medicare SELECT Insurance Policies May be Issued — General notice with comment period. See also correction at 56 FR 65269, December 16, 1991.

57 FR 37980, August 21, 1992: Medicare Program; HHS' Recognition of NAIC Model Standards for Regulation of Medigap Policies — Notice. 57 FR 58507, December 10, 1992: Privacy Act of 1974; Report of New System — Notice of new system of records (pertaining to data necessary to evaluate the Medicare SELECT program).

58 FR 35017, June 30, 1993: Medicare Program; Revised Designation of States In Which Medicare SELECT Insurance Policies May Be Issued — Notice.

58 FR 54159, October 20, 1993: HCFA Public Information Collection Requirements Submitted to the Office of Management and Budget (OMB) for Clearance (pertaining to CLIA certification recommendation; CLIA laboratory personnel report; Medigap complaint data base; certification as a rural health clinic (RHC) and RHC survey report form; screening mammography services data report; ambulatory surgical center request for certification and survey report form; blood bank inspection checklist and report; Medicaid program budget report form; supplier of ESRD services form; and grantee data collection instrument) — Notice.

58 FR 60204, November 15, 1993: HCFA Public Information Collection Requirements Submitted to the Office of Management and Budget (OMB) for Clearance (pertaining to procedures for transmitting information between Medicare carriers and Medicare supplemental insurers; Medicare physician or supplier agreement; patient intake data form for the National Home Health Agency; agency characteristics form for the National Home Health Agency prospective payment demonstration; intake and assessment survey package for the community nursing organization demonstration; comprehensive outpatient rehabilitation facility (CORF eligibility and survey forms and information collection requirements) — Notice.

59 FR 30941, June 16, 1994: HCFA Public Information Collection Requirements Submitted to the Office of Management and Budget (OMB) for Clearance (pertaining to evaluation of Medicare SELECT amendments; and hospital and hospital health care complex cost report forms).

60 FR 30877, June 12, 1995: Medicare Program; HHS' Approval of NAIC Statements Relating to Duplication of Medicare Benefits — Notice.

61 FR 40422, August 2, 1996: HCFA Agency Information Collection Activities: Proposed Collection; Comment request (pertaining to survey and certification of ambulatory surgical centers; the Medigap complaint database; fiscal intermediaries' provider overpayment actions; and hospital standards for potentially HIV infectious blood and blood products).

61 FR 57688, November 7, 1996: HCFA Agency Information Collection Activities: Comment request (pertaining to clinical laboratory surveys; clinical laboratory personnel qualifications; Medicare/Medicaid hospital survey report forms; beneficiary disenrollment from HMOs and CMPs; survey reports for ambulatory

surgical centers; the Medigap complaint database; and survey forms for comprehensive outpatient rehabilitation facilities).

62 FR 31612, June 10, 1997: HCFA Agency Information Collection Activities; Proposed Collection; Comment request (pertaining to request for termination of premium hospital and/or supplementary medical insurance).

63 FR 67078, December 4, 1998: Medicare Program; Recognition of NAIC Model Standards for Regulation of Medicare Supplemental Insurancee — Notice.

1999

64 FR 23087, April 29, 1999: HCFA Emergency Clearance: Public Information Collection Requirements Submitted to the Office of Management and Budget (OMB) (pertaining to Medigap comparison data available of the Medicare web site medicare.gov).

2000

65 FR 11588, March 3, 2000: HCFA Agency Information Collection Activities: Proposed Collection; Comment request (pertaining to Medigap compare).

65 FR 18999, April 10, 2000: Medicare Program; Deductible Amount for Medigap High Deductible Options for Calendar Year 2000 — Notice.

65 FR 25460, May 2, 2000: Medicare and State Health Care Programs: Fraud and Abuse; Civil Money Penalty Safe Harbor to Protect Payment of Medicare Supplemental Insurance and Medigap Premiums for ESRD Beneficiaries — Notice of proposed rulemaking affecting 42 CFR Part 1003.

65 FR 35946, June 6, 2000: HCFA Agency Information Collection Activities: Submission for OMB Review; Comment request (pertaining to Medigap compare).

2001

66 FR 9858, February 12, 2001: HCFA Privacy Act of 1974; Report of New System (pertaining to complaints against health insurance issuers and health plans).

66 FR 15122, March 15, 2001: HCFA Agency Information Collection Activities: Proposed Collection; Comment request (pertaining to Medigap compare data form).

66 FR 33102, June 20, 2001: HCFA Agency Information Collection Activities; Submission for OMB Review; Comment request (pertaining to "Medigap Compare" data).

See § 2:47.

§ 6:48 SELLING MEDICARE BENEFICIARIES SUPPLEMENTAL HEALTH INSURANCE POLICIES THAT DUPLICATE MEDICARE BENEFITS/NOT OBTAINING A VALID BUYER'S STATEMENT/NOT PREPARING SELLER'S ACKNOWLEDGMENT/FAILING TO COMPLY WITH DISCLOSURE REQUIREMENTS — Section 1882(d)(3) [42 U.S.C.A. 1395ss(d)(3)]

Regulations

42 CFR Part 402 — Civil Money Penalties, Assessments, and Exclusions

42 CFR Part 403, Subpart B — Medicare Supplemental Policies

42 CFR Part 409 — Hospital Insurance Benefits

42 CFR Part 410 — Supplementary Medical Insurance (SMI) Benefits

42 CFR Part 420 — Program Integrity: Medicare

42 CFR Chapter V — Office of Inspector General — Health Care, Department of Health and Human Services

Subchapter A — General Provisions

Part 1000 — Introduction; General Definitions

Subchapter B — OIG Authorities

Part 1001 — Program Integrity: Medicare amd State Health Care Programs

Part 1003 — Civil Money Penalties, Assessments and Exclusions

Part 1005 — Appeals of Exclusions, Civil Money Penalties and Assessments

Part 1006 — Investigational Inquiries

56 FR 47763, September 20, 1991: Medicare Program; Conditional Designation of States in Which Medicare SELECT Insurance Policies May be Issued — General notice with comment period. See also correction at 56 FR 65269, December 16, 1991.

57 FR 37980, August 21, 1992: Medicare Program; HHS' Recognition of NAIC Model Standards for Regulation of Medigap Policies — Notice. 57 FR 58507, December 10, 1992: Privacy Act of 1974; Report of New System — Notice of new system of records (per-

taining to data necessary to evaluate the Medicare SELECT program).

58 FR 35017, June 30, 1993: Medicare Program; Revised Designation of States In Which Medicare SELECT Insurance Policies May Be Issued — Notice.

58 FR 54159, October 20, 1993: HCFA Public Information Collection Requirements Submitted to the Office of Management and Budget (OMB) for Clearance (pertaining to CLIA certification recommendation; CLIA laboratory personnel report; Medigap complaint data base; certification as a rural health clinic (RHC) and RHC survey report form; screening mammography services data report; ambulatory surgical center request for certification and survey report form; blood bank inspection checklist and report; Medicaid program budget report form; supplier of ESRD services form; and grantee data collection instrument) — Notice.

58 FR 60204, November 15, 1993: HCFA Public Information Collection Requirements Submitted to the Office of Management and Budget (OMB) for Clearance (pertaining to procedures for transmitting information between Medicare carriers and Medicare supplemental insurers; Medicare physician or supplier agreement; patient intake data form for the National Home Health Agency; agency characteristics form for the National Home Health Agency prospective payment demonstration; intake and assessment survey package for the community nursing organization demonstration; comprehensive outpatient rehabilitation facility (CORF eligibility and survey forms and information collection requirements) — Notice.

59 FR 30941, June 16, 1994: HCFA Public Information Collection Requirements Submitted to the Office of Management and Budget (OMB) for Clearance (pertaining to evaluation of Medicare SELECT amendments; and hospital and hospital health care complex cost report forms).

60 FR 30877, June 12, 1995: Medicare Program; HHS' Approval of NAIC Statements Relating to Duplication of Medicare Benefits — Notice.

61 FR 40422, August 2, 1996: HCFA Agency Information Collection Activities: Proposed Collection; Comment request (pertaining to survey and certification of ambulatory surgical centers; the Medigap complaint database; fiscal intermediaries' provider overpayment actions; and hospital standards for potentially HIV infectious blood and blood products).

61 FR 57688, November 7, 1996: HCFA Agency Information Collection Activities: Comment request (pertaining to clinical laboratory surveys; clinical laboratory personnel qualifications; Medicare/Medicaid hospital survey report forms; beneficiary disenrollment from HMOs and CMPs; survey reports for ambulatory surgical centers; the Medigap complaint database; and survey forms for comprehensive outpatient rehabilitation facilities).

62 FR 31612, June 10, 1997: HCFA Agency Information Collection Activities; Proposed Collection; Comment request (pertaining to request for termination of premium hospital and/or supplementary medical insurance).

63 FR 67078, December 4, 1998: Medicare Program; Recognition of NAIC Model Standards for Regulation of Medicare Supplemental Insurancee — Notice.

1999

64 FR 23087, April 29, 1999: HCFA Emergency Clearance: Public Information Collection Requirements Submitted to the Office of Management and Budget (OMB) (pertaining to Medigap comparison data available of the Medicare web site medicare.gov).

2000

65 FR 11588, March 3, 2000: HCFA Agency Information Collection Activities: Proposed Collection; Comment request (pertaining to Medigap compare).

65 FR 18999, April 10, 2000: Medicare Program; Deductible Amount for Medigap High Deductible Options for Calendar Year 2000 — Notice.

65 FR 25460, May 2, 2000: Medicare and State Health Care Programs: Fraud and Abuse; Civil Money Penalty Safe Harbor to Protect Payment of Medicare Supplemental Insurance and Medigap Premiums for ESRD Beneficiaries — Notice of proposed rulemaking affecting 42 CFR Part 1003.

65 FR 35946, June 6, 2000: HCFA Agency Information Collection Activities: Submission for OMB Review; Comment request (pertaining to Medigap compare).

2001

66 FR 9858, February 12, 2001: HCFA Privacy Act of 1974; Report of New System (pertaining to complaints against health insurance issuers and health plans).

66 FR 15122, March 15, 2001: HCFA Agency Information Collection Activities: Proposed Collection; Comment request (pertaining to Medigap compare data form).

66 FR 33102, June 20, 2001: HCFA Agency Information Collection Activities; Submission for OMB Review; Comment request (pertaining to "Medigap Compare" data).

See § 2:48.

§ 6:49 USING THE MAIL TO MARKET MEDICARE SUPPLEMENTAL HEALTH INSURANCE POLICIES WHICH HAVE NOT BEEN STATE-APPROVED — Section 1882(d)(4) [42 U.S.C.A. 1395ss(d)(4)]

Regulations

42 CFR Part 402 — Civil Money Penalties, Assessments, and Exclusions

42 CFR Part 403, Subpart B — Medicare Supplemental Policies

42 CFR Part 409 — Hospital Insurance Benefits

42 CFR Part 410 — Supplementary Medical Insurance (SMI) Benefits

42 CFR Part 420 — Program Integrity: Medicare

42 CFR Chapter V — Office of Inspector General — Health Care, Department of Health and Human Services

Subchapter A — General Provisions Part 1000 — Introduction; General Definitions

Subchapter B — OIG Authorities

Part 1001 — Program Integrity: Medicare and State Health Care Programs

Part 1003 — Civil Money Penalties, Assessments and Exclusions

Part 1005 — Appeals of Exclusions, Civil Money Penalties and Assessments

Part 1006 — Investigational Inquiries

56 FR 47763, September 20, 1991: Medicare Program; Conditional Designation of States in Which Medicare SELECT Insurance Policies May be Issued — General notice with comment period. See also correction at 56 FR 65269, December 16, 1991.

57 FR 37980, August 21, 1992: Medicare Program; HHS' Recognition of NAIC Model Standards for Regulation of Medigap Policies — Notice. 57 FR 58507, December 10, 1992: Privacy Act of 1974; Report of New System — Notice of new system of records (pertaining to data necessary to evaluate the Medicare SELECT program).

58 FR 35017, June 30, 1993: Medicare Program; Revised Designation of States In Which Medicare SELECT Insurance Policies May Be Issued — Notice.

58 FR 54159, October 20, 1993: HCFA Public Information Collection Requirements Submitted to the Office of Management and Budget (OMB) for Clearance (pertaining to CLIA certification recommendation; CLIA laboratory personnel report; Medigap complaint data base; certification as a rural health clinic (RHC) and RHC survey report form; screening mammography services data report; ambulatory surgical center request for certification and survey report form; blood bank inspection checklist and report; Medicaid program budget report form; supplier of ESRD services form; and grantee data collection instrument) — Notice.

58 FR 60204, November 15, 1993: HCFA Public Information Collection Requirements Submitted to the Office of Management and Budget (OMB) for Clearance (pertaining to procedures for transmitting information between Medicare carriers and Medicare supplemental insurers; Medicare physician or supplier agreement; patient intake data form for the National Home Health Agency; agency characteristics form for the National Home Health Agency prospective payment demonstration; intake and assessment survey package for the community nursing organization demonstration; comprehensive outpatient rehabilitation facility (CORF eligibility and survey forms and information collection requirements) — Notice.

59 FR 30941, June 16, 1994: HCFA Public Information Collection Requirements Submitted to the Office of Management and Budget (OMB) for Clearance (pertaining to evaluation of Medicare SELECT amendments; and hospital and hospital health care complex cost report forms).

60 FR 30877, June 12, 1995: Medicare Program; HHS' Approval of NAIC Statements Relating to Duplication of Medicare Benefits — Notice.

61 FR 40422, August 2, 1996: HCFA Agency Information Collection Activities: Proposed Collection; Comment request (pertaining to

survey and certification of ambulatory surgical centers; the Medigap complaint database; fiscal intermediaries' provider overpayment actions; and hospital standards for potentially HIV infectious blood and blood products).

61 FR 57688, November 7, 1996: HCFA Agency Information Collection Activities: Comment request (pertaining to clinical laboratory surveys; clinical laboratory personnel qualifications; Medicare/Medicaid hospital survey report forms; beneficiary disenrollment from HMOs and CMPs; survey reports for ambulatory surgical centers; the Medigap complaint database; and survey forms for comprehensive outpatient rehabilitation facilities).

62 FR 31612, June 10, 1997: HCFA Agency Information Collection Activities; Proposed Collection; Comment request (pertaining to request for termination of premium hospital and/or supplementary medical insurance).

63 FR 67078, December 4, 1998: Medicare Program; Recognition of NAIC Model Standards for Regulation of Medicare Supplemental Insurance — Notice.

1999

64 FR 23087, April 29, 1999: HCFA Emergency Clearance: Public Information Collection Requirements Submitted to the Office of Management and Budget (OMB) (pertaining to Medigap comparison data available of the Medicare web site medicare.gov).

2000

65 FR 11588, March 3, 2000: HCFA Agency Information Collection Activities: Proposed Collection; Comment request (pertaining to Medigap compare).

65 FR 18999, April 10, 2000: Medicare Program; Deductible Amount for Medigap High Deductible Options for Calendar Year 2000 — Notice.

65 FR 25460, May 2, 2000: Medicare and State Health Care Programs: Fraud and Abuse; Civil Money Penalty Safe Harbor to Protect Payment of Medicare Supplemental Insurance and Medigap Premiums for ESRD Beneficiaries — Notice of proposed rulemaking affecting 42 CFR Part 1003.

65 FR 35946, June 6, 2000: HCFA Agency Information Collection Activities: Submission for OMB Review; Comment request (pertaining to Medigap compare).

2001

66 FR 9858, February 12, 2001: HCFA Privacy Act of 1974; Report of New System (pertaining to complaints against health insurance issuers and health plans).

66 FR 15122, March 15, 2001: HCFA Agency Information Collection Activities: Proposed Collection; Comment request (pertaining to Medigap compare data form).

66 FR 33102, June 20, 2001: HCFA Agency Information Collection Activities; Submission for OMB Review; Comment request (pertaining to "Medigap Compare" data).

See § 2:49.

§ 6:50 ISSUING OR SELLING MEDICARE SUPPLEMENTAL HEALTH INSURANCE POLICIES THAT DO NOT COMPLY WITH FORM AND CONTENT REQUIREMENTS — Section 1882(p)(8) [42 U.S.C.A. 1395ss(p)(8)]

Regulations

42 CFR Part 402 — Civil Money Penalties, Assessments, and Exclusions

42 CFR Part 403, Subpart B — Medicare Supplemental Policies

42 CFR Part 409 — Hospital Insurance Benefits

42 CFR Part 410 — Supplementary Medical Insurance (SMI) Benefits

42 CFR Part 420 — Program Integrity: Medicare

42 CFR Chapter V — Office of Inspector General — Health Care, Department of Health and Human Services

Subchapter A — General Provisions Part 1000 — Introduction; General Definitions

Subchapter B — OIG Authorities

Part 1001 — Program Integrity: Medicare and State Health Care Programs

Part 1003 — Civil Money Penalties, Assessments and Exclusions

Part 1005 — Appeals of Exclusions, Civil Money Penalties and Assessments

Part 1006 — Investigational Inquiries

56 FR 47763, September 20, 1991: Medicare Program; Conditional Designation of States in Which Medicare SELECT Insurance Poli-

cies May be Issued — General notice with comment period. See also correction at 56 FR 65269, December 16, 1991.

57 FR 37980, August 21, 1992: Medicare Program; HHS' Recognition of NAIC Model Standards for Regulation of Medigap Policies — Notice. 57 FR 58507, December 10, 1992: Privacy Act of 1974; Report of New System — Notice of new system of records (pertaining to data necessary to evaluate the Medicare SELECT program).

58 FR 35017, June 30, 1993: Medicare Program; Revised Designation of States In Which Medicare SELECT Insurance Policies May Be Issued — Notice.

58 FR 54159, October 20, 1993: HCFA Public Information Collection Requirements Submitted to the Office of Management and Budget (OMB) for Clearance (pertaining to CLIA certification recommendation; CLIA laboratory personnel report; Medigap complaint data base; certification as a rural health clinic (RHC) and RHC survey report form; screening mammography services data report; ambulatory surgical center request for certification and survey report form; blood bank inspection checklist and report; Medicaid program budget report form; supplier of ESRD services form; and grantee data collection instrument) — Notice.

58 FR 60204, November 15, 1993: HCFA Public Information Collection Requirements Submitted to the Office of Management and Budget (OMB) for Clearance (pertaining to procedures for transmitting information between Medicare carriers and Medicare supplemental insurers; Medicare physician or supplier agreement; patient intake data form for the National Home Health Agency; agency characteristics form for the National Home Health Agency prospective payment demonstration; intake and assessment survey package for the community nursing organization demonstration; comprehensive outpatient rehabilitation facility (CORF eligibility and survey forms and information collection requirements) — Notice.

59 FR 30941, June 16, 1994: HCFA Public Information Collection Requirements Submitted to the Office of Management and Budget (OMB) for Clearance (pertaining to evaluation of Medicare SELECT amendments; and hospital and hospital health care complex cost report forms).

60 FR 30877, June 12, 1995: Medicare Program; HHS' Approval of NAIC Statements Relating to Duplication of Medicare Benefits — Notice.

61 FR 40422, August 2, 1996: HCFA Agency Information Collection Activities: Proposed Collection; Comment request (pertaining to survey and certification of ambulatory surgical centers; the Medigap complaint database; fiscal intermediaries' provider overpayment actions; and hospital standards for potentially HIV infectious blood and blood products).

61 FR 57688, November 7, 1996: HCFA Agency Information Collection Activities: Comment request (pertaining to clinical laboratory surveys; clinical laboratory personnel qualifications; Medicare/Medicaid hospital survey report forms; beneficiary disenrollment from HMOs and CMPs; survey reports for ambulatory surgical centers; the Medigap complaint database; and survey forms for comprehensive outpatient rehabilitation facilities).

62 FR 31612, June 10, 1997: HCFA Agency Information Collection Activities; Proposed Collection; Comment request (pertaining to request for termination of premium hospital and/or supplementary medical insurance).

63 FR 67078, December 4, 1998: Medicare Program; Recognition of NAIC Model Standards for Regulation of Medicare Supplemental Insurance — Notice.

1999

64 FR 23087, April 29, 1999: HCFA Emergency Clearance: Public Information Collection Requirements Submitted to the Office of Management and Budget (OMB) (pertaining to Medigap comparison data available of the Medicare web site medicare.gov).

2000

65 FR 11588, March 3, 2000: HCFA Agency Information Collection Activities: Proposed Collection; Comment request (pertaining to Medigap compare).

65 FR 18999, April 10, 2000: Medicare Program; Deductible Amount for Medigap High Deductible Options for Calendar Year 2000 — Notice.

65 FR 25460, May 2, 2000: Medicare and State Health Care Programs: Fraud and Abuse; Civil Money Penalty Safe Harbor to Protect Payment of Medicare Supplemental Insurance and Medigap Premiums for ESRD Beneficiaries — Notice of proposed rulemaking affecting 42 CFR Part 1003.

65 FR 35946, June 6, 2000: HCFA Agency Information Collection Activities: Submission for OMB Review; Comment request (pertaining to Medigap compare).

2001

66 FR 9858, February 12, 2001: HCFA Privacy Act of 1974; Report of New System (pertaining to complaints against health insurance issuers and health plans).

66 FR 15122, March 15, 2001: HCFA Agency Information Collection Activities: Proposed Collection; Comment request (pertaining to Medigap compare data form).

66 FR 33102, June 20, 2001: HCFA Agency Information Collection Activities; Submission for OMB Review; Comment request (pertaining to "Medigap Compare" data).

See § 2:50.

§ 6:51 FAILURE TO OFFER A MEDICARE SUPPLEMENTAL HEALTH INSURANCE POLICY THAT PROVIDES ONLY THE CORE GROUP OF BASIC BENEFITS — Section 1882(p)(9)(C) [42 U.S.C.A. 1395ss(p)(9)(C)]

Regulations

42 CFR Part 402 — Civil Money Penalties, Assessments, and Exclusions

42 CFR Part 403, Subpart B — Medicare Supplemental Policies

42 CFR Part 409 — Hospital Insurance Benefits

42 CFR Part 410 — Supplementary Medical Insurance (SMI) Benefits

42 CFR Part 420 — Program Integrity: Medicare

42 CFR Chapter V — Office of Inspector General — Health Care, Department of Health and Human Services

Subchapter A — General Provisions

Part 1000 — Introduction; General Definitions

Subchapter B — OIG Authorities

Part 1001 — Program Integrity: Medicare and State Health Care Programs

Part 1003 — Civil Money Penalties, Assessments and Exclusions

Part 1005 — Appeals of Exclusions, Civil Money Penalties and Assessments

Part 1006 — Investigational Inquiries

56 FR 47763, September 20, 1991: Medicare Program; Conditional Designation of States in Which Medicare SELECT Insurance Policies May be Issued — General notice with comment period. See also correction at 56 FR 65269, December 16, 1991.

57 FR 37980, August 21, 1992: Medicare Program; HHS' Recognition of NAIC Model Standards for Regulation of Medigap Policies — Notice. 57 FR 58507, December 10, 1992: Privacy Act of 1974; Report of New System — Notice of new system of records (pertaining to data necessary to evaluate the Medicare SELECT program).

58 FR 35017, June 30, 1993: Medicare Program; Revised Designation of States In Which Medicare SELECT Insurance Policies May Be Issued — Notice.

58 FR 54159, October 20, 1993: HCFA Public Information Collection Requirements Submitted to the Office of Management and Budget (OMB) for Clearance (pertaining to CLIA certification recommendation; CLIA laboratory personnel report; Medigap complaint data base; certification as a rural health clinic (RHC) and RHC survey report form; screening mammography services data report; ambulatory surgical center request for certification and survey report form; blood bank inspection checklist and report; Medicaid program budget report form; supplier of ESRD services form; and grantee data collection instrument) — Notice.

58 FR 60204, November 15, 1993: HCFA Public Information Collection Requirements Submitted to the Office of Management and Budget (OMB) for Clearance (pertaining to procedures for transmitting information between Medicare carriers and Medicare supplemental insurers; Medicare physician or supplier agreement; patient intake data form for the National Home Health Agency; agency characteristics form for the National Home Health Agency prospective payment demonstration; intake and assessment survey package for the community nursing organization demonstration; comprehensive outpatient rehabilitation facility (CORF eligibility and survey forms and information collection requirements) — Notice.

59 FR 30941, June 16, 1994: HCFA Public Information Collection Requirements Submitted to the Office of Management and Budget (OMB) for Clearance (pertaining to evaluation of Medicare SELECT amendments; and hospital and hospital health care complex cost report forms).

60 FR 30877, June 12, 1995: Medicare Program; HHS' Approval of NAIC Statements Relating to Duplication of Medicare Benefits — Notice.

61 FR 40422, August 2, 1996: HCFA Agency Information Collection Activities: Proposed Collection; Comment request (pertaining to survey and certification of ambulatory surgical centers; the Medigap complaint database; fiscal intermediaries' provider overpayment actions; and hospital standards for potentially HIV infectious blood and blood products).

61 FR 57688, November 7, 1996: HCFA Agency Information Collection Activities: Comment request (pertaining to clinical laboratory surveys; clinical laboratory personnel qualifications; Medicare/Medicaid hospital survey report forms; beneficiary disenrollment from HMOs and CMPs; survey reports for ambulatory surgical centers; the Medigap complaint database; and survey forms for comprehensive outpatient rehabilitation facilities).

62 FR 31612, June 10, 1997: HCFA Agency Information Collection Activities; Proposed Collection; Comment request (pertaining to request for termination of premium hospital and/or supplementary medical insurance).

63 FR 67078, December 4, 1998: Medicare Program; Recognition of NAIC Model Standards for Regulation of Medicare Supplemental Insurance — Notice.

1999

64 FR 23087, April 29, 1999: HCFA Emergency Clearance: Public Information Collection Requirements Submitted to the Office of Management and Budget (OMB) (pertaining to Medigap comparison data available of the Medicare web site medicare.gov).

2000

65 FR 11588, March 3, 2000: HCFA Agency Information Collection Activities: Proposed Collection; Comment request (pertaining to Medigap compare).

65 FR 18999, April 10, 2000: Medicare Program; Deductible Amount for Medigap High Deductible Options for Calendar Year 2000 — Notice.

65 FR 25460, May 2, 2000: Medicare and State Health Care Programs: Fraud and Abuse; Civil Money Penalty Safe Harbor to Protect Payment of Medicare Supplemental Insurance and Medigap

Premiums for ESRD Beneficiaries — Notice of proposed rulemaking affecting 42 CFR Part 1003.

65 FR 35946, June 6, 2000: HCFA Agency Information Collection Activities: Submission for OMB Review; Comment request (pertaining to Medigap compare).

2001

66 FR 9858, February 12, 2001: HCFA Privacy Act of 1974; Report of New System (pertaining to complaints against health insurance issuers and health plans).

66 FR 15122, March 15, 2001: HCFA Agency Information Collection Activities: Proposed Collection; Comment request (pertaining to Medigap compare data form).

66 FR 33102, June 20, 2001: HCFA Agency Information Collection Activities; Submission for OMB Review; Comment request (pertaining to "Medigap Compare" data).

See § 2:51.

§ 6:52 FAILURE TO PROVIDE REINSTATEMENT RIGHTS TO PURCHASERS OF MEDICARE SUPPLEMENTAL HEALTH INSURANCE POLICIES WHO BECOME ELIGIBLE FOR MEDICAID — Section 1882(q)(5) [42 U.S.C.A. 1395ss(q)(5)]

Regulations

42 CFR Part 402 — Civil Money Penalties, Assessments, and Exclusions

42 CFR Part 403, Subpart B — Medicare Supplemental Policies

42 CFR Part 409 — Hospital Insurance Benefits

42 CFR Part 410 — Supplementary Medical Insurance (SMI) Benefits

42 CFR Part 420 — Program Integrity: Medicare

42 CFR Chapter V — Office of Inspector General — Health Care, Department of Health and Human Services

Subchapter A — General Provisions Part 1000 — Introduction; General Definitions

Subchapter B — OIG Authorities

Part 1001 — Program Integrity: Medicare and State Health Care Programs

Part 1003 — Civil Money Penalties, Assessments and Exclusions

Part 1005 — Appeals of Exclusions, Civil Money Penalties and Assessments

Part 1006 — Investigational Inquiries

56 FR 47763, September 20, 1991: Medicare Program; Conditional Designation of States in Which Medicare SELECT Insurance Policies May be Issued — General notice with comment period. See also correction at 56 FR 65269, December 16, 1991.

57 FR 37980, August 21, 1992: Medicare Program; HHS' Recognition of NAIC Model Standards for Regulation of Medigap Policies — Notice. 57 FR 58507, December 10, 1992: Privacy Act of 1974; Report of New System — Notice of new system of records (pertaining to data necessary to evaluate the Medicare SELECT program).

58 FR 35017, June 30, 1993: Medicare Program; Revised Designation of States In Which Medicare SELECT Insurance Policies May Be Issued — Notice.

58 FR 54159, October 20, 1993: HCFA Public Information Collection Requirements Submitted to the Office of Management and Budget (OMB) for Clearance (pertaining to CLIA certification recommendation; CLIA laboratory personnel report; Medigap complaint data base; certification as a rural health clinic (RHC) and RHC survey report form; screening mammography services data report; ambulatory surgical center request for certification and survey report form; blood bank inspection checklist and report; Medicaid program budget report form; supplier of ESRD services form; and grantee data collection instrument) — Notice.

58 FR 60204, November 15, 1993: HCFA Public Information Collection Requirements Submitted to the Office of Management and Budget (OMB) for Clearance (pertaining to procedures for transmitting information between Medicare carriers and Medicare supplemental insurers; Medicare physician or supplier agreement; patient intake data form for the National Home Health Agency; agency characteristics form for the National Home Health Agency prospective payment demonstration; intake and assessment survey package for the community nursing organization demonstration; comprehensive outpatient rehabilitation facility (CORF eligibility and survey forms and information collection requirements) — Notice.

59 FR 30941, June 16, 1994: HCFA Public Information Collection Requirements Submitted to the Office of Management and Budget (OMB) for Clearance (pertaining to evaluation of Medicare SELECT

amendments; and hospital and hospital health care complex cost report forms).

60 FR 30877, June 12, 1995: Medicare Program; HHS' Approval of NAIC Statements Relating to Duplication of Medicare Benefits — Notice.

61 FR 40422, August 2, 1996: HCFA Agency Information Collection Activities: Proposed Collection; Comment request (pertaining to survey and certification of ambulatory surgical centers; the Medigap complaint database; fiscal intermediaries' provider overpayment actions; and hospital standards for potentially HIV infectious blood and blood products).

61 FR 57688, November 7, 1996: HCFA Agency Information Collection Activities: Comment request (pertaining to clinical laboratory surveys; clinical laboratory personnel qualifications; Medicare/Medicaid hospital survey report forms; beneficiary disenrollment from HMOs and CMPs; survey reports for ambulatory surgical centers; the Medigap complaint database; and survey forms for comprehensive outpatient rehabilitation facilities).

62 FR 31612, June 10, 1997: HCFA Agency Information Collection Activities; Proposed Collection; Comment request (pertaining to request for termination of premium hospital and/or supplementary medical insurance).

63 FR 67078, December 4, 1998: Medicare Program; Recognition of NAIC Model Standards for Regulation of Medicare Supplemental Insurance — Notice.

1999

64 FR 23087, April 29, 1999: HCFA Emergency Clearance: Public Information Collection Requirements Submitted to the Office of Management and Budget (OMB) (pertaining to Medigap comparison data available of the Medicare web site medicare.gov).

2000

65 FR 11588, March 3, 2000: HCFA Agency Information Collection Activities: Proposed Collection; Comment request (pertaining to Medigap compare).

65 FR 18999, April 10, 2000: Medicare Program; Deductible Amount for Medigap High Deductible Options for Calendar Year 2000 — Notice.

65 FR 25460, May 2, 2000: Medicare and State Health Care Programs: Fraud and Abuse; Civil Money Penalty Safe Harbor to Protect Payment of Medicare Supplemental Insurance and Medigap Premiums for ESRD Beneficiaries — Notice of proposed rulemaking affecting 42 CFR Part 1003.

65 FR 35946, June 6, 2000: HCFA Agency Information Collection Activities: Submission for OMB Review; Comment request (pertaining to Medigap compare).

2001

66 FR 9858, February 12, 2001: HCFA Privacy Act of 1974; Report of New System (pertaining to complaints against health insurance issuers and health plans).

66 FR 15122, March 15, 2001: HCFA Agency Information Collection Activities: Proposed Collection; Comment request (pertaining to Medigap compare data form).

66 FR 33102, June 20, 2001: HCFA Agency Information Collection Activities; Submission for OMB Review; Comment request (pertaining to "Medigap Compare" data).

See § 2:52.

§ 6:53 FAILURE BY ISSUERS OF MEDICARE SUPPLEMENTAL HEALTH INSURANCE POLICIES TO MEET REQUIREMENTS FOR PREEXISTING CONDITIONS, WAITING PERIODS, ELIMINATION PERIODS, PROBATIONARY PERIODS, AND PRICE AND COVERAGE NONDISCRIMINATION — Section 1882(s)(3) [42 U.S.C.A. 1395ss(s)(3)]

Regulations

42 CFR Part 402 — Civil Money Penalties, Assessments, and Exclusions

42 CFR Part 403, Subpart B — Medicare Supplemental Policies

42 CFR Part 409 — Hospital Insurance Benefits

42 CFR Part 410 — Supplementary Medical Insurance (SMI) Benefits

42 CFR Part 420 — Program Integrity: Medicare

42 CFR Chapter V — Office of Inspector General — Health Care, Department of Health and Human Services

Subchapter A — General Provisions

Part 1000 — Introduction; General Definitions

Subchapter B — OIG Authorities

Part 1001 — Program Integrity: Medicare and State Health Care Programs

Part 1003 — Civil Money Penalties, Assessments and Exclusions

Part 1005 — Appeals of Exclusions, Civil Money Penalties and Assessments

Part 1006 — Investigational Inquiries

56 FR 47763, September 20, 1991: Medicare Program; Conditional Designation of States in Which Medicare SELECT Insurance Policies May be Issued — General notice with comment period. See also correction at 56 FR 65269, December 16, 1991.

57 FR 37980, August 21, 1992: Medicare Program; HHS' Recognition of NAIC Model Standards for Regulation of Medigap Policies — Notice. 57 FR 58507, December 10, 1992: Privacy Act of 1974; Report of New System — Notice of new system of records (pertaining to data necessary to evaluate the Medicare SELECT program).

58 FR 35017, June 30, 1993: Medicare Program; Revised Designation of States In Which Medicare SELECT Insurance Policies May Be Issued — Notice.

58 FR 54159, October 20, 1993: HCFA Public Information Collection Requirements Submitted to the Office of Management and Budget (OMB) for Clearance (pertaining to CLIA certification recommendation; CLIA laboratory personnel report; Medigap complaint data base; certification as a rural health clinic (RHC) and RHC survey report form; screening mammography services data report; ambulatory surgical center request for certification and survey report form; blood bank inspection checklist and report; Medicaid program budget report form; supplier of ESRD services form; and grantee data collection instrument) — Notice.

58 FR 60204, November 15, 1993: HCFA Public Information Collection Requirements Submitted to the Office of Management and Budget (OMB) for Clearance (pertaining to procedures for transmitting information between Medicare carriers and Medicare supplemental insurers; Medicare physician or supplier agreement; patient intake data form for the National Home Health Agency; agency characteristics form for the National Home Health Agency prospective payment demonstration; intake and assessment survey package for the community nursing organization demonstration; comprehensive outpatient rehabilitation facility (CORF eligibility

and survey forms and information collection requirements) — Notice.

59 FR 30941, June 16, 1994: HCFA Public Information Collection Requirements Submitted to the Office of Management and Budget (OMB) for Clearance (pertaining to evaluation of Medicare SELECT amendments; and hospital and hospital health care complex cost report forms).

60 FR 30877, June 12, 1995: Medicare Program; HHS' Approval of NAIC Statements Relating to Duplication of Medicare Benefits — Notice.

61 FR 40422, August 2, 1996: HCFA Agency Information Collection Activities: Proposed Collection; Comment request (pertaining to survey and certification of ambulatory surgical centers; the Medigap complaint database; fiscal intermediaries' provider overpayment actions; and hospital standards for potentially HIV infectious blood and blood products).

61 FR 57688, November 7, 1996: HCFA Agency Information Collection Activities: Comment request (pertaining to clinical laboratory surveys; clinical laboratory personnel qualifications; Medicare/Medicaid hospital survey report forms; beneficiary disenrollment from HMOs and CMPs; survey reports for ambulatory surgical centers; the Medigap complaint database; and survey forms for comprehensive outpatient rehabilitation facilities).

62 FR 31612, June 10, 1997: HCFA Agency Information Collection Activities; Proposed Collection; Comment request (pertaining to request for termination of premium hospital and/or supplementary medical insurance).

63 FR 67078, December 4, 1998: Medicare Program; Recognition of NAIC Model Standards for Regulation of Medicare Supplemental Insurance — Notice.

1999

64 FR 23087, April 29, 1999: HCFA Emergency Clearance: Public Information Collection Requirements Submitted to the Office of Management and Budget (OMB) (pertaining to Medigap comparison data available of the Medicare web site medicare.gov).

2000

65 FR 11588, March 3, 2000: HCFA Agency Information Collection Activities: Proposed Collection; Comment request (pertaining to Medigap compare).

65 FR 18999, April 10, 2000: Medicare Program; Deductible Amount for Medigap High Deductible Options for Calendar Year 2000 — Notice.

65 FR 25460, May 2, 2000: Medicare and State Health Care Programs: Fraud and Abuse; Civil Money Penalty Safe Harbor to Protect Payment of Medicare Supplemental Insurance and Medigap Premiums for ESRD Beneficiaries — Notice of proposed rulemaking affecting 42 CFR Part 1003.

65 FR 35946, June 6, 2000: HCFA Agency Information Collection Activities: Submission for OMB Review; Comment request (pertaining to Medigap compare).

2001

66 FR 9858, February 12, 2001: HCFA Privacy Act of 1974; Report of New System (pertaining to complaints against health insurance issuers and health plans).

66 FR 15122, March 15, 2001: HCFA Agency Information Collection Activities: Proposed Collection; Comment request (pertaining to Medigap compare data form).

66 FR 33102, June 20, 2001: HCFA Agency Information Collection Activities; Submission for OMB Review; Comment request (pertaining to "Medigap Compare" data).

See § 2:53.

§ 6:54 SPECIAL OBLIGATIONS FOR ISSUERS OF MEDICARE SUPPLEMENTAL HEALTH INSURANCE POLICIES WHO PROVIDE BENEFITS THROUGH CONTRACTS WITH NETWORKS OF PROVIDERS (MEDICARE SELECT) — Section 1882(t)(2) [42 U.S.C.A. 1395ss(t)(2)]

Regulations

42 CFR Part 402 — Civil Money Penalties, Assessments, and Exclusions

42 CFR Part 403, Subpart B — Medicare Supplemental Policies

42 CFR Part 409 — Hospital Insurance Benefits

42 CFR Part 410 — Supplementary Medical Insurance (SMI) Benefits

42 CFR Part 420 — Program Integrity: Medicare

42 CFR Chapter V — Office of Inspector General — Health Care, Department of Health and Human Services

Subchapter A — General Provisions

Part 1000 — Introduction; General Definitions

Subchapter B — OIG Authorities

Part 1001 — Program Integrity: Medicare and State Health Care Programs

Part 1003 — Civil Money Penalties, Assessments and Exclusions

Part 1005 — Appeals of Exclusions, Civil Money Penalties and Assessments

Part 1006 — Investigational Inquiries

56 FR 47763, September 20, 1991: Medicare Program; Conditional Designation of States in Which Medicare SELECT Insurance Policies May be Issued — General notice with comment period. See also correction at 56 FR 65269, December 16, 1991.

57 FR 37980, August 21, 1992: Medicare Program; HHS' Recognition of NAIC Model Standards for Regulation of Medigap Policies — Notice. 57 FR 58507, December 10, 1992: Privacy Act of 1974; Report of New System — Notice of new system of records (pertaining to data necessary to evaluate the Medicare SELECT program).

58 FR 35017, June 30, 1993: Medicare Program; Revised Designation of States In Which Medicare SELECT Insurance Policies May Be Issued — Notice.

58 FR 54159, October 20, 1993: HCFA Public Information Collection Requirements Submitted to the Office of Management and Budget (OMB) for Clearance (pertaining to CLIA certification recommendation; CLIA laboratory personnel report; Medigap complaint data base; certification as a rural health clinic (RHC) and RHC survey report form; screening mammography services data report; ambulatory surgical center request for certification and survey report form; blood bank inspection checklist and report; Medicaid program budget report form; supplier of ESRD services form; and grantee data collection instrument) — Notice.

58 FR 60204, November 15, 1993: HCFA Public Information Collection Requirements Submitted to the Office of Management and Budget (OMB) for Clearance (pertaining to procedures for transmitting information between Medicare carriers and Medicare supplemental insurers; Medicare physician or supplier agreement; patient intake data form for the National Home Health Agency; agency characteristics form for the National Home Health Agency prospective payment demonstration; intake and assessment survey package for the community nursing organization demonstration;

comprehensive outpatient rehabilitation facility (CORF eligibility and survey forms and information collection requirements) —Notice.

59 FR 30941, June 16, 1994: HCFA Public Information Collection Requirements Submitted to the Office of Management and Budget (OMB) for Clearance (pertaining to evaluation of Medicare SELECT amendments; and hospital and hospital healthcare complex cost report forms).

60 FR 30877, June 12, 1995: Medicare Program; HHS' Approval of NAIC Statements Relating to Duplication of Medicare Benefits — Notice.

61 FR 40422, August 2, 1996: HCFA Agency Information Collection Activities: Proposed Collection; Comment request (pertaining to survey and certification of ambulatory surgical centers; the Medigap complaint database; fiscal intermediaries' provider overpayment actions; and hospital standards for potentially HIV infectious blood and blood products).

61 FR 57688, November 7, 1996: HCFA Agency Information Collection Activities: Comment request (pertaining to clinical laboratory surveys; clinical laboratory personnel qualifications; Medicare/Medicaid hospital survey report forms; beneficiary disenrollment from HMOs and CMPs; survey reports for ambulatory surgical centers; the Medigap complaint database; and survey forms for comprehensive outpatient rehabilitation facilities).

62 FR 31612, June 10, 1997: HCFA Agency Information Collection Activities; Proposed Collection; Comment request (pertaining to request for termination of premium hospital and/or supplementary medical insurance).

63 FR 67078, December 4, 1998: Medicare Program; Recognition of NAIC Model Standards for Regulation of Medicare Supplemental Insurance — Notice.

1999

64 FR 23087, April 29, 1999: HCFA Emergency Clearance: Public Information Collection Requirements Submitted to the Office of Management and Budget (OMB) (pertaining to Medigap comparison data available of the Medicare web site medicare.gov).

2000

65 FR 11588, March 3, 2000: HCFA Agency Information Collection Activities: Proposed Collection; Comment request (pertaining to Medigap compare).

65 FR 18999, April 10, 2000: Medicare Program; Deductible Amount for Medigap High Deductible Options for Calendar Year 2000 — Notice.

65 FR 25460, May 2, 2000: Medicare and State Health Care Programs: Fraud and Abuse; Civil Money Penalty Safe Harbor to Protect Payment of Medicare Supplemental Insurance and Medigap Premiums for ESRD Beneficiaries — Notice of proposed rulemaking affecting 42 CFR Part 1003.

65 FR 35946, June 6, 2000: HCFA Agency Information Collection Activities: Submission for OMB Review; Comment request (pertaining to Medigap compare).

2001

66 FR 9858, February 12, 2001: HCFA Privacy Act of 1974; Report of New System (pertaining to complaints against health insurance issuers and health plans).

66 FR 15122, March 15, 2001: HCFA Agency Information Collection Activities: Proposed Collection; Comment request (pertaining to Medigap compare data form).

66 FR 33102, June 20, 2001: HCFA Agency Information Collection Activities; Submission for OMB Review; Comment request (pertaining to "Medigap Compare" data).

See § 2:54.

§ 6:55 TERMINATING PROVIDER AGREEMENTS OF HOSPITAL PROVIDERS OF EXTENDED CARE SERVICES — Section 1883 [42 U.S.C.A. 1395tt]

Regulations

42 CFR Part 402 — Civil Money Penalties, Assessments, and Exclusions

42 CFR Part 405, Subpart K — Conditions of Participation; Skilled Nursing Facilities

42 CFR Part 424 — Conditions for Medicare Payment

42 CFR Part 440 — Services: General Provisions [Medicaid]

42 CFR Part 442 — Standards for Payment for Nursing Facilities and Intermediate Care Facilities [Medicaid]

42 CFR Part 447 — Payment for Services [Medicaid]

42 CFR Part 456 — Utilization Control

42 CFR Part 476 — Utilization and Quality Control Review

42 CFR Part 482 — Conditions of Participation for Hospitals

42 CFR Part 483 — Requirements for States and Long Term Care Facilities

42 CFR Part 488 — Survey, Certification and Enforcement Procedures

42 CFR Part 489 — Provider Agreements and Supplier Approval

42 CFR Part 498 — Appeals Procedures for Determinations that Affect Participation in the Medicare Program and for Determinations that Affect the Participation of ICF's/MR and Certain NF's in the Medicaid Program

54 FR 5316, February 2, 1989: Medicare and Medicaid; Requirements for Long Term Care Facilities — Final rule with comment period, amending 42 CFR Parts 405, 442, 447, 483, 488, 489, and 498. See also delay in effective date at 54 FR 29717, July 14, 1989; corrections at 54 FR 8361, February 27, 1989, and 54 FR 37466, September 11, 1989; and final rule delaying effective date from January 1, 1990, to October 1, 1990, at 54 FR 53611, December 29, 1989.

55 FR 10256, March 20, 1990: Medicare and Medicaid; Charges to Residents' Funds in Nursing Homes — Proposed rule to amend 42 CFR Part 483. See also final rule at 57 FR 53572, November 12, 1992.

55 FR 10938, March 23, 1990: Medicare and Medicaid Programs; Nurse Aide Training and Competency Evaluation Programs — Proposed rule to amend 42 CFR Parts 431, 433, and 483.

55 FR 10951, March 23, 1990: Medicare and Medicaid Programs; Preadmission Screening and Annual Resident Review — Proposed rule to amend 42 CFR Parts 405, 431, and 483.

55 FR 46104, November 1, 1990: Medicare Program; Inpatient Hospital Deductible and Hospital and Skilled Nursing Facility Coinsurance Amounts for 1991 — Notice.

56 FR 13317, April 1, 1991: Medicare Program; Schedule of Limits for Skilled Nursing Facility Inpatient Routine Service Costs — Final notice with comment period. See also correction published at 56 FR 22053, May 13, 1991.

56 FR 31666, July 11, 1991: Medicare Program; Revised Procedures for Paying Claims from Providers of Services (re direct deposits) — Notice with comment period.

FR 48826, September 26, 1991: Medicare and Medicaid; Requirements for Long Term Care Facilities — Final rule affecting 42 CFR Parts 422, 447, 483, 488, 489, and 498. See also correction at 57 FR 43922, September 23, 1992.

56 FR 48880, September 26, 1991: Medicare and Medicaid Programs; Nurse Aide Training and Competency Evaluation Programs — Final rule affecting 42 CFR Parts 431, 433, and 483. See also correction at 56 FR 59331, November 25, 1991.

56 FR 54539, October 22, 1991: Medicare Program; Swing-Bed Program Changes — Final rule affecting 42 CFR Parts 413, 482, 483.

56 FR 55382, October 25, 1991: Medicare Program; Essential Access Community Hospitals (EACHs) and Rural Primary Care Hospitals (RPCHs) — Proposed rule affecting 42 CFR Parts 400, 409, 410, 411, 412, 413, 424, 440, 485, 488, 489. See also final rule affecting those Parts and Part 498 at 58 FR 30630, May 26, 1993.

57 FR 4516, February 5, 1992: Medicare and Medicaid Programs; Omnibus Nursing Home Requirements — Proposed rule affecting 42 CFR Parts 418, 440, 441, 482, 483, and 488. See also correction at 57 FR 8961, March 13, 1992.

57 FR 8194, March 6, 1992: Medicare and Medicaid Programs; Advance Directives — Interim final rule with comment period, affecting 42 CFR Parts 417, 431, 434, 483, 484, 489, and 498.

57 FR 39278, August 28, 1992: Medicare and Medicaid Programs; Survey, Certification and Enforcement of Skilled Nursing Facilities and Nursing Facilities — Proposed rule affecting 42 CFR Parts 431, 442, 488, and 489.

57 FR 46177, October 7, 1992: Medicare Program; Schedule of Limits for Skilled Nursing Facility Inpatient Routine Service Costs — Final notice with comment period.

57 FR 46362, October 8, 1992: Medicare and Medicaid Programs; Revised Effective Date of Medicare/Medicaid Provider Agreement and Supplier Participation — Proposed rule affecting 42 CFR Parts 431, 440, 442, 488, 489, and 498.

57 FR 46865, October 13, 1992: HCFA Public Information Collection Requirements Submitted to the Office of Management and Budget for Clearance (pertaining to impact of home health care plan management and evaluation; end-stage renal disease medical case review; Medicare/Medicaid hospital swing-bed survey report form; quarterly Medicaid statement of expenditures; Medicaid program budget report; information collection requirements in final peer

review organization sanction regulations; appeals procedures for determinations that affect participation in Medicare; request for medical review information for Part B intermediary outpatient therapy bills and other Part B outpatient bills; and Medicaid limitations on provider-related donations and health care-related taxes, and limitations on payment to disproportionate share hospitals).

57 FR 48033, October 21, 1992: Medicare Program; Revised Procedures for Paying Claims From Providers of Services — Final notice.

57 FR 54710, November 20, 1992: Medicaid Program; Elimination of Certain Written Documentation Pertaining to Medicaid Long-Term Care Facilities — Final rule affecting 42 CFR Part 442.

57 FR 56450, November 30, 1992: Medicare and Medicaid Programs; Preadmission Screening and Annual Resident Review — Final rule with comment period, affecting 42 CFR Parts 405, 431, 433, and 483. See also correction published at 58 FR 25784, April 28, 1993.

57 FR 61614, December 28, 1992: Medicare and Medicaid; Resident Assessment in Long Term Care Facilities — Proposed rule affecting 42 CFR Parts 456 and 483.

58 FR 21174, April 19, 1993: HCFA Public Information Collection Requirements Submitted to the Office of Management and Budget for Clearance re end stage renal disease survey forms; municipal health services cost reports forms; advance directives; withholding Medicare payments to recover Medicaid overpayments; home office cost statements; and statistical report on medical care.

59 FR 762, January 6, 1994: Medicare Program; Schedule of Limits for Skilled Nursing Facility Inpatient Routine Service Costs — Final notice with comment period.

59 FR 26955, May 25, 1994: Medicare Program; Self-implementing Coverage and Payment Provisions: 1993 Legislation — Final rule with comment period (pertaining to reductions in payments for skilled nursing facility services — return on equity; reductions in payments for hospice services; reduction in Part A premium for certain individuals with 30 or more quarters of Social Security coverage; extension of 10 percent reduction in payments for capital-related costs of outpatient hospital services; extension of reduction in payments for other costs for outpatient hospital services; reduction in payments for intraocular lenses; payment for parenteral and enteral nutrients, supplies and equipment during 1994 and 1995; increase in annual cap on amount of Medicare payment for outpatient physical therapy and occupational therapy

services; rural health clinics and Federally qualified health centers; reduction in payments for Epoetin; and changes in Part B premium.)

59 FR 29578, June 8, 1994: Medicare Program; Optional Payment System for Low Medicare Volume Skilled Nursing Facilities — Proposed rule affecting 42 CFR Part 413.

59 FR 56116, November 10, 1994: Medicare and Medicaid Programs; Survey, Certification and Enforcement of Skilled Nursing Facilities and Nursing Facilities — Final rule affecting 42 CFR Parts 401, 431, 435, 440, 441, 442, 447, 483, 488, 489, and 498. See also correcting amendment, effective July 1, 1995, at 62 FR 44221, August 20, 1997.

59 FR 64141, December 13, 1994: Medicare and Medicaid Programs; Revisions to Conditions of Participation for Hospitals — Final rule affecting 42 CFR Parts 405 and 482.

59 FR 66969, December 28, 1994: HCFA Public Information Collection Requirements Submitted to the Office of Management and Budget (OMB) for Clearance (pertaining to physician certification in skilled nursing facilities, and criteria for Medicare coverage of adult liver transplants.

60 FR 21525, May 2, 1995: HCFA Public Information Collection Requirements Submitted to the Office of Management and Budget (OMB) for Clearance (pertaining to intermediary requests for information from skilled nursing facilities, reimbursement for CLIA compliance surveys, patient outcome data in home health agencies, common claim forms for Medicare/Medicaid reimbursement, and a study of childhood immunization costs).

60 FR 37590, July 21, 1995: Medicare Program; Optional Payment System for Low Medicare Volume Skilled Nursing Facilities — Final rule affecting 42 CFR Part 413.

60 FR 40847, August 10, 1995: Office of Inspector General: Publication of OIG Special Fraud Alerts: Home Health Fraud, and Fraud and Abuse in the Provision of Medical Supplies to Nursing Facilities — Notice.

60 FR 50115, September 28, 1995: Medicare and Medicaid Programs; Survey, Certification and Enforcement of Skilled Nursing Facilities and Nursing Facilities — Final rule and correction to final regulations, affecting 42 CFR Parts 431, 440, 442, 488, 489, and 498. See also corrections at 60 FR 52731, October 10, 1995, and at 60 FR 534456, October 13, 1995.

60 FR 58088, November 24, 1995: HCFA Public Information Collection Requirements Submitted for Public Comment and

Recommendations (pertaining to skilled nursing facility (SNF) and skilled nursing facility health care complex cost reports).

60 FR 62237, December 5, 1995: Medicare Program; Uniform Electronic Cost Reporting for Skilled Nursing Facilities and Home Health Agencies — Proposed rule affecting 42 CFR Part 413.

60 FR 64167, December 14, 1995: HCFA Public Information Collection Requirements Submitted for Public Comment and Recommendations (pertaining to home health care; Medicare/Medicaid certification of physical therapy and speech pathology services; certification as suppliers of Portable X-ray Services; certification of organ procurement organizations; certification for physical therapists in independent practice; and approval as a hospital provider of extended care services (swing bed)).

61 FR 11214, March 19, 1996: HCFA Agency Information Collection Activities: Proposed Collection; Comment Request (pertaining to conditions of coverage for organ procurement organizations; and skilled nursing facility and skilled nursing facility healthcare complex forms).

61 FR 14798, April 3, 1996: HCFA Agency Information Collection Activities: Proposed Collection; Comment Request (pertaining to statistical reports on medical care eligibility, payments and services under Medicaid; State survey agency lists of positions and schedule of equipment purchases; granting and withdrawing of deeming authority to national accreditation organizations; maximizing the effectiveness of home health care; requests for certification in the Medicare or Medicaid program to provide outpatient physical therapy and/or speech pathology services; physical therapists in independent practice; requests for provider approval as a hospital provider of extended care services (swing bed) under Medicare and Medicaid; and requests for designation as an organ procurement organization).

61 FR 17677, April 22, 1996: Medicare and Medicaid Programs; New Payment Methodology for Routine Extended Care Services Provided in a Swing-bed Hospital — Proposed rule affecting 42 CFR Part 413.

61 FR 30623, June 17, 1996: Office of Inspector General Publication of OIG Special Fraud Alert: Fraud and Abuse in the Provision of Services in Nursing Homes — Notice.

61 FR 34855, July 3, 1996: HCFA Agency Information Collection Activities: Submission for OMB Review; Comment Request (pertain-

ing to information collection requirements for hospital conditions of participation in Medicare).

61 FR 35231, July 5, 1996: HCFA Agency Information Collection Activities: Proposed Collection; Comment Request (pertaining to Medicaid payment standards for inpatient hospital or long-term care services).

61 FR 51611, October 3, 1996: Medicare and Medicaid Programs; New Payment Methodology for Routine Extended Care Services Provided in a Swing-bed Hospital — Final Rule affecting 42 CFR Part 413. See also correction at 61 FR 58631, November 18, 1996.

61 FR 57688, November 7, 1996: HCFA Agency Information Collection Activities: Comment request (pertaining to clinical laboratory surveys; clinical laboratory personnel qualifications; Medicare/Medicaid hospital survey report forms; beneficiary disenrollment from HMOs and CMPs; survey reports for ambulatory surgical centers; the Medigap complaint database; and survey forms for comprehensive outpatient rehabilitation facilities).

61 FR 68270, December 27, 1996: HCFA Agency Information Collection Activities: Submission for OMB Review; Comment request (pertaining to a facility identification and screening form for hospital providers of extended care services (swing-beds) in the Medicare and Medicaid programs).

62 FR 3902, January 27, 1997: HCFA Agency Information Collection Activities: Proposed Collection; Comment request (pertaining to hospice survey and deficiencies report form).

62 FR 7467, February 19, 1997: HCFA Agency Information Collection Activities: Proposed Collection; Comment request (pertaining to form for a hospital request for certification in the Medicare and Medicaid programs).

62 FR 8252, February 24, 1997: HCFA Agency Information Collection Activities: Submission for OMB Review; Comment request (pertaining to conditions of participation for rural health clinics).

62 FR 8744, February 26, 1997: HCFA Agency Information Collection Activities: Submission for OMB Review; Comment request (pertaining to Medicare provider/supplier enrollment application).

62 FR 11214, March 11, 1997: HCFA Agency Information Collection Activities: Submission for OMB Review; Comment request (pertaining to intermediate care facility for the mentally retarded or persons with related conditions survey report forms).

62 FR 18639, April 16, 1997: HCFA Agency Information Collection Activities: Proposed Collection; Comment request (pertaining to the

hospital request for certification in the Medicare and Medicaid programs form).

62 FR 30603, June 4, 1997: HCFA Agency Information Collection Activities: Submission for OMB Review; Comment request (pertaining to skilled nursing facility and skilled nursing facility health care complex cost reports; and hospital conditions of participation).

62 FR 43931, August 18, 1997: Medicare and Medicaid Programs: Effective Dates of Provider Agreements and Supplier Approvals — Final rule affecting 42 CFR Parts 431, 442, 488, 489, and 498.

62 FR 47182, September 8, 1997: Office of Inspector General: Health Care Programs: Fraud and Abuse; Revised OIG Exclusion Authorities Resulting from Public Law 104–191 — Notice of Proposed rulemaking, affecting 42 CFR Parts 1000, 1001, 1002, and 1005.

62 FR 51536, October 1, 1997: Medicare Program; Schedules of Limits and Prospectively Determined Payment Rates for Skilled Nursing Facility Inpatient Routine Service Costs — Final notice with comment period.

62 FR 51551, October 1, 1997: Medicare Program; Adjustments to Cost Limits for Skilled Nursing Facility Inpatient Routine service Costs — Proposed notice.

62 FR 55410, October 24, 1997: Office of Inspector General: Criteria for Implementing Permissive Exclusion Authority under Section 1128(b)(7) of the Social Security Act — Notice.

62 FR 48736, October 30, 1997: HCFA Agency Information Collection Activities: Submission for OMB Review; Comment request (pertaining to prospective payment for skilled nursing facilities).

62 FR 66376, December 18, 1997: HCFA Emergency Clearance: Public Information Collection Requirements Submitted to the Office of Management and Budget (OMB) (pertaining to Medicare and other Federal health care program enrollment forms for providers and suppliers).

62 FR 66726, December 19, 1997: Medicare and Medicaid Programs; Hospital Conditions of Participation; Provider Agreements and Supplier Approval — Proposed rule affecting 42 CFR Parts 416, 482, 485, and 489.

62 FR 67174, December 23, 1997: Medicare and Medicaid; Resident Assessment in Long Term Care Facilities — Final rule affecting 42 CFR Part 483.

62 FR 67392, December 24, 1997: Office of Inspector General: Criteria for Implementing Permissive Exclusion Authority under Section 1128(b)(7) of the Social Security Act — Notice.

63 FR 2926, January 20, 1998: Medicare Program; Additional Supplier Standards — Proposed rule affecting 42 CFR Part 424.

63 FR 7743, February 17, 1998: Medicare and Medicaid Programs; Hospital Conditions of Participation; Provider Agreements and Supplier Approval — Notice of extension of comment period, affecting 42 CFR Parts 416, 482, 485, and 489.

63 FR 8987, February 23, 1998: Office of Inspector General: Publication of the OIG Compliance Program for Hospitals — Notice.

63 FR 9844, February 26, 1998: HCFA Emergency Clearance: Public Information Collection Requirements Submitted to the Office of Management and Budget (OMB) (pertaining to development of an assessment system for post acute care).

63 FR 10920, March 5, 1998: HCFA Emergency Clearance: Public Information Collection Requirements Submitted to the Office of Management and Budget (OMB) (pertaining to Medicare and other Federal health care program provider and supplier application forms).

63 FR 14719, March 26, 1998: HCFA Agency Information Collection Activities: Proposed Collection; Comment request (pertaining to physician certification and re-certification in skilled nursing facilities).

63 FR 19502, April 20, 1998: HCFA Agency Information Collection Activities: Proposed collection; Comment request (pertaining to annual early and periodic screening, diagnostic, and treatment services (EPSDT) participation report; Medicare and other health care programs provider/supplier enrollment application; and research and analytic support for implementing performance measurement in Medicare fee for service).

63 FR 20415, April 24, 1998: Office of Inspector General: Publication of OIG Special Fraud Alert: Fraud and Abuse in Nursing Home Arrangements with Hospices — Notice.

63 FR 26810, May 14, 1998: HCFA Agency Information Collection Activities: Proposed Collection; Comment request (pertaining to development of an assessment system for post-acute care).

63 FR 28396, May 22, 1998: HCFA Privacy Act of 1974 — Notice of New System of Records (pertaining to the long term care minimum data set).

63 FR 29648, June 1, 1998: Medicare and Medicaid Programs; Surety Bond Requirements for Home Health Agencies — Final rule affecting 42 CFR Parts 441 and 489.

63 FR 31123, June 8, 1998: Medicare Program; Incentive Programs — Fraud and Abuse — Final rule affecting 42 CFR Part 420.

63 FR 46676, September 2, 1998: Office of Inspector General: Health Care Programs; Fraud and Abuse; Revised OIG Exclusion Authorities Resulting from Public Law 104–191 — Final rule affecting 42 CFR Parts 1000, 1001, 1002, and 1005. See also correction at 63 FR 57918, October 29, 1998.

63 FR 46736, September 2, 1998: Office of Inspector General: Health Care Programs; Fraud and Abuse; Revised OIG Sanction Authorities Resulting from Public Law 105–33 — Notice of proposed rulemaking affecting 42 CFR 1001, 1002, and 1003.

63 FR 58341, October 30, 1998: Office of Inspector General: Health Care Fraud and Abuse Data Collection Program: Reporting of Final Adverse Actions — Notice of proposed rulemaking under section 1128E of the Social Security Act, affecting 45 CFR 61.

63 FR 58399, October 30, 1998: Office of Inspector General: Publication of the OIG's Provider Self-Disclosure Protocol — Notice.

63 FR 60356, November 9, 1998: HCFA Agency Information Collection activities: Proposed Collection; Comment request (pertaining to skilled nursing facility resident assessment MDS data).

63 FR 66551, December 2, 1998: HCFA Agency Information Collection Activities: Submission for OMB review; Comment request (pertaining to EverCare coverage for nursing home residents under Medicare).

63 FR 70137, December 18, 1998: Office of Inspector General: Solicitation of Information and Recommendations for Developing OIG Compliance Program Guidance for the Nursing Home Industry — Notice.

63 FR 71819, December 30, 1998: Office of Inspector General; Health Care Fraud and Abuse Data Collection Program; Reporting under section 1128E of the Social Security Act of Final Adverse Actions — Notice of proposed rule-making; extension of comment period, affecting 45 CFR 61.

63 FR 72317, December 31, 1998: HCFA Agency Information Collection Activities: Proposed Collection; Comment request (pertaining to advanced directives under Medicare and Medicaid; and Medicare/Medicaid disclosure of ownership and control interests).

63 FR 72318, December 31, 1998: HCFA Agency Information Collection Activities: Proposed Collection; Comment request (pertaining to fire safety survey report forms for health care facilities).

1999

64 FR 6664, February 10, 1999: HCFA Agency Information Collection Activities: Submission for OMB Review; Comment request (pertaining to skilled nursing facility (SNF) resident assessment MDS data).

64 FR 13354, March 18, 1999: Medicare and Medicaid Programs; Civil Money Penalties for Nursing Homes (SNF/NF), Change in Notice Requirements, and Expansion of Discretionary Remedy Delegation — Final rule with comment period, affecting 42 CFR Part 488.

64 FR 13997, March 23, 1999: HCFA Agency Information Collection Activities: Submission for OMB Review; Comment request (pertaining to Medicare and Medicaid requirements for advanced directives, and disclosure of ownership and financial control interest).

64 FR 17184, April 8, 1999: HCFA Medicare Program; April 23, 1999 Open Town Hall Meeting to Discuss the Skilled Nursing Facility Prospective Payment System (SNF/PPS) and Quality of Care in Nursing Facilities — Notice of meeting.

64 FR 36070, July 2, 1999: Medicare and Medicaid Programs; Hospital Conditions of Participation: Patient Rights — Interim final rule with comment, affecting 42 CFR 482.

64 FR 39517, July 22, 1999: HCFA Agency Information Collection Activities: Submission for OMB Review; Comment request (pertaining to Medicare participating physician or supplier agreement form HCFA-460).

64 FR 39934, July 23, 1999: Medicare and Medicaid Program; Appeal of the Loss of Nurse Aide Training Programs — Interim final rule with comment period, affecting 42 CFR Parts 431 and 498. See also correction at 64 FR 43295, August 10, 1999.

64 FR 41644, July 30, 1999: Medicare Program; Prospective Payment System and Consolidated Billing for Skilled Nursing Facilities — Final rule affecting 42 CFR Parts 409, 411, 413, and 489. See also correction at 64 FR 60122, November 4, 1999.

64 FR 41684, July 30, 1999: Medicare Program; Prospective Payment System and Consolidated Billing for Skilled Nursing

Facilities — Update — Notice. See also correction at 64 FR 54030, October 5, 1999

64 FR 42610, August 5, 1999: Medicare Program; Revision of the Procedures for Requesting Exceptions to Cost Limits for Skilled Nursing Facilities and Elimination of Reclassifications — Final rule.

64 FR 54263, October 6, 1999: Medicaid Program; Flexibility in Payment Methods for Services of Hospitals, Nursing Facilities, and Intermediate Care Facilities for the Mentally Retarded — Proposed rule affecting 42 CFR Part 447.

64 FR 55949, October 15, 1999: HCFA Agency Information Collection Activities: Proposed Collection; Comment request (pertaining to physician certifications and re-certifications about the necessity for skilled nursing facility care).

64 FR 57103, October 22, 1999: Medicare Program; Inpatient Hospital Deductible and Hospital and Extended Care Services Coinsurance Amounts for 2000 — Notice.

64 FR 62679, November 17, 1999: HCFA Agency Information Collection Activities: Proposed Collection; Comment request (pertaining to hospital conditions of participation).

64 FR 66482, November 26, 1999: HCFA Agency Information Collection Activities: Proposed Collection; Comment request (pertaining to resident assessment in skilled nursing facilities).

64 FR 69271, December 10, 1999: HCFA Agency Information Collection Activities: Proposed Collection; Comment request (pertaining to hospital providers of extender care (swing bed) services in Medicare and Medicaid).

64 FR 69273, December 10, 1999: HCFA Agency Information Collection Activities: Submission for OMB Review; Comment request (pertaining to Medicare/Medicaid hospital survey reports).

2000

65 FR 2186, January 13, 2000: HCFA Agency Information Collection Activities; Submission for OMB Review; Comment request (pertaining to physician certifications/re-certifications in skilled nursing facilities).

65 FR 8727, February 22, 2000: Medicare and Medicaid Programs; Recognition of the American Osteopathic Association (AOA) for Continued Approval of Deeming Authority for Hospitals — Final notice.

65 FR 11589, March 3, 2000: Office of Inspector General: Health Care Integrity and Protection Data Bank under Section 1128E of the Social Security Act: Announcement of Opening Date for Querying and User Fees — Notice.

65 FR 12556, March 9, 2000: HCFA Agency Information Collection Activities: Proposed Collection; Comment request (pertaining to hospital request for certification in the Medicare/Medicaid program).

65 FR 12560, March 9, 2000: HCFA Agency Information Collection Activities: Submission for OMB Review; Comment request (pertaining to hospital provider of extended care services (swing beds) in the Medicare and Medicaid programs).

65 FR 14289, March 16, 2000: Office of Inspector General: Publication of the OIG Compliance Program Guidance for Nursing Facilities — Notice.

65 FR 14986, March 20, 2000: HCFA Agency Information Collection Activities: Submission for OMB Review; Comment request (pertaining to skilled nursing facility resident assessment MDS data).

65 FR 19187, April 10, 2000: Medicare Program; Prospective Payment System and Consolidated Billing for Skilled Nursing Facilities; Update- — Proposed rule affecting 42 CFR Parts 411 and 489.

65 FR 34986, June 1, 2000: Office of Inspector General; Privacy Act; Implementation (exempting the Healthcare Integrity and Protection Data Bank under Section 1128C of the Social Security Act from certain provisions of the Privacy Act (5 U.S.C.A. 552a) — Final rule affecting 45 CFR Part 5b.

65 FR 35654, June 5, 2000: HCFA Agency Information Collection Activities: Submission for OMB Review; Comment request (pertaining to hospital request for certification in Medicare and Medicaid).

65 FR 35945, June 6, 2000: HCFA Agency Information Collection Activities: Proposed Collection; Comment request (pertaining to SNF cost reports).

See § 2:55.

65 FR 50548, August 18, 2000: HCFA Privacy Act of 1974; Report of New System (pertaining to Medicare Provider Analysis and Review (MEDPAR) of all services rendered to a beneficiary from admission to discharge for hospital inpatient and SNF stays).

65 FR 54856, September 11, 2000: HCFA Agency Information Collection Activities: Submission for OMB Review; Comment request (pertaining to skilled nursing facility cost reports).

65 FR 54857, September 11, 2000: HCFA Agency Information Collection Activities: Submission for OMB Review; Comment request (pertaining to ICF/MR survey report forms).

65 FR 64227, October 26, 2000: HCFA Agency Information Collection Activities: Proposed Collection; Comment request (pertaining to home health agency cost reports; skilled nursing facility cost reports; and hospital cost reports).

2001

66 FR 3148, January 12, 2001: Medicaid Program; Revision to Medicaid Upper Payment Limit Requirements for Hospital Services, Nursing Facility Services, Intermediate Care Facility Services for the Mentally Retarded, and Clinic Services—Final rule affecting 42 CFR Part 447.

66 FR 3497, January 16, 2001: Medicare Program; Prospective Payment System and Consolidated Billing for Skilled Nursing Facilities—Update; Correction notice affecting 42 FR Parts 411, 313, and 489. See FR Doc. 00–19004, July 31, 2000.

66 FR 7919, January 26, 2001: HCFA Agency Information Collection Activities: Proposed Collection; Comment request (pertaining to provider Medicare agreements).

66 FR 8807, February 2, 2001: HCFA Agency Information Collection Activities: Proposed Collection; Comment request (pertaining to Medicare Federal health care programs provider/supplier enrollment application).

66 FR 9587, February 8, 2001: HCFA Agency Information Collection Activities: Proposed Collection; Comment request (pertaining to a project to develop an outcome–reporting of restraints and seclusion deaths by hospitals).

66 FR 16062, March 23, 2001: HCFA Agency Information Collection Activities: Submission for OMB Review; Comment request (pertaining to SNF cost report forms).

66 FR 17657, April 3, 2001: Medicaid Program; Modification of the Medicaid Upper Payment Limit Transition Period for Inpatient Hospital Services, Outpatient Hospital Services, Nursing Facility Services, Intermediate Care Facility Services for the Mentally Retarded and Clinic Services—Proposed rule affecting 42 CFR Part 447.

66 FR 27151, May 16, 2001: HCFA Agency Information Collection Activities: Proposed Collection; Comment request (pertaining to the Long Term Care Awareness Project).

See § 2:55.

§ 6:56 WITHHOLDING MEDICARE PAYMENTS FROM OVERPAID MEDICAID PROVIDERS — Section 1885 [42 U.S.C.A. 1395vv]

Regulations

42 CFR Part 401, Subpart F — Claims Collection and Compromise

42 CFR Part 405, Subpart C — Recovery of Overpayments and Suspension of Payment; and Subpart R — Provider Reimbursement Determinations and Appeals

42 CFR Part 447 — Payments for Services [Medicaid]

42 CFR Part 455 — Program Integrity: Medicaid

56 FR 31332, July 10, 1991: Medicare Program; Changes Concerning Interest Rates Charged on Overpayments and Underpayments — Final rule. See also correction at 56 FR 41726, August 22, 1991.

56 FR 31666, July 11, 1991: Medicare Program; Revised Procedures for Paying Claims from Providers of Services (re direct deposits) — Notice with comment period.

57 FR 43462, September 21, 1992: Health Care Financing Administration Public Information Collection Requirements Submitted to the Office of Management and Budget for Clearance (pertaining to sole community home health agencies; physician/supplier overpayment reports; physician or supplier Medicare agreements; conditions of participation for rural health clinics; Medicare provider refunds; conditions of participation for comprehensive outpatient rehabilitation facilities; Medicaid income and eligibility verification system; Medicaid integrated review schedule; provider overpayment report; financial statement of Medicare provider debtors; negative case action review schedule for Medicaid quality control; outpatient resource costing study; Medicaid intermediate care facility for the mentally retarded or persons with related conditions survey report form; installment agreement of beneficiary refund of overpayment; PRO assumption of responsibilities; Medicare contractor administrative budget and cost reporting system forms; fire safety survey report forms; medical records review under prospective payment

system; and Qualified Medicare Beneficiary supplement to the Medicare current beneficiary survey).

58 FR 21174, April 19, 1993: HCFA Public Information Collection Requirements Submitted to the Office of Management and Budget for Clearance re end stage renal disease survey forms; municipal health services cost reports forms; advance directives; withholding Medicare payments to recover Medicaid overpayments; home office cost statements; and statistical report on medical care.

61 FR 29406, June 10, 1996: HCFA Agency Information Collection Activities: proposed Collection; Comment Request (pertaining to end stage renal disease application and survey and certification report forms; withholding Medicare payments to recover Medicaid overpayments; acquisition, protection, and disclosure of PRO information; clinical laboratory certification and recertification survey forms; CLIA laboratory personnel report forms; prepaid health plan cost reports; Medicare credit balance reporting requirements; statement of deficiencies and plan of correction requirements for organ procurement organizations; Medicare/Medicaid hospital survey report forms; advance directive requirements for Medicare and Medicaid; payment adjustments for sole community hospitals; survey reports for physical therapists in independent practice; HMO and CMP national data reporting requirements; identification of extension units of outpatient physical therapy and outpatient speech pathology providers; and fire safety survey reports).

61 FR 40422, August 2, 1996: HCFA Agency Information Collection Activities: Proposed Collection; Comment request (pertaining to survey and certification of ambulatory surgical centers; the Medigap complaint database; fiscal intermediaries' provider overpayment actions; and hospital standards for potentially HIV infectious blood and blood products).

61 FR 43062, August 20, 1996: HCFA Agency Information Collection Activities: Submission for OMB Review; Comment request (pertaining to withholding Medicare payments to recover Medicaid overpayments; acquisition, protection, and disclosure of Peer Review Organization (PRO) information; cost reports for HMOs; and collection of credit balance information from health care providers).

61 FR 49269, September 19, 1996: Medicare Program; Waiver of Recovery of Overpayment — Final rule affecting 42 CFR Parts 401 and 405. See also correction at 61 FR 69034, December 31, 1996.

63 FR 20639, April 27, 1998: HCFA Agency Information Collection Activities: Proposed Collection; Comment request (pertaining to

financial reports to evaluate requests from physicians or suppliers to pay debts under extended repayment schedule or to compromise a debt for less than the full amount).

63 FR 25320, May 7, 1998: HCFA National Standard Health Care Provider Identifier — Proposed Rule affecting 45 CFR Part 142.

63 FR 36249, July 2, 1998: HCFA Agency Information Collection Activities: Submission for OMB Review; Comment request (pertaining to requests from physicians/suppliers to pay indebtedness under extended repayment schedule, or to compromise a debt for less than the full amount).

63 FR 40297, July 28, 1998: HCFA Privacy Act of 1974; Report of New System (pertaining to establishment of the National Provider System (NPS) database).

1999

64 FR 15775, April 1, 1999: HCFA Agency Information Collection Activities: Proposed Collection; Comment request (pertaining to withholding Medicare payments to recover Medicaid overpayments).

64 FR 39517, July 22, 1999: HCFA Agency Information Collection Activities: Submission for OMB Review; Comment request (pertaining to Medicare participating physician or supplier agreement form HCFA-460).

64 FR 51128, September 21, 1999: HCFA Agency Information Collection Activities: Submission for OMB Review; Comment request (pertaining to withholding Medicare payments to recover Medicaid overpayments).

2001

66 FR 23944, May 10, 2001: HCFA Agency Information Collection Activities: Proposed Collection; Comment request (pertaining to financial reports for providers indebted to Medicare who want to repay over time).

See § 2:56.

§ 6:57 DISCONTINUING AND REDUCING PAYMENTS TO HOSPITALS FOR INPATIENT HOSPITAL SERVICES IN STATES WHICH HAVE ALTERNATIVE (NON-FEDERAL DRG) HOSPITAL REIMBURSEMENT SYSTEMS — Section 1886(c) [42 U.S.C.A. 1395ww(c)]

Regulations

42 CFR Part 403, Subpart C — Recognition of State Reimbursement Control Systems

42 CFR Part 412 — Prospective Payment System for Inpatient Hospital Services

56 FR 31666, July 11, 1991: Medicare Program; Revised Procedures for Paying Claims from Providers of Services (re direct deposits) — Notice with comment period.

56 FR 41110, August 19, 1991: Medicare Program; Uniform Electronic Cost Reporting System for Hospitals — Proposed rule affecting 42 CFR Part 413.

56 FR 55382, October 25, 1991: Medicare Program; Essential Access Community Hospitals (EACHs) and Rural Primary Care Hospitals (RPCHs) — Proposed rule affecting 42 CFR Parts 400, 409, 410, 411, 412, 413, 424, 440, 485, 488, 489. See also final rule affecting those Parts and Part 498 at 58 FR 30630, May 26, 1993.

57 FR 36006, August 12, 1992: Medicare Program; Self-implementing Coverage and Payments Provisions: 1990 Legislation — Final rule with comment period, affecting 42 CFR Parts 405, 406, 409, 420, 411, 412, 413, 418, and 489. Pertains to capital-related inpatient hospital costs; capital-related outpatient hospital costs; non-capital related outpatient hospital costs; payment for physician pathology services; payment for services of physicians as assistants-at-surgery; payments for ambulatory surgical procedures in hospital outpatient departments; payments for radiology services performed in hospital outpatient departments; hospice benefit extension; enrollment of HMO members in Medicare Part A; coverage of ostomy supplies; application of pre-entitlement stay in psychiatric hospital to limit on payment for inpatient hospital services; payments to dialysis facilities; payment rates for erythropoietin (EPO); and Medicare secondary payer provision for individuals with ESRD. See also confirmation of final rule at 58 FR 58502, November 2, 1993.

58 FR 4705, January 15, 1993: Medicare Program: Uniform Hospital Billing and Payment Mechanisms — Proposed notice.

58 FR 30630, May 26, 1993: Medicare Program; Essential Access Community Hospitals (EACHs) and Rural Primary Care Hospitals (RPCHs) — Final rule affecting 42 CFR Parts 400, 409, 410, 411, 412, 413, 424, 440, 485, 488, 489, and 498. See also correction at 58 FR 49934, September 24, 1993.

58 FR 43156, August 13, 1993: Medicaid Program; Limitations on Provider-Related Donations and Health Care-Related Donations and Health Care-Related Taxes; Limitations on Payments to Disproportionate Share Hospitals — Final rule affecting 42 CFR parts 433 and 447. See also correction at 58 FR 44536, August 23, 1993 as corrected at 58 FR 51130, September 30, 1993, and see also 62 FR 53571, October 15, 1997, for revision of waiver criteria for tax programs based exclusively on regional variations; a correction affecting 42 CFR Part 433.

58 FR 43184, August 13, 1993: Medicaid Program; Limitation on Aggregate Payments to Disproportionate Share Hospitals; Federal Fiscal Year 1993 — Notice.

58 FR 46270, September 1, 1993: Medicare Program; Changes to the Hospital Inpatient Prospective Payment Systems and Fiscal Year 1994 Rates — Final rule with comment period. See also correction at 58 FR 67350, December 21, 1993.

58 FR 54045, October 20, 1993: Medicare Program; Demonstration Project to Develop a Uniform Cost Reporting System for Hospitals — Final Rule affecting 42 CFR Part 403.

59 FR 760, January 6, 1994: Medicare Program; Elimination of Additional Payments for Administrative and General Costs of Hospital-Based Home Health Agencies — Final notice with comment period.

59 FR 4717, February 1, 1994: Medicaid Program; Limitations on Aggregate Payments to Disproportionate Share Hospitals: Federal Fiscal year 1994 — Notice.

59 FR 14865, March 30, 1994: HCFA Public Information Collection Requirements Submitted to the Office of Management and Budget (OMB) for Clearance (pertaining to home health agency Medicare and Medicaid survey report forms for conditions of participation; conditions of participation for rural health clinics; Medicaid re-evaluation of assets for determining payment rates to hospitals and nursing homes; statistical report on medical care, eligible, recipients, payments, and services.)

59 FR 22764, May 2, 1994: Medicaid Program; Limitations on Aggregate Payments to Disproportionate Share Hospitals: Federal Fiscal Year 1994 — Notice. See also correction at 59 FR 28133, May 31, 1994.

59 FR 50762, October 5, 1994: HCFA Public Information Collection Requirements Submitted to the Office of Management and Budget (OMB) for Clearance (pertaining to reimbursement of hospital costs for residents and interns, criteria for psychiatric and rehabilitation hospital units' reimbursement under the prospective payment system, disclosure of owners and managers of suppliers for fraud and abuse detection purposes, reimbursement of municipal health services clinics, survey form for hospital compliance with anti-dumping requirements, and evaluation of patient and physician satisfaction with the Medicare participating heart bypass center demonstration).

60 FR 3250, January 13, 1995: Medicaid Program; Limitations on Aggregate Payments to Disproportionate Share Hospitals: Federal Fiscal Year 1995 — Notice.

60 FR 19405, April 18, 1995: HCFA Public Information Collection Requirements Submitted to the Office of Management and Budget (OMB) for Clearance (pertaining to Medicaid limitations on provider related donations and health care related taxes and limitations on payments to disproportionate share hospitals).

60 FR 33123, June 27, 1995: Medicare Program; Uniform Electronic Cost Reporting System for Hospitals — Final rule affecting 42 CFR Part 413.

60 FR 33126, June 27, 1995: Medicare Program; Clarification of Medicare's Accrual Basis of Accounting Policy — Final rule affecting 42 CFR Part 413.

60 FR 33137, June 27, 1995: Medicare Program; Date for Filing Medicare Cost Reports — Final rule affecting 42 CFR Part 413.

60 FR 39403, August 2, 1995: HCFA Public Information Collection Requirements Submitted for Public Comment and Recommendations (pertaining to PRO reporting forms; Oregon Medicaid reform demonstration; review functions of PRO's; medical records review under PPS; evaluation of Medicare cataract surgery alternate payment demonstration; home health agency survey and deficiencies report; CLIA survey forms; field testing of uniform needs assessment instrument for hospital discharge planning).

60 FR 45487, August 31, 1995: HCFA Public Information Collection Requirements Submitted for Public Comment and

Recommendations (pertaining to the standardized form for applying for Medicare reimbursement by providers).

60 FR 46838, September 8, 1995: Medicaid Program; Limitations on Aggregate Payments to Disproportionate Share Hospitals: Federal Year 1995 — Notice.

61 FR 9186, March 7, 1996: HCFA Agency Information Collection Activities; Proposed Collection; Comment Request (pertaining to hospital and hospital healthcare complex cost reports).

61 FR 10000, March 12, 1996: HCFA Agency Information Collection Activities: Proposed Collection; Comment Request (pertaining to payment adjustments for sole community hospitals).

61 FR 17710, April 22, 1996: HCFA Agency Information Collection Activities: Proposed Collection; Comment Request (pertaining to payment adjustments for sole community hospitals; conditions of participation for portable x-ray suppliers; and cost reports for independent rural health centers and freestanding Federally qualified health centers).

61 FR 21195, May 9, 1996: Medicaid Program; Limitations on Aggregate Payments to Disproportionate Share Hospitals: Federal Fiscal Year 1996 — Notice. See also correction at 61 FR 29418, June 10, 1996.

61 FR 21969, May 13, 1996: Medicare and Medicaid Program; Criteria for a Rural Hospital to Be Designated as an Essential Access Community Hospital (EACH) — Final rule with comment period, affecting 42 CFR Part 412.

61 FR 24310, May 14, 1996: HCFA Agency Information Collection Activities: Proposed Collection; Comment Request (pertaining to distribution of the brochure "An Important Message from Medicare" by hospitals; Conditions of participation for coverage for physical therapists in independent practice; and the Medicare disproportionate share adjustment procedure and criteria).

61 FR 27087, May 30, 1996: HCFA Agency Information Collection Activities; Submission for OMB Review; Comment Request (pertaining to hospital and hospital healthcare complex cost reports).

61 FR 29406, June 10, 1996: HCFA Agency Information Collection Activities: proposed Collection; Comment Request (pertaining to end stage renal disease application and survey and certification report forms; withholding Medicare payments to recover Medicaid overpayments; acquisition, protection, and disclosure of PRO information; clinical laboratory certification and recertification survey forms; CLIA laboratory personnel report forms; prepaid health plan cost

reports; Medicare credit balance reporting requirements; statement of deficiencies and plan of correction requirements for organ procurement organizations; Medicare/Medicaid hospital survey report forms; advance directive requirements for Medicare and Medicaid; payment adjustments for sole community hospitals; survey reports for physical therapists in independent practice; HMO and CMP national data reporting requirements; identification of extension units of outpatient physical therapy and outpatient speech pathology providers; and fire safety survey reports).

61 FR 42257, August 14, 1996: HCFA Proposals Submitted for Collection of Public Comment: Submission for OMB Review (pertaining to third-party liability in Medicaid programs; surveys of federally qualified health centers (FQHCs); distribution of Medicare information by hospitals; Medicare reimbursement for hospitals with a disproportionate share of Medicare inpatients; Medicaid quality control; and the National Payer Identifier).

61 FR 51295, October 1, 1996: HCFA Public Information Requirements Submitted for Collection of Public Comment: Submission for OMB Review (pertaining to approval of Medicaid payment rates for inpatient hospital or long term care services).

61 FR 51611, October 3, 1996: Medicare and Medicaid Programs; New Payment Methodology for Routine Extended Care Services Provided in a Swing-bed Hospital — Final Rule affecting 42 CFR Part 413. See also correction at 61 FR 58631, November 18, 1996.

61 FR 54209, October 17, 1996: HCFA Agency Information Collection Activities: Proposed Collection; Comment request (pertaining to hospital eligibility for swing-bed status).

61 FR 68270, December 27, 1996: HCFA Agency Information Collection Activities: Submission for OMB Review; Comment request (pertaining to a facility identification and screening form for hospital providers of extended care services (swing-beds) in the Medicare and Medicaid programs).

62 FR 4772, January 31, 1997: Medicaid Program; Preliminary Limitations on Aggregate Payments to Disproportionate Share Hospitals: Federal Fiscal Year 1997 — Notice.

62 FR 18639, April 16, 1997: HCFA Agency Information Collection Activities: Proposed Collection; Comment request (pertaining to the hospital request for certification in the Medicare and Medicaid programs form).

62 FR 48292, September 15, 1997: Medicaid Program; Final Limitations on Aggregate Payments to Disproportionate Share Hospitals: Federal Fiscal Year 1997 — Notice.

63 FR 1379, January 9, 1998: Medicare Program; Limit on the Valuation of a Depreciable Asset Recognized as an Allowance for Depreciation and Interest on Capital Indebtedness after a Change of Ownership — Final rule with comment period, affecting 42 CFR Part 413.

63 FR 8987, February 23, 1998: Office of Inspector General: Publication of the OIG Compliance Program for Hospitals — Notice.

63 FR 9843, February 26, 1998: HCFA Agency Information Collection Activities: Proposed Collection; Comment request (pertaining to Medicare provider cost report reimbursement questionnaire and supporting regulations).

63 FR 10920, March 5, 1998: HCFA Emergency Clearance: Public Information Collection Requirements Submitted to the Office of Management and Budget (OMB) (pertaining to Medicare and other Federal health care program provider and supplier application forms).

63 FR 20652, April 27, 1998: HCFA Agency Information Collection Activities: Proposed Collection; Comment request (pertaining to information collection requirements applicable to the obligation of hospitals to examine and treat emergency medical conditions and women in labor).

63 FR 25576, May 8, 1998: Medicare Program; Changes to the Hospital Inpatient Prospective Payment Systems and Fiscal Year 1999 Rates — Proposed rule affecting 42 CFR Parts 405, 412, and 413. See also correction at 63 FR 26565, May 13, 1998.

63 FR 26318, May 12, 1998: Medicare Program Changes to the Hospital Inpatient Prospective Payment Systems and Fiscal Year 1998 Rates — Final Rule, affecting 42 CFR Parts 410, 412, 413, 415, and 485.

63 FR 27303, May 18, 1998: HCFA Agency Information Collection Activities: Submission for OMB Review; Comment request (pertaining to Medicare provider cost report reimbursement questionnaire).

63 FR 32234, June 12, 1998: HCFA Agency Information Collection Activities: Submission for OMB Review; Comment request (pertaining to Medicare/Medicaid psychiatric hospital survey data).

63 FR 33856, June 22, 1998: Medicare and Medicaid Programs; Hospital Conditions of Participation; Identification of Potential

Organ Tissue, and Eye Donors and Transplant Hospitals' Provision of Transplant-Related Data — Final rule affecting 42 CFR Part 482.

1999

64 FR 1025, January 7, 1999: HCFA Agency Information Collection Activities: Proposed Collection; Comment request (pertaining to payment adjustment for sole community hospitals).

64 FR 5665, February 4, 1999: HCFA Agency Information Collection Activities: Proposed Collection; Comment request (pertaining to Medicaid disproportionate share hospital payments for institutions for mental disease).

64 FR 6665, February 10, 1999: HCFA Agency Information Collection Activities: Proposed Collection; Comment request (pertaining to sole community home health agencies (HHS)).

64 FR 14455, March 25, 1999: HCFA Agency Information Collection Activities: Submission for OMB Review; Comment request (pertaining to payment adjustment for sole community hospitals).

64 FR 19544, April 21, 1999: HCFA Agency Information Collection Activities: Submission for OMB Review; Comment request (pertaining to home health agency cost reports, and Medicaid disproportionate share hospital payments for institutions for mental disease).

64 FR 24666, May 7, 1999: HCFA Agency Information Collection Activities: Proposed Collection; Comment request (pertaining to Medicare disproportionate share adjustment procedure).

64 FR 36320, July 6, 1999: Medicare Program; Prospective Payment System for Hospital Outpatient Services — Notice of extension of comment period for proposed rule affecting 42 CFR Parts 409, 410, 411, 412, 413, 419, 489, 498, and 1003.

64 FR 37985, July 14, 1999: Office of Inspector General; Publication of the OIG Special Advisory Bulletin on Gainsharing Arrangements and CMPs for Hospital Payments to Physicians to Reduce or Limit Services to Beneficiaries — Notice.

64 FR 40612, July 27, 1999: HCFA Agency Information Collection Activities: Submission for OMB Review; Comment request (pertaining to Medicare disproportionate share adjustment procedure and criteria for hospitals).

64 FR 41490, July 30, 1999: Medicare Program; Changes to the Hospital Inpatient Prospective Payment Systems and FY 2000 Rates — Final rule affecting 42 CFR Parts 412, 413, 483, and 485.

64 FR 51908, September 27, 1999: Medicare Program; Revision to the Accrual Basis of Accounting Policy—Final rule affecting 42 CFR Part 413.

64 FR 62679, November 17, 1999: HCFA Agency Information Collection Activities: Proposed Collection; Comment request (pertaining to hospital conditions of participation).

64 FR 69271, December 10, 1999: HCFA Agency Information Collection Activities: Proposed Collection; Comment request (pertaining to hospital providers of extender care (swing bed) services in Medicare and Medicaid).

64 FR 69273, December 10, 1999: HCFA Agency Information Collection Activities: Submission for OMB Review; Comment request (pertaining to Medicare/Medicaid hospital survey reports).

2000

65 FR 2967, January 20, 2000: Medicare Program; Medicare Inpatient Disproportionate Share Hospital (DSH) Adjustment Calculation: Change in the Treatment of Certain Medicaid Patient Days in States with 1115 Expansion Waivers—Interim final rule with comment period, affecting 42 CFR Part 412.

65 FR 8727, February 22, 2000: Medicare and Medicaid Programs; Recognition of the American Osteopathic Association (AOA) for Continued Approval of Deeming Authority for Hospitals— Final notice.

65 FR 10098, February 25, 2000: HCFA Agency Information Collection Activities: Proposed Collection; Comment request (pertaining to study to support development and refinement of a classification system and prospective payment system for patients in inpatient rehabilitation hospitals and exempt rehabilitation units).

65 FR 12556, March 9, 2000: HCFA Agency Information Collection Activities: Proposed Collection; Comment request (pertaining to hospital request for certification in the Medicare/Medicaid program).

65 FR 12560, March 9, 2000: HCFA Agency Information Collection Activities: Submission for OMB Review; Comment request (pertaining to hospital provider of extended care services (swing beds) in the Medicare and Medicaid programs).

65 FR 18341, April 7, 2000: Medicare Program; Process for Requesting Recognition of New Technologies and Certain Drugs, Biologicals, and Medical Devices for Special Payment under the Hospital Outpatient Prospective Payment System-—Notice.

65 FR 18434, April 7, 2000: Office of Inspector General, Medicare Program; Prospective Payment System for Hospital Outpatient Ser-

vices — Final rule with comment period, affecting 42 CFR Parts 409, 410, 411, 412, 413, 419, 424, 489, 498, and 1003.

65 FR 35652, June 5, 2000: HCFA Agency Information Collection Activities: Proposed Collection; Comment request (pertaining to hospital and health care complex cost reports).

65 FR 35654, June 5, 2000: HCFA Agency Information Collection Activities: Submission for OMB Review; Comment request (pertaining to hospital request for certification in Medicare and Medicaid).

65 FR 40535, June 30, 2000: Medicare Program; Prospective Payment System for Hospital Outpatient Services; Delay of Effective Date - Notice affecting 42 CFR Parts 409, 410, 411, 412, 413, 419, 424, 489, 498, and 1003. See also correction at 65 FR 59748, October 6, 2000.

65 FR 42022, July 7, 2000: Medicare Program; Question and Answer Session on July 24, 2000, to Discuss Remaining Concerns about the Implementation of the Hospital Outpatient Prospective Payment System (PPS) — Notice of meeting.

65 FR 45992, July 26, 2000: HCFA Agency Information Collection Activities: Proposed Collection; Comment request (pertaining to psychiatric unit, rehabilitation unit, and rehabilitation hospital criteria worksheets).

C65 FR 47026, August 1, 2000: Medicare Program; Provisions of the Balanced Budget Refinement Act of 1999; Hospital Inpatient Payments and Rates and Costs of Graduate Medical Education-Interim final rule with comment period, affecting 42 CFR Parts 410, 412, 413, 482, and 485.

65 FR 47054, August 1, 2000: Medicare Program; Changes to the Hospital Inpatient Prospective Payment Systems and Fiscal Year 2001 Rates — Final rule affecting 42 CFR Parts 410, 412, 413, and 485. See also correction at 66 FR 13020 and 13021, March 2, 2001.

65 FR 47670, August 3, 2000: Medicare Program; Prospective Payment System for Hospital Outpatient Services: Revisions to Criteria to Define New or Innovative Medical Devices, Drugs, and Biologicals Eligible for Pass-Through Payments and Corrections to the Criteria for the Grandfather Provision for Certain Federally Qualified Health Centers-Interim final rule with comment period, affecting 42 CFR Parts 413 and 419.

65 FR 47706, August 3, 2000: Medicare Program; Prospective Payment System for Hospital Outpatient Services: Revision of the Provider-based Location Criteria for Certain PPS-exempt Facilities — Proposed rule affecting 42 CFR Part 413.

65 FR 58919, October 3, 2000: Medicare Program; Prospective Payment System for Hospital Outpatient Services: Provider-Based Criteria; Delay of Effective Date and Correction — Notice. See also correction at 66 FR 1599, January 9, 2001 (affects 42 CFR Parts 413 and 498). See also 65 FR 18434, April 7, 2000.

65 FR 61171, October 16, 2000: HCFA Agency Information Collection Activities: Submission for OMB Review; Comment request (pertaining to psychiatric unit, rehabilitation unit, and rehabilitation hospital criteria worksheets).

65 FR 67798, November 13, 2000: Medicare Program; Prospective Payment System for Hospital Outpatient Services-Interim final rule with comment period, affecting 42 CFR Part 419.

2001

66 FR 1996, January 10, 2001: HCFA Agency Information Collection Activities; Comment request (pertaining to Medicare uniform institutional provider bill for reimbursement of covered services by all providers that accept assignment of claims).

66 FR 3148, January 12, 2001: Medicaid Program; Revision to Medicaid Upper Payment Limit Requirements for Hospital Services, Nursing Facility Services, Intermediate Care Facility Services for the Mentally Retarded, and Clinic Services—Final rule affecting 42 CFR Part 447.

66 FR 7919, January 26, 2001: HCFA Agency Information Collection Activities: Proposed Collection; Comment request (pertaining to provider Medicare agreements).

66 FR 15352, March 19, 2001: Medicare and Medicaid Programs; Hospital Conditions of Participation: Anesthesia Services: Delay of Effective Date—Final rule; delay of effective date, affecting 42 CFR Parts 416, 482, and 485.

66 FR 16063, March 23, 2001: HCFA Agency Information Collection Activities: Submission for OMB Review; Comment request (pertaining to hospital and health care complex cost report form).

66 FR 17657, April 3, 2001: Medicaid Program; Modification of the Medicaid Upper Payment Limit Transition Period for Inpatient Hospital Services, Outpatient Hospital Services, Nursing Facility Services, Intermediate Care Facility Services for the Mentally Retarded and Clinic Services—Proposed rule affecting 42 CFR Part 447.

66 FR 34222, June 27, 2001: HCFA Agency Information Collection Activities: Proposed Collection; Comment request (pertaining to lim-

itation on provider–related donations and health care-related taxes; and limitations on payments to disproportionate share hospitals).

See § 2:57.

§ 6:58 UNNECESSARY HOSPITAL ADMISSIONS AND OTHER INAPPROPRIATE PRACTICES BY HOSPITALS TO CIRCUMVENT REIMBURSEMENT REQUIREMENTS — Section 1886(f) [42 U.S.C.A. 1395ww(f)]

Regulations

42 CFR Part 402 — Civil Money Penalties, Assessments, and Exclusions

42 CFR Part 405, Subpart C — Recovery of Overpayments and Suspension of Payment

42 CFR Part 409 — Hospital Insurance Benefits

42 CFR Part 412 — Prospective Payment System for Inpatient Hospital Services

42 CFR Part 424 — Conditions for Medicare Payment

42 CFR Part 447 — Payment for Services [Medicaid]

42 CFR Part 456 — Utilization Control

42 CFR Part 473 — Reconsiderations and Appeals

42 CFR Part 476 — Utilization and Quality Control Review

42 CFR Part 482 — Conditions of Participation for Hospitals

42 CFR Part 488 — Survey, Certification, and Enforcement Procedures

42 CFR Part 489 — Provider Agreements and Supplier Approval

42 CFR Part 498 — Appeals Procedures for Determinations that Affect Participation in the Medicare Program and for Determinations that Affect the Participation of ICF's/MR and Certain NF's in the Medicaid Program

42 CFR Chapter V — Office of Inspector General — Health Care, Department of Health and Human Services

Subchapter A — General Provisions

Part 1000 — Introduction; General Definitions

Subchapter B — OIG Authorities

Part 1001 — Program Integrity: Medicare and State Health Care Programs

Part 1003 — Civil Money Penalties, Assessments and Exclusions

Part 1004 — Imposition of Sanctions on Health Care Practitioners and Providers of Health Care Services by a Peer Review Organization

Part 1005 — Appeals of Exclusions, Civil Money Penalties and Assessments

Part 1006 — Investigational Inquiries

56 FR 55382, October 25, 1991: Medicare Program; Essential Access Community Hospitals (EACHs) and Rural Primary Care Hospitals (RPCHs) — Proposed rule affecting 42 CFR Parts 400, 409, 410, 411, 412, 413, 424, 440, 485, 488, 489. See also final rule affecting those Parts and Part 498 at 58 FR 30630, May 26, 1993.

57 FR 36006, August 12, 1992: Medicare Program; Self-implementing Coverage and Payments Provisions: 1990 Legislation — Final rule with comment period, affecting 42 CFR Parts 405, 406, 409, 420, 411, 412, 413, 418, and 489. Pertains to capital-related inpatient hospital costs; capital-related outpatient hospital costs; non-capital related outpatient hospital costs; payment for physician pathology services; payment for services of physicians as assistants-at-surgery; payments for ambulatory surgical procedures in hospital outpatient departments; payments for radiology services performed in hospital outpatient departments; hospice benefit extension; enrollment of HMO members in Medicare Part A; coverage of ostomy supplies; application of pre-entitlement stay in psychiatric hospital to limit on payment for inpatient hospital services; payments to dialysis facilities; payment rates for erythropoietin (EPO); and Medicare secondary payer provision for individuals with ESRD. See also confirmation of final rule at 58 FR 58502, November 2, 1993.

57 FR 46362, October 8, 1992: Medicare and Medicaid Programs; Revised Effective Date of Medicare/Medicaid Provider Agreement and Supplier Participation — Proposed rule affecting 42 CFR Parts 431, 440, 442, 488, 489, and 498.

57 FR 46865, October 13, 1992: HCFA Public Information Collection Requirements Submitted to the Office of Management and Budget for Clearance (pertaining to impact of home health care plan management and evaluation; end-stage renal disease medical case review; Medicare/Medicaid hospital swing-bed survey report form; quarterly Medicaid statement of expenditures; Medicaid program budget report; information collection requirements in final peer review organization sanction regulations; appeals procedures for determinations that affect participation in Medicare; request for

medical review information for Part B intermediary outpatient therapy bills and other Part B outpatient bills; and Medicaid limitations on provider-related donations and health care-related taxes, and limitations on payment to disproportionate share hospitals).

58 FR 4705, January 15, 1993: Medicare Program: Uniform Hospital Billing and Payment Mechanisms — Proposed notice.

58 FR 30630, May 26, 1993: Medicare Program; Essential Access Community Hospitals (EACHs) and Rural Primary Care Hospitals (RPCHs) — Final rule affecting 42 CFR Parts 400, 409, 410, 411, 412, 413, 424, 440, 485, 488, 489, and 498. See also correction at 58 FR 49934, September 24, 1993.

58 FR 43156, August 13, 1993: Medicaid Program; Limitations on Provider-Related Donations and Health Care-Related Donations and Health Care-Related Taxes; Limitations on Payments to Disproportionate Share Hospitals — Final rule affecting 42 CFR parts 433 and 447. See also correction at 58 FR 44536, August 23, 1993 as corrected at 58 FR 51130, September 30, 1993.

58 FR 43184, August 13, 1993: Medicaid Program; Limitation on Aggregate Payments to Disproportionate Share hospitals; Federal Fiscal Year 1993 — Notice.

58 FR 54045, October 20, 1993: Medicare Program; Demonstration Project to Develop a Uniform Cost Reporting System for Hospitals — Final Rule affecting 42 CFR Part 403.

59 FR 760, January 6, 1994: Medicare Program; Elimination of Additional Payments for Administrative and General Costs of Hospital-Based Home Health Agencies — Final notice with comment period.

59 FR 4717, February 1, 1994: Medicaid Program; Limitations on Aggregate Payments to Disproportionate Share Hospitals: Federal Fiscal year 1994 — Notice.

59 FR 14865, March 30, 1994: HCFA Public Information Collection Requirements Submitted to the Office of Management and Budget (OMB) for Clearance (pertaining to home health agency Medicare and Medicaid survey report forms for conditions of participation; conditions of participation for rural health clinics; Medicaid re-evaluation of assets for determining payment rates to hospitals and nursing homes; statistical report on medical care, eligible, recipients, payments, and services.)

59 FR 22764, May 2, 1994: Medicaid Program; Limitations on Aggregate Payments to Disproportionate Share Hospitals: Federal

Fiscal Year 1994 — Notice. See also correction at 59 FR 28133, May 31, 1994.

59 FR 50762, October 5, 1994: HCFA Public Information Collection Requirements Submitted to the Office of Management and Budget (OMB) for Clearance (pertaining to reimbursement of hospital costs for residents and interns, criteria for psychiatric and rehabilitation hospital units' reimbursement under the prospective payment system, disclosure of owners and managers of suppliers for fraud and abuse detection purposes, reimbursement of municipal health services clinics, survey form for hospital compliance with anti-dumping requirements, and evaluation of patient and physician satisfaction with the Medicare participating heart bypass center demonstration).

60 FR 3250, January 13, 1995: Medicaid Program; Limitations on Aggregate Payments to Disproportionate Share Hospitals: Federal Fiscal Year 1995 — Notice.

60 FR 19405, April 18, 1995: HCFA Public Information Collection Requirements Submitted to the Office of Management and Budget (OMB) for Clearance (pertaining to Medicaid limitations on provider related donations and health care related taxes and limitations on payments to disproportionate share hospitals).

60 FR 33123, June 27, 1995: Medicare Program; Uniform Electronic Cost Reporting System for Hospitals — Final rule affecting 42 CFR Part 413.

60 FR 33126, June 27, 1995: Medicare Program; Clarification of Medicare's Accrual Basis of Accounting Policy — Final rule affecting 42 CFR Part 413.

60 FR 33137, June 27, 1995: Medicare Program; Date for Filing Medicare Cost Reports — Final rule affecting 42 CFR Part 413.

60 FR 39403, August 2, 1995: HCFA Public Information Collection Requirements Submitted for Public Comment and Recommendations (pertaining to PRO reporting forms; Oregon Medicaid reform demonstration; review functions of PRO's; medical records review under PPS; evaluation of Medicare cataract surgery alternate payment demonstration; home health agency survey and deficiencies report; CLIA survey forms; field testing of uniform needs assessment instrument for hospital discharge planning).

60 FR 45487, August 31, 1995: HCFA Public Information Collection Requirements Submitted for Public Comment and Recommendations (pertaining to the standardized form for applying for Medicare reimbursement by providers).

60 FR 46838, September 8, 1995: Medicaid Program; Limitations on Aggregate Payments to Disproportionate Share Hospitals: Federal Year 1995 — Notice.

61 FR 9186, March 7, 1996: HCFA Agency Information Collection Activities; Proposed Collection; Comment Request (pertaining to hospital and hospital healthcare complex cost reports).

61 FR 10000, March 12, 1996: HCFA Agency Information Collection Activities: Proposed Collection; Comment Request (pertaining to payment adjustments for sole community hospitals).

61 FR 17710, April 22, 1996: HCFA Agency Information Collection Activities: Proposed Collection; Comment Request (pertaining to payment adjustments for sole community hospitals; conditions of participation for portable x-ray suppliers; and cost reports for independent rural health centers and freestanding Federally qualified health centers).

61 FR 21195, May 9, 1996: Medicaid Program; Limitations on Aggregate Payments to Disproportionate Share Hospitals: Federal Fiscal Year 1996 — Notice. See also correction at 61 FR 29418, June 10, 1996.

61 FR 21969, May 13, 1996: Medicare and Medicaid Program; Criteria for a Rural Hospital to Be Designated as an Essential Access Community Hospital (EACH) — Final rule with comment period, affecting 42 CFR Part 412.

61 FR 24310, May 14, 1996: HCFA Agency Information Collection Activities: Proposed Collection; Comment Request (pertaining to distribution of the brochure "An Important Message from Medicare" by hospitals; Conditions of participation for coverage for physical therapists in independent practice; and the Medicare disproportionate share adjustment procedure and criteria).

61 FR 27087, May 30, 1996: HCFA Agency Information Collection Activities; Submission for OMB Review; Comment Request (pertaining to hospital and hospital healthcare complex cost reports).

61 FR 29406, June 10, 1996: HCFA Agency Information Collection Activities: proposed Collection; Comment Request (pertaining to end stage renal disease application and survey and certification report forms; withholding Medicare payments to recover Medicaid overpayments; acquisition, protection, and disclosure of PRO information; clinical laboratory certification and recertification survey forms; CLIA laboratory personnel report forms; prepaid health plan cost reports; Medicare credit balance reporting requirements; statement of deficiencies and plan of correction requirements for organ procure-

ment organizations; Medicare/Medicaid hospital survey report forms; advance directive requirements for Medicare and Medicaid; payment adjustments for sole community hospitals; survey reports for physical therapists in independent practice; HMO and CMP national data reporting requirements; identification of extension units of outpatient physical therapy and outpatient speech pathology providers; and fire safety survey reports).

61 FR 42257, August 14, 1996: HCFA Proposals Submitted for Collection of Public Comment: Submission for OMB Review (pertaining to third-party liability in Medicaid programs; surveys of federally qualified health centers (FQHCs); distribution of Medicare information by hospitals; Medicare reimbursement for hospitals with a disproportionate share of Medicare inpatients; Medicaid quality control; and the National Payer Identifier).

61 FR 51295, October 1, 1996: HCFA Public Information Requirements Submitted for Collection of Public Comment: Submission for OMB Review (pertaining to approval of Medicaid payment rates for inpatient hospital or long term care services).

61 FR 51611, October 3, 1996: Medicare and Medicaid Programs; New Payment Methodology for Routine Extended Care Services Provided in a Swing-bed Hospital — Final Rule affecting 42 CFR Part 413. See also correction at 61 FR 58631, November 18, 1996.

61 FR 54209, October 17, 1996: HCFA Agency Information Collection Activities: Proposed Collection; Comment request (pertaining to hospital eligibility for swing-bed status).

61 FR 68270, December 27, 1996: HCFA Agency Information Collection Activities: Submission for OMB Review; Comment request (pertaining to a facility identification and screening form for hospital providers of extended care services (swing-beds) in the Medicare and Medicaid programs).

62 FR 4772, January 31, 1997: Medicaid Program; Preliminary Limitations on Aggregate Payments to Disproportionate Share Hospitals: Federal Fiscal Year 1997 — Notice.

62 FR 18639, April 16, 1997: HCFA Agency Information Collection Activities: Proposed Collection; Comment request (pertaining to the hospital request for certification in the Medicare and Medicaid programs form).

62 FR 48292, September 15, 1997: Medicaid Program; Final Limitations on Aggregate Payments to Disproportionate Share Hospitals: Federal Fiscal Year 1997 — Notice.

63 FR 1379, January 9, 1998: Medicare Program; Limit on the Valuation of a Depreciable Asset Recognized as an Allowance for Depreciation and Interest on Capital Indebtedness after a Change of Ownership — Final rule with comment period, affecting 42 CFR Part 413.

63 FR 8987, February 23, 1998: Office of Inspector General: Publication of the OIG Compliance Program for Hospitals — Notice.

63 FR 9843, February 26, 1998: HCFA Agency Information Collection Activities: Proposed Collection; Comment request (pertaining to Medicare provider cost report reimbursement questionnaire and supporting regulations).

63 FR 10920, March 5, 1998: HCFA Emergency Clearance: Public Information Collection Requirements Submitted to the Office of Management and Budget (OMB) (pertaining to Medicare and other Federal health care program provider and supplier application forms).

63 FR 20652, April 27, 1998: HCFA Agency Information Collection Activities: Proposed Collection; Comment request (pertaining to information collection requirements applicable to the obligation of hospitals to examine and treat emergency medical conditions and women in labor).

63 FR 27303, May 18, 1998: HCFA Agency Information Collection Activities: Submission for OMB Review; Comment request (pertaining to Medicare provider cost report reimbursement questionnaire).

63 FR 32234, June 12, 1998: HCFA Agency Information Collection Activities: Submission for OMB Review; Comment request (pertaining to Medicare/Medicaid psychiatric hospital survey data).

63 FR 38413, July 16, 1998: HCFA Agency Information Collection Activities: Submission for OMB Review; Comment request (pertaining to Clinical Laboratory Improvement Act certification requirements; EPSDT participation reports; limitations on provider-related donations and health care-related taxes, and limitations on payments to disproportionate share hospitals; and Medicare+Choice provider sponsored organization waiver requests forms).

1999

64 FR 1025, January 7, 1999: HCFA Agency Information Collection Activities: Proposed Collection; Comment request (pertaining to payment adjustment for sole community hospitals).

64 FR 5665, February 4, 1999: HCFA Agency Information Collection Activities: Proposed Collection; Comment request (pertaining to Medicaid disproportionate share hospital payments for institutions for mental disease).

64 FR 14455, March 25, 1999: HCFA Agency Information Collection Activities: Submission for OMB Review; Comment request (pertaining to payment adjustment for sole community hospitals).

64 FR 19544, April 21, 1999: HCFA Agency Information Collection Activities: Submission for OMB Review; Comment request (pertaining to home health agency cost reports, and Medicaid disproportionate share hospital payments for institutions for mental disease).

64 FR 36070, July 2, 1999: Medicare and Medicaid Programs; Hospital Conditions of Participation: Patient Rights — Interim final rule with comment, affecting 42 CFR 482.

64 FR 36320, July 6, 1999: Medicare Program; Prospective Payment System for Hospital Outpatient Services — Notice of extension of comment period for proposed rule affecting 42 CFR Parts 409, 410, 411, 412, 413, 419, 489, 498, and 1003.

FR 37985, July 14, 1999: Office of Inspector General; Publication of the OIG Special Advisory Bulletin on Gainsharing Arrangements and CMPs for Hospital Payments to Physicians to Reduce or Limit Services to Beneficiaries — Notice.

64 FR 40612, July 27, 1999: HCFA Agency Information Collection Activities: Submission for OMB Review; Comment request (pertaining to Medicare disproportionate share adjustment procedure and criteria for hospitals).

64 FR 41490, July 30, 1999: Medicare Program; Changes to the Hospital Inpatient Prospective Payment Systems and FY 2000 Rates — Final rule affecting 42 CFR Parts 412, 413, 483, and 485.

64 FR 69271, December 10, 1999: HCFA Agency Information Collection Activities: Proposed Collection; Comment request (pertaining to hospital providers of extender care (swing bed) services in Medicare and Medicaid).

64 FR 69273, December 10, 1999: HCFA Agency Information Collection Activities: Submission for OMB Review; Comment request (pertaining to Medicare/Medicaid hospital survey reports).

2000

65 FR 2967, January 20, 2000: Medicare Program; Medicare Inpatient Disproportionate Share Hospital (DSH) Adjustment

Calculation: Change in the Treatment of Certain Medicaid Patient Days in States with 1115 Expansion Waivers — Interim final rule with comment period, affecting 42 CFR Part 412.

65 FR 8727, February 22, 2000: Medicare and Medicaid Programs; Recognition of the American Osteopathic Association (AOA) for Continued Approval of Deeming Authority for Hospitals — Final notice.

65 FR 10098, February 25, 2000: HCFA Agency Information Collection Activities: Proposed Collection; Comment request (pertaining to study to support development and refinement of a classification system and prospective payment system for patients in inpatient rehabilitation hospitals and exempt rehabilitation units).

65 FR 12556, March 9, 2000: HCFA Agency Information Collection Activities: Proposed Collection; Comment request (pertaining to hospital request for certification in the Medicare/Medicaid program).

65 FR 12560, March 9, 2000: HCFA Agency Information Collection Activities: Submission for OMB Review; Comment request (pertaining to hospital provider of extended care services (swing beds) in the Medicare and Medicaid programs).

65 FR 18341, April 7, 2000: Medicare Program; Process for Requesting Recognition of New Technologies and Certain Drugs, Biologicals, and Medical Devices for Special Payment under the Hospital Outpatient Prospective Payment System- — Notice.

65 FR 18434, April 7, 2000: Office of Inspector General, Medicare Program; Prospective Payment System for Hospital Outpatient Services — Final rule with comment period, affecting 42 CFR Parts 409, 410, 411, 412, 413, 419, 424, 489, 498, and 1003.

65 FR 35652, June 5, 2000: HCFA Agency Information Collection Activities: Proposed Collection; Comment request (pertaining to hospital and health care complex cost reports).

65 FR 35654, June 5, 2000: HCFA Agency Information Collection Activities: Submission for OMB Review; Comment request (pertaining to hospital request for certification in Medicare and Medicaid).

65 FR 40535, June 30, 2000: Medicare Program; Prospective Payment System for Hospital Outpatient Services; Delay of Effective Date - Notice affecting 42 CFR Parts 409, 410, 411, 412, 413, 419, 424, 489, 498, and 1003. See also correction at 65 FR 59748, October 6, 2000.

65 FR 42022, July 7, 2000: Medicare Program; Question and Answer Session on July 24, 2000, to Discuss Remaining Concerns about the Implementation of the Hospital Outpatient Prospective Payment System (PPS) — Notice of meeting.

65 FR 45992, July 26, 2000: HCFA Agency Information Collection Activities: Proposed Collection; Comment request (pertaining to psychiatric unit, rehabilitation unit, and rehabilitation hospital criteria worksheets).

C65 FR 47026, August 1, 2000: Medicare Program; Provisions of the Balanced Budget Refinement Act of 1999; Hospital Inpatient Payments and Rates and Costs of Graduate Medical Education-Interim final rule with comment period, affecting 42 CFR Parts 410, 412, 413, 482, and 485.

65 FR 47054, August 1, 2000: Medicare Program; Changes to the Hospital Inpatient Prospective Payment Systems and Fiscal Year 2001 Rates — Final rule affecting 42 CFR Parts 410, 412, 413, and 485.

65 FR 47670, August 3, 2000: Medicare Program; Prospective Payment System for Hospital Outpatient Services: Revisions to Criteria to Define New or Innovative Medical Devices, Drugs, and Biologicals Eligible for Pass-Through Payments and Corrections to the Criteria for the Grandfather Provision for Certain Federally Qualified Health Centers-Interim final rule with comment period, affecting 42 CFR Parts 413 and 419.

65 FR 47706, August 3, 2000: Medicare Program; Prospective Payment System for Hospital Outpatient Services: Revision of the Provider-based Location Criteria for Certain PPS-exempt Facilities — Proposed rule affecting 42 CFR Part 413.

65 FR 58919, October 3, 2000: Medicare Program; Prospective Payment System for Hospital Outpatient Services: Provider-Based Criteria; Delay of Effective Date and Correction — Notice.

65 FR 61171, October 16, 2000: HCFA Agency Information Collection Activities: Submission for OMB Review; Comment request (pertaining to psychiatric unit, rehabilitation unit, and rehabilitation hospital criteria worksheets).

65 FR 67798, November 13, 2000: Medicare Program; Prospective Payment System for Hospital Outpatient Services-Interim final rule with comment period, affecting 42 CFR Part 419.

2001

66 FR 1996, January 10, 2001: HCFA Agency Information Collection Activities; Comment request (pertaining to Medicare uniform institutional provider bill for reimbursement of covered services by all providers that accept assignment of claims).

66 FR 3148, January 12, 2001: Medicaid Program; Revision to Medicaid Upper Payment Limit Requirements for Hospital Services, Nursing Facility Services, Intermediate Care Facility Services for the Mentally Retarded, and Clinic Services—Final rule affecting 42 CFR Part 447.

66 FR 7919, January 26, 2001: HCFA Agency Information Collection Activities: Proposed Collection; Comment request (pertaining to provider Medicare agreements).

66 FR 15352, March 19, 2001: Medicare and Medicaid Programs; Hospital Conditions of Participation: Anesthesia Services: Delay of Effective Date—Final rule; delay of effective date, affecting 42 CFR Parts 416, 482, and 485.

66 FR 16063, March 23, 2001: HCFA Agency Information Collection Activities: Submission for OMB Review; Comment request (pertaining to hospital and health care complex cost report form).

66 FR 17657, April 3, 2001: Medicaid Program; Modification of the Medicaid Upper Payment Limit Transition Period for Inpatient Hospital Services, Outpatient Hospital Services, Nursing Facility Services, Intermediate Care Facility Services for the Mentally Retarded and Clinic Services—Proposed rule affecting 42 CFR Part 447.

66 FR 34222, June 27, 2001: HCFA Agency Information Collection Activities: Proposed Collection; Comment request (pertaining to limitation on provider-related donations and health care-related taxes; and limitations on payments to disproportionate share hospitals).

See § 2:58.

§ 6:59 GIVING A HOME HEALTH AGENCY ADVANCE NOTICE OF A STANDARD SURVEY — Section 1891(c)(1) [42 U.S.C.A. 1395bbb(c)(1)]

Regulations

42 CFR Part 402 — Civil Money Penalties, Assessments, and Exclusions

42 CFR Part 409 — Hospital Insurance Benefits, Subpart E — Home Health Services under Hospital Insurance

42 CFR Part 410 — Supplementary Medical Insurance (SMI) Benefits, Subpart C — Home Health Services under SMI

42 CFR Part 424 — Conditions for Medicare Payment

42 CFR Part 440 — Services: General Provisions [Medicaid]

42 CFR Part 441 — Services: Requirements and Limits Applicable to Specific Services [Medicaid]

42 CFR Part 476 — Utilization and Quality Control Review

42 CFR Part 484 — Conditions of Participation: Home Health Agencies

42 CFR Part 488 — Survey, Certification, and Enforcement Procedures

42 CFR Part 489 — Provider Agreements and Supplier Approval

42 CFR Part 498 — Appeals Procedures for Determinations that Affect Participation in the Medicare Program and for Determinations that Affect the Participation of ICF's/MR and Certain NF's in the Medicaid Program

42 CFR Chapter V — Office of Inspector General — Health Care, Department of Health and Human Services

Subchapter A — General Provisions

Part 1000 — Introduction; General Definitions

Subchapter B — OIG Authorities

Part 1001 — Program Integrity: Medicare and State Health Care Programs

Part 1002 — Program Integrity: State–initiated Exclusion from Medicaid

Part 1003 — Civil Money Penalties, Assessments and Exclusions

Part 1004 — Imposition of Sanctions on Health Care Practitioners and Providers of Health Care Services by a Peer Review Organization

Part 1005 — Appeals of Exclusions, Civil Money Penalties and Assessments

Part 1006 — Investigational Inquiries

Part 1007 — State Medicaid Fraud Control Units

Part 1008 — Advisory Opinions by the OIG

53 FR 46015, November 15, 1988: Medicare Program; Schedule of Limits on Home Health Agency Costs Per Visit for Cost Reporting on or after July 1, 1988 — Correction. See also correction and notice with comment period at 53 FR 3685, January 25, 1989.

54 FR 33354, August 14, 1989: Medicare Program; Home Health Agencies: Conditions of Participation and Reduction in Recordkeeping Requirements — Interim final rule with comment period, to amend and redesignate 42 CFR Part 405, Subpart L as 42 CFR Part 484. See also correction at 54 FR 35131, August 23, 1989.

56 FR 12934, March 28, 1991: Medicare Program; Schedule of Limits on Home Health Agency Costs Per Visit for Cost Reporting

Periods Beginning on or after July 1, 1989 — Final notice. See also correction published at 56 FR 14424, April 9, 1991.

56 FR 30927, July 8, 1991: Privacy Act of 1974; Report of New System (re Quality Assurance for the Home Health Agency (HHA) Prospective Payment Demonstration) — Notice.

56 FR 32967, July 18, 1991: Medicare Program; Home Health Agencies: Conditions of Participation — Final rule. See also correction at 56 FR 51334, October 11, 1991, affecting 42 CFR Part 484.

56 FR 37054, August 2, 1991: Medicare and Medicaid Programs; Survey and Enforcement Requirements and Alternative Sanctions for Home Health Agencies — Proposed rule affecting 42 CFR Parts 441, 488, and 489.

56 FR 43929, September 5, 1991: Medicare and Medicaid Programs; Recognition of the Community Health Accreditation Program Standards for Home Care Organizations — Proposed notice.

56 FR 49154, September 27, 1991: Medicare Program; Medicare Coverage of Home Health Services, Medicare Conditions of Participation, and Home Health Aide Supervision — Proposed rule affecting 42 CFR Parts 409, 418, and 484.

56 FR 50542, October 7, 1991: Medicare Program; "Confined to the Home" Requirements for Home Health Services — Proposed rule affecting 42 CFR Part 409.

56 FR 64256, December 9, 1991: Medicare Program; Schedule of Limits on Home Health Agency Costs Per Visit for Cost Reporting Periods Beginning On or After July 1, 1991 — Notice with comment period. See also correction at 57 FR 749, January 8, 1992.

57 FR 4044, February 3, 1992: Medicare Program; Recognition of the Joint Commission of the Accreditation of Healthcare Organizations' Standards for Home Care Organizations — Proposed notice.

57 FR 22773, May 29, 1992: Medicare Program; Recognition of Community Health Accreditation Program Standards for Home Care Organizations — Final notice.

57 FR 29142, June 30, 1992: Medicaid Program; Home and Community-Based Services Waivers for Individuals Age 65 or Older — Interim final rule with comment period, affecting 42 CFR Parts 400, 435, 436, 440, and 441.

57 FR 29325, July 1, 1992: HCFA Public Information Collection Requirements Submitted to the Office of Management and Budget for Clearance (pertaining to outpatient physical therapy and/or speech pathology services; conditions of coverage for organ procure-

ment organizations; and home and community-based services waiver requirements for individuals age 65 or older).

57 FR 29410, July 1, 1992: Medicare Program; Schedule of Limits on Home Health Agency Costs Per Visit for Cost Reporting Periods Beginning on or after July 1, 1992, affecting 42 CFR Part 413. See also corrections at 57 FR 38959, August 27, 1992, and 57 FR 43004, September 17, 1992.

57 FR 32798, July 23, 1992: HCFA Public Information Collection Requirements Submitted to the Office of Management and Budget for Clearance (pertaining to attending physician's certification of medical necessity for home oxygen therapy).

57 FR 43462, September 21, 1992: Health Care Financing Administration Public Information Collection Requirements Submitted to the Office of Management and Budget for Clearance (pertaining to sole community home health agencies; physician/supplier overpayment reports; physician or supplier Medicare agreements; conditions of participation for rural health clinics; Medicare provider refunds; conditions of participation for comprehensive outpatient rehabilitation facilities; Medicaid income and eligibility verification system; Medicaid integrated review schedule; provider overpayment report; financial statement of Medicare provider debtors; negative case action review schedule for Medicaid quality control; outpatient resource costing study; Medicaid intermediate care facility for the mentally retarded or persons with related conditions survey report form; installment agreement of beneficiary refund of overpayment; PRO assumption of responsibilities; Medicare contractor administrative budget and cost reporting system forms; fire safety survey report forms; medical records review under prospective payment system; and Qualified Medicare Beneficiary supplement to the Medicare current beneficiary survey).

57 FR 46362, October 8, 1992: Medicare and Medicaid Programs; Revised Effective Date of Medicare/Medicaid Provider Agreement and Supplier Participation — Proposed rule affecting 42 CFR Parts 431, 440, 442, 488, 489, and 498.

57 FR 46865, October 13, 1992: HCFA Public Information Collection Requirements Submitted to the Office of Management and Budget for Clearance (pertaining to impact of home health care plan management and evaluation; end-stage renal disease medical case review; Medicare/Medicaid hospital swing-bed survey report form; quarterly Medicaid statement of expenditures; Medicaid program budget report; information collection requirements in final peer

review organization sanction regulations; appeals procedures for determinations that affect participation in Medicare; request for medical review information for Part B intermediary outpatient therapy bills and other Part B outpatient bills; and Medicaid limitations on provider-related donations and health care-related taxes, and limitations on payment to disproportionate share hospitals).

58 FR 21174, April 19, 1993: HCFA Public Information Collection Requirements Submitted to the Office of Management and Budget for Clearance re end stage renal disease survey forms; municipal health services cost reports forms; advance directives; withholding Medicare payments to recover Medicaid overpayments; home office cost statements; and statistical report on medical care.

58 FR 36748, July 8, 1993: Medicare Program; Schedule of Limits on Home Health Agency Costs Per Visit for Cost Reporting Periods Beginning on or After July 1, 1993 — Notice with comment period.

58 FR 38579, July 19, 1993: HCFA Public Information Collection Requirements Submitted to the Office of Management and Budget (OMB) for Clearance re survey of home health agencies; CLIA survey report form; validation of state surveys; Medicaid listing of participating home health agencies; financial information regarding Medicare benefits from Medicare contractors; and third-party liability under Medicaid.

58 FR 46198, September 1, 1993: HCFA Public Information Collection Requirements (ICR) Submitted to the Office of Management and Budget (OMB) for Clearance (pertaining to prenatal services and assistance screening; home health agency treatment forms; conditions of participation for intermediate care facilities for the mentally retarded; State Medicaid eligibility quality control sample selection lists; prepaid health plan cost report; hospital survey report form; procedures for determining whether providers, practitioners, or other suppliers of services are liable for certain noncovered services; Medicare credit balance reporting requirements; Medicare provider cost report questionnaire form; Medicare current beneficiary survey rounds 7-10; sterilization regulation/consent form; PRO reconsideration and appeals information requirements; information collection requirements in HSQ-110, acquisition, protection and disclosure of PRO information; Medicare/Medicaid organ procurement organization's (OPO) request for certification) — Notice.

58 FR 59270, November 8, 1993: HCFA Public Information Collection Requirements Submitted to the Office of Management and

Budget (OMB) for Clearance (pertaining to formats for utilization and quality control peer review organizations (PROs); home health agency plan of treatment forms; State survey agency budget expenditure report and certification workload report; home health agency cost report; recordkeeping requirements in provider reimbursement manual; quarterly Medicaid statement of expenditures; Medicare contract application for Federally qualified health maintenance organizations; hospice survey and deficiencies report form; organ procurement agency/histocompatibility laboratory statement of reimbursable costs) — Notice.

58 FR 60204, November 15, 1993: HCFA Public Information Collection Requirements Submitted to the Office of Management and Budget (OMB) for Clearance (pertaining to procedures for transmitting information between Medicare carriers and Medicare supplemental insurers; Medicare physician or supplier agreement; patient intake data form for the National Home Health Agency; agency characteristics form for the National Home Health Agency prospective payment demonstration; intake and assessment survey package for the community nursing organization demonstration; comprehensive outpatient rehabilitation facility (CORF eligibility and survey forms and information collection requirements) — Notice.

59 FR 760, January 6, 1994: Medicare Program; Elimination of Additional Payments for Administrative and General Costs of Hospital-Based Home Health Agencies — Final notice with comment period.

59 FR 41330, August 11, 1994: HCFA Public Information Collection Requirements Submitted to the Office of Management and Budget (OMB) for Clearance (pertaining to home dialysis forms, patient drug utilization data, and home health agency reimbursement).

59 FR 50762, October 5, 1994: HCFA Public Information Collection Requirements Submitted to the Office of Management and Budget (OMB) for Clearance (pertaining to reimbursement of hospital costs for residents and interns, criteria for psychiatric and rehabilitation hospital units' reimbursement under the prospective payment system, disclosure of owners and managers of suppliers for fraud and abuse detection purposes, reimbursement of municipal health services clinics, survey form for hospital compliance with anti-dumping requirements, and evaluation of patient and physician

satisfaction with the Medicare participating heart bypass center demonstration).

59 FR 65482, December 20, 1994: Medicare Program; Medicare Coverage of Home Health Services, Medicare Conditions of Participation, and Home Health Aide Supervision — Final rule affecting 42 CFR Parts 409, 413, 418, and 484. See also correction at 60 FR 39122, August 1, 1995.

60 FR 7774, February 9, 1995: HCFA Public Information Collection Requirements Submitted to the Office of Management and Budget (OMB) for Clearance (pertaining to justification for ESRD composite rates for outpatient dialysis services, and home health agency compliance with health and safety requirements).

60 FR 8389, February 14, 1995: Medicare Program; Schedule of Limits on Home Health Agency Costs Per Visit — Notice with comment period.

60 FR 12770, March 8, 1995: HCFA Public Information Collection Requirements Submitted to the Office of Management and Budget (OMB) for Clearance (pertaining to survey forms for compliance with CLIA; CLIA application forms for testing on human specimens, and forms for outcome-based quality assurance programs for home health agencies).

60 FR 17538, April 6, 1995: Medicare and Medicaid Programs; Quarterly Listing of Program.

60 FR 21525, May 2, 1995: HCFA Public Information Collection Requirements Submitted to the Office of Management and Budget (OMB) for Clearance (pertaining to intermediary requests for information from skilled nursing facilities, reimbursement for CLIA compliance surveys, patient outcome data in home health agencies, common claim forms for Medicare/Medicaid reimbursement, and a study of childhood immunization costs).

60 FR 40847, August 10, 1995: Office of Inspector General: Publication of OIG Special Fraud Alerts: Home Health Fraud, and Fraud and Abuse in the Provision of Medical Supplies to Nursing Facilities — Notice.

60 FR 62237, December 5, 1995: Medicare Program; Uniform Electronic Cost Reporting for Skilled Nursing Facilities and Home Health Agencies — Proposed rule affecting 42 CFR Part 413.

60 FR 64167, December 14, 1995: HCFA Public Information Collection Requirements Submitted for Public Comment and Recommendations (pertaining to home health care; Medicare/Medicaid certification of physical therapy and speech pathology

services; certification as suppliers of Portable X-ray Services; certification of organ procurement organizations; certification for physical therapists in independent practice; and approval as a hospital provider of extended care services (swing bed)).

61 FR 7012, February 23, 1996: HCFA Notice Submitted for Collection of Public Comment: Submission for OMB Review (pertaining to granting and withdrawing of deeming authority to private non-profit Accreditation organizations and the Clinical Laboratory Improvement Act Exemption under State laboratory programs; and the rules for participation of home health agencies to participate as sole community home health agencies).

61 FR 14798, April 3, 1996: HCFA Agency Information Collection Activities: Proposed Collection; Comment Request (pertaining to statistical reports on medical care eligibility, payments and services under Medicaid; State survey agency lists of positions and schedule of equipment purchases; granting and withdrawing of deeming authority to national accreditation organizations; maximizing the effectiveness of home health care; requests for certification in the Medicare or Medicaid program to provide outpatient physical therapy and/or speech pathology services; physical therapists in independent practice; requests for provider approval as a hospital provider of extended care services (swing bed) under Medicare and Medicaid; and requests for designation as an organ procurement organization).

61 FR 25229, May 20, 1996: HCFA Agency Information Collection Activities: Proposed Collection; Comment Request (pertaining to evaluation of the Oregon reform demonstration; evaluation of the per-episode home health prospective payment demonstration; and the blood bank inspection checklist instrument used by State agencies to determine compliance with CLIA).

61 FR 32347, June 24, 1996: Medicare and Medicaid Programs; Provider Appeals: Technical Amendments — Final rule with comment period, affecting 42 CFR Parts 405, 417, 431, 473, and 498).

61 FR 34344, July 1, 1996: Medicare Program: Schedule of Limits on Home Health Agency Costs Per Visit for Cost Reporting Periods Beginning on or after July 1, 1996: Notice with comment period.

61 FR 49271, September 19, 1996: Medicare Program; Part B Advance Payments to Suppliers Furnishing Items or Services under Medicare Part B — Final rule affecting 42 CFR Part 421.

61 FR 56963, November 5, 1996: HCFA Agency Information Collection Activities: Proposed Collection; Comment request (pertaining

to geographic adjustment factors for existing payment localities used in calculating the Medicare fee schedule; demonstration project to test capitated payments for home health services, medical devices, durable medical equipment, and certain ambulatory care under Medicare; and certification of medical necessity forms for durable medical equipment and supplies).

62 FR 26, January 2, 1997: Medicare Program; Electronic Cost Reporting for Skilled Nursing Facilities and Home Health Agencies — Final Rule. See also correction at 62 FR 27210, May 19, 1997.

62 FR 3514, January 23, 1997: Submitted for Collection of Public Comment: Submission for OMB Review (pertaining to Home and Community-based Services Waiver Requests).

62 FR 5632, February 6, 1997: HCFA Agency Information Collection Activities: Proposed Collection; Comment request (pertaining to data collection for a project to develop a case-mix adjustment system for a national home health prospective payment program).

62 FR 7350, February 19, 1997: Office of Inspector General: Medicare and State Health Care Programs: Fraud and Abuse; Issuance of Advisory Opinions by the OIG — Interim final rule with comment period, affecting 42 CFR Part 1008.

62 FR 8744, February 26, 1997: HCFA Agency Information Collection Activities: Submission for OMB Review; Comment request (pertaining to Medicare provider/supplier enrollment application).

62 FR 11004, March 10, 1997: Medicare and Medicaid Programs; Revision of the Conditions of Participation for Home Health Agencies and Use of the Outcome and Assessment Information Set (OASIS) as Part of the Revised Conditions of Participation for Home Health Agencies — Introduction to proposed rules, affecting 42 CFR Part 484.

62 FR 11005, March 10, 1997: Medicare and Medicaid Programs; Conditions of Participation for Home Health Agencies — Proposed rule affecting 42 CFR Part 484. See also correction at 62 FR 11953, March 13, 1997.

62 FR 11035, March 10, 1997: Medicare and Medicaid Programs; Use of the OASIS as Part of the Conditions of Participation for Home Health Agencies — Proposed rule.

62 FR 13389, March 20, 1997: HCFA Agency Information Collection Activities: Proposed Collection; Comment request (pertaining to home health agency cost report form).

62 FR 19582, April 22, 1997: HCFA Emergency Clearance: Public Information Collection Requirements Submitted to the Office of

Management and Budget (pertaining to attending physicians' certification of medical necessity for home oxygen therapy).

62 FR 23140, April 29, 1997: Office of Inspector General: Health Care Programs: Fraud and Abuse; Revised PRO Sanctions for Failing to Meet Statutory Obligations — Final rule.

62 FR 29730, June 2, 1997: HCFA Agency Information Collection Activities: Submission for OMB Review; Comment request (pertaining to home health agency cost reports).

62 FR 39848, July 24, 1997: HCFA Agency Information Collection Activities; Proposed Collection; Comment request (pertaining to home health certification and plan of care forms for reimbursement; and Medicare/Medicaid disclosure of ownership and control forms).

62 FR 43931, August 18, 1997: Medicare and Medicaid Programs: Effective Dates of Provider Agreements and Supplier Approvals — Final rule affecting 42 CFR Parts 431, 442, 488, 489, and 498.

62 FR 45672, August 28, 1997: HCFA Agency Information Collection Activities: Proposed Collection; Comment request (pertaining to conditions of participation for home health agencies; and negative case action review process annual reports for States).

62 FR 51874, October 3, 1997: HCFA Agency Information Collection Activities: Submission for OMB Review; Comment request (pertaining to home health services certification and plan of care).

62 FR 65049, December 10, 1997: Office of Inspector General: Solicitation of New Safe Harbors and Special Fraud Alerts — Notice of intent to develop regulations, affecting 42 CFR Part 1001.

62 FR 66376, December 18, 1997: HCFA Emergency Clearance: Public Information Collection Requirements Submitted to the Office of Management and Budget (OMB) (pertaining to Medicare and other Federal health care program enrollment forms for providers and suppliers).

63 FR 89, January 2, 1998: Medicare Program; Schedule of Limits on Home Health Agency Costs Per Visit for Cost Reporting Periods Beginning on or after October 1, 1997 — Notice with comment period.

63 FR 291, January 5, 1998: Medicare and Medicaid Programs; Surety Bond and Capitalization Requirements for Home Health Agencies; Final rule affecting 42 CFR Parts 413, 440, 441, and 489.

63 FR 2926, January 20, 1998: Medicare Program; Additional Supplier Standards — Proposed rule affecting 42 CFR Part 424.

63 FR 5958, February 5, 1998: HCFA Agency Information Collection Activities: Proposed Collection; Comment request (pertaining to

quality assurance for phase II of the home agency prospective payment demonstration).

63 FR 7743, February 17, 1998: Medicare and Medicaid Programs; Hospital Conditions of Participation; Provider Agreements and Supplier Approval — Notice of extension of comment period, affecting 42 CFR Parts 416, 482, 485, and 489.

63 FR 10730, March 4, 1998: Medicare and Medicaid Programs; Surety Bond Requirements for Home Health Agencies — Final rule affecting 42 CFR Parts 441 and 489.

63 FR 10732, March 4, 1998: Medicare and Medicaid Programs; Surety Bond Requirements for Home Health Agencies — Notice of Intent to Amend Regulations.

63 FR 10920, March 5, 1998: HCFA Emergency Clearance: Public Information Collection Requirements Submitted to the Office of Management and Budget (OMB) (pertaining to Medicare and other Federal health care program provider and supplier application forms).

63 FR 15718, March 31, 1998: Medicare Program; Schedule of Per-beneficiary Limitations on Home Health Agency Costs for Cost Reporting Periods Beginning on or after October 1, 1997 — Final rule with comment period, affecting 42 CFR Part 413.

63 FR 16563, April 3, 1998: HCFA Agency Information Collection Activities: Submission for OMB Review; Comment request (pertaining to quality assurance for phase II of the home agency prospective payment demonstration).

63 FR 17877, April 10, 1998: HCFA Agency Information Collection Activities: Proposed Collection; Comment request (pertaining to home health agency cost reports).

63 FR 19502, April 20, 1998: HCFA Agency Information Collection Activities: Proposed Collection; Comment request (pertaining to Medicare home health quality assurance demonstration).

63 FR 19502, April 20, 1998: HCFA Agency Information Collection Activities: Proposed collection; Comment request (pertaining to annual early and periodic screening, diagnostic, and treatment services (EPSDT) participation report; Medicare and other health care programs provider/supplier enrollment application; and research and analytic support for implementing performance measurement in Medicare fee for service).

63 FR 29648, June 1, 1998: Medicare and Medicaid Programs; Surety Bond Requirements for Home Health Agencies — Final rule affecting 42 CFR Parts 441 and 489.

63 FR 38414, July 16, 1998: HCFA Privacy Act of 1974; Report of Altered System (pertaining to disclosure of individual-specific information to combat fraud or abuse in health benefit programs).

63 FR 38839, July 20, 1998: HCFA Agency Information Collection Activities: Submission for OMB Review; Comment request (pertaining to Medicare home health quality assurance demonstration).

63 FR 41170, July 31, 1998: Medicare and Medicaid Programs; Surety Bond Requirements for Home Health Agencies — Final rule affecting 42 CFR Parts 441 and 489.

63 FR 42410, August 7, 1998: Office of Inspector General: Publication of the OIG Compliance Program Guidance for Home Health Agencies — Notice.

63 FR 42912, August 11, 1998: Medicare Program; Schedules of Per-visit and Per-beneficiary Limitations on Home Health Agency Costs for Cost Reporting Periods Beginning on or after October 1, 1998 — Notice with comment period. See also correction at 63 FR 57698, October 28, 1998.

63 FR 48734, September 11, 1998: HCFA Agency Information Collection Activities: Proposed Collection; Comment request (pertaining to medical review activities under PPS by Peer Review Organizations; and survey and deficiency reports for home health agencies).

63 FR 63478, November 13, 1998: HCFA Agency Information Collection Activities: Proposed Collection; Comment request (pertaining to processing Medicare+Choice disenrollment requests from beneficiaries; creation of the Utilization and Quality Control Peer Review Organization; and rules for participation of HHA's in Medicare and review of plans of care for home health services).

63 FR 65601, November 27, 1998: HCFA Agency Information Collection Activities: Submission for OMB Review; Comment request (pertaining to medical records review under PPS; and home health agency survey and deficiencies reports, and home health functional assessment instruments).

1999

64 FR 1813, January 12, 1999: Office of Inspector General Publication of OIG Special Fraud Alert on Physician Liability for Certifications in the Provision of Medical Equipment and Supplies and Home Health Services — Notice.

64 FR 2228, January 13, 1999: Office of Inspector General: Solicitation of Information and Recommendations for Developing OIG Compliance Program Guidance for the Hospice Industry — Notice.

64 FR 6665, February 10, 1999: HCFA Agency Information Collection Activities: Proposed Collection; Comment request (pertaining to sole community home health agencies (HHS)).

64 FR 10305, March 3, 1999: HCFA Agency Information Collection Activities: Proposed Collection; Comment request (pertaining to attending physician's certification of medical necessity for home oxygen therapy).

64 FR 13997, March 23, 1999: HCFA Agency Information Collection Activities: Submission for OMB Review; Comment request (pertaining to Medicare and Medicaid requirements for advanced directives, and disclosure of ownership and financial control interest).

64 FR 17673, April 12, 1999: HCFA Agency Information Collection Activities: Proposed Collection; Comment request (pertaining to Medicare participating physician or supplier agreements).

64 FR 23846, May 4, 1999: HCFA Emergency Clearance: Public Information Collection Requirements Submitted to the Office of Management and Budget (OMB) (pertaining to the outcome and assessment information set (OASIS) for home health care agencies).

64 FR 24956, May 10, 1999: Medicare and Medicaid Programs; Effective Dates of Provider Agreements and Supplier Approvals-Correction restoring regulations inadvertently removed when a final rule concerning effective dates for provider agreements and supplier approvals was published at 62 FR 43931, August 18, 1997.

64 FR 32984, June 18, 1999: Medicare and Medicaid Programs; Mandatory Use, Collection, Encoding, and Transmission of Outcome and Assessment Information Set (OASIS) for Home Health Agencies — Notice.

64 FR 32992, June 18, 1999: HCFA Privacy Act of 1974; Report of New System (pertaining to a new system of records containing data on the physical, mental, functional, and psychosocial status of all patients receiving the services of home health agencies (HHAs) approved to participate in Medicare or Medicaid).

64 FR 36887, July 8, 1999: HCFA Agency Information Collection Activities: Proposed Collection; Comment request (pertaining to reporting outcome and assessment information data set (OASIS) as part of the conditions of participation for home health agencies).

64 FR 38203, July 15, 1999: HCFA Agency Information Collection Activities: Submission for OMB Review; Comment request (pertaining to attending physician's certification of medical necessity for home oxygen therapy).

64 FR 39517, July 22, 1999: HCFA Agency Information Collection Activities: Submission for OMB Review; Comment request (pertaining to Medicare participating physician or supplier agreement form HCFA-460).

64 FR 42766, August 5, 1999: Medicare Program; Schedules of Per-visit and Per-Beneficiary Limitations on Home Health Agency Costs for Cost Reporting Periods Beginning on or after October 1, 1999, and Portions of Cost Reporting Periods Beginning before October 1, 2000 — Notice with comment period. See also correction at 64 FR 57101, October 22, 1999.

64 FR 49197, September 10, 1999: Medicare and Medicaid Programs; Application of the Joint Commission for Accreditaton of Healthcare Organizations (JCAHO) for Continued Approval of Deeming Authority for Home Health Agencies — Proposed notice.

64 FR 49198, September 10, 1999: Medicare and Medicaid Programs; Application of the Community Health Accreditation Program, Incorporated, CHAP) for Continued Approval of Deeming Authority for Home Health Agencies — Proposed notice.

64 FR 51328, September 22, 1999: HCFA Emergency Clearance: Public Information Collection Requirements Submitted to the Office of Management and Budget (OMB) (pertaining to the obligation of home health agencies to give beneficiaries advance written notice of noncovered care or of reducing or terminating ongoing care).

64 FR 57431, October 25, 1999: Medicare Program; Appeals of Carrier Determinations that a Supplier Fails to Meet the Requirements for Medicare Billing Privileges — Proposed rule affecting 42 CFR Part 405.

64 FR 57612, October 26, 1999: Medicare Program; Open Town Hall Meeting on November 8, 1999, to Present and Overview of the Home Health Prospective Payment System Proposed Rule Followed by a General Home Health Listening Session — Notice of Meeting.

64 FR 58134, October 28, 1999: Medicare Program; Prospective Payment System for Home Health Agencies — Proposed rule affecting 42 CFR Parts 409, 410, 411, 413, 424, and 484.

2000

65 FR 135, January 3, 2000: HCFA Agency Information Collection Activities: proposed Collection; Comment request (pertaining to home health advance beneficiary notices). See also correction at 65 FR 2967, January 19, 2000.

65 FR 1400, January 10, 2000: HCFA Agency Information Collection Activities: Submission for OMB Review; Comment request (pertaining to reporting outcome and assessment information set (OASIS) data set as a condition of participation for HHAs).

65 FR 8722, February 22, 2000: Medicaid Program; Additional Comment Period for the Schedules of Per-visit and Per-beneficiary Limitations on Home Health Agency Costs for Cost Reporting Periods Beginning on or after October 1, 1999, and Portions of Cost Reporting Periods Beginning October 1, 2000 — Notice of an additional 15-day comment period.

65 FR 8722, February 22, 2000: Medicare and Medicaid Programs; Re-approval of the Deeming Authority of the Joint Commission on Accreditation of Healthcare Organizations (JCAHO) for Home Health Agencies (HHAs) — Final notice.

65 FR 8725, February 22, 2000: Medicare and Medicaid Programs; Reapproval of the Deeming Authority of the Community Health Accreditation Program, Incorporated (CHAP) for Home Health Agencies (HHAs) — Final notice.

65 FR 24217, April 25, 2000: HCFA Agency Information Collection Activities: Submission for OMB Review; Comment request (pertaining to home health advance beneficiary notices).

65 FR 24400, April 26, 2000: Office of Inspector General; Health Care Programs: Fraud and Abuse; Revised OIG Civil Money Penalties Resulting from Public Law 104-191 (HIPAA) — Final rule affecting 42 CFR Parts 1001, 1003, 1005, and 1006. See also correction at 65 FR 35583, June 5, 2000.

65 FR 34986, June 1, 2000: Office of Inspector General; Privacy Act; Implementation (exempting the Healthcare Integrity and Protection Data Bank under Section 1128C of the Social Security Act from certain provisions of the Privacy Act (5 U.S.C.A. 552a) — Final rule affecting 45 CFR Part 5b.

65 FR 35652, June 5, 2000: HCFA Agency Information Collection Activities: Proposed Collection; Comment request (pertaining to home health agency cost reports).

65 FR 41128, July 3, 2000: Medicare Program; Prospective Payment System for Home Health Agencies — Final rule affecting 42 CFR Parts 409, 410, 411, 413, 424, and 484. See also correction at 66 FR 32777, June 18, 2001.

65 FR 42021, July 7, 2000: HCFA Agency Information Collection Activities: Proposed Collection; Comment request (pertaining to notice to providers, suppliers, and practitioners about non-covered services to beneficiaries).

65 FR 45091, July 20, 2000: HCFA Intent of Emergency Clearance: Public Information Collection Meeting to Discuss Requirements to Be Resubmitted to the Office of Management and Budget (OMB) Concerning the Home Health Agency Beneficiary Notices).

65 FR 50713, August 21, 2000: HCFA Agency Information Collection Activities: Proposed Collection; Comment request (pertaining to home health services under hospital insurance manual).

65 FR 53963, September 6, 2000: Medicare Program: Appeals of Carrier Determinations that a Physician or Other Supplier Fails to Meet the Requirements for Medicare Billing Privileges; Reopening of Comment Period — Notice of reopening of comment period for proposed rule affecting 42 CFR Part 405.

65 FR 59858, October 6, 2000: HCFA Notice of Extension of Emergency Office of Management and Budget Clearance of Agency Information Collection Activities (pertaining to notices and demand bills from home health agencies).

65 FR 60366, October 11, 2000: Medicare Program; Additional Supplier Standards — Final rule with comment period, affecting 42 CFR Part 424.

65 FR 64227, October 26, 2000: HCFA Agency Information Collection Activities: Proposed Collection; Comment Request; Public Information Collection Meeting to Discuss Proposed Revisions (pertaining to notice requirements from suppliers, physicians, and practitioners to beneficiaries when Medicare Part B payment may be denied).

65 FR 65860, November 2, 2000: HCFA Agency Information Collection Activities: Proposed Collection; Comment request (pertaining to reporting outcome and assessment (OASIS) data as part of conditions of participation for home health agencies).

2001

66 FR 1996, January 10, 2001: HCFA Agency Information Collection Activities; Comment request (pertaining to Medicare uniform institutional provider bill for reimbursement of covered services by all providers that accept assignment of claims).

66 FR 1997, January 10, 2001: HCFA Notice of OMB Approval (pertaining to uniform home health advance beneficiary notice).

66 FR 2912, January 12, 2001: HCFA Agency Information Collection Activities: Proposed Collection; Comment request (pertaining to Medicare/Medicaid health insurance common claim form).

66 FR 8807, February 2, 2001: HCFA Agency Information Collection Activities: Proposed Collection; Comment request (pertaining to Medicare Federal health care programs provider/supplier enrollment application).

66 FR 13327, March 5, 2001: HCFA Agency Information Activities Collection Activities: Submission for OMB Review; Comment request (pertaining to home health agency cost report form).

66 FR 13547, March 6, 2001: HCFA Agency Information Collection Activities: Proposed Collection; Comment request (pertaining to hospice request for certification as a provider).

66 FR 18645, April 10, 2001: HCFA Agency Information Collection Activities: Submission for OMB Review; Comment request (pertaining to Medicare and Medicaid outcome and assessment information set (OASIS) as part of the conditions of participation for home health agencies).

66 FR 18646, April 10, 2001: HCFA Agency Information Collection Activities: Submission for OMB Review; Comment request (pertaining to Medicare/Medicaid health insurance common claim form).

66 FR 18959, April 12, 2001: HCFA Agency Information Collection Activities: Submission for OMB Review; Comment request (pertaining to home health services under Part A).

66 FR 19507, April 16, 2001: HCFA Agency Information Collection Activities: Proposed Collection; Comment request (pertaining to conflict of interest and ownership and control information form).

66 FR 20316, April 20, 2001: HCFA Agency Information Collection Activities: Submission for OMB Review; Comment request (pertaining to advance beneficiary notice by physicians, practitioners, suppliers, and providers about items and services denied by Medicare as not reasonable and necessary).

66 FR 20997, April 26, 2001: HCFA Agency Information Collection Activities: Submission for OMB Review; Comment request (pertaining to health insurance provider agreement form).

66 FR 21770, May 1, 2001: HCFA Agency Information Collection Activities: Submission for OMB Review; Comment request (pertaining to Medicare uniform institutional provider bill form).

66 FR 33102, June 20, 2001: HCFA Agency Information Collection Activities; Submission for OMB Review; Comment request (pertaining to provider/supplier enrollment application form).

See § 2:59.

§ 6:60 FAILURE BY A HOME HEALTH AGENCY TO COMPLY WITH MEDICARE CONDITIONS OF PARTICIPATION — Sections 1891(e) and (f) [42 U.S.C.A. 1395bbb(e)and (f)]

Regulations

42 CFR Part 402 — Civil Money Penalties, Assessments, and Exclusions

42 CFR Part 409 — Hospital Insurance Benefits, Subpart E — Home Health Services under Hospital Insurance

42 CFR Part 410 — Supplementary Medical Insurance (SMI) Benefits, Subpart C — Home Health Services under SMI

42 CFR Part 424 — Conditions for Medicare Payment

42 CFR Part 440 — Services: General Provisions [Medicaid]

42 CFR Part 441 — Services: Requirements and Limits Applicable to Specific Services [Medicaid]

42 CFR Part 466 — Utilization and Quality Control Review

42 CFR Part 484 — Conditions of Participation: Home Health Agencies

42 CFR Part 488 — Survey, Certification and Enforcement Procedures

42 CFR Part 489 — Provider Agreements and Supplier Approval

42 CFR Part 498 — Appeals Procedures for Determinations that Affect Participation in the Medicare Program and for Determinations that Affect the Participation of ICF's/MR and Certain NF's in the Medcaid Program

42 CFR Chapter V — Office of Inspector General — Health Care, Department of Health and Human Services

Subchapter A — General Provisions

Part 1000 — Introduction; General Definitions

Subchapter B — OIG Authorities

Part 1001 — Program Integrity: Medicare and State Health Care Programs

Part 1002 — Program Integrity: State–initiated Exclusion from Medicaid

Part 1003 — Civil Money Penalties, Assessments and Exclusions

Part 1004 — Imposition of Sanctions on Health Care Practitioners and Providers of Health Care Services by a Peer Review Organization

Part 1005 — Appeals of Exclusions, Civil Money Penalties and Assessments

Part 1006 — Investigational Inquiries

Part 1007 — State Medicaid Fraud Control Units

Part 1008 — Advisory Opinions by the OIG

53 FR 46015, November 15, 1988: Medicare Program; Schedule of Limits on Home Health Agency Costs Per Visit for Cost Reporting on or after July 1, 1988 — Correction. See also correction and notice with comment period at 53 FR 3685, January 25, 1989.

54 FR 33354, August 14, 1989: Medicare Program; Home Health Agencies: Conditions of Participation and Reduction in Recordkeeping Requirements — Interim final rule with comment period, to amend and redesignate 42 CFR Part 405, Subpart L as 42 CFR Part 484. See also correction at 54 FR 35131, August 23, 1989.

56 FR 12934, March 28, 1991: Medicare Program; Schedule of Limits on Home Health Agency Costs Per Visit for Cost Reporting Periods Beginning on or after July 1, 1989 — Final notice. See also correction published at 56 FR 14424, April 9, 1991.

56 FR 30927, July 8, 1991: Privacy Act of 1974; Report of New System (re Quality Assurance for the Home Health Agency (HHA) Prospective Payment Demonstration) — Notice.

56 FR 32967, July 18, 1991: Medicare Program; Home Health Agencies: Conditions of Participation — Final rule. See also correction at 56 FR 51334, October 11, 1991, affecting 42 CFR Part 484.

56 FR 37054, August 2, 1991: Medicare and Medicaid Programs; Survey and Enforcement Requirements and Alternative Sanctions for Home Health Agencies — Proposed rule affecting 42 CFR Parts 441, 488, and 489.

56 FR 43929, September 5, 1991: Medicare and Medicaid Programs; Recognition of the Community Health Accreditation Program Standards for Home Care Organizations — Proposed notice.

56 FR 49154, September 27, 1991: Medicare Program; Medicare Coverage of Home Health Services, Medicare Conditions of Participation, and Home Health Aide Supervision —Proposed rule affecting 42 CFR Parts 409, 418, and 484.

56 FR 50542, October 7, 1991: Medicare Program; "Confined to the Home" Requirements for Home Health Services— Proposed rule affecting 42 CFR Part 409.

56 FR 64256, December 9, 1991: Medicare Program; Schedule of Limits on Home Health Agency Costs Per Visit for Cost Reporting Periods Beginning On or After July 1, 1991—Notice with comment period. See also correction at 57 FR 749, January 8, 1992.

57 FR 4044, February 3, 1992: Medicare Program; Recognition of the Joint Commission of the Accreditation of Healthcare Organizations' Standards for Home Care Organizations—Proposed notice.

57 FR 22773, May 29, 1992: Medicare Program; Recognition of Community Health Accreditation Program Standards for Home Care Organizations—Final notice.

57 FR 29142, June 30, 1992: Medicaid Program; Home and Community-Based Services Waivers for Individuals Age 65 or Older—Interim final rule with comment period, affecting 42 CFR Parts 400, 435, 436, 440, and 441.

57 FR 29325, July 1, 1992: HCFA Public Information Collection Requirements Submitted to the Office of Management and Budget for Clearance (pertaining to outpatient physical therapy and/or speech pathology services; conditions of coverage for organ procurement organizations; and home and community-based services waiver requirements for individuals age 65 or older).

57 FR 29410, July 1, 1992: Medicare Program; Schedule of Limits on Home Health Agency Costs Per Visit for Cost Reporting Periods Beginning on or after July 1, 1992, affecting 42 CFR Part 413.

57 FR 32798, July 23, 1992: HCFA Public Information Collection Requirements Submitted to the Office of Management and Budget for Clearance (pertaining to attending physician's certification of medical necessity for home oxygen therapy).

57 FR 43462, September 21, 1992: Health Care Financing Administration Public Information Collection Requirements Submitted to the Office of Management and Budget for Clearance (pertaining to sole community home health agencies; physician/supplier overpayment reports; physician or supplier Medicare agreements; conditions of participation for rural health clinics; Medicare provider refunds; conditions of participation for comprehensive outpatient

rehabilitation facilities; Medicaid income and eligibility verification system; Medicaid integrated review schedule; provider overpayment report; financial statement of Medicare provider debtors; negative case action review schedule for Medicaid quality control; outpatient resource costing study; Medicaid intermediate care facility for the mentally retarded or persons with related conditions survey report form; installment agreement of beneficiary refund of overpayment; PRO assumption of responsibilities; Medicare contractor administrative budget and cost reporting system forms; fire safety survey report forms; medical records review under prospective payment system; and Qualified Medicare Beneficiary supplement to the Medicare current beneficiary survey).

57 FR 46362, October 8, 1992: Medicare and Medicaid Programs; Revised Effective Date of Medicare/Medicaid Provider Agreement and Supplier Participation — Proposed rule affecting 42 CFR Parts 431, 440, 442, 488, 489, and 498.

57 FR 46865, October 13, 1992: HCFA Public Information Collection Requirements Submitted to the Office of Management and Budget for Clearance (pertaining to impact of home health care plan management and evaluation; end-stage renal disease medical case review; Medicare/Medicaid hospital swing-bed survey report form; quarterly Medicaid statement of expenditures; Medicaid program budget report; information collection requirements in final peer review organization sanction regulations; appeals procedures for determinations that affect participation in Medicare; request for medical review information for Part B intermediary outpatient therapy bills and other Part B outpatient bills; and Medicaid limitations on provider-related donations and health care-related taxes, and limitations on payment to disproportionate share hospitals).

58 FR 21174, April 19, 1993: HCFA Public Information Collection Requirements Submitted to the Office of Management and Budget for Clearance re end stage renal disease survey forms; municipal health services cost reports forms; advance directives; withholding Medicare payments to recover Medicaid overpayments; home office cost statements; and statistical report on medical care.

58 FR 36748, July 8, 1993: Medicare Program; Schedule of Limits on Home Health Agency Costs Per Visit for Cost Reporting Periods Beginning on or After July 1, 1993 — Notice with comment period.

58 FR 38579, July 19, 1993: HCFA Public Information Collection Requirements Submitted to the Office of Management and Budget (OMB) for Clearance re survey of home health agencies; CLIA survey

report form; validation of state surveys; Medicaid listing of participating home health agencies; financial information regarding Medicare benefits from Medicare contractors; and third-party liability under Medicaid.

58 FR 46198, September 1, 1993: HCFA Public Information Collection Requirements (ICR) Submitted to the Office of Management and Budget (OMB) for Clearance (pertaining to prenatal services and assistance screening; home health agency treatment forms; conditions of participation for intermediate care facilities for the mentally retarded; State Medicaid eligibility quality control sample selection lists; prepaid health plan cost report; hospital survey report form; procedures for determining whether providers, practitioners, or other suppliers of services are liable for certain noncovered services; Medicare credit balance reporting requirements; Medicare provider cost report questionnaire form; Medicare current beneficiary survey rounds 7-10; sterilization regulation/consent form; PRO reconsideration and appeals information requirements; information collection requirements in HSQ-110, acquisition, protection and disclosure of PRO information; Medicare/Medicaid organ procurement organization's (OPO) request for certification)—Notice.

58 FR 59270, November 8, 1993: HCFA Public Information Collection Requirements Submitted to the Office of Management and Budget (OMB) for Clearance (pertaining to formats for utilization and quality control peer review organizations (PROs); home health agency plan of treatment forms; State survey agency budget expenditure report and certification workload report; home health agency cost report; recordkeeping requirements in provider reimbursement manual; quarterly Medicaid statement of expenditures; Medicare contract application for Federally qualified health maintenance organizations; hospice survey and deficiencies report form; organ procurement agency/histocompatibility laboratory statement of reimbursable costs)—Notice.

58 FR 60204, November 15, 1993: HCFA Public Information Collection Requirements Submitted to the Office of Management and Budget (OMB) for Clearance (pertaining to procedures for transmitting information between Medicare carriers and Medicare supplemental insurers; Medicare physician or supplier agreement; patient intake data form for the National Home Health Agency; agency characteristics form for the National Home Health Agency prospective payment demonstration; intake and assessment survey

package for the community nursing organization demonstration; comprehensive outpatient rehabilitation facility (CORF eligibility and survey forms and information collection requirements) — Notice.

59 FR 760, January 6, 1994: Medicare Program; Elimination of Additional Payments for Administrative and General Costs of Hospital-Based Home Health Agencies — Final notice with comment period.

59 FR 41330, August 11, 1994: HCFA Public Information Collection Requirements Submitted to the Office of Management and Budget (OMB) for Clearance (pertaining to home dialysis forms, patient drug utilization data, and home health agency reimbursement).

59 FR 50762, October 5, 1994: HCFA Public Information Collection Requirements Submitted to the Office of Management and Budget (OMB) for Clearance (pertaining to reimbursement of hospital costs for residents and interns, criteria for psychiatric and rehabilitation hospital units' reimbursement under the prospective payment system, disclosure of owners and managers of suppliers for fraud and abuse detection purposes, reimbursement of municipal health services clinics, survey form for hospital compliance with anti-dumping requirements, and evaluation of patient and physician satisfaction with the Medicare participating heart bypass center demonstration).

59 FR 65482, December 20, 1994: Medicare Program; Medicare Coverage of Home Health Services, Medicare Conditions of Participation, and Home Health Aide Supervision — Final rule affecting 42 CFR Parts 409, 413, 418, and 484. See also correction at 60 FR 39122, August 1, 1995.

60 FR 7774, February 9, 1995: HCFA Public Information Collection Requirements Submitted to the Office of Management and Budget (OMB) for Clearance (pertaining to justification for ESRD composite rates for outpatient dialysis services, and home health agency compliance with health and safety requirements).

60 FR 8389, February 14, 1995: Medicare Program; Schedule of Limits on Home Health Agency Costs Per Visit — Notice with comment period.

60 FR 12770, March 8, 1995: HCFA Public Information Collection Requirements Submitted to the Office of Management and Budget (OMB) for Clearance (pertaining to survey forms for compliance with CLIA; CLIA application forms for testing on human specimens, and

forms for outcome-based quality assurance programs for home health agencies).

60 FR 21525, May 2, 1995: HCFA Public Information Collection Requirements Submitted to the Office of Management and Budget (OMB) for Clearance (pertaining to intermediary requests for information from skilled nursing facilities, reimbursement for CLIA compliance surveys, patient outcome data in home health agencies, common claim forms for Medicare/Medicaid reimbursement, and a study of childhood immunization costs).

60 FR 40847, August 10, 1995: Office of Inspector General: Publication of OIG Special Fraud Alerts: Home Health Fraud, and Fraud and Abuse in the Provision of Medical Supplies to Nursing Facilities — Notice.

60 FR 62237, December 5, 1995: Medicare Program; Uniform Electronic Cost Reporting for Skilled Nursing Facilities and Home Health Agencies — Proposed rule affecting 42 CFR Part 413.

60 FR 64167, December 14, 1995: HCFA Public Information Collection Requirements Submitted for Public Comment and Recommendations (pertaining to home health care; Medicare/Medicaid certification of physical therapy and speech pathology services; certification as suppliers of Portable X-ray Services; certification of organ procurement organizations; certification for physical therapists in independent practice; and approval as a hospital provider of extended care services (swing bed)).

61 FR 7012, February 23, 1996: HCFA Notice Submitted for Collection of Public Comment: Submission for OMB Review (pertaining to granting and withdrawing of deeming authority to private non-profit Accreditation organizations and the Clinical Laboratory Improvement Act Exemption under State laboratory programs; and the rules for participation of home health agencies to participate as sole community home health agencies).

61 FR 14798, April 3, 1996: HCFA Agency Information Collection Activities: Proposed Collection; Comment Request (pertaining to statistical reports on medical care eligibility, payments and services under Medicaid; State survey agency lists of positions and schedule of equipment purchases; granting and withdrawing of deeming authority to national accreditation organizations; maximizing the effectiveness of home health care; requests for certification in the Medicare or Medicaid program to provide outpatient physical therapy and/or speech pathology services; physical therapists in independent practice; requests for provider approval as a hospital

provider of extended care services (swing bed) under Medicare and Medicaid; and requests for designation as an organ procurement organization).

61 FR 25229, May 20, 1996: HCFA Agency Information Collection Activities: Proposed Collection; Comment Request (pertaining to evaluation of the Oregon reform demonstration; evaluation of the per-episode home health prospective payment demonstration; and the blood bank inspection checklist instrument used by State agencies to determine compliance with CLIA).

61 FR 32347, June 24, 1996: Medicare and Medicaid Programs; Provider Appeals: Technical Amendments — Final rule with comment period, affecting 42 CFR Parts 405, 417, 431, 473, and 498.

61 FR 34344, July 1, 1996: Medicare Program: Schedule of Limits on Home Health Agency Costs Per Visit for Cost Reporting Periods Beginning on or after July 1, 1996: Notice with comment period.

61 FR 49271, September 19, 1996: Medicare Program; Part B Advance Payments to Suppliers Furnishing Items or Services under Medicare Part B — Final rule affecting 42 CFR Part 421.

61 FR 56963, November 5, 1996: HCFA Agency Information Collection Activities: Proposed Collection; Comment request (pertaining to geographic adjustment factors for existing payment localities used in calculating the Medicare fee schedule; demonstration project to test capitated payments for home health services, medical devices, durable medical equipment, and certain ambulatory care under Medicare; and certification of medical necessity forms for durable medical equipment and supplies).

62 FR 26, January 2, 1997: Medicare Program; Electronic Cost Reporting for Skilled Nursing Facilities and Home Health Agencies — Final Rule. See also correction at 62 FR 27210, May 19, 1997.

62 FR 5632, February 6, 1997: HCFA Agency Information Collection Activities: Proposed Collection; Comment request (pertaining to data collection for a project to develop a case-mix adjustment system for a national home health prospective payment program).

62 FR 7350, February 19, 1997: Office of Inspector General: Medicare and State Health Care Programs: Fraud and Abuse; Issuance of Advisory Opinions by the OIG — Interim final rule with comment period, affecting 42 CFR Part 1008.

62 FR 8744, February 26, 1997: HCFA Agency Information Collection Activities: Submission for OMB Review; Comment request (pertaining to Medicare provider/supplier enrollment application).

62 FR 11004, March 10, 1997: Medicare and Medicaid Programs; Revision of the Conditions of Participation for Home Health Agencies and Use of the Outcome and Assessment Information Set (OASIS) as Part of the Revised Conditions of Participation for Home Health Agencies — Introduction to proposed rules, affecting 42 CFR Part 484.

62 FR 11005, March 10, 1997: Medicare and Medicaid Programs; Conditions of Participation for Home Health Agencies — Proposed rule affecting 42 CFR Part 484. See also correction at 62 FR 11953, March 13, 1997.

62 FR 11035, March 10, 1997: Medicare and Medicaid Programs; Use of the OASIS as Part of the Conditions of Participation for Home Health Agencies — Proposed rule.

62 FR 13389, March 20, 1997: HCFA Agency Information Collection Activities: Proposed Collection; Comment request (pertaining to home health agency cost report form).

62 FR 19582, April 22, 1997: HCFA Emergency Clearance: Public Information Collection Requirements Submitted to the Office of Management and Budget (pertaining to attending physicians' certification of medical necessity for home oxygen therapy).

62 FR 23140, April 29, 1997: Office of Inspector General: Health Care Programs: Fraud and Abuse; Revised PRO Sanctions for Failing to Meet Statutory Obligations — Final rule.

62 FR 29730, June 2, 1997: HCFA Agency Information Collection Activities: Submission for OMB Review; Comment request (pertaining to home health agency cost reports).

62 FR 39848, July 24, 1997: HCFA Agency Information Collection Activities; Proposed Collection; Comment request (pertaining to home health certification and plan of care forms for reimbursement; and Medicare/Medicaid disclosure of ownership and control forms).

62 FR 43931, August 18, 1997: Medicare and Medicaid Programs: Effective Dates of Provider Agreements and Supplier Approvals — Final rule affecting 42 CFR Parts 431, 442, 488, 489, and 498.

62 FR 45672, August 28, 1997: HCFA Agency Information Collection Activities: Proposed Collection; Comment request (pertaining to conditions of participation for home health agencies; and negative case action review process annual reports for States).

62 FR 51874, October 3, 1997: HCFA Agency Information Collection Activities: Submission for OMB Review; Comment request (pertaining to home health services certification and plan of care).

62 FR 55410, October 24, 1997: Office of Inspector General: Criteria for Implementing Permissive Exclusion Authority under Section 1128(b)(7) of the Social Security Act — Notice.

62 FR 65049, December 10, 1997: Office of Inspector General: Solicitation of New Safe Harbors and Special Fraud Alerts — Notice of intent to develop regulations, affecting 42 CFR Part 1001.

62 FR 66376, December 18, 1997: HCFA Emergency Clearance: Public Information Collection Requirements Submitted to the Office of Management and Budget (OMB) (pertaining to Medicare and other Federal health care program enrollment forms for providers and suppliers).

63 FR 89, January 2, 1998: Medicare Program; Schedule of Limits on Home Health Agency Costs Per Visit for Cost Reporting Periods Beginning on or after October 1, 1997 — Notice with comment period.

63 FR 291, January 5, 1998: Medicare and Medicaid Programs; Surety Bond and Capitalization Requirements for Home Health Agencies; Final rule affecting 42 CFR Parts 413, 440, 441, and 489.

63 FR 2926, January 20, 1998: Medicare Program; Additional Supplier Standards — Proposed rule affecting 42 CFR Part 424.

63 FR 5958, February 5, 1998: HCFA Agency Information Collection Activities: Proposed Collection; Comment request (pertaining to quality assurance for phase II of the home agency prospective payment demonstration).

63 FR 7743, February 17, 1998: Medicare and Medicaid Programs; Hospital Conditions of Participation; Provider Agreements and Supplier Approval — Notice of extension of comment period, affecting 42 CFR Parts 416, 482, 485, and 489.

63 FR 10730, March 4, 1998: Medicare and Medicaid Programs; Surety Bond Requirements for Home Health Agencies — Final rule affecting 42 CFR Parts 441 and 489.

63 FR 10732, March 4, 1998: Medicare and Medicaid Programs; Surety Bond Requirements for Home Health Agencies — Notice of Intent to Amend Regulations.

63 FR 10920, March 5, 1998: HCFA Emergency Clearance: Public Information Collection Requirements Submitted to the Office of Management and Budget (OMB) (pertaining to Medicare and other Federal health care program provider and supplier application forms).

63 FR 15718, March 31, 1998: Medicare Program; Schedule of Per-beneficiary Limitations on Home Health Agency Costs for Cost

Reporting Periods Beginning on or after October 1, 1997— Final rule with comment period, affecting 42 CFR Part 413.

63 FR 16563, April 3, 1998: HCFA Agency Information Collection Activities: Submission for OMB Review; Comment request (pertaining to quality assurance for phase II of the home agency prospective payment demonstration).

63 FR 17877, April 10, 1998: HCFA Agency Information Collection Activities: Proposed Collection; Comment request (pertaining to home health agency cost reports).

63 FR 19502, April 20, 1998: HCFA Agency Information Collection Activities: Proposed Collection; Comment request (pertaining to Medicare home health quality assurance demonstration).

63 FR 19502, April 20, 1998: HCFA Agency Information Collection Activities: Proposed collection; Comment request (pertaining to annual early and periodic screening, diagnostic, and treatment services (EPSDT) participation report; Medicare and other health care programs provider/supplier enrollment application; and research and analytic support for implementing performance measurement in Medicare fee for service).

63 FR 29648, June 1, 1998: Medicare and Medicaid Programs; Surety Bond Requirements for Home Health Agencies — Final rule affecting 42 CFR Parts 441 and 489.

63 FR 38414, July 16, 1998: HCFA Privacy Act of 1974; Report of Altered System (pertaining to disclosure of individual-specific information to combat fraud or abuse in health benefit programs).

63 FR 38839, July 20, 1998: HCFA Agency Information Collection Activities: Submission for OMB Review; Comment request (pertaining to Medicare home health quality assurance demonstration).

63 FR 41170, July 31, 1998: Medicare and Medicaid Programs; Surety Bond Requirements for Home Health Agencies — Final rule affecting 42 CFR Parts 441 and 489.

63 FR 42410, August 7, 1998: Office of Inspector General: Publication of the OIG Compliance Program Guidance for Home Health Agencies — Notice.

63 FR 42912, August 11, 1998: Medicare Program; Schedules of Per-visit and Per-beneficiary Limitations on Home Health Agency Costs for Cost Reporting Periods Beginning on or after October 1, 1998 — Notice with comment period. See also correction at 63 FR 57698, October 28, 1998.

63 FR 48734, September 11, 1998: HCFA Agency Information Collection Activities: Proposed Collection; Comment request (per-

taining to medical review activities under PPS by Peer Review Organizations; and survey and deficiency reports for home health agencies).

63 FR 63478, November 13, 1998: HCFA Agency Information Collection Activities: Proposed Collection; Comment request (pertaining to processing Medicare+Choice disenrollment requests from beneficiaries; creation of the Utilization and Quality Control Peer Review Organization; and rules for participation of HHA's in Medicare and review of plans of care for home health services).

63 FR 65601, November 27, 1998: HCFA Agency Information Collection Activities: Submission for OMB Review; Comment request (pertaining to medical records review under PPS; and home health agency survey and deficiencies reports, and home health functional assessment instruments).

1999

64 FR 1813, January 12, 1999: Office of Inspector General Publication of OIG Special Fraud Alert on Physician Liability for Certifications in the Provision of Medical Equipment and Supplies and Home Health Services — Notice.

64 FR 2228, January 13, 1999: Office of Inspector General: Solicitation of Information and Recommendations for Developing OIG Compliance Program Guidance for the Hospice Industry — Notice.

64 FR 6665, February 10, 1999: HCFA Agency Information Collection Activities: Proposed Collection; Comment request (pertaining to sole community home health agencies (HHS)).

64 FR 10305, March 3, 1999: HCFA Agency Information Collection Activities: Proposed Collection; Comment request (pertaining to attending physician's certification of medical necessity for home oxygen therapy).

64 FR 13997, March 23, 1999: HCFA Agency Information Collection Activities: Submission for OMB Review; Comment request (pertaining to Medicare and Medicaid requirements for advanced directives, and disclosure of ownership and financial control interest).

64 FR 17673, April 12, 1999: HCFA Agency Information Collection Activities: Proposed Collection; Comment request (pertaining to Medicare participating physician or supplier agreements).

64 FR 23846, May 4, 1999: HCFA Emergency Clearance: Public Information Collection Requirements Submitted to the Office of

Management and Budget (OMB) (pertaining to the outcome and assessment information set (OASIS) for home health care agencies).

64 FR 24956, May 10, 1999: Medicare and Medicaid Programs; Effective Dates of Provider Agreements and Supplier Approvals-Correction restoring regulations inadvertently removed when a final rule concerning effective dates for provider agreements and supplier approvals was published at 62 FR 43931, August 18, 1997.

64 FR 32984, June 18, 1999: Medicare and Medicaid Programs; Mandatory Use, Collection, Encoding, and Transmission of Outcome and Assessment Information Set (OASIS) for Home Health Agencies — Notice.

64 FR 32992, June 18, 1999: HCFA Privacy Act of 1974; Report of New System (pertaining to a new system of records containing data on the physical, mental, functional, and psychosocial status of all patients receiving the services of home health agencies (HHAs) approved to participate in Medicare or Medicaid).

64 FR 36887, July 8, 1999: HCFA Agency Information Collection Activities: Proposed Collection; Comment request (pertaining to reporting outcome and assessment information data set (OASIS) as part of the conditions of participation for home health agencies).

64 FR 38203, July 15, 1999: HCFA Agency Information Collection Activities: Submission for OMB Review; Comment request (pertaining to attending physician's certification of medical necessity for home oxygen therapy).

64 FR 39517, July 22, 1999: HCFA Agency Information Collection Activities: Submission for OMB Review; Comment request (pertaining to Medicare participating physician or supplier agreement form HCFA-460).

64 FR 42766, August 5, 1999: Medicare Program; Schedules of Per-visit and Per-Beneficiary Limitations on Home Health Agency Costs for Cost Reporting Periods Beginning on or after October 1, 1999, and Portions of Cost Reporting Periods Beginning before October 1, 2000 — Notice with comment period. See also correction at 64 FR 57101, October 22, 1999.

64 FR 49197, September 10, 1999: Medicare and Medicaid Programs; Application of the Joint Commission for Accreditaton of Healthcare Organizations (JCAHO) for Continued Approval of Deeming Authority for Home Health Agencies — Proposed notice.

64 FR 49198, September 10, 1999: Medicare and Medicaid Programs; Application of the Community Health Accreditation

Program, Incorporated, CHAP) for Continued Approval of Deeming Authority for Home Health Agencies — Proposed notice.

64 FR 51328, September 22, 1999: HCFA Emergency Clearance: Public Information Collection Requirements Submitted to the Office of Management and Budget (OMB) (pertaining to the obligation of home health agencies to give beneficiaries advance written notice of noncovered care or of reducing or terminating ongoing care).

64 FR 57431, October 25, 1999: Medicare Program; Appeals of Carrier Determinations that a Supplier Fails to Meet the Requirements for Medicare Billing Privileges — Proposed rule affecting 42 CFR Part 405.

64 FR 57612, October 26, 1999: Medicare Program; Open Town Hall Meeting on November 8, 1999, to Present and Overview of the Home Health Prospective Payment System Proposed Rule Followed by a General Home Health Listening Session — Notice of Meeting.

64 FR 58134, October 28, 1999: Medicare Program; Prospective Payment System for Home Health Agencies — Proposed rule affecting 42 CFR Parts 409, 410, 411, 413, 424, and 484.

2000

65 FR 135, January 3, 2000: HCFA Agency Information Collection Activities: proposed Collection; Comment request (pertaining to home health advance beneficiary notices). See also correction at 65 FR 2967, January 19, 2000.

65 FR 1400, January 10, 2000: HCFA Agency Information Collection Activities: Submission for OMB Review; Comment request (pertaining to reporting outcome and assessment information set (OASIS) data set as a condition of participation for HHAs).

65 FR 8722, February 22, 2000: Medicaid Program; Additional Comment Period for the Schedules of Per-visit and Per-beneficiary Limitations on Home Health Agency Costs for Cost Reporting Periods Beginning on or after October 1, 1999, and Portions of Cost Reporting Periods Beginning October 1, 2000 — Notice of an additional 15-day comment period.

65 FR 8722, February 22, 2000: Medicare and Medicaid Programs; Re-approval of the Deeming Authority of the Joint Commission on Accreditation of Healthcare Organizations (JCAHO) for Home Health Agencies (HHAs) — Final notice.

65 FR 8725, February 22, 2000: Medicare and Medicaid Programs; Reapproval of the Deeming Authority of the Community Health

Accreditation Program, Incorporated (CHAP) for Home Health Agencies (HHAs) — Final notice.

65 FR 24217, April 25, 2000: HCFA Agency Information Collection Activities: Submission for OMB Review; Comment request (pertaining to home health advance beneficiary notices).

65 FR 24400, April 26, 2000: Office of Inspector General; Health Care Programs: Fraud and Abuse; Revised OIG Civil Money Penalties Resulting from Public Law 104-191 (HIPAA) — Final rule affecting 42 CFR Parts 1001, 1003, 1005, and 1006. See also correction at 65 FR 35583, June 5, 2000.

65 FR 34986, June 1, 2000: Office of Inspector General; Privacy Act; Implementation (exempting the Healthcare Integrity and Protection Data Bank under Section 1128C of the Social Security Act from certain provisions of the Privacy Act (5 U.S.C.A. 552a) — Final rule affecting 45 CFR Part 5b.

65 FR 35652, June 5, 2000: HCFA Agency Information Collection Activities: Proposed Collection; Comment request (pertaining to home health agency cost reports).

65 FR 41128, July 3, 2000: Medicare Program; Prospective Payment System for Home Health Agencies — Final rule affecting 42 CFR Parts 409, 410, 411, 413, 424, and 484.

65 FR 42021, July 7, 2000: HCFA Agency Information Collection Activities: Proposed Collection; Comment request (pertaining to notice to providers, suppliers, and practitioners about non-covered services to beneficiaries).

65 FR 45091, July 20, 2000: HCFA Intent of Emergency Clearance: Public Information Collection Meeting to Discuss Requirements to Be Resubmitted to the Office of Management and Budget (OMB) Concerning the Home Health Agency Beneficiary Notices).

65 FR 50713, August 21, 2000: HCFA Agency Information Collection Activities: Proposed Collection; Comment request (pertaining to home health services under hospital insurance manual).

65 FR 53963, September 6, 2000: Medicare Program: Appeals of Carrier Determinations that a Physician or Other Supplier Fails to Meet the Requirements for Medicare Billing Privileges; Reopening of Comment Period — Notice of reopening of comment period for proposed rule affecting 42 CFR Part 405.

65 FR 59858, October 6, 2000: HCFA Notice of Extension of Emergency Office of Management and Budget Clearance of Agency

Information Collection Activities (pertaining to notices and demand bills from home health agencies).

65 FR 60366, October 11, 2000: Medicare Program; Additional Supplier Standards — Final rule with comment period, affecting 42 CFR Part 424.

65 FR 64227, October 26, 2000: HCFA Agency Information Collection Activities: Proposed Collection; Comment Request; Public Information Collection Meeting to Discuss Proposed Revisions (pertaining to notice requirements from suppliers, physicians, and practitioners to beneficiaries when Medicare Part B payment may be denied).

65 FR 65860, November 2, 2000: HCFA Agency Information Collection Activities: Proposed Collection; Comment request (pertaining to reporting outcome and assessment (OASIS) data as part of conditions of participation for home health agencies).

2001

66 FR 1996, January 10, 2001: HCFA Agency Information Collection Activities; Comment request (pertaining to Medicare uniform institutional provider bill for reimbursement of covered services by all providers that accept assignment of claims).

66 FR 1997, January 10, 2001: HCFA Notice of OMB Approval (pertaining to uniform home health advance beneficiary notice).

66 FR 2912, January 12, 2001: HCFA Agency Information Collection Activities: Proposed Collection; Comment request (pertaining to Medicare/Medicaid health insurance common claim form).

66 FR 8807, February 2, 2001: HCFA Agency Information Collection Activities: Proposed Collection; Comment request (pertaining to Medicare Federal health care programs provider/supplier enrollment application).

66 FR 13327, March 5, 2001: HCFA Agency Information Activities Collection Activities: Submission for OMB Review; Comment request (pertaining to home health agency cost report form).

66 FR 13547, March 6, 2001: HCFA Agency Information Collection Activities: Proposed Collection; Comment request (pertaining to hospice request for certification as a provider).

66 FR 18645, April 10, 2001: HCFA Agency Information Collection Activities: Submission for OMB Review; Comment request (pertaining to Medicare and Medicaid outcome and assessment information

set (OASIS) as part of the conditions of participation for home health agencies).

66 FR 18646, April 10, 2001: HCFA Agency Information Collection Activities: Submission for OMB Review; Comment request (pertaining to Medicare/Medicaid health insurance common claim form).

66 FR 18959, April 12, 2001: HCFA Agency Information Collection Activities: Submission for OMB Review; Comment request (pertaining to home health services under Part A).

66 FR 19507, April 16, 2001: HCFA Agency Information Collection Activities: Proposed Collection; Comment request (pertaining to conflict of interest and ownership and control information form).

66 FR 20316, April 20, 2001: HCFA Agency Information Collection Activities: Submission for OMB Review; Comment request (pertaining to advance beneficiary notice by physicians, practitioners, suppliers, and providers about items and services denied by Medicare as not reasonable and necessary).

66 FR 20997, April 26, 2001: HCFA Agency Information Collection Activities: Submission for OMB Review; Comment request (pertaining to health insurance provider agreement form).

66 FR 21770, May 1, 2001: HCFA Agency Information Collection Activities: Submission for OMB Review; Comment request (pertaining to Medicare uniform institutional provider bill form).

66 FR 33102, June 20, 2001: HCFA Agency Information Collection Activities; Submission for OMB Review; Comment request (pertaining to provider/supplier enrollment application form).

See § 2:60.

§ 6:61 OFFSETTING MEDICARE PAYMENTS TO INDIVIDUALS TO COLLECT PAST-DUE OBLIGATIONS ARISING FROM BREACH OF SCHOLARSHIP AND LOAN CONTRACTS — Section 1892 [42 U.S.C.A. 1395ccc]

Regulations

42 CFR Part 401, Subpart F — Claims Collection and Compromise

42 CFR Part 405, Subpart C — Suspension of Payment, Recovery of Overpayments, and Repayment of Scholarships and Loans

42 CFR Part 420 — Program Integrity: Medicare

42 CFR Chapter V — Office of Inspector General — Health Care, Department of Health and Human Services

Subchapter A — General Provisions

Part 1000 — Introduction; General Definitions

Subchapter B — OIG Authorities

Part 1001 — Program Integrity: Medicare

55 FR 46685, November 6, 1990: Medicare Program; Offset Medicare Payments to Individuals to Collect Past-Due Obligations Arising from Breach of Scholarship and Loan Contracts — Proposed rule to amend 42 CFR Part 405.

57 FR 19089, May 4, 1992: Medicare Program; Offset of Medicare Payments to Individuals to Collect Past-Due Obligations Arising From Breach of Scholarship and Loan Contracts — Final rule affecting 42 CFR Part 405.

63 FR 20639, April 27, 1998: HCFA Agency Information Collection Activities: Proposed Collection; Comment request (pertaining to financial reports to evaluate requests from physicians or suppliers to pay debts under extended repayment schedule or to compromise a debt for less than the full amount).

63 FR 36249, July 2, 1998: HCFA Agency Information Collection Activities: Submission for OMB Review; Comment request (pertaining to requests from physicians/suppliers to pay indebtedness under extended repayment schedule, or to compromise a debt for less than the full amount).

2001

66 FR 23944, May 10, 2001: HCFA Agency Information Collection Activities: Proposed Collection; Comment request (pertaining to financial reports for providers indebted to Medicare who want to repay over time).

See § 2:61.

§ 6:62 TERMINATION OF PACE PROVIDER AGREEMENTS — Section 1894 [42 U.S.C. A. 1395eee]

Regulations

42 CFR Part 417 — Health Maintenance Organizations, Competitive Medical Plans, and Health Care Prepayment Plans

42 CFR Part 420 — Program Integrity: Medicare

42 CFR Part 460 — Programs of All–inclusive Care for the Elderly (PACE)

42 CFR Chapter V — Office of Inspector General — Health Care, Department of Health and Human Services

Subchapter A — General Provisions

Part 1000 — Introduction; General Definitions

Subchapter B — OIG Authorities

Part 1001 — Program Integrity: Medicare and State Health Care Programs

Part 1003 — Civil Money Penalties, Assessments and Exclusions

Part 1004 — Imposition of Sanctions on Health Care Practitioners and Providers of Health Care Services by a Peer Review Organization

Part 1005 — Appeals of Exclusions, Civil Money Penalties and Assessments

Part 1006 — Investigational Inquiries

Part 1007 — State Medicaid Fraud Control Units

Part 1008 — Advisory Opinions by the OIG

62 FR 45426, August 27, 1997: HCFA Agency Information Collection Activities: Submission for OMB Review; Comment request (pertaining to qualification applications for competitive medical plans and Federally qualified HMOs).

62 FR 49016, September 18, 1997: HCFA Agency Information Collection Activities: Submission for OMB Review; Comment Request (pertaining to managed care incentive arrangement disclosure forms).

62 FR 51873, October 3, 1997: HCFA Agency Information Collection Activities: Proposed Collection; Comment request (pertaining to survey of primary care givers for the District of Columbia managed care demonstration).

62 FR 66375, December 18, 1997: HCFA Agency Information Collection Activities: Proposed Collection; Comment request (pertaining to ESRD cost report forms; evaluation of the Oregon Medicaid reform demonstration; and qualification of new HMOs and CMPs).

62 FR 66376, December 18, 1997: HCFA Emergency Clearance: Public Information Collection Requirements Submitted to the Office of Management and Budget (OMB) (pertaining to Medicare and other Federal health care program enrollment forms for providers and suppliers).

63 FR 7175, February 12, 1998: HCFA Emergency Clearance: Public Information Collection Requirements Submitted to the Office of Managment and Budget (OMB) (pertaining to managed care adjusted community rate (ACR) proposal).

63 FR 12475, March 13, 1998: HCFA Agency Information Collection Activities; Submission for OMB Review; Comment request

(pertaining to HMO and CMP national data reporting requirements).

63 FR 18924, April 16, 1998: HCFA Emergency Clearance: Public Information Collection Requirements Submitted to the Office of Management and Budget (OMB) (pertaining to collection of managed care data using the uniform institutional providers form).

63 FR 26811, May 14, 1998: Medicare and Medicaid Programs: Request for Public Comments on the Quality Improvement System for Managed Care — Solicitation of comments; notice of public meeting.

63 FR 42409, August 7, 1998: HCFA Agency Information Collection Activities: Proposed Collection; Comment request (pertaining to health plan data and information consumer assessment survey).

63 FR 43187, August 12, 1998: HCFA Privacy Act of 1974; System of Records — Notice of new system of records pertaining to indicators of the performance of health plans.

63 FR 58059, October 29, 1998: HCFA Agency Information Collection Activities: Submission for OMB Review; Comment request (pertaining to consumer assessment of managed care plans).

63 FR 58399, October 30, 1998: Office of Inspector General: Publication of the OIG's Provider Self-Disclosure Protocol — Notice.

1999

64 FR 6664, February 10, 1999: HCFA Agency Information Collection Activities: Proposed Collection; Comment request (pertaining to Medicare agreement applications for health care prepayment plans).

64 FR 25891, May 13, 1999: HCFA Agency Information Collection Activities: Submission for OMB Review; Comment request (pertaining to Medicare agreement application for health care prepayment plans under section 1833).

64 FR 32508, June 17, 1999: HCFA Agency Information Collection Activities: Submission for OMB Review; Comment Request (pertaining to the quality improvement system for managed care (QISMC)).

64 FR 43707, August 11, 1999: HCFA Agency Information Collection Activities: Proposed Collection; Comment request (pertaining to cost reports for prepaid health plans (HMOs and CMPs)).

64 FR 46919, August 27, 1999: HCFA Emergency Clearance: Public Information Collection Requirements Submitted to the Office of Management and Budget (OMB) (pertaining to survey of disenrollment by Medicare beneficiaries from alternative health plans).

64 FR 58418, October 29, 1999: HCFA Agency Information Collection Activities: Proposed Collection; Comment request (pertaining to outcome based continuous quality improvement (OBCQI) approach for the PACE program).

64 FR 66234, November 24, 1999: Medicare and Medicaid Programs; Programs of All-inclusive Care for the Elderly (PACE) — Interim final rule with comment period, affecting 42 CFR Parts 460, 462, 466, 473, and 476.

64 FR 67223, December 1, 1999: Medicaid Program; External Quality Review of Medicaid Managed Care Organizations — Proposed rule affecting 42 CFR Parts 433 and 438.

2000

65 FR 6614, February 10, 2000: HCFA Agency Information Collection Activities: Proposed Collection; Comment request (pertaining to Medicare managed care disenrollment form).

65 FR 8370, February 18, 2000: HCFA Agency Information Collection Activities: Submission for OMB Review; Comment request (pertaining to a project to develop an outcome-based continuous quality improvement system for PACE).

65 FR 16924, March 30, 2000: HCFA Agency Information Collection Activities: Proposed Collection; Comment request (pertaining to a survey of beneficiaries who have disenrolled from their health care services plans).

65 FR 25737, May 3, 2000: HCFA Agency Information Collection Activities: Proposed Collection; Comment request (pertaining to managed care disenrollment form).

65 FR 25738, May 3, 2000: HCFA Emergency Clearance: Public Informatiion Collection Requirements Submitted to the Office of Management and Budget (OMB) (pertaining to the Medicare managed care CAHPS Survey).

65 FR 26618, May 5, 2000: HCFA Emergency Clearance: Public Information Collection Requirements Submitted to the Office of Management and Budget (OMB) (pertaining to Medicare consumer assessment survey of health plans).

65 FR 40111, June 29, 2000: HCFA Agency Information Collection Activities: Proposed Collection; comment request (pertaining to qualification applications for prepaid health plans (HMOs).

65 FR 40668, June 30, 2000: HCFA Agency Information Collection Activities: Submission for OMB Review; Comment request (pertaining to Medicare comprehensive health plan disenrollment).

65 FR 50713, August 21, 2000: HCFA Agency Information Collection Activities: Proposed Collection; Comment request (pertaining to social HMO demonstration payment methodology)

65 FR 53319, September 1, 2000: HCFA Agency Information Collection Activities: Proposed Collection; Comment request (pertaining to incentive arrangement disclosure form for managed care organizations and their related medical groups and physicians).

65 FR 57195, September 21, 2000: HCFA Agency Information Collection Activities; Proposed Collection; Comment request (pertaining to Medicare managed care CAHPS survey for quality of care purposes).

65 FR 79867, December 20, 2000: HCFA Agency Information Collection Activities: Proposed Collection; Comment request (pertaining to quality improvement system for managed care).

65 FR 79868, December 20, 2000: HCFA Agency Information Collection Activities: Proposed Collection; Comment request (pertaining to Medicare consumer assessment survey of health plans).

65 FR 79868, December 20, 2000: HCFA Emergency Clearance: Public Information Collection Requirements Submitted to the Office of Management and Budget (OMB) (pertaining to survey of beneficiaries who involuntarily disenroll from their managed care plan).

2001

66 FR 9586, February 8, 2001: HCFA Agency Information Collection Activities: Proposed Collection; Comment request (pertaining to a project to develop an outcome–based continuous quality improvement system for PACE).

66 FR 9858, February 12, 2001: HCFA Privacy Act of 1974; Report of New System (pertaining to complaints against health insurance issuers and health plans).

66 FR 11546, February 26, 2001: Medicaid Program; Medicaid Managed Care: Delay of Effective Date—Final rule delay, affecting 42 CFR Parts 400, 430, 431, 434, 435, 438, 440, and 447.

66 FR 15122, March 15, 2001: HCFA Agency Information Collection Activities: Submission for OMB Review; Comment request (pertaining to quality improvement system for managed care).

66 FR 16678, March 27, 2001: HCFA Agency Information Collection Activities: Submission for OMB Review; Comment request (pertaining to Medicare managed care CAHPS survey).

66 FR 23945, May 10, 2001: HCFA Agency Information Collection Activities: Submission for OMB Review; Comment request (pertaining to development of an outcome–based continuous quality improvement system for PACE).

66 FR 28916, May 25, 2001: HCFA Agency Information Collection Activities: Proposed Collection; Comment request (pertaining to collection of managed care data using the uniform institutional providers form).

66 FR 32776, June 18, 2001: Medicaid Program; Medicaid Managed Care: Further Delay of Effective Date for Final Rule affecting 42 CFR Parts 400, 430, 431, 434, 435, 438, 440, and 447.

See 2:62.

Chapter 7

REGULATIONS: SANCTIONS IN THE MEDICAID STATUTE

§ 7:1 PUBLICIZING FINDINGS OF STATE SURVEYS OF HEALTH CARE FACILITIES — Section 1902(a)(36) [42 U.S.C.A. 1396a(a)(36)]

Regulations

42 CFR Part 401, Subpart B — Confidentiality and Disclosure

42 CFR Part 402 — Civil Money Penalties, Assessments, and Exclusions

42 CFR Part 405, Subpart U — Conditions for Coverage of Suppliers of End-Stage Renal Disease (ESRD) Services; and Subpart

X — Rural Health Clinic and Federally Qualified Health Center Services

42 CFR Part 411, Subpart J — Physician Ownership of, and Referral of Patients or Laboratory Specimens to, Entities Furnishing Clinical Laboratory or Other Health Services

42 CFR Part 418 — Hospice Care [Medicare]

42 CFR Part 420 — Program Integrity [Medicare]

42 CFR Part 431 — State Organization and General Administration [Medicaid]

42 CFR Part 440 — Services: General Provisions [Medicaid]

42 CFR Part 442 — Standards for Payment for Nursing Facilities and Intermediate Care Facilities for the Mentally Retarded [Medicaid]

42 CFR Part 447 — Payment for Services [Medicaid]

42 CFR Part 455 — Program Integrity [Medicaid]

42 CFR Part 456 — Utilization Control

42 CFR Part 460 — Programs of All–Inclusive Care for the Elderly (PACE)

42 CFR Part 476 — Utilization and Quality Control Review

42 CFR Part 478 — Reconsiderations and Appeals

42 CFR Part 480 — Acquisition, Protection, and Disclosure of Peer Review Information

42 CFR Part 482 — Conditions of Participation for Hospitals [Medicare]

42 CFR Part 483 — Requirements for States and Long Term Care Facilities [Medicare]

42 CFR Part 484 — Conditions of Participation: Home Health Agencies

42 CFR Part 485 — Conditions of Participation and Conditions for Coverage: Specialized Providers and Suppliers

42 CFR Part 486 — Conditions for Coverage of Specialized Services Furnished by Suppliers

42 CFR Part 488 — Survey, Certification, and Enforcement Procedures [Medicare]

42 CFR Part 489 — Provider Agreements and Supplier Approval

42 CFR Part 491 — Certification of Certain Health Facilities

42 CFR Part 493 — Laboratory Requirements

42 CFR Part 498 — Appeals Procedures for Determinations that Affect Participation in the Medicare Program and for Determinations that Affect the Participation of ICF's/MR and Certain NF's in the Medicaid Program

54 FR 5316, February 2, 1989: Medicare and Medicaid; Requirements for Long Term Care Facilities — Final rule with comment period, amending 42 CFR Parts 405, 442, 447, 483, 488, 489, and 498. See also delay in effective date at 54 FR 29717, July 14, 1989; corrections at 54 FR 8361, February 27, 1989, and 54 FR 37466, September 11, 1989; and final rule delaying effective date from January 1, 1990, to October 1, 1990, at 54 FR 53611, December 29, 1989.

54 FR 33354, August 14, 1989: Medicare Program; Home Health Agencies: Conditions of Participation and Reduction in Recordkeeping Requirements — Interim final rule with comment period, amending and redesignating 42 CFR Part 405, Subpart L, as Part 484.

54 FR 35131, August 23, 1989: Medicare Program; Home Health Care Agencies: Conditions of Participation and Reduction in Recordkeeping Requirements — Correction of notice published August 14, 1989.

55 FR 9538, March 14, 1990: Medicare, Medicaid and CLIA Programs; Revision of the Laboratory Regulations for the Medicare, Medicaid, and Clinical Laboratories Improvement Act of 1967 Programs — Final rule with comment period, amending 42 CFR Parts 74, 405, 416, 440, 482, 483, 488, and 493.

55 FR 10256, March 20, 1990: Medicare and Medicaid; Charges to Residents' Funds in Nursing Homes — Proposed rule to amend 42 CFR Part 483. See also final rule at 57 FR 53572, November 12, 1992.

55 FR 10938, March 23, 1990: Medicare and Medicaid Programs; Nurse Aide Training and Competency Evaluation Programs — Proposed rule to amend 42 CFR Parts 431, 433, and 483.

55 FR 10951, March 23, 1990: Medicare and Medicaid Programs; Preadmission Screening and Annual Resident Review — Proposed rule to amend 42 CFR Parts 405, 431, and 483.

55 FR 20896, May 21, 1990: Medicare, Medicaid and CLIA Programs; Regulations Implementing the Clinical Laboratory Improvement Amendments of 1988 (CLIA '88) — Proposed rule. See also extension of time for public comment to September 21, 1990, published at 55 FR 34289 on August 22, 1990.

55 FR 42907, October 24, 1990: Medicare Program; Standards Applied by Utilization and Quality Control Peer Review Organizations: Consideration of Remote Rural Location and Other Relevant Factors — Notice of policy and request for comments.

55 FR 50831, December 11, 1990: Medicare Program; Hospice Care Amendments: Medicare — Final rule with comment period, amends 42 CFR Part 418.

56 FR 13430, April 2, 1991: Medicare and Laboratory Certification Programs; Enforcement Procedures for Laboratories — Proposed rule.

56 FR 30696, July 5, 1991: Medicaid Program; Correction and Reduction Plans for Intermediate Care Facilities for the Mentally Retarded — Final rule affecting 42 CFR Part 442. See also correction at 56 FR 49147, September 27, 1991.

56 FR 32967, July 18, 1991: Medicare Program; Home Health Agencies: Conditions of Participation — Final rule. See also correction at 56 FR 51334, October 11, 1991, affecting 42 CFR Part 484.

56 FR 37054, August 2, 1991: Medicare and Medicaid Programs; Survey and Enforcement Requirements and Alternative Sanctions for Home Health Agencies — Proposed rule affecting 42 CFR Parts 441, 488, and 489.

56 FR 43929, September 5, 1991: Medicare and Medicaid Programs; Recognition of the Community Health Accreditation Program Standards for Home Care Organizations — Proposed notice.

56 FR 46559, September 13, 1991: Medicare Program; Review of Information Collection and Recordkeeping Requirements for Providers of Outpatient Physical Therapy and/or Speech Pathology Services — Final rule affecting 42 CFR Part 405.

56 FR 48112, September 24, 1991: Medicaid Program; Community Supported Living Arrangements Services — Interim final rule with comment period, affecting 42 CFR Part 441.

56 FR 48826, September 26, 1991: Medicare and Medicaid; Requirements for Long Term Care Facilities — Final rule affecting 42 CFR Parts 422, 447, 483, 488, 489, and 498. See also correction at 57 FR 43922, September 23, 1992.

56 FR 48880, September 26, 1991: Medicare and Medicaid Programs; Nurse Aide Training and Competency Evaluation Programs — Final rule affecting 42 CFR Parts 431, 433, and 483. See also correction at 56 FR 59331, November 25, 1991.

56 FR 49154, September 27, 1991: Medicare Program; Medicare Coverage of Home Health Services, Medicare Conditions of Participation, and Home Health Aide Supervision — Proposed rule affecting 42 CFR Parts 409, 418, and 484.

56 FR 50542, October 7, 1991: Medicare Program; "Confined to the Home" Requirements for Home Health Services — Proposed rule affecting 42 CFR Part 409.

57 FR 4044, February 3, 1992: Medicare Program; Recognition of the Joint Commission of the Accreditation of Healthcare Organizations' Standards for Home Care Organizations Proposed notice.

57 FR 4516, February 5, 1992: Medicare and Medicaid Programs; Omnibus Nursing Home Requirements — Proposed rule affecting 42 CFR Parts 418, 440, 441, 482, 483, and 488. See also correction at 57 FR 8961, March 13, 1992.

57 FR 7002, February 28, 1992: Medicare, Medicaid and CLIA Programs; Regulations Implementing the Clinical Laboratory Improvement Amendments of 1988 (CLIA) — Final rule with comment period, affecting 42 CFR Parts 405, 410, 416, 417, 418, 440, 482, 483, 484, 485, 488, 491, 493, and 494. See also correction at 57 FR 35760, August 11, 1992, and correction amendments at 58 FR 5212, January 19, 1993.

57 FR 7188, February 28, 1992: Clinical Laboratory Improvement Act Program Fee Collection — Final rule with comment affecting 42 CFR Part 493. See also correction at 57 FR 31664, July 17, 1992, and correction amendments at 58 FR 5212, January 19, 1993.

57 FR 7218, February 28, 1992: Medicare Program; Medicare and Laboratory Certification Program; Enforcement Procedures for Laboratories — Final rule affecting 42 CFR Part 493. See also correction amendments at 58 FR 5212, January 19, 1993.

57 FR 8194, March 6, 1992: Medicare and Medicaid Programs; Advance Directives — Interim final rule with comment period, affecting 42 CFR Parts 417, 431, 434, 483, 484, 489, and 498.

57 FR 8588, March 11, 1992: Medicare Program; Physician Ownership of, and Referrals to, Health Care Entities that Furnish Clinical Laboratory Services — Proposed rule affecting 42 CFR Part 411.

57 FR 22773, May 29, 1992: Medicare Program; Recognition of Community Health Accreditation Program Standards for Home Care Organizations — Final notice.

57 FR 33992, July 31, 1992: Clinical Laboratories Improvement Act Program; Granting and Withdrawal of Deeming Authority to Private Nonprofit Accreditation Organizations and of CLIA Exemption under State Laboratory Programs — Final rule.

57 FR 39278, August 28, 1992: Medicare and Medicaid Programs; Survey, Certification and Enforcement of Skilled Nursing Facilities

and Nursing Facilities — Proposed rule affecting 42 CFR Parts 431, 442, 488, and 489.

57 FR 43462, September 21, 1992: Health Care Financing Administration Public Information Collection Requirements Submitted to the Office of Management and Budget for Clearance (pertaining to sole community home health agencies; physician/supplier overpayment reports; physician or supplier Medicare agreements; conditions of participation for rural health clinics; Medicare provider refunds; conditions of participation for comprehensive outpatient rehabilitation facilities; Medicaid income and eligibility verification system; Medicaid integrated review schedule; provider overpayment report; financial statement of Medicare provider debtors; negative case action review schedule for Medicaid quality control; outpatient resource costing study; Medicaid intermediate care facility for the mentally retarded or persons with related conditions survey report form; installment agreement of beneficiary refund of overpayment; PRO assumption of responsibilities; Medicare contractor administrative budget and cost reporting system forms; fire safety survey report forms; medical records review under prospective payment system; and Qualified Medicare Beneficiary supplement to the Medicare current beneficiary survey).

57 FR 46362, October 8, 1992: Medicare and Medicaid Programs; Revised Effective Date of Medicare/Medicaid Provider Agreement and Supplier Participation — Proposed rule affecting 42 CFR Parts 431, 440, 442, 488, 489, and 498.

57 FR 46865, October 13, 1992: HCFA Public Information Collection Requirements Submitted to the Office of Management and Budget for Clearance (pertaining to impact of home health care plan management and evaluation; end-stage renal disease medical case review; Medicare/Medicaid hospital swing-bed survey report form; quarterly Medicaid statement of expenditures; Medicaid program budget report; information collection requirements in final peer review organization sanction regulations; appeals procedures for determinations that affect participation in Medicare; request for medical review information for Part B intermediary outpatient therapy bills and other Part B outpatient bills; and Medicaid limitations on provider-related donations and health care-related taxes, and limitations on payment to disproportionate share hospitals).

57 FR 54710, November 20, 1992: Medicaid Program; Elimination of Certain Written Documentation Pertaining to Medicaid Long-Term Care Facilities — Final rule affecting 42 CFR Part 442.

57 FR 56450, November 30, 1992: Medicare and Medicaid Programs; Preadmission Screening and Annual Resident Review — Final rule with comment period, affecting 42 CFR Parts 405, 431, 433, and 483. See also correction published at 58 FR 25784, April 28, 1993.

57 FR 61614, December 28, 1992: Medicare and Medicaid; Resident Assessment in Long Term Care Facilities — Proposed rule affecting 42 CFR Parts 456 and 483.

58 FR 5215, January 19, 1993: Medicare, Medicaid and CLIA Programs; Regulations Implementing the Clinical Laboratory Improvement Amendments of 1988 (CLIA) and Clinical Laboratory Improvement Act Program Fee Collection — Final rule with comment period, affecting 42 CFR Part 493. See also correction published at 58 FR 39154, July 22, 1993.

58 FR 21174, April 19, 1993: HCFA Public Information Collection Requirements Submitted to the Office of Management and Budget for Clearance re end stage renal disease survey forms; municipal health services cost reports forms; advance directives; withholding Medicare payments to recover Medicaid overpayments; home office cost statements; and statistical report on medical care.

58 FR 29416, May 20, 1993: HCFA Public Information Collection Requirements Submitted to the Office of Management and Budget (OMB) for Clearance re cataract surgery; Medicaid utilization management initiatives; Medicare coverage of screening mammography; psychiatric unit criteria worksheet and rehabilitation unit criteria worksheet; Medicare secondary payor forms; ambulatory surgical center survey forms; ambulance service compliance with State and local requirements; and early and periodic screening, diagnostic and treatment reports.

58 FR 38579, July 19, 1993: HCFA Public Information Collection Requirements Submitted to the Office of Management and Budget (OMB) for Clearance re survey of home health agencies; CLIA survey report form; validation of state surveys; Medicaid listing of participating home health agencies; financial information regarding Medicare benefits from Medicare contractors; and third-party liability under Medicaid.

58 FR 46198, September 1, 1993: HCFA Public Information Collection Requirements (ICR) Submitted to the Office of Management and Budget (OMB) for Clearance (pertaining to prenatal services and assistance screening; home health agency treatment forms; conditions of participation for intermediate care facilities for the

mentally retarded; State Medicaid eligibility quality control sample selection lists; prepaid health plan cost report; hospital survey report form; procedures for determining whether providers, practitioners, or other suppliers of services are liable for certain noncovered services; Medicare credit balance reporting requirements; Medicare provider cost report questionnaire form; Medicare current beneficiary survey rounds 7–10; sterilization regulation/consent form; PRO reconsideration and appeals information requirements; information collection requirements in HSQ-110, acquisition, protection and disclosure of PRO information; Medicare/Medicaid organ procurement organization's (OPO) request for certification) — Notice.

58 FR 52112, October 6, 1993: Medicare, Medicaid, and CLIA Programs; Clinical Laboratory Improvement Amendments of 1988 Exemption of Laboratories Licensed by the State of Washington — Notice.

58 FR 54159, October 20, 1993: HCFA Public Information Collection Requirements Submitted to the Office of Management and Budget (OMB) for Clearance (pertaining to CLIA certification recommendation; CLIA laboratory personnel report; Medigap complaint data base; certification as a rural health clinic (RHC) and RHC survey report form; screening mammography services data report; ambulatory surgical center request for certification and survey report form; blood bank inspection checklist and report; Medicaid program budget report form; supplier of ESRD services form; and grantee data collection instrument) — Notice.

58 FR 59270, November 8, 1993: HCFA Public Information Collection Requirements Submitted to the Office of Management and Budget (OMB) for Clearance (pertaining to formats for utilization and quality control peer review organizations (PROs); home health agency plan of treatment forms; State survey agency budget expenditure report and certification workload report; home health agency cost report; recordkeeping requirements in provider reimbursement manual; quarterly Medicaid statement of expenditures; Medicare contract application for Federally qualified health maintenance organizations; hospice survey and deficiencies report form; organ procurement agency/histocompatibility laboratory statement of reimbursable costs) — Notice.

58 FR 60204, November 15, 1993: HCFA Public Information Collection Requirements Submitted to the Office of Management and Budget (OMB) for Clearance (pertaining to procedures for transmit-

ting information between Medicare carriers and Medicare supplemental insurers; Medicare physician or supplier agreement; patient intake data form for the National Home Health Agency; agency characteristics form for the National Home Health Agency prospective payment demonstration; intake and assessment survey package for the community nursing organization demonstration; comprehensive outpatient rehabilitation facility (CORF eligibility and survey forms and information collection requirements) — Notice.

58 FR 63533, December 2, 1993: Medicare Program; Required Laboratory Procedures for Rural Health Clinics — Final rule with comment period, affecting 42 CFR Part 491.

59 FR 5201, February 3, 1994: HCFA Public Information Collection Requirements Submitted to the Office of Management and Budget (OMB) for Clearance (pertaining to evaluation of the Medicare case management demonstration; evaluation of the Medicaid uninsured demonstrations; Internal Revenue Service, Social Security Administration, and HCFA data match; survey of physician owned medical liability insurers for use in computing the input component of the physician liability component of the Geographic Practice Cost Index and the Medicare Economic Index; emergency and foreign hospital services for Canadian travel claims; CLIA survey report form; Medicaid management information system (MMIS) data form) — Notice.

59 FR 6228, February 10, 1994: Medicare Program; Change in Provider Agreement Regulations Related to Federal Employee Health Benefits — Proposed rule affecting 42 CFR Part 489.

59 FR 14865, March 30, 1994: HCFA Public Information Collection Requirements Submitted to the Office of Management and Budget (OMB) for Clearance (pertaining to home health agency Medicare and Medicaid survey report forms for conditions of participation; conditions of participation for rural health clinics; Medicaid re-evaluation of assets for determining payment rates to hospitals and nursing homes; statistical report on medical care, eligible, recipients, payments, and services.)

59 FR 23069, May 4, 1994: HCFA Public Information Collection Requirements Submitted to the Office of Management and Budget (OMB) for Clearance (pertaining to clinical laboratory improvement amendments (CLIA) flexible survey protocol form; application for health insurance benefits under Medicare for individual with chronic renal disease form; Medicare Qualification Statement for

Federal employees form; attending physician's statement and documentation of Medicare emergency form; request for Part B Medicare hearing by an Administrative Law Judge forms; CLIA adverse action extract; and medicare and Medicaid coverage data bank reports form.)

59 FR 25460, May 16, 1994: HCFA Public Information Collection Requirements Submitted to the Office of Management and Budget (OMB) for Clearance (pertaining to Medicare uniform institutional provider bill; hospice survey and deficiencies report form; HMO financial information reports to members; hospital request for certification in Medicare and Medicaid form.)

59 FR 27023, May 25, 1994: HCFA Public Information Collection Requirements Submitted to the Office of Management and Budget (OMB) for Clearance (pertaining to Medicare beneficiary survey of influenza vaccination form; Medicaid integrated quality control review worksheet; post laboratory survey questionnaire form; and post laboratory survey questionnaire — surveyor form).

59 FR 46500, September 8, 1994: Medicare and Medicaid Programs; Conditions of Coverage for Organ Procurement Organizations — Interim final rule with comment, affecting 42 CFR Parts 405, 482, and 485.

59 FR 50762, October 5, 1994: HCFA Public Information Collection Requirements Submitted to the Office of Management and Budget (OMB) for Clearance (pertaining to reimbursement of hospital costs for residents and interns, criteria for psychiatric and rehabilitation hospital units' reimbursement under the prospective payment system, disclosure of owners and managers of suppliers for fraud and abuse detection purposes, reimbursement of municipal health services clinics, survey form for hospital compliance with anti-dumping requirements, and evaluation of patient and physician satisfaction with the Medicare participating heart bypass center demonstration).

59 FR 52129, October 14, 1994: Medicare Program; Hospice Services under Medicare Program; Intent to Form Negotiated Rulemaking Committee — Notice.

59 FR 52178, October 14, 1994: HCFA Public Information Collection Requirements Submitted to the Office of Management and Budget (OMB) for Clearance (pertaining to Medicare reimbursement for outpatient services, cost reports for free-standing skilled nursing facilities; Medicare coverage criteria for adult heart transplants, drug rebates for Medicaid, optional prospective payment cost

report for certain skilled nursing facilities, reimbursable costs for organ procurement agencies, distribution and use of end stage renal disease treatment sources, conditions of coverage for ambulatory surgical centers, and waivers for home and community based services).

59 FR 54197, October 28, 1994: HCFA Public Information Collection Requirements Submitted to the Office of Management and Budget (OMB) for Clearance (pertaining to Medicare beneficiary surveys, estimated acquisition costs of injectable drugs, reconsideration of adverse determinations made on Part A claims, beneficiary and supplier or physician hearing requests, and compliance with hospital anti-dumping requirements).

59 FR 56116, November 10, 1994: Medicare and Medicaid Programs; Survey, Certification and Enforcement of Skilled Nursing Facilities and Nursing Facilities — Final rule affecting 42 CFR Parts 401, 431, 435, 440, 441, 442, 447, 483, 488, 489, and 498. See also correcting amendment, effective July 1, 1995, at 62 FR 44221, August 20, 1997.

59 FR 56500, November 14, 1994: HCFA Public Information Collection Requirements Submitted to the Office of Management and Budget (OMB) for Clearance (pertaining to monitoring and evaluation of Medicare cataract surgery alternate payment demonstration, form for listing deficiencies for laboratory surveys, form for personnel requirements for laboratory CLIA certification, and CLIA reinstatement form).

59 FR 65482, December 20, 1994: Medicare Program; Medicare Coverage of Home Health Services, Medicare Conditions of Participation, and Home Health Aide Supervision — Final rule affecting 42 CFR Parts 409, 413, 418, and 484. See also correction at 60 FR 39122, August 1, 1995.

59 FR 66314, December 23, 1994: Medicare, Medicaid, and CLIA Programs; Clinical Laboratory Improvement Amendments of 1988 Continuance of Exemption of Laboratories Licensed by the State of Washington — Notice.

60 FR 130, January 3, 1995: HCFA; CLIA Program: Approval of the Joint Commission on Accreditation of Healthcare Organizations as an Accrediting Organization — Notice.

60 FR 2325, January 9, 1995: Medicare Program; Providers and Suppliers of Specialized Services: Technical Amendments — Final rule with comment period, affecting 42 CFR Parts 400, 405, 410, 484,

485, 486, and 498. See also correction at 60 FR 11632, March 2, 1995, and 60 FR 45086, August 30, 1995.

60 FR 21525, May 2, 1995: HCFA Public Information Collection Requirements Submitted to the Office of Management and Budget (OMB) for Clearance (pertaining to intermediary requests for information from skilled nursing facilities, reimbursement for CLIA compliance surveys, patient outcome data in home health agencies, common claim forms for Medicare/Medicaid reimbursement, and a study of childhood immunization costs).

60 FR 26445, May 17, 1995: HCFA Public Information Collection Requirements Submitted to the Office of Management and Budget (OMB) for Clearance (pertaining to Medicare/Medicaid psychiatric hospital survey data, and hospice requests for Medicare certification).

60 FR 39403, August 2, 1995: HCFA Public Information Collection Requirements Submitted for Public Comment and Recommendations (pertaining to PRO reporting forms; Oregon Medicaid reform demonstration; review functions of PRO's; medical records review under PPS; evaluation of Medicare cataract surgery alternate payment demonstration; home health agency survey and deficiencies report; CLIA survey forms; field testing of uniform needs assessment instrument for hospital discharge planning).

60 FR 40184, August 7, 1995: HCFA Public Information Collection Requirements Submitted for Public Comment and Recommendations (pertaining to CLIA alternative quality assessment survey forms; and data collection and analysis for generating procedure specific physician cost estimates).

60 FR 50115, September 28, 1995: Medicare and Medicaid Programs; Survey, Certification and Enforcement of Skilled Nursing Facilities and Nursing Facilities — Final rule and correction to final regulations, affecting 42 CFR Parts 431, 440, 442, 488, 489, and 498. See also corrections at 60 FR 52731, October 10, 1995, and at 60 FR 534456, October 13, 1995.

60 FR 50630, September 29, 1995: HCFA Public Information Collection Requirements Submitted for Public Comment and Recommendations (pertaining to sole community home health agencies).

60 FR 55719, November 2, 1995: HCFA Public Information Collection Requirements Submitted for Public Comment and Recommendations (pertaining to evaluation of the Oregon Medicaid reform demonstration; field testing of the uniform needs assessment

instrument for hospital discharge planning; survey of physician practice costs; evaluation of the Medicare cataract surgery alternate payment demonstration; and alternative CLIA quality assessment surveys).

60 FR 64167, December 14, 1995: HCFA Public Information Collection Requirements Submitted for Public Comment and Recommendations (pertaining to home health care; Medicare/Medicaid certification of physical therapy and speech pathology services; certification as suppliers of Portable X-ray Services; certification of organ procurement organizations; certification for physical therapists in independent practice; and approval as a hospital provider of extended care services (swing bed)).

61 FR 2255, January 25, 1996: HCFA Public Information Collection Requirements Submitted for Public Comment and Recommendations (pertaining to survey forms about health and safety requirements for physical therapists in independent practice; and national data reporting requirements for HMOs and CMPs).

61 FR 6645, February 21, 1996: HCFA Agency Information Collection Activities: Proposed Collection; Comment Request (pertaining to survey forms to evaluate Federally qualified health centers; and the Medicare Carrier provider/supplier application form).

61 FR 7012, February 23, 1996: HCFA Notice Submitted for Collection of Public Comment: Submission for OMB Review (pertaining to granting and withdrawing of deeming authority to private non-profit accreditation organizations and the Clinical Laboratory Improvement Act Exemption under State laboratory programs; and the rules for participation of home health agencies to participate as sole community home health agencies).

61 FR 14798, April 3, 1996: HCFA Agency Information Collection Activities: Proposed Collection; Comment Request (pertaining to statistical reports on medical care eligibility, payments and services under Medicaid; State survey agency lists of positions and schedule of equipment purchases; granting and withdrawing of deeming authority to national accreditation organizations; maximizing the effectiveness of home health care; requests for certification in the Medicare or Medicaid program to provide outpatient physical therapy and/or speech pathology services; physical therapists in independent practice; requests for provider approval as a hospital provider of extended care services (swing bed) under Medicare and Medicaid; and requests for designation as an organ procurement organization).

61 FR 16925, April 18, 1996: HCFA Agency Information Collection Activities: Proposed Collection; Comment Request (pertaining to Medicare participating physician or supplier agreements; and hospital conditions of participation).

61 FR 17710, April 22, 1996: HCFA Agency Information Collection Activities: Proposed Collection; Comment Request (pertaining to payment adjustments for sole community hospitals; conditions of participation for portable x-ray suppliers; and cost reports for independent rural health centers and freestanding Federally qualified health centers).

61 FR 25229, May 20, 1996: HCFA Agency Information Collection Activities: Proposed Collection; Comment Request (pertaining to evaluation of the Oregon reform demonstration; evaluation of the per-episode home health prospective payment demonstration; and the blood bank inspection checklist instrument used by State agencies to determine compliance with CLIA).

61 FR 26914, May 29, 1996: HCFA Emergency Clearance: Public Information Collection Requirements Submitted to the Office of Management and Budget (OMB) (pertaining to re-designation, certification and recertification of organ procurement organizations).

61 FR 29406, June 10, 1996: HCFA Agency Information Collection Activities: proposed Collection; Comment Request (pertaining to end stage renal disease application and survey and certification report forms; withholding Medicare payments to recover Medicaid overpayments; acquisition, protection, and disclosure of PRO information; clinical laboratory certification and recertification survey forms; CLIA laboratory personnel report forms; prepaid health plan cost reports; Medicare credit balance reporting requirements; statement of deficiencies and plan of correction requirements for organ procurement organizations; Medicare/Medicaid hospital survey report forms; advance directive requirements for Medicare and Medicaid; payment adjustments for sole community hospitals; survey reports for physical therapists in independent practice; HMO and CMP national data reporting requirements; identification of extension units of outpatient physical therapy and outpatient speech pathology providers; and fire safety survey reports).

61 FR 30072, June 13, 1996: HCFA Agency Information Collection Activities: Proposed Collection; Comment Request (pertaining to conditions of coverage for organ procurement organizations).

61 FR 31141, June 19, 1996: HCFA Agency Information Collection Activities: Proposed Collection; Comment Request (pertaining to

authorization agreements for electronic funds transfer; applications for health insurance under Medicare for individuals with chronic renal disease; CLIA application forms; forms for surveyors to evaluate laboratory survey processes; post laboratory survey questionnaires for laboratories to evaluate the survey process).

61 FR 34437, July 2, 1996: HCFA Agency Information Collection Activities: Submission for OMB Review; Comment Request (pertaining to Peer Review Organization procedures for reconsideration of initial decisions; Part B enrollment forms; certification of rural health clinics for Medicare participation; Medicaid utilization review requirements for home health agencies; State listings of Medicaid recipients in institutions and procedures for State inspection of care review; procedures for disenrollment of beneficiaries from HMOs or CMPs; effectiveness of telemedicine services; formats for PROs to submit data to HCFA; and request for accelerated payments forms for providers).

61 34855, July 3, 1996: HCFA Agency Information Collection Activities: Submission for OMB Review; Comment Request (pertaining to information collection requirements for hospital conditions of participation in Medicare).

61 FR 37487, July 18, 1996: HCFA Agency Information Collection Activities: Submission for OMB Review; Comment request (pertaining to cost reports for independent rural health centers and freestanding federally qualified health centers; and conditions of participation for portable x-ray suppliers).

61 FR 40847, August 6, 1996: HCFA Agency Information Collection Activities: Proposed Collection; Comment request (pertaining to survey and certification of comprehensive outpatient rehabilitation facilities (CORFs)).

61 FR 41417, August 8, 1996: HCFA Agency Information Collection Activities: Submission for OMB Review; Comment request (pertaining to prospective payment for home health care; and Medicare standards for hospices).

61 FR 42257, August 14, 1996: HCFA Proposals Submitted for Collection of Public Comment: Submission for OMB Review (pertaining to third-party liability in Medicaid programs; surveys of federally qualified health centers (FQHCs); distribution of Medicare information by hospitals; Medicare reimbursement for hospitals with a disproportionate share of Medicare inpatients; Medicaid quality control; and the National Payer Identifier).

61 FR 43373, August 22, 1996: HCFA Agency Information Collection Activities: Proposed Collection; Comment request (pertaining to hospital claims for inpatient care for statutorily excluded services; and hospice standards for Medicare participation).

61 FR 43374, August 22, 1996: HCFA Agency Information Collection Activities: Submission for OMB Review; Comment request (pertaining to conditions of participation for rehabilitation agencies and conditions for coverage for physical therapist in independent practice).

61 FR 46814, September 5, 1996: HCFA Agency Information Collection Activities: Submission for OMB Review; Comment request (pertaining to authorization agreements for electronic funds transfers; entitlement to Medicare for individuals with chronic renal disease; application forms for clinical laboratories; and clinical laboratory survey questionnaires).

61 FR 47131, September 6, 1996: HCFA Agency Information Collection Activities: Submission for OMB Review; Comment request (pertaining to conditions of coverage for organ procurement organizations; and statements of deficiencies and plan of correction forms for organ procurement organizations).

61 FR 48157, September 12, 1996: HCFA Agency Information Collection Activities: Submission for OMB Review; Comment request (pertaining to authorization agreement for electronic funds transfer; entitlement to Medicare for individuals with chronic renal disease; application forms for clinical laboratories; and clinical laboratory survey forms).

61 FR 57688, November 7, 1996: HCFA Agency Information Collection Activities: Comment request (pertaining to clinical laboratory surveys; clinical laboratory personnel qualifications; Medicare/Medicaid hospital survey report forms; beneficiary disenrollment from HMOs and CMPs; survey reports for ambulatory surgical centers; the Medigap complaint database; and survey forms for comprehensive outpatient rehabilitation facilities).

61 FR 64913, December 9, 1996: HCFA Agency Information Collection Activities: Proposed Collection; Comment request (pertaining to survey report forms for ICF/MRs; and current Medicare beneficiary surveys).

61 FR 67041, December 19, 1996: Medicare Program; Recognition of the Ambulatory Surgical Center Standards of the Joint Commission on the Accreditation of Healthcare Organizations and the

Accreditation Association for Ambulatory Health Care — Final notice.

62 FR 3514, January 23, 1997: Submitted for Collection of Public Comment: Submission for OMB Review (pertaining to Home and Community-based Services Waiver Requests).

62 FR 3902, January 27, 1997: HCFA Agency Information Collection Activities: Proposed Collection; Comment request (pertaining to hospice survey and deficiencies report form).

62 FR 7467, February 19, 1997: HCFA Agency Information Collection Activities: Proposed Collection; Comment request (pertaining to form for a hospital request for certification in the Medicare and Medicaid programs).

62 FR 8026, February 21, 1997: HCFA Agency Information Collection Activities: Proposed Collection; Comment request (pertaining to Clinical Laboratory Improvement Act adverse action extract).

62 FR 8252, February 24, 1997: HCFA Agency Information Collection Activities: Submission for OMB Review; Comment request (pertaining to conditions of participation for rural health clinics).

62 FR 8744, February 26, 1997: HCFA Agency Information Collection Activities: Submission for OMB Review; Comment request (pertaining to Medicare provider/supplier enrollment application).

62 FR 9435, March 3, 1997: Office of Inspector General: Publication of the OIG Model Compliance Plan for Clinical Laboratories — Notice.

62 FR 10285, March 6, 1997: HCFA Agency Information collection Activities: Submission for OMB Review; Comment request (pertaining to end stage renal disease (ESRD) application and survey and certification report form).

62 FR 11004, March 10, 1997: Medicare and Medicaid Programs; Revision of the Conditions of Participation for Home Health Agencies and Use of the Outcome and Assessment Information Set (OASIS) as Part of the Revised Conditions of Participation for Home Health Agencies — Introduction to proposed rules, affecting 42 CFR Part 484.

62 FR 11005, March 10, 1997: Medicare and Medicaid Programs; Conditions of Participation for Home Health Agencies — Proposed rule affecting 42 CFR Part 484. See also correction at 62 FR 11953, March 13, 1997.

62 FR 11035, March 10, 1997: Medicare and Medicaid Programs; Use of the OASIS as Part of the Conditions of Participation for Home Health Agencies — Proposed rule.

62 FR 11213, March 11, 1997: HCFA Agency Information Collection Activities: Proposed Collection; Comment request (pertaining to post-laboratory survey questionnaire).

62 FR 11214, March 11, 1997: HCFA Agency Information Collection Activities: Submission for OMB Review; Comment request (pertaining to intermediate care facility for the mentally retarded or persons with related conditions survey report forms).

62 FR 17850, April 11, 1997: HCFA Agency Information Collection Activities: Proposed Collection; Comment request (pertaining to the Medicaid EPSDT program).

62 FR 18639, April 16, 1997: HCFA Agency Information Collection Activities: Proposed Collection; Comment request (pertaining to the hospital request for certification in the Medicare and Medicaid programs form).

62 FR 23140, April 29, 1997: Office of Inspector General: Health Care Programs: Fraud and Abuse; Revised PRO Sanctions for Failing to Meet Statutory Obligations — Final rule.

62 FR 25636, May 9, 1997: HCFA Agency Information Collection Activities: Proposed Collection; Comment request (pertaining to information collection requirements about examination and treatment for emergency medical conditions and women in labor).

62 FR 25855, May 12, 1997: Medicare, Medicaid, and CLIA Programs; Clinical Laboratory Requirements — Extension of Certain Effective Dates for Clinical Laboratory Requirements under CLIA — Final rule with comment period, affecting 42 CFR Part 493.

62 FR 28057, May 22, 1997: HCFA Agency Information Collection Activities: Submission for OMB Review; Comment request (pertaining to post laboratory survey questionnaire).

62 FR 30603, June 4, 1997: HCFA Agency Information Collection Activities: Submission for OMB Review; Comment request (pertaining to skilled nursing facility and skilled nursing facility health care complex cost reports; and hospital conditions of participation).

62 FR 32615, June 17, 1997: Medicare Program; Ambulance Services — Proposed rule affecting 42 CFR Parts 410 and 424.

62 FR 39848, July 24, 1997: HCFA Agency Information Collection Activities; Proposed Collection; Comment request (pertaining to home health certification and plan of care forms for reimbursement; and Medicare/Medicaid disclosure of ownership and control forms).

62 FR 43931, August 18, 1997: Medicare and Medicaid Programs: Effective Dates of Provider Agreements and Supplier Approvals — Final rule affecting 42 CFR Parts 431, 442, 488, 489, and 498.

62 FR 45672, August 28, 1997: HCFA Agency Information Collection Activities: Proposed Collection; Comment request (pertaining to conditions of participation for home health agencies; and negative case action review process annual reports for States).

62 FR 48666, September 16, 1997: HCFA Agency Information Collection Activities: Submission for OMB Review; Comment request (pertaining to conditions of coverage for ambulatory surgical centers).

62 FR 48871, September 17, 1997: HCFA Agency Information Collection Activities: Proposed Collection; Comment request (pertaining to conditions of coverage of supplier of ESRD services).

62 FR 63551, December 1, 1997: HCFA Agency Information Collection Activities: Proposed Collection; Comment request (pertaining to conditions of coverage of suppliers of ESRD services).

62 FR 66119, December 17, 1997: HCFA Agency Information Collection Activities: Proposed Collection; Comment request (pertaining to clinical laboratory compliance inspections).

62 FR 66726, December 19, 1997: Medicare and Medicaid Programs; Hospital Conditions of Participation; Provider Agreements and Supplier Approval — Proposed rule affecting 42 CFR Parts 416, 482, 485, and 489.

62 FR 67881, December 30, 1997: HCFA Agency Information Collection activities: Proposed Collection; Comment request (pertaining to clinical laboratory survey forms).

63 FR 2926, January 20, 1998: Medicare Program; Additional Supplier Standards — Proposed rule affecting 42 CFR Part 424.

63 FR 7743, February 17, 1998: Medicare and Medicaid Programs; Hospital Conditions of Participation; Provider Agreements and Supplier Approval — Notice of extension of comment period, affecting 42 CFR Parts 416, 482, 485, and 489.

63 FR 8987, February 23, 1998: Office of Inspector General: Publication of the OIG Compliance Program for Hospitals — Notice.

63 FR 10920, March 5, 1998: HCFA Emergency Clearance: Public Information Collection Requirements Submitted to the Office of Management and Budget (OMB) (pertaining to Medicare and other Federal health care program provider and supplier application forms).

63 FR 12474, March 13, 1998: HCFA Agency Information Collection Activities: Proposed Collection; Comment request (pertaining to hospice request for certification in the Medicare program and Medicare/Medicaid psychiatric hospital survey data).

63 FR 12474, March 13, 1998: HCFA Agency Information Collection Activities: Submission for OMB Review; Comment request (pertaining to requirements for clinical laboratory testing on human specimens).

63 FR 12475, March 13, 1998: HCFA Agency Information Collection Activities; Submission for OMB Review; Comment request (pertaining to HMO and CMP national data reporting requirements).

63 FR 12476, March 13, 1998: HCFA Agency Information Collection Activities: Submission for OMB Review; Comment request (pertaining to alternate quality assessment form for clinical laboratories with good performance records).

63 FR 19502, April 20, 1998: HCFA Agency Information Collection Activities: Proposed collection; Comment request (pertaining to annual early and periodic screening, diagnostic, and treatment services (EPSDT) participation report; Medicare and other health care programs provider/supplier enrollment application; and research and analytic support for implementing performance measurement in Medicare fee for service).

63 FR 23790, April 30, 1998: Medicare and Medicaid Programs; Recognition of the American Association for Accreditation of Ambulatory Surgery Facilities, Inc., for Ambulatory Surgical Centers — Proposed notice.

63 FR 25214, May 7, 1998: HCFA Agency Information Collection Activities: Proposed Collection; Comment request (pertaining to organ procurement organization statement of deficiencies and plan of correction forms).

63 FR 26722, May 14, 1998: HCFA CLIA Program; Simplifying CLIA Regulations Relating to Accreditation, Exemption of Laboratories under a State Licensure Program, Proficiency Testing, and Inspection — Final rule affecting 42 CFR Part 493. See also correction at 63 FR 32699, June 15, 1998.

63 FR 28396, May 22, 1998: HCFA Privacy Act of 1974 — Notice of New System of Records (pertaining to the long term care minimum data set).

63 FR 29415, May 29, 1998: HCFA Agency Information Collection Activities: Submission for OMB Review; Comment request (pertaining to hospice request for certification in the Medicare program).

63 FR 32234, June 12, 1998: HCFA Agency Information Collection Activities: Submission for OMB Review; Comment request (pertaining to Medicare/Medicaid psychiatric hospital survey data).

63 FR 33856, June 22, 1998: Medicare and Medicaid Programs; Hospital Conditions of Participation; Identification of Potential Organ Tissue, and Eye Donors and Transplant Hospitals' Provision of Transplant-Related Data — Final rule affecting 42 CFR Part 482.

63 FR 34903, June 26, 1998: HCFA Agency Information Collection Activities: Proposed Collection; Comment request (pertaining to collection of managed care data using the institutional providers form).

63 FR 37129, July 9, 1998: HCFA Agency Information Collection Activities; Submission for OMB Review; Comment request (pertaining to organ procurement organization requests for participation in Medicare and Medicaid).

63 FR 38413, July 16, 1998: HCFA Agency Information Collection Activities: Submission for OMB Review; Comment request (pertaining to Clinical Laboratory Improvement Act certification requirements; EPSDT participation reports; limitations on provider-related donations and health care-related taxes, and limitations on payments to disproportionate share hospitals; and Medicare+Choice provider sponsored organization waiver requests forms).

63 FR 40723, July 30, 1998: HCFA Agency Information Collection Activities: Proposed Collection; Comment request (pertaining to requirements for health care prepayment plan (HCPP) eligibility under Section 1833 of the Social Security Act).

63 FR 42796, August 11, 1998: Medicare Program; Negotiated Rulemaking; Coverage and Administrative Policies for Clinical Diagnostic Laboratory Tests; Change in Meeting Time — Notice of meetings.

63 FR 45249, August 25, 1998: HCFA Agency Information Collection Activities: Submission for OMB Review; Comment request (pertaining to development of an assessment system for post-acute care in rehabilitation facilities).

63 FR 48734, September 11, 1998: HCFA Agency Information Collection Activities: Proposed Collection; Comment request (pertaining to medical review activities under PPS by Peer Review Organizations; and survey and deficiency reports for home health agencies).

63 FR 48735, September 11, 1998: Medicare and Medicaid Programs; Recognition of the Community Health Accreditation Program, Inc. (CHAP) and Joint Commission for Accreditation of Healthcare Organizations (JCAHO) for Hospices — Proposed notice.

63 FR 55031, October 14, 1998: Medicare, Medicaid, and CLIA Programs; Extension of Certain Effective Dates for Clinical Laboratory Requirements under CLIA — Final rule with comment period, affecting 42 CFR 493.

63 FR 58058, October 29, 1998: HCFA Emergency Clearance: Public Information Collection Requirements Submitted to the Office of Management and Budget (OMB) (pertaining to on-site inspection for durable medical equipment (DME) suppliers).

63 FR 60356, November 9, 1998: HCFA Agency Information Collection activities: Proposed Collection; Comment request (pertaining to skilled nursing facility resident assessment MDS data).

63 FR 63478, November 13, 1998: HCFA Agency Information Collection Activities: Proposed Collection; Comment request (pertaining to processing Medicare+Choice disenrollment requests from beneficiaries; creation of the Utilization and Quality Control Peer Review Organization; and rules for participation of HHA's in Medicare and review of plans of care for home health services).

63 FR 65601, November 27, 1998: HCFA Agency Information Collection Activities: Submission for OMB Review; Comment request (pertaining to medical records review under PPS; and home health agency survey and deficiencies reports, and home health functional assessment instruments).

63 FR 66554, December 2, 1998: Medicare Program; Recognition of the American Association for Accreditation of Ambulatory Surgery Facilities, Inc., for Ambulatory Surgical Centers Program — Final notice.

63 FR 72318, December 31, 1998: HCFA Agency Information Collection Activities: Proposed Collection; Comment request (pertaining to fire safety survey report forms for health care facilities).

1999

64 FR 1024, January 7, 1999: HCFA Agency Information Collection Activities: Proposed Collection; Comment request (pertaining to granting and withdrawal of deeming authority to national accreditation organizations).

64 FR 1810, January 12, 1999: HCFA Agency Information Collection Activities: Proposed Collection; Comment request (pertaining to Medicaid eligibility quality control MEQC) samples; identification of extension units of outpatient physical therapy (OPT) and outpatient speech pathology (OSP) providers; request for certification in the

Medicare and/or Medicaid program(s) to provide OPT or OSP services; and request for certification as a supplier of portable X-ray services under Medicare and/or Medicaid).

64 FR 3303, January 21, 1999: HCFA Agency Information Collection Activities: Proposed Collection; Comment request (pertaining to on-site inspection for durable medical equipment suppliers).

64 FR 3304, January 21, 1999: HCFA Agency Information Collection Activities: Proposed Collection; Comment request (pertaining to field testing of the uniform needs assessment instrument for patients discharged from hospitals).

64 FR 3748, January 25, 1999: Medicare and Medicaid Programs: Reporting Outcome and Assessment Information Set (OASIS) Data as Part of the Conditions of Participation for Home Health Agencies-Interim final rule with comment period, affecting 42 CFR Parts 484 and 488.

64 FR 3764, January 25, 1999: Medicare and Medicaid Programs: Comprehensive Assessment and Use of the OASIS as Part of the Conditions of Participation for Home Health Agencies — Final rule affecting 42 CFR Part 484.

64 FR 4435, January 28, 1999: HCFA Agency Information Collection Activities; Submission for OMB Review; Comment request (pertaining to home and community-based services waiver requests).

64 FR 6664, February 10, 1999: HCFA Agency Information Collection Activities: Submission for OMB Review; Comment request (pertaining to skilled nursing facility (SNF) resident assessment MDS data).

64 FR 6665, February 10, 1999: HCFA Agency Information Collection Activities: Proposed Collection; Comment request (pertaining to sole community home health agencies (HHS)).

64 FR 10479, March 4, 1999: HCFA Agency Information Collection Activities: Proposed Collection; Comment request (pertaining to conditions of participation for portable X-ray suppliers).

64 FR 13354, March 18, 1999: Medicare and Medicaid Programs; Civil Money Penalties for Nursing Homes (SNF/NF), Change in Notice Requirements, and Expansion of Discretionary Remedy Delegation — Final rule with comment period, affecting 42 CFR Part 488.

64 FR 13997, March 23, 1999: HCFA Agency Information Collection Activities: Submission for OMB Review; Comment request (pertaining to Medicare and Medicaid requirements for advanced

directives, and disclosure of ownership and financial control interest).

64 FR 14454, March 25, 1999: HCFA Agency Information Collection Activities: Proposed Collection; Comment request (pertaining to blood bank inspection checklist under CLIA).

64 FR 14454, March 25, 1999: HCFA Agency Information Collection Activities: Submission for OMB Review; Comment request (pertaining to Medicaid eligibility quality control sampling; fire safety survey report forms; and income and eligibility verification systems under Medicaid).

64 FR 17184, April 8, 1999: HCFA Medicare Program; April 23, 1999 Open Town Hall Meeting to Discuss the Skilled Nursing Facility Prospective Payment System (SNF/PPS) and Quality of Care in Nursing Facilities — Notice of meeting.

64 FR 17673, April 12, 1999: HCFA Agency Information Collection Activities: Proposed Collection; Comment request (pertaining to Medicare participating physician or supplier agreements).

64 FR 19375, April 20, 1999: HCFA Agency Information Collection Activities: Proposed Collection; Comment request (pertaining to acquisition, protection, and disclosure of peer review organization (PRO) information).

64 FR 19376, April 20, 1999: Medicare Program; Recognition of the Community Health Accreditation Program, Inc. (CHAP) for Hospices).

64 FR 23846, May 4, 1999: HCFA Emergency Clearance: Public Information Collection Requirements Submitted to the Office of Management and Budget (OMB) (pertaining to the outcome and assessment information set (OASIS) for home health care agencies).

64 FR 24956, May 10, 1999: Medicare and Medicaid Programs; Effective Dates of Provider Agreements and Supplier Approvals-Correction restoring regulations inadvertently removed when a final rule concerning effective dates for provider agreements and supplier approvals was published at 62 FR 43931, August 18, 1997.

64 FR 25892, May 13, 1999: HCFA Agency Information Collection Activities: Submission for OMB Review; Comment request (pertaining to granting and withdrawal of deeming authority to national accreditation organizations).

64 FR 29048, May 28, 1999: HCFA Agency Information Collection Activities: Proposed Collection; Comment request (pertaining to certification as a rural health clinic).

64 FR 29050, May 28, 1999: HCFA Emergency Clearance: Public Information Collection Requirements Submitted to the Office of Management and Budget (OMB) (pertaining to the community mental health center site visit assessment tool).

64 FR 30340, June 7, 1999: HCFA Agency Information Collection Activities: Submission for OMB Review; Comment request (pertaining to information collection requirements in the final peer review organization (PRO) sanction regulations).

64 FR 32239, June 16, 1999: HCFA Agency Information Collection Activities: Proposed Collection; Comment request (pertaining to conditions of coverage for organ procurement organizations).

64 FR 32240, June 16, 1999: HCFA Agency Information Collection Activities: Submission for OMB Review; Comment request (pertaining to conditions of participation for portable x-ray suppliers).

64 FR 32881, June 18, 1999: Medicare Program; Recognition of the Joint Commission for Accreditation of Healthcare Organizations (JCAHO) for Hospices — Final notice.

64 FR 32984, June 18, 1999: Medicare and Medicaid Programs; Mandatory Use, Collection, Encoding, and Transmission of Outcome and Assessment Information Set (OASIS) for Home Health Agencies — Notice.

64 FR 32992, June 18, 1999: HCFA Privacy Act of 1974; Report of New System (pertaining to a new system of records containing data on the physical, mental, functional, and psychosocial status of all patients receiving the services of home health agencies (HHAs) approved to participate in Medicare or Medicaid).

64 FR 36070, July 2, 1999: Medicare and Medicaid Programs; Hospital Conditions of Participation: Patient Rights — Interim final rule with comment, affecting 42 CFR 482.

64 FR 36887, July 8, 1999: HCFA Agency Information Collection Activities: Proposed Collection; Comment request (pertaining to reporting outcome and assessment information data set (OASIS) as part of the conditions of participation for home health agencies).

64 FR 37142, July 9, 1999: HCFA Agency Information Collection Activities: Submission for OMB Review; Comment request (pertaining to request for certification in the Medicare/Medicaid program to provide outpatient physical therapy and/or speech-language pathology and the outpatient physical therapy and/or speech-language pathology survey report form; request for certification as a supplier of portable X-ray services); and procedures for making national coverage decisions).

64 FR 38202, July 15, 1999: HCFA Agency Information Collection Activities: Proposed Collection; Comment request (pertaining to CLIA personnel reports; and CLIA certification for tests on human specimens).

64 FR 38910, July 20, 1999: HCFA Agency Information Collection Activities: Proposed Collection; Comment request (pertaining to comprehensive outpatient rehabilitation facility (CORF) eligibility requirements).

64 FR 39517, July 22, 1999: HCFA Agency Information Collection Activities: Submission for OMB Review; Comment request (pertaining to Medicare participating physician or supplier agreement form HCFA-460).

64 FR 39934, July 23, 1999: Medicare and Medicaid Program; Appeal of the Loss of Nurse Aide Training Programs — Interim final rule with comment period, affecting 42 CFR Parts 431 and 498. See also correction at 64 FR 43295, August 10, 1999.

64 FR 40017, July 23, 1999: HCFA Agency Information Collection Activities: Submission for OMB Review; Comment request (pertaining to acquisition, protection and disclosure of peer review organization (PRO) information).

64 FR 49196, September 10, 1999: HCFA Agency Information Collection Activities; Submission for OMB Review; Comment request (pertaining to conditions of coverage for organ procurement organizations).

64 FR 49197, September 10, 1999: Medicare and Medicaid Programs; Application of the Joint Commission for Accreditaton of Healthcare Organizations (JCAHO) for Continued Approval of Deeming Authority for Home Health Agencies — Proposed notice.

64 FR 49198, September 10, 1999: Medicare and Medicaid Programs; Application of the Community Health Accreditation Program, Incorporated, CHAP) for Continued Approval of Deeming Authority for Home Health Agencies — Proposed notice.

64 FR 49199, September 10, 1999: Medicare and Medicaid Programs; Reapplication of the American Osteopathic Association (AOA) for Continued Approval of Deeming Authority for Hospitals — Proposed notice.

64 FR 57431, October 25, 1999: Medicare Program; Appeals of Carrier Determinations that a Supplier Fails to Meet the Requirements for Medicare Billing Privileges — Proposed rule affecting 42 CFR Part 405.

64 FR 57619, October 26, 1999: Office of Inspector General; Privacy Act; Exempt Record System, Pertaining to the Healthcare Integrity and Protection Data Bank (HIPDB) — Notice of proposed rulemaking affecting 45 CFR Part 5b.

64 FR 57740, October 26, 1999: Office of Inspector General; Healthcare Fraud and Abuse Data Collection Program: Reporting of Final Adverse Actions - Final rule affecting 45 CFR Part 61. See also correction at 65 FR 70506, November 24, 2000. 2000

64 FR 57902, October 27, 1999: HCFA Agency Information Collection Activites: Proposed Collection; Comment request (pertaining to evaluation of new Medicare+Choice plans).

64 FR 58418, October 29, 1999: HCFA Agency Information Collection Activities: Proposed Collection; Comment request (pertaining to outcome based continuous quality improvement (OBCQI) approach for the PACE program).

64 FR 58851, November 1, 1999: Office of Inspector General; Healthcare Integrity and Protection Data Bank: Announcement of Opening Date for Reporting and Self-query Fee — Notice.

64 FR 62679, November 17, 1999: HCFA Agency Information Collection Activities: Proposed Collection; Comment request (pertaining to hospital conditions of participation).

64 FR 62679, November 17, 1999: HCFA Agency Information Collection Activities: Proposed Collection; Comment request (pertaining to surveys of end stage renal disease facilities).

64 FR 62680, November 17, 1999: HCFA Agency Information Collection Activities: Submission for OMB Review; Comment request (pertaining to hospice care eligibility standards, reimbursement procedures, and conditions of participation).

64 FR 62681, November 17, 1999: HCFA Agency Information Collection Activities: Submission for OMB Review; Comment request (pertaining to peer review organization (PRO) reconsiderations and appeals).

64 FR 66482, November 26, 1999: HCFA Agency Information Collection Activities: Proposed Collection; Comment request (pertaining to resident assessment in skilled nursing facilities).

64 FR 67223, December 1, 1999: Medicaid Program; External Quality Review of Medicaid Managed Care Organizations — Proposed rule affecting 42 CFR Parts 433 and 438.

64 FR 67918, December 3, 1999: HCFA Agency Information Collection Activities: Proposed Collection; Comment request (pertaining to conditions of participation for rural health clinics).

64 FR 69272, December 10, 1999: HCFA Agency Information Collection Activities: Submission for OMB Review; Comment request (pertaining to community mental health center site visit assessment tools).

64 FR 69272, December 10, 1999: HCFA Agency Information Collection Activities: Submission for OMB Review; Comment request (pertaining to comprehensive outpatient rehabilitation facility (CORF) eligibility and survey forms).

64 FR 69273, December 10, 1999: HCFA Agency Information Collection Activities: Submission for OMB Review; Comment request (pertaining to Medicare/Medicaid hospital survey reports).

64 FR 69273, December 10, 1999: HCFA Agency Information Collection Activities: Submission for OMB Review; Comment request (pertaining to HCFA-377 ambulatory surgical center survey report form).

64 FR 73563, December 30, 1999: HCFA Agency Information Collection Activities: Submission for OMB Review; Comment request pertaining to Medicare program integrity organizational conflict of interest disclosure certificates).

2000

65 FR 1400, January 10, 2000: HCFA Agency Information Collection Activities: Submission for OMB Review; Comment request (pertaining to reporting outcome and assessment information set (OASIS) data set as a condition of participation for HHAs).

65 FR 4437, January 27, 2000: HCFA Agency Information Collection Activities: Proposed Collection; Comment request (pertaining to durable medical equipment regional carrier certificate of medical necessity).

65 FR 4824, February 1, 2000: HCFA Agency Information Collection Activities: Submission for OMB Review; Comment request (pertaining to clinical laboratory personnel reports).

65 FR 8722, February 22, 2000: Medicare and Medicaid Programs; Re-approval of the Deeming Authority of the Joint Commission on Accreditation of Healthcare Organizations (JCAHO) for Home Health Agencies (HHAs) — Final notice.

65 FR 8725, February 22, 2000: Medicare and Medicaid Programs; Reapproval of the Deeming Authority of the Community Health Accreditation Program, Incorporated (CHAP) for Home Health Agencies (HHAs) — Final notice.

65 FR 8727, February 22, 2000: Medicare and Medicaid Programs; Recognition of the American Osteopathic Association (AOA) for Continued Approval of Deeming Authority for Hospitals — Final notice.

65 FR 8983, February 23, 2000: HCFA Agency Information collection Activities: Submission for OMB Review; Comment request (pertaining to conditions of participation for rural health clinics).

65 FR 10450, February 28, 2000: Medicare Program; Rural Health Clinics: Amendments to Participation Requirements and Payment Provisions; and Establishment of a Quality Assessment and Performance Improvement Program — Proposed rule affecting 42 CFR Parts 405 and 491.

65 FR 11589, March 3, 2000: HCFA Agency Information Collection Activities: Submission for OMB Review; Comment request (pertaining to end stage renal disease medical information system/ESRD facility survey).

65 FR 12556, March 9, 2000: HCFA Agency Information Collection Activities: Proposed Collection; Comment request (pertaining to hospital request for certification in the Medicare/Medicaid program).

65 FR 12560, March 9, 2000: HCFA Agency Information Collection Activities: Submission for OMB Review; Comment request (pertaining to hospital provider of extended care services (swing beds) in the Medicare and Medicaid programs).

65 FR 13082, March 10, 2000: Medicare Program; Negotiated Rulemaking: Coverage and Administrative Policies for Clinical Diagnostic Laboratory Services — Proposed rule affecting 42 CFR Part 410.

65 FR 14288, March 16, 2000: HCFA Agency Information Collection Activities: Proposed Collection; Comment request (pertaining to end stage renal disease application and survey and certification).

65 FR 14289, March 16, 2000: Office of Inspector General: Publication of the OIG Compliance Program Guidance for Nursing Facilities — Notice.

65 FR 14986, March 20, 2000: HCFA Agency Information Collection Activities: Submission for OMB Review; Comment request (pertaining to skilled nursing facility resident assessment MDS data).

65 FR 25738, May 3, 2000: HCFA Emergency Clearance: Public Informatiion Collection Requirements Submitted to the Office of Management and Budget (OMB) (pertaining to the Medicare managed care CAHPS Survey).

65 FR 26618, May 5, 2000: HCFA Emergency Clearance: Public Information Collection Requirements Submitted to the Office of Management and Budget (OMB) (pertaining to Medicare consumer assessment survey of health plans).

65 FR 30415, May 11, 2000: HCFA Agency Information Collection Activities: Submission for OMB Review; Comment request (pertaining to conflict of interest and ownership and control information).

65 FR 35652, June 5, 2000: HCFA Agency Information Collection Activities: Proposed Collection; Comment request (pertaining to hospital conditions of participation; identification of potential organ, tissue, and eye donors and transplant hospitals' provision of transplant-related data).

65 FR 35653, June 5, 2000: HCFA Agency Information Collection Activities: Proposed Collection; Comment request (pertaining to ICF/MR survey forms).

65 FR 35654, June 5, 2000: HCFA Agency Information Collection Activities: Submission for OMB Review; Comment request (pertaining to hospital request for certification in Medicare and Medicaid).

65 FR 37566, June 15, 2000: HCFA Agency Information Collection Activities: Submission for OMB Review; Comment request (pertaining to hospice survey and deficiencies report form).

65 FR 37566, June 15, 2000: HCFA Agency Information Collection Activities: Submission for OMB Review; Comment request (pertaining to post-laboratory survey questionnaire under CLIA).

65 FR 40111, June 29, 2000: HCFA Agency Information Collection Activities: Proposed Collection; comment request (pertaining to qualification applications for prepaid health plans (HMOs).

65 FR 45992, July 26, 2000: HCFA Agency Information Collection Activities: Proposed Collection; Comment request (pertaining to psychiatric unit, rehabilitation unit, and rehabilitation hospital criteria worksheets).

65 FR 47739, August 3, 2000: HCFA Agency Information Collection Activities: Submission for OMB Review; Comment request (pertaining to CLIA adverse action extract).

65 FR 54857, September 11, 2000: HCFA Agency Information Collection Activities: Submission for OMB Review; Comment request (pertaining to ICF/MR survey report forms).

65 FR 54857, September 11, 2000: HCFA Agency Information Collection Activities: Submission for OMB Review; Comment request (pertaining to hospital conditions of participa-

tion-identification of potential organ, tissue, and eye donors, and transplant hospitals' provision of transplant-related data).

65 FR 57195, September 21, 2000: HCFA Agency Information Collection Activities; Proposed Collection; Comment request (pertaining to Medicare managed care CAHPS survey for quality of care purposes).

65 FR 58279, September 28, 2000: HCFA Agency Information Collection Activities: Proposed Collection; Comment request (pertaining to Medicare consumer assessment survey of health plans-CAHPS).

65 FR 59431, October 5, 2000: HCFA Agency Information Collection Activities: Proposed Collection; Comment request (pertaining to conditions for coverage of suppliers of end stage renal disease services).

65 FR 59432, October 5, 2000: HCFA Agency Information Collection Activities: Submission for OMB Review; Comment request (pertaining to end stage renal disease application and survey and certification report).

65 FR 69416, November 16, 2000: Medicare and Medicaid Programs; Hospital Conditions of Participation: Laboratory Services — Proposed rule affecting 42 CFR Part 482.

65 FR 69942, November 21, 2000: HCFA Agency Information Collection Activities: Proposed Collection; Comment request (pertaining to restraints/seclusion death reporting by hospitals).

65 FR 76647, December 7, 2000: HCFA Agency Information Collection Activities: Proposed Collection; Comment request (pertaining to alternate quality assessment survey in lieu of onsite survey for CLIA labs with good performance).

65 FR 79867, December 20, 2000: HCFA Agency Information Collection Activities: Proposed Collection; Comment request (pertaining to home health Medicare conditions of participation information collection requirements).

65 FR 79867, December 20, 2000: HCFA Agency Information Collection Activities: Proposed Collection; Comment request (pertaining to quality improvement system for managed care).

65 FR 79868, December 20, 2000: HCFA Agency Information Collection Activities: Proposed Collection; Comment request (pertaining to Medicare consumer assessment survey of health plans).

65 FR 82941, December 29, 2000: Medicare, Medicaid, and CLIA Programs; Extension of Certain Effective Dates for Clinical Labora-

tory Requirements under CLIA — Final rule with comment period, affecting 42 CFR Part 493.

2001

66 FR 2912, January 12, 2001: HCFA Agency Information Collection Activities: Proposed Collection; Comment request (pertaining to clinical laboratory ICRs contained in supporting regulations at 42 CFR section 493.1–.2001).

66 FR 6629, January 22, 2001: HCFA Agency Information Collection Activities: Submission for OMB Review; Comment request (pertaining to Medicare Integrity Program Organizational Conflict of Interest Disclosure Certificate).

66 FR 7919, January 26, 2001: HCFA Agency Information Collection Activities: Proposed Collection; Comment request (pertaining to provider Medicare agreements).

66 FR 8807, February 2, 2001: HCFA Agency Information Collection Activities: Proposed Collection; Comment request (pertaining to Medicare Federal health care programs provider/supplier enrollment application).

66 FR 9586, February 8, 2001: HCFA Agency Information Collection Activities: Proposed Collection; Comment request (pertaining to a project to develop an outcome–based continuous quality improvement system for PACE).

66 FR 9587, February 8, 2001: HCFA Agency Information Collection Activities: Proposed Collection; Comment request (pertaining to a project to develop an outcome–reporting of restraints and seclusion deaths by hospitals).

66 FR 9865, February 12, 2001: Office of Inspector General: Privacy Act of 1974; Amendment to the Health Care Program Violations System of Records—Notice and comment period (pertaining to including Social Security numbers of sanctioned individual in the Health Care Program Violations record).

66 FR 13546, March 6, 2001: HCFA Agency Information Collection Activities: Proposed Collection; Comment request (pertaining to independent diagnostic testing facility documentation of proficiency of medical personnel and resources).

66 FR 13547, March 6, 2001: HCFA Agency Information Collection Activities: Proposed Collection; Comment request (pertaining to Medicare/Medicaid psychiatric hospital survey data).

66 FR 13547, March 6, 2001: HCFA Agency Information Collection Activities: Proposed Collection; Comment request (pertaining to hospice request for certification as a provider).

66 FR 14156, March 9, 2001: HCFA Agency Information Collection Activities: Proposed Collection; Comment request (pertaining to oxygen consumer survey).

66 FR 14157, March 9, 2001: HCFA Agency Information Collection Activities: Submission for OMB review; Comment request (pertaining to home health Medicare conditions of participation information collection requirements).

66 FR 14157, March 9, 2001: HCFA Agency Information Collection Activities: Submission for OMB review; Comment request (pertaining to alternate quality assessment form for CLIA compliance).

66 FR 14906, March 14, 2001: Medicare and Medicaid Programs; Recognition of the American Osteopathic Association for Ambulatory Surgical Centers Program—Proposed notice.

66 FR 15352, March 19, 2001: Medicare and Medicaid Programs; Hospital Conditions of Participation: Anesthesia Services: Delay of Effective Date—Final rule; delay of effective date, affecting 42 CFR Parts 416, 482, and 485.

66 FR 16480, March 26, 2001: HCFA Agency Information Collection Activities; Proposed Collection; Comment request (pertaining to conditions of coverage of suppliers of end stage renal disease services). See also correction at 66 FR 18096, April 5, 2001.

66 FR 18645, April 10, 2001: HCFA Agency Information Collection Activities: Submission for OMB Review; Comment request (pertaining to Medicare and Medicaid outcome and assessment information set (OASIS) as part of the conditions of participation for home health agencies).

66 FR 18647, April 10, 2001: HCFA Agency Information Collection Activities: Submission for OMB Review; Comment request (pertaining to CLIA compliance).

66 FR 18958, April 12, 2001: HCFA Agency Information Collection Activities: Submission for OMB Review; Comment request (pertaining to information collection requirements for ambulance services).

66 FR 18959, April 12, 2001: HCFA Agency Information Collection Activities: Submission for OMB Review; Comment request (pertaining to organ procurement organization requests for designation).

66 FR 19507, April 16, 2001: HCFA Agency Information Collection Activities: Proposed Collection; Comment request (pertaining to conflict of interest and ownership and control information form).

66 FR 19508, April 16, 2001: HCFA Agency Information Collection Activities: Proposed Collection; Comment request (pertaining to on site inspection for durable medical equipment (DME) suppliers).

66 FR 19509, April 16, 2001: Medicare and Medicaid Programs; Application by the American Osteopathic Association (AOF) for Approval of Deeming Authority for Critical Access Hospitals—Proposed notice.

66 FR 20315, April 20, 2001: HCFA Agency Information Collection Activities: Submission for OMB Review; Comment request (pertaining to DMEPOS supplier standards).

66 FR 20316, April 20, 2001: HCFA Agency Information Collection Activities: Submission for OMB Review; Comment request (pertaining to DMEPOS supplier survey).

66 FR 20997, April 26, 2001: HCFA Agency Information Collection Activities: Submission for OMB Review; Comment request (pertaining to health insurance provider agreement form).

66 FR 22242, May 3, 2001: HCFA Agency Information Collection Activities: Proposed Collection; Comment request (pertaining to CLIA certification requirements).

66 FR 23945, May 10, 2001: HCFA Agency Information Collection Activities: Submission for OMB Review; Comment request (pertaining to development of an outcome–based continuous quality improvement system for PACE).

66 FR 27598, May 18, 2001: Medicare and Medicaid Programs; Hospital Conditions of Participation; Anesthesia Services: Delay of Effective Date—Notice of final rule affecting 42 CFR Parts 416, 482, and 485.

66 FR 31245, June 11, 2001: Office of Inspector General; Healthcare Integrity and Protection Data Bank: Change in User Fees—Notice.

66 FR 33102, June 20, 2001: HCFA Agency Information Collection Activities; Submission for OMB Review; Comment request (pertaining to provider/supplier enrollment application form).

66 FR 34223, June 27, 2001: Medicare Program; Application by the American Diabetes Association (ADA) for Recognition as a National Accreditation Program for Accrediting Entities that Furnish Outpatient Diabetes Self–management Training—Proposed notice.

66 FR 34457, June 28, 2001: HCFA Agency Information Collection Activities: Proposed Collection; Comment request (pertaining to

durable medical equipment and prosthetics, orthotics, and supplies supplier survey).

See § 3:1.

§ 7:2 ADDITIONAL PENALTIES FOR PERSONS OR ENTITIES SANCTIONED BY EXCLUSION UNDER SECTION 1128 OR UNDER SECTION 1128A — Section 1902(a)(39) [42 U.S.C.A. 1396a(a)(39)]

Regulations

42 CFR Part 420 — Program Integrity: Medicare

42 CFR Part 455 — Program Integrity: Medicaid

42 CFR Part 498 — Appeals Procedures for Determinations that Affect Participation in the Medicare Program and for Determinations that Affect the Participation of ICF's/MR and Certain NF's in the Medicaid Program

42 CFR Chapter V — Office of Inspector General — Health Care, Department of Health and Human Services

Subchapter A — General Provisions

Part 1000 — Introduction; General Definitions

Subchapter B — OIG Authorities

Part 1001 — Program Integrity: Medicare and State Health Care Programs

Part 1002 — Program Integrity: State-initiated Exclusion from Medicaid

Part 1003 — Civil Money Penalties, Assessments and Exclusions

Part 1004 — Imposition of Sanctions on Health Care Practitioners and Providers of Health Care Services by a Peer Review Organization

Part 1005 — Appeals of Exclusions, Civil Money Penalties and Assessments

Part 1006 — Investigational Inquiries

Part 1007 — State Medicaid Fraud Control Units

Part 1008 — Advisory Opinions by the OIG

55 FR 12205, April 2, 1990: Health Care Programs: Fraud and Abuse; Amendments to OIG Exclusion and CMP Authorities Resulting from Public Law 100–93, the Medicare and Medicaid Patient and Program Protection Act of 1987, Public Law 99–272, the Consolidated Omnibus Budget Reconciliation Act of 1985, and Public Law 100–360, the Medicare Catastrophic Coverage Act of 1988 — Proposed rule to amend 42 CFR Parts 1000, 1001, 1002, 1003, 1004,

1005, 1006, and 1007. See also correction published at 55 FR 17461, April 25, 1990.

57 FR 3298, January 29, 1992: Health Care Programs: Fraud and Abuse; Amendments to OIG Exclusion and CMP Authorities Resulting From Public Law 100–93 — Final rule affecting 42 CFR Parts 1001, 1002, 1003, 1004, 1005, 1006, and 1007. See also final rule and correction at 57 FR 9669, March 20, 1992; final rule affecting 42 CFR Parts 1001and 1005, with clarification at 58 FR 5617, January 22, 1993; and final rule affecting 42 CFR Part 1001, with correction, at 58 FR 40752, July 30, 1993.

57 FR 46865, October 13, 1992: HCFA Public Information Collection Requirements Submitted to the Office of Management and Budget for Clearance (pertaining to impact of home health care plan management and evaluation; end-stage renal disease medical case review; Medicare/Medicaid hospital swing-bed survey report form; quarterly Medicaid statement of expenditures; Medicaid program budget report; information collection requirements in final peer review organization sanction regulations; appeals procedures for determinations that affect participation in Medicare; request for medical review information for Part B intermediary outpatient therapy bills and other Part B outpatient bills; and Medicaid limitations on provider-related donations and health care-related taxes, and limitations on payment to disproportionate share hospitals).

63 FR 14393, March 25, 1998: Office of Inspector General: Health Care Programs: Fraud and Abuse; Revised OIG Civil Money Penalties Resulting from the Health Insurance Portability and Accountability Act of 1996 — Notice of proposed rulemaking, affecting 42 CFR Parts 1003, 1005, and 1006.

63 FR 46676, September 2, 1998: Office of Inspector General: Health Care Programs; Fraud and Abuse; Revised OIG Exclusion Authorities Resulting from Public Law 104–191 — Final rule affecting 42 CFR Parts 1000, 1001, 1002, and 1005. See also correction at 63 FR 57918, October 29, 1998.

63 FR 46736, September 2, 1998: Office of Inspector General: Health Care Programs; Fraud and Abuse; Revised OIG Sanction Authorities Resulting from Public Law 105–33 — Notice of proposed rulemaking affecting 42 CFR 1001, 1002, and 1003.

63 FR 58341, October 30, 1998: Office of Inspector General: Health Care Fraud and Abuse Data Collection Program: Reporting of Final Adverse Actions — Notice of proposed rulemaking under section 1128E of the Social Security Act, affecting 45 CFR 61.

63 FR 71819, December 30, 1998: Office of Inspector General; Health Care Fraud and Abuse Data Collection Program; Reporting under section 1128E of the Social Security Act of Final Adverse Actions — Notice of proposed rule-making; extension of comment period, affecting 45 CFR 61.

1999

64 FR 6753, February 16, 1999: Office of Inspector General: Privacy Act; Notification of New System of Records in Conjunction with the Healthcare Integrity and Protection Data Bank — Notice of a new system of records.

64 FR 39420, July 22, 1999: Office of Inspector General; Health Care Programs; Fraud and Abuse; Revised OIG Sanction Authorities Resulting from P.L. 105–33, the Balanced Budget Act of 1997 — Final rule affecting 42 CFR Parts 1001, 1002, and 1003. See also correction at 64 FR 42174, August 3, 1999.

64 FR 42791, September 30, 1999: Office of Inspector General; Publication of the OIG Special Advisory Bulletin on the Effect of Exclusion from Participation in Federal Health Care Programs — Notice. See also correction at 64 FR 55484, October 13, 1999.

64 FR 57619, October 26, 1999: Office of Inspector General; Privacy Act; Exempt Record System, Pertaining to the Healthcare Integrity and Protection Data Bank (HIPDB) — Notice of proposed rulemaking affecting 45 CFR Part 5b.

64 FR 57740, October 26, 1999: Office of Inspector General; Healthcare Fraud and Abuse Data Collection Program: Reporting of Final Adverse Actions - Final rule affecting 45 CFR Part 61. See also correction at 65 FR 70506, November 24, 2000.

64 FR 58851, November 1, 1999: Office of Inspector General; Healthcare Integrity and Protection Data Bank: Announcement of Opening Date for Reporting and Self-query Fee — Notice.

2000

65 FR 11589, March 3, 2000: Office of Inspector General: Health Care Integrity and Protection Data Bank under Section 1128E of the Social Security Act: Announcement of Opening Date for Querying and User Fees — Notice.

65 FR 24400, April 26, 2000: Office of Inspector General; Health Care Programs: Fraud and Abuse; Revised OIG Civil Money Penalties Resulting from Public Law 104-191 (HIPAA) — Final rule

affecting 42 CFR Parts 1001, 1003, 1005, and 1006. See also correction at 65 FR 35583, June 5, 2000.

65 FR 34986, June 1, 2000: Office of Inspector General; Privacy Act; Implementation (exempting the Healthcare Integrity and Protection Data Bank under Section 1128C of the Social Security Act from certain provisions of the Privacy Act (5 U.S.C. 552a) — Final rule.

65 FR 63035, October 20, 2000: Office of Inspector General: Medicare and State Health Care Programs: Fraud and Abuse; Revisions and Technical Corrections — Proposed rule affecting 42 CFR Parts 1001, 1003, 1005, and 1008.

2001

66 FR 9865, February 12, 2001: Office of Inspector General: Privacy Act of 1974; Amendment to the Health Care Program Violations System of Records—Notice and comment period (pertaining to including Social Security numbers of sanctioned individual in the Health Care Program Violations record).

66 FR 31245, June 11, 2001: Office of Inspector General; Healthcare Integrity and Protection Data Bank: Change in User Fees—Notice.

See § 3:2.

§ 7:3 DISCLOSING INFORMATION ABOUT SANCTIONS AGAINST HEALTH CARE PRACTITIONERS AND PROVIDERS — Section 1902(a)(49) and Section 1921 [42 U.S.C.A. 1396a(a)(49)and 42 U.S.C.A. 1396r-2]

Regulations

42 CFR Part 420 — Program Integrity: Medicare

42 CFR Part 455 — Program Integrity: Medicaid

42 CFR Part 466 — Utilization and Quality Control Review

42 CFR Chapter V — Office of Inspector General — Health Care, Department of Health and Human Services

Subchapter A — General Provisions

Part 1000 — Introduction; General Definitions

Subchapter B — OIG Authorities

Part 1001 — Program Integrity: Medicare and State Health Care Programs

Part 1002 — Program Integrity: State-initiated Exclusion from Medicaid

Part 1003 — Civil Money Penalties, Assessments and Exclusions

Part 1004 — Imposition of Sanctions on Health Care Practitioners and Providers of Health Care Services by a Peer Review Organization

Part 1005 — Appeals of Exclusions, Civil Money Penalties and Assessments

Part 1006 — Investigational Inquiries

Part 1007 — State Medicaid Fraud Control Units

Part 1008 — Advisory Opinions by the OIG

45 CFR Part 60 — National Data Bank for Adverse Information on Physicians and Health Care Practitioners

55 FR 12205, April 2, 1990: Health Care Programs: Fraud and Abuse; Amendments to OIG Exclusion and CMP Authorities Resulting from Public Law 100–93, the Medicare and Medicaid Patient and Program Protection Act of 1987, Public Law 99–272, the Consolidated Omnibus Budget Reconciliation Act of 1985, and Public Law 100–360, the Medicare Catastrophic Coverage Act of 1988 — Proposed rule to amend 42 CFR Parts 1000, 1001, 1002, 1003, 1004, 1005, 1006, and 1007. See also correction published at 55 FR 17461, April 25, 1990.

57 FR 3298, January 29, 1992: Health Care Programs: Fraud and Abuse; Amendments to OIG Exclusion and CMP Authorities Resulting From Public Law 100–93 — Final rule affecting 42 CFR Parts 1001, 1002, 1003, 1004, 1005, 1006, and 1007. See also final rule and correction at 57 FR 9669, March 20, 1992; final rule affecting 42 CFR Parts 1001and 1005, with clarification at 58 FR 5617, January 22, 1993; and final rule affecting 42 CFR Part 1001, with correction, at 58 FR 40752, July 30, 1993.

57 FR 46865, October 13, 1992: HCFA Public Information Collection Requirements Submitted to the Office of Management and Budget for Clearance (pertaining to impact of home health care plan management and evaluation; end-stage renal disease medical case review; Medicare/Medicaid hospital swing-bed survey report form; quarterly Medicaid statement of expenditures; Medicaid program budget report; information collection requirements in final peer review organization sanction regulations; appeals procedures for determinations that affect participation in Medicare; request for medical review information for Part B intermediary outpatient therapy bills and other Part B outpatient bills; and Medicaid limitations on provider-related donations and health care-related taxes, and limitations on payment to disproportionate share hospitals).

59 FR 50762, October 5, 1994: HCFA Public Information Collection Requirements Submitted to the Office of Management and Budget (OMB) for Clearance (pertaining to reimbursement of hospital costs for residents and interns, criteria for psychiatric and rehabilitation hospital units' reimbursement under the prospective payment system, disclosure of owners and managers of suppliers for fraud and abuse detection purposes, reimbursement of municipal health services clinics, survey form for hospital compliance with anti-dumping requirements, and evaluation of patient and physician satisfaction with the Medicare participating heart bypass center demonstration).

63 FR 58341, October 30, 1998: Office of Inspector General: Health Care Fraud and Abuse Data Collection Program: Reporting of Final Adverse Actions — Notice of proposed rulemaking under section 1128E of the Social Security Act, affecting 45 CFR 61.

63 FR 58399, October 30, 1998: Office of Inspector General: Publication of the OIG's Provider Self-Disclosure Protocol — Notice.

63 FR 71819, December 30, 1998: Office of Inspector General; Health Care Fraud and Abuse Data Collection Program; Reporting under section 1128E of the Social Security Act of Final Adverse Actions — Notice of proposed rule-making; extension of comment period, affecting 45 CFR 61.

1999

64 FR 6753, February 16, 1999: Office of Inspector General: Privacy Act; Notification of New System of Records in Conjunction with the Healthcare Integrity and Protection Data Bank — Notice of a new system of records.

64 FR 10478, March 4, 1999: HCFA Agency Information Collection Activities: Proposed Collection; Comment request (pertaining to information collection requirements in final peer review organization (PRO) sanction regulations).

64 FR 19375, April 20, 1999: HCFA Agency Information Collection Activities: Proposed Collection; Comment request (pertaining to acquisition, protection, and disclosure of peer review organization (PRO) information).

64 FR 30340, June 7, 1999: HCFA Agency Information Collection Activities: Submission for OMB Review; Comment request (pertaining to information collection requirements in the final peer review organization (PRO) sanction regulations).

64 FR 40017, July 23, 1999: HCFA Agency Information Collection Activities: Submission for OMB Review; Comment request (pertaining to acquisition, protection and disclosure of peer review organization (PRO) information).

64 FR 57619, October 26, 1999: Office of Inspector General; Privacy Act; Exempt Record System, Pertaining to the Healthcare Integrity and Protection Data Bank (HIPDB)—Notice of proposed rulemaking affecting 45 CFR Part 5b.

64 FR 57740, October 26, 1999: Office of Inspector General; Healthcare Fraud and Abuse Data Collection Program: Reporting of Final Adverse Actions — Final rule affecting 45 CFR Part 61.

64 FR 58851, November 1, 1999: Office of Inspector General; Healthcare Integrity and Protection Data Bank: Announcement of Opening Date for Reporting and Self-query Fee — Notice.

64 FR 73563, December 30, 1999: HCFA Agency Information Collection Activities: Submission for OMB Review; Comment request pertaining to Medicare program integrity organizational conflict of interest disclosure certificates).

2000

65 FR 11589, March 3, 2000: Office of Inspector General: Health Care Integrity and Protection Data Bank under Section 1128E of the Social Security Act: Announcement of Opening Date for Querying and User Fees — Notice.

65 FR 24400, April 26, 2000: Office of Inspector General; Health Care Programs: Fraud and Abuse; Revised OIG Civil Money Penalties Resulting from Public Law 104-191 (HIPAA)—Final rule affecting 42 CFR Parts 1001, 1003, 1005, and 1006. See also correction at 65 FR 35583, June 5, 2000.

65 FR 34986, June 1, 2000: Office of Inspector General; Privacy Act; Implementation (exempting the Healthcare Integrity and Protection Data Bank under Section 1128C of the Social Security Act from certain provisions of the Privacy Act (5 U.S.C. 552a)—Final rule.

65 FR 63035, October 20, 2000: Office of Inspector General: Medicare and State Health Care Programs: Fraud and Abuse; Revisions and Technical Corrections — Proposed rule affecting 42 CFR Parts 1001, 1003, 1005, and 1008.

2001

66 FR 9865, February 12, 2001: Office of Inspector General: Privacy Act of 1974; Amendment to the Health Care Program Violations System of Records—Notice and comment period (pertaining to including Social Security numbers of sanctioned individual in the Health Care Program Violations record).

66 FR 31245, June 11, 2001: Office of Inspector General; Healthcare Integrity and Protection Data Bank: Change in User Fees—Notice.

Office of Inspector General Notices of Program Exclusions

58 FR 41794, August 5, 1993: For March through June 1993.

58 FR 44686, August 24, 1993: For July 1993.

58 FR 48073, September 14, 1993: For August 1993.

58 FR 53519, October 15, 1993: For September 1993.

58 FR 60205, November 15, 1993: For October 1993.

58 FR 66007, December 17, 1993: For November 1993.

58 FR 3862, January 27, 1994: For December 1993.

59 FR 6285, February 10, 1994: For January 1994.

59 FR 15919, April 5, 1994: For February 1994.

59 FR 21769, April 26, 1994: For March 1994.

59 FR 25951, May 18, 1994: For April 1994.

59 FR 31255, June 17, 1994: For May 1994.

59 FR 35941, July 14, 1994: For June 1994.

59 FR 41776, August 15, 1994: For July 1994.

59 FR 47341, September 15, 1994: For August 1994.

59 FR 52973, October 20, 1994: For September 1994.

59 FR 60155, November 22, 1994: For October 1994.

59 FR 65371, December 19, 1994: For November 1994.

60 FR 4179, January 20, 1995: For December 1994.

60 FR 7780, February 9, 1995: For January 1995.

60 FR 14763, March 20, 1995: For February 1995.

60 FR 19072, April 14, 1995: For March 1995.

60 FR 27532, May 24, 1995: For April 1995.

60 FR 32016, June 19, 1995: For May 1995.

60 FR 37459, July 20, 1995: For June 1995.

60 FR 46296, September 6, 1995: For July 1995.

60 FR 48999, September 21, 1995: For August 1995.

60 FR 54880, October 26, 1995: For September 1995.

60 FR 57448, November 15, 1995: For October 1995.

60 FR 64174, December 14, 1995: For November 1995.

61 FR 6017, February 15, 1996: For December 1995 and January 1996.
61 FR 11055, March 18, 1996: For February 1996.
61 FR 17711, April 22, 1996: For March 1996.
61 FR 24502, May 15, 1996: For April 1996.
61 FR 30243, June 14, 1996: For May 1996.
61 FR 38455, July 24, 1996: For June 1996.
61 FR 42258, August 14, 1996: For July 1996.
61 FR 48710, September 16, 1996: For August 1996.
61 FR 53231, October 10, 1996: For September 1996.
61 FR 59102, November 20, 1996: For October 1996.
61 FR 66285, December 17, 1996: For November 1996.
62 FR 4315, January 29, 1997: For December 1996.
62 FR 8028, February 21, 1997: For January 1997.
62 FR 13888, March 24, 1997: For February 1997.
62 FR 19340, April 21, 1997: For March, 1997.
62 FR 26807, May 15, 1997: For April, 1997.
62 FR 33663, June 20, 1997: For May, 1997.
62 FR 41064, July 31, 1997: For June 1997.
62 FR 43177, August 12, 1997: For July 1997.
62 FR 48873, September 17, 1997: For August 1997.
62 FR 53642, October 15, 1997: For September 1997.
62 FR 60903, November 13, 1997: For October 1997.
62 FR 66377, December 18, 1997: For November 1997.
63 FR 2989, January 20, 1998: For December 1997.

1998

63 FR 8998, February 23, 1998: For January 1998.
63 FR 12477, March 13, 1998: For February 1998.
63 FR 17431, April 9, 1998: For March 1998.
63 FR 26812, May 14, 1998: For April 1998.
63 FR 32109, June 11, 1998: For May 1998.
63 FR 37891, July 14, 1998: For June 1998.
63 FR 43404, August 13, 1998: For July 1998.
63 FR 49703, September 17, 1998: For August 1998.
63 FR 55133, October 14, 1998: For September 1998.
63 FR 60357, November 9, 1998: For October 1998.
63 FR 69638, December 17, 1998: For November 1998.

1999

64 FR 3525, January 22, 1999: For December 1998.

64 FR 8390, February 19, 1999: For January 1999.
64 FR 14456, March 25, 1999: For February 1999.
64 FR 17185, April 8, 1999: For March 1999.
64 FR 25509, May 12, 1999: For April 1999.
64 FR 31007, June 9, 1999: For May 1999.
64 FR 38205, July 15, 1999: For June 1999.
64 FR 43708, August 11, 1999: For July 1999.
64 FR 51128, September 21, 1999: For August 1999.
64 FR 55740, October 14, 1999: For September 1999.
64 FR 62682, November 17, 1999: For October 1999.
64 FR 69539, December 13, 1999: For November 1999.
65 FR 3728, January 24, 2000: For December 1999.

2000

65 FR 8376, February 18, 2000: For January 2000.
65 FR 14986, March 20, 2000: For February 2000.
65 FR 19006, April 10, 2000: For March 2000.
65 FR 30415, May 11, 2000: For April 2000.
65 FR 37156, June 13, 2000: For May 2000.
65 FR 45093, July 20, 2000: For June 2000.
65 FR 53321, September 1, 2000: For July 2000.
65 FR 57358, September 22, 2000: For August 2000.
65 FR 61172, October 16, 2000: For September 2000.
65 FR 68153, November 14, 2000: For October 2000.
65 FR 77884, December 13, 2000: For November 2000.
66 FR 6634, January 22, 2001: For December 2000.

2001

66 FR 10305, February 14, 2001: For January 2001.
66 FR 14591, March 13, 2001: For February 2001.
66 FR 18962, April 12, 2001: For March 2001.
66 FR 27520, May 17, 2001: For April 2001.
66 FR 31941, June 13, 2001: For May, 2001.
See § 3:3.

§ 7:4 BILLING MEDICAID ELIGIBLES OR FINANCIALLY RESPONSIBLE RELATIVES OR REPRESENTATIVES FOR MEDICAL EXPENSES WHEN THIRD PARTIES ARE LIABLE TO PAY — Sections 1902(g) and 1902(a)(25) [42 U.S.C.A. 1396a(g) and 1396a(a)(25)]

Regulations

42 CFR Part 405, Subpart C — Recovery of Overpayment and Suspension of Payment [Medicare]

42 CFR Part 430 — Grants to States for Medical Assistance Programs

42 CFR Part 431 — State Organization and General Administration

42 CFR Part 433 — State Fiscal Administration

42 CFR Part 440 — Services: General Provisions

42 CFR Part 441 — Services: Requirements and Limits Applicable to Specific Services

55 FR 1432, January 16, 1990: Medicaid Program; State plan Requirements and Other Provisions Relating to State Third Party Liability Programs — Final rule. See also correction published at 55 FR 5118, February 13, 1990.

58 FR 38579, July 19, 1993: HCFA Public Information Collection Requirements Submitted to the Office of Management and Budget (OMB) for Clearance re survey of home health agencies; CLIA survey report form; validation of state surveys; Medicaid listing of participating home health agencies; financial information regarding Medicare benefits from Medicare contractors; and third-party liability under Medicaid.

64 FR 44031, August 12, 1999: HCFA Agency Information Collection Activites: Submission for OMB Review; Comment request (pertaining to survey and certification of rural health clinics; and determining third party liability in Medicaid programs).

See § 3:4.

§ 7:5 FAILURE BY AN INTERMEDIATE CARE FACILITY FOR THE MENTALLY RETARDED TO COMPLY WITH MEDICAID CONDITIONS FOR PARTICIPATION — Section 1902(i) [42 U.S.C.A. 1396a(i)]

Regulations

42 CFR Part 440 — Services: General Provisions

42 CFR Part 441 — Services: Requirements and Limits Applicable to Specific Services

42 CFR Part 442 — Standards for Payment for Nursing Facilities and Intermediate Care Facilities for the Mentally Retarded [Medicaid]

42 CFR Part 447 — Payment for Services

42 CFR Part 483, especially Subpart I — Conditions of Participation for Intermediate Care Facilities for the Mentally Retarded

56 FR 30696, July 5, 1991: Medicaid Program; Correction and Reduction Plans for Intermediate Care Facilities for the Mentally Retarded — Final rule affecting 42 CFR Part 442. See also correction at 56 FR 49147, September 27, 1991.

57 FR 43462, September 21, 1992: Health Care Financing Administration Public Information Collection Requirements Submitted to the Office of Management and Budget for Clearance (pertaining to sole community home health agencies; physician/supplier overpayment reports; physician or supplier Medicare agreements; conditions of participation for rural health clinics; Medicare provider refunds; conditions of participation for comprehensive outpatient rehabilitation facilities; Medicaid income and eligibility verification system; Medicaid integrated review schedule; provider overpayment report; financial statement of Medicare provider debtors; negative case action review schedule for Medicaid quality control; outpatient resource costing study; Medicaid intermediate care facility for the mentally retarded or persons with related conditions survey report form; installment agreement of beneficiary refund of overpayment; PRO assumption of responsibilities; Medicare contractor administrative budget and cost reporting system forms; fire safety survey report forms; medical records review under prospective payment system; and Qualified Medicare Beneficiary supplement to the Medicare current beneficiary survey).

58 FR 46198, September 1, 1993: HCFA Public Information Collection Requirements (ICR) Submitted to the Office of Management and Budget (OMB) for Clearance (pertaining to prenatal services and assistance screening; home health agency treatment forms; conditions of participation for intermediate care facilities for the mentally retarded; State Medicaid eligibility quality control sample selection lists; prepaid health plan cost report; hospital survey report form; procedures for determining whether providers, practitioners, or other suppliers of services are liable for certain noncovered services; Medicare credit balance reporting require-

ments; Medicare provider cost report questionnaire form; Medicare current beneficiary survey rounds 7–10; sterilization regulation/consent form; PRO reconsideration and appeals information requirements; information collection requirements in HSQ-110, acquisition, protection and disclosure of PRO information; Medicare/Medicaid organ procurement organization's (OPO) request for certification) — Notice.

60 FR 37066, July 19, 1995: HCFA Public Information Collection Requirements Submitted to the Office of Management and Budget (OMB) for Clearance (pertaining to actuarial forecasts for Medicaid utilization and cost, employers identified through a match of IRS, SSA, and Medicare records for purposes of the Medicare Secondary Payer provision, health and safety requirements for portable X-ray suppliers, and evaluation of Intermediate Care Facilities for Persons with Mental Retardation — establishing psychoactive drug use baselines).

62 FR 11214, March 11, 1997: HCFA Agency Information Collection Activities: Submission for OMB Review; Comment request (pertaining to intermediate care facility for the mentally retarded or persons with related conditions survey report forms).

1999

64 FR 54263, October 6, 1999: Medicaid Program; Flexibility in Payment Methods for Services of Hospitals, Nursing Facilities, and Intermediate Care Facilities for the Mentally Retarded — Proposed rule affecting 42 CFR Part 447.

2000

65 FR 35653, June 5, 2000: HCFA Agency Information Collection Activities: Proposed Collection; Comment request (pertaining to ICF/MR survey forms).

65 FR 54857, September 11, 2000: HCFA Agency Information Collection Activities: Submission for OMB Review; Comment request (pertaining to ICF/MR survey report forms).

65 FR 60151, October 10, 2000: Medicaid Program; Revision to Medicaid Upper Payment Limit Requirements for Hospital Services, Nursing Facility Services, Intermediate Care Facility Services for the Mentally Retarded, and Clinic Services — Proposed rule affecting 42 CFR Part 447.

2001

66 FR 3148, January 12, 2001: Medicaid Program; Revision to Medicaid Upper Payment Limit Requirements for Hospital Services, Nursing Facility Services, Intermediate Care Facility Services for the Mentally Retarded, and Clinic Services—Final rule affecting 42 CFR Part 447.

66 FR 17657, April 3, 2001: Medicaid Program; Modification of the Medicaid Upper Payment Limit Transition Period for Inpatient Hospital Services, Outpatient Hospital Services, Nursing Facility Services, Intermediate Care Facility Services for the Mentally Retarded and Clinic Services—Proposed rule affecting 42 CFR Part 447.

See § 3:5.

§ 7:5.1 OVERCHARGING MEDICAID ELIGIBLES WHO ARE QUALIFIED MEDICARE BENEFICIARIES — Section 1902(n)(3) [42 U.S.C.A. 1396a(n)(3)]

Regulations

42 CFR Part 420 — Program Integrity: Medicare

42 CFR Part 455 — Program Integrity: Medicaid

42 CFR Chapter V — Office of Inspector General — Health Care, Department of Health and Human Services

Subchapter A — General Provisions

Part 1000 — Introduction; General Definitions

Subchapter B — OIG Authorities

Part 1001 — Program Integrity: Medicare and State Health Care Programs

Part 1002 — Program Integrity: State-initiated Exclusion from Medicaid

Part 1003 — Civil Money Penalties, Assessments and Exclusions

Part 1004 — Imposition of Sanctions on Health Care Practitioners and Providers of Health Care Services by a Peer Review Organization

Part 1005 — Appeals of Exclusions, Civil Money Penalties and Assessments

Part 1006 — Investigational Inquiries

Part 1007 — State Medicaid Fraud Control Units

Part 1008 — Advisory Opinions by the OIG

See § 3:5.1.

§ 7:6 PROVIDING MEDICAID EXCLUSIONS FOR THE SAME GROUNDS AS MEDICARE EXCLUSIONS — Section 1902(p)(1) [42 U.S.C.A. 1396a(p)(1)]

Regulations

42 CFR Part 402 — Civil Money Penalties, Assessments, and Exclusions

42 CFR Part 420 — Program Integrity: Medicare

42 CFR Part 455 — Program Integrity: Medicaid

42 CFR Chapter V — Office of Inspector General — Health Care, Department of Health and Human Services

Subchapter A — General Provisions

Part 1000 — Introduction; General Definitions

Subchapter B — OIG Authorities

Part 1001 — Program Integrity: Medicare and State Health Care Programs

Part 1002 — Program Integrity: State-initiated Exclusion from Medicaid

Part 1003 — Civil Money Penalties, Assessments and Exclusions

Part 1004 — Imposition of Sanctions on Health Care Practitioners and Providers of Health Care Services by a Peer Review Organization

Part 1005 — Appeals of Exclusions, Civil Money Penalties and Assessments

Part 1006 — Investigational Inquiries

Part 1007 — State Medicaid Fraud Control Units

Part 1008 — Advisory Opinions by the OIG

55 FR 12205, April 2, 1990: Health Care Programs: Fraud and Abuse; Amendments to OIG Exclusion and CMP Authorities Resulting from Public Law 100–93, the Medicare and Medicaid Patient and Program Protection Act of 1987, Public Law 99–272, the Consolidated Omnibus Budget Reconciliation Act of 1985, and Public Law 100–360, the Medicare Catastrophic Coverage Act of 1988 — Proposed rule to amend 42 CFR Parts 1000, 1001, 1002, 1003, 1004, 1005, 1006, and 1007. See also correction published at 55 FR 17461, April 25, 1990.

57 FR 3298, January 29, 1992: Health Care Programs: Fraud and Abuse; Amendments to OIG Exclusion and CMP Authorities Resulting From Public Law 100–93 — Final rule affecting 42 CFR Parts 1001, 1002, 1003, 1004, 1005, 1006, and 1007. See also final rule and correction at 57 FR 9669, March 20, 1992; final rule affecting 42 CFR

Parts 1001and 1005, with clarification at 58 FR 5617, January 22, 1993; and final rule affecting 42 CFR Part 1001, with correction, at 58 FR 40752, July 30, 1993.

63 FR 14393, March 25, 1998: Office of Inspector General: Health Care Programs: Fraud and Abuse; Revised OIG Civil Money Penalties Resulting from the Health Insurance Portability and Accountability Act of 1996 — Notice of proposed rulemaking, affecting 42 CFR Parts 1003, 1005, and 1006.

63 FR 46676, September 2, 1998: Office of Inspector General: Health Care Programs; Fraud and Abuse; Revised OIG Exclusion Authorities Resulting from Public Law 104–191 — Final rule affecting 42 CFR Parts 1000, 1001, 1002, and 1005. See also correction at 63 FR 57918, October 29, 1998.

63 FR 46736, September 2, 1998: Office of Inspector General: Health Care Programs; Fraud and Abuse; Revised OIG Sanction Authorities Resulting from Public Law 105–33 — Notice of proposed rulemaking affecting 42 CFR 1001, 1002, and 1003.

63 FR 58341, October 30, 1998: Office of Inspector General: Health Care Fraud and Abuse Data Collection Program: Reporting of Final Adverse Actions — Notice of proposed rulemaking under section 1128E of the Social Security Act, affecting 45 CFR 61.

63 FR 68687, December 14, 1998: Medicare and Medicaid Program; Civil Money Penalties, Assessments, Exclusions, and Related Appeals Procedures — Final rule with comment period, affecting 42 CFR 400 and 402.

63 FR 71819, December 30, 1998: Office of Inspector General; Health Care Fraud and Abuse Data Collection Program; Reporting under section 1128E of the Social Security Act of Final Adverse Actions — Notice of proposed rule-making; extension of comment period, affecting 45 CFR 61.

1999

64 FR 6753, February 16, 1999: Office of Inspector General: Privacy Act; Notification of New System of Records in Conjunction with the Healthcare Integrity and Protection Data Bank — Notice of a new system of records.

64 FR 39420, July 22, 1999: Office of Inspector General; Health Care Programs; Fraud and Abuse; Revised OIG Sanction Authorities Resulting from P.L. 105–33, the Balanced Budget Act of

1997 — Final rule affecting 42 CFR Parts 1001, 1002, and 1003. See also correction at 64 FR 42174, August 3, 1999.

64 FR 42791, September 30, 1999: Office of Inspector General; Publication of the OIG Special Advisory Bulletin on the Effect of Exclusion from Participation in Federal Health Care Programs — Notice. See also correction at 64 FR 55484, October 13, 1999.

64 FR 57619, October 26, 1999: Office of Inspector General; Privacy Act; Exempt Record System, Pertaining to the Healthcare Integrity and Protection Data Bank (HIPDB) — Notice of proposed rulemaking affecting 45 CFR Part 5b.

64 FR 57740, October 26, 1999: Office of Inspector General; Healthcare Fraud and Abuse Data Collection Program: Reporting of Final Adverse Actions — Final rule affecting 45 CFR Part 61.

64 FR 58851, November 1, 1999: Office of Inspector General; Healthcare Integrity and Protection Data Bank: Announcement of Opening Date for Reporting and Self-query Fee — Notice.

2000

65 FR 11589, March 3, 2000: Office of Inspector General: Health Care Integrity and Protection Data Bank under Section 1128E of the Social Security Act: Announcement of Opening Date for Querying and User Fees — Notice.

65 FR 24400, April 26, 2000: Office of Inspector General; Health Care Programs: Fraud and Abuse; Revised OIG Civil Money Penalties Resulting from Public Law 104-191 (HIPAA) — Final rule affecting 42 CFR Parts 1001, 1003, 1005, and 1006. See also correction at 65 FR 35583, June 5, 2000.

65 FR 34986, June 1, 2000: Office of Inspector General; Privacy Act; Implementation (exempting the Healthcare Integrity and Protection Data Bank under Section 1128C of the Social Security Act from certain provisions of the Privacy Act (5 U.S.C. 552a) — Final rule.

65 FR 50552, August 18, 2000: HCFA Privacy Act of 1974; Report of Modified or Altered System (pertaining to revision of language in global fraud and abuse routine uses).

65 FR 63035, October 20, 2000: Office of Inspector General: Medicare and State Health Care Programs: Fraud and Abuse; Revisions and Technical Corrections — Proposed rule affecting 42 CFR Parts 1001, 1003, 1005, and 1008.

2001

66 FR 9865, February 12, 2001: Office of Inspector General: Privacy Act of 1974; Amendment to the Health Care Program Violations System of Records—Notice and comment period (pertaining to including Social Security numbers of sanctioned individual in the Health Care Program Violations record).

66 FR 31245, June 11, 2001: Office of Inspector General; Healthcare Integrity and Protection Data Bank: Change in User Fees—Notice.

See § 3:6.

§ 7:7 EXCLUDING HEALTH MAINTENANCE ORGANIZATIONS AND OTHER ENTITIES AUTHORIZED TO IMPLEMENT PRIMARY CARE CASE MANAGEMENT OR SPECIALTY PHYSICIAN SERVICES — Section 1902(p)(2) [42 U.S.C.A. 1396a(p)(2)]

Regulations

42 CFR Part 417 — Health Maintenance Organizations, Competitive Medical Plans, and Health Care Prepayment Plans

42 CFR Part 420 — Program Integrity: Medicare

42 CFR Part 434 — Contracts

42 CFR Part 455 — Program Integrity: Medicaid

42 CFR Chapter V — Office of Inspector General — Health Care, Department of Health and Human Services

Subchapter A — General Provisions

Part 1000 — Introduction; General Definitions

Subchapter B — OIG Authorities

Part 1001 — Program Integrity: Medicare and State Health Care Programs

Part 1002 — Program Integrity: State-initiated Exclusion from Medicaid

Part 1003 — Civil Money Penalties, Assessments and Exclusions

Part 1005 — Appeals of Exclusions, Civil Money Penalties and Assessments

Part 1006 — Investigational Inquiries

Part 1007 — State Medicaid Fraud Control Units

Part 1008 — Advisory Opinions by the OIG

55 FR 12205, April 2, 1990: Health Care Programs: Fraud and Abuse; Amendments to OIG Exclusion and CMP Authorities Result-

ing from Public Law 100–93, the Medicare and Medicaid Patient and Program Protection Act of 1987, Public Law 99–272, the Consolidated Omnibus Budget Reconciliation Act of 1985, and Public Law 100–360, the Medicare Catastrophic Coverage Act of 1988 — Proposed rule to amend 42 CFR Parts 1000, 1001, 1002, 1003, 1004, 1005, 1006, and 1007. See also correction published at 55 FR 17461, April 25, 1990.

55 FR 12738, June 12, 1990: Waiver of Certain Membership Requirements for Certain Health Maintenance Organizations, (HMOs), and State Option for Disenrollment Restrictions for Certain HMOs under Medicaid — Final rule affecting 42 CFR Parts 434 and 435. See also corrections published at 55 FR 25774, June 22, 1990, and 55 FR 33407, August 15, 1990.

56 FR 30723, July 5, 1991: Health Maintenance Organizations; Conforming Health Maintenance Organization Rules to Statutory Requirements — Proposed rule.

56 FR 31597, July 11, 1991: Health Maintenance Organizations; Group Specific Ratings — Notice of proposed rulemaking. See also correction at 56 FR 38485, August 13, 1991.

56 FR 33403, July 22, 1991: Medicare and State Health Care Programs: Fraud and Abuse; Civil Monetary Penalties and Intermediate Sanctions for Certain Violations by Health Maintenance Organizations and Competitive Medical Plans — Proposed rule.

56 FR 46562, September 13, 1991: Medicare Program; Explanation of Enrollee Rights and Other Provisions Applicable to Health Maintenance Organizations and Competitive Medical Plans — Final rule affecting 42 CFR Part 417.

57 FR 3298, January 29, 1992: Health Care Programs: Fraud and Abuse; Amendments to OIG Exclusion and CMP Authorities Resulting From Public Law 100–93 — Final rule affecting 42 CFR Parts 1001, 1002, 1003, 1004, 1005, 1006, and 1007. See also final rule and correction at 57 FR 9669, March 20, 1992; final rule affecting 42 CFR Parts 1001and 1005, with clarification at 58 FR 5617, January 22, 1993; and final rule affecting 42 CFR Part 1001, with correction, at 58 FR 40752, July 30, 1993.

58 FR 5402, January 21, 1993: Health Maintenance Organizations; HMO Qualification Determinations and Compliance Actions — Notice.

58 FR 31407, June 2, 1993: Health Maintenance Organizations: Qualification Determinations and Compliance Actions for Calendar Year 1992, Fourth Quarter — Notice.

58 FR 38170, July 15, 1993: Health Maintenance Organizations: Organizational Structure and Services — Notice of proposed rulemaking, affecting 42 CFR Part 417.

58 FR 39820, July 26, 1993: Health Maintenance Organizations: Qualification Determinations and Compliance Actions During the Period January 1, 1993, through March 31, 1993 — Notice.

58 FR 38062, July 15, 1993: Medicare Program, Health Maintenance Organizations: Technical Amendments — Final rule with comment period, affecting 42 CFR Part 417.

58 FR 38170, July 15, 1993: Health Maintenance Organizations: Organizational Structure and Services — Notice of proposed rulemaking, affecting 42 CFR Part 417. See also correction at 58 FR 46925, September 3, 1993.

58 FR 39820, July 26, 1993: Health Maintenance Organizations: Qualification Determinations and Compliance Actions During the Period January 1, 1993, through March 31, 1993 — Notice.

58 FR 68366, December 27, 1993: Medicare Program; Retroactive Enrollment and Disenrollment in Risk Health Maintenance Organizations and Competitive Medical Plans — Proposed rule affecting 42 CFR Part 417.

59 FR 8429, February 22, 1994: Medicare Program; Health Maintenance Organization and Competitive Medical Plan National Coverage Decisions — Proposed rule affecting 42 CFR Part 417.

59 FR 8435, February 22, 1994: Medicare Program; Limits on Payment to Health Maintenance Organizations (HMOs), Competitive Medical Plans (CMPs), and Health Care Prepayment Plans (HCPPs) — Proposed rule affecting 42 CFR Part 417.

59 FR 11230, March 10, 1994: Medicare Program; Post Contract Protections and Other Coordinated Care Issues (involving HMOs and CMPs that cease to furnish services under Medicare risk or cost contracts) — Proposed rule affecting 42 CFR Part 417.

59 FR 18820, April 20, 1994: HCFA: Health Maintenance Organizations: Qualification Determinations and Compliance Actions During the Period October 1, 1993, through December 31, 1993.

59 FR 23820, May 9, 1994: Medicaid Program; Requirements for Certain Health Insuring Organizations and OBRA '90 Technical Amendments, affecting 42 CFR Parts 434 and 435.

59 FR 25460, May 16, 1994: HCFA Public Information Collection Requirements Submitted to the Office of Management and Budget (OMB) for Clearance (pertaining to Medicare uniform institutional provider bill; hospice survey and deficiencies report form; HMO

financial information reports to members; hospital request for certification in Medicare and Medicaid form).

59 FR 36072, July 15, 1994: Medicare and State Health Care Programs: Fraud and Abuse, Civil Money Penalties and Intermediate Sanctions for Certain Violations by Health Maintenance Organizations and Competitive Medical Plans — Final rule affecting 42 CFR Parts 417, 431, 434, and 1003. See also correction at 59 FR 48566, September 22, 1994.

59 FR 49834, September 30, 1994: Medicare Program; Qualified Health Maintenance Organizations; Technical Amendments — Final rule with comment period, affecting 42 CFR Part 417.

59 FR 59933, November 21, 1994: Medicare Program; Appeal Rights and Procedures for Beneficiaries Enrolled in Prepaid Health Care Plans — Final rule affecting 42 CFR Part 417.

60 FR 14435, March 17, 1995: HCFA Public Information Collection Requirements Submitted to the Office of Management and Budget (OMB) for Clearance (pertaining to Medicaid drug rebates, termination of enrollment in Federally Qualified HMOs, imposition of cost-sharing charges in Medicaid, Medicare current beneficiary surveys, and forms for establishing entitlement to hospital insurance).

60 FR 34885, July 5, 1995: HCFA Full Reporting by Health Maintenance Organizations (HMOs) and Competitive Medical Plans (CMPs) Paid on a Cost Basis — Final rule affecting 42 CFR Part 417. See also correction at 60 FR 45372, August 31, 1995.

60 FR 45673, September 1, 1995: Medicare Program; Contracts with Health Maintenance Organizations (HMOs) and Competitive Medical Plans (CMPs) — Final rule with comment period, affecting 42 CFR Part 417.

60 FR 46228, September 6, 1995: Medicare Program; Payments of HMOs and CMPs and Appeals: Technical Amendments — Final rule with comment period, affecting 42 CFR Part 417.

61 FR 2122, January 25, 1996: Medicare and State Health Care Programs; Fraud and Abuse; Safe Harbors for Protecting Health Plans — Final rule.

61 FR 2255, January 25, 1996: HCFA Public Information Collection Requirements Submitted for Public Comment and Recommendations (pertaining to survey forms about health and safety requirements for physical therapists in independent practice; and national data reporting requirements for HMOs and CMPs).

61 FR 27282, May 31, 1996: HCFA Health Maintenance Organizations: Employer Contribution to HMOs — Final rule affecting 42 CFR Part 417

61 FR 29406, June 10, 1996: HCFA Agency Information Collection Activities: proposed Collection; Comment Request (pertaining to end stage renal disease application and survey and certification report forms; withholding Medicare payments to recover Medicaid overpayments; acquisition, protection, and disclosure of PRO information; clinical laboratory certification and recertification survey forms; CLIA laboratory personnel report forms; prepaid health plan cost reports; Medicare credit balance reporting requirements; statement of deficiencies and plan of correction requirements for organ procurement organizations; Medicare/Medicaid hospital survey report forms; advance directive requirements for Medicare and Medicaid; payment adjustments for sole community hospitals; survey reports for physical therapists in independent practice; HMO and CMP national data reporting requirements; identification of extension units of outpatient physical therapy and outpatient speech pathology providers; and fire safety survey reports).

61 FR 34437, July 2, 1996: HCFA Agency Information Collection Activities: Submission for OMB Review; Comment Request (pertaining to Peer Review Organization procedures for reconsideration of initial decisions; Part B enrollment forms; certification of rural health clinics for Medicare participation; Medicaid utilization review requirements for home health agencies; State listings of Medicaid recipients in institutions and procedures for State inspection of care review; procedures for disenrollment of beneficiaries from HMOs or CMPs; effectiveness of telemedicine services; formats for PROs to submit data to HCFA; and request for accelerated payments forms for providers).

61 FR 58568, November 15, 1996: Office of Inspector General; Publication of the Medicare Beneficiary Advisory Bulletin on HMO Arrangements — Notice.

61 FR 67566, December 23, 1996: HCFA Emergency Clearance: Public Information Collection Requirements Submitted to OMB (pertaining to assessment of health plans).

61 FR 69034, December 30, 1996: Medicare and Medicaid Programs; Requirements for Physician Incentive Plans in Prepaid Health Care Organizations — Final rule affecting 42 CFR Parts 417 and 434.

62 FR 12834, March 18, 1997: HCFA Correction Notice: Agency Information Collection Activities: Submission for Emergency OMB Review; Comment request (pertaining to managed care organization incentive arrangement disclosure form).

62 FR 23368, April 30, 1997: Medicare Program; Establishment of an Expedited Review process for Medicare Beneficiaries Enrolled in Health Maintenance Organizations, Competitive Medical Plans, and Health Care Prepayment Plans — Final rule with comment period, affecting 42 CFR Part 417.

62 FR 23781, May 1, 1997: HCFA Agency Information Collection Activities: Proposed Collection; Comment request (pertaining to requirement to disclose HMO financial information to members).

62 FR 28410, May 23, 1997: Office of Inspector General: Health Care Programs: Fraud and Abuse — Notice of Intent to Form the Negotiated Rulemaking Committee for the Shared Risk Exception (statutory exceptions to the anti-kickback statute) — affecting 42 CFR Part 1001.

62 FR 34761, June 27, 1997: HCFA Agency Information Collection activities: Proposed Collection; Comment request (pertaining to managed care organization, incentive arrangement disclosure forms; and qualification application form for competitive medical plans, and Medicare contract application for Federally qualified HMO's.

62 FR 45263, August 26, 1997: HCFA Agency Information Collection Activities: Proposed Collection; Comment request (pertaining to physician certification of medical necessity for home oxygen therapy; and consumer assessment of health plans).

62 FR 45426, August 27, 1997: HCFA Agency Information Collection Activities: Submission for OMB Review; Comment request (pertaining to qualification applications for competitive medical plans and Federally qualified HMOs).

62 FR 49016, September 18, 1997: HCFA Agency Information Collection Activities: Submission for OMB Review; Comment Request (pertaining to managed care incentive arrangement disclosure forms).

62 FR 50390, September 25, 1997: HCFA Agency Information Collection Activities: Submission for OMB Review; Comment request (pertaining to disclosure of HMO financial information).

62 FR 51873, October 3, 1997: HCFA Agency Information Collection Activities: Proposed Collection; Comment request (pertaining to

survey of primary care givers for the District of Columbia managed care demonstration).

62 FR 55410, October 24, 1997: HCFA Agency Information Collection Activities: Submission for OMB Review; Comment request (pertaining to Medicare/Medicaid disclosure of ownership and control forms).

62 FR 55410, October 24, 1997: Office of Inspector General: Criteria for Implementing Permissive Exclusion Authority under Section 1128(b)(7) of the Social Security Act — Notice.

62 FR 61825, November 19, 1997: HCFA Agency Information Collection Activities; Submission for OMB Review; Comment request (pertaining to survey forms for consumer assessment of health plans).

62 FR 62063, November 20, 1997: HCFA Agency Information Collection Activities: Proposed Collection; Comment request (pertaining to managed care of ESRD).

62 FR 65049, December 10, 1997: Office of Inspector General: Solicitation of New Safe Harbors and Special Fraud Alerts — Notice of intent to develop regulations, affecting 42 CFR Part 1001.

62 FR 66375, December 18, 1997: HCFA Agency Information Collection Activities: Proposed Collection; Comment request (pertaining to ESRD cost report forms; evaluation of the Oregon Medicaid reform demonstration; and qualification of new HMOs and CMPs).

62 FR 67392, December 24, 1997: Office of Inspector General: Criteria for Implementing Permissive Exclusion Authority under Section 1128(b)(7) of the Social Security Act — Notice.

63 FR 187, January 5, 1998: Office of Inspector General; Negotiated Rulemaking Committee on the Shared Risk Exception — Notice of meeting.

63 FR 7175, February 12, 1998: HCFA Emergency Clearance: Public Information Collection Requirements Submitted to the Office of Managment and Budget (OMB) (pertaining to managed care adjusted community rate (ACR) proposal).

63 FR 11263, March 6, 1998: HCFA Agency Information Collection Activities: Submission for OMB Review; Comment request (pertaining to end stage renal disease managed care demonstration.

63 FR 12475, March 13, 1998: HCFA Agency Information Collection Activities; Submission for OMB Review; Comment request (pertaining to HMO and CMP national data reporting requirements).

63 FR 14393, March 25, 1998: Office of Inspector General: Health Care Programs: Fraud and Abuse; Revised OIG Civil Money Penalties Resulting from the Health Insurance Portability and Accountability Act of 1996 — Notice of proposed rulemaking, affecting 42 CFR Parts 1003, 1005, and 1006.

63 FR 18924, April 16, 1998: HCFA Emergency Clearance: Public Information Collection Requirements Submitted to the Office of Management and Budget (OMB) (pertaining to collection of managed care data using the uniform institutional providers form).

63 FR 26811, May 14, 1998: Medicare and Medicaid Programs: Request for Public Comments on the Quality Improvement System for Managed Care — Solicitation of comments; notice of public meeting.

63 FR 38311, July 16, 1998: Office of Inspector General: Medicare and State Health Care Programs: Fraud and Abuse; Issuance of Advisory Opinions by the OIG — Final rule affecting 42 CFR 1008. See also correction at 63 FR 43449, August 13, 1998.

63 FR 42409, August 7, 1998: HCFA Agency Information Collection Activities: Proposed Collection; Comment request (pertaining to health plan data and information consumer assessment survey).

63 FR 43187, August 12, 1998: HCFA Privacy Act of 1974; System of Records — Notice of new system of records pertaining to indicators of the performance of health plans.

63 FR 46676, September 2, 1998: Office of Inspector General: Health Care Programs; Fraud and Abuse; Revised OIG Exclusion Authorities Resulting from Public Law 104–191 — Final rule affecting 42 CFR Parts 1000, 1001, 1002, and 1005. See also correction at 63 FR 57918, October 29, 1998.

63 FR 46736, September 2, 1998: Office of Inspector General: Health Care Programs; Fraud and Abuse; Revised OIG Sanction Authorities Resulting from Public Law 105–33 — Notice of proposed rulemaking affecting 42 CFR 1001, 1002, and 1003.

63 FR 58059, October 29, 1998: HCFA Agency Information Collection Activities: Submission for OMB Review; Comment request (pertaining to consumer assessment of managed care plans).

63 FR 58341, October 30, 1998: Office of Inspector General: Health Care Fraud and Abuse Data Collection Program: Reporting of Final Adverse Actions — Notice of proposed rulemaking under section 1128E of the Social Security Act, affecting 45 CFR 61.

63 FR 58399, October 30, 1998: Office of Inspector General: Publication of the OIG's Provider Self-Disclosure Protocol — Notice.

63 FR 68223, December 10, 1998: Office of Inspector General; Solicitation of New Safe Harbors and Special Fraud Alerts — Notice of intent to develop regulations, affecting 42 CFR 1001.

63 FR 68687, December 14, 1998: Medicare and Medicaid Program; Civil Money Penalties, Assessments, Exclusions, and Related Appeals Procedures — Final rule with comment period, affecting 42 CFR 400 and 402.

63 FR 71819, December 30, 1998: Office of Inspector General; Health Care Fraud and Abuse Data Collection Program; Reporting under section 1128E of the Social Security Act of Final Adverse Actions — Notice of proposed rule-making; extension of comment period, affecting 45 CFR 61.

1999

64 FR 6664, February 10, 1999: HCFA Agency Information Collection Activities: Proposed Collection; Comment request (pertaining to Medicare agreement applications for health care prepayment plans).

64 FR 6753, February 16, 1999: Office of Inspector General: Privacy Act; Notification of New System of Records in Conjunction with the Healthcare Integrity and Protection Data Bank — Notice of a new system of records.

64 FR 25891, May 13, 1999: HCFA Agency Information Collection Activities: Submission for OMB Review; Comment request (pertaining to Medicare agreement application for health care prepayment plans under section 1833).

64 FR 32508, June 17, 1999: HCFA Agency Information Collection Activities: Submission for OMB Review; Comment Request (pertaining to the quality improvement system for managed care (QISMC)).

64 FR 37985, July 14, 1999: Office of Inspector General; Publication of the OIG Special Advisory Bulletin on Gainsharing Arrangements and CMPs for Hospital Payments to Physicians to Reduce or Limit Services to Beneficiaries — Notice.

64 FR 39420, July 22, 1999: Office of Inspector General; Health Care Programs; Fraud and Abuse; Revised OIG Sanction Authorities Resulting from P.L. 105–33, the Balanced Budget Act of 1997 — Final rule affecting 42 CFR Parts 1001, 1002, and 1003. See also correction at 64 FR 42174, August 3, 1999.

64 FR 42791, September 30, 1999: Office of Inspector General; Publication of the OIG Special Advisory Bulletin on the Effect of Exclusion from Participation in Federal Health Care Pro-

grams — Notice. See also correction at 64 FR 55484, October 13, 1999.

64 FR 57619, October 26, 1999: Office of Inspector General; Privacy Act; Exempt Record System, Pertaining to the Healthcare Integrity and Protection Data Bank (HIPDB) — Notice of proposed rulemaking affecting 45 CFR Part 5b.

64 FR 57740, October 26, 1999: Office of Inspector General; Healthcare Fraud and Abuse Data Collection Program: Reporting of Final Adverse Actions - Final rule affecting 45 CFR Part 61. See also correction at 65 FR 70506, November 24, 2000.

64 FR 58851, November 1, 1999: Office of Inspector General; Healthcare Integrity and Protection Data Bank: Announcement of Opening Date for Reporting and Self-query Fee — Notice.

64 FR 63504, November 19, 1999: Office of Inspector General; Fraud and Abuse; Statutory Exception to the Anti-kickback Statute for Shared Risk Arrangements — Interim final rule with request for comment, affection 42 CFR Part 1001. See also correction at 64 FR 71317, December 21, 1999.

64 FR 63518, November 19, 1999: Office of Inspector General; Fraud and Abuse; Clarification of the Initial OIG Safe Harbor Provisions and Establishment of Additional Safe Harbor Provisions under the Anti-kickback Statute — Final rule affecting 42 CFR Part 1001.

64 FR 69217, December 10, 1999: Office of Inspector General; Solicitation of New Safe Harbors and Special Fraud Alerts — Intent to develop regulations affecting 42 CFR Part 1001.

2000

65 FR 11589, March 3, 2000: Office of Inspector General: Health Care Integrity and Protection Data Bank under Section 1128E of the Social Security Act: Announcement of Opening Date for Querying and User Fees — Notice.

65 FR 24400, April 26, 2000: Office of Inspector General; Health Care Programs: Fraud and Abuse; Revised OIG Civil Money Penalties Resulting from Public Law 104-191 (HIPAA) — Final rule affecting 42 CFR Parts 1001, 1003, 1005, and 1006. See also correction at 65 FR 35583, June 5, 2000.

65 FR 25737, May 3, 2000: HCFA Agency Information Collection Activities: Proposed Collection; Comment request (pertaining to managed care disenrollment form).

65 FR 25738, May 3, 2000: HCFA Emergency Clearance: Public Informatiion Collection Requirements Submitted to the Office of

Management and Budget (OMB) (pertaining to the Medicare managed care CAHPS Survey).

65 FR 26618, May 5, 2000: HCFA Emergency Clearance: Public Information Collection Requirements Submitted to the Office of Management and Budget (OMB) (pertaining to Medicare consumer assessment survey of health plans).

65 FR 34986, June 1, 2000: Office of Inspector General; Privacy Act; Implementation (exempting the Healthcare Integrity and Protection Data Bank under Section 1128C of the Social Security Act from certain provisions of the Privacy Act (5 U.S.C. 552a) — Final rule.

65 FR 40111, June 29, 2000: HCFA Agency Information Collection Activities: Proposed Collection; comment request (pertaining to qualification applications for prepaid health plans (HMOs).

65 FR 40668, June 30, 2000: HCFA Agency Information Collection Activities: Submission for OMB Review; Comment request (pertaining to Medicare comprehensive health plan disenrollment).

65 FR 50713, August 21, 2000: HCFA Agency Information Collection Activities: Proposed Collection; Comment request (pertaining to social HMO demonstration payment methodology)

65 FR 53319, September 1, 2000: HCFA Agency Information Collection Activities: Proposed Collection; Comment request (pertaining to incentive arrangement disclosure form for managed care organizations and their related medical groups and physicians).

65 FR 57195, September 21, 2000: HCFA Agency Information Collection Activities; Proposed Collection; Comment request (pertaining to Medicare managed care CAHPS survey for quality of care purposes).

65 FR 79867, December 20, 2000: HCFA Agency Information Collection Activities: Proposed Collection; Comment request (pertaining to quality improvement system for managed care).

65 FR 79868, December 20, 2000: HCFA Agency Information Collection Activities: Proposed Collection; Comment request (pertaining to Medicare consumer assessment survey of health plans).

65 FR 79868, December 20, 2000: HCFA Emergency Clearance: Public Information Collection Requirements Submitted to the Office of Management and Budget (OMB) (pertaining to survey of beneficiaries who involuntarily disenroll from their managed care plan).

2001

66 FR 6228, January 19, 2001: Medicaid Program; Medicaid Managed Care—Final rule with comment period, affecting 42 CFR Part 400, 430, 431, 435, 438, 440, and 447.

66 FR 9858, February 12, 2001: HCFA Privacy Act of 1974; Report of New System (pertaining to complaints against health insurance issuers and health plans).

66 FR 11546, February 26, 2001: Medicaid Program; Medicaid Managed Care: Delay of Effective Date—Final rule delay, affecting 42 CFR Parts 400, 430, 431, 434, 435, 438, 440, and 447.

66 FR 15122, March 15, 2001: HCFA Agency Information Collection Activities: Submission for OMB Review; Comment request (pertaining to quality improvement system for managed care).

66 FR 16678, March 27, 2001: HCFA Agency Information Collection Activities: Submission for OMB Review; Comment request (pertaining to Medicare managed care CAHPS survey).

66 FR 28916, May 25, 2001: HCFA Agency Information Collection Activities: Proposed Collection; Comment request (pertaining to collection of managed care data using the uniform institutional providers form).

66 FR 32776, June 18, 2001: Medicaid Program; Medicaid Managed Care: Further Delay of Effective Date for Final Rule affecting 42 CFR Parts 400, 430, 431, 434, 435, 438, 440, and 447.

See § 3:7.

§ 7:8 TERMINATION OF MEDICAID CERTIFICATION OF AND INTERMEDIATE SANCTIONS FOR PSYCHIATRIC HOSPITALS — Section 1902(y) [42 U.S.C.A. 1396a(y)]

Regulations

42 CFR Part 402 — Civil Money Penalties, Assessments, and Exclusions

42 CFR Part 440 — Services: General Provisions

42 CFR Part 441 — Services: Requirements and Limits Applicable to Specific Services

42 CFR Part 447 — Payments for Services

42 CFR Part 455 — Program Integrity: Medicaid

42 CFR Part 456 — Utilization Control

42 CFR Part 489 — Provider Agreements and Supplier Approval

57 FR 36006, August 12, 1992: Medicare Program; Self-implementing Coverage and Payments Provisions: 1990 Legis-

lation — Final rule with comment period, affecting 42 CFR Parts 405, 406, 409, 420, 411, 412, 413, 418, and 489. Pertains to capital-related inpatient hospital costs; capital-related outpatient hospital costs; non-capital related outpatient hospital costs; payment for physician pathology services; payment for services of physicians as assistants-at-surgery; payments for ambulatory surgical procedures in hospital outpatient departments; payments for radiology services performed in hospital outpatient departments; hospice benefit extension; enrollment of HMO members in Medicare Part A; coverage of ostomy supplies; application of pre-entitlement stay in psychiatric hospital to limit on payment for inpatient hospital services; payments to dialysis facilities; payment rates for erythropoietin (EPO); and Medicare secondary payer provision for individuals with ESRD. See also confirmation of final rule at 58 FR 58502, November 2, 1993.

57 FR 46362, October 8, 1992: Medicare and Medicaid Programs; Revised Effective Date of Medicare/Medicaid Provider Agreement and Supplier Participation — Proposed rule affecting 42 CFR Parts 431, 440, 442, 488, 489, and 498.

60 FR 26445, May 17, 1995: HCFA Public Information Collection Requirements Submitted to the Office of Management and Budget (OMB) for Clearance (pertaining to Medicare/Medicaid psychiatric hospital survey data, and hospice requests for Medicare certification).

63 FR 7743, February 17, 1998: Medicare and Medicaid Programs; Hospital Conditions of Participation; Provider Agreements and Supplier Approval — Notice of extension of comment period, affecting 42 CFR Parts 416, 482, 485, and 489.

63 FR 8987, February 23, 1998: Office of Inspector General: Publication of the OIG Compliance Program for Hospitals — Notice.

63 FR 12474, March 13, 1998: HCFA Agency Information Collection Activities: Proposed Collection; Comment request (pertaining to hospice request for certification in the Medicare program and Medicare/Medicaid psychiatric hospital survey data).

63 FR 19502, April 20, 1998: HCFA Agency Information Collection Activities: Proposed collection; Comment request (pertaining to annual early and periodic screening, diagnostic, and treatment services (EPSDT) participation report; Medicare and other health care programs provider/supplier enrollment application; and research and analytic support for implementing performance measurement in Medicare fee for service).

63 FR 32234, June 12, 1998: HCFA Agency Information Collection Activities: Submission for OMB Review; Comment request (pertaining to Medicare/Medicaid psychiatric hospital survey data).

63 FR 64195, November 19, 1998: Medicaid Program; Inpatient Psychiatric Services Benefit for Individuals under Age 21 —Final rule affecting 42 CFR 440and 441.

1999

64 FR 17673, April 12, 1999: HCFA Agency Information Collection Activities: Proposed Collection; Comment request (pertaining to Medicare participating physician or supplier agreements).

64 FR 24956, May 10, 1999: Medicare and Medicaid Programs; Effective Dates of Provider Agreements and Supplier Approvals-Correction restoring regulations inadvertently removed when a final rule concerning effective dates for provider agreements and supplier approvals was published at 62 FR 43931, August 18, 1997.

64 FR 39517, July 22, 1999: HCFA Agency Information Collection Activities: Submission for OMB Review; Comment request (pertaining to Medicare participating physician or supplier agreement form HCFA-460).

64 FR 42791, September 30, 1999: Office of Inspector General; Publication of the OIG Special Advisory Bulletin on the Effect of Exclusion from Participation in Federal Health Care Programs—Notice. See also correction at 64 FR 55484, October 13, 1999.

64 FR 57619, October 26, 1999: Office of Inspector General; Privacy Act; Exempt Record System, Pertaining to the Healthcare Integrity and Protection Data Bank (HIPDB)—Notice of proposed rulemaking affecting 45 CFR Part 5b.

64 FR 57740, October 26, 1999: Office of Inspector General; Healthcare Fraud and Abuse Data Collection Program: Reporting of Final Adverse Actions - Final rule affecting 45 CFR Part 61. See also correction at 65 FR 70506, November 24, 2000.

64 FR 58851, November 1, 1999: Office of Inspector General; Healthcare Integrity and Protection Data Bank: Announcement of Opening Date for Reporting and Self-query Fee—Notice.

2000

65 FR 11589, March 3, 2000: Office of Inspector General: Health Care Integrity and Protection Data Bank under Section 1128E of the

Social Security Act: Announcement of Opening Date for Querying and User Fees — Notice.

65 FR 34986, June 1, 2000: Office of Inspector General; Privacy Act; Implementation (exempting the Healthcare Integrity and Protection Data Bank under Section 1128C of the Social Security Act from certain provisions of the Privacy Act (5 U.S.C. 552a) — Final rule.

65 FR 45992, July 26, 2000: HCFA Agency Information Collection Activities: Proposed Collection; Comment request (pertaining to psychiatric unit, rehabilitation unit, and rehabilitation hospital criteria worksheets).

65 FR 61171, October 16, 2000: HCFA Agency Information Collection Activities: Submission for OMB Review; Comment request (pertaining to psychiatric unit, rehabilitation unit, and rehabilitation hospital criteria worksheets).

65 FR 69942, November 21, 2000: HCFA Agency Information Collection Activities: Proposed Collection; Comment request (pertaining to restraints/seclusion death reporting by hospitals).

2001

66 FR 7147, January 22, 2001: Medicaid Program; Use of Restraint and Seclusion in Psychiatric Residential Treatment Facilities Providing Psychiatric Services to Individuals Under Age 21—Final rule affecting 42 CFR Parts 441 and 483.

66 FR 9865, February 12, 2001: Office of Inspector General: Privacy Act of 1974; Amendment to the Health Care Program Violations System of Records—Notice and comment period (pertaining to including Social Security numbers of sanctioned individual in the Health Care Program Violations record).

66 FR 13547, March 6, 2001: HCFA Agency Information Collection Activities: Proposed Collection; Comment request (pertaining to Medicare/Medicaid psychiatric hospital survey data).

66 FR 15800, March 21, 2001: Medicare Program; Use of Restraint and Seclusion in Residential Treatment Facilities Providing Inpatient Psychiatric Services to Individuals under Age 21: Delay of effective date, affecting 42 CFR Parts 441 and 483.

66 FR 28110, May 22, 2001: Medicaid Program; Use of Restraint and Seclusion in Psychiatric Residential Treatment Facilities Providing Inpatient Psychiatric Services to Individuals under Age

21—Interim final rule, amendment and clarification with request for comment, affecting 42 CFR Parts 441 and 483.

66 FR 31245, June 11, 2001: Office of Inspector General; Healthcare Integrity and Protection Data Bank: Change in User Fees—Notice.

See § 3:8.

§ 7:9 FAILURE BY HEALTH MAINTENANCE ORGANIZATIONS TO COMPLY WITH MEDICAID REQUIREMENTS — Section 1903(m)(5) [42 U.S.C.A. 1396b(m)(5)]

Regulations

42 CFR Part 417 — Health Maintenance Organizations, Competitive Medical Plans, and Health Care Prepayment Plans

42 CFR Part 420 — Program Integrity: Medicare

42 CFR Part 434 — Contracts

42 CFR Part 455 — Program Integrity: Medicaid

42 CFR Chapter V — Office of Inspector General — Health Care, Department of Health and Human Services

Subchapter A — General Provisions

Part 1000 — Introduction; General Definitions

Subchapter B — OIG Authorities

Part 1001 — Program Integrity: Medicare and State Health Care Programs

Part 1002 — Program Integrity: State-initiated Exclusion from Medicaid

Part 1003 — Civil Money Penalties, Assessments and Exclusions

Part 1005 — Appeals of Exclusions, Civil Money Penalties and Assessments

Part 1006 — Investigational Inquiries

Part 1007 — State Medicaid Fraud Control Units

Part 1008 — Advisory Opinions by the OIG

55 FR 12738, June 12, 1990: Waiver of Certain Membership Requirements for Certain Health Maintenance Organizations, (HMOs), and State Option for Disenrollment Restrictions for Certain HMOs under Medicaid — Final rule affecting 42 CFR Parts 434 and 435. See also corrections published at 55 FR 25774, June 22, 1990, and 55 FR 33407, August 15, 1990.

56 FR 30723, July 5, 1991: Health Maintenance Organizations; Conforming Health Maintenance Organization Rules to Statutory Requirements — Proposed rule.

56 FR 31597, July 11, 1991: Health Maintenance Organizations; Group Specific Ratings — Notice of proposed rulemaking. See also correction at 56 FR 38485, August 13, 1991.

56 FR 33403, July 22, 1991: Medicare and State Health Care Programs: Fraud and Abuse; Civil Monetary Penalties and Intermediate Sanctions for Certain Violations by Health Maintenance Organizations and Competitive Medical Plans — Proposed rule.

56 FR 46562, September 13, 1991: Medicare Program; Explanation of Enrollee Rights and Other Provisions Applicable to Health Maintenance Organizations and Competitive Medical Plans — Final rule affecting 42 CFR Part 417.

57 FR 33202, July 27, 1992: Health Maintenance Organizations; HMO Qualification Determinations and Compliance Actions — Notice. See also correction at 57 FR 41810, September 11, 1992.

57 FR 36006, August 12, 1992: Medicare Program; Self-implementing Coverage and Payments Provisions: 1990 Legislation — Final rule with comment period, affecting 42 CFR Parts 405, 406, 409, 420, 411, 412, 413, 418, and 489. Pertains to capital-related inpatient hospital costs; capital-related outpatient hospital costs; non-capital related outpatient hospital costs; payment for physician pathology services; payment for services of physicians as assistants-at-surgery; payments for ambulatory surgical procedures in hospital outpatient departments; payments for radiology services performed in hospital outpatient departments; hospice benefit extension; enrollment of HMO members in Medicare Part A; coverage of ostomy supplies; application of pre-entitlement stay in psychiatric hospital to limit on payment for inpatient hospital services; payments to dialysis facilities; payment rates for erythropoietin (EPO); and Medicare secondary payer provision for individuals with ESRD.

57 FR 46119, October 7, 1992: Medicare Program; Appeal Rights and Procedures for Beneficiaries Enrolled in Prepaid Health Care Plans — Notice of proposed rulemaking affecting 42 CFR Part 417.

57 FR 52723, November 5, 1992: Medicare and State Health Care Programs: Fraud and Abuse; Safe Harbors for Protecting Health Plans — Interim final rule with request for comment. See also extension of comment period at 58 FR 2989, January 7, 1993, affecting 42 CFR 1001.

57 FR 59024, December 14, 1992: Medicare and Medicaid Programs; Requirements for Physician Incentive Plans in Prepaid

Health Care Organizations — Proposed rule affecting 42 CFR Parts 417 and 434 (HCFA) and 42 CFR Part 1003 (Office of Inspector General). See also extension of comment period at 58 FR 8568, February 16, 1993.

58 FR 31407, June 2, 1993: Health Maintenance Organizations: Qualification Determinations and Compliance Actions for Calendar Year 1992, Fourth Quarter — Notice.

58 FR 38062, July 15, 1993: Medicare Program, Health Maintenance Organizations: Technical amendments — Final rule with comment period, affecting 42 CFR Part 417.

58 FR 38170, July 15, 1993: Health Maintenance Organizations: Organizational Structure and Services — Notice of proposed rulemaking, affecting 42 CFR Part 417.

58 FR 39820, July 26, 1993: Health Maintenance Organizations: Qualification Determinations and Compliance Actions During the Period January 1, 1993, through March 31, 1993 — Notice.

58 FR 38062, July 15, 1993: Medicare Program, Health Maintenance Organizations: Technical Amendments — Final rule with comment period, affecting 42 CFR Part 417.

58 FR 38170, July 15, 1993: Health Maintenance Organizations: Organizational Structure and Services — Notice of proposed rulemaking, affecting 42 CFR Part 417. See also correction at 58 FR 46925, September 3, 1993.

58 FR 39820, July 26, 1993: Health Maintenance Organizations: Qualification Determinations and Compliance Actions During the Period January 1, 1993, through March 31, 1993 — Notice.

58 FR 68366, December 27, 1993: Medicare Program; Retroactive Enrollment and Disenrollment in Risk Health Maintenance Organizations and Competitive Medical Plans — Proposed rule affecting 42 CFR Part 417.

59 FR 8429, February 22, 1994: Medicare Program; Health Maintenance Organization and Competitive Medical Plan National Coverage Decisions — Proposed rule affecting 42 CFR Part 417.

59 FR 8435, February 22, 1994: Medicare Program; Limits on Payment to Health Maintenance Organizations (HMOs), Competitive Medical Plans (CMPs), and Health Care Prepayment Plans (HCPPs) — Proposed rule affecting 42 CFR Part 417.

59 FR 11230, March 10, 1994: Medicare Program; Post Contract Protections and Other Coordinated Care Issues (involving HMOs and CMPs that cease to furnish services under Medicare risk or cost contracts) — Proposed rule affecting 42 CFR Part 417.

59 FR 18820, April 20, 1994: HCFA: Health Maintenance Organizations: Qualification Determinations and Compliance Actions During the Period October 1, 1993, through December 31, 1993.

59 FR 23820, May 9, 1994: Medicaid Program; Requirements for Certain Health Insuring Organizations and OBRA '90 Technical Amendments, affecting 42 CFR Parts 434 and 435.

59 FR 25460, May 16, 1994: HCFA Public Information Collection Requirements Submitted to the Office of Management and Budget (OMB) for Clearance (pertaining to Medicare uniform institutional provider bill; hospice survey and deficiencies report form; HMO financial information reports to members; hospital request for certification in Medicare and Medicaid form).

59 FR 36072, July 15, 1994: Medicare and State Health Care Programs: Fraud and Abuse, Civil Money Penalties and Intermediate Sanctions for Certain Violations by Health Maintenance Organizations and Competitive Medical Plans — Final rule affecting 42 CFR Parts 417, 431, 434, and 1003. See also correction at 59 FR 48566, September 22, 1994.

59 FR 49834, September 30, 1994: Medicare Program; Qualified Health Maintenance Organizations; Technical Amendments — Final rule with comment period, affecting 42 CFR Part 417.

59 FR 59933, November 21, 1994: Medicare Program; Appeal Rights and Procedures for Beneficiaries Enrolled in Prepaid Health Care Plans — Final rule affecting 42 CFR Part 417.

60 FR 14435, March 17, 1995: HCFA Public Information Collection Requirements Submitted to the Office of Management and Budget (OMB) for Clearance (pertaining to Medicaid drug rebates, termination of enrollment in Federally Qualified HMOs, imposition of cost-sharing charges in Medicaid, Medicare current beneficiary surveys, and forms for establishing entitlement to hospital insurance).

60 FR 34885, July 5, 1995: HCFA Full Reporting by Health Maintenance Organizations (HMOs) and Competitive Medical Plans (CMPs) Paid on a Cost Basis — Final rule affecting 42 CFR Part 417. See also correction at 60 FR 45372, August 31, 1995.

60 FR 45673, September 1, 1995: Medicare Program; Contracts with Health Maintenance Organizations (HMOs) and Competitive Medical Plans (CMPs) — Final rule with comment period, affecting 42 CFR Part 417.

60 FR 46228, September 6, 1995: Medicare Program; Payments of HMOs and CMPs and Appeals: Technical Amendments — Final rule with comment period, affecting 42 CFR Part 417.

61 FR 2122, January 25, 1996: Medicare and State Health Care Programs; Fraud and Abuse; Safe Harbors for Protecting Health Plans — Final rule.

61 FR 2255, January 25, 1996: HCFA Public Information Collection Requirements Submitted for Public Comment and Recommendations (pertaining to survey forms about health and safety requirements for physical therapists in independent practice; and national data reporting requirements for HMOs and CMPs).

61 FR 29406, June 10, 1996: HCFA Agency Information Collection Activities: proposed Collection; Comment Request (pertaining to end stage renal disease application and survey and certification report forms; withholding Medicare payments to recover Medicaid overpayments; acquisition, protection, and disclosure of PRO information; clinical laboratory certification and recertification survey forms; CLIA laboratory personnel report forms; prepaid health plan cost reports; Medicare credit balance reporting requirements; statement of deficiencies and plan of correction requirements for organ procurement organizations; Medicare/Medicaid hospital survey report forms; advance directive requirements for Medicare and Medicaid; payment adjustments for sole community hospitals; survey reports for physical therapists in independent practice; HMO and CMP national data reporting requirements; identification of extension units of outpatient physical therapy and outpatient speech pathology providers; and fire safety survey reports).

61 FR 34437, July 2, 1996: HCFA Agency Information Collection Activities: Submission for OMB Review; Comment Request (pertaining to Peer Review Organization procedures for reconsideration of initial decisions; Part B enrollment forms; certification of rural health clinics for Medicare participation; Medicaid utilization review requirements for home health agencies; State listings of Medicaid recipients in institutions and procedures for State inspection of care review; procedures for disenrollment of beneficiaries from HMOs or CMPs; effectiveness of telemedicine services; formats for PROs to submit data to HCFA; and request for accelerated payments forms for providers).

61 FR 58568, November 15, 1996: Office of Inspector General; Publication of the Medicare Beneficiary Advisory Bulletin on HMO Arrangements — Notice.

61 FR 67566, December 23, 1996: HCFA Emergency Clearance: Public Information Collection Requirements Submitted to OMB (pertaining to assessment of health plans).

61 FR 69034, December 30, 1996: Medicare and Medicaid Programs; Requirements for Physician Incentive Plans in Prepaid Health Care Organizations — Final rule affecting 42 CFR Parts 417 and 434.

62 FR 12834, March 18, 1997: HCFA Correction Notice: Agency Information Collection Activities: Submission for Emergency OMB Review; Comment request (pertaining to managed care organization incentive arrangement disclosure form).

62 FR 23368, April 30, 1997: Medicare Program; Establishment of an Expedited Review process for Medicare Beneficiaries Enrolled in Health Maintenance Organizations, Competitive Medical Plans, and Health Care Prepayment Plans — Final rule with comment period, affecting 42 CFR Part 417.

62 FR 23781, May 1, 1997: HCFA Agency Information Collection Activities: Proposed Collection; Comment request (pertaining to requirement to disclose HMO financial information to members).

62 FR 28410, May 23, 1997: Office of Inspector General: Health Care Programs: Fraud and Abuse — Notice of Intent to Form the Negotiated Rulemaking Committee for the Shared Risk Exception (statutory exceptions to the anti-kickback statute) — affecting 42 CFR Part 1001.

62 FR 34761, June 27, 1997: HCFA Agency Information Collection activities: Proposed Collection; Comment request (pertaining to managed care organization, incentive arrangement disclosure forms; and qualification application form for competitive medical plans, and Medicare contract application for Federally qualified HMO's.

62 FR 45263, August 26, 1997: HCFA Agency Information Collection Activities: Proposed Collection; Comment request (pertaining to physician certification of medical necessity for home oxygen therapy; and consumer assessment of health plans).

62 FR 45426, August 27, 1997: HCFA Agency Information Collection Activities: Submission for OMB Review; Comment request (pertaining to qualification applications for competitive medical plans and Federally qualified HMOs).

62 FR 49016, September 18, 1997: HCFA Agency Information Collection Activities: Submission for OMB Review; Comment

Request (pertaining to managed care incentive arrangement disclosure forms).

62 FR 50390, September 25, 1997: HCFA Agency Information Collection Activities: Submission for OMB Review; Comment request (pertaining to disclosure of HMO financial information).

62 FR 51873, October 3, 1997: HCFA Agency Information Collection Activities: Proposed Collection; Comment request (pertaining to survey of primary care givers for the District of Columbia managed care demonstration).

62 FR 55410, October 24, 1997: HCFA Agency Information Collection Activities: Submission for OMB Review; Comment request (pertaining to Medicare/Medicaid disclosure of ownership and control forms).

62 FR 55410, October 24, 1997: Office of Inspector General: Criteria for Implementing Permissive Exclusion Authority under Section 1128(b)(7) of the Social Security Act — Notice.

62 FR 61825, November 19, 1997: HCFA Agency Information Collection Activities; Submission for OMB Review; Comment request (pertaining to survey forms for consumer assessment of health plans).

62 FR 65049, December 10, 1997: Office of Inspector General: Solicitation of New Safe Harbors and Special Fraud Alerts — Notice of intent to develop regulations, affecting 42 CFR Part 1001.

62 FR 66375, December 18, 1997: HCFA Agency Information Collection Activities: Proposed Collection; Comment request (pertaining to ESRD cost report forms; evaluation of the Oregon Medicaid reform demonstration; and qualification of new HMOs and CMPs).

63 FR 187, January 5, 1998: Office of Inspector General; Negotiated Rulemaking Committee on the Shared Risk Exception — Notice of meeting.

63 FR 7175, February 12, 1998: HCFA Emergency Clearance: Public Information Collection Requirements Submitted to the Office of Managment and Budget (OMB) (pertaining to managed care adjusted community rate (ACR) proposal).

63 FR 11263, March 6, 1998: HCFA Agency Information Collection Activities: Submission for OMB Review; Comment request (pertaining to end stage renal disease managed care demonstration).

63 FR 12475, March 13, 1998: HCFA Agency Information Collection Activities; Submission for OMB Review; Comment request (pertaining to HMO and CMP national data reporting requirements).

63 FR 18924, April 16, 1998: HCFA Emergency Clearance: Public Information Collection Requirements Submitted to the Office of Management and Budget (OMB) (pertaining to collection of managed care data using the uniform institutional providers form).

63 FR 26811, May 14, 1998: Medicare and Medicaid Programs: Request for Public Comments on the Quality Improvement System for Managed Care — Solicitation of comments; notice of public meeting.

63 FR 38414, July 16, 1998: HCFA Privacy Act of 1974; Report of Altered System (pertaining to disclosure of individual-specific information to combat fraud or abuse in health benefit programs).

63 FR 40723, July 30, 1998: HCFA Agency Information Collection Activities: Proposed Collection; Comment request (pertaining to requirements for health care prepayment plan (HCPP) eligibility under Section 1833 of the Social Security Act).

63 FR 42409, August 7, 1998: HCFA Agency Information Collection Activities: Proposed Collection; Comment request (pertaining to health plan data and information consumer assessment survey).

63 FR 43187, August 12, 1998: HCFA Privacy Act of 1974; System of Records — Notice of new system of records pertaining to indicators of the performance of health plans.

63 FR 58059, October 29, 1998: HCFA Agency Information Collection Activities: Submission for OMB Review; Comment request (pertaining to consumer assessment of managed care plans).

63 FR 58341, October 30, 1998: Office of Inspector General: Health Care Fraud and Abuse Data Collection Program: Reporting of Final Adverse Actions — Notice of proposed rulemaking under section 1128E of the Social Security Act, affecting 45 CFR 61.

63 FR 58399, October 30, 1998: Office of Inspector General: Publication of the OIG's Provider Self-Disclosure Protocol — Notice.

63 FR 68223, December 10, 1998: Office of Inspector General; Solicitation of New Safe Harbors and Special Fraud Alerts — Notice of intent to develop regulations, affecting 42 CFR 1001.

63 FR 71819, December 30, 1998: Office of Inspector General; Health Care Fraud and Abuse Data Collection Program; Reporting under section 1128E of the Social Security Act of Final Adverse Actions — Notice of proposed rule-making; extension of comment period, affecting 45 CFR 61.

1999

64 FR 32508, June 17, 1999: HCFA Agency Information Collection Activities: Submission for OMB Review; Comment Request (pertaining to the quality improvement system for managed care (QISMC)).

64 FR 6753, February 16, 1999: Office of Inspector General: Privacy Act; Notification of New System of Records in Conjunction with the Healthcare Integrity and Protection Data Bank — Notice of a new system of records.

64 FR 37985, July 14, 1999: Office of Inspector General; Publication of the OIG Special Advisory Bulletin on Gainsharing Arrangements and CMPs for Hospital Payments to Physicians to Reduce or Limit Services to Beneficiaries — Notice.

64 FR 39420, July 22, 1999: Office of Inspector General; Health Care Programs; Fraud and Abuse; Revised OIG Sanction Authorities Resulting from P.L. 105–33, the Balanced Budget Act of 1997 — Final rule affecting 42 CFR Parts 1001, 1002, and 1003. See also correction at 64 FR 42174, August 3, 1999.

64 FR 42791, September 30, 1999: Office of Inspector General; Publication of the OIG Special Advisory Bulletin on the Effect of Exclusion from Participation in Federal Health Care Programs — Notice. See also correction at 64 FR 55484, October 13, 1999.

64 FR 57619, October 26, 1999: Office of Inspector General; Privacy Act; Exempt Record System, Pertaining to the Healthcare Integrity and Protection Data Bank (HIPDB) — Notice of proposed rulemaking affecting 45 CFR Part 5b.

64 FR 57740, October 26, 1999: Office of Inspector General; Healthcare Fraud and Abuse Data Collection Program: Reporting of Final Adverse Actions - Final rule affecting 45 CFR Part 61. See also correction at 65 FR 70506, November 24, 2000.

64 FR 58851, November 1, 1999: Office of Inspector General; Healthcare Integrity and Protection Data Bank: Announcement of Opening Date for Reporting and Self-query Fee — Notice.

64 FR 63504, November 19, 1999: Office of Inspector General; Fraud and Abuse; Statutory Exception to the Anti-kickback Statute for Shared Risk Arrangements — Interim final rule with request for comment, affection 42 CFR Part 1001. See also correction at 64 FR 71317, December 21, 1999.

64 FR 63518, November 19, 1999: Office of Inspector General; Fraud and Abuse; Clarification of the Initial OIG Safe Harbor Provi-

sions and Establishment of Additional Safe Harbor Provisions under the Anti-kickback Statute — Final rule affecting 42 CFR Part 1001.

64 FR 69217, December 10, 1999: Office of Inspector General; Solicitation of New Safe Harbors and Special Fraud Alerts — Intent to develop regulations affecting 42 CFR Part 1001.

2000

65 FR 9274, February 24, 2000: Office of Inspector General: Publication of OIG Special Fraud Alert on Rental of Space in Physician Offices by Persons or Entities to Which Physicians Refer — Notice.

65 FR 11589, March 3, 2000: Office of Inspector General: Health Care Integrity and Protection Data Bank under Section 1128E of the Social Security Act: Announcement of Opening Date for Querying and User Fees — Notice.

65 FR 24400, April 26, 2000: Office of Inspector General; Health Care Programs: Fraud and Abuse; Revised OIG Civil Money Penalties Resulting from Public Law 104-191 (HIPAA) — Final rule affecting 42 CFR Parts 1001, 1003, 1005, and 1006. See also correction at 65 FR 35583, June 5, 2000.

65 FR 32060, May 22, 2000: Office of Inspector General Medicare and State Health Care Programs: Fraud and Abuse: Ambulance Restocking Safe Harbor under the Anti-kickback Statute — Notice of proposed rulemaking affecting 42 CFR 1001.

65 FR 34986, June 1, 2000: Office of Inspector General; Privacy Act; Implementation (exempting the Healthcare Integrity and Protection Data Bank under Section 1128C of the Social Security Act from certain provisions of the Privacy Act (5 U.S.C. 552a) — Final rule.

65 FR 50713, August 21, 2000: HCFA Agency Information Collection Activities: Proposed Collection; Comment request (pertaining to social HMO demonstration payment methodology)

65 FR 53319, September 1, 2000: HCFA Agency Information Collection Activities: Proposed Collection; Comment request (pertaining to incentive arrangement disclosure form for managed care organizations and their related medical groups and physicians).

65 FR 57195, September 21, 2000: HCFA Agency Information Collection Activities; Proposed Collection; Comment request (pertaining to Medicare managed care CAHPS survey for quality of care purposes).

65 FR 63035, October 20, 2000: Office of Inspector General: Medicare and State Health Care Programs: Fraud and Abuse; Revisions and Technical Corrections — Proposed rule affecting 42 CFR Parts 1001, 1003, 1005, and 1008.

65 FR 79867, December 20, 2000: HCFA Agency Information Collection Activities: Proposed Collection; Comment request (pertaining to quality improvement system for managed care).

65 FR 79868, December 20, 2000: HCFA Agency Information Collection Activities: Proposed Collection; Comment request (pertaining to Medicare consumer assessment survey of health plans).

65 FR 79868, December 20, 2000: HCFA Emergency Clearance: Public Information Collection Requirements Submitted to the Office of Management and Budget (OMB) (pertaining to survey of beneficiaries who involuntarily disenroll from their managed care plan).

2001

66 FR 6228, January 19, 2001: Medicaid Program; Medicaid Managed Care—Final rule with comment period, affecting 42 CFR Part 400, 430, 431, 435, 438, 440, and 447.

66 FR 6629, January 22, 2001: HCFA Agency Information Collection Activities: Submission for OMB Review; Comment request (pertaining to Medicare Integrity Program Organizational Conflict of Interest Disclosure Certificate).

66 FR 9858, February 12, 2001: HCFA Privacy Act of 1974; Report of New System (pertaining to complaints against health insurance issuers and health plans).

66 FR 9865, February 12, 2001: Office of Inspector General: Privacy Act of 1974; Amendment to the Health Care Program Violations System of Records—Notice and comment period (pertaining to including Social Security numbers of sanctioned individual in the Health Care Program Violations record).

66 FR 11546, February 26, 2001: Medicaid Program; Medicaid Managed Care: Delay of Effective Date—Final rule delay, affecting 42 CFR Parts 400, 430, 431, 434, 435, 438, 440, and 447.

66 FR 15122, March 15, 2001: HCFA Agency Information Collection Activities: Submission for OMB Review; Comment request (pertaining to quality improvement system for managed care).

66 FR 16678, March 27, 2001: HCFA Agency Information Collection Activities: Submission for OMB Review; Comment request (pertaining to Medicare managed care CAHPS survey).

66 FR 19507, April 16, 2001: HCFA Agency Information Collection Activities: Proposed Collection; Comment request (pertaining to conflict of interest and ownership and control information form).

66 FR 28916, May 25, 2001: HCFA Agency Information Collection Activities: Proposed Collection; Comment request (pertaining to collection of managed care data using the uniform institutional providers form).

66 FR 31245, June 11, 2001: Office of Inspector General; Healthcare Integrity and Protection Data Bank: Change in User Fees—Notice.

66 FR 32776, June 18, 2001: Medicaid Program; Medicaid Managed Care: Further Delay of Effective Date for Final Rule affecting 42 CFR Parts 400, 430, 431, 434, 435, 438, 440, and 447.

See § 3:9.

§ 7:10 FAILURE BY STATES TO MEET MEDICAID PLAN REQUIREMENTS — Section 1904 [42 U.S.C.A. 1396c]

Regulations

42 CFR Part 430 — Grants to States for Medical Assistance Programs

42 CFR Part 431 — State Organization and General Administration

42 CFR Part 432 — State Personnel Administration

42 CFR Part 433 — State Fiscal Administration

42 CFR Part 434 — Contracts

42 CFR Part 435 — Eligibility in the States, District of Columbia, the Northern Mariana Islands, and American Samoa

42 CFR Part 436 — Eligibility in Guam, Puerto Rico, and the Virgin Islands

42 CFR Part 440 — Services: General Provisions

42 CFR Part 441 — Services: Requirements and Limits Applicable to Specific Services

42 CFR Part 442 — Standards for Payment for Nursing Facilities and Intermediate Care Facilities for the Mentally Retarded [Medicaid]

42 CFR Part 447 — Payment for Services

42 CFR Part 455 — Program Integrity: Medicaid

42 CFR Part 456 — Utilization Control

42 CFR Part 476 — Utilization and Quality Control Review

53 FR 38032, September 29, 1988: Medicaid Program; Eligibility of Aliens for Medicaid — Notice.

53 FR 48314, December 2, 1988: Medicare and Medicaid Programs; Medicare, Medicaid, and Clinical Laboratories Improvement Act (CLIA) Patient Confidentiality Rules — Final rule amending 42 CFR Parts 74, 405, and 441.

53 FR 48645, December 2, 1988: Medicare and Medicaid Programs; Medicare, Medicaid, and Clinical Laboratories Improvement Act (CLIA) Patient Confidentiality Rules — Final rule amending 42 CFR Parts 74, 405, and 441.

53 FR 50293, December 14, 1988: Medicare and Medicaid Programs; Health Care Financing Research and Demonstration; Availability of Funds for Cooperative Agreements and Grants, Medicare Catastrophic Coverage Act of 1988.

54 FR 1956, January 18, 1989: Medicare and Medicaid Programs; Denial of Payment for Substandard Quality Care and Review of Beneficiary Complaints — Proposed rule to amend 42 CFR Parts 405, 424, 462, 466, 473, 476, and 489.

54 FR 4023, January 27, 1989: Miscellaneous Medicare and Medicaid Amendments — Final rule amending 42 CFR Parts 409, 410, 416, 421, 424, 441, and 489.

54 FR 5316, February 2, 1989: Medicare and Medicaid; Requirements for Long Term Care Facilities — Final rule with comment period, amending 42 CFR Parts 405, 442, 447, 483, 488, 489, and 498. See also delay in effective date at 54 FR 29717, July 14, 1989; corrections at 54 FR 8361, February 27, 1989, and 54 FR 37466, September 11, 1989; and final rule delaying effective date from January 1, 1990, to October 1, 1990, at 54 FR 53611, December 29, 1989.

54 FR 5452, February 3, 1989: Medicaid Program; Refunding of Federal Share of Overpayments Made to Medicaid Providers — Final regulations amending 42 CFR Part 433. See also correction at 54 FR 5452, February 28, 1989.

54 FR 7798, February 23, 1989: Medicaid Program; Eligibility Groups, Coverage, and Conditions of Eligibility; Legislative Changes Under OBRA '87, COBRA, and TEFRA — Notice of proposed rulemaking to amend 42 CFR Parts 431, 433, 435, 436, 440, and 447.

54 FR 8738, March 2, 1989: Medicaid Program; Targeting Information for Income and Eligibility Verification Systems — Interim final rule with comment period to amend 42 CFR Parts 433 and 435.

54 FR 9995, March 9, 1989: Medicare and Medicaid Programs; Fraud and Abuse; Administrative Adjudication of Certain Health Care Exclusion Cases — Final rule amending 42 CFR 1001.

54 FR 21065, May 16, 1989: Medicare and Medicaid; Approved Information Collection Requirements and Federal Medical Assistance Percentage Computation — Final rule and technical correction.

54 FR 27755, June 30, 1989: Medicaid Program; MMIS System Performance Review Revisions — Proposed notice.

54 FR 39421, September 26, 1989: Medicaid Program; Eligibility and Coverage Requirements — Proposed rule to amend 42 CFR Parts 435, 436, and 440.

54 FR 41966, October 13, 1989: Medicaid Program; Medicaid Management Information System: Revised Definition of "Mechanized Claims Processing and Information Retrieval System" — Final rule with comment period.

55 FR 1432, January 16, 1990: Medicaid Program; State plan Requirements and Other Provisions Relating to State Third Party Liability Programs — Final rule. See also correction published at 55 FR 5118, February 13, 1990.

55 FR 9538, March 14, 1990: Medicare, Medicaid and CLIA Programs; Revision of the Laboratory Regulations for the Medicare, Medicaid, and Clinical Laboratories Improvement Act of 1967 Programs — Final rule with comment period, amending 42 CFR Parts 74, 405, 416, 440, 482, 483, 488, and 493.

55 FR 10256, March 20, 1990: Medicare and Medicaid; Charges to Residents' Funds in Nursing Homes — Proposed rule to amend 42 CFR Part 483. See also final rule at 57 FR 53572, November 12, 1992.

55 FR 10938, March 23, 1990: Medicare and Medicaid Programs; Nurse Aide Training and Competency Evaluation Programs — Proposed rule to amend 42 CFR Parts 431, 433, and 483.

55 FR 10951, March 23, 1990: Medicare and Medicaid Programs; Preadmission Screening and Annual Resident Review — Proposed rule to amend 42 CFR Parts 405, 431, and 483.

55 FR 12205, April 2, 1990: Health Care Programs: Fraud and Abuse; Amendments to OIG Exclusion and CMP Authorities Resulting from Public Law 100–93, the Medicare and Medicaid Patient and Program Protection Act of 1987, Public Law 99–272, the Consolidated Omnibus Budget Reconciliation Act of 1985, and Public Law 100–360, the Medicare Catastrophic Coverage Act of 1988 — Pro-

posed rule to amend 42 CFR Parts 1000, 1001, 1002, 1003, 1004, 1005, 1006, and 1007. See also correction published at 55 FR 17461, April 25, 1990.

55 FR 20896, May 21, 1990: Medicare, Medicaid and CLIA Programs; Regulations Implementing the Clinical Laboratory Improvement Amendments of 1988 (CLIA '88) — Proposed rule. See also extension of time for public comment to September 21, 1990, published at 55 FR 34289 on August 22, 1990.

55 FR 12738, June 12, 1990: Waiver of Certain Membership Requirements for Certain Health Maintenance Organizations, (HMOs), and State Option for Disenrollment Restrictions for Certain HMOs under Medicaid — Final rule affecting 42 CFR Parts 434 and 435. See also corrections published at 55 FR 25774, June 22, 1990, and 55 FR 33407, August 15, 1990.

55 FR 31758, August 3, 1990: Clinical Laboratory Improvement Act Programs; Fee Collection — Proposed rule affecting 42 CFR Part 493.

55 FR 48601, November 21, 1990: Medicaid Program; Eligibility Groups, Coverage, and Conditions of Eligibility; Legislative Changes under OBRA '87, COBRA, and TEFRA — Final rule amends 42 CFR Parts 433, 435, 436, 440, and 447. See also corrections at 55 FR 52130, December 19, 1990, 56 FR 10807, March 14, 1991.

55 FR 51292, December 13, 1990: Medicaid Program; Modification of Certain Requirements for Health Insuring Organizations — Final rule.

56 FR 7049, February 21, 1991: Medicaid Program; Drug Rebate Agreement — Notice with comment period. See also 56 FR 9012, March 4, 1991.

56 FR 8832, March 1, 1991: Medicare and Medicaid Programs; OBRA '87 Conforming Amendments — Final rule with comment period, amends 42 CFR Parts 400, 405, 406, 408, 409, 410, 413, 416, 417, 424, 430, 431, 435, 436, 440, 441, 447, 455, 482, 485, 489, 491, and 498. See also correction published at 56 FR 23021, May 20, 1991.

56 FR 13430, April 2, 1991: Medicare and Laboratory Certification Programs; Enforcement Procedures for Laboratories — Proposed rule.

56 FR 30696, July 5, 1991: Medicaid Program; Correction and Reduction Plans for Intermediate Care Facilities for the Mentally Retarded — Final rule affecting 42 CFR Part 442. See also correction at 56 FR 49147, September 27, 1991.

56 FR 33403, July 22, 1991: Medicare and State Health Care Programs: Fraud and Abuse; Civil Monetary Penalties and Intermediate Sanctions for Certain Violations by Health Maintenance Organizations and Competitive Medical Plans — Proposed rule.

56 FR 37054, August 2, 1991: Medicare and Medicaid Programs; Survey and Enforcement Requirements and Alternative Sanctions for Home Health Agencies — Proposed rule affecting 42 CFR Parts 441, 488, and 489.

56 FR 38074, August 12, 1991: Medicare and Medicaid; Eligibility for Premium Hospital Insurance; State Buy-in Agreements — Final rule with comment period affecting 42 CFR Parts 400, 406, and 407. See also correction at 56 FR 50058, October 3, 1991.

56 FR 43929, September 5, 1991: Medicare and Medicaid Programs; Recognition of the Community Health Accreditation Program Standards for Home Care Organizations — Proposed notice.

56 FR 46380, September 12, 1991: Medicaid Program; State Share of Financial Participation — Interim final rule with comment, affecting 42 CFR Part 433.

56 FR 48112, September 24, 1991: Medicaid Program; Community Supported Living Arrangements Services — Interim final rule with comment period, affecting 42 CFR Part 441.

56 FR 48826, September 26, 1991: Medicare and Medicaid; Requirements for Long Term Care Facilities — Final rule affecting 42 CFR Parts 422, 447, 483, 488, 489, and 498. See also correction at 57 FR 43922, September 23, 1992.

56 FR 48880, September 26, 1991: Medicare and Medicaid Programs; Nurse Aide Training and Competency Evaluation Programs — Final rule affecting 42 CFR Parts 431, 433, and 483. See also correction at 56 FR 59331, November 25, 1991.

56 FR 56141, October 31, 1991: Medicaid Program; Standards for Defining Disproportionate Share Hospitals — Proposed rule affecting 42 CFR Part 447. Withdrawn, 56 FR 64228, December 9, 1991.

56 FR 65490, December 17, 1991: Medicaid Program; Model Medicaid Application Form — Notice.

56 FR 65853, December 19, 1991: Medicaid Program: Medicaid Eligibility Quality Control Program — Response to comments on final rule issued May 31, 1990, affecting 42 CFR Part 431.

56 FR 66392, December 23, 1991: Medicaid Program; Required Coverage of Nurse Practitioner Services — Proposed rule affecting

42 CFR Parts 440 and 441. See also correction at 57 FR 4085, February 3, 1992.

57 FR 3298, January 29, 1992: Health Care Programs: Fraud and Abuse; Amendments to OIG Exclusion and CMP Authorities Resulting From Public Law 100–93 — Final rule affecting 42 CFR Parts 1001, 1002, 1003, 1004, 1005, 1006, and 1007. See also final rule and correction at 57 FR 9669, March 20, 1992; final rule affecting 42 CFR Parts 1001 and 1005, with clarification at 58 FR 5617, January 22, 1993; and final rule affecting 42 CFR Part 1001, with correction, at 58 FR 40752, July 30, 1993.

57 FR 4516, February 5, 1992: Medicare and Medicaid Programs; Omnibus Nursing Home Requirements — Proposed rule affecting 42 CFR Parts 418, 440, 441, 482, 483, and 488. See also correction at 57 FR 8961, March 13, 1992.

57 FR 7002, February 28, 1992: Medicare, Medicaid and CLIA Programs; Regulations Implementing the Clinical Laboratory Improvement Amendments of 1988 (CLIA) — Final rule with comment period, affecting 42 CFR Parts 405, 410, 416, 417, 418, 440, 482, 483, 484, 485, 488, 491, 493, and 494. See also correction at 57 FR 35760, August 11, 1992, and correction amendments at 58 FR 5212, January 19, 1993.

57 FR 7218, February 28, 1992: Medicare Program; Medicare and Laboratory Certification Program; Enforcement Procedures for Laboratories — Final rule affecting 42 CFR Part 493. See also correction amendments at 58 FR 5212, January 19, 1993.

57 FR 8194, March 6, 1992: Medicare and Medicaid Programs; Advance Directives — Interim final rule with comment period, affecting 42 CFR Parts 417, 431, 434, 483, 484, 489, and 498.

57 FR 8588, March 11, 1992: Medicare Program; Physician Ownership of, and Referrals to, Health Care Entities that Furnish Clinical Laboratory Services — Proposed rule affecting 42 CFR Part 411.

57 FR 13106, April 15, 1992: Medicare and Medicaid Programs; Small Business Innovation Research Grants for Fiscal Year 1992 — Notice.

57 FR 28100, June 24, 1992: Medicaid Program; Coordination of Medicaid with Special Supplemental Food Program for Women, Infants, and Children (WIC) — Final regulations affecting 42 CFR Part 431.

57 FR 28183, June 24, 1992: Medicare and Medicaid Programs; Small Business Innovation Research Grants for Fiscal Year 1992; Correction — Notice.

57 FR 29142, June 30, 1992: Medicaid Program; Home and Community-Based Services Waivers for Individuals Age 65 or Older — Interim final rule with comment period, affecting 42 CFR Parts 400, 435, 436, 440, and 441.

57 FR 33992, July 31, 1992: Clinical Laboratories Improvement Act Program; Granting and Withdrawal of Deeming Authority to Private Nonprofit Accreditation Organizations and of CLIA Exemption under State Laboratory Programs — Final rule.

57 FR 38778, August 27, 1992: Medicaid Program; Medicaid Management Information System (MMIS) Performance Review; Notification Procedures for Changes in Requirements, Performance Standards, and Re-approval Conditions — Final notice affecting 42 CFR Part 433. See also correction at 57 FR 45112, September 30, 1992.

57 FR 39278, August 28, 1992: Medicare and Medicaid Programs; Survey, Certification and Enforcement of Skilled Nursing Facilities and Nursing Facilities — Proposed rule affecting 42 CFR Parts 431, 442, 488, and 489.

57 FR 43462, September 21, 1992: Health Care Financing Administration Public Information Collection Requirements Submitted to the Office of Management and Budget for Clearance (pertaining to sole community home health agencies; physician/supplier overpayment reports; physician or supplier Medicare agreements; conditions of participation for rural health clinics; Medicare provider refunds; conditions of participation for comprehensive outpatient rehabilitation facilities; Medicaid income and eligibility verification system; Medicaid integrated review schedule; provider overpayment report; financial statement of Medicare provider debtors; negative case action review schedule for Medicaid quality control; outpatient resource costing study; Medicaid intermediate care facility for the mentally retarded or persons with related conditions survey report form; installment agreement of beneficiary refund of overpayment; PRO assumption of responsibilities; Medicare contractor administrative budget and cost reporting system forms; fire safety survey report forms; medical records review under prospective payment system; and Qualified Medicare Beneficiary supplement to the Medicare current beneficiary survey).

57 FR 46362, October 8, 1992: Medicare and Medicaid Programs; Revised Effective Date of Medicare/Medicaid Provider Agreement and Supplier Participation — Proposed rule affecting 42 CFR Parts 431, 440, 442, 488, 489, and 498.

57 FR 46865, October 13, 1992: HCFA Public Information Collection Requirements Submitted to the Office of Management and Budget for Clearance (pertaining to impact of home health care plan management and evaluation; end-stage renal disease medical case review; Medicare/Medicaid hospital swing-bed survey report form; quarterly Medicaid statement of expenditures; Medicaid program budget report; information collection requirements in final peer review organization sanction regulations; appeals procedures for determinations that affect participation in Medicare; request for medical review information for Part B intermediary outpatient therapy bills and other Part B outpatient bills; and Medicaid limitations on provider-related donations and health care-related taxes, and limitations on payment to disproportionate share hospitals).

57 FR 47587, October 19, 1992: Medicare and Medicaid Programs; Use of Standardized Federal Claims Processing Forms and ProceduresAdvance notice of proposed rulemaking.

57 FR 59397, November 2, 1992: Medicaid Program; Drug Use Review Program and Electronic Claims Management System for Outpatient Drug ClaimsInterim final rule with comment period, affecting 42 CFR Part 456.

57 FR 54705, November 20, 1992: Medicaid Program; Prohibitions of FFP for Educational and Vocational Training for Institutionalized IndividualsFinal rule affecting 42 CFR Part 441.

57 FR 54710, November 20, 1992: Medicaid Program; Elimination of Certain Written Documentation Pertaining to Medicaid Long-Term Care FacilitiesFinal rule affecting 42 CFR Part 442.

57 FR 55118, November 24, 1992: Medicaid Program; Limitations on Provider-Related Donations and Health Care-Related Taxes; Limitations on Payments to Disproportionate Share HospitalsInterim final rule with comment period, affecting 42 CFR Parts 433 and 447.

57 FR 55261, November 24, 1992: Medicaid Program; Limitations on Aggregate Payments to Disproportionate Share Hospitals: Fiscal Year 1993Notice.

57 FR 56294, November 27, 1992: Extension of Medicaid When Support Collection Results in Termination of EligibilityNotice of

proposed rulemaking affecting 42 CFR Parts 435 and 436 and 45 CFR Part 233.

57 FR 56450, November 30, 1992: Medicare and Medicaid Programs; Preadmission Screening and Annual Resident ReviewFinal rule with comment period, affecting 42 CFR Parts 405, 431, 433, and 483. See also correction published at 58 FR 25784, April 28, 1993.

57 FR 56996, December 2, 1992: Medicare and Medicaid Programs; Approved Information Collection Requirements and HCFA's Claims Collection AuthorityFinal rule with comment period, affecting 42 CFR Parts 400, 401, and 405.

57 FR 57403, December 4, 1992: Medicaid Program: Computer Matching and Privacy Protection for Medicaid Eligibility — Proposed rule affecting 42 CFR Part 435.

57 FR 59024, December 14, 1992: Medicare and Medicaid Programs; Requirements for Physician Incentive Plans in Prepaid Health Care Organizations — Proposed rule affecting 42 CFR Parts 417 and 434 (HCFA) and 42 CFR Part 1003 (Office of Inspector General). See also extension of comment period at 58 FR 8568, February 16, 1993.

57 FR 60818, December 22, 1992: HCFA, Privacy Act of 1974; Systems of Records — Notice of proposed new routine use for existing system of records (pertaining to Medicaid and the group health plan system for dual eligibles).

57 FR 61614, December 28, 1992: Medicare and Medicaid; Resident Assessment in Long Term Care Facilities — Proposed rule affecting 42 CFR Parts 456 and 483.

58 FR 4904, January 19, 1993: Medicaid Program; Exemption of Poverty Level Pregnant Women from the Cooperation Requirements of Establishing Paternity and Obtaining Medical Support and Payments as a Condition of Eligibility; Technical Correction — Final rule with comment period, affecting 42 CFR Parts 433, 435, and 436.

58 FR 4908, January 19, 1993: Medicare Program; Eligibility and Coverage Requirements — Final rule with comment period, affecting 42 CFR Parts 435, 436, and 440. See also corrections published at 58 FR 26185 and 58 FR 39092.

58 FR 5212, January 19, 1993: Medicare, Medicaid and CLIA Programs; CLIA Program Fee Collection; Correction Amendments — Correcting 57 FR 7002–7186 and 57 FR 7188–7218 and 57 FR 7218–7243, published February 28, 1992, affecting 42 CFR Part 493. See also correction at 58 FR 48323, September 15, 1993.

58 FR 5215, January 19, 1993: Medicare, Medicaid and CLIA Programs; Regulations Implementing the Clinical Laboratory Improvement Amendments of 1988 (CLIA) and Clinical Laboratory Improvement Act Program Fee Collection — Final rule with comment period, affecting 42 CFR Part 493. See also correction published at 58 FR 39154, July 22, 1993.

58 FR 9120, February 19, 1993: Medicaid Program; Eligibility and Coverage Requirements — Notice of delay of effective dates and compliance dates, affecting 42 CFR Parts 435, 436, and 440.

58 FR 21174, April 19, 1993: HCFA Public Information Collection Requirements Submitted to the Office of Management and Budget for Clearance re end stage renal disease survey forms; municipal health services cost reports forms; advance directives; withholding Medicare payments to recover Medicaid overpayments; home office cost statements; and statistical report on medical care.

58 FR 29416, May 20, 1993: HCFA Public Information Collection Requirements Submitted to the Office of Management and Budget (OMB) for Clearance re cataract surgery; Medicaid utilization management initiatives; Medicare coverage of screening mammography; psychiatric unit criteria worksheet and rehabilitation unit criteria worksheet; Medicare secondary payor forms; ambulatory surgical center survey forms; ambulance service compliance with State and local requirements; and early and periodic screening, diagnostic and treatment reports.

58 FR 38579, July 19, 1993: HCFA Public Information Collection Requirements Submitted to the Office of Management and Budget (OMB) for Clearance re survey of home health agencies; CLIA survey report form; validation of state surveys; Medicaid listing of participating home health agencies; financial information regarding Medicare benefits from Medicare contractors; and third-party liability under Medicaid.

58 FR 43241, August 9, 1993: HCFA, Privacy Act of 1974; Report of New System — Pertaining to Evaluation of Medicaid Demonstration for Improving Access to Care for Substance Abusing Pregnant Women — Notice.

58 FR 43156, August 13, 1993: Medicaid Program; Limitations on Provider-Related Donations and Health Care-Related Donations and Health Care-Related Taxes; Limitations on Payments to Disproportionate Share Hospitals — Final rule affecting 42 CFR parts 433 and 447. See also correction at 58 FR 44536, August 23, 1993 as corrected at 58 FR 51130, September 30, 1993. And see correction at

62 FR 53571, October 15, 1997: Revision of Waiver Criteria for Tax Programs Based Exclusively on Regional Variations, affecting 42 CFR Part 433.

58 FR 43184, August 13, 1993: Medicaid Program; Limitation on Aggregate Payments to Disproportionate Share hospitals; Federal Fiscal Year 1993 — Notice.

58 FR 43832, August 18, 1993: Medicare and Medicaid Programs; Payment for Clinical Diagnostic Laboratory Tests — Proposed rule affecting 42 CFR Parts 405, 413, 414, 424, 431, and 447.

58 FR 44457, August 23, 1993: Medicaid Program; Eligibility and Coverage Requirements — Notice of delay of effective dates and compliance dates affecting 42 CFR Parts 435, 436, and 440.

58 FR 46198, September 1, 1993: HCFA Public Information Collection Requirements (ICR) Submitted to the Office of Management and Budget (OMB) for Clearance (pertaining to prenatal services and assistance screening; home health agency treatment forms; conditions of participation for intermediate care facilities for the mentally retarded; State Medicaid eligibility quality control sample selection lists; prepaid health plan cost report; hospital survey report form; procedures for determining whether providers, practitioners, or other suppliers of services are liable for certain noncovered services; Medicare credit balance reporting requirements; Medicare provider cost report questionnaire form; Medicare current beneficiary survey rounds 7–10; sterilization regulation/consent form; PRO reconsideration and appeals information requirements; information collection requirements in HSQ-110, acquisition, protection and disclosure of PRO information; Medicare/Medicaid organ procurement organization's (OPO) request for certification) — Notice.

58 FR 47904, September 13, 1993: HCFA, Public Information Collection Requirements (ICR) Submitted to the Office of Management and Budget (OMB) for Clearance (pertaining to chronic renal disease medical evidence report; Medicare common claims form; Social Security Office report of State buy-in problem; Medicare physician survey form; beneficiary survey form; Medicaid payment rate changes for inpatient hospital or long term care services; home and community-based services: waiver requirements; Medicare peer review organizations reporting forms; uniform institutional provider claim form) — Notice.

58 FR 47905, September 13, 1993: Reconsideration of Disapproval of New York State Plan Amendment — Notice of hearing.

58 FR 48611, September 17, 1993: Medicaid Program; Qualified Family Members — Final rule affecting 42 CFR Parts 435 and 436.

58 FR 49272, September 22, 1993: Medicaid Program; Referrals to Child Support Enforcement Agencies of Medicaid Families — Proposed rule affecting 42 CFR Part 433.

58 FR 51288, October 1, 1993: Medicaid Program; Early and Periodic Screening, Diagnosis, and Treatment Services Defined — Proposed rule affecting 42 CFR Parts 440 and 441.

58 FR 52112, October 6, 1993: Medicare, Medicaid, and CLIA Programs; Clinical Laboratory Improvement Amendments of 1988 Exemption of Laboratories Licensed by the State of Washington — Notice.

58 FR 53481, October 15, 1993: Medicaid Program; Case Management — Proposed rule affecting 42 CFR Parts 431, 440, 441 and 447.

58 FR 54096, October 20, 1993: Office of Inspector General: Civil Money Penalties for Prohibited Referrals to Entities Providing Clinical Laboratory Services and for Prohibited Arrangements and Schemes — Proposed rule affecting 42 CFR Part 1003.

58 FR 61692, November 22, 1993: Medicaid Program; Revised Medicaid Management Information Systems (MMIS) Functional Requirements — Proposed notice.

58 FR 54159, October 20, 1993: HCFA Public Information Collection Requirements Submitted to the Office of Management and Budget (OMB) for Clearance (pertaining to CLIA certification recommendation; CLIA laboratory personnel report; Medigap complaint data base; certification as a rural health clinic (RHC) and RHC survey report form; screening mammography services data report; ambulatory surgical center request for certification and survey report form; blood bank inspection checklist and report; Medicaid program budget report form; supplier of ESRD services form; and grantee data collection instrument) — Notice.

59 FR 1659, January 12, 1994: Medicaid program; Deduction of Incurred Medical Expenses (Spend down) — Final rule with comment period, affecting 42 CFR Parts 435 and 436.

59 FR 4252, January 31, 1994: Medicaid Program: Computer Matching and Privacy Protection for Medicaid Eligibility — Final rule affecting 42 CFR Part 435.

59 FR 4284, January 31, 1994: HCFA Reconsideration of Disapproval of California State Plan Amendment — Notice of hearing.

59 FR 4717, February 1, 1994: Medicaid Program; Limitations on Aggregate Payments to Disproportionate Share Hospitals: Federal Fiscal year 1994 — Notice.

59 FR 4880, February 2, 1994: Medicaid Program; Third Party Liability (TPL) Cost-Effectiveness Waivers — Proposed rule affecting 42 CFR Part 433.

59 FR 5201, February 3, 1994: HCFA Public Information Collection Requirements Submitted to the Office of Management and Budget (OMB) for Clearance (pertaining to evaluation of the Medicare case management demonstration; evaluation of the Medicaid uninsured demonstrations; Internal Revenue Service, Social Security Administration, and HCFA data match; survey of physician owned medical liability insurers for use in computing the input component of the physician liability component of the Geographic Practice Cost Index and the Medicare Economic Index; emergency and foreign hospital services for Canadian travel claims; CLIA survey report form; Medicaid management information system (MMIS) data form) — Notice.

59 FR 13666, March 23, 1994: Medicaid Program; Low-Income Eligibility Groups and Coverage of Services; Legislative Changes — Proposed rule affecting 42 CFR Parts 431, 435, 436, 440, and 447.

59 FR 14865, March 30, 1994: HCFA Public Information Collection Requirements Submitted to the Office of Management and Budget (OMB) for Clearance (pertaining to home health agency Medicare and Medicaid survey report forms for conditions of participation; conditions of participation for rural health clinics; Medicaid re-evaluation of assets for determining payment rates to hospitals and nursing homes; statistical report on medical care, eligible, recipients, payments, and services.)

59 FR 18138, April 15, 1994: HCFA Reconsideration of Disapproval of Ohio State Plan Amendment (SPA) — Notice of hearing.

59 FR 22764, May 2, 1994: Medicaid Program; Limitations on Aggregate Payments to Disproportionate Share Hospitals: Federal Fiscal Year 1994 — Notice. See also correction at 59 FR 28133, May 31, 1994.

59 FR 23069, May 4, 1994: HCFA Public Information Collection Requirements Submitted to the Office of Management and Budget (OMB) for Clearance (pertaining to clinical laboratory improvement amendments (CLIA) flexible survey protocol form; application for health insurance benefits under Medicare for individual with

chronic renal disease form; Medicare Qualification Statement for Federal employees form; attending physician's statement and documentation of Medicare emergency form; request for Part B Medicare hearing by an Administrative Law Judge forms; CLIA adverse action extract; and Medicare and Medicaid coverage data bank reports form.)

59 FR 23820, May 9, 1994: Medicaid Program; Requirements for Certain Health Insuring Organizations and OBRA '90 Technical Amendments, affecting 42 CFR Parts 434 and 435.

59 FR 24167, May 10, 1994: Medicare and Medicaid Programs; Medicare-Medicaid Coverage Data Bank Requirements: Preliminary Guidance — Notice (pertaining to reports employers must make about individuals covered by group health plans).

59 FR 27023, May 25, 1994: HCFA Public Information Collection Requirements Submitted to the Office of Management and Budget (OMB) for Clearance (pertaining to Medicare beneficiary survey of influenza vaccination form; Medicaid integrated quality control review worksheet; post laboratory survey questionnaire form; and post laboratory survey questionnaire — surveyor form).

59 FR 29430, June 7, 1994: HCFA Public Information Collection Requirements Submitted to the Office of Management and Budget (OMB) for Clearance (pertaining to systems performance review forms for State Medicaid Management Information Systems).

59 FR 31569, June 20, 1994: Medicaid Program; Requirements for Enrollment in or Payment for Certain Employer Group Health Plans — Proposed rule affecting 42 CFR Parts 435 and 436.

59 FR 36072, July 15, 1994: Medicare and State Health Care Programs: Fraud and Abuse, Civil Money Penalties and Intermediate Sanctions for Certain Violations by Health Maintenance Organizations and Competitive Medical Plans — Final rule affecting 42 CFR Parts 417, 431, 434, and 1003. See also correction at 59 FR 52682, October 19, 1994.

59 FR 36419, July 18, 1994: Medicaid Program: Nurse-Midwife Services — Proposed rule affecting 42 CFR Part 440.

59 FR 37702, July 25, 1994: Medicaid Program; Home and Community-Based Services and Respiratory Care for Ventilator-Dependent Individuals — Final rule with comment period affecting 42 CFR Parts 435, 440, and 441.

59 FR 39296, August 2, 1994: Medicare and Medicaid; Approved Information Collection Requirements — Final Rule with comment period, affecting 42 CFR Part 400.

59 FR 41327, August 11, 1994: HCFA Privacy Act of 1974; System of Records (pertaining to Medicaid Statistical Information System).

59 FR 46500, September 8, 1994: Medicare and Medicaid Programs; Conditions of Coverage for Organ Procurement Organizations — Interim final rule with comment, affecting 42 CFR Parts 405, 482, and 485.

59 FR 48805, September 23, 1994: Medicaid Program; Outstation Intake Locations for Certain Low-Income Pregnant Women, Infants, and Children Under Age 19 — Interim final rule with comment period, affecting 42 CFR Parts 435 and 436.

59 FR 48811, September 23, 1994: Medicaid Program; Drug use Review Program and Electronic Claims Management System for Outpatient Drug Claims — Final rule affecting 42 CFR Part 456.

59 FR 49080, September 26, 1994: Office of Inspector General; Performance Standards for State Medicaid Fraud Control Units — Notice.

59 FR 49249, September 27, 1994: Medicaid Program; Demonstration Proposals Pursuant to Section 1115(a) of the Social Security Act; Policies and Procedures — Notice.

59 FR 50235, October 3, 1994: Medicaid Program; Charges for Vaccine Administration Under the Vaccines for Children (VFC) Program — Notice with comment period. See also correction at 59 FR 51989, October 13, 1994.

59 FR 50246, October 3, 1994: Medicare and Medicaid Programs; Small Business Innovation Research Grants for Fiscal Year 1995 — Notice.

59 FR 56116, November 10, 1994: Medicare and Medicaid Programs; Survey, Certification and Enforcement of Skilled Nursing Facilities and Nursing Facilities — Final rule affecting 42 CFR Parts 401, 431, 435, 440, 441, 442, 447, 483, 488, 489, and 498. See also correcting amendment, effective July 1, 1995, at 62 FR 44221, August 20, 1997.

59 FR 59241, November 16, 1994: Medicare and Medicaid Programs; Delay in Implementation of the Medicare-Medicaid Coverage Data Bank Requirements — Notice.

59 FR 49372, November 17, 1994: Medicaid Program; Aid to Families with Dependent Children; Extension of Medicaid when Support Collection Results in Termination of Eligibility Final rule affecting 42 CFR Parts 435 and 436.

9 FR 59624, November 17, 1994: Medicaid Program; Inpatient Psychiatric Services for Individuals under Age 21 — Proposed rule affecting 42 CFR Parts 440, 441, 447, and 483.

59 FR 62606, December 6, 1994: Medicare, Medicaid, and CLIA Programs; Extension of Certain Effective Dates for Clinical Laboratory Requirements and Personnel Requirements for Cytologists — Final rule with comment period, affecting 42 CFR Part 493.

59 FR 64141, December 13, 1994: Medicare and Medicaid Programs; Revisions to Conditions of Participation for Hospitals — Final rule affecting 42 CFR Parts 405 and 482.

59 FR 66314, December 23, 1994: Medicare, Medicaid, and CLIA Programs; Clinical Laboratory Improvement Amendments of 1988 Continuance of Exemption of Laboratories Licensed by the State of Washington — Notice.

60 FR 3250, January 13, 1995: Medicaid Program; Limitations on Aggregate Payments to Disproportionate Share Hospitals: Federal Fiscal Year 1995 — Notice.

60 FR 6714, February 3, 1995: HCFA Public Information Collection Requirements Submitted to the Office of Management and Budget (OMB) for Clearance (pertaining to Medicaid eligibility quality control, and approval of State plan material).

60 FR 14435, March 17, 1995: HCFA Public Information Collection Requirements Submitted to the Office of Management and Budget (OMB) for Clearance (pertaining to Medicaid drug rebates, termination of enrollment in Federally Qualified HMOs, imposition of cost-sharing charges in Medicaid, Medicare current beneficiary surveys, and forms for establishing entitlement to hospital insurance).

60 FR 18136, April 10, 1995: Medicaid Program; Rescission of the Guidelines for Documenting Medicaid Recipient Access to Immunizations Under the Vaccines for Children (VFC) Program — Notice.

60 FR 19405, April 18, 1995: HCFA Public Information Collection Requirements Submitted to the Office of Management and Budget (OMB) for Clearance (pertaining to Medicaid limitations on provider related donations and health care related taxes and limitations on payments to disproportionate share hospitals).

60 FR 19856, April 21, 1995: Medicaid Program; Required Coverage of Nurse Practitioner Services — Final rule affecting 42 CFR Parts 440 and 441.

60 FR 21525, May 2, 1995: HCFA Public Information Collection Requirements Submitted to the Office of Management and Budget (OMB) for Clearance (pertaining to intermediary requests for information from skilled nursing facilities, reimbursement for CLIA compliance surveys, patient outcome data in home health agencies, common claim forms for Medicare/Medicaid reimbursement, and a study of childhood immunization costs).

60 FR 35498, July 10, 1995: Medicaid Program; Third Party Liability (TPL) Cost-effectiveness Waivers — Final rule affecting 42 CFR Part 433.

60 FR 42888, August 17, 1995: HCFA Public Information Collection Requirements Submitted for Public Comment and Recommendations (pertaining to evaluation of the Medicare cataract surgery alternate payment demonstration and Medicaid eligibility quality control).

60 FR 44503, August 28, 1995: Medicare, Medicaid, and CLIA Programs; Clinical Laboratory Improvement Amendments of 1988 Exemption of Permit-holding Laboratories in the State of New York — Notice.

60 FR 46838, September 8, 1995: Medicaid Program; Limitations on Aggregate Payments to Disproportionate Share Hospitals: Federal Year 1995 — Notice.

60 FR 48442, September 19, 1995: Medicaid Program; Payment for Covered Outpatient Drugs under Drug Rebate Agreements with Manufacturers — Proposed rule affecting 42 CFR Parts 441 and 447.

60 FR 50443, September 29, 1995: Medicare and Medicaid Programs; Approved Information Collection Requirements (pertaining to valid OMB control numbers for 42 CFR) — Technical final rule.

60 FR 55719, November 2, 1995: HCFA Public Information Collection Requirements Submitted for Public Comment and Recommendations (pertaining to evaluation of the Oregon Medicaid reform demonstration; field testing of the uniform needs assessment instrument for hospital discharge planning; survey of physician practice costs; evaluation of the Medicare cataract surgery alternate payment demonstration; and alternative CLIA quality assessment surveys).

60 FR 61483, November 30, 1995: Medicaid Program: Nurse-midwife Services — Final rule affecting 42 CFR Part 440.

60 FR 64167, December 14, 1995: HCFA Public Information Collection Requirements Submitted for Public Comment and Recommendations (pertaining to Medicaid drug rebates).

60 FR 64167, December 14, 1995: HCFA Public Information Collection Requirements Submitted for Public Comment and Recommendations (pertaining to home health care; Medicare/Medicaid certification of physical therapy and speech pathology services; certification as suppliers of Portable X-ray Services; certification of organ procurement organizations; certification for physical therapists in independent practice; and approval as a hospital provider of extended care services (swing bed)).

61 FR 5402, February 12, 1996: HCFA Agency Information Collection Activities: Proposed Collection: Comment Request (pertaining to examination and treatment for emergency medical conditions and women in labor; hospice core service waiver requests; home office cost reports; and State Medicaid eligibility quality control samples).

61 FR 7522, February 28, 1996: HCFA Public Information Collection Requirements Submitted for Public Comment and Recommendations (pertaining to Medicare and Medicaid disclosure of ownership and control interest statements).

61 FR 9405, March 8, 1996: Medicaid Program; Coverage of Personal Care Services — Proposed rule affecting 42 CFR Part 440.

61 FR 13508, March 27, 1996: HCFA Proposed Collection of Public Comment; Submission for OMB Review (pertaining to reconciliation of State invoices for the Medicaid drug rebate program).

61 FR 13430, March 27, 1996: Medicare and Medicaid Programs; Requirements for Physician Incentive Plans in Prepaid Health Care Organizations — Final rule with comment period, affecting 42 CFR Parts 417, 434, and 1003. See also correction at 61 FR 46384, September 3, 1996.

61 FR 14798, April 3, 1996: HCFA Agency Information Collection Activities: Proposed Collection; Comment Request (pertaining to statistical reports on medical care eligibility, payments and services under Medicaid; State survey agency lists of positions and schedule of equipment purchases; granting and withdrawing of deeming authority to national accreditation organizations; maximizing the effectiveness of home health care; requests for certification in the Medicare or Medicaid program to provide outpatient physical therapy and/or speech pathology services; physical therapists in independent practice; requests for provider approval as a hospital provider of extended care services (swing bed) under Medicare and

Medicaid; and requests for designation as an organ procurement organization).

61 FR 17677, April 22, 1996: Medicare and Medicaid Programs; New Payment Methodology for Routine Extended Care Services Provided in a Swing-bed Hospital — Proposed rule affecting 42 CFR Part 413.

61 FR 19722, May 2, 1996: Medicare and Medicaid Programs; Conditions of Coverage for Organ Procurement Organizations (OPOs) — Final rule with comment period, affecting 42 CFR Parts 405 and 486.

61 FR 20833, May 8, 1996: HCFA Agency Information Collection Activities: Proposed Collection: Comment Request (pertaining to State Medicaid eligibility quality control sample selection lists).

61 FR 21195, May 9, 1996: Medicaid Program; Limitations on Aggregate Payments to Disproportionate Share Hospitals: Federal Fiscal Year 1996 — Notice. See also correction at 61 FR 29418, June 10, 1996.

61 FR 21969, May 13, 1996: Medicare and Medicaid Program; Criteria for a Rural Hospital to Be Designated as an Essential Access Community Hospital (EACH) — Final rule with comment period, affecting 42 CFR Part 412.

61 FR 25229, May 20, 1996: HCFA Agency Information Collection Activities: Proposed Collection; Comment Request (pertaining to evaluation of the Oregon reform demonstration; evaluation of the per-episode home health prospective payment demonstration; and the blood bank inspection checklist instrument used by State agencies to determine compliance with CLIA).

61 FR 25873, May 23, 1996: HCFA Agency Information Collection Activities: Submission for OMB Review; Comment Request (pertaining to State Medicaid eligibility quality control sampling plans).

61 FR 25883, May 23, 1996: HCFA Agency Information Collection Activities: Proposed Collection; Comment Request (pertaining to certification of Medicaid eligibility quality control payment error rates).

61 FR 29406, June 10, 1996: HCFA Agency Information Collection Activities: proposed Collection; Comment Request (pertaining to end stage renal disease application and survey and certification report forms; withholding Medicare payments to recover Medicaid overpayments; acquisition, protection, and disclosure of PRO information; clinical laboratory certification and recertification survey forms; CLIA laboratory personnel report forms; prepaid health plan cost

reports; Medicare credit balance reporting requirements; statement of deficiencies and plan of correction requirements for organ procurement organizations; Medicare/Medicaid hospital survey report forms; advance directive requirements for Medicare and Medicaid; payment adjustments for sole community hospitals; survey reports for physical therapists in independent practice; HMO and CMP national data reporting requirements; identification of extension units of outpatient physical therapy and outpatient speech pathology providers; and fire safety survey reports).

61 FR 29409, June 10, 1996: HCFA New and Pending Demonstration Project Proposals Submitted

61 FR 30072, June 13, 1996: Medicare, Medicaid, and CLIA Programs; Clinical Laboratory Improvement Amendments of 1988 Exemption of Laboratories in the State of Oregon Notice.

61 FR 32347, June 24, 1996: Medicare and Medicaid Programs; Provider Appeals: Technical Amendments — Final rule with comment period, affecting 42 CFR Parts 405,417, 431, 473, and 498). See also corrections at 61 FR 35307, July 5, 1996, 61 FR 42385, August 15, 1996, and 61 FR 51021, September 30, 1996.

61 FR 34437, July 2, 1996: HCFA Agency Information Collection Activities: Submission for OMB Review; Comment Request (pertaining to Peer Review Organization procedures for reconsideration of initial decisions; Part B enrollment forms; certification of rural health clinics for Medicare participation; Medicaid utilization review requirements for home health agencies; State listings of Medicaid recipients in institutions and procedures for State inspection of care review; procedures for disenrollment of beneficiaries from HMOs or CMPs; effectiveness of telemedicine services; formats for PROs to submit data to HCFA; and request for accelerated payments forms for providers).

61 FR 35231, July 5, 1996: HCFA Agency Information Collection Activities: Proposed Collection; Comment Request (pertaining to Medicaid payment standards for inpatient hospital or long-term care services).

61 FR 37278, July 17, 1996: HCFA Public Information Requirements Submitted for Collection of Public Comment: Submission for OMB Review (pertaining to statistical reports of medical care and eligibility for Medicaid recipients).

61 FR 38395, July 24, 1996: Medicaid Program; Medicaid Eligibility Quality Control, Progressive Reductions in Federal Financial Participation for FYs 1982–1984, Payment for Physician Billing for

Clinical Laboratory Services, and Utilization Control of Skilled Nursing Facility Services: Removal of Obsolete Requirements — Final rule.

61 FR 42257, August 14, 1996: HCFA Proposals Submitted for Collection of Public Comment: Submission for OMB Review (pertaining to third-party liability in Medicaid programs; surveys of federally qualified health centers (FQHCs); distribution of Medicare information by hospitals; Medicare reimbursement for hospitals with a disproportionate share of Medicare inpatients; Medicaid quality control; and the National Payer Identifier).

61 FR 43062, August 20, 1996: HCFA Agency Information Collection Activities: Submission for OMB Review; Comment request (pertaining to withholding Medicare payments to recover Medicaid overpayments; acquisition, protection, and disclosure of Peer Review Organization (PRO) information; cost reports for HMOs; and collection of credit balance information from health care providers).

61 FR 43373, August 22, 1996: HCFA Public Information Requirements Submitted for Public Comment: Submission for OMB Review (pertaining to certification of Medicaid eligibility quality control payment error rates).

61 FR 47423, September 9, 1996: Medicare and Medicaid Programs; Hospital Standard for Potentially HIV Infectious Blood and Blood Products — Final rule, affecting 42 CFR Part 482.

61 FR 49781, September 23, 1996: Medicaid Program; Final Limitations on Aggregate Payments to Disproportionate Share Hospitals: Federal Fiscal Year 1966 — Notice.

61 FR 50492, September 26, 1996: HCFA Agency Information Collection Activities: Proposed Collection; Comment request (pertaining to resolution of beneficiary complaints regarding State buy-ins for Medicare entitlement).

61 FR 51295, October 1, 1996: HCFA Public Information Requirements Submitted for Collection of Public Comment: Submission for OMB Review (pertaining to approval of Medicaid payment rates for inpatient hospital or long term care services).

61 FR 51611, October 3, 1996: Medicare and Medicaid Programs; New Payment Methodology for Routine Extended Care Services Provided in a Swing-bed Hospital — Final Rule affecting 42 CFR Part 413. See also correction at 61 FR 58631, November 18, 1996.

61 FR 52299, October 7, 1996: Office of Inspector General; Medicare and State Health Care Programs and Program Fraud Civil

Remedies: Fraud and Abuse; Civil Money Penalties Inflation Adjustments — Final rule affecting 42 CFR Part 1003.

61 FR 52951, October 9, 1996: HCFA Agency Information Collection Activities: Submission for OMB Review; Comment request (pertaining to Peer Review Organization Reconsiderations and Appeals; Part B enrollment forms; certification as a Rural Health Clinic; Medicaid utilization control programs; lists of Medicaid recipients in institutions; and business proposal formats for PROs).

61 FR 55155, October 24, 1996: HCFA Agency Information Collection Activities: Proposed Collection; Comment request (pertaining to Medicare/Medicaid common claim forms and instructions).

61 FR 55155, October 24, 1996: HCFA Emergency Clearance: Agency Public.

61 FR 57688, November 7, 1996: HCFA Agency Information Collection Activities: Comment request (pertaining to clinical laboratory surveys; clinical laboratory personnel qualifications; Medicare/Medicaid hospital survey report forms; beneficiary disenrollment from HMOs and CMPs; survey reports for ambulatory surgical centers; the Medigap complaint database; and survey forms for comprehensive outpatient rehabilitation facilities).

61 FR 57876, November 8, 1996: Medicare and Medicaid Programs; Announcement of Additional Application from Hospital Requesting Waivers for Organ Procurement Service Area and Technical Correction — Notice with comment period.

61 FR 58140, November 13, 1996: Medicaid and Aid to Families with Dependent Children; Certain Provisions of the National Voter Registration Act of 1993 — Final rule affecting 42 CFR Part 431.

61 FR 59198, November 21, 1996: Medicaid Program: Family Planning Services and Supplies for Individuals of Child-bearing Age — Correcting amendment affecting 42 CFR Part 440.

61 FR 68048, December 26, 1996: HCFA Agency Information Collection: Proposed Collection; Comment request (pertaining to the Medicaid management information system).

61 FR 68270, December 27, 1996: HCFA Agency Information Collection Activities: Submission for OMB Review; Comment request (pertaining to a facility identification and screening form for hospital providers of extended care services (swing-beds) in the Medicare and Medicaid programs).

61 FR 69034, December 30, 1996: Medicare and Medicaid Programs; Requirements for Physician Incentive Plans in Prepaid

Health Care Organizations — Final rule affecting 42 CFR Parts 417 and 434.

62 FR 1682, January 13, 1997: Medicaid Program; Redeterminations of Medicaid Eligibility Due to Welfare Reform — Final rule with comment period, affecting 42 CFR Part 435.

62 FR 3514, January 23, 1997: Submitted for Collection of Public Comment: Submission for OMB Review (pertaining to Home and Community‐based Services Waiver Requests).

62 FR 4304, January 29, 1997: HCFA Emergency Clearance: Public Information Collection Requirements Submitted to the Office of Management and Budget (OMB) (pertaining to Medicare/Medicaid health insurance common claim form).

62 FR 4311, January 29, 1997: Medicaid Program; New and Pending Demonstration Project Proposals Submitted Pursuant to Section 1115(a) of the Social Security Act: August and September 1995; October 1995; November 1995; July 1996; and October 1996; Correction.

62 FR 7467, February 19, 1997: HCFA Agency Information Collection Activities: Proposed Collection; Comment request (pertaining to form for a hospital request for certification in the Medicare and Medicaid programs).

62 FR 9435, March 3, 1997: Office of Inspector General: Publication of the OIG Model Compliance Plan for Clinical Laboratories — Notice.

62 FR 10285, March 6, 1997: HCFA Agency Information collection Activities: Submission for OMB Review; Comment request (pertaining to end stage renal disease (ESRD) application and survey and certification report form).

62 FR 11004, March 10, 1997: Medicare and Medicaid Programs; Revision of the Conditions of Participation for Home Health Agencies and Use of the Outcome and Assessment Information Set (OASIS) as Part of the Revised Conditions of Participation for Home Health Agencies — Introduction to proposed rules, affecting 42 CFR Part 484.

62 FR 11005, March 10, 1997: Medicare and Medicaid Programs; Conditions of Participation for Home Health Agencies — Proposed rule affecting 42 CFR Part 484. See also correction at 62 FR 11953, March 13, 1997.

62 FR 11035, March 10, 1997: Medicare and Medicaid Programs; Use of the OASIS as Part of the Conditions of Participation for Home Health Agencies — Proposed rule.

62 FR 11214, March 11, 1997: HCFA Agency Information Collection Activities: Submission for OMB Review; Comment request (pertaining to intermediate care facility for the mentally retarded or persons with related conditions survey report forms).

62 FR 12834, March 18, 1997: HCFA Submittal for Collection of Public Comment: Submission for OMB Review (pertaining to the Medicaid management information system).

62 FR 14155, March 25, 1997: HCFA Agency Information Collection Activities: Proposed Collection; Comment request (pertaining to Medicaid drug utilization review; Medicaid management information systems; and the Medicaid post-eligibility process for FFP).

62 FR 14156, March 25, 1997: HCFA Submittal for Collection of Public Comment: Submission for OMB Review (pertaining to statistical report on medical care for Medicaid recipients).

62 FR 14156, March 25, 1997: HCFA Agency Information Collection Activities: Submission for OMB Review; Comment request (pertaining to Social Security office buy-in problems).

62 FR 17197, April 9, 1997: HCFA Agency Information Collection Activities: Proposed Collection; Comment request (pertaining to evaluation of five State health care reform demonstrations and evaluation of the Medicaid State health reform demonstrations).

62 FR 17197, April 9, 1997: HCFA Agency Information Collection Activities: Proposed Collection; Comment request (pertaining to the Medicaid drug rebate program).

62 FR 17850, April 11, 1997: HCFA Agency Information Collection Activities: Proposed Collection; Comment request (pertaining to the Medicaid EPSDT program).

62 FR 18639, April 16, 1997: HCFA Agency Information Collection Activities: Proposed Collection; Comment request (pertaining to the hospital request for certification in the Medicare and Medicaid programs form).

62 FR 19326, April 21, 1997: Medicare and Medicaid Programs; Announcement of Additional Applications from Hospitals Requesting Waivers for Organ Procurement Service Area — Notice with comment period.

62 FR 19328, April 21, 1997: Medicare and Medicaid Programs; Quarterly Listing of Program Issuances, Third Quarter 1996 — Notice.

62 FR 23140, April 29, 1997: Medicaid Program; Third Party Liability (TPL) Cost-effectiveness Waivers — Correcting Amendment to 60 FR 35498, July 10, 1995.

62 FR 23140, April 29, 1997: Office of Inspector General: Health Care Programs: Fraud and Abuse; Revised PRO Sanctions for Failing to Meet Statutory Obligations — Final rule.

62 FR 23251, April 29, 1997: Medicare Program: Initiative Involving Facilities that Furnish Hemodialysis Treatments — Notice.

62 FR 25855, May 12, 1997: Medicare, Medicaid, and CLIA Programs; Clinical Laboratory Requirements — Extension of Certain Effective Dates for Clinical Laboratory Requirements under CLIA — Final rule with comment period, affecting 42 CFR Part 493.

62 FR 26545, May 14, 1997: Medicaid Program; Allocation of Enhanced Federal matching Funds for Increased Administrative Costs Resulting from Welfare Reform — Notice with comment period. See also correction at 62 FR 33459, June 19, 1997.

62 FR 28056, May 22, 1997: HCFA Agency Information Collection Activities: Proposed Collection; Comment request (pertaining to Medicaid report on payables and receivables).

62 FR 28057, May 22, 1997: HCFA Agency Information Collection Activities: Submission for OMB Review; Comment request (pertaining to post laboratory survey questionnaire).

62 FR 29729, June 2, 1997: HCFA Agency Information Collection Activities: Proposed Collection; Comment request (pertaining to Medicaid integrated quality control review worksheet).

62 FR 29730, June 2, 1997: HCFA Submitted for Collection of Public comment: Submission for OMB Review (pertaining to performance review for Medicaid management information systems; Medicaid post-eligibility pre-print; and Medicaid drug utilization review).

62 FR 31613, June 10, 1997: HCFA Agency Information Collection Activities: Proposed Collection; Comment request (pertaining to organ procurement organization/histocompatibility laboratory statement of reimbursable cost form; and outpatient rehabilitation cost report form).

62 FR 39848, July 24, 1997: HCFA Agency Information Collection Activities; Proposed Collection; Comment request (pertaining to home health certification and plan of care forms for reimbursement; and Medicare/Medicaid disclosure of ownership and control forms).

62 FR 42259, August 6, 1997: HCFA Agency Information Collection Activities: Submission for OMB Review; Comment request (pertaining to accounting data from States regarding Medicaid payables and receivables).

62 FR 43931, August 18, 1997: Medicare and Medicaid Programs: Effective Dates of Provider Agreements and Supplier Approvals — Final rule affecting 42 CFR Parts 431, 442, 488, 489, and 498.

62 FR 44283, August 20, 1997: HCFA Emergency Clearance: Public Information Collection Requirements Submitted to the Office of Management and Budget (OMB) (pertaining to Medicare/Medicaid common claim forms and instructions). See also correction at 62 FR 45264, August 26, 1997.

62 FR 44478, August 21, 1997: HCFA Agency Information Collection Activities: Proposed Collection; Comment request (pertaining to sterilization consent forms for Medicaid eligibles).

62 FR 47896, September 11, 1997: Medicaid Program; Coverage of Personal Care Services — Final rule affecting 42 CFR Part 440. See also correction at 62 FR 49726, September 23, 1997.

62 FR 48292, September 15, 1997: Medicaid Program; Final Limitations on Aggregate Payments to Disproportionate Share Hospitals: Federal Fiscal Year 1997 — Notice.

62 FR 48872, September 17, 1997: Medicare and Medicaid Programs; Announcement of Additional Applications from Hospitals Requesting Waivers for Organ Procurement Service Area — Notice with comment period.

62 FR 49696, September 23, 1997: HCFA Agency Information Collection Activities: Proposed Collection; Comment request (pertaining to Medicaid drug rebate program).

62 FR 51115, September 30, 1997: HCFA Agency Information Collection Activities: Submission for OMB Review; Comment request (pertaining to evaluation of the Oregon Medicaid reform demonstration).

62 FR 55410, October 24, 1997: HCFA Agency Information Collection Activities: Submission for OMB Review; Comment request (pertaining to Medicare/Medicaid disclosure of ownership and control forms).

62 FR 58736, October 30, 1997: HCFA Agency Information Collection Activities: Proposed Collection; Comment request (pertaining to Medicaid budget reports).

62 FR 63953, December 3, 1997: HCFA Agency Information Collection Activities: Proposed Collection Comment request (pertaining to annual report form for home and community based services waivers).

62 FR 65085, December 10, 1997: HCFA Agency Information Collection Activities: Proposed Collection; Comment request (pertaining to Medicaid quality control).

62 FR 66375, December 18, 1997: HCFA Agency Information Collection Activities: Proposed Collection; Comment request (pertaining to amendment of State Medicaid plans).

62 FR 66376, December 18, 1997: HCFA Agency Information Collection Activities: Proposed Collection; Comment request (pertaining to imposition of cost sharing charges under Medicaid).

62 FR 66726, December 19, 1997: Medicare and Medicaid Programs; Hospital Conditions of Participation; Provider Agreements and Supplier Approval — Proposed rule affecting 42 CFR Parts 416, 482, 485, and 489.

62 FR 67174, December 23, 1997: Medicare and Medicaid; Resident Assessment in Long Term Care Facilities — Final rule affecting 42 CFR Part 483.

63 FR 291, January 5, 1998: Medicare and Medicaid Programs; Surety Bond and Capitalization Requirements for Home Health Agencies; Final rule affecting 42 CFR Parts 413, 440, 441, and 489.

63 FR 1114, January 8, 1998: HCFA Agency Information Collection Activities: Submission for OMB Review; Comment request (pertaining to improved data exchange between States and drug labelers).

63 FR 1115, January 8, 1998: HCFA Agency Information Collection Activities: Submission for OMB Review; Comment request (pertaining to survey of primary care givers for the District of Columbia's managed care demonstration for disabled and special needs children).

63 FR 1646, January 9, 1998: Medicare Program; Physicians' Referrals; Issuance of Advisory Opinions — Final rule with comment period, affecting 42 CFR Part 411.

63 FR 1659, January 9, 1998: Medicare and Medicaid Programs; Physicians' Referrals to Health Care Entities with Which They Have Financial Relationships — Proposed rule affecting 42 CFR Parts 411, 424, 435, and 455.

63 FR 3752, January 26, 1998: Medicaid Program; State Allotments for Payment of Medicare Part B Premiums for Qualifying Individuals; Federal Fiscal Year 1998 — Notice with comment period.

63 FR 4459, January 29, 1998: HCFA Emergency Clearance: Public Information Collection Requirements Submitted to the Office

of Management and Budget (OMB) (pertaining to Medicare/Medicaid health insurance common claim form and instructions).

63 FR 4645, January 30, 1998: HCFA Agency Information Collection Activities: Proposed Collection; Comment request (pertaining to statistical report on medical care: eligibles, recipients, payments, and services).

63 FR 5106, January 30, 1998: Medicare and Medicaid Programs; Salary Equivalency Guidelines for Physical Therapy, Respiratory Therapy, Speech Language Pathology, and Occupational Therapy Services — Final rule affecting 42 CFR Part 413. See also revised effective date and technical correction at 63 FR 15315, March 31, 1998.

63 FR 7743, February 17, 1998: Medicare and Medicaid Programs; Hospital Conditions of Participation; Provider Agreements and Supplier Approval — Notice of extension of comment period, affecting 42 CFR Parts 416, 482, 485, and 489.

63 FR 9845, February 26, 1998: HCFA Agency Information Collection Activities: Submission for OMB Review; Comment request (pertaining to annual report on home and community based services waivers).

63 FR 10400, March 3, 1998: HCFA Agency Information Collection Activities: Submission for OMB Review; Comment request (pertaining to Medicaid State plan material, and cost sharing charges under Medicaid).

63 FR 10400, March 3, 1998: Medicaid Program; State Allotments for Additional Federal Funding of Emergency Health Services Furnished to Undocumented Aliens: Federal Fiscal Years 1998 through 2001 — Notice.

63 FR 10730, March 4, 1998: Medicare and Medicaid Programs; Surety Bond Requirements for Home Health Agencies — Final rule affecting 42 CFR Parts 441 and 489.

63 FR 10732, March 4, 1998: Medicare and Medicaid Programs; Surety Bond Requirements for Home Health Agencies — Notice of Intent to Amend Regulations.

63 FR 11649, March 10, 1998: Medicare and Medicaid Programs; Physicians' Referrals to Health Care Entities with Which They Have Financial Relationships — Notice of extension of comment period for proposed rule.

63 FR 11687, March 10, 1998: Medicare and Medicaid Programs; Announcement of Additional Application from Hospital Requesting

Waiver for Organ Procurement Service Area — Notice with comment period.

63 FR 12474, March 13, 1998: HCFA Agency Information Collection Activities: Proposed Collection; Comment request (pertaining to hospice request for certification in the Medicare program and Medicare/Medicaid psychiatric hospital survey data).

63 FR 14393, March 25, 1998: Office of Inspector General: Health Care Programs: Fraud and Abuse; Revised OIG Civil Money Penalties Resulting from the Health Insurance Portability and Accountability Act of 1996 — Notice of proposed rulemaking, affecting 42 CFR Parts 1003, 1005, and 1006.

63 FR 14720, March 26, 1998: HCFA Agency Information Collection Activities: Submission for OMB Review; Comment request (pertaining to Medicaid program budget report).

63 FR 14720, March 26, 1998: HCFA Agency Information Collection Activities: Submission for OMB Review; Comment request (pertaining to quarterly Medicaid statement of expenditures for the Medical assistance program).

63 FR 17878, April 10, 1998: HCFA Agency Information Collection Activities: Proposed Collection; Comment request (pertaining to Medicaid post-eligibility preprint).

63 FR 19503, April 20, 1998: HCFA Agency Information Collection Activities: Submission for OMB Review; Comment request (pertaining to Medicaid integrated quality control review manual instructions).

63 FR 20640, April 27, 1998: HCFA Agency Information Collection Activities: Submission for OMB Review; Comment request — State child health plan information collection requirements).

63 FR 23790, April 30, 1998: Medicare and Medicaid Programs; Recognition of the American Association for Accreditation of Ambulatory Surgery Facilities, Inc., for Ambulatory Surgical Centers — Proposed notice.

63 FR 26811, May 14, 1998: Medicare and Medicaid Programs: Request for Public Comments on the Quality Improvement System for Managed Care — Solicitation of comments; notice of public meeting.

63 FR 27990, May 21, 1998: HCFA Agency Information Collection Activities: Proposed Collection; Comment request (pertaining to multi-state evaluation of dual eligibles, i.e., persons eligible for both Medicare and Medicaid).

63 FR 28394, May 22, 1998: HCFA Agency Information Collection Activities: Proposed Collection; Comment request (pertaining to Medicaid termination of enrollment information collection requirements).

63 FR 29648, June 1, 1998: Medicare and Medicaid Programs; Surety Bond Requirements for Home Health Agencies — Final rule affecting 42 CFR Parts 441 and 489.

63 FR 32888, June 16, 1998: HCFA Agency Information Collection Activities: Proposed Collection; Comment request (pertaining to Medicare secondary payer reports; and drug utilization review for Medicaid patients).

63 FR 33376, June 18, 1998: HCFA Agency Information Collection Activities; Submission for OMB Review; Comment request (pertaining to Medicaid post-eligibility pre-print report form).

63 FR 33856, June 22, 1998: Medicare and Medicaid Programs; Hospital Conditions of Participation; Identification of Potential Organ Tissue, and Eye Donors and Transplant Hospitals' Provision of Transplant-Related Data — Final rule affecting 42 CFR Part 482.

63 FR 36924, July 8, 1998: HCFA Notice of Hearing: Reconsideration of Disapproval of New York Title XXI State Plan Amendment — Notice of hearing.

63 FR 37129, July 9, 1998: HCFA Agency Information Collection Activities; Submission for OMB Review; Comment request (pertaining to organ procurement organization requests for participation in Medicare and Medicaid).

63 FR 38311, July 16, 1998: Office of Inspector General: Medicare and State Health Care Programs: Fraud and Abuse; Issuance of Advisory Opinions by the OIG — Final rule affecting 42 CFR 1008. See also correction at 63 FR 43449, August 13, 1998.

63 FR 38413, July 16, 1998: HCFA Agency Information Collection Activities: Submission for OMB Review; Comment request (pertaining to Clinical Laboratory Improvement Act certification requirements; EPSDT participation reports; limitations on provider-related donations and health care-related taxes, and limitations on payments to disproportionate share hospitals; and Medicare+Choice provider sponsored organization waiver requests forms).

63 FR 38414, July 16, 1998: HCFA Privacy Act of 1974; Report of Altered System (pertaining to disclosure of individual-specific information to combat fraud or abuse in health benefit programs).

63 FR 39583, July 23, 1998: HCFA Agency Information Collection Activities; Proposed Collection; Comment request (pertaining to Medicaid agencies report forms on children's health insurance expenditures).

63 FR 41170, July 31, 1998: Medicare and Medicaid Programs; Surety Bond Requirements for Home Health Agencies — Final rule affecting 42 CFR Parts 441 and 489.

63 FR 42054, August 6, 1998: HCFA Agency Information Collection Activities: Submission for OMB Review; Comment Request (pertaining to Medicare/Medicaid/CLIA conditions of participation).

63 FR 42270, August 7, 1998: Medicaid and Title IV-E Programs; Revision to the Definition of an Unemployed Parent — Final rule with comment period, affecting 45 CFR 233.

63 FR 42638, August 10, 1998: HCFA Agency Information Collection Activities: Submission for OMB Review; Comment request (pertaining to multi-state evaluation of dual eligibles demonstration (Medicare/Medicaid)).

63 FR 46676, September 2, 1998: Office of Inspector General: Health Care Programs; Fraud and Abuse; Revised OIG Exclusion Authorities Resulting from Public Law 104–191 — Final rule affecting 42 CFR Parts 1000, 1001, 1002, and 1005. See also correction at 63 FR 57918, October 29, 1998.

63 FR 46736, September 2, 1998: Office of Inspector General: Health Care Programs; Fraud and Abuse; Revised OIG Sanction Authorities Resulting from Public Law 105–33 — Notice of proposed rulemaking affecting 42 CFR 1001, 1002, and 1003.

63 FR 48735, September 11, 1998: Medicare and Medicaid Programs; Recognition of the Community Health Accreditation Program, Inc. (CHAP) and Joint Commission for Accreditation of Healthcare Organizations (JCAHO) for Hospices — Proposed notice.

63 FR 52022, September 29, 1998: Medicaid Program; Medicaid Managed Care — Proposed rule affecting 42 CFR Parts 400, 430, 431, 434, 435, 438, 440, and 447.

63 FR 54142, October 8, 1998: Medicaid Program; Disproportionate share Hospital Payments-Institutions for Mental Disease — Notice.

63 FR 55031, October 14, 1998: Medicare, Medicaid, and CLIA Programs; Extension of Certain Effective Dates for Clinical Laboratory Requirements under CLIA — Final rule with comment period, affecting 42 CFR 493.

63 FR 56656, October 22, 1998: HCFA Agency Information Collection Activities: Submission for OMB Review; Comment request (pertaining to drug utilization review for Medicaid).

63 FR 57697, October 28, 1998: HCFA Agency Information Collection Activities; Proposed Collection; Comment request (pertaining to EPSDT participation report).

63 FR 58341, October 30, 1998: Office of Inspector General: Health Care Fraud and Abuse Data Collection Program: Reporting of Final Adverse Actions — Notice of proposed rulemaking under section 1128E of the Social Security Act, affecting 45 CFR 61.

63 FR 68687, December 14, 1998: Medicare and Medicaid Program; Civil Money Penalties, Assessments, Exclusions, and Related Appeals Procedures — Final rule with comment period, affecting 42 CFR 400 and 402.

63 FR 69635, December 17, 1998: HCFA Agency Information Collection Activities: Proposed Collection; Comment request (pertaining to Medicaid eligibility quality control sampling).

63 FR 71819, December 30, 1998: Office of Inspector General; Health Care Fraud and Abuse Data Collection Program; Reporting under section 1128E of the Social Security Act of Final Adverse Actions — Notice of proposed rule-making; extension of comment period, affecting 45 CFR 61.

63 FR 72317, December 31, 1998: HCFA Agency Information Collection Activities: Proposed Collection; Comment request (pertaining to advanced directives under Medicare and Medicaid; and Medicare/Medicaid disclosure of ownership and control interests).

63 FR 72318, December 31, 1998: HCFA Agency Information Collection Activities: Proposed Collection; Comment request (pertaining to fire safety survey report forms for health care facilities).

1999

64 FR 1810, January 12, 1999: HCFA Agency Information Collection Activities: Proposed Collection; Comment request (pertaining to Medicaid eligibility quality control MEQC) samples; identification of extension units of outpatient physical therapy (OPT) and outpatient speech pathology (OSP) providers; request for certification in the Medicare and/or Medicaid program(s) to provide OPT or OSP services; and request for certification as a supplier of portable X-ray services under Medicare and/or Medicaid).

64 FR 1811, January 12, 1999: Medicare and Medicaid Programs; Announcement of Additional Applications from Hospitals Request-

ing Waivers for Organ Procurement Service Area Assignments — Notice with comment period.

64 FR 3748, January 25, 1999: Medicare and Medicaid Programs: Reporting Outcome and Assessment Information Set (OASIS) Data as Part of the Conditions of Participation for Home Health Agencies-Interim final rule with comment period, affecting 42 CFR Parts 484 and 488.

64 FR 3764, January 25, 1999: Medicare and Medicaid Programs: Comprehensive Assessment and Use of the OASIS as Part of the Conditions of Participation for Home Health Agencies — Final rule affecting 42 CFR Part 484.

64 FR 4435, January 28, 1999: HCFA Agency Information Collection Activities; Submission for OMB Review; Comment request (pertaining to home and community-based services waiver requests).

64 FR 5666, February 4, 1999: HCFA Emergency Clearance: Public Information Collection Requirements Submitted to the Office of Management and Budget (OMB) (pertaining to the Medicare/Medicaid health insurance common claim form).

64 FR 6664, February 10, 1999: HCFA Agency Information Collection Activities: Submission for OMB Review; Comment request (pertaining to skilled nursing facility (SNF) resident assessment MDS data).

64 FR 9336, February 25, 1999: HCFA Agency Information Collection Activities: Submission for OMB Review; Comment request (pertaining to home office cost reports for chain organizations; ambulance requests for Medicare payment; a supplement to the Medicare current beneficiary survey; and the Medicaid program budget report prepared by State Medicaid agencies).

64 FR 13354, March 18, 1999: Medicare and Medicaid Programs; Civil Money Penalties for Nursing Homes (SNF/NF), Change in Notice Requirements, and Expansion of Discretionary Remedy Delegation — Final rule with comment period, affecting 42 CFR Part 488.

64 FR 13432, March 18, 1999: HCFA Agency Information Collection Activities: Submission for OMB Review; Comment request (pertaining to Medicaid eligibility quality control sampling).

64 FR 13997, March 23, 1999: HCFA Agency Information Collection Activities: Submission for OMB Review; Comment request (pertaining to Medicare and Medicaid requirements for advanced

directives, and disclosure of ownership and financial control interest).

64 FR 20008, April 23, 1999: HCFA Agency Information Collection Activities: Submission for OMB Review; Comment request (pertaining to annual early and periodic screening, diagnostic, and treatment (EPSDT) services).

64 FR 24956, May 10, 1999: Medicare and Medicaid Programs; Effective Dates of Provider Agreements and Supplier Approvals-Correction restoring regulations inadvertently removed when a final rule concerning effective dates for provider agreements and supplier approvals was published at 62 FR 43931, August 18, 1997.

64 FR 27798, May 21, 1999: HCFA Agency Information Collection Activities: Proposed collection; Comment request (pertaining to determining third party liability (TPL) by State Medicaid agencies).

64 FR 29048, May 28, 1999: HCFA Agency Information Collection Activities: Proposed Collection; Comment request (pertaining to certification as a rural health clinic).

64 FR 32984, June 18, 1999: Medicare and Medicaid Programs; Mandatory Use, Collection, Encoding, and Transmission of Outcome and Assessment Information Set (OASIS) for Home Health Agencies — Notice.

64 FR 32992, June 18, 1999: HCFA Privacy Act of 1974; Report of New System (pertaining to a new system of records containing data on the physical, mental, functional, and psychosocial status of all patients receiving the services of home health agencies (HHAs) approved to participate in Medicare or Medicaid).

64 FR 36070, July 2, 1999: Medicare and Medicaid Programs; Hospital Conditions of Participation: Patient Rights — Interim final rule with comment, affecting 42 CFR 482.

64 FR 37985, July 14, 1999: Office of Inspector General; Publication of the OIG Special Advisory Bulletin on Gainsharing Arrangements and CMPs for Hospital Payments to Physicians to Reduce or Limit Services to Beneficiaries — Notice.

64 FR 39934, July 23, 1999: Medicare and Medicaid Program; Appeal of the Loss of Nurse Aide Training Programs — Interim final rule with comment period, affecting 42 CFR Parts 431 and 498. See also correction at 64 FR 43295, August 10, 1999.

64 FR 43198, August 9, 1999: Medicare and Medicaid Programs; Announcement of Additional Applications from Hospitals Requesting Waivers for Organ Procurement Service Areas — Notice with comment period.

64 FR 44030, August 12, 1999: HCFA Agency Information Collection Activites: Submission for OMB Review; Comment request (pertaining to blood bank inspection checklists and reports under CLIA; and Medicaid eligibility quality control).

64 FR 44031, August 12, 1999: HCFA Agency Information Collection Activites: Submission for OMB Review; Comment request (pertaining to survey and certification of rural health clinics; and determining third party liability in Medicaid programs).

64 FR 49121, September 10, 1999: Medicaid Program; Optional Coverage of Certain Tuberculosis-related Services to TB-Infected Individual — Proposed rule affecting 42 CFR Parts 435, 436, and 440.

64 FR 49197, September 10, 1999: Medicare and Medicaid Programs; Application of the Joint Commission for Accreditaton of Healthcare Organizations (JCAHO) for Continued Approval of Deeming Authority for Home Health Agencies — Proposed notice.

64 FR 49198, September 10, 1999: Medicare and Medicaid Programs; Application of the Community Health Accreditation Program, Incorporated, CHAP) for Continued Approval of Deeming Authority for Home Health Agencies — Proposed notice.

64 FR 49199, September 10, 1999: Medicare and Medicaid Programs; Reapplication of the American Osteopathic Association (AOA) for Continued Approval of Deeming Authority for Hospitals — Proposed notice.

64 FR 42791, September 30, 1999: Office of Inspector General; Publication of the OIG Special Advisory Bulletin on the Effect of Exclusion from Participation in Federal Health Care Programs — Notice. See also correction at 64 FR 55484, October 13, 1999.

64 FR 54263, October 6, 1999: Medicaid Program; Flexibility in Payment Methods for Services of Hospitals, Nursing Facilities, and Intermediate Care Facilities for the Mentally Retarded — Proposed rule affecting 42 CFR Part 447.

64 FR 58418, October 29, 1999: HCFA Agency Information Collection Activities: Proposed Collection; Comment request (pertaining to outcome based continuous quality improvement (OBCQI) approach for the PACE program).

64 FR 59185, November 2, 1999: Medicare and Medicaid Programs; Quarterly Listing of Program Issuances — Fourth Quarter, 1998 — Notice.

64 FR 66234, November 24, 1999: Medicare and Medicaid Programs; Programs of All-inclusive Care for the Elderly (PACE) — Interim final rule with comment period, affecting 42 CFR Parts 460, 462, 466, 473, and 476.

64 FR 66482, November 26, 1999: HCFA Agency Information Collection Activities: Proposed Collection; Comment request (pertaining to resident assessment in skilled nursing facilities).

64 FR 67028, November 30, 1999: Medicare and Medicaid Programs; Religious Nonmedical Health Care Institutions and Advance Directives — Interim final rule with comment period, affecting 42 CFR Parts 403, 412, 431, 440, 442, 446, 456, 488, and 489.

64 FR 67223, December 1, 1999: Medicaid Program; External Quality Review of Medicaid Managed Care Organizations — Proposed rule affecting 42 CFR Parts 433 and 438.

64 FR 69271, December 10, 1999: HCFA Agency Information Collection Activities: Proposed Collection; Comment request (pertaining to hospital providers of extender care (swing bed) services in Medicare and Medicaid).

64 FR 69273, December 10, 1999: HCFA Agency Information Collection Activities: Submission for OMB Review; Comment request (pertaining to Medicare/Medicaid hospital survey reports).

2000

65 FR 1400, January 10, 2000: HCFA Agency Information Collection Activities: Submission for OMB Review; Comment request (pertaining to reporting outcome and assessment information set (OASIS) data set as a condition of participation for HHAs).

65 FR 2186, January 13, 2000: HCFA Agency Information Collection Activities; Submission for OMB Review; Comment request (pertaining to physician certifications/re-certifications in skilled nursing facilities).

65 FR 5354, February 3, 2000: HCFA Agency Information Collection Activities: Proposed Collection; Comment request (pertaining to standardized Medicare/Medicaid claim form for reimbursement of covered services).

65 FR 5354, February 3, 2000: HCFA Agency Information Collection Activities: Proposed Collection; Comment request (pertaining to State buy-in programs).

65 FR 8370, February 18, 2000: HCFA Agency Information Collection Activities: Submission for OMB Review; Comment request

(pertaining to a project to develop an outcome-based continuous quality improvement system for PACE).

65 FR 8722, February 22, 2000: Medicaid Program; Additional Comment Period for the Schedules of Per-visit and Per-beneficiary Limitations on Home Health Agency Costs for Cost Reporting Periods Beginning on or after October 1, 1999, and Portions of Cost Reporting Periods Beginning October 1, 2000 — Notice of an additional 15-day comment period.

65 FR 8722, February 22, 2000: Medicare and Medicaid Programs; Re-approval of the Deeming Authority of the Joint Commission on Accreditation of Healthcare Organizations (JCAHO) for Home Health Agencies (HHAs) — Final notice.

65 FR 8725, February 22, 2000: Medicare and Medicaid Programs; Reapproval of the Deeming Authority of the Community Health Accreditation Program, Incorporated (CHAP) for Home Health Agencies (HHAs) — Final notice.

65 FR 8727, February 22, 2000: Medicare and Medicaid Programs; Recognition of the American Osteopathic Association (AOA) for Continued Approval of Deeming Authority for Hospitals — Final notice.

65 FR 12556, March 9, 2000: HCFA Agency Information Collection Activities: Proposed Collection; Comment request (pertaining to hospital request for certification in the Medicare/Medicaid program).

65 FR 12556, March 9, 2000: HCFA Agency Information Collection Activities: Proposed Collection; Comment request (pertaining to Medicaid drug rebate).

65 FR 12560, March 9, 2000: HCFA Agency Information Collection Activities: Submission for OMB Review; Comment request (pertaining to hospital provider of extended care services (swing beds) in the Medicare and Medicaid programs).

65 FR 14986, March 20, 2000: HCFA Agency Information Collection Activities: Submission for OMB Review; Comment request (pertaining to skilled nursing facility resident assessment MDS data).

65 FR 19187, April 10, 2000: Medicare Program; Prospective Payment System and Consolidated Billing for Skilled Nursing Facilities; Update- — Proposed rule affecting 42 CFR Parts 411 and 489.

65 FR 25460, May 2, 2000: Medicare and State Health Care Programs: Fraud and Abuse; Civil Money Penalty Safe Harbor to Protect Payment of Medicare Supplemental Insurance and Medigap Premiums for ESRD Beneficiaries — Notice of proposed rulemaking affecting 42 CFR Part 1003.

65 FR 25492, May 2, 2000: Medicare, Medicaid and CLIA Programs; Clinical Laboratory Improvement Amendments of 1988 Removal of Exemption of Laboratories in the State of Oregon — Notice.

65 FR 34478, May 30, 2000: Medicaid Program; State Allotments for Payment of Medicare Part B Premiums for Qualifying Individuals: Federal Fiscal Year 2000 — Notice.

65 FR 34715, May 31, 2000: Medicaid Infrastructure Grant Program to Support the Competitive Employment of People with Disabilities — Notice.

65 FR 34986, June 1, 2000: Office of Inspector General; Privacy Act; Implementation (exempting the Healthcare Integrity and Protection Data Bank under Section 1128C of the Social Security Act from certain provisions of the Privacy Act (5 U.S.C. 552a) — Final rule affecting 45 CFR Part 5b.

65 FR 35652, June 5, 2000: HCFA Agency Information Collection Activities: Proposed Collection; Comment request (pertaining to hospital conditions of participation; identification of potential organ, tissue, and eye donors and transplant hospitals' provision of transplant-related data).

65 FR 35652, June 5, 2000: HCFA Agency Information Collection Activities: Proposed Collection; Comment request (pertaining to home health agency cost reports).

65 FR 35653, June 5, 2000: HCFA Agency Information Collection Activities: Proposed Collection; Comment request (pertaining to ICF/MR survey forms).

65 FR 35653, June 5, 2000: HCFA Agency Information Collection Activities: Submission for OMB Review; Comment request (pertaining to model application template for State child health plan under Medicaid and the State Children's Health Insurance Program).

65 FR 35654, June 5, 2000: HCFA Agency Information Collection Activities: Submission for OMB Review; Comment request (pertaining to hospital request for certification in Medicare and Medicaid).

65 FR 40669, June 30, 2000: HCFA Agency Information Collection Activities: Submission for OMB Review; Comment request (pertaining to Medicaid drug rebate program).

65 FR 49001, August 10, 2000: HCFA Emergency Clearance: Public Information Collection Requirements Submitted to the Office of Management and Budget (OMB) (pertaining to quality improvement system for managed care).

65 FR 50373, August 17, 2000: HCFA; Health Insurance Reform: Announcement of Designated Standard Maintenance Organizations — Notice.

65 FR 50713, August 21, 2000: HCFA Agency Information Collection Activities: Proposed Collection; Comment request (pertaining to social HMO demonstration payment methodology)

65 FR 53319, September 1, 2000: HCFA Agency Information Collection Activities: Proposed Collection; Comment request (pertaining to incentive arrangement disclosure form for managed care organizations and their related medical groups and physicians).

65 FR 54857, September 11, 2000: HCFA Agency Information Collection Activities: Submission for OMB Review; Comment request (pertaining to ICF/MR survey report forms).

65 FR 54857, September 11, 2000: HCFA Agency Information Collection Activities: Submission for OMB Review; Comment request (pertaining to hospital conditions of participation-identification of potential organ, tissue, and eye donors, and transplant hospitals' provision of transplant-related data).

65 FR 60105, October 10, 2000: Medicaid Program; Home and Community-based Services — Final rule with comment period, affecting 42 CFR Parts 440 and 441.

65 FR 60151, October 10, 2000: Medicaid Program; Revision to Medicaid Upper Payment Limit Requirements for Hospital Services, Nursing Facility Services, Intermediate Care Facility Services for the Mentally Retarded, and Clinic Services — Proposed rule affecting 42 CFR Part 447.

65 FR 61171, October 16, 2000: HCFA Agency Information Collection Activities: Submission for OMB Review; Comment request (pertaining to Medicaid sterilization regulations and consent forms).

65 FR 63081, October 20, 2000: HCFA Agency Information Collection Activities: Submission for OMB Review; Comment request (pertaining to Medicaid report on payables and receivables, and municipal health services cost report form).

65 FR 64226, October 26, 2000: HCFA Agency Information Collection Activities: Proposed Collection; Comment request (pertaining to reconciliation of State invoices for drug rebate agreements).

65 FR 64919, October 31, 2000: Medicaid Program; Change in Application of Federal Financial Participation Limits — Proposed rule affecting 42 CFR Part 435.

65 FR 64966, October 31, 2000: Medicare, Medicaid, and CLIA Programs; Continuance of the Approval of COLA as a CLIA Accredi-

tation Organization — Notice. See also correction at 65 FR 70575, November 24, 2000.

65 FR 66255, November 3, 2000: HCFA Agency Information Collection Activities: Proposed Collection; Comment request (pertaining to survey of Medicaid home and community-based services waiver and personal care option recipients).

65 FR 69416, November 16, 2000: Medicare and Medicaid Programs; Hospital Conditions of Participation: Laboratory Services — Proposed rule affecting 42 CFR Part 482.

65 FR 69942, November 21, 2000: HCFA Agency Information Collection Activities: Proposed Collection; Comment request (pertaining to restraints/seclusion death reporting by hospitals).

65 FR 79868, December 20, 2000: HCFA Emergency Clearance: Public Information Collection Requirements Submitted to the Office of Management and Budget (OMB) (pertaining to survey of beneficiaries who involuntarily disenroll from their managed care plan).

65 FR 82941, December 29, 2000: Medicare, Medicaid, and CLIA Programs; Extension of Certain Effective Dates for Clinical Laboratory Requirements under CLIA — Final rule with comment period, affecting 42 CFR Part 493.

2001

66 FR 2316, January 11, 2001: Medicaid Program; Change in Application of Federal Financial Participation Limits—Final rule affecting 42 CFR Part 435.

66 FR 2532, January 11, 2001: Medicaid Program; Infrastructure Grant Program to Support the Competitive Employment of People with Disabilities—Notice.

66 FR 2912, January 12, 2001: HCFA Agency Information Collection Activities: Proposed Collection; Comment request (pertaining to Medicare/Medicaid health insurance common claim form).

66 FR 3148, January 12, 2001: Medicaid Program; Revision to Medicaid Upper Payment Limit Requirements for Hospital Services, Nursing Facility Services, Intermediate Care Facility Services for the Mentally Retarded, and Clinic Services—Final rule affecting 42 CFR Part 447.

66 FR 4674, January 18, 2001: Medicare and Medicaid Programs; Hospital Conditions of Participation: Anesthesia—Final rule affecting 42 CFR Parts 416, 482, and 485.

66 FR 6228, January 19, 2001: Medicaid Program; Medicaid Managed Care—Final rule with comment period, affecting 42 CFR Part 400, 430, 431, 435, 438, 440, and 447.

66 FR 6629, January 22, 2001: HCFA Agency Information Collection Activities: Submission for OMB Review; Comment request (pertaining to Medicaid drug rebate program).

66 FR 7147, January 22, 2001: Medicaid Program; Use of Restraint and Seclusion in Psychiatric Residential Treatment Facilities Providing Psychiatric Services to Individuals Under Age 21—Final rule affecting 42 CFR Parts 441 and 483.

66 FR 9588, February 8, 2001: HCFA Agency Information Collection Activities: Proposed Collection; Comment request (pertaining to imposition of cost–sharing charges under Medicaid).

66 FR 11546, February 26, 2001: Medicaid Program; Medicaid Managed Care: Delay of Effective Date—Final rule delay, affecting 42 CFR Parts 400, 430, 431, 434, 435, 438, 440, and 447.

66 FR 13328, March 5, 2001: Medicare, Medicaid, and CLIA Programs; Continuance of the Approval of the American Society for Histocompatibility and Immunogenetics as a CLIA Accreditation Organization—Notice.

66 FR 13547, March 6, 2001: HCFA Agency Information Collection Activities: Proposed Collection; Comment request (pertaining to Medicare/Medicaid psychiatric hospital survey data).

66 FR 14343, March 12, 2001: Medicaid Program; Change in Application of Federal Financial Participation Limits: Delay of Effective Date—Final rule affecting 42 CFR Part 435.

66 FR 15352, March 19, 2001: Medicare and Medicaid Programs; Hospital Conditions of Participation: Anesthesia Services: Delay of Effective Date—Final rule; delay of effective date, affecting 42 CFR Parts 416, 482, and 485.

66 FR 16268, March 23, 2001: HCFA Agency Information Collection Activities; Proposed Collection; Comment request (pertaining to Medicaid post–eligibility preprint).

66 FR 16268, March 23, 2001: HCFA Agency Information Collection Activities: Submission for OMB Review; Comment request (pertaining to survey of home and community–based services waivers and personal care option recipients for the multi–site study of Medicaid home and community–based services).

66 FR 17657, April 3, 2001: Medicaid Program; Modification of the Medicaid Upper Payment Limit Transition Period for Inpatient Hospital Services, Outpatient Hospital Services, Nursing Facility

Services, Intermediate Care Facility Services for the Mentally Retarded and Clinic Services—Proposed rule affecting 42 CFR Part 447.

66 FR 18645, April 10, 2001: HCFA Agency Information Collection Activities: Submission for OMB Review; Comment request (pertaining to Medicare and Medicaid outcome and assessment information set (OASIS) as part of the conditions of participation for home health agencies).

66 FR 18646, April 10, 2001: HCFA Agency Information Collection Activities: Submission for OMB Review; Comment request (pertaining to transmittal and notice of approval of state plan material).

66 FR 18646, April 10, 2001: HCFA Agency Information Collection Activities: Submission for OMB Review; Comment request (pertaining to Medicare/Medicaid health insurance common claim form).

66 FR 19509, April 16, 2001: Medicare and Medicaid Programs; Application by the American Osteopathic Association (AOF) for Approval of Deeming Authority for Critical Access Hospitals—Proposed notice.

66 FR 20314, April 20, 2001: HCFA Agency Information Collection Activities: Proposed Collection; Comment request (pertaining to survey of Medicaid home and community-based services waiver and personal care option recipients).

66 FR 27598, May 18, 2001: Medicare and Medicaid Programs; Hospital Conditions of Participation; Anesthesia Services: Delay of Effective Date—Notice of final rule affecting 42 CFR Parts 416, 482, and 485.

66 FR 28110, May 22, 2001: Medicaid Program; Use of Restraint and Seclusion in Psychiatric Residential Treatment Facilities Providing Inpatient Psychiatric Services to Individuals under Age 21—Interim final rule, amendment and clarification with request for comment, affecting 42 CFR Parts 441 and 483.

66 FR 28183, May 22, 2001: Medicaid Program; Infrastructure Grant Program to Support the Design and Delivery of Long Term Services and Supports that Permit People of Any Age Who Have a Disability or Long–term Illness to Live in the Community—Notice of funding availability.

66 FR 32360, June 14, 2001: HCFA Agency Information Collection Activities: Proposed Collection; Comment request (pertaining to evaluation of the BadgerCare Medicaid demonstration in Wisconsin).

66 FR 32776, June 18, 2001: Medicaid Program; Medicaid Managed Care: Further Delay of Effective Date for Final Rule affecting 42 CFR Parts 400, 430, 431, 434, 435, 438, 440, and 447.

66 FR 33103, June 20, 2001: HCFA Agency Information Collection Activities; Submission for OMB Review; Comment request (pertaining to Medicaid post–eligibility form).

See § 3:10.

§ 7:11 CANCELLING CERTIFICATION AND APPROVAL OF SKILLED NURSING FACILITIES, INTERMEDIATE CARE FACILITIES, AND INTERMEDIATE CARE FACILITIES FOR THE MENTALLY RETARDED — Section 1910 [42 U.S.C.A. 1396i]

Regulations

42 CFR Part 420 — Program Integrity: Medicare

42 CFR Part 431, Subpart D — Appeals Process for SNF's and ICF's

42 CFR Part 442 — Standards for Payment for Nursing Facilities and Intermediate Care Facilities for the Mentally Retarded [Medicaid]

42 CFR Part 447 — Payments for Services

42 CFR Part 455 — Program Integrity: Medicaid

42 CFR Part 456 — Utilization Control

42 CFR Part 483 — Requirements for States and Long Term Care Facilities

42 CFR Part 488 — Survey, Certification, and Enforcement Procedures

42 CFR Part 489 — Provider Agreements and Supplier Approval

42 CFR Part 498 — Appeals Procedures for Determinations that Affect Participation in the Medicare Program and for Determinations that Affect the Participation of ICF's/MR and Certain NF's in the Medicaid Program

42 CFR Chapter V — Office of Inspector General — Health Care, Department of Health and Human Services

Subchapter A — General Provisions

Part 1000 — Introduction; General Definitions

Subchapter B — OIG Authorities

Part 1001 — Program Integrity: Medicare and State Health Care Programs

Part 1002 — Program Integrity: State-initiated Exclusion from Medicaid

Part 1003 — Civil Money Penalties, Assessments and Exclusions

Part 1004 — Imposition of Sanctions on Health Care Practitioners and Providers of Health Care Services by a Peer Review Organization

Part 1005 — Appeals of Exclusions, Civil Money Penalties and Assessments

Part 1006 — Investigational Inquiries

Part 1007 — State Medicaid Fraud Control Units

Part 1008 — Advisory Opinions by the OIG

54 FR 5316, February 2, 1989: Medicare and Medicaid; Requirements for Long Term Care Facilities — Final rule with comment period, amending 42 CFR Parts 405, 442, 447, 483, 488, 489, and 498. See also delay in effective date at 54 FR 29717, July 14, 1989; corrections at 54 FR 8361, February 27, 1989, and 54 FR 37466, September 11, 1989; and final rule delaying effective date from January 1, 1990, to October 1, 1990, at 54 FR 53611, December 29, 1989.

55 FR 10256, March 20, 1990: Medicare and Medicaid; Charges to Residents' Funds in Nursing Homes — Proposed rule to amend 42 CFR Part 483. See also final rule at 57 FR 53572, November 12, 1992.

55 FR 10938, March 23, 1990: Medicare and Medicaid Programs; Nurse Aide Training and Competency Evaluation Programs — Proposed rule to amend 42 CFR Parts 431, 433, and 483.

55 FR 10951, March 23, 1990: Medicare and Medicaid Programs; Preadmission Screening and Annual Resident Review — Proposed rule to amend 42 CFR Parts 405, 431, and 483.

56 FR 13317, April 1, 1991: Medicare Program; Schedule of Limits for Skilled Nursing Facility Inpatient Routine Service Costs — Final notice with comment period. See also correction published at 56 FR 22053, May 13, 1991.

56 FR 30696, July 5, 1991: Medicaid Program; Correction and Reduction Plans for Intermediate Care Facilities for the Mentally Retarded — Final rule affecting 42 CFR Part 442. See also correction at 56 FR 49147, September 27, 1991.

56 FR 48826, September 26, 1991: Medicare and Medicaid; Requirements for Long Term Care Facilities — Final rule affecting 42 CFR Parts 422, 447, 483, 488, 489, and 498. See also correction at 57 FR 43922, September 23, 1992.

56 FR 48880, September 26, 1991: Medicare and Medicaid Programs; Nurse Aide Training and Competency Evaluation Programs — Final rule affecting 42 CFR Parts 431, 433, and 483. See also correction at 56 FR 59331, November 25, 1991.

57 FR 4516, February 5, 1992: Medicare and Medicaid Programs; Omnibus Nursing Home Requirements — Proposed rule affecting 42 CFR Parts 418, 440, 441, 482, 483, and 488. See also correction at 57 FR 8961, March 13, 1992.

57 FR 39278, August 28, 1992: Medicare and Medicaid Programs; Survey, Certification and Enforcement of Skilled Nursing Facilities and Nursing Facilities — Proposed rule affecting 42 CFR Parts 431, 442, 488, and 489.

57 FR 43462, September 21, 1992: Health Care Financing Administration Public Information Collection Requirements Submitted to the Office of Management and Budget for Clearance (pertaining to sole community home health agencies; physician/supplier overpayment reports; physician or supplier Medicare agreements; conditions of participation for rural health clinics; Medicare provider refunds; conditions of participation for comprehensive outpatient rehabilitation facilities; Medicaid income and eligibility verification system; Medicaid integrated review schedule; provider overpayment report; financial statement of Medicare provider debtors; negative case action review schedule for Medicaid quality control; outpatient resource costing study; Medicaid intermediate care facility for the mentally retarded or persons with related conditions survey report form; installment agreement of beneficiary refund of overpayment; PRO assumption of responsibilities; Medicare contractor administrative budget and cost reporting system forms; fire safety survey report forms; medical records review under prospective payment system; and Qualified Medicare Beneficiary supplement to the Medicare current beneficiary survey).

57 FR 46362, October 8, 1992: Medicare and Medicaid Programs; Revised Effective Date of Medicare/Medicaid Provider Agreement and Supplier Participation — Proposed rule affecting 42 CFR Parts 431, 440, 442, 488, 489, and 498.

57 FR 48033, October 21, 1992: Medicare Program; Revised Procedures for Paying Claims From Providers of Services — Final notice.
57 FR 53572, November 12, 1992: Medicare and Medicaid; Charges to Residents' Funds in Nursing Homes — Final rule affecting 42 CFR Part 483.

57 FR 54710, November 20, 1992: Medicaid Program; Elimination of Certain Written Documentation Pertaining to Medicaid Long-Term Care Facilities — Final rule affecting 42 CFR Part 442.

57 FR 56450, November 30, 1992: Medicare and Medicaid Programs; Preadmission Screening and Annual Resident Review — Final rule with comment period, affecting 42 CFR Parts 405, 431, 433, and 483. See also correction published at 58 FR 25784, April 28, 1993.

57 FR 61614, December 28, 1992: Medicare and Medicaid; Resident Assessment in Long Term Care Facilities — Proposed rule affecting 42 CFR Parts 456 and 483.

58 FR 38579, July 19, 1993: HCFA Public Information Collection Requirements Submitted to the Office of Management and Budget (OMB) for Clearance re survey of home health agencies; CLIA survey report form; validation of state surveys; Medicaid listing of participating home health agencies; financial information regarding Medicare benefits from Medicare contractors; and third-party liability under Medicaid.

58 FR 46198, September 1, 1993: HCFA Public Information Collection Requirements (ICR) Submitted to the Office of Management and Budget (OMB) for Clearance (pertaining to prenatal services and assistance screening; home health agency treatment forms; conditions of participation for intermediate care facilities for the mentally retarded; State Medicaid eligibility quality control sample selection lists; prepaid health plan cost report; hospital survey report form; procedures for determining whether providers, practitioners, or other suppliers of services are liable for certain noncovered services; Medicare credit balance reporting requirements; Medicare provider cost report questionnaire form; Medicare current beneficiary survey rounds 7–10; sterilization regulation/consent form; PRO reconsideration and appeals information requirements; information collection requirements in HSQ-110, acquisition, protection and disclosure of PRO information; Medicare/Medicaid organ procurement organization's (OPO) request for certification) — Notice.

59 FR 762, January 6, 1994: Medicare Program; Schedule of Limits for Skilled Nursing Facility Inpatient Routine Service Costs — Final notice with comment period.

59 FR 26955, May 25, 1994: Medicare Program; Self-implementing Coverage and Payment Provisions: 1993 Legislation — Final rule with comment period (pertaining to reductions in

payments for skilled nursing facility services — return on equity; reductions in payments for hospice services; reduction in Part A premium for certain individuals with 30 or more quarters of Social Security coverage; extension of 10 percent reduction in payments for capital-related costs of outpatient hospital services; extension of reduction in payments for other costs for outpatient hospital services; reduction in payments for intraocular lenses; payment for parenteral and enteral nutrients, supplies and equipment during 1994 and 1995; increase in annual cap on amount of Medicare payment for outpatient physical therapy and occupational therapy services; rural health clinics and Federally qualified health centers; reduction in payments for Epoetin; and changes in Part B premium.)

59 FR 29578, June 8, 1994: Medicare Program; Optional Payment System for Low Medicare Volume Skilled Nursing Facilities — Proposed rule affecting 42 CFR Part 413.

59 FR 52178, October 14, 1994: HCFA Public Information Collection Requirements Submitted to the Office of Management and Budget (OMB) for Clearance (pertaining to Medicare reimbursement for outpatient services, cost reports for free-standing skilled nursing facilities; Medicare coverage criteria for adult heart transplants, drug rebates for Medicaid, optional prospective payment cost report for certain skilled nursing facilities, reimbursable costs for organ procurement agencies, distribution and use of end stage renal disease treatment sources, conditions of coverage for ambulatory surgical centers, and waivers for home and community based services).

59 FR 56116, November 10, 1994: Medicare and Medicaid Programs; Survey, Certification and Enforcement of Skilled Nursing Facilities and Nursing Facilities — Final rule affecting 42 CFR Parts 401, 431, 435, 440, 441, 442, 447, 483, 488, 489, and 498. See also correcting amendment, effective July 1, 1995, at 62 FR 44221, August 20, 1997.

59 FR 66969, December 28, 1994: HCFA Public Information Collection Requirements Submitted to the Office of Management and Budget (OMB) for Clearance (pertaining to physician certification in skilled nursing facilities, and criteria for Medicare coverage of adult liver transplants).

60 FR 21525, May 2, 1995: HCFA Public Information Collection Requirements Submitted to the Office of Management and Budget (OMB) for Clearance (pertaining to intermediary requests for information from skilled nursing facilities, reimbursement for CLIA

compliance surveys, patient outcome data in home health agencies, common claim forms for Medicare/Medicaid reimbursement, and a study of childhood immunization costs).

60 FR 37590, July 21, 1995: Medicare Program; Optional Payment System for Low Medicare Volume Skilled Nursing Facilities — Final rule affecting 42 CFR Part 413.

60 FR 50115, September 28, 1995: Medicare and Medicaid Programs; Survey, Certification and Enforcement of Skilled Nursing Facilities and Nursing Facilities — Final rule and correction to final regulations, affecting 42 CFR Parts 431, 440, 442, 488, 489, and 498. See also corrections at 60 FR 52731, October 10, 1995, and at 60 FR 534456, October 13, 1995.

60 FR 37066, July 19, 1995: HCFA Public Information Collection Requirements Submitted to the Office of Management and Budget (OMB) for Clearance (pertaining to actuarial forecasts for Medicaid utilization and cost, employers identified through a match of IRS, SSA, and Medicare records for purposes of the Medicare Secondary Payer provision, health and safety requirements for portable X-ray suppliers, and evaluation of Intermediate Care Facilities for Persons with Mental Retardation — establishing psychoactive drug use baselines).

61 FR 11214, March 19, 1996: HCFA Agency Information Collection Activities: Proposed Collection; Comment Request (pertaining to conditions of coverage for organ procurement organizations; and skilled nursing facility and skilled nursing facility healthcare complex forms).

61 FR 35231, July 5, 1996: HCFA Agency Information Collection Activities: Proposed Collection; Comment Request (pertaining to Medicaid payment standards for inpatient hospital or long-term care services).

61 FR 38395, July 24, 1996: Medicaid Program; Medicaid Eligibility Quality Control, Progressive Reductions in Federal Financial Participation for FYs 1982–1984, Payment for Physician Billing for Clinical Laboratory Services, and Utilization Control of Skilled Nursing Facility Services: Removal of Obsolete Requirements — Final rule.

61 FR 46466, September 3, 1996: Medicare Program; Schedule of Prospectively Determined Payment Rates for Skilled Nursing Facility Inpatient Routine Service Costs — Final rule with comment period.

61 FR 51295, October 1, 1996: HCFA Public Information Requirements Submitted for Collection of Public Comment: Submission for OMB Review (pertaining to approval of Medicaid payment rates for inpatient hospital or long term care services).

61 FR 51611, October 3, 1996: Medicare and Medicaid Programs; New Payment Methodology for Routine Extended Care Services Provided in a Swing-bed Hospital — Final Rule affecting 42 CFR Part 413. See also correction at 61 FR 58631, November 18, 1996.

61 FR 54209, October 17, 1996: HCFA Agency Information Collectio Activities: Proposed Collection; Comment request (pertaining to hospital eligibility for swing-bed status).

61 FR 64913, December 9, 1996: HCFA Agency Information Collection Activities: Proposed Collection; Comment request (pertaining to survey report forms for ICF/MRs; and current Medicare beneficiary surveys).

61 FR 68270, December 27, 1996: HCFA Agency Information Collection Activities: Submission for OMB Review; Comment request (pertaining to a facility identification and screening form for hospital providers of extended care services (swing-beds) in the the Medicare and Medicaid programs).

62 FR 26, January 2, 1997: Medicare Program; Electronic Cost Reporting for Skilled Nursing Facilities and Home Health Agencies — Final Rule. See also correction at 62 FR 27210, May 19, 1997.

62 FR 11214, March 11, 1997: HCFA Agency Information Collection Activities: Submission for OMB Review; Comment request (pertaining to intermediate care facility for the mentally retarded or persons with related conditions survey report forms).

62 FR 11458, March 12, 1997: HCFA Agency Information Collection Activities: Proposed Collection; Comment request (pertaining to skilled nursing facility and skilled nursing facility health care complex cost report form).

62 FR 30603, June 4, 1997: HCFA Agency Information Collection Activities: Submission for OMB Review; Comment request (pertaining to skilled nursing facility and skilled nursing facility health care complex cost reports; and hospital conditions of participation).

62 FR 33095, June 18, 1997: HCFA Agency Information Collection Activities: Proposed Collection; Comment request (pertaining to skilled nursing facility prospective payment system cost report form).

62 FR 23140, April 29, 1997: Office of Inspector General: Health Care Programs: Fraud and Abuse; Revised PRO Sanctions for Failing to Meet Statutory Obligations — Final rule.

62 FR 43931, August 18, 1997: Medicare and Medicaid Programs: Effective Dates of Provider Agreements and Supplier Approvals — Final rule affecting 42 CFR Parts 431, 442, 488, 489, and 498.

62 FR 51536, October 1, 1997: Medicare Program; Schedules of Limits and Prospectively Determined Payment Rates for Skilled Nursing Facility Inpatient Routine Service Costs — Final notice with comment period.

62 FR 55410, October 24, 1997: HCFA Agency Information Collection Activities: Submission for OMB Review; Comment request (pertaining to Medicare/Medicaid disclosure of ownership and control forms).

62 FR 48736, October 30, 1997: HCFA Agency Information Collection Activities: Submission for OMB Review; Comment request (pertaining to prospective payment for skilled nursing facilities).

62 FR 66726, December 19, 1997: Medicare and Medicaid Programs; Hospital Conditions of Participation; Provider Agreements and Supplier Approval — Proposed rule affecting 42 CFR Parts 416, 482, 485, and 489.

62 FR 67174, December 23, 1997: Medicare and Medicaid; Resident Assessment in Long Term Care Facilities — Final rule affecting 42 CFR Part 483.

63 FR 14719, March 26, 1998: HCFA Agency Information Collection Activities: Proposed Collection; Comment request (pertaining to physician certification and re-certification in skilled nursing facilities).

63 FR 20415, April 24, 1998: Office of Inspector General: Publication of OIG Special Fraud Alert: Fraud and Abuse in Nursing Home Arrangements with Hospices — Notice.

63 FR 26252, May 12, 1998: Medicare Program: Prospective Payment System and Consolidated Billing for Skilled Nursing Facilities — Final rule, affecting 42 CFR Parts 409, 410, 411, 413, 424, 483, and 489. See also correction at 63 FR 53301, October 5, 1998.

63 FR 28395, May 22, 1998: HCFA Agency Information Collection Activities: Submission for OMB Review; Comment request (pertaining to physician certifications and recertifications in skilled nursing facilities).

63 FR 28396, May 22, 1998: HCFA Privacy Act of 1974 —Notice of New System of Records (pertaining to the long term care minimum data set).

63 FR 37498, July 13, 1998: Medicare Program; Prospective Payment System and Consolidated Billing for Skilled Nursing Facilities — Notice of extension of comment period for interim final rule, affecting 42 CFR 409, 410, 411,413, 424, 483, and 489.

63 FR 42797, August 11, 1998: Medicare Program; Revision of the Procedures for Requesting Exceptions to Cost Limits for Skilled Nursing Facilities and Elimination of Reclassifications — Proposed rule affecting 42 CFR Part 413.

63 FR 58399, October 30, 1998: Office of Inspector General: Publication of the OIG's Provider Self-Disclosure Protocol —Notice.

63 FR 60356, November 9, 1998: HCFA Agency Information Collection activities: Proposed Collection; Comment request (pertaining to skilled nursing facility resident assessment MDS data).

63 FR 68290, December 10, 1998: HCFA Agency Information Collection Activities: Submission for OMB Review; Comment request (pertaining to outpatient rehabilitation cost reports; SNF and SNF health care complex cost reports).

63 FR 70137, December 18, 1998: Office of Inspector General: Solicitation of Information and Recommendations for Developing OIG Compliance Program Guidance for the Nursing Home Industry — Notice.

63 FR 72317, December 31, 1998: HCFA Agency Information Collection Activities: Proposed Collection; Comment request (pertaining to advanced directives under Medicare and Medicaid; and Medicare/Medicaid disclosure of ownership and control interests).

63 FR 72318, December 31, 1998: HCFA Agency Information Collection Activities: Proposed Collection; Comment request (pertaining to fire safety survey report forms for health care facilities).

1999

64 FR 6664, February 10, 1999: HCFA Agency Information Collection Activities: Submission for OMB Review; Comment request (pertaining to skilled nursing facility (SNF) resident assessment MDS data).

64 FR 6753, February 16, 1999: Office of Inspector General: Privacy Act; Notification of New System of Records in Conjunction with

the Healthcare Integrity and Protection Data Bank— Notice of a new system of records.

64 FR 13354, March 18, 1999: Medicare and Medicaid Programs; Civil Money Penalties for Nursing Homes (SNF/NF), Change in Notice Requirements, and Expansion of Discretionary Remedy Delegation—Final rule with comment period, affecting 42 CFR Part 488.

64 FR 13997, March 23, 1999: HCFA Agency Information Collection Activities: Submission for OMB Review; Comment request pertaining to Medicare and Medicaid requirements for advanced directives, and disclosure of ownership and financial control interest).

64 FR 17184, April 8, 1999: HCFA Medicare Program; April 23, 1999 Open Town Hall Meeting to Discuss the Skilled Nursing Facility Prospective Payment System (SNF/PPS).

64 FR 24956, May 10, 1999: Medicare and Medicaid Programs; Effective Dates of Provider Agreements and Supplier Approvals—Correction restoring regulations inadvertently removed when a final rule concerning effective dates for provider agreements and supplier approvals was published at 62 FR 43931, August 18, 1997.

64 FR 39934, July 23, 1999: Medicare and Medicaid Program; Appeal of the Loss of Nurse Aide Training Programs— Interim final rule with comment period, affecting 42 CFR Parts 431 and 498. See also correction at 64 FR 43295, August 10, 1999.

64 FR 39517, July 22, 1999: HCFA Agency Information Collection Activities: Submission for OMB Review; Comment request (pertaining to Medicare participating physician or supplier agreement form HCFA-460).

64 FR 41644, July 30, 1999: Medicare Program; Prospective Payment System and Consolidated Billing for Skilled Nursing Facilities—Final rule affecting 42 CFR Parts 409, 411, 413, and 489. See also correction at 64 FR 60122, November 4, 1999

64 FR 41684, July 30, 1999: Medicare Program; Prospective Payment System and Consolidated Billing for Skilled Nursing Facilities—Update—Notice. See also correction at 64 FR 54030, October 5, 1999.

64 FR 42610, August 5, 1999: Medicare Program; Revision of the Procedures for Requesting Exceptions to Cost Limits for Skilled Nursing Facilities and Elimination of Reclassifications Final rule.

64 FR 54263, October 6, 1999: Medicaid Program; Flexibility in Payment Methods for Services of Hospitals, Nursing Facilities, and

Intermediate Care Facilities for the Mentally Retarded— Proposed rule affecting 42 CFR Part 447.

64 FR 55949, October 15, 1999: HCFA Agency Information Collection Activities: Proposed Collection; Comment request (pertaining to physician certifications and re-certifications about the necessity for skilled nursing facility care).

64 FR 66482, November 26, 1999: HCFA Agency Information Collection Activities: Proposed Collection; Comment request (pertaining to resident assessment in skilled nursing facilities).

64 FR 67028, November 30, 1999: Medicare and Medicaid Programs; Religious Nonmedical Health Care Institutions and Advance Directives — Interim final rule with comment period, affecting 42 CFR Parts 403, 412, 431, 440, 442, 446, 456, 488, and 489.

64 FR 69271, December 10, 1999: HCFA Agency Information Collection Activities: Proposed Collection; Comment request (pertaining to hospital providers of extender care (swing bed) services in Medicare and Medicaid).

2000

65 FR 2186, January 13, 2000: HCFA Agency Information Collection Activities; Submission for OMB Review; Comment request (pertaining to physician certifications/re-certifications in skilled nursing facilities).

65 FR 12560, March 9, 2000: HCFA Agency Information Collection Activities: Submission for OMB Review; Comment request (pertaining to hospital provider of extended care services (swing beds) in the Medicare and Medicaid programs).

65 FR 14289, March 16, 2000: Office of Inspector General: Publication of the OIG Compliance Program Guidance for Nursing Facilities — Notice.

65 FR 14986, March 20, 2000: HCFA Agency Information Collection Activities: Submission for OMB Review; Comment request (pertaining to skilled nursing facility resident assessment MDS data).

65 FR 19187, April 10, 2000: Medicare Program; Prospective Payment System and Consolidated Billing for Skilled Nursing Facilities; Update- — Proposed rule affecting 42 CFR Parts 411 and 489.

65 FR 35653, June 5, 2000: HCFA Agency Information Collection Activities: Proposed Collection; Comment request (pertaining to ICF/MR survey forms).

65 FR 54856, September 11, 2000: HCFA Agency Information Collection Activities: Submission for OMB Review; Comment request (pertaining to skilled nursing facility cost reports).

65 FR 54857, September 11, 2000: HCFA Agency Information Collection Activities: Submission for OMB Review; Comment request (pertaining to ICF/MR survey report forms).

65 FR 60151, October 10, 2000: Medicaid Program; Revision to Medicaid Upper Payment Limit Requirements for Hospital Services, Nursing Facility Services, Intermediate Care Facility Services for the Mentally Retarded, and Clinic Services — Proposed rule affecting 42 CFR Part 447.

65 FR 64227, October 26, 2000: HCFA Agency Information Collection Activities: Proposed Collection; Comment request (pertaining to home health agency cost reports; skilled nursing facility cost reports; and hospital cost reports).

2001

66 FR 3148, January 12, 2001: Medicaid Program; Revision to Medicaid Upper Payment Limit Requirements for Hospital Services, Nursing Facility Services, Intermediate Care Facility Services for the Mentally Retarded, and Clinic Services—Final rule affecting 42 CFR Part 447.

66 FR 3497, January 16, 2001: Medicare Program; Prospective Payment System and Consolidated Billing for Skilled Nursing Facilities—Update; Correction notice affecting 42 FR Parts 411, 313, and 489. See FR Doc. 00–19004, July 31, 2000.

66 FR 16062, March 23, 2001: HCFA Agency Information Collection Activities: Submission for OMB Review; Comment request (pertaining to SNF cost report forms).

66 FR 17657, April 3, 2001: Medicaid Program; Modification of the Medicaid Upper Payment Limit Transition Period for Inpatient Hospital Services, Outpatient Hospital Services, Nursing Facility Services, Intermediate Care Facility Services for the Mentally Retarded and Clinic Services—Proposed rule affecting 42 CFR Part 447.

66 FR 27151, May 16, 2001: HCFA Agency Information Collection Activities: Proposed Collection; Comment request (pertaining to the Long Term Care Awareness Project).

See § 3:11.

§ 7:12 DISAPPROVING RURAL HEALTH CLINIC APPLICATIONS FOR CERTIFICATION — Section 1910(a) [42 U.S.C.A. 1396i(a)]

Regulations

42 CFR Part 405, Subpart X — Rural Health Clinic and Federally Qualified Health Care Services [Medicare]

42 CFR Part 420 — Supplementary Medical Insurance (SMI) Benefits

42 CFR Part 424 — Conditions for Medicare Payment

42 CFR Part 440 — Services: General Provisions

42 CFR Part 447 — Payment for Services

42 CFR Part 476 — Utilization and Quality Control Review

42 CFR Part 488 — Survey, Certification, and Enforcement Procedures

42 CFR Part 491 — Certification of Certain Health Facilities

42 CFR Part 498 — Appeals Procedures for Determinations that Affect Participation in the Medicare Program and for Determinations that Affect the Participation of ICF's/MR and Certain NF's in the Medicaid Program.

57 FR 43462, September 21, 1992: Health Care Financing Administration Public Information Collection Requirements Submitted to the Office of Management and Budget for Clearance (pertaining to sole community home health agencies; physician/supplier overpayment reports; physician or supplier Medicare agreements; conditions of participation for rural health clinics; Medicare provider refunds; conditions of participation for comprehensive outpatient rehabilitation facilities; Medicaid income and eligibility verification system; Medicaid integrated review schedule; provider overpayment report; financial statement of Medicare provider debtors; negative case action review schedule for Medicaid quality control; outpatient resource costing study; Medicaid intermediate care facility for the mentally retarded or persons with related conditions survey report form; installment agreement of beneficiary refund of overpayment; PRO assumption of responsibilities; Medicare contractor administrative budget and cost reporting system forms; fire safety survey report forms; medical records review under prospective payment system; and Qualified Medicare Beneficiary supplement to the Medicare current beneficiary survey).

57 FR 46362, October 8, 1992: Medicare and Medicaid Programs; Revised Effective Date of Medicare/Medicaid Provider Agreement

and Supplier Participation — Proposed rule affecting 42 CFR Parts 431, 440, 442, 488, 489, and 498.

57 FR 48033, October 21, 1992: Medicare Program; Revised Procedures for Paying Claims From Providers of Services — Final notice.

58 FR 54159, October 20, 1993: HCFA Public Information Collection Requirements Submitted to the Office of Management and Budget (OMB) for Clearance (pertaining to CLIA certification recommendation; CLIA laboratory personnel report; Medigap complaint data base; certification as a rural health clinic (RHC) and RHC survey report form; screening mammography services data report; ambulatory surgical center request for certification and survey report form; blood bank inspection checklist and report; Medicaid program budget report form; supplier of ESRD services form; and grantee data collection instrument) — Notice.

58 FR 63533, December 2, 1993: Medicare Program; Required Laboratory Procedures for Rural Health Clinics — Final rule with comment period, affecting 42 CFR Part 491.

59 FR 14865, March 30, 1994: HCFA Public Information Collection Requirements Submitted to the Office of Management and Budget (OMB) for Clearance (pertaining to home health agency Medicare and Medicaid survey report forms for conditions of participation; conditions of participation for rural health clinics; Medicaid re-evaluation of assets for determining payment rates to hospitals and nursing homes; statistical report on medical care, eligible, recipients, payments, and services.)

59 FR 26955, May 25, 1994: Medicare Program; Self‐implementing Coverage and Payment Provisions: 1993 Legislation — Final rule with comment period (pertaining to reductions in payments for skilled nursing facility services — return on equity; reductions in payments for hospice services; reduction in Part A premium for certain individuals with 30 or more quarters of Social Security coverage; extension of 10 percent reduction in payments for capital-related costs of outpatient hospital services; extension of reduction in payments for other costs for outpatient hospital services; reduction in payments for intraocular lenses; payment for parenteral and enteral nutrients, supplies and equipment during 1994 and 1995; increase in annual cap on amount of Medicare payment for outpatient physical therapy and occupational therapy services; rural health clinics and Federally qualified health centers; reduction in payments for Epoetin; and changes in Part B premium.)

61 FR 6645, February 21, 1996: HCFA Agency Information Collection Activities: Proposed Collection; Comment Request (pertaining to survey forms to evaluate Federally qualified health centers; and the Medicare Carrier provider/supplier application form).

61 FR 14640, April 3, 1996: Medicare Program; Payment for Federally Qualified Health Center Services — Final rule affecting 42 CFR Parts 405 and 491.

61 FR 17710, April 22, 1996: HCFA Agency Information Collection Activities: Proposed Collection; Comment Request (pertaining to payment adjustments for sole community hospitals; conditions of participation for portable x-ray suppliers; and cost reports for independent rural health centers and freestanding Federally qualified health centers).

61 FR 37487, July 18, 1996: HCFA Agency Information Collection Activities: Submission for OMB Review; Comment request (pertaining to cost reports for independent rural health centers and freestanding federally qualified health centers; and conditions of participation for portable x-ray suppliers).

61 FR 52951, October 9, 1996: HCFA Agency Information Collection Activities: Submission for OMB Review; Comment request (pertaining to Peer Review Organization Reconsiderations and Appeals; Part B enrollment forms; certification as a rural health clinic; Medicaid utilization control programs; lists of Medicaid recipients in institutions; and business proposal formats for PROs).

61 FR 66284, December 17, 1996: HCFA Agency Information Collection Activities: Proposed Collection; Comment request (pertaining to conditions of participation for rural health clinics).

62 FR 8252, February 24, 1997: HCFA Agency Information Collection Activities: Submission for OMB Review; Comment request (pertaining to conditions of participation for rural health clinics).

63 FR 2926, January 20, 1998: Medicare Program; Additional Supplier Standards — Proposed rule affecting 42 CFR Part 424.

63 FR 7743, February 17, 1998: Medicare and Medicaid Programs; Hospital Conditions of Participation; Provider Agreements and Supplier Approval — Notice of extension of comment period, affecting 42 CFR Parts 416, 482, 485, and 489.

63 FR 10920, March 5, 1998: HCFA Emergency Clearance: Public Information Collection Requirements Submitted to the Office of Management and Budget (OMB) (pertaining to Medicare and other Federal health care program provider and supplier application forms).

63 FR 36250, July 2, 1998: HCFA Agency Information Collection Activities; Submission for OMB review; Comment request (pertaining to provider/supplier enrollment applications).

1999

64 FR 29048, May 28, 1999: HCFA Agency Information Collection Activities: Proposed Collection; Comment request (pertaining to certification as a rural health clinic).

64 FR 39517, July 22, 1999: HCFA Agency Information Collection Activities: Submission for OMB Review; Comment request (pertaining to Medicare participating physician or supplier agreement form HCFA-460).

64 FR 52332, September 28, 1999: HCFA Agency Information Collection Activities: Submission for OMB Review; Comment request (pertaining to cost reports for independent rural health centers and free-standing Federally qualified health centers).

64 FR 67918, December 3, 1999: HCFA Agency Information Collection Activities: Proposed Collection; Comment request (pertaining to conditions of participation for rural health clinics).

2000

65 FR 8983, February 23, 2000: HCFA Agency Information collection Activities: Submission for OMB Review; Comment request (pertaining to conditions of participation for rural health clinics).

65 FR 10450, February 28, 2000: Medicare Program; Rural Health Clinics: Amendments to Participation Requirements and Payment Provisions; and Establishment of a Quality Assessment and Performance Improvement Program — Proposed rule affecting 42 CFR Parts 405 and 491.

65 FR 50312, August 17, 2000: HCFA; Health Insurance Reform: Standards for Electronic Transactions — Final rule affecting 45 CFR Parts 160 and 162.

65 FR 60366, October 11, 2000: Medicare Program; Additional Supplier Standards — Final rule with comment period, affecting 42 CFR Part 424.

65 FR 64227, October 26, 2000: HCFA Agency Information Collection Activities: Proposed Collection; Comment Request; Public Information Collection Meeting to Discuss Proposed Revisions (pertaining to notice requirements from suppliers, physicians, and practitioners to beneficiaries when Medicare Part B payment may be denied).

2001

66 FR 20316, April 20, 2001: HCFA Agency Information Collection Activities: Submission for OMB Review; Comment request (pertaining to advance beneficiary notice by physicians, practitioners, suppliers, and providers about items and services denied by Medicare as not reasonable and necessary).

66 FR 20997, April 26, 2001: HCFA Agency Information Collection Activities: Submission for OMB Review; Comment request (pertaining to health insurance provider agreement form).

See § 3:12.

§ 7:13 REQUIRING STATES TO WITHHOLD MEDICAID UNDERPAYMENTS TO OFFSET MEDICARE OVERPAYMENTS — Section 1914 [42 U.S.C.A. 1396m]

Regulations

42 CFR Part 405, Subpart C — Recovery of Overpayments and Suspension of Payment

42 CFR Part 447 — Payment for Services

58 FR 21174, April 19, 1993: HCFA Public Information Collection Requirements Submitted to the Office of Management and Budget for Clearance re end stage renal disease survey forms; municipal health services cost reports forms; advance directives; withholding Medicare payments to recover Medicaid overpayments; home office cost statements; and statistical report on medical care.

61 FR 40422, August 2, 1996: HCFA Agency Information Collection Activities: Proposed Collection; Comment request (pertaining to survey and certification of ambulatory surgical centers; the Medigap complaint database; fiscal intermediaries' provider overpayment actions; and hospital standards for potentially HIV infectious blood and blood products).

61 FR 43062, August 20, 1996: HCFA Agency Information Collection Activities: Submission for OMB Review; Comment request (pertaining to withholding Medicare payments to recover Medicaid overpayments; acquisition, protection, and disclosure of Peer Review Organization (PRO) information; cost reports for HMOs; and collection of credit balance information from health care providers).

63 FR 20639, April 27, 1998: HCFA Agency Information Collection Activities: Proposed Collection; Comment request (pertaining to financial reports to evaluate requests from physicians or suppliers to

pay debts under extended repayment schedule or to compromise a debt for less than the full amount).

1999

64 FR 15775, April 1, 1999: HCFA Agency Information Collection Activities: Proposed Collection; Comment request (pertaining to withholding Medicare payments to recover Medicaid overpayments).

64 FR 29049, May 28, 1999: HCFA Agency Information Collection Activities: Proposed Collection; Comment request (pertaining to Medicare credit balance reporting requirements for Medicare providers who have been overpaid).

64 FR 45267, August 19, 1999: HCFA Agency Information Collection Activities: Submission for OMB Review; Comment request (pertaining to Medicare credit balance reporting requirements).

64 FR 51128, September 21, 1999: HCFA Agency Information Collection Activities: Submission for OMB Review; Comment request (pertaining to withholding Medicare Payments to recover Medicaid overpayments).

See § 3:13.

§ 7:14 FAILURE BY NURSING FACILITIES TO COMPLY WITH MEDICAID REQUIREMENTS FOR RESIDENT ASSESSMENTS — Section 1919(b) [42 U.S.C.A. 1396r(b)]

Regulations

42 CFR Part 402 — Civil Money Penalties, Assessments, and Exclusions

42 CFR Part 420 — Program Integrity: Medicare

42 CFR Part 431, Subpart D — Appeals Process for NF's and ICF's/MR

42 CFR Part 440 — Services: General Provisions

42 CFR Part 442 — Standards for Payment for Nursing Facilities and Intermediate Care Facilities for the Mentally Retarded [Medicaid]

42 CFR Part 447 — Payment for Services

42 CFR Part 455 — Program Integrity: Medicaid

42 CFR Part 456 — Utilization Control

42 CFR Part 483 — Requirements for States and Long Term Care Facilities

42 CFR Part 488 — Survey, Certification, and Enforcement Procedures

42 CFR Part 489 — Provider Agreements and Supplier Approval

42 CFR Part 498 — Appeals Procedures for Determinations that Affect Participation in the Medicare Program and for Determinations that Affect the Participation of ICF's/MR and Certain NF's in the Medicaid Program

42 CFR Chapter V — Office of Inspector General — Health Care, Department of Health and Human Services

Subchapter A — General Provisions

Part 1000 — Introduction; General Definitions

Subchapter B — OIG Authorities

Part 1001 — Program Integrity: Medicare and State Health Care Programs

Part 1002 — Program Integrity: State-initiated Exclusion from Medicaid

Part 1003 — Civil Money Penalties, Assessments and Exclusions

Part 1004 — Imposition of Sanctions on Health Care Practitioners and Providers of Health Care Services by a Peer Review Organization

Part 1005 — Appeals of Exclusions, Civil Money Penalties and Assessments

Part 1006 — Investigational Inquiries

Part 1007 — State Medicaid Fraud Control Units

Part 1008 — Advisory Opinions by the OIG

54 FR 5316, February 2, 1989: Medicare and Medicaid; Requirements for Long Term Care Facilities — Final rule with comment period, amending 42 CFR Parts 405, 442, 447, 483, 488, 489, and 498. See also delay in effective date at 54 FR 29717, July 14, 1989; corrections at 54 FR 8361, February 27, 1989, and 54 FR 37466, September 11, 1989; and final rule delaying effective date from January 1, 1990, to October 1, 1990, at 54 FR 53611, December 29, 1989.

55 FR 10256, March 20, 1990: Medicare and Medicaid; Charges to Residents' Funds in Nursing Homes — Proposed rule to amend 42 CFR Part 483. See also final rule at 57 FR 53572, November 12, 1992.

55 FR 10938, March 23, 1990: Medicare and Medicaid Programs; Nurse Aide Training and Competency Evaluation Programs — Proposed rule to amend 42 CFR Parts 431, 433, and 483.

55 FR 10951, March 23, 1990: Medicare and Medicaid Programs; Preadmission Screening and Annual Resident Review — Proposed rule to amend 42 CFR Parts 405, 431, and 483.

55 FR 12205, April 2, 1990: Health Care Programs: Fraud and Abuse; Amendments to OIG Exclusion and CMP Authorities Resulting from Public Law 100–93, the Medicare and Medicaid Patient and Program Protection Act of 1987, Public Law 99–272, the Consolidated Omnibus Budget Reconciliation Act of 1985, and Public Law 100–360, the Medicare Catastrophic Coverage Act of 1988 — Proposed rule to amend 42 CFR Parts 1000, 1001, 1002, 1003, 1004, 1005, 1006, and 1007. See also correction published at 55 FR 17461, April 25, 1990.

56 FR 30696, July 5, 1991: Medicaid Program; Correction and Reduction Plans for Intermediate Care Facilities for the Mentally Retarded — Final rule affecting 42 CFR Part 442. See also correction at 56 FR 49147, September 27, 1991.

56 FR 48826, September 26, 1991: Medicare and Medicaid; Requirements for Long Term Care Facilities — Final rule affecting 42 CFR Parts 422, 447, 483, 488, 489, and 498. See also correction at 57 FR 43922, September 23, 1992.

56 FR 48880, September 26, 1991: Medicare and Medicaid Programs; Nurse Aide Training and Competency Evaluation Programs — Final rule affecting 42 CFR Parts 431, 433, and 483. See also correction at 56 FR 59331, November 25, 1991.

57 FR 3298, January 29, 1992: Health Care Programs: Fraud and Abuse; Amendments to OIG Exclusion and CMP Authorities Resulting From Public Law 100–93 — Final rule affecting 42 CFR Parts 1001, 1002, 1003, 1004, 1005, 1006, and 1007. See also final rule and correction at 57 FR 9669, March 20, 1992; final rule affecting 42 CFR Parts 1001and 1005, with clarification at 58 FR 5617, January 22, 1993; and final rule affecting 42 CFR Part 1001, with correction, at 58 FR 40752, July 30, 1993.

57 FR 4516, February 5, 1992: Medicare and Medicaid Programs; Omnibus Nursing Home Requirements — Proposed rule affecting 42 CFR Parts 418, 440, 441, 482, 483, and 488. See also correction at 57 FR 8961, March 13, 1992.

57 FR 8194, March 6, 1992: Medicare and Medicaid Programs; Advance Directives — Interim final rule with comment period, affecting 42 CFR Parts 417, 431, 434, 483, 484, 489, and 498.

57 FR 39278, August 28, 1992: Medicare and Medicaid Programs; Survey, Certification and Enforcement of Skilled Nursing Facilities and Nursing Facilities — Proposed rule affecting 42 CFR Parts 431, 442, 488, and 489.

57 FR 43462, September 21, 1992: Health Care Financing Administration Public Information Collection Requirements Submitted to the Office of Management and Budget for Clearance (pertaining to sole community home health agencies; physician/supplier overpayment reports; physician or supplier Medicare agreements; conditions of participation for rural health clinics; Medicare provider refunds; conditions of participation for comprehensive outpatient rehabilitation facilities; Medicaid income and eligibility verification system; Medicaid integrated review schedule; provider overpayment report; financial statement of Medicare provider debtors; negative case action review schedule for Medicaid quality control; outpatient resource costing study; Medicaid intermediate care facility for the mentally retarded or persons with related conditions survey report form; installment agreement of beneficiary refund of overpayment; PRO assumption of responsibilities; Medicare contractor administrative budget and cost reporting system forms; fire safety survey report forms; medical records review under prospective payment system; and Qualified Medicare Beneficiary supplement to the Medicare current beneficiary survey).

57 FR 46362, October 8, 1992: Medicare and Medicaid Programs; Revised Effective Date of Medicare/Medicaid Provider Agreement and Supplier Participation — Proposed rule affecting 42 CFR Parts 431, 440, 442, 488, 489, and 498.

57 FR 54710, November 20, 1992: Medicaid Program; Elimination of Certain Written Documentation Pertaining to Medicaid Long-Term Care Facilities — Final rule affecting 42 CFR Part 442.

57 FR 56450, November 30, 1992: Medicare and Medicaid Programs; Preadmission Screening and Annual Resident Review — Final rule with comment period, affecting 42 CFR Parts 405, 431, 433, and 483. See also correction published at 58 FR 25784, April 28, 1993.

57 FR 61614, December 28, 1992: Medicare and Medicaid; Resident Assessment in Long Term Care Facilities — Proposed rule affecting 42 CFR Parts 456 and 483.

58 FR 21174, April 19, 1993: HCFA Public Information Collection Requirements Submitted to the Office of Management and Budget for Clearance re end stage renal disease survey forms; municipal health services cost reports forms; advance directives; withholding Medicare payments to recover Medicaid overpayments; home office cost statements; and statistical report on medical care.

59 FR 52178, October 14, 1994: HCFA Public Information Collection Requirements Submitted to the Office of Management and Budget (OMB) for Clearance (pertaining to Medicare reimbursement for outpatient services, cost reports for free-standing skilled nursing facilities; Medicare coverage criteria for adult heart transplants, drug rebates for Medicaid, optional prospective payment cost report for certain skilled nursing facilities, reimbursable costs for organ procurement agencies, distribution and use of end stage renal disease treatment sources, conditions of coverage for ambulatory surgical centers, and waivers for home and community based services).

59 FR 56116, November 10, 1994: Medicare and Medicaid Programs; Survey, Certification and Enforcement of Skilled Nursing Facilities and Nursing Facilities— Final rule affecting 42 CFR Parts 401, 431, 435, 440, 441, 442, 447, 483, 488, 489, and 498. See also correcting amendment, effective July 1, 1995, at 62 FR 44221, August 20, 1997.

59 FR 66969, December 28, 1994: HCFA Public Information Collection Requirements Submitted to the Office of Management and Budget (OMB) for Clearance (pertaining to physician certification in skilled nursing facilities, and criteria for Medicare coverage of adult liver transplants).

60 FR 16580, March 31, 1995: Office of Inspector General: Civil Money Penalties for Referrals to Entities and for Prohibited Arrangements and Schemes— Final rule with comment period, affecting 42 CFR Part 1003.

60 FR 21525, May 2, 1995: HCFA Public Information Collection Requirements Submitted to the Office of Management and Budget (OMB) for Clearance (pertaining to intermediary requests for information from skilled nursing facilities, reimbursement for CLIA compliance surveys, patient outcome data in home health agencies, common claim forms for Medicare/Medicaid reimbursement, and a study of childhood immunization costs).

60 FR 32916, June 26, 1995: Office of Inspector General; Health Care Programs; Fraud and Abuse; Technical Revision to the Scope and Effect of the OIG Exclusion Regulations— Final rule affecting 42 CFR Part 1001.

60 FR 37066, July 19, 1995: HCFA Public Information Collection Requirements Submitted to the Office of Management and Budget (OMB) for Clearance (pertaining to actuarial forecasts for Medicaid utilization and cost, employers identified through a match of IRS,

SSA, and Medicare records for purposes of the Medicare Secondary Payer provision, health and safety requirements for portable X-ray suppliers, and evaluation of Intermediate Care Facilities for Persons with Mental Retardation — establishing psychoactive drug use baselines).

60 FR 37590, July 21, 1995: Medicare Program; Optional Payment System for Low Medicare Volume Skilled Nursing Facilities — Final rule affecting 42 CFR Part 413.

60 FR 50115, September 28, 1995: Medicare and Medicaid Programs; Survey, Certification and Enforcement of Skilled Nursing Facilities and Nursing Facilities — Final rule and correction to final regulations, affecting 42 CFR Parts 431, 440, 442, 488, 489, and 498. See also corrections at 60 FR 52731, October 10, 1995, and at 60 FR 534456, October 13, 1995.

60 FR 58088, November 24, 1995: HCFA Public Information Collection Requirements Submitted for Public Comment and Recommendations (pertaining to skilled nursing facility (SNF) and skilled nursing facility health care complex cost reports).

60 FR 62237, December 5, 1995: Medicare Program; Uniform Electronic Cost Reporting for Skilled Nursing Facilities and Home Health Agencies — Proposed rule affecting 42 CFR Part 413.

61 FR 11214, March 19, 1996: HCFA Agency Information Collection Activities: Proposed Collection; Comment Request (pertaining to conditions of coverage for organ procurement organizations; and skilled nursing facility and skilled nursing facility healthcare complex forms).

61 FR 14798, April 3, 1996: HCFA Agency Information Collection Activities: Proposed Collection; Comment Request (pertaining to statistical reports on medical care eligibility, payments and services under Medicaid; State survey agency lists of positions and schedule of equipment purchases; granting and withdrawing of deeming authority to national accreditation organizations; maximizing the effectiveness of home health care; requests for certification in the Medicare or Medicaid program to provide outpatient physical therapy and/or speech pathology services; physical therapists in independent practice; requests for provider approval as a hospital provider of extended care services (swing bed) under Medicare and Medicaid; and requests for designation as an organ procurement organization).

61 FR 17677, April 22, 1996: Medicare and Medicaid Programs; New Payment Methodology for Routine Extended Care Services Pro-

vided in a Swing-bed Hospital— Proposed rule affecting 42 CFR Part 413.

61 FR 30623, June 17, 1996: Office of Inspector General Publication of OIG Special Fraud Alert: Fraud and Abuse in the Provision of Services in Nursing Homes — Notice.

61 FR 35231, July 5, 1996: HCFA Agency Information Collection Activities: Proposed Collection; Comment Request (pertaining to Medicaid payment standards for inpatient hospital or long-term care services).

61 FR 38395, July 24, 1996: Medicaid Program; Medicaid Eligibility Quality Control, Progressive Reductions in Federal Financial Participation for FYs 1982–1984, Payment for Physician Billing for Clinical Laboratory Services, and Utilization Control of Skilled Nursing Facility Services: Removal of Obsolete Requirements — Final rule.

61 FR 46466, September 3, 1996: Medicare Program; Schedule of Prospectively Determined Payment Rates for Skilled Nursing Facility Inpatient Routine Service Costs— Final rule with comment period.

61 FR 51295, October 1, 1996: HCFA Public Information Requirements Submitted for Collection of Public Comment: Submission for OMB Review (pertaining to approval of Medicaid payment rates for inpatient hospital or long term care services).

61 FR 51611, October 3, 1996: Medicare and Medicaid Programs; New Payment Methodology for Routine Extended Care Services Provided in a Swing-bed Hospital— Final Rule affecting 42 CFR Part 413. See also correction at 61 FR 58631, November 18, 1996.

61 FR 54209, October 17, 1996: HCFA Agency Information Collectio Activities: Proposed Collection; Comment request (pertaining to hospital eligibility for swing-bed status).

61 FR 64913, December 9, 1996: HCFA Agency Information Collection Activities: Proposed Collection; Comment request (pertaining to survey report forms for ICF/MRs; and current Medicare beneficiary surveys).

61 FR 68270, December 27, 1996: HCFA Agency Information Collection Activities: Submission for OMB Review; Comment request (pertaining to a facility identification and screening form for hospital providers of extended care services (swing-beds) in the the Medicare and Medicaid programs).

62 FR 26, January 2, 1997: Medicare Program; Electronic Cost Reporting for Skilled Nursing Facilities and Home Health Agencies — Final Rule. See also correction at 62 FR 27210, May 19, 1997.

62 FR 11214, March 11, 1997: HCFA Agency Information Collection Activities: Submission for OMB Review; Comment request (pertaining to intermediate care facility for the mentally retarded or persons with related conditions survey report forms).

62 FR 11458, March 12, 1997: HCFA Agency Information Collection Activities: Proposed Collection; Comment request (pertaining to skilled nursing facility and skilled nursing facility health care complex cost report form).

62 FR 23140, April 29, 1997: Office of Inspector General: Health Care Programs: Fraud and Abuse; Revised PRO Sanctions for Failing to Meet Statutory Obligations — Final rule.

62 FR 30603, June 4, 1997: HCFA Agency Information Collection Activities: Submission for OMB Review; Comment request (pertaining to skilled nursing facility and skilled nursing facility health care complex cost reports; and hospital conditions of participation).

62 FR 33095, June 18, 1997: HCFA Agency Information Collection Activities: Proposed Collection; Comment request (pertaining to skilled nursing facility prospective payment system cost report form).

62 FR 43931, August 18, 1997: Medicare and Medicaid Programs: Effective Dates of Provider Agreements and Supplier Approvals — Final rule affecting 42 CFR Parts 431, 442, 488, 489, and 498.

62 FR 47182, September 8, 1997: Office of Inspector General: Health Care Programs: Fraud and Abuse; Revised OIG Exclusion Authorities Resulting from Public Law 104–191 — Notice of Proposed rulemaking, affecting 42 CFR Parts 1000, 1001, 1002, and 1005.

62 FR 51536, October 1, 1997: Medicare Program; Schedules of Limits and Prospectively Determined Payment Rates for Skilled Nursing Facility Inpatient Routine Service Costs — Final notice with comment period.

62 FR 55410, October 24, 1997: HCFA Agency Information Collection Activities: Submission for OMB Review; Comment request (pertaining to Medicare/Medicaid disclosure of ownership and control forms).

62 FR 55410, October 24, 1997: Office of Inspector General: Criteria for Implementing Permissive Exclusion Authority under Section 1128(b)(7) of the Social Security Act — Notice.

62 FR 48736, October 30, 1997: HCFA Agency Information Collection Activities: Submission for OMB Review; Comment request (pertaining to prospective payment for skilled nursing facilities).

62 FR 67174, December 23, 1997: Medicare and Medicaid; Resident Assessment in Long Term Care Facilities — Final rule affecting 42 CFR Part 483.

62 FR 67392, December 24, 1997: Office of Inspector General: Criteria for Implementing Permissive Exclusion Authority under Section 1128(b)(7) of the Social Security Act — Notice.

63 FR 9844, February 26, 1998: HCFA Agency Information Collection Activities: Proposed Collection; Comment request (pertaining to procedures for advisory opinions concerning physician referrals and supporting regulations in 42 CFR Sections 411.370- 411.389).

63 FR 14393, March 25, 1998: Office of Inspector General: Health Care Programs: Fraud and Abuse; Revised OIG Civil Money Penalties Resulting from the Health Insurance Portability and Accountability Act of 1996 — Notice of proposed rulemaking, affecting 42 CFR Parts 1003, 1005, and 1006.

63 FR 14719, March 26, 1998: HCFA Agency Information Collection Activities: Proposed Collection; Comment request (pertaining to physician certification and re-certification in skilled nursing facilities).

63 FR 20415, April 24, 1998: Office of Inspector General: Publication of OIG Special Fraud Alert: Fraud and Abuse in Nursing Home Arrangements with Hospices — Notice.

63 FR 26252, May 12, 1998: Medicare Program: Prospective Payment System and Consolidated Billing for Skilled Nursing Facilities — Final rule, affecting 42 CFR Parts 409, 410, 411, 413, 424, 483, and 489. See also correction at 63 FR 53301, October 5, 1998.

63 FR 28395, May 22, 1998: HCFA Agency Information Collection Activities: Submission for OMB Review; Comment request (pertaining to procedures for advisory opinions concerning physician referrals and supporting regulations in 42 CFR 411.370 through 411.389).

63 FR 28395, May 22, 1998: HCFA Agency Information Collection Activities: Submission for OMB Review; Comment request (pertaining to physician certifications and recertifications in skilled nursing facilities).

63 FR 28396, May 22, 1998: HCFA Privacy Act of 1974 — Notice of New System of Records (pertaining to the long term care minimum data set).

63 FR 46676, September 2, 1998: Office of Inspector General: Health Care Programs; Fraud and Abuse; Revised OIG Exclusion Authorities Resulting from Public Law 104–191 — Final rule affecting 42 CFR Parts 1000, 1001, 1002, and 1005. See also correction at 63 FR 57918, October 29, 1998.

63 FR 46736, September 2, 1998: Office of Inspector General: Health Care Programs; Fraud and Abuse; Revised OIG Sanction Authorities Resulting from Public Law 105–33 — Notice of proposed rulemaking affecting 42 CFR 1001, 1002, and 1003.

63 FR 58399, October 30, 1998: Office of Inspector General: Publication of the OIG's Provider Self-Disclosure Protocol — Notice.

63 FR 60356, November 9, 1998: HCFA Agency Information Collection activities: Proposed Collection; Comment request (pertaining to skilled nursing facility resident assessment MDS data).

63 FR 68223, December 10, 1998: Office of Inspector General; Solicitation of New Safe Harbors and Special Fraud Alerts — Notice of intent to develop regulations, affecting 42 CFR 1001.

63 FR 68687, December 14, 1998: Medicare and Medicaid Program; Civil Money Penalties, Assessments, Exclusions, and Related Appeals Procedures — Final rule with comment period, affecting 42 CFR 400 and 402.

63 FR 70137, December 18, 1998: Office of Inspector General: Solicitation of Information and Recommendations for Developing OIG Compliance Program Guidance for the Nursing Home Industry — Notice.

63 FR 72317, December 31, 1998: HCFA Agency Information Collection Activities: Proposed Collection; Comment request (pertaining to advanced directives under Medicare and Medicaid; and Medicare/Medicaid disclosure of ownership and control interests).

63 FR 72318, December 31, 1998: HCFA Agency Information Collection Activities: Proposed Collection; Comment request (pertaining to fire safety survey report forms for health care facilities).

1999

64 FR 6664, February 10, 1999: HCFA Agency Information Collection Activities: Submission for OMB Review; Comment request

(pertaining to skilled nursing facility (SNF) resident assessment MDS data).

64 FR 13354, March 18, 1999: Medicare and Medicaid Programs; Civil Money Penalties for Nursing Homes (SNF/NF), Change in Notice Requirements, and Expansion of Discretionary Remedy Delegation — Final rule with comment period, affecting 42 CFR Part 488.

64 FR 13997, March 23, 1999: HCFA Agency Information Collection Activities: Submission for OMB Review; Comment request (pertaining to Medicare and Medicaid requirements for advanced directives, and disclosure of ownership and financial control interest).

64 FR 17184, April 8, 1999: HCFA Medicare Program; April 23, 1999 Open Town Hall Meeting to Discuss the Skilled Nursing Facility Prospective Payment System (SNF/PPS).

64 FR 39420, July 22, 1999: Office of Inspector General; Health Care Programs; Fraud and Abuse; Revised OIG Sanction Authorities Resulting from P.L. 105–33, the Balanced Budget Act of 1997 — Final rule affecting 42 CFR Parts 1001, 1002, and 1003. See also correction at 64 FR 42174, August 3, 1999.

64 FR 39517, July 22, 1999: HCFA Agency Information Collection Activities: Submission for OMB Review; Comment request (pertaining to Medicare participating physician or supplier agreement form HCFA-460).

64 FR 39934, July 23, 1999: Medicare and Medicaid Program; Appeal of the Loss of Nurse Aide Training Programs — Interim final rule with comment period, affecting 42 CFR Parts 431 and 498. See also correction at 64 FR 43295, August 10, 1999.

64 FR 41644, July 30, 1999: Medicare Program; Prospective Payment System and Consolidated Billing for Skilled Nursing Facilities — Final rule affecting 42 CFR Parts 409, 411, 413, and 489. See also correction at 64 FR 60122, November 4, 1999.

64 FR 41684, July 30, 1999: Medicare Program; Prospective Payment System and Consolidated Billing for Skilled Nursing Facilities — Update — Notice. See also correction at 64 FR 54030, October 5, 1999.

64 FR 42610, August 5, 1999: Medicare Program; Revision of the Procedures for Requesting Exceptions to Cost Limits for Skilled Nursing Facilities and Elimination of Reclassifications — Final rule.

64 FR 42791, September 30, 1999: Office of Inspector General; Publication of the OIG Special Advisory Bulletin on the Effect of Exclusion from Participation in Federal Health Care Programs — Notice. See also correction at 64 FR 55484, October 13, 1999.

64 FR 54263, October 6, 1999: Medicaid Program; Flexibility in Payment Methods for Services of Hospitals, Nursing Facilities, and Intermediate Care Facilities for the Mentally Retarded — Proposed rule affecting 42 CFR Part 447.

64 FR 55949, October 15, 1999: HCFA Agency Information Collection Activities: Proposed Collection; Comment request (pertaining to physician certifications and re-certifications about the necessity for skilled nursing facility care).

64 FR 58419, October 29, 1999: Office of Inspector General; Draft OIG Compliance Program Guidance for Nursing Facilities — Notice and comment period.

64 FR 63518, November 19, 1999: Office of Inspector General; Fraud and Abuse; Clarification of the Initial OIG Safe Harbor Provisions and Establishment of Additional Safe Harbor Provisions under the Anti-kickback Statute — Final rule affecting 42 CFR Part 1001.

64 FR 66482, November 26, 1999: HCFA Agency Information Collection Activities: Proposed Collection; Comment request (pertaining to resident assessment in skilled nursing facilities).

64 FR 67028, November 30, 1999: Medicare and Medicaid Programs; Religious Nonmedical Health Care Institutions and Advance Directives — Interim final rule with comment period, affecting 42 CFR Parts 403, 412, 431, 440, 442, 446, 456, 488, and 489.

64 FR 69217, December 10, 1999: Office of Inspector General; Solicitation of New Safe Harbors and Special Fraud Alerts — Intent to develop regulations affecting 42 CFR Part 1001.

64 FR 69271, December 10, 1999: HCFA Agency Information Collection Activities: Proposed Collection; Comment request (pertaining to hospital providers of extender care (swing bed) services in Medicare and Medicaid).

2000

65 FR 2186, January 13, 2000: HCFA Agency Information Collection Activities; Submission for OMB Review; Comment request (pertaining to physician certifications/re-certifications in skilled nursing facilities).

65 FR 12560, March 9, 2000: HCFA Agency Information Collection Activities: Submission for OMB Review; Comment request (pertaining to hospital provider of extended care services (swing beds) in the Medicare and Medicaid programs).

65 FR 14289, March 16, 2000: Office of Inspector General: Publication of the OIG Compliance Program Guidance for Nursing Facilities — Notice.

65 FR 14986, March 20, 2000: HCFA Agency Information Collection Activities: Submission for OMB Review; Comment request (pertaining to skilled nursing facility resident assessment MDS data).

65 FR 19187, April 10, 2000: Medicare Program; Prospective Payment System and Consolidated Billing for Skilled Nursing Facilities; Update--Proposed rule affecting 42 CFR Parts 411 and 489.

65 FR 24400, April 26, 2000: Office of Inspector General; Health Care Programs: Fraud and Abuse; Revised OIG Civil Money Penalties Resulting from Public Law 104-191 (HIPAA) — Final rule affecting 42 CFR Parts 1001, 1003, 1005, and 1006. See also correction at 65 FR 35583, June 5, 2000.

65 FR 54856, September 11, 2000: HCFA Agency Information Collection Activities: Submission for OMB Review; Comment request (pertaining to skilled nursing facility cost reports).

65 FR 54857, September 11, 2000: HCFA Agency Information Collection Activities: Submission for OMB Review; Comment request (pertaining to ICF/MR survey report forms).

65 FR 60151, October 10, 2000: Medicaid Program; Revision to Medicaid Upper Payment Limit Requirements for Hospital Services, Nursing Facility Services, Intermediate Care Facility Services for the Mentally Retarded, and Clinic Services-Proposed rule affecting 42 CFR Part 447.

65 FR 64227, October 26, 2000: HCFA Agency Information Collection Activities: Proposed Collection; Comment request (pertaining to home health agency cost reports; skilled nursing facility cost reports; and hospital cost reports).

2001

66 FR 856, January 4, 2001: Medicare and Medicaid Programs; Physicians Referrals to Health Care Entities with which They Have Financial Relationships—Final rule with comment period, affecting 42 CFR Parts 411 and 424.

66 FR 3148, January 12, 2001: Medicaid Program; Revision to Medicaid Upper Payment Limit Requirements for Hospital Services, Nursing Facility Services, Intermediate Care Facility Services for the Mentally Retarded, and Clinic Services—Final rule affecting 42 CFR Part 447.

66 FR 3497, January 16, 2001: Medicare Program; Prospective Payment System and Consolidated Billing for Skilled Nursing Facilities—Update; Correction notice affecting 42 FR Parts 411, 313, and 489. See FR Doc. 00-19004, July 31, 2000.

66 FR 6629, January 22, 2001: HCFA Agency Information Collection Activities: Submission for OMB Review; Comment request (pertaining to Medicare Integrity Program Organizational Conflict of Interest Disclosure Certificate).

66 FR 8771, February 2, 2001: Medicare and Medicaid Programs; Physicians' Referrals to Health Care Entities with which They Have Financial Relationships: Delay of Effective Date of Final Rule and Technical Amendment, affecting 42 CFR Parts 411 and 424.

66 FR 16062, March 23, 2001: HCFA Agency Information Collection Activities: Submission for OMB Review; Comment request (pertaining to SNF cost report forms).

66 FR 17657, April 3, 2001: Medicaid Program; Modification of the Medicaid Upper Payment Limit Transition Period for Inpatient Hospital Services, Outpatient Hospital Services, Nursing Facility Services, Intermediate Care Facility Services for the Mentally Retarded and Clinic Services—Proposed rule affecting 42 CFR Part 447.

66 FR 17813, April 4, 2001: Medicare and Medicaid Programs; Physicians' Referrals to Health Care Entities with which They Have Financial Relationships; Extension of Comment period—Notice, affecting 42 CFR Parts 411 and 424.

66 FR 19507, April 16, 2001: HCFA Agency Information Collection Activities: Proposed Collection; Comment request (pertaining to conflict of interest and ownership and control information form).

66 FR 27151, May 16, 2001: HCFA Agency Information Collection Activities: Proposed Collection; Comment request (pertaining to the Long Term Care Awareness Project).

66 FR 28916, May 25, 2001: HCFA Agency Information Collection Activities; Proposed Collection; Comment request (pertaining to procedures for advisory opinions concerning physician referrals under section 1877 of the Social Security Act).

66 FR 31245, June 11, 2001: Office of Inspector General; Health-care Integrity and Protection Data Bank: Change in User Fees—Notice.

See § 3:14.

§ 7:15 ABUSE OR NEGLECT OF NURSING FACILITY RESIDENTS OR MISAPPROPRIATION OF THE IR PROPERTY — Section 1919(g)(1)(C) [42 U.S.C.A. 1396r(g)(1)(C)]

Regulations

42 CFR Part 402 — Civil Money Penalties, Assessments, and Exclusions

42 CFR Part 420 — Program Integrity: Medicare

42 CFR Part 431, Subpart D — Appeals Process for NF's and ICF's/MR

42 CFR Part 440 — Services: General Provisions

42 CFR Part 442 — Standards for Payment for Nursing Facilities and Intermediate Care Facilities for the Mentally Retarded [Medicaid]

42 CFR Part 447 — Payment for Services

42 CFR Part 455 — Program Integrity: Medicaid

42 CFR Part 456 — Utilization Control

42 CFR Part 483 — Requirements for States and Long Term Care Facilities

42 CFR Part 488 — Survey, Certification, and Enforcement Procedures

42 CFR Part 489 — Provider Agreements and Supplier Approval

42 CFR Part 498 — Appeals Procedures for Determinations that Affect Participation in the Medicare Program and for Determinations that Affect the Participation of ICF's/MR and Certain NF's in the Medicaid Program

42 CFR Chapter V — Office of Inspector General — Health Care, Department of Health and Human Services

Subchapter A — General Provisions

Part 1000 — Introduction; General Definitions

Subchapter B — OIG Authorities

Part 1001 — Program Integrity: Medicare and State Health Care Programs

Part 1002 — Program Integrity: State-initiated Exclusion from Medicaid

Part 1003 — Civil Money Penalties, Assessments and Exclusions

Part 1004 — Imposition of Sanctions on Health Care Practitioners and Providers of Health Care Services by a Peer Review Organization

Part 1005 — Appeals of Exclusions, Civil Money Penalties and Assessments

Part 1006 — Investigational Inquiries

Part 1007 — State Medicaid Fraud Control Units

Part 1008 — Advisory Opinions by the OIG

54 FR 5316, February 2, 1989: Medicare and Medicaid; Requirements for Long Term Care Facilities — Final rule with comment period, amending 42 CFR Parts 405, 442, 447, 483, 488, 489, and 498. See also delay in effective date at 54 FR 29717, July 14, 1989; corrections at 54 FR 8361, February 27, 1989, and 54 FR 37466, September 11, 1989; and final rule delaying effective date from January 1, 1990, to October 1, 1990, at 54 FR 53611, December 29, 1989.

55 FR 10256, March 20, 1990: Medicare and Medicaid; Charges to Residents' Funds in Nursing Homes — Proposed rule to amend 42 CFR Part 483. See also final rule at 57 FR 53572, November 12, 1992.

55 FR 10938, March 23, 1990: Medicare and Medicaid Programs; Nurse Aide Training and Competency Evaluation Programs — Proposed rule to amend 42 CFR Parts 431, 433, and 483.

55 FR 10951, March 23, 1990: Medicare and Medicaid Programs; Preadmission Screening and Annual Resident Review — Proposed rule to amend 42 CFR Parts 405, 431, and 483.

55 FR 12205, April 2, 1990: Health Care Programs: Fraud and Abuse; Amendments to OIG Exclusion and CMP Authorities Resulting from Public Law 100–93, the Medicare and Medicaid Patient and Program Protection Act of 1987, Public Law 99–272, the Consolidated Omnibus Budget Reconciliation Act of 1985, and Public Law 100–360, the Medicare Catastrophic Coverage Act of 1988 — Proposed rule to amend 42 CFR Parts 1000, 1001, 1002, 1003, 1004, 1005, 1006, and 1007. See also correction published at 55 FR 17461, April 25, 1990.

56 FR 30696, July 5, 1991: Medicaid Program; Correction and Reduction Plans for Intermediate Care Facilities for the Mentally Retarded — Final rule affecting 42 CFR Part 442. See also correction at 56 FR 49147, September 27, 1991.

56 FR 48826, September 26, 1991: Medicare and Medicaid; Requirements for Long Term Care Facilities — Final rule affecting

42 CFR Parts 422, 447, 483, 488, 489, and 498. See also correction at 57 FR 43922, September 23, 1992.

56 FR 48880, September 26, 1991: Medicare and Medicaid Programs; Nurse Aide Training and Competency Evaluation Programs — Final rule affecting 42 CFR Parts 431, 433, and 483. See also correction at 56 FR 59331, November 25, 1991.

57 FR 3298, January 29, 1992: Health Care Programs: Fraud and Abuse; Amendments to OIG Exclusion and CMP Authorities Resulting From Public Law 100–93 — Final rule affecting 42 CFR Parts 1001, 1002, 1003, 1004, 1005, 1006, and 1007. See also final rule and correction at 57 FR 9669, March 20, 1992; final rule affecting 42 CFR Parts 1001and 1005, with clarification at 58 FR 5617, January 22, 1993; and final rule affecting 42 CFR Part 1001, with correction, at 58 FR 40752, July 30, 1993.

57 FR 4516, February 5, 1992: Medicare and Medicaid Programs; Omnibus Nursing Home Requirements — Proposed rule affecting 42 CFR Parts 418, 440, 441, 482, 483, and 488. See also correction at 57 FR 8961, March 13, 1992.

57 FR 8194, March 6, 1992: Medicare and Medicaid Programs; Advance Directives — Interim final rule with comment period, affecting 42 CFR Parts 417, 431, 434, 483, 484, 489, and 498.

57 FR 39278, August 28, 1992: Medicare and Medicaid Programs; Survey, Certification and Enforcement of Skilled Nursing Facilities and Nursing Facilities — Proposed rule affecting 42 CFR Parts 431, 442, 488, and 489.

57 FR 43462, September 21, 1992: Health Care Financing Administration Public Information Collection Requirements Submitted to the Office of Management and Budget for Clearance (pertaining to sole community home health agencies; physician/supplier overpayment reports; physician or supplier Medicare agreements; conditions of participation for rural health clinics; Medicare provider refunds; conditions of participation for comprehensive outpatient rehabilitation facilities; Medicaid income and eligibility verification system; Medicaid integrated review schedule; provider overpayment report; financial statement of Medicare provider debtors; negative case action review schedule for Medicaid quality control; outpatient resource costing study; Medicaid intermediate care facility for the mentally retarded or persons with related conditions survey report form; installment agreement of beneficiary refund of overpayment; PRO assumption of responsibilities; Medicare contractor administrative budget and cost reporting system forms; fire safety survey

report forms; medical records review under prospective payment system; and Qualified Medicare Beneficiary supplement to the Medicare current beneficiary survey).

57 FR 46362, October 8, 1992: Medicare and Medicaid Programs; Revised Effective Date of Medicare/Medicaid Provider Agreement and Supplier Participation — Proposed rule affecting 42 CFR Parts 431, 440, 442, 488, 489, and 498.

57 FR 54710, November 20, 1992: Medicaid Program; Elimination of Certain Written Documentation Pertaining to Medicaid Long-Term Care Facilities — Final rule affecting 42 CFR Part 442.

57 FR 56450, November 30, 1992: Medicare and Medicaid Programs; Preadmission Screening and Annual Resident Review — Final rule with comment period, affecting 42 CFR Parts 405, 431, 433, and 483. See also correction published at 58 FR 25784, April 28, 1993.

57 FR 61614, December 28, 1992: Medicare and Medicaid; Resident Assessment in Long Term Care Facilities — Proposed rule affecting 42 CFR Parts 456 and 483.

58 FR 21174, April 19, 1993: HCFA Public Information Collection Requirements Submitted to the Office of Management and Budget for Clearance re end stage renal disease survey forms; municipal health services cost reports forms; advance directives; withholding Medicare payments to recover Medicaid overpayments; home office cost statements; and statistical report on medical care.

59 FR 52178, October 14, 1994: HCFA Public Information Collection Requirements Submitted to the Office of Management and Budget (OMB) for Clearance (pertaining to Medicare reimbursement for outpatient services, cost reports for free-standing skilled nursing facilities; Medicare coverage criteria for adult heart transplants, drug rebates for Medicaid, optional prospective payment cost report for certain skilled nursing facilities, reimbursable costs for organ procurement agencies, distribution and use of end stage renal disease treatment sources, conditions of coverage for ambulatory surgical centers, and waivers for home and community based services).

59 FR 56116, November 10, 1994: Medicare and Medicaid Programs; Survey, Certification and Enforcement of Skilled Nursing Facilities and Nursing Facilities — Final rule affecting 42 CFR Parts 401, 431, 435, 440, 441, 442, 447, 483, 488, 489, and 498. See also correcting amendment, effective July 1, 1995, at 62 FR 44221, August 20, 1997.

59 FR 66969, December 28, 1994: HCFA Public Information Collection Requirements Submitted to the Office of Management and Budget (OMB) for Clearance (pertaining to physician certification in skilled nursing facilities, and criteria for Medicare coverage of adult liver transplants).

60 FR 16580, March 31, 1995: Office of Inspector General: Civil Money Penalties for Referrals to Entities and for Prohibited Arrangements and Schemes — Final rule with comment period, affecting 42 CFR Part 1003.

60 FR 21525, May 2, 1995: HCFA Public Information Collection Requirements Submitted to the Office of Management and Budget (OMB) for Clearance (pertaining to intermediary requests for information from skilled nursing facilities, reimbursement for CLIA compliance surveys, patient outcome data in home health agencies, common claim forms for Medicare/Medicaid reimbursement, and a study of childhood immunization costs).

60 FR 32916, June 26, 1995: Office of Inspector General; Health Care Programs; Fraud and Abuse; Technical Revision to the Scope and Effect of the OIG Exclusion Regulations — Final rule affecting 42 CFR Part 1001.

60 FR 37066, July 19, 1995: HCFA Public Information Collection Requirements Submitted to the Office of Management and Budget (OMB) for Clearance (pertaining to actuarial forecasts for Medicaid utilization and cost, employers identified through a match of IRS, SSA, and Medicare records for purposes of the Medicare Secondary Payer provision, health and safety requirements for portable X-ray suppliers, and evaluation of Intermediate Care Facilities for Persons with Mental Retardation — establishing psychoactive drug use baselines).

60 FR 37590, July 21, 1995: Medicare Program; Optional Payment System for Low Medicare Volume Skilled Nursing Facilities — Final rule affecting 42 CFR Part 413.

60 FR 50115, September 28, 1995: Medicare and Medicaid Programs; Survey, Certification and Enforcement of Skilled Nursing Facilities and Nursing Facilities — Final rule and correction to final regulations, affecting 42 CFR Parts 431, 440, 442, 488, 489, and 498. See also corrections at 60 FR 52731, October 10, 1995, and at 60 FR 534456, October 13, 1995.

60 FR 58088, November 24, 1995: HCFA Public Information Collection Requirements Submitted for Public Comment and

Recommendations (pertaining to skilled nursing facility (SNF) and skilled nursing facility health care complex cost reports).

60 FR 62237, December 5, 1995: Medicare Program; Uniform Electronic Cost Reporting for Skilled Nursing Facilities and Home Health Agencies — Proposed rule affecting 42 CFR Part 413.

61 FR 11214, March 19, 1996: HCFA Agency Information Collection Activities: Proposed Collection; Comment Request (pertaining to conditions of coverage for organ procurement organizations; and skilled nursing facility and skilled nursing facility healthcare complex forms).

61 FR 14798, April 3, 1996: HCFA Agency Information Collection Activities: Proposed Collection; Comment Request (pertaining to statistical reports on medical care eligibility, payments and services under Medicaid; State survey agency lists of positions and schedule of equipment purchases; granting and withdrawing of deeming authority to national accreditation organizations; maximizing the effectiveness of home health care; requests for certification in the Medicare or Medicaid program to provide outpatient physical therapy and/or speech pathology services; physical therapists in independent practice; requests for provider approval as a hospital provider of extended care services (swing bed) under Medicare and Medicaid; and requests for designation as an organ procurement organization).

61 FR 17677, April 22, 1996: Medicare and Medicaid Programs; New Payment Methodology for Routine Extended Care Services Provided in a Swing-bed Hospital — Proposed rule affecting 42 CFR Part 413.

61 FR 30623, June 17, 1996: Office of Inspector General Publication of OIG Special Fraud Alert: Fraud and Abuse in the Provision of Services in Nursing Homes — Notice.

61 FR 35231, July 5, 1996: HCFA Agency Information Collection Activities: Proposed Collection; Comment Request (pertaining to Medicaid payment standards for inpatient hospital or long-term care services).

61 FR 38395, July 24, 1996: Medicaid Program; Medicaid Eligibility Quality Control, Progressive Reductions in Federal Financial Participation for FYs 1982–1984, Payment for Physician Billing for Clinical Laboratory Services, and Utilization Control of Skilled Nursing Facility Services: Removal of Obsolete Requirements — Final rule.

61 FR 46466, September 3, 1996: Medicare Program; Schedule of Prospectively Determined Payment Rates for Skilled Nursing Facility Inpatient Routine Service Costs — Final rule with comment period.

61 FR 51295, October 1, 1996: HCFA Public Information Requirements Submitted for Collection of Public Comment: Submission for OMB Review (pertaining to approval of Medicaid payment rates for inpatient hospital or long term care services).

61 FR 51611, October 3, 1996: Medicare and Medicaid Programs; New Payment Methodology for Routine Extended Care Services Provided in a Swing-bed Hospital — Final Rule affecting 42 CFR Part 413. See also correction at 61 FR 58631, November 18, 1996.

61 FR 54209, October 17, 1996: HCFA Agency Information Collectio Activities: Proposed Collection; Comment request (pertaining to hospital eligibility for swing-bed status).

61 FR 64913, December 9, 1996: HCFA Agency Information Collection Activities: Proposed Collection; Comment request (pertaining to survey report forms for ICF/MRs; and current Medicare beneficiary surveys).

61 FR 68270, December 27, 1996: HCFA Agency Information Collection Activities: Submission for OMB Review; Comment request (pertaining to a facility identification and screening form for hospital providers of extended care services (swing-beds) in the the Medicare and Medicaid programs).

62 FR 26, January 2, 1997: Medicare Program; Electronic Cost Reporting for Skilled Nursing Facilities and Home Health Agencies — Final Rule. See also correction at 62 FR 27210, May 19, 1997.

62 FR 11214, March 11, 1997: HCFA Agency Information Collection Activities: Submission for OMB Review; Comment request (pertaining to intermediate care facility for the mentally retarded or persons with related conditions survey report forms).

62 FR 11458, March 12, 1997: HCFA Agency Information Collection Activities: Proposed Collection; Comment request (pertaining to skilled nursing facility and skilled nursing facility health care complex cost report form).

62 FR 23140, April 29, 1997: Office of Inspector General: Health Care Programs: Fraud and Abuse; Revised PRO Sanctions for Failing to Meet Statutory Obligations — Final rule.

62 FR 30603, June 4, 1997: HCFA Agency Information Collection Activities: Submission for OMB Review; Comment request (pertain-

ing to skilled nursing facility and skilled nursing facility health care complex cost reports; and hospital conditions of participation).

62 FR 33095, June 18, 1997: HCFA Agency Information Collection Activities: Proposed Collection; Comment request (pertaining to skilled nursing facility prospective payment system cost report form).

62 FR 43931, August 18, 1997: Medicare and Medicaid Programs: Effective Dates of Provider Agreements and Supplier Approvals — Final rule affecting 42 CFR Parts 431, 442, 488, 489, and 498.

62 FR 47182, September 8, 1997: Office of Inspector General: Health Care Programs: Fraud and Abuse; Revised OIG Exclusion Authorities Resulting from Public Law 104–191 — Notice of Proposed rulemaking, affecting 42 CFR Parts 1000, 1001, 1002, and 1005.

62 FR 51536, October 1, 1997: Medicare Program; Schedules of Limits and Prospectively Determined Payment Rates for Skilled Nursing Facility Inpatient Routine Service Costs — Final notice with comment period.

62 FR 55410, October 24, 1997: HCFA Agency Information Collection Activities: Submission for OMB Review; Comment request (pertaining to Medicare/Medicaid disclosure of ownership and control forms).

62 FR 55410, October 24, 1997: Office of Inspector General: Criteria for Implementing Permissive Exclusion Authority under Section 1128(b)(7) of the Social Security Act — Notice.

62 FR 48736, October 30, 1997: HCFA Agency Information Collection Activities: Submission for OMB Review; Comment request (pertaining to prospective payment for skilled nursing facilities).

62 FR 67174, December 23, 1997: Medicare and Medicaid; Resident Assessment in Long Term Care Facilities — Final rule affecting 42 CFR Part 483.

62 FR 67392, December 24, 1997: Office of Inspector General: Criteria for Implementing Permissive Exclusion Authority under Section 1128(b)(7) of the Social Security Act — Notice.

63 FR 9844, February 26, 1998: HCFA Agency Information Collection Activities: Proposed Collection; Comment request (pertaining to procedures for advisory opinions concerning physician referrals and supporting regulations in 42 CFR Sections 411.370- 411.389).

63 FR 14393, March 25, 1998: Office of Inspector General: Health Care Programs: Fraud and Abuse; Revised OIG Civil Money Penalties Resulting from the Health Insurance Portability and

Accountability Act of 1996 — Notice of proposed rulemaking, affecting 42 CFR Parts 1003, 1005, and 1006.

63 FR 14719, March 26, 1998: HCFA Agency Information Collection Activities: Proposed Collection; Comment request (pertaining to physician certification and re-certification in skilled nursing facilities).

63 FR 20415, April 24, 1998: Office of Inspector General: Publication of OIG Special Fraud Alert: Fraud and Abuse in Nursing Home Arrangements with Hospices — Notice.

63 FR 26252, May 12, 1998: Medicare Program: Prospective Payment System and Consolidated Billing for Skilled Nursing Facilities — Final rule, affecting 42 CFR Parts 409, 410, 411, 413, 424, 483, and 489. See also correction at 63 FR 53301, October 5, 1998.

63 FR 28395, May 22, 1998: HCFA Agency Information Collection Activities: Submission for OMB Review; Comment request (pertaining to procedures for advisory opinions concerning physician referrals and supporting regulations in 42 CFR 411.370 through 411.389).

63 FR 28395, May 22, 1998: HCFA Agency Information Collection Activities: Submission for OMB Review; Comment request (pertaining to physician certifications and recertifications in skilled nursing facilities).

63 FR 28396, May 22, 1998: HCFA Privacy Act of 1974 — Notice of New System of Records (pertaining to the long term care minimum data set).

63 FR 46676, September 2, 1998: Office of Inspector General: Health Care Programs; Fraud and Abuse; Revised OIG Exclusion Authorities Resulting from Public Law 104–191 — Final rule affecting 42 CFR Parts 1000, 1001, 1002, and 1005. See also correction at 63 FR 57918, October 29, 1998.

63 FR 46736, September 2, 1998: Office of Inspector General: Health Care Programs; Fraud and Abuse; Revised OIG Sanction Authorities Resulting from Public Law 105–33 — Notice of proposed rulemaking affecting 42 CFR 1001, 1002, and 1003.

63 FR 58399, October 30, 1998: Office of Inspector General: Publication of the OIG's Provider Self-Disclosure Protocol — Notice.

63 FR 60356, November 9, 1998: HCFA Agency Information Collection activities: Proposed Collection; Comment request (pertaining to skilled nursing facility resident assessment MDS data).

63 FR 68223, December 10, 1998: Office of Inspector General; Solicitation of New Safe Harbors and Special Fraud Alerts — Notice of intent to develop regulations, affecting 42 CFR 1001.

63 FR 68687, December 14, 1998: Medicare and Medicaid Program; Civil Money Penalties, Assessments, Exclusions, and Related Appeals Procedures — Final rule with comment period, affecting 42 CFR 400 and 402.

63 FR 70137, December 18, 1998: Office of Inspector General: Solicitation of Information and Recommendations for Developing OIG Compliance Program Guidance for the Nursing Home Industry — Notice.

63 FR 72317, December 31, 1998: HCFA Agency Information Collection Activities: Proposed Collection; Comment request (pertaining to advanced directives under Medicare and Medicaid; and Medicare/Medicaid disclosure of ownership and control interests).

63 FR 72318, December 31, 1998: HCFA Agency Information Collection Activities: Proposed Collection; Comment request (pertaining to fire safety survey report forms for health care facilities).

1999

64 FR 6664, February 10, 1999: HCFA Agency Information Collection Activities: Submission for OMB Review; Comment request (pertaining to skilled nursing facility (SNF) resident assessment MDS data).

64 FR 13354, March 18, 1999: Medicare and Medicaid Programs; Civil Money Penalties for Nursing Homes (SNF/NF), Change in Notice Requirements, and Expansion of Discretionary Remedy Delegation — Final rule with comment period, affecting 42 CFR Part 488.

64 FR 13997, March 23, 1999: HCFA Agency Information Collection Activities: Submission for OMB Review; Comment request (pertaining to Medicare and Medicaid requirements for advanced directives, and disclosure of ownership and financial control interest).

64 FR 17184, April 8, 1999: HCFA Medicare Program; April 23, 1999 Open Town Hall Meeting to Discuss the Skilled Nursing Facility Prospective Payment System (SNF/PPS).

64 FR 39420, July 22, 1999: Office of Inspector General; Health Care Programs; Fraud and Abuse; Revised OIG Sanction Authorities Resulting from P.L. 105–33, the Balanced Budget Act of

1997 — Final rule affecting 42 CFR Parts 1001, 1002, and 1003. See also correction at 64 FR 42174, August 3, 1999.

64 FR 39517, July 22, 1999: HCFA Agency Information Collection Activities: Submission for OMB Review; Comment request (pertaining to Medicare participating physician or supplier agreement form HCFA-460).

64 FR 39934, July 23, 1999: Medicare and Medicaid Program; Appeal of the Loss of Nurse Aide Training Programs — Interim final rule with comment period, affecting 42 CFR Parts 431 and 498. See also correction at 64 FR 43295, August 10, 1999.

64 FR 41644, July 30, 1999: Medicare Program; Prospective Payment System and Consolidated Billing for Skilled Nursing Facilities — Final rule affecting 42 CFR Parts 409, 411, 413, and 489. See also correction at 64 FR 60122, November 4, 1999.

64 FR 41684, July 30, 1999: Medicare Program; Prospective Payment System and Consolidated Billing for Skilled Nursing Facilities — Update — Notice. See also correction at 64 FR 54030, October 5, 1999.

64 FR 42610, August 5, 1999: Medicare Program; Revision of the Procedures for Requesting Exceptions to Cost Limits for Skilled Nursing Facilities and Elimination of Reclassifications — Final rule.

64 FR 42791, September 30, 1999: Office of Inspector General; Publication of the OIG Special Advisory Bulletin on the Effect of Exclusion from Participation in Federal Health Care Programs — Notice. See also correction at 64 FR 55484, October 13, 1999.

64 FR 54263, October 6, 1999: Medicaid Program; Flexibility in Payment Methods for Services of Hospitals, Nursing Facilities, and Intermediate Care Facilities for the Mentally Retarded — Proposed rule affecting 42 CFR Part 447.

64 FR 55949, October 15, 1999: HCFA Agency Information Collection Activities: Proposed Collection; Comment request (pertaining to physician certifications and re-certifications about the necessity for skilled nursing facility care).

64 FR 58419, October 29, 1999: Office of Inspector General; Draft OIG Compliance Program Guidance for Nursing Facilities — Notice and comment period.

64 FR 63518, November 19, 1999: Office of Inspector General; Fraud and Abuse; Clarification of the Initial OIG Safe Harbor Provi-

sions and Establishment of Additional Safe Harbor Provisions under the Anti-kickback Statute — Final rule affecting 42 CFR Part 1001.

64 FR 66482, November 26, 1999: HCFA Agency Information Collection Activities: Proposed Collection; Comment request (pertaining to resident assessment in skilled nursing facilities).

64 FR 67028, November 30, 1999: Medicare and Medicaid Programs; Religious Nonmedical Health Care Institutions and Advance Directives — Interim final rule with comment period, affecting 42 CFR Parts 403, 412, 431, 440, 442, 446, 456, 488, and 489.

64 FR 69217, December 10, 1999: Office of Inspector General; Solicitation of New Safe Harbors and Special Fraud Alerts — Intent to develop regulations affecting 42 CFR Part 1001.

64 FR 69271, December 10, 1999: HCFA Agency Information Collection Activities: Proposed Collection; Comment request (pertaining to hospital providers of extender care (swing bed) services in Medicare and Medicaid).

2000

65 FR 2186, January 13, 2000: HCFA Agency Information Collection Activities; Submission for OMB Review; Comment request (pertaining to physician certifications/re-certifications in skilled nursing facilities).

65 FR 12560, March 9, 2000: HCFA Agency Information Collection Activities: Submission for OMB Review; Comment request (pertaining to hospital provider of extended care services (swing beds) in the Medicare and Medicaid programs).

65 FR 14289, March 16, 2000: Office of Inspector General: Publication of the OIG Compliance Program Guidance for Nursing Facilities — Notice.

65 FR 14986, March 20, 2000: HCFA Agency Information Collection Activities: Submission for OMB Review; Comment request (pertaining to skilled nursing facility resident assessment MDS data).

65 FR 19187, April 10, 2000: Medicare Program; Prospective Payment System and Consolidated Billing for Skilled Nursing Facilities; Update--Proposed rule affecting 42 CFR Parts 411 and 489.

65 FR 24400, April 26, 2000: Office of Inspector General; Health Care Programs: Fraud and Abuse; Revised OIG Civil Money Penalties Resulting from Public Law 104-191 (HIPAA) — Final rule

affecting 42 CFR Parts 1001, 1003, 1005, and 1006. See also correction at 65 FR 35583, June 5, 2000.

65 FR 54856, September 11, 2000: HCFA Agency Information Collection Activities: Submission for OMB Review; Comment request (pertaining to skilled nursing facility cost reports).

65 FR 54857, September 11, 2000: HCFA Agency Information Collection Activities: Submission for OMB Review; Comment request (pertaining to ICF/MR survey report forms).

65 FR 60151, October 10, 2000: Medicaid Program; Revision to Medicaid Upper Payment Limit Requirements for Hospital Services, Nursing Facility Services, Intermediate Care Facility Services for the Mentally Retarded, and Clinic Services-Proposed rule affecting 42 CFR Part 447.

65 FR 64227, October 26, 2000: HCFA Agency Information Collection Activities: Proposed Collection; Comment request (pertaining to home health agency cost reports; skilled nursing facility cost reports; and hospital cost reports).

2001

66 FR 856, January 4, 2001: Medicare and Medicaid Programs; Physicians Referrals to Health Care Entities with which They Have Financial Relationships—Final rule with comment period, affecting 42 CFR Parts 411 and 424.

66 FR 3148, January 12, 2001: Medicaid Program; Revision to Medicaid Upper Payment Limit Requirements for Hospital Services, Nursing Facility Services, Intermediate Care Facility Services for the Mentally Retarded, and Clinic Services—Final rule affecting 42 CFR Part 447.

66 FR 3497, January 16, 2001: Medicare Program; Prospective Payment System and Consolidated Billing for Skilled Nursing Facilities—Update; Correction notice affecting 42 FR Parts 411, 313, and 489. See FR Doc. 00–19004, July 31, 2000.

66 FR 6629, January 22, 2001: HCFA Agency Information Collection Activities: Submission for OMB Review; Comment request (pertaining to Medicare Integrity Program Organizational Conflict of Interest Disclosure Certificate).

66 FR 8771, February 2, 2001: Medicare and Medicaid Programs; Physicians' Referrals to Health Care Entities with which They Have Financial Relationships: Delay of Effective Date of Final Rule and Technical Amendment, affecting 42 CFR Parts 411 and 424.

66 FR 16062, March 23, 2001: HCFA Agency Information Collection Activities: Submission for OMB Review; Comment request (pertaining to SNF cost report forms).

66 FR 17657, April 3, 2001: Medicaid Program; Modification of the Medicaid Upper Payment Limit Transition Period for Inpatient Hospital Services, Outpatient Hospital Services, Nursing Facility Services, Intermediate Care Facility Services for the Mentally Retarded and Clinic Services—Proposed rule affecting 42 CFR Part 447.

66 FR 17813, April 4, 2001: Medicare and Medicaid Programs; Physicians' Referrals to Health Care Entities with which They Have Financial Relationships; Extension of Comment period—Notice, affecting 42 CFR Parts 411 and 424.

66 FR 19507, April 16, 2001: HCFA Agency Information Collection Activities: Proposed Collection; Comment request (pertaining to conflict of interest and ownership and control information form).

66 FR 27151, May 16, 2001: HCFA Agency Information Collection Activities: Proposed Collection; Comment request (pertaining to the Long Term Care Awareness Project).

66 FR 28916, May 25, 2001: HCFA Agency Information Collection Activities; Proposed Collection; Comment request (pertaining to procedures for advisory opinions concerning physician referrals under section 1877 of the Social Security Act).

66 FR 31245, June 11, 2001: Office of Inspector General; Healthcare Integrity and Protection Data Bank: Change in User Fees—Notice.

See § 3:15.

§ 7:16 GIVING NURSING FACILITIES ADVANCE NOTICE OF A SURVEY — Section 1919(g)(2)(A)(i) [42 U.S.C.A. 1396r(g)(2)(A)(i)]

Regulations

42 CFR Part 402 — Civil Money Penalties, Assessments, and Exclusions

42 CFR Part 420 — Program Integrity: Medicare

42 CFR Part 431, Subpart D — Appeals Process for NF's and ICF's/MR

42 CFR Part 440 — Services: General Provisions

42 CFR Part 442 — Standards for Payment for Nursing Facilities and Intermediate Care Facilities for the Mentally Retarded

42 CFR Part 447 — Payment for Services

42 CFR Part 455 — Program Integrity: Medicaid

42 CFR Part 456 — Utilization Control

42 CFR Part 483 — Requirements for States and Long Term Care Facilities

42 CFR Part 488 — Survey, Certification, and Enforcement Procedures

42 CFR Part 489 — Provider Agreements and Supplier Approval

42 CFR Part 498 — Appeals Procedures for Determinations that Affect Participation in the Medicare Program and for Determinations that Affect the Participation of ICF's/MR and Certain NF's in the Medicaid Program

42 CFR Chapter V — Office of Inspector General — Health Care, Department of Health and Human Services

Subchapter A — General Provisions

Part 1000 — Introduction; General Definitions

Subchapter B — OIG Authorities

Part 1001 — Program Integrity: Medicare and State Health Care Programs

Part 1002 — Program Integrity: State-initiated Exclusion from Medicaid

Part 1003 — Civil Money Penalties, Assessments and Exclusions

Part 1004 — Imposition of Sanctions on Health Care Practitioners and Providers of Health Care Services by a Peer Review Organization

Part 1005 — Appeals of Exclusions, Civil Money Penalties and Assessments

Part 1006 — Investigational Inquiries

Part 1007 — State Medicaid Fraud Control Units

Part 1008 — Advisory Opinions by the OIG

54 FR 5316, February 2, 1989: Medicare and Medicaid; Requirements for Long Term Care Facilities — Final rule with comment period, amending 42 CFR Parts 405, 442, 447, 483, 488, 489, and 498. See also delay in effective date at 54 FR 29717, July 14, 1989; corrections at 54 FR 8361, February 27, 1989, and 54 FR 37466, September 11, 1989; and final rule delaying effective date from January 1, 1990, to October 1, 1990, at 54 FR 53611, December 29, 1989.

55 FR 10256, March 20, 1990: Medicare and Medicaid; Charges to Residents' Funds in Nursing Homes — Proposed rule to amend 42 CFR Part 483. See also final rule at 57 FR 53572, November 12, 1992.

55 FR 10938, March 23, 1990: Medicare and Medicaid Programs; Nurse Aide Training and Competency Evaluation Programs — Proposed rule to amend 42 CFR Parts 431, 433, and 483.

55 FR 10951, March 23, 1990: Medicare and Medicaid Programs; Preadmission Screening and Annual Resident Review — Proposed rule to amend 42 CFR Parts 405, 431, and 483.

55 FR 12205, April 2, 1990: Health Care Programs: Fraud and Abuse; Amendments to OIG Exclusion and CMP Authorities Resulting from Public Law 100–93, the Medicare and Medicaid Patient and Program Protection Act of 1987, Public Law 99–272, the Consolidated Omnibus Budget Reconciliation Act of 1985, and Public Law 100–360, the Medicare Catastrophic Coverage Act of 1988 — Proposed rule to amend 42 CFR Parts 1000, 1001, 1002, 1003, 1004, 1005, 1006, and 1007. See also correction published at 55 FR 17461, April 25, 1990.

56 FR 30696, July 5, 1991: Medicaid Program; Correction and Reduction Plans for Intermediate Care Facilities for the Mentally Retarded — Final rule affecting 42 CFR Part 442. See also correction at 56 FR 49147, September 27, 1991.

56 FR 48826, September 26, 1991: Medicare and Medicaid; Requirements for Long Term Care Facilities — Final rule affecting 42 CFR Parts 422, 447, 483, 488, 489, and 498. See also correction at 57 FR 43922, September 23, 1992.

56 FR 48880, September 26, 1991: Medicare and Medicaid Programs; Nurse Aide Training and Competency Evaluation Programs — Final rule affecting 42 CFR Parts 431, 433, and 483. See also correction at 56 FR 59331, November 25, 1991.

57 FR 3298, January 29, 1992: Health Care Programs: Fraud and Abuse; Amendments to OIG Exclusion and CMP Authorities Resulting From Public Law 100–93 — Final rule affecting 42 CFR Parts 1001, 1002, 1003, 1004, 1005, 1006, and 1007. See also final rule and correction at 57 FR 9669, March 20, 1992; final rule affecting 42 CFR Parts 1001and 1005, with clarification at 58 FR 5617, January 22, 1993; and final rule affecting 42 CFR Part 1001, with correction, at 58 FR 40752, July 30, 1993.

57 FR 4516, February 5, 1992: Medicare and Medicaid Programs; Omnibus Nursing Home Requirements — Proposed rule affecting 42 CFR Parts 418, 440, 441, 482, 483, and 488. See also correction at 57 FR 8961, March 13, 1992.

57 FR 8194, March 6, 1992: Medicare and Medicaid Programs; Advance Directives — Interim final rule with comment period, affecting 42 CFR Parts 417, 431, 434, 483, 484, 489, and 498.

57 FR 39278, August 28, 1992: Medicare and Medicaid Programs; Survey, Certification and Enforcement of Skilled Nursing Facilities and Nursing Facilities — Proposed rule affecting 42 CFR Parts 431, 442, 488, and 489.

57 FR 43462, September 21, 1992: Health Care Financing Administration Public Information Collection Requirements Submitted to the Office of Management and Budget for Clearance (pertaining to sole community home health agencies; physician/supplier overpayment reports; physician or supplier Medicare agreements; conditions of participation for rural health clinics; Medicare provider refunds; conditions of participation for comprehensive outpatient rehabilitation facilities; Medicaid income and eligibility verification system; Medicaid integrated review schedule; provider overpayment report; financial statement of Medicare provider debtors; negative case action review schedule for Medicaid quality control; outpatient resource costing study; Medicaid intermediate care facility for the mentally retarded or persons with related conditions survey report form; installment agreement of beneficiary refund of overpayment; PRO assumption of responsibilities; Medicare contractor administrative budget and cost reporting system forms; fire safety survey report forms; medical records review under prospective payment system; and Qualified Medicare Beneficiary supplement to the Medicare current beneficiary survey).

57 FR 46362, October 8, 1992: Medicare and Medicaid Programs; Revised Effective Date of Medicare/Medicaid Provider Agreement and Supplier Participation — Proposed rule affecting 42 CFR Parts 431, 440, 442, 488, 489, and 498.

57 FR 54710, November 20, 1992: Medicaid Program; Elimination of Certain Written Documentation Pertaining to Medicaid Long-Term Care Facilities — Final rule affecting 42 CFR Part 442.

57 FR 56450, November 30, 1992: Medicare and Medicaid Programs; Preadmission Screening and Annual Resident Review — Final rule with comment period, affecting 42 CFR Parts 405, 431, 433, and 483. See also correction published at 58 FR 25784, April 28, 1993.

57 FR 61614, December 28, 1992: Medicare and Medicaid; Resident Assessment in Long Term Care Facilities — Proposed rule affecting 42 CFR Parts 456 and 483.

58 FR 21174, April 19, 1993: HCFA Public Information Collection Requirements Submitted to the Office of Management and Budget for Clearance re end stage renal disease survey forms; municipal health services cost reports forms; advance directives; withholding Medicare payments to recover Medicaid overpayments; home office cost statements; and statistical report on medical care.

59 FR 52178, October 14, 1994: HCFA Public Information Collection Requirements Submitted to the Office of Management and Budget (OMB) for Clearance (pertaining to Medicare reimbursement for outpatient services, cost reports for free-standing skilled nursing facilities; Medicare coverage criteria for adult heart transplants, drug rebates for Medicaid, optional prospective payment cost report for certain skilled nursing facilities, reimbursable costs for organ procurement agencies, distribution and use of end stage renal disease treatment sources, conditions of coverage for ambulatory surgical centers, and waivers for home and community based services).

59 FR 56116, November 10, 1994: Medicare and Medicaid Programs; Survey, Certification and Enforcement of Skilled Nursing Facilities and Nursing Facilities — Final rule affecting 42 CFR Parts 401, 431, 435, 440, 441, 442, 447, 483, 488, 489, and 498. See also correcting amendment, effective July 1, 1995, at 62 FR 44221, August 20, 1997.

59 FR 66969, December 28, 1994: HCFA Public Information Collection Requirements Submitted to the Office of Management and Budget (OMB) for Clearance (pertaining to physician certification in skilled nursing facilities, and criteria for Medicare coverage of adult liver transplants).

60 FR 16580, March 31, 1995: Office of Inspector General: Civil Money Penalties for Referrals to Entities and for Prohibited Arrangements and Schemes — Final rule with comment period, affecting 42 CFR Part 1003.

60 FR 21525, May 2, 1995: HCFA Public Information Collection Requirements Submitted to the Office of Management and Budget (OMB) for Clearance (pertaining to intermediary requests for information from skilled nursing facilities, reimbursement for CLIA compliance surveys, patient outcome data in home health agencies, common claim forms for Medicare/Medicaid reimbursement, and a study of childhood immunization costs).

60 FR 32916, June 26, 1995: Office of Inspector General; Health Care Programs; Fraud and Abuse; Technical Revision to the Scope

and Effect of the OIG Exclusion Regulations — Final rule affecting 42 CFR Part 1001.

60 FR 37066, July 19, 1995: HCFA Public Information Collection Requirements Submitted to the Office of Management and Budget (OMB) for Clearance (pertaining to actuarial forecasts for Medicaid utilization and cost, employers identified through a match of IRS, SSA, and Medicare records for purposes of the Medicare Secondary Payer provision, health and safety requirements for portable X-ray suppliers, and evaluation of Intermediate Care Facilities for Persons with Mental Retardation — establishing psychoactive drug use baselines).

60 FR 37590, July 21, 1995: Medicare Program; Optional Payment System for Low Medicare Volume Skilled Nursing Facilities — Final rule affecting 42 CFR Part 413.

60 FR 50115, September 28, 1995: Medicare and Medicaid Programs; Survey, Certification and Enforcement of Skilled Nursing Facilities and Nursing Facilities — Final rule and correction to final regulations, affecting 42 CFR Parts 431, 440, 442, 488, 489, and 498. See also corrections at 60 FR 52731, October 10, 1995, and at 60 FR 534456, October 13, 1995.

60 FR 58088, November 24, 1995: HCFA Public Information Collection Requirements Submitted for Public Comment and Recommendations (pertaining to skilled nursing facility (SNF) and skilled nursing facility health care complex cost reports).

60 FR 62237, December 5, 1995: Medicare Program; Uniform Electronic Cost Reporting for Skilled Nursing Facilities and Home Health Agencies — Proposed rule affecting 42 CFR Part 413.

61 FR 11214, March 19, 1996: HCFA Agency Information Collection Activities: Proposed Collection; Comment Request (pertaining to conditions of coverage for organ procurement organizations; and skilled nursing facility and skilled nursing facility healthcare complex forms).

61 FR 14798, April 3, 1996: HCFA Agency Information Collection Activities: Proposed Collection; Comment Request (pertaining to statistical reports on medical care eligibility, payments and services under Medicaid; State survey agency lists of positions and schedule of equipment purchases; granting and withdrawing of deeming authority to national accreditation organizations; maximizing the effectiveness of home health care; requests for certification in the Medicare or Medicaid program to provide outpatient physical therapy and/or speech pathology services; physical therapists in

independent practice; requests for provider approval as a hospital provider of extended care services (swing bed) under Medicare and Medicaid; and requests for designation as an organ procurement organization).

61 FR 17677, April 22, 1996: Medicare and Medicaid Programs; New Payment Methodology for Routine Extended Care Services Provided in a Swing-bed Hospital— Proposed rule affecting 42 CFR Part 413.

61 FR 30623, June 17, 1996: Office of Inspector General Publication of OIG Special Fraud Alert: Fraud and Abuse in the Provision of Services in Nursing Homes — Notice.

61 FR 35231, July 5, 1996: HCFA Agency Information Collection Activities: Proposed Collection; Comment Request (pertaining to Medicaid payment standards for inpatient hospital or long-term care services).

61 FR 38395, July 24, 1996: Medicaid Program; Medicaid Eligibility Quality Control, Progressive Reductions in Federal Financial Participation for FYs 1982–1984, Payment for Physician Billing for Clinical Laboratory Services, and Utilization Control of Skilled Nursing Facility Services: Removal of Obsolete Requirements — Final rule.

61 FR 46466, September 3, 1996: Medicare Program; Schedule of Prospectively Determined Payment Rates for Skilled Nursing Facility Inpatient Routine Service Costs — Final rule with comment period.

61 FR 51295, October 1, 1996: HCFA Public Information Requirements Submitted for Collection of Public Comment: Submission for OMB Review (pertaining to approval of Medicaid payment rates for inpatient hospital or long term care services).

61 FR 51611, October 3, 1996: Medicare and Medicaid Programs; New Payment Methodology for Routine Extended Care Services Provided in a Swing-bed Hospital— Final Rule affecting 42 CFR Part 413. See also correction at 61 FR 58631, November 18, 1996.

61 FR 54209, October 17, 1996: HCFA Agency Information Collectio Activities: Proposed Collection; Comment request (pertaining to hospital eligibility for swing-bed status).

61 FR 64913, December 9, 1996: HCFA Agency Information Collection Activities: Proposed Collection; Comment request (pertaining to survey report forms for ICF/MRs; and current Medicare beneficiary surveys).

61 FR 68270, December 27, 1996: HCFA Agency Information Collection Activities: Submission for OMB Review; Comment request (pertaining to a facility identification and screening form for hospital providers of extended care services (swing-beds) in the the Medicare and Medicaid programs).

62 FR 26, January 2, 1997: Medicare Program; Electronic Cost Reporting for Skilled Nursing Facilities and Home Health Agencies — Final Rule. See also correction at 62 FR 27210, May 19, 1997.

62 FR 11214, March 11, 1997: HCFA Agency Information Collection Activities: Submission for OMB Review; Comment request (pertaining to intermediate care facility for the mentally retarded or persons with related conditions survey report forms).

62 FR 11458, March 12, 1997: HCFA Agency Information Collection Activities: Proposed Collection; Comment request (pertaining to skilled nursing facility and skilled nursing facility health care complex cost report form).

62 FR 23140, April 29, 1997: Office of Inspector General: Health Care Programs: Fraud and Abuse; Revised PRO Sanctions for Failing to Meet Statutory Obligations — Final rule.

62 FR 30603, June 4, 1997: HCFA Agency Information Collection Activities: Submission for OMB Review; Comment request (pertaining to skilled nursing facility and skilled nursing facility health care complex cost reports; and hospital conditions of participation).

62 FR 33095, June 18, 1997: HCFA Agency Information Collection Activities: Proposed Collection; Comment request (pertaining to skilled nursing facility prospective payment system cost report form).

62 FR 43931, August 18, 1997: Medicare and Medicaid Programs: Effective Dates of Provider Agreements and Supplier Approvals — Final rule affecting 42 CFR Parts 431, 442, 488, 489, and 498.

62 FR 47182, September 8, 1997: Office of Inspector General: Health Care Programs: Fraud and Abuse; Revised OIG Exclusion Authorities Resulting from Public Law 104–191 — Notice of Proposed rulemaking, affecting 42 CFR Parts 1000, 1001, 1002, and 1005.

62 FR 51536, October 1, 1997: Medicare Program; Schedules of Limits and Prospectively Determined Payment Rates for Skilled Nursing Facility Inpatient Routine Service Costs — Final notice with comment period.

62 FR 55410, October 24, 1997: HCFA Agency Information Collection Activities: Submission for OMB Review; Comment request

(pertaining to Medicare/Medicaid disclosure of ownership and control forms).

62 FR 55410, October 24, 1997: Office of Inspector General: Criteria for Implementing Permissive Exclusion Authority under Section 1128(b)(7) of the Social Security Act — Notice.

62 FR 48736, October 30, 1997: HCFA Agency Information Collection Activities: Submission for OMB Review; Comment request (pertaining to prospective payment for skilled nursing facilities).

62 FR 67174, December 23, 1997: Medicare and Medicaid; Resident Assessment in Long Term Care Facilities — Final rule affecting 42 CFR Part 483.

62 FR 67392, December 24, 1997: Office of Inspector General: Criteria for Implementing Permissive Exclusion Authority under Section 1128(b)(7) of the Social Security Act — Notice.

63 FR 9844, February 26, 1998: HCFA Agency Information Collection Activities: Proposed Collection; Comment request (pertaining to procedures for advisory opinions concerning physician referrals and supporting regulations in 42 CFR Sections 411.370- 411.389).

63 FR 14393, March 25, 1998: Office of Inspector General: Health Care Programs: Fraud and Abuse; Revised OIG Civil Money Penalties Resulting from the Health Insurance Portability and Accountability Act of 1996 — Notice of proposed rulemaking, affecting 42 CFR Parts 1003, 1005, and 1006.

63 FR 14719, March 26, 1998: HCFA Agency Information Collection Activities: Proposed Collection; Comment request (pertaining to physician certification and re-certification in skilled nursing facilities).

63 FR 20415, April 24, 1998: Office of Inspector General: Publication of OIG Special Fraud Alert: Fraud and Abuse in Nursing Home Arrangements with Hospices — Notice.

63 FR 26252, May 12, 1998: Medicare Program: Prospective Payment System and Consolidated Billing for Skilled Nursing Facilities — Final rule, affecting 42 CFR Parts 409, 410, 411, 413, 424, 483, and 489. See also correction at 63 FR 53301, October 5, 1998.

63 FR 28395, May 22, 1998: HCFA Agency Information Collection Activities: Submission for OMB Review; Comment request (pertaining to procedures for advisory opinions concerning physician referrals and supporting regulations in 42 CFR 411.370 through 411.389).

63 FR 28395, May 22, 1998: HCFA Agency Information Collection Activities: Submission for OMB Review; Comment request (pertaining to physician certifications and recertifications in skilled nursing facilities).

63 FR 28396, May 22, 1998: HCFA Privacy Act of 1974 —Notice of New System of Records (pertaining to the long term care minimum data set).

63 FR 46676, September 2, 1998: Office of Inspector General: Health Care Programs; Fraud and Abuse; Revised OIG Exclusion Authorities Resulting from Public Law 104–191 — Final rule affecting 42 CFR Parts 1000, 1001, 1002, and 1005. See also correction at 63 FR 57918, October 29, 1998.

63 FR 46736, September 2, 1998: Office of Inspector General: Health Care Programs; Fraud and Abuse; Revised OIG Sanction Authorities Resulting from Public Law 105–33 — Notice of proposed rulemaking affecting 42 CFR 1001, 1002, and 1003.

63 FR 58399, October 30, 1998: Office of Inspector General: Publication of the OIG's Provider Self-Disclosure Protocol —Notice.

63 FR 60356, November 9, 1998: HCFA Agency Information Collection activities: Proposed Collection; Comment request (pertaining to skilled nursing facility resident assessment MDS data).

63 FR 68223, December 10, 1998: Office of Inspector General; Solicitation of New Safe Harbors and Special Fraud Alerts —Notice of intent to develop regulations, affecting 42 CFR 1001.

63 FR 68687, December 14, 1998: Medicare and Medicaid Program; Civil Money Penalties, Assessments, Exclusions, and Related Appeals Procedures — Final rule with comment period, affecting 42 CFR 400 and 402.

63 FR 70137, December 18, 1998: Office of Inspector General: Solicitation of Information and Recommendations for Developing OIG Compliance Program Guidance for the Nursing Home Industry — Notice.

63 FR 72317, December 31, 1998: HCFA Agency Information Collection Activities: Proposed Collection; Comment request (pertaining to advanced directives under Medicare and Medicaid; and Medicare/Medicaid disclosure of ownership and control interests).

63 FR 72318, December 31, 1998: HCFA Agency Information Collection Activities: Proposed Collection; Comment request (pertaining to fire safety survey report forms for health care facilities).

1999

64 FR 6664, February 10, 1999: HCFA Agency Information Collection Activities: Submission for OMB Review; Comment request (pertaining to skilled nursing facility (SNF) resident assessment MDS data).

64 FR 13354, March 18, 1999: Medicare and Medicaid Programs; Civil Money Penalties for Nursing Homes (SNF/NF), Change in Notice Requirements, and Expansion of Discretionary Remedy Delegation — Final rule with comment period, affecting 42 CFR Part 488.

64 FR 13997, March 23, 1999: HCFA Agency Information Collection Activities: Submission for OMB Review; Comment request (pertaining to Medicare and Medicaid requirements for advanced directives, and disclosure of ownership and financial control interest).

64 FR 17184, April 8, 1999: HCFA Medicare Program; April 23, 1999 Open Town Hall Meeting to Discuss the Skilled Nursing Facility Prospective Payment System (SNF/PPS).

64 FR 39420, July 22, 1999: Office of Inspector General; Health Care Programs; Fraud and Abuse; Revised OIG Sanction Authorities Resulting from P.L. 105–33, the Balanced Budget Act of 1997 — Final rule affecting 42 CFR Parts 1001, 1002, and 1003. See also correction at 64 FR 42174, August 3, 1999.

64 FR 39517, July 22, 1999: HCFA Agency Information Collection Activities: Submission for OMB Review; Comment request (pertaining to Medicare participating physician or supplier agreement form HCFA-460).

64 FR 39934, July 23, 1999: Medicare and Medicaid Program; Appeal of the Loss of Nurse Aide Training Programs — Interim final rule with comment period, affecting 42 CFR Parts 431 and 498. See also correction at 64 FR 43295, August 10, 1999.

64 FR 41644, July 30, 1999: Medicare Program; Prospective Payment System and Consolidated Billing for Skilled Nursing Facilities — Final rule affecting 42 CFR Parts 409, 411, 413, and 489. See also correction at 64 FR 60122, November 4, 1999.

64 FR 41684, July 30, 1999: Medicare Program; Prospective Payment System and Consolidated Billing for Skilled Nursing Facilities — Update — Notice. See also correction at 64 FR 54030, October 5, 1999.

64 FR 42610, August 5, 1999: Medicare Program; Revision of the Procedures for Requesting Exceptions to Cost Limits for Skilled Nursing Facilities and Elimination of Reclassifications —Final rule.

64 FR 42791, September 30, 1999: Office of Inspector General; Publication of the OIG Special Advisory Bulletin on the Effect of Exclusion from Participation in Federal Health Care Programs—Notice. See also correction at 64 FR 55484, October 13, 1999.

64 FR 54263, October 6, 1999: Medicaid Program; Flexibility in Payment Methods for Services of Hospitals, Nursing Facilities, and Intermediate Care Facilities for the Mentally Retarded— Proposed rule affecting 42 CFR Part 447.

64 FR 55949, October 15, 1999: HCFA Agency Information Collection Activities: Proposed Collection; Comment request (pertaining to physician certifications and re-certifications about the necessity for skilled nursing facility care).

64 FR 58419, October 29, 1999: Office of Inspector General; Draft OIG Compliance Program Guidance for Nursing Facilities— Notice and comment period.

64 FR 63518, November 19, 1999: Office of Inspector General; Fraud and Abuse; Clarification of the Initial OIG Safe Harbor Provisions and Establishment of Additional Safe Harbor Provisions under the Anti-kickback Statute—Final rule affecting 42 CFR Part 1001.

64 FR 66482, November 26, 1999: HCFA Agency Information Collection Activities: Proposed Collection; Comment request (pertaining to resident assessment in skilled nursing facilities).

64 FR 67028, November 30, 1999: Medicare and Medicaid Programs; Religious Nonmedical Health Care Institutions and Advance Directives—Interim final rule with comment period, affecting 42 CFR Parts 403, 412, 431, 440, 442, 446, 456, 488, and 489.

64 FR 69217, December 10, 1999: Office of Inspector General; Solicitation of New Safe Harbors and Special Fraud Alerts —Intent to develop regulations affecting 42 CFR Part 1001.

64 FR 69271, December 10, 1999: HCFA Agency Information Collection Activities: Proposed Collection; Comment request (pertaining to hospital providers of extender care (swing bed) services in Medicare and Medicaid).

2000

65 FR 2186, January 13, 2000: HCFA Agency Information Collection Activities; Submission for OMB Review; Comment request (pertaining to physician certifications/re-certifications in skilled nursing facilities).

65 FR 12560, March 9, 2000: HCFA Agency Information Collection Activities: Submission for OMB Review; Comment request (pertaining to hospital provider of extended care services (swing beds) in the Medicare and Medicaid programs).

65 FR 14289, March 16, 2000: Office of Inspector General: Publication of the OIG Compliance Program Guidance for Nursing Facilities — Notice.

65 FR 14986, March 20, 2000: HCFA Agency Information Collection Activities: Submission for OMB Review; Comment request (pertaining to skilled nursing facility resident assessment MDS data).

65 FR 19187, April 10, 2000: Medicare Program; Prospective Payment System and Consolidated Billing for Skilled Nursing Facilities; Update--Proposed rule affecting 42 CFR Parts 411 and 489.

65 FR 24400, April 26, 2000: Office of Inspector General; Health Care Programs: Fraud and Abuse; Revised OIG Civil Money Penalties Resulting from Public Law 104-191 (HIPAA) — Final rule affecting 42 CFR Parts 1001, 1003, 1005, and 1006. See also correction at 65 FR 35583, June 5, 2000.

65 FR 54856, September 11, 2000: HCFA Agency Information Collection Activities: Submission for OMB Review; Comment request (pertaining to skilled nursing facility cost reports).

65 FR 54857, September 11, 2000: HCFA Agency Information Collection Activities: Submission for OMB Review; Comment request (pertaining to ICF/MR survey report forms).

65 FR 60151, October 10, 2000: Medicaid Program; Revision to Medicaid Upper Payment Limit Requirements for Hospital Services, Nursing Facility Services, Intermediate Care Facility Services for the Mentally Retarded, and Clinic Services-Proposed rule affecting 42 CFR Part 447.

65 FR 64227, October 26, 2000: HCFA Agency Information Collection Activities: Proposed Collection; Comment request (pertaining to home health agency cost reports; skilled nursing facility cost reports; and hospital cost reports).

2001

66 FR 856, January 4, 2001: Medicare and Medicaid Programs; Physicians Referrals to Health Care Entities with which They Have Financial Relationships—Final rule with comment period, affecting 42 CFR Parts 411 and 424.

66 FR 3148, January 12, 2001: Medicaid Program; Revision to Medicaid Upper Payment Limit Requirements for Hospital Services, Nursing Facility Services, Intermediate Care Facility Services for the Mentally Retarded, and Clinic Services—Final rule affecting 42 CFR Part 447.

66 FR 3497, January 16, 2001: Medicare Program; Prospective Payment System and Consolidated Billing for Skilled Nursing Facilities—Update; Correction notice affecting 42 FR Parts 411, 313, and 489. See FR Doc. 00–19004, July 31, 2000.

66 FR 6629, January 22, 2001: HCFA Agency Information Collection Activities: Submission for OMB Review; Comment request (pertaining to Medicare Integrity Program Organizational Conflict of Interest Disclosure Certificate).

66 FR 8771, February 2, 2001: Medicare and Medicaid Programs; Physicians' Referrals to Health Care Entities with which They Have Financial Relationships: Delay of Effective Date of Final Rule and Technical Amendment, affecting 42 CFR Parts 411 and 424.

66 FR 16062, March 23, 2001: HCFA Agency Information Collection Activities: Submission for OMB Review; Comment request (pertaining to SNF cost report forms).

66 FR 17657, April 3, 2001: Medicaid Program; Modification of the Medicaid Upper Payment Limit Transition Period for Inpatient Hospital Services, Outpatient Hospital Services, Nursing Facility Services, Intermediate Care Facility Services for the Mentally Retarded and Clinic Services—Proposed rule affecting 42 CFR Part 447.

66 FR 17813, April 4, 2001: Medicare and Medicaid Programs; Physicians' Referrals to Health Care Entities with which They Have Financial Relationships; Extension of Comment period—Notice, affecting 42 CFR Parts 411 and 424.

66 FR 19507, April 16, 2001: HCFA Agency Information Collection Activities: Proposed Collection; Comment request (pertaining to conflict of interest and ownership and control information form).

66 FR 27151, May 16, 2001: HCFA Agency Information Collection Activities: Proposed Collection; Comment request (pertaining to the Long Term Care Awareness Project).

66 FR 28916, May 25, 2001: HCFA Agency Information Collection Activities; Proposed Collection; Comment request (pertaining to procedures for advisory opinions concerning physician referrals under section 1877 of the Social Security Act).

66 FR 31245, June 11, 2001: Office of Inspector General; Healthcare Integrity and Protection Data Bank: Change in User Fees—Notice.

See § 3:16.

§ 7:17 FAILING A NURSING FACILITY SURVEY — Section 1919(g)(5), 1919(h), and 1919(i) [42 U.S.C.A. 1396r(g)(5), 1396r(h), and 1396r(i)]

Regulations

42 CFR Part 402 — Civil Money Penalties, Assessments, and Exclusions

42 CFR Part 420 — Program Integrity: Medicare

42 CFR Part 431, Subpart D — Appeals Process for NF's and ICF's/MR

42 CFR Part 440 — Services: General Provisions

42 CFR Part 442 — Standards for Payment for Nursing Facilities and Intermediate Care Facilities for the Mentally Retarded [Medicaid]

42 CFR Part 447 — Payment for Services

42 CFR Part 455 — Program Integrity: Medicaid

42 CFR Part 456 — Utilization Control

42 CFR Part 483 — Requirements for States and Long Term Care Facilities

42 CFR Part 488 — Survey, Certification, and Enforcement Procedures

42 CFR Part 489 — Provider Agreements and Supplier Approval

42 CFR Part 498 — Appeals Procedures for Determinations that Affect Participation in the Medicare Program and for Determinations that Affect the Participation of ICF's/MR and Certain NF's in the Medicaid Program

42 CFR Chapter V — Office of Inspector General — Health Care, Department of Health and Human Services

Subchapter A — General Provisions

Part 1000 — Introduction; General Definitions

Subchapter B — OIG Authorities

Part 1001 — Program Integrity: Medicare and State Health Care Programs

Part 1002 — Program Integrity: State-initiated Exclusion from Medicaid

Part 1003 — Civil Money Penalties, Assessments and Exclusions

Part 1004 — Imposition of Sanctions on Health Care Practitioners and Providers of Health Care Services by a Peer Review Organization

Part 1005 — Appeals of Exclusions, Civil Money Penalties and Assessments

Part 1006 — Investigational Inquiries

Part 1007 — State Medicaid Fraud Control Units

Part 1008 — Advisory Opinions by the OIG

54 FR 5316, February 2, 1989: Medicare and Medicaid; Requirements for Long Term Care Facilities — Final rule with comment period, amending 42 CFR Parts 405, 442, 447, 483, 488, 489, and 498. See also delay in effective date at 54 FR 29717, July 14, 1989; corrections at 54 FR 8361, February 27, 1989, and 54 FR 37466, September 11, 1989; and final rule delaying effective date from January 1, 1990, to October 1, 1990, at 54 FR 53611, December 29, 1989.

55 FR 10256, March 20, 1990: Medicare and Medicaid; Charges to Residents' Funds in Nursing Homes — Proposed rule to amend 42 CFR Part 483. See also final rule at 57 FR 53572, November 12, 1992.

55 FR 10938, March 23, 1990: Medicare and Medicaid Programs; Nurse Aide Training and Competency Evaluation Programs — Proposed rule to amend 42 CFR Parts 431, 433, and 483.

55 FR 10951, March 23, 1990: Medicare and Medicaid Programs; Preadmission Screening and Annual Resident Review — Proposed rule to amend 42 CFR Parts 405, 431, and 483.

55 FR 12205, April 2, 1990: Health Care Programs: Fraud and Abuse; Amendments to OIG Exclusion and CMP Authorities Resulting from Public Law 100–93, the Medicare and Medicaid Patient and Program Protection Act of 1987, Public Law 99–272, the Consolidated Omnibus Budget Reconciliation Act of 1985, and Public Law 100–360, the Medicare Catastrophic Coverage Act of 1988 — Proposed rule to amend 42 CFR Parts 1000, 1001, 1002, 1003, 1004, 1005, 1006, and 1007. See also correction published at 55 FR 17461, April 25, 1990.

56 FR 30696, July 5, 1991: Medicaid Program; Correction and Reduction Plans for Intermediate Care Facilities for the Mentally

Retarded — Final rule affecting 42 CFR Part 442. See also correction at 56 FR 49147, September 27, 1991.

56 FR 48826, September 26, 1991: Medicare and Medicaid; Requirements for Long Term Care Facilities — Final rule affecting 42 CFR Parts 422, 447, 483, 488, 489, and 498. See also correction at 57 FR 43922, September 23, 1992.

56 FR 48880, September 26, 1991: Medicare and Medicaid Programs; Nurse Aide Training and Competency Evaluation Programs — Final rule affecting 42 CFR Parts 431, 433, and 483. See also correction at 56 FR 59331, November 25, 1991.

57 FR 3298, January 29, 1992: Health Care Programs: Fraud and Abuse; Amendments to OIG Exclusion and CMP Authorities Resulting From Public Law 100–93 — Final rule affecting 42 CFR Parts 1001, 1002, 1003, 1004, 1005, 1006, and 1007. See also final rule and correction at 57 FR 9669, March 20, 1992; final rule affecting 42 CFR Parts 1001and 1005, with clarification at 58 FR 5617, January 22, 1993; and final rule affecting 42 CFR Part 1001, with correction, at 58 FR 40752, July 30, 1993.

57 FR 4516, February 5, 1992: Medicare and Medicaid Programs; Omnibus Nursing Home Requirements — Proposed rule affecting 42 CFR Parts 418, 440, 441, 482, 483, and 488. See also correction at 57 FR 8961, March 13, 1992.

57 FR 8194, March 6, 1992: Medicare and Medicaid Programs; Advance Directives — Interim final rule with comment period, affecting 42 CFR Parts 417, 431, 434, 483, 484, 489, and 498.

57 FR 39278, August 28, 1992: Medicare and Medicaid Programs; Survey, Certification and Enforcement of Skilled Nursing Facilities and Nursing Facilities — Proposed rule affecting 42 CFR Parts 431, 442, 488, and 489.

57 FR 43462, September 21, 1992: Health Care Financing Administration Public Information Collection Requirements Submitted to the Office of Management and Budget for Clearance (pertaining to sole community home health agencies; physician/supplier overpayment reports; physician or supplier Medicare agreements; conditions of participation for rural health clinics; Medicare provider refunds; conditions of participation for comprehensive outpatient rehabilitation facilities; Medicaid income and eligibility verification system; Medicaid integrated review schedule; provider overpayment report; financial statement of Medicare provider debtors; negative case action review schedule for Medicaid quality control; outpatient resource costing study; Medicaid intermediate care facility for the

mentally retarded or persons with related conditions survey report form; installment agreement of beneficiary refund of overpayment; PRO assumption of responsibilities; Medicare contractor administrative budget and cost reporting system forms; fire safety survey report forms; medical records review under prospective payment system; and Qualified Medicare Beneficiary supplement to the Medicare current beneficiary survey).

57 FR 46362, October 8, 1992: Medicare and Medicaid Programs; Revised Effective Date of Medicare/Medicaid Provider Agreement and Supplier Participation — Proposed rule affecting 42 CFR Parts 431, 440, 442, 488, 489, and 498.

57 FR 54710, November 20, 1992: Medicaid Program; Elimination of Certain Written Documentation Pertaining to Medicaid Long-Term Care Facilities — Final rule affecting 42 CFR Part 442.

57 FR 56450, November 30, 1992: Medicare and Medicaid Programs; Preadmission Screening and Annual Resident Review — Final rule with comment period, affecting 42 CFR Parts 405, 431, 433, and 483. See also correction published at 58 FR 25784, April 28, 1993.

57 FR 61614, December 28, 1992: Medicare and Medicaid; Resident Assessment in Long Term Care Facilities — Proposed rule affecting 42 CFR Parts 456 and 483.

58 FR 21174, April 19, 1993: HCFA Public Information Collection Requirements Submitted to the Office of Management and Budget for Clearance re end stage renal disease survey forms; municipal health services cost reports forms; advance directives; withholding Medicare payments to recover Medicaid overpayments; home office cost statements; and statistical report on medical care.

59 FR 52178, October 14, 1994: HCFA Public Information Collection Requirements Submitted to the Office of Management and Budget (OMB) for Clearance (pertaining to Medicare reimbursement for outpatient services, cost reports for free-standing skilled nursing facilities; Medicare coverage criteria for adult heart transplants, drug rebates for Medicaid, optional prospective payment cost report for certain skilled nursing facilities, reimbursable costs for organ procurement agencies, distribution and use of end stage renal disease treatment sources, conditions of coverage for ambulatory surgical centers, and waivers for home and community based services).

59 FR 56116, November 10, 1994: Medicare and Medicaid Programs; Survey, Certification and Enforcement of Skilled Nursing

Facilities and Nursing Facilities — Final rule affecting 42 CFR Parts 401, 431, 435, 440, 441, 442, 447, 483, 488, 489, and 498. See also correcting amendment, effective July 1, 1995, at 62 FR 44221, August 20, 1997.

59 FR 66969, December 28, 1994: HCFA Public Information Collection Requirements Submitted to the Office of Management and Budget (OMB) for Clearance (pertaining to physician certification in skilled nursing facilities, and criteria for Medicare coverage of adult liver transplants).

60 FR 16580, March 31, 1995: Office of Inspector General: Civil Money Penalties for Referrals to Entities and for Prohibited Arrangements and Schemes — Final rule with comment period, affecting 42 CFR Part 1003.

60 FR 21525, May 2, 1995: HCFA Public Information Collection Requirements Submitted to the Office of Management and Budget (OMB) for Clearance (pertaining to intermediary requests for information from skilled nursing facilities, reimbursement for CLIA compliance surveys, patient outcome data in home health agencies, common claim forms for Medicare/Medicaid reimbursement, and a study of childhood immunization costs).

60 FR 32916, June 26, 1995: Office of Inspector General; Health Care Programs; Fraud and Abuse; Technical Revision to the Scope and Effect of the OIG Exclusion Regulations — Final rule affecting 42 CFR Part 1001.

60 FR 37066, July 19, 1995: HCFA Public Information Collection Requirements Submitted to the Office of Management and Budget (OMB) for Clearance (pertaining to actuarial forecasts for Medicaid utilization and cost, employers identified through a match of IRS, SSA, and Medicare records for purposes of the Medicare Secondary Payer provision, health and safety requirements for portable X-ray suppliers, and evaluation of Intermediate Care Facilities for Persons with Mental Retardation — establishing psychoactive drug use baselines).

60 FR 37590, July 21, 1995: Medicare Program; Optional Payment System for Low Medicare Volume Skilled Nursing Facilities — Final rule affecting 42 CFR Part 413.

60 FR 50115, September 28, 1995: Medicare and Medicaid Programs; Survey, Certification and Enforcement of Skilled Nursing Facilities and Nursing Facilities — Final rule and correction to final regulations, affecting 42 CFR Parts 431, 440, 442, 488, 489, and 498.

See also corrections at 60 FR 52731, October 10, 1995, and at 60 FR 534456, October 13, 1995.

60 FR 58088, November 24, 1995: HCFA Public Information Collection Requirements Submitted for Public Comment and Recommendations (pertaining to skilled nursing facility (SNF) and skilled nursing facility health care complex cost reports).

60 FR 62237, December 5, 1995: Medicare Program; Uniform Electronic Cost Reporting for Skilled Nursing Facilities and Home Health Agencies — Proposed rule affecting 42 CFR Part 413.

61 FR 11214, March 19, 1996: HCFA Agency Information Collection Activities: Proposed Collection; Comment Request (pertaining to conditions of coverage for organ procurement organizations; and skilled nursing facility and skilled nursing facility healthcare complex forms).

61 FR 14798, April 3, 1996: HCFA Agency Information Collection Activities: Proposed Collection; Comment Request (pertaining to statistical reports on medical care eligibility, payments and services under Medicaid; State survey agency lists of positions and schedule of equipment purchases; granting and withdrawing of deeming authority to national accreditation organizations; maximizing the effectiveness of home health care; requests for certification in the Medicare or Medicaid program to provide outpatient physical therapy and/or speech pathology services; physical therapists in independent practice; requests for provider approval as a hospital provider of extended care services (swing bed) under Medicare and Medicaid; and requests for designation as an organ procurement organization).

61 FR 17677, April 22, 1996: Medicare and Medicaid Programs; New Payment Methodology for Routine Extended Care Services Provided in a Swing-bed Hospital — Proposed rule affecting 42 CFR Part 413.

61 FR 30623, June 17, 1996: Office of Inspector General Publication of OIG Special Fraud Alert: Fraud and Abuse in the Provision of Services in Nursing Homes — Notice.

61 FR 35231, July 5, 1996: HCFA Agency Information Collection Activities: Proposed Collection; Comment Request (pertaining to Medicaid payment standards for inpatient hospital or long-term care services).

61 FR 38395, July 24, 1996: Medicaid Program; Medicaid Eligibility Quality Control, Progressive Reductions in Federal Financial Participation for FYs 1982–1984, Payment for Physician Billing for

Clinical Laboratory Services, and Utilization Control of Skilled Nursing Facility Services: Removal of Obsolete Requirements — Final rule.

61 FR 46466, September 3, 1996: Medicare Program; Schedule of Prospectively Determined Payment Rates for Skilled Nursing Facility Inpatient Routine Service Costs — Final rule with comment period.

61 FR 51295, October 1, 1996: HCFA Public Information Requirements Submitted for Collection of Public Comment: Submission for OMB Review (pertaining to approval of Medicaid payment rates for inpatient hospital or long term care services).

61 FR 51611, October 3, 1996: Medicare and Medicaid Programs; New Payment Methodology for Routine Extended Care Services Provided in a Swing-bed Hospital — Final Rule affecting 42 CFR Part 413. See also correction at 61 FR 58631, November 18, 1996.

61 FR 54209, October 17, 1996: HCFA Agency Information Collectio Activities: Proposed Collection; Comment request (pertaining to hospital eligibility for swing-bed status).

61 FR 64913, December 9, 1996: HCFA Agency Information Collection Activities: Proposed Collection; Comment request (pertaining to survey report forms for ICF/MRs; and current Medicare beneficiary surveys).

61 FR 68270, December 27, 1996: HCFA Agency Information Collection Activities: Submission for OMB Review; Comment request (pertaining to a facility identification and screening form for hospital providers of extended care services (swing-beds) in the the Medicare and Medicaid programs).

62 FR 26, January 2, 1997: Medicare Program; Electronic Cost Reporting for Skilled Nursing Facilities and Home Health Agencies — Final Rule. See also correction at 62 FR 27210, May 19, 1997.

62 FR 11214, March 11, 1997: HCFA Agency Information Collection Activities: Submission for OMB Review; Comment request (pertaining to intermediate care facility for the mentally retarded or persons with related conditions survey report forms).

62 FR 11458, March 12, 1997: HCFA Agency Information Collection Activities: Proposed Collection; Comment request (pertaining to skilled nursing facility and skilled nursing facility health care complex cost report form).

62 FR 23140, April 29, 1997: Office of Inspector General: Health Care Programs: Fraud and Abuse; Revised PRO Sanctions for Failing to Meet Statutory Obligations — Final rule.

62 FR 30603, June 4, 1997: HCFA Agency Information Collection Activities: Submission for OMB Review; Comment request (pertaining to skilled nursing facility and skilled nursing facility health care complex cost reports; and hospital conditions of participation).

62 FR 33095, June 18, 1997: HCFA Agency Information Collection Activities: Proposed Collection; Comment request (pertaining to skilled nursing facility prospective payment system cost report form).

62 FR 43931, August 18, 1997: Medicare and Medicaid Programs: Effective Dates of Provider Agreements and Supplier Approvals — Final rule affecting 42 CFR Parts 431, 442, 488, 489, and 498.

62 FR 47182, September 8, 1997: Office of Inspector General: Health Care Programs: Fraud and Abuse; Revised OIG Exclusion Authorities Resulting from Public Law 104–191 — Notice of Proposed rulemaking, affecting 42 CFR Parts 1000, 1001, 1002, and 1005.

62 FR 51536, October 1, 1997: Medicare Program; Schedules of Limits and Prospectively Determined Payment Rates for Skilled Nursing Facility Inpatient Routine Service Costs — Final notice with comment period.

62 FR 55410, October 24, 1997: HCFA Agency Information Collection Activities: Submission for OMB Review; Comment request (pertaining to Medicare/Medicaid disclosure of ownership and control forms).

62 FR 55410, October 24, 1997: Office of Inspector General: Criteria for Implementing Permissive Exclusion Authority under Section 1128(b)(7) of the Social Security Act — Notice.

62 FR 48736, October 30, 1997: HCFA Agency Information Collection Activities: Submission for OMB Review; Comment request (pertaining to prospective payment for skilled nursing facilities).

62 FR 67174, December 23, 1997: Medicare and Medicaid; Resident Assessment in Long Term Care Facilities — Final rule affecting 42 CFR Part 483.

62 FR 67392, December 24, 1997: Office of Inspector General: Criteria for Implementing Permissive Exclusion Authority under Section 1128(b)(7) of the Social Security Act — Notice.

63 FR 9844, February 26, 1998: HCFA Agency Information Collection Activities: Proposed Collection; Comment request (pertaining to procedures for advisory opinions concerning physician referrals and supporting regulations in 42 CFR Sections 411.370–411.389).

63 FR 14393, March 25, 1998: Office of Inspector General: Health Care Programs: Fraud and Abuse; Revised OIG Civil Money Penalties Resulting from the Health Insurance Portability and Accountability Act of 1996 — Notice of proposed rulemaking, affecting 42 CFR Parts 1003, 1005, and 1006.

63 FR 14719, March 26, 1998: HCFA Agency Information Collection Activities: Proposed Collection; Comment request (pertaining to physician certification and re-certification in skilled nursing facilities).

63 FR 20415, April 24, 1998: Office of Inspector General: Publication of OIG Special Fraud Alert: Fraud and Abuse in Nursing Home Arrangements with Hospices — Notice.

63 FR 26252, May 12, 1998: Medicare Program: Prospective Payment System and Consolidated Billing for Skilled Nursing Facilities — Final rule, affecting 42 CFR Parts 409, 410, 411, 413, 424, 483, and 489. See also correction at 63 FR 53301, October 5, 1998.

63 FR 28395, May 22, 1998: HCFA Agency Information Collection Activities: Submission for OMB Review; Comment request (pertaining to procedures for advisory opinions concerning physician referrals and supporting regulations in 42 CFR 411.370 through 411.389).

63 FR 28395, May 22, 1998: HCFA Agency Information Collection Activities: Submission for OMB Review; Comment request (pertaining to physician certifications and recertifications in skilled nursing facilities).

63 FR 28396, May 22, 1998: HCFA Privacy Act of 1974 — Notice of New System of Records (pertaining to the long term care minimum data set).

63 FR 46676, September 2, 1998: Office of Inspector General: Health Care Programs; Fraud and Abuse; Revised OIG Exclusion Authorities Resulting from Public Law 104–191 — Final rule affecting 42 CFR Parts 1000, 1001, 1002, and 1005. See also correction at 63 FR 57918, October 29, 1998.

63 FR 46736, September 2, 1998: Office of Inspector General: Health Care Programs; Fraud and Abuse; Revised OIG Sanction Authorities Resulting from Public Law 105–33 — Notice of proposed rulemaking affecting 42 CFR 1001, 1002, and 1003.

63 FR 58399, October 30, 1998: Office of Inspector General: Publication of the OIG's Provider Self-Disclosure Protocol — Notice.

63 FR 60356, November 9, 1998: HCFA Agency Information Collection activities: Proposed Collection; Comment request (pertaining to skilled nursing facility resident assessment MDS data).

63 FR 68223, December 10, 1998: Office of Inspector General; Solicitation of New Safe Harbors and Special Fraud Alerts — Notice of intent to develop regulations, affecting 42 CFR 1001.

63 FR 68687, December 14, 1998: Medicare and Medicaid Program; Civil Money Penalties, Assessments, Exclusions, and Related Appeals Procedures — Final rule with comment period, affecting 42 CFR 400 and 402.

63 FR 70137, December 18, 1998: Office of Inspector General: Solicitation of Information and Recommendations for Developing OIG Compliance Program Guidance for the Nursing Home Industry — Notice.

63 FR 72317, December 31, 1998: HCFA Agency Information Collection Activities: Proposed Collection; Comment request (pertaining to advanced directives under Medicare and Medicaid; and Medicare/Medicaid disclosure of ownership and control interests).

63 FR 72318, December 31, 1998: HCFA Agency Information Collection Activities: Proposed Collection; Comment request (pertaining to fire safety survey report forms for health care facilities).

1999

64 FR 6664, February 10, 1999: HCFA Agency Information Collection Activities: Submission for OMB Review; Comment request (pertaining to skilled nursing facility (SNF) resident assessment MDS data).

64 FR 13354, March 18, 1999: Medicare and Medicaid Programs; Civil Money Penalties for Nursing Homes (SNF/NF), Change in Notice Requirements, and Expansion of Discretionary Remedy Delegation — Final rule with comment period, affecting 42 CFR Part 488.

64 FR 13997, March 23, 1999: HCFA Agency Information Collection Activities: Submission for OMB Review; Comment request (pertaining to Medicare and Medicaid requirements for advanced directives, and disclosure of ownership and financial control interest).

64 FR 17184, April 8, 1999: HCFA Medicare Program; April 23, 1999 Open Town Hall Meeting to Discuss the Skilled Nursing Facility Prospective Payment System (SNF/PPS).

64 FR 39420, July 22, 1999: Office of Inspector General; Health Care Programs; Fraud and Abuse; Revised OIG Sanction Authorities Resulting from P.L. 105–33, the Balanced Budget Act of 1997 — Final rule affecting 42 CFR Parts 1001, 1002, and 1003. See also correction at 64 FR 42174, August 3, 1999.

64 FR 39517, July 22, 1999: HCFA Agency Information Collection Activities: Submission for OMB Review; Comment request (pertaining to Medicare participating physician or supplier agreement form HCFA-460).

64 FR 39934, July 23, 1999: Medicare and Medicaid Program; Appeal of the Loss of Nurse Aide Training Programs — Interim final rule with comment period, affecting 42 CFR Parts 431 and 498. See also correction at 64 FR 43295, August 10, 1999.

64 FR 41644, July 30, 1999: Medicare Program; Prospective Payment System and Consolidated Billing for Skilled Nursing Facilities — Final rule affecting 42 CFR Parts 409, 411, 413, and 489. See also correction at 64 FR 60122, November 4, 1999.

64 FR 41684, July 30, 1999: Medicare Program; Prospective Payment System and Consolidated Billing for Skilled Nursing Facilities — Update — Notice. See also correction at 64 FR 54030, October 5, 1999.

64 FR 42610, August 5, 1999: Medicare Program; Revision of the Procedures for Requesting Exceptions to Cost Limits for Skilled Nursing Facilities and Elimination of Reclassifications — Final rule.

64 FR 42791, September 30, 1999: Office of Inspector General; Publication of the OIG Special Advisory Bulletin on the Effect of Exclusion from Participation in Federal Health Care Programs — Notice. See also correction at 64 FR 55484, October 13, 1999.

64 FR 54263, October 6, 1999: Medicaid Program; Flexibility in Payment Methods for Services of Hospitals, Nursing Facilities, and Intermediate Care Facilities for the Mentally Retarded — Proposed rule affecting 42 CFR Part 447.

64 FR 55949, October 15, 1999: HCFA Agency Information Collection Activities: Proposed Collection; Comment request (pertaining to physician certifications and re-certifications about the necessity for skilled nursing facility care).

64 FR 58419, October 29, 1999: Office of Inspector General; Draft OIG Compliance Program Guidance for Nursing Facilities — Notice and comment period.

64 FR 63518, November 19, 1999: Office of Inspector General; Fraud and Abuse; Clarification of the Initial OIG Safe Harbor Provisions and Establishment of Additional Safe Harbor Provisions under the Anti-kickback Statute — Final rule affecting 42 CFR Part 1001.

64 FR 66482, November 26, 1999: HCFA Agency Information Collection Activities: Proposed Collection; Comment request (pertaining to resident assessment in skilled nursing facilities).

64 FR 67028, November 30, 1999: Medicare and Medicaid Programs; Religious Nonmedical Health Care Institutions and Advance Directives — Interim final rule with comment period, affecting 42 CFR Parts 403, 412, 431, 440, 442, 446, 456, 488, and 489.

64 FR 69217, December 10, 1999: Office of Inspector General; Solicitation of New Safe Harbors and Special Fraud Alerts — Intent to develop regulations affecting 42 CFR Part 1001.

64 FR 69271, December 10, 1999: HCFA Agency Information Collection Activities: Proposed Collection; Comment request (pertaining to hospital providers of extender care (swing bed) services in Medicare and Medicaid).

2000

65 FR 2186, January 13, 2000: HCFA Agency Information Collection Activities; Submission for OMB Review; Comment request (pertaining to physician certifications/re-certifications in skilled nursing facilities).

65 FR 12560, March 9, 2000: HCFA Agency Information Collection Activities: Submission for OMB Review; Comment request (pertaining to hospital provider of extended care services (swing beds) in the Medicare and Medicaid programs).

65 FR 14289, March 16, 2000: Office of Inspector General: Publication of the OIG Compliance Program Guidance for Nursing Facilities — Notice.

65 FR 14986, March 20, 2000: HCFA Agency Information Collection Activities: Submission for OMB Review; Comment request (pertaining to skilled nursing facility resident assessment MDS data).

65 FR 19187, April 10, 2000: Medicare Program; Prospective Payment System and Consolidated Billing for Skilled Nursing Facilities; Update--Proposed rule affecting 42 CFR Parts 411 and 489.

65 FR 24400, April 26, 2000: Office of Inspector General; Health Care Programs: Fraud and Abuse; Revised OIG Civil Money Penalties Resulting from Public Law 104-191 (HIPAA) — Final rule

affecting 42 CFR Parts 1001, 1003, 1005, and 1006. See also correction at 65 FR 35583, June 5, 2000.

65 FR 54856, September 11, 2000: HCFA Agency Information Collection Activities: Submission for OMB Review; Comment request (pertaining to skilled nursing facility cost reports).

65 FR 54857, September 11, 2000: HCFA Agency Information Collection Activities: Submission for OMB Review; Comment request (pertaining to ICF/MR survey report forms).

65 FR 60151, October 10, 2000: Medicaid Program; Revision to Medicaid Upper Payment Limit Requirements for Hospital Services, Nursing Facility Services, Intermediate Care Facility Services for the Mentally Retarded, and Clinic Services-Proposed rule affecting 42 CFR Part 447.

65 FR 64227, October 26, 2000: HCFA Agency Information Collection Activities: Proposed Collection; Comment request (pertaining to home health agency cost reports; skilled nursing facility cost reports; and hospital cost reports).

2001

66 FR 856, January 4, 2001: Medicare and Medicaid Programs; Physicians Referrals to Health Care Entities with which They Have Financial Relationships—Final rule with comment period, affecting 42 CFR Parts 411 and 424.

66 FR 3148, January 12, 2001: Medicaid Program; Revision to Medicaid Upper Payment Limit Requirements for Hospital Services, Nursing Facility Services, Intermediate Care Facility Services for the Mentally Retarded, and Clinic Services—Final rule affecting 42 CFR Part 447.

66 FR 3497, January 16, 2001: Medicare Program; Prospective Payment System and Consolidated Billing for Skilled Nursing Facilities—Update; Correction notice affecting 42 FR Parts 411, 313, and 489. See FR Doc. 00–19004, July 31, 2000.

66 FR 6629, January 22, 2001: HCFA Agency Information Collection Activities: Submission for OMB Review; Comment request (pertaining to Medicare Integrity Program Organizational Conflict of Interest Disclosure Certificate).

66 FR 8771, February 2, 2001: Medicare and Medicaid Programs; Physicians' Referrals to Health Care Entities with which They Have Financial Relationships: Delay of Effective Date of Final Rule and Technical Amendment, affecting 42 CFR Parts 411 and 424.

66 FR 16062, March 23, 2001: HCFA Agency Information Collection Activities: Submission for OMB Review; Comment request (pertaining to SNF cost report forms).

66 FR 17657, April 3, 2001: Medicaid Program; Modification of the Medicaid Upper Payment Limit Transition Period for Inpatient Hospital Services, Outpatient Hospital Services, Nursing Facility Services, Intermediate Care Facility Services for the Mentally Retarded and Clinic Services—Proposed rule affecting 42 CFR Part 447.

66 FR 17813, April 4, 2001: Medicare and Medicaid Programs; Physicians' Referrals to Health Care Entities with which They Have Financial Relationships; Extension of Comment period—Notice, affecting 42 CFR Parts 411 and 424.

66 FR 19507, April 16, 2001: HCFA Agency Information Collection Activities: Proposed Collection; Comment request (pertaining to conflict of interest and ownership and control information form).

66 FR 27151, May 16, 2001: HCFA Agency Information Collection Activities: Proposed Collection; Comment request (pertaining to the Long Term Care Awareness Project).

66 FR 28916, May 25, 2001: HCFA Agency Information Collection Activities; Proposed Collection; Comment request (pertaining to procedures for advisory opinions concerning physician referrals under section 1877 of the Social Security Act).

66 FR 31245, June 11, 2001: Office of Inspector General; Healthcare Integrity and Protection Data Bank: Change in User Fees—Notice.

See § 3:17.

§ 7:18 FAILURE BY INTERMEDIATE CARE FACILITIES FOR THE MENTALLY RETARDED TO MEET FEDERAL STANDARDS — Section 1922 [42 U.S.C.A. 1396r-3]

Regulations

42 CFR Part 440 — Services: General Provisions

42 CFR Part 441 — Services: Requirements and Limits Applicable to Specific Services

42 CFR Part 442 — Standards for Payment for Nursing Facilities and Intermediate Care Facilities for the Mentally Retarded

42 CFR Part 447 — Payment for Services

42 CFR Part 483, Subpart I — Conditions of Participation for Intermediate Care Facilities for the Mentally Retarded

56 FR 30696, July 5, 1991: Medicaid Program; Correction and Reduction Plans for Intermediate Care Facilities for the Mentally Retarded — Final rule affecting 42 CFR Part 442. See also correction at 56 FR 49147, September 27, 1991.

57 FR 43462, September 21, 1992: Health Care Financing Administration Public Information Collection Requirements Submitted to the Office of Management and Budget for Clearance (pertaining to sole community home health agencies; physician/supplier overpayment reports; physician or supplier Medicare agreements; conditions of participation for rural health clinics; Medicare provider refunds; conditions of participation for comprehensive outpatient rehabilitation facilities; Medicaid income and eligibility verification system; Medicaid integrated review schedule; provider overpayment report; financial statement of Medicare provider debtors; negative case action review schedule for Medicaid quality control; outpatient resource costing study; Medicaid intermediate care facility for the mentally retarded or persons with related conditions survey report form; installment agreement of beneficiary refund of overpayment; PRO assumption of responsibilities; Medicare contractor administrative budget and cost reporting system forms; fire safety survey report forms; medical records review under prospective payment system; and Qualified Medicare Beneficiary supplement to the Medicare current beneficiary survey).

57 FR 54710, November 20, 1992: Medicaid Program; Elimination of Certain Written Documentation Pertaining to Medicaid Long-Term Care Facilities — Final rule affecting 42 CFR Part 442.

58 FR 46198, September 1, 1993: HCFA Public Information Collection Requirements (ICR) Submitted to the Office of Management and Budget (OMB) for Clearance (pertaining to prenatal services and assistance screening; home health agency treatment forms; conditions of participation for intermediate care facilities for the mentally retarded; State Medicaid eligibility quality control sample selection lists; prepaid health plan cost report; hospital survey report form; procedures for determining whether providers, practitioners, or other suppliers of services are liable for certain noncovered services; Medicare credit balance reporting requirements; Medicare provider cost report questionnaire form; Medicare current beneficiary survey rounds 7–10; sterilization regulation/consent form; PRO reconsideration and appeals information requirements; information collection requirements in HSQ-110, acquisition, protection and disclosure of PRO information; Medi-

care/Medicaid organ procurement organization's (OPO) request for certification) — Notice.

60 FR 37066, July 19, 1995: HCFA Public Information Collection Requirements Submitted to the Office of Management and Budget (OMB) for Clearance (pertaining to actuarial forecasts for Medicaid utilization and cost, employers identified through a match of IRS, SSA, and Medicare records for purposes of the Medicare Secondary Payer provision, health and safety requirements for portable X-ray suppliers, and evaluation of Intermediate Care Facilities for Persons with Mental Retardation — establishing psychoactive drug use baselines).

62 FR 11214, March 11, 1997: HCFA Agency Information Collection Activities: Submission for OMB Review; Comment request (pertaining to intermediate care facility for the mentally retarded or persons with related conditions survey report forms).

64 FR 54263, October 6, 1999: Medicaid Program; Flexibility in Payment Methods for Services of Hospitals, Nursing Facilities, and Intermediate Care Facilities for the Mentally Retarded — Proposed rule affecting 42 CFR Part 447.

2000

65 FR 35653, June 5, 2000: HCFA Agency Information Collection Activities: Proposed Collection; Comment request (pertaining to ICF/MR survey forms).

65 FR 54857, September 11, 2000: HCFA Agency Information Collection Activities: Submission for OMB Review; Comment request (pertaining to ICF/MR survey report forms).

65 FR 60151, October 10, 2000: Medicaid Program; Revision to Medicaid Upper Payment Limit Requirements for Hospital Services, Nursing Facility Services, Intermediate Care Facility Services for the Mentally Retarded, and Clinic Services-Proposed rule affecting 42 CFR Part 447.

2001

66 FR 3148, January 12, 2001: Medicaid Program; Revision to Medicaid Upper Payment Limit Requirements for Hospital Services, Nursing Facility Services, Intermediate Care Facility Services for the Mentally Retarded, and Clinic Services—Final rule affecting 42 CFR Part 447.

66 FR 17657, April 3, 2001: Medicaid Program; Modification of the Medicaid Upper Payment Limit Transition Period for Inpatient Hos-

pital Services, Outpatient Hospital Services, Nursing Facility Services, Intermediate Care Facility Services for the Mentally Retarded and Clinic Services—Proposed rule affecting 42 CFR Part 447.

See § 3:18.

§ 7:19 FAILURE BY DRUG MANUFACTURERS AND WHOLESALERS TO COMPLY WITH MEDICAID DRUG REBATE REQUIREMENTS — Section 1927 [42 U.S.C.A. 1396s]

Regulations

42 CFR Part 402 — Civil Money Penalties, Assessments, and Exclusions

42 CFR Part 440 — Services: General Provisions

42 CFR Part 441 — Services: Requirements and Limits Applicable to Specific Services

42 CFR Part 455 — Program Integrity: Medicaid

42 CFR Chapter V — Office of Inspector General — Health Care, Department of Health and Human Services

Subchapter A — General Provisions

Part 1000 — Introduction; General Definitions

Subchapter B — OIG Authorities

Part 1002 — Program Integrity: State-initiated Exclusion from Medicaid

Part 1003 — Civil Money Penalties, Assessments and Exclusions

Part 1005 — Appeals of Exclusions, Civil Money Penalties and Assessments

Part 1006 — Investigational Inquiries

Part 1007 — State Medicaid Fraud Control Units

Part 1008 — Advisory Opinions by the OIG

59 FR 48811, September 23, 1994: Medicaid Program; Drug Use Review Program and Electronic Claims Management System for Outpatient Drug Claims — Final rule affecting 42 CFR Part 456.

59 FR 65372, December 19, 1994: Office of Inspector General — Notice of Publication of Special Fraud Alerts (pertaining to joint venture arrangements, routine waiver of Medicare Part B copayments and deductibles, hospital incentives to referring physicians, prescription drug marketing practices, and arrangements for provision of clinical laboratory services).

60 FR 48442, September 19, 1995: Medicaid Program; Payment for Covered Outpatient Drugs under Drug Rebate Agreements with Manufacturers — Proposed rule affecting 42 CFR Parts 441 and 447.

60 FR 64167, December 14, 1995: HCFA Public Information Collection Requirements Submitted for Public Comment and Recommendations (pertaining to Medicaid drug rebates).

61 FR 13508, March 27, 1996: HCFA Proposed Collection of Public Comment; Submission for OMB Review (pertaining to reconciliation of State invoices for the Medicaid drug rebate program).

62 FR 17197, April 9, 1997: HCFA Agency Information Collection Activities: Proposed Collection; Comment request (pertaining to the Medicaid drug rebate program).

62 FR 32890, June 23, 1997: HCFA Submitted for Collection of Public comment: Submission for OMB review (pertaining to Medicaid drug rebate program).

62 FR 49696, September 23, 1997: HCFA Agency Information Collection Activities: Proposed Collection; Comment request (pertaining to Medicaid drug rebate program).

63 FR 1114, January 8, 1998: HCFA Agency Information Collection Activities: Submission for OMB Review; Comment request (pertaining to improved data exchange between States and drug labelers).

63 FR 56656, October 22, 1998: HCFA Agency Information Collection Activities: Submission for OMB Review; Comment request (pertaining to drug utilization review for Medicaid).

2000

65 FR 12556, March 9, 2000: HCFA Agency Information Collection Activities: Proposed Collection; Comment request (pertaining to Medicaid drug rebate).

65 FR 40669, June 30, 2000: HCFA Agency Information Collection Activities: Submission for OMB Review; Comment request (pertaining to Medicaid drug rebate program).

65 FR 64226, October 26, 2000: HCFA Agency Information Collection Activities: Proposed Collection; Comment request (pertaining to reconciliation of State invoices for drug rebate agreements).

2001

66 FR 6629, January 22, 2001: HCFA Agency Information Collection Activities: Submission for OMB Review; Comment request (pertaining to Medicaid drug rebate program).

See § 3:19.

§ 7:20 GIVING ADVANCE NOTICE OF A SURVEY TO A COMMUNITY CARE SETTING FOR FUNCTIONALLY DISABLED ELDERLY INDIVIDUALS — Section 1929(i)(3)(A) [42 U.S.C.A. 1396u(i)(3)(A)]

Regulations

42 CFR Part 440 — Services: General Provisions (Medicaid)

42 CFR Part 441 — Services: Requirements and Limits Applicable to Specific Services (Medicaid)

42 CFR Part 455 — Program Integrity: Medicaid

42 CFR Chapter V — Office of Inspector General — Health Care, Department of Health and Human Services

Subchapter A — General Provisions

Part 1000 — Introduction; General Definitions

Subchapter B — OIG Authorities

Part 1002 — Program Integrity: State-initiated Exclusion from Medicaid

Part 1003 — Civil Money Penalties, Assessments and Exclusions

Part 1005 — Appeals of Exclusions, Civil Money Penalties and Assessments

Part 1006 — Investigational Inquiries

Part 1007 — State Medicaid Fraud Control Units

Part 1008 — Advisory Opinions by the OIG

56 FR 31647, July 11, 1991: Public Information Collection Requirements Submitted to the Office of Management and Budget for Clearance (re community supported living arrangements, and physician financial interest in clinical laboratories survey) — Notice.

56 FR 48112, September 24, 1991: Medicaid Program; Community Supported Living Arrangements Services — Interim final rule with comment period, affecting 42 CFR Part 441.

57 FR 22773, May 29, 1992: Medicare Program; Recognition of Community Health Accreditation Program Standards for Home Care Organizations — Final notice.

57 FR 29142, June 30, 1992: Medicaid Program; Home and Community-Based Services Waivers for Individuals Age 65 or Older — Interim final rule with comment period, affecting 42 CFR Parts 400, 435, 436, 440, and 441.

58 FR 47904, September 13, 1993: HCFA, Public Information Collection Requirements (ICR) Submitted to the Office of Management and Budget (OMB) for Clearance (pertaining to chronic renal disease medical evidence report; Medicare common claims form; Social Security Office report of State buy-in problem; Medicare physician survey form; beneficiary survey form; Medicaid payment rate changes for inpatient hospital or long term care services; home and community-based services: waiver requirements; Medicare peer review organizations reporting forms; uniform institutional provider claim form) — Notice.

59 FR 52178, October 14, 1994: HCFA Public Information Collection Requirements Submitted to the Office of Management and Budget (OMB) for Clearance (pertaining to Medicare reimbursement for outpatient services, cost reports for free-standing skilled nursing facilities; Medicare coverage criteria for adult heart transplants, drug rebates for Medicaid, optional prospective payment cost report for certain skilled nursing facilities, reimbursable costs for organ procurement agencies, distribution and use of end stage renal disease treatment sources, conditions of coverage for ambulatory surgical centers, and waivers for home and community based services).

60 FR 6714, February 3, 1995: HCFA Public Information Collection Requirements Submitted to the Office of Management and Budget (OMB) for Clearance (pertaining to criteria for Medicare coverage of lung transplants, evaluation of drug use review demonstrations projects, and evaluation of the community supported living arrangements program).

60 FR 45487, August 31, 1995: HCFA Public Information Collection Requirements Submitted to the Office of Management and Budget (OMB) for Clearance (pertaining to the annual report on home and community-based waivers).

60 FR 64068, December 13, 1995: HCFA Public Information Collection Requirements Submitted for Public Comment and Recommendations (pertaining to annual reports on home and community-based services waivers).

61 FR 10586, March 14, 1996: HCFA Submitted for Collection of Public Comment: Submission for OMB Review (pertaining to home

and community-based services waiver requests; and income and eligibility verification system information collection requirements).

61 FR 58567, November 15, 1996: HCFA Agency Information Collection Activities: Proposed Collection; Comment request (pertaining to home and community based waiver requests).

62 FR 3514, January 23, 1997: Submitted for Collection of Public Comment: Submission for OMB Review (pertaining to home and community-based services waiver requests).

62 FR 63953, December 3, 1997: HCFA Agency Information Collection Activities: Proposed Collection Comment request (pertaining to annual report form for home and community based services waivers).

63 FR 9845, February 26, 1998: HCFA Agency Information Collection Activities: Submission for OMB Review; Comment request (pertaining to annual report on home and community based services waivers).

63 FR 44629, August 20, 1998: HCFA Agency Information Collection Activities: Proposed Collection; Comment request (pertaining to home and community-based services waiver requests).

1999

64 FR 4435, January 28, 1999: HCFA Agency Information Collection Activities; Submission for OMB Review; Comment request (pertaining to home and community-based services waiver requests).

2000

65 FR 66255, November 3, 2000: HCFA Agency Information Collection Activities: Proposed Collection; Comment request (pertaining to survey of Medicaid home and community-based services waiver and personal care option recipients).

2001

66 FR 14906, March 14, 2001: HCFA Agency Information Collection Activities: Proposed Collection; Comment request (pertaining to annual report on home and community based services waivers).

66 FR 16268, March 23, 2001: HCFA Agency Information Collection Activities: Submission for OMB Review; Comment request (pertaining to survey of home and community–based services waiv-

ers and personal care option recipients for the multi–site study of Medicaid home and community–based services).

66 FR 19508, April 16, 2001: HCFA Agency Information Collection Activities: Proposed Collection; Comment request (pertaining to real choice systems change grants, nursing facility transition/access housing grants, community personal assistance service and supports grants, national technical assistance and learning collaborative grants to support systems change for community living).

66 FR 20314, April 20, 2001: HCFA Agency Information Collection Activities: Proposed Collection; Comment request (pertaining to survey of Medicaid home and community–based services waiver and personal care option recipients).

See § 3:20.

§ 7:21 NEGLECT AND ABUSE AND MISAPPROPRIATION OF PROPERTY OF INDIVIDUALS IN HOME AND COMMUNITY CARE SETTINGS FOR FUNCTIONALLY DISABLED ELDERLY INDIVIDUALS — Section 1929(i)(5) [42 U.S.C.A. 1396u(i)(5)]

Regulations

42 CFR Part 440 — Services: General Provisions (Medicaid)

42 CFR Part 441 — Services: Requirements and Limits Applicable to Specific Services (Medicaid)

42 CFR Part 455 — Program Integrity: Medicaid

42 CFR Chapter V — Office of Inspector General — Health Care, Department of Health and Human Services

Subchapter A — General Provisions

Part 1000 — Introduction; General Definitions

Subchapter B — OIG Authorities

Part 1002 — Program Integrity: State-initiated Exclusion from Medicaid

Part 1003 — Civil Money Penalties, Assessments and Exclusions

Part 1005 — Appeals of Exclusions, Civil Money Penalties and Assessments

Part 1006 — Investigational Inquiries

Part 1007 — State Medicaid Fraud Control Units

Part 1008 — Advisory Opinions by the OIG

56 FR 31647, July 11, 1991: Public Information Collection Requirements Submitted to the Office of Management and Budget for Clearance (re community supported living arrangements, and

physician financial interest in clinical laboratories survey) — Notice.

56 FR 48112, September 24, 1991: Medicaid Program; Community Supported Living Arrangements Services — Interim final rule with comment period, affecting 42 CFR Part 441.

57 FR 22773, May 29, 1992: Medicare Program; Recognition of Community Health Accreditation Program Standards for Home Care Organizations — Final notice.

57 FR 29142, June 30, 1992: Medicaid Program; Home and Community-Based Services Waivers for Individuals Age 65 or Older — Interim final rule with comment period, affecting 42 CFR Parts 400, 435, 436, 440, and 441.

58 FR 47904, September 13, 1993: HCFA, Public Information Collection Requirements (ICR) Submitted to the Office of Management and Budget (OMB) for Clearance (pertaining to chronic renal disease medical evidence report; Medicare common claims form; Social Security Office report of State buy-in problem; Medicare physician survey form; beneficiary survey form; Medicaid payment rate changes for inpatient hospital or long term care services; home and community-based services: waiver requirements; Medicare peer review organizations reporting forms; uniform institutional provider claim form) — Notice.

59 FR 52178, October 14, 1994: HCFA Public Information Collection Requirements Submitted to the Office of Management and Budget (OMB) for Clearance (pertaining to Medicare reimbursement for outpatient services, cost reports for free-standing skilled nursing facilities; Medicare coverage criteria for adult heart transplants, drug rebates for Medicaid, optional prospective payment cost report for certain skilled nursing facilities, reimbursable costs for organ procurement agencies, distribution and use of end stage renal disease treatment sources, conditions of coverage for ambulatory surgical centers, and waivers for home and community based services).

60 FR 6714, February 3, 1995: HCFA Public Information Collection Requirements Submitted to the Office of Management and Budget (OMB) for Clearance (pertaining to criteria for Medicare coverage of lung transplants, evaluation of drug use review demonstrations projects, and evaluation of the community supported living arrangements program).

60 FR 45487, August 31, 1995: HCFA Public Information Collection Requirements Submitted to the Office of Management and

Budget (OMB) for Clearance (pertaining to the annual report on home and community-based waivers).

60 FR 64068, December 13, 1995: HCFA Public Information Collection Requirements Submitted for Public Comment and Recommendations (pertaining to annual reports on home and community-based services waivers).

61 FR 10586, March 14, 1996: HCFA Submitted for Collection of Public Comment: Submission for OMB Review (pertaining to home and community-based services waiver requests; and income and eligibility verification system information collection requirements).

61 FR 58567, November 15, 1996: HCFA Agency Information Collection Activities: Proposed Collection; Comment request (pertaining to home and community based waiver requests).

62 FR 3514, January 23, 1997: Submitted for Collection of Public Comment: Submission for OMB Review (pertaining to home and community-based services waiver requests).

62 FR 63953, December 3, 1997: HCFA Agency Information Collection Activities: Proposed Collection Comment request (pertaining to annual report form for home and community based services waivers).

63 FR 9845, February 26, 1998: HCFA Agency Information Collection Activities: Submission for OMB Review; Comment request (pertaining to annual report on home and community based services waivers).

63 FR 44629, August 20, 1998: HCFA Agency Information Collection Activities: Proposed Collection; Comment request (pertaining to home and community-based services waiver requests).

1999

64 FR 4435, January 28, 1999: HCFA Agency Information Collection Activities; Submission for OMB Review; Comment request (pertaining to home and community-based services waiver requests).

2000

65 FR 66255, November 3, 2000: HCFA Agency Information Collection Activities: Proposed Collection; Comment request (pertaining to survey of Medicaid home and community-based services waiver and personal care option recipients).

2001

66 FR 14906, March 14, 2001: HCFA Agency Information Collection Activities: Proposed Collection; Comment request (pertaining to annual report on home and community based services waivers).

66 FR 16268, March 23, 2001: HCFA Agency Information Collection Activities: Submission for OMB Review; Comment request (pertaining to survey of home and community–based services waivers and personal care option recipients for the multi–site study of Medicaid home and community–based services).

66 FR 19508, April 16, 2001: HCFA Agency Information Collection Activities: Proposed Collection; Comment request (pertaining to real choice systems change grants, nursing facility transition/access housing grants, community personal assistance service and supports grants, national technical assistance and learning collaborative grants to support systems change for community living).

66 FR 20314, April 20, 2001: HCFA Agency Information Collection Activities: Proposed Collection; Comment request (pertaining to survey of Medicaid home and community–based services waiver and personal care option recipients).

See § 3:21.

§ 7:22 DISCLOSURE OF INSPECTION REPORTS AND ACTIVITIES RELATED TO HOME AND COMMUNITY CARE SETTINGS FOR FUNCTIONALLY DISABLED ELDERLY INDIVIDUALS — Section 1929(i)(6) [42 U.S.C.A. 1396u(i)(6)]

Regulations

42 CFR Part 440 — Services: General Provisions (Medicaid)

42 CFR Part 441 — Services: Requirements and Limits Applicable to Specific Services (Medicaid)

42 CFR Part 455 — Program Integrity: Medicaid

42 CFR Chapter V — Office of Inspector General — Health Care, Department of Health and Human Services

Subchapter A — General Provisions

Part 1000 — Introduction; General Definitions

Subchapter B — OIG Authorities

Part 1002 — Program Integrity: State-initiated Exclusion from Medicaid

Part 1003 — Civil Money Penalties, Assessments and Exclusions

Part 1005 — Appeals of Exclusions, Civil Money Penalties and Assessments

Part 1006 — Investigational Inquiries

Part 1007 — State Medicaid Fraud Control Units

Part 1008 — Advisory Opinions by the OIG

56 FR 31647, July 11, 1991: Public Information Collection Requirements Submitted to the Office of Management and Budget for Clearance (re community supported living arrangements, and physician financial interest in clinical laboratories survey) — Notice.

56 FR 48112, September 24, 1991: Medicaid Program; Community Supported Living Arrangements Services — Interim final rule with comment period, affecting 42 CFR Part 441.

57 FR 22773, May 29, 1992: Medicare Program; Recognition of Community Health Accreditation Program Standards for Home Care Organizations — Final notice.

57 FR 29142, June 30, 1992: Medicaid Program; Home and Community-Based Services Waivers for Individuals Age 65 or Older — Interim final rule with comment period, affecting 42 CFR Parts 400, 435, 436, 440, and 441.

58 FR 47904, September 13, 1993: HCFA, Public Information Collection Requirements (ICR) Submitted to the Office of Management and Budget (OMB) for Clearance (pertaining to chronic renal disease medical evidence report; Medicare common claims form; Social Security Office report of State buy-in problem; Medicare physician survey form; beneficiary survey form; Medicaid payment rate changes for inpatient hospital or long term care services; home and community-based services: waiver requirements; Medicare peer review organizations reporting forms; uniform institutional provider claim form) — Notice.

59 FR 52178, October 14, 1994: HCFA Public Information Collection Requirements Submitted to the Office of Management and Budget (OMB) for Clearance (pertaining to Medicare reimbursement for outpatient services, cost reports for free-standing skilled nursing facilities; Medicare coverage criteria for adult heart transplants, drug rebates for Medicaid, optional prospective payment cost report for certain skilled nursing facilities, reimbursable costs for organ procurement agencies, distribution and use of end stage renal disease treatment sources, conditions of coverage for ambulatory surgical centers, and waivers for home and community based services).

60 FR 6714, February 3, 1995: HCFA Public Information Collection Requirements Submitted to the Office of Management and Budget (OMB) for Clearance (pertaining to criteria for Medicare coverage of lung transplants, evaluation of drug use review demonstrations projects, and evaluation of the community supported living arrangements program).

60 FR 45487, August 31, 1995: HCFA Public Information Collection Requirements Submitted to the Office of Management and Budget (OMB) for Clearance (pertaining to the annual report on home and community-based waivers).

60 FR 64068, December 13, 1995: HCFA Public Information Collection Requirements Submitted for Public Comment and Recommendations (pertaining to annual reports on home and community-based services waivers).

61 FR 10586, March 14, 1996: HCFA Submitted for Collection of Public Comment: Submission for OMB Review (pertaining to home and community-based services waiver requests; and income and eligibility verification system information collection requirements).

61 FR 58567, November 15, 1996: HCFA Agency Information Collection Activities: Proposed Collection; Comment request (pertaining to home and community based waiver requests).

62 FR 3514, January 23, 1997: Submitted for Collection of Public Comment: Submission for OMB Review (pertaining to home and community-based services waiver requests).

62 FR 63953, December 3, 1997: HCFA Agency Information Collection Activities: Proposed Collection Comment request (pertaining to annual report form for home and community based services waivers).

63 FR 9845, February 26, 1998: HCFA Agency Information Collection Activities: Submission for OMB Review; Comment request (pertaining to annual report on home and community based services waivers).

63 FR 44629, August 20, 1998: HCFA Agency Information Collection Activities: Proposed Collection; Comment request (pertaining to home and community-based services waiver requests).

1999

64 FR 4435, January 28, 1999: HCFA Agency Information Collection Activities; Submission for OMB Review; Comment request

(pertaining to home and community-based services waiver requests).

2000

65 FR 66255, November 3, 2000: HCFA Agency Information Collection Activities: Proposed Collection; Comment request (pertaining to survey of Medicaid home and community-based services waiver and personal care option recipients).

2001

66 FR 14906, March 14, 2001: HCFA Agency Information Collection Activities: Proposed Collection; Comment request (pertaining to annual report on home and community based services waivers).

66 FR 16268, March 23, 2001: HCFA Agency Information Collection Activities: Submission for OMB Review; Comment request (pertaining to survey of home and community–based services waivers and personal care option recipients for the multi–site study of Medicaid home and community–based services).

66 FR 19508, April 16, 2001: HCFA Agency Information Collection Activities: Proposed Collection; Comment request (pertaining to real choice systems change grants, nursing facility transition/access housing grants, community personal assistance service and supports grants, national technical assistance and learning collaborative grants to support systems change for community living).

66 FR 20314, April 20, 2001: HCFA Agency Information Collection Activities: Proposed Collection; Comment request (pertaining to survey of Medicaid home and community–based services waiver and personal care option recipients).

See § 3:22.

§ 7:23 FAILURE BY HOME AND COMMUNITY CARE SETTINGS FOR FUNCTIONALLY DISABLED ELDERLY INDIVIDUALS TO COMPLY WITH MEDICAID REQUIREMENTS — Section 1929(j) [42 U.S.C.A. 1396u(j)]

Regulations

42 CFR Part 440 — Services: General Provisions (Medicaid)

42 CFR Part 441 — Services: Requirements and Limits Applicable to Specific Services (Medicaid)

42 CFR Part 455 — Program Integrity: Medicaid

42 CFR Chapter V — Office of Inspector General — Health Care, Department of Health and Human Services

Subchapter A — General Provisions

Part 1000 — Introduction; General Definitions

Subchapter B — OIG Authorities

Part 1002 — Program Integrity: State-initiated Exclusion from Medicaid

Part 1003 — Civil Money Penalties, Assessments and Exclusions

Part 1005 — Appeals of Exclusions, Civil Money Penalties and Assessments

Part 1006 — Investigational Inquiries

Part 1007 — State Medicaid Fraud Control Units

Part 1008 — Advisory Opinions by the OIG

56 FR 31647, July 11, 1991: Public Information Collection Requirements Submitted to the Office of Management and Budget for Clearance (re community supported living arrangements, and physician financial interest in clinical laboratories survey) — Notice.

56 FR 48112, September 24, 1991: Medicaid Program; Community Supported Living Arrangements Services — Interim final rule with comment period, affecting 42 CFR Part 441.

57 FR 22773, May 29, 1992: Medicare Program; Recognition of Community Health Accreditation Program Standards for Home Care Organizations — Final notice.

57 FR 29142, June 30, 1992: Medicaid Program; Home and Community-Based Services Waivers for Individuals Age 65 or Older — Interim final rule with comment period, affecting 42 CFR Parts 400, 435, 436, 440, and 441.

58 FR 47904, September 13, 1993: HCFA, Public Information Collection Requirements (ICR) Submitted to the Office of Management and Budget (OMB) for Clearance (pertaining to chronic renal disease medical evidence report; Medicare common claims form; Social Security Office report of State buy-in problem; Medicare physician survey form; beneficiary survey form; Medicaid payment rate changes for inpatient hospital or long term care services; home and community-based services: waiver requirements; Medicare peer review organizations reporting forms; uniform institutional provider claim form) — Notice.

59 FR 52178, October 14, 1994: HCFA Public Information Collection Requirements Submitted to the Office of Management and Budget (OMB) for Clearance (pertaining to Medicare reimburse-

ment for outpatient services, cost reports for free-standing skilled nursing facilities; Medicare coverage criteria for adult heart transplants, drug rebates for Medicaid, optional prospective payment cost report for certain skilled nursing facilities, reimbursable costs for organ procurement agencies, distribution and use of end stage renal disease treatment sources, conditions of coverage for ambulatory surgical centers, and waivers for home and community based services).

60 FR 6714, February 3, 1995: HCFA Public Information Collection Requirements Submitted to the Office of Management and Budget (OMB) for Clearance (pertaining to criteria for Medicare coverage of lung transplants, evaluation of drug use review demonstrations projects, and evaluation of the community supported living arrangements program).

60 FR 45487, August 31, 1995: HCFA Public Information Collection Requirements Submitted to the Office of Management and Budget (OMB) for Clearance (pertaining to the annual report on home and community-based waivers).

60 FR 64068, December 13, 1995: HCFA Public Information Collection Requirements Submitted for Public Comment and Recommendations (pertaining to annual reports on home and community-based services waivers).

61 FR 10586, March 14, 1996: HCFA Submitted for Collection of Public Comment: Submission for OMB Review (pertaining to home and community-based services waiver requests; and income and eligibility verification system information collection requirements).

61 FR 58567, November 15, 1996: HCFA Agency Information Collection Activities: Proposed Collection; Comment request (pertaining to home and community based waiver requests).

62 FR 3514, January 23, 1997: Submitted for Collection of Public Comment: Submission for OMB Review (pertaining to home and community-based services waiver requests).

62 FR 63953, December 3, 1997: HCFA Agency Information Collection Activities: Proposed Collection Comment request (pertaining to annual report form for home and community based services waivers).

63 FR 9845, February 26, 1998: HCFA Agency Information Collection Activities: Submission for OMB Review; Comment request (pertaining to annual report on home and community based services waivers).

63 FR 44629, August 20, 1998: HCFA Agency Information Collection Activities: Proposed Collection; Comment request (pertaining to home and community-based services waiver requests).

1999

64 FR 4435, January 28, 1999: HCFA Agency Information Collection Activities; Submission for OMB Review; Comment request (pertaining to home and community-based services waiver requests).

2000

65 FR 66255, November 3, 2000: HCFA Agency Information Collection Activities: Proposed Collection; Comment request (pertaining to survey of Medicaid home and community-based services waiver and personal care option recipients).

2001

66 FR 14906, March 14, 2001: HCFA Agency Information Collection Activities: Proposed Collection; Comment request (pertaining to annual report on home and community based services waivers).

66 FR 16268, March 23, 2001: HCFA Agency Information Collection Activities: Submission for OMB Review; Comment request (pertaining to survey of home and community–based services waivers and personal care option recipients for the multi–site study of Medicaid home and community–based services).

66 FR 19508, April 16, 2001: HCFA Agency Information Collection Activities: Proposed Collection; Comment request (pertaining to real choice systems change grants, nursing facility transition/access housing grants, community personal assistance service and supports grants, national technical assistance and learning collaborative grants to support systems change for community living).

66 FR 20314, April 20, 2001: HCFA Agency Information Collection Activities: Proposed Collection; Comment request (pertaining to survey of Medicaid home and community–based services waiver and personal care option recipients).

See § 3:23.

§ 7:24 FAILURE BY PROVIDERS OF COMMUNITY SUPPORTED LIVING ARRANGEMENTS SERVICES TO COMPLY WITH STATUTORY REQUIREMENTS — Section 1930(h)(2) [42 U.S.C.A. 1396v(h)(2)]

Regulations

42 CFR Part 430 — Grants to States for Medical Assistance Programs

42 CFR Part 440 — Services: General Provisions

42 CFR Part 455 — Program Integrity: Medicaid

42 CFR Chapter V — Office of Inspector General — Health Care, Department of Health and Human Services

Subchapter A — General Provisions

Part 1000 — Introduction; General Definitions

Subchapter B — OIG Authorities

Part 1002 — Program Integrity: State-initiated Exclusion from Medicaid

Part 1003 — Civil Money Penalties, Assessments and Exclusions

Part 1005 — Appeals of Exclusions, Civil Money Penalties and Assessments

Part 1006 — Investigational Inquiries

Part 1007 — State Medicaid Fraud Control Units

Part 1008 — Advisory Opinions by the OIG

56 FR 31647, July 11, 1991: Public Information Collection Requirements Submitted to the Office of Management and Budget for Clearance (re community supported living arrangements, and physician financial interest in clinical laboratories survey) — Notice.

56 FR 48112, September 24, 1991: Medicaid Program; Community Supported Living Arrangements Services — Interim final rule with comment period, affecting 42 CFR Part 441.

57 FR 22773, May 29, 1992: Medicare Program; Recognition of Community Health Accreditation Program Standards for Home Care Organizations — Final notice.

57 FR 29142, June 30, 1992: Medicaid Program; Home and Community-Based Services Waivers for Individuals Age 65 or Older — Interim final rule with comment period, affecting 42 CFR Parts 400, 435, 436, 440, and 441.

58 FR 47904, September 13, 1993: HCFA, Public Information Collection Requirements (ICR) Submitted to the Office of Management and Budget (OMB) for Clearance (pertaining to chronic renal disease

medical evidence report; Medicare common claims form; Social Security Office report of State buy-in problem; Medicare physician survey form; beneficiary survey form; Medicaid payment rate changes for inpatient hospital or long term care services; home and community-based services: waiver requirements; Medicare peer review organizations reporting forms; uniform institutional provider claim form) — Notice.

59 FR 52178, October 14, 1994: HCFA Public Information Collection Requirements Submitted to the Office of Management and Budget (OMB) for Clearance (pertaining to Medicare reimbursement for outpatient services, cost reports for free-standing skilled nursing facilities; Medicare coverage criteria for adult heart transplants, drug rebates for Medicaid, optional prospective payment cost report for certain skilled nursing facilities, reimbursable costs for organ procurement agencies, distribution and use of end stage renal disease treatment sources, conditions of coverage for ambulatory surgical centers, and waivers for home and community based services).

60 FR 6714, February 3, 1995: HCFA Public Information Collection Requirements Submitted to the Office of Management and Budget (OMB) for Clearance (pertaining to criteria for Medicare coverage of lung transplants, evaluation of drug use review demonstrations projects, and evaluation of the community supported living arrangements program).

60 FR 45487, August 31, 1995: HCFA Public Information Collection Requirements Submitted to the Office of Management and Budget (OMB) for Clearance (pertaining to the annual report on home and community-based waivers).

60 FR 64068, December 13, 1995: HCFA Public Information Collection Requirements Submitted for Public Comment and Recommendations (pertaining to annual reports on home and community-based services waivers).

61 FR 10586, March 14, 1996: HCFA Submitted for Collection of Public Comment: Submission for OMB Review (pertaining to home and community-based services waiver requests; and income and eligibility verification system information collection requirements).

61 FR 58567, November 15, 1996: HCFA Agency Information Collection Activities: Proposed Collection; Comment request (pertaining to home and community based waiver requests).

62 FR 3514, January 23, 1997: Submitted for Collection of Public Comment: Submission for OMB Review (pertaining to home and community-based services waiver requests).

62 FR 63953, December 3, 1997: HCFA Agency Information Collection Activities: Proposed Collection Comment request (pertaining to annual report form for home and community based services waivers).

63 FR 9845, February 26, 1998: HCFA Agency Information Collection Activities: Submission for OMB Review; Comment request (pertaining to annual report on home and community based services waivers).

63 FR 44629, August 20, 1998: HCFA Agency Information Collection Activities: Proposed Collection; Comment request (pertaining to home and community-based services waiver requests).

1999

64 FR 4435, January 28, 1999: HCFA Agency Information Collection Activities; Submission for OMB Review; Comment request (pertaining to home and community-based services waiver requests).

2000

65 FR 66255, November 3, 2000: HCFA Agency Information Collection Activities: Proposed Collection; Comment request (pertaining to survey of Medicaid home and community-based services waiver and personal care option recipients).

2001

66 FR 14906, March 14, 2001: HCFA Agency Information Collection Activities: Proposed Collection; Comment request (pertaining to annual report on home and community based services waivers).

66 FR 16268, March 23, 2001: HCFA Agency Information Collection Activities: Submission for OMB Review; Comment request (pertaining to survey of home and community–based services waivers and personal care option recipients for the multi–site study of Medicaid home and community–based services).

66 FR 19508, April 16, 2001: HCFA Agency Information Collection Activities: Proposed Collection; Comment request (pertaining to real choice systems change grants, nursing facility transition/access housing grants, community personal assistance service and supports

grants, national technical assistance and learning collaborative grants to support systems change for community living).

66 FR 20314, April 20, 2001: HCFA Agency Information Collection Activities: Proposed Collection; Comment request (pertaining to survey of Medicaid home and community–based services waiver and personal care option recipients).

See § 3:24.

§ 7:25 FAILURE BY MEDICAID MANAGED CARE ORGANIZATIONS TO COMPLY WITH FRAUD AND ABUSE PROTECTION REQUIREMENTS — Sections 1932(d) and (e) [42 U.S.C.A. 1396u-2(e)]

Regulations

42 CFR Part 417 — Health Maintenance Organizations, Competitive Medical Plans, and Health Care Prepayment Plans

42 CFR Part 420 — Program Integrity: Medicare

42 CFR Part 434 — Contracts [Medicaid]

42 CFR Part 455 — Program Integrity: Medicaid

62 FR 45426, August 27, 1997: HCFA Agency Information Collection Activities: Submission for OMB Review; Comment request (pertaining to qualification applications for competitive medical plans and Federally qualified HMOs).

62 FR 61825, November 19, 1997: HCFA Agency Information Collection Activities; Submission for OMB Review; Comment request (pertaining to survey forms for consumer assessment of health plans).

62 FR 41063, July 31, 1997: HCFA Emergency Clearance: Public Information Collection Requirements Submitted to the Office of Management and Budget (OMB) (pertaining to performance measures for the Medicare Managed Care Program).

62 FR 45263, August 26, 1997: HCFA Agency Information Collection Activities: Proposed Collection; Comment request (pertaining to physician certification of medical necessity for home oxygen therapy; and consumer assessment of health plans).

62 FR 45426, August 27, 1997: HCFA Agency Information Collection Activities: Submission for OMB Review; Comment request (pertaining to qualification applications for competitive medical plans and Federally qualified HMOs).

62 FR 49016, September 18, 1997: HCFA Agency Information Collection Activities: Submission for OMB Review; Comment

Request (pertaining to managed care incentive arrangement disclosure forms).

62 FR 62063, November 20, 1997: HCFA Agency Information Collection Activities: Proposed Collection; Comment request (pertaining to managed care of ESRD).

63 FR 7175, February 12, 1998: HCFA Emergency Clearance: Public Information Collection Requirements Submitted to the Office of Managment and Budget (OMB) (pertaining to managed care adjusted community rate (ACR) proposal).

63 FR 11263, March 6, 1998: HCFA Agency Information Collection Activities: Submission for OMB Review; Comment request (pertaining to end stage renal disease managed care demonstration.

63 FR 12475, March 13, 1998: HCFA Agency Information Collection Activities; Submission for OMB Review; Comment request (pertaining to HMO and CMP national data reporting requirements).

63 FR 18924, April 16, 1998: HCFA Emergency Clearance: Public Information Collection Requirements Submitted to the Office of Management and Budget (OMB) (pertaining to collection of managed care data using the uniform institutional providers form).

63 FR 26811, May 14, 1998: Medicare and Medicaid Programs: Request for Public Comments on the Quality Improvement System for Managed Care — Solicitation of comments; notice of public meeting.

63 FR 38414, July 16, 1998: HCFA Privacy Act of 1974; Report of Altered System (pertaining to disclosure of individual-specific information to combat fraud or abuse in health benefit programs).

63 FR 42409, August 7, 1998: HCFA Agency Information Collection Activities: Proposed Collection; Comment request (pertaining to health plan data and information consumer assessment survey).

63 FR 43187, August 12, 1998: HCFA Privacy Act of 1974; System of Records — Notice of new system of records pertaining to indicators of the performance of health plans.

63 FR 58059, October 29, 1998: HCFA Agency Information Collection Activities: Submission for OMB Review; Comment request (pertaining to consumer assessment of managed care plans).

63 FR 58341, October 30, 1998: Office of Inspector General: Health Care Fraud and Abuse Data Collection Program: Reporting of Final Adverse Actions — Notice of proposed rulemaking under section 1128E of the Social Security Act, affecting 45 CFR 61.

63 FR 58399, October 30, 1998: Office of Inspector General: Publication of the OIG's Provider Self-Disclosure Protocol — Notice.

63 FR 68223, December 10, 1998: Office of Inspector General; Solicitation of New Safe Harbors and Special Fraud Alerts — Notice of intent to develop regulations, affecting 42 CFR 1001.

63 FR 71819, December 30, 1998: Office of Inspector General; Health Care Fraud and Abuse Data Collection Program; Reporting under section 1128E of the Social Security Act of Final Adverse Actions — Notice of proposed rule-making; extension of comment period, affecting 45 CFR 61.

1999

64 FR 6664, February 10, 1999: HCFA Agency Information Collection Activities: Proposed Collection; Comment request (pertaining to Medicare agreement applications for health care prepayment plans).

64 FR 6753, February 16, 1999: Office of Inspector General: Privacy Act; Notification of New System of Records in Conjunction with the Healthcare Integrity and Protection Data Bank — Notice of a new system of records.

64 FR 25891, May 13, 1999: HCFA Agency Information Collection Activities: Submission for OMB Review; Comment request (pertaining to Medicare agreement application for health care prepayment plans under section 1833).

64 FR 32508, June 17, 1999: HCFA Agency Information Collection Activities: Submission for OMB Review; Comment Request (pertaining to the quality improvement system for managed care (QISMC)).

64 FR 43707, August 11, 1999: HCFA Agency Information Collection Activities: Proposed Collection; Comment request (pertaining to cost reports for prepaid health plans (HMOs and CMPs)).

64 FR 67223, December 1, 1999: Medicaid Program; External Quality Review of Medicaid Managed Care Organizations — Proposed rule affecting 42 CFR Parts 433 and 438.

2000

65 FR 11589, March 3, 2000: Office of Inspector General: Health Care Integrity and Protection Data Bank under Section 1128E of the Social Security Act: Announcement of Opening Date for Querying and User Fees — Notice.

65 FR 25737, May 3, 2000: HCFA Agency Information Collection Activities: Proposed Collection; Comment request (pertaining to managed care disenrollment form).

65 FR 34986, June 1, 2000: Office of Inspector General; Privacy Act; Implementation (exempting the Healthcare Integrity and Protection Data Bank under Section 1128C of the Social Security Act from certain provisions of the Privacy Act (5 U.S.C. 552a)—Final rule.

65 FR 40111, June 29, 2000: HCFA Agency Information Collection Activities: Proposed Collection; comment request (pertaining to qualification applications for prepaid health plans (HMOs).

65 FR 50713, August 21, 2000: HCFA Agency Information Collection Activities: Proposed Collection; Comment request (pertaining to social HMO demonstration payment methodology)

65 FR 53319, September 1, 2000: HCFA Agency Information Collection Activities: Proposed Collection; Comment request (pertaining to incentive arrangement disclosure form for managed care organizations and their related medical groups and physicians).

65 FR 79867, December 20, 2000: HCFA Agency Information Collection Activities: Proposed Collection; Comment request (pertaining to quality improvement system for managed care).

65 FR 79868, December 20, 2000: HCFA Emergency Clearance: Public Information Collection Requirements Submitted to the Office of Management and Budget (OMB) (pertaining to survey of beneficiaries who involuntarily disenroll from their managed care plan).

2001

66 FR 6228, January 19, 2001: Medicaid Program; Medicaid Managed Care—Final rule with comment period, affecting 42 CFR Part 400, 430, 431, 435, 438, 440, and 447.

66 FR 9858, February 12, 2001: HCFA Privacy Act of 1974; Report of New System (pertaining to complaints against health insurance issuers and health plans).

66 FR 11546, February 26, 2001: Medicaid Program; Medicaid Managed Care: Delay of Effective Date—Final rule delay, affecting 42 CFR Parts 400, 430, 431, 434, 435, 438, 440, and 447.

66 FR 15122, March 15, 2001: HCFA Agency Information Collection Activities: Submission for OMB Review; Comment request (pertaining to quality improvement system for managed care).

66 FR 16678, March 27, 2001: HCFA Agency Information Collection Activities: Submission for OMB Review; Comment request (pertaining to Medicare managed care CAHPS survey).

66 FR 28916, May 25, 2001: HCFA Agency Information Collection Activities: Proposed Collection; Comment request (pertaining to collection of managed care data using the uniform institutional providers form).

66 FR 32776, June 18, 2001: Medicaid Program; Medicaid Managed Care: Further Delay of Effective Date for Final Rule affecting 42 CFR Parts 400, 430, 431, 434, 435, 438, 440, and 447.

See § 3:25.

§ 7:26 TERMINATION OF MEDICAID CONTRACTS WITH MANAGED CARE ENTITIES — Section 1932(e)(4) [42 U.S.C.A. 1396u-2(e)(4)]

Regulations

42 CFR Part 417 — Health Maintenance Organizations, Competitive Medical Plans, and Health Care Prepayment Plans

42 CFR Part 420 — Program Integrity: Medicare

42 CFR Part 434 — Contracts [Medicaid]

42 CFR Part 455 — Program Integrity: Medicaid

62 FR 45426, August 27, 1997: HCFA Agency Information Collection Activities: Submission for OMB Review; Comment request (pertaining to qualification applications for competitive medical plans and Federally qualified HMOs).

62 FR 61825, November 19, 1997: HCFA Agency Information Collection Activities; Submission for OMB Review; Comment request (pertaining to survey forms for consumer assessment of health plans).

62 FR 41063, July 31, 1997: HCFA Emergency Clearance: Public Information Collection Requirements Submitted to the Office of Management and Budget (OMB) (pertaining to performance measures for the Medicare Managed Care Program).

62 FR 45263, August 26, 1997: HCFA Agency Information Collection Activities: Proposed Collection; Comment request (pertaining to physician certification of medical necessity for home oxygen therapy; and consumer assessment of health plans).

62 FR 45426, August 27, 1997: HCFA Agency Information Collection Activities: Submission for OMB Review; Comment request

(pertaining to qualification applications for competitive medical plans and Federally qualified HMOs).

62 FR 49016, September 18, 1997: HCFA Agency Information Collection Activities: Submission for OMB Review; Comment Request (pertaining to managed care incentive arrangement disclosure forms).

62 FR 62063, November 20, 1997: HCFA Agency Information Collection Activities: Proposed Collection; Comment request (pertaining to managed care of ESRD).

63 FR 7175, February 12, 1998: HCFA Emergency Clearance: Public Information Collection Requirements Submitted to the Office of Managment and Budget (OMB) (pertaining to managed care adjusted community rate (ACR) proposal).

63 FR 11263, March 6, 1998: HCFA Agency Information Collection Activities: Submission for OMB Review; Comment request (pertaining to end stage renal disease managed care demonstration.

63 FR 12475, March 13, 1998: HCFA Agency Information Collection Activities; Submission for OMB Review; Comment request (pertaining to HMO and CMP national data reporting requirements).

63 FR 18924, April 16, 1998: HCFA Emergency Clearance: Public Information Collection Requirements Submitted to the Office of Management and Budget (OMB) (pertaining to collection of managed care data using the uniform institutional providers form).

63 FR 26811, May 14, 1998: Medicare and Medicaid Programs: Request for Public Comments on the Quality Improvement System for Managed Care — Solicitation of comments; notice of public meeting.

63 FR 38414, July 16, 1998: HCFA Privacy Act of 1974; Report of Altered System (pertaining to disclosure of individual-specific information to combat fraud or abuse in health benefit programs).

63 FR 42409, August 7, 1998: HCFA Agency Information Collection Activities: Proposed Collection; Comment request (pertaining to health plan data and information consumer assessment survey).

63 FR 43187, August 12, 1998: HCFA Privacy Act of 1974; System of Records — Notice of new system of records pertaining to indicators of the performance of health plans.

63 FR 58059, October 29, 1998: HCFA Agency Information Collection Activities: Submission for OMB Review; Comment request (pertaining to consumer assessment of managed care plans).

63 FR 58341, October 30, 1998: Office of Inspector General: Health Care Fraud and Abuse Data Collection Program: Reporting of Final Adverse Actions — Notice of proposed rulemaking under section 1128E of the Social Security Act, affecting 45 CFR 61.

63 FR 58399, October 30, 1998: Office of Inspector General: Publication of the OIG's Provider Self-Disclosure Protocol — Notice.

63 FR 68223, December 10, 1998: Office of Inspector General; Solicitation of New Safe Harbors and Special Fraud Alerts — Notice of intent to develop regulations, affecting 42 CFR 1001.

63 FR 71819, December 30, 1998: Office of Inspector General; Health Care Fraud and Abuse Data Collection Program; Reporting under section 1128E of the Social Security Act of Final Adverse Actions — Notice of proposed rule-making; extension of comment period, affecting 45 CFR 61.

1999

64 FR 6664, February 10, 1999: HCFA Agency Information Collection Activities: Proposed Collection; Comment request (pertaining to Medicare agreement applications for health care prepayment plans).

64 FR 6753, February 16, 1999: Office of Inspector General: Privacy Act; Notification of New System of Records in Conjunction with the Healthcare Integrity and Protection Data Bank — Notice of a new system of records.

64 FR 25891, May 13, 1999: HCFA Agency Information Collection Activities: Submission for OMB Review; Comment request (pertaining to Medicare agreement application for health care prepayment plans under section 1833).

64 FR 32508, June 17, 1999: HCFA Agency Information Collection Activities: Submission for OMB Review; Comment Request (pertaining to the quality improvement system for managed care (QISMC)).

64 FR 43707, August 11, 1999: HCFA Agency Information Collection Activities: Proposed Collection; Comment request (pertaining to cost reports for prepaid health plans (HMOs and CMPs)).

64 FR 67223, December 1, 1999: Medicaid Program; External Quality Review of Medicaid Managed Care Organizations — Proposed rule affecting 42 CFR Parts 433 and 438.

2000

65 FR 11589, March 3, 2000: Office of Inspector General: Health Care Integrity and Protection Data Bank under Section 1128E of the

Social Security Act: Announcement of Opening Date for Querying and User Fees — Notice.

65 FR 25737, May 3, 2000: HCFA Agency Information Collection Activities: Proposed Collection; Comment request (pertaining to managed care disenrollment form).

65 FR 34986, June 1, 2000: Office of Inspector General; Privacy Act; Implementation (exempting the Healthcare Integrity and Protection Data Bank under Section 1128C of the Social Security Act from certain provisions of the Privacy Act (5 U.S.C. 552a) — Final rule.

65 FR 40111, June 29, 2000: HCFA Agency Information Collection Activities: Proposed Collection; comment request (pertaining to qualification applications for prepaid health plans (HMOs).

65 FR 50713, August 21, 2000: HCFA Agency Information Collection Activities: Proposed Collection; Comment request (pertaining to social HMO demonstration payment methodology)

65 FR 53319, September 1, 2000: HCFA Agency Information Collection Activities: Proposed Collection; Comment request (pertaining to incentive arrangement disclosure form for managed care organizations and their related medical groups and physicians).

65 FR 79867, December 20, 2000: HCFA Agency Information Collection Activities: Proposed Collection; Comment request (pertaining to quality improvement system for managed care).

65 FR 79868, December 20, 2000: HCFA Emergency Clearance: Public Information Collection Requirements Submitted to the Office of Management and Budget (OMB) (pertaining to survey of beneficiaries who involuntarily disenroll from their managed care plan).

2001

66 FR 6228, January 19, 2001: Medicaid Program; Medicaid Managed Care—Final rule with comment period, affecting 42 CFR Part 400, 430, 431, 435, 438, 440, and 447.

66 FR 9858, February 12, 2001: HCFA Privacy Act of 1974; Report of New System (pertaining to complaints against health insurance issuers and health plans).

66 FR 11546, February 26, 2001: Medicaid Program; Medicaid Managed Care: Delay of Effective Date—Final rule delay, affecting 42 CFR Parts 400, 430, 431, 434, 435, 438, 440, and 447.

66 FR 15122, March 15, 2001: HCFA Agency Information Collection Activities: Submission for OMB Review; Comment request (pertaining to quality improvement system for managed care).

66 FR 16678, March 27, 2001: HCFA Agency Information Collection Activities: Submission for OMB Review; Comment request (pertaining to Medicare managed care CAHPS survey).

66 FR 28916, May 25, 2001: HCFA Agency Information Collection Activities: Proposed Collection; Comment request (pertaining to collection of managed care data using the uniform institutional providers form).

66 FR 32776, June 18, 2001: Medicaid Program; Medicaid Managed Care: Further Delay of Effective Date for Final Rule affecting 42 CFR Parts 400, 430, 431, 434, 435, 438, 440, and 447.

See § 3:26.

§ 7:27 TERMINATION OF MEDICAID PACE PROVIDER AGREEMENTS — Section 1934(e)(5) [42 U.C.S.C. 1396u-4(e)(5)]

Regulations

42 CFR Part 417 — Health Maintenance Organizations, Competitive Medical Plans, and Health Care Prepayment Plans

42 CFR Part 420 — Program Integrity: Medicare

42 CFR Part 434 — Contracts [Medicaid]

42 CFR Part 455 — Program Integrity: Medicaid

62 FR 45426, August 27, 1997: HCFA Agency Information Collection Activities: Submission for OMB Review; Comment request (pertaining to qualification applications for competitive medical plans and Federally qualified HMOs).

62 FR 61825, November 19, 1997: HCFA Agency Information Collection Activities; Submission for OMB Review; Comment request (pertaining to survey forms for consumer assessment of health plans).

62 FR 41063, July 31, 1997: HCFA Emergency Clearance: Public Information Collection Requirements Submitted to the Office of Management and Budget (OMB) (pertaining to performance measures for the Medicare Managed Care Program).

62 FR 45263, August 26, 1997: HCFA Agency Information Collection Activities: Proposed Collection; Comment request (pertaining to physician certification of medical necessity for home oxygen therapy; and consumer assessment of health plans).

62 FR 45426, August 27, 1997: HCFA Agency Information Collection Activities: Submission for OMB Review; Comment request

(pertaining to qualification applications for competitive medical plans and Federally qualified HMOs).

62 FR 49016, September 18, 1997: HCFA Agency Information Collection Activities: Submission for OMB Review; Comment Request (pertaining to managed care incentive arrangement disclosure forms).

62 FR 62063, November 20, 1997: HCFA Agency Information Collection Activities: Proposed Collection; Comment request (pertaining to managed care of ESRD).

63 FR 7175, February 12, 1998: HCFA Emergency Clearance: Public Information Collection Requirements Submitted to the Office of Managment and Budget (OMB) (pertaining to managed care adjusted community rate (ACR) proposal).

63 FR 11263, March 6, 1998: HCFA Agency Information Collection Activities: Submission for OMB Review; Comment request (pertaining to end stage renal disease managed care demonstration.

63 FR 12475, March 13, 1998: HCFA Agency Information Collection Activities; Submission for OMB Review; Comment request (pertaining to HMO and CMP national data reporting requirements).

63 FR 18924, April 16, 1998: HCFA Emergency Clearance: Public Information Collection Requirements Submitted to the Office of Management and Budget (OMB) (pertaining to collection of managed care data using the uniform institutional providers form).

63 FR 26811, May 14, 1998: Medicare and Medicaid Programs: Request for Public Comments on the Quality Improvement System for Managed Care — Solicitation of comments; notice of public meeting.

63 FR 38414, July 16, 1998: HCFA Privacy Act of 1974; Report of Altered System (pertaining to disclosure of individual-specific information to combat fraud or abuse in health benefit programs).

63 FR 42409, August 7, 1998: HCFA Agency Information Collection Activities: Proposed Collection; Comment request (pertaining to health plan data and information consumer assessment survey).

63 FR 43187, August 12, 1998: HCFA Privacy Act of 1974; System of Records — Notice of new system of records pertaining to indicators of the performance of health plans.

63 FR 58059, October 29, 1998: HCFA Agency Information Collection Activities: Submission for OMB Review; Comment request (pertaining to consumer assessment of managed care plans).

63 FR 58341, October 30, 1998: Office of Inspector General: Health Care Fraud and Abuse Data Collection Program: Reporting of Final Adverse Actions — Notice of proposed rulemaking under section 1128E of the Social Security Act, affecting 45 CFR 61.

63 FR 58399, October 30, 1998: Office of Inspector General: Publication of the OIG's Provider Self-Disclosure Protocol — Notice.

63 FR 68223, December 10, 1998: Office of Inspector General; Solicitation of New Safe Harbors and Special Fraud Alerts — Notice of intent to develop regulations, affecting 42 CFR 1001.

63 FR 71819, December 30, 1998: Office of Inspector General; Health Care Fraud and Abuse Data Collection Program; Reporting under section 1128E of the Social Security Act of Final Adverse Actions — Notice of proposed rule-making; extension of comment period, affecting 45 CFR 61.

1999

64 FR 6664, February 10, 1999: HCFA Agency Information Collection Activities: Proposed Collection; Comment request (pertaining to Medicare agreement applications for health care prepayment plans).

64 FR 6753, February 16, 1999: Office of Inspector General: Privacy Act; Notification of New System of Records in Conjunction with the Healthcare Integrity and Protection Data Bank — Notice of a new system of records.

64 FR 25891, May 13, 1999: HCFA Agency Information Collection Activities: Submission for OMB Review; Comment request (pertaining to Medicare agreement application for health care prepayment plans under section 1833).

64 FR 32508, June 17, 1999: HCFA Agency Information Collection Activities: Submission for OMB Review; Comment Request (pertaining to the quality improvement system for managed care (QISMC)).

64 FR 37985, July 14, 1999: Office of Inspector General; Publication of the OIG Special Advisory Bulletin on Gainsharing Arrangements and CMPs for Hospital Payments to Physicians to Reduce or Limit Services to Beneficiaries — Notice.

64 FR 39420, July 22, 1999: Office of Inspector General; Health Care Programs; Fraud and Abuse; Revised OIG Sanction Authorities Resulting from P.L. 105–33, the Balanced Budget Act of 1997 — Final rule affecting 42 CFR Parts 1001, 1002, and 1003. See also correction at 64 FR 42174, August 3, 1999.

64 FR 43707, August 11, 1999: HCFA Agency Information Collection Activities: Proposed Collection; Comment request (pertaining to cost reports for prepaid health plans (HMOs and CMPs)).

64 FR 42791, September 30, 1999: Office of Inspector General; Publication of the OIG Special Advisory Bulletin on the Effect of Exclusion from Participation in Federal Health Care Programs — Notice. See also correction at 64 FR 55484, October 13, 1999.

64 FR 57619, October 26, 1999: Office of Inspector General; Privacy Act; Exempt Record System, Pertaining to the Healthcare Integrity and Protection Data Bank (HIPDB) — Notice of proposed rulemaking affecting 45 CFR Part 5b.

64 FR 57740, October 26, 1999: Office of Inspector General; Healthcare Fraud and Abuse Data Collection Program: Reporting of Final Adverse Actions — Final rule affecting 45 CFR Part 61.

64 FR 58418, October 29, 1999: HCFA Agency Information Collection Activities: Proposed Collection; Comment request (pertaining to outcome based continuous quality improvement (OBCQI) approach for the PACE program).

64 FR 58851, November 1, 1999: Office of Inspector General; Healthcare Integrity and Protection Data Bank: Announcement of Opening Date for Reporting and Self-query Fee — Notice.

64 FR 63504, November 19, 1999: Office of Inspector General; Fraud and Abuse; Statutory Exception to the Anti-kickback Statute for Shared Risk Arrangements — Interim final rule with request for comment, affection 42 CFR Part 1001. See also correction at 64 FR 71317, December 21, 1999.

64 FR 63518, November 19, 1999: Office of Inspector General; Fraud and Abuse; Clarification of the Initial OIG Safe Harbor Provisions and Establishment of Additional Safe Harbor Provisions under the Anti-kickback Statute — Final rule affecting 42 CFR Part 1001.

64 FR 66234, November 24, 1999: Medicare and Medicaid Programs; Programs of All-inclusive Care for the Elderly (PACE) — Interim final rule with comment period, affecting 42 CFR Parts 460, 462, 466, 473, and 476.

64 FR 67223, December 1, 1999: Medicaid Program; External Quality Review of Medicaid Managed Care Organizations — Proposed rule affecting 42 CFR Parts 433 and 438.

64 FR 69217, December 10, 1999: Office of Inspector General; Solicitation of New Safe Harbors and Special Fraud Alerts — Intent to develop regulations affecting 42 CFR Part 1001.

2000

65 FR 8370, February 18, 2000: HCFA Agency Information Collection Activities: Submission for OMB Review; Comment request (pertaining to a project to develop an outcome-based continuous quality improvement system for PACE).

65 FR 11589, March 3, 2000: Office of Inspector General: Health Care Integrity and Protection Data Bank under Section 1128E of the Social Security Act: Announcement of Opening Date for Querying and User Fees — Notice.

65 FR 25737, May 3, 2000: HCFA Agency Information Collection Activities: Proposed Collection; Comment request (pertaining to managed care disenrollment form).

65 FR 34986, June 1, 2000: Office of Inspector General; Privacy Act; Implementation (exempting the Healthcare Integrity and Protection Data Bank under Section 1128C of the Social Security Act from certain provisions of the Privacy Act (5 U.S.C. 552a) — Final rule.

65 FR 40111, June 29, 2000: HCFA Agency Information Collection Activities: Proposed Collection; comment request (pertaining to qualification applications for prepaid health plans (HMOs).

65 FR 50713, August 21, 2000: HCFA Agency Information Collection Activities: Proposed Collection; Comment request (pertaining to social HMO demonstration payment methodology)

65 FR 53319, September 1, 2000: HCFA Agency Information Collection Activities: Proposed Collection; Comment request (pertaining to incentive arrangement disclosure form for managed care organizations and their related medical groups and physicians).

65 FR 79867, December 20, 2000: HCFA Agency Information Collection Activities: Proposed Collection; Comment request (pertaining to quality improvement system for managed care).

65 FR 79868, December 20, 2000: HCFA Emergency Clearance: Public Information Collection Requirements Submitted to the Office of Management and Budget (OMB) (pertaining to survey of beneficiaries who involuntarily disenroll from their managed care plan).

2001

66 FR 6629, January 22, 2001: HCFA Agency Information Collection Activities: Submission for OMB Review; Comment request (pertaining to Medicare Integrity Program Organizational Conflict of Interest Disclosure Certificate).

66 FR 9586, February 8, 2001: HCFA Agency Information Collection Activities: Proposed Collection; Comment request (pertaining to a project to develop an outcome-based continuous quality improvement system for PACE).

66 FR 9858, February 12, 2001: HCFA Privacy Act of 1974; Report of New System (pertaining to complaints against health insurance issuers and health plans).

66 FR 9865, February 12, 2001: Office of Inspector General: Privacy Act of 1974; Amendment to the Health Care Program Violations System of Records—Notice and comment period (pertaining to including Social Security numbers of sanctioned individual in the Health Care Program Violations record).

66 FR 11546, February 26, 2001: Medicaid Program; Medicaid Managed Care: Delay of Effective Date—Final rule delay, affecting 42 CFR Parts 400, 430, 431, 434, 435, 438, 440, and 447.

66 FR 15122, March 15, 2001: HCFA Agency Information Collection Activities: Submission for OMB Review; Comment request (pertaining to quality improvement system for managed care).

66 FR 16678, March 27, 2001: HCFA Agency Information Collection Activities: Submission for OMB Review; Comment request (pertaining to Medicare managed care CAHPS survey).

66 FR 19507, April 16, 2001: HCFA Agency Information Collection Activities: Proposed Collection; Comment request (pertaining to conflict of interest and ownership and control information form).

66 FR 23945, May 10, 2001: HCFA Agency Information Collection Activities: Submission for OMB Review; Comment request (pertaining to development of an outcome–based continuous quality improvement system for PACE).

66 FR 28916, May 25, 2001: HCFA Agency Information Collection Activities: Proposed Collection; Comment request (pertaining to collection of managed care data using the uniform institutional providers form).

66 FR 31245, June 11, 2001: Office of Inspector General; Healthcare Integrity and Protection Data Bank: Change in User Fees—Notice.

66 FR 32776, June 18, 2001: Medicaid Program; Medicaid Managed Care: Further Delay of Effective Date for Final Rule affecting 42 CFR Parts 400, 430, 431, 434, 435, 438, 440, and 447.

See § 3:27

§ 7:28 INTERMEDIATE SANCTIONS FOR MEDICAID PACE PROVIDERS — Section 1934(e)(6)(B) [42 U.S.C.A. 1396u-4(e)(6)(B)]

Regulations

42 CFR Part 417 — Health Maintenance Organizations, Competitive Medical Plans, and Health Care Prepayment Plans

42 CFR Part 420 — Program Integrity: Medicare

42 CFR Part 434 — Contracts [Medicaid]

42 CFR Part 455 — Program Integrity: Medicaid

62 FR 45426, August 27, 1997: HCFA Agency Information Collection Activities: Submission for OMB Review; Comment request (pertaining to qualification applications for competitive medical plans and Federally qualified HMOs).

62 FR 61825, November 19, 1997: HCFA Agency Information Collection Activities; Submission for OMB Review; Comment request (pertaining to survey forms for consumer assessment of health plans).

62 FR 41063, July 31, 1997: HCFA Emergency Clearance: Public Information Collection Requirements Submitted to the Office of Management and Budget (OMB) (pertaining to performance measures for the Medicare Managed Care Program).

62 FR 45263, August 26, 1997: HCFA Agency Information Collection Activities: Proposed Collection; Comment request (pertaining to physician certification of medical necessity for home oxygen therapy; and consumer assessment of health plans).

62 FR 45426, August 27, 1997: HCFA Agency Information Collection Activities: Submission for OMB Review; Comment request (pertaining to qualification applications for competitive medical plans and Federally qualified HMOs).

62 FR 49016, September 18, 1997: HCFA Agency Information Collection Activities: Submission for OMB Review; Comment Request (pertaining to managed care incentive arrangement disclosure forms).

62 FR 62063, November 20, 1997: HCFA Agency Information Collection Activities: Proposed Collection; Comment request (pertaining to managed care of ESRD).

63 FR 7175, February 12, 1998: HCFA Emergency Clearance: Public Information Collection Requirements Submitted to the Office of Managment and Budget (OMB) (pertaining to managed care adjusted community rate (ACR) proposal).

63 FR 11263, March 6, 1998: HCFA Agency Information Collection Activities: Submission for OMB Review; Comment request (pertaining to end stage renal disease managed care demonstration.

63 FR 12475, March 13, 1998: HCFA Agency Information Collection Activities; Submission for OMB Review; Comment request (pertaining to HMO and CMP national data reporting requirements).

63 FR 18924, April 16, 1998: HCFA Emergency Clearance: Public Information Collection Requirements Submitted to the Office of Management and Budget (OMB) (pertaining to collection of managed care data using the uniform institutional providers form).

63 FR 26811, May 14, 1998: Medicare and Medicaid Programs: Request for Public Comments on the Quality Improvement System for Managed Care — Solicitation of comments; notice of public meeting.

63 FR 38414, July 16, 1998: HCFA Privacy Act of 1974; Report of Altered System (pertaining to disclosure of individual-specific information to combat fraud or abuse in health benefit programs).

63 FR 42409, August 7, 1998: HCFA Agency Information Collection Activities: Proposed Collection; Comment request (pertaining to health plan data and information consumer assessment survey).

63 FR 43187, August 12, 1998: HCFA Privacy Act of 1974; System of Records — Notice of new system of records pertaining to indicators of the performance of health plans.

63 FR 58059, October 29, 1998: HCFA Agency Information Collection Activities: Submission for OMB Review; Comment request (pertaining to consumer assessment of managed care plans).

63 FR 58341, October 30, 1998: Office of Inspector General: Health Care Fraud and Abuse Data Collection Program: Reporting of Final Adverse Actions — Notice of proposed rulemaking under section 1128E of the Social Security Act, affecting 45 CFR 61.

63 FR 58399, October 30, 1998: Office of Inspector General: Publication of the OIG's Provider Self-Disclosure Protocol — Notice.

63 FR 68223, December 10, 1998: Office of Inspector General; Solicitation of New Safe Harbors and Special Fraud Alerts — Notice of intent to develop regulations, affecting 42 CFR 1001.

63 FR 71819, December 30, 1998: Office of Inspector General; Health Care Fraud and Abuse Data Collection Program; Reporting under section 1128E of the Social Security Act of Final Adverse Actions — Notice of proposed rule-making; extension of comment period, affecting 45 CFR 61.

1999

64 FR 6664, February 10, 1999: HCFA Agency Information Collection Activities: Proposed Collection; Comment request (pertaining to Medicare agreement applications for health care prepayment plans).

64 FR 6753, February 16, 1999: Office of Inspector General: Privacy Act; Notification of New System of Records in Conjunction with the Healthcare Integrity and Protection Data Bank — Notice of a new system of records.

64 FR 25891, May 13, 1999: HCFA Agency Information Collection Activities: Submission for OMB Review; Comment request (pertaining to Medicare agreement application for health care prepayment plans under section 1833).

64 FR 32508, June 17, 1999: HCFA Agency Information Collection Activities: Submission for OMB Review; Comment Request (pertaining to the quality improvement system for managed care (QISMC)).

64 FR 37985, July 14, 1999: Office of Inspector General; Publication of the OIG Special Advisory Bulletin on Gainsharing Arrangements and CMPs for Hospital Payments to Physicians to Reduce or Limit Services to Beneficiaries — Notice.

64 FR 39420, July 22, 1999: Office of Inspector General; Health Care Programs; Fraud and Abuse; Revised OIG Sanction Authorities Resulting from P.L. 105–33, the Balanced Budget Act of 1997 — Final rule affecting 42 CFR Parts 1001, 1002, and 1003. See also correction at 64 FR 42174, August 3, 1999.

64 FR 43707, August 11, 1999: HCFA Agency Information Collection Activities: Proposed Collection; Comment request (pertaining to cost reports for prepaid health plans (HMOs and CMPs)).

64 FR 42791, September 30, 1999: Office of Inspector General; Publication of the OIG Special Advisory Bulletin on the Effect of Exclusion from Participation in Federal Health Care Programs — Notice. See also correction at 64 FR 55484, October 13, 1999.

64 FR 57619, October 26, 1999: Office of Inspector General; Privacy Act; Exempt Record System, Pertaining to the Healthcare Integrity and Protection Data Bank (HIPDB) — Notice of proposed rulemaking affecting 45 CFR Part 5b.

64 FR 57740, October 26, 1999: Office of Inspector General; Healthcare Fraud and Abuse Data Collection Program: Reporting of Final Adverse Actions — Final rule affecting 45 CFR Part 61.

64 FR 58418, October 29, 1999: HCFA Agency Information Collection Activities: Proposed Collection; Comment request (pertaining to outcome based continuous quality improvement (OBCQI) approach for the PACE program).

64 FR 58851, November 1, 1999: Office of Inspector General; Healthcare Integrity and Protection Data Bank: Announcement of Opening Date for Reporting and Self-query Fee — Notice.

64 FR 63504, November 19, 1999: Office of Inspector General; Fraud and Abuse; Statutory Exception to the Anti-kickback Statute for Shared Risk Arrangements — Interim final rule with request for comment, affection 42 CFR Part 1001. See also correction at 64 FR 71317, December 21, 1999.

64 FR 63518, November 19, 1999: Office of Inspector General; Fraud and Abuse; Clarification of the Initial OIG Safe Harbor Provisions and Establishment of Additional Safe Harbor Provisions under the Anti-kickback Statute — Final rule affecting 42 CFR Part 1001.

64 FR 66234, November 24, 1999: Medicare and Medicaid Programs; Programs of All-inclusive Care for the Elderly (PACE) — Interim final rule with comment period, affecting 42 CFR Parts 460, 462, 466, 473, and 476.

64 FR 67223, December 1, 1999: Medicaid Program; External Quality Review of Medicaid Managed Care Organizations — Proposed rule affecting 42 CFR Parts 433 and 438.

64 FR 69217, December 10, 1999: Office of Inspector General; Solicitation of New Safe Harbors and Special Fraud Alerts — Intent to develop regulations affecting 42 CFR Part 1001.

2000

65 FR 8370, February 18, 2000: HCFA Agency Information Collection Activities: Submission for OMB Review; Comment request (pertaining to a project to develop an outcome-based continuous quality improvement system for PACE).

65 FR 11589, March 3, 2000: Office of Inspector General: Health Care Integrity and Protection Data Bank under Section 1128E of the Social Security Act: Announcement of Opening Date for Querying and User Fees — Notice.

65 FR 25737, May 3, 2000: HCFA Agency Information Collection Activities: Proposed Collection; Comment request (pertaining to managed care disenrollment form).

65 FR 34986, June 1, 2000: Office of Inspector General; Privacy Act; Implementation (exempting the Healthcare Integrity and Pro-

tection Data Bank under Section 1128C of the Social Security Act from certain provisions of the Privacy Act (5 U.S.C. 552a)—Final rule.

65 FR 40111, June 29, 2000: HCFA Agency Information Collection Activities: Proposed Collection; comment request (pertaining to qualification applications for prepaid health plans (HMOs).

65 FR 50713, August 21, 2000: HCFA Agency Information Collection Activities: Proposed Collection; Comment request (pertaining to social HMO demonstration payment methodology)

65 FR 53319, September 1, 2000: HCFA Agency Information Collection Activities: Proposed Collection; Comment request (pertaining to incentive arrangement disclosure form for managed care organizations and their related medical groups and physicians).

65 FR 79867, December 20, 2000: HCFA Agency Information Collection Activities: Proposed Collection; Comment request (pertaining to quality improvement system for managed care).

65 FR 79868, December 20, 2000: HCFA Emergency Clearance: Public Information Collection Requirements Submitted to the Office of Management and Budget (OMB) (pertaining to survey of beneficiaries who involuntarily disenroll from their managed care plan).

2001

66 FR 6629, January 22, 2001: HCFA Agency Information Collection Activities: Submission for OMB Review; Comment request (pertaining to Medicare Integrity Program Organizational Conflict of Interest Disclosure Certificate).

66 FR 9586, February 8, 2001: HCFA Agency Information Collection Activities: Proposed Collection; Comment request (pertaining to a project to develop an outcome-based continuous quality improvement system for PACE).

66 FR 9858, February 12, 2001: HCFA Privacy Act of 1974; Report of New System (pertaining to complaints against health insurance issuers and health plans).

66 FR 9865, February 12, 2001: Office of Inspector General: Privacy Act of 1974; Amendment to the Health Care Program Violations System of Records—Notice and comment period (pertaining to including Social Security numbers of sanctioned individual in the Health Care Program Violations record).

66 FR 11546, February 26, 2001: Medicaid Program; Medicaid Managed Care: Delay of Effective Date—Final rule delay, affecting 42 CFR Parts 400, 430, 431, 434, 435, 438, 440, and 447.

66 FR 15122, March 15, 2001: HCFA Agency Information Collection Activities: Submission for OMB Review; Comment request (pertaining to quality improvement system for managed care).

66 FR 16678, March 27, 2001: HCFA Agency Information Collection Activities: Submission for OMB Review; Comment request (pertaining to Medicare managed care CAHPS survey).

66 FR 19507, April 16, 2001: HCFA Agency Information Collection Activities: Proposed Collection; Comment request (pertaining to conflict of interest and ownership and control information form).

66 FR 23945, May 10, 2001: HCFA Agency Information Collection Activities: Submission for OMB Review; Comment request (pertaining to development of an outcome–based continuous quality improvement system for PACE).

66 FR 28916, May 25, 2001: HCFA Agency Information Collection Activities: Proposed Collection; Comment request (pertaining to collection of managed care data using the uniform institutional providers form).

66 FR 31245, June 11, 2001: Office of Inspector General; Healthcare Integrity and Protection Data Bank: Change in User Fees—Notice.

66 FR 32776, June 18, 2001: Medicaid Program; Medicaid Managed Care: Further Delay of Effective Date for Final Rule affecting 42 CFR Parts 400, 430, 431, 434, 435, 438, 440, and 447.

See § 3:28.

Chapter 8

REGULATIONS: SANCTIONS IN TITLE XI

§ 8:1 DISCLOSURE OF INFORMATION IN THE POSSESSION OF THE SECRETARY OF HEALTH AND HUMAN SERVICES — Section 1106 [42 U.S.C.A. 1306]

Regulations

20 CFR Part 401 — Disclosure of Official Records and Information [Social Security]

42 CFR Part 401, Subpart B — Confidentiality and Disclosure

42 CFR Part 417 — Health Maintenance Organizations, especially Section 417.482: Access to facilities and records; and Section 417.486: Disclosure of information and confidentiality

42 CFR Part 420 — Program Integrity: Medicare

42 CFR Part 431, Subpart C — Administrative Requirements: Provider Relations, especially Section 431.115: Disclosure of survey information and provider or contractor evaluation; and Subpart F — Safeguarding Information on Applicants and Recipients

42 CFR Part 455 — Program Integrity: Medicaid

42 CFR Part 456, Subpart C — Utilization Control: Hospitals, Section 446.112: Records and reports, and Section 456.113: Confidentiality; Subpart D — Utilization Control: Mental Hospitals, Section 456.212: Records and reports, and Section 456.213: Confidentiality; Subpart E — Utilization Control: Skilled Nursing Facilities, Section 456.312: Records and reports, and Section 456.313: Confidentiality; Subpart F — Utilization Control: Intermediate Care Facilities, Section 456.412: Records and reports, and Section 456.413: Confidentiality

42 CFR Part 476 — Acquisition, Protection, and Disclosure of Peer Review Information

56 FR 47758, September 20, 1991: Medicare Program; Criteria and Standards for Evaluating Intermediary and Carrier Performance — General notice with comment period.

57 FR 46865, October 13, 1992: HCFA Public Information Collection Requirements Submitted to the Office of Management and Budget for Clearance (pertaining to impact of home health care plan

management and evaluation; end-stage renal disease medical case review; Medicare/Medicaid hospital swing-bed survey report form; quarterly Medicaid statement of expenditures; Medicaid program budget report; information collection requirements in final peer review organization sanction regulations; appeals procedures for determinations that affect participation in Medicare; request for medical review information for Part B intermediary outpatient therapy bills and other Part B outpatient bills; and Medicaid limitations on provider-related donations and health care-related taxes, and limitations on payment to disproportionate share hospitals).

57 FR 53760, November 12, 1992: Privacy Act of 1974; Report of Altered System — Notice of alteration of an existing system of records (pertaining to peer review organization data management information).

57 FR 53763, November 12, 1992: Privacy Act of 1974; Altered system of records — Notice of proposed name change and additional routine uses for existing system of records (pertaining to the Medicare bill file and the Medicare enrollment system and the national claim history).

57 FR 57403, December 4, 1992: Medicaid Program: Computer Matching and Privacy Protection for Medicaid Eligibility — Proposed rule affecting 42 CFR Part 435.

57 FR 58507, December 10, 1992: Privacy Act of 1974; Report of New System — Notice of new system of records (pertaining to data necessary to evaluate the Medicare SELECT program).

57 FR 60818, December 22, 1992: HCFA, Privacy Act of 1974; Systems of Records — Notice of proposed new routine use for existing system of records (pertaining to Medicaid and the group health plan system for dual eligibles).

58 FR 29416, May 20, 1993: HCFA Public Information Collection Requirements Submitted to the Office of Management and Budget (OMB) for Clearance re cataract surgery; Medicaid utilization management initiatives; Medicare coverage of screening mammography; psychiatric unit criteria worksheet and rehabilitation unit criteria worksheet; Medicare secondary payor forms; ambulatory surgical center survey forms; ambulance service compliance with State and local requirements; and early and periodic screening, diagnostic and treatment reports.

58 FR 38579, July 19, 1993: HCFA Public Information Collection Requirements Submitted to the Office of Management and Budget (OMB) for Clearance re survey of home health agencies; CLIA survey

report form; validation of state surveys; Medicaid listing of participating home health agencies; financial information regarding Medicare benefits from Medicare contractors; and third-party liability under Medicaid.

58 FR 46198, September 1, 1993: HCFA Public Information Collection Requirements (ICR) Submitted to the Office of Management and Budget (OMB) for Clearance (pertaining to prenatal services and assistance screening; home health agency treatment forms; conditions of participation for intermediate care facilities for the mentally retarded; State Medicaid eligibility quality control sample selection lists; prepaid health plan cost report; hospital survey report form; procedures for determining whether providers, practitioners, or other suppliers of services are liable for certain noncovered services; Medicare credit balance reporting requirements; Medicare provider cost report questionnaire form; Medicare current beneficiary survey rounds 7–10; sterilization regulation/consent form; PRO reconsideration and appeals information requirements; information collection requirements in HSQ-110, acquisition, protection and disclosure of PRO information; Medicare/Medicaid organ procurement organization's (OPO) request for certification) — Notice.

58 FR 47904, September 13, 1993: HCFA, Public Information Collection Requirements (ICR) Submitted to the Office of Management and Budget (OMB) for Clearance (pertaining to chronic renal disease medical evidence report; Medicare common claims form; Social Security Office report of State buy-in problem; Medicare physician survey form; beneficiary survey form; Medicaid payment rate changes for inpatient hospital or long term care services; home and community-based services: waiver requirements; Medicare peer review organizations reporting forms; uniform institutional provider claim form) — Notice.

58 FR 59270, November 8, 1993: HCFA Public Information Collection Requirements Submitted to the Office of Management and Budget (OMB) for Clearance (pertaining to formats for utilization and quality control peer review organizations (PROs); home health agency plan of treatment forms; State survey agency budget expenditure report and certification workload report; home health agency cost report; recordkeeping requirements in provider reimbursement manual; quarterly Medicaid statement of expenditures; Medicare contract application for Federally qualified health maintenance organizations; hospice survey and deficiencies report form; organ

procurement agency/histocompatibility laboratory statement of reimbursable costs) — Notice.

58 FR 60204, November 15, 1993: HCFA Public Information Collection Requirements Submitted to the Office of Management and Budget (OMB) for Clearance (pertaining to procedures for transmitting information between Medicare carriers and Medicare supplemental insurers; Medicare physician or supplier agreement; patient intake data form for the National Home Health Agency; agency characteristics form for the National Home Health Agency prospective payment demonstration; intake and assessment survey package for the community nursing organization demonstration; comprehensive outpatient rehabilitation facility (CORF eligibility and survey forms and information collection requirements) — Notice.

58 FR 67795, December 22, 1993: HCFA Public Information Collection Requirements Submitted to the Office of Management and Budget (OMB) for Clearance (pertaining to clinical laboratory improvement amendments; third party premium billing request form; ambulatory surgical center payment rate survey; online survey, certification and reporting system (OSCAR); conditions of participation for rehabilitation agencies and conditions for coverage for physical therapists in independent practice) — Notice.

59 FR 5201, February 3, 1994: HCFA Public Information Collection Requirements Submitted to the Office of Management and Budget (OMB) for Clearance (pertaining to evaluation of the Medicare case management demonstration; evaluation of the Medicaid uninsured demonstrations; Internal Revenue Service, Social Security Administration, and HCFA data match; survey of physician owned medical liability insurers for use in computing the input component of the physician liability component of the Geographic Practice Cost Index and the Medicare Economic Index; emergency and foreign hospital services for Canadian travel claims; CLIA survey report form; Medicaid management information system (MMIS) data form) — Notice.

59 FR 14865, March 30, 1994: HCFA Public Information Collection Requirements Submitted to the Office of Management and Budget (OMB) for Clearance (pertaining to home health agency Medicare and Medicaid survey report forms for conditions of participation; conditions of participation for rural health clinics; Medicaid re-evaluation of assets for determining payment rates to hospitals

and nursing homes; statistical report on medical care, eligible, recipients, payments, and services.)

59 FR 19181, April 22, 1994: HCFA Privacy Act of 1974 —Notice of Proposed Expansion of System Purpose and New Routine Uses for Existing System of Records. Pertains to routine release of information from the National Claims History (NCH) to assist a variety of health initiatives; involves release to other Federal agencies to comply with a statute or regulation and to States to support administration of health care programs when necessary to enable a State to comply with a statute or regulation. See also correction at 59 FR 28554, June 2, 1994.

59 FR 23069, May 4, 1994: HCFA Public Information Collection Requirements Submitted to the Office of Management and Budget (OMB) for Clearance (pertaining to clinical laboratory improvement amendments (CLIA) flexible survey protocol form; application for health insurance benefits under Medicare for individual with chronic renal disease form; Medicare Qualification Statement for Federal employees form; attending physician's statement and documentation of Medicare emergency form; request for Part B Medicare hearing by an Administrative Law Judge forms; CLIA adverse action extract; and Medicare and Medicaid coverage data bank reports form.)

59 FR 25460, May 16, 1994: HCFA Public Information Collection Requirements Submitted to the Office of Management and Budget (OMB) for Clearance (pertaining to Medicare uniform institutional provider bill; hospice survey and deficiencies report form; HMO financial information reports to members; hospital request for certification in Medicare and Medicaid form.)

59 FR 27023, May 25, 1994: HCFA Public Information Collection Requirements Submitted to the Office of Management and Budget (OMB) for Clearance (pertaining to Medicare beneficiary survey of influenza vaccination form; Medicaid integrated quality control review worksheet; post laboratory survey questionnaire form; and post laboratory survey questionnaire — surveyor form).

59 FR 29430, June 7, 1994: HCFA Public Information Collection Requirements Submitted to the Office of Management and Budget (OMB) for Clearance (pertaining to systems performance review forms for State Medicaid Management Information Systems).

59 FR 30941, June 16, 1994: HCFA Public Information Collection Requirements Submitted to the Office of Management and Budget (OMB) for Clearance (pertaining to evaluation of Medicare SELECT

amendments; and hospital and hospital health care complex cost report forms).

59 FR 35739, July 13, 1994: HCFA Public Information Collection Requirements Submitted to the Office of Management and Budget (OMB) for Clearance (pertaining to current beneficiary survey forms; and Medicare independent renal dialysis facility cost report forms).

59 FR 36204, July 15, 1994: HCFA Public Information Collection Requirements Submitted to the Office of Management and Budget (OMB) for Clearance (pertaining to Medicare common claims form; and HMO qualification applications form).

59 FR 37046, July 20, 1994: HCFA Public Information Collection Requirements Submitted to the Office of Management and Budget (OMB) for Clearance (pertaining to notification to providers, practitioners, and suppliers that they are liable for certain noncovered services; medical review of Part B intermediary outpatient therapy claims; end stage renal disease network cost report forms; hospital request for certification in the Medicare/Medicaid programs form; and end stage renal disease network business proposal forms).

59 FR 37243, July 21, 1994: HCFA Privacy Act of 1974; System of Records (pertaining to new routine use disclosure of carrier and intermediary claims records and beneficiary information to providers or their banks for account management purposes).

59 FR 39296, August 2, 1994: Medicare and Medicaid; Approved Information Collection Requirements — Final Rule with comment period, affecting 42 CFR Part 400.

59 FR 41327, August 11, 1994: HCFA Privacy Act of 1974; System of Records (pertaining to Medicaid Statistical Information System).

59 FR 41329, August 11, 1994: HCFA Privacy Act of 1974; System of Records (pertaining to individuals authorized access to HCFA's data center).

59 FR 50762, October 5, 1994: HCFA Public Information Collection Requirements Submitted to the Office of Management and Budget (OMB) for Clearance (pertaining to reimbursement of hospital costs for residents and interns, criteria for psychiatric and rehabilitation hospital units' reimbursement under the prospective payment system, disclosure of owners and managers of suppliers for fraud and abuse detection purposes, reimbursement of municipal health services clinics, survey form for hospital compliance with anti-dumping requirements, and evaluation of patient and physician

satisfaction with the Medicare participating heart bypass center demonstration).

59 FR 52171, October 14, 1994: HCFA Public Information Collection Requirements Submitted to the Office of Management and Budget (OMB) for Clearance (pertaining to end stage renal disease medical eligibility data).

59 FR 52178, October 14, 1994: HCFA Public Information Collection Requirements Submitted to the Office of Management and Budget (OMB) for Clearance (pertaining to Medicare reimbursement for outpatient services, cost reports for free-standing skilled nursing facilities; Medicare coverage criteria for adult heart transplants, drug rebates for Medicaid, optional prospective payment cost report for certain skilled nursing facilities, reimbursable costs for organ procurement agencies, distribution and use of end stage renal disease treatment sources, conditions of coverage for ambulatory surgical centers, and waivers for home and community based services).

59 FR 54197, October 28, 1994: HCFA Public Information Collection Requirements Submitted to the Office of Management and Budget (OMB) for Clearance (pertaining to Medicare beneficiary surveys, estimated acquisition costs of injectable drugs, reconsideration of adverse determinations made on Part a claims, beneficiary and supplier or physician hearing requests, and compliance with hospital anti-dumping requirements).

59 FR 56500, November 14, 1994: HCFA Public Information Collection Requirements Submitted to the Office of Management and Budget (OMB) for Clearance (pertaining to monitoring and evaluation of Medicare cataract surgery alternate payment demonstration, form for listing deficiencies for laboratory surveys, form for personnel requirements for laboratory CLIA certification, and CLIA reinstatement form).

59 FR 66969, December 28, 1994: HCFA Public Information Collection Requirements Submitted to the Office of Management and Budget (OMB) for Clearance (pertaining to physician certification in skilled nursing facilities, and criteria for Medicare coverage of adult liver transplants).

60 FR 4176, January 20, 1995: HCFA Privacy Act of 1974; System of Records (pertaining to supplemental medical insurance accounting collection and enrollment system).

60 FR 5940, January 31, 1995: HCFA Public Information Collection Requirements Submitted to the Office of Management and

Budget (OMB) for Clearance (pertaining to quarterly Medicaid expenditures, and the Medicaid post-eligibility pre-print).

60 FR 6714, February 3, 1995: HCFA Public Information Collection Requirements Submitted to the Office of Management and Budget (OMB) for Clearance (pertaining to criteria for Medicare coverage of lung transplants, evaluation of drug use review demonstrations projects, and evaluation of the community supported living arrangements program).

60 FR 7205, February 7, 1995: HCFA Public Information Collection Requirements Submitted to the Office of Management and Budget (OMB) for Clearance (pertaining to race and ethnicity surveys for the Medicare enrollment database).

60 FR 7774, February 9, 1995: HCFA Public Information Collection Requirements Submitted to the Office of Management and Budget (OMB) for Clearance (pertaining to justification for ESRD composite rates for outpatient dialysis services, and home health agency compliance with health and safety requirements).

60 FR 12770, March 8, 1995: HCFA Public Information Collection Requirements Submitted to the Office of Management and Budget (OMB) for Clearance (pertaining to survey forms for compliance with CLIA; CLIA application forms for testing on human specimens, and forms for outcome-based quality assurance programs for home health agencies).

60 FR 14435, March 17, 1995: HCFA Public Information Collection Requirements Submitted to the Office of Management and Budget (OMB) for Clearance (pertaining to Medicaid drug rebates, termination of enrollment in Federally Qualified HMO's, imposition of cost-sharing charges in Medicaid, Medicare current beneficiary surveys, and forms for establishing entitlement to hospital insurance).

60 FR 19405, April 18, 1995: HCFA Public Information Collection Requirements Submitted to the Office of Management and Budget (OMB) for Clearance (pertaining to Medicaid limitations on provider related donations and health care related taxes and limitations on payments to disproportionate share hospitals).

60 FR 21525, May 2, 1995: HCFA Public Information Collection Requirements Submitted to the Office of Management and Budget (OMB) for Clearance (pertaining to intermediary requests for information from skilled nursing facilities, reimbursement for CLIA compliance surveys, patient outcome data in home health agencies,

common claim forms for Medicare/Medicaid reimbursement, and a study of childhood immunization costs).

60 FR 26445, May 17, 1995: HCFA Public Information Collection Requirements Submitted to the Office of Management and Budget (OMB) for Clearance (pertaining to Medicare/Medicaid psychiatric hospital survey data, and hospice requests for Medicare certification).

60 FR 33811, June 29, 1995: HCFA Public Information Collection Requirements Submitted to the Office of Management and Budget (OMB) for Clearance (pertaining to early and periodic screening, diagnostic and treatment (EPSDT) reports).

60 FR 37066, July 19, 1995: HCFA Public Information Collection Requirements Submitted to the Office of Management and Budget (OMB) for Clearance (pertaining to actuarial forecasts for Medicaid utilization and cost, employers identified through a match of IRS, SSA, and Medicare records for purposes of the Medicare Secondary Payer provision, health and safety requirements for portable X-ray suppliers, and evaluation of Intermediate Care Facilities for Persons with Mental Retardation — establishing psychoactive drug use baselines).

60 FR 38565, July 27, 1995: HCFA Privacy Act of 1974; Report of New System — Notice of system pertaining to evaluation of, and external quality assurance for, the community nursing organization (CNO) demonstration.

60 FR 39403, August 2, 1995: HCFA Public Information Collection Requirements Submitted for Public Comment and Recommendations (pertaining to PRO reporting forms; Oregon Medicaid reform demonstration; review functions of PRO's; medical records review under PPS; evaluation of Medicare cataract surgery alternate payment demonstration; home health agency survey and deficiencies report; CLIA survey forms; field testing of uniform needs assessment instrument for hospital discharge planning).

60 FR 40184, August 7, 1995: HCFA Public Information Collection Requirements Submitted for Public Comment and Recommendations (pertaining to CLIA alternative quality assessment survey forms; and data collection and analysis for generating procedure specific physician cost estimates).

60 FR 41914, August 14, 1995: Medicare Program; Physician Financial Relationships with, and Referrals to, Health Care Entities that Furnish Clinical Laboratory Services; Financial Relationship Reporting Requirements — Final rule affecting 42 CFR Part 411.

60 FR 42887, August 17, 1995: HCFA Public Information Collection Requirements Submitted for Public Comment and Recommendations (pertaining to national provider identifier and Medicare payment of ambulance service charges).

60 FR 42888, August 17, 1995: HCFA Public Information Collection Requirements Submitted for Public Comment and Recommendations (pertaining to evaluation of the Medicare cataract surgery alternate payment demonstration and Medicaid eligibility quality control).

60 FR 45487, August 31, 1995: HCFA Public Information Collection Requirements Submitted for Public Comment and Recommendations (pertaining to the standardized form for applying for Medicare reimbursement by providers).

60 FR 45487, August 31, 1995: HCFA Public Information Collection Requirements Submitted to the Office of Management and Budget (OMB) for Clearance (pertaining to the annual report on home and community-based waivers).

60 FR 50443, September 29, 1995: Medicare and Medicaid Programs; Approved Information Collection Requirements (pertaining to valid OMB control numbers for 42 CFR) — Technical final rule.

60 FR 50630, September 29, 1995: HCFA Public Information Collection Requirements Submitted for Public Comment and Recommendations (pertaining to sole community home health agencies).

60 FR 52530, October 6, 1995: HCFA Public Information Collection Requirements Submitted to the Office of Management and Budget (OMB) for Clearance (pertaining to durable medical equipment regional carriers and certificates of medical necessity).

60 FR 53383, October 13, 1995: HCFA Public Information Collection Requirements Submitted for Public Comment and Recommendations (pertaining to durable medical equipment regional carriers and certificates of medical necessity).

60 FR 53877, October 24, 1995: HCFA Public Information Collection Requirements Submitted for Public Comment and Recommendations (pertaining to sole community home health agencies).

60 FR 55719, November 2, 1995: HCFA Public Information Collection Requirements Submitted for Public Comment and Recommendations (pertaining to evaluation of the Oregon Medicaid reform demonstration; field testing of the uniform needs assessment instrument for hospital discharge planning; survey of physician

practice costs; evaluation of the Medicare cataract surgery alternate payment demonstration; and alternative CLIA quality assessment surveys).

60 FR 58088, November 24, 1995: HCFA Public Information Collection Requirements Submitted for Public Comment and Recommendations (pertaining to skilled nursing facility (SNF) and skilled nursing facility health care complex cost reports).

60 FR 58088, November 24, 1995: HCFA Public Information Collection Requirements Submitted for Public Comment and Recommendations (pertaining to granting and withdrawal of deeming authority to private nonprofit accreditation organizations and the CLIA exemption under State laboratory programs).

60 FR 58365, November 27, 1995: HCFA Public Information Collection Requirements Submitted for Public Comment and Recommendations (pertaining to Medicare carrier provider/supplier enrollment applications).

60 FR 58631, November 28, 1995: HCFA Public Information Collection Requirements Submitted for Public Comment and Recommendations (pertaining to Medicaid eligibility quality control).

60 FR 61263, November 29, 1995: HCFA Public Information Collection Requirements Submitted for Public Comment and Recommendations (pertaining to Medicare uniform institutional provider bills, and end stage renal disease medical evidence reports for Medicare entitlement and patient registration).

60 FR 64067, December 13, 1995: HCFA Public Information Collection Requirements Submitted for Public Comment and Recommendations (pertaining to Medicare payment for ambulance services).

60 FR 64068, December 13, 1995: HCFA Public Information Collection Requirements Submitted for Public Comment and Recommendations (pertaining to annual reports on home and community-based services waivers).

60 FR 64167, December 14, 1995: HCFA Public Information Collection Requirements Submitted for Public Comment and Recommendations (pertaining Medicaid drug rebates).

60 FR 64167, December 14, 1995: HCFA Public Information Collection Requirements Submitted for Public Comment and Recommendations (pertaining to home health care; Medicare/Medicaid certification of physical therapy and speech pathology services; certification as suppliers of Portable X-ray Services; certifi-

cation of organ procurement organizations; certification for physical therapists in independent practice; and approval as a hospital provider of extended care services (swing bed)).

61 FR 1940, January 24, 1996: HCFA Public Information Collection Requirements Submitted for Public Comment and Recommendations (pertaining to eligibility of an end stage renal disease claimant).

61 FR 2255, January 25, 1996: HCFA Public Information Collection Requirements Submitted for Public Comment and Recommendations (pertaining to survey forms about health and safety requirements for physical therapists in independent practice; and national data reporting requirements for HMOs and CMPs).

61 FR 3715, February 1, 1996: HCFA Emergency Clearance: Public Information Collection Requirements Submitted to the Office of Management and Budget (OMB) (pertaining to requirements for examination and treatment for emergency medical conditions and women in labor).

61 FR 4278, February 5, 1996: HCFA Public Information Collection Requirements Submitted for Public Comment and Recommendations (pertaining to a national provider system numbers to replace the enumeration functions of the Medicare Online Survey, Certification and Reporting system, Clinical Laboratories Improvement Amendments of 1988, and National Supplier Clearing House provider numbering systems).

61 FR 4786, February 8, 1996: HCFA Public Information Collection Requirements Submitted for Public Comment and Recommendations (pertaining to identification of extension units of outpatient physical therapy and outpatient speech pathology providers).

61 FR 4787, February 8, 1996: HCFA Public Information Collection Requirements Submitted for Public Comment: Submission for OMB Review (pertaining to Peer Review Organization reporting forms).

61 FR 5402, February 12, 1996: HCFA Agency Information Collection Activities: Proposed Collection: Comment Request (pertaining to examination and treatment for emergency medical conditions and women in labor; hospice core service waiver requests; home office cost reports; and State Medicaid eligibility quality control samples).

61 FR 6645, February 21, 1996: HCFA Agency Information Collection Activities: Proposed Collection; Comment Request (pertaining

to survey forms to evaluate Federally qualified health centers; and the Medicare Carrier provider/supplier application form).

61 FR 6645, February 21, 1996: HCFA Privacy Act of 1974; Systems of Records — Notice of revision of system to allow disclosure of information to the Social Security Administration as a routine use, to enable HCFA to implement and maintain Medicare and Medicaid.

61 FR 7012, February 23, 1996: HCFA Notice Submitted for Collection of Public Comment: Submission for OMB Review (pertaining to granting and withdrawing of deeming authority to private non-profit Accreditation organizations and the Clinical Laboratory Improvement Act Exemption under State laboratory programs; and the rules for participation of home health agencies to participate as sole community home health agencies).

61 FR 7522, February 28, 1996: HCFA Public Information Collection Requirements Submitted for Public Comment and Recommendations (pertaining to Medicare and Medicaid disclosure of ownership and control interest statements).

61 FR 9186, March 7, 1996: HCFA Agency Information Collection Activities; Proposed Collection; Comment Request (pertaining to hospital and hospital healthcare complex cost reports).

61 FR 10000, March 12, 1996: HCFA Agency Information Collection Activities: Proposed Collection; Comment Request (pertaining to payment adjustments for sole community hospitals).

61 FR 10586, March 14, 1996: HCFA Submitted for Collection of Public Comment: Submission for OMB Review (pertaining to home and community-based services waiver requests; and income and eligibility verification system information collection requirements).

61 FR 11214, March 19, 1996: HCFA Agency Information Collection Activities: Proposed Collection; Comment Request (pertaining to conditions of coverage for organ procurement organizations; and skilled nursing facility and skilled nursing facility healthcare complex forms).

61 FR 11646, March 21, 1996: HCFA Agency Information Collection Activities: Proposed Collection; Comment Request (pertaining to advance directives; video display terminal (VDT) operators eye care program; peer review organization sanction regulations; and deficiency correction status information under CLIA).

61 FR 13205, March 26, 1996: HCFA Agency Information Collection Activities: Submission for OMB Review; Comment Request (pertaining to Medicare standardized forms for reimbursement of covered services by all providers that accept Medicare assignment).

61 FR 13508, March 27, 1996: HCFA Proposed Collection of Public Comment; Submission for OMB Review (pertaining to reconciliation of State invoices for the Medicaid drug rebate program).

61 FR 14798, April 3, 1996: HCFA Agency Information Collection Activities: Proposed Collection; Comment Request (pertaining to statistical reports on medical care eligibility, payments and services under Medicaid; State survey agency lists of positions and schedule of equipment purchases; granting and withdrawing of deeming authority to national accreditation organizations; maximizing the effectiveness of home health care; requests for certification in the Medicare or Medicaid program to provide outpatient physical therapy and/or speech pathology services; physical therapists in independent practice; requests for provider approval as a hospital provider of extended care services (swing bed) under Medicare and Medicaid; and requests for designation as an organ procurement organization).

61 FR 16804, April 17, 1996: HCFA Agency Information Collection Activities: Proposed Collection; Comment Request (pertaining to the Medicare current beneficiary survey; and the Medicare geographical classification review board procedures and criteria).

61 FR 16925, April 18, 1996: HCFA Agency Information Collection Activities: Proposed Collection; Comment Request (pertaining to Medicare participating physician or supplier agreements; and hospital conditions of participation).

61 FR 17710, April 22, 1996: HCFA Agency Information Collection Activities: Proposed Collection; Comment Request (pertaining to payment adjustments for sole community hospitals; conditions of participation for portable x-ray suppliers; and cost reports for independent rural health centers and freestanding Federally qualified health centers).

61 FR 19077, April 30, 1996: HCFA Agency Information Collection Activities: Proposed Collection; Comment Request (pertaining to the national payer identifier (PAYER-ID)).

61 FR 19628, May 2, 1996: HCFA Agency Information Collection Activities: Proposed Collection; Comment Request (pertaining to permissible billing for physicians that do not accept Medicare assignments).

61 FR 20528, May 7, 1996: HCFA Privacy Act of 1974; System of Records (pertaining to the Medicare physician identification and eligibility system).

61 FR 20833, May 8, 1996: HCFA Agency Information Collection Activities: Proposed Collection: Comment Request (pertaining to State Medicaid eligibility quality control sample selection lists).

61 FR 21474, May 10, 1996: HCFA Agency Information Collection Activities; Submission for OMB Review; Comment Request (pertaining to waiver requests affecting hospice core services).

61 FR 24310, May 14, 1996: HCFA Agency Information Collection Activities: Proposed Collection; Comment Request (pertaining to distribution of the brochure "An Important Message from Medicare" by hospitals; Conditions of participation for coverage for physical therapists in independent practice; and the Medicare disproportionate share adjustment procedure and criteria).

61 FR 24804, May 16, 1996: HCFA Agency Information Collection Activities: Submission for OMB review; Comment Request (pertaining to Medicare claims for home office costs by chain organizations).

61 FR 25229, May 20, 1996: HCFA Agency Information Collection Activities: Proposed Collection; Comment Request (pertaining to evaluation of the Oregon reform demonstration; evaluation of the per-episode home health prospective payment demonstration; and the blood bank inspection checklist instrument used by State agencies to determine compliance with CLIA).

61 FR 25873, May 23, 1996: HCFA Agency Information Collection Activities: Submission for OMB Review; Comment Request (pertaining to State Medicaid eligibility quality control sampling plans).

61 FR 25883, May 23, 1996: HCFA Agency Information Collection Activities: Proposed Collection; Comment Request (pertaining to certification of Medicaid eligibility quality control payment error rates).

61 FR 26914, May 29, 1996: HCFA Emergency Clearance: Public Information Collection Requirements Submitted to the Office of Management and Budget (OMB) (pertaining to re-designation, certification and recertification of organ procurement organizations).

61 FR 27087, May 30, 1996: HCFA Agency Information Collection Activities; Submission for OMB Review; Comment Request (pertaining to hospital and hospital healthcare complex cost reports).

61 FR 28882, June 6, 1996: HCFA Agency Information Collection Activities: Submission for OMB Review; Comment Request (pertaining to end stage renal disease medical evidence reports to determine Medicare eligibility; and examination and treatment for emergency medical conditions and women in labor).

61 FR 29406, June 10, 1996: HCFA Agency Information Collection Activities: proposed Collection; Comment Request (pertaining to end stage renal disease application and survey and certification report forms; withholding Medicare payments to recover Medicaid overpayments; acquisition, protection, and disclosure of PRO information; clinical laboratory certification and recertification survey forms; CLIA laboratory personnel report forms; prepaid health plan cost reports; Medicare credit balance reporting requirements; statement of deficiencies and plan of correction requirements for organ procurement organizations; Medicare/Medicaid hospital survey report forms; advance directive requirements for Medicare and Medicaid; payment adjustments for sole community hospitals; survey reports for physical therapists in independent practice; HMO and CMP national data reporting requirements; identification of extension units of outpatient physical therapy and outpatient speech pathology providers; and fire safety survey reports).

61 FR 30072, June 13, 1996: HCFA Agency Information Collection Activities: Proposed Collection; Comment Request (pertaining to conditions of coverage for organ procurement organizations).

61 FR 31141, June 19, 1996: HCFA Agency Information Collection Activities: Proposed Collection; Comment Request (pertaining to authorization agreements for electronic funds transfer; applications for health insurance under Medicare for individuals with chronic renal disease; CLIA application forms; forms for surveyors to evaluate laboratory survey processes; post laboratory survey questionnaires for laboratories to evaluate the survey process).

61 FR 31142, June 19, 1996: HCFA Agency Information Collection Activities: Proposed Collection; Comment Request (pertaining to Medicare current beneficiary surveys; and criteria for Medicare).

61 FR 31142, June 19, 1996: HCFA Agency Information Collection Activities: Proposed Collection; Comment Request (pertaining to criteria for Medicare coverage of heart transplants).

61 FR 33532, June 27, 1996: HCFA Agency Information Collection Activities: Submission for OMB Review; Comment Request (pertaining to information collection requirements in PRO sanction regulations).

61 FR 33752, June 28, 1996: HCFA Agency Information Collection Activities: Submission for OMB Review; Comment Request (pertaining to end stage renal disease medical information systems; and end stage renal disease death notifications).

61 FR 34437, July 2, 1996: HCFA Agency Information Collection Activities: Submission for OMB Review; Comment Request (pertaining to Peer Review Organization procedures for reconsideration of initial decisions; Part B enrollment forms; certification of rural health clinics for Medicare participation; Medicaid utilization review requirements for home health agencies; State listings of Medicaid recipients in institutions and procedures for State inspection of care review; procedures for disenrollment of beneficiaries from HMOs or CMPs; effectiveness of telemedicine services; formats for PROs to submit data to HCFA; and request for accelerated payments forms for providers).

61 FR 34855, July 3, 1996: HCFA Agency Information Collection Activities: Submission for OMB Review; Comment Request (pertaining to information collection requirements for hospital conditions of participation in Medicare).

61 FR 35231, July 5, 1996: HCFA Agency Information Collection Activities: Proposed Collection; Comment Request (pertaining to Medicaid payment standards for inpatient hospital or long-term care services).

61 FR 35231, July 5, 1996: HCFA Agency Information Collection Activities: Submission for OMB Review; Comment Request (pertaining to Medicare geographical classification review board procedures and criteria).

61 FR 37278, July 17, 1996: HCFA Agency Information Collection Activities: Proposed Collection; Comment request (pertaining to Medicare provider/supplier enrollment forms).

61 FR 37278, July 17, 1996: HCFA Public Information Requirements Submitted for Collection of Public Comment: Submission for OMB Review (pertaining to statistical reports of medical care and eligibility for Medicaid recipients).

61 FR 37486, July 18, 1996: HCFA Agency Information Collection Activities: Proposed Collection Activity; Comment request (pertaining to dissemination of information on the internet).

61 FR 37487, July 18, 1996: HCFA Agency Information Collection Activities: Submission for OMB Review; Comment request (pertaining to cost reports for independent rural health centers and freestanding federally qualified health centers; and conditions of participation for portable x-ray suppliers).

61 FR 38454, July 24, 1996: HCFA Agency Information Collection Activities: Submission for OMB Review; Comment request (pertaining to physicians who do not accept Medicare assignment).

61 FR 40422, August 2, 1996: HCFA Agency Information Collection Activities: Proposed Collection; Comment request (pertaining to survey and certification of ambulatory surgical centers; the Medigap complaint database; fiscal intermediaries’ provider overpayment actions; and hospital standards for potentially HIV infectious blood and blood products).

61 FR 40847, August 6, 1996: HCFA Agency Information Collection Activities: Proposed Collection; Comment request (pertaining to survey and certification of comprehensive outpatient rehabilitation facilities (CORFs)).

61 FR 41417, August 8, 1996: HCFA Agency Information Collection Activities: Submission for OMB Review; Comment request (pertaining to prospective payment for home health care; and Medicare standards for hospices).

61 FR 42257, August 14, 1996: HCFA Proposals Submitted for Collection of Public Comment: Submission for OMB Review (pertaining to third-party liability in Medicaid programs; surveys of federally qualified health centers (FQHCs); distribution of Medicare information by hospitals; Medicare reimbursement for hospitals with a disproportionate share of Medicare inpatients; Medicaid quality control; and the National Payer Identifier).

61 FR 43062, August 20, 1996: HCFA Agency Information Collection Activities: Submission for OMB Review; Comment request (pertaining to withholding Medicare payments to recover Medicaid overpayments; acquisition, protection, and disclosure of Peer Review Organization (PRO) information; cost reports for HMOs; and collection of credit balance information from health care providers).

61 FR 43373, August 22, 1996: HCFA Agency Information Collection Activities: Proposed Collection; Comment request (pertaining to hospital claims for inpatient care for statutorily excluded services; and hospice standards for Medicare participation).

61 FR 43373, August 22, 1996: HCFA Public Information Requirements Submitted for Public Comment: Submission for OMB Review (pertaining to certification of Medicaid eligibility quality control payment error rates).

61 FR 43374, August 22, 1996: HCFA Agency Information Collection Activities: Submission for OMB Review; Comment request (pertaining to conditions of participation for rehabilitation agencies and conditions for coverage for physical therapist in independent practice).

61 FR 43774, August 26, 1996: HCFA Agency Information Collection Activities: Proposed collection; Comment request (pertaining to national provider information numbers).

61 FR 46655, September 4, 1996: HCFA Agency Information Collection Activities: Submission for OMB Review; Comment request (pertaining to criteria for Medicare coverage of heart transplants).

61 FR 46814, September 5, 1996: HCFA Agency Information Collection Activities: Submission for OMB Review; Comment request (pertaining to authorization agreements for electronic funds transfers; entitlement to Medicare for individuals with chronic renal disease; application forms for clinical laboratories; and clinical laboratory survey questionnaires).

61 FR 47131, September 6, 1996: HCFA Agency Information Collection Activities: Proposed Collection; Comment request (pertaining to Medicare Part B appeal rights).

61 FR 47131, September 6, 1996: HCFA Agency Information Collection Activities: Submission for OMB Review; Comment request (pertaining to conditions of coverage for organ procurement organizations; and statements of deficiencies and plan of correction forms for organ procurement organizations).

61 FR 48157, September 12, 1996: HCFA Agency Information Collection Activities: Proposed Collection; Comment request (pertaining to hospital standard for potentially HIV infections blood and blood products).

61 FR 48157, September 12, 1996: HCFA Agency Information Collection Activities: Submission for OMB Review; Comment request (pertaining to authorization agreement for electronic funds transfer; entitlement to Medicare for individuals with chronic renal disease; application forms for clinical laboratories; and clinical laboratory survey forms).

61 FR 49781, September 23, 1996: HCFA Agency Information Collection Activities; Submission for OMB Review; Comment request (pertaining to provider eligibility for accelerated payments; and maximizing the effective use of telemedicine).

61 FR 50492, September 26, 1996: HCFA Agency Information Collection Activities: Proposed Collection; Comment request (pertaining to resolution of beneficiary complaints regarding State buy-ins for Medicare entitlement).

61 FR 51295, October 1, 1996: HCFA Public Information Requirements Submitted for Collection of Public Comment: Submission for

OMB Review (pertaining to approval of Medicaid payment rates for inpatient hospital or long term care services).

61 FR 52951, October 9, 1996: HCFA Agency Information Collection Activities: Submission for OMB Review; Comment request (pertaining to Peer Review Organization Reconsiderations and Appeals; Part B enrollment forms; certification as a Rural Health Clinic; Medicaid utilization control programs; lists of Medicaid recipients in institutions; and business proposal formats for PROs).

61 FR 53228, October 10, 1996: HCFA Agency Information Collection Activities: Proposed Collection: Comment request (pertaining to emergency and foreign hospital services claims forms for medical care in Canada).

61 FR 54209, October 17, 1996: HCFA Agency Information Collection Activities: Proposed Collection; Comment request (pertaining to hospital eligibility for swing-bed status).

61 FR 55155, October 24, 1996: HCFA Agency Information Collection Activities: Proposed Collection; Comment request (pertaining to Medicare/Medicaid common claim forms and instructions).

61 FR 55155, October 24, 1996: HCFA Emergency Clearance: Agency Public Information Collection Requirements Submitted to OMB (pertaining to employer identifiers to ensure compliance with Medicare secondary payor requirements).

61 FR 56689, November 4, 1996: HCFA Agency Information Collection Activities: Proposed Collection; Comment request (pertaining to employer identifiers to ensure compliance with Medicare secondary payor requirements).

61 FR 56963, November 5, 1996: HCFA Agency Information Collection Activities: Proposed Collection; Comment request (pertaining to geographic adjustment factors for existing payment localities used in calculating the Medicare fee schedule; demonstration project to test capitated payments for home health services, medical devices, durable medical equipment, and certain ambulatory care under Medicare; and certification of medical necessity forms for durable medical equipment and supplies).

61 FR 46964, November 5, 1996: HCFA Agency Information Collection Activities: Submission for OMB Review; Comment request (pertaining to hospice conditions of participation in Medicare).

61 FR 57688, November 7, 1996: HCFA Agency Information Collection Activities: Comment request (pertaining to clinical laboratory surveys; clinical laboratory personnel qualifications; Medicare/Medicaid hospital survey report forms; beneficiary dis-

enrollment from HMOs and CMPs; survey reports for ambulatory surgical centers; the Medigap complaint database; and survey forms for comprehensive outpatient rehabilitation facilities).

61 FR 58199, November 13, 1996: HCFA Agency Information Collection Activities: Proposed Collection; Comment request (pertaining to Medicare uniform institutional provider bill Form 1450 (UB-92) and instructions).

61 FR 58200, November 13, 1996: HCFA Emergency Clearance: Public Information Collection Requirements Submitted to OMB (pertaining to auditable financial statements for Medicaid reports on payables and receivables).

61 FR 58200, November 13, 1996: HCFA Agency Information Collection Activities: Proposed Collection: Comment request (pertaining to procedures for ordering Medicare/Medicaid forms and program manuals).

61 FR 58567, November 15, 1996: HCFA Agency Information Collection Activities: Proposed Collection; Comment request (pertaining to home and community based waiver requests).

61 FR 59451, November 22, 1996, HCFA Agency Information Collection Activities: Submission for OMB Review; Comment request (pertaining to Medicare hospital standard for potentially HIV infectious blood and blood products; and pertaining to emergency and foreign hospital services claims forms for medical care in Canada).

61 FR 60290, November 27, 1996: HCFA Agency Information Collection Activities; Submission for OMB Review; Comment request (pertaining to Medicare Part B requests for review of initial determinations).

61 FR 64913, December 9, 1996: HCFA Agency Information Collection Activities: Proposed Collection; Comment request (pertaining to survey report forms for ICF/MRs; and current Medicare beneficiary surveys).

61 FR 66284, December 17, 1996: HCFA Agency Information Collection Activities: Proposed Collection; Comment request (pertaining to conditions of participation for rural health clinics).

61 FR 67566, December 23, 1996: HCFA Emergency Clearance: Public Information Collection Requirements Submitted to OMB (pertaining to assessment of health plans).

61 FR 68048, December 26, 1996: HCFA Agency Information Collection: Proposed Collection; Comment request (pertaining to the Medicaid management information system).

61 FR 68270, December 27, 1996: HCFA Agency Information Collection Activities: Submission for OMB Review; Comment request (pertaining to a facility identification and screening form for hospital providers of extended care services (swing-beds) in the Medicare and Medicaid programs).

61 FR 68758, December 30, 1996: HCFA Agency Information Collection Activities: Submission for OMB Review; Comment request (pertaining to the national provider identification system).

62 FR 1338, January 9, 1997: HCFA Agency Information Collection Activities: Proposed Collection: Comment request (pertaining to statistical reports on Medicare eligibles).

62 FR 3514, January 23, 1997: Submitted for Collection of Public Comment: Submission for OMB Review (pertaining to Home and Community-based Services Waiver Requests).

62 FR 3902, January 27, 1997: HCFA Agency Information Collection Activities: Proposed Collection; Comment request (pertaining to hospice survey and deficiencies report form).

62 FR 4304, January 29, 1997: HCFA Emergency Clearance: Public Information Collection Requirements Submitted to the Office of Management and Budget (OMB) (pertaining to Medicare/Medicaid health insurance common claim form).

62 FR 4538, January 30, 1997: HCFA Agency Information Collection Activities: Submission for OMB Review; Comment request (pertaining to intake and assessment survey package for the Community Nursing Organization Demonstration).

62 FR 4772, January 31, 1997: HCFA Agency Information Collection Activities: Submission for OMB Review; Comment request (pertaining to analysis of malpractice premium data).

62 FR 5433, February 5, 1997: HCFA Agency Information Collection Activities: Submission for OMB Review; Comment request (pertaining to Internal Revenue Service/Social Security Administration/Health Care Financing Administration data match).

62 FR 5632, February 6, 1997: HCFA Agency Information Collection Activities: Proposed Collection; Comment request (pertaining to data collection for a project to develop a case-mix adjustment system for a national home health prospective payment program).

62 FR 6550, February 12, 1997: HCFA Agency Information Collection Activities: Submission for OMB Review; Comment request (pertaining to intermediary request to hospitals for medical information on inpatient claims for statutorily excluded services).

62 FR 7240, February 18, 1997: HCFA Agency Information Collection Activities: Submission for OMB Review; Comment request (pertaining to Medicare current beneficiary survey form).

62 FR 7467, February 19, 1997: HCFA Agency Information Collection Activities: Proposed Collection; Comment request (pertaining to form for a hospital request for certification in the Medicare and Medicaid programs).

62 FR 7791, February 20, 1997: HCFA Emergency Clearance: Public Information Collection Requirements Submitted to the Office of Management and Budget (OMB) (pertaining to Medicare current beneficiary survey form).

62 FR 8026, February 21, 1997: HCFA Agency Information Collection Activities: Proposed Collection; Comment request (pertaining to Clinical Laboratory Improvement Act adverse action extract).

62 FR 8026, February 21, 1997: HCFA Agency Information Collection Activities: Submission for OMB Review; Comment request (pertaining to durable medical equipment regional carrier certificate of medical necessity).

62 FR 8252, February 24, 1997: HCFA Agency Information Collection Activities: Submission for OMB Review; Comment request (pertaining to conditions of participation for rural health clinics).

62 FR 8450, February 25, 1997: HCFA Agency Information Collection Activities: Submission for OMB Review; Comment request (pertaining to Medicare current beneficiary survey form).

62 FR 8744, February 26, 1997: HCFA Agency Information Collection Activities: Submission for OMB Review; Comment request (pertaining to Medicare provider/supplier enrollment application).

62 FR 10285, March 6, 1997: HCFA Agency Information collection Activities: Submission for OMB Review; Comment request (pertaining to end stage renal disease (ESRD) application and survey and certification report form).

62 FR 11213, March 11, 1997: HCFA Agency Information Collection Activities: Proposed Collection; Comment request (pertaining to post-laboratory survey questionnaire).

62 FR 11214, March 11, 1997: HCFA Agency Information Collection Activities: Submission for OMB Review; Comment request (pertaining to intermediate care facility for the mentally retarded or persons with related conditions survey report forms).

62 FR 11458, March 12, 1997: HCFA Agency Information Collection Activities: Proposed Collection; Comment request (pertaining to

skilled nursing facility and skilled nursing facility health care complex cost report form).

62 FR 12834, March 18, 1997: HCFA Submittal for Collection of Public Comment: Submission for OMB Review (pertaining to the Medicaid management information system).

62 FR 12834, March 18, 1997: HCFA Correction Notice: Agency Information Collection Activities: Submission for Emergency OMB Review; Comment request (pertaining to managed care organization incentive arrangement disclosure form).

62 FR 13389, March 20, 1997: HCFA Agency Information Collection Activities: Proposed Collection; Comment request (pertaining to home health agency cost report form).

62 FR 14155, March 25, 1997: HCFA Agency Information Collection Activities: Proposed Collection; Comment request (pertaining to voluntary customer surveys to determine satisfaction with the quality of HCFA programs).

62 FR 14155, March 25, 1997: HCFA Agency Information Collection Activities: Proposed Collection; Comment request (pertaining to Medicaid drug utilization review; Medicaid management information systems; and the Medicaid post-eligibility process for FFP).

62 FR 14156, March 25, 1997: HCFA Submittal for Collection of Public Comment: Submission for OMB Review (pertaining to statistical report on medical care for Medicaid recipients).

62 FR 14156, March 25, 1997: HCFA Agency Information Collection Activities: Submission for OMB Review; Comment request (pertaining to Social Security office buy-in problems).

62 FR 14918, March 28, 1997: HCFA Agency Information Collection Activities: Proposed Collection; Comment request (pertaining to Part B Medicare claim request for hearing forms).

62 FR 15914, April 3, 1997: HCFA Agency Information Collection Activities: Proposed Collection; Comment request (pertaining to data collection for the second generation social health maintenance organization demonstration).

62 FR 15914, April 3, 1997: HCFA Agency Information Collection Activities: Submission for OMB Review; Comment request (pertaining to data collection forms for a project to develop a case-mix adjustment system for a national home health prospective payment program).

62 FR 16863, April 8, 1997: HCFA Agency Information Collection Activities: Submission for OMB Review; Comment request (pertaining to hospice survey and deficiencies report form).

62 FR 16894, April 8, 1997: Internal Revenue Service, Pension and Welfare Benefits.

62 FR 17197, April 9, 1997: HCFA Agency Information Collection Activities: Proposed Collection; Comment request (pertaining to evaluation of five State health care reform demonstrations and evaluation of the Medicaid State health reform demonstrations).

62 FR 17197, April 9, 1997: HCFA Agency Information Collection Activities: Proposed Collection; Comment request (pertaining to the Medicaid drug rebate program).

62 FR 17850, April 11, 1997: HCFA Agency Information Collection Activities: Proposed Collection; Comment request (pertaining to the Medicaid EPSDT program).

62 FR 18638, April 16, 1997: HCFA Agency Information Collection Activities: Proposed Collection; Comment request (pertaining to the hospital and hospital health care complex cost report form).

62 FR 18639, April 16, 1997: HCFA Agency Information Collection Activities: Proposed Collection; Comment request (pertaining to the hospital request for certification in the Medicare and Medicaid programs form).

62 FR 18776, April 17, 1997: HCFA New and Pending Demonstration Project Proposals Submitted Pursuant to Section 1115(a) of the Social Security Act: February 1997 — Notice.

62 FR 19326, April 21, 1997: Medicare and Medicaid Programs; Announcement of Additional Applications from Hospitals Requesting Waivers for Organ Procurement Service Area — Notice with comment period.

62 FR 19328, April 21, 1997: Medicare and Medicaid Programs; Quarterly Listing of Program Issuances, Third Quarter 1996 — Notice.

62 FR 19582, April 22, 1997: HCFA Emergency Clearance: Public Information Collection Requirements Submitted to the Office of Management and Budget (pertaining to attending physicians’ certification of medical necessity for home oxygen therapy).

62 FR 23251, April 29, 1997: Medicare Program: Initiative Involving Facilities that Furnish Hemodialysis Treatments — Notice.

62 FR 23781, May 1, 1997: HCFA Agency Information Collection Activities: Proposed Collection; Comment request (pertaining to requirement to disclose HMO financial information to members).

62 FR 23782, May 1, 1997: HCFA Agency Information Collection Activities: Proposed Collection; Comment request (pertaining to

methodology for estimating waiver costs of HCFA demonstration projects).

62 FR 25636, May 9, 1997: HCFA Agency Information Collection Activities: Proposed Collection; Comment request (pertaining to information collection requirements about examination and treatment for emergency medical conditions and women in labor).

62 FR 26806, May 15, 1997: HCFA Agency Information Collection Activities: Proposed collection; Comment request (pertaining to Medicare qualification statement for Federal Employees).

62 FR 28056, May 22, 1997: HCFA Agency Information Collection Activities: Proposed Collection; Comment request (pertaining to Medicaid report on payables and receivables).

62 FR 28057, May 22, 1997: HCFA Agency Information Collection Activities: Submission for OMB Review; Comment request (pertaining to post laboratory survey questionnaire).

62 FR 28884, May 28, 1997: HCFA Agency Information Collection Activities: Proposed Collection; Comment request (pertaining to end stage renal disease beneficiary selection).

62 FR 28884, May 28, 1997: HCFA Agency Information Collection Activities: Proposed Collection; Comment request (pertaining to partnership/regulated entity customer survey generic clearance).

62 FR 29729, June 2, 1997: HCFA Agency Information Collection Activities: Proposed Collection; Comment request (pertaining to Medicaid integrated quality control review worksheet).

62 FR 29730, June 2, 1997: HCFA Submitted for Collection of Public comment: Submission for OMB Review (pertaining to performance review for Medicaid management information systems; Medicaid post-eligibility pre-print; and Medicaid drug utilization review).

62 FR 29730, June 2, 1997: HCFA Agency Information Collection Activities: Submission for OMB Review; Comment request (pertaining to home health agency cost reports).

62 FR 30603, June 4, 1997: HCFA Agency Information Collection Activities: Submission for OMB Review; Comment request (pertaining to skilled nursing facility and skilled nursing facility health care complex cost reports; and hospital conditions of participation).

62 FR 31121, June 6, 1997: HCFA Agency Information Collection Activities: Submission for OMB Review; Comment request (pertaining to voluntary customer surveys about quality of HCFA programs).

62 FR 31612, June 10, 1997: HCFA Agency Information Collection Activities; Proposed Collection; Comment request (pertaining to

request for termination of premium hospital and/or supplementary medical insurance).

62 FR 31613, June 10, 1997: HCFA Agency Information Collection Activities: Proposed Collection; Comment request (pertaining to organ procurement organization/histocompatibility laboratory statement of reimbursable cost form; and outpatient rehabilitation cost report form).

62 FR 31613, June 10, 1997: HCFA Agency Information Collection Activities: Submission for OMB Review; Comment request (pertaining to requests for hearing for Part B claims; requests for hearings for Part A benefits; requests for a Part A Medicare hearing by an administrative law judge; requests for a Part B Medicare hearing by an administrative law judge; and information about provider refunds when claims are denied by Medicare).

62 FR 31614, June 10, 1997: HCFA Agency Information Collection Activities: Submission for OMB Review; Comment request (pertaining to data collection for the second generation social health maintenance organization demonstration).

62 FR 32358, June 13, 1997: HCFA Agency Information Collection Activities: Proposed Collection; Comment request (pertaining to municipal health services cost report form).

62 FR 33095, June 18, 1997: HCFA Agency Information Collection Activities: Proposed Collection; Comment request (pertaining to skilled nursing facility prospective payment system cost report form).

62 FR 32890, June 23, 1997: HCFA Agency Information Collection Activities: Proposed Collection: Comment request (pertaining to Medicaid integrated quality control review worksheet).

62 FR 32890, June 23, 1997: HCFA Submitted for Collection of Public comment: Submission for OMB review (pertaining to Medicaid drug rebate program).

62 FR 34761, June 27, 1997: HCFA Agency Information Collection activities: Proposed Collection; Comment request (pertaining to managed care organization, incentive arrangement disclosure forms; and qualification application form for competitive medical plans, and Medicare contract application for Federally qualified HMO's.

62 FR 35214, June 30, 1997: HCFA Agency Information Collection Activities: Submission for OMB Review; Comment request (pertaining to CLIA adverse actions).

62 FR 35823, July 2, 1997: HCFA Agency Information Collection Activities: Submission for OMB Review; Comment request (pertaining to estimating costs of waivers for HCFA demonstrations).

62 FR 35823, July 2, 1997: HCFA Agency Information Collection Activities: Submission for OMB Review; Comment request (pertaining to verification of ambulance eligibility for reimbursement under Medicare; and determining final payment for hospitals and related complexes under Medicare).

62 FR 36068, July 3, 1997: HCFA Agency Information Collection Activities; Proposed Collection; Comment request (pertaining to ESRD Network semi-annual cost report forms, and ESRD Network contract proposals).

62 FR 39849, July 24, 1997: HCFA Agency Information Collection Activities; Proposed Collection; Comment request (pertaining to deferment request forms for the National Health Service Corps and Native Hawaiian Health scholarship programs).

62 FR 40537, July 29, 1997: HCFA Agency Information Collection Activities: Proposed Collection; Comment request (pertaining to Medicare current beneficiary survey forms).

62 FR 41063, July 31, 1997: HCFA Emergency Clearance: Public Information Collection Requirements Submitted to the Office of Management and Budget (OMB) (pertaining to performance measures for the Medicare Managed Care Program).

62 FR 42258, August 6, 1997: HCFA Agency Information Collection Activities: Proposed Collection; Comment request (pertaining to provider and supplier liability for certain noncovered services; and data about interns and residents for medical education reimbursement to hospitals).

62 FR 42259, August 6, 1997: HCFA Agency Information Collection Activities: Submission for OMB Review; Comment request (pertaining to accounting data from States regarding Medicaid payables and receivables).

62 FR 43738, August 15, 1997: HCFA Agency Information Collection Activities: Proposed Collection; Comment request (pertaining to criteria for excluding psychiatric units from PPS; and reconciliation report forms for drub labelers to assure accurate drug rebate payments).

62 FR 43738, August 15, 1997: HCFA Agency Information Collection Activities: Submission for OMB Review; Comment request (pertaining to the third party premium billing request form).

62 FR 44283, August 20, 1997: HCFA Emergency Clearance: Public Information Collection Requirements Submitted to the Office of Management and Budget (OMB) (pertaining to Medicare/Medicaid common claim forms and instructions). See also correction at 62 FR 45264, August 26, 1997.

62 FR 44478, August 21, 1997: HCFA Agency Information Collection Activities: Proposed Collection; Comment request (pertaining to sterilization consent forms for Medicaid eligibles).

62 FR 44478, August 21, 1997: HCFA Agency Information Collection Activities; Submission for OMB Review; Comment request (pertaining to reimbursable costs for organ procurement organizations).

62 FR 44701, August 22, 1997: HCFA Agency Information Collection Activities: Submission for OMB Review; Comment request (pertaining to cost reports for municipal health services programs).

62 FR 44976, August 25, 1997: HCFA Agency Information Collection Activities: Submission for OMB Review; Comment request (pertaining to beneficiary termination from hospital and/or supplementary medical insurance; outpatient rehabilitation cost report forms; and data collection regarding examination and treatment for emergency medical conditions and women in labor).

62 FR 45263, August 26, 1997: HCFA Agency Information Collection Activities: Proposed Collection; Comment request (pertaining to physician certification of medical necessity for home oxygen therapy; and consumer assessment of health plans).

62 FR 45426, August 27, 1997: HCFA Agency Information Collection Activities: Submission for OMB Review; Comment request (pertaining to qualification applications for competitive medical plans and Federally qualified HMOs).

62 FR 45672, August 28, 1997: HCFA Agency Information Collection Activities: Proposed Collection; Comment request (pertaining to conditions of participation for home health agencies; and negative case action review process annual reports for States).

62 FR 45673, August 28, 1997: HCFA Agency Information Collection Activities: Submission for OMB Review; Comment request (pertaining to evaluation of five State health care reform demonstrations).

62 FR 46980, September 5, 1997: HCFA Emergency Clearance: Public Information Collection Requirements Submitted to the Office of Management and Budget (OMB) (pertaining to State application for funds to initiate and expand provision of child health insurance).

62 FR 48666, September 16, 1997: HCFA Agency Information Collection Activities: Submission for OMB Review; Comment request (pertaining to conditions of coverage for ambulatory surgical centers).

62 FR 48871, September 17, 1997: HCFA Agency Information Collection Activities: Proposed Collection; Comment request (pertaining to conditions of coverage of supplier of ESRD services).

62 FR 49016, September 18, 1997: HCFA Agency Information Collection Activities: Submission for OMB Review; Comment Request (pertaining to managed care incentive arrangement disclosure forms).

62 FR 49017, September 18, 1997: HCFA Agency Information Collection Activities: Submission for OMB Review; Comment request (pertaining to ESRD network semi-annual cost reports; and ESRD business proposal forms).

62 FR 49696, September 23, 1997: HCFA Agency Information Collection Activities: Proposed Collection; Comment request (pertaining to Medicaid drug rebate program).

62 FR 50390, September 25, 1997: HCFA Agency Information Collection Activities: Submission for OMB Review; Comment request (pertaining to disclosure of HMO financial information).

62 FR 51114, September 30, 1997: HCFA Agency Information Collection Activities: Proposed Collection; Comment request (pertaining to State child health plans).

62 FR 51115, September 30, 1997: HCFA Agency Information Collection Activities: Submission for OMB Review; Comment request (pertaining to evaluation of the Oregon Medicaid reform demonstration).

62 FR 51669, October 2, 1997: HCFA Agency Information Collection Activities: Submission for OMB Review; Comment request (pertaining to Medicare reimbursement options for ESRD patients).

62 FR 51873, October 3, 1997: HCFA Agency Information Collection Activities: Proposed Collection; Comment request (pertaining to survey of primary care givers for the District of Columbia managed care demonstration).

62 FR 51874, October 3, 1997: HCFA Agency Information Collection Activities: Submission for OMB Review; Comment request (pertaining to home health services certification and plan of care).

62 FR 52566, October 8, 1997: HCFA Agency Information Collection Activities: Submission for OMB Review; Comment request (pertaining to reimbursement for psychiatric units; and procedures

for determining liability of providers, practitioners, and suppliers for noncovered services).

62 FR 52566, October 8, 1997: HCFA Agency Information Collection Activities: Submission for OMB Review; Comment request (pertaining to reimbursement of teaching hospitals for interns and residents).

62 FR 55410, October 24, 1997: HCFA Agency Information Collection Activities: Submission for OMB Review; Comment request (pertaining to Medicare/Medicaid disclosure of ownership and control forms).

62 FR 55820, October 28, 1997: HCFA Agency Information Collection Activities: Submission for OMB Review; Comment request (pertaining to Medicare beneficiary survey forms).

62 FR 58736, October 30, 1997: HCFA Agency Information Collection Activities: Proposed Collection; Comment request (pertaining to Medicaid budget reports).

62 FR 48736, October 30, 1997: HCFA Agency Information Collection Activities: Submission for OMB Review; Comment request (pertaining to prospective payment for skilled nursing facilities).

62 FR 59714, November 4, 1997: HCFA Agency Information Collection Activities; Proposed Collection; Comment request (pertaining to ESRD reimbursement).

62 FR 61825, November 19, 1997: HCFA Agency Information Collection Activities; Submission for OMB Review; Comment request (pertaining to survey forms for consumer assessment of health plans).

62 FR 62063, November 20, 1997: HCFA Agency Information Collection Activities: Proposed Collection; Comment request (pertaining to managed care of ESRD).

62 FR 62064, November 20, 1997: HCFA Agency Information Collection Activities: Proposed Collection; Comment request (pertaining to quarterly statements of Medicaid expenditures).

62 FR 62064, November 20, 1997: HCFA Agency Information Collection Activities: Proposed Collection; Comment request (pertaining to Medicaid quality control worksheets).

62 FR 62065, November 20, 1997: HCFA Agency Information Collection Activities; Submission for OMB Review; Comment request (pertaining to Medicare for Federal employees).

62 FR 63551, December 1, 1997: HCFA Agency Information Collection Activities: Proposed Collection; Comment request (pertaining to conditions of coverage of suppliers of ESRD services).

62 FR 63552, December 1, 1997: HCFA Agency Information Collection Activities: Proposed Collection; Comment request (pertaining to criteria for Medicare coverage of lung transplants; and criteria for coverage of liver transplants).

62 FR 63953, December 3, 1997: HCFA Agency Information Collection Activities: Proposed Collection Comment request (pertaining to annual report form for home and community based services waivers).

62 FR 64851, December 9, 1997: HCFA Agency Information Collection Activities: Submission for OMB Review; Comment request (pertaining to physician certification of medical necessity for home oxygen therapy).

62 FR 65085, December 10, 1997: HCFA Agency Information Collection Activities: Proposed Collection; Comment request (pertaining to Medicaid quality control).

62 FR 66119, December 17, 1997: HCFA Agency Information Collection Activities: Proposed Collection; Comment request (pertaining to clinical laboratory compliance inspections).

62 FR 66119, December 17, 1997: HCFA Emergency Clearance: Public Information Collection Requirements Submitted to the Office of Management and Budget (OMB) (pertaining to portability from group to individual insurance coverage).

62 FR 66375, December 18, 1997: HCFA Agency Information Collection Activities: Proposed Collection; Comment request (pertaining to ESRD cost report forms; evaluation of the Oregon Medicaid reform demonstration; and qualification of new HMOs and CMPs).

62 FR 66375, December 18, 1997: HCFA Agency Information Collection Activities: Proposed Collection; Comment request (pertaining to amendment of State Medicaid plans).

62 FR 66376, December 18, 1997: HCFA Agency Information Collection Activities: Proposed Collection; Comment request (pertaining to imposition of cost sharing charges under Medicaid).

62 FR 66376, December 18, 1997: HCFA Emergency Clearance: Public Information Collection Requirements Submitted to the Office of Management and Budget (OMB) (pertaining to Medicare and other Federal health care program enrollment forms for providers and suppliers).

62 FR 67085, December 23, 1997: HCFA Agency Information Collection Activities: Submission for OMB Review; Comment request (pertaining to Medicare negative case action reviews).

62 FR 67388, December 24, 1997: HCFA Emergency Clearance: Public Information Collection Requirements Submitted to the Office of Management and Budget (OMB) (pertaining to collection of inpatient data for Medicare+Choice organizations).

62 FR 67389, December 24, 1997: HCFA Announcement of Office of Management and Budget (OMB) Control Numbers for Agency Information Collections Approved under the Paperwork Reduction Act of 1995.

62 FR 67881, December 30, 1997: HCFA Agency Information Collection activities: Proposed Collection; Comment request (pertaining to clinical laboratory survey forms).

63 FR 1114, January 8, 1998: HCFA Agency Information Collection Activities: Proposed Collection; Comment request (pertaining to survey of physicians to determine their information needs regarding Medicare and Medicaid).

63 FR 1114, January 8, 1998: HCFA Agency Information Collection Activities: Submission for OMB Review; Comment request (pertaining to improved data exchange between States and drug labelers).

63 FR 1115, January 8, 1998: HCFA Agency Information Collection Activities: Submission for OMB Review; Comment request (pertaining to survey of primary care givers for the District of Columbia's managed care demonstration for disabled and special needs children).

63 FR 2405, January 15, 1998: HCFA Agency Information Collection Activities: Submission for OMB Review; Comment request (pertaining to request for exception to ESRD composite rates).

63 FR 3329, January 22, 1998: HCFA Agency Information Collection Activities: Proposed Collection; Comment request (pertaining to evaluation of the Medicare Choices Demonstration).

63 FR 4459, January 29, 1998: HCFA Agency Information Collection Activities: Proposed Collection; Comment request (pertaining to peer review organization contracts and solicitation of statements of interest from In-State Organizations).

63 FR 4459, January 29, 1998: HCFA Emergency Clearance: Public Information Collection Requirements Submitted to the Office of Management and Budget (OMB) (pertaining to Medicare/Medicaid health insurance common claim form and instructions).

63 FR 4645, January 30, 1998: HCFA Agency Information Collection Activities: Proposed Collection; Comment request (pertaining to

statistical report on medical care: eligibles, recipients, payments, and services).

63 FR 5958, February 5, 1998: HCFA Agency Information Collection Activities: Proposed Collection; Comment request (pertaining to end stage renal disease medical evidence report Medicare entitlement and patient registration).

63 FR 5958, February 5, 1998: HCFA Agency Information Collection Activities: Proposed Collection; Comment request (pertaining to quality assurance for phase II of the home agency prospective payment demonstration).

63 FR 7175, February 12, 1998: HCFA Emergency Clearance: Public Information Collection Requirements Submitted to the Office of Managment and Budget (OMB) (pertaining to managed care adjusted community rate (ACR) proposal).

63 FR 7175, February 12, 1998: HCFA Emergency Clearance: Public Information Collection Requirements Submitted to the Office of Management and Budget (OMB) (pertaining to research and analytic support for implementing performance measurement in fee for service Medicare and group practices).

63 FR 7421, February 13, 1998: HCFA Agency Information Collection Activities: Submission for OMB Review; Comment request (pertaining to criteria for Medicare coverage of lung transplants).

63 FR 7811, February 17, 1998: HCFA Agency Information Collection Activities: Submission for OMB Review; Comment request (pertaining to criteria for Medicare coverage of liver transplants).

63 FR 9843, February 26, 1998: HCFA Agency Information Collection Activities: Proposed Collection; Comment request (pertaining to Medicare provider cost report reimbursement questionnaire and supporting regulations).

63 FR 9844, February 26, 1998: HCFA Emergency Clearance: Public Information Collection Requirements Submitted to the Office of Management and Budget (OMB) (pertaining to development of an assessment system for post acute care).

63 FR 9844, February 26, 1998: HCFA Agency Information Collection Activities: Proposed Collection; Comment request (pertaining to procedures for advisory opinions concerning physician referrals and supporting regulations in 42 CFR Sections 411.370- 411.389).

63 FR 9845, February 26, 1998: HCFA Agency Information Collection Activities: Proposed Collection; Comment request (pertaining to CLIA budget workload reports).

63 FR 9845, February 26, 1998: HCFA Agency Information Collection Activities: Submission for OMB Review; Comment request (pertaining to annual report on home and community based services waivers).

63 FR 10400, March 3, 1998: HCFA Agency Information Collection Activities: Submission for OMB Review; Comment request (pertaining to Medicaid State plan material, and cost sharing charges under Medicaid).

63 FR 10920, March 5, 1998: HCFA Emergency Clearance: Public Information Collection Requirements Submitted to the Office of Management and Budget (OMB) (pertaining to Medicare and other Federal health care program provider and supplier application forms).

63 FR 10921, March 5, 1998: Medicare Program; HCFA Market Research for Providers and Other Partners.

63 FR 11263, March 6, 1998: HCFA Agency Information Collection Activities: Submission for OMB Review; Comment request (pertaining to end stage renal disease managed care demonstration).

63 FR 12474, March 13, 1998: HCFA Agency Information Collection Activities: Proposed Collection; Comment request (pertaining to hospice request for certification in the Medicare program and Medicare/Medicaid psychiatric hospital survey data).

63 FR 12474, March 13, 1998: HCFA Agency Information Collection Activities: Submission for OMB Review; Comment request (pertaining to requirements for clinical laboratory testing on human specimens).

63 FR 12475, March 13, 1998: HCFA Agency Information Collection Activities; Submission for OMB Review; Comment request (pertaining to HMO and CMP national data reporting requirements).

63 FR 12475, March 13, 1998: HCFA Agency Information Collection Activities: Submission for OMB Review; Comment request (pertaining to independent renal dialysis facility cost report forms).

63 FR 12476, March 13, 1998: HCFA Emergency Clearance: Public Information Collection Requirements Submitted to the Office of Management and Budget (OMB) (pertaining to Medicare+Choice Provider Sponsored Organization (PSO) waiver request forms).

63 FR 12476, March 13, 1998: HCFA Agency Information Collection Activities: Submission for OMB Review; Comment request

(pertaining to alternate quality assessment form for clinical laboratories with good performance records).

63 FR 14719, March 26, 1998: HCFA Agency Information Collection Activities: Proposed Collection; Comment request (pertaining to physician certification and re-certification in skilled nursing facilities).

63 FR 14720, March 26, 1998: HCFA Agency Information Collection Activities: Submission for OMB Review; Comment request (pertaining to Medicaid program budget report).

63 FR 14720, March 26, 1998: HCFA Agency Information Collection Activities: Submission for OMB Review; Comment request (pertaining to quarterly Medicaid statement of expenditures for the Medical assistance program).

63 FR 14720, March 26, 1998: HCFA Agency Information Collection Activities: Submission for OMB Review; Comment request (pertaining to Medicare Physician Communication Survey).

63 FR 16563, April 3, 1998: HCFA Agency Information Collection Activities: Submission for OMB Review; Comment request (pertaining to end stage renal disease medical evidence report Medicare entitlement and/or patient registration).

63 FR 16563, April 3, 1998: HCFA Agency Information Collection Activities: Submission for OMB Review; Comment request (pertaining to evaluation of Medicare Choices demonstration).

63 FR 16563, April 3, 1998: HCFA Agency Information Collection Activities: Submission for OMB Review; Comment request (pertaining to quality assurance for phase II of the home agency prospective payment demonstration).

63 FR 17877, April 10, 1998: HCFA Agency Information Collection Activities: Proposed Collection; Comment request (pertaining to home health agency cost reports).

63 FR 17877, April 10, 1998: HCFA Agency Information Collection Activities: Proposed Collection; Comment request (pertaining to outpatient rehabilitation cost reports).

63 FR 17878, April 10, 1998: HCFA Agency Information Collection Activities: Proposed Collection; Comment request (pertaining to Medicaid post-eligibility preprint).

63 FR 18924, April 16, 1998: HCFA Emergency Clearance: Public Information Collection Requirements Submitted to the Office of Management and Budget (OMB) (pertaining to collection of managed care data using the uniform institutional providers form).

63 FR 19502, April 20, 1998: HCFA Agency Information Collection Activities: Proposed Collection; Comment request (pertaining to Medicare home health quality assurance demonstration).

63 FR 19502, April 20, 1998: HCFA Agency Information Collection Activities: Proposed collection; Comment request (pertaining to annual early and periodic screening, diagnostic, and treatment services (EPSDT) participation report; Medicare and other health care programs provider/supplier enrollment application; and research and analytic support for implementing performance measurement in Medicare fee for service).

63 FR 19503, April 20, 1998: HCFA Agency Information Collection Activities: Submission for OMB Review; Comment request (pertaining to evaluation of the Oregon Medicaid reform demonstration).

63 FR 19503, April 20, 1998: HCFA Agency Information Collection Activities: Submission for OMB Review; Comment request (pertaining to Medicaid integrated quality control review manual instructions).

63 FR 19504, April 20, 1998: HCFA Agency Information Collection Activities: Submission for OMB Review; Comment request (pertaining to peer review organization contracts; solicitation of statements of interest from in-State organizations).

63 FR 20204, April 23, 1998: HCFA Agency Information Collection Activities: Proposed Collection; Comment request (pertaining to distribution of the pamphlet "An Important Message from Medicare" by hospitals to beneficiaries).

63 FR 20204, April 23, 1998: HCFA Agency Information Collection Activities: Proposed Collection; Comment request (pertaining to organ procurement organization (OPO) designation).

63 FR 20205, April 23, 1998: HCFA Agency Information Collection Activities: Submission for OMB Review; Comment request (pertaining to statistical report on medical care: eligibles, recipients, payments and services).

63 FR 20639, April 27, 1998: HCFA Agency Information Collection Activities: Proposed Collection; Comment request (pertaining to financial reports to evaluate requests from physicians or suppliers to pay debts under extended repayment schedule or to compromise a debt for less than the full amount).

63 FR 20639, April 27, 1998: HCFA Agency Information Collection Activities: Submission for OMB Review; Comment request

(pertaining to peer review organization contracts and solicitation of statements of interest from in-State organizations).

63 FR 20640, April 27, 1998: HCFA Agency Information Collection Activities: Submission for OMB Review; Comment request — State child health plan information collection requirements).

63 FR 20652, April 27, 1998: HCFA Agency Information Collection Activities: Proposed Collection; Comment request (pertaining information collection requirements applicable to the obligation of hospitals to examine and treat emergency medical conditions and women in labor).

63 FR 25214, May 7, 1998: HCFA Agency Information Collection Activities: Proposed Collection; Comment request (pertaining to organ procurement organization statement of deficiencies and plan of correction forms).

63 FR 25215, May 7, 1998: HCFA Agency Information Collection Activities: Proposed Collection; Comment request (pertaining to clinical laboratory improvement amendments application forms; limits on provider-related donations and health care-related taxes and payments to disproportionate share hospitals; and Medicare+Choice provider sponsored organization waiver request forms).

63 FR 25215, May 7, 1998: HCFA Agency Information Collection Activities: Proposed Collection; Comment request (pertaining to disclosure and privacy protection for HCFA data).

63 FR 26810, May 14, 1998: HCFA Agency Information Collection Activities: Proposed Collection; Comment request (pertaining to development of an assessment system for post-acute care).

63 FR 26810, May 14, 1998: HCFA Emergency Clearance: Public Information Collection Requirements Submitted to the Office of Management and Budget (OMB) (pertaining to Medicare secondary payer information collection).

63 FR 27303, May 18, 1998: HCFA Agency Information Collection Activities: Submission for OMB Review; Comment request (pertaining to Medicare provider cost report reimbursement questionnaire).

63 FR 27990, May 21, 1998: HCFA Agency Information Collection Activities: Proposed Collection; Comment request (pertaining to multi-state evaluation of dual eligibles, i.e., persons eligible for both Medicare and Medicaid).

63 FR 28394, May 22, 1998: HCFA Agency Information Collection Activities: Proposed Collection; Comment request (pertaining to

Medicaid termination of enrollment information collection requirements).

63 FR 28394, May 22, 1998: HCFA Agency Information Collection Activities: Proposed Collection; Comment request (pertaining to application for health insurance forms).

63 FR 28394, May 22, 1998: HCFA Agency Information Collection Activities: Submission for OMB Review; Comment request (pertaining to CLIA budget workload reports).

63 FR 28395, May 22, 1998: HCFA Agency Information Collection Activities: Submission for OMB Review; Comment request (pertaining to procedures for advisory opinions concerning physician referrals).

63 FR 28395, May 22, 1998: HCFA Agency Information Collection Activities: Submission for OMB Review; Comment request (pertaining to physician certifications and recertifications in skilled nursing facilities).

63 FR 29415, May 29, 1998: HCFA Agency Information Collection Activities: Submission for OMB Review; Comment request (pertaining to hospice request for certification in the Medicare program).

63 FR 32234, June 12, 1998: HCFA Agency Information Collection Activities: Submission for OMB Review; Comment request (pertaining to Medicare/Medicaid psychiatric hospital survey data).

63 FR 32888, June 16, 1998: HCFA Agency Information Collection Activities: Proposed Collection; Comment request (pertaining to Medicare secondary payer reports; and drug utilization review for Medicaid patients).

63 FR 33376, June 18, 1998: HCFA Agency Information Collection Activities; Submission for OMB Review; Comment request (pertaining to Medicaid post-eligibility pre-print report form).

63 FR 33377, June 18, 1998: HCFA Emergency Clearance: Public Information Collection Requirements Submitted to the Office of Management and Budget (OMB) (pertaining to the children's health insurance program budget).

63 FR 34442, June 24, 1998: HCFA Agency Information Collection Activities: Submission for OMB Review; Comment request (pertaining to Medicaid eligibility quality control).

63 FR 34903, June 26, 1998: HCFA Agency Information Collection Activities: Proposed Collection; Comment request (pertaining to collection of managed care data using the institutional providers form).

63 FR 34904, June 26, 1998: HCFA Agency Information Collection Activities: Proposed Collection; Comment request (pertaining to health care prepayment plan Medicare application agreement).

63 FR 36249, July 2, 1998: HCFA Agency Information Collection Activities: Submission for OMB Review; Comment request (pertaining to requests from physicians/suppliers to pay indebtedness under extended repayment schedule, or to compromise a debt for less than the full amount).

63 FR 36249, July 2, 1998: HCFA Emergency Clearance: Public Information Collection Requirements Submitted to the Office of Management and Budget (OMB) (pertaining to HMO mandatory contract provisions under section 1876 of the Social Security Act).

63 FR 36250, July 2, 1998: HCFA Agency Information Collection Activities; Submission for OMB review; Comment request (pertaining to provider/supplier enrollment applications).

63 FR 37129, July 9, 1998: HCFA Agency Information Collection Activities: Submission for OMB Review; Comment request (pertaining to examination and treatment for emergency medical conditions and women in labor).

63 FR 37129, July 9, 1998: HCFA Agency Information Collection Activities; Submission for OMB Review; Comment request (pertaining to organ procurement organization requests for participation in Medicare and Medicaid).

63 FR 38413, July 16, 1998: HCFA Agency Information Collection Activities: Submission for OMB Review; Comment request (pertaining to Clinical Laboratory Improvement Act certification requirements; EPSDT participation reports; limitations on provider-related donations and health care-related taxes, and limitations on payments to disproportionate share hospitals; and Medicare+Choice provider sponsored organization waiver requests forms).

63 FR 38414, July 16, 1998: HCFA Privacy Act of 1974; Report of Altered System (pertaining to disclosure of individual-specific information to combat fraud or abuse in health benefit programs).

63 FR 38838, July 20, 1998: HCFA Agency Information Collection Activities: Proposed Collection; Comment request (pertaining to Medicare beneficiary surveys).

63 FR 38838, July 20, 1998: HCFA Agency Information Collection Activities: Proposed Collection; Comment request (pertaining to children's health insurance program).

63 FR 38839, July 20, 1998: HCFA Agency Information Collection Activities: Submission for OMB Review; Comment request (pertaining to Medicare home health quality assurance demonstration).

63 FR 39101, July 21, 1998: HCFA Privacy Act of 1974; Report of New System (pertaining to end stage renal disease managed care demonstration).

63 FR 39583, July 23, 1998: HCFA Agency Information Collection Activities; Proposed Collection; Comment request (pertaining to Medicaid agencies report forms on children's health insurance expenditures).

63 FR 39585, July 23, 1998: HCFA Agency Information Collection Activities: Submission for OMB Review; Comment request (pertaining to privacy restrictions on disclosure of HCFA data).

63 FR 39880, July 24, 1998: HCFA Agency Information Collection Activities: Proposed Collection; Comment request (pertaining to Medicare secondary payer information collection).

63 FR 39881, July 24, 1998: HCFA Agency Information Collection Activities: Submission for OMB Review; Comment request (pertaining to beneficiary applications for Medicare hospital insurance).

63 FR 40297, July 28, 1998: HCFA Privacy Act of 1974; Report of New System (pertaining to establishment of the National Provider System (NPS) database).

63 FR 40723, July 30, 1998: HCFA Agency Information Collection Activities: Proposed Collection; Comment request (pertaining to hospice cost reports).

63 FR 40723, July 30, 1998: HCFA Agency Information Collection Activities: Proposed Collection; Comment request (pertaining to requirements for health care prepayment plan (HCPP) eligibility under Section 1833 of the Social Security Act).

63 FR 42054, August 6, 1998: HCFA Agency Information Collection Activities: Submission for OMB Review; Comment Request (pertaining to Medicare/Medicaid/CLIA conditions of participation).

63 FR 42409, August 7, 1998: HCFA Agency Information Collection Activities: Proposed Collection; Comment request (pertaining to health plan data and information consumer assessment survey).

63 FR 42638, August 10, 1998: HCFA Agency Information Collection Activities: Submission for OMB Review; Comment request (pertaining to multi-state evaluation of dual eligibles demonstration (Medicare/Medicaid)).

63 FR 43187, August 12, 1998: HCFA Privacy Act of 1974; System of Records — Notice of new system of records pertaining to indicators of the performance of health plans.

63 FR 43403, August 13, 1998: HCFA Emergency Clearance: Public Information Collection Requirements Submitted to the Office of Management and Budget (OMB) (pertaining to the Medicare and You survey form to collect information from internet users accessing the Medicare+Choice Handbook on the Medicare.gov web site).

63 FR 44265, August 18, 1998: HCFA Announcement of Office of Management and Budget (OMB) Control numbers for Agency Information Collections Approved under the Paperwork Reduction Act of 1995.

63 FR 44629, August 20, 1998: HCFA Agency Information Collection Activities: Proposed Collection; Comment request (pertaining to home and community-based services waiver requests).

63 FR 45249, August 25, 1998: HCFA Agency Information Collection Activities: Submission for OMB Review; Comment request (pertaining to development of an assessment system for post-acute care in rehabilitation facilities).

63 FR 45828, August 27, 1998: HCFA Emergency Clearance: Public Information Collection Requirements Submitted to the Office of Management and Budget (OMB) (pertaining to surveys of the effectiveness of the Medicare+Choice education campaign).

63 FR 45829, August 27, 1998: HCFA Emergency Clearance: Public Information Collection Requirements Submitted to the Office of Management and Budget (OMB) (pertaining to a survey of callers to determine consumer satisfaction with the Medicare+Choice toll-free information line).

63 FR 48734, September 11, 1998: HCFA Agency Information Collection Activities: Proposed Collection; Comment request (pertaining to medical review activities under PPS by Peer Review Organizations; and survey and deficiency reports for home health agencies).

63 FR 53923, October 7, 1998: HCFA Emergency Clearance: Public Information Collection Requirements Submitted to the Office of Management and Budget (OMB) (pertaining to Medicare+Choice requirements for quality assurance and enrollee services).

63 FR 55631, October 16, 1998: HCFA Emergency Clearance: Public Information Collection Requirements Submitted to the Office

of Management and Budget (OMB) (pertaining to DMEPOS supplier competitive bidding demonstration).

63 FR 56655, October 22, 1998: HCFA Agency Information Collection Activities: Submission for OMB Review; Comment request (pertaining to Medicare beneficiary survey).

63 FR 56656, October 22, 1998: HCFA Agency Information Collection Activities: Submission for OMB Review; Comment request (pertaining to drug utilization review for Medicaid).

63 FR 57301, October 27, 1998: HCFA Agency Information Collection Activities; Submission for OMB Review; Comment request (pertaining to survey of callers to Medicare+Choice toll-free line).

63 FR 57697, October 28, 1998: HCFA Agency Information Collection Activities; Proposed Collection; Comment request (pertaining to EPSDT participation report).

63 FR 58058, October 29, 1998: HCFA Emergency Clearance: Public Information Collection Requirements Submitted to the Office of Management and Budget (OMB) (pertaining to on-site inspection for durable medical equipment (DME) suppliers).

63 FR 58059, October 29, 1998: HCFA Agency Information Collection Activities: Submission for OMB Review; Comment request (pertaining to consumer assessment of managed care plans).

63 FR 59795, November 5, 1998: HCFA Emergency Clearance: Public Information Collection Requirements Submitted to the Office of Management and Budget (OMB) (pertaining to Medicare coordinated care demonstration project).

63 FR 60356, November 9, 1998: HCFA Agency Information Collection Activities: Proposed Collection; Comment request (pertaining to collection of information on resource utilization by Medicare providers, suppliers, and CLIA laboratories).

63 FR 60356, November 9, 1998: HCFA Agency Information Collection activities: Proposed Collection; Comment request (pertaining to skilled nursing facility resident assessment MDS data).

63 FR 60357, November 9, 1998: HCFA Agency Information Collection Activities: Submission for OMB Review; Comment request (pertaining to Medicare secondary payer information collection).

63 FR 63478, November 13, 1998: HCFA Agency Information Collection Activities: Proposed Collection; Comment request (pertaining to processing Medicare+Choice disenrollment requests from beneficiaries; creation of the Utilization and Quality Control

Peer Review Organization; and rules for participation of HHA's in Medicare and review of plans of care for home health services).

63 FR 63936, November 17, 1998: HCFA Emergency Clearance: Public Information Collection Requirements Submitted to the Office of Management and Budget (OMB) (pertaining to collection of DMEPOS supplier data in support of the Medicare DMEPOS competitive bidding demonstration).

63 FR 64724, November 23, 1998: HCFA Agency Information Collection Activities: Proposed Collection; Comment request (pertaining to Medicare beneficiary surveys; and Medicaid budget reports).

63 FR 65213, November 25, 1998: HCFA Agency Information Collection Activities: Proposed Collection; Comment request (pertaining to chain organization home office cost statements; and requests for reimbursement for ambulance services under Medicare Part B).

63 FR 65601, November 27, 1998: HCFA Agency Information Collection Activities: Submission for OMB Review; Comment request (pertaining to medical records review under PPS; and home health agency survey and deficiencies reports, and home health functional assessment instruments).

63 FR 66551, December 2, 1998: HCFA Agency Information Collection Activities: Submission for OMB review; Comment request (pertaining to EverCare coverage for nursing home residents under Medicare).

63 FR 66552, December 2, 1998: HCFA Agency Information Collection Activities: Submission for OMB Review; Comment request (pertaining to Medicaid statements of expenditures.

63 FR 67908, December 9, 1998: HCFA; Announcement of Office of Management and Budget (OMB) Control Numbers for Agency Information Collections Approved under the Paperwork Reduction Act of 1995 — Notice.

63 FR 68290, December 10, 1998: HCFA Agency Information Collection Activities: Submission for OMB Review; Comment request (pertaining to outpatient rehabilitation cost reports; SNF and SNF health care complex cost reports).

63 FR 68464, December 11, 1998: Medicare Program; Criteria and Standards for Evaluating Intermediary and Carrier Performance: Millennium Compliance — Notice with comment period.

63 FR 69079, December 15, 1998: HCFA Agency Information Collection Activities: Proposed Collection; Comment request (per-

taining to Managed care adjusted community rate for Medicare+Choice organizations).

63 FR 69635, December 17, 1998: HCFA Agency Information Collection Activities: Proposed Collection; Comment request (pertaining to Medicaid eligibility quality control sampling).

63 FR 69635, December 17, 1998: HCFA Emergency Clearance: Public Information Collection Requirements Submitted to the Office of Management and Budget (OMB) (pertaining to collecting information from internet users as they exit from certain Medicare and DHHS web sites).

63 FR 69637, December 17, 1998: HCFA Emergency Clearance: Public Information Collection Requirements Submitted to the Office of Management and Budget (OMB) (pertaining to access to the individual insurance market for individuals under the Health Insurance Portability and Accountability Act).

63 FR 71654, December 29, 1998: HCFA Emergency Clearance: Public Information Collection Requirements Submitted to the Office of Management and Budget (OMB) (pertaining to evaluation of competitive bidding demonstration for durable medical equipment and prosthetics, orthotics, and supplies).

63 FR 72317, December 31, 1998: HCFA Agency Information Collection Activities: Proposed Collection; Comment request (pertaining to advanced directives under Medicare and Medicaid; and Medicare/Medicaid disclosure of ownership and control interests).

63 FR 72318, December 31, 1998: HCFA Agency Information Collection Activities: Proposed Collection; Comment request (pertaining to fire safety survey report forms for health care facilities).

1999

64 FR 1810, January 12, 1999: HCFA Agency Information Collection Activities: Proposed Collection; Comment request (pertaining to Medicaid eligibility quality control MEQC) samples; identification of extension units of outpatient physical therapy (OPT) and outpatient speech pathology (OSP) providers; request for certification in the Medicare and/or Medicaid program(s) to provide OPT or OSP services; and request for certification as a supplier of portable X-ray services under Medicare and/or Medicaid).

64 FR 1811, January 12, 1999: Medicare and Medicaid Programs; Announcement of Additional Applications from Hospitals Requesting Waivers for Organ Procurement Service Area Assignments — Notice with comment period.

64 FR 2907, January 19, 1999: HCFA Agency Information Collection Activities: Submission for OMB Review; Comment request (pertaining to call-back survey of callers to Medicare+Choice toll-free line).

64 FR 3303, January 21, 1999: HCFA Agency Information Collection Activities: Proposed Collection; Comment request (pertaining to on-site inspection for durable medical equipment suppliers).

64 FR 3304, January 21, 1999: HCFA Agency Information Collection Activities: Proposed Collection; Comment request (pertaining to field testing of the uniform needs assessment instrument for patients discharged from hospitals).

64 FR 3305, January 21, 1999: HCFA Emergency Clearance: Public Information Collection Requirements Submitted to the Office of Management and Budget (OMB) (pertaining to Y2K compliance status of HCFA business partners).

64 FR 3748, January 25, 1999: Medicare and Medicaid Programs: Reporting Outcome and Assessment Information Set (OASIS) Data as Part of the Conditions of Participation for Home Health Agencies-Interim final rule with comment period, affecting 42 CFR Parts 484 and 488.

64 FR 3764, January 25, 1999: Medicare and Medicaid Programs: Comprehensive Assessment and Use of the OASIS as Part of the Conditions of Participation for Home Health Agencies — Final rule affecting 42 CFR Part 484.

64 FR 4435, January 28, 1999: HCFA Agency Information Collection Activities: Submission for OMB Review; Comment request (pertaining to hospice cost reports).

64 FR 4435, January 28, 1999: HCFA Agency Information Collection Activities; Submission for OMB Review; Comment request (pertaining to home and community-based services waiver requests).

64 FR 6664, February 10, 1999: HCFA Agency Information Collection Activities: Proposed Collection; Comment request (pertaining to Medicare agreement applications for health care prepayment plans).

64 FR 6664, February 10, 1999: HCFA Agency Information Collection Activities: Submission for OMB Review; Comment request (pertaining to skilled nursing facility (SNF) resident assessment MDS data).

64 FR 6665, February 10, 1999: HCFA Agency Information Collection Activities: Proposed Collection; Comment request (pertaining to sole community home health agencies (HHS)).

64 FR 6905, February 11, 1999: HCFA Agency Information Collection Activities: Proposed Collection; Comment request (pertaining to suggestion program on methods to improve Medicare efficiency).

64 FR 6906, February 11, 1999: HCFA Agency Information Collection Activities: Proposed Collection; Comment request (pertaining to collection of assessment information on three government web sites (medicare.gov, 4woman.gov, and healthfinder.gov), and a feedback questionnaire for the Educational and Health Promotion Group (EHPG)).

64 FR 6907, February 11, 1999: HCFA Agency Information Collection Activities: Submission for OMB Review; Comment request (pertaining to the annual early and periodic screening, diagnostic, and treatment services (EPSDT) participation report).

64 FR 6753, February 16, 1999: Office of Inspector General: Privacy Act; Notification of New System of Records in Conjunction with the Healthcare Integrity and Protection Data Bank — Notice of a new system of records.

64 FR 9160, February 24, 1999: HCFA Agency Information Collection Activities: Proposed Collection; Comment request (pertaining to Medicare DMEPOS competitive bidding demonstration).

64 FR 9161, February 24, 1999: HCFA Agency Information Collection Activities: Proposed Collection; Comment request (pertaining Medicare DMEPOS competitive bidding demonstration).

64 FR 9335, February 25, 1999: HCFA Agency Information Collection Activities: Proposed Collection; Comment request (pertaining to evaluation of competitive bidding demonstration for DMEPOS).

64 FR 9336, February 25, 1999: HCFA Agency Information Collection Activities: Submission for OMB Review; Comment request (pertaining to home office cost reports for chain organizations; ambulance requests for Medicare payment; a supplement to the Medicare current beneficiary survey; and the Medicaid program budget report prepared by State Medicaid agencies).

64 FR 10478, March 4, 1999: HCFA Agency Information Collection Activities: Proposed Collection; Comment request (pertaining to information collection requirements in final peer review organization (PRO) sanction regulations).

64 FR 10479, March 4, 1999: HCFA Agency Information Collection Activities: Proposed Collection; Comment request (pertaining to conditions of participation for portable X-ray suppliers).

64 FR 13432, March 18, 1999: HCFA Agency Information Collection Activities: Submission for OMB Review; Comment request (pertaining to Medicaid eligibility quality control sampling).

64 FR 13997, March 23, 1999: HCFA Agency Information Collection Activities: Submission for OMB Review; Comment request (pertaining to Medicare and Medicaid requirements for advanced directives, and disclosure of ownership and financial control interest).

64 FR 14454, March 25, 1999: HCFA Agency Information Collection Activities: Proposed Collection; Comment request (pertaining to blood bank inspection checklist under CLIA).

64 FR 14454, March 25, 1999: HCFA Agency Information Collection Activities: Submission for OMB Review; Comment request (pertaining to Medicaid eligibility quality control sampling; fire safety survey report forms; and income and eligibility verification systems under Medicaid).

64 FR 17184, April 8, 1999: HCFA Medicare Program; April 23, 1999 Open Town Hall Meeting to Discuss the Skilled Nursing Facility Prospective Payment System (SNF/PPS) and Quality of Care in Nursing Facilities — Notice of meeting.

64 FR 17673, April 12, 1999: HCFA Agency Information Collection Activities: Proposed Collection; Comment request (pertaining to Medicare participating physician or supplier agreements).

64 FR 19375, April 20, 1999: HCFA Agency Information Collection Activities: Proposed Collection; Comment request (pertaining to acquisition, protection, and disclosure of peer review organization (PRO) information).

64 FR 19544, April 21, 1999: HCFA Agency Information Collection Activities: Submission for OMB Review; Comment request (pertaining to assessment of three government web sites (medicare.gov, 4woman.gov, and healthfinder.gov); feedback questionnaire for the educational and health promotion group; and evaluation of Medicare+Choice medical savings demonstration).

64 FR 20008, April 23, 1999: HCFA Agency Information Collection Activities: Submission for OMB Review; Comment request (pertaining to annual early and periodic screening, diagnostic, and treatment (EPSDT) services).

64 FR 23087, April 29, 1999: HCFA Emergency Clearance: Public Information Collection Requirements Submitted to the Office of Management and Budget (OMB) (pertaining to Medigap comparison data available of the Medicare web site medicare.gov).

64 FR 23845, May 4, 1999: HCFA Agency Information Collection Activities: Proposed Collection; Comment request (pertaining to the national Medicare education program community survey of Medicare beneficiaries).

64 FR 23845, May 4, 1999: HCFA Agency Information Collection Activities: Proposed Collection; Comment request (pertaining to Medicare geographical classification review board procedures).

64 FR 23846, May 4, 1999: HCFA Emergency Clearance: Public Information Collection Requirements Submitted to the Office of Management and Budget (OMB) (pertaining to the outcome and assessment information set (OASIS) for home health care agencies).

64 FR 23847, May 4, 1999: HCFA Agency Information Collection Activities: Submission for OMB Review; Comment request (pertaining to uniform needs assessment instrument (UNIA) for patients being discharged from Medicare-certified hospitals).

64 FR 24716, May 7, 1999: Medicare Program; Changes to the Hospital Inpatient Prospective Payment Systems and Fiscal Year 2000 Rates — Proposed rule affecting 42 CFR 412, 413,483, and 485. See also correction at 64 FR 31995, June 15, 1999.

64 FR 24666, May 7, 1999: HCFA Agency Information Collection Activities: Proposed Collection; Comment request (pertaining to Medicare disproportionate share adjustment procedure).

64 FR 25891, May 13, 1999: HCFA Agency Information Collection Activities: Submission for OMB Review; Comment request (pertaining to Medicare DMEPOS competitive bidding demonstration).

64 FR 25891, May 13, 1999: HCFA Agency Information Collection Activities: Submission for OMB Review; Comment request (pertaining to Medicare agreement application for health care prepayment plans under section 1833).

64 FR 25892, May 13, 1999: HCFA Agency Information Collection Activities: Submission for OMB Review; Comment request (pertaining to managed care organization Y2K readiness).

64 FR 25892, May 13, 1999: HCFA Agency Information Collection Activities: Submission for OMB Review; Comment request (pertaining to granting and withdrawal of deeming authority to national accreditation organizations).

64 FR 27584, May 20, 1999: HCFA Emergency Clearance: Public Information Collection Requirements Submitted to the Office of Management and Budget (OMB) (pertaining to state and local government retirement benefit information of individuals to determine eligibility for Medicare Part A).

64 FR 27798, May 21, 1999: HCFA Agency Information Collection Activities: Proposed collection; Comment request (pertaining to determining third party liability (TPL) by State Medicaid agencies).

64 FR 28826, May 27, 1999: HCFA Agency Information Collection Activities: Submission for OMB Review; Comment request (pertaining to evaluation of competitive bidding demonstration for durable medical equipment and prosthetics, orthotics, and supplies (DMEPOS)).

64 FR 29048, May 28, 1999: HCFA Agency Information Collection Activities: Proposed Collection; Comment request (pertaining to certification as a rural health clinic).

64 FR 29049, May 28, 1999: HCFA Agency Information Collection Activities: Proposed Collection; Comment request (pertaining to Medicare credit balance reporting requirements for Medicare providers who have been overpaid).

64 FR 29050, May 28, 1999: HCFA Emergency Clearance: Public Information Collection Requirements Submitted to the Office of Management and Budget (OMB) (pertaining to the community mental health center site visit assessment tool).

64 FR 29657, June 2, 1999: HCFA Emergency Clearance: Public Information Collection requirements Submitted to the Office of Management and Budget (OMB) (pertaining to survey of Medicare beneficiaries for the national Medicare and You Handbook.

64 FR 30042, June 4, 1999: HCFA Agency Information Activities: Proposed Collection; Comment request (pertaining to IRS/SSA/HCFA Medicare secondary payor data match).

64 FR 30340, June 7, 1999: HCFA Agency Information Collection Activities: Submission for OMB Review; Comment request (pertaining to information collection requirements in the final peer review organization (PRO) sanction regulations).

64 FR 32239, June 16, 1999: HCFA Agency Information Collection Activities: Proposed Collection; Comment request (pertaining to conditions of coverage for organ procurement organizations).

64 FR 32240, June 16, 1999: HCFA Agency Information Collection Activities: Submission for OMB Review; Comment request (pertaining to conditions of participation for portable x-ray suppliers).

64 FR 32508, June 17, 1999: HCFA Agency Information Collection Activities: Submission for OMB Review; Comment Request (pertaining to the quality improvement system for managed care (QISMC)).

64 FR 32984, June 18, 1999: Medicare and Medicaid Programs; Mandatory Use, Collection, Encoding, and Transmission of Outcome

and Assessment Information Set (OASIS) for Home Health Agencies — Notice.

64 FR 32992, June 18, 1999: HCFA Privacy Act of 1974; Report of New System (pertaining to a new system of records containing data on the physical, mental, functional, and psychosocial status of all patients receiving the services of home health agencies (HHAs) approved to participate in Medicare or Medicaid).

64 FR 36887, July 8, 1999: HCFA Agency Information Collection Activities: Proposed Collection; Comment request (pertaining to reporting outcome and assessment information data set (OASIS) as part of the conditions of participation for home health agencies).

64 FR 37142, July 9, 1999: HCFA Agency Information Collection Activities: Proposed Collection; Comment request (pertaining to *Medicare and You* brochure feedback postcard).

64 FR 37142, July 9, 1999: HCFA Agency Information Collection Activities: Submission for OMB Review; Comment request (pertaining to request for certification in the Medicare/Medicaid program to provide outpatient physical therapy and/or speech-language pathology and the outpatient physical therapy and/or speech-language pathology survey report form; request for certification as a supplier of portable X-ray services); and procedures for making national coverage decisions).

64 FR 37551, July 12, 1999: HCFA Emergency Clearance; Public Information Collection Requirements Submitted to the Office of Management and Budget (OMB) (pertaining to Medicare lifestyle modification program demonstration).

64 FR 38202, July 15, 1999: HCFA Agency Information Collection Activities: Proposed Collection; Comment request (pertaining to requests for accelerated payments of Medicare reimbursement when providers have financial difficulties).

64 FR 38202, July 15, 1999: HCFA Agency Information Collection Activities: Proposed Collection; Comment request (pertaining to CLIA personnel reports; and CLIA certification for tests on human specimens).

64 FR 38203, July 15, 1999: HCFA Agency Information Collection Activities: Submission for OMB Review; Comment request (pertaining to attending physician's certification of medical necessity for home oxygen therapy).

64 FR 38204, July 15, 1999: HCFA Agency Information Collection Activities: Submission for OMB review; Comment request (pertaining to national hospital malpractice insurance survey).

64 FR 38204, July 15, 1999: HCFA Agency Information Collection Activities: Submission for OMB Review; Comment request (pertaining to the national Medicare education program survey about Medicare+Choice awareness).

64 FR 38910, July 20, 1999: HCFA Agency Information Collection Activities: Proposed Collection; Comment request (pertaining to comprehensive outpatient rehabilitation facility (CORF) eligibility requirements).

64 FR 39517, July 22, 1999: HCFA Agency Information Collection Activities: Submission for OMB Review; Comment request (pertaining to Medicare participating physician or supplier agreement form HCFA-460).

64 FR 40017, July 23, 1999: HCFA Agency Information Collection Activities: Submission for OMB Review; Comment request (pertaining to Medicare geographical classification review board procedures and criteria).

64 FR 40017, July 23, 1999: HCFA Agency Information Collection Activities: Submission for OMB Review; Comment request (pertaining to acquisition, protection and disclosure of peer review organization (PRO) information).

64 FR 40612, July 27, 1999: HCFA Agency Information Collection Activities: Submission for OMB Review; Comment request (pertaining to Medicare disproportionate share adjustment procedure and criteria for hospitals).

64 FR 40888, July 28, 1999: HCFA Agency Information Collection Activities: Proposed Collection; Comment request (pertaining to community mental health center site visit assessment tool).

64 FR 41444, July 30, 1999: HCFA Agency Information Collection Activities: Proposed Collection; Comment request (pertaining to ambulatory surgical center survey report form).

64 FR 41444, July 30, 1999: HCFA Agency Information Collection Activities: Proposed Collection; Comment request (pertaining to criteria for Medicare coverage of heart transplants; and the Medicaid statistical information system (MSIS)).

64 FR 41445, July 30, 1999: HCFA Emergency Clearance: Public Information Collection Requirements Submitted to the Office of Management and Budget (OMB) (pertaining to Medicare+Choice organization appeals and grievance data collection and reporting requirements).

64 FR 42702, August 5, 1999: HCFA Agency Information Collection Activities: Proposed Collection; Comment request (pertaining to

access to individual health insurance markets/information collection requirements in the Health Insurance Portability and Accountability Act.)

64 FR 42702, August 5, 1999: HCFA Agency Information Collection Activities: Proposed Collection; Comment request (pertaining to multi-state evaluation of dual eligibles demonstration — Wisconsin partnership program).

64 FR 43707, August 11, 1999: HCFA Agency Information Collection Activities: Proposed Collection; Comment request (pertaining to cost reports for prepaid health plans (HMOs and CMPs)).

64 FR 44030, August 12, 1999: HCFA Agency Information Collection Activities: Proposed Collection; Comment request (pertaining to market survey of fraud, waste and abuse detection software).

64 FR 44030, August 12, 1999: HCFA Agency Information Collection Activites: Submission for OMB Review; Comment request (pertaining to blood bank inspection checklists and reports under CLIA; and Medicaid eligibility quality control).

64 FR 44031, August 12, 1999: HCFA Agency Information Collection Activites: Submission for OMB Review; Comment request (pertaining to survey and certification of rural health clinics; and determining third party liability in Medicaid programs).

64 FR 45266, August 19, 1999: HCFA Agency Information Collection Activities: Proposed Collection; Comment request (pertaining to PRO reconsiderations and appeals).

64 FR 45266, August 19, 1999: HCFA Agency Information Collection Activities: Proposed Collection; Comment request (pertaining to business proposal formats for utilization and quality control peer review organizations (PROs)).

64 FR 45267, August 19, 1999: HCFA Agency Information Collection Activities: Submission for OMB Review; Comment request (pertaining to Medicare credit balance reporting requirements).

64 FR 46400, August 25, 1999: HCFA Agency Information Collection Activities: Proposed Collection; Comment request (pertaining to hospice information collection requirements).

64 FR 46401, August 25, 1999: HCFA Agency Information Collection Activities: Submission for OMB Review; Comment request (pertaining to SSA/IRS/HCFA data match to implement the Medicare secondary payer provisions).

64 FR 46694, August 26, 1999: HCFA Emergency Clearance: Public Information Collection Requirements Submitted to the Office of

Management and Budget (OMB) (pertaining to the Medicare telephone call center customer satisfaction study).

64 FR 46919, August 27, 1999: HCFA Emergency Clearance: Public Information Collection Requirements Submitted to the Office of Management and Budget (OMB) (pertaining to survey of disenrollment by Medicare beneficiaries from alternative health plans).

64 FR 48844, September 8, 1999: HCFA Agency Information Collection Activities: Proposed Collection; Comment request (pertaining to requests for retirement benefit information).

64 FR 49196, September 10, 1999: HCFA Agency Information Collection Activities; Submission for OMB Review; Comment request (pertaining to conditions of coverage for organ procurement organizations).

64 FR 49196, September 10, 1999: HCFA Emergency Clearance: Public Information Collection Requirements Submitted to the Office of Management and Budget (OMB) (pertaining to survey of Medicare beneficiaries for the national *Medicare and You Handbook 2000 evaluation).*

64 FR 51128, September 21, 1999: HCFA Agency Information Collection Activities: Submission for OMB Review; Comment request (pertaining to withholding Medicare Payments to recover Medicaid overpayments).

64 FR 51328, September 22, 1999: HCFA Emergency Clearance: Public Information Collection Requirements Submitted to the Office of Management and Budget (OMB) (pertaining to the obligation of home health agencies to give beneficiaries advance written notice of noncovered care or of reducing or terminating ongoing care).

64 FR 52332, September 28, 1999: HCFA Agency Information Collection Activities: Submission for OMB Review; Comment request (pertaining to cost reports for independent rural health centers and free-standing Federally qualified health centers).

64 FR 54029, October 5, 1999: HCFA Agency Information Collection Activities: Submission for OMB Review; Comment request (pertaining to provider requests for accelerated payment of Medicare reimbursements).

64 FR 55483, October 13, 1999: HCFA Agency Information Collection Activities: Proposed Collection; Comment request (pertaining to forms used to determine whether Medicare beneficiaries have coverage under an employer group health plan based on current employment).

64 FR 55737, October 14, 1999: HCFA Agency Information Collection Activities: Proposed Collection; Comment request (pertaining to the adjusted community rate proposal for Medicare+Choice plans).

64 FR 55948, October 15, 1999: HCFA Agency Information Collection Activities: Proposed Collection; Comment request (pertaining to form HCFA-4040, which is used to request enrollment in Medicare Part B).

64 FR 55949, October 15, 1999: HCFA Agency Information Collection Activities: Proposed Collection; Comment request (pertaining to physician certifications and re-certifications about the necessity for skilled nursing facility care).

64 FR 57902, October 27, 1999: HCFA Agency Information Collection Activites: Proposed Collection; Comment request (pertaining to evaluation of new Medicare+Choice plans).

64 FR 58418, October 29, 1999: HCFA Agency Information Collection Activities: Proposed Collection; Comment request (pertaining to outcome based continuous quality improvement (OBCQI) approach for the PACE program).

64 FR 58851, November 1, 1999: HCFA Agency Information Collection Activities: Proposed Collection; Comment request (pertaining to emergency foreign hospital services).

64 FR 59184, November 2, 1999: HCFA Agency Information Collection Activities: Submission for OMB Review; Comment request (pertaining to multi-state evaluation of dual eligibles demonstrations; Wisconsin partnership program).

64 FR 59184, November 2, 1999: HCFA Agency Information Collection Activities: Submission for OMB Review; Comment Request (pertaining to HIPAA requirements for the individual health insurance market).

64 FR 60213, November 4, 1999: HCFA Agency Information Collection Activities: Submission for OMB Review; Comment request (pertaining to cost reports for prepaid health plans).

64 FR 60450, November 5, 1999: HCFA Agency Information Collection Activities: Submission for OMB Review; Comment request (pertaining to feedback postcard for *Medicare and You 2000* brochure).

64 FR 62679, November 17, 1999: HCFA Agency Information Collection Activities: Proposed Collection; Comment request (pertaining to surveys of end stage renal disease facilities).

64 FR 62680, November 17, 1999: HCFA Agency Information Collection Activities: Submission for OMB Review; Comment request

(pertaining to hospice care eligibility standards, reimbursement procedures, and conditions of participation).

64 FR 62680, November 17, 1999: HCFA Agency Information Collection Activities: Proposed Collection; Comment request (pertaining to applications for Medicare benefits for chronic renal disease).

64 FR 63680, November 17, 1999: HCFA Agency Information Collection Activities: Proposed Collection; Comment request (pertaining to end stage renal disease death notices).

64 FR 62681, November 17, 1999: HCFA Agency Information Collection Activities: Submission for OMB Review; Comment request (pertaining to peer review organization (PRO) reconsiderations and appeals).

64 FR 62681, November 17, 1999: HCFA Agency Information Collection Activities: Submission for OMB Review; Comment request (pertaining business proposal formats for utilization and quality control peer review organizations (PRO's)).

64 FR 66482, November 26, 1999: HCFA Agency Information Collection Activities: Proposed Collection; Comment request (pertaining to resident assessment in skilled nursing facilities).

64 FR 67291, December 1, 1999: HCFA Agency Information Collection Activities: Submission for OMB Review; Comment request (pertaining to forms to determine whether individual receive retirement payments based on State or local government employment or whether individual's employers subsidize Medicare Part A premiums).

64 FR 67918, December 3, 1999: HCFA Agency Information Collection Activities: Proposed Collection; Comment request (pertaining to conditions of participation for rural health clinics).

64 FR 67919, December 3, 1999: HCFA Agency Information Collection Activities: Proposed Collection; Comment request (pertaining to Medicare lifestyle modification program demonstration).

64 FR 67919, December 3, 1999: HCFA Agency Information Collection Activities: Proposed Collection; Comment request (pertaining to request for review of an initial determination of a Medicare Part B claim).

64 FR 68698, December 8, 1999: HCFA Agency Information Collection Activities: Submission for OMB Review; Comment request (pertaining to market survey of waste, fraud and abuse detection software).

64 FR 69021, December 9, 1999: HCFA Agency Information Collection Activities: Proposed Collection; Comment request (pertaining

to analysis of malpractice premium data to compute the physician fee schedule).

64 FR 69271, December 10, 1999: HCFA Agency Information Collection Activities: Proposed Collection; Comment request (pertaining to hospital providers of extender care (swing bed) services in Medicare and Medicaid).

64 FR 69272, December 10, 1999: HCFA Agency Information Collection Activities: Submission for OMB Review; Comment request (pertaining to community mental health center site visit assessment tools).

64 FR 69272, December 10, 1999: HCFA Agency Information Collection Activities: Submission for OMB Review; Comment request (pertaining to comprehensive outpatient rehabilitation facility (CORF) eligibility and survey forms).

64 FR 69273, December 10, 1999: HCFA Agency Information Collection Activities: Submission for OMB Review; Comment request (pertaining to Medicare/Medicaid hospital survey reports).

64 FR 69273, December 10, 1999: HCFA Agency Information Collection Activities: Submission for OMB Review; Comment request (pertaining to website bounceback forms for medicare.gov/nmpe).

64 FR 69273, December 10, 1999: HCFA Agency Information Collection Activities: Submission for OMB Review; Comment request (pertaining to HCFA-377 ambulatory surgical center survey report form).

64 FR 71148, December 20, 1999: HCFA Agency Information Collection Activities: Submission for OMB Review; Comment request (pertaining to CLIA survey reports).

64 FR 71797, December 22, 1999: HCFA Agency Information Collection Activities: Proposed Collection; Comment request (pertaining to electronic forms transfer to facilitate funds bank transfers for providers).

64 FR 73057, December 29, 1999: HCFA Office of Strategic Planning; Statement of Organization, Functions, and Delegations of Authority.

64 FR 73563, December 30, 1999: HCFA Agency Information Collection Activities: Submission for OMB Review; Comment request pertaining to Medicare program integrity organizational conflict of interest disclosure certificates).

2000

65 FR 135, January 3, 2000: HCFA Agency Information Collection Activities: proposed Collection; Comment request (pertaining to home health advance beneficiary notices). See also correction at 65 FR 2967, January 19, 2000.

65 FR 1161, January 7, 2000: HCFA Emergency Clearance: Public Information Collection Requirements submitted to the Office of Management and Budget (OMB) (pertaining to Medicare DMEPOS competitive bidding demonstration--site 2).

65 FR 1400, January 10, 2000: HCFA Agency Information Collection Activities: Submission for OMB Review; Comment request (pertaining to reporting outcome and assessment information set (OASIS) data set as a condition of participation for HHAs).

65 FR 2186, January 13, 2000: HCFA Agency Information Collection Activities; Submission for OMB Review; Comment request (pertaining to request for enrollment in supplementary Medical insurance).

65 FR 2186, January 13, 2000: HCFA Agency Information Collection Activities; Submission for OMB Review; Comment request (pertaining to physician certifications/re-certifications in skilled nursing facilities).

65 FR 2186, January 13, 2000: HCFA Agency Information Collection Activities; Submission for OMB Review; Comment request (pertaining to request for employment information from employers to determine whether a Medicare beneficiary's coverage under a group health plan is based on current employment.

65 FR 3724, January 24, 2000: HCFA Agency Information Collection Activities: Submission for OMB Review; Comment request (pertaining to evaluation by new Medicare members of Medicare+Choice plans).

65 FR 3725, January 24, 2000: HCFA Agency Information Collection Activities: submission for OMB Review; Comment request (pertaining to the adjusted community rate proposal for Medicare+Choice plan benefit packages).

65 FR 4437, January 27, 2000: HCFA Agency Information Collection Activities: Proposed Collection; Comment request (pertaining to durable medical equipment regional carrier certificate of medical necessity).

65 FR 4438, January 27, 2000: HCFA Agency Information Collection Activities: Submission for OMB Review; Comment request

(pertaining to emergency and foreign hospital services beneficiary statement in Canadian travel claims).

65 FR 4824, February 1, 2000: HCFA Agency Information Collection Activities: Submission for OMB Review; Comment request (pertaining to clinical laboratory personnel reports).

65 FR 5354, February 3, 2000: HCFA Agency Information Collection Activities: Proposed Collection; Comment request (pertaining to standardized Medicare/Medicaid claim form for reimbursement of covered services).

65 FR 5354, February 3, 2000: HCFA Agency Information Collection Activities: Proposed Collection; Comment request (pertaining to State buy-in programs).

65 FR 6614, February 10, 2000: HCFA Agency Information Collection Activities: Proposed Collection; Comment request (pertaining to Medicare managed care disenrollment form).

65 FR 8367, February 18, 2000: HCFA Agency Information Collection Activities: Proposed Collection; Comment request (pertaining to health care services for deaf and hard of hearing adults).

65 FR 8367, February 18, 2000: HCFA announcement of Office of Management and Budget (OMB) Control Numbers for Agency Information Collections Approved under the Paperwork Reduction Act of 1995.

65 FR 8370, February 18, 2000: HCFA Agency Information Collection Activities: Submission for OMB Review; Comment request (pertaining to a project to develop an outcome-based continuous quality improvement system for PACE).

65 FR 8983, February 23, 2000: HCFA Agency Information collection Activities: Submission for OMB Review; Comment request (pertaining to conditions of participation for rural health clinics).

65 FR 8983, February 23, 2000: HCFA Agency Information collection Activities: Submission for OMB Review; Comment request (pertaining to Medicare lifestyle modification program demonstration).

65 FR 10098, February 25, 2000: HCFA Agency Information Collection Activities: Proposed Collection; Comment request (pertaining to conflict of interest and ownership and control information with respect to fiscal intermediaries and carriers).

65 FR 10098, February 25, 2000: HCFA Agency Information Collection Activities: Proposed Collection; Comment request (pertaining to study to support development and refinement of a classification

system and prospective payment system for patients in inpatient rehabilitation hospitals and exempt rehabilitation units).

65 FR 11587, March 3, 2000: HCFA Agency Information Collection Activities: Proposed Collection; Comment request (pertaining to maximizing the effective use of telemedicine).

65 FR 11588, March 3, 2000: HCFA Agency Information Collection Activities: Proposed Collection; Comment request (pertaining to Medigap compare).

65 FR 11588, March 3, 2000: HCFA Agency Information Collection Activities: Submission for OMB Review; Comment request (pertaining to application for health insurance benefits under Medicare for individuals with chronic renal disease).

65 FR 11589, March 3, 2000: HCFA Agency Information Collection Activities: Submission for OMB Review; Comment request (pertaining to end stage renal disease medical information system/ESRD facility survey).

65 FR 11786, March 6, 2000: HCFA Notice of Hearing: Reconsideration of Disapproval of Utah State Children's Health Insurance Program (SCHIP) State Plan Amendment (SPA)—Notice of hearing.

65 FR 12556, March 9, 2000: HCFA Agency Information Collection Activities: Proposed Collection; Comment request (pertaining to individual market-guarantee issue election packet under HIPAA).

65 FR 12556, March 9, 2000: HCFA Agency Information Collection Activities: Proposed Collection; Comment request (pertaining to hospital request for certification in the Medicare/Medicaid program).

65 FR 12556, March 9, 2000: HCFA Agency Information Collection Activities: Proposed Collection; Comment request (pertaining to Medicaid drug rebate).

65 FR 12558, March 9, 2000: HCFA Agency Information Collection Activities: Proposed Collection; Comment request (pertaining to model application template for State child health plan under Title XXI of the Social Security Act).

65 FR 12559, March 9, 2000: HCFA Agency Information Collection Activities: Submission for OMB Review; Comment request (pertaining to end stage renal disease death notification).

65 FR 12559, March 9, 2000: HCFA Agency Information Collection Activities: Submission for OMB Review; Comment request (pertaining to authorization agreement for electronic forms transfer).

65 FR 12560, March 9, 2000: HCFA Agency Information Collection Activities: Submission for OMB Review; Comment request (pertain-

ing to hospital provider of extended care services (swing beds) in the Medicare and Medicaid programs).

65 FR 14288, March 16, 2000: HCFA Agency Information Collection Activities: Proposed Collection; Comment request (pertaining to end stage renal disease application and survey and certification).

65 FR 14986, March 20, 2000: HCFA Agency Information Collection Activities: Submission for OMB Review; Comment request (pertaining to skilled nursing facility resident assessment MDS data).

65 FR 15912, March 24, 2000: HCFA Agency Information Collection Activities: Submission for OMB Review; Comment request (pertaining to Medicare uniform institutional provider claim forms).

65 FR 15912, March 24, 2000: HCFA Agency Information Collection Activities: Submission for OMB Review; Comment request (pertaining to malpractice premium data).

65 FR 16924, March 30, 2000: HCFA Agency Information Collection Activities: Proposed Collection; Comment request (pertaining to a survey of beneficiaries who have disenrolled from their health care services plans).

65 FR 19382, April 11, 2000: HCFA Agency Information Collection Activities: Proposed Collection; Comment request (pertaining to evaluation of qualified Medicare Beneficiary (QMB) and specified low-income Medicare beneficiary (SLMB) outreach activities.

65 FR 19382, April 11, 2000: HCFA Emergency Clearance: Public Information Collection Requirements Submitted to the Office of Management and Budget (OMB) (pertaining to adjusted community rate for Medicare+Choice organizations.

65 FR 19782, April 12, 2000: HCFA Agency Information Collection Activities: Proposed Collection; Comment request (pertaining to methodology for estimating waiver costs of HCFA demonstration projects).

65 FR 19782, April 12, 2000: HCFA Agency Information Collection Activities: Proposed Collection; Comment request (pertaining to Medicare+Choice beneficiary notices).

65 FR 19783, April 12, 2000: HCFA Agency Information Collection Activities: Proposed Collection; Comment request (pertaining to pamphlet "Important Message About Medicare Rights: Admission, Discharge, and Appeals").

65 FR 19783, April 12, 2000: HCFA Emergency Clearance: Public Information Collection Requirements Submitted to the Office of

Management and Budget (OMB) (pertaining to Medicare+Choice beneficiary notices).

65 FR 24217, April 25, 2000: HCFA Agency Information Collection Activities: Submission for OMB Review; Comment request (pertaining to home health advance beneficiary notices).

65 FR 24707, April 27, 2000: HCFA Agency Information Collection Activities: Proposed Collection; Comment request (pertaining to collection of data on physician encounters from Medicare+Choice organizations).

65 FR 25736, May 3, 2000: HCFA Agency Information Collection Activities: Proposed Collection; Comment request (pertaining to Medicare DMEPOS competitive bidding demonstration; follow-up to original survey).

65 FR 25737, May 3, 2000: HCFA Agency Information Collection Activities: Proposed Collection; Comment request (pertaining to managed care disenrollment form).

65 FR 25737, May 3, 2000: HCFA Agency Information Collection Activities: Submission for OMB Review; Comment request (pertaining to health care services for deaf and hard of hearing adults).

65 FR 25738, May 3, 2000: HCFA Emergency Clearance: Public Informatiion Collection Requirements Submitted to the Office of Management and Budget (OMB) (pertaining to the Medicare managed care CAHPS Survey).

65 FR 25939, May 4, 2000: HCFA Agency Information Collection Activities: Proposed Collection; Comment request (pertaining to ambulatory surgical center payment rate survey).

65 FR 26218, May 5, 2000: HCFA Agency Information Collection Activities: Proposed Collection; Comment request (pertaining to CLIA amendments adverse action extract).

65 FR 26218, May 5, 2000: HCFA Agency Information Collection Activities: Submission for OMB Review; Comment request (pertaining to report of State buy-in problems).

65 FR 26618, May 5, 2000: HCFA Emergency Clearance: Public Information Collection Requirements Submitted to the Office of Management and Budget (OMB) (pertaining to Medicare consumer assessment survey of health plans).

65 FR 30414, May 11, 2000: HCFA Agency Information Collection Activities: Submission for OMB Review; Comment request (pertaining to health insurance common claims form).

65 FR 30415, May 11, 2000: HCFA Agency Information Collection Activities: Submission for OMB Review; Comment request (pertaining to conflict of interest and ownership and control information).

65 FR 31576, May 18, 2000: HCFA Agency Information Collection Activities: Submission for OMB Review; Comment request (pertaining to maximizing the effective use of telemedicine).

65 FR 34715, May 31, 2000: HCFA Agency Information Collection Activities: Submission for OMB Review; Comment request (pertaining to HIPAA individual market guarantee issue election packet).

65 FR 35379, June 2, 2000: HCFA Agency Information Collection Activities: Proposed Collection; Comment request (pertaining to requests for hearing of Medicare Part B claims and requests for reconsideration of Medicare Part A claims).

65 FR 35652, June 5, 2000: HCFA Agency Information Collection Activities: Proposed Collection; Comment request (pertaining to hospital and health care complex cost reports).

65 FR 35652, June 5, 2000: HCFA Agency Information Collection Activities: Proposed Collection; Comment request (pertaining to hospital conditions of participation; identification of potential organ, tissue, and eye donors and transplant hospitals' provision of transplant-related data).

65 FR 35652, June 5, 2000: HCFA Agency Information Collection Activities: Proposed Collection; Comment request (pertaining to home health agency cost reports).

65 FR 35653, June 5, 2000: HCFA Agency Information Collection Activities: Proposed Collection; Comment request (pertaining to ICF/MR survey forms).

65 FR 35653, June 5, 2000: HCFA Agency Information Collection Activities: Submission for OMB Review; Comment request (pertaining to model application template for State child health plan under Medicaid and the State Children's Health Insurance Program).

65 FR 35654, June 5, 2000: HCFA Agency Information Collection Activities: Submission for OMB Review; Comment request (pertaining to hospital request for certification in Medicare and Medicaid).

65 FR 35945, June 6, 2000: HCFA Agency Information Collection Activities: Proposed Collection; Comment request (pertaining to SNF cost reports).

65 FR 35946, June 6, 2000: HCFA Agency Information Collection Activities: Submission for OMB Review; Comment request (pertaining to Medigap compare).

65 FR 35946, June 6, 2000: HCFA Emergency Clearance: Public Information Collection Requirements Submitted to the Office of Management and Budget (OMB) (pertaining to the Ticket to Work and Work Incentives Act).

65 FR 35948, June 6, 2000: HCFA Privacy Act of 1974; System of Records (pertaining to Medicare enrollment records statistics).

65 FR 36453, June 8, 2000: HCFA Agency Information Collection Activities: Proposed Collection; Comment request (pertaining to Medicare+Choice beneficiary appeal notices and denials of medical services and denials of payment).

65 FR 36454, June 8, 2000: HCFA Agency Information Collection Activities: Proposed Collection; Comment request (pertaining to third party premium billing requests).

65 FR 36454, June 8, 2000: HCFA Agency Information Collection Activities: Proposed Collection; Comment request (pertaining to organ procurement organization histocompatibility laboratory statement of reimbursable costs).

65 FR 37566, June 15, 2000: HCFA Agency Information Collection Activities: Submission for OMB Review; Comment request (pertaining to hospice survey and deficiencies report form).

65 FR 37566, June 15, 2000: HCFA Agency Information Collection Activities: Submission for OMB Review; Comment request (pertaining to post-laboratory survey questionnaire under CLIA).

65 FR 37792, June 16, 2000: HCFA Privacy Act of 1974; Report of Altered System — Notice of the modification or alteration to 20 systems of records).

65 FR 38836, June 22, 2000: HCFA Emergency Clearance: Public Information Collection Requirements Submitted to the Office of Management and Budget (OMB) (pertaining to recognition of new technology/pass-through items under PPS for hospital outpatient services).

65 FR 39416, June 26, 2000: HCFA Agency Information Collection Activities: Proposed Collection; Comment request (pertaining to Medicare+Choice organization appeals and grievance data disclosure requirements).

65 FR 39417, June 26, 2000: HCFA Agency Information Collection Activities: Proposed Collection; Comment request (pertaining to Ticket to Work and Work Incentives: Medicaid infrastructure grants).

65 FR 40111, June 29, 2000: HCFA Emergency Clearance: Public Information Collection Requirements Submitted to the Office of

Management and Budget (OMB) (pertaining to health aging smoking cessation demonstration).

65 FR 40111, June 29, 2000: HCFA Agency Information Collection Activities: Proposed Collection; comment request (pertaining to qualification applications for prepaid health plans (HMOs).

65 FR 40668, June 30, 2000: HCFA Agency Information Collection Activities: Proposed Collection; Comment request (pertaining to request for termination of premium for hospital and/or supplementary medical insurance).

65 FR 40668, June 30, 2000: HCFA Agency Information Collection Activities: Submission for OMB Review; Comment request (pertaining to Medicare comprehensive health plan disenrollment).

65 FR 40669, June 30, 2000: HCFA Agency Information Collection Activities: Submission for OMB Review; Comment request (pertaining to Medicaid drug rebate program).

65 FR 42021, July 7, 2000: HCFA Agency Information Collection Activities: Proposed Collection; Comment request (pertaining to notice to providers, suppliers, and practitioners about non-covered services to beneficiaries).

65 FR 43025, July 12, 2000: HCFA Agency Information Collection Activities: Proposed Collection; Comment request (pertaining to indirect medical education of interns and residents).

65 FR 43026, July 12, 2000: HCFA Agency Information Collection Activities: Submission for OMB Review; Comment request (pertaining to collection of data on physician encounters from Medicare+Choice organizations).

65 FR 44798, July 19, 2000: HCFA Agency Information Collection Activities: Submission for OMB Review; Comment request (pertaining to Medicare DMEPOS competitive bidding demonstrations follow-up to original survey).

65 FR 45090, July 20, 2000: HCFA Agency Information Collection Activities: Proposed Collection; Comment request (pertaining to Medicare DMEPOS competitive bidding demonstration).

65 FR 45090, July 20, 2000: HCFA Agency Information Collection Activities; Proposed Collection; Comment request (pertaining to end stage renal disease (ESRD) network business proposal forms).

65 FR 45091, July 20, 2000: HCFA Intent of Emergency Clearance: Public Information Collection Meeting to Discuss Requirements to Be Resubmitted to the Office of Management and Budget (OMB) Concerning the Home Health Agency Beneficiary Notices).

65 FR 45091, July 2000: HCFA Agency Information Collection Activities: Submission for OMB Review; Comment request (pertaining to methodology for estimating waiver costs of HCFA demonstration projects).

65 FR 45992, July 26, 2000: HCFA Agency Information Collection Activities: Proposed Collection; Comment request (pertaining to psychiatric unit, rehabilitation unit, and rehabilitation hospital criteria worksheets).

65 FR 47738, August 3, 2000: HCFA Agency Information Collection Activities: Proposed Collection; Comment request (pertaining to Medicare beneficiary survey for Michigan PRO).

65 FR 47738, August 3, 2000: HCFA Agency Information Collection Activities: Proposed Collection; Comment request (pertaining to sterilization regulations and consent form).

65 FR 47739, August 3, 2000: HCFA Agency Information Collection Activities: Proposed Collection; Comment request (pertaining to municipal health services cost report form).

65 FR 47739, August 3, 2000: HCFA Agency Information Collection Activities: Submission for OMB Review; Comment request (pertaining to CLIA adverse action extract).

65 FR 47995, August 4, 2000: HCFA Agency Information Collection Activities: Proposed Collection; Comment request (pertaining to evaluation of the qualified Medicare Beneficiary (QMB) and specified low-income Medicare beneficiary (SLMB) programs).

65 FR 47995, August 4, 2000: HCFA Privacy Act of 1974; Report of New System (pertaining to the national emphysema treatment trial).

65 FR 48000, August 4, 2000: HCFA Privacy Act of 1974; Report of Modified or Altered System (pertaining to the explanation of Medicare benefits records).

65 FR 48003, August 4, 2000: HCFA Agency Information Collection Activities: Proposed Collection; Comment request (pertaining to Ricky Ray hemophilia relief fund program).

65 FR 49001, August 10, 2000: HCFA Emergency Clearance: Public Information Collection Requirements Submitted to the Office of Management and Budget (OMB) (pertaining to quality improvement system for managed care).

65 FR 49002, August 10, 2000: HCFA Emergency Clearance: Public Information Collection Requirements Submitted to the Office of Management and Budget (OMB) (pertaining to oxygen consumer survey for medical equipment and supplies).

65 FR 50544, August 18, 2000: HCFA Privacy Act of 1974; Report of New System (pertaining to links of Social Security Administration and HCFA data).

65 FR 50548, August 18, 2000: HCFA Privacy Act of 1974; Report of New System (pertaining to Medicare Provider Analysis and Review (MEDPAR) of all services rendered to a beneficiary from admission to discharge for hospital inpatient and SNF stays).

65 FR 50552, August 18, 2000: HCFA Privacy Act of 1974; Report of Modified or Altered System (pertaining to revision of language in global fraud and abuse routine uses).

65 FR 50713, August 21, 2000: HCFA Agency Information Collection Activities: Proposed Collection; Comment request (pertaining to social HMO demonstration payment methodology)

65 FR 50713, August 21, 2000: HCFA Agency Information Collection Activities: Proposed Collection; Comment request (pertaining to home health services under hospital insurance manual).

65 FR 50714, August 21, 2000: HCFA Agency Information Collection Activities: Submission for OMB Review; Comment request (pertaining to a study to develop and refine a classification system and prospective payment system for patients in in-patient rehabilitation hospitals and exempt rehabilitation units).

65 FR 53019, August 31, 2000: HCFA Agency Information Collection Activities: Proposed Collection; Comment request (pertaining to Medicare current beneficiary survey).

65 FR 53319, September 1, 2000: HCFA Agency Information Collection Activities: Proposed Collection; Comment request (pertaining to incentive arrangement disclosure form for managed care organizations and their related medical groups and physicians).

65 FR 53727, September 5, 2000: HCFA Agency Information Collection Activities: Proposed Collection; Comment request (pertaining to ambulance services reimbursement request form for physicians, suppliers, and beneficiaries).

65 FR 54535, September 8, 2000: HCFA Emergency Clearance: Public Information Collection Requirements Submitted to the Office of Management and Budget (OMB) (pertaining to stages of change survey for informed choice in the Medicare population).

65 FR 54536, September 8, 2000: HCFA Agency Information Collection Activities: Submission for OMB Review; Comment request (pertaining to reasonable costs incurred to furnish treatment to end stage renal disease patients by organ procurement organizations

and histocompatibility laboratories; and third party premium billing request forms).

65 FR 54856, September 11, 2000: HCFA Agency Information Collection Activities: Submission for OMB Review; Comment request (pertaining to skilled nursing facility cost reports).

65 FR 54856, September 11, 2000: HCFA Agency Information Collection Activities: Submission for OMB Review; Comment request (pertaining to hospital and health care complex cost reports).

65 FR 54857, September 11, 2000: HCFA Agency Information Collection Activities: Submission for OMB Review; Comment request (pertaining to ICF/MR survey report forms).

65 FR 54857, September 11, 2000: HCFA Agency Information Collection Activities: Submission for OMB Review; Comment request (pertaining to hospital conditions of participation-identification of potential organ, tissue, and eye donors, and transplant hospitals' provision of transplant-related data).

65 FR 55635, September 14, 2000: HCFA Agency Information Collection Activities: Submission for OMB Review; Comment request (pertaining to qualification application form for prepaid health plans; and request for termination of premium hospital and/or supplementary medical insurance).

65 FR 55982, September 15, 2000: HCFA Agency Information Collection Activities: Submission for OMB Review; Comment request (pertaining to Ticket to Work and Work Incentives).

65 FR 57195, September 21, 2000: HCFA Agency Information Collection Activities; Proposed Collection; Comment request (pertaining to Medicare managed care CAHPS survey for quality of care purposes).

65 FR 57356, September 22, 2000: HCFA Agency Information Collection Activities: Submission for OMB Review; Comment request (pertaining to requests for hearings under Medicare Part B; requests for reconsideration under Part A; requests for Part A hearing by an administrative law judge; and requests for Part B Medicare hearing by an administrative law judge).

65 FR 57821, September 26, 2000: HCFA Agency Information Collection Activities: Submission for OMB Review; Comment request (pertaining to the booklet, Important Message from Medicare).

65 FR 57821, September 26, 2000: HCFA Emergency Clearance: Public Information Collection Requirements Submitted to the Office

of Management and Budget (OMB) (pertaining to home health advanced beneficiary notices of liability).

65 FR 58279, September 28, 2000: HCFA Agency Information Collection Activities: Proposed Collection; Comment request (pertaining to Medicare consumer assessment survey of health plans, CAHPS).

65 FR 59193, October 4, 2000: HCFA Privacy Act of 1974; report of New System (pertaining to HCFA employee parking privileges).

65 FR 59431, October 5, 2000: HCFA Agency Information Collection Activities: Proposed Collection; Comment request (pertaining to conditions for coverage of suppliers of end stage renal disease services).

65 FR 59432, October 5, 2000: HCFA Agency Information Collection Activities: Submission for OMB Review; Comment request (pertaining to end stage renal disease application and survey and certification report).

65 FR 59432, October 5, 2000: HCFA Agency Information Collection Activities: Submission for OMB Review; Comment request (pertaining to Medicare DMEPOS competitive bidding demonstration).

65 FR 59433, October 5, 2000: HCFA Agency Information Collection Activities: Submission for OMB Review; Comment request (pertaining to HCFA employee building pass applications).

65 FR 59757, October 6, 2000: HCFA Agency Information Collection Activities: Proposed Collection; Comment request (pertaining to stages of change survey for informed choice in the Medicare population).

65 FR 59757, October 6, 2000: HCFA Agency Information Collection Activities: Proposed Collection; Comment request (pertaining to end stage renal disease provisions in provider reimbursement manual).

65 FR 59858, October 6, 2000: HCFA Notice of Extension of Emergency Office of Management and Budget Clearance of Agency Information Collection Activities (pertaining to notices and demand bills from home health agencies).

65 FR 59859, October 6, 2000: HCFA Agency Information Collection Activities: Submission for OMB Review; Comment request (pertaining to indirect medical education costs).

65 FR 60674, October 12, 2000: HCFA Agency Information Collection Activities: Submission for OMB Review; Comment request

(pertaining to Medicare+Choice organization appeals and grievance data disclosure requirements).

65 FR 60969, October 13, 2000: HCFA Agency Information Collection Activities: Proposed Collection; Comment request (pertaining to Ticket to Work and Work Incentives Act grants).

65 FR 60969, October 13, 2000: HCFA Emergency Clearance: Public Information Collection Requirements Submitted to the Office of Management and Budget (OMB) (pertaining to testing the effectiveness of three possible Medicare smoking cessation benefits).

65 FR 61171, October 16, 2000: HCFA Agency Information Collection Activities: Submission for OMB Review; Comment request (pertaining to psychiatric unit, rehabilitation unit, and rehabilitation hospital criteria worksheets).

65 FR 61171, October 16, 2000: HCFA Agency Information Collection Activities: Submission for OMB Review; Comment request (pertaining to Medicaid sterilization regulations and consent forms).

65 FR 62724, October 19, 2000: HCFA Notice of Emergency Clearance and Public Meeting: Public Information Collection Requirements Submitted to the Office of Management and Budget (OMB) (pertaining to Medicare secondary payment requirements).

65 FR 63080, October 20, 2000: HCFA Agency Information Collection Activities: Submission for OMB Review; Comment request (pertaining to evaluation of the qualified Medicare beneficiary and specified low-income Medicare beneficiary programs).

65 FR 63081, October 20, 2000: HCFA Agency Information Collection Activities: Submission for OMB Review; Comment request (pertaining to Medicaid report on payables and receivables, and municipal health services cost report form).

65 FR 64226, October 26, 2000: HCFA Agency Information Collection Activities: Proposed Collection; Comment request (pertaining to reconciliation of State invoices for drug rebate agreements).

65 FR 64227, October 26, 2000: HCFA Agency Information Collection Activities: Proposed Collection; Comment request (pertaining to home health agency cost reports; skilled nursing facility cost reports; and hospital cost reports).

65 FR 64227, October 26, 2000: HCFA Agency Information Collection Activities: Proposed Collection; Comment Request; Public Information Collection Meeting to Discuss Proposed Revisions (pertaining to notice requirements from suppliers, physicians, and practitioners to beneficiaries when Medicare Part B payment may be denied).

65 FR 64228, October 26, 2000: HCFA Agency Information Collection Activities: Proposed Collection; Comment request (pertaining to collection of data on physician encounters from Medicare+Choice organizations).

65 FR 64229, October 26, 2000: HCFA Emergency Clearance: Public Information Collection Requirements Submitted to the Office of Management and Budget (OMB) (pertaining to DMEPOS supplier survey).

65 FR 65860, November 2, 2000: HCFA Agency Information Collection Activities: Proposed Collection; Comment request (pertaining to follow-up of Medicare+Choice disenrollees receiving fee-for service inpatient hospital care).

65 FR 65860, November 2, 2000: HCFA Agency Information Collection Activities: Proposed Collection; Comment request (pertaining to reporting outcome and assessment (OASIS) data as part of conditions of participation for home health agencies).

65 FR 65861, November 2, 2000: HCFA Agency Information Collection Activities: Proposed Collection; Comment request (pertaining to conflict of interest disclosure requirements for Medicare program integrity).

65 FR 66255, November 3, 2000: HCFA Agency Information Collection Activities: Proposed Collection; Comment request (pertaining to survey of Medicaid home and community-based services waiver and personal care option recipients).

65 FR 66255, November 3, 2000: HCFA Agency Information Collection Activities: Proposed Collection; Comment request (pertaining to Medicare qualification for Federal employees).

65 FR 67751, November 13, 2000: HCFA Agency Information Collection Activities: Submission for OMB Review; Comment request (pertaining to Medicare beneficiary line survey).

65 FR 69942, November 21, 2000: HCFA Agency Information Collection Activities: Proposed Collection; Comment request (pertaining to restraints/seclusion death reporting by hospitals).

65 FR 69942, November 21, 2000: HCFA Agency Information Collection Activities: Proposed Collection; Comment request (pertaining to healthy aging smoking cessation demonstration).

65 FR 69942, November 21, 2000: HCFA Agency Information Collection Activities: Proposed Collection; Comment request (pertaining to Medicare beneficiary customer service survey).

65 FR 69943, November 21, 2000: HCFA Agency Information Collection Activities: Proposed Collection; Comment request (pertaining to imposition of cost sharing charges under Medicaid).

65 FR 69943, November 21, 2000: HCFA Agency Information Collection Activities: Proposed Collection; Comment request (pertaining to suggestion program on methods to improve Medicare efficiency).

65 FR 69944, November 21, 2000: HCFA Agency Information Collection Activities: Proposed Collection; Comment request (pertaining to additional DMEPOS supplier standards).

65 FR 69944, November 21, 2000: HCFA Agency Information Collection Activities: Proposed Collection; Comment request (pertaining to Medicare current beneficiary survey).

65 FR 75943, December 5, 2000: HCFA Agency Information Collection Activities: Submission for OMB Review; Comment Request (pertaining to Medicare payment for ambulance services); end stage renal disease reimbursement; and evaluation of the State Medicaid reform demonstrations).

65 FR 76647, December 7, 2000: HCFA Agency Information Collection Activities: Proposed Collection; Comment request (pertaining to alternate quality assessment survey in lieu of onsite survey for CLIA labs with good performance).

65 FR 76648, December 7, 2000: HCFA Agency Information Collection Activities: Proposed Collection; Comment (pertaining to Medicare coverage of liver transplants).

65 FR 76648, December 7, 2000: HCFA Agency Information Collection Activities: Proposed Collection; Comment (pertaining to criteria for Medicare coverage of lung transplants).

65 FR 77035, December 8, 2000: HCFA Agency Information Collection Activities: Proposed Collection; Comment request (pertaining to DMEPOS supplier survey).

65 FR 79867, December 20, 2000: HCFA Agency Information Collection Activities: Proposed Collection; Comment request (pertaining to home health Medicare conditions of participation information collection requirements).

65 FR 79867, December 20, 2000: HCFA Agency Information Collection Activities: Proposed Collection; Comment request (pertaining to quality improvement system for managed care).

65 FR 79868, December 20, 2000: HCFA Agency Information Collection Activities: Proposed Collection; Comment request (pertaining to Medicare consumer assessment survey of health plans).

65 FR 79868, December 20, 2000: HCFA Emergency Clearance: Public Information Collection Requirements Submitted to the Office of Management and Budget (OMB) (pertaining to survey of beneficiaries who involuntarily disenroll from their managed care plan).

2001

66 FR 1995, January 10, 2001: HCFA Agency Information Collection Activities: Proposed Collection; Comment request (pertaining to hospital outpatient encounters from Medicare+Choice programs).

66 FR 1996, January 10, 2001: HCFA Agency Information Collection Activities; Comment request (pertaining to Medicare uniform institutional provider bill for reimbursement of covered services by all providers that accept assignment of claims).

66 FR 1996, January 10, 2001: HCFA Agency Information Collection Activities; Proposed Collection; Comment request (pertaining to transmittal and notice of approval of State plan material and supporting regulations).

66 FR 1997, January 10, 2001: HCFA Notice of OMB Approval (pertaining to uniform home health advance beneficiary notice).

66 FR 2912, January 12, 2001: HCFA Agency Information Collection Activities: Proposed Collection; Comment request (pertaining to clinical laboratory ICRs contained in supporting regulations at 42 CFR section 493.1–.2001).

66 FR 2912, January 12, 2001: HCFA Agency Information Collection Activities: Proposed Collection; Comment request (pertaining to Medicare/Medicaid health insurance common claim form).

66 FR 2913, January 12, 2001: HCFA Agency Information Collection Activities: Proposed Collection; Comment request (pertaining to Ticket to Work and Work Incentives Act demonstration to maintain independence and employment grants).

66 FR 2913, January 12, 2001: HCFA Agency Information Collection Activities: Submission for OMB Review; Comment request (pertaining to collection of data about physician encounters from Medicare+Choice organizations).

66 FR 6628, January 22, 2001: HCFA Agency Information Collection Activities: Proposed Collection; Comment request (pertaining to ambulance supplier claim forms).

66 FR 6629, January 22, 2001: HCFA Agency Information Collection Activities: Submission for OMB Review; Comment request (pertaining to Medicaid drug rebate program).

66 FR 6629, January 22, 2001: HCFA Agency Information Collection Activities: Submission for OMB Review; Comment request (pertaining to Medicare Integrity Program Organizational Conflict of Interest Disclosure Certificate).

66 FR 7919, January 26, 2001: HCFA Agency Information Collection Activities: Proposed Collection; Comment request (pertaining to provider Medicare agreements).

66 FR 8806, February 2, 2001: HCFA Agency Information Collection Activities: Proposed Collection; Comment request (pertaining to national Medicare practitioner and provider survey about educational needs).

66 FR 8807, February 2, 2001: HCFA Agency Information Collection Activities: Proposed Collection; Comment request (pertaining to Medicare Federal health care programs provider/supplier enrollment application).

66 FR 8807, February 2, 2001: HCFA Agency Information Collection Activities: Submission for OMB Review; Comment request (pertaining to follow–up of Medicare+Choice disenrollees receiving fee–for–service inpatient hospital care).

66 FR 8808, February 2, 2001: HCFA Agency Information Collection Activities: Submission for OMB Review; Comment request (pertaining to suggestion program on methods to improve Medicare efficiency and supporting regulations).

66 FR 9586, February 8, 2001: HCFA Agency Information Collection Activities: Proposed Collection; Comment request (pertaining to negative case action process to determine the accuracy of ineligible determinations).

66 FR 9586, February 8, 2001: HCFA Agency Information Collection Activities: Proposed Collection; Comment request (pertaining to a project to develop an outcome–based continuous quality improvement system for PACE).

66 FR 9587, February 8, 2001: HCFA Agency Information Collection Activities: Proposed Collection; Comment request (pertaining to a project to develop an outcome–reporting of restraints and seclusion deaths by hospitals).

66 FR 9588, February 8, 2001: HCFA Agency Information Collection Activities: Proposed Collection; Comment request (pertaining to healthy aging smoking cessation demonstration).

66 FR 9588, February 8, 2001: HCFA Agency Information Collection Activities: Proposed Collection; Comment request (pertaining to imposition of cost–sharing charges under Medicaid).

66 FR 9712, February 9, 2001: HCFA Agency Information Collection Activities: Proposed Collection; Comment request (pertaining to Medicare customer service study for the Medicare Integrity Program).

66 FR 9858, February 12, 2001: HCFA Privacy Act of 1974; Report of New System (pertaining to complaints against health insurance issuers and health plans).

66 FR 10702, February 16, 2001: HCFA Agency Information Collection Activities: Submission for OMB Review; Comment request (pertaining to Medicare qualification statement for Federal employees).

66 FR 10702, February 16, 2001: HCFA Agency Information Collection Activities: Submission for OMB Review; Comment request (pertaining to stages of change survey for informed choice in the Medicare population).

66 FR 11035, February 21, 2001: HCFA Agency Information Collection Activities: Submission for OMB Review; Comment request (pertaining to reimbursement for ESRD providers).

66 FR 11591, February 26, 2001: HCFA Agency Information Collection Activities: Proposed Collection; Comment request (pertaining to Medicare+Choice program requirements).

66 FR 12940, March 1, 2001: HCFA Agency Information Collection Activities: Proposed Collection, Comment request (pertaining to independent renal dialysis facility cost report form).

66 FR 13327, March 5, 2001: HCFA Agency Information Activities Collection Activities: Submission for OMB Review; Comment request (pertaining to home health agency cost report form).

66 FR 13327, March 5, 2001: HCFA Agency Information Activities Collection Activities: Submission for OMB Review; Comment request (pertaining to criteria for Medicare coverage of liver transplants).

66 FR 13328, March 5, 2001: HCFA Agency Information Activities Collection Activities: Submission for OMB Review; Comment request (pertaining to criteria for Medicare coverage of lung transplants).

66 FR 13546, March 6, 2001: HCFA Agency Information Collection Activities: Proposed Collection; Comment request (pertaining to independent diagnostic testing facility documentation of proficiency of medical personnel and resources).

66 FR 13547, March 6, 2001: HCFA Agency Information Collection Activities: Proposed Collection; Comment request (pertaining to Medicare/Medicaid psychiatric hospital survey data).

66 FR 13547, March 6, 2001: HCFA Agency Information Collection Activities: Proposed Collection; Comment request (pertaining to hospice request for certification as a provider).

66 FR 14155, March 9, 2001: HCFA Agency Information Collection Activities: Proposed Collection; Comment request (pertaining to end stage renal disease medical evidence report for Medicare entitlement and/or patient registration).

66 FR 14156, March 9, 2001: HCFA Agency Information Collection Activities: Proposed Collection; Comment request (pertaining to oxygen consumer survey).

66 FR 14157, March 9, 2001: HCFA Agency Information Collection Activities: Submission for OMB review; Comment request (pertaining to home health Medicare conditions of participation information collection requirements).

66 FR 14157, March 9, 2001: HCFA Agency Information Collection Activities: Submission for OMB review; Comment request (pertaining to alternate quality assessment form for CLIA compliance).

66 FR 14392, March 12, 2001: HCFA Agency Information Collection Activities: Proposed Collection; Comment request (pertaining to recognition of new technology pass–through items under PPS for hospital outpatient services).

66 FR 14906, March 14, 2001: HCFA Agency Information Collection Activities: Proposed Collection; Comment request (pertaining to annual report on home and community based services waivers).

66 FR 15122, March 15, 2001: HCFA Agency Information Collection Activities: Proposed Collection; Comment request (pertaining to Medigap compare data form).

66 FR 15122, March 15, 2001: HCFA Agency Information Collection Activities: Submission for OMB Review; Comment request (pertaining to Medicare beneficiary customer service survey).

66 FR 15122, March 15, 2001: HCFA Agency Information Collection Activities: Submission for OMB Review; Comment request (pertaining to quality improvement system for managed care).

66 FR 15264, March 16, 2001: HCFA Agency Information Collection Activities; Proposed Collection; Comment request (pertaining to State health insurance assistance program (SHIP) client contact form).

66 FR 15264, March 16, 2001: HCFA Privacy Act of 1974; report of Modified or Altered System (pertaining to record of individuals authorized to enter HCFA buildings via card key access system).

66 FR 15496, March 19, 2001: HCFA Privacy Act of 1974; Report of Modified or Altered System (pertaining to "A Current Beneficiary Survey").

66 FR 16061, March 22, 2001: HCFA Agency Information Collection Activities: Proposed Collection; Comment request (pertaining to private contracts of physicians who opt out of Medicare).

66 FR 16062, March 23, 2001: HCFA Agency Information Collection Activities: Submission for OMB Review; Comment request (pertaining to Medicare+Choice beneficiary appeal notices).

66 FR 16062, March 23, 2001: HCFA Agency Information Collection Activities: Submission for OMB Review; Comment request (pertaining to SNF cost report forms).

66 FR 16063, March 23, 2001: HCFA Agency Information Collection Activities: Submission for OMB Review; Comment request (pertaining to hospital and health care complex cost report form).

66 FR 16268, March 23, 2001: HCFA Agency Information Collection Activities; Proposed Collection; Comment request (pertaining to data collection to support policy analysis of choices offered to Medicare+Choice enrollees and choices made by enrollees).

66 FR 16268, March 23, 2001: HCFA Agency Information Collection Activities; Proposed Collection; Comment request (pertaining to Medicaid post–eligibility preprint).

66 FR 16268, March 23, 2001: HCFA Agency Information Collection Activities: Submission for OMB Review; Comment request (pertaining to survey of home and community–based services waivers and personal care option recipients for the multi–site study of Medicaid home and community–based services).

66 FR 16480, March 26, 2001: HCFA Agency Information Collection Activities; Proposed Collection; Comment request (pertaining to hospital outpatient encounters from Medicare+Choice programs).

66 FR 16480, March 26, 2001: HCFA Agency Information Collection Activities; Proposed Collection; Comment request (pertaining to conditions of coverage of suppliers of end stage renal disease services). See also correction at 66 FR 18096, April 5, 2001.

66 FR 16481, March 26, 2001: HCFA Agency Information Collection Activities: Submission for OMB Review; Comment request (pertaining to managed care adjusted community rate proposal for Medicare+Choice organizations).

66 FR 16678, March 27, 2001: HCFA Agency Information Collection Activities: Submission for OMB Review; Comment request (pertaining to Medicare managed care CAHPS survey).

66 FR 16679, March 27, 2001: HCFA Privacy Act of 1974; Report of New System of Records (pertaining to "1–800 Medicare Choices Helpline")—Notice.

66 FR 17431, March 30, 2001: HCFA Agency Information Collection Activities: Proposed Collection; Comment request (pertaining to data collection of quality indicators for congestive heart failure submitted by Medicare+Choice organizations requesting extra payments in CY 2002 and CY 2003).

66 FR 18096, April 5, 2001: HCFA Agency Information Collection Activities: Proposed Collection; Comment request (pertaining to employment information for Medicare enrollment purposes).

66 FR 18645, April 10, 2001: HCFA Agency Information Collection Activities: Submission for OMB Review; Comment request (pertaining to Medicare and Medicaid outcome and assessment information set (OASIS) as part of the conditions of participation for home health agencies).

66 FR 18646, April 10, 2001: HCFA Agency Information Collection Activities: Submission for OMB Review; Comment request (pertaining to transmittal and notice of approval of state plan material).

66 FR 18646, April 10, 2001: HCFA Agency Information Collection Activities: Submission for OMB Review; Comment request (pertaining to Medicare/Medicaid health insurance common claim form).

66 FR 18647, April 10, 2001: HCFA Agency Information Collection Activities: Submission for OMB Review; Comment request (pertaining to CLIA compliance).

66 FR 18781, April 11, 2001: HCFA Agency Information Collection Activities: Proposed Collection; Comment request (pertaining to Peer Review Organization contracts and solicitation of statements of interest).

66 FR 18958, April 12, 2001: HCFA Agency Information Collection Activities: Submission for OMB Review; Comment request (pertaining to information collection requirements for ambulance services).

66 FR 18958, April 12, 2001: HCFA Agency Information Collection Activities: Submission for OMB Review; Comment request (pertaining to survey instrument for special populations).

66 FR 18959, April 12, 2001: HCFA Agency Information Collection Activities: Submission for OMB Review; Comment request (pertaining to organ procurement organization requests for designation).

66 FR 18959, April 12, 2001: HCFA Agency Information Collection Activities: Submission for OMB Review; Comment request (pertaining to home health services under Part A).

66 FR 19507, April 16, 2001: HCFA Agency Information Collection Activities: Proposed Collection; Comment request (pertaining to conflict of interest and ownership and control information form).

66 FR 19508, April 16, 2001: HCFA Agency Information Collection Activities: Proposed Collection; Comment request (pertaining to on site inspection for durable medical equipment (DME) suppliers).

66 FR 19508, April 16, 2001: HCFA Agency Information Collection Activities: Proposed Collection; Comment request (pertaining to real choice systems change grants, nursing facility transition/access housing grants, community personal assistance service and supports grants, national technical assistance and learning collaborative grants to support systems change for community living).

66 FR 19789, April 17, 2001: HCFA Agency Information Collection Activities: Proposed Collection; Comment request (pertaining to Medicare provider cost report reimbursement questionnaire).

66 FR 20314, April 20, 2001: HCFA Agency Information Collection Activities: Proposed Collection; Comment request (pertaining to survey of Medicaid home and community–based services waiver and personal care option recipients).

66 FR 20314, April 20, 2001: HCFA Agency Information Collection Activities: Proposed Collection; Comment request (pertaining to informatics, telemedicine, and education demonstration).

66 FR 20315, April 20, 2001: HCFA Agency Information Collection Activities: Proposed Collection; Comment request (pertaining to inpatient rehabilitation assessment instrument).

66 FR 20315, April 20, 2001: HCFA Agency Information Collection Activities: Submission for OMB Review; Comment request (pertaining to DMEPOS supplier standards).

66 FR 20316, April 20, 2001: HCFA Agency Information Collection Activities: Submission for OMB Review; Comment request (pertaining to DMEPOS supplier survey).

66 FR 20316, April 20, 2001: HCFA Agency Information Collection Activities: Submission for OMB Review; Comment request (pertaining to advance beneficiary notice by physicians, practitioners, suppliers, and providers about items and services denied by Medicare as not reasonable and necessary).

66 FR 20997, April 26, 2001: HCFA Agency Information Collection Activities: Proposed Collection; Comment request (pertaining to maximizing the effective use of telemedicine).

66 FR 20997, April 26, 2001: HCFA Agency Information Collection Activities: Submission for OMB Review; Comment request (pertaining to health insurance provider agreement form).

66 FR 21770, May 1, 2001: HCFA Agency Information Collection Activities: Submission for OMB Review; Comment request (pertaining to Medicare uniform institutional provider bill form).

66 FR 21987, May 2, 2001: HCFA Agency Information Collection Activities: Proposed Collection; Comment request (pertaining to Medicare+Choice provider sponsored organization (PSO) waiver request form).

66 FR 22242, May 3, 2001: HCFA Agency Information Collection Activities: Proposed Collection; Comment request (pertaining to CLIA certification requirements).

66 FR 22242, May 3, 2001: HCFA Agency Information Collection Activities: Proposed Collection; Comment request (pertaining to application form to establish entitlement to hospital insurance and supplementary health insurance).

66 FR 23944, May 10, 2001: HCFA Agency Information Collection Activities: Proposed Collection; Comment request (pertaining to financial reports for providers indebted to Medicare who want to repay over time).

66 FR 23944, May 10, 2001: HCFA Agency Information Collection Activities: Proposed Collection; Comment request (pertaining to examination and treatment for emergency conditions and women in labor).

66 FR 23945, May 10, 2001: HCFA Agency Information Collection Activities: Submission for OMB Review; Comment request (pertaining to development of an outcome–based continuous quality improvement system for PACE).

66 FR 23945, May 10, 2001: HCFA Agency Information Collection Activities: Submission for OMB Review; Comment request (pertaining to Medicare program integrity study to improve customer satisfaction).

66 FR 23946, May 10, 2001: HCFA Emergency Clearance: Public Information Collection Requirements Submitted to the Office of Management and Budget (OMB) (pertaining to provision of community–based services for persons with disabilities who would otherwise receive services in an institutional setting).

66 FR 24146, May 11, 2001: HCFA Agency Information Collection Activities: Proposed Collection; Comment request (pertaining to survey of Medicare beneficiaries in medically underserved areas).

66 FR 24391, May 14, 2001: HCFA Agency Information Collection Activities: Submission for OMB Review; Comment request (pertaining to Medicare+Choice program requirements).

66 FR 26869, May 15, 2001: HCFA Agency Information Collection Activities: Proposed Collection; Comment request (pertaining to data use agreement and information collection requirements for protecting privacy).

66 FR 27151, May 16, 2001: HCFA Agency Information Collection Activities: Proposed Collection; Comment request (pertaining to the Long Term Care Awareness Project).

66 FR 27519, May 17, 2001: HCFA Agency Information Collection Activities: Submission for OMB Review; Comment request (pertaining to independent renal dialysis facility cost report form).

66 FR 28188, May 22, 2001: HCFA Privacy Act of 1974; Computer Matching Program (Match Number 2001–04)—Notice.

66 FR 28916, May 25, 2001: HCFA Agency Information Collection Activities; Proposed Collection; Comment request (pertaining to procedures for advisory opinions concerning physician referrals under section 1877 of the Social Security Act).

66 FR 28916, May 25, 2001: HCFA Agency Information Collection Activities: Proposed Collection; Comment request (pertaining to collection of managed care data using the uniform institutional providers form).

66 FR 29581, May 31, 2001: HCFA Agency Information Collection Activities: Submission for OMB Review; Comment request (pertaining to national Medicare Practitioner and Provider survey).

66 FR 29823, June 1, 2001: HCFA Agency Information Collection Activities: Proposed Collection; Comment request (pertaining to data reporting requirements for managed care organizations in the Medicare+Choice program).

66 FR 29823, June 1, 2001: HCFA Agency Information Collection Activities: Submission for OMB review; Comment request (pertaining to medical equipment and supplies consumer survey).

66 FR 29824, June 1, 2001: HCFA Agency Information Collection Activities: Submission for OMB review; Comment request (pertaining to end stage renal disease medical evidence report for Medicare entitlement and patient registration).

66 FR 30739, June 7, 2001: HCFA Agency Information Collection Activities: Submission for OMB Review; Comment request (pertaining to PRO contract solicitation).

66 FR 32360, June 14, 2001: HCFA Agency Information Collection Activities: Proposed Collection; Comment request (pertaining to evaluation of the BadgerCare Medicaid demonstration in Wisconsin).

66 FR 32360, June 14, 2001: HCFA Agency Information Collection Activities: Proposed Collection; Comment request (pertaining to end stage renal disease death notification).

66 FR 32630, June 15, 2001: HCFA Agency Information Collection Activities; Submission for OMB Review; Comment request (pertaining to contracts by practitioners and physicians who opt–out of Medicare).

66 FR 33102, June 20, 2001: HCFA Agency Information Collection Activities; Submission for OMB Review; Comment request (pertaining to provider/supplier enrollment application form).

66 FR 33102, June 20, 2001: HCFA Agency Information Collection Activities; Submission for OMB Review; Comment request (pertaining to "Medigap Compare" data).

66 FR 33103, June 20, 2001: HCFA Agency Information Collection Activities; Submission for OMB Review; Comment request (pertaining to Medicaid post–eligibility form).

66 FR 34222, June 27, 2001: HCFA Agency Information Collection Activities: Proposed Collection; Comment request (pertaining to limitation on provider–related donations and health care–related taxes; and limitations on payments to disproportionate share hospitals).

66 FR 34222, June 27, 2001: HCFA Agency Information Collection Activities: Proposed Collection; Comment request (pertaining to CLIA budget workload reports).

66 FR 34223, June 27, 2001: HCFA Agency Information Collection Activities: Submission for OMB Review; Comment request (pertaining to data on quality indicators for congestive heart failure submitted by Medicare+Choice organizations seeking extra payment).

66 FR 34457, June 28, 2001: HCFA Agency Information Collection Activities: Proposed Collection; Comment request (pertaining to durable medical equipment and prosthetics, orthotics, and supplies supplier survey).

See § 4:1.

§ 8:2 FALSE REPRESENTATIONS ABOUT REQUIREMENTS OF THE SOCIAL SECURITY ACT — Section 1107(a) [42 U.S.C.A. 1307]

Regulations

None

See § 4:2.

§ 8:3 FALSE REPRESENTATIONS TO ELICIT INFORMATION FROM THE SECRETARY OF HEALTH AND HUMAN SERVICES — Section 1107(b) [42 U.S.C.A. 1307(b)]

Regulations

20 CFR Part 401 — Disclosure of Official Records and Information [Social Security]

42 CFR Part 401, Subpart B — Confidentiality and Disclosure

See § 4:3.

§ 8:4 FAILURE TO COMPLY WITH STATE HEALTH PLANNING REQUIREMENTS — Section 1122 [42 U.S.C.A. 1320a-1]

Regulations

42 CFR Subchapter I — Medical Care Quality and Cost Containment, Part 100 — Cost Containment and Quality Control

42 CFR Part 405, Subpart R — Provider Reimbursement Determinations and Appeals, especially Section 405.1890: Appeals from a determination under section 1122 of the Act

[Note: Find CFR as of October 1, 1988.]

See § 4:4.

§ 8:5 FAILURE TO COMPLY WITH SUBPOENAS ISSUED BY THE COMPTROLLER GENERAL — Section 1125(b) [42 U.S.C.A. 1320a-4(b)]

Regulations

20 CFR Part 401 — Disclosure of Official Records and Information [Social Security]

42 CFR Part 401, Subpart B — Confidentiality and Disclosure

42 CFR Part 417 — Health Maintenance Organizations, especially Section 417.482: Access to facilities and records; and Section 417.486: Disclosure of information and confidentiality

42 CFR Part 420 — Program Integrity: Medicare

42 CFR Part 431, Subpart C —Administrative Requirements: Provider Relations, especially Section 431.115: Disclosure of survey information and provider or contractor evaluation; and Subpart F — Safeguarding Information on Applicants and Recipients

42 CFR Part 455 — Program Integrity: Medicaid

42 CFR Part 456, Subpart C —Utilization Control: Hospitals, Section 446.112: Records and reports, and Section 456.113: Confidentiality; Subpart D — Utilization Control: Mental Hospitals, Section 456.212: Records and reports, and Section 456.213: Confidentiality; Subpart E — Utilization Control: Skilled Nursing Facilities, Section 456.312: Records and reports, and Section 456.313: Confidentiality; Subpart F — Utilization Control: Intermediate Care Facilities, Section 456.412: Records and reports, and Section 456.413: Confidentiality

42 CFR Part 475 — Peer Review Organizations

42 CFR Part 476 — Utilization and Quality Control Review

42 CFR Part 480 — Acquisition, Protection, and Disclosure of Peer Review Information

See § 4:5.

§ 8:6 EXCLUSION FROM MEDICARE AND STATE HEALTH CARE PROGRAMS — Section 1128 [42 U.S.C.A. 1320a-6]

Regulations

42 CFR Part 402 — Civil Money Penalties, Assessments, and Exclusions

42 CFR Part 405, Subpart C — Suspension of Payment, Recovery of Overpayments, and Repayment of Scholarships and Loans

42 CFR Part 411 — Exclusions from Medicare and Limitations on Medicare Payment

42 CFR Part 420 — Program Integrity: Medicare

42 CFR Part 455 — Program Integrity: Medicaid

42 CFR Part 498 — Appeals Procedures for Determinations that Affect Participation in the Medicare Program and for Determinations that Affect the Participation of ICF's/MR and Certain NF's in the Medicaid Program

42 CFR Chapter V — Office of Inspector General — Health Care, Department of Health and Human Services

Subchapter A - General Provisions

Part 1000 - Introduction; General Definitions

Subchapter B - OIG Authorities

Part 1001 - Program Integrity: Medicare and State Health Care Programs

Part 1002 - Program Integrity: State-initiated Exclusion from Medicaid

Part 1003 - Civil Money Penalties, Assessments and Exclusions

Part 1004 — Imposition of Sanctions on Health Care Practitioners and Providers of Health Care Services by a Peer Review Organization

Part 1005 — Appeals of Exclusions, Civil Money Penalties and Assessments

Part 1006 — Investigational Inquiries

Part 1007 — State Medicaid Fraud Control Units

Part 1008 — Advisory Opinions by the OIG

55 FR 3986, February 6, 1990: Medicare and Social Security: Fraud and Abuse; Civil Money Penalties for Misuse of Certain Terms, Symbols and Emblems — Proposed rule.

55 FR 12205, April 2, 1990: Health Care Programs: Fraud and Abuse; Amendments to OIG Exclusion and CMP Authorities Resulting from Public Law 100–93, the Medicare and Medicaid Patient and Program Protection Act of 1987, Public Law 99–272, the Consolidated Omnibus Budget Reconciliation Act of 1985, and Public Law 100–360, the Medicare Catastrophic Coverage Act of 1988 — Proposed rule to amend 42 CFR Parts 1000, 1001, 1002, 1003, 1004, 1005, 1006, and 1007. See also correction published at 55 FR 17461, April 25, 1990.

56 FR 33403, July 22, 1991: Medicare and State Health Care Programs: Fraud and Abuse; Civil Monetary Penalties and Intermediate Sanctions for Certain Violations by Health Maintenance Organizations and Competitive Medical Plans — Proposed rule.

56 FR 35952, July 29, 1991: Medicare and State Health Care Programs: Fraud and Abuse; OIG Anti-Kickback Provisions — Final rule.

56 FR 37054, August 2, 1991: Medicare and Medicaid Programs; Survey and Enforcement Requirements and Alternative Sanctions for Home Health Agencies — Proposed rule affecting 42 CFR Parts 441, 488, and 489.

56 FR 61374, December 3, 1991: Medicare Program; Reporting Requirements for Financial Relationships Between Physicians and Health Care Entities That Furnish Selected Items and Ser-

vices — Interim final rule with comment period affecting 42 CFR Part 411.

57 FR 3298, January 29, 1992: Health Care Programs: Fraud and Abuse; Amendments to OIG Exclusion and CMP Authorities Resulting From Public Law 100–93 — Final rule affecting 42 CFR Parts 1001, 1002, 1003, 1004, 1005, 1006, and 1007. See also final rule and correction at 57 FR 9669, March 20, 1992; final rule affecting 42 CFR Parts 1001and 1005, with clarification at 58 FR 5617, January 22, 1993; and final rule affecting 42 CFR Part 1001, with correction, at 58 FR 40752, July 30, 1993.

57 FR 8588, March 11, 1992: Medicare Program; Physician Ownership of, and Referrals to, Health Care Entities that Furnish Clinical Laboratory Services — Proposed rule affecting 42 CFR Part 411.

57 FR 19089, May 4, 1992: Medicare Program; Offset of Medicare Payments to Individuals to Collect Past-Due Obligations Arising From Breach of Scholarship and Loan Contracts — Final rule affecting 42 CFR Part 405.

57 FR 46865, October 13, 1992: HCFA Public Information Collection Requirements Submitted to the Office of Management and Budget for Clearance (pertaining to impact of home health care plan management and evaluation; end-stage renal disease medical case review; Medicare/Medicaid hospital swing-bed survey report form; quarterly Medicaid statement of expenditures; Medicaid program budget report; information collection requirements in final peer review organization sanction regulations; appeals procedures for determinations that affect participation in Medicare; request for medical review information for Part B intermediary outpatient therapy bills and other Part B outpatient bills; and Medicaid limitations on provider-related donations and health care-related taxes, and limitations on payment to disproportionate share hospitals).

57 FR 52723, November 5, 1992: Medicare and State Health Care Programs: Fraud and Abuse; Safe Harbors for Protecting Health Plans — Interim final rule with request for comment. See also extension of comment period at 58 FR 2989, January 7, 1993, affecting 42 CFR 1001.

57 FR 59024, December 14, 1992: Medicare and Medicaid Programs; Requirements for Physician Incentive Plans in Prepaid Health Care Organizations — Proposed rule affecting 42 CFR Parts 417 and 434 (HCFA) and 42 CFR Part 1003 (Office of Inspector

General). See also extension of comment period at 58 FR 8568, February 16, 1993.

59 FR 9452, February 28, 1994: Office of Inspector General: Health Care Programs; Fraud and Abuse; Revisions to the PRO Sanctions Process — Proposed rule affecting 42 CFR Part 1004.

59 FR 36072, July 15, 1994: Medicare and State Health Care Programs: Fraud and Abuse, Civil Money Penalties and Intermediate Sanctions for Certain Violations by Health Maintenance Organizations and Competitive Medical Plans — Final rule affecting 42 CFR Parts 417, 431, 434, and 1003. See also correction at 59 FR 48566, September 22, 1994.

59 FR 37202, July 21, 1994: Medicare and State Health Care Programs; Fraud and Abuse; Clarification of the OIG Safe Harbor Anti-kickback Provisions — Proposed rule affecting 42 CFR Part 1001.

59 FR 50762, October 5, 1994: HCFA Public Information Collection Requirements Submitted to the Office of Management and Budget (OMB) for Clearance (pertaining to reimbursement of hospital costs for residents and interns, criteria for psychiatric and rehabilitation hospital units' reimbursement under the prospective payment system, disclosure of owners and managers of suppliers for fraud and abuse detection purposes, reimbursement of municipal health services clinics, survey form for hospital compliance with anti-dumping requirements, and evaluation of patient and physician satisfaction with the Medicare participating heart bypass center demonstration).

59 FR 61571, December 1, 1994: Office of Inspector General; Fraud and Abuse; Civil Money Penalties for Hospital Physician Incentive Plans — Proposed rule affecting 42 CFR Part 1003.

59 FR 65372, December 19, 1994: Office of Inspector General — Notice of Publication of Special Fraud Alerts (pertaining to joint venture arrangements, routine waiver of Medicare Part B copayments and deductibles, hospital incentives to referring physicians, prescription drug marketing practices, and arrangements for provision of clinical laboratory services).

60 FR 16580, March 31, 1995: Office of Inspector General: Civil Money Penalties for Referrals to Entities and for Prohibited Arrangements and Schemes — Final rule with comment period, affecting 42 CFR Part 1003.

60 FR 32916, June 26, 1995: Office of Inspector General; Health Care Programs; Fraud and Abuse; Technical Revision to the Scope

and Effect of the OIG Exclusion Regulations — Final rule affecting 42 CFR Part 1001.

60 FR 40847, August 10, 1995: Office of Inspector General: Publication of OIG Special Fraud Alerts: Home Health Fraud, and Fraud and Abuse in the Provision of Medical Supplies to Nursing Facilities — Notice.

60 FR 41914, August 14, 1995: Medicare Program; Physician Financial Relationships with, and Referrals to, Health Care Entities that Furnish Clinical Laboratory Services; Financial Relationship Reporting Requirements — Final rule affecting 42 CFR Part 411.

60 FR 55721, November 2, 1995: Office of Inspector General Publication of the Medicare Advisory Bulletin on Hospice Benefits — Notice.

60 FR 58239, November 27, 1995: Office of Inspector General; Health Care Programs: Fraud and Abuse; Revisions to the Civil Money Penalty Provisions Relating to the Misuse of Certain Names, Symbols and Emblems — Final rule affecting 42 CFR Part 1003.

60 FR 63634, December 12, 1995: Office of Inspector General; Health Care Programs: Fraud and Abuse; Revisions to the PRO Sanctions Process — Final rule. See also correction at 61 FR 1841, January 24, 1996.

61 FR 2122, January 25, 1996: Medicare and State Health Care Programs; Fraud and Abuse; Safe Harbors for Protecting Health Plans — Final rule.

61 FR 7522, February 28, 1996: HCFA Public Information Collection Requirements Submitted for Public Comment and Recommendations (pertaining to Medicare and Medicaid disclosure of ownership and control interest statements).

61 FR 13430, March 27, 1996: Medicare and Medicaid Programs; Requirements for Physician Incentive Plans in Prepaid Health Care Organizations — Final rule with comment period, affecting 42 CFR Parts 417, 434, and 1003.

61 FR 30623, June 17, 1996: Office of Inspector General Publication of OIG Special Fraud Alert: Fraud and Abuse in the Provision of Services in Nursing Homes — Notice.

61 FR 33532, June 27, 1996: HCFA Agency Information Collection Activities: Submission for OMB Review; Comment Request (pertaining to information collection requirements in PRO sanction regulations).

61 FR 52299, October 7, 1996: Office of Inspector General; Medicare and State Health Care Programs and Program Fraud Civil

Remedies: Fraud and Abuse; Civil Money Penalties Inflation Adjustments — Final rule affecting 42 CFR Part 1003.

61 FR 58568, November 15, 1996: Office of Inspector General; Publication of the Medicare Beneficiary Advisory Bulletin on HMO Arrangements — Notice.

61 FR 69060, December 31, 1996: Office of Inspector General: Solicitation of New Safe Harbors and Modifications to Existing Safe Harbors — Notice of intent to develop regulations, affecting 42 CFR Part 1001.

62 FR 7350, February 19, 1997: Office of Inspector General: Medicare and State Health Care Programs: Fraud and Abuse; Issuance of Advisory Opinions by the OIG — Interim final rule with comment period, affecting 42 CFR Part 1008.

62 FR 23140, April 29, 1997: Office of Inspector General: Health Care Programs: Fraud and Abuse; Revised PRO Sanctions for Failing to Meet Statutory Obligations — Final rule.

62 FR 39798, July 24, 1997: Office of Inspector General: Negotiated Rulemaking Committee on the Shared Risk Exception (affecting 42 CFR Part 1001) — Notice of meeting.

62 FR 47182, September 8, 1997: Office of Inspector General: Health Care Programs: Fraud and Abuse; Revised OIG Exclusion Authorities Resulting from Public Law 104–191 — Notice of Proposed rulemaking, affecting 42 CFR Parts 1000, 1001, 1002, and 1005.

62 FR 47195, September 8, 1997: Office of Inspector General: Negotiated Rulemaking Committee on the Shared Risk Exception (affecting 42 CFR Part 1001) — Notice of meeting.

62 FR 55410, October 24, 1997: Office of Inspector General: Criteria for Implementing Permissive Exclusion Authority under Section 1128(b)(7) of the Social Security Act — Notice.

62 FR 63689, December 2, 1997: Office of Inspector General: Negotiated Rulemaking Committee on the Shared Risk Exception — Notice of meeting, affecting 42 CFR Part 1001.

62 FR 65049, December 10, 1997: Office of Inspector General: Solicitation of New Safe Harbors and Special Fraud Alerts — Notice of intent to develop regulations, affecting 42 CFR Part 1001.

62 FR 67392, December 24, 1997: Office of Inspector General: Criteria for Implementing Permissive Exclusion Authority under Section 1128(b)(7) of the Social Security Act — Notice.

63 FR 187, January 5, 1998: Office of Inspector General; Negotiated Rulemaking Committee on the Shared Risk Exception — Notice of meeting.

63 FR 8987, February 23, 1998: Office of Inspector General: Publication of the OIG Compliance Program for Hospitals — Notice.

63 FR 9844, February 26, 1998: HCFA Agency Information Collection Activities: Proposed Collection; Comment request (pertaining to procedures for advisory opinions concerning physician referrals and supporting regulations in 42 CFR Sections 411.370- 411.389).

63 FR 14393, March 25, 1998: Office of Inspector General: Health Care Programs: Fraud and Abuse; Revised OIG Civil Money Penalties Resulting from the Health Insurance Portability and Accountability Act of 1996 — Notice of proposed rulemaking, affecting 42 CFR Parts 1003, 1005, and 1006.

63 FR 20415, April 24, 1998: Office of Inspector General: Publication of OIG Special Fraud Alert: Fraud and Abuse in Nursing Home Arrangements with Hospices — Notice.

63 FR 28395, May 22, 1998: HCFA Agency Information Collection Activities: Submission for OMB Review; Comment request (pertaining to procedures for advisory opinions concerning physician referrals and supporting regulations in 42 CFR 411.370 through 411.389).

63 FR 31123, June 8, 1998: Medicare Program; Incentive Programs — Fraud and Abuse — Final rule affecting 42 CFR Part 420.

63 FR 38311, July 16, 1998: Office of Inspector General: Medicare and State Health Care Programs: Fraud and Abuse; Issuance of Advisory Opinions by the OIG — Final rule affecting 42 CFR 1008. See also correction at 63 FR 43449, August 13, 1998.

63 FR 38414, July 16, 1998: HCFA Privacy Act of 1974; Report of Altered System (pertaining to disclosure of individual-specific information to combat fraud or abuse in health benefit programs).

63 FR 42409, August 7, 1998: Office of Inspector General: Solicitation of Information and Recommendations for Developing OIG Compliance Program Guidance for the Durable Medical Equipment Industry — Notice.

63 FR 42410, August 7, 1998: Office of Inspector General: Publication of the OIG Compliance Program Guidance for Home Health Agencies — Notice.

63 FR 45076, August 24, 1998: Office of Inspector General — Publication of OIG Compliance Program Guidance for Clinical Laboratories.

63 FR 46676, September 2, 1998: Office of Inspector General: Health Care Programs; Fraud and Abuse; Revised OIG Exclusion Authorities Resulting from Public Law 104–191 — Final rule affecting 42 CFR Parts 1000, 1001, 1002, and 1005. See also correction at 63 FR 57918, October 29, 1998.

63 FR 46736, September 2, 1998: Office of Inspector General: Health Care Programs; Fraud and Abuse; Revised OIG Sanction Authorities Resulting from Public Law 105–33 — Notice of proposed rulemaking affecting 42 CFR 1001, 1002, and 1003.

63 FR 50577, September 22, 1998: Office of Inspector General: Solicitation of Information and Recommendations for Developing OIG Compliance Program Guidance for Certain Medicare+Choice Organizations — Notice.

63 FR 58341, October 30, 1998: Office of Inspector General: Health Care Fraud and Abuse Data Collection Program: Reporting of Final Adverse Actions — Notice of proposed rulemaking under section 1128E of the Social Security Act, affecting 45 CFR 61.

63 FR 58399, October 30, 1998: Office of Inspector General: Publication of the OIG's Provider Self-Disclosure Protocol — Notice.

63 FR 67486, December 7, 1998: Office of Inspector General and HCFA; Solicitation of Comments on the OIG/HCFA Special Advisory Bulletin on the Patient Anti-Dumping Statute — Notice.

63 FR 68223, December 10, 1998: Office of Inspector General; Solicitation of New Safe Harbors and Special Fraud Alerts — Notice of intent to develop regulations, affecting 42 CFR 1001.

63 FR 68687, December 14, 1998: Medicare and Medicaid Program; Civil Money Penalties, Assessments, Exclusions, and Related Appeals Procedures — Final rule with comment period, affecting 42 CFR 400 and 402.

63 FR 70137, December 18, 1998: Office of Inspector General: Solicitation of Information and Recommendations for Developing OIG Compliance Program Guidance for the Nursing Home Industry — Notice.

63 FR 70138, December 18, 1998: Office of Inspector General: Publication of the OIG Compliance Program Guidance for Third-party Medical Billing Companies — Notice.

63 FR 71819, December 30, 1998: Office of Inspector General; Health Care Fraud and Abuse Data Collection Program; Reporting under section 1128E of the Social Security Act of Final Adverse Actions — Notice of proposed rule-making; extension of comment period, affecting 45 CFR 61.

1999

64 FR 1813, January 12, 1999: Office of Inspector General Publication of OIG Special Fraud Alert on Physician Liability for Certifications in the Provision of Medical Equipment and Supplies and Home Health Services — Notice.

64 FR 2228, January 13, 1999: Office of Inspector General: Solicitation of Information and Recommendations for Developing OIG Compliance Program Guidance for the Hospice Industry — Notice.

64 FR 6753, February 16, 1999: Office of Inspector General: Privacy Act; Notification of New System of Records in Conjunction with the Healthcare Integrity and Protection Data Bank — Notice of a new system of records.

64 FR 10478, March 4, 1999: HCFA Agency Information Collection Activities: Proposed Collection; Comment request (pertaining to information collection requirements in final peer review organization (PRO) sanction regulations).

64 FR 13997, March 23, 1999: HCFA Agency Information Collection Activities: Submission for OMB Review; Comment request (pertaining to Medicare and Medicaid requirements for advanced directives, and disclosure of ownership and financial control interest).

64 FR 19375, April 20, 1999: HCFA Agency Information Collection Activities: Proposed Collection; Comment request (pertaining to acquisition, protection, and disclosure of peer review organization (PRO) information).

64 FR 24956, May 10, 1999: Medicare and Medicaid Programs; Effective Dates of Provider Agreements and Supplier Approvals — Correction restoring regulations inadvertently removed when a final rule concerning effective dates for provider agreements and supplier approvals was published at 62 FR 43931, August 18, 1997.

64 FR 30340, June 7, 1999: HCFA Agency Information Collection Activities: Submission for OMB Review; Comment request (pertaining to information collection requirements in the final peer review organization (PRO) sanction regulations).

64 FR 36368, July 6, 1999: Office of Inspector General Publication of OIG Compliance Program Guidance for the Durable Medical Equipment, Prosthetics, Orthotics and Supply Industry — Notice.

64 FR 37985, July 14, 1999: Office of Inspector General; Publication of the OIG Special Advisory Bulletin on Gainsharing

Arrangements and CMPs for Hospital Payments to Physicians to Reduce or Limit Services to Beneficiaries — Notice.

64 FR 39150, July 21, 1999: Office of Inspector General; Draft OIG Compliance Program Guidance for Hospices — Notice and comment period.

64 FR 39420, July 22, 1999: Office of Inspector General; Health Care Programs; Fraud and Abuse; Revised OIG Sanction Authorities Resulting from P.L. 105–33, the Balanced Budget Act of 1997 — Final rule affecting 42 CFR Parts 1001, 1002, and 1003. See also correction at64 FR 42174, August 3, 1999.

64 FR 48846, September 8, 1999: Office of Inspector General: Solicitation of Information and Recommendations for Developing OIG Compliance Program Guidance for Individual Physicians and Small Group Practices — Notice.

64 FR 42791, September 30, 1999: Office of Inspector General; Publication of the OIG Special Advisory Bulletin on the Effect of Exclusion from Participation in Federal Health Care Programs — Notice. See also correction at64 FR 55484, October 13, 1999.

64 FR 57619, October 26, 1999: Office of Inspector General; Privacy Act; Exempt Record System, Pertaining to the Healthcare Integrity and Protection Data Bank (HIPDB) — Notice of proposed rulemaking affecting 45 CFR Part 5b.

64 FR 57740, October 26, 1999: Office of Inspector General; Healthcare Fraud and Abuse Data Collection Program: Reporting of Final Adverse Actions - Final rule affecting 45 CFR Part 61. See also correction at 65 FR 70506, November 24, 2000.

64 FR 58419, October 29, 1999: Office of Inspector General; Draft OIG Compliance Program Guidance for Nursing Facilities — Notice and comment period.

64 FR 58851, November 1, 1999: Office of Inspector General; Healthcare Integrity and Protection Data Bank: Announcement of Opening Date for Reporting and Self-query Fee — Notice.

64 FR 61353, November 10, 1999: Office of Inspector General/HCFA; OIG/HCFA Special Advisory Bulletin on the Patient Anti-dumping Statute.

64 FR 61893, November 15, 1999: Office of Inspector General; Publication of the OIG's Compliance Program Guidance for Medicare+Choice Organizations Offering Coordinated Care Plans — Notice.

64 FR 63504, November 19, 1999: Office of Inspector General; Fraud and Abuse; Statutory Exception to the Anti-kickback Statute for Shared Risk Arrangements — Interim final rule with request for comment, affection 42 CFR Part 1001. See also correction at 64 FR 71317, December 21, 1999.

64 FR 63518, November 19, 1999: Office of Inspector General; Fraud and Abuse; Clarification of the Initial OIG Safe Harbor Provisions and Establishment of Additional Safe Harbor Provisions under the Anti-kickback Statute — Final rule affecting42 CFR Part 1001.

64 FR 69217, December 10, 1999: Office of Inspector General; Solicitation of New Safe Harbors and Special Fraud Alerts — Intent to develop regulations affecting 42 CFR Part 1001.

2000

65 FR 9274, February 24, 2000: Office of Inspector General: Publication of OIG Special Fraud Alert on Rental of Space in Physician Offices by Persons or Entities to Which Physicians Refer — Notice.

65 FR 11589, March 3, 2000: Office of Inspector General: Health Care Integrity and Protection Data Bank under Section 1128E of the Social Security Act: Announcement of Opening Date for Querying and User Fees — Notice.

65 FR 14289, March 16, 2000: Office of Inspector General: Publication of the OIG Compliance Program Guidance for Nursing Facilities — Notice.

65 FR 24400, April 26, 2000: Office of Inspector General; Health Care Programs: Fraud and Abuse; Revised OIG Civil Money Penalties Resulting from Public Law 104-191 (HIPAA) — Final rule affecting 42 CFR Parts 1001, 1003, 1005, and 1006. See also correction at 65 FR 35583, June 5, 2000.

65 FR 32060, May 22, 2000: Office of Inspector General Medicare and State Health Care Programs: Fraud and Abuse: Ambulance Restocking Safe Harbor under the Anti-kickback Statute — Notice of proposed rulemaking affecting 42 CFR 1001.

65 FR 34986, June 1, 2000: Office of Inspector General; Privacy Act; Implementation (exempting the Healthcare Integrity and Protection Data Bank under Section 1128C of the Social Security Act from certain provisions of the Privacy Act (5 U.S.C. 552a) — Final rule.

65 FR 36818, June 12, 2000: Office of Inspector General: Draft OIG Compliance Program for Individual and Small Group Physician Practices — Notice and comment period.

65 FR 50204, August 17, 2000: Office of Inspector General: Solicitation of Information and Recommendations for Developing a Compliance Risk Guidance for the Ambulance Industry — Notice.

65 FR 50552, August 18, 2000: HCFA Privacy Act of 1974; Report of Modified or Altered System (pertaining to revision of language in global fraud and abuse routine uses). 65 FR 59434, October 5, 2000: Office of Inspector General Compliance Program for Individual and Small Group Physician Practices — Notice.

65 FR 63035, October 20, 2000: Office of Inspector General: Medicare and State Health Care Programs: Fraud and Abuse; Revisions and Technical Corrections — Proposed rule affecting 42 CFR Parts 1001, 1003, 1005, and 1008.

65 FR 78124, December 14, 2000: Office of Inspector General: Solicitation of New Safe Harbors and Special Fraud Alerts — Notice of intent to develop regulations.

2001

66 FR 856, January 4, 2001: Medicare and Medicaid Programs; Physicians Referrals to Health Care Entities with which They Have Financial Relationships—Final rule with comment period, affecting 42 CFR Parts 411 and 424.

66 FR 6629, January 22, 2001: HCFA Agency Information Collection Activities: Submission for OMB Review; Comment request (pertaining to Medicare Integrity Program Organizational Conflict of Interest Disclosure Certificate).

66 FR 8771, February 2, 2001: Medicare and Medicaid Programs; Physicians' Referrals to Health Care Entities with which They Have Financial Relationships: Delay of Effective Date of Final Rule and Technical Amendment, affecting 42 CFR Parts 411 and 424.

66 FR 9858, February 12, 2001: HCFA Privacy Act of 1974; Report of New System (pertaining to complaints against health insurance issuers and health plans).

66 FR 9865, February 12, 2001: Office of Inspector General: Privacy Act of 1974; Amendment to the Health Care Program Violations System of Records—Notice and comment period (pertaining to including Social Security numbers of sanctioned individual in the Health Care Program Violations record).

66 FR 17813, April 4, 2001: Medicare and Medicaid Programs; Physicians' Referrals to Health Care Entities with which They Have Financial Relationships; Extension of Comment period—Notice, affecting 42 CFR Parts 411 and 424.

66 FR 19507, April 16, 2001: HCFA Agency Information Collection Activities: Proposed Collection; Comment request (pertaining to conflict of interest and ownership and control information form).

66 FR 23944, May 10, 2001: HCFA Agency Information Collection Activities: Proposed Collection; Comment request (pertaining to financial reports for providers indebted to Medicare who want to repay over time).

66 FR 28916, May 25, 2001: HCFA Agency Information Collection Activities; Proposed Collection; Comment request (pertaining to procedures for advisory opinions concerning physician referrals under section 1877 of the Social Security Act).

66 FR 31245, June 11, 2001: Office of Inspector General; Healthcare Integrity and Protection Data Bank: Change in User Fees—Notice.

66 FR 31246, June 11, 2001: Office of Inspector General; Solicitation of Information and Recommendations for Developing a Compliance Program Guidance for the Pharmaceutical Industry—Notice.

Office of Inspector General Notices of Program Exclusions

58 FR 41794, August 5, 1993: For March through June 1993.

58 FR 44686, August 24, 1993: For July 1993.

58 FR 48073, September 14, 1993: For August 1993.

58 FR 53519, October 15, 1993: For September 1993.

58 FR 60205, November 15, 1993: For October 1993.

58 FR 66007, December 17, 1993: For November 1993.

58 FR 3862, January 27, 1994: For December 1993.

59 FR 6285, February 10, 1994: For January 1994.

59 FR 15919, April 5, 1994: For February 1994.

59 FR 21769, April 26, 1994: For March 1994.

59 FR 25951, May 18, 1994: For April 1994.

59 FR 31255, June 17, 1994: For May 1994.

59 FR 35941, July 14, 1994: For June 1994.

59 FR 41776, August 15, 1994: For July 1994

59 FR 47341, September 15, 1994: For August 1994

59 FR 52973, October 20, 1994: For September 1994

59 FR 60155, November 22, 1994: For October 1994.

59 FR 65371, December 19, 1994: For November 1994.

60 FR 4179, January 20, 1995: For December 1994.
60 FR 7780, February 9, 1995: For January 1995.
60 FR 14763, March 20, 1995: For February 1995.
60 FR 19072, April 14, 1995: For March 1995.
60 FR 27532, May 24, 1995: For April 1995.
60 FR 32016, June 19, 1995: For May 1995.
60 FR 37459, July 20, 1995: For June 1995.
60 FR 46296, September 6, 1995: For July 1995.
60 FR 48999, September 21, 1995: For August 1995.
60 FR 54880, October 26, 1995: For September 1995.
60 FR 57448, November 15, 1995: For October 1995.
60 FR 64174, December 14, 1995: For November 1995.
61 FR 6017, February 15, 1996: For December 1995.
61 FR 6017, February 15, 1996: For January 1996.
61 FR 11055, March 18, 1996: For February 1996.
61 FR 17711, April 22, 1996: For March 1996.
61 FR 24502, May 15, 1996: For April 1996.
61 FR 30243, June 14, 1996: For May 1996.
61 FR 38455, July 24, 1996: For June 1996.
61 FR 42258, August 14, 1996: For July 1996.
61 FR 48710, September 16, 1996: For August 1996.
61 FR 53231, October 10, 1996: For September 1996.
61 FR 59102, November 20, 1996: For October 1996.
61 FR 66285, December 17, 1996: For November 1996.
62 FR 4315, January 29, 1997: For December 1996.
62 FR 8028, February 21, 1997: For January 1997.
62 FR 13888, March 24, 1997: For February 1997.
62 FR 19340, April 21, 1997: For March, 1997.
62 FR 26807, May 15, 1997: For April, 1997.
62 FR 33663, June 20, 1997: For May, 1997.
62 FR 41064, July 31, 1997: For June 1997.
62 FR 43177, August 12, 1997: For July 1997.
62 FR 48873, September 17, 1997: For August 1997.
62 FR 53642, October 15, 1997: For September 1997.
62 FR 60903, November 13, 1997: For October 1997.
62 FR 66377, December 18, 1997: For November 1997.
63 FR 2989, January 20, 1998: For December 1997.
63 FR 8998, February 23, 1998: For January 1998.
63 FR 12477, March 13, 1998: For February 1998.
63 FR 17431, April 9, 1998: For March 1998.
63 FR 26812, May 14, 1998: For April 1998.

63 FR 32109, June 11, 1998: For May 1998.
63 FR 37891, July 14, 1998: For June 1998.
63 FR 43404, August 13, 1998: For July 1998.
63 FR 49703, September 17, 1998: For August 1998.
63 FR 55133, October 14, 1998: For September 1998.
63 FR 60357, November 9, 1998: For October 1998.
63 FR 69638, December 17, 1998: For November 1998.
64 FR 3525, January 22, 1999: For December 1998.

1999

64 FR 8390, February 19, 1999: For January 1999.
64 FR 3525, January 22, 1999: For December 1998.
64 FR 8390, February 19, 1999: For January 1999.
64 FR 14456, March 25, 1999: For February 1999.
64 FR 17185, April 8, 1999: For March 1999.
64 FR 25509, May 12, 1999: For April 1999.
64 FR 31007, June 9, 1999: For May 1999.
64 FR 38205, July 15, 1999: For June 1999.
64 FR 43708, August 11, 1999: For July 1999.
64 FR 51128, September 21, 1999: For August 1999.
64 FR 55740, October 14, 1999: For September 1999.
64 FR 62682, November 17, 1999: For October 1999.
64 FR 69539, December 13, 1999: For November 1999.
65 FR 3728, January 24, 2000: For December 1999.

2000

65 FR 8376, February 18, 2000: For January 2000.
65 FR 14986, March 20, 2000: For February 2000.
65 FR 19006, April 10, 2000: For March 2000.
65 FR 30415, May 11, 2000: For April 2000.
65 FR 37156, June 13, 2000: For May 2000.
65 FR 45093, July 20, 2000: For June 2000.
65 FR 53321, September 1, 2000: For July 2000.
65 FR 57358, September 22, 2000: For August 2000.
65 FR 61172, October 16, 2000: For September 2000.
65 FR 68153, November 14, 2000: For October 2000.
65 FR 77884, December 13, 2000: For November 2000.
66 FR 6634, January 22, 2001: For December 2000.

2001

66 FR 10305, February 14, 2001: For January 2001.
66 FR 14591, March 13, 2001: For February 2001.
66 FR 18962, April 12, 2001: For March 2001.
66 FR 27520, May 17, 2001: For April 2001.
66 FR 31941, June 13, 2001: For May 2001.
See § 4:6.

§ 8:7 DISCLOSURE BY INSTITUTIONS, ORGANIZATIONS, AND AGENCIES OF OWNERS AND OTHER INDIVIDUALS SANCTIONED OR CONVICTED AND OF CERTAIN BUSINESS RELATIONSHIPS — Sections 1128(b)(9) and (10), 1124, 1124A, and 1126 [42 U.S.C.A. 1320a-7(b)(9) and (10), 1320a-3, 1320a-3a, and 1320a-5]

Regulations

20 CFR Part 401 — Disclosure of Official Records and Information [Social Security]

42 CFR Part 401, Subpart B — Confidentiality and Disclosure

42 CFR Part 402 — Civil Money Penalties, Assessments, and Exclusions

42 CFR Part 411 — Exclusions from Medicare and Limitations on Medicare Payment

42 CFR Part 417, Subpart B — Health Maintenance Organizations, especially Section 417.236: Information access and disclosure requirements; Section 417.482: Access to facilities and records; and Section 417.486: Disclosure of information and confidentiality

42 CFR Part 420 — Program Integrity: Medicare

42 CFR Part 431, Subpart C — Administrative Requirements: Provider Relations, especially Section 431.115: Disclosure of survey information and provider or contractor evaluation; and Subpart F — Safeguarding Information on Applicants and Recipients

42 CFR Part 455 — Program Integrity: Medicaid

42 CFR Part 456, Subpart C — Utilization Control: Hospitals, Section 446.112: Records and reports, and Section 456.113: Confidentiality; Subpart D — Utilization Control: Mental Hospitals, Section 456.212: Records and reports, and Section 456.213: Confidentiality; Subpart E — Utilization Control: Skilled Nursing Facilities, Section 456.312: Records and reports, and Section 456.313: Confidentiality; Subpart F — Utilization Control: Interme-

diate Care Facilities, Section 456.412: Records and reports, and Section 456.413: Confidentiality

42 CFR Part 475 — Peer Review Organizations

42 CFR Part 476 — Utilization and Quality Control Review

42 CFR Part 480 — Acquisition, Protection, and Disclosure of Peer Review Information

42 CFR Part 498 — Appeals Procedures for Determinations that Affect Participation in the Medicare Program and for Determinations that Affect the Participation of ICF's/MR and Certain NF's in the Medicaid Program

42 CFR Chapter V — Office of Inspector General — Health Care, Department of Health and Human Services

Subchapter A — General Provisions Part 1000 — Introduction; General Definitions

Subchapter B — OIG Authorities

Part 1001 — Program Integrity: Medicare and State Health Care Programs

Part 1002 — Program Integrity: State-initiated Exclusion from Medicaid

Part 1003 — Civil Money Penalties, Assessments and Exclusions

Part 1004 — Imposition of Sanctions on Health Care Practitioners and Providers of Health Care Services by a Peer Review Organization

Part 1005 — Appeals of Exclusions, Civil Money Penalties and Assessments

Part 1006 — Investigational Inquiries

Part 1007 — State Medicaid Fraud Control Units

Part 1008 — Advisory Opinions by the OIG

55 FR 3986, February 6, 1990: Medicare and Social Security: Fraud and Abuse; Civil Money Penalties for Misuse of Certain Terms, Symbols and Emblems — Proposed rule.

55 FR 12205, April 2, 1990: Health Care Programs: Fraud and Abuse; Amendments to OIG Exclusion and CMP Authorities Resulting from Public Law 100–93, the Medicare and Medicaid Patient and Program Protection Act of 1987, Public Law 99–272, the Consolidated Omnibus Budget Reconciliation Act of 1985, and Public Law 100–360, the Medicare Catastrophic Coverage Act of 1988 — Proposed rule to amend 42 CFR Parts 1000, 1001, 1002, 1003, 1004, 1005, 1006, and 1007. See also correction published at 55 FR 17461, April 25, 1990.

56 FR 61374, December 3, 1991: Medicare Program; Reporting Requirements for Financial Relationships Between Physicians and Health Care Entities That Furnish Selected Items and Services — Interim final rule with comment period affecting 42 CFR Part 411.

57 FR 3298, January 29, 1992: Health Care Programs: Fraud and Abuse; Amendments to OIG Exclusion and CMP Authorities Resulting From Public Law 100–93 — Final rule affecting 42 CFR Parts 1001, 1002, 1003, 1004, 1005, 1006, and 1007. See also final rule and correction at 57 FR 9669, March 20, 1992; final rule affecting 42 CFR Parts 1001and 1005, with clarification at 58 FR 5617, January 22, 1993; and final rule affecting 42 CFR Part 1001, with correction, at 58 FR 40752, July 30, 1993.

57 FR 8588, March 11, 1992: Medicare Program; Physician Ownership of, and Referrals to, Health Care Entities that Furnish Clinical Laboratory Services — Proposed rule affecting 42 CFR Part 411.

58 FR 49008, September 21, 1993: Office of Inspector General: Additional Safe Harbor Provisions under the OIG Anti-Kickback Statute — Proposed rule pertaining to investment interests in rural areas, in ambulatory surgical centers, and in group practices composed exclusively of active investors; practitioner recruitment; obstetrical malpractice insurance subsidies; referral agreements for specialty services; and cooperative hospital service organizations.

58 FR 54096, October 20, 1993: Office of Inspector General: Civil Money Penalties for Prohibited Referrals to Entities Providing Clinical Laboratory Services and for Prohibited Arrangements and Schemes — Proposed rule affecting 42 CFR Part 1003.

59 FR 37202, July 21, 1994: Medicare and State Health Care Programs; Fraud and Abuse; Clarification of the OIG Safe Harbor Anti-kickback Provisions — Proposed rule affecting 42 CFR Part 1001.

59 FR 50762, October 5, 1994: HCFA Public Information Collection Requirements Submitted to the Office of Management and Budget (OMB) for Clearance (pertaining to reimbursement of hospital costs for residents and interns, criteria for psychiatric and rehabilitation hospital units' reimbursement under the prospective payment system, disclosure of owners and managers of suppliers for fraud and abuse detection purposes, reimbursement of municipal health services clinics, survey form for hospital compliance with anti-dumping requirements, and evaluation of patient and physician

satisfaction with the Medicare participating heart bypass center demonstration).

59 FR 61571, December 1, 1994: Office of Inspector General; Fraud and Abuse; Civil Money Penalties for Hospital Physician Incentive Plans — Proposed rule affecting 42 CFR Part 1003.

59 FR 65372, December 19, 1994: Office of Inspector General — Notice of Publication of Special Fraud Alerts (pertaining to joint venture arrangements, routine waiver of Medicare Part B copayments and deductibles, hospital incentives to referring physicians, prescription drug marketing practices, and arrangements for provision of clinical laboratory services).

60 FR 16580, March 31, 1995: Office of Inspector General: Civil Money Penalties for Referrals to Entities and for Prohibited Arrangements and Schemes — Final rule with comment period, affecting 42 CFR Part 1003.

60 FR 32916, June 26, 1995: Office of Inspector General; Health Care Programs; Fraud and Abuse; Technical Revision to the Scope and Effect of the OIG Exclusion Regulations — Final rule affecting 42 CFR Part 1001.

60 FR 41914, August 14, 1995: Medicare Program; Physician Financial Relationships with, and Referrals to, Health Care Entities that Furnish Clinical Laboratory Services; Financial Relationship Reporting Requirements — Final rule affecting 42 CFR Part 411.

61 FR 2122, January 25, 1996: Medicare and State Health Care Programs; Fraud and Abuse; Safe Harbors for Protecting Health Plans — Final rule.

61 FR 7522, February 28, 1996: HCFA Public Information Collection Requirements Submitted for Public Comment and Recommendations (pertaining to Medicare and Medicaid disclosure of ownership and control interest statements).

61 FR 13430, March 27, 1996: Medicare and Medicaid Programs; Requirements for Physician Incentive Plans in Prepaid Health Care Organizations — Final rule with comment period, affecting 42 CFR Parts 417, 434, and 1003.

62 FR 7350, February 19, 1997: Office of Inspector General: Medicare and State Health Care Programs: Fraud and Abuse; Issuance of Advisory Opinions by the OIG — Interim final rule with comment period, affecting 42 CFR Part 1008.

62 FR 23140, April 29, 1997: Office of Inspector General: Health Care Programs: Fraud and Abuse; Revised PRO Sanctions for Failing to Meet Statutory Obligations — Final rule.

62 FR 28410, May 23, 1997: Office of Inspector General: Health Care Programs: Fraud and Abuse — Notice of Intent to Form the Negotiated Rulemaking Committee for the Shared Risk Exception (statutory exceptions to the anti-kickback statute) — affecting42 CFR Part 1001.

62 FR 35214, June 30, 1997: HCFA Agency Information Collection Activities: Submission for OMB Review; Comment request (pertaining to CLIA adverse actions).

62 FR 39848, July 24, 1997: HCFA Agency Information Collection Activities; Proposed Collection; Comment request (pertaining to home health certification and plan of care forms for reimbursement; and Medicare/Medicaid disclosure of ownership and control forms).

62 FR 47182, September 8, 1997: Office of Inspector General: Health Care Programs: Fraud and Abuse; Revised OIG Exclusion Authorities Resulting from Public Law 104–191 — Notice of Proposed rulemaking, affecting 42 CFR Parts 1000, 1001, 1002, and 1005.

62 FR 49016, September 18, 1997: HCFA Agency Information Collection Activities: Submission for OMB Review; Comment Request (pertaining to managed care incentive arrangement disclosure forms).

62 FR 55410, October 24, 1997: HCFA Agency Information Collection Activities: Submission for OMB Review; Comment request (pertaining to Medicare/Medicaid disclosure of ownership and control forms).

62 FR 55410, October 24, 1997: Office of Inspector General: Criteria for Implementing Permissive Exclusion Authority under Section 1128(b)(7) of the Social Security Act — Notice.

62 FR 65049, December 10, 1997: Office of Inspector General: Solicitation of New Safe Harbors and Special Fraud Alerts — Notice of intent to develop regulations, affecting 42 CFR Part 1001.

62 FR 67392, December 24, 1997: Office of Inspector General: Criteria for Implementing Permissive Exclusion Authority under Section 1128(b)(7) of the Social Security Act — Notice.

63 FR 1646, January 9, 1998: Medicare Program; Physicians' Referrals; Issuance of Advisory Opinions — Final rule with comment period, affecting 42 CFR Part 411.

63 FR 1659, January 9, 1998: Medicare and Medicaid Programs; Physicians' Referrals to Health Care Entities with Which They Have Financial Relationships — Proposed rule affecting 42 CFR Parts 411, 424, 435, and 455.

63 FR 8987, February 23, 1998: Office of Inspector General: Publication of the OIG Compliance Program for Hospitals — Notice.

63 FR 9844, February 26, 1998: HCFA Agency Information Collection Activities: Proposed Collection; Comment request (pertaining to procedures for advisory opinions concerning physician referrals and supporting regulations in 42 CFR Sections 411.370- 411.389).

63 FR 11649, March 10, 1998: Medicare and Medicaid Programs; Physicians' Referrals to Health Care Entities with Which They Have Financial Relationships — Notice of extension of comment period for proposed rule.

63 FR 14393, March 25, 1998: Office of Inspector General: Health Care Programs: Fraud and Abuse; Revised OIG Civil Money Penalties Resulting from the Health Insurance Portability and Accountability Act of 1996 — Notice of proposed rulemaking, affecting 42 CFR Parts 1003, 1005, and 1006.

63 FR 20415, April 24, 1998: Office of Inspector General: Publication of OIG Special Fraud Alert: Fraud and Abuse in Nursing Home Arrangements with Hospices — Notice.

63 FR 28395, May 22, 1998: HCFA Agency Information Collection Activities: Submission for OMB Review; Comment request (pertaining to procedures for advisory opinions concerning physician referrals and supporting regulations in 42 CFR 411.370 through 411.389).

63 FR 31123, June 8, 1998: Medicare Program; Incentive Programs — Fraud and Abuse — Final rule affecting 42 CFR Part 420.

63 FR 38311, July 16, 1998: Office of Inspector General: Medicare and State Health Care Programs: Fraud and Abuse; Issuance of Advisory Opinions by the OIG — Final rule affecting 42 CFR 1008. See also correction at 63 FR 43449, August 13, 1998.

63 FR 38414, July 16, 1998: HCFA Privacy Act of 1974; Report of Altered System (pertaining to disclosure of individual-specific information to combat fraud or abuse in health benefit programs).

63 FR 42409, August 7, 1998: Office of Inspector General: Solicitation of Information and Recommendations for Developing OIG Compliance Program Guidance for the Durable Medical Equipment Industry — Notice.

63 FR 42410, August 7, 1998: Office of Inspector General: Publication of the OIG Compliance Program Guidance for Home Health Agencies — Notice.

63 FR 45076, August 24, 1998: Office of Inspector General — Publication of OIG Compliance Program Guidance for Clinical Laboratories.

63 FR 46676, September 2, 1998: Office of Inspector General: Health Care Programs; Fraud and Abuse; Revised OIG Exclusion Authorities Resulting from Public Law 104–191 — Final rule affecting 42 CFR Parts 1000, 1001, 1002, and 1005. See also correction at 63 FR 57918, October 29, 1998.

63 FR 46736, September 2, 1998: Office of Inspector General: Health Care Programs; Fraud and Abuse; Revised OIG Sanction Authorities Resulting from Public Law 105–33 — Notice of proposed rulemaking affecting 42 CFR 1001, 1002, and 1003.

63 FR 50577, September 22, 1998: Office of Inspector General: Solicitation of Information and Recommendations for Developing OIG Compliance Program Guidance for Certain Medicare+Choice Organizations — Notice.

63 FR 58341, October 30, 1998: Office of Inspector General: Health Care Fraud and Abuse Data Collection Program: Reporting of Final Adverse Actions — Notice of proposed rulemaking under section 1128E of the Social Security Act, affecting 45 CFR 61.

63 FR 58399, October 30, 1998: Office of Inspector General: Publication of the OIG's Provider Self-Disclosure Protocol — Notice.

63 FR 67486, December 7, 1998: Office of Inspector General and HCFA; Solicitation of Comments on the OIG/HCFA Special Advisory Bulletin on the Patient Anti-Dumping Statute — Notice.

63 FR 68223, December 10, 1998: Office of Inspector General; Solicitation of New Safe Harbors and Special Fraud Alerts — Notice of intent to develop regulations, affecting 42 CFR 1001.

63 FR 68687, December 14, 1998: Medicare and Medicaid Program; Civil Money Penalties, Assessments, Exclusions, and Related Appeals Procedures — Final rule with comment period, affecting 42 CFR 400 and 402.

63 FR 70137, December 18, 1998: Office of Inspector General: Solicitation of Information and Recommendations for Developing OIG Compliance Program Guidance for the Nursing Home Industry — Notice.

63 FR 70138, December 18, 1998: Office of Inspector General: Publication of the OIG Compliance Program Guidance for Third-party Medical Billing Companies — Notice.

63 FR 71819, December 30, 1998: Office of Inspector General; Health Care Fraud and Abuse Data Collection Program; Reporting

under section 1128E of the Social Security Act of Final Adverse Actions — Notice of proposed rule-making; extension of comment period, affecting 45 CFR 61.

1999

64 FR 1813, January 12, 1999: Office of Inspector General Publication of OIG Special Fraud Alert on Physician Liability for Certifications in the Provision of Medical Equipment and Supplies and Home Health Services — Notice.

64 FR 2228, January 13, 1999: Office of Inspector General: Solicitation of Information and Recommendations for Developing OIG Compliance Program Guidance for the Hospice Industry — Notice.

64 FR 6753, February 16, 1999: Office of Inspector General: Privacy Act; Notification of New System of Records in Conjunction with the Healthcare Integrity and Protection Data Bank — Notice of a new system of records.

64 FR 10478, March 4, 1999: HCFA Agency Information Collection Activities: Proposed Collection; Comment request (pertaining to information collection requirements in final peer review organization (PRO) sanction regulations).

64 FR 13997, March 23, 1999: HCFA Agency Information Collection Activities: Submission for OMB Review; Comment request (pertaining to Medicare and Medicaid requirements for advanced directives, and disclosure of ownership and financial control interest).

64 FR 19375, April 20, 1999: HCFA Agency Information Collection Activities: Proposed Collection; Comment request (pertaining to acquisition, protection, and disclosure of peer review organization (PRO) information).

64 FR 24956, May 10, 1999: Medicare and Medicaid Programs; Effective Dates of Provider Agreements and Supplier Approvals — Correction restoring regulations inadvertently removed when a final rule concerning effective dates for provider agreements and supplier approvals was published at 62 FR 43931, August 18, 1997.

64 FR 30340, June 7, 1999: HCFA Agency Information Collection Activities: Submission for OMB Review; Comment request (pertaining to information collection requirements in the final peer review organization (PRO) sanction regulations).

64 FR 36368, July 6, 1999: Office of Inspector General Publication of OIG Compliance Program Guidance for the Durable Medical Equipment, Prosthetics, Orthotics and Supply Industry — Notice.

64 FR 37985, July 14, 1999: Office of Inspector General; Publication of the OIG Special Advisory Bulletin on Gainsharing Arrangements and CMPs for Hospital Payments to Physicians to Reduce or Limit Services to Beneficiaries — Notice.

64 FR 39150, July 21, 1999: Office of Inspector General; Draft OIG Compliance Program Guidance for Hospices — Notice and comment period.

64 FR 39420, July 22, 1999: Office of Inspector General; Health Care Programs; Fraud and Abuse; Revised OIG Sanction Authorities Resulting from P.L. 105–33, the Balanced Budget Act of 1997 — Final rule affecting 42 CFR Parts 1001, 1002, and 1003. See also correction at64 FR 42174, August 3, 1999.

64 FR 48846, September 8, 1999: Office of Inspector General: Solicitation of Information and Recommendations for Developing OIG Compliance Program Guidance for Individual Physicians and Small Group Practices — Notice.

64 FR 42791, September 30, 1999: Office of Inspector General; Publication of the OIG Special Advisory Bulletin on the Effect of Exclusion from Participation in Federal Health Care Programs — Notice. See also correction at64 FR 55484, October 13, 1999.

64 FR 57619, October 26, 1999: Office of Inspector General; Privacy Act; Exempt Record System, Pertaining to the Healthcare Integrity and Protection Data Bank (HIPDB) — Notice of proposed rulemaking affecting 45 CFR Part 5b.

64 FR 57740, October 26, 1999: Office of Inspector General; Healthcare Fraud and Abuse Data Collection Program: Reporting of Final Adverse Actions — Final rule affecting 45 CFR Part 61.

64 FR 58419, October 29, 1999: Office of Inspector General; Draft OIG Compliance Program Guidance for Nursing Facilities — Notice and comment period.

64 FR 58851, November 1, 1999: Office of Inspector General; Healthcare Integrity and Protection Data Bank: Announcement of Opening Date for Reporting and Self-query Fee — Notice.

64 FR 61353, November 10, 1999: Office of Inspector General/HCFA; OIG/HCFA Special Advisory Bulletin on the Patient Anti-dumping Statute.

64 FR 61893, November 15, 1999: Office of Inspector General; Publication of the OIG's Compliance Program Guidance for Medicare+Choice Organizations Offering Coordinated Care Plans — Notice.

64 FR 63504, November 19, 1999: Office of Inspector General; Fraud and Abuse; Statutory Exception to the Anti-kickback Statute for Shared Risk Arrangements — Interim final rule with request for comment, affection 42 CFR Part 1001. See also correction at 64 FR 71317, December 21, 1999.

64 FR 63518, November 19, 1999: Office of Inspector General; Fraud and Abuse; Clarification of the Initial OIG Safe Harbor Provisions and Establishment of Additional Safe Harbor Provisions under the Anti-kickback Statute — Final rule affecting42 CFR Part 1001.

64 FR 69217, December 10, 1999: Office of Inspector General; Solicitation of New Safe Harbors and Special Fraud Alerts — Intent to develop regulations affecting 42 CFR Part 1001.

64 FR 73563, December 30, 1999: HCFA Agency Information Collection Activities: Submission for OMB Review; Comment request pertaining to Medicare program integrity organizational conflict of interest disclosure certificates).

2000

65 FR 9274, February 24, 2000: Office of Inspector General: Publication of OIG Special Fraud Alert on Rental of Space in Physician Offices by Persons or Entities to Which Physicians Refer — Notice.

65 FR 11589, March 3, 2000: Office of Inspector General: Health Care Integrity and Protection Data Bank under Section 1128E of the Social Security Act: Announcement of Opening Date for Querying and User Fees — Notice.

65 FR 14289, March 16, 2000: Office of Inspector General: Publication of the OIG Compliance Program Guidance for Nursing Facilities — Notice.

65 FR 24400, April 26, 2000: Office of Inspector General; Health Care Programs: Fraud and Abuse; Revised OIG Civil Money Penalties Resulting from Public Law 104-191 (HIPAA) — Final rule affecting 42 CFR Parts 1001, 1003, 1005, and 1006. See also correction at 65 FR 35583, June 5, 2000.

65 FR 32060, May 22, 2000: Office of Inspector General Medicare and State Health Care Programs: Fraud and Abuse: Ambulance

Restocking Safe Harbor under the Anti-kickback Statute— Notice of proposed rulemaking affecting 42 CFR 1001.

65 FR 34986, June 1, 2000: Office of Inspector General; Privacy Act; Implementation (exempting the Healthcare Integrity and Protection Data Bank under Section 1128C of the Social Security Act from certain provisions of the Privacy Act (5 U.S.C. 552a)—Final rule.

65 FR 36818, June 12, 2000: Office of Inspector General: Draft OIG Compliance Program for Individual and Small Group Physician Practices—Notice and comment period.

65 FR 50204, August 17, 2000: Office of Inspector General: Solicitation of Information and Recommendations for Developing a Compliance Risk Guidance for the Ambulance Industry— Notice.

65 FR 50552, August 18, 2000: HCFA Privacy Act of 1974; Report of Modified or Altered System (pertaining to revision of language in global fraud and abuse routine uses).

65 FR 53319, September 1, 2000: HCFA Agency Information Collection Activities: Proposed Collection; Comment request (pertaining to incentive arrangement disclosure form for managed care organizations and their related medical groups and physicians).

65 FR 59434, October 5, 2000: Office of Inspector General Compliance Program for Individual and Small Group Physician Practices—Notice.

65 FR 63035, October 20, 2000: Office of Inspector General: Medicare and State Health Care Programs: Fraud and Abuse; Revisions and Technical Corrections—Proposed rule affecting 42 CFR Parts 1001, 1003, 1005, and 1008.

65 FR 65861, November 2, 2000: HCFA Agency Information Collection Activities: Proposed Collection; Comment request (pertaining to conflict of interest disclosure requirements for Medicare program integrity).

65 FR 78124, December 14, 2000: Office of Inspector General: Solicitation of New Safe Harbors and Special Fraud Alerts —Notice of intent to develop regulations.

2001

66 FR 856, January 4, 2001: Medicare and Medicaid Programs; Physicians Referrals to Health Care Entities with which They Have Financial Relationships—Final rule with comment period, affecting 42 CFR Parts 411 and 424.

66 FR 6629, January 22, 2001: HCFA Agency Information Collection Activities: Submission for OMB Review; Comment request (pertaining to Medicare Integrity Program Organizational Conflict of Interest Disclosure Certificate).

66 FR 8771, February 2, 2001: Medicare and Medicaid Programs; Physicians' Referrals to Health Care Entities with which They Have Financial Relationships: Delay of Effective Date of Final Rule and Technical Amendment, affecting 42 CFR Parts 411 and 424.

66 FR 9858, February 12, 2001: HCFA Privacy Act of 1974; Report of New System (pertaining to complaints against health insurance issuers and health plans).

66 FR 9865, February 12, 2001: Office of Inspector General: Privacy Act of 1974; Amendment to the Health Care Program Violations System of Records-Notice and comment period (pertaining to including Social Security numbers of sanctioned individual in the Health Care Program Violations record).

66 FR 17813, April 4, 2001: Medicare and Medicaid Programs; Physicians' Referrals to Health Care Entities with which They Have Financial Relationships; Extension of Comment period—Notice, affecting 42 CFR Parts 411 and 424.

66 FR 19507, April 16, 2001: HCFA Agency Information Collection Activities: Proposed Collection; Comment request (pertaining to conflict of interest and ownership and control information form).

66 FR 23944, May 10, 2001: HCFA Agency Information Collection Activities: Proposed Collection; Comment request (pertaining to financial reports for providers indebted to Medicare who want to repay over time).

66 FR 28916, May 25, 2001: HCFA Agency Information Collection Activities; Proposed Collection; Comment request (pertaining to procedures for advisory opinions concerning physician referrals under section 1877 of the Social Security Act).

66 FR 31245, June 11, 2001: Office of Inspector General; Healthcare Integrity and Protection Data Bank: Change in User Fees—Notice.

66 FR 31246, June 11, 2001: Office of Inspector General; Solicitation of Information and Recommendations for Developing a Compliance Program Guidance for the Pharmaceutical Industry—Notice.

See § 4:7.

§ 8:8 CIVIL MONEY PENALTIES — Section 1128A [42 U.S.C.A. 1320a-7a]

Regulations

42 CFR Part 402 — Civil Money Penalties, Assessments, and Exclusions

42 CFR Part 420 — Program Integrity: Medicare

42 CFR Part 455 — Program Integrity: Medicaid

42 CFR Part 498 — Appeals Procedures for Determinations that Affect Participation in the Medicare Program and for Determinations that Affect the Participation of ICF's/MR and Certain NF's in the Medicaid Program

42 CFR Chapter V — Office of Inspector General — Health Care, Department of Health and Human Services

Subchapter A — General Provisions

Part 1000 — Introduction; General Definitions

Subchapter B — OIG Authorities

Part 1001 — Program Integrity: Medicare and State Health Care Programs

Part 1002 — Program Integrity: State-initiated Exclusion from Medicaid

Part 1003 — Civil Money Penalties, Assessments and Exclusions

Part 1004 — Imposition of Sanctions on Health Care Practitioners and Providers of Health Care Services by a Peer Review Organization

Part 1005 — Appeals of Exclusions, Civil Money Penalties and Assessments

Part 1006 — Investigational Inquiries

Part 1007 — State Medicaid Fraud Control Units

Part 1008 — Advisory Opinions by the OIG

55 FR 12205, April 2, 1990: Health Care Programs: Fraud and Abuse; Amendments to OIG Exclusion and CMP Authorities Resulting from Public Law 100–93, the Medicare and Medicaid Patient and Program Protection Act of 1987, Public Law 99–272, the Consolidated Omnibus Budget Reconciliation Act of 1985, and Public Law 100–360, the Medicare Catastrophic Coverage Act of 1988 — Proposed rule to amend 42 CFR Parts 1000, 1001, 1002, 1003, 1004, 1005, 1006, and 1007. See also correction published at 55 FR 17461, April 25, 1990.

56 FR 33403, July 22, 1991: Medicare and State Health Care Programs: Fraud and Abuse; Civil Monetary Penalties and Interme-

diate Sanctions for Certain Violations by Health Maintenance Organizations and Competitive Medical Plans — Proposed rule.

56 FR 37054, August 2, 1991: Medicare and Medicaid Programs; Survey and Enforcement Requirements and Alternative Sanctions for Home Health Agencies — Proposed rule affecting 42 CFR Parts 441, 488, and 489.

57 FR 3298, January 29, 1992: Health Care Programs: Fraud and Abuse; Amendments to OIG Exclusion and CMP Authorities Resulting From Public Law 100–93 — Final rule affecting 42 CFR Parts 1001, 1002, 1003, 1004, 1005, 1006, and 1007. See also final rule and correction at 57 FR 9669, March 20, 1992; final rule affecting 42 CFR Parts 1001and 1005, with clarification at 58 FR 5617, January 22, 1993; and final rule affecting 42 CFR Part 1001, with correction, at 58 FR 40752, July 30, 1993.

57 FR 46865, October 13, 1992: HCFA Public Information Collection Requirements Submitted to the Office of Management and Budget for Clearance (pertaining to impact of home health care plan management and evaluation; end-stage renal disease medical case review; Medicare/Medicaid hospital swing-bed survey report form; quarterly Medicaid statement of expenditures; Medicaid program budget report; information collection requirements in final peer review organization sanction regulations; appeals procedures for determinations that affect participation in Medicare; request for medical review information for Part B intermediary outpatient therapy bills and other Part B outpatient bills; and Medicaid limitations on provider-related donations and health care-related taxes, and limitations on payment to disproportionate share hospitals).

59 FR 36072, July 15, 1994: Medicare and State Health Care Programs: Fraud and Abuse, Civil Money Penalties and Intermediate Sanctions for Certain Violations by Health Maintenance Organizations and Competitive Medical Plans — Final rule affecting 42 CFR Parts 417, 431, 434, and 1003. See also correction at 59 FR 48566, September 22, 1994.

59 FR 50762, October 5, 1994: HCFA Public Information Collection Requirements Submitted to the Office of Management and Budget (OMB) for Clearance (pertaining to reimbursement of hospital costs for residents and interns, criteria for psychiatric and rehabilitation hospital units' reimbursement under the prospective payment system, disclosure of owners and managers of suppliers for fraud and abuse detection purposes, reimbursement of municipal health services clinics, survey form for hospital compliance with

anti-dumping requirements, and evaluation of patient and physician satisfaction with the Medicare participating heart bypass center demonstration).

59 FR 61571, December 1, 1994: Office of Inspector General; Fraud and Abuse; Civil Money Penalties for Hospital Physician Incentive Plans — Proposed rule affecting 42 CFR Part 1003.

59 FR 65372, December 19, 1994: Office of Inspector General — Notice of Publication of Special Fraud Alerts (pertaining to joint venture arrangements, routine waiver of Medicare Part B copayments and deductibles, hospital incentives to referring physicians, prescription drug marketing practices, and arrangements for provision of clinical laboratory services).

61 FR 2122, January 25, 1996: Medicare and State Health Care Programs; Fraud and Abuse; Safe Harbors for Protecting Health Plans — Final rule.

61 FR 13430, March 27, 1996: Medicare and Medicaid Programs; Requirements for Physician Incentive Plans in Prepaid Health Care Organizations — Final rule with comment period, affecting 42 CFR Parts 417, 434, and 1003.

61 FR 30623, June 17, 1996: Office of Inspector General Publication of OIG Special Fraud Alert: Fraud and Abuse in the Provision of Services in Nursing Homes — Notice.

61 FR 52299, October 7, 1996: Office of Inspector General; Medicare and State Health Care Programs and Program Fraud Civil Remedies: Fraud and Abuse; Civil Money Penalties Inflation Adjustments — Final rule affecting 42 CFR Part 1003.

61 FR 58568, November 15, 1996: Office of Inspector General; Publication of the Medicare Beneficiary Advisory Bulletin on HMO Arrangements — Notice.

61 FR 69060, December 31, 1996: Office of Inspector General: Solicitation of New Safe Harbors and Modifications to Existing Safe Harbors — Notice of intent to develop regulations, affecting 42 CFR Part 1001.

62 FR 7350, February 19, 1997: Office of Inspector General: Medicare and State Health Care Programs: Fraud and Abuse; Issuance of Advisory Opinions by the OIG — Interim final rule with comment period, affecting 42 CFR Part 1008.

62 FR 9435, March 3, 1997: Office of Inspector General: Publication of the OIG Model Compliance Plan for Clinical Laboratories — Notice.

62 FR 23140, April 29, 1997: Office of Inspector General: Health Care Programs: Fraud and Abuse; Revised PRO Sanctions for Failing to Meet Statutory Obligations — Final rule.

62 FR 28410, May 23, 1997: Office of Inspector General: Health Care Programs: Fraud and Abuse — Notice of Intent to Form the Negotiated Rulemaking Committee for the Shared Risk Exception (statutory exceptions to the anti-kickback statute) — affecting42 CFR Part 1001.

62 FR 39798, July 24, 1997: Office of Inspector General: Negotiated Rulemaking Committee on the Shared Risk Exception (affecting 42 CFR Part 1001) — Notice of meeting.

62 FR 47182, September 8, 1997: Office of Inspector General: Health Care Programs: Fraud and Abuse; Revised OIG Exclusion Authorities Resulting from Public Law 104–191 — Notice of Proposed rulemaking, affecting 42 CFR Parts 1000, 1001, 1002, and 1005.

62 FR 47195, September 8, 1997: Office of Inspector General: Negotiated Rulemaking Committee on the Shared Risk Exception (affecting 42 CFR Part 1001) — Notice of meeting.

62 FR 55410, October 24, 1997: Office of Inspector General: Criteria for Implementing Permissive Exclusion Authority under Section 1128(b)(7) of the Social Security Act — Notice.

62 FR 63689, December 2, 1997: Office of Inspector General: Negotiated Rulemaking Committee on the Shared Risk Exception — Notice of meeting, affecting 42 CFR Part 1001.

62 FR 65049, December 10, 1997: Office of Inspector General: Solicitation of New Safe Harbors and Special Fraud Alerts — Notice of intent to develop regulations, affecting 42 CFR Part 1001.

62 FR 67392, December 24, 1997: Office of Inspector General: Criteria for Implementing Permissive Exclusion Authority under Section 1128(b)(7) of the Social Security Act — Notice.

63 FR 187, January 5, 1998: Office of Inspector General; Negotiated Rulemaking Committee on the Shared Risk Exception — Notice of meeting.

63 FR 1646, January 9, 1998: Medicare Program; Physicians' Referrals; Issuance of Advisory Opinions — Final rule with comment period, affecting 42 CFR Part 411.

63 FR 1659, January 9, 1998: Medicare and Medicaid Programs; Physicians' Referrals to Health Care Entities with Which They Have Financial Relationships — Proposed rule affecting 42 CFR Parts 411, 424, 435, and 455.

63 FR 8987, February 23, 1998: Office of Inspector General: Publication of the OIG Compliance Program for Hospitals — Notice.

63 FR 9844, February 26, 1998: HCFA Agency Information Collection Activities: Proposed Collection; Comment request (pertaining to procedures for advisory opinions concerning physician referrals and supporting regulations in 42 CFR Sections 411.370- 411.389).

63 FR 11649, March 10, 1998: Medicare and Medicaid Programs; Physicians' Referrals to Health Care Entities with Which They Have Financial Relationships — Notice of extension of comment period for proposed rule.

63 FR 14393, March 25, 1998: Office of Inspector General: Health Care Programs: Fraud and Abuse; Revised OIG Civil Money Penalties Resulting from the Health Insurance Portability and Accountability Act of 1996 — Notice of proposed rulemaking, affecting 42 CFR Parts 1003, 1005, and 1006.

63 FR 20415, April 24, 1998: Office of Inspector General: Publication of OIG Special Fraud Alert: Fraud and Abuse in Nursing Home Arrangements with Hospices — Notice.

63 FR 28395, May 22, 1998: HCFA Agency Information Collection Activities: Submission for OMB Review; Comment request (pertaining to procedures for advisory opinions concerning physician referrals and supporting regulations in 42 CFR 411.370 through 411.389).

63 FR 31123, June 8, 1998: Medicare Program; Incentive Programs — Fraud and Abuse — Final rule affecting 42 CFR Part 420.

63 FR 38311, July 16, 1998: Office of Inspector General: Medicare and State Health Care Programs: Fraud and Abuse; Issuance of Advisory Opinions by the OIG — Final rule affecting 42 CFR 1008. See also correction at 63 FR 43449, August 13, 1998.

63 FR 38414, July 16, 1998: HCFA Privacy Act of 1974; Report of Altered System (pertaining to disclosure of individual-specific information to combat fraud or abuse in health benefit programs).

63 FR 42409, August 7, 1998: Office of Inspector General: Solicitation of Information and Recommendations for Developing OIG Compliance Program Guidance for the Durable Medical Equipment Industry — Notice.

63 FR 42410, August 7, 1998: Office of Inspector General: Publication of the OIG Compliance Program Guidance for Home Health Agencies — Notice.

63 FR 45076, August 24, 1998: Office of Inspector General — Publication of OIG Compliance Program Guidance for Clinical Laboratories.

63 FR 46676, September 2, 1998: Office of Inspector General: Health Care Programs; Fraud and Abuse; Revised OIG Exclusion Authorities Resulting from Public Law 104–191 — Final rule affecting 42 CFR Parts 1000, 1001, 1002, and 1005. See also correction at 63 FR 57918, October 29, 1998.

63 FR 46736, September 2, 1998: Office of Inspector General: Health Care Programs; Fraud and Abuse; Revised OIG Sanction Authorities Resulting from Public Law 105–33 — Notice of proposed rulemaking affecting 42 CFR 1001, 1002, and 1003.

63 FR 50577, September 22, 1998: Office of Inspector General: Solicitation of Information and Recommendations for Developing OIG Compliance Program Guidance for Certain Medicare+Choice Organizations — Notice.

63 FR 58341, October 30, 1998: Office of Inspector General: Health Care Fraud and Abuse Data Collection Program: Reporting of Final Adverse Actions — Notice of proposed rulemaking under section 1128E of the Social Security Act, affecting 45 CFR 61.

63 FR 58399, October 30, 1998: Office of Inspector General: Publication of the OIG's Provider Self-Disclosure Protocol — Notice.

63 FR 67486, December 7, 1998: Office of Inspector General and HCFA; Solicitation of Comments on the OIG/HCFA Special Advisory Bulletin on the Patient Anti-Dumping Statute — Notice.

63 FR 68223, December 10, 1998: Office of Inspector General; Solicitation of New Safe Harbors and Special Fraud Alerts — Notice of intent to develop regulations, affecting 42 CFR 1001.

63 FR 68687, December 14, 1998: Medicare and Medicaid Program; Civil Money Penalties, Assessments, Exclusions, and Related Appeals Procedures — Final rule with comment period, affecting 42 CFR 400 and 402.

63 FR 70137, December 18, 1998: Office of Inspector General: Solicitation of Information and Recommendations for Developing OIG Compliance Program Guidance for the Nursing Home Industry — Notice.

63 FR 70138, December 18, 1998: Office of Inspector General: Publication of the OIG Compliance Program Guidance for Third-party Medical Billing Companies — Notice.

63 FR 71819, December 30, 1998: Office of Inspector General; Health Care Fraud and Abuse Data Collection Program; Reporting

under section 1128E of the Social Security Act of Final Adverse Actions — Notice of proposed rule-making; extension of comment period, affecting 45 CFR 61.

1999

64 FR 1813, January 12, 1999: Office of Inspector General Publication of OIG Special Fraud Alert on Physician Liability for Certifications in the Provision of Medical Equipment and Supplies and Home Health Services — Notice.

64 FR 2228, January 13, 1999: Office of Inspector General: Solicitation of Information and Recommendations for Developing OIG Compliance Program Guidance for the Hospice Industry — Notice.

64 FR 6753, February 16, 1999: Office of Inspector General: Privacy Act; Notification of New System of Records in Conjunction with the Healthcare Integrity and Protection Data Bank — Notice of a new system of records.

64 FR 10478, March 4, 1999: HCFA Agency Information Collection Activities: Proposed Collection; Comment request (pertaining to information collection requirements in final peer review organization (PRO) sanction regulations).

64 FR 13997, March 23, 1999: HCFA Agency Information Collection Activities: Submission for OMB Review; Comment request (pertaining to Medicare and Medicaid requirements for advanced directives, and disclosure of ownership and financial control interest).

64 FR 19375, April 20, 1999: HCFA Agency Information Collection Activities: Proposed Collection; Comment request (pertaining to acquisition, protection, and disclosure of peer review organization (PRO) information).

64 FR 24956, May 10, 1999: Medicare and Medicaid Programs; Effective Dates of Provider Agreements and Supplier Approvals — Correction restoring regulations inadvertently removed when a final rule concerning effective dates for provider agreements and supplier approvals was published at 62 FR 43931, August 18, 1997.

64 FR 30340, June 7, 1999: HCFA Agency Information Collection Activities: Submission for OMB Review; Comment request (pertaining to information collection requirements in the final peer review organization (PRO) sanction regulations).

64 FR 36368, July 6, 1999: Office of Inspector General Publication of OIG Compliance Program Guidance for the Durable Medical Equipment, Prosthetics, Orthotics and Supply Industry — Notice.

64 FR 37985, July 14, 1999: Office of Inspector General; Publication of the OIG Special Advisory Bulletin on Gainsharing Arrangements and CMPs for Hospital Payments to Physicians to Reduce or Limit Services to Beneficiaries — Notice.

64 FR 39150, July 21, 1999: Office of Inspector General; Draft OIG Compliance Program Guidance for Hospices — Notice and comment period.

64 FR 39420, July 22, 1999: Office of Inspector General; Health Care Programs; Fraud and Abuse; Revised OIG Sanction Authorities Resulting from P.L. 105–33, the Balanced Budget Act of 1997 — Final rule affecting 42 CFR Parts 1001, 1002, and 1003. See also correction at64 FR 42174, August 3, 1999.

64 FR 48846, September 8, 1999: Office of Inspector General: Solicitation of Information and Recommendations for Developing OIG Compliance Program Guidance for Individual Physicians and Small Group Practices — Notice.

64 FR 42791, September 30, 1999: Office of Inspector General; Publication of the OIG Special Advisory Bulletin on the Effect of Exclusion from Participation in Federal Health Care Programs — Notice. See also correction at64 FR 55484, October 13, 1999.

64 FR 57619, October 26, 1999: Office of Inspector General; Privacy Act; Exempt Record System, Pertaining to the Healthcare Integrity and Protection Data Bank (HIPDB) — Notice of proposed rulemaking affecting 45 CFR Part 5b.

64 FR 57740, October 26, 1999: Office of Inspector General; Healthcare Fraud and Abuse Data Collection Program: Reporting of Final Adverse Actions — Final rule affecting 45 CFR Part 61.

64 FR 58419, October 29, 1999: Office of Inspector General; Draft OIG Compliance Program Guidance for Nursing Facilities — Notice and comment period.

64 FR 58851, November 1, 1999: Office of Inspector General; Healthcare Integrity and Protection Data Bank: Announcement of Opening Date for Reporting and Self-query Fee — Notice.

64 FR 61353, November 10, 1999: Office of Inspector General/HCFA; OIG/HCFA Special Advisory Bulletin on the Patient Anti-dumping Statute.

64 FR 61893, November 15, 1999: Office of Inspector General; Publication of the OIG's Compliance Program Guidance for Medicare+Choice Organizations Offering Coordinated Care Plans — Notice.

64 FR 63504, November 19, 1999: Office of Inspector General; Fraud and Abuse; Statutory Exception to the Anti-kickback Statute for Shared Risk Arrangements — Interim final rule with request for comment, affection 42 CFR Part 1001. See also correction at 64 FR 71317, December 21, 1999.

64 FR 63518, November 19, 1999: Office of Inspector General; Fraud and Abuse; Clarification of the Initial OIG Safe Harbor Provisions and Establishment of Additional Safe Harbor Provisions under the Anti-kickback Statute — Final rule affecting42 CFR Part 1001.

64 FR 69217, December 10, 1999: Office of Inspector General; Solicitation of New Safe Harbors and Special Fraud Alerts — Intent to develop regulations affecting 42 CFR Part 1001.

64 FR 73563, December 30, 1999: HCFA Agency Information Collection Activities: Submission for OMB Review; Comment request pertaining to Medicare program integrity organizational conflict of interest disclosure certificates).

2000

65 FR 9274, February 24, 2000: Office of Inspector General: Publication of OIG Special Fraud Alert on Rental of Space in Physician Offices by Persons or Entities to Which Physicians Refer — Notice.

65 FR 11589, March 3, 2000: Office of Inspector General: Health Care Integrity and Protection Data Bank under Section 1128E of the Social Security Act: Announcement of Opening Date for Querying and User Fees — Notice.

65 FR 14289, March 16, 2000: Office of Inspector General: Publication of the OIG Compliance Program Guidance for Nursing Facilities — Notice.

65 FR 24400, April 26, 2000: Office of Inspector General; Health Care Programs: Fraud and Abuse; Revised OIG Civil Money Penalties Resulting from Public Law 104-191 (HIPAA) — Final rule affecting 42 CFR Parts 1001, 1003, 1005, and 1006. See also correction at 65 FR 35583, June 5, 2000.

65 FR 32060, May 22, 2000: Office of Inspector General Medicare and State Health Care Programs: Fraud and Abuse: Ambulance Restocking Safe Harbor under the Anti-kickback Statute — Notice of proposed rulemaking affecting 42 CFR 1001.

65 FR 34986, June 1, 2000: Office of Inspector General; Privacy Act; Implementation (exempting the Healthcare Integrity and Protection Data Bank under Section 1128C of the Social Security Act

from certain provisions of the Privacy Act (5 U.S.C. 552a) — Final rule.

65 FR 36818, June 12, 2000: Office of Inspector General: Draft OIG Compliance Program for Individual and Small Group Physician Practices — Notice and comment period.

65 FR 50204, August 17, 2000: Office of Inspector General: Solicitation of Information and Recommendations for Developing a Compliance Risk Guidance for the Ambulance Industry — Notice.

65 FR 50552, August 18, 2000: HCFA Privacy Act of 1974; Report of Modified or Altered System (pertaining to revision of language in global fraud and abuse routine uses).

65 FR 53319, September 1, 2000: HCFA Agency Information Collection Activities: Proposed Collection; Comment request (pertaining to incentive arrangement disclosure form for managed care organizations and their related medical groups and physicians).

65 FR 59434, October 5, 2000: Office of Inspector General Compliance Program for Individual and Small Group Physician Practices — Notice.

65 FR 63035, October 20, 2000: Office of Inspector General: Medicare and State Health Care Programs: Fraud and Abuse; Revisions and Technical Corrections — Proposed rule affecting 42 CFR Parts 1001, 1003, 1005, and 1008.

65 FR 65861, November 2, 2000: HCFA Agency Information Collection Activities: Proposed Collection; Comment request (pertaining to conflict of interest disclosure requirements for Medicare program integrity).

65 FR 78124, December 14, 2000: Office of Inspector General: Solicitation of New Safe Harbors and Special Fraud Alerts — Notice of intent to develop regulations.

2001

66 FR 856, January 4, 2001: Medicare and Medicaid Programs; Physicians Referrals to Health Care Entities with which They Have Financial Relationships—Final rule with comment period, affecting 42 CFR Parts 411 and 424.

66 FR 6629, January 22, 2001: HCFA Agency Information Collection Activities: Submission for OMB Review; Comment request (pertaining to Medicare Integrity Program Organizational Conflict of Interest Disclosure Certificate).

66 FR 8771, February 2, 2001: Medicare and Medicaid Programs; Physicians' Referrals to Health Care Entities with which They Have Financial Relationships: Delay of Effective Date of Final Rule and Technical Amendment, affecting 42 CFR Parts 411 and 424.

66 FR 9858, February 12, 2001: HCFA Privacy Act of 1974; Report of New System (pertaining to complaints against health insurance issuers and health plans).

66 FR 9865, February 12, 2001: Office of Inspector General: Privacy Act of 1974; Amendment to the Health Care Program Violations System of Records-Notice and comment period (pertaining to including Social Security numbers of sanctioned individual in the Health Care Program Violations record).

66 FR 17813, April 4, 2001: Medicare and Medicaid Programs; Physicians' Referrals to Health Care Entities with which They Have Financial Relationships; Extension of Comment period—Notice, affecting 42 CFR Parts 411 and 424.

66 FR 19507, April 16, 2001: HCFA Agency Information Collection Activities: Proposed Collection; Comment request (pertaining to conflict of interest and ownership and control information form).

66 FR 23944, May 10, 2001: HCFA Agency Information Collection Activities: Proposed Collection; Comment request (pertaining to financial reports for providers indebted to Medicare who want to repay over time).

66 FR 28916, May 25, 2001: HCFA Agency Information Collection Activities; Proposed Collection; Comment request (pertaining to procedures for advisory opinions concerning physician referrals under section 1877 of the Social Security Act).

66 FR 31245, June 11, 2001: Office of Inspector General; Healthcare Integrity and Protection Data Bank: Change in User Fees—Notice.

66 FR 31246, June 11, 2001: Office of Inspector General; Solicitation of Information and Recommendations for Developing a Compliance Program Guidance for the Pharmaceutical Industry—Notice.

See § 4:8.

§ 8:9 CRIMINAL PENALTIES: FALSE STATEMENTS, FALSE REPRESENTATIONS, CONCEALMENT, FAILURE TO DISCLOSE, AND CONVERSION WITH RESPECT TO BENEFITS AND PAYMENTS — Section 1128B(a) [42 U.S.C.A. 1320a-7b(a)]

Regulations

42 CFR Part 420 — Program Integrity: Medicare

42 CFR Part 455 — Program Integrity: Medicaid

42 CFR Chapter V — Office of Inspector General — Health Care, Department of Health and Human Services

Subchapter A — General Provisions

Part 1000 — Introduction; General Definitions

Subchapter B — OIG Authorities

Part 1001 — Program Integrity: Medicare and State Health Care Programs

Part 1002 — Program Integrity: State-initiated Exclusion from Medicaid

Part 1003 — Civil Money Penalties, Assessments and Exclusions

Part 1005 — Appeals of Exclusions, Civil Money Penalties and Assessments

Part 1006 — Investigational Inquiries

Part 1007 — State Medicaid Fraud Control Units

Part 1008 — Advisory Opinions by the OIG

55 FR 12205, April 2, 1990: Health Care Programs: Fraud and Abuse; Amendments to OIG Exclusion and CMP Authorities Resulting from Public Law 100–93, the Medicare and Medicaid Patient and Program Protection Act of 1987, Public Law 99–272, the Consolidated Omnibus Budget Reconciliation Act of 1985, and Public Law 100–360, the Medicare Catastrophic Coverage Act of 1988 — Proposed rule to amend 42 CFR Parts 1000, 1001, 1002, 1003, 1004, 1005, 1006, and 1007. See also correction published at 55 FR 17461, April 25, 1990.

57 FR 3298, January 29, 1992: Health Care Programs: Fraud and Abuse; Amendments to OIG Exclusion and CMP Authorities Resulting From Public Law 100–93 — Final rule affecting 42 CFR Parts 1001, 1002, 1003, 1004, 1005, 1006, and 1007. See also final rule and correction at 57 FR 9669, March 20, 1992; final rule affecting 42 CFR Parts 1001and 1005, with clarification at 58 FR 5617, January 22, 1993; and final rule affecting 42 CFR Part 1001, with correction, at 58 FR 40752, July 30, 1993.

62 FR 47182, September 8, 1997: Office of Inspector General: Health Care Programs: Fraud and Abuse; Revised OIG Exclusion Authorities Resulting from Public Law 104–191 — Notice of Proposed rulemaking, affecting 42 CFR Parts 1000, 1001, 1002, and 1005.

62 FR 55410, October 24, 1997: Office of Inspector General: Criteria for Implementing Permissive Exclusion Authority under Section 1128(b)(7) of the Social Security Act — Notice.

62 FR 67392, December 24, 1997: Office of Inspector General: Criteria for Implementing Permissive Exclusion Authority under Section 1128(b)(7) of the Social Security Act — Notice.

63 FR 14393, March 25, 1998: Office of Inspector General: Health Care Programs: Fraud and Abuse; Revised OIG Civil Money Penalties Resulting from the Health Insurance Portability and Accountability Act of 1996 — Notice of proposed rulemaking, affecting 42 CFR Parts 1003, 1005, and 1006.

63 FR 31123, June 8, 1998: Medicare Program; Incentive Programs — Fraud and Abuse — Final rule affecting 42 CFR Part 420.

63 FR 46676, September 2, 1998: Office of Inspector General: Health Care Programs; Fraud and Abuse; Revised OIG Exclusion Authorities Resulting from Public Law 104–191 — Final rule affecting 42 CFR Parts 1000, 1001, 1002, and 1005. See also correction at 63 FR 57918, October 29, 1998.

63 FR 46736, September 2, 1998: Office of Inspector General: Health Care Programs; Fraud and Abuse; Revised OIG Sanction Authorities Resulting from Public Law 105–33 — Notice of proposed rulemaking affecting 42 CFR 1001, 1002, and 1003.

63 FR 58341, October 30, 1998: Office of Inspector General: Health Care Fraud and Abuse Data Collection Program: Reporting of Final Adverse Actions — Notice of proposed rulemaking under section 1128E of the Social Security Act, affecting 45 CFR 61.

63 FR 68223, December 10, 1998: Office of Inspector General; Solicitation of New Safe Harbors and Special Fraud Alerts — Notice of intent to develop regulations, affecting 42 CFR 1001.

63 FR 68687, December 14, 1998: Medicare and Medicaid Program; Civil Money Penalties, Assessments, Exclusions, and Related Appeals Procedures — Final rule with comment period, affecting 42 CFR 400 and 402.

63 FR 71819, December 30, 1998: Office of Inspector General; Health Care Fraud and Abuse Data Collection Program; Reporting under section 1128E of the Social Security Act of Final Adverse Actions — Notice of proposed rule-making; extension of comment period, affecting 45 CFR 61.

1999

64 FR 6753, February 16, 1999: Office of Inspector General: Privacy Act; Notification of New System of Records in Conjunction with the Healthcare Integrity and Protection Data Bank — Notice of a new system of records.

64 FR 13997, March 23, 1999: HCFA Agency Information Collection Activities: Submission for OMB Review; Comment request (pertaining to Medicare and Medicaid requirements for advanced directives, and disclosure of ownership and financial control interest).

64 FR 24956, May 10, 1999: Medicare and Medicaid Programs; Effective Dates of Provider Agreements and Supplier Approvals — Correction restoring regulations inadvertently removed when a final rule concerning effective dates for provider agreements and supplier approvals was published at 62 FR 43931, August 18, 1997].

64 FR 39420, July 22, 1999: Office of Inspector General; Health Care Programs; Fraud and Abuse; Revised OIG Sanction Authorities Resulting from P.L. 105–33, the Balanced Budget Act of 1997 — Final rule affecting 42 CFR Parts 1001, 1002, and 1003. See also correction at64 FR 42174, August 3, 1999.

64 FR 42791, September 30, 1999: Office of Inspector General; Publication of the OIG Special Advisory Bulletin on the Effect of Exclusion from Participation in Federal Health Care Programs — Notice. See also correction at64 FR 55484, October 13, 1999.

64 FR 57619, October 26, 1999: Office of Inspector General; Privacy Act; Exempt Record System, Pertaining to the Healthcare Integrity and Protection Data Bank (HIPDB) — Notice of proposed rulemaking affecting 45 CFR Part 5b.

64 FR 57740, October 26, 1999: Office of Inspector General; Healthcare Fraud and Abuse Data Collection Program: Reporting of Final Adverse Actions — Final rule affecting 45 CFR Part 61.

64 FR 58851, November 1, 1999: Office of Inspector General; Healthcare Integrity and Protection Data Bank: Announcement of Opening Date for Reporting and Self-query Fee — Notice.

2000

65 FR 9274, February 24, 2000: Office of Inspector General: Publication of OIG Special Fraud Alert on Rental of Space in Physician Offices by Persons or Entities to Which Physicians Refer — Notice.

65 FR 11589, March 3, 2000: Office of Inspector General: Health Care Integrity and Protection Data Bank under Section 1128E of the Social Security Act: Announcement of Opening Date for Querying and User Fees — Notice.

65 FR 14289, March 16, 2000: Office of Inspector General: Publication of the OIG Compliance Program Guidance for Nursing Facilities — Notice.

65 FR 24400, April 26, 2000: Office of Inspector General; Health Care Programs: Fraud and Abuse; Revised OIG Civil Money Penalties Resulting from Public Law 104-191 (HIPAA) — Final rule affecting 42 CFR Parts 1001, 1003, 1005, and 1006. See also correction at 65 FR 35583, June 5, 2000.

65 FR 32060, May 22, 2000: Office of Inspector General Medicare and State Health Care Programs: Fraud and Abuse: Ambulance Restocking Safe Harbor under the Anti-kickback Statute — Notice of proposed rulemaking affecting 42 CFR 1001.

65 FR 34986, June 1, 2000: Office of Inspector General; Privacy Act; Implementation (exempting the Healthcare Integrity and Protection Data Bank under Section 1128C of the Social Security Act from certain provisions of the Privacy Act (5 U.S.C. 552a) — Final rule.

65 FR 36818, June 12, 2000: Office of Inspector General: Draft OIG Compliance Program for Individual and Small Group Physician Practices — Notice and comment period.

65 FR 50204, August 17, 2000: Office of Inspector General: Solicitation of Information and Recommendations for Developing a Compliance Risk Guidance for the Ambulance Industry — Notice.

65 FR 50552, August 18, 2000: HCFA Privacy Act of 1974; Report of Modified or Altered System (pertaining to revision of language in global fraud and abuse routine uses).

65 FR 53319, September 1, 2000: HCFA Agency Information Collection Activities: Proposed Collection; Comment request (pertaining to incentive arrangement disclosure form for managed care organizations and their related medical groups and physicians).

65 FR 59434, October 5, 2000: Office of Inspector General Compliance Program for Individual and Small Group Physician Practices — Notice.

65 FR 63035, October 20, 2000: Office of Inspector General: Medicare and State Health Care Programs: Fraud and Abuse; Revisions and Technical Corrections — Proposed rule affecting 42 CFR Parts 1001, 1003, 1005, and 1008.

65 FR 65861, November 2, 2000: HCFA Agency Information Collection Activities: Proposed Collection; Comment request (pertaining to conflict of interest disclosure requirements for Medicare program integrity).

65 FR 78124, December 14, 2000: Office of Inspector General: Solicitation of New Safe Harbors and Special Fraud Alerts — Notice of intent to develop regulations.

2001

66 FR 856, January 4, 2001: Medicare and Medicaid Programs; Physicians Referrals to Health Care Entities with which They Have Financial Relationships—Final rule with comment period, affecting 42 CFR Parts 411 and 424.

66 FR 6629, January 22, 2001: HCFA Agency Information Collection Activities: Submission for OMB Review; Comment request (pertaining to Medicare Integrity Program Organizational Conflict of Interest Disclosure Certificate).

66 FR 8771, February 2, 2001: Medicare and Medicaid Programs; Physicians' Referrals to Health Care Entities with which They Have Financial Relationships: Delay of Effective Date of Final Rule and Technical Amendment, affecting 42 CFR Parts 411 and 424.

66 FR 9858, February 12, 2001: HCFA Privacy Act of 1974; Report of New System (pertaining to complaints against health insurance issuers and health plans).

66 FR 9865, February 12, 2001: Office of Inspector General: Privacy Act of 1974; Amendment to the Health Care Program Violations System of Records—Notice and comment period (pertaining to including Social Security numbers of sanctioned individual in the Health Care Program Violations record).

66 FR 17813, April 4, 2001: Medicare and Medicaid Programs; Physicians' Referrals to Health Care Entities with which They Have Financial Relationships; Extension of Comment period—Notice, affecting 42 CFR Parts 411 and 424.

66 FR 19507, April 16, 2001: HCFA Agency Information Collection Activities: Proposed Collection; Comment request (pertaining to conflict of interest and ownership and control information form).

66 FR 23944, May 10, 2001: HCFA Agency Information Collection Activities: Proposed Collection; Comment request (pertaining to financial reports for providers indebted to Medicare who want to repay over time).

66 FR 28916, May 25, 2001: HCFA Agency Information Collection Activities; Proposed Collection; Comment request (pertaining to procedures for advisory opinions concerning physician referrals under section 1877 of the Social Security Act).

66 FR 31245, June 11, 2001: Office of Inspector General; Healthcare Integrity and Protection Data Bank: Change in User Fees—Notice.

66 FR 31246, June 11, 2001: Office of Inspector General; Solicitation of Information and Recommendations for Developing a Compliance Program Guidance for the Pharmaceutical Industry—Notice.

See § 4:9.

§ 8:10 CRIMINAL PENALTIES: KICKBACKS, BRIBES, AND REBATES — Section 1128B(b) [42 U.S.C.A. 1320a-7b(b)]

Regulations

42 CFR Part 402 — Civil Money Penalties, Assessments, and Exclusions

42 CFR Part 420 — Program Integrity: Medicare

42 CFR Part 455 — Program Integrity: Medicaid

42 CFR Chapter V — Office of Inspector General — Health Care, Department of Health and Human Services

Subchapter A — General Provisions

Part 1000 — Introduction; General Definitions

Subchapter B — OIG Authorities

Part 1001 — Program Integrity: Medicare and State Health Care Programs

Part 1002 — Program Integrity: State-initiated Exclusion from Medicaid

Part 1005 — Appeals of Exclusions, Civil Money Penalties and Assessments

Part 1006 — Investigational Inquiries

Part 1007 — State Medicaid Fraud Control Units

Part 1008 — Advisory Opinions by the OIG

53 FR 51856, December 23, 1988: Medicare and Medicaid Programs; Fraud and Abuse; OIG Anti-Kickback Provisions — Proposed rule to amend 42 CFR Part 1001.

53 FR 52448, December 28, 1988: Medicare and Medicaid Programs; Fraud and Abuse OIG Anti-Kickback

Provisions — Withdrawal of proposed rulemaking set forth at 53 FR 51856.

54 FR 3088, January 23, 1989: Medicare and Medicaid Programs; Fraud and Abuse OIG Anti-Kickback Provisions — Proposed rule to amend 42 CFR Part 1001.

55 FR 12205, April 2, 1990: Health Care Programs: Fraud and Abuse; Amendments to OIG Exclusion and CMP Authorities Resulting from Public Law 100–93, the Medicare and Medicaid Patient and Program Protection Act of 1987, Public Law 99–272, the Consolidated Omnibus Budget Reconciliation Act of 1985, and Public Law 100–360, the Medicare Catastrophic Coverage Act of 1988 — Proposed rule to amend 42 CFR Parts 1000, 1001, 1002, 1003, 1004, 1005, 1006, and 1007. See also correction published at 55 FR 17461, April 25, 1990.

56 FR 35952, July 29, 1991: Medicare and State Health Care Programs: Fraud and Abuse; OIG Anti-Kickback Provisions — Final rule.

57 FR 3298, January 29, 1992: Health Care Programs: Fraud and Abuse; Amendments to OIG Exclusion and CMP Authorities Resulting From Public Law 100–93 — Final rule affecting 42 CFR Parts 1001, 1002, 1003, 1004, 1005, 1006, and 1007. See also final rule and correction at 57 FR 9669, March 20, 1992; final rule affecting 42 CFR Parts 1001and 1005, with clarification at 58 FR 5617, January 22, 1993; and final rule affecting 42 CFR Part 1001, with correction, at 58 FR 40752, July 30, 1993.

57 FR 52723, November 5, 1992: Medicare and State Health Care Programs: Fraud and Abuse; Safe Harbors for Protecting Health Plans — Interim final rule with request for comment. See also extension of comment period at 58 FR 2989, January 7, 1993, affecting 42 CFR 1001.

57 FR 59024, December 14, 1992: Medicare and Medicaid Programs; Requirements for Physician Incentive Plans in Prepaid Health Care Organizations — Proposed rule affecting 42 CFR Parts 417 and 434 (HCFA) and 42 CFR Part 1003 (Office of Inspector General). See also extension of comment period at 58 FR 8568, February 16, 1993.

58 FR 49008, September 21, 1993: Office of Inspector General: Additional Safe Harbor Provisions under the OIG Anti-Kickback Statute — Proposed rule pertaining to investment interests in rural areas, in ambulatory surgical centers, and in group practices composed exclusively of active investors; practitioner recruitment;

obstetrical malpractice insurance subsidies; referral agreements for specialty services; and cooperative hospital service organizations.

58 FR 54096, October 20, 1993: Office of Inspector General: Civil Money Penalties for Prohibited Referrals to Entities Providing Clinical Laboratory Services and for Prohibited Arrangements and Schemes — Proposed rule affecting 42 CFR Part 1003.

59 FR 37202, July 21, 1994: Medicare and State Health Care Programs; Fraud and Abuse; Clarification of the OIG Safe Harbor Anti-kickback Provisions — Proposed rule affecting 42 CFR Part 1001.

59 FR 50762, October 5, 1994: HCFA Public Information Collection Requirements Submitted to the Office of Management and Budget (OMB) for Clearance (pertaining to reimbursement of hospital costs for residents and interns, criteria for psychiatric and rehabilitation hospital units' reimbursement under the prospective payment system, disclosure of owners and managers of suppliers for fraud and abuse detection purposes, reimbursement of municipal health services clinics, survey form for hospital compliance with anti-dumping requirements, and evaluation of patient and physician satisfaction with the Medicare participating heart bypass center demonstration).

59 FR 61571, December 1, 1994: Office of Inspector General; Fraud and Abuse; Civil Money Penalties for Hospital Physician Incentive Plans — Proposed rule affecting 42 CFR Part 1003.

59 FR 65372, December 19, 1994: Office of Inspector General — Notice of Publication of Special Fraud Alerts (pertaining to joint venture arrangements, routine waiver of Medicare Part B copayments and deductibles, hospital incentives to referring physicians, prescription drug marketing practices, and arrangements for provision of clinical laboratory services).

60 FR 16580, March 31, 1995: Office of Inspector General: Civil Money Penalties for Referrals to Entities and for Prohibited Arrangements and Schemes — Final rule with comment period, affecting 42 CFR Part 1003.

60 FR 32916, June 26, 1995: Office of Inspector General; Health Care Programs; Fraud and Abuse; Technical Revision to the Scope and Effect of the OIG Exclusion Regulations — Final rule affecting 42 CFR Part 1001.

60 FR 40847, August 10, 1995: Office of Inspector General: Publication of OIG Special Fraud Alerts: Home Health Fraud, and Fraud

and Abuse in the Provision of Medical Supplies to Nursing Facilities — Notice.

60 FR 41914, August 14, 1995: Medicare Program; Physician Financial Relationships with, and Referrals to, Health Care Entities that Furnish Clinical Laboratory Services; Financial Relationship Reporting Requirements — Final rule affecting 42 CFR Part 411.

60 FR 55721, November 2, 1995: Office of Inspector General Publication of the Medicare Advisory Bulletin on Hospice Benefits — Notice.

61 FR 2122, January 25, 1996: Medicare and State Health Care Programs; Fraud and Abuse; Safe Harbors for Protecting Health Plans — Final rule.

61 FR 13430, March 27, 1996: Medicare and Medicaid Programs; Requirements for Physician Incentive Plans in Prepaid Health Care Organizations — Final rule with comment period, affecting 42 CFR Parts 417, 434, and 1003.

61 FR 30623, June 17, 1996: Office of Inspector General Publication of OIG Special Fraud Alert: Fraud and Abuse in the Provision of Services in Nursing Homes — Notice.

61 FR 52299, October 7, 1996: Office of Inspector General; Medicare and State Health Care Programs and Program Fraud Civil Remedies: Fraud and Abuse; Civil Money Penalties Inflation Adjustments — Final rule affecting 42 CFR Part 1003.

61 FR 58568, November 15, 1996: Office of Inspector General; Publication of the Medicare Beneficiary Advisory Bulletin on HMO Arrangements — Notice.

61 FR 69060, December 31, 1996: Office of Inspector General: Solicitation of New Safe Harbors and Modifications to Existing Safe Harbors — Notice of intent to develop regulations, affecting 42 CFR Part 1001.

Programs: Fraud and Abuse; Issuance of Advisory Opinions by the OIG — Interim final rule with comment period, affecting 42 CFR Part 1008.

62 FR 23140, April 29, 1997: Office of Inspector General: Health Care Programs: Fraud and Abuse; Revised PRO Sanctions for Failing to Meet Statutory Obligations — Final rule.

62 FR 28410, May 23, 1997: Office of Inspector General: Health Care Programs: Fraud and Abuse — Notice of Intent to Form the Negotiated Rulemaking Committee for the Shared Risk Exception (statutory exceptions to the anti-kickback statute) — affecting42 CFR Part 1001.

62 FR 39798, July 24, 1997: Office of Inspector General: Negotiated Rulemaking Committee on the Shared Risk Exception (affecting 42 CFR Part 1001) — Notice of meeting.

62 FR 47182, September 8, 1997: Office of Inspector General: Health Care Programs: Fraud and Abuse; Revised OIG Exclusion Authorities Resulting from Public Law 104–191 — Notice of Proposed rulemaking, affecting 42 CFR Parts 1000, 1001, 1002, and 1005.

62 FR 47195, September 8, 1997: Office of Inspector General: Negotiated Rulemaking Committee on the Shared Risk Exception (affecting 42 CFR Part 1001) — Notice of meeting.

62 FR 55410, October 24, 1997: Office of Inspector General: Criteria for Implementing Permissive Exclusion Authority under Section 1128(b)(7) of the Social Security Act — Notice.

62 FR 63689, December 2, 1997: Office of Inspector General: Negotiated Rulemaking Committee on the Shared Risk Exception — Notice of meeting, affecting 42 CFR Part 1001.

62 FR 65049, December 10, 1997: Office of Inspector General: Solicitation of New Safe Harbors and Special Fraud Alerts — Notice of intent to develop regulations, affecting 42 CFR Part 1001.

62 FR 67392, December 24, 1997: Office of Inspector General: Criteria for Implementing Permissive Exclusion Authority under Section 1128(b)(7) of the Social Security Act — Notice.

63 FR 187, January 5, 1998: Office of Inspector General; Negotiated Rulemaking Committee on the Shared Risk Exception — Notice of meeting.

63 FR 1646, January 9, 1998: Medicare Program; Physicians' Referrals; Issuance of Advisory Opinions — Final rule with comment period, affecting 42 CFR Part 411.

63 FR 1659, January 9, 1998: Medicare and Medicaid Programs; Physicians' Referrals to Health Care Entities with Which They Have Financial Relationships — Proposed rule affecting 42 CFR Parts 411, 424, 435, and 455.

63 FR 8987, February 23, 1998: Office of Inspector General: Publication of the OIG Compliance Program for Hospitals — Notice.

63 FR 9844, February 26, 1998: HCFA Agency Information Collection Activities: Proposed Collection; Comment request (pertaining to procedures for advisory opinions concerning physician referrals and supporting regulations in 42 CFR Sections 411.370- 411.389).

63 FR 11649, March 10, 1998: Medicare and Medicaid Programs; Physicians' Referrals to Health Care Entities with Which They Have

Financial Relationships — Notice of extension of comment period for proposed rule.

63 FR 14393, March 25, 1998: Office of Inspector General: Health Care Programs: Fraud and Abuse; Revised OIG Civil Money Penalties Resulting from the Health Insurance Portability and Accountability Act of 1996 — Notice of proposed rulemaking, affecting 42 CFR Parts 1003, 1005, and 1006.

63 FR 20415, April 24, 1998: Office of Inspector General: Publication of OIG Special Fraud Alert: Fraud and Abuse in Nursing Home Arrangements with Hospices — Notice.

63 FR 28395, May 22, 1998: HCFA Agency Information Collection Activities: Submission for OMB Review; Comment request (pertaining to procedures for advisory opinions concerning physician referrals and supporting regulations in 42 CFR 411.370 through 411.389).

63 FR 31123, June 8, 1998: Medicare Program; Incentive Programs — Fraud and Abuse — Final rule affecting 42 CFR Part 420.

63 FR 38311, July 16, 1998: Office of Inspector General: Medicare and State Health Care Programs: Fraud and Abuse; Issuance of Advisory Opinions by the OIG — Final rule affecting 42 CFR 1008. See also correction at 63 FR 43449, August 13, 1998.

63 FR 38414, July 16, 1998: HCFA Privacy Act of 1974; Report of Altered System (pertaining to disclosure of individual-specific information to combat fraud or abuse in health benefit programs).

63 FR 42409, August 7, 1998: Office of Inspector General: Solicitation of Information and Recommendations for Developing OIG Compliance Program Guidance for the Durable Medical Equipment Industry — Notice.

63 FR 42410, August 7, 1998: Office of Inspector General: Publication of the OIG Compliance Program Guidance for Home Health Agencies — Notice.

63 FR 45076, August 24, 1998: Office of Inspector General — Publication of OIG Compliance Program Guidance for Clinical Laboratories.

63 FR 46676, September 2, 1998: Office of Inspector General: Health Care Programs; Fraud and Abuse; Revised OIG Exclusion Authorities Resulting from Public Law 104–191 — Final rule affecting 42 CFR Parts 1000, 1001, 1002, and 1005. See also correction at 63 FR 57918, October 29, 1998.

63 FR 46736, September 2, 1998: Office of Inspector General: Health Care Programs; Fraud and Abuse; Revised OIG Sanction

Authorities Resulting from Public Law 105–33 — Notice of proposed rulemaking affecting 42 CFR 1001, 1002, and 1003.

63 FR 50577, September 22, 1998: Office of Inspector General: Solicitation of Information and Recommendations for Developing OIG Compliance Program Guidance for Certain Medicare+Choice Organizations — Notice.

63 FR 58341, October 30, 1998: Office of Inspector General: Health Care Fraud and Abuse Data Collection Program: Reporting of Final Adverse Actions — Notice of proposed rulemaking under section 1128E of the Social Security Act, affecting 45 CFR 61.

63 FR 58399, October 30, 1998: Office of Inspector General: Publication of the OIG's Provider Self-Disclosure Protocol — Notice.

63 FR 67486, December 7, 1998: Office of Inspector General and HCFA; Solicitation of Comments on the OIG/HCFA Special Advisory Bulletin on the Patient Anti-Dumping Statute — Notice.

63 FR 68223, December 10, 1998: Office of Inspector General; Solicitation of New Safe Harbors and Special Fraud Alerts — Notice of intent to develop regulations, affecting 42 CFR 1001.

63 FR 68687, December 14, 1998: Medicare and Medicaid Program; Civil Money Penalties, Assessments, Exclusions, and Related Appeals Procedures — Final rule with comment period, affecting 42 CFR 400 and 402.

63 FR 70137, December 18, 1998: Office of Inspector General: Solicitation of Information and Recommendations for Developing OIG Compliance Program Guidance for the Nursing Home Industry — Notice.

63 FR 70138, December 18, 1998: Office of Inspector General: Publication of the OIG Compliance Program Guidance for Third-party Medical Billing Companies — Notice.

63 FR 71819, December 30, 1998: Office of Inspector General; Health Care Fraud and Abuse Data Collection Program; Reporting under section 1128E of the Social Security Act of Final Adverse Actions — Notice of proposed rule-making; extension of comment period, affecting 45 CFR 61.

1999

64 FR 1813, January 12, 1999: Office of Inspector General Publication of OIG Special Fraud Alert on Physician Liability for Certifications in the Provision of Medical Equipment and Supplies and Home Health Services — Notice.

64 FR 2228, January 13, 1999: Office of Inspector General: Solicitation of Information and Recommendations for Developing OIG Compliance Program Guidance for the Hospice Industry — Notice.

64 FR 6753, February 16, 1999: Office of Inspector General: Privacy Act; Notification of New System of Records in Conjunction with the Healthcare Integrity and Protection Data Bank — Notice of a new system of records.

64 FR 10478, March 4, 1999: HCFA Agency Information Collection Activities: Proposed Collection; Comment request (pertaining to information collection requirements in final peer review organization (PRO) sanction regulations).

64 FR 13997, March 23, 1999: HCFA Agency Information Collection Activities: Submission for OMB Review; Comment request (pertaining to Medicare and Medicaid requirements for advanced directives, and disclosure of ownership and financial control interest).

64 FR 19375, April 20, 1999: HCFA Agency Information Collection Activities: Proposed Collection; Comment request (pertaining to acquisition, protection, and disclosure of peer review organization (PRO) information).

64 FR 30340, June 7, 1999: HCFA Agency Information Collection Activities: Submission for OMB Review; Comment request (pertaining to information collection requirements in the final peer review organization (PRO) sanction regulations).

64 FR 36368, July 6, 1999: Office of Inspector General Publication of OIG Compliance Program Guidance for the Durable Medical Equipment, Prosthetics, Orthotics and Supply Industry — Notice.

64 FR 37985, July 14, 1999: Office of Inspector General; Publication of the OIG Special Advisory Bulletin on Gainsharing Arrangements and CMPs for Hospital Payments to Physicians to Reduce or Limit Services to Beneficiaries — Notice.

64 FR 39150, July 21, 1999: Office of Inspector General; Draft OIG Compliance Program Guidance for Hospices — Notice and comment period.

64 FR 39420, July 22, 1999: Office of Inspector General; Health Care Programs; Fraud and Abuse; Revised OIG Sanction Authorities Resulting from P.L. 105–33, the Balanced Budget Act of 1997 — Final rule affecting 42 CFR Parts 1001, 1002, and 1003. See also correction at64 FR 42174, August 3, 1999.

64 FR 48846, September 8, 1999: Office of Inspector General: Solicitation of Information and Recommendations for Developing

OIG Compliance Program Guidance for Individual Physicians and Small Group Practices — Notice.

64 FR 42791, September 30, 1999: Office of Inspector General; Publication of the OIG Special Advisory Bulletin on the Effect of Exclusion from Participation in Federal Health Care Programs — Notice. See also correction at64 FR 55484, October 13, 1999.

64 FR 57619, October 26, 1999: Office of Inspector General; Privacy Act; Exempt Record System, Pertaining to the Healthcare Integrity and Protection Data Bank (HIPDB) — Notice of proposed rulemaking affecting 45 CFR Part 5b.

64 FR 57740, October 26, 1999: Office of Inspector General; Healthcare Fraud and Abuse Data Collection Program: Reporting of Final Adverse Actions — Final rule affecting 45 CFR Part 61.

64 FR 58419, October 29, 1999: Office of Inspector General; Draft OIG Compliance Program Guidance for Nursing Facilities — Notice and comment period.

64 FR 58851, November 1, 1999: Office of Inspector General; Healthcare Integrity and Protection Data Bank: Announcement of Opening Date for Reporting and Self-query Fee — Notice.

64 FR 61353, November 10, 1999: Office of Inspector General/HCFA; OIG/HCFA Special Advisory Bulletin on the Patient Anti-dumping Statute.

64 FR 61893, November 15, 1999: Office of Inspector General; Publication of the OIG's Compliance Program Guidance for Medicare+Choice Organizations Offering Coordinated Care Plans — Notice.

64 FR 63504, November 19, 1999: Office of Inspector General; Fraud and Abuse; Statutory Exception to the Anti-kickback Statute for Shared Risk Arrangements — Interim final rule with request for comment, affection 42 CFR Part 1001. See also correction at 64 FR 71317, December 21, 1999.

64 FR 63518, November 19, 1999: Office of Inspector General; Fraud and Abuse; Clarification of the Initial OIG Safe Harbor Provisions and Establishment of Additional Safe Harbor Provisions under the Anti-kickback Statute — Final rule affecting42 CFR Part 1001.

64 FR 69217, December 10, 1999: Office of Inspector General; Solicitation of New Safe Harbors and Special Fraud Alerts — Intent to develop regulations affecting 42 CFR Part 1001.

64 FR 73563, December 30, 1999: HCFA Agency Information Collection Activities: Submission for OMB Review; Comment request

pertaining to Medicare program integrity organizational conflict of interest disclosure certificates).

2000

65 FR 9274, February 24, 2000: Office of Inspector General: Publication of OIG Special Fraud Alert on Rental of Space in Physician Offices by Persons or Entities to Which Physicians Refer — Notice.

65 FR 11589, March 3, 2000: Office of Inspector General: Health Care Integrity and Protection Data Bank under Section 1128E of the Social Security Act: Announcement of Opening Date for Querying and User Fees — Notice.

65 FR 14289, March 16, 2000: Office of Inspector General: Publication of the OIG Compliance Program Guidance for Nursing Facilities — Notice.

65 FR 24400, April 26, 2000: Office of Inspector General; Health Care Programs: Fraud and Abuse; Revised OIG Civil Money Penalties Resulting from Public Law 104-191 (HIPAA) — Final rule affecting 42 CFR Parts 1001, 1003, 1005, and 1006. See also correction at 65 FR 35583, June 5, 2000.

65 FR 32060, May 22, 2000: Office of Inspector General Medicare and State Health Care Programs: Fraud and Abuse: Ambulance Restocking Safe Harbor under the Anti-kickback Statute — Notice of proposed rulemaking affecting 42 CFR 1001.

65 FR 34986, June 1, 2000: Office of Inspector General; Privacy Act; Implementation (exempting the Healthcare Integrity and Protection Data Bank under Section 1128C of the Social Security Act from certain provisions of the Privacy Act (5 U.S.C. 552a) — Final rule.

65 FR 36818, June 12, 2000: Office of Inspector General: Draft OIG Compliance Program for Individual and Small Group Physician Practices — Notice and comment period.

65 FR 50204, August 17, 2000: Office of Inspector General: Solicitation of Information and Recommendations for Developing a Compliance Risk Guidance for the Ambulance Industry — Notice.

65 FR 50552, August 18, 2000: HCFA Privacy Act of 1974; Report of Modified or Altered System (pertaining to revision of language in global fraud and abuse routine uses).

65 FR 53319, September 1, 2000: HCFA Agency Information Collection Activities: Proposed Collection; Comment request (pertaining

to incentive arrangement disclosure form for managed care organizations and their related medical groups and physicians).

65 FR 59434, October 5, 2000: Office of Inspector General Compliance Program for Individual and Small Group Physician Practices — Notice.

65 FR 63035, October 20, 2000: Office of Inspector General: Medicare and State Health Care Programs: Fraud and Abuse; Revisions and Technical Corrections — Proposed rule affecting 42 CFR Parts 1001, 1003, 1005, and 1008.

65 FR 65861, November 2, 2000: HCFA Agency Information Collection Activities: Proposed Collection; Comment request (pertaining to conflict of interest disclosure requirements for Medicare program integrity).

65 FR 78124, December 14, 2000: Office of Inspector General: Solicitation of New Safe Harbors and Special Fraud Alerts — Notice of intent to develop regulations.

2001

66 FR 856, January 4, 2001: Medicare and Medicaid Programs; Physicians Referrals to Health Care Entities with which They Have Financial Relationships—Final rule with comment period, affecting 42 CFR Parts 411 and 424.

66 FR 6629, January 22, 2001: HCFA Agency Information Collection Activities: Submission for OMB Review; Comment request (pertaining to Medicare Integrity Program Organizational Conflict of Interest Disclosure Certificate).

66 FR 8771, February 2, 2001: Medicare and Medicaid Programs; Physicians' Referrals to Health Care Entities with which They Have Financial Relationships: Delay of Effective Date of Final Rule and Technical Amendment, affecting 42 CFR Parts 411 and 424.

66 FR 9858, February 12, 2001: HCFA Privacy Act of 1974; Report of New System (pertaining to complaints against health insurance issuers and health plans).

66 FR 9865, February 12, 2001: Office of Inspector General: Privacy Act of 1974; Amendment to the Health Care Program Violations System of Records—Notice and comment period (pertaining to including Social Security numbers of sanctioned individual in the Health Care Program Violations record).

66 FR 17813, April 4, 2001: Medicare and Medicaid Programs; Physicians' Referrals to Health Care Entities with which They Have

Financial Relationships; Extension of Comment period—Notice, affecting 42 CFR Parts 411 and 424.

66 FR 19507, April 16, 2001: HCFA Agency Information Collection Activities: Proposed Collection; Comment request (pertaining to conflict of interest and ownership and control information form).

66 FR 23944, May 10, 2001: HCFA Agency Information Collection Activities: Proposed Collection; Comment request (pertaining to financial reports for providers indebted to Medicare who want to repay over time).

66 FR 28916, May 25, 2001: HCFA Agency Information Collection Activities; Proposed Collection; Comment request (pertaining to procedures for advisory opinions concerning physician referrals under section 1877 of the Social Security Act).

66 FR 31245, June 11, 2001: Office of Inspector General; Healthcare Integrity and Protection Data Bank: Change in User Fees—Notice.

66 FR 31246, June 11, 2001: Office of Inspector General; Solicitation of Information and Recommendations for Developing a Compliance Program Guidance for the Pharmaceutical Industry—Notice.

See § 4:10.

§ 8:11 CRIMINAL PENALTIES: FALSE STATEMENTS AND FALSE REPRESENTATIONS TO QUALIFY FOR PROVIDER STATUS — Section 1128B(c) [42 U.S.C.A. 1320a-7b(c)]

Regulations

42 CFR Part 402 — Civil Money Penalties, Assessments, and Exclusions

42 CFR Part 405, Subpart U — Conditions for Coverage of Suppliers of End-Stage Renal Disease (ESRD) Services

42 CFR Part 411, Subpart J — Physician Ownership of, and Referral of Patients or Laboratory Specimens to, Entities Furnishing Clinical Laboratory or Other Health Services

42 CFR Part 416 — Ambulatory Surgical Services

42 CFR Part 417 — Health Maintenance Organizations, Competitive Medical Plans, and Health Care Prepayment Plans

42 CFR Part 418 — Hospice Care

42 CFR Part 420 — Program Integrity: Medicare

42 CFR Part 442 — Standards for Payment for Nursing Facilities and Intermediate Care Facilities for the Mentally Retarded

42 CFR Part 455 — Program Integrity: Medicaid

42 CFR Part 462 — Peer Review Organizations

42 CFR Part 482 — Conditions of Participation for Hospitals

42 CFR Part 483 — Requirements for States and Long Term Care Facilities

42 CFR Part 484 — Conditions of Participation: Home Health Agencies

42 CFR Part 485 — Conditions of Participation: Specialized Providers

42 CFR Part 486 — Conditions for Coverage of Specialized Services Furnished by Suppliers

42 CFR Part 488 — Survey, Certification, and Enforcement Procedures

42 CFR Part 489 — Provider Agreements and Supplier Approval

42 CFR Part 491 — Certification of Certain Health Facilities

42 CFR Part 493 — Laboratory Requirements

42 CFR Part 498 — Appeals Procedures for Determinations that Affect Participation in the Medicare Program and for Determinations that Affect the Participation of ICF's/MR and Certain NF's in the Medicaid Program

42 CFR Chapter V — Office of Inspector General — Health Care, Department of Health and Human Services

Subchapter A — General Provisions

Part 1000 — Introduction; General Definitions

Subchapter B — OIG Authorities

Part 1001 — Program Integrity: Medicare and State Health Care Programs

Part 1002 — Program Integrity: State-initiated Exclusion from Medicaid

Part 1005 — Appeals of Exclusions, Civil Money Penalties and Assessments

Part 1006 — Investigational Inquiries

Part 1007 — State Medicaid Fraud Control Units

Part 1008 — Advisory Opinions by the OIG

54 FR 5316, February 2, 1989: Medicare and Medicaid; Requirements for Long Term Care Facilities — Final rule with comment period, amending 42 CFR Parts 405, 442, 447, 483, 488, 489, and 498. See also delay in effective date at 54 FR 29717, July 14, 1989; corrections at 54 FR 8361, February 27, 1989, and 54 FR 37466,

September 11, 1989; and final rule delaying effective date from January 1, 1990, to October 1, 1990, at 54 FR 53611, December 29, 1989.

54 FR 33354, August 14, 1989: Medicare Program; Home Health Agencies: Conditions of Participation and Reduction in Recordkeeping Requirements — Interim final rule with comment period, amending and redesignating 42 CFR Part 405, Subpart L as 42 CFR Part 484.

54 FR 35131, August 23, 1989: Medicare Program; Home Health Care Agencies: Conditions of Participation and Reduction in Recordkeeping Requirements — Correction of notice published Monday August 14, 1989

55 FR 9538, March 14, 1990: Medicare, Medicaid and CLIA Programs; Revision of the Laboratory Regulations for the Medicare, Medicaid, and Clinical Laboratories Improvement Act of 1967 Programs — Final rule with comment period, amending 42 CFR Parts 74, 405, 416, 440, 482, 483, 488, and 493.

55 FR 12205, April 2, 1990: Health Care Programs: Fraud and Abuse; Amendments to OIG Exclusion and CMP Authorities Resulting from Public Law 100–93, the Medicare and Medicaid Patient and Program Protection Act of 1987, Public Law 99–272, the Consolidated Omnibus Budget Reconciliation Act of 1985, and Public Law 100–360, the Medicare Catastrophic Coverage Act of 1988 — Proposed rule to amend 42 CFR Parts 1000, 1001, 1002, 1003, 1004, 1005, 1006, and 1007. See also correction published at 55 FR 17461, April 25, 1990.

55 FR 20896, May 21, 1990: Medicare, Medicaid and CLIA Programs; Regulations Implementing the Clinical Laboratory Improvement Amendments of 1988 (CLIA '88) — Proposed rule. See also extension of time for public comment to September 21, 1990, published at 55 FR 34289 on August 22, 1990.

55 FR 50831, December 11, 1990: Medicare Program; Hospice Care Amendments: Medicare — Final rule with comment period, amends 42 CFR Part 418.

56 FR 13430, April 2, 1991: Medicare and Laboratory Certification Programs; Enforcement Procedures for Laboratories — Proposed rule.

56 FR 30696, July 5, 1991: Medicaid Program; Correction and Reduction Plans for Intermediate Care Facilities for the Mentally Retarded — Final rule affecting 42 CFR Part 442. See also correction at 56 FR 49147, September 27, 1991.

56 FR 32967, July 18, 1991: Medicare Program; Home Health Agencies: Conditions of Participation — Final rule. See also correction at 56 FR 51334, October 11, 1991, affecting 42 CFR Part 484.

56 FR 33403, July 22, 1991: Medicare and State Health Care Programs: Fraud and Abuse; Civil Monetary Penalties and Intermediate Sanctions for Certain Violations by Health Maintenance Organizations and Competitive Medical Plans — Proposed rule.

56 FR 37054, August 2, 1991: Medicare and Medicaid Programs; Survey and Enforcement Requirements and Alternative Sanctions for Home Health Agencies — Proposed rule affecting 42 CFR Parts 441, 488, and 489.

56 FR 46562, September 13, 1991: Medicare Program; Explanation of Enrollee Rights and Other Provisions Applicable to Health Maintenance Organizations and Competitive Medical Plans — Final rule affecting 42 CFR Part 417.

56 FR 48112, September 24, 1991: Medicaid Program; Community Supported Living Arrangements Services — Interim final rule with comment period, affecting 42 CFR Part 441.

56 FR 48826, September 26, 1991: Medicare and Medicaid; Requirements for Long Term Care Facilities — Final rule affecting 42 CFR Parts 422, 447, 483, 488, 489, and 498. See also correction at 57 FR 43922, September 23, 1992.

56 FR 49154, September 27, 1991: Medicare Program; Medicare Coverage of Home Health Services, Medicare Conditions of Participation, and Home Health Aide Supervision — Proposed rule affecting 42 CFR Parts 409, 418, and 484.

56 FR 56141, October 31, 1991: Medicaid Program; Standards for Defining Disproportionate Share Hospitals — Proposed rule affecting 42 CFR Part 447. Withdrawn, 56 FR 64228, December 9, 1991.

56 FR 61374, December 3, 1991: Medicare Program; Reporting Requirements for Financial Relationships Between Physicians and Health Care Entities That Furnish Selected Items and Services — Interim final rule with comment period affecting 42 CFR Part 411.

57 FR 3298, January 29, 1992: Health Care Programs: Fraud and Abuse; Amendments to OIG Exclusion and CMP Authorities Resulting From Public Law 100–93 — Final rule affecting 42 CFR Parts 1001, 1002, 1003, 1004, 1005, 1006, and 1007. See also final rule and correction at 57 FR 9669, March 20, 1992; final rule affecting 42 CFR Parts 1001and 1005, with clarification at 58 FR 5617, January 22,

1993; and final rule affecting 42 CFR Part 1001, with correction, at 58 FR 40752, July 30, 1993.

57 FR 4516, February 5, 1992: Medicare and Medicaid Programs; Omnibus Nursing Home Requirements — Proposed rule affecting 42 CFR Parts 418, 440, 441, 482, 483, and 488. See also correction at 57 FR 8961, March 13, 1992.

57 FR 7002, February 28, 1992: Medicare, Medicaid and CLIA Programs; Regulations Implementing the Clinical Laboratory Improvement Amendments of 1988 (CLIA) — Final rule with comment period, affecting 42 CFR Parts 405, 410, 416, 417, 418, 440, 482, 483, 484, 485, 488, 491, 493, and 494. See also correction at 57 FR 35760, August 11, 1992, and correction amendments at 58 FR 5212, January 19, 1993.

57 FR 7218, February 28, 1992: Medicare Program; Medicare and Laboratory Certification Program; Enforcement Procedures for Laboratories — Final rule affecting 42 CFR Part 493. See also correction amendments at 58 FR 5212, January 19, 1993.

57 FR 8588, March 11, 1992: Medicare Program; Physician Ownership of, and Referrals to, Health Care Entities that Furnish Clinical Laboratory Services — Proposed rule affecting 42 CFR Part 411.

57 FR 22773, May 29, 1992: Medicare Program; Recognition of Community Health Accreditation Program Standards for Home Care Organizations — Final notice.

57 FR 33202, July 27, 1992: Health Maintenance Organizations; HMO Qualification Determinations and Compliance Actions — Notice. See also correction at 57 FR 41810, September 11, 1992.

57 FR 33992, July 31, 1992: Clinical Laboratories Improvement Act Program; Granting and Withdrawal of Deeming Authority to Private Nonprofit Accreditation Organizations and of CLIA Exemption under State Laboratory Programs — Final rule.

57 FR 39278, August 28, 1992: Medicare and Medicaid Programs; Survey, Certification and Enforcement of Skilled Nursing Facilities and Nursing Facilities — Proposed rule affecting 42 CFR Parts 431, 442, 488, and 489.

57 FR 43462, September 21, 1992: Health Care Financing Administration Public Information Collection Requirements Submitted to the Office of Management and Budget for Clearance (pertaining to sole community home health agencies; physician/supplier overpayment reports; physician or supplier Medicare agreements;

conditions of participation for rural health clinics; Medicare provider refunds; conditions of participation for comprehensive outpatient rehabilitation facilities; Medicaid income and eligibility verification system; Medicaid integrated review schedule; provider overpayment report; financial statement of Medicare provider debtors; negative case action review schedule for Medicaid quality control; outpatient resource costing study; Medicaid intermediate care facility for the mentally retarded or persons with related conditions survey report form; installment agreement of beneficiary refund of overpayment; PRO assumption of responsibilities; Medicare contractor administrative budget and cost reporting system forms; fire safety survey report forms; medical records review under prospective payment system; and Qualified Medicare Beneficiary supplement to the Medicare current beneficiary survey).

58 FR 5215, January 19, 1993: Medicare, Medicaid and CLIA Programs; Regulations Implementing the Clinical Laboratory Improvement Amendments of 1988 (CLIA) and Clinical Laboratory Improvement Act Program Fee Collection — Final rule with comment period, affecting 42 CFR Part 493. See also correction published at 58 FR 39154, July 22, 1993.

58 FR 38579, July 19, 1993: HCFA Public Information Collection Requirements Submitted to the Office of Management and Budget (OMB) for Clearance re survey of home health agencies; CLIA survey report form; validation of state surveys; Medicaid listing of participating home health agencies; financial information regarding Medicare benefits from Medicare contractors; and third-party liability under Medicaid.

58 FR 46198, September 1, 1993: HCFA Public Information Collection Requirements (ICR) Submitted to the Office of Management and Budget (OMB) for Clearance (pertaining to prenatal services and assistance screening; home health agency treatment forms; conditions of participation for intermediate care facilities for the mentally retarded; State Medicaid eligibility quality control sample selection lists; prepaid health plan cost report; hospital survey report form; procedures for determining whether providers, practitioners, or other suppliers of services are liable for certain noncovered services; Medicare credit balance reporting requirements; Medicare provider cost report questionnaire form; Medicare current beneficiary survey rounds 7–10; sterilization regulation/consent form; PRO reconsideration and appeals information requirements; information collection requirements in HSQ-110,

acquisition, protection and disclosure of PRO information; Medicare/Medicaid organ procurement organization's (OPO) request for certification) — Notice.

58 FR 54096, October 20, 1993: Office of Inspector General: Civil Money Penalties for Prohibited Referrals to Entities Providing Clinical Laboratory Services and for Prohibited Arrangements and Schemes — Proposed rule affecting 42 CFR Part 1003.

58 FR 54159, October 20, 1993: HCFA Public Information Collection Requirements Submitted to the Office of Management and Budget (OMB) for Clearance (pertaining to CLIA certification recommendation; CLIA laboratory personnel report; Medigap complaint data base; certification as a rural health clinic (RHC) and RHC survey report form; screening mammography services data report; ambulatory surgical center request for certification and survey report form; blood bank inspection checklist and report; Medicaid program budget report form; supplier of ESRD services form; and grantee data collection instrument) — Notice.

59 FR 14865, March 30, 1994: HCFA Public Information Collection Requirements Submitted to the Office of Management and Budget (OMB) for Clearance (pertaining to home health agency Medicare and Medicaid survey report forms for conditions of participation; conditions of participation for rural health clinics; Medicaid re-evaluation of assets for determining payment rates to hospitals and nursing homes; statistical report on medical care, eligible, recipients, payments, and services.)

59 FR 18820, April 20, 1994: HCFA: Health Maintenance Organizations: Qualification Determinations and Compliance Actions During the Period October 1, 1993 through December 31, 1993.

59 FR 25460, May 16, 1994: HCFA Public Information Collection Requirements Submitted to the Office of Management and Budget (OMB) for Clearance (pertaining to Medicare uniform institutional provider bill; hospice survey and deficiencies report form; HMO financial information reports to members; hospital request for certification in Medicare and Medicaid form.)

59 FR 27023, May 25, 1994: HCFA Public Information Collection Requirements Submitted to the Office of Management and Budget (OMB) for Clearance (pertaining to Medicare beneficiary survey of influenza vaccination form; Medicaid integrated quality control review worksheet; post laboratory survey questionnaire form; and post laboratory survey questionnaire — surveyor form).

59 FR 50762, October 5, 1994: HCFA Public Information Collection Requirements Submitted to the Office of Management and Budget (OMB) for Clearance (pertaining to reimbursement of hospital costs for residents and interns, criteria for psychiatric and rehabilitation hospital units' reimbursement under the prospective payment system, disclosure of owners and managers of suppliers for fraud and abuse detection purposes, reimbursement of municipal health services clinics, survey form for hospital compliance with anti-dumping requirements, and evaluation of patient and physician satisfaction with the Medicare participating heart bypass center demonstration).

59 FR 56116, November 10, 1994: Medicare and Medicaid Programs; Survey, Certification and Enforcement of Skilled Nursing Facilities and Nursing Facilities — Final rule affecting 42 CFR Parts 401, 431, 435, 440, 441, 442, 447, 483, 488, 489, and 498.

59 FR 56500, November 14, 1994: HCFA Public Information Collection Requirements Submitted to the Office of Management and Budget (OMB) for Clearance (pertaining to monitoring and evaluation of Medicare cataract surgery alternate payment demonstration, form for listing deficiencies for laboratory surveys, form for personnel requirements for laboratory CLIA certification, and CLIA reinstatement form).

59 FR 65482, December 20, 1994: Medicare Program; Medicare Coverage of Home Health Services, Medicare Conditions of Participation, and Home Health Aide Supervision — Final rule affecting 42 CFR Parts 409, 413, 418, and 484.

60 FR 6714, February 3, 1995: HCFA Public Information Collection Requirements Submitted to the Office of Management and Budget (OMB) for Clearance (pertaining to criteria for Medicare coverage of lung transplants, evaluation of drug use review demonstrations projects, and evaluation of the community supported living arrangements program).

60 FR 12770, March 8, 1995: HCFA Public Information Collection Requirements Submitted to the Office of Management and Budget (OMB) for Clearance (pertaining to survey forms for compliance with CLIA; CLIA application forms for testing on human specimens, and forms for outcome-based quality assurance programs for home health agencies).

60 FR 21525, May 2, 1995: HCFA Public Information Collection Requirements Submitted to the Office of Management and Budget (OMB) for Clearance (pertaining to intermediary requests for infor-

mation from skilled nursing facilities, reimbursement for CLIA compliance surveys, patient outcome data in home health agencies, common claim forms for Medicare/Medicaid reimbursement, and a study of childhood immunization costs).

60 FR 26445, May 17, 1995: HCFA Public Information Collection Requirements Submitted to the Office of Management and Budget (OMB) for Clearance (pertaining to Medicare/Medicaid psychiatric hospital survey data, and hospice requests for Medicare certification).

60 FR 37066, July 19, 1995: HCFA Public Information Collection Requirements Submitted to the Office of Management and Budget (OMB) for Clearance (pertaining to actuarial forecasts for Medicaid utilization and cost, employers identified through a match of IRS, SSA, and Medicare records for purposes of the Medicare Secondary Payer provision, health and safety requirements for portable X-ray suppliers, and evaluation of Intermediate Care Facilities for Persons with Mental Retardation — establishing psychoactive drug use baselines).

60 FR 38565, July 27, 1995: HCFA Privacy Act of 1974; Report of New System — Notice of system pertaining to evaluation of, and external quality assurance for, the community nursing organization (CNO) demonstration.

60 FR 39403, August 2, 1995: HCFA Public Information Collection Requirements Submitted for Public Comment and Recommendations (pertaining to PRO reporting forms; Oregon Medicaid reform demonstration; review functions of PRO's; medical records review under PPS; evaluation of Medicare cataract surgery alternate payment demonstration; home health agency survey and deficiencies report; CLIA survey forms; field testing of uniform needs assessment instrument for hospital discharge planning).

60 FR 41914, August 14, 1995: Medicare Program; Physician Financial Relationships with, and Referrals to, Health Care Entities that Furnish Clinical Laboratory Services; Financial Relationship Reporting Requirements — Final rule affecting 42 CFR Part 411.

60 FR 45673, September 1, 1995: Medicare Program; Contracts with Health Maintenance Organizations (HMOs) and Competitive Medical Plans (CMPs) — Final rule with comment period, affecting 42 CFR Part 417.

60 FR 50115, September 28, 1995: Medicare and Medicaid Programs; Survey, Certification and Enforcement of Skilled Nursing Facilities and Nursing Facilities — Final rule and correction to final

regulations, affecting 42 CFR Parts 431, 440, 442, 488, 489, and 498. See also corrections at 60 FR 52731, October 10, 1995, and at 60 FR 534456, October 13, 1995.

60 FR 55719, November 2, 1995: HCFA Public Information Collection Requirements Submitted for Public Comment and Recommendations (pertaining to evaluation of the Oregon Medicaid reform demonstration; field testing of the uniform needs assessment instrument for hospital discharge planning; survey of physician practice costs; evaluation of the Medicare cataract surgery alternate payment demonstration; and alternative CLIA quality assessment surveys).

60 FR 58088, November 24, 1995: HCFA Public Information Collection Requirements Submitted for Public Comment and Recommendations (pertaining to granting and withdrawal of deeming authority to private nonprofit accreditation organizations and the CLIA exemption under State laboratory programs).

60 FR 58365, November 27, 1995: HCFA Public Information Collection Requirements Submitted for Public Comment and Recommendations (pertaining to Medicare carrier provider/supplier enrollment applications).

60 FR 63440, December 11, 1995: Medicare Program; Additional Supplier Standards — Final rule with comment period, affecting 42 CFR Parts 411 and 424.

60 FR 64167, December 14, 1995: HCFA Public Information Collection Requirements Submitted for Public Comment and Recommendations (pertaining to home health care; Medicare/Medicaid certification of physical therapy and speech pathology services; certification as suppliers of Portable X-ray Services; certification of organ procurement organizations; certification for physical therapists in independent practice; and approval as a hospital provider of extended care services (swing bed)).

61 FR 6645, February 21, 1996: HCFA Agency Information Collection Activities: Proposed Collection; Comment Request (pertaining to survey forms to evaluate Federally qualified health centers; and the Medicare Carrier provider/supplier application form).

61 FR 7012, February 23, 1996: HCFA Notice Submitted for Collection of Public Comment: Submission for OMB Review (pertaining to granting and withdrawing of deeming authority to private non-profit Accreditation organizations and the Clinical Laboratory Improvement Act Exemption under State laboratory programs; and

the rules for participation of home health agencies to participate as sole community home health agencies).

61 FR 7522, February 28, 1996: HCFA Public Information Collection Requirements Submitted for Public Comment and Recommendations (pertaining to Medicare and Medicaid disclosure of ownership and control interest statements).

61 FR 11214, March 19, 1996: HCFA Agency Information Collection Activities: Proposed Collection; Comment Request (pertaining to conditions of coverage for organ procurement organizations; and skilled nursing facility and skilled nursing facility healthcare complex forms).

61 FR 14798, April 3, 1996: HCFA Agency Information Collection Activities: Proposed Collection; Comment Request (pertaining to statistical reports on medical care eligibility, payments and services under Medicaid; State survey agency lists of positions and schedule of equipment purchases; granting and withdrawing of deeming authority to national accreditation organizations; maximizing the effectiveness of home health care; requests for certification in the Medicare or Medicaid program to provide outpatient physical therapy and/or speech pathology services; physical therapists in independent practice; requests for provider approval as a hospital provider of extended care services (swing bed) under Medicare and Medicaid; and requests for designation as an organ procurement organization).

61 FR 16925, April 18, 1996: HCFA Agency Information Collection Activities: Proposed Collection; Comment Request (pertaining to Medicare participating physician or supplier agreements; and hospital conditions of participation).

61 FR 17710, April 22, 1996: HCFA Agency Information Collection Activities: Proposed Collection; Comment Request (pertaining to payment adjustments for sole community hospitals; conditions of participation for portable x-ray suppliers; and cost reports for independent rural health centers and freestanding Federally qualified health centers).

61 FR 21969, May 13, 1996: Medicare and Medicaid Program; Criteria for a Rural Hospital to Be Designated as an Essential Access Community Hospital (EACH)— Final rule with comment period, affecting 42 CFR Part 412.

61 FR 24310, May 14, 1996: HCFA Agency Information Collection Activities: Proposed Collection; Comment Request (pertaining to distribution of the brochure "An Important Message from Medicare" by

hospitals; Conditions of participation for coverage for physical therapists in independent practice; and the Medicare disproportionate share adjustment procedure and criteria).

61 FR 29406, June 10, 1996: HCFA Agency Information Collection Activities: proposed Collection; Comment Request (pertaining to end stage renal disease application and survey and certification report forms; withholding Medicare payments to recover Medicaid overpayments; acquisition, protection, and disclosure of PRO information; clinical laboratory certification and recertification survey forms; CLIA laboratory personnel report forms; prepaid health plan cost reports; Medicare credit balance reporting requirements; statement of deficiencies and plan of correction requirements for organ procurement organizations; Medicare/Medicaid hospital survey report forms; advance directive requirements for Medicare and Medicaid; payment adjustments for sole community hospitals; survey reports for physical therapists in independent practice; HMO and CMP national data reporting requirements; identification of extension units of outpatient physical therapy and outpatient speech pathology providers; and fire safety survey reports).

61 FR 30072, June 13, 1996: HCFA Agency Information Collection Activities: Proposed Collection; Comment Request (pertaining to conditions of coverage for organ procurement organizations).

61 FR 31141, June 19, 1996: HCFA Agency Information Collection Activities: Proposed Collection; Comment Request (pertaining to authorization agreements for electronic funds transfer; applications for health insurance under Medicare for individuals with chronic renal disease; CLIA application forms; forms for surveyors to evaluate laboratory survey processes; post laboratory survey questionnaires for laboratories to evaluate the survey process).

61 FR 34437, July 2, 1996: HCFA Agency Information Collection Activities: Submission for OMB Review; Comment Request (pertaining to Peer Review Organization procedures for reconsideration of initial decisions; Part B enrollment forms; certification of rural health clinics for Medicare participation; Medicaid utilization review requirements for home health agencies; State listings of Medicaid recipients in institutions and procedures for State inspection of care review; procedures for disenrollment of beneficiaries from HMOs or CMPs; effectiveness of telemedicine services; formats for PROs to submit data to HCFA; and request for accelerated payments forms for providers).

61 FR 34855, July 3, 1996: HCFA Agency Information Collection Activities: Submission for OMB Review; Comment Request (pertaining to information collection requirements for hospital conditions of participation in Medicare).

61 FR 37278, July 17, 1996: HCFA Agency Information Collection Activities: Proposed Collection; Comment request (pertaining to Medicare provider/supplier enrollment forms).

61 FR 37487, July 18, 1996: HCFA Agency Information Collection Activities: Submission for OMB Review; Comment request (pertaining to cost reports for independent rural health centers and freestanding federally qualified health centers; and conditions of participation for portable x-ray suppliers).

61 FR 40422, August 2, 1996: HCFA Agency Information Collection Activities: Proposed Collection; Comment request (pertaining to survey and certification of ambulatory surgical centers; the Medigap complaint database; fiscal intermediaries’ provider overpayment actions; and hospital standards for potentially HIV infectious blood and blood products).

61 FR 40847, August 6, 1996: HCFA Agency Information Collection Activities: Proposed Collection; Comment request (pertaining to survey and certification of comprehensive outpatient rehabilitation facilities (CORFs)).

61 FR 41417, August 8, 1996: HCFA Agency Information Collection Activities: Submission for OMB Review; Comment request (pertaining to prospective payment for home health care; and Medicare standards for hospices).

61 FR 43373, August 22, 1996: HCFA Agency Information Collection Activities: Proposed Collection; Comment request (pertaining to hospital claims for inpatient care for statutorily excluded services; and hospice standards for Medicare participation).

61 FR 43374, August 22, 1996: HCFA Agency Information Collection Activities: Submission for OMB Review; Comment request (pertaining to conditions of participation for rehabilitation agencies and conditions for coverage for physical therapist in independent practice).

61 FR 46814, September 5, 1996: HCFA Agency Information Collection Activities: Submission for OMB Review; Comment request (pertaining to authorization agreements for electronic funds transfers; entitlement to Medicare for individuals with chronic renal disease; application forms for clinical laboratories; and clinical laboratory survey questionnaires).

61 FR 47131, September 6, 1996: HCFA Agency Information Collection Activities: Submission for OMB Review; Comment request (pertaining to conditions of coverage for organ procurement organizations; and statements of deficiencies and plan of correction forms for organ procurement organizations).

61 FR 52951, October 9, 1996: HCFA Agency Information Collection Activities: Submission for OMB Review; Comment request (pertaining to Peer Review Organization Reconsiderations and Appeals; Part B enrollment forms; certification as a Rural Health Clinic; Medicaid utilization control programs; lists of Medicaid recipients in institutions; and business proposal formats for PROs).

61 FR 57688, November 7, 1996: HCFA Agency Information Collection Activities: Comment request (pertaining to clinical laboratory surveys; clinical laboratory personnel qualifications; Medicare/Medicaid hospital survey report forms; beneficiary disenrollment from HMOs and CMPs; survey reports for ambulatory surgical centers; the Medigap complaint database; and survey forms for comprehensive outpatient rehabilitation facilities).

61 FR 58567, November 15, 1996: HCFA Agency Information Collection Activities: Proposed Collection; Comment request (pertaining to home and community based waiver requests).

61 FR 64913, December 9, 1996: HCFA Agency Information Collection Activities: Proposed Collection; Comment request (pertaining to survey report forms for ICF/MRs; and current Medicare beneficiary surveys).

61 FR 66284, December 17, 1996: HCFA Agency Information Collection Activities: Proposed Collection; Comment request (pertaining to conditions of participation for rural health clinics).

62 FR 3902, January 27, 1997: HCFA Agency Information Collection Activities: Proposed Collection; Comment request (pertaining to hospice survey and deficiencies report form).

62 FR 8252, February 24, 1997: HCFA Agency Information Collection Activities: Submission for OMB Review; Comment request (pertaining to conditions of participation for rural health clinics).

62 FR 9435, March 3, 1997: Office of Inspector General: Publication of the OIG Model Compliance Plan for Clinical Laboratories — Notice.

62 FR 10285, March 6, 1997: HCFA Agency Information collection Activities: Submission for OMB Review; Comment request (pertaining to end stage renal disease (ESRD) application and survey and certification report form).

62 FR 11004, March 10, 1997: Medicare and Medicaid Programs; Revision of the Conditions of Participation for Home Health Agencies and Use of the Outcome and Assessment Information Set (OASIS) as Part of the Revised Conditions of Participation for Home Health Agencies — Introduction to proposed rules, affecting 42 CFR Part 484.

62 FR 11005, March 10, 1997: Medicare and Medicaid Programs; Conditions of Participation for Home Health Agencies — Proposed rule affecting 42 CFR Part 484. See also correction at 62 FR 11953, March 13, 1997.

62 FR 11035, March 10, 1997: Medicare and Medicaid Programs; Use of the OASIS as Part of the Conditions of Participation for Home Health Agencies — Proposed rule.

62 FR 11213, March 11, 1997: HCFA Agency Information Collection Activities: Proposed Collection; Comment request (pertaining to post-laboratory survey questionnaire).

62 FR 11214, March 11, 1997: HCFA Agency Information Collection Activities: Submission for OMB Review; Comment request (pertaining to intermediate care facility for the mentally retarded or persons with related conditions survey report forms).

62 FR 16863, April 8, 1997: HCFA Agency Information Collection Activities: Submission for OMB Review; Comment request (pertaining to hospice survey and deficiencies report form).

62 FR 18639, April 16, 1997: HCFA Agency Information Collection Activities: Proposed Collection; Comment request (pertaining to the hospital request for certification in the Medicare and Medicaid programs form).

62 FR 30603, June 4, 1997: HCFA Agency Information Collection Activities: Submission for OMB Review; Comment request (pertaining to skilled nursing facility and skilled nursing facility health care complex cost reports; and hospital conditions of participation).

62 FR 32615, June 17, 1997: Medicare Program; Ambulance Services — Proposed rule affecting 42 CFR Parts 410 and 424.

62 FR 39848, July 24, 1997: HCFA Agency Information Collection Activities; Proposed Collection; Comment request (pertaining to home health certification and plan of care forms for reimbursement; and Medicare/Medicaid disclosure of ownership and control forms).

62 FR 47182, September 8, 1997: Office of Inspector General: Health Care Programs: Fraud and Abuse; Revised OIG Exclusion Authorities Resulting from Public Law 104–191 — Notice of Pro-

posed rulemaking, affecting 42 CFR Parts 1000, 1001, 1002, and 1005.

62 FR 49016, September 18, 1997: HCFA Agency Information Collection Activities: Submission for OMB Review; Comment Request (pertaining to managed care incentive arrangement disclosure forms).

62 FR 55410, October 24, 1997: Office of Inspector General: Criteria for Implementing Permissive Exclusion Authority under Section 1128(b)(7) of the Social Security Act — Notice.

62 FR 55410, October 24, 1997: HCFA Agency Information Collection Activities: Submission for OMB Review; Comment request (pertaining to Medicare/Medicaid disclosure of ownership and control forms).

62 FR 65049, December 10, 1997: Office of Inspector General: Solicitation of New Safe Harbors and Special Fraud Alerts — Notice of intent to develop regulations, affecting 42 CFR Part 1001.

62 FR 67392, December 24, 1997: Office of Inspector General: Criteria for Implementing Permissive Exclusion Authority under Section 1128(b)(7) of the Social Security Act — Notice.

63 FR 1646, January 9, 1998: Medicare Program; Physicians' Referrals; Issuance of Advisory Opinions — Final rule with comment period, affecting 42 CFR Part 411.

63 FR 1659, January 9, 1998: Medicare and Medicaid Programs; Physicians' Referrals to Health Care Entities with Which They Have Financial Relationships — Proposed rule affecting 42 CFR Parts 411, 424, 435, and 455.

63 FR 2926, January 20, 1998: Medicare Program; Additional Supplier Standards — Proposed rule affecting 42 CFR Part 424.

63 FR 7743, February 17, 1998: Medicare and Medicaid Programs; Hospital Conditions of Participation; Provider Agreements and Supplier Approval — Notice of extension of comment period, affecting 42 CFR Parts 416, 482, 485, and 489.

63 FR 9844, February 26, 1998: HCFA Agency Information Collection Activities: Proposed Collection; Comment request (pertaining to procedures for advisory opinions concerning physician referrals and supporting regulations in 42 CFR Sections 411.370- 411.389).

63 FR 10920, March 5, 1998: HCFA Emergency Clearance: Public Information Collection Requirements Submitted to the Office of Management and Budget (OMB) (pertaining to Medicare and other Federal health care program provider and supplier application forms).

63 FR 11649, March 10, 1998: Medicare and Medicaid Programs; Physicians' Referrals to Health Care Entities with Which They Have Financial Relationships — Notice of extension of comment period for proposed rule.

63 FR 12474, March 13, 1998: HCFA Agency Information Collection Activities: Proposed Collection; Comment request (pertaining to hospice request for certification in the Medicare program and Medicare/Medicaid psychiatric hospital survey data).

63 FR 14393, March 25, 1998: Office of Inspector General: Health Care Programs: Fraud and Abuse; Revised OIG Civil Money Penalties Resulting from the Health Insurance Portability and Accountability Act of 1996 — Notice of proposed rulemaking, affecting 42 CFR Parts 1003, 1005, and 1006.

63 FR 23790, April 30, 1998: Medicare and Medicaid Programs; Recognition of the American Association for Accreditation of Ambulatory Surgery Facilities, Inc., for Ambulatory Surgical Centers — Proposed notice.

63 FR 25214, May 7, 1998: HCFA Agency Information Collection Activities: Proposed Collection; Comment request (pertaining to organ procurement organization statement of deficiencies and plan of correction forms).

63 FR 26722, May 14, 1998: HCFA CLIA Program; Simplifying CLIA Regulations Relating to Accreditation, Exemption of Laboratories under a State Licensure Program, Proficiency Testing, and Inspection — Final rule affecting 42 CFR Part 493. See also correction at 63 FR 32699, June 15, 1998.

63 FR 28395, May 22, 1998: HCFA Agency Information Collection Activities: Submission for OMB Review; Comment request (pertaining to procedures for advisory opinions concerning physician referrals).

63 FR 29415, May 29, 1998: HCFA Agency Information Collection Activities: Submission for OMB Review; Comment request (pertaining to hospice request for certification in the Medicare program).

63 FR 32234, June 12, 1998: HCFA Agency Information Collection Activities: Submission for OMB Review; Comment request (pertaining to Medicare/Medicaid psychiatric hospital survey data).

63 FR 33856, June 22, 1998: Medicare and Medicaid Programs; Hospital Conditions of Participation; Identification of Potential Organ Tissue, and Eye Donors and Transplant Hospitals' Provision of Transplant-Related Data — Final rule affecting 42 CFR Part 482.

63 FR 34904, June 26, 1998: HCFA Agency Information Collection Activities: Proposed Collection; Comment request (pertaining to health care prepayment plan Medicare application agreement).

63 FR 36250, July 2, 1998: HCFA Agency Information Collection Activities; Submission for OMB review; Comment request (pertaining to provider/supplier enrollment applications).

63 FR 38311, July 16, 1998: Office of Inspector General: Medicare and State Health Care Programs: Fraud and Abuse; Issuance of Advisory Opinions by the OIG— Final rule affecting 42 CFR 1008. See also correction at 63 FR 43449, August 13, 1998.

63 FR 38414, July 16, 1998: HCFA Privacy Act of 1974; Report of Altered System (pertaining to disclosure of individual-specific information to combat fraud or abuse in health benefit programs).

63 FR 40297, July 28, 1998: HCFA Privacy Act of 1974; Report of New System (pertaining to establishment of the National Provider System (NPS) database).

63 FR 40723, July 30, 1998: HCFA Agency Information Collection Activities: Proposed Collection; Comment request (pertaining to requirements for health care prepayment plan (HCPP) eligibility under Section 1833 of the Social Security Act).

63 FR 42054, August 6, 1998: HCFA Agency Information Collection Activities: Submission for OMB Review; Comment Request (pertaining to Medicare/Medicaid/CLIA conditions of participation).

63 FR 46676, September 2, 1998: Office of Inspector General: Health Care Programs; Fraud and Abuse; Revised OIG Exclusion Authorities Resulting from Public Law 104–191—Final rule affecting 42 CFR Parts 1000, 1001, 1002, and 1005. See also correction at 63 FR 57918, October 29, 1998.

63 FR 46736, September 2, 1998: Office of Inspector General: Health Care Programs; Fraud and Abuse; Revised OIG Sanction Authorities Resulting from Public Law 105–33—Notice of proposed rulemaking affecting 42 CFR 1001, 1002, and 1003.

63 FR 58341, October 30, 1998: Office of Inspector General: Health Care Fraud and Abuse Data Collection Program: Reporting of Final Adverse Actions— Notice of proposed rulemaking under section 1128E of the Social Security Act, affecting 45 CFR 61.

63 FR 58399, October 30, 1998: Office of Inspector General: Publication of the OIG's Provider Self-Disclosure Protocol —Notice.

63 FR 68223, December 10, 1998: Office of Inspector General; Solicitation of New Safe Harbors and Special Fraud Alerts —Notice of intent to develop regulations, affecting 42 CFR 1001.

63 FR 68687, December 14, 1998: Medicare and Medicaid Program; Civil Money Penalties, Assessments, Exclusions, and Related Appeals Procedures — Final rule with comment period, affecting 42 CFR 400 and 402.

63 FR 71819, December 30, 1998: Office of Inspector General; Health Care Fraud and Abuse Data Collection Program; Reporting under section 1128E of the Social Security Act of Final Adverse Actions — Notice of proposed rule-making; extension of comment period, affecting 45 CFR 61.

63 FR 72317, December 31, 1998: HCFA Agency Information Collection Activities: Proposed Collection; Comment request (pertaining to advanced directives under Medicare and Medicaid; and Medicare/Medicaid disclosure of ownership and control interests).

1999

64 FR 1810, January 12, 1999: HCFA Agency Information Collection Activities: Proposed Collection; Comment request (pertaining to Medicaid eligibility quality control MEQC) samples; identification of extension units of outpatient physical therapy (OPT) and outpatient speech pathology (OSP) providers; request for certification in the Medicare and/or Medicaid program(s) to provide OPT or OSP services; and request for certification as a supplier of portable X-ray services under Medicare and/or Medicaid).

64 FR 1813, January 12, 1999: Office of Inspector General Publication of OIG Special Fraud Alert on Physician Liability for Certifications in the Provision of Medical Equipment and Supplies and Home Health Services — Notice.

64 FR 2228, January 13, 1999: Office of Inspector General: Solicitation of Information and Recommendations for Developing OIG Compliance Program Guidance for the Hospice Industry — Notice.

64 FR 3303, January 21, 1999: HCFA Agency Information Collection Activities: Proposed Collection; Comment request (pertaining to on-site inspection for durable medical equipment suppliers).

64 FR 4435, January 28, 1999: Office of Inspector General: Draft Compliance Guidance for the Durable Medical Equipment, Prosthetics, Orthotics and Supply Industry — Notice and comment period.

64 FR 5666, February 4, 1999: HCFA Emergency Clearance: Public Information Collection Requirements Submitted to the Office of Management and Budget (OMB) (pertaining to the Medicare/Medicaid health insurance common claim form).

64 FR 6664, February 10, 1999: HCFA Agency Information Collection Activities: Proposed Collection; Comment request (pertaining to Medicare agreement applications for health care prepayment plans).

64 FR 6753, February 16, 1999: Office of Inspector General: Privacy Act; Notification of New System of Records in Conjunction with the Healthcare Integrity and Protection Data Bank — Notice of a new system of records.

64 FR 10305, March 3, 1999: HCFA Agency Information Collection Activities: Proposed Collection; Comment request (pertaining to attending physician's certification of medical necessity for home oxygen therapy).

64 FR 10479, March 4, 1999: HCFA Agency Information Collection Activities: Proposed Collection; Comment request (pertaining to conditions of participation for portable X-ray suppliers).

64 FR 11922, March 10, 1999: HCFA Agency Information Collection Activities: Proposed Collection; Comment request (pertaining to attending physician's statement and documentation regarding medical emergency care).

64 FR 13997, March 23, 1999: HCFA Agency Information Collection Activities: Submission for OMB Review; Comment request (pertaining to Medicare and Medicaid requirements for advanced directives, and disclosure of ownership and financial control interest).

64 FR 14454, March 25, 1999: HCFA Agency Information Collection Activities: Proposed Collection; Comment request (pertaining to blood bank inspection checklist under CLIA).

64 FR 17673, April 12, 1999: HCFA Agency Information Collection Activities: Proposed Collection; Comment request (pertaining to Medicare participating physician or supplier agreements).

64 FR 24956, May 10, 1999: Medicare and Medicaid Programs; Effective Dates of Provider Agreements and Supplier Approvals — Correction restoring regulations inadvertently removed when a final rule concerning effective dates for provider agreements and supplier approvals was published at 62 FR 43931, August 18, 1997.

64 FR 25891, May 13, 1999: HCFA Agency Information Collection Activities: Submission for OMB Review; Comment request (pertaining to Medicare agreement application for health care prepayment plans under section 1833).

64 FR 29048, May 28, 1999: HCFA Agency Information Collection Activities: Proposed Collection; Comment request (pertaining to certification as a rural health clinic).

64 FR 29050, May 28, 1999: HCFA Emergency Clearance: Public Information Collection Requirements Submitted to the Office of Management and Budget (OMB) (pertaining to the community mental health center site visit assessment tool).

64 FR 30340, June 7, 1999: HCFA Agency Information Collection Activities: Submission for OMB Review; Comment request (pertaining to attending physicians statement and documentation of medical emergencies).

64 FR 32239, June 16, 1999: HCFA Agency Information Collection Activities: Proposed Collection; Comment request (pertaining to conditions of coverage for organ procurement organizations).

64 FR 32240, June 16, 1999: HCFA Agency Information Collection Activities: Submission for OMB Review; Comment request (pertaining to conditions of participation for portable x-ray suppliers).

64 FR 36368, July 6, 1999: Office of Inspector General Publication of OIG Compliance Program Guidance for the Durable Medical Equipment, Prosthetics, Orthotics and Supply Industry — Notice.

64 FR 36887, July 8, 1999: HCFA Agency Information Collection Activities: Proposed Collection; Comment request (pertaining to reporting outcome and assessment information data set (OASIS) as part of the conditions of participation for home health agencies).

64 FR 37142, July 9, 1999: HCFA Agency Information Collection Activities: Submission for OMB Review; Comment request (pertaining to request for certification in the Medicare/Medicaid program to provide outpatient physical therapy and/or speech-language pathology and the outpatient physical therapy and/or speech-language pathology survey report form; request for certification as a supplier of portable X-ray services); and procedures for making national coverage decisions).

64 FR 37985, July 14, 1999: Office of Inspector General; Publication of the OIG Special Advisory Bulletin on Gainsharing Arrangements and CMPs for Hospital Payments to Physicians to Reduce or Limit Services to Beneficiaries — Notice.

64 FR 38202, July 15, 1999: HCFA Agency Information Collection Activities: Proposed Collection; Comment request (pertaining to CLIA personnel reports; and CLIA certification for tests on human specimens).

64 FR 38910, July 20, 1999: HCFA Agency Information Collection Activities: Proposed Collection; Comment request (pertaining to comprehensive outpatient rehabilitation facility (CORF) eligibility requirements).

64 FR 39150, July 21, 1999: Office of Inspector General; Draft OIG Compliance Program Guidance for Hospices — Notice and comment period.

64 FR 39420, July 22, 1999: Office of Inspector General; Health Care Programs; Fraud and Abuse; Revised OIG Sanction Authorities Resulting from P.L. 105–33, the Balanced Budget Act of 1997 — Final rule affecting 42 CFR Parts 1001, 1002, and 1003. See also correction at64 FR 42174, August 3, 1999.

64 FR 39517, July 22, 1999: HCFA Agency Information Collection Activities: Submission for OMB Review; Comment request (pertaining to Medicare participating physician or supplier agreement form HCFA-460).

64 FR 39934, July 23, 1999: Medicare and Medicaid Program; Appeal of the Loss of Nurse Aide Training Programs — Interim final rule with comment period, affecting 42 CFR Parts 431 and 498. See also correction at 64 FR 43295, August 10, 1999.

64 FR 41444, July 30, 1999: HCFA Agency Information Collection Activities: Proposed Collection; Comment request (pertaining to ambulatory surgical center survey report form).

64 FR 43198, August 9, 1999: Medicare and Medicaid Programs; Announcement of Additional Applications from Hospitals Requesting Waivers for Organ Procurement Service Areas — Notice with comment period.

64 FR 44031, August 12, 1999: HCFA Agency Information Collection Activites: Submission for OMB Review; Comment request (pertaining to survey and certification of rural health clinics; and determining third party liability in Medicaid programs).

64 FR 48846, September 8, 1999: Office of Inspector General: Solicitation of Information and Recommendations for Developing OIG Compliance Program Guidance for Individual Physicians and Small Group Practices — Notice.

64 FR 49196, September 10, 1999: HCFA Agency Information Collection Activities; Submission for OMB Review; Comment request (pertaining to conditions of coverage for organ procurement organizations).

64 FR 42791, September 30, 1999: Office of Inspector General; Publication of the OIG Special Advisory Bulletin on the Effect of Exclusion from Participation in Federal Health Care Programs — Notice. See also correction at64 FR 55484, October 13, 1999.

64 FR 54031, October 5, 1999: Office of Inspector General; Publication of the OIG Compliance Program, Guidance for Hospices — Notice.

64 FR 57619, October 26, 1999: Office of Inspector General; Privacy Act; Exempt Record System, Pertaining to the Healthcare Integrity and Protection Data Bank (HIPDB) — Notice of proposed rulemaking affecting 45 CFR Part 5b.

64 FR 57740, October 26, 1999: Office of Inspector General; Healthcare Fraud and Abuse Data Collection Program: Reporting of Final Adverse Actions - Final rule affecting 45 CFR Part 61. See also correction at 65 FR 70506, November 24, 2000.

64 FR 61893, November 15, 1999: Office of Inspector General; Publication of the OIG's Compliance Program Guidance for Medicare+Choice Organizations Offering Coordinated Care Plans — Notice.

64 FR 62679, November 17, 1999: HCFA Agency Information Collection Activities: Proposed Collection; Comment request (pertaining to hospital conditions of participation).

64 FR 62679, November 17, 1999: HCFA Agency Information Collection Activities: Proposed Collection; Comment request (pertaining to surveys of end stage renal disease facilities).

64 FR 62680, November 17, 1999: HCFA Agency Information Collection Activities: Submission for OMB Review; Comment request (pertaining to hospice care eligibility standards, reimbursement procedures, and conditions of participation).

64 FR 63504, November 19, 1999: Office of Inspector General; Fraud and Abuse; Statutory Exception to the Anti-kickback Statute for Shared Risk Arrangements — Interim final rule with request for comment, affection 42 CFR Part 1001. See also correction at 64 FR 71317, December 21, 1999.

64 FR 63518, November 19, 1999: Office of Inspector General; Fraud and Abuse; Clarification of the Initial OIG Safe Harbor Provisions and Establishment of Additional Safe Harbor Provisions under the Anti-kickback Statute — Final rule affecting42 CFR Part 1001.

64 FR 66482, November 26, 1999: HCFA Agency Information Collection Activities: Proposed Collection; Comment request (pertaining to resident assessment in skilled nursing facilities).

64 FR 67918, December 3, 1999: HCFA Agency Information Collection Activities: Proposed Collection; Comment request (pertaining to conditions of participation for rural health clinics).

64 FR 69217, December 10, 1999: Office of Inspector General; Solicitation of New Safe Harbors and Special Fraud Alerts — Intent to develop regulations affecting 42 CFR Part 1001.

64 FR 69272, December 10, 1999: HCFA Agency Information Collection Activities: Submission for OMB Review; Comment request (pertaining to community mental health center site visit assessment tools).

64 FR 69272, December 10, 1999: HCFA Agency Information Collection Activities: Submission for OMB Review; Comment request (pertaining to comprehensive outpatient rehabilitation facility (CORF) eligibility and survey forms).

64 FR 69273, December 10, 1999: HCFA Agency Information Collection Activities: Submission for OMB Review; Comment request (pertaining to Medicare/Medicaid hospital survey reports).

64 FR 69273, December 10, 1999: HCFA Agency Information Collection Activities: Submission for OMB Review; Comment request (pertaining to HCFA-377 ambulatory surgical center survey report form).

64 FR 71148, December 20, 1999: HCFA Agency Information Collection Activities: Submission for OMB Review; Comment request (pertaining to CLIA survey reports).

64 FR 71148, December 20, 1999: Medicare Program; Adjustment in Payment Amounts for New Technology Intraocular Lenses Furnished by Ambulatory Surgical Centers — Notice with comment period.

64 FR 73563, December 30, 1999: HCFA Agency Information Collection Activities: Submission for OMB Review; Comment request pertaining to Medicare program integrity organizational conflict of interest disclosure certificates).

2000

65 FR 1400, January 10, 2000: HCFA Agency Information Collection Activities: Submission for OMB Review; Comment request (pertaining to reporting outcome and assessment information set (OASIS) data set as a condition of participation for HHAs).

65 FR 8983, February 23, 2000: HCFA Agency Information collection Activities: Submission for OMB Review; Comment request (pertaining to conditions of participation for rural health clinics).

65 FR 10450, February 28, 2000: Medicare Program; Rural Health Clinics: Amendments to Participation Requirements and Payment Provisions; and Establishment of a Quality Assessment and Per-

formance Improvement Program — Proposed rule affecting 42 CFR Parts 405 and 491.

65 FR 11589, March 3, 2000: HCFA Agency Information Collection Activities: Submission for OMB Review; Comment request (pertaining to end stage renal disease medical information system/ESRD facility survey).

65 FR 11589, March 3, 2000: Office of Inspector General: Health Care Integrity and Protection Data Bank under Section 1128E of the Social Security Act: Announcement of Opening Date for Querying and User Fees — Notice.

65 FR 12556, March 9, 2000: HCFA Agency Information Collection Activities: Proposed Collection; Comment request (pertaining to hospital request for certification in the Medicare/Medicaid program).

65 FR 12560, March 9, 2000: HCFA Agency Information Collection Activities: Submission for OMB Review; Comment request (pertaining to hospital provider of extended care services (swing beds) in the Medicare and Medicaid programs).

65 FR 13082, March 10, 2000: Medicare Program; Negotiated Rulemaking: Coverage and Administrative Policies for Clinical Diagnostic Laboratory Services — Proposed rule affecting 42 CFR Part 410.

65 FR 14288, March 16, 2000: HCFA Agency Information Collection Activities: Proposed Collection; Comment request (pertaining to end stage renal disease application and survey and certification).

65 FR 14986, March 20, 2000: HCFA Agency Information Collection Activities: Submission for OMB Review; Comment request (pertaining to skilled nursing facility resident assessment MDS data).

65 FR 24400, April 26, 2000: Office of Inspector General; Health Care Programs: Fraud and Abuse; Revised OIG Civil Money Penalties Resulting from Public Law 104-191 (HIPAA) — Final rule affecting 42 CFR Parts 1001, 1003, 1005, and 1006. See also correction at 65 FR 35583, June 5, 2000.

65 FR 25738, May 3, 2000: HCFA Emergency Clearance: Public Informatiion Collection Requirements Submitted to the Office of Management and Budget (OMB) (pertaining to the Medicare managed care CAHPS Survey).

65 FR 25939, May 4, 2000: HCFA Agency Information Collection Activities: Proposed Collection; Comment request (pertaining to ambulatory surgical center payment rate survey).

65 FR 26218, May 5, 2000: HCFA Agency Information Collection Activities: Proposed Collection; Comment request (pertaining to CLIA amendments adverse action extract).

65 FR 26618, May 5, 2000: HCFA Emergency Clearance: Public Information Collection Requirements Submitted to the Office of Management and Budget (OMB) (pertaining to Medicare consumer assessment survey of health plans).

65 FR 34986, June 1, 2000: Office of Inspector General; Privacy Act; Implementation (exempting the Healthcare Integrity and Protection Data Bank under Section 1128C of the Social Security Act from certain provisions of the Privacy Act (5 U.S.C. 552a)—Final rule affecting 45 CFR Part 5b.

65 FR 35652, June 5, 2000: HCFA Agency Information Collection Activities: Proposed Collection; Comment request (pertaining to hospital conditions of participation; identification of potential organ, tissue, and eye donors and transplant hospitals' provision of transplant-related data).

65 FR 35653, June 5, 2000: HCFA Agency Information Collection Activities: Proposed Collection; Comment request (pertaining to ICF/MR survey forms).

65 FR 35654, June 5, 2000: HCFA Agency Information Collection Activities: Submission for OMB Review; Comment request (pertaining to hospital request for certification in Medicare and Medicaid).

65 FR 37566, June 15, 2000: HCFA Agency Information Collection Activities: Submission for OMB Review; Comment request (pertaining to hospice survey and deficiencies report form).

65 FR 40111, June 29, 2000: HCFA Agency Information Collection Activities: Proposed Collection; comment request (pertaining to qualification applications for prepaid health plans (HMOs).

65 FR 47739, August 3, 2000: HCFA Agency Information Collection Activities: Submission for OMB Review; Comment request (pertaining to CLIA adverse action extract).

65 FR 49002, August 10, 2000: HCFA Emergency Clearance: Public Information Collection Requirements Submitted to the Office of Management and Budget (OMB) (pertaining to oxygen consumer survey for medical equipment and supplies).

65 FR 50204, August 17, 2000: Office of Inspector General: Solicitation of Information and Recommendations for Developing a Compliance Risk Guidance for the Ambulance Industry— Notice.

65 FR 50552, August 18, 2000: HCFA Privacy Act of 1974; Report of Modified or Altered System (pertaining to revision of language in global fraud and abuse routine uses).

65 FR 53319, September 1, 2000: HCFA Agency Information Collection Activities: Proposed Collection; Comment request (pertaining to incentive arrangement disclosure form for managed care organizations and their related medical groups and physicians).

65 FR 53963, September 6, 2000: Medicare Program: Appeals of Carrier Determinations that a Physician or Other Supplier Fails to Meet the Requirements for Medicare Billing Privileges; Reopening of Comment Period — Notice of reopening of comment period for proposed rule affecting 42 CFR Part 405.

65 FR 54857, September 11, 2000: HCFA Agency Information Collection Activities: Submission for OMB Review; Comment request (pertaining to ICF/MR survey report forms).

65 FR 54857, September 11, 2000: HCFA Agency Information Collection Activities: Submission for OMB Review; Comment request (pertaining to hospital conditions of participation-identification of potential organ, tissue, and eye donors, and transplant hospitals' provision of transplant-related data).

65 FR 57195, September 21, 2000: HCFA Agency Information Collection Activities; Proposed Collection; Comment request (pertaining to Medicare managed care CAHPS survey for quality of care purposes).

65 FR 58279, September 28, 2000: HCFA Agency Information Collection Activities: Proposed Collection; Comment request (pertaining to Medicare consumer assessment survey of health plans-CAHPS).

65 FR 59431, October 5, 2000: HCFA Agency Information Collection Activities: Proposed Collection; Comment requet (pertaining to conditions for coverage of suppliers of end stage renal disease services).

65 FR 59432, October 5, 2000: HCFA Agency Information Collection Activities: Submission for OMB Review; Comment request (pertaining to end stage renal disease application and survey and certification report).

65 FR 59434, October 5, 2000: Office of Inspector General Compliance Program for Individual and Small Group Physician Practices — Notice.

65 FR 59757, October 6, 2000: HCFA Agency Information Collection Activities: Proposed Collection; Comment request (pertaining to

stages of change survey for informed choice in the Medicare population).

65 FR 60366, October 11, 2000: Medicare Program; Additional Supplier Standards — Final rule with comment period, affecting 42 CFR Part 424.

65 FR 61171, October 16, 2000: HCFA Agency Information Collection Activities: Submission for OMB Review; Comment request (pertaining to psychiatric unit, rehabilitation unit, and rehabilitation hospital criteria worksheets).

65 FR 63035, October 20, 2000: Office of Inspector General: Medicare and State Health Care Programs: Fraud and Abuse; Revisions and Technical Corrections — Proposed rule affecting 42 CFR Parts 1001, 1003, 1005, and 1008.

65 FR 65860, November 2, 2000: HCFA Agency Information Collection Activities: Proposed Collection; Comment request (pertaining to reporting outcome and assessment (OASIS) data as part of conditions of participation for home health agencies).

65 FR 65861, November 2, 2000: HCFA Agency Information Collection Activities: Proposed Collection; Comment request (pertaining to conflict of interest disclosure requirements for Medicare program integrity).

65 FR 66255, November 3, 2000: HCFA Agency Information Collection Activities: Proposed Collection; Comment request (pertaining to survey of Medicaid home and community-based services waiver and personal care option recipients).

65 FR 76647, December 7, 2000: HCFA Agency Information Collection Activities: Proposed Collection; Comment request (pertaining to alternate quality assessment survey in lieu of onsite survey for CLIA labs with good performance).

65 FR 77035, December 8, 2000: HCFA Agency Information Collection Activities: Proposed Collection; Comment request (pertaining to DMEPOS supplier survey).

65 FR 78124, December 14, 2000: Office of Inspector General: Solicitation of New Safe Harbors and Special Fraud Alerts — Notice of intent to develop regulations.

65 FR 79867, December 20, 2000: HCFA Agency Information Collection Activities: Proposed Collection; Comment request (pertaining to home health Medicare conditions of participation information collection requirements).

65 FR 79867, December 20, 2000: HCFA Agency Information Collection Activities: Proposed Collection; Comment request (pertaining to quality improvement system for managed care).

65 FR 79868, December 20, 2000: HCFA Agency Information Collection Activities: Proposed Collection; Comment request (pertaining to Medicare consumer assessment survey of health plans).

65 FR 82941, December 29, 2000: Medicare, Medicaid, and CLIA Programs; Extension of Certain Effective Dates for Clinical Laboratory Requirements under CLIA — Final rule with comment period, affecting 42 CFR Part 493.

2001

66 FR 2912, January 12, 2001: HCFA Agency Information Collection Activities: Proposed Collection; Comment request (pertaining to clinical laboratory ICRs contained in supporting regulations at 42 CFR section 493.1–.2001).

66 FR 4674, January 18, 2001: Medicare and Medicaid Programs; Hospital Conditions of Participation: Anesthesia—Final rule affecting 42 CFR Parts 416, 482, and 485.

66 FR 6629, January 22, 2001: HCFA Agency Information Collection Activities: Submission for OMB Review; Comment request (pertaining to Medicare Integrity Program Organizational Conflict of Interest Disclosure Certificate).

66 FR 7919, January 26, 2001: HCFA Agency Information Collection Activities: Proposed Collection; Comment request (pertaining to provider Medicare agreements).

66 FR 8807, February 2, 2001: HCFA Agency Information Collection Activities: Proposed Collection; Comment request (pertaining to Medicare Federal health care programs provider/supplier enrollment application).

66 FR 9586, February 8, 2001: HCFA Agency Information Collection Activities: Proposed Collection; Comment request (pertaining to a project to develop an outcome–based continuous quality improvement system for PACE).

66 FR 9587, February 8, 2001: HCFA Agency Information Collection Activities: Proposed Collection; Comment request (pertaining to a project to develop an outcome-reporting of restraints and seclusion deaths by hospitals).

66 FR 13547, March 6, 2001: HCFA Agency Information Collection Activities: Proposed Collection; Comment request (pertaining to hospice request for certification as a provider).

66 FR 14157, March 9, 2001: HCFA Agency Information Collection Activities: Submission for OMB review; Comment request (pertaining to home health Medicare conditions of participation information collection requirements).

66 FR 14157, March 9, 2001: HCFA Agency Information Collection Activities: Submission for OMB review; Comment request (pertaining to alternate quality assessment form for CLIA compliance).

66 FR 14906, March 14, 2001: Medicare and Medicaid Programs; Recognition of the American Osteopathic Association for Ambulatory Surgical Centers Program—Proposed notice.

66 FR 15352, March 19, 2001: Medicare and Medicaid Programs; Hospital Conditions of Participation: Anesthesia Services: Delay of Effective Date—Final rule; delay of effective date, affecting 42 CFR Parts 416, 482, and 485.

66 FR 16480, March 26, 2001: HCFA Agency Information Collection Activities; Proposed Collection; Comment request (pertaining to conditions of coverage of suppliers of end stage renal disease services). See also correction at 66 FR 18096, April 5, 2001.

66 FR 18645, April 10, 2001: HCFA Agency Information Collection Activities: Submission for OMB Review; Comment request (pertaining to Medicare and Medicaid outcome and assessment information set (OASIS) as part of the conditions of participation for home health agencies).

66 FR 18647, April 10, 2001: HCFA Agency Information Collection Activities: Submission for OMB Review; Comment request (pertaining to CLIA compliance).

66 FR 19507, April 16, 2001: HCFA Agency Information Collection Activities: Proposed Collection; Comment request (pertaining to conflict of interest and ownership and control information form).

66 FR 19508, April 16, 2001: HCFA Agency Information Collection Activities: Proposed Collection; Comment request (pertaining to on site inspection for durable medical equipment (DME) suppliers).

66 FR 19509, April 16, 2001: Medicare and Medicaid Programs; Application by the American Osteopathic Association (AOF) for Approval of Deeming Authority for Critical Access Hospitals—Proposed notice.

66 FR 20315, April 20, 2001: HCFA Agency Information Collection Activities: Proposed Collection; Comment request (pertaining to inpatient rehabilitation assessment instrument).

66 FR 20315, April 20, 2001: HCFA Agency Information Collection Activities: Submission for OMB Review; Comment request (pertaining to DMEPOS supplier standards).

66 FR 20316, April 20, 2001: HCFA Agency Information Collection Activities: Submission for OMB Review; Comment request (pertaining to DMEPOS supplier survey).

66 FR 20997, April 26, 2001: HCFA Agency Information Collection Activities: Submission for OMB Review; Comment request (pertaining to health insurance provider agreement form).

66 FR 22242, May 3, 2001: HCFA Agency Information Collection Activities: Proposed Collection; Comment request (pertaining to CLIA certification requirements).

66 FR 23945, May 10, 2001: HCFA Agency Information Collection Activities: Submission for OMB Review; Comment request (pertaining to development of an outcome–based continuous quality improvement system for PACE).

66 FR 27598, May 18, 2001: Medicare and Medicaid Programs; Hospital Conditions of Participation; Anesthesia Services: Delay of Effective Date—Notice of final rule affecting 42 CFR Parts 416, 482, and 485.

66 FR 33102, June 20, 2001: HCFA Agency Information Collection Activities; Submission for OMB Review; Comment request (pertaining to provider/supplier enrollment application form).

See § 4:11.

§ 8:12 CRIMINAL PENALTIES: EXCESSIVE MEDICAID CHARGES AND UNLAWFUL FINANCIAL PRECONDITIONS FOR CARE IN HOSPITALS AND NURSING FACILITIES — Section 1128B(d) [42 U.S.C.A. 1320a-7b(d)]

Regulations

42 CFR Part 420 — Program Integrity: Medicare

42 CFR Part 424 — Conditions for Medicare Payment

42 CFR Part 440 — Services: General Provisions [Medicaid]

42 CFR Part 442 — Standards for Payment for Nursing Facilities and Intermediate Care Facilities for the Mentally Retarded [Medicaid]

42 CFR Part 447 — Payment for Services [Medicaid]
42 CFR Part 455 — Program Integrity: Medicaid
42 CFR Part 482 — Conditions of Participation for Hospitals
42 CFR Part 483 — Requirements for States and Long Term Care Facilities
42 CFR Part 488 — Survey, Certification, and Enforcement Procedures
42 CFR Part 489 — Provider Agreements and Supplier Approval
42 CFR Chapter V — Office of Inspector General — Health Care, Department of Health and Human Services
Subchapter A — General Provisions
Part 1000 — Introduction; General Definitions
Subchapter B — OIG Authorities
Part 1001 — Program Integrity: Medicare and State Health Care Programs
Part 1002 — Program Integrity: State-initiated Exclusion from Medicaid
Part 1003 — Civil Money Penalties, Assessments and Exclusions
Part 1004 — Imposition of Sanctions on Health Care Practitioners and Providers of Health Care Services by a Peer Review Organization
Part 1005 — Appeals of Exclusions, Civil Money Penalties and Assessments
Part 1006 — Investigational Inquiries
Part 1007 — State Medicaid Fraud Control Units
Part 1008 — Advisory Opinions by the OIG

57 FR 53572, November 12, 1992: Medicare and Medicaid; Charges to Residents' Funds in Nursing Homes — Final rule affecting 42 CFR Part 483.

See § 4:12.

§ 8:13 CRIMINAL PENALTIES: VIOLATING A PHYSICIAN OR SUPPLIER PARTICIPATION AGREEMENT OR A MEDICARE ASSIGNMENT OF BENEFITS AGREEMENT — Section 1128B(e) [42 U.S.C.A. 1320a-7b(e)]

Regulations

42 CFR Part 402 — Civil Money Penalties, Assessments, and Exclusions
42 CFR Part 410 — Supplementary Medical Insurance (SMI) Benefits

42 CFR Part 414 — Payment for Part B Medical and Other Health Services

42 CFR Part 420 — Program Integrity: Medicare

42 CFR Part 424 — Conditions for Medicare Payment

42 CFR Part 456 — Utilization Control

42 CFR Part 476 — Utilization and Quality Control Review

42 CFR Part 489 — Provider Agreements and Supplier Approval

42 CFR Part 498 — Appeals Procedures for Determinations that Affect Participation in the Medicare Program and for Determinations that Affect the Participation of ICF's/MR and Certain NF's in the Medicaid Program

42 CFR Chapter V — Office of Inspector General — Health Care, Department of Health and Human Services

Subchapter A — General Provisions

Part 1000 — Introduction; General Definitions

Subchapter B — OIG Authorities

Part 1001 — Program Integrity: Medicare and State Health Care Programs

Part 1003 — Civil Money Penalties, Assessments and Exclusions

Part 1004 — Imposition of Sanctions on Health Care Practitioners and Providers of Health Care Services by a Peer Review Organization

Part 1005 — Appeals of Exclusions, Civil Money Penalties and Assessments

Part 1006 — Investigational Inquiries

Part 1007 — State Medicaid Fraud Control Units

Part 1008 — Advisory Opinions by the OIG

57 FR 36006, August 12, 1992: Medicare Program; Self-implementing Coverage and Payments Provisions: 1990 Legislation — Final rule with comment period, affecting 42 CFR Parts 405, 406, 409, 420, 411, 412, 413, 418, and 489. Pertains to capital-related inpatient hospital costs; capital-related outpatient hospital costs; non-capital related outpatient hospital costs; payment for physician pathology services; payment for services of physicians as assistants-at-surgery; payments for ambulatory surgical procedures in hospital outpatient departments; payments for radiology services performed in hospital outpatient departments; hospice benefit extension; enrollment of HMO members in Medicare Part A; coverage of ostomy supplies; application of pre-entitlement stay in psychiatric hospital to limit on payment for inpatient hospital services; payments to dialysis facilities; payment rates for

erythropoietin (EPO); and Medicare secondary payer provision for individuals with ESRD.

57 FR 43462, September 21, 1992: Health Care Financing Administration Public Information Collection Requirements Submitted to the Office of Management and Budget for Clearance (pertaining to sole community home health agencies; physician/supplier overpayment reports; physician or supplier Medicare agreements; conditions of participation for rural health clinics; Medicare provider refunds; conditions of participation for comprehensive outpatient rehabilitation facilities; Medicaid income and eligibility verification system; Medicaid integrated review schedule; provider overpayment report; financial statement of Medicare provider debtors; negative case action review schedule for Medicaid quality control; outpatient resource costing study; Medicaid intermediate care facility for the mentally retarded or persons with related conditions survey report form; installment agreement of beneficiary refund of overpayment; PRO assumption of responsibilities; Medicare contractor administrative budget and cost reporting system forms; fire safety survey report forms; medical records review under prospective payment system; and Qualified Medicare Beneficiary supplement to the Medicare current beneficiary survey).

57 FR 46362, October 8, 1992: Medicare and Medicaid Programs; Revised Effective Date of Medicare/Medicaid Provider Agreement and Supplier Participation — Proposed rule affecting 42 CFR Parts 431, 440, 442, 488, 489, and 498.

57 FR 46865, October 13, 1992: HCFA Public Information Collection Requirements Submitted to the Office of Management and Budget for Clearance (pertaining to impact of home health care plan management and evaluation; end-stage renal disease medical case review; Medicare/Medicaid hospital swing-bed survey report form; quarterly Medicaid statement of expenditures; Medicaid program budget report; information collection requirements in final peer review organization sanction regulations; appeals procedures for determinations that affect participation in Medicare; request for medical review information for Part B intermediary outpatient therapy bills and other Part B outpatient bills; and Medicaid limitations on provider-related donations and health care-related taxes, and limitations on payment to disproportionate share hospitals).

57 FR 47587, October 19, 1992: Medicare and Medicaid Programs; Use of Standardized Federal Claims Processing Forms and Procedures — Advance notice of proposed rulemaking.

57 FR 48033, October 21, 1992: Medicare Program; Revised Procedures for Paying Claims From Providers of Services — Final notice.

58 FR 46198, September 1, 1993: HCFA Public Information Collection Requirements (ICR) Submitted to the Office of Management and Budget (OMB) for Clearance (pertaining to prenatal services and assistance screening; home health agency treatment forms; conditions of participation for intermediate care facilities for the mentally retarded; State Medicaid eligibility quality control sample selection lists; prepaid health plan cost report; hospital survey report form; procedures for determining whether providers, practitioners, or other suppliers of services are liable for certain noncovered services; Medicare credit balance reporting requirements; Medicare provider cost report questionnaire form; Medicare current beneficiary survey rounds 7–10; sterilization regulation/consent form; PRO reconsideration and appeals information requirements; information collection requirements in HSQ-110, acquisition, protection and disclosure of PRO information; Medicare/Medicaid organ procurement organization's (OPO) request for certification) — Notice.

58 FR 60204, November 15, 1993: HCFA Public Information Collection Requirements Submitted to the Office of Management and Budget (OMB) for Clearance (pertaining to procedures for transmitting information between Medicare carriers and Medicare supplemental insurers; Medicare physician or supplier agreement; patient intake data form for the National Home Health Agency; agency characteristics form for the National Home Health Agency prospective payment demonstration; intake and assessment survey package for the community nursing organization demonstration; comprehensive outpatient rehabilitation facility (CORF eligibility and survey forms and information collection requirements) — Notice.

59 FR 6228, February 10, 1994: Medicare Program; Change in Provider Agreement Regulations Related to Federal Employee Health Benefits — Proposed rule affecting 42 CFR Part 489.

61 FR 13205, March 26, 1996: HCFA Agency Information Collection Activities: Submission for OMB Review; Comment Request (pertaining to Medicare standardized forms for reimbursement of covered services by all providers that accept Medicare assignment).

61 FR 16925, April 18, 1996: HCFA Agency Information Collection Activities: Proposed Collection; Comment Request (pertaining to

Medicare participating physician or supplier agreements; and hospital conditions of participation).

61 FR 19628, May 2, 1996: HCFA Agency Information Collection Activities: Proposed Collection; Comment Request (pertaining to permissible billing for physicians that do not accept Medicare assignments).

61 FR 20528, May 7, 1996: HCFA Privacy Act of 1974; System of Records (pertaining to the Medicare physician identification and eligibility system).

61 FR 37278, July 17, 1996: HCFA Agency Information Collection Activities: Proposed Collection; Comment request (pertaining to Medicare provider/supplier enrollment forms).

61 FR 38454, July 24, 1996: HCFA Agency Information Collection Activities: Submission for OMB Review; Comment request (pertaining to physicians who do not accept Medicare assignment).

62 FR 8744, February 26, 1997: HCFA Agency Information Collection Activities: Submission for OMB Review; Comment request (pertaining to Medicare provider/supplier enrollment application).

62 FR 66376, December 18, 1997: HCFA Emergency Clearance: Public Information Collection Requirements Submitted to the Office of Management and Budget (OMB) (pertaining to Medicare and other Federal health care program enrollment forms for providers and suppliers).

62 FR 66726, December 19, 1997: Medicare and Medicaid Programs; Hospital Conditions of Participation; Provider Agreements and Supplier Approval — Proposed rule affecting 42 CFR Parts 416, 482, 485, and 489.

63 FR 2926, January 20, 1998: Medicare Program; Additional Supplier Standards — Proposed rule affecting 42 CFR Part 424.

63 FR 4459, January 29, 1998: HCFA Emergency Clearance: Public Information Collection Requirements Submitted to the Office of Management and Budget (OMB) (pertaining to Medicare/Medicaid health insurance common claim form and instructions).

63 FR 7743, February 17, 1998: Medicare and Medicaid Programs; Hospital Conditions of Participation; Provider Agreements and Supplier Approval — Notice of extension of comment period, affecting 42 CFR Parts 416, 482, 485, and 489.

63 FR 14393, March 25, 1998: Office of Inspector General: Health Care Programs: Fraud and Abuse; Revised OIG Civil Money Penalties Resulting from the Health Insurance Portability and

Accountability Act of 1996 — Notice of proposed rulemaking, affecting 42 CFR Parts 1003, 1005, and 1006.

63 FR 19502, April 20, 1998: HCFA Agency Information Collection Activities: Proposed collection; Comment request (pertaining to annual early and periodic screening, diagnostic, and treatment services (EPSDT) participation report; Medicare and other health care programs provider/supplier enrollment application; and research and analytic support for implementing performance measurement in Medicare fee for service).

63 FR 25320, May 7, 1998: HCFA National Standard Health Care Provider Identifier — Proposed Rule affecting 45 CFR Part 142.

63 FR 34904, June 26, 1998: HCFA Agency Information Collection Activities: Proposed Collection; Comment request (pertaining to health care prepayment plan Medicare application agreement).

63 FR 36250, July 2, 1998: HCFA Agency Information Collection Activities; Submission for OMB review; Comment request (pertaining to provider/supplier enrollment applications).

63 FR 37129, July 9, 1998: HCFA Agency Information Collection Activities; Submission for OMB Review; Comment request (pertaining to organ procurement organization requests for participation in Medicare and Medicaid).

63 FR 38414, July 16, 1998: HCFA Privacy Act of 1974; Report of Altered System (pertaining to disclosure of individual-specific information to combat fraud or abuse in health benefit programs).

63 FR 42054, August 6, 1998: HCFA Agency Information Collection Activities: Submission for OMB Review; Comment Request (pertaining to Medicare/Medicaid/CLIA conditions of participation).

1999

64 FR 1813, January 12, 1999: Office of Inspector General Publication of OIG Special Fraud Alert on Physician Liability for Certifications in the Provision of Medical Equipment and Supplies and Home Health Services — Notice.

64 FR 6753, February 16, 1999: Office of Inspector General: Privacy Act; Notification of New System of Records in Conjunction with the Healthcare Integrity and Protection Data Bank — Notice of a new system of records.

64 FR 17673, April 12, 1999: HCFA Agency Information Collection Activities: Proposed Collection; Comment request (pertaining to Medicare participating physician or supplier agreements).

64 FR 24956, May 10, 1999: Medicare and Medicaid Programs; Effective Dates of Provider Agreements and Supplier Approvals — Correction restoring regulations inadvertently removed when a final rule concerning effective dates for provider agreements and supplier approvals was published at 62 FR 43931, August 18, 1997.

64 FR 37142, July 9, 1999: HCFA Agency Information Collection Activities: Submission for OMB Review; Comment request (pertaining to request for certification in the Medicare/Medicaid program to provide outpatient physical therapy and/or speech-language pathology and the outpatient physical therapy and/or speech-language pathology survey report form; request for certification as a supplier of portable X-ray services); and procedures for making national coverage decisions).

64 FR 39517, July 22, 1999: HCFA Agency Information Collection Activities: Submission for OMB Review; Comment request (pertaining to Medicare participating physician or supplier agreement form HCFA-460).

64 FR 48846, September 8, 1999: Office of Inspector General: Solicitation of Information and Recommendations for Developing OIG Compliance Program Guidance for Individual Physicians and Small Group Practices — Notice.

64 FR 57619, October 26, 1999: Office of Inspector General; Privacy Act; Exempt Record System, Pertaining to the Healthcare Integrity and Protection Data Bank (HIPDB) — Notice of proposed rulemaking affecting 45 CFR Part 5b.

64 FR 57740, October 26, 1999: Office of Inspector General; Healthcare Fraud and Abuse Data Collection Program: Reporting of Final Adverse Actions - Final rule affecting 45 CFR Part 61. See also correction at 65 FR 70506, November 24, 2000.

2000

65 FR 5354, February 3, 2000: HCFA Agency Information Collection Activities: Proposed Collection; Comment request (pertaining to standardized Medicare/Medicaid claim form for reimbursement of covered services).

65 FR 11589, March 3, 2000: Office of Inspector General: Health Care Integrity and Protection Data Bank under Section 1128E of the Social Security Act: Announcement of Opening Date for Querying and User Fees — Notice.

65 FR 15912, March 24, 2000: HCFA Agency Information Collection Activities: Submission for OMB Review; Comment request (pertaining to Medicare uniform institutional provider claim forms).

65 FR 24400, April 26, 2000: Office of Inspector General; Health Care Programs: Fraud and Abuse; Revised OIG Civil Money Penalties Resulting from Public Law 104-191 (HIPAA) — Final rule affecting 42 CFR Parts 1001, 1003, 1005, and 1006. See also correction at 65 FR 35583, June 5, 2000.

65 FR 30414, May 11, 2000: HCFA Agency Information Collection Activities: Submission for OMB Review; Comment request (pertaining to health insurance common claims form).

65 FR 34986, June 1, 2000: Office of Inspector General; Privacy Act; Implementation (exempting the Healthcare Integrity and Protection Data Bank under Section 1128C of the Social Security Act from certain provisions of the Privacy Act (5 U.S.C. 552a) — Final rule.

65 FR 36818, June 12, 2000: Office of Inspector General: Draft OIG Compliance Program for Individual and Small Group Physician Practices — Notice and comment period.

65 FR 42021, July 7, 2000: HCFA Agency Information Collection Activities: Proposed Collection; Comment request (pertaining to notice to providers, suppliers, and practitioners about non-covered services to beneficiaries).

65 FR 50204, August 17, 2000: Office of Inspector General: Solicitation of Information and Recommendations for Developing a Compliance Risk Guidance for the Ambulance Industry — Notice.

65 FR 50312, August 17, 2000: HCFA; Health Insurance Reform: Standards for Electronic Transactions — Final rule affecting 45 CFR Parts 160 and 162.

65 FR 53727, September 5, 2000: HCFA Agency Information Collection Activities: Proposed Collection; Comment request (pertaining to ambulance services reimbursement request form for physicians, suppliers, and beneficiaries).

65 FR 53963, September 6, 2000: Medicare Program: Appeals of Carrier Determinations that a Physician or Other Supplier Fails to Meet the Requirements for Medicare Billing Privileges; Reopening of Comment Period — Notice of reopening of comment period for proposed rule affecting 42 CFR Part 405.

65 FR 60366, October 11, 2000: Medicare Program; Additional Supplier Standards — Final rule with comment period, affecting 42 CFR Part 424.

65 FR 64227, October 26, 2000: HCFA Agency Information Collection Activities: Proposed Collection; Comment Request; Public Information Collection Meeting to Discuss Proposed Revisions (pertaining to notice requirements from suppliers, physicians, and practitioners to beneficiaries when Medicare Part B payment may be denied).

2001

66 FR 1996, January 10, 2001: HCFA Agency Information Collection Activities; Comment request (pertaining to Medicare uniform institutional provider bill for reimbursement of covered services by all providers that accept assignment of claims).

66 FR 6629, January 22, 2001: HCFA Agency Information Collection Activities: Submission for OMB Review; Comment request (pertaining to Medicare Integrity Program Organizational Conflict of Interest Disclosure Certificate).

66 FR 7919, January 26, 2001: HCFA Agency Information Collection Activities: Proposed Collection; Comment request (pertaining to provider Medicare agreements).

66 FR 8807, February 2, 2001: HCFA Agency Information Collection Activities: Proposed Collection; Comment request (pertaining to Medicare Federal health care programs provider/supplier enrollment application).

66 FR 9712, February 9, 2001: HCFA Agency Information Collection Activities: Proposed Collection; Comment request (pertaining to Medicare customer service study for the Medicare Integrity Program).

66 FR 9865, February 12, 2001: Office of Inspector General: Privacy Act of 1974; Amendment to the Health Care Program Violations System of Records—Notice and comment period (pertaining to including Social Security numbers of sanctioned individual in the Health Care Program Violations record).

66 FR 13547, March 6, 2001: HCFA Agency Information Collection Activities: Proposed Collection; Comment request (pertaining to hospice request for certification as a provider).

66 FR 16061, March 22, 2001: HCFA Agency Information Collection Activities: Proposed Collection; Comment request (pertaining to private contracts of physicians who opt out of Medicare).

66 FR 19507, April 16, 2001: HCFA Agency Information Collection Activities: Proposed Collection; Comment request (pertaining to conflict of interest and ownership and control information form).

66 FR 20997, April 26, 2001: HCFA Agency Information Collection Activities: Submission for OMB Review; Comment request (pertaining to health insurance provider agreement form).

66 FR 28916, May 25, 2001: HCFA Agency Information Collection Activities; Proposed Collection; Comment request (pertaining to procedures for advisory opinions concerning physician referrals under section 1877 of the Social Security Act).

66 FR 31245, June 11, 2001: Office of Inspector General; Healthcare Integrity and Protection Data Bank: Change in User Fees—Notice.

66 FR 32630, June 15, 2001: HCFA Agency Information Collection Activities; Submission for OMB Review; Comment request (pertaining to contracts by practitioners and physicians who opt–out of Medicare).

66 FR 33102, June 20, 2001: HCFA Agency Information Collection Activities; Submission for OMB Review; Comment request (pertaining to provider/supplier enrollment application form).

See § 4:13.

§ 8:13.1 FAILURE TO REPORT INFORMATION ABOUT FINAL ADVERSE ACTIONS AGAINST HEALTH CARE PROVIDERS, SUPPLIERS, AND PRACTITIONERS TO THE NATIONAL HEALTH CARE FRAUD AND ABUSE DATA COLLECTION PROGRAM: Section 1128E(b)(6) [42 U.S.C.A. 1320a-7e(b)(6)]

Regulations

42 CFR Part 420 — Program Integrity: Medicare

42 CFR Part 455 — Program Integrity: Medicaid

42 CFR Chapter V — Office of Inspector General — Health Care, Department of Health and Human Services

Subchapter A — General Provisions

Part 1000 — Introduction; General Definitions

Subchapter B — OIG Authorities

Part 1001 — Program Integrity: Medicare and State Health Care Programs

Part 1002 — Program Integrity: State-initiated Exclusion from Medicaid

Part 1003 — Civil Money Penalties, Assessments and Exclusions

Part 1005 — Appeals of Exclusions, Civil Money Penalties and Assessments

Part 1006 — Investigational Inquiries

Part 1007 — State Medicaid Fraud Control Units

Part 1008 — Advisory Opinions by the OIG

63 FR 58341, October 30, 1998: Office of Inspector General: Health Care Fraud and Abuse Data Collection Program: Reporting of Final Adverse Actions — Notice of proposed rulemaking under section 1128E of the Social Security Act, affecting 45 CFR 61.

63 FR 71819, December 30, 1998: Office of Inspector General; Health Care Fraud and Abuse Data Collection Program; Reporting under section 1128E of the Social Security Act of Final Adverse Actions — Notice of proposed rule-making; extension of comment period, affecting 45 CFR 61.

1999

64 FR 6753, February 16, 1999: Office of Inspector General: Privacy Act; Notification of New System of Records in Conjunction with the Healthcare Integrity and Protection Data Bank — Notice of a new system of records.

64 FR 57619, October 26, 1999: Office of Inspector General; Privacy Act; Exempt Record System, Pertaining to the Healthcare Integrity and Protection Data Bank (HIPDB) — Notice of proposed rulemaking affecting 45 CFR Part 5b.

64 FR 57740, October 26, 1999: Office of Inspector General; Healthcare Fraud and Abuse Data Collection Program: Reporting of Final Adverse Actions - Final rule affecting 45 CFR Part 61. See also correction at 65 FR 70506, November 24, 2000.

2000

65 FR 11589, March 3, 2000: Office of Inspector General: Health Care Integrity and Protection Data Bank under Section 1128E of the Social Security Act: Announcement of Opening Date for Querying and User Fees — Notice.

65 FR 34986, June 1, 2000: Office of Inspector General; Privacy Act; Implementation (exempting the Healthcare Integrity and Protection Data Bank under Section 1128C of the Social Security Act from certain provisions of the Privacy Act (5 U.S.C. 552a) — Final rule.

2001

66 FR 9865, February 12, 2001: Office of Inspector General: Privacy Act of 1974; Amendment to the Health Care Program Violations System of Records—Notice and comment period (pertaining to including Social Security numbers of sanctioned individual in the Health Care Program Violations record).

66 FR 31245, June 11, 2001: Office of Inspector General; Healthcare Integrity and Protection Data Bank: Change in User Fees—Notice.

See § 4:13.1.

§ 8:14 MISUSE OF FEDERAL GOVERNMENT NAMES, SYMBOLS, AND EMBLEMS — Section 1140 [42 U.S.C.A. 1320b-10]

Regulations

42 CFR Part 420 — Program Integrity: Medicare

42 CFR Part 455 — Program Integrity: Medicaid

42 CFR Chapter V — Office of Inspector General — Health Care, Department of Health and Human Services

Subchapter A — General Provisions

Part 1000 — Introduction; General Definitions

Subchapter B — OIG Authorities

Part 1001 — Program Integrity: Medicare and State Health Care Programs

Part 1002 — Program Integrity: State-initiated Exclusion from Medicaid

Part 1003 — Civil Money Penalties, Assessments and Exclusions

Part 1005 — Appeals of Exclusions, Civil Money Penalties and Assessments

Part 1006 — Investigational Inquiries

Part 1007 — State Medicaid Fraud Control Units

Part 1008 — Advisory Opinions by the OIG

55 FR 3986, February 6, 1990: Medicare and Social Security: Fraud and Abuse; Civil Money Penalties for Misuse of Certain Terms, Symbols and Emblems — Proposed rule.

60 FR 58239, November 27, 1995: Office of Inspector General; Health Care Programs: Fraud and Abuse; Revisions to the Civil Money Penalty Provisions Relating to the Misuse of Certain Names, Symbols and Emblems — Final rule affecting 42 CFR Part 1003.

See § 4:14.

§ 8:15 [RESERVED]

§ 8:16 VIOLATING REPORTING AND DISCLOSURE OBLIGATIONS REGARDING THE MEDICARE AND MEDICAID COVERAGE DATA BANK — Section 1144 [42 U.S.C.A. 1320b-14] — NOTE: This sanction was repealed effective October 2, 1996, by section 1(a) of the Medicare/Medicaid Data Bank Elimination Act of 1996, P.L. 104–226.

Regulations

42 CFR Part 411 — Exclusions from Medicare and Limitations on Medicare Payment

42 CFR Part 433, Subpart D — Third Party Liability [Medicaid]

42 CFR Chapter V — Office of Inspector General — Health Care, Department of Health and Human Services

Subchapter A — General Provisions

Part 1000 — Introduction; General Definitions

Subchapter B — OIG Authorities

Part 1001 — Program Integrity: Medicare and State Health Care Programs

Part 1003 — Civil Money Penalties, Assessments and Exclusions

Part 1005 — Appeals of Exclusions, Civil Money Penalties and Assessments

Part 1006 — Investigational Inquiries

Part 1007 — State Medicaid Fraud Control Units

Part 1008 — Advisory Opinions by the OIG

54 FR 41716, October 11, 1989: Medicare as Secondary Payer and Medicare Recovery Against Third Parties — Final rule.

54 FR 47678, November 16, 1989: Medicare Program; Medicare as Secondary Payer and Medicare Recovery Against Third Parties; Publication of Court Orders — Publication of court orders.

55 FR 1432, January 16, 1990: Medicaid Program; State Plan Requirements and Other Provisions Relating to State Third Party Liability Programs — Final rule. See also correction published at 55 FR 5118, February 13, 1990.

55 FR 1819, January 19, 1990: Medicare as Secondary Payer and Medicare Recovery Against Third Parties — Correction of final rule published at 54 FR 41716, October 11, 1989.

55 FR 8491, March 8, 1990: Medicare Program; Medicare Secondary Payer for Disabled Active Individuals — Proposed rule to amend 42 CFR Part 411.

55 FR 11019, March 26, 1990: Medicare Program; Medicare as Secondary Payer and Medicare Recovery Against Third Parties — Final rule and reinstatement of regulations published at 54 FR 41716 on October 11, 1989.

56 FR 1200, January 11, 1991: Changes to Medicare Secondary Payer (MSP) Provisions — Notice.

56 FR 31952, July 12, 1991: Medicare Program; Medicare Secondary Payer Data Match — Notice.

58 FR 29416, May 20, 1993: HCFA Public Information Collection Requirements Submitted to the Office of Management and Budget (OMB) for Clearance re cataract surgery; Medicaid utilization management initiatives; Medicare coverage of screening mammography; psychiatric unit criteria worksheet and rehabilitation unit criteria worksheet; Medicare secondary payor forms; ambulatory surgical center survey forms; ambulance service compliance with State and local requirements; and early and periodic screening, diagnostic and treatment reports.

58 FR 38579, July 19, 1993: HCFA Public Information Collection Requirements Submitted to the Office of Management and Budget (OMB) for Clearance re survey of home health agencies; CLIA survey report form; validation of state surveys; Medicaid listing of participating home health agencies; financial information regarding Medicare benefits from Medicare contractors; and third-party liability under Medicaid.

59 FR 4285, January 31, 1994: Medicare Program; Medicare Secondary Payment — General notice.

59 FR 23069, May 4, 1994: HCFA Public Information Collection Requirements Submitted to the Office of Management and Budget (OMB) for Clearance (pertaining to clinical laboratory improvement amendments (CLIA) flexible survey protocol form; application for health insurance benefits under Medicare for individual with chronic renal disease form; Medicare Qualification Statement for Federal employees form; attending physician's statement and documentation of Medicare emergency form; request for Part B Medicare hearing by an Administrative Law Judge forms; CLIA adverse action extract; and Medicare and Medicaid coverage data bank reports form.)

59 FR 24167, May 10, 1994: Medicare and Medicaid Programs; Medicare-Medicaid Coverage Data Bank Requirements: Preliminary Guidance — Notice (pertaining to reports employers must make about individuals covered by group health plans).

59 FR 59241, November 16, 1994: Medicare and Medicaid Programs; Delay in Implementation of the Medicare-Medicaid Coverage Data Bank Requirements — Notice.

60 FR 37066, July 19, 1995: HCFA Public Information Collection Requirements Submitted to the Office of Management and Budget (OMB) for Clearance (pertaining to actuarial forecasts for Medicaid utilization and cost, employers identified through a match of IRS, SSA, and Medicare records for purposes of the Medicare Secondary Payer provision, health and safety requirements for portable X-ray suppliers, and evaluation of Intermediate Care Facilities for Persons with Mental Retardation — establishing psychoactive drug use baselines).

60 FR 45344, August 31, 1995: Medicare Program; Medicare Secondary Payer for Individuals Entitled to Medicare and Also Covered under Group Health Plans — Final rule with comment period affecting 42 CFR Parts 400and 411. See also correction at 60 FR 48749, September 30, 1995. See also correction at 60 FR 53876, October 18, 1995.

See § 4:16.

§ 8:16.1 PUBLIC ACCESS TO INFORMATION ABOUT HOSPITAL FINANCIAL INTERESTS IN ENTITIES TO WHICH REFERRALS OF PATIENTS ARE MADE — Sections 1146 and 1866(a)(1)(S) [42 U.S.C.A. 1320b-16 and 1395cc(a)(1)(S)]

Regulations

42 CFR Part 420 — Program Integrity: Medicare

42 CFR Part 455 — Program Integrity: Medicaid

42 CFR Chapter V — Office of Inspector General — Health Care, Depratment of Health and Human Services

Subchapter A — General Provisions

Part 1000 — Introduction; General Definitions

Subchapter B — OIG Authorities

Part 1001 — Program Integrity: Medicare and State Health Care Programs

Part 1002 — Program Integrity: State-initiated Exclusion from Medicaid

Part 1003 — Civil Money Penalties, Assessments and Exclusions

Part 1005 — Appeals of Exclusions, Civil Money Penalties and Assessments

Part 1006 — Investigational Inquiries

Part 1007 — State Medicaid Fraud Control Units

Part 1008 — Advisory Opinions by the OIG

63 FR 1646, January 9, 1998: Medicare Program; Physicians' Referrals; Issuance of Advisory Opinions — Final rule with comment period, affecting 42 CFR Part 411.

63 FR 1659, January 9, 1998: Medicare and Medicaid Programs; Physicians' Referrals to Health Care Entities with Which They Have Financial Relationships — Proposed rule affecting 42 CFR Parts 411, 424, 435, and 455.

63 FR 8987, February 23, 1998: Office of Inspector General: Publication of the OIG Compliance Program for Hospitals — Notice.

63 FR 9844, February 26, 1998: HCFA Agency Information Collection Activities: Proposed Collection; Comment request (pertaining to procedures for advisory opinions concerning physician referrals and supporting regulations in 42 CFR Sections 411.370- 411.389).

63 FR 11649, March 10, 1998: Medicare and Medicaid Programs; Physicians' Referrals to Health Care Entities with Which They Have Financial Relationships — Notice of extension of comment period for proposed rule.

63 FR 20415, April 24, 1998: Office of Inspector General: Publication of OIG Special Fraud Alert: Fraud and Abuse in Nursing Home Arrangements with Hospices — Notice.

63 FR 28395, May 22, 1998: HCFA Agency Information Collection Activities: Submission for OMB Review; Comment request (pertaining to procedures for advisory opinions concerning physician referrals and supporting regulations in 42 CFR 411.370 through 411.389).

1999

64 FR 13997, March 23, 1999: HCFA Agency Information Collection Activities: Submission for OMB Review; Comment request (pertaining to Medicare and Medicaid requirements for advanced directives, and disclosure of ownership and financial control interest).

64 FR 73563, December 30, 1999: HCFA Agency Information Collection Activities: Submission for OMB Review; Comment request pertaining to Medicare program integrity organizational conflict of interest disclosure certificates).

2000

65 FR 9274, February 24, 2000: Office of Inspector General: Publication of OIG Special Fraud Alert on Rental of Space in Physician Offices by Persons or Entities to Which Physicians Refer —Notice.

65 FR 10098, February 25, 2000: HCFA Agency Information Collection Activities: Proposed Collection; Comment request (pertaining to conflict of interest and ownership and control information with respect to fiscal intermediaries and carriers).

65 FR 30415, May 11, 2000: HCFA Agency Information Collection Activities: Submission for OMB Review; Comment request (pertaining to conflict of interest and ownership and control information).

65 FR 53319, September 1, 2000: HCFA Agency Information Collection Activities: Proposed Collection; Comment request (pertaining to incentive arrangement disclosure form for managed care organizations and their related medical groups and physicians).

65 FR 65861, November 2, 2000: HCFA Agency Information Collection Activities: Proposed Collection; Comment request (pertaining to conflict of interest disclosure requirements for Medicare program integrity).

2001

66 FR 856, January 4, 2001: Medicare and Medicaid Programs; Physicians Referrals to Health Care Entities with which They Have Financial Relationships—Final rule with comment period, affecting 42 CFR Parts 411 and 424.

66 FR 6629, January 22, 2001: HCFA Agency Information Collection Activities: Submission for OMB Review; Comment request (pertaining to Medicare Integrity Program Organizational Conflict of Interest Disclosure Certificate).

66 FR 8771, February 2, 2001: Medicare and Medicaid Programs; Physicians' Referrals to Health Care Entities with which They Have Financial Relationships: Delay of Effective Date of Final Rule and Technical Amendment, affecting 42 CFR Parts 411 and 424.

66 FR 9865, February 12, 2001: Office of Inspector General: Privacy Act of 1974; Amendment to the Health Care Program Violations System of Records—Notice and comment period (pertaining to including Social Security numbers of sanctioned individual in the Health Care Program Violations record).

66 FR 17813, April 4, 2001: Medicare and Medicaid Programs; Physicians' Referrals to Health Care Entities with which They Have

Financial Relationships; Extension of Comment period—Notice, affecting 42 CFR Parts 411 and 424.

66 FR 19507, April 16, 2001: HCFA Agency Information Collection Activities: Proposed Collection; Comment request (pertaining to conflict of interest and ownership and control information form).

66 FR 28916, May 25, 2001: HCFA Agency Information Collection Activities; Proposed Collection; Comment request (pertaining to procedures for advisory opinions concerning physician referrals under section 1877 of the Social Security Act).

66 FR 31245, June 11, 2001: Office of Inspector General; Healthcare Integrity and Protection Data Bank: Change in User Fees—Notice.

See § 4:16.1.

§ 8:17 TERMINATING CONTRACTS WITH PEER REVIEW ORGANIZATIONS — Section 1153 [42 U.S.C.A. 1320c-2]

Regulations

42 CFR Part 405, Subpart C — Suspension of Payment, Recovery of Overpayments, and Repayment of Scholarships and Loans; Subpart G — Reconsiderations and Appeals Under Medicare Part A; Subpart H — Appeals Under the Medicare Part B Program; Subpart R — Provider Reimbursement Determinations and Appeals

42 CFR Part 456 — Utilization Control

42 CFR Part 462 — Peer Review Organizations

42 CFR Part 476 — Utilization and Quality Control Review

42 CFR Part 478 — Reconsiderations and Appeals

42 CFR Part 480 — Acquisition, Protection, and Disclosure of Peer Review Information

42 CFR Chapter V — Office of Inspector General — Health Care, Department of Health and Human Services

Subchapter A — General Provisions

Part 1000 — Introduction; General Definitions

Subchapter B — OIG Authorities

Part 1001 — Program Integrity: Medicare and State Health Care Programs

Part 1002 — Program Integrity: State-initiated Exclusion from Medicaid

Part 1003 — Civil Money Penalties, Assessments and Exclusions

Part 1004 — Imposition of Sanctions on Health Care Practitioners and Providers of Health Care Services by a Peer Review Organization

Part 1005 — Appeals of Exclusions, Civil Money Penalties and Assessments

Part 1006 — Investigational Inquiries

Part 1007 — State Medicaid Fraud Control Units

Part 1008 — Advisory Opinions by the OIG

55 FR 42907, October 24, 1990: Medicare Program; Standards Applied by Utilization and Quality Control Peer Review Organizations: Consideration of Remote Rural Location and Other Relevant Factors — Notice of policy and request for comments.

56 FR 29967, July 1, 1991: Medicare Peer Review Organization contracts: Solicitation of Statements of Interest from In-State Organizations (AK, ID, Me, VT, DC) — Notice.

56 FR 43790, September 4, 1991: Medicare Program; Peer Review Organizations: Revised Scopes of Work for Delaware, Missouri, Montana, Nebraska, New Jersey, Nevada, Oklahoma, Rhode Island, South Carolina, Washington, and Wyoming — Final notice.

57 FR 26871, June 16, 1992: Medicare Program; Peer Review Organizations: Revised Scopes of Work for the District of Columbia, Puerto Rico, the Virgin Islands, and All States Except Delaware, Florida, Missouri, Montana, Nebraska, Nevada, Oklahoma, Rhode Island, South Carolina, Washington, and Wyoming — Final notice. See also correction at 57 FR 35837, August 11, 1992.

57 FR 43462, September 21, 1992: Health Care Financing Administration Public Information Collection Requirements Submitted to the Office of Management and Budget for Clearance (pertaining to sole community home health agencies; physician/supplier overpayment reports; physician or supplier Medicare agreements; conditions of participation for rural health clinics; Medicare provider refunds; conditions of participation for comprehensive outpatient rehabilitation facilities; Medicaid income and eligibility verification system; Medicaid integrated review schedule; provider overpayment report; financial statement of Medicare provider debtors; negative case action review schedule for Medicaid quality control; outpatient resource costing study; Medicaid intermediate care facility for the mentally retarded or persons with related conditions survey report form; installment agreement of beneficiary refund of overpayment; PRO assumption of responsibilities; Medicare contractor administrative budget and cost reporting system forms; fire safety survey

report forms; medical records review under prospective payment system; and Qualified Medicare Beneficiary supplement to the Medicare current beneficiary survey).

57 FR 46865, October 13, 1992: HCFA Public Information Collection Requirements Submitted to the Office of Management and Budget for Clearance (pertaining to impact of home health care plan management and evaluation; end-stage renal disease medical case review; Medicare/Medicaid hospital swing-bed survey report form; quarterly Medicaid statement of expenditures; Medicaid program budget report; information collection requirements in final peer review organization sanction regulations; appeals procedures for determinations that affect participation in Medicare; request for medical review information for Part B intermediary outpatient therapy bills and other Part B outpatient bills; and Medicaid limitations on provider-related donations and health care-related taxes, and limitations on payment to disproportionate share hospitals).

57 FR 47779, October 20, 1992: Medicare Program; Payment to Hospitals for Furnishing Photocopies to Peer Review Organizations — Final rule affecting 42 CFR Parts 412 and 466.

57 FR 53760, November 12, 1992: Privacy Act of 1974; Report of Altered System — Notice of alteration of an existing system of records (pertaining to peer review organization data management information).

58 FR 12042, March 2, 1993: Medicare Program; Peer Review Organizations: New PRO Contracts for All States and Territories and the District of Columbia — Notice.

58 FR 17417, April 2, 1993: Medicare Program; Peer Review Organization Contracts: Solicitation of Statements of Interest From In-State Organizations — Kentucky — General notice.

58 FR 46198, September 1, 1993: HCFA Public Information Collection Requirements (ICR) Submitted to the Office of Management and Budget (OMB) for Clearance (pertaining to prenatal services and assistance screening; home health agency treatment forms; conditions of participation for intermediate care facilities for the mentally retarded; State Medicaid eligibility quality control sample selection lists; prepaid health plan cost report; hospital survey report form; procedures for determining whether providers, practitioners, or other suppliers of services are liable for certain noncovered services; Medicare credit balance reporting requirements; Medicare provider cost report questionnaire form; Medicare current beneficiary survey rounds 7–10; sterilization regula-

tion/consent form; PRO reconsideration and appeals information requirements; information collection requirements in HSQ-110, acquisition, protection and disclosure of PRO information; Medicare/Medicaid organ procurement organization's (OPO) request for certification) — Notice.

58 FR 47904, September 13, 1993: HCFA, Public Information Collection Requirements (ICR) Submitted to the Office of Management and Budget (OMB) for Clearance (pertaining to chronic renal disease medical evidence report; Medicare common claims form; Social Security Office report of State buy-in problem; Medicare physician survey form; beneficiary survey form; Medicaid payment rate changes for inpatient hospital or long term care services; home and community-based services: waiver requirements; Medicare peer review organizations reporting forms; uniform institutional provider claim form) — Notice.

58 FR 59270, November 8, 1993: HCFA Public Information Collection Requirements Submitted to the Office of Management and Budget (OMB) for Clearance (pertaining to formats for utilization and quality control peer review organizations (PROs); home health agency plan of treatment forms; State survey agency budget expenditure report and certification workload report; home health agency cost report; recordkeeping requirements in provider reimbursement manual; quarterly Medicaid statement of expenditures; Medicare contract application for Federally qualified health maintenance organizations; hospice survey and deficiencies report form; organ procurement agency/histocompatibility laboratory statement of reimbursable costs) — Notice.

58 FR 65186, December 13, 1993: Medicare Program; Peer Review Organization, General Criteria and Standards for Evaluating Performance of Contract Obligations — Notice with comment period.

60 FR 21824, May 3, 1995: Medicare Program; Peer Review Organization Contracts: Solicitation of Statements of Interest From In-State Organizations — Alaska, Delaware, the District of Columbia, Idaho, Kentucky, Maine, Nebraska, Nevada, South Carolina, Vermont, and Wyoming — Notice.

60 FR 39403, August 2, 1995: HCFA Public Information Collection Requirements Submitted for Public Comment and Recommendations (pertaining to PRO reporting forms; Oregon Medicaid reform demonstration; review functions of PRO's; medical records review under PPS; evaluation of Medicare cataract surgery alternate payment demonstration; home health agency survey and deficiencies

report; CLIA survey forms; field testing of uniform needs assessment instrument for hospital discharge planning).

60 FR 63634, December 12, 1995: Office of Inspector General; Health Care Programs: Fraud and Abuse; Revisions to the PRO Sanctions Process — Final rule. See also correction at 61 FR 1841, January 24, 1996.

61 FR 4787, February 8, 1996: HCFA Public Information Collection Requirements Submitted for Public Comment: Submission for OMB Review (pertaining to Peer Review Organization reporting forms).

61 FR 29406, June 10, 1996: HCFA Agency Information Collection Activities: proposed Collection; Comment Request (pertaining to end stage renal disease application and survey and certification report forms; withholding Medicare payments to recover Medicaid overpayments; acquisition, protection, and disclosure of PRO information; clinical laboratory certification and recertification survey forms; CLIA laboratory personnel report forms; prepaid health plan cost reports; Medicare credit balance reporting requirements; statement of deficiencies and plan of correction requirements for organ procurement organizations; Medicare/Medicaid hospital survey report forms; advance directive requirements for Medicare and Medicaid; payment adjustments for sole community hospitals; survey reports for physical therapists in independent practice; HMO and CMP national data reporting requirements; identification of extension units of outpatient physical therapy and outpatient speech pathology providers; and fire safety survey reports).

61 FR 33532, June 27, 1996: HCFA Agency Information Collection Activities: Submission for OMB Review; Comment Request (pertaining to information collection requirements in PRO sanction regulations).

61 FR 34437, July 2, 1996: HCFA Agency Information Collection Activities: Submission for OMB Review; Comment Request (pertaining to Peer Review Organization procedures for reconsideration of initial decisions; Part B enrollment forms; certification of rural health clinics for Medicare participation; Medicaid utilization review requirements for home health agencies; State listings of Medicaid recipients in institutions and procedures for State inspection of care review; procedures for disenrollment of beneficiaries from HMOs or CMPs; effectiveness of telemedicine services; formats for PROs to submit data to HCFA; and request for accelerated payments forms for providers).

61 FR 43062, August 20, 1996: HCFA Agency Information Collection Activities: Submission for OMB Review; Comment request (pertaining to withholding Medicare payments to recover Medicaid overpayments; acquisition, protection, and disclosure of Peer Review Organization (PRO) information; cost reports for HMOs; and collection of credit balance information from health care providers).

61 FR 52951, October 9, 1996: HCFA Agency Information Collection Activities: Submission for OMB Review; Comment request (pertaining to Peer Review Organization Reconsiderations and Appeals; Part B enrollment forms; certification as a Rural Health Clinic; Medicaid utilization control programs; lists of Medicaid recipients in institutions; and business proposal formats for PROs).

62 FR 23140, April 29, 1997: Office of Inspector General: Health Care Programs: Fraud and Abuse; Revised PRO Sanctions for Failing to Meet Statutory Obligations — Final rule.

62 FR 35824, July 2, 1997: Medicare Program; Description of the Health Care Financing Administration's Evaluation Methodology for the Peer Review Organization 5th Scope of Work Contracts — Notice with comment period.

63 FR 4459, January 29, 1998: HCFA Agency Information Collection Activities: Proposed Collection; Comment request (pertaining to peer review organization contracts and solicitation of statements of interest from In-State Organizations).

63 FR 19504, April 20, 1998: HCFA Agency Information Collection Activities: Submission for OMB Review; Comment request (pertaining to peer review organization contracts; solicitation of statements of interest from in-State organizations).

63 FR 20639, April 27, 1998: HCFA Agency Information Collection Activities: Submission for OMB Review; Comment request (pertaining to peer review organization contracts and solicitation of statements of interest from in-State organizations).

63 FR 40534, July 29, 1998: Medicare Program; Peer Review Organization Contracts: Solicitation of Statements of Interest from In-state Organizations — Alaska, Delaware, the District of Columbia, Hawaii, Idaho, Illinois, Kentucky, Maine, Nebraska, Nevada, South Carolina, Vermont, and Wyoming — Notice.

63 FR 48734, September 11, 1998: HCFA Agency Information Collection Activities: Proposed Collection; Comment request (pertaining to medical review activities under PPS by Peer Review Organizations; and survey and deficiency reports for home health agencies).

63 FR 63478, November 13, 1998: HCFA Agency Information Collection Activities: Proposed Collection; Comment request (pertaining to processing Medicare+Choice disenrollment requests from beneficiaries; creation of the Utilization and Quality Control Peer Review Organization; and rules for participation of HHA's in Medicare and review of plans of care for home health services).

1999

64 FR 5665, February 4, 1999: HCFA Agency Information Collection Activities: Proposed Collection; Comment request (pertaining to Medicare+Choice disenrollment forms, and utilization and quality control peer review organizations (PROs)).

64 FR 10478, March 4, 1999: HCFA Agency Information Collection Activities: Proposed Collection; Comment request (pertaining to information collection requirements in final peer review organization (PRO) sanction regulations).

64 FR 30340, June 7, 1999: HCFA Agency Information Collection Activities: Submission for OMB Review; Comment request (pertaining to information collection requirements in the final peer review organization (PRO) sanction regulations).

64 FR 36021, July 2, 1999: Medicare Program; July 19, 1999 Open Town Hall Meeting to Discusss the Implementation of the Peer Review Organizations' (PROs) Sixth Round Contract Activities — Notice of meeting.

64 FR 40017, July 23, 1999: HCFA Agency Information Collection Activities: Submission for OMB Review; Comment request (pertaining to acquisition, protection and disclosure of peer review organization (PRO) information).

64 FR 45266, August 19, 1999: HCFA Agency Information Collection Activities: Proposed Collection; Comment request (pertaining to PRO reconsiderations and appeals).

64 FR 45266, August 19, 1999: HCFA Agency Information Collection Activities: Proposed Collection; Comment request (pertaining to business proposal formats for utilization and quality control peer review organizations (PROs)).

64 FR 62681, November 17, 1999: HCFA Agency Information Collection Activities: Submission for OMB Review; Comment request (pertaining to peer review organization (PRO) reconsiderations and appeals).

64 FR 62681, November 17, 1999: HCFA Agency Information Collection Activities: Submission for OMB Review; Comment request (pertaining business proposal formats for utilization and quality control peer review organizations (PRO's)).

2000

65 FR 24971, April 28, 2000: Medicare Program; Open Town Hall Meeting to Promote and Establish Partnerships between the Medicare Peer Review Organizations(PROs) and Entities in the Health Care Community to Foster Health Care Quality Improvement — May 15, 2000 — Notice of meeting.

65 FR 47738, August 3, 2000: HCFA Agency Information Collection Activities: Proposed Collection; Comment request (pertaining to Medicare beneficiary survey for Michigan PRO).

2001

66 FR 18781, April 11, 2001: HCFA Agency Information Collection Activities: Proposed Collection; Comment request (pertaining to Peer Review Organization contracts and solicitation of statements of interest).

66 FR 20997, April 26, 2001: Medicare program; Evaluation Criteria and Standards for Peer Review Organization 6th Round Contract—Notice

See § 4:17.

§ 8:18 DISALLOWANCE OF MEDICARE CLAIMS BY PEER REVIEW ORGANIZATIONS — Section 1154 [42 U.S.C.A. 1320c-3]

Regulations

42 CFR Part 405, Subpart C — Suspension of Payment, Recovery of Overpayments, and Repayment of Scholarships and Loans; Subpart G — Reconsiderations and Appeals Under Medicare Part A; Subpart H — Appeals Under the Medicare Part B Program; Subpart R — Provider Reimbursement Determinations and Appeals

42 CFR Part 456 — Utilization Control

42 CFR Part 475 — Peer Review Organizations

42 CFR Part 476 — Utilization and Quality Control Review

42 CFR Part 478 — Reconsiderations and Appeals

42 CFR Part 480 — Acquisition, Protection, and Disclosure of Peer Review Information

42 CFR Chapter V — Office of Inspector General — Health Care, Department of Health and Human Services

Subchapter A — General Provisions

Part 1000 — Introduction; General Definitions

Subchapter B — OIG Authorities

Part 1001 — Program Integrity: Medicare and State Health Care Programs

Part 1002 — Program Integrity: State-initiated Exclusion from Medicaid

Part 1003 — Civil Money Penalties, Assessments and Exclusions

Part 1004 — Imposition of Sanctions on Health Care Practitioners and Providers of Health Care Services by a Peer Review Organization

Part 1005 — Appeals of Exclusions, Civil Money Penalties and Assessments

Part 1006 — Investigational Inquiries

Part 1007 — State Medicaid Fraud Control Units

Part 1008 — Advisory Opinions by the OIG

55 FR 42907, October 24, 1990: Medicare Program; Standards Applied by Utilization and Quality Control Peer Review Organizations: Consideration of Remote Rural Location and Other Relevant Factors — Notice of policy and request for comments.

56 FR 29967, July 1, 1991: Medicare Peer Review Organization contracts: Solicitation of Statements of Interest from In-State Organizations (AK, ID, Me, VT, DC) — Notice.

56 FR 43790, September 4, 1991: Medicare Program; Peer Review Organizations: Revised Scopes of Work for Delaware, Missouri, Montana, Nebraska, New Jersey, Nevada, Oklahoma, Rhode Island, South Carolina, Washington, and Wyoming — Final notice.

57 FR 26871, June 16, 1992: Medicare Program; Peer Review Organizations: Revised Scopes of Work for the District of Columbia, Puerto Rico, the Virgin Islands, and All States Except Delaware, Florida, Missouri, Montana, Nebraska, Nevada, Oklahoma, Rhode Island, South Carolina, Washington, and Wyoming — Final notice. See also correction at 57 FR 35837, August 11, 1992.

57 FR 43462, September 21, 1992: Health Care Financing Administration Public Information Collection Requirements Submitted to the Office of Management and Budget for Clearance (pertaining to sole community home health agencies; physician/supplier overpayment reports; physician or supplier Medicare agreements; conditions of participation for rural health clinics; Medicare provider

refunds; conditions of participation for comprehensive outpatient rehabilitation facilities; Medicaid income and eligibility verification system; Medicaid integrated review schedule; provider overpayment report; financial statement of Medicare provider debtors; negative case action review schedule for Medicaid quality control; outpatient resource costing study; Medicaid intermediate care facility for the mentally retarded or persons with related conditions survey report form; installment agreement of beneficiary refund of overpayment; PRO assumption of responsibilities; Medicare contractor administrative budget and cost reporting system forms; fire safety survey report forms; medical records review under prospective payment system; and Qualified Medicare Beneficiary supplement to the Medicare current beneficiary survey).

57 FR 46865, October 13, 1992: HCFA Public Information Collection Requirements Submitted to the Office of Management and Budget for Clearance (pertaining to impact of home health care plan management and evaluation; end-stage renal disease medical case review; Medicare/Medicaid hospital swing-bed survey report form; quarterly Medicaid statement of expenditures; Medicaid program budget report; information collection requirements in final peer review organization sanction regulations; appeals procedures for determinations that affect participation in Medicare; request for medical review information for Part B intermediary outpatient therapy bills and other Part B outpatient bills; and Medicaid limitations on provider-related donations and health care-related taxes, and limitations on payment to disproportionate share hospitals).

57 FR 47779, October 20, 1992: Medicare Program; Payment to Hospitals for Furnishing Photocopies to Peer Review Organizations — Final rule affecting 42 CFR Parts 412 and 466.

57 FR 53760, November 12, 1992: Privacy Act of 1974; Report of Altered System — Notice of alteration of an existing system of records (pertaining to peer review organization data management information).

58 FR 12042, March 2, 1993: Medicare Program; Peer Review Organizations: New PRO Contracts for All States and Territories and the District of Columbia — Notice.

58 FR 17417, April 2, 1993: Medicare Program; Peer Review Organization Contracts: Solicitation of Statements of Interest From In-State Organizations — Kentucky — General notice.

58 FR 46198, September 1, 1993: HCFA Public Information Collection Requirements (ICR) Submitted to the Office of Management

and Budget (OMB) for Clearance (pertaining to prenatal services and assistance screening; home health agency treatment forms; conditions of participation for intermediate care facilities for the mentally retarded; State Medicaid eligibility quality control sample selection lists; prepaid health plan cost report; hospital survey report form; procedures for determining whether providers, practitioners, or other suppliers of services are liable for certain noncovered services; Medicare credit balance reporting requirements; Medicare provider cost report questionnaire form; Medicare current beneficiary survey rounds 7–10; sterilization regulation/consent form; PRO reconsideration and appeals information requirements; information collection requirements in HSQ-110, acquisition, protection and disclosure of PRO information; Medicare/Medicaid organ procurement organization's (OPO) request for certification) — Notice.

58 FR 47904, September 13, 1993: HCFA, Public Information Collection Requirements (ICR) Submitted to the Office of Management and Budget (OMB) for Clearance (pertaining to chronic renal disease medical evidence report; Medicare common claims form; Social Security Office report of State buy-in problem; Medicare physician survey form; beneficiary survey form; Medicaid payment rate changes for inpatient hospital or long term care services; home and community-based services: waiver requirements; Medicare peer review organizations reporting forms; uniform institutional provider claim form) — Notice.

58 FR 59270, November 8, 1993: HCFA Public Information Collection Requirements Submitted to the Office of Management and Budget (OMB) for Clearance (pertaining to formats for utilization and quality control peer review organizations (PROs); home health agency plan of treatment forms; State survey agency budget expenditure report and certification workload report; home health agency cost report; recordkeeping requirements in provider reimbursement manual; quarterly Medicaid statement of expenditures; Medicare contract application for Federally qualified health maintenance organizations; hospice survey and deficiencies report form; organ procurement agency/histocompatibility laboratory statement of reimbursable costs) — Notice.

58 FR 65186, December 13, 1993: Medicare Program; Peer Review Organization, General Criteria and Standards for Evaluating Performance of Contract Obligations — Notice with comment period.

60 FR 21824, May 3, 1995: Medicare Program; Peer Review Organization Contracts: Solicitation of Statements of Interest From In-State Organizations — Alaska, Delaware, the District of Columbia, Idaho, Kentucky, Maine, Nebraska, Nevada, South Carolina, Vermont, and Wyoming — Notice.

60 FR 39403, August 2, 1995: HCFA Public Information Collection Requirements Submitted for Public Comment and Recommendations (pertaining to PRO reporting forms; Oregon Medicaid reform demonstration; review functions of PRO's; medical records review under PPS; evaluation of Medicare cataract surgery alternate payment demonstration; home health agency survey and deficiencies report; CLIA survey forms; field testing of uniform needs assessment instrument for hospital discharge planning).

60 FR 63634, December 12, 1995: Office of Inspector General; Health Care Programs: Fraud and Abuse; Revisions to the PRO Sanctions Process — Final rule. See also correction at 61 FR 1841, January 24, 1996.

61 FR 4787, February 8, 1996: HCFA Public Information Collection Requirements Submitted for Public Comment: Submission for OMB Review (pertaining to Peer Review Organization reporting forms).

61 FR 29406, June 10, 1996: HCFA Agency Information Collection Activities: proposed Collection; Comment Request (pertaining to end stage renal disease application and survey and certification report forms; withholding Medicare payments to recover Medicaid overpayments; acquisition, protection, and disclosure of PRO information; clinical laboratory certification and recertification survey forms; CLIA laboratory personnel report forms; prepaid health plan cost reports; Medicare credit balance reporting requirements; statement of deficiencies and plan of correction requirements for organ procurement organizations; Medicare/Medicaid hospital survey report forms; advance directive requirements for Medicare and Medicaid; payment adjustments for sole community hospitals; survey reports for physical therapists in independent practice; HMO and CMP national data reporting requirements; identification of extension units of outpatient physical therapy and outpatient speech pathology providers; and fire safety survey reports).

61 FR 33532, June 27, 1996: HCFA Agency Information Collection Activities: Submission for OMB Review; Comment Request (pertaining to information collection requirements in PRO sanction regulations).

61 FR 34437, July 2, 1996: HCFA Agency Information Collection Activities: Submission for OMB Review; Comment Request (pertaining to Peer Review Organization procedures for reconsideration of initial decisions; Part B enrollment forms; certification of rural health clinics for Medicare participation; Medicaid utilization review requirements for home health agencies; State listings of Medicaid recipients in institutions and procedures for State inspection of care review; procedures for disenrollment of beneficiaries from HMOs or CMPs; effectiveness of telemedicine services; formats for PROs to submit data to HCFA; and request for accelerated payments forms for providers).

61 FR 43062, August 20, 1996: HCFA Agency Information Collection Activities: Submission for OMB Review; Comment request (pertaining to withholding Medicare payments to recover Medicaid overpayments; acquisition, protection, and disclosure of Peer Review Organization (PRO) information; cost reports for HMOs; and collection of credit balance information from health care providers).

61 FR 52951, October 9, 1996: HCFA Agency Information Collection Activities: Submission for OMB Review; Comment request (pertaining to Peer Review Organization Reconsiderations and Appeals; Part B enrollment forms; certification as a Rural Health Clinic; Medicaid utilization control programs; lists of Medicaid recipients in institutions; and business proposal formats for PROs).

62 FR 23140, April 29, 1997: Office of Inspector General: Health Care Programs: Fraud and Abuse; Revised PRO Sanctions for Failing to Meet Statutory Obligations — Final rule.

62 FR 35824, July 2, 1997: Medicare Program; Description of the Health Care Financing Administration's Evaluation Methodology for the Peer Review Organization 5th Scope of Work Contracts — Notice with comment period.

63 FR 4459, January 29, 1998: HCFA Agency Information Collection Activities: Proposed Collection; Comment request (pertaining to peer review organization contracts and solicitation of statements of interest from In-State Organizations).

63 FR 19504, April 20, 1998: HCFA Agency Information Collection Activities: Submission for OMB Review; Comment request (pertaining to peer review organization contracts; solicitation of statements of interest from in-State organizations).

63 FR 20639, April 27, 1998: HCFA Agency Information Collection Activities: Submission for OMB Review; Comment request (pertain-

ing to peer review organization contracts and solicitation of statements of interest from in-State organizations).

63 FR 40534, July 29, 1998: Medicare Program; Peer Review Organization Contracts: Solicitation of Statements of Interest from In-state Organizations — Alaska, Delaware, the District of Columbia, Hawaii, Idaho, Illinois, Kentucky, Maine, Nebraska, Nevada, South Carolina, Vermont, and Wyoming — Notice.

63 FR 48734, September 11, 1998: HCFA Agency Information Collection Activities: Proposed Collection; Comment request (pertaining to medical review activities under PPS by Peer Review Organizations; and survey and deficiency reports for home health agencies).

63 FR 63478, November 13, 1998: HCFA Agency Information Collection Activities: Proposed Collection; Comment request (pertaining to processing Medicare+Choice disenrollment requests from beneficiaries; creation of the Utilization and Quality Control Peer Review Organization; and rules for participation of HHA's in Medicare and review of plans of care for home health services).

1999

64 FR 5665, February 4, 1999: HCFA Agency Information Collection Activities: Proposed Collection; Comment request (pertaining to Medicare+Choice disenrollment forms, and utilization and quality control peer review organizations (PROs)).

64 FR 10478, March 4, 1999: HCFA Agency Information Collection Activities: Proposed Collection; Comment request (pertaining to information collection requirements in final peer review organization (PRO) sanction regulations).

64 FR 30340, June 7, 1999: HCFA Agency Information Collection Activities: Submission for OMB Review; Comment request (pertaining to information collection requirements in the final peer review organization (PRO) sanction regulations).

64 FR 36021, July 2, 1999: Medicare Program; July 19, 1999 Open Town Hall Meeting to Discusss the Implementation of the Peer Review Organizations' (PROs) Sixth Round Contract Activities — Notice of meeting.

64 FR 40017, July 23, 1999: HCFA Agency Information Collection Activities: Submission for OMB Review; Comment request (pertaining to acquisition, protection and disclosure of peer review organization (PRO) information).

64 FR 45266, August 19, 1999: HCFA Agency Information Collection Activities: Proposed Collection; Comment request (pertaining to PRO reconsiderations and appeals).

64 FR 45266, August 19, 1999: HCFA Agency Information Collection Activities: Proposed Collection; Comment request (pertaining to business proposal formats for utilization and quality control peer review organizations (PROs)).

64 FR 62681, November 17, 1999: HCFA Agency Information Collection Activities: Submission for OMB Review; Comment request (pertaining to peer review organization (PRO) reconsiderations and appeals).

64 FR 62681, November 17, 1999: HCFA Agency Information Collection Activities: Submission for OMB Review; Comment request (pertaining business proposal formats for utilization and quality control peer review organizations (PROs)).

2000

65 FR 24971, April 28, 2000: Medicare Program; Open Town Hall Meeting to Promote and Establish Partnerships between the Medicare Peer Review Organizations (PROs) and Entities in the Health Care Community to Foster Health Care Quality Improvement — May 15, 2000 — Notice of meeting.

65 FR 47738, August 3, 2000: HCFA Agency Information Collection Activities: Proposed Collection; Comment request (pertaining to Medicare beneficiary survey for Michigan PRO).

2001

66 FR 18781, April 11, 2001: HCFA Agency Information Collection Activities: Proposed Collection; Comment request (pertaining to Peer Review Organization contracts and solicitation of statements of interest).

66 FR 20997, April 26, 2001: Medicare program; Evaluation Criteria and Standards for Peer Review Organization 6th Round Contract—Notice

See § 4:18.

§ 8:19 SANCTIONS RECOMMENDED BY PEER REVIEW ORGANIZATIONS — Section 1156 [42 U.S.C.A. 1320c-5]

Regulations

42 CFR Part 456 — Utilization Control
42 CFR Part 475 — Peer Review Organizations
42 CFR Part 476 — Utilization and Quality Control Review
42 CFR Part 478 — Reconsiderations and Appeals
42 CFR Part 480 — Acquisition, Protection, and Disclosure of Peer Review Information
42 CFR Chapter V — Office of Inspector General — Health Care, Department of Health and Human Services
Subchapter A — General Provisions
Part 1000 — Introduction; General Definitions
Subchapter B — OIG Authorities
Part 1001 — Program Integrity: Medicare and State Health Care Programs
Part 1002 — Program Integrity: State-initiated Exclusion from Medicaid
Part 1003 — Civil Money Penalties, Assessments and Exclusions
Part 1004 — Imposition of Sanctions on Health Care Practitioners and Providers of Health Care Services by a Peer Review Organization
Part 1005 — Appeals of Exclusions, Civil Money Penalties and Assessments
Part 1006 — Investigational Inquiries
Part 1007 — State Medicaid Fraud Control Units
Part 1008 — Advisory Opinions by the OIG

55 FR 12205, April 2, 1990: Health Care Programs: Fraud and Abuse; Amendments to OIG Exclusion and CMP Authorities Resulting from Public Law 100–93, the Medicare and Medicaid Patient and Program Protection Act of 1987, Public Law 99–272, the Consolidated Omnibus Budget Reconciliation Act of 1985, and Public Law 100–360, the Medicare Catastrophic Coverage Act of 1988 — Proposed rule to amend 42 CFR Parts 1000, 1001, 1002, 1003, 1004, 1005, 1006, and 1007. See also correction published at 55 FR 17461, April 25, 1990.

55 FR 42907, October 24, 1990: Medicare Program; Standards Applied by Utilization and Quality Control Peer Review Organizations: Consideration of Remote Rural Location and Other Relevant Factors — Notice of policy and request for comments.

56 FR 29967, July 1, 1991: Medicare Peer Review Organization contracts: Solicitation of Statements of Interest from In-State Organizations (AK, ID, Me, VT, DC) — Notice.

56 FR 43790, September 4, 1991: Medicare Program; Peer Review Organizations: Revised Scopes of Work for Delaware, Missouri, Montana, Nebraska, New Jersey, Nevada, Oklahoma, Rhode Island, South Carolina, Washington, and Wyoming — Final notice.

57 FR 3298, January 29, 1992: Health Care Programs: Fraud and Abuse; Amendments to OIG Exclusion and CMP Authorities Resulting From Public Law 100–93 — Final rule affecting 42 CFR Parts 1001, 1002, 1003, 1004, 1005, 1006, and 1007. See also final rule and correction at 57 FR 9669, March 20, 1992; final rule affecting 42 CFR Parts 1001and 1005, with clarification at 58 FR 5617, January 22, 1993; and final rule affecting 42 CFR Part 1001, with correction, at 58 FR 40752, July 30, 1993.

57 FR 26871, June 16, 1992: Medicare Program; Peer Review Organizations: Revised Scopes of Work for the District of Columbia, Puerto Rico, the Virgin Islands, and All States Except Delaware, Florida, Missouri, Montana, Nebraska, Nevada, Oklahoma, Rhode Island, South Carolina, Washington, and Wyoming — Final notice. See also correction at 57 FR 35837, August 11, 1992.

57 FR 43462, September 21, 1992: Health Care Financing Administration Public Information Collection Requirements Submitted to the Office of Management and Budget for Clearance (pertaining to sole community home health agencies; physician/supplier overpayment reports; physician or supplier Medicare agreements; conditions of participation for rural health clinics; Medicare provider refunds; conditions of participation for comprehensive outpatient rehabilitation facilities; Medicaid income and eligibility verification system; Medicaid integrated review schedule; provider overpayment report; financial statement of Medicare provider debtors; negative case action review schedule for Medicaid quality control; outpatient resource costing study; Medicaid intermediate care facility for the mentally retarded or persons with related conditions survey report form; installment agreement of beneficiary refund of overpayment; PRO assumption of responsibilities; Medicare contractor administrative budget and cost reporting system forms; fire safety survey report forms; medical records review under prospective payment system; and Qualified Medicare Beneficiary supplement to the Medicare current beneficiary survey).

57 FR 46865, October 13, 1992: HCFA Public Information Collection Requirements Submitted to the Office of Management and Budget for Clearance (pertaining to impact of home health care plan management and evaluation; end-stage renal disease medical case

review; Medicare/Medicaid hospital swing-bed survey report form; quarterly Medicaid statement of expenditures; Medicaid program budget report; information collection requirements in final peer review organization sanction regulations; appeals procedures for determinations that affect participation in Medicare; request for medical review information for Part B intermediary outpatient therapy bills and other Part B outpatient bills; and Medicaid limitations on provider-related donations and health care-related taxes, and limitations on payment to disproportionate share hospitals).

57 FR 47779, October 20, 1992: Medicare Program; Payment to Hospitals for Furnishing Photocopies to Peer Review Organizations — Final rule affecting 42 CFR Parts 412 and 466.

57 FR 53760, November 12, 1992: Privacy Act of 1974; Report of Altered System — Notice of alteration of an existing system of records (pertaining to peer review organization data management information).

58 FR 12042, March 2, 1993: Medicare Program; Peer Review Organizations: New PRO Contracts for All States and Territories and the District of Columbia — Notice.

58 FR 17417, April 2, 1993: Medicare Program; Peer Review Organization Contracts: Solicitation of Statements of Interest From In-State Organizations — Kentucky — General notice.

58 FR 46198, September 1, 1993: HCFA Public Information Collection Requirements (ICR) Submitted to the Office of Management and Budget (OMB) for Clearance (pertaining to prenatal services and assistance screening; home health agency treatment forms; conditions of participation for intermediate care facilities for the mentally retarded; State Medicaid eligibility quality control sample selection lists; prepaid health plan cost report; hospital survey report form; procedures for determining whether providers, practitioners, or other suppliers of services are liable for certain noncovered services; Medicare credit balance reporting requirements; Medicare provider cost report questionnaire form; Medicare current beneficiary survey rounds 7–10; sterilization regulation/consent form; PRO reconsideration and appeals information requirements; information collection requirements in HSQ-110, acquisition, protection and disclosure of PRO information; Medicare/Medicaid organ procurement organization's (OPO) request for certification) — Notice.

58 FR 47904, September 13, 1993: HCFA, Public Information Collection Requirements (ICR) Submitted to the Office of Management

and Budget (OMB) for Clearance (pertaining to chronic renal disease medical evidence report; Medicare common claims form; Social Security Office report of State buy-in problem; Medicare physician survey form; beneficiary survey form; Medicaid payment rate changes for inpatient hospital or long term care services; home and community-based services: waiver requirements; Medicare peer review organizations reporting forms; uniform institutional provider claim form) — Notice.

58 FR 59270, November 8, 1993: HCFA Public Information Collection Requirements Submitted to the Office of Management and Budget (OMB) for Clearance (pertaining to formats for utilization and quality control peer review organizations (PROs); home health agency plan of treatment forms; State survey agency budget expenditure report and certification workload report; home health agency cost report; recordkeeping requirements in provider reimbursement manual; quarterly Medicaid statement of expenditures; Medicare contract application for Federally qualified health maintenance organizations; hospice survey and deficiencies report form; organ procurement agency/histocompatibility laboratory statement of reimbursable costs) — Notice.

58 FR 65186, December 13, 1993: Medicare Program; Peer Review Organization, General Criteria and Standards for Evaluating Performance of Contract Obligations — Notice with comment period.

60 FR 21824, May 3, 1995: Medicare Program; Peer Review Organization Contracts: Solicitation of Statements of Interest From In-State Organizations — Alaska, Delaware, the District of Columbia, Idaho, Kentucky, Maine, Nebraska, Nevada, South Carolina, Vermont, and Wyoming — Notice.

60 FR 39403, August 2, 1995: HCFA Public Information Collection Requirements Submitted for Public Comment and Recommendations (pertaining to PRO reporting forms; Oregon Medicaid reform demonstration; review functions of PRO's; medical records review under PPS; evaluation of Medicare cataract surgery alternate payment demonstration; home health agency survey and deficiencies report; CLIA survey forms; field testing of uniform needs assessment instrument for hospital discharge planning).

60 FR 63634, December 12, 1995: Office of Inspector General; Health Care Programs: Fraud and Abuse; Revisions to the PRO Sanctions Process — Final rule. See also correction at 61 FR 1841, January 24, 1996.

61 FR 4787, February 8, 1996: HCFA Public Information Collection Requirements Submitted for Public Comment: Submission for OMB Review (pertaining to Peer Review Organization reporting forms).

61 FR 29406, June 10, 1996: HCFA Agency Information Collection Activities: proposed Collection; Comment Request (pertaining to end stage renal disease application and survey and certification report forms; withholding Medicare payments to recover Medicaid overpayments; acquisition, protection, and disclosure of PRO information; clinical laboratory certification and recertification survey forms; CLIA laboratory personnel report forms; prepaid health plan cost reports; Medicare credit balance reporting requirements; statement of deficiencies and plan of correction requirements for organ procurement organizations; Medicare/Medicaid hospital survey report forms; advance directive requirements for Medicare and Medicaid; payment adjustments for sole community hospitals; survey reports for physical therapists in independent practice; HMO and CMP national data reporting requirements; identification of extension units of outpatient physical therapy and outpatient speech pathology providers; and fire safety survey reports).

61 FR 33532, June 27, 1996: HCFA Agency Information Collection Activities: Submission for OMB Review; Comment Request (pertaining to information collection requirements in PRO sanction regulations).

61 FR 34437, July 2, 1996: HCFA Agency Information Collection Activities: Submission for OMB Review; Comment Request (pertaining to Peer Review Organization procedures for reconsideration of initial decisions; Part B enrollment forms; certification of rural health clinics for Medicare participation; Medicaid utilization review requirements for home health agencies; State listings of Medicaid recipients in institutions and procedures for State inspection of care review; procedures for disenrollment of beneficiaries from HMOs or CMPs; effectiveness of telemedicine services; formats for PROs to submit data to HCFA; and request for accelerated payments forms for providers).

61 FR 43062, August 20, 1996: HCFA Agency Information Collection Activities: Submission for OMB Review; Comment request (pertaining to withholding Medicare payments to recover Medicaid overpayments; acquisition, protection, and disclosure of Peer Review Organization (PRO) information; cost reports for HMOs; and collection of credit balance information from health care providers).

61 FR 52951, October 9, 1996: HCFA Agency Information Collection Activities: Submission for OMB Review; Comment request (pertaining to Peer Review Organization Reconsiderations and Appeals; Part B enrollment forms; certification as a Rural Health Clinic; Medicaid utilization control programs; lists of Medicaid recipients in institutions; and business proposal formats for PROs).

62 FR 23140, April 29, 1997: Office of Inspector General: Health Care Programs: Fraud and Abuse; Revised PRO Sanctions for Failing to Meet Statutory Obligations — Final rule.

62 FR 35824, July 2, 1997: Medicare Program; Description of the Health Care Financing Administration's Evaluation Methodology for the Peer Review Organization 5th Scope of Work Contracts — Notice with comment period.

63 FR 4459, January 29, 1998: HCFA Agency Information Collection Activities: Proposed Collection; Comment request (pertaining to peer review organization contracts and solicitation of statements of interest from In-State Organizations).

63 FR 19504, April 20, 1998: HCFA Agency Information Collection Activities: Submission for OMB Review; Comment request (pertaining to peer review organization contracts; solicitation of statements of interest from in-State organizations).

63 FR 20639, April 27, 1998: HCFA Agency Information Collection Activities: Submission for OMB Review; Comment request (pertaining to peer review organization contracts and solicitation of statements of interest from in-State organizations).

63 FR 40534, July 29, 1998: Medicare Program; Peer Review Organization Contracts: Solicitation of Statements of Interest from In-state Organizations — Alaska, Delaware, the District of Columbia, Hawaii, Idaho, Illinois, Kentucky, Maine, Nebraska, Nevada, South Carolina, Vermont, and Wyoming — Notice.

63 FR 48734, September 11, 1998: HCFA Agency Information Collection Activities: Proposed Collection; Comment request (pertaining to medical review activities under PPS by Peer Review Organizations; and survey and deficiency reports for home health agencies).

63 FR 63478, November 13, 1998: HCFA Agency Information Collection Activities: Proposed Collection; Comment request (pertaining to processing Medicare+Choice disenrollment requests from beneficiaries; creation of the Utilization and Quality Control Peer Review Organization; and rules for participation of HHA's in Medicare and review of plans of care for home health services).

1999

64 FR 5665, February 4, 1999: HCFA Agency Information Collection Activities: Proposed Collection; Comment request (pertaining to Medicare+Choice disenrollment forms, and utilization and quality control peer review organizations (PROs)).

64 FR 10478, March 4, 1999: HCFA Agency Information Collection Activities: Proposed Collection; Comment request (pertaining to information collection requirements in final peer review organization (PRO) sanction regulations).

64 FR 30340, June 7, 1999: HCFA Agency Information Collection Activities: Submission for OMB Review; Comment request (pertaining to information collection requirements in the final peer review organization (PRO) sanction regulations).

64 FR 36021, July 2, 1999: Medicare Program; July 19, 1999 Open Town Hall Meeting to Discusss the Implementation of the Peer Review Organizations' (PROs) Sixth Round Contract Activities — Notice of meeting.

64 FR 40017, July 23, 1999: HCFA Agency Information Collection Activities: Submission for OMB Review; Comment request (pertaining to acquisition, protection and disclosure of peer review organization (PRO) information).

64 FR 45266, August 19, 1999: HCFA Agency Information Collection Activities: Proposed Collection; Comment request (pertaining to PRO reconsiderations and appeals).

64 FR 45266, August 19, 1999: HCFA Agency Information Collection Activities: Proposed Collection; Comment request (pertaining to business proposal formats for utilization and quality control peer review organizations (PROs)).

64 FR 62681, November 17, 1999: HCFA Agency Information Collection Activities: Submission for OMB Review; Comment request (pertaining to peer review organization (PRO) reconsiderations and appeals).

64 FR 62681, November 17, 1999: HCFA Agency Information Collection Activities: Submission for OMB Review; Comment request (pertaining business proposal formats for utilization and quality control peer review organizations (PROs)).

2000

65 FR 24971, April 28, 2000: Medicare Program; Open Town Hall Meeting to Promote and Establish Partnerships between the Medicare Peer Review Organizations (PROs) and Entities in the Health

Care Community to Foster Health Care Quality Improvement — May 15, 2000 — Notice of meeting.

65 FR 47738, August 3, 2000: HCFA Agency Information Collection Activities: Proposed Collection; Comment request (pertaining to Medicare beneficiary survey for Michigan PRO).

2001

66 FR 18781, April 11, 2001: HCFA Agency Information Collection Activities: Proposed Collection; Comment request (pertaining to Peer Review Organization contracts and solicitation of statements of interest).

66 FR 20997, April 26, 2001: Medicare program; Evaluation Criteria and Standards for Peer Review Organization 6th Round Contract—Notice

See § 4:19.

§ 8:20 UNLAWFUL DISCLOSURE OF INFORMATION OBTAINED BY PEER REVIEW ORGANIZATIONS — Section 1160 [42 U.S.C.A. 1320c-9]

Regulations

42 CFR Part 456 — Utilization Control

42 CFR Part 475 — Peer Review Organizations

42 CFR Part 476 — Utilization and Quality Control Review

42 CFR Part 478 — Reconsiderations and Appeals

42 CFR Part 480 — Acquisition, Protection, and Disclosure of Peer Review Information

42 CFR Chapter V — Office of Inspector General — Health Care, Department of Health and Human Services

Subchapter A — General Provisions

Part 1000 — Introduction; General Definitions

Subchapter B — OIG Authorities

Part 1001 — Program Integrity: Medicare and State Health Care Programs

Part 1002 — Program Integrity: State-initiated Exclusion from Medicaid

Part 1004 — Imposition of Sanctions on Health Care Practitioners and Providers of Health Care Services by a Peer Review Organization

Part 1005 — Appeals of Exclusions, Civil Money Penalties and Assessments

Part 1006 — Investigational Inquiries

Part 1007 — State Medicaid Fraud Control Units

Part 1008 — Advisory Opinions by the OIG

55 FR 12205, April 2, 1990: Health Care Programs: Fraud and Abuse; Amendments to OIG Exclusion and CMP Authorities Resulting from Public Law 100–93, the Medicare and Medicaid Patient and Program Protection Act of 1987, Public Law 99–272, the Consolidated Omnibus Budget Reconciliation Act of 1985, and Public Law 100–360, the Medicare Catastrophic Coverage Act of 1988 — Proposed rule to amend 42 CFR Parts 1000, 1001, 1002, 1003, 1004, 1005, 1006, and 1007. See also correction published at 55 FR 17461, April 25, 1990.

55 FR 42907, October 24, 1990: Medicare Program; Standards Applied by Utilization and Quality Control Peer Review Organizations: Consideration of Remote Rural Location and Other Relevant Factors — Notice of policy and request for comments.

56 FR 29967, July 1, 1991: Medicare Peer Review Organization contracts: Solicitation of Statements of Interest from In-State Organizations (AK, ID, Me, VT, DC) — Notice.

56 FR 43790, September 4, 1991: Medicare Program; Peer Review Organizations: Revised Scopes of Work for Delaware, Missouri, Montana, Nebraska, New Jersey, Nevada, Oklahoma, Rhode Island, South Carolina, Washington, and Wyoming — Final notice.

57 FR 3298, January 29, 1992: Health Care Programs: Fraud and Abuse; Amendments to OIG Exclusion and CMP Authorities Resulting From Public Law 100–93 — Final rule affecting 42 CFR Parts 1001, 1002, 1003, 1004, 1005, 1006, and 1007. See also final rule and correction at 57 FR 9669, March 20, 1992; final rule affecting 42 CFR Parts 1001and 1005, with clarification at 58 FR 5617, January 22, 1993; and final rule affecting 42 CFR Part 1001, with correction, at 58 FR 40752, July 30, 1993.

57 FR 26871, June 16, 1992: Medicare Program; Peer Review Organizations: Revised Scopes of Work for the District of Columbia, Puerto Rico, the Virgin Islands, and All States Except Delaware, Florida, Missouri, Montana, Nebraska, Nevada, Oklahoma, Rhode Island, South Carolina, Washington, and Wyoming — Final notice. See also correction at 57 FR 35837, August 11, 1992.

57 FR 43462, September 21, 1992: Health Care Financing Administration Public Information Collection Requirements Submitted to

the Office of Management and Budget for Clearance (pertaining to sole community home health agencies; physician/supplier overpayment reports; physician or supplier Medicare agreements; conditions of participation for rural health clinics; Medicare provider refunds; conditions of participation for comprehensive outpatient rehabilitation facilities; Medicaid income and eligibility verification system; Medicaid integrated review schedule; provider overpayment report; financial statement of Medicare provider debtors; negative case action review schedule for Medicaid quality control; outpatient resource costing study; Medicaid intermediate care facility for the mentally retarded or persons with related conditions survey report form; installment agreement of beneficiary refund of overpayment; PRO assumption of responsibilities; Medicare contractor administrative budget and cost reporting system forms; fire safety survey report forms; medical records review under prospective payment system; and Qualified Medicare Beneficiary supplement to the Medicare current beneficiary survey).

57 FR 46865, October 13, 1992: HCFA Public Information Collection Requirements Submitted to the Office of Management and Budget for Clearance (pertaining to impact of home health care plan management and evaluation; end-stage renal disease medical case review; Medicare/Medicaid hospital swing-bed survey report form; quarterly Medicaid statement of expenditures; Medicaid program budget report; information collection requirements in final peer review organization sanction regulations; appeals procedures for determinations that affect participation in Medicare; request for medical review information for Part B intermediary outpatient therapy bills and other Part B outpatient bills; and Medicaid limitations on provider-related donations and health care-related taxes, and limitations on payment to disproportionate share hospitals).

57 FR 47779, October 20, 1992: Medicare Program; Payment to Hospitals for Furnishing Photocopies to Peer Review Organizations — Final rule affecting 42 CFR Parts 412 and 466.

57 FR 53760, November 12, 1992: Privacy Act of 1974; Report of Altered System — Notice of alteration of an existing system of records (pertaining to peer review organization data management information).

58 FR 12042, March 2, 1993: Medicare Program; Peer Review Organizations: New PRO Contracts for All States and Territories and the District of Columbia — Notice.

58 FR 17417, April 2, 1993: Medicare Program; Peer Review Organization Contracts: Solicitation of Statements of Interest From In-State Organizations — Kentucky — General notice.

58 FR 46198, September 1, 1993: HCFA Public Information Collection Requirements (ICR) Submitted to the Office of Management and Budget (OMB) for Clearance (pertaining to prenatal services and assistance screening; home health agency treatment forms; conditions of participation for intermediate care facilities for the mentally retarded; State Medicaid eligibility quality control sample selection lists; prepaid health plan cost report; hospital survey report form; procedures for determining whether providers, practitioners, or other suppliers of services are liable for certain noncovered services; Medicare credit balance reporting requirements; Medicare provider cost report questionnaire form; Medicare current beneficiary survey rounds 7–10; sterilization regulation/consent form; PRO reconsideration and appeals information requirements; information collection requirements in HSQ-110, acquisition, protection and disclosure of PRO information; Medicare/Medicaid organ procurement organization's (OPO) request for certification) — Notice.

58 FR 47904, September 13, 1993: HCFA, Public Information Collection Requirements (ICR) Submitted to the Office of Management and Budget (OMB) for Clearance (pertaining to chronic renal disease medical evidence report; Medicare common claims form; Social Security Office report of State buy-in problem; Medicare physician survey form; beneficiary survey form; Medicaid payment rate changes for inpatient hospital or long term care services; home and community-based services: waiver requirements; Medicare peer review organizations reporting forms; uniform institutional provider claim form) — Notice.

58 FR 59270, November 8, 1993: HCFA Public Information Collection Requirements Submitted to the Office of Management and Budget (OMB) for Clearance (pertaining to formats for utilization and quality control peer review organizations (PROs); home health agency plan of treatment forms; State survey agency budget expenditure report and certification workload report; home health agency cost report; recordkeeping requirements in provider reimbursement manual; quarterly Medicaid statement of expenditures; Medicare contract application for Federally qualified health maintenance organizations; hospice survey and deficiencies report form; organ

procurement agency/histocompatibility laboratory statement of reimbursable costs) — Notice.

58 FR 65186, December 13, 1993: Medicare Program; Peer Review Organization, General Criteria and Standards for Evaluating Performance of Contract Obligations — Notice with comment period.

60 FR 21824, May 3, 1995: Medicare Program; Peer Review Organization Contracts: Solicitation of Statements of Interest From In-State Organizations — Alaska, Delaware, the District of Columbia, Idaho, Kentucky, Maine, Nebraska, Nevada, South Carolina, Vermont, and Wyoming — Notice.

60 FR 39403, August 2, 1995: HCFA Public Information Collection Requirements Submitted for Public Comment and Recommendations (pertaining to PRO reporting forms; Oregon Medicaid reform demonstration; review functions of PRO's; medical records review under PPS; evaluation of Medicare cataract surgery alternate payment demonstration; home health agency survey and deficiencies report; CLIA survey forms; field testing of uniform needs assessment instrument for hospital discharge planning).

60 FR 63634, December 12, 1995: Office of Inspector General; Health Care Programs: Fraud and Abuse; Revisions to the PRO Sanctions Process — Final rule. See also correction at 61 FR 1841, January 24, 1996.

61 FR 4787, February 8, 1996: HCFA Public Information Collection Requirements Submitted for Public Comment: Submission for OMB Review (pertaining to Peer Review Organization reporting forms).

61 FR 29406, June 10, 1996: HCFA Agency Information Collection Activities: proposed Collection; Comment Request (pertaining to end stage renal disease application and survey and certification report forms; withholding Medicare payments to recover Medicaid overpayments; acquisition, protection, and disclosure of PRO information; clinical laboratory certification and recertification survey forms; CLIA laboratory personnel report forms; prepaid health plan cost reports; Medicare credit balance reporting requirements; statement of deficiencies and plan of correction requirements for organ procurement organizations; Medicare/Medicaid hospital survey report forms; advance directive requirements for Medicare and Medicaid; payment adjustments for sole community hospitals; survey reports for physical therapists in independent practice; HMO and CMP national data reporting requirements; identification of extension

units of outpatient physical therapy and outpatient speech pathology providers; and fire safety survey reports).

61 FR 33532, June 27, 1996: HCFA Agency Information Collection Activities: Submission for OMB Review; Comment Request (pertaining to information collection requirements in PRO sanction regulations).

61 FR 34437, July 2, 1996: HCFA Agency Information Collection Activities: Submission for OMB Review; Comment Request (pertaining to Peer Review Organization procedures for reconsideration of initial decisions; Part B enrollment forms; certification of rural health clinics for Medicare participation; Medicaid utilization review requirements for home health agencies; State listings of Medicaid recipients in institutions and procedures for State inspection of care review; procedures for disenrollment of beneficiaries from HMOs or CMPs; effectiveness of telemedicine services; formats for PROs to submit data to HCFA; and request for accelerated payments forms for providers).

61 FR 43062, August 20, 1996: HCFA Agency Information Collection Activities: Submission for OMB Review; Comment request (pertaining to withholding Medicare payments to recover Medicaid overpayments; acquisition, protection, and disclosure of Peer Review Organization (PRO) information; cost reports for HMOs; and collection of credit balance information from health care providers).

61 FR 52951, October 9, 1996: HCFA Agency Information Collection Activities: Submission for OMB Review; Comment request (pertaining to Peer Review Organization Reconsiderations and Appeals; Part B enrollment forms; certification as a Rural Health Clinic; Medicaid utilization control programs; lists of Medicaid recipients in institutions; and business proposal formats for PROs).

62 FR 23140, April 29, 1997: Office of Inspector General: Health Care Programs: Fraud and Abuse; Revised PRO Sanctions for Failing to Meet Statutory Obligations — Final rule.

62 FR 35824, July 2, 1997: Medicare Program; Description of the Health Care Financing Administration's Evaluation Methodology for the Peer Review Organization 5th Scope of Work Contracts — Notice with comment period.

63 FR 4459, January 29, 1998: HCFA Agency Information Collection Activities: Proposed Collection; Comment request (pertaining to peer review organization contracts and solicitation of statements of interest from In-State Organizations).

63 FR 19504, April 20, 1998: HCFA Agency Information Collection Activities: Submission for OMB Review; Comment request (pertaining to peer review organization contracts; solicitation of statements of interest from in-State organizations).

63 FR 20639, April 27, 1998: HCFA Agency Information Collection Activities: Submission for OMB Review; Comment request (pertaining to peer review organization contracts and solicitation of statements of interest from in-State organizations).

63 FR 40534, July 29, 1998: Medicare Program; Peer Review Organization Contracts: Solicitation of Statements of Interest from In-state Organizations — Alaska, Delaware, the District of Columbia, Hawaii, Idaho, Illinois, Kentucky, Maine, Nebraska, Nevada, South Carolina, Vermont, and Wyoming — Notice.

63 FR 48734, September 11, 1998: HCFA Agency Information Collection Activities: Proposed Collection; Comment request (pertaining to medical review activities under PPS by Peer Review Organizations; and survey and deficiency reports for home health agencies).

63 FR 63478, November 13, 1998: HCFA Agency Information Collection Activities: Proposed Collection; Comment request (pertaining to processing Medicare+Choice disenrollment requests from beneficiaries; creation of the Utilization and Quality Control Peer Review Organization; and rules for participation of HHA's in Medicare and review of plans of care for home health services).

1999

64 FR 5665, February 4, 1999: HCFA Agency Information Collection Activities: Proposed Collection; Comment request (pertaining to Medicare+Choice disenrollment forms, and utilization and quality control peer review organizations (PROs)).

64 FR 10478, March 4, 1999: HCFA Agency Information Collection Activities: Proposed Collection; Comment request (pertaining to information collection requirements in final peer review organization (PRO) sanction regulations).

64 FR 30340, June 7, 1999: HCFA Agency Information Collection Activities: Submission for OMB Review; Comment request (pertaining to information collection requirements in the final peer review organization (PRO) sanction regulations).

64 FR 36021, July 2, 1999: Medicare Program; July 19, 1999 Open Town Hall Meeting to Discusss the Implementation of the Peer

Review Organizations' (PROs) Sixth Round Contract Activities — Notice of meeting.

64 FR 40017, July 23, 1999: HCFA Agency Information Collection Activities: Submission for OMB Review; Comment request (pertaining to acquisition, protection and disclosure of peer review organization (PRO) information).

64 FR 45266, August 19, 1999: HCFA Agency Information Collection Activities: Proposed Collection; Comment request (pertaining to PRO reconsiderations and appeals).

64 FR 45266, August 19, 1999: HCFA Agency Information Collection Activities: Proposed Collection; Comment request (pertaining to business proposal formats for utilization and quality control peer review organizations (PROs)).

64 FR 62681, November 17, 1999: HCFA Agency Information Collection Activities: Submission for OMB Review; Comment request (pertaining to peer review organization (PRO) reconsiderations and appeals).

64 FR 62681, November 17, 1999: HCFA Agency Information Collection Activities: Submission for OMB Review; Comment request (pertaining business proposal formats for utilization and quality control peer review organizations (PROs)).

2000

65 FR 24971, April 28, 2000: Medicare Program; Open Town Hall Meeting to Promote and Establish Partnerships between the Medicare Peer Review Organizations (PROs) and Entities in the Health Care Community to Foster Health Care Quality Improvement — May 15, 2000 — Notice of meeting.

65 FR 47738, August 3, 2000: HCFA Agency Information Collection Activities: Proposed Collection; Comment request (pertaining to Medicare beneficiary survey for Michigan PRO).

2001

66 FR 18781, April 11, 2001: HCFA Agency Information Collection Activities: Proposed Collection; Comment request (pertaining to Peer Review Organization contracts and solicitation of statements of interest).

66 FR 20997, April 26, 2001: Medicare program; Evaluation Criteria and Standards for Peer Review Organization 6th Round Contract—Notice

See § 4:20.

§ 8:21 DISQUALIFICATION OF PHYSICIANS FROM GIVING SECOND OPINIONS ABOUT SURGERY — Section 1164(b)(4)(D) [42 U.S.C.A. 1320c-3(b)(4)(D)] — NOTE: This sanction was repealed effective October 31, 1994, by section 156(a)(1) of the Social Security Act Amendments of 1994, P.L. 103–432.

Regulations

42 CFR Part 456 — Utilization Control

42 CFR Part 462 — Peer Review Organizations

42 CFR Part 466 — Utilization and Quality Control Review

42 CFR Part 473 — Reconsiderations and Appeals

42 CFR Part 476 — Acquisition, Protection, and Disclosure of Peer Review Information

42 CFR Chapter V — Office of Inspector General — Health Care, Department of Health and Human Services

Subchapter A — General Provisions

Part 1000 — Introduction; General Definitions

Subchapter B — OIG Authorities

Part 1001 — Program Integrity: Medicare and State Health Care Programs

Part 1002 — Program Integrity: State-initiated Exclusion from Medicaid

Part 1004 — Imposition of Sanctions on Health Care Practitioners and Providers of Health Care Services by a Peer Review Organization

Part 1005 — Appeals of Exclusions, Civil Money Penalties and Assessments

Part 1006 — Investigational Inquiries

Part 1007 — State Medicaid Fraud Control Units

Part 1008 — Advisory Opinions by the OIG

55 FR 12205, April 2, 1990: Health Care Programs: Fraud and Abuse; Amendments to OIG Exclusion and CMP Authorities Resulting from Public Law 100–93, the Medicare and Medicaid Patient and Program Protection Act of 1987, Public Law 99–272, the Consolidated Omnibus Budget Reconciliation Act of 1985, and Public Law 100–360, the Medicare Catastrophic Coverage Act of 1988 — Proposed rule to amend 42 CFR Parts 1000, 1001, 1002, 1003, 1004, 1005, 1006, and 1007. See also correction published at 55 FR 17461, April 25, 1990.

55 FR 42907, October 24, 1990: Medicare Program; Standards Applied by Utilization and Quality Control Peer Review Organizations: Consideration of Remote Rural Location and Other Relevant Factors — Notice of policy and request for comments.

56 FR 29967, July 1, 1991: Medicare Peer Review Organization contracts: Solicitation of Statements of Interest from In-State Organizations (AK, ID, Me, VT, DC) — Notice.

56 FR 43790, September 4, 1991: Medicare Program; Peer Review Organizations: Revised Scopes of Work for Delaware, Missouri, Montana, Nebraska, New Jersey, Nevada, Oklahoma, Rhode Island, South Carolina, Washington, and Wyoming — Final notice.

57 FR 3298, January 29, 1992: Health Care Programs: Fraud and Abuse; Amendments to OIG Exclusion and CMP Authorities Resulting From Public Law 100–93 — Final rule affecting 42 CFR Parts 1001, 1002, 1003, 1004, 1005, 1006, and 1007. See also final rule and correction at 57 FR 9669, March 20, 1992; final rule affecting 42 CFR Parts 1001and 1005, with clarification at 58 FR 5617, January 22, 1993; and final rule affecting 42 CFR Part 1001, with correction, at 58 FR 40752, July 30, 1993.

57 FR 26871, June 16, 1992: Medicare Program; Peer Review Organizations: Revised Scopes of Work for the District of Columbia, Puerto Rico, the Virgin Islands, and All States Except Delaware, Florida, Missouri, Montana, Nebraska, Nevada, Oklahoma, Rhode Island, South Carolina, Washington, and Wyoming — Final notice. See also correction at 57 FR 35837, August 11, 1992.

57 FR 43462, September 21, 1992: Health Care Financing Administration Public Information Collection Requirements Submitted to the Office of Management and Budget for Clearance (pertaining to sole community home health agencies; physician/supplier overpayment reports; physician or supplier Medicare agreements; conditions of participation for rural health clinics; Medicare provider refunds; conditions of participation for comprehensive outpatient rehabilitation facilities; Medicaid income and eligibility verification system; Medicaid integrated review schedule; provider overpayment report; financial statement of Medicare provider debtors; negative case action review schedule for Medicaid quality control; outpatient resource costing study; Medicaid intermediate care facility for the mentally retarded or persons with related conditions survey report form; installment agreement of beneficiary refund of overpayment; PRO assumption of responsibilities; Medicare contractor administrative budget and cost reporting system forms; fire safety survey

report forms; medical records review under prospective payment system; and Qualified Medicare Beneficiary supplement to the Medicare current beneficiary survey).

57 FR 46865, October 13, 1992: HCFA Public Information Collection Requirements Submitted to the Office of Management and Budget for Clearance (pertaining to impact of home health care plan management and evaluation; end-stage renal disease medical case review; Medicare/Medicaid hospital swing-bed survey report form; quarterly Medicaid statement of expenditures; Medicaid program budget report; information collection requirements in final peer review organization sanction regulations; appeals procedures for determinations that affect participation in Medicare; request for medical review information for Part B intermediary outpatient therapy bills and other Part B outpatient bills; and Medicaid limitations on provider-related donations and health care-related taxes, and limitations on payment to disproportionate share hospitals).

57 FR 47779, October 20, 1992: Medicare Program; Payment to Hospitals for Furnishing Photocopies to Peer Review Organizations — Final rule affecting 42 CFR Parts 412 and 466.

57 FR 53760, November 12, 1992: Privacy Act of 1974; Report of Altered System — Notice of alteration of an existing system of records (pertaining to peer review organization data management information).

58 FR 12042, March 2, 1993: Medicare Program; Peer Review Organizations: New PRO Contracts for All States and Territories and the District of Columbia — Notice.

58 FR 17417, April 2, 1993: Medicare Program; Peer Review Organization Contracts: Solicitation of Statements of Interest From In-State Organizations — Kentucky — General notice.

58 FR 46198, September 1, 1993: HCFA Public Information Collection Requirements (ICR) Submitted to the Office of Management and Budget (OMB) for Clearance (pertaining to prenatal services and assistance screening; home health agency treatment forms; conditions of participation for intermediate care facilities for the mentally retarded; State Medicaid eligibility quality control sample selection lists; prepaid health plan cost report; hospital survey report form; procedures for determining whether providers, practitioners, or other suppliers of services are liable for certain noncovered services; Medicare credit balance reporting requirements; Medicare provider cost report questionnaire form; Medicare current beneficiary survey rounds 7–10; sterilization regula-

tion/consent form; PRO reconsideration and appeals information requirements; information collection requirements in HSQ-110, acquisition, protection and disclosure of PRO information; Medicare/Medicaid organ procurement organization's (OPO) request for certification) — Notice.

58 FR 47904, September 13, 1993: HCFA, Public Information Collection Requirements (ICR) Submitted to the Office of Management and Budget (OMB) for Clearance (pertaining to chronic renal disease medical evidence report; Medicare common claims form; Social Security Office report of State buy-in problem; Medicare physician survey form; beneficiary survey form; Medicaid payment rate changes for inpatient hospital or long term care services; home and community-based services: waiver requirements; Medicare peer review organizations reporting forms; uniform institutional provider claim form) — Notice.

58 FR 59270, November 8, 1993: HCFA Public Information Collection Requirements Submitted to the Office of Management and Budget (OMB) for Clearance (pertaining to formats for utilization and quality control peer review organizations (PROs); home health agency plan of treatment forms; State survey agency budget expenditure report and certification workload report; home health agency cost report; recordkeeping requirements in provider reimbursement manual; quarterly Medicaid statement of expenditures; Medicare contract application for Federally qualified health maintenance organizations; hospice survey and deficiencies report form; organ procurement agency/histocompatibility laboratory statement of reimbursable costs) — Notice.

58 FR 65186, December 13, 1993: Medicare Program; Peer Review Organization, General Criteria and Standards for Evaluating Performance of Contract Obligations — Notice with comment period.

See § 4:21.

Chapter 9

REGULATIONS: SANCTIONS IN THE HEALTH CARE QUALITY IMPROVEMENT ACT OF 1986

§ 9:1 FAILURE BY HEALTH CARE ENTITIES TO REPORT ADVERSE ACTIONS AGAINST PHYSICIANS — Section 411(b) and Section 423(c)(1) [42 U.S.C.S. 11111(b) and 11133(c)(1)]

Regulations

42 CFR Part 401, Subpart B — Confidentiality and Disclosure
42 CFR Part 420 — Program Integrity: Medicare
42 CFR Part 455 — Program Integrity: Medicaid

42 CFR Part 456 — Utilization Control

42 CFR Part 462 — Peer Review Organizations

42 CFR Part 466 — Utilization and Quality Control Review

42 CFR Part 476 — Acquisition, Protection, and Disclosure of Peer Review Information

42 CFR Chapter V — Office of Inspector General — Health Care, Department of Health and Human Services

Subchapter A — General Provisions

Part 1000 — Introduction; General Definitions

Subchapter B — OIG Authorities

Part 1001 — Program Integrity: Medicare and State Health Care Programs

Part 1002 — Program Integrity: State–initiated Exclusion from Medicaid

Part 1003 — Civil Money Penalties, Assessments and Exclusions

Part 1004 — Imposition of Sanctions on Health Care Practitioners and Providers of Health Care Services by a Peer Review Organization

Part 1005 — Appeals of Exclusions, Civil Money Penalties and Assessments

Part 1006 — Investigational Inquiries

Part 1007 — State Medicaid Fraud Control Units

Part 1008 — Advisory Opinions by the OIG

54 FR 42722, October 17, 1989: National Practitioner Data Bank for Adverse Information on Physicians and Other Health Care Practitioners — Final regulations [45 CFR Part 60]

56 FR 28488, June 21, 1991: Civil Money Penalties for Failure to Report Medical Malpractice Payments and for Breaching the Confidentiality of Information — Final rule affecting 42 CFR Part 1003.

61 FR 4788, February 8, 1996: Health Resources and Services Administration National Practitioner Data Bank: Change in User Fee—Notice.

63 FR 4460, January 29, 1998: Health Resources and Services Administration: National Practitioner Data Bank; Change in User Fee and Elimination of Diskette Queries.

63 FR 5811, February 4, 1998: Health Resources and Services Administration: National Practitioner Data Bank; Change in User Fee and Elimination of Diskette Queries. See also withdrawal at 63 FR 7421, February 13, 1998.

63 FR 7812, February 17, 1998: Health Resources and Services Administration: National Practitioner Data Bank for Adverse Infor-

mation on Physicians and Other Health Care Practitioners: Availability of and Fee for Public Use Data File.

1999

64 FR 6753, February 16, 1999: Office of Inspector General: Privacy Act; Notification of New System of Records in Conjunction with the Healthcare Integrity and Protection Data Bank — Notice of a new system of records.

See § 5:1.

§ 9:2 FAILURE TO REPORT MEDICAL MALPRACTICE PAYMENTS — Section 421 [42 U.S.C.S. 11131]

Regulations

42 CFR Part 401, Subpart B — Confidentiality and Disclosure
42 CFR Part 420 — Program Integrity: Medicare
42 CFR Part 455 — Program Integrity: Medicaid
42 CFR Part 456 — Utilization Control
42 CFR Part 462 — Peer Review Organizations
42 CFR Part 466 — Utilization and Quality Control Review
42 CFR Part 476 — Acquisition, Protection, and Disclosure of Peer Review Information
42 CFR Chapter V — Office of Inspector General — Health Care, Department of Health and Human Services
Subchapter A — General Provisions
Part 1000 — Introduction; General Definitions
Subchapter B — OIG Authorities
Part 1001 — Program Integrity: Medicare and State Health Care Programs
Part 1002 — Program Integrity: State–initiated Exclusion from Medicaid
Part 1003 — Civil Money Penalties, Assessments and Exclusions
Part 1004 — Imposition of Sanctions on Health Care Practitioners and Providers of Health Care Services by a Peer Review Organization
Part 1005 — Appeals of Exclusions, Civil Money Penalties and Assessments
Part 1006 — Investigational Inquiries
Part 1007 — State Medicaid Fraud Control Units
Part 1008 — Advisory Opinions by the OIG

54 FR 42722, October 17, 1989: National Practitioner Data Bank for Adverse Information on Physicians and Other Health Care Practitioners — Final regulations [45 CFR Part 60]

56 FR 28488, June 21, 1991: Civil Money Penalties for Failure to Report Medical Malpractice Payments and for Breaching the Confidentiality of Information — Final rule affecting 42 CFR Part 1003.

61 FR 4788, February 8, 1996: Health Resources and Services Administration National Practitioner Data Bank: Change in User Fee—Notice.

63 FR 4460, January 29, 1998: Health Resources and Services Administration: National Practitioner Data Bank; Change in User Fee and Elimination of Diskette Queries.

63 FR 5811, February 4, 1998: Health Resources and Services Administration: National Practitioner Data Bank; Change in User Fee and Elimination of Diskette Queries. See also withdrawal at 63 FR 7421, February 13, 1998.

63 FR 7812, February 17, 1998: Health Resources and Services Administration: National Practitioner Data Bank for Adverse Information on Physicians and Other Health Care Practitioners: Availability of and Fee for Public Use Data File.

1999

64 FR 6753, February 16, 1999: Office of Inspector General: Privacy Act; Notification of New System of Records in Conjunction with the Healthcare Integrity and Protection Data Bank — Notice of a new system of records.

See § 5:2.

§ 9:3 FAILURE BY MEDICAL EXAMINER BOARDS TO REPORT INFORMATION ABOUT ADVERSE ACTIONS TAKEN BY HEALTH CARE ENTITIES AGAINST PHYSICIANS AND ABOUT HEALTH CARE ENTITIES THAT FAIL TO MAKE SUCH REPORTS — Sections 422 and 423(c)(2) [42 U.S.C.S. 11132 and 11133(c)(2)]

Regulations

42 CFR Part 401, Subpart B — Confidentiality and Disclosure
42 CFR Part 420 — Program Integrity: Medicare
42 CFR Part 455 — Program Integrity: Medicaid
42 CFR Part 456 — Utilization Control

42 CFR Part 462 — Peer Review Organizations

42 CFR Part 466 — Utilization and Quality Control Review

42 CFR Part 476 — Acquisition, Protection, and Disclosure of Peer Review Information

42 CFR Chapter V — Office of Inspector General — Health Care, Department of Health and Human Services

Subchapter A — General Provisions

Part 1000 — Introduction; General Definitions

Subchapter B — OIG Authorities

Part 1001 — Program Integrity: Medicare and State Health Care Programs

Part 1002 — Program Integrity: State–initiated Exclusion from Medicaid

Part 1003 — Civil Money Penalties, Assessments and Exclusions

Part 1004 — Imposition of Sanctions on Health Care Practitioners and Providers of Health Care Services by a Peer Review Organization

Part 1005 — Appeals of Exclusions, Civil Money Penalties and Assessments

Part 1006 — Investigational Inquiries

Part 1007 — State Medicaid Fraud Control Units

Part 1008 — Advisory Opinions by the OIG

54 FR 42722, October 17, 1989: National Practitioner Data Bank for Adverse Information on Physicians and Other Health Care Practitioners — Final regulations [45 CFR Part 60]

56 FR 28488, June 21, 1991: Civil Money Penalties for Failure to Report Medical Malpractice Payments and for Breaching the Confidentiality of Information — Final rule affecting 42 CFR Part 1003.

61 FR 4788, February 8, 1996: Health Resources and Services Administration National Practitioner Data Bank: Change in User Fee—Notice.

63 FR 4460, January 29, 1998: Health Resources and Services Administration: National Practitioner Data Bank; Change in User Fee and Elimination of Diskette Queries.

63 FR 5811, February 4, 1998: Health Resources and Services Administration: National Practitioner Data Bank; Change in User Fee and Elimination of Diskette Queries. See also withdrawal at 63 FR 7421, February 13, 1998.

63 FR 7812, February 17, 1998: Health Resources and Services Administration: National Practitioner Data Bank for Adverse Infor-

mation on Physicians and Other Health Care Practitioners: Availability of and Fee for Public Use Data File.

1999

64 FR 6753, February 16, 1999: Office of Inspector General: Privacy Act; Notification of New System of Records in Conjunction with the Healthcare Integrity and Protection Data Bank — Notice of a new system of records.

See § 5:3.

§ 9:4 FAILURE BY HOSPITALS TO OBTAIN ADVERSE INFORMATION ABOUT PHYSICIANS FROM THE SECRETARY OF HEALTH AND HUMAN SERVICES AND FROM STATE MEDICAL EXAMINER BOARDS — Section 425 [42 U.S.C.S. 11135]

Regulations

42 CFR Part 401, Subpart B — Confidentiality and Disclosure

42 CFR Part 420 — Program Integrity: Medicare

42 CFR Part 455 — Program Integrity: Medicaid

42 CFR Part 456 — Utilization Control

42 CFR Part 462 — Peer Review Organizations

42 CFR Part 466 — Utilization and Quality Control Review

42 CFR Part 476 — Acquisition, Protection, and Disclosure of Peer Review Information

42 CFR Chapter V — Office of Inspector General — Health Care, Department of Health and Human Services

Subchapter A — General Provisions

Part 1000 — Introduction; General Definitions

Subchapter B — OIG Authorities

Part 1001 — Program Integrity: Medicare and State Health Care Programs

Part 1002 — Program Integrity: State–initiated Exclusion from Medicaid

Part 1003 — Civil Money Penalties, Assessments and Exclusions

Part 1004 — Imposition of Sanctions on Health Care Practitioners and Providers of Health Care Services by a Peer Review Organization

Part 1005 — Appeals of Exclusions, Civil Money Penalties and Assessments

Part 1006 — Investigational Inquiries

Part 1007 — State Medicaid Fraud Control Units
Part 1008 — Advisory Opinions by the OIG

54 FR 42722, October 17, 1989: National Practitioner Data Bank for Adverse Information on Physicians and Other Health Care Practitioners — Final regulations [45 CFR Part 60]

56 FR 28488, June 21, 1991: Civil Money Penalties for Failure to Report Medical Malpractice Payments and for Breaching the Confidentiality of Information — Final rule affecting 42 CFR Part 1003.

61 FR 4788, February 8, 1996: Health Resources and Services Administration National Practitioner Data Bank: Change in User Fee—Notice.

63 FR 4460, January 29, 1998: Health Resources and Services Administration: National Practitioner Data Bank; Change in User Fee and Elimination of Diskette Queries.

63 FR 5811, February 4, 1998: Health Resources and Services Administration: National Practitioner Data Bank; Change in User Fee and Elimination of Diskette Queries. See also withdrawal at 63 FR 7421, February 13, 1998.

63 FR 7812, February 17, 1998: Health Resources and Services Administration: National Practitioner Data Bank for Adverse Information on Physicians and Other Health Care Practitioners: Availability of and Fee for Public Use Data File.

1999

64 FR 6753, February 16, 1999: Office of Inspector General: Privacy Act; Notification of New System of Records in Conjunction with the Healthcare Integrity and Protection Data Bank — Notice of a new system of records.

See § 5:4.

§ 9:5 UNLAWFUL DISCLOSURE OF INFORMATION COLLECTED PURSUANT TO THE HEALTH CARE QUALITY IMPROVEMENT ACT — Section 427 [42 U.S.C.S. 11137]

Regulations

42 CFR Part 401, Subpart B — Confidentiality and Disclosure
42 CFR Part 420 — Program Integrity: Medicare
42 CFR Part 455 — Program Integrity: Medicaid
42 CFR Part 456 — Utilization Control
42 CFR Part 462 — Peer Review Organizations

42 CFR Part 466 — Utilization and Quality Control Review

42 CFR Part 476 — Acquisition, Protection, and Disclosure of Peer Review Information

42 CFR Chapter V — Office of Inspector General — Health Care, Department of Health and Human Services

Subchapter A — General Provisions

Part 1000 — Introduction; General Definitions

Subchapter B — OIG Authorities

Part 1001 — Program Integrity: Medicare and State Health Care Programs

Part 1002 — Program Integrity: State–initiated Exclusion from Medicaid

Part 1003 — Civil Money Penalties, Assessments and Exclusions

Part 1004 — Imposition of Sanctions on Health Care Practitioners and Providers of Health Care Services by a Peer Review Organization

Part 1005 — Appeals of Exclusions, Civil Money Penalties and Assessments

Part 1006 — Investigational Inquiries

Part 1007 — State Medicaid Fraud Control Units

Part 1008 — Advisory Opinions by the OIG

54 FR 42722, October 17, 1989: National Practitioner Data Bank for Adverse Information on Physicians and Other Health Care Practitioners — Final regulations [45 CFR Part 60]

56 FR 28488, June 21, 1991: Civil Money Penalties for Failure to Report Medical Malpractice Payments and for Breaching the Confidentiality of Information — Final rule affecting 42 CFR Part 1003.

61 FR 4788, February 8, 1996: Health Resources and Services Administration National Practitioner Data Bank: Change in User Fee—Notice.

63 FR 4460, January 29, 1998: Health Resources and Services Administration: National Practitioner Data Bank; Change in User Fee and Elimination of Diskette Queries.

63 FR 5811, February 4, 1998: Health Resources and Services Administration: National Practitioner Data Bank; Change in User Fee and Elimination of Diskette Queries. See also withdrawal at 63 FR 7421, February 13, 1998.

63 FR 7812, February 17, 1998: Health Resources and Services Administration: National Practitioner Data Bank for Adverse Information on Physicians and Other Health Care Practitioners: Availability of and Fee for Public Use Data File.

1999

64 FR 6753, February 16, 1999: Office of Inspector General: Privacy Act; Notification of New System of Records in Conjunction with the Healthcare Integrity and Protection Data Bank—Notice of a new system of records.

See § 5:5.

PART III
APPENDIXES

APPENDIX A

FALSE CLAIMS AND CIVIL ACTIONS FOR FALSE CLAIMS [31 U.S.C.S. 3729-3733]

31 U.S.C.S. 3729. False claims

(a) Liability for certain acts.—Any person who—

(1) knowingly presents, or causes to be presented, to an officer or employee of the United States Government or a member of the Armed Forces of the United States a false or fraudulent claim for payment or approval;

(2) knowingly makes, uses, or causes to be made or used, a false record or statement to get a false or fraudulent claim paid or approved by the Government;

(3) conspires to defraud the Government by getting a false or fraudulent claim allowed or paid;

(4) has possession, custody, or control of property or money used, or to be used, by the government and, intending to defraud the Government or willfully to conceal the property, delivers, or causes to be delivered, less property than the amount for which the person receives a certificate or receipt;

(5) authorized to make or deliver a document certifying receipt of property used, or to be used, by the Government and, intending to defraud the Government, makes or delivers the receipt without completely knowing that the information on the receipt is true;

(6) knowingly buys or receives as a pledge of an obligation or debt, public property from an officer or employee of the Government, or a member of the Armed Forces, who lawfully may not sell or pledge the property; or

(7) knowingly makes, uses, or causes to be made or used, a false record or statement to conceal, avoid, or decrease an obligation to pay or transmit money or property to the Govern-

ment, is liable to the United States Government for a civil penalty of not less than $5,000 and not more than $10,000, plus 3 times the amount of damages which the Government sustains because of the act of that person, except that if the court finds that—

(A) the person committing the violation of this subsection furnished officials of the United States responsible for investigating false claims violations with all information known to such person about the violation within 30 days after the date on which the defendant first obtained the information;

(B) such person fully cooperated with any Government investigation of such violation; and

(C) at the time such person furnished the United States with the information about the violation, no criminal prosecution, civil action, or administrative action had commenced under this title with respect to such violation, and the person did not have actual knowledge of the existence of an investigation into such violation; the court may assess not less than 2 times the amount of damages which the Government sustains because of the act of the person. A person violating this subsection shall also be liable to the United States Government for the costs of a civil action brought to recover any such penalty or damages.

(b) Knowing and knowingly defined.—For purposes of this section, the terms "knowing" and "knowingly" mean that a person, with respect to information—

(1) has actual knowledge of the information;

(2) acts in deliberate ignorance of the truth or falsity of the information; or

(3) acts in reckless disregard of the truth or falsity of the information,

and no proof of specific intent to defraud is required.

(c) Claim defined.—For purposes of this section, "claim" includes any request or demand, whether under a contract or otherwise, for money or property which is made to a contractor, grantee, or other recipient if the United States Government provides any portion of the money or property which is requested or demanded, or if the Government will reimburse such contractor, grantee, or other recipient for any portion of the money or property which is requested or demanded.

(d) Exemption from disclosure.—Any information furnished pursuant to subparagraphs (A) through (C) of subsection (a) shall be exempt from disclosure under section 552 of title 5 [which is the Freedom of Information Act].

(e) Exclusion.—This section does not apply to claims, records, or statements made under the Internal Revenue Code of 1986. [P.L. 103-272, changed the year from 1954].

31 U.S.C.S. 3730. Civil actions for false claims

(a) Responsibilities of the attorney general.—The Attorney General diligently shall investigate a violation under section 3729. If the Attorney General finds that a person has violated or is violating section 3729, the Attorney General may bring a civil action under this section against the person.

(b) Actions by private persons.—(1) A person may bring a civil action for a violation of section 3729 for the person and for the United States Government. The action shall be brought in the name of the Government. The action may be dismissed only if the court and the Attorney General give written consent to the dismissal and their reasons for consenting.

(2) A copy of the complaint and written disclosure of substantially all material evidence and information the person possesses shall be served on the Government pursuant to Rule 4(d)(4) of the Federal Rules of Civil Procedure. The complaint shall be filed in camera, shall remain under seal for at least 60 days, and shall not be served on the defendant until the court so orders. The Government may elect to intervene and proceed with the action within 60 days after it receives both the complaint and the material evidence and information.

(3) The Government may, for good cause shown, move the court for extensions of the time during which the complaint remains under seal under paragraph (2). Any such motions may be supported by affidavits or other submissions in camera. The defendant shall not be required to respond to any complaint filed under this section until 20 days after the complaint is unsealed and served upon the defendant pursuant to Rule 4 of the Federal Rules of Civil Procedure.

(4) Before the expiration of the 60-day period or any extensions obtained under paragraph (3), the Government shall—

(A) proceed with the action, in which case the action shall be conducted by the Government; or

(B) notify the court that it declines to take over the action, in which case the person bringing the action shall have the right to conduct the action.

(5) When a person brings an action under this subsection, no person other than the Government may intervene or bring a related action based on the facts underlying the pending action.

(c) Rights of the parties to Qui Tam actions.—(1) If the Government proceeds with the action, it shall have the primary responsibility for prosecuting the action, and shall not be bound by an act of the person bringing the action. Such person shall have the right to continue as a party to the action, subject to the limitations set forth in paragraph (2).

(2)(A) The Government may dismiss the action notwithstanding the objections of the person initiating the action if the person has been notified by the Government of the filing of the motion and the court has provided the person with an opportunity for a hearing on the motion.

(B) The Government may settle the action with the defendant notwithstanding the objections of the person initiating the action if the court determines, after a hearing, that the proposed settlement is fair, adequate, and reasonable under all the circumstances. Upon a showing of good cause, such hearing may be held in camera.

(C) Upon a showing by the Government that unrestricted participation during the course of the litigation by the person initiating the action would interfere with or unduly delay the government's prosecution of the case, or would be repetitious, irrelevant, or for purposes of harassment, the court may, in its discretion, impose limitations on the person's participation, such as—

(i) limiting the number of witnesses the person may call;

(ii) limiting the length of the testimony of such witnesses;

(iii) limiting the person's cross-examination of witnesses; or

(iv) otherwise limiting the participation by the person in the litigation.

(D) Upon a showing by the defendant that unrestricted participation during the course of the litigation by the person initiating the action would be for purposes of harassment or would cause the defendant undue burden or unnecessary expense, the court may limit the participation by the person in the litigation.

(3) If the Government elects not to proceed with the action, the person who initiated the action shall have the right to conduct the action. If the Government so requests, it shall be served with copies of all pleadings filed in the action and shall be supplied with copies of all deposition transcripts (at the Government's expense). When a person proceeds with the action, the court, without limiting the status and rights of the person initiating the action, may nevertheless permit the Government to intervene at a later date upon a showing of good cause.

(4) Whether or not the Government proceeds with the action, upon a showing by the Government that certain actions of discovery by the person initiating the action would interfere with the Government's investigation or prosecution of a criminal or civil matter arising out of the same facts, the court may stay such discovery for a period of not more than 60 days. Such a showing shall be conducted in camera. The court may extend the 60-day period upon a further showing in camera that the Government has pursued the criminal or civil investigation or proceedings with reasonable diligence and any proposed discovery in the civil action will interfere with the ongoing criminal or civil investigation or proceedings.

(5) Notwithstanding subsection (b), the Government may elect to pursue its claim through any alternate remedy available to the Government, including any administrative proceeding to determine a civil money penalty. If any such alternate remedy is pursued in another proceeding, the person initiating the action shall have the same rights in such proceeding as such person would have had if the action had continued under this section. Any finding of fact or conclusion

of law made in such other proceeding that has become final shall be conclusive on all parties to an action under this section. For purposes of the preceding sentence, a finding or conclusion is final if it has been finally determined on appeal to the appropriate court of the United States, if all time for filing such an appeal with respect to the finding or conclusion has expired, or if the finding or conclusion is not subject to judicial review.

(d) Award to Qui Tam plaintiff.—

(1) If the Government proceeds with an action brought by a person under subsection (b), such person shall, subject to the second sentence of this paragraph, receive at least 15 percent but not more than 25 percent of the proceeds of the action or settlement of the claim, depending upon the extent to which the person substantially contributed to the prosecution of the action. Where the action is one which the court finds to be based primarily on disclosures of specific information (other than information provided by the person bringing the action) relating to allegations or transactions in a criminal, civil, or administrative hearing, in a congressional, administrative, or Government Accounting Office report, hearing, audit, or investigation, or from the news media, the court may award such sums as it considers appropriate, but in no case more than 10 percent of the proceeds, taking into account the significance of the information and the role of the person bringing the action in advancing the case to litigation. Any payment to a person under the first or second sentence of this paragraph shall be made from the proceeds. Any such person shall also receive an amount for reasonable expenses which the court finds to have been necessarily incurred, plus reasonable attorneys' fees and costs. All such expenses, fees, and costs shall be awarded against the defendant.

(2) If the Government does not proceed with an action under this section, the person bringing the action or settling the claim shall receive an amount which the court decides is reasonable for collecting the civil penalty and damages. The amount shall be not less than 25 percent and not more than 30 percent of the proceeds of the action or settlement and shall be paid out of such proceeds. Such person shall also receive an amount for reasonable expenses which the court finds to have

been necessarily incurred, plus reasonable attorneys' fees and costs. All such expenses, fees, and costs shall be awarded against the defendant.

(3) Whether or not the Government proceeds with the action, if the court finds that the action was brought by a person who planned and initiated the violation of section 3729 upon which the action was brought, then the court may, to the extent the court considers appropriate, reduce the share of the proceeds of the action which the person would otherwise receive under paragraph (1) or (2) of this subsection, taking into account the role of that person in advancing the case to litigation and any relevant circumstances pertaining to the violation. If the person bringing the action is convicted of criminal conduct arising from his or her role in the violation of section 3729, that person shall be dismissed from the civil action and shall not receive any share of the proceeds of the action. Such dismissal shall not prejudice the right of the United States to continue the action, represented by the Department of Justice.

(4) If the Government does not proceed with the action and the person bringing the action conducts the action, the court may award to the defendant its reasonable attorneys' fees and expenses if the defendant prevails in the action and the court finds that the claim of the person bringing the action was clearly frivolous, clearly vexatious, or brought primarily for purposes of harassment.

(e) Certain actions barred.—(1) No court shall have jurisdiction over an action brought by a former or present member of the armed forces under subsection (b) of this section against a member of the armed forces arising out of such person's service in the armed forces.

(2)(A) No court shall have jurisdiction over an action brought under subsection (b) against a Member of Congress, a member of the judiciary, or a senior executive branch official if the action is based on evidence or information known to the Government when the action was brought[.]

(B) For purposes of this paragraph, "senior executive branch official" means any officer or employee listed in paragraphs (1) through (8) of section 101(f) of the Ethics in Government Act of 1978 (5 U.S.C.S. App.) [Prior to amendment by P.L. 101-280 “section 201(f)” appeared in place of “paragraphs (1) through (8) of section 101(f)”. P.L. 103-272 deleted the superfluous word "section" which preceded paragraphs, effective July 5, 1994.]

(3) In no event may a person bring an action under subsection (b) which is based upon allegations or transactions which are the subject of a civil suit or an administrative civil money penalty proceeding in which the Government is already a party.

(4)(A) No court shall have jurisdiction over an action under this section based upon the public disclosure of allegations or transactions in a criminal, civil, or administrative hearing, in a congressional, administrative, or Government Accounting Office report, hearing, audit, or investigation, or from the news media, unless the action is brought by the Attorney General or the person bringing the action is an original source of the information.

(B) For purposes of this paragraph, “original source” means an individual who has direct and independent knowledge of the information on which the allegations are based and has voluntarily provided the information to the Government before filing an action under this section which is based on the information.

(f) Government not liable for certain expenses.—The Government is not liable for expenses which a person incurs in bringing an action under this section.

(g) Fees and expenses to prevailing defendant.—In civil actions brought under this section by the United States, the provisions of section 2412(d) of title 28 shall apply [which is the Equal Access to Justice Act].

(h) Any employee who is discharged, demoted, suspended, threatened, harassed, or in any other manner discriminated against in the terms and conditions of employment by his or her employer because of lawful acts done by the employee on behalf of the employee or others in furtherance of an action under this section, including investigation for, initiation of, testimony for, or assistance in an action filed or to be filed under this section, shall be entitled to all relief necessary to make the employee whole. Such relief shall include reinstatement with the same seniority status such employee would have had but for the discrimination, 2 times the amount of back pay, interest on the

[Text Continued on Page App. A-9]

back pay, and compensation for any special damages sustained as a result of the discrimination, including litigation costs and reasonable attorneys' fees. An employee may bring an action in the appropriate district court of the United States for the relief provided in this subsection.

31 U.S.C.S. 3731. False claims procedure

(a) A subpena requiring the attendance of a witness at a trial or hearing conducted under section 3730 of this title may be served at any place in the United States.

(b) A civil action under section 3730 may not be brought—

(1) more than 6 years after the date on which the violation of section 3729 is committed, or

(2) more than 3 years after the date when facts material to the right of action are known or reasonably should have been known by the official of the United States charged with responsibility to act in the circumstances, but in no event more than 10 years after the date on which the violation is committed,

whichever occurs last.

(c) In any action brought under section 3730, the United States shall be required to prove all essential elements of the cause of action, including damages, by a preponderance of the evidence.

(d) Notwithstanding any other provision of law, the Federal Rules of Criminal Procedure, or the Federal Rules of Evidence, a final judgment rendered in favor of the United States in any criminal proceeding charging fraud or false statements, whether upon a verdict after trial or upon a plea of guilty or nolo contendere, shall estop the defendant from denying the essential elements of the offense in any action which involves the same transaction as in the criminal proceeding and which is brought under subsection (a) or (b) of section 3730.

31 U.S.C.S. 3732. False claims jurisdiction

(a) Actions under section 3730.—Any action under section 3730 may be brought in any judicial district in which the defendant or, in the case of multiple defendants, any one defendant can be found, resides, transacts business, or in which any act proscribed by section 3729 occurred. A summons as required by the

Federal Rules of Civil Procedure shall be issued by the appropriate district court and served at any place within or outside the United States.

(b) Claims under state law.—The district courts shall have jurisdiction over any action brought under the laws of any State for the recovery of funds paid by a State or local government if the action arises from the same transaction or occurrence as an action brought under section 3730.

31 U.S.C 3733. Civil investigative demands

(a) In general.—

(1) Issuance and service.—Whenever the Attorney General has reason to believe that any person may be in possession, custody, or control of any documentary material or information relevant to a false claims law investigation, the Attorney General may, before commencing a civil proceeding under section 3730 or other false claims law, issue in writing and cause to be served upon such person, a civil investigative demand requiring such person—

(A) to produce such documentary material for inspection and copying,

(B) to answer in writing written interrogatories with respect to such documentary material or information,

(C) to give oral testimony concerning such documentary material or information, or

(D) to furnish any combination of such material, answers, or testimony.

The Attorney General may not delegate the authority to issue civil investigative demands under this subsection. Whenever a civil investigative demand is an express demand for any product of discovery, the Attorney General, the Deputy Attorney General, or an Assistant Attorney General shall cause to be served, in any manner authorized by this section, a copy of such demand upon the person from whom the discovery was obtained and shall notify the person to whom such demand is issued of the date on which such copy was served.

(2) Contents and deadlines.—

(A) Each civil investigative demand issued under paragraph (1) shall state the nature of the conduct constituting the alleged violation of a false claims law which is under investigation, and the applicable provision of law alleged to be violated.

(B) If such demand is for the production of documentary material, the demand shall—

(i) describe each class of documentary material to be produced with such definiteness and certainty as to permit such material to be fairly identified;

(ii) prescribe a return date for each such class which will provide a reasonable period of time within which the material so demanded may be assembled and made available for inspection and copying; and

(iii) identify the false claims law investigator to whom such material shall be made available.

(C) If such demand is for answers to written interrogatories, the demand shall—

(i) set forth with specificity the written interrogatories to be answered;

(ii) prescribe dates at which time answers to written interrogatories shall be submitted; and

(iii) identify the false claims law investigator to whom such answers shall be submitted.

(D) If such demand is for the giving of oral testimony, the demand shall—

(i) prescribe a date, time, and place at which oral testimony shall be commenced;

(ii) identify a false claims law investigator who shall conduct the examination and the custodian to whom the transcript of such examination shall be submitted;

(iv) notify the person receiving the demand of the right to be accompanied by an attorney and any other representative; and

(v) describe the general purpose for which the demand is being issued and the general nature of the testimony, including the primary areas of inquiry, which will be taken pursuant to the demand.

(E) Any civil investigative demand issued under this section which is an express demand for any product of discovery shall not be returned or returnable until 20 days after a copy of such demand has been served upon the person from whom the discovery was obtained.

(F) The date prescribed for the commencement of oral testimony pursuant to a civil investigative demand issued under this section shall be a date which is not less than seven days after the date on which demand is received, unless the Attorney General or an Assistant Attorney General designated by the Attorney General determines that exceptional circumstances are present which warrant the commencement of such testimony within a lesser period of time.

(G) The Attorney General shall not authorize the issuance under this section of more than one civil investigative demand for oral testimony by the same person unless the person requests otherwise or unless the Attorney General, after investigation, notifies that person in writing that an additional demand for oral testimony is necessary. The Attorney General may not, notwithstanding section 510 of title 28 [which pertains to delegation of the Attorney General's authority], authorize the performance, by any other officer, employee, or agency, of any function vested in the Attorney General under this subparagraph.

(b) Protected material or information.—

(1) In general.—A civil investigative demand issued under subsection (a) may not require the production of any documentary material, the submission of any answers to written interrogatories, or the giving of any oral testimony if such material, answers or testimony would be protected from disclosure under—

(A) the standards applicable to subpoenas or subpoenas duces tecum issued by a court of the United States to aid in a grand jury investigation; or

(B) the standards applicable to discovery requests under the Federal Rules of Civil Procedure, to the extent that the application of such standards to any such demand is appropriate and consistent with the provisions and purposes of this section.

(2) Effect on other orders, rules, and laws.—Any such demand which is an express demand for any product of discovery supersedes any inconsistent order, rule, or provision of law (other than this section) preventing or restraining disclosure of such product of discovery to any person. Disclosure of any product of discovery pursuant to any such express demand does not constitute a waiver of any right or privilege which the person making such disclosure may be entitled to invoke to resist discovery of trial preparation materials.

(c) Service; jurisdiction.—

(1) By whom served.—Any civil investigative demand issued under subsection (a) may be served by a false claims law investigator, or by a United States marshal or a deputy marshal, at any place within the territorial jurisdiction of any court of the United States.

(2) Service in foreign countries.—Any such demand or any petition filed under subsection (j) may be served upon any person who is not found within the territorial jurisdiction of any court of the United States in such manner as the Federal Rules of Civil Procedure prescribe for service in a foreign country. To the extent that the courts of the United States can assert jurisdiction over any such person consistent with due process, the United States District Court for the District of Columbia shall have the same jurisdiction to take any action respecting compliance with the section by any such person that such court would have if such person were personally within the jurisdiction of such court.

(d) Service upon legal entities and natural persons.—

(1) Legal entities.—Service of any civil investigative demand issued under subsection (a) or of any petition filed under subsection (j) may be made upon a partnership, corporation, association, or other legal entity by—

(A) delivering an executed copy of such demand or petition to any partner, executive officer, managing agent, or general agent of the partnership, corporation, association, or entity, or to any agent authorized by appointment or by law to receive service of process on behalf of such partnership, corporation, association, or entity;

(B) delivering an executed copy of such demand or petition to the principal office or place of business of the partnership, corporation, association, or entity; or

(C) depositing an executed copy of such demand or petition in the United States mails by registered or certified mail, with a return receipt requested, addressed to such partnership, corporation, association, or entity at its principal office or place of business.

(2) Natural persons.—Service of any such demand or petition may be made upon any natural person by—

(A) delivering an executed copy of such demand or petition to the person; or

(B) depositing an executed copy of such demand or petition in the United States mails by registered or certified mail, with a return receipt requested, addressed to the person at the person's residence or principal office or place of business.

(e) Proof of service.—A verified return by the individual serving any civil investigative demand issued under subsection (a) or any petition filed under subsection (j) setting forth the manner of such service shall be proof of such service. In the case of service by registered or certified mail, such return shall be accompanied by the return post office receipt of delivery of such demand.

(f) Documentary material.—

(1) Sworn certificates.—The production of documentary material in response to a civil investigative demand served under this section shall be made under a sworn certificate, in such form as the demand designates, by—

(A) in the case of a natural person, the person to whom the demand is directed, or

(B) in the case of a person other than a natural person, a person having knowledge of the facts and circumstances relating to such production and authorized to act on behalf of such person.

The certificate shall state that all of the documentary material required by the demand and in the possession, custody, or control of the person to whom the demand is directed has been produced and made available to the false claims law investigator identified in the demand.

(2) Production of materials.—Any person upon whom any civil investigative demand for the production of documentary material has been served under this section shall make such material available for inspection and copying to the false claims law investigator identified in such demand at the principal place of business of such person, or at such other place as the false claims law investigator and the person thereafter may agree and prescribe in writing, or as the court may direct under subsection (j)(1). Such material shall be made so available on the return date specified in such demand, or on such later date as the false claims law investigator may prescribe in writing. Such person may upon written agreement between the person and the false claims law investigator, substitute copies for originals of all or any part of such material.

(g) Interrogatories.—Each interrogatory in a civil investigative demand served under this section shall be answered separately and fully in writing under oath and shall be submitted under a sworn certificate, in such form as the demand designates by—

(1) in the case of a natural person, the person to whom the demand is directed, or

(2) in the case of a person other than a natural person, the person or persons responsible for answering each interrogatory.

If any interrogatory is objected to, the reasons for the objection shall be stated in the certificate instead of an answer. The certificate shall state that all information required by the demand and in the possession, custody, control, or knowledge of the person to whom the demand is directed has been submitted. To the extent that any information is not furnished, the information shall be identified and reasons set forth with particularity regarding the reasons why the information was not furnished.

(h) Oral examinations.—

(1) Procedures.—The examination of any person pursuant to a civil investigative demand for oral testimony served under this section shall be taken before an officer authorized to administer oaths and affirmations by the laws of the United States or of the place where the examination is held. The

officer before whom the testimony is to be taken shall put the witness on oath or affirmation and shall, personally or by someone acting under the direction of the officer and in the officer's presence, record the testimony of the witness. The testimony shall be taken stenographically and shall be transcribed. When the testimony is fully transcribed, the officer before whom the testimony is taken shall promptly transmit a copy of the transcript of the testimony to the custodian. This subsection shall not preclude the taking of testimony by any means authorized by, and in a manner consistent with, the Federal Rules of Civil Procedure.

(2) Persons present.—The false claims law investigator conducting the examination shall exclude from the place where the examination is held all persons except the person giving the testimony, the attorney for and any other representative of the person giving the testimony, the attorney for the Government, any person who may be agreed upon by the attorney for the Government and the person giving the testimony, the officer before whom the testimony is to be taken, and any stenographer taking such testimony.

(3) Where testimony taken.—The oral testimony of any person taken pursuant to a civil investigative demand served under this section shall be taken in the judicial district of the United States within which such person resides, is found or transacts business, or in such other place as may be agreed upon by the false claims law investigator conducting the examination and such person.

(4) Transcript of testimony.—When the testimony is fully transcribed, the false claims law investigator or the officer before whom the testimony is taken shall afford the witness, who may be accompanied by counsel, a reasonable opportunity to examine and read the transcript, unless such examination and reading are waived by the witness. Any changes in form or substance which the witness desires to make shall be entered and identified upon the transcript by the officer or the false claims law investigator, with a statement of the reasons given by the witness for making such changes. The transcript shall then be signed by the witness, unless the witness in writing waives the signing, is ill, cannot be found, or refuses to sign. If the transcript is not signed by

the witness within 30 days after being afforded a reasonable opportunity to examine it, the officer or the false claims law investigator shall sign it and state on the record the fact of the waiver, illness, absence of the witness, or the refusal to sign, together with the reasons, if any, given therefor.

(5) Certification and delivery to custodian.—The officer before whom the testimony is taken shall certify on the transcript that the witness was sworn by the officer and that the transcript is a true record of the testimony given by the witness, and the officer or false claims law investigator shall promptly deliver the transcript, or send the transcript by registered or certified mail, to the custodian.

(6) Furnishing or inspection of transcript by witness.—Upon payment of reasonable charges therefor, the false claims law investigator shall furnish a copy of the transcript to the witness only, except that the Attorney General, the Deputy Attorney General, or an Assistant Attorney General may, for good cause, limit such witness to inspection of the official transcript of the witness' testimony.

(7) Conduct of oral testimony.—

(A) Any person compelled to appear for oral testimony under a civil investigative demand issued under subsection (a) may be accompanied, represented, and advised by counsel. Counsel may advise such person, in confidence, with respect to any question asked of such person. Such person or counsel may object on the record to any question, in whole or in part, and shall briefly state for the record the reason for the objection. An objection may be made, received, and entered upon the record when it is claimed that such person is entitled to refuse to answer the question on the grounds of any constitutional or other legal right or privilege, including the privilege against self-incrimination. Such person may not otherwise object to or refuse to answer any question, and may not directly or through counsel otherwise interrupt the oral examination. If such person refuses to answer any question, a petition may be filed in the district court of the United States under subsection (j)(1) for an order compelling such person to answer such question.

(B) If such person refuses to answer any question on the grounds of the privilege against self-incrimination, the testimony of such person may be compelled in accordance with provisions of part V of title 18.

(8) Witness fees and allowances.—Any person appearing for oral testimony under a civil investigative demand issued under subsection (a) shall be entitled to the same fees and allowances which are paid to witnesses in the district courts of the United States.

(i) Custodians of documents, answers, and transcripts.

(1) Designation.—The Attorney General shall designate a false claims law investigator to serve as custodian of documentary material, answers to interrogatories, and transcripts of oral testimony received under this section, and shall designate such additional false claims law investigators as the Attorney General determines from time to time to be necessary to serve as deputies to the custodian.

(2) Responsibility for materials; disclosure.—

(A) A false claims law investigator who receives any documentary material, answers to interrogatories, or transcripts of oral testimony under this section shall transmit them to the custodian. The custodian shall take physical possession of such material, answers, or transcripts and shall be responsible for the use made of them and for the return of documentary material under paragraph (4).

(B) The custodian may cause the preparation of such copies of such documentary material, answers to interrogatories, or transcripts of oral testimony as may be required for official use by any false claims law investigator, or other officer or employee of the Department of Justice, who is authorized for such use under regulations which the Attorney General shall issue. Such material, answers, and transcripts may be used by any such authorized false claims law investigator or other officer or employee in connection with the taking of oral testimony under this section.

(C) Except as otherwise provided in this subsection, no documentary material, answers to interrogatories, or transcripts of oral testimony, or copies thereof, while in the possession of the custodian, shall be available for examination by any individual other than a false claims law investigator or other officer or employee of the Department of Justice authorized under subparagraph (B). The prohibition in the preceding sentence on the availability of material, answers, or transcripts shall not apply if consent is given by the person who produced such material, answers, or transcripts, or, in the case of any product of discovery produced pursuant to an express demand for such material, consent is given by the person from whom the discovery was obtained. Nothing in this subparagraph is intended to prevent disclosure to the Congress, including any committee or subcommittee of the Congress, or to any other agency of the United States for use by such agency in furtherance of its statutory responsibilities. Disclosure of information to any such other agency shall be allowed only upon showing substantial need for the use of the information by such agency in furtherance of its statutory responsibilities.

(D) While in the possession of the custodian and under such reasonable terms and conditions as the Attorney General shall prescribe—

(i) documentary material and answers to interrogatories shall be available for examination by the person who produced such material or answers, or by a representative of that person authorized by that person to examine such material and answers; and

(ii) transcripts of oral testimony shall be available for examination by the person who produced such testimony, or by a representative of that person authorized by that person to examine such transcripts.

(3) Use of material, answers, or transcripts in other proceedings.—Whenever any attorney of the Department of Justice has been designated to appear before any court, grand jury, or Federal agency in any case or proceeding, the custodian of any documentary material, answers to interrogatories, or transcripts of oral testimony received under this section may deliver to such attorney such material, answers, or transcripts for official use in connection with any such case or proceeding as such attorney determines to be required. Upon

the completion of any such material, answers, or transcripts so delivered which have not passed into the control of such court, grand jury, or agency through introduction into the record of such case or proceeding.

(4) Conditions for return of material.—If any documentary material has been produced by any person in the course of any false claims law investigation pursuant to a civil investigative demand under this section, and—

(A) any case or proceeding before the court or grand jury arising out of such investigation, or any proceeding before any Federal agency involving such material, has been completed, or

(B) no case or proceeding in which such material may be used has been commenced within a reasonable time after completion of the examination and analysis of all documentary material and other information assembled in the course of such investigation,

the custodian shall, upon written request of the person who produced such material, return to such person any such material (other than copies furnished to the false claims law investigator under subsection (f)(2) or made for the Department of Justice under paragraph (2)(B) which has not passed into the control of any court, grand jury, or agency through introduction into the record of such case or proceeding.

(5) Appointment of successor custodians.—In the event of the death, disability, or separation from service in the Department of Justice of the custodian of any documentary material, answers to interrogatories, or transcripts of oral testimony produced pursuant to a civil investigative demand under this section, or in the event of the official relief of such custodian from responsibility for the custody and control of such material, answers, or transcripts, the Attorney General shall promptly—

(A) designate another false claims law investigator to serve as custodian of such material, answers, or transcripts, and

(B) transmit in writing to the person who produced such material, answers, or testimony notice of the identity and address of the successor so designated.

Any person who is designated to be a successor under this paragraph shall have, with regard to such material, answers, or transcripts, the same duties and responsibilities as were imposed by this section upon that person's predecessor in office, except that the successor shall not be held responsible for any default or dereliction which occurred before that designation.

(j) Judicial proceedings.—

(1) Petition for enforcement.—Whenever any person fails to comply with any civil investigative demand issued under subsection (a), or whenever satisfactory copying or reproduction of any material requested in such demand cannot be done and such person refuses to surrender such material, the Attorney General may file, in the district court of the United States for any judicial district in which such person resides, is found, or transacts business, and serve upon such person a petition for an order of such court for the enforcement of the civil investigative demand.

(2) Petition to modify or set aside demand.—

(A) Any person who has received a civil investigative demand issued under subsection (a) may file, in the district court of the United States for the judicial district within which such person resides, is found, or transacts business, and serve upon the false claims law investigator identified in such demand a petition for an order of the court to modify or set aside such demand. In the case of a petition addressed to an express demand for any product of discovery, a petition to modify or set aside such demand may be brought only in the district court of the United States for the judicial district in which the proceeding in which such discovery was obtained is or was last pending. Any petition under this subparagraph must be filed—

(i) within 20 days after the date of service of the civil investigative demand, or at any time before the return date specified in the demand, whichever is earlier, or

(ii) within such longer period as may be prescribed in writing by any false claims law investigator identified in the demand.

(B) The petition shall specify each ground upon which the petitioner relies in seeking relief under subparagraph (A), and may be based upon any failure of the demand to comply with the provisions of this section or upon any constitutional or other legal right or privilege of such person. During the pendency of the petition in the court, the court may stay, as it deems proper, the running of the time allowed for compliance with the demand, in whole or in part, except that the person filing the petition shall comply with any portions of the demand not sought to be modified or set aside.

(3) Petition to modify or set aside demand for product of discovery.—

(A) In the case of any civil investigative demand issued under subsection (a) which is an express demand for any product of discovery, the person from whom such discovery was obtained may file, in the district court of the United States for the judicial district in which the proceeding in which such discovery was obtained is or was last pending, and serve upon any false claims law investigator identified in the demand and upon the recipient of the demand, a petition for an order of such court to modify or set aside those portions of the demand requiring production of any such product of discovery. Any petition under this subparagraph must be filed—

(i) within 20 days after the date of service of the civil investigative demand, or at any time before the return date specified in the demand, whichever date is earlier, or

(ii) within such longer period as may be prescribed in writing by any false claims law investigator identified in the demand.

(B) The petition shall specify each ground upon which the petitioner relies in seeking relief under subparagraph (A), and may be based upon any failure of the portions of the demand from which relief is sought to comply with the provisions of this section, or upon any constitutional or other legal right or privilege of the petitioner. During the pendency of the petition, the court may stay, as it deems proper, compliance with the demand and the running of the time allowed for compliance with the demand.

(4) Petition to require performance by custodian of duties.—At any time during which any custodian is in custody or control of any documentary material or answers to interrogatories produced, or transcripts of oral testimony given, by any person in compliance with any civil investigative demand issued under subsection (a), such person, and in the case of an express demand for any product of discovery, the person from whom such discovery was obtained, may file, in the district court of the United States for the judicial district within which the office of such custodian is situated, and serve upon such custodian, a petition for an order of such court to require the performance by the custodian of any duty imposed upon the custodian by this section.

(5) Jurisdiction.—Whenever any petition is filed in any district court of the United States under this subsection, such court shall have jurisdiction to hear and determine the matter so presented, and to enter such order or orders as may be required to carry out the provisions of this section. Any final order so entered shall be subject to appeal under section 1291 of title 28 [which pertains to appellate court review of district court decisions]. Any disobedience of any final order entered under this section by any court shall be punished as a contempt of the court.

(6) Applicability of federal rules of civil procedure.—The Federal Rules of Civil Procedure shall apply to any petition under this subsection, to the extent that such rules are not inconsistent with the provisions of this section.

(k) Disclosure exemption.—Any documentary material, answers to written interrogatories, or oral testimony provided under any civil investigative demand issued under subsection (a) shall be exempt from disclosure under section 552 of title 5 [which is the Freedom of Information Act].

(l) Definitions.—For purposes of this section—

(1) the term "false claims law" means—

(A) this section and section 3729 through 3732; and

(B) any Act of Congress enacted after the date of the enactment of this section which prohibits, or makes available to the United States in any court of the United States any civil remedy with respect to, any false claim against, bribery of, or corruption of any officer or employee of the United States;

(2) the term "false claims law investigation" means any inquiry conducted by any false claims law investigator for the purpose of ascertaining whether any person is or has been engaged in any violation of a false claims law;

(3) the term "false claims law investigator" means any attorney or investigator employed by the Department of Justice who is charged with the duty of enforcing or carrying into effect any false claims law, or any officer or employee of the United States acting under the direction and supervision of such attorney or investigator in connection with a false claims law investigation;

(4) the term "person" means any natural person, partnership, corporation, association, or other legal entity, including any State or political subdivision of a State;

(5) the term "documentary material" includes the original or any copy of any book, record, report, memorandum, paper, communication, tabulation, chart, or other document, or data compilations stored in or accessible through computer of other information retrieval systems, together with instructions and all other materials necessary to use or interpret such data compilations, and any product of discovery;

(6) the term "custodian" means the custodian, or any deputy custodian, designated by the Attorney General under subsection (i)(1); and

(7) the term "product of discovery" includes—

(A) the original or duplicate of any deposition, interrogatory, document, thing, result of the inspection of land or other property, examination, or admission, which is obtained by any method of discovery in any judicial or administrative proceeding of an adversarial nature;

(B) any digest, analysis, selection, compilation, or derivation of any item listed in subparagraph (A); and

(C) any index or other manner of access to any item listed in subparagraph (A).

APPENDIX B

THE PROGRAM FRAUD CIVIL REMEDIES ACT OF 1986— P.L. 99-509, 31 U.S.C.S. 3801-3812

31 U.S.C.S. 3801. Definitions

(a) For purposes of this chapter—

(1) "authority" means—

(A) an executive department;

(B) a military department;

(C) an establishment (as such term is defined in section 11(2) of the Inspector General Act of 1978) which is not an executive department; and

(D) the United States Postal Service;

(2) "authority head" means—

(A) the head of an authority; or

(B) an official or employee of the authority designated, in regulations promulgated by the head of the authority, to act on behalf of the head of the authority;

(3) "claim" means any request, demand, or submission—

(A) made to an authority for property, services, or money (including money representing grants, loans, insurance, or benefits);

(B) made to a recipient of property, services, or money from an authority or to a party to a contract with an authority—

(i) for property of [sic or] services if the United States—

(I) provided such property or services;

(II) provided any portion of the funds for the purchase of such property or services; or

(III) will reimburse such recipient or party for the purchase of such property or services; or

(ii) for the payment of money (including money representing grants, loans, insurance, or benefits) if the United States—

(I) provided any portion of the money requested or demanded; or

(II) will reimburse such recipient or party for any portion of the money paid on such request or demand; or

(C) made to an authority which has the effect of decreasing an obligation to pay or account for property, services, or money, except that such term does not include any claim made in any return of tax imposed by the Internal Revenue Code of 1954;

(4) "investigating official" means an individual who—

(A)(i) in the case of an authority in which an Office of Inspector General is established by the Inspector General Act of 1978 or by any other Federal law, is the Inspector General of that authority or an officer or employee of such Office designated by the Inspector General;

(ii) in the case of an authority in which an Office of Inspector General is not established by the Inspector General Act of 1978 or by any other Federal law, is an officer or employee of the authority designated by the authority head to conduct investigations under section 3803(a)(1) of this title; or

(iii) in the case of a military department, is the Inspector General of the Department of Defense or an officer or employee of the Office of Inspector General of the Department of Defense who is designated by the Inspector General; and

(B) who, if a member of the Armed Forces of the United States on active duty, is serving in grade 0-7 or above or, if a civilian employee, is serving in a position for which the rate of basic pay is not less than the minimum rate of basic pay for grade GS-16 under the General Schedule;

(5) "knows or has reason to know", for purposes of establishing liability under section 3802, means that a person, with respect to a claim or statement—

(A) has actual knowledge that the claim or statement is false, fictitious, or fraudulent;

(B) acts in deliberate ignorance of the truth or falsity of the claim or statement; or

(C) acts in reckless disregard of the truth or falsity of the claim or statement,

and no proof of specific intent to defraud is required;

(6) "person" means any individual, partnership, corporation, association, or private organization;

(7) "presiding officer" means—

(A) in the case of an authority to which the provisions of subchapter II of chapter 5 of title 5 apply, an administrative law judge appointed in the authority pursuant to section 3105 of such title or detailed to the authority pursuant to section 3344 of such title; or

(B) in the case of an authority to which the provisions of such subchapter do not apply, an officer or employee of the authority who—

(i) is selected under chapter 33 of title 5 pursuant to the competitive examination process applicable to administrative law judges;

(ii) is appointed by the authority head to conduct hearings under section 3803 of this title [Prior to amendment effective July 5, 1994, "this title" read "such title".]

(iii) is assigned to cases in rotation so far as practicable;

(iv) may not perform duties inconsistent with the duties and responsibilities of a presiding officer;

(v) is entitled to pay prescribed by the Office of Personnel Management independently of ratings and recommendations made by the authority and in accordance with chapter 51 of such title and subchapter III of chapter 53 of such title;

(vi) is not subject to performance appraisal pursuant to chapter 43 of such title; and

(vii) may be removed, suspended, furloughed, or reduced in grade or pay only for good cause established and determined by the Merit Systems Protection Board on the record after opportunity for hearing by such Board;

(8) "reviewing official" means any officer or employee of an authority—

(A) who is designated by the authority head to make the determination required under section 3803(a)(2) of this title;

(B) who, if a member of the Armed Forces of the United States on active duty, is serving in grade 0-7 or above or, if a civilian employee, is serving in a position for which the basic pay is not less than the minimum rate of basic pay for grade GS-16 under the General Schedule; and

(C) who is—

(i) not subject to supervision by, or required to report to, the investigating official; and

(ii) not employed in the organizational unit of the authority in which the investigating official is employed; and

(9) "statement" means any representation, certification, affirmation, document, record, or accounting or bookkeeping entry made—

(A) with respect to a claim or to obtain the approval or payment of a claim (including relating to eligibility to make a claim); or

(B) with respect to (including relating to eligibility for)—

(i) a contract with, or a bid or proposal for a contract with; or

(ii) a grant, loan, or benefit from,

an authority, or any State, political subdivision of a State, or other party, if the United States Government provides any portion of the money or property under such contract or for such grant, loan, or benefit, or if the Government will reimburse such State, political subdivision, or party for any portion of the money or property under such contract or for such grant, loan, or benefit,

except that such term does not include any statement made in any return of tax imposed by the Internal revenue Code of 1954.

(b) For purposes of paragraph (3) of subsection (a)—

(1) each voucher, invoice, claim form, or other individual request or demand for property, services, or money constitutes a separate claim;

(2) each claim for property, services, or money is subject to this chapter regardless of whether such property, services, or money is actually delivered or paid; and

(3) a claim shall be considered made, presented, or submitted to an authority, recipient, or party when such claim is actually made to an agent, fiscal intermediary, or other entity, including any State or political subdivision thereof, acting for or on behalf of such authority, recipient, or party.

(c) for purposes of paragraph (9) of subsection (a)—

(1) each written representation, certification, or affirmation constitutes a separate statement; and

(2) a statement shall be considered made, presented, or submitted to an authority when such statement is actually made to an agent, fiscal intermediary, or other entity, including any State or political subdivision thereof, acting for or on behalf of such authority.

31 U.S.C.S. 3802. False claims and statements; liability

(a)(1) Any person who makes, presents, or submits, or causes to be made presented, or submitted, a claim that the person knows or has reason to know—

(A) is false, fictitious, or fraudulent;

(B) includes or is supported by any written statement which asserts a material fact which is false, fictitious, or fraudulent;

(C) includes or is supported by any written statement that—

(i) omits a material fact;

(ii) is false, fictitious, or fraudulent as a result of such omission; and

(iii) is a statement in which the person making, presenting, or submitting such statement has a duty to include such material fact; or

(D) is for payment for the provision of property or services which the person has not provided as claimed, shall be subject to, in addition to any other remedy that may be prescribed by law, a civil penalty of not more than $5,000 for each such claim. Except as provided in paragraph (3) of this subsection, such person shall also be subject to an assessment in lieu of damages sustained by the United States because of such claim, of not more than twice the amount of such claim, or the portion of such claim, which is determined under this chapter to be in violation of the preceding sentence.

(2) Any person who makes, presents, or submits, or causes to be made, presented or submitted, a written statement that—

(A) the person knows or has reason to know—

(i) asserts a material fact which is false, fictitious, or fraudulent; or

(ii)(I) omits a material fact; and

(II) is false, fictitious, or fraudulent as a result of such omission;

(B) in the case of a statement described in clause (ii) of subparagraph (A), is a statement in which the person making, presenting, or submitting such statement has a duty to include such material fact; and

(C) contains or is accompanied by an express certification or affirmation of the truthfulness and accuracy of the contents of the statement,

shall be subject to, in addition to any other remedy that may be prescribed by law, a civil penalty of not more than $5,000 for each such statement.

(3) An assessment shall not be made under the second sentence of paragraph (1) with respect to a claim if payment by the Government has not been made on such claim.

(b)(1) Except as provided in paragraphs (2) and (3) of this subsection—

(A) a determination under section 3803(a)(2) of this title that there is adequate evidence to believe that a person is liable under subsection (a) of this section; or

(B) a determination under section 3803 of this title that a person is liable under subsection (a) of this section, may provide the authority with grounds for commencing any administrative or contractual action against such person which is authorized by law and which is in addition to any action against such person under this chapter.

(2) A determination referred to in paragraph (1) of this subsection may be used by the authority, but shall not require such authority, to commence any administrative or contractual action which is authorized by law.

(3) In the case of an administrative or contractual action to suspend or debar any person who is eligible to enter into contracts with the Federal Government, a determination referred to in paragraph (1) of this subsection shall not be considered as a conclusive determination of such person's responsibility pursuant to Federal procurement laws and regulations.

31 U.S.C.S. 3803. Hearing and determinations

(a)(1) The investigating official of an authority may investigate allegations that a person is liable under section 3802 of this title and shall report the findings and conclusions of such investigation to the reviewing official of the authority. The preceding sentence does not modify any responsibility of an investigating official to report violations of criminal law to the Attorney General.

(2) If the reviewing official of an authority determines, based upon the report of the investigating official under paragraph (1) of this subsection, that there is adequate evidence to believe that a person is liable under section 3802 of this title, the reviewing official shall transmit to the Attorney General a written notice of the intention of such official to refer the allegations of such liability to a presiding officer of such authority. Such notice shall include—

(A) a statement of the reasons of the reviewing official for the referral of such allegations;

(B) a statement specifying the evidence which supports such allegations;

(C) a description of the claims or statements for which liability under section 3802 of this title is alleged;

(D) an estimate of the amount of money or the value of property or services requested or demanded in violation of section 3802 of this title; and

(E) a statement of any exculpatory or mitigating circumstances which may relate to such claims or statements.

(b)(1) Within 90 days after receipt of a notice from a reviewing official under paragraph (2) of subsection (a), the Attorney General or an Assistant Attorney General designated by the Attorney General shall transmit a written statement to the reviewing official which specifies—

(A) that the Attorney General or such Assistant Attorney General approves or disapproves the referral to a presiding officer of the allegations of liability stated in such notice;

(B) in any case in which the referral of allegations is approved, that the initiation of a proceeding under this section with respect to such allegations is appropriate; and

(C) in any case in which the referral of allegations is disapproved, the reasons for such disapproval.

(2) A reviewing official may refer allegations of liability to a presiding officer only if the Attorney General or an Assistant Attorney General designated by the Attorney General approves the referral of such allegations in a written statement described in paragraph (1) of this subsection.

(3) If the Attorney General or an Assistant Attorney General designated by the Attorney General transmits to an authority head a written finding that the continuation of any hearing under this section with respect to a claim or statement may adversely affect any pending or potential criminal or civil action related to such claim or statement, such hearing shall be immediately stayed and may be resumed only upon written authorization of the Attorney General.

(c)(1) No allegations of liability under section 3802 of this title with respect to any claim made, presented, or submitted by any person shall be referred to a presiding officer under paragraph (2) of subsection (b) if the reviewing official determines that—

(A) an amount of money in excess of $150,000; or

(B) property or services with a value in excess of $150,000, is requested or demanded in violation of section 3802 of this title in such claim or in a group of related claims which are submitted at the time such claim is submitted.

(2)(A) Except as provided in subparagraph (B) of this paragraph, no allegations of liability against an individual under section 3802 of this title with respect to any claim or statement made, presented, or submitted, or caused to be made, presented or submitted, by such individual relating to any benefits received by such individual shall be referred to a presiding officer under paragraph (2) of subsection (b).

(B) Allegations of liability against an individual under section 3802 of this title with respect to any claim or statement made, presented, or submitted, or caused to be made, presented, or submitted, by such individual relating to any benefits received by such individual may be referred to a presiding officer under paragraph (2) of subsection (b) if—

(i) such claim or statement is made by such individual in making application for such benefits;

(ii) such allegations relate to the eligibility of such individual to receive such benefits; and

(iii) with respect to such claim or statement, the individual—

(I) has actual knowledge that the claim or statement is false, fictitious, or fraudulent;

(II) acts in deliberate ignorance of the truth or falsity of the claim or statement; or

(III) acts in reckless disregard of the truth or falsity of the claim or statement.

(C) For purposes of this subsection, the term "benefits" means—

(i) benefits under the supplemental security income program under title XVI of the Social Security Act;

(ii) old age, survivors, and disability insurance benefits under title II of the Social Security Act;

(iii) benefits under title XVIII of the Social Security Act;

(iv) aid to families with dependent children under a State plan approved under section 402(a) of the Social Security Act;

(v) medical assistance under a State plan approved under section 1902(a) of the Social Security Act;

(vi) benefits under title XX of the Social Security Act;

(vii) benefits under the food stamp program (as defined in section 3(h) of the Food Stamp Act of 1977);

(viii) benefits under chapters 11, 13, 15, 17, and 21 of title 38;

(ix) benefits under the Black Lung Benefits Act;

(x) benefits under the special supplemental nutrition P.L. 103-448 substituted "nutrition" for "food", effective November 2, 1994.] program for women, infants, and children established under section 17 of the Child Nutrition Act of 1966;

(xi) benefits under section 336 of the Older Americans Act;

(xii) any annuity or other benefit under the Railroad Retirement Act of 1974;

(xiii) benefits under the National School Lunch Act;

(xiv) benefits under any housing assistance program for lower income families or elderly or handicapped persons which is administered by the Secretary of Housing and Urban Development or the Secretary of Agriculture;

(xv) benefits under the Low-Income Home Energy Assistance Act of 1981; and

(xvi) benefits under part A of the Energy Conservation in Existing Buildings Act of 1976,

which are intended for the personal use of the individual who receives the benefits or for a member of the individual's family.

(d)(1) On or after the date on which a reviewing official is permitted to refer allegations of liability to a presiding officer under subsection (b) of this section, the reviewing official shall mail, by registered or certified mail, or shall deliver, a notice to the person alleged to be liable under section 3802 of this title. Such notice shall specify the allegations of liability against such person and shall state the right of such person to request a hearing with respect to such allegations.

(2) If, within 30 days after receiving a notice under paragraph (1) of this subsection, the person receiving such notice

[Text Continued on Page App. B-11]

requests a hearing with respect to the allegations contained in such notice—

(A) the reviewing official shall refer such allegations to a presiding officer for the commencement of such hearing; and

(B) the presiding officer shall commence such hearing by mailing by registered or certified mail, or by delivery of, a notice which complies with paragraphs (2)(A) and (3)(B)(i) of subsection (g) to such person.

(e)(1)(A) Except as provided in subparagraph (B) of this paragraph, at any time after receiving a notice under paragraph (2)(B) of subsection (d), the person receiving such notice shall be entitled to review, and upon payment of a reasonable fee for duplication, shall be entitled to obtain a copy of, all relevant and material documents, transcripts, records, and other materials, which relate to such allegations and upon which the findings and conclusions of the investigating official under paragraph (1) of subsection (a) are based.

(B) A person is not entitled under subparagraph (A) to review and obtain a copy of any document, transcript, record, or material which is privileged under Federal law.

(2) At any time after receiving a notice under paragraph (2)(B) of subsection (d), the person receiving such notice shall be entitled to obtain all exculpatory information in the possession of the investigating official or the reviewing official relating to the allegations contained in such notice. The provisions of subparagraph (B) of paragraph (1) do not apply to any document, transcript, record, or other material, or any portion thereof, in which such exculpatory information is contained.

(f) Any hearing commenced under paragraph (2) of subsection (d) shall be conducted by the presiding officer on the record in order to determine—

(1) the liability of a person under section 3802 of this title; and

(2) if a person is determined to be liable under such section, the amount of any civil penalty or assessment to be imposed on such person.

Any such determination shall be based on the preponderance of the evidence.

(g)(1) Each hearing under subsection (f) of this section shall be conducted—

(A) in the case of an authority to which the provisions of subchapter II of chapter 5 of title 5 apply, in accordance with—

(i) the provisions of such subchapter to the extent that such provisions are not inconsistent with the provisions of this chapter; and

(ii) procedures promulgated by the authority head under paragraph (3) of this subsection; or

(B) in the case of an authority to which the provisions of such subchapter do not apply, in accordance with procedures promulgated by the authority head under paragraphs (2) and (3) of this subsection.

(2) An authority head of an authority described in subparagraph (B) of paragraph (1) shall by regulation promulgate procedures for the conduct of hearings under this chapter. Such procedures shall include:

(A) The provision of written notice of the hearing to any person alleged to be liable under section 3802 of this title, including written notice of—

(i) the time, place, and nature of the hearing;

(ii) the legal authority and jurisdiction under which the hearing is to be held; and

(iii) the matters of facts and law to be asserted.

(B) The provision to any person alleged to be liable under section 3802 of this title of opportunities for the submission of facts, arguments, offers of settlement, or proposals of adjustment.

(C) Procedures to ensure that the presiding officer shall not, except to the extent required for the disposition of ex parte matters as authorized by law—

(i) consult a person or party on a fact in issue, unless on notice and opportunity for all parties to the hearing to participate; or

(ii) be responsible to or subject to the supervision or direction of the investigating official or the reviewing official.

(D) Procedures to ensure that the investigating official and the reviewing official do not participate or advise in the decision required under subsection (h) of this section or the review of the decision by the authority head under subsection (i) of this section, except as provided in subsection (j) of this section.

(E) The provision to any person alleged to be liable under section 3802 of this title of opportunities to present such person's case through oral or documentary evidence, to submit rebuttal evidence, and to conduct such cross-examination as may be required for a full and true disclosure of the facts.

(F) Procedures to permit any person alleged to be liable under section 3802 of this title to be accompanied, represented, and advised by counsel or such other qualified representative as the authority head may specify in such regulations.

(G) Procedures to ensure that the hearing is conducted in an impartial manner, including procedures to—

(i) permit the presiding officer to at any time disqualify himself; and

(ii) permit the filing, in good faith, of a timely and sufficient affidavit alleging personal bias or another reason for disqualification of a presiding officer or a reviewing official.

(3)(A) Each authority head shall promulgate by regulation procedures described in subparagraph (B) of this paragraph for the conduct of hearings under this chapter. Such procedures shall be in addition to the procedures described in paragraph (1) or paragraph (2) of this subsection, as the case may be.

(B) The procedures referred to in subparagraph (A) of this paragraph are:

(i) Procedures for the inclusion, in any written notice of a hearing under this section to any person alleged to be liable under section 3802 of this title, of a description of the procedures for the conduct of the hearing.

(ii) Procedures to permit discovery by any person alleged to be liable under section 3802 of this title only to the extent that the presiding officer determines that such discovery is necessary for the expeditious, fair, and reasonable consideration of the issues, except that such procedures shall not apply to documents, transcripts, records, or other material which a person is entitled to review under paragraph (1) of subsection (e) or to information to which a person is entitled under paragraph (2) of such subsection. Procedures promulgated under this clause shall prohibit the discovery of the notice required under subsection (a)(2) of this section.

(4) Each hearing under subsection (f) of this section shall be held—

(A) in the judicial district of the United States in which the person alleged to be liable under section 3802 of this title resides or transacts business;

(B) in the judicial district of the United States in which the claim or statement upon which the allegation of liability under such section was made, presented, or submitted; or

(C) in such other place as may be agreed upon by such person and the presiding officer who will conduct such hearing.

(h) The presiding officer shall issue a written decision, including findings and determinations, after the conclusion of the hearing. Such decision shall include the findings of fact and conclusions of law which the presiding officer relied upon in determining whether a person is liable under this chapter. The presiding officer shall promptly send to each party to the hearing a copy of such decision and a statement describing the right of any person determined to be liable under section 3802 of this title to appeal the decision of the presiding officer to the authority head under paragraph (2) of subsection (i).

(i)(1) Except as provided in paragraph (2) of this subsection and section 3805 of this title, the decision, including the findings and determinations, of the presiding officer issued under subsection (h) of this section are final.

(2)(A)(i) Except as provided in clause (ii) of this subparagraph, within 30 days after the presiding officer issues a decision under subsection (h) of this section, any person determined in such decision to be liable under section 3802 of this title may appeal such decision to the authority head.

(ii) If, within the 30-day period described in clause (i) of this subparagraph, a person determined to be liable under this chapter requests the authority head for extension of such 30-day period to file an appeal of a decision issued by the presiding officer under subsection (h) of this section, the authority head may extend such period if such person demonstrates good cause for such extension.

(B) Any authority head reviewing under this section the decision, findings, and determinations of a presiding officer shall not consider any objection that was not raised in the hearing conducted pursuant to subsection (f) of this section unless a demonstration is made of extraordinary circumstances causing the failure to raise the objection. If any party demonstrates to the satisfaction of the authority head that additional evidence not presented at such hearing is material and that there were reasonable grounds for the failure to present such evidence at such hearing, the authority head shall remand the matter to the presiding officer for consideration of such additional evidence.

(C) The authority head may affirm, reduce, reverse, compromise, remand, or settle any penalty or assessment determined by the presiding officer pursuant to this section. The authority head shall promptly send to each party to the appeal a copy of the decision of the authority head and a statement describing the right of any person determined to be liable under section 3802 of this title to judicial review under section 3805 of this title.

(j) The reviewing official has the exclusive authority to compromise or settle any allegations of liability under section 3802 of this title against a person without the consent of the presiding officer at any time after the date on which the reviewing official is permitted to refer allegations of liability to a presiding officer under subsection (b) of this section and prior to the date on which the presiding officer issues a decision under subsection (h) of this section. Any such compromise or settlement shall be in writing.

31 U.S.C.S. 3804. Subpoena authority

(a) For the purposes of an investigation under section 3803(a)(1) of this title, an investigating official is authorized to require by subpoena the production of all information, documents, reports, answers, records, accounts, papers, and data not otherwise reasonably available to the authority.

(b) For the purposes of conducting a hearing under section 3803(f) of this title, a presiding officer is authorized—

(1) to administer oaths or affirmations; and

(2) to require by subpoena the attendance and testimony of witnesses and the production of all information, documents, reports, answers, records, accounts, papers, and other data and documentary evidence which the presiding officer considers relevant and material to the hearing.

(c) In the case of contumacy or refusal to obey a subpoena issued pursuant to subsection (a) or (b) of this section, the district courts of the United States shall have jurisdiction to issue an appropriate order for the enforcement of any such subpoena. Any failure to obey such order of the court is punishable by such court as contempt. In any case in which an authority seeks the enforcement of a subpoena issued pursuant to subsection (a) or (b) of this section, the authority shall request the Attorney General to petition any district court in which a hearing under this chapter is being conducted, or in which the person receiving the subpoena resides or conducts business, to issue such an order.

31 U.S.C.S. 3805. Judicial review

(a)(1) A determination by a reviewing official under section 3803 of this title shall be final and shall not be subject to judicial review.

(2) Unless a petition is filed under this section, a determination under section 3803 of this title that a person is liable under section 3802 of this title shall be final and shall not be subject to judicial review.

(b)(1)(A) Any person who has been determined to be liable under section 3802 of this title pursuant to section 3803 of this title may obtain review of such determination in—

(i) the United States district court for the district in which such person resides or transacts business;

(ii) the United States district court for the district in which the claim or statement upon which the determination of liability is based was made, presented, or submitted; or

(iii) the United States District Court for the District of Columbia.

(B) Such review may be obtained by filing in any such court a written petition that such determination be modified or set aside. Such petition shall be filed—

(i) only after such person has exhausted all administrative remedies under this chapter; and

(ii) within 60 days after the date on which the authority head sends such person a copy of the decision of such authority head under section 3803(i)(2) of this title.

(2) The clerk of the court shall transmit a copy of a petition filed under paragraph (1) of this subsection to the authority and to the Attorney General. Upon receipt of the copy of such petition, the authority shall transmit to the Attorney General the record in the proceeding resulting in the determination of liability under section 3802 of this title. Except as otherwise provided in this section, the district courts of the United States shall have jurisdiction to review the decision, findings, and determinations in issue and to affirm, modify, remand for further consideration, or set aside, in whole or in part, the decision, findings, and determinations of the authority, and to enforce such decision, findings, and determinations to the extent that such decision, findings, and determinations are affirmed or modified.

(c) The decisions, findings, and determinations of the authority with respect to questions of fact shall be final and conclusive, and shall not be set aside unless such decisions, findings, and determinations are found by the court to be unsupported by substantial evidence. In concluding whether the decisions, findings, and determinations of an authority are unsupported by substantial evidence, the court shall review the whole record or those parts of it cited by a party, and due account shall be taken of the rule of prejudicial error.

(d) Any district court reviewing under this section the decision, findings, and determinations of an authority shall not consider any objection that was not raised in the hearing conducted pursuant to section 3803(f) of this title unless a demonstration is made of extraordinary circumstances causing the failure to raise the objection. If any party demonstrates to the satisfaction of the court that additional evidence not presented at such hearing is material and that there were reasonable grounds for the failure to present such evidence at such hearing, the court shall remand the matter to the authority for consideration of such additional evidence.

(e) Upon a final determination by the district court that a person is liable under section 3802 of this title, the court shall enter a final judgment for the appropriate amount in favor of the United States.

31 U.S.C.S. 3806. Collection of civil penalties and assessments

(a) The Attorney General shall be responsible for judicial enforcement of any civil penalty or assessment imposed pursuant to the provisions of this chapter.

(b) Any penalty or assessment imposed in a determination which has become final pursuant to this chapter may be recovered in a civil action brought by the Attorney General. In any such action, no matter that was raised or that could have been raised in a hearing conducted under section 3803(f) of this title or pursuant to judicial review under section 3805 of this title may be raised as a defense, and the determination of liability and the determination of amounts of penalties and assessments shall not be subject to review.

(c) The district courts of the United States shall have jurisdiction of any action commenced by the United States under subsection (b) of this section.

(d) Any action under subsection (b) of this section may, without regard to venue requirements, be joined and consolidated with or asserted as a counterclaim, cross-claim, or setoff by the United States in any other civil action which includes as parties the United States and the person against whom such action may be brought.

(e) The United States Claims Court shall have jurisdiction of any action under subsection (b) of this section to recover any penalty or assessment if the cause of action is asserted by the United States as a counterclaim in a matter pending in such court.

(f) The Attorney General shall have exclusive authority to compromise or settle any penalty or assessment the determination of which is the subject of a pending petition pursuant to section 3805 of this title or a pending action to recover such penalty or assessment pursuant to this section.

(g)(1) Except as provided in paragraph (2) of this subsection, any amount of penalty or assessment collected under this chapter shall be deposited as miscellaneous receipts in the Treasury of the United States.

(2)(A) Any amount of a penalty or assessment imposed by the United States Postal Service under this chapter shall be deposited in the Postal Service Fund established by section 2003 of title 39

(B) Any amount of a penalty or assessment imposed by the Secretary of Health and Human Services under this chapter with respect to a claim or statement made in connection with old age and survivors benefits under title II of the Social Security Act shall be deposited in the Federal Old-Age and Survivors Insurance Trust Fund.

(C) Any amount of a penalty or assessment imposed by the Secretary of Health and Human Services under this chapter with respect to a claim or statement made in connection with disability benefits under title II of the Social Security Act shall be deposited in the Federal Disability Insurance Trust Fund.

(D) Any amount of a penalty or assessment imposed by the Secretary of Health and Human Services under this chapter with respect to a claim or statement made in connection with benefits under part A of title XVIII of the Social Security Act shall be deposited in the Federal Hospital Insurance Trust Fund.

(E) Any amount of a penalty or assessment imposed by the Secretary of Health and Human Services under this chapter with respect to a claim or statement made in connection with benefits under part B of title XVIII of the Social Security Act shall be deposited in the Federal Supplementary Medical Insurance Trust Fund.

31 U.S.C 3807. Right to administrative offset

(a) The amount of any penalty or assessment which has become final under section 3803 of this title, or for which a judgment has been entered under section 3805(e) or 3806 of this title, or any amount agreed upon in a settlement or compromise under section 3803(j) or 3806(f) of this title, may be collected by administrative offset under section 3716 of this title, except that an administrative offset may not be made under this subsection against a refund of an overpayment of Federal taxes, then or later owing by the United States to the person liable for such penalty or assessment.

(b) All amounts collected pursuant to this section shall be remitted to the Secretary of the Treasury for deposit in accordance with section 3806(g) of this title.

31 U.S.C.S. 3808. Limitations

(a) A hearing under section 3803(d)(2) of this title with respect to a claim or statement shall be commenced within 6 years after the date on which such claim or statement is made, presented, or submitted.

(b) A civil action to recover a penalty or assessment under section 3806 of this title shall be commenced within 3 years after the date on which the determination of liability for such penalty or assessment becomes final.

(c) If at any time during the course of proceedings brought pursuant to this chapter the authority head receives or discovers any specific information regarding bribery, gratuities, conflict of interest, or other corruption or similar activity in relation to a false claim or statement, the authority head shall immediately report such information to the Attorney General, and in the case of an authority in which an Office of Inspector General is established by the Inspector General Act of 1978 or by any other Federal law, to the Inspector General of that authority.

referrals, services furnished, or the amount of business otherwise generated from that investor to the entity.

(ii) At least one-third of each surgeon investor's medical practice income from all sources for the previous fiscal year or previous 12-month period must be derived from the surgeon's performance of procedures (as defined in this paragraph).

(iii) The entity or any investor (or other individual or entity acting on behalf of the entity or any investor) must not loan funds to or guarantee a loan for an investor if the investor uses any part of such loan to obtain the investment interest.

(iv) The amount of payment to an investor in return for the investment must be directly proportional to the amount of the capital investment (including the fair market value of any pre-operational services rendered) of that investor.

(v) All ancillary services for Federal health care program beneficiaries performed at the entity must be directly and integrally related to primary procedures performed at the entity, and none may be separately billed to Medicare or other Federal health care programs.

(vi) The entity and any surgeon investors must treat patients receiving medical benefits or assistance under any Federal health care program in a nondiscriminatory manner.

(2) Single-Specialty ASCs — If all of the investors are physicians engaged in the same medical practice specialty who are in a position to refer patients directly to the entity and perform procedures on such referred patients; group practices (as defined in this paragraph) composed exclusively of such physicians; or investors who are not employed by the entity or by any investor, are not in a position to provide items or services to the entity or any of its investors, and are not in a position to make or influence referrals directly or indirectly to the entity or any of its investors, all of the following six standards must be met —

(i) The terms on which an investment interest is offered to an investor must not be related to the previous or expected volume of referrals, services furnished, or the amount of business otherwise generated from that investor to the entity.

(ii) At least one-third of each physician investor's medical practice income from all sources for the previous fiscal year or previous 12-month period must be derived from the surgeon's performance of procedures (as defined in this paragraph).

(iii) The entity or any investor (or other individual or entity acting on behalf of the entity or any investor) must not loan funds to or guarantee a loan for an investor if the investor uses any part of such loan to obtain the investment interest.

(iv) The amount of payment to an investor in return for the investment must be directly proportional to the amount of the capital investment (including the fair market value of any pre-operational services rendered) of that investor.

(v) All ancillary services for Federal health care program beneficiaries performed at the entity must be directly and integrally related to primary procedures performed at the entity, and none may be separately billed to Medicare or other Federal health care programs.

(vi) The entity and any physician investors must treat patients receiving medical benefits or assistance under any Federal health care program in a nondiscriminatory manner.

(3) Multi-Specialty ASCs — If all of the investors are physicians who are in a position to refer patients directly to the entity and perform procedures on such referred patients; group practices, as defined in this paragraph, composed exclusively of such physicians; or investors who are not employed by the entity or by any investor, are not in a position to provide items or services to the entity or any of its investors, and are not in a position to make or influence referrals directly or indirectly to the entity or any of its investors, all of the following seven standards must be met —

(i) The terms on which an investment interest is offered to an investor must not be related to the previous or expected volume of referrals, services furnished, or the amount of business otherwise generated from that investor to the entity.

(ii) At least one-third of each physician investor's medical practice income from all sources for the previous fiscal year or previous 12-month period must be derived from the physician's performance of procedures (as defined in this paragraph).

(iii) At least one-third of the procedures (as defined in this paragraph) performed by each physician investor for the previous fiscal year or previous 12-month period must be performed at the investment entity.

(iv) The entity or any investor (or other individual or entity acting on behalf of the entity or any investor) must not loan funds to or guarantee a loan for an investor if the investor uses any part of such loan to obtain the investment interest.

(v) The amount of payment to an investor in return for the investment must be directly proportional to the amount of the capital investment (including the fair market value of any pre-operational services rendered) of that investor.

(vi) All ancillary services for Federal health care program beneficiaries performed at the entity must be directly and integrally related to primary procedures performed at the entity, and none may be separately billed to Medicare or other Federal health care programs.

(vii) The entity and any physician investors must treat patients receiving medical benefits or assistance under any Federal health care program in a nondiscriminatory manner.

(4) Hospital/Physician ASCs — If at least one investor is a hospital, and all of the remaining investors are physicians who meet the requirements of paragraphs (r)(1), (r)(2) or (r)(3) of this section; group practices (as defined in this paragraph) composed of such physicians; surgical group practices (as defined in this paragraph); or investors who are not employed by the entity or by any investor, are not in a position to provide items or services to the entity or any of its investors, and are not in a position to refer patients directly or indirectly to the entity or any of its investors, all of the following eight standards must be met —

(i) The terms on which an investment interest is offered to an investor must not be related to the previous or expected volume of referrals, services furnished, or the amount of business otherwise generated from that investor to the entity.

(ii) The entity or any investor (or other individual or entity acting on behalf of the entity or any investor) must not loan funds to or guarantee a loan for an investor if the investor uses any part of such loan to obtain the investment interest.

(iii) The amount of payment to an investor in return for the investment must be directly proportional to the amount of the capital investment (including the fair market value of any pre-operational services rendered) of that investor.

(iv) The entity and any hospital or physician investor must treat patients receiving medical benefits or assistance under any Federal health care program in a nondiscriminatory manner.

(v) The entity may not use space, including, but not limited to, operating and recovery room space, located in or owned by any hospital investor, unlesssuch space is leased from the hospital in accordance with a lease that complies with all the standards of the space rental safe harbor set forth in paragraph (b) of this section; nor may it use equipment owned by or services provided by the hospital unless such equipment is leased in accordance with a lease that complies with the equipment rental safe harbor set forth in paragraph (c) of this section, and such services are provided in accordance with a contract that complies with the personal services and management contracts safe harbor set forth in paragraph (d) of this section.

(vi) All ancillary services for Federal health care program beneficiaries performed at the entity must be directly and integrally related to primary procedures performed at the entity, and none may be separately billed to Medicare or other Federal health care programs.

(vii) The hospital may not include on its cost report or any claim for payment from a Federal health care program any costs associated with the ASC (unless such costs are required to be included by a Federal health care program).

(viii) The hospital may not be in a position to make or influence referrals directly or indirectly to any investor or the entity.

(5) For purposes of paragraph (r) of this section, procedures means any procedure or procedures on the list of Medicare-covered procedures for ambulatory surgical centers in accordance with regulations issued by the Department and group practice means a group practice that meets all of the standards of paragraph (p) of this section. Surgical group practice means a group practice that meets all of the standards of paragraph (p) of this section and is composed exclusively of surgeons who meet the requirements of paragraph (r)(1) of this section.

(s) Referral agreements for specialty services. As used in section 1128B of the Act, remuneration does not include any exchange of value among individuals and entities where one party agrees to refer a patient to the other party for the provision of a specialty service payable in whole or in part under Medicare or a State health care program in return for an agreement on the part of the other party to refer that patient back at a mutually agreed upon time or circumstance as long as the following four standards are met—

(1) The mutually agreed upon time or circumstance for referring the patient back to the originating individual or entity is clinically appropriate.

(2) The service for which the referral is made is not within the medical expertise of the referring individual or entity, but is within the special expertise of the other party receiving the referral.

(3) The parties receive no payment from each other for the referral and do not share or split a global fee from any Federal health care program in connection with the referred patient.

(4) Unless both parties belong to the same group practice as defined in paragraph (p) of this section, the only exchange of value between the parties is the remuneration the parties receive directly from third-party payors or the patient compensating the parties for the services they each have furnished to the patient.

Dated: February 4, 1999.

June Gibbs Brown, Inspector General.

Approved: June 9, 1999.

Donna E. Shalala,Secretary.

[FR Doc. 99–29989 Filed 11–18–99; 8:45 am]

BILLING CODE 4150–04-P

APPENDIX F8.1

Statutory Exception to the Anti-Kickback Statute for Shared Risk Arrangements; Final Rule; 64 FR 63504, November 19, 1999

[Federal Register: November 19, 1999 (Volume 64, Number 223)][Rules and Regulations]

Part IV

Department of Health and Human Services

Office of Inspector General

42 CFR Part 1001

Federal Health Care Programs: Fraud and Abuse; Statutory Exception to the Anti-Kickback Statute for Shared Risk Arrangements; Final Rule

DEPARTMENT OF HEALTH AND HUMAN SERVICES

Office of Inspector General

42 CFR Part 1001

RIN 0991-AA91

Federal Health Care Programs: Fraud and Abuse; Statutory Exception to the Anti-Kickback Statute for Shared Risk Arrangements

AGENCY: Office of Inspector General (OIG), HHS

ACTION: Interim final rule with request for comment.

SUMMARY: In accordance with section 216 of the Health Insurance Portability and Accountability Act of 1996 (HIPAA), and section 14 of the Medicare and Medicaid Patient and Program Protection Act of 1987, this interim final rule establishes two new safe harbors from the anti-kickback law (section 1128B(b) of the Social Security Act) to provide protection for certain managed care arrangements. The first safe harbor protects certain financial arrangements between managed care plans and individuals or entities with whom they contract for the provision of health care items and services, where Federal health care programs pay such plans on a capitated basis. The second safe harbor protects certain financial arrangements between managed care plans (including employer-sponsored group health plans) and individuals or entities with whom they contract for health care items and services with respect to services reimbursed on a fee-for-service basis by a Federal health care program provided that such individuals and entities are placed at substantial financial risk for the cost or utilization of items or services furnished to Federal health care program beneficiaries. Each of these safe harbors set forth standards that will result in the particular arrangement being protected from criminal prosecution and civil or administrative sanctions under the anti-kickback provisions.

DATES: Effective date: This rule is effective on November 19, 1999. Comment period: To assure consideration, public comments must be delivered to the address provided below by no later than 5 p.m. on January 18, 2000.

ADDRESSES: Please mail or deliver your written comments to the following address: Office of Inspector General, Department of Health and Human Services, Attention: OIG-54-IFC, Room 5246, Cohen Building 330 Independence Avenue, S.W., Washington, D.C. 20201.

FOR FURTHER INFORMATION CONTACT:

Julie E. Kass, Senior Counsel, Office of Counsel to the Inspector General, (202) 205–9501; or Joel Schaer, Regulations Officer, Office of Counsel to the Inspector General, (202) 619–1306.

SUPPLEMENTARY INFORMATION:

I. Background

A. The Anti-Kickback Statute

Section 1128B(b) of the Social Security Act (the Act) (42 U.S.C. 1320a-7b(b)) provides criminal penalties for individuals or entities that knowingly and willfully offer, pay, solicit or receive remuneration to induce the referral of business reimbursable under a Federal health care program (including Medicare and Medicaid). The offense is a felony punishable by fines of up to $25,000 and imprisonment for up to 5 years. Section 2 of the Medicare and Medicaid Patient and Program Protection Act of 1987 (MMPPPA) authorizes the exclusion of an individual or entity from participation in the Medicare and State health care programs if it is determined that the party has violated the anti-kickback statute. In addition, the Balanced Budget Act of 1997, Public Law 105–33, amended section 1128A(a) of the Act to include an administrative civil money penalty provision for violating the anti-kickback statute. The administrative sanction is $50,000 for each act and an assessment of not more than 3 times the amount of remuneration offered, paid, solicited or received, without regard to whether a portion of such remuneration was offered, paid, solicited or received for a lawful purpose. (See section 1128A(a)(7) of the Act; 42 U.S.C. 1320a-7a(a)(7)).

The anti-kickback statute contains five statutory exceptions from the statutory prohibitions. The exceptions are for certain discounts obtained by a provider and disclosed to the Federal health care program, compensation paid to a bona fide employee by an employer, amounts paid to a group purchasing organization by a vendor subject to certain conditions, waivers of coinsurance by Federally qualified health centers, and remuneration paid as part of a risk-sharing arrangement. The last exception is the subject of this rulemaking.

Section 14 of MMPPPA also required the OIG to promulgate regulations specifying those payment and business practices that, although potentially capable of inducing referrals of business under the Medicare and State health care programs, would not be subject to criminal prosecution under section 1128B of the Act and that will not provide a basis for administrative sanctions under sections 1128 (b)(7) or 1128A(a)(7) of the Act. (See section 2 of Pub. L. 100–93.) Congress intended that the regulations setting forth various "safe harbors" would be periodically updated to reflect changing business practices and technologies in the health care industry.

The failure of an arrangement to fit inside a safe harbor or statutory exception does not mean that the arrangement is illegal. It is incorrect to assume that arrangements outside of a safe harbor are suspect due to that fact alone. That an arrangement does not meet a safe harbor only means that the arrangement does not have guaranteed protection and must be evaluated on a case-by-case basis.

The anti-kickback statute potentially applies to many managed care arrangements because a common strategy of these arrangements is to offer physicians, hospitals and other providers increased patient volume in return for substantial fee discounts. Because discounts to managed care plans can constitute "remuneration" within the meaning of the anti-kickback statute, a number of health care providers and managed care plans have expressed concern that many relatively innocuous, or even beneficial, commercial managed care arrangements implicate the statute and may subject them to criminal prosecution and administrative sanctions. In response to these concerns, we issued final safe harbor regulations for managed care arrangements on January 25, 1996 (61 FR 2122) to protect certain managed care arrangements that we did not believe posed any significant risk of fraud or abuse. (See 42 CFR 1001.952(m)). We are soliciting comments on whether the current managed care safe harbor should be removed in light of this rulemaking so as to avoid confusion.

We recognize that many managed care arrangements exist in the marketplace today that do not fall within a safe harbor, but are not illegal under the anti-kickback statute. Such arrangements must be analyzed on a case-by-case basis. Any individual or entity with questions regarding whether a specific arrangement violates the anti-kickback statute may submit an advisory opinion request to the OIG in accordance with regulations set forth in 42 CFR part 1008.

B. Section 216 of HIPAA

1. Summary of Statutory Provision

In section 216 of HIPAA, Congress created a new statutory exception to the anti-kickback statute that covers remuneration in accordance with two categories of risk-sharing arrangements. The first category is "any remuneration between an organization and an individual or entity providing items or services, or a combination thereof, pursuant to a written agreement between the organization and the individual or entity if the organization is an eligible organization under section 1876 (of the Social Security Act) * * *" The second category is "any remuneration between an organization and an individual or entity providing items or services, or a combination thereof, pursuant to a written agreement between the organization and the individual or entity * * * if the written agreement, through a risk-sharing arrangement, places the individual or entity at substantial financial risk for the cost or utilization of the items or services, or a combination thereof, which the individual or entity is obligated to provide." Congress directed the Department to develop regulations implementing the exceptions using a negotiated rulemaking process.2. Negotiated Rulemaking Process

The negotiated rulemaking process began in the spring of 1997, and on March 7, 1997, a facilitator with the Department's Departmental Appeals Board issued a convening report to the Inspector General, setting out findings and recommendations on the use of a negotiated rulemaking process for these regulations and identifying industry and consumer representatives who, based on their interests, should serve on the committee. On May 23, 1997, the OIG issued a notice of intent to form a Negotiated Rulemaking Committee, in accordance with the Negotiated Rulemaking Act of 1990, Public Law 101–648, as amended by Public Law 102–354 (5 U.S.C. 561 et seq.), and requested public comments on whether those interests affected by the key issues of the negotiated rulemaking had been identified (62 FR 28410). After review of the comments, the Secretary appointed a committee consisting of 23 parties representing all of the major groups identified as having a significant interest in these regulations. The negotiated rulemaking committee was comprised of the following groups:

- American Association of Retired Persons
- American Hospital Association
- American Health Care Association
- American Medical Association
- American Medical Group Association
- Blue Cross Blue Shield Association
- Consumer Coalition for Quality Health Care
- Coordinated Care Coalition
- Department of Justice
- Federation of American Health Systems
- Health Insurance Association of America
- Health Insurance Manufacturers Association
- Independent Insurance Agents of America/National Association of Health
- Underwriters/National Association of Life Underwriters
- National Association of Chain Drug Stores
- National Association of Community Health Centers
- National Association of Insurance Commissioners
- National Association of Medicaid Fraud Control Units
- National Association of State Medicaid Directors
- National Rural Health Association
- Office of Inspector General, DHHS
- Pharmaceutical Research and Manufacturers of America
- The IPA Association of America

The committee was charged with reaching consensus on the basic content of interim final regulations relating to section 216 of HIPAA. Committee consensus was defined as a unanimous concurrence of all committee members, provided that there was a quorum of two-thirds of the committee members present. Unanimous concurrence with respect to a committee decision meant only that the committee members "could live with" the particular decision.

The committee held seven multi-day negotiating sessions beginning in June 1997. During the sessions, the committee made significant progress in developing new regulations. On January 22, 1998, the committee unanimously concurred on the committee statement that formed the basis of this rulemaking when considered as a whole. A copy of the committee statement can be found on the OIG web site at http://www.dhhs.gov/progorg/oig.

C. Basis for Interim Final Rulemaking

These interim final regulations will be effective upon publication. For a number of reasons, we find that good cause exists for an immediate effective date for these regulations. First, Congress specifically mandated that the regulations implementing section 216 of HIPAA should be published as interim final regulations. Second, those portions of the rule that are technically outside of the scope of section 216 of HIPAA were discussed in a public forum during the negotiated rulemaking sessions and are integral to the protections afforded under the portions of the regulation implementing section 216 of HIPAA. In addition, safe harbors do not create any affirmative obligation on any individuals or entities. They only exempt certain conduct from potential criminal and administrative sanctions. As a result, we find that the benefit conferred on the public by this rule's immediate promulgation provides good cause for it to be effective upon publication.

II. Provisions of the Interim Final Rule

In this section, we discuss the purpose and scope of the safe harbors, summarize the provisions of this interim final rule, and describe general issues that arose during the negotiated rulemaking. We then describe the individual provisions of the rulemaking and related issues discussed by the committee.

A. Purpose

The rule is intended to implement section 216 of HIPAA by creating two new regulatory safe harbors that correspond to the two categories of managed care arrangements identified in that statutory provision. The first safe harbor, set forth in Sec. 1001.952(t), protects various financial arrangements between managed care entities that receive a fixed or capitated amount from the Federal health care programs and individuals and entities with whom the managed care entity contracts for the provision of health care items or services.

The second safe harbor, set forth in Sec. 1001.952(u), protects contractual relationships between managed care entities and their contractors and subcontractors where the contractors and subcontractors are at substantial financial risk for the cost or utilization of items or services they provide or order for Federal health care program beneficiaries. As explained in detail below, the negotiated rulemaking committee recognized that there are few existing managed care arrangements that would qualify under newly-established Sec. 1001.952(u) that are not otherwise covered by the safe harbor in newly-established Sec. 1001.952(t). In practice, most managed care arrangements, such as employer-sponsored health plans, do not place their contractors and subcontractors at substantial financial risk for the cost or utilization of items or services provided to Federal healthcare program beneficiaries. Typically, the contractors and subcontractors to such health plans are reimbursed directly by the Federal payor on a fee-for-service basis. Notwithstanding the fee-for-service payment arrangements, Sec. 1001.952(u) identifies a category of arrangements that could qualify for protection.

B. Scope of the Safe Harbors

The safe harbors established in Secs. 1001.952(t) and (u) protect remuneration between parties where the remuneration is a price reduction for the provision of health care items or services. Other remuneration, such as profit distributions from investment interests in an entity with a risk sharing arrangement, is not protected by these safe harbors. Individuals or entities seeking safe harbor protection for such arrangements may meet the requirements of another safe harbor, such as the safe harbor for investment interests in small entities set forth in Sec. 1001.952(a)(2).

In addition, if an arrangement covers both remuneration that qualifies for protection under either Sec. 1001.952(t) or (u), and remuneration that is not qualified for protection, the former remuneration remains protected. For example, a managed care plan may "carve out" transplant services from its capitated payment methodology and pay for those services on a fee-for-service basis. The remuneration for the transplant services would not be protected under these safe harbors. However, protection for the items or services covered by the capitation, assuming all safe harbor conditions are otherwise met, would not be lost. Further, an arrangement that potentially falls within more than one safe harbor need only meet the requirements of one safe harbor. The remuneration for the transplant services may be protected under a separate safe harbor, such as the personal services safe harbor (Sec. 1001.952(d)).

Finally, compliance with a safe harbor only provides protection from the Federal anti-kickback criminal statute and related administrative sanction authorities. Safe harbors do not apply to other laws, such as State licensure laws, antitrust laws or other Federal and State health care fraud laws. Further, the terms and definitions in these safe harbors do not apply to other laws, including but not limited to the anti-trust laws.

C. General Issues Discussed By The Committee

The literal language of section 216 of HIPAA presented several threshold problems. First, the two categories of managed care arrangements identified by section 216 of HIPAA were narrow and did not provide protection for other managed care arrangements that the committee believed presented similar low risks of fraud or abuse. For example, section 216 was passed prior to the enactment of the Balanced Budget Act of 1997, which provides both for the phasing out of section 1876 managed care contracts, and the creation of Medicare+Choice programs under the new Medicare Part C. Many of the new Medicare+Choice organizations are similar to section 1876 organizations and deserve the same extensive protection. Nevertheless, while Congress in the Balanced Budget Act changed many of the references to section 1876 in the Act to the new Medicare Part C, it did not change the reference in section 216 of HIPAA.

A similar issue arose with respect to the second category of arrangements protected by section 216. The statutory language was limited to arrangements in which the provider or supplier is at substantial financial risk for items or services that it is obligated to provide. However, as a practical matter, many effective managed care systems place the physicians at substantial risk, not for the physician services they provide directly, but for the ancillary and hospital services they order. Furthermore, the financial incentives in most managed care plans are based not on the individual performance of a physician, but on the aggregate performance of a group of physicians.

Given the shortcomings of the statutory language, the Department determined that it would exercise its authority under section 14 of the MMPPPA to expand these safe harbors beyond the legal confines of section 216. Again, section 14 of MMPPPA allows the Secretary to promulgate regulations to protect arrangements that the Department determines may technically violate the anti-kickback statute, but which pose a low risk of program fraud or abuse. Exercise of this authority permits protection of certain types of managed care arrangements that are not encompassed within the statutory language of section 216 of HIPAA. The committee statement includes these expanded provisions and specifically identifies them as areas outside of the scope of section 216.

A final conceptual issue was the definition of "substantial financial risk." Some committee members wanted the rule to set forth clear "bright line" standards, so that both law enforcement officers and the industry would know whether a particular arrangement was protected or not. While bright line tests can potentially "chill" the development of some innovative managed care arrangements, any ambiguity in the scope of protection could be exploited by unscrupulous individuals or entities to engage in abusive or fraudulent activities, especially in light of the high burden of proof on the Government in criminal proceedings. Plans have the option of submitting advisory opinion requests for arrangements that do not fit within these safe harbors. Furthermore, the Department annually solicits suggestions for additions to the anti-kickback safe harbors (62 FR 65049; December 10, 1997). Moreover, we have agreed to review the target payment percentages of the numeric substantial financial risk test as more research and data become available.

D. Section 1001.952(t)—Price Reductions Offered to Eligible Managed Care Organizations

1. Overview

This safe harbor corresponds to the first category of arrangements identified in section 216 of HIPAA, which exempts certain arrangements involving "eligible organizations under section 1876" of the Act. Section 1876 of the Act provides for the Health Care Financing Administration (HCFA) to enter into managed care contracts with Federally-qualified health maintenance organizations (HMOs) and certain competitive medical plans that have characteristics similar to Federally-qualified HMOs. As used in section 1876 of the Act and the implementing regulations, an "eligible organization" encompasses both (i) Federally-qualified HMOs and competitive medical plans that have entered into either risk or cost-based managed care contracts with HCFA, and (ii) Federally-qualified HMOs that have not entered into risk or cost-based managed care contracts with HCFA.

This safe harbor recognized that eligible organizations with risk contracts under section 1876 of the Act presented little or no risk of overutilization or increased costs to the Federal health care programs, given applicable payment arrangements and regulatory oversight. When plans are paid a capitated amount for all of the services they provide regardless of the dates, frequency or type of services, there is no incentive to overutilize. In any event, even if overutilization occurs, the Federal health care programs are not at risk for these increased costs.

The safe harbor set forth in Sec. 1001.952(t) extends protection from the anti-kickback statute beyond themanaged care arrangements under section 1876 of the Act that are specifically protected by section 216 of HIPAA. The expansion includes other programs where the Federal health care programs pay on a capitated or fixed aggregate basis, such as certain Medicare Part C plans. Further, it extends safe harbor protection "downstream" to cover subcontracts with other providers and entities to provide items and services in accordance with a protected managed care arrangement. So long as the Federal health care programs' aggregate financial exposure is fixed in accordance with its contract with the managed care organization, these subcontracting arrangements are protected regardless of the payment methodology, subject to the limitations set forth below.

2. Limitations

While Sec. 1001.952(t) broadens the statutory exception in important respects, there are some important limitations. First, the broad protection for arrangements with subcontractors is limited to risk-based managed care plans that do not claim any payment from a Federal health care program other than the capitated amount set forth in the managed care plan's agreement with the Federal health care program. Where the managed care plan, its contractors or its subcontractors are permitted to seek additional payments from any of the Federal health care programs, the regulatory safe harbor protection is significantly more limited. For example, protection is not extended to arrangements with subcontractors when the contract under section 1876 of the Act is cost-based or where the prime contract is protected solely because the contracting entity is a Federally-qualified HMO. In the first instance, reimbursement from the Federal health care program is based on costs, and in the latter case, services for Medicare enrollees are reimbursed on a fee-for-service basis. In both instances, reimbursement will increase with utilization, thus providing the same incentive to overutilize as any fee-for-service payment methodology.

A second limitation on the regulatory safe harbor protection is that it only applies to remuneration for health care items and services and those items or services reasonably related to the provision of health care items and services. Section 1001.952(t) does not cover marketing services or any services provided prior to a beneficiary's enrollment in a health plan. This limitation also applies to the other new safe harbor in Sec. 1001.952(u).

Another significant limitation is that there is no protection if the financial arrangements under the managed care agreement are implicitly or explicitly part of a broader agreement to steer fee-for-service Federal health care program business to the entity giving the discount to induce the referral of managed care business. Specifically, we understand that most managed care plans have multiple relationships with their contractors and subcontractors for the provision of services for various product lines, including non-federal HMOs, preferred provider organizations (PPOs) and point of service networks. Consequently, although neither a managed care plan receiving a capitated payment from a Federal health care program nor its contractors or subcontractors has an incentive to overutilize items or services or pass additional costs back to the Federal health care programs under the capitated arrangement, we are concerned that a managed care plan or contractor may offer (or be offered) a reduced rate for its items or services in the Federal capitated arrangement in order to have the opportunity to participate in other product lines that do not have stringent payment or utilization constraints. This practice is a form of a practice that has become known as "swapping"; in the case of managed care arrangements low capitation rates could be traded for access to additional fee-for-service lines of business. We are concerned when these discounts are in exchange for access to fee-for-service lines of business, where there is an incentive to overutilize services provided to Federal health care program beneficiaries.

For example, we would have concerns where an HMO with a Medicare risk contract under Medicare Part C also has an employer-sponsored PPO that includes retirees and requires participating providers to accept a low capitation rate for the Medicare HMO risk patients in exchange for access to the Medicare fee-for-service patients in the PPO. Although in such circumstances the cost to the Medicare program for the risk based HMO beneficiaries will not be increased, there may be increased expenditures for Medicare beneficiaries in the PPO arrangement, since the providers may have an incentive to increase services to the Medicare enrollees in the PPO to offset the discounted rates to the Medicare HMO. Accordingly, such arrangements could violate the anti-kickback statute and should not be protected.3. Analysis of Sec. 1001.952(t)

a. Arrangements between eligible managed care organizations and first tier contractors. Section 1001.952(t)(1) is divided into two parts and sets out the substantive standards that arrangements must meet in order to receive safe harbor protection. Paragraph (t)(1)(i) of this section sets out the standards for arrangements between the eligible managed care organization (EMCO) and any individual or entity that contracts directly with the EMCO. These direct or "first tier" contractors are the only parties that are protected by the literal language of section 216 of HIPAA. Accordingly, the regulation treats these first tier contractors differently than individuals or entities that provide health care items or services in accordance with subcontracts with these first tier entities. We refer to these subcontractors as "downstream" contractors or providers. Paragraph (t)(1)(ii) of this section sets out the standards which must be met in order for arrangements between first tier contractors and any downstream subcontractor or between successive tiers of downstream subcontractors to be protected.

Under Sec. 1001.952(t)(1)(i)(A), the EMCO and any first tier contractor must have an agreement that is written and signed by the parties, specifies the items and services covered under the agreement, and has a term of at least one year. These requirements are similar to the requirements for written agreements in other safe harbor provisions. In paragraph (1)(i)(A)(IV) of this section, there is a requirement that neither party will receive any additional payment for covered services from the Federal health care programs. This requirement is intended to insure that there is an incentive to control costs by eliminating the ability on the part of the first tier contractor to offset losses incurred through the capitated methodology.

There are three exceptions to this general prohibition on the plan's receipt of additional Federal health care payments. These exceptions, set out in Sec. 1001.952(t)(1)(i)(A)(IV) are:

- HMOs and CMPs that have Medicare cost-based contracts under section 1876 of the Act;

- Federally-qualified HMOs without a HCFA contract; and
- Federally qualified health centers that claim supplemental payments from a Federal health care program.

For Federally-qualified HMOs and Medicare cost-based HMOs/CMPs, the billing arrangement under which they receive additional Federal health program payments must be set forth in

the written agreement. With respect to Federally-qualified HMOs and Medicare cost-based HMOs/CMPs, the language of section 216 of HIPAA expressly requires this exception, since they are "eligible organizations" in section 1876 of the Act. The exception for Federally-qualified health centers is beyond the language of section 216. Nevertheless, an exception for Federally-qualified health centers recognizes the special role they play in health care delivery systems in many medically underserved areas. We wish to make clear, however, that the safe harbor protects only the provision of health care items or services by (1) individuals or entities that contract directly with the HMOs and CMPs with cost-based contracts under section 1876 of the Act, or with Federally-qualified HMOs that do not have a risk-based contract with the Medicare program, i.e., first tier providers, or (2) in the case of a Federally-qualified health center, by the health center itself.

As part of this interim final rule, we are soliciting comments concerning coverage of arrangements where a Medicaid managed care plan or an individual or entity under such a plan bills another Federal health care program on a fee-for-service basis for a person that is dually eligible for Medicare and Medicaid. One possibility would be to extend safe harbor protection in instances where (1) the Medicaid plan bills the Federal health care program; (2) the individual or entity is paid by the Medicaid plan in the same amount and in the same way as for those enrollees who are not subject to the coordination of benefits; and (3) neither the plan nor the individual or entity otherwise shifts the burden of such an arrangement to the extent that increased payments are claimed from a Federal health care program.

The last two standards in Sec. 1001.952(t)(1)(i) insure that the discounts by the providers do not increase the risk of overutilization or increased costs in other Federal health care programs. As explained in the overview section, this safe harbor does not protect situations where one party gives or receives a discount or other remuneration in return for or to induce the provision or acceptance of business (other than that covered by the arrangement) for which payment may be made by the Federal health care programs on a fee-for-service basis. In addition, in accordance with paragraph (1)(i)(C) of this section, the arrangement cannot shift the financial burden to the extent that increased payments are claimed from Federal health care programs.

b. Arrangements between first tier contractors and downstream contractors. Except as discussed below, arrangements between a first tier contractor and a downstream contractor, or between successive tiers of downstream contractors, are protected as long as the arrangement is for the provision of health care items or services that are covered by the arrangement between the first tier contractor and the EMCO. In addition, arrangements between the first tier contractor and subcontractor, or between such subcontractors and subcontractors farther downstream, must meet the same requirements as apply to arrangements between EMCOs and first tier contractors.

The one exception to the generally broad safe harbor protection for "downstream" providers is for arrangements between providers for health care items or services that are downstream from (1) Federally-qualified health centers receiving supplemental payments, (2) HMOs or CMPs with cost-based contracts under section 1876 of the Act; or (3) Federally-qualified HMOs (unless they are provided in accordance with a risk-based contract under section 1876 of the Act or Medicare Part C). Reimbursement to these entities is not strictly risk-based and presents some risk of overutilization and increased Federal program costs. However, the safe harbor does protect entities that are providing items or services in accordance with a contract or subcontract with Federally-qualified health centers if the health centers do not receive any supplemental payments from the State. In such situations, the Federally-qualified health center has a strong financial incentive to guard against overutilization or excessive costs.

c. Definitions. For purposes of Sec. 1001.952(t), we have set forth the definition for several terms. Rather than discuss the definitions in alphabetical order (as they appear in the regulation), they are discussed below in logical order, grouping the definitions that apply to various contracting parties together.

Eligible Managed Care Organization — Eligible managed care organizations are Medicare risk-based or cost-based contractors under section 1876 of the Act, Medicare Part C health plans (except for medical savings accounts and fee-for-service plans), certain

Medicaid managed care organizations (as described below), most Programs For All Inclusive Care For The Elderly (PACE) and Federally-qualified HMOs.

Section 1001.952(t)(2)(ii)(C)-(D) identify the Medicaid managed care organizations that fall within the definition of eligible managed care organization. Protected arrangements are those defined in section 1903(m)(1)(A) of the Act that provide or arrange for services for Medicaid enrollees under a contract in accordance with section 1903 (m). These plans are paid by the State Medicaid agency on a capitated basis. In addition, the safe harbor provision protects other plans with risk-based contracts with a State agency to provide or arrange for items or services to Medicaid enrollees, provided that contracts are subject to the upper payment limit in 42 CFR 447.361 or any equivalent cap approved by the Secretary.

The safe harbor also protects most PACE programs. These programs provide a capitated amount for medical and certain social services for the elderly. The BBA changed not-for-profit PACE programs from demonstration status to covered services under Medicare and Medicaid. PACE programs that still have demonstration status (i.e., certain for-profit programs) are not protected by this safe harbor.

We are soliciting comments on whether the Department of Defense's TriCare program should also be included within the definition of "eligible managed care organization" and, if included, to what extent protection should be granted. The committee statement includes TriCare within the types of organizations that should receive protection through the Department's regulatory authority. However, TriCare is a relatively new health care program for the active status military and their dependents, and has a more complex reimbursement methodology than Medicare risk contracts and retains important elements of cost-based, retrospective methodologies. Accordingly, it is unclear whether there are financial safeguards to control overutilization and limit costs to the Federal Government that are sufficient to warrant per se protection from the anti-kickback statute.

First Tier Contractors — A first tier contractor is an individual or entity that has a contract to provide or arrange for items or services directly with an eligible managed care organization.

Downstream Contractor — A downstream contractor is an individual or entity that provides or arranges for items or services in accordance with a subcontract with either (1) a party that is contracting directly with an EMCO, or (2) another party for the provision or arrangement of items or services that arecovered in accordance with a contract between the parties in (1).

Items and Services — The term "items and services" is defined for purposes of this section to mean health care items, devices, supplies or services or those items or services that are reasonably related to such services, such as non-emergency transportation, patient education, attendant services, disease management, case management and utilization review and quality assurance. "Items and services" does not include marketing services or any similar pre-enrollment activities. The exclusion of marketing services is not meant to apply to nurse call-in lines or value-added services for current enrollees.

E. Section 1001.952(u) — Price Reductions Offered to Qualified Managed Care Plans

1. Overview

An overview of this new safe harbor, a summary of several major issues that arose during the committee's discussions, and an outline of the new provisions of this safe harbor are set forth below.

While Sec. 1001.952(t) protects certain arrangements based upon the "status" of the parties, e.g., designation as an eligible organization for purposes of section 1876 of the Act or participation in the PACE program, Sec. 1001.952(u) provides safe harbor protection for arrangements that qualify under the functional test identified in section 216 of HIPAA, that is, risk-sharing arrangements that place a health care provider under substantial financial risk for the cost or utilization of health care services the provider is obligated to provide.2. Limitations

Section 216 of HIPAA contains two important qualifications that substantially narrow the universe of arrangements that can potentially qualify for protection using the functional test. The most important constraint is that the provider has to be at substantial financial risk for items or services provided to Federal health care program beneficiaries. However, except for providers participating in the Medicare and Medicaid managed care plans that are already covered by the new safe harbor in Sec. 1001.952(t), almost all other providers are reimbursed by Federal health care programs on a fee-for-service basis.

However, according to information presented to the committee, most managed care arrangements that cover Federal health care program beneficiaries and are not paid on a risk basis are employer-sponsored health plans that cover retirees who may also qualify for Medicare. In these managed care arrangements, the participating providers typically submit claims for services provided to enrollees who have primary coverage under Medicare directly to the Medicare carriers and intermediaries and receive reimbursement on a fee-for-service basis. In other words, services to Medicare beneficiaries typically are "carved out" of the risk-sharing arrangements these plans have with their participating providers. In accordance with section 216 of HIPAA, these providers are not at "substantial financial risk" for the cost or utilization of services they provide to Medicare patients. Therefore, such arrangements do not merit protection under the statutory criteria.

The second major limitation in section 216 is that the providers must be at risk for the cost or utilization of items or services they are "obligated to provide." Many risk sharing arrangements with physicians are based on the cost or utilization of items and services they order but that are actually provided by other entities (e.g., physician bonuses based on the number of hospital admissions). Accordingly, this requirement also substantially narrows the universe of arrangements that could potentially qualify for protection under Sec. 1001.952(u).

Working within these two constraints, the committee determined to protect financial arrangements that:

- Are part of a comprehensive managed care arrangement in which at least fifty percent of the enrollees do not have primary coverage under Medicare.
- Place providers at substantial financial risk for the cost or utilization of health care items and services for all enrollees.
- Use the identical risk and payment methodologies to reimburse providers for services provided to enrollees with primary coverage paid by Federal health care programs as is used for all other enrollees. In other words, payments from the plan to its providers must be the same for identical items or services provided to people with similar health status.
- Allow payment differentials only when they are related to utilization patterns and/or costs of providing items or services to the relevant population.3. Major Issues.

a. Definition of an "organization". The statutory language exempts "remuneration between an organization and an individual or entity." Some committee members believed the term "organization" could refer to any entity that provides health care services. However, other committee members were concerned that if the term "organization" meant any health care entity or individual, it would be easy for two parties to camouflage an illegal kickback arrangement as a risk sharing arrangement that could meet the requirements of the safe harbor. For example, the entity paying the kickback could agree to a capitation payment below fair market value for one service or group of patients, i.e., the "remuneration," in exchange for referrals of fee-for-service patients. The scheme would be a variant of providing a deep discount on a good not reimbursable by Medicare to induce the purchase of other goods that are reimbursable by Medicare. We have previously stated that such arrangements potentially implicate the anti-kickback statute (61 FR 2130; January 25, 1996).

The committee members opposed to a broad reading of the term "organization" contended that the term in section 216 of HIPAA had to be read in context of the entirety of section 216. Under their reading, the term "organization" referred back to the term "eligible organization," which preceded it in the same sentence, and should be construed consistent with that term. In other words, an "organization" in section 216 of HIPAA should have many of the characteristics of an "eligible organization" under section 1876 of the Act. The committee statement, as a whole, reflects this view.

Accordingly, in order to qualify under Sec. 1001.952(u), the risk sharing arrangement must be part of a comprehensive managed care plan. We use the term "qualified managed care plan" (QMCP) to describe such plans. These plans must be health plans, as defined in current safe harbor regulations (Sec. 1001.952(l)(2)), and provide a comprehensive range of health services. In addition, a QMCP must include certain elements in its arrangement with providers to assure that the health care services are managed, including utilization review, quality assurance and grievance procedure requirements. These requirements are derived from the current regulatory requirements for "eligible organizations" under section 1876 of the Act. Some of the representatives at the negotiating sessions expressed concern that while some of a QMCP's arrangements with providers will meet the above requirements, others will not. The committee concluded that thosearrangements that meet the requirements could receive protection under the safe harbor, even though the other arrangements could not.

Further, the committee statement, which was adopted as a whole, reflects the view that the QMCP had to be at some financial risk for the cost or utilization of services provided to enrollees. This requirement was especially important because, for the reasons discussed above in section II.E.1 of this preamble, the providers generally are not actually at risk for the items or services being provided to Medicare enrollees. Accordingly, protection for such plans is premised on (1) the plans being at risk for services to their non-Medicare enrollees, and (2) the plans reimbursing providers for items or services to Medicare beneficiaries on the same basis as for other plan enrollees. Given the variety of employer arrangements, the regulations set out two alternative methods by which the QMCP can meet this risk requirement.

The first option is that the QMCP can receive a premium payment that is fixed in advance. This requirement would cover all insurance arrangements in which, by definition, the plan assumes risk. Under this option, 50 percent of the enrollees cannot have primary coverage under Medicare. Alternatively, even where the QMCP is not paid on a premium basis, it can qualify if less than ten percent of the plan's enrollees have primary coverage under Medicare. This alternative will permit many self-funded ERISA plans that provide health care items or services in accordance with arrangements with third party administrators (TPAs) or contracts with insurers for administrative services only (ASOs) to qualify. In these arrangements, an employer pays the TPA or ASO separately for administering the plan and retains responsibility for payments to the providers. In such arrangements, the TPA or ASO may not have a financial incentive to control utilization or costs. Moreover, because the rule requires the providers to reassign any proceeds from Federal health care programs to the employer, the employer may actually profit on services to Medicare beneficiaries. By limiting Federal health care beneficiaries to less than 10 percent of total enrollment, the regulations substantially limit the ability of the employer to offset costs for its employees with Medicare reassignment.

In addition to these requirements, the regulations also would not protect a QMCP that is receiving premiums from setting its premiums based on the number of Federal health care program beneficiaries in the health plan or the amount of services provided to such beneficiaries. Some committee members believed that such a requirement was necessary to prevent employers from receiving lower rates for non-federal health care program beneficiaries because the plan expects to make up the difference on utilization by the Federal health care program beneficiaries for whom they receive fee-for-service payments.

b. Substantial financial risk. Developing a definition for "substantial financial risk" was one of the most difficult and time consuming tasks for the committee. Several suggestions were offered, and two caucuses were held and developed options. One caucus discussed a numerical approach to the definition, while the other tried to find a non-numerical approach. Much of the discussion over the suggested definitions concerned whether a non-numerical definition could be clear and precise enough for individuals and entities to know definitively whether they met the safe harbor requirements. Suggestions that did not provide enough assurances were discarded, and after some joint discussion, the elements of each approach were combined. The committee statement and these regulations reflect that determination.

For purposes of the rule, the methods to determine substantial financial risk were grouped into three standards:

- The payment methodology standard protects certain payment methodologies that are commonly used to place an individual or entity at substantial financial risk, including capitation, percentage of premium arrangements and payments based on certain diagnostic related groupings, so long as the reimbursement is reasonable given the historical utilization patterns and costs for the same or comparable population in similar managed care arrangements. Hybrid payment systems that combine a periodic fixed fee per patient with other incentives, such as withholds and bonuses, should be analyzed under the numeric standard.
- The numeric standard includes bonuses and withhold arrangements that meet certain criteria.
- The physician incentive plan standard protects arrangements that meet all of the requirements for HCFA's physician incentive plan rules under 42 CFR 417.479.

These provisions are discussed in greater detail in the section-by-section analysis that follows.

c. Downstream arrangements. The committee also discussed whether the rule would protect only arrangements between the QMCP and its direct or "first tier" contractors, or whether it would also protect arrangements between the first tier contractors and their downstream subcontractors and arrangements between those subcontractors and providers farther downstream. The committee statement, when taken as a whole, reflects the view that, with some exceptions, the rule should protect all written agreements between downstream subcontractors, as well as those between the QMCP and its first tier contractors. However, in order to prevent fee-for-service or cost-based kickbacks disguised as risk-sharing arrangements by contractors that are not at substantial financial risk, subcontractors are only protected if both parties to the subcontract are at substantial financial risk for the items or services covered by the agreement. In other words, if either party to an agreement is not paid on a substantial financial risk basis, the contract is not protected for either party.

Situations in which a subcontractor has an investment interest in its contractor raise other considerations. In such situations, the financial disincentive for overutilization created by a risk sharing arrangement might be offset by a return on the investment interest. Where both parties have to be at substantial financial risk in order to qualify for protection, the parties continue to have the necessary financial risk to protect against overutilization. However, where a first tier contractor has an investment interest in a QMCP, amounts received as a return on investment could offset the controls and safeguards of the risk-sharing arrangement. This result is possible because the QMCP may be receiving fee-for-service payments for services to Medicare enrollees on a reassignment basis. Therefore, the rule does not protect remuneration between a QMCP and a first tier contractor that has an investment interest in the QMCP, unless it qualifies under the large entity investment safe harbor (Sec. 1001.952(a)).4. Analysis of Sec. 1001.952(u)

a. Arrangements between QMCPs and first tier contractors. In order to qualify for protection, a contractual arrangement must be directly between a QMCP and a first tier contractor. The definition of a QMCP is set forth in Sec. 1001.952(u)(2)(vi). There are three standards that apply to the arrangements between the QMCP and first tier contractors. First, Sec. 1001.952(u)(1)(i)(A) requires that the contracts must be set out in writing and contain certain information, including the payment methodology. These requirements facilitate verification ofcompliance with the substantive requirements of the regulation.

Second, Sec. 1001.965(u)(2)(i)(B) makes clear that where a first tier contractor has an investment interest in the QMCP, the investment interest must meet the safe harbor requirements of Sec. 1001.952(a)(1). This condition addresses the concern that the contractor's substantial financial risk may be offset by returns on its ownership interest in the organization and therefore undermine protections against overutilization. We want to emphasize that, while arrangements in which providers have investment interests in a QMCP may not qualify for safe harbor protection, such arrangements do not necessarily violate the anti-kickback statute.

Third, Sec. 1001.952(u)(1)(i)(C) defines "substantial financial risk" by four alternative methodologies. The first three methods (paragraphs (u)(1)(i)(C)(I) -(III)) provides protection for several payment methodologies that historically have been used by plans and HMOs to transfer risk to providers: Capitation, percentage of premiums and inpatient reimbursement based on Federal health care program diagnostic related groupings (DRGs). Under any of these methods, the payment amounts must be reasonable given the historical utilization patterns and costs for the same or comparable populations in similar managed care arrangements. We are requesting comments on the extent to which the risk of full capitation is diminished by the purchase of commercial stop loss insurance or contractual provisions regarding the limitation of financial liability.

The exception for DRGs is limited to Federal health care program DRGs, since these are the only DRG methodologies with which we have significant experience and data for Federal health care program beneficiaries. Inpatient psychiatric DRGs are not covered because, based on the experience of the Medicare and Medicaid programs, these groupings are not sufficient to deter unnecessary admissions or to protect patients seeking those services. We emphasize that, although the plan must reimburse providers for items and services to other enrollees using the same DRG system, the amount of payment may vary so long as it is based on adequate utilization and cost data for the covered population that justifies the difference.

The definition of substantial financial risk also includes a numeric standard for certain bonus and withhold arrangements (paragraph (u)(1)(i)(C)(IV)). In the case of a physician provider, the requirement for substantial financial risk will also be satisfied if the arrangement places the physician at risk for an amount that exceeds the substantial financial risk threshold of the physician incentive payment rule (42 CFR 417.479(f)), and the arrangement is in compliance with the stop-loss and beneficiary survey requirements of 42 CFR 417.479(g). Although the committee statement requires the patient panel size to be less than 25,000 covered lives to meet the substantial financial risk element, we determined that this requirement does not provide significant additional protection and, therefore, it is not included in this rule. A bonus or withhold arrangement can also qualify if the target payment is at least 20 percent greater than the minimum payment for individuals or non-institutional entities, or is at least ten percent greater than the minimum payment in the case of institutional entities, specifically, hospitals and nursing homes. We are requesting data on the appropriateness of different target payment percentages for institutional and non-institutional entities. In addition, we also seek comments on whether additional individuals and entities, such as pharmacy providers, manufacturers and federally qualified health centers, should be considered institutional entities for purposes of this paragraph.

The "minimum payment" is defined in Sec. 1001.952(u)(2)(v). Generally, it represents the minimum amount a contractor will receive under a contract, regardless of utilization. In addition, the bonus or withhold must be earned in direct proportion to the ratio of the actual to the target utilization. For example, if the provider's utilization is only 80 percent of the target, the provider receives 80 percent of the difference between the target payment and the minimum payment. This requirement should protect against sham arrangements that provide a penalty or bonus conditioned entirely upon achieving a utilization level that is unreasonable. Finally, in calculating the substantial financial risk percentage, the target payment and the minimum payment must both include any bonus for performance (e.g., timely submission of paperwork, continuing medical education, meeting attendance) that is given to at least 75 percent of the participating individuals or entities who are paid a performance bonus based on the same bonus structure under the arrangement. This requirement is necessary to prevent plans from reallocating their compensation to performance bonuses, thereby increasing the apparent percentage of risk on the remaining compensation. In year one of an arrangement, it is not necessary to include the performance bonus in the substantial financial risk calculation.

Section 1001.952(u)(1)(i)(D) provides that the QMCP (or, in the case of a self-funded ERISA plan, the employer) must bill the Federal health care programs directly for covered services and compensate the provider for such services on the same basis as services to similar enrollees without primary coverage from a Federal health care program. Two examples of such arrangements are (1) staff model HMOs where the physicians are salaried, and (2) a plan that, in accordance with a reassignment agreement, bills Medicare for Part B services and pays the provider under the same bonus arrangement applicable to other enrollees. Because Medicare requires hospitals to claim payment directly, the rule is applicable where a hospital submits claims directly to a Federal health care program on a DRG basis and the plan pays the hospital for the plan's other enrollees using the same methodology.

Section 1001.952(u)(1)(i)(E) does not protect parties to a contract from trading discounted business for more remunerative fee-for-service business.

b. Arrangements with downstream contractors. Section 1001.952 (u)(1)(ii) provides that subcontracting arrangements between first tier contractors and downstream contractors (and any arrangements with providers farther downstream) are protected if both parties are paid in accordance with one of the substantial financial risk methodologies identified in this section. This provides assurances that both parties have a financial incentive to control utilization. In addition, the individual or entity providing items or services in accordance with the contract must be paid for items and services to Federal health care program beneficiaries in the same manner as for other enrollees. Finally, as discussed above, the arrangement cannot involve remuneration in return for, or to include the provision or acceptance of other Federal health care program business and cannot shift the financial burden of the arrangement to the Federal health care programs.

c. Definitions. Most of the defined terms in Sec. 1001.952(u) have the same meaning as those set forth in Sec. 1001.952(t). The additional defined terms are discussed below.

Minimum Payment — The minimum payment is the guaranteed amount that an individual or entity is entitled to receive under a risk-sharing contract for purposes of calculating substantialfinancial risk under the numeric standard. The minimum payment is the lowest amount a provider can reasonably be expected to receive based on past or expected performance.

Obligated To Provide — The statute requires individuals or entities to be placed at substantial financial risk for the cost or utilization of services they are "obligated to provide." A strict reading of the statutory language would not include many risk arrangements that are currently used to give incentives to physicians. Accordingly, for purposes of this regulation, the term is defined broadly and includes any items or services (as defined in this regulation) for which the individual or entity is financially responsible, makes referrals, or receives incentives based on the provider, group or health plan's performance.

Qualified Managed Care Plan — As discussed above, the committee statement, which was adopted as a whole, reflects the view that protection should apply to only those risk-sharing arrangements for the provision of health care items or services that were part of an comprehensive managed health care plan. For purposes of these regulations, we have defined such plans as "qualified managed care plans." Section 1001.952(u)(2)(vi) requires that the items and services be provided under agreement by an entity that qualifies as a health plan under Sec. 1001.952(1)(2), and Sec. 1001.952(u)(2)(vi)(A) requires that the QMCP provide a comprehensive range of health services. Section 1001.952(u)(2)(vi)(B) requires that the organization provide or arrange for (1) reasonable utilization goals and a utilization review program; (2) a quality assurance program that promotes the coordination of care, protects against underutilization and specifies patient goals, including measurable outcomes where appropriate; (3) grievance and hearing procedures; (4) protection for its members from incurring financial liability other than copayments and deductibles; and (5) assurances that treatment for Federal health care program beneficiaries is no different than for other enrollees due to their status as Federal health care program beneficiaries. These requirements are derived from current regulations under section 1876 of the Act and assure that basic indicia of a managed care plan exist. Finally, the requirement that there be at least 50 percent non-federal health care program enrollees reduces the likelihood that Federal health care program beneficiaries will receive disparate treatment either in insured or ERISA plans as compared to other enrollees.

Target Payment — The target payment is defined as the fair market value payment consistent with arms-length negotiations that will be earned by an individual or entity depending on the individual or entity's meeting a utilization target or range of utilization targets that are consistent with historical utilization rates for the same or comparable populations in similar managed care arrangements. The utilization target may not be a precise number, but rather a range. In order to protect against undue incentives to underutilize, the rule provides that if a provider's utilization falls below or surpasses the utilization target (whether a fixed number or range), any payment amounts attributable to performance beyond (or below) the utilization target will not be included in the calculation of substantial financial risk. Arrangements where the target payment is set at a level that is unrealistic would always produce the appearance of substantial financial risk and, accordingly, will not be protected.

III. Regulatory Impact Statement

Executive Order 12866, the Unfunded Mandates Reform Act and the Regulatory Flexibility Act

The Office of Management and Budget (OMB) has reviewed this interim final rule in accordance with the provisions of Executive Order 12866 and the Regulatory Flexibility Act (5 U.S.C. 601–612), and has determined that it does not meet the criteria for a significant regulatory action. Executive Order 12866 directs agencies to assess all costs and benefits of available regulatory alternatives and, when rulemaking is necessary, to select regulatory approaches that maximize net benefits (including potential economic, environmental, public health, safety distributive and equity effects). The Unfunded Mandates Reform Act, Public Law 104–4, requires that agencies prepare an assessment of anticipated costs and benefits on any rulemaking that may result in an annual expenditure by State, local or tribal government, or by the private sector of $100 million or more. In addition, under the Regulatory Flexibility Act, if a rule has a significant economic effect on a substantial number of small businesses, the Secretary must specifically consider the economic effect of rule on small business entities and analyze regulatory options that could lessen the impact of the rule.

Executive Order 12866 requires that all regulations reflect consideration of alternatives, costs, benefits, incentives, equity and available information. Regulations must meet certain standards, such as avoiding unnecessary burden. The safe harbor provisions set forth in this rulemaking are designed to permit individuals and entities to freely engage in business practices and arrangements that encourage competition, innovation and economy. In doing so, these regulations impose no requirements on any party. Health care providers and others may voluntarily seek to comply with these provisions so that they have the assurance that their business practices are not subject to any enforcement actions under the anti-kickback statute. We believe that any aggregate economic effect of these safe harbor regulations will be minimal and will impact only those limited few who engage in prohibited behavior in violation of the statute. As such, we believe that the aggregate economic impact of these regulations is minimal and will have no effect on the economy or on Federal or State expenditures.

Additionally, in accordance with the Unfunded Mandates Reform Act of 1995, we have determined that there are no significant costs associated with these safe harbor guidelines that would impose any mandates on States, local or tribal governments, or the private sector, that will result in an annual expenditure of $100 million or more, and that a full analysis under the Act is not necessary.

Further, in accordance with the Regulatory Flexibility Act (RFA) of 1980, and the Small Business Regulatory Enforcement Act of 1996, which amended the RFA, we are required to determine if this rule will have a significant economic effect on a substantial number of small entities and, if so, to identify regulatory options that could lessen the impact. While these safe harbor provisions may have an impact on small entities, we believe that the aggregate economic impact of this rulemaking should be minimal, since it is the nature of the violation and not the size of the entity that will result in a violation of the anti-kickback statute. Since the vast majority of individuals and entities potentially affected by these regulations do not engage in prohibited arrangements, schemes or practices in violation of the law, we have concluded that these interim final regulations should not have a significant economic impact on a number of small business entities, and that a regulatory flexibility analysis is not required for this rulemaking.

Paperwork Reduction Act

As indicated above, the provisions of these interim final regulations are voluntary and impose no new reporting or recordkeeping requirements on health care providers necessitating clearance by OMB.

IV. Public Inspection of Comments

Comments will be available for public inspection beginning December 10, 1999, in Room 5518 of the Office of Inspector General at 330 Independence Avenue, SW, Washington, DC, on Monday through Friday of each week from 8:00 a.m. 4:30 p.m., (202) 619–0089.

List of Subjects in 42 CFR Part 1001

Administrative practice and procedure, Fraud, Grant programs — health, Health facilities, Health professions, Maternal and child health, Medicaid, Medicare.

Accordingly, 42 CFR part 1001 is amended as follows:

PART 1001 — [AMENDED]

1. The authority citation for part 1001 continues to read as follows:

Authority: 42 U.S.C. 1302, 1320a-7, 1320a-7b, 1395u(j), 1395u(k), 1395y(d), 1395y(e), 1395cc(b)(2)(D),(E) and (F), and 1395hh; and sec.2455, Pub.L. 103–355, 108 Stat. 3327 (31 U.S.C. 6101 note).

2. Section 1001.952 is amended by republishing the introductory text; by reserving paragraphs (n) through (s); and by adding new paragraphs (t) and (u) to read as follows:

Sec. 1001.952 Exceptions.

The following payment practices shall not be treated as a criminal offense under section 1128B of the Act and shall not serve as the basis for an exclusion:* * * * *

(n)-(s) [Reserved]

(t) Price reductions offered to eligible managed care organizations. (1) As used in section 1128(B) of the Act, "remuneration" does not include any payment between:

(i) An eligible managed care organization and any first tier contractor for providing or arranging for items or services, as long as the following three standards are met —

(A) The eligible managed care organization and the first tier contractor have an agreement that:

(1) Is set out in writing and signed by both parties;

(2) Specifies the items and services covered by the agreement;

(3) Is for a period of at least one year; and

(4) Specifies that the first tier contractor cannot claim payment in any form directly or indirectly from a Federal health care program for items or services covered under the agreement, except for:

(i) HMOs and competitive medical plans with cost-based contracts under section 1876 of the Act where the agreement with the eligible managed care organization sets out the arrangements in accordance with which the first tier contractor is billing the Federal health care program;

(ii) Federally qualified HMOs without a contract under sections 1854 or 1876 of the Act, where the agreement with the eligible managed care organization sets out the arrangements in accordance with which the first tier contractor is billing the Federal health care program; or

(iii) First tier contractors that are Federally qualified health centers that claim supplemental payments from a Federal health care program.

(B) In establishing the terms of the agreement, neither party gives or receives remuneration in return for or to induce the provision or acceptance of business (other than business covered by the agreement) for which payment may be made in whole or in part by a Federal health care program on a fee-for-service basis.

(C) Neither party to the agreement shifts the financial burden of the agreement to the extent that increased payments are claimed from a Federal health care program.

(ii) A first tier contractor and a downstream contractor or between two downstream contractors to provide or arrange for items or services, as long as the following four standards are met—

(A) The parties have an agreement that:

(1) Is set out in writing and signed by both parties;

(2) Specifies the items and services covered by the agreement; (3) Is for a period of at least one year; and

(4) Specifies that the party providing the items or services cannot claim payment in any form from a Federal health care program for items or services covered under the agreement.

(B) In establishing the terms of the agreement, neither party gives or receives remuneration in return to induce the provision or acceptance of business (other than business covered by the agreement) for which payment may be made in whole or in part by a Federal health care program on a fee-for-service basis.

(C) Neither party shifts the financial burden of the agreement to the extent that increased payments are claimed from a Federal health care program.

(D) The agreement between the eligible managed care organization and first tier contractor covering the items or services that are covered by the agreement between the parties does not involve:

(1) A Federally qualified health center receiving supplemental payments;

(2) A HMO or CMP with a cost-based contract under section 1876 of the Act; or

(3) A Federally qualified HMO, unless the items or services are covered by a risk based contract under sections 1854 or 1876 of the Act.

(2) For purposes of this paragraph, the following terms are defined as follows:

(i) Downstream contractor means an individual or entity that has a subcontract directly or indirectly with a first tier contractor for the provision or arrangement of items or services that are covered by an agreement between an eligible managed care organization and the first tier contractor.

(ii) Eligible managed care organization [1] means —

(A) A HMO or CMP with a risk or cost based contract in accordance with section 1876 of the Act;

(B) Any Medicare Part C health plan that receives a capitated payment from Medicare and which must have its total Medicare beneficiary cost sharing approved by HCFA under section 1854 of the Act;

(C) Medicaid managed care organizations as defined in section 1903(m)(1)(A) that provide or arrange for items or services for Medicaid enrollees under a contract in accordance with section 1903(m) of the Act (except for fee-for-service plans or medical savings accounts);

(D) Any other health plans that provide or arrange for items and services for Medicaid enrollees in accordance with a risk-based contract with a State agency subject to the upper payment limits in Sec. 447.361 of this title or an equivalent payment cap approved by the Secretary;

(E) Programs For All Inclusive Care For The Elderly (PACE) under sections 1894 and 1934 of the Act, except for for-profit demonstrations under sections 4801(h) and 4802(h) of Pub. L. 105–33; or

(F) A Federally qualified HMO.

(iii) First tier contractor means an individual or entity that has a contract directly with an eligible managed care organization to provide or arrange for items or services.

(iv) Items and services means health care items, devices, supplies or services or those services reasonably related to the provision of health care items, devices, supplies or services including, but not limited to, non-emergencytransportation, patient education, attendant services, social services (e.g., case management), utilization review and quality assurance. Marketing and other pre-enrollment activities are not "items or services" for purposes of this section.

(u) Price reductions offered by contractors with substantial financial risk to managed care organizations. (1) As used in section 1128 (B) of the Act, "remuneration" does not include any payment between:

(i) A qualified managed care plan and a first tier contractor for providing or arranging for items or services, where the following five standards are met —

---

[1] The eligible managed care organizations in paragraphs (u)(2)(ii)(A)-(F) of this section are only eligible with respect to items or services covered by the contracts specified in those paragraphs.

(A) The agreement between the qualified managed care plan and first tier contractor must:

(1) Be in writing and signed by the parties;

(2) Specify the items and services covered by the agreement;

(3) Be for a period of a least one year;

(4) Require participation in a quality assurance program that promotes the coordination of care, protects against underutilization and specifies patient goals, including measurable outcomes where appropriate; and

(5) Specify a methodology for determining payment that is commercially reasonable and consistent with fair market value established in an arms-length transaction and includes the intervals at which payments will be made and the formula for calculating incentives and penalties, if any.

(B) If a first tier contractor has an investment interest in a qualified managed care plan, the investment interest must meet the criteria of paragraph (a)(1) of this section.

(C) The first tier contractor must have substantial financial risk for the cost or utilization of services it is obligated to provide through one of the following four payment methodologies:

(1) A periodic fixed payment per patient that does not take into account the dates services are provided, the frequency of services, or the extent or kind of services provided;

(2) Percentage of premium;

(3) Inpatient Federal health care program diagnosis-related groups (DRGs) (other than those for psychiatric services);

(4) Bonus and withhold arrangements, provided—

(i) The target payment for first tier contractors that are individuals or non-institutional providers is at least 20 percent greater than the minimum payment, and for first tier contractors that are institutional providers, i.e., hospitals and nursing homes, is at least 10 percent greater than the minimum payment;

(ii) The amount at risk, i.e., the bonus or withhold, is earned by a first tier contractor in direct proportion to the ratio of the contractor's actual utilization to its target utilization;

(iii) In calculating the percentage in accordance with paragraph (u)(1)(i)(C)(4)(i) of this section, both the target payment amount and the minimum payment amount include any performance bonus, e.g., payments for timely submission of paperwork, continuing medical education, meeting attendance, etc., at a level achieved by 75 percent of the first tier contractors who are eligible for such payments;

(iv) Payment amounts, including any bonus or withhold amounts, are reasonable given the historical utilization patterns and costs for the same or comparable populations in similar managed care arrangements; and

(v) Alternatively, for a first tier contractor that is a physician, the qualified managed care plan has placed the physician at risk for referral services in an amount that exceeds the substantial financial risk threshold set forth in 42 CFR 417.479(f) and the arrangement is in compliance with the stop-loss and beneficiary survey requirements of 42 CFR 417.479(g).

(D) Payments for items and services reimbursable by Federal health care program must comply with the following two standards —

(1) The qualified managed care plan (or in the case of a self-funded employer plan that contracts with a qualified managed care plan to provide administrative services, the self-funded employer plan) must submit the claims directly to the Federal health care program, in accordance with a valid reassignment agreement, for items or services reimbursed by the Federal health care program. (Notwithstanding the foregoing, inpatient hospital services, other than psychiatric services, will be deemed to comply if the hospital is reimbursed by a Federal health care program under a DRG methodology.)

(2) Payments to first tier contractors and any downstream contractors for providing or arranging for items or services reimbursed by a Federal health care program must be identical to payment arrangements to or between such parties for the same items or services provided to other beneficiaries with similar health status, provided that such payments may be adjusted where the adjustments are related to utilization patterns or costs of providing items or services to the relevant population.

(E) In establishing the terms of an arrangement —

(1) Neither party gives or receives remuneration in return for or to induce the provision or acceptance of business (other than business covered by the arrangement) for which payment may be made in whole or in part by a Federal health care program on a fee-for-service or cost basis; and

(2) Neither party to the arrangement shifts the financial burden of such arrangement to the extent that increased payments are claimed from a Federal health care program.

(ii) A first tier contractor and a downstream contractor, or between downstream contractors, to provide or arrange for items or services, as long as the following three standards are met—

(A) Both parties are being paid for the provision or arrangement of items or services in accordance with one of the payment methodologies set out in paragraph (u)(1)(i)(C) of this section;

(B) Payment arrangements for items and services reimbursable by a Federal health care program comply with paragraph (u)(1)(i)(D) of this section; and

(C) In establishing the terms of an arrangement —

(1) Neither party gives or receives remuneration in return for or to induce the provision or acceptance of business (other than business covered by the arrangement) for which payment may be made in whole or in part by a Federal health care program on a fee-for-service or cost basis; and

(2) Neither party to the arrangement shifts the financial burden of the arrangement to the extent that increased payments are claimed from a Federal health care program.

(2) For purposes of this paragraph, the following terms are defined as follows:

(i) Downstream contractor means an individual or entity that has a subcontract directly or indirectly with a first tier contractor for the provision or arrangement of items or services that are covered by an agreement between a qualified managed care plan and the first tier contractor.

(ii) First tier contractor means an individual or entity that has a contract directly with a qualified managed care plan to provide or arrange for items or services.

(iii) Is obligated to provide for a contractor refers to items or services:

(A) Provided directly by an individual or entity and its employees;

(B) For which an individual or entity is financially responsible, but which are provided by downstream contractors;

(C) For which an individual or entity makes referrals or arrangements; or

(D) For which an individual or entity receives financial incentives based onits own, its provider group's, or its qualified managed care plan's performance (or combination thereof).

(iv) Items and services means health care items, devices, supplies or services or those services reasonably related to the provision of health care items, devices, supplies or services including, but not limited to, non-emergency transportation, patient education, attendant services, social services (e.g., case management), utilization review and quality assurance. Marketing or other pre-enrollment activities are not "items or services" for purposes of this definition in this paragraph.

(v) Minimum payment is the guaranteed amount that a provider is entitled to receive under an agreement with a first tier or downstream contractor or a qualified managed care plan.

(vi) Qualified managed care plan means a health plan as defined in paragraph (l)(2) of this section that:

(A) Provides a comprehensive range of health services;

(B) Provides or arranges for —

(1) Reasonable utilization goals to avoid inappropriate utilization;

(2) An operational utilization review program;

(3) A quality assurance program that promotes the coordination of care, protects against underutilization, and specifies patient goals, including measurable outcomes where appropriate;

(4) Grievance and hearing procedures;

(5) Protection of enrollees from incurring financial liability other than copayments and deductibles; and

(6) Treatment for Federal health care program beneficiaries that is not different than treatment for other enrollees because of their status as Federal health care program beneficiaries; and

(C) Covers a beneficiary population of which either —

(1) No more than 10 percent are Medicare beneficiaries, not including persons for whom a Federal health care program is the secondary payer; or (2) No more than 50 percent are Medicare beneficiaries (not including persons for whom a Federal health care program is the secondary payer), provided that payment of premiums is on a periodic basis that does not take into account the dates services are rendered, the frequency of services, or the extent or kind of services rendered, and provided further that such periodic payments for the non-Federal health care program beneficiaries do not take into account the number of Federal health care program fee-for-service beneficiaries covered by the agreement or the amount of services generated by such beneficiaries.

(vii) Target payment means the fair market value payment established through arms length negotiations that will be earned by an individual or entity that:

(A) Is dependent on the individual or entity's meeting a utilization target or range of utilization targets that are set consistent with historical utilization rates for the same or comparable populations in similar managed care arrangements, whether based on its own, its provider group's or the qualified managed care plan's utilization (or a combination thereof); and

(B) Does not include any bonus or fees that the individual or entity may earn from exceeding the utilization target.

Dated: February 11, 1999.

June Gibbs Brown,Inspector General.

Approved: June 8, 1999.

Donna E. Shalala, Secretary.

[FR Doc. 99–29988 Filed 11–18–99; 8:45 am]

BILLING CODE 4150–04-P

APPENDIX F8.2

Solicitation of New Safe Harbors and Special Fraud Alerts; 64 FR 69217, December 10, 1999

[Federal Register: December 10, 1999 (Volume 64, Number 237)]
[Proposed Rules]

DEPARTMENT OF HEALTH AND HUMAN SERVICES

Office of Inspector General

42 CFR Part 1001

Solicitation of New Safe Harbors and Special Fraud Alerts

AGENCY: Office of Inspector General (OIG), HHS.

ACTION: Intent to develop regulations.

SUMMARY: In accordance with section 205 of the Health Insurance Portability and Accountability Act (HIPAA) of 1996, this annual document solicits proposals and recommendations for developing new and modifying existing safe harbor provisions under the Federal and State health care programs' anti-kickback statute, as well as developing new OIG Special Fraud Alerts.

DATES: To assure consideration, public comments must be delivered to the address provided below by no later than 5 p.m. on February 8, 2000.

ADDRESSES: Please mail or deliver your written comments to the following address: Office of Inspector General, Department of Health and Human Services, Attention: OIG-41-N, Room 5246, Cohen Building, 330 Independence Avenue, SW., Washington, DC 20201.

We do not accept comments by facsimile (FAX) transmission. In commenting, please refer to file code OIG-41-N. Comments received timely will be available for public inspection as they are received, generally beginning approximately three weeks after publication of a document, in Room 5541 of the Office of Inspector General at 330 Independence Avenue, SW., Washington, DC, on Monday through Friday of each week from 8 a.m. to 4:30 p.m.

FOR FURTHER INFORMATION CONTACT:

Joel Schaer, (202) 619–0089, OIG Regulations Officer.

SUPPLEMENTARY INFORMATION:

I. Background

A. The OIG Safe Harbor Provisions

Section 1128B(b) of the Social Security Act (the Act) (42 U.S.C. 1320a-7b(b)) provides criminal penalties for individuals or entities that knowingly and willfully offer, pay, solicit or receive remuneration in order to induce business reimbursed under the Federal or State health care programs. The offense is classified as a felony, and is punishable by fines of up to $25,000 and imprisonment for up to 5 years. The OIG may also impose administrativesanctions or exclude violators from the Federal or State health care programs.

The types of remuneration covered specifically include kickbacks, bribes, and rebates, whether made directly or indirectly, overtly or covertly, or in cash or in kind. In addition, prohibited conduct includes not only remuneration intended to induce referrals of patients, but remuneration intended to induce the arranging for or the purchasing, leasing or ordering of any good, facility, service, or item paid for by Federal or State health care programs.

Since the statute on its face is so broad, concern has been expressed for many years that some relatively innocuous commercial arrangements are technically covered by the statute and are, therefore, subject to criminal prosecution. As a response to the above concern, the Medicare and Medicaid Patient and Program Protection Act of 1987, section 14 of Public Law 100–93, specifically required the development and promulgation of regulations, the so-called "safe harbor" provisions, designed to specify various payment and business practices which, although potentially capable of inducing referrals of business under the Federal and State health care programs, would not be treated as criminal offenses under the anti-kickback statute (section 1128B(b) of the Act; 42 U.S.C. 1320a-7b(b)) and would not serve as a basis for a program exclusion under section 1128(b)(7) of the Act; 42 U.S.C. 1320a-7(b)(7). The OIG safe harbor provisions have been developed "to limit the reach of the statute somewhat by permitting certain non-abusive arrangements, while encouraging beneficial and innocuous arrangements" (56 FR 35952, July 29, 1991). Health care providers and others may voluntarily seek to comply with these provisions so that they have the assurance that their business practices are not subject to any enforcement action under the anti-kickback statute or program exclusion authority.

To date, the OIG has developed and codified in 42 CFR 1001.952 a total of 21 final safe harbors that describe practices that are sheltered from liability. The OIG is also currently developing a proposed safe harbor rule addressing ambulance restocking arrangements.

B. OIG Special Fraud Alerts

In addition, the OIG has also periodically issued Special Fraud Alerts to give continuing guidance to health care providers with respect to practices the OIG regards as unlawful. These Special Fraud Alerts serve to notify the health care industry that the OIG has become aware of certain abusive practices that the OIG plans to pursue and prosecute, or to bring civil and administrative action, as appropriate. The Special Fraud Alerts also serve as a tool to encourage industry compliance by giving providers an opportunity to examine their own practices. The OIG Special Fraud Alerts are intended for extensive distribution directly to the health care provider community, as well as those charged with administering the Medicare and Medicaid programs.

In developing these Special Fraud Alerts, the OIG has relied on a number of sources and has consulted directly with experts in the subject field, including those within the OIG, other agencies of the Department, other Federal and State agencies, and those in the health care industry. To date, ten individual Special Fraud Alerts have been issued by the OIG and subsequently reprinted in the Federal Register.[1]

C. Section 205 of Public Law 104–191

In accordance with the Health Insurance Portability and Accountability Act of 1996 (Pub. L. 104–191), the Department is now required to provide additional formal guidance regarding the application of the anti-kickback statute and the safe harbor provisions, as well as other OIG health care fraud and abuse sanctions. In addition to accepting and responding to requests for advisory opinions from outside parties regarding the interpretation and applicability of certain statutes relating to the Federal and State health care programs, section 205 of Public Law 104–191 requires the Department to

[1] See 59 FR 65372 (December 19, 1994); 60 FR 40847 (August 10, 1995); 61 FR 30623 (June 17, 1996); 63 FR 20415 (April 24, 1998); and 64 FR 1813 (January 12, 1999). The OIG has also issued three Special Advisory Bulletins — 64 FR 37985 (July 14, 1999); 64 FR 52791 (September 30, 1999); and 64 FR 61353 (November 10, 1999).

develop and publish an annual notice in the Federal Register formally soliciting proposals for modifying existing safe harbors to the anti-kickback statute and for developing new safe harbors and Special Fraud Alerts. In accordance with this requirement, the OIG has published notices in the Federal Register on December 31, 1996 (61 FR 69060); December 10, 1997 (62 FR 65049) and December 7, 1998 (63 FR 67486), soliciting such proposals.

In developing safe harbors for a criminal statute, the OIG is compelled to engage in a complete and thorough review of the range of factual circumstances that may fall within the proposed safe harbor subject area so as to uncover all potential opportunities for fraud and abuse. Only then can the OIG determine, in consultation with the Department of Justice, whether it can effectively develop regulatory limitations and controls that will permit beneficial and innocuous arrangements within a subject area while, at the same time, protecting the Federal health care programs and their beneficiaries from abusive practices.

II. Solicitation of Additional New Recommendations and Proposals

In accordance with the requirements of section 205 of Public Law 104–191, the OIG is continuing to study safe harbor and Special Fraud Alert proposals submitted in response to the annual solicitations. Some of those suggestions have been addressed in the safe harbor rulemakings recently published on November 19, 1999 (64 FR 63504 and 64 FR 63518) or are already under development. In response to the previously-issued Federal Register solicitation notices, a status report of the public comments received for new and modified safe harbors is set forth annually in an appendix to the OIG's Semiannual Report covering the period April through September.[2] The OIG is currently taking the recommendations listed in the appendix under advisement and is not seeking additional public comment on those proposals at this time. Rather, this notice seeks additional recommendations from affected provider, practitioner, supplier and beneficiary representatives regarding the development of proposed or modified safe harbor regulations and new Special Fraud Alerts beyond those summarized in the appendix to the OIG Semiannual Report referenced above.

Criteria for Modifying and Establishing Safe Harbor Provisions

---

[2] The OIG Semiannual Report can be accessed through the OIG web site at http://www.dhhs.gov/oig/semann/index.htm.

In accordance with the statute, we will consider a number of factors in reviewing proposals for new or modified safe harbor provisions, such as the extent to which the proposals would effect an increase or decrease in —

- Access to health care services;
- The quality of care services;
- Patient freedom of choice among health care providers;
- Competition among health care providers;
- The cost to Federal health care programs;
- The potential overutilization of the health care services; and
- The ability of health care facilities to provide services in medically underserved areas or to medically underserved populations.

In addition, we will also take into consideration the existence (or nonexistence) of any potential financial benefit to health care professionals or providers that may vary based on their decisions whether to (1) order a health care item or service, or (2) arrange for a referral of health care items or services to a particular practitioner or provider.

Criteria for Developing Special Fraud Alerts

In determining whether to issue additional Special Fraud Alerts, we will also consider whether, and to what extent, those practices that would be identified in new Special Fraud Alerts may result in any of the consequences set forth above, and the volume and frequency of the conduct that would be identified in these Special Fraud Alerts.

A detailed explanation of justifications or empirical data supporting the suggestion, and sent to the address indicated above, would prove helpful in our considering and drafting new or modified safe harbor regulations and Special Fraud Alerts.

Dated: November 29, 1999.June Gibbs Brown,Inspector General.[FR Doc. 99–32025 Filed 12-9-99; 8:45 am]BILLING CODE 4150–04-P

APPENDIX F8.2A

Solicitation of New Safe Harbors and Special Fraud Alerts

[Federal Register: December 14, 2000 (Volume 65, Number 241)] [Proposed Rules]

DEPARTMENT OF HEALTH AND HUMAN SERVICES

Office of Inspector General

42 CFR Part 1001

AGENCY: Office of Inspector General (OIG), HHS.

ACTION: Notice of intent to develop regulations.

SUMMARY: In accordance with section 205 of the Health Insurance Portability and Accountability Act (HIPAA) of 1996, this annual notice solicits proposals and recommendations for developing new and modifying existing safe harbor provisions under the Federal and State health care programs' anti-kickback statute, as well as developing new OIG Special Fraud Alerts.

DATES: To assure consideration, public comments must be delivered to the address provided below by no later than 5 p.m. on February 12, 2001.

ADDRESSES: Please mail or deliver your written comments to the following address: Office of Inspector General, Department of Health and Human Services, Attention: OIG-51-N, Room 5246, Cohen Building, 330 Independence Avenue, SW., Washington, DC 20201.

We do not accept comments by facsimile (FAX) transmission. In commenting, please refer to file code OIG-51-N. Comments received timely will be available for public inspection as they are received, generally beginning approximately 3 weeks after publication of a document, in Room 5541 of the Office of Inspector General at 330 Independence Avenue, SW., Washington, DC, on Monday through Friday of each week from 8:00 a.m. to 4:30 p.m.

FOR FURTHER INFORMATION CONTACT: Joel Schaer, (202) 619–0089, OIG Regulations Officer.

SUPPLEMENTARY INFORMATION:

I. Background

A. The OIG Safe Harbor Provisions

Section 1128B(b) of the Social Security Act (the Act) (42 U.S.C. 1320a-7b(b)) provides criminal penalties for individuals or entities that knowingly and willfully offer, pay, solicit or receive remuneration in order to induce business reimbursed under the Federal or State health care programs. The offense is classified as a felony, and is punishable by fines of up to $25,000 and imprisonment for up to 5 years. The OIG may also impose administrative sanctions or exclude violators from the Federal or State health care programs.

The types of remuneration covered specifically include kickbacks, bribes, and rebates, whether made directly or indirectly, overtly or covertly, or in cash or in kind. In addition, prohibited conduct includes not only remuneration intended to induce referrals of patients, but remuneration intended to induce the arranging for or the purchasing, leasing or ordering of any good, facility, service, or item paid for by Federal or State health care programs.

Since the statute on its face is so broad, concern has been expressed for many years that some relatively innocuous commercial arrangements are technically covered by the statute and are, therefore, subject to criminal prosecution. As a response to the above concern, the Medicare and Medicaid Patient and Program Protection Act of 1987, section 14 of Public Law 100–93, specifically required the development and promulgation of regulations, the so-called "safe harbor" provisions, designed to specify various payment and business practices which, although potentially capable of inducing referrals of business under the Federal and State health care programs, would not be treated as criminal offenses under the anti-kickback statute (section 1128B(b) of the Act; 42 U.S.C. 1320a-7b(b)) and would not serve as a basis for a program exclusion under section 1128(b)(7) of the Act; 42 U.S.C. 1320a-7(b)(7). The OIG safe harbor provisions have been developed "to limit the reach of the statute somewhat by permitting certain non-abusive arrangements, while encouraging beneficial and innocuous arrangements" (56 FR 35952, July 29, 1991). Health care providers and others may voluntarily seek to comply with these provisions so that they have the assurance that their business practices are not subject to any enforcement action under the anti-kickback statute or program exclusion authority.

To date, the OIG has developed and codified in 42 CFR 1001.952 a total of 21 final safe harbors that describe practices that are sheltered from liability. The OIG is also currently developing a final safe harbor rule addressing ambulance restocking arrangements.

B. OIG Special Fraud Alerts

In addition, the OIG has also periodically issued Special Fraud Alerts to give continuing guidance to health care providers with respect to practices the OIG regards as unlawful. These Special Fraud Alerts serve to notify the health care industry that the OIG has become aware of certain abusive practices that the OIG plans to pursue and prosecute, or to bring civil and administrative action, as appropriate. The Special Fraud Alerts also serve as a tool to encourage industry compliance by giving providers an opportunity to examine their own practices. The OIG Special Fraud Alerts are intended for extensive distribution directly to the health care provider community, as well as those charged with administering the Medicare and Medicaid programs.

In developing these Special Fraud Alerts, the OIG has relied on a number of sources and has consulted directly with experts in the subject field, including those within the OIG, other agencies of the Department, other Federal and State agencies, and those in the health care industry. To date, ten individual Special Fraud Alerts have been issued by the OIG and subsequently reprinted in the **Federal Register**.[1]

C. Section 205 of Public Law 104–191

Section 205 of Public Law 104–191 requires the Department to develop and publish an annual notice in the Federal Register formally soliciting proposals for modifying existing safe harbors to the anti-kickback statute and for developing new safe harbors and Special Fraud Alerts.

---

[1] See 59 FR 65372 (December 19, 1994); 60 FR 40847 (August 10, 1995); 61 FR 30623 (June 17, 1996); 63 FR 20415 (April 24, 1998); and 64 FR 1813 (January 12, 1999). The OIG has also issued three Special Advisory Bulletins — 64 FR 37985 (July 14, 1999); 64 FR 52791 (September 30, 1999); and 64 FR 61353 (November 10, 1999).

In developing safe harbors for a criminal statute, the OIG is compelled to engage in a complete and thorough review of the range of factual circumstances that may fall within the proposed safe harbor subject area so as to uncover all potential opportunities for fraud and abuse. Only then can the OIG determine, in consultation with the Department of Justice, whether it can effectively develop regulatory limitations and controls that will permit beneficial and innocuous arrangements within a subject area while, at the same time, protecting the Federal health care programs and their beneficiaries from abusive practices.

II. Solicitation of Additional New Recommendations and Proposals

In accordance with the requirements of section 205 of Public Law 104–191, the OIG is continuing to study safe harbor and Special Fraud Alert proposals submitted in response to the annual solicitations. Some of those suggestions have been addressed in the safe harbor rulemakings published on November 19, 1999 (64 FR 63504 and 64 FR 63518) or are already under development. The OIG last published a Federal Register solicitation notice for developing new safe harbors and Special Fraud Alerts on December 10, 1999 (64 FR 69217). The OIG received 17 timely-filed responses from a cross-section of organizations, associations and other interested parties. In response to that and previously-issued Federal Register solicitation notices, a status report of the public comments received for new and modified safe harbors is set forth in Appendix G to the OIG's Semiannual Report covering the period April 1, 2000 through September, 30, 2000.[2] OIG is currently taking the recommendations listed in the appendix under advisement and is not seeking additional public comment on those proposals at this time. Rather, this notice seeks additional recommendations from affected provider, practitioner, supplier and beneficiary representatives regarding the development of proposed or modified safe harbor regulations and new Special Fraud Alerts beyond those summarized in the appendix to the OIG Semiannual Report referenced above.

---

[2] The OIG Semiannual Report can be accessed through the OIG web site at http://www.dhhs.gov/oig/semann/index.htm.

Criteria for Modifying and Establishing Safe Harbor Provisions

In accordance with the statute, we will consider a number of factors in reviewing proposals for new or modified safe harbor provisions, such as the extent to which the proposals would effect an increase or decrease in —

- Access to health care services;
- The quality of care services;
- Patient freedom of choice among health care providers;
- Competition among health care providers;
- The cost to Federal health care programs;
- The potential overutilization of the health care services; and
- The ability of health care facilities to provide services in medically underserved areas or to medically underserved populations.

In addition, we will also take into consideration the existence (or nonexistence) of any potential financial benefit to health care professionals or providers that may vary based on their decisions whether to (1) order a health care item or service, or (2) arrange for a referral of health care items or services to a particular practitioner or provider.

Criteria for Developing Special Fraud Alerts

In determining whether to issue additional Special Fraud Alerts, we will also consider whether, and to what extent, those practices that would be identified in new Special Fraud Alerts may result in any of the consequences set forth above, and the volume and frequency of the conduct that would be identified in these Special Fraud Alerts.

A detailed explanation of justifications or empirical data supporting the suggestion, and sent to the address indicated above, would prove helpful in our considering and drafting new or modified safe harbor regulations and Special Fraud Alerts.

Dated: December 7, 2000.

June Gibbs Brown,

Inspector General.

[FR Doc. 00–31808 Filed 12–13–00; 8:45 am]

BILLING CODE 4152–01–P

APPENDIX F8.3

Civil Money Penalty Safe Harbor to Protect Payment of Medicare Supplemental Insurance and Medigap Premiums for ESRD Beneficiaries, Proposed Rule; 65 FR 25460, May 2, 2000

[Federal Register: May 2, 2000 (Volume 65, Number 85)][Proposed Rules] [Page 25460–25463]

DEPARTMENT OF HEALTH AND HUMAN SERVICES

Office of Inspector General

42 CFR Part 1003

RIN 0991-AB04

Medicare and State Health Care Programs: Fraud and Abuse; Civil Money Penalty Safe Harbor To Protect Payment of Medicare Supplemental Insurance and Medigap Premiums for ESRD Beneficiaries

AGENCY: Office of Inspector General (OIG), HHS.

ACTION: Notice of proposed rulemaking.

SUMMARY: In accordance with section 5201 of the Omnibus Consolidated and Emergency Supplemental Appropriations Act for Fiscal Year 1999, this proposed rule would set forth in the OIG's civil money penalty provisions in 42 CFR part 1003 a new safe harbor for unlawful inducements to beneficiaries to provide protection for independent dialysis facilities that pay, in whole or in part, premiums for Supplementary Medical Insurance (Medicare Part B) or Medicare Supplemental Health Insurance policies (Medigap) for financially needy Medicare beneficiaries with end-stage renal disease (ESRD). This safe harbor would specifically establish various standards and guidelines that, if met, would result in the particular arrangement being protected from civil sanctions under section 1128A(a)(5) of the Social Security Act.

DATES: To assure consideration, public comments on this proposed rule must be delivered to the address provided below by no later than 4:30 p.m. on July 3, 2000.

ADDRESSES: Please mail or deliver your written comments to the following address: Office of Inspector General, Department of Health and Human Services, Attention: OIG-699-P, Room 5546, Cohen Building, 330 Independence Avenue, S.W., Washington, D.C. 20201. We do not accept comments by facsimile (FAX) transmission. In commenting, please refer to code OIG-699-P.

FOR FURTHER INFORMATION CONTACT: Julie Kass (202) 205–9501 or Joel Schaer (202) 619–0089, Office of Counsel to the Inspector General.

SUPPLEMENTARY INFORMATION:

I. Background

A. Section 1128A(a)(5) of the Social Security Act

The Health Insurance Portability and Accountability Act of 1996 (HIPAA), Public Law 104–191, amended the Social Security Act (Act) to prohibit providers from offering patients any inducement to order or receive items or services from a particular provider, practitioner or supplier. Specifically, section 231(h) of HIPAA established a new provision — section 1128A(a)(5) of the Act — to provide for the imposition of a civil money penalty (CMP) against any person who:

> Offers or transfers remuneration to any individual eligible for benefits under [Medicare or Medicaid] that such person knows or should know is likely to influence such individual to order or receive from a particular provider, practitioner, or supplier any item or service for which payment may be made, in whole or in part, under [Medicare or Medicaid].

Section 231(h) of HIPAA also created a new section 1128A(i)(6) of the Act to define the term "remuneration" for purposes of the new CMP. The section defines "remuneration," in relevant part, as "transfers of items or services for free or for other than fair market value." Remuneration does not include certain enumerated practices, including waivers of coinsurance and deductible amounts, if the waiver: (1) Is not advertised; (2) is not routinely offered; and (3) is made following an individualized good faith assessment of financial need or is made after reasonable efforts to collect the coinsurance or deductible amounts have failed. There is no exception for the payment of Medicare Part B or Medigap insurance premiums on behalf of beneficiaries even when the same criteria are met.

[Page 25461]

On October 21, 1998, Congress enacted the Omnibus Consolidated and Emergency Supplemental Appropriations Act for Fiscal Year 1999 (OCESAA), Public Law 105–277. Section 5201 of OCESAA specifically authorized the Secretary to issue regulations establishing "safe harbors" under section 1128A(a)(5) of the Act for payment practices that would otherwise run afoul of the statute. (In addition to this provision, the Secretary is vested with the authority to issue advisory opinions providing legal and regulatory guidance to providers under this section.) With respect to the payment of Medicare Part B and Medigap premiums for ESRD patients, Congress required any exception to be established through a rulemaking process and limited it to the two-year period beginning on the date the final rule is promulgated. In addition, if the Secretary promulgates a safe harbor for ESRD premiums, Congress required the Comptroller General of the United States to conduct a study of any disproportionate impact on specific issuers of Medigap insurance policies due to adverse selection in enrolling Medicare ESRD beneficiaries. The Comptroller report would include a recommendation as to whether the time limit on the safe harbor should be extended.

B. End-Stage Renal Disease and Medicare's Dialysis Benefit

End-stage renal disease is a chronic disease that requires regular renal replacement therapy, such as dialysis treatments, as well as regular monitoring of laboratory values, diet and medication. In addition to irreversible renal failure, ESRD patients commonly suffer from certain co-morbid conditions, such as diabetes, anemia, hypertension and congestive heart failure. Without ongoing dialysis treatment or a transplant, ESRD is a fatal condition. End-stage renal disease affects a disproportionate share of minority populations that also have a higher than average incidence of poverty.

In 1978, Congress amended title 11 of the Act to create a special Medicare benefit under Public Law 95–292 for eligible individuals with ESRD (or dependents of those who are eligible). In accordance with section 226A of the Act, eligible persons are entitled to benefits under Medicare Part A and are eligible to enroll under Part B of the Medicare program. End-stage renal disease benefits include all Part A and Part B items and services covered under the Medicare program, and ESRD beneficiaries are subject to all the regular deductible, premium and coinsurance provisions of Part A and Part B.

Medicare pays a composite rate to dialysis facilities for each dialysis treatment. The composite rate includes: (1) Medically necessary dialysis equipment, (2) home dialysis support services, (3) all necessary dialysis supplies, (4) routine ESRD-related laboratory tests and (5) all dialysis services furnished by the dialysis facility's staff. Certain other ESRD services, such as non-routine laboratory tests, may be paid to the facility outside of the composite rate.

Medicare Part B payments generally cover 80 percent of the composite rate. End-stage renal disease patients are responsible for the remaining 20 percent coinsurance and any deductibles. Typically, ESRD patients are responsible for approximately $5,000 per year in coinsurance for their dialysis treatments alone. This amount does not include the cost of coinsurance associated with hospital and physician services. In addition, ESRD patients must pay for a number of related drugs that are not covered by Medicare. On average the cost of Medigap insurance can range from approximately $1,200 to $3,600, depending on what the policy covers.

C. Effects of Section 1128A(a)(5) on the ESRD Population

After the enactment of HIPAA, representatives of a number of ESRD providers informed the OIG that many ESRD providers had been paying for Medicare Part B premiums and Medigap policies for financially needy patients who could not afford to purchase such insurance. Under the new statutory CMP provision, the OIG concluded that such premium subsidies could be unlawful in many circumstances, and dialysis providers subsequently suspended the purchase of Medigap policies and payment of Medicare Part B premiums for their patients. However, some providers entered into arrangements with nonprofit organizations that agreed to pay premiums on behalf of needy ESRD patients.

To date, in accordance with statutory authority under section 1128D(b) of the Act, the OIG has issued three advisory opinions approving the payment by unrelated entities of insurance premiums for financially needy ESRD patients. In the first opinion, the American Kidney Fund (AKF) — a *bona fide* section 501(c)(3) charitable and educational organization — and a number of dialysis providers established an arrangement whereby providers make contributions to the AKF which, in turn, independently screens candidates for financial need and then pays Medicare Part B and Medigap premiums on behalf of qualifying patients.[1] We have indicated that this system does not violate the CMP provision because the dialysis providers are not making payments to patients or on their patients' behalf, and there is no "pass through" of specific payments to specific patients. The two other advisory opinion requests, which were also approved, involved a State-funded program and a Statewide program modeled on the AKF arrangement.[2]

Providers claim that these new premium payment programs are unwieldy, create delays and uncertainty for beneficiaries, and create unnecessary paperwork and bureaucracy. In addition, the provider community has indicated that the risks to the Medicare and Medicaid programs and to the patients do not appear to differ significantly from when dialysis providers paid the premiums directly.

II. Provisions of the Proposed Rule

We are proposing an exception to section 1128A(a)(5) of the Act for independent dialysis facilities, as defined in 42 CFR 413.174, that pay for Medicare Part B and Medigap premiums for financially needy ESRD patients when:

- The payment is not advertised;
- The dialysis facility does not routinely make payments for such policies; and
- The dialysis facility makes a good faith determination that the individual is financially needy.

Protection would not extend to the payment of Medicare Part B or Medigap premiums on behalf of any other beneficiaries (i.e., beneficiaries without ESRD) or by any other provider, conduct which section 1128A(a)(5) of the Act specifically prohibits.

The OIG is concerned that by offering to provide financial assistance to ESRD patients as part of an advertisement or solicitation, providers might influence a beneficiary's choice of provider. Therefore, to fit within the proposed exception, independent dialysis

---

1 See OIG Advisory Opinion 97–1.

2 See OIG Advisory Opinions 97–2 and 98–17.

facilities would have to refrain from advertising any offer to make such payments. Without advertising the payment of premiums, the likelihood increases that ESRD patients will have selected their dialysis provider prior to receiving the offer of payment for Medicare Part B or Medigap premiums.

Moreover, we believe that it is inappropriate for health care providers

[Page 25462]

to pay Medicare Part B or Medigap premiums *routinely* on behalf of ESRD beneficiaries, rather than to make payment decisions on a case-by-case basis. In this proposed rule, we are not specifying any particular method of determining financial need, since what may constitute "financial need" will vary depending on various factors and circumstances. What is important is that providers make determinations of financial need on an individualized, case-by-case basis in accordance with a reasonable set of income guidelines uniformly applied in all cases. The guidelines should be based on objective criteria and appropriate for the applicable locality. We believe that it is not appropriate to apply inflated income guidelines that result in waivers of copayments for persons not in genuine financial need.

Limited applicability. Despite the similarity of the criteria for the proposed payment of premium safe harbor to the statutory criteria for the waiver of copayment exception, we wish to emphasize that the proposed regulatory protection would apply only to payments by independent dialysis facilities that have no hospital, physician or other provider or supplier ownership. While waivers of copayments are themselves suspect, the payment of insurance premiums by a provider or supplier who is paid on a fee-for-service basis significantly increases the incentive for overutilization and other abuse.

In the case of dialysis, providers are paid a prospectively fixed payment for the dialysis services provided to each patient. Thus, there is less incentive to overutilize or provide unnecessary services, notwithstanding the additional insurance coverage. By contrast, we believe that a provider or supplier that is treating a patient with a chronic condition on a fee-for-service basis has a strong incentive to recoup its outlay for the premium by providing additional services. In the case of a hospital-based dialysis facility or independent dialysis facility in which a hospital, physician or other provider or supplier has an ownership interest, we are concerned that these providers or suppliers would have the same incentive as other providers or suppliers paid on a fee-for-service basis, especially given the substantial amount of health care services required by ESRD patients for co-morbid conditions. Accordingly, we are excluding from this proposed exception hospital-based dialysis facilities and independent dialysis facilities, owned in whole or in part by a hospital, physician or other provider or supplier paid on a fee-for-service basis, and seek specific comments on this exclusion from the exception. We are also concerned with the potential impact of adverse selection on the Medigap insurance market, and seek specific comments concerning the potential effects this provision may have on Medigap plans.

III. Regulatory Impact Statement

Executive Order 12866, the Unfunded Mandates Reform Act and the Regulatory Flexibility Act

The Office of Management and Budget (OMB) has reviewed this proposed rule in accordance with the provisions of Executive Order 12866 and the Regulatory Flexibility Act (5 U.S.C. 601–612), and has determined that the rulemaking does not meet the criteria for a significant regulatory action. Executive Order 12866 directs agencies to assess all costs and benefits of available regulatory alternatives and, when rulemaking is necessary, to select regulatory approaches that maximize net benefits, including potential economic, health and equity effects. The Unfunded Mandates Reform Act (Public Law 104–4) requires that agencies prepare an assessment of anticipated costs and benefits on any rulemaking that may result in an expenditure by State, local or tribal government, or by the private sector of $100 million or more in any given year. In addition, under the Regulatory Flexibility Act, if a rule has a significant economic effect on a substantial number of small businesses, the Secretary must specifically consider the economic effect of a rule on small business entities and analyze regulatory options that could lessen the impact of the rule.

Executive Order 12866

Executive Order 12866 requires that all regulations reflect consideration of alternatives, costs, benefits, incentives, equity and available information. Regulations must meet certain standards, such as avoiding unnecessary burden. We believe that this proposed rule would have no significant economic impact. The proposed safe harbor provision being set forth is designed to permit individuals and entities to freely engage in business practice and arrangements that encourage competition, choice and economy. In doing so, the rule would impose no requirements on any party. Independent dialysis facilities may voluntarily seek to comply with this proposed provision so that their business practice is not subject to enforcement actions under the civil money penalty statute. Any aggregate economic effect of this safe harbor rule would be minimal, allowing independent dialysis facilities to do directly what some dialysis facilities are already allowed to do indirectly through the AKF (in accordance with OIG Advisory Opinion 97–1). As such, we believe that the aggregate economic impact of this proposed safe harbor rule would be minimal and would have no effect on the economy or on Federal or State expenditures.

Unfunded Mandates Reform Act

Additionally, in accordance with the Unfunded Mandates Reform Act of 1995, since there are no significant costs associated with this proposed safe harbor guideline that would impose any mandates on State, local or tribal governments, or the private sector that would result in an expenditure of $100 million or more in any given year, we have determined that a full analysis under the Act is not necessary.

Regulatory Flexibility Act

In accordance with Regulatory Flexibility Act (RFA) of 1980, and the Small Business Regulatory Enforcement Act of 1996, which amended the RFA, we have determined that this proposed rule would have no significant economic effect on a substantial number of small entities. While this proposed safe harbor may have an impact on some small entities, we believe that the aggregate economic impact of this rulemaking should be minimal, since it is the nature of a violation and not the size of the entity that determines whether the OIG will pursue a sanction action. Since this proposed safe harbor would offer individuals and entities greater flexibility in their business arrangements, we believe that the proposed regulations should not have a significant economic impact on a number of small business providers, and that a regulatory flexibility analysis is not required for this rulemaking.

IV. Public Inspection of Comments

Comments will be available for public inspection beginning on May 16, 2000 in Room 5518 of the Office of Inspector General at 330 Independence Avenue, SW., Washington, DC, on Monday through Friday of each week from 8:00 a.m. to 4:30 p.m., (202) 619–0089. Because of the large number of comments we normally receive on regulations, we cannot acknowledge or respond to them individually. However, we will consider all timely and appropriate comments when developing the final rule.

List of Subjects in 42 CFR Part 1003

Administrative practice and procedure, Fraud, Grant programs — health, Health facilities, Health

[Page 25463]

professions, Maternal and child health, Medicare, Medicaid, Penalties.

Accordingly, 42 CFR part 1003 would be amended as set forth below:

PART 1003 — [AMENDED]

1. The authority citation for part 1003 would be revised to read as follows:

Authority: 42 U.S.C. 1302, 1320–7, 1320a-7a, 1320b-10, 1395u(j), 1395u(k), 1395dd(d)(1), 1395mm, 1395nn, 1395ss(d), 1396b(m), 11131(c), 11137(b)(2).

2. Section 1003.101 would be amended by:

a. Republishing the introductory text; and

b. Amending the definition of renumeration by revising the introductory text and paragraphs (3) and (4), and by adding a new paragraph (5).

§ 1003.101 Definitions.

For purposes of this part:

* * * * *

Remuneration, as set forth in § 1003.102(b)(12) of this part, is consistent with the definition contained in section 1128A(i)(6) of the Act, and includes the waiver of coinsurance and deductible amounts (or any part thereof) and transfers of items or services for free or for other than fair market value. The term "remuneration" does not include—

* * * * *

(3) Differentials in coinsurance and deductible amounts as part of a benefit plan design (as long as the differentials have been disclosed in writing to all beneficiaries, third party payers and providers), to whom claims are presented;

(4) Incentives given to individuals to promote the delivery of preventive care services where the delivery of such services is not tied (directly or indirectly) to the provision of other services reimbursed in whole or in part by Medicare or an applicable State health care program. Such incentives may include the provision of preventive care, but may not include—

(i) Cash or instruments convertible to cash; or

(ii) An incentive the value of which is disproportionately large in relationship to the value of the preventive care service (i.e., either the value of the service itself or the future health care costs reasonably expected to be avoided as a result of the preventive care); or

(5) Any payments for Supplementary Medical Insurance (Medicare Part B) or Medicare Supplemental Health Insurance (Medigap) premium amounts (or any parts thereof) by an independent dialysis facility, as defined in § 413.174 of this title, that is not owned in whole or in part by a hospital, physician, or other provider or supplier paid on a fee-for-service basis, as long as all of the following three standards are met —

(i) The payment is not offered as part of any advertisement or solicitation;

(ii) The facility does not routinely make payments for such premiums; and

(iii) The facility makes the payment for such premiums only after determining in good faith that the individual on behalf of whom such payment is made is in financial need.

* * * * *

Dated: August 9, 1999.

June Gibbs Brown,

Inspector General.

Approved: September 2, 1999.

Editorial Note: This document was received at the Office of the **Federal Register** on April 25, 2000.

Donna E. Shalala,

Secretary.

[FR Doc. 00–10695 Filed 5–1-00; 8:45 am]

BILLING CODE 4152–01-P

APPENDIX F8.4

Ambulance Restocking Safe Harbor Under the Anti-Kickback Statute, Proposed Rule; 65 FR 32060, May 22, 2000

[Federal Register: May 22, 2000 (Volume 65, Number 99)]
[Proposed Rules] [Page 32060–32065]

DEPARTMENT OF HEALTH AND HUMAN SERVICES

Office of Inspector General

42 CFR Part 1001

RIN 0991-AB05

Medicare and State Health Care Programs: Fraud and Abuse; Ambulance Restocking Safe Harbor Under the Anti-Kickback Statute

AGENCY: Office of Inspector General (OIG), HHS.

ACTION: Notice of proposed rulemaking.

SUMMARY: This proposed rule would set forth a new safe harbor, as authorized under section 14 of the Medicare and Medicaid Patient and Program Protection Act of 1987, to protect certain arrangements involving hospitals that replenish drugs and medical supplies used by ambulance providers when

[Page 32061]

transporting emergency patients to the hospitals.

DATES: To assure consideration, public comments must be delivered to the address provided below by no later than 5 p.m. on July 21, 2000.

ADDRESSES: Please mail or deliver your written comments to the following address: Department of Health and Human Services,

Office of Inspector General, 330 Independence Avenue, SW, Room 5246, Attention: OIG-62-P, Washington, DC 20201.

Because of staffing and resource limitations, we cannot accept comments by facsimile (FAX) transmission. In commenting, please refer to file OIG-62-P.

FOR FURTHER INFORMATION CONTACT: Vicki L. Robinson, Senior Counsel, Office of Counsel to the Inspector General, (202) 619–0335.

SUPPLEMENTARY INFORMATION:

I. Background

Section 1128B(b) of the Social Security Act (the Act) (42 U.S.C. 1320a-7b(b)) provides criminal penalties for individuals or entities that knowingly and willfully offer, pay, solicit or receive remuneration in order to induce the referral of business reimbursable under the Federal or State health care programs. The offense is classified as a felony and is punishable by fines of up to $25,000 and imprisonment for up to five years. Violations of the anti-kickback statute may also result in the imposition of a civil money penalty (CMP) under section 1128A(a)(7) of the Act (42 U.S.C. 1320a-7a(a)(7)) or program exclusion under section 1128(b)(7) of the Act (42 U.S.C. 1320a-7(b)(7)).

The types of remuneration covered specifically include kickbacks, bribes and rebates, whether made directly or indirectly, overtly or covertly, in cash or in kind. In addition, prohibited conduct includes not only the payment of remuneration intended to induce referrals of patients, but also the payment of remuneration intended to induce the purchasing, leasing or ordering of any good, facility, service or item reimbursable by any Federal or State health care program.

Establishing the Original Safe Harbors

Since the statute on its face is so broad, concern had been expressed that some relatively innocuous commercial arrangements were technically covered by the statute and therefore were subject to criminal prosecution. As a response to the above concern, section 14 of the Medicare and Medicaid Patient and Program Protection Act of 1987, Public Law 100–93, specifically required the development and promulgation of regulations, the so-called "safe harbor" provisions, designed to specify various payment and business practices which, although potentially capable of inducing referrals of business under the Federal and State health care programs, would not be treated as criminal offenses under the anti-kickback statute. Beginning in July 29, 1991, we have published in the Federal Register a series of final regulations establishing "safe harbors" in various areas.[1] These OIG safe harbor provisions have been developed to limit the reach of the statute somewhat by permitting certain non-abusive arrangements, while encouraging beneficial and innocuous arrangements.

Health care providers and others may voluntarily seek to comply with these provisions so that they have the assurance that their business practices are not subject to any enforcement action under the anti-kickback statute, the CMP provision for anti-kickback violations or program exclusion authority related to kickbacks. In giving the Department the authority to protect certain arrangements and payment practices under the anti-kickback statute, Congress intended the safe harbor regulations to be evolving rules that would be updated periodically to reflect changing business practices and technologies in the health care industry.

OIG Advisory Opinions on Restocking Ambulance Supplies

The OIG has issued four advisory opinions regarding arrangements between hospitals and other facilities providing emergency medical supplies, *i.e.*, "receiving facilities" and ambulance companies, under which the receiving facilities replenish ambulances with drugs and medical supplies used during the transport of *emergency* patients to the receiving facilities. In many of these arrangements, the drugs and supplies are replenished without charge to the ambulance company.

In OIG Advisory Opinion 97–6 (October 8, 1997), we responded to a request for an advisory opinion involving an ambulance replenishing arrangement that presented a specific set of facts clearly implicating the anti-kickback statute. The arrangement, as presented in the facts certified by the requesting party, contained no appropriate safeguards against fraud and abuse of the Federal health care programs and their beneficiaries. Accordingly, we concluded that the arrangement potentially violated the anti-kickback statute.

Subsequently, in 1998, we received several additional advisory opinion requests that involved ambulance replenishing arrangements, and issued three additional advisory opinions *approving*

[1] 56 FR 35952 (July 29, 1991); 61 FR 2122 (January 25, 1996); 64 FR 63518 (November 19, 1999); and 64 FR 63504 (November 19, 1999).

ambulance replenishing arrangements.[2] The facts of those three arrangements differed significantly from the facts that led to OIG Advisory Opinion 97–6. Specifically, the latter three opinions involved ambulance replenishing programs conducted in accordance with comprehensive, coordinated emergency medical delivery systems involving all of an area's ambulance providers and hospitals (as well as other components of the emergency medical system, such as physicians and local government officials). The OIG approved the three arrangements (with the limited exception of a portion of one of the three programs), persuaded that the arrangements posed little risk of Federal health care program fraud or abuse and that the arrangements promoted comprehensive and coordinated efforts to improve emergency medical care.

Since the release of OIG Advisory Opinion 98–14 in October 1998, the OIG has received no further advisory opinion requests on the topic of ambulance replenishing and few informal follow-up inquiries regarding these arrangements.

II. Provisions of the Proposed Rule

The OIG believes that, in general, the ambulance and hospital industries understand the distinction between the first unfavorable advisory opinion and the subsequent three favorable opinions and are generally able to assess and structure arrangements accordingly. However, the OIG is aware of anecdotal reports that some receiving facilities are curbing or eliminating ambulance replenishing programs in order to cut emergency room costs, while other receiving facilities feel pressured to participate in ambulance replenishment arrangements. Some receiving facilities would like to implement or continue operating replenishing programs, but are concerned about possible liability under the anti-kickback statute.

We continue to believe that properly structured replenishing arrangements serve a significant public interest by providing a means of ensuring that ambulances are fully stocked with current medications, sanitary linens and

---

[2] OIG Advisory opinion 98–7 (June 11, 1998); OIG Advisory Opinion 98–13 (September 30, 1998); and OIG Advisory Opinion 98–14 (October 28, 1998).

[Page 32062]

appropriate supplies, and that those supplies are compatible with equipment used in local emergency rooms so as to expedite the transfer of critically ill or injured patients to emergency room systems. Such replenishing arrangements are consistent with Federal policy established over the past 25 years. [3]

In an effort to further assure those providers engaged in innocuous and beneficial replenishing arrangements, we are proposing a new safe harbor under § 1001.952 of our regulations to protect certain arrangements between receiving facilities (including hospitals) and ambulance companies under which the receiving facilities replenish ambulances with drugs and medical supplies used during the transport of emergency patients to the receiving facilities. Under this proposed rule, we would provide safe harbor protection for ambulance replenishing arrangements that satisfy all of the conditions in one of two categories established by the safe harbor. Both categories pertain only to emergency ambulance services; the safe harbor would not protect replenishing of ambulance supplies, linens or medications following routine ambulance transports.

Replenishing Arrangements Where Ambulance Provider Pays Receiving Facility Fair Market Value

The first new proposed safe harbor would protect replenishing arrangements where an ambulance provider pays the receiving facility fair market value, based on an arms-length transaction, for replenished drugs or supplies (including linens) used in connection with the transport of an emergency patient. Payment would not need to be made at the time of the replenishing, provided commercially

[3] See, e.g., Emergency Medical Services Systems Act of 1973 (EMSSA), Public Law 93–154 (providing Federal funding for the development of regional Emergency Medical Services (EMS) systems at the State, regional, and local levels, and defining "emergency medical services system" as "a system which provides for the arrangement of personnel, facilities and equipment for the effective and coordinated delivery in an appropriate geographical area of health care services under emergency conditions * * * and which is administered by a public or nonprofit private entity which has the authority and the resources to provide effective administration of the system."); Highway Safety Act of 1966, Public Law 89–594 (establishing an EMS program in the Department of Transportation); Emergency Medical Services for Children Program, under the Public Health Act, Public Law 98–555 (providing funds for enhancing pediatric EMS); and Trauma Care Systems Planning and Development Act of 1990, Public Law 101–590.

reasonable and appropriate payment arrangements have been made in advance. For linens, an exchange of a comparable quantity of laundered linens for soiled linens would be considered fair market value, notwithstanding any economic value attributable to the laundering of linens by receiving facilities, which often have specialized laundering equipment needed for compliance with sanitation requirements. A non-profit receiving facility would be protected under this safe harbor if it sells replenished drugs or medical supplies to a non-profit ambulance provider at cost in order to comply with the Non-Profit Institutions Act. [4]

Remuneration in the Form of Contemporaneous Replenishing of Drugs or Medical Supplies

The second proposed safe harbor would protect remuneration in the form of contemporaneous replenishing of drugs or medical supplies (including linens) used during an emergency transport of a patient to the receiving facility, even if the replenishing is for free or at reduced prices. We are proposing that the following seven conditions be met in order to qualify for protection under this safe harbor:

(1) Receiving facilities must provide replenishing on an equal basis for all ambulance providers who bring emergency patients to the receiving facility. This condition is intended to prevent receiving facilities from inappropriately using replenishing to attract or reward high referring ambulance providers.

(2) The replenishing arrangement must be part of a comprehensive and coordinated effort to improve the EMS delivery system in the relevant service area and must be open to all emergency ambulance providers and receiving facilities operating in the service area. It must be implemented with the participation of, and monitored by, a regional EMS Council or functionally similar entity, organization or association (the Oversight Entity). The Oversight Entity must be a non-profit entity composed of representatives of a broad array of participants in a service area's emergency medical system, such as hospitals, ambulance providers, emergency room physicians and nurses, public safety organizations, paramedics, local educational institutions and community residents. The involvement of a wide

[4] 15 U.S.C. 13(c) exception to the Robinson-Patman Act (15 U.S.C. 13(a)-(f)). Inquiries as to the applicability of, or compliance with, the Non-Profit Institutions Act or the Robinson-Patman Act should be directed to the Federal Trade Commission.

range of representatives of the local EMS community provides substantial assurance that the replenishment arrangement is intended to benefit the local community, rather than a single provider or group of providers. Participation in the Oversight Entity should be open to all interested parties in the service area on equal terms and conditions, i.e., the Oversight Entity cannot be composed solely of representatives of a single health system. Typically, Oversight Entities will engage in the following types of activities:

- Standardization of EMS practices and equipment;
- Education and training for pre-hospital care providers;
- Ongoing evaluation and improvement of EMS capabilities in the service area;
- Public information campaigns; and
- Other activities designed to promote EMS care for the service area.

We recognize that the size, composition, structure and scope of activities of Oversight Entities may necessarily vary depending on the size and resources of the particular service area. We would expect, for example, an Oversight Entity in a small rural area with one hospital, a few physicians and one ambulance provider to look and operate differently than one in a densely populated urban area with several hospitals, a number of transport providers and diverse physicians, teaching facilities, Government agencies and the like. Oversight Entities should be part of a comprehensive and coordinated regional EMS system appropriate to the size and resources of the service area. We are not specifying any particular structure or legal form for the Oversight Entity; it must simply be functionally similar to a regional EMS Counsel. The participants in the Oversight Entity should be representative of the service area's EMS system. We are specifically soliciting comments on our proposal that safe harbored replenishing arrangements must be a part of a comprehensive and consolidated regional EMS system.

(3) The replenishing arrangement must be memorialized in writing, whether through a contract signed under the auspices of the Oversight Entity by all participating ambulance providers and receiving facilities or by a generally applicable plan or protocol promulgated or approved by the Oversight Entity. The replenishing arrangement must in practice comport with the terms of the written documentation.

(4) The receiving facility must not bill any Federal health care program or Federal program beneficiary for the replenished drugs or supplies, or write off such drugs or supplies as bad debt. The purpose of this requirement is to

[Page 32063]

prevent double payments by Medicare, which pays hospitals under Part A (through fiscal intermediaries), but which typically pays ambulance providers for drugs and supplies used during emergency transports under Part B (through carriers).

(5) In order to prevent "double dipping," ambulance providers may not bill any Federal health care program or Federal beneficiary separately for the replenished drugs or supplies.

(6) The receiving facility and the ambulance provider must maintain records of the replenished drugs or supplies and make those records available to the Secretary upon request.

(7) The receiving facility and ambulance provider must otherwise comply with all Federal, State and local laws regulating emergency medical care and the provision of drugs and medical supplies, including laws relating to the handling of controlled substances such as morphine.

Nothing in this preamble or the proposed regulations is intended to express any view as to the appropriate billing of the Federal health care programs for supplies used during emergency transport services. Parties seeking to comply with these proposed safe harbors would still need to comply with all relevant billing and claims filing rules. The fifth and sixth conditions described above for the second proposed safe harbor merely set forth criteria for determining whether a particular arrangement qualifies for safe harbor protection under the anti-kickback statute; the conditions do not purport to establish any reimbursement rule. Questions regarding reimbursement under the Medicare and Medicaid programs should be addressed to the Health Care Financing Administration or the party's relevant fiscal intermediary or carrier.

As with the existing safe harbor provisions currently codified in § 1001.952, compliance with these proposed safe harbors would be voluntary. Failure to fit into one of these safe harbors would not mean that an ambulance replenishment arrangement is illegal. Rather, it would simply mean that the arrangement would need to be evaluated on a case-by-case basis.

Meeting the Criteria for Establishing New Safe Harbors

Section 205 of the Health Insurance Portability and Accountability Act, Public Law 104–191, established certain criteria that the Secretary may consider when modifying or establishing safe harbors to the anti-kickback statute. We indicated our intent to consider these criteria in evaluating proposals for new safe harbors in our Notice of Intent to Develop Regulations (61 FR 69061; December 31, 1996). We have considered these criteria in developing this proposed rulemaking, and we believe, for the reasons described above, that the proposed safe harbor for certain ambulance replenishing arrangements is likely to: (1) Increase or have no effect on access for needy patients to health care services; (2) increase the quality of health care services for needy patients; (3) have little or no effect on the cost of Federal health care programs; (4) have little or no effect on competition; and (5) have little or no effect on the quantity of services provided in underserved areas. We further believe the proposed safe harbor contains safeguards that limit the potential for overutilization and assure that patients retain their freedom of choice of service providers.

III. Regulatory Impact Statement

Executive Order 12866, the Unfunded Mandates Reform Act, Executive Order 13132, and the Regulatory Flexibility Act

The Office of Management and Budget (OMB) has reviewed this proposed rule in accordance with the provisions of Executive Order 12866 and the Regulatory Flexibility Act (5 U.S.C. 601–612), and has determined that it does not meet the criteria for a significant regulatory action. Executive Order 12866 directs agencies to assess all costs and benefits of available regulatory alternatives and, when rulemaking is necessary, to select regulatory approaches that maximize net benefits, including potential economic, environmental, public health, safety distributive and equity effects. Section 202 of the Unfunded Mandates Reform Act, Public Law 104–4, requires that agencies prepare an assessment of anticipated costs and benefits on any rulemaking that may result in an expenditure by State, local or tribal Government, or by the private sector of $100 million or more in any given year. Further, Executive Order 13132, Federalism, requires agencies to determine if a rule will have a significant affect on States, on their relationship with the Federal Government, and on the distribution of power and responsibility among the various levels of government.

In addition, under the Small Business Enforcement Act (SBEA) of 1996, if a rule has a significant economic effect on a substantial number of small businesses, the Secretary must specifically consider the economic effect of a rule on small business entities and analyze regulatory options that could lessen the impact of the rule. In addition, under the Regulatory Flexibility Act, if a rule has a significant economic effect on a substantial number of small businesses, the Secretary must specifically consider the economic effect of a rule on small business entities and analyze regulatory options that could lessen the impact of the rule.

Executive Order 12866 requires that all regulations reflect consideration of alternatives, costs, benefits, incentives, equity and available information. Regulations must meet certain standards, such as avoiding unnecessary burden. We believe that this proposed rule would have no significant economic impact. The proposed safe harbor provisions set forth in this rulemaking are designed to permit individuals and entities to freely engage in business practices and arrangements that encourage competition, innovation and economy. As indicated above, in doing so, these regulations impose no requirements on any party. Health care providers and others may voluntarily seek to comply with these provisions so that they have the assurance that their business practices are not subject to any enforcement actions under the anti-kickback statute. We believe that any aggregate economic effect of these safe harbor regulations would be minimal and would impact only those limited few who engage in prohibited behavior in violation of the statute. As such, we believe that the aggregate economic impact of these proposed regulations is minimal and would have no effect on the economy or on Federal or State expenditures

Additionally, in accordance with the Unfunded Mandates Reform Act of 1995, we believe that there are no significant costs associated with these proposed safe harbor guidelines that would impose any mandates on State, local or tribal governments, or the private sector that will result in an expenditure of $100 million or more in any given year. Further, in reviewing this rule under the threshold criteria of Executive Order 13132, Federalism, we have determined that this rule would not significantly affect the rights, roles and responsibilities of States, and that a full analysis under these Acts are not necessary.

Further, in accordance with the Regulatory Flexibility Act (RFA) of 1980, and the Small Business Regulatory Enforcement Act of 1996, which amended the RFA, we are required to determine if this rule will have a significant economic effect on a substantial number of small entities and, if so, to identify regulatory options that could lessen the impact. While

[Page 32064]

these safe harbor provisions may have an impact on small entities, we believe that the aggregate economic impact of this rulemaking would be minimal, since it is the nature of the violation and not the size of the entity that will result in a violation of the anti-kickback statute. Since the vast majority of individuals and entities potentially affected by these regulations do not engage in prohibited arrangements, schemes or practices in violation of the law, we believe that these proposed regulations would not have a significant economic impact on a number of small business entities, and that a regulatory flexibility analysis is not required for this rulemaking.

Paperwork Reduction Act

In accordance with section 3506(c)(2)(A) of the Paperwork Reduction Act (PRA) of 1995, we are required to solicit public comments, and receive final OMB approval, on any information collection requirements set forth in rulemaking. While compliance with the provisions in this safe harbor rule would be voluntary, proposed § 1001.952(v)(3) contains information collection requirements that would require approval by OMB. As such, we are required to solicit public comments under section 3506(c)(2)(A) of the PRA on these requirements. Specifically, in order to qualify for safe harbor protection for ambulance restocking arrangements under § 1001.952(v)(3), the regulations would require that replenishing agreements be set forth in writing in the form of (1) a contract signed under the auspices of the oversight entity by all participating ambulance providers and receiving facilities or (2) a generally applicable plan or protocol promulgated or approved by the oversight entity. There is no obligation to submit these agreements to the Secretary, however, in order to achieve initial compliance with the safe harbor. In addition, to qualify for safe harbor protection for ambulance restocking arrangements under § 1001.952(v)(3), the receiving facility and the ambulance provider must maintain records of the replenished drugs and medical supplies (including linens) and make those records available to the Secretary promptly upon request. However, as indicated above, the safe harbor does not require any submission of reports, data collection or other documents in order to be in compliance with the anti-kickback statute.

In accordance with the PRA requirements, we are inviting comments on (1) whether the proposed collection of information is necessary for the proper performance of the functions of the agency, including whether the information will have practical utility; (2) the accuracy of the estimate of the burden of the proposed collection of information; (3) ways to enhance the quality, utility and clarity of the information collected; and (4) ways to minimize the burden of the collection of information on parties, including through the use of automated collection techniques or other forms of information technology. As part of the OMB approval for the collection of information contained in this rule, we are soliciting public comments on this requirement, thereby initiating the normal PRA clearance.

Title: Ambulance Restocking Safe Harbor Under the Anti-Kickback Statute.

Summary of the collection of information: Proposed § 1001.952(v) would set forth a new statutory exception to the anti-kickback statute that covers any gift or transfer of drugs or medical supplies (including linens) by a hospital or other receiving facility to an ambulance provider for the purpose of replenishing comparable drugs or medical supplies (including linens) used by the ambulance provider in connection with the transport of an emergency patient to the hospital or other receiving facility. Safe harbors do not create any affirmative obligation on any individuals or entities. Seeking protection under these safe harbor provisions is purely voluntary.

The aggregate information burden for the information collection requirements contained in this proposed rulemaking is set forth below.

Respondents: In accordance with proposed § 1001.952(v), the respondents for the collection of information described in these regulations are parties involved in written agreements between (1) a hospital or other receiving facility that replenishes drugs and medical supplies, and (2) ambulance providers who bring emergency patients to the receiving facility.

Estimated number of respondents: The safe harbor being proposed in § 1001.952(v) would protect those restocking arrangements between receiving facilities that replenish drugs and medical supplies on an equal basis to all ambulance providers who transport their emergency patients to the receiving facility. Virtually all such replenishing arrangements already are memorialized in written contracts as a matter of prudent business practice, irrespective of the existence of the proposed safe harbor. We believe that few, if any, parties will enter into written arrangements specifically for the purposes of safe harbor protection. Accordingly, we estimate that the number of parties entering into written agreements to qualify for safe harbor protection will be negligible.

Estimated number of responses per respondent: None.

Estimated total annual burden on respondents: We believe that the burden of preparing written agreements and the aggregate information burden for the information collection requirements contained in this proposed rulemaking would be minimal. As indicated above, in most, if not all, cases the parties already have written agreements as part of the parties' replenishing arrangements, independent of the safe harbor requirements. Accordingly, any burden imposed by these proposed regulations would impose no burden on such parties.

Comments on this information collection activity should be sent to: Allison Herron Eydt, OIG Desk Officer, Office of Management and Budget, Room 10235, New Executive Office Building, 725 17th Street. NW, Washington, DC 20053, FAX: (202) 395–6974.

Comments on these paperwork reduction requirements may be submitted to the above-cited individual within 60 days following the **Federal Register** publication of this proposed rule.

IV. Public Inspection of Comments and Response to Comments

Comments will be available for public inspection June 5, 2000 in Room 5518, Office of Counsel to the Inspector General, at 330 Independence Avenue, SW, Washington, DC on Monday through Friday of each week (Federal holidays excepted) between the hours of 9 a.m. and 4 p.m., (202) 619–0089.

Because of the large number of items of correspondence we normally receive on **Federal Register** documents published for comment, we are not able to acknowledge or respond to them individually. We will consider all comments we receive by the date and time specified in the DATES section of this preamble, and will respond to the comments in the preamble of the final rule.

List of Subjects in 42 CFR Part 1001

Administrative practice and procedure, Fraud, Grant programs — health, Health facilities, Health professions, Maternal and child health, Medicaid, Medicare.

Accordingly, 42 CFR part 1001 would be amended as set forth below:

[Page 32065]

PART 1001 — [AMENDED]

1. The authority citation for part 1001 would continue to read as follows:

Authority: 42 U.S.C. 1302, 1320a-7, 1320a-7b, 1395u(h), 1395u (j), 1395u(k), 1395y(d), 1395y(e), 1395cc(b)(2)(D), (E) and (F), and 1395hh; and sec. 2455, Pub.L. 103–355, 108 Stat. 3327 (31 U.S.C. 6101 note).

2. Section 1001.952 would be amended by republishing the introductory text and by adding a new paragraph (v) to read as follows:

§ 1001.952 Exceptions

The following payment practices shall not be treated as a criminal offense under section 1128B of the Act and shall not serve as the basis for an exclusion:

* * * * *

(v) Ambulance restocking. (1) As used in section 1128B of the Act, "remuneration" does not include any gift or transfer of drugs or medical supplies (including linens) by a hospital or other receiving facility to an ambulance provider for the purpose of replenishing comparable drugs or medical supplies (including linens) used by the ambulance provider in connection with the transport of an emergency patient to the hospital or other receiving facility if all of the applicable standards in either paragraph (v)(2) or (v)(3) of this section are satisfied.

(2)(i) Except as otherwise provided in paragraph (v)(2)(ii) of this section, the ambulance provider pays the receiving facility fair market value, based on an arms-length transaction, for the replenished drugs or medical supplies (including linens). A non-profit receiving facility will be deemed to meet this standard if it sells replenished drugs or medical supplies to a non-profit ambulance provider at cost in order to comply with the Non-Profit Institutions Act (15 U.S.C. 13 (c)), exception to the Robinson-Patman Act (15 U.S.C. 3(a)-(f)).

(ii) If payment is not made contemporaneously with the replenishing of the drugs or medical supplies (including linens), the receiving facility and the ambulance provider make commercially reasonable payment arrangements in advance.

(3)(i) The receiving facility replenishes drugs and medical supplies (including linens) on an equal basis for all ambulance providers who bring emergency patients to the receiving facility.

(ii) The replenishing arrangement must be implemented with the participation of, and monitored by, an oversight entity (as defined in paragraph (v)(4)(ii) of this section) as part of a comprehensive and coordinated regional emergency medical system appropriate to the size and resources of the service area and must be open and available to all emergency ambulance providers and receiving facilities in the service area.

(iii) The replenishing arrangement must be memorialized in writing. The writing may be in the form of—

(A) A contract signed under the auspices of the oversight entity by all participating ambulance providers and receiving facilities or

(B) A generally applicable plan or protocol promulgated or approved by the oversight entity.

(iv) The receiving facility refrains from billing any Federal health care program or Federal health care program beneficiary for the replenished drugs or medical supplies (including linens) and does not write off the cost of such drugs or medical supplies (including linens) as bad debt.

(v) The ambulance provider refrains from billing any Federal health care program or Federal health care program beneficiary separately for the replenished drugs or medical supplies (including linens).

(vi) The receiving facility and the ambulance provider maintain records of the replenished drugs and medical supplies (including linens) and make those records available to the Secretary promptly upon request.

(vii) The receiving facility and the ambulance provider otherwise comply with all Federal, State and local laws regulating emergency medical care and the provision of drugs and medical supplies, including, but not limited to, laws relating to the handling of controlled substances.

(4) For purposes of paragraph (v)(3) of this section —

(i) A "receiving facility" is a hospital or other facility that provides emergency medical services; and

(ii) An "oversight entity" is a regional emergency medical services council or functionally similar entity, association or organization that—

(A) Is described in section 501(c)(3) or 501(c)(4) of the Internal Revenue Code and exempt from taxation under section 501(a) of that Code;

(B) Includes, or is composed of, representatives of a broad array of participants in a service area's emergency medical system (e.g., hospitals, ambulance providers, emergency room physicians, paramedics, public safety organizations, local educational institutions and community residents);

(C) Is open to all interested parties in the service area on equal terms and conditions; and

(D) Has as its mission the improvement of the emergency medical services delivery system in the relevant service area.

Dated: November 2, 1999.

June Gibbs Brown,

Inspector General.

Approved: November 18, 1999.

Donna E. Shalala,

Secretary.

[FR Doc. 00–12697 Filed 5–19–00; 8:45 am]

BILLING CODE 4150–04-P

APPENDIX F9

Advisory Opinion No. 97-1

[Names and addresses of Requestors have been redacted]

Re: Advisory Opinion No. 97–1

Dear [Names have been redacted]:

We are writing in response to your request for an advisory opinion, which we accepted pursuant to 42 C.F.R. § 1008.41 on April 11, 1997. Your request asks whether donations by renal dialysis providers to an independent 501(c)(3) charitable organization for the purpose of funding a program to pay for Supplementary Medical Insurance Program ("Medicare Part B") or Medicare Supplementary Health Insurance ("Medigap") premiums for financially needy Medicare beneficiaries with end-stage renal disease where such beneficiaries may be receiving treatment from the donor-dialysis providers (the "Proposed Arrangement") would constitute grounds for the imposition of a civil monetary penalty under Section 231(h) of the Health Insurance Portability and Accountability Act of 1996 ("HIPAA").

You have certified that all of the information you provided in your request, including all supplementary letters, is true and correct, and constitutes a complete description of the facts and agreements among the parties regarding the Proposed Arrangement. You have also certified that upon our approval of the Proposed Arrangement, you will undertake to effectuate the Proposed Arrangement.

In issuing this opinion, we have relied solely on the facts and information you presented to us. We have not undertaken an independent investigation of such information. This opinion is limited to the facts presented. If material facts have not been disclosed, this opinion is without force and effect.

Based on the information provided and subject to certain conditions described below, we have determined that the Proposed Arrangement would not constitute grounds for the imposition of civil monetary penalties under Section 231(h) of HIPAA. This opinion may not be relied on by any person other than the addressees and is further qualified as set out in Part III below and in 42 C.F.R. Part 1008.

I. FACTUAL BACKGROUND

The American Kidney Fund and Company A, Company B, Company C, Company D, Company E, and Company F, (collectively the "Companies") have made the following representations with respect to the Proposed Arrangement. The American Kidney Fund and the Companies are collectively the "Requestors".

A. End-Stage Renal Disease and Medicare's Dialysis Benefit

End-stage renal disease ("ESRD") is a chronic disease that requires regular dialysis, as well as monitoring of laboratory values, diet, and medication. In addition to chronic renal failure, ESRD patients also commonly suffer from certain co-morbid conditions, including diabetes, anemia, hypertension, and congestive heart failure.

In 1972, Congress created a special Medicare ESRD benefit. This benefit is for all individuals with ESRD who have earned a certain level of eligibility for Social Security benefits (or are dependents of those who have attained that level). People in this category are entitled to benefits under Medicare Part A and are eligible to enroll in Medicare Part B. Medicare Part B payments on behalf of ESRD patients generally cover eighty percent of the composite rate for Medicare-covered maintenance dialysis services, as well as eighty percent of physician services and certain ancillary services.[1] Medigap insurance can be purchased to cover a patient's annual Medicare coinsurance obligations for Medicare-covered services.

B. Parties to the Proposed Arrangement

1. The Companies

[Material redacted] [The companies have formed an association] to address issues that affect the dialysis industry and to improve the way the renal dialysis industry performs as a whole. While the Companies [as an association] have worked with the American Kidney Fund to develop the proposed arrangement, the individual providers have applied for the advisory opinion in their separate capacities.

2. American Kidney Fund

---

[1] We note that Medicare reimbursement for some medical services provided to ESRD patients, such as certain lab services, are not covered under the composite rate.

The American Kidney Fund ("AKF") is a *bona fide*, 501(c)(3) charitable and educational organization that has been in existence for over twenty-five years. AKF, a public charity, is governed by a board of twenty-five members. The board bylaws provide that membership on the board should be comprised of representatives involved with ESRD issues, including nephrology physicians, nephrology nurses, nephrology social workers, patients or family members of ESRD patients, and community leaders. Vacancies on the board are filled by vote of the remaining board members. Although two members of the current board are employees of subsidiaries of one Company, the AKF board is not directly or indirectly controlled by any Company or Companies. AKF has established a subcommittee of the board's Program and Grant Committee to have primary oversight authority for the Health

Insurance Premium Program; membership on such subcommittee will be restricted to exclude any employees, officers, shareholders, or owners of any dialysis provider.

In addition to its educational efforts on behalf of those suffering from renal failure, AKF provides direct financial support in the form of grants to needy persons with ESRD for items such as transportation, medication, and insurance premiums. In the past, AKF has funded 100 percent of all eligible grant requests from ESRD patients. In 1995, AKF assisted over 12,000 patients with ESRD and received over $5 million in donations. Of that amount, less than ten percent was contributed by the Companies. The largest percentage of AKF's funds was directed towards patient aid. AKF disseminates information about its patient assistance and other programs throughout the national dialysis provider community, especially to social workers who work with ESRD patients.

C. Health Insurance Premium Program

AKF's Health Insurance Premium Program ("HIPP") provides financial assistance to financially needy ESRD patients for the costs of medicine, transportation, and health insurance premiums, including Medicare Part B and Medigap premiums. Assistance is available to all eligible patients on an equal basis. In general, eligibility for participation in AKF's assistance programs requires a physician certification, a referral letter signed by a social worker or administrator at a dialysis provider, and an individual Patient Grant Application. The Patient Grant Application requires patients to provide detailed financial information for their entire household.[2] While a patient can apply directly to AKF for a grant, most applications are submitted on the patient's behalf by dialysis providers or social workers employed by a dialysis provider.

Upon receipt of a patient's application, a member of AKF's staff reviews the application, gathers additional information, if necessary, and makes an initial recommendation as to the disposition of the application based upon AKF's needs assessment and eligibility criteria. A senior staff employee reviews the recommendation and makes a final determination. All determinations are made by AKF employees who have no financial interest in the Companies or other dialysis providers and are based on their good faith assessment that the applicant is in financial need and eligible for assistance. If AKF determines that a patient is eligible for assistance, AKF notifies the dialysis provider's social worker that the insurance premium has been paid in order to ensure that the patient's billing information is accurate.

Because of AKF's limited financial resources, an AKF patient assistance grant is provided for a specific time period. Upon expiration of the period, the patient must submit another grant application. Grant requests are reviewed on a first-come, first-served basis to the extent funding is available.

D. The Proposed Arrangement

AKF proposes to expand significantly its patient assistance grants to financially needy ESRD patients for payment of medical insurance premiums through HIPP. Additional funding will be donated primarily by the Companies. Medical social workers at each Company's dialysis facility will assist patients in identifying all available sources of assistance for which they qualify, which may include assistance from HIPP, and if appropriate, will refer financially needy patients to AKF for such assistance. However, the Companies will not advertise the availability of possible financial assistance to the public and will not disclose directly or indirectly to individual

---

[2] The information required includes: assets held in checking and savings accounts; the value of a home, stocks and bonds, and automobiles; monthly income (which is made up of take-home pay of the patient and spouse, social security, welfare, retirement income, veterans benefits, etc.); and monthly expenses for rent, mortgage, food, utilities, transportation, medical expenses, insurance, charge accounts, and loans. AKF further requires that the patient disclose all sources of alternative assistance available, such as Medicare, Medicaid, and state renal programs.

patients they refer that such members have contributed to AKF to fund the grants.

AKF will continue to use its current procedures in assessing the financial need and eligibility of all patients, whether self-referred or referred by the Companies, or other non-donor dialysis providers. Determinations will be made solely on AKF's good faith assessment of a patient's financial need. AKF staff involved in awarding patient grants will not take the identity of the referring facility or the amount of any provider's donation into consideration when assessing patient applications or making grant determinations.

Under the Proposed Arrangement, the Companies will be free to determine whether to make contributions to AKF and, if so, how much to contribute. All the Companies have certified that they will not track the amount that AKF pays on behalf of patients dialyzing at their facilities in order to calculate future contributions. However, in calculating their contributions to AKF, the Companies have indicated that they may consider what they would have otherwise paid on behalf of financially needy patients utilizing their facilities. The Companies will not disclose to each other, or other dialysis providers, the amount or method of calculating their respective contributions to AKF, and AKF will not disclose one Company's contribution to another Company or to other dialysis providers.

Contributions will be made without any restrictions or conditions placed on the donation. The Companies have acknowledged that "contributions . . . will be gifts without any guarantee or promise on the part of AKF that patients referred to AKF for possible financial assistance with their insurance premiums will receive such assistance. AKF's discretion as to the uses of contributions will be absolute, independent, and autonomous."

II. LEGAL ANALYSIS

Section 231(h) of HIPAA, effective January 1, 1997, provides for the imposition of civil monetary penalties against any person who:

offers or transfers remuneration to any individual eligible for benefits under [Federal health care programs (including Medicare or Medicaid)] that such person knows or should know is likely to influence such individual to order or receive from a particular provider, practitioner, or supplier any item or service for which payment may be made, in whole or in part, [by a Federal health care program].

Section 231(h) defines "remuneration", in relevant part, as "transfers of items or services for free or for other than fair market value."[3]

We conclude that the Proposed Arrangement would not constitute grounds for the imposition of civil monetary penalties under Section 231(h) of HIPAA. A violation of Section 231(h) requires that something of value be given to a beneficiary, either directly or on his or her behalf. Simply put, the contributions to AKF by the Companies are not made to or on behalf of beneficiaries.[4]

Moreover, while the premium payments by AKF may constitute remuneration to beneficiaries, they are not likely to influence patients to order or receive services from particular providers. To the contrary, the insurance coverage purchased by AKF will follow a patient regardless of which provider the patient selects, thereby enhancing patient freedom of choice in health care providers.

A. Donations By The Companies Do Not Constitute Remuneration To An Eligible Beneficiary

The Companies' contributions to AKF would not constitute grounds for the imposition of civil monetary penalties under Section 231(h), because such contributions are not made to or on behalf of an individual eligible for Federal heath care program benefits. AKF is a bona fide, independent, publicly-funded, 501(c)(3) charitable organization whose charitable purposes include aiding ESRD patients and their families and is not subject to control, directly or indirectly, by any Company or Companies. Under the Proposed Arrangement, AKF will have absolute discretion regarding the use of provider contributions made to AKF.

Moreover, eligibility for HIPP assistance is available to any financially needy ESRD patient regardless of provider; it is not limited to patients of the companies. AKF will make all AKF eligibility determinations using its own criteria, and AKF staff will not take into account the identity of the referring provider or the amount of any donation to AKF by such provider.

Finally, as an additional safeguard, the Companies have represented that they will not track the amounts that AKF pays on behalf of patients dialyzing at their facilities in order to calculate amounts

[3] The statutory definition of remuneration provides an exception, not applicable here, for certain waivers of coinsurance and deductible amounts.

[4] The Proposed Arrangement differs from an arrangement where a renal dialysis provider directly pays premiums for beneficiaries, thus potentially influencing them to continue to use that particular dialysis provider in order to ensure continuing payment of premiums.

of future contributions, although donations may take into account the amounts that the Companies would have otherwise expended on financially needy patients. Contributions will not be earmarked for the use of particular beneficiaries or groups of beneficiaries. The Companies may change the amount of their contributions or discontinue contributing to AKF at any time. The Companies have represented that they will individually determine the amount of their contributions without consulting with the other Companies or other contributing dialysis providers.

In sum, the interposition of AKF, a **bona fide**, independent, charitable organization, and its administration of HIPP provides sufficient insulation so that the premium payments should not be attributed to the Companies. The Companies who contribute to AKF will not be assured that the amount of HIPP assistance their patients receive bears any relationship to the amount of their donations. Indeed, the Companies are not guaranteed that beneficiaries they refer to HIPP will receive any assistance at all. In these circumstances, we do not believe that the donations by the Companies to AKF can reasonably be construed as payments to eligible beneficiaries of a Federal health care program.

B. AKF's Purchase of Premiums Is Not Likely to Influence A Beneficiary's Choice of a Particular Provider

Section 231(h) prohibits payments to or on behalf of Federal health care program beneficiaries only if the payments are likely to influence such beneficiaries to use a particular provider. In the circumstances presented by the Proposed Arrangement, we believe that AKF's payments of premiums on behalf of financially needy beneficiaries is not likely to influence a beneficiary's selection of a particular provider.

As part of the application process for HIPP, AKF requires certain medical and financial certifications from the applicant's physician and social worker. While patients may apply directly to AKF, more commonly, the dialysis provider makes the application on behalf of the patient. Thus, a patient will often have already selected a provider prior to submitting his or her application for assistance or the initial payment of premiums by AKF. As an additional safeguard, HIPP will not be advertised to the public by the Companies; this should reduce the probability that a beneficiary would select a Company based on its participation in HIPP. Most importantly, once in possession of Medicare Part B or Medigap coverage, a beneficiary will be able to select any provider of his or her choice. Simply put,

AKF's payment of premiums will expand, rather than limit, beneficiaries' freedom of choice.

III. LIMITATIONS

The limitations applicable to this opinion include the following:

- This advisory opinion is issued only to AKF, Company A, Company B, Company C, Company D, Company E, and Company F, which are the Requestors of this opinion. This advisory opinion has no application, and cannot be relied upon, by any other individual or entity.
- This advisory opinion does not address any other current or past arrangement for the payment of Part B or Medigap premiums by any dialysis provider or any other charitable or non-profit organization. The U.S. Department of Health and Human Services does not accept or acquiesce in any characterizations of the propriety of such arrangements in the materials submitted by the Requestors.
- This advisory opinion may not be introduced into evidence in any matter involving an entity or individual that is not a Requestor to this opinion.
- This advisory opinion is applicable only to the statutory provision specifically noted above. No opinion is herein expressed or implied with respect to the application of any other Federal, state, or local statute, rule, regulation, ordinance, or other law that may be applicable to the Proposed Arrangement, including any laws relating to insurance or insurance contracts.
- This advisory opinion will not bind or obligate any agency other than the U.S. Department of Health and Human Services.
- This advisory opinion is prospective only. It has no application to conduct which precedes the date of this opinion.
- This advisory opinion is limited in scope to the specific arrangement described in this letter and has no applicability to other arrangements, even those which appear similar in nature or scope.

This opinion is also subject to any additional limitations set forth at 42 C.F.R. Part 1008.

The OIG will not proceed against the Requestors with respect to any action taken in good faith reliance upon this advisory opinion as long as all of the material facts have been fully, completely, and accurately presented, and the arrangement in practice comports with the information provided. The OIG reserves the right to reconsider the questions and issues raised in this advisory opinion and, where the public interest requires, modify or terminate this opinion. In the event that this advisory opinion is modified or terminated, the OIG will not proceed against the requestors with respect to any action taken in good faith reliance upon this advisory opinion, where all of the relevant facts were fully, completely, and accurately presented and where such action was promptly discontinued upon notification of the modification or termination of this advisory opinion.

Sincerely,

/S/

D. McCarty Thornton

Chief Counsel to the Inspector General

APPENDIX F10

Advisory Opinion No. 97-2

[name and address redacted]

Re: [name redacted]

Advisory Opinion No. 97–2

Dear [redacted]:

We are writing in response to your request for an advisory opinion, which we accepted pursuant to 42 C.F.R. Part 1008.41 on April 28, 1997. Your request asks whether a state-funded program that pays for insurance premiums for financially needy Medicare beneficiaries with end-stage renal disease (the "Arrangement") would constitute grounds for the imposition of a civil monetary penalty under Section 231(h) of the Health Insurance Portability and Accountability Act of 1996 ("HIPAA") [42 U.S.C. § 1320a-7a(a)(5)].

You have certified that all of the information you provided in your request, including all supplementary letters, is true and correct, and constitutes a complete description of the facts and agreements among the parties regarding the Arrangement.

In issuing this opinion, we have relied solely on the facts and information you presented to us. We have not undertaken any independent investigation of such information. This opinion is limited to the facts presented. If material facts have not been disclosed, this opinion is without force and effect.

Based on the information provided and subject to certain conditions described below, we conclude that the Arrangement would not constitute grounds for the imposition of civil monetary penalties under Section 231(h) of HIPAA. This opinion may not be relied on by any person other than the addressee and is further qualified as set out in Part III below and in 42 C.F.R. Part 1008.

I. FACTUAL BACKGROUND

Program X is a State-funded program administered by University A. Program X receives an annual appropriation from the State of Y to fund a variety of programs that assist financially needy State residents to obtain treatment for end-stage renal disease ("ESRD"), including dialysis and kidney transplant services. Program X programs are programs of last resort intended to be used when no other sources of funding for treatment are available. Funds appropriated to Program X can be used only for medical expenses related to ESRD. Program X distributes State funds to qualifying health care providers pursuant to written contracts ("Facility Agreements") that specify the maximum amount of funds granted to each contract facility and the categorical purposes for which the funds are allocated. Funds are disbursed to contract facilities by Program X in accordance with monthly or quarterly statements submitted by the contract facilities. Any variation from the budget set forth in the Facility Agreement must be approved in advance by Program X. Program X has Facility Agreements with all chronic dialysis providers in the State.

Among the programs administered by Program X is an Insurance Premium Program ("IPP", also referred to as the "Arrangement"). Under IPP, Program X reimburses its contract facilities for payment of Medicare Part B, Medigap, and major medical insurance premiums paid on behalf of indigent ESRD patients.[1] IPP funds are available to all contract facilities; the amount allocated to each contract facility is set forth in the facility's Facility Agreement. Under IPP, a qualifying patient may have his or her premiums paid without regard to where he or she receives treatment, but must apply for IPP benefits through a participating provider. Because the amount of money budgeted to each facility for IPP is fixed in advance, funding may not always be available for otherwise qualifying patients at specific facilities. Patients who receive IPP benefits at one facility and subsequently change providers remain eligible for IPP, but must reapply for funds through the new facility.[2]

To qualify for IPP benefits, patients must meet residency, citizenship, medical condition, and financial eligibility tests prescribed by Program X in a Contract Guidelines and Billing Manual (the "Manual"). Social workers at the contract facilities assess patients' eligibility for Program X programs, including IPP, using guidelines

---

[1] Premiums are not reimbursed for policies that exclude renal benefits, except for waiting periods for pre-existing conditions.

[2] Program X is working to implement a system that will enable it to allocate IPP funds in a manner that will permit funding to follow patients who switch providers without requiring a reapplication for benefits. Currently, facility changes are infrequent and handled on a case-by-case basis.

in the Manual. All patients are screened for financial eligibility in accordance with Program X's specific income-expense-total assets means test. Program X also requires that all prospective IPP beneficiaries who appear to be eligible for Medicaid apply for Medicaid benefits; those who qualify for Medicaid are automatically deemed financially eligible for IPP. When evaluating whether to provide IPP benefits to individual patients, contract facilities are required to consider the cost savings that will accrue to Program X. Program X reserves the right to decline to reimburse a contract facility for premium payments where there are no cost savings to Program X and no net benefit to the patient. Contract facility social workers also assist qualifying patients in completing application forms for Program X benefits.

II. LEGAL ANALYSIS

Section 231(h) of HIPAA, effective January 1, 1997, provides for the imposition of civil monetary penalties against any person who:

> offers or transfers remuneration to any individual eligible for benefits under [Federal health care programs (including Medicare or Medicaid)] that such person knows or should know is likely to influence such individual to order or receive from a particular provider, practitioner, or supplier any item or service for which payment may be made, in whole or in part, [by a Federal health care program].

Section 231(h) defines "remuneration", in relevant part, as "transfers of items or services for free or for other than fair market value."[3]

We conclude that the Arrangement does not constitute grounds for the imposition of civil monetary penalties under Section 231(h) of HIPAA. A violation of Section 231(h) requires that something of value be given to a beneficiary, either directly or on his or her behalf, that the donor knows or should know is likely to influence the beneficiary's choice of a particular provider. All funds for IPP premium payments are provided by the State and are made available to all chronic dialysis facilities in the State and to all eligible patients. In these circumstances, we do not believe that the State-financed IPP premium payments are likely to influence individual patients in their selection of particular providers. For ease of administration, the State uses the contract facilities as conduits for IPP funds and has them perform certain ministerial functions in accordance with specific guidelines established by Program X. The contract facilities

[3] The statutory definition of remuneration provides an exception, not applicable here, for certain waivers of coinsurance and deductible amounts.

do not have any substantial discretion regarding patient eligibility. To the extent a patient qualifies and premium payments are made, the State, rather than the contract facility, is providing the remuneration. Accordingly, we do not believe that the contract facilities acting within the scope of IPP are providing prohibited remuneration under Section 231(h).[4]

III. LIMITATIONS

The limitations applicable to this opinion include the following:

- This advisory opinion is issued only to Program X, which is the Requestor of this opinion. This advisory opinion has no application, and cannot be relied upon, by any other individual or entity.
- This advisory opinion may not be introduced into evidence in any matter involving an entity or individual that is not a Requestor to this opinion.
- This advisory opinion is applicable only to the statutory provision specifically noted above. No opinion is herein expressed or implied with respect to the application of any other Federal, state, or local statute, rule, regulation, ordinance, or other law that may be applicable to the Arrangement.
- This advisory opinion will not bind or obligate any agency other than the U.S. Department of Health and Human Services.
- This advisory opinion is limited in scope to the specific arrangement described in this letter and has no applicability to other arrangements, even those which appear similar in nature or scope.

This opinion is also subject to any additional limitations set forth at 42 C.F.R. Part 1008.

The OIG will not proceed against the Requestor with respect to any action taken in good faith reliance upon this advisory opinion as long as all of the material facts have been fully, completely, and accurately presented, and the arrangement in practice comports with the information provided. The OIG reserves the right to reconsider the questions and issues raised in this advisory opinion and, where the public interest requires, modify or terminate this opinion. In the event that this advisory opinion is modified or terminated, the OIG will not proceed against the Requestor with respect to any

[4] We express no opinion on the legality of any premium payments that are not reimbursable by Program X under the IPP program.

action taken in good faith reliance upon this advisory opinion, where all of the relevant facts were fully, completely, and accurately presented and where such action was promptly discontinued upon notification of the modification or termination of this advisory opinion.

Sincerely,
D. McCarty Thornton
Chief Counsel to the Inspector General

APPENDIX F11

Advisory Opinion No. 97-3

[names redacted]

Re: Advisory Opinion No. 97–3

Dear [names redacted]:

We are writing in response to your request for an advisory opinion, which we accepted pursuant to 42 C.F.R. Part 1008.41 on June 11, 1997. Your request asks whether Mrs. P's transfer of assets to her nephew, Mr. S, and subsequent application for Medicaid benefits (the "Arrangement"), subjects her to sanction under 42 U.S.C. 1320a-7b(a)(6), which prohibits certain dispositions of assets for the purpose of qualifying for Medicaid.[1] Mr. N advised Mrs. P to transfer her assets and assisted in the transfer process. You may be collectively referred to in this opinion as the "Requestors".

You have certified that all of the information you provided in your request, including all supplementary letters, is true and correct, and constitutes a complete description of the facts regarding the Arrangement. In issuing this opinion, we have relied solely on the facts and information you presented to us. We have not undertaken any independent investigation of such information. This opinion is limited to the facts presented. If material facts have not been disclosed, this opinion is without force and effect.

Based on the information provided and subject to certain conditions described below, we conclude that the Arrangement would not constitute grounds for the imposition of sanctions under 42 U.S.C. 1320a-7b(a)(6). This opinion may not be relied on by any person other than the addressee and is further qualified as set out in Part III below and in 42 C.F.R. Part 1008.

I. FACTUAL BACKGROUND

Mrs. P, an 87-year-old widow residing in a nursing home in the State of Oregon, is in need of long term nursing home care. On February 12, 1997, Mrs. P transferred $7,785 to her great-nephew,

[1] For the reasons set forth in our letter dated June 11, 1997, we have declined to opine as to other questions set forth in your request.

Mr. S, who orally agreed to hold and use the assets for her personal needs in the future. Because the average monthly private nursing home cost in Oregon is $2,595, this transfer of assets created a three month period during which Mrs. P would have been ineligible for Medicaid had she applied. *See* 42 U.S.C. 1396p(c), OAR 461–140–295(2). Between February 12, 1997, and May 13, 1997, Mrs. P spent the remainder of her assets for her continuing care and personal needs until less than $2,000 remained. Mrs. P applied for prospective Medicaid benefits on May 13, 1997, more than three months after the disposition of her assets to her great-nephew. The application is pending with the State of Oregon Department of Health and Human Services. The parties anticipate that Mrs. P will be deemed eligible for benefits. The Oregon Department of Human Resources has stated that the State of Oregon will not impose a period of ineligibility for Medicaid based on the circumstances of the reported transfer of assets, provided that Mrs. P waited a "durational penalty period" before applying for benefits.[2]

II. LEGAL ANALYSIS

42 U.S.C. § 1320a-7b(a)(6) applies to any individual who:

> knowingly and willfully disposes of assets (including any transfer in trust) in order for an individual to become eligible for medical assistance under a State plan under title XIX [42 U.S.C.S. §§ 1396 et seq.], if disposing of the assets results in the imposition of a period of ineligibility for such assistance under section 1917(c) [42 U.S.C.S. § 1396p(c)].

42 U.S.C. § 1396 *et seq.* established the Federal-state health program commonly known as Medicaid. Medicaid benefits are available to persons who meet certain criteria, including financial need. Eligible persons may not have assets that exceed certain thresholds. Pursuant to section 1396p(c), applicants who transfer assets for less

[2] Mrs. P and Mr. N previously submitted a request for an advisory opinion regarding the transfer of assets at issue here, which request was rejected pursuant to 42 C.F.R. § 1008.15(c) because the same or substantially same course of action was the subject of an ongoing court proceeding involving the U.S. Department of Justice. That proceeding, a declaratory judgment action filed by Mrs. P and Mr. N in the United States District Court of the District of Oregon (Civ. Action No. [redacted]), was subsequently dismissed for lack of subject matter jurisdiction. Copies of certain pleadings and the court's order and opinion, along with a copy of a letter from the Oregon Department of Human Resources filed with the court regarding the period of ineligibility, were included with the Requestors' present request.

than fair market value for the purpose of qualifying for nursing facility, home health, or other long term care services within three years of applying for benefits are temporarily for these long term care services.[3] The length of the period of ineligibility, which is calculated at the state's option either from the first day of the month in which assets were transferred or the first day of the month following the transfer date is determined by dividing the value of the transferred assets by the statewide monthly nursing home cost as determined by the state.

For purposes of this opinion, the key portion of 42 U.S.C. § 1320a-7b(a)(6) is the last phrase, "if disposing of the assets results in the imposition of a period of ineligibility for such assistance." The State of Oregon has represented that it will not impose a period of ineligibility if Mrs. P waits to apply for Medicaid benefits until after the expiration of the period of time during which she would otherwise have been ineligible for benefits under the statute. The Requestors have represented that, given the value of the transferred assets and the applicable monthly nursing home cost for Oregon, the three month period of ineligibility that would have applied to Mrs. P had she sought Medicaid benefits at the time of her asset transfer expired prior to May 13, 1997. Accordingly, based on the State's representation and assuming, as represented by the Requestors, that three months is the correct ineligibility period under Oregon law, the requestors will not be subject to sanction under 42 U.S.C. § 1320a-7b(a)(6), because no period of ineligibility will be imposed because of Mrs. P's disposition of assets.

III. LIMITATIONS

The limitations applicable to this opinion include the following:

- This advisory opinion is issued only to [names redacted] who are the Requestors of this opinion. This advisory opinion has no application, and cannot be relied upon, by any other individual or entity.
- This advisory opinion may not be introduced into evidence in any matter involving an entity or individual that is not a Requestor to this opinion.

---

[3] The statute contains exceptions, not applicable here, for certain assets transferred to spouses, children, or siblings, and for certain transfers where the transferee intended to dispose of assets at fair market value, where the transfer was exclusively for a purpose other than qualifying for benefits, or where the assets have been returned to the transferee. States have discretion to waive the period of ineligibility in cases of undue hardship.

- This advisory opinion is applicable only to the statutory provision specifically noted above. No opinion is herein expressed or implied with respect to the application of any other Federal, state, or local statute, rule, regulation, ordinance, or other law that may be applicable to the Proposed Arrangement.
- This advisory opinion will not bind or obligate any agency other than the U.S. Department of Health and Human Services.
- This advisory opinion is limited in scope to the specific arrangement described in this letter and has no applicability to other arrangements, even those which appear similar in nature or scope.

This opinion is also subject to any additional limitations set forth at 42 C.F.R. Part 1008.

The OIG will not proceed against the Requestors with respect to any action taken in good faith reliance upon this advisory opinion as long as all of the material facts have been fully, completely, and accurately presented, and the arrangement in practice comports with the information provided. The OIG reserves the right to reconsider the questions and issues raised in this advisory opinion and, where the public interest requires, modify or terminate this opinion. In the event that this advisory opinion is modified or terminated, the OIG will not proceed against the requestors with respect to any action taken in good faith reliance upon this advisory opinion, where all of the relevant facts were fully, completely, and accurately presented and where such action was promptly discontinued upon notification of the modification or termination of this advisory opinion.

Sincerely,
D. McCarty Thornton
Chief Counsel to the Inspector General

APPENDIX F12

[September 25, 1997]

[name redacted]

Re: [name redacted]

Advisory Opinion No. 97–4

Dear [name redacted]:

We are writing in response to your request for an advisory opinion, in which you ask whether declining to pursue collection of copayments from certain patients who have employer-sponsored Medicare complementary coverage constitutes grounds for imposition of sanctions under Section 231(h) of the Health Insurance Portability and Accountability Act ("HIPAA") [42 U.S.C. § 1320a-7a(a)(5)] or under Sections 1128B(b) (the anti-kickback statute) or 1128A(7) (relating to payment of kickbacks) of the Social Security Act [42 U.S.C. §§ 1320a-7b(b) and 1320a-7(b)(7)].

You have certified that all of the information you provided in your request, including all supplementary letters, is true and correct, and constitutes a complete description of the facts and agreements among the parties regarding the proposed arrangement. In issuing this opinion, we have relied solely on the facts and information you presented to us. We have not undertaken any independent investigation of such information. This opinion is limited to the facts presented. If material facts have not been disclosed, this opinion is without force and effect.

Based on the information provided and subject to certain conditions described below, we conclude that the proposed arrangement may constitute grounds for the imposition of civil monetary penalties under Section 231(h) of HIPAA. We further conclude that the proposed arrangement may constitute grounds for the imposition of criminal penalties under 1128B(b) and for exclusion under 1128(b)(7) (as it relates to kickbacks) of the Social Security Act. This opinion may not be relied on by any person other than the addressee and is further qualified as set out in Part III below and in 42 C.F.R. Part 1008.

I. FACTUAL BACKGROUND

Company A (the "Requestor") is a Michigan limited liability company doing business as Center B. Center B is a Medicare-certified ambulatory surgical center ("ASC") licensed by the State of Michigan Department of Community Health and accredited by the Accreditation Association for Ambulatory Health Care. Center B limits the scope of its services to the provision of endoscopy services. Center B believes that it provides endoscopy services to patients in a manner that is more convenient, cost-effective, and of higher quality than the provision of comparable services in a hospital inpatient or outpatient setting.

Medicare payment for ASC services consists of a facility fee and a professional fee. The facility fee is a prospectively determined rate; the professional fee is based on the Medicare physician fee schedule. Both fees are subject to Medicare Part B coinsurance and deductible amounts (collectively, the "Medicare Copayment").

Certain current and prospective Center B patients are retirees who have Medicare complementary coverage furnished by their former employer to cover the cost of the Medicare Copayment. The employer contracts with Company X to administer the complementary coverage. In administering the complementary coverage, Company X pays the Medicare Copayment attributable to the professional fee to the physician who performs the endoscopy services, but declines to pay the Medicare Copayment attributable to the facility fee to Center B. Company X denies payment of the facility fee copayment on the ground that Center B is not an ambulatory surgical facility participating with Company X.[1] Center B has represented that this policy adversely affects Medicare beneficiaries and the Medicare program, because beneficiaries are denied the choice of receiving health care services at Center B. Center B asserts that receiving services at its facility is more convenient and less costly than receiving comparable services in a hospital setting.

The Proposed Arrangement that is the subject of Center B's request for an advisory opinion is as follows. Center B would pursue payment of the facility fee Medicare Copayment exclusively from Company X, including any appeal rights within Company X. Center

---

[1] Center B contends that Company X's denial of the facility fee copayment is contrary to Medicare payment principles. In support of this view, it has submitted an Order from the Wayne County (Michigan) Circuit Court in the matter of *Greater Lansing Ambulatory Center Company et al. v. Blue Cross and Blue Shiled of Michigan*, No. 96–635927-CZ (March 1, 1997).

B has provided a copy of a proposed form of appeal letter that would be sent in response to each denied claim. However, if Company X were to continue to deny payment, Center B would not pursue payment from the covered beneficiaries. Center B is concerned that this Proposed Arrangement may constitute a prohibited waiver of the Medicare Copayment in violation of Section 231(h) of HIPAA and the anti-kickback statute.

II. LEGAL ANALYSIS

The Proposed Arrangement May Constitute a Violation of Section 231(h) of HIPAA.

Section 231(h) of HIPAA, effective January 1, 1997, provides for the imposition of civil monetary penalties against any person who:

> offers or transfers remuneration to any individual eligible for benefits under [Federal health care programs (including Medicare or Medicaid)] that such person knows or should know is likely to influence such individual to order or receive from a particular provider, practitioner, or supplier any item or service for which payment may be made, in whole or in part, [by a Federal health care program].

Section 231(h) defines "remuneration" as including, inter alia, the waiver of coinsurance and deductible amounts (or any part thereof). Waivers of coinsurance and deductible amounts are excepted from the definition of remuneration if:

(i) the waiver is not offered as part of any advertisement or solicitation;
(ii) the person making the waiver does not routinely waive coinsurance or deductible amounts; and
(iii) the person making the waiver (I) waives the coinsurance and deductible amounts after determining in good faith that the individual is in financial need; or (II) fails to collect coinsurance or deductible amounts after making reasonable collection efforts.

See 42 U.S.C. § 1320a-7a(i)(6), as amended by section 4331 of the Balanced Budget Act of 1997, P.L. 105–33.[2] Subsections (i), (ii), and

[2] The statute, as amended, contains three further exceptions, not applicable here, for: (i) certain permissible waivers specified in section 1128B(b)(3) of the Social Security Act or in regulations issued by the Secretary; (ii) certain differentials in coinsurance and deductible amounts as part of a benefit plan design; and (iii) certain incentives given to individuals to promote the delivery of preventive care.

at least one prong of subsection (iii) must be satisfied for the exception to apply.

Based on our review of the Proposed Arrangement as represented in the request letter, we first conclude that the Proposed Arrangement may fall within the general proscription against inducements to Federal health care program beneficiaries set forth in section 231 (h) of HIPAA. Prohibited "remuneration" for purposes of section 231 (h) specifically includes a waiver of coinsurance and deductible amounts that a provider knows or should know is likely to influence a beneficiary's choice of a particular provider. Medicare beneficiaries are obligated to pay Medicare Copayments; therefore any waiver of that obligation constitutes remuneration to the beneficiary. According to the request letter, Center B's proposal to refrain from pursuing collection of the Medicare Copayment from beneficiaries is intended, at least in part, to encourage covered beneficiaries to obtain services at Center B's facility. The Proposed Arrangement would therefore potentially be subject to sanction under section 231 (h).

We further conclude that the Proposed Arrangement does not meet the criteria for the exception under section 231(h), because it does not satisfy either prong of subsection (iii) of the exception. The Proposed Arrangement does not satisfy the first prong, because it does not provide for individualized determinations of financial hardship. The only remaining issue is whether the Proposed Arrangement satisfies the second prong by constituting "reasonable collection efforts."

Reasonable collection efforts are those efforts that a reasonable provider would undertake to collect amounts owed for items and services provided to patients. These efforts should include a *bona fide* attempt to bill and collect from the patient if the patient's insurer refuses to pay. [3] When an insurer has taken a consistent position with the provider that a category of claims are not covered, the provider's continued submission of such claims, including subsequent appeals, is not a *bona fide* collection effort. In such circumstances, the provider must make reasonable efforts to collect the Medicare Copayment from the patient.

In the absence of reasonable collection efforts or individualized determinations of financial need, the Proposed Arrangement fails to meet either prong of subsection (iii) of § 1320a-7(i)(6). Thus, the

[3] *See, e.g.*, 42 C.F.R. § 413.80; Prov. Reimb. Man., Part I, §§ 308, 310.

Proposed Arrangement may constitute unlawful remuneration for the purpose of influencing beneficiaries to select Center B as their provider in contravention of section 231(h) of HIPAA.

The Proposed Arrangement May Constitute a Violation of the Anti-Kickback Statute.

The anti-kickback statute, 42 U.S.C. § 1320a-7b(b), makes it a criminal offense knowingly and willfully to offer, pay, solicit, or receive any remuneration to induce the referral of business that may be paid for by a Federal health care program. Specifically, the statute provides that

> Whoever knowingly and willfully offers or pays [or solicits or receives] any remuneration (including any kickback, bribe, or rebate) directly or indirectly, overtly or covertly, in cash or in kind to any person to induce such person — to refer an individual to a person for the furnishing or arranging for the furnishing of any item or service for which payment may be made in whole or in part under a Federal health care program, or to purchase, lease, order, or arrange for or recommend purchasing, leasing, or ordering any good, facility, service, or item for which payment may be made in whole or in part under a Federal health care program, shall be guilty of a felony.

42 U.S.C. § 1320a-7b(b). In other words, the statute prohibits payments made purposefully to induce referrals of business paid for by a Federal health care program. The statute ascribes liability to both sides of an impermissible "kickback" transaction. The statute has been interpreted to cover any arrangement where one purpose of the remuneration was to obtain money for the referral of services or to induce further referrals. United States v. Kats, 871 F.2d 105 (9th Cir. 1989); United States v. Greber, 760 F.2d 68 (3d Cir.), cert. denied, 474 U.S. 988 (1985). "Remuneration" for purposes of the anti-kickback statute includes the transfer of any thing of value, in cash or in-kind, directly or indirectly, covertly or overtly.

We have said previously that providers who routinely waive Medicare Copayments may be held liable under the anti-kickback statute. *See* Special Fraud Alert, 59 Fed. Reg. 242 (1994). [4] When providers forgive financial obligations for reasons other than genuine financial hardship of the particular patient, they unlawfully may be inducing

---

[4] Although the Special Fraud Alert addressed charge-based providers, we expressly stated that the Special Fraud Alert should not be interpreted to legitimize routine waiver of Medicare copayments with respect to providers paid under prospective payment or cost-based systems.

the patient to purchase items or services in violation of the anti-kickback statute's proscription against offering or paying something of value as an inducement to generate business payable by a Federal health care program. Thus, except in those special cases of financial hardship, providers must make a good faith effort to collect Medicare Copayments. One indicator of a suspect waiver is the failure to collect Medicare Copayments for a specific group of Medicare patients for reasons unrelated to indigency.

Here, the Proposed Arrangement is suspect because it would effectively waive the Medicare Copayment for the specific group of Medicare patients covered by the Company X complementary coverage, if Company X continues to deny payment. Moreover, an inference can be drawn that the Proposed Arrangement's waiver of the Medicare Copayment for reasons unrelated to individualized financial hardship may unlawfully induce patients to purchase services from Center B that are reimbursable by Medicare. For these reasons, the Proposed Arrangement may be subject to sanction under the anti-kickback statute, 42 U.S.C. § 1320a-7b(b).

III. LIMITATIONS

The limitations applicable to this opinion include the following:

- This advisory opinion is issued only to Company A, which is theRequestor of this opinion. This advisory opinion has no application, and cannot be relied upon, by any other individual or entity.
- This advisory opinion may not be introduced into evidence in any matter involving an entity or individual that is not a Requestor to this opinion.
- This advisory opinion is applicable only to the statutory provisions specifically noted above. No opinion is herein expressed or implied with respect to the application of any other Federal, state, or local statute, rule, regulation, ordinance, or other law that may be applicable to the Arrangement.
- This advisory opinion will not bind or obligate any agency other than the U.S. Department of Health and Human Services.
- This advisory opinion is limited in scope to the specific arrangement described in this letter and has no applicability to other arrangements, even those which appear similar in nature or scope.

This opinion is also subject to any additional limitations set forth at 42 C.F.R. Part 1008.

The OIG will not proceed against the Requestor with respect to any action taken in good faith reliance upon this advisory opinion as long as all of the material facts have been fully, completely, and accurately presented, and the arrangement in practice comports with the information provided. The OIG reserves the right to reconsider the questions and issues raised in this advisory opinion and, where the public interest requires, modify or terminate this opinion. In the event that this advisory opinion is modified or terminated, the OIG will not proceed against the Requestor with respect to any action taken in good faith reliance upon this advisory opinion, where all of the relevant facts were fully, completely, and accurately presented and where such action was promptly discontinued upon notification of the modification or termination of this advisory opinion.

Sincerely,
D. McCarty Thornton
Chief Counsel to the Inspector General

APPENDIX F13

October 6, 1997

[Names and addresses of Requestors have been redacted]

Re: Advisory Opinion No. 97–5

Dear Sirs:

We are writing in response to your request for an advisory opinion on behalf of Radiology Group X and Hospital System A. The request asks whether an outpatient radiology imaging center joint venture owned by a medical group specializing in radiology and a hospital care provider (i) generates prohibited remuneration within the meaning of the anti-kickback statute, Section 1128B of the Social Security Act ("Act"); (ii) constitutes grounds for the imposition of an exclusion under Section 1128(b)(7) of the Act (as it applies to kickbacks); (iii) constitutes grounds for criminal sanctions under Section 1128B(b) of the Act; and/or (iv) satisfies the criteria set out in Section 1128B(b)(3) of the Act or associated regulations, 42 C.F.R. § 1001.952.

Radiology Group X and Hospital System A have certified that all of the information provided in the request, including all supplementary letters, is true and correct, and constitutes a complete description of the relevant facts and agreements among the parties regarding the joint venture ("Proposed Arrangement". Radiology Group X and Hospital System A have also certified that upon our approval, they will undertake to effectuate the Proposed Arrangement.

In issuing this opinion, we have relied solely on the facts and information presented to us. We have not undertaken an independent investigation of such information. This opinion is limited to the facts presented. If material facts have not been disclosed, this opinion is without force and effect.

Based on the information provided and subject to certain conditions described below, we have determined that the Proposed Arrangement does not meet any of the statutory or regulatory safe harbors set out in Section 1128B(b)(3) of the Act or 42 C.F.R. § 1001.952. However, we also conclude that the Proposed Arrangement would not generate prohibited remuneration within the meaning of the anti-kickback statute, Section Page 2 1128B of the Act, and therefore, does not constitute grounds for the imposition of either an exclusion under Section 1128(b)(7) of the Act (as it applies to kickbacks) or criminal sanctions under Section 1128B(b) of the Act.

This opinion may not be relied on by any person or entity other than the addressees and is further qualified as set out in Part III below and in 42 C.F.R. Part 1008.

I. FACTUAL BACKGROUND

Radiology Group X and Hospital System A have made the following representations with respect to the Proposed Arrangement. Radiology Group X and Hospital System A are collectively the "Requestors".

A. Parties to the Proposed Arrangement.

Hospital System A. Hospital System A operates three hospitals in State C: Hospital 1, Hospital 2, and Hospital 3. Hospital 1, located in State C, is licensed for 351 beds and is the largest hospital in the several counties surrounding City D. Hospital 1 has a full range of radiological equipment at its facility, including a CT scanner, ultrasound equipment, fluoroscopic radiographic equipment, nuclear radiographic equipment, and magnetic resonance imaging ("MRI" equipment. Hospital 1 will continue to operate its radiology department after the Proposed Arrangement is implemented.

Hospital System A employs three physicians directly or through its subsidiary organizations. These physicians will not make referrals to the Proposed Arrangement's joint venture imaging center, nor will any such referrals be accepted if made.

Radiology Group X. Radiology Group X is a medical group specializing in radiology. It is a State C professional corporation owned and controlled by five radiologists. Dr. Y, serves as the President of Radiology Group X.

The shareholders of Radiology Group X are also the members of Radiology Group X's affiliate, Company Z. Ownership and control interests in Radiology Group X and Company Z are identical. Company Z is a newly-formed State C limited liability company and one of the members of the Proposed Arrangement's joint venture company, Imaging Center [defined below].

Current Relationship Between Radiology Group X and Hospital 1. Radiology Group X and Hospital 1 have represented that they have an informal, unwritten arrangement whereby Radiology Group X provides professional radiology services to the hospital, while hospital employees provide the technical services. The hospital owns all of the radiological equipment and is responsible for employing qualified technicians. As part of Page 3 this arrangement, Radiology Group X's president, Dr. Y, serves as Hospital 1's Director of the Department of Radiology. His duties are set forth in the hospital's Medical and Dental Staff By-Laws. In addition, Hospital 1 provides Radiology Group X with space in its facility to perform radiologic interpretations. [1]

While there is no written agreement, the hospital has certified that the fair market value of the space used by Radiology Group X is substantially equal to the fair market value for compensation of Dr. Y's duties as the Director of the Department of Radiology. Further, the arrangements whereby Radiology Group X and Dr. Y provide services to Hospital 1 and Hospital 1 provides Radiology Group X with space in its facility are separate from, and not dependent on, the terms and conditions of the Proposed Arrangement.

B. Proposed Arrangement.

Radiology Group X, through its affiliate Company Z, and Hospital System A have proposed to enter into a joint venture to establish an outpatient radiology imaging center ("Imaging Center". The Imaging Center will be located in the Village of E, at the western edge of City D. The Imaging Center will offer a full range of state-of-the-art imaging techniques, including X-ray equipment, fluoroscope equipment, a superconducting open MRI system, a computerized tomography scanner, and an ultrasound system.

The Imaging Center will be owned and operated by a State C limited liability company, Company B. The members of Company B will be Company Z and Hospital System A. Company Z and Hospital System A will make capital contributions of $204,000 and $196,000, respectively. In return, each member will receive voting and distribution rights proportional to its investment. Additional capital contributions will be apportioned to Company Z and Hospital System A based upon their respective ownership interests. [2]

---

[1] Radiology Group X does not have any non-hospital based office space.

[2] If either member of Company B is unable or unwilling to make any part of an additional capital contribution, the other member has a right to make up the difference, treat such amount as either an additional capital contribution or as a loan, and adjust the proportional percentages of ownership accordingly. For purposes of this opinion, we have assumed that any loan would be at fair market value.

The Imaging Center will be staffed by employees hired by Company B. Radiology Group X radiologists will be the exclusive providers of professional services to the Imaging Center. The president of Radiology Group X, or his designee, will be in charge of supervising and administering all aspects of the clinical services rendered at the Imaging Center, including quality assurance. The Radiology Group X radiologists will not be employees of the Imaging Center, but will enter into a service provider agreement with Company B. Under the service agreement, Radiology Group X will not receive any compensation from the Imaging Center. Radiology Group X will bill patients and third-party payers, including Medicare and Medicaid, for the professional component of radiological services directly. The Imaging Center will bill separately its technical component to patients and third-party payers.

II. LEGAL ANALYSIS

The anti-kickback statute makes it a criminal offense knowingly and willfully to offer, pay, solicit or receive any remuneration to induce referrals of items or services reimbursed by Federal health care programs. 42 U.S.C. § 1320a-7b(b). Where remuneration is paid purposefully in exchange for referrals of items or services paid for by a Federal health care program, the kickback statute is violated. By its terms, the statute ascribes criminal liability to parties on both sides of an impermissible "kickback" transaction.

The statute has been interpreted to cover any arrangement where *one* purpose of the remuneration is to obtain money for the referral of services or to induce further referrals. United States v. Kats, 871 F.2d 105 (9th Cir. 1989); United States v. Greber, 760 F.2d 68 (3d Cir.), cert. denied, 476 U.S. 988 (1985). Violations of the statute constitute a felony punishable by a maximum fine of $25,000, imprisonment up to five years or both. Conviction will also lead to automatic exclusion from Federal health care programs including Medicare and Medicaid.

The Office of Inspector General may also initiate an administrative proceeding to exclude an individual from Federal health care programs for fraud, kickbacks and other prohibited activities. Section 1128(b)(7) of the Act. Because both the criminal and administrative sanctions related to the Proposed Arrangement are based on the anti-kickback statute, the analysis is the same under either provision.

Health care joint ventures in which investors are also sources of referrals or suppliers of items or services to the joint venture raise many questions under the anti-kickback statute. In 1989, the Office of Inspector General issued a "Special Fraud Alert" specifically discussing joint venture arrangements that may violate the anti-kickback statute.[3] In general, joint ventures between radiologists and health care providers in a position to order imaging services may be suspect, because distributions from the joint ventures may be disguised remuneration paid in return for referrals. Like any kickback scheme, these arrangements can lead to overutilization of such services, increased costs for Federal health care programs, corruption of professional judgment, and unfair competition.

A. The Proposed Joint Venture Does Not Meet the Safe Harbor For Investment Interests in Small Entities.

In 1991, the Department of Health and Human Services ("Department" published safe harbor regulations which define practices that are not subject to the anti-kickback statute because such arrangements would be unlikely to result in fraud or abuse. Failure to comply with a safe harbor provision does not make an arrangement per se illegal. Rather, the safe harbors set forth specific conditions that, if fully met, would assure the entities involved of not being prosecuted or sanctioned for the arrangement qualifying for the safe harbor. The only safe harbor regulation potentially available to the Proposed Arrangement addresses investment interests in small entities. See 42 C.F.R. § 1001.952(a)(2).[4]

The safe harbor for investments in small entities has eight elements, each of which must be satisfied in order for the arrangement to qualify for the exception. The eight elements address three areas of concern in abusive joint ventures: (i) how investors are selected and retained; (ii) the nature of the business structure; and (iii) the financing and profit distributions. The eight elements are:

- no more than forty percent of the investment interests may be held by investors who are in a position to make or influence

[3] *See* Special Fraud Alert, "Joint Venture Arrangements" (OIG-89-4), *reprinted in* 59 Fed. Reg. 65373 (December 19, 1994).

[4] The Requestors had suggested that the "shared risk" statutory exception to the anti-kickback statute added by Section 216 of the Health Insurance Portability and Accountability Act, Pub. Law No. 104–191 (Aug. 21, 1996), potentially applied. That provision, however, applies only to contractual arrangements where a person supplying items or services is at risk for the cost or utilization of such items or services and is obligated to provide them, as in some managed care contracts.

referrals, furnish items or services, or generate business ("Interested Investors";

- interests offered to passive investors who are Interested Investors cannot be made on terms different from those offered to other investors;
- the terms on which an investment is offered to Interested Investors cannot take into account any previous or expected volume of referrals, services furnished, or amount of business generated from such investors;
- there is no requirement that a passive investor make referrals to, or otherwise generate business for, the entity as a condition of remaining an investor;
- the entity cannot market or furnish the items or services differently to passive investors and non-investors;
- no more than forty percent of the gross revenue of the entity may come from Interested Investors;
- the entity cannot loan or guarantee funds to an Interested Investor if the loan or guarantee is used to obtain the investment interest; and
- an investor's return on investment must be directly proportional to the amount of capital investment of that investor.

Strict compliance with all elements is required. *See* 56 Fed. Reg. 35952, 35954 (July 29, 1991).

The Proposed Arrangement fails to meet at least one of the eight elements. More than 40% of the investment interest is owned by persons who furnish items or services to the new venture; Radiology Group X owns 51% of the entity and will provide the professional services to the venture. Accordingly, the Proposed Arrangement does not meet the only relevant safe harbor.

B. The Proposed Arrangement Will Not Result in Prohibited Remuneration.

Even though the Proposed Arrangement does not fall within a safe harbor, it does not necessarily violate the anti-kickback statute. With respect to joint ventures, the major concern is that the profit distributions to investors in the joint venture, who are also referral sources to the joint venture, may potentially represent remuneration for those referrals. A related concern is that, where the investing parties have a referral relationship wholly apart from the joint venture, distributions from the joint venture could potentially represent remuneration to one party for referrals to the other party based on those independent relationships. Accordingly, all aspects of all relationships between the parties must be examined.

1. There Is No Prohibited Remuneration For Referrals To The Imaging Center.

Our initial inquiry is whether the distributions from the joint venture may be "disguised" remuneration for referrals by the investors to the joint venture. Based upon the information and representations provided, we find that neither Radiology Group X nor Hospital System A will be able to generate referrals to the joint venture.

A threshold issue is the proper characterization of Hospital System A's role in relationship to the joint venture. In many instances, hospitals are capable of influencing, and do influence, referrals to other health care providers, such as through discharge planning with respect to post-discharge care. In addition, hospitals are in a position to influence the flow of radiology work performed at the hospital, because the hospital controls to whom radiologic interpretations are referred. *See Financial Arrangements Between Hospitals and Hospital-Based Physicians*, OEI-09–89–00330, 1991. In this instance, however, and subject to the conditions set out below, we do not believe that the Hospital System A hospitals will be able to generate referrals to the Imaging Center.

First, Hospital System A has represented that its employed physicians will make no referrals to the Imaging Center, and the Imaging Center will not accept any referrals from those physicians. *Second*, Hospital System A has agreed that it will take no actions, either overt or covert, financial or otherwise, to induce its medical staff (i.e., any physician with admitting or staff privileges) to use the Imaging Center. *Third*, Hospital System A has agreed that it will inform the medical staff of the preceding agreement. *Fourth*, physician referrals to the Imaging Center will not be tracked by Hospital System A, its hospitals, Company Z, or Radiology Group X. *Fifth*, Hospital System A hospitals will continue to operate and use their own radiology units. In these circumstances, referrals from physicians with admitting or staff privileges at the Hospital System A hospitals would not be attributable to Hospital System A.

Moreover, the Radiology Group X radiologists are also unlikely to be able to generate an appreciable number of referrals to the Imaging Center. In general, radiologists do not order the radiological tests they perform; such tests are ordered by a patient's attending physician. Although there may be situations in which a radiologist can recommend additional testing to the attending physician during the course of a consultation and, as a practical matter, indirectly generate some additional business, those tests must be approved by the patient's attending physician.[5] In these limited circumstances — the recommendation of additional testing by a radiologist to an attending physician with whom the radiologist has no financial arrangements and pursuant to a *bona fide* medical consultation — we conclude that a Radiology Group X radiologist's recommendation is not prohibited under the anti-kickback statute.[6]

In sum, since neither Radiology Group X nor Hospital System A will be in a position to generate or influence an appreciable number of referrals to the Imaging Center, the distributions of any profits would not constitute illegal remuneration in exchange for referrals.

2. There Is No Prohibited Remuneration For Referrals Outside Of The Joint Venture.

Radiology Group X derives a substantial amount of its revenues from its position as the exclusive provider of professional radiology services for Hospital 1.[7] This raises the possibility that the joint venture may be a vehicle by which Radiology Group X may indirectly reward Hospital System A for revenues Radiology Group X receives as a result of its arrangement with Hospital 1.[8]

In determining whether the joint venture may be a vehicle for illegally remunerating one investor for referrals to another investor, we examine initially whether the party making the referrals receives

---

[5] See 61 Fed. Reg. 59490, 59497 (November 22, 1996) (with respect to when Medicare will cover diagnostic tests, the Health Care Financing Administration has stated, "we believe that the physician interpreting the diagnostic tests has an obligation to discuss any changes in or additions to the original order with the patient's physician.").

[6] Radiology Group X radiologists receive no remuneration from patients= attending physicians, and none of the attending physicians which refer to Radiology Group X have any financial relationships with Radiology Group X.

[7] Radiology Group X radiologists are not in a position to make referrals to the Hospital System A hospitals for the same reasons that they cannot make appreciable referrals to the Imaging Center. Accordingly, the potential profit distributions from the Imaging Center to the Radiology Group X radiologists would not represent disguised remuneration for any possible referrals to Hospital System A hospitals.

[8] Specific problems with financial arrangements between hospital-based physicians, such as radiologists, and hospitals were discussed in a 1991 Management Advisory Report entitled *Financial Arrangements Between Hospitals and Hospital-Based Physicians*, OEI-09–89–00330 (1991).

a disproportionate return on its investment compared to the return on the investment of the party receiving the referrals. Any excess or disproportionate return on the investment may be remuneration for referrals. Based on the facts and circumstances as represented by Radiology Group X and Hospital System A, both parties have made substantial financial investments in the venture, and control of the venture and Page 10 distribution of profits will be in direct proportion to such investments. Thus, both parties= return on investment is commensurate with their undertakings and would not appear to include any "unearned" remuneration to Hospital 1 attributable to its arrangements with Radiology Group X. Accordingly, any profit distributions from the Proposed Arrangement would not appear to represent compensation to Hospital System A or Hospital 1 for their referrals to Radiology Group X.

Moreover, based on the representations by Radiology Group X and Hospital System A that the value of the premises and equipment provided to Radiology Group X are substantially equal to the value of Dr. Y's services to Hospital 1, we conclude that any profit distribution from the Imaging Center will not represent illegal remuneration for the use of space and equipment at Hospital 1.[9]

However, even in situations where each party's return is proportionate with its investment, the mere opportunity to invest (and consequently receive profit distributions) may in certain circumstances constitute illegal remuneration if offered in exchange for past or future referrals. Such situations may include arrangements where one or several investors in a joint venture control a sufficiently large stream of referrals to make the venture's financial success highly likely, or where one investor has an established track record with similar ventures or the financial investment required is so small that the investors have little or no real risk. By contrast, there are no such indicia that the Proposed Arrangement will generate any profits for its investors, since neither party is in a position to influence appreciable referrals to the joint venture nor has successfully operated a freestanding imaging center before. In light of the substantial financial investment being made by Hospital System A, we find no evidence that the mere opportunity to participate as an investor in the Imaging Center constitutes illegal remuneration to Hospital System A.

III. CONCLUSION

---

[9] We are not, however, making any independent finding as to the legality of the current arrangement between Radiology Group X and Hospital 1.

For the above reasons, we have determined that the Proposed Arrangement does not contain any prohibited remuneration within the meaning of the anti-kickback statute, 1128B of the Social Security Act ("Act", and consequently does not constitute grounds for the imposition of either an exclusion under section 1128(b)(7) of the Act (as it applies to kickbacks) or criminal sanction under 1128B(b) of the Act.

IV. LIMITATIONS

The limitations applicable to this opinion include the following:

- This advisory opinion is issued only to the Radiology Group X and Hospital System A, which are the Requestors of this opinion. This advisory opinion has no application, and cannot be relied upon, by any other individual or entity.
- This advisory opinion may not be introduced into evidence in any matter involving an entity or individual that is not a Requestor to this opinion.
- This advisory opinion is applicable only to the statutory provisions specifically noted above. No opinion is herein expressed or implied with respect to the application of any other Federal, state, or local statute, rule, regulation, ordinance, or other law that may be applicable to the Proposed Arrangement, including any laws relating to insurance or insurance contracts.
- This advisory opinion will not bind or obligate any agency other than the U.S. Department of Health and Human Services.
- This advisory opinion is prospective only. It has no application to conduct which precedes the date of this opinion.
- This advisory opinion does not make any determination as to whether any amounts paid by one party to another are representative of fair market value.
- This advisory opinion is limited in scope to the specific arrangement described in this letter and has no applicability to other arrangements, even those which appear similar in nature or scope.

This opinion is also subject to any additional limitations set forth at 42 C.F.R. Part 1008.

The OIG will not proceed against the Requestors with respect to any action taken in good faith reliance upon this advisory opinion as long as all of the material facts have been fully, completely, and accurately presented, and the arrangement in practice comports with the information provided. The OIG reserves the right to reconsider the questions and issues raised in this advisory opinion and, where the public interest requires, modify or terminate this opinion. In the event that this advisory opinion is modified or terminated, the OIG will not proceed against the Requestors with respect to any action taken in good faith reliance upon this advisory opinion, where all of the relevant facts were fully, completely, and accurately presented and where such action was promptly discontinued upon notification of the modification or termination of this advisory opinion.

Sincerely,

/S/

D. McCarty Thornton

Chief Counsel to the Inspector General

APPENDIX F14

Advisory Opinion No. 97–6

[October 8, 1997]

[name and address redacted]

Re: [name redacted]

Advisory Opinion No. 97–6

Ladies and Gentlemen:

We are writing in response to your request for an advisory opinion, in which you asked whether a proposed arrangement for restocking ambulance supplies and medications (the "Proposed Arrangement" would constitute illegal remuneration as defined in the anti-kickback statute, 42 U.S.C.A. § 1320a-7b(b).

You have certified that all of the information you provided in your request, including all supplementary letters, is true and correct, and constitutes a complete description of the facts and agreements among the parties regarding the Proposed Arrangement.

In issuing this opinion, we have relied solely on the facts and information you presented to us. We have not undertaken any independent investigation of such information. This opinion is limited to the facts presented. If material facts have not been disclosed, this opinion is without force and effect.

Based on the information provided and subject to certain conditions described below, we conclude that the Proposed Arrangement would likely constitute prohibited remuneration under 42 U.S.C.A. § 1320a-7b(b).

I. FACTUAL BACKGROUND

Company X owns and operates two acute care hospitals (the "Hospitals" located in the City Y area. Ambulance services operated by local municipalities frequently transport patients to the Hospitals. Under the Proposed Arrangement, the Hospitals would, without charge, restock the local ambulance squads with any supplies or medications used while transporting patients to the Hospitals. Neither Company X nor the Hospitals would bill any Federal health care program,[1] and the ambulance services would receive no other reimbursement for the items supplied.

Ambulance services in State Z are regulated pursuant to a State Z administrative regulation, [citation redacted], which provides, in pertinent part, that an ambulance service must transfer a patient to a hospital emergency room selected by the patient or the patient's physician, unless the ambulance attendant determines that transport to another facility is necessary to save the patient's life or limb or the ambulance service is operating under a governmentally-approved local or regional diversion plan or medical triage protocol.

II. LEGAL ANALYSIS

The anti-kickback statute, 42 U.S.C.A. § 1320a-7b(b), makes it a criminal offense knowingly and willfully to offer, pay, solicit, or receive any remuneration to induce the referral of business covered by a Federal health care program. Specifically, the statute provides that:

> Whoever knowingly and willfully offers or pays [or solicits or receives] any remuneration (including any kickback, bribe, or rebate) directly or indirectly, overtly or covertly, in cash or in kind to any person to induce such person — to refer an individual to a person for the furnishing or arranging for the furnishing of any item or service for which payment may be made in whole or in part under a Federal health care program, or to purchase, lease, order, or arrange for or recommend purchasing, leasing, or ordering any good, facility, service, or item for which payment may be made in whole or in part under a Federal health care program, shall be guilty of a felony.

42 U.S.C.A. § 1320a-7b(b). In other words, the statute prohibits payments made purposefully to induce referrals of business paid for by a Federal health care program. The statute ascribes liability to both sides of an impermissible "kickback" transaction. The statute has

---

[1] Federal health care programs are any plans or programs that provide health benefits, whether directly, through insurance, or otherwise, that are funded directly, in whole or in part, by the United States government (other than the health insurance program under chapter 89 of title 5, United States Code), or any State health care program as defined at 42 U.S.C.A. § 1320a-7 (h). *See* 42 U.S.C.A. § 1320a-7b(f).

been interpreted to cover *any* arrangement where *one* purpose of the remuneration was to obtain money for the referral of services or to induce further referrals. *United States v. Kats,* 871 F.2d 105 (9th Cir. 1989); *United States v. Greber,* 760 F.2d 68 (3d Cir.), *cert. denied,* 474 U.S. 988 (1985). "Remuneration" for purposes of the anti-kickback statute includes the transfer of anything of value, in cash or in-kind, directly or indirectly, covertly or overtly.

The Hospitals'proposed provision of free supplies and medications to the municipal ambulance services fits squarely within the meaning of remuneration for purposes of the anti-kickback statute. An inference may be drawn that at least one purpose of this remuneration may be to induce the ambulance services to bring patients to the Hospitals. To the extent those patients include beneficiaries of Federal health care programs who require covered hospital services, the anti-kickback statute may be implicated.

Company X asserts that the Proposed Arrangement would not be abusive because it would not lead to increased costs for the Federal health care programs. This argument misses the mark. As we have said elsewhere, increased cost to the programs is not the only criteria used in determining whether a particular business arrangement is abusive. *See, e.g.,* 56 Fed. Reg. 35952, 35954 (July 29, 1991). Others include preventing overutilization of health care items and services, ensuring quality of care for Federal program beneficiaries, preserving patient freedom of choice, and safeguarding fair competition in the health care marketplace.

The Proposed Arrangement poses a risk of improper steering of patients and unfair competition. With regard to the former, State Z administrative regulation [citation redacted] requires ambulance services to transport patients to the facility of the patient's choice, except in certain exigent circumstances. However, compliance with State Z administrative regulation [citation redacted] is not sufficient to deter the abuses addressed by the anti-kickback statute. Patients in need of ambulance services are often in a vulnerable state, and their choice of emergency room may be influenced by ambulance service personnel. In these circumstances, where the payments relate directly to the delivery of patients, remuneration paid by a hospital to an ambulance service, including the provision of free goods, would be highly suspect.

Accordingly, for the above-stated reasons, we conclude that the Proposed Arrangement would likely constitute prohibited remuneration under 42 U.S.C.A. § 1320a-7b(b).

III. LIMITATIONS

The limitations applicable to this opinion include the following:

- This advisory opinion is applicable only to the statutory provision specifically noted above. No opinion is herein expressed or implied with respect to the application of any other Federal, state, or local statute, rule, regulation, ordinance, or other law that may be applicable to the Arrangement. In particular, no opinion is herein expressed or implied with respect to [State Z administrative regulation, citation redacted].
- This advisory opinion will not bind or obligate any agency other than the U.S. Department of Health and Human Services.

This opinion is also subject to any additional limitations set forth at 42 C.F.R. Part 1008.

The OIG reserves the right to reconsider the questions and issues raised in this advisory opinion and, where the public interest requires, modify or terminate this opinion.

Sincerely,

/S/

D. McCarty Thornton
Chief Counsel to the Inspector General

APPENDIX F15

HCFA Final Rule: Medicare Program; Physicians' Referrals; Issuance of Advisory Opinions

Federal Register: January 9, 1998 (Volume 63, Number 6)
Final Rule
Page 1645-1658

DEPARTMENT OF HEALTH AND HUMAN SERVICES

Health Care Financing Administration

42 CFR Part 411

RIN 0938-AI38

Medicare Program; Physicians' Referrals; Issuance of Advisory Opinions

AGENCY: Health Care Financing Administration (HCFA), HHS.
ACTION: Final rule with comment period.

SUMMARY: This final rule with comment period incorporates into HCFA's regulations the provisions of section 1877(g)(6) of the Social Security Act (the Act), as added by section 4314 of the Balanced Budget Act of 1997. Section 1877(g)(6) requires that the Secretary issue written advisory opinions to outside parties concerning whether the referral of a Medicare patient by a physician for certain designated health services (other than clinical laboratory services) is prohibited under the physician referral provisions in section 1877 of the Act. Section 1877 not only prohibits certain referrals under the Medicare program, but also affects Federal financial participation payments to States under the Medicaid program for medical assistance consisting of designated health services furnished as the result of certain physician referrals. This final rule sets forth the specific procedures HCFA will use to issue advisory opinions.

EFFECTIVE DATES: The regulations are effective January 9, 1998.

Comment Date: Comments will be considered if we receive them at the appropriate address as provided below, no later than 5 p.m on March 10, 1998.

ADDRESSES: Mail written comments (1 original and 3 copies) to the following address: Health Care Financing Administration, Department of Health and Human Services, Attention: HCFA-1902-IFC, P.O. Box 26688, Baltimore, MD 21207.

If you prefer, you may deliver your written comments (1 original and 3 copies) to one of the following addresses: Room 309-G, Hubert H. Humphrey Building, 200 Independence Avenue, S.W., Washington, DC 20201, or Room C5–09–26, 7500 Security Boulevard, Baltimore, MD 21244–1850.

Comments may also be submitted electronically to the following e-mail address: hcfa1902ifc.hcfa.gov. E-mail comments must include the full name and address of the sender and must be submitted to the referenced address in order to be considered. All comments must be incorporated in the e-mail message because we may not be able to access attachments. Because of staffing and resource limitations, we cannot accept comments by facsimile (FAX) transmission. In commenting, please refer to file code HCFA-1902-IFC. Comments received timely will be available for public inspection as they are received, generally beginning approximately 3 weeks after publication of a document, in Room 309-G of the Department's offices at 200 Independence Avenue, S.W., Washington, DC, on Monday through Friday of each week from 8:30 a.m. to 5 p.m. (phone: (202) 690–7890).

Copies: To order copies of the Federal Register containing this document, send your request to: New Orders, Superintendent of Documents, P.O. Box 371954, Pittsburgh, PA 15250–7954. Specify the date of the issue requested and enclose a check or money order payable to the Superintendent of Documents, or enclose your Visa or Master Card number and expiration date. Credit card orders can also be placed by calling the order desk at (202) 783–3238 or by faxing to (202) 275-6802. The cost for each copy is $8. As an alternative, you can view and photocopy the Federal Register document at most libraries designated as Federal Depository Libraries and at many other public and academic libraries throughout the country that receive the Federal Register.

This Federal Register document is also available from the Federal Register online database through GPO Access, a service of the U.S.

Government Printing Office. Free public access is available on a Wide Area Information Server (WAIS) through the Internet and via asynchronous dial-in. Internet users can access the database by using the World Wide Web; the Superintendent of Documents home page address is http://www.access.gpo.gov/su__docs/, by using local WAIS client software, or by telnet to swais.access.gpo.gov, then log in as guest (no password required). Dial-in users should use communications software and modem to call (202) 512–1661; type swais, then log in as guest (no password required).

FOR FURTHER INFORMATION CONTACT: Joanne Sinsheimer (410) 786–4620.

SUPPLEMENTARY INFORMATION:

I. Background

A. Legislative History of Section 1877

Section 6204 of the Omnibus Budget Reconciliation Act of 1989 (OBRA '89), Public Law 101–239, enacted on December 19, 1989, added section 1877 to the Social Security Act (the Act). (Unless we indicate otherwise, all references in this document to sections of the law are references to the Act.) In general, section 1877 as it read under OBRA '89 provided that, if a physician (or an immediate family member of a physician) had a financial relationship with a clinical laboratory, that physician could not make a referral to the laboratory for the furnishing of clinical laboratory services for which Medicare might otherwise pay. It also provided that the laboratory could not present or cause to be presented a Medicare claim or bill to any individual, third party payer, or other entity for clinical laboratory services furnished under the prohibited referral. Additionally, it required a refund of any amount collected from an individual as the result of billing for an item or service furnished under a prohibited referral. These provisions were effective for referrals made on or after January 1, 1992.

The statute defined "financial relationship" as an ownership or investment interest in the entity providing clinical laboratory services or a compensation arrangement between the physician (or immediate family member) and the entity. The statute provided a number of exceptions to the prohibition. Some of these exceptions applied to both ownership/investment interests and compensation arrangements, while other exceptions applied to only one or the other of these. Additionally, the statute imposed reporting requirements relating to a physician's (or family member's) financial relationships and provided for sanctions.

Section 4207(e) of the Omnibus Budget Reconciliation Act of 1990 (OBRA '90), Public Law 101–508, enacted on November 5, 1990, amended certain provisions of section 1877 to clarify the definitions in section 1877(h), alter the reporting requirements, and to provide an additional exception to the prohibition.

Section 1877 was extensively revised by section 13562 of the Omnibus Budget Reconciliation Act of 1993 (OBRA '93, Public Law 103–66, enacted on August 10, 1993). It modified the prior law to apply to referrals for ten "designated health services" in addition to clinical laboratory services, modified some exceptions, and added new ones. Some of the amendments were retroactively effective to January 1, 1992, while others (such as the expansion to the additional designated health services) did not become effective until January 1, 1995. Section 152 of the Social Security Act Amendments of 1994 (SSA '94), Public Law 103-432, enacted on October 31, 1994, amended the list of designated services, effective January 1, 1995. It also changed the reporting requirements in section 1877(f) and amended some of the effective dates of the OBRA '93 provisions. The amended list of designated health services includes:

- Clinical laboratory services.
- Physical therapy services.
- Occupational therapy services.
- Radiology services, including magnetic resonance imaging, computerized axial tomography scans, and ultrasound services.
- Radiation therapy services and supplies.
- Durable medical equipment and supplies.
- Parenteral and enteral nutrients, equipment, and supplies.
- Prosthetics, orthotics, and prosthetic devices and supplies.
- Home health services.
- Outpatient prescription drugs.
- Inpatient and outpatient hospital services.

Section 13624 of OBRA '93 extended aspects of the referral prohibition to the Medicaid program, adding a new paragraph (s) to section 1903 of the Social Security Act. This provision denies Federal financial participation (FFP) payment under the Medicaid program to a State for certain expenditures for designated health services. A State cannot receive FFP for designated health services furnished to an individual on the basis of a physician referral that would result in a denial of payment under the Medicare program if Medicare covered the services to the same extent and under the same terms and conditions as under the State Medicaid plan. Section 13624 also specified that the reporting requirements in section 1877(f) and the civil money penalty provision in section 1877(g)(5) (which relates to reporting) apply to a provider of a designated health service for which payment may be made under Medicaid in the same manner as they apply to a provider of a designated health service for which payment may be made under Medicare. Section 1903(s) applies to a physician's referrals made on or after December 31, 1994.

B. Regulations Relating to Section 1877

On March 11, 1992, we published a proposed rule (57 FR 8588) setting forth the self-referral prohibition and exceptions to the prohibition in section 1877, as enacted by OBRA '89 and amended by OBRA '90, relating to a physician's referrals for clinical laboratory services.

On August 14, 1995, we published, at 60 FR 41914, a final rule with comment period that incorporated into the Medicare regulations the provisions of section 1877 that relate to the prohibition on physician referrals for clinical laboratory services. The August 1995 final rule contains revisions to the March 11, 1992, proposal based on comments submitted by the public. Further, it incorporates the amendments and exceptions created by OBRA '93 and the amendments in SSA '94 that relate to referrals for clinical laboratory services. It addresses only those changes that had a retroactive effective date of January 1, 1992; it does not incorporate those modifications to section 1877 that became effective for referrals made on or after January 1, 1995. (Even though the August 1995 final rule incorporates OBRA '93 and SSA '94 provisions, it generally only reiterates them without interpreting them. We interpreted the new provisions only in a few instances in which it was necessary to do so in order to implement the statute at all.)

We are publishing elsewhere in this same issue of the Federal Register a proposed rule that interprets the OBRA '93 and SSA '94 provisions described above and incorporates and interprets the provisions of section 1877 that became effective on January 1, 1995, and concern the other designated health services. This proposed rule also addresses the application of sections 1877 and 1903(s) to the Medicaid program.

C. Advisory Opinions: Section 4314 of Public Law 105–33

Section 4314 of the Balanced Budget Act of 1997, Public Law 105–33, enacted on August 5, 1997, added section 1877(g)(6) to the Act. This provision requires that the Department provide additional formal guidance to outside parties regarding the application of the physician referral statute.

Section 1877(g)(6)(A) requires that the Secretary issue written advisory opinions concerning whether a referral relating to designated health services (other than clinical laboratory services) is prohibited under the provisions in section 1877. This paragraph states that each advisory opinion issued by the Secretary will be binding on the Secretary and the party or parties who requested the opinion.

Section 1877(g)(6)(B) requires the Secretary, in issuing physician referral advisory opinions, to apply the rules in paragraphs (b)(3) and (4) of section 1128D of the Act, to the extent practicable. Section 1128D was added to the Act by section 205 of the Health Insurance Portability and Accountability Act of 1996, Public Law 104–191, effective August 21, 1996. It requires the Secretary, in consultation with the Attorney General, to issue written advisory opinions to particular parties on certain specified matters involved in applying the anti-kickback statute in section 1128B(b) of the Act, the safe harbor provisions in 42 CFR 1001.952, as well as other health care fraud and abuse sanctions handled by the Office of Inspector General (OIG).

Section 1128D(b)(3)(A) prohibits the OIG in its advisory opinions from addressing whether fair market value will be or was paid or received for any goods, services, or property. Section 1128D(b)(3)(B) prohibits the OIG from addressing whether an individual is a bona fide employee within the requirements of section 3121(d)(2) of the Internal Revenue Code of 1986. As noted above, HCFA is required to apply these provisions "to the extent practicable." We are incorporating these provisions in their entirety into our own advisory opinion rules.

Section 1128D(b)(4)(A) states that the OIG advisory opinions are binding on the Secretary and the party or parties requesting the opinion. Section 1128D(b)(4)(B) provides that if a party fails to seek an advisory opinion, this fact may not be introduced into evidence to prove that the party intended to violate the provisions of sections 1128, 1128A, or 1128B. We are also required to apply these provisions "to the extent practicable." We are incorporating section 1128D(b)(4)(B) in its entirety. However, we are not incorporating section 1128D(b)(4)(A) because we believe that it is redundant with our own advisory authority in section 1877(g)(6)(A). This provision states that each advisory opinion issued by the Secretary will be binding on the Secretary and on the party or parties requesting the opinion.

Section 1877(g)(6)(B) also requires us to take into account the regulations promulgated by the OIG to cover advisory opinions, issued by the OIG under the authority of section 1128D(b)(5). We believe that "take into account" means that we should use the OIG regulations as our model, but that we are not bound to follow them. We have attempted to follow the OIG regulations as closely as possible in each instance in which we believed that it was reasonable to do so.

Section 1128D(b)(5)(A) states that the OIG's regulations must provide for —

- The procedure to be followed by a party applying for an advisory opinion;
- The procedure to be followed by the Secretary in responding to a request for an advisory opinion;
- The interval in which the Secretary will respond;
- The reasonable fee to be charged to the party requesting an advisory opinion; and
- The manner in which advisory opinions will be made available to the public.

Under section 1128D(b)(5)(B), the OIG is required to issue an advisory opinion to a party by not later than 60 days after receiving the request for the opinion and to charge the requesting party a fee that is equal to the costs the Secretary incurs in responding to the request.

The OIG's procedures for advisory opinions are set forth in 42 CFR part 1008. They were published as an interim final rule with comment period on February 19, 1997 (62 FR 7350). In section III. of this preamble, we discuss each of the elements required by section 1128D(b)(5)(A) (for the OIG's regulations). Many of our procedures are based on those articulated in the OIG regulations.

II. Provisions of the Interim Final Rule with Comment Period

A. Overview of the Advisory Opinion Requirement

This interim final rule with comment period creates regulations at sections 411.370 through 411.389 that establish procedures for the advisory opinions described in section 1877(g)(6). These advisory opinions will provide the public with meaningful advice regarding whether, based on specific facts, a physician's referrals for a designated health service (other than a clinical laboratory service) are prohibited by the referral provisions in section 1877. The advisory opinion process will be meaningful to any parties who are interested in learning whether a particular business arrangement involving a physician (or a physician's immediate family member) will result in the physician being prohibited from making certain referrals under the Medicare program. This process also could prove significant to parties who are interested in the status of a physician's referrals under the Medicaid program. That is because the FFP provision in section 1903(s) of the Act depends upon whether a physician's referrals would be prohibited under the Medicare rules if the Medicare program covered a designated health service in the same manner as it is covered under the State Medicaid plan.

In an advisory opinion, we will restate the material facts known to us, present our analysis, and provide conclusions about how we believe the law applies to the facts presented. We will base our analysis on our interpretation of the provisions in section 1877.

Section 1877(g)(6) requires advisory opinions only on the issue of whether a referral relating to designated health services (other than clinical laboratory services) is a prohibited referral under section 1877. If a physician has an unexcepted financial relationship with an entity, as defined by the statute and our regulations, then that physician's referrals for designated health services for a Medicare patient would be prohibited, regardless of the intent of any of the parties involved in the arrangement. Thus, our advisory opinions will be fact-based, and will contain no discussions about what we believe the parties knew when they entered into the arrangement or what they may have intended.

While section 1877 is primarily a payment ban that is effective regardless of the intent of the parties involved, there are additional sanctions under section 1877(g)(3) and (g)(4) that include elements of knowledge or intent. Section 1877(g)(4), in fact, imposes a penalty for certain referrals that might not otherwise be prohibited, if the parties involved in an arrangement have a particular purpose in mind. This provision applies to any physician or other entity that enters into an arrangement or scheme (such as a cross-referral arrangement) that the physician or entity knows or should know has a principal purpose of ensuring referrals by the physician to a particular entity that, if the physician directly made referrals to that entity, would be in violation of section 1877. Sanctions under this provision include potentially significant civil money penalties and possible exclusion from the Medicare and other health care programs.

We do not believe that section 1877(g)(6) requires us to express any opinion about what the parties to an arrangement knew or intended, for purposes of any of the sanctions in section 1877(g) (3) and (4). Even if we wished to comment on any intent-based aspect of the referral provisions, we believe that it is not practical for us to make an independent determination of the subjective intent of the parties based only upon written materials that have been submitted by the requestor. While we expect requestors to submit complete written descriptions of their arrangements and transactions, along with relevant portions of documents, these materials do not afford a satisfactory basis upon which we could make a reliable determination of subjective intent.

Section 1877(g)(6)(A) states that an advisory opinion shall be binding on the Secretary and on the party or parties requesting an opinion. It is also our view that an advisory opinion may legally be relied upon only by the requestors.

We believe that advisory opinions are capable of being misused by persons not a party to the transaction in question in order to inappropriately escape liability. Advisory opinions are intended only to address the facts of a particular arrangement. A third party may implement an arrangement that appears similar to the arrangement described in the advisory opinion, but the third party may introduce additional factors that may make a difference in the outcome of an advisory opinion.

As set forth below, this interim final rule with comment period has been developed primarily to address the following issues:

- The procedure to be followed by a party applying for an advisory opinion.
- The procedure we will follow in responding to a request.

- The interval within in which we will respond to a request for an advisory opinion.
- The reasonable fee we will charge to the party requesting an advisory opinion.
- The manner in which we will make advisory opinions available to the public.

This final rule with comment period does not address the substance or the content of advisory opinions issued by us.

B. Responsibilities of Outside Parties Seeking Advisory Opinions

1. Who Can Request an Advisory Opinion

Any individual or entity may submit a request to us for a written advisory opinion about whether a physician's referral relating to a designated health service, other than a clinical laboratory service, is prohibited under section 1877. We anticipate that most requests will involve financial relationships that involve health care business arrangements. Therefore, for purposes of this discussion, we will generally use the term "arrangement" to refer to the factual circumstances that are involved in a request for an advisory opinion, even though some requests might involve facts that are not related to a business arrangement.

As indicated above, the advisory opinion process is designed to provide authoritative guidance to participants in particular arrangements. Therefore, the arrangement in question must either be in existence at the time of the request for an advisory opinion or, with respect to prospective arrangements, there must be a good faith intention to enter into the described arrangement in the near future. (With respect to prospective conduct, we are stating that the requestor can declare the intention to enter into the arrangement contingent upon receiving a favorable advisory opinion from us or from both us and the OIG.)

Requestors who are not individuals are required to disclose certain ownership information, so that we can check to ensure that the matter which is the subject of the advisory opinion request is not under current investigation. We are also requiring that requestors inform us, to the best of their knowledge, about whether the arrangement involved in the request is the subject of any current investigations.

2. Matters Not Subject to an Advisory Opinion

As explained above, even if a party requests it, we will not address the issue of whether fair market value was, or will be, paid or received for any goods, services, or property or the issue of whether an individual is a bona fide employee within the requirements of section 3121(d)(2) of the Internal Revenue Code of 1986.

In addition, we do not believe that it is appropriate to provide advisory opinions to persons *not* involved in the arrangement in question. For example, we believe that a description of a competitor's arrangement is not the proper subject of an advisory opinion since the participants to the particular transaction would not be involved in the request. A party to an actual arrangement — either existing or about to be entered into — is in a position to provide full and complete information regarding the facts in question. By contrast, third parties are not in a position to provide a reliable statement about the facts of a particular arrangement in which the third party is not a participant. In addition, it is unclear who would be bound by an advisory opinion on an arrangement that does not involve the requestor.

Similarly, we do not believe it is appropriate to provide advisory opinions on hypothetical or generalized arrangements. Section 1877(g)(6) requires the Secretary to issue advisory opinions concerning "whether a referral relating to designated health services (other than clinical laboratory services) is prohibited under this section." (Emphasis added.) We interpret this provision to mean a specific referral involving a physician in a specific situation. We also believe there are reasons to avoid opinions on generalized arrangements. Because of the complexity of the business arrangements that exist in today's health care community, physician referral cases are not likely to be the same in all material respects. The introduction by a party of any *additional* factors could make a material difference in the resulting opinion. We believe it would not be possible for an advisory opinion to reliably identify all the possible hypothetical factors that might lead to different results.

3. Initiating the Process for an Advisory Opinion

A requestor must submit a written request for an advisory opinion in order to initiate the process. The request must clearly and thoroughly present a complete description of the situation that is the subject of the advisory opinion. The request should include all facts that would be relevant in determining whether a particular situation could result in a physician's referrals being prohibited under section 1877. To the extent that the request provides the necessary information in a clear and orderly manner, we will be better able to process it.

We are requiring any submission to include copies of all relevant documents or relevant portions of documents, such as financial statements, contracts, leases, employment agreements and court documents (requestors may withhold irrelevant portions), as well as descriptions of any other arrangements or relationships that may affect the documents or our analysis. In addition, the submission should include a narrative description of the arrangement. In making the request, a requestor must include the identities (including names and addresses) of the requestor and all other actual and potential parties to the arrangement, to the extent known to the requestor. In addition, the request must include the Taxpayer Identification Number (TIN) of the requestor. The Debt Collection Improvement Act of 1996 (section 31001 of Public Law 104–134) requires agencies to collect the TIN from all persons or businesses "doing business with a Federal agency." (See 31 U.S.C.A. 7701(c).) We believe that requesting, receiving, and paying for our work on an advisory opinion fits into the category of "doing business with a Federal agency." Therefore, a request for an advisory opinion must include the TIN of the requestor. The TIN will be used for purposes of collecting and reporting on any delinquent amounts arising out of the requestor's failure to render proper payment for the advisory opinion. In addition to the above information, we are also requiring the requestor to identify a designated contact person who will be available to communicate with us.

We are also requiring that requestors make two certifications as part of their request for an advisory opinion. If the requestor is an individual, the individual must sign the certification; if the requestor is a corporation, it must be signed by the Chief Executive Officer, or a comparable officer; if the requestor is a partnership, it must be signed by a managing partner; and, if the requestor is a limited liability company, the certification must be signed by a managing member. The responsible individual must certify that all of the information provided as part of the request is true and correct, and constitutes a complete description of the facts regarding which an advisory opinion is being sought, to the best of the requestor's knowledge. If the request relates to prospective conduct, the regulations state that the request must also include a certification that the requestor intends in good faith to enter into the arrangement described in the request. A requestor may make this certification contingent upon receiving a favorable advisory opinion from us or from both us and the OIG.

While all submissions should include the above categories of information, we cannot in these interim final regulations provide complete details on exactly what information a requestor must provide. We anticipate that we will receive requests that involve a wide variety of business arrangements, some of which may be quite complex. At a minimum, any request must describe the entities and parties involved in an arrangement, the specific terms of the arrangement, and the direct or indirect relationship between the physician (or a physician's immediate relative) and any entity that furnishes designated health services. Requestors should also include any information they believe demonstrates that the arrangement meets one of the exceptions to the referral prohibition.

We are soliciting public comment and input on any other types of information that a requestor should routinely provide and intend to address this point further in any revised final rulemaking. In the interim, prior to submitting a request for an advisory opinion, *we strongly advise* that a requestor contact us to inquire about the information HCFA will need to process a request of the type the requestor intends to submit. Inquiries can be made by telephoning Joanne Sinsheimer at (410) 786-4620. We may, depending on the subject matter of the inquiry, informally provide parties with preliminary questions to help them structure their requests. Our goal is to help ensure that the requests include the factual information we will need to respond to them. Requestors should (but are not required to) answer these questions in their requests for an advisory opinion. If the information we need is in the first submission, we will be better able to render a prompt, concise, and appropriate advisory opinion. We welcome comments on this approach.

The regulation also requires that a requestor inform us about whether the parties involved in the request have also asked for or are planning to ask for an advisory opinion on the arrangement in question from the OIG under section 1128D(b) of the Act. We plan to routinely exchange information with the OIG on requests that we receive and on our intended responses. We plan, in particular, to establish a system that will help guarantee adequate coordination when parties have asked for opinions from both us and the OIG.

4. Fees charged to requesting parties

There is no express authority for us to charge a user fee to individuals who request an advisory opinion under section 4314 of the Balanced Budget Act of 1997. However, in the absence of express authority for this particular purpose, we can rely on the authority for collecting such a fee provided by the Independent Offices Appropriations Act of 1952 (IOAA), 31 U.S.C.A. 9701. That statute generally governs Federal agencies' imposition and collection of user fees. In § 9701(a), the Congress expressed its intent that each service or thing of value provided by a Government agency to a person is to be self-sustaining to the extent possible. Section 9701(b) authorizes agencies to prescribe regulations establishing the fee for a service or thing of value provided by the agency. The fee must be "fair" and based on the cost to the government of providing the service or thing, the value of the service or thing to the recipient, public policy or interest served, and other relevant facts. 31 U.S.C.A. 9701(b).

In 1974, the Supreme Court ruled that the user fee statute must be read narrowly as authorizing not a "tax" (which may be levied only by Congress and need not relate to benefits bestowed on the taxpayer), but a "fee" for a particular benefit. *National Cable Television Ass'n, Inc. v. United States,* 415 U.S. 336 (1974)(FCC had authority to impose fees; costs that inure to the public's benefit should not be included in the fee imposed). In a companion case, *Federal Power Commission v. New England Power Company,* 415 U.S. 345 (1974), the Court opined that the Office of Management and Budget (OMB) had properly construed the user fee statute in a 1959 circular, which stated that a reasonable charge "should be made to each identifiable recipient for a measurable unit or amount of government service or property from which he derives a special benefit." *Id.* at 349. The OMB Circular A-25 was revised in 1993, and currently provides under the heading "General policy" that a user charge "will be assessed against each identifiable recipient for special benefits derived from Federal activities beyond those received by the general public." 58 FR 38142, 38144. The language of currently applicable OMB guidance to agencies about when a "special benefit" will be considered to accrue for purposes of imposing a charge is virtually identical to that cited by the Court with approval. *Id.* at 349, fn. 3.

More recent appellate court decisions addressing agencies' authority to impose user fees similarly examine the extent to which there is a "*specific* service that confers a *special* private benefit on an *identifi-*

able beneficiary." *Seafarers Int'l Union of N. Am. v. Coast Guard,* 81 F.3d 179, 184 (D.C. Cir. 1996) (emphasis in original). *See, also, Engine Mfrs. Ass'n v. EPA,* 20 F.2d 1177 (D.C. Cir. 1994) and *Central & Southern Motor Freight Tariff Ass'n v. United States,* 777 F.2d 722 (D.C. Cir. 1985). We believe that the advisory opinions we must provide under section 4314 fall squarely into this category. That is, they are an "extra" service that an interested party can request from the Secretary, they relate to the party's own, unique situation, and they are binding on the Secretary and the requesting party alone, with no general application.

Section 411.372(b)(9) requires that a requestor make payment for an advisory opinion directly to us. We believe that HCFA has the authority to both collect and retain the fees. Annual appropriations acts have since 1996 authorized our retention of otherwise authorized user fees, and this authority would apply to all user fees we are authorized to collect. The retention language appears in the most recent appropriations act, enacted on November 13, 1997, Public Law 105–78, in the paragraphs covering appropriations for our program management. This language states that, in carrying out titles XVIII and XIX of the Act, the Secretary is authorized to use a specific amount of money that will be transferred from the Federal Hospital Insurance and the Federal Supplementary Medical Insurance Trust Funds, together with "such sums as may be collected from authorized user fees and the sale of data, which shall remain available until expended, * * *."

Since section 1877(g)(6) of the Act requires that we take into account the OIG regulations implementing section 1128D(b)(5), we have modeled our user fee on the fee that appears in those regulations. Under section 1128D(b)(5)(A)(iv), the OIG regulations must provide for a "reasonable fee" to be charged to the party requesting an advisory opinion. Section 1128D(b)(5)(B)(ii) requires that requestors be charged a fee equal to the costs incurred by the Department in responding to the request.

We have adopted the "actual cost" fee from the OIG regulations. Section 411.375(b) of our regulations indicates that in determining the actual costs, we will factor in the salary, benefits, and overhead costs of policy analysts, attorneys, and others who may work on analyzing requests and writing advisory opinions, including administrative and supervisory support for these individuals. Because we expect that requests may range widely in their complexity, we do not believe it is possible to calculate or accurately estimate the cost of providing an advisory opinion in advance. In fact, the OIG has interpreted section 1128D(b)(5)(B)(ii) to require a fee that represents the *actual* costs that it has incurred in processing each individual request. We are also reflecting this concept in our regulations.

We have included in our regulations the OIG's requirement that, once the advisory opinion process is complete, either because we have issued the opinion or the request has been withdrawn, the requestor is responsible for paying an amount equal to the costs incurred by the Government in responding to the request.

Although we cannot reliably project the processing costs in advance, we can make broad estimates that may be of use to prospective requestors. We estimate that, currently, the actual cost of processing a request, including salaries, benefits and overhead, would be approximately $75 an hour. We must include in our estimate the time of technical staff, attorneys, supervisors, and support staff, as well as others with whom we may consult on various issues.

The time it will take us to process a request will depend on the complexity of the request and the quality of the submission. Simple requests might only take a few hours. For example, a request concerning whether a physician can refer patients to his wife, who works for a physical therapy facility, may take approximately three hours to analyze and produce a written opinion. On the other hand, a request involving the application of the physician referral rules to a large, multi-party, intricate business arrangement may take us in excess of forty hours to fully analyze and produce a written advisory opinion.

We believe that it is reasonable to expect that requests for an advisory opinion will, at present, cost at least $250 for initial processing. It will take time for us to carefully read and analyze every request for an advisory opinion and to ensure that we have accurately understood all the material facts in each request. Accordingly, the regulations provide for a nonrefundable payment of $250 that must accompany any request for an advisory opinion that we receive through the end of 1998. Once we have gained experience in estimating the resources we will need and have factored in any inflation in our costs, we may need to revise our initial fee through a program issuance. We expect to revise the fee periodically after December 31, 1998.

Because we do not believe that we can accurately estimate our costs in advance for a particular request, we intend to try to accommodate requestors who may want to limit the costs of receiving an advisory opinion. The regulations provide that requestors may designate a "triggering dollar amount" in their requests for an advisory opinion. If we calculate that the cost of processing a request has reached, or is likely to exceed, that triggering amount, we will stop processing the request and promptly notify the requestor. The requestor may then decide to either authorize us to continue or withdraw the request. We believe we will be able to more accurately reflect costs in advance once we have gained experience. In the interim, this triggering mechanism should be useful in helping to ensure that requestors do not pay costs far in excess of what they expect to pay when they submit their requests.

Section 411.375(c)(4) of the regulations specifically indicates that, while a requestor may withdraw a request for an advisory opinion at any time, he or she will be responsible for any costs we incurred in processing the request before it was withdrawn.

When we have completed the advisory opinion as discussed below, or the requestor has withdrawn the request, we will calculate the total costs that we incurred in processing the request. In calculating this amount, we will take into account any previous payments associated with the request, such as the initial $250 fee, and then notify the requestor of the amount he or she still owes. Once the requestor has paid the full cost, we will release the opinion to the requestor.

We believe that our approach for payment and release will be sufficient for the vast majority of requests for advisory opinions. However, we also believe that we need an additional procedure for cases in which the request will necessitate that we acquire expert advice. We may, for example, need to consult with accountants or with business professionals in order to better understand complex financial relationships.

Because such expert reviews will entail additional time and expense, we believe that we should treat differently any request that requires outside consultation rather than just a standard application of the governing law to a given set of facts. If we determine that we require an expert opinion, we will obtain an estimate for the costs of the opinion and provide the requestor with that estimate. The requestor may then decide to either pay the estimated cost of the expert review or withdraw the request. If the requestor pays the estimated cost, we will promptly refer the matter to the expert for review. Once the outside expert has provided us with the review, we will continue the advisory opinion process by applying the expert evaluation to the legal questions at issue. If the expert evaluation ultimately costs more than the estimated cost, we will bill the requestor for the additional expense as part of the Department's overall costs in responding to the request. These additional costs will be included when we determine whether we are approaching a requestor's "triggering dollar amount."

We intend to begin processing requests as soon as we receive them. However, although we will be charging user fees for the cost to the Government for responding to these requests, we will not be adding staff until we determine the volume of requests and the complexity of the legal issues and fact patterns. Once we have had some experience processing requests for advisory opinions, we intend to reconsider the method described in this section for calculating fees. We are specifically soliciting comments on our methodology for determining costs.

C. HCFA's Responsibilities

1. Reviewing Requests for Advisory Opinions

Once we receive a request for an advisory opinion, we will promptly examine it to determine if it appears to contain sufficient information for us to form the basis for an informed advisory opinion. (Generally speaking, a request is most likely to be sufficient if the requestor sought our advice before submitting a formal request, and the request contains responses to any preliminary questions we may have posed at that time.) If a request does not appear to us to be sufficient, we will promptly notify the requestor about the additional information we need. On the other hand, if the request appears to be sufficient, we will accept the request. In all cases, we will either ask for additional information or accept the request within fifteen working days after we receive the request. If we have requested additional information and the requestor resubmits the advisory opinion request, we will assess the resubmission within fifteen working days to determine whether it can be accepted or whether we still need further information. At the point when we accept the request, we will notify the requestor by U.S. mail of the date of our acceptance.

We believe that this approach will provide us with a reasonable amount of time to identify requests that do not contain sufficient information. We are limiting the time period for this initial assessment in order to ensure that we promptly process requests that appear to be complete. We are interested in public comments on whether we have developed an appropriate method for screening advisory opinion requests before we accept them.

Even in situations in which we have accepted a request, we reserve the right to later determine that we need additional information. If we decide that additional information is necessary, we will notify the requestor in the same manner as we would notify a requestor before accepting a request. The time period between when we notify the requestor about the additional information we need and when we receive the requested information will not be counted as part of the time within which we must issue an opinion.

Because we believe that we may need to make fact-intensive inquiries in order to render many advisory opinions, we anticipate that we may need to request additional information from many requestors. In responding, the requestor should provide us with the necessary information and include with it a certification from the same individual who certified the original request for an advisory opinion (or, if the requestor is an entity, from an individual who is in a comparable position).

2. Timeframe for Issuing Advisory Opinions

Section 1128D(b)(5)(B) of the Act requires that the OIG issue an advisory opinion within 60 days after it has received the request for the opinion. The OIG has reflected this timeframe in its regulations at 42 CFR 1008.43. Because section 1877(g)(6) does not impose any deadline, we have established our own 90-day timeframe for most requests. In addition, for requests that we determine, in our discretion, involve complex legal issues or highly complicated fact patterns, we reserve the right to issue an advisory opinion within a reasonable timeframe. We have created this timeframe based upon our perception that we will receive many requests for advisory opinions and that a large percentage will involve complex fact patterns. This perception is based on the quantity and the nature of phone calls we have received, on a daily basis, over many years. We believe that the number of requests will be affected by the fact that the referral provisions in section 1877 apply to many parties because they can be triggered regardless of the intent of the parties. In addition, if an arrangement involves a physician who has a problematic financial relationship with an entity that furnishes designated health services, the parties must know that the arrangement meets an exception before that physician can refer. We have also based our timeframe on staffing limitations.

Although we will be charging user fees for the cost to the Government for responding to these requests, we will not be adding staff until we determine the volume of requests and the complexity of the legal issues and fact patterns.

Once we have had some experience processing requests for advisory opinions, we intend to reevaluate the timeframe to ensure that it is fair and to determine whether more staff is necessary. We are specifically soliciting comments on this issue.

We intend to begin processing requests as soon as we receive them. Once we receive a request that appears to meet all the submission criteria, we will promptly accept the request and our 90-day period for issuing an opinion will begin. We will send the advisory opinion to the requestor by regular U.S. mail by the end of the 90-day period and once the requestor has paid all the required fees.

We believe that under certain circumstances the running of our 90-day period for issuing an opinion should be tolled (suspended). The suspended periods will only reflect time when we cannot work on analyzing the request. If we notify a requestor that the costs have reached, or are likely to exceed, the triggering amount designated by that requestor, we will stop processing the request until the requestor instructs us to continue. Similarly, if we notify a requestor of the need for, and estimated cost of, an outside expert opinion on a nonlegal issue, the regulations state that we will stop processing the request until the requestor pays the estimated cost and the outside expert provides its opinion. Likewise, in those instances in which we request additional information from the requestor that we believe is necessary for us to issue the advisory opinion, we will stop processing the opinion until we receive the additional information.

The time period for issuing an advisory opinion does not include the time after we notify the requestor that the advisory opinion is complete and the requestor must pay the full balance due for the cost of the opinion.

While we intend to issue advisory opinions within 90 days of receiving the request, we do not believe that the 90-day time period should include delays in the processing of the request that are not within our control. With the exception of the delay that occurs while we wait for a necessary outside expert opinion, all of the possible events that can suspend the period are under the exclusive control of the requestor. We believe that for the vast majority of advisory opinion requests, the 90-day period will only be suspended for those periods during which the requestor has not paid a required fee or has not provided the information we need to process the request.

We will issue an advisory opinion to the requestor after we have considered the complete description of all the facts the requestor has provided to us. In the opinion, we will restate the material facts known to us, present our analysis, and provide conclusions about how we believe the law applies to the facts presented to us.

3. Dissemination of Advisory Opinions

Section 1128D(b)(5)(A)(v) requires that the OIG's regulations describe the manner in which advisory opinions will be made available to the public. We have adopted the OIG's policy as follows: As set forth in § 411.384(b) of these regulations, once we issue an advisory opinion to a requestor, we will promptly make a copy of that opinion available for public inspection (in Room 309-G of the Department's offices at 200 Independence Avenue, S.W., Washington, DC (phone: 202–690–7890)) during our normal hours of operation and on our web site (http://www.hcfa.gov/regs/aop/). We also anticipate that commercial publishers and trade groups are likely to make advisory opinions widely available to interested members of the public. We welcome public comments and additional suggestions about disseminating advisory opinions to the public.

We will make available documents that are related to a request for an advisory opinion and have been submitted to us and any related internal government documents, to the extent we are required to do so by the Freedom of Information Act (FOIA) (5 U.S.C.A. 552). If a requestor provides information it believes is not subject to disclosure under FOIA, such as items that the requestor believes are trade secrets or privileged and confidential commercial or financial information, the requestor should identify this information in the manner described in 45 CFR 5.65 (c) and (d). The requestor's assertions about the nature of the information, however, are not controlling.

In addition, although a document may be exempt from disclosure under FOIA, facts reflected in that document may become part of the advisory opinion that HCFA will provide to the public. We will describe the material facts of the arrangement in question in the body of each advisory opinion, which will be made fully available to the public. To the extent that it may be necessary to reveal specific facts that could be regarded as confidential information, we believe we have the authority to do so under sections 1106(a) and 1877(g)(6) of the Act. We do not intend to release any such facts unless we believe it is necessary to do so.

4. Rescission of an Advisory Opinion

Section 411.382 reserves our right to rescind or revoke an advisory opinion after we issue it, in limited circumstances. For example, we can rescind an opinion if we learn after issuing it that the arrangement in question may lead to fraud and abuse. In such a situation, we will notify the requestor that we have rescinded and make the notice available to the same extent as an advisory opinion. The requestor would not be subject to sanctions for any actions it took prior to the notice of rescission, if the requestor relied in good faith on the advisory opinion (unless we establish that the requestor failed to provide us with material information when it submitted the request for the opinion) and where the parties promptly discontinue the action upon receiving notice that we have rescinded or revoked our approval. We would also allow the parties to discontinue the action within what we believe is a reasonable "wind down" period, if we believe that the business arrangement is one that cannot be discontinued immediately. We are specifically soliciting comments on whether this approach reasonably balances the Government's need to ensure that advisory opinions are legally correct and the requestor's interest in finality.

5. Scope and Effect of Advisory Opinions

Section 411.387 of these regulations addresses the scope and effect of advisory opinions. When we issue an advisory opinion under this process, it is legally binding on the Department and the requestor, but only with respect to the specific conduct of the particular requestor. Section 1877(g)(6)(A) requires only that an advisory opinion issued by the Secretary be binding upon the Secretary and the party or parties requesting the opinion. In light of this provision, the Department is not legally bound with respect to the conduct of a third party, even if the conduct of that party appears similar to the conduct of the requestor. Thus, under these regulations, no third parties are bound by nor may they rely upon an advisory opinion. Each advisory opinion will apply legal standards to a set of facts involving certain known persons who provide specific statements about key factual issues. A third party may create a look-alike arrangement, but any *additional* characteristics could lead to an unfavorable opinion. Therefore, by their very nature, advisory opinions cannot be applied generally.

We believe that even if a party has received a favorable advisory opinion from us regarding a particular arrangement, the Government is not totally prevented from commencing an action against a party to that arrangement. For example, this could occur if a requestor has failed to disclose a material fact. In any such action under sections 1128, 1128A or 1128B of the Act, an individual or entity who has requested and received an advisory opinion from us regarding the arrangement in question may seek to introduce the advisory opinion into evidence in the proceeding.

III. Regulatory Impact Analysis

We have examined the impact of this rule as required by Executive Order 12866 and the Regulatory Flexibility Act (RFA) (Pub. L. 96–354). Executive Order 12866 directs agencies to assess all costs and benefits of available regulatory alternatives and, when regulation is necessary, to select regulatory approaches that maximize net benefits (including potential economic, environmental, public health and safety effects, distributive impacts, and equity). The RFA requires agencies to analyze options for regulatory relief of small businesses. For purposes of the RFA, most hospitals, and most other providers, physicians, and health care suppliers are small entities, either by nonprofit status or by having revenues of $5 million or less annually.

Section 1102(b) of the Social Security Act requires us to prepare a regulatory impact analysis for any proposed rule that may have a significant impact on the operations of a substantial number of small rural hospitals. This analysis must conform to the provisions of section 603 of the RFA. For purposes of section 1102(b) of the Act, we define a small rural hospital as a hospital that is located outside a Metropolitan Statistical Area and has fewer than fifty beds.

This rule establishes procedures for us to receive, review, and respond to requests for advisory opinions on the issue of whether a physician's referrals for certain designated health services are prohibited under section 1877 of the Social Security Act. This rule does not address the substance of section 1877 nor the substance or content of the advisory opinions we may issue in the future. Any effect an advisory opinion may have on the behavior of health care providers is the result of the substantive content of section 1877 and of the advisory opinions themselves, and not this rule.

Parties interested in advisory opinions will incur certain costs in requesting the opinions. However, it is the law that allows us to require that requestors pay cost-based fees for advisory opinions. This rule merely lays out procedures for paying the costs.

Estimated number of respondents: Many individuals and entities that provide certain designated health services that may be paid for by Medicare or Medicaid could potentially have questions regarding the referral provisions in section 1877.

We estimate that, within the last year, we received an average of eight telephone calls each day regarding the physician self-referral provisions. We believe that some percentage of calls involved issues and situations about which the callers would be unlikely to request written advisory opinions. Nevertheless, we believe that we can use the number of inquiries as a basis for estimating the number of requests we are likely to receive for advisory opinions. Using this basis, we estimate that 200 physicians, health care entities, and other entities or individuals will request advisory opinions within the first year following publication of this rule. We also anticipate that the number of requests will decline in subsequent years, unless there are significant changes in the law. The costs to these requestors will vary depending on the complexity of each request. Compared, however, to the costs of seeking private legal advice, we believe that the fees charged for our review will not be substantial, and in many cases will not exceed the $250 minimum payment.

Obviously, the actual number of requests could be larger since, for the first time, formal written opinions are available. Conversely, the numbers could be smaller for a combination of many unquantifiable reasons, such as the desire not to subject an arrangement to official scrutiny.

Under the Regulatory Flexibility Act (5 U.S.C.A. 601–612), if a rule has a significant economic effect on a substantial number of small businesses, the Secretary must specifically consider the effects of the rule on small business entities and analyze regulatory options that could lessen the impact of the rule. As stated above, this rule does not address the substance of section 1877 of the Act or the substance of advisory opinions that may be issued in the future. It describes the process by which an individual or entity may receive an opinion about how section 1877 applies to particular business practices. The aggregate economic impact of this rulemaking on small business entities should, therefore, be minimal.

Thus, we have concluded, and the Secretary certifies, that this final rule will not have a significant economic impact on a substantial number of small business entities, and that a regulatory flexibility analysis is not required for this rulemaking.

In accordance with the provisions of E.O. 12866, this regulation was reviewed by the Office of Management and Budget.

IV. Authority for an Interim Final Rule with Comment Period, and Waiver of Delayed Effective Date

We ordinarily publish a general notice of proposed rulemaking in the Federal Register and invite public comment on the proposed rule. That rule would have included a reference to the legal authority under which we are proposing it, and the terms and substance of the proposed rule or a description of the subjects and issues involved. Further, we generally provide for final rules to be effective no sooner than thrity days after the date of publication unless we find good cause to waive the delay.

In order to implement the provisions in section 1877(g)(6) in a timely manner, section 1877(g)(6)(C) gives us the authority to promulgate regulations that take effect on an interim basis after notice and pending opportunity for public comment. We have chosen to exercise this authority for the following reasons. We believe that the statutory requirement that we accept requests for advisory opinions that are submitted on or after November 4, 1997, makes it imperative that, by that date, we have in place specific procedures to address how we will receive and process advisory opinion requests. It would be contrary to the public interest for us to receive and process advisory opinions without first setting forth procedural guidelines. We also believe that the 60-day period for public comment established by this interim final rule will protect the public's interest in this rulemaking, while providing us with additional input and recommendations, without unduly delaying the advisory opinion process. We are therefore publishing the advisory opinion procedures as an interim final rule with comment period. We also find that for good cause it would be against the public interest to delay the effective date of this rule. We will respond to all appropriate and relevant public comments that we receive during the 60-day comment period, and we will make any necessary revisions to these regulations through a revised final rule.

V. Collection of Information Requirements

In order to provide appropriate advisory opinions, we will need certain information from the parties who request advisory opinions. Sections 411.372, 411.373, and 411.378 of this interim final rule contain information collection requirements that require approval by OMB. We are required to solicit public comments under section 3506(c)(2)(A) of the Paperwork Reduction Act of 1995. Specifically, comments are invited on (1) whether the proposed collection of information is necessary for the proper performance of the functions of the agency, including whether the information will have practical utility; (2) the accuracy of the estimate of the burden of the proposed collection of information; (3) ways to enhance the quality, utility and clarity of the information collected; and (4) ways to minimize the burden of the collection of information on respondents, including through the use of automated collection techniques or other forms of information technology.

We are requesting an emergency review of this interim final rule with comment period. In compliance with section 3506(c)(2)(A) of the Paperwork Reduction Act of 1995, we are submitting to OMB the collection of information requirements described below for emergency review. We are requesting an emergency review because the collection of this information is needed before the expiration of the normal time limits under OMB's regulations at 5 CFR part 1320, to ensure compliance with section 1877(g)(6)(D) of the Act, which was added by section 4314 of the Balanced Budget Act of 1997. Section 1877(g)(6)(D) requires us to respond to requests for advisory opinions that are submitted after November 3, 1997. We cannot reasonably comply with normal clearance procedures because of the statutory deadline and public harm is likely to result if the agency cannot provide for advisory opinions.

We are providing a 3-day public comment period from the date of publication of this interim final rule, with OMB review and approval 4 days from the date of publication, and a 180-day approval. During this 180-day period, we will publish a separate Federal Register notice announcing the initiation of an extensive 60-day agency review and public comment period on these requirements. We will submit the requirements for OMB review and an extension of this emergency approval.

Title: HCFA Advisory Opinion Procedure.

Summary of the collection of information: Section 4314 of Public Law 105–33, in establishing section 1877(g)(6) of the Act, requires the Department to provide advisory opinions to the public regarding whether a physician's referrals for certain designated health services are prohibited under the other provisions in section 1877 of the Act. These regulations provide the procedures under which members of the public may request advisory opinions from HCFA. Because all requests for advisory opinions are purely voluntary, respondents will only be required to provide information to us that is relevant to their individual requests.

The following discussion describes the aggregate effect of the collections of information included in the text of this interim final rule.

Respondents: The "respondents" for the collection of information described in these regulations will be self-selected individuals and entities that choose to submit requests for advisory opinions to HCFA. We anticipate that the respondents will include health care providers of many types, from physicians who are sole practitioners to large diversified publicly-traded corporations.

Estimated number of respondents: 200. This estimate is based on the number of telephone calls we have received regarding the physician referral provisions.

Estimated number of responses per respondent: 1.

Estimated total annual burden on respondents: We believe that the burden of preparing a request for an advisory opinion will vary widely depending upon the size and complexity of the business transactions in question. We estimate that the average burden for each submitted request for an advisory opinion will be in the range of 2 to 40 hours. We further believe that the burden for most requests will be closer to the lower end of the range, with an average burden of 10 hours per respondent. Total burden for this proposed information collection is estimated to be 2000 hours.

We are requiring that requests for advisory opinions involve existing conduct, or conduct in which the requestor intends to engage. We anticipate that most requests will involve business arrangements into which the requesting party intends to enter. Because the facts will relate to business plans, we believe the requesting party in many cases will already have collected and analyzed all or almost all of the information we will need in order to review the request. Therefore, in order to request an advisory opinion, the requestor will most likely simply need to compile for our examination information that the requestor has already collected and reviewed. In some cases, however, the requestor may need to expend a more significant amount of time in order to submit information relating to a complex arrangement that involves a large number of parties.

Comments on this information collection should be sent to both: Health Care Financing Administration, Office of Information Services, Information Technology Investment Management Group, Division of HCFA Enterprise Standards, Attn: HCFA-1902-IFC, Room C2–26–17, 7500 Security Boulevard, Baltimore, MD 21244–1850

and

Allison Herron Eydt, HCFA Desk Officer, Office of Management and Budget, Room 10235, New Executive Office Building, 725 17th Street, N.W., Washington, DC 20503.

You may also fax comments on these paperwork reduction requirements to the Health Care Financing Administration at (410) 786–1415 and to Ms. Eydt at (202) 395–6974. All comments should refer to file code HCFA-1902-IFC.

To be considered, you must submit comments on these paperwork reduction requirements to the individuals listed above within 3 days after this interim final rule is published in the Federal Register.

List of Subjects in 42 CFR Part 411

Administrative practice and procedures, Fraud, Grant programs— health, Health facilities, Health professions, Medicaid, Medicare, Penalties.

42 CFR part 411 is amended as set forth below:

PART 411 —EXCLUSIONS FROM MEDICARE AND LIMITATIONS ON MEDICARE PAYMENT

1. The authority citation for part 411 continues to read as follows:

Authority: §§ 1102 and 1871 of the Social Security Act (42 U.S.C.A. 1302 and 1395hh).

2. Sections 411.370, 411.372, 411.373, 411.375, 411.377 through 411.380, 411.382, 411.384, and 411.386 through 411.389 are added to subpart J to read as follows:

§ 411.370 Advisory Opinions Relating to Physician Referrals.

(a) *Period during which HCFA will accept requests.* The provisions of §§ 411.370 through 411.389 apply to requests for advisory opinions that are submitted to HCFA after November 3, 1997, and before August 21, 2000, and to any requests submitted during any other time period during which HCFA is required by law to issue the advisory opinions described in this subpart.

(b) *Matters that qualify for advisory opinions and who may request one.* Any individual or entity may request a written advisory opinion from HCFA concerning whether a physician's referral relating to designated health services (other than clinical laboratory services) is prohibited under section 1877 of the Act. In the advisory opinion, HCFA determines whether a business arrangement described by the parties to that arrangement appears to constitute a "financial relationship" (as defined in section 1877(a)(2) of the Act) that could potentially restrict a physician's referrals, and whether the arrangement or the designated health services at issue appear to qualify for any of the exceptions to the referral prohibition described in section 1877 of the Act.

(1) The request must involve an existing arrangement or one into which the requestor, in good faith, specifically plans to enter. The planned arrangement may be contingent upon the party or parties receiving a favorable advisory opinion. HCFA does not consider, for purposes of an advisory opinion, requests that present a general question of interpretation, pose a hypothetical situation, or involve the activities of third parties.

(2) The requestor must be a party to the existing or proposed arrangement.

(c) *Matters not subject to advisory opinions.* HCFA does not address through the advisory opinion process —

(1) Whether the fair market value was, or will be, paid or received for any goods, services, or property; and

(2) Whether an individual is a bona fide employee within the requirements of section 3121(d)(2) of the Internal Revenue Code of 1986.

(d) *Facts subject to advisory opinions.* HCFA considers requests for advisory opinions that involve applying specific facts to the subject matter described in paragraph (b) of this section. Requestors must include in the advisory opinion request a complete description of the arrangement that the requestor is undertaking, or plans to undertake, as described in § 411.372.

(e) *Requests that will not be accepted.* HCFA does not accept an advisory opinion request or issue an advisory opinion if —

(1) The request is not related to a named individual or entity;
(2) HCFA is aware that the same, or substantially the same, course of action is under investigation, or is or has been the subject of a proceeding involving the Department of Health and Human Services or another governmental agency; or
(3) HCFA believes that it cannot make an informed opinion or could only make an informed opinion after extensive investigation, clinical study, testing, or collateral inquiry.

(f) *Effects of an advisory opinion on other Governmental authority.* Nothing in this part limits the investigatory or prosecutorial authority of the OIG, the Department of Justice, or any other agency of the Government. In addition, in connection with any request for an advisory opinion, HCFA, the OIG, or the Department of Justice may conduct whatever independent investigation it believes appropriate.

§ 411.372 Procedure for Submitting a Request.

(a) *Format for a request.* A party or parties must submit a request for an advisory opinion to HCFA in writing, including an original request and 2 copies. The request must be addressed to: Health Care Financing Administration, Department of Health and Human Services, Attention: Advisory Opinions, P.O. Box 26505, Baltimore, MD 21207.
(b) *Information HCFA requires with all submissions.* The request must include the following:

(1) The name, address, telephone number, and Taxpayer Identification Number of the requestor.
(2) The names and addresses, to the extent known, of all other actual and potential parties to the arrangement that is the subject of the request.
(3) The name, title, address, and daytime telephone number of a contact person who will be available to discuss the request with HCFA on behalf of the requestor.
(4) A complete and specific description of all relevant information bearing on the arrangement, including —

(i) A complete description of the arrangement that the requestor is undertaking, or plans to undertake, including: the purpose of the arrangement; the nature of each party's (including each entity's) contribution to the arrangement; the direct or indirect relationships between the parties, with an emphasis on the relationships between physicians involved in the arrangement (or their immediate family members who are involved) and any entities that provide designated health services; the types of services for which a physician wishes to refer, and whether the referrals will involve Medicare or Medicaid patients;

(ii) Complete copies of all relevant documents or relevant portions of documents that affect or could affect the arrangement, such as personal services or employment contracts, leases, deeds, pension or insurance plans, financial statements, or stock certificates (or, if these relevant documents do not yet exist, a complete description, to the best of the requestor's knowledge, of what these documents are likely to contain);

(iii) Detailed statements of all collateral or oral understandings, if any; and

(iv) Descriptions of any other arrangements or relationships that could affect HCFA's analysis.

(5) Complete information on the identity of all entities involved either directly or indirectly in the arrangement, including their names, addresses, legal form, ownership structure, nature of the business (products and services) and, if relevant, their Medicare and Medicaid provider numbers. The requestor must also include a brief description of any other entities that could affect the outcome of the opinion, including those with which the requestor, the other parties, or the immediate family members of involved physicians, have any financial relationships (either direct or indirect, and as defined in section 1877(a)(2) of the Act and § 411.351), or in which any of the parties holds an ownership or control interest as defined in section 1124(a)(3) of the Act.

(6) A discussion of the specific issues or questions the requestor would like HCFA to address including, if possible, a description of why the requestor believes the referral prohibition in section 1877 of the Act might or might not be triggered by the arrangement and which, if any, exceptions to the prohibition the requestor believes might apply. The requestor

should attempt to designate which facts are relevant to each issue or question raised in the request and should cite the provisions of law under which each issue or question arises.

(7) An indication of whether the parties involved in the request have also asked for or are planning to ask for an advisory opinion on the arrangement in question from the OIG under section 1128D(b) of the Act (42 U.S.C.A. 1320a-7d(b)) and whether the arrangement is or is not, to the best of the requestor's knowledge, the subject of an investigation.

(8) The certification(s) described in § 411.373. The certification(s) must be signed by—

(i) The requestor, if the requestor is an individual;

(ii) The chief executive officer, or comparable officer, of the requestor, if the requestor is a corporation;

(iii) The managing partner of the requestor, if the requestor is a partnership; or

(iv) A managing member, if the requestor is a limited liability company.

(9) A check or money order payable to HCFA in the amount described in § 411.375(a).

(c) *Additional information HCFA might require.* If the request does not contain all of the information required by paragraph (b) of this section, or, if either before or after accepting the request, HCFA believes it needs more information in order to render an advisory opinion, it may request whatever additional information or documents it deems necessary. Additional information must be provided in writing, signed by the same person who signed the initial request (or by an individual in a comparable position), and be certified as described in § 411.373.

§ 411.373 Certification.

(a) Every request must include the following signed certification: "With knowledge of the penalties for false statements provided by 18 U.S.C.A. 1001 and with knowledge that this request for an advisory opinion is being submitted to the Department of Health and Human Services, I certify that all of the information provided is true and correct, and constitutes a complete description of the facts regarding which an advisory opinion is sought, to the best of my knowledge and belief."

(b) If the advisory opinion relates to a proposed arrangement, in addition to the certification required by paragraph (a) of this section, the following certification must be included and signed by the requestor: "The arrangement described in this request for an advisory opinion is one into which [the requestor], in good faith, plans to enter." This statement may be made contingent on a favorable advisory opinion, in which case the requestor should add one of the following phrases to the certification:

(1) "if HCFA issues a favorable advisory opinion."
(2) "if HCFA and the OIG issue favorable advisory opinions."

§ 411.375 Fees for the Cost of Advisory Opinions.

(a) *Initial payment.* Parties must include with each request for an advisory opinion submitted through December 31, 1998, a check or money order payable to HCFA for $250. For requests submitted after this date, parties must include a check or money order in this amount, unless HCFA has revised the amount of the initial fee in a program issuance, in which case, the requestor must include the revised amount. This initial payment is nonrefundable.
(b) *How costs are calculated.* Before issuing the advisory opinion, HCFA calculates the costs the Department has incurred in responding to the request. The calculation includes the costs of salaries, benefits, and overhead for analysts, attorneys, and others who have worked on the request, as well as administrative and supervisory support for these individuals.
(c) *Agreement to pay all costs.* (1) By submitting the request for an advisory opinion, the requestor agrees, except as indicated in paragraph (c)(3) of this section, to pay all costs the Department incurs in responding to the request for an advisory opinion.

(2) In its request for an advisory opinion, the requestor may designate a triggering dollar amount. If HCFA estimates that the costs of processing the advisory opinion request have reached or are likely to exceed the designated triggering dollar amount, HCFA notifies the requestor.
(3) If HCFA notifies the requestor that the actual or estimated cost of processing the request has reached or is likely to exceed the triggering dollar amount, HCFA stops processing the request until the requestor makes a written request for HCFA to continue. If HCFA is delayed in processing the

request for an advisory opinion because of this procedure, the time within which HCFA must issue an advisory opinion is suspended until the requestor asks HCFA to continue working on the request.

(4) If the requestor chooses not to pay for HCFA to complete an advisory opinion, or withdraws the request, the requestor is still obligated to pay for all costs HCFA has identified as costs it incurred in processing the request for an advisory opinion, up to that point.

(5) If the costs HCFA has incurred in responding to the request are greater than the amount the requestor has paid, HCFA, before issuing the advisory opinion, notifies the requestor of any additional amount that is due. HCFA does not issue an advisory opinion until the requestor has paid the full amount that is owed. Once the requestor has paid HCFA the total amount due for the costs of processing the request, HCFA issues the advisory opinion. The time period HCFA has for issuing advisory opinions is suspended from the time HCFA notifies the requestor of the amount owed until the time HCFA receives full payment.

(d) *Fees for outside experts.* (1) In addition to the fees identified in this section, the requestor also must pay any required fees for expert opinions, if any, from outside sources, as described in § 411.377.

(2) The time period for issuing an advisory opinion is suspended from the time that HCFA notifies the requestor that it needs an outside expert opinion until the time HCFA receives that opinion.

§ 411.377 Expert Opinions from Outside Sources.

(a) HCFA may request expert advice from qualified sources if HCFA believes that the advice is necessary to respond to a request for an advisory opinion. For example, HCFA may require the use of accountants or business experts to assess the structure of a complex business arrangement or to ascertain a physician's or immediate family member's financial relationship with entities that provide designated health services.

(b) If HCFA determines that it needs to obtain expert advice in order to issue a requested advisory opinion, HCFA notifies the requestor of that fact and provides the identity of the appropriate expert and an estimate of the costs of the expert advice. As indicated in § 411.375(d), the requestor must pay the estimated cost of the expert advice.

(c) Once HCFA has received payment for the estimated cost of the expert advice, HCFA arranges for the expert to provide a prompt review of the issue or issues in question. HCFA considers any additional expenses for the expert advice, beyond the estimated amount, as part of the costs HCFA has incurred in responding to the request, and the responsibility of the requestor, as described in § 411.375(c).

§ 411.378 Withdrawing a Request.

The party requesting an advisory opinion may withdraw the request before HCFA issues a formal advisory opinion. This party must submit the withdrawal in writing to the same address as the request, as indicated in § 411.372(a). Even if the party withdraws the request, the party must pay the costs the Department has expended in processing the request, as discussed in § 411.375. HCFA reserves the right to keep any request for an advisory opinion and any accompanying documents and information, and to use them for any governmental purposes permitted by law.

§ 411.379 When HCFA Accepts a Request.

(a) Upon receiving a request for an advisory opinion, HCFA promptly makes an initial determination of whether the request includes all of the information it will need to process the request.

(b) Within fifteen working days of receiving the request, HCFA —

(1) Formally accepts the request for an advisory opinion;

(2) Notifies the requestor about the additional information it needs, or

(3) Declines to formally accept the request.

(c) If the requestor provides the additional information HCFA has requested, or otherwise resubmits the request, HCFA processes the resubmission in accordance with paragraphs (a) and (b) of this section as if it were an initial request for an advisory opinion.

(d) Upon accepting the request, HCFA notifies the requestor by regular U.S. mail of the date that HCFA formally accepted the request.

(e) The 90-day period that HCFA has to issue an advisory opinion set forth in § 411.380(c) does not begin until HCFA has formally accepted the request for an advisory opinion.

§ 411.380 When HCFA Issues a Formal Advisory Opinion.

(a) HCFA considers an advisory opinion to be issued once it has received payment and once the opinion has been dated, numbered, and signed by an authorized HCFA official.

(b) An advisory opinion contains a description of the material facts known to HCFA that relate to the arrangement that is the subject of the advisory opinion, and states HCFA's opinion about the subject matter of the request based on those facts. If necessary, HCFA includes in the advisory opinion material facts that could be considered confidential information or trade secrets within the meaning of 18 U.S.C.A. 1095.

(c) (1) HCFA issues an advisory opinion, in accordance with the provisions of this part, within 90 days after it has formally accepted the request for an advisory opinion, or, for requests that HCFA determines, in its discretion, involve complex legal issues or highly complicated fact patterns, within a reasonable time period.

(2) If the 90th day falls on a Saturday, Sunday, or Federal holiday, the time period ends at the close of the first business day following the weekend or holiday;

(3) The 90-day period is suspended from the time HCFA—

(i) Notifies the requestor that the costs have reached or are likely to exceed the triggering amount as described in § 411.375(c)(2) until HCFA receives written notice from the requestor to continue processing the request;

(ii) Requests additional information from the requestor until HCFA receives the additional information;

(iii) Notifies the requestor of the full amount due until HCFA receives payment of this amount; and

(iv) Notifies the requestor of the need for expert advice until HCFA receives the expert advice.

(d) After HCFA has notified the requestor of the full amount owed and has received full payment of that amount, HCFA issues the advisory opinion and promptly mails it to the requestor by regular first class U.S. mail.

§ 411.382 HCFA's Right to Rescind Advisory Opinions.

Any advice HCFA gives in an opinion does not prejudice its right to reconsider the questions involved in the opinion and, if it determines that it is in the public interest, to rescind or revoke the opinion. HCFA provides notice to the requestor of its decision to rescind or revoke the opinion so that the requestor and the parties involved in the requestor's arrangement may discontinue any course of action they have taken in accordance with the advisory opinion. HCFA does not proceed against the requestor with respect to any action the requestor and the involved parties have taken in good faith reliance upon HCFA's advice under this part, provided—

(a) The requestor presented to HCFA a full, complete and accurate description of all the relevant facts; and

(b) The parties promptly discontinue the action upon receiving notice that HCFA had rescinded or revoked its approval, or discontinue the action within a reasonable "wind down" period, as determined by HCFA.

§ 411.384 Disclosing Advisory Opinions and Supporting Information.

(a) Advisory opinions that HCFA issues and releases in accordance with the procedures set forth in this subpart are available to the public.

(b) Promptly after HCFA issues an advisory opinion and releases it to the requestor, HCFA makes available a copy of the advisory opinion for public inspection during its normal hours of operation and on the DHHS/HCFA web site.

(c) Any predecisional document, or part of such predecisional document, that is prepared by HCFA, the Department of Justice, or any other Department or agency of the United States in connection with an advisory opinion request under the procedures set forth in this part is exempt from disclosure under 5 U.S.C.A. 552, and will not be made publicly available.

(d) Documents submitted by the requestor to HCFA in connection with a request for an advisory opinion are available to the public to the extent they are required to be made available by 5 U.S.C.A. 552, through procedures set forth in 45 CFR part 5.

(e) Nothing in this section limits HCFA's obligation, under applicable laws, to publicly disclose the identity of the requesting party or parties, and the nature of the action HCFA has taken in response to the request.

§ 411.386 HCFA's Advisory Opinions as Exclusive.

The procedures described in this subpart constitute the only method by which any individuals or entities can obtain a binding advisory opinion on the subject of a physician's referrals, as described in § 411.370. HCFA has not and does not issue a binding advisory opinion on the subject matter in § 411.370, in either oral or written form, except through written opinions it issues in accordance with this subpart.

§ 411.387 Parties Affected by Advisory Opinions.

An advisory opinion issued by HCFA does not apply in any way to any individual or entity that does not join in the request for the opinion. Individuals or entities other than the requestor(s) may not rely on an advisory opinion.

§ 411.388 When Advisory Opinions are not Admissible Evidence.

The failure of a party to seek or to receive an advisory opinion may not be introduced into evidence to prove that the party either intended or did not intend to violate the provisions of sections 1128, 1128A or 1128B of the Act.

§ 411.389 Range of the Advisory Opinion.

(a) An advisory opinion states only HCFA's opinion regarding the subject matter of the request. If the subject of an advisory opinion is an arrangement that must be approved by or is regulated by any other agency, HCFA's advisory opinion cannot be read to indicate HCFA's views on the legal or factual issues that may be raised before that agency.
(b) An advisory opinion that HCFA issues under this part does not bind or obligate any agency other than the Department. It does not affect the requestor's, or anyone else's, obligations to any other agency, or under any statutory or regulatory provision other than that which is the specific subject matter of the advisory opinion.

(Catalog of Federal Domestic Assistance Program No. 93.773, Medicare—Hospital Insurance; and Program No. 93.774, Medicare— Supplementary Medical Insurance Program)

Dated: December 2, 1997.

Nancy-Ann Min DeParle,

Administrator, Health Care Financing Administration.

Dated: December 30, 1997.

Donna E. Shalala,

Secretary.

[FR Doc. 98–270 Filed 1–5-98; 8:45 am]

BILLING CODE 4120-01-P

APPENDIX F16

HCFA Final Rule: Medicare and Medicaid Programs; Physicians' Referrals to Health Care Entities With Which They Have Financial Relationships

DEPARTMENT OF HEALTH AND HUMAN SERVICES
Health Care Financing Administration
42 CFR Parts 411 and 424
[HCFA-1809-FC]
RIN 0938-AG80

AGENCY: Health Care Financing Administration (HCFA), HHS.

ACTION: Final rule with comment period.

SUMMARY: This final rule with 90-day comment period (Phase I of this rulemaking) incorporates into regulations the provisions in paragraphs (a), (b), and (h) of section 1877 of the Social Security Act (the Act). Under section 1877, if a physician or a member of a physician's immediate family has a financial relationship with a health care entity, the physician may not make referrals to that entity for the furnishing of designated health services (DHS) under the Medicare program, unless an exception applies. The following services are DHS: clinical laboratory services; physical therapy services; occupational therapy services; radiology services, including magnetic resonance imaging, computerized axial tomography scans, and ultrasound services; radiation therapy services and supplies; durable medical equipment and supplies; parenteral and enteral nutrients, equipment, and supplies; prosthetics, orthotics, and prosthetic devices and supplies; home health services; outpatient prescription drugs; and inpatient and outpatient hospital services.

In addition, section 1877 of the Act provides that an entity may not present or cause to be presented a Medicare claim or bill to any individual, third party payer, or other entity for DHS furnished under a prohibited referral, nor may we make payment for a designated health service furnished under a prohibited referral.

Paragraph (a) of section 1877 of the Act includes the general prohibition. Paragraph (b) of the Act includes exceptions that pertain to both ownership and compensation relationships, including an in-office ancillary services exception. Paragraph (h) includes definitions that are used throughout section 1877 of the Act, including the group practice definition and the definitions for each of the DHS.

We intend to publish a second final rule with comment period (Phase II of this rulemaking) shortly addressing, to the extent necessary, the remaining sections of the Act. Phase II of this rulemaking will address comments concerning the ownership and investment exceptions in paragraphs (c) and (d) and the compensation exceptions in paragraph (e) of section 1877 of the Act. Phase II of this rulemaking will also address comments concerning the reporting requirements and sanctions provided by paragraphs (f) and (g) of the Act, respectively, and include further consideration of the general exception to the referral prohibition related to both ownership/investment and compensation for services furnished in an ambulatory surgical center (ASC), end-stage renal dialysis facility, or by a hospice in Sec. 411.355(d) of the regulations (this exception presently is in force and effect as to clinical laboratory services). In addition, Phase II of this rulemaking will address section 1903(s) of the Act, which extends aspects of the referral prohibition to the Medicaid Program. Phase II will also address comments received in response to this rulemaking, as appropriate, and certain proposals for new exceptions to section 1877 of the Act not included in the 1998 proposed rulemaking, but suggested in the public comments.

DATES: Effective date: The regulations delineated in Phase I of this rulemaking are effective on January 4, 2002 except for Sec. 424.22(d), which is effective on February 5, 2001.

Comment date: We will consider comments if we receive them at the appropriate address, as provided below, no later than 5 p.m. on April 4, 2001.

ADDRESSES: Mail written comments (one original and three copies) to the following address only: Health Care Financing Administration, Department of Health and Human Services, Attn: HCFA-1809-FC, P.O. Box 8013, Baltimore, MD 21244–8013.

Since comments must be received by the date specified above, please allow sufficient time for mailed comments to be received timely in the event of delivery delays. If you prefer, you may deliver your written comments (one original and three copies) by courier to one of the following addresses: Room 443-G, Hubert H. Humphrey

Building, 200 Independence Avenue, SW., Washington, DC 20201, or C5–15–03, Central Building, 7500 Security Boulevard, Baltimore, MD 21244–1850. Comments mailed to the two addresses provided in this paragraph may be delayed and received too late to be considered.

Because of staffing and resource limitations, we cannot accept comments by facsimile (FAX) transmission. In commenting, please refer to file code HCFA-1809-FC.

Comments received timely will be available for public inspection as they are received, generally beginning approximately 3 weeks after publication of a document, in Room 443-G of the Department's offices at 200 Independence Avenue, SW., Washington, DC 20201, on Monday through Friday of each week from 8:30 a.m. to 5 p.m. (phone: (202) 690–7890).

Copies: To order copies of the **Federal Register** containing this document, send your request to: New Orders, Superintendent of Documents, P.O. Box 371954, Pittsburgh, PA 15250–7954. Specify the date of the issue requested and enclose a check or money order payable to the Superintendent of Documents, or enclose your Visa or Master Card number and expiration date. Credit card orders can also be placed by calling the order desk at (202) 512–1800 or by faxing to (202) 512–2250. The cost for each copy is $8. As an alternative, you can view and photocopy the **Federal Register** document at most libraries designated as Federal Depository Libraries and at many other public and academic libraries throughout the country that receive the **Federal Register**.

FOR FURTHER INFORMATION CONTACT: Joanne Sinsheimer, (410) 786–4620.

SUPPLEMENTARY INFORMATION: This **Federal Register** document is also available from the **Federal Register** online database through GPO Access, a service of the U.S. Government Printing Office. Free public access is available on a Wide Area Information Server (WAIS) through the Internet and via asynchronous dial-in. Internet users can access the database by using the World Wide Web; the Superintendent of Documents home page address is http://www.access.gpo.gov/nara_docs/, by using local WAIS client software, or by telnet to swais.access.gpo.gov, then login as guest (no password required). Dial-in users should use communications software and modem to call (202) 512–1661; type swais, then login as guest (no password required).

At the time that we forward our regulations and notices to the Office of the **Federal Register** (OFR) for publication, we announce them on our Internet website (http://www.hcfa.gov/regs/regsnotices.htm) as a service to the public. We began providing this service on May 30, 2000. We note that the OFR may make minor editorial changes to a document before publishing it. While we provide a document on our website, the document that we publish in the **Federal Register** is the official HCFA publication.

To help readers locate information in this final rule, we are providing the following Table of Contents:

I. Background

A. Legislative and Regulatory History

1. Section 1877 of the Act

Section 6204 of the Omnibus Budget Reconciliation Act of 1989 (Pub. L. 101–239) (OBRA 1989), enacted on December 19, 1989, added section 1877 to the Act. Section 1877 of the Act prohibited a physician from referring a patient to an entity for clinical laboratory services for which Medicare might otherwise pay, if the physician or the physician's immediate family member had a financial relationship with the entity. The statute defined "financial relationship" as an ownership or investment interest in the entity or a compensation arrangement between the physician (or the physician's immediate family member) and the entity. The statute provided for several exceptions to the prohibition. Some applied to ownership/investment interests and compensation arrangements; others applied only to ownership/investment interests or only to compensation arrangements.

The statute further prohibited an entity from presenting or causing to be presented a Medicare claim or bill to any individual, third party payer, or other entity for clinical laboratory services furnished under a prohibited referral. Additionally, the statute mandated refunding any amount collected under a bill for an item or service furnished under a prohibited referral. Finally, the statute imposed reporting requirements and provided for sanctions, including civil monetary penalty provisions. Section 1877 of the Act became effective on January 1, 1992.

Section 4207(e) of the Omnibus Budget Reconciliation Act of 1990 (Pub. L. 101–508) (OBRA 1990), enacted on November 5, 1990, amended certain provisions of section 1877 of the Act to clarify definitions and reporting requirements relating to physician ownership and referral and to provide an additional exception to the prohibition.

Several subsequent laws further changed section 1877 of the Act. Section 13562 of the Omnibus Budget Reconciliation Act of 1993 (Pub. L. 103–66) (OBRA 1993), enacted on August 10, 1993, expanded the referral prohibition to cover 10 "designated health services," in addition to clinical laboratory services, modified some of the existing statutory exceptions, and added new exceptions. Section 152 of the Social Security Act Amendments of 1994 (SSA 1994) (Pub. L. 103–432), enacted on October 31, 1994, amended the list of designated services, effective January 1, 1995, changed the reporting requirements at section 1877(f) of the Act, and modified some of the effective dates established by OBRA 1993. Some provisions relating to referrals for clinical laboratory services were effective retroactively to January 1, 1992, while other provisions became effective on January 1, 1995.

2. Section 1903(s) of the Act

Title XIX of the Act established the Medicaid program to provide medical assistance to individuals who meet certain income and resource requirements. The States operate Medicaid programs in accordance with Federal laws and regulations and with a State plan that we approve. Though States administer the Medicaid programs, the Federal and State governments jointly finance them. We call the Federal government's share of medical assistance expenditures "Federal financial participation" (FFP).

Until OBRA 1993, there were no statutory or regulatory requirements affecting a physician's referrals for services covered under the Medicaid program. Section 13624 of OBRA 1993, entitled "Application of Medicare Rules Limiting Certain Physician Referrals," added a new paragraph (s) to section 1903 of the Act, that extends aspects of the Medicare prohibition on physician referrals to Medicaid. This provision bars FFP in State expenditures for DHS furnished to an individual based on a physician referral that would result in a denial of payment for the services under the Medicare program if Medicare covered the services to the same extent and under the same terms and conditions as under the State Medicaid plan. The statute also made certain reporting requirements in section 1877(f) of the Act and a civil monetary penalty provision in section 1877(g)(5) (related to the reporting requirements) applicable to providers of DHS for which payment may be made under Medicaid in the same manner as they apply to providers of such services for which payment may be made under Medicare. Section 1903(s) of the Act applies to a physician's referrals made on or after December 31, 1994.

B. Regulations History

1. Regulations Published by HCFA and the Office of the Inspector General (OIG) Relating to Section 1877 of the Act

The following is a summary of the series of regulations we have published in the **Federal Register** over the past several years to implement the provisions of section 1877 of the Act, as amended, and section 1903(s) of the Act:

On December 3, 1991, we issued an interim final rule with comment period (54 FR 61374) to set forth the reporting requirements under section 1877(f) of the Act.

On March 11, 1992, we issued a proposed rule (57 FR 8588) to implement the self-referral prohibition and exceptions related to referrals for clinical laboratory services established by section 1877 of the Act, and amended by OBRA 1990.

On August 14, 1995, we issued a final rule with comment period (60 FR 41914) incorporating the provisions of OBRA 1993 and SSA

1994 that relate to referrals for clinical laboratory services under section 1877 of the Act, effective January 1, 1992, and revising the March 11, 1992 proposal based on the public comments we received.

On January 9, 1998, we issued a proposed rule (63 FR 1659) to amend the provisions of the August 1995 final rule and to reflect other changes in section 1877 of the Act enacted by OBRA 1993 and SSA 1994 that were effective January 1, 1995. These include, among other changes, the expansion of the referral prohibition to the 10 additional DHS, and the Medicaid expansion.

On January 9, 1998, we published a final rule with comment period (63 FR 1846) incorporating into our regulations the specific procedures we will use to issue advisory opinions, as required under section 1877(g)(6) of the Act. Section 1877(g)(6) of the Act requires that we issue written advisory opinions to outside parties concerning whether the referral of a Medicare patient by a physician for DHS (other than clinical laboratory services) is prohibited under section 1877 of the Act.

We also note that on October 20, 1993, the OIG published a proposed rule (58 FR 54096) to implement the civil money penalty provisions under sections 1877(g)(3) and (g)(4) of the Act. The OIG followed with publication of a final rule with comment period (60 FR 16580) on March 31, 1995.

2. Details About Prior Related Regulations

On August 14, 1995, we published in the **Federal Register** a final rule with comment period (60 FR 41914) that incorporated into regulations the provisions of section 1877 of the Act prohibiting physician referrals for clinical laboratory services under the Medicare program. That rule incorporated certain expansions and exceptions created by OBRA 1993, and the amendments in SSA 1994. It included only the expansions and other changes that related to prohibited referrals for clinical laboratory services that were retroactively effective to January 1, 1992, and interpreted the new provisions only in a few limited instances in which it was essential to implement the law. That rule also included our responses to the public comments we received on both the December 3, 1991 interim final rule with comment period (56 FR 61374) that established the reporting requirements under section 1877(f) of the Act, and the March 11, 1992 proposed rule (57 FR 8588) that covered section 1877 of the Act, as amended by OBRA 1990, and related to referrals for clinical laboratory services.

Because the August 1995 rule addressed only those changes made by OBRA 1993 and SSA 1994 that had a retroactive effective date of January 1, 1992, we explained our intent to later publish a proposed rule to fully implement the extensive revisions to section 1877 of the Act made by OBRA 1993 and SSA 1994, and to interpret those provisions when necessary. In the later proposed rule, we intended to include the revisions that relate to referrals for the additional DHS (including clinical laboratory services) that became effective January 1, 1995, and to implement the Medicaid expansion in section 1903(s) of the Act that became effective for referrals made on or after December 31, 1994.

As intended, on January 9, 1998, we published the proposed rule (63 FR 1659). The rule was organized as follows: In section I (63 FR 1661 through 1663), we summarized the problems associated with physician self-referrals and the relevant legislative and regulatory background. In section II (63 FR 1663 through 1673), part A, we summarized the provisions of our proposed rule and described how we proposed to alter the final regulation covering referrals for clinical laboratory services to apply it to the additional DHS and to reflect the statutory changes in section 1877 of the Act that were effective on January 1, 1995. In section II, part B, we described the changes we proposed to make to the Medicaid regulations to incorporate section 1903(s) of the Act. In section III (63 FR 1673 through 1705), we discussed in detail how we proposed to interpret any provisions in sections 1877 and 1903(s) of the Act that we believed were ambiguous, incomplete, or that provided us with discretion. We also discussed policy changes or clarifications we proposed to make to the August 1995 rule covering referrals for clinical laboratory services. Section IV (63 FR 1705 through 1715) of the proposed rule included our responses to some of the most common questions concerning physician referrals that we received from physicians, providers, and others in the health care community. We included our interpretations of how the law applies in the situations described to us. Section V (63 FR 1715 through 1719) included a Regulatory Impact Analysis, and section VI (63 FR 1719 through 1720) covered our policy on responding to comments. The proposed regulation text appeared at 63 FR 1720 through 1728.

In the January 1998 proposed rule, we proposed to incorporate the Medicaid expansion in section 1903(s) of the Act into Sec. 435.1012(a) (Limitation to FFP related to prohibited referrals). Section 435.1012(a) stated that no FFP was available for a State's expenditures for certain DHS, as they are defined in proposed Sec. 411.351, furnished to an individual under the State plan. No FFP is available if the services are those furnished on the basis of a physician referral that would, if Medicare provided for coverage of the services to the same extent and under the same terms and conditions as under the State plan, result in the denial of Medicare payment for the services under Secs. 411.351 through 411.360. In Sec. 435.1012(c), we included a cross reference to the procedures we established for individuals or entities to request advisory opinions from us on whether a physician's referrals relating to DHS (other than clinical laboratory services) are prohibited under section 1877 of the Act. Although these advisory opinions were meant to reflect our interpretation of section 1877 of the Act, they can potentially affect FFP payments to States under the Medicaid program.

Section 1877(b)(3) of the Act excepts from the referral prohibition services furnished to enrollees of certain "prepaid" health plans; however, these exceptions extend only to services furnished to Medicare beneficiaries under Medicare contracts and demonstration projects. As a result, the exception for prepaid arrangements does not apply to physicians who wish to refer in the context of the Medicaid program. In order to give effect to this exception in the Medicaid context, we included, in the January 1998 proposed rule, in Sec. 435.1012(b) an exception for DHS furnished by managed care entities analogous to the Medicare entities excepted under section 1877(b)(3) of the Act. The new exception was meant to cover entities that provide services to Medicaid-eligible enrollees under contract with State Medicaid agencies and under certain demonstration projects. (We discussed these analogous entities in detail in the proposed rule at 63 FR 1697.)

To accommodate the Congress's subsequent creation of the Medicare+Choice (M+C) Program in the Balanced Budget Act of 1997 (Pub. L. 105–33) (BBA 1997), we included an amendment to the physician referral regulations as part of the June 26, 1998 interim final rule with comment period (63 FR 35066) establishing the M+C Program. We amended the final physician self-referral regulations covering referrals for clinical laboratory services by adding an exception in Sec. 411.355(c)(5) for services furnished to prepaid enrollees by a coordinated care plan. We defined a coordinated care plan as such a plan, within the meaning of section 1851(a)(2)(A) of the Act, offered by an organization in accordance with a contract with us under section 1857 of the Act and the M+C regulations. We are reprinting that provision in Phase I of this rulemaking.

II. Development of Phase I of This Final Rulemaking

A. Technical Explanation of Bifurcation of the Regulation

Phase I of this rulemaking implements subsections (a) and (b) of section 1877 of the Act, and related definitions, as applied to the Medicare program. We intend to issue Phase II of this rulemaking to cover the remainder of section 1877 of the Act, including its application to the Medicaid program, shortly.

Phase I of This Rulemaking

Given the importance of subsections (a) and (b), and the substantial changes we are making to the January 1998 proposed rule, we are proceeding with the issuance of Phase I of this rulemaking at this time. Further, we are issuing Phase I for comment and delaying its effective date for 1 year to allow individuals and entities engaged in business arrangements affected by Phase I time to restructure those arrangements to comply with the provisions of Phase I, except for Sec. 424.22(d), which is effective February 5, 2001. The statutory provisions interpreted by Phase I remain in effect, as they have been since 1989 for clinical laboratory services and 1993 for all other DHS.

Phase I of this rulemaking differs substantially from the January 1998 proposed rule in several major respects, which include the following:

Clarification of the definitions of DHS.

Clarification of the concept of "indirect financial relationship" and creation of a new exception for indirect compensation arrangements.

Substantial broadening of the in-office ancillary services exception by easing the criteria for qualifying as a group practice and conforming the supervision requirements to HCFA coverage and payment policies for the specific services.

Expansion of the in-office ancillary services exception to cover certain DME provided in physicians' offices to patients to assist them in ambulating, and blood glucose monitors.

Allowance of shared facilities in the same building where physicians routinely provide services that are in addition to Federal and private pay DHS.

Exclusion of services personally performed by the referring physician from the definition of "referral."

Creation of a new exception for compensation of faculty in academic medical centers.

Addition of a new "risk-sharing" exception for commercial and employer-sponsored managed care plans.

Interpretation of the "volume or value" standard for purposes of section 1877 of the Act as permitting unit of service or unit of time-based payments, so long as the unit of service or unit of time-based payment is fair market value and does not vary over time. (The details of these and other changes are explained at length in section VI of this preamble.)

Creation of an exception where DHS are furnished by entities that did not know of or have reason to suspect the identity of the referring physician.

In developing Phase I of this rulemaking, we have carefully reconsidered the January 1998 proposed rule given both the history and structure of section 1877 of the Act and the extensive comments we received on the January 1998 proposed regulation. We believe that Phase I of this rulemaking addresses many of the industry's primary concerns, is consistent with the statute's goals and directives, and protects beneficiaries of Federal health care programs.

Our paramount concern is to implement section 1877 of the Act consistent with congressional intent. Prior to enactment of section 1877, there were a number of studies, primarily in academic literature, that consistently found that physicians who had ownership or investment interests in entities to which they referred ordered more services than physicians without those financial relationships (some of these studies involved compensation as well). Increased utilization occurred whether the physician owned shares in a separate company that provided ancillary services or owned the equipment and provided the services as part of his or her medical practice. This correlation between financial ties and increased utilization was the impetus for section 1877 of the Act.

The approach chosen by the Congress in enacting section 1877 of the Act is preventive because it essentially prohibits many financial arrangements between physicians and entities providing DHS. Specifically, section 1877 of the Act imposes a blanket prohibition on the submission of Medicare claims (and payment to the States of FFP under the Medicaid program) for certain DHS when the service provider has a financial relationship with the referring physician, unless the financial relationship fits into one of several relatively specific exceptions. Significantly, no wrongful intent or culpable conduct is required. The primary remedy is simply nonpayment by the program, without penalties. In other words, the basic remedy is recoupment of overpayments by the program. (Of course, wrongful conduct, such as knowingly submitting a claim in violation of the prohibition, can be punished through recoupment of overpayments and imposition of penalties, the False Claims Act, and other Federal statutory and common law remedies.)

The effect of this statutory scheme is that failure to comply with section 1877 of the Act can have a substantial financial result. For example, if a hospital has a $5,000 consulting contract with a surgeon and the contract does not fit in an exception, every claim submitted by the hospital for Medicare beneficiaries admitted or referred by that surgeon is not payable, since all inpatient and outpatient hospital services are DHS.

While the statutory scheme of the physician self-referral prohibition is, in large part, the key to its effectiveness, it obligates us to proceed carefully in determining the scope of activities that are prohibited. In Phase I of this rulemaking, we have attempted to minimize the impact of the rule on many common physician group governance and compensation arrangements.

The potential impact of the regulation was further confirmed by the voluminous comments we received from the public and health care community in response to the January 1998 proposed rule. In addition to specific complaints and objections about the January 1998 proposed rule, the commenters expressed several general concerns, which include the following:

The rule inappropriately intruded into the organization and delivery of medical care within physicians' offices.

The rule, in many respects, was counter to our other long-standing policies on coverage and similar issues.

The rule was unclear in many areas and that given the potentially serious consequences (for example, payment denial), "bright line" rules were essential.

Some aspects of the rule, such as its treatment of indirect financial relationships, were administratively impractical or would have been prohibitively costly in terms of monitoring compliance.

With these overall considerations in mind, we have developed several criteria for evaluating our regulatory options. First, we have tried in Phase I of this rulemaking to interpret the prohibitions narrowly and the exceptions broadly, to the extent consistent with the statutory language and intent. As a practical matter, we believe that, while the statute must be implemented to achieve its intent, we should be cautious in interpreting its reach so broadly as to prohibit potentially beneficial financial arrangements. Accordingly, we have tried to focus the regulation on financial relationships that may result in overutilization, which we believe was the main abuse at which the statute was aimed. Some provisions of the January 1998 proposed rule did not appear to address overutilization so much as other potential abuses, such as unfair competition. At the same time, we do not believe the Congress intended us to review every possible designated health service to determine its potential for overutilization. The Congress has already made that determination, and we believe that compliance with the exceptions in Phase I of this rulemaking should not cause undue disruption of the health care delivery system.

Second, a corollary of the above interpretation is that the Congress only intended section 1877 of the Act to establish a minimum threshold for acceptable financial relationships, and that potentially abusive financial relationships that may be permitted under section 1877 of the Act could still be addressed through other statutes that address health care fraud and abuse, including the anti-kickback statute (section 1128B(b) of the Act). In some instances, financial relationships that are permitted by section 1877 of the Act might merit prosecution under section 1128B(b) of the Act. Conversely, conduct that may be proscribed by section 1877 of the Act may not violate the anti-kickback statute.

Third, we have attempted to ensure that Phase I of this rulemaking will not adversely impact the medical care of Federal health care beneficiaries or other patients. In those instances in which we have determined that the provisions of Phase I of this rulemaking may impact current arrangements under which patients are receiving medical care, we have attempted to verify that there are other ways available to structure the arrangement so that patients could continue to receive the care in the same location. In almost all cases, we believe the provisions of Phase I of this rulemaking should not require substantial changes in delivery arrangements, although they may affect the referring physician's or group practice's ability to bill for the care. In other words, while the provisions of Phase I of this rulemaking may affect a physician's ability to profit financially from the provision of some services, there should be alternative providers available to provide the services in the same setting or alternative business structures that would permit the services to be provided (again, possibly without physician financial interest).

Fourth, we have revised the provisions of our January 1998 proposed rule to conform, as much as possible, to our other policies that affect the same or similar activity. For example, we are dropping the requirement that an in-office ancillary service be supervised under the strict "direct supervision" standards of the "incident to" billing rules in favor of requiring the level of supervision that is mandated under Medicare payment and coverage rules applicable to particular DHS.

Fifth, we have attempted, as much as possible, to establish "bright line" rules so that physicians and health care entities can ensure compliance and minimize administrative costs. We agree with the commenters that as a payment rule, the regulations implementing section 1877 of the Act should establish clear standards, and we have attempted to do so within the constraints of the statutory and regulatory scheme.

We believe Phase I of this rulemaking substantially addresses the concerns raised by the commenters and, yet, is consistent with the statute. Given the breadth of the statute and the myriad of financial relationships to which it applies, it is impossible to satisfy all concerns in all instances. We have attempted to read the statute narrowly to avoid adversely impacting potentially beneficial arrangements. However, we will continue to monitor financial arrangements in the health care industry and will revisit particular regulatory decisions if we determine there is abuse or overutilization.

B. General Comments Regarding the January 1998 Proposed Rule and Responses

Comment: Many commenters echoed the general views expressed by a major physician trade association. The trade association noted that section 1877 of the Act significantly impacts the manner in which physicians deliver health care services and the manner in which they relate to one another and to other health care providers. The trade association urged us to give physicians and other providers clear direction on how to structure their financial arrangements, while providing sufficient flexibility for physicians and providers practicing in numerous and varying arrangements throughout the health care industry. The trade association and other commenters expressed concern that the January 1998 proposed rule failed to reflect the fundamental changes occurring in the health care marketplace — especially the consolidation and integration of physician practices, hospitals, and other health care entities. Indeed, the commenters perceived the proposed regulations as hostile to those changes. The trade association and others believe that section 1877 of the Act and our regulations should focus on passive ownership and referral arrangements and not on partially and fully integrated practices demanded by the current competitive marketplace.

In addition, some commenters, including the trade association, thought that the provisions of the January 1998 proposed rule exceeded our statutory authority and imposed unnecessary and costly burdens on physicians that would harm patient access to health care facilities and services, with no apparent public benefit. In their view, the provisions of the January 1998 proposed rule (1) micro-managed physician practices in situations that do not pose a real potential for abuse, (2) limited proper and reasonable management practices, and (3) inappropriately interfered with the practice of medicine. Finally, a number of commenters suggested that, instead of promulgating a set of regulations that micro-manage the business of medicine, we could better control overutilization of DHS by monitoring the medical necessity of such services and the competency of those providing them.

Response: In developing Phase I of this rulemaking, we have been mindful of the criticism that the provisions of the January 1998 proposed rule inappropriately micro-managed physician practices. Given the purpose, structure, and scope of section 1877 of the Act, some impact on physician practices is inevitable and, frankly, intended. In Phase I of this rulemaking, we have endeavored to create "bright line" rules that are easily applied, while providing the health care industry with as much flexibility as possible. Where possible, we have tried to simplify the requirements in Phase I of this rulemaking, consistent with the clear congressional mandate to prohibit certain physician referrals tainted by physician financial self-interest. We believe Phase I of this rulemaking offers adequate flexibility to physician practices as they integrate and consolidate. For example, the revised unified business test, in the group practice definition, no longer bars cost-center or location-based distribution of a group practice's revenues from services that are not DHS. Another example: the in-office ancillary services exception covers certain ancillary services provided in facilities shared by practitioners in the same building in which they practice.

The provisions of Phase I of this rulemaking do not prevent physicians from directly providing their patients with convenient, cost-effective DHS. Consistent with the purpose of the statute, however, the provisions of Phase I of this rulemaking do restrict the circumstances under which physicians can financially benefit from DHS they order that are provided by others. This distinction is important. Section 1877 of the Act regulates the financial relationship between referring physicians and the provider of the DHS. If a physician determines not to provide access to such services in the absence of personal profit, the decision is the physician's, not the statute's. Nothing in section 1877 of the Act restricts patient access to those services.

Finally, we cannot agree with the claim that medical necessity reviews are always an effective control on overutilization. Medical necessity reviews alone cannot control unnecessary utilization and contain health care costs. These reviews are costly and only effective in controlling the most aberrant behavior. Most importantly, the statute does not permit us — nor would we choose — to override the Congress' judgement by substituting medical necessity reviews for existing statutory standards.

Comment: Other commenters expressed concern that neither the statute nor the January 1998 proposed rule goes far enough in preventing abusive referral arrangements. Several commenters complained that allowing physicians to provide ancillary services competitively disadvantages independent ancillary services providers that are not owned or controlled by physicians. These commenters believe that an obvious referral-for-profit scheme occurs when a physician employs his or her own ancillary personnel. While most commenters who expressed this view were independent ancillary services providers, one physician also complained about fellow physicians who "churn" patients through CT/MRI machines in their offices, resulting in what the commenter termed, a "cash spigot." The commenter expressed the view that such machines are not standard in a physician's office and are solely added to physicians' offices to generate profits. Commenters also expressed concern that, in some cases, physicians do not have appropriate oversight or credentialing for the ancillary services they provide. One commenter suggested that physicians should only be permitted to provide ancillary services if no other provider is available in the area.

Response: While we believe the commenters raised valid concerns about abuses in the health care system, the plain language of the statute makes clear that the Congress did not intend section 1877 of the Act to bar all physician-owned ancillary services facilities. To the contrary, these facilities are expressly allowed under certain specific circumstances (see sections 1877(b), (c), and (d) of the Act). Simply stated, the law is meant to prevent only the most egregious financial relationships; it does not address every potential act of fraud and abuse. As we caution throughout this preamble, section 1877 of the Act provides only a threshold check against fraud and abuse; many arrangements that are lawful under section 1877 of the Act may still violate other fraud and abuse laws, including the Federal anti-kickback statute (section 1128B(b) of the Act).

Comment: Several commenters believe that section 1877 of the Act and implementing regulations would not permit patients to receive services, such as x-rays, physical therapy, or crutches, at a physician's office or in a long term care facility where the patient resides. The commenters observed that requiring patients to seek services related to their diagnoses or treatment at several different locations is an inconvenience to patients and may require them to travel long distances to obtain services, thus, discouraging elderly or disabled patients from seeking needed health care services.

Response: The commenters misunderstand section 1877 of the Act. Section 1877 of the Act regulates financial relationships; it does not regulate the delivery of services. Section 1877 of the Act does not bar the provision of ancillary services in a physician's office, in a long term care facility, or at nearby, convenient locations. The law only imposes restrictions on a physician who makes a referral for a designated health service if he or she has a financial relationship with the ancillary services provider, such as an employment contract, an office space lease, or an ownership interest. Depending on the structure of the financial relationship, the physician may be able to profit from ordering ancillary services, thereby creating a risk that his or her orders may be motivated, in part, by personal financial considerations. Statutory and regulatory exceptions are designed to enable physicians to make ancillary services available on-site to their own patients, provided they meet the conditions set forth in the applicable exception. However, nothing in the law prevents physicians from making available convenient ancillary services when the physician has no financial interest in the provision of the services. For example, a physician may arrange for a diagnostic services provider to perform diagnostic tests in the physician's office for which the diagnostic services provider bills, provided that any rental arrangement meets the rental exception in Sec. 411.357(b) and does not violate the anti-kickback statute. Section 1877 of the Act reflects the Congress' unmistakable intent to recognize and accommodate the traditional role played by physicians in the delivery of ancillary services to their patients, while constraining the abuse of the public fisc that results when physician referrals are driven by financial incentives. These regulations reflect that policy balance.

Comment: One commenter stated that we had not informed Medicare beneficiaries about the potential restrictions on their access to care under section 1877 of the Act and its regulations, or informed Medicare providers about the potential restrictions on their ability to provide ancillary services.

Response: Once both Phase I and Phase II of this rulemaking are published, we intend to educate providers further about the new regulations. Providers have been on notice as to section 1877 of the Act since 1989 with respect to clinical laboratory services and 1993 with respect to all other DHS. We intend to provide general information to beneficiaries as well. However, we do not believe beneficiaries will face the restrictions on access that the commenters contemplate. Indeed, these regulations do not restrict the provision of services to Medicare beneficiaries. If a physician chooses not to make services available to patients if he or she cannot personally benefit financially from services he or she orders, but which are provided by others, the physician is responsible for restricting access. Finally, Phase I of this rulemaking is being, and Phase II of this rulemaking will be, published in the **Federal Register** and noted on the Department's website, which serves as notice to the affected community. We believe most providers will also be informed through their trade press, trade associations, and other sources.

Comment: Two commenters expressed concern that section 1877 of the Act and associated regulations would criminalize common conduct in physicians' offices.

Response: Section 1877 of the Act is a civil, not a criminal, statute. A violation of section 1877 of the Act results in nonpayment of claims and monetary sanctions. Criminal penalties or deprivation of liberty are not authorized by section 1877 of the Act.

Comment: Given the alleged complexity of the physician self-referral law and regulations and their impact on physicians' traditional business practices, several commenters requested that the effective date of the regulation be delayed to allow a reasonable time for physicians to familiarize themselves with the law and that the regulations be applied prospectively only. One commenter asked that we issue compliance guidelines. Another commenter inquired about penalties if physicians ignore the physician self-referral law.

Response: We agree with the commenters that the health care providers engaged in business arrangements affected by Phase I of this rulemaking may need time to restructure those arrangements to comply with Phase I of this rulemaking where it proscribes conduct not previously prohibited. We are, therefore, delaying the effective date of Phase I of this rulemaking for 1 year, except for Sec. 424.22(d), which is effective February 5, 2001. In the meantime, the statute, in its entirety, remains in full force and effect with respect to all DHS listed in section 1877(h)(6) of the Act. Until the effective date of these new final regulations, the August 1995 final rule covering referrals for clinical laboratory services remains in full force and effect with respect to clinical laboratory services referrals and claims for services. Any party or parties who do not comply with the provisions of the statute, the August 1995 final rule covering referrals for clinical laboratory services, or the provisions of Phase I of this rulemaking (when it becomes effective one year from the date of publication of this **Federal Register** notice) are subject to all applicable penalties and sanctions, including those that appear in section 1877(g) of the Act. (Section 1877(g)(3) and (g)(4) sanctions are covered in an OIG regulation that was published at 60 FR 16580 on March 31, 1995.)

Because of the significant changes we are making in Phase I of this rulemaking, we are publishing these regulations in final form with a 90-day comment period. We are interested in the industry's views as to the changes we have incorporated into these regulations. Any further changes we deem necessary based on comments will be addressed in Phase II of this rulemaking or shortly thereafter.

Regarding the issue of compliance guidelines, we often issue guidelines in the form of manual provisions or operational policy letters when we find that the statute and regulations do not address particular issues in sufficient detail.

Comment: A number of commenters objected to what they perceived as disparate treatment of solo and group practitioners. One commenter, for example, complained that under the proposed rule, a solo practitioner could provide, and keep the profits from, unlimited ancillary services provided to his or her patients, regardless of how much the physician self-refers in his or her own office, whereas a group practitioner could not.

Response: Certain disparities between the treatment of group and solo practitioners are inherent in the statutory language and structure. For example, the Congress expressly limited profit shares for group practice members to methodologies that do not directly take into account the member's DHS referrals. For obvious reasons, solo practitioners cannot be similarly limited. On the other hand, the statute allows group practices greater flexibility in terms of the locations where they can provide DHS to their patients and still come within the in-office ancillary services exception. To the extent possible, and consistent with the statute, we have tried in Phase I of this rulemaking to minimize the regulatory disparities between group and solo practitioners.

Comment: In noting that the January 1998 proposed regulation interpreted the statute to minimize any risk of fraud or abuse, several commenters stated that the marginal anti-fraud benefit of this approach is low because of additional post-1993 fraud and abuse legislation, the implementation of the anti-kickback statute, computer claims payment edits instituted by our carriers, and the creation of the National Practitioners Data Bank. The Health Insurance Portability and Accountability Act of 1996 (HIPAA) increased funding for Medicare program safeguards such as increased coordination between Federal, State, and local authorities; investigations, audits, and inspections; and guidance to the industry. HIPAA also established the Medicare Integrity Program to encourage private entities to engage in anti-fraud activities. The BBA in 1997 also created more severe criminal penalties for health care fraud. The commenters stated that the January 1998 proposed regulation prohibits many otherwise appropriate relationships in order to deter a small proportion of inappropriate practices. The commenters asked that the final rule be more flexible and not overcompensate for potential risks because the commenters believe that post-1993 legislation and enforcement efforts can address any inappropriate practices that may or may not be deterred by the physician self-referral law.

Response: As described above, the approach taken by the Congress in enacting section 1877 of the Act results in important differences between it and other anti-fraud and abuse measures, especially the criminal anti-kickback statute (section 1128B(b) of the Act). The laws are complementary and, although overlapping in some aspects, not redundant. We believe the Congress intended to create an array of fraud and abuse authorities to enable the government to protect the public fisc, beneficiaries of Federal programs, and honest health care providers from the corruption of the health care system by unscrupulous providers. We have revisited the January 1998 proposed rule in significant respects that minimize any unnecessary impact on providers.

Comment: A number of commenters objected to the inclusion in several of the proposed regulatory exceptions, such as the exception for fair market value transactions, of a requirement that the transaction be in compliance with the anti-kickback statute. According to the commenters, the two statutes are separate and, since the anti-kickback statute is intent-based, it would be impossible to determine with certainty whether a transaction meets the exceptions.

Response: We recognize that section 1877 of the Act and the anti-kickback statute, section 1128B(b) of the Act, are different statutes and compliance with one does not depend on compliance with the other in most situations. Notwithstanding, the Secretary's authority to create additional regulatory exceptions to section 1877 of the Act is limited by the requirement in section 1877(b)(4) that she determine that the excepted financial relationship "does not pose a risk of program or patient abuse." Section 1877 of the Act sets a minimum standard for acceptable financial relationships; many relationships that may not merit blanket prohibition under section 1877 of the Act can, in some circumstances and given necessary intent, violate the anti-kickback statute. If the requirement that a financial relationship comply with the anti-kickback statute were dropped, unscrupulous physicians and entities could potentially protect intentional unlawful and abusive conduct by complying with the minimal requirements of a regulatory exception created under section 1877(b)(4) of the Act. (By contrast, the statutory exceptions require no finding by the Secretary and, thus, carry no presumptive protection under the anti-kickback statute.) In addition, some arrangements may pose a risk of improper billing or claims submission.

As a practical matter, the statutory language authorizing exceptions leaves us two choices: (1) we can limit the exceptions to those situations that pose no risk of fraud or abuse — a very stringent standard that few, if any, of the proposed regulatory exceptions meet; or (2) we can protect arrangements that, in most situations, would not pose a risk, and rely on the anti-kickback statute or other fraud and abuse laws to address any residual risk. Given the commenters' expressed preference for flexibility, we have chosen the latter alternative. Moreover, since the parties should be in compliance with the anti-kickback statute, the additional regulatory burden is minimal. In the interest of simplification, we are considering an additional exception under section 1877 of the Act for any arrangement that fits squarely in an anti-kickback "safe harbor" (section 1001.952 (Exceptions)) and plan to address the matter further in Phase II of this rulemaking.

III. The General Prohibition Under Section 1877 of the Act

Section 1877(a) of the Act establishes the basic structure and elements of the statutory prohibition: A physician cannot (1) refer patients to an entity (2) for the furnishing of DHS (3) if there is a financial relationship between the referring physician (or an immediate family member of the referring physician) and the entity, (4) unless the financial relationship fits within one of the specific exceptions in the statute or regulations issued by the Secretary. (DHS are defined in Sec. 411.351 and discussed at length in section VIII.A of this preamble.) In this section, we discuss our interpretations of what constitutes a financial relationship, especially an indirect financial relationship, and what constitutes a referral, including an indirect referral.

Existing Law: Subject to certain exceptions, section 1877(a)(1) of the Act prohibits a physician from making a referral to an entity for the furnishing of DHS for which Medicare would otherwise pay, if the physician (or an immediate family member) has a financial relationship with the DHS entity, and prohibits the DHS entity from billing Medicare or any individual (including, but not limited to, the beneficiary), third party payer, or other entity for those services. A financial relationship is (i) either an ownership or investment interest in the DHS entity (or in another entity that holds an ownership or investment interest in the entity) or (ii) a compensation arrangement with the DHS entity, either directly or indirectly. An ownership or investment interest may exist through equity, debt, or other means.

As defined by section 1877(h)(5) of the Act, a "referral" means a request by a physician for an item or service for which payment may be made under Medicare Part B, including a request for a consultation (including any tests or procedures ordered or performed by the consulting physician or under the supervision of the consulting physician), and the request or establishment of a plan of care by a physician that includes the furnishing of DHS, with certain exceptions for consultations by pathologists, diagnostic radiologists, and radiation oncologists.

Proposed Rule: In general, we proposed interpreting the concept of "indirect financial relationship" very broadly. In the January 1998 proposed rule, we proposed including within the reach of section 1877 of the Act any ownership or investment interest, including ownership or investment interests through intermediate entities, no matter how indirect, and we proposed to include indirect compensation relationships by tracing compensation paid by an entity furnishing DHS through other entities, regardless of how the compensation might be transformed.

We similarly proposed a broad interpretation of the phrase "referral to an entity." As defined in the statute, a referral is a "request" by a physician for a DHS. We proposed defining a "request" as any step taken after a physician performs an initial examination or a physician service on a patient that indicates that the physician believes the DHS is necessary. Under this broad reading, a referral could be either written or oral, made on medical charts or records, or indicated by a prescription or written order. We also proposed that a referral could be direct or indirect, meaning that a physician would be considered to have made a referral if he or she caused the referral to have been made by someone else (for example, an employee, a hospital discharge planner, or a staff member of a company that the physician owns or controls). We interpreted "referrals" to include DHS services subsequently performed by the referring physician.

The Final Rule: Given the significance of the general prohibition, we received many comments related to various aspects of the January 1998 proposed rule. In particular, commenters sought clarification of fundamental statutory concepts, including direct and indirect compensation and ownership or investment arrangements. In addition, many commenters took issue with our interpretation of several of the key terms, including "referral," "consultation," and "furnishing."

We are making a number of significant changes to the general prohibition sections in Phase I of this rulemaking. These revisions include the following:

Clarification as to what constitutes a "direct" versus an "indirect" financial arrangement, including the addition of a "knowledge" element for indirect financial relationships.

Creation of a new exception for indirect compensation arrangements.

Clarification that payment obligations that are secured, including those secured by a revenue stream, are among the relationships considered to be ownership or investment interests.

Revision of the definition of "referral" to exclude services personally performed by the referring physician.

Creation of an exception under section 1877 of the Act for entities submitting claims for DHS that did not know of and did not have reason to suspect the identity of the physician who made the DHS referral to the entity.

These changes are discussed in greater detail below. First, we address the definition of a "financial relationship;" second, we address the definition of "referral." These two aspects of the general prohibition under section 1877 of the Act are analytically distinct and require separate analyses. In general, we believe a sensible approach is to ask two questions: (1) Is there a direct or indirect financial relationship between the referring physician and the entity furnishing DHS? (2) Is there a referral for DHS from the physician to the entity? If the answer to both questions is affirmative, section 1877 of the Act is violated, unless an exception applies.

A. When Is There a Financial Relationship Between the Physician and the Entity?

The existence of a financial relationship between the referring physician (or an immediate family member) and the entity furnishing DHS is the factual predicate for triggering the application of section 1877 of the Act. Section 1877(a)(2) defines a financial relationship as: (1) An ownership or investment interest of a referring physician (or immediate family member) in the entity furnishing DHS, or (2) a compensation arrangement between the referring physician (or an immediate family member) and the entity furnishing DHS. Any financial relationship between the referring physician and the DHS entity triggers application of the statute, even if the financial relationship is wholly unrelated to a designated health service payable by Medicare. In many instances, the financial relationship will not relate to DHS. Unless the financial relationship fits into a statutory or regulatory exception, however, referrals for DHS are prohibited.

The statute expressly contemplates that "financial relationships" include both direct and indirect ownership and investment interests and direct and indirect compensation arrangements between referring physicians and DHS entities (sections 1877(a)(2) and 1877(h)(1) of the Act, respectively). We consider a "direct" financial relationship to be an arrangement between the entity furnishing DHS and a referring physician or immediate family member with no person or entity (other than agents) interposed between them. While some commenters inquired whether particular arrangements or relationships, such as stock options or vesting in retirement plans, could be characterized as ownership or compensation arrangements, there were no substantive comments as to the underlying definition of a direct financial relationship. The specific questions raised by the commenters are addressed in the comments and responses that follow.

With respect to "indirect" financial relationships, in the preamble to the January 1998 proposed rule, we proposed to include as an "indirect" financial relationship any ownership or investment interest, including ownership or investment interests through intermediate entities, no matter how indirect, and we proposed to include indirect compensation relationships by tracing compensation paid by an entity furnishing DHS through other entities, regardless of how the compensation might be transformed. In short, we proposed very broad interpretations of indirect financial relationships.

We have generally adopted the overall interpretations of "financial relationship" in the January 1998 proposed rule, with the important exception of "indirect" financial relationships. Many commenters objected to the discussions in the preamble to the January 1998 proposed regulations relating to indirect financial relationships on the grounds that the discussions were confusing, inconsistent, administratively impracticable, or unfair. We have responded to the commenters by substantially revising the regulations pertaining to indirect financial relationships, especially indirect compensation arrangements. As described in the paragraphs that follow, we have added a knowledge element to the definitions of "indirect" financial relationships. We have also made other significant changes in the treatment of indirect compensation arrangements.

Knowledge Element for Establishing the Existence of an Indirect Financial Arrangement

We are amending the definitions of (i) "indirect ownership or investment interest" and (ii) "indirect compensation arrangement" in Sec. 411.354 to include a knowledge element. Many commenters expressed concern that by extending liability for indirect financial relationships to relationships involving any number of intermediate persons or entities, the January 1998 proposed regulation imposed an unfair burden on entities furnishing DHS affirmatively to ferret out and discover potential indirect financial relationships or else risk submitting improper claims because of relationships they knew nothing about. While we believe that, in most circumstances, the referring physician (or his or her immediate family member) will only be one or two degrees of separation from the entity furnishing the DHS, we have nevertheless modified the January 1998 proposed regulation to add a "knowledge" element in cases of indirect financial relationships. This modification limits exposure under section 1877 of the Act to those circumstances in which the entity furnishing DHS has actual knowledge of an indirect financial relationship or acts in reckless disregard or deliberate ignorance as to the existence of an indirect financial relationship. (We sometimes refer to this "actual knowledge or reckless disregard or deliberate ignorance" standard in this preamble by the shorthand phrase "knows or has reason to suspect.") We define the "knowledge" element in a manner consistent with Federal law, as described below.

In order to satisfy this "knowledge" element in the case of an indirect ownership or investment interest, the DHS entity need only know or have reason to suspect that the referring physician (or immediate family member) has some ownership or investment interest in the entity furnishing the DHS (or in an entity that holds an ownership or investment interest in the DHS entity). Likewise, to satisfy this "knowledge" element in the case of an indirect compensation arrangement, the DHS entity need only know or have reason to suspect that the referring physician (or immediate family member) is receiving some aggregate compensation that varies with, or otherwise reflects, the volume or value of referrals or other business generated by the referring physician for the entity furnishing DHS. In other words, we are not requiring that the DHS entity have knowledge of every link in the chain of entities having financial relationships that connects the DHS entity to the referring physician (or immediate family member).

Specifically, we are providing that, in the case of indirect financial relationships, referrals will only be prohibited (and claims disallowed) if the DHS entity (i) has actual knowledge that the referring physician (or immediate family member) has an indirect financial relationship (that is, that the referring physician or immediate family member (a) has some ownership or investment interest in the DHS entity or (b) receives aggregate compensation that takes into account or otherwise reflects referrals or other business generated by the referring physician for the entity furnishing DHS), or (ii) acts in reckless disregard or deliberate ignorance of whether such an indirect financial relationship exists. Essentially, we are adopting a "knowledge" element comparable to the scienter standard in the Civil Monetary Penalty Law, section 1128A of the Act. This "knowledge" element generally imposes a duty of reasonable inquiry on providers. In the specific context of indirect financial relationships under section 1877 of the Act, we wish to make clear that, given the impracticability of investigating every possible indirect financial relationship involving a referring physician, the knowledge element does not impose an affirmative obligation to inquire as to indirect financial relationships. A duty of reasonable inquiry does require, however, that providers in possession of facts that would lead a reasonable person to suspect the existence of an indirect financial relationship take reasonable steps to determine whether such a financial relationship exists and, if so, whether that indirect financial relationship falls within an exception to the statute (such as the new exception for certain indirect compensation arrangements in Sec. 411.354) or whether the DHS being furnished fall within an exception (such as the in-office ancillary services exception) before submitting a claim for the referred item or service or making a referral. The reasonable steps to be taken will depend on the circumstances. Reasonable steps may include the DHS entity obtaining, in good faith, a good faith, written assurance from the referring physician (or immediate family member, as applicable) or the entity from which the referring physician (or immediate family member) receives direct compensation that the physician's or immediate family member's aggregate compensation is fair market value for services furnished and does not take into account or otherwise reflect referrals or other business generated by the referring physician for the DHS entity, so as to qualify under the new exception for certain indirect financial relationships in Sec. 411.354 (discussed below). A written assurance is not determinative, however, especially if the DHS entity has knowledge of, or reason to suspect, other, contradictory evidence or information.

The addition of a knowledge requirement as an element of an improper indirect financial relationship addresses the concerns expressed by many commenters that it would be impossible continuously to investigate and uncover indirect financial relationships of every referring physician and his or her immediate family members. While the "knowing" element we are adopting may allow more claims to be paid than a requirement that would interpret the statute to impose an absolute duty to investigate (and may impose a higher evidentiary burden on the government in an enforcement action), we believe that incorporating a knowledge element in the definition of indirect financial relationships more fairly balances the burden of compliance against the risk of abuse the statute was intended to prevent. We iterate that for purposes of section 1877 of the Act, the DHS entity has no affirmative duty to inquire or investigate whether an indirect financial relationship with a referring physician (or immediate family member) exists, absent some information that would put a reasonable person on alert, and that the duty that is imposed is one of reasonable inquiry in the circumstances.

Indirect Compensation Arrangements

We have substantially revised the January 1998 proposed regulations by restructuring our approach to indirect compensation arrangements. In the January 1998 proposed regulation, we had proposed to trace compensation paid by an entity furnishing DHS through any number of other persons or entities, regardless of how the compensation might be transformed. Many commenters complained that the examples provided in different parts of the preamble to the January 1988 proposed rule were inconsistent or unclear. Upon reviewing the comments and the preamble, we understand the commenters' confusion and have revised the provisions that apply to indirect compensation arrangements by:

Defining "indirect compensation arrangement" to establish a "bright line" test, including the "knowing" element described above; and

Creating a new exception under section 1877(b)(4) of the Act for certain indirect compensation arrangements that is generally consistent with the new "fair market value" exception for direct compensation arrangements.

This treatment of indirect compensation arrangements more clearly parallels the analysis and regulatory treatment of direct compensation arrangements by (i) defining the universe of financial relationships that potentially triggers disallowance of claims (that is, the definition of "indirect compensation arrangement"); and (ii) creating an exception for the subset of "indirect compensation arrangements" that will not trigger disallowance. The standards in the new exception for indirect compensation arrangements are based in large part on the standards found in the various statutory and proposed regulatory exceptions for direct compensation arrangements, especially the fair market value exception proposed in the January 1998 proposed regulations, which was received favorably by the commenters and has been incorporated into the final regulations in Sec. 411.354(d).

The definition of an "indirect compensation arrangement" and the new exception are discussed in detail below.

Definition of "Indirect Compensation Arrangement." We have developed a simple test to identify whether an indirect compensation relationship exists. We are adopting in Phase I of this rulemaking, a definition of "indirect compensation arrangement" that has three elements: (1) There must exist between the referring physician (or immediate family member) and the DHS entity an unbroken chain of persons or entities that have financial relationships between them (that is, each link in the chain has either an ownership or investment interest or compensation arrangement with the preceding link); (2) the aggregate compensation received by the referring physician (or immediate family member) from the person or entity in the chain with which the physician has a direct financial relationship varies with, or otherwise reflects, the volume or value of referrals or other business generated by the referring physician for the entity furnishing DHS; and (3) the DHS entity must have actual knowledge that the aggregate compensation received by the referring physician (or immediate family member) from the entity with which the physician has a direct financial relationship varies with, or otherwise reflects, the volume or value of referrals or other business generated by the referring physician for the entity furnishing DHS, or act in reckless disregard or deliberate ignorance of the existence of such relationship.

The first element of the indirect compensation arrangement definition is met if there is an unbroken chain of financial relationships from the DHS entity to the referring physician (or immediate family member), regardless of the form or purpose of the payments or their relationship to the DHS referrals. This element is relatively straightforward. The unbroken chain that creates an indirect compensation arrangement can consist of any combination of excepted or unexcepted financial relationships, whether ownership or investment interests or compensation arrangements.

One issue raised by several commenters was whether an ownership or investment interest could also create a compensation arrangement. An ownership or investment interest creates a direct compensation arrangement between the owner/investor and the owned/investment entity, since the ownership or investment establishes an arrangement for the distribution of any profits or other benefits (for example, tax benefits in the case of a pass-through entity) from the venture to the owners/investors. However, when the ownership or investment interest itself meets a specific statutory exception under section 1877 of the Act, any anticipated return on investment or other remuneration flowing from the ownership or investment is similarly excepted, provided the return or other remuneration is bona fide and not a sham (sham returns would include, for example, use of loan proceeds to make distributions in the absence of bona fide profits from the venture).

An excepted financial relationship may still constitute a link in a chain that establishes an indirect compensation arrangement between a referring physician and a DHS entity. For example, if a referring physician owns an interest in a hospital that meets the exception under section 1877(d)(3) of the Act (which allows a referring physician to own an interest in a hospital as a whole, but not in a subdivision of the hospital), and the hospital contracts for services with a clinical laboratory to which the physician refers, there would exist a chain of persons or entities having financial relationships between the referring physician and the DHS entity (referring physician whole hospital clinical laboratory), even though the financial relationship between the referring physician and the hospital fits in an exception. We address this issue further in the responses to comments that follow.

The second element of the definition of indirect compensation arrangement is that the aggregate compensation received by the referring physician (or immediate family member) from the person or entity in the chain with which the referring physician (or immediate family member) has a direct financial relationship varies with, or otherwise reflects, the value or volume of referrals or other business generated by the referring physician for the entity furnishing DHS. For the purpose of the definition of indirect compensation arrangements, we are looking at whether aggregate compensation in the direct financial relationship varies with, or otherwise reflects, the value or volume of referrals or other business generated by the referring physician for the entity furnishing DHS. Accordingly, for purposes of this element, any "per service" or "per use" payment arrangement between the physician and the person or entity with which the physician has the direct relationship that is based, in whole or in part, on referrals or other business generated for the DHS entity would satisfy this element. So too, any payment or other remuneration conditioned more generally on referrals or business generated for the DHS entity would satisfy this element of the definition of "indirect compensation arrangement," except as described in Sec. 411.354(d)(5) (describing limited circumstances when an entity may condition compensation on referrals). (For a discussion of Sec. 411.354(d)(5), see section V of this preamble).

If the financial arrangement between the physician (or immediate family member) and the person or entity in the chain with which the physician has the direct financial relationship is an ownership or investment interest, we will look at the relationship between that person or entity (that is, the "owned entity") and the next person or entity in the chain with which the owned entity has a direct financial relationship (if that financial relationship is also an ownership or investment interest, we will look to the next direct financial relationship in the chain, and so forth, until we reach a compensation arrangement with an "unowned" entity with which there is a compensation arrangement — a chain consisting entirely of owned entities is an indirect ownership or investment interest, not an indirect compensation arrangement). The inquiry then becomes whether the aggregate compensation the owned entity receives varies with, or otherwise reflects, the volume or value of referrals or other business generated by the referring physician for the entity furnishing DHS.

The third element in the definition of indirect compensation arrangement is that the entity furnishing DHS must know or have reason to suspect that the referring physician's (or immediate family member's) aggregate compensation varies with, or otherwise reflects, the value or volume of referrals or other business generated by the referring physician for the entity furnishing the DHS. As discussed above, reason to suspect a financial relationship will trigger a duty to make an inquiry into the relationship that is reasonable in the circumstances. In the context of indirect compensation arrangements, in most cases, the referring physician (or immediate family member) will have knowledge of the basis for his or her compensation and be in the best position to assure compliance with section 1877 of the Act. Thus, as noted above, reasonable inquiry by the DHS entity may include obtaining, in good faith, a good faith, written assurance from the referring physician (or immediate family member, as applicable) or the entity from which the referring physician (or immediate family member) receives direct compensation that the physician's or immediate family member's aggregate compensation falls within the indirect compensation arrangement exception in Sec. 411.354 (that is, the compensation is fair market value for services furnished and does not take into account or otherwise reflect referrals or other business generated by the referring physician for the DHS entity). As discussed below, we are creating a new exception for indirect compensation arrangements, for which we believe most nonabusive indirect compensation arrangements can readily qualify.

Exception for Indirect Compensation Arrangements. While the definition of an "indirect compensation arrangement" identifies the universe of potentially improper arrangements, we recognize that many of those indirect compensation arrangements may be substantially similar to direct compensation arrangements that fit in one of the existing statutory exceptions in section 1877 of the Act or one of the regulatory exceptions we proposed in January 1998. However, many of these indirect compensation arrangements cannot fit in those direct compensation arrangement exceptions, because the arrangements are with persons or entities that are not the person or entity furnishing DHS. Accordingly, we are creating a new exception, using the Secretary's authority under section 1877(b)(4) of the Act, to provide an exception for certain indirect compensation arrangements. The new exception would protect an indirect compensation arrangement if the following conditions are satisfied:

The compensation received by the referring physician (or immediate family member) from the person or entity in the chain with which the referring physician (or immediate family member) has the direct financial relationship is fair market value for the items or services provided under the arrangement and does not take into account the value or volume of referrals or other business generated by the referring physician for the entity furnishing DHS;

The compensation arrangement between the referring physician (or immediate family member) and the person or entity in the chain with which the physician (or immediate family member) has the direct financial relationship is set out in writing, signed by the parties, and specifies the services covered by the arrangement (in the case of a bona fide employment relationship, the arrangement need not be set out in a written contract, but it must be for identifiable services and be commercially reasonable even if no referrals are made to the employer);

The compensation arrangement does not violate the anti-kickback statute or any laws or regulations governing billing or claims submission.

Where the financial relationship between the physician and the person or entity with whom he or she has a direct financial relationship is an ownership or investment interest, we will apply the requirements of this exception to the first compensation arrangement in the chain of relationships between the physician and the entity furnishing DHS.

For purposes of the new exception, in determining whether compensation takes into account the value or volume of referrals or other business generated by the referring physician for the DHS entity, we will apply the tests for "volume or value of referrals" and "other business generated" that are discussed in section V of this preamble and set forth in Sec. 411.354(d) of these regulations. This is consistent with our determination to interpret those phrases uniformly in all exceptions in which they appear. Thus, "per service" or "per use" compensation arrangements can fit in the new exception for indirect compensation arrangements, provided the "per use" or "per service" payments are fair market value for the items or services provided (and do not include any additional amount that might be attributable to the volume or value of referrals or other business generated between the referring physician and the entity furnishing DHS) and the payments do not vary during the term of the compensation arrangement in any manner that takes into account referrals to the DHS entity.

Some of the statutory and regulatory exceptions operate to exclude certain categories of services from the reach of section 1877 of the Act, when certain criteria are satisfied. In effect, services described in these exceptions are not DHS for purposes of the statute. These service-based exceptions include the physicians' services exception, in-office ancillary services exception, prepaid plans exception, and academic medical center exception, in Sec. 411.355 of these regulations. Thus, even if there is an indirect compensation arrangement between a referring physician and an entity furnishing DHS, these exceptions may apply to referrals of the particular services described in the exception. Referrals of DHS that do not fit in a services-based exception would be prohibited unless the indirect compensation arrangement fits in the new exception for indirect compensation arrangements.

Finally, we are not adopting our interpretation in the January 1998 proposed rule with regard to common ownership or investment in the same entity (which is not the entity furnishing DHS) by the referring physician (or immediate family member) and the entity furnishing DHS. In the January 1998 proposed rule, we proposed that such common ownership would not create a compensation arrangement between the referring physician and the DHS entity. However, in the light of our modified and more limited definitions of indirect financial relationships, we have revisited the issue of common ownership. We believe that such relationships should be analyzed in the same manner as any indirect financial relationship.

We are also making the following changes in the general prohibition sections of the regulations:

Clarification that an ownership or investment interest in a subsidiary corporation will not be considered a direct ownership or investment interest in the parent or a sibling corporation. However, an owner of a subsidiary corporation may have an indirect financial relationship with the parent or sibling company that could trigger a violation of section 1877 of the Act.

Treatment of stock options as creating a compensation relationship and not an ownership interest until such time as the options are exercised.

Clarification that payment obligations that are secured, including those that are secured by a revenue stream, are considered ownership or investment interests.

In the following paragraphs, we address the specific comments we received on the discussion and proposed interpretations of financial relationships set out in the January 1998 proposed rule and our responses to them.

Comment: A number of commenters objected to the concept of "tracing" compensation from, and ownership or investment interests in, an entity furnishing DHS through any number of intermediate entities to a referring physician. According to these commenters, the administrative burden of trying to comply would be costly and ultimately impossible. These commenters believe that our proposed interpretation would place the entities furnishing the services, as well as physicians making referrals, at risk for what was unknowable given potentially complex business arrangements. One commenter suggested that we keep the same definition of financial relationship as the August 1995 final rule, which the commenter stated was limited to direct ownership and compensation arrangements.

Response: The commenter who suggested that the August 1995 final rule was limited to direct financial relationships is mistaken. In the August 1995 final rule, we defined financial relationship to include indirect financial relationships. We did not, however, expand on how we would interpret and apply the term "indirect." We believe that limiting the statutory prohibition to direct ownership and compensation arrangements would seriously weaken the statute. Unscrupulous physicians and entities furnishing DHS would simply interpose entities between themselves and funnel the money through them. Furthermore, as we stated in the preamble to the January 1998 proposed rule, the statute, by its terms, applies to indirect ownership and investment interests and compensation arrangements.

As discussed above, we have revised the treatment of indirect compensation arrangements. First, we are no longer requiring any tracing of payments. The initial screen is simply whether there is an unbroken chain of persons or entities having financial relationships between the referring physician (or an immediate family member) and the entity furnishing DHS, regardless of the nature of the payments or financial relationships. Second, we have limited liability to instances in which the DHS entity knows or has reason to suspect that aggregate compensation received by the referring physician (or immediate family member) varies with, or otherwise reflects, the volume or value of referrals or other business generated for the DHS entity. Finally, we have made clear that absent information that would put a reasonable person on alert, a DHS entity has no affirmative duty to inquire or investigate such arrangements.

Comment: A major trade association representing physicians (and other commenters) claimed that our explanations of how we would treat several types of situations involving indirect financial relationships appeared inconsistent. Specifically, the association referred to the example of a hospital contracting with a group practice to furnish physician services and to staff the hospital, and the hospital paying the group practice for these services, and with the group practice, in turn, compensating the physicians through salaries that "in some way" reflect the hospital services. According to the January 1998 proposed rule, the physicians would have an indirect compensation relationship with the hospital that would require an exception. The commenter complained that this position is inconsistent with another example in the preamble in which we stated that, when a physician who owned a physical therapy (PT) company referred patients for treatment including PT to a skilled nursing facility (SNF) that contracted with the physician's PT company, we would equate the physician with the PT provider.

Response: We believe the new provisions for indirect compensation arrangements address the commenters' concerns.

In the example cited by the commenter involving the payments by a hospital to a group practice that, in turn, pays its employees a salary, we would not require evidence that the salary is "in some way" related to the hospital payment. It is enough that the hospital has a financial relationship (that is, a personal services contract) with the medical group, which, in turn, has a financial relationship with its employees. Since there is an unbroken chain of financial relationships between the referring physician and the DHS entity, the first element in the indirect compensation definition is satisfied.

The second element of the definition of an indirect compensation arrangement would be satisfied if the aggregate compensation to the referring physician from the medical group varied with, or otherwise reflected, the volume or value of referrals or other business generated by the referring physician for the DHS entity (that is, the hospital) — a fact that should be relatively easy to establish.

The final element in the definition of an indirect compensation relationship requires that the hospital (that is, the DHS entity) (i) have actual knowledge or reason to suspect that the referring physician is receiving compensation from the medical group (that is, the entity in the chain with which the referring physician has a direct financial relationship) that varies with, or otherwise reflects, the volume or value of referrals or other business generated for the hospital.

Indirect compensation arrangements that do not fit in the new exception for such arrangements can be restructured or abandoned. Arrangements under which a referring physician receives compensation tied to the volume or value of his or her referrals or other business generated for a DHS entity are the very arrangements at which section 1877 of the Act is targeted.

Commenters claimed that our discussion at 63 FR 1710 in the preamble of the January 1998 proposed rule was confusing because of the way we described a physician's referrals to a SNF, which, in turn, referred the patients to a PT company in which the referring physician had an ownership interest and which billed Medicare directly for services to SNF patients. In that example, the referring physician had a direct financial relationship (ownership) with the PT company. There was no indirect financial relationship involving the SNF. Rather, the referring physician had a referral arrangement with the SNF, but not a financial relationship, and the SNF had a referral arrangement with the PT provider, but not a financial relationship. We think the issue in the example is whether, by sending patients to the SNF, the physician is making referrals to the PT provider, with which the physician has a direct financial relationship. We discuss that issue in the following section on referrals.

However, we think it useful to reconsider the example in light of consolidated billing for SNFs. (We note that consolidated billing should not be confused with composite rate payments. Consolidated billing is a process for submitting claims while composite rate payment constitutes a distinct payment methodology.) Under consolidated billing, the SNF in the example will be billing the PT services directly to Medicare. In this situation, there would be an indirect compensation relationship between the SNF—which is now the DHS entity—and the referring physician. Since the SNF would be purchasing PT services from the PT company owned by the referring physician, a financial relationship would exist between the SNF and the PT company, and the physician's ownership interest in the PT company would complete the chain (SNF PT company referring physician). Thus, the first element of the definition of an indirect compensation arrangement would be satisfied. With respect to the second element, the financial relationship between the referring physician and the person or entity in the chain with which the referring physician has a direct financial relationship (that is, the PT company) is an investment interest. Accordingly, we look to the compensation paid by the SNF to the owned entity (that is, the PT company) in order to see if the second element is satisfied. Since the PT company is compensated on a per service basis that reflects referrals by the referring physician to the SNF, the second element is met. Assuming knowledge on the part of the SNF, there would be an indirect compensation arrangement, and the issue becomes whether the indirect compensation arrangement satisfies the new exception for indirect compensation arrangements in Sec. 411.354.

Comment: Several commenters stated that when there is a chain of payments that begins with a payment by a provider of DHS to another entity controlled by it, the first payment outside the entities under common control should be the arrangement that has to meet an exception. For example, in looking at payments from a hospital to a physician group practice that is wholly owned by the hospital for hospital staffing and subsequent payments from the group to its employed physicians, the payments that would need to qualify for an exception are the payments to the employed physicians. One commenter proposed that when tracing indirect financial relationships, the inquiry should end any time a payment in the chain meets an exception.

Response: The first commenters' suggested approach is problematic because the "volume or value" standard for the employed physician's compensation is measured based on referrals to the physician's employer, the medical group. Applying the commenters' proposed test to the example, the medical group could pay the physician employees based on the volume and value of referrals and business generated for the hospital and still comply with the employment exception. Phase I of this rulemaking would require that the compensation to the physicians not vary with or otherwise reflect either referrals to the group (to comply with the employee exception) or referrals to, or other business generated for, the hospital (so that it does not qualify as an indirect compensation relationship). To the extent that the compensation paid to the physicians did vary based on referrals or other business generated for the hospital, the arrangement would still be protected if it complied with the new indirect compensation arrangements exception in Sec. 411.354.

We also considered, but ultimately rejected, the second commenter's proposal that the inquiry end any time a financial relationship fits in an exception. The fact that one financial arrangement meets an exception does not necessarily prevent the referring physician from receiving payments based on DHS referrals to a DHS entity. For example, if a person or entity owns both a group practice and a DHS entity, a compensation arrangement with a physician employee of the group practice could fit in an exception so long as it did not take into account referrals between the employee and the group practice. The exception would not, however, prevent the compensation arrangement from taking into account referrals or other business generated by the physician employee for the DHS entity.

Having considered the several views of the commenters, we believe that Phase I of this rulemaking strikes a balance that protects the Medicare program while limiting the reach of the regulation to abusive relationships. Under Phase I of this rulemaking, there would be an unbroken chain of financial relationships (the DHS entity the owner medical group referring physician). However, unless the compensation received by the employed physician varies with or otherwise reflects his or her referrals to, or other business generated for, the DHS entity, and the DHS entity has the requisite knowledge, there would not be an indirect compensation arrangement. If there were, the arrangement would have to meet an applicable exception.

Comment: One commenter asked whether there would be an indirect compensation arrangement if an employed physician refers patients for DHS to an entity that has an ownership or investment interest in the physician's employer.

Response: There may be an indirect compensation arrangement if a physician refers patients for DHS to an entity that has an ownership or investment interest in the physician's employer, since the physician would be referring to a DHS entity that has a financial relationship (ownership or investment) with an entity that has a financial relationship (compensation) with the physician. If the referring physician's compensation from his or her employer reflected DHS referrals or other business generated by the referring physician for the entity providing the DHS, and the DHS entity had actual knowledge or reason to suspect that the physician's aggregate compensation reflected the volume or value of referrals or other business for the DHS entity, there would be an indirect compensation arrangement. Unless the arrangement fit in the new indirect compensation arrangements or another exception, referrals to the entity would be prohibited.

Comment: Another commenter asked whether a physician's referrals would be prohibited in a situation involving a physician practice management company (PPMC). Specifically, the commenter asked about a referring physician who has an ownership or investment interest in a PPMC, which, in turn, controls a captive professional corporation (PC) through a web of legal agreements, including a long-term management contract. The physician refers patients for DHS to the captive professional corporation.

Response: In the scenario described by the commenter, there is very likely an indirect compensation arrangement, since the captive PC has a financial relationship with the PPMC (the management contract), which has a financial relationship (ownership or investment) with the referring physician. Since the financial relationship between the physician and the entity in the chain of financial relationships with which the physician has a direct financial relationship (that is, the PPMC) is an ownership or investment interest, we look to the compensation arrangement between the owned entity (that is, the PPMC) and the next entity in the chain, in this case, the captive PC, to determine whether the second element of the test for an indirect compensation arrangement is met. Accordingly, if the entity furnishing the DHS (the captive PC in this example) knows or has reason to suspect that the PPMC's compensation from the captive PC varies with, or otherwise reflects, the value or volume of the captive PC's business (and consequently varies, in the aggregate, based on the referring physician's DHS referrals to the captive PC), there would be an indirect financial relationship between the captive PC and the referring physician. Unless the indirect compensation arrangement fits in the new indirect compensation arrangements or another exception, the physician could not refer DHS to the captive PC, and the captive PC could not submit claims for those DHS referrals.

Comment: Several commenters objected to our proposal that a physician can receive indirect compensation through a nonprofit enterprise if the enterprise is controlled by an individual who is in a position to "influence" the physician's referrals. The example was the owner of a clinical laboratory who is also the director of research at a nonprofit research facility that could provide physician research grants in exchange for referrals to the laboratory.

Response: The issue is whether there is a prohibited indirect financial relationship between the DHS entity (the clinical laboratory) and the referring physician. Assuming there is a financial relationship between the owner of the clinical laboratory and the nonprofit research facility, there would be a chain of persons or entities with financial relationships (clinical laboratory research director not-for-profit referring physician), and the issues become (i) whether the aggregate amount of the research grants to the referring physician varies with, or otherwise reflects, the value or volume of referrals or other business generated by the referring physician for the clinical laboratory, (ii) whether the clinical laboratory knows of or has reason to suspect that the referring physician's aggregate compensation under the research grants varies with, or otherwise reflects, the volume or value of referrals or other business generated for the clinical laboratory, and (iii) if there is an indirect financial relationship, whether an exception applies. Of course, even if there is no financial relationship between the clinical laboratory and the nonprofit research facility, there could be a violation of the anti-kickback statute, section 1128B(b) of the Act, in the situation described in the comment.

Comment: Several commenters stated that compensation derived from an ownership or investment interest (for example, a return on an investment interest or a dividend) should not give rise to indirect compensation. To support this position, they referred to discussions in the preamble to the January 1998 proposed rule and in the preamble to the August 1995 final regulations, in which we stated that compensation derived from, or ancillary to, an investment interest that qualified for an investment exception under sections 1877 (b) through (d) of the Act would not also have to meet a compensation exception.

Response: We agree with the commenters that dividends or profit distributions from an ownership or investment interest that qualifies for an ownership or investment interest exception under sections 1877(b) through (d) of the Act do not also have to meet a separate compensation exception. In other words, the ownership and investment exceptions in the statute protect the ownership or investment interest and any corresponding return on the excepted investment. Our discussion in the preamble to the January 1998 proposed rule specifically referenced and clarified the August 1995 final rule preamble discussion, which was limited to the issue of whether distributions from an excepted investment interest (that is, an ownership or investment interest protected under sections 1877(b) through (d) of the Act) had to meet an additional exception for compensation arrangements. Nothing in either preamble discussion was intended to be interpreted as saying that any other ownership or investment interests (that is, ownership or investment interests that are not specifically excepted) are not compensation arrangements. We believe that an ownership or investment interest (including distributions from the interest) creates a compensation arrangement, as defined in section 1877(h)(1)(A) of the Act, between the owner/investor and the owned/investment entity and can be part of a chain of persons or entities having financial relationships that create an indirect compensation arrangement.

Without this interpretation, unscrupulous physicians could evade section 1877 of the Act by simply interposing a shell entity, which they own, between themselves and the DHS entity (which they do not own) and taking out the compensation as dividends. In short, they would simply launder the compensation through the shell investment entity.

Comment: Another commenter suggested that a loan and any interest payments should be treated as either ownership or compensation, but not both.

Response: We agree with the commenter. If a loan qualifies as a protected ownership or investment interest, the interest payments do not create a separate compensation arrangement. Accordingly, the interest payments need not satisfy a separate compensation exception.

Comment: A number of commenters asked that we clarify that an investment in a subsidiary that does not furnish DHS is not necessarily an ownership interest in the parent or a sibling corporation.

Response: An ownership or investment interest in a subsidiary company is neither an ownership or investment interest in the parent company, nor in any other subsidiary of the parent, unless the subsidiary company itself has an ownership or investment interest in the parent or such other subsidiaries. However, an owner of a subsidiary company may have an indirect financial relationship with the parent or sibling company that could trigger a violation of section 1877 of the Act.

Comment: One commenter objected to the suggestion in the preamble to the January 1998 proposed rule that an interest in a retirement plan might be treated as an ownership or investment interest. Another commenter stated that an unsecured loan that was subordinated to an entity's credit facility should not be treated as an ownership or investment interest.

(d) Proceeding commenced by State; contract term or written instructions of agency

In the case of a proceeding referred to in subsection (a) of this section that is commenced by a State, the head of the executive agency that awarded the covered contract involved in the proceeding may allow the costs incurred by the contractor in connection with such proceeding as reimbursable costs if the agency head determines, under regulations prescribed by such agency head, that the costs were incurred as a result of (1) a specific term or condition of the contract, or (2) specific written instructions of the agency.

(e) Amount; regulations; other proceedings

(1) Except as provided in paragraph (3), costs incurred by a contractor in connection with a criminal, civil, or administrative proceeding commenced by the United States or a State in connection with a covered contract may be allowed as reimbursable costs under the contract if such costs are not disallowable under subsection (a) of this section, but only to the extent provided in paragraph (2).

(2)(A) The amount of the costs allowable under paragraph (1) in any case may not exceed the amount equal to 80 percent of the amount of the costs incurred, to the extent that such costs are determined to be otherwise allowable and allocable under the single Government-wide procurement regulation issued pursuant to section 403(4)(a) of this title.

(B) Regulations issued for the purpose of subparagraph (A) shall provide for appropriate consideration of the complexity of procurement litigation, generally accepted principles governing the award of legal fees in civil actions involving the United States as a party, and such other factors as may be appropriate.

(3) In the case of a proceeding referred to in paragraph (1), contractor costs otherwise allowable as reimbursable costs under this subsection are not allowable if (A) such proceeding involves the same contractor misconduct alleged as the basis of another criminal, civil, or administrative proceeding, and (B) the costs of such other proceeding are not allowable under subsection (a) of this section.

(f) Definitions

allowable as reimbursable costs under a covered contract if the proceeding (1) relates to a violation of, or a failure to comply with a Federal or State statute or regulation, and (2) results in a disposition described in subsection (b) of this section.

(b) Dispositions

A disposition referred to in subsection (a)(2) of this section is any of the following:

(1) In the case of a criminal proceeding, a conviction (including a conviction pursuant to a plea of nolo contendere) by reason of the violation or failure referred to in subsection (a) of this section.

(2) In the case of a civil or administrative proceeding involving an allegation of fraud or similar misconduct, a determination of contractor liability on the basis of the violation or failure referred to in subsection (a) of this section.

(3) In the case of any civil or administrative proceeding, the imposition of a monetary penalty by reason of the violation or failure referred to in subsection (a) of this section.

(4) A final decision by an appropriate official of an executive agency—

(A) to debar or suspend the contractor;

(B) to rescind or void the contract; or

(C) to terminate the contract for default, by reason of the violation or failure referred to in subsection (a) of this section.

(5) A disposition of the proceeding by consent or compromise if such action could have resulted in a disposition described in paragraph (1), (2), (3), or (4).

(c) Proceeding commenced by United States; consent or compromise

In the case of a proceeding referred to in subsection (a) of this section that is commenced by the United States and is resolved by consent or compromise pursuant to an agreement entered into by a contractor and the United States, the costs incurred by the contractor in connection with such proceeding that are otherwise not allowable as reimbursable costs under such subsection may be allowed to the extent specifically provided in such agreement.

services incurred by a contractor in connection with such proceeding shall not be allowed in excess of the rate specified in the Equal Access to Justice Act (28 U.S.C.S. 2412(D)(2)(a); 5 U.S.C.S. 504(a)) unless the responsible contracting officer finds that a special factor (such as the limited availability of qualified attorneys or agents) justifies an award of higher rates.

(c) For purposes of this section—

(1) the term "covered contract" means a contract for an amount more than $100,000 entered into by a department or agency of the United States other than a fixed-price contract without cost incentives;

(2) the term "proceeding" means a civil, criminal, or an administrative investigation, prosecution, or proceeding; and

(3) the term "proceeding costs" means all costs relating to a proceeding incurred before, during, or after the commencement of the proceeding, and such term includes—

(A) administrative and clerical expenses;

(B) the cost of legal services (whether performed by an employee of the contractor or otherwise);

(C) the cost of the services of accountants and consultants retained by a contractor; and

(D) the salaries and wages of employees, including officers and directors.

In addition, section 3(c) of P.L. 100-700 (see footnote to 18 U.S.C.S. 293) provides:

(c) APPLICABILITY.—The amendments made by this section shall apply to contracts entered into after the date of the enactment of this Act [which was November 19, 1988].

Section 8 of P.L. 100-700 amended the Federal Property and Administrative Services Act of 1949 to read:

41 U.S.C.S. 256. Limitations on allowability of costs incurred by contractors in certain proceedings

(a) Violation of Federal or State statute or regulation except as otherwise provided in this section, costs incurred by a contractor in connection with any criminal, civil, or administrative proceeding commenced by the United States or a State are not

lines, or shall amend existing guidelines, to provide for appropriate penalty enhancements, where conscious or reckless risk of serious personal injury resulting from the fraud has occurred. The Commission shall consider the appropriateness of assigning to such a defendant an offense level under Chapter Two of the sentencing guidelines that is at least two levels greater than the level that would have been assigned had conscious or reckless risk of serious personal injury not resulted from the fraud.

In addition, section 3 of P.L. 100-700 added section 293 to Chapter 15 of Title 18. Prior to its repeal by section 3(a) of P.L. 101-123, which repeal was deemed effective retroactive to the date of enactment of P.L. 100-700, it read:

18 U.S.C.S. 293. Limitation on Government contract costs

(a) Any proceeding costs incurred in connection with any proceeding brought by the United States or a State government that relates to a violation of, or failure to comply with, any Federal or State law or regulation on the part of the contractor are not allowable costs in a covered contract if the proceeding results in any of the following:

(1) an indictment by a Federal grand jury, or a conviction (including a conviction pursuant to a plea of nolo contendere) by reason of such violation or failure to comply;

(2) the assessment of a monetary penalty by reason of a civil or administrative finding of such violation or failure to comply;

(3) a civil judgment containing a finding of liability, or an administrative finding of liability, by reason of such violation or failure to comply, if the charges which are the subject of the proceeding involve fraud or similar offenses;

(4) a decision to debar or suspend the contractor or rescind, void, or terminate a contract for default, by reason of such violation or failure to comply; or

(5) the resolution of the proceeding by consent or compromise, where the penalty or relief sought by the government included the actions described in paragraphs (1) through (5).

(b) In any proceeding brought by the United States or a State government that does not result in any of the actions described in paragraphs (1) through (5) of subsection (a), costs for legal

source" means an individual who has direct and independent knowledge of the information on which the allegations are based and has voluntarily provided the information to the Government; or

(D) that individual participated in the violation of this section with respect to which such payment would be made.

(3) The failure of the Attorney General to authorize a payment shall not be subject to judicial review.

(h) Any individual who—

(1) is discharged, demoted, suspended, threatened, harassed, or in any other manner discriminated against in the terms and conditions of employment by an employer because of lawful acts done by the employee on behalf of the employee or others in furtherance of a prosecution under this section (including investigation for, initiation of, testimony for, or assistance in such prosecution), and

(2) was not a participant in the unlawful activity that is the subject of said prosecution, may, in a civil action, obtain all relief necessary to make such individual whole. Such relief shall include reinstatement with the same seniority status such individual would have had but for the discrimination, 2 times the amount of back pay, interest on the back pay, and compensation for any special damages sustained as a result of the discrimination, including litigation costs and reasonable attorney's fees.

NOTE: P.L. 103-322, redesignated former paragraph (g) as paragraph (h), and added new paragraph (g), effective September 13, 1994.

Section 2(b) of P.L. 100-700, provides in a footnote to 18 U.S.C.S. 1031:

Pursuant to its authority under section 994(p) of title 28, United States Code and section 21 of the Sentencing Act of 1987, the United States Sentencing Commission shall promulgate guide-

[Text Continued on Page App. E-3]

3571(d) [which authorizes that penalty as an alternative fine based on gain or loss].

(e) In determining the amount of the fine, the court shall consider the factors set forth in 18 U.S.C.S. sections 3553 [which deals with imposition of a sentence] and 3572 [which deals with imposition of a sentence of fine and related matters], and the factors set forth in the guidelines and policy statements of the United States Sentencing Commission, including—

(1) the need to reflect the seriousness of the offense, including the harm or loss to the victim and the gain to the defendant;

(2) whether the defendant previously has been fined for a similar offense; and

(3) any other pertinent equitable considerations.

(f) A prosecution of an offense under this section may be commenced any time not later than 7 years after the offense is committed, plus any additional time otherwise allowed by law.

(g)(1) In special circumstances and in his or her sole discretion, the Attorney General is authorized to make payments from funds appropriated to the Department of Justice to persons who furnish information relating to a possible prosecution under this section. The amount of such payment shall not exceed $250,000. Upon application by the Attorney General, the court may order that the Department shall be reimbursed for a payment from a criminal fine imposed under this section.

(2) An individual is not eligible for such a payment if—

(A) that individual is an officer or employee of a Government agency who furnishes information or renders service in the performance of official duties;

(B) that indivuidual failed to furnish the information to the individual's employer prior to furnishing it to law enforcement authorities, unless the court determines the individual has justifiable reasons for that failure;

(C) the furnished information is based upon public disclosure of allegations ro transactions in a criminal, civil, or administrative hearing, in a congressional, administrative, or GAO report, hearing, audit or investigation, or from the news media unless the person is the original source of the information. For the purposes of this subsection, "original

APPENDIX E

P.L. 100-700: THE MAJOR FRAUD ACT OF 1988

18 U.S.C.S. 1031. Major fraud against the United States

(a) Whoever knowingly executes, or attempts to execute, any scheme or artifice with the intent—

(1) to defraud the United States; or

(2) to obtain money or property by means of false or fraudulent pretenses, representations, or promises,

in any procurement of property or services as a prime contractor with the United States or as a subcontractor or supplier on a contract in which there is a prime contract with the United States, if the value of the contract, subcontract, or any constituent part thereof, for such property or services is $1,000,000 or more shall, subject to the applicability of subsection (c) of this section, be fined not more than $1,000,000, or imprisoned not more than 10 years, or both.

(b) The fine imposed for an offense under this section may exceed the maximum otherwise provided by law, if such fine does not exceed $5,000,000 and—

(1) the gross loss to the Government or the gross gain to a defendant is $500,000 or greater, or

(2) the offense involves a conscious or reckless risk of serious personal injury.

(c) The maximum fine imposed upon a defendant for a prosecution including a prosecution with multiple counts under this section shall not exceed $10,000,000.

(d) Nothing in this section shall preclude a court from imposing any other sentences available under this title, including without limitation a fine up to twice the amount of the gross loss or gross gain involved in the offense pursuant to 18 U.S.C.S. section

APPENDIX D

STATEMENTS OR ENTRIES GENERALLY

18 U.S.C.S. 1001. Statements or entries generally

Whoever, in any matter within the jurisdiction of any department or agency of the United States knowingly and willfully falsifies, conceals or covers up by any trick, scheme, or device a material fact, or makes any false, fictitious or fraudulent statements or representations, or makes or uses any false writing or document knowing the same to contain any false, fictitious or fraudulent statement or entry, shall be fined not more than $10,000 or imprisoned not more than five years, or both.

APPENDIX C

FALSE, FICTITIOUS OR FRAUDULENT CLAIMS

18 U.S.C.S. 287. False, fictitious or fraudulent claims

Whoever makes or presents to any person or officer in the civil, military, or naval service of the United States, or to any department or agency thereof, any claim upon or against the United States, or any department or agency thereof, knowing such claim to be false, fictitious, or fraudulent, shall be imprisoned not more than five years and shall be subject to a fine in the amount provided in this title.

relate to the allegations and on which the government relies in bringing the case must be disclosed except those privileged under federal law. Thus, those materials that would not be available under the Federal Rules of Evidence or Civil Procedure are not subject to disclosure. The conferees deleted the specific reference to inter-agency and intra-agency materials only because such materials are considered privileged.

The conference agreement modifies the Senate provision by vesting judicial review in the district court rather [sic rather than] the court of appeals. In addition, the agreement narrows the standard for judicial review to comport with the "substantial evidence" standard provided under the Administrative Procedure Act for administrative adjudications.

These modifications to the judicial review provision are not to be interpreted, under any circumstance, to allow for de novo judicial review. Providing such review would not only contradict, but totally undermine, the purpose of these provisions by requiring the Justice Department to relitigate the factual and legal issues which had already been adjudicated through the administrative process.

The conference agreement provides that the administrative remedy established by the Senate provision will be included in Title 31 as a new chapter 38.

Finally, the conference agreement also makes numerous technical, conforming, and clarifying changes to the Senate provisions.

thoughtlessness, or inadvertence. The definition clarifies, therefore, that a person who makes a false claim or statement through mere negligence does not meet the requisite scienter requirement and would not be held liable under the Act. Only those individuals who are extremely reckless, who demonstrate an extreme departure from ordinary care, would be subject to liability.

House provision

No comparable provision.

Conference agreement

The conference agreement retains the major elements of the Senate provisions with a number of changes.

The conferees agreed to raise the jurisdictional cap from $100,000 to $150,000 under which an agency may initiate administrative action.

The conference agreement modifies the coverage of false statements that are unrelated to claims. Under the agreement, the administrative remedy will be available for such statements if they are submitted to establish eligibility for contracts or benefits, such as statements relating to eligibility to be considered a minority contractor for the purpose of bidding for contracts under minority set-aside programs. Coverage of statements related to claims is not affected by this modification.

Under the conference agreement, the maximum penalty that may be imposed under the administrative procedure is lowered from $10,000 to $5,000.

The conference agreement deletes the Senate provision which would have granted testimonial subpoena authority to the Inspectors General.

The conference agreement modifies the application of these provisions to the beneficiaries of certain federal programs. The administrative remedy established by these provisions would apply only to those beneficiaries who misrepresent their basic eligibility to participate in the enumerated programs. The exemption applies only to individuals who are receiving benefits and does not apply to providers who may receive or are assigned benefits by recipients.

The conference agreement clarifies the type of government materials available for discovery under this administrative procedure. The agreement states that all relevant and material documents which

IG's findings would be transmitted to the agency's reviewing official, who would independently evaluate the allegations to determine whether there is adequate evidence to believe that a false claim or statement has been submitted.

If so, the matter would be referred to the Justice Department for consideration. This procedure ensures that the Department will have an opportunity to review the charges and elect, if it so chooses, to litigate in federal court. An agency may only commence administrative proceedings against the person alleged to be liable if the Justice Department approves initiation of such proceedings. In those cases, the reviewing official would notify the person of the charges and of his or her right to a hearing.

An Administrative Law Judge—an independent, trained hearing examiner—would conduct the hearing to determine whether or not the person is liable and the amount of penalty and assessment, if any, to be imposed. The hearing itself would be conducted pursuant to the due process safeguards of the Administrative Procedure Act, which entitles the person to a written notice of the allegations, the right to be represented by counsel, and the right to present evidence on his or her own behalf. The provision even goes beyond these APA protections by providing the person discovery rights.

Finally, the person alleged to be liable has the right to appeal the hearing examiner's decision to the agency head and then, having exhausted all administrative remedies, the right to seek judicial review in a U.S. Court of Appeals.

In establishing liability under this administrative remedy, the government would not only have to prove that a claim or statement is false, but also that the person "knows or has reason to know" that the claim or statement is false. The provision defines this knowledge standard to cover those persons who either have actual knowledge that a claim or statement submitted is false, act in deliberate ignorance of the truth of [sic or] falsity of the claim or statement, or act in reckless disregard of the truth or falsity of the claims or statement. The penalty and assessment, if the person is found liable, would be up to $10,000 for each false claim or statement, plus double the amount falsely claimed.

The "knows or has reason to know" standard for establishing liability under this section is intended to capture those persons who recklessly disregard facts which are known or readily discoverable upon reasonable inquiry, while excluding those persons who submit false claims or make false statements through mistake, momentary

31 U.S.C.S. 3811. Effect on other law

(a) This chapter does not diminish the responsibility of any agency to comply with the provisions of chapter 35 of title 44.

(b) This chapter does not supersede the provisions of section 3512 of title 44.

(c) For purposes of this section, the term "agency" has the same meaning as in section 3502(1) of title 44.

31 U.S.C.S. 3812. Prohibition against delegation

Any function, duty, or responsibility which this chapter specifies be carried out by the Attorney General or an Assistant Attorney General designated by the Attorney General, shall not be delegated to, or carried out by, any other officer or employee of the Department of Justice.

EXCERPTS FROM THE LEGISLATIVE HISTORY

U.S. Code Congressional and Administrative News
1986, pp. 3902-3905

Senate provision

Part C of section 7 establishes an administrative remedy for false claim and false statement cases under $100,000 that the Department of Justice has declined to litigate. This remedy is based on legislation, S. 1134, the Program Fraud Civil Remedies Act of 1986, that was reported by the Senate Governmental Affairs Committee on November 19, 1985 (report 99-212).

While judicial remedies are available to penalize and deter fraud against the government, the cost of litigation often exceeds the amount recovered, thus making it economically impractical for the Justice Department to go to court. The government is frequently left without an adequate remedy for the small-dollar cases.

The consequence, according to the Justice Department, is that the federal government loses "tens, if not hundreds, of millions of dollars" to fraud each year. Beyond the actual monetary loss, fraud in federal programs also erodes public confidence in the administration of these programs by allowing ineligible persons to participate.

Under the administrative remedy set forth in this provision, a typical case would begin with an investigation conducted by the agency's investigating official, usually the Inspector General. The

31 U.S.C.S. 3809. Regulations

Within 180 days after the date of enactment of this chapter, each authority head shall promulgate rules and regulations necessary to implement the provisions of this chapter. Such rules and regulations shall—

(1) ensure that investigating officials and reviewing officials are not responsible for conducting the hearing required in section 3803(f) of this title, making the determinations required by subsections (f) and (h) of section 3803 of this title, or making collections under section 3806 of this title; and

(2) require a reviewing official to include in any notice required by section 3803(a)(2) of this title a statement which specifies that the reviewing official has determined that there is a reasonable prospect of collecting, from a person with respect to whom the reviewing official is referring allegations of liability in such notice, the amount for which such person may be liable.

31 U.S.C.S. 3810. Reports

Not later than October 31 of each year, each authority head shall prepare and transmit to the appropriate committees and subcommittees of the Congress an annual report summarizing actions taken under this chapter during the most recent 12-month period ending the previous September 30. Such report shall include—

(1) a summary of matters referred by the investigating official of the authority to the reviewing official of the authority under section 3803(a)(1) of this title during such period;

(2) a summary of matters transmitted to the Attorney General under section 3803(a)(2) of this title during such period;

(3) a summary of all hearings conducted by presiding officers under section 3803(f) of this title, and the results of such hearings, during such period; and

(4) a summary of the actions taken during such period to collect any civil penalty or assessment imposed under this chapter.

As used in this section:

(1) The term "covered contract" means a contract for an amount more than $100,000 entered into by an executive agency other than a fixed-price contract without cost incentives.

(2) The term "proceeding" includes an investigation.

(3) The term "costs", with respect to a proceeding—

(A) means all costs incurred by a contractor, whether before or after the commencement of such proceeding; and

(B) includes—

(i) administrative and clerical expenses;

(ii) the cost of legal services, including legal services performed by an employee of the contractor;

(iii) the cost of the services of accountants and consultants retained by the contractor; and

(iv) the pay of directors, officers, and employees of the contractor for time devoted by such directors, officers, and employees to such proceeding.

(4) The term "penalty" does not include restitution, reimbursement, or compensatory damages.

Finally, section 8(b) of P.L. 100-700 amended 10 U.S.C.S. 2324 principally by including language similar to that of 41 U.S.C.S. 256, quoted above; however, 10 U.S.C.S. 2324 pertains to allowable costs under defense contracts.

APPENDIX F

SAFE HARBOR PROVISIONS

APPENDIX F1

INITIAL SAFE HARBOR REGULATIONS, JULY 29, 1991

federal register

Monday
July 29, 1991

Part III

Department of Health and Human Services

Office of Inspector General

42 CFR Part 1001

Medicare and State Health Care Programs: Fraud and Abuse; OIG Anti-Kickback Provisions; Rule

DEPARTMENT OF HEALTH AND HUMAN SERVICES

Office of Inspector General

42 CFR Part 1001

RIN 0991-AA49

Medicare and State Health Care Programs: Fraud and Abuse; OIG Anti-Kickback Provisions

AGENCY: Office of Inspector General (OIG), HHS.

ACTION: Final rule.

SUMMARY: This final rule implements section 14 of Public Law 100-93, the Medicare and Medicaid Patient and Program Protection Act of 1987, by specifying various payment practices which, although potentially capable of inducing referrals of business under Medicare or a State health care program, will be protected from criminal prosecution or civil sanctions under the anti-kickback provisions of the statute.

EFFECTIVE DATE: This regulation is effective on July 29, 1991.

FOR FURTHER INFORMATION CONTACT:

Thomas S. Crane or D. McCarty Thornton, Office of the General Counsel, (202) 619-0335.

Joel Schaer, Office of Inspector General, (202) 619-3270.

SUPPLEMENTARY INFORMATION:

I. Background

A. The Medicare Anti-Kickback Statute

Section 1128B(b) of the Social Security Act (42 U.S.C. 1320a-7b(b)), previously codified at sections 1877 and 1909 of the Act, provides criminal penalties for individuals or entities that knowingly and willfully offer, pay, solicit or receive remuneration in order to induce business reimbursed under the Medicare or State health care programs. The offense is classified as a felony, and is punishable by fines of up to $25,000 and imprisonment for up to 5 years.

This provision is extremely broad. The types of remuneration covered specifically include kickbacks, bribes, and rebates made directly or indirectly, overtly or covertly, or in cash or in kind. In addition, prohibited conduct includes not only remuneration intended to induce referrals of patients, but remuneration also intended to induce the purchasing, leasing, ordering, or arranging for any good, facility, service, or item paid for by Medicare or State health care programs.

Since the statute on its face is so broad, concern has arisen among a number of health care providers that many relatively innocuous, or even beneficial, commercial arrangements are technically covered by the statute and are, therefore, subject to criminal prosecution.

B. Public Law 100-93

Public Law 100-93, the Medicare and Medicaid Patient and Program Protection Act of 1987, added two new provisions addressing the anti-kickback statute. Section 2 specifically provided new authority to the Office of Inspector General (OIG) to exclude an individual or entity from participation in the Medicare and State health care programs if it is determined that the party has engaged in a prohibited remuneration scheme. (Section 1128(b)(7) of the Act, 42 U.S.C. 1320a-7(b)(7)) This new sanction authority is intended to provide an alternative civil remedy, short of criminal prosecution, that will be a more effective way of regulating abusive business practices than is the case under criminal law.

In addition, section 14 of Public Law 100-93 requires the promulgation of regulations specifying those payment practices that will not be subject to criminal prosecution under section 1128B of the Act and that will not provide a basis for exclusion from the Medicare program or from the State health care programs under section 1128(b)(7) of the Act.

C. Notice of Intent

The legislative history of section 14 of Public Law 100-93 indicates that Congress expected the Department of Health and Human Services to consult with affected provider, practitioner, supplier and beneficiary representatives before promulgating regulations. In order to most effectively address issues related to this provision, we published a notice of intent to develop regulations (52 FR 38794, October 19, 1987) soliciting comments from interested parties prior to developing a proposed regulation. As a result of that notice, the OIG received a number of public comments, recommendations and suggestions on generic criteria that can be applied to particular types of business arrangements in order to determine if such arrangements are inappropriate for civil or criminal sanctions.

D. Notice of Proposed Rulemaking

The proposed regulation designed to implement section 14 of Public Law 100-93 was developed by the OIG and published in the Federal Register on January 23, 1989 (54 FR 3033). The regulation sets forth various proposed business and payment practices, or "safe harbors," that would not be treated as criminal offenses under section 1128B(b) of the Act and would not serve as a basis for a program exclusion under section 1128(b)(7) of the Act. As a result of that proposed rulemaking, we received a total of 754 public comments for consideration.

II. Summary of the Proposed Rule

A. Business Arrangements Not Exempt

The proposed regulation indicated that in order for a business arrangement to comply with one of the ten safe harbors, each standard of that safe harbor provision would have to be met. The proposed rule stated that if the business arrangement involves payments for different purposes (for example a single payment for personal services and for equipment rental) then each payment purpose would be analyzed to determine if all the standards of each applicable safe harbor provision have been fulfilled. The proposed rule further specified that where individuals and entities have entered into arrangements that are covered by the statute and where they have chosen not to fully comply with one of the exemptions proposed in these regulations, they would risk scrutiny by the OIG and may be subject to civil or criminal enforcement action.

B. Need for Continuing Guidance

Since there may be a need for the Department to respond to changes in health care delivery or business arrangements more quickly and informally than through the regulatory process to keep the industry abreast of our enforcement policy, the proposed rule invited public comment on how we can best achieve the dual goals of keeping the industry aware of our views of particular business practices, and assuring that our regulations remain current with new developments.

C. Notice to Beneficiaries

While we considered including in several of the proposed safe harbor provisions a requirement that a person notify each Medicare or Medicaid patient he or she refers to a related entity of the financial relationship that exists, we indicated that such notice requirements may be unduly burdensome compared with the potential benefits and, therefore, did not include the requirement in the safe harbors in the proposed regulation. Instead, we invited public comments on this issue.

D. Preferred Provider Organizations

We cited the increasing variety of arrangements among entities grouped under the generic headings "preferred provider organizations" (PPOs) or "managed care," and that unlike HMOs, there is often no single entity that is recognized as the "health care provider." The proposed regulations did not specifically delineate a safe harbor provision for these arrangements since we believed that one or more of the other proposed safe harbors would often cover relationships in preferred provider and managed care networks. We invited comments from the public, however, on the idea of adding additional safe harbors that would provide further protection to HMOs, PPOs, and other managed care plans.

E. Waiver of Coinsurance and Deductible Amounts for Inpatient Hospital Care

We noted that with the advent in 1983 of the prospective payment system for paying hospitals for inpatient care, some hospitals have advertised the routine waiver of Medicare coinsurance and deductible amounts as a means of attracting patients to their facilities. We solicited comments on defining a safe harbor for waiving coinsurance and deductible amounts that would be limited to inpatient hospital care, be available to all Medicare beneficiaries without regard to diagnosis or length of stay, and assure that any costs to the hospital of waiving the coinsurance and deductible amounts would not be passed on to any Federal program as a bad debt or in any other way.

F. Proposed Safe Harbors

The regulation published on January 23, 1989, proposing to amend 42 CFR part 1001 by adding a new § 1001.952, set forth "safe harbors" in ten broad areas:

1. Investment Interests

To reflect the view that Congress did not intend to bar all investments by physicians in other health care entities to which they refer patients, a safe harbor provision was proposed for investment interests in large public corporations where such investments are available to the general public. This safe harbor described a minimum number of shareholders and a minimum number of assets the company must have in order to qualify under this provision.

Safe harbors for limited and managing partnerships were considered under the proposed regulation, but were not included. These areas were discussed in the preamble of the proposed rule, and we specifically requested public comments on adopting these practices as safe harbors.

2. Space Rental

While many rental arrangements are legitimate, many situations exist where rental payments are simply a device used to mask illegal payments intended to induce referrals. Accordingly, a safe harbor provision was proposed for rental arrangements if: (a) Access to the space is for periodic intervals and such intervals are set in advance in the lease, rather than based on the number of referred patients; (b) the lease is for at least one year so it cannot be readjusted on too frequent a basis to reflect prior referrals; and (c) the charges reflect fair market value.

3. Equipment Rental

With the understanding that the payment for the use of diagnostic and other medical equipment may simply be a vehicle to provide reimbursement for referrals, a safe harbor was proposed for certain situations involving equipment rentals similar to those applied to real estate rentals cited above.

4. Personal Services and Management Contracts

While health care providers often have arrangements to perform services for each other on a mutually beneficial basis, some of these arrangements may vary the payment with the volume of referrals. The proposed regulation set forth a safe harbor provision for joint ventures and other arrangements involving payments for personal services or management contracts, but only if certain standards are met that limit the opportunity to provide financial incentives in exchange for referrals. This proposed provision required the services to be paid at fair market value, and was predicated on requirements similar to those set forth in the provisions for space and equipment rental.

5. Sale of Practice

Unlike the traditional sale of a practice by a retiring physician, a physician may sell, or appear to sell, a practice to a hospital while continuing to practice on its staff. A safe harbor provision was proposed for the sale of physician practices when occurring as the result of retirement or some other event that removes the physician from the practice of medicine or from the service area in which he or she was practicing, but not when the sale is for the purpose of obtaining an ongoing source of patient referrals.

6. Referral Services

Professional societies and other consumer-oriented groups often operate referral services for a fee. Because such a service fee could be construed as a payment in order to obtain a referral, we concluded that it was appropriate to establish a specific safe harbor for this type of practice. In order to safeguard against abuse, however, the provision is only available when several standards are met.

7. Warranties

It is in the public interest to have companies offer warranties as an inducement to the consumer to purchase a product. A safe harbor was proposed for such purposes.

8. Discounts

Safe harbors relating to discounts, employees and group purchasing organizations are specifically required by statute. The discount exception was intended to encourage price competition that benefits the Medicare and Medicaid programs. The proposed discount provision was limited in application to reductions in the amount a seller charges for a good or service to the buyer. The discount could take the form of a specified price break, or the inclusion of an extra quantity of the item purchased "at no extra charge." We did not propose to protect many kinds of marketing incentive programs such as cash rebates, free goods or services, redeemable coupons, or credits.

9. Employees

The proposed exception for employees permitted an employer to pay an employee in whatever manner he or she chose for having that employee assist in the solicitation of program business and applied only to bona fide employee-employer relationships.

10. Group Purchasing Organizations

The proposed group purchasing organization (GPO) exception was designed to apply to payments from vendors to entities authorized to act as a GPO for individuals or entities who are furnishing Medicare or Medicaid services. The proposed exception required a written agreement between the GPO and the individual or entity that specifies the amounts vendors will pay the GPO.

III. Response to Comments and Summary of Revisions

As indicated above, in response to the proposed rulemaking we received 754 public comments from various provider groups, medical facilities, professional and business organizations and associations, medical societies, State and local government entities, private practitioners and concerned citizens. The comments included both general and broadreaching concerns regarding the impact of this regulation, and specific comments on those areas and safe harbor provisions about which we requested public input. A summary of the comments received and our responses to those comments follows.

A. General Comments

Comment: A large number of commenters expressed concern about the implication of engaging in a business arrangement that does not comply fully with a provision of this regulation. Some of these commenters expressed the view that the safe harbor provisions are narrowly drawn and leave many lawful business arrangements unprotected. Moreover, the preamble to the proposed rule warns: "[W]here individuals and entities have entered into arrangements that are covered by the statute, where they have chosen not to comply fully with one of the exemptions in these regulations, they would risk scrutiny by the OIG * * *." These commenters urged the OIG to make clear that the failure to comply fully with a safe harbor provision is not *per se* illegal, and does not mean that prosecution will automatically follow. In addition, they requested safe harbor protection for business arrangements where there has only been a "technical violation" of the statute, where there has been "substantial compliance" with this regulation, or where the remuneration in question is "de minimis."

Response: This regulation covers many categories of business arrangements, providing standards to be met within each safe harbor provision. If a person participates in an arrangement that fully complies with a given provision, he or she will be assured of not being prosecuted criminally or civilly for the arrangement that is the subject of that provision.

This regulation does not expand the scope of activities that the statute prohibits. The statute itself describes the scope of illegal activities. The legality of a particular business arrangement must be determined by comparing the particular facts to the proscriptions of the statute.

The failure to comply with a safe harbor can mean one of three things. First, as we stated in the preamble to the proposed rule, it may mean that the arrangement does not fall within the ambit of the statute. In other words, the arrangement is not intended to induce the referral of business reimbursable under Medicare or Medicaid; so there is no reason to comply with the safe harbor standards, and no risk of prosecution.

Second, at the other end of the spectrum, the arrangement could be a clear statutory violation and also not qualify for safe harbor protection. In that case, assuming the arrangement is obviously abusive, prosecution would be very likely.

Third, the arrangement may violate the statute in a less serious manner, although not be in compliance with a safe harbor provision. Here there is no way to predict the degree of risk. Rather, the degree of the risk depends on an evaluation of the many factors which are part of the decision-making process regarding case selection for investigation and prosecution. Certainly, in many (but not necessarily all) instances, prosecutorial discretion would be exercised not to pursue cases where the participants appear to have acted in a genuine good-faith attempt to comply with the terms of a safe harbor, but for reasons beyond their control are not in compliance with the terms of that safe harbor. In other instances, there may not even be an applicable safe harbor, but the arrangement may appear innocuous. But in other instances, we will want to take appropriate action.

We do not believe the Medicare and Medicaid programs would be properly served if we assured protection in all instances of "substantial compliance," "technical violations," or "de minimis" payments. Unfortunately, these are vague concepts, subject to differing interpretations. In this requlation, we have attempted to provide bright lines, to the extent possible, for safe harbors in order to provide clarity and predictability as to what conduct is immune from government action. Our endorsement of the concepts mentioned above would only serve to blur these lines and produce litigation as to what "substantial," "technical" and "de minimis" really mean. The OIG therefore declines to adopt these concepts.

A recent decision of the United States Court of Appeals for the First Circuit provides an indication of the litigation problems that could arise if "substantial compliance" with a safe harbor provision was all that was required. *United States* v. *Bay State Ambulance and Hospital Rental Service, Inc.*, 874 F.2d 20 (1st Cir., 1989) involved an arrangement between an employee of a city owned hospital (Felci) and an ambulance company (Bay State). Felci was involved in the administration of the city's ambulance service contract. During this period, Bay State retained Felci as a consultant, provided him with two automobiles, and paid Felci's consulting company several thousand dollars. When it came time for renewal of the ambulance contract, Felci used his position and influence at the city hospital to assist Bay State in securing the new contract. Felci was prosecuted and convicted under the statute.

In affirming Felci's conviction (as well as that of Bay State's president, Kotzen), the First Circuit rejected Felci's contention that he had substantially complied with this regulation as published as a notice of proposed rulemaking, and thus should not be prosecuted. The court found: "The proposed regulation does not exempt every transaction in which the amount paid for services is an amount consistent with fair market value; rather it exempts only a small subset of such transactions * * *. [U]nder the circumstances such as the present case where the consulting arrangement is not full-time, * * * stringent requirements are necessary to meet the exemption from criminal liability. HHS has thus decided *not* to create a safe harbor for transactions such as the present case." (Emphasis in original; footnote omitted) *Id.* 874 F.2d at 31.

Comment: Several commenters described business arrangements that technically may violate the statute, but do not increase costs to the Medicare or Medicaid programs, or otherwise injure beneficiaries. They requested safe harbor protection for these arrangements because of concern of their risk of being scrutinized.

Response: Increased cost to the Medicare and Medicaid programs and harm to beneficiaries are not the only criteria we look at in determining whether a particular business arrangement is abusive. As the court in *United States* v. *Ruttenberg*, 625 F.2d 173, 177, n.9 (7th Cir. 1980) noted:

> [T]he law does not make increased cost to the government the sole criterion of corruption. In prohibiting "kickbacks," Congress need not have spelled out the obvious truisms that, while unnecessary expenditure of money earned and contributed by taxpaying fellow citizens may exacerbate the result of the crime, kickback schemes can freeze competing suppliers from the system, can mask the possibility of government price reductions, can misdirect program funds, and, when proportional, can erect strong temptations to order more drugs and supplies than needed.

Furthermore, it is unfortunately not possible to provide safe harbor protections for all business arrangements that are not abusive. There are certain arrangements that, although themselves legitimate, are structurally so similar to abusive arrangements that protection by way of new safe harbor provisions will inevitably also protect abusive practices as well. For example, equipment rental arrangements made between parties in a position to make and accept referrals do not receive safe harbor protection if the payments are based on utilization (sometimes known as a "wear and tear" clause). We recognize that equipment becomes less valuable the more it is used, and that its owner deserves compensation for such wear and tear. However, it is also a relatively easy matter to disguise such a wear and tear payment as a payment for referrals. Thus, we need to examine the intent of the parties on a case-by-case basis even though a large majority of such payments may represent only legitimate compensation to the owner of the equipment.

The recent case, *United States* v. *Bay State Ambulance and Hospital Rental Service, Inc.*, discussed above, emphasizes that the gravamen of a violation of the statute is "inducement" and not necessarily the structure of the arrangement. *Id.* 874 F.2d at 29. Thus, such case by case inquiries must necessarily focus on the intent of the parties.

The *Bay State Ambulance* case also illustrates the risk health care providers engage in when they enter into a business arrangement that violates the statute, but try to argue that the arrangement does not increase program costs or result in overutilization. The First Circuit rejected the defendants' arguments that there would have been no fiscal drain on public programs because ambulance services and Medicare reimbursement would have been required no matter which ambulance service company had received the contract. The court noted that it was unclear whether Medicare paid Bay State more for these services than it would have paid to the losing bidder even though that bidder's charges were lower. The court observed: "Although the reason for enacting the statute was to prevent drains on the public fisc, the statute does not require that there be a drain on the public fisc in order for payments to be illegal." *Id.* n.21, 874 F.2d at 32.

Comment: Numerous commenters expressed concern about the difficulty in revising a business arrangement that they entered into with a good-faith belief that the arrangement did not violate the statute, but which they now find does not qualify under one of the safe harbor provisions. They suggested that the OIG either "grandfather" these arrangements or provide a reasonable period of time before initiating enforcement action to enable health care providers to restructure their arrangements to meet the safe harbor provisions.

Response: The failure of a particular business arrangement to comply with these provisions does not determine whether or not the arrangement violates the statute because, as we stated above, this regulation does not make conduct illegal. Any conduct that could be construed to be illegal after the promulgation of this rule would have been illegal at any time since the current law was enacted in 1977. Thus illegal arrangements entered into in the past were undertaken with a risk of prosecution. This regulation is intended to provide a formula for avoiding risk in the future.

We also recognize, however, that many health care providers have structured their business arrangements based on the advice of an attorney and in good-faith believed that the arrangement was legal. In the event that they now find that the arrangement does not comply fully with a particular safe harbor provision and are working with diligence and good faith to restructure it so that it does comply, we will use our discretion to be fair to the parties to such arrangements.

Nonetheless, we believe that it would be inappropriate for us to provide a blanket protection, even for a limited period of time, for all business arrangements that do not qualify for a safe harbor. As we stated above, certain business arrangements that do not qualify may warrant immediate enforcement action.

Comment: Many commenters discussed the interrelationships between these safe harbor provisions and reimbursement rules promulgated by the Health Care Financing Administration (HCFA). A few of these commenters appeared to suggest that if a health care provider complied with a particular safe harbor provision, then its reimbursement may be affected.

Response: We wish to emphasize that nothing in this regulation changes reimbursement rules promulgated by HCFA or a State health care program. Clearly if a provider chooses to engage in one course of conduct in order to comply with these safe harbor provisions, such action may very well have reimbursement implications. However, such reimbursement is governed exclusively by HCFA or State regulations, and not by this regulation.

Comment: Several commenters requested that the OIG publish this regulation with an additional comment period because of the complexity of the issues involved and the revisions or additions of new safe harbor provisions created as a result of the comments.

Response: We believe that the disadvantages of providing an additional comment period outweigh the benefits. As we stated above, we received extensive comments in response to this proposed rule. In addition, due to the novelty and complexity of these issues, we started this process with a special notice of intent to develop regulations, (52 FR 38794, October 19, 1987) and received over 150 comments, which we used to develop the proposed rule.

Also weighing against any benefit of receiving additional comments on this rule is the desirability of providing the level of certainty that accompanies a final rule. This will permit individuals and entities to structure business arrangements under the provisions of this rule with the assurance that it will not change in the near future. Such assurance is delayed somewhat by providing an additional comment period.

We acknowledge the congressional expectation that we should "formally re-evaluate the anti-kickback regulations on a periodic basis, and, in so doing, * * * solicit public comment at the outset of the review process." H.R. Rep. No. 85, part 2, 100th Cong. 1st Sess. 27 (1987). We believe it is most appropriate to allow all parties time to obtain experience with these safe harbor provisions in their final form before we solicit additional public comments to start our formal re-evaluation process.

Nonetheless, we received many comments requesting safe harbor protection for a number of business arrangements, many of which deserve safe harbor protection. As discussed in more detail below in section III.B.3. of this preamble, the comments we received on HMOs, PPOs, and other managed care plans warrant the creation of two new safe harbor provisions. Because of the lack of specificity in those comments, we expect to publish these provisions as a separate interim final regulation at a later date. While this provision will be effective upon publication, the public will have an opportunity to submit their specific comments and concerns regarding this new safe harbor.

In addition, as discussed in more detail below in section III.B. of this preamble, many other arrangements brought to our attention were for arrangements on which we did not solicit comments. Because some of these arrangements may deserve safe harbor protection, we anticipate publishing additional safe harbor provisions in a separate notice of proposed rulemaking. Any discussion below indicating that we are considering a new safe harbor provision should in no way be construed as legalizing the business arrangement at this time.

Comment: Numerous commenters suggested that the OIG should employ a cease and desist mechanism. Some suggested that the OIG should be required to employ such a mechanism before it initiates a criminal prosecution or program exclusion. Others supported the use of this mechanism because they believed that many business arrangements that violate the statute do not warrant prosecution but should be stopped.

Response: We do not have the authority to seek or issue a legally enforceable order directing a person to cease and desist from a particular unlawful kickback activity. We recognize that there may be situations where it may be appropriate to inform a person that he or she is violating the statute, and request that the unlawful activity be stopped. Where the person takes immediate action to conform his activity to the law, we may decide that no further action is warranted. However, there may be other situations where criminal prosecution is appropriate even though the person has stopped the illegal activity. Since we lack the power to issue or seek a legally enforceable cease and desist order, we cannot rely on that mechanism as a significant enforcement tool.

Comment: Three commenters suggested that because many business arrangements will not meet the safe harbor provisions, the regulation was of limited value. They suggested that health care providers would be better aided if the OIG would provide examples of arrangements that violate the statute.

Response: As we stated above, the purpose of this regulation is not to describe illegal conduct, but rather to set forth standards for certain safe harbors. If an individual or entity engages in a business arrangement that is the subject of a safe harbor provision and complies with all of its provisions, that individual will be assured that he or she will not be prosecuted. However, we recognize the desirability of communicating to the public the existence of other business practices and arrangements that we believe are subject to serious abuse. Accordingly, we issued a special OIG Fraud Alert on joint venture arrangements that described various suspect features of these business ventures that may result in a violation of the statute. As the need arises, we intend to issue other fraud alerts that will provide guidance to the public on other types of arrangements.

Comment: In seeking guidance with respect to transactions or practices not covered by any specific safe harbor provision, many commenters requested the OIG to include within this regulation a list of generic criteria it would consider in evaluating business arrangements under the statute. These commenters cite a variety of positive and negative factors as relevant generic criteria, including on the positive side whether the arrangement has "a legitimate business purpose" or promotes the delivery of needed services, particularly to indigent, elderly, or rural populations; and on the negative side whether the arrangement promotes overutilization, interferes with patient freedom of choice, diminishes the quality of care provided, or increases costs to beneficiaries or to the government. Some commenters pointed out that the legislative history of Public Law 100-93 directs the Department to include in the rules "any generic criteria that might apply to business arrangements generally." H.R. Rep. No. 85, part 2, 100th Cong., 1st Sess. 27 (1987).

Response: We believe the same generic criteria applicable to all business arrangements would not provide useful guidance to the extent that they are based on value judgments regarding the relative advantages (e.g., lower cost or improved accessibility) and disadvantages (e.g., higher cost or overutilization) of the arrangement. It would be virtually impossible to set forth rules describing how we intend to apply them. For example, the determination of whether a joint venture has a legitimate business purpose, is a matter of subjective judgment, and we believe the use of such criteria would invite litigation because health care providers will not be sure if they are complying with them.

An example of the problems in using these types of generic criteria can be seen if we attempted to provide safe harbor protection for business arrangements that have a "legitimate business purpose." The statute proscribes the giving of rebates as a form of remuneration to induce referrals. Yet rebates are legitimate and common business practices outside the health care services business sector. For the numerous people who engage in both health care and non-health care lines of business, they may have become accustomed to providing various inducements to others in their non-health care activities. They may now start to provide similar inducements in their health care lines of business in a manner that violates the statute. To them, these inducements have a "legitimate business purpose," that is, to gain referrals and thereby make money, yet the practice is expressly prohibited by the statute.

We believe that Congress did not require us to specify such generic criteria. The House Committee Report so often cited by commenters directs us to promulgate rules that, "to the extent practical, contain * * * any generic criteria that might apply to business arrangements generally." *Id.* We believe that we have done so. It was only practical to include generic criteria for specific categories of arrangements, such as "fair market value" in the "space rental" safe harbor. We have concluded, however, that a single set of standards for all business arrangements would be of extremely limited value because the subjectivity or arbitrariness in applying the standards to individual fact situations would make such standards of extremely limited value.

We recognize that some of the factors cited by commenters are useful in determining the extent to which a particular arrangement is abusive, and therefore likely to be prosecuted. For example, the more an arrangement involving remuneration offered to induce referrals increases Medicare or Medicaid program costs or results in unnecessary utilization, the more likely it would be that we would have an interest in prosecuting the offense. It must be emphasized that these are not the only factors upon which a determination regarding prosecution is based, and as we have noted "the statute does not require that there be a drain on the public fisc in order for payments to be illegal." *United States* v. *Bay State Ambulance and Hospital Rental Service, Inc., supra,* 874 F.2d at 32, n. 21.

Comment: Several commenters objected to the regulation because they believed that the OIG had exceeded its statutory authority. In particular, they commented that the OIG does not have authority under section 14 of Public Law 100-93 to narrow the scope of the statutory exceptions, particularly the "discount" exception of section 1128B(b)(3)(A) of the Act. They cited the last sentence of section 14(a) which states, "Any practices specified in regulations pursuant to [sec. 14 of Pub. L. 100-93] shall be in addition to the practices described in subparagraphs (A) through (C) of section 1128B(b)(3)." This sentence led some commenters to conclude that our regulatory authority does not permit us to refine or clarify the statutory exceptions.

Response: We believe that these commenters have misconstrued the intent of this sentence. The plain language of the first sentence of section 14(a) of Public Law 100–93 requires the Secretary to promulgate regulations "specifying payment practices that shall not be treated as a criminal offense under section 1128B(b) of the Social Security Act and shall not serve as the basis for an exclusion under section 1128(b)(7) of such Act." We believe that the second sentence, which was quoted by many commenters, requires us to add to the exceptions provided in section 1128B(b)(3) of the Act. But we do not believe the intent of this sentence is to prohibit us from interpreting statutory terms used in these exceptions. The clear congressional intent behind the development of these safe harbor provisions is to define innocuous arrangements that should not be prosecuted, including the statutory exceptions. We believe it is in the public interest to provide the health care community with our interpretation of the meaning of certain important statutory terms, for example, "appropriately reflect" in the discount exception or "bona fide employment relationship" in the employee-employer exception.

Comment: One commenter asked the OIG to clarify how it expects health care providers to comply with this regulation when it engages in a business arrangement that may be covered by two or more of the provisions of this regulation.

Response: This comment addresses two potential situations. The first situation arises where a payment practice serves a single purpose (e.g., compensation for personal services), but potentially fits into more than one safe harbor (e.g., the employer-employee safe harbor and the personal services and management contracts safe harbor). In this situation, if the payment practice fits into either one of the safe harbors, it is exempt from criminal prosecution and program exclusion. In the example given, if the payment practice does not qualify as a bona fide employment relationship, it still may receive safe harbor protection under the personal services and management contract safe harbor.

The second situation arises where a payment practice serves multiple purposes (e.g., a payment to recompensate another party for personal services and equipment rental). Under these circumstances, it will be necessary to examine each aspect of the payment practice to determine compliance with each respective safe harbor provision. A person engaged in a "multi-purpose" payment practice who seeks protection will need to document separately his or her compliance with the safe harbor applicable to each purpose being served by the payment practice. Compliance with one provision (for one of the purposes of the payment practice) would not insulate the entire payment practice from criminal prosecution or program exclusion, where another purpose of the payment practice is implemented in a manner which violates the statute.

In the provision-by-provision analysis in section III.C. below, we will discuss specific comments and our responses to other special issues regarding the interrelationships of these provisions.

Comment: Two commenters requested that the OIG clarify the relationship between the statute and various State laws.

Response: Issues of state law are completely independent of the federal anti-kickback statute and these regulations. There is no federal preemption provision under the statute. Thus, conduct that is lawful under the federal anti-kickback statute or this regulation may still be illegal under State law. Conversely, conduct that is lawful under State law may still be illegal under the federal anti-kickback statute.

Comment: We received many comments on the proposed "Ethics in Patient Referrals Act" then pending in Congress aimed at restricting physicians from referring patients to entities in which they have a financial interest, the so-called "Stark Bill." Many of these commenters asked the OIG to either support or oppose this legislation. Others asked the OIG to clarify the relationship of this legislation to the anti-kickback statute and this regulation.

Response: This legislation was enacted as section 6204 of the Omnibus Budget Reconciliation Act of 1989, Public Law 101–239, adding a new section 1877 to the Act. With numerous exceptions, it generally restricts physicians from making referrals for clinical laboratory services to entities in which they have an ownership or other compensation arrangement. These referral restrictions become effective on January 1, 1992.

The legislation, although in many respects aimed at the same problems as we are addressing in this regulation, requires different elements of proof and has different remedies than under the anti-kickback statute. Generally, section 1877 is violated when a "financial relationship" exists between an entity furnishing clinical laboratory services and a physician, and a referral is made or a claim or bill is presented. For the anti-kickback statute to be violated, it must be shown that the remuneration between the two parties was intended to induce the referral of business payable under Medicare or Medicaid. Whereas the anti-kickback statute contains criminal penalties, violations under section 1877 will result in a denial of payment and may result in the imposition of civil money penalties and program exclusions under section 1128A of the Act.

Because of these differences between the two provisions, the conference report includes the following clarification:

> The conferees wish to clarify that any prohibition, exemption, or exception authorized under this provision in no way alters (or reflects on) the scope and application of the anti-kickback provisions in section 1128B of the Social Security Act. The conferees do not intend that this provision should be construed as affecting, or in any way interfering, with the efforts of the Inspector General to enforce current law, such as cases described in the recent Fraud Alert issued by the Inspector General. In particular, entities which would be eligible for a specific exemption would be subject to all of the provisions of current law.

H.R. Conf. Rep. 239, 101st Cong., 1st sess. 856 (1989).

This clear expression of legislative intent to keep enforcement under the anti-kickback statute separate from enforcement under section 1877 makes it inappropriate to adjust our safe harbor provisions to take into account any exception or prohibition under section 1877.

Comment: Thirty-three commenters reacted to our comments in the preamble of the proposed rule regarding the breadth and scope of the statute. Fourteen commenters suggested that these regulations should in no way undermine the scope or strength of the statute. These commenters believe that by adding the civil exclusion remedy for the kickback violations as part of Public Law 100–93, Congress sent a clear and appropriate message to the health care community not to place financial considerations above beneficiaries' interests. Two commenters requested that the statute's term "to refer" should be defined. Other commenters were concerned that diminishing the reach of the statute would create conflicts of interest between health care providers and their patients, and impugn the professional image of physicians. A few commenters opposed the implementation of any safe harbor provisions whatsoever.

Response: Our charge from Congress under section 14 of Public Law 100-93 is to clarify what payment practices will not subject a person to criminal prosecution or exclusion from the Medicare or State health care programs. The process involves both a determination of the scope of the statute and decisions as to how to draft the safe harbor provisions so that they protect only non-abusive relationships.

With respect to the scope of the statute, we do not believe that it is necessary to define any of the statute's terms in the regulation itself. However, the meaning of two of its terms deserve comment (1) "any remuneration (including any kickback, bribe, or rebate) directly or indirectly, overtly or covertly, in cash or in kind;" and (2) "to induce." These terms demonstrate congressional intent to create a very broadly worded prohibition. Our comments in the preamble to the proposed rule reflected our belief that Congress ratified this intent in their mandate to create these safe harbor provisions.

Congress's intent in placing the term "remuneration" in the statute in 1977 was to cover the transferring of anything of value in any form or manner whatsoever. The statute's language makes clear that illegal payments are prohibited beyond merely "bribes," "kickbacks," and "rebates," which were the three terms used in the original 1972 statute. The language "directly or indirectly, overtly or covertly, in cash or in kind" makes clear that the form or manner of the payment includes indirect, covert, and in kind transactions. Moreover, the statutory exception for discounts demonstrates that Congress prohibited transactions where there is no direct payment at all from the party receiving the referrals. The remuneration in a discount is merely a lowered price that a purchaser would otherwise obtain from a seller, which is made as an inducement to purchase larger quantities.

The statute's legislative history supports this reading of the term "remuneration," and makes clear that the fundamental analysis required of a trier of fact is "to recognize that the substance rather than simply the form of a transaction should be controlling" (123 Cong. Rec. 30,280 (1977), Statement of Chairman of the House Committee on Ways and Means and principal author of H.R. 3, Representative Rostenkowski). Also see H.R. Rep. No. 393, part II, 95th Cong., lst Sess. 53; reprinted in (1977) U.S. Code Cong. & Ad. News 3056; S.Rep. No. 453, 95th Cong., lst Sess. 12 (1977).

The meaning of the term "to induce," which describes the intent of those who offer or pay remuneration in paragraph (2) of the statute, is found in the ordinary dictionary definition: "to lead or move by influence or persuasion" (The American Heritage Dictionary (2d College Ed. 1982)).

The OIG's interpretation of the statute is fully supported by its case law. At the time that the proposed rule was issued, the leading case interpreting the breadth of the statute was *United States* v. *Greber*, 760 F.2d 68 (3d Cir.) *cert. denied*, 474 U.S. 988 (1985). Since publication of the notice of proposed rulemaking on January 23, 1989, two other circuit courts have lent further support to a broad reading of the statute: *Bay State Ambulance*, which was discussed above, and *United States* v. *Kats*, 871 F.2d 105 (9th Cir. 1989).

Kats involved an arrangement between physician offices or clinics, a phlebotomy service ("THC"), and a clinical diagnostic laboratory ("Tech-Lab"). Under the arrangement, THC collected blood and urine samples from physician offices and medical clinics, and forwarded these laboratory specimens to Tech-Lab. Tech-Lab performed the laboratory tests and billed the respective insurance programs, including Medicare and Medicaid. Tech-Lab kicked back 50 percent of its proceeds to THC, which in turn kicked back part of its proceeds to the various physician offices and clinics, including a clinic owned by Yan Kats. Kats and others were prosecuted and convicted under the statute.

In upholding Kats's conviction, the United States Court of Appeals for the Ninth Circuit became the first court specifically to adopt the holding in *Gerber* that "if one purpose of the payment is to induce future referrals, the [M]edicare statute has been violated." 760 F.2d at 69. The *Kats* court held that the statute is violated unless the payments are "wholly and not incidentally attributable to the delivery of goods or services." *Id.* 871 F.2d at 108. The court upheld a jury instruction that read, in part, "It is not a defense that there might have been other reasons for the solicitation of a remuneration by the defendants, if you find that one of the material purposes for the solicitation was to obtain money for the referral of services." *Id.* 871 F.2d at 108, n.1.

Because the statute is broad, the payment practices described in these safe harbor provisions would be prohibited by the statute but for their inclusion here. In mandating this regulation, Congress directed us to limit the reach of the statute somewhat by permitting certain non-abusive arrangements, while encouraging beneficial or innocuous arrangements. We believe that we have accomplished this task in a manner that will not restrict our ability to prosecute, either criminally or civilly, abusive schemes that violate the statute. However, these safe harbor provisions do not constitute a guarantee that a health care provider whose practice conforms to a particular safe harbor will not engage in abusive practices. For this reason, we intend to monitor business arrangements that comply with the terms of these safe harbor provisions, particularly investment interests (see section III.C.1.b.ii. below), to determine whether abusive arrangements exist within the parameter of a particular safe harbor. If abusive arrangements are found to exist, we will entirely withdraw or modify any provision as appropriate.

Comment: A small number of commenters requested clarification as to whether the statute prohibits remuneration in return for referrals or other arrangements to induce services or items reimbursed under Medicare alone, or whether the conduct prohibited by the statute includes referrals or other arrangements to induce services or items reimbursed by Medicaid and other State health care programs.

Response: We agree that clarification is needed, and have amended the final rule to make clear that the statute, and hence these safe harbor provisions, apply to items or services which may be paid in whole or in part under Medicare or a federally funded State health care program, such as Medicaid. However, because commenters have expressed particular concern about the applicability of these provisions to items and services payable under the Medicare and Medicaid programs, our discussion of comments and responses often refer solely to these two programs.

B. Comments on Areas That the OIG Invited Comments

In this section, we discuss four issues on which we specifically invited public comments: continuing guidance, notice to beneficiaries, preferred provider organizations (PPOs), and waiver of coinsurance and deductible amounts for inpatient hospital care. We also requested comments on suggested standards for two additional investment interest provisions that would protect investors, such as limited and general partners, investing in small entities. Our discussion of those comments and our responses are contained in the provision-by-provision analysis of investment interests (see section III.C.1. below).

1. Continuing Guidance

Comment: We received a large number of responses to our invitation for comments on how the OIG can best inform health care providers about fraudulent practices, and can best ensure that the safe harbor regulation remains current as new health care business practices develop. Many of these commenters suggested that the Department issue advisory opinions about the legality of proposed business arrangements under the statute. Some commenters requested that the Department implement a mechanism for informing health care providers about business practices that raise problems under the statute.

Proponents of advisory opinions argued that such a mechanism would provide guidance concerning activities unaddressed by the safe harbor regulation, curb illegal payment practices, and keep the Department informed of industry developments. These commenters asserted that the Department has authority to issue advisory opinions pursuant to its general statutory authority to promulgate regulations, and pursuant to the specific authority under Public Law 100-93 to promulgate this regulation. The commenters contended that advisory opinion rulings would not hamper the Department of Justice's prosecutorial discretion under the statute, because the immunizing effects of advice given would be limited to the facts disclosed. The commenters also claimed that several other agencies employ advisory opinion procedures in administering laws under their respective jurisdictions.

Response: We understand and appreciate providers' desire for legal security in their business relations. Consistent with our mandate under Public Law 100-93, we will continue to make efforts to inform health care providers about business practices that may subject them to criminal prosecution or program exclusion.

We have concluded that we will not provide a mechanism responding to individual requests for advisory opinions about the legality of a particular business arrangement under the statute. The statute is primarily a criminal statute, and the Department of Justice is vested with exclusive authority to enforce all criminal laws of the United States. See sections 516, 519 and 547 of title 28 of the United States Code. A plethora of case law holds that this exclusive authority extends to all decisions to initiate, or to decline to initiate, criminal prosecutions. See *Smith* v. *United States*, 375 F.2d 243, 247 (4th Cir. 1967), *cert. denied* 389 U.S. 841; *Powell* v. *Katzenbach*, 359 F.2d 234 (D.C. Cir. 1965), *cert. denied* 384 U.S. 906; *United States* v. *Wong Kim Bo*, 466 F.2d 1298 (5th Cir. 1972); *United States* v. *Kysar*, 459 F. 2d 422 (10th Cir. 1972). For these reasons, this Department cannot, through advisory opinions, immunize health care providers from criminal prosecution under the statute.

The general or specific statutory authorizations cited by commenters do not supersede the case law cited above. The Department's general authority as an executive agency to promulgate regulations governing conduct within the Department's jurisdiction does not, implicitly or explicitly, include authority to make judgments that are within the exclusive domain of another agency. Neither does our mandate, under Public Law 100-93, to promulgate this regulation provide such authority. Our charge to immunize, by regulation, conduct and arrangements potentially falling under the statute does not include judging whether the conduct of particular individuals violates the statute.

Aside from these legal impediments, it is impossible as a practical matter to give meaningful advice with respect to liability under the statute in the context of a letter ruling. The statute requires proof of a knowing and willful intent to induce or arrange for referrals or for other business reimbursable under the Medicare or Medicaid programs. See *United States* v. *Bay State Ambulance and Hospital Rental Service, Inc., supra*, 874 F.2d at 29 ("The gravamen of Medicare Fraud is inducement"); *United States* v. *Greber*, 760 F. 2d 68 at 71 ("The statute is aimed at the inducement factor"). Thus, the extent to which conduct is motivated by inducing or arranging for referrals will, in large part, determine liability under the statute. The types of factual summaries that typically accompany requests for advisory opinions—descriptions of proposed management contracts or lease agreements, or prospectuses of joint ventures—are likely, however, to be insufficient for purposes of understanding the motives of the parties.

In our experience, assessing whether parties to a particular scheme intend to induce referrals requires substantial investigation resources. Requests for advice typically do not furnish complete and objective accounts of all the facts necessary to determine the subjective intent of the parties. In addition, requests for advice involving business arrangements not yet consummated are especially difficult to analyze because the motives of the parties to induce referrals often become apparent only when the arrangement is operational.

Furthermore, we do not believe that an advisory opinion process is a necessary or appropriate mechanism for keeping the Department aware of new developments in industry business practices, and ensuring that the regulation remains current. As we have discussed above, the legislative history of Public Law 100-93 clearly directs the Secretary to "formally re-evaluate the anti-kickback regulations on a periodic basis and, in so doing, * * * solicit public comment at the outset of the review process." H.R. Rep. No. 85, *supra*, at 27. We believe that periodic updating of this regulation, with the opportunity for public input, is the best way to ensure that these regulations remain practical and relevant in the face of changes in health care delivery and payment arrangements. The need to clarify, interpret, fine tune, expand, or otherwise alter this regulation in response to public and industry input will provide an occasion for us to respond to unanticipated, newly developing, or other beneficial arrangements.

Despite commenters' arguments that other Federal agencies offer the public mechanisms for obtaining advisory opinions, only one other agency of which we are aware, the Federal Elections Commission (FEC), provides any advice with respect to a statutory provision that prohibits "knowing and willful" conduct. The FEC issues such advice under specific statutory authority (2 U.S.C. 437d(a)(7)). It is our understanding, however, that the FEC's advisory opinions do not inquire into whether any conduct is knowing and willful. Thus, the FEC's practice follows the general rule that agencies will refrain from rendering prospective advice on issues of intent. For example, the IRS has stated that it will not issue advice as to the "due diligence" or "good-faith" of parties. See Rev. Proc. 88-3, 1988-1 IRB 29.

As an alternative, we believe that OIG fraud alerts are the best mechanism for imparting practical and continuing guidance to individuals and entities seeking to avoid violations of the statute. The fraud alert program, implemented in March of 1984, was designed to increase our effectiveness in preventing fraud in this Department's programs by highlighting conduct likely to be illegal. Since 1984, we have issued over 100 fraud alerts on subjects unrelated to the anti-kickback statute. On April 24, 1989, we initiated distribution of a Special Fraud Alert on Joint Venture Arrangements to all individuals and entities participating in Medicare, which gave examples of specific characteristics of provider-owned entities that, in our view, might result in abusive or unlawful business arrangements. By identifying what we consider to be suspect features of limited partnerships and other joint ventures (including potentially abusive practices for selecting and retaining investors, for structuring the legal entity or entities involved, and for distributing profits), the Special Fraud Alert communicated our views about the legitimacy of potential or existing ownership arrangements. We believe that fraud alerts can be equally as educational about other areas of enforcement of the statute, and plan to distribute similar information as the need arises.

Comment: A few commenters inquired about the binding effect of advisory letters written by HCFA in the 1970s, when that agency was responsible for enforcing the statute. The commenters suggested that these letters may serve to protect health care providers who engage in a particular business arrangement that was approved by HCFA at that time even though the OIG has not now proposed a safe harbor for that arrangement.

Response: No person in the Department or with the fiscal intermediaries or carriers is, or ever has been, authorized to permit a practice that the statute makes illegal. The Department's lack of authority to provide legal advice on the application of the statute to specific factual situations has been consistently communicated to the public for years. Consequently, no person may reasonably rely on any such advice, especially when that advice is a letter written to a third party about a business arrangement different from the one in which the party is engaging. In sum, the so-called advisory letters may not be regarded in any way as authoritative.

The only authority to legalize conduct is this safe harbor regulation. This regulation supersedes any prior communications from the Department regarding business practices considered not subject to prosecution, and is the only formal mechanism to set forth business arrangements or payment practices that will not be prosecuted under the statute.

Comment: Two commenters requested the OIG to issue selective opinions on issues affecting a class of providers that arise under the statute and safe harbor regulations, even if we decline to provide advice about specific business arrangements or activities.

Response: As we have said, we plan to provide guidance on generic issues through fraud alerts distributed to the provider community. In addition, we remain open to examining the usefulness of other mechanisms for informing the public and health care provider groups about the types of new business arrangements to which the OIG will give investigative priority.

2. Notice to Beneficiaries

Comment: Commenters overwhelmingly supported requiring health care providers to disclose to patients any financial relationships with sources of referral. They argued that such disclosure would not be burdensome, and that many codes of professional ethics, as well as many state statutes, already mandate such disclosure.

Response: With one exception, we have decided not to require such disclosure to qualify under a particular safe harbor provision. First, the activities covered under each safe harbor provision are by definition activities that we deem have a low potential for abuse. Second, disclosure in and of itself would not provide a significant additional assurance that abuse would not occur, even though disclosure may reduce the potential for abuse somewhat by increasing consumer awareness of the relationship between health care providers. Finally, it is possible for a health care provider to cast a disclosure to fit that provider's promotional objective, which is exactly the opposite result from that which we would want to achieve.

The one provision in which we condition safe harbor protection on disclosure is that of referral services. Referral services help beneficiaries make their initial contact with the health care system before a relationship of trust is established with a particular health care provider. Without disclosure of the manner in which a provider of services was selected or rejected by a referral service and the relationship between the service and health care providers, a consumer has very little information upon which to base his or her trust in the practitioner to whom the consumer is being referred. For example, a consumer may well decide to put more trust in a surgeon referred by the referral service if the consumer knew that the referral service only uses board certified physicians. On the other hand, a consumer may feel less confidence in a referral if any physician, no matter what his or her disciplinary record, were one of the referral service's members. Consequently, we are confident that, in this instance, disclosure represents a meaningful added protection.

Although we are not requiring disclosure of financial interests under the other safe harbor provisions, we consider disclosure of financial interests in entities to which health care providers refer patients an ethical duty (See, for example, rule 8.03 of the Current Opinions of the Council on Ethical and Judicial Affairs of the American Medical Association, Chicago, Ill. 1989). Also, to the extent that disclosure affects a patient's freedom of choice and quality of care, it may be necessary to enable a patient to give informed consent.

3. Health Maintenance Organizations, Preferred Provider Organizations and Other Managed Care Plans

We received a number of responses to our invitation to comment on how to protect health maintenance organizations (HMOs), preferred provider organizations (PPOs), and other managed care plans. In addition, we received many other comments regarding HMOs that waive coinsurance and deductible amounts, and price reduction agreements negotiated by these and other types of health benefit plans. We are including these comments in this section.

Comment: Two commenters requested safe harbor protection for HMOs that waive the beneficiary's obligation to pay coinsurance and deductible amounts. They believed that this was a common practice among HMOs. In addition, a few commenters pointed out that some PPOs negotiate agreements with contract health care providers for those providers not to charge the health plan or enrollee for some or all of the coinsurance and deductible amounts they are owed for furnishing services to enrollees. Under such an agreement, when the contract provider bills the Medicare program directly (and not the health plan) and agrees to waive all coinsurance and deductibles, the commenters typically phrased the agreement as one "to accept Medicare payment as payment in full." One commenter specifically objected to this practice.

Response: We agree that protection should be given to prepaid plans with contracts and agreements with HCFA and State agencies for waiver of beneficiary obligations to pay coinsurance and deductible amounts. However, as will be discussed below, we do not agree that such protection is warranted at this time for PPOs and prepaid plans that do not have contracts or agreements with HCFA or State agencies.

Health plans offer a variety of incentives to attract beneficiaries to become enrollees. In many instances, HCFA permits such HMOs and competitive medical plans (CMPs) to waive the premiums attributable to the coinsurance and deductible amounts. Further, HMOs and CMPs under a risk contract with HCFA are required under certain circumstances to reduce coinsurance and deductible amounts or offer additional benefit options.

The routine waiver by a prepaid health plan of beneficiaries' obligation to pay coinsurance and deductible amounts is clearly distinguishable from such routine waiver by other health care providers, such as hospital outpatient departments, physicians, or durable medical equipment suppliers. Two principal characteristics distinguish a health plan's routine waiver of cost-sharing amounts from that of other health care providers. First, a health plan's routine waiver program is inextricably intertwined with the offering of a comprehensive package of covered benefits, and is not offered for the purchase of an individual item or service. Quite often, in the case of prepaid plans, the routine waiver of cost-sharing amounts is made in the form of a reduction or waiver of the beneficiary's premium and may also be combined with the offering of increased covered benefits. Thus, the routine waiver of cost-sharing amounts is generally not an incentive to use a particular item or service at the time it is furnished.

Second, although cost-sharing requirements can serve to control utilization, HMOs and other health plans under contract with HCFA or a State agency have built-in incentives to control unnecessary utilization, or have their utilization and costs monitored by HCFA or the State agency. Thus, the issue of potential overutilization (with increased costs to the programs) is adequately dealt with without resort to imposing the obligation on beneficiaries to pay coinsurance and deductible amounts.

Therefore, we expect to publish at a later date an additional safe harbor provision to protect prepaid health plans that have a contract or agreement with HCFA or a State agency where the health plan offers beneficiaries increased benefits coverage, reduced cost-sharing amounts (coinsurance, deductibles, or copayments), or reduced premiums where certain standards are met. Because of the limited scope of the comments we received on HMOs, PPOs and managed care plans, we expect to publish at a later date an interim final rule in order to solicit additional comments from the public on this new safe harbor provision.

This new safe harbor provision will not protect incentives offered to beneficiaries by health plans, such as PPOs, that are not operating under a contract or agreement with HCFA or a State agency. Unlike health plans with such contracts or agreements, we are not confident that all PPOs that engage in these negotiated waiver agreements properly protect the Medicare and Medicaid programs against overutilization. And we did not receive sufficient comments on the different types of PPOs for us to distinguish the characteristics of a PPO engaging in these negotiated waiver agreements where the Medicare and Medicaid programs are properly protected.

Comment: Several commenters requested the OIG to protect a variety of arrangements between HMOs, PPOs, competitive medical plans (CMPs), managed care plans, and other health plans on the one hand, and medical groups and other health care providers who furnish items and services to the health plans at a reduced price on the other hand. A few of these commenters observed the benefits that can be achieved when a health care provider offers discounts to these organizations. Several commenters recommended special treatment for relationships between HMOs and health care providers, such as physicians and hospitals, involving the leasing of space and equipment and contracting for personal services. One commenter requested special safe harbor protection for "[a]ll transactions between an HMO and contracting medical groups * * * if the medical group provides over 90 percent of its services to HMO members."

Response: We agree that there is a need to provide safe harbor protection for certain practices between managed care plans and health care providers. Thus, we are expecting to publish a rule that will protect many of these price reduction arrangements where certain standards are met. For the same reasons as stated above, we are expecting to publish this safe harbor provision as an interim final rule with an opportunity for additional comments from the public.

The safe harbor provision we are expecting to publish will only protect agreements between health plans and contract health care providers for the sole purpose of furnishing items and services covered by the health plan, Medicare, or Medicaid. In other words, for the reasons explained below, we are not protecting in this provision the contracts between health plans and contract health care providers for these providers to furnish services other than covered benefits, such as peer review and management services.

As with all safe harbor provisions, where two parties engage in a multi-faceted payment arrangement where protection is sought from more than one safe harbor, we expect separate justifications to be clearly set forth for each provision for which protection is sought. Where HMOs contract with physicians and other health care providers for the furnishing of services other than covered health care services, we believe that HMOs, PPOs and other prepaid health plans will be able to conform their arrangements to the appropriate safe harbor provisions. For example, many contract health care providers furnish peer review, marketing services, or pre-enrollment screening for HMOs. For the remuneration attributable to the furnishing of such services to be protected, it must comply with the personal service/management contracts safe harbor provision. Also for example, the remuneration attributable to the lease of space or equipment must comply with those respective safe harbor provisions.

We are not convinced that merely because a medical group has a large majority of its business with an HMO that a special across-the-board exemption for all transactions is warranted. HMOs operate under a variety of payment mechanisms, both with respect to the Medicare and Medicaid payments they receive and the payments they make to physicians. Although in many cases the incentive structure in which HMOs operate is designed to protect against overutilization of service, this incentive structure may not extend to fee-for-service arrangements.

Further, even though many HMOs have generally operated largely free of fraud and abuse problems, we are aware of some HMOs that have abused their contractual relationships with medical groups, where individuals in the groups have engaged in abusive activities on behalf of the HMO, or where the medical group has compromised the interest of beneficiaries in order to keep the vital HMO contract. In at least one case, a criminal conviction was obtained for such a practice. Although safe harbor protection is warranted for certain contractual relationships between health plans and contract health care providers, we also intend to use our authorities aggressively to monitor closely and, where appropriate, penalize any abusive relationships between these parties to assure that medically necessary services of a high quality are available and accessible to all enrollees.

4. Waiver of Beneficiary Deductible and Coinsurance Amounts

Comment: The OIG received numerous comments on the establishment of a safe harbor for waiver of hospital inpatient coinsurance and deductible (copayment) amounts owed by program beneficiaries. Many commenters requested the OIG to provide safe harbor protection for routine hospital waiver or partial reduction of inpatient fees not subsequently claimed as bad debts because the practice would benefit hospital inpatients without increasing program costs. Some commenters urged the OIG to protect the submission of bad debt claims where copayments were routinely waived for limited categories of patients, such as seniors. On the other hand, several commenters were concerned that permitting hospital waiver of inpatient copayments would encourage overutilization of hospital services and promote cost-shifting to patients with nongovernmental insurance policies.

Response: Since October 1, 1983, when the prospective payment system (PPS) for reimbursing hospital inpatient services was implemented, we have been aware of hospitals that routinely waive Medicare beneficiary deductibles and coinsurance charges for inpatient hospital services in order to attract patients. Because the waiver of patient charges constitutes an inducement to use services in exchange for something of value (the forgiveness of financial obligation), this practice violates the statute. However, assuming the waived amounts are not later claimed as bad debt, the practice appears to cause no direct financial harm to the Medicare program because hospitals receive a pre-determined payment amount under PPS regardless of their costs or charges. Moreover, due to hospital peer review requirements and the relatively fixed level of patient demand for hospital inpatient services, waiver of inpatient beneficiary fees is not likely to increase utilization significantly. Furthermore, if hospital waiver policies do not discriminate on the basis of length of stay or type of disease, the potential for program abuse appears minimal.

In addition, we know of no data, nor have commenters produced or referred us to any, indicating that routine hospital waivers of inpatient copayments owed by program beneficiaries will shift the costs of care to non-Medicare patients. Rather, we assume that most hospitals that choose to waive these amounts do so because the hospital more than makes up in increased volume for any initial "loss" resulting from not collecting the full amount to which it is entitled. Although we believe there is little risk of "cost-shifting" to the non-Medicare population, the first standard in this provision makes clear that any such cost-shifting is not protected.

We do not agree, however, that health care providers who choose to waive copayment amounts routinely for some or all of their patients should be permitted to claim such amounts as bad debt. Such a rule would muddle two very distinct Medicare policies. Traditionally, Medicare health care providers are reimbursed for uncollectible payments owed by beneficiaries. See 42 CFR 413.80. This rule requires, among other things, that health care providers make an indigence determination on a case-by-case basis, or reasonable collection efforts, prior to recouping bad debt losses from the program. See also Provider Reimbursement Manual, sections 310, 312, HCFA Pub. No. 15–1. Thus, payment of Medicare bad debts, unlike routine waivers of Medicare cost sharing amounts protected under this safe harbor regulation, are only authorized under certain conditions pertaining to the uncollectability of payments and the indigence of beneficiaries. Health care providers who routinely waive beneficiary copayments in accordance with this safe harbor regulation, and do not make case-by-case indigence determinations or otherwise prove uncollectability under 42 CFR 413.80, cannot deduct expenses as bad debt. Where such an unlawful expense is claimed, the hospital may be subject to civil or criminal prosecution.

Comment: Many commenters requested the OIG to extend safe harbor protection to waiver of patient fees imposed for a wide array of provider services. Several commenters sought protection for waiver of beneficiary copayments for part A services furnished by other cost-based health care providers, such as skilled nursing facilities and home health agencies. These commenters argued that where services are paid on a reasonable cost basis, just as where services are reimbursed under PPS, waiver of beneficiary copayments causes no financial harm to the program. Other commenters sought still broader protection under the safe harbor for copayments for services under part B, arguing that the limited protection granted for inpatient hospital copayments was discriminatory.

Response: We believe that protection is uniquely appropriate for waiver of patient charges related to hospital inpatient services. A routine waiver program will not likely increase patient demand for these services, since beneficiaries cannot admit themselves, and hospital overnight stays are inherently undesirable from a patient's perspective. Thus, it is unlikely that a routine waiver program will affect utilization. By contrast, cost-based fee-for-service health care providers, such as home health agencies and nursing homes, may be able to offset their losses resulting from their waiver of copayments by increasing their Medicare allowable costs. Such manipulation of reimbursement amounts would be virtually impossible to prevent. Thus, we do not believe that the protection offered under this safe harbor provision should be extended to routine waiver of beneficiary copayments by cost-based fee-for-service health care providers.

Routine waiver of beneficiary copayments by individuals or entities reimbursed on the basis of reasonable charges even more clearly affects program costs. When charge-based health care providers routinely fail to collect all or part of beneficiary copayments authorized by law, and then submit actual charges to Medicare as if copayment amounts were collected, these charges increase customary and prevailing rates which, in turn, inflate program costs. The Medicare Carriers Manual makes clear that in these situations, a health care provider is required to reduce his or her actual charge. See section 5220, HCFA Pub. No. 14. Thus, we believe that individuals and entities who fail to reduce actual charges submitted to Medicare are misrepresenting their charges, and may be subject to civil and criminal liability for submitting false claims.

We are aware that some local government health care providers, including county hospital outpatient departments, routinely reduce beneficiary payments at the time of service for the extremely indigent populations they serve. For these health care providers, offering patients the option of reduced payment at time of service may be a more successful collection strategy than subsequently billing patients for the entire copayment. This practice, while not protected by this safe harbor regulation, would not likely violate the statute so long as the partial forgiveness of the copayment obligation was strictly a pragmatic financial decision and not an inducement to patients to purchase medical services. We see no purpose in interfering in the mission of local governments or other hospitals that serve primarily indigent populations when they reduce beneficiary fees for those unable to pay. Such health care providers, typically, have no need to engage in sophisticated marketing strategies to induce more business.

Comment: One commenter advised the OIG that in accordance with 42 U.S.C. 254b(f)(3)(F) and 254c(e)(3)(F), federally qualified migrant and community health care centers are required to develop a sliding fee schedule for patients based upon ability to pay, which could result in waiver of part or all of the Medicare coinsurance and deductible amounts. These commenters argued that such waivers, although mandated under Public Health Service Act grant programs, could be deemed a violation of the statute.

Response: In section 4161(a)(4) of Public Law 101-508, the Omnibus Budget Reconciliation Act of 1990, Congress enacted a fourth statutory exception to the statute, which exempts a waiver of any Medicare Part B coinsurance by a Federally qualified health care center to any individual who qualifies for subsidized services under the Public Health Services Act. Thus, we are providing a safe harbor provision for this exception. In addition, we are making this safe harbor applicable to similarly situated individuals who receive services under the Maternal and Child Health Service Block Grant program (see section 505(2)(D) of the Act; 42 U.S.C. 705(2)(D), or who are Medicaid beneficiaries.

Comment: Six commenters argued that protecting routine waiver of beneficiary payments for inpatient hospital services would discourage competition from ambulatory surgical centers (ASCs).

Response: Although the granting of safe harbor protection for the waiver of inpatient copayments gives practitioners or their patients an incentive to choose inpatient hospital settings over outpatient settings, we believe that the activities of the PROs reasonably ensure that services are furnished in outpatient settings where appropriate. Therefore, we believe that the granting of safe harbor protection only for inpatient services is unlikely to draw patients away from ASCs and other outpatient settings.

Comment: A few commenters requested the OIG to protect waiver or discounts of inpatient copayments where hospitals and physicians offer this benefit not to patients directly, but to insurance companies, HMOs, or employer or union medical service plans, that have assumed liability for the beneficiary portion of payment under the terms of their insurance policies. Insurers offering these insurance benefits may attempt to negotiate with hospitals to reduce or eliminate the beneficiary portion of reimbursement in exchange for endorsing the hospital as a preferred provider or offering other tangible benefits.

Response: This safe harbor provision protects the waiver by hospitals of inpatient copayment amounts only where these amounts would otherwise be paid by Medicare beneficiaries themselves. In paragraph (k)(1)(iii), we have expressly made this provision inapplicable to negotiated price reduction agreements between health care providers and third-party payers, even where the reduction involves beneficiary copayments for which the third party payor has assumed liability as part of a Medigap policy. As we discussed in the section immediately above, we are expecting to publish an additional safe harbor provision to protect HMOs, CMPs and HCPPs under contract with HCFA or a State agency that waive coinsurance and deductible amounts owed by beneficiaries where certain standards are met.

Comment: Two commenters sought protection for the waiver of patient copayment amounts for the first eight days of care in a skilled nursing facility (SNF) after discharge from a hospital under the same ownership. These commenters stated that protection was needed to enable the smooth transfer of patients who were ill, and to allow hospital beds to be vacated for sicker patients.

Response: We understand that health care providers operating both hospitals and SNFs may, for entirely legitimate reasons, wish to continue waiving SNF copayment amounts when transferring hospital patients into the SNF for a brief period. In section III.D. below, we discuss in more detail the special considerations that exist where the hospital and SNF are wholly owned by a single "parent" entity, or where one of the facilities is the sole owner of the other.

Comment: One commenter requested the OIG to expand the safe harbor provision for waiver of hospital inpatient copayments to cover the provision of free items or services such as meals or presurgical overnight stays, samples of products from manufacturers, or blood screening and other testing services. The commenter suggested that such free gifts benefit patients without causing harm to the program, so long as there is no obligation to purchase additional items or services upon receipt of the free gifts.

Response: We decline to protect the offer of free gifts to beneficiaries within this safe harbor provision, as we have declined to protect this practice within the safe harbor provision governing discounts. The statute clearly contemplates that illicit remuneration may involve payments "in cash or in kind." The practice of offering free gifts may well induce beneficiaries to purchase additional or unnecessary items or services. Such inducements could easily become excessive, and there is no distinct financial or other cut-off point below which we could be sure that gifts remained non-abusive. Because we understand that such inducements are an area of significant abuse, we believe that protection of this practice would be unwarranted.

C. Provision-by-Provision Analysis of Safe Harbors

1. Investment Interests—§ 1001.952(a)

The OIG received close to three hundred comments on the issue of providing safe harbor protection for payments from investment interests. These comments are divided into three broad categories: (a) Comments on the proposed safe harbor provision for payments from investments in large publicly traded entities; (b) suggestions for safe harbors for payments from investments in small entities such as limited partnerships, about which we solicited comments, and (c) proposals for protecting payments from other investment interests. For convenience, we are discussing all of these comments in this section. Before discussing the comments and responses for these three broad categories of investment interests, we will discuss general issues raised with respect to investment interests.

Comment: We received a number of comments asking the OIG to clarify the types of investors and investment interests to be protected. In particular, we received many comments urging the OIG to protect indirect investment interests held by family members and to protect debt as well as equity investments.

Response: We are adding a definition of the terms "investor" and "investment interests" to this safe harbor provision. We are defining an "investor" to include both individuals and entities who either directly or indirectly hold an investment interest in an entity. Our definition includes examples, which are not intended to be an exhaustive list of ways that investment interests may be indirectly held. For example, a family member of a referring physician may hold the investment interest in the joint venture entity, or a referring physician may have a legal or beneficial interest in an entity, such as his or her group practice, a trust or a holding company, where that entity directly holds the investment interest in the joint venture entity. In both cases, we view the physician as having the ownership interest in the joint venture entity.

In many cases we distinguish investors who do business with the entity in which they have invested from other investors who are exclusively seeking a return on their investment. We call an investor who does business with the entity as "an investor who is in a position to make or influence referrals to, furnish items or services to, or otherwise generate business for the entity." This classification is meant to include all investors who do business in any manner with the entity. Except as noted below, we do not limit this category to investors who actually make referrals. Rather, our focus is on the status of the investor and the ability to make or influence the referral stream or level of business activity for the entity. Such investors include not only physicians, but hospitals and other entities capable of influencing referrals.

We note that this category of investor doing business with the entity also includes those investors who furnish items and services to the entity as well as those investors who otherwise generate business for the entity. Thus for example, if a durable medical equipment (DME) supplier and hospital both enter into a joint venture to furnish DME to patients when they leave the hospital, both the DME supplier and the hospital fit within this category of investor doing business with the entity.

There are some very limited situations where, because of the special status or location of the investor, he or she does not fit within this category of investor doing business with the entity. For example, for the most part, retired physicians no longer make or influence referrals. In addition, typically a physician who resides and practices in a separate service area from the entity is similarly not "in a position to make or influence referrals." Or an investor could simply make an agreement barring him or her from actually making or influencing referrals to the entity. In all three examples, the determination whether an investor should be classified as doing business with the entity in which he or she has invested is a factual question. However, we will accept a written stipulation that for the life of the investment the investor will not make referrals to, furnish items or services for, or otherwise generate business for the entity. We emphasize that, because of the potential for abuse of this stipulation agreement, the investor must be bound to this agreement for the life of the investment as long as he or she remains an investor.

Finally, our definition of the term "investment interest" makes clear that debt as well as equity investments are protected.

a. *Large Publicly Traded Entities. Comment:* Several commenters questioned the relationship of this proposed safe harbor provision to the rules of the Securities and Exchange Commission (SEC) for the registration of securities. For example, some suggested that the OIG should exempt all investment interests that are traded on a publicly regulated exchange, while another suggested that public trading be an additional condition for protection. In addition, a variety of comments were received regarding the standards adopted from the SEC rules that, in order for payments from investment interests in an entity to be protected, the assets of the entity must exceed $5 million and the number of shareholders must exceed 500 persons (the so-called "$5 million asset/500 investor rule"). While some suggested the $5 million test was too high, one suggested that it was too low. One commenter suggested that the 500 shareholder test was too high, and another suggested that the OIG require either $5 million in assets or 500 shareholders, but not both. Finally, another commenter suggested that the OIG protect an investment in an entity any time the asset level was greater than $5 million.

Response: We intended to protect profit distributions made to referring investors in large publicly traded corporations where the investment interest was obtained at fair market value through trading on a publicly regulated exchange. The remuneration received by these investors is so tangentially related to their referrals that the potential for abuse is minimal.

As we stated in the preamble of the proposed rule, we adopted the SEC registration rules from 15 U.S.C. 78/(g) and 17 CFR 240.12g–1, which generally require entities with more than $5 million in assets and more than 500 investors to register with the SEC. At the time, we had believed that such a test would protect payments from only those entities that are actively traded on a national securities exchange.

Based on the comments we received and our experience in enforcing the statute, we believe that in many respects the SEC rules are not applicable for the purposes of protecting against abuse. In particular, the $5 million threshold is too low. An entity that owns two magnetic resonance imaging (MRI) machines may well meet this test. Thus, we are changing the asset threshold level from $5 million to $50 million. Publicly traded entities of this size are sufficiently large to assure that abuse is minimal.

In addition, the SEC's other criteria of 500 investors does not provide meaningful protection against abuse. We recognize that in many cases a large number of investors can dilute the influence of one investor's referral patterns on the level of payments that he or she receives. However, it has been our experience that many sham joint ventures try to obtain many investors, each of whom contribute nominal investments, as a mechanism to lock-in the loyalties of as many physicians as possible. Thus, depending on the factual circumstances of a particular joint venture, a large number of investors could either be abusive or minimize abuse.

We are making other revisions to this first investment interest safe harbor provision to provide greater clarity consistent with our original intent. Thus this safe harbor as revised contains two definitional prerequisites in paragraph (a)(1) for the type of entity we are protecting, and is followed by five standards, all of which must be met to the extent they apply to the investment interest in question.

For an entity to be protected under this safe harbor, it must meet two definitional prerequisites. The first prerequisite to qualify for protection is that the assets of the entity must be measured any time within the previous fiscal year or the previous 12 month period. This time period is different from the SEC rule, which we believe to be overly restrictive for the purposes of this safe harbor. The time period for measuring compliance which we are adopting will mean for all practical purposes that growing entities will be protected as soon as they reach compliance with all the preconditions and standards in this safe harbor, rather than having to wait for the next fiscal year as the SEC requires. In addition, the time period we are specifying permits an entity to retain safe harbor protection for a limited time period even though it is no longer in compliance with the $50 million asset threshold in this rule. During this time period, an entity will have the opportunity to bring itself back into compliance.

The second definitional prerequisite is that the entity must possess $50 million in the form of undepreciated net tangible assets. This clarification of what we mean by $50 million in assets removes many assets which we never intended to include within the scope of protection. We are excluding all intangible assets such as the company's valuation of its name recognition and stock and other forms of goodwill. We are excluding such assets because their valuation is too subject to "creative" accounting or appraisal techniques. The assets must also be reduced by any liabilities. Thus, a corporation only has $1 million of net tangible assets when it buys a $5 million piece of equipment with a $4 million loan. However, we are excluding from the calculation of assets any reductions in the value of assets due to depreciation. We believe it is inappropriate for an entity to lose safe harbor protection as a result of the aging of its assets. Further, we do not want to create incentives to replace equipment unnecessarily merely for the entity to regain safe harbor protection based on the value of new equipment. We are also clarifying that the reporting of net tangible assets must be based on net acquisition costs of purchasing such assets from an unrelated entity. The use of net acquisition costs in this rule is a generally accepted accounting principle, and makes clear that, for the purposes of this rule, we will not accept a company's use of current market valuations of assets. Further, we intend to use the Medicare related party rule, 42 CFR 413.17, to assure that the acquisition costs from the purchase of an asset is only based on a bona fide purchase through an arm's length transaction. Our final clarification in how to apply the $50 million asset test is that assets unrelated to a company's health care line of business cannot be used in the calculation of assets. For example, a nursing home corporation could be a subsidiary of a hotel chain. The hotel assets cannot be used for purposes of qualifying for the $50 million asset test. However, with the exception of the related party rule, it is not our intent to require corporations to be familiar with cost reimbursement rules of 42 CFR part 413. Tangible assets used in furnishing items and services may be counted even though they may not be allowable costs under part 413. The information necessary to determine compliance with this $50 million asset test is readily available in the accounting books of entities, and the accounting methods for determining compliance are fully consistent with generally accepted accounting principles. Thus, an independent certified public accountant should have little trouble certifying an entity's compliance with these requirements.

This safe harbor contains five standards, not all of which may be applicable in every instance. The first two standards, paragraphs (a)(1) (i)–(ii), which will be discussed here, focus on the nature of the investment interest. (The three remaining standards are being added in response to other comments which will be discussed below.)

The first standard (see paragraph (a)(1)(i)) applies only to an investment interest in an equity security, and requires such a security to be registered with the SEC under 15 U.S.C. 78*l* (b) or (g). We had considered but are rejecting an alternative standard that the investment interest must merely meet the SEC registration qualifications. This requirement of actual registration provides a clear bright-line rule, and is an indication of good-faith entry into the public securities markets, which is a significant factor underlying the rationale for this safe harbor. In addition, we are requiring the investment interest actually to be registered with the SEC because many exemptions exist to the SEC's $5 million asset/500 investor rule, which permit many entities to be actively traded but not to be registered with the SEC, and thus not under its oversight. See 15 U.S.C. 78*l*(g)(2). However, the SEC's reasons for granting an exception may not be consistent with the purposes of this rule, and thus we see no particular reason to protect securities simply because they qualify for an SEC exemption. We note that one such exemption under 15 U.S.C. 78*l*(g)(2) is for securities listed and registered on a national securities exchange. Such securities must comply with 15 U.S.C. 78*l*(b), and for the purposes of this rule we are requiring such securities to be registered with the SEC.

We are not applying the registration requirement to investment interests that involve debt securities because we believe that the extra safeguard of SEC registration is unnecessary. Publicly traded debt instruments, although protected under this safe harbor, are not the type of investment interests that are the focal point of this rule. Although the potential for abuse is present, we have not been apprised of the actual occurrence of abuse relating to these investment interests, and believe that their usefulness as instruments for inducing investors' referrals is more limited than equity investment interests.

The second standard (see paragraph (a)(1)(ii)) responds to the commenters' suggestions regarding public trading. We are adding a standard to this provision requiring the investment interest of an investor in a position to make or influence referrals to, furnish items and services to, or otherwise generate business for the entity to be obtained on terms equally available to the public through a registered national securities exchange, such as the New York Stock Exchange or the American Stock Exchange, or through the National Association of Securities Dealers Automated Quotation (NASDAQ) system. We note that we specifically intend to preclude safe harbor protection for securities traded through the so-called "pink sheets" or those "non-NASDAQ" securities that are traded through the OTC Bulletin Board Service. See. Securities Exchange Act Release No. 34–27975, May 1, 1990. This standard follows our original intent to assure that the investment interests of physicians or others in a position to influence referrals must be obtained through the kind of arms length trading that is normally associated with actively traded public securities at the fair market value through a publicly regulated exchange. Such public trading assures that the entity does not obtain capital by self-selecting investors based on their status as sources of referrals.

Although we are not requiring investment interests of other investors to be obtained through public trading, physicians and others in a position to influence referrals must strictly comply with this standard. We plan to closely scrutinize attempts to circumvent this standard. For example, any investment interest obtained before an entity becomes publicly traded is not protected under this provision. In addition, an investor is not protected by exchanging a limited partnership interest for shares in a newly formed entity that is publicly traded. Further, this standard precludes protection of payments from securities where physicians are afforded the opportunity to buy the available shares of an entity before other members of the public have the opportunity to invest in that entity. Such an entity would have only physicians as investors, and it is not our intent to protect payments from such entities. We expect the public to be afforded a genuine opportunity to invest in these publicly traded entities. Where referring sources (or their immediate families) hold a large proportion of the shares, we will presume that this standard has not been met.

Comment: A number of commenters suggested that the OIG expand this provision in a variety of ways to protect remuneration from debt as well as equity instruments and from entities other than corporations, such as partnerships.

Response: As discussed above, this safe harbor protects debt as well as equity instruments. We recognize that an ambiguity existed in our proposed rule in that our 500 investor test applied only to "a class of equity security" and thus appeared to prohibit debt instruments from qualifying under this safe harbor provision. However, this ambiguity is resolved by eliminating the 500 investor test. In addition as discussed above, we are exempting debt instruments from the SEC registration requirement contained in the first standard.

We also agree that investments in partnerships should be protected, and we are revising this provision accordingly, by adding a definition of investment interest.

Comment: A few commenters expressed concern that entities meeting the requirements contained in the proposed safe harbor provision could still be engaging in abusive relationships with individuals in a position to make referrals. One commenter suggested that we specifically protect against fraudulent cross-referral arrangements whereby investors in entity "A" are explicitly or implicitly encouraged to refer to entity "B" in return for entity "A" receiving the referrals from the investors of entity "B."

Response: We agree with the thrust of these comments, and are adding three standards (see paragraphs (a)(1) (iii)–(v)) to clarify our original intent and assure that investment interests are not used as inducements for referrals. One, the entity or any investor must not market or furnish the entity's items or services to passive investors in any manner differently than to non-investors. In other words, although an entity may seek referrals or other business from passive investors, it must promote and furnish its items or services to investors and non-investors in the same manner. An entity may not use a separate marketing approach or provide a different level of service to passive investors as opposed to non-investors. For example, in its promotional efforts, the entity may not in any manner appeal to or refer to such investor's position as an investor, and in serving customers it may not offer special arrangements to investors that are not available or are offered on different terms to non-investors. Any distribution to passive investors of individual or aggregate investor referral patterns would also not be protected under this provision. In addition, the entity or any investor must not promote the items or services of other entities as part of a cross referral agreement. One type of cross referral arrangement we are not protecting is the sham transaction described in the above comment.

Two, the entity must not loan funds to or guarantee a loan for an investor to use for the purpose of obtaining the investment interest. We do not believe protection should be afforded where an investor is loaned money from the entity, or from a parent or subsidiary corporation (or is guaranteed a loan by the entity or a related organization), and the investor makes an investment based on that loan. In such a situation, the investor is adding no real capital to the entity. We note, however, that safe harbor protection is available where the investor borrows from other sources, such as from his or her broker or a bank.

And three, the amount of payment in return for the investment interest must be directly proportional to the amount of the capital investment. Such payments are consistent with the type of corporate dividend payment that we are trying to protect.

We believe that these minor revisions, which are fully consistent with our original intent, should offer reasonable protection against the possibility of significant abuses without unduly restricting the types of entities that may qualify under this provision.

b. *Small Entities.* In the notice of proposed rulemaking we solicited comments on expanding the proposed investment interest safe harbor to protect payments from investments in small entities, particularly limited and general partnership interests. For limited partnership interests we suggested four standards for protection: (1) A bona fide opportunity to invest is made on an equal basis without regard to the investor's ability to make referrals, (2) no requirement is imposed on the investor to make referrals, (3) disclosure is made to the referred patient, and (4) payments are not related to referrals. As conditions for protection of payments from investments in general partnership interests, we suggested that disclosure of the investment interest be made to a referred patient and payments not be related to referrals.

Comment: A large number of people commented that, in view of the OIG's interpretation of the statute as not prohibiting all referrals to entities in which a physician has an investment interest, safe harbor protection should be provided for legitimate arrangements. While some commenters suggested that the OIG adopt generic criteria for analyzing these arrangements, others commented more directly on the proposed standards we suggested in the proposed rule. A few commenters suggested that any safe harbor protections should treat indirect ownership interests held by family members in the same manner as direct ownership interests to assure that investors who make referrals to that entity do not circumvent the intent of these requirements by having investments held in the name of family members instead of their own names.

The enormous response to this invitation for comment reflected the polarization of the health care community on this issue. Those supporting safe harbor protection emphasized that physician-investor joint ventures promote competition, provide quality services, promote patient convenience, bring needed services to communities, are cost effective, do not lead to over-utilization, do not compromise ethics, and enable services to be provided outside hospitals and physician offices. Those urging no safe harbor protection or expressing a need for stringent safeguards argued that these joint ventures hurt competition, compromise quality of care, are not in patients' best interests, increase costs, lead to over-utilization, and create conflict of interests between health care providers and patients.

A large number of commenters generally supported safe harbor protection for payments to those with managing partnership interests and agreed with the OIG's two suggested conditions for protection. However, a few commenters opposed such protection. In addition, a few commenters suggested that the OIG define which individuals would be protected under this provision.

Response: Because of the significant business investment activity in these small entities—typically joint ventures—and the advantages of permitting them in certain situations, we believe that safe harbor protection is warranted. However, we have also observed widespread abuses in many of these joint ventures. In particular, we believe that a large number of these newly formed entities are designed to have physicians as investors specifically to induce them to use the entity in which they have invested. Therefore, any safe harbor protection must include significant safeguards to minimize any corrupting influence the investment interest may have on the physician-investor's decision where to refer a patient. We are including a second investment interest provision (paragraph (a)(2)) that protects payments to investors who are limited and general partners, shareholders, or holders of debt securities where eight standards are met. We will discuss some of the definitional categories of persons who are protected under this provision, our response to comments recommending special protection for managing partnership interests, and our three categories that provide structure for the eight standards in this safe harbor.

We have classified "investors" as either "passive" or "active" because some of the standards apply only to those defined as "passive" investors. The definition of an "active" investor includes two categories of persons. The first category is modeled after a bona fide general partner in a partnership under the Uniform Partnership Act who is responsible for the day-to-day management of the entity.

We are including a second way to qualify as an "active" investor: the individual or entity must agree in writing to undertake the liability for the partnership, including the acts of its agents acting within the scope of their agency. We believe that such an affirmative act will assure that the individual or entity performs many of the same functions that general partners do who actively manage the day-to-day operations of the joint venture entity. For example, these active investors undertake the business risk that a typical general partner does, and will be interested in assuring that the day-to-day managers of the entity engage in sound business practices and not run afoul of the statute as well as other Federal and State laws and regulations.

"Passive" investors are those investors who are not active investors, such as limited partners in a partnership or shareholders in a corporation.

This second investment interest safe harbor provision includes some standards that must be met by both passive and active investors, and some standards that need only be met by passive investors, to the extent any exist in the joint venture. If an entity contains only active investors, the standards applicable only to passive investors would, of course, not apply. It must be emphasized, however, that the standards for this safe harbor must be met by all the investors in the entity. To the extent that one class of investors, such as active investors, qualifies, but the passive investors do not meet one of the standards, safe harbor protection is not given to payments to any investors in the entity.

In this regard, special attention must be paid to cases involving ownership interests held indirectly through other entities. Take a situation, for example, where a group of individuals are passive investors in entity "A", which in turn is the active investor in entity "B." For entity "B" to qualify under this safe harbor provision, entity "A" must meet all the requirements for active investor in entity "B," and the individual investors of entity "A" must meet all the requirements as passive investors in entity "B."

We believe that this provision will protect investment interests of those with managing partnership interests who establish limited partnerships that meet the standards of this provision. We have decided not to include a third investment interest provision at this time that would place fewer requirements on business structures composed entirely of active investors. We recognize that there are many legitimate small businesses structured in this manner where a group of individuals come together and all of them participate as hands-on managers in the day-to-day operations of the business and undertake personal liability for the entity. Historically, many hospitals were formed in this manner. And currently many group practices and other innovative health care delivery systems are being formed on a bona fide basis in this same manner. However, there are many new entities that have the same business structure, but that may be subject to abuse under the statute. Consequently, we have determined that it is inappropriate to implement a safe harbor provision at this time for entities composed exclusively of active investors that would not have to meet the standards we are implementing in this second investment interest provision. However, we are considering a new safe harbor provision for such investment interests which we anticipate publishing as a separate regulation.

The safe harbor provision we are including in this rule for investment interests in small entities was developed based on the standards we suggested in the proposed rule, the comments we received on our proposals and our continuing experience in enforcing the statute. This experience includes investigations of abusive joint venture arrangements, our Fraud Alert describing suspect features of these arrangements, and our Report to Congress entitled "Financial Arrangements Between Physicians and Health Care Businesses" (OIG, Office of Analysis and Inspections, May 1989). The Report to Congress disclosed in detail both the extensive ownership of joint ventures by physicians, and the additional services received by patients of these physicians as compared to all Medicare patients in general.

The standards for this provision are structured into three categories that we have identified as being of concern to us in joint venture arrangements: (1) The manner in which investors are selected and retained, (2) the nature of their business structure, and (3) the financing and profit distributions. To the extent possible, we have adopted bright line rules. We believe that this approach will facilitate compliance because investors will be able to determine easily whether they meet the conditions of safe harbor protection. As discussed in section III.A. above, we are not accepting commenters' suggestions for generic criteria. We believe that such criteria do not provide sufficient protection against abusive arrangements, nor do they provide meaningful guidance to delineate when a provider has complied with them.

The following discussion will be structured along the lines of the three problem areas we have identified.

(i) *Manner in which investors are selected and retained.* In this section we discuss the comments and our responses regarding the problem of the manner in which investors are selected and retained. The first five standards of this investment interest provision protecting small entities (paragraphs (a)(2)(i)–(v)) relate to this problem area.

Comment: The OIG received mixed comments on the first standard suggested in the proposed rule, that a bona fide opportunity to invest be provided on an equal basis to all investors without regard to their ability to make referrals. A large number of commenters expressed concern about the meaning and workability of this standard, particularly that it is vague and would be difficult to police. Several commenters construed this first suggested standard as a results-oriented test requirement, in other words, that joint ventures must be owned partly by individuals not in a position to make referrals. Some suggested that the OIG place a limit on the percentage of ownership of an entity that can be held by such referring investors. The percentages ranged from 5 percent to 85 percent ownership by referring investors. Others suggested that the OIG should not require these entities to have some amount of non-referring investors. One commenter specifically objected to a requirement that a joint venture have a majority of the ownership interests held by non-referring investors. Five commenters expressed concern that any requirement that investment interests be offered to non-referring individuals may be construed as requiring a public offering, thus triggering the necessity of complying with SEC rules (such as Regulation D governing the limited offering and sale of securities without registration under the Securities Act of 1933, 17 CFR 230.501 *et seq.*) or State "blue sky" laws which require public securities registration.

Response: We agree with the concerns expressed by most of the commenters about our first suggested standard. Thus, we are replacing it with three standards (paragraphs (a)(2)(i)–(iii)) in order to better address problems concerning the manner in which investors are selected. To comply with our first standard, investors who make referrals or who are in a position to make referrals or furnish items or services cannot own more than 40 percent of the value of investment interests within each class of investments in the entity. This standard requires not only that a bona fide opportunity to invest has been afforded to people not in a position to make referrals, but that these individuals hold at least 60 percent of the value of the investment interests in each class of investments.

In essence, we are switching a process measure with an outcome measure. As several commenters observed, our proposed standard of equal opportunity to invest contemplated that an equal number of referring and non-referring individuals would be given an opportunity to invest. Such a process-orientated test would have been virtually impossible to monitor. For example, such a standard would have required a joint venture to monitor all marketing solicitations, and determine the referral status of everyone who was solicited to make sure that an equal number of referring and non-referring potential investors were given the opportunity to invest. The alternative outcome measure we are adopting will provide a bright line test which will assist all the parties to the joint venture and the Department in determining whether compliance with this first standard has been achieved.

Although compliance with this "60–40 percent investment" standard will necessitate some monitoring data, we want to minimize the burden. Therefore, the joint venture is free to use any internal accounting principles it chooses to adopt so long as it uses such principles consistently over time so that it is not manipulating the data to obscure its noncompliance. In addition, we are establishing two alternative time periods in which compliance is to be measured. The measurement period can either be a joint venture's prior fiscal year or the previous 12 month period. For example, if a joint venture uses a calendar year as its fiscal year and wants to know in April 1990 whether it is in compliance with this standard, it may either look at the number and status of investors in 1989, or it may use its investor data from March 1989 through March 1990.

We expect that the parties to a joint venture will find it far preferable to use its prior fiscal year data because if that year's data shows compliance with this standard then the joint venture is in compliance for the entire current fiscal year. The alternative approach of a rolling 12 month average will enable a joint venture to reach compliance sometime within the current fiscal year so that it does not have to remain out of compliance for a full year. However, we also recognize that a joint venture using this rolling 12 month average that is being operated close to this 40 percent line may find itself in compliance one month and then out of compliance the next month. We emphasize that it is highly unlikely we will pursue an investigation of a joint venture where it complies with all the other standards in this safe harbor, is out of compliance with this 60–40 percent investment standard based on its prior fiscal year data, but is making a good-faith effort to reach compliance with this standard based on data showing compliance on a monthly basis for the most recent months of operation.

As previously discussed, for the purposes of complying with this 60–40 percent investment standard, we are classifying investors who provide items and services together with investors who make or influence referrals to the entity. This classification is necessary to preclude a supplier, such as a DME company, from forming a joint venture with referring physicians, giving them a 39 percent interest in the entity. It would be inappropriate to grant safe harbor protection to such an entity because all of the owners would be doing business with the joint venture by either furnishing items or making referrals. In order to remedy this problem, the DME supplier is classified with the referring physicians for the purposes of this 60–40 percent investment standard. Thus, for example, if a DME supplier and its referral sources want to be investors in an entity with which they will do business, to comply with this first standard, at least 60 percent of the value of the investment interests must be held by investors who will neither make referrals nor engage in business activity with the entity.

The second and third standards of this provision address the problems of discriminatory marketing strategies that result in the offer of better deals, for example, more shares or a better price, to individuals who will refer a high volume of patients. The second standard focuses on the *status* of investor and bars safe harbor protection where the terms of investment opportunities depend on whether a passive investor is in a position to influence referrals, furnish items or services, or otherwise generate business for the entity. The entity can offer investments to such investors only on the same terms as those offered to other passive investors not in a position to influence the flow of business to the entity. We are not imposing this standard on active investors because we recognize that it is precisely because of a physician's familiarity with the health care field that he or she may be chosen as a general partner and offered different investment terms from those offered to passive investors.

The third standard assumes that an investment interest is being offered to a person in a position to make referrals, but bars the offering of favorable terms based on his or her past or expected referrals or amount of business otherwise generated for the entity. This standard applies both to active and passive investors because we believe it is inappropriate to protect all investment interests where any investor, even general partners, can obtain more shares because they can be expected to generate more business for the entity. We recognize that there may be situations where it is not abusive to offer more shares based on this consideration, but we also believe that such a practice can have a serious potential for abuse.

With respect to the potential triggering of a public registration requirement under SEC rules or State "blue sky" laws, we believe that there is nothing in this provision that would compel such a result. Thus, we see no need to modify this provision.

Comment: In response to the OIG's proposal that no requirement be imposed on the investor to make referrals, many comments dealt with the issue of how investors are retained. Specifically, many commenters objected to requirements, which entities commonly place on investors, that investors must divest their interest if they no longer are able to make referrals to that entity. One commenter suggested that the OIG prohibit entities from distributing any information to investors about their referral patterns to that entity.

Response: We generally agree with these comments and have addressed them in the fourth and fifth standards of this safe harbor provision. (Paragraphs (a) (2) (iv) and (v)). The fourth standard bars the entity from requiring passive investors to make referrals or remain in a position to make referrals as a condition for retaining their investment. The fifth standard parallels the new standard for publicly traded entities and requires the entity and investors not to market or furnish items or services to passive investors in any manner differently than to non-investors. Some examples of practices that would not be protected are provided in the discussion above on the parallel provision for publicly traded entities. These two standards apply only to passive investors because, as we stated, we recognize that active investors are often sought out because they will help generate business for the joint venture.

This fifth standard also requires the entity and any investor not to promote the services of other entities as part of a cross referral agreement. As we noted in the previous section on publicly traded entities, an example of a cross referral arrangement that would not comply with this standard exists when investors in entity "A" are explicitly or implicitly encouraged to refer to entity "B" in return for entity "A" receiving the referrals from the investors of entity "B."

Comment: A large number of commenters supported the OIG's third proposal that disclosure of the investment interest be made to individuals for which a referral is made. However, some were opposed to such a requirement.

Response: For the reasons discussed in section III.B.2. above, we decline to adopt a disclosure requirement.

(ii) *Business structure.* In this section we discuss the comments and our responses regarding the problem of the nature of the business structure of joint ventures. The sixth standard (paragraph (a)(2)(vi)) relates to this problem area.

Comment: The OIG received a large number of comments relating to the business structure of joint ventures, and particularly on the problem that many abusive joint ventures exist primarily on the referrals from their investors. Many of these commenters alleged that such joint ventures are unable to compete for business in the open market on the basis of cost, quality and convenience. These commenters alleged that such joint ventures thereby hurt competition by unfairly "locking in" referrals from investors. However, one trade association reported from a survey of its members that, on average, 47 percent of the referrals to entities operated by its members came from non-investors. Many commenters also expressed concern that abusive joint ventures have no real business purpose, and that the four standards we suggested will not prevent abuse. Four commenters suggested that safe harbor protection be provided where the costs to Medicare and Medicaid are not increased. One commenter observed that, in many cases, the apparent lower costs of joint ventures are illusory because their hours of operation are shorter than those of hospitals. To assure that joint ventures do not raise costs or operate in an abusive manner, a large number of commenters suggested that the OIG require utilization review.

Response: We agree with the concern that entities protected under this safe harbor provision should not exist by relying on their business coming from referrals from investing physicians. In our experience, a large number of joint ventures are formed with the intent to encourage investors to refer patients to the joint venture. In many cases, the referrals from investing physicians dominate the joint venture's business so that it is does not have to compete for outside business and that it cannot survive without such referrals from its investing physicians. At that point, the business purpose of the joint venture becomes suspect.

We also agree with commenters who believed that the standards we suggested in the proposed rule will not sufficiently protect against abuse. Although some protection is afforded by the fifth standard we are promulgating which is discussed immediately above (that the entity may not treat a passive investor differently than non-investors), we believe that an additional bright line rule is necessary as a condition of safe harbor protection.

Therefore, the sixth standard in this provision requires that no more than 40 percent of an entity's gross revenue comes from referrals from, or items or services furnished by, investors. This "60–40 percent revenue" standard is reasonable, and, at least according to one commenter's survey of its members, appears to be achievable for many joint ventures.

This standard, as well as the first standard in this safe harbor provision, provide clear rules which assure that no protection is afforded to joint ventures that operate primarily on the referrals of physician investors. By requiring that no more than 40 percent of the joint venture's revenue come from investors' referrals, we help assure that revenues of these joint ventures come from a wider group than referrals from physician investors. And by limiting the number of investors who make referrals, we help assure that the profits from these entities are distributed to a wider group than referring physician investors. Thus, these two standards will help assure that joint ventures are not dependent on the capital and referrals of physician-investors.

As part of the Department's program to monitor business arrangements' compliance with these safe harbor provisions (see section III.A. above), we will report to the Secretary on the compliance with these two 60–40 rules (see § 1001.953). This report, which will be issued within 180 days of the publication of this rule, will evaluate whether compliance with these two 60–40 rules adequately controls abusive arrangements or whether more stringent requirements are needed.

As with the first 60–40 percent standard, we are permitting a joint venture to use any internal accounting principles it chooses to adopt so long as it uses such principles consistently over time so that it is not manipulating the data to obscure its non-compliance. In addition, we are establishing the same two alternative time periods in which compliance is to be measured. The measurement period can either be a joint venture's prior fiscal year or the previous 12 month period. Again, as with the first 60–40 percent standard, it is highly unlikely we will pursue an investigation of a joint venture where it complies with all the other standards in this safe harbor, is out of compliance with this 60–40 percent standard based on its prior fiscal year data, but is making a good-faith effort to reach compliance with this standard based on data showing compliance on a monthly basis for the most recent months of operation.

As noted above in the discussion of our definition of the term "investor," in applying these two 60–40 rules in situations where the joint venture entity is owned by other entities, we will examine the ownership structure of these other entities to determine whether they are owned by physicians who are referring to the joint venture entity. In such a situation, these physicians are considered to be investors of the joint venture entity, and their ownership interest must be offset by non-referring owners and the revenue they generate for the joint venture must be offset by referrals from non-investors.

We believe the suggestion that we require protected joint ventures to provide services at lower costs to Medicare and Medicaid is unworkable. Although such a feature is obviously a desirable goal, we believe that any analysis of the relative costs of services can only be accomplished meaningfully on a case-by-case basis. Examples of some of the areas such an analysis must examine include: (1) The reimbursement methodology of the service, (2) the patient population being served, (3) the hours of operation, (4) the bad debt and free care policies, and (5) the impact on costs and charges of depreciation of new equipment. These factors must be analyzed for both the joint venture entity and other competing entities to which a comparison is being drawn.

We believe that utilization review should be encouraged. However, there are many variables that distinguish a successful utilization review program from a sham. For example, utilization review may be conducted under contract by a Peer Review Organization or another independent contractor, or it may be conducted in-house. A critical feature of utilization review is that follow-up or corrective action occurs when a determination is made that a particular practitioner who is under review is engaging in aberrant or substandard behavior. Obviously this action can take many forms, ranging from barring the practitioner from further practice to taking no action at all. Because there are so many variables to an effective utilization review program, we believe it would be overly prescriptive and largely unproductive to impose such a requirement. Thus, we decline to include a utilization review requirement as part of this safe harbor.

(iii) *Financing and profit distributions.* In this section we discuss the comments and our responses regarding the problem of the financing and profit distribution of joint ventures. The last two standards (paragraphs (a)(2) (vii) and (viii)) relate to this problem area.

Comment: As discussed above, a large number of commenters argued that physician involvement in joint ventures is necessary because physicians provide needed capital. Several commenters, however, questioned whether investors are really generating capital for the joint ventures in which they invest. Many suggested that the OIG only protect an investor's capital in cases where the capital was genuinely at risk. In other words, if the investor's interest is obtained through a no-interest loan paid off through deductions from future dividend distributions, there was never really any capital placed in risk. Some suggested that the OIG protect investment interests even where the entity loans the investor funds which are then used to make the capital investment. One commenter reported results from a survey of its members that, on average, 60 percent of the investment from referring physician owners came in the form on non-cash investments (including debt guarantees).

Response: We agree that a new condition of safe harbor protection is needed to assure that the investments are bona fide, i.e., that investors' funds are genuinely at risk. Thus, the seventh standard of this provision parallels the new standard for the provision dealing with investments in large publicly traded entities: These entities cannot lend the funds or guarantee loans used to make the investment. Consistent with our first investment interest provision, other debt relationships are permitted. For example, the entity may borrow from the investor, and investors may borrow from other sources to obtain funds to use for the capital investment. But as we discussed above, where investors make their investment with money loaned from the entity, they are adding no real capital to it. Thus, this standard will help assure that physicians and other investors in fact provide new needed capital and that the joint venture is not in reality a sham to facilitate the distribution of payments for referrals.

Comment: The OIG received a large number of comments suggesting other protections to assure non-abusive financing arrangements and, in particular, urging the OIG to protect "nominal" investments. Many suggested that the OIG specify an upper limit on the amount an individual may invest, either in terms of a dollar amount or a percentage interest in the entity. Some specifically suggested a 5 percent limit. Three commenters took another approach and suggested a minimum capitalization amount, pointing out that many of the more abusive arrangements have minimal capital needs.

Response: We believe that individuals with a small investment in an entity may be just as likely as those with a large investment stake to be influenced to make referrals to the entity. Many of the more abusive joint venture arrangements of which we are aware offer only nominal investments to physicians. We believe that, in many cases, these nominal investment interests are designed to induce referrals or encourage the investor to otherwise generate business for the entity. In addition, by distributing the benefits of ownership to as wide a base of physician investors as possible, these joint ventures seek to lock-up their market, and thus operate in an insulated business environment largely free from normal competitive pressures such as pricing constraints.

We believe that it is not useful to impose a minimum capitalization requirement. Because each joint venture has different capital needs, it is not possible to specify one level of capitalization that would represent a reasonable floor for all joint ventures. For example, requiring at least $500,000 in capitalization would obviously be viewed very differently by a laboratory joint venture than by a magnetic resonance imaging joint venture. We do believe, however, that it is useful to analyze joint ventures on a case-by-case basis to determine what the real capital needs of the project are, and whether the capital that has been invested is merely a sham to pay investors for referrals.

Comment: We received a large number of comments on one of the standards suggested in the preamble to the proposed rule, that payments not be related to referrals. We also received other comments relating to the general problem of the manner in which profits are distributed. Many commenters suggested that the OIG limit the return on investment which will be subject to protection. Some suggested merely that the return be "reasonable," while another commenter stressed that there is no realistic way to determine an appropriate cut-off for a return on investment that would still be classified as "reasonable." One commenter suggested that, because there is less potential for abuse with repayments on debt instruments, the OIG should treat these payments differently from profit distributions.

Response: The eighth standard in this provision is that the amount of payment to each investor must be directly proportional to his or her capital investment. In other words, to receive protection, dividend payments can only be tied to the number of shares owned by an investor, and not to his or her referrals. Where investors, such as general partners, contribute capital in the form of pre-operational services or sweat equity, their dividend payments may reflect the fair market value of those services rendered.

This standard in no way protects payments to active investors for operational services they provide to the joint venture. By its very terms, this provision only protects payments that represent a return on investment. Safe harbor protection for the personal services that an active investor renders would be governed by the "personal services and management contracts" provisions (paragraph (d)).

With respect to limiting the return on investment, we believe that it would be arbitrary to specify a limitation applicable for all joint ventures, and that it would be meaningless to merely specify as a general criterion that the return "be reasonable." As many commenters pointed out, a reasonable return can be appropriately measured only in light of the risk of the investment. An investor would surely expect a much higher return from an investment in an expensive piece of diagnostic equipment that might soon become obsolete than from an investment in a relatively inexpensive piece of equipment that can be expected to generate a steady profit stream for the foreseeable future.

With respect to repayments on debt instruments, we believe that it is unnecessary to create a separate provision for debt instruments, but, as discussed in section III.C.1.a. above, this provision is written to protect a variety of payments in securities, including debt instruments.

c. Proposals for New Safe Harbor Provisions

A large number of comments were received urging the OIG to provide special protection for investments in certain special circumstances which would not qualify under the safe harbor provisions suggested in the proposed rule.

Note: Any discussion below indicating that we are considering a new safe harbor provision should in no way be construed as legalizing the business arrangement at this time.

Comment: A large majority of these commenters requested protection for ambulatory surgical centers (ASCs). Many of these commenters believed that the OIG was attempting to eliminate ASCs. In presenting the benefits of ASCs, these commenters made many of the same arguments discussed in section III.C1.b. above, regarding the positive features of joint ventures in general. In addition, many commenters emphasized the unique features of ASCs: (1) They are subject to peer review; (2) they provide services at lower prices than hospitals; (3) they were formed to a very large extent by physicians, and (4) in many cases, they are really an extension of a physician's practice. Several other commenters suggested protection for payments from other types of entities based on a rationale similar to this latter "extension of practice" argument. For example, commenters wanted protection for physicians providing inpatient services for their patients, nephrologists performing services at renal dialysis facilities, pathologists examining test results in laboratories, and radiation therapy oncologists performing radiation therapy services at outpatient centers.

Response: We understand that a special situation may exist when a physician sees a patient in his or her office, makes a referral to an entity in which he or she has an ownership interest and performs the service for which the referral is made. In such a situation, Medicare makes payment to the facility for the service it furnishes, which may result in a profit distribution to the physician. And the physician may also receive reimbursement from the program for performing the professional service.

We believe that, with respect to the physician's own fee, such a referral is simply a referral to oneself. It should not matter whether the patient is first seen at the office or at the facility. Consequently, we believe that, in this situation, both the professional service fee and the profit distribution from the associated facility fee that are generated from this referral may warrant protection. However, we remain concerned about the investing physician's ability to profit from any diagnostic testing that is generated from the services he or she performs. We are also concerned about the extent to which we should modify this second investment interest safe harbor to protect a physician-investor's profit in other joint venture entities where he or she both makes a referral and performs some level of service for the referred patient at the entity. Therefore, we are considering a safe harbor provision, that we anticipate publishing as a separate regulation to protect these payments where there is no likelihood of abuse.

We believe that a broader exemption at this time for payments from ASCs and similar entities is not appropriate. We recognize that many of these entities, and ASCs in particular, have operated under the Medicare and Medicaid programs largely without abuse and have saved these programs money when compared to some alternative treatment settings, particularly inpatient hospital care. We also recognize that one of the fundamental purposes of the statute is to prevent abusive business arrangements that increase cost to the Medicare and Medicaid programs. However, our approach is one of providing standards that define categories of business arrangements and business practices that will be given safe harbor protection. Our approach is not one of providing protection to particular categories of health care providers who earn it by being lawful or cost-effective.

We remain concerned about the widespread apprehension expressed by those commenters with an ownership interest in ASCs. Many commenters did not understand that the investment interest safe harbor provisions upon which we invited comment would protect many of the situations about which the commenters claimed no protection was being offered. In addition, as we made clear in section III.A. above, when an investment interest does not qualify under one of the safe harbor provisions, it does not mean that prosecution is imminent. The business arrangement may not even violate the statute, or, after examination on a case-by-case basis, we may conclude that prosecution is not warranted. Our disinclination to provide blanket protection for all investment interests in ASCs does not mean that we hold them in disfavor.

2. Space and Equipment Rental and Personal Services and Management Contracts—§§ 1001.952 (b), (c), and (d)

Comment: An overwhelming number of commenters criticized the restrictive definition of fair market value in the safe harbor provision for space rental. Many expressed concern that the safe harbor does not exempt rental payments that take into account added value attributable to a rental property's intended use as a facility for furnishing medical, laboratory, or other health services. Some were disappointed that this safe harbor provision does not appear to allow adjustments in rental charges for special construction or renovation costs incurred by the lessor to make the space suitable for furnishing medical services. Other commenters argued that the added value to providers of locating in a building or area proximate and convenient to other health care providers is a legitimate factor in calculating rent and may bear no relationship to prospective referrals of Medicare or Medicaid program business. They contended that the close proximity of rental property to other health care providers justifies elevated rent because both providers and their patients view such location as a convenience.

Response: The safe harbor provision for space rental does not contemplate a single figure for fair market value. Rather, it contemplates a rental fee falling within a reasonable commercial range, but not taking into account any value attached by either party based upon the property's proximity or convenience to referral sources. To the extent there is a nexus between the location of property and the opportunity to engage in business reimbursable under Medicare or Medicaid, rental charges that take location into account may impermissibly generate referrals or other health care business. For example, we believe that a fair inference may be drawn that impermissible payments are being made when a group of doctors owns a medical arts building and rents space in that building to a diagnostic laboratory, and the rent is substantially above the laboratory' s cost of renting the same sized space at a nearby location.

Consequently, we decline to extend safe harbor protection to space rental charges that take into account any value attached to property due to the proximity of referral sources. We have modified the definition of fair market value in this provision to clarify that protection does not extend to rental charges reflecting the value attributed by either party to the proximity or convenience of property to potential sources of referrals or other business from the other party. However, we would note that where the lessor is a real estate developer or other entity not involved in the delivery of health care services, any arrangements that encourage referrals between the lessee and other third parties would not likely be scrutinized by the OIG.

However, we recognize that there may be instances where rental fees for medical, laboratory or other health related office space are justifiably higher than the market price for comparable commercial property. For example, we agree with commenters who stated that the cost of leasehold improvements needed to make space suitable for the furnishing of medical services (such as extra plumbing or electrical costs) should be considered within the provision's definition of fair market value. Accordingly, we have further amended this safe harbor's definition of fair market value to delete the requirement that fair market value not take into account the intended use of rental space. However, we have retained the requirement that rental payments be commensurate with the fair market value of equivalent commercial property, and decline to extend blanket safe harbor protection to rental arrangements that reflect the added value a hospital places on having referring physicians located in a medical building the hospital owns on its property. We recognize that this requirement will preclude safe harbor protection for many health care providers who lease space to physicians or suppliers at a reduced rate due to the favorable location of the property. In particular, hospitals that give rent concessions to staff physicians leasing private office space may not fall within the safe harbor. For a discussion of how such payments may qualify as part of a physician recruitment effort, see section III.D. below.

Comment: A few commenters inquired whether rental arrangements involving both the use of office space and the furnishing of personal or management services must meet the requirements of both safe harbor provisions in order to be protected from liability under the statute.

Response: In section III.A. above, we addressed generally the circumstances under which the requirements of two relevant safe harbor provisions must be met in order to be protected under this regulation. However, because several commenters specifically requested guidance about contracts involving the rental of space and the furnishing of personal services, we are responding to their comments here.

To the extent that office rental payments include the value of other personal services furnished as part of a business arrangement, the payments must reflect the fair market value of the rent and these personal services in order to qualify under the safe harbor regulation. To be exempt from kickback liability, arrangements involving remuneration for rental and personal services must meet the conditions of each provision. For example, where a mobile business provides diagnostic services to patients in physicians' offices, and contracts for diagnostic equipment or for cleaning, billing or other services in addition to renting office space from these physicians, the arrangement must qualify under the provisions for space and equipment rental and personal services and management contracts.

Comment: Several commenters, expressing support for a strong and effective anti-kickback statute, stated that sham office leases in which the space is not actually used are among the most common and abusive kickback schemes. Examples of such abusive schemes cited by commenters included physicians who entered into office rental contracts with other referring physicians, solely in order to obtain the referrals, and diagnostic services companies and clinical laboratories that lease space from physicians which the laboratories in reality do not use, as kickbacks for the physicians' patient referrals.

Response: We agree that sham contracts in which remuneration is exchanged for property that does not exist or space which is not used are among the most egregious kickback arrangements. We have become aware of office rental arrangements in which the "space" rented may not be large enough or otherwise suitable to perform any services for which rent could legitimately be paid. For example, a physician may rent office space to a clinical laboratory, allegedly in order to provide space to furnish laboratory services, when the space (often a closet or anteroom not useable for such purposes) is not actually occupied by laboratory personnel at any time. If the physician refers most or all laboratory work to this lessee, the "rent" is simply remuneration for referring laboratory work.

We believe, however, that these safe harbor provisions are sufficient to protect against this abuse. These provisions require that the amount of payments for rent, equipment or personal services contracts not take into account the volume or value of referrals or other business generated between the parties. If a sham contract is entered into, which on paper looks like it complies with these provisions, but where there is no intent to have the space or equipment used or the services provided, then clearly we will look behind the contract and find that in reality payments are based on referrals. Thus, these contracts would not be protected under these provisions.

Comment: Two commenters stated that the safe harbor requirements for determining fair market value of rental space should be the same requirements of section 501(c)(3) of title 26 of the United States Code, the Internal Revenue Code section governing tax exemptions for nonprofit institutions. Under this section, fair market value assessments are necessary to determine whether hospital/physician arrangements result in the prohibited inurement of private benefit to individuals.

Response: We do not believe that procedures for assessing the fair market value of hospital/physician arrangements under the Internal Revenue Code are relevant to safe harbor requirements under the anti-kickback statute. The anti-kickback statute is concerned with prohibiting fraud and abuse by individuals and entities participating in the Medicare and Medicaid programs; a statute providing tax exemptions to nonprofit institutions under specified conditions does not share this focus. The requirements we have set forth for determining fair market value under the safe harbor regulation are not undermined by the fact that they do not replicate the requirements under the Internal Revenue Code. Moreover, we cannot see, nor has any commenter adequately explained, how these regulations impede health care providers' ability to obtain tax exempt status under the Internal Revenue Code.

Comment: Commenters requested clarification as to whether these safe harbor provisions protect any types of percentage, "per use" or "per procedure" leases or contracts in which the amount of compensation fluctuates in accordance with the actual use of premises or equipment, or the frequency of services performed. A few commenters inquired whether percentage leases between parties in a position to refer Medicare or Medicaid business were a *per se* violation of the statute. Many commenters urged the OIG to extend safe harbor protection to per use equipment leases, and to percentage contracts for personal services, in which total business, in contrast to referral business, is the basis for payment. With regard to equipment leases, several commenters argued that these provisions should protect equipment lessors who receive higher rent based on increased use, because the useful life and value of equipment depreciates with use.

Response: As we explained in section III.A. above, in discussing wear and tear clauses, percentage or per use agreements between health care providers in a position to refer Medicare or Medicaid business threaten to violate the statute because the payments in these arrangements are directly tied to the volume of business or amount of revenue generated, providing an improper incentive to refer. Moreover, historically, percentage leases and contracts have been rife with abuse.

These sorts of arrangements need to be examined on a case-by-case basis. For example, a lease to a hospital of major medical equipment, such as a magnetic resonance imaging scanner, may specify that higher rent is to be paid when more than a predetermined number of procedures is performed. Such an arrangement can be troublesome if the lessor is a partnership of radiologists on the hospital's medical staff, because the incentive for overutilization is clear. It is the nature of the relationship, if any, between overall volume of use and referrals, that triggers the statute. Thus, if the owner of equipment were not in a position to make referrals to the lessee, the agreement would not violate the statute.

For these reasons, we specifically decline to protect rental charges or compensation for personal services where the aggregate amounts of payments are not set out in advance. This does not mean, however, that percentage or per use leases and contracts that are based on overall volume (including business from referral sources with no financial interest to motivate them), are *per se* violations of the statute. We recognize that legitimate considerations, such as the depreciation of equipment, could result in some part of the payment to be based on a percentage or "per use" payment arrangement without these payments influencing or being influenced by Medicare or Medicaid referrals. However, the more the payments appear to reflect the volume of referrals from the financially-interested party, the more suspect the arrangement becomes and the more likely we will need to examine it carefully.

Comment: Many commenters were opposed to the condition that space and equipment leases and personal services and management contracts run for periods of not less than one year. They argued that the one year condition was superfluous, given additional restrictions relating to fair market value and referral relationships between the parties. They also argued that the one year rule would preclude many legitimate short-term arrangements, such as leases of state-of-the-art imaging equipment by health care providers who could not afford a full year's lease. Some health care providers claimed that the rule would cause them to forsake good business judgment in order to obtain needed equipment or services.

Commenters were most concerned about the one year requirement in the context of personal services and management contracts. Several commenters argued that many professional services typically contracted for by health care providers, from medical or surgical consulting services to peer review functions, involve projects or activities that require less than one year to complete. They argued that it is inefficient and wasteful for health care providers to enter into contracts for periods of one year under these circumstances. Additionally, a few commenters sought clarification as to the effect of the one year rule on leases terminated for cause prior to the expiration of a contract extending one year or longer. In particular, there was concern that the conditions of the space rental safe harbor not conflict with Internal Revenue Service guidelines governing advance determinations of tax exempt status. These guidelines require tax exempt facilities to be able to terminate, within 90 days notice, contracts with non-exempt persons where compensation is based on fees charged for services furnished by the non-exempt persons.

Response: We have retained the one year contract requirement as a condition for safe harbor protection under the space rental, equipment rental, and personal services and management contracts safe harbor provisions. We included the one year rule limitation in these provisions because we are concerned about abuse resulting from periodic renegotiation of ostensibly short term agreements, in response to changes in referral patterns. For example, if a health care provider rents office space to another individual or entity with whom he or she is in an ongoing referral relationship, and these providers alter their rental terms with frequency, the volume or value of referrals can influence the size of renegotiated rental payments. When rental charges are constantly subject to modification, the threat to the lessor of receiving reduced rent, or the threat to the lessee of paying higher rent, may improperly induce increased referrals. However, we recognize that health care providers may enter into short-term leases or services contracts for legitimate business reasons and not on account of referral opportunities. For example, an academic physician who spends one semester or school year visiting at another medical university may need to rent office space from the medical university for less than a year.

Several commenters expressed concern that contracts for the performance of activities or services that, by their very nature, take less than one year, would necessarily fall outside the safe harbor provision for personal services and management contracts. However, the one year contract requirement restricts the period within which contract terms may not be changed, and not the time within which services under a contract may be performed. So long as contract terms are not altered within a one year period, an agreement that is performed in less than one year's time will meet the one year requirement in the safe harbor provision.

With regard to the comments we received concerning early termination clauses in leases or contracts extending not less than one year, we acknowledge the customary use of such provisions for tax and other legitimate business purposes. The legitimacy of an early termination clause in a lease or contract which otherwise meets the conditions of these three provisions depends on the parties' intent. Termination "for cause" clauses drafted in compliance with Internal Revenue Service or other legal or regulatory requirements should not jeopardize safe harbor status, if the purpose of the termination clause is to comply with those requirements, and not to facilitate renegotiation of contract terms. If a contract is terminated in accordance with a legally enforceable termination clause, the failure to renew the contract would provide evidence that the termination was effectuated for a legitimate purpose.

Comment: The safe harbor provisions governing space and equipment rental and personal services and management contracts provide that when the property or service is to be provided on a periodic, sporadic or part-time basis, the agreement must specify precisely the timing and duration of rental periods and compensation charged for each period. Numerous commenters were troubled by these requirements. They argued that furnishing professional services and leasing space and equipment on an "as needed" basis are commercially acceptable, cost-effective business practices that should be protected so long as the rate of compensation is commercially reasonable. They also stated that under many periodic lease and contract arrangements, precise intervals of activity or use, and the exact compensation for these intervals, cannot feasibly be specified in advance. In addition, there was concern that requiring specificity of time intervals and compensation as conditions for safe harbor protection would interfere with the flexibility necessary to accommodate changing demand, and would increase costs in situations where the demand proved lower than expected at the time the contract was made. Finally, a few commenters asked for clarification of the meaning of the word "periodicity" in these three provisions when the space or equipment lease or personal services agreement is not on a full-time basis.

Response: Part-time contractual arrangements and periodic access leases between health care providers are especially vulnerable to abuse because they are subject to modification based on changing referral patterns between the parties. For example, an optometrist who pays *ad hoc* "rent" to an ophthalmologist for the time spent in the physician's office examining only referred patients, is impermissibly paying for the referrals. In order to avoid the potential for abuse inherent in part-time business arrangements between parties in actual or potential referral relationships, we have limited safe harbor protection under these three provisions to periodic leases and contracts which set forth the timing, frequency, and length of services or intervals of use.

We recognize that health care providers, for various reasons, may be unable to specify the timing or duration of business arrangements, or the precise compensation involved. For example, compensation under a management contract requiring the furnishing of supplies and the hiring of personnel may need to vary depending on the costs of the supplies and number of personnel. Or, a health care provider may contract with an allied health practitioner group (such as a physical therapy group) to pay a specific amount per hour of care provided, without being able to anticipate the scheduling of services in advance. We believe that part-time leases or service arrangements that do not meet safe harbor standards need to be analyzed on a case-by-case basis under the statute. Many periodic contracts of this sort would fall outside the statute because the compensation involved is not linked to referral opportunities. A contract to serve as medical director of a small clinic on a part-time basis, for example, is not likely to involve activities or compensation tied to the referral of patients or to arrangement for services reimbursable under Medicare or Medicaid programs.

Finally, we are deleting the word "periodicity" from these three provisions because it duplicates the requirements that the rental or equipment lease or personal services agreement specify the schedule of intervals, their precise length, and payments for the intervals.

Comment: Three commenters requested the OIG to protect marketing and advertising activities because such activities either promote competition or do not violate the statute.

Response: The statute on its face prohibits the offering or acceptance of remuneration, *inter alia*, for the purposes of "arranging for or recommending purchasing, leasing, or ordering any. . . service or item" payable under Medicare or Medicaid. Thus, we believe that many marketing and advertising activities may involve at least technical violations of the statute. We, of course, recognize that many of these advertising and marketing activities do not warrant prosecution in part because (1) they are passive in nature, i.e., the activities do not involve direct contact with program beneficiaries, or (2) the individual or entity involved in these promotions is not involved in the delivery of health care. Such individuals or entities are not in a position of public trust in the same manner as physicians or other health care professionals who recommend or order products and services for their patients. Thus, we agree that many advertising and marketing activities warrant safe harbor protection under the personal services and management contracts safe harbor.

However, we have experienced many instances where promoters and consultants have become involved in marketing activities that encourage health care providers and others to violate the statute, such as to develop impermissible joint venture arrangements or to routinely waive coinsurance and deductible amounts owed under Medicare Part B. It would be inappropriate to allow such activities to receive safe harbor protection.

Thus, we are adding paragraph (d)(6) to this safe harbor provision to make clear that the service that is contracted for is not protected if it involves the counselling or promotion of a business arrangement or other activity which itself constitutes a violation of any State or Federal law. However, the safe harbor (revised as indicated) protects contracts where the individual paid under the contract counsels or promotes business arrangements or other activities that are either specifically exempted under one of the provisions of this regulation or otherwise do not violate the statute.

Comment: Four commenters sought specific protection for commission sales arrangements between health care providers and independent contractors.

Response: We see no reason, nor has any commenter claimed to have provided one, for treating commission sales agreements differently under these regulations from other types of contracts for personal services performed by independent contractors. Therefore, commission sales agreements must meet the conditions of the safe harbor provisions governing personal services and management contracts.

3. Sale of Practice—§ 1001.952(e)

Comment: While many commenters supported the one-year limitation on the completion of a sale of a practice, others believed that it is too short. One commenter asserted that such a limitation would effectively ban ption agreements on sales of physicians' practices.

Response: We decline to protect option agreements or sales which extend beyond one year because, as we stated in the preamble to the proposed rule, we believe that this is an area of significant abuse. Often, sales and option agreements are designed solely to ensure referrals, and payments for the sale or option agreement are actually payments for referrals. The one-year limit serves to protect sales where the sale occurs because the physician is no longer going to be practicing and not because the purchaser seeks an ongoing stream of referrals. To the extent that one can enter into an option agreement, exercise that option and complete the purchase of the practice within one year from the date the option agreement is entered into, this aspect of the transaction will fall within this safe harbor provision.

Many commenters appeared confused about whether the provision requires payments from the sale to be completed within one year. This provision does not preclude a purchaser from making payments to a practitioner beyond the one-year period as long as the other conditions of this provision have been met.

Comment: Many commenters strongly supported the one-year grace period from the date of a purchase agreement to complete the purchase, and during which time referrals would be permissible. One commenter believed this period should be shortened to six months, but others stated that it should be longer than one year.

Response: We were presented with no persuasive reason to extend or shorten this one-year period and we therefore decline to revise this limitation period.

Comment: Several hospitals requested protection for their purchases of the practices of retiring physicians.

Response: When a hospital purchases a physician's practice and thereafter there are no referrals from that physician to the hospital, the statute would not appear to be implicated. Accordingly, in ordinary circumstances, a hospital is not in violation of the statute if it purchases the practice of a retiring physician who no longer makes referrals to that hospital.

However, many hospitals engage in this practice as part of a physician recruitment effort. Such activities do implicate the statute, but we are considering a new safe harbor provision, that we anticipate publishing as a separate regulation, to protect many such recruitment activities.

Comment: Several hospitals requested that their practice of buying physicians' practices for fair market value and then retaining the physicians on staff be afforded the protection of a safe harbor. They asserted that the financial pressures of maintaining private practices have drawn physicians to hospitals in order to get management assistance and capital.

Response: As we stated in the preamble of the proposed rule, hospitals often purchase physicians' practices in order to ensure the hospital of a steady stream of referrals. We continue to believe that such practices lead to increased program costs and potential conflicts between the patient's best interests and the physician's business relationship to the hospital. Accordingly, we decline to protect a practice that often leads to the very abuses that the statute is designed to prevent.

Comment: Several commenters requested safe harbor protection for the sale of an individual's practice to a group practice or the sale of part of a practice to another physician or group practice when the physician chooses to change the scope of his or her practice.

Response: We recognize that some buy-out arrangements are not abusive, and we would not want to prosecute such arrangements. However, we are also aware of abusive purchase arrangements, such as between ophthalmologists and optometrists, where one practitioner or group practice seeks to buy another practitioner's practice as a condition for continuing to make referrals. In essence, the sale becomes another mechanism for the buyer to profit from the stream of referrals made to the seller who previously practiced independently without dividing profits with the new "partner." No commenter proposed standards for a safe harbor provision that would cover only arrangements that are not abusive, and we are skeptical that such standards can be formulated. Accordingly, we have not protected this very diverse category of sales of practices. Rather, we are considering a limited new safe harbor provision for the purchase of group practices that we anticipate publishing as a separate regulation.

Comment: Two commenters asked the OIG to clarify the relationship between the safe harbor provision for the sale of a practice and the employee exception.

Response: Where a practitioner purchases another practitioner's practice, makes payments to that other practitioner which continue for some period of time, and retains that other practitioner on his or her staff as an employee, we believe that such payments are not protected under this provision or the employee exception. They do not qualify under this provision because the practitioner who sold the practice remains in a position to make referrals. The payments are not protected by the employee exception because that provision only protects payments "for employment in the provision of covered items or services * * *." These payments, however, relate to the purchase of a practice and not to services provided pursuant to employment for the provision of items or services. Of course, the employing practitioner who has bought out the other practitioner is making other payments for such employment services, and if a bona fide employment relationship as defined in 26 U.S.C. 3121(d)(2) exists, then these payments are protected under the employee safe harbor provision. As noted in the General comments section in section III.A. above, where parties are attempting to comply with two safe harbor provisions, we would expect separate justifications for compliance with each provision.

4. Referral Services—§ 1001.952(f)

Comment: Many commenters urged the OIG to extend this safe harbor provision beyond only physicians to include payments by chiropractors, dentists, podiatrists, psychologists, nursing homes and other health care providers to entities that refer members of the public to them.

Response: We agree and have revised this provision to protect payments by practitioners and other health care providers who utilize referral services.

Comment: Many commenters requested that the OIG define the term "qualified" with respect to the requirement that a referral service not exclude any "qualified" health care provider from participation in the service.

Response: Whether a particular health care provider is "qualified" as a participant in a referral service will vary depending on how the service is organized. For instance, to be qualified as a participant in a referral service run by a hospital, it may be necessary that the participant be an employee of that hospital. On the other hand, a referral service run by a professional organization may require only that the participant be a dues-paying member of that organization to qualify for participation. The determination as to whether a particular health care provider is "qualified" to participate in the service may be made by the referral service according to its own criteria. To be protected under this safe harbor, the referral service must apply the eligibility criteria equally to all participants in the referral service.

In addition, the referral service must disclose to all persons seeking a referral the criteria it uses to determine who is qualified as a participant. The information that must be disclosed includes the manner in which it selects the pool of participants. In other words, if a pregnant woman calls a hospital's referral service, the referral service must disclose how it selects obstetricians to be qualified to receive referrals and whether the obstetrician has paid a fee to participate. The referral service must also disclose how the particular obstetrician is selected for the referral, for example, on a rotation basis. In addition, the referral service must disclose the relationship between the participant and the referral service, for example, that the obstetrician is on the active medical staff. Finally, the referral service must disclose what criteria it uses to exclude an individual or entity from continuing as a participant, for example, if a malpractice allegation is raised against the obstetrician or if he or she refuses to treat a certain level of uncompensated care cases.

The referral service must maintain a written record certifying that such disclosures have been made to each person seeking a referral. Such a record must be signed by either the person seeking the referral or by the individual making the disclosure on behalf of the referral service. This requirement will not be met if the referral service merely maintains a blank copy of the disclosure form or instructions to staff on how to make the disclosure.

Comment: One commenter suggested that a referral service should be permitted to require the practitioners or providers to charge clients that are referred by the service the same fees as they charge other clients.

Response: We agree and have revised paragraph (f)(3) to permit referral services to bar participants from engaging in discriminatory pricing practices.

Comment: A few commenters were uncertain about what fees could be charged for the referral service. They questioned whether the referral fee must be paid prior to the referral and whether a set amount could be charged for each referral.

Response: This provision protects fee payments that are related only to the cost of operating the referral service. This provision explicitly does not protect fees that in any manner are based on the volume or value of Medicare or Medicaid referrals or business otherwise generated by the participant for the referral service. While a referral fee need not be paid in full before any referrals are made, paragraph (f)(2) specifies that referral fees may not be based on the volume of referrals to the practitioner or provider.

Comment: One commenter asked whether the disclosure requirements of this provision could be satisfied by sending a letter to the referred person after the referral is made.

Response: Although the method of disclosure is not prescribed, to meet the requirements of this provision any disclosure must constitute effective disclosure. Effective disclosure requires that the relevant information is communicated in time for the information to be used by the beneficiary before an important decision is made. Accordingly, it is unlikely that disclosure after the referral has been made would constitute effective disclosure if the beneficiary had already seen the health care provider, or in some cases, if the appointment had already been made.

Comment: Several commenters questioned whether the statute and, therefore, this safe harbor provision, applies to referral services where health care providers are not charged for the services or where the services are provided pursuant to association dues.

Response: The statute applies to such referral services. The statute is implicated not only where direct payments are made in return for referrals, but also where indirect forms of remuneration are given for referrals. For example, hospitals often operate free referral services for members of their medical staffs as one of the benefits that comes with being on that hospital's staff. In return for the benefits of staff privileges (including the free referral service), physicians have a variety of obligations, such as sitting on various hospital committees. Depending on the circumstances, the services physicians furnish a hospital to assist in its operations may constitute a form of remuneration to the hospital for providing the referral service, and would be covered by the statute. As the United States Court of Appeals for the First Circuit found: "Giving a person an opportunity to earn money may well be an inducement to that person to channel potential Medicare payments towards a particular recipient." *United States* v. *Bay State Ambulance and Hospital Rental Service, Inc., supra*, 874 F.2d at 29. Therefore, staff physicians and hospitals seeking safe harbor protection must comply with this provision when they are engaged in a referral service that does not charge a specific fee.

5. Warranties—§ 1001.952(g)

Comment: Two commenters objected to the requirement that as a condition for protection the warranty include payments to compensate for any costs associated with the replacement of the product that is the subject of the warranty. These commenters pointed out that virtually no warranties now in existence pay for such expenses and that this requirement will necessitate the revision of warranty policies, which in turn must be paid for by price increases to cover this additional liability expense.

Response: We agree with the concern over the potential that this standard will increase costs, and are deleting it. We are revising this provision based on the Federal Trade Commission interpretation of 15 U.S.C. 2301(6), which does not require the manufacturer to make full payment to compensate for all costs associated with its defective product.

Comment: One pacemaker manufacturer noted that a particular warranty complied with the discount exception, implying that it need not comply with this warranty provision.

Response: We do not believe that warranty arrangements fit within the "discount" safe harbor provision, and are revising that provision accordingly. However, we agree that some of the policies underlying the discount exception should apply to warranties. Consequently, with respect to any reductions of equipment prices offered as part of a warranty agreement, we are requiring the same disclosure requirements as contained in the discount provision.

Comment: Two commenters urged the OIG to expand this safe harbor provision to protect "competitive replacement agreements." Under such an agreement, for example, a company offers various inducements to encourage hospitals (or other entities such as ASCs) and physicians to replace a defective pacemaker with one made by the company offering the inducements. These commenters argued that these arrangements should be protected because they make it easier to purchase the latest available technology. In addition, the comments pointed out that there is little potential for abuse because Peer Review organizations review virtually every pacemaker implant decision, and because competitive replacement programs put the beneficiary only in the same financial position he or she would be in if he or she purchased a replacement pacemaker from the original manufacturer pursuant to that manufacturer's warranty.

Response: We generally agree with these comments, but we remain concerned that many of these programs either provide additional incentives beyond the original warranty or impose additional costs on the Medicare and Medicaid programs. For example, while some competitive replacement programs replace the item, such as a pacemaker, only on the same terms as those in the warranty of the original manufacturer, others replace the item under other conditions as well; while some provide the replacement item free of charge, others provide a discount on the replacement item capped at a specified dollar amount; and while some make no payments for medical expenses, others assist patients (either directly or by paying the health care provider) with their unreimbursed medical expenses up to a specified dollar amount. Depending on the original manufacturer's warranty, some of these programs do much more than merely put the beneficiary in the same position he or she would be in if he or she bought a replacement item from the original manufacturer under the terms of that warranty.

We believe that safe harbor protection is proper where a replacement program honors the original manufacturer's warranty, which qualifies by itself under this provision, and the agreement provides remuneration on the same terms as the original manufacturer's warranty without providing additional incentives or shifting additional costs to the Medicare and Medicaid programs. Under such programs, any incentive to replace a product under warranty stems from the original warranty, and not from the competitive replacement agreement.

We remain concerned about potential abuse in one additional area. Some competitive replacement agreements pay the health care provider or practitioner directly for the beneficiary's medical expenses. We believe that such direct payments are potentially abusive because the health care provider or practitioner knows that the warranty insures against beneficiaries' bad debts. Thus, we are adding paragraph (g)(4) so that safe harbor protection is not provided when payments are made to any health care provider (such as a hospital or ASC) for expenses such as medical, surgical or hospital expenses incurred by the beneficiary. Payments made to the health care provider or practitioner for the item itself, or price reductions on that item, are protected.

Comment: One commenter suggested that the OIG should provide safe harbor protection for payments made by manufacturers or suppliers to settle claims or to satisfy judgments arising out of product liability claims regardless of whether such payments were included in the warranty at the time of the original sale of the item.

Response: Where such payments are not part of a warranty made at the time of the original sale of an item, they do not appear to be intended to induce the purchase of that item, and hence are not covered by the statute. Where such payments are included in a warranty given at the time of sale, they would only be protected if they were made as part of a warranty that complied with this provision.

Comment: One commenter suggested that the OIG should not provide safe harbor protection for middlemen suppliers that expand the protection afforded by the manufacturer' s warranty.

Response: We believe that warranties generally benefit consumers as well as the Medicare and Medicaid program, even though they may constitute a technical violation of the statute. As long as a supplier acting as a middleman wholesaler complies with this safe harbor provision, we fail to see the harm when it provides greater benefits than those provided by the manufacturer. Such expanded warranties are commonly provided by middlemen in industries other than health care, for example, by automobile dealers, and we believe such expanded warranties should be encouraged.

6. Discounts—§ 1001.952(h)

Comment: A few commenters expressed concern about the meaning of the word "discount." For example, four commenters asked us to clarify whether a discount includes a general price reduction offered across the board to all buyers. One commenter argued that a marketing strategy similar to a warranty, but not falling within that safe harbor provision was, in fact, a discount.

Response: We believe that this first statutory exception is intended to cover discounts and other price reductions offered by a seller through an arms length transaction to induce a buyer to order or purchase goods (including items) or services for which the discount applies or other goods or services payable under Medicare or Medicaid. A discount typically is the difference in the price at which a good or service is normally sold compared to the price at which it is actually sold when the inducement is given.

The statutory discount exception applies only to discounts obtained by health care providers who submit claims to the Medicare and Medicaid programs. We believe that this exception was not intended to cover the offering of discounts by health care providers who submit claims, for example, to beneficiaries as part of a routine waiver program for coinsurance and deductible amounts. We have changed the definition of the term "discount" to clarify the limited scope of this exception. A discussion of the limited safe harbor protection we are providing for routine waivers is found in section III.B.4. In addition, as discussed in section III.B.3., price reductions negotiated by HMOs, preferred provider organizations and other health care plans to protect such discounted fee arrangements are expected to be addressed at a later date in a separate interim final rule.

We believe discounts are distinct from across-the-board price reductions offered to all buyers where the inducement that is made is so diffuse that it does not appear intended to encourage a particular buyer to purchase or order a particular good or service payable under Medicare or Medicaid.

In addition, we believe that Congress did not intend for this discount exception to apply to price reductions offered to one payor but not to Medicare or Medicaid. For example, we are aware of cases where laboratories offer a discount to physicians who then bill the patient, but do not offer the same discount to the Medicare program. In some of these cases, the discount offered to the physician is explicitly conditioned on the physician's referral of all of his or her laboratory business. Such a "discount" does not benefit Medicare, and is therefore inconsistent with the statutory intent for discounts to be reported to the programs with costs and charges reduced appropriately to reflect the discounts.

Another problem exists when an entity, which is both a provider or supplier of items or services and a joint venture partner with referring physicians, makes discounts to the joint venture as a way to share its profits with the physician partners. Very often this entity furnishes items or services to the joint venture, and also acts as the joint venture's general partner or provides management services to the joint venture. For example, in some cases a reference laboratory performs testing for another laboratory at a discount price in accordance with a management contract. In other cases, the services the reference laboratory provides are paid on the basis of a percentage of revenues that the joint venture receives from Medicare. These arrangements are not arms length transactions where the joint venture entity shops around for the best price on a good or service. Rather, it has entered into a collusive arrangement with a particular provider or supplier of items or services that seeks to share its profits with referring physician partners. To clarify that we do not intend to protect these types of transactions which are sometimes made to appear as "discounts," we are clarifying the definition of "discounts" in paragraph (h)(3) of this section to permit only transactions made on an arms length basis.

Since many of these illegal transactions are made as part of personal services or management contracts, we are clarifying the definition of "discounts" to preclude discounts made as part of such transactions. We are making this revision for the additional reason that Congress did not intend to exempt such arrangements merely because those services were provided at a "discount." Since we believe that contracts for personal or management services do not fit within the ambit of the statutory discount exception, such arrangements must be analyzed under the respective safe harbor provision for those contracts. Of course, to the extent that the failure to report the actual price of the management contract implicates the civil monetary penalties law (section 1128A of the Act) liability may be imposed under that statute.

With respect to warranties, as we discussed in the warranty section immediately above, warranties are not discounts. Therefore to provide clearer guidance, we have modified the definition of the term "discount" in paragraph (h)(3) to exclude warranties and other examples of arrangements that do not constitute "discounts."

Comment: Many commenters urged the OIG to expand this safe harbor provision to include a variety of other discounting practices where the benefit received relates to something other than the specific good or service purchased or provided. Examples of the suggested permissible arrangements include bundled goods closely related to the purchased goods, such as free "surgical packs" (including such items as sutures, Healon, viscoelastics, and disposable gloves provided with purchases of intraocular lenses (IOLs), or credits toward free computers or other items that are useful in a physician's practice.

Response: We believe that such an interpretation goes well beyond the legislative intent of this statutory exception, and vitiates its purpose. We believe that Congress did not intend to include within this provision the practice of a seller giving away, or reducing the price of, one good in connection with the purchase of a different good. Such arrangements, for the most part, do not represent price reductions where the value of the goods received can be measured and fully reported to the Medicare and Medicaid programs.

Although there are many instances where these practices are cost effective arrangements that benefit the health care provider, there is enormous potential for abuse. One of the most common features of a serious kickback violation exists when a seller offers a valuable good, for example a car or a trip, to a person in return for that person's participation in activity prohibited under the statute, for example, referral of business payable by the Medicare and Medicaid programs. Thus, these commenters, while pointing to some potentially beneficial arrangements, are asking us to permit a broad class of arrangements that would include acts which have resulted in criminal convictions and at least one pending criminal prosecution. See *e.g., United States v. Bay State Ambulance and Hospital Rental Service, Inc., supra.*

Even where the particular item that is being given away may result in a more effective means of delivering the supplies to the health care provider, these types of "discounts" cause problems because they often shift costs among reimbursement systems or distort the true costs of all the items. As a result, it may be difficult for the Medicare and Medicaid programs to determine the proper reimbursement levels.

For example, in developing accurate pricing data to assist HCFA in setting the amount of reimbursement for IOLs, we found that bundled pricing arrangements similar to those suggested by our commenters were common, and made it difficult to determine the true acquisition cost of IOLs. (See Medicare certified Ambulatory Surgical Centers, Cataract Surgery Costs and Related Issues, at 9–12, March 1988, OAI–09–88–00490.) In addition, HCFA determined that its IOL pricing data obtained from the ASCs "revealed significant inconsistencies in reporting net IOL costs." 53 FR 31476. The necessity of accurately reporting the true acquisition costs of IOLs undistorted by bundling arrangements is underscored by HCFA's stated policy in its final rule promulgating a $200 add-on rate: "to continue to collect data on IOL acquisition costs and purchasing arrangements to ensure that the IOL rate appropriately reflects lens acquisition costs." 55 FR 436.

Finally, this practice of bundling IOLs with other goods is of sufficient seriousness that it is the subject of at least one pending criminal prosecution.

For these reasons, we decline to broaden the scope of this provision to include discounts on bundled goods and have clarified the definition of the term "discount" to specifically exclude such arrangements. Of course, where discounts are offered on goods that are unbundled and the discount otherwise complies with the rules of this provision, safe harbor protection is granted.

For purchasing practices involving the free provision of another type of item, we will examine the surrounding circumstances to determine the desirability of prosecuting that arrangement. Examples of potential factors which we may consider include: (1) The amount of the benefit that was reported and passed along to the programs, (2) whether the good is separately reimbursable, and (3) the intent behind the arrangement.

A related issue is the practice of giving away free computers. In some cases the computer can only be used as part of a particular service that is being provided, for example, printing out the results of laboratory tests. In this situation, it appears that the computer has no independent value apart from the service that is being provided and that the purpose of the free computer is not to induce an act prohibited by the statute. Rather, the computer is part of a package of services provided at a price that can be accurately reported to the programs. In contrast, sometimes the computer that is given away is a regular personal computer, which the physician is free to use for a variety of purposes in addition to receiving test results. In that situation the computer has a definite value to the physician, and, depending on the circumstances, may well constitute an illegal inducement.

Comment: A large number of commenters urged the OIG to broaden this safe harbor provision to include other reductions in price, such as "rebates" and "credits." These commenters argued that such programs are equivalent to price reductions and are capable of being properly reported.

Response: We generally agree with the thrust of these comments and have revised the definition of discount in paragraph (h)(3) to protect rebate checks, redeemable coupons and credits, subject to the following conditions. First, because of our continued concern about the potential for improper use of redeemable coupons, we are limiting the ability of recipients of such discounts to negotiate these instruments to third parties. As revised, this provision requires these instruments to be redeemed only by the seller. Second, the rebate check, redeemable coupon, or credit can only be applied to the same good or service that was purchased or provided. Thus, a redeemable coupon or credit obtained on the purchase of one good cannot be used toward the purchase of a different good. Third, like other discounts covered under this provision, these forms of discounts must be fully and accurately reported. Finally, except as noted below, such discounts must be given at the time the good or service was purchased or provided.

The reporting of credits presents an unusual situation because the monetary value of the credit only applies to future purchases of goods or services. Thus, to comply with this provision, the buyer must report the credits on the applicable cost report or claim form covering the goods or services for which the credit is being used.

Comment: A large number of commenters urged the OIG to expand this safe harbor provision to include other types of discount mechanisms where the value of the discount is not calculated until after some period of time has passed. Examples of such a discount mechanism include end-of-year discounts and prompt pay discounts. These commenters believed that these discounting mechanisms encourage legitimate, beneficial business practices that do not harm the program. In addition, many commenters pointed out that such discounting practices have long been encouraged through HCFA's prudent buyer guidelines. (Provider Reimbursement Manual, part I section 2103, HCFA Pub. No. 15–1)

Response: We recognize that there are many legitimate discount programs where the value of the discount is only reported after the good is purchased or the service is provided. Unfortunately, due to the nature of some reimbursement systems, it is sometimes not possible to determine retrospectively how much such discounts reduce the price of the goods or services previously purchased or provided. For example, it would be virtually impossible to take the numerous claims for cataract surgery submitted by a physician in a given year and determine the true acquisition cost of an IOL provided to that physician when the discount is only calculated at year end. Thus, paragraph (h)(1)(iii) of this section, which governs discounts on items and services paid on the basis of charges or acquisition costs, does not permit end-of-year discounts. On the other hand, where the Department or a State agency requires a health care provider to maintain cost reports (including HMOs, CMPs and health care prepayment plans (HCPPs pursuant to agreements under sections 1876(h) or 1833 of the Act), we believe that end of year calculations of discounts on purchases of the same good or service can be fully and accurately reported, as well as those discounts obtained at the time of the purchase.

Therefore, we are revising this provision in paragraph (h)(1)(i) of this section (which applies only to cost report providers) to protect such end-of-year discounts when all of the following conditions are met. One, end-of-year discounts can only be calculated based on purchases of the same good or service in a single fiscal year. Of course, the discount may be obtained at the time of purchase as well. Two, the entity must claim the benefit of the discount from the seller in the fiscal year in which the discount is earned or the following year. In many cases, a seller will be able to calculate the amount of the discount and give the buyer the benefit of the discount (for example, in a credit or reduced price on future purchases of that same good) in the same fiscal year in which the credit was earned. However, in many other cases, the seller may take several weeks after the end of a fiscal year to give the buyer the necessary information. Under either circumstance, this prong of the safe harbor is satisfied. Three, the buyer must fully and accurately report the discount in the cost report for the fiscal year in which the benefit of the discount is received. And four, if the Secretary or a State Medicaid agency requests information, the buyer must provide the appropriate invoices from the seller. (See discussion below of seller's separate reporting requirements.)

We believe that this revision complies with the most important statutory requirement of the discount exception—full reporting—and accommodates many of these end-of-year discounting programs. In addition, we believe that this revision is consistent with HCFA's prudent buyer rules, which are not applicable to charge-based health care providers.

With respect to prompt pay discounts, we have made no change to include such discount arrangements. No change is necessary because, by definition, they are designed to induce prompt payment, and thus do not appear to violate the statute. Of course, we will continue to scrutinize closely "prompt pay" discounts to make sure that they are not payments made for an illegal purpose cloaked under a legitimate label.

Comment: Three commenters requested the OIG to provide various kinds of special treatment for HMOs and PPOs. For example, one commenter urged the OIG to broaden this provision as it applies to HMOs to permit cash grants and training assistance. Another commenter urged the OIG to change the definition of discount to permit discounts offered to HMOs and PPOs by contract health care providers.

Response: We recognize that HMOs and CMPs paid in accordance with a risk contract with HCFA or a State health care program deserve special attention, and paragraph (h)(1)(ii) follows the proposed rule recognizing their special status. These HMOs and CMPs need not report discounts they receive except as may otherwise be required under their risk contract.

In addition, we have expanded this provision in significant ways that should be of assistance to all health care providers, including HMOs. However, we do not believe that it would be appropriate to provide special safe harbor protection for purchasing arrangements that go beyond the intended purpose of this statutory exception. As with all arrangements that drift from a safe harbor out to sea, we will examine them on a case-by-case basis to determine whether the statute has been violated in such a way as to warrant prosecution.

With respect to discounts offered to HMOs, CMPs and PPOs by contract health care providers, as discussed in section III.B.3. above, we are expecting to promulgate a new interim final safe harbor provision to protect arrangements between these parties for the furnishing of covered items and services to beneficiaries where certain standards are met.

Comment: Many commenters objected on a variety of grounds to the requirement that charge-based health care providers reduce their charges by the full amount of the discount. These commenters pointed out that historically the Medicare program has not sought to regulate the discrete components that make up a particular charge. In addition, many suggested that the OIG will destroy the incentive of obtaining discounts if it requires health care providers to pass along the full amount of the discount to the programs. Another rationale for suggesting a change in this safe harbor provision is that the OIG should treat cost and charge-based health care providers in the same manner, and because this safe harbor provision does not require a reduction in reported costs for cost-based health care providers, no parallel requirement should be placed on charge-based health care providers.

Response: We agree with the thrust of these comments, and are revising paragraph (h)(1)(iii) of this safe harbor provision to delete the requirement that charge-based health care providers reduce their charges by the full amount of the discount. Such a provision would be largely unenforceable. As many commenters pointed out, the Department has never monitored the various input costs that make up a health care provider's charge. Therefore, we are not in a position to know a health care provider's base from which he or she was reducing the charge. Thus, for example, if a physician receives a discount as defined in this provision valued at $4 per service, the physician could argue that he or she is not required to reduce the charge by that amount because other costs included in that charge had increased to offset the $4 discount. We are generally not in a position to prove otherwise.

Although we continue to believe that individuals and entities have an obligation to pass along to the Medicare and Medicaid programs the value of discounts they receive, we believe that the actual savings that would result from requiring such charge reductions would be offset by the cost of enforcement. In many areas of reimbursement, for example, physician or laboratory services and purchases of IOLs, Congress has steadily moved away from charge-based reimbursement or has imposed limitations on charges. We believe that those statutory reforms are better suited to address the problem of excessive charging practices. Nonetheless, even though we are deleting this requirement for the purposes of this safe harbor provision, we strongly encourage charge-based health care providers to pass along discounts to the programs.

With respect to the different treatment of health care providers based on the type of reimbursement system, we believe that reasonable safe harbor rules for discounts must be closely tailored to the various reimbursement principles and cost reporting mechanisms. Just as we believe it is appropriate to treat HMOs reimbursed on a capitated basis differently from other health care providers, we now believe that it is appropriate to treat charge-based health care providers differently from cost-based health care providers for the purposes of requiring the discount to be passed along to the program. Such an approach is far preferable than a blind adherence to uniform treatment of health care providers. We believe that such a position is a reasonable reading of the statutory requirement that "the reduction in price [be] * * * appropriately reflected in the costs claimed or charges made by the provider or entity * * *." (Section 1128B(b)(3)(A) of the Act.)

We emphasize, however, that paragraph (h)(1)(iii) still requires charge-based health care providers to comply with the respective rules regarding full and accurate reporting of discounts as defined in this provision. This reporting requirement is limited to items or services that are separately claimed as a line item for payment with the Department or a State agency. As discussed below, under paragraph (h)(1)(iii) of this section, we will not require health care providers to report discounts they receive on goods purchased for which a line item charge is not separately made, but rather is included within their professional charge.

In addition, we note that some commenters were confused about the requirements we are placing on health care providers reimbursed on the basis of costs. The regulation need not specify that a health care provider must separately reduce its cost by the amount of the discount because the cost reporting requirements accomplish the statutory purpose of having the amount of the discount "appropriately reflected in the costs claimed." Whether a provider submits cost reports (and complies with paragraph (h)(1)(i) of this section) or submits a seller's invoice to demonstrate its acquisition costs (and complies with paragraph (h)(1)(iii) of this section), the amount of the discount is passed along to the Medicare and Medicaid programs. As a result, this revised discount provision treats items and services reimbursed on the basis of charges differently from those reimbursed on the basis of costs, because costs will be reduced by the amounts of discounts whereas charges will not be affected.

Finally, although we have attempted to tailor this discount provision to make sense within the context of the varying reimbursement rules, as we have explained in section III.A. above, compliance with this safe harbor provision in no way affects Medicare or Medicaid reimbursement rules.

Comment: Five commenters discussed the requirement in the proposed rule that the discount appear on the seller's invoice or statement and the consequent liability of the seller for failing to make such disclosure. They questioned the apparent inconsistency with the preamble to the proposed rule that no requirements need be placed on sellers in order for their discounts to qualify under this exemption.

Response: We agree with the comments that we should clarify the requirement for a seller to report the value of the discount on the invoice or statement provided to a purchaser, and we are modifying this provision in paragraph (h)(2) accordingly. As discussed above, such standards are necessary to assist the Department and State agencies in verifying that the buyer has fully and accurately reported the value of the discount.

This paragraph describes the requirements we are placing on sellers. With respect to those who sell goods or services to risk contract HMOs and CMPs at a discount, paragraph (h)(2)(i) makes clear that the seller is under no obligation to report the discount to the HMO or CMP for purposes of this safe harbor. Paragraph (h)(2)(ii) sets out the seller's requirements with respect to its sales to all other health care providers. It must either fully and accurately report the discount on the invoice or statement. In addition, it must inform the buyer of its obligations under paragraph (h)(1). With respect to permissible end-of-year discounts, this paragraph, as revised, requires the seller's invoice or statement to show clearly the existence of a discount program, and the seller must inform the buyer of its obligations under paragraph (h)(1). The seller is also required to provide the buyer with a separate document, such as a reconciliation statement, showing the calculation of the discount and identifying the specific goods or services purchased to which the discount is attributed.

It was our original intent not to hold sellers liable for the reporting omissions of health care providers, and we believe such a policy remains appropriate. However, we agree with the commenters that some rules should apply to sellers. We believe that the limited conditions we are placing on sellers seeking safe harbor protection will not place an undue burden on them, but are sufficient to prevent them from avoiding liability when they engage in unlawful schemes disguised as discounts.

Comment: Many commenters questioned what information must be reported to the programs and the methods to be used in reporting such information. Among the questions that were asked is whether the list price, discount, and final actual price all need to be reported on the invoice, claim, or statement. In addition, many commenters suggested that it was unrealistic to require practitioners to report all discounts on goods they purchase, such as office supplies and surgical gloves, for which they do not charge separately, but rather include within their professional service charge.

Response: The fundamental test for complying with the reporting requirement is whether the actual purchase price net of any discount is fully and accurately reported by the seller on the invoice or statement (or, where applicable for end-of-year discounts, on a reconciliation statement) and by the purchaser on the claim or request for payment submitted to Medicare and Medicaid. We do not necessarily require all the information in the calculation of the discount to be noted specifically on the invoice, statement, claim or request for payment; rather, a notation may be made that the actual purchase price is "net discount." Such reporting is acceptable for the purpose of satisfying this provision.

We agree that no purpose would be accomplished if we were to require practitioners to report the discounts they receive on office supplies where there is no requirement to separately report the item on which the discount is received. Thus, we are clarifying the requirements for reporting discounts under paragraph (h)(1)(iii) of this section to make clear that where a practitioner obtains a discount, defined in this provision, for a good that is included as part of his or her professional service charge, such discounts need not be reported. Where a practitioner, however, purchases an item or service at a discount and such item or service is separately claimed as a line item on the applicable claim form, the discounted price must be fully and accurately reported. For example, where a surgeon performs cataract surgery in his or her office and implants an intraocular lens (IOL), the surgeon must report any discount received on the price of the IOL.

Finally, it is noted that where the discount in question does not qualify as a discount under this provision, no safe harbor protection applies. For example, as we stated above, we are not expanding this safe harbor provision to protect the offering of a free good different from the one that is being purchased. Thus, consistent with that position, we are not willing to protect the offering of free computers even when named as "office supplies" to induce the purchase of other items that are reimbursable separately.

7. Employees—§ 1001.952(i)

Comment: Many commenters urged the OIG to extend this exception to apply to independent contractors paid on a commission basis. Two commenters asserted that the legislative history of the statute makes clear that Congress intended to include independent contractors in the employee exception. In support of this contention, they quoted remarks made by Representative Rostenkowski when the House was considering the Medicare-Medicaid Anti-Fraud and Abuse Amendments of 1977. (123 Cong. Rec. 30,280 (1977))

Response: We continue to reject this approach because of the existence of widespread abusive practices by salespersons who are independent contractors and, therefore, who are not under appropriate supervision and control. Although two commenters asserted that they could achieve appropriate supervision and control of independent contractors by including restrictive terms in the contract, we cannot expand this provision to cover such relationships unless we can predict with reasonable certainty that they will not be abusive. We are confident that the employer-employee relationship is unlikely to be abusive, in part because the employer is generally fully liable for the actions of its employees and is therefore more motivated to supervise and control them.

Furthermore, we believe that Representative Rostenkowski's remarks do not reflect congressional intent in this case. His comments related to the House version of the employee exception that was rejected by the Conference Committee. Instead, Congress passed the Senate version, which expressly limited the exception to bona fide employment relationships (See H.Conf.Rep. No. 673, 95th Cong., 1st Sess. 41 (1977)). Consequently, we find no support for the position that Congress intended to cover independent contractors under this exception.

Comment: Two commenters questioned the wisdom of the employee exception, stating that health care providers should not be able to refer patients to other health care providers within their own offices because abuse could be worse than when individuals or entities make referrals to outside sources.

Response: The exception for bona fide employment relationships is clear on the face of the statute, and we are not free to ignore that statutory mandate.

Comment: One commenter asserted that we do not have the statutory authority to limit the definition of "employee" to the meaning it has under 26 U.S.C. 3121(d)(2).

Response: As we have discussed, Congress expressly limited the scope of the employee exception to "bona fide employment relationship[s]" between an employer and an employee. The Secretary clearly has the power, and indeed the duty, to establish the criteria for a bona fide employment relationship. The Internal Revenue Service's (IRS) definition of employee is a longstanding one that has been developed by both agency and court rulings. Furthermore, this definition is sufficiently narrow that it excludes certain types of relationships that we believe tend to be associated with violations of the statute. We are clarifying this safe harbor provision to make clear that the meaning of the term "employee" is defined not only by 26 U.S.C. 3121(d)(2) itself, but also by the IRS's interpretation of that provision as codified in its regulations and other interpretive sources.

Comment: One commenter inquired whether a part-time employee paid on a commission-only basis falls within the employee exception.

Response: As long as a bona fide employer-employee relationship exists between the part-time employee and the employer, such a relationship falls within the scope of this provision.

Comment: Some commenters asserted that many legitimate employment relationships that are common in the health care industry are not protected from prosecution under this exception. One commenter suggested that the employee exception include independent contractors where beneficiaries are being induced to participate in cost-containment programs because such programs are beneficial to Medicare and State health care programs, and therefore should be protected.

Response: We recognize that this provision does not cover some types of personal service arrangements, but our position is necessary to protect the program from abuse to a reasonable degree. However, many of these other arrangements could be protected under the personal services and management contracts safe harbor provision.

Comment: One commenter stated that hospitals are often compelled by State "corporate practice of medicine" requirements to employ physicians and other health care personnel as independent contractors, and that these employment relationships should be afforded safe harbor protection.

Response: We understand that there may be circumstances where, because of State laws, health care providers may not be able to enter into arrangements with health care personnel that comply with the IRS definition of employee. In such cases, however, health care providers may obtain protection for payments from these arrangements by drafting their personal contracts to satisfy the safe harbor provision for personal services and management contracts.

8. Group Purchasing Organizations—§ 1001.952(j)

Comment: One commenter urged the OIG to further define what constitutes a group purchasing organization (GPO) for purposes of this provision. This commenter specifically questioned whether a nursing home chain that requested percentage payments from laboratories as "GPO fees" in return for the referral of laboratory services from member nursing homes fit this definition.

Response: As stated in the preamble to the proposed rule, this exception applies to payments made by a vendor of goods or services to a person authorized to act on behalf of a group of individuals or entities who are furnishing Medicare or Medicaid services. Our definition of the term "GPO" makes clear that a nursing home chain requesting fees for referrals would not qualify for this safe harbor because a chain of nursing homes that are wholly owned subsidiaries of a single corporate entity for all practical purposes constitutes a single entity and not a "group" of entities. As we discuss in section III.D. below, because of the special relationship wholly-owned subsidiaries have with their parent corporation, we are considering separate protection for payments between these entities. However, following this reasoning, we do not believe it appropriate for a nursing home chain to qualify as a GPO and request "GPO fees" for referrals. If a nursing home directly requested such a fee it would appear to represent an illegal inducement. We see no reason how such a solicitation sanitizes the illegality when it is made indirectly by a wholly-owned subsidiary of the nursing home, instead of directly by the nursing home itself.

In addition, we believe that Congress did not intend this exception to apply where it is the vendor and not the health care provider who is furnishing services and directly billing the Medicare or Medicaid program. For example, in addition to services furnished by the nursing home, other health care providers furnish many part B services to nursing home patients, such as laboratory services and durable medical equipment (DME). We believe that a GPO, acting on behalf of a group of nursing homes, is not serving as a GPO when it receives a "GPO fee" from a laboratory or DME supplier that is supplying goods or services to nursing home patients and billing Medicare or Medicaid directly.

Comment: Several commenters objected to the requirement that a purchasing agent, i.e., a GPO, have a written agreement with each individual or entity in the group that specifies the amount the agent will be paid by each vendor. This requirement, they asserted, would be burdensome and expensive.

Response: We agree with the general thrust of these comments and have modified paragraph (j)(1)(ii). The statutory exception requires that written contracts specify the amount the GPO will be paid by the vendor. We believe that this statutory mandate is satisfied if the GPO discloses to a health care provider the fees it will receive from only those vendors that provide goods or services to that provider. This obviates the need for the GPO to divulge fees from vendors that do not provide goods or services to that particular individual or entity.

Comment: To promote administrative convenience, efficiency, and cost-containment purposes, several commenters requested that the GPO should be permitted to specify the range of fees to be paid by the potential vendors instead of the actual amount. One commenter asserted that because of the varying contracts between GPOs and their vendors, it was impossible to determine and disclose in advance the amount the GPO would receive from its vendors.

Response: We agree that it is not necessary, in all circumstances, to specify the exact fees the GPO will receive from its vendors as a result of a particular member's purchases. The legislative history to this exception, however, shows Congress's concern for excessive GPO fees, particularly those exceeding 3 percent. (See, H.Conf. Rep. 1012, 99th Cong., 2d Sess. 310–11 (1986)) For this reason, we are revising this provision (see paragraph (j)(1)(i)) so that a GPO needs to specify the administrative fee it is paid from vendors only if any fee will be above 3 percent.

In the event that the fee cannot be ascertained at the time of the contract or the fee is not fixed at 3 percent or less, the contract must state the maximum amount that could be paid to the GPO by the vendor. This mechanism will permit some flexibility in payments made to the GPO, yet retain the focus on excessive fees about which Congress was concerned.

Comment: Several commenters questioned the interrelationship of this provision to the discount safe harbor.

Response: Several commenters appeared confused about the relationship between these two provisions. This is an example of an arrangement where two safe harbor provisions could apply, i.e., one applicable to discounts, and one applicable to GPOs. However, the GPO provision applies only to payments made by a vendor of goods or services to a person authorized to act as a GPO. Payments, such as discounts, made by vendors of goods or services to health care providers must qualify under the discount exception.

D. Comments on Proposals for New Safe Harbor Provisions

In sections III.B.3. and III.C.1. we discussed proposals and our responses regarding new safe harbor provisions for negotiated price reductions and investment interests. In this section we discuss the remaining proposals and our responses regarding potential new safe harbors.

Note: Any discussion below indicating that we are considering a new safe harbor provision should in no way be construed as legalizing the business arrangement at this time.

Comment: A large number of commenters urged the OIG to adopt a safe harbor provision to protect certain physician recruitment activities. They commented that subsidy payments to physicians for recruitment purposes provide important benefits to many communities that have difficulty in obtaining and retaining physicians. Some urged that we also protect hospital recruitment activities even though a physician does not need to move his or her residence to join the medical staff of the new hospital. Others urged a variety of other provisions, for example, that we not require the physician to disclose to his or her patients the relationship between the physician and the hospital, and that we not specify how long the payments may continue.

Response: We agree with the need to protect some recruitment activities for physicians and other practitioners, and we are considering a new safe harbor provision for practitioner recruitment that we anticipate publishing as a separate regulation.

Comment: Three commenters requested the OIG to adopt a safe harbor provision that will protect all payments that subsidize malpractice premiums. These commenters stressed that such payments have an overwhelming public benefit with limited potential for abuse. One of these commenters argued that obstetrician-gynecologists are facing significant difficulty in paying for malpractice insurance, and suggested that many communities are facing a cut-off of obstetrical services as a result.

Response: We understand the need to assist certain physicians in making malpractice insurance more affordable, and we are considering a new safe harbor provision which we anticipate publishing as a separate regulation, that would protect certain arrangements that subsidize the costs of a practitioner's malpractice insurance premiums where there is no likelihood of abuse.

Comment: Several commenters asked the OIG to provide a new safe harbor provision to protect different types of cross-referral arrangements where no money is exchanged between the parties, for example, traditional referral patterns between a primary care practitioner and specialist, between a hospital and nursing home, and among practitioners within a group practice.

Response: We agree that a large majority of these relationships benefit patients by assuring either proper continuity of care or convenient access to a specialist in whom the primary care physician has confidence. Thus, we are considering a new safe harbor provision, that we anticipate publishing as a separate regulation, that would protect many such arrangements where there is no likelihood of abuse.

Comment: Two commenters suggested that the regulation protect payments related to cooperative hospital service organizations qualified under section 501(e) of the Internal Revenue Code of 1986. Under this statute and implementing Internal Revenue Service regulation, these organizations are formed by one or more hospitals (known as "patron-hospitals") to provide specifically enumerated services, such as purchasing, billing, and clinical services solely for the benefit of its patron-hospitals. In addition, these entities are required to distribute "all net earnings to patrons on the basis of services performed." (26 U.S.C. 501(e)(2)) The commenters believed that although such a distribution requirement runs afoul of the anti-kickback statute, the services they perform are beneficial to rural communities in particular, and there has been no indication of abuse by these organizations.

Response: We agree and are considering a new safe harbor provision, that we anticipate publishing as a separate regulation, that would protect payments between cooperative hospital service organizations and patron-hospitals.

Comment: Many commenters requested the OIG to clarify that payments between corporations which have common ownership are not subject to the statute. Commenters cited as examples intracorporate discounts and payments between two wholly-owned subsidiaries. Some commenters argued that referral arrangements between two related corporations do not constitute "referrals" within the meaning of the statute, and suggested that the OIG define the word "referral" to exclude such activity.

Response: We agree that much of the activity described in these comments is either not covered by the statute or deserves safe harbor protection. We believe that the statute is not implicated when payments are transferred within a single entity, for example, from one division to another. Thus, no explicit safe harbor protection is needed for such payments.

Because the statute is implicated when payments are made from one entity to another even though the payments are made between entities with common ownership, we believe that safe harbor protection may be appropriate. However, we remain concerned about wholly-owned shell entities that are established for a fraudulent purpose, for example, to help hide the identity of the owners or to shield assets. Nonetheless, we are considering a new safe harbor provision, that we anticipate publishing as a separate regulation, that would protect payments between wholly owned subsidiaries and other payments between entities where exclusive ownership control is present and the practice is not otherwise abusive.

We do not, however, believe that the situations commenters described require us to define the word "referral." The commenters do not appear concerned with any unusual conduct that warrants special attention. Rather the commenters have focused on the source and recipient of the payment in question. Thus, our consideration in any proposed rule will be focused on the relationship of the parties making and receiving payments.

IV. Additional Information

A. Regulatory Impact Statement

Executive Order 12291 requires us to prepare and publish a final regulatory impact analysis for any regulation that meets one of the Executive Order criteria for a "major rule," that is, that which would be likely to result in (1) an annual effect on the economy of $100 million or more; (2) a major increase in costs or prices for consumers, individuals, industries, Federal, State, or local government agencies or geographic regions; or, (3) significant adverse effects on competition, employment, investment, productivity, innovation, or on the ability of United States-based enterprises to compete with foreign-based enterprises in domestic or export markets. In addition, we generally prepare a regulatory flexibility analysis that is consistent with the Regulatory Flexibility Act (5 U.S.C. 601–612), unless the Secretary certifies that a final regulation would not have a significant economic impact on a substantial number of small entities.

In the proposed rule published on January 23, 1989, we indicated that this provision was designed to specify the various business and payment practices that would not be considered a kickback for purposes of criminal or civil remedies, and served to clarify departmental policy as to the legality of various commercial arrangements. We stated that the great majority of health care providers and practitioners do not engage in illegal remuneration schemes, and that the aggregate economic impact of this provision should, in effect, be minimal, affecting only those who have chosen to engage in prohibited payment schemes in violation of the statutory intent. As indicated in the proposed regulation's impact statement, the rulemaking is a result of a statutory requirement and not a Department initiative.

The two comments we received on the cost impact indicated that the safe harbors for discounts and personnel services contracts would cast a cloud over a substantial number of legitimate business practices and existing contractual arrangements. Both commenters believed that a comprehensive regulatory flexibility analysis should be performed and a statement added disclosing the possible financial impact of this rulemaking.

Consistent with the intent of the statute, this regulation has been designed to permit individuals and entities to freely engage in business practices and arrangements that encourage competition, innovation and economy. However, the regulation imposes no requirements on anyone. Health care providers and others may voluntarily seek to comply with these provisions so that they have the assurance that their business practices are not subject to any enforcement action under the anti-kickback statute. Thus, it is impossible to predict how many individuals and entities will be affected by this regulation. For these reasons, we have determined that a regulatory impact analysis is not required. Further we have determined, and the Secretary certifies, that this final rule will not have a significant economic impact on a number of small business entities, and we have, therefore, not prepared a regulatory flexibility analysis.

B. Department of Justice Review

In accordance with the provisions of Public Law 100-93, this regulation has been developed in consultation with the Department of Justice.

List of Subjects in 42 CFR Part 1001

Administrative practice and procedure, Fraud, Health facilities, Health professions, Medicare.

TITLE 42—PUBLIC HEALTH

CHAPTER V—OFFICE OF INSPECTOR GENERAL—HEALTH CARE, DEPARTMENT OF HEALTH AND HUMAN SERVICES

42 CFR part 1001 is amended as set forth below:

1. The heading for part 1001 is revised to read as follows:

PART 1001—PROGRAM INTEGRITY—MEDICARE AND STATE HEALTH CARE PROGRAMS

2. The authority citation for part 1001 is revised to read as follows:

Authority: 42 U.S.C. 1302, 1320a–7, 1320a–7b, 1395u(j), 1395u(k), 1395y(e), and 1395hh, and section 14 of Public Law 100-93, unless otherwise noted.

3. Section 1001.1 is revised to read as follows:

§ 1001.1 Scope and purpose.

(a) This part sets forth provisions for the detection of fraud and abuse in the Medicare and certain State health care programs. It implements statutory sections, specifically identified in each subpart, aimed at protecting the integrity of the Medicare and certain State health care programs.

(b) This part also sets forth provisions addressing the OIG's authority to exclude any individual and entity that it determines has committed an act described in section 1128B of the Social Security Act, subject to the exceptions set forth in this part.

4. A new Subpart E is added to read as follows:

Subpart E—Permissive Exclusions

Sec.
1001.951 Fraud, kickbacks and other prohibited activities.
1001.952 Exceptions.
1001.953 OIG report on compliance with investment interest safe harbor.

Subpart E—Permissive Exclusions

§ 1001.951 Fraud, kickbacks and other prohibited activities.

The OIG may exclude any individual or entity that it determines has committed an act described in section 1128B of the Social Security Act, subject to the exceptions set forth in § 1001.952.

§ 1001.952 Exceptions.

The following payment practices shall not be treated as a criminal offense under section 1128B of the Act and shall not serve as the basis for an exclusion:

(a) *Investment Interests.* As used in section 1128B of the Act, "remuneration" does not include any payment that is a return on an investment interest, such as a dividend or interest income, made to an investor as long as all of the applicable standards are met within one of the following two categories of entities:

(1) If, within the previous fiscal year or previous 12 month period, the entity possesses more than $50,000,000 in undepreciated net tangible assets (based on the net acquisition cost of purchasing such assets from an unrelated entity) related to the furnishing of items and services, all of the following five applicable standards must be met—

(i) With respect to an investment interest that is an equity security, the equity security must be registered with the Securities and Exchange Commission under 15 U.S.C. 78l(b) or (g).

(ii) The investment interest of an investor in a position to make or influence referrals to, furnish items or services to, or otherwise generate business for the entity must be obtained on terms equally available to the public through trading on a registered national securities exchange, such as the New York Stock Exchange or the American Stock Exchange, or on the National Association of Securities Dealers Automated Quotation System.

(iii) The entity or any investor must not market or furnish the entity's items or services (or those of another entity as part of a cross referral agreement) to passive investors differently than to non-investors.

(iv) The entity must not loan funds to or guarantee a loan for an investor who is in a position to make or influence referrals to, furnish items or services to, or otherwise generate business for the entity if the investor uses any part of such loan to obtain the investment interest.

(v) The amount of payment to an investor in return for the investment interest must be directly proportional to the amount of the capital investment of that investor.

(2) If the entity possesses investment interests that are held by either active or passive investors, all of the following eight applicable standards must be met—

(i) No more than 40 percent of the value of the investment interests of each class of investments may be held in the previous fiscal year or previous 12 month period by investors who are in a position to make or influence referrals to, furnish items or services to, or otherwise generate business for the entity.

(ii) The terms on which an investment interest is offered to a passive investor, if any, who is in a position to make or influence referrals to, furnish items or services to, or otherwise generate business for the entity must be no different from the terms offered to other passive investors.

(iii) The terms on which an investment interest is offered to an investor who is in a position to make or influence referrals to, furnish items or services to, or otherwise generate business for the entity must not be related to the previous or expected volume of referrals, items or services furnished, or the amount of business otherwise generated from that investor to the entity.

(iv) There is no requirement that a passive investor, if any, make referrals to, be in a position to make or influence referrals to, furnish items or services to, or otherwise generate business for the entity as a condition for remaining as an investor.

(v) The entity or any investor must not market or furnish the entity's items or services (or those of another entity as part of a cross referral agreement) to passive investors differently than to non-investors.

(vi) No more than 40 percent of the gross revenue of the entity in the previous fiscal year or previous 12 month period may come from referrals, items or services furnished, or business otherwise generated from investors.

(vii) The entity must not loan funds to or guarantee a loan for an investor who is in a position to make or influence referrals to, furnish items or services to, or otherwise generate business for the entity if the investor uses any part of such loan to obtain the investment interest.

(viii) The amount of payment to an investor in return for the investment interest must be directly proportional to the amount of the capital investment (including the fair market value of any pre-operational services rendered) of that investor.

For purposes of paragraph (a) of this section, the following terms apply. *Active investor* means an investor either who is responsible for the day-to-day management of the entity and is a bona fide general partner in a partnership under the Uniform Partnership Act or who agrees in writing to undertake liability for the actions of the entity's agents acting within the scope of their agency. *Investment interest* means a security issued by an entity, and may include the following classes of investments: Shares in a corporation, interests or units of a partnership, bonds, debentures, notes, or other debt instruments. *Investor* means an individual or entity either who directly holds an investment interest in an entity, or who holds such investment interest indirectly by, including but not limited to, such means as having a family member hold such investment interest or holding a legal or beneficial interest in another entity (such as a trust or holding company) that holds such investment interest. *Passive investor* means an investor who is not an active investor, such as a limited partner in a partnership under the Uniform Partnership Act, a shareholder in a corporation, or a holder of a debt security.

(b) *Space Rental.* As used in section 1128B of the Act, "remuneration" does not include any payment made by a lessee to a lessor for the use of premises, as long as all of the following five standards are met—

(1) The lease agreement is set out in writing and signed by the parties.

(2) The lease specifies the premises covered by the lease.

(3) If the lease is intended to provide the lessee with access to the premises for periodic intervals of time, rather than on a full-time basis for the term of the lease, the lease specifies exactly the schedule of such intervals, their precise length, and the exact rent for such intervals.

(4) The term of the lease is for not less than one year.

(5) The aggregate rental charge is set in advance, is consistent with fair market value in arms-length transactions and is not determined in a manner that takes into account the volume or value of any referrals or business otherwise generated between the parties for which payment may be made in whole or in part under Medicare or a State health care program.

For purposes of paragraph (b) of this section, the term *fair market value* means the value of the rental property for general commercial purposes, but shall not be adjusted to reflect the additional value that one party (either the prospective lessee or lessor) would attribute to the property as a result of its proximity or convenience to sources of referrals or business otherwise generated for which payment may be made in whole or in part under Medicare or a State health care program.

(c) *Equipment rental.* As used in section 1128B of the Act, "remuneration" does not include any payment made by a lessee of equipment to the lessor of the equipment for the use of the equipment, as long as all of the following five standards are met—

(1) The lease agreement is set out in writing and signed by the parties.

(2) The lease specifies the equipment covered by the lease.

(3) If the lease is intended to provide the lessee with use of the equipment for periodic intervals of time, rather than on a full-time basis for the term of the lease, the lease specifies exactly the schedule of such intervals, their precise length, and the exact rent for such interval.

(4) The term of the lease is for not less than one year.

(5) The aggregate rental charge is set in advance, is consistent with fair market value in arms-length transactions and is not determined in a manner that takes into account the volume or value of any referrals or business otherwise generated between the parties for which payment may be made in whole or in part under Medicare or a State health care program.

For purposes of paragraph (c) of this section, the term *fair market value* means the value of the equipment when obtained from a manufacturer or professional distributor, but shall not be adjusted to reflect the additional value one party (either the prospective lessee or lessor) would attribute to the equipment as a result of its proximity or convenience to sources of referrals or business otherwise generated for which payment may be made in whole or in part under Medicare or a State health care program.

(d) *Personal services and management contracts.* As used in section 1128B of the Act, "remuneration" does not include any payment made by a principal to an agent as compensation for the services of the agent, as long as all of the following six standards are met—

(1) The agency agreement is set out in writing and signed by the parties.

(2) The agency agreement specifies the services to be provided by the agent.

(3) If the agency agreement is intended to provide for the services of the agent on a periodic, sporadic or part-time basis, rather than on a full-time basis for the term of the agreement, the agreement specifies exactly the schedule of such intervals, their precise length, and the exact charge for such intervals.

(4) The term of the agreement is for not less than one year.

(5) The aggregate compensation paid to the agent over the term of the agreement is set in advance, is consistent with fair market value in arms-length transactions and is not determined in a manner that takes into account the volume or value of any referrals or business otherwise generated between the parties for which payment may be made in whole or in part under Medicare or a State health care program.

(6) The services performed under the agreement do not involve the counseling or promotion of a business arrangement or other activity that violates any State or Federal law.

For purposes of paragraph (d) of this section, an agent of a principal is any person, other than a bona fide employee of the principal, who has an agreement to perform services for, or on behalf of, the principal.

(e) *Sale of practice.* As used in section 1128B of the Act, "remuneration" does not include any payment made to a practitioner by another practitioner where the former practitioner is selling his or her practice to the latter practitioner, as long as both of the following two standards are met—

(1) The period from the date of the first agreement pertaining to the sale to the completion of the sale is not more than one year.

(2) The practitioner who is selling his or her practice will not be in a professional position to make referrals to, or otherwise generate business for, the purchasing practitioner for which payment may be made in whole or in part under Medicare or a State health care program after one year from the date of the first agreement pertaining to the sale.

(f) *Referral services.* As used in section 1128B of the Act, "remuneration" does not include any payment or exchange of anything of value between an individual or entity ("participant") and another entity serving as a referral service ("referral service"), as long as all of the following four standards are met—

(1) The referral service does not exclude as a participant in the referral service any individual or entity who meets the qualifications for participation.

(2) Any payment the participant makes to the referral service is assessed equally against and collected equally from all participants, and is only based on the cost of operating the referral service, and not on the volume or value of any referrals to or business otherwise generated by the participants for the referral service for which payment may be made in whole or in part under Medicare or a State health care program.

(3) The referral service imposes no requirements on the manner in which the participant provides services to a referred person, except that the referral service may require that the participant charge the person referred at the same rate as it charges other persons not referred by the referral service, or that these services be furnished free of charge or at reduced charge.

(4) The referral service makes the following five disclosures to each person seeking a referral, with each such disclosure maintained by the referral service in a written record certifying such disclosure and signed by either such person seeking a referral or by the individual making the disclosure on behalf of the referral service—

(i) The manner in which it selects the group of participants in the referral service to which it could make a referral;

(ii) Whether the participant has paid a fee to the referral service;

(iii) The manner in which it selects a particular participant from this group for that person;

(iv) The nature of the relationship between the referral service and the group of participants to whom it could make the referral; and

(v) The nature of any restrictions that would exclude such an individual or entity from continuing as a participant.

(g) *Warranties.* As used in section 1128B of the Act, "remuneration" does not include any payment or exchange of anything of value under a warranty provided by a manufacturer or supplier of an item to the buyer (such as a health care provider or beneficiary) of the item, as long as the buyer complies with all of the following standards in paragraphs (g)(1) and (g)(2) of this section and the manufacturer or supplier complies with all of the following standards in paragraphs (g)(3) and (g)(4) of this section—

(1) The buyer must fully and accurately report any price reduction of the item (including a free item), which was obtained as part of the warranty, in the applicable cost reporting mechanism or claim for payment filed with the Department or a State agency.

(2) The buyer must provide, upon request by the Secretary or a State agency, information provided by the manufacturer or supplier as specified in paragraph (g)(3) of this section.

(3) The manufacturer or supplier must comply with either of the following two standards—

(i) The manufacturer or supplier must fully and accurately report the price reduction of the item (including a free item), which was obtained as part of the warranty, on the invoice or statement submitted to the buyer, and inform the buyer of its obligations under paragraphs (a)(1) and (a)(2) of this section.

(ii) Where the amount of the price reduction is not known at the time of sale, the manufacturer or supplier must fully and accurately report the existence of a warranty on the invoice or statement, inform the buyer of its obligations under paragraphs (g)(1) and (g)(2) of this section, and, when the price reduction becomes known, provide the buyer with documentation of the calculation of the price reduction resulting from the warranty.

(4) The manufacturer or supplier must not pay any remuneration to any individual (other than a beneficiary) or entity for any medical, surgical, or hospital expense incurred by a beneficiary other than for the cost of the item itself.

For purposes of paragraph (g) of this section, the term *warranty* means either an agreement made in accordance with the provisions of 15 U.S.C. 2301(6), or a manufacturer's or supplier's agreement to replace another manufacturer's or supplier's defective item (which is covered by an agreement made in accordance with this statutory provision), on terms equal to the agreement that it replaces.

(h) *Discounts.* As used in section 1128B of the Act, "remuneration" does not include a discount, as defined in paragraph (h)(3) of this section, on a good or service received by a buyer, which submits a claim or request for payment for the good or service for which payment may be made in whole or in part under Medicare or a State health care program, from a seller as long as the buyer complies with the applicable standards of paragraph (h)(1) of this section and the seller complies with the applicable standards of paragraph (h)(2) of this section:

(1) With respect to the following three categories of buyers, the buyer must comply with all of the applicable standards within each category—

(i) If the buyer is an entity which reports its costs on a cost report required by the Department or a State agency, it must comply with all of the following four standards—

(A) the discount must be earned based on purchases of that same good or service bought within a single fiscal year of the buyer;

(B) the buyer must claim the benefit of the discount in the fiscal year in which the discount is earned or the following year;

(C) the buyer must fully and accurately report the discount in the applicable cost report; and

(D) the buyer must provide, upon request by the Secretary or a State agency, information provided by the seller as specified in paragraph (h)(2)(ii) of this section.

(ii) If the buyer is an entity which is a health maintenance organization or competitive medical plan acting in accordance with a risk contract under section 1876(g) or 1903(m) of the Act, or under another State health care program, it need not report the discount except as otherwise may be required under the risk contract.

(iii) If the buyer is not an entity described in paragraphs (h)(1)(i) or (h)(1)(ii) of this section, it must comply with all of the following three standards—

(A) the discount must be made at the time of the original sale of the good or service;

(B) where an item or service is separately claimed for payment with the Department or a State agency, the buyer must fully and accurately report the discount on that item or service; and

(C) the buyer must provide, upon request by the Secretary or a State agency, information provided by the seller as specified in paragraph (h)(2)(ii)(A) of this section.

(2) With respect to either of the following two categories of buyers, the seller must comply with all of the applicable standards within each category—

(i) If the buyer is an entity described in paragraph (h)(1)(ii) of this section, the seller need not report the discount to the buyer for purposes of this provision.

(ii) If the buyer is any other individual or entity, the seller must comply with either of the following two standards—

(A) where a discount is required to be reported to the Department or a State agency under paragraph (h)(1) of this section, the seller must fully and accurately report such discount on the invoice or statement submitted to the buyer, and inform the buyer of its obligations to report such discount; or

(B) where the value of the discount is not known at the time of sale, the seller must fully and accurately report the existence of a discount program on the invoice or statement submitted to the buyer, inform the buyer of its obligations under paragraph (h)(1) of this section and, when the value of the discount becomes known, provide the buyer with documentation of the calculation of the discount identifying the specific goods or services purchased to which the discount will be applied.

(3) For purposes of this paragraph, the term *discount* means a reduction in the amount a seller charges a buyer (who buys either directly or through a wholesaler or a group purchasing organization) for a good or service based on an arms length transaction. The term *discount* may include a rebate check, credit or coupon directly redeemable from the seller only to the extent that such reductions in price are attributable to the original good or service that was purchased or furnished. The term *discount* does not include—

(i) Cash payment;

(ii) Furnishing one good or service without charge or at a reduced charge in exchange for any agreement to buy a different good or service;

(iii) A reduction in price applicable to one payor but not to Medicare or a State health care program;

(iv) A reduction in price offered to a beneficiary (such as a routine reduction or waiver of any coinsurance or deductible amount owed by a program beneficiary);

(v) Warranties;

(vi) Services provided in accordance with a personal or management services contract; or

(vii) Other remuneration in cash or in kind not explicitly described in this paragraph.

(i) *Employees.* As used in section 1128B of the Act, "remuneration" does not include any amount paid by an employer to an employee, who has a bona fide employment relationship with the employer, for employment in the furnishing of any item or service for which payment may be made in whole or in part under Medicare or a State health care program. For purposes of paragraph (i) of this section, the term *employee* has the same meaning as it does for purposes of 26 U.S.C. 3121(d)(2):

(j) *Group purchasing organizations.* As used in section 1128B of the Act, "remuneration" does not include any payment by a vendor of goods or services to a group purchasing organization (GPO), as part of an agreement to furnish such goods or services to an individual or entity as long as both of the following two standards are met—

(1) The GPO must have a written agreement with each individual or entity, for which items or services are furnished, that provides for either of the following—

(i) The agreement states that participating vendors from which the individual or entity will purchase goods or services will pay a fee to the GPO of 3 percent or less of the purchase price of the goods or services provided by that vendor.

(ii) In the event the fee paid to the GPO is not fixed at 3 percent or less of the purchase price of the goods or services, the agreement specifies the amount (or if not known, the maximum amount) the GPO will be paid by each vendor (where such amount may be a fixed sum or a fixed percentage of the value of purchases made from the vendor by the members of the group under the contract between the vendor and the GPO).

(2) Where the entity which receives the good or service from the vendor is a health care provider of services, the GPO must disclose in writing to the entity at least annually, and to the Secretary upon request, the amount received from each vendor with respect to purchases made by or on behalf of the entity.

For purposes of paragraph (j) of this section, the term *group purchasing organization* (GPO) means an entity authorized to act as a purchasing agent for a group of individuals or entities who are furnishing services for which payment may be made in whole or in part under Medicare or a State health care program, and who are neither wholly-owned by the GPO nor subsidiaries of a parent corporation that wholly owns the GPO (either directly or through another wholly-owned entity).

(k) *Waiver of beneficiary coinsurance and deductible amounts.* As used in section 1128B of the Act, "remuneration" does not include any reduction or waiver of a Medicare or a State health care program beneficiary's obligation to pay coinsurance or deductible amounts as long as all of the standards are met within either of the following two categories of health care providers:

(1) If the coinsurance or deductible amounts are owed to a hospital for inpatient hospital services for which Medicare pays under the prospective payment system, the hospital must comply with all of the following three standards—

(i) The hospital must not later claim the amount reduced or waived as a bad debt for payment purposes under Medicare or otherwise shift the burden of the reduction or waiver onto Medicare, a State health care program, other payers, or individuals.

(ii) The hospital must offer to reduce or waive the coinsurance or deductible amounts without regard to the reason for admission, the length of stay of the beneficiary, or the diagnostic related group for which the claim for Medicare reimbursement is filed.

(iii) The hospital's offer to reduce or waive the coinsurance or deductible amounts must not be made as part of a price reduction agreement between a hospital and a third-party payor.

(2) If the coinsurance or deductible amounts are owed by an individual who qualifies for subsidized services under a provision of the Public Health Services Act or under titles V or XIX of the Act to a federally qualified health care center or other health care facility under any Public Health Services Act grant program or under title V of the Act, the health care center or facility may reduce or waive the coinsurance or deductible amounts for items or services for which payment may be made in whole or in part under part B of Medicare or a State health care program.

§ 1001.953 OIG report on compliance with investment interest safe harbor.

Within 180 days of the effective date of this subpart, the OIG will report to the Secretary on the compliance with §§ 1001.952(a)(2)(i) and 1001.952(a)(2)(vi).

Dated: July 19, 1991.

R.P. Kusserow,

Inspector General, Department of Health and Human Services.

Approved: July 22, 1991.

Louis W. Sullivan,

Secretary.

[FR Doc. 91-17891 Filed 7-26-91; 8:45 am]

BILLING CODE 4150-04-M

APPENDIX F2

ADDITIONAL SAFE HARBOR REGULATIONS, NOVEMBER 5, 1992

DEPARTMENT OF HEALTH AND HUMAN SERVICES

Office of Inspector General

42 CFR Part 1001

RIN 0991–AA59

Medicare and State Health Care Programs: Fraud and Abuse; Safe Harbors for Protecting Health Plans

AGENCY: Office of Inspector General (OIG), HHS.

ACTION: Interim final rule with request for comment.

SUMMARY: In accordance with section 14 of the Medicare and Medicaid Patient and Program Protection Act of 1987, this interim final rule establishes two new safe harbors and amends one existing safe harbor to provide protection for certain health care plans, such as health maintenance organizations and preferred provider organizations. The first new provision protects certain incentives to enrollees (including waiver of coinsurance and deductible amounts) paid by health care plans. The second new provision protects certain negotiated price reduction agreements between health care plans and contract health care providers. Finally, an existing safe harbor has been amended to protect certain agreements entered into between hospitals and Medicare SELECT insurers. These safe harbors specifically set forth various standards and guidelines that, if met, will result in the particular arrangement being protected from criminal prosecution or civil sanctions under the anti-kickback provisions of the statute.

DATES: Effective date: This rule is effective on November 5, 1992. Comment period: Although this rule is final, we will consider comments on this regulatory revision delivered to the address provided below by 5 p.m., January 4, 1993. Comments are available for public inspection on November 19, 1992.

ADDRESSES: Address comments to: Office of Inspector General, Department of Health and Human Services, Attention: LRR–28–FC, room 5246, 330 Independence Avenue, SW., Washington, DC 20201. If you prefer, you may deliver your comments to Room 5551, 330 Independence Avenue, SW., Washington, DC. In commenting, please refer to file code LRR–28–FC. Comments are available for public inspection in room 5551, 330 Independence Avenue, SW., Washington, DC on Monday through Friday of each week from 9 a.m. to 5 p.m., (202) 619–3270.

FOR FURTHER INFORMATION CONTACT:
Linda Grabel or D. McCarty Thornton, Office of the General Counsel, (202) 619–0335.
Joel Schaer, Office of Inspector General, (202) 619–3270.

For paperwork reduction and information collection requirements write to: Allison Eydt, Office of Management and Budget, New Executive Office Building, room 3001, 725 17th Street, NW., Washington, DC 20503.

SUPPLEMENTARY INFORMATION:

I. Background

Section 14 of Public Law 100–93 requires the promulgation of regulations specifying those payment practices that will not be subject to criminal prosecution under section 1128B(b) of the Social Security Act (the Act), 42 U.S.C. 1320a–7b(b), and that will not provide a basis for exclusion from

Medicare or the State health care programs under section 1128(b)(7) of the Act. 42 U.S.C. 1320a–7(b)(7). State health care programs are the Medicaid program, the Maternal and Child Health Services Block Grant program, and the Social Services Block Grant program.

Proposed regulations designed to implement section 14 of Public Law 100–93 were developed by the Office of Inspector General (OIG) and published in the Federal Register on January 23, 1989 (54 FR 3088). The regulations set forth various proposed business and payment practices, or "safe harbors," that would not be treated as criminal offenses under section 1128B(b) of the Act and would not serve as a basis for a program exclusion under section 1128(b)(7) of the Act.

In that proposed rulemaking, we did not specifically delineate a safe harbor provision for a variety of arrangements grouped under the generic headings of "managed care" plans for "preferred provider organizations" (PPOs) because we believed that one or more of the other proposed safe harbors would protect relationships in managed care and PPO networks. However, we did invite public comments on the question of adding additional safe harbors that would provide further protections to health maintenance organizations (HMOs), PPOs and other managed care plans. Although we received a number of responsive comments, we did not publish a specific safe harbor in this area in the final rule published on July 29, 1991 (56 FR 35952). As was true then, we could publish the two new safe harbors related to managed care in final form without an opportunity for further public comment. In addition, as discussed in section III.C. of this preamble, we find that good cause exists to publish the amendment regarding Medicare SELECT without a prior comment period. Therefore, further public comment is not required before publication of this rule. However, we will accept public comments submitted within 60 days of the publication of this interim final rule.

These interim final regulations will be effective upon publication. We find that good cause exists for an immediate effective date due to the nature of these safe harbor regulations. This rule places no affirmative obligation on any individual or entity. Indeed, by expanding safe harbor protection, this rule exempts certain conduct from potential criminal and administrative sanctions. We find that the benefit conferred on the public by this rule's publication provides good cause for it to be effective upon publication.

We wish to emphasize that nothing in this final regulation changes reimbursement rules promulgated by the Health Care Financing Administration (HCFA) or a State health care program. If a provider chooses to engage in one course of conduct in order to comply with these safe harbor provisions, such action may very well have reimbursement implications. However, such reimbursement is governed exclusively by HCFA or State regulations, and not by this rulemaking.

II. Summary of Comments Received

As a result of our request for comments in the proposed rulemaking published on January 23, 1989, we received numerous responses on how best to protect HMOs, PPOs and other managed care plans. The following is a summary of the various issues raised through that public comment process. In the following section, we will discuss our responses to the comments we received.

Two commenters requested safe harbor protection for HMOs that waive the beneficiary's obligation to pay coinsurance and deductible amounts. They believed that this was a common practice among HMOs. In addition, a few commenters pointed out that some PPOs negotiate agreements with contract health care providers for those providers not to change the health plan or enrollee for some or all of the coinsurance and deductible amounts they are owed for furnishing services to enrollees. Under such an agreement, when the contract provider bills the Medicare program directly (and not the health plan) and agrees to waive all coinsurance and deductibles, the commenters typically phrased the agreement as one "to accept Medicare payment as payment in full." One commenter specifically objected to this practice.

Several commenters requested the OIG to protect a variety of arrangements between HMOs, PPOs, competitive medical plans (CMPs) as defined in 42 CFR part 417, managed care plans, and other health plans on the one hand, and medical groups and other health care providers who furnish items and services to the health plans at a reduced price on the other hand. A few of these commenters indicated that benefits can be achieved when a health care provider offers discounts to these organizations.

III. Provisions of the Interim Final Rule

In this section, we discuss our responses to the comments indicated above, and set forth the provisions of this interim final rule.

Many program beneficiaries are now served by a wide variety of managed care plans, such as various models of HMOs, CMPs, and health care prepayment plans (HCPPs) as defined in 42 CFR part 417, and prepaid health plans (PHPs) as defined in 42 CFR part 434, as well as PPOs, and we agree that additional safe harbor protection is warranted. We are promulgating two safe harbor provisions to protect the essential activities of prepaid health plans ("health plans"). The first provision protects the various marketing incentives that health plans offer to attract "enrollees" through increased benefits coverage, reduced cost-sharing amounts (coinsurance, deductibles, or copayments), or reduced premiums. The second provision protects the contractual relationships between health plans and "contract health care providers" for the furnishing of covered items and services at reduced prices. Before discussing the specific features of these two safe harbor provisions, we will discuss our specific use of the terms "health plan," "contract health care provider," and "enrollee," all of which are defined in § 1001.952(1)(2).

Definition of Terms

Health Plan

For an entity to be classified as a "health plan", it must either (1) furnish, or arrange under agreement with contract health care providers for the furnishing of, items or services to enrollees or, (2) as with some PPOs, furnish health insurance coverage for the provision of such items or services. In either case, it must charge a premium (with exceptions noted below) for these covered benefits. Such premiums may be paid by a variety of sources, including HCFA, a State agency, an employer, or the enrollee. In addition, the health plan must either be operating under a contract or agreement with HCFA or a State health care program, or be subject to State regulation of its premium structure.

Where the health plans do not operate in accordance with a contract or agreement with HCFA or State health care program, we require the regulation of the premium structures because of our experience with phony insurance plans created by providers where for a $1 "premium" all Medicare coinsurance and deductibles are covered. The premium structure of these "insurance plans" is not based on a bona fide assessment of the liability risk of providing health benefits to enrollees. Therefore, such health plans are not legitimate forms of health insurance or prepaid health care, and we consider them to be unlawful routine copayment waiver programs.

Such health plans with regulated premium structures must operate under the oversight to State insurance laws or a State enabling statute governing HMOs or PPOs. Many such health plans may be federally qualified HMOs under 42 U.S.C. 300e or may operate under the Employee Retirement Income Security Act of 1974. Such health plans also may exist in a variety of other forms. They may be established as provider-based plans, or be independent of providers (such as union-sponsored plans or company plans). In addition, they may be Medicare supplemental (Medigap) policies, such as a Medicare SELECT plan issued under the terms of section 1881(t)(1) of the Act.

Contract Health Care Provider

Under these safer harbor provisions, the term "contract health care provider" means an individual or entity under contract with a health plan to furnish to the health plan's enrollees items or services that are covered by the health plan, Medicare, or a State health care program. Although such health care providers may have contractual relationships with health plans to perform a variety of other functions, such as marketing or peer review, the term "contract health care provider" under these two safe harbor provisions is limited to contractual relations for the furnishing of covered items and services.

Enrollee

The third defined term for these two safe harbor provisions is "enrollee," meaning an individual who has entered into a contractual relationship with a health plan (or on whose behalf an employer, or other private or governmental entity has entered into such a relationship) under which the individual is entitled to receive specified health care items and services, or insurance coverage for such items and services, in return for payment of a premium.

Set forth below is a discussion of the specific features of these two safe harbor provisions, and the amendments to existing § 1001.952(k) involving the protection of certain waivers of Medicare copayments for inpatient hospital services under Medicare SELECT.

A. Increased Coverage, Reduced Cost-sharing Amounts, or Reduced Premium Amounts Offered by Health Plans

The first of these safe harbor provisions protecting health plans deals with the relationship of health plans to enrollees. Although the anti-kickback statute is generally not implicated when a health plan offers a premium to a Medicare or State health care program beneficiary to provide an insurance package, the statute is implicated when discounts on premiums or other incentives are offered.

Health plans offer a variety of incentives to attract beneficiaries to enroll. Under these incentives a health plan may increase covered benefits, reduce or eliminate the beneficiary's obligation to pay cost-sharing amounts (such as coinsurance, deductibles, and copayments), or reduce or eliminate the beneficiary's obligation to pay the premium amounts attributable to the costs of furnishing the covered benefits. The first new safer harbor covers health plans operating pursuant to a contract or agreement with HCFA or a State health care program and is divided into two parts. The first part of the safe harbor (§ 1001.952(l)(1)(i)) protects HMOs, PHPs, CMPs and other health plan under risk contract, and the second part of the safe harbor (§ 1001.952(l)(1)(i)) protects HMOs, CMPs, PHPs, HCPPs and other health plans paid on a reasonable cost or similar basis. Before discussing the standards contained in these two parts of the safe harbors, we will briefly discuss the types of incentives these health plans offer enroilees and why we believe safe harbor protection is appropriate.

In some cases, incentives to enrollees are either mandated under the Social Security Act or are provided with the approval of HCFA. For example, under section 1876 of the Act and implementing regulations, beneficiaries who enroll in HMOs and CMPs are financially responsible for paying the Medicare coinsurance and deductible amounts. Further, section 1876 permits HMOs and CMPs to charge beneficiaries monthly premiums to cover such coinsurance and deductible amounts. HCFA must approve the premiums that are charged, and it regularly permits health plans to waive these premiums. Further, under certain conditions, section 1876 mandates HMOs and CMPs to offer additional benefits or reduce beneficiary cost-sharing amounts. The decision regarding the mix between additional benefits and reduced cost-sharing amounts, however, is left up to the discretion of the health plan.

The routine waiver of a beneficiary's obligation to pay coinsurance and deductible amounts by a prepaid health plan is clearly distinguishable from such routine waiver by other health care providers, such as hospital outpatient departments, physicians, or durable medical equipment suppliers. Two principal characteristics distinguish a health plan's routine waiver of cost-sharing amounts from that of other health care providers. First, a health plan's routine waiver program is inextricably intertwined with the offering of a comprehensive package of covered benefits, and is not offered for the purchase of an individual item or service. Quite often, in the case of prepaid plans, the routine waiver of cost-sharing amounts is made in the form of a waiver of the beneficiary's premium and may also be combined with the offering of increased covered benefits. Thus, the routine waiver of cost-sharing amounts is generally not an incentive to use a particular item or service at the time it is furnished.

Second, although cost-sharing requirements can serve to control utilization, HMOs and other health plans under contract with HCFA or a State health care program have built-in incentives to control unnecessary utilization, or have their utilization and costs monitored by HCFA or the State health care program. Thus, the issue of potential overutilization (with increased costs to the Medicare and Medicaid programs) is adequately dealt with without report to imposing the obligation on beneficiaries to pay coinsurance and deductible amounts.

As discussed above, both parts of this safe harbor protect health plans that are acting in accordance with a contract or agreement with HCFA or a State health care program. As stated above, the first part of this safe harbor protects incentives offered by risk-based contract health plans, such as HMOs, CMPs and PHPs, operating in accordance with section 1876(g) or 1903(m) of the Act, under a Federal statutory demonstration authority, or under other Federal statutory or regulatory authority. The only standard for such health plans is that the health plan may not discriminate in the offering of these incentives, but must offer the same incentives to all enrollees unless otherwise specifically approved by HCFA or a State health care program. This standard will minimize the possibility for the health plan to improperly favor certain healthy beneficiaries or to use incentives to improperly encourage utilization at the time the item or service is furnished.

The second part of the safe harbor protects incentives offered to enrollees by HMOs, CMPs, PHPs and HCPPs that are under contract with HCFA or a State health care program, and that are paid on a reasonable cost or similar basis. For these plans, two standards must be met. One, the same incentives must be offered to all enrollees for all covered services. And two, the health plan may not claim the cost of these incentives as bad debts or otherwise shift the burden of these incentives onto Medicare, Medicaid, other payors, or individuals. We impose this second standard because the incentives a health plan offers to its enrollees should make economic sense for the health plan, and should not be motivated by a desire to shift costs. In addition, it is noted that claiming such costs as Medicare bad debts is not authorized under 42 CFR 413.80 and 417.536 of the Medicare regulations. And where such a claim is presented unlawfully, an entity may be subject to civil or criminal prosecution.

This new safe harbor does not protect incentives to enrollees offered by health plans that do *not* have a contractual relationship with HCFA or a State health care program. [Note: As indicated above, we are amending existing § 1001.952(k) to protect certain waivers of Medicare copayments for inpatient hospital services under Medicare SELECT. See section III.C. of this preamble below.] An example of some of the incentives we are not protecting is an agreement between a PPO and a contract health care provider whereby that provider agrees not to charge the health plan or enrollee all or part of the coinsurance and deductible amounts. When the contract provider bills the program directly (and not the health plan) and agrees to waive all coinsurance and deductibles, the agreement typically is characterized as an agreement to "accept Medicare payment as payment in full." Although such waiver programs may be offered in conjunction with a package of health care benefits and thus have some features similar to the other waiver programs we are protecting in this safe harbor provision, we are not convinced that the Medicare and Medicaid programs are properly protected against overutilization. As discussed above, when a health plan under contract with HCFA or a State health care program waives cost-sharing amounts, utilization and costs are controlled or monitored. This is not necessarily the case with HMOs and PPOs or their providers that bill the Medicare and Medicaid programs on a fee-for-service basis.

For this reason, we are soliciting comments on whether safe harbor protection should be afforded health plans, which do not have a contract or agreement with HCFA or a State health care program, to waive cost-sharing amounts as part of their agreements with contract providers.

B. Price Reductions Offered to Health Plans

This second safe harbor provision for health plans protects the price reductions offered to them by contract health care providers pursuant to an agreement to furnish or arrange for the furnishing of covered items and services. Typically, health care providers will contract with health plans and agree to furnish items and services to enrollees of the health plan at a discount from the provider's usual fee in return for obtaining a large volume of patients.

As with the safe harbor provision discussed above protecting incentives to enrollees, this safe harbor provision is divided into two separate parts for risk-based and cost-reimbursed health plans that operate in accordance with a contract or agreement with HCFA or a State health care program. In addition, this price reduction safe harbor provision contains a third part protecting other health plans that do not have contracts or agreements with HCFA or State health care programs where additional standards are met.

Before discussing the standards to be met in each of these three price reduction safe harbors, we will discuss three definitional prerequisites in § 1001.952(m)(1). The first prerequisite is that the protected remuneration is the contract health care provider's reduction of its usual charges for the services. This safe harbor does not cover reductions which are applicable only to a specific part or portion of the health care provider's charge, such as coinsurance and deductibles, but only applies to reductions in the total amount charged by the health care provider as its usual fee. Furthermore, we are only protecting the remuneration which represents the price reduction offered by the contract health care provider to make clear that any other forms of remuneration offered or paid by a contract health care provider to a health plan are not protected under this safe harbor provision. Indeed, we will closely review any forms of other such remuneration to ensure that improper payments are not employed to induce the health plan to issue a contract or otherwise steer patients to the person paying the remuneration.

The second prerequisite is that the terms of the agreement between the parties must be in writing. This prerequisite is intended to assist the Department in understanding the intent of the parties. Obviously, if need be, we will look behind the contract to determine if the real intent of the parties is not fully disclosed in the written agreement.

The third prerequisite is that the agreement must be for the sole purpose of having the contract health care provider furnish to enrollees items or services that are covered by the health plan, Medicare, or Medicaid. In other words, this provision does not protect contracts between health plans and contract health care providers for these providers to furnish services other than covered benefits. For example, many contract health care providers furnish peer review, marketing services, or pre-enrollment screening. We note that health plans with HCFA contracts under section 1876 of the Act are not permitted to engage in such pre-enrollment screening as a means of denying or discouraging relatively sick beneficiaries from enrolling (sections 1876(c)(3) and (i)(6) of the Act). For the remuneration attributable to the furnishing of other than covered services to be protected, it must comply with the personal service/management contracts safe harbor (§ 1001.952(d)) as set forth in the safe harbor regulations published in the Federal Register on July 29, 1991 (56 FR 35952). And as with all safe harbor provisions, where two parties engage in a multi-faceted payment arrangement where protection is sought from more than one safe harbor, separate justifications must be clearly set forth for each provision for which protection is sought.

We are imposing this third prerequisite because of our experience with some HMOs that have abused their contractual relationships with medical groups where individuals in the groups have engaged in abusive or illegal activities on behalf of the HMO, for example, by conducting pre-enrollment screening. In at least one case such activities have resulted in a criminal conviction. We intend to use our authorities aggressively to monitor closely and penalize where appropriate any abusive relationships between health plans and contract health care providers to assure the medically necessary services of a high quality are available and accessible to all enrollees.

We now discuss the standards in each of the three parts of the price reduction safe harbor. The first part of this safe harbor (§ 1001.952(m)(1)(i)) protects risk-based HMOs, PHPs and CMPs under contract with HCFA or a State health care program, and operating in accordance with section 1876(g) or 1903(m) of the Act, under a Federal statutory demonstration authority, or under other Federal statutory or regulatory authority. Risk-based contract health plans must meet the three fundamental prerequisites discussed above. Additionally, except as specifically authorized by HCFA or the State health care program, contract health care providers may not separately bill Medicare, Medicaid or another State health care program for items or services furnished under the agreement with the health plan. Nor may the contract health care provider otherwise shift the burden of the agreement onto Medicare, Medicaid, other payors, or individuals.

The second part of the price reduction safe harbor (§ 1001.952(m)(1)(ii)) protects health plans that have executed a contract or agreement with HCFA or a State health care program to have payment made on a reasonable cost or similar basis. Price reduction agreements with contract health care providers will be protected as long as four standards are met. One, the term of the agreement may not be for less than one year. Two, the agreement must specify in advance the covered items and services that the contract health care provider will furnish to enrollees and the methodology for computing the payment to the contract health care provider. Three, the health plan must fully and accurately report to HCFA or the State health care program the amount it has paid the contract health care provider pursuant to the agreement. And four, the contract health care provider may not claim payment in any form unless specifically authorized by HCFA or the State health care program, or otherwise shift the burden of such an agreement onto Medicare, Medicaid, other payors, or individuals for the costs of furnishing the items and services. Any claim for reimbursement made directly to Medicare, Medicaid or other State health care program for items or services for which payment was made by the health plan would constitute an unlawful false claim.

The third part of the price reduction safe harbor (§ 1001.952(m)(1)(iii)) protects price reductions offered by contract health care providers to all other health plans where six standards are met. One, the term of the price reduction agreement may not be for less than one year. Two, the agreement must specify in advance the covered items and services, which party is to file claims or requests for payment with Medicare, Medicaid and the other State health care programs, and the schedule of fees that contract provider will be paid. In other words, to meet this second standard, although it does not matter whether the health plan or the contract health care provider bills Medicare, Medicaid or another State health care program, the parties must agree to a set fee schedule. Three, unless a fee update is specifically authorized by Medicare or a State health care program, the fee schedule must remain in effect throughout the term of the agreement. Four, the party submitting claims for items or services furnished under the agreement may not claim or request payment for amounts in excess of the fee schedule. This fourth standard should not be misconstrued as a "lowest charge" provision in that it does not restrict the contract provider from claiming or requesting payment in amounts in excess of this fee schedule when it negotiates a different fee schedule with another health plan or when it is furnishing items or services directly to enrollees on a fee-for-service basis. Five, full and accurate reporting of costs must be made by the health plan or the contract health care provider. And six, to help assure that false claims are not filed, we prohibit the party which is not responsible under the agreement for seeking reimbursement from Medicare, Medicaid and any other State health care program from claiming payment or otherwise shifting the burden of the price reduction onto Medicare, Medicaid, other payors, or individuals.

C. Waiver of Part A Deductible and Coinsurance Amounts Pursuant to an Agreement Between a Hospital and a Medicare SELECT Insurer

The Department has designated 15 States in which State insurance regulators may approve the issuance of Medicare supplemental (Medigap) insurance policies that restrict Medigap benefits to services provided through a network of providers if the standards in section 1882(t)(1) of the Act are met. (See Pub. L. 101-508, section 4358.) Under this authority, known as Medicare SELECT, approved insurers may contract with health care provider entities to furnish items or services to policyholders. Subject to the approval of the State insurance commissioner, the Medicare SELECT insurer may pay less than full Medigap benefits for services obtained outside this provider network.

In return for becoming a preferred provider under the Medicare SELECT plan, the provider would presumably be willing to accept less payment for its treatment of Medicare SELECT beneficiaries. The Medicare SELECT insurer, in turn, should be able to provide health care to its beneficiaries at a lower price. The beneficiary will, in theory, relinquish some freedom of choice in selecting health care providers in return for lower Medigap insurance premiums.

The arrangements between Medicare SELECT insurers and provider entities might implicate the anti-kickback statute. The provider may offer or pay remuneration (in the form of reducing its charges) to induce the referral of Medicare patients by the insurer to the provider. Likewise, the insurer may solicit or receive remuneration from the provider in return for the insurer's referral of Medicare beneficiaries. We believe that some potential arrangements between Medicare SELECT insurers and providers should be granted safe harbor protection while other potential arrangements could be abusive and do not deserve protection.

We have identified two types of arrangements between Medicare SELECT insurers and providers that may implicate the statute but deserve safe harbor protection. First, payments between Medicare SELECT insurers and health care providers may be protected under the newly established safe harbor for price reductions offered to health plans (§ 1001.952(m)). Second, waivers or reduction of inpatient hospital coinsurance and deductible by a hospital pursuant to an agreement with a Medicare SELECT insurer will be protected under the amendment to the safe harbor set forth below.

On July 29, 1991, the Department published final regulations which, among other provisions, included a safe harbor for the reduction or waiver of coinsurance or deductible amounts for inpatient hospital services paid for under the prospective payment system (§ 1001.952(k)(1)). To receive safe harbor protection, three standards must be met: (1) The hospital may not claim the waived amount as bad debt or otherwise shift the cost of the waiver; (2) the hospital may not discriminate in offering reductions or waivers based on the patient's reason for admission; and (3) the reduction or waiver may not result from an agreement between the hospital and a third-party payor. The Department concluded that waivers of coinsurance and deductibles for inpatient hospital services that comply with these standards will not increase costs to the Medicare program, shift costs to other payors, or increase patient demand for inpatient hospital services.

We are amending this existing safe harbor to accommodate the waiver or reduction of inpatient hospital coinsurance or deductible amounts made pursuant to a contract between the hospital and a Medicare SELECT insurer. Specifically, the third standard in this safe harbor will now exempt agreements that are part of a contract between a hospital and a Medicare SELECT insurer for the furnishing of items or services to Medicare SELECT beneficiaries. To qualify for protection under this safe harbor, the insurer must have issued a Medicare SELECT insurance policy under the terms of section 1882(t)(1) of the Act. In other words, the Medicare SELECT policy must meet all of the requirements of section 1882(t)(1), and must be approved by a State insurance commissioner for use in one of the 15 States designated by the Secretary. Furthermore, to be protected by this safe harbor, the waiver of coinsurance or deductible amounts provided for under the agreement must be limited to beneficiaries covered by the insurer's Medicare SELECT policy.

The other requirements of the safe harbor still apply to such waivers or reductions. We believe that this amendment will allow Medicare SELECT insurers to enter into advantageous contracts with hospitals, while continuing to ensure that hospital waivers do not increase costs to Medicare or other payors, or promote over utilization. The evaluation of Medicare SELECT to be completed in 1994 (see Pub. L. 101–508, section 4358(d)) will enable us to determine whether this amendment has had any of these undesirable effects.

In contrast, we will provide safe harbor protection for other types of arrangements between Medicare SELECT insurers and providers that may implicate the anti-kickback statute. For example, we continue to consider routine waivers of coinsurance and deductibles under Part B of Medicare to be an area of potential abuse. Any provider that routinely waives coinsurance and deductible under Part B is subject to criminal liability and civil and administrative sanctions under Federal false claims and false statements statutes as well as the anti-kickback statute. (See OIG's Special Fraud Alert on Routine Waiver of Copayments or Deductibles Under Medicare Part B.) Section 1882(t) of the Act does not provide any safeguards against the abuse of Part B waivers. Therefore, we will not grant any safe harbor protection for the waiver or reduction of Part B coinsurance or deductibles by Medicare SELECT providers.

We find good cause to publish this amendment in interim final form with a comment period rather than as a proposed rule. We find that the delay that would result from soliciting public comment prior to publications would be impracticable, unnecessary and contrary to the public interest. Medicare SELECT only applies to Medicare supplemental (Medigap) insurers who meet specific statutory criteria in one of 15 States designated by the Secretary during the three year period commencing on January 1, 1992. Because the Medicare SELECT program has already started and is only authorized to continue to the end of 1994, the amendment must be published promptly in final form in order to have its intended effect, that is, to protect certain transactions involving Medicare SELECT providers. Furthermore, the amendment is quite limited in scope since it merely broadens one standard in an existing safe harbor to accommodate certain actions taken in accordance with agreements between hospitals and Medicare SELECT insurers. Finally, the amendment by expanding a safe harbor, places no affirmative obligations on any individuals or entities. Rather, the amendment expands a safe harbor to enable some entities to more easily immunize themselves from potential criminal and administrative sanctions.

IV. Additional Information

A. Regulatory Impact Statement

Executive Order 12291 requires us to prepare and publish a final regulatory impact analysis for any regulation that meets one of the Executive Order criteria for a "major rule," that is, that which would be likely to result in (1) an annual effect on the economy of $100 million or more; (2) a major increase in costs or prices for consumers, individuals, industries, Federal, State, or local government agencies or geographic regions; or, (3) significant adverse effects on competition, employment, investment, productivity, innovation, or on the ability of United States-based enterprises to compete with foreign-based enterprises in domestic or export markets. In addition, we generally prepare a regulatory flexibility analysis that is consistent with the Regulatory Flexibility Act (5 U.S.C. 601–612), unless the Secretary certifies that a final regulation would not have a significant economic impact on a substantial number of small entities.

In the proposed rule published on January 23, 1989, we indicated that this provision was designed to specify business and payment practices that would not be considered a kickback for purposes of criminal or civil remedies, and served to clarify departmental policy as to the legality of various commercial arrangements. We stated that the great majority of health care providers and practitioners do not engage in illegal remuneration schemes, and that the aggregate economic impact of this provision should, in effect, be minimal, affecting only those who have chosen to engage in prohibited payment schemes in violation of the statutory intent. As indicated above, this interim final rulemaking serves to further expand the safe harbor provisions to enable entities to more easily immunize themselves from potential criminal and administrative sanctions, and to eliminate potential barriers to the provision of coordinated health care under the Medicare and State health care programs.

Consistent with the intent of the statute, this regulation has been designed to permit individuals and entities to freely engage in business practices and arrangements that encourage competition, innovation and economy. Compliance with these provisions may require that certain individuals and entities change their business practices or arrangements. It is impossible to predict how many individuals and entities will be affected by this regulation. We believe, however, that the number will be insignificant.

For this reason, we have determined that a regulatory impact analysis is not required. Further, we have determined, and the Secretary certifies, that this final rule will not have a significant economic impact on a number of small business entities, and we have, therefore, not prepared a regulatory flexibility analysis.

B. Information Collection Requirements

Sections 1001.952(m)(1)(ii) and 1001.952(m)(1)(iii) of this rule contain information collection requirements which are subject to Office of Management and Budget review under the Paperwork Reduction Act of 1980. These sections are currently approved under OMB control number 0938–0165 (HCFA–276). Comments on these requirements may be forwarded to the individual whose name appears in the address section of this preamble.

C. Department of Justice Review

In accordance with the provisions of Public Law 100–93, these regulations have been developed in consultation with the Department of Justice.

D. Response to Comments

Because of the large number of comments we normally receive on regulations, we cannot acknowledge or respond to them individually. However, we will consider all comments received timely and the appropriateness of revising this interim final rule.

List of Subjects in 42 CFR Part 1001

Administrative practice and procedure, Fraud, Health facilities, Health professions, Medicare.

TITLE 42—PUBLIC HEALTH

CHAPTER V—OFFICE OF INSPECTOR GENERAL—HEALTH CARE, DEPARTMENT OF HEALTH AND HUMAN SERVICES

42 CFR Part 1001 is amended as set forth below:

PART 1001—PROGRAM INTEGRITY—MEDICARE AND STATE HEALTH CARE PROGRAMS

1. The authority citation for part 1001 is revised to read as follows:

Authority: 42 U.S.C. 1302, 1320a-7, 1320a-7b, 1395u(j), 1395u(k), 1395y(e), and 1395hh.

2. Section 1001.952 is amended by revising paragraph (k)(1)(iii) and republishing the introductory text of the section, paragraph (k) introductory text and paragraph (k)(1) introductory text, and adding new paragraphs (l) and (m) to read as follows:

§ 1001.952 Exceptions.

The following payment practices shall not be treated as a criminal offense under section 1128B of the Act and shall not serve as the basis for an exclusion:

* * * * *

(k) *Waiver of beneficiary coinsurance and deductible amounts.* As used in section 1128B of the Act, "remuneration" does not include any reduction or waiver of a Medicare or a State health care program beneficiary's obligation to pay coinsurance or deductible amounts as long as all of the standards are met within either of the following two categories of health care providers:

(1) If the coinsurance or deductible amounts are owed to a hospital for inpatient hospital services for which Medicare pays under the prospective payment system, the hospital must comply with all of the following three standards—

* * * * *

(iii) This hospital's offer to reduce or waive the coinsurance or deductible amounts must not be made as part of a price reduction agreement between a hospital and a third-party payor, unless the agreement is part of a contract for the furnishing of items or services to a beneficiary of a Medicare supplemental policy issued under the terms of section 1882(t)(1) of the Act.

* * * * *

(l) *Increased coverage, reduced cost-sharing amounts, or reduced premium amounts offered by health plans.* (1) As used in section 1128B of the Act, "remuneration" does not include the additional coverage of the any item or service offered by a health plan to an enrollee or the reduction of some or all of the enrollee's obligation to pay the health plan or a contract health care provider for cost-sharing amounts (such as coinsurance, deductible, or copayment amounts) or for premium amounts attributable to items or services covered by the health plan, the Medicare program, or a State health care program, as long as the health plan complies with all of the standards within one of the following two categories of health plans:

(i) If the health plan is a risk-based health maintenance organization, competitive medical plan, prepaid health plan, or other health plan under contact with HCFA or a State health care program and operating in accordance with section 1876(g) or 1903(m) of the Act, under a Federal statutory demonstration authority, or under other Federal statutory or regulatory authority, it must offer the same increased coverage or reduced cost-sharing or premium amounts to all enrollees unless otherwise approved by HCFA or by a State health care program.

(ii) If the health plan is a health maintenance organization, competitive medical plan, health care prepayment plan, prepaid health plan or other health plan that has executed a contract or agreement with HCFA or with a State health care program to receive payment for enrollees on a reasonable cost or similar basis, it must comply with both of the following two standards—

(A) The health plan must offer the same increased coverage or reduced cost-sharing or premium amounts to all enrollees unless otherwise approved by HCFA or by a State health care program; and

(B) The health plan must not claim the costs of the increased coverage or the reduced cost-sharing or premium amounts as a bad debt for payment purposes under Medicare or a State health care program or otherwise shift the burden of the increased coverage or reduced cost-sharing or premium amounts onto Medicare, a State health care program, other payors, or individuals.

(2) For purposes of paragraph (l) of this section, the terms—

Contract health care provider means an individual or entity under contract with a health plan to furnish items or services to enrollees who are covered by the health plan, Medicare, or a State health care program.

Enrollee means an individual who has entered into a contractual relationship with a health plan (or on whose behalf an employer, or other private or governmental entity has entered into such a relationship) under which the individual is entitled to receive specified health care items and services, or insurance coverage for such items and services, in return for payment of a premium.

Health plan means an entity that furnishes or arranges under agreement with contract health care providers for the furnishing of items or services to enrollees, or furnishes insurance coverage for the provision of such items and services, in exchange for a premium, where such entity either operates in accordance with a contract, agreement or statutory demonstration authority approved by HCFA or a State health care program, or has its premium structure regulated under a State insurance statute or a State enabling statute governing health maintenance organizations or preferred provider organizations.

(m) *Price reductions offered to health plans.* (1) As used in section 1128B of the Act, "remuneration" does not include a reduction in price a contract health care provider offers to a health plan in accordance with the terms of a written agreement between the contract health care provider and the health plan for the sole purpose of furnishing to enrollees items or services that are covered by the health plan, Medicare, or a State health care program, as long as both the health plan and contract health care provider comply with all of the applicable standards within one of the following three categories of health plans:

(i) If the health plan is a health maintenance organization, competitive medical plan, or prepaid health plan under contract with HCFA or a State agency and operating in accordance with section 1876(g) or 1903(m) of the Act, under a Federal statutory demonstration authority, or under other Federal statutory or regulatory authority, the contract health care provider must not claim payment in any form from the Department or the State agency for items or services furnished in accordance with the agreement except as approved by HCFA or the State health care program, or otherwise shift the burden of such an agreement onto Medicare, a State health care program, other payors, or individuals.

(ii) If the health plan is a health maintenance organization, competitive medical plan, health care prepayment plan, prepaid health plan, or other health plan that has executed a contract or agreement with HCFA or a State health care program to receive payment for enrollees on a reasonable cost or similar basis, the health plan and contract health care provider must comply with all of the following four standards—

(A) The term of the agreement between the health plan and the contract health care provider must be for not less than one year;

(B) The agreement between the health plan and the contract health care provider must specify in advance the covered items and services to be furnished to enrollees, and the methodology for computing the payment to the contract health care provider;

(C) The health plan must fully and accurately report, on the applicable cost report or other claim form filed with the Department or the State health care program, the amount it has paid the contract health care provider under the agreement for the covered items and services furnished to enrollees; and

(D) The contract health care provider must not claim payment in any form from the Department or the State health care program for items or services furnished in accordance with the agreement except as approved by HCFA or the State health care program, or otherwise shift the burden of such an agreement onto Medicare, a State health care program, other payors, or individuals.

(iii) If the health plan is not described in paragraphs (m)(1)(i) or (m)(1)(ii) of this section, both the health plan and contract health care provider must comply with all of the following six standards—

(A) The term of the agreement between the health plan and the contract health care provider must be for not less than one year;

(B) The agreement between the health plan and the contract health care provider must specify in advance the covered items and services to be furnished to enrollees, which party is to file claims or requests for payment with Medicare or the State health care program for such items and services, and the schedule of fees the contract health care provider will charge for furnishing such items and services to enrollees;

(C) The fee schedule contained in the agreement between the health plan and the contract health care provider must remain in effect throughout the term of the agreement, unless a fee increase results directly from a payment update authorized by Medicare or the State health care program;

(D) The party submitting claims or requests for payment from Medicare or the State health care program for items and services furnished in accordance with the agreement must not claim or request payment for amounts in excess of the fee schedule;

(E) The contract health care provider and the health plan must fully and accurately report on any cost report filed with Medicare or a State health care program the fee schedule amounts charged in accordance with the agreement; and

(F) The party to the agreement, which does not have the responsibility under the agreement for filing claims or requests for payment, must not claim or request payment in any form from the Department of the State health care program for items or services furnished in accordance with the agreement, or otherwise shift the burden of such an agreement onto Medicare, a state health care program, other payors, or individuals.

(2) For purposes of this paragraph, the terms *contract health care provider, enrollee,* and *health plan* have the same meaning as in paragraph (l)(2) of this section.

Dated: August 12, 1992.

Bryan B. Mitchell,

Principal Deputy Inspector General.

Approved: October 6, 1992.

Louis W. Sullivan,

Secretary.

[FR Doc. 92–26802 Filed 11–4–92; 8:45 am]

BILLING CODE 4150-04-M

DEPARTMENT OF HEALTH AND HUMAN SERVICES

Office of Inspector General

42 CFR Part 1001

[RIN 0991–AA69]

Medicare and State Health Care Programs; Fraud and Abuse; Safe Harbors for Protecting Health Plans—Extension of Comment Period

AGENCY: Office of Inspector General (OIG), HHS.

ACTION: Interim final rule with request for comment; extension of comment period.

SUMMARY: On November 5, 1992, we published an interim final rule establishing two new safe harbors, and amended one existing safe harbor, to provide protection for certain health care plans, such as health maintenance organizations and preferred provider organizations (57 FR 52723). We are extending the comment period at the request of several organizations.

DATES: Comments may be submitted until March 5, 1993.

ADDRESSES: Comments should be submitted to: Office of Inspector General, Department of Health and Human Services, Attention: LRR–28–FC, room 5246, 330 Independence Avenue, SW., Washington, DC 20201.

FOR FURTHER INFORMATION CONTACT: Joel Schaer, Office of Inspector General, (202) 619–0089.

SUPPLEMENTARY INFORMATION: These safe harbors specifically set forth various standards and guidelines that, if met, will result in the particular arrangement being protected from criminal prosecution or civil sanctions under the anti-kickback provisions of the statute. Although this rule was issued in final form and became effective on the date of publication, we indicated in the preamble of that document that we were allowing a 60-day public comment period during which time interested parties could submit their comments and concerns regarding these safe harbors to the Office of Inspector General. The OIG agreed to consider all comments received on or before January 4, 1993.

Since publication of that final rule, we have received requests from several outside organizations to extend the existing comment period beyond the 60-day period. Specifically, because of our desire to work with affected outside groups in considering innovative suggestions and ideas in establishing practical and workable safe harbors, and concerns made known to us by some parties that the holiday season has hampered their ability to poll their constituents in a timely and effective manner to provide necessary and comprehensive information, we have agreed to extend the public comment period on this interim final rulemaking until March 5, 1992. We note that even though we are formally extending the comment period by an additional 60 days, those managed care safe harbor provision regulations have the effect of a final rule and such extension will not have an effect on the current implication of this rule.

Dated: December 18, 1992.

Approved: December 31, 1992.

Bryan B. Mitchell,

Principal Deputy Inspector General.

Louis W. Sullivan,

Secretary.

[FR Doc. 93–272 Filed 1–4–93; 11:52 am]

BILLING CODE 4150-04-M

APPENDIX F3

ADDITIONAL SAFE HARBOR PROVISIONS UNDER THE OIG ANTI-KICKBACK STATUTE, SEPTEMBER 21, 1993

DEPARTMENT OF HEALTH AND HUMAN SERVICES

Office of Inspector General

42 CFR Part 1001

RIN 0991-AA66

Health Care Programs: Fraud and Abuse; Additional Safe Harbor Provisions Under the OIG Anti-Kickback Statute

AGENCY: Office of Inspector General, HHS.

ACTION: Proposed rule.

SUMMARY: This proposed regulation is designed to set forth an expanded listing of safe harbor provisions as authorized under section 14 of the Medicare and Medicaid Patient and Program Protection Act of 1987. This new listing of proposed safe harbors delineates additional payment and business practices under Medicare and State health care programs that would be protected from criminal prosecution or civil sanctions under the anti-kickback provisions of the statute.

DATES: To assure consideration, public comments must be mailed or delivered to the address provided below by November 22, 1993. Comments are available for public inspection October 5, 1993.

ADDRESSES: Address comments in writing to: Office of Inspector General, Department of Health and Human Services, Attention: LRR-27-P, room 5246, 330 Independence Avenue, SW., Washington, DC 20201.

If you prefer, you may deliver your comments to room 5551, 330 Independence Avenue, SW., Washington, DC. In commenting, please refer to file code LRR-27-P. Comments will be available for public inspection in room 5551, 330 Independence Avenue, SW., Washington, DC on Monday through Friday of each week from 9 a.m. to 5 p.m., (202) 619-3270.

FOR FURTHER INFORMATION CONTACT: Joel Schaer, Office of Inspector General; (202) 619-3270.

SUPPLEMENTARY INFORMATION:

I. Background

Public Law 100-93

Section 14 of Public Law 100-93, the Medicare and Medicaid Patient and Program Protection Act of 1987, requires the promulgation of regulations specifying those payment and business practices which, although potentially capable of inducing referrals of business under the Medicare and State health care programs, would not be treated as criminal offenses under section 1128B(b) of the Social Security Act (42 U.S.C. 1320a-7b(b)) and would not serve as a basis for a program exclusion under section 1128(b)(7) of the Act (42 U.S.C. 1320a-7(b)(7)).

Congress intended that the regulations setting forth various "safe harbors" would be evolving rules that would be periodically updated to reflect changing business practices and technologies in the health care industry. As evidenced in the House Committee Report accompanying Public Law 100-93, the Committee stated that it believed that periodic public input was necessary:

> * * * to ensure that the regulations remain relevant in light of changes in health care delivery and payment and to ensure that published interpretations of the law are not impeding legitimate and beneficial activities. Accordingly, the Committee expects that the Secretary will formally re-evaluate the anti-kickback regulations on a periodic basis and, in doing so, will solicit public comments at the outset of the review process.

Initial Proposed Rulemaking

On January 23, 1989, we published a notice of proposed rulemaking setting forth various business and payment practices that we proposed to exempt from the anti-kickback statute, and the rationale for their inclusion in a listing of "safe harbor" provisions (54 FR 3088). The rulemaking proposed the establishment of safe harbors in ten broad areas: investment interests, space rental, equipment rental, personal services/management contracts, sales of practice, referral services, warranties, discounts, employees and group purchasing.

In response to the proposed rulemaking, we received over 750 public comments that included both general and broad-reaching concerns regarding the impact of these regulations. The majority of the comments received specifically addressed the ten proposed safe harbors. A summary of these comments and our analysis and response to those concerns are set out in the preamble to the final regulation that was published in the **Federal Register** on July 29, 1991 (56 FR 35952). In addition, the public comments contained several suggestions for the consideration and adoption of additional safe harbor provisions under 42 CFR 1001.952. Set forth below are seven proposed new safe harbor provisions. We invite public comment on these new provisions.

We wish to emphasize that nothing in this proposed regulation changes reimbursement rules promulgated by the Health Care Financing Administration (HCFA) or a State health care program. If a provider chooses to engage in a particular course of conduct in order to comply with these safe harbor provisions, such action may very well have reimbursement implications; however, such reimbursement is governed exclusively by HCFA or State regulations, and not by this rulemaking.

In addition, because this is simply a notice of proposed rulemaking, compliance with either the terms of this proposed rule or standards discussed in this preamble does not provide safe harbor protection at the present time. The only way to protect behavior which implicates the anti-kickback statute is compliance with a safe harbor provision which has been published in final form.

II. Provisions of the Proposed Rule

Set forth below is a description of the additional payment practices that we are proposing to exempt under § 1001.952 of our regulations and the rationale for their inclusion in this proposed rulemaking.

A. Additional Investment Interests

We are proposing three additional investment interest safe harbor provisions in § 1001.952(a) to protect payments to investors who engage in business with the entity in which they have invested.

1. Investment Interests in Rural Areas

We have been informed that many rural areas have particular problems that make it difficult for them to comply with the two 60-40 rules of the "small entity" investment interest safe harbor provision as currently set forth in §§ 1001.952(a)(2) (i) and (vi). The first 60-40 rule, known as the "60-40 investor rule," requires that no more than 40 percent of the investment interests of the entity be held by investors who are in a position to make or influence referrals to, furnish items or services to, or otherwise generate business for the entity. The second 60-40 rule, known as the "60-40 revenue rule," requires that no more than 40 percent of the gross revenue of the entity may come from referrals or business otherwise generated from investors. Rural areas have an especially difficult time complying with these two standards in many cases because physicians may be the only source of capital, and they may have no alternative facility to which they can refer.

Consequently, in a third investment interest safe harbor, § 1001.952(a)(3), we are proposing to eliminate these two 60-40 rules for entities serving rural areas. This safe harbor would apply to entities located in rural areas as defined by the Office of Management and Budget and used by the Bureau of the Census. According to the 1991 Statistical Abstract of the United States, 22.5 percent of the population in 1990 reside in such areas. We are soliciting comments on the appropriateness of this definition of a rural area, and we will consider comments on how the definition could be adapted to further the intent of this proposed safe harbor. We stress, however, that the method used for designating rural areas must ensure that this safe harbor only protects entities that truly serve a rural population. One alternative would be to adopt the definition of rural area found in 42 CFR 412.62(f)(1)(ii).

We are not proposing, however, to modify any of the other six standards in the small investment interest safe harbor for rural areas that are set forth in §§ 1001.952(a)(2) (ii)–(v), (vii), and (viii). These six standards provide fundamental assurances against abuse, and we have not been apprised of any particular difficulty that rural entities are experiencing with these other standards. Therefore, we are not requesting public comments regarding the applicability of these six standards to the proposed small investment interest safe harbor for rural areas.

In place of the 60–40 *investor* rule we are proposing a more flexible standard that will still assure that referring sources, physicians in particular, are not inappropriately selected as investors. We are proposing to require the entity to make a bona fide offer of the investment interest to any individual or entity irrespective of whether such prospective investor is in a position to make or influence referrals to, furnish items or services to, or otherwise generate business for the entity. In other words, the entity may comply with this first standard by offering the opportunity for investment in a good faith, nondiscriminatory manner to any individuals or entities who are potential sources of capital.

Although we are eliminating the 60–40 *revenue* rule, we remain concerned that a sham joint venture structure could be established that does not intend to serve the rural area in which it is located. Consequently, we are proposing to incorporate a standard that would require that at least 85 percent of the dollar volume of the entity's business in the previous fiscal year or previous 12 month period must be derived from the service of persons who reside in a rural area. In the case of an entity that has not yet been in business for 12 months, compliance with this standard will be determined by examining the composition of the entity's business over the entire period of its existence.

2. Investment Interests in Ambulatory Surgical Centers

In a fourth investment interest safe harbor, § 1001.952(a)(4), we are proposing to protect payments to investors in ambulatory surgical centers (ASCs) who are surgeons who refer patients directly to the ASC and perform surgery themselves on these referred patients.

As stated in the preamble of the original set of safe harbor provisions published on July 29, 1991 (56 FR 35971):

> A special situation may exist when a physician sees a patient in his or her office, makes a referral to an entity in which he or she has an ownership interest and performs the service for which the referral is made.

This concept is often referred to as an extension of the physician's office practice. In the above situation, the physician-investor receives two payments: (1) the professional fee for furnishing the service, and (2) the profit distribution from the entity based on the program payment the entity receives that was generated from the referral. We do not consider the statute to be implicated by the first payment. However, we believe that the second payment is potentially covered by the statute.

As with any investment interest held by a potential referral source, the profit distribution provides some financial incentive to refer patients to the entity. To the extent this payment has the potential to induce physician-investors to overutilize the entity, no safe harbor protection is warranted.

In contrast, where these payments do not constitute a significant inducement to make referrals, they may merit safe harbor protection. Where the professional fee generated by a referral is substantially greater than the facility fee generated by the referral, we believe that the profit distribution payment (which results from the facility fee) does not constitute a significant improper inducement. Only where a great disparity between the facility and professional fees exists will the incremental increase in profit distribution from a referral be so small as to be inconsequential when compared to the corresponding professional fee. Therefore, we will only consider providing safe harbor protection to types of extensions of practice that receive facility fees from referrals that are greatly disparate from the professional fee generated by the referral.

Because we believe that ASCs generally fit this criterion, we have proposed a safe harbor for certain investment interests in ASCs. When a patient is referred to an ASC for surgery, there is a great disparity between the surgeon's professional fee and the ASC's facility fee. Therefore, we propose to protect the payment of profit distributions from the ASC to investors where all investors in the ASC are surgeons in a position to refer to the ASC and perform services.

This proposed safe harbor applies only to ASCs certified under 42 CFR part 416. We are not proposing to protect ASCs located on the premises of a hospital that share their operating or recovery room space with the hospital for treatment of the hospital's inpatients or outpatients.

This proposed fourth investment interest provision contains five standards. The first standard precludes an investor from being afforded better investment terms based on past or expected referrals or amount of services furnished to the entity. The second standard requires that a passive investor not be required to make referrals to the entity in order to continue as an investor. The third standard prohibits the entity or any investor from loaning funds to the investor for use in obtaining an investment interest. Standard four requires that payments not be based on referrals. Finally, the practitioner must agree to treat Medicare and Medicaid patients.

In contrast to the other investment interest safe harbors which seek to limit investment by individuals in a position to refer, this proposed ASC safe harbor only protects entities whose investment interests are held entirely by such individuals. With that distinction in mind, four of the five proposed standards have been adapted from those in the small entity safe harbor at § 1001.952(a)(2). We believe these standards provide fundamental assurances against abuse; however, we are soliciting comments on the extent to which other standards are appropriate to safeguard against potential abuse.

Further, while this proposed safe harbor only applies to ASCs certified under 42 CFR part 416, we are also soliciting comments on whether this rationale is applicable to entities other than ASCs. Specifically, we are soliciting comments on what degree of disparity should exist between the professional fees and facility fees generated by referrals to a type of entity for that type of entity to receive safe harbor protection.

The rationale underlying this safe harbor does not extend to investment interests held by physicians who are not in a position to refer patients directly to the ASC and perform surgery. Such physicians do not receive a professional fee as a result of services performed by the entity. An example to illustrate the potential perils of protecting profit distributions to such investors would be where a non-surgeon physician investor may refer a patient to a surgeon-investor who may, in turn, refer the patient to the ASC where the surgeon-investor may perform the surgery. In this scenario, the non-surgeon investor would receive a return, through the ASC's profit distribution, for the "indirect referral" of the patient. Because of the potential for improper inducement of referrals illustrated in this example, we do not think investment interests held by non-surgeon investors merit safe harbor protection.

3. Investment Interests in Group Practices Composed Exclusively of Active Investors

We are considering promulgating a fifth investment interest safe harbor to protect payments to investors in entities composed only of active investors in a group practice. Although there may be other types of joint ventures composed exclusively of active investors which should receive safe harbor protection, we do not propose to protect them at this time. Rather, we are presently soliciting comments on how to expand this limited safe harbor provision.

This fifth investment interest safe harbor, § 1001.952(a)(5), would protect the investment interests of members of group practices that meet two prerequisites and three standards. The two prerequisites are that all the investors must meet our definition of "active investor," and all the investors must be physician members of a "group practice."

We propose to adopt the definition of group practice contained in section 1877(h)(4) of the Act (as added by section 6204(a) of the Omnibus Budget Reconciliation Act of 1989, Public Law 101–239), which restricts physicians from making referrals for clinical laboratory services to entities with which they have an ownership interest or other compensation arrangement. This definition requires (a) physician members of the group to provide substantially the full range of their services through the shared use of office space, facilities, equipment and personnel; (b) substantially all of the services of the members to be provided through the group, billed through the group, with payments received as receipts of the group; and (c) overhead expenses and income of the group to be distributed in accordance with a predetermined formula. We intend principally to protect investors who are individuals who qualify as "physicians" under this definition. However, because our definition of investor includes entities as well as individuals, our definition of group practice permits physicians to invest as a professional corporation, but only to the extent that the corporation is exclusively owned by the physicians. We are soliciting comments on the appropriateness of using this definition of "group practice" for the purposes of this safe harbor provision. One alternative would be to adopt the definition contained in the regulations implementing section 1877(h)(4) of the Act when that regulation is published in final form (see 57 FR 8588, March 11, 1992). Another alternative would be to use the definition currently set forth in 42 CFR 417.100.

The three standards in this safe harbor are derived directly from the second investment interest safe harbor in § 1001.952(a)(2). First, we are requiring that the terms of the investment interest not be preferentially given to certain physicians in the group practice based on their expected referrals. Second, the entity or another investor cannot loan or guarantee a loan to the investors to be used to obtain the investment interest. And third, the amount of return must be directly proportional to the capital invested. We are specifically inviting comments on the appropriateness of applying these standards to group practices. In particular, we are soliciting information in the types of compensation arrangements that exist within group practices, and the extent to which they create inappropriate incentives that distort the professional judgment of the members of the group.

We recognize that there may be other non-abusive joint ventures consisting exclusively of active investors. Typically, such entities are partnerships consisting of general partner investors. The general partners are involved in the day-to-day operation of the entity, and undertake personal liability. However, entities structured in this manner can have a variety of different characteristics. For example, as discussed above, the entity can be a physicians group practice where all the physicians are general partners, or the entity can be a joint venture between two other entities, such as a hospital and durable medical equipment (DME) supplier or a DME manufacturer and a DME distributor. In addition, the entity may be a subchapter S corporation instead of a partnership.

In view of the wide variety of types of entities that may warrant protection, and the varying degree of safeguards that may be warranted for different types, we are soliciting comments on whether we should protect other types of joint ventures composed exclusively of active investors, and the extent to which we should adopt the standards we have included in the second investment interest safe harbor (§ 1001.952(a)(2)). Among the areas about which we are specifically soliciting comments are the varying degree of safeguards that are needed when the general partners are entities as opposed to individuals, the extent to which such a provision should apply in the context of a subchapter S corporation or other business structure, and the extent to which protection should be afforded to these entities when they have passive investors who are not in a position to make referrals.

B. Practitioner Recruitment

We are proposing a safe harbor provision for certain payments or benefits offered by rural hospitals and entities in their efforts to recruit physicians and other practitioners to join their staffs. It has come to our attention that hospitals located in rural areas have been encountering problems in helping to attract physicians needed by the community. With this proposed safe harbor we hope to address this problem without protecting arrangements designed to channel Medicare and Medicaid business to recruiting hospitals. We have proposed to limit the safe harbor to hospitals and other entities located in "rural areas" as that term is defined in the proposed investment interest safe harbor for entities located in rural areas. We are soliciting comments on alternative geographic criteria for protecting recruitment of physicians under this safe harbor. One example may be limiting the safe harbor to recruitment of practitioners by hospitals and entities located in areas which are health professional shortage areas for the practitioner's specialty category.

We are proposing to protect recruitment activities aimed at only two types of health care providers: (1) A practitioner who will need to relocate to a new geographic area and start a new practice, or (2) a new practitioner to assist him or her in starting a practice or specialty after completing an internship or residency program. Not covered within this safe harbor are arrangements between hospitals and physicians that are, in reality, payments to obtain the referrals of established practitioners who work at least in part at another hospital in the same area.

For the recruitment activity to be protected, we propose seven standards: (1) the arrangement and its terms must be in writing; (2) if a practitioner is leaving an established practice, the physical location of the new primary place of practice must be not less than 100 miles from the location of the established primary place of practice and at least 85 percent of the revenue of the new practice must be generated from new patients not previously seen by the practitioner at his or her former practice; (3) unless the practitioner's new primary place of practice is designated as a health professional shortage area (HPSA) for the practitioner's HPSA specialty category during the entire duration of the payments or benefits, the duration of the payments or benefits cannot exceed 3 years; (4) the entity providing the benefits cannot condition the agreement on the practitioner's referral of business to the entity; (5) the practitioner cannot be restricted from establishing staff privileges at another entity or referring business to another entity; (6) the entity cannot vary, adjust or renegotiate the amount or value of benefits based on the volume of business the practitioner generates for the entity; and (7) the practitioner must treat medicare and medicaid patients.

Hospitals would not fall within this safe harbor if they use recruitment efforts as a means of offering compensation to physicians as inducements for referrals. Thus, we do not propose to protect subsidy payments beyond the 3-year period. However, after three years, hospitals may still engage in financial relationships with these physicians that qualify under other safe harbor provisions, such as space rental, personal services/ management contracts, or the safe harbor proposed below on malpractice insurance.

The one exception to the 3-year limit on payments or benefits would be where the practitioner has been recruited to a HPSA. The designated shortage would have to be in the practitioner's HPSA specialty category. In addition, in order to be exempted from the 3-year limit, the area would have to be designated a HPSA during the duration of the relationship between the entity and the practitioner.

We are also soliciting comments on how to protect payments designed to retain physicians already practicing in an area that has been designated a HPSA for the physician's specialty category.

C. Obstetrical Malpractice Insurance Subsidies

We are proposing a new safe harbor provision that would permit a hospital or other entity to pay all or part of the malpractice insurance premiums for practitioners engaging in obstetrical practice in primary care health professional shortage areas. For the purposes of this provision, "practitioner" includes a "certified nurse-midwife" as defined in section 1861(gg) of the Act. Seven standards would need to be met. The first five standards are adopted from concepts in the rural investment interest and practitioner recruitment safe harbor provisions proposed above. These standards require that: (1) the agreement must be set forth in writing; (2) at least 85 percent of the practitioner's obstetrical patients treated under the coverage of the malpractice insurance reside in the shortage area or be a part of a designated shortage area population; (3) there is no requirement that the practitioner refer any level of patients to the entity; (4) there is no restriction placed on the practitioner from establishing staff privileges at, referring patients to, or otherwise generating business for other entities; and (5) the amount of the payment may not vary based on referrals made by the practitioner to the entity.

Two additional standards are also being proposed. The sixth standard attempts to assure access to Medicaid patients seeking obstetrical care by requiring the practitioner, as a condition of safe harbor protection, to treat such patients. Finally, the seventh standard requires bona fide insurance policies to assure that this provision is not used as a mechanism to disguise improper inducements to physicians or other practitioners. Such insurance policies are regulated under State law and are exempt from antitrust and Federal Trade Commission enforcement in accordance with 15 U.S.C. 1012.

Under this proposed safe harbor provision, entities would be permitted to limit the coverage of the malpractice insurance to services performed at that entity. Although we are concerned that such restrictive policies have the effect of limiting a practitioner's professional mobility, we recognize that there are important reasons for such restrictions. Often a hospital's malpractice policy is limited to insure against misconduct on its premises. Although a hospital can provide reasonable assurances to its underwriter that it is overseeing the conduct of its medical staff, it has little ability to make any assurances of the conduct of its staff when they are working at other hospitals. Thus, the underwriter could be engaging in a much higher risk, and therefore might legitimately charge a much higher premium, if it were to provide insurance for the hospital's medical staff when it furnishes services off-site. Finally, we believe that any potential for influencing the practitioner's choice of where to practice that may result from this standard is mitigated by other standards within this proposed provision that limit the ability of the entity to use malpractice subsidies to control the stream of referrals from that practitioner.

As we noted above, nothing in this proposed rule should be construed as authorizing Medicare payment to hospitals or other institutional providers for the cost they may incur for such malpractice insurance. Any allowable costs for such insurance is governed strictly by Medicare and Medicaid rules.

We recognize the narrowness of this safe harbor provision, which is limited to malpractice subsidies for obstetrical care in HPSAs. Although the malpractice problem affects many more practitioners than those we are proposing to protect here, we remain concerned that such subsidies may lead to inappropriate incentives and loyalties created by such incentives. However, we are soliciting comments on specific, narrowly drawn circumstances where this safe harbor provision could be expanded to help assure beneficiary access to services that may be significantly affected by the cost of malpractice insurance premiums. In addition, we are soliciting views regarding the feasibility of expanding this provision to protect malpractice insurance programs that are not regulated under State law, but which are operated directly by providers.

D. Referral Agreements for Specialty Services

We are proposing to protect arrangements under which an individual or entity agrees to refer a patient to another individual or entity for specialty services in return for an agreement on the part of the party receiving the referral to refer that patient back at a certain time or under certain circumstances. For example, a primary care physician and a specialist may agree that, when their patient reaches a particular stage of recovery, the primary care physician should resume treatment of the patient.

The first standard we are proposing clarifies what is meant by specialty services; that is, the service for which the referral is made may not be within the medical expertise of the referring individual or entity, but is within the special expertise of the other party receiving the referral. The second standard we are proposing prohibits any actual *payment* to be made between the parties for the referral. The third standard requires that the only exchange of value between the parties, with one exception to be discussed below, is the opportunity to obtain monetary remuneration directly from third-party payors or the patient, as compensation for his or her respective professional services. As the United States Court of Appeals for the First Circuit has recognized: "Giving a person an opportunity to earn money may well be an inducement to that person to channel potential Medicare payments toward a particular recipient." *United States* v. *Bay State Ambulance and Hospital Rental Service, Inc.*, 874 F.2d 20, 29 (1st Cir. 1989). Since the opportunity to generate a fee may constitute the requisite remuneration under the statute, generally speaking, we believe that the statute is implicated in many of these agreements. However, we also believe that these relationships benefit patients by assuring proper continuity of care or convenient access to a specialist in whom the primary care physician has confidence.

The one exception where we are proposing to permit remuneration between the parties is where both parties belong to the same group practice. Obviously in such situations revenues are shared between members of the group practice, and thus it appears that the referring physician receives remuneration for the referral. However, such financial benefits are an inherent part of belonging to a group practice, and therefore we are proposing to protect such remuneration.

As discussed in sections II.A.2. and B. above, we are concerned about potentially abusive combinations of physicians that are a "group practice" in name only. Consequently, we are proposing to use the same definition of group practice as we are proposing for the fourth investment interest safe harbor. This definition is the same definition of "group practice" as is contained in section 1877(h)(4) of the Act, as added by section 6204(a) of Public Law 101–239.

E. Cooperative Hospital Service Organizations

We are proposing to provide a new safe harbor provision for most cooperative hospital service organizations (CHSOs) that qualify under section 501(c)(3) of the Internal Revenue Code. Under this statute and the implementing regulation (26 CFR 1.501(e)–1)), these organizations are formed by two or more tax exempt hospitals (known as "patron-hospitals") to provide specifically enumerated services, such as purchasing, billing, and clinical services solely for the benefit of its patron-hospitals. In addition, these entities are required to distribute "all net earnings to patrons on the basis of services performed" (26 U.S.C. 501(e)(2)).

Where a health care provider engages in an activity which is specifically required by another statutory provision and the provider is afforded no discretion in the manner of compliance, such a requirement is a valid defense to an alleged violation of the anti-kickback statute. However, where the health care provider is engaging in the activity to fulfill a general statutory obligation, but is afforded discretion in the manner of compliance, such a defense is not available because the provider's choice in the method of compliance may be motivated by an intent to generate program-related business. With respect to the payments the CHSO makes to its patron-hospitals, we believe that the level of discretion given to these providers as to what payment formula to use warrants safe harbor protection. However, we specifically invite comments regarding the various types of payment formula (which comply with the Internal Revenue Service (IRS) rules) that are used, but some of which may be more abusive than others.

This proposed provision would protect payments from a patron-hospital to a CHSO to support the CHSO's operational costs and those payments from a CHSO to a patron-hospital that are required under IRS rules. This proposed provision requires as a condition of protection that the CHSO must be wholly owned by its patron-hospitals. Such a condition protects against potentially abusive joint venture arrangements that are formed under the guise of CHSOs.

To the extent a CHSO acts as a group purchasing organization or a patron-hospital obtains discounts as a result of the CHSO's activities, CHSOs and patron-hospitals must comply with the respective safe harbor provisions applicable to group purchasing organizations and discounts to be fully protected.

We are soliciting comments on the extent to which we should expand this provision to protect other similar entities specifically organized and protected under Federal or State laws.

III. Solicitation of Comments for Modifying the Sale of Practice Safe Harbor

In addition to the proposed provisions discussed above, we are soliciting comments on the desirability of modifying the existing sale of practice safe harbor set forth in § 1001.952(e) to accommodate transactions involving the rural hospital purchase of practice as part of a practitioner recruitment program.

The sale of practice safe harbor set forth in § 1001.952(e) does not protect a hospital purchasing the practice of a retiring physician. We have been informed that many rural hospitals, as part of their efforts to recruit practitioners, buy and "hold" the practice of a retiring physician, often using *locum tenens* physicians until a new physician can be recruited to replace the retiring one. We are soliciting comments on the desirability of modifying the existing sale of practice safe harbor to permit such a practice where the recruitment program complies with any safe harbor we establish to protect practitioner recruitment.

IV. Regulatory Impact Statement

Executive Order 12291 requires us to prepare and publish an initial regulatory impact analysis for any proposed regulation that meets one of the Executive Order criteria for a "major rule," that is, that would be likely to result in (1) an annual effect on the economy of $100 million or more; (2) a major increase in costs or prices for consumers, individuals, industries, Federal, State, or local government agencies or geographic areas; or (3) significant adverse effects on competition, employment, investment, productivity, innovation, or on the ability of United States-based enterprises to compete with foreign-based enterprises in domestic or export markets. In addition, we generally prepare a regulatory flexibility analysis that is consistent with the Regulatory Flexibility Act (5 U.S.C. 601 through 612), unless the Secretary certifies that a proposed regulation would not have a significant economic impact on a substantial number of small entities.

For the reasons set forth in the final rule published on July 29, 1991 (56 FR 35952), we have determined that a regulatory impact analysis is not required. Further we have determined, and the Secretary certifies, that this proposed rule would not have a significant economic impact on a number of small business entities. Therefore, we have not prepared a regulatory flexibility analysis.

V. Additional Information

Response to Comments

Because of the large number of comments we normally receive on proposed regulations, we cannot acknowledge or respond to them individually. However, in preparing the final rule, we will consider all comments received timely and respond to the major issues in the preamble of that rule.

List of Subjects in 42 CFR Part 1001

Administrative practice and procedure, Fraud, Health facilities, Health professions, Medicaid, Medicare.

TITLE 42—PUBLIC HEALTH

CHAPTER V—OFFICE OF INSPECTOR GENERAL—HEALTH CARE, DEPARTMENT OF HEALTH AND HUMAN SERVICES

42 CFR Chapter V, Part 1001 would be amended as set forth below:

PART 1001—PROGRAM INTEGRITY—MEDICARE AND STATE HEALTH CARE PROGRAMS

1. The authority citation for part 1001 continues to read as follows:

Authority: 42 U.S.C. 1302, 1320a–7, 1320a–7b, 1395u(j), 1395u(k), 1395y(e), 1395cc(b)(2)(D), (E) and (F), and 1395hh, and section 14 of Pub. L. 100–93.

2. Section 1001.952 would be amended by revising paragraph (a) introductory text, paragraph (a)(1) introductory text, paragraphs (a)(1)(v) and (a)(2)(viii); by adding paragraphs (a)(3) through (a)(5); by revising paragraph (a) concluding text; and by adding paragraphs (n) through (q) to read as follows:

§ 1001.952 Exceptions.

* * * * *

(a) *Investment Interests.* As used in section 1128B of the Act, "remuneration" does not include any payment that is a return on an investment interest, such as a dividend or interest income, made to an investor as long as all of the applicable standards are met within one of the following five categories of entities:

(1) If, within the previous fiscal year or previous 12 month period, the entity possesses more than $50,000,000 in undepreciated net tangible assets (based on the net acquisition cost of purchasing such assets from an unrelated entity) related to the furnishing of items and services, all of the following five standards must be met—

* * * * *

(v) The amount of payment to an investor in return for the investment interest must be directly proportional to the amount of the capital investment of that investor.

(2) * * *

(viii) The amount of payment to an investor in return for the investment interest must be directly proportional to the amount of the capital investment (including the fair market value of any pre-operational services rendered) of that investor.

(3) If the entity possesses investment interests that are held by either active or passive investors and is located in a rural area, all of the following eight standards must be met—

(i) The entity must offer equal and bona fide opportunities to acquire investment interests to individuals or entities irrespective of whether such prospective investor is in a position to make or influence referrals to, furnish items or services to, or otherwise generate business for the entity.

(ii) The terms on which an investment interest is offered to a passive investor, if any, who is in a position to make or influence referrals to, furnish items or services to, or otherwise generate business for the entity must be no different from the terms offered to other passive investors.

(iii) The terms on which an investment interest is offered to an investor who is in a position to make or influence referrals to, furnish items or services to, or otherwise generate business for the entity must not be related to the previous or expected volume of referrals, items or services furnished, or the amount of business otherwise generated from that investor to the entity.

(iv) There is no requirement that a passive investor, if any, make referrals to, be in a position to make or influence referrals to, furnish items or services to, or otherwise generate business for the entity as a condition for remaining as an investor.

(v) The entity or any investor must not market or furnish the entity's items or services (or those of another entity as part of a cross referral agreement) to passive investors differently than to non-investors.

(vi) At least 85 percent of the dollar volume of the entity's business in the previous fiscal year or previous 12-month period must be derived from the service of persons who reside in a rural area.

(vii) The entity or any investor must not loan funds to or guarantee a loan for an investor who is in a position to make or influence referrals to, furnish items or services to, or otherwise generate business for the entity if the investor uses any part of such loan to obtain the investment interest.

(viii) The amount of payment to an investor in return for the investment interest must be directly proportional to the amount of the capital investment (including the fair market value of any pre-operational services rendered) of that investor.

(4) If the entity is a certified ambulatory surgical center (ASC) under part 416 of this title, whose operating and recovery room space is dedicated exclusively to the ASC (and not a part of a hospital), and all of the investors are surgeons who are in a position to refer patients directly to the entity and perform surgery on such referred patients, all of the following five standards must be met—

(i) The terms on which an investment interest is offered to an investor must not be related to the previous or expected volume of referrals, services furnished, or the amount of business otherwise generated from that investor to the entity.

(ii) There is no requirement that a passive investor, if any, make referrals to the entity as a condition for remaining as an investor.

(iii) The entity or any investor must not loan funds to or guarantee a loan for an investor if the investor uses any part of such loan to obtain the investment interest.

(iv) The amount of payment to an investor in return for the investment interest must be directly proportional to the amount of the capital investment (including the fair market value of any pre-operational services rendered) of that investor.

(v) The practitioner must agree to treat patients receiving medical benefits or assistance under title XVIII or XIX of the Act.

(5) If the entity possesses investment interests all of which are held by active investors and all of these investors are physician members of a group practice, all of the following three standards must be met—

(i) The terms on which an investment interest is offered to the investor must not be related to the previous or expected volume or referrals of business, items or services furnished, or the amount of business otherwise generated from that investor to the entity.

(ii) The entity or any investor must not loan funds to or guarantee a loan for the investor if the investor uses any part of such loan to obtain the investment interest;

(iii) The amount of payment to the investor in return for the investment interest must be directly proportional to the amount of the capital investment (including the fair market value of any pre-operational services rendered) of that investor.

For purposes of paragraph (a) of this section, the following terms apply. *Active investor* means an investor either who is responsible for the day-to-day management of the entity and is a bona fide general partner in a partnership under the Uniform Partnership Act or who agrees in writing to undertake liability for the actions of the entity's agents acting within the scope of their agency. *Group practice* means a group of two or more physicians that meets the definition of group practice under section 1877(h)(4) of the Act. *Investment interest* means a security issued by an entity, and may include the following classes of investments: shares in a corporation, interests or units of a partnership, bonds, debentures, notes, or other debt instruments. *Investor* means an individual or entity either who directly holds an investment interest in an entity, or who holds such investment indirectly by, including but not limited to, such means as having a family member hold such investment interest or holding a legal or beneficial interest in another entity (such as a trust or holding company) that holds such investment interest. *Passive investor* means an investor who is not an active investor, such as a limited partner in a partnership under the Uniform Partnership Act, a shareholder in a corporation, or a holder of a debt security. *Rural area* means any defined geographic area that is not a metropolitan area as defined by the Office of Management and Budget.

* * * * *

(n) *Practitioner recruitment.* As used in section 1128B of the Act, "remuneration" does not include any payment or exchange of anything of value by an entity located in rural areas (as defined in paragraph (a) of this section) in order to induce a practitioner who has been practicing within his or her current specialty for less than one year to establish staff privileges at the entity, or to induce any other practitioner to relocate his or her primary place of practice to the geographic area served by the entity, as long as all of the following seven standards are met—

(1) The arrangement is set forth in a written agreement that specifies the benefits provided by the entity, the terms under which the benefits are to be provided, and the obligations of each party.

(2) If a practitioner is leaving an established practice, the physical location of the new primary place of practice must be no less than 100 miles from the location of the established primary place of practice and at least 85 percent of the revenues of the new practices must be generated from new patients not previously seen by the practitioner at his or her former practice.

(3) The benefits are provided by the entity for a period not in excess of 3 years, and the terms of the agreement are not renegotiated during this 3 year period in any substantial aspect, unless the practitioner's new primary place of practice is designated as a health professional shortage area (HPSA) for the practitioner's specialty category during the entire duration of the relationship between the practitioner and the entity.

(4) There is no requirement that the practitioner make referrals to, be in a position to make or influence referrals to, or otherwise generate business for the entity as a condition for receiving the benefits.

(5) The practitioner is not restricted from establishing staff privileges at, referring any service to, or otherwise generating any business for any other entity of his or her choosing.

(6) The amount or value of the benefits provided by the entity may not vary (or be adjusted or renegotiated) in any manner based on the volume or value of any expected referrals to or business otherwise generated for the entity by the practitioner for which payment may be made in whole or in part under Medicare or a State health care program.

(7) The practitioner agrees to treat patients receiving medical benefits or assistance under title XVIII or XIX of the Act.

(o) *Obstetrical malpractice insurance subsidies.* As used in section 1128B of the Act, "remuneration" does not include any payment made by a hospital or other entity to another entity that is providing malpractice insurance regulated by State law, where such payment is used to pay for some or all of the costs of malpractice insurance premiums for a practitioner who engages in obstetrical practice (including a certified nurse-midwife as defined in section 1861(gg) of the Act) in primary care HPSAs, as long as all of the following eight standards are met—

(1) The payment is made in accordance with a written agreement between the entity paying the premiums and the practitioner, which sets out the payments to be made by the entity, and the terms under which the payments are to be provided.

(2) At least 85 percent of the practitioner's obstetrical patients treated under the coverage of the malpractice insurance must either—

(i) Reside in an area designated by the Secretary under part 5 of this title as having a shortage of primary medical care manpower, or

(ii) Be part of a population group designated by the Secretary under part 5 of this title as having a shortage of primary medical care manpower.

(3) There is no requirement that the practitioner make referrals to, be in a position to make or influence referrals to, or otherwise generate business for the entity as a condition for receiving the benefits.

(4) The practitioner is not restricted from establishing staff privileges at, referring any service to, or otherwise generating any business for any other entity of his or her choosing.

(5) The amount of payment may not vary based on the volume or value of any previous or expected referrals to or business otherwise generated for the entity by the practitioner for which payment may be made in whole or in part under Medicare or a State health care program.

(6) The practitioner agrees to treat obstetrical patients who receive medical assistance under title XIX of the Act.

(7) The insurance premium is calculated based on a bona fide assessment of the liability risk covered under the insurance policy.

(p) *Referral agreements for specialty services.* As used in section 1128B of the Act, "remuneration" does not include any exchange of value among individuals and entities where one party agrees to refer a patient to the other party for the provision of a specialty service payable in whole or in part under Medicare or a State health care program in return for an agreement on the part of the other party to refer that patient back at a mutually agreed upon time or circumstance as long as the following three standards are met—

(1) The service for which the referral is made is not within the medical expertise of the referring individual or entity, but is within the special expertise of the other party receiving the referral.

(2) The parties receive no payment from each other for the referral.

(3) Unless both parties belong to the same group practice as defined in paragraph (a) of this section, the only exchange of value between the parties is

the remuneration the parties receive directly from third-party payors or the patient compensating the parties for the services they each have furnished to the patient.

(q) *Cooperative hospital service organizations.* As used in section 1128B of the Act, "remuneration" does not include any payment made between a cooperative hospital service organization (CHSO) and its patron-hospital, both of which are described in section 501(e) of the Internal Revenue Code of 1986 and are tax-exempt under section 501(c)(3) of the Internal Revenue Code, where the CHSO is wholly owned by two or more patron-hospitals, as long as all of the standards are met within either of the following two categories of payments—

(1) If the patron-hospital makes a payment to the CHSO, it must be for the purpose of paying for the bona fide operating expenses of the CHSO.

(2) If the CHSO makes a payment to the patron-hospital, it must be for the purpose of paying a distribution of net earnings required to be made under section 501(e)(2) of the Internal Revenue Code of 1986.

Dated: February 17, 1993.

Bryan B. Mitchell,

Principal Deputy Inspector General.

Approved: June 28, 1993.

Donna E. Shalala,

Secretary, Department of Health and Human Services.

[FR Doc. 93-22871 Filed 9-20-93; 8:45 am]

BILLING CODE 4150-04-M

APPENDIX F4

CLARIFICATION OF THE OIG SAFE HARBOR ANTI-KICKBACK PROVISIONS, JULY 21, 1994

DEPARTMENT OF HEALTH AND HUMAN SERVICES

Office of Inspector General

42 CFR Part 1001

RIN 0991–AA74

Medicare and State Health Care Programs: Fraud and Abuse; Clarification of the OIG Safe Harbor Anti-Kickback Provisions

AGENCY: Office of Inspector General (OIG), HHS.

ACTION: Proposed rule.

SUMMARY: This proposed rule would clarify various aspects of safe harbor provisions originally published in the Federal Register on July 29, 1991 as a final rule (56 FR 35952). The safe harbor provisions have been specifically designed to set forth those payment practices and business arrangements that will be protected from criminal prosecution and civil sanctions under the anti-kickback provisions of the statute. This proposed rule would modify the original set of final safe harbor provisions to give greater clarity to the rulemaking's original intent.

DATES: To assure consideration, public comments must be delivered to the address provided below by September 19, 1994. Comments are available for public inspection August 4, 1994.

ADDRESSES: Address comments to: Office of Inspector General, Department of Health and Human Services, Attention: LRR-35-P, room 5246, 330 Independence Ave., SW., Washington, DC 20201.

If you prefer, you may deliver your comments to room 5551, 330 Independence Avenue, SW., Washington, DC. In commenting, please refer to file code LRR-35-P. Comments are available for public inspection in room 5551 330 Independence Avenue, SW., Washington, DC, on Monday through Friday each week from 9 a.m. to 5 p.m., (202) 619-3270.

FOR FURTHER INFORMATION CONTACT:
Sandra Sands, Office of the General Counsel, (202) 619-1306
Joel Schaer, Office of Inspector General, (202) 619-3270

SUPPLEMENTARY INFORMATION:

I. Background

On July 29, 1991, we published in the Federal Register a final rule setting forth various safe harbor provisions to the Medicare and Medicaid anti-kickback statute (56 FR 35952). This regulation was authorized under section 14 of Public Law 100-93, the Medicare and Medicaid Patient and Program Protection Act of 1987. The final rule specified those payment practices that will not be subject to criminal prosecution under section 1128B(b) of the Social Security Act (the Act) (42 U.S.C. 1320a-7b(b)), and that will not provide a basis for exclusion from Medicare or the State health care programs under section 1128(b)(7) of the Act (42 U.S.C. 1320a-7(b)(7)).

Since publication of the final rule, we have become aware of a limited number of ambiguities that have created uncertainties for health care providers trying to comply with the safe harbor provisions. We have also become aware of certain instances where our intent, either to protect or preclude protection for particular business arrangements, is not fully reflected in the text of the regulation even though it is reflected in the preamble. This proposed rule would serve to modify the text of the July 29, 1991 final rule to conform to the rulemaking's original intent.

The clarifications contained in this proposed rule do not represent an attempt to reevaluate the wisdom of the original safe-harbor decisions. Instead, the changes set forth in this proposed rule would serve only to protect business practices originally intended to be protected by removing ambiguities in the regulatory language. This clarity should aid the formation of legal business practices without establishing any new significant legal obligations on the parties affected by the regulations.

II. Summary of the Proposed Changes

A. Clarification to the General Comments Section of Preamble

- Several individuals have commented that the following sentence in the preamble has created confusion:

"Because the statute is broad, the payment practices described in these safe harbor provisions would be prohibited by the statute but for their inclusion here." (56 FR 35958)

This sentence was not meant to imply that, *in all instances irrespective of the parties intent*, the government could prosecute conduct described in the regulation, but for its inclusion in the regulation. Whether a particular payment practice violates the statute is a question that can only be resolved by an analysis of the elements of the statute as applied to that set of facts. Generally speaking, however, the original final rule did describe payment practices that would be prohibited, where the unlawful intent exists, but for the safe harbor protection that has been granted.

- In discussing the space and equipment rental and personal services and management contracts, we stated that if a "sham contract is entered into * * * we will look behind the contract" to its substance in evaluating whether the arrangement qualifies for safe-harbor protection (56 FR 35972). We received numerous inquiries as to whether we would similarly look behind the form of other arrangements to determine whether the substance of the arrangement fits within a particular safe harbor.

In some cases, such inquiries have led us to clarify particular safe harbors, as is illustrated by the following discussions of the safe harbors for investment interests, space and equipment rental, and personal services and management contracts. However, because of the broad variety of transactions subject to the Medicare and Medicaid anti-kickback statute and the ability of individuals to manipulate the safe harbors in ways not contemplated, we believe that a general rule preventing sham arrangements from receiving safe harbor protection would be appropriate. Thus, we are proposing adding a new § 1001.954 to the regulations. Such an approach has several precedents. The Federal Trade Commission (FTC) with the concurrence of the Department of Justice promulgated § 801.90 of the FTC's rules implementing the Hart-Scott-Rodino Antitrust Improvements Act of 1976 (16 CFR 801.90), which disregards sham transactions entered into for the purpose of avoiding obligations under the Act. In addition, other Federal agencies (such as the Securities Exchange Commission and the Internal Revenue Service) have promulgated regulations and policies that seek to protect the government from making enforcement decisions based on information that does not accurately reflect the substance of the transaction. (See, for example, 17 CFR 240.12b-20; *Estate of Korman* versus *Comm.*, TC Memo 1987-120; and Rev. Rul. 81-149, 1981-1 CB 77.) Moreover, the courts have historically disregarded sham arrangements when examining the rights and obligations of the parties in tax cases. (See, for example, *Knetsch* versus *United States*, 364 U.S. 361 (1960); and *Thompson* versus *Commissioner of Internal Revenue*, 631 F.2d 642 (9th Cir. 1981), *cert. denied*, 452 U.S. 961 (1981).)

B. Clarifications to Investment Interests Safe Harbor (§ 1001.952(a))

- *Health Care Assets and Revenues*

In qualifying for the "large entity" or "small entity" investment interest safe harbors, the monetary value or amount of certain assets and revenues must be determined. Specifically, the safe harbors include: (1) The $50,000,000 asset threshold in § 1001.952(a)(1); and (2) the gross revenues in the "60-40 revenue rule" in § 1001.952(a)(2)(vi). In these cases, *only the assets or revenues related to the furnishing of health care items or services will be counted for the purposes of qualifying for these safe harbor requirements.* It would be an obvious sham, inconsistent with our original intent, if a joint venture could merge with a non-health care business and have those non-health care assets, and the revenues derived from that non-health care line of business counted for the purposes of qualifying for safe harbor protection. We are thus proposing to revise these safe harbor provisions to further clarify our original intent that only health care assets and revenues will be counted in determining these values and amounts.

• *Acquisition of Investment Interests*

As set forth in § 1001.952(a)(1)(ii), an "interested" investor (who is in a position to make or influence referrals to, furnish items or services to, or otherwise generate business for the entity) must obtain his or her investment interest through trading on a registered national securities exchange on terms equally available to the public. This does not mean that an interested investor may acquire his or her interest in any way other than the methods available to the general public to acquire investment interests. We believe that the investor must acquire his or her investment interest in the *same way* as members of the public—directly off of a registered national securities exchange through a broker—and it must be the same type of investment interest that is available to the public. For example, a transaction in which the interested investor receives restricted or "lettered" stock from the entity would not be considered a valid acquisition of investment interests under this requirement.

The discussion above does not represent a change in this standard. Rather, it serves only to emphasize that the investment interest "*must be obtained* on terms equally available to the public through trading on a registered national securities exchange * * *" (§ 1001.952(a)(1)(ii)) (Emphasis added). Moreover, to obtain an investment interest "on terms equally available to the public," there cannot be any side agreements that require stock to be purchased or that restrict in any manner the investor's ability to dispose of the stock. Any such agreement would constitute a sham transaction which would disqualify dividend payments to that investor from safe harbor protection.

• *Loans for the Purchase of the Investment Interest*

One of the standards in the large and small entity investment interest safe harbors prohibits the entity from loaning an investor funds that are used by the investor to purchase his or her investment interest. (See §§ 1001.952(a)(1)(iv) and 1001.952(a)(2)(vii).) We are proposing to change this standard to prohibit other investors, individuals or entities as well as the entity from making such loans.

• *Class of Investment Interests*

In the 60–40 investor rule in the small entity investment interest safe harbor (§ 1001.952(a)(2)(i)), we established two categories of investors: (1) "untainted" or "disinterested" investors are those who do no business with the entity, but hold the investment interest purely as an investment; and (2) "tainted" or "interested" investors are those who are in a position to make or influence referrals to, furnish items or services to, or otherwise generate business for the entity. For purposes of determining in which category to place an investor, we require "each class of investments" to meet the 60–40 apportionment between the two categories.

We have become aware of the difficulty in applying the 60–40 rule to each class of investors in a joint venture where the general partners hold a separate class of stock or investment interest from the limited partners. In such a situation, that class of investment interest for the general partners consists of 100 percent "tainted" or "interested" investors since the general partners are providing services to the entity. Therefore, we believe that the entire joint venture does not qualify for safe harbor protection.

While it is not always true that an active investor holds a different class of investment interest from a passive investor, we have found that it is unnecessarily restrictive to have this 60–40 investor rule only apply to *each* class of investment interest. Thus, we are proposing to modify this first investment interest standard to allow an alternative to the class-by-class analysis. The new alternative would allow equity investment interests to be combined together or debt investment interests to be combined together (separate from the equity investments) for purposes of apportioning investors into "untainted" and "tainted" pools and meeting the 60–40 test. Only equivalent classes of equity investment interests could be combined, and only equivalent classes of debt investment interests could be combined. That is, the classes of investment interests combined would have to be similar in all material respects. For example, the classes to be combined would have to have equivalent returns in proportion to amounts invested. In addition, if one class is given preferential treatment (e.g., in the case of disposition), such an interest could not be combined with subservient interests for purposes of compliance with the 60–40 investor rule.

If a limited partnership has a general partner who holds 20 percent of the value of the investment interests, referring physicians hold 20 percent, and all the other investors have no business relationship with the partnerships, then the 60–40 investor rule would be met, as long as all other requirements are satisfied.

The 60–40 investor rule would not be met if any of the other disinterested investors in the above example holds a debt instrument instead of an equity instrument. For example, if a joint venture raises one-third of its capital through a debt instrument held by disinterested investors, with the remaining two thirds of its capital derived from equity instruments held equally by interested (physicians and general partners) and disinterested investors, the safe harbor would not be met. In this example, even though interested investors hold only one-third of all the investment interests, they hold one-half of the *equity* investment interests, and thus no safe harbor protection would be available.

We note that other standards in this small entity safe harbor preclude protection for abusive schemes to give referring investors preferential treatment *in any way* by creating different classes of investment. For example, if a joint venture creates two classes of stock, with one of the classes reserved for referring physicians who receive a higher dividend per share than non-referring investors in the other class, such an arrangement would not comply with at least sections 1001.952(a)(2) (ii), (iii) and (viii).

• *Items or Services Furnished by an Investor*

As discussed above, when an investor furnishes items or services to the joint venture, such as management services, he or she is a tainted or interested investor for the purposes of complying with the 60–40 investor rule (§ 1001.952(a)(2)(vi)). It was not our intent to have any revenues that the joint venture derives from this investor's services to be considered tainted for the purpose of qualifying for the 60–40 revenue rule.

Because of the apparent confusion caused by the language "items or services furnished" in this safe harbor standard, we are proposing striking it. The focus of the inquiry in this standard is *where* the business and clients are coming from. In other words, the revenues are tainted, and may not exceed 40 percent of total revenues, if they are derived "from referrals * * * or business otherwise generated from investors." We note that the language we are proposing to strike—"items or services furnished"—is superfluous because, if the revenue is "generated" (i.e., induced *to come to* the joint venture for items or services *by an investor*), it is tainted. Thus, the language we are proposing to delete appears not to have added anything and merely caused confusion.

The following example demonstrates the confusion and our solution. If a radiologist holds an investment interest in an imaging center and reads all the films at the center, his or her reading of the film does not taint all the revenues from the referrals by non-investors. However, we have received a few questions from people who read the 60–40 revenue rule as making such referrals tainted because the investor furnished services at the joint venture.

We emphasize that if a radiologist-investor is reading the film *and* making referrals or otherwise generating business, then the revenues the joint venture derives from that activity would become tainted. For example, revenues would be tainted when a radiologist-investor takes part in a consultation with a non-investor internist, and during that consultation the radiologist recommends a procedure which is performed at the joint venture.

C. Clarifications to Space and Equipment Rental and Personal Services and Management Contracts Safe Harbors (§§ 1001.952 (b), (c) and (d))

• In the preamble discussing the safe harbor provisions for space and equipment rental and personal services and management contracts (56 FR 35971–74), we made clear that one of our concerns was that health care providers in a position to make referrals to each other who engaged in these business arrangements could renegotiate their contracts on a regular basis depending on the volume of business generated. It is for this reason that we require the leases or contracts be for a term of not less than one year. (See §§ 1001.952(b)(4), 1001.952(c)(4), and 1001.952(d)(4).)

It has come to our attention that a small number of health care providers believe they are complying with the literal terms of these safe harbor provisions, but are circumventing our intent not to protect agreements that are renegotiated based on the volume of business generated between the parties. They believe that they are protected if they enter into multiple agreements, each of which is for a period of one year, but when all the agreements are viewed together renegotiations are taking place more frequently (e.g., every month), with the terms of the additional agreements based in part on the volume of business being generated between the parties under existing agreements. For example, a one year personal services contract between a hospital and a high-volume referring physician is created for the physician to perform certain services. The next month a *new* one year contract is created for a slightly different service, with the amount of payment influenced by the previous months referrals.

This scenario does not comply with the requirement in each of these safe harbor provisions that the compensation not take "into account the volume or value of any referrals or business otherwise generated between the parties * * * ." (§§ 1001.952(b)(5), 1001.952(c)(5), and 1001.952(d)(5)). However, because the principal problem in this situation is that the parties are creating multiple overlapping agreements, we are proposing to revise these three safe harbor provisions to expressly preclude such schemes.

In addition, it appears that some health care providers are attempting to pay for referrals by renting more space than they actually need from referral sources. Although such an arrangement would not fit within a safe harbor because the aggregate rental charge would be determined in a manner that would account for the volume or value of referrals or business otherwise generated between the parties, we are proposing to revise the safe harbor provisions in §§ 1001.952 (b)(5), (c)(5) and (d)(5) to expressly preclude this practice.

D. Clarifications to Referral Services Safe-Harbor (§ 1001.952(f))

• One of the standards in the referral services safe harbor provision requires that any fee the referral service charges the participant be "based on the cost of operating the referral service, and not on the volume or value of any referrals to or business otherwise generated *by the participants* for the referral service * * * ." (Emphasis added) (§ 1001.952(f)(2)). This language precludes protection where a referral service, such as one operated by a hospital, *lowers* its referral service fee to one of its staff physicians who participates in the service because that physician is a high-volume referrer.

This language creates an ambiguity where the referral service tries to adjust its fee based on the volume of referrals *it makes to the participant*. Thus, we propose clarifying the second prong to preclude safe harbor protection for payments that are based on the volume or value of referrals to or business otherwise generated by either party for the other party.

E. Clarifications To Discount Safe Harbor (§ 1001.952(h))

• Many people requested clarification of the safe harbor for discounts. Because there has been some uncertainty over what obligations individuals or entities have to meet in order to receive protection under this safe harbor, we propose dividing the parties into three groups: buyers, sellers, and offerors of discounts. In describing each party's obligations, we would revise paragraphs (h)(1) and (h)(2), and add a new paragraph (h)(3).

In addition, through a proposed new paragraph (h)(4), we would clarify that, for purposes of this regulation, a "rebate" is any discount which is not given at the time of sale. Consequently, a rebate transaction may be covered within the safe harbor if it involves a buyer under § 1001.952 (h)(1)(i) or (h)(1)(ii), but it is not covered if it involves a buyer under § 1001.952(h)(1)(iii) because, under that provision, *all discounts must be given at the time of sale.*

We also wish to clarify what has to happen for sellers to receive safe harbor protection. In the safe harbor regulation itself, we state that discounts will be safe harbored if both the seller "and" the buyer comply with the applicable standards as described in the rule. Yet in the preamble we state that sellers should not be held liable for the omissions of buyers. If a seller has done everything that it reasonably could under the circumstances to ensure that the buyer understands its obligations to accurately report the discount, the seller is safe harbored irrespective of the omissions of the buyer. To receive such protection, however, the seller must report the discount to the buyer and inform the buyer of its obligation to report the discount. To emphasize that the seller's obligations require more than superficial compliance with the safe harbor, we propose to add to that the seller must inform the buyer "in an effective manner" of its obligations to report the discount. We also propose adding a requirement that the seller "refrain from doing anything that would impede the buyer from meeting its obligations under this paragraph." Thus, if the seller, in good faith, meets its obligations under the safe harbor and the buyer does not meet its obligations due to no fault of the seller, the seller would receive safe harbor protection. However, when the seller submits a claim or request for payment on behalf of the buyer, the seller must fully and accurately report the discount to

Medicare or the State health care program. Likewise, when an offeror of a discount meets its obligations under § 1001.952(h)(3), and the buyer or seller does not meet its obligations due to no fault of the offeror, the offeror would receive safe harbor protection.

In addition, we are proposing to clarify whether any reduction in price offered to a *beneficiary* could be safe harbored under this regulation. Congress protected "a discount or other reduction in price *obtained by a provider of services or other entity*" (emphasis added) and made no provision for such discounts obtained by a beneficiary. In § 1001.952(h)(3)(iv) of the regulation, we removed from safe harbor protection a "reduction in price offered to a beneficiary * * * ." In that section, all we intended to remove from this safe harbor was "routine reduction or waiver of any coinsurance or deductible-amount owed by a program beneficiary." Thus, to the extent that a discount is offered to a beneficiary and all other applicable standards in the safe harbor are met, such a discount would receive safe harbor protection.

Many people have expressed confusion regarding the relationship between the safe harbor for discounts and the statutory exception for discounts. (See section 1128B(b)(3)(A) of the Act.) Specifically, we are asked if there are any practices involving discounts which were protected by Congress under the statutory exception which do not fit within the safe harbor for discounts. Our intention is that *all* the discounts or reductions in price that Congress intended to protect under the statutory exception for discounts are protected under the safe harbor for discounts. Moreover, as is illustrated by the discussion above regarding discounts to beneficiaries, we are proposing to expand the safe harbor for discounts to include additional practices that we do not consider abusive.

In the preamble to the final regulation, we stated that when reporting a discount, one only need report the actual purchase price and note that it is a "net discount" (56 FR 35981). However, for purposes of submitting a claim or request for payment, what is necessary is that the value of the discount is accurately reflected in the actual purchase price. It is not necessary to distinguish whether this price is the result of a discount, or to state "net discount." Consequently, buyers who were uncertain about how and where to report on a particular form the fact that the price was due to a discount need not be concerned with reporting that fact, as long as the actual purchase price accurately reflects the discount.

Finally, we are proposing some minor editorial changes that do not affect the substance of the provision, but hopefully make it easier to understand.

F. Technical Correction

- A typographical error at 56 FR 35978 gave a citation to a HCFA rule on payment for intraocular lenses as "55 FR 436." We would correct this citation to the HCFA rule to read as "55 FR 4536."
- We are proposing the deletion of § 1001.953 which calls for the completion of an OIG report on compliance with the investment interest safe harbor at § 1001.952(a)(2)(i) and 1001.952(a)(2)(vi) within a specified period of time after publication of the original safe harbor provisions. While the OIG is continuing its work on evaluating this safe harbor provision, we believe completion of this report to be an internal administrative process that need not be set forth in the regulations.

III. Regulatory Impact Statement

As we indicated in the original safe harbor final rule published on July 29, 1991, consistent with the intent of the statute, the original safe harbor rulemaking and these proposed clarifications are designed to permit individuals and entities to freely engage in business practices and arrangements that encourage competition, innovation and economy. In doing so, the regulations impose no requirements on any party. Health care providers and others may voluntarily seek to comply with these provisions so that they have the assurance that their business practices are not subject to any enforcement action under the anti-kickback statute. We believe that the economic impact of these provisions would be minimal.

In addition, we generally prepare a regulatory flexibility analysis that is consistent with the Regulatory Flexibility Act (5 U.S.C. 601–612). We have determined, and the Secretary certifies, that this proposed regulation would not have a significant economic impact on a substantial number of small business entities, and we have, therefore, not prepared a regulatory flexibility analysis.

List of Subjects in 42 CFR Part 1001

Administrative practice and procedure, Fraud, Health facilities, Health professions, Medicaid, Medicare.

TITLE 42—PUBLIC HEALTH

CHAPTER V—OFFICE OF INSPECTOR GENERAL—HEALTH CARE, DEPARTMENT OF HEALTH AND HUMAN SERVICES

42 CFR part 1001 would be amended as set forth below:

PART 1001—PROGRAM INTEGRITY—MEDICARE AND STATE HEALTH CARE PROGRAMS

1. The authority citation for part 1001 would continue to read as follow:

Authority: 42 U.S.C. 1302, 1320a-7, 1320a-7b, 1395u(j), 1395u(k), 1395y(d), 1395y(e), 1395cc(b)(2)(D), (E) and (F), and 1395hh, and section 14 of Public Law 100–93.

2. Section 1001.952 would be amended by:

a. republishing the introductory text for this section;
b. republishing the introductory text for paragraph (a)(1), and by revising paragraphs (a)(1)(iv), (a)(2)(i), (a)(2)(vi) and (a)(2)(vii);
c. revising paragraphs (b)(2) and (b)(5);
d. adding a new paragraph (b)(6);
e. revising paragraphs (c)(2) and (c)(5);
f. adding a new paragraph (c)(6);
g. revising paragraphs (d)(2), (d)(5) and (d)(6);
h. adding a new paragraph (d)(7);
i. revising paragraphs (f)(2); and
j. revising paragraph (h), to read as follows—

§ 1001.952 Exceptions.

The following payment practices shall not be treated as a criminal offense under section 1128B of the Act and shall not serve as the basis for an exclusion:

(a) *Investment interests.* * * *

(1) If, within the previous fiscal year or previous 12 month period, the entity possesses more than $50,000,000 in undepreciated net tangible assets (based on the net acquisition cost of purchasing such assets from an unrelated entity) related to the furnishing of health care items and services, all of the following five applicable standards must be met—

* * * * *

(iv) The entity or any investor (or other individual or entity acting on behalf of the entity or any investor in the entity) must not loan funds to or guarantee a loan for an investor who is in a position to make or influence referrals to, furnish items or services to, or otherwise generate business for the entity if the investor uses any part of such loan to obtain the investment interest.

* * * * *

(2) * * *

(i) No more than 40 percent of the value of the investment interests of each class of investment interests may be held in the previous fiscal year or previous 12 month period by investors who are in a position to make or influence referrals to, furnish items or services to, or otherwise generate business for the entity. (For purposes of § 1001.952(a)(2)(i), equivalent classes of equity investments may be combined, and equivalent classes of debt instruments may be combined.)

* * * * *

(vi) No more than 40 percent of the entity's gross revenue related to the furnishing of health care items and services in the previous fiscal year or previous 12 month period may come from referrals, or business otherwise generated from investors.

(vii) The entity or any investor must not loan funds to or guarantee a loan for an investor who is in a position to make or influence referrals to, furnish items or services to, or otherwise generate business for the entity if the investor uses any part of such loan to obtain the investment interest.

* * * * *

(b) *Space rental.* * * *

(2) The lease covers all of the premises leased between the parties for the period of the lease and specifies the premises covered by the lease.

* * * * *

(5) The aggregate space rented does not exceed that which is reasonably necessary to accomplish the legitimate business purpose of the rental.

(6) The aggregate rental charge is set in advance, is consistent with fair market value in arms-length transactions and is not determined in a manner that takes into account the volume or value of any referrals or business otherwise generated between the parties for which payment may be made in whole or in part under Medicare or a State health care program.

* * * * *

(c) *Equipment rental.*

* * * * *

(2) The lease covers all of the equipment leased between the parties for the period of the lease and specifies the equipment covered by the lease.

* * * * *

(5) The aggregate equipment rental does not exceed that which is reasonably necessary to accomplish the legitimate business purpose of the rental.

(6) The aggregate rental charge is set in advance, is consistent with fair market value in arms-length transactions and is not determined in a manner that takes into account the volume or value of any referrals or business otherwise generated between the parties for which payment may be made in whole or in part under Medicare or a State health care program.

* * * * *

(d) *Personal services and management contracts.*

* * * * *

(2) The agency agreement covers all of the services the agent provides to the principal for the period of the agreement and specifies the services to be provided by the agent.

* * * * *

(5) The aggregate services contracted for do not exceed those which are reasonably necessary to accomplish the legitimate business purpose of the services.

(6) The aggregate compensation paid to the agent over the term of the agreement is set in advance, is consistent with fair market value in arms-length transactions and is not determined in a manner that takes into account the volume or value of any referrals or business otherwise generated between the parties for which payment may be made in whole or in part under Medicare or a State health care program.

(7) The services performed under the agreement do not involve the counseling or promotion of a business arrangement or other activity that violates any State or Federal law.

* * * * *

(f) *Referral services.* * * *

(2) Any payment the participant makes to the referral service is assessed equally against and collected equally from all participants, and is only based on the cost of operating the referral service, and not on the volume or value of any referrals to or business otherwise generated by either party for the other party for which payment may be made in whole or in part under Medicare or a State health care program.

* * * * *

(h) *Discounts.* As used in section 1128B of the Act, "remuneration" does not include a discount, as defined in paragraph (h)(5) of this section, on an item or service for which payment may be made, in whole or in part, under Medicare or a State health care program for a *buyer* as long as the buyer complies with the applicable standards of paragraph (h)(1) of this section; a *seller* as long as the seller complies with the applicable standards of paragraph (h)(2) of this section; and an *offeror* of a discount who is not a seller under paragraph (h)(2) of this section so long as such offeror complies with the applicable standards of paragraph (h)(3) of this section:

(1) With respect to the following three categories of *buyers*, the buyer must comply with all of the applicable standards within one of the three following categories—

(i) If the buyer is an entity which is a health maintenance organization or a competitive medical plan acting in accordance with a risk contract under section 1876(g) or 1903(m) of the Act, or under another State health care program, it need not report the discount except as otherwise may be required under the risk contract.

(ii) If the buyer is an entity which reports its costs on a cost report required by the Department or a State health care program, it must comply with all of the following four standards—

(A) the discount must be earned based on purchases of that same good or service bought within a single fiscal year of the buyer.

(B) the buyer must claim the benefit of the discount in the fiscal year in which the discount is earned or the following year.

(C) the buyer must fully and accurately report the discount in the applicable cost report; and

(D) the buyer must provide, upon request by the Secretary or a State agency, information provided by the seller as specified in paragraph (h)(2)(ii) of this section, or information provided by the offeror as specified in paragraph (h)(3)(ii) of this section.

(iii) If the buyer is an individual or entity in whose name a claim or request for payment is submitted for an item or service for which payment may be made, in whole or in part, under Medicare or a State health care program (not including individuals or entities receiving items or services from entities defined as buyers in paragraph (h)(1)(i) or (h)(1)(ii) of this section), the buyer must comply with all of the following three standards—

(A) the discount must be made at the time of the sale of the good or service (rebates are therefore not allowable);

(B) where an item or service is separately claimed for payment with the Medicare program or a State health care program, the buyer (if submitting the claim) must fully and accurately report the discount on that item or service; and

(C) the buyer (if submitting the claim) must provide, upon request by the Secretary or a State agency, information provided by the seller as specified in paragraph (h)(2)(iii)(B) of this section, or information provided by the offeror as specified in paragraph (h)(3)(iii)(A) of this section.

(2) The seller is an individual or entity that furnishes an item or service

for which payment may be made, in whole or in part, under Medicare or a State health care program to the buyer and who permits a discount to be taken off the buyer's purchase price. The seller must comply with all of the applicable standards within the following three categories—

(i) If the buyer is an entity which is a health maintenance organization or a competitive medical plan acting in accordance with a risk contract under section 1876(g) or 1903(m) of the Act, or under another State health care program, the seller need not report the discount to the buyer for purposes of this provision.

(ii) If the buyer, is an entity that reports its costs on a cost report required by the Department or a State agency, the seller must comply with either of the following two standards—

(A) where a discount is required to be reported to Medicare or a State health care program under paragraph (h)(1) of this section, the seller must fully and accurately report such discount on the invoice, coupon or statement submitted to the buyer, inform the buyer in an effective manner of its obligations to report such discount, and refrain from doing anything which would impede the buyer from meeting its obligations under this paragraph; or

(B) where the value of the discount is not known at the time of sale, the seller must fully and accurately report the existence of a discount program on the invoice, coupon or statement submitted to the buyer, inform the buyer in an effective manner of its obligations to report such discount under paragraph (h)(1) of this section and, when the value of the discount becomes known, provide the buyer with documentation of the calculation of the discount identifying the specific goods or services purchased to which the discount will be applied, and refrain from doing anything which would impede the buyer from meeting its obligations under this paragraph.

(iii) If the buyer is an individual or entity not included in paragraph (h)(2)(i) or (h)(2)(ii) of this section, the seller must comply with either of the following two standards—

(A) where the seller submits a claim or request for payment on behalf of the buyer and the item or service is separately claimed, the seller must fully and accurately report the discount on the claim or request for payment to Medicare or a State health care program and the seller must provide, upon request by the Secretary or a State agency, information provided by the offeror as specified in paragraph (h)(3)(iii)(A) of this section; or

(B) where the buyer submits a claim, the seller must fully and accurately report such discount on the invoice, coupon or statement submitted to the buyer; inform the buyer in an effective manner of its obligations to report such discount; and refrain from doing anything that would impede the buyer from meeting its obligations under this paragraph.

(3) The offeror of a discount is an individual or entity who is not a seller under paragraph (h)(2) of this section, but promotes the purchase of an item or service by a buyer under paragraph (h)(1) of this section at a reduced price for which payment may be made, in whole or in part, under Medicare or a State health care program. The offeror must comply with all of the applicable standards within the following three categories—

(i) If the buyer is an entity which is a health maintenance organization or a competitive medical plan acting in accordance with a risk contract under section 1876(g) or 1903(m) of the Act, or under another State health care program, the offeror need not report the discount to the buyer for purposes of this provision.

(ii) If the buyer is an entity that reports its costs on a cost report required by the Department or a State agency, the offeror must comply with the following two standards—

(A) the offeror must inform the buyer in an effective manner of its obligation to report such a discount; and

(B) the offeror of the discount must refrain from doing anything that would impede the buyer's ability to meet its obligations under this paragraph.

(iii) If the buyer is an individual or entity in whose name a request for payment is submitted for an item or service for which payment may be made, in whole or in part, under Medicare or a State health care program (not including individuals or entities defined as buyers in paragraph (h)(1)(i) or (h)(1)(ii) of this section), the offeror must comply with the following two standards—

(A) the offeror must inform the individual or entity submitting the claim or request for payment in an effective manner of their obligations to report such a discount; and

(B) the offeror of the discount must refrain from doing anything that would impede the buyer's or seller's ability to meet its obligations under this paragraph.

(4) For purposes of this paragraph (a), a *rebate* is any discount which is not given at the time of sale.

(5) For purposes of this paragraph (a), the term *discount* means a reduction in the amount a buyer (who buys either directly or through a wholesaler or a group purchasing organization) is charged for an item or service based on an arms-length transaction. The term *discount* does not include—

(i) Cash payment;

(ii) Furnishing one good or service without charge or at a reduced charge to include the purchase of a different good or service;

(iii) A reduction in price applicable to one payer but not to Medicare or a State health care program;

(iv) A routine reduction or waiver of any coinsurance or deductible amount owned by a program beneficiary;

(v) Warranties;

(vi) Services provided in accordance with a personal or management services contract; or

(vii) Other remuneration, in cash or in kind, not explicitly described in this paragraph (a)(5).

* * * * *

§ 1001.953 [Removed]

3. Section 1001.953 would be removed.

4. Section 1001.954 would be added to read as follows:

§ 1001.954 Sham Transactions or Devices.

Any transaction or other device entered into or employed for the purpose of appearing to fit within a safe harbor when the substance of the transaction or device is not accurately reflected by the form will be disregarded, and whether the arrangement receives the protection of a safe harbor will be determined by the substance of the transaction or device.

Dated: March 14, 1994.

June Gibbs Brown,

Inspector General.

Approved: April 22, 1994.

Donna E. Shalala,

Secretary, Department of Health and Human Services.

[FR Doc. 94-16873 Filed 7-20-94; 8:45 am]

BILLING CODE 4150-04-M

APPENDIX F5

NEW SAFE HARBOR FOR PROTECTING HEALTH PLANS, JANUARY 25, 1996

2122 Federal Register / Vol. 61, No. 17 / Thursday, January 25, 1996 / Rules and Regulations

DEPARTMENT OF HEALTH AND HUMAN SERVICES

Office of Inspector General

42 CFR Part 1001

RIN 0991–AA69

Medicare and State Health Care Programs: Fraud and Abuse; Safe Harbors for Protecting Health Plans

AGENCY: Office of Inspector General (OIG), HHS.

ACTION: Final rule.

SUMMARY: In accordance with section 14 of the Medicare and Medicaid Patient and Program Protection Act of 1987, this final rule sets forth various standards and guidelines for safe harbor provisions designed to protect certain health care plans, such as health maintenance organizations and preferred provider organizations, under the Medicare and State health care programs' anti-kickback statute. These safe harbor provisions were originally published in the Federal Register on November 5, 1992 in interim final form. In response to the various public comments received, this final rule revises and clarifies various aspects of that earlier rulemaking.

EFFECTIVE DATE: This rule is effective on January 25, 1996.

FOR FURTHER INFORMATION CONTACT:
Linda Grabel or Tom Hoffman, Office of the General Counsel, (202) 619–0335
Joel Schaer, Office of Inspector General, (202) 619–3270.

Please send comments regarding the paperwork reduction and information collection requirements discussed in section IV.B. of this preamble in writing to: Joel Schaer, Regulations Officer, Office of Inspector General, Room 5550 Cohen Building, 330 Independence Avenue SW., Washington, D.C. 20201.

SUPPLEMENTARY INFORMATION:

I. Background

On November 5, 1992, we published an interim final rule with comment period establishing two new safe harbors, and amending one existing safe harbor, to provide protection for certain health care plans, such as health maintenance organizations (HMOs) and preferred provider organizations (PPOs) (57 FR 52723). The first new safe harbor provision, set forth in § 1001.952(l), protects certain incentives to enrollees (including waiver of coinsurance and deductible amounts) paid by health care plans. The second new provision, set forth in § 1001.952(m), protects certain negotiated price reduction agreements between health care plans and contract health care providers. In addition, the existing safe harbor addressing the waiver of beneficiary coinsurance and deductible amounts, codified in § 1001.952(k), was amended to protect certain agreements entered into between hospitals and Medicare SELECT insurers.

These safe harbors set forth various standards and guidelines that, if met, allow specific business arrangements and payment practices of certain health care plans *not* to be treated as criminal offenses under section 1128B(b) of the Social Security Act (the Act) and *not* to serve as a basis for a program exclusion under section 1128(b)(7) of the Act. As with the other safe harbor provisions codified in § 1001.95 of the regulations, these new safe harbors placed no affirmative obligation on any individual or entity.

Although the regulations were issued in final form and became effective on their date of publication, we indicated in the preamble of that November 5, 1992 document that we were allowing a 60-day public comment period during which time interested parties could submit comments and concerns regarding these safe harbors. An additional 60-day extension to the public comment period was published in the Federal Register on January 7, 1993 (58 FR 2989).

II. Summary of the Interim Final Rule

A. Section 1001.952(l)—Increased Coverage, Reduced Cost-Sharing Amounts, or Reduced Premium Amounts Offered by Health Plan

As indicated above, a new safe harbor, set forth in § 1001.952(l), was created to protect certain incentives to enrollees (including increased benefits and waiver of deductible and coinsurance amounts) offered by health plans. This safe harbor contained two parts designed to protect incentives offered by health care plans under contract with the Health Care Financing Administration (HCFA) or a State health care program.

The first part of this safe harbor protected risk-based health plans, like HMOs, competitive medical plans (CMPs) and prepaid health plans (PHPs), under contract with HCFA or a State health care program; and operating (i) in accordance with section 1876(g) or 1903(m) of the Act, (ii) under a Federal statutory demonstration authority, or (iii) under other Federal statutory or regulatory authority. Under this part, the only standard for such health plans was that the health care plan could not discriminate in the offering of these incentives, but must offer the same incentives to all enrollees unless otherwise specifically approved by HCFA or a State health care program.

The second part of this safe harbor protected incentives offered to enrollees by HMOs, CMPs, PHPs and health care prepaid plans (HCPPs) that are under contract with HCFA or a State health care program, and that are paid on a reasonable cost or similar basis. For these plans to be under the safe harbor, two standards had to be met—(1) the same incentives must be offered to all enrollees for all covered services, and (2) the health plan may not claim the cost of these incentives as bad debts or otherwise shift the burden of these incentives onto Medicare, the State health care programs, other payers or individuals.

B. Section 1001.952(m)—Price Reductions Offered to Health Plans

The safe harbor in § 1001.952(m) was created to protect certain negotiated price reduction agreements between health care plans and contract health care providers, and was set forth in three parts. The first two parts were designed to protect risk-based and cost-reimbursed health care plans that operate in accordance with a contract or agreement with HCFA or a State health care program; the third part established additional standards to protect health plans that do not have contracts or agreements with HCFA or State health care programs. In order to comply with this price reduction safe harbor, three fundamental prerequisites were to be met in all cases—(1) the protected remuneration was the contract health care provider's reduction of its usual charges for the services; (2) the terms of the agreement between the parties must be in writing; and (3) the agreement must be for the sole purpose of having the contract health care provider furnish enrollees items or services that are covered by the health plan, Medicare or the State health care program.

The first part of this safe harbor (§ 1001.952(m)(1)(i)) protected risk-based HMOs, CMPs and PHPs under contract with HCFA or a State health care program; and operating (i) in accordance with section 1876(g) or 1903(m) of the Act, (ii) under a Federal demonstration authority, or (iii) under other Federal statutory or regulatory authority. In addition to the three prerequisites mentioned above, in order to be covered under the safe harbor risk-based contract health plans under this part could not separately bill Medicare, Medicaid or another State health care program for items and services furnished under the agreement with the health plan (except as specifically authorized by HCFA or the State health care program), and could not otherwise shift the burden of the agreement onto Medicare, Medicaid, other payers or individuals.

The second part (§ 1001.952(m)(1)(ii)) protected health care plans that have executed a contract or agreement with HCFA or a State health care program to have payment made on a reasonable cost or similar basis. In addition to the three prerequisites, price reduction agreements with contract health care providers under this safe harbor were protected if (1) the term of the agreement was not less than one year; (2) the agreement specified in advance the covered items and services that the contract health care provider will furnish to enrollees and the methodology for computing the payment to the contract health care provider; (3) the health plan fully and accurately reported to HCFA or the State health care program the amount it paid the contract health care provider in accordance with the agreement; and (4) the contract health care provider could not claim payment in any form unless specifically authorized by HCFA or the State health care program.

Lastly, the third part of this safe harbor (§ 1001.952(m)(1)(iii)) protected reductions offered by contract health care providers to all other health plans when six standards, in addition to the three prerequisites, were met. The six standards set forth required (1) the term of the price reduction agreement not be less than one year; (2) the agreement specify in advance the covered items and services, which party is to file claims or requests for payment with Medicare, Medicaid and other State health care programs, and the schedule of fees that contract provider will be paid; (3) the schedule remain in effect throughout the term of the agreement (unless a fee update is specifically authorized by HCFA or a State health care program); (4) the party submitting claims for items or services under the agreement not claim or request payment for amounts in excess of the fee schedule; (5) full and accurate reporting of costs be made by the health plan or the contract health care provider; and (6) a prohibition on the party that is not responsible under the agreement for seeking reimbursement from Medicare, Medicaid and any other State health care program from claiming payment or otherwise shifting the burden of the price reduction onto Medicare, Medicaid, other payers or individuals.

C. Section 1001.952(k)—Waiver of Beneficiary Coinsurance and Deductible Amounts

The existing safe harbor in § 1001.952(k), the waiver of coinsurance and deductible amounts, was also amended to protect certain agreements entered into between hospitals and Medicare SELECT insurers. Medicare SELECT is a type of supplemental policy under which reduced benefits may be paid for the use of an out-of-network health care provider. Under this amended safe harbor, waivers or reductions of inpatient hospital coinsurance and deductibles by a hospital in accordance with an agreement with a Medicare SELECT insurer were protected by amending the third of the existing 3 standards set forth in § 1001.952(k)(1). The prior standard required that the reduction or waiver not result from an agreement between a hospital and a third-party payer. The amended standard exempted agreements that are part of a contract between a hospital and a Medicare SELECT insurer for furnishing items or services to Medicare SELECT beneficiaries when (1) the insurer issued a Medicare SELECT insurance policy under the terms of section 1882(t)(1) of the Act, and (2) the waiver of coinsurance or deductible amounts provided under the agreement were limited to beneficiaries covered by the insurer's Medicare SELECT policy. The other requirements of the existing safe harbor still apply to such waivers or reductions.

III. Response to Comments and Summary of Revisions

As a result of our request for comments, we received a total of 42 timely-filed public comments from various health care associations, health care plans and medical groups, professional and business organizations, and insurance companies on how best to protect HMOs, PPOs and other managed care plans. The comments included both general and broad concerns about the impact of the regulations, and specific comments on those areas and the safe harbor provisions about which we invited public input. The following is a summary of the issues raised through that public comment process, our response to those various comments, and a summary of the specific revisions and clarifications being made to these regulations.

A. General Comments

Comment: Commenters generally objected that the safe harbors would inhibit or "chill" existing activities in which managed care plans engage and thereby jeopardize numerous arrangements. They specifically asserted that should HMOs and PPOs not receive safe harbor protection, vast networks of providers would be at risk and would therefore refuse to enter into discount arrangements with such entities.

Response: The commenters have misconstrued the effect of the safe harbor provisions. The interim final rule did not expand the zone of illegal conduct under the anti-kickback statute. Legally and logically, the safe harbors can only make the zone of illegal conduct smaller. As indicated above, compliance with the safe harbors is completely voluntary. If a practice or arrangement does not fall within a safe harbor, it has precisely the same legal risk that it had before the safe harbor was promulgated. The safe harbors are designed to provide a means through which plans and providers can be assured that their arrangements are immune from potential criminal and administrative sanctions under the anti-kickback statute.

Comment: Several commenters wrote that the regulations do not address numerous activities that managed care entities engage in, and thus imply that such activities could be considered unlawful or would be subject to heightened scrutiny.

Response: Commenters should not infer that because a safe harbor provision does not specifically refer to a particular arrangement or activity, it is unlawful. Nor should they interpret that lack of a safe harbor to mean that these activities will be subjected to heightened scrutiny. Moreover, the safe harbors do not create affirmative obligations on individuals or entities since compliance with these safe harbors is purely voluntary. The failure to comply with a safe harbor means only that the practice or arrangement does not have the absolute assurance of protection from anti-kickback liability.

Comment: Certain commenters argued that the statute does not apply to particular arrangements. For instance, one commenter claimed that a hospital's agreement with a managed care plan to forego a deductible or coinsurance does not violate the statute because "payment" is made to a third party payer. Other commenters contended that since the statute confers exempt status on health plans for all discounted transactions, a safe harbor for price reduction agreements is unnecessary. Some commenters further indicated that the statute does not apply to the enrollment of persons in a health plan. These commenters opined that the regulations erroneously indicate that HMOs, especially independent practitioner association models, are "providers" in a position to refer patients.

Response: We believe that the anti-kickback statute is broad enough to potentially cover each of these types of arrangements. The statute prohibits any remuneration which is in return for, or which is designed to induce, the flow of Medicare and Medicaid program-related business. Therefore, it could cover a hospital's agreement to forego or reduce coinsurance or deductibles in exchange for increased program-related business. It does not matter that the payment is made to a third party rather than the beneficiary.

The current discount statutory exception and the discount safe harbor are generally not applicable to the discounts involved in managed care plans. The statutory exception covers discounts obtained by buyers which are to be reported to the programs by such buyers with costs and charges reduced appropriately to reflect the discounts. In managed care plans, the provider is the "seller" who provides a discount to the plan/patient "buyer." Where the provider/seller submits a claim to the program, the statutory requirements have not been met and therefore, the discount is not exempted. The discount safe harbor (which encompasses all conduct under the statutory discount exception) also requires that the discount be offered to Medicare and Medicaid. In the case of managed care contracts with providers, the discount is offered only to the managed care plan. Since the discounted fees are not offered to Medicare or Medicaid, the arrangement does not fall within the parameters of the safe harbor. An additional safe harbor is therefore necessary to protect discounts between managed care plans and providers.

Enrollment in a health plan falls within the scope of the anti-kickback statute where such enrollment involves Medicare or Medicaid beneficiaries and results from various incentives offered to these individuals by the managed care plan. The incentives offered to beneficiaries constitute remuneration with the meaning of the statute. Once enrolled, the plan is entitled to receive Medicare or Medicaid reimbursement for the services directly provided to program beneficiaries. Alternatively, the plan steers enrollees to certain providers who furnish reimbursable services. The incentives offered to program beneficiaries can be in return for obtaining reimbursable program business and, therefore, are covered by the statute.

Moreover, one does not have to be a "provider" or make an actual "referral" to be covered by the anti-kickback statute. The statute covers any persons who offer, pay, solicit, or receive any unlawful remuneration. The scope of prohibited conduct includes not only that which is intended to induce referrals, but also that which is intended to induce the purchasing, leasing, ordering or arranging for any good, facility, service or item paid for by Medicare or Medicaid. Accordingly, the statute covers recommendations on which providers to use, and would include the preferred or approved provider lists of HMOs or PPOs, especially where such providers have agreed to discount their fees in return for such designations.

Comment: Some commenters wanted the OIG to obtain industry input before finalizing these safe harbor regulations.

Response: The interim final rule originally provided for a 60-day public comment period. The OIG subsequently agreed to extend the comment period an additional 60 days. Consequently, we do not believe that further public comment is necessary before the regulations are revised to take into account the public comments received.

Comment: One commenter requested that the OIG provide a mechanism by which members of the public could seek advance rulings on whether practices violate the anti-kickback statute or fall within the safe harbor regulations.

Response: As we explained in the July 29, 1991 final safe regulations setting forth the original safe harbor provisions, we understand and appreciate the desire for legal security in parties' business relations. However, we are unable to provide a mechanism responding to individual requests for advisory opinions about the legality of a particular business arrangement under the statute for several reasons. The Department of Justice (DOJ) has exclusive authority to enforce all criminal laws of the United States such as the anti-kickback statute. (See 28 U.S.C. 516, 519 and 547.) Any advisory opinions that we would issue would not be binding on DOJ and could serve to impede the prosecution of a particular case. Moreover, the statute requires proof of knowing and willful intent, which is generally impossible to evaluate on the basis of written submissions from interested requestors.

Comment: Certain commenters wrote that the OIG should publish a new safe harbor exempting managed care entities from the 60/40 investor and revenue provisions of the small entity safe harbor on investment interests.

Response: These issues lie beyond the scope of this rulemaking and would require separate notice and public comment in order to be adopted. The OIG will consider whether circumstances warrant the future revision of that safe harbor for managed care entities.

Comment: Some commenters addressed the issue of independent agents and brokers in the managed care arena. They asserted that the OIG should revise the existing safe harbor on personal or management services or create an additional safe harbor to protect an HMO's or PPO's use of independent agents and brokers. They believed that independent broker representatives have been the most effective marketing tool for Medicare coverage products. These commenters stated that HMOs or PPOs cannot meet the personal services safe harbor because they cannot establish the aggregate compensation element in advance of a transaction.

Response: This issue is beyond the scope of the interim final rule and would require separate notice and public comment in order to be adopted. In addition, we disagree that the OIG should protect independent agents or brokers used by HMOs or PPOs. Widespread abusive practices have occurred in several States involving independent contractors who misrepresent the nature of a plan's coverage in attempting to enroll individuals. As discussed in the preamble to the July 29, 1991 final safe harbor regulations, we are unpersuaded that such contractors would be subject to adequate supervision or control unless they become employees. We recognize that various personal services arrangements are not covered by these regulations but reiterate that the OIG must reasonably protect the Medicare and State health care programs from abuse.

Comment: Some commenters requested that the OIG seek to amend the anti-kickback statute to clarify its parameters and provide ample scope to managed care entities for their contracting and pricing practices.

Response: The OIG clearly lacks authority in these regulations to amend the anti-kickback statute, which only Congress may do. Therefore, the commenters' suggestion falls outside the scope of this rulemaking. The OIG will, however, continue to consider from time to time whether additional safe harbors are appropriate or whether other specific managed care contracting or pricing practices should be protected.

Comment: One commenter stated that the revised final rule should clearly prohibit providers from balance billing Medicare patients any amounts which exceed either Federal or State law. The commenter noted that currently Federal law permits providers generally to balance bill their patients up to 115 percent of the Medicare allowable amount and that some States do not allow any balance billing whatsoever.

Response: The commenter raises an issue which is beyond the purview of these managed care safe harbor regulations. Neither the new safe harbors nor the amended Medicare SELECT provision addresses the balance billing practices of providers. As the commenter indicates, Federal law precludes providers from charging beneficiaries more than 15 percent above the fee schedule or other allowable charge. The Medicare statute includes a specific remedy for violations of the limitations on balance billing. Moreover, some States like New York absolutely ban balance billing and have mechanisms to enforce those requirements. Therefore, we believe that both Federal and State law already adequately regulate balance billing practices.

B. Comments Applicable to the Two New Safe Harbors

1. The Definition of "Health Plan"

Comment: The vast majority of commenters objected to the scope of the definition of health plan used in the regulations as being too narrow and requested that it be broadened. Commenters specifically requested that the definition should be expanded to include ERISA plans, employer self-funded plans, union welfare funds, non-premium or uninsured HMOs, exclusive provider organizations (EPOs), physician/hospital organizations (PHOs), and PPOs which serve as intermediaries between providers and plans or between providers and employers.

Response: We agree that the definition of health plan should be broadened and have revised the definition to include two additional categories of entities. We had not intended to exclude ERISA plans or other company or union sponsored health plans, and we had specifically mentioned these types of plans as legitimate health plans in the preamble to the interim final rule. As we discussed in that preamble, our primary concern in requiring a health plan to charge a premium and in requiring State regulation of that premium was to exclude phony insurance plans from protection. We still believe it is necessary for the definition to exclude such phony insurance plans because if such plans were not excluded, we would have lost a major tool to combat them and, if they were immunized from liability under the anti-kickback statute, we would have only limited ability to take effective action against these types of abusive arrangements. For example, the requirement is necessary to prevent entities from establishing "insurance plans" that charge only minimal premiums, such as $1.00, that are unrelated to the cost or level of services provided. Often, such plans are merely an attempt to legitimize an unlawful waiver of coinsurance or deductibles. The requirement is also necessary to prevent the creation and use of "shell" entities, which would qualify as a health plan and would, in turn, subcontract all of its responsibilities to other entities or insurance companies. We believe the revisions we have made to the definition of health plan will allow a wide variety of legitimate managed care health plans to qualify for protection.

The revised definition maintains the requirement that the entity furnish or arrange for the furnishing of items or services to enrollees of the plan through contracts or agreements with health care providers, or furnish insurance coverage for the provision of such items or services. However, we have broadened the definition to provide that the entity must furnish or arrange for the provision of items or services to enrollees in exchange for either a premium or a fee. The fee is designed to cover those situations where a premium is not charged, such as where an employer negotiates directly with providers the fees it will pay for the provision of health care services. It would also cover situations where an entity establishes a network of providers and markets that network to an employer or an insurance company, in return for a fee for administering the plan. The fee must reflect the fair market value of administering the plan or the network.

Additionally, in order to qualify as a health plan, the entity must fall within one of four categories. The entity must (1) operate in accordance with a contract, agreement, or statutory demonstration authority approved by HCFA or a State health care program; (2) charge a premium and have its premium structure regulated under a State insurance statute or a State enabling statute governing HMOs or PPOs; (3) be an employer or a union welfare fund whose enrollees are current or retired employees or union members, respectively; or (4) be licensed in the State, be under contract with an employer, a union welfare fund, or a health insurance company, which meets the requirements of (2) or (3), and be paid a fee for the administration of the plan. The first two categories were included in the original definition of health plan. The third category is designed to cover ERISA plans, or other employer or union plans which are self-insured or self-funded and which contract directly with health care providers or insurance companies. In order to exclude bogus or sham entities, we have required that the enrollees of such plans be limited to current or retired employees or current union members, and their families. By union welfare funds, we mean those funds which are operated by bona fide labor organizations. The fourth category is designed to cover entities such as PPOs that act as intermediaries between contract health care providers and employers, union welfare funds or insurance companies. Again, to exclude entities that are not bona fide intermediaries, we have required that the entity be furnishing or arranging for services under contract with a bona fide insurance company, employer, or union welfare fund.

We elected to broaden the definition of health plan by referring to categories of entities based on how they operate or arrange for services rather than by specifically naming different types of common managed care entities, such as HMOs, PPOs, EPOs, or PHOs. We believe this is a preferable approach because there are no single or commonly recognized definitions of each of these types of entities. Any definition we might choose to use would likely be viewed as arbitrary and would likely exclude some otherwise legitimate arrangements. We believe that the majority of legitimate managed care entities will be able to fit into one of the four categories contained in the definition.

We would also point out that the broadening of the definition of health plan to cover preferred provider organizations which act as intermediaries does not provide automatic safe harbor protection for the arrangement between the organization and the insurance company, employer, or union welfare fund. It only enables such organizations to qualify as a health plan for purposes of negotiating protected price reduction agreements with contract health care providers. In order for the PPO's intermediary arrangement to qualify for safe harbor protection, it must meet the requirements of the personal services and management contracts safe harbor in § 1001.952(d).

Comment: A number of commenters argued that legitimate managed care health plans can be identified through the accreditation process by AAPI or NCQA or by requiring non-accredited entities to meet the requirements of those bodies. They believed that the definition of health plan should be revised to include all managed care plans and that the safe harbor should require accreditation or that entities meet the standards for such accreditation.

Response: We do not believe that it is appropriate to require health plans to seek accreditation from private companies or require them to comply with the standards developed by such private companies. We would have no way to determine compliance with those standards if an entity did not seek accreditation. Moreover, accreditation is not a widespread practice and the standards used by such companies are not universally recognized or accepted as minimum standards that should be required for all managed care plans. Finally, we are not aware of any evidence that health plans or entities that do not meet these accreditation standards are abusive or illegitimate, nor do we have any evidence that accredited plans are less likely than other managed care plan to engage in practices that may violate the anti-kickback statute. Therefore, we have declined to require or incorporate accreditation as a part of the definition of a health plan or as a requirement of a safe harbor.

Comment: Some commenters believed that the OIG should pursue "sham" arrangements via "selective enforcement" of Fraud Alert standards rather than through limiting the definition of a health plan.

Response: We disagree that the OIG should allow any managed care entity to qualify as a health plan because the OIG can effectively pursue sham transactions through the selective enforcement of the Fraud Alert standards. First, the Fraud Alerts issued by the OIG do not establish standards which can be enforced. The standards that exist are established by the anti-kickback statute or other federal statutes and regulations. The Fraud Alerts only set forth practices that have been identified as abusive or that may be potentially abusive depending on the circumstances and the intent of the parties. The Fraud Alerts are intended to provide guidance to the public on how they can avoid violations of the statute. Second, the purpose of the safe harbor regulations is both to identify practices or arrangements that fall within the broad scope of the anti-kickback statute but that are not abusive, and to immunize those practices or arrangements from criminal or civil liability. Our intent in establishing these safe harbors is to include only those practices or arrangements that we are confident are not abusive. Accordingly, we believe it is appropriate to limit the definition of health plans to exclude sham managed care plans or phony insurance plans to ensure that such plans do not qualify for protection under a safe harbor.

2. Shifting the Burden

Comment: The commenters universally objected to the interim final rule's prohibition against plans "shifting the burden" of increased coverage, reduced cost-sharing or price reductions onto other payers. Most commenters asserted that this standard was unclear and imposed a burdensome requirement on health plans that the government should not be imposing. They argued that without the ability to shift the revenue loss from incentives or discounts across their entire customer base, health plans would be unable to offer incentives and providers would be unwilling or unable to offer discounts.

Response: We continue to believe that enrollee incentives and provider price reductions should be economically sensible, i.e., they should not be driven by a motive to shift costs to the government or other payers. A health plan should not be offering incentives or provider discounts unless they believe the cost of those incentives or discounts can be recovered through lower operating costs resulting from increased volume, economies of scale or other efficiencies. We also believe that practices should be protected only if they do not cause harm to the Medicare and Medicaid programs. Accordingly, we are only willing to protect incentives and price reductions that do not result in increased costs to the programs. In order to ensure that result, we believe it is necessary to include a requirement which prohibits cost shifting to the Medicare and Medicaid programs. We recognize that the prohibition as originally drafted went beyond what was necessary to protect these Federal programs. We have therefore narrowed the scope of the prohibition against cost shifting to the Medicare and State health care programs and have clarified the circumstances when cost shifting is considered to have occurred, i.e. when an arrangement or agreement results in increased payments being claimed from the Medicare or State health care programs.

Comment: Some commenters requested that the OIG set standards establishing when cost shifting has occurred. They complained that plans and providers have no way to tell if they are in compliance with this requirement.

Response: We do not believe it would be possible to provide a complete or exhaustive list of situations where cost shifting has occurred. We believe that plans and providers make judgments that they expect to forego income to maintain market share, or that they expect to recover lost income resulting from incentives to enrollees or discounts to plans. These plans and providers make judgments whether those means involve allocating increased costs to other customers or payers. Certainly, in any case where a plan or provider raises its costs or fees to others or reduces the services it provides to others as a result of an incentive or a discount, prohibited cost shifting has occurred. Claiming certain costs, such as waivers of coinsurance or deductibles, as bad debt would also constitute impermissible cost shifting.

C. Provision-by-Provision Analysis of Safe Harbors

1. Waiver of Part A Deductible and Coinsurance Amounts in Accordance With an Agreement Between a Hospital and a Medicare SELECT Insurer

Comment: Several commenters objected to the expansion of this safe harbor provision being limited to Medicare SELECT plans for a variety of different reasons. These included the fact that Medicare SELECT is only available in 15 States; that other Medigap plans or preferred provider plans provide no greater risk of abuse than do Medicare SELECT plans; that Medicare SELECT was not intended to be the exclusive mechanism for allowing new and innovative Medigap benefits; and that preferred provider plans that existed prior to the enactment of Medicare SELECT and that now have frozen enrollments due to the standardization of Medigap policies should be allowed to continue to arrange for waivers through agreements with hospitals.

Response: We believe that it continues to be appropriate to limit the amendment of the safe harbor on inpatient hospital waivers of coinsurance and deductibles to Medicare SELECT. As we noted in the preamble to the interim final rule, the Medicare SELECT program is a demonstration project, authorized in only 15 States, and scheduled to operate only from January 1, 1992 until the end of 1994. In order to provide any protection during the demonstration period, it was necessary to publish the safe harbor promptly and in final form. Since we had not previously received comments on this issue from managed care entities, we did not believe a broad waiver was appropriate without subjecting the proposal to notice and comment. Therefore, a limited waiver was included in order to permit the demonstration projects to enter into agreements with hospitals for the waiver of inpatient deductibles and coinsurance amounts without fear of prosecution under the anti-kickback statute. We also believe that the amendment was appropriately limited to Medicare SELECT because the demonstration project included an evaluation and report that would enable the OIG to determine whether the amendment had any undesirable effects. We believe that such evaluation will also provide a factual basis for the OIG to decide whether the amendment should be continued or expanded to other similar types of arrangements.

The demonstration project is still in progress and no final report has yet been issued evaluating the different Medicare SELECT plans that are operating in the 15 States participating in the demonstration project. However, we have reviewed some of the preliminary results of the evaluation. While the data indicate that most beneficiaries who purchase a Medicare SELECT policy pay a lower premium than they would pay for the same package of benefits under a regular supplemental policy, in most cases the lower premiums are the result of the waiver of inpatient hospital deductibles and coinsurance by hospitals rather than the result of reduced utilization or improved management of care. The amendment to the safe harbor permitting agreements between hospitals and Medicare SELECT insurers for the waiver of these cost sharing obligations seems to be the variable that enables Medicare SELECT insurers to reduce claims and thereby offer lower premiums to beneficiaries.

The evaluation of service utilization by beneficiaries with Medicare SELECT policies is expected to take several months to complete. We expect that this part of the evaluation will provide information as to whether the amendment has affected costs to the Medicare program or other payers, or whether it promotes or helps to control overutilization or inappropriate utilization of inpatient hospital or other services. Additionally, it will provide information on whether the Medicare SELECT program is fulfilling the legislative intent of establishing a "managed care" Medicare supplement alternative. Specifically, the intent of Medicare SELECT was to give beneficiaries some of the benefits of a managed care plan enrollment, that is, case management, a primary care physician and cost effective care; it was not intended to be a mere discounting arrangement between hospitals and insurers.

Accordingly, we believe it is appropriate to reserve the option of expanding, revising or rescinding the amendment until we have had an opportunity to consider the complete results of the Medicare SELECT evaluation report.

We do not see any basis for providing safe harbor protection to non-SELECT plans which offer preferred provider provisions merely because such plans predate the enactment of the Medicare SELECT program or because their enrollment is frozen as the result of the new standardized Medigap program rules. The mere existence of a practice or arrangement is not a sufficient basis to exempt that practice or arrangement from the reach of the anti-kickback statute. Our position is that we will not provide safe harbor protection for any practice or arrangement unless we are confident the practice or arrangement is not abusive. We do not currently have any evidence to show that the waivers negotiated by these plans are not abusive or harmful to the programs. The fact that enrollment in these plans is frozen does not make the waivers any less potentially abusive or any less risky. The enactment of Medicare

SELECT and the standardization of Medigap benefits and policies did nothing to affect or change the legal status of routine waivers of coinsurance or deductibles. Consequently, they do not provide any justification for an extension of the existing safe harbor.

We believe that the Medicare SELECT demonstration project is also distinguishable from other preferred provider arrangements on other grounds. First, section 1882(t) of the Social Security Act establishes certain minimum standards that Medicare SELECT plans must meet. These standards include a provider network to provide all services with sufficient access, full benefits for emergency care, an ongoing quality assurance program, and provisions to ensure that beneficiaries are fully informed about the benefits and restrictions of the plan. Medicare SELECT plans are also subject to the imposition of civil monetary penalties for the failure to meet certain requirements, including the failure to provide medically necessary services within the provider network. No other Medigap plans or preferred provider plans are subject to these standards or penalties. Finally, the Medicare SELECT program is subject to ongoing evaluation and expires at the end of 1994. We believe the requirements imposed on Medicare SELECT plans and the time-limited nature of the demonstration provide substantially more protection and less risk to both the Medicare program and Medicare beneficiaries than do other plans.

Contrary to one commenter's belief, we do not view the Medicare SELECT program to be the exclusive vehicle for providing new or innovative Medigap benefit packages. Since it is an existing program, we considered whether it was appropriate to provide any safe harbor protection. To the extent that a State approves a new or innovative Medigap benefit package, we would similarly consider whether any additional safe harbor protection was necessary or appropriate. While States may have the authority to approve the sale of certain non-standardized benefit packages, they do not have the authority to exempt any such benefit packages from the prohibitions of the anti-kickback statute. As we were unwilling to provide a blanket exemption for the Medicare SELECT program, we are unwilling to commit in advance to a blanket exemption for any State-approved innovative benefit package. The approval of additional benefits as part of a Medigap policy would not necessarily implicate the anti-kickback statute and therefore no automatic protection would be necessary. However, the arrangements that insurers may enter into in order to be able to furnish those benefits economically or without additional premium costs could be violative of the anti-kickback statute.

Comment: Some commenters believed that this safe harbor should allow inpatient waivers for agreements with third party payers for all managed care entities. Other commenters requested that safe harbor protection be extended to entities having risk or cost contracts with HCFA.

Response: We disagree. At the present time, we do not believe there is sufficient evidence to demonstrate that waivers that result from agreements between hospitals and third party payers, such as insurers or health plans, are not abusive. We believe there are significant differences between waivers of deductibles and coinsurance offered by hospitals directly to beneficiaries and those negotiated between hospitals and health plans. When we promulgated the original safe harbor provision, we noted that there is a limited risk of abuse because of various factors. First, the Medicare program is not directly harmed since hospitals receive a predetermined amount under the prospective payment system for each admission regardless of their costs or charges. Second, hospital admissions are subject to peer review and there is a relatively fixed level of patient demand for hospital services. Third, physicians, rather than patients, make the decision whether admission is medically indicated and their practice patterns and admitting privileges also affect the decision as to which hospital will be selected. Therefore, we believed that a waiver of inpatient beneficiary fees would not be likely to increase utilization significantly, especially if hospitals could not discriminate on the basis of length of stay or type of diagnosis.

These limiting factors do not exist where waivers result from agreements between hospitals and insurers or plans. In contrast to the effect of a waiver given to a beneficiary which affects only a single admission, health plans or insurers have the capacity to direct the flow of large numbers of admissions to specific hospitals by designating them as preferred or exclusive providers in return for an agreement to waive coinsurance and deductibles. Where this flow results from the hospital's agreement to waive inpatient beneficiary fees or to reduce its charges, or both, the practice can be abusive and anti-competitive. Hospital reimbursement rates differ and the designation of certain hospitals as preferred or exclusive providers in a particular geographic area could result in a direct increase in the amounts paid by the Medicare program for inpatient hospital costs. Thus, while the plan or insurer would save money, the Medicare program would not. Similarly, a health plan or insurer's designation of certain hospitals could result in substantial decreases in the number of admissions to other area hospitals and might eventually result in the closure of some facilities, thus lessening competition. Reduced competition could lead to increased charges by the remaining hospitals. Additionally, the waiver of beneficiary fees or reduced charges that the hospital has agreed to in order to obtain the health plan or insurer's business may ultimately be passed along to the Medicare program or other payers. Finally, we are concerned about the possibility of overutilization or inappropriate use of services that may result from a waiver of beneficiary fees. Where Medicare is the primary payer, a hospital's waiver of inpatient deductible and coinsurance amounts results in the insurer or health plan having no financial liability. Since the plan or insurer has no financial stake, it may be less concerned about guarding against the overutilization or inappropriate utilization of services.

We have made, however, a minor change to the regulation to clarify the meaning of "third party payer." There has been some question as to whether that term would include PPOs that serve as intermediaries between health care providers and insurers or employers, but who are not responsible for the payment of claims for services provided to beneficiaries. We have revised the regulation to indicate that a third party payer includes any entity that meets the definition of a health plan set forth in § 1001.952(l)(2) of the regulation. With the limited exception for Medicare SELECT, it is our intent, as discussed in the preamble to the July 29, 1991 final safe harbor regulations, to protect only those waivers that are given by hospitals directly to beneficiaries. We did not intend to protect any waivers that resulted from contractual agreements entered into by hospitals.

Comment: A number of commenters, including some who are Medicare SELECT insurers, raised objections to the effect that even where Medicare SELECT is in place, the safe harbor does not permit waiver of coinsurance for a large number of services that are essential to cost-efficient managed care networks (e.g., hospital outpatient services, ambulatory surgical centers, physician services) because it is limited to inpatient hospital services. They urged that the safe harbor be expanded to cover services reimbursed under Part B of Medicare.

Response: We do not believe that safe harbor protection is appropriate for routine waivers of coinsurance and deductibles for outpatient services covered under the Medicare Part B program. We also do not believe that such waivers are necessary or essential to the efficient or cost-effective operation of managed care plans. Managed care plans are free to seek discounts or price reductions from providers that lower the costs of providing services, as long as those reductions are reflected as a lowering of the provider's total charge for the service. We have expressly provided protection for this type of discount in the safe harbor on price reductions offered to health plans.

As we indicated in the preamble to the interim final rule, routine waivers of coinsurance and deductibles are an area of significant abuse in the Medicare program. Such waivers result in the submission of false claims to the Medicare program because providers misstate their charges on claims submitted to the program. For example, if a provider's usual charge is $100 and he or she routinely waives the 20 percent coinsurance, then the provider's actual charge for providing the service is really only $80, the amount he or she expects to receive as payment for the service. If the provider submits a claim to the Medicare program for $100, he or she has misrepresented the actual charge and the Medicare program will reimburse the provider a higher than appropriate amount. If the Medicare program reimburses the provider $80, then the program will have paid for the entire cost of providing the service, rather than the 80 percent authorized by law. In this single instance, the program would have overpaid the provider by $16 (the difference between $80 and $64, which is 80 percent of the provider's actual fee of $80). Thus, the waiver of coinsurance results in substantially higher costs to the Medicare program. Similar problems may arise with cost-based health care providers. We would also note that the Secretary's authority to grant safe harbor protection extends only to violations of the anti-kickback statute. The Secretary has no authority to provide protection from criminal, civil, or administrative liability arising from the submission of false claims to the Medicare program.

We also believe that the routine waiver of coinsurance and deductibles may result in overutilization or inappropriate utilization of services. Cost sharing is an essential element of the Medicare program. To the extent that beneficiaries have a financial stake in the cost of services, they have a direct interest in seeking the most efficient and economical providers and are deterred from seeking unnecessary services. As a result, Medicare program expenditures are lower. Where Medicare beneficiaries have no financial stake because a provider has waived their coinsurance amount, they are less likely to be concerned over whether the charge for the service is $10 or $100, and are less likely to question the medical necessity of the item or service provided or ordered. Similarly, where a health plan (or insurer) is responsible for paying a Medicare beneficiary's coinsurance or deductible amounts, it is concerned about the cost or necessity of the services provided to their enrollees. However, where a health plan negotiates a waiver of Medicare coinsurance or deductible amounts with providers, it no longer has a financial stake because there are no costs it incurs for the services provided by that provider to Medicare beneficiaries. Once again, the Medicare program ends up paying for the full cost of care.

We have no evidence to indicate that Medicare SELECT plans are significantly different from other Medigap plans or other types of managed care health plans in this respect, or that they will adequately protect the Medicare program from higher costs or inappropriate expenditures. Section 1882(t) of the Act does not provide any specific safeguards against the abuses that occur from the waiver of Medicare Part B coinsurance or deductibles. Thus, we continue to decline to provide any expanded protection for Medicare SELECT plans.

Comment: One commenter indicated that the False Claims Act and other laws, but not this rule, should address situations where waivers of coinsurance and deductibles might result in inaccurate charges billed to Medicare program.

Response: We disagree that abuses arising from the waiver of coinsurance and deductibles should be addressed through the use of the False Claims Act and other laws and regulations. One of the primary purposes of the anti-kickback statute is to protect the Medicare program from higher costs and overutilization that occur when financial incentives are offered or given in order to obtain Medicare program business. Thus, the anti-kickback statute is an appropriate mechanism to deal with higher program costs resulting from inaccurate charges and claims submitted to the Medicare program.

Moreover, the purpose of the safe harbor regulations is to exempt from criminal or civil liability those practices which, although they violate the anti-kickback statute, are not harmful to the Medicare or State health care programs. As discussed above, routine waivers of Medicare Part B coinsurance and deductible amounts are harmful and abusive because they regularly lead to false claims and increased costs and because they encourage overutilization or inappropriate utilization of services. Thus, safe harbor protection is unwarranted and inappropriate.

Finally, another purpose of the safe harbor regulations is to provide standards which providers and other persons or entities can comply with and be assured that they will not be subject to criminal or civil prosecution or exclusion from program participation. We actively encourage providers to come into compliance with applicable safe harbor provisions. It would be unfair and misleading, if not an abuse of discretion, for us to provide an exception under the anti-kickback statute for certain behavior when compliance with that exception would subject providers and plans or insurers to the very same criminal, civil, and administrative sanctions under the False Claims Act or other provisions. The mission of the OIG is to prevent fraud and abuse, not to encourage it.

Comment: One commenter indicated that the OIG should, at a minimum, publish a new Federal Register notice that lists examples of coinsurance waiver arrangements that may not qualify for safe harbor protection, but "probably would not be pursued criminally or civilly by the OIG."

Response: We do not believe that there are any specific types of situations involving a routine waiver of coinsurance or deductibles that we would decline to pursue as a general rule. Thus, we believe that publication of a new Federal Register notice is not necessary. In the OIG Fraud Alert on this subject, we have indicated that waivers were only appropriate on a case-by-case basis in consideration of a patient's financial hardship or where a good faith effort to collect has been made. We have not changed our position.

2. Incentives to All Enrollees

Comment: Some commenters maintained that a literal reading of the enrollee incentive safe harbor would necessitate uniformity among all products, thereby eliminating any incentive. The commenters encouraged the OIG to eliminate the provision or restrict it to all enrollees of a particular product.

2130 Federal Register / Vol. 61, No. 17 / Thursday, January 25, 1996 / Rules and Regulations

Response: The purpose of the requirement that incentives be provided to all enrollees was to restrict the ability of health plans to target particular Medicare or Medicaid beneficiaries or groups of such beneficiaries and induce them to enroll in the plan by providing incentives. We were concerned that plans would target healthy beneficiaries by offering them increased services or reductions in cost sharing and attempt to avoid older or sicker beneficiaries or those with expensive or chronic health conditions requiring a high utilization of services by offering only the same services available through a fee-for-service plan. Accordingly, we are reluctant to eliminate this requirement from the safe harbor. We are also reluctant to limit the regulation to a product-specific approach because we are concerned that the same type of abuses could occur where health plans offered several different products.

Comment: A number of commenters urged the OIG to restrict the scope of "enrollee" only to members of the Medicare or State health care programs. They believed that the inclusion of all enrollees was unwarranted and exceeded the scope of the Medicare and Medicaid Patient Program Protection Act (MMPPPA) of 1987.

Response: Although we do not agree that the scope of the provision exceeded our authority under MMPPPA, we believe that these concerns can be adequately addressed by limiting the provision to all enrollees who are also beneficiaries of the Medicare and State health care programs. Accordingly, we have revised the safe harbor on incentives to enrollees to require that incentives offered by health plans be offered to all Medicare or State health care program enrollees of the plan. We believe that this limitation will adequately safeguard against the possibility that health plans may improperly favor certain healthy beneficiaries or use incentives to improperly encourage utilization when the item or service is furnished.

3. Incentives by Non-Contract Health Plans

Comment: Several commenters believed that safe harbor protection should be given to any managed care plan that offers a higher level of benefits or services obtained from a contract provider. They believed that protection should be given for all incentives by managed care plans, including those providing Medicare supplemental coverage. Other commenters indicated that coinsurance waivers and other financial incentives to encourage the use of a preferred provider panel were historically legitimate managed care incentives that do not cause harm to Medicare or Medicaid and should therefore be recognized.

Response: We remain unpersuaded at this time that safe harbor protection is appropriate for health plans that are not under contract with HCFA or a Medicaid State agency. Unlike contract plans that are limited to a few types of arrangements, non-contract plans consist of widely varying arrangements and widely differing scopes of benefits. These plans are subject to little oversight. Most of the commenters who requested a broadening of the safe harbor failed to provide any discussion of precisely how the Medicare and Medicaid programs would or could be protected against abuses if all managed care plans were permitted to offer any kind of incentives free of anti-kickback liability. Nor did they provide any substantive evidence that the majority of the existing managed care plans have effective mechanisms and controls that would adequately protect the Medicare and Medicaid programs against higher costs or overutilization. Finally, the commenters did not suggest any standards we could impose which would eliminate plans that do not have in effect adequate mechanisms to protect the Medicare or Medicaid programs from abuse.

Moreover, we believe that the fact that the Medicare and Medicaid programs reimburse services provided to enrollees of non-contract plans on a fee-for-service basis makes these situations subject to the same potential abuses and risks as exist with incentives offered by non-managed care plans or providers. Where a health care provider who is part of a preferred provider network treats a beneficiary and will be paid for each service that he or she provides on a fee-for-service basis by Medicare or Medicaid, that provider has no built-in incentive not to overutilize. To the extent that the provider has agreed to accept reduced fees for the treatment of plan enrollees, he or she may have a direct incentive to increase the number of services to make up for the reduction in fees. Similarly, if the beneficiary has reduced or no cost sharing obligations, the beneficiary faces no disincentive to overutilization. The plan does not prevent reimbursement for these unnecessary services because the claims are directly submitted to and paid by Medicare or Medicaid. Finally, where managed care providers agree to accept Medicare payment as payment in full, the burden of the reduced cost sharing incentives offered to beneficiaries comes at the expense of the Medicare program, because the program will end up paying 100 percent of the provider's fee. Thus, these incentives can cause harm to the Medicare and Medicaid programs.

Comment: Some commenters argued that incentives by non-contract plans should be allowed because most managed care plans adequately monitor for overutilization, and that many non-contract plans are monitored either as Federally-qualified HMOs or as a result of accreditation by independent organizations. They also argued that Medicare and Medicaid patients cannot be carved out of a managed care plan's incentive programs, and that a loss of administrative efficiencies could result if plans need to handle program beneficiaries differently than others covered under group plans.

Response: We do not believe that existing utilization review mechanisms are sufficient to protect the Medicare and Medicaid programs against abuses associated with self-referral. One major problem is that there are no widely accepted definitions or standards governing utilization review. This presents a major barrier to drafting a safe harbor with clear, well-defined standards. Additionally, most utilization review activity is focused on expensive procedures or on patterns of care, and therefore does not address individual physician decisions on diagnostic or other treatment services, where many self-referral abuses occur. Utilization review is also designed to identify and address medical care that falls outside of accepted medical parameters or norms. Most of the problems we have observed in the area of self-referral involve physician treatment decisions that are within the range of accepted parameters or norms, but where financial incentives may improperly influence or affect physician judgments. Accordingly, we are not at all confident that utilization review will cure or prevent self-referral problems that the anti-kickback statute was intended to address. Therefore, it would be unwise to adopt utilization review mechanisms as an appropriate standard for safe harbor protection.

Where Medicare or Medicaid are responsible for paying for a portion of the care rendered to enrollees of a managed care plan, the plan must already have some procedures that are different from those used where the plan is solely responsible for the cost of care. For example, separate claims must be submitted to those programs either before or after claims are submitted to the managed care health plan. We believe that managed care plans can handle potential differences between Medicare's and the plan's coinsurance amounts in ways that are efficient and economical as well as in compliance with the requirements of Federal law.

Comment: One commenter specifically urged that safe harbor protection should be limited to plans under contract with HCFA or a State agency, arguing that if it is broadened it will result in unfair competitive practices and illegal waivers of coinsurance and deductibles. A second commenter agreed, but believed an exception should be made for situations where dual coverage exists and the second plan adopts a non-duplication of benefits or preservation of deductibles and coinsurance posture.

Response: We share the concerns of the commenters that expansion of the safe harbor provision could result in abusive or illegal practices. As we indicated in an earlier response, we remain concerned that because services provided to enrollees of non-contract plans are reimbursed on a fee-for-service basis, the plans would pose the same risks to the Medicare and Medicaid programs as typical fee-for-service plans. In the case of contract plans, the reimbursement formulae take into account the cost sharing obligations of beneficiaries that the Medicare or Medicaid programs may require, so there is no problem with illegal waivers of coinsurance or deductibles. We also believe that the rules applicable to contract plans and the oversight provided by HCFA or a State Medicaid agency should be sufficient to prevent anti-competitive or other abusive practices from occurring in contract plans.

We do not believe that a special safe harbor provision is necessary or warranted at this time to deal with dual coverage situations. Dual coverage is where a person is covered by more than one health insurance policy. An example would be where a husband and wife are both employed and each is covered by an employer policy that includes family members. We do not believe that dual coverage (to be distinguished from Medicare supplemental or Medigap coverage) is a problem that affects significant numbers of Medicare or Medicaid beneficiaries. Companies are expressly prohibited by law from selling Medicare beneficiaries health insurance coverage that duplicates any existing coverage that they may have. Medicaid is a payer of last resort and will not pay for services covered by other health insurance or plans.

4. Price Reduction Agreements

Comment: One commenter questioned why the price reduction safe harbor applicable to plans not under contract with HCFA or a Medicaid State agency was drafted on a fee-for-service concept.

Response: The safe harbor was drafted in this manner because that is how the Medicare and Medicaid programs almost exclusively pay for services furnished to program beneficiaries by non-contract managed care health plans or by providers who are affiliated with non-contract plans. Such plans and providers are reimbursed for each separate covered service provided to Medicare or Medicaid beneficiaries on the basis of fee schedules or allowable charges. Capitated payment arrangements and reasonable cost-related reimbursement are only directly allowed in plans which are under contract. We have dealt with those types of arrangements in the first two parts of the price reduction safe harbor dealing with plans under contract with HCFA or a Medicaid State agency. Therefore, we did not believe it was necessary or appropriate to provide for safe harbor protection for other types of payment mechanisms in the price reduction safe harbor for non-contract plans.

Comment: Many commenters objected to the fact that this safe harbor exempted only remuneration in the form of a reduction in the provider's usual charge for the service, thereby not protecting capitation agreements, bonuses, and withhold arrangements. These commenters believed that the safe harbor should protect all HMO or PPO compensation arrangements, including risk incentive pools and volume rebates, so long as they were not linked to referrals of Medicare or Medicaid patients.

Response: We have reconsidered our position that we did not need to address capitated arrangements in the safe harbor for price reductions in non-contract health plans. Although the Medicare and Medicaid programs may pay for services on a fee-for-service basis, some health plans contract with individual health care providers for the provision of services using a variety of different mechanisms, including capitation. Since the amount paid to a provider under a capitated arrangement may represent a reduction in the amount he or she would otherwise receive for treating a particular patient and the provider agrees to accept such payment amount in return for an agreed upon or anticipated flow of patients, the anti-kickback statute may be implicated. Therefore, we believe that some protection for these arrangements may be warranted.

Our experience has indicated that the most common risks that the anti-kickback statute is directed toward preventing are not present in the case of at-risk, capitated payment mechanisms. Where a provider is paid a fixed amount for all the services provided to a patient, there is no incentive for overutilization. If anything, there is an incentive to underutilize. Accordingly, the Medicare and Medicaid programs face little risk of overutilization or the increased costs that accompany such overutilization where services are provided by a provider who is paid solely on an at-risk or capitated basis. For these reasons, we believe it would be appropriate for us to provide safe harbor protection for such arrangements.

Accordingly, we have revised the price reduction safe harbor to add a new category of price reduction agreement applicable to capitated payment arrangements to providers. In order to qualify for safe harbor protection, both the health plan and the contract health care provider must comply with five standards. First, the term of the agreement must be for not less than one year. Second, the agreement must specify the covered items or services that will be furnished to enrollees of the plan and the total amount per enrollee that the provider will be paid for such covered items or services, including any copayments to be paid by enrollees. The amount the provider will be paid per enrollee may be expressed in a per month or other time period basis. Third, the payment amount set forth in the agreement must remain in effect throughout the term of the agreement. Fourth, the health plan and the provider must fully and accurately report to the Medicare and State health care programs upon request, the terms of the agreement and the amounts paid in accordance with the agreement. Finally, the provider must not claim or request payment in any form from the Department, a State health care program or an enrollee (other than specified copayment amounts) for covered items or services. Similarly, the health plan must not pay the provider in excess of the amounts provided by the agreement for the provision of covered items or services.

For the most part, the conditions applicable to this new category of price reduction agreement are the same or comparable to those applicable to fee-for-service arrangements. We believe these conditions are necessary to prevent plans or providers from manipulating the terms of the agreed upon arrangement and adjusting the level of reimbursement or the scope of covered services for improper or illegal purposes. We believe that providers and plans should take steps to ensure that they have sufficient information concerning the costs of providing services and the frequency and types of services that will be required for the plan's enrollees before they enter into these types of arrangements. We believe that the restrictions on seeking or paying additional amounts for covered services and the requirements for disclosure are necessary to ensure that the Medicare and Medicaid programs are not being charged excessive or inappropriate amounts.

We have declined to provide specific safe harbor protection to withhold pools, risk incentive pools, or other types of incentive programs offered by non-contract managed care plans. One problem we have with these types of arrangements is that there are no uniform standards or definitions applicable to each of these different types of mechanisms. Each health plan sets its own standards or risk pools and determines the amounts that will be paid or withheld. Because these types of arrangements vary so widely in amounts and scope, and because there are no commonly accepted minimum standards as to what criteria an incentive plan should include, we do not believe that it would be feasible for us to set adequate or appropriate minimum standards for a safe harbor. Moreover, because these types of payment mechanisms offer additional remuneration to providers that is related to the volume or value of services provided, their use is particularly vulnerable to abuse. They can be used to manipulate provider payment levels and can be used to inappropriately affect the flow of Medicare and Medicaid reimbursable business. We are not confident that we could create a safe harbor where we would be reasonably certain that any individual incentive plan qualifying for protection would be non-abusive.

We also believe that withhold arrangements present additional problems. We are concerned that in some cases providers subject to a withhold may be submitting false claims to the Medicare and Medicaid programs. If the provider does not ultimately receive the withheld amount or does not have a reasonable expectation of receiving it, and includes the full amount of the potential fee on the claim form, he or she has misrepresented the amount of his or her fee and stands to be overpaid by the Medicare or Medicaid programs. For example, if a provider's agreed upon fee is $100 but the health plan has a 20 percent withhold in place, he or she is only assured of receiving $80 in payment for the services provided. If that provider submits a claim to the Medicare program for $100 and is paid $80, that provider will have received full payment from the Medicare program unless he or she also receives the withheld amount. The net effect is the same as an express waiver of coinsurance.

In some cases involving withholds, there is little likelihood that the payment amounts withheld will actually be made to providers. We are unwilling to protect any practice that may result in the submission of false or improper claims to the programs.

Comment: Some commenters objected to the fact that this safe harbor provision does not recognize compensation based on reasonable and customary allowances, such as a discount from usual charges.

Response: We believe that reasonable and customary or usual charges have no fixed meaning and are subject to change at the provider's discretion and, therefore, subject to manipulation and abuse. We believe it is necessary to have a fixed and identifiable list of charges and services in order to be able to determine compliance with the terms of the safe harbor. If the provider had a list of his or her reasonable and customary or usual charges that was incorporated as a part of the agreement with the health plan, and the agreement specified that the agreed upon payment rate would be 80 percent of the charges on the list, we believe that would be acceptable under the terms of the safe harbor because the price for each service would be a fixed and readily ascertainable amount. Of course, it would be the reduced amount that is the provider's charge for services to the plan's enrollees, not the reasonable and customary or usual charge, and that reduced amount would be required to be submitted on any claims or requests for payment to the Medicare or Medicaid programs for services rendered to plan enrollees.

Comment: Some commenters objected to the prohibition against submitting a claim in excess of the fee schedule because it prohibits plans or intermediaries that operate by negotiating discounts with providers and marking up the fees to the purchaser. This is the PPO's mechanism for defraying its costs. They indicated that such arrangements should be allowed because fees are still less than what the purchaser would otherwise pay. Specifically, commenters stated that the safe harbor should cover fees to providers that are a percentage of charges billed by the contracting provider and are attributable to the PPO's marketing services to third party payers.

Response: We believe any arrangements that set fees based on the volume or value of services provided to patients are subject to abuse and therefore, we decline blanket protection for them. We have seen instances where such payments are really only thinly disguised attempts to pay for referrals. Moreover, there is also no guarantee that the marked-up charges submitted to the Medicare and Medicaid programs would be any lower than the provider's usual charges to the programs. Thus, there is no guarantee that the programs will benefit from allowing such arrangements. We believe that there are enough other options a PPO can employ to cover its administrative or marketing costs. The PPO can include such costs in the premiums charged to plan enrollees or in fees charged to insurers or employers where the PPO administers the plan for such entities. The PPO is also free to enter into separate contracts with providers for management services. Of course, in order to qualify for safe harbor protection, such contracts would have to meet the terms of the safe harbor on management or personal services contracts. We also wish to emphasize that by not protecting such payment mechanisms under the safe harbor, we do not prohibit them, as the commenters believe. The failure to fall within a safe harbor means only that they are subject to the anti-kickback statute in precisely the same manner that they were prior to the issuance of the safe harbor.

Comment: Some commenters opposed the regulation's "sole purpose" requirement as being inconsistent with the structures of managed care plans. These commenters argued that providers qualifying for the safe harbors should be allowed to contribute activities such as pre-enrollment screening, utilization review and quality assurance services.

Response: Our intent in creating the safe harbor for price reduction agreements was to protect only those discounts given by contract health care providers for the items and services they furnish to enrollees. In order to ensure that we can determine whether the discounts given by providers comply with all of the requirements of the safe harbor, it is necessary to have a separate agreement that covers only the discounted arrangements that fall within the scope of the safe harbor. We have not prohibited managed care entities from entering into separate agreements with providers for other activities such as utilization review, pre-enrollment screening or even marketing activities. However, contracts for such activities will be scrutinized separately and will only be afforded safe harbor protection if they meet the requirements of the existing management and personal services safe harbor.

We are unwilling to expand the price reduction safe harbor to cover these activities because, as we noted in the preamble to the interim final rule, we have observed that some HMOs have abused their contractual relationships with medical groups where individuals in the groups have conducted abusive or illegal activities on behalf of the HMO. For instance, various contract health plans have engaged in pre-enrollment screening in order to deny or discourage relatively sick beneficiaries from enrolling. Such activities in at least one case resulted in a criminal conviction. Additionally, it is easy to manipulate agreements for the provision of utilization review services and other activities to make payments to reward providers for certain actions or to provide additional reimbursement to certain providers in violation of the anti-kickback statute. For these reasons, we believe the standards of the management and personal services safe harbor should continue to be applied to personal services contracts between managed care entities and contract health care providers.

Comment: A number of commenters wanted the OIG to protect volume-sensitive fee schedules, subject to "possible pricing adjustments," if the schedule is stated in the contract and not increased during its term. These commenters would like to render higher payment to providers who service a greater number of managed care patients to ensure access to care.

Response: We decline to protect volume-sensitive fee schedules. We have found that volume-sensitive reimbursement levels are often extremely abusive. These types of schedules offer increased incentives for providers to overutilize, since the payments they receive will be higher if they provide more services to more patients. We are not sure what one of the commenters meant specifically by the term "possible pricing adjustments," but we are concerned that any such adjustments could create a referral-driven mechanism that would not serve the interests of the programs. We believe that other mechanisms exist through which health plans may ensure that providers give adequate coverage to patients or through which plans could reimburse providers who agree to treat a larger number of plan enrollees. For example, plans could require that providers agree to treat minimum numbers of enrollees and set the amount of compensation based on that number. Alternatively, providers could agree to treat all plan enrollees who need services up to a certain number, with higher reimbursement levels for larger numbers of patients.

Comment: Several commenters took exception to the one-year term minimum requirement, contending that it excludes common contract terms, such as reciprocal termination clauses and inhibits plans, that may need to contract with a particular provider for less than one year. Other commenters argued that the requirement unduly restricts HMOs and does not allow for alterations based on changed circumstances. These commenters asserted that a change during the contract year in the percentage of fee schedule an HMO will pay is not a means of inducing referrals of patients enrolled in a plan.

Response: We have found that reciprocal termination clauses can result in parties engaging in "sham" contracts whereby they terminate the contract and renegotiate terms to gain more favorable financial positions. Alternatively, they may terminate contracts in order to enter into contracts with more favorable financial terms with other providers. These renegotiations may affect the flow of Medicare or Medicaid reimbursable business. We believe it is necessary for the contracts to have a fixed term of at least one year in order to avoid such manipulations. We have adopted a one-year term for all of the safe harbor provisions involving contracts. The commenters have not demonstrated any reasons why managed care contracts necessitate a different length. Accordingly, if parties alter contractual terms based on purportedly changed circumstances, that alteration will not enjoy safe harbor protection. Termination "for cause" clauses drafted in compliance with Internal Revenue Service or other legal or regulatory requirements should not jeopardize safe harbor status if the purpose of the termination clause is to comply with these requirements and not to facilitate renegotiation of contract terms. If a contract is terminated in accordance with a legally enforceable termination clause, the failure to renew the contract would indicate that the termination was effectuated for a legitimate business purpose. As to other types of termination clauses, the OIG will examine such conduct on a case-by-case basis to assess whether it is abusive and harmful.

We acknowledge that health care providers may enter into short-term service contracts for legitimate business reasons and not because of referral opportunities. However, we cannot ensure that only legitimate short-term contracts will be covered if we delete the one-year requirement. We would also note that the one-year term does not refer to the length of time that services will be necessarily provided, but rather to the length of time within which the fees for the services covered by the agreement may not be changed. So long as the contract terms are not altered within a one-year period, an agreement that is performed in less than one year will meet the one-year requirement in the safe harbor provision.

Comment: Some commenters requested that the price reductions allowed under the safe harbor should be limited to a specific amount, e.g., a Medicare-approved rate or a percentage. They claimed that this restriction is necessary to prevent providers from accepting below-cost prices and increasing prices for non-managed care Medicare patients and others.

Response: We understand that providers negotiate discounted prices with health plans in order to increase the number of patients in their practices. Providers may expect that they can make up for the reductions in their charges by providing services to a greater number of patients. Generally, providers may anticipate a certain number of new patients as a result of entering into a contract with a managed care plan. However, the commenters raise a valid concern that the price reductions given, if great enough, may shift the burden of the price reduction to others by resulting in increased prices for non-managed care Medicare patients. We have specifically addressed that concern in the safe harbor by including a prohibition against cost-shifting onto the Medicare or State health care programs. Therefore, we are not convinced that setting limitations on the amount of a discount a provider may offer is necessary to prevent abuse. We also believe that the wide variations in providers' rates and costs make identifying a fixed "below-cost" point virtually impossible. We would have to assess a provider's entire billing practice to determine whether, in a given case, services were offered at rates below actual cost.

Comment: A number of commenters contended that managed care plans cannot reasonably ensure that its contract providers are not submitting claims which violate the contract's terms or claims that exceed the fee schedule. According to these commenters, Medicare should recoup the amounts erroneously paid to the provider rather than deprive both the provider and the plan of safe harbor protection.

Response: We believe it is appropriate to condition the granting of safe harbor protection on compliance by both plans and providers. Managed care health plans have an ongoing relationship with contract health care providers that includes monitoring and utilization review of the services provided to plan enrollees. This relationship is different from the usual relationship between buyers and sellers. Because of this special, ongoing relationship, health plans have a greater ability to monitor and ensure compliance with the requirements of the safe harbor regarding the submission of claims to the Medicare or Medicaid programs. Unless plans are held accountable in some way for the propriety of claims submitted to the programs, they will have no interest in ensuring the accuracy of those claims.

We also believe that health plans have available to them several ways to monitor or ensure compliance. For example, plans may require that the plan submit all claims to the Medicare or Medicaid programs. Alternatively, as part of their contracts with providers, plans have the ability to require providers to furnish copies of claims submitted to the programs for plan enrollees or to allow a review of their billing records. Plans can include as a contract term the requirement to submit program claims according to the agreed upon fee schedule and provide for termination of the contract for non-compliance. We would also expect plans to report to the Medicare or Medicaid programs any contract-related violations of which they become aware so the programs can take appropriate steps to deal with the improper billing, including recovery of any overpayments made to the provider. We would consider the actions taken by the health plan in deciding whether any action was warranted under the anti-kickback statute.

Comment: Several commenters wrote that the price reduction safe harbor imposes unnecessary and impractical standards regarding advance disclosure of covered fees and services, fee schedules and cost shifting that will impede negotiations and increase costs. These commenters urged the OIG to permit other methods of describing covered items or services, such as incorporation by reference of benefit summaries.

Response: We are uncertain how the requirement that the agreement spell out the agreed-upon fees will result in an increase in costs or will impede negotiations between health plans and providers. This safe harbor merely requires that the agreement specify in writing what the parties have already agreed upon, i.e., the items and services that will be furnished to plan enrollees and the prices that the provider will charge for them. We have no objections if the parties wish to reference the covered items and services and the schedule of fees for those services in an attachment to the contract. However, those attachments must clearly indicate the specific amounts that will be paid to the provider for each of the covered items and services he or she furnishes to plan enrollees in order to comply with the safe harbor. General summaries of plan benefit coverage and references to percentages of usual charges will not suffice. We reserve the right to closely scrutinize these attachments to ensure that the parties have adequately identified these items or services. We believe it is important for both the providers and the plans to know what the contract covers and the amounts they are entitled to bill the plan, the Medicare and Medicaid programs and the program beneficiaries.

Comment: One commenter objected to the safe harbor requirements on the grounds that managed care contracts with providers rarely establish fees for services covered by others nor do they specify billing procedures for services not billable to the managed care plan.

Response: We believe that the commenter has misconstrued the safe harbor's requirements. The safe harbor does not broaden the scope of managed care plans' coverage to services covered by other plans nor does it require a price reduction agreement between a managed care plan and a provider to establish fees for services provided by others or for services not billable to the plan. The agreement need only identify those services that the provider will be paid for by the plan and only those services that are covered by the plan and provided to plan enrollees.

IV. Additional Information

A. Regulatory Impact Statement

The Office of Management and Budget (OMB) has reviewed this revised final rule in accordance with the provisions of Executive Order 12866. As indicated in the original safe harbor provisions published on July 29, 1991 and the interim final rule for these safe harbors published on November 5, 1992, the safe harbor provisions set forth in this rulemaking are designed to permit individuals and entities to freely engage in business practices and arrangements that encourage competition, innovation and economy. In doing so, these regulations impose no requirements on any party. Health care providers and others may voluntarily seek to comply with these provisions so that they have the assurance that their business practices are not subject to any enforcement action under the anti-kickback statute. As such, we believe that the economic impact of these regulations is minimal and have no effect on the economy or on Federal or State expenditures.

In addition, we generally prepare a regulatory flexibility analysis that is consistent with the Regulatory Flexibility Act (5 U.S.C. 601–612). We believe that the majority of health care providers and practitioners do not engage in illegal remuneration schemes, and that the aggregate economic impact of this provision should, in effect, be minimal, affecting only those who have chosen to engage in prohibited payment schemes in violation of the statutory intent. As indicated above, this revised final rule serves to clarify various aspects of the safe harbor provisions originally published on November 5, 1992 to enable entities to more easily immunize themselves from potential criminal and administrative sanctions, and to eliminate potential barriers to the provision of coordinated health care under the Medicare and State health care programs. As a result, we have determined, and the Secretary certifies, that this final rule will not have a significant economic impact on a number of small business entities, and we have, therefore, not prepared a regulatory flexibility analysis.

B. Paperwork Reduction Act

Under the Paperwork Reduction Act of 1995, agencies are required to provide 60-day notice in the Federal Register and solicit public comment before a collection of information requirement is submitted to OMB for review and approval. In order to fairly evaluate whether an information collection should be approved by OMB, section 3506(c)(2)(A) of the Paperwork Reduction Act of 1995 requires that we solicit comments on the following issues:

- Whether the information collection is necessary and useful to carry out the proper functions of the agency;
- The accuracy of the agency's estimate of the information collection burden;
- The quality, utility and clarity of the information to be collected; and
- Recommendations to minimize the information collection burden on the affected public, including automated collection techniques.

As a result, we are soliciting public comment on the information collection requirements being set forth in sections

1001.952(m)(1) (ii), (iii) and (iv) of these regulations.

Under the safe harbor for price reductions offered to health plans, if a health plan is an HMO, competitive medical plan, health care prepayment plan, prepaid health plan or other health plan that has executed a contract or agreement with HCFA or a State health care program to receive payment for enrollees on a reasonable cost or similar basis, the health plan and the contract health care provider must comply with four standards. One of those standards is that the plan must fully and accurately report the amount it has paid the contract health care provider under the agreement for the covered items and services furnished to enrollees on the applicable cost report or other claim form filed with the Department or the State health care program (§ 1001.952(m)(1)(ii)).

Similarly, if a health plan is not described in section 1001.952(m)(1) (i) and (ii) of the regulations, and the contract health care provider is not paid on an at-risk, capitated basis, both the plan and contract provider must, among the six standards set forth, fully and accurately report any cost report filed with Medicare or a State health care program the fee schedule amounts charged in accordance with the agreement (§ 1001.952(m)(1)(iii)).

In addition, under sections 1001.952(m)(1) (iii) and (iv), both the health plan and the provider, upon request, must report to the Medicare or State health care program the terms of the agreement and amounts paid in accordance with the agreement.

We estimate that the current burden associated with the submitting the data would be minimal, i.e., less than one hour per request. Specifically, we anticipate that any data request will not involve the creation of any new documents or the calculation of new figures by entities. Rather, we would be seeking only copies of those agreements that have already been executed by entities and those amounts paid to individual providers that are already maintained for general business and tax purposes. Since most plans maintain such information on electronic data bases and have these contracts on file, we believe such requests can be produced and provided in less than one hour's time. Further, we believe that only a very small number of plans and providers—less than 3 percent of the nation's health care plans and contract providers—would be potentially impacted by this request. Accordingly, we estimate that the total number of requests will be no more than 10 to 12 per year since they will be made only where there is a question of whether a specific plan or provider has violated the statute and claims immunity based on these safe harbor regulations. Based on an estimate of less than one dozen requests per year, the estimated total burden on these entities will be under 20 hours.

This information collection and recordkeeping requirement is not effective until it has been approved by OMB. A notice will be published in the Federal Register when approval is obtained. As indicated in the INFORMATION CONTACT section at the beginning of this preamble, organizations and individuals wishing to submit comments on this information collection and recordkeeping requirement should direct them to the Office of Inspector General, Office of Management and Policy, Room 5550, Cohen Building, Washington, D.C. 20201, Attention: Joel Schaer, Regulations Officer.

C. Department of Justice Review

In accordance with the provisions of Public Law 100–93, these regulations have been developed in consultation with the Department of Justice.

List of Subjects in 42 CFR Part 1001

Administrative practice and procedure, Fraud, Health facilities, Health professions, Medicare.

TITLE 42—PUBLIC HEALTH

CHAPTER V—OFFICE OF INSPECTOR GENERAL—HEALTH CARE, DEPARTMENT OF HEALTH AND HUMAN SERVICES

42 CFR Part 1001 is amended as set forth below:

PART 1001—PROGRAM INTEGRITY—MEDICARE AND STATE HEALTH CARE PROGRAMS

1. The authority citation for part 1001 is revised to read as follows:

Authority: 42 U.S.C. 1302, 1320a–7, 1320a–7b, 1395u(j), 1395u(k), 1395y(e), and 1395hh.

2. Section 1001.952 is amended by republishing the introductory text of both paragraph (k) and (k)(1) and revising paragraphs (k)(1)(iii), (l), and (m) to read as follows:

§ 1001.952 Exceptions.

* * * * *

(k) *Waiver of beneficiary coinsurance and deductible amounts.* As used in section 1128B of the Act, "remuneration" does not include any reduction or waiver of a Medicare or a State health care program beneficiary's obligation to pay coinsurance or deductible amounts as long as all of the standards are met within either of the following two categories of health care providers:

(1) If the coinsurance or deductible amounts are owed to a hospital for inpatient hospital services for which Medicare pays under the prospective payment system, the hospital must comply with all of the following three standards—

* * * * *

(iii) The hospital's offer to reduce or waive the coinsurance or deductible amounts must not be made as part of a price reduction agreement between a hospital and a third-party payer (including a health plan as defined in paragraph (l)(2) of this section), unless the agreement is part of a contract for the furnishing of items or services to a beneficiary of a Medicare supplemental policy issued under the terms of section 1882(t)(1) of the Act.

* * * * *

(l) *Increased coverage, reduced cost-sharing amounts, or reduced premium amounts offered by health plans.* (1) As used in section 1128B of the Act, "remuneration" does not include the additional coverage of any item or service offered by a health plan to an enrollee or the reduction of some or all of the enrollee's obligation to pay the health plan or a contract health care provider for cost-sharing amounts (such as coinsurance, deductible, or copayment amounts) or for premium amounts attributable to items or services covered by the health plan, the Medicare program, or a State health care program, as long as the health plan complies with all of the standards within one of the following two categories of health plans:

(i) If the health plan is a risk-based health maintenance organization, competitive medical plan, prepaid health plan, or other health plan under contract with HCFA or a State health care program and operating in accordance with section 1876(g) or 1903(m) of the Act, under a Federal statutory demonstration authority, or under other Federal statutory or regulatory authority, it must offer the same increased coverage or reduced cost-sharing or premium amounts to all Medicare or State health care program enrollees covered by the contract unless otherwise approved by HCFA or by a State health care program.

(ii) If the health plan is a health maintenance organization, competitive medical plan, health care prepayment plan, prepaid health plan or other health plan that has executed a contract or agreement with HCFA or with a State health care program to receive payment for enrollees on a reasonable cost or similar basis, it must comply with both of the following two standards—

(A) The health plan must offer the same increased coverage or reduced cost-sharing or premium amounts to all Medicare or State health care program enrollees covered by the contract or agreement unless otherwise approved by HCFA or by a State health care program; and

(B) The health plan must not claim the costs of the increased coverage or the reduced cost-sharing or premium amounts as a bad debt for payment purposes under Medicare or a State health care program or otherwise shift the burden of the increased coverage or reduced cost-sharing or premium amounts to the extent that increased payments are claimed from Medicare or a State health care program.

(2) For purposes of paragraph (l) of this section, the terms—

Contract health care provider means an individual or entity under contract with a health plan to furnish items or services to enrollees who are covered by the health plan, Medicare, or a State health care program.

Enrollee means an individual who has entered into a contractual relationship with a health plan (or on whose behalf an employer, or other private or governmental entity has entered into such a relationship) under which the individual is entitled to receive specified health care items and services, or insurance coverage for such items and services, in return for payment of a premium or a fee.

Health plan means an entity that furnishes or arranges under agreement with contract health care providers for the furnishing of items or services to enrollees, or furnishes insurance coverage for the provision of such items and services, in exchange for a premium or a fee, where such entity:

(i) Operates in accordance with a contract, agreement or statutory demonstration authority approved by HCFA or a State health care program;

(ii) Charges a premium and its premium structure is regulated under a State insurance statute or a State enabling statute governing health maintenance organizations or preferred provider organizations;

(iii) Is an employer, if the enrollees of the plan are current or retired employees, or is a union welfare fund, if the enrollees of the plan are union members; or

(iv) Is licensed in the State, is under contract with an employer, union welfare fund, or a company furnishing health insurance coverage as described in conditions (ii) and (iii) of this definition, and is paid a fee for the administration of the plan which reflects the fair market value of those services.

(m) *Price reductions offered to health plans.* (1) As used in section 1128B of the Act, "remuneration" does not include a reduction in price a contract health care provider offers to a health plan in accordance with the terms of a written agreement between the contract health care provider and the health plan for the sole purpose of furnishing to enrollees items or services that are covered by the health plan, Medicare, or a State health care program, as long as both the health plan and contract health care provider comply with all of the applicable standards within one of the following four categories of health plans:

(i) If the health plan is a risk-based health maintenance organization, competitive medical plan, or prepaid health plan under contract with HCFA or a State agency and operating in accordance with section 1876(g) or 1903(m) of the Act, under a Federal statutory demonstration authority, or under other Federal statutory or regulatory authority, the contract health care provider must not claim payment in any form from the Department or the State agency for items or services furnished in accordance with the agreement except as approved by HCFA or the State health care program, or otherwise shift the burden of such an agreement to the extent that increased payments are claimed from Medicare or a State health care program.

(ii) If the health plan is a health maintenance organization, competitive medical plan, health care prepayment plan, prepaid health plan, or other health plan that has executed a contract or agreement with HCFA or a State health care program to receive payment for enrollees on a reasonable cost or similar basis, the health plan and contract health care provider must comply with all of the following four standards—

(A) The term of the agreement between the health plan and the contract health care provider must be for not less than one year;

(B) The agreement between the health plan and the contract health care provider must specify in advance the covered items and services to be furnished to enrollees, and the methodology for computing the payment to the contract health care provider;

(C) The health plan must fully and accurately report, on the applicable cost report or other claim form filed with the Department or the State health care program, the amount it has paid the contract health care provider under the agreement for the covered items and services furnished to enrollees; and

(D) The contract health care provider must not claim payment in any form from the Department or the State health care program for items or services furnished in accordance with the agreement except as approved by HCFA or the State health care program, or otherwise shift the burden of such an agreement to the extent that increased payments are claimed from Medicare or a State health care program.

(iii) If the health plan is not described in paragraphs (m)(1)(i) or (m)(1)(ii) of this section and the contract health care provider is not paid on an at-risk, capitated basis, both the health plan and contract health care provider must comply with all of the following six standards—

(A) The term of the agreement between the health plan and the contract health care provider must be for not less than one year;

(B) The agreement between the health plan and the contract health care provider must specify in advance the covered items and services to be furnished to enrollees, which party is to file claims or requests for payment with Medicare or the State health care program for such items and services, and the schedule of fees the contract health care provider will charge for furnishing such items and services to enrollees;

(C) The fee schedule contained in the agreement between the health plan and the contract health care provider must remain in effect throughout the term of the agreement, unless a fee increase results directly from a payment update authorized by Medicare or the State health care program;

(D) The party submitting claims or requests for payment from Medicare or the State health care program for items and services furnished in accordance with the agreement must not claim or request payment for amounts in excess of the fee schedule;

(E) The contract health care provider and the health plan must fully and accurately report on any cost report filed with Medicare or a State health care program the fee schedule amounts charged in accordance with the agreement and, upon request, will report to the Medicare or a State health care program the terms of the agreement and the amounts paid in accordance with the agreement; and

(F) The party to the agreement, which does not have the responsibility under the agreement for filing claims or requests for payment, must not claim or request payment in any form from the Department or the State health care program for items or services furnished in accordance with the agreement, or otherwise shift the burden of such an agreement to the extent that increased payments are claimed from Medicare or a State health care program.

(iv) If the health plan is not described in paragraphs (m)(1)(i) or (m)(1)(ii) of this section, and the contract health care provider is paid on an at-risk, capitated basis, both the health plan and contract health care provider must comply with all of the following five standards—

(A) The term of the agreement between the health plan and the contract health provider must be for not less than one year;

(B) The agreement between the health plan and the contract health provider must specify in advance the covered items and services to be furnished to enrollees and the total amount per enrollee (which may be expressed in a per month or other time period basis) the contract health care provider will be paid by the health plan for furnishing such items and services to enrollees and must set forth any copayments, if any, to be paid by enrollees to the contract health care provider for covered services;

(C) The payment amount contained in the agreement between the health care plan and the contract health care provider must remain in effect throughout the term of the agreement;

(D) The contract health care provider and the health plan must fully and accurately report to the Medicare and State health care program upon request, the terms of the agreement and the amounts paid in accordance with the agreement; and

(E) The contract health care provider must not claim or request payment in any form from the Department, a State health care program or an enrollee (other than copayment amounts described in paragraph (m)(2)(iv)(B) of this section) and the health plan must not pay the contract care provider in excess of the amounts described in paragraph (m)(2)(iv)(B) of this section for items and services covered by the agreement.

(2) For purposes of this paragraph, the terms *contract health care provider*, *enrollee*, and *health plan* have the same meaning as in paragraph (l)(2) of this section.

Dated: June 21, 1995.
June Gibbs Brown,
Inspector General.

Approved: September 12, 1995.
Donna E. Shalala,
Secretary, Department of Health and Human Services.

[FR Doc. 96–1073 Filed 1–24–96; 8:45 am]

BILLING CODE 4150–04–P

APPENDIX F6

SOLICITATIONS OF NEW SAFE HARBORS AND MODIFICATIONS TO EXISTING SAFE HARBORS

69060 Federal Register / Vol. 61, No. 252 / Tuesday, December 31, 1996 / Proposed Rules

DEPARTMENT OF HEALTH AND HUMAN SERVICES

Office of Inspector General

42 CFR Part 1001

Solicitation of New Safe Harbors and Modifications to Existing Safe Harbors

AGENCY: Office of Inspector General (OIG), HHS.

ACTION: Notice of intent to develop regulations.

SUMMARY: In accordance with section 205 of the Health Insurance Portability and Accountability Act of 1996, this notice solicits proposals and recommendations for developing new and modifying existing safe harbor provisions under the Medicare and State health care programs' anti-kickback statute, as well as developing new OIG Special Fraud Alerts.

DATES: To assure consideration, public comments must be delivered to the address provided below by no later than 5 p.m. on March 3, 1997.

ADDRESSES: Please mail or deliver your written comments to the following

Federal Register / Vol. 61, No. 252 / Tuesday, December 31, 1996 / Proposed Rules 69061

address: Office of Inspector General, Department of Health and Human Services, Attention: OIG–11–N, Room 5246, Cohen Building, 330 Independence Avenue, S.W. Washington, DC 20201.

Because of staffing and resource limitations, we cannot accept comments by facsimile (FAX) transmission. In commencing, please refer to file code OIG–11–N. Comments received timely will be available for public inspection as they are received, generally beginning approximately 3 weeks after publication of a document, in Room 5541 of the Office of Inspector General at 330 Independence Avenue, S.W., Washington, D.C., on Monday through Friday of each week from 8:00 a m. to 4:30 p.m.

FOR FURTHER INFORMATION CONTACT: Joel Schaer, (202) 619–0089, OIG Regulations Officer.

SUPPLEMENTARY INFORMATION:

I. Background

A. The OIG Safe Harbor Provisions

Section 1128B(b) of the Social Security Act (42 U.S.C. 1320a–7b(b)) provides criminal penalties for individuals or entities that knowingly and willfully offer, pay, solicit or relieve remuneration in order to induce business reimbursed under the Medicare or State health care programs. The offense is classified as a felony, and is punishable by fines of up to $25,000 and imprisonment for up to 5 years.

The types of remuneration covered specifically include kickbacks, bribes, and rebates, whether made directly or indirectly, overtly or covertly, or in cash or in kind. In addition, prohibited conduct includes not only remuneration intended to induce referrals of patients, but remuneration intended to induce the purchasing, leasing, ordering, or arranging for any good, facility, service, or item paid for by Medicare or State health care programs.

Since the statute on its face is so broad, concern has been expressed for many years that some relatively innocuous commercial arrangements are technically covered by the statute and are, therefore, subject to criminal prosecution. As a response to the above concern, the Medicare and Medicaid Patient and Program Protection Act of 1987, section 14 of Public Law 100–93, specifically required the development and promulgation of regulations, the so-called "safe harbor" provisions, designed to specify various payment and business practices which, although potentially capable of inducing referrals of business under the Medicare and State health care programs, would not be treated as criminal offenses under the anti-kickback statute (section 1128B(b) of the Social Security Act; 42 U.S.C. 1320a–7b(b)) and would not serve as a basis for a program exclusion under section 1128(b)(7) of the Social Security Act; 42 U.S.C. 1320a–7(b)(7). The OIG safe harbor provisions have been developed "to limit the reach of the statute somewhat by permitting certain non-abusive arrangements, while encouraging beneficial and innocuous arrangements" (56 FR 35952, July 29, 1991). Health care providers and others may voluntarily seek to comply with these provisions so that they have the assurance that their business practices are not subject to any enforcement action under the anti-kickback statute or program exclusion authority.

To date, the OIG has developed and codified in 42 CFR 1001.952 a total of 13 final safe harbors that describe practices that are sheltered from liability, and is continuing to finalize 8 additional safe harbor provisions (see the OIG notice of proposed rulemaking at 58 FR 49008, September 21, 1993).

B. OIG Special Fraud Alerts

In addition, the OIG has also periodically issued Special Fraud Alerts to give continuing guidance to health care providers with respect to practices the OIG regards as unlawful. These Special Fraud Alerts provide the OIG with a means of notifying the health care industry that we have become aware of certain abusive practices which we plan to pursue and prosecute, or bring civil and administrative action, as appropriate. The Special Fraud Alerts also serve as a tool to encourage industry compliance by giving providers an opportunity to examine their own practices. The OIG Special Fraud Alerts are intended for extensive distribution directly to the health care provider community, as well as those charged with administering the Medicare and Medicaid programs.

In developing these Special Fraud Alerts, the OIG has relied on a number of sources and has consulted directly with experts in the subject field, including those within the OIG, other agencies of the Department, other Federal and State agencies, and from those in the health care industry. To date, eight individual Special Fraud Alerts have been issued by the OIG and subsequently reprinted in the **Federal Register** on December 19, 1994 (59 FR 65372), August 10, 1995 (60 FR 40847) and June 17, 1996 (61 FR 30623)

II. Section 205 of Public Law 104–191

The Health Insurance Portability and Accountability Act of 1996, Public Law 104-191, effective August 21, 1996, now requires the Department to provide additional formal guidance regarding the application of the anti-kickback statute and the safe harbor provisions, as well as other OIG health care fraud and abuse sanctions. Among the provisions set forth in section 205 of Public Law 104–191 is the requirement that the Department develop and publish an annual notice in the **Federal Register** formally soliciting proposals for (1) modifying existing safe harbors, (2) developing new safe harbors and OIG Special Fraud Alerts, and (3) issuing requests for advisory opinions. After considering such proposals and recommendations, the Department, in consultation with the Department of Justice, will consider the issuance of new and modified safe harbor regulations, as appropriate. In addition, the OIG will consider the issuance of additional Special Fraud Alerts. Finally, in accordance with the statute, the OIG will formally begin accepting requests for advisory opinions on February 21, 1997. Regulations establishing the procedures and a process for accepting and issuing advisory opinions are being prepared for separate publication in the **Federal Register** and will be issued in the near future.

Criteria for Modifying and Establishing Safe Harbor Provisions

In accordance with the statute, we will consider a number of factors in considering proposals for new or modified safe harbor provisions, such as the extent to which the proposals would affect an increase or decrease in—

- Access to health care services;
- The quality of health care services;
- Patient freedom of choice among health care providers;
- Competition among health care providers;
- The cost to Federal health care programs;
- The potential overutilization of the health care services; and
- The ability of health care facilities to provide services in medically underserved areas or to medically underserved populations.

In addition, we will also take into consideration the existence (or nonexistence) of any potential financial benefit to a health care professional or provider that may vary based on their decisions of whether to (1) order a health care item or service, or (2) arrange for a referral of health care items or services to a particular practitioner or provider.

Criteria for Developing Special Fraud Alerts

In determining whether to issue additional Special Fraud Alerts, we will also consider whether, and to what extent, those practices that would be identified in new Fraud Alerts may result in any of the consequences set forth above, and the volume and frequency of the conduct that would be identified in these Special Fraud Alerts.

III. Solicitation of Public Comments

In order to address the requirements of section 205 of Public Law 104–191, we are requesting public comments from affected provider, practitioner, supplier and beneficiary representatives regarding the development of proposed or modified safe harbor regulations and new Special Fraud Alerts. A detailed explanation of justification or empirical data supporting the suggestion would prove helpful in our considering and drafting new or modified safe harbor regulations and Special Fraud Alerts.

Dated: December 20, 1996.

June Gibbs Brown,

Inspector General, Department of Health and Human Services.

Approved: December 20, 1996.

Donna E. Shalala,

Secretary.

[FR Doc. 96–33277 Filed 12–30–96; 8:45 am]

BILLING CODE 4150-04-M

APPENDIX F7

OIG Notice, Health Care Programs, Fraud and Abuse; Intent to Form the Negotiated Rulemaking Committee for Shared Risk Exception

Federal Register: May 23, 1997 (Volume 62, Number 100)
Proposed Rules
Pages 28410–28413

DEPARTMENT OF HEALTH AND HUMAN SERVICES

Office of Inspector General

42 CFR Part 1001

RIN 0991-AA91

Health Care Programs, Fraud and Abuse; Intent To Form the Negotiated Rulemaking Committee for the Shared Risk Exception

AGENCY: Office of Inspector General (OIG), HHS.

ACTION: Intent to form negotiated rulemaking committee and notice of meetings.

SUMMARY: We have been statutorily-mandated under section 216 of the Health Insurance Portability and Accountability Act (HIPAA) of 1996, to establish a negotiated rulemaking committee in accordance with the Negotiated Rulemaking Act and the Federal Advisory Committee Act (FACA). The committee's purpose would be to negotiate the development of the interim final rule addressing the shared risk exception, in section 216 of HIPAA, to the Federal health care programs' anti-kickback provisions. The committee will consist of representatives of interests that are likely to be significantly affected by the interim rule. The committee will be assisted by an impartial facilitator. We are requesting public comments on whether we have properly identified interests that will be affected by key issues discussed below.

DATES: Comments will be considered if we receive them at the address provided below by no later than 5 p.m. on June 9, 1997.

The meetings will be held at 9:00 a.m. on June 17–18, 1997, and July 28–30, 1997.

ADDRESSES: Please mail or deliver your written comments (1 original and 3 copies) to the following address: Office of Inspector General, Department of Health and Human Services, Attention: OIG-33-NOI, Room 5246, Cohen Building, 330 Independence Avenue, SW., Washington, DC 20201.

Because of staffing and resource limitations, we cannot accept comments by facsimile (FAX) transmission. In commenting, please refer to file code OIG-33-NOI. Comments received timely will be available for public inspections as they are received, generally beginning approximately 2 weeks after publication of a document, in Room 5550 of the Office of Inspector General at 330 Independence Avenue, S.W., Washington, D.C., on Monday through Friday of each week from 8:00 a.m. to 4:30 p.m., (202) 619–0335.

The meetings will be held at the Holiday Inn Capitol, 550 C Street, SW., Washington, DC 20024.

FOR FURTHER INFORMATION CONTACT:

Joel Schaer, (202) 619–0089, OIG Regulations Officer; Judy Ballard, (202) 690–7419, Convener.

SUPPLEMENTARY INFORMATION:

I. Negotiated Rulemaking Act

The Negotiated Rulemaking Act, Public Law 101–648 (5 U.S.C. 561–569), establishes a framework for the conduct of negotiated rulemaking and encourages agencies to use negotiated rulemaking to enhance the informal rulemaking process. Under the Act, the head of an agency must consider whether —

- There is a need for a rule;
- There are a limited number of identifiable interests that will be significantly affected by the rule;
- There is a reasonable likelihood that a committee can be convened with a balanced representation of person who (1) Can adequately represent the interests identified, and (2) are willing to negotiate in good faith to reach a consensus on the rulemaking;

- There is reasonable likelihood that a committee will reach a consensus on the rulemaking within a fixed period of time;
- The negotiated rulemaking process will not unreasonably delay the development and issuance of a final rule;
- The agency has adequate resources and is willing to commit such resources, including technical assistance, to the committee; and
- The agency, to the maximum extent possible consistent with the legal obligations of the agency, will use the consensus of the committee with respect to developing the rule proposed by the agency for notice and comment.

Negotiations are conducted by a committee chartered under the FACA (5 U.S.C. App. 2). The committee includes an agency representative and is assisted by an impartial facilitator. The goal of the committee is to reach consensus on the language or issues involved in a rule. If consensus is reached, it is used as the basis of the interim final rule. The process does not affect otherwise procedural requirements of the FACA, the Administrative Procedure Act and other statutes.

II. Subject and Scope of the Rule

A. Need for the Rule

Section 216 of HIPAA (Public Law 104–191) mandates a negotiated rulemaking process for establishing standards for a statutory exception to the anti-kickback statute.

B. Subject and Scope of the Rule

The Federal health care programs' anti-kickback statute, set forth in section 1128B(b) of the Social Security Act (the Act), provides criminal penalties for individuals or entities that knowingly and willfully offer, pay, solicit or receive bribes, kickbacks or other remuneration in order to induce business reimbursed by Medicare or other Federal health care programs. In addition, for violations of section 1128B(b), the Department has the authority to exclude a person or entity from participation in the Medicare or State health care programs, in accordance with section 1128(b)(7) of the Act.

Because the statutory language of the anti-kickback statute is quite broad, there was concern that many innocuous or even beneficial arrangements would be covered by the statute. As a result, section 14 of Public Law 100–93, the Medicare and Medicaid Patient and Program Protection Act of 1987, authorized the promulgation of regulations specifying payment practices that shall not be treated as a criminal offense under section 1128B(b) of the Social Security Act and shall not serve as the basis for an exclusion under section 1128(b)(7) of such Act." These have come to be known as the ̀safe harbor" regulations. To date, we have promulgated two final rules that have established 13 specific areas for ̀safe harbor" protection under the anti-kickback statute (July 21, 1991 (56 FR 35952) and January 25, 1996 (61 FR 2122)).

Section 216 of HIPAA specifically amends section 128B(b)(3)(F) of the Act to include a new statutory exception for risk-sharing arrangements. The provision establishes a new statutory exception from liability under the anti-kickback statute for remuneration between an eligible organization under section 1876 of the Act and an individual or entity providing items or services, or any combination thereof, in accordance with a written agreement between these parties. The provision also allows remuneration between an organization and an individual or entity if a written agreement places the individual or entity at ̀substantial financial risk" for the cost or utilization of the items or services provided. Section 216 requires the Department, in consultation with the Department of Justice, to engage in a negotiated rulemaking process to establish standards related to this exception for risk-sharing arrangements. The factors to be considered are (1) The level of risk appropriate to the size and type of arrangement; (2) the frequency of assessment and distribution of incentives; (3) the level of capital contribution; and (4) the extent to which the risk-sharing arrangement provides incentives to control the cost and quality of health care services.

C. Issues and Questions To Be Resolved

We anticipate some discussions about the basic approach to the rule, including what policy issues are properly considered in determining whether arrangements should be excepted from the anti-kickback provisions, whether flexibility or certainty in the rule is more important, and whether the definitions of terms used in the exception must be consistent with use of those terms in other contexts. In addition, we anticipate discussion on a limited number of specific issues.

Specific Issues for Discussion

The negotiated rulemaking will address the following specific issues.

How is the term ̀written agreement" to be defined?

We expect discussion on whether the agreement should be of minimum duration, what the agreement should contain and whether unwritten side agreements should be prohibited.

What does the term èligible organization under section 1876 of the Social Security Act" mean?

We expect discussion on whether this phrase is limited to Medicare risk contractors (and to arrangements for services provided under Medicare contracts) or has a broader meaning. In addition, we expect discussions on whether the first part of the exception applies to remuneration only if it is in accordance with an agreement where an èligible organization" is a party, or also if in accordance with lower level" agreements, such as one between a physician and a physician group practice that has an agreement with a health maintenance organization. There may also be some discussion of the term òrganization" as used in the second part of the exception.

What is an ìndividual or entity providing items or services or a combination thereof"?

We expect discussion on whether this includes entities such as drug companies or device manufacturers providing combinations of items and services, and when this constitutes bundling" that would be harmful to the Federal health care programs without further protections. We also expect to address whether the services must be health care services or could be other services, such as marketing services.

What constitutes substantial financial risk for the cost of utilization of items or service"?

The legislative history of the exception lists certain factors (such as the level of capital contribution) to be taken into account in determining whether the risk is substantial. We expect discussion on how these factors should be taken into account, what constitutes risk (for example, should bonuses and withholds be treated the same), and whether special treatment should be given to encourage providers to assume risk where they do not ordinarily do so or where risk is difficult to measure. In addition, we anticipate discussion about how to take into account the total risk-sharing arrangement between the parties.

Issues Outside the Scope of the Rule

With regard to parameters outside the scope of the rule, the OIG does not plan to negotiate the following issues —

- Whether any existing regulatory exceptions to the anti-kickback provisions (safe harbors) should be amended, or proposed safe harbors enacted;
- Whether any other new safe harbors should be enacted; or

- How the OIG should implement a requirement that it issue advisory opinions.

In addition, the OIG will not agree to adopt any practices or concepts that do not contain adequate controls on potential abuse or manipulation.

We invite public comment on issues not identified.

III. Affected Interests and Potential Participants

The convener has proposed, and we have agreed to accept, the following organizations as negotiation participants. We believe these organizations represent an appropriate mix of interests and backgrounds affected.

American Association of Health Plans
American Association of Retired Persons
American Health Care Association
American Hospital Association
American Medical Association
American Medical Group Association
Blue Cross Blue Shield Association
Consumer Coalition on Quality in Health Care
Coordinated Care Coalition
Department of Justice
Federation of American Health Systems
Health Industry Manufacturers Association
Heath Insurance Association of America
National Association of Community Health Centers
Independent Insurance Agents of America/National Association of Health Underwriters
National Association of Medicaid Fraud Control Units
National Association of State Medicaid Directors
Nation Rural Health Association
Pharmaceutical Research and Manufacturers Association
The IPA Association of America

The interests identified included law enforcement agencies, health programs, health plans, provider organizations, health care professionals and consumers. In determining whether the potential effect of the rule on provider and professional groups which sought to participate is significant," we considered the extent to which —

- Items or services provided by group members are covered by the relevant programs;
- Group members are entering into risk-sharing arrangements;

- The anti-kickback provisions have been applied to prosecute or prohibit arrangements which group members have used or considered using (either where one party is an èligible organization" or where risk-sharing may be involved); and
- The group actively lobbied for the exception or commented on related provisions. We also sought to reflect differences in the type of risk that might be assumed and in the ways individuals or entities organize to provide items or services.

The intent in establishing the negotiating committee is that all interests are represented, not necessarily all parties. We believe this proposed list of participants represents all interests associated with the rule to be negotiated. We invite comment on this list of negotiation participants.

IV. Schedule for the Negotiation

We have set a deadline of 6 months beginning with the date of the first meeting for the committee to complete work on developing the interim final rule. We intend to terminate the activities of the committee if it does not appear likely to reach consensus within this time period.

The first meeting is schedule for June 17–18, 1997 at the Holiday Inn Capitol, 550 C Street, S.W., Washington, D.C. 20024. The first day's meeting will begin at 9:00 a.m. The purpose of this meeting will be discuss in detail how the negotiations will proceed and how the committee will function. The committee will —

- Agree to ground rules for committee operation;
- Hear presentations on the anti-kickback statute and related provisions, as well as what risk-sharing arrangements are being developed;
- Determine how best to address the principal issues; and
- If time permits, begin to address those issues.

A second meeting is scheduled for July 28–30, 1997 at the Holiday Inn Capitol, 550 C Street, S.W., Washington, D.C. 20024, beginning at 9:00 a.m. We expect that by this meeting the committee can complete action on any procedural matters outstanding from the organizational meeting, and either begin or continue to address the issues.

Subsequent meetings of the committee would be held approximately one month apart, in the Washington, D.C. area.

V. Formation of the Negotiating Committee

A. Procedure for Establishing an Advisory Committee

As a general rule, an agency of the Federal Government is required to comply with the requirements of FACA when it establishes or uses a group that includes nonfederal members as a source of advice. Under FACA, an advisory committee is established once the charter has been approved by the Secretary. We will not begin negotiations until the charter is approved.

B. Participants

The number of participants in the group should not exceed 25. A number larger than this could make it difficult to conduct effective negotations. One purpose of this notice to help determine whether the interim final rule would significantly affect interests not adequately represented by the proposed participants. We do not believe that each potentially affected organization or individual must necessarily have its own representative. However, each interest must be adequately represented. Moreover, we must be satisfied that the group as a whole reflects a proper balance and mix of interests.

C. Requests for Representation

If, in response to this notice, an additional individual or representative of an interest requests membership or representation in the negotiating group, we will determine, in consultation with the convener, whether that individual or representative should be added to the group. We will make that decision based on whether the individual or interest —

- Would be significantly affected by the rule; and
- Is already adequately represented in the negotiating group.

D. Establishing the Committee

After reviewing any comments on this notice and any requests for representation, we will take the final steps to form the committee.

VI. Negotiation Procedures

When the committee is formed, the following procedures and guidelines will apply, unless they are modified as a result of comments received on this notice or during the negotiating process.

A. Facilitator

We will use an impartial facilitator. The facilitator will not be involved with the substantive development or enforcement of the regulation. The facilitator's role is to —

- Chair negotiating sessions;
- Help the negotiation process run smoothly; and
- Help participants define and reach consensus.

B. Good Faith Negotiations

Participants must be willing to negotiate in good faith and be authorized to do so. We believe this must be accomplished by selection of senior officials as participants. We believe senior officials are best suited to represent the interests and viewpoint of their organizations. This applies to the OIG as well, and we are designating

D. McCarty Thornton, Chief Counsel to the Inspector General, to represent the OIG.

C. Administrative Support

We will supply logistical, administrative and management support. If deemed necessary and appropriate, we will provide technical support to the committee in gathering and analyzing additional data or information.

D. Meetings

Meetings will be held at the Holiday Inn Capitol, 550 C Street, S.W., Washington, D.C. 20024 at the convenience of the committee. We are announcing the first two meetings through this notice, and will announce committee meetings and agendas through further notices in the **Federal Register**. Unless announced otherwise, meetings are open to the public.

E. Committee Procedures

Under the general guidance and direction of the facilitator, and subject to any applicable legal requirements, the members will establish the detailed procedures for committee meetings that they consider most appropriate.

F. Defining Consensus

The goal of the negotiating process is consensus. Under the Negotiated Rulemaking Act, consensus means that each interest concurs in the result, unless the term is defined otherwise by the committee. We expect the participants to fashion their working definition of this term.

G. Failure of Advisory Committee To Reach Consensus

If the committee is unable to reach consensus, the OIG will proceed to develop an interim final rule. Parties to the negotiation may withdraw at any time. If this happens, the remaining committee members and the OIG will evaluate whether the committee should continue.

H. Record of Meetings

In accordance with FACA's requirements, minutes of all committee meetings will be kept. The minutes will be placed in the public rulemaking record.

I. Other Information

In accordance with the provisions of Executive Order 12866, this notice was reviewed by the Office of Management and Budget.

Dated: April 11, 1997.

June Gibbs Brown,

Inspector General.

Approved: May 19, 1997.

Donna E. Shalala,

Secretary.

[FR Doc. 97–13718 Filed 5–21–97; 10:02 am]

BILLING CODE 4150–04-M

APPENDIX F8

Clarification of the Initial OIG Safe Harbor Provisions and Establishment of Additional Safe Harbor Provisions Under the Anti-Kickback Statute; Final Rule

Federal Register: November 19, 1999 (Volume 64, Number 223)
Rules and Regulations
Part V

DEPARTMENT OF HEALTH AND HUMAN SERVICES

Office of Inspector General

42 CFR Part 1001

Medicare and State Health Care Programs: Fraud and Abuse; Clarification of the Initial OIG Safe Harbor Provisions and Establishment of Additional Safe Harbor Provisions Under the Anti-Kickback Statute

DEPARTMENT OF HEALTH AND HUMAN SERVICES
Office of Inspector General
42 CFR Part 1001
RIN 0991-AA66 (Also incorporating RIN 0991-AA74)
AGENCY: Office of Inspector General (OIG), HHS.
ACTION: Final rule.

SUMMARY: This final rule serves both to add new safe harbor provisions under the Federal and State health care programs' anti-kickback statute, as authorized under section 14 of Public Law 100–93, the Medicare and Medicaid Patient and Program Protection Act of 1987, and to clarify various aspects of the original safe harbor provisions now codified in 42 CFR part 1001 (originally proposed in RIN 0991-AA74). Specifically, this final rule modifies the original set of final safe harbor provisions codified in 42 CFR 1001.952 to give greater clarity to that rulemaking's original intent. In addition, this final rule sets forth an expanded set of safe harbor provisions designed to protect additional payment and business practices from criminal prosecution or civil sanctions under the anti-kickback provisions of the statute.

EFFECTIVE DATE: This rulemaking is effective November 19, 1999.

FOR FURTHER INFORMATION CONTACT:

Vicki L. Robinson, Office of Counsel to the Inspector General (202) 619–0335Joel Schaer, Office of Counsel to the Inspector General (202) 619–1306

SUPPLEMENTARY INFORMATION:

I. Background

Section 1128B(b) of the Social Security Act (the "Act") (42 U.S.C. 1320a-7b(b)) provides criminal penalties for individuals or entities that knowingly and willfully offer, pay, solicit or receive remuneration in order to induce business reimbursable under the Federal or State health care programs. The offense is classified as a felony and is punishable by fines of up to $25,000 and imprisonment for up to 5 years. Violations of the anti-kickback statute may also result in the imposition of a civil money penalty (CMP) under section 1128A(a)(7) of the Act (42 U.S.C. 1320a-7a(a)(7)) or program exclusion under section 1128 of the Act (42 U.S.C. 1320a-7).

The types of remuneration covered specifically include kickbacks, bribes, and rebates, whether made directly or indirectly, overtly or covertly, in cash or in kind. In addition, prohibited conduct includes not only remuneration intended to induce referrals of patients, but remuneration intended to induce the purchasing, leasing or ordering, or arranging of any good, facility, service, or item paid for by Federal or State health care programs.

Establishing the Original Safe Harbors

Since the statute on its face is so broad, concern had been expressed that some relatively innocuous commercial arrangements were technically covered by the statute and therefore were subject to criminal prosecution. As a response to the above concern, the Medicare and Medicaid Patient and Program Protection Act (MMPPPA) of 1987, section 14 of Public Law 100–93, specifically required the development and promulgation of regulations, the so-called "safe harbor" provisions, designed to specify various payment and business practices which, although potentially capable of inducing referrals of business under the Federal and State health care programs, would not be treated as criminal offenses under the anti-kickback statute. The OIG safe harbor provisions have been developed "to limit the reach of the statute somewhat by permitting certain non-abusive arrangements, while encouraging beneficial and innocuous arrangements."[1] Health care providers and others may voluntarily seek to comply with these provisions so that they have the assurance that their business practices are not subject to any enforcement action under the anti-kickback statute, the CMP provision for anti-kickback violations, or the program exclusion authority related to kickbacks.

On July 29, 1991, we published in the Federal Register the 1991 final rule (56 FR 35952) setting forth various safe harbor provisions to the Medicare and Medicaid anti-kickback statute. The rulemaking was authorized under section 14 of Public Law 100–93, MMPPPA of 1987, and specified certain payment practices that will not be subject to criminal prosecution under section 1128B(b) of the Social Security Act (42 U.S.C. 1320a-7b(b)), and that will not provide a basis for exclusion from Medicare or the State health care programs under section 1128(b)(7) of the Act (42 U.S.C. 1320a-7(b)(7)). The initial final rulemaking established "safe harbors' ' in ten broad areas: investment interests, space rental, equipment rental, personal services and management contracts, sales of practices, referral services, warranties, discounts, employees, and group purchasing organizations. However, in giving the Department the authority to protect certain arrangements and payment practices under the anti-kickback statute, Congress intended the regulations to be evolving rules that would be updated periodically to reflect changing business practices and technologies in the health care industry.

Establishing Additional Safe Harbors

The public comments in response to the original proposed rule establishing the safe harbor provisions contained suggestions for the consideration and adoption of additional safe harbor provisions under 42 CFR 1001.952. As a result of those comments, on September 21, 1993, the OIG published a proposed rule (58 FR 49008) (the "1993 proposed rule") formally requesting public comments on seven new areas of safe harbor protection under the anti-kickback statute, as well as proposed modifications to the existing safe harbor for sales of practices. The proposals for new safe harbors addressed investment interests in rural areas; ambulatory surgical centers; group

[1] 56 FR 35952; July 21, 1991.

practices; practitioner recruitment; obstetrical malpractice insurance subsidies; referral agreements for specialty services; and cooperative hospital service organizations described in section 501 (e) of the Internal Revenue Code.

Clarifying the Original Safe Harbor Provisions

After publication of the 1991 final rule, the OIG became aware of a limited number of issues that had created uncertainties for health care providers trying to comply with the original safe harbor provisions, and of certain instances where our intent, either to protect or preclude protection for particular business arrangements, was not fully reflected in the text of the regulation, even though it was reflected in the preamble. As a result, the OIG developed and published a new notice of proposed rulemaking on July 21, 1994 (59 FR 37202) (the "1994 proposed clarifications") intended to modify the text of 1991 final rule to conform to the rulemaking's original intent. The clarifications contained in the proposed rule did not represent an attempt to reevaluate the basic judgments that led to the original safe harbors, but rather were designed to protect business practices originally intended to be protected by making the regulatory language more precise.

Annual Solicitations for Suggestions for Modified and New Safe Harbors

In accordance with section 205 of the Health Insurance Portability and Accountability Act (HIPAA) of 1996 (Pub. L. 104–191), the Department is now required to develop and publish an annual notice in the Federal Register formally soliciting proposals for modifying existing safe harbors and promulgating new safe harbors and OIG special fraud alerts. The Department will review the proposals and, in consultation with the Department of Justice (DoJ), consider issuing new or modified safe harbor regulations, where appropriate. On December 31, 1996, we published the first of these notices in the Federal Register (61 FR 69060), soliciting public comment regarding "the development of proposed or modified safe harbor regulations," including the pending proposals for new and modified safe harbors (61 FR 69062). We published additional annual notices on December 10, 1997 (62 FR 65050) and December 10, 1998 (63 FR 68223). (These notices are referred to in this preamble collectively as the "annual solicitations.") Respondents to the annual solicitations suggested a number of areas for new or modified safe harbor protection; additionally, a number of respondents commented on the 1993 proposed rule and the 1994 proposed clarifications. This rulemaking is based on the comments received in response to the 1993 proposed rule, the 1994 proposed clarifications, and the annual solicitations insofar as the latter addressed the new and modified safe harbor proposals contained in the 1993 proposed rule and the 1994 proposed clarifications. Other suggestions for new and modified safe harbors are under review and will be the subject of annual reports to Congress made as part of the Inspector General's year-end semiannual report, as required by HIPAA.

Shared-Risk Exception

Section 216 of HIPAA created an exception to the anti-kickback statute for certain risk-sharing arrangements and directed the Department to use a negotiated rulemaking process to establish companion regulations. Specifically, section 216 of HIPAA created an exception for certain managed care arrangements, involving remuneration (i) between eligible organizations under section 1876 of the Social Security Act (certain health maintenance organizations and competitive medical plans) and individuals or entities providing items or services and (ii) between any organization and an individual or entity that has a risk-sharing arrangement, if a written agreement places the individual or entity at "substantial financial risk" for the cost or utilization of the items or services provided.

On January 22, 1998, the negotiated rulemaking committee comprised of 21 industry representatives, a representative from the DoJ, and an OIG representative representing the Department, reached consensus on a final proposal for two new safe harbors.[2] Issues raised in comments to the 1993 proposed rule and the 1994 proposed clarifications that pertain to matters covered by the two shared-risk exception safe harbors are not considered in this final rulemaking.

II. Summary of Proposed Rules, Response to Public Comments and Summary of Revisions

In response to the 1993 proposed rule and the 1994 proposed clarifications, we received a total of 313 timely-filed public comments on the additional safe harbors proposed rule and 28 timely-filed public comments on the safe harbor clarifications proposed rule from various provider groups, medical facilities, professional and business organizations and associations, medical societies, State and local government entities, private practitioners, and concerned citizens. We received 32 comments in response to the annual

[2] The OIG's interim final rule addressing the safe harbors for shared-risk arrangements is published in today's edition of the Federal Register.

solicitations that were relevant to the issues addressed in this rulemaking. A summary of the comments and our responses to those comments follow.

A. General Comments

1. Conformity With Stark Law

Comment: Several commenters urged the OIG to conform existing and proposed safe harbors to the statutory exceptions to section 1877 of the Act, otherwise known as the "Stark Law." These commenters believe that payment arrangements permitted under the Stark Law should be protected under the anti-kickback statute. They argue that it is confusing for the industry to be subject to two separate bodies of fraud and abuse law applicable to arrangements involving physician self-referrals. At minimum, these commenters urge that the safe harbors be made consistent with the Stark exceptions with respect to physician compliance with the anti-kickback statute.

Response: The Stark Law is a civil statute that generally (i) prohibits physicians from making referrals for clinical laboratory or other designated health services to entities in which the physicians have ownership or other financial interests and (ii) prohibits entities from presenting or causing to be presented claims or bills to any individual, third party payor, or other entity for designated health services furnished pursuant to a prohibited referral. (42 U.S.C. 1395nn(a)(1)). The anti-kickback statute, on the other hand, is a criminal statute that prohibits the knowing and willful offer, payment, solicitation, or receipt of remuneration to induce Federal health care program business. Both laws are directed at the problem of inappropriate financial incentives influencing medical decision-making. This similarity notwithstanding, the statutes are different in scope and structural approach. Under the Stark Law, physicians may not refer patients for certain designated health services to entities from which the physicians receive financial benefits, except as allowed in enumerated exceptions. A transaction must fall entirely within an exception to be lawful under the Stark Law. The anti-kickback statute, on the other hand, establishes an intent-based criminal prohibition with optional statutory and regulatory "safe harbors" that do not purport to define the full range of lawful activity. Rather, safe harbors provide a means of assuring that payment practices are not illegal. Payment practices that do not fully comply with a safe harbor may still be lawful if no purpose of the payment practice is to induce referrals of Federal health care program business. Because the two statutory schemes are fundamentally different, the conference report for the Stark Law included language clarifying that "any prohibition, exemption, or exception authorized under this provision in no way alters (or reflects on) the scope and application of the anti-kickback provisions in section 1128B of the Social Security Act" (H.R. Conf. Rep. 239, 101st Cong., 1st sess. 856 (1989)).

We are mindful that it may sometimes be burdensome for parties to review their arrangements under two separate statutory schemes. However, it would be inappropriate to adjust our safe harbor provisions in a manner that would prejudice enforcement of the anti-kickback statute merely to conform the safe harbors to an exception or prohibition under section 1877 of the Act. This is particularly the case in view of the clear legislative intent to keepenforcement under the anti-kickback statute separate from enforcement under section 1877 of the Act. Moreover, variation between the Stark Law exceptions and anti-kickback safe harbors is reasonable in light of the schematic differences between the two statutes. To the extent the anti-kickback statute and the Stark Law address the same conduct, the Stark Law acts as a structural bar to arrangements that contain a per se conflict of interest. However, even if an arrangement passes muster under the Stark Law, it may still constitute a violation of the anti-kickback statute, if the requisite intent to induce referrals is present.

2. Integrated Delivery Systems and Managed Care

Comment: Several commenters urged the OIG to modify existing safe harbors and develop new safe harbors to protect and encourage the development of integrated health care delivery systems and managed care arrangements. For example, several commenters urged the OIG to provide specific safe harbor protection for payments between wholly-owned entities, including parent entities and their wholly-owned subsidiaries. Some commenters questioned whether the anti-kickback statute is an appropriate method of regulating business arrangements in the health care industry, particularly in the context of managed care.

Response: The anti-kickback statute is very broad and potentially covers many managed care arrangements that are common in the marketplace today. However, we have recognized that many of these arrangements do not create the potential for fraud or abuse under the anti-kickback statute and have created safe harbors aimed at those managed care arrangements. Currently, for example, a safe harbor protects certain price reductions offered to health plans (Sec.

1001.952(m)). In addition, Congress enacted in HIPAA a statutory shared-risk exception for certain managed care plans and arrangements that put individuals or entities at substantial financial risk.[3]

With respect to integrated delivery systems and payments between wholly-owned entities, we have stated previously that the anti-kickback statute is not implicated when payments are transferred within a single corporate entity, for example, from one division to another, and therefore no explicit safe harbor is needed for such payments (56 FR 35983). We recognize that there are many lawful integrated delivery system arrangements and arrangements between wholly-owned entities in the marketplace today and that many of these arrangements may be beneficial to the Federal health care programs and their beneficiaries. We are concerned, however, that integrated delivery systems, including arrangements involving wholly-owned subsidiaries, may present opportunities for the payment of improper financial incentives that result in overutilization of services and increased program costs and that may adversely affect quality of care and patient freedom of choice among providers. This is primarily of concern where payment by the Federal health care programs is on a fee-for-service basis, as may occur, for example, with a hospital's referrals to a wholly-owned home health care agency (see, for example, Medicare Hospital Discharge Planning, OEI-02–94–00320 (December 1997)). Accordingly, we do not anticipate providing safe harbor protection for integrated delivery systems and arrangements between wholly-owned entities at this time. The advisory opinion process (42 CFR part 1008) is available for parties wishing to obtain OIG review of their particular integrated delivery or wholly-owned arrangements.

3. Additional Safe Harbors

Comment: Several commenters urged the OIG to demonstrate renewed commitment to issuing clarifying interpretations of the anti-kickback statute in a regular and timely manner.

Response: The OIG recognizes the need to work closely with the industry to combat fraud and abuse in the Federal health care programs through meaningful industry guidance consistent with our law enforcement obligations. As part of HIPAA, the OIG received substantial additional funding for its fraud-fighting efforts. A portion of that funding has been used for a number of industry guidance purposes, including the creation of an Industry Guidance Branch in

[3] See footnote 2.

the Office of Counsel to the Inspector General, which is tasked with issuing advisory opinions and promulgating safe harbor regulations and special fraud alerts. As part of our mandate under HIPAA, we have canvassed the industry through annual notices in the Federal Register soliciting public suggestions for new and modified safe harbors and special fraud alerts. The suggestions received in response to those notices, as well as other suggestions received from the industry or generated internally, are under review, and we anticipate further rulemaking periodically in connection with some of these safe harbor suggestions. We have reported to Congress on the status of the suggestions in the OIG semiannual report to be issued shortly. In addition, the ongoing issuance of advisory opinions, model compliance guidance, special fraud alerts and special advisory bulletins is providing the industry with meaningful guidance on the scope and application of the anti-kickback statute in a regular and timely manner.

4. Transition Period

Comment: Several commenters urged the OIG to afford providers who entered into arrangements with a good faith belief that the arrangements did not violate the anti-kickback statute a reasonable grace period to restructure existing arrangements to conform to the final safe harbors contained in these regulations. In particular, several commenters expressed concern that the 1994 clarifications would be interpreted to be retroactive to the date of the original safe harbors, with no provision for "grandfathering" arrangements that providers believed in good faith complied with the safe harbors as set forth in the 1991 final rule. For example, these commenters note that it was not clear that only "health care" assets could be counted for purposes of qualifying for the large entity investment safe harbor (Sec. 1001.952(a)(i)). Specifically, one commenter proposed implementation of a one year grace period.

Response: We recognize that many providers have in good faith attempted to structure lawful arrangements under the anti-kickback statute that may not fit squarely within these final safe harbor rules. In this regard, we repeat our response to similar comments in our preamble to the 1991 final rule. There we stated:

The failure of a particular business arrangement to comply with these provisions does not determine whether or not the arrangement violates the statute because * * * this regulation does not make conduct illegal. Any conduct that could be construed to be illegal after the promulgation of this rule would have been illegal at any time since the current law was enacted in 1977. Thus illegal arrangements entered into in the past were undertaken with a risk of prosecution. This regulation is intended to provide a formula for avoiding risk in the future.

We also recognize, however, that many health care providers have structured their business arrangements based on the advice of an attorney and in good-faith belief that the arrangement was legal. In the event that they now find that the arrangement does not comply fully with a particular safe harbor provision and are working with diligence and good faith to restructure it so that it does comply, we will use our discretion to be fair to the parties to such arrangements. (56 FR 35955).

These same principles apply with respect to arrangements structured in good faith in accordance with the 1991 final rule. Thus, to the extent that parties reasonably believed that they complied with a safe harbor based on the 1991 final rule and work with diligence and good faith to restructure their arrangements so that they comply with the safe harbor as clarified in this final rule, we will exercise our discretion to be fair to the parties. We are not setting a specific "grace period," as we believe that the reasonable time period for restructuring an arrangement will vary depending on the type and complexity of the arrangement.5. Meaning of Safe Harbors

Comment: Several commenters asked the OIG to clarify that the failure to meet the conditions of a safe harbor does not mean that an arrangement is suspect under the anti-kickback statute. One commenter expressed concern that members of the public view arrangements that do not comply with a safe harbor as suspect arrangements.

Response: The issue of the scope and effect of the safe harbors is important and often misunderstood. We addressed this issue in our preamble to the 1991 final rule:

This (safe harbor) regulation does not expand the scope of activities that the statute prohibits. The statute itself describes the scope of illegal activities. The legality of a particular business arrangement must be determined by comparing the particular facts to the proscriptions of the statute.

The failure to comply with a safe harbor can mean one of three things. First * * * it may mean that the arrangement does not fall within the ambit of the statute. In other words, the arrangement is not intended to induce the referral of business reimbursable under (a

Federal health care program); so there is no reason to comply with the safe harbor standards, and no risk of prosecution.

Second, at the other end of the spectrum, the arrangement could be a clear statutory violation and also not qualify for safe harbor protection. In that case, assuming the arrangement is obviously abusive, prosecution would be very likely.

Third, the arrangement may violate the statute in a less serious manner, although not be in compliance with a safe harbor provision. Here there is no way to predict the degree of risk. Rather, the degree of risk depends on an evaluation of the many factors which are part of the decision-making process regarding case selection for investigation and prosecution. Certainly, in many (but not necessarily all) instances, prosecutorial discretion would be exercised not to pursue cases where the participants appear to have acted in a genuine good-faith attempt to comply with the terms of a safe harbor, but for reasons beyond their control are not in compliance with the terms of the safe harbor. In other instances, there may not even be an applicable safe harbor, but the arrangement may appear innocuous. But in other instances, we will want to take appropriate action. (56 FR 35954)

Thus, it is not true that every arrangement that does not comply with a safe harbor is suspect under the anti-kickback statute, though such arrangements may be suspect in particular circumstances. Parties seeking guidance about their specific arrangements may request an OIG advisory opinion in accordance with the regulations set forth at 42 CFR part 1008.

B. 1994 Clarifications to Existing Safe Harbors

In general, the 1994 proposed clarifications were designed to clarify various aspects of the original safe harbor provisions. Set forth below are a summary of the proposed clarifications for each safe harbor provision, a summary of the final clarifications adopted in this rulemaking, summaries of the public comments received, and our responses to those comments.1. Investment Interests

Summary of Proposed Clarifications: We proposed five clarifications to the investment interests safe harbor, as follows

- First, we proposed that only assets or revenues related to the furnishing of health care items or services will be counted for purposes of qualifying for either the $50,000,000 asset threshold for "large entities" (Sec. 1001.952(a)(1)) or the 60–40 gross revenue test for "small entities" (Sec. 1001.952(a)(2)(vi)). The purpose of this modification is to make clear our original intent that only assets and revenues derived from health care lines of business will be considered for purposes of qualifying for safe harbor protection.

- Second, we proposed revising the standards that prohibit an entity from loaning funds to an investor to be used to purchase the investor's investment interest in the entity. (Secs. 1001.952 (a)(1)(iv) and 952(a)(2)(vii)). The revised standard would make clear that the prohibition also includes any such loan from another investor or a person acting on behalf of the entity or any investor.
- Third, we proposed modifying the first investment interest standard to the small entity investment safe harbor (the 60–40 investor test) to allow an alternative to the existing requirement of class-by-class analysis. Under the current rule, "each class of investments" must meet the 60–40 investor test. Upon review, we found this class-by-class analysis unnecessarily restrictive. Accordingly, the proposed alternative would allow equivalent classes of equity investment interests to be combined together or equivalent classes of debt investment interests to be combined together (separate from the equity investments) in order to apportion investors into "untainted" and "tainted" pools for purposes of meeting the 60–40 investor test.
- Fourth, we proposed striking the language "items or services furnished" from the 60–40 revenue rule (Sec. 1001.952(a)(2)(vi)) in the small entity investment safe harbor to make clear that we did not intend for revenues that the joint venture derives from items or services furnished by an investor to the joint venture (such as management services) to be considered tainted for purposes of satisfying the 60–40 revenue test.
- Fifth, we proposed a clarification in the preamble to the 1994 proposed clarification to the effect that an interested investor must obtain his or her investment interest in the same way as members of the public (i.e., directly off a registered national securities exchange through a broker) and the investment interest must be the same type of investment interest that is available to the public. In this regard, we stated that there cannot be any side agreements that require stock to be purchased or that restrict in any manner an investor's ability to dispose of the stock. We proposed no change in the language of the existing safe harbor, which states that the investment

interest of an interested investor "must be obtained on terms equally available to the public thorough trading on a registered national securities exchange * * * or on the National Association of Securities Dealers Automated Quotation Service" (Sec. 1001.952(a)(1)(ii)).

Summary of the Final Rule: We are adopting the clarifications to the large and small entity investment safe harbors as proposed in the 1994 proposed clarifications and described above, with the following modifications in response to comments received (unless otherwise noted):

- We have added language to Sec. 1001.952(a)(2)(vii) clarifying that, for purposes of the small entity investment safe harbor, loans to an investor may not be made by individuals or entities acting on behalf of the investment entity or any of its investors. This language is the same as language proposed to be added to Sec. 1001.952(a)(1)(iv) in the large entity investment safe harbor in the 1994 proposed clarifications and was described as applying to the small entity investment safe harbor in the preamble to the 1994 proposed clarifications. It was inadvertently omitted from the regulatory language published in the notice of proposed rulemaking.
- We have revisited the meaning of "on terms equally available" in the second standard of the large entity investment safe harbor and have concluded that an investment interest is obtained on equally available terms if it is obtained at the same price as is available to the general public trading on a registered securities exchange through a broker and is not subject to restrictions on transferability.

Comments and Responses

a. Large Entity Investments

Comment: In response to our clarification that only assets or revenues "related to the furnishing of health care items or services'' will be counted for purposes of qualifying for either the $50,000,000 asset threshold for "large entities" or the 60–40 gross revenue test for "small entities," several commenters sought guidance regarding what constitutes "health care items or services." For example, some commenters wondered whether a managed care organization would be considered a health care business if it does not furnish health care services. Some commenters objected to the proposal, arguing that requiring items and services to be health care related would actually increase the incentives for improper referrals. They reason, for example, that a large entity entirely composed of health-care related businesses would be more susceptible to the lure of paying kickbacks for referrals than a diversified entity less dependent on health care derived profits.

Response: By using the term "health care items or services," we mean (i) health care items, devices, supplies, and services and (ii) items or services reasonably related to the furnishing of health care items, devices, supplies, or services, including, but not limited to, non-emergency transportation, patient education, attendant services, social services (e.g., case management), utilization review, quality assurance, and practice management services. Marketing services are not included. In this context, we believe that a managed care company would count as a health care related asset for purposes of the large entity investment threshold test and that revenue derived from a managed care company would count as "tainted" revenue for purposes of the 60–40 revenue test in the small entity investment safe harbor.

While we agree that diversified assets may, in some circumstances, indirectly minimize financial incentives for referrals from investor referral sources, we continue to believe that arrangements involving ventures between health care businesses and non-health care business pose an increased risk of program abuse. As we stated in the preamble to the 1994 clarifications, "[i]t would be an obvious sham, inconsistent with our original intent, if a joint venture could merge with a non-health care business and have those non-health care assets, and the revenues derived from that non-health care line of business counted for the purposes of qualifying for safe harbor protection" (59 FR 37203–37204).

Comment: Several commenters expressed concern about our clarification of the phrase "on terms equally available to the public" in the safe harbor condition that describes how interested investors must obtain their investment interests in order to receive safe harbor protection (Sec. 1001.952(a)(1)(ii)). We indicated that the phrase should be interpreted to mean that the interested investor must obtain his or her investment interest in the same way as investors from the general public. Several commenters urged that this interpretation was too narrow and imposed unwarranted limitations on investment in large entities. These commenters argued, for example, that a large entity should be permitted to purchase a physician's practice using stock in addition to cash, provided that the value of the stock plus all other consideration paid to the physician equals the fair market value for the practice. For example, one commenter asked why it would be acceptable for an entity to purchase a practice for $1 million in cash (assuming fair market value to be $1 million), but not to do so for $500,000 in cash and $500,000 worth of stock. These commenters suggest that the phrase "on terms equally available" should mean that the stock is not lettered, restricted, subject to side agreements, or otherwise subject to limited transferability. One commenter proposed an alternative safe harbor condition that would deny safe harbor protection to an interested investor's holding of publicly-traded stock that is subject to transfer restrictions that are not applicable to the stock when held by members of the public.

Response: We have two significant concerns regarding interested investors' investments in large entities that are in health care related businesses. First, we are concerned that limited transferability or other restrictions on the sale or disposition of stock may serve to "lock" interested investors into specific investments, thereby increasing the incentives for those investors to refer Federal health care program business to the investment entity. Second, we are concerned that interested investors who are potential referral sources for the investment entity not be permitted to obtain their investment interests at insider prices or at prices more favorable than those available to the general public when purchasing stock from a registered national securities exchange through a broker. Such favorable treatment could potentially be disguised remuneration for referrals. For example, we are aware of certain public offerings of health care companies that involve simultaneous acquisitions of physician practices in exchange for stock in the newly-public company, with the stock valued in a manner that results in the selling physician obtaining the stock at a lower price or on more advantageous terms than offered to the public. The economic benefit conferred on the physician in such an arrangement potentially violates the anti-kickback statute if one purpose of the benefit is to reward or induce referrals. The investment would not fall within the large entity investment safe harbor.

Notwithstanding, upon further consideration of this issue, we are persuaded that requiring stock acquired by interested investors to be obtained in the same way as the same stock acquired by members of the public imposes an unduly restrictive interpretation on the existing safe harbor language. Accordingly, we are adding language to make clear that an investment interest will not qualify for safe harbor protection as "obtained on terms equally available to the public" if (i) the investment interest is subject to restrictions or limited transferability (including side agreements) not applicable to the same investment interest when held by members of the public and/or (ii) the investment interest is not obtained for the same price that is available to the general public when trading on a registered national securities exchange through a broker. Thus, in the example cited by the commenter above, the investment interest would be protected if $1 million is the fair market value for the physician practice (not taking into account the value of any referrals) and the stock obtained by the physician is valued at $500,000 based on the price per share then available to the general public trading on a registered nationalsecurities exchange through a broker. However, the public stock offering described in the preceding paragraph would not be protected.

b. Small Entity Investments

Comment: Some commenters asked that we clarify which investors constitute referral sources for purposes of the small entity safe harbor. One commenter recommended that we amend the small entity safe harbor to make clear that only physicians (using the Medicare program definition of that term) are capable of making referrals or influencing the flow of business. In this commenter's view, the current OIG position that referral source investors may include hospitals and other entities means that safe harbor protection is unavailable for various integrated delivery system models that involve joint ownership and investment. Another commenter requested that we clarify that manufacturers that invest in health care entities and sell products to those entities are rarely in a position to refer patients, and thus should not fall within the pool of "tainted" investors for purposes of the investment interests safe harbors.

Response: We continue to believe that the appropriate focus under this safe harbor is the status of the investors and the ability of the investors to make or influence the investment entity's referral stream or level of business activity. Investors that furnish items or services to the entity, as well as investors that refer patients or otherwise generate business for the entity, are "tainted" investors doing business with the entity for purposes of the 60–40 investor test. Thus, to iterate the example provided in the preamble to the 1991 final rule, if a durable medical equipment (DME) supplier and hospital enter into a joint venture to furnish DME to patients when they leave the hospital, both the DME supplier and the hospital fit within the category of investors doing business with the entity (56 FR 35968).

We are not persuaded that hospitals, nursing homes, skilled nursing facilities, or other institutions are incapable of influencing referrals of Federal health care program business. To the contrary, we are aware of instances of referrals that are in fact controlled by these institutions' employees or agents. (See, e.g., Medicare Hospital Discharge Planning, OEI-02-94-00320 (December 1997); Special Fraud Alert: Fraud and Abuse in Nursing Home Arrangements with Hospices, 63 FR 20415 (April 24, 1998)). Similarly, we believe that managed care companies and physician practice plans may control referrals in certain circumstances. We agree, however, that in many circumstances manufacturers that invest in health care entities and sell products to those entities may not be in a position to refer patients to, or generate business for, those entities for purposes of the 60–40 revenue test (Sec. 1001.952(a)(2)(vi)). However, in other circumstances, investor manufacturers may fall within the pool of "tainted" investors, and thus each arrangement must be evaluated on a case-by-case basis. In short, manufacturers may be "tainted" investors for purposes of the 60–40 investor test (Sec. 1001.952(a)(2)(i)), where they are in a position to furnish items or services to the investment entity or to influence the flow of referrals to the entity.

Comment: One commenter who supported our proposal to aggregate similar classes of investment interests sought clarification of the proposed condition that classes of investment interests be "similar in all material respects" for purposes of the 60–40 investor test, particularly as the condition applies to debt investment interests. For example, the commenter noted that the OIG is willing to treat general partners' and limited partners' interests as sufficiently similar for safe harbor purposes (56 FR 37204), even though general partner and limited partner interests are not similar in a number of arguably material respects, such as fiduciary obligations and assumption of liability. With respect to debt interests, the commenter questioned whether differing redemption rights would result in otherwise similar classes of debt being deemed too dissimilar to aggregate. Similarly, the commenter questioned whether debt instruments with different interest rates could be aggregated (especially if the different interest rates accurately reflect market rates at the time the instruments issued) and whether secured debt instruments could be aggregated with unsecured debt instruments.

Response: Our use of the phrase "similar in all material respects" was not intended to suggest that for purposes of aggregation, classes of investment interests must be similar in all respects that might be material to a partner or to a lender or a borrower, but only that classes of investment interests must be similar in all respects material to the purposes of the safe harbor. The focus is on the potential for remuneration to investors who are existing or potential referral sources; material investment terms are those terms that create, or relate to the creation of, potential value for investors. For example, classes of investment interests may be aggregated where the classes have similar rights with respect to the entity's income and assets, where investors receive equivalent returns in proportion to amounts invested, and, most importantly, where there is no preferential treatment of referral source investors, including, but not limited to, preferences that take effect in the event of a disposition of entity assets.

Comment: One commenter expressed concern about our treatment of general partners for purposes of the 60–40 investor rule. We have previously stated that general partners — who have fiduciary obligations to manage a partnership so as to make a profit and who are liable for losses incurred due to gross mismanagement — provide services to a partnership and are, therefore, "tainted" or "interested" investors for purposes of the 60–40 investor rule. The commenter observed that this interpretation serves to disqualify many partnerships from safe harbor protection and that our proposal to permit classes of investment interests to be aggregated for purposes of determining compliance with the 60–40 investor rule does not adequately address this issue. According to the commenter, even under our proposed aggregation test, safe harbor protection is only available if general partners hold a minority interest in the partnership, even if the partnership has no potential referral source investors. Thus, for example, a hospital owned entirely by a partnership composed of non-referral source investors would not qualify for safe harbor protection if the general partners owned more than 40 percent of any class of investment interest.

Response: As we explained in our preamble to the 1991 final rule, it would be inappropriate to grant safe harbor protection, for example, to a joint venture composed of a DME supplier and physicians, because all of the owners would be doing business with the joint venture by either furnishing items or services or making referrals (56 FR 35968). We recognize that there may be circumstances, such as those posited by the commenter, where the fact that an investor is furnishing items or services to the investment entity may not pose an increased risk of improper referrals comparable to the risk posed in our DME/physician joint venture example. However, we find that it is not feasible to craft a rule that would clearly distinguish among types of investors furnishing items or services, while excluding potentially abusive arrangements from safe harbor protection.

Distributions to investors in partnerships that have no existing or potential referral source investors may not implicate the anti-kickback statute at all, since the crux of the statute is a prohibition on remuneration to induce or reward referrals of Federal health care program business. To the extent the statute is implicated, partnerships that do not comply fully with all safe harbor conditions will have to be evaluated on a case-by-case basis. Our advisory opinion process is also available to parties contemplating such partnerships (42 CFR part 1008).

Comment: Several commenters supported our proposal to change the 60–40 revenue test by striking "items or services furnished" (Sec. 1001.952(a)(2)(vi)). However, these commenters asked for clarification of the term "business otherwise generated" as used in the safe harbor standard. We have previously explained that revenue is "generated" if it is "induced to come to the joint venture for items or services by an investor" (56 FR 37205) (emphasis in original). These commenters requested that we clarify that "by an investor" means by an investor who is a licensed professional with legal authority to order items and services, for instance, an investor with legal authority to refer or induce a person to obtain care from a participating provider.

Response: We disagree that the definition of an investor for these purposes should be as narrow as the commenters suggest. Certain investors that are arguably not "licensed professionals," such as hospitals, long-term care facilities, home health agencies, managed care companies, and physician practice management companies, may be in a position to generate business for an entity in which they have an investment interest and to receive distributions that may be remuneration for that business. We recognize that there may be occasional instances where business is generated by investors who would not ordinarily be considered as potential referral sources. This might occur, for example, if an investor is not in a health care related line of business, but happens to refer friends or relatives to a joint venture entity in which he or she has invested. However, we think that these situations are likely to be infrequent and, in most circumstances, are not likely to generate appreciable revenue.

Comment: As described above, several commenters questioned our clarification that the term "revenue" for purposes of the 60–40 revenue test means revenue related to the furnishing of health care items or services. In addition, two commenters expressed concern about an example involving radiologists that we used to illustrate our discussion of the revenue rule in the preamble to the 1994 proposed clarifications. Specifically, the example stated that:

If a radiologist holds an investment interest in an imaging center and reads all the films at the center, his or her reading of the film does not taint all the revenues from the referrals by non-investors. However, we have received a few questions from people who read the 60–40 revenue rule as making such referrals tainted because the investor furnished services at the joint venture.

We emphasize that if a radiologist-investor is reading the film and making referrals or otherwise generating business, then the revenues the joint venture derives from that activity would become tainted. For example, revenues would be tainted when a radiologist-investor takes part in a consultation with a non-investor internist, and during that consultation the radiologist recommends a procedure which is performed at the joint venture. (59 FR 37205).

Commenters complained that in light of this example, a radiologist-investor seeking safe harbor protection would essentially be prohibited from practicing medicine, because he or she would be precluded from recommending follow-up procedures. Moreover, the commenters argued that compliance with the example would not be feasible because of the record keeping and administrative burden associated with tracking all recommendations to determine if recommended follow-up studies were later performed at the radiologist-investor's facility. These commenters asked that we clarify our position regarding radiologist-investors.

Response: We continue to be persuaded that it is appropriate and consistent with our original intent that only health care related revenues be counted for purposes of the 60–40 revenue test. The purpose of the test is to limit the number of investor referrals to a safe harbor protected joint venture, thereby minimizing the risk that profit distributions might be disguised payments for investor referrals.

Our use of the example in the preamble to the 1994 proposed clarifications was merely intended to illustrate the difference between providing items and services to an entity (which does not result in "tainted" revenue) and generating business for the entity (which does result in "tainted" revenue). In retrospect, our focus on radiologists in the example may have led to some confusion about the anti-kickback implications specifically for radiologists' practice of medicine. In the unique circumstances of radiologists, we wish to clarify that the occasional recommendation of additional testing by a radiologist to an attending physician with whom the radiologist has no financial arrangements and pursuant to a bona fide medical consultation is not prohibited under the anti-kickback statute. Accordingly, for purposes of the 60–40 revenue test, such consultative recommendations would not "taint" revenue derived from tests performed at the joint venture entity as a result of a subsequent referral of the patient by his or her attending physician for the recommended tests.

Comment: One commenter supported our proposed clarification regarding the prohibition on loans from entities or their investors that are used by investors to purchase their investment interests (Sec. 1001.952(a)(2)(vii)). Another commenter requested that we make clear that we do not intend to prohibit loans from banks or other unrelated parties.

Response: The seventh investment interest standard addressing loans is not intended to apply to loans from banks or other unrelated third parties that are not equity investors in the entity seeking safe harbor protection and that are not acting on behalf of the entity or any of its investors, even if the loan is used in whole or in part by a prospective investor to purchase an investment interest. On the other hand, the safe harbor condition is intended to preclude from protection loan guarantees, collateral assignments or other arrangements made by an investment entity or any of its investors, or by individuals or entities acting on their behalf, to secure a loan from a bank or other unrelated third party, if the loan is used in whole or in part by an investor to obtain an investment interest in the entity.

Comment: The remaining comments to the existing investment interest safe harbors addressed various aspects of the safe harbors not specifically covered by the proposed clarifications. Two commenters argued that the safe harbor's two 60–40 tests unnecessarily limit potential investors for, and referral sources to, legitimate, cost-effective, high-quality health care ventures. In one commenter's view, the 60–40 tests prevent potential joint ventures from attracting necessary capital and cause investors to refrain from using the venture's services, even when the venture offers higher quality, lower prices, or better patient convenience than competing providers. This commenter noted that the two 60–40 tests are particularly problematic in rural and underserved areas, where alternative sources of capital and alternative providers are often in short supply.

Response: Except as otherwise noted above, we are adopting the proposed clarifications to the investment interests safe harbor as set forth in our 1994 proposed clarifications. Aside from clarifying that "revenue" refers to health care related revenue and deleting the phrase "items or services furnished" in Sec. 1001.952(a)(2)(vi), we are not persuaded at this time that there is a need to revisit the two 60–40 tests for small entity investments. Elsewhere in this rulemaking, we address a new safe harbor for investments in rural and urban undeserved areas (Sec. 1001.952(a)(3)) that eliminates the 60–40 revenue test and incorporates a modified 60–40 investor test.2. Space and Equipment Rental and Personal Services and Management Contracts Summary of Proposed Clarifications

We proposed 2 clarifications to the space and equipment rental and personal services and management contracts safe harbors (Secs. 1001.952(b), (c), and (d)). First, we proposed revising these safe harbors expressly to preclude schemes involving the use of multiple overlapping contracts to circumvent the safe harbor requirement that space and equipment rental and personal services and management contracts be for terms of at least 1 year. This requirement was intended to prevent regular renegotiation of contracts based on the volume of referrals or business generated between the parties. Second, we proposed revising these safe harbors to preclude safe harbor protection for health care providers that rent more space or equipment or purchase more services than they actually need as a means of paying for referrals.

Summary of Final Rule: We are adopting the clarifications to the space and equipment rental and personal services and management contracts safe harbors as proposed in the 1994 proposed clarifications and described above, with the following modifications in response to comments received:

- We are substituting the word "term" for the word "period" in the second condition of each safe harbor to be more consistent with customary business terminology;

- We are replacing the phrase "legitimate business purpose" with the phrase "commercially reasonable business purpose" in each safe harbor to make clear that the test is not whether a business arrangement is lawful, but whether it serves a commercially reasonable business purpose, that is, whether the space and equipment leased or services purchased have intrinsic commercial value to the lessee or purchaser.Comments and Responses.

Comment: A commenter expressed concern that the safe harbor condition that a lease cover all equipment leased between parties and specify the equipment leased would jeopardize many common commercial equipment leasing transactions. This commenter asserted that manufacturers and lessors typically lease capital equipment to health care providers at different times, but under leases that cover the same time period, in whole or in part. The commenter opined that other safe harbor conditions, including those prescribing aggregate compensation, fair market value, and arms-length negotiations, are sufficient safeguards against abuse.

Response: We recognize that some lawful equipment contracts will not qualify for safe harbor protection and will need to be analyzed on a case-by-case basis. The existence of a safe harbor for a particular set of business arrangements does not jeopardize other types of arrangements under the anti-kickback statute. Many multiple contract arrangements are legitimate business arrangements that do not violate the statute; however, some multiple contract arrangements are essentially shams that operate to reward and encourage referrals. We are unable to provide safe harbor protection for such arrangements, in view of the potential abuse of multiple overlapping contracts described above. The advisory opinion process (42 CFR part 1008) is available to parties seeking individualized legal opinions regarding the legality of their leasing arrangements under the anti-kickback statute.

Comment: One commenter suggested that for purposes of clarity and consistency with customary business terminology we substitute the word "term" for the word "period" as used in Secs. 1001.952(b)(2), (c)(2), and (d)(2).

Response: We agree that substituting the word "term" for "period" in Secs. 1001.952(b)(2), (c)(2), and (d)(2) would provide clarity and consistency in the context of leases and service contracts.

Comment: One commenter approved of our proposal that the aggregate space, equipment, or services contracted for not exceed "that which is reasonably necessary to accomplish the legitimate business purpose" of the party renting the space or equipment or purchasing the services. This commenter believed that the clarification would inhibit lessors with greater bargaining power from coercing lessees into contracting for more space than needed to conduct business. However, several commenters suggested that the language of our proposed clarification is ambiguous, duplicative, and confusing, and, in the words of one commenter, would open a "Pandora's Box of potentially conflicting interpretations." For example, one commenter observed that many arrangements in today's health care arena, such as cost-sharing or risk-sharing arrangements, joint research initiatives, and data collection arrangements, may not reflect "traditional" business purposes, but are legitimate and reasonable in responding to insurers' growing demands for cost-effectiveness. One commenter recommended replacing the word "legitimate" with the word "reasonable."

Response: We believe the proposed clarification further ensures that protected leases and personal services contracts will provide for fair market value compensation. However, we agree that the term "legitimate" may be misconstrued. Thus, in the final rule we are substituting the phrase "commercially reasonable business purpose" for "legitimate business purpose" to make clear that the test is not merely whether a business purpose is legal or illegal. The "commercially reasonable business purpose" test is intended to preclude safe harbor protection for health care providers that surreptitiously pay for referrals — whether because of coercion or by their own initiative — by renting more space or equipment or purchasing more services than they actually need from referral sources. By "commercially reasonable business purpose," we mean that the purpose must be reasonably calculated to further the business of the lessee or purchaser. In other words, the rental or the purchase must be of space, equipment, or services that the lessee or purchaser needs, intends to utilize, and does utilize in furtherance of its commercially reasonable business objectives. Thus, for example, a space rental contract between a physician and a DME supplier for space in the physician's office that includes extra office space that the DME supplier neither occupies nor uses for its DME business would not be protected by this safe harbor. Nor would the safe harbor protect the lease of more space than would reasonably be rented by a similarly-situated DME supplier negotiating in an arms-length transaction with a non-referral source lessor. Cost-sharing or risk-sharing arrangements, joint research initiatives,and data collection arrangements may qualify as commercially reasonable business purposes in many circumstances. However, we are aware of abusive arrangements involving contracts with referral sources for data collection services or research projects where the data to be collected or research to be performed have no value to the entity paying for them and are merely pretexts for payments for referrals. Such arrangements do not comply with the safe harbor and are highly suspect under the anti-kickback statute.

Comment: The remaining comments we received regarding clarification of this safe harbor addressed matters not covered by the proposed clarifications. Several commenters described difficulties in meeting the safe harbor for part-time arrangements— including time-share office leases, per use equipment leases, and personal services contracts with hourly compensation —caused by the requirement that the "aggregate" contract price be set in advance (Secs. 1001.952(b)(5), (c)(5), and (d)(5)). One commenter noted that these types of arrangements typically contain compensation methods that are set in advance and that can be made consistent with fair market value and unrelated to the volume or value of referrals. Along these lines, one commenter suggested that the OIG permit "aggregate" payments that are not set in advance, if they are calculated in accordance with specific and predetermined formulas set forth in the written agreement. Similarly, several commenters expressed concern about the impracticality of the requirement that protected contracts specify the exact schedule of intervals for the use of space or equipment or the rendering of services for many part-time or as-needed arrangements.

Response: We continue to believe that both the "aggregate" and the "specific schedule of intervals" requirements are necessary to ensure that safe harbor protection is not afforded to arrangements that include payments that are adjusted periodically on the basis of the volume or value of referrals or business otherwise generated from a referral source. We recognize that these requirements may raise practical problems for certain providers seeking safe harbor protection for part-time or as-needed arrangements. Nevertheless, we are aware of many instances of abuse in these types of arrangements; therefore, for purposes of granting protection from prosecution, we believe it is appropriate to protect only those arrangements that can meet the safe harbor's strict standards. However, as we have stated numerous times, safe harbors do not define the scope of legal activities under the anti-kickback statute.

Part-time, as-needed, and other similar arrangements that cannot fit within the safe harbor may be lawful, if no payments are made, directly or indirectly, to induce referrals of Federal health care program business.

Comment: One commenter sought clarification regarding the effect of a termination provision in a lease or contract in light of the safe harbor requirement that leases or contracts be for at least a 1-year term. This commenter specifically asked whether the 1-year term requirement is satisfied (i) if the lease or contract allows for "for cause" termination by either party, or (ii) if the lease or contract permits termination by either party with or without cause upon advance written notice, provided there is a concurrent contractual provision that restricts parties that terminate without cause from entering into any further relationships for the balance of the required 1-year period.

Response: The 1-year term requirement ensures that protected leases or contracts cannot be readjusted frequently based on the number of referrals between the parties. Although not specifically stated in the safe harbor regulation, a "for cause" termination clause that (i) specifies the conditions under which the contract may be terminated "for cause," and (ii) operates in conjunction with an absolute prohibition on any renegotiation of the lease or contract or further financial arrangements between the parties for the duration of the original 1-year term would satisfy the 1-year term requirement. We remain concerned, however, that "without cause" termination provisions could be used by unscrupulous parties to create sham leases and contracts. This could occur, for example, where the parties enter into an agreement to pay a sum of money upfront for services to be performed over a period of time. Parties could disguise payments for referrals by terminating the agreement without cause after payment, but before performance of any services. A 1-year prohibition on renegotiation or further financial arrangements would be meaningless in such circumstances.

3. Referral Services

Summary of Proposed Clarifications: The referral services safe harbor requires that any fee a referral service charges a participant be "based on the cost of operating the referral service, and not on the volume or value of any referrals to or business otherwise generated by the participants for the referral service * * *" (Sec. 1001.952(f)(2)) (emphasis added). This language created an unintended ambiguity when a referral service tries to adjust its fee based on the volume of referrals it makes to the participants. We proposed clarifying that the safe harbor precludes protection for payments from participants to referral services that are based on the volume or value of referrals to, or business otherwise generated by, either party for the other party.

Summary of Final Rule: We received one comment in favor of our proposed clarification to the referral services safe harbor and none opposed. We are adopting the proposed clarification as set forth in the 1994 proposed clarifications.

4. Discounts

Summary of Proposed Clarifications: As a general rule, discounts for health care items and services are encouraged under the Federal health care programs so long as the Federal health care programs share in the discount where appropriate, and as appropriate, to the reimbursement methodology. Arrangements in accordance with which Federal programs get less than their proportional share of cost-savings on items or services payable by the programs are seriously abusive. Such arrangements result in the programs being overcharged and are not protected by either the statutory exception or regulatory safe harbor for discounts.

Because of expressed industry uncertainty over what obligations individuals or entities have to meet in order to receive protection under this safe harbor, we proposed clarifying the discount safe harbor by dividing the parties to a discount arrangement into three groups — buyers, sellers, and offerors of discounts — with descriptions of each party's obligations in separate paragraphs. In addition, we proposed clarifying the definition of "rebate" for purposes of this safe harbor. A rebate under our proposal would be defined as any discount not given at the time of sale. Consequently, a rebate transaction would not be covered by the safe harbor if it involves a buyer under Sec. 1001.952(h)(1)(iii) that is neither a cost-reporter nor a HMO or CMP, because for such buyers, all discounts must be given at the time of sale.

We also proposed clarifying the scope of safe harbor protection for sellers in situations where buyers have not fully complied with their obligations under the safe harbor provisions. If a seller has done everything that it reasonably could under the circumstances to ensure that the buyer understands its obligation toreport the discount accurately, the seller is protected irrespective of the buyer's omissions. To receive such protection, however, the seller must report the discount to the buyer and inform the buyer of its obligation to report the discount. To emphasize that the seller's obligations require more than perfunctory compliance with the safe harbor, we proposed adding that the seller must inform the buyer "in an effective manner." We also proposed adding a requirement that the seller "refrain from doing anything that would impede the buyer from meeting its obligations under this paragraph." Thus, if the seller, in good faith, meets its obligations under the safe harbor and the buyer does not meet its obligations due to no fault of the seller, the seller would receive safe harbor protection. However, when a seller submits a claim or request for payment on behalf of the buyer, the seller must fully and accurately report the discount to the appropriate Federal or State health care program. An offeror of a discount would similarly receive safe harbor protection if it meets all of its safe harbor obligations, but its buyer or seller does not meet its obligations due to no fault of the offeror.

We further proposed clarifying whether any reduction in price offered to a beneficiary could be safe harbored under this regulation. To the extent that a discount is offered to a beneficiary and all other applicable standards in the safe harbor are met, such a discount would receive safe harbor protection. However, discounts to beneficiaries in the form of routine reductions or waivers of any coinsurance or deductible amount owned by the beneficiaries do not meet the safe harbor conditions and are not protected.

The preamble to the 1991 final rule stated that when reporting a discount, one only need report the actual purchase price and note that it is "net discount." However, for purposes of submitting a claim or request for payment, we proposed clarifying that what is necessary is that the value of the discount be accurately reflected in the actual purchase price. It is not necessary to distinguish whether this price is the result of a discount or to state "net discount." Consequently, parties who were uncertain about how or where to report on a particular form the fact that the price was due to a discount need not be concerned with reporting that fact, as long as the actual purchase price accurately reflects the discount.

Finally, we proposed some minor editorial changes that do not affect the substance of the provision, but hopefully make it easier to understand.

Summary of Final Rule: We are adopting the clarifications to the discount safe harbor as proposed in the 1994 proposed clarifications and described above, with the following modifications in response to comments received (unless otherwise noted):

- In paragraphs (h)(2) and (h)(5)(ii), we are changing the words "furnishes" to "supplies" and "furnishing" to "supplying," respectively, to clarify the role of sellers under the discount safe harbor and to avoid confusion with other regulatory uses of the word "furnishes."
- We are modifying our proposal that sellers and offerors give buyers "effective notice" of their obligations to report discounts by requiring instead that sellers and offerors provide buyers with notice in a manner that is reasonably calculated to give the buyers notice of their reporting obligations, including their obligation to provide information to the Secretary upon request under Sec. 1001.952(h)(1). The intent of this modification is to make clear that safe harbor protection for sellers and offerors who fully comply with the safe harbor conditions is conditioned on the actions of the sellers and offerors, and not on the buyers' compliance.
- We are modifying our proposed definition of a "rebate" to include any discount the terms of which are fixed at the time of the sale of the good or service and disclosed to the buyer, but which is not received at the time of the sale of the good or service. This modification will enable us to extend safe harbor protection to certain charge-based buyers and buyers reimbursed on the basis of fee schedules who obtain rebates. We are eliminating the requirement that charge-based buyers report discounts on claims submitted to the Federal programs; however, we are retaining the requirement that such buyers provide documentation of discounts to the Secretary upon request.
- We are clarifying that credits and coupons may qualify for safe harbor protection if they meet all of the safe harbor criteria; however, credits or coupons that are, in essence, cash equivalents are not discounts for safe harbor purposes.
- We are clarifying that, in certain circumstances described in more detail below, discounts on multiple items may qualify as a "discount" for safe harbor purposes where the reimbursement methodology for all discounted items or services is the same and where the discount can be fully disclosed to the Federal health care programs and accurately reflected where appropriate, and as appropriate, to the reimbursement methodology.

- We are correcting a technical error in the prop osed clarifications by changing the word "include" in Sec. 1001.952(h)(5)(ii) to "induce."Comment and Response.

Comment: Many commenters questioned the relationship between the regulatory safe harbor for discounts and the statutory exception for discounts, which provides for protection for "a discount or other reduction in price obtained by a provider of services or other entity under a Federal health care program, if the reduction in price is properly disclosed and appropriately reflected in the costs claimed or charges made by the provider or entity under a Federal health care program" (42 U.S.C. 1320a-7b(b)(3)(A)). In the preamble to the 1991 final rule, we stated that the regulatory safe harbor includes all discounts Congress intended to protect under the statutory exception (56 FR 37206). Commenters expressed concern that this statement means that failure to qualify under the discount safe harbor is a statutory violation if items or services payable by a Federal health care program are involved, since intent to induce business is always present in a discount arrangement. Under this interpretation, according to commenters, numerous forms of discount pricing, such as pricing one product dependent on the price of another, discount package pricing, and certain capitation arrangements, would be prohibited without the case-by-case analysis generally afforded other types of arrangements that do not fit squarely within a safe harbor. These commenters also urge that limiting permissible discounts to those that comply with the safe harbor "freezes" the health care industry into a particular way of doing business, thereby chilling innovations in discount pricing that could result in reductions in health care costs, especially as the market moves from fee-for-service arrangements to managed care. These commenters argue that Congress did not give the OIG authority to constrict the reach of the statutory exception. One commenter observed that Congress unequivocally stated that practices protected under the safe harbors were to be in addition to existing statutory protections (Pub. L. 100–93, section 14(a)), and therefore the regulatory discount safe harbor should create a class of protected practices in addition to practices protected under the statutory exception.

Response: As stated in the preamble to the 1994 proposed clarifications, it continues to be our position that theregulatory safe harbor protects all discounts or reductions in price protected by Congress in the statutory exception (see 59 FR 37206). The Secretary is vested with the authority to make and publish rules, not inconsistent with the Social Security Act, necessary to the efficient administration of her functions under the Social Security Act (42 U.S.C. 1302). The anti-kickback statute, including all exceptions thereto, are codified as part of the Social Security Act. Moreover, the regulatory safe harbor expands upon the statutory safe harbor by defining additional discounting practices not included in the statutory exception that are not abusive, such as certain discounts to beneficiaries (other than routine waivers of cost-sharing amounts) that meet all applicable safe harbor standards. In sum, the regulatory safe harbor both incorporates and enlarges upon the statutory exception.

Comment: One commenter questioned the safe harbor exclusion of reductions in price that are available to one payer but not to Medicare or Medicaid (Sec. 1001.952(h)(3)(iii)), noting that it is unclear how failure to provide a discount to Medicare or Medicaid gives rise to a question under the anti-kickback statute, which prohibits remuneration to induce referrals of items or services payable by a Federal health care program. The commenter further argued that there is no basis in the statutory discount safe harbor for a requirement that Medicare and Medicaid patients receive the same prices as other patients.

Response: The safe harbor excludes from the definition of a protected "discount" price reductions that apply to one payer but not to the Federal health care programs. This exclusion is necessary to protect against abusive arrangements in which remuneration in the form of discounts on items or services for private pay patients is offered to a provider to induce referrals of Federal health care program patients. For example, as noted in the preamble to the 1991 final rule, we are aware of clinical laboratories that offer price reductions to physicians for laboratory work for private pay patients on the condition that the physicians refer all of their Medicare and Medicaid business to the laboratory. Such "swapping" arrangements, which essentially shift costs to the Federal health care programs, continue to be of concern to this office. We do not believe that Congress intended to except such schemes from the anti-kickback statute. Nor do we believe that Congress intended for the Federal health care programs to pay premium prices and thus serve as de facto subsidy programs for other reimbursement systems.

Comment: Several commenters generally supported the clarification of the discount safe harbor to recognize 3 groups: Buyers, sellers and offerors. However, a number of commenters requested further clarification regarding the meaning of "offeror" and how an "offeror" differs from a "seller". Specifically, commenters asked about the application of the "offeror" category to wholesalers and other brokers, as well as to managed care plans, group purchasing organizations and preferred provider organizations.

Response: An "offeror" may be any individual or entity that provides a discount on an item or service to a buyer, but that is not the seller of the item or service. For example, many pharmaceutical manufacturers sell some or all of their products through wholesalers, which, in turn, sell the products to hospitals, retail pharmacies, HMOs, and other providers. A manufacturer may offer a discount in the form of a rebate to the ultimate purchaser that is in addition to any discount from the wholesaler to the retailer. For purposes of this regulation, the manufacturer would be the "offeror," the wholesaler the "seller," and the retailer the "buyer." While we believe that typically the wholesaler would be the "seller" and its retail customer the "buyer," if a wholesaler offers a discount to a retail purchaser that has purchased the discounted product from another party, the wholesaler could qualify as an "offeror."

Nothing in these regulations precludes a managed care organization, including a preferred provider organization, from being eligible as an "offeror" in accordance with the safe harbor. However, in many situations, discounts offered by managed care organizations will not fit within the scope of the discount safe harbor, because the buyers who obtain the discounts will not be providers of services that claim payment for costs or charges associated with the discounted items or services under a Federal health care program. For example, the recipient of a preferred provider organization discount is typically an employer or other payer or patient. However, some discount arrangements offered by a managed care organization may be eligible for safe harbor protection under the discount safe harbor, provided all conditions of the safe harbor are satisfied. In addition, managed care "discounts" are potentially protected by the shared-risk exception (42 U.S.C. 1320a-7b(b)(3)(F)), and the existing safe harbors for managed care arrangements (Secs. 1001.952(l) and (m)).

Comment: One commenter objected to the safe harbor's portrayal of the role of "sellers." This commenter maintained that sellers do not generally "furnish" items or services, nor do they "permit" buyers to take discounts off the purchase price. Rather, sellers sell, lease, transfer, or otherwise arrange for the use of products, in some cases involving discounts or reductions in price. This commenter noted that other OIG regulations define "furnish" as referring to items and services provided directly by or under the direct supervision of, or ordered by, a practitioner or other individual, or ordered or prescribed by a physician (either as an employee or in his or her own capacity), a provider, or other supplier of services (see Sec. 000.10). In addition, the preamble to the OIG final rule addressing amendments to the OIG's exclusion and CMP authorities resulting from Public Law 100–93 states that manufacturers who do not receive payment directly or indirectly from Medicare or Medicaid do not "furnish" items in the context of that definition (57 FR 3298 and 3300). For consistency and to avoid confusion, the commenter suggests that the term "furnished" should be replaced by the term "supplies."

Response: To avoid confusion with other regulatory definitions, we agree that the term "supplies" should be substituted for "furnishes" in Secs. 1001.952(h)(2) and (h)(5)(ii).

Comment: Several commenters commented that the proposed language clarifying the seller's obligation to disclose the discount properly to the buyer is beyond the scope of the statutory exception and confuses rather than clarifies the seller's obligations. A number of commenters suggested that the requirement that sellers provide effective notice would lead to mistrust between buyers and sellers and disputes about whether "effective notice" was provided. One commenter suggested that the requirement inappropriately saddles a seller with the responsibility of being the buyer's "brother's keeper." Some commenters requested clarification of what qualifies as "notice." Others questioned the intention of the added language requiring sellers to "refrain from impeding" the buyer's performance of its obligations. One commenter objected that this requirement imposed an undue burden on sellers, because sellers would have to know all of an individual buyer's specific billing activities and possible obligations in order to be in a position to refrain from doing anythingthat could impede the buyer in meeting its obligations.

Response: As we stated in the preamble to the 1991 final rule (56 FR 35958), we believe the statute permits us to interpret statutory terms used in the statutory exceptions, including the phrase "appropriately reflect" in the discount exception (also see 42 U.S.C. 1302).

We note that the statutory exception does not protect any seller if the purchaser has not appropriately reflected the discount. Thus, the objection based on the statute is misplaced.

With respect to the substance of the comments, the proposed clarification would require that the seller inform the buyer "in an effective manner" of the buyer's obligation to report the discount and refrain from doing anything to impede the buyer from fulfilling its obligations. We agree that the phrase "in an effective manner" perhaps unintentionally focuses on the buyer's conduct and might inappropriately be interpreted to mean that a seller is only protected when the buyer, in fact, fulfills its obligation to report the discount. This was not our intention. Accordingly, we have decided to modify the language to require the seller to inform the buyer of its obligations "in a manner that is reasonably calculated to give notice to the buyer." We believe this language provides the seller with an objective standard by which to measure the sufficiency of its notice. We are further clarifying that for safe harbor purposes one of the buyer's obligations is to provide information about discounts to the Secretary upon request in accordance with Sec. 1001.952(h)(1).

We are not prescribing a specific form of notice. The form of notice appropriate in particular situations may vary. Our intention in adding the "refrain from impeding" standard is to make clear that a seller will only be protected by the safe harbor if it is not complicit in a buyer's noncompliance with its obligations to report discounts accurately to the Federal health care programs. We are not making any change to the requirement that the seller not impede the buyer's compliance because we believe the language is clear. The same standard applies to offerors; they will not be protected by the safe harbor if they are complicit in either buyer or seller noncompliance.

Comment: A number of commenters objected to our bar on safe harbor protection for rebates offered to charge-based providers. Our proposed definition of "rebate" defined a rebate as a discount not given at the time of sale. Under our proposed clarification, safe harbor protection would only be extended to charge-based providers for discounts made at the time of sale of a good or service. The commenters point out, for example, that the regulation precludes retail pharmacies and outpatient clinics from being eligible for price reductions on the same basis as hospitals (cost reporters) and other large purchasers (e.g., HMOs). Moreover, the commenters note that there may be situations in which adjustments to previous billings or other errors could result in a rebate. The commenters also maintain that where payment is based on the lesser of actual charges or a fee schedule amount, fee schedules could be adjusted to reflect the availability of volume discounting. The commenters argue that excluding rebates for charge-based providers lacks a statutory basis, since the statutory exception refers to a "reduction in price obtained by a provider," without any reference to when the reduction must be obtained. The commenters further argue that there is no sound basis for not protecting delayed discounts to physicians, since we are not requiring physicians to reduce their charges for the amount of a discount, even where there is a separately claimed item. Thus, the commenters urge that rebates be covered so long as the amount is fully disclosed to the Federal health care programs and the other safe harbor conditions are satisfied.

Response: The most important aspect of the discount safe harbor is that the Federal health care programs share in the discount in proportion to the percentage the programs pay of the total cost. Congress intended only to protect discounts that could fairly benefit the Federal health care programs. It is our intention in these regulations to ensure that the only discounts protected are those where the Federal programs receive such benefit.

Having considered the comments received about rebates, we have concluded that excluding safe harbor protection for all rebates to charge-based buyers or buyers that are reimbursed based on Federal program fee schedules is unnecessarily restrictive and may prevent the Federal health care programs from realizing indirect benefits that may accrue from rebates to charge-based providers.

Accordingly, we are defining a "rebate" for purposes of the safe harbor as a discount, the terms of which are fixed at the time of the sale and disclosed to the buyer at the time of sale, but which is not given at the time of sale. "Terms" refers to the methodology that will be used to calculate the rebate (e.g., a percentage of sales or a fixed amount per item purchased during a given period of time). The terms of the rebate must be set at the time of the sale and disclosed to the buyer, even though the exact dollar amount of the rebate may not be known until the rebate is paid. In some circumstances, a rebate may be paid only after some number of successive purchases of particular goods or services; in such circumstances, the terms of the rebate must be fixed and disclosed to the buyer at the time of the first sale of a good or service to which the rebate applies. We are eliminating the safe harbor requirement that charge-based buyers (and sellers if submitting claims on behalf of charge-based buyers) disclose the amount of discounts on claims submitted to the Federal programs. We are retaining the existing requirement that buyers (and sellers submitting claims on their behalf) must provide information documenting the discount upon request of the Secretary.

Comment: The proposed clarifications eliminated a reference to credits and coupons in the definition of a "discount" (Sec. 1001.952 (h)(3)). Two commenters expressed concern that this deletion indicated an intent to prohibit safe harbor protection for credits and coupons.

Response: To the contrary, our revised definition of "discount" applies to any reduction in the price a buyer who buys directly or through a wholesaler or group purchasing organization is charged for an item or service based on an arms-length transaction, except for certain forms of price reduction expressly not included in the definition (e.g., no cash or cash equivalents, no routine waivers of copayments). If a coupon or credit fits within the definition of a discount, it is included within the safe harbor (assuming all safe harbor conditions are satisfied). However, we did not intend to protect credits or coupons that are merely surrogate cash payments, such as credits or coupons that can be used like cash to purchase unspecified goods or services from the seller or offeror. Thus, a coupon good for a reduced price on a designated item could be included in the definition, so long as it meets all of the other requirements of the regulation; however, a coupon good for a certain dollar amount off any goods sold by the seller is not included in the definition. We are, therefore, adding clarifying language to the definition of "discount" to make clear that cash equivalents are not discounts for purposes of the safe harbor.

Comment: One commenter objected to a "discount" for purposes of the safe harbor being limited to discounts offered to buyers who buy directly or through wholesalers or group purchasing organizations. This commenter urged that this limitation fails to accommodate new distribution arrangements, many of which contribute to purchasing economies. For example, hospitals, physicians or ambulatory surgical centers may buy items and services through HMOs or other brokering-type suppliers.

Response: In general, if a discount is negotiated with a bona fide seller of the item or service, including an entity that aggregates provider demand to obtain access to volume discounts, in accordance with an arms-length transaction, and if the discount otherwise meets all safe harbor requirements, we believe that the discount would come within the safe harbor definition of discount. However, there may be arrangements that do not fit the definition where access to a seller's favorable discount rates is itself an inducement or reward for referrals, e.g., providing certain physician practices access to a hospital's employee health benefits plan in order to reduce the physician's employee insurance costs.

Comment: Several commenters expressed concern about the exclusion from the definition of "discount" of price reductions furnished on one good or service without or at a reduced charge to induce the purchase of a different good or service. These commenters assert that this restriction was intended to preclude furnishing a good at a reduced price in exchange for any agreement to buy a good which was reimbursed under a different reimbursement methodology, in such a way that discounts would not be passed along to the Medicare program. For example, the safe harbor was not intended to protect a discount on hospital supplies covered by a Diagnostic Related Group (DRG) payment in exchange for the purchase at the full price of capital equipment separately reimbursed by Medicare on a reasonable cost basis in accordance with a hospital's cost report. Nor was it intended to protect a discount earned on products reimbursed by Medicare but applied to products reimbursed by non-Medicare payers. However, these commenters argue that the safe harbor should not exclude discounts on multiple products when the net value of the discounts could be properly reported to, and benefit, the Medicare program. For example, commenters believe that safe harbor protection should be available for a discount to a hospital for sterile gauze pads in exchange for the purchase of surgical tape, both of which are included in the hospital's DRG payment and recorded on the hospital's cost report as routine costs not separately reimbursable. These commenters expressed concern that the discount safe harbor's limitation on discounts for bundled or multiple items or services fails to recognize the diversity of cost controls inherent in such reimbursement methodologies as DRGs; physician payment under the RBRVS system; national limitation amounts for clinical laboratory tests; fee schedules for DME, prosthetics, orthotics, and other supplies; and fixed rates for ASCs. Finally, commenters noted that by restricting discounts on multiple items, the safe harbors may prevent the Federal health care programs from benefitting from purchasing economies that result from volume purchasing and group discounts.

Response: We agree that one purpose of the limitation on discounts for bundled items or services is to preclude protection for discounts that do not benefit the Federal health care programs, but which are used to induce purchases of other products for which the Federal health care programs pay the full price. These discounts are problematic, because they shift costs among reimbursement systems or distort the true costs of all items. As a result, it may be difficult for the Federal health care programs to determine proper reimbursement levels. (See 56 FR 35987, for example, citing the example of the development of accurate pricing data for intraocular lenses.)

However, we are persuaded that in certain circumstances, discounts offered on one good or service to induce the purchase of a different good or service where the net value can be properly reported do not pose a risk of program abuse and may benefit the programs through lower costs or charges achieved through volume purchasing and other economies of scale. Such circumstances exist where the goods and services are reimbursed by the same Federal health care program in the same manner, such as under a DRG payment.

Comment: Several commenters questioned our intent in changing certain language in the definition of discount from "in exchange for any agreement to buy a different good or service" to "to include (induce) the purchase of a different good or service." (See Sec. 1001.952(h)(5)(ii)).

Response: We changed this language to be consistent with the anti-kickback statute, which prohibits inducements to refer Federal health care program business, even if there is no actual referral made or agreement to refer. We are correcting an editorial error in the proposed rule, which incorrectly used the word "include" instead of "induce" in Sec. 1001.952(h)(5)(ii).5. Sham Transactions or Devices

Summary: We proposed a new provision to clarify that any arrangement entered into or employed for the purpose of appearing to fit within a safe harbor when the substance of the arrangement is not accurately reflected by its form will be disregarded, and the substance of the arrangement will determine whether safe harbor protection is warranted.

Comment: Although one commenter supported the proposed sham transactions rule, many commenters objected to it. These commenters argued that the proposed sham transactions rule was vague, lacked clear objective criteria, and did not provide any examples of sham transactions.

Response: Upon further consideration, we have decided to withdraw this proposal. We emphasize, however, that for purposes of determining compliance with the safe harbors, we will evaluate both the form and substance of arrangements. To be protected, the form must accurately reflect the substance. As we have explained in the context of space and equipment rentals:

If a sham contract is entered into, which on paper looks like it complies with these provisions, but where there is no intent to have the space or equipment used or the services provided, then clearly we will look behind the contract and find that in reality payments are based on referrals. Thus, these contracts would not be protected under these provisions. (56 FR 35972)

This same general principle would apply in determining compliance with other safe harbors.

C. 1993 Proposed Safe Harbors

The 1993 proposed rule set forth new safe harbor regulations in the subject areas described below. Each description includes a summary of the proposed rule; a summary of the final rule, including a summary of significant changes between the proposed and final rules; and a summary of comments received and our responses.1. Investment Interests in Underserved Areas

Summary of Proposed Rule: It had come to our attention that it is difficult for entities located in many rural areas to comply with the two 60–40 tests set forth in the "small entity" investment interest safe harbor. The first 60–40 rule (Sec. 1001.952(a)(2)(i)) requires that no more than 40 percent of the investment interests of the entity be held byinvestors who are in a position to make or influence referrals to, furnish items or services to, or otherwise generate business for the entity (the "60–40 investor rule"). The second 60–40 rule (Sec. 1001.952(a)(2)(vi)) requires that no more than 40 percent of the gross revenue of the entity may come from referrals or business otherwise generated from investors (the "60–40 revenue rule"). Entities located in rural areas may have an especially difficult time complying with these two standards, because in many cases physicians may be the primary sources of capital in the area, and those physicians may have no alternative facility to which they can refer.

Consequently, we proposed an additional safe harbor for investments in entities located in rural areas that would have eliminated the two 60–40 rules. We proposed defining the rural areas included in the safe harbor in accordance with the standards set by the Office of Management and Budget (OMB) and used by the Bureau of the Census. We solicited comments on the appropriateness of this definition of rural area. We stressed that the method for designating rural areas must ensure that this safe harbor only protects entities that truly serve a rural population. We suggested that one alternative would be to adopt the definition of "rural" found at 42 CFR 412.62(f)(1)(ii), which is the definition used by HCFA in its DRG reimbursement rules. We proposed leaving in place the remaining six standards for small entity investments for purposes of the new safe harbor. These six standards provide substantial assurances against abuse, and we had not been apprised of any particular difficulty that rural entities were experiencing with these standards.

In place of the 60–40 tests, we proposed a more flexible standard that would still assure that referring sources, physicians in particular, were not inappropriately selected as investors. First, we proposed requiring the entity to make a bona fide offer of the investment interest to any individual or entity irrespective of whether such prospective investor is in a position to make or influence referrals to, furnish items or services to, or otherwise generate business for the entity. Thus, we proposed requiring that opportunities for investment be offered in a good faith, non-discriminatory manner to any individuals or entities that are potential sources of capital. Second, to exclude the possibility of sham business structures not intended to serve the rural areas in which they are located, we proposed incorporating a standard that would require that at least 85 percent of the dollar volume of the entity's business in the previous fiscal year or twelve month period be derived from items and services provided to persons residing in the rural area. For entities that have not been in business for 12 months, compliance with this standard would be determined by examining the composition of the entity's business over the entire period of its existence.

Methods of Classifying Geographic Areas: Depending on its purpose, the Government uses several methodologies to define whether certain geographic areas are "urban" or "rural" and whether certain geographic areas or populations have inadequate access to health care services. Among them, the following are relevant to this preamble discussion:

- OMB Methodology: The OMB defines a Metropolitan Statistical Area (MSA) as a group of counties (or, in New England, a group of townships) surrounding and related to an urban core area containing a large population nucleus. The core of an MSA is a city with a population of at least 50,000 people and/or an urbanized area with a total population of at least 100,000 (75,000 in New England). The OMB defines a county as part of the MSA if it contains the core city or contains part of a continuous urbanized area around the core city, even if outlying areas of the county are rural in character. Using this methodology, an area may be considered "rural" if it is not metropolitan, e.g., not part of an OMB-defined MSA (see 44 U.S.C. 3504).

- HCFA DRG Definition: For purposes of establishing DRG payments, HCFA defines "rural" areas as all areas outside the metropolitan areas (MSAs) defined by OMB (Sec. 412.62(f)(1)(ii)).
- Medically Underserved Areas/Populations (MUA/MUPs): The MUA/MUP system was developed in the 1970s in accordance with section 330(b)(3) of the Public Health Service (PHS) Act to identify areas and populations eligible to participate in the Community Health Center Program. MUAs and MUPs are designated by the Health Resources and Services Administration (HRSA). An MUA is either a rural or urban area designated by the Secretary as having a shortage of health care services; an MUP is a population group designated as having such a shortage, such as certain migrant farmworkers or homeless populations. Factors HRSA considers as part of the existing MUA/MUP designation process include population-to-primary care physician ratios, infant mortality rates, poverty rates, and the percentage of the population aged 65 or over. The regulations governing MUA/MUPs are currently set forth at 42 CFR part 51c.
- Health Professional Shortage Areas (HPSAs): HRSA developed HPSAs to meet the statutory requirement in section 332 of the PHS Act to designate areas, population groups and facilities with a shortage of health professionals eligible for placement of National Health Services Corps personnel. HPSA designations are currently based primarily on measurements of area population-to-provider ratios for specific geographic service areas (or population groups within those areas), together with indicators that provider resources in adjoining areas are overutilized, excessively distant (e.g., more than 30 minutes travel time away for primary care) or otherwise inaccessible (42 CFR part

5). A HPSA can be designated based on shortages of (1) providers in a geographic area; (2) providers willing to treat a specific population within a defined area; or (3) providers for a public or nonprofit facility serving a designated area or population group (which could include a hospital). HPSAs are identified for three types of provider shortages: primary care, dental care and mental health care. The current primary care HPSA criteria define a "primary care physician" as a physician in one of the following specialties: general practice, family practice, pediatrics, general internal medicine or obstetrics/gynecology. Mental health providers covered by mental health HPSA designations include psychiatrists, clinical psychologists, psychiatric nurses, psychiatric social workers and marriage counselors.

- Notice of Proposed Rulemaking on MUA/MUPs and HPSAs. HRSA has proposed revising the MUA/MUP and HPSA regulations to improve the current designation process by combining the two designation processes; automating the scoring process and simplifying it by maximizing the use of national data; expanding States' roles in identification of rational service areas for designation; and incorporating better measures or correlates of health status and lack of access, including measures of minorities and isolated rural areas (63 FR 46538). In response to public comments, HRSA has announced its intention to issue a second notice of proposed rulemaking following a period of evaluation of comments received, analysis of alternative approaches and impact testing (64 FR 28831). Following an additional public comment period, new regulations governing MUA/MUPs andHPSAs are expected to be codified at 42 CFR part 5.

Summary of Final Rule: Paramount among OIG's concerns is that beneficiaries have adequate access to quality health care. We are aware that certain communities experience shortages of health care services that affect Federal program beneficiaries and others. This rule for investments in underserved areas is designed to balance the interests of those communities in facilitating the development of health care services with the anti-fraud interests that are the basis of the anti-kickback statute.

Health care joint ventures in underserved areas raise the same basic anti-kickback concerns as other joint ventures: First, is the joint venture a bona fide business enterprise? Second, are distributions from the joint venture really payments for referrals to the joint venture from investors? Third, are the distributions really payments for referrals from one investor to another? For this reason, it is important that any safe harbor contain adequate safeguards and conditions against fraud and abuse.

This new safe harbor for investments in joint ventures in underserved areas is designed to provide additional flexibility for investments in underserved areas that may experience a shortage of available capital from non-referral source investors. The safe harbor includes specific criteria that substantially reduce the risk of inappropriate payments for referrals and exclude from protection entities that do not serve the health care needs of people living in the underserved areas in which the entities are located. Because the safe harbor affords protection for a broader range of investments in joint ventures in underserved areas, we hope it will promote the development of needed health care ventures.

Based on our review of the comments received from, and concerns expressed by, various commenters, we have made several significant changes to the proposed safe harbor, all of which are described in more detail in the responses to comments section below.

- First, we have expanded safe harbor protection to include urban, as well as rural, underserved areas. We are persuaded that joint ventures in urban underserved areas often experience the same difficulties in qualifying for safe harbor protection as their rural counterparts. We are defining an underserved area as any defined geographic area that is designated as a MUA in accordance with the regulations at 42 CFR part 51c (or, if and when applicable, 42 CFR part 5).
- Second, we have reduced from 85 percent to 75 percent the volume of the investment entity's business that must be derived from residents of underserved areas.
- Third, we have provided a "grace" period for investment entities that qualify for safe harbor protection at the time of the initial investment, but subsequently find themselves located in areas that have ceased to meet the safe harbor definition of an underserved area.
- Fourth, we have incorporated a modified investor rule that requires that at least half of the investment interests in the entity be held by non-referral source investors. Here, we were in part persuaded by comments from health care entities that are currently located in underserved areas and that have no or

> few referral source investors. These entities expressed concern about unfair competition from new entities entirely composed of referral source investors (primarily physicians) in markets with few referral sources. We were also concerned about limiting inappropriate financial incentives.Comments and Responses.

Comment: We solicited comments regarding the appropriateness of our proposal to define "rural" with reference to the OMB standards for MSAs. In response, several commenters urged us to adopt our alternative proposal to use the rural definition employed by HCFA for purposes of reimbursing hospitals located in rural areas under DRG payment rates (42 CFR 412.62(f)(1)(iii)). A number of commenters urged us to extend the investment interest safe harbor for rural entities to equally qualified underserved urban areas.

Response: One of the important issues in designing this safe harbor is how to define geographically the scope of investments to which it applies. After consideration and examination of various approaches to defining "rural" for purposes of this safe harbor, we have decided to limit this safe harbor to investment interests in entities located in areas defined by HRSA as MUAs (that otherwise meet all safe harbor eligibility standards). This decision responds to requests for safe harbor protection to facilitate investment in areas demonstrably experiencing difficulty in attracting needed health care services. Unlike OMB's MSAs, which merely measure geographic distributions of population, MUAs identify areas experiencing health care shortages by accounting for such factors as poverty levels, infant mortality, and population age. Thus, we are amending the rule to substitute MUAs for the existing definition of "rural" to more closely tailor the safe harbor to protect investment interests in entities located in underserved areas.

In addition to more accurately targeting rural areas with shortages of health care services, protecting investments in MUAs offers a means of expanding safe harbor protection to urban underserved areas. We are persuaded that many urban underserved areas experience difficulties in attracting investments in health care services that are comparable to those experienced in rural areas. Because one of our objectives in creating this safe harbor is to foster the development of needed health care services, we believe it makes sense to protect qualified investments in defined shortage areas without regard to density of population.

At the time of publication of this rulemaking, HRSA's final regulations on the new process for designating MUAs are still pending. Although we anticipate that those regulations will be finalized, we are persuaded that, even in the absence of that rule, and notwithstanding certain concerns we have regarding the administration of the current program, our selection of MUAs as a basis for this safe harbor is sound and more consistent with the stated purpose of the safe harbor than either of our original proposals for identifying the covered areas.

We anticipate that, if finally promulgated, HRSA's new rule for evaluating and designating MUAs may result in some areas presently classified as MUAs losing their classifications. Moreover, HRSA has indicated its intent to review MUA classifications regularly, resulting in the possibility that some areas could periodically lose their classifications. Given this potential, it is incumbent on us to address the effect of the loss of a MUA designation on an entity protected by the safe harbor for investments in underserved areas. If an entity that meets all of the safe harbor standards were located in an area that loses its designation as a MUA after the entity has initially qualified for the safe harbor, the entity would technically no longer fit squarely within the safe harbor and would lose its protection. However, we are mindful of the need investors have for reasonable certainty in their arrangements and the significant effect a sudden loss of safe harbor protection resulting from circumstances outside their direct control may have on investors. Accordingly, we are including in this safe harbor a 3-year grace period during which such entities will be protected, provided they continue to meet all of the other safe harborconditions. This grace period will afford entities that wish to maintain safe harbor protection an opportunity to restructure so as to qualify for the small entity investment interest safe harbor at Sec. 1001.952(a)(2). We wish to iterate that loss of safe harbor protection does not mean that a joint venture arrangement becomes unlawful.

Comment: Several commenters expressed concern about our proposal to eliminate the 60–40 tests of the small entity investment safe harbor for purposes of this safe harbor. One commenter advocated that the 60–40 rules should continue to apply to facilities located in rural areas to prevent a proliferation of unnecessary facilities, especially laboratories, that are dependent on referrals from investor-physicians. Another commenter supported restricting the safe harbor only to rural areas where alternative sources of a particular service are not otherwise available. These commenters argued that a proliferation of protected entities with large numbers of referral source investors could adversely affect existing entities in rural communities. One commenter suggested that we use a "demonstrated community need" standard instead of limiting safe harbor protection to defined geographic areas. This commenter further recommended that entities that meet such a "demonstrated community need" test be required to disclose to patients a referring physician's ownership interest and to conduct utilization review of an entity's services.

Response: Having considered these comments, we are persuaded that eliminating both 60–40 rules, and in particular the 60–40 investor rule, may lead to inappropriate financial incentives and unfair competition in some areas by allowing referral source investors, primarily physicians, to "lock up" the market for particular services in those areas. Ensuring fair competition in the health care marketplace is one of the goals of the anti-kickback statute. We are also concerned that an excessive proliferation of particular services in rural or urban underserved areas could lead to overutilization by entities competing for scarce revenue and could prompt protected entities to develop revenue streams from patients not residing in underserved areas, in contravention of the intent and spirit of the safe harbor.

MUA designations are not made on a service-specific basis; thus, an area may qualify as a MUA based on an overall shortage of health care services even if it has a sufficient supply of a particular heath care service. As we stated in the preamble to the 1993 proposed rule, one of the purposes of this safe harbor is to ensure adequate access to medical care for patients in underserved areas. Our intent was to design a safe harbor that would accomplish this purpose, while excluding ventures that do not serve the underserved areas in which they are located. We remain persuaded that there are many rural and urban underserved areas with legitimate shortages of health care services and limited sources of potential investors. However, while we believe that market competition should minimize the number of duplicative ventures in a particular underserved area, we are persuaded that safe harbor protection should be limited, to the extent practicable, to ventures that fill a genuine health care need of area residents.

In light of our intention to minimize safe harbor protection for redundant health care services owned by referral source investors in otherwise underserved areas, reduce inappropriate financial incentives, and maintain fair competition for providers that are not owned by referral source investors, we have revisited our original proposal to eliminate both of the 60–40 tests of the small entity investment safe harbor for purposes of this safe harbor. In this final rule, we are adopting our original proposal to eliminate the 60–40 revenue rule, but we are retaining a modified limitation on the number of interested investors. Specifically, we are requiring, as a condition for protection, that investors who make referrals or who are in a position to make referrals or furnish items or services to the entity not own more than 50 percent of the value of investment interests within each class of investments in the entity. As with the 60–40 investor rule in the small entity investment safe harbor, we are permitting equivalent classes of stock to be aggregated for purposes of determining safe harbor compliance.

We believe that eliminating the 60–40 revenue rule, thereby permitting entities to draw 100 percent of their revenue from referrals by investor-owners, should make investment in such entities sufficiently attractive to non-referral source investors so as to permit the entities to meet the new 50–50 investor test. We recognize that this safe harbor may not fully answer all of the concerns raised by the commenters and that there may be particular circumstances in which ventures with parties to existing health care entities can not qualify for safe harbor protection. Some of these ventures may be appropriate for protection through an advisory opinion (42 CFR part 1008). In addition, joint ventures in underserved areas may still qualify for protection under the small entity investment interest safe harbor at Sec. 1001.951(a)(2).

We are not adopting the suggestion that we promulgate a "demonstrated community need" standard for this safe harbor. Such a standard would not create a sufficiently clear rule and would be unenforceable in practice. Moreover, the additional two standards suggested by one commenter — public disclosure of ownership interests and utilization review — while good practices, are not, in our experience, effective deterrents to fraud and abuse.

Comment: One commenter urged us to allow compliance with the rural investment safe harbor if an entity certified its inability to comply with the 60–40 rules in the small entity safe harbor despite its best efforts.

Response: A mere "best efforts" exception to the small entity investment interests safe harbor based on a certification from the investment entity would be insufficient to protect against abusive arrangements and would be impractical in application. Like all parties that cannot comply with a safe harbor, parties that are unable to comply with the 50–50 investor rule have recourse to the advisory opinion process for guidance about their specific arrangements.

Comment: One commenter requested that the OIG incorporate a "fair market value" principle more explicitly into the proposed rural investment safe harbor.

Response: The principle of "fair market value" is included in this investment safe harbor at Sec. 1001.952(a)(3)(viii).

Comment: One commenter expressed concern that a rural referral center (RRC) that had been reclassified as located in an urban area by the Medicare Geographic Classification Review Board for purposes of Medicare payment (42 CFR 412.230) would not be eligible to receive protection under the rural investment interest safe harbor. RRCs are Medicare participating acute care hospitals that are located in rural areas and that qualify under HCFA rules as referral centers (see 42 CFR 412.96). Under certain circumstances, an individual hospital, including a referral center, may be redesignated from a rural area to an urban area for purposes of using the urban area's standardized amount for inpatient operating costs, wage index value, or both. (42 CFR 413.230).

Response: A RRC located in a MUA would be eligible for protection under the rural investment interest safe harbor, provided it meets all of the conditions of the safe harbor. Reclassification as"urban" for Medicare payment purposes would not bar safe harbor protection.

Comment: Several commenters asked us to further explain how facilities can comply with the requirement that an entity must offer equal and bona fide opportunities to acquire investment interests to individuals or entities irrespective of whether such prospective investors are in a position to make or influence referrals to, furnish item or services to, or otherwise generate business for the entity (Sec. 1001.952(a)(3)(i)). In the alternative, a commenter requested that this provision be deleted. One commenter expressed concern that the "broad" terms of the proposed safe harbor would make it difficult for parties to identify "potential sources of capital" and inquired whether satisfying the safe harbor required investment opportunities to be registered under Federal and State securities laws as public offerings. Another commenter expressed concern about publicizing investment opportunities in rural areas where investors often do not wish to be publicly identified.

Response: Our intent in proposing the "equal and bona fide opportunities" standard was to ensure that investment opportunities are offered in a good faith, nondiscriminatory manner to any individuals or entities that are potential sources of capital, so that referral source investors are not inappropriately selected as investors. In light of our decision to require that at least 50 percent of the investment interests be held by non-referral source investors, we have concluded that this standard is not necessary. Accordingly, we are not adopting it in the final rule.

Comment: The sixth standard of the proposed safe harbor required that at least 85 percent of the dollar volume of the entity's business in the previous fiscal year or previous 12-month period be derived from services provided to persons residing in the underserved area. One commenter asked us to lower the 85 percent dollar volume requirement to 40 percent in order to make the threshold more attainable and allow more investment interests to qualify for protection.

Response: As we explained in the preamble to the 1993 proposed rule, although we proposed eliminating the 60–40 revenue rule for investments for purposes of the proposed safe harbor, we remained concerned that a sham joint venture structure could be established that does not intend to serve the underserved area in which it is located. This safe harbor responds to requests for assistance in facilitating investment in underserved areas. It is not unreasonable to offer this safe harbor protection only to investments in entities that will primarily serve underserved populations by providing services needed in their communities. We are persuaded, however, that lowering the required percentage to 75 percent would adequately protect against abuses and further the purpose of this safe harbor. Accordingly, we are requiring that at least 75 percent of the dollar volume of the entity's business in the previous fiscal year or previous 12-month period be derived from services provided to persons residing in an underserved area or persons who are members of a MUP (as defined by HRSA).

2. Ambulatory Surgical Centers

Summary of Proposed Rule: We proposed a fourth investment interest safe harbor to protect payments to investors in ambulatory surgical centers (ASCs) who are surgeons who refer patients directly to the ASC and perform surgery themselves on these referred patients. What we intended to protect is often understood conceptually as an extension of the physician's office space. We further explained that a safe harbor for investment interests in ASCs was warranted because the professional fee generated by a referral from a physician-investor to the ASC is substantially greater than the facility fee generated by the referral, and therefore profit distributions to physician-investors, which are derived from the facility fee, do not constitute a significant improper inducement to make referrals. The rationale underlying the proposed safe harbor would not extend to investment interests held by physicians who are not in a position to refer patients directly to the ASC and perform surgery. We explained that the concern with investments by such physicians is the potential for indirect kickbacks, because they might receive a return, through the ASC's profit distribution, for referrals of patients to other investors who perform surgical procedures at the ASC. We solicited comments on whether the rationale underlying this safe harbor is applicable to entities other than ASCs. We also specifically solicited comments on what degree of disparity should exist between the professional fee and the facility fee generated by referrals to a type of entity for that type of entity to receive safe harbor protection.

The proposed safe harbor applied only to ASCs certified under 42 CFR part 416. We did not propose protecting ASCs located on the premises of a hospital that share operating or recovery room space with the hospital for treatment of the hospital's inpatients or outpatients. The proposed safe harbor contained the following 5 standards:

- The terms on which an investment interest is offered to an investor must not be related to the previous or expected volume of referrals, services furnished or the amount of business otherwise generated from that investor to the entity.
- There is no requirement that a passive investor, if any, make referrals to the entity as a condition for remaining an investor.
- Neither the entity nor any investor may loan funds to, or guarantee a loan for, an investor if the investor uses any part of such loan to obtain the investment interest.
- The amount of payment to an investor in return for the investment interest must be directly proportional to the amount of the capital investment (including the fair market value of any pre-operational services rendered) of that investor.
- Each investor must agree to treat patients receiving Medicare or Medicaid benefits.

In contrast to the other investment interest safe harbors that limit investment by individuals in a position to refer, the proposed ASC safe harbor would have only protected entities whose investment interests were held entirely by such individuals. With that distinction in mind, four of the five standards were adapted from the standards in the small entity safe harbor (Sec. 1001.952(a)(2)). We solicited comments on the extent to which other standards were appropriate to safeguard against potential abuse.

Summary of Final Rule: The OIG received nearly two hundred comments relating to the proposed safe harbor for investment interests in ASCs. As a result of these comments, we have significantly reworked this safe harbor to provide, in general, expanded safe harbor protection for investments in ASCs.

As an initial matter, our proposed placement of the ASC safe harbor with the investment interests safe harbor appears to have caused confusion as to the safe harbor's purpose and scope. Our proposed ASC safe harbor contemplated a joint venture composed entirely of referral source investors. Placing these regulations alongside the large entity safe harbor, which limits safe harbor protection to investments that are so small as to be, at most, tangentially related to referrals, and the small entity investment safe harbor, which limits safe harbor protection to ventures composed of no more than 40 percent referral source investors, ledsome commenters to question why an ASC with 100 percent referral source investors would pose less risk of fraud and abuse than another type of investment entity with a smaller percentage of referral source investors. The answer is that ASC investments do not necessarily pose less risk. Rather, as described in more detail below, investments in ASCs raise concerns that are different from those addressed by the small entity investment safe harbor; therefore, investments in ASCs warrant different safe harbor criteria, including different safeguards, limitations and controls.

The new ASC safe harbor has four categories: Surgeon-Owned ASCs, Single-Specialty ASCs, Multi-Specialty ASCs, and Hospital/Physician ASCs. Safe harbor protection requires full compliance with all of the standards of any one category. All four categories have the following requirements in common: (i) The ASC must be certified under 42 CFR part 416; (ii) loans from the entity or other investors for the purpose of investing are prohibited; (iii) investment interests must be offered on terms not related to the volume or value of referrals; (iv) all ancillary services must be directly and integrally related to primary procedures performed at the ASC and none may be separately billed to Medicare or other Federal health care programs; and (v) neither the ASC nor physicians practicing at the ASC can discriminate against Federal health care program beneficiaries. Additional specific standards apply to particular categories. Moreover, in the interest of ensuring patient freedom of choice and promoting informed decision-making by patients, we have included a requirement in each category that patients referred to the ASC by an investor be fully informed of the investor's investment interest.

The four categories are summarized here and described in greater detail in the responses to comments below:

- Surgeon-Owned ASCs. The first category is designed to protect ASC investments where all of the physician investors are either general surgeons or surgeons engaged in the same surgical specialty. Specifically, category one protects certain investments in entities where all of the investors are either (i) general surgeons or surgeons engaged in the same surgical specialty, all of whom are in a position to refer patients directly to the ASC and perform procedures on such referred patients; (ii) group practices that are composed of such surgeons and that meet all of the requirements of the group practice safe harbor (Sec. 1001.952(p)); or (iii) investors who (a) do not provide items or services to the ASC or its investors, (b) are not employed by the ASC or any investor, and (c) are not in a position to refer patients directly or indirectly to, or generate business for, the ASC or any of its investors. A surgeon is considered to be in a position to refer patients directly and perform procedures if he or she derives at least one-third of his or her medical practice income from all sources for the previous fiscal year or previous 12-month period from his or her own performance of procedures that require an ASC or hospital surgical setting in accordance with Medicare reimbursement rules (the "one-third practice income" test).
- Single-Specialty ASCs. The second category is similar to the first category, except that it is designed to protect ASC investments where all of the physician investors are engaged in the same medical practice specialty (e.g., gastroenterologists), provided that they perform ASC procedures as a significant part of their medical practices. The physicians that qualify under this category need not be traditional surgeons. Specifically, category

two protects certain investments in entities where all of the investors are either (i) physicians engaged in the same medical practice specialty who are in a position to refer patients directly to the ASC and perform procedures on such referred patients; (ii) group practices that are composed of such physicians and that meet all of the requirements of the group practice safe harbor (Sec. 1001.952(p)); or (iii) investors who (a) do not provide items or services to the ASC or its investors, (b) are not employed by the ASC or any investor, and (c) are not in a position to refer patients directly or indirectly to, or generate business for, the ASC or any of its investors. As with category one (Surgeon-Owned ASCs), physician investors must meet the "one-third practice income" test.

- Multi-Specialty ASCs. The third category is similar to the first two categories, but it allows a mix of the types of physicians addressed in those categories. Thus, the third category protects certain investments in entities where all of the investors are either (i) physicians (surgeons or non-surgeons) who are in a position to refer patients directly to the ASC and perform procedures on such referred patients; (ii) group practices that are composed of such physicians and that meet all of the requirements of the group practice safe harbor (Sec. 1001.952(p)); or (iii) investors who (a) do not provide items or services to the ASC or its investors, (b) are not employed by the ASC or any investor, and (c) are not in a position to refer patients directly or indirectly to, or generate business for, the ASC or any of its investors. The physicians must meet the "one-third practice income" test described in the preceding paragraphs. In addition, physicians in this category must meet a second standard related to practice income because of the increased risk of remuneration for referrals among physicians with different specialties. Specifically, the rule requires that at least one-third of the physician's procedures that require an ASC or hospital surgical setting (in accordance with Medicare reimbursement rules) be performed at the ASC in which he or she is investing. We believe that for physicians who meet the "one-third/one-third" test, an investment in an ASC truly qualifies as an extension of the physician's office. We believe such physician investors are unlikely to have significant incentives to generate referrals for other investors because of the minimal additional return on investment derived from such referrals.

- Hospital/Physician ASCs. The fourth category protects certain investments by hospitals in ASCs. To qualify for the safe harbor, at least one investor must be a hospital and the other investors must be (i) physicians or group practices that otherwise qualify under the safe harbor or (ii) non-referral source investors. The hospital must not be in a position to refer patients directly or indirectly to the ASC or any physician investor. The ASC space must be dedicated exclusively to the ASC and not used by the hospital for the treatment of the hospital's inpatients or outpatients. The ASC may lease space that is located in or owned by a hospital investor, if the space lease qualifies for protection under the space rental safe harbor. Equipment and personal services provided by the hospital must similarly meet safe harbor requirements.

In this final rule, we are expressly departing from the underlying rationale for our original safe harbor proposal, which was the professional fee/facility fee differential. The existence of a significant disparity between the facility fee and the professional fee, such that the facility fee is significantly smaller than the professional fee, minimizes the risk of improper incentives for referrals; however, we are aware that professional and facility fees have changed and may continue to change over time and that the ratio between them will not always, by itself, provide a clear basis for safe harbor protection. So although the fee differential was meaningful at the time, we will in the future look more broadly for indicia that an ASC investment represents the extension of a physician'soffice space and not a means to profit from referrals.

The gravamen of an anti-kickback offense is payment of remuneration to induce the referral of Federal health care program business. In the context of an ASC, our chief concern is that a return on an investment in an ASC might be a disguised payment for referrals. Two examples illustrate the potential problem. First, primary care physicians could be offered an investment interest in an ASC for a nominal capital contribution as an incentive to refer patients to surgeon owners of the ASC. The primary care physicians would not perform any services at the ASC, but would profit from any referrals they make. Second, physicians in specialties that typically refer to one another could jointly invest in an ASC so that they are positioned to earn a profit from such referrals or so that one physician specialty provides the ASC services and the other provides the referrals. In such cases, medical decision-making may be corrupted by financial incentives offered to potential referral sources who stand to profit from services provided by another physician.

With the above concern in mind, we are still able to provide safe harbor protection for certain non-surgeon physicians, group practices and hospitals that meet certain requirements set forth in the safe harbor. These requirements are designed to preclude protection for investors who might have incentives to generate returns on their investments through referrals to other investors or to other physicians who perform procedures at the ASC. The safe harbor will also protect some investment interests held by persons who are not in a position to make or influence referrals either directly or indirectly to the ASC or to any of its investors.

However, except as otherwise described in the regulations, we are not protecting investment interests held by any party that provides items or services to, is in a position to influence the flow of referrals directly or indirectly to, or generates business for, the entity or any investor. Notwithstanding, investments by these parties are not necessarily unlawful, provided that payments made in return for the investment are not for the purpose of inducing or rewarding referrals.

Indeed, we recognize that some legitimate ASC arrangements may not fit precisely in the final ASC safe harbor. Those that do not fit may be eligible for safe harbor protection under the small entity investments safe harbor (Sec. 1001.952(a)(2)) or the new safe harbor for investments in underserved areas (Sec. 1001.952(a)(3)). Alternatively, current or potential investors may request an OIG advisory opinion in accordance with section 1128D(b) of the Act and the regulations at 42 CFR part 1008.

Our responses to public comments are summarized below.

Comments and Responses

Comment: Many commenters commended the OIG for proposing a safe harbor to shield ASCs from prosecution under the anti-kickback statute. Many commenters noted that ASCs have saved Medicare hundreds of millions of dollars, forcing hospitals to become more competitive, because ASC payment rates are typically lower than hospital payment rates for the same procedures. Several commenters stated that ASCs foster patient access to care, particularly in medically underserved regions. Moreover, many commenters observed that patients generally prefer outpatient surgical care at an ASC to hospital care.

Response: We agree that ASCs can significantly reduce costs for Federal health care programs, while simultaneously benefitting patients. The HCFA has promoted the use of ASCs as cost-effective alternatives to higher cost settings, such as hospital inpatient surgery. Where the ASC is functionally an extension of a physician's office, so that the physician personally performs services at the ASC on his or her own patients as a substantial part of his or her medical practice, we believe that the ASC serves a bona fide business purpose and that the risk of improper payments for referrals is relatively low. Where the criteria set forth in the safe harbor are satisfied, we do not consider investments in ASCs to be a likely source of overutilization of services payable by the Federal health care programs or increased program costs. We are concerned, however, that patient freedom of choice be protected and informed decision-making promoted in situations where a physician is required to refer to an entity that he or she owns in order to qualify for safe harbor protection. Accordingly, we are adding a requirement that the existence of the ownership interest be disclosed to patients. We note that such disclosure in and of itself does not provide sufficient assurance against fraud and abuse of the Federal health care programs. This conclusion derives from our observation that a disclosure of financial interest is often part of a testimonial, i.e., a reason why the patient should patronize that facility. Thus, often patients are not put on guard against the potential conflict of interest, i.e., the possible effect of financial considerations on the physician's medical judgment.

Comment: Many commenters questioned our proposal to limit safe harbor protection to physicians who are "surgeons", given that many procedures or services performed in ASCs are performed by physicians not commonly called surgeons (i.e., cardiologists, gastroenterologists, radiologists or pathologists). Many commenters argued that the "extension of practice?" rationale would apply to surgeons and such other physicians alike.

A number of commenters proposed that we adopt a definition of "surgeon" that would include any physician who performs procedures classified as surgical by HCFA regulations. For example, many kinds of endoscopy are classified as surgical procedures in accordance with 42 CFR 416.65 and various updates to the list of HCFA-approved ASC surgical procedures published in the Federal Register (see 42 CFR 416.65(c); 63 FR 32290 (1998) (to be codified at 42 CFR parts 416 and 488)). One commenter suggested that physicians who refer to an ASC, but do not perform services at the ASC, should be permitted in the safe harbor as long as they meet the safe harbor's five enumerated requirements.

Response: As discussed above, we agree that limiting the safe harbor to investors who are physicians traditionally termed "surgeons" is unnecessarily restrictive, especially in light of advancing technology and the scope of HCFA's approved list of ASC procedures. In light of the many comments received on this topic, we have revised the safe harbor to protect investments in ASCs certified under 42 CFR part 416 by non-surgeon physicians, group practices, hospitals and non-referral source investors that meet certain conditions. Investments by group practices and hospitals are discussed in responses to separate comments below.

With respect to physicians, we are promulgating three categories of safe harbor criteria, each designed to protect different types of physician investment. All of the categories protect combinations of qualifying physicians, which generally are those physicians who perform a substantial number of procedures listed on the HCFA ASC surgical procedures list as part of their medical practices. Specifically, at least one-third of each physician investor's medical practice income from all sources for the previous fiscal year or previous 12-month period must be derived from the physician's performance of procedures that require an ASC or hospital surgical setting. Inaddition, where there is a risk of referrals among physicians or surgeons in different specialties, we are requiring that each perform at least one third of his or her procedures that require an ASC or hospital surgical setting at the investment ASC. We believe these standards ensure that a physicians investment in an ASC will truly represent an extension of his or her office. Where physicians own an ASC in which they will personally perform a significant number of procedures, obvious and legitimate business and professional reasons exist for the ownership, including convenience, professional autonomy, accountability and quality control. Moreover, any risk of overutilization or unnecessary surgery is already present by reason of the opportunity for a surgeon to generate his professional fee; the additional financial return from the ASC is not likely to increase the risk of overutilization of procedures significantly. We believe that the "one-third/one-third" standards in the safe harbor ensure that physician investors will have no significant incentive beyond receipt of their professional fees to refer to the entity or any of its investors, because any return on investment will be attributable primarily to legitimate business and only tangentially to possible referrals of ASC business.

Because of the risk of remuneration for referrals, investments by other physicians, such as anesthesiologists, radiologists and pathologists, or by non-physician providers, such as certified registered nurse anesthetists, are not protected by the safe harbor if the physician or provider is in a position to provide items or services to, refer patients directly or indirectly to, or generate business for, the ASC or any of its investors. The determination whether an investor should be classified as a potential referral source is a factual question. As is the case for investments in small entities (56 FR 35964), we will accept a written stipulation that for the life of the investment the investor will not make referrals to, furnish items or services to, or otherwise generate business for, the entity or any of its investors, provided that, in fact, the investor's actions comport with the written stipulation. We wish to make clear that investments by these physicians and other providers do not necessarily implicate the anti-kickback statute. Finally, we note that we do not consider an investment by a physician's own wholly-owned professional corporation to be an excluded non-physician investment.

Comment: Many commenters also objected to our proposal to protect only ASCs owned entirely by surgeons who practice there. These commenters asserted that non-surgeons, and more specifically non-physicians, should be allowed safe harbor protection for investments in ASCs. Many commenters advocated a rule that would allow surgeon investors to transfer ownership to family members and other non-surgeons upon retirement or death without jeopardizing the ASC's safe harbor protection. Commenters also expressed concern that the safe harbor did not protect investments held by administrative staff at the ASC. Many commenters asserted that co-ownership with administrative staff would enable these individuals to make long-term commitments to providing better services in a cost-effective manner. Many commenters further expressed the view that anyone who is not in a position to refer patients to the ASC, including corporate entities such as for-profit management companies, should be eligible to invest in the ASC. Some commenters urged that investments held by a physician's retirement plan be protected.

Response: We are extending safe harbor protection to investors who are not in a position to provide items or services to the ASC or any of its investors and who are not in a position directly or indirectly to generate referrals for the entity or any of its investors.

There is minimal risk that a payment made to such a non-referral source investor would implicate the anti-kickback statute, and accordingly investments by such investors do not taint the ASC investment. However, we believe that hospitals, skilled nursing facilities, home health agencies, managed care companies, physician practice management companies, and similar entities may be referral sources in some circumstances. By way of example only, a hospital may be in a position to influence referrals when it employs physicians who make referrals, when it owns surgical practices, or when it is affiliated with a "friendly" or "captive" professional corporation owned or controlled by its employees. We further believe that some employees, such as certain marketing and administrative staff, may be referral sources.

Comment: Many commenters argued that the scope of the safe harbor should be expanded to include facilities that are not traditionally considered "surgical" centers, such as lithotripsy facilities, end-stage renal disease (ESRD) facilities, comprehensive outpatient rehabilitation facilities (CORFs), radiation oncology facilities, cardiac catheterization centers and optical dispensing facilities. Many commenters argued that such facilities, like ASCs, are part of the physician's practice and are not simply vehicles for passive investment and self-referral. A number of commenters stated that such facilities would not encourage overutilization, would increase access to care, would reduce costs, and would maintain or improve quality of care. Several commenters averred that investments in such facilities offer little inducement because each investor makes very little profit from investments in such facilities, in part because in some facilities, each physician's investment is a small percentage of the whole. Other commenters stated that the cost of operating these facilities is so high that each investor's net revenues from the facility investment is marginal. Many commenters argued that existing regulation by Federal and State agencies and by physician associations creates sufficient checks on fraud and abuse.

Response: Our regulatory treatment of ASCs recognizes the Department's historical policy of promoting greater utilization of ASCs because of the substantial cost savings to Federal health care programs when procedures are performed in ASCs rather than in more costly hospital inpatient or outpatient facilities. Physician investment in ASCs was an important corollary to the Department's efforts to promote ASCs because physicians were natural sources of capital, since many hospitals were reluctant to open or invest in

ASCs that competed with their own outpatient and inpatient surgery departments. Accordingly, many of the early ASCs were financed and owned by surgeons and other physicians who worked in them. Currently, HCFA's goal is to set payment rates that are consistent across different sites of service.[4] However, currently surgeries in ASCs generally continue to be reimbursed at lower rates.

Safe harbor protection for ASCs derives in large measure from this longstanding policy encouraging freestanding ASCs as a less costly alternative to hospitals for appropriate surgeries. In addition, Medicare's uniform, prospectively-established ASC payment methodology and the safe harbor's restriction on billing Medicare separately for ancillary services provide further assurance against abuse.

Investments by referring physicians or combinations of referring physicians and hospitals in non-ASC clinical joint ventures, including, but not limited to, cardiac catheterization laboratories, radiation oncology centers or ESRD facilities, do not share the same policy background and are not subject to the same reimbursement structure as investments by physicians in ASCs. Such clinical joint ventures may raise concerns not present with ASCs. In short, to qualify under this safe harbor, a facility must be a certified ASC under 42 CFR part 416. The existing small entity investment safe harbor (Sec. 1001.952(a)(2)) may be applicable for other joint ventures (assuming all safe harbor conditions are satisfied). In addition, we are not prepared at this time to extend safe harbor protection to non-HCFA-certified ASCs. Industry-promulgated standards, while welcome and often helpful in combating fraud and abuse, may not be sufficient to safeguard the Federal health care programs.

Comment: Several commenters asserted that hospitals with investment interests in ASCs should also be protected under the proposed ASC safe harbor. One commenter expressed the view that hospitals have no financial incentive to refer outpatient surgeries to ASCs because ASC net collections would be significantly lower than hospital net collections for the same procedures. By contrast, several other commenters suggested that hospitals would refer outpatient procedures to ASCs to enable the hospitals to focus resources on

---

[4] See e.g., Update of Ratesetting Methodology, Payment Rates, Payment Policies, and the List of Covered Surgical Procedures for Ambulatory Surgical Centers Effective October 1, 1998, 63 FR 32290, 32307 (to be codified at 42 CFR parts 416 and 488) (proposed June 12, 1998).

inpatient operations and treatments and the development of integrated delivery systems. Several commenters asserted that a hospital referral of a patient to an ASC would be an extension of the hospital's practice analogous to a surgeon's referral of a patient to an ASC. A number of commenters asserted that patients would benefit from using an ASC in close proximity to a hospital, and that creating an ASC would make efficient use of surplus hospital space.

Response: After reviewing the comments, we are persuaded that safe harbor protection should be extended to ASCs jointly owned by hospitals and physicians who qualify under the terms of this safe harbor. Although joint ventures between hospitals and physicians are often susceptible to fraud and abuse, precluding all safe harbor protection for hospital investors in ASCs may unnecessarily place hospitals at a competitive disadvantage if they are forced to compete with ASCs owned by physicians, who principally control referrals.

To be protected by the safe harbor, a hospital investment must meet all of the conditions set forth in the safe harbor. The hospital must not be in a position to make or influence referrals directly or indirectly to the ASC or to any of its physician investors. Whether this condition is met will depend on the facts and circumstances of particular arrangements. Any space used by the ASC that is located in, or owned by, the hospital must be leased in accordance with a lease arrangement that satisfies all of the criteria of the space rental safe harbor (Sec. 1001.952(b)). Similarly, any hospital equipment used by the ASC must be leased under an arrangement that satisfies the equipment rental safe harbor (Sec. 1001.952(c)), and any personal services provided by the hospital must be provided in accordance with a contract that complies with the personal services and management contracts safe harbor (Sec. 1001.952(d)). To further mitigate the risk of improper cost-shifting, in no event may operating or recovery room space be shared with the hospital for the treatment of the hospital's inpatients or outpatients, nor may the hospital reflect or include any costs associated with developing or operating the ASC on any Federal health care program claim or cost report (except such non-reimbursable costs as may be required by the programs).

Comment: Many commenters expressed the view that a safe harbor that protects an investment where 100 percent of the investors are physicians would be inconsistent with the 60–40 investor rule in the existing investment interest in small entities safe harbor. Several commenters argued that imposing a new 100 percent rule would be burdensome on those investors who diligently tried to comply with the 40 percent rule.

Response: We are not changing the rules for those ASCs that meet the criteria for the "small entity" safe harbor. However, many existing ASCs that are owned entirely or predominantly by the physicians who practice there cannot fit within the "small entity" safe harbor and thus are not currently afforded safe harbor protection. Depending on the circumstances, either this new safe harbor, the "small entity" safe harbor (Sec. 1001.952(a)(2)), or the new "underserved areas" safe harbor (Sec. 1001.952(a)(3)) may offer protection to investors in an ASC.

Comment: Several commenters requested clarification of the requirement that a participating practitioner "must agree to treat" Medicare and Medicaid patients. Some commenters noted that it was unclear what level of participation in these Federal health care programs would satisfy the requirement. One commenter questioned whether the safe harbor would require treating Medicare and Medicaid patients to the exclusion of other patients if capacity were limited. Two commenters questioned whether it was sufficient to "agree to treat" instead of actually treating Medicare and Medicaid patients. Another commenter wondered whether all investors in the facility must treat Medicare and Medicaid patients. One commenter suggested that the requirement be deleted from the safe harbor. Another suggested that each ASC maintain records, on an annual basis, to show that it actually provided services to Medicare and Medicaid patients in proportion to those patients in the community. Several commenters noted that the requirement to treat Medicare and Medicaid patients is unnecessary because the anti-kickback statute is implicated only when Federal health care program reimbursement is requested.

Response: The requirement that all protected investors agree to treat Medicare and Medicaid patients is intended to ensure Medicare and Medicaid patients access to care at ASCs on a non-discriminatory basis. Thus, decisions whether to accept and treat Federal health care program beneficiaries must be made on a nondiscriminatory basis. This requirement is further intended to promote cost savings for the programs by encouraging investors to provide services for Federal program beneficiaries in ASCs rather than hospitals in medically appropriate circumstances. We do not intend to exclude from protection physicians who are not accepting any new patients. We are not adopting the suggestion that ASCs demonstrate that they provide services to Medicare and Medicaid patients in proportion to the numbers of those patients in the community. We find that requirement to be too limiting. We are clarifying the language of the safe harbor to make clear its anti-discrimination purpose, and we are expanding it to require non-discriminatory treatment of all Federal health care program beneficiaries.

The commenter is correct that the anti-kickback statute would not be implicated, and no safe harbor protection required, if the investor physicians were not in a position to make referrals of or otherwise generate business payable in whole or in part under a Federal health care program. However, given the number of Federal health care programs, which includeMedicare, Medicaid, TRICARE, Veterans' Administration, Public Health Service, Indian Health Service, and children's health insurance under Title XXI of the Act, we think it likely that most investor physicians will potentially be in a position to refer Federal program business.

Comment: One commenter was concerned that States might interpret State self-referral prohibitions as also prohibiting surgeons in ASCs from referring patients to the ASC for related laboratory, radiology and other ancillary services, and asked that we clarify that, under this safe harbor, such "self-referrals" would be permissible.

Response: We are not in a position to comment on State self-referral prohibitions. The ASC safe harbor is not intended to protect payments derived from ancillary services performed at or by the ASC, unless such services are directly and integrally related to the primary procedure performed at the ASC. Thus, for example, payments in connection with invasive radiology (a procedure in which an imaging modality is used to guide a needle, probe, or catheter accurately) would be protected, while payments for diagnostic or therapeutic radiology would not be protected. To clarify the safe harbor on this point, we have added a requirement that all ancillary services for Federal health care program beneficiaries performed at or by the ASC be directly and integrally related to primary procedures performed at the ASC and that no ancillary services be separately billed to the programs. Simply stated, because of the risk of overutilization of ancillary services, this safe harbor does not protect ancillary services joint ventures married to ASCs. Payments to providers of ancillary services may be protected under the employee compensation or personal services contract safe harbors, if the arrangements meet all applicable criteria.

Comment: A number of commenters expressed the opinion that integrated multispecialty or single-specialty group practices, as well as HMOs, should be able to develop ASCs as part of the practice network or HMO. With respect to HMO ownership and operation of ASCs, one commenter requested that the safe harbor permit such ownership even if physicians own the HMO and would be referral sources for the ASC.

Response: We have revised the safe harbor to protect explicitly group practice investments in qualifying ASCs. To be protected, a group practice investor must meet the requirements for the group practices safe harbor at Sec. 1001.952(p) and be composed entirely of physicians who meet all of the criteria for protection as individual investors under the ASC safe harbor. Nothing in these regulations is intended to preclude the development of ASCs by HMOs, provided such arrangements do not include impermissible payments of remuneration to induce or reward referrals of Federal program business. These rules merely describe a certain subset of lawful practices that are deemed protected from prosecution under the anti-kickback statute.

Comment: At least one commenter suggested that the safe harbor be expanded for ASCs in rural areas, so that any individual or entity who is financially able to invest may do so, on the ground that there is a great need for ASCs and limited ability to capitalize them in rural areas.

Response: We believe that the provisions of this safe harbor will permit most investors who are in a position to capitalize ASCs in rural areas to do so. No special exception is necessary. Investors in an ASC located in a rural area may qualify for safe harbor protection under the investment interests in ASCs safe harbor, the investment interests in small entities safe harbor, or the new investment interests in underserved areas safe harbor. Investors in ASCs need only satisfy one safe harbor to qualify returns on their investments for protection from prosecution under the anti-kickback statute.

3. Investment Interests In Group Practices

Summary of Proposed Rule: We proposed a new safe harbor to protect payments to investors in entities composed only of active investors in a group practice. This safe harbor would have protected the investment interests of members of group practices that met certain prerequisites and standards. We proposed adopting the definition of group practice contained in the Stark Law at section 1877 (h)(4) of the Act. The Stark Law prohibits Medicare payment where physicians make referrals for designated health services to entities in which they have an ownership interest or with which they have a compensation arrangement, unless that interest or arrangement meets the strict terms of a statutory exception. In the proposed safe harbor, we intended principally to protect investors who are individuals who qualify as "physicians" under the Stark Law definition; however, our definition of group practice permitted a physician to invest as a professional corporation, if the corporation were exclusively owned by the physician. The proposed safe harbor was intended to protect any payment that is a return on an investment interest (such as a dividend or interest income) made to a physician member of a group practice who is an "active investor" in the investment entity, as long as all of the standards in the safe harbor were satisfied. For example, the safe harbor would have protected any payments resulting from the ownership of an interest in the group practice itself. It also could have been read — although it was not intended — to protect dividends from an investment in an MRI facility to which the physician-investors referred patients, if the investment met the terms of the safe harbor. The proposed safe harbor was not intended to protect other payments made by group practices, such as salary payments to employees of a group practice or payments to independent contractors.

We solicited comments on the appropriateness of our definition of group practice. We further solicited comments on the appropriateness of incorporating standards from the second investment interest safe harbor (Sec. 1001.952(a)(2)), including the prohibition on preferential terms of an investment interest being offered to certain physicians based on expected referrals; the prohibition on loans or loan guarantees from the entity or another investor used to obtain the investment interest; and the requirement that the amount of the return on an investor's investment must be directly proportional to the capital invested. In particular, we solicited information regarding the types of compensation arrangements that exist within group practices and the extent to which such compensation arrangements create inappropriate incentives that might distort the professional judgement of the members of the group. Lastly, we solicited comments on how we might expand the proposed safe harbor to other types of joint ventures composed exclusively of active investors.

We received over a dozen comments on this proposal. While some commenters supported the safe harbor and some opposed it, most questioned the need for the safe harbor and indicated that it would cause confusion among existing group practices. Moreover, it became apparent from reviewing the comments that the intended scope of the safe harbor was not clear. Some commenters understood the safe harbor to protect investments in group practices; others believed it protected investments by group practice members in other entities. A few commenters believed it covered both types of investments.

Summary of Final Rule: Because of the evident confusion caused by the proposed safe harbor, and for reasons more fully explained below, we have decided not to promulgate the safe harbor in the form it was originally proposed. Instead, we are adopting a simpler, although perhaps narrower, safe harbor that protects returns on investments in the group practice itself (i.e., not in separately owned health care services), if the group practice meets the Stark Law definition of a group practice (section 1877(h)(4) of the Act) and if the group practice investors are all licensed professionals who practice in the group. The safe harbor also protects investments in solo practices where the practice is conducted through the solo practitioner's professional corporation or other separate legal entity. The anti-kickback statute is not otherwise implicated for investments by solo practitioners in their practices. The safe harbor protects returns derived from in-office ancillary services that qualify for the exception for "in-office ancillary services" under the Stark Law (section 1877(b)(2) of the Act). This safe harbor does not protect investments made jointly by group members in separate entities. The general parameters of this new safe harbor were suggested in comments submitted by a group practice trade association as a less complicated alternative to our proposed safe harbor language.

Specifically, the new safe harbor imposes four criteria. First, the equity interests in the practice or group must be held by licensed professionals who practice in the practice or group. The equity interests may be held by an individual professional corporation if the corporation is exclusively owned by a single individual. Second, the equity interests must be in the practice or group itself, and not some subdivision of the practice or group. Third, the practice (unless a solo practice) must meet the definition of "group practice" in section 1877(h)(4) of the Act and implementing regulations. Fourth, profit distributions derived from in-office ancillary services are only protected if the services meet the definition of "in-office ancillary services' ' in section 1877(b)(2) of the Act and implementing regulations. We believe these conditions will offer reasonably broad safe harbor coverage for integrated medical practices, while at the same time minimizing financial incentives that could lead to inappropriate utilization and increased program costs.

Conceptually, this new safe harbor is consistent with the accommodation for referrals between group practice members contained in the safe harbor for specialty referral arrangements (Sec. 1001.952 (s)). In our preamble to the 1993 proposed rule, we explained that revenues shared between members of a group practice as a result of a referral from one member of the group to another are an inherent part of belonging to a group practice. This safe harbor protects such payments, provided all safe harbor conditions are satisfied.

We want to emphasize our view that under section 1877(h)(4) of the Act, a group practice must consist of one legal entity and must be a unified business with centralized decision-making, pooling of expenses and revenues, and a distribution system that is not based on satellite offices operating as if they were separate enterprises or profit centers. This safe harbor is not intended to protect group practices that are not legally organized, but instead only hold themselves out as groups. Nor is this safe harbor intended to protect multiple groups of physicians that remain in many ways separate, but join together for selective purposes, such as taking advantage of the exceptions in section 1877 of the Act that apply to group practices. For purposes of these regulations, a group practice may be one legal entity if it is composed of owners who are individual professional corporations or is owned by physicians who are individually incorporated.

Comments and Responses

Comment: One commenter supported a safe harbor based on the definition of "group practice" contained in section 1877(h)(4) of the Act, but objected to the application of any other standards or conditions. This commenter argued that a bona fide group practice can be equated, for fraud and abuse purposes, with sole-practitioner medical practices in that any remuneration shared or exchanged among the members of the group and any investment made jointly by the group in an entity to which the members of the group practice may make referrals and which can be considered as "extension" of the group practice should be regarded as a self-referral. On the other hand, some commenters expressed concern regarding the anti-competitive effects of protecting group practice investments in ancillary services and the attendant increased risk of abusive practices, including overutilization. Commenters suggested that the safe harbor include a requirement for public notice of group practice investment in ancillary services entities and notices to patients identifying alternative service providers.

Response: We agree that, generally speaking, safe harbor protection is warranted for remuneration shared or exchanged among the members of a group practice that meets the definition of a group practice under the Stark Law (section 1877(h)(4) of the Act). However, we are persuaded that investments by group practice members in entities that provide ancillary services may have anti-competitive effects and may result in abusive arrangements and incentives to overutilize those ancillary services. Accordingly, we do not believe that safe harbor protection is warranted for group practice investments in ancillary services at this time. Of course, investments in ancillary services may be covered by the small entity investment safe harbor. This new safe harbor for investments in group practices protects remuneration derived from in-office ancillary services, as defined in section 1877(b)(2) of the Act and implementing regulations.

Comment: Some commenters questioned the need to protect physicians' investments in their own group practice, and suggested that the anti-kickback statute is not implicated by a physician's ownership of his or her own professional practice.

Response: The plain language of the anti-kickback statute is sufficiently broad so as potentially to include payments from a group practice to an investor in the practice, even if the investor is a physician member of the group practice. However, our promulgation of this safe harbor is not an indication that we view investments in group practices as suspect per se under the anti-kickback statute. Similarly, we do not view investments in solo practices as suspect per se.

Comment: Some commenters urged that the proposed safe harbor would have excluded from protection most existing group practices. First, the proposed safe harbor required all investment interests in the group to be held by physicians. "Investment interests' ' was broadly defined to include bonds, notes and other debt instruments. Thus, if a group practice borrowed from a bank or other entity, the bank or other entity would have had an investment interest that precluded safe harbor protection. Second, the proposed safe harbor required all investors to be "active investors." One commenter noted that in most groups, the responsibility for the day-to-day management of the entity is given to one physician or to a practice manager operating under the supervision of a managing physician. This commenter stated that it is not possible or desirable for every physician partner to be responsible for the day-to-day operation of the practice. Another commenterobserved that many group practices are corporations in which the members are shareholders and thus not "active investors" in the corporation.

Response: We agree that inclusion of debt interests and the requirement that all investors be "active investors" as defined in our investment interests safe harbor unnecessarily limited the proposed group practice safe harbor. The new safe harbor, which applies only to investors who practice in a group practice that meets the group practice definition in the Stark Law, looks only to equity interests owned by physicians for purposes of measuring safe harbor compliance. Moreover, the new safe harbor does not require all group members be "active investors" as defined in the small entity investment interests safe harbor. Thus, the fact that all group members do not participate in the day-to-day management of the group practice will not disqualify a group practice from safe harbor protection.

Comment: One commenter expressed concern about the proposed restriction on investment terms being related to the previous or expected volume of referrals, noting that many physicians who previously practiced in solo or small groups have joined group practices or merged into large groups precisely because of the professional relationships between and among the physicians involved.

Response: We agree that a restriction on the terms of an investment interest being related to previous or expected volume of referrals is not necessary in the context of investments in group practices that meet the definition of a group practice under the Stark Law. Our revised safe harbor language does not contain such a requirement. However, the return on the investment interest must comply with the Stark Law, which limits compensation to physician investors that is based on the volume or value of referrals by the physician (section 1877(h)(4)(A)(iv) of the Act and implementing regulations).

Comment: One commenter expressed concern about the prohibition on group practices making loans to, or guaranteeing loans for, investors, if the loans are used to acquire an interest in the group. This commenter believed that this provision could create a problem for physicians who are given the opportunity to buy into an existing practice over time, if a deferred capital contribution were viewed as a loan.

Response: Our new safe harbor does not contain a prohibition on loans from group practices or group practice members used to acquire interests in the group practice.

Comment: One commenter suggested that the safe harbor should be expanded by adding protection for in-office ancillary services (such as a laboratory) shared by physicians who are not part of the same group practice, where the physicians sharing the in-office laboratory bill independently of one another and do not benefit from the volume or value of referrals made by their partners. According to the commenter, these arrangements are common, practical, and cost-effective.

Response: We agree that these arrangements are often practical and cost-effective for physicians. However, as indicated above, we are not prepared to provide safe harbor protection for investments in separately-owned ancillary services at this time, whether the ownership is by group practice members or others. We remain concerned that investments in ancillary services may create incentives for overutilization and lead to increased program costs. This is not to say that all such arrangements are unlawful under the anti-kickback statute. However, we do not believe that it would be possible to craft a sufficiently circumscribed safe harbor that would protect legitimate investments, while at the same time excluding from protection sham investments that are in reality vehicles for the payment of kickbacks.

Comment: One commenter recommended that the safe harbor apply to all practitioners within the reach of the anti-kickback statute, including nurse practitioners, certified nurse-midwives, clinical nurse specialists and certified registered nurse anesthesiologists.

Response: For now, we are limiting the safe harbor to group practices as defined in the Stark Law. The Stark Law definition of group practices applies only to physicians. We may consider an expansion to non-physician practitioners in future rulemaking.4. Practitioner Recruitment

Summary of Proposed Rule: We proposed a safe harbor for certain payments or benefits offered by rural hospitals and entities in their efforts to recruit physicians and other practitioners. It had come to our attention that some hospitals located in rural areas encounter difficulties in attracting physicians to their communities. Our proposed safe harbor was designed to address this problem without protecting recruitment arrangements intended to channel Federal health care program beneficiaries to recruiting hospitals and entities.

We proposed limiting the practitioner recruitment safe harbor to entities located in rural areas as defined in our proposed safe harbor for investments in rural areas. However, we solicited comments on alternative geographic criteria. One alternative we suggested was limiting safe harbor protection to recruitment of practitioners located in areas that are health professional shortage areas (HPSAs) for the practitioner's specialty category.

To ensure that we did not protect arrangements designed to channel Federal program business to recruiting hospitals or entities, we proposed protecting recruitment of 2 types of practitioners: (1) Practitioners relocating at least 100 miles to a new geographic area and starting a new practice, and (2) new practitioners starting practices or specialties after completing an internship or residency program. We proposed seven standards that would have to be met to qualify for safe harbor protection. We also solicited comments about protecting payments designed to retain physicians already practicing in an area that has been designated as a HPSA for the physician's specialty category.

Summary of Final Rule: The intent of the practitioner recruitment safe harbor is to promote beneficiary access to quality health care by permitting communities that have difficulty attracting needed medical professionals to offer inducements to those professionals without running afoul of the anti-kickback statute. This safe harbor is intended to apply only to areas with a demonstrated need for practitioners and only to practitioners who actually serve the residents of such areas. We are adopting the proposed safe harbor with the following modifications:

- We are expanding the safe harbor to cover practitioner recruitment in urban, as well as rural, underserved areas. Specifically, the safe harbor applies to recruitment activities where the recruited practitioner's primary place of practice will be located in a HPSA for the practitioner's specialty area in accordance with 42 CFR part 5.
- We have eliminated the "100 mile" rule.
- We have reduced the required new patient revenues from 85 percent to 75 percent.

- At least 75 percent of the revenues of the new practice must be generated from patients residing in a HPSA or a MUA or who are members of a MUP (as defined by HRSA).
- The benefits may be provided for a term of up to 3 years, provided there is a written agreement, and the benefits donot directly or indirectly benefit other referral sources. If the HPSA ceases to be a HPSA during the term of the written agreement, the recruitment arrangement will not lose its safe harbor protection.
- The recruited practitioner must agree to treat Federal health care program patients in a non-discriminatory manner.
- We are not requiring the entity doing the recruiting to be located in the underserved area.
- We are not requiring new practitioners to establish staff privileges at the recruiting entity.Comments and Responses.

Comment: Commenters expressed a range of views regarding our proposed definition of "rural" for purposes of this safe harbor. Some urged us to adopt the definition of rural used by HCFA to reimburse hospitals located in rural areas under DRG payment rates (42 CFR 412.62(f)(1)(iii)). Others urged that an entity be protected under the safe harbor if it qualifies as a disproportionate share hospital (DSH) under Medicare payment policy. Some commenters suggested that we use HRSA's designations of HPSAs as a means of limiting protection afforded by the safe harbor. Several commenters recommended use of HRSA's designation of MUAs (42 CFR part 51c). One commenter suggested that we substitute a "demonstrated community need" standard for the geographic criteria. In addition, many commenters suggested that we extend the practitioner recruitment safe harbor to underserved urban areas. Several commenters proposed that we conform the safe harbor to the Stark Law exception for physician recruitment by eliminating geographic criteria.

Response: We are not prepared to expand this safe harbor by protecting practitioner recruitment wherever it occurs. In many areas, hospitals and other recruiting entities can attract sufficient numbers of qualified practitioners. In such areas, we see no need to protect additional payments or benefits that may in reality be disguised bonuses for high referrers. We recognize, however, that many hospitals in rural and urban underserved areas have legitimate problems attracting physicians and other practitioners and may need to offer additional financial incentives to acquire adequate staff. After carefully reviewing the suggested options, we have concluded that the most sensible approach — one that fairly balances the need to address practitioner shortages with the need to guard against abusive practices — is to extend safe harbor protection to recruitment payments and benefits provided to new and relocating practitioners who establish their primary place of practice in a HPSA in the practitioner's specialty area (see discussion of HPSAs above). The choice of HPSAs has the advantage of (i) including urban underserved areas, which we are persuaded often experience comparable difficulties attracting health care practitioners as rural areas, and (ii) targeting areas that have demonstrated a shortage of practitioners in particular specialties, and, consequently a need for additional recruitment.

We are not adopting the definition of "rural" used by HCFA for purposes of reimbursing rural hospitals under DRG payment rates. As discussed above, that definition is derived from the OMB definition of "rural" that is used by the Bureau of Census. The OMB methodology is not as closely tailored to the purpose of this safe harbor as is HRSA's HPSA methodology. Moreover, the OMB methodology would not identify underserved urban areas. We also concluded that the use of MUAs would create a broader safe harbor than is needed to facilitate the type of practitioner recruitment we intend to protect. Unlike HPSAs, which target practitioner shortages, MUAs measure shortages of health care services generally.

Similarly, we are not adopting the proposal to use DSH payments as a criterion for safe harbor protection. Although they are an indicator of the number of low-income patients a hospital treats, DSH payments do not necessarily indicate practitioner shortages. A "demonstrated community need" standard, while appealing in theory, presents too many difficulties in application to produce consistent and predictable safe harbor protection.

Comment: One commenter asked us to clarify whether the safe harbor protected payments made by recruiting entities that are not located in an rural area to practitioners who are practicing in a rural area. This commenter observed that some hospitals in "non-rural" areas serve patients who live in "rural" areas.

Response: The safe harbor provides that an entity will be protected if the practitioner's primary place of practice is located in a HPSA for the practitioner's specialty area. Consistent with our intent to facilitate recruitment of health care practitioners to serve the needs of underserved populations, we are not requiring that the recruiting entity also be located in a HPSA.

Comment: One commenter wondered whether a rural referral center (RRC) that had been reclassified by HCFA as urban for purposes of Medicare payment would be eligible for protection under the practitioner recruitment safe harbor.

Response: A RRC recruiting a practitioner whose primary place of practice will be located in a HPSA for the practitioner's specialty area would be eligible for protection under the rural investment interest safe harbor provided it met all of the conditions of the safe harbor.

Comment: The proposed safe harbor applies to new and relocating practitioners who derive 85 percent of their patient revenue from new patients not previously seen by the practitioner at his or her former place of practice. One commenter urged that the threshold be lowered to 50 percent to expand safe harbor protection. One commenter questioned the ability to measure compliance with the 85 percent revenue standard prospectively. Another commenter inquired whether a hospital would be required to audit a recruited physician's practice to ensure compliance with the 85 percent revenue test. One commenter suggested that the 85 percent revenue test be eliminated for urban providers.

Response: A dollar volume standard is necessary to ensure that safe harbor protection is granted only to new practitioners and those genuinely relocating and starting new practices. This safe harbor is intended to protect recruitment activities, not payments to retain physicians in existing practices. The safe harbor does not cover arrangements between hospitals and physicians that may be, in reality, payments to obtain the referrals of established practitioners. However, upon further consideration, we agree that the 85 percent standard we proposed is too high. We are, therefore, lowering the required percentage to 75 percent, which we believe will be sufficient to deter abuses. We recognize that determining compliance with the safe harbor may be problematic in some circumstances, such as during the first year of practice. However, we think that new and relocating practitioners should be able to achieve a reasonable degree of certainty that they have complied with the regulations. Parties to recruitment arrangements may use any reasonable method for establishing compliance, provided they use the same principles consistently over time, so as to avoid manipulating data to obscure noncompliance.

Comment: Several commenters suggested that we use a patient population test instead of a revenue test as a basis for ensuring that the practice is truly new or relocated.

Response: A revenue-based test more accurately measures whether services are, in fact, being provided to new patients than does a test based on the numbers of patients in a practitioner's practice. We do not intend to protect relocating practitioners who establish practices in HPSAs, but who continue primarily to treat patients from the practitioner's former practice.

Comment: The proposed safe harbor contained a requirement that a relocating practitioner's physical primary place of practice be at least 100 miles from his or her previous primary place of practice. Several commenters urged us to eliminate the 100 mile rule altogether or reduce the distance required. These commenters pointed out that the 100 mile requirement would produce arbitrary results in some circumstances and that some rural areas with practitioner shortages were located less than 100 miles from urban areas with pools of potential practitioners from which to recruit. Moreover, the 100 mile rule made it more difficult for urban undeserved areas to qualify for safe harbor protection. One commenter suggested using a travel distance of one and a half hours as a means of ensuring a majority of the practitioner's patients will be new. In the alternative, a commenter suggested making the 100 mile rule an alternative test to the 85 percent new patient revenue rule.

Response: The 100 mile rule was intended to ensure that the safe harbor protected recruitment of new or relocating practitioners only. However, we are persuaded that the proposed 100 mile rule would be impractical and lead to arbitrary results in some circumstances and would unnecessarily limit the protection afforded by this safe harbor. We also recognize that the 100 mile rule would make it difficult for entities in urban underserved areas to enter into recruitment arrangements that qualify for the safe harbor. Accordingly, we are eliminating the 100 mile rule, thereby enabling some recruitment arrangements to qualify for the safe harbor even if the practitioner relocates his or her primary place of practice only a short distance to a HPSA.

We are concerned, however, about the possibility of abuse by experienced practitioners, particularly in urban settings, who may "relocate" their offices short distances to underserved areas in order to qualify for the safe harbor and therefore receive recruitment payments that may, in fact, be rewards for referrals. The 75 percent new patient revenue test does not adequately guard against such abuse, because it measures whether patients are new to the practice and not whether patients are part of an underserved population. To ensure that safe harbor protection is not available for practitioners who relocate but do not serve the populations intended to benefit from this safe harbor, we are adding a requirement that 75 percent of the revenues of the new practice must be generated from patients residing in a HPSA or a MUA or who are members of a MUP. The patients do not necessarily have to reside in the specific HPSA in which the practitioner's new practice is located, but may reside instead in a nearby MUA or HPSA. In sum, to qualify for the safe harbor, a new or relocating physician must substantially treat patients who are new to the physician's practice and who reside in underserved areas, or are members of medically-underserved populations designated by HRSA.

Comment: A number of commenters discussed the third proposed safe harbor standard, which would have imposed certain time limits on payments and benefits protected by the safe harbor. One commenter recommended extending the time limit for protected recruitment payments in non-HPSA rural areas from 3 years to 5 years. Several commenters urged us to allow protected recruitment payments for practitioners in HPSAs for as long as an area is designated as a HPSA. Some commenters questioned what would happen if a HPSA designation was revoked during the term of the recruitment contact. These commenters recommended that the contract continue to be protected for its term.

Response: Our original proposed safe harbor contemplated a 3 year limit on benefits, unless the practitioner was located in a HPSA, in which case recruitment benefits would be protected for the entire duration of the relationship between the practitioner and the recruiting entity. Given that we have limited the scope of this safe harbor to HPSAs, the 3 year limit for non-HPSA rural areas originally proposed no longer pertains.

However, our experience over the past few years has shown that practitioner recruitment is an area frequently subject to abusive practices. The risk of kickbacks is mitigated when payments are made to new or relocating physicians who do not have established referrals streams that can be locked up through inappropriate incentives and loyalties. Thus, we have concluded that protected payments under this safe harbor should not be of unlimited duration or subject to renegotiation that may be based on the volume or value of referrals. We believe that 3 years is a reasonable time period for recruitment benefits. Accordingly, we are amending the third standard to read as follows: "the benefits are provided by the entity for a period not to exceed 3 years, and the terms of the agreement are not renegotiated during this 3 year period in any substantial aspect." By "any substantial aspect," we mean in any manner that materially affects the payments and benefits to be made to the recruited practitioners under the written agreement. We have also revised the safe harbor to make clear that if the HPSA designation is revoked during the term of the contract, the payments will remain protected for the term of the contract (which term may not exceed 3 years), provided all other safe harbor conditions are satisfied.

We understand that limiting recruitment payments and benefits raises the question of incentives to retain physicians in HPSAs beyond an initial 3 year period. Because of the increased risk of kickbacks, payments for retention purposes require closer scrutiny than initial recruitment payments. We solicited comments regarding development of a physician retention safe harbor. We received several comments in support of such a safe harbor. A physician retention safe harbor may be the subject of future rulemaking.

Comment: Several commenters had concerns about the fourth proposed standard of the physician recruitment safe harbor, which would require that "the entity providing the benefits cannot condition the agreement on the practitioner's referral of business to the entity." Specifically, one commenter inquired if this meant that the hospital could not condition the recruitment payments on the practitioner having and maintaining staff privileges at the recruiting entity.

Response: This requirement is derived from the small entity investment interests safe harbor at Sec. 1001.952(a)(2)(iv) and is intended to ensure that the agreement is not conditioned on the referral of business from the practitioner to the entity. Consistent with this provision, hospitals may require a practitioner to have and maintain staff privileges; however, a hospital may not prohibit the practitioner from obtaining or maintaining staff privileges at other facilities. A hospital may not condition recruitment payments on aggregate admissions by the practitioner, nor may it require a recruited practitioner to admit a proportionate share of his or her patients to the hospital. A hospital may impose conditions intended to ensure quality of patient care, such as requiring that a physician have performed a minimum number of a particular type ofprocedure before performing the procedure at the hospital.

Comment: Some commenters questioned the need for the requirement that practitioners agree to treat Medicare and Medicaid patients. One commenter suggested that the regulations require a recruited physician to treat all patients referred by the hospital, regardless of a patient's insurance status or ability to pay. A similar comment suggested that the regulations for physician recruitment require the physician to become a participating provider in the Medicare and Medicaid programs.

Response: We have generally addressed this issue in our discussion above. To impose a standard requiring a practitioner to treat all patients referred by a hospital would exceed our regulatory authority. Likewise, we are not requiring recruited practitioners to become participating providers in the Medicare and Medicaid programs. However, if they participate in any Federal health care program, they must treat all program beneficiaries in a nondiscriminatory manner.

Comment: A number of commenters requested that we further define the terms "payment" and "benefit" as used in Secs. 1001.952 (n)(1), (3), and (6) of the proposed physician recruitment safe harbor. Some commenters sought guidance regarding which specific payment practices are protected by the safe harbor.

Response: We decline to specify in these regulations any particular set of payment practices covered by this safe harbor. Recruitment practices necessarily vary depending on specific circumstances. Accordingly, whether payment practices are protected by this safe harbor must be evaluated on a case-by-case basis. In particular, the amount or value of the benefits provided by the entity may not vary (or be adjusted or renegotiated) in any manner based on the volume or value of any expected referrals to, or business otherwise generated for, the recruiting entity by the practitioner for which payment may be made in whole or in part under a Federal health care program.

Comment: A commenter urged that the final regulations make clear that compliance with the recruitment safe harbor exempts parties from having to comply with other safe harbor regulations, including the personal services, space and equipment rental and obstetrical malpractice insurance safe harbors.

Response: This comment addresses a situation where a recruitment agreement may involve more than one safe harbor (e.g., the space rental and obstetrical malpractice safe harbors). If the recruitment agreement as a whole meets the criteria of the recruitment safe harbor, then the agreement as a whole is exempt from criminal prosecution. If, however, the agreement does not fit within the recruitment safe harbor, certain payments made in accordance with it may still be protected under the other safe harbors, if the other individual safe harbor criteria are met.

Comment: Several commenters requested that we clarify whether the safe harbor protects joint recruitment efforts between hospitals and group practices or between hospitals and individual physicians who may employ new physicians in their practices. Along these same lines, one commenter asked us to protect the indirect recruitment activities of managed care organizations, which frequently conduct physician recruitment in conjunction with participating hospitals.

Response: We are aware that an increasing amount of physician recruitment is being conducted through joint arrangements between hospitals and group practices or solo practitioners. Typically, these arrangements involve payments from hospitals to group practices or solo practitioners to assist the group practice or solo practitioner in recruiting a new physician. Managed care organizations are also involved in joint practitioner recruitment activities with hospitals and physician practices. On the one hand, these arrangements can be efficient and cost effective means of recruiting needed practitioners to an underserved community. Moreover, many new practitioners prefer joining an existing group practice to starting a solo practice. On the other hand, these arrangements can be used to disguise payments for referrals from the group practice or solo practice to the hospital.

We are not persuaded that a safe harbor can be crafted that would protect legitimate joint recruiting arrangements of the type described above without sweeping in sham arrangements that are actually disguised payments for referrals. However, we want to make clear that joint recruitment arrangements are not necessarily illegal and must be evaluated on a case-by-case basis. Parties seeking further guidance about their joint recruitment activities may apply for an advisory opinion.

Comment: One commenter stated that the sixth standard of the proposed safe harbor for physician recruitment, which prohibits benefits that vary based on the volume or value of expected referrals, would eliminate income guarantees from safe harbor protection, since the amount of the funds advanced against the guarantee are generally not determined until the new physician has commenced his or her practice and the initial income from the practice has been determined. According to the commenter, income guarantees are among the most common recruitment incentives.

Response: The anti-kickback statute prohibits payment of any remuneration to induce referrals for which payment may be made in whole or in part by a Federal health care program. To this end, this safe harbor, like others, prohibits payments that are based on the volume or value of expected referrals. Recruitment incentives tied to volume or value of referrals generated are not immunized by this safe harbor. However, where the maximum amount of the income guarantee and the formula for determining payment under the guarantee are set in advance and not subject to renegotiation, the formula is not tied to volume or value of referrals, and the income guarantee otherwise meets the safe harbor requirements, the fact that the actual amount that will be paid to the practitioner under the guarantee is not known in advance will not disqualify the income guarantee from safe harbor protection.

Comment: One commenter requested clarification as to how the recruitment safe harbor would apply to physicians recruited to fill medical director positions where, in most cases, the physician is not an employee of the facility and is not generally perceived as a source of referrals.

Response: In many circumstances, medical directors are potential referral sources and medical director contracts serve as a means to reward referrals. There is no special protection for medical directors under the practitioner recruitment safe harbor. To be protected, a recruitment arrangement must meet all of the standards of the safe harbor, including the new patient and underserved patient revenue tests (Secs. 1001.952(n)(2) and (8)). In the alternative, a contract for medical director services may qualify for protection under the employee compensation or personal services contract safe harbors (Secs. 1001.952(i) and (d)).

Comment: Several commenters urged us to make the safe harbor consistent with IRS Revenue Ruling 97–21 on physician recruitment.

Response: The IRS Revenue Ruling 97–21 on physician recruitment by a tax-exempt hospital is intended to provide guidance on recruitment activities that are consistent with a hospital's operations as a tax-exempt entity. The revenue ruling sets forth standards for determining whether atax-exempt hospital's practitioner recruitment activities jeopardize its tax-exempt status. Under the revenue ruling, a hospital does not jeopardize its tax-exempt status if its recruitment payments are reasonably related to its tax-exempt purpose. However, this standard is an insufficient safeguard against improper payments for referrals. A payment that is reasonably related to a hospital's tax-exempt purpose, but is tied to the volume or value of expected referrals, will likely run afoul of the anti-kickback statute and is not appropriate for safe harbor protection.

Comment: One commenter asked us to reaffirm that not all physician recruitment activities necessarily violate the anti-kickback statute, and that recruitment programs not meeting the safe harbor criteria will be analyzed on a case-by-case basis.

Response: The failure of a particular arrangement to comply with the safe harbor does not determine whether or not the arrangement violates the anti-kickback statute. Neither does such failure determine whether an enforcement action is warranted. As a general rule, remuneration to physicians, including recruitment, should be consistent with fair market value for necessary services rendered by the physician. The practitioner recruitment safe harbor protects certain payment practices that may depart from this general rule if particular criteria established by the safe harbor are met. Arrangements that do not qualify for the safe harbor must be evaluated on a case-by-case basis to determine whether there has been a violation and whether an enforcement proceeding is warranted.

5. Obstetrical Malpractice Insurance Subsidies

Summary of Proposed Rule: We proposed a new safe harbor to permit a hospital or other entity to pay all or part of the malpractice insurance premiums for practitioners engaging in obstetrical practice in primary health care professional shortage areas. For purposes of this safe harbor, we included certified nurse midwives as defined in section 1861(gg) of the Act in the definition of "practitioner." We limited this safe harbor to the provision of malpractice insurance regulated by State law. We explained that nothing in the safe harbor would authorize payment by the Federal health care programs to hospitals or other institutional providers for costs they may incur in providing malpractice insurance. Any allowable costs for such insurance are governed strictly by Federal health care program rules.

We solicited comments on specific, narrowly-drawn circumstances where this safe harbor provision could be expanded to help assure beneficiary access to services that may be significantly affected by the cost of malpractice insurance premiums. In addition, we solicited views regarding the feasibility of expanding this safe harbor to protect malpractice insurance programs that are not regulated under State law, but which are operated directly by providers.

Summary of Final Rule: This safe harbor is intended to facilitate access to obstetrical services for Federal health care program beneficiaries in primary care health professional shortage areas by protecting from the reach of the anti-kickback statute subsidized malpractice insurance for practitioners who are primarily engaged in obstetrical practices in those areas. We have adopted the proposed safe harbor with the following modifications:

- We are expanding the safe harbor to cover self-funded insurance plans.
- We are reducing from 85 percent to 75 percent the proportion of the practitioner's obstetrical patients who must be treated under the subsidized insurance coverage.
- We are eliminating the phrase "be in a position to make or influence referrals" from Sec. 1001.952(o)(3), since most, if not all, insurers require practitioners to be in a position to perform obstetrical services as a condition of coverage.
- We are requiring that protected practitioners be engaged in obstetrics as a routine part of their practices. Full subsidies for obstetrical malpractice insurance may be paid for full-time obstetricians or nurse midwives; for part-time practitioners in obstetrics, the safe harbor protects only costs attributable to the obstetrical portion of their practices.Comments and Responses.

Comment: One commenter recommended expanding the phrase "practitioners engaging in obstetrical practice" to include explicitly family practitioners and other physicians who may deliver babies, in order to make clear that the safe harbor covers insurance subsidies for such individuals.

Response: We agree that limited safe harbor protection is appropriate for family practitioners and other physicians and certified nurse midwives who deliver babies as a routine part of their medical practices. Accordingly, we are amending the proposed regulation to provide for limited coverage for "a practitioner who engages in obstetrical practice as a routine part of his or her medical practice." For purposes of this safe harbor, by "routine" we mean that the practitioner must provide substantial and regular obstetrical services; we do not intend to protect obstetrical insurance subsidies for practitioners who practice obstetrical medicine on only an occasional basis.

For practitioners who are not full-time obstetricians or certified nurse midwives, we will protect payments for obstetrical malpractice insurance only. We will not protect subsidies for other types of medical malpractice liability insurance. Thus, for these practitioners the protected subsidy will be the difference between the cost of malpractice insurance that includes obstetrical coverage and the cost of malpractice insurance that does not include such coverage. Similarly, the safe harbor will protect certain insurance subsidies paid on behalf of practitioners engaged in obstetrical practices part-time in a HPSA and part-time elsewhere. We have in mind, in particular, urban obstetricians who may practice several days in an inner-city clinic (in a HPSA) and several days in areas that are not underserved. For these practitioners, the safe harbor protects insurance subsidies for obstetrical malpractice insurance coverage related exclusively to services provided in the HPSA. If the practitioner is covered by a single insurance policy or program, the safe harbor covers subsidies for that portion of the insurance premium that is reasonably allocable to obstetrical services provided in a HPSA.

Comment: We solicited comments on specific, narrowly-drawn circumstances where this safe harbor provision could be expanded to help assure beneficiary access to services that may be significantly affected by the cost of malpractice insurance premiums. In response, one commenter recommended expanding this safe harbor to include neuro, cardiovascular and orthopedic surgeons. Two commenters recommended enlarging the safe harbor to cover malpractice insurance coverage for pediatricians. A commenter also recommended expanding the safe harbor to cover emergency room coverage by high risk medical specialists in situations where a hospital is able to certify that a viable panel of specialists is only possible if the hospital can provide this benefit. One hospital association expressed concern that a safe harbor only for insurance subsidies for obstetrical practitioners may create unnecessary concern in the industry that all other types of practitioner malpractice insurance subsidies may be suspect. Theassociation recommended greatly expanding the proposed safe harbor or deleting it as written.

Response: This safe harbor is intended to promote access to obstetrical services for Federal health care program beneficiaries and others in underserved areas. Although we solicited comments on expanding this safe harbor, we are not persuaded at this time that there are compelling reasons to expand it beyond malpractice insurance subsidies for practitioners engaging in obstetrical practices. This safe harbor does not call into question the legality of all other types of practitioner malpractice insurance subsidies. Such subsidies may qualify for protection under other safe harbors, such as practitioner recruitment, personal services contracts or employee compensation (Secs. 1001.952(n), (d), and (i)). Moreover, as we have previously stated, the fact that a payment practice does not fall within the ambit of a safe harbor does not necessarily mean that the practice violates the anti-kickback statute. At the same time, we note that malpractice insurance subsidies paid to or on behalf of potential referral sources may be suspect under the anti-kickback statute. These arrangements are subject to a case-by-case evaluation. The advisory opinion process is available for parties seeking OIG guidance on the anti-kickback implications of particular insurance subsidy arrangements (See 42 CFR part 1008).

Comment: Several commenters offered views on the geographic scope of the safe harbor. One commenter recommended that we expand the scope of the safe harbor to protect subsidies in primary care HPSAs and in rural areas as defined in 42 CFR 412.62(f)(1)(iii). Another urged application of the safe harbor in urban areas. Some commenters noted that the HPSA designation process is a volatile, on-going process, and that the list of shortage areas is rarely an accurate reflection of actual need for health care professionals at a particular point in time. Moreover, these commenters believed that dependence on Federal designations fails to recognize the role of states in identifying and remedying health professional shortage areas. One commenter suggested focusing on emergency room admissions of obstetrics patients who have no designated primary care practitioner rather than on HPSA data to measure community need.

One commenter raised the question of what happens when the offer of subsidized malpractice insurance induces a physician to relocate to a HPSA, but the physician's relocation itself serves to remove the community's HPSA designation. This commenter proposed substituting a "need" standard, with the appropriate documentation of need for the subsidized practitioner left up to the entity providing the subsidy. This commenter observed that many current safe harbors use the concept of "fair market value" without requiring any particular fair market value standard to be met, and the health care community for the most part understands that documentation is critical to prove fair market value in the event a particular transaction is later scrutinized. Examples of documentation of "need" could include determinations by State legislatures, as well as any other appropriate indications of need for a particular type of health care professional.

Response: As described in greater detail above in our responses to comments on the practitioner recruitment safe harbor, primary care HPSAs may be located in rural or urban areas. We are limiting this safe harbor to primary care HPSAs so as to ensure as much as possible that the benefits protected by this safe harbor are extended to practitioners in areas where there is a well-founded, documented shortage of obstetrical practitioners. We are aware that there are and have been problems with the HPSA process. We expect that the Department's anticipated revision of the process should address many of those problems, including providing States with greater input in designating shortage areas. We believe that a general "need" standard could be manipulated in ways that would permit abusive payments in the guise of insurance subsidies. We note that nothing in this safe harbor prevents protection of malpractice insurance subsidies for practitioners engaged in practice outside primary care HPSAs as part of an arms-length, fair market value compensation package that meets the requirements of the personal services safe harbor or the employee compensation exception to the anti-kickback statute (Secs. 1001.952(d) and (c); 42 U.S.C. 1320a-7b (b)(3)(B)).

Comment: One commenter questioned the feasibility of the requirement that 85 percent of the practitioner's obstetrical patients treated under the insurance coverage must come from certain defined underserved populations, noting that compliance with the standard can only be determined after the payment of the insurance premium subsidy. The commenter observed that obtaining liability coverage necessarily precedes treatment of any patients under that coverage. Documenting compliance with the standard is particularly problematic where insurance subsidies are used as recruiting devices for new or relocating practitioners who do not have established patient pools that can be measured. One commenter suggested that this problem could be solved by deeming the 85 percent test satisfied if the practitioner provides a written stipulation that the 85 percent test will be met.

Response: Upon further review, we believe that an 85 percent test is unnecessarily restrictive. Accordingly, we have amended the safe harbor to provide that 75 percent of the patients treated must come from underserved populations, that is, they must reside in a HPSA or a MUA or be part of a MUP, all as defined by HRSA and described above. Moreover, we agree that under the test as drafted in the proposed rule, it would not be possible for parties seeking safe harbor protection to determine whether a payment for an insurance subsidy satisfies the safe harbor prior to making the payment. However, we believe that a practitioner stipulation is insufficient by itself to ensure that appropriate populations are benefitting from the increased access to obstetrical care contemplated by this safe harbor. Accordingly, we have amended the safe harbor to provide that for the initial coverage period, which will be limited to one year, the practitioner must certify that he or she has a reasonable basis for believing that he or she will meet the 75 percent test for the duration of the coverage period. Thereafter, for payments of insurance premiums to be protected, the 75 percent standard must have been met for the period covered by the preceding insurance premium payment, which coverage period may not exceed one year.

Comment: One commenter recommended eliminating the requirement that the insurance subsidy be paid to the insurance provider, rather than the subsidized practitioner.

Response: The requirement that the subsidy be paid to the insurance provider is a reasonable means of ensuring that the payment is used for the purposes intended by this safe harbor. Permitting a direct cash payment to the subsidized practitioner increases the risk that the "subsidy" payment may in fact be a disguised payment for referrals. We are not persuaded that payment directly to insurance providers is impractical or unduly burdensome on subsidizing entities or subsidized practitioners.

Comment: One commenter believed that the requirement that practitionerstreat Medicaid patients is superfluous, because the anti-kickback statute is only implicated where Medicaid and Medicare referrals are in fact made. Another commenter recommended amending the requirement to provide that a physician may not discriminate against Medicaid patients to the extent the physician is able to see new patients in his or her practice. Otherwise, the safe harbor would preclude protection for physicians whose current practices may be full.

Response: These issues are addressed above with respect to the safe harbor regarding physician recruitment.

Comment: A commenter observed that some professional liability underwriters, especially in states with harsh liability climates, do not have the surpluses required to provide coverage beyond certain minimum limits, and suggested that the safe harbor should protect hospital underwriting of all physician liability above certain limits in order to protect physicians against large awards against them. The commenter suggested limits of $100,000 to $300,000.

Response: This proposal, which essentially would cover the entire range of practitioner services, does not meet our requirements for proposals of specific, narrowly-drawn circumstances where the safe harbor could be expanded to help assure beneficiary access to services significantly affected by the cost of malpractice insurance premiums.

Comment: Several commenters suggested the safe harbor be extended to protect payment of premiums or establishment of reserves in self-funded programs underwritten and operated by hospitals and other providers, including risk-retention groups. These commenters point out that many hospitals and other entities elect self-insurance programs for physicians on the medical staff, instead of purchasing commercial insurance from independent third parties. The commenters noted that self-insurance programs, including risk-retention groups, were established in response to the unavailability or unaffordability of malpractice insurance for certain areas or specialities. Commenters believed that these programs keep health care costs to a more reasonable level and ought to be encouraged and protected. They argued that the benefit to the physician is the same whether insurance is provided through a self-funded program or commercial third party insurance, and thus hospitals or other health care providers with self-funded programs should not be deprived of protection. Self-insured hospitals are not in a position to make payments to another entity that provides insurance. To assure that only bona fide programs are shielded, one commenter recommended that only programs that have been certified by a qualified actuary as adequate relative to the risk assumed should be afforded safe harbor protection. Finally, several commenters suggested expanding the safe harbor to include offshore insurance products.

Response: We solicited comments regarding the feasibility of expanding the safe harbor to protect subsidies for insurance under programs operated directly by providers. As indicated in the preamble to the 1993 proposed rule, our concern was that the subsidized insurance policies be bona fide to ensure that this safe harbor is not used as a mechanism to disguise improper inducements to practitioners. The requirement that the insurance be bona fide also protects practitioners and patients. We agree that from the practitioner's perspective, the benefit derived from an insurance subsidy is the same whether the insurance is provided by commercial third party insurance or a self-funded program. Accordingly, we have amended the safe harbor to extend protection to bona fide self-funded obstetrical malpractice insurance programs, including risk-retention groups that qualify under the Liability Risk Retention Act, 15 U.S.C. 3901, and to bona fide offshore insurance products. Although we are not defining the full scope of bona fide insurance products, we believe that certification by a qualified actuary that the program is adequate relative to the risk insured would be an indicator of a bona fide insurance program.

Comment: One commenter suggested that the prohibition on requiring a physician to "be in a position to make or influence referrals" limits the ability of facilities to require that physicians maintain medical licenses and be in a position to practice medicine and recommended that the prohibition be eliminated.

Response: Nothing in these safe harbor regulations is intended to prevent hospitals and other health care facilities from requiring that physicians and other practitioners who perform services at or for such facilities be fully licensed and able to practice medicine. In particular, we recognize that proper licensure and qualifications to practice medicine are prerequisites for obtaining malpractice insurance. We are persuaded that the language "be in a position to make or influence referrals to" is unnecessary in the context of a safe harbor for obstetrical malpractice insurance subsidies. Therefore, we have amended the third condition of the safe harbor to prohibit any requirement that practitioners "make referrals to, or otherwise generate business for, the entity as a condition for receiving the benefits."

Comment: One commenter expressed concern that the safe harbor does not adequately protect group practices.

Response: A group practice that provides obstetrical malpractice insurance subsidies may qualify as an "entity" for purposes of this safe harbor. Moreover, as indicated above, we have amended the safe harbor to permit entities to subsidize insurance through self-funded insurance programs. This safe harbor is not intended to protect group practices for any payment practice that does not satisfy all of the safe harbor criteria, including the requirements that the subsidized practitioner practice in a primary care HPSA and that 75 percent of the obstetrical patients treated reside in underserved areas.6. Referral Agreements for Specialty Services

Summary of Proposed Rule: We proposed a new safe harbor for referral agreements for specialty services. This safe harbor would protect arrangements under which an individual or entity agrees to refer a patient to another individual or entity for specialty services in return for an agreement on the part of the party receiving the referral to refer the patient back at a certain time or under certain circumstances. For example, a primary care physician and a specialist (to whom the primary care physician has made a referral) may agree that, when their patient reaches a particular stage of recovery, the primary care physician should resume treatment of the patient.

We proposed three standards that such a referral arrangement would have to meet to fit within the safe harbor. First, the service for which the initial referral is made must not be within the medical expertise of the referring party and must be within the special expertise of the party receiving the referral. Second, the parties could receive no payment from each other for the referral. Third, the only exchange of value permitted between the parties would be the monetary remuneration each party would receive directly from third-party payers or the patient as compensation for professional services furnished by each party to the patient.

We proposed an accommodation in this safe harbor for members of the same group practice who refer to one another. Where the referring and receiving physicians belong to the same group practice, revenues are shared amongmembers of the group practice, and thus it appears that the referring physician receives remuneration for the referral. However, such financial benefits are an inherent part of belonging to a group practice, and therefore we proposed protecting such remuneration if the group practice met the definition of "group practice" in section 1877(h)(4) of the Act.

Summary of Final Rule: Because of the potential for abuse when the referring physician and the specialty physician receiving the referral split a global payment from a Federal health care program, we are revising the regulation specifically to exclude remuneration received in such circumstances from the safe harbor. We are also adding a requirement that the condition for the referral back to the originating referral source must be clinically appropriate. We are otherwise promulgating the safe harbor as proposed.

Comments and Responses

Comment: A number of commenters generally supported the approach of the proposed safe harbor, stating that it would adequately protect legitimate referral arrangements while sufficiently discouraging illegitimate ones. They suggested that the safe harbor would be useful because it would assure convenient access to follow-up care in communities where there are no specialists. However, several commenters suggested that insulating referrals for specialty services from the kickback statute would encourage arrangements that might compromise the quality of patient care, because arrangements between the primary physician and the referral specialist might require a patient to be referred back to the primary physician, regardless of whether it would be clinically appropriate. Further, specialty referral arrangements could deny patients the right to choose their providers.

Response: We share the commenters' concerns that patient referrals be made only under clinically appropriate circumstances. Indeed, clinical appropriateness should be the touchstone of all referrals, specialty or otherwise. To emphasize the importance of clinical appropriateness as a consideration, we are revising the safe harbor to reflect that the "mutually agreed upon time or circumstance" for the receiving specialist to return the patient must be clinically appropriate. We are not further defining "clinically appropriate," however, because whether a referral is clinically appropriate will depend on the particular facts and circumstances. Depending on circumstances, an agreement to refer a patient back on a date certain, without regard to medical condition, would be questionable.

We also share the commenters' concerns regarding the preservation of patient freedom of choice. Patient freedom of choice may be compromised, however, if patients are not given access to needed specialty care. There is a legitimate concern if physicians are disinclined to refer patients to specialists because of fear of losing patients to those specialists permanently. Thus, for example, the safe harbor would protect an agreement between a general cardiologist and a cardiologist with special expertise on a particular medical condition whereby (i) the general cardiologist would refer a patient to the specialist for treatment of the particular medical condition about which the specialist has expertise, and (ii) the specialist — who also has a general cardiology practice — would refer the patient back to the originating cardiologist upon completion of the specialty treatment.

We want to make clear that protection under this safe harbor is limited to referral arrangements for patients of the physician making referrals to the specialist. The safe harbor does not protect generalized cross-referral arrangements of the "you send me your patients and I'll send you mine" variety. Rather, the safe harbor protects an agreement to refer patients to a specialist in return for an agreement or understanding that the specialist will refer those same patients back at the agreed upon time or circumstance (e.g., completion of the specialist services for which the patient was referred). In other words, assuming all safe harbor conditions are satisfied (and there is no split of a global fee, as discussed below), the safe harbor will protect agreements along the lines of "I'll send you my patients who need your specialist services if you agree to send them back to me upon completion of your services."

On balance, we believe that a safe harbor under the anti-kickback statute for referrals for specialty services is appropriate and will protect many legitimate referral arrangements that benefit patients, including those living in remote areas. Where no payment is made between the referring and receiving parties (and there is no splitting of a Federal health care program global fee, as discussed below), we believe the specialty referral arrangements protected by the safe harbor pose no more than a minimal risk of illegal remuneration for referrals in violation of the anti-kickback statute.

Comment: Ophthalmology providers were especially concerned that the proposed safe harbor may encourage the development of potentially abusive referral arrangements with optometrists, who wish to receive the post-operative portion of the Medicare global fee for eye surgery. The ophthalmologists allege that many optometrists refer patients to ophthalmologists on the condition that patients be referred back to the optometrists for post-surgical care, often without regard to clinical appropriateness. Some ophthalmologists claimed that optometrists generally control referrals and therefore ophthalmologists, for whom surgical procedures are the mainstay of their practices, must acquiesce to these return referral arrangements in order to get patients. One commenter described a situation where an optometrist/ophthalmologist network referred patients for cataract surgery only to ophthalmologists who would agree to split the global surgical fee by referring the patient back to the optometrist for post-operative care. The optometrists referred their patients to an ophthalmologic surgery center 200 miles away when there were at least 50 available ophthalmologists from 7 to 35 miles away.

In such circumstances, the ophthalmologists do not do any of the follow-up care for the patients and the post-operative portion of the global fee is paid to the optometrists. The commenter, an ophthalmologist, had provided some of the patients referred by the optometrist network with a second opinion and found that none required surgery.

Response: The serious issues raised by the ophthalmologists about apparently routine or blanket agreements to split global Medicare fees with referring optometrists (as well as other information that has come to our attention from industry and Government sources) has caused us to modify the scope of this safe harbor. We have revised the safe harbor regulation to preclude protection for arrangements between parties that share or split a global or bundled payment from a Federal health care program for the referred patient. Thus, for example, the safe harbor does not protect referral arrangements where the parties bill Medicare using the 54/55 modifiers to indicate an 80 percent-20 percent split of the surgical fee for cataract surgery.

By limiting the safe harbor, we do not mean to suggest that all specialty referral arrangements involving splitting of global fees are illegal under the anti-kickback statute. Whether a particularreferral arrangement for specialty services violates the anti-kickback statute depends on a case-by-case analysis of all of the facts and circumstances, including, but not limited to, whether the specialty services are medically necessary, whether the timing of the referrals is clinically appropriate, and whether the services performed are commensurate with the portion of the global fee received.

Comment: One commenter questioned whether the anti-kickback statute applies to specialty referral arrangements where no kickback, rebate or other consideration is made for the referral.

Response: As the United States Court of Appeals for the First Circuit has recognized, the opportunity to generate a fee may constitute the requisite remuneration under the statute, even if no payment or rebate is paid for a referral. For instance, the opportunity to split a global surgical fee, as in the hypothetical described in the previous comment, is an example of a circumstance in which an opportunity to generate a fee is something of value to a referring party apart from any payment for the referral. Giving a person an opportunity to earn money may well be an inducement to that person to channel potential Medicare patients toward a particular recipient.

(See United States v. Bay State Ambulance and Hospital Rental Service, Inc., 874 F.2d 20, 29 (1st Cir. 1989)).

Comment: A managed care organization trade association commented that managed care organization arrangements often require the referral of patients to other contracting providers as a condition of the provider's compensation and that the anti-kickback statute should not be construed so broadly as to encompass these types of managed care arrangements. In addition, a managed care plan commented that the safe harbor should be expanded to exempt expressly referrals made within an HMO, or that the OIG should establish a new safe harbor for referrals made by HMO-participating physicians.

Response: The anti-kickback statute is broad and technically may cover many managed care arrangements that are common in the marketplace today. However, we have recognized that most of these arrangements involving HMOs do not create the potential for fraud or abuse and have created safe harbors aimed at those arrangements. Currently, Sec. 1001.952(m) protects certain price reductions offered to health plans. In addition, as part of HIPAA, Congress enacted a statutory exception for managed care arrangements that put individuals or entities at substantial financial risk (42 U.S.C. 1320a-7b(b)(3)(F)).[5] These safe harbors offer broad protection under the anti-kickback statute to HMOs.

Comment: One commenter urged that we clarify the safe harbor to make clear that it covers primary care practitioners in rural areas who do not belong to group practices.

Response: The safe harbor applies to solo practitioners, as well as members of group practices. To be protected by the safe harbor, solo practitioners may not give anything of value to a specialist in exchange for the referral back of his or her original patient, except for the opportunity to receive compensation for services directly from third parties or patients. Members of bona fide group practices who refer among themselves are not similarly restricted; they may share revenues from specialty services performed as a result of the intra-group referrals.7. Cooperative Hospital Service Organizations

Summary of Proposed Rule: We proposed a new safe harbor to protect cooperative hospital service organizations (CHSOs) that qualify under section 501(e) of the Internal Revenue Code. These organizations are formed by two or more tax exempt hospitals (known as "patron hospitals") to provide specifically enumerated

[5] See footnote 2.

services, such as purchasing, billing, and clinical services solely for the benefit of patron hospitals. These entities are required by law to distribute all of their net earnings to patrons on the basis of services performed (26 U.S.C. 501(e)(2)).

The safe harbor would protect payments from a patron hospital to a CHSO to support the CHSO's operational costs and those payments from a CHSO to a patron hospital that are required by IRS rules. As a condition of protection, the CHSO must be wholly owned by its patron hospitals, in order to avoid potentially abusive joint venture arrangements formed under the guise of CHSOs. To the extent a CHSO acts as a group purchasing agent or a patron hospital obtains discounts as a result of the CHSO's activities, CHSOs and patron hospitals must comply with the respective safe harbor provisions applicable to group purchasing organization and discounts (Secs. 1001.952(j) and (h)) to be fully protected. We solicited comments regarding the various types of payment formula (which comply with the IRS rules) that are used by CHSOs, but did not receive any comments on this issue.

Summary of Final Rule: We are adopting the rule as proposed, with some minor technical changes.Comments and Responses

Comment: We requested comments on the extent to which we should expand this provision to protect other similar entities specifically organized under Federal or State laws. Four comments were submitted suggesting that the safe harbor be expanded to include other types of cooperative organizations that qualify under subchapter T of the Internal Revenue Code (sections 1381 to 1388). One commenter also requested that the safe harbor be expanded to include other types of hospital cooperative organizations.

Response: We decline to extend safe harbor protection to cooperative organizations that do not qualify under section 501(e). Unlike CHSOs complying with that section, there are few limitations applicable to cooperative organizations qualifying under subchapter T. There are no limits on the types of services that may be shared, nor are there restrictions on the identity of shareholders. The conditions and limitations imposed on tax-exempt entities, including the limits on private inurement, do not apply to subchapter T organizations. We believe the limitations imposed under section 501(e) are necessary to protect against potentially abusive joint ventures or referral arrangements. Additionally, in view of the small number of comments we received concerning non-hospital cooperatives and the fact that we received only a single comment requesting broader hospital coverage, we are not persuaded of the need to broaden the safe harbor to other types of hospital or non-hospital cooperatives. Accordingly, we are adopting the proposed safe harbor for CHSOs without modification.8. Modification of Sale of Practice Safe Harbor

Summary of Proposed Rule: We solicited comments on the desirability of modifying the existing sale of practice safe harbor set forth in Sec. 1001.952(e) to accommodate transactions involving the rural hospital purchase of a physician practice as part of a practitioner recruitment program that complies with the safe harbor we are establishing to protect practitioner recruitment. The existing sale of practice safe harbor did not protect such purchases. We had been informed that many rural hospitals buy and “hold” the practice of a retiring physician, often using locum tenensphysicians until a new physician can be recruited to replace the retiring one.

Summary of Final Rule: We are modifying the existing sale of practice safe harbor to protect payments made to a practitioner by a hospital or other entity to purchase the practitioner’s practice where the following conditions are satisfied:

- The sale is completed within 3 years.
- After completion of the sale, the practitioner who is selling his or her practice will not be in a professional position to make referrals to, or otherwise generate business for, the purchasing entity for which payment may be made by a Federal health care program.
- The practice being acquired must be located in a HPSA for the practitioner’s specialty area.
- Commencing at the time of the sale, the purchasing entity must diligently and in good faith engage in recruitment activities that (i) may reasonably be expected to result in the recruitment of a new practitioner to take over the acquired practice within 1 year of completion of the sale, and (ii) satisfy the conditions of the new practitioner recruitment safe harbor (Sec. 1001.952 (n)).Comments and Responses.

Comment: Commenters generally supported our proposed modification to the sale of practice safe harbor. Some commenters urged that the safe harbor be extended to sales of practices in urban underserved areas. One commenter stated that the problem of preserving and maintaining a retiring physician’s practice until a new physician can be recruited and established exists in both urban and rural HPSAs. Because of these difficulties, a hospital may find itself in the position of "holding" a practice for some time. One commenter suggested that in the case of small, rural hospitals with tight cash flow, the payment period under the safe harbor should be 3 to 5 years, rather than 1 year as set forth in the existing safe harbor.

Several commenters stated that the existing sale of practice safe harbor is too narrow. Some commenters suggested that the safe harbor be expanded to include entities other than hospitals, such as hospital systems and other health care organizations. These commenters urged the OIG to modify the safe harbor to protect, among other arrangements, sales of practices in accordance with fair market value transactions and sales of practices to entities in connection with the process of creating integrated health care delivery systems. One commenter urged the OIG to modify the safe harbor to provide that reasonable valuation of all assets, tangible and intangible, may be used to determine the market value of the practice.

Response: Based on the comments we received to our solicitation and after further consideration, we are persuaded that a need exists to protect certain practice acquisitions by hospitals and other entities located in rural and urban underserved areas that are engaged in practitioner recruitment programs, and that these arrangements can be protected without concurrently immunizing potentially fraudulent or abusive practices. Specifically, we are modifying the sale of practice safe harbor to protect acquisitions of the practices of physicians in underserved areas who are retiring or relocating a distance that would preclude them from being in a position to make referrals to the purchasing entity, if the acquisitions occur as part of a practitioner recruitment program that qualifies for protection under the safe harbor for practitioner recruitment contained in these regulations. We are requiring that the physician be retired from the practice of medicine or otherwise no longer in a position to generate referrals for the hospital. A purchase of a practice from a physician potentially still in a position to make referrals to the purchasing entity might result in abusive payments to induce referrals of business from the physician's new practice. Relocation a significant distance from the practice being sold is an indicator that a physician is no longer in a position to refer patients. We agree that a longer payment period is appropriate in the context of this safe harbor; accordingly, we are establishing a 3 year period for completion of the sale from the date of the first agreement pertaining to the sale.

As a result, to be protected, a sale of practice by a practitioner must meet all of the following conditions: (1) The period from the date of the first agreement pertaining to the sale to the completion of the sale is not more than 3 years; (2) following the sale, the practitioner may not be in a position to make or influence referrals to, or otherwise generate business for, the purchasing entity for which payment may be made in whole or in part under a Federal health care program; (3) the practice being acquired must be located in a HPSA for the practitioner's specialty area; (4) commencing at the time of the first agreement pertaining to the sale, the purchasing entity must diligently and in good faith engage in commercially reasonable recruitment activities that (i) may reasonably be expected to result in the recruitment of a new practitioner to take over the acquired practice within a 1 year period, and (ii) will satisfy the conditions of the practitioner recruitment safe harbor at Sec. 1001.952(n).

We are not inclined at this time to modify the sale of practice safe harbor further. While we do not intend to stand in the way of integrated delivery system acquisitions of practices, we are concerned that many such arrangements may provide incentives for overutilization, increased billings to the Federal programs, and inappropriate steering of patients in circumstances where the Federal health care programs pay on a fee-for-service basis. Moreover, we remain of the opinion that payments for "intangibles'' can easily be used to disguise payments for referrals of Federal health care program business, and therefore we are unwilling to provide safe harbor protection for any particular valuation methodology.

III. Regulatory Impact Statement

Executive Order 12866, the Unfunded Mandates Reform Act and Regulatory Flexibility Act

The Office of Management and Budget has reviewed this final rule in accordance with the provisions of Executive Order 12866 and the Regulatory Flexibility Act (5 U.S.C. 601–612), and has determined that it does not meet the criteria for an economically significant regulatory action. Executive Order 12866 direct agencies to assess all costs and benefits of available regulatory alternatives and, when rulemaking is necessary, to select regulatory approaches that maximize net benefits (including potential economic, environmental, public health, safety distributive and equity effects). The Unfunded Mandates Reform Act, Public Law 104–4, requires that agencies prepare an assessment of anticipated costs and benefits on any rulemaking that may result in an annual expenditure by State, local or tribal government, or by the private sector of $100 million or more. In addition, under the Regulatory Flexibility Act, if a rule has a significant economic effect on a substantial number of small businesses, the Secretary must specifically consider the economic effect of a rule on small business entities and analyze regulatory options that could lessen the impact of the rule.

Executive Order 12866 requires that all regulations reflect consideration of alternatives, costs, benefits, incentives, equity and available information. Regulations must meet certain standards, such as avoiding unnecessaryburden. We believe that this final rule should have no significant economic impact. The safe harbor provisions set forth in this rulemaking are designed to permit individuals and entities to freely engage in business practices and arrangements that encourage competition, innovation and economy. In doing so, these regulations impose no requirements on any party. Health care providers and others may voluntarily seek to comply with these provisions so that they have the assurance that their business practices are not subject to any enforcement actions under the anti-kickback statute.

We believe that any aggregate economic effect of these safe harbor regulations will be minimal and will impact only those limited few who engage in prohibited behavior in violation of the statute. As such, we believe that the aggregate economic impact of these regulations is minimal and will have no effect on the economy or on Federal or State expenditures.

Additionally, in accordance with the Unfunded Mandates Reform Act of 1995, we have determined that there are no significant costs associated with these safe harbor guidelines that would impose any mandates on State, local or tribal governments, or the private sector that will result in an annual expenditure of $100 million or more, and that a full analysis under the Act is not necessary.

Further, in accordance with the Regulatory Flexibility Act (RFA) of 1980, and the Small Business Regulatory Enforcement Act of 1996, which amended the RFA, we are required to determine if this rule will have a significant economic effect on a substantial number of small entities and, if so, to identify regulatory options that could lessen the impact. While some of these safe harbor provisions may have an impact on small entities, we believe that the aggregate economic impact of this rulemaking should be minimal, since it is the nature of the violation and not the size of the entity that will result in a violation of the anti-kickback statute. Since the vast majority of individuals and entities potentially affected by these regulations do not engage in prohibited arrangements, schemes or practices in violation of the law, we have concluded that these final regulations should not have a significant economic impact on a number of small business entities, and that a regulatory flexibility analysis is not required for this rulemaking.

Paperwork Reduction Act

As indicated above, the provisions of these final regulations are voluntary and impose no new reporting or recordkeeping requirements on health care providers necessitating clearance by OMB.

List of Subjects in 42 CFR Part 1001

Administrative practice and procedure, Fraud, Grant programs — health, Health facilities, Health professions, Maternal and child health, Medicaid, Medicare.

Accordingly, 42 CFR part 1001 is amended as set forth below:

PART 1001 — [AMENDED]

1. The authority citation for part 1001 continues to read as follows:

Authority: 42 U.S.C. 1302, 1320a-7, 1320a-7b, 1395u(j), 1395u(k), 1395y(d), 1395y(e), 1395cc(b)(2) (D), (E) and (F), and 1395hh; and sec. 2455, Pub.L. 103–355, 108 Stat. 3327 (31 U.S.C. 6101 note).

2. Section 1001.952 is amended as follows:

a. By republishing the introductory text;

b. Revising paragraph (a), introductory text;

c. Republishing paragraph (a)(1), introductory text;

d. Revising paragraphs (a)(1)(ii) and (iv), (a)(2)(i), (vi) and (vii);

e. Adding a new paragraph (a)(3)

f. Redesignating the closing definitional paragraph in paragraph (a); as paragraph (a)(4) and revising it;

g. Revising paragraph (b), and introductory text, and paragraph (b)(2) and adding a new paragraph (b)(6);

h. Revising paragraph (c), and introductory text, and paragraph (c)(2) and adding a new paragraph (c)(6);

i. Revising paragraph (d), introductory text, and paragraph (d)(2) and adding a new paragraph (d)(7);

j. Revising paragraph (e);

k. Republishing paragraph (f), introductory text, and revising paragraph (f)(2); l. Revising paragraph (h); and

m. Adding new paragraphs (n) through (s).

The additions and revisions to Sec. 1001.952 read as follows:

Sec. 1001.952 Exceptions.

The following payment practices shall not be treated as a criminal offense under section 1128B of the Act and shall not serve as the basis for an exclusion:

(a) Investment interests. As used in section 1128B of the Act, "remuneration" does not include any payment that is a return on an investment interest, such as a dividend or interest income, made to an investor as long as all of the applicable standards are met within one of the following three categories of entities:

(1) If, within the previous fiscal year or previous 12 month period, the entity possesses more than $50,000,000 in undepreciated net tangible assets (based on the net acquisition cost of purchasing such assets from an unrelated entity) related to the furnishing of health care items and services, all of the following five standards must be met — * * * * *

(ii) The investment interest of an investor in a position to make or influence referrals to, furnish items or services to, or otherwise generate business for the entity must be obtained on terms (including any direct or indirect transferability restrictions) and at a price equally available to the public when trading on a registered securities exchange, such as the New York Stock Exchange or the American Stock Exchange, or in accordance with the National Association of Securities Dealers Automated Quotation System.* * * * *

(iv) The entity or any investor (or other individual or entity acting on behalf of the entity or any investor in the entity) must not loan funds to or guarantee a loan for an investor who is in a position to make or influence referrals to, furnish items or services to, or otherwise generate business for the entity if the investor uses any part of such loan to obtain the investment interest.* * * * *

(2) * * *

(i) No more than 40 percent of the value of the investment interests of each class of investment interests may be held in the previous fiscal year or previous 12 month period by investors who are in a position to make or influence referrals to, furnish items or services to, or otherwise generate business for the entity. (For purposes of paragraph (a)(2)(i) of this section, equivalent classes of equity investments may be combined, and equivalent classes of debt instruments may be combined.)* * * * *

(vi) No more than 40 percent of the entity's gross revenue related to the furnishing of health care items and services in the previous fiscal year or previous 12-month period may come from referrals or business otherwise generated from investors.

(vii) The entity or any investor (or other individual or entity acting on behalf of the entity or any investor in the entity) must not loan funds to or guarantee a loan for an investor who is in a position to make or influence referrals to, furnish items or services to, or otherwise generate business for theentity if the investor uses any part of such loan to obtain the investment interest.* * * * *

(3)(i) If the entity possesses investment interests that are held by either active or passive investors and is located in an underserved area, all of the following eight standards must be met—

(A) No more than 50 percent of the value of the investment interests of each class of investments may be held in the previous fiscal year or previous 12-month period by investors who are in a position to make or influence referrals to, furnish items or services to, or otherwise generate business for, the entity. (For purposes of paragraph (a)(3)(i)(A) of this section, equivalent classes of equity investments may be combined, and equivalent classes of debt instruments may be combined.)

(B) The terms on which an investment interest is offered to a passive investor, if any, who is in a position to make or influence referrals to, furnish items or services to, or otherwise generate business for the entity must be no different from the terms offered to other passive investors.

(C) The terms on which an investment interest is offered to an investor who is in a position to make or influence referrals to, furnish items or services to, or otherwise generate business for the entity must not be related to the previous or expected volume of referrals, items or services furnished, or the amount of business otherwise generated from that investor to the entity.

(D) There is no requirement that a passive investor, if any, make referrals to, be in a position to make or influence referrals to, furnish items or services to, or otherwise generate business for the entity as a condition for remaining as an investor.

(E) The entity or any investor must not market or furnish the entity's items or services (or those of another entity as part of a cross-referral agreement) to passive investors differently than to non-investors.

(F) At least 75 percent of the dollar volume of the entity's business in the previous fiscal year or previous 12-month period must be derived from the service of persons who reside in an underserved area or are members of medically underserved populations.

(G) The entity or any investor (or other individual or entity acting on behalf of the entity or any investor in the entity) must not loan funds to or guarantee a loan for an investor who is in a position to make or influence referrals to, furnish items or services to, or otherwise generate business for the entity if the investor uses any part of such loan to obtain the investment interest.

(H) The amount of payment to an investor in return for the investment interest must be directly proportional to the amount of the capital investment (including the fair market value of any pre-operational services rendered) of that investor.

(ii) If an entity that otherwise meets all of the above standards is located in an area that was an underserved area at the time of the initial investment, but subsequently ceases to be an underserved area, the entity will be deemed to comply with paragraph (a)(3)(i) of this section for a period equal to the lesser of:

(A) The current term of the investment remaining after the date upon which the area ceased to be an underserved area or

(B) Three years from the date the area ceased to be an underserved area.

(4) For purposes of paragraph (a) of this section, the following terms apply. Active investor means an investor either who is responsible for the day-to-day management of the entity and is a bona fide general partner in a partnership under the Uniform Partnership Act or who agrees in writing to undertake liability for the actions of the entity's agents acting within the scope of their agency. Investment interest means a security issued by an entity, and may include the following classes of investments: shares in a corporation, interests or units in a partnership or limited liability company, bonds, debentures, notes, or other debt instruments. Investor means an individual or entity either who directly holds an investment interest in an entity, or who holds such investment interest indirectly by, including but not limited to, such means as having a family member hold such investment interest or holding a legal or beneficial interest in another entity (such as a trust or holding company) that holds such investment interest. Passive investor means an investor who is not an active investor, such as a limited partner in a partnership under the Uniform Partnership Act, a shareholder in a corporation, or a holder of a debt security. Underserved area means any defined geographic area that is designated as a Medically Underserved Area (MUA) in accordance with regulations issued by the Department. Medically underserved population means a Medically Underserved

Population (MUP) in accordance with regulations issued by the Department.

(b) Space rental. As used in section 1128B of the Act, "remuneration" does not include any payment made by a lessee to a lessor for the use of premises, as long as all of the following six standards are met — * * * * *

(2) The lease covers all of the premises leased between the parties for the term of the lease and specifies the premises covered by the lease.* * * * *

(6) The aggregate space rented does not exceed that which is reasonably necessary to accomplish the commercially reasonable business purpose of the rental.* * * * *

(c) Equipment rental. As used in section 1128B of the Act, "remuneration" does not include any payment made by a lessee of equipment to the lessor of the equipment for the use of the equipment, as long as all of the following six standards are met — * * * * *

(2) The lease covers all of the equipment leased between the parties for the term of the lease and specifies the equipment covered by the lease.* * * * *

(6) The aggregate equipment rental does not exceed that which is reasonably necessary to accomplish the commercially reasonable business purpose of the rental.* * * * *

(d) Personal services and management contracts. As used in section 1128B of the Act, "remuneration" does not include any payment made by a principal to an agent as compensation for the services of the agent, as long as all of the following seven standards are met — * * * * *

(2) The agency agreement covers all of the services the agent provides to the principal for the term of the agreement and specifies the services to be provided by the agent.* * * * *

(7) The aggregate services contracted for do not exceed those which are reasonably necessary to accomplish the commercially reasonable business purpose of the services.* * * * *

(e) Sale of practice. (1) As used in section 1128B of the Act, "remuneration" does not include any payment made to a practitioner by another practitioner where the former practitioner is selling his or her practice to the latter practitioner, as long as both of the following two standards are met —

(i) The period from the date of the first agreement pertaining to the sale to the completion of the sale is not more than one year.

(ii) The practitioner who is selling his or her practice will not be in a professional position to make referrals to, or otherwise generate business for, the purchasing practitioner for which payment may be made in whole or in part under Medicare or a State health care program after one year from the date of the first agreement pertaining to the sale.

(2) As used in section 1128B of the Act, "remuneration" does not include any payment made to a practitioner by a hospital or other entity where the practitioner is selling his or her practice to the hospital or other entity, so long as the following four standards are met:

(i) The period from the date of the first agreement pertaining to the sale to the completion date of the sale is not more than three years.

(ii) The practitioner who is selling his or her practice will not be in a professional position after completion of the sale to make or influence referrals to, or otherwise generate business for, the purchasing hospital or entity for which payment may be made in whole or in part under Medicare or a State health care program.

(iii) The practice being acquired must be located in a Health Professional Shortage Area (HPSA), as defined in Departmental regulations, for the practitioner's specialty area.

(iv) Commencing at the time of the first agreement pertaining to the sale, the purchasing hospital or entity must diligently and in good faith engage in commercially reasonable recruitment activities that:

(A) May reasonably be expected to result in the recruitment of a new practitioner to take over the acquired practice within a one year period and

(B) Will satisfy the conditions of the practitioner recruitment safe harbor in accordance with paragraph (n) of this section.

(f) Referral services. As used in section 1128B of the Act, "remuneration" does not include any payment or exchange of anything of value between an individual or entity ("participant") and another entity serving as a referral service ("referral service"), as long as all of the following four standards are met — * * * * *

(2) Any payment the participant makes to the referral service is assessed equally against and collected equally from all participants, and is only based on the cost of operating the referral service, and not on the volume or value of any referrals to or business otherwise generated by either party for the other party for which payment may

be made in whole or in part under Medicare or a State health care program.* * * * *

(h) Discounts. As used in section 1128B of the Act, "remuneration" does not include a discount, as defined in paragraph (h)(5) of this section, on an item or service for which payment may be made, in whole or in part, under Medicare or a State health care program for a buyer as long as the buyer complies with the applicable standards of paragraph (h)(1) of this section; a seller as long as the seller complies with the applicable standards of paragraph (h)(2) of this section; and an offeror of a discount who is not a seller under paragraph (h)(2) of this section so long as such offeror complies with the applicable standards of paragraph (h)(3) of this section:

(1) With respect to the following three categories of buyers, the buyer must comply with all of the applicable standards within one of the three following categories —

(i) If the buyer is an entity which is a health maintenance organization (HMO) or a competitive medical plan (CMP) acting in accordance with a risk contract under section 1876(g) or 1903(m) of the Act, or under another State health care program, it need not report the discount except as otherwise may be required under the risk contract.

(ii) If the buyer is an entity which reports its costs on a cost report required by the Department or a State health care program, it must comply with all of the following four standards —

(A) The discount must be earned based on purchases of that same good or service bought within a single fiscal year of the buyer;

(B) The buyer must claim the benefit of the discount in the fiscal year in which the discount is earned or the following year;

(C) The buyer must fully and accurately report the discount in the applicable cost report; and

(D) the buyer must provide, upon request by the Secretary or a State agency, information provided by the seller as specified in paragraph (h)(2)(ii) of this section, or information provided by the offeror as specified in paragraph (h)(3)(ii) of this section.

(iii) If the buyer is an individual or entity in whose name a claim or request for payment is submitted for the discounted item or service and payment may be made, in whole or in part, under Medicare or a State health care program (not including individuals or entities defined as buyers in paragraph (h)(1)(i) or (h)(1)(ii) of this section), the buyer must comply with both of the following standards —

(A) The discount must be made at the time of the sale of the good or service or the terms of the rebate must be fixed and disclosed in writing to the buyer at the time of the initial sale of the good or service; and

(B) the buyer (if submitting the claim) must provide, upon request by the Secretary or a State agency, information provided by the seller as specified in paragraph (h)(2)(iii)(B) of this section, or information provided by the offeror as specified in paragraph (h)(3)(iii)(A) of this section.

(2) The seller is an individual or entity that supplies an item or service for which payment may be made, in whole or in part, under Medicare or a State health care program to the buyer and who permits a discount to be taken off the buyer's purchase price. The seller must comply with all of the applicable standards within the following three categories —

(i) If the buyer is an entity which is an HMO a CMP acting in accordance with a risk contract under section 1876(g) or 1903(m) of the Act, or under another State health care program, the seller need not report the discount to the buyer for purposes of this provision.

(ii) If the buyer is an entity that reports its costs on a cost report required by the Department or a State agency, the seller must comply with either of the following two standards —

(A) Where a discount is required to be reported to Medicare or a State health care program under paragraph (h)(1) of this section, the seller must fully and accurately report such discount on the invoice, coupon or statement submitted to the buyer; inform the buyer in a manner that is reasonably calculated to give notice to the buyer of its obligations to report such discount and to provide information upon request under paragraph (h)(1) of this section; and refrain from doing anything that would impede the buyer from meeting its obligations under this paragraph; or

(B) Where the value of the discount is not known at the time of sale, the seller must fully and accurately report the existence of a discount program on the invoice, coupon or statement submitted to the buyer; inform the buyer in a manner reasonably calculated to give notice to the buyer of its obligations to report such discount and to provide information upon request under paragraph (h)(1) of this section; when the value of the discount becomesknown, provide the buyer with documentation of the calculation of the discount identifying the specific goods or services purchased to which the discount will be applied; and refrain from doing anything which would impede the buyer from meeting its obligations under this paragraph.

(iii) If the buyer is an individual or entity not included in paragraph (h)(2)(i) or (h)(2)(ii) of this section, the seller must comply with either of the following two standards —

(A) Where the seller submits a claim or request for payment on behalf of the buyer and the item or service is separately claimed, the seller must provide, upon request by the Secretary or a State agency, information provided by the offeror as specified in paragraph (h)(3)(iii)(A) of this section; or

(B) Where the buyer submits a claim, the seller must fully and accurately report such discount on the invoice, coupon or statement submitted to the buyer; inform the buyer in a manner reasonably calculated to give notice to the buyer of its obligations to report such discount and to provide information upon request under paragraph (h)(1) of this section; and refrain from doing anything that would impede the buyer from meeting its obligations under this paragraph.

(3) The offeror of a discount is an individual or entity who is not a seller under paragraph (h)(2) of this section, but promotes the purchase of an item or service by a buyer under paragraph (h)(1) of this section at a reduced price for which payment may be made, in whole or in part, under Medicare or a State health care program. The offeror must comply with all of the applicable standards within the following three categories —

(i) If the buyer is an entity which is an HMO or a CMP acting in accordance with a risk contract under section 1876(g) or 1903(m) of the Act, or under another State health care program, the offeror need not report the discount to the buyer for purposes of this provision.

(ii) If the buyer is an entity that reports its costs on a cost report required by the Department or a State agency, the offeror must comply with the following two standards —

(A) The offeror must inform the buyer in a manner reasonably calculated to give notice to the buyer of its obligations to report such a discount and to provide information upon request under paragraph (h)(1) of this section; and

(B) The offeror of the discount must refrain from doing anything that would impede the buyer's ability to meet its obligations under this paragraph.

(iii) If the buyer is an individual or entity in whose name a request for payment is submitted for the discounted item or service and payment may be made, in whole or in part, under Medicare or a

State health care program (not including individuals or entities defined as buyers in paragraph (h)(1)(i) or (h)(1)(ii) of this section), the offeror must comply with the following two standards —

(A) The offeror must inform the individual or entity submitting the claim or request for payment in a manner reasonably calculated to give notice to the individual or entity of its obligations to report such a discount and to provide information upon request under paragraphs (h)(1) and (h)(2) of this section; and

(B) The offeror of the discount must refrain from doing anything that would impede the buyer's or seller's ability to meet its obligations under this paragraph.

(4) For purposes of this paragraph, a rebate is any discount the terms of which are fixed and disclosed in writing to the buyer at the time of the initial purchase to which the discount applies, but which is not given at the time of sale.

(5) For purposes of this paragraph, the term discount means a reduction in the amount a buyer (who buys either directly or through a wholesaler or a group purchasing organization) is charged for an item or service based on an arms-length transaction. The term discount does not include —

(i) Cash payment or cash equivalents (except that rebates as defined in paragraph (h)(4) of this section may be in the form of a check);

(ii) Supplying one good or service without charge or at a reduced charge to induce the purchase of a different good or service, unless the goods and services are reimbursed by the same Federal health care program using the same methodology and the reduced charge is fully disclosed to the Federal health care program and accurately reflected where appropriate, and as appropriate, to the reimbursement methodology;

(iii) A reduction in price applicable to one payer but not to Medicare or a State health care program;

(iv) A routine reduction or waiver of any coinsurance or deductible amount owed by a program beneficiary;

(v) Warranties;

(vi) Services provided in accordance with a personal or management services contract; or

(vii) Other remuneration, in cash or in kind, not explicitly described in paragraph (h)(5) of this section.

(n) Practitioner recruitment. As used in section 1128B of the Act, "remuneration" does not include any payment or exchange of anything of value by an entity in order to induce a practitioner who has been practicing within his or her current specialty for less than one year to locate, or to induce any other practitioner to relocate, his or her primary place of practice into a HPSA for his or her specialty area, as defined in Departmental regulations, that is served by the entity, as long as all of the following nine standards are met —

(1) The arrangement is set forth in a written agreement signed by the parties that specifies the benefits provided by the entity, the terms under which the benefits are to be provided, and the obligations of each party.

(2) If a practitioner is leaving an established practice, at least 75 percent of the revenues of the new practice must be generated from new patients not previously seen by the practitioner at his or her former practice.

(3) The benefits are provided by the entity for a period not in excess of 3 years, and the terms of the agreement are not renegotiated during this 3-year period in any substantial aspect; provided, however, that if the HPSA to which the practitioner was recruited ceases to be a HPSA during the term of the written agreement, the payments made under the written agreement will continue to satisfy this paragraph for the duration of the written agreement (not to exceed 3 years).

(4) There is no requirement that the practitioner make referrals to, be in a position to make or influence referrals to, or otherwise generate business for the entity as a condition for receiving the benefits; provided, however, that for purposes of this paragraph, the entity may require as a condition for receiving benefits that the practitioner maintain staff privileges at the entity.

(5) The practitioner is not restricted from establishing staff privileges at, referring any service to, or otherwise generating any business for any other entity of his or her choosing.

(6) The amount or value of the benefits provided by the entity may not vary (or be adjusted or renegotiated) in any manner based on the volume or value of any expected referrals to or business otherwise generated for the entity by the practitioner for which payment may be made in whole or in part under Medicare or a State health care program.

(7) The practitioner agrees to treat patients receiving medical benefits or assistance under any Federal health careprogram in a nondiscriminatory manner.

(8) At least 75 percent of the revenues of the new practice must be generated from patients residing in a HPSA or a Medically Underserved Area (MUA) or who are part of a Medically Underserved Population (MUP), all as defined in paragraph (a) of this section.

(9) The payment or exchange of anything of value may not directly or indirectly benefit any person (other than the practitioner being recruited) or entity in a position to make or influence referrals to the entity providing the recruitment payments or benefits of items or services payable by a Federal health care program.

(o) Obstetrical malpractice insurance subsidies. As used in section 1128B of the Act, "remuneration" does not include any payment made by a hospital or other entity to another entity that is providing malpractice insurance (including a self-funded entity), where such payment is used to pay for some or all of the costs of malpractice insurance premiums for a practitioner (including a certified nurse-midwife as defined in section 1861(gg) of the Act) who engages in obstetrical practice as a routine part of his or her medical practice in a primary care HPSA, as long as all of the following seven standards are met —

(1) The payment is made in accordance with a written agreement between the entity paying the premiums and the practitioner, which sets out the payments to be made by the entity, and the terms under which the payments are to be provided.

(2)(i) The practitioner must certify that for the initial coverage period (not to exceed one year) the practitioner has a reasonable basis for believing that at least 75 percent of the practitioner's obstetrical patients treated under the coverage of the malpractice insurance will either —

(A) Reside in a HPSA or MUA, as defined in paragraph (a) of this section; or

(B) Be part of a MUP, as defined in paragraph (a) of this section.

(ii) Thereafter, for each additional coverage period (not to exceed one year), at least 75 percent of the practitioner's obstetrical patients treated under the prior coverage period (not to exceed one year) must have —

(A) Resided in a HPSA or MUA, as defined in paragraph (a) of this section; or

(B) Been part of a MUP, as defined in paragraph (a) of this section.

(3) There is no requirement that the practitioner make referrals to, or otherwise generate business for, the entity as a condition for receiving the benefits.

(4) The practitioner is not restricted from establishing staff privileges at, referring any service to, or otherwise generating any business for any other entity of his or her choosing.

(5) The amount of payment may not vary based on the volume or value of any previous or expected referrals to or business otherwise generated for the entity by the practitioner for which payment may be made in whole or in part under Medicare or a State health care program.

(6) The practitioner must treat obstetrical patients who receive medical benefits or assistance under any Federal health care program in a nondiscriminatory manner.

(7) The insurance is a bona fide malpractice insurance policy or program, and the premium, if any, is calculated based on a bona fide assessment of the liability risk covered under the insurance. For purposes of paragraph (o) of this section, costs of malpractice insurance premiums means:

(i) For practitioners who engage in obstetrical practice full-time, any costs attributable to malpractice insurance; or

(ii) For practitioners who engage in obstetrical practice on a part-time or sporadic basis, the costs:

(A) Attributable exclusively to the obstetrical portion of the practitioner's malpractice insurance and

(B) Related exclusively to obstetrical services provided in a primary care HPSA.

(p) Investments in group practices. As used in section 1128B of the Act, "remuneration" does not include any payment that is a return on an investment interest, such as a dividend or interest income, made to a solo or group practitioner investing in his or her own practice or group practice if the following four standards are met —

(1) The equity interests in the practice or group must be held by licensed health care professionals who practice in the practice or group.

(2) The equity interests must be in the practice or group itself, and not some subdivision of the practice or group.

(3) In the case of group practices, the practice must:

(i) Meet the definition of "group practice" in section 1877(h)(4) of the Social Security Act and implementing regulations; and

(ii) Be a unified business with centralized decision-making, pooling of expenses and revenues, and a compensation/profit distribution system that is not based on satellite offices operating substantially as if they were separate enterprises or profit centers.

(4) Revenues from ancillary services, if any, must be derived from "in-office ancillary services" that meet the definition of such term in section 1877(b)(2) of the Act and implementing regulations.

(q) Cooperative hospital service organizations. As used in section 1128B of the Act, "remuneration" does not include any payment made between a cooperative hospital service organization (CHSO) and its patron-hospital, both of which are described in section 501(e) of the Internal Revenue Code of 1986 and are tax-exempt under section 501(c)(3) of the Internal Revenue Code, where the CHSO is wholly owned by two or more patron-hospitals, as long as the following standards are met —

(1) If the patron-hospital makes a payment to the CHSO, the payment must be for the purpose of paying for the bona fide operating expenses of the CHSO, or

(2) If the CHSO makes a payment to the patron-hospital, the payment must be for the purpose of paying a distribution of net earnings required to be made under section 501(e)(2) of the Internal Revenue Code of 1986.

(r) Ambulatory surgical centers. As used in section 1128B of the Act, "remuneration" does not include any payment that is a return on an investment interest, such as a dividend or interest income, made to an investor, as long as the investment entity is a certified ambulatory surgical center (ASC) under part 416 of this title, whose operating and recovery room space is dedicated exclusively to the ASC, patients referred to the investment entity by an investor are fully informed of the investor's investment interest, and all of the applicable standards are met within one of the following four categories —

(1) Surgeon-owned ASCs — If all of the investors are general surgeons or surgeons engaged in the same surgical specialty, who are in a position to refer patients directly to the entity and perform surgery on such referred patients; surgical group practices (as defined in this paragraph) composed exclusively of such surgeons; or investors who are not employed by the entity or by any investor, are not in a position to provide items or services to the entity or any of its investors, and are not in a position to make or influence referrals directly or indirectly to the entity or any of its investors, all of the following six standards must be met —

(i) The terms on which an investment interest is offered to an investor must not be related to the previous orexpected volume of

Response: We are persuaded by the logic of the commenter and, accordingly, we withdraw the statement in the preamble to the January 1998 proposed rule that an interest in a retirement plan might be treated as an ownership or investment interest for purposes of section 1877 of the Act. We will consider contributions (including employer contributions) to retirement plans to be part of an employee's overall compensation arrangement with his or her employer. We also agree that an unsecured loan that is subordinated to a credit facility is a compensation arrangement and not an ownership or investment interest for purposes of section 1877 of the Act.

Comment: Another commenter stated that secured debt given by a not-for-profit hospital, as part of its acquisition of medical practices, should not be treated as an ownership or investment interest in the hospital, but as compensation.

Response: Section 1877(a)(2) of the Act provides that "an ownership or investment interest * * * may be through equity, debt or other means." Accordingly, we believe that loans, bonds, or other financial instruments that are secured with an entity's property or revenue, or a portion thereof, constitute investment interests within the meaning of section 1877 of the Act. In addition, a contrary reading would result in disparate treatment of entities based on their organizational status.

Comment: One commenter asserted that stock options should be treated as either ownership or investment interests or compensation arrangements, but not both. Another commenter stated that stock options should be treated as compensation and not ownership since they do not carry voting rights or the right to dividends and must be sold upon conversion.

Response: In Phase I of this rulemaking, we are revising the rule to treat stock options as compensation at the time they are awarded. At the time they are exercised or converted, they create an ownership or investment interest and must meet an appropriate exception. Any dividends or profit distributions derived from an excepted stock ownership or investment interest would not have to meet a separate compensation exception.

Comment: Another commenter stated that stock options could be structured to discourage referrals for DHS.

Response: The fact that a particular financial arrangement might be structured to discourage referrals does not provide a basis for creating an exception. The statute is intended to remove incentives to overutilize by prohibiting certain financial relationships. If application of the statute required a case-by-case examination to determine the effect of the financial relationship, the statute's efficacy would be undermined.

Comment: One commenter suggested that the determination of whether a convertible security is a compensation arrangement or an ownership or investment interest should depend on which party has the right to convert the security. According to the commenter, if the DHS entity has the right to convert the security, the interest should be treated as compensation until conversion.

Response: We are applying the same approach to convertible securities as we are applying to stock options, and we will classify them as compensation until they are converted into equity. However, many convertible securities are bonds that can be converted into stock. Since bonds are typically secured debt, bonds will be treated as an ownership or investment interest.

B. When Does a Physician Make a Referral?

As defined by section 1877(h)(5) of the Act, a "referral" means a request by a physician for an item or service for which payment may be made under Medicare Part B, including a request for a consultation (including any tests or procedures ordered or performed by the consulting physician or under the supervision of the consulting physician), and the request or establishment of a plan of care by a physician that includes the furnishing of DHS, with certain exceptions for consultations by pathologists, diagnostic radiologists, and radiation oncologists. In the January 1998 proposed rule, we interpreted "referral" to mean any request by a physician for a service, including services subsequently performed by the physician. We proposed defining a "request" as any step taken after a physician performs an initial examination or a physician service on a patient that indicates that the physician believes the service is necessary. Under this broad definition, a referral could be either written or oral, made on medical charts or records, or indicated by a prescription or written order. We also proposed that a referral could be direct or indirect, meaning that a physician would be considered to have made a referral if he or she caused the referral to have been made by someone else (for example, an employee, a hospital discharge planner, or a staff member of a company that the physician owns or controls). As a general principle, we proposed that a physician may "cause" a referral to be made if he or she has the ability to control or influence the individual who selects the entity that furnishes the DHS.

In response to the public comments, we are making several significant changes to the definition of "referral" in Phase I of this rulemaking. These changes include the following:

Revision of the definition of "referral" to exclude services performed personally by the referring physician. Simply stated, we are persuaded that a physician cannot make a "request" of himself or herself for services he or she personally performs. However, a physician can make a "request" of others, including, without limitation, his or her employees, co-workers, or independent contractors. These requests are "referrals" under section 1877 of the Act (although many of them will fit in an exception). We continue to believe that a referral can occur in a wide variety of formats, written, oral, or electronic, depending on the particular service.

Adding an exception using our regulatory authority under section 1877(b)(4) of the Act for certain referrals of DHS to an entity with which the referring physician has a prohibited financial relationship that are "indirect" referrals (for example, when a physician has caused a referral to be made by someone else or has directed or routed a referral through an intermediary) or are oral referrals (that is, no written request or other documentation that would identify the referring physician is required). A claim by the entity furnishing the DHS may be paid for purposes of section 1877 of the Act if the entity did not know or have reason to suspect the identity of the referring physician. In these circumstances, there is minimal risk of patient or program abuse by the entity submitting the claim (provided that the claim is otherwise valid).

Clarification of the definition of a "consultation." In light of the clarifications relating to indirect and oral referrals described above, the practical significance of the definition of a "consultation" is substantially reduced.

We believe that these changes address many of the concerns expressed by commenters. In particular, we have endeavored to respond to the perceived harshness of section 1877 of the Act by creating a narrow exception under our section 1877(b)(4) authority. If the entity furnishing DHS knows of or has reason to suspect the identity of the physician who prescribed or ordered the DHS or made the referral, the DHS entity may not submit a claim for the services. If the physician who prescribes or orders a DHS is someone with whom the DHS entity has a prohibited financial relationship, we think a reasonable DHS entity should suspect that the physician referred the patient to the entity, absent some credible evidence to the contrary.

In the following paragraphs, we discuss and respond to the comments we received on the proposed interpretations of "referral" and "consultation" as published in the January 1998 proposed rule.

1. "Referral"

Comment: Many commenters objected to our interpretation in the January 1998 proposed rule that a service ordered and personally performed by a physician is a referral within the meaning of section 1877 of the Act. Commenters asked us to clarify that there is no referral if the referring physician personally performs the service. Similarly, some commenters sought clarification that there is no referral if the services are "incident to" services personally performed by the referring physician.

Response: We are persuaded by the commenters that a physician does not make a "request," in the ordinary sense of that term, if he or she personally performs a designated health service. We agree it does not make sense to consider work that a referring physician initiates and personally performs as a referral to an entity. Thus, we are amending our definition of "referral" to exclude services that are personally performed by the referring physician (that is, the referring physician physically performs the service), and we are revising our definition of "entity" to clarify that the referring physician himself or herself is not an entity for purposes of section 1877 of the Act (although the physician's practice is an entity). All other Medicare-covered DHS performed at the request of a referring physician are "referrals" for purposes of section 1877 of the Act. A service performed by a hospital for which the hospital bills the technical or facility component of the charge would be a referred service. In such circumstances, however, the physician's service performed at the hospital for which the physician would bill Part B would not be a referred service.

With respect to services performed by others, including a physician's employees, we think the issue is more complicated. Services performed by others are reasonably considered to be performed as a result of a "request." Moreover, the statutory language in section 1877(h)(4)(B)(i) of the Act indicates that the Congress considered there to be a difference between personally performed services and services performed by others. On balance, we have chosen to include services performed by others, including a physician's employees, in the definition of referral. We are concerned that a blanket rule exempting services performed by a physician's employees from the definition of "referral" could, in some circumstances, undermine the intent of section 1877 of the Act. For example, by stationing employees in off-site DHS facilities, a physician practice could circumvent the statutory "building" requirements of the in-office ancillary services exception.

Even the more limited suggestion made by some commenters that there should be no "referral" if an employee's services are properly billable as "incident to" a physician's personally performed services could result in circumvention of the "building" requirements in some cases.

However, we believe the definition of "referral" we are adopting here — in conjunction with the in-office ancillary services exception — strikes an appropriate balance. Under the final rule, services performed by anyone other than the referring physician (whether an employee, a staff member, or a member of the physician's group practice) is a "referral" for purposes of section 1877 of the Act. Thus, services performed by a physician's employees will be considered "referrals". However, in most cases, such referrals will be permitted under the in-office ancillary services exception, which is substantially broader in this final rule than in the 1998 proposed rule. Services performed by employees that do not meet the "same building" or "centralized building" tests (as applicable, depending on whether the physician is a solo or group practitioner) will be prohibited unless another exception applies.

We recognize that, in many cases, services performed by a physician's employees are, for practical purposes, tantamount to services performed by the physician (for example, a physician's assistant applying a neck brace ordered by a physician for an individual who has been in an auto accident, when the face-to-face encounter with the patient, including the physical examination by the physician, indicates the need for a properly adjusted neck brace). While such services are included in the definition of "referral" under this final rule, given the significance of this issue, we are soliciting comments as to whether, and under what conditions, services performed by a physician's employees could be treated as the physician's personally performed services under section 1877 of the Act.

Comment: A commenter asked that we clarify that a plan of care that includes the provision of DHS by the physician establishing the plan of care is not a referral. If not clarified as suggested, the commenter believes that the physician would effectively be barred from treating his or her own patients.

Response: If the DHS are personally performed by the physician who established the plan of care, there would be no referral as to those personally performed services.

Comment: Some commenters objected to our proposed presumption that a physician has referred his or her patient to an entity for the furnishing of DHS if the patient obtains the services from the entity with which the physician has a financial relationship. One commenter described the following scenario: A physician orally tells a patient or another person that the patient needs a designated health service. The patient obtains the service from an entity with which the physician has a prohibited financial relationship. The entity does not know (and cannot know) that the physician orally told the patient (or other person) that the service was needed. The commenter sought clarification as to the application of section 1877 of the Act in these circumstances.

Response: We are establishing an exception for indirect and oral referrals. When there is no written order or other documentation of the referral, the issue is whether the DHS provider knows or has reason to suspect the identity of the physician who prescribed or ordered the DHS or made the referral.

Comment: Several commenters sought clarification that a physician's ordering, dispensing, or prescribing of drugs does not constitute a referral to the manufacturer of the drugs. The commenters noted that the manufacturers are not entities that furnish DHS (that is, outpatient prescription drugs) to patients. Rather, furnishing of DHS is performed by physicians, pharmacies, hospitals, and clinics.

Response: We agree that, in most cases, drug manufacturers are not entities that furnish DHS to patients for purposes of section 1877 of the Act, and, therefore, the ordering, dispensing, or prescribing of drugs would not constitute a referral to the manufacturer of the drugs. However, manufacturer-owned or -affiliated retail pharmacy operations, or other health care providers may be entities for purposes of section 1877 of the Act, if they furnish DHS to patients.

Comment: A commenter recommended that activities that a solo practitioner performs as a customary and integral part of patient treatment should not be considered a "referral."

Response: We find the commenter's proposed language too vague to be used in creating a standard. We believe our revised definition of "referral" that excludes personally performed services and our changes to the in-office ancillary services exception (see section VII.B.1 of this preamble) adequately address the commenter's concerns.

Comment: A commenter stated that referrals for DHS by a nonphysician professional employee of a group practice, such as a nurse practitioner or a physician assistant, should not be imputed to a physician member of the group practice, when the nonphysician is authorized and licensed to prescribe treatment on his or her own and can make independent decisions regarding referrals. For example, if a nurse practitioner, staffing a group practice office without a physician member present, orders and performs a plain x-ray, the referral for the x-ray should not be imputed to a physician member of the group practice. If the referral is imputed, the service may not qualify under the in-office ancillary services exception, because it is not personally performed by the referring physician, another physician in the group practice, or a person who is directly supervised by the referring physician or another group practice physician. Alternatively, the commenter suggested that we modify the "direct supervision" standard to mirror our payment and coverage requirements to enable "imputed" referrals by a nurse practitioner and a physician assistant to fit in the in-office ancillary services exception.

Response: As previously stated, we are revising the "direct supervision" standard in the in-office ancillary services exception to mirror our payment and coverage requirements. (See discussion in section VI.B.2 of this preamble.) This change should address the concern identified by the commenter.

We believe that the question of whether a referral by a nurse practitioner or a physician assistant should be imputed to an employer physician will depend on the facts and circumstances of the referral. The inquiry is whether the physician controls or influences the nonphysician's referral. The Congress and HHS have recognized that many nurse practitioners and physician assistants are independent providers authorized and licensed to prescribe treatment and make independent decisions regarding referrals. However, these practitioners do not always act independently of their employers.

For example, sometimes services of a nonphysician practitioner are billed "incident to" a physician service rather than directly under the nonphysician's independent billing number. In short, we are concerned that physicians could attempt to circumvent section 1877 of the Act by funneling referrals through nonphysician practitioners. We believe the change in the supervision requirement affords sufficient protection for legitimate arrangements.

Comment: Several commenters were confused by our discussion in the preamble to the January 1998 proposed rule at 63 FR 1710 of a situation in which a physician who owned a physical therapy (PT) company referred patients for treatment, including PT, to a skilled nursing facility (SNF) that contracted with the physician's PT company. In the preamble, we indicated that we would analyze the arrangement as an indirect compensation arrangement and equate the physician with the PT provider.

Response: In the preamble of the January 1998 proposed rule, we suggested that the critical factor would be the degree of control the physician had over the PT provider and the extent of the PT provider's relationship with the SNF. We are abandoning that analysis. We think the proper focus is whether the physician is making a referral to the PT provider within the meaning of section 1877 of the Act. In other words, we believe that a physician can make a referral of DHS "to an entity" even though the referral is first directed or routed through another person or entity, provided the physician has reason to know the identity of the actual provider of the service. In the SNF/PT provider example, the relevant inquiry is whether the physician has made a referral, directly or indirectly, to the entity furnishing DHS, in other words, whether he or she is referring "to" that entity. Accordingly, if the physician referring the patient to the SNF knows that the PT company in which he or she has an investment interest will furnish DHS to the patient or could reasonably be expected to know that the PT company will actually furnish DHS to the patient, the referral is a referral "to the entity" and is prohibited, unless an exception applies. Similarly, where the PT company knows or has reason to suspect that the referral for DHS came from a referring physician with whom the PT company has a prohibited financial relationship, the PT company cannot submit the claim for the DHS. The PT/SNF example will be affected by the advent of full consolidated billing for SNFs, as described above in the responses to comments on indirect compensation arrangements.

To trigger section 1877 of the Act, the direction or steering of a patient "to an entity" does not need to be in writing, nor does it have to be absolute; it need only be reasonably intended to result in the patient receiving the service from the entity. Thus, for example, when a physician provides an order or prescription for a DHS to a patient that ostensibly can be filled by any of a number of entities and then suggests or informs the patient that the order can be serviced by a particular entity, there would be a referral "to" that entity. Given the administrative burden on entities presenting claims, in the context of an indirect financial relationship, we believe a claim for DHS should be subject to nonpayment unless the entity does not know that, and does not have reason to suspect that, the referring physician had directed the patient to the entity.

2. Consultation

The Existing Law: Section 1877(h)(5)(C) of the Act excepts from the definition of a "referral" by a "referring physician" a request by a pathologist for clinical laboratory tests or pathological examination services, a request by a radiologist for diagnostic radiology services, and a request by a radiation oncologist for radiation therapy, if the services are furnished by, or under the supervision of, the specialist, pursuant to a consultation requested by another physician. Section 1877(h)(5)(C) creates a narrow exception from the definition of "referral" for a small subset of services provided or ordered by certain specialists pursuant to a consultation requested by another physician (the referring physician).

The Proposed Rule: In the preamble to the 1998 proposed rule, we referred to the interpretation of consultation that appeared in the March 1992 proposed rule for clinical laboratory services (57 FR 8595). There, we interpreted a consultation to be:

A professional service furnished to a patient by a physician (the consultant) at the request of the patient's attending physician. A consultation includes the history and examination of the patient as well as a written report that is transmitted to the attending physician for inclusion in the patient's permanent record. If, in the course of that consultation, the consulting physician deems it necessary to order clinical laboratory services, those services may not be ordered from a laboratory in which the referring [attending] physician has a financial interest. Other referrals, such as sending a patient to a specialist who assumes responsibility for furnishing the appropriate treatment, or providing a list of referrals for a second opinion, are not "consultations" or "referrals" that would trigger the [physician referral provision]. We did not add anything to this definition in the August 1995 final rule concerning referrals for clinical laboratory services.

Commenters to the 1998 proposed rule took issue with this interpretation for several reasons, including the requirement that the consulting physician examine and take a history of the patient, and the interpretation's failure to demarcate clearly when a consultant takes over treatment of the patient.

The Final Rule: The final rule adopts a very broad interpretation of a consultation. We want to make clear that this definition is only for the very limited purpose of determining when a pathologist's, diagnostic radiologist's, or radiation oncologist's ordering of DHS from a facility with which he or she has an otherwise prohibited financial relationship will not prohibit submission of a claim to Medicare. Most importantly, this definition is not intended to, and has no bearing on, coverage or payment rules relating to consultations. Coverage and payment rules related to consultations raise many issues that are irrelevant for the very limited application of the term in section 1877 of the Act. Simply put, while there may be many difficult issues in determining when certain specialty services are consultations, as opposed to routine treatment, such difficulties are relatively rare in the context of the three exceptions in section 1877(h)(5)(C) of the Act (namely, a request by a pathologist for clinical laboratory services or pathological examination services, a request by a radiologist for diagnostic radiology services, or a request by a radiation oncologist for radiation therapy).

As a preliminary matter, we think it important to recognize that section 1877 of the Act defines referrals very broadly. Section 1877(h)(5) specifically includes referrals or requests for services made by the referring physician, as well as any DHS provided pursuant to a consultation with another physician, including DHS provided by the consulting physician or any DHS ordered by the consulting physician.

Section 1877(h)(5)(A) of the Act having established that a referral includes all DHS ordered by a consulting physician, section 1877(h)(5)(C) then carves out: (i) A request by a pathologist for clinical laboratory services or pathological examination services, (ii) a request by a radiologist for diagnostic radiology services, and (iii) a request by a radiation oncologist for radiation therapy, if the services are furnished by, or under the supervision of, the pathologist, radiologist, or radiation oncologist pursuant to a consultation requested by another physician.

The final rule adopts the following criteria to identify a consultation for purposes of section 1877:

(1) A consultation is provided by a physician whose opinion or advice regarding evaluation and/or management of a specific medical problem is requested by another physician.

(2) The request and need for the consultation is documented in the patient's medical record.

(3) After the consultation is provided, the consulting physician prepares a written report of his or her findings, which is provided to the physician who requested the consultation.

(4) With respect to radiation therapy services provided by a radiation oncologist, a course of radiation treatments over a period of time will be considered to be pursuant to a consultation, provided the radiation oncologist communicates with the referring physician on a regular basis about the patient's course of treatment and progress.

Finally, we want to make clear that the exception in section 1877(h)(5)(C) of the Act only protects the referral of DHS from the pathologist, diagnostic radiologist, or radiation oncologist to the DHS provider. If the DHS provider— (1) knows or has reason to suspect that the referral originated from the referring physician, and (2) has a direct or indirect financial relationship with the referring physician, the DHS provider cannot submit a claim to Medicare for the DHS unless the financial relationship fits into an exception. Moreover, the referring physician may not make the referral to the consultant if he or she knows or has reason to suspect that the consultant will order DHS from an entity with which the referring physician has a direct or indirect financial relationship to which no exception applies.

Comment: A commenter suggested that the "diagnostic radiology" exception should be expanded to include other DHS performed or supervised by nonradiologist physicians to assure quality of care and access to a broad variety of services. The commenter asked that we broaden the consultation exception to include all DHS used to diagnose disease that are ordered pursuant to a consultation initiated by another physician.

Response: We agree that section 1877(h)(5)(C) of the Act creates an exception for the referrals of some specialists and not others. However, the Congress specifically excepted the requests of radiologists for diagnostic radiology services if the services are furnished by, or under the supervision of, the radiologist, pursuant to a consultation requested by another physician. It is our view that the Congress regarded most radiologists in this situation and the other excepted specialists as physicians who were not instigating a referral for services, but merely implementing the request of another physician who has already determined that the patient is likely to need radiology services. The Congress believes that, in general, a radiologist in this situation would not be likely to overutilize services.

We do not believe that we have the authority to extend this exception to other specialists, some of whom provide separate physician services to patients and would be in a position to instigate the referral for radiology.

Comment: One commenter was concerned about our willingness to exempt pathologists, radiologists, and radiation oncologists, yet require other arrangements and physicians to alter their referral methods. The commenter asserted that pathologists will order further stains or studies on specimens to aid in a diagnosis. Radiologists, not infrequently, recommend further studies as part of their interpretation, again to help make a diagnosis. The commenter stated that given the current medico-legal atmosphere, it is rare that he does not follow the suggestions of these consultants. In addition, the commenter stated that he has seen cancer patients with new or progressive diseases who are being treated by radiation oncologists without any direct input from attending or primary care physicians. In the commenter's view, these examples are standard medical practice and self-serving. Since radiologists often have an ownership interest in the diagnostic facility and pathologists in a laboratory facility, they are doubly benefitted by the referral.

Response: The statute clearly establishes special rules for diagnostic radiologists, pathologists, and radiation oncologists.

Comment: A number of commenters explained their problems with distinguishing a consultation from a referral based on their particular speciality area. For example, one commenter stated that during an active phase of an oncologic, hematologic, or pneumatologic illness, the care of the patient specific to that illness may be managed by the subspecialist and the overall care of the patient may be managed by the referring physician using the information obtained from the consultation. This commenter believes that a referral would occur only if the total care of the patient were transferred.

Another commenter asserted that rarely does a treating physician completely give up the care of a patient to another physician, and rarely does the treating physician completely retain responsibility for the care of the patient. Rather, a physician will send a patient to a specialist for testing, diagnosis, and initial treatment, and then the originating physician will take over the care of the patient.

Representing specialists who frequently perform consultations and assume the neurological care of patients at the request of referring physicians, one commenter asserted that it is appropriate to bill for a consultation when care is transferred, rather than a lower-paying evaluation and management visit, because of the extra work for the consulting physician involved in preparing a report for the attending physician.

Response: We agree with the commenters that it can be difficult to determine whether a first physician initiating a visit to a second physician should constitute a referral to another physician or the request for a consultation with that physician. However, as discussed above, in the three specific instances identified in the statute, we think there will be little disagreement in determining when there is a consultation. In any event, for purposes of section 1877(h)(5)(C) of the Act, we are adopting a broader interpretation of a consultation than is in the coverage rules. Finally, payment and coverage for consultations are not addressed or affected by this rule.

Comment: One commenter, representing an association of radiologists, discussed the case of what happens when a patient is sent to a radiation oncologist for treatment of a tumor. The commenter stated that radiation oncology treatment occurs over a period of weeks or months, and is provided within a continuum of care involving the radiation oncologist, the referring physician, and even other physicians.

Response: We agree with the commenter and have clarified the definition to recognize that radiation therapy may extend over a prolonged period of time and still be considered to be pursuant to a consultation, provided the radiation oncologist regularly communicates with the referring physician as to the patient's care.

Comment: Commenters stated that when a referring physician sends a patient to a radiation oncologist for radiation therapy, the referring physician may not see the patient for some time. The radiation oncologist may decide during this time that the patient needs services other than radiation therapy services. The commenter asked whether the radiation oncologist's referrals for nonradiation therapy services falls within the scope of the consultation exception.

Response: Under section 1877(h)(5)(C) of the Act, for radiation oncology, only a request for radiation therapy by a radiation oncologist is not considered to be a referral. We understand that in some situations when a patient is undergoing radiation therapy, the patient's care is not supervised by a physician other than the radiation oncologist. However, the radiation oncologist cannot send the patient for DHS other than radiation therapy services to an entity with which the radiation oncologist has a financial relationship without meeting an appropriate exception.

Comment: Section 1877(h)(5)(C) of the Act excepts DHS provided by consulting pathologists, diagnostic radiologists, and radiation oncologists if the services are furnished by, or under the supervision of, the consulting physician. A commenter inquired whether the required supervision could be delegated to a member of the consulting physician's group practice.

Response: The plain language of section 1877(h)(5)(C) of the Act does not allow for supervision by anyone other than the consulting physician. However, we are broadly interpreting the supervision requirement in this section to be consistent with the supervision requirements elsewhere in these regulations. Thus, the level of supervision required is whatever level is required under the applicable Medicare payment and coverage requirements. Furthermore, the in-office ancillary services exception may be available for services supervised by a physician in the consulting physician's group practice.

Comment: A commenter stated that neither diagnostic radiologists nor pathologists perform physical examinations on patients. An association representing certain specialists stated that the definition of a consultation should be modified so as not to require a patient history and physical examination except when appropriate; for example, diagnostic radiologists and nuclear medicine physicians generally do not take a patient's history or perform a medical examination. However, a nuclear medicine physician would perform a history and physical examination when a patient is referred for therapy. In addition, an association representing clinical laboratories declared that it is unlikely that a pathologist would ever see a patient or take a history from a patient. An association representing radiologists asserted that diagnostic radiologists generally do not take a patient's history or conduct a medical examination; therefore, we should clarify that a history and examination of the patient is not required as part of a radiologic consultation.

Response: For purposes of section 1877 of the Act, we agree that a consultation does not necessarily include either taking the history of a patient or performing a physical examination. Certainly, pathologists would rarely see a patient. We do expect that, on occasion, a consulting physician, such as a radiologist, might interview a patient to gain additional information about the patient's condition, but this might not amount to a full scale history. Similarly, the radiologist might examine a patient, but focus only on a particular area of concern. We are amending our description of a "consultation" to clarify that there is no requirement that these steps be performed.

Comment: A commenter asked whether the prohibition under section 1877 of the Act is triggered when a physician, who has no financial relationship with a diagnostic imaging center, initiates a referral to the imaging center rather than to a particular radiologist.

Response: We understand the commenter to be asking whether the consultation exception set forth in section 1877(h)(5)(C) of the Act applies if the request for the consultation is made to the entity that employs or contracts with a consulting radiologist rather than to the consulting radiologist. The commenter's main concern seemed to be whether a subsequent request by the employed or contractor radiologist for diagnostic radiology services furnished by the imaging center would be protected under section 1877(h)(5)(C) of the Act. We believe that under section 1877(h)(5)(C) of the Act, the request for a consultation can be made to either a particular radiologist or an entity. Also, if the referring physician does not have a financial relationship with the diagnostic imaging center, the referral to the center is not prohibited under the general prohibition in section 1877(a) of the Act.

IV. Physician Compensation Under Section 1877 of the Act: An Overview

Many public comments addressed physician compensation issues. The statute touches on physician compensation in several places: the definition of group practice, the employee exception, and the personal services exception. The interplay of section 1877 of the Act and physician compensation is one of the most significant aspects of the self-referral law.

Obviously, the issue of physician compensation is of critical importance to the physician community. As a starting point, we do not believe that the Congress intended section 1877 of the Act to regulate physician compensation practices, except as necessary to minimize financial incentives to refer DHS to entities with which the physicians have financial relationships. Having carefully studied the public comments and having reconsidered the statutory provisions, the legislative history, and our January 1998 regulatory proposals, we believe the following general principles govern the application of the statute to the manner in which physicians are paid:

First, as explained in section III.B of this preamble, for purposes of section 1877 of the Act, the term "referral" does not include DHS that are personally performed by the physician. As a practical matter, the statutory language and structure indicate Congressional recognition that physicians are commonly compensated based on productivity with respect to services they personally perform.

Second, with respect to group practices, the Congress intended to confer group practice status on bona fide group practices and not on loose confederations of physicians who come together as a "group" substantially in order to capture the profits of DHS under the in-office ancillary services exception to section 1877 of the Act. To that end, we proposed adding a "unified business" standard to the group practice definition, using the statutory authority the Congress conferred on the Secretary to impose additional standards on group practices. However, in response to comments, we have reconsidered the test for a "unified business"; the final regulations under Phase I of this rulemaking adopt a considerably more flexible approach to the same end. Under Phase I of this rulemaking, one of several characteristics of a "unified business" is that the group's physician compensation methodologies are established by the centralized management of the group practice. For the limited purposes of establishing that a group practice is a unified business, we think it is appropriate to look at physician compensation derived from all sources, not just from DHS. However, location- and specialty-based compensation practices are expressly permitted with respect to the distribution of revenues derived from services that are not DHS. Such practices may also be allowed for DHS, depending on the circumstances. (See the discussion of the group practice definition in section VI.C of this preamble.)

Third, except for the limited purpose of determining whether a group practice is a unified business, the physician compensation provisions for group practices under section 1877 of the Act only affect the distribution of revenues derived from DHS. In general, these revenues are likely to comprise a relatively small portion of the total revenues of most group practices. As we indicated in 1998, section 1877 of the Act does not affect the distribution of monies earned from other services. From a practical business standpoint, however, some group practices may find it impractical to segregate DHS revenues. These parties may find it more expedient to allocate compensation in accordance with the methods permitted for DHS revenues under section 1877 of the Act.

Fourth, the statute implicitly recognizes that solo practitioners will keep all the profits from DHS that fit in the in-office ancillary services exception, whether performed personally or by others.

Fifth, section 1877 of the Act contemplates that physicians — whether group practice members, independent contractors, or employees — can be paid in a manner that directly correlates to their own personal labor, including labor in the provision of DHS. In other words, "productivity," as used in the statute, refers to the quantity and intensity of a physician's own work, but does not include the physician's fruitfulness in generating DHS performed by others (that is, the fruits of passive activity). "Incident to" services are not included in productivity bonuses under the statute unless the services are incident to services personally performed by a referring physician who is in a bona fide group practice. ("Incident to" services must meet the requirements of section 1861(s)(2)(A) of the Act and section 2050, "Services and Supplies," of the Medicare Carriers Manual (HCFA Pub. 14–3), Part 3 — Claims Process.) In the case of independent contractors under the personal service arrangements exception and employees under the bona fide employment exception, the amount of compensation for personal productivity is limited to fair market value for the services they personally perform. The fair market value standard in these exceptions acts as an additional check against inappropriate financial incentives. (The personal service arrangements exception, as well as several other exceptions, contains additional restrictions on compensation that varies based on the volume or value of referrals. The volume or value standard is discussed in section V of this preamble.)

Sixth, the Congress recognized that in the case of group practices, revenues derived from DHS must be distributed to the group practice members in some fashion, even though the members generate the DHS revenue. However, the Congress wished to minimize the economic incentives to generate unnecessary referrals of DHS.

Accordingly, the Congress permitted group practice members (and independent contractors who qualify as "physicians in the group practice") to receive shares of the overall profits of the group, so long as those shares do not directly correlate to the volume or value of referrals generated by the member or "physician in the group practice" for DHS performed by someone else. In addition, the Congress permitted groups to pay their physicians productivity bonuses based directly on personal productivity (including services incident to personally performed services), but precluded groups from paying group practice physicians any productivity bonus based directly on referrals of DHS performed by someone else. As detailed below, we are establishing under Phase I of this rulemaking certain methodologies that describe compensation practices that will be deemed to be indirectly related to the volume or value of DHS referrals for purposes of section 1877(h)(4)(B)(i) of the Act and therefore allowable under section 1877 of the Act. Groups are free to develop their own indirect methodologies, but such methodologies are subject to case-by-case review.

V. "Volume or Value" of Referrals and "Other Business Generated" Standards: An Overview

Many of the exceptions in section 1877 of the Act covering specific kinds of compensation arrangements include as one element of the exception a requirement that the compensation not take into account the volume or value of any referrals and, in some of the exceptions, the further requirement that the compensation not take into account other business generated between the parties.

In the preamble to the January 1998 proposed regulation, we had interpreted this volume or value standard as follows:

Compensation could be based on units of service (for example, "per use" equipment rentals) so long as the units of service did not include services provided to patients who were referred by the physician receiving the payment. For example, a physician who owned a lithotripter could rent it to a hospital on a per procedure basis, except for lithotripsies for patients referred by the physician-owner; payments for the use of the lithotripter for those patients would have to use a methodology that did not vary with referrals.

The language "or other business generated between the parties" meant that the payment in an arrangement had to be fair market value for the services expressly covered by the arrangement and could not include any payment for services not covered by the arrangement.

Physician compensation arrangements that were fixed in amount but conditioned either expressly or implicitly on the physicians referring patients to a particular provider or supplier took into account the value or volume of referrals within the meaning of the statute.

After reviewing the comments received, we are substantially revising the regulation with respect to the scope of the volume or value standard. Most importantly, we are permitting time-based or unit-of-service-based payments, even when the physician receiving the payment has generated the payment through a DHS referral. We have reviewed the legislative history with respect to the exception for space and equipment leases and concluded that the Congress intended that time-based or unit-of-service-based payments be protected, so long as the payment per unit is at fair market value at inception and does not subsequently change during the lease term in any manner that takes into account DHS referrals. In the case of those exceptions that include the additional restriction that the payment not take into account "other business generated between the parties," the per unit payment also may not take into account any other business, including non-Federal health care business, generated by the referring physician. We are interpreting the phrase "generated between the parties" to mean business generated by the referring physician for purposes of section 1877 of the Act.

Applying Phase I of this rulemaking to the lithotripter example noted above, the "per use" rental payments would be protected, even for lithotripsies performed on patients referred by the physician-owner, provided that the "per use" rental payment was at fair market value, did not vary over the lease term, and met the other requirements of the rental exception. In other words, if the "per use" payment is fair market value, we will not require a separate payment arrangement for use of the equipment on patients referred by the physician-owner. In determining whether the initial "per use" payment is at "fair market value," we will generally look to the price a hospital would pay to rent the equipment from a company that did not have any physician ownership or investment (and thus was not in a position to generate referrals or other business — DHS or otherwise — for the hospital) in an arm's-length transaction. In some cases, all the available comparables or market values may involve transactions between entities that are in a position to refer or generate other business. In such situations, we would look to alternative valuation methodologies, including, but not limited to, cost plus reasonable rate of return on investment on leases of comparable medical equipment from disinterested lessors. (The definition of fair market value is discussed in more detail in section VII.B of this preamble.)

In the light of our interpretation of the volume or value standard as permitting unit of service or unit of time-based payments, we have determined that the additional limiting phrase "not taking into account * * * other business generated between the parties" means simply that the fixed, fair market value payment cannot take into account, or vary with, referrals of Medicare or Medicaid DHS or any other business generated by the referring physician, including other Federal and private pay business. Simply stated, section 1877 of the Act establishes a straightforward test that compensation arrangements should be at fair market value for the work or service performed or the equipment or space leased — not inflated to compensate for the physician's ability to generate other revenues.

In order to establish a "bright line" rule, we are applying this interpretation of the volume or value standard uniformly to all provisions under section 1877 of the Act and part 411 where the language appears (for example, the employee, personal service arrangements, rental of office space/equipment, fair market value, non-monetary compensation under $300, hospital medical staff benefits, academic medical center exceptions, indirect compensation arrangements, and the group practice definition). The "other business generated" restriction applies only to those exceptions in which it expressly appears.

Consistent with this interpretation, we have determined that we will not consider the volume or value standard implicated by otherwise acceptable compensation arrangements for physician services solely because the arrangement requires the physician to refer to a particular provider as a condition of payment. So long as the payment is fixed in advance for the term of the agreement, is consistent with fair market value for the services performed (that is, the payment does not take into account the volume or value of the anticipated or required referrals), and otherwise complies with the requirements of the applicable exception, the fact that an employer or a managed care contract requires referrals to certain providers will not vitiate the exception. Any such contract, however, must expressly provide exceptions (1) when the patient expresses a different choice, (2) when the patient's insurer determines the provider, or

(3) when the referral is not in the best medical interest of the patient in the physician's judgment. We caution that these mandatory arrangements could still implicate the anti-kickback statute, depending on the facts and circumstances.

Finally, we want to clarify that ownership or investment interests that are not protected under sections 1877(b) through (d) of the Act (and are therefore compensation arrangements under section 1877(h)(1)(A) of the Act) are deemed to take into account the value or volume of referrals. We believe this view is consistent with the general prohibition on investment and ownership interests in the statute.

Our responses to comments follow below:

Comment: One commenter asked us to clarify the statement in the preamble of the January 1998 proposed rule at 63 FR 1780 that the volume or value standard that is in the compensation and other exceptions is uniformly meant to cover (and thus exclude from an exception) other business generated between the parties. Another commenter asked us to clarify that the requirement that the compensation not take into account the volume or value of referrals or other business generated between the parties refers only to referrals of DHS.

Response: The discussion of the phrase "other business generated between the parties" in the preamble to the January 1998 proposed rule caused confusion. Based on our review of the legislative history, we believe that the Congress intended the language to be a limitation on the compensation or payment formula parallel to the statutory and regulatory prohibition on taking into account referrals of DHS business. Simply stated, in the provisions in which the phrase appears, affected payments cannot be based or adjusted in any way on referrals of DHS or on any other business referred by the physician, including other Federal and private pay business.

Comment: One commenter urged us to amend the language of the regulation to correspond to the extensive discussion of the volume or value standard in the preamble.

Response: We are modifying the regulation to clarify the meaning of the volume or value standard.

Comment: One commenter asked us to clarify that a valuation of a physician's practice could include the value of self-generated DHS in the purchase price as long as the purchase agreement was not contingent on future referrals.

Response: For purposes of section 1877 of the Act, the valuation of a physician practice could include the value of DHS in the purchase price if the DHS provided by the selling physician fit into an exception, such as the in-office ancillary services exception, and the purchase agreement (and purchase price) is not contingent on future referrals. Depending on the identity of the purchaser, however, the inclusion of the value of ancillary revenues could implicate the anti-kickback statute.

Comment: Several commenters asked us to clarify that the language requiring that the payment be fixed in advance and not be determined in a manner that takes into account the value or volume of referrals or other business generated between the parties does not require that the aggregate compensation be established in advance, but only that the methodology (for example, a rental per use, or payment per service) be fixed in advance.

Response: We are modifying the regulation to make it clear that the aggregate payment need not be specified in advance. However, if the aggregate amount is not specified, the amount of the payment on a "per use," "per service," or "per time period" basis must be fixed in advance. For example, a contract could include a fee schedule for services, provided the fee schedule is uniformly applied to all services provided to the contracting party. In addition, the payment must be fair market value compensation not taking into account the volume or value of referrals or other business generated by the referring physician either at inception or during the term of the agreement.

Comment: Commenters also wished us to clarify whether the following arrangements take into account the volume or value of referrals or other business generated between the parties: (1) Payments based on a percentage of gross revenues; (2) payments based on a percentage of collections; (3) payments based on a percentage of expenses; and (4) payments based on a percentage of a fee schedule.

Response: A compensation arrangement does not take into account the volume or value of referrals or other business generated between the parties if the compensation is fixed in advance and will result in fair market value compensation, and the compensation does not vary over the term of the arrangement in any manner that takes into account referrals or other business generated. The first three arrangements described by the commenters are neither aggregate fixed compensation amounts, nor fixed "per service," "per use," or "per time period" payment amounts. Percentage compensation that is determined by calculating a percentage of a fluctuating or indeterminate amount, such as revenues, collections, or expenses, is not fixed in advance. Accordingly, the first three arrangements do not meet the requirement that compensation be fixed in advance. Whether the fourth arrangement mentioned by the commenters — a percentage of a fee schedule — is fixed in advance compensation depends on the circumstances. If the percentage payments are based on a single fee schedule, such that there is, in effect, a single fixed fee for each service, the arrangement meets the requirement that the compensation be fixed in advance. However, a percentage of fee schedule arrangement that bases payments on multiple fee schedules, such that there may be different fees for a particular service depending on the ultimate payer, is not fixed in advance. Thus, for example, if a physician has a contract for services with a hospital that has a chargemaster for all services, the physician can be paid a fixed percentage of that chargemaster fee schedule for each service. However, when the hospital accepts different payment amounts from different payers for a service, the physician cannot be paid a percentage of those varying amounts.

Comment: Several commenters requested that the final rule make clear that payments based on "per use" or "per service" meet the volume or value standard in the exceptions so long as the payments are at fair market value and the "per use" or "per service" amount does not change over the term of the contract based on the value or volume of referrals of DHS. The commenters stated that their position was consistent with the intent of the Congress and supported their position with language from the Conference Committee report.

Response: As described above, we are modifying the regulation to reflect the Conference Committee report, H. Rep. No. 213, 103rd Cong., 1st Sess. 814 (1993). The "per use," "per service," or "per time period" amount must reflect fair market value at inception not taking into account the volume or value of referrals and must not change over the term of the contract based on the volume or value of DHS referrals, or, when applicable, other business (that is, other Federal or private pay business) generated by the referring physician.

Comment: One commenter specifically objected to our proposed interpretation that a "per use" payment was acceptable except when the payment was for a referral from a physician with an ownership or investment interest in the equipment. According to the commenter, the physician's ownership or investment interest should not matter so long as the physician does not have a controlling interest.

Response: We believe equipment rental arrangements are subject to abuse whether the payment received is only a small portion of the rental or the entire amount. Control is irrelevant; it is the financial incentive that has been shown repeatedly to result in overutilization. Despite the obvious potential for abuse, given the clearly expressed congressional intent in the legislative history, we are permitting "per use" payments even when the physician is generating the referrals. We wish to make clear that these arrangements may violate the anti-kickback statute.

Comment: A commenter asked that we clarify that a hospital can lease equipment on a "per use" basis to a physician for use in the physician's practice.

Response: A hospital can lease equipment to a physician for use in the physician's practice on a "per use" basis, provided the lease arrangement otherwise fits in the rental exception. As noted above, these arrangements may violate the anti-kickback statute.

Comment: Many commenters objected to our proposed interpretation in the preamble that fixed payments to a physician could be determined to take into account the volume or value of referrals if a condition or requirement for receiving the payment was that the physician refer DHS to a given entity, such as an employer or an affiliated entity. A number of commenters stated that we did not have statutory authority for our proposed interpretation. Some commenters said these arrangements were necessary to develop integrated networks and ensure quality control. Another commenter stated that the proposal would interfere with exclusive hospital-based physician relationships. One commenter argued that the proposed interpretation was inconsistent with the employee exception, while yet another stated the position was inconsistent with the common law duty of loyalty owed by an employee to his or her employer and the employer's right to set the terms and conditions of employment. Another commenter stated that the proposed interpretation would adversely impact managed care arrangements by, in effect, requiring all managed care arrangements to meet the physician incentive plan regulations. Finally, a commenter proposed that we allow entities to require physicians to refer to a particular provider as part of a contract, except (1) when the patient expresses a different choice, (2) when the patient's insurer determines the provider, or (3) when the referral is against the physician's judgment.

Response: While we believe that payments tied to referral requirements can be abused, we agree that the proposed interpretation potentially would have had far-reaching effects, especially for managed care arrangements and group practices. We are adopting in modified form the one commenter's suggestion for appropriate conditions listed in the last sentence of the comment. We believe the suggested conditions will not impose a significant burden, since they are likely to be required anyway under existing laws, professional codes, and most contracts. Thus, so long as the referral requirement does not apply if a patient expresses a different choice, the patient's insurer determines the provider, or the referral is not in the best medical interest of the patient in the physician's judgment and the payment to the physician is fixed in advance at fair market value for the services actually rendered and does not vary based on referrals or, when applicable, other business generated by the physician, the fact that referrals may be required to be made to specific providers will not nullify an exception.

Comment: One commenter stated that the final rule should not prohibit primary care case management arrangements.

Response: As discussed in the preceding comment, we are no longer viewing these arrangements as violating the volume or value standard simply because referrals may be required to be made to certain providers. The arrangement would have to meet the other provisions of an exception.

Comment: According to two commenters, many covenants not to compete could be called into question by the proposed interpretation that fixed payments tied to referral requirements can violate the volume or value standard, a component of many of the exceptions. The commenters argued that these covenants are necessary adjuncts to many business acquisitions and personal services or management arrangements and urged us to affirm their legitimacy.

Response: The commenters were unclear as to how the proposed interpretation would have adversely impacted covenants not to compete. A requirement to refer to a specific provider is different from an agreement not to establish a competing business. In other words, a covenant not to compete might prevent a physician from setting up a private practice or offering services that compete with the entity that purchased his or her practice. If an agreement also included the requirement that the physician refer business to the purchaser, the agreement would be suspect under the anti-kickback statute.

Comment: One commenter asked us to clarify that the discussion in the preamble about the volume or value standard applies not only to its interpretation in the context of the compensation exceptions, but also to its interpretation in the other exceptions in which the same language appears.

Response: The meaning of the volume or value standard as set forth in the preamble and regulations text under Phase I of this rulemaking applies to the standard wherever it appears in the statute and regulations.

Comment: One commenter stated that the interpretation of the volume or value standard in the January 1998 proposed rule at 63 FR 1701 would permit hospitals to pressure physicians to refer to network and other providers that the hospitals own or control.

Response: It is not clear from the comment what aspect of the proposed rule would lead the commenter to believe that this kind of coercion would occur. Nonetheless, section 1877 of the Act is limited in its application and does not address every abuse in the health care industry. The fact that a particular arrangement is not prohibited by section 1877 of the Act does not mean that the arrangement is not abusive; it simply means that a referral and submission of a claim for DHS is not prohibited under section 1877 of the Act.

VI. Exceptions Applicable to Ownership and Compensation Arrangements (Section 1877(b) of the Act)

A. Physician Services (Section 1877(b)(1) of the Act)

The Existing Law: Section 1877(b)(1) of the Act specifies that the general prohibition under section 1877 of the Act does not apply to services furnished on a referral basis, if the services are physician services, as defined in section 1861(q) of the Act, and are furnished (1) personally by another physician in the same group practice as the referring physician or (2) under the personal supervision of another physician in the same group practice as the referring physician. Section 1861(q) defines "physicians' services" as "professional services performed by physicians, including surgery, consultation, and home, office, and institutional calls (but not including services described in subsection (b)(6) [certain intern and resident services])." A physician is defined in the Act as a duly licensed and authorized doctor of medicine or osteopathy, doctor of dental surgery or dental medicine, doctor of podiatric medicine, doctor of optometry, or chiropractor who meets certain qualifications specified in the Act. (See section 1861(r) of the Act.)

The August 1995 final rule incorporated this provision in Sec. 411.355 (General exceptions to the referral prohibition related to both ownership/investment and compensation), paragraph (a) (Physician services), covering physician services as defined in Sec. 410.20 (Physicians' services), paragraph (a) (Included services). The definition of a physician service in Sec. 410.20(a) generally parallels the definition in section 1861(r) of the Act, with the addition of diagnosis and therapy services. Under the August 1995 final rule, physician services need not be performed in any specific location.

The Proposed Rule: The January 1998 proposed rule retained Sec. 411.355(a) as set forth in the August 1995 final rule. In the preamble to the January 1998 proposed rule, we noted that the exception would apply to physician services that constitute DHS under section 1877 of the Act and regulations and that the exception in the Medicare context would not apply to services performed by nonphysicians, even though furnished under a physician's supervision, such as ancillary or "incident to" services. We interpreted "personal supervision" to mean that the group practice physician must be legally responsible for monitoring the results of any test or other designated health service and must be available to assist the individual who is furnishing the service, even though the group practice physician need not be present while the service is being furnished.

The Final Rule: In general, we believe that the physician services exception is of limited application. However, the physician services exception does afford protection for referrals of the narrow class of physician services that are included in the definitions of DHS, especially in the area of radiology. (See discussion in section VIII.A of this preamble.) The physician services exception enables physicians in group practices to make referrals for physician services that are DHS within their group practices. In addition, the in-office ancillary services exception may also apply, depending on the circumstances. We are interpreting the physician services exception to apply to referrals to (or referral services supervised by) a member of the group practice or an independent contractor who qualifies as a "physician in the group" as defined in Sec. 411.351 (Definitions).

In particular, we are incorporating the physician services exception in Sec. 411.355(a) as proposed in our January 1998 proposed rule, with the following modifications:

First, we are interpreting "personal supervision" to correspond with our revised interpretation of "direct supervision" in the context of the in-office ancillary services exception. (See discussion in section VI.B.2 of this preamble.) We can discern no compelling reason to have separate and potentially inconsistent supervision standards in the exceptions under section 1877 of the Act. Accordingly, the level of supervision required under the physician services exception is the level of supervision required under the payment and coverage rules applicable to the particular physician service at issue.

Second, as noted above, we are expressly interpreting the exception to apply to referrals to (or physician's services supervised by) a member of the group practice or an independent contractor who qualifies as a "physician in the group" as defined in Sec. 411.351.

Finally, as many have pointed out, the physician services exception (unlike the in-office ancillary services exception) does not cover referred services that are performed by the referring physician. We believe this narrower scope of the physician services exception is evidence that personally performed physician services fall outside the scope of section 1877 of the Act. For this and other reasons expressed elsewhere in this preamble, in Sec. 411.351 of Phase I of this rulemaking, we are defining a "referral" for purposes of section 1877 of the Act to exclude referrals for work personally performed by the referring physician, and we have made clear that a referring physician is not himself or herself an entity to which he or she makes referrals.

Comment: A commenter asked that the regulations include a clear provision for providing compensation for professional reading fees within an outpatient group practice for diagnostic procedures such as EKG, pulmonary function testing, EEG, etc.

Response: To the extent that the professional reading fees mentioned by the commenter are DHS (see Sec. 411.351), the rules set forth in these regulations apply. (We note, however, that pulmonary function testing and EKGs and ECGs typically will not be DHS unless furnished in a hospital setting.) First, if the professional reading is performed personally by the referring physician, no referral occurs for purposes of section 1877 of the Act (though there may still be a referral of the technical component). Second, if the professional reading is performed by a physician other than the referring physician, the physician services and in-office ancillary services exceptions are available. In the case of a group practice, physician compensation will be governed by the rules in Sec. 411.352 (Group practice). Subject to those rules, the physician performing the professional reading may be paid directly based on his or her personal performance of professional services.

Comment: A commenter expressed the view that all physician services are excluded from the scope of section 1877 of the Act. The commenter asserted that no evidence exists that the Congress intended to include in section 1877 of the Act physician services within the meaning of section 1861(s)(1) of the Act. The commenter, therefore, concluded that including professional components of services is beyond the scope of section 1877 and our regulatory authority.

Response: We disagree. A number of the DHS enumerated by the Congress in section 1877(h)(6) of the Act include substantial physician services components, and the Congress provided no exclusion or carve out. Indeed, we believe the physician services exception itself clearly evidences the Congress's recognition that the DHS categories set forth in section 1877(h)(6) of the Act include some physician services. At the very least, the Congress anticipated that there might be situations in which it would be difficult to demarcate clearly professional and technical components of the DHS. For those situations, the Congress provided an exception that makes clear that group practice physicians may refer physician services within their group practices when the conditions of the exception are satisfied.

Comment: A commenter inquired whether the physician services exception applies to services performed by a nonphysician. In the commenter's view, if the exception does not apply to these services, the exception would conflict directly with our other rules on the practice parameters applicable to nonphysician practitioners.

Response: We are cognizant of the expanding and evolving role of nonphysician practitioners in the health care delivery system for Medicare beneficiaries. Notwithstanding, we are not persuaded that an expansion of the physicians' services exception is appropriate or, in the light of other interpretations set forth in these regulations, necessary to accommodate the commenter's concerns.

Section 1877(b)(1) expressly applies only to physicians' services as defined in section 1861(q) of the Act. Section 1861(q) of the Act provides that physician services are "professional services performed by physicians." The Act provides for Medicare coverage for certain services that would be physicians' services if furnished by a physician when such services are performed by a physician assistant (under the supervision of a physician) or a nurse practitioner or clinical nurse specialist (working in collaboration with a physician) (see sections 1861(s)(K)(i) and (s)(K)(ii) of the Act.) However, while such services may be identical to physicians' services, they are not physicians' services under section 1861(q) of the Act. Congress has provided for separate treatment of such services under the payment rules. To define nonphysician services as physician services for purposes of section 1877(b)(1) of the Act would distort Medicare's overall payment and coverage scheme.

We are also concerned that expanding the physicians' services exception, which has no building or billing requirements, to include nonphysician practitioners' services would permit group practices to circumvent the requirements of the in-office ancillary services exception.

However, while we are not including nonphysician services under section 1877(b)(1) of the Act, we have made other changes in the regulations that address the commenter's concerns. Specifically, we have interpreted the direct supervision requirement of the in-office ancillary services exception as requiring the level of supervision mandated under the relevant Medicare payment and coverage rules. See section VII.B.2 of this preamble. In other words, in the case of nonphysician practitioners, the supervision requirement of the in-office ancillary services exception corresponds to the supervision requirements applicable to such practitioners. Thus, the in-office ancillary services exception will cover most referral DHS provided by nonphysician practitioners in a group practice setting (provided the exception's building and billing requirements are also satisfied), without imposing additional supervision requirements on such practitioners.

Moreover, referrals made by nonphysician practitioners generally do not implicate section 1877 of the Act, which focuses exclusively on referrals by physicians. However, if a referral made by a physician assistant or nurse practitioner (or other nonphysician) is directed or controlled by a physician, we are treating the referral as an indirect referral made by the directing or controlling physician, who is, in fact, the "referring physician." This interpretation is necessary to prevent the use of nonphysician practitioners to circumvent section 1877 of the Act.

We believe these interpretations adequately address the commenter's concerns and are consistent with the statutory language and structure. However, we invite public comments as to the need for a further exception for referred DHS performed by nonphysician practitioners in a group practice setting.

Comment: A commenter sought clarification as to the treatment of "incident to" services under the physicians' services exception. The commenter believed that unless "incident to" services are included in the exception, the exception would conflict with other payment and coverage rules.

Response: We are interpreting the physicians' services exception to apply only to "incident to" services (as defined in Sec. 411.351) that are physician services under section 1861(q). All other "incident to" services would need to qualify under the in-office ancillary services or another exception.

Comment: A commenter suggested that the term "physician" should be defined in the regulations.

Response: The Act defines "physician" in section 1861(r). We agree that it would be helpful to incorporate this definition into these regulations and are doing so.

B. In-office Ancillary Services (Section 1877(b)(2) of the Act)

The Existing Law: We have divided our discussion of the in-office ancillary services exception into four subsections that correspond with the statutory structure: DHS included in the in-office ancillary services exception, supervision, building requirements, and billing requirements. The relevant provisions of the existing law are described in each subsection below.

The Proposed Rule: The relevant provisions of the proposed rule are described in each subsection below.

The Final Rule: Many commenters were highly critical of the January 1998 proposed rule's interpretation of the exception for in-office ancillary services, contending that the rule was arbitrary, inconsistent with our existing policies, and inefficient. We have revisited the premises of the January 1998 proposed rule, reexamined the statutory language and legislative history, and restructured the exception. The in-office ancillary services exception in Phase I of this rulemaking is consistent with the language of section 1877 of the Act and the organization and operation of many modern physicians' offices. While in most respects the exception is broader and administratively simpler than the proposed exception, we have substantially limited the ability of group practices to use part-time arrangements to provide DHS in buildings or facilities in which they do not routinely provide a wide range of services other than Federal or private pay DHS.

In revising the exception, we were cognizant of several key considerations. First, the Congress clearly was concerned with regulating physicians' ordering of DHS, even in the context of their own practices; otherwise, a detailed exception would not have been necessary. Second, the Congress intended to protect some in-office ancillary services provided they were truly ancillary to the medical services being provided by the physician or group; otherwise, the Congress would not have created the exception. Finally, we believe the boundaries of the exception as intended by the Congress are best expressed in the building requirement in section 1877(b)(2)(A)(ii) of the Act, which permits DHS to be provided in the same building where the physicians provide their regular medical services, or, in the case of a group practice, in a central DHS building.

Based on those considerations, we have revised the in-office ancillary services exception to permit the provision of DHS in the same building in which a group or a physician routinely provides the full range of the group's or physician's medical services with a minimum of restrictions. In general, the final exception will protect shared DHS facilities, so long as the physicians or groups that share the facility also routinely provide their full range of services in the same building. Moreover, in certain circumstances, part-time practitioners would be permitted to share the DHS facility, as long as they are also providing medical services they routinely provide that are not DHS (whether Federal or private pay). Coupled with a relaxation of the proposed supervision requirement described below, we believe the final exception captures what the Congress intended to protect.

What will not be protected by Phase I of this rulemaking are a number of part-time, intermittent arrangements that functionally are nothing more than shared off-site facilities. Many of these part-time, off-site ancillary services arrangements are inconvenient for patients both as to location and time, and are created by physicians principally to capture revenue rather than to enhance patient care. To preclude such arrangements, and as a counter-balance to allowing certain shared facilities, we have interpreted the same building requirement as including a "full range of services" condition, and the centralized building requirement as requiring exclusivity. These interpretations are consistent with the statutory language and structure. To the extent the January 1998 proposed rule would have permitted these arrangements, it is no longer operative. To qualify under the "centralized building" standard, Phase I of this rulemaking will require, among other things, the group practice to own or lease and use the space exclusively on a full-time basis.

In addition to the changes to the "building" requirements, the exception for in-office ancillary services under Phase I of this rulemaking contains a number of other significant changes (all described in more detail in the relevant comments and responses sections that follow):

Significantly expanding the scope of services potentially included in the in-office ancillary services exception by — (1) making clear that outpatient prescription drugs may be "furnished" in the office, even if they are used by the patient at home; (2) explicitly permitting external ambulatory infusion pumps that are DME to be provided under the in-office ancillary services exception; (3) making clear that chemotherapy infusion drugs may be provided under the in-office ancillary services exception through the administration or dispensing of the drugs to patients in the physician's office; and (4) creating a new exception for certain items of durable medical equipment (DME) furnished in a physician's office for the convenience of the physician's patients.

Substantially modifying the "direct supervision" requirement to conform it to relevant Medicare and Medicaid payment and coverage rules for the specific service, in keeping with our premise that the Congress did not intend to revamp radically the provision of ancillary services in physicians' offices.

Allowing independent contractors to provide the requisite supervision, provided they are "physicians in the group practice," meaning that they have contracted with the group practice to treat group practice patients on group premises and have reassigned their claims to the group under Sec. 424.80 of these regulations (as further explained in section 3060, "Reassignment," of the Medicare Carriers Manual (HCFA Pub. 14–3), Part 3 — Claims Process).

Additional revisions and modifications to the rule are addressed in the discussion below. The discussion is divided into four subparts: the scope of DHS, supervision, building requirements, and billing requirements. The discussion of each subpart contains summaries of public comments and our responses to them.

1. Scope of Designated Health Services That Can Be In-Office Ancillary Services

The Existing Law: As a threshold matter, the DHS that are potentially protected by the in-office ancillary services exception are any of the DHS enumerated in section 1877(h)(6) of the Act, except DHS specifically excluded from the exception under section 1877(b)(2) of the Act. Excluded are all parenteral and enteral nutrients, equipment, and supplies (PEN) and DME (except for infusion pumps, which remain eligible for the exception). Referrals — in-office or otherwise — for services that are not DHS need not fit in the exception, since they do not implicate the statute. The scope of services that are considered to be DHS is discussed in section VIII.A of this preamble.

The Proposed Rule: We proposed that DHS would be considered furnished in the location where the service was actually performed or where a patient receives and begins using an item. We also proposed expanding the category of DHS included in the in-office ancillary services exception to include crutches, provided the physician does not mark up the cost of the crutches.

The Final Rule: First, we are revising the rule to provide that services will be considered "furnished" for purposes of the exception (1) in the location where the service is actually performed upon a patient or (2) when an item is dispensed to a patient in a manner that is sufficient to meet Medicare billing and coverage rules. This change will make application of the rule clearer in the case of outpatient prescription drugs and ambulatory infusion pumps that are DME. Second, in the interests of patient convenience, we are using our regulatory authority under section 1877(b)(4) of the Act to expand the exception to include certain DME, including crutches, canes, walkers, and folding manual wheelchairs, that meet conditions set forth in the regulations. (Braces and collars are orthotics and, thus, may already qualify under the statute for the in-office ancillary services exception.) These conditions generally will require that — (1) the items are DME, such as canes, crutches, walkers, and folding wheelchairs, that a patient uses to ambulate in order to leave the physician's office; (2) the items are furnished in a building that meets the "same building" requirements of section 1877(b)(2) of the Act and Sec. 411.355(b)(2)(i) as part of the treatment for the specific condition for which the physician-patient encounter occurred; (3) the items must be furnished personally by the physician who ordered the DME, by another physician in the group practice, or by an employee of the physician or the group practice; (4) the physician who furnishes the DME must meet all DME supplier standards; (5) the arrangement does not violate the anti-kickback statute; (6) the billing and claims submission for the DME complies with all applicable laws and regulations; and (7) all other requirements of the in-office ancillary services exception are satisfied. We are similarly excepting blood glucose monitors.

We are withdrawing our proposal that physicians not mark up these items when provided in-office to their patients; we believe the current DME Regional Carrier (DMERC) reimbursement provisions provide sufficient cost containment controls. We believe these limited modifications to the DME exclusion will promote quality of patient care without any significant increased risk of patient or program abuse.

Finally, with respect to infusion pumps (other than pumps that are PEN equipment or supplies), we are including, under Phase I of this rulemaking, the furnishing of external ambulatory infusion pumps as in-office ancillary services covered by the exception (which uses the generic term "infusion pumps"), provided all other conditions of the exception are satisfied. Because they are specifically included in the statutory exception, external ambulatory infusion pumps need not meet the added requirements for DME outlined in the preceding paragraph.

Comment: A hospital-based pathologist in a hospital with a full-service laboratory urged that the in-office ancillary services exception should not protect laboratories based in physicians' offices. The pathologist asserted that these laboratories are merely enterprises that enable physicians to profit from referrals for laboratory tests and create unfair competition for pathology laboratories that are not owned by physicians. The pathologist expressed skepticism about the justification proffered by many physicians that in-office laboratories exist for the convenience of patients, noting that, in his case, his hospital laboratory is located directly across the street from the offices of physicians with in-office laboratories.

Response: Despite the fact that physician-owned or controlled laboratories and other DHS facilities may competitively disadvantage entities that do not have physician ownership or control, the Congress made a policy determination not to apply the prohibition under section 1877 of the Act to DHS referrals that occur within the parameters of a physician's or group practices' own medical practice, provided these referrals fit squarely in an exception under section 1877 of the Act.

Comment: The in-office ancillary services exception applies to DHS that are "furnished" in accordance with certain statutory conditions. A number of commenters objected to our interpretation that the term "furnished" excluded items provided to a patient (or delivered to a patient's home) that are meant to be used at home rather than in the physician's office. The commenters observed that such a rule does not make sense in the case of outpatient prescription drugs, which are commonly dispensed to patients for later consumption at home.

Response: In general, we believe the Congress intended to exclude from the reach of the statute only items and services provided (or used, as the case may be) in the physician's office. However, we believe that our definition of those circumstances can be simplified to accommodate the provision of outpatient prescription drugs, as well as ambulatory infusion pumps that are DME. Accordingly, we are revising the rule to provide that services will be considered "furnished," for purposes of the exception, in the location where the service is actually performed upon a patient or where an item is dispensed to a patient in a manner that is sufficient to meet the Medicare billing and coverage rules.

Comment: One commenter suggested that we should make clear that so long as the in-office ancillary services exception is met, discounts on drugs do not need to be passed on to Medicare.

Response: Nothing in section 1877 of the Act or these regulations is intended to require physicians to pass discounts on to the Medicare program. Whether a discount must be passed on to the program by physicians or others remains the subject of other statutory and regulatory provisions.

Comment: Commenters requested clarification that the furnishing of chemotherapy drugs can meet the in-office ancillary services exception. Commenters also sought clarification with respect to chemotherapy-related laboratory tests, x-rays, and prescription drugs that are secondary to the provision of chemotherapy.

Response: Chemotherapy infusion drugs and ancillary laboratory tests, x-rays, and prescription drugs are DHS for purposes of section 1877 of the Act that may be provided by physicians as in-office ancillary services if all of the conditions of the exception are satisfied. In light of the changes we are making in Phase I of this rulemaking — including revisions to the definition of "furnish" and to the supervision requirement in Sec. 411.355(b)(5)—we believe the exception is sufficiently broad to accommodate virtually all existing arrangements for the provision of chemotherapy drugs and related services to patients in physicians' offices. Under Phase I of this rulemaking, referrals for chemotherapy infusion drugs may be protected by the in-office ancillary services exception if they are administered or dispensed to patients in the referring physician's office (or through the referring physician's group practice) in accordance with the supervision requirements already imposed by the Medicare program. We anticipate no appreciable disruption of chemotherapy services to Medicare or other patients as a result of Phase I of this rulemaking.

Comment: A commenter sought clarification whether the furnishing of allergen treatment sets would be protected under the in-office ancillary services exception.

Response: The provision of allergen treatment sets is protected by the in-office ancillary services exception so long as all of the conditions of the exception are satisfied. We believe that the changes in Phase I of this rulemaking to the definition of "furnish" in Sec. 411.355(b)(5) and the supervision requirements make clear that allergen treatment sets may be furnished to patients under the in-office ancillary services exception.

Comment: A number of commenters questioned the scope of our proposed extension of the in-office ancillary services exception to include the furnishing of crutches (DME being otherwise excluded by statute). The proposed extension would permit physicians to provide crutches if they make no profit on them and otherwise meet certain criteria. We proposed that the physician could bill only for the cost of acquiring and supplying the crutches. Commenters were confused as to how these costs would be determined and found the proposal to be unnecessarily restrictive. In addition, commenters wondered why crutches were included, but not canes, walkers, collars, splints, and the like. Other commenters variously sought inclusion of other DME, including DME for rheumatological conditions, orthopedic DME, and blood glucose monitors. Commenters suggested various measures for determining when DME should be permitted as an in-office ancillary service. One commenter proposed that whatever test we adopt should take into account the following: (1) the intended use of the item (that is, whether the item is an integral element in the customary continuum of patient care); (2) the cost of the item (that is, fair market value or a dollar cap); (3) the life-expectancy of the item (that is, whether items are limited to one-time prescriptions for 5 or 6 weeks); and (4) physician instruction (that is, whether some physician instruction in the use of the item is required). Other commenters proposed dollar caps as a means of excluding from the exception physician-directed sales of expensive wheelchairs, beds, and other pieces of equipment on which markups are significant.

Response: In the interest of patient convenience, we are using our regulatory authority under section 1877(b)(4) of the Act to expand the in-office ancillary services exception to include certain DME, including crutches, canes, walkers, and folding wheelchairs, that meet conditions set forth in the regulation (in our January 1998 proposed rule, we proposed a more limited exception for crutches only). (Braces and collars are classified as orthotics and already potentially qualify under the statute for the in-office ancillary services exception; splints are covered under section 1861(s)(5) of the Act and are not included in any category of DHS.) In doing so, we are concerned primarily with enabling the patient to depart from the physician's office. The narrow scope of this expansion and the fact that the need for ambulation equipment is objectively verifiable mitigate the potential for overutilization.

For somewhat different reasons, we are also creating an exception to permit blood glucose monitors (and one starter set of testing strips and lancets, consisting of no more than 100 of each; this number is at least one month's supply) to be provided under the in-office ancillary services exception (under the authority granted in section 1877(b)(4) of the Act). In light of section 4105 of the BBA 1997, which added a Medicare benefit for diabetes self-management training services, we do not believe that the Congress intended the physician self-referral law to interfere with a physician's efforts to provide blood glucose monitors to patients. Therefore, the in-office ancillary services exception may be used by a physician or group practice to furnish a blood glucose monitor and a starter set of strips and lancets if the physician or group furnishes outpatient diabetes self-management training to patients for whom the blood glucose monitors are furnished.

While commenters sought the inclusion in this exception of various other items of DME, we decline to extend the in-office ancillary services exception further. To do so would, in essence, vitiate the congressional determination to exclude DME from the in-office ancillary services exception. We do not find — and we believe that the

Congress did not find — that the in-office furnishing of other DME would pose no risk of fraud or abuse, as required under section 1877(b)(4) of the Act.

Having considered the various suggestions made by the commenters, we are adopting the following conditions for DME provided as an in-office ancillary service (these conditions being in addition to all other conditions of the exception):

The item is one that a patient requires for the purposes of ambulating, uses in order to depart from the physician's office, or is a blood glucose monitor (including one starter set of test strips and lancets).

The item is furnished in a building that meets the "same building" requirements in the in-office ancillary services exception as part of the treatment for the specific condition for which the physician-patient encounter occurred.

The item is furnished personally by the physician who ordered the DME, by another physician in the group practice, or by an employee of the physician or the group practice.

A physician or group practice that furnishes the DME meets all DME supplier standards located in paragraph (c) of Sec. 424.57 (Special payment rules for items furnished by DMEPOS suppliers and issuance of DMEPOS supplier billing numbers).

The arrangement does not violate the anti-kickback statute or any law or regulation governing billing and claims submission. (This condition is necessary to meet the "no risk of fraud or abuse" standard in 1877(b)(4) of the Act.)

All other requirements of the in-office ancillary services exception are satisfied.

We agree with the commenters that our proposal with respect to not marking up costs was confusing and unnecessarily restrictive, and we are not adopting it. While we find the commenters' suggestions for dollar caps on DME items attractive, we have concluded that it is not feasible to devise dollar caps that would appropriately include low-value DME and exclude high-value DME in all cases (for example, a $150 limit might be high for some types of DME and low for others). Upon further reflection, we believe the current DMERC reimbursement provisions provide sufficient cost containment controls, with respect to these items of DME we are including in the exception. We believe the modifications to the DME exclusion that we are making will promote quality of patient care without any significant increased risk of patient or program abuse.

Finally, we note with respect to DME furnished in physicians' offices that these arrangements remain subject to our conditions of participation for DME suppliers and other applicable payment and coverage rules.

Comment: A commenter asked that the final rule address whether the use of consignment closets as a means of providing DME in a physician's office implicates section 1877 of the Act. For example, a surgeon enters into an arrangement for a DME supplier to rent space (for example, a closet) in the surgeon's office at fair market value under a lease that meets the rental exception. The technician who measures for braces or DME supplies is a shared employee of the surgeon's practice and the supplier, with the supplier paying for the time the technician spends measuring the braces and supplying DME. The billing is done by the supplier. The commenter asserted that in this example, there is no financial relationship because the surgeon does not bill Medicare.

Response: If the lease fits squarely in the rental exception and the arrangement for the personal services of the technician fits squarely in the personal service arrangements exception, the "consignment closet" arrangement described in the preceding comment may not create a prohibited financial relationship under section 1877 of the Act. We wish to clarify that this result does not depend on whether the physician bills Medicare. To the contrary, the essential prohibition under section 1877 of the Act is on physicians making referrals to entities with which they have prohibited financial relationships and on those entities billing Medicare. Nothing in this rule is intended to, or should be interpreted as, legitimizing consignment closet arrangements. These arrangements raise significant questions under other legal authorities, including the anti-kickback statute and our supplier standards. Physicians and suppliers who are considering "consignment closet" arrangements would be well-advised to read the OIG's Special Fraud Alert on the Rental of Physician Office Space by Persons or Entities to Which They Refer published in the **Federal Register** on February 24, 2000 (65 FR 9274).

Comment: One commenter expressed concern about the interaction of section 1877 of the Act and the proposed surety bond rule that would exempt physicians from the surety bond requirement if they provide DME incident to patient care. Specifically, the commenter asked whether we believe that physicians are allowed to disburse DME, orthotics, and prosthetics incident to patient care without violating the provisions of section 1877 of the Act and whether these provisions are applicable if a physician has a surety bond.

Response: Section 1877 requirements under the exception exist wholly apart from other requirements of law that may apply. In addition, the commenter is mistaken in asserting that we proposed to exempt physicians who furnish DME in their offices from the proposed surety bond requirements that would apply to all suppliers. We assume that the commenter is referring to our proposed rule concerning supplier standards that was published on January 20, 1998 (63 FR 2926). Such an exception is not included in the proposed rule.

Comment: Oncologists complained that the proposed regulations — which interpreted the in-office ancillary services exception as applying only to infusion pumps that are implanted in a physician's office — would prohibit them from furnishing external ambulatory infusion pumps to their patients, contravening clear congressional intent and causing substantial inconvenience to patients. External ambulatory infusion pumps are used to administer chemotherapy agents and pain medication to cancer patients. The pumps are typically filled in the oncologist's office, and the drug flow is ordinarily initiated before the patient leaves the office. The statutory in-office ancillary services exception excludes DME (which typically is used by patients in their homes), but includes "infusion pumps." Thus, the commenters asserted that the plain language of the exception indicates clear congressional intent to authorize physicians to furnish a certain category of DME — infusion pumps — to patients, even though those pumps will be used at home.

Response: We agree. The statute uses the general term "infusion pumps." We are revising the regulation in Sec. 411.355(b) to make clear that the in-office ancillary services exception protects external ambulatory infusion pumps (other than pumps that are PEN equipment or supplies) that are filled or serviced in the physician's office, even though the patient uses them at home. However, the in-office ancillary services exception does not protect an infusion pump that is used to deliver PEN because that pump is not classified as DME, but is considered PEN. PEN is categorically excluded from the exception under section 1877(b)(2) of the Act. The statutory language addressing infusion pumps in the in-office ancillary services exception applies only to DME.

Comment: Two commenters requested clarification as to the application of the in-office ancillary services exception to home care physicians who primarily treat patients in their homes. These commenters asserted that home care physicians play an important role in the delivery of cost-effective, quality care to patients and provide services that, in some cases, preclude the need for more expensive hospitalizations. These commenters believe that section 1877 of the Act should not apply to home visits. In the alternative, these commenters requested clarification of the following issues:

Are DHS performed in a patient's home concurrently with the performance of a physician service included in the in-office ancillary services exception (for example, a physician uses a hand-held portable laboratory during a physician visit in the home)? Can a technician accompanying the physician perform the DHS during the home visit?

What is the application of section 1877 of the Act to group practices that own home health agencies that in turn provide DHS to group patients?

Are referrals from medical directors of home health agencies protected by the employee or another exception?

Response: We find nothing in the statute that excludes referrals for DHS by home care physicians from the reach of the statute. To the contrary, the Congress expressly included home health services as a designated health service. That said, we generally agree with the commenters that the provision of DHS in a patient's home should be protected by the in-office ancillary services exception, provided that all of the conditions of the exception are satisfied. However, in many cases, services provided by home care physicians will not fit neatly into the in-office ancillary services exception. For example, under the "same building" requirements, we are requiring that physicians provide substantial physician services unrelated to DHS in the building and that the services provided there be the full range of the physicians' services. We believe that a home care physician meets these "same building" tests if his or her principal medical practice consists of treating patients in their private homes (for purposes of determining whether a physician is principally a home care physician, private homes do not include nursing, long term care, or other facilities), and the physician (or a staff member accompanying him or her) provides a designated health service in a private home contemporaneously with a physician service (provided by the referring physician) that is not a designated health service and the other exception requirements are met. (DHS provided in facilities, such as nursing homes, by home care or other physicians may qualify under the in-office ancillary services exception if all conditions of the exception are satisfied.) We have concluded that it may be appropriate to develop additional rules for home care physicians under the in-office ancillary services exception. We are expressly soliciting comments on this issue and will consider it further in Phase II of this rulemaking.

As to the commenter's second question, section 1877 of the Act applies to a group practice's ownership of a home health agency in the same manner it applies to the ownership by a group practice of any DHS entity. Referrals to the entity by the group practice or by members of the group must qualify under an ownership exception, such as the in-office ancillary services exception. In general, we do not believe that the furnishing of most home health services will meet the requirements of the in-office ancillary services exception. Unless a physician in the group personally conducts the home visit and provides a physician service unrelated to the furnishing of DHS, the "same building" requirements will not be satisfied (we see no plausible way for home health services to qualify under the "centralized building" option under section 1877(b)(2)(A)(ii)(II) of the Act). In some cases, the "rural provider" exception may apply (that exception will be discussed in the Phase II rulemaking).

Finally, with respect to referrals from medical directors of home health agencies, these referrals may be protected by the employee exception or the personal service arrangements exception, depending on the facts and circumstances of the medical director's relationship with the home health agency. However, if the medical director is an owner of a group practice that owns the home health agency, an ownership exception would still need to apply.

Comment: A commenter sought clarification as to whether a referral to a physician spouse in another group practice, who subsequently orders a designated health service for the referred patient, could come within the in-office ancillary services exception. The commenter observed that there are many two-physician marriages in the health care industry and that many spouses engage in different specialities and practice in different group practices. The commenter argued that the referrals between physician spouses to each other's group practices should not constitute prohibited referrals, so long as either the referring physician or the physician spouse accepting the referral complies with an exception. In our January 1998 proposed rule, we took the position that a physician in one group practice will be prohibited from referring to his or her physician spouse in another group practice because the referring physician cannot meet the in-office ancillary services exception. The commenter found this interpretation overly restrictive and narrow. In the commenter's view, if the physician receiving the referral meets the in-office ancillary services exception, he or she should be able to accept the referral, because the accepting spouse and not the referring spouse is ordering the designated health service.

Response: On reconsideration, we generally agree with the commenter, with one important distinction. We believe that the referral to a spouse should be allowed, if the referral is for a physician service unrelated to the furnishing of a designated health service (that is, a designated health service is not the reason for the referral) and any subsequent DHS referrals by the spouse fit within the in-office ancillary services exception with respect to the spouse receiving the referral. We recognize that there may be some circumstances, particularly in underserved areas, where a spouse may be the only qualified provider of a particular DHS. We are considering whether a limited additional exception is warranted and will address the issue further in Phase II of this rulemaking. We invite comments on this issue.

2. Direct Supervision

The Existing Law: Section 1877(b)(2) of the Act provides an exception for in-office ancillary services. To qualify as in-office ancillary services, the services must, among other things, be furnished personally by a referring physician or another physician member in the same group practice, or be furnished by individuals who are "directly supervised" by the referring physician or another physician in the group practice. The August 1995 final rule covering referrals for clinical laboratory services defined "direct supervision" in Sec. 411.351 as supervision by a physician who is present in the office suite and immediately available to provide assistance and direction throughout the time services are being performed.

The Proposed Rule: The January 1998 proposed rule retained this definition, with several clarifications and changes. In the preamble to the January 1998 proposed regulation, we expressed our view that the Congress intended the in-office ancillary services exception to apply to services that are closely attached to the activities of the referring physician. Consistent with this interpretation, we used the definition of "direct supervision" that appears in section 2050, "Services and Supplies," of the Medicare Carriers Manual (HCFA Pub. 14–3), Part 3 — Claims Process, which describes services that are incident to a physician's professional services under section 1861(s)(2)(A) of the Act. Under this rule, supervision must be provided by a physician who is present in the office suite in which the services are being furnished, throughout the time they are being furnished, and who is immediately available to provide assistance and direction. The definition in the proposed rule also clarified the meaning of the term "present in the office suite" to mean that the physician is actually physically present. However, we would still have considered the physician "present" during brief unexpected absences, as well as during routine absences of a short duration (such as during a lunch break), provided the absences occur during time periods in which the physician is otherwise scheduled and ordinarily expected to be present and the absences do not conflict with any other requirements in the Medicare program for a particular level of physician supervision.

The Final Rule: Our interpretation of the "direct supervision" standard produced the largest number of public comments about the in-office ancillary services exception, virtually all suggesting that our proposal would be overly burdensome, result in enigmatic technical rules, and require wasteful and inefficient practices.

We have revisited the direct supervision requirement and are now interpreting "directly supervised" in the statute to mean that the supervision meets the supervision requirements under applicable Medicare and Medicaid payment or coverage rules for the specific services at issue. Upon further review and consideration, we concluded that the Congress did not use the phrase "directly supervised" in any technical sense. Rather, the Congress sought to establish a nexus between the referring physician and the individual performing the ancillary services in order to limit the exception to services that are truly "ancillary" to the referring physician's medical practice. We believe that the Congress did not intend section 1877 of the Act to supersede or replicate existing statutory and regulatory structures that address supervision of services from the perspective of quality of care or patient safety. This interpretation is consistent with the often cited legislative history for section 1877 of the Act indicating that the Congress did not intend to require physicians to be present at all times that ancillary services were being performed. (See Conference Report for OBRA 1993, H. Rep. No. 213, 103d Congress 810 (1993).) Instead, we believe a sensible approach is to defer to existing Medicare and Medicaid supervision requirements. (Those rules are not addressed in Phase I of this rulemaking.)

In our January 1998 proposed rule with respect to the group practice definition, we proposed eliminating independent contractors as members of the group practice. This created the prospect that independent contractors would not be able to provide the supervision required under the in-office ancillary services exception. The statute provides that physicians "in the group practice" may supervise the furnishing of ancillary services to patients of a referring physician who is a member of the group practice. Under Phase I of this rulemaking, physicians "in the group practice" include owners of the group practice, employees of the group practice, and independent contractors who are "in the group practice." Owners and employees may also be members of the group; independent contractors may not. We will consider an independent contractor physician to be "in the group practice" if he or she has a contractual arrangement to provide services to the group's patients in the group practice's facilities and the independent contractor's arrangement with the group complies with the reassignment rules in Sec. 424.80(b)(3) of these regulations and in section 3060.3, "Payment to Health Care Delivery System," of the Medicare Carriers Manual (HCFA Pub. 14–3), Part 3 — Claims Process. Independent contractors who qualify as physicians "in the group practice" may receive overall profit shares and productivity bonuses described in section 1877(h)(4)(B)(i) of the Act, as implemented by these regulations, and may provide the supervision required under the in-office ancillary services exception.

Comment: Many commenters raised concerns about the level of supervision required under the in-office ancillary services exception. Many commenters objected to our proposed interpretation of the direct supervision requirement, which would have adopted the supervision requirement applicable to "incident to" services in section 2050, "Services and Supplies," of the Medicare Carriers Manual (HCFA Pub. 14–3), Part 3 — Claims Process, including a "present in the office suite" requirement, with an exception for brief absences by the physician. These commenters variously found the "presence" requirement overly burdensome, impractical, confusing, and unclear. Commenters believe that a general requirement of a physician's physical presence for all ancillary services would create unnecessary inefficiencies in the delivery of health care services, drive up costs, and inconvenience patients. For example, some commenters noted that tests are often scheduled in the mornings when physicians are making rounds or attending hospital meetings, with the physicians interpreting the tests when they arrive later at the office. Some commenters observed that they could discern no obvious connection between direct supervision and curtailing fraud and abuse. Others noted that a strict direct supervision requirement does not guarantee that DHS are medically appropriate and are not simply being performed for financial gain.

Commenters suggested various alternative standards, including "appropriate supervision," "professional responsibility," "general supervision," and "employee status." The vast majority of commenters, however, urged that the in-office ancillary services exception "direct supervision" requirement be interpreted to comport with the applicable supervision requirements under our other payment and coverage rules. These commenters stressed that these rules adequately take into account quality concerns and the health and safety of patients and that there is no justification for imposing an additional layer of supervision requirements.

Response: Upon further review and consideration of the statute, the legislative history, and the public comments, we have concluded that the Congress did not use the phrase "directly supervised" in any technical sense in the statute. Rather, we believe the Congress sought to establish a nexus between the referring physician and the individual performing the ancillary services in order to limit the exception to services that are truly "ancillary" to the referring physician's medical practice. We believe that the Congress did not intend section 1877 of the Act to supersede or replicate existing statutory and regulatory structures that address supervision of services from the perspective of quality of care or patient safety. This interpretation is consistent with the often cited legislative history indicating that the Congress did not intend in the context of section 1877 of the Act to require physicians to be present at all times that ancillary services were being performed ("The conferees intend that the requirement for direct supervision by a physician would be met if the lab is in the physician's office which is personally supervised by a lab director, or a physician, even if the physician is not always on site" (H. Rep. No. 213, 103d Cong. 810 (1993)). We are persuaded that a more sensible approach is to defer to existing Medicare and Medicaid supervision requirements. (Those rules are not addressed in Phase I of this rulemaking.) Thus, the in-office ancillary services exception supervision requirements will be satisfied if the level of supervision provided meets all applicable Medicare or Medicaid payment and coverage requirements.

Comment: One commenter viewed the strict "direct supervision" standard established in the August 1995 final rule as an important check on inappropriate referrals and objected to any liberalization of the requirement, arguing that it would allow the connection between a physician's activities and DHS to "grow too thin." The commenter believes it is appropriate for us to impose higher standards of care to protect patients who are referred for DHS, because these services have been determined to present a particularly high risk of inappropriate referrals. The commenter further noted that as the health and safety rationale for supervision declines (supervision being less necessary for certain low-risk services), the risk of unnecessary referrals and overutilization increases. The commenter recommended that we retain the "incident to" direct supervision standard. In the alternative, the commenter proposed a "sphere of service" test under which a physician would be allowed to refer a patient for services only if that physician, and not another licensed practitioner, normally would perform the services. According to the commenter, this approach would eliminate physician incentives to establish "backroom" practices to provide services that could be provided more efficiently elsewhere.

Response: We share this commenter's concerns about inappropriate financial incentives driving the provision of DHS. We are concerned that heightened downward pressure on physician incomes will generate increased upward pressure to expand in-office ancillary services as a means of offsetting income losses. However, we believe the Congress clearly articulated a policy determination to allow in-office ancillary services that meet certain statutory criteria. While the stricter "incident to" supervision standard might serve to reduce the risk of overutilization somewhat, on balance, we believe that using section 1877 of the Act to superimpose a separate supervision requirement on existing regulatory structures governing appropriate levels of supervision would be overly burdensome, inefficient, and inconsistent with the overall design of the statute. We note, however, that physicians wishing to bill DHS "incident to" (and group practice physicians wishing to obtain productivity bonuses for services incident to their personally performed physician services) must comply with the "incident to" supervision requirements, including the "present and available" requirement and the employee requirement, as set forth in section 2050, "Services and Supplies," of the Medicare Carriers Manual (HCFA Pub. 14–3), Part 3 — Claims Process.

Comment: One commenter asked whether technicians must be directly supervised if a group practice provides technician services to a hospital. If so, the commenter requested that we clarify whether the group practice must follow self-referral supervision standards or hospital supervision standards.

Response: If a hospital is billing for the services, as this commenter implied, the in-office ancillary services exception does not apply (along with its supervision requirement). Any hospital standards would always apply, since any requirement for supervision under section 1877 of the Act is separate and distinct from other supervision requirements under the Medicare and Medicaid statute and regulations.

Comment: While many commenters approved of our proposal to exclude independent contractors as members of a group practice for purposes of complying with the definitional tests for a group practice (making it easier for many groups, especially smaller groups, to qualify as a group practice for purposes of section 1877 of the Act), many commenters also urged that independent contractors be included as members of a group practice for purposes of the direct supervision requirement of the in-office ancillary services exception. Many commenters expressed concern that our bar on direct supervision by independent contractors would undercut the ability of group practices to deliver necessary health care services in situations in which employment of the physician is not possible or desirable. To support their claim that the statute does not require that the direct supervision be provided by a "member" of the group, commenters observed that section 1877(b)(2)(A)(i) of the Act only requires supervision "by the [referring] physician or by another physician in the group." One commenter noted that this language is consistent with section 3060.3, "Payment to the Health Care Delivery System," of the Medicare Carriers Manual (HCFA Pub. 14–3), Part 3 — Claims Process, which treats independent contractors as "in the group" for reassignment purposes. Another commenter suggested that an independent contractor could properly be considered "in the group" if the physician provides services to the group practice's patients in the group practice's facility under a contract with the group, and the services are billed by the group.

Response: Having reviewed the comments and reconsidered the statutory language, we are persuaded that independent contractors may be physicians "in the group" for purposes of the in-office ancillary services exception. We are considering an independent contractor physician to be "in the group practice" if (1) he or she has a contractual arrangement to provide services to the group's patients in the group practice's facilities, (2) the contract contains compensation terms that are the same as those that apply to group members under section 1877(h)(4)(iv) of the Act or the contract fits in the personal services exception, and (3) the contract complies with the reassignment rules at Sec. 424.80(b)(3) of these regulations and in section 3060.3, "Payment to the Health Care Delivery System," of the Medicare Carriers Manual (HCFA Pub. 14–3), Part 3 — Claims Process, so that his or her services are billed by the group practice. We are codifying this new test in Sec. 411.351 of the regulations. This latter requirement presents a technical problem under the plain language of the statute, which we address as follows. The billing requirements under section 1877(b)(2)(B) of the Act do not provide for billing by the group practice when a supervising physician is "a physician in the group practice," rather than a member of the group. Given the statutory structure and language, particularly the language of the direct supervision requirement under section 1877(b)(2)(A)(i)of the Act, we are interpreting the billing requirements to extend to billing by the group practice when the supervising physician is "in the group practice" in order to effectuate the direct supervision requirement. Independent contractors who qualify as "physicians in the group practice" may receive overall profit shares and productivity bonuses described in section 1877(h)(4)(B)(i) of the Act, as implemented by these regulations. As discussed in section VI.C.3 of this preamble, independent contractors are not "members" of the group.

Comment: Several commenters sought clarification with respect to the application of the in-office ancillary services exception to referrals for DHS from an independent contractor to the group practice with which he or she contracts (for example, referrals from an independent contractor to the group's in-office laboratory).

Response: Independent contractor physicians will have compensation relationships with the group practices with which they contract. In order for an independent contractor to refer DHS to the group practice, an exception must apply. Possible exceptions, depending on the circumstances, include the in-office ancillary services exception for independent contractors who are "physicians in the group", the physicians" services exception, the personal service arrangements exception, or the risk-sharing exception for services provided to certain managed care enrollees. We note that under the in-office ancillary services exception, the furnishing of DHS would have to take place in a "same building" location under section 1877(b)(2)(A)(ii)(I) of the Act, as the "centralized building" provision (section 1877(b)(2)(A)(ii)(II) of the Act) only applies to referring physicians who are group members.

Comment: Several practitioners of ultrasonography commented that a direct supervision requirement that mandates physician presence for in-office ancillaries unfairly benefits radiologists, who are generally available on-site because they do not have "patients" to see or other responsibilities, while disadvantaging vascular laboratories that operate without physicians on-site. The commenters suggested that the rule require that ultrasound examinations and interpretations be performed in accordance with standards set by independent professional associations. However, another commenter — radiologist — urged us to retain the direct supervision requirement in the interest of patient health and safety.

Response: As noted above, we are modifying the direct supervision requirement under the in-office ancillary services exception to apply the requisite supervision requirements under Medicare and Medicaid payment and coverage rules.

3. The Building Requirements

The Existing Law: Under section 1877(b)(2)(A)(ii) of the Act, in-office ancillary services must be furnished in a building in which the referring physician, or another physician who is a member of the same group practice, furnishes physician services unrelated to the furnishing of DHS. Alternatively, in the case of a referring physician who is a member of a group practice, the in-office ancillary services can be furnished in another building that is used by the group practice for the provision of some or all of the group's clinical laboratory services, or for the centralized provision of the group's DHS (other than clinical laboratory services). (The existing regulations address the same and other building requirements only with respect to clinical laboratory services.)

The Proposed Rule: In our January 1998 proposed rule, we proposed defining the "same building" in Sec. 411.355(b)(2)(i) as the same physical structure, with one address, and not multiple structures connected by tunnels or walkways.

The Final Rule: The building requirements are designed to ensure that the DHS qualifying for the exception are truly "in-office" (that is, part of the physician's routine medical office practice) and not provided as part of a separate business enterprise. The location requirements do not pertain to the furnishing of DHS that are not payable by Medicare or Medicaid; these services may be furnished anywhere, subject to any restrictions in other applicable Federal, State, or local laws.

In general, the structure of the statutory language suggests that the Congress had two main objectives: permitting the provision of in-office ancillary services for the convenience of patients during their patient visits and, in the group practice context, permitting the provision of in-office ancillary services in a dedicated building used for these services (for example, a central clinical laboratory). By contrast, we believe the Congress did not intend to protect part-time rentals of ancillary services facilities under this exception.

Upon further consideration, we believe that the Congress did not intend the application of the in-office ancillary services exception to turn on the nuances of architectural design. Thus, for purposes of Phase I of this rulemaking, a "building" is defined as a structure with, or combination of structures that share, a single street address as assigned by the U.S. Postal Service. For purposes of this rule, the "same building" does not include exterior spaces, such as courtyards, lawns, driveways, or parking lots, or interior parking garages. The building could include a SNF or other facility or a patient's home, provided all other conditions of the exception are satisfied. A mobile van or trailer is not a building or a part of a building.

The statute implements congressional intent by offering two location options: the "same building" option, available to solo practitioners and group practices, and the "centralized building" option, available only to groups. (See section 1877(b)(2)(A)(ii)(I) and (b)(2)(A)(ii)(II) of the Act.)

"Same Building"

Under section 1877(b)(2)(A)(ii)(I) of the Act, services qualify for the in-office ancillary services exception if they are furnished "in a building in which the referring physician (or another physician who is a member of the same group practice) furnishes physician services unrelated to the furnishing of designated health services." We believe the underlying intent of this provision is to allow physicians to furnish DHS that are ancillary to the physician's core medical practice in the location where the core medical services are routinely delivered. We believe the Congress did not intend to permit the wholesale provision of DHS in locations in which physicians perform only token services that are not related to the furnishing of DHS (that is, only token physician services that are not Federal or private pay DHS). Simply stated, the DHS should be ancillary to physician services that are not DHS, and not the other way around. The exception was intended as an accommodation to physicians' customary practice of medicine and not as a loophole for physicians and group practices to operate DHS enterprises that are unconnected — or only marginally connected — to their medical practices. In addition, the significant easing of the "direct supervision" requirement described above necessitates a somewhat stricter interpretation of the location standards than we proposed in our January 1998 proposed rule, in order to ensure an adequate nexus between in-office ancillary DHS and the physician's core medical practice. Thus, we are making the following changes (except where noted) in the "same building" requirements:

In our January 1998 proposed rule, we proposed interpreting the rule as allowing any quantity of services unrelated to DHS to be furnished in the same building. We are revising the rule to require that the referring physician (or another physician who is a member of the same group practice) must furnish in the same building substantial physician services unrelated to the furnishing of Federal or private pay DHS. We are defining the phrase "services unrelated to the furnishing of designated health services" to mean physician services that are neither Federal nor private pay DHS, even if the physician service leads to the ordering of DHS. In addition, to preclude single-service DHS enterprises from the in-office ancillary services exception, we are requiring that the unrelated physician services furnished in the building represent substantially the full range of physician services unrelated to the furnishing of DHS that the physician routinely provides (or, in the case of a member of a group practice, the full range of physician services that the physician routinely provides for the group practice).

We are adding a requirement that the DHS furnished in the building be furnished to patients whose primary nexus with the referring physician (or his or her group practice) is the receipt of physician services unrelated to the furnishing of DHS. Simply stated, obtaining DHS should not be the main reason the patient has contact with the referring physician (or his or her group practice). Again, this standard will ensure that self-referred DHS are ancillary and not primary services for the patients who receive them. Thus, for example, a physician who provides physician services and DHS for his or her patients in a nursing home may not also provide token physician services to other nursing home patients in order to provide DHS under the in-office ancillary services exception.

The space in the building in which the DHS are provided need not be adjacent to the space in which services that are not DHS are provided (subject to the dictates of any Medicare or Medicaid payment or coverage supervision rules).

Shared facilities in the same building are permitted to the extent they comply with the supervision, location, and billing requirements of the in-office ancillary services exception; we are not, however, creating a broader shared-facility exception.

We believe that a home care physician whose principal medical practice consists of treating patients in their private homes meets the "same building" requirements if the physician (or a staff member accompanying the physician) provides a designated health service contemporaneously with a physician service (provided by the referring physician) that is not a designated health service in the patient's private home and the other exception requirements are met. Because the location requirements of the in-office ancillary services exception may disadvantage home care physicians, we are considering whether special rules should be developed under the "same building" requirements for physicians who primarily practice as home care physicians. We are soliciting comments on that issue and intend to address it further in Phase II of this rulemaking.

"Centralized Building"

Under section 1877(b)(2)(A)(ii)(II) of the Act, in the case of a referring physician who is a member of a group practice, services qualify for the in-office ancillary services exception if they are furnished "in another building which is used by the group practice * * * for the provision of some or all of the group's clinical laboratory services, or * * * for the centralized provision of the group's designated health services (other than clinical laboratory services)." We believe that this statutory provision — which allows group practices to have "off-site" DHS locations — was intended to accommodate the concerns of group practices with multiple office locations that wanted to consolidate DHS operations for cost containment purposes. However, in permitting group practices to provide centralized DHS, the Congress did not intend to eviscerate the "in-office" element of the exception. We are therefore interpreting the "centralized building" standard as follows:

The space (whether an entire building, subpart of a building, or mobile unit) used for the provision of the group practice's clinical laboratory services or centralized DHS qualifies for the exception only if it is used exclusively by the group, that is, it is wholly owned by the group practice or leased by the group practice on a full-time basis (that is, 24 hours per day, 7 days per week). To preclude part-time arrangements in the form of one-day rentals, we are requiring that the centralized building be owned or leased exclusively by the group practice for at least 6 months. This rule precludes facilities shared by group practices in off-site buildings.

Part-time "centralized" DHS arrangements are precluded. For example, a group practice may not rent a magnetic resonance imaging (MRI) facility 1 day per week and treat that facility as a "centralized" building under section 1877(b)(2)(A)(ii)(II) of the Act.

Under the authority granted to the Secretary in the unnumbered paragraph that follows section 1877(b)(2)(A)(ii)(II)(bb) of the Act (that allows the Secretary to determine other terms and conditions related to section 1877(b)(2)(A)(ii)(II)(bb) under which the provision of DHS does not present a risk of program or patient abuse), we are determining that a mobile facility (for example, an x-ray van) owned and used exclusively by a group practice (24 hours per day, 7 days per week, for at least six months) will be considered to meet the "centralized building" standard, even though a mobile facility is not a building.

Group practices may lease or sublease DHS facility space (including mobile units) to or from other group practices or solo practitioners on a part-time basis, but DHS provided to patients of part-time lessee or sublessee group practices will not fit in the in-office ancillary services exception, unless the "same building" requirements are met.

Referrals for ancillary services from other physicians or group practices that are not affiliated with the group practice providing the DHS do not implicate section 1877 of the Act, provided there are no impermissible financial relationships between the parties. A referral for a designated health service does not create a financial relationship.

These building rules are designed to give physicians and group practices a meaningful opportunity to provide bona fide in-office ancillary DHS to their patients, while preventing group practices from using the in-office ancillary services exception to operate enterprises that are functionally nothing more than self-referred DHS enterprises, providing minimal services that are not DHS so as to comply nominally with the exception and capture DHS profits. We believe the Congress did not intend the exception to include these operations. Far from promoting patient convenience and quality of care, these arrangements pose a significant risk of overutilization of services and shuttling of patients to DHS locations for the economic betterment of the physicians, without regard to the patient's best interests.

Comment: Many commenters found the proposed regulations and interpretations of the "building" requirements to be confusing, over broad, potentially contradictory, and, in the words of one commenter, "metaphysical." With respect to our proposed "physical structure" requirements, many commenters urged us not to place the agency or physicians into surveying real estate to determine whether a structure is one building. Commenters variously observed that while some walkways or tunnels between commercial medical office buildings may be sidewalks between distinct and separate buildings, other walkways or tunnels are part of the modern architecture of these buildings or are required to comply with zoning, land use, open space, or other real estate laws or to surmount natural barriers present on the site of the building.

There were a number of suggestions for revising the requirement. One group of commenters urged us to adopt a mailing address rule stating that a building would be considered as one building for all suites or room numbers located inside that are required by the U.S. Postal Service to use the same street address, regardless of suite number. Under this rule, suites operated by the same group practice or solo physician in buildings that use separate street addresses would be treated as separate buildings for the purposes of the in-office ancillary services exception. Other commenters objected to a street address test, noting that physicians have no control over the manner in which their buildings are assigned street addresses and that the parameters for assigning street addresses may vary by State and locality. One commenter expressed concern about buildings located on corner lots that might have two street addresses.

A second approach proposed by one commenter was to revise the regulations to allow connected buildings or portions of buildings that are owned or controlled by the same group practice. Still other commenters claimed that the emphasis should be on the proximity of the supervising physician to the patient during the performance of DHS. Under this view, the location requirement of the in-office ancillary services exception should focus on whether the physician is "immediately available" to the support personnel and not on an artificially imposed physical design constraint. Along these lines, several commenters proposed that services be considered in the "same building" if the physician is within a certain number of minutes (for example, 10 minutes) from the patient or if the physician is "close at hand."

Response: We regard the building requirement of the in-office ancillary services exception, in combination with the supervision and billing requirements, as the Congress's attempt to circumscribe the exception so that it applies only to services provided within the referring physician's actual sphere of practice. Without these requirements, physicians could refer to, and profit from, almost any entity, with the claim that somehow the referred services are "in-office" services that are being supervised from some remote place.

Notwithstanding, we realize that our proposed definition of a "building"—which attempted to define a building in architectural terms—could cause practical problems for some physicians and that a clearer, "bright line" rule would be preferable. Accordingly, having considered the various alternatives suggested by the commenters, we have concluded that for purposes of Phase I of this rulemaking, we are defining a "building" as a structure with, or combination of structures that share, a single street address as assigned by the U.S. Postal Service. A building will be considered as one building for all suites or room numbers located inside that are required by the U.S. Postal Service to use the same street address, regardless of the suite number. Under this rule, suites used by the same group practice or solo physician in buildings with separate street addresses will be treated as separate buildings for the purposes of the in-office ancillary services exception. While we recognize that this mailing address rule may result in an occasional anomaly, we are persuaded that it creates a "bright line" rule that will be easy to apply and will produce fair results in the vast majority of cases. Questionable cases may be appropriate candidates for an advisory opinion.

The space in the building in which the DHS are provided need not be adjacent to the space in which services that are not DHS are provided (subject to the dictates of any Medicare or Medicaid payment or coverage supervision rules). Shared facilities in the same building are permitted under section 1877 of the Act to the extent they comply with the supervision, location, and billing requirements of the in-office ancillary services exception; we are not creating a broader shared facility exception.

Because of the increased risk of abuse, we do not intend to protect DHS provided by mobile vans or other mobile facilities under the in-office ancillary services exception, except in very limited circumstances described in section VI.B.3 of this preamble. Thus, we wish to make clear that for purposes of this rule, a "building" does not include exterior spaces, such as courtyards or parking lots, nor does it include interior parking garages. For purposes of the in-office ancillary services exception, a building consists of usable professional office space and common areas such as lobbies, corridors, elevator banks, and restrooms.

In light of the changes we are making in the supervision standard, we believe it is necessary to revisit the building standards in order to effectuate congressional intent to limit the scope of the in-office ancillary services exception to services that are truly ancillary to physician services and are not a primary business of the practice. Thus, we are revising the "same building" requirements to more definitively tie in-office ancillary services to the referring physician's core medical practice. Simply stated, we want to ensure that services covered by the exception are, in fact, furnished "in office." Under section 1877(b)(2)(A)(ii)(I) of the Act, services qualify for the in-office ancillary services exception if they are furnished "in a building in which the referring physician (or another physician who is a member of the same group practice) furnishes physicians' services unrelated to the furnishing of designated health services." We believe the underlying intent of this provision is to allow physicians to furnish DHS that are ancillary to the physician's core medical practice in the location where the core medical practice occurs. We believe the Congress did not intend to permit the wholesale provision of DHS in locations in which physicians perform only token services unrelated to the furnishing of DHS. Thus, we are interpreting the "same building" requirements as follows:

The referring physician (or another physician who is a member of the same group practice) must furnish in the same building substantial physician services unrelated to the furnishing of DHS. In addition, we are requiring that the unrelated physician services furnished in the building represent substantially the full range of physician services unrelated to the furnishing of DHS that the physician routinely provides (or, in the case of a member of a group practice, the full range of physician services that the physician routinely provides for the group practice). Independent contractors are not members of a group practice for purposes of section 1877 of the Act; thus, their activities do not count for purposes of compliance with the substantial physician services test or the full range of services test under the "same building" requirements, unless they are the referring physician. (See discussion in section VI.B.3 of this preamble.)

For purposes of this exception, we are defining the phrase "services unrelated to the furnishing of designated health services" to mean physician services that are neither Federal nor private pay DHS, even if the services might generate orders or referrals of DHS. Thus, for example, a cardiologist who examines a patient and thereafter orders a diagnostic radiology test has performed a service unrelated to the furnishing of DHS. On the other hand, a cardiologist who reads the results of a diagnostic radiology test (such as, for example, a transthoracic echocardiography for congenital cardiac anomalies, CPT code 93303) (whether for a Federal or private pay patient) has performed a service that is related to the furnishing of DHS.

The DHS furnished in the building are furnished to patients whose primary nexus with the referring physician (or the group practice of which the referring physician is a member) is the receipt of physician services unrelated to the furnishing of DHS. Thus, for example, a physician who provides physician services and DHS for his or her patients in a nursing home may not also provide token physician services to other nursing home patients in order to provide those services under the in-office ancillary services exception.

Comment: One commenter believes that our proposed interpretation of the "same building" requirements contradicts the purpose of section 1877(b)(2)(A)(ii) of the Act. The commenter focused on the part of this provision that requires that ancillary services be furnished in a building "in which the referring physician * * * furnishes physicians' services unrelated to the furnishing of designated health services." The proposed rule regarded a physician's examination and diagnosis of a patient that leads to the physician requesting a designated health service as acts that are "unrelated to the furnishing of designated health services." The commenter is concerned that this interpretation would allow a physician's office to be a single specialty "mill" in which the physician could quickly generate a large quantity of referrals for profit. In other words, the exception could apply to a physician who does little more than conduct cursory evaluations and refer patients for a particular designated health service (for example, physical therapy). The commenter believes that, instead, the physician's office is meant to be a location in which the physician provides bona fide diagnostic and curative services to individuals presenting a variety of conditions.

Response: We share the commenter's general concern about inappropriate DHS arrangements, although we believe that the statute does not require us to include in the in-office ancillary services exception only services referred by physicians who treat a variety of conditions. The focus of the exception, in our view, is the requirement that the services be provided or performed in conjunction with a physician's own professional activities or as adjuncts to physician services, in a location in which the physician (or a member of his or her group practice) practices. If we were to limit this exception as the commenter suggested, some physician specialists might be prohibited from referring within their own practices. On the other hand, we agree that some restriction in the definition is appropriate to preclude physicians from providing virtually nothing more than referrals for DHS. Thus, as discussed above, in Phase I of this rulemaking, we are requiring that the unrelated physician services furnished in the building represent substantially the full range of physician services unrelated to the furnishing of DHS that the physician routinely provides (or, in the case of a member of a group practice, the full range of physician services that the physician routinely provides for the group practice).

Comment: Several commenters believe that our proposal to have our regional carriers determine whether the building requirements are satisfied was unworkable and impractical and would result in inequitable application of the law. Commenters noted that local carriers are often reluctant to express opinions on these issues and disinclined to provide written opinions. If the proposal survives, one commenter urged us, at a minimum, to give carriers explicit authority and direction to issue these written opinions.

Response: We have endeavored to develop regulations that provide sufficiently clear rules so that parties can determine compliance without resorting to a regional carrier's determination.

Comment: A commenter expressed concern about DHS performed by physicians who travel to see patients. The commenter is a physician in a group practice of six physiatrists who perform electromyography and nerve conduction studies in a midwestern State. The group travels to rural counties in the State in which it practices to evaluate patients for musculoskeletal and neurologic problems. The patients often need nerve testing, and the group's physiatrists are often the only health care professionals in the county able to perform this testing. The commenter expressed concern that the regulations would prohibit the physiatrists from providing needed medical assessment and care to patients in these circumstances.

Response: Electromyography and nerve conduction studies are not physical therapy services under our definition in Sec. 411.351; therefore, referrals for these services do not implicate section 1877 of the Act. Nonetheless, we wish to address the commenter's underlying question regarding traveling practitioners. Assuming that the physiatrist group meets the definition of a group practice under section 1877(h)(4) of the Act and the DHS are performed in the same building where the physiatrist (or a member of the group) also performs substantial physician services unrelated to the furnishing of Federal or private pay DHS, we believe the in-office ancillary services exception may apply in the situation described by the commenter. As noted elsewhere, we are soliciting comments on problems faced by physicians who principally practice in patients' homes and may be disadvantaged by the location requirements of the in-office ancillary services exception. We note also that the rural provider exception (to be addressed in Phase II of this rulemaking) may apply in the situation described by the commenter.

Comment: A commenter asked that we make clear that if a solo practitioner provides a designated health service for his or her own patients in the solo practitioner's own office, then the solo practitioner is not in violation of section 1877 of the Act.

Response: In the vast majority of situations we can envision, if a solo practitioner provides a designated health service for his or her own patients in the solo practitioner's own office, then the solo practitioner will not violate section 1877 of the Act. First, we are revising the definition of a "referral" for purposes of section 1877 of the Act to exclude DHS personally performed by the referring physician. Second, with respect to DHS performed by employees of the solo practitioner (including "incident to" services), we believe the Congress intended for the in-office ancillary services exception to apply to solo practitioners as well as group practices. Thus, so long as a solo practitioner's provision of DHS meets the in-office ancillary services exception, section 1877 of the Act would not be violated.

Comment: Commenters were divided about the provision of ancillary services through mobile units. Some believe that the use of mobile units and equipment leads to abusive arrangements. Other commenters supported the use of mobile units as cost-efficient means of sharing expensive DHS resources, particularly in rural areas. One commenter noted that State certificate of necessity (CON) volume requirements would be nearly impossible to meet without mobile units. The same commenter argued that sharing equipment is a critical part of cost containment, because idle equipment may lead to overutilization. One commenter pointed out that Federal antitrust agencies approve joint ownership of high technology equipment and that Blue Cross/Blue Shield has many policy provisions requiring joint ownership. These commenters generally advocated that mobile units be permitted and that mobile units qualify as a centralized location for the provision of DHS. A commenter observed that under the January 1998 proposed rule, a group practice could move any piece of equipment from office to office and, applying the "same building" requirements, use that piece of equipment for the provision of DHS. In light of this, the commenter questioned whether it made sense for the group practice to be prohibited from transporting the piece of equipment in a mobile vehicle to the various practice sites and using the equipment in the vehicle, if the mobile unit were exclusively used by the group practice and is not leased to any other health care provider. The commenter requested clarification that in these circumstances, the mobile unit would meet either the "same building" requirements or "centralized building" standard. Other commenters urged a broader exception for mobile units, for example, including them if they are parked in the parking lot of a physician's medical office building or treating the units themselves as buildings.

Response: The treatment of mobile units presents difficult questions under section 1877 of the Act. On the one hand, we have serious concerns about the potential for fraud and abuse when services are provided with mobile units. These are the same concerns we have (and believe the Congress shares) about all shared physician-owned or controlled ancillary services facilities. We believe that section 1877 of the Act is aimed at arrangements that enable physicians to profit from referrals to free-standing, money-making services ventures that are not central to their medical practices. On the other hand, we agree that the statute clearly permits services provided by mobile units that qualify under the "same building" requirements. Thus, we agree with the commenter that a group practice can move any piece of equipment from office to office and use that "in-office" piece of equipment for the provision of DHS in a location that meets the "same building" requirements. Because we are defining "building" narrowly to exclude parking lots and interior parking garages, services provided in mobile vans or trailers will not comply with the "same building" requirements. We believe it reasonable to conclude that these services are not "in-office" when a van circulates among various physicians' offices and is rented serially by each. These arrangements would seem to be calculated to enhance physician revenues, rather than patient convenience, since patients would likely be encouraged, if not required, to schedule appointments on the day that the physician stands to profit from the services.

That said, we believe that mobile services can constitute an important part of the health care delivery system for many patients. Nothing in the statute or these regulations precludes a physician or group practice from arranging for a mobile provider to treat the physician's patients at his or her office location, so long as the financial arrangement, if any, between the physician or group practice and the ancillary services provider fits in an exception under section 1877 of the Act. In addition, in rural areas, the "rural provider" exception (to be addressed in Phase II of this rulemaking) may apply to protect some physician-owned mobile service providers. Finally, we are persuaded that the risk is low if a group practice exclusively owns and uses its own mobile van or trailer that circulates among its group practice locations. In that limited circumstance, we are treating the mobile unit as akin to a "centralized" building under section 1877(b)(2)(A)(ii)(II) of the Act.

Comment: Several commenters sought clarification in the regulations text that group practices can have more than one centralized location for the provision of DHS. However, one commenter offered a contrary view. This commenter expressed the view that the Congress intended that the in-office ancillary services exception be interpreted narrowly with respect to centralized, free-standing locations. Specifically, the commenter cites the Conference Report for OBRA 1993 in H. Rep. No. 213, 1st Sess., 810 (1993), which states: "The conference agreement includes an exception for clinical laboratory services provided by a group practice with multiple office locations. For all other DHS the exception for group practices applies only if the services are provided in a centralized location" (emphasis added). Based on this language, the commenter believes that the Congress intended to permit group practices to have a single centralized location to provide DHS, but not to permit group practices to establish multiple wholly owned locations or franchises for DHS.

Response: Under section 1877(b)(2)(A)(ii)(II) of the Act, in the case of a referring physician who is a member of a group practice, services qualify for the in-office ancillary services exception if they are furnished "in another building which is used by the group practice * * * for the provision of some or all of the group's clinical laboratory services, or * * * for the centralized provision of the group's designated health services (other than clinical laboratory services)." Neither the statute nor the legislative history for this provision specifically requires one single centralized location for a group to provide DHS. In addition, we see no compelling reason to impose such a requirement. We are interpreting the word "centralized" to apply when a group practice has established a separate facility for furnishing DHS to patients, without the requirement that it service all of the practice's offices or provide all of the practice's DHS. We are incorporating this interpretation into the regulations text.

If we were to require only one centralized facility for DHS, a group practice could be in the position of having to send patients from some offices to inconvenient locations or to house a variety of different kinds of ancillary services in one location, such as combining all physical therapy, laboratory services, and x-rays in one building. It may be entirely impractical for a group practice to house the equipment and staff for such diverse services in one location. We believe the Congress meant to allow groups to use this kind of "central" or dedicated location in situations in which the facility is convenient to some of the different offices, but as a result may not be physically attached to any one of them. Thus, the facility is "central" to multiple offices, rather than attached to just one.

Comment: Several commenters sought clarification that a group practice with a single office location for the delivery of services that are not DHS can have a separate, centralized building for the delivery of DHS.

Response: While we believe that the "centralized building" provision — which allows group practices to have "off-site" DHS locations — was intended to accommodate the concerns of group practices with multiple office locations that wanted to consolidate DHS operations for cost containment purposes, we can discern nothing in the statute or legislative history that would prevent a group practice with only one office location from using a centralized building for the provision of DHS.

However, we are concerned that allowing single and multi-office group practices to have multiple off-site locations for DHS would effectively gut the in-office ancillary services exception without additional controls. Accordingly, we are modifying the "centralized building" standard to ensure that DHS referrals protected by the in-office ancillary services exception are truly part of the group practice's medical practice. First, we are requiring that the centralized office space (whether an entire building, subpart of a building, or mobile unit) used for the provision of the group practice's clinical laboratory services or DHS qualifies for the exception only if it is used exclusively by the group practice or group practice physicians, that is, it is wholly owned by the group practice (other than a security interest held by an unrelated lender or mortgagor) or is leased or subleased by the group practice on a full-time basis (that is, 24 hours per day, 7 days per week, for at least 6 months). This rule precludes group practice shared facilities in off-site buildings. Second, part-time "centralized" DHS arrangements are precluded. For example, a group practice may not rent an MRI facility one day per week and treat that facility as a "centralized" building. Third, a mobile facility (for example, an x-ray van) owned and used exclusively by the group practice will be considered a "centralized building."

Notwithstanding, group practices may lease or sublease DHS facility space (including mobile units) to or from other group practices or solo practitioners on a part-time basis. However, DHS provided to patients of part-time lessee or sublessee group practices will not fit in the in-office ancillary services exception, unless the "same building" requirements are met. Finally, referrals for ancillary services to a group practice from physicians not in the group practice or other group practices do not implicate section 1877 of the Act, provided there are no impermissible financial relationships between the parties. A referral for a designated health service does not create a financial relationship.

Comment: Many commenters urged us to establish a separate exception for shared facilities. Several commenters argued that shared facilities pose no greater risk of overutilization than DHS furnished by solo practices or group practices. Moreover, commenters believe that shared facilities overseen by referring physicians are likely to be more convenient, efficient, and accountable than other facilities. A number of commenters suggested that failure to protect shared facilities would disrupt existing arrangements that are widespread in the industry (as one commenter stated, shared facilities are the "reality of what's going on"), leaving many solo practitioners with only two options: merge with others to form group practices or disband their shared facilities. One physician commenter believes that if his shared radiology and clinical laboratory facilities are not permitted, the result would be a shift of income to commercial laboratory ventures, pathologists, and radiologists, further "dichotomizing" the incomes of primary care physicians and specialists. The physician claimed that his income would drop by 25 percent and that he would have to fire employees and default on a lease. Commenters representing the interests of solo practitioners asserted that there is no meaningful distinction between DHS facilities shared by solo practitioners and group practice-owned DHS facilities.

A physician-oriented trade association and other commenters urged us to add a new exception to allow the legitimate use of shared office facilities by physicians modeled on language included in BBA 1997, but never enacted. Other commenters offered different formulations, including allowing shared facilities if they are in the same building or complex of buildings as the solo practitioners' office practices.

Response: In the August 1995 final rule and the preamble to the January 1998 proposed regulation, we observed that the in-office ancillary services exception would allow certain shared facility arrangements among solo practitioners who do not wish to become a group practice. For example, we noted that two solo practitioners who share an office and jointly own a laboratory can continue to refer to that laboratory, as long as each physician (1) furnishes physician services unrelated to the furnishing of DHS in the office (that is, the arrangement meets the "same building" requirements), (2) directly supervises the laboratory services for his or her own Medicare or Medicaid patients while they are being furnished, and (3) bills for the services. We further noted that if only one of the solo practitioners owns the laboratory in a shared office, the nonowning physician can refer to the laboratory as long as he or she is not receiving compensation from the owner in exchange for referrals. We solicited comments on the effects of section 1877 of the Act on other shared facility arrangements.

After careful review of the public comments, we are persuaded that our original approach in the January 1998 proposed regulations is most consistent with the purposes of section 1877 of the Act. Under that approach, shared facilities are permitted if they comply with the supervision, location, and billing requirements of the in-office ancillary services exception. With respect to the location of the shared facility, Phase I of this rulemaking permits shared facilities that meet the "same building" requirements. (However, shared facilities do not qualify under the "centralized building" standard because they will not meet the exclusively used requirement). Thus, as noted above, two solo practitioners who share an office and jointly own a laboratory can continue to refer to that laboratory, as long as each physician furnishes substantial physician services unrelated to the furnishing of DHS in the building where the laboratory is located, provides (directly or through an independent contractor if permitted under applicable payment and coverage rules) the appropriate level of supervision for DHS for his or her own Medicare or Medicaid patients, and bills for the services. We believe the relaxation of the direct supervision requirement under these regulations will enable additional shared facilities to come within the exception. Additionally, if only one of the solo practitioners owns the laboratory in a shared facility arrangement, the nonowning physician can refer to the laboratory as long as he or she is not compensated by the owner in exchange for referrals.

We are not persuaded, however, that a separate exception for shared facilities is warranted. The BBA 1997 language that several commenters proffered would apply to services that are furnished—

Personally by the referring physician who is a shared facility physician or personally by an individual directly employed or under the general supervision of such a physician;

By a shared facility in a building in which the referring physician furnishes substantially all of the services of the physician that are unrelated to the furnishing of shared facility services;

To a patient of a shared facility physician; and

That are billed by the referring physician or a group practice of which the physician is a member.

Given that we are revising the supervision standards under the in-office ancillary services exception, we believe that the in-office ancillary services exception will cover most, if not all, of the nonabusive shared facility arrangements that would have been protected by this commenter's proposed additional exception.

Comment: A commenter questioned the application of the proposed regulations if physicians who share a building, but for legal or personal reasons are not formally organized into a professional structure (that is, a "single legal entity"), form a joint venture to establish a clinical laboratory or other ancillary service provider.

Response: As explained above, solo practitioners may own and operate shared DHS facilities so long as they fit in the in-office ancillary services exception. If the practitioners form a separate joint venture to provide the services, they may run into problems complying with the billing requirements of the in-office ancillary services exception, if the joint venture does the billing (that is, the joint venture will not qualify as a wholly owned entity and, therefore, will not fit into any of the in-office ancillary billing requirements under section 1877(b)(2)(B) of the Act or Sec. 411.355(b)).

4. The Billing Requirement

The Existing Law: To qualify for the in-office ancillary services exception under the statute, the DHS must be billed by one of the following:

The physician performing or supervising the service;

The group practice of which such physician is a member, under that group practice's billing number; or

An entity that is wholly owned by the referring or supervising physician or the referring or supervising physician's group practice.

The Proposed Rule: In the proposed regulation, we interpreted the billing requirements to allow a single group to bill under more than one billing number assigned to the group and to allow an agent to bill for the group in the group's name, using the group's number, provided the billing arrangement meets the requirements in Sec. 424.80(b)(6). We further interpreted the "wholly owned" entity provision to mean that a physician or group practice can establish a wholly owned provider of DHS that can bill Medicare or Medicaid on its own behalf, under its own billing number that is not a group billing number.

The Final Rule: As with the other requirements in this exception, the billing requirements serve to tie the ancillary services for which self-referrals will be permitted to the physician's routine medical practice. Phase I of this rulemaking incorporates the OBRA 1993 amendment clarifying that in-office ancillary services that are billed by a group practice of which the referring or supervising physician is a member must be billed under a billing number assigned to the group practice. However, group practices may have, and bill under, multiple group practice billing numbers, subject to any applicable Medicare or Medicaid program restrictions. Wholly owned entities that qualify to do the billing under the rule may use their own billing numbers and need not use a number assigned to the physician or group practice that owns them. The entities must be wholly owned either by the physician performing or supervising the services or by the group practice; joint ventures between group practices and individual group practice physicians or that include other providers or investors do not qualify as wholly owned entities.

Billing may be done by independent third party billing companies if they are acting as agents of a solo practitioner, group practice, or entity, but the billing must be done under billing numbers assigned to the solo practitioner, group practice, or entity, and the services may not be separately billed under a billing company's number. The billing arrangements must meet the requirements of Sec. 424.80(b)(6).

The express billing requirements of section 1877(b)(2)(B) of the Act contain no billing method applicable to supervising independent contractor physicians who are "physician in the group" under section 1877(b)(2)(A)(i) of the Act and Sec. 411.351, but who are not members of the group under Sec. 411.351 (these physicians cannot bill themselves as the supervising physician because they are required to reassign their billing rights to the group in order to qualify as "physicians in the group"). We believe the Congress intended the billing requirements of section 1877(b)(2)(B) of the Act to correspond with the supervision requirements of section 1877(b)(2)(a)(i) of the Act and that this omission was simply a legislative drafting oversight. Accordingly, we are interpreting the billing requirements to be consistent with the supervision requirements, which permit supervision by a "physician in the group." Therefore, the billing conditions will be satisfied if the DHS are billed by the group practice when the supervising physician is a "physician in the group."

In summary, under the regulations in Phase I of this rulemaking, to qualify for the in-office ancillary services exception, DHS must be billed by one of the following:

The physician performing or supervising the service.

The group practice of which such physician is a member, under that group practice's billing number.

The group practice if the physician is a "physician in the group practice," under that group practice's billing number.

An entity that is wholly owned by the referring or supervising physician or the referring or supervising physician's group practice.

Comment: One commenter objected to our interpretation of the "wholly owned" entity provision as unsupported by the statute. The commenter believes that allowing separate and distinct entities to provide services and bill on their own behalf would frustrate efforts to detect fraud and abuse, because the provider numbers of the physician making the referral and the entity providing the DHS would not be clearly linked on a claim form. The commenter believes that the Congress likely intended to exempt only wholly owned entities that primarily provide administrative and billing services.

Response: We find nothing in the statutory language that would limit wholly owned entities under section 1877(b)(2)(B) of the Act to entities that provide only administrative and billing services. Rather, we believe the wholly owned entity provision can be read reasonably to permit group practices to provide DHS and bill through these entities. A narrower interpretation would seem to imply that the group practices could only bill using third party billing companies if these companies were wholly owned by the group. We believe it unlikely that the Congress intended such an interpretation.

Comment: A commenter suggested that the billing provisions in the in-office ancillary services exception be changed to include billing by a hospital for physician services furnished under arrangements. This change would allow physician services for hospital patients to come within the in-office ancillary services exception.

Response: The in-office ancillary services exception is designed to exempt from the referral prohibition certain DHS that are provided within a group practice. As discussed in section VIII of this preamble, DHS provided under arrangements with a hospital are inpatient or outpatient hospital services for purposes of the statute. We believe the Congress did not intend to protect inpatient and outpatient hospital services under the in-office ancillary services exception. In fact, in describing the in-office ancillary services exception in H. Rep. No. 111, 103d Congress, 1st Sess. 546 (1993), the Congress pointed out that services provided by a hospital or other provider "under arrangement" with a group practice are not protected under the general exception for in-office ancillary services. "Under arrangements" issues are further discussed in section VIII.M of this preamble.

C. Group Practice Definition (Section 1877(h)(4) of the Act)

The Existing Law: As defined in section 1877(h)(4) of the Act, a "group practice" is a group of two or more physicians legally organized as a partnership, professional corporation, foundation, not-for-profit corporation, faculty practice plan, or similar association, that meets certain conditions. Section 1877(h)(4) of the Act was promulgated as part of the original section 1877 law and later amended by OBRA 1993. The current law contains the following conditions applicable to "group practices" for purposes of section 1877 (those conditions added by OBRA 1993 are so noted):

Each physician member of the group furnishes substantially the full range of services that the physician routinely furnishes, including medical care, consultation, diagnosis, or treatment, through the joint use of shared office space, facilities, equipment, and personnel (the "full range of services" test).

Substantially all of the services of the physician members of the group are furnished through the group, are billed under a billing number assigned to the group, and amounts so received are treated as receipts of the group (the "substantially all test") (revised by OBRA 1993).

The overhead expenses of and the income from the practice are distributed in accordance with methods previously determined (modified by OBRA 1993).

No physician member of the group directly or indirectly receives compensation based on the volume or value of referrals by the physician, with the exception of certain profits and productivity bonuses (added by OBRA 1993).

Members of the group personally conduct at least 75 percent of the physician-patient encounters of the group practice (the "75 percent physician-patient encounters test") (added by OBRA 1993).

The group practice complies with all other standards established by the Secretary in regulations.

In addition, section 1877(h)(4)(B) of the Act establishes two "Special Rules" —

A physician in a group practice may be paid a share of the overall profits of the group, or a productivity bonus based on services personally performed or services incident to the personally performed services, so long as the share or bonus is not determined in any manner that is directly related to the volume or value of referrals by the physician (added by OBRA 1993); and

In the case of a faculty practice plan associated with a hospital, institution of higher education, or medical school with an approved medical residency training program in which physician members may furnish a variety of different specialty services and furnish professional services both within and outside the group, as well as perform other tasks such as research, the conditions contained in the definition of "group practice" apply only with respect to the services furnished within the faculty practice plan.

Our August 1995 final rule covering clinical laboratory services referrals defined "group practice" at Sec. 411.351 based on the statute as it read effective January 1, 1992. At that time, we interpreted the "substantially all test" to mean that at least 75 percent of the patient care services (defined as services addressing the medical needs of specific patients) of the group practice members must be furnished through the group. We interpreted members of the group to include owners, employees, and independent contractors. We required that the group practice be "a single legal entity." Finally, we stated that the "substantially all test" would not apply to any group practice that is located solely in a health professional shortage area (HPSA). For group practices located outside of a HPSA, the rule provided that any time spent by group practice members providing services in a HPSA would not be used to calculate whether the group practice located outside the HPSA had met the "substantially all test."

The Proposed Rule: We proposed several changes to the definition of "group practice" in Sec. 411.351 to incorporate OBRA 1993 changes. We also proposed several other significant changes. First, we proposed a "unified business test" — targeted at sham group practices — that would require group practices to exhibit "centralized decision making, a pooling of expenses and revenues, and a distribution system that is not based on each satellite office operating as if it were a separate enterprise." Second, we proposed excluding independent contractors as members of the group to ease compliance with the "substantially all test." Third, we proposed expanding our definition of "patient care services" to include any of a physician's tasks that address the medical needs of specific patients or patients in general or that benefit the group practice.

Final Rule: As with the in-office ancillary services exception, we have been guided in developing the final definition of "group practice" by twin goals: (1) To minimize the regulatory intrusiveness of the definition while giving meaning to the statutory language and intent; and (2) to provide clear guidance as to what constitutes a "group practice" for purposes of section 1877 of the Act. We understand the importance of group practice status to physicians: simply stated, it allows group members to refer patients to one another (or to the group itself) for DHS payable by Medicare or Medicaid, and it allows group members to share in profits derived from such DHS. Section 1877 of the Act recognizes that referrals within groups are commonplace and may be appropriate adjuncts to a group's core medical practice.

As an initial matter, the definition of "group practice" promulgated in the statute and these regulations applies only for purposes of section 1877 of the Act and may have little or no bearing for purposes of other Medicare or Medicaid provisions. For example, the definition of a "physician group" under the physician incentive plan rules is broader than the definition of "group practice" under section 1877 of the Act.

A common complaint about our January 1998 proposed regulation was that it would exclude many bona fide group practices, intrude too far into the business and financial operations of physician practices, and chill group practice integration that is crucial in an increasingly managed care environment. We have been mindful of these concerns in developing Phase I of this rulemaking. It is not our intent to micro-manage group practices or dictate their organization or operation; rather, our intent is to define "group practice" so as to create, consistent with our understanding of the statutory intent, a meaningful exception to the general referral prohibition under section 1877 of the Act, an exception that permits certain traditional and commonplace referral patterns within group practices, without permitting the exception to swallow the rule. In general, Phase I of this rulemaking is more expansive than our January 1998 proposed rule and affords physicians substantial flexibility in designing and managing their medical practices (subject, of course, to any other legal impediments imposed by Federal or State law).

We believe the group practice definition set forth in section 1877(h)(4) of the Act is premised on two assumptions. First, internal group practice referrals should only be protected under the physician services or in-office ancillary services exceptions (both of which apply in specific ways to group practices) if the group practice is a bona fide group practice and not a loose confederation of individual physicians bound together primarily to profit from DHS referrals. We believe the Congress intended a true group practice to consist of physicians whose practices are fully integrated, medically and economically. In short, the physicians practice medicine together in a single group, not separately, and their financial prospects are interdependent. Thus, the Congress imposed certain tests that demonstrate the requisite integration and gave the Secretary regulatory authority to impose additional tests. If true integration is present, we do not believe the Congress otherwise intended to regulate the formal structure and operation of the group. Second, the financial incentives for group practice physicians to generate referrals of Medicare or Medicaid payable DHS for the group should be attenuated. Thus, the group practice definition provides that group practice physicians may not be paid directly or indirectly based on the volume or value of DHS referrals, unless the compensation is a profit share or productivity bonus that is only indirectly related to those referrals.

With these precepts in mind, Phase I of this rulemaking incorporates the following significant revisions:

Broadening of the types of arrangements that qualify as a "single legal entity" to include, among other things, multi-entity legal structures and structures owned by a single physician.

Adoption of our proposal to exclude independent contractors from the definition of a "member of the group." However, independent contractors who meet the conditions set forth at Sec. 411.351 may qualify as "physicians in the group practice" who may receive profit shares and productivity bonuses under section 1877(h)(4)(B)(i) of the Act.

Adoption of our proposed expanded definition of "patient care services" so that patient care services include all services a physician performs that address the medical needs of specific patients or patients in general or benefit the group practice (for example, administrative services for the group).

Expansion of our 1998 proposal to gauge compliance with the "substantially all test" by measuring a physician's actual time spent on patient care services by permitting groups to adopt other reasonable methods for determining compliance.

Creation of a substantially more flexible definition of a "unified business" that will permit group practices to use cost- and location-based accounting with respect to services that are not DHS, and, in some cases, with respect to services that are DHS if the compensation method is not directly related to the volume or value of the physician's referrals and other conditions are satisfied.

Revision of the productivity bonus rules so that group practices may pay member physicians and independent contractors who qualify as "physicians in the group" productivity bonuses based directly on the physician's personal productivity (including services incident to such personally performed services that meet the requirements of section 1861(s)(2)(A) of the Act and section 2050 of the Medicare Carriers Manual, Part 3), but may not pay such physicians any bonus based directly on their referrals of DHS that are performed by someone else.

Promulgation of specific methods for ensuring that compensation for DHS is only indirectly related to referral income. In addition, parties may use other methods that are reasonable and documented.

Elimination of the group practice attestation requirement.

These revisions and others are discussed in the comments and responses that follow. Each comment and response section begins with an overview of the relevant provision in the group practice definition and a summary of the final rule relating to that provision. The sections are divided as follows: General comments, the single legal entity requirement, members of the group, the "full range of services" test, the "substantially all" test, and the "75% physician-patient encounters" test.

1. General Comments

Comment: Many commenters, including a group practice trade association, criticized the proposed regulations for group practices as overly intrusive into the internal operations of physician practices, unnecessarily complex, and incapable of implementation in a fair and reasonable manner. The association and other commenters believe that the Congress intended the group practice provisions in the law predominately to regulate the external ownership, compensation, and referral arrangements of physicians and not the inner workings of group practices themselves. The association and other commenters protested that the rules create arbitrary distinctions among different types of physicians. These commenters contended that no tenable reason exists to treat group practices, pathologists, radiologists, and radiation oncologists — all of whom are permitted under the statute or various exceptions to make referrals to entities with which they have financial relationships under certain circumstances — differently than other physicians, since they have an equal incentive to self-refer.

Response: As indicated above, in preparing Phase I of this rulemaking, we have been mindful of the commenters' concerns about the intrusiveness of the proposed rule, and have sought to minimize the regulatory impact of the group practice definition and to provide clear guidance as to what constitutes a "group practice" for purposes of section 1877 of the Act. We do not intend to use these regulations to micro-manage group practices or to dictate their organization or operation, except as is necessary to give effect to the statutory intent of the Congress to create a limited exception to the general referral prohibition for DHS referrals by physicians within their own group practices. In general, Phase I of this rulemaking is broader than the January 1998 proposed rule and affords physicians substantial flexibility in designing and managing their medical practices.

While we have endeavored to apply these rules as equally as possible to solo and group practitioners and among various types of practitioners, some differences in regulation and outcomes are unavoidable, and in some cases desired, given the wide array of arrangements to which the statute applies and the distinctions inherent in the statutory scheme. For example, the Congress included a specific exception for referrals by consulting pathologists, diagnostic radiologists, and radiation oncologists that does not apply in the case of other consulting physicians. The Congress intended disparate treatment of these consulting physicians, reasonably, we believe, because of the limited ability of pathologists, diagnostic radiologists, and radiation oncologists to generate patient referrals of services they either perform or supervise. Similarly, the Congress judged referrals within group practices (and solo practices) deserving of special consideration based, we believe, on a recognition of physicians' traditional practice of delivering DHS in their own offices to their own patients.

Comment: A commenter sought clarification as to whether a group practice was exempt from section 1877 of the Act. Several commenters observed that group practice status does not, by itself, protect against the risk of overutilization of ancillary services provided by the group.

Response: A group practice is not exempt from section 1877 of the Act by virtue of being a "group practice" under the definition in section 1877(h)(4) of the Act and Sec. 411.352 of these regulations. A relevant exception, such as the in-office ancillary services or the physician services exceptions, must still apply.

Comment: Several commenters suggested that section 1877 of the Act and the regulations should focus on referrals of medically unnecessary tests to entities with which physicians have prohibited financial relationships. Some commenters suggested that we use our utilization data to develop norms for each physician specialty that could be the basis for measuring appropriate utilization and preventing inappropriate referrals.

Response: We disagree that section 1877 of the Act should apply only to referrals of unnecessary items and services. While overutilization is a principal concern of the statute, and a primary focus of this rule, nothing in the statute suggests that the Congress intended to limit the statute's reach to referrals of medically unnecessary tests or procedures. Rather, the statute applies to all referrals of DHS to entities with which a referring physician has a prohibited financial relationship. The statute is designed to create a bright line that prohibits a high risk category of financial relationships and relieves the government from having to "look behind" every physician referral.

2. Single Legal Entity Requirement

The Existing Law: Under the statute, a group practice must consist of "two or more physicians who are legally organized as a partnership, professional corporation (PC), foundation, not-for-profit corporation, faculty practice plan, or similar association." The August 1995 final rule took the position that a group practice could consist of only one legal entity and that any individual or entity could organize, operate, or control a group practice, as long as two or more physicians had a role in providing services and the group met all of the other specific requirements for being a group practice under section 1877 of the Act. Thus, for example, a hospital could "own or operate" a group practice, provided no State law prohibited it.

The Proposed Rule: The January 1998 proposed regulations retained the interpretation of the single legal entity requirement from the August 1995 rule, requiring the legally organized group practice to consist of a "single legal entity", that is, one legal entity identified as the group practice that meets all of the group practice definitional tests. In addition, the January 1998 proposed regulations proposed allowing individual physicians who are incorporated as individual professional corporations to form a group practice, subject to meeting the remaining conditions of the group practice definition.

The Final Rule: We are retaining and incorporating into the regulations text the "bright line" rule that a group practice must be a single legal entity. The single legal entity can assume any form recognized by the State in which the entity achieves its legal status, including, but not limited to, a corporation (for-profit, professional, or nonprofit), partnership, foundation, faculty practice plan, or limited liability company. The single legal entity can be legally organized by any party or parties, including, but not limited to, physicians, health care facilities, or other persons or entities. The single legal entity must be formed primarily for the purpose of being a physician group practice. Hence, for example, a hospital that employs physicians is not a "group practice" for purposes of section 1877 of the Act, although the hospital can form or acquire a group practice that is a separate single legal entity. The following structures are among those that may qualify under Phase I of this rulemaking, assuming all other requirements of the group practice definition are satisfied:

A partnership between two or more physicians.

A partnership between one physician and another party, provided that the partnership employs at least one other physician. (Similarly, a partnership between two nonphysician parties can qualify if it employs at least two physicians).

A corporation or limited liability company with one or more physician shareholders or members, provided that a corporation or limited liability company with only one physician shareholder or member employs at least one other physician.

A corporation or limited liability company owned by nonphysicians, provided it employs at least two physicians.

A single legal entity owned by two or more physicians through their individual professional corporations.

A solo practitioner who is organized as a legal entity (for example, a professional corporation) and employs at least one other full-time physician.

A single legal entity (whether a corporation, limited liability company, or other form) owned by one or more other legal entities (that is, a multi-entity arrangement) that involves two or more physicians through employment or indirect ownership, provided that the "investing" or "owner" entities are not themselves functioning group practices. (In other words, existing groups may not band together to form a group practice primarily to share in-office ancillary referrals.) It is our understanding that the prevalent practice in these kinds of arrangements is for the physicians who own the investing entities to become employees of the new group practice, and for the investing entities themselves to cease functioning as group practices.

This list is illustrative only, and other variations are possible. What is essential is that there must be one identifiable legal entity that is a bona fide group practice of two or more physicians. The definition of group practice does not include a loose confederation of physicians, a substantial purpose of which is to share profits from referrals (sometimes referred to as a "group practice without walls"), or separate group practices under common ownership or control through a physician practice management company, hospital, or health care system, or other entity or organization.

We have responded to public comments regarding problems faced by faculty practice plans under section 1877 of the Act by using our regulatory authority under section 1877(b)(4) of the Act to create a new exception applicable to faculty practice plans. This new exception is discussed in section VII.A of this preamble.

While several commenters requested accommodation in the group practice definition for bifurcated foundation-model group practices (that is, arrangements between a nonprofit entity that provides health care services and a physician group, typically used in States that restrict the corporate practice of medicine), we have determined that those arrangements are better addressed by the personal service arrangements exception. As noted elsewhere in this preamble, we intend to apply our uniform interpretation of the volume or value standard to all exceptions in which it appears. (See the discussion in section V of this preamble.)

Comment: Many commenters concurred with our position that a group practice can be organized by any individual or entity, but took issue with other aspects of our group practice organizational tests. As a threshold matter, a number of commenters maintained that the statute does not require a "single legal entity." These commenters generally fell into three categories: (1) Commenters seeking protection for foundation model "groups" in States that follow the corporate practice of medicine doctrine, (2) commenters seeking protection for physician "groups" practicing in academic medical settings, and (3) commenters seeking protection for "groups" that are under common ownership or control, but that are not bound together in a single legal entity. Comments on the first two issues — foundation models and academic medical settings — are summarized and addressed elsewhere in this section and in section VII.A of this preamble.

As to the third category — common ownership and control — commenters generally requested that we recognize organizations under common control as a single unit or group practice, as we do in our definition of "hospital" in Sec. 411.351 (Definitions) of the regulations. (Section 411.351 reads as follows: "Hospital * * * refers to any separate legally-organized operating entity plus any subsidiary, related entity, or other entities that perform services for the hospital's patients and for which the hospital bills.") Specifically, the commenters suggested we interpret this portion of the group practice definition as covering a single legal entity that includes any separate, legally-organized operating entity plus any subsidiary, related entity, or other entities that perform services for the group practice's patients and for which the group practice bills. Some commenters noted that the ability to have subsidiaries is important for groups for valid, nonabusive business reasons, such as to operate in more than one State when States have different corporate requirements, to organize components of the continuum of care such as home health or skilled nursing care, and to operate as multi-entity integrated delivery systems. Some commenters indicated that some State laws require physicians to practice in a different entity when working in a bordering State. Also noted was that complex corporate structures are sometimes required for a variety of other legitimate business reasons, such as allowing groups to meet State licensing requirements, to allocate the risk of liability, to comply with inconsistent State regulations, or to meet corporate practice of medicine requirements. Similarly, these commenters maintained that an aggregation of groups managed by the same physician practice management company or multiple groups owned by the same hospital should be considered a "group practice" for purposes of section 1877 of the Act.

Response: Having considered the comments, we iterate our view that a group practice must be a "single legal entity." A standard that would allow entities under common ownership or control to be a group practice under section 1877(h)(4) of the Act does not sufficiently protect against sham group practice arrangements or loose confederations of physicians operating as a group practice substantially for purposes of profiting from DHS referrals. We find nothing in the statute that suggests that the Congress intended for a "group practice" to be so broadly construed as to include multiple group practices that happen to use the services of the same management company or that happen to be affiliated with the same health system. Single legal entities owned by multiple entities are permitted, as discussed in the response to the next comment. We address the special needs of foundation-based practices and faculty practice plans in this section and in section VII.A of this preamble, respectively.

Comment: Many commenters considered our proposed parameters for the composition of the "single legal entity" too restrictive, taking issue, in particular, with our statement that "the statute specifically requires that a partnership consist of two or more physicians who are partners and that a PC consist of two or more physicians who are incorporated together." While several commenters commended our proposal to allow group practices to include individual professional corporations that employ their own shareholders, commenters generally espoused expanding the group practice definition to include any physician group (regardless of its ownership) that is organized as a distinct legal entity and that employs more than one physician, provided that all of the other group practice definitional tests are met.

In these commenters' view, prohibiting a sole practitioner from owning a group practice that employs multiple physicians is unfair, inconsistent, anticompetitive, and not supported by the statutory language. The commenters pointed out that, under our January 1998 proposed rule, a hospital could own a group practice, but an individual physician could not. Commenters believe that the other requirements for meeting the group practice definition prevent any sham practice arrangements and that an interpretation requiring direct ownership by two physicians does not further Federal fraud and abuse policy.

A number of commenters asked that we clarify that a group practice may be owned by any legal corporate structure or arrangement including, but not limited to, limited liability companies, multi-member professional corporations, sole physician shareholder companies that employ at least one physician, hospitals that employ physicians, entities owned jointly by physicians and a hospital (for example, a physician hospital organization (PHO)), or general corporations that employ two physicians without any physician ownership. This interpretation is consistent with the August 1995 final rule. In particular, several commenters observed that group practices commonly are formed through the merger of existing group practices. The merging practices typically contribute assets and transfer physicians and other employees to the new group practice entity, which bills for the physician services under a group billing number and treats amounts received as receipts of the new group practice, and which meets the other group practice definitional requirements. The commenter urged that the new group practice entity should qualify for group practice status, without having to dissolve the merging shareholder entities, which are often maintained for tax or other purposes unrelated to Medicare or the fraud and abuse laws.

To prevent sham group practices, one commenter suggested that, in the case of a new group practice formed by the merger of existing group practices or professional corporations, we should require the new group practice to employ its members rather than allowing the multiple professional corporations (PCs) that formed the new group to continue employing practice members (except in the case of an individual professional corporation that employs a physician and owns a stake in a group practice). Similarly, another commenter recommended requiring all group practices (regardless of layers of composition) to be fully integrated into a single operating medical business at the top or "group" level. A group practice would be deemed fully integrated if it met the group practice definitional tests and presented itself as a single medical business whose equity holders operate as a single business by sharing such things as contracts, liability, facilities, equipment, support personnel, management, and a pension plan. A fully-integrated group would be required to employ or contract with all physicians at the group level so that physician compensation and accounts receivable of all members of the group would be "at risk" in the event of losses due to poor management of the group or in the event of a malpractice claim against any member of the group.

Response: We generally agree with the commenters. We have reconsidered the statutory language and believe that the provision requiring "a group of 2 or more physicians legally organized as a partnership, professional corporation, foundation, not-for-profit corporation, faculty practice plan, or similar association — " can be interpreted in several ways. It can reasonably be read to mean that a group must consist of some kind of legally organized entity, owned by virtually any combination of individuals or other entities, provided that there are at least two physicians providing services to patients as group practitioners. We have amended the definition of a group practice accordingly in Sec. 411.351. We believe this interpretation allows us to treat all practices, regardless of who owns or operates them, more uniformly. The introduction to this section provides an illustrative list of possible group practice organizational structures.

We are adopting the commenters' suggestion that no entity that owns all or part of a group practice (that is, no equity holder in the group) may itself function or qualify as a group practice (whether a group practice under section 1877(h)(4) of the Act or otherwise). Thus, for example, in the case of a new group practice formed through the merger of existing group practices, the merging or defunct group practices may not themselves operate as medical group practices (that is, they may not furnish or bill for health care services); however, the defunct practices are not required to dissolve. The merging group practices should transfer all medical assets to the new group practice, and the new group practice should employ the physicians and bill for their services, treating receipts as receipts of the new group practice.

We also generally agree that a group practice should consist of a single medical business whose equity holders operate as a single business by sharing such things as contracts, liability, facilities, equipment, support personnel, management, and a pension plan. This aspect of a group practice is addressed by the unified business test in Sec. 411.352 of the regulations. (See section VI.C.7 of this preamble for additional information).

Comment: Commenters questioned whether a hospital could qualify as the "single legal entity" needed to establish group practice status. In the August 1995 regulations, we stated that "* * * if a clinic (or other facility) is legally organized to include two or more physicians and provides the services of physicians, it is a group practice, even if it is established, operated, and controlled by a nonphysician group or corporation. This would be so regardless of who employs the physicians (in the scenario presented by the commenter, the clinic physicians were employed by the hospital that established the clinic)." (60 FR 41937) One commenter interpreted this language to mean that a hospital, which is itself a legal entity, could employ physicians and, therefore, qualify as a group practice if the other requirements of the group practice definition were met. Thus, the hospital would not need to establish a separate legal entity for its employed physicians to be considered a group practice. A related concern was whether a single hospital could encompass multiple group practices. According to the commenter, the ability of hospitals to establish multiple groups is especially important for a hospital entity that may operate several campuses in different cities as unincorporated divisions, a situation likely to increase as providers consolidate into regional networks.

Response: We believe the commenter's interpretation would stretch the meaning of a "group practice" too far. We do not believe that a hospital can reasonably be construed as a "group practice." We find no basis to conclude that the Congress thought otherwise. The statement from the August 1995 regulations was made in response to a comment regarding an arrangement in which a tax-exempt hospital had affiliated group practices and established a separate tax-exempt physician-directed clinic as the group practice's operating entity, but employed the physicians in the affiliated groups directly. In responding to the comment, we attempted to make two points: (1) That a group practice need not be legally organized by physicians; and (2) that a physician-directed clinic could qualify as a group practice.

We iterate that a group practice may be legally organized by a hospital or other nonphysician person or entity; however, neither the hospital itself nor any other facility the primary purpose of which is something other than to operate a physician group medical practice, can be a group practice. A hospital may establish multiple group practices through subsidiaries or affiliated entities that are separate legal entities. Each entity may be a group practice for purposes of section 1877 of the Act, although the aggregation of groups will not be. Exceptions, such as the in-office ancillary services exception, would only apply to referrals within one of those groups and not across multiple groups within the same hospital entity.

Comment: A commenter noted that the August 1998 proposed rule clearly states that a hospital may own and operate a group practice (assuming there is no State law impediment to such ownership) and that physicians may own a group indirectly through individual professional corporations. In light of these statements, the commenter sought clarification on three points: (1) Whether a single legal entity owned jointly by physicians and the parent company of a hospital could qualify as a group practice, provided all of the other conditions in the definition were satisfied; (2) whether the "single legal entity" test could be met by a limited liability company; and (3) whether several physicians organized as a limited liability company could, in turn, own another entity (for example, a second limited liability company) that could qualify as a group practice.

Response: In responding to the commenter's questions, we apply the principles described above. First, a single legal entity owned jointly by physicians and the parent company of a hospital could qualify as a group practice, provided all of the other conditions in the definition were satisfied. Second, a limited liability company duly organized under applicable State law could qualify as a "single legal entity." Third, several physicians organized as a limited liability company could, in turn, own another entity that could qualify as a group practice provided that the first limited liability company is not, and does not operate as, a group practice. In this last case, the physician members of the first limited liability company would be considered members of the group by virtue of their indirect ownership interest in the second entity.

Comment: Commenters note that health systems, management companies, hospitals, and other nonprofit and for-profit corporations must comply with State laws governing the corporate practice of medicine. In some States, these laws restrict or prohibit a corporation from directly employing physicians. In some cases, the corporations form a "captive" or "friendly" professional corporation with one physician owner who holds the ownership rights to the professional corporation in trust for the corporation. The friendly professional corporation directly employs physicians who then form the group practice. The corporation manages the business of the group practice, with the sole physician shareholder acting primarily as a "figurehead." The arrangement ensures that the corporation only indirectly employs the physicians and does not violate the corporate practice of medicine rules. Commenters noted that typically only one physician is a shareholder in the friendly professional corporation so that day-to-day transactions are less cumbersome.

Response: Since we have amended the group practice definition to cover groups that consist of one physician owner and one or more physician employees, we believe that the types of "captive" or "friendly" professional corporations described in the comment can both meet our definition and comply with corporate practice of medicine requirements. Groups must continue to meet all of the other criteria in the group practice definition in section 1877(h)(4) of the Act and Sec. 411.351.

Comment: Several commenters asked that we clarify whether the "single legal entity" requirement precludes a group practice from having subsidiary entities that, for example, own real estate or equipment, provide billing services, or operate ancillary services.

Response: As we noted in the August 1995 final regulations, we believe that the statute does not preclude a single group practice from owning other legal entities for the purposes of providing services to the group practice. Thus, to cite the example in the August 1995 final regulation at 60 FR 41936, a group practice could wholly own and separately incorporate a laboratory facility that provides laboratory services to a group practice or other patients. The physicians could qualify for the in-office ancillary services exception provided they meet the requirements for supervision, location, and billing. The billing requirement in section 1877(b)(2)(B) of the Act allows services to be billed by the referring or supervising physician, the group practice, or an entity wholly owned by the group practice. The exception appears to anticipate that a group practice may wholly own separate legal entities for billing or for providing ancillary services. Parties should be aware, however, that the group practice safe harbor under the anti-kickback statute (Sec. 1001.952(p) of this title), does not protect group practice ownership of ancillary services; for purposes of the anti-kickback statute, these arrangements are evaluated on a case-by-case basis.

3. Members of the Group

The Existing Law: Under the August 1995 final regulations, owners, employees, and independent contractors were all considered "members of a group" practice for purposes of the group practice definitional tests.

The Proposed Rule: The proposed regulations proposed modifying the definition of the term "members of the group" to include only physician partners, shareholders, and full-time and part-time physician employees. Independent contractors would no longer be considered members of the group. This change was proposed to aid group practices attempting to comply with the 75 percent "substantially all test." Physicians would be considered members of the group during the time that they furnish patient care services to the group.

The Final Rule: We are adopting our January 1998 proposal to define a member of a group practice as any physician who owns, or is employed by, the group practice. In the case of a group practice owned by professional corporations or defunct group practices, the physicians who own those entities will be considered members of the group practice. Also, those physicians who own all or part of the group practice through their own professional corporations and who are employed by their own professional corporations (which contract with the group practice to provide physician services) will be considered members of the group. Physicians are members of the group during the time they furnish "patient care services" (as defined at Sec. 411.351) to patients of the group or for the benefit of the group, even if those services cannot be billed by the group (for example, certain administrative services, pro bono services).

Independent contractors and leased employees will not be considered members of the group. The exclusion of independent contractors is intended to aid many group practices in complying with the "substantially all test" described below. Although not group practice members, under certain circumstances, independent contractors may provide the required supervision for the in-office ancillary services exception, as described in section VI.B.2 of this preamble.

While nonphysicians, such as nurse practitioners and physicians assistants, may be group practice "members" for general purposes under section 1877 of the Act, their membership will have no practical effect, since they are not "physicians" for purposes of the three group practice "tests" (the "full range of services," "substantially all," and "75 percent physician-patient encounters" test), nor for purposes of the profits and productivity bonuses provisions. While referrals by nurse practitioners and physician assistants generally do not trigger section 1877 of the Act, which applies only to physicians (as defined at section 1861(r) of the Act), referrals made by nonphysician health care professionals may implicate the statute if those referrals are directed or controlled by a physician. In other words, a physician or group practice cannot channel referrals through a nurse practitioner, physician assistant, or other nonphysician health care professional in order to circumvent the prohibition under section 1877, and any channeled referrals would be imputed to the responsible physician.

Comment: Many commenters supported our proposal to count owners and employees as members of the group, but not independent contractors. This change would facilitate compliance with the group practice definition by group practices that use part-time independent contractor physicians to supplement and expand the range of services the group offers to patients. Some commenters recommended that independent contractors be excluded only for purposes of the "substantially all test," but not for other purposes, including the direct supervision requirement of the in-office ancillary services exception and the 75 percent physician-patient encounters test. Some commenters objected to excluding independent contractors from the definition of "members of the group" because they perceived that such exclusion would prevent group practices from paying independent contractors productivity bonuses for the work they personally perform under section 1877(h)(4)(B)(i) of the Act.

Response: We are retaining our proposal to exclude independent contractors from the definition of "members of the group practice." On balance, we believe this change will benefit many group practices that wish to qualify for group practice status. As to the other concerns raised by commenters, we believe those concerns have largely been addressed by other changes in these regulations. We have liberalized the direct supervision standard in the in-office ancillary services exception to permit supervision by independent contractors who meet certain conditions that establish that the independent contractors are "physicians in the group practice." (See discussion in section VI.B.2 of this preamble). As discussed below, in greater detail, we are permitting group practices to pay productivity bonuses to independent contractors who are "physicians in the group practice." (See discussion in section VI.C.8 of this preamble).

Comment: A number of commenters advocated a flexible approach to the definition of "member of the group," urging that groups be permitted to elect whether to include independent contractors as members on an annual or other basis. These elections would apply uniformly for purposes of qualifying under all of the group practice definitional tests and the in-office ancillary services exception, and would be reported to us.

Response: The election process described by the commenters strikes us as unnecessary given the significant changes in this final rule with respect to the treatment of independent contractors under the in-office ancillary services exception and the group practice productivity bonus provisions. In our view, an election process would impose an additional administrative burden on groups and the government, with minimal offsetting benefit.

Comment: To accommodate multi-entity group arrangements, a commenter suggested that "members of a group" should include owners of the group, employees of the group, and owners of any sole or multiple shareholder professional corporation that has an ownership interest in the group (that is, indirect owners).

Response: For purposes of the definition of "members of the group," we are including any physician owners of a sole or multiple shareholder PC or other entity that has an ownership interest in the group. In essence, we intend to "look through" any corporate or entity owners to the ultimate physician owners. Thus, members of the group include physicians who are owners (directly or indirectly) and bona fide employees of the group.

Comment: Several commenters suggested that independent contractors be permitted to qualify as group practice members on a locum tenens basis. Thus, for example, a group would be allowed to use independent contractors to provide coverage when a member of the group is ill and unable to practice medicine temporarily. Other reasons to use locum tenens physicians could include death or disability of a physician, resignation of a physician, accommodating seasonal increases in patient loads, and "trial runs" of physicians being recruited to join a practice. According to commenters, locum tenens providers are typically paid on a fee-for-time basis by the staffing organizations with which they are affiliated. Thus, they typically have no direct financial relationships with any of the health care entities to which they are assigned. The health care entities retain all patient receipts and, when possible, Medicare payments are reassigned to the health care entity.

Response: Nothing in section 1877 of the Act or these regulations prevents the use of locum tenens physicians in situations like those described in the comments. The issue raised, however, is how these physicians should be treated for purposes of a group practice's compliance with the group practice definition and how referrals by such physicians should be treated under the general prohibition under section 1877. As to the first issue, we believe an appropriate use of locum tenens physicians in exigent situations should not prevent a group practice that otherwise complies with the definition at section 1877(h)(4) and Sec. 411.352 of these regulations from qualifying for group practice status. We are applying the rules at section 3060 "Reassignment," of the Medicare Carrier's Manual (HCFA Pub. 14–3), Part 3 — Claims Process (the reassignment provisions) as the test for whether a physician is a locum tenens physician. A locum tenens physician will be considered as "standing in the shoes" of the regular physician (as defined in section 3060.7) if he or she replaces the regular physician in accordance with section 3060.7. We note that section 3060.7 does not treat a physician hired on a "trial run" basis as a locum tenens physician.

Comment: One commenter sought clarification that on-call physicians who are independent contractors would be exempted from the group member and group practice requirements but would be able to provide and supervise care on behalf of a group member. On-call physicians for one group may be members of other group practices. They may or may not be compensated for their services or bill under the group practice billing number of the group for which they are serving in an on-call capacity. According to the commenter, on-call arrangements are commonplace, especially among groups that do not have sufficient numbers of specialists to cover for each other. The commenter requested a specific exemption under the statute so that on-call physicians do not impede groups from meeting the group practice definition and are not precluded from ordering DHS when they are serving in an on-call capacity. The commenter suggested an on-call physician be treated as "standing in the shoes" of the member while providing on-call services for purposes of the "substantially all test," the 75 percent physician-patient encounters test, and the supervision requirement of the in-office ancillary services exception.

Response: We agree that it is appropriate to treat on-call physicians as "standing in the shoes" of the member while providing on-call services for purposes of the "substantially all test," the 75 percent physician-patient encounters test, and the supervision requirement of the in-office ancillary services exception, provided that the services are billed by the practice for which the physician is serving on an on-call basis.

Comment: Several commenters questioned whether nurse practitioners, physician assistants, or other nonphysician providers could be group members, and if so, whether their services would count in the calculation of the 75 percent physician-patient encounters test.

Response: We perceive nothing in the statute that would prevent group practices from admitting nurse practitioners, physician assistants, or others as members of the group for purposes other than section 1877 of the Act. However, the definition of a "group practice" in section 1877(h)(4) of the Act contains several requirements that apply specifically to physician members of the group. Provisions of the in-office ancillary services exception and the physician services exception also refer specifically to physician members or physicians in the same group practice. The term "physician" is specifically defined under the Medicare statute at section 1861(r) of the Act and does not include nurse practitioners or physician assistants. Any services that these individuals provide are not counted under the "substantially all test" or under any other part of the group practice requirements or exceptions that apply to physician members.

The referral prohibition in section 1877 of the Act applies only to referrals that are made by a physician to an entity with which that physician, or an immediate family member, has a financial relationship. If a nonphysician practitioner is referring a physician's patients at the physician's suggestion or in lieu of the treating physician, we would impute the referrals to the physician. Simply stated, physicians may not delegate their own referrals to avoid the referral prohibition. On the other hand, we would not impute the referrals if the nurse practitioner or the physician assistant is independently treating the patients and initiates the referrals on his or her own. We think the determination will depend on the specific facts and circumstances.

Comment: One commenter asked that we exclude from the definition of members of the group any employees who provide interpretation or supervision services only and are not otherwise involved in patient care.

Response: Given the revisions we have made in Phase I of this rulemaking to the in-office ancillary services exception and the group practice definition, we see no need for a special exclusion for physicians who provide interpretation or supervision services only. We recognize that these physicians may affect, among other things, a group practice's ability to comply with the 75 percent physician-patient encounters test because they generally do not see patients. But to exclude physicians who generally do not see patients would undermine the purpose of the test, which is to ensure that group practices are first, and foremost, joint medical practices for the provision of physician services to patients and not primarily designated health care services enterprises. The Congress addressed the special circumstances of pathologists, diagnostic radiologists, and radiation oncologists in a separate provision. (See discussion of section 1877(h)(5)(C) in section III.B of this preamble).

Comment: A commenter sought clarification that physicians who are employees of their own individual professional corporations instead of the group practice are considered "group members." The definition of a group member in Sec. 411.351 already includes physicians whose ownership interest in the group is held through an individual professional corporation. Many physicians wish to not only hold ownership interests in an individual professional corporation, but to be employees of these corporations for pension and tax reasons. To avoid potential abuse, the commenter suggested that we add the following parenthetical to the definition of "member of group" in Sec. 411.351: "(including physicians who are employed by an individual professional corporation, as long as the group has legal authority over the terms of the physician's employment and is legally responsible for services provided by the physician on the group's behalf)."

Response: We agree with the commenter that these physicians are "members" of the group. If a physician already qualifies as an "owner" of the group through his or her individual professional corporation, then his or her status as an employee or contractor is irrelevant for purposes of qualifying for group practice status. The amendatory language proposed by the commenter is not necessary, although we are revising the regulations text to clarify that a physician who is employed by an individual professional corporation that has an ownership interest in the group practice is a "member of the group." Physicians who are employed by their own individual professional corporations and who have no ownership interest in the group (directly or through an individual professional corporation), but provide services to the group, are independent contractors and therefore not members of the group.

Comment: A commenter suggested that a physician who opts out of, and is not receiving any payments from, the Medicare program should not be bound by the limitations in section 1877 of the Act, and, thus, should be able to refer to entities with which he or she has a financial relationship. The commenter also asked that we clarify whether a physician who opts out of the Medicare program pursuant to the private contracting authority in the BBA 1997, but continues to practice with a particular group of physicians, is a group "member" for purposes of the physician self-referral law. The commenter reported that we have elsewhere stated that a group physician's opting out does not affect the ability of the rest of the group members to provide and bill for services they furnish to Medicare beneficiaries. The commenter stated that physicians who reassign benefits to organizations that participate in Medicare may not opt out, and that consequently physicians who belong to groups that participate in Medicare and who opt out may not bill and accept payments from Medicare beneficiaries through the group practice unless the entire group practice opts out. Thus, a physician who opts out would have to bill under his or her own name instead of through the group.

The commenter also questioned whether a physician's time spent treating Medicare beneficiaries that is billed through the physician's own name must be counted against the amount of time the physician has spent treating other patients of the group practice. (We assume this means that, for the "substantially all test," the commenter wishes to know whether the physician's private billing constitutes "patient care services" provided outside the group context that would affect whether the physician provides substantially all of his or her services through the group and bills substantially all of his or her services under a billing number assigned to the group.)

The commenter urged that we consider physicians who have opted out as "members" of the group practice only for those services furnished through the group, but not count the physician services in calculating whether the group has met the "substantially all test."

Response: We agree with the commenter that a physician who opts out of the Medicare program and is not receiving any payments from the Medicare program is not bound by the limitations in section 1877 of the Act and, therefore, can refer to entities with which he or she has a financial relationship. Section 1877 prohibits only referrals for services "for which payment otherwise may be made under Medicare," and Medicare would not otherwise pay for services under a private contract. The commenter also is correct in stating that when a group physician has opted out, it does not affect the ability of the rest of the group members to furnish and bill for services they furnish to Medicare beneficiaries.

The commenter is not correct, however, that when a group physician has opted out, the group may not bill in its own name for services provided by the opt-out physician under a private contract. The Medicare statute does not prevent an opt-out physician's group — regardless of whether the group has a participation agreement with Medicare — from billing payers other than Medicare for services furnished under a private contract. Of course, neither the physician nor the group is allowed to bill Medicare for services furnished under a private contract. Thus, a physician who opts out can remain a group member during the time he or she provides services to group patients, provided the services are billed through the group practice to payers other than Medicare. We believe the requirements in the group practice definition are meant to demonstrate that the physicians involved in the group are actually practicing medicine together. A physician can demonstrate a significant level of participation by treating either program or nonprogram patients, as long as they are group patients.

We also believe that any services the physician bills in his or her own name are not group services and, therefore, should be factored into the "substantially all test" as outside patient care services.

Comment: Several commenters were concerned about the proposed rule's effects on nonprofit medical foundations, particularly in light of our statement that a group practice can consist of only one legal entity. One commenter was specifically concerned about medical foundations in California, where such entities are established so that practices can comply with the corporate practice of medicine prohibition. One of the key exceptions to the prohibition allows nonphysician ("lay") participation in arranging for the delivery of physician services if the nonphysician is a qualified medical foundation. (These entities are nonprofit and exempt from Federal income taxation under section 501(c)(3) of the Internal Revenue Code). In California, for example, these foundations provide patient care through a separate, contracted medical group that is comprised of at least 40 physicians who collectively practice in at least 10 specialty areas. A chief concern was that our proposed rules would prevent the nonprofit foundation-model group practice from furnishing DHS under the in-office ancillary services exception because it has no employed physicians or physician owners who can qualify as "members of the group" for purposes of the group practices definitional tests.

The commenter considers the California nonprofit medical foundation to be, in essence, one bifurcated medical services provider that should be treated as a "single legal entity" for purposes of section 1877 of the Act. That is, under California law, the medical foundation is itself a health care provider; yet this can only work if the medical foundation encompasses the physicians who contract to provide the professional services. The IRS currently regards the physician-foundation relationship as comprising an integrated whole and grants tax-exempt status to those truly integrated foundations as providers of professional medical care. The foundation operates and owns all elements of the practice, but cannot provide the physician services, and the physicians have agreed to furnish all patient care services through the foundation model; it is the foundation, and not the physicians, who own the medical practice.

The commenter stated that entities such as management service organizations do not merit tax-exempt status because they support the provision of services, but do not actually provide services, while the foundations actually provide services. The IRS scrutinizes the entire foundation relationship to assure that its interdependent functions and operations comply with the fundamental requirements for tax exemption.

Response: As an initial matter, that an arrangement is subject to IRS regulation is not determinative under section 1877 of the Act. The IRS's goals in regulating business structures do not necessarily take into account preventing fraud and abuse in the Medicare and Medicaid programs. As to foundation-model practices in corporate practice of medicine States, we recognize that they present special problems under section 1877 of the Act. On the one hand, section 1877(h)(4)(A) clearly authorizes group practices that are "foundations." On the other hand, in the typical foundation-model arrangement, the physicians are not legally organized as a "foundation."

In reviewing the statute and legislative history, we have reached the following conclusions. First, the Congress used the term "foundation" in the group practice definition in a generic sense to cover any situations in which the single legal entity, that is, the group practice, consists of a foundation; the reference was not necessarily intended to encompass bifurcated foundation-model arrangements. Second, the Congress intended for foundation-model arrangements to be excepted under the personal service arrangements exception. The OBRA 1993 Conference Report states that the "conferees intend that this exception [personal service arrangements] would apply to payments made by a nonprofit Medical Foundation under a contract with physicians to provide health care services and which conducts medical research." H. Rep. No. 213, 103d Cong., 1st Sess. 814 (1993).

The personal service arrangements exception should provide foundation-model arrangements with additional flexibility in structuring their arrangements and that most foundation-model arrangements will be able to fit in the exception, in accordance with the congressional intent. The "volume or value of referrals" and "other business generated" standards will apply uniformly to all exceptions in which they are included. (See the discussion in section V of this preamble and the regulations at Sec. 411.354(d).)

Comment: Several commenters noted that another arrangement commonly used in corporate practice of medicine States is the use of "friendly" or "captive" PCs to create hospital-affiliated group practices in States that prohibit hospitals from employing physicians directly. For example, a commenter explained that in Ohio, a single physician may own stock in a PC, but hold the stock in trust for a hospital or other nonprofit corporation. The PC itself employs physicians who operate as a group practice and would fulfill all of the other group practice requirements. The commenter suggested that this arrangement would satisfy section 1877 of the Act if the rule were changed to permit groups to be owned by a single physician owner.

Response: As noted in section VI.C.2 of this preamble, we have made the change suggested by the commenter. Group practices may be owned by a single physician provided that the group practice employs at least one other physician. Therefore, we believe that "friendly" or "captive" PCs can qualify as group practices if they meet all of the other conditions of the group practice definition.

Comment: Several commenters noted that the sole owner of the "captive" or "friendly" PC may be a hospital-based physician who does not practice medicine as part of the group. These commenters wondered whether a nonparticipating physician owner would be a member of the group for purposes of the group practice definitional tests, particularly the "substantially all test."

Response: We believe that a hospital-based physician, who does not practice medicine as part of the group, is not a member of the group practice for purposes of the definitional tests. However, that means that the physician is not a member for any other purpose either. Thus, for example, a captive or friendly PC owned by such a physician would need to employ at least two physicians to qualify as a group practice. In addition, the sole physician owner described in the comment would not be eligible for sharing in overall profits or productivity bonuses under section 1877(h)(4)(B)(i) of the Act and Sec. 411.352(i) of the regulations.

Comment: Commenters generally supported our position in the proposed regulations that a physician's financial relationship with an entity under section 1877 of the Act would not be imputed to his or her group practice. Thus, other members of the group practice could continue to make referrals to the entity, provided that the members did not have financial relationships with the entity and the physician with the financial relationship was not in a position to control the referrals of other group members. However, one commenter suggested that we include as members (who could continue to make referrals) physicians who are employed by their own PC (instead of the group) as long as the group has legal authority over the terms of the physician's employment and is legally responsible for services provided by the physician on behalf of the group. This commenter noted that for tax and pension reasons, many physicians prefer to be employed by their PCs rather than the group practice entity.

Response: We are adopting the position we discussed in the proposed regulations, that is, that a physician's financial relationship with an entity under section 1877 of the Act will not be imputed to his or her group practice. Thus, other members of the group practice can continue to make referrals to the entity, provided that the members do not have financial relationships with the entity and the physician with the financial relationship is not in a position to control the referrals of other group members. As we have indicated elsewhere in this preamble, physicians who are employed by their own individual PCs are considered members of the group if the PC has an ownership interest in the group. If not, the physician would be considered an independent contractor who is not a member of the group.

4. The "Full Range of Services Test"

Existing Law: The definition of a group practice in section 1877(h)(4)(A)(i) of the Act provides that, among other requirements, each physician who is a member of the group must provide substantially the full range of services that the physician routinely provides, including medical care, consultation, diagnosis, or treatment, through the joint use of shared office space, facilities, equipment, and personnel. In the August 1995 final rule covering referrals for clinical lab services, we required physician members to furnish the full range of "patient care services," defined as services addressing the medical needs of specific patients.

The Proposed Rule: In the January 1998 proposed rule, we proposed expanding "patient care services" to include any physician's tasks that address the medical needs of specific patients or patients in general or that benefit the practice. These activities could include, for example, time spent training group staff members, arranging for equipment, or performing administrative or management tasks, as long as these activities benefit the operation of the group practice. Services wholly outside the group's medical practice, such as teaching, do not count as patient care services. This proposed test was designed to ensure that a physician is actually practicing medicine as he or she ordinarily would as part of the group and has not simply joined the group in name only. It further ensures that physicians are practicing as part of the group and not simply using the group to profit from DHS referrals.

The Final Rule: We are promulgating the test as proposed in the January 1998 proposed rule.

Comment: Commenters generally favored our proposal to revise the definition of "patient care services" to include any physician task that addresses the medical needs of specific patients or patients in general, or that benefits the group practice. However, commenters requested clarification whether activities that are conducted outside the group practice, such as teaching, overseeing residents, or conducting medical research, but that nonetheless benefit patients in general, are covered within the definition. Other similar activities might include administrative positions within hospital systems or independent physicians' associations that involve oversight of patients beyond those of the group practice.

Response: It does not appear to us that the activities listed by the commenter would particularly benefit group practice patients, except possibly in a very attenuated way. (The answer might change if the group itself was contracted to perform these "outside" tasks.) Therefore, we would generally not regard them as patient care services performed for the group. Instead, they might qualify as patient care services provided outside of the group. For example, the physician could be supervising residents in a hospital while the residents treat patients, the volunteer activities might involve treating indigent patients, or the administrative work could involve overseeing the efficient delivery of care to patients.

If the physician furnishes patient care services exclusively within the group, then whatever services he or she furnishes should constitute the full range of that physician's routine patient care services. If the physician furnishes patient care services both inside and outside of the group, then the services for the group's patients should be comparable in scope to those provided outside of the group setting. Any of a physician's services that do not involve caring for patients should not affect this test. For example, if a physician teaches medicine outside of the practice, but does not oversee patient care, we would not expect that the physician would also be performing teaching services as part of his or her group services.

5. The "Substantially All Test"

The Existing Law: Under the definition of a "group practice" in section 1877(h)(4)(A)(ii) of the Act, substantially all of the services of the physician members must be provided through the group and billed under a billing number assigned to the group, and amounts so received must be treated as receipts of the group. In Sec. 411.351, we interpreted "substantially all" to mean at least 75 percent of the total patient care services of the group practice's members. We promulgated special rules for group practices located solely in HPSAs and for physician members' time spent providing services in HPSAs.

The Proposed Rule: We proposed measuring patient care services (using the same definition of "patient care services" applied in the full range of services test described above) by the "total patient care time" each member spends on these services. We concluded that patient care time was the most straightforward and least burdensome method for measuring a physician's patient care services, but we solicited comments on other viable methodologies. Again, this test ensures that physicians who are members of the group practice are economically bound to the group for other than DHS referrals and are not just members of the group for purposes of profiting from DHS referrals.

The Final Rule: We are promulgating this test as proposed in our January 1998 proposed rule, except as discussed in this preamble. As proposed in our January 1998 proposed rule, the "substantially all test" could be measured based on the member physician's actual time spent performing patient care services, whether performed inside or outside the group practice. Having reviewed the comments regarding alternative methods for meeting the test, we are amending the "substantially all test" to allow group practices greater flexibility. While "actual time spent" remains the default standard, group practices may adopt alternative measures, provided those measures are reasonable, fixed in advance of the performance of the services being measured (that is, no ex post facto methods), uniformly applied over time, verifiable, and documented. Independent contractors and leased employees are not defined under the final rule as members of the group; therefore, their services need not be counted for purposes of complying with the "substantially all test."

Comment: Many commenters appreciated our expansion of the definition of patient care services to include services that benefit group patients in general or the group practice itself, but suggested that group practices be allowed to adopt alternative methods for measuring compliance with the 75 percent "substantially all test," depending on the particular circumstances of the group and the most reasonable manner available for the group. These commenters pointed out that many physicians do not maintain time records and to do so would create an unnecessary administrative burden. Additionally, some commenters believe that it would be difficult or misleading to calculate the exact number of patient care hours as we suggested in the proposed regulations because many full-time physicians tend to work more than 40 hours per week. (Data submitted by a major physician trade association reflected that the "average" physician works 57.9 hours a week, with 53.2 hours spent on patient care activities). For example, one physician in a practice may work a full-time schedule of 40 hours per week for the group and another 60 hours per week; it would be inconsistent to count both as furnishing the same 100 percent of their time to the practice. Alternatively, a physician may work a full 40-hour week at his or her practice and then an additional 20 hours at a hospital or clinic. To count this physician as working only two-thirds time for the group, based on a straight calculation of hours, would be unreasonable. One commenter thought that the regulations should establish a presumption that 40 hours per week of patient care time for physicians equals 100 percent of such time for purposes of calculating the 75 percent "substantially all test"; any hours spent beyond 40 hours on professional patient care time would fall outside of the 75 percent "substantially all test." Some groups expressed a preference for using relative value units (RVUs) to measure patient care services, while others preferred a revenue based calculation or a test based on patient encounters furnished and billed through the group. One commenter thought that the "patient care time" standard was ambiguous and not objectively verifiable, since physician timekeeping often does not account for time spent on activities not involving direct patient care.

Response: We are persuaded that it would be appropriate to permit group practices additional flexibility in measuring compliance with the "substantially all test" based on their unique circumstances. The "actual time spent" standard described in the preamble of the January 1998 proposed rule remains the default standard. Group practices that employ that standard can be assured that they are appropriately measuring "patient care services." As we noted in the January 1998 proposed rule, we are not requiring that physicians use detailed time sheets or time cards; in most cases, appointment calendars, personal schedules, billing records, or other existing sources will be sufficient to establish the time spent on patient care services. Group practices may adopt alternative means of satisfying the "substantially all test," provided the means used are (1) reasonable, (2) fixed in advance of the performance of the services being measured (that is, no ex post facto methods), (3) uniformly applied over time, and (4) verifiable. The data used to calculate compliance with the "substantially all test" and supporting documentation must be made available to the Secretary upon request.

Comment: Several commenters sought clarification whether the 75 percent "substantially all test" for patient care services is measured based on total patient services across all specialities in a group or whether it is measured on a specialty-by-specialty basis.

Response: Section 1877(h)(4)(A)(ii) of the Act provides that a group practice is a legally organized entity "for which substantially all of the services of the physicians who are members * * * are provided through the group * * * ." In Sec. 411.351, we interpreted "substantially all" to mean at least 75 percent of the total patient care services of each of the group practice's members. It is our view that a group practice should aggregate all of the patient care services that each of its members provides, both inside and outside of the practice, including all varieties of patient care services, to determine whether 75 percent of those services are furnished through the group. However, any services that are provided by a group through independent contractors would not be figured into the test. The test is designed to demonstrate that the activities of each member are conducted through the group. Services performed by independent contractors would have no bearing on this measure.

Comment: One commenter sought clarification in applying the 75 percent rule to new group practices that may be owned by, or employ, part-time physicians who are practicing elsewhere during the group's initial 12-month start-up period. In some cases, these groups will not meet the group practice definition during the start-up period.

Response: We agree with the commenter that some accommodation should be made for new group practices. Nothing in the statutory language precludes such accommodation. Accordingly, the final regulations provide that during the "start up" period for a new group practice (not to exceed 12 months), a group practice must make a reasonable, good faith effort to ensure that the group practice complies with the "substantially all test" as soon as practicable, but no later than 12 months from the date of the initial formation of the group practice. This "start up" provision does not apply when an existing group practice admits a new member or when an existing group practice reorganizes.

Comment: A commenter related the following scenario: A specialist provides professional services for a hospital outpatient under a contract with the hospital that allows a hospital employee to perform the technical component of the service. The specialist reassigns his or her payments for the professional services to the hospital. The hospital then bills Medicare for a global payment that includes the professional and technical components. Under this arrangement, the hospital pays the specialist a contractual amount for the professional component. The commenter requested that we explicitly permit the professional component of these types of services to be counted as part of the 75 percent requirement for purposes of the "substantially all test," even though the hospital and not the group practice bills Medicare for the specialist's services. Alternatively, commenters recommended that we change the two compensation exceptions that deal with hospitals (located in regulations in Secs. 411.357(g) and (h)) to exclude compensation paid to a physician for professional services.

Response: We agree that a group practice should be able to count the professional component of services provided by a member physician under a global payment when calculating the "75 percent of patient care services requirement" for purposes of the "substantially all test," even though the hospital actually bills Medicare directly for the physician services. We regard the "substantially all test" as designed to guarantee that a physician is providing a substantial amount of his or her own services through the group practice. If the group's business includes providing professional services to another entity, which, in turn, pays the group for those services, it is our view that these are services that should count as services a physician provides through the group. We are, therefore, interpreting the requirement that substantially all of a physician's services be provided through the group and be billed "under a billing number assigned to the group" and amounts so received treated as receipts of the group to include any physicians' professional services billed by a group under any group billing number regardless of the payer of the services, provided the receipts are treated as receipts of the group. In other words, the phrase "billed under a billing number assigned to the group" in section 1877(h)(4)(A)(ii) of the Act does not refer exclusively to Medicare or Medicaid billing numbers.

Comment: Several commenters objected to the proposed regulation because they believe it would require groups to bill under a group billing number and would force physicians in a group to bill individually when a patient has been seen in the hospital.

Response: While we are somewhat unclear as to the commenters' concern, we see nothing in these regulations that affects how group practice physicians bill for services provided to their own patients seen in a hospital.

6. The "Seventy-Five Percent Physician-Patient Encounters Test"

The Existing Law: Under section 1877(h)(4)(A)(v) of the Act, physician members of a group practice must personally conduct at least 75 percent of the group practice's patient encounters (measured per capita, not by time). The test ensures that the group practice is a legitimate medical practice and not primarily a business for the provision of lucrative ancillary services.

The Proposed Rule: The proposed rule would exclude independent contractors or leased employees from the test because they would not be considered members of the group.

The Final Rule: We are promulgating this test as proposed in our January 1998 proposed rule.

Comment: A commenter requested confirmation that bona fide employed physicians count for purposes of the 75 percent physician-patient encounters test.

Response: As discussed in section VI.C.3 of this preamble, members of a group practice include employed physicians. Thus, patient encounters by bona fide employed physicians count for purposes of the 75 percent physician-patient encounters test.

7. Unified Business Test

The Existing Law: For purposes of the group practice definition, section 1877(h)(4)(A)(iii) of the Act requires that "the overhead expenses of and the income from the group practice are distributed in accordance with methods previously determined."

The Proposed Rule: In our January 1998 proposed rule, we proposed exercising our discretion under section 1877(h)(4)(vi) of the Act to impose an additional standard under the definition of group practice that would require groups to be a "unified business." Our purpose was to ensure that group practices are substantially integrated business operations and that their allocation of group expenses and income to members reflect this. Absent a unified business test, we are concerned about the development of sham groups that are formed primarily for the purpose of profiting from self-referrals, but not for other, bona fide purposes. Thus, in the proposed regulations, we interpreted section 1877(h)(4)(A)(iii) of the Act as requiring that the group's overhead expenses and income be distributed according to methods that are —

Determined prior to the time period during which the group has earned the income or incurred the costs, and

Distributed according to methods indicating that the group practice is a unified business.

We indicated that the methods must reflect "centralized decision making, a pooling of expenses and revenues, and a distribution system that is not based on each satellite office operating as if it were a separate enterprise."

The Final Rule: The statute requires that the overhead expenses of, and income from, the group practice be distributed in accordance with methods "previously determined." Unlike the January 1998 proposed rule, which interpreted "previously determined" as meaning before the group earned the income or incurred the cost, the final rule treats a distribution methodology as "previously determined" if it is determined prior to receipt of payment for the services giving rise to the overhead expense or producing the income. Apart from this limitation, the rule does not prevent group practices from adjusting their compensation methodologies prospectively as frequently as they desire (subject to the restrictions on the distribution of DHS revenues in section 1877(h)(4)(B)(i) of the Act).

Commenters were nearly uniform in their criticism of the proposed unified business test, claiming that it invalidated many bona fide and common group practice compensation structures and discouraged beneficial integration of group practices. Reflecting these comments, Phase I of this rulemaking retains the general unified business test, but offers groups considerable additional flexibility in satisfying the requirement. Importantly, Phase I of this rulemaking permits many forms of cost center and location-based accounting, provided that compensation formulae with respect to DHS revenues otherwise meet the requirements of the law. To meet the unified business test, a group practice must be organized and operated on a bona fide basis as a single integrated business enterprise with legal and organizational integration. Essential elements are: (1) Centralized decision making by a body representative of the practice that maintains effective control over the group's assets and liabilities (including budgets, compensation, and salaries); (2) consolidated billing, accounting, and financial reporting; and (3) centralized utilization review (for example, utilization review conducted on a group-wide basis). We designed the rule to preclude group practice status for loose confederations of physicians that are group practices in name, but not operation. As adopted in Phase I of this rulemaking, the unified business test sets general parameters indicative of integration, but does not dictate specific compensation practices. Compensation, with respect to DHS, is subject to separate limitations described in these regulations.

Comment: Many commenters objected to our proposal to interpret the phrase "previously determined" to mean that the methodology for setting group members" compensation must be fixed before the group has earned the income or incurred the costs of providing the designated health care services. One commenter stated that this proposed interpretation would overly restrict a group practice's ability to adjust physician compensation periodically to reflect a physician's contribution to the group practice or to pay discretionary bonuses. Some commenters observed that groups have traditionally used ad hoc compensation systems that allow groups to "wait and see how the year goes." These systems afford groups flexibility to deal with business realities as they occur without, in the commenters' view, increasing the risk of self-referral compensation. In lieu of our proposed "prior to incurrence" rule, a number of commenters favored a "prior to distribution" rule. One commenter recommended coupling a "prior to distribution" rule with a requirement that distributions not relate to the volume or value of Medicare or Medicaid DHS referrals and that distributions not be retroactively adjusted in a manner that establishes a relationship between compensation and referrals. Another commenter suggested that "previously determined" be interpreted to mean that the compensation formula must be reported at the same time groups report their financial relationships to us.

Response: It is a statutory requirement that a group's compensation methodology be determined in advance. Unrestricted ad hoc compensation systems would allow groups to compensate physicians directly based on the number of designated health care services referrals they generate — the very conduct the statute is intended to prohibit. A "prior to distribution" rule would be circular, since any distribution scheme would be determined prior to the distribution. We agree, however, that groups should have some flexibility in designing and implementing compensation systems that are responsive to changing circumstances. It is our understanding that most groups operate on a cash basis. In the final rule, we are requiring that group practices determine the methodology for distributing overhead expenses of, and income from, the provision of designated health care services prior to the receipt of payment for those services. The methodology may be determined at any time until payment has been received, even if the income has been earned or costs incurred. This rule permits groups to adjust their methodologies prospectively as often as they deem appropriate. We believe Phase I of this rulemaking provides groups with sufficient flexibility to respond to business realities, while complying with the statutory requirement that the distribution system be "previously determined."

Section 1877(h)(4)(A)(iv) of the Act prohibits a physician member of the group from being compensated in a manner that takes into account the volume or value of DHS referrals, except as provided in section 1877(h)(4)(B)(i) of the Act. Thus, a compensation method that directly relates to the volume or value of Medicare referrals or is retroactively adjusted would violate section 1877(h)(4)(A)(iv) of the Act.

Comment: A commenter asked whether a group practice can distribute unexpected income which, by its nature, was not "previously" part of the group's distribution methodology. The commenter cited as an example a group practice opening a new site without specifically determining in advance how revenues or profits would be distributed to group members.

Response: We are unclear as to the circumstances under which a group practice would open a new office without considering distribution of the revenues or profits from that new office. We see no reason to deviate from the "prior to payment" rule established in these regulations for "unexpected income."

Comment: Although many commenters generally recognized the appropriateness of precluding group practice status for groups that are merely confederations of independent, unintegrated medical groups, many commenters expressed concerns about the unified business requirement promulgated in the proposed regulations. First, commenters questioned our legal authority to graft this new condition onto the statutory group practice definition. Second, commenters expressed the view that the unified business standard as proposed would have a chilling effect on legitimate group practices and discourage beneficial integration. Of particular concern was the perception that the regulations would completely prohibit or unduly complicate the group practices' use of profit and cost center or location-based accounting and distribution of expenses and income. In this regard, many commenters argued that site-specific or specialty-specific accountability encourages efficient management of expenses and practice patterns and eliminates a "free rider" problem that impedes cost effective integration, which groups find increasingly important with the growth of managed care. One commenter, representing a physician practice management company, noted that one reason groups prefer cost center accounting is that many physicians in newly-acquired group practices want to minimize changes in income levels they have historically realized; cost center accounting facilitates more absolute integration over time.

Instead of barring cost center or location-based accounting and distribution of expenses and income, commenters encouraged us to rely on other indicators of integration. One commenter suggested that we could address our concern about loose confederations of groups by revising the rule to require that a group practice be organized and operated on a bona fide basis as a single business enterprise integrated legally and operationally. According to the commenters, while many legitimately integrated medical practices allow their satellite offices to make day-to-day, local practice decisions, almost all significant decisions, such as hiring and firing physicians and approval of annual operating budgets, are made by the entire practice's governing body. Moreover, the costs of central business activities such as billing, collections, managed care contracting, and purchasing of some products and services are, in most cases, shared by all practice sites, either per capita or based on a generally applied formula. Commenters offered numerous suggestions as to relevant criteria for ascertaining that a group practice is a unified business.

Response: Our statutory authority to impose a unified business test resides in section 1877(h)(4)(A)(vi) of the Act, which vests in the Secretary the ability to impose additional standards on group practices by regulation. Upon further consideration, we agree with the commenters that our proposed unified business test was too restrictive. The unified business test was designed to ensure that group practices are substantially integrated business operations and that their distribution of group expenses and income to members reflects this. The unified business test guards against the development of sham groups formed primarily for the purpose of profiting from self-referrals.

Phase I of this rulemaking, described in detail above, retains the general unified business test, but offers groups considerable flexibility in satisfying the requirement. Importantly, many forms of cost center and location-based accounting are permitted, provided that compensation formulae with respect to the distribution of DHS revenues otherwise meet the requirements of the law.

Comment: A physician trade association asked whether groups that compensate their physicians under more than one methodology can qualify as a "unified business." This issue is especially significant for larger groups that have expanded through the acquisition of other existing group practices, each of which may have negotiated different compensation arrangements. Typically, the methodology for compensating each new physician who joins the group is set in advance, based on the negotiations between the parties and approved by the governing body of the acquiring group (or an authorized committee of the governing body).

Response: We see no impediment in the revised unified business test to groups like those described in the comment from qualifying as a unified business. In order to qualify for group practice status, the group would have to meet all of the other group practice tests, including the limitations on compensation based directly or indirectly on the volume or value of referrals and the restrictions on profit sharing and productivity bonuses. (See the discussion in section VI.C.8 of this preamble.)

Comment: One commenter expressed concern that the proposed unified business standard could be interpreted to prevent integrated medical practices from compensating their physicians on an individual collections minus expenses basis. A commenter urged that groups be allowed to compensate physicians based on their own productivity (excluding any revenue or expense related to the group's DHS), and that it be permissible to calculate the physician's compensation by allocating to the physician all of the physician's direct medical expenses of practice (including, but not limited to, for example, malpractice insurance, continuing medical education, space cost, supplies) and his or her pro rata share of general overhead not based on any volume or value of his or her referrals (for example, administrative and management costs). Similarly, another commenter stated that it is common practice for groups to compensate their members according to formulae that take into account "office profits," described as collected revenues attributable to a physician's medical services performed by that physician or personnel under his supervision, not including revenues for DHS or direct or indirect expenses of that physician.

Response: Distribution of group practice revenues derived from DHS is subject to the compensation rules set forth at Sec. 411.352. With respect to income derived from other sources, groups are free to divide it in any manner they choose, provided they can demonstrate that they are a unified business under the three principles discussed in section VI.C.7 of this preamble. Depending on individual circumstances, we believe that most of the compensation methodologies described in the comment can be accommodated within the parameters of the revised unified business test.

Comment: One commenter questioned whether a total contingent revenue pool, distributed on an aggregate basis (after subtracting expenses that include allocated central practice or "home office" expenses) to the practitioners in a given branch or satellite office of a larger statewide PC according to a predetermined formula, would meet the requirements of the unified business test.

Response: Whether the described scheme fits in the exception would depend on whether the three factors described above are present. The scheme would also have to meet the requirements of sections 1877(h)(4)(A)(iv) (compensation for group members) and (h)(4)(B)(i) (profits and productivity bonuses) of the Act with respect to DHS. In particular, under the overall profit shares rule as set forth in Phase I of this rulemaking, as discussed in section VI.C.8, overall profit shares must be derived from aggregations of the entire practice or a component of the practice consisting of at least five physicians.

Comment: A commenter sought clarification as to whether the financial allocation requirements under the unified business standard apply solely to the DHS furnished by the group or whether they extend more broadly to all health care services furnished by the group. The commenter viewed the latter approach as beyond the statutory authority, which applies only to furnishing DHS, and as contrary to our own statements in the preamble to the proposed regulations that compensation arrangements for services that are not DHS are outside the scope of the statute and regulations.

Response: The Congress specifically conferred on the Secretary in section 1877(h)(4)(A)(vi) of the Act authority to impose additional standards in the definition of a group practice. For the limited purposes of establishing that a group practice is a unified business, we believe it is appropriate to consider the group practice's methods of distributing revenues derived from all sources, not just DHS. Group practices can distribute the revenues from services that are not Medicare-DHS in any manner they wish. However, if the payment methods do not indicate a unified business (or indicate a business that is unified solely with respect to the provision of DHS), the group may not qualify as a group practice under section 1877(h)(4) of the Act and Sec. 411.352. Compensation paid to a physician creates a compensation arrangement within the meaning of Sec. 411.354, even if the compensation relates only to services that are not DHS. Absent an applicable exception (for example, the in-office ancillary services or employee exceptions), this compensation arrangement triggers the self-referral prohibition as to any of the physician's referrals of DHS.

8. Profit Shares and Productivity Bonuses

The Existing Law: In general, the statute provides that a physician who is a member of the group may not be compensated directly or indirectly based on the volume or value of his or her referrals of DHS. In addition, the statute provides that a "physician in a group practice" may receive shares of overall profits of the group or a productivity bonus based on services personally performed or incident to such personally performed services, provided the share or bonus is not determined in a manner that is directly related to the volume or value of referrals by such physician. In other words, group practice compensation formulae that are only indirectly related to the volume or value of referrals of DHS are permissible.

The Proposed Rule: We proposed to interpret the statute to mean that productivity bonuses could only relate to work personally performed by the physician that results from referrals from other physicians in the group, and could not relate (directly or indirectly) to work that results from self-referrals or DHS referrals to other physicians and other office personnel. Thus, we said that a physician could only receive compensation for his or her own DHS referrals through the aggregation that occurs as part of the overall sharing of group profits. As to the overall sharing of profits, we indicated that profits must be aggregated at the group level and not at a component level.

The Final Rule: In section IV of this preamble, we provide an overview of the physician compensation provisions of section 1877 of the Act. In general, a group practice can segregate its DHS revenues from its other revenues for purposes of compensating physicians; section 1877 of the Act applies only to a practice's DHS revenues. Generally, this income is likely to comprise a relatively small portion of the total revenues of most practices.

Under Phase I of this rulemaking, group practices may pay member physicians and independent contractors who qualify as "physicians in the group" productivity bonuses based directly on the physician's personal productivity (including services incident to such personally performed services that meet the requirements of section 1861(s)(2)(A) of the Act and section 2050 of the Medicare Carriers Manual, Part 3), but may not pay these physicians any bonus based directly on their referrals of DHS that are performed by someone else. The statute also permits group practice members (and independent contractors who qualify as "physicians in the group") to receive shares of the overall profits of the group, so long as those shares do not directly correlate to the volume or value of DHS referrals generated by the physician that are provided by someone else. We are defining "share of overall profits" as meaning a share of the entire profits of the entire group or any component of the group that consists of at least 5 physicians derived from DHS.

Under the statutory scheme, revenues generated by DHS may be distributed to group practice members and physicians in the group in accordance with methods that indirectly take into account DHS referrals. In general, we believe a compensation structure does not directly take into account the volume or value of referrals if there is no direct correlation between the total amount of a physician's compensation and the volume or value of the physician's DHS referrals (regardless of whether the services are personally performed). Phase I of this rulemaking contains specific methodologies that describe compensation methods that are deemed to be indirect. In addition, Phase I of this rulemaking contains additional provisions that allow group practices to devise other reasonable indirect compensation methodologies.

The distribution methods for overall profit shares are as follows:

(1) A per capita (that is, per physician) division of the overall profits.

(2) A distribution of DHS revenues based on the distribution of the group practice's revenues attributable to services that are not DHS payable by Federal or private payers.

(3) Any distribution of DHS revenues if the group practice's DHS revenues are less than 5 percent of the group practice's total revenues and no physician's allocated portion of those revenues is more than 5 percent of the physician's total compensation from the group practice.

The methods for productivity bonuses are as follows:

A productivity bonus based on the physician's total patient encounters or RVUs.

A productivity bonus based on the allocation of the physician's compensation that is attributable to services that are not DHS payable by Federal or private payers.

Any productivity bonus that includes DHS revenues if the group practice's DHS revenues are less than 5 percent of the group practice's total revenues and no physician's allocated portion of those revenues is more than 5 percent of the physician's total compensation from the group.

Comment: Many commenters objected to our proposed interpretation of the statute to mean that productivity bonuses can relate only to work personally performed that results from referrals from other physicians in the group, and cannot relate (directly or indirectly) to work that results from self-referrals. Commenters protested that this interpretation barred any compensation based on a physician's personal productivity for self-referred DHS and was, therefore, contrary to clear statutory intent. Several commenters explained that our interpretation would produce anomalous results in some circumstances. For example, an internist refers a patient with a gastrointestinal complaint to a gastrointestinal specialist, and the specialist evaluates the patient at an initial visit. The specialist subsequently performs an endoscopy on the patient. Under the proposed January 1998 regulations, the endoscopy would be a self-referral by the specialist, and the specialist could not receive a productivity bonus for performing the endoscopy. However, if the specialist referred the patient to another physician in the same group practice for the endoscopy, the specialist could receive compensation indirectly based on that endoscopy. Thus, in the commenter's view, the rule creates a disincentive to perform services and an incentive to refer (which may be contrary to good patient care and not cost effective). The commenter further noted that specialists who perform substantial amounts of DHS are disadvantaged by the proposed interpretation because they cannot be rewarded for personal productivity, while their counterparts, for whom the performance of DHS is a less significant part of their practices, can.

Commenters suggested an interpretation that would permit productivity bonuses for DHS personally performed by the referring physician, but not for DHS referred to others. The commenters generally requested that the final rule allow group practices to compensate members of the group based upon the volume or value of DHS, so long as the services are personally performed by the physician or are incident to the physician's personally performed services. One commenter noted that ancillary services (including "incident to" services) performed for one's own patients are more "personal" to the ordering or supervising physician than are services he or she performs on colleagues' patients. Commenters also complained that our proposed interpretation would lead to disparate treatment of solo and group practitioners, since solo practitioners could receive the profits from personally performed DHS that they self-refer, whereas group practitioners could not. One commenter thought that this discrepancy would make solo practitioners reluctant to join group practices, thereby discouraging beneficial market integration.

Finally, some commenters noted that many group practices have insufficient information technology systems to track whether a service performed by a physician resulted from a self-referral or a referral from another physician. Commenters asserted that our proposed interpretation would impose a significant additional administrative burden on those groups.

Response: In light of the comments, the changes we have made to our interpretation of the definition of a "referral" and the volume or value standard, and our further review of the statutory language, we are persuaded that our proposed interpretation of the scope of productivity bonuses was unnecessarily restrictive. Accordingly, we have revised the regulation to make clear that group practices may pay member physicians (and independent contractors who qualify as "physicians in the group") productivity bonuses based directly on the physician's personal productivity (including services "incident to" such personally performed services that meet the requirements of section 1861(s)(2)(A) of the Act and section 2050, "Services and Supplies," of the Medicare Carrier's Manual (HCFA Pub. 14–3), Part 3 — Claims Process), but may not pay these physicians any bonus based directly on their referrals of DHS that are performed by someone else.

Comment: Commenters sought clarification about the treatment of productivity bonuses for "incident to" services. One commenter observed that according to long-standing regulatory policies, "incident to" services are services that are an incidental although integral part of a physician's personal, professional service to a patient. Thus, in the commenter's view, there cannot be a referral for "incident to" services in any ordinary sense, since what the ancillary service provider does is part of the physician's service itself. Several commenters expressed their belief that one purpose of the productivity bonus provision was to allow physicians to receive "credit" for "incident to" services in their compensation. One commenter pointed out that it would be hard to exclude "incident to" services in the calculation of productivity bonuses since claim forms typically do not indicate who performed the "incident to" service (that is, whether the service was performed by the supervising physician or someone else). Other commenters interpreted the statutory reference as equating "incident to" services with "in-office ancillary" services. Under this view, commenters asserted that the statutory language plainly allows productivity bonuses based indirectly on the volume or value of the physician's in-office ancillary services and opposed our proposed interpretation that prohibited any compensation based on referrals for in-office ancillary services.

Response: We agree with the essence of these comments with respect to group practices. Under the final regulation, group practice physicians can receive compensation directly related to the physician's personal productivity and to services incident to the physician's personally performed services, provided the "incident to" services comply with the requirements of section 1861(s)(2)(A) of the Act and section 2050, "Services and Supplies," of the Medicare Carrier's Manual (HCFA Pub. 14–3), Part 3 — Claims Process, and any subsequent or additional HHS rules or regulations affecting "incident to" billing. This means that the "incident to" services must be directly supervised by the physician. In other words, the physician (or another clinic physician in the case of a physician-directed clinic) must be present in the office suite and immediately available to provide assistance and direction. Moreover, the person performing the "incident to" services must be an employee of the physician (or the physician-directed clinic). We believe that the heightened supervision requirement imposed by the "incident to" rules provides some assurance that the "incident to" DHS will not be the primary incentive for the self-referral. However, we may revisit the issue of compensation tied to "incident to" services if we find that abuses are occurring, especially in the area of physician-directed clinics.

Comment: We received a number of comments seeking clarification related to the methods of paying compensation that are not directly based on the volume or value of referrals. First, commenters urged that we allow pooling of revenues that are not DHS revenues, because such revenues are not governed by the statute. Second, a number of commenters objected to our position in the proposed regulations that overall profits are not profits that "belong only to a particular specialty or subspecialty group" (even if the group is located in several States or has several locations in one State) because "the narrower the pooling, the more likely it will be that a physician will receive compensation for his or her own referrals." Commenters urged that pooling at practice sites with more than a few physicians should not result in any individual's compensation being directly related to the volume or value of his or her referrals, even if DHS revenues are included in the pool. Commenters generally advocated that we allow pooling if at least three physicians are included in the pool and the distribution formula is not related to DHS referrals. Third, commenters offered a variety of suggestions about how to calculate "indirect" compensation. For example, one commenter suggested that compensation be considered "indirect" if the referrals have no mathematical effect on compensation. Others suggested that compensation be considered "indirect" if it is based on per capita calculations, RVUs, patient encounters, hours worked, ownership shares in the practice, or seniority.

Response: First, we are persuaded that we should permit some additional flexibility related to the distribution of shares of overall profits by group practices. Thus, we are defining a "share of overall profits" to mean a share of the entire profits derived from DHS of the entire group practice or any component of the group that consists of at least five physicians. We believe a threshold of at least five physicians is likely to be broad enough to attenuate the ties between compensation and referrals. We are rejecting the suggestion to use a threshold of three physicians because we believe that the lesser threshold would result in pooling that would be too narrow and, therefore, potentially too closely related to DHS referrals. Second, we recognize the need for clear guidance as to appropriate indirect compensation methodologies. For that reason, we are including in

Phase I of this rulemaking methodologies that describe compensation distribution systems that we deem to be indirect. In other words, if a group practice wants absolute assurance that its productivity bonuses or profit shares are not directly related to referrals, the group practice may employ one of the regulatory methodologies set forth in Sec. 411.352 of the regulations. Group practices are not required, however, to use these methods. The regulations clarify that other methods (including distributions based on ownership interests or seniority) are acceptable so long as they are reasonable, objectively verifiable, and indirectly related to referrals. These compensation methods should be adequately documented and supporting information must be made available to the Secretary upon request. Under this latter "catch-all" provision, the group practice essentially bears the risk of noncompliance.

Comment: Several commenters sought clarification as to whether an independent contractor could be compensated under the productivity bonus provision of the group practice definition as a "physician in the group", even though independent contractors are not members of the group.

Response: Independent contractors who qualify as "physicians in the group" under the provisions of Sec. 411.351 can receive productivity bonuses under section 1877(h)(4)(B)(i) of the Act.

Comment: One commenter sought clarification as to how providers should treat capitation payments that cover more than one service for purposes of allocating profit shares and productivity bonuses.

Response: In general, we believe that capitation payments are not likely to lead to increased utilization. Parties may use any reasonable allocation method with respect to such payments.

Comment: On page 1691 of the preamble to the January 1998 proposed regulations, we explained our view that "profits should not be pooled and divided between group members so that they relate directly to the number of designated health services for Medicare or Medicaid patients physicians referred to themselves or the value of those self-referrals (such as a value based on complexity of the service)." A commenter objected to the parenthetical statement, asserting that barring consideration of the complexity of the service is contrary to other Medicare payment provisions, which take into consideration the level of training necessary to perform, and difficulty of, certain procedures.

Response: Given our revised interpretation, we believe the parenthetical statement ("such as value based on complexity of the service") is no longer relevant to these regulations. Group practice members can be compensated directly based on their personal productivity (that is, the fruits of their own labors), but not on their productivity in generating referrals. They may only be compensated based indirectly on DHS referrals to other physicians or providers. So long as the compensation is only indirectly related to the volume or value of DHS referrals, we believe it makes little difference if the value of the DHS referrals reflects the complexity of the services.

Comment: A commenter sought clarification that when a physician is a member of a group practice and is also an employee of the group practice, his or her compensation may be determined under the group practice's rules without regard to the employee exception.

Response: We agree that when a physician is a member of a group practice, his or her compensation need only comply with the group practice rules. Meeting the group practice definition allows physicians in the group to refer within the group under the in-office ancillary services exception or the physicians' services exception. However, nothing prevents a physician and group practice from using the employee exception instead. It is important to remember that referrals of DHS are only permitted if an exception, such as the in-office ancillary services exception or employee exception, applies.

Comment: Several commenters were confused by our use of the terms "revenues" and "profits" throughout the preamble to the January 1998 proposed regulations. For example, on page 1691 we stated that "the referring physician can receive a portion of the group's overall pooled revenues from these services as long as the group does not share these profits in a manner that relates directly to who made the referrals for them." Similarly, on the same page we stated that we "regard 'over-all profits of the group' to mean all of the profits or revenues a group can distribute in any form to group members * * *." These commenters requested that the terms "profits" and "revenues" be used in a manner that is consistent with their generally accepted meanings or that definitions of the terms be provided in the regulations.

Response: We agree that the terms "revenues" and "profits" were used inconsistently in the January 1998 proposed regulation. In Phase I of this rulemaking, we have endeavored to use those terms consistent with their generally accepted meanings.

9. Group Practice Attestations

The Existing Law: In Sec. 411.360 of the August 1995 final rule covering referrals for clinical laboratory services, we included the requirement that group practices provide their carriers with a written statement annually to attest that, during the most recent 12-month period, 75 percent of the total patient care services of group members was furnished through the group. Any group that intended to meet the definition of a group practice in order to qualify for one of the exceptions provided in the regulations was required to submit the required attestation to its carrier by December 12, 1995. On December 11, 1995, we published in the **Federal Register**, at 6/0 FR 63438, a final rule that delays the date by which a group of physicians must file an attestation statement. The December final rule amended Sec. 411.360 to require that a group that intends to meet the definition of a group practice must submit an attestation statement to its carrier no later than 60 days after the group receives attestation instructions from its carrier. The preamble to the December rule points out that a group could regard itself as a group practice in the interim period before it receives attestation instructions, provided the group believes that it meets the definition of a group practice under Sec. 411.351.

The Proposed Rule: The proposed rule retained Sec. 411.360, as amended by the December 1995 final rule, with several minor changes.

The Final Rule: We have eliminated the attestation requirement.

Comment: One commenter suggested that group practice attestations not be required until 1 year after final regulations are published, while another recommended 1\1/2\ years after publication of the final rule. Otherwise, the commenter stated, a group practice would have to attest to membership requirements for the previous 12 months, without benefit of having had the membership requirements published in advance and an opportunity to comply with them.

One commenter also questioned whether we will actually use the information gained from group practice attestations. The commenter believes that imposing a civil money penalty for failing to submit an attestation is overly harsh when compared to the minimal benefit that may be derived from the attestations. The commenter recommended that we remove the requirement for attestations or, at least, reduce the related penalties.

Response: We agree with the commenters. After reviewing the attestation requirement, we have concluded that it would impose an unwarranted burden on group practices. We intend instead to allow groups to treat the information they need to establish that they are a group practice in the same manner as any information a furnishing entity must provide to us under the reporting requirements in Sec. 411.361. In order to make reporting requirements more manageable, we intend to develop a streamlined "reporting" system that does not require entities to retain and submit large quantities of data. We believe instead that entities should retain enough records to demonstrate, in the event of an audit, that particular relationships are excepted under the law. In the case of the in-office ancillary services exception and physician services exceptions in section 1877(b)(1) and (b)(2), an entity may need to establish that the services it provided were referred by members of a genuine group practice. Thus, a group should retain records that demonstrate that it meets the requirements in section 1877(h)(4) of the Act and Sec. 411.351.

D. Prepaid Plans (Section 1877(b)(3) of the Act)

The Existing Law: In the August 1995 final rule, we interpreted the prepaid plan exception, section 1877(b)(3) of the Act, as creating an exception to the general prohibition on referrals for services furnished by certain prepaid health plans to their enrollees, including Federally qualified health maintenance organizations (HMOs) or prepaid health care organizations with a contract or agreement under sections 1876 or 1833(a)(1)(A) of the Act, or organizations participating in demonstration projects under section 402(a) of the Social Security Amendments of 1967 or section 222(a) of the Social Security Amendments of 1972. The August 1995 final rule incorporated section 1877(b)(3) into the regulations in Sec. 411.355(c), concerning clinical laboratory services furnished by an organization (or its contractors or subcontractors) to enrollees of these prepaid health plans (not including services provided to enrollees in any other plan or line of business offered or administered by the same organization).

The Proposed Rule: The January 1998 proposed rule proposed an additional exception for services provided by organizations participating in the Medicaid program that are analogous to those cited in section 1877(b)(3) of the Act, including managed care organizations (MCOs) that contract with Medicaid under section 1903(m) of the Act, entities operating under a demonstration project under section

1115(a) of the Act, prepaid health plans contracting with a State, and health insuring organizations furnishing services as managed care contractors. (Although we proposed including demonstration projects under section 1115(a) of the Act in the preamble of the January 1998 proposed rule at 63 FR 1697, they were not listed in proposed Sec. 435.1012 as the result of a drafting error. We will include a technical correction for this section in Phase II of this rulemaking.) In addition, the rule proposed to extend the protection of section 1877(b)(3) of the Act to providers, suppliers, and other entities that provided services to enrollees of the protected organizations under contracts with these organizations, either directly or indirectly.

The January 1998 proposed rule also took a number of other positions that directly affected physicians' financial relationships with managed care entities and plans other than Medicare and Medicaid managed care plans. Most importantly, we proposed that MCOs would be deemed to be entities "furnishing" DHS provided by other entities if the MCOs billed Medicare for DHS provided to Medicare patients by providers and suppliers pursuant to a contractual arrangement with the MCOs (other than services under a plan protected under section 1877(b)(3) of the Act or other protected arrangement).

The preamble of the January 1998 proposed rule also discussed whether an MCO network physician could refer private fee-for-service patients to other physicians and providers that were participating in an MCO network. According to the preamble, a physician who had a contractual relationship with an MCO could refer a nonenrolled Medicare fee-for-service patient for a designated health service to another physician who also had a contract with the MCO provided that the physician to whom he or she referred the patient was not otherwise affiliated with the MCO. However, if the same physician referred the same patient to a laboratory owned by the MCO, the general prohibition would apply and the financial arrangement between the MCO and the physician would have to qualify for an exception. In other words, the referring physician would not have a financial relationship with the second physician, but he would have one with the laboratory. Of course, the arrangement could still be protected under the personal service arrangements exception.

The M+C interim final rule (63 FR 35066) amended Sec. 411.355(c) of the regulations covering referrals for clinical laboratory services to include a new paragraph (5). This paragraph added to the list of prepaid plans coordinated care plans (within the meaning of section 1851(a)(2)(A) of the Act) offered by an organization in accordance with a contract with us under section 1857 of the Act. Section 1877(b)(3) of the Act was also amended by section 524(a) of the Balanced Budget Refinement Act of 1999 (BBRA) (Pub. L. 106–113, enacted on November 29, 1999), which added a new paragraph (E). Paragraph (E) includes in the prepaid plans exception services referred by a physician to an organization that is an M+C organization under Part C that is offering a coordinated care plan described in section 1851 of the Act [42 U.S.C. 1395w-21(a)(2)(A)] to an individual enrolled with the organization.

The Final Rule: Virtually all commenters agreed with our decision to interpret the prepaid plan exception to protect any referrals by physicians for DHS covered by the listed Medicare managed care plans to an MCO that has a Medicare managed care contract or any entity, provider, or supplier furnishing these services under a contract or subcontract with the MCO, directly or indirectly ("downstream providers"). Several commenters asked that we amend the regulations text to reflect the interpretation. We are amending the text of Sec. 411.355(c) to make clear that downstream providers are protected.

We are not finalizing at this time the proposed new Sec. 435.1012 (Limitation on FFP related to prohibited referrals), paragraph (b) (Exception for services furnished to enrollees on a predetermined, capitated basis), which would have extended the protection to certain prepaid plans under Medicaid. A number of commenters agreed with our proposed exception for services provided by organizations analogous to those cited in section 1877(b)(3) of the Act. These and other commenters suggested that a number of other Medicare or Medicaid arrangements be included in the exception, including M+C coordinated care plans, Medicaid managed care plans under the BBA 1997, Medicaid managed care entities operating under a waiver pursuant to section 1115 of the Act, any demonstration project approved by us, including primary care case management programs (PCCMs) and managed long term care programs (MLTCs), programs of all-inclusive care for the elderly (PACE), capitated Medicare demonstration programs (including social health maintenance organizations (SHMOs), the Medicare subvention demonstration, and the Medicare prepaid competitive pricing demonstration). The commenters pointed out that although the preamble to the January

1998 proposed rule had proposed to include some of the above programs in the new exception, they had not been referenced in the regulations text. We agree with the commenters on adding the Medicaid organizations that are analogous to those in section 1877(b)(3) of the Act as described in the January 1998 proposed rule and on some of the other listed areas; however, we will address Medicaid managed care, and potentially other suggestions related to Medicaid managed care raised by the commenters, in Phase II of this rulemaking.

We are also revising in Phase I of this rulemaking the proposed regulations in response to comments expressing concerns about the impact of the January 1998 proposed rule on commercial and employer-provided managed care arrangements. First, we are creating a new compensation exception for remuneration pursuant to a bona fide "risk-sharing arrangement" between a physician and a health plan for the provision of items or services to enrollees of the health plan, even when such an arrangement does not fall within existing statutory exceptions. (We note that the new risk-sharing arrangement exception differs from the shared risk exception to the anti-kickback statute at Secs. 1001.952(t) and (u); for example, unlike the anti-kickback exception, the new exception under section 1877 of the Act contains no conditions related to the volume of Medicare beneficiaries enrolled in the health plan or the quantification of the financial risk.) Physicians generally are compensated for services to managed care enrollees in one of three ways, the first two of which do not vary based on the volume or value of referrals: (1) A salary in the case of a physician who is an employee, (2) a "fee-for-service" contractual arrangement under which the physician assumes no risk, or (3) a risk-sharing arrangement, under which the physician assumes risk for the costs of services, either through a capitation arrangement, or through a withhold, bonus, or risk-corridor approach. The first two compensation arrangements are eligible for the statutory exceptions for bona fide employment relationships and personal service arrangements, while the third is potentially eligible for the new risk-sharing arrangement exception we are creating in this final rule in Sec. 411.357(n).

Second, we are revising the definition of "entity" in Sec. 411.351 to permit physician ownership of network-type HMOs, MCOs, provider-sponsored organizations ("PSOs") and independent practice associations ("IPAs"). Specifically, we are clarifying the definition of entity furnishing DHS, to provide that a person or entity is considered to be furnishing DHS if it is the person or entity to which we make payment for the DHS, directly or upon assignment on the patient's behalf, except that if the person or entity has reassigned its right to payment to (i) an employer pursuant to Sec. 424.80(b)(1), (ii) a facility pursuant to Sec. 424.80(b)(2), or (iii) a health care delivery system, including clinics, pursuant to Sec. 424.80(b)(3) (other than a health care delivery system that is a health plan (as defined in Sec. 1000.952(l)), and other than any MCO, PSO, or IPA with which a health plan contracts for services provided to plan enrollees), the person or entity furnishing DHS is the person or entity to which payment has been reassigned. We are providing further that a health plan, MCO, PSO, or IPA that employs a supplier or operates a facility that could accept reassignment from a supplier pursuant to Secs. 424.80(b)(1) and (b)(2) is the entity furnishing DHS for any services provided by such supplier.

We believe these changes address the comments we received from the commercial and employer-sponsored managed care plans.

Comment: While commenters uniformly welcomed the broad protection given in the January 1998 proposed rule to referrals for services covered by Medicare prepaid health plans, several commenters stated that we interpreted several provisions of the statute in a manner that, taken together, would severely limit MCOs' use of physician incentive plans, whether under commercial or Medicare contracts. The commenters strongly objected to our statement that the prohibition on DHS referrals applies to referrals to entities that arrange for the furnishing of the DHS to Medicare or Medicaid patients by contracting with other providers, whenever the arranging entity also bills Medicare or Medicaid for the services. (See 63 FR 1706.) The commenters explained that this view, when joined with our interpretation of section 1877(e)(3)(B) of the Act (the physician incentive plan provision in the personal service arrangements exception), could effectively preclude the use of risk-sharing arrangements with physicians in any health plan, including commercial plans. The commenters explained the problem as follows:

Physicians that participate in a managed care network will have a compensation arrangement with the MCO for payment for services to the MCO's enrollees. That payment arrangement will create a financial relationship for purposes of section 1877 of the Act. (Even participation in the network of an organization eligible for the Medicare prepaid plans exception would not entirely avoid this result, since the prepaid plans exception only protects referrals for DHS furnished to beneficiaries enrolled under the Medicare contract). Many of these compensation arrangements use withholds, capitation, bonuses, or other methodologies that take into account, directly or indirectly, the volume or value of referrals or other business generated by the referring physician.

Most, if not all, commercial or employer-provided group health plans offered by MCOs include some enrollees who are Medicare beneficiaries. Typically, these enrollees either are retired employees who have expanded benefits under an employer-provided plan (in which case Medicare is the primary insurer and the employer plan secondary) or are beneficiaries who have group health plan coverage based on current employment status (in which case the employer plan is the primary insurer and Medicare secondary). Even the MCOs that have Medicare managed care lines of business that are protected by the prepaid plans exception commonly have commercial lines of business that include some Medicare beneficiaries who are not enrolled under the organization's Medicare contract (that is, Medicare's payment is made on a fee-for-service basis under the traditional Medicare program).

When a Medicare beneficiary is enrolled in a commercial or employer-provided group health plan, Medicare often pays for services provided by the plan to the beneficiary/enrollee on a fee-for-service basis. In such a case, if Medicare is the primary insurer, it will reimburse the provider according to the same provisions as any fee-for-service provider; if Medicare is the secondary insurer, it will pay based on a formula prescribed by law.

Generally, if an enrollee of a commercial or employer-provided health plan has primary coverage under Medicare, the network physician or supplier (not the MCO) will submit the claim to Medicare directly, since Medicare is the primary insurance. However, many, if not all, such MCOs will occasionally bill Medicare for services provided by network providers to these Medicare beneficiaries. Most often, the purpose of the billing is to coordinate with Medicare when Medicare is the secondary payer. Occasionally, the MCOs may bill Medicare as the primary payer; for example, when there has been a recent change in beneficiary status, such as when a beneficiary's group health plan coverage ceases being based on current employment status because the beneficiary retires and Medicare becomes the primary insurer. Of course, MCOs may bill and be paid by Medicare only where the MCO meets the criteria for direct payment, assignment of benefits or reassignment of benefits. (See Secs. 424.73 and 424.80 of these regulations.)

Accordingly, under the interpretation in the January 1998 proposed rule, a physician in the MCO network will be deemed to make a referral to the MCO for the provision of a DHS whenever the physician refers an enrollee of the MCO's commercial plan who also happens to be a Medicare beneficiary to another network provider for DHS. (Referrals of enrollees in any of the excepted prepaid plans would not be affected since they are not referrals of DHS by virtue of the prepaid plans exception.)

As a result, unless all of the MCO's payment arrangements with network physicians, regardless of the line of business, fit in an exception under section 1877 of the Act, the referral of any enrollee with primary or secondary coverage under Medicare for a designated health service would be prohibited.

The only kinds of physician compensation arrangements that are protected by the personal service arrangements exception in the proposed rule are (1) fixed per-service payments based on fair market value (for example, discounted fee-for-service arrangements) or (2) payment arrangements that incorporate risk-sharing elements, such as bonuses or withholds, provided they qualify as a physician incentive plan under section 1877(e)(3)(B) of the Act.

However, many payment arrangements in commercial or employer-provided health plans contain risk-sharing elements that take into account a physician's referrals or the volume of services provided but that do not currently comply with the physician incentive plan regulations. These arrangements would have to be restructured. Moreover, even if restructured, the physician incentive plan regulations contain a number of requirements that would require revision if they are to be implemented with respect to non-M+C plans.

Lastly, in the preamble to our January 1998 proposed rule, we stated that section 1877(e)(3)(B) of the Act only applied to compensation arrangements directly between the "entity" (that is, the MCO) and the physician; any compensation arrangements between a physician and party other than the MCO, such as an IPA or other subcontractor, would not qualify as a physician incentive plan.

The commenters asserted that the net effect of our interpretation in the January 1998 proposed rule of when an entity was furnishing DHS provided by another entity would be the total disruption of commercial and employer-provided health plans. The only way an

MCO could assure that its physician compensation arrangements were in compliance with section 1877 of the Act would be to restructure all its payment arrangements to pay all physicians for all lines of business on a discounted fee-for-service basis. Moreover, since the MCOs and, in many instances, subcontractors such as IPAs would also be entities furnishing DHS, any physician ownership of such entities would be a prohibited investment interest unless an appropriate exception applied.

Response: Nothing in the legislative history suggests that section 1877 of the Act was intended by the Congress to require the wholesale restructuring of commercial managed care arrangements with physicians. Accordingly, we are making two major changes to the January 1998 proposed rule that we believe will address the commenters' concerns. First, as noted above, we are creating a new compensation exception for bona fide risk-sharing arrangements between a health plan and providers for services provided to plan enrollees that do not otherwise qualify for an existing statutory exception. This exception will address concerns related to the prohibition on compensation arrangements in section 1877 of the Act. Second, we are revising our definition of "entity" to clarify that a person or entity is considered to be furnishing DHS if it is the person or entity to which we make payment for the DHS, directly or upon assignment on the patient's behalf, except that if the person or entity has reassigned its right to payment to (i) an employer pursuant to Sec. 424.80(b)(1), (ii) a facility pursuant to Sec. 424.80(b)(2), or (iii) a health care delivery system, including clinics, pursuant to Sec. 424.80(b)(3) (other than a health care delivery system that is a health plan (as defined in Sec. 1000.952(l)), and other than any MCO, PSO, or IPA with which a health plan contracts for services provided to plan enrollees), the person or entity furnishing DHS is the person or entity to which payment has been reassigned. We are providing further that a health plan, MCO, PSO, or IPA that employs a supplier or operates a facility that could accept reassignment from a supplier pursuant to Secs. 424.80(b)(1) and (b)(2) is the entity furnishing DHS for any services provided by such supplier. We believe this change should address the possible adverse impact on physician ownership of MCOs and IPAs.

With respect to the first change, we are creating in Sec. 411.357(n) a new exception under section 1877(b)(4) of the Act for bona fide risk-sharing compensation arrangements between an MCO and a physician (either directly or indirectly through a subcontractor) for services to enrollees of a health plan. (For purposes of the new exception, we are incorporating the definitions of "health plan" and "enrollees" found in Sec. 1001.952(l).) The vast majority of Medicare and Medicaid beneficiaries in managed care plans are either in M+C plans or Medicaid managed care plans, both of which are already required to comply with the physician incentive plan regulations. As to the relatively small number of Medicare beneficiaries in commercial or employer-sponsored plans that do not necessarily satisfy physician incentive plan requirements, or otherwise qualify for an existing exception under section 1877 of the Act, we are not currently aware of any fraud or abuse involving the Medicare program or Medicare beneficiaries arising from physician risk-sharing arrangements in these commercial or employer-provided health plans. Given the potential for the unintended disruption of these arrangements described by the commenters and the administrative need for "bright line" rules, we believe the new physician risk-sharing arrangements exception to section 1877 of the Act is needed. We will continue to monitor these arrangements for possible abuse and, if necessary, may revisit the issue in the future.

With respect to the second change, the potential impact of the January 1998 proposed rule on physician ownership of MCOs and IPAs was attributable to our interpretation that an MCO or IPA was an entity furnishing DHS provided by another entity whenever it billed for the services provided by another entity pursuant to a contract with the MCO or IPA. As noted above, in response to the above comment, we are amending the definition of "entity" in Sec. 411.351 to clarify that a health plan, or an MCO, PSO, or IPA with which the plan contracts directly or indirectly for services to plan enrollees, will only be considered to be furnishing DHS when the health plan, MCO, PSO, or IPA furnishes the services directly (that is, through an employee), or otherwise is the entity to which we make payment for the DHS, either directly or upon assignment on the patient's behalf, or pursuant to a valid reassignment under the Medicare rules and regulations to (i) an employer pursuant to Sec. 424.80(b)(1), (ii) a facility pursuant to Sec. 424.80(b)(2), or (iii) a health care delivery system, including clinics, pursuant to Sec. 424.80(b)(3) (other than a health care delivery system that is a health plan (as defined in Sec. 1000.952(l)), and other than any MCO, PSO, or IPA with which a health plan contracts for services provided to plan enrollees). We are providing further that a health plan, MCO, PSO, or IPA that employs a supplier or operates a facility that could accept reassignment from a supplier pursuant to Secs. 424.80(b)(1) and (b)(2) is the entity furnishing DHS for any services provided by such supplier.

We believe this change should allow for physician ownership of most types of network IPAs and MCOs. Ownership or investment interests in entities, including MCOs and IPAs, that provide DHS directly would still be prohibited (absent an applicable exception). Moreover, any indirect financial arrangements between physicians and the entities directly providing DHS would need to be analyzed to ensure there are no prohibited indirect financial relationships. For example, an MCO may have an investment interest in a lab, and a physician that contracts with that MCO may refer a Medicare beneficiary to that lab for DHS, for which Medicare is billed on a fee-for-service basis. While the MCO would not be considered to be furnishing the DHS for purposes of section 1877 of the Act, the lab in which the MCO has an investment interest would be furnishing DHS. Since the physician has a financial relationship with the MCO, and the MCO has an investment interest in the lab, there may be an indirect financial relationship that would then have to fit in an exception, most likely the indirect compensation arrangement exception or the risk-sharing arrangement exception. (See discussion in section III.A of this preamble.)

Finally, in Phase II of this rulemaking, we expect to amend the January 1998 proposed regulations for the personal service arrangements exception to reflect that risk-sharing compensation arrangements between entities downstream of a Medicare MCO can qualify as physician incentive plans within the meaning of section 1877(e)(3)(B) of the Act; this interpretation is consistent with our interpretation in the Medicare physician incentive plan regulations in Secs. 422.208 and 422.210.

We believe these provisions will address the commenters' concerns.

Comment: One commenter stated that even if the MCO itself directly provided DHS pursuant to a physician referral, the MCO's compensation arrangement with the referring physician should not be deemed to take into account the volume or value of referrals for DHS unless the risk-sharing arrangement was based in part on the utilization or cost of the DHS provided directly by the MCO.

Response: For purposes of the personal service arrangements exception, the compensation from the MCO does not take into account "the volume or value of referrals or other business generated between the parties" unless the compensation varies based on the volume or value of the MCO's business that is generated by the physician. (See the discussion of "volume or value" and "other business generated" in section V of this preamble.) We have addressed the issue of physician risk-sharing arrangements (including, but not limited to, capitation payments, bonuses, and withholds) with commercial and employer-sponsored managed care plans by creating a new exception under section 1877(b)(4) of the Act for bona fide risk-sharing compensation arrangements between an MCO and a physician (either directly or indirectly through a subcontractor) for services to enrollees of a health plan.

Comment: Several commenters were unclear whether physicians who participate in a managed care network would be prohibited from referring Medicare fee-for-service patients who are not enrollees of a managed care plan for DHS to other providers in the managed care network simply because both providers had contractual relationships with the same MCO.

Response: Physicians who participate in a managed care network would not be prohibited from referring Federal fee-for-service patients who are not enrollees of a managed care plan for DHS to other providers with contractual relationships with the same MCO solely on the basis of the parallel contractual arrangement with the MCO. In other words, two physicians who contract with an MCO do not have a financial relationship with each other for purposes of section 1877 of the Act on that basis alone. However, they may have other financial relationships (including indirect financial relationships) that would bar their referrals (in the absence of an applicable exception).

Comment: Several commenters asked that we create an exception for nongovernment plans that include any significant cost-sharing elements. This exception would be similar to the exception in the Federal anti-kickback statute for risk-sharing arrangements.

Response: As discussed earlier, we have created a new exception for bona fide risk-sharing compensation arrangements between health plans and physicians. The exception we are creating is substantially broader than the shared risk exception in the Federal anti-kickback statute.

Comment: Another commenter asked that we create an exception to permit public hospitals to enter into incentive arrangements with physician groups for the treatment of the public hospital's patients. One commenter also suggested that we create an exception for commercial managed care product lines that serve fewer than 20 percent Medicare patients as part of the group and that are not marketed directly to Medicare patients.

Response: As described above, we have created a risk-sharing arrangements exception in Sec. 411.357(n) that should address the commenter's concern regarding commercial managed care arrangements. With respect to the request to create an exemption for public hospital patients, the commenter provided no explanation of the types of arrangements proposed to be excepted, and we see no reason why these arrangements could not be subject to abuse.

Comment: Two commenters asked us to clarify that the prepaid plan exception protects any DHS provided to any enrollee of any plan (including commercial or employer-sponsored plans) offered by an entity that either is a Federally-qualified HMO or has a contract under one of the programs cited in section 1877(b)(3) of the Act. One of the commenters asked us to clarify that services to persons covered under an employer self-funded health plan that is administered by an entity with a qualified contract under section 1877(b)(3) of the Act and uses the MCO's network of providers would also be exempt under the prepaid plan exception.

Response: We believe that the Congress intended that the exception in section 1877(b)(3) of the Act protect only the financial arrangements for services to enrollees of the prepaid plans identified in section 1877(b)(3). We see no basis for concluding that because an entity has one contract covering a specific population, there is any protection against abusive relationships in other product lines. Accordingly, we are clarifying the regulation to state that the protection extends only to financial arrangements for the services to enrollees of the plans specifically identified in the regulation and does not protect enrollees in any other plan or line of business furnished by the MCO or to which the MCO provides administrative services.

Comment: One commenter suggested that we use the definition of health plan and enrollee set forth in the managed care safe harbor regulations to the Federal anti-kickback statute, Sec. 1001.952 (Exceptions), paragraph (l) (Increased coverage, reduced cost-sharing amounts, or reduced premium amounts offered by health plans). The commenter stated that it was unclear from the preamble of the January 1998 proposed rule whether employees covered by an employer self-funded plan that utilized a commercial insurer to administer the plan would be considered "enrollees" of the commercial insurer for purposes of the prepaid plan exception and for application of the physician incentive plan provision of the personal service arrangements exception.

Response: We agree that employer self-funded plans should be able to qualify for protection of their physician compensation arrangements. We believe the new risk-sharing compensation exception will address the commenters' concerns. For purposes of the new exception, we are incorporating the definitions of "health plan" and "enrollee" from the safe harbor regulations for certain health plans set forth in Sec. 1001.952(l)(2). This definition would result in equal treatment for self-funded plans and insured plans.

Comment: One commenter requested that we interpret section 1877 of the Act to "grandfather" any pre-existing managed care arrangements. The same commenter asked that we broaden the exception for personal service arrangements to protect quality-related incentive plans that take into account the volume or value of DHS referrals.

Response: The statutory provisions clearly envision their application to managed care plans. Accordingly, a blanket "grandfather" provision for these plans is inappropriate. With respect to the request for protection of quality-related incentive plans, the commenter did not provide any details as to the kind of incentives being described. We do not perceive any impediment in the regulation that would preclude basing compensation on quality measures unrelated to the value or volume of DHS referrals or other business generated by the physician. However, absent further clarification, we are not inclined to protect any arrangement that takes into account referrals or business generated by the physician.

Comment: One commenter requested that we create a new exception for payer-directed services. According to the commenter, in managed care arrangements, the payer is the party that directs the referrals for DHS and not the physician who is contractually obligated to refer in the network. Another commenter stated that, in the managed care environment, our proposed presumption in the January 1998 proposed rule that a physician has referred a patient to an entity with which he or she has a financial relationship if the patient, in fact, procures the services from this entity — even if there is no order or written plan of care — should not be applied.

Response: We believe the changes we have made to accommodate various financial relationships between managed care organizations and physicians should address the referral issues in the managed care environment.

Comment: Several commenters asked that the provision in the group practice definition permitting employees to receive productivity bonuses be expanded to permit remuneration based on volume or value of DHS referrals if the arrangement complies with the physician incentive plan regulations as permitted in the personal service arrangements exception. The commenters noted that in some arrangements, the employed physicians have separate contracts with the MCO, while in others the contract is between the MCO and the group, making it important to permit the group to incentivize its employed physicians. According to the commenters, employers should have at least as much latitude in structuring their compensation arrangements with employees as with independent contractors. The commenters suggested that the group practice definition already expressly permits productivity bonuses indirectly tied to referrals — a greater concern since overutilization is the primary concern of section 1877 of the Act. In light of that provision, one commenter believes it is incongruous to prohibit physician incentive plan arrangements that discourage utilization if they comply with the physician incentive plan regulations.

Response: We agree that, at least in the managed care environment, there is little reason to impose a more restrictive requirement on compensation arrangements between a group and its employees than on arrangements between the group and its independent contractors. However, this concern is only one aspect of the broader relationship between the group practice, personal service arrangement, and bona fide employment relationship exceptions that is discussed in sections IV and VI.C.8 of this preamble.

Comment: Several commenters asked that we clarify the reporting obligations of plans that are not technically subject to the physician incentive plan regulations, since they are not Medicare or Medicaid managed care plans (or M+C plans), but that are complying with the regulations to qualify their financial arrangements with physicians for the personal service arrangements exception in section 1877 of the Act.

Response: The various reporting requirements associated with, or triggered by, the regulation will be addressed in Phase II of this rulemaking.

VII. New Regulatory Exceptions

This section describes new regulatory exceptions that are not in the statute, but which appeared in the January 1998 proposed rule or that we have created in response to comments and pursuant to statutory authority conferred on the Secretary. The new exceptions discussed here include: Academic medical centers, fair market value, and non-monetary compensation up to $300 (and medical staff benefits). Other new exceptions described elsewhere in this preamble include: Implants in an ASC (Sec. 411.355(e); section VIII.J of this preamble); EPO and other dialysis-related drugs (Sec. 411.355(f); section VIII.L of this preamble); preventive screening tests, immunizations, and vaccines (Sec. 411.355(h); section VIII.L of this preamble); risk-sharing arrangements (Sec. 411.357(n); section VI.D of this preamble); compliance training programs (Sec. 411.357(o); section VII.C of this preamble); eyeglasses and contact lenses (Sec. 411.355(i); section VIII.J of this preamble); and indirect compensation arrangements (Sec. 411.354(c)(3); section III.A of this preamble).

A. Academic Medical Centers

The Existing Law: Section 1877(h)(4) of the Act contains a special rule for faculty practice plans. The rule provides that "in the case of a faculty practice plan associated with a hospital, institution of higher education, or medical school with an approved medical residency training program in which physician members may provide a variety of different specialty services and provide professional services both within and outside the group, as well as perform other tasks such as research, subparagraph (A) [the definition of "group practice"] shall be applied only with respect to the services provided within the faculty practice plan."

Several commenters to the August 1995 final rule suggested that we create a separate exception for faculty practice plans, since these plans are typically involved in complex organizational arrangements that do not fit comfortably — or at all — in the group practice definition. At the time of the August 1995 final rule, we rejected the suggestion for a new exception based on our view that the personal service arrangements exception and the employment exception would provide physicians in academic medical settings with appropriate protection under section 1877 of the Act.

The Proposed Rule: We proposed no changes.

The Final Rule: We have revisited our prior position. The comments have persuaded us that academic medical practices raise numerous questions under section 1877 of the Act that are not adequately addressed by existing exceptions.

Though the relevant provision in the group practice definition is somewhat obscure, we believe it demonstrates congressional intent to address the circumstances of physicians practicing in academic medical settings. We do not believe, however, that the core problem of how to treat academic medical practices under section 1877 of the Act is amenable to resolution under the group practice definition; the problem lies elsewhere.

Academic medical settings often involve multiple affiliated entities that jointly deliver health care services to patients (for example, a faculty practice plan, medical school, teaching hospital, outpatient clinics). There are frequent referrals and monetary transfers between these various entities, and these relationships raise the possibility of indirect remuneration for referrals. The exceptions under section 1877 of the Act do not easily apply. For example, faculty practice plan physicians refer patients for ancillary services to entities that are outside of (and not wholly owned by) the single legal entity in which they conduct their medical practices (that is, the "group practice"), but with which they may have direct or indirect compensation relationships (for example, part of the physician's compensation may come from an affiliated medical school or teaching hospital). These referrals typically will not qualify under the in-office ancillary services exception, and it may be difficult to structure compensation relationships for faculty practice plan physicians that securely fit in the personal service arrangements exception because the physician's compensation often comes directly or indirectly from several separate sources.

Having reviewed the comment letters addressing the problems facing faculty practice plans under section 1877 of the Act, we believe the fundamental need of faculty practice plans is for a separate compensation exception for payments to faculty of academic medical centers that takes into account the unique circumstances of a faculty practice, including the symbiotic relationship among faculty, medical centers, and teaching institutions, and the educational and research roles of faculty in these settings. Therefore, we are using our regulatory authority under section 1877(b)(4) of the Act to create a separate compensation exception for payments to faculty of academic medical centers that meet certain conditions that ensure that the arrangement poses essentially no risk of fraud or abuse. This exception is in addition to other exceptions that may apply in particular circumstances; an arrangement need only fit in one available exception.

The conditions applicable under the new exception in Sec. 411.355(e)(1)(i) are that the referring physician is a bona fide employee of a component of an academic medical center on a full-time or substantial part-time basis, is licensed to practice medicine in the State, has a bona fide faculty appointment at the affiliated medical school, and provides either substantial academic or substantial clinical teaching services for which the faculty member receives compensation as part of his or her employment relationship with the academic medical center. The purpose of this condition is to ensure that protected physicians are truly engaged in an academic medical practice. The exception does not apply to payments to physicians who provide only occasional academic or clinical teaching services or who are principally community rather than academic medical center practitioners.

Under the new exception in Sec. 411.355(e)(1)(i)(A), a "component" of an academic medical center means an affiliated medical school, faculty practice plan, hospital, teaching facility, institution of higher education, or departmental professional corporation. For purposes of this exception, an academic medical center may have some, but need not have all, of these components. As indicated in the preceding provision, however, the minimum requirements are a medical school, a faculty practice plan, and a hospital.

Under the new exception in Sec. 411.355(e)(1)(ii), the total compensation paid for the previous 12-month period (or fiscal year or calendar year) from all academic medical center components to the referring physician is set in advance and, in the aggregate, does not exceed fair market value for the services provided, and is not determined in a manner that takes into account the volume or value of any referrals or other business generated within the academic medical center. As with the corresponding provisions in the personal service arrangements, employee, and fair market value exceptions, this provision requires that remuneration to physicians be for bona fide services provided by the physicians and not for referrals. In determining fair market value for services in an academic medical practice, we believe the relevant comparison is aggregate compensation paid to physicians practicing in similar academic settings located in similar environments. Relevant factors include geographic location, size of the academic institutions, scope of clinical and academic programs offered, and the nature of the local health care marketplace. Nothing in this regulation is intended to preclude productivity bonuses paid to academic medical center physicians on the basis of services they personally perform.

Under the new exception in Sec. 411.355(e)(2), the "academic medical center" for purposes of this section shall consist of—(1) an accredited medical school (including a university, when appropriate); (2) an affiliated faculty practice plan that is a nonprofit, tax-exempt organization under section 501(c)(3) or (c)(4) of the Internal Revenue Code (or is a part of such an organization under an umbrella designation); and (3) one or more affiliated hospital(s) in which a majority of the hospital medical staff consists of physicians who are faculty members, and where a majority of all hospital admissions are made by physicians who are faculty members. This provision ensures that the exception only protects physician compensation in genuine academic medical settings. This new exception reflects our view that the predominant purpose of an academic medical center is to teach new physicians and to run medical practices that support the teaching mission.

To fit within the new exception in Sec. 411.355(e)(3), the academic medical center must meet the following conditions:

All transfers of money between components of the academic medical center must directly or indirectly support the missions of teaching, indigent care, research, or community service. This provision ensures that the academic medical center is bona fide and that transfers of funds are not inappropriate payments of indirect compensation for referrals. We believe that patient care is integral to an academic medical center's community service mission.

The relationship of the components of the academic medical center must be set forth in a written agreement that has been adopted by the governing body of each component. This provision requires a bona fide affiliation between the medical center components.

All money paid to a referring physician for research must be used solely to support bona fide research. We are concerned that research funding could be used to disguise additional payments for referrals. We are including this provision to ensure that money earmarked (intended or designated) for research is used solely for research purposes.

Under the new exception in Sec. 411.355(e)(4), the referring physician's compensation arrangement must not violate the anti-kickback statute (section 1128B(b) of the Act) and billing and claims submission must be proper. As with all exceptions created under section 1877(b)(4) of the Act, this provision is necessary to ensure that the arrangement poses no risk of fraud or abuse.

Comment: As noted above, commenters pointed out that the structure of faculty practice plans can be very complicated; for example, physicians in a faculty practice plan may be compensated by one entity, but conduct their medical practice through a separate entity and order laboratory and other ancillary services from additional related entities (for example, the teaching hospital, the university's research laboratory for highly specialized testing, in-office laboratories within the faculty departments that may or may not be incorporated as professional corporations). As a result, arrangements between and among the various sub-entities of such faculty practice plans can raise a number of issues under section 1877 of the Act. In particular, the question arises whether each separate legal entity and relationship among legal entities must meet an exception under section 1877 of the Act.

Commenters appealed for a separate exception for faculty practice plans, insisting that faculty practice plans pose a minimal risk of abuse under section 1877 of the Act. First, they asserted that physicians in faculty practice plans are less likely to make abusive referrals than their more entrepreneurial counterparts in private practice because they practice in a setting that focuses on academic pursuits and patient care at affiliated teaching hospitals and clinics. Second, they stated that many faculty practice plans include not-for-profit organizations that are regulated under IRS rules that forbid private inurement and private benefit.

Response: As explained in the introduction to this section of the preamble, we have revisited the issue of academic medical practices and are persuaded that academic medical practices present unique concerns under section 1877 of the Act that warrant a separate exception. Our new exception is described in the introduction. We believe that faculty practice plans will pose little risk of fraud or abuse under the conditions set forth in the new exception. We are not persuaded that physicians in faculty practice plans are necessarily less economically-motivated than their private practice counterparts or that regulation under IRS rules, though beneficial, is sufficient to prevent fraud or abuse.

Comment: A commenter suggested that the group practice definition and the requirements of the in-office ancillary services exception or personal service arrangements exception should be applied only at the level of the "umbrella" organization (that is, the organization that encompasses all the physicians within the faculty practice plan) for the entire faculty practice, thus obviating the need for each legal entity within the same academic setting to meet the provisions of section 1877 of the Act.

Response: In light of the new exception, we see no need to create new rules under existing exceptions for faculty practice plans. Parties may use the new exception or existing exceptions, depending on their individual circumstances.

Comment: As an alternative to a separate exception for faculty practice plans, one commenter urged that faculty practice plans be permitted to have independent contractors as "members" during the time they are providing services to the group. The commenter expressed the view that this solution would be preferable to requiring the faculty practice plan to employ such individuals.

Response: In light of the new compensation exception for physicians in faculty practice plans, we see no need to alter the definition of "member of the group" for academic medical practices. The definition of a "group practice" expressly includes a "faculty practice plan," and any faculty practice plan that fits in the definition is a "group practice" for purposes of section 1877 of the Act.

Comment: A commenter observed that under section 1877(b)(4)(B)(ii) of the Act a faculty practice plan qualifies as a group practice based solely on the services provided and revenue generated by the participating physicians within the faculty practice plan, regardless of the outside activities of those physicians. The commenter sought clarification that the converse would also be true, that time and revenue allocable to a physician's faculty practice would not count against the "group practice" status of his outside medical group.

Response: The outside medical group must qualify for group practice status under the tests described in section 1877(h)(4) of the Act (Sec. 411.352 of the regulations) and in this preamble at VI.C. Time and revenue allocable to a physician's faculty practice would be treated as all other outside time and revenue for purposes of those tests. In other words, such time and revenue would be treated no differently than time group practice physicians who are not in faculty practice plans spend supervising residents or conducting research.

B. Fair Market Value (Sec. 411.357(l))

The Proposed Rule. This proposed rule created an exception for compensation relationships that are based upon fair market value and meet certain other criteria. This exception is available for compensation arrangements between an entity and either a physician (or immediate family member) or any group of physicians (even if the group does not meet the definition of group practice set forth in Sec. 411.351), as long as the compensation arrangement—

Is in writing, is signed by the parties, and covers only identifiable items or services, all of which are specified in the agreement;

Covers all of the items and services to be provided by the physician (or immediate family member) to the entity or, alternatively, cross refers to any other agreements for items or services between these parties;

Specifies the time frame for the arrangement, which can be for any period of time and contain a termination clause, provided the parties enter into only one arrangement covering the same items or services during the course of a year. An arrangement made for less than 1 year may be renewed any number of times if the terms of the arrangement and the compensation for the same items or services do not change;

Specifies the compensation that will be provided under the arrangement, which has been set in advance. The compensation must be consistent with fair market value and not be determined in a manner that takes into account the volume or value of any referrals (as defined in Sec. 411.351), payment for referrals for medical services that are not covered under Medicare or Medicaid, or other business generated between the parties;

Involves a transaction that is commercially reasonable and furthers the legitimate business purposes of the parties; and

Meets a safe harbor under the anti-kickback statute or otherwise is in compliance with the anti-kickback provisions in section 1128B(b) of the Act.

The Final Rule: Except for the revisions described below, Phase I of this rulemaking adopts the proposed regulation. The revisions include:

Elimination of the requirement that the written document cross-reference other agreements between the parties.

Revision of the "set in advance" language to conform the exception to other exceptions in which that language appears. "Set in advance," as used in the fair market value exception, will have the uniform meaning described in section V of this preamble and Sec. 411.354(d) of the regulations.

Revision of Sec. 411.357(l)(3) to conform to our uniform interpretation of the volume or value standard in Sec. 411.354(d) (discussed at section V of this preamble).

Revision of the proposal in Sec. 411.357(l)(5) that required "compliance with" the anti-kickback statute. Under the final regulations, the compensation arrangement must—(1) not violate the anti-kickback statute, (2) comply with a statutory or regulatory anti-kickback safe harbor, or (3) have been approved by the OIG pursuant to a favorable advisory opinion issued in accordance with part 1008 (Advisory Opinions of the OIG) of this chapter. In addition, billing and claims submission must be proper.

Addition of a provision to mirror section 1877(e)(3)(A)(vi) of the Act, which clarifies that the services performed under the agreement cannot involve the counseling or promotion of a business arrangement or other activity that violates Federal or State law. While we believe this condition is implied throughout the statute, we are conforming the new fair market value exception to the Congress's inclusion of this same standard in the personal service arrangements exception.

Comment: Several commenters objected to the requirement that an arrangement must meet a safe harbor under the anti-kickback statute or otherwise be in compliance with the anti-kickback provisions in section 1128B(b) of the Act. First, commenters pointed out that the anti-kickback statute is an intent-based statute that prohibits certain knowing and willful conduct, whereas section 1877 of the Act is not based upon intent. In addition, one commenter was concerned that a violation of the anti-kickback statute by one party would preclude both parties from using the fair market value exception. Thus, the innocent party who might be unaware of the other party's violation of the anti-kickback statute and relying on the fair market value exception could unknowingly violate section 1877 of the Act. Second, several commenters stated that few arrangements would meet the requirements necessary to obtain safe harbor protection under the anti-kickback statute. Therefore, such arrangements would be excepted from section 1877 of the Act only if they met the standard of being "in compliance with the anti-kickback statute." These commenters were concerned that "being in compliance with the anti-kickback statute" was a nebulous standard that could only be accomplished with certainty by obtaining an OIG advisory opinion.

Response: In response to the concerns of commenters, we have revised Sec. 411.357(l)(5) of the regulations to make it clear that for a compensation arrangement to qualify for the fair market value exception, it must meet one of the following criteria:

It must not violate the anti-kickback statute.

It must comply with a statutory or regulatory anti-kickback safe harbor.

It must have been approved by the OIG pursuant to a favorable advisory opinion issued in accordance with part 1008 of this title.

This revision is both a clarification of the text set forth in the January 1998 proposed rule and an expansion of the types of arrangements that may qualify for the fair market value exception. In particular, we are changing the requirement from "being in compliance with" the anti-kickback statute to requiring that the arrangement not violate the anti-kickback statute. The revised language is more appropriate with respect to a criminal statute, such as the anti-kickback statute. In addition, since the broad statutory language of the anti-kickback statute technically covers some relatively innocuous commercial arrangements, and since the OIG has promulgated regulations granting safe harbor protection for some of these arrangements (Sec. 1001.952 of this title), we are revising the criteria to permit compensation arrangements that comply fully with a regulatory safe harbor. Arrangements that comply with the statutory exceptions at section 1128B(b)(3) of the Act also satisfy the new criteria. Finally, any compensation arrangement that has been approved by the OIG pursuant to a favorable advisory opinion issued in accordance with part 1008 of this title would meet the criteria of Sec. 411.357(l)(5). (We caution, however, that only the requestor of an OIG advisory opinion may rely on the opinion for any purposes, including, without limitation, the fulfillment of this criteria. Therefore, all parties that intend to rely on the advisory opinion should be included as requestors.)

Finally, we address the scenario where only one party has the requisite intent (that is, acting knowingly and willfully) to violate the anti-kickback statute. In such a case, only the party with the requisite intent would have violated the anti-kickback statute. However, if both parties relied on meeting the "not in violation of the anti-kickback statute" standard to qualify for the fair market value exception, the anti-kickback statute violation would preclude the use of the fair market value exception to section 1877 of the Act and both parties would have violated section 1877 of the Act. Although we understand the dilemma, we believe that it would be unusual that only one party to a compensation arrangement would have the requisite intent for violation of the anti-kickback statute. If any one purpose of remuneration is to induce or reward referrals of Federal health care program business, the statute is violated. (See United States v. Kats, 871 F.2d 105 (9th Cir. 1989); United States v. Greber, 760 F.2d 68 (3d Cir.), cert. denied, 474 U.S. 988 (1985).) Also, if the "innocent" party knows that the compensation arrangement would violate the anti-kickback statute but for the lack of the requisite intent, that party should be aware of the risk he or she is facing and take action to ensure that prohibited payments are not made. In that situation, we would advise structuring the arrangement to fit within a safe harbor, if possible, or obtaining an OIG advisory opinion.

For a discussion on the differences between section 1877 of the Act and the anti-kickback statute, together with an analysis of the impact that the anti-kickback statute has on these regulatory exceptions, see section II of this preamble.

Comment: Some commenters requested clarification regarding whether services provided by an entity to a physician would fit within the fair market value exception. One commenter was confused by the fact that the preamble to the January 1998 proposed rule implied that the exception would cover any compensation arrangements based upon fair market value, but the rule itself implied that it only covered arrangements where the physician (or immediate family member) provided items or services.

Response: This fair market value exception only covers items or services provided by a physician or any immediate family member to an entity. Depending on the facts, payments made by a physician to an entity for items or services furnished by the entity might qualify for the exception for payments by a physician which is set forth under Sec. 411.357(i), provided that the compensation is consistent with fair market value and the payments are not specifically excepted under another provision in Secs. 411.355 through 411.357.

Comment: One commenter requested clarification regarding whether this exception would be available if another exception could apply.

Response: In the preamble to the January 1998 proposed rule, we stated that parties involved in a compensation arrangement should use the fair market value exception if they have doubts about whether they meet the requirements in the other exceptions listed in Sec. 411.357. We have reconsidered our position. The parties may use the fair market value exception even if another exception potentially applies. We believe that the safeguards against overutilization included in the fair market value exception are sufficient to cover various types of compensation arrangements, including some arrangements that are covered by other exceptions.

Comment: A couple of commenters expressed concern regarding the application of the fair market value exception to legitimate physician recruitment practices that do not otherwise qualify for exception under the physician recruitment exception set forth at Sec. 411.357(e). One commenter was concerned that in order to meet the "commercially reasonable" and "legitimate business purposes" prerequisites, hospitals would be forced to obtain costly experts' reports regarding recruiting incentives provided in comparable situations. Another commenter sought clarification regarding whether the "commercially reasonable" prerequisite was based upon the specific business in which the parties are involved or business in general. This commenter was concerned that some arrangements (for example, loan forgiveness programs) might be commercially reasonable in the context of hospital/physician relationships, but might not be commercially reasonable from a general business perspective.

Response: Physician recruitment arrangements might be covered by this fair market value exception or the physician recruitment exception, depending on the specific facts involved. However, we recognize that many physician recruitment arrangements that offer "extra" payments to induce physicians to relocate will not be covered by the fair market value exception, because compensation offered for the physician's services exceeds the fair market value for such services. We will consider the comments on the recruitment exception in Phase II of this final rule.

With respect to determining what is "commercially reasonable," any reasonable method of valuation is acceptable, and the determination should be based upon the specific business in which the parties are involved, not business in general. In addition, we strongly suggest that the parties maintain good documentation supporting valuation. Finally, with respect to difficult cases, the parties could seek an advisory opinion under section 1877 of the Act. (See Sec. 411.370.) However, we cannot express opinions on whether compensation represents fair market value. (See Sec. 411.370(c)(1).) For further discussion of "fair market value", see section VIII.B.3 of this preamble.

Comment: One commenter thought that it would be burdensome to require inclusion of all items and services provided by the physician (or immediate family member) or a cross reference to other pertinent agreements. First, the commenter noted that there may be no written agreement for certain bona fide employment arrangements. Therefore, if an immediate family member of a physician is employed by the entity and there is no written employment agreement, the physician's compensation arrangement with the entity could not satisfy this requirement of the fair market value exception. Second, the commenter stated that arrangements between an entity and a physician (or immediate family member) may change from time to time as a result of new arrangements, terminations, renewals, etc. Therefore, the list of other agreements would become outdated quickly. Third, the commenter asserted that the requirement duplicated the information that was already required under the reporting requirements. To rectify the foregoing problems, the commenter suggested that the exception should only require a reference to a master list of contracts that could be updated periodically. Finally, the commenter requested clarification regarding what contracts must be cross-referenced when there is a compensation arrangement between an entity and a member of a physician group practice. The commenter questioned, with respect to a contract between an entity and an immediate family member of a physician who is a member of a group practice, whether the contract must cross-reference arrangements between the entity and—(1) the group practice, (2) each member of that group practice, and (3) any family member of a member of the group practice.

Response: We agree that it is burdensome to require that the written agreement either cover all items and services to be provided by the physician or immediate family member to the entity, or cross refer to any other agreements for items or services between any of these parties. To alleviate this burden, we are eliminating the requirement that the agreement cross refer to any other agreements. Nevertheless, we note that cross-referencing other agreements and arrangements is a good practice and will enable contracting entities, as well as auditors, to review more efficiently the full scope of a physician's relationship to the entity. In cases where a physician or an immediate family member of a physician is employed by the entity and there is no written employment agreement, the commenter's conclusion that the physician's compensation arrangement with the entity could not satisfy this requirement of the fair market value exception is correct. Another exception, such as the employment exception, may apply, since it does not require a written agreement.

Comment: Some commenters were concerned that by requiring that the compensation not be related to the volume or value of program referrals, non-program referrals, or other business generated between the parties, we had undermined the usefulness of the fair market value exception, as well as many other exceptions which are subject to the same restriction. One commenter suggested that an arrangement should not pose a risk of abuse as long as the compensation does not reflect the volume or value of the physician's own referrals.

Response: For a discussion of the "value or volume of referrals" standard, refer to the discussion at section V of this preamble. We are conforming the language of the new fair market value exception to our uniform interpretation of the standard, which is discussed at section V of this preamble.

C. Non-Monetary Compensation up to $300 (and Medical Staff Benefits (Secs. 411.357(k) and (m))

The Proposed Rule. Physicians and their immediate family members are often given noncash items or services that have a relatively low value and are not part of a formal, written agreement. For example, a physician might receive free samples of certain drugs or chemicals from a laboratory or free coffee mugs or note pads from a hospital. Although these free or discounted items and services fall within the definition of "compensation arrangement," we believe that such compensation is unlikely to cause overutilization, if held within reasonable limits. Therefore, we proposed a new exception, titled De Minimis Compensation, for compensation from an entity in the form of items or services that would not exceed $50 per gift and an aggregate of $300 per year. In addition, to qualify for the proposed exception, the entity providing the compensation would have to make it available to all similarly situated individuals, regardless of whether these individuals refer patients to the entity for services, and the compensation could not be determined in any way that would take into account the volume or value of the physician's referrals to the entity.

The Final Rule. Except for the revisions discussed below, the regulations in Phase I of this rulemaking are the same as the proposed rule:

Changing the name of this exception from "De Minimis Compensation" to "Non-Monetary Compensation Up To $300" to avoid any unintentional implication that the dollar limits set forth in the exception are minimal or inconsequential in all circumstances. That is, although the $300 dollar limit may be relatively low when compared to the average physician's annual income, we believe the amount could be sufficient to induce referrals. However, we believe that the dollar limit, together with the other conditions of the exception, are sufficient to protect against abuse.

Elimination of the $50 per gift limit. Therefore, if the other conditions of the exception are met, an entity can give a physician one noncash gift per year valued up to $300 or two or more noncash gifts per year, as long as the annual aggregate value of the gifts does not exceed $300.

Addition of a provision that precludes protection for gifts solicited by physicians to prevent physicians from making such gifts a condition or expectation of doing business.

Elimination of the "similarly situated" standard. This standard was designed to ensure that compensation was not paid primarily to reward high referrers. To ensure the same end, we are augmenting the standard that prohibits compensation that takes into account the volume or value of referrals by also prohibiting compensation that takes into account the volume or value of any other business generated between the parties.

Addition of a new exception (Sec. 411.357(m)) to allow certain incidental benefits of low value provided by hospitals to their medical staffs.

Comment: Several commenters argued that section 1877 of the Act does not apply to relationships between physicians and drug manufacturers, because a drug manufacturer is not an "entity" that furnishes health services to which a physician purchasing drugs makes a "referral" under section 1877 of the Act. Applying this interpretation, commenters concluded that free drug samples, free training, and other gifts (for example, pens, notepads, and other items) provided to physicians by drug manufacturers are not prohibited by section 1877 of the Act, and, therefore, do not need to qualify for any of the exceptions. Also, many expressed concern that, if section 1877 of the Act is interpreted as applying to physicians' relationships with drug manufacturers, then free drug samples and training provided to physicians by pharmaceutical companies would be prohibited, because they would exceed the proposed per gift and annual dollar limits of the de minimis exception. They reasoned that free drug samples should be exempt from section 1877 of the Act, because they are extensively regulated by Federal law that restricts their use and prohibits their sale, and, therefore, free drug samples pose little risk of abuse. They also stressed that free training given in connection with free samples should be exempt, because it is part of the sales effort which benefits patients, as well as physicians.

Response: We agree that drug manufacturers typically are not "entities" that furnish health services to which physicians purchasing drugs make "referrals" under section 1877 of the Act. (See section VIII.B of this preamble.) Therefore, as a general rule, neither free drugs, free training, nor gifts provided to physicians by drug manufacturers are prohibited by section 1877 of the Act. We caution, however, that free or discounted items or services provided by drug manufacturers to physicians must be scrutinized to ensure compliance with other applicable laws and regulations, including, without limitation, the anti-kickback statute and the Federal laws restricting the sale and distribution of drug samples, 21 U.S.C. Sec. 353(c) through (d).

Comment: Many commenters expressed concern regarding the per gift and annual dollar limits. In particular, they stated that the dollar limits were so low that they precluded protection for many legitimate compensation arrangements. For example, many commenters were concerned that no protection would be provided for free or discounted benefits provided by a hospital for its medical staff. Commenters believe that free or discounted benefits (for example, free or discounted meals and refreshments, free or discounted parking, free continuing medical education or other training, free computer/Internet access, free laboratory coats, free or discounted malpractice insurance, free transcription of medical records, and free photocopying) would add up and exceed the dollar limits quickly. Concern was also expressed about the administrative burden of tracking the exact dollar amounts for benefits provided to each medical staff physician.

Finally, one commenter questioned whether, with respect to group practices, the dollar limit would apply to each individual member of the group or to the group as a whole. Another commenter suggested that the dollar limits should be indexed for inflation.

Response: First, we have added a new exception (Sec. 411.357(m)) for incidental benefits given to a hospital's medical staff members. The question of incidental benefits given by a hospital to members of its medical staff was addressed previously in the preamble to the January 1998 proposed rule at 63 FR 1713–1714. In particular, we noted that:

Entities, such as hospitals, often provide physicians with certain incidental benefits, such as their malpractice insurance, or with reduced or free parking, meals or other incidental benefits. We believe the answer to this question hinges on the nature of any other financial relationship the physician has with the entity. For example, if a physician receives free "extras" such as malpractice insurance, parking, or meals while he or she serves as the entity's employee, then these extras might qualify as part of the compensation that the physician receives under a bona fide employment relationship, provided they are specified in the employment agreement. If the physician or entity can demonstrate that the extras constitute part of the payment that such entities typically provide to physicians, regardless of whether they make referrals to the entity, the extras constitute payment that is consistent with fair market value, and that furthers the entity's legitimate business purposes. If an incidental benefit cannot meet the requirements under a statutory exception or the new general exception for compensation arrangements we have included in Sec. 411.357(l), it might still meet the de minimis exception we have included in Sec. 411.357(k) if it has limited value. We have also been asked about parking spaces that a hospital provides to physicians who have privileges to treat their patients in the hospital. It is our view that, while a physician is making rounds, the parking benefits both the hospital and its patients, rather than providing the physician with any personal benefit. Thus, we do not intend to regard parking for this purpose as remuneration furnished by the hospital to the physician, but instead as part of the physician's privileges. However, if a hospital provides parking to a physician for periods of time that do not coincide with his or her rounds, that parking could constitute remuneration.

We recognize that many of the incidental benefits that hospitals provide to medical staff members do not qualify for the employment exception because most members of a hospital's medical staff are not hospital employees, and do not qualify for the fair market value exception because, to the extent that the medical staff membership is the only relationship between the hospital and certain physicians, there is no written agreement between the parties to which these incidental benefits could be added. While we still believe that medical staff incidental benefits could be structured in a way that would reward physicians for referrals and, thereby, lead to overutilization, we also recognize that many medical staff incidental benefits are customary industry practices that are intended to benefit the hospital and its patients. For example, free computer/Internet access benefits the hospital and its patients by facilitating the maintenance of up-to-date, accurate medical records and the availability of cutting edge medical information. Consequently, we have added a new exception (Sec. 411.357(m)), which provides that medical staff incidental benefits are excepted from section 1877 of the Act, if the benefits in question are—

Offered by a hospital to all members of the medical staff without regard to the volume or value of referrals or other business generated between the parties;

Offered only during periods when the medical staff members are making rounds or performing other duties that benefit the hospital and its patients;

Provided by the hospital and used by the medical staff members only on the hospital's campus;

Reasonably related to the provision of, or designed to facilitate directly or indirectly the delivery of, medical services at the hospital;

Consistent with the types of benefits offered to medical staff members by other hospitals within the same local region or, if no such hospitals exist, by comparable hospitals located in comparable regions; and

Of low value (that is, less than $25) with respect to each occurrence of the benefit (for example, each benefit must be of low value).

Regardless of compliance with the foregoing, we caution that medical staff incidental benefits should be reviewed to ensure compliance with other applicable laws and regulations, including, without limitation, the anti-kickback statute.

Medical staff incidental benefits that do not meet the foregoing conditions could constitute prohibited remuneration and, therefore, would be permitted under section 1877 of the Act only if an exception applies. For example, malpractice insurance offered by a hospital only to its emergency room physicians would not meet the foregoing conditions. Therefore, to be exempt from section 1877 of the Act, it would have to qualify for one of the exceptions. Malpractice insurance would not qualify for the exception for non-monetary compensation up to $300, because it would exceed the applicable dollar limits. Nor would it qualify for the exception for remuneration unrelated to the provision of DHS, because such payments would be related to the provision of emergency services, which are included in the definition of inpatient hospital services and, therefore, are DHS. Malpractice insurance provided to emergency room physicians might qualify for the employee exception if the physician is employed by the hospital and the insurance is part of the employment agreement. Similarly, we do not believe medical transcription services are an incidental benefit of nominal value.

We are aware that some hospitals are offering compliance training programs for physicians on their medical staffs or in their local communities. Because we believe such programs are beneficial and do not pose a risk of fraud or abuse, we are creating a new exception for such compliance training programs.

We intentionally set the dollar limits in the proposed exception at a low level to decrease the likelihood that the items or services would influence utilization. However, in response to the comments, we have eliminated the $50 per gift dollar limit. Therefore, under the final rule, an entity could give a physician either one noncash gift per year of up to $300 in value or two or more noncash gifts per year, as long as the annual aggregate value of the gifts does not exceed $300. This change permits larger one-time gifts. For example, a noncash gift valued at $150 would have exceeded the per gift dollar limit of the proposed rule, but would be permitted under the final rule, as long as the annual aggregate does not exceed $300 and the other conditions of the exception are met.

The exception for non-monetary compensation up to $300 only protects gifts to individual physicians. Thus, gifts given to a group practice would not qualify for this exception. Noncash gifts could, however, be given to one member, several individual members, or each member of a group practice, if each such gift meets all of the conditions of the exception for non-monetary compensation up to $300. We caution, however, that the exception will not apply to gifts, such as holiday parties or office equipment or supplies, that are valued at not more than $300 per physician in the group, but are, in effect, given or used as a group gift. Notwithstanding the foregoing, we recognize that the aggregate dollar amount could be substantial for gifts to individual physician members of very large groups. For example, if a group consists of 50 physicians, each physician of the group could be given an aggregate of $300 in non-cash gifts within a given year, equaling a total of $15,000 from one entity. Such a large gift could provide an economic incentive for overutilization. Therefore, to counter-balance the removal of the $50 per gift limit and to further guard against abuse, we have added a provision that excludes gifts solicited by the receiving physicians or their group practice. This change also serves to clarify that our use of the term "gift" refers to the ordinary meaning of the term; that is, a gift must involve a voluntary transfer made without consideration or compensation expected or received in return. This new provision prevents members of group practices, as well as solo practitioners, from making noncash gifts a condition of doing business with a particular entity. We intend to monitor the provision of gifts to group practice physicians under this exception and may revisit our position if abuses occur. Such gifts remain subject to the anti-kickback statute.

Finally, we have decided not to index the $300 annual aggregate dollar limit for inflation. Removal of the per gift dollar limit gives entities much greater flexibility with respect to the value of noncash gifts. That is, under the proposed rule, a single gift could not exceed $50; whereas, under the final rule, the value of a single gift could be up to $300, as long as the other conditions are met. We believe that this revision decreases the need for adjustment for inflation. In addition, we think it would create confusion as to the actual limit in succeeding years if we were to provide for an inflation adjuster. The rule as it stands creates an easy-to-follow bright line. However, we will continue to monitor the effect of the $300 limit and may revisit the limit in the future.

Comment: One commenter asked for clarification regarding the relationship between the de minimis exception and the statute's exception for remuneration provided by a hospital to a physician "if such remuneration does not relate to the provision of designated health services." (See section 1877(e)(4) of the Act.)

Response: The exception for non-monetary compensation up to $300 and the statutory exception for remuneration unrelated to the provision of DHS are totally separate exceptions with different criteria. The determination as to which of these exceptions, if any, is applicable depends on the facts and circumstances of the case involved.

Comment: One commenter questioned whether the requirement that compensation must be made available to all similarly situated individuals would prohibit hospitals from hosting meals on a person-to-person basis. Another commenter suggested that the similarly situated requirement should be eliminated because the type of promotional items that would be covered by the exception would probably be provided only to referrers or potential referrers, and such minimal gifts were unlikely to cause overutilization.

Response: We agree that, on balance, the "similarly situated" test does not add significantly to the protections of the exception. Accordingly, we have eliminated the "similarly situated" standard. This standard was designed to ensure that compensation was not paid primarily to reward high referrers. To ensure the same end, we are augmenting the standard that prohibits compensation that takes into account the volume or value of referrals by also prohibiting compensation that takes into account the volume or value of any other business generated by the referring physician.

Comment: Two commenters questioned how professional courtesy discounts (that is, free or discounted services provided to physicians) would be handled under section 1877 of the Act. One of the commenters suggested that professional courtesy discounts should not violate section 1877 of the Act, because they fall within the non-monetary compensation up to $300 exception or they do not constitute "remuneration."

Response: The term "professional courtesy" is used (or misused) to describe a number of analytically different practices, including the practice by a physician of waiving the entire fee for services provided to the physician's office staff, other physicians, and/or their families (the traditional meaning); the waiver of coinsurance obligations or other out-of-pocket expenses for physicians or their families (that is, insurance only billing); and similar payment arrangements by hospitals or other institutions for services provided to their medical staffs or employees. Therefore, we cannot generalize about the application of section 1877 of the Act to such arrangements. Some such arrangements may fit in an existing exception, depending on the circumstances (for example, the non-monetary compensation up to $300 exception if the value of the courtesy services is less than $300 and the other conditions of the exception are satisfied). However, some such arrangements may not fit in an exception. We are considering whether an exception could be developed for such arrangements and will address the matter further in Phase II of this rulemaking. We are soliciting comments about appropriate conditions for such an exception and an appropriate definition of "professional courtesy." In addition to conducting an analysis of professional courtesy arrangements under section 1877 of the Act, these arrangements must be analyzed with respect to other fraud and abuse, as well as payment, authorities, including the anti-kickback statute, the False Claims Act (31 U.S.C. Sec. 3729 et seq.), and the prohibition of inducements to beneficiaries (section 1128A(a)(5) of the Act).

VIII. Definitions of the Designated Health Services

A. General Principles

Basis for the Definitions

As we pointed out in the preamble to the January 1998 proposed rule (63 FR 1673), section 1877(h)(6) of the Act lists the DHS, but does not define them. Moreover, the list in section 1877(h)(6) of the Act does not necessarily correspond to specific service categories as they are defined under either Medicare or Medicaid. For example, section 1877(h)(6)(D) of the Act uses the phrase, "[r]adiology services, including magnetic resonance imaging, computerized axial tomography scans, and ultrasound services," although ultrasound is not usually considered a radiology service. In defining the DHS in Sec. 411.351 of the January 1998 proposed rule, we stated that we chose, as much as possible, to base the definitions in section 1877 of the Act on existing definitions in the Medicare program. We also explained that in situations in which it was not clear whether a service was included, we would look to the intent of the statute. In general, we believe the Congress meant to include specific services that are or could be subject to abuse.

Because we had received a number of inquiries from individuals who were confused about whether a particular service fell under one of the DHS categories, we proposed defining the DHS whenever we could by cross-referencing existing definitions in the Medicare statute, regulations, or manuals or by including specific language whenever we believed the definitions should deviate from standard Medicare definitions.

Many of the comments we received on the proposed rule reflected that commenters were still unclear about which services fall under the DHS categories. Many commenters specifically requested that we establish a "bright line" test for identifying these services, and suggested that we base the services on an established list, such as the Current Procedural Terminology (CPT) codes. We agree that more precise definitions will make it much easier administratively for physicians and entities to comply with the law.

Accordingly, we have determined that we will define certain DHS (clinical laboratory services, physical therapy, occupational therapy, radiology and certain other imaging services, and radiation therapy services (sections 1877(h)(6)(A)through (h)(6)(E) of the Act) by publishing specific lists of CPT and HCFA Common Procedure Coding System (HCPCS) codes that physicians and providers most commonly associate with a given designated health service. The lists of codes will define the entire scope of the designated services category for purposes of section 1877 of the Act. While the definitions section of the regulations will contain a general explanation of the principles used to select the codes, in all cases the published list of codes will be controlling.

For services described in section 1877(h)(6) of the Act, paragraphs (F) through (K), we will not be publishing a service-by-service list. The codes for these services may be just one component used for identifying the service; the codes may be all those that appear in a specific "level," such as all HCPCS level 2 codes, for a service; or the service is not defined using HCPCS codes at all. The definitions for the services in paragraphs (F) through (K) are explained in detail below under each service category.

The HCPCS is a collection of codes and descriptors that represent procedures, supplies, products, and services that may be provided to Medicare beneficiaries and to individuals enrolled in private health insurance programs. We believe that these codes will already be familiar to many in the health care industry. These codes must be used when billing Medicare for Part B services and supplies. The codes are divided into three levels, the first two of which are used in this final rule and are described below; they are listed in HCPCS 2001:

Level I: Codes and descriptors copyrighted by the American Medical Association in its Current Procedural Terminology, Fourth Edition (CPT-4). These are 5-position numeric codes primarily representing physician services.

Level II: These are 5-position alpha-numeric codes representing primarily items and nonphysician services that are not represented in the level I codes. Included are codes and descriptors copyrighted by the American Dental Association's Current Dental Terminology, Second Edition (CDT-2). These are 5-position alpha-numeric codes comprising the "D" series. All other level II codes and descriptors are approved and maintained jointly by the alpha-numeric editorial panel (consisting of HCFA, the Health Insurance Association of America, and the Blue Cross and Blue Shield Association).

Because these specific codes change and can quickly become out-of-date, we are not including the lists of DHS codes in the regulations text, but rather in an accompanying attachment. The definitions of specific services in the regulations text will cross refer to a comprehensive table that will appear initially in the **Federal Register** along with Phase I of this rulemaking and thereafter in an addendum to the annual final rule concerning payment policies under the physician fee schedule rule. This list titled, "List of CPT/HCPCS Codes Used to Describe Certain Designated Health Services Under the Physician Referral Provisions (Section 1877 of the Social Security Act)," will also be posted on the HCFA web site at http://www.hcfa.gov on the date of **Federal Register** publication of this final rule. The table published each year will be a comprehensive listing of all codes for DHS and not merely a listing of changes to the prior year's table. The updates will also be posted on the HCFA web site. The physician fee schedule rule is generally published in late October or early November. We will consider comments on each year's revised list if we receive them during the applicable comment period for that rule. If any changes are made, we will then publish a revised table and respond to any public comments that we receive. This approach will provide an annual comprehensive list of codes for those DHS noted above (sections 1877(h)(6)(A)through (h)(6)(E) of the Act).

We are not providing lists of codes for the following categories of DHS (sections 1877(h)(6)(F) through (h)(6)(K) of the Act): Durable medical equipment and supplies; parenteral and enteral nutrients, equipment, and supplies; prosthetics, orthotics, and prosthetic devices and supplies; home health services; outpatient prescription drugs; or inpatient and outpatient hospital services. We believe the definitions in Phase I of this rulemaking for these DHS provide sufficiently clear "bright line" rules.

In the preamble to the January 1998 proposed rule, we had stated that we believed the Congress intended to include specific services that are or could be subject to abuse and that we would attempt to define the services accordingly. In the January 1998 proposed rule preamble and regulations text, we then attempted in some cases to include or exclude services or types of services based on our view as to their potential for abuse. Many commenters disagreed with our views about particular services (for example, lithotripsy), and many more argued that the particular service they provided should also be excluded because it was not overutilized. In light of these comments and upon further review of the statutory scheme, we have decided that the Congress did not intend that we categorize DHS by determining the potential for overutilization or abuse on a service-by-service basis. Accordingly, in Phase I of this rulemaking, we are including all services that we believe come within the general categories; we have created limited exceptions for a few specific cases (that is, implants in ambulatory surgical centers, legislatively mandated preventive screening tests and immunizations subject to frequency limits, eyeglasses and contact lenses subject to frequency limits, and erythropoietin (EPO) provided by end-stage renal disease (ESRD) facilities) for which we believe an exception poses a limited risk of abuse and is necessary to avoid needless disruption of patient care. However, even for those rare exceptions, we will continue to monitor the services for abuse and, if necessary, revisit the exclusions.

We also stated in the preamble to the January 1998 proposed rule (63 FR 1673) that we consider a service to be a designated health service, even if it is billed as something else or is subsumed within another service category by being bundled with other services for billing purposes. We gave as an example skilled nursing facility (SNF) services, which can encompass a variety of DHS, such as physical therapy (PT), occupational therapy (OT), or laboratory services. Commenters complained that this interpretation would result in an expansion of the DHS beyond the services specifically listed in the law. According to the commenters, when the Congress intended to cover specific Medicare services (including composite rate services, such as hospital or home health services), it did so expressly. Upon review, we agree with the commenters. Under the final rule, services that would otherwise constitute DHS, but that are paid by Medicare as part of a composite payment for a group of services as a separate benefit (for example, ambulatory surgical center (ASC) or SNF rate), are not DHS for purposes of section 1877 of the Act. (As expressly provided in section 1877(h)(6) of the Act, hospital and home health services remain DHS although they are paid through a composite rate.) We note, however, that because of SNF consolidated billing, most, if not all, SNFs will also be considered entities providing DHS (for example, PT or OT) under Part B to SNF patients who have exhausted their Part A benefit or to other nursing home residents (that is, patients for whom the services are not covered as part of a composite rate). The consolidated billing requirement places with the SNF the Medicare billing responsibility for most of the services that a SNF resident receives (except for certain practitioner services and a limited number of other services) under Part A and under Part B. (Presently, consolidated billing is in effect only for patients in a covered Part A stay, but will become effective for Part B services in the near future.) Accordingly, a physician will not be able to refer Medicare patients who will require DHS to a SNF in which he or she has an ownership or investment interest, unless the interest is protected under an exception to section 1877 of the Act.

In the August 1995 final rule relating to clinical laboratory services, we created an exception for laboratory services furnished in an ASC or ESRD facility or by a hospice if the services were included in a composite rate or per diem hospice charge. (See Sec. 411.355(d)). In the January 1998 proposed rule, we had proposed extending this composite rate exception to include all DHS furnished in an ASC or ESRD facility or by a hospice if payment is included in the ASC payment rate, the ESRD composite payment rate, or as part of the hospice payment rate. This proposal was intended to address problems faced by ASCs, ESRD facilities, and hospices in the light of our proposed stance on DHS subsumed by bundled payments. However, since under the final rule DHS that are subsumed by a bundled payment do not implicate section 1877 of the Act, we have not adopted our proposal to extend Sec. 411.355(d) beyond clinical laboratory services. Moreover, given our final interpretation, we are reconsidering the need for Sec. 411.355(d) as applied to clinical laboratory services and intend to address the matter further in Phase II of this rulemaking. We are soliciting comments on this issue.

B. General Comment: Professional Services as Designated Health Services

Comment: Many commenters expressed the view that the professional component of DHS (particularly clinical laboratory and radiology services) should not implicate section 1877 of the Act. Commenters asserted that the Congress did not intend for professional services to come within the physician self-referral law prohibition and that we exceeded our authority to promulgate regulations by including them. Commenters also contended that limiting DHS under section 1877 of the Act solely to the technical components of services would sufficiently control the risk of program or patient abuse. Other commenters stated that if we included professional components of some DHS, we should do so for all DHS. The commenters pointed out that our proposed position on productivity bonuses (that is, that they may not reflect the volume or value of any DHS referrals) would require special bookkeeping to segregate professional fees when calculating bonuses that will burden practices, without serving a public policy purpose.

Response: We believe that it was not the intent of the statute to exclude all professional services from the list of DHS. Many of the DHS, such as radiology and radiation therapy, have substantial physician service components. If the Congress intended to exclude them, we would expect the statute to specifically do so. While some services are not viewed as having a professional component that is paid separately, Medicare still requires professional supervision of them to qualify for Medicare payment.

We agree to some extent that limiting referrals for the technical component of a service should greatly reduce the number of unnecessary referrals. Nonetheless, there are some DHS that consist only of a professional component (for example, some radiation therapy services) or are primarily professional in nature, and these would not otherwise be subject to the law if we carved out all professional components.

We agree with the commenters that we should include professional components when relevant in all DHS categories. Therefore, we have revised the definitions of each of the DHS to include the professional components in each case in which a professional component is included in the CPT or HCPCS codes that represent one of those services.

We understand that these rules may impose an administrative burden on some group practices, depending on how they choose to comply with section 1877 of the Act. We think Phase I of this rulemaking has a number of substantive changes that will ease the administrative burden of compliance, including the exception from the definition of "referral" for personally performed services and the greater flexibility afforded group practices over their distribution of revenues. As a practical matter, the professional component of many of these services will be excluded from the definition of a referral as services personally performed by the referring physician.

Individual Designated Health Services

We discuss below each designated health service category in the order in which it appears in section 1877(h)(6) of the Act. Each discussion includes a general summary of the category, summaries of the relevant public comments, and our responses.

C. Clinical Laboratory Services

In the August 1995 final rule covering a physician's referrals for clinical laboratory services, we defined these services in Sec. 411.351 as—

The biological, microbiological, serological, chemical, immunohematological, hematological, biophysical, cytological, pathological, or other examination of materials derived from the human body for the purpose of providing information for the diagnosis, prevention, or treatment of any disease or impairment of, or the assessment of the health of, human beings. These examinations also include procedures to determine, measure, or otherwise describe the presence or absence of various substances or organisms in the body.

We had stated in the August 1995 final rule, in response to a commenter who requested a definition of clinical laboratory services, that we believed the most appropriate way for a physician or clinical laboratory to determine if a diagnostic test is a clinical laboratory test subject to the requirements of section 1877 of the Act, is to find out if the test is subject to categorization under the Clinical Laboratory Improvement Act (CLIA). We pointed out that there is a list of clinical laboratory test systems, assays, and examinations categorized by complexity and published by the Center for Disease Control (CDC). We also stated that, given this definition, CPT codes would not be the sole references to identify clinical laboratory services for physician referral purposes.

Commenters also had asked about the professional components of laboratory services. We stated that we believed that CLIA covers the actual examination of materials, their analysis, and any interpretation and reporting of the results that are performed by a facility that qualifies as a laboratory, as defined in Sec. 493.2 (Definitions). However, if a laboratory sent test results to an independent physician, any interpretation performed by the physician would not be performed by the laboratory facility. As a result, the services would not constitute part of the clinical laboratory test.

We stated in the January 1998 proposed rule covering referrals for the other DHS that we would retain the definition of clinical laboratory services that was incorporated into our regulations by the August 1995 final rule. However, in line with our revised approach for identifying the DHS in this final rule, we have amended the rule to refer specifically to CPT and HCPCS codes. We have included as DHS the professional components of laboratory tests when they are listed as such in the codes. It is our belief that the specification of the codes in the attachment to this final rule is consistent with, although not identical to, the definition of clinical laboratory services in our January 1998 proposed rule.

D. Physical Therapy Services

We proposed to define physical therapy services in Sec. 411.351 as those outpatient physical therapy services (including speech-language pathology services) described at section 1861(p) of the Act and in Sec. 410.100 (Included services), paragraphs (b) and (d). Under section 1861(p) of the Act, the term "outpatient physical therapy services" specifically includes speech-language pathology services. Because section 1877(h)(6) of the Act lists physical therapy services in general, and not just outpatient services, we also included in the definition any other services with the characteristics described in Sec. 410.100(b) and (d) that are covered under Medicare Part A or Part B, regardless of who provides them, the location in which they are provided, or how they are billed.

We pointed out that services that are essentially the same as "outpatient physical therapy services" are also covered by Medicare in other contexts and in different settings, and may be billed under different categories. For example, we have a longstanding policy of covering physical therapy and occupational therapy as diagnostic or therapeutic inpatient hospital services. Similarly, these services can also be covered as SNF services, and can be furnished as "incident to" physician services under section 1861(s)(2)(A) of the Act. (Section 1877 implications for DHS provided by SNFs are discussed earlier in this section.)

It was our view in the January 1998 proposed rule that covered outpatient physical therapy services basically included three types of services, which were best described in Sec. 410.100(b) (which specifically concerns services provided by a comprehensive rehabilitation facility (CORF)). This definition covers the testing and measurement of the function or dysfunction of the neuromuscular, musculoskeletal, cardiovascular, and respiratory systems; assessment and treatment related to dysfunction caused by illness or injury and aimed at preventing or reducing disability or pain and restoring lost function; and the establishment of a maintenance therapy program for an individual whose restoration has been reached. Many commenters asserted that the proposed definition was imprecise or improperly included some procedures that are not generally considered physical therapy services.

We have responded to these concerns by redefining physical therapy services, as some commenters suggested, by using a list of HCPCS codes. We believe the list is limited to services that are more traditionally regarded as physical therapy. In general, these services are described in the "Physical Medicine and Rehabilitation" section (the 97000 series) of the CPT and in other relevant sections of the HCPCS.

In the January 1998 proposed rule, we also included speech-language pathology services as a designated health service since section 1861(p) of the Act includes "speech-language pathology services" in the definition of "outpatient physical therapy services." These services are defined in section 1861(ll)(1) of the Act as speech, language, and related function assessment and rehabilitation services furnished by a qualified speech-language pathologist as this pathologist is legally authorized to perform under State law (or the State regulatory mechanism) as would otherwise be covered if furnished by a physician. Section 1861(ll)(3) of the Act defines a "qualified speech-language pathologist."

We used in the proposed rule the brief description of speech-language pathology services in Sec. 410.100(d), which applies to services provided in CORFs, as those services that are necessary for the diagnosis and treatment of speech and language disorders that create difficulties in communication. In an effort to furnish a "bright line" test, we are defining the services in Phase I of this rulemaking by the specific codes that correspond to the services that we consider to be speech-language pathology services.

As we developed the list of CPT and HCPCS codes relevant to speech-language pathology, we realized that our proposed definition, which cross-refers to the CORF definition in Sec. 410.100(d), did not encompass the full range of services that are commonly considered to be speech-language pathology services. It failed to recognize that speech-language difficulties can be caused by cognitive disorders and failed to recognize that speech-language pathology may be used to treat swallowing and other oral-motor dysfunctions. Therefore, in developing the list of codes for speech pathology in Phase I of this rulemaking, we included the diagnosis and treatment of cognitive disorders including swallowing and other oral-motor dysfunctions.

Finally, because of the overlap between physical therapy, occupational therapy, and speech-language pathology services, we are listing the codes for all three services together. We believe that this set of HCPCS codes represents what most clinicians would define as PT/OT/speech therapy services that are covered by the Medicare program. The list is set out in the attachment to this final rule.

Comment: A number of commenters were particularly concerned that the proposed definition of physical therapy services implies that physical therapists can perform diagnostic testing and measurements, such as electromyography tests (EMGs). These tests are used primarily to provide medical diagnostic information regarding neuromuscular diseases and occasionally to measure neuromuscular function. Although some States permit physical therapists to perform these tests, the commenters believe that EMGs are typically performed by a physician as part of a physical examination to determine whether a patient is a surgical candidate or if some other course of treatment is warranted.

In addition, other commenters stated that the proposed definition of physical therapy services could be interpreted to include therapeutic procedures such as nerve blocks and arthrocentesis that the commenters believe are physician services. One commenter, a physician who practices physical medicine and rehabilitation, asserted that our proposed definition of physical therapy included services that could be administered by physicians and physical therapists. He feared that this could prohibit him from treating patients he diagnoses. Several commenters responded to the inclusion in the definition of physical therapy of any "assessment and treatment" designed to alleviate pain or disability. The commenters asserted that this phrase captures a large portion of modern medicine, given that pain is the most common presenting symptom in a physician's office, and virtually any assessment or treatment following therefrom would have as its purpose the alleviation of that pain.

Response: Nothing in the proposed definition affected the scope of any practitioner's practice. We agree with the commenters that only in certain States are physical therapists licensed to perform EMGs. Additionally, we agree that therapeutic procedures such as nerve blocks and arthrocentesis are typically performed by a physician and are not generally considered to be a part of physical therapy. These procedures are not included on the list of codes that defines the scope of physical therapy for purposes of section 1877(h)(6)(B) of the Act. In the January 1998 proposed rule, we did not intend to convey the message that what is generally considered physical therapy would change. We proposed to use an existing definition of physical therapy (in Sec. 410.100(b), which covers physical therapy services in CORFs) precisely because we did not want to change the existing perception of physical therapy.

In order to avoid confusion, we are revising our proposed definition by providing a list of CPT and HCPCS codes that are, collectively, the PT/OT/speech-language therapy DHS. This list of codes defines the entire scope of PT/OT/speech-language therapy services for purposes of section 1877 of the Act. Finally, we note that under Phase I of this rulemaking, if a physician personally provides a designated health service to his or her patient, there is no "referral" for purposes of section 1877(a)(1) of the Act. See section III.B of this preamble.

Comment: One commenter asserted that pulmonary function tests are for the measurement of the function of the respiratory system and have nothing to do with physical therapy. However, another commenter recommended that the definition of physical therapy include the neuromuscular and pulmonary function tests that test for functional capacity ratings and that are usually performed by a physical therapist without the direct supervision of a physician.

Response: We agree with the commenter that pulmonary function tests for the measurement of the function of the respiratory system are not physical therapy. The only pulmonary function test that may be considered to be a physical therapy service is pulse oximetry testing, CPT code 94762, when it is used to test for functional capacity ratings. A pulse oximetry test that is performed to determine whether a patient has enough oxygen to perform certain activities of daily living is, for example, a physical therapy service.

Comment: One commenter recommended that we define physical therapy as those therapeutic exercises and physical medicine modalities described in the 97000 series of the CPT codes, included in the patient's written plan of physical therapy treatment, and provided by a physical therapist or physical therapy aide.

Response: We agree with the commenter that PT services should be based on the CPT codes and have modified the rule accordingly. With respect to which professionals can provide a given service, we defer in this rule to existing Medicare policy. Many of these DHS can be provided by physicians.

Comment: A number of commenters opposed the inclusion of speech-language pathology services in the definition of physical therapy services. The commenters stated that the Congress did not intend to include these services within the ban on physician referrals and asserted that including these services as DHS is unnecessary (although they did not state why this would be the case). One commenter asserted that when the Congress intended to include outpatient speech-language pathology services within the category of outpatient physical therapy services, the Congress enacted explicit language that made that intention clear. The commenter pointed to section 4541(a)(1) of the BBA 1997, which added paragraph (8)(A) to section 1833(a) of the Act. That provision states that, for covered individuals, amounts will be paid from the Medicare Trust Fund for "outpatient physical therapy services (which includes outpatient speech-language pathology services) and outpatient occupational therapy services furnished — " * * * by certain entities.

Response: The definition of "outpatient physical therapy services" in section 1861(p) of the Act specifically states that "the term 'outpatient physical therapy services' also includes speech-language pathology services furnished by a provider of services, a clinic, rehabilitation agency, or by a public health agency, or by others. * * *" Thus, by definition, speech-language pathology services are a subset of outpatient physical therapy services under the Medicare statute. We believe that the parenthetical language under the BBA 1997 simply confirms our interpretation.

E. Occupational Therapy Services

In the January 1998 proposed regulations text, we proposed to include those OT services described in section 1861(g) of the Act and the CORF regulations in Sec. 410.100(c). We proposed that occupational therapy services would also include any other services with the characteristics described in Sec. 410.100(c) that are covered under Medicare Part A or Part B, regardless of who furnishes them, the location in which they are furnished, or how they are billed. In proposed Sec. 411.351, OT services included the following:

Teaching of compensatory techniques to permit an individual with a physical impairment or limitation to engage in daily activities.

Evaluation of an individual's level of independent functioning.

Selection and teaching of task-oriented therapeutic activities to restore sensory-integrative function.

Assessment of an individual's vocational potential, except when the assessment is related solely to vocational rehabilitation.

As discussed in the preceding section, we are revising our proposed definition by providing a list of CPT and HCPCS codes that collectively are the PT/OT/speech therapy DHS. Also, as described above, we are excluding from the definition of DHS any designated health service that is paid for as part of a "bundled" payment (for example, services covered by the SNF Part A rate or the ASC rate), unless the statute otherwise provides that a "bundled" set of services is itself a designated health service (for example, home health services and inpatient and outpatient hospital services).

Comment: A major OT association asserted that the definition of OT is too narrow because it does not adequately capture the scope of the OT benefit. For example, OT is furnished to patients with cognitive impairments as well as to patients with physical impairments and limitations. As another example, OT may also be furnished in partial hospitalization programs for patients with a psychiatric illness. The commenter believes that it is important for the definition in Sec. 411.351 to be as complete and accurate as possible to assure appropriate compliance with the law, and that Sec. 410.100(c) is too narrow to be used as the complete definition of OT services for purposes of these regulations. The commenter suggested that we broaden the definition by adding to it the coverage guidelines stated in section 3101.9, "Occupational Therapy Furnished by the Hospital or by Others under Arrangements with the Hospital and under its Supervision," of the Medicare Intermediary Manual (HCFA Pub. 13–3), Part 3 — Claims Process, and section 2217, "Covered Occupational Therapy," of the Medicare Carriers Manual (HCFA Pub. 14–3), Part 3 — Claims Process. The commenter recommended that we use the following definition for OT in Sec. 411.351:

Occupational therapy services means those services described at section 1861(g) of the Act, Sec. 410.100(c) of this chapter, and in the occupational therapy coverage guidelines contained in section 3101.9 of the Medicare Intermediary Manual and section 2217 of the Medicare Carriers Manual. Occupational therapy services also include any other services with the characteristics described in Sec. 410.100(c) and the occupational therapy coverage guidelines that are covered under Medicare Part A or B, regardless of who furnishes them, the location in which they are furnished, or how they are billed.

Response: We agree with the commenter that the proposed definition does not clearly recognize that OT is furnished to patients with cognitive impairments. As we have stated previously in this preamble, we did not intend to change what is commonly regarded as OT. We referred to the existing definition in Sec. 410.100(c) so that we would not be proposing any change. However, as the commenter pointed out, the existing definition at Sec. 410.100(c) is not complete. Therefore, we are expanding the proposed definition by including codes for the "teaching of compensatory techniques to permit an individual with a physical or cognitive impairment or limitation to engage in daily activities."

However, the commenter is correct that a partial hospitalization program may provide OT services. This is in accordance with section 1861(ff) of the Act, which defines "partial hospitalization services" and specifically includes OT as a partial hospitalization service. However, with respect to partial hospitalization, we have determined that services provided as part of a group of services paid under a bundled rate are not DHS. Partial hospitalization services are paid under a bundled rate. Therefore, partial hospitalization services (including OT services provided as part of the partial hospitalization benefit) furnished by a community mental health center are not DHS. However, partial hospitalization services furnished by a hospital are outpatient hospital services, which is a category of DHS.

In order to eliminate any confusion the January 1998 proposed regulations may have caused and to make Phase I of this rulemaking clear, we are defining OT by a list of specific HCPCS/CPT codes. In light of the changes we have made in Phase I of this rulemaking, it is not necessary for us to include the references to the intermediary and carrier manuals that the commenter suggested.

Occupational therapy services may be furnished by an occupational therapist, an occupational therapy aide who is supervised by an occupational therapist, or by a physician. Section 1861(r) of the Act allows a physician to furnish any medical service that his or her State allows the physician to furnish.

F. Radiology and Certain Other Imaging Services

In the January 1998 proposed rule, we combined the DHS in section 1877(h)(6)(D) of the Act — "radiology services, including magnetic resonance imaging, computerized axial tomography, and ultrasound services"—and 1877(h)(6)(E) of the Act—"radiation therapy services and supplies" into the following definition:

Radiology services and radiation therapy and supplies means any diagnostic test or therapeutic procedure using X-rays, ultrasound or other imaging services, computerized axial tomography, magnetic resonance imaging, radiation, or nuclear medicine, and diagnostic mammography services, as covered under section 1861(s)(3) and (4) of the Act and Secs. 410.32(a), 410.34, and 410.35 of this chapter, including the professional component of these services, but excluding any invasive radiology procedure in which the imaging modality is used to guide a needle, probe, or a catheter accurately.

Commenters found the proposed definition to be confusing in two main respects:

The definition both combined two different categories of radiology-related services (that is, radiology and radiation therapy and supplies) and included other services not commonly considered to be radiology-related (ultrasound and nuclear medicine). Many commenters thought that all services not strictly considered radiology should be excluded.

At different places in the January 1998 proposed regulation preamble, we stated that we were excluding DHS that were peripheral, incidental, or secondary to a nondesignated health service. In the proposed definition, however, we only excluded imaging modalities used to "guide a needle, probe, or catheter." Many commenters thought the scope of excluded radiology and other imaging services should be broader than just guidance, while others thought the distinction between primary and secondary services would be difficult to apply in practice.

Based on the comments, we have redefined this category of DHS in a manner that should provide greater clarity. First, we have segregated radiation therapy and supplies from radiology and other imaging services and returned them to a separate category, as in the statute. (We discuss comments relating to radiation therapy services in section VIII.G of this preamble). Second, we are excluding nuclear medicine since those services are not commonly considered to be radiology. Third, for purposes of these regulations we have renamed the category of services covered by section 1877(h)(6)(D) of the Act "Radiology and Certain Other Imaging Services" to make clear the Congress's intent to include in subsection (D) some imaging services other than radiology. Fourth, consistent with the approach we are following with several other of the DHS categories, we are defining the entire scope of covered services under section 1877(h)(6)(D) of the Act by using lists of CPT and HCPCS codes, which lists control in all circumstances. The lists include those services typically considered as radiology or ultrasound services, or as constituting an MRI or a computerized axial tomography (CAT) scan. Fifth, we have excluded certain covered preventive screening procedures, such as screening mammography, that are subject to HCFA-imposed frequency limits that mitigate the potential for abuse. In these circumstances, we believe the Congress did not intend the physician self-referral law to interfere with a physician's or entity's attempts to provide these preventive procedures to Medicare patients.

Sixth, based on the comments we received, we concluded that the terms "invasive" radiology and radiology "incidental" or "secondary" to a non-DHS procedure used in our proposed definition of "radiology services" created confusion and uncertainty. We agree with commenters that "invasive" radiology includes more than just those procedures used to "guide a needle, probe or catheter." Consequently, we are revising our definition of radiology and certain other imaging services to exclude from the definitional list of codes x-ray, fluoroscopy, and ultrasound services that are themselves invasive procedures that require the insertion of a needle, catheter, tube, or probe. Thus, cardiac catheterizations and endoscopies will not fall within the scope of "radiology services" for purposes of section 1877 of the Act. All MRIs or CAT scans, however, are within the scope of DHS because excluding some on the basis that they are "invasive" tests would have the effect of excluding all MRIs and CAT scans that use contrast injection. The use of contrast is not mandatory for the performance of a scan, as it is for the performance of a barium enema, excretory urogram, or traditional vascular angiography. Thus, an exclusion from the DHS definition of contrast for MRIs and CAT scans could have the effect of encouraging the use of contrast when it is not necessary.

In addition, we have concluded that radiology procedures that are integral to the performance of, and performed during, a nonradiology medical procedure are not within the scope of DHS. The list of codes that defines the scope of "radiology and certain other imaging services" will make this distinction clear. Examples of these integral services include, but are not limited to, imaging guidance procedures and radiology procedures used to determine, during surgery, whether surgery is being conducted successfully. In the CPT, these radiology procedures are identified as cross-references to the principle procedures with which they are associated. A radiology procedure, such as a CAT scan or a chest x-ray, performed before or after another procedure, such as a lung cancer resection, is considered to be a diagnostic radiology procedure that is not integral to the principle procedure (that is, the lung cancer resection). While these radiology procedures are essential to the performance of the principle procedure, physicians have discretion in choosing which entity provides the radiology service independent of the entity providing the principle surgical service. These nonconcurrent services are DHS.

Regardless of our definition of "radiology and certain other imaging services," some services that are not within the scope of that definition may still be DHS if they are inpatient or outpatient hospital services, a separate category of DHS under section 1877(h)(6)(K) of the Act. These services would be subject to the physician referral rule if the referring physician has a financial relationship with the hospital. We anticipate most of these financial arrangements will meet an exception under section 1877 of the Act (for example, the exception for hospital ownership or either the employment or personal service arrangements exception).

We address comments related to the definition of services covered by section 1877(h)(6)(D) of the Act below. To the extent some commenters raised issues such as the general effects of section 1877 of the Act on physicians' practices or on medicine in general, those issues are addressed elsewhere in the preamble, where relevant.

Comment: Several commenters asserted that the proposed definition of "radiology services" that included all sound-based or imaging-based technologies is contrary to congressional intent. The commenters argued that the Congress intended to limit the definition by removing original language that included the phrase "other diagnostic services" along with radiology services.

Response: The phrase "radiology, or other diagnostic services" was added in section 1877(h)(6)(D) of the Act by OBRA 1993 as one of the categories of DHS the Congress chose to cover in addition to clinical laboratory services. This one set of services appeared to include the extremely broad category of "other diagnostic services," in addition to radiology services. The Congress narrowed this category in section 152 of the Social Security Act Amendments of 1994 (SSA 1994), Public Law 103–432, enacted on October 31, 1994, perhaps because it realized the huge scope of "diagnostic services." The amendments revised section 1877(h)(6)(D) of the Act, effective January 1, 1995, by replacing the category with "radiology services, including magnetic resonance imaging, computerized axial tomography, and ultrasound services." While all of these services might not be subsumed in the category "radiology services," the Congress clearly intended to include them as DHS. We have renamed the category "radiology and certain other imaging services" to reflect the Congress's intent.

Comment: One commenter questioned why cardiac, vascular, and obstetric ultrasound procedures could not be referred. The commenter stated that in most institutions these procedures are not considered radiology procedures since radiologists may never supervise or interpret them. Another commenter argued that although echocardiography is a type of ultrasound procedure, it should not be considered a radiology service because echocardiography is a service developed and performed primarily by cardiologists, billed under cardiology CPT codes, and furnished to cardiac patients. As a result, the commenter argued that it is inaccurate and inappropriate to include echocardiography within the definition of radiology services.

Response: Cardiac, vascular, and obstetric ultrasound procedures are subject to the physician self-referral provisions because section 1877(h)(6)(D) of the Act specifically includes ultrasound as a designated health service, not because they are ordinarily considered to be "radiology services." Simply stated, the term "radiology services" as applied to the services described by section 1877(h)(6)(D) of the Act is a misnomer. Section 1877(h)(6)(D) of the Act includes any services that are traditionally regarded as "radiology" services, as well as MRIs, CAT scans, and ultrasound services. Cardiac echography and vascular echography are clearly ultrasound services. Nothing in the regulation would prohibit a vascular surgeon, neurologist, or other specialist from ordering a particular service from an entity with which he or she has no prohibited financial relationship.

Comment: Several commenters were opposed to our proposal to exclude as "invasive" radiology only those invasive procedures used to guide a needle, probe, or catheter accurately. Two of the commenters were concerned that invasive radiology procedures, which use an imaging modality not only to guide a needle, probe or catheter, but also to record an accurate picture of the areas of the body being probed or catheterized, would be included in the definition of radiology. (An example of this would be an ultrasound device placed at the end of a catheter or endoscope.)

Response: We agree and have not included x-ray, fluoroscopy, and ultrasound services that require the insertion of a needle, catheter, tube, or probe on the list of HCPCS/CPT codes that defines the full scope of radiology and other imaging services for purposes of section 1877 of the Act. Some of these services may still be DHS when they fall within the category of inpatient and outpatient hospital services.

Comment: Several commenters objected to our proposal to exclude radiology services that were "merely incidental or secondary" to another procedure that the physician has ordered. (See our January 1998 proposed rule, 63 FR 1676.) Some commenters noted that it is generally not possible to establish, based on the CPT code used, whether or not the primary purpose of the procedure was the interventional procedure itself (with the imaging being an adjunct procedure) or whether the primary purpose was to take a picture with an imaging modality. Because it is extremely difficult and impractical in the commenters' view to separate the radiology component from the underlying procedure, the commenters recommended that we exclude all invasive radiology services, encompassing those procedures that may include an adjunct radiology procedure performed at the same time as the interventional procedure. Other commenters thought that the definition of radiology services should also exclude imaging services when they are performed before and/or after a surgical procedure. For example, a commenter requested that we add language to the proposed definition of radiology to exclude any radiology procedure in which the imaging modality is used to plan the invasive procedure. The commenter noted that for many invasive procedures, an ultrasound before the actual procedure might be routinely necessary in order to plan the manner in which the needle, catheter, or probe would be guided during the actual invasive procedure. In these circumstances, the patient already has received the diagnosis that the invasive procedure is necessary. The commenter believes that we should maintain the view that a physician would not refer a patient for these procedures in order to profit from unnecessary radiology services. Another commenter stated that under our proposed interpretation of invasive procedures, an echocardiogram that showed a need for bypass surgery would be a designated health service, while one that ruled out surgery would not, since there would be no surgical procedure to which the imaging service would be "incidental." Finally, a neurologist commented that there are a number of radiology procedures performed by neurologists that are incidental to other procedures, particularly certain surgical services. One of the examples given by the commenter was carotid duplex or transcranial Doppler ultrasound, which are tests performed after carotid endarterectomy to look for clots. The commenter believes these radiology services should be excluded.

Response: We agree with the commenter that the "incidental/secondary" test in the January 1998 proposed rule has led to some confusion and uncertainty and have abandoned it in Phase I of this rulemaking. We believe the list of codes set forth in Phase I of this rulemaking (and annually thereafter in the physician fee schedule rule) will create a "bright line" test that will ease compliance. In selecting the codes for radiology and ultrasound, we are not including any codes for radiology or ultrasound procedures that have an invasive component; that is, that include the insertion of a needle, catheter, tube, or probe through the skin or into a body orifice. ("Invasive" would encompass radiology services involving contrast that must be injected, but not contrast materials that are ingested by the patients themselves.) In addition, we are not including radiology and ultrasound procedures that are integral to and performed during the time a nonradiology procedure is being performed, such as ultrasound used to provide guidance for biopsies and major surgical procedures or used to determine, during surgery, whether surgery is being conducted successfully. Phase I of this rulemaking requires that to be considered integral to a nonradiology procedure (and therefore not a radiology or other imaging service for purposes of section 1877(h)(6)(D) of the Act), the imaging procedure must be performed during the nonradiology procedure. A radiology or ultrasound procedure performed before or after another procedure (for example, a scan or a chest x-ray before a lung cancer resection, an echocardiogram before a bypass, or a duplex carotid ultrasound before or after surgery) is a diagnostic radiology procedure that is not integral to another procedure and therefore is a radiology or other imaging service under section 1877(h)(6)(D) of the Act. In the case of services performed before or after a procedure, referring physicians have discretion in choosing the entity that provides the radiology service independent of the entity providing the surgical service. Depending on the facts, referrals for these services to entities with which the referring physician has a financial relationship may be protected under the various exceptions to the statute.

In all cases, the definitional list of codes controls in determining whether a service falls within the scope of "radiology or certain other imaging services" for purposes of section 1877 of the Act.

Comment: Two commenters were opposed to our proposal to exclude "invasive" or "interventional" radiology procedures from the definition of radiology services. The commenters believe that these procedures should be included as DHS in order to safeguard against overutilization and ensure that appropriately trained physicians perform the services. One commenter argued that as a clinical matter, "invasive" or "interventional" radiology services rarely are performed in an office setting. Typically, interventional radiologists perform such procedures as angiography or angioplasty in a hospital because they involve significant and delicate work on a patient's cardiovascular system. Patients who undergo invasive procedures must then be monitored for a period of time in an appropriate medical setting. Consequently, that commenter, as well as another, objected to our statement in the preamble to the January 1998 proposed rule (63 FR 1676) that invasive procedures ordinarily are "merely incidental or secondary to another procedure that the physician has ordered." One of the commenters stated that the radiology services are neither incidental nor secondary, but a vital and integral part of the invasive procedure performed. The procedures are as much radiological as they are any other portion. One commenter stated that if invasive procedures occur in an office, they should be performed by a radiologist. The commenter believes that excluding invasive or interventional radiology procedures could result in certain referral arrangements by physicians that might pose some risk of patient or program abuse. One of the commenters noted that when interventional radiologists perform invasive radiology procedures, there is no risk of program or patient abuse. This is because interventional radiologists do not typically make referrals; they merely perform the invasive radiology procedures and return the patient to the care of the referring physician. The commenter believes, however, that physicians other than interventional radiologists may have an incentive to self-refer.

Response: We agree with the commenter that we were incorrect to characterize interventional radiology as "secondary" to many procedures, when it can in fact be a vital and integral part of the invasive procedure being performed. It is not the purpose of the physician self-referral law to discourage any physicians from furnishing their own services, such as interventional radiology, within their own practices, provided the physicians are functioning within the scope of their license to practice.

Comment: Many commenters asserted that all or particular invasive cardiology services should be excluded from the definition because they are not subject to program or patient abuse. Another commenter asked that we be consistent with regard to all forms of cardiac catheterizations and endoscopy procedures. The commenter stated that providers want to be able to perform all endoscopy services or cardiac catheterization services in the same setting and not have to limit their services.

Response: Cardiac catheterizations and endoscopy procedures are not included on the CPT code list that defines the scope of "radiology and certain other imaging services," because they do not involve imaging services that are covered under any of the categories in section 1877(h)(6)(D) of the Act. These services may still constitute DHS as inpatient or outpatient hospital services.

Comment: Two commenters noted that in the preamble to the January 1998 proposed rule (63 FR 1676), we stated that percutaneous transluminal angioplasty was an example of an invasive radiology procedure that we would exclude from the definition of radiology. The commenters stated that this procedure is not commonly considered to involve "invasive radiology."

Response: The commenters are correct in stating that percutaneous transluminal angioplasty is not fundamentally radiological in nature; it is predominantly a therapeutic intervention. Our wording in the examples for invasive radiology may have been confusing. We intended to convey that the imaging procedures associated with percutaneous transluminal angioplasty would be considered integral to the performance of the angioplasty. However, by using specific CPT codes to define the scope of services covered by section 1877(h)(6)(D) of the Act, we have now narrowed the definition of radiology services so that it does not include radiology that is integral to interventional procedures, such as angioplasty.

Comment: One commenter supported our proposal to exclude screening mammography from the definition of DHS. The commenter believes that we should expand the exclusion to cover all DHS for which we have specified coverage or frequency limits. The commenter stated that screening tests by definition are not subject to overutilization.

Response: We agree with this commenter and have modified Phase I of this rulemaking to exclude from the reach of section 1877 of the Act certain legislatively mandated preventive screening and immunization services that are subject to HCFA-imposed frequency limits and are paid based on a fee schedule. The preventive services to which this exception applies are identified in Appendix A. We will add codes for new preventive screening tests and immunizations, as appropriate, through the annual updating of the attachment to this final rule.

Comment: One commenter recommended that all mammography be excluded from the definition of "radiology services." The commenter argued that generally diagnostic mammography procedures are performed only when a woman has clinical indications for a diagnostic mammogram. Thus, any risk of program or patient abuse is significantly reduced, if not eliminated. The commenter also mentioned that the quality-centered requirements of the Mammography Quality Standards Act of 1992 minimize the risk of potential overutilization of mammography services. Another commenter recommended the exclusion of "diagnostic" mammography services because he stated that it is necessary to perform the mammography on the same equipment for purposes of comparing the initial screening with the second diagnostic mammography. To prohibit patients from using the same facility adds an unnecessary element of potential error to the equation.

Response: Diagnostic mammography is clearly a radiological service under section 1877(h)(6)(D) of the Act, and it could be subject to abuse. It is our understanding that most women receive mammography from a radiologist who is requesting diagnostic radiology services. These physicians have not made a referral under section 1877(h)(5)(C) of the Act if they request diagnostic mammography as the result of a consultation requested by another physician. We are regarding this exception as applying to diagnostic mammography that results when a radiologist has first performed a screening mammography as the result of a consultation, and then recommends follow-up diagnostic mammography, or begins his or her consultation with diagnostic mammography. (The physician who initiated the consultation with the radiologist has made a referral that could fall within the scope of the physician self-referral law if he or she has a financial relationship with the radiology facility.)

Comment: A commenter asked if stress tests are DHS. The commenter noted that some stress tests use nuclear medicine procedures.

Response: Stress tests are generally considered to be a physician service that does not involve radiology, and stress tests are not specifically listed in the law as DHS. Some stress tests use nuclear medicine procedures to create an image of the heart. Because these services are not included on the definitional CPT code list for radiology or other imaging services, they are not DHS.

Comment: One commenter stated that unless changed or clarified, the proposed regulations could inhibit the development and application of telemedicine technology to populations covered by the physician referral rules. Of specific concern was the area of ultrasound and a "unified" payment (that is, a combined payment for the technical and professional components of the service). The commenter asserted that Medicare and many State Medicaid programs provide a unified payment for ultrasound. The commenter described the problems of a unified payment with an example of a community physician performing the technical component of an ultrasound service and a distant tertiary hospital's physician performing the professional component. If the tertiary provider billed for the ultrasound service under a "unified" (that is, global) fee-for-service payment to cover the professional component of the ultrasound service, the tertiary facility logically should determine a payment for the technical component to pay the community physician who provides that service. However, since the community physician would be referring to the tertiary facility for the ultrasound study, such a payment could violate the physician referral regulations (that is, it would not fall within an exception).

At the time of the comment period for the January 1998 proposed rule, the commenter was aware that we were considering the publication of a separate proposed rule that would specify an appropriate "split" of global payments in the area of telemedicine; that is, it would specify separate payment amounts for the technical and professional components of services. The commenter suggested that if we did issue those regulations, we should also recognize in the physician referral rules that payment by the tertiary provider to the referring community physician for providing the technical component of an ultrasound service performed via telemedicine should be exempted if it is under a HCFA-designated, or insurer-designated, allocation between the two aspects of an otherwise "global" payment.

Response: We believe that Phase I of this rulemaking addresses this issue satisfactorily. The basic principle of Phase I of this rulemaking is that any payment from an entity furnishing a designated health service to a referring physician must be at fair market value, not taking into account the volume or value of any referrals or other business generated by the referring physician (when this latter language is included in an exception). We are revising Phase I of this rulemaking to make clear that "per service" payments are allowed, even with respect to DHS ordered by the physician, provided the payment meets the fair market value standard. In the situation described by the commenter, the split is determined by the Medicare program based on its independent view of the value of the services provided. Of course, any split between a referring physician and another provider may also raise concerns under the Federal anti-kickback statute.

With respect to Medicare reimbursement for telehealth services, we published a proposed rule on June 22, 1998 (63 FR 33882) and final rule on November 2, 1998 (63 FR 58814) to implement section 4206 of the BBA 1997. Specifically, the November 1998 final rule permitted payment for professional consultations via interactive telecommunication systems in rural HPSAs and established separate payment amounts for the referring and consulting practitioners of a teleconsultation in a rural HPSA. As we noted in the preamble (63 FR 58883) to that November 1998 final rule, the rule specifies that the consulting practitioner must submit the claim for the consultation service and must share 25 percent of the total payment with the referring practitioner.

We clarified in the November 1998 telehealth final rule that these provisions only apply to teleconsultation services. Under Medicare, a teleconsultation is a consultation service delivered via telemedicine. These services are represented by CPT codes 99241 through 99275. Diagnostic ultrasound (CPT code 76506) on the other hand, is a radiology service and would not fall within the purview of a teleconsultation under Medicare. Therefore, the payment methodology requiring the sharing of payment between the consulting and referring practitioners would not apply to diagnostic ultrasound services. In the case of diagnostic ultrasound, the physician providing the interpretation of the image typically would bill for the interpretation, while the technical component (that is, conducting the test) is billed by the practitioner or facility that captured the ultrasound image. Medicare has no national rule stating that the professional and technical components of a service, including ultrasound services, must be billed in a "global" manner. In fact, in the annual update to the physician fee schedule, separate codes for the professional component as well as the technical component of a service are listed, including the diagnostic ultrasound codes. Of course, in those cases in which there is no technical component, one code is used for Medicare payment and billing.

G. Radiation Therapy

Section 1877(h)(6)(E) of the Act includes radiation therapy services and supplies. In the January 1998 proposed rule, we combined radiation therapy with radiology in a single definition.

Because commenters found the combined definition to be confusing, we are amending the January 1998 proposed regulation so that radiology services and radiation therapy services are now separate categories (as in section 1877 of the Act itself). This change makes it clear that the two categories are actually very separate kinds of services. We are basing our definition of radiation therapy services and supplies on section 1861(s)(4) of the Act. This provision includes, as "medical and other health services" covered by Medicare, "x-ray, radium, and radioactive isotope therapy, including materials and services of technicians." However, we want to clarify that, for physician referral purposes, the list of codes that defines "radiation therapy services and supplies" in Phase I of this rulemaking does not include nuclear medicine services. While nuclear medicine involves the injection of radioactive isotopes directly into a patient's bloodstream, these services are not generally regarded as radiation therapy, they involve different equipment and procedures, and physicians who provide nuclear medicine have a separate certification. We have included in the attachment to this final rule a list of codes that will define radiation therapy services and supplies. This list will be updated and reprinted in full annually as part of the physician fee schedule.

Comment: A commenter noted that because the January 1998 proposed regulations bundle radiology services and radiation therapy and supplies into a single category of DHS, the professional component of radiation therapy services has also been included within the definition of DHS. The commenter stated that some radiation oncologists would effectively be precluded from being paid on a productivity basis for their services, given that virtually all of the professional services that some physicians perform are radiation therapy services for Medicare patients. The commenter believes that the Congress did not intend this result.

Response: The law excludes from the definition of a "referral" any request by a radiation oncologist for radiation therapy if these services are furnished by (or under the supervision of) the radiation oncologist pursuant to a consultation requested by another physician. In addition, we are amending the definition of a "referral" to exclude any professional components personally performed by referring physicians themselves. Together, these provisions should largely address the commenter's concerns.

Comment: Several commenters recommended that we exclude prostate brachytherapy from the definition of radiation therapy. Prostate brachytherapy is the placement of radioactive sources into the prostate, through ultrasound guidance, for the purpose of treating prostate cancer. The commenters argued that this procedure should be excluded because it is performed once and is only performed on persons with a biopsy-proven diagnosis of prostate cancer. They advocated the use of physician ownership of brachytherapy facilities and equipment because it means that the urologists and radiation oncologists involved are actually performing the procedure themselves in a facility contracting with those physicians. The design of this model includes the supervision of every case by an experienced brachytherapist present in the operating room. According to the commenter, physician ownership of the equipment also ensures quality of physician education and of surgical technique.

The commenters asserted that we should allow multiple physicians to own brachytherapy equipment because centralized planning for radiation physics results in all cases being planned in a controlled and uniform fashion. Uniformity eliminates many empirical physician decisions that in the past led to dosimetry errors. In addition, having two or more physicians owning the equipment encourages reporting of outcome data collection to a central agency, resulting in a continuous and rapid review of treatment results and complications. Commenters pointed out that experts have published restrictive dose guidelines for the various stages of prostate cancer treated with brachytherapy, so there is no risk of overutilization. Also, brachytherapy is less expensive and has a lower complication rate than the other forms of treatment (radical prostatectomy or external beam radiation therapy).

The commenters believe that because of all of these factors the procedure has little potential for program or patient abuse and should be exempt from the physician self-referral prohibition.

Response: We are aware of no logical or empirical evidence that physician ownership improves quality of services or physicians' skills. On the other hand, brachytherapy is one of several therapy options for certain prostate conditions. We believe that ownership of a brachytherapy center by urologists could well influence their recommended therapy and, therefore, affect utilization. In short, the relationship is exactly the type of financial relationship section 1877 of the Act is intended to address. The law excludes from the definition of a "referral" any request by a radiation oncologist for radiation therapy if these services are furnished by (or under the supervision of) the radiation oncologist pursuant to a consultation requested by another physician. In addition, we have amended the definition of a "referral" to exclude any professional components performed by referring physicians themselves.

H. Durable Medical Equipment (DME)

In Sec. 411.351 of the January 1998 proposed rule, we defined DME as having the meaning given in section 1861(n) of the Act and Sec. 414.202 (Definitions). In the preamble to the January 1998 proposed rule (63 FR 1677 through 1678), we offered explanations of the terms and a list of the general DME categories. However, we stated in the preamble (63 FR 1677) that because the number of items considered to be DME was so extensive, we could not in the proposed rule identify all of them. Commenters were concerned about our failure to articulate a "bright-line" definition of DME. The commenters stated that if we could not do that, physicians would have to assume that the dispensing of all DME falls under the referral prohibition.

The most frequent complaint was the difficulty the commenters had in determining whether a given item was DME or a prosthetic, prosthetic device or orthotic. (The distinction is significant since under section 1877(b)(2) of the Act prosthetics, prosthetic devices, and orthotics may be provided to a patient by a physician under the in-office ancillary services exception, while DME (other than infusion pumps) cannot.) The easiest way to determine the proper classification of an item is to consult the Durable Medical Equipment, Prosthetics/Orthotics, and Supplies (DMEPOS) fee schedule, which is updated quarterly and available on the internet under HCFA's public use files (www.hcfa.gov/stats/pufiles.htm). Under the DMEPOS fee schedule, items are identified by their HCPCS code and also include a category designation that identifies whether the item is DME, prosthetics, orthotics, or prosthetic devices. DME items include the following categories:

CR, capped rental DME.

FS, DME requiring frequent and substantial servicing.

IN, inexpensive or routinely purchased DME.

OX, oxygen and oxygen equipment.

SU, DME supplies.

TE, transcutaneous electrical (or electronic) nerve stimulator.

Additionally, DME includes the HCPCS code E1399. This code covers a number of miscellaneous DME items, but does not appear on HCFA's national fee schedule. Each DMERC (regional DME carrier) is responsible for creating a fee schedule for individual items that are not included on HCFA's fee schedule.

We note that Phase I of this rulemaking does not change existing definitions for DME, prosthetics, prosthetic devices, or orthotics. Thus, the existing classification of an item (that is, its classification as either DME, prosthetic, prosthetic device, or orthotic) will remain the same.

In sum, if, after reviewing the definitions and accompanying explanations that we provided in the January 1998 proposed rule, as well as the DMEPOS fee schedule and the HCPCS codes covering miscellaneous items, physicians and their staffs still have questions about whether a specific item is considered to be DME, we would suggest that they contact their local carrier or DMERC for clarification.

Comment: One commenter asked for clarification on whether prosthetic and orthotic devices that seem to meet the criteria for DME are considered DME supplies and whether they could be provided under the in-office ancillary services exception. The commenter expressed some confusion regarding whether crutches are DME or a prosthetic or orthotic device.

Response: The categories of prosthetics, orthotics, prosthetic devices or DME are mutually exclusive; no item can fall into more than one of these categories. If individuals are concerned about a particular type of equipment or a supply, we would suggest that they review the HCPCS codes or DMEPOS fee schedule or contact their local carrier or DMERC for clarification. Again, we note that DMERCs process more than DME claims. They also are responsible for claims for other types of devices and supplies. Crutches are DME.

Comment: A commenter recommended that we exempt crutches from the definition of DME. The commenter suggested that crutches are provided as peripheral parts of a major service (that is, a diagnosis of a broken leg) and that it is unlikely a physician would over-prescribe crutches for a diagnosis of a broken leg just so that the physician can bill for the crutches. The commenter believes that having the physician provide the crutches and instruct the patient on how to use them helps to prevent further damage to the patient and is essential to good patient care.

Response: We believe that crutches are clearly DME and therefore DHS under section 1877(h)(6)(F) of the Act. As we stated in the January 1998 proposed rule, although we cannot justify excluding crutches as a designated health service, we recognize that including crutches could greatly inconvenience patients if physicians were barred from providing them to patients who need them to ambulate following treatment for an injury or an incapacitating procedure. For this reason, we proposed expanding the in-office ancillary services exception to cover crutches when furnished in a manner that meets the in-office ancillary services exception requirements and in which the physician realizes no direct or indirect profit from furnishing the crutches. We have adopted the proposal in an expanded and modified form — without the proposed profit restriction — as described in section VI.B.1 of this preamble.

Comment: Several commenters opposed the inclusion of DME as a designated health service and argued that the inclusion of DME will result in additional delays in treatment and barriers to access for the nation's poor and elderly populations. Two of the commenters urged us to support a legislative change to remove DME from the DHS list, while others urged us to revise the January 1998 proposed rule to remove DME entirely as a designated health service. Those commenters argued that when DME is furnished as an in-office service, it has not been associated with program abuse and offers little or no opportunity for overutilization. One of the commenters contended that an unintended effect of the inclusion of DME on the DHS list would be underutilization, because physicians would be prohibited from furnishing DME in their offices.

Response: We believe that we cannot create a separate exception for DME because we cannot guarantee that such an exception would always be free from program or patient abuse. The Congress explicitly included DME as a designated health service in section 1877(h)(6)(F) of the Act; we have no authority to vitiate that judgment. We note that physicians would only be prohibited from furnishing DME services when they have an unexcepted financial relationship with the DME supplier. Moreover, although we are not removing DME from the list of DHS, we are substantially revising the manner in which the in-office ancillary services exception applies to DME. These changes will expand the provision of DME under the in-office ancillary services exception as detailed in section VI.B.1 of this preamble.

I. Parenteral and Enteral Nutrients, Equipment and Supplies

Section 1877(h)(6)(G) of the Act includes as DHS the category of parenteral and enteral nutrients, equipment, and supplies (PEN). Enteral and parenteral therapy as a Medicare Part B benefit is provided under the prosthetic device benefit provision in section 1861(s)(8) of the Act. The regulations cover prosthetic devices in Sec. 410.36 (Medical suppliers, appliances, and devices: Scope), paragraph (a)(2). Details for enteral and parenteral therapy are set forth in section 65–10, "Enteral and Parenteral Nutritional Therapy Covered as Prosthetic Device," of the Medicare Coverage Issues Manual (HCFA Pub. 6). When the coverage requirements for enteral or parenteral nutritional therapy are met, Medicare also covers related supplies, equipment, and nutrients.

We proposed in Sec. 411.351 of the January 1998 rule to define "enteral nutrients, equipment, and supplies" as items and supplies needed to provide enteral nutrition to a patient with a functioning gastrointestinal tract who, due to pathology to or nonfunction of the structures that normally permit food to reach the digestive tract, cannot maintain weight and strength commensurate with his or her general condition. (See section 65–10, "Enteral and Parenteral Nutritional Therapy Covered as Prosthetic Device," of the Medicare Coverage Issues Manual (HCFA Pub. 6) for additional information.)

We proposed in Sec. 411.351 to define "parenteral nutrients, equipment, and supplies" as items and supplies needed to provide nutriment to a patient with permanent, severe pathology of the alimentary tract that does not allow absorption of sufficient nutrients to maintain strength commensurate with the patient's general condition, as described in section 65–10, "Enteral and Parenteral Nutritional Therapy Covered as Prosthetic Device," of the Medicare Coverage Issues Manual (HCFA Pub. 6).

We are clarifying in Phase I of this rulemaking that this category includes all HCPCS level 2 codes for these services. We believe this list will address any uncertainties that physicians and providers might have about what constitutes PEN, and is consistent with our definition in the proposed rule.

We also pointed out in the preamble to the January 1998 proposed rule that, like DME, section 1877(b)(2) of the Act specifically excludes PEN as services that can qualify for the in-office ancillary services exception.

Comment: A physician representing himself and an infusion therapy association asserted that physicians should be allowed to prescribe, provide, and be reimbursed for parenteral nutrition for their own patients as an extension of their practices. The commenter asserted that there has been no evidence of abuse, while there have been major problems with fraud and abuse and excessive profits by nonphysician home infusion providers, which function essentially without physician control and minimal input from physicians. The commenter believes that because patients with increasingly complex medical problems are sent home earlier from the hospital, the role of the physician office-based model is increasingly important. The January 1998 proposed referral regulations, the payment schedule for medications, and the restriction on physician reimbursement for ambulatory infusion pumps all discourage a physician's involvement in these services.

Response: Section 1877 of the Act does not prohibit physicians from prescribing enteral and parenteral nutrition for their own patients; nor does it prohibit infusion companies from contracting with expert or knowledgeable physicians for consulting services provided the remuneration is fair market value and does not take into account referrals or other business between the parties. Section 1877 of the Act does, however, prohibit a physician from furnishing enteral and parenteral nutrition in his or her own office and billing for it unless the physician's arrangement qualifies for an exception, such as the rural provider exception in section 1877(d)(2) of the Act. The Congress specifically excluded the provision of enteral and parenteral nutrition and durable medical equipment (DME, other than infusion pumps) from the in-office ancillary services exception in section 1877(b)(2)of the Act.

We have the authority to create additional exceptions to the referral prohibition for financial relationships under section 1877(b)(4) of the Act, but only if we determine that there is no risk of program or patient abuse. However, we believe that physicians could potentially over-prescribe parenteral nutrition if they have the financial incentive to do so.

We only cover parenteral nutrition when there is a permanent need (except when covered under the home health benefit). (See the Medicare Coverage Issues Manual (HCFA Pub. 6), section 65–10, “Enteral and Parenteral Nutritional Therapy Covered as Prosthetic Device,” for additional information. Because coverage of nutritional therapy as a Part B benefit is provided under the prosthetic device benefit provision, the patient must have a permanently inoperative internal body organ or function.) We see no reason why a patient should have to go to a physician's office regularly to receive parenteral nutrition. Medicare already covers parenteral nutrition delivered in the home through the home health benefit or the prosthetic device benefit. Because enteral nutrition is widely available through grocery stores, drug stores, and other retail outlets, we see no reason why a patient must purchase enteral nutrition from a physician. A patient can purchase certain more specialized types of enteral nutrition that are not widely available from a DME supplier.

If a patient is to receive nutrition via an infusion pump, the in-office ancillary services exception cannot be used for the furnishing of the pump, since this exception only allows physicians' offices to furnish infusion pumps that are DME. See section VI.B.1 of this preamble for more details about infusion pumps. (To furnish an infusion pump that is DME for use in the home, a physician would have to meet all of the supplier requirements in Sec. 424.57.)

As for the commenter's concerns about the payment schedule for medications, that issue is not addressed by the physician referral regulation.

J. Prosthetics, Orthotics, and Prosthetic Devices and Supplies

Prosthetics, orthotics, and prosthetic devices and supplies are included as DHS under section 1877(h)(6)(H) of the Act. We proposed in the January 1998 rule to define “prosthetics” at Sec. 411.351 as artificial legs, arms, and eyes, as described in section 1861(s)(9) of the Act. We defined “orthotics” as leg, arm, back, and neck braces, as listed in section 1861(s)(9) of the Act. We proposed to define a “prosthetic device” as a device (other than a dental device) listed in section 1861(s)(8) of the Act that replaces all or part of an internal body organ, including colostomy bags and including one pair of conventional eyeglasses or contact lenses furnished subsequent to each cataract surgery with insertion of an intraocular lens, as well as services necessary to design the device, select materials and components, measure, fit, and align the device, and instruct patients in its proper usage. We proposed defining "prosthetic supplies" as "supplies that are necessary for the effective use of a prosthetic device (including supplies directly related to colostomy care)."

We are clarifying in Phase I of this rulemaking that this category includes all HCPCS level 2 codes for these services that are covered under Medicare. Physicians and other persons can readily determine the classification of an item by consulting the DMEPOS fee schedule. However, as with DME, there are several specific HCPCS codes representing miscellaneous items classified as prosthetics, orthotics, or prosthetic devices that do not appear in the fee schedule.

We explained in the preamble of the January 1998 proposed rule (63 FR 1678) that Medicare regards intraocular lenses (IOLs) used as part of cataract surgery as prosthetic devices. We also stated in the preamble that if these lenses are implanted in an ASC, they would be covered under the ASC payment rate and would have been excluded under the exception we proposed to create in Sec. 411.355(d). As explained above, we are no longer considering DHS that are included in a bundled ASC payment to be DHS. Accordingly, when an IOL is included in an ASC bundled payment rate, it will not be considered to be a designated health service.

We are also addressing a number of commenters' requests by creating exceptions (through our authority under section 1877(b)(4) of the Act) for prosthetic devices that are implanted in a Medicare-certified ASC and for eyeglasses or contact lenses that are prescribed after cataract surgery. We explain our reasons for these exceptions in our responses to specific comments.

Comment: One commenter asserted that the final rule should allow physicians to provide durable medical equipment, orthotics, and prosthetics directly to patients when they are medically necessary. Physicians currently supply splints, braces, or other devices directly to patients who have injuries, thereby ensuring that the patient gets the appropriate device, that the item is properly fitted, and that the patient is properly instructed in its use. To require a patient with an injury to leave the office, go to a DME supplier, purchase the necessary equipment, and return to the physician's office for fitting or placement and instructions on use, would be unwise, inconvenient, and could frequently cause unnecessary pain or further injury.

Response: The splints, casts, and other devices used to treat fractures and dislocations the commenter mentions are covered under section 1861(s)(5) of the Act, a benefit category that is different from the benefit categories that include DME, prosthetics, orthotics, and prosthetic devices. They are therefore not DHS under section 1877(h)(6) of the Act. Leg, arm, back, and neck braces are considered to be "orthotics" and are thus included as DHS. These can be provided by a physician within his or her own practice under the in-office ancillary services exception in section 1877(b)(2) of the Act, which excepts a physician's referral if the services meet certain supervision, location, and billing requirements. This exception could apply to referrals for any prosthetics, orthotics, or prosthetic devices. As modified by these regulations, the in-office ancillary exception could also apply to referrals for certain DME services. (See section VI.B.1 of this preamble.)

Comment: A number of commenters favored our proposal to exclude IOLs implanted during cataract surgery performed in an ASC because the IOLs are included in the ASC payment rate. The commenters asserted that a substantial number of ASCs are owned by the physicians who perform surgical procedures in them and that these physicians are not members of one group practice. The commenters see the ASCs as an extension of the physician's own office and believe they provide a high quality, low cost setting for outpatient surgery.

Commenters requested that we exempt from the physician self-referral prohibition other prosthetic devices implanted in conjunction with surgical procedures because the provision of the prosthetic devices is incidental to the provision of ASC facility services, which are exempt from the physician self-referral prohibition. The commenter asserted that, as we noted in the January 1998 proposed rule, a physician would not unnecessarily subject patients to a surgical procedure to profit from the implant. In addition, there is no risk of program abuse because the Medicare payment for prosthetic devices implanted in conjunction with ASC facility services is limited to the lower of the actual charge for the device or a fee schedule amount. Commenters emphasized that the use of implanted prosthetic devices in reconstructive surgery is immensely beneficial to patients.

Response: We agree with the commenters that all prosthetic devices implanted in a Medicare-certified ASC by the referring physician or a member of the referring physician's group practice should be excluded. We have chosen this position because, if surgeons refer to an ASC in which they have an ownership interest, there will, in many cases, be no exception that would apply to their financial relationship with the ASC. Implanted prosthetic devices, implanted prosthetics, and implanted DME are not included in the bundled ASC payment rate and thus would retain their character as DHS even when implanted in an ASC. As a practical matter, the absence of an exception for all of these items implanted in ASCs is likely to result in these procedures moving to more costly hospital outpatient settings. We believe that the exclusion of these implants from the reach of section 1877 of the Act (using our authority under section 1877(b)(4)) will not increase the risk of overutilization beyond what is already presented by the surgeon's Part B physician fee and is consistent with the Congress's decision not to include ambulatory surgical services as a specific designated health service. We are specifically providing that the exception does not protect items implanted in other settings. Nor does it protect arrangements between physicians and manufacturers or distributors of implants where the manufacturers or distributors furnish DHS, for example, through subsidiaries or affiliates. We are providing that the arrangement for the provision of the implant in the ASC may not violate the anti-kickback statute and all billing and claims submission must be proper.

Comment: Some commenters recommended that we exclude some or all implants to assure that there is no chilling of the ability and opportunity of Medicare patients to obtain the most appropriate and up to date technology that will be both effective and cost efficient. In addition, commenters pointed out that invasive surgery always entails a risk to the patient and is not undertaken without a physician seriously evaluating that risk in relation to the therapeutic or diagnostic benefit likely to be brought by the device to be implanted and determining what specialized model and brand of device will be most effective. Commenters believe that including implants in the definition of prosthetic devices will have the counterproductive effect of preventing surgeons from participating in research and development of these products, thereby curtailing research activity and blunting future development. This chilling effect would dramatically affect the quality of patient life and severely limit progress in reducing the cost to patients.

Response: Surgeons should be able to provide implants to their patients in any appropriate setting by meeting exceptions to the physician self-referral law. As we described in responses to earlier comments, we are creating an exception for implants that are performed in Medicare-certified ASCs. As to implants in other settings or those in ASCs that do not meet the new exception, other exceptions may still apply. Physicians who perform implants within their own practices may be able to use the in-office ancillary services exception in section 1877(b)(2) of the Act, which is discussed in section VI.B.1 of this preamble. If a physician performs the surgery in a hospital, and the hospital bills for the implant, the service would be a designated hospital service, regardless of whether the implant is a prosthetic or prosthetic device. In these cases, any financial relationship between the physician and the hospital would have to fit in an exception or the physician could not perform the surgery, much less the implant, since all hospital services are DHS. There are several exceptions that apply to referrals for hospital services.

The commenters seem to be under the misapprehension that section 1877 of the Act would prevent financial relationships between the manufacturer of an implant and a physician. These financial relationships would not be subject to section 1877 of the Act unless the manufacturer were an entity that bills Medicare directly. However, arrangements between physicians and manufacturers may be problematic under other legal authorities, including, for example, the Federal anti-kickback statute.

Comment: One commenter believes that we should not interpret the definition of prosthetics, orthotics, and prosthetic devices and supplies for physician referral purposes to include hip and knee implants. The commenter believes that hip and knee implants do not fall within the definitions of prosthetics, orthotics, and prosthetic devices and supplies that we included in the January 1998 proposed rule. The commenter pointed out that "prosthetics" is defined as artificial legs, arms, and eyes, that "orthotics" is defined as leg, arm, back and neck braces, and "prosthetic devices" is defined as devices that replace all or part of an internal body organ. The commenter believes that hip and knee replacements do not fall under any of these categories.

The commenter further stated that, if hip and knee implants are somehow considered as prosthetic devices under Medicare, they should be excluded from the referral prohibition on the basis that they are only a component of a primary surgical procedure meant to repair damaged or painful joints. The commenter believes physicians will not ask patients to undergo painful and debilitating surgery for the sake of implanting an unnecessary artificial knee or hip implant. Also, if these items are billed as part of the hospital diagnosis-related group (DRG) payment for a surgical procedure, there is no financial incentive to use more costly or unnecessary implants and there is no increased cost to the program if one implant is chosen over another.

Response: Knee implants are considered to be "prosthetics." They are components of the artificial legs that are identified as prosthetics under section 1861(s)(9) of the Act. Artificial hips are only furnished to hospital inpatients under Medicare Part A, so we consider them to be a component of an inpatient hospital service. If a physician sends a patient to a hospital for a hip or knee implant or the insertion of a prosthetic device, all the services billed by the hospital would qualify as DHS under section 1877(h)(6)(K) of the Act because they are "inpatient or outpatient hospital services." The implants would therefore be subject to the physician self-referral law, even if we excluded them from the separate category of "prosthetics, orthotics, or prosthetic devices and supplies."

Comment: A commenter asserted that we should exclude cochlear implants from the definition of prosthetic devices. In the January 1998 proposed rule, we had indicated our concern that a physician would choose a particular device because he or she had supplied it to the ASC where the patient's implant surgery was performed or because the physician receives money from a supplier for ordering the particular device. The commenter stated that the professional association he represents is unaware of any abuses in this area and, if there were abuses, they would be subject to the anti-kickback law.

Another commenter from an association of audiologists agreed with us that cochlear implants are a type of prosthetic device that is properly within the scope of the proposed rule. The commenter regards a cochlear implant as clearly being a prosthetic device because it replaces all or part of an internal body organ. A cochlear implant is an electronic device specifically designed to replace the function of a damaged cochlea.

Response: We agree with the second commenter that cochlear implants are covered as prosthetic devices under Medicare and are categorized as such in the CPT codes in the attachment to this final rule. As noted above, we are excepting all implants performed in a Medicare-certified ASC by the referring physician or a member of the referring physician's group practice, subject to certain conditions set forth in the exception.

Comment: A commenter noted that in the January 1998 proposed rule we stated that a prosthetic device includes services necessary to design the device, select materials and components, measure, fit, and align the device, and instruct patients in its proper usage. The commenter requested that we expressly clarify that certain services provided to patients after a cochlear implant are subject to the physician self-referral provisions. These services include device mapping, aural rehabilitation programs for adults to enable them to learn to use the device, and aural habilitation programs for children to maximize speech and language development.

The commenter asserted that these postsurgical services are provided by audiologists without physician involvement or supervision of any kind. In addition, the commenter stated that cochlear rehabilitation services are not included in the global fee for cochlear implantation surgery. Instead, these services are billed under a unique CPT code, 92510.

Response: The Medicare definition of a prosthetic device ordinarily includes the services necessary to design the device, select materials and components, measure, fit, and align the device, and instruct patients in its proper usage. In fact, the costs of delivery, fitting, measuring and instructing the patient are bundled into the fee schedule payment amount for not only prosthetic devices, but for DME, orthotics, and prosthetics as well. However, cochlear implants are somewhat unique. Because it can be particularly difficult for a patient to learn to use the implant, cochlear rehabilitation services are categorized separately as speech-language pathology services. These services are billed under CPT code 92510 (which is included as a PT service because it is a speech-language pathology service). Therefore, all of these services qualify as "designated health services," but under different categories.

Comment: A commenter pointed out that items such as rib belts, slings, and basic braces (those not custom-fitted) are in the prosthetic/orthotic section of the HCPCS. The commenter asked whether these items would be considered orthotics or DME, since the patient would be wearing the item home. The commenter believes that, in either case, it would be inappropriate to prevent a physician from supplying and billing for these items when the patient has come to the office with an injury. The commenter asserted that requiring a patient to leave the physician's office to purchase necessary equipment is inconvenient and unwise because it may result in unnecessary pain or injury to the patient.

Response: The items described as "rib belts" and "slings" are not included in any DHS category. The items described as "basic braces" are orthotics. Nothing in Phase I of this rulemaking moves any item or device from one coverage category to another coverage category. If the items qualify as in-office ancillary services under section 1877(b)(2) of the Act, a physician who supplies them in his or her office in the course of seeing a patient should be able to use the in-office ancillary services exception in order to provide them to the patient, even if the patient takes the items home. We regard the physician as "furnishing" an item in his or her office if the physician dispenses the item to the patient there.

Comment: Several commenters urged us to exclude eyeglasses and contact lenses from the definition of prosthetic devices. Commenters noted that there is no incentive to overutilize or abuse this benefit because we acknowledge that one pair of conventional eyeglasses or contact lenses is medically necessary after cataract surgery; Medicare coverage is limited to one pair of conventional eyeglasses or contact lenses; and Medicare payment is on a reasonable charge basis.

Response: We agree with the commenters that eyeglasses and contact lenses should be excluded from the reach of section 1877 of the Act for purposes of Medicare referrals. The Medicare coverage of these items is unique in that it is limited to one pair of either item after each cataract surgery and is available to any patient who has had this surgery. In that respect, the coverage is similar to the coverage of preventive screening services that are subject to frequency limits, as discussed earlier in this section. In addition, the Medicare-approved amount of payment does not vary based on the expense of a particular pair of glasses or contact lenses. Medicare pays fixed amounts for eyeglasses and contact lenses that are single focal, and fixed amounts for eyeglasses and contact lenses that are bifocal. In sum, we see little opportunity or incentive for a physician to either under or overutilize these items in the Medicare program. Accordingly, we are creating a new exception under the authority in section 1877(b)(4) of the Act for eyeglasses and contact lenses after cataract surgery. Like other section 1877(b)(4) exceptions, the new exception is subject to there being no violation of the anti-kickback statute or any billing or claims submission law or regulation.

K. Home Health Services

In the January 1998 proposed rule, we proposed to define home health services as the services described in section 1861(m) of the Act and part 409, subpart E. We included in the preamble to that rule (63 FR 1679), a discussion of how we proposed to reconcile section 1877 of the Act and the physician certification requirements for home health services in Sec. 424.22 (Requirements for home health services), paragraph (d) (Limitations on the performance of certification and plan of treatment functions). In that discussion, we explained that the home health agency (HHA) rule and its exceptions have been superseded by section 1877 of the Act. Phase I of this rulemaking reflects this change. Our responses to comments mostly serve to clarify how the modified home health rule will work.

Comment: Four commenters supported our proposal to reconcile the physician self-referral law with the physician certification requirements for home health services contained in Sec. 424.22(d). One commenter specifically expressed agreement with our proposed position that the exceptions to the physician self-referral law would also apply to physician certification requirements for home health services. Another commenter specifically supported the proposed changes that would eliminate the 5 percent ownership and $25,000 financial or contractual relationship limits and replace them with the prohibition on self-referral contained in section 1877 of the Act. The commenter stated that this change would allow HHAs to provide for medical oversight by a salaried physician as permitted under the Medicare hospice benefit. (We believe that commenter meant that the proposed elimination of the $25,000 financial or contractual relationship provision would allow an HHA to pay a physician medical director more than $25,000 as long as the HHA meets relevant ownership and compensation exceptions described in the proposed rule.) Another commenter asked that we clarify whether the current $25,000 limit on financial or contractual relationships as it relates to medical directors of home care agencies will be removed.

Response: We are removing the current 5 percent ownership limit and the $25,000 limit on financial or contractual relationships from Sec. 424.22(d). The new Sec. 424.22(d) appears exactly as we proposed it: "The need for home health services to be provided by an HHA may not be certified or recertified, and a plan of treatment may not be established and reviewed, by any physician who has a financial relationship, as defined in Sec. 411.351 of this chapter,

'Definitions,' with that HHA, unless the physician's relationship meets one of the exceptions in Secs. 411.355 through 411.357 of this chapter * * *." The elimination of the $25,000 financial or contractual relationship provision will allow an HHA to pay a physician medical director more than $25,000 as long as the financial relationship meets a relevant ownership or compensation exception under section 1877 of the Act.

Although we are delaying the effective date for most of Phase I of this rulemaking for 1 year, we are making the change in Sec. 424.22(d) effective February 5, 2001. Having weighed the alternatives, we believe an effective date of February 5, 2001 for the revision of Sec. 424.22(d) is desirable, even though the revisions to Secs. 411.355 and 411.357 will not be effective until later. In the interim, the references to Secs. 411.355 and 411.357 will cross-refer to the statutory exceptions set forth in section 1877 of the Act. It is our view that during the interim period, the exceptions set forth in those sections would apply under Sec. 424.22(d) for services other than laboratory services.

Comment: One commenter requested that we retain the provisions in Sec. 424.22(e) (Exceptions to limitations), (f) (Procedures for classification as a sole community HHA) and (g) (Basis for classification as a sole community HHA) that except governmental entities and sole community HHAs from the prohibition on certification of need for home health services by related physicians. The commenter noted that keeping this language would remove the threat of unfair competition for agencies that have historically been the sole providers in their communities. The commenter explained that the "rural provider" exception to the physician self-referral law would permit an urban physician to establish a new HHA in a rural area, as long as the agency's service population is at least 75 percent rural. This would create new and unfair competition for many rural agencies that are small, nonprofit organizations.

Response: We realize that eliminating the exceptions for governmental entities and sole community HHAs in combination with the ownership exception for rural providers under the physician self-referral law may create new competition for small, nonprofit HHAs. Nonetheless, we believe that we do not have the legal authority to retain these exceptions in any meaningful way. As we pointed out in the preamble to the January 1998 proposed rule (63 FR 1680), even if a physician and an HHA are involved in an arrangement that meets one of the home health exceptions at issue, the arrangement simultaneously remains subject to the requirements in section 1877 of the Act. That is, if an exception under the HHA certification regulations is subsumed within the exceptions in section 1877 of the Act, a physician will be able to refer; if it is not, the arrangement will disqualify the physician from referring in spite of Sec. 424.22. Thus, the HHA exceptions have been superseded by section 1877 of the Act.

The Secretary does have the authority to create additional exceptions to the referral prohibition under section 1877(b)(4) of the Act, but only in situations in which she determines that there is no risk of program or patient abuse. We believe that the fact that an entity is run by the government or is a sole community HHA does not guarantee that there will be no unnecessary referrals. In addition, it is our view that we should treat all providers equally and allow them an equal opportunity to compete, particularly in areas where there have historically been too few providers. In fact, the purpose of the "rural provider" exception in section 1877(d)(2) of the Act is to encourage physicians to invest in or remain invested in under-served areas. (Note that hospitals do not have similar exceptions for governmental entities or sole community hospitals.) Therefore, we do not intend to include the exceptions for governmental entities and sole community providers in the revised HHA certification regulations because we believe that our proposed approach provides the best protection against possible program abuse and fulfills the intent of the law.

Comment: A commenter representing home care physicians asked that we clarify whether physicians making home visits are providing services that qualify as DHS under the January 1998 proposed regulations.

Response: Under the Medicare program, when a physician performs a physician service, including a visit to a home health patient, the physician service is billed as a physician service and is not considered a home health service. This is the case even when the physician has an employment contract with the HHA, such as when a physician is employed as a medical director. Thus, the commenter is correct in noting that physician home visits are not themselves on the list of DHS in section 1877(h)(6) of the Act, and would only qualify as such if the physician was actually performing a specific designated health service (for example, performing physical therapy). In these cases, the service would still be protected if it is personally performed by the referring physician, since it would not be considered a referral under the final rule. (See section III.B of this preamble.) In addition, some in-home services provided by a home care physician may qualify under the in-office ancillary services exception. (See section VI.B of this preamble.)

L. Outpatient Prescription Drugs

Section 1877(h)(6)(J) of the Act provides that "designated health services" includes the category of "outpatient prescription drugs," but does not define this term. Because Medicare does not cover a category of services called "outpatient prescription drugs," we proposed to define this term in the regulation. We proposed to include only drugs (including biologicals) defined or listed under section 1861 (s) and (t) of the Act, and in part 410, furnished under the Medicare Part B benefit that patients can obtain from a pharmacy with a prescription, even if patients can only receive the drug under medical supervision. In the preamble to the January 1998 proposed regulation (63 FR 1680), we included as an example oncology drugs that are routinely furnished in a physician's office, under the physician's direct supervision, provided the drugs could be obtained by prescription from a pharmacy.

We proposed specifically to exclude from the definition of "outpatient prescription drugs" erythropoietin (EPO) and other drugs furnished as part of a dialysis treatment for an individual who dialyzes at home or in a facility.

Upon further review of the law, existing regulations, and the public comments, we have concluded that our proposed definition of "outpatient prescription drugs" was not clear enough. In Phase I of this rulemaking, we are revising the definition of outpatient prescription drugs to make clear that it includes all prescription drugs covered by Medicare Part B. We are not excluding any outpatient prescription drugs from the DHS category of "outpatient prescription drugs." Including all outpatient prescription drugs is consistent with our policy throughout these final regulations of avoiding carving services out of DHS definitions through service-by-service analyses of the potential for fraud and abuse. Our definition of outpatient prescription drugs provides physicians and DHS entities with a "bright line," common sense rule. Moreover, the breadth of the definition is ameliorated to a very large extent by our expansion of the exception for in-office ancillary services, which includes much greater flexibility with respect to the direct supervision requirement, and our promulgation of a new limited exception under section 1877(b)(4) of the Act for the provision of EPO and certain other dialysis-related drugs by or in ESRD facilities (described in greater detail below). Those changes, together with the changes in the definition of "group practice" and "referral," should permit a physician to furnish patients with covered drugs, either by administering or dispensing the drugs to patients in his or her office or, in the case of EPO and other specific dialysis drugs, by furnishing the drugs in or through a physician-owned ESRD facility. We wish to make clear that nothing in this regulation affects, or is intended to affect, current or future coverage of any particular prescription drug.

We are creating an exception for EPO and certain other specific drugs that are required for the efficacy of dialysis when they are furnished by an ESRD facility with which the referring physician has a financial arrangement. We are similarly excepting certain vaccinations, immunizations, and preventive screening tests that are subject to HCFA-imposed frequency limits. We are also clarifying that physicians who provide drugs in their own offices are not required to pass on to Medicare discounts they receive in purchasing these drugs, unless otherwise required to do so by the Medicare program. These issues are discussed in detail below.

Comment: A number of commenters raised the issue of whether drugs and biologicals provided incident to physician services are included in the definition of outpatient prescription drugs. The commenters pointed out that most drugs and biologicals are covered under Medicare Part B only if they require administration by a physician, and thus typically are covered in the physician office setting only if furnished as "incident to" physician services. Thus, the resulting "self referral" is effectively a requirement for Medicare coverage. In the commenters' view, excluding drugs furnished incident to physician services from the definition of "outpatient prescription drugs" would ensure that the physician self-referral law does not discourage the types of "referrals" that are prerequisites to Medicare coverage.

One commenter asserted that drugs that are covered under Medicare only as a component of a physician service should be excluded because physician services were never intended to be included within the referral prohibition. Another commenter recommended that we make all injectable drugs exempt from the referral prohibition under the in-office ancillary services exception.

Several commenters were particularly concerned about antigens and serums that a patient receives in a physician's office, stating that they should be excluded from the category of outpatient prescription drugs, along with chemotherapy. Another commenter pointed out that if our definition of outpatient prescription drugs includes drugs administered during a patient's office visit, patients could have serious access problems to such drugs as antibiotics, renal therapy, and vaccines. Another commenter recommended that we limit outpatient prescription drugs to those that are self-administered, such as oral cancer drugs, oral antiemetics, and immunosuppressives, for which there is Medicare coverage that does not depend on administration in a physician's office.

Response: We believe the commenters are conflating two issues: (1) What drugs fit in the term "outpatient prescription drugs" in section 1877(h)(6)(J) of the Act and (2) the scope of the in-office ancillary services exception in section 1877(b)(2) of the Act. Upon review, for purposes of defining "outpatient prescription drugs" under section 1877(h)(6)(J) of the Act, we can ascertain no meaningful distinction between prescription drugs dispensed by pharmacies or those mixed and administered in a physician's office. To the extent the latter is permitted, it is through the vehicle of the in-office ancillary services exception. The scope of that exception is discussed in section VI.B.1 of this preamble.

Comment: Many commenters stated that oncology drugs administered to patients by injection or infusion in a physician's office should be excluded from the definition of outpatient drugs because a patient essentially cannot obtain these drugs from a pharmacy before visiting his or her physician. When a patient comes to a physician's office for chemotherapy, the patient receives a series of blood tests to determine the patient's physiological state. Based on these tests, the chemotherapy agents are mixed and tailored by the oncologist's staff to address the patient's current health status. Therefore, a patient cannot pick up from a pharmacy the medication he or she needs before visiting the physician. We may have misunderstood how chemotherapy drugs are actually administered.

In addition, the commenters pointed out that a great majority of retail pharmacies are not currently prepared to provide chemotherapeutic mixing and dispensing services for infusion drugs. That is because Federal regulations and accepted standards of practice for physicians, oncology nurses, technicians, and pharmacists require that the preparation, storage, transportation, and disposal of chemotherapy drugs and applicable supportive agents be conducted under the most rigorously controlled circumstances.

Response: We agree that chemotherapy agents are not commonly available from retail pharmacies, but are prepared for individual patients. However, these drugs are outpatient prescription drugs; they are available only upon a physician's order and are provided in an outpatient setting. (When provided in an inpatient setting, they would be inpatient hospital services under section 1877(h)(6)(K) of the Act.) We believe these drugs are usually administered in oncologists' offices and typically should qualify for the in-office ancillary services exception. (See discussion in section VI.B.1 of this preamble.)

Comment: Several commenters have stated that in-office x-rays and laboratory tests that are performed in conjunction with the provision of chemotherapy should be excluded from the definition of DHS. The commenters seemed particularly concerned that if these services are regarded as DHS, a physician would have to directly supervise them. The commenters expressed concern that requiring a physician to be present during the times these services are provided would run directly counter to common practice in oncology offices and would greatly inconvenience patients.

These commenters asserted that it is extremely unlikely that a physician would refer a patient for chemotherapy simply to obtain the revenue from the x-ray and laboratory tests that are performed in conjunction with the provision of chemotherapy. They regard as a precedent for this exception our proposals to exclude from the definition of radiology certain invasive radiology services in which an imaging modality is used to guide a needle, probe, or catheter properly and to exclude EPO from the definition of outpatient prescription drugs when EPO is provided incidental to dialysis treatment. We had proposed to exclude these invasive radiology procedures and EPO because they are merely furnished incidental to, or secondary to, another procedure that the physician has ordered.

Response: The Congress has imposed certain constraints on physicians' financial arrangements with entities to which they refer patients for DHS. The provision of chemotherapy is a designated health service, as is the provision of radiology and clinical laboratory services. In order for a physician to refer patients to an entity with which the referring physician has a financial arrangement, the physician's financial relationship with the entity must come within an exception to section 1877 of the Act.

As discussed elsewhere, we are not prepared to limit the scope of DHS under section 1877(h)(6) of the Act except in rare situations. We believe that most arrangements for the provision of chemotherapy and related ancillary services by physicians to their patients can be restructured to come within the in-office ancillary services exception as modified by this final rule. (See section VI.B of this preamble.) As discussed above, we are abandoning the "peripheral/incidental" test that was proposed in the January 1998 proposed rule; we point out that even under that test, the primary procedure could not itself be a designated health service.

Finally, we wish to clarify that we are excepting EPO under certain circumstances because we believe that the Congress did not intend to preclude physician ownership of ESRD facilities. Commenters have noted that when the Congress intended to cover specific Medicare services, including composite rate services, it did so expressly. We agree. The Congress did not list ESRD facility services under section 1877(h)(6) of the Act, while it did list home health services and hospital services. Therefore, we do not regard services furnished under a composite rate by an ESRD facility as DHS. Given the high correlation between EPO and ESRD services, the inclusion of EPO as a DHS would vitiate the Congress' apparent intent. Accordingly, we are excepting from the reach of the statute under our section 1877(b)(4) of the Act authority EPO or other drugs required for dialysis when furnished in or by an ESRD facility owned by physicians. The list of these drugs is set forth in the attachment to this final rule. Given the strict utilization and coverage criteria for EPO in particular and ESRD in general, we conclude this narrow exception presents no quantifiable risk of fraud or abuse. We are not protecting any physician investment in a home dialysis supply company or other entity that supplies EPO to ESRD facilities or that supplies EPO to patients pursuant to a contract with an ESRD facility; in such situations, the physician's investment in the dialysis supply company is no different from any other investment in a DHS entity and there is no indication in the legislative history that home dialysis supply companies were not meant to be covered by the statute.

Comment: A substantial number of commenters requested that we not require physicians to pass on to Medicare discounts they receive in purchasing oncology drugs. Commenters pointed out that the proposed regulations appear to require this result. Some commenters believe that this proposed requirement conflicts with section 1877(e)(8)(B) of the Act, which excepts any payment made by a physician for items and services if the price is consistent with fair market value.

Response: Nothing in this section 1877 of the Act or these regulations is intended to impose on physicians a requirement to pass discounts on drugs on to the Medicare and Medicaid programs; whether a discount must be passed on to a Federal health care program by physicians or others, however, remains the subject of other statutory and regulatory provisions.

Comment: One commenter asked that we confirm that the definition of "outpatient prescription drugs" would apply only to those drugs that are furnished to "outpatients" of any facility, including a SNF or nursing facility. The commenter believes that if the Congress had intended that the statute cover drugs provided to "inpatients" of facilities, it could have easily written the statute to do so. The commenter pointed out that drugs provided to "inpatients" are generally covered under Medicare Part A and are peripheral components of the services being provided and billed for, particularly under the prospective payment system for SNFs under which SNFs receive a per diem rate for virtually all items and services furnished to a Medicare Part A patient.

Response: In the January 1998 proposed rule, we proposed to include only drugs furnished to an individual under the Medicare Part B benefit and to exclude drugs furnished by providers under Medicare Part A. We have reflected this in Phase I of this rulemaking. A patient may reside in a SNF under a Part A stay or a patient may reside in a SNF without being covered under Part A. If the stay is not covered under Part A, it is possible that the patient may receive some drugs under the Part B benefit that are considered "outpatient prescription drugs" under these physician self-referral provisions. In addition, under section 1835(a) of the Act, a SNF may furnish services to an individual who is not a SNF inpatient. That is, it is possible for a SNF to provide services to an individual who does not reside in the SNF. For example, a SNF with an x-ray machine may furnish x-ray services to a nonresident if the individual has a referral for an x-ray and he or she wishes to receive the x-ray at this location. We assume the individuals who receive these services are the "outpatients" to whom the commenter is referring. (We note that drugs provided to patients in a hospital setting would be inpatient or outpatient hospital services under section 1877(h)(6)(K) of the Act.)

Patients in nursing facilities are typically covered under the Medicaid program. We intend to address all Medicaid-related physician referral issues in a separate rulemaking.

Comment: A commenter requested that we amend the January 1998 proposed rule to clarify that immunizations are not DHS under the definition of "outpatient prescription drugs." The commenter pointed out that immunizations, particularly in pediatric and family care practices, are often personally administered by a physician to his or her own patients or are furnished on an "incident to" basis under the physician's direct supervision. In the adult population, there is also an increasing public awareness of the need for preventive immunizations, such as pneumococcal vaccine and influenza vaccine. These immunizations are widely and actively promoted in this country as constituting good preventive medicine. The commenter believes that the January 1998 proposed regulation could discourage immunizations because under the proposed interpretation of productivity bonuses in the group practice definition, a physician would be unable to share in a productivity bonus based on his or her own administration of, or direct supervision of, these immunizations.

Response: The commenter raised issues relating to immunizations that are covered by Medicare under section 1861(s)(10) of the Act, which covers pneumococcal vaccine and influenza vaccine and their administration, as well as hepatitis B vaccine and its administration if furnished to an individual who is at high or intermediate risk of contracting hepatitis B. Under our authority to create additional exceptions in section 1877(b)(4), we are excluding from the reach of section 1877 of the Act certain immunizations and vaccines covered under section 1861(s)(10) of the Act that are subject to HCFA-imposed frequency limits and that are paid by Medicare on the basis of a fee schedule. We believe that under the terms of the exception the risk of abuse for these services is extremely low and that this exclusion is consistent with the statutory language and structure and the expressed Congressional intent to provide preventive care to Medicare beneficiaries.

In referring to drugs furnished in pediatric and family practices, we assume that the commenter was interested in the definition of outpatient prescription drugs under the Medicaid program. We intend to address the effects of the physician self-referral prohibition on the Medicaid program in Phase II of this rulemaking.

Comment: A commenter raised questions about our decision to exclude EPO and other drugs furnished as part of a dialysis treatment from the definition of "outpatient prescription drugs." The commenter considered this exclusion ambiguous and requested clarification about whether a particular drug provided by a facility is "part of a dialysis treatment." The commenter pointed out that EPO and other pharmaceuticals are typically administered during the course of treatment to avoid the painful process of injecting the patient multiple times, but that it could be argued that these pharmaceuticals are not "part of" the treatment itself. Therefore, the commenter requested that we revise the exclusion of "other drugs furnished as part of the dialysis treatment" to instead apply to "other drugs furnished to an individual who dialyzes at home or in a facility, as part of an ESRD patient's plan of care."

Response: When we carved out of the definition of "outpatient prescription drugs, EPO and other drugs furnished as part of the dialysis treatment," we did not aim to carve out the far broader category of all "other drugs furnished * * * as part of an ESRD patient's plan of care." We regard "other drugs furnished as part of the dialysis treatment" to be those furnished so that the dialysis treatment can be effective and to counteract the problems that can be caused directly by dialysis. For example, dialysis makes some patients anemic, so EPO is provided to deal with this dialysis-related problem. In addition, iron therapy is covered to make EPO therapy effective and Vitamin D hormone therapy is covered to correct for bone density loss caused by dialysis. Other drugs furnished to an individual who dialyzes at home or in a facility may include drugs that a patient uses for reasons other than to make the dialysis treatment effective. In fact, these other drugs may have nothing whatsoever to do with a patient's renal problems.

Comment: Another commenter agreed with our proposal to exclude EPO in the January 1998 proposed rule because it would allow physicians who own a dialysis facility to prescribe Medicare-covered medications to patients of the dialysis facility on the basis that the drugs are an integral part of the dialysis procedure. The commenter asked that we clarify that self-administered medications for home dialysis such as EPO can only be furnished by the dialysis provider or a supplier that has an agreement with the dialysis provider (a Method II supplier) and cannot be provided through the referring physician's office. The commenter contended that teaching the home dialysis patients to self-administer medications and monitoring the effects of self-administered medications is the responsibility of the dialysis facility.

Response: We agree with the commenter. As provided in Sec. 414.335 (Payment for EPO furnished to a home dialysis patient for use in the home), medications for home dialysis can only be furnished by the dialysis provider or a Method II supplier that has an agreement with a provider. If a referring physician has a financial agreement with a Method II supplier, the arrangement must meet an exception.

Comment: A commenter asked that immunosuppressant drugs prescribed for patients following organ transplants and covered by Medicare be excluded from the definition of "outpatient prescription drugs." The commenter believes that the rationale for excluding these drugs is similar to the rationale for excluding EPO, since the use of these drugs is peripheral to the transplant surgery, but medically integral to the success of the surgery.

The commenter contended that excluding immunosuppressants from the definition will not provide an opportunity for program or patient abuse because their cost is an economically minor, though medically critical, part of a large and immensely complicated treatment. In addition, the commenter believes that physicians have no motivation to overprescribe these drugs, because the drugs are only used for transplant patients according to clinically accepted protocols that are designed to prevent organ rejection while avoiding unnecessarily high levels of toxicity. The commenter believes that the transplant community adheres to the prevailing standards of medical care with only minor deviations. In addition, each transplant center is required to report its transplant survival rates to an HHS contractor. Centers with survival rates below established thresholds can lose their certification.

Response: Immunosuppressant drugs furnished in an outpatient setting are "outpatient prescription drugs" under Phase I of this rulemaking. (They are inpatient or outpatient hospital services when furnished in a hospital setting.) We are not persuaded that an exception is appropriate or necessary. We believe that to the extent physicians provide transplant drugs to patients in their offices, they will generally be able to do so under the in-office ancillary services exception. If a referring physician has an ownership or investment interest in a free-standing transplant pharmacy or other pharmacy that provides transplant drugs to his or her patients pursuant to a referral, the financial relationship would have to fit in an applicable exception.

M. Inpatient and Outpatient Hospital Services

In Sec. 411.351 of the January 1998 proposed rule, we defined inpatient hospital services as services that a hospital provides for its patients that are furnished either by the hospital or by others "under arrangements" with the hospital. For outpatient services, we explained in the preamble of the January 1998 proposed rule (63 FR 1683) that we would consider all covered services (either diagnostic or therapeutic) performed on hospital outpatients that are billed by the hospital to Medicare (including arranged for services) as outpatient hospital services. We have revised the definition of outpatient hospital services in the regulations text to clarify that it includes services furnished "under arrangements." Inpatient services are not coded by HCPCS codes. Any outpatient hospital service, regardless of the HCPCS code, is a designated health service.

In the January 1998 proposed rule, we requested comment on whether we should exclude lithotripsy from the definition of inpatient or outpatient hospital services on the theory that it could not be overutilized, since the procedure itself apparently documents the medical necessity to prescribe it. Commenters were also concerned about physician services that are "bundled" into hospital payments and about services furnished by a hospital "under arrangements" with an outside facility. We discuss each of these topics below.

Comment: We received hundreds of comments on the subject of lithotripsy, mostly from urologists who have ownership interests in a lithotriptor that a hospital rents. These commenters requested that lithotripsy be excluded from the definition of inpatient and outpatient hospital services so that they could continue to refer to the hospitals without being concerned about how the hospital compensates them. According to these commenters, urologist-owned lithotriptors increased quality of care and patient access without any risk of overutilization of lithotripsy. We also received comments on this topic from individual hospitals, a State and national hospital trade association, and nonphysicians who rented lithotriptors to hospitals in competition with physician owners. These commenters asserted that hospitals pay more for the use of physician-owned lithotriptors than hospitals pay for the use of their own lithotriptors or lithotriptors owned by nonphysicians and urged us to include lithotripsy in the definition of inpatient and outpatient hospital services.

Response: We have determined that there is no reason to treat lithotripsy any differently than other inpatient or outpatient hospital services. As we have said elsewhere in the preamble, we believe the Congress did not intend that we make service-by-service decisions on whether a service is a designated health service based on the service's potential for overutilization. Even were we able to determine that there is no potential for overutilization of lithotripsy (including comparisons to alternative treatments), there is a substantial potential for urologists who own lithotriptors to extract higher than market rate rents for their equipment or for the financial arrangement between the lessor urologists and the lessee hospital to encourage overutilization of other hospital services. Commenters provided no evidence to support their claims that physician ownership of lithotriptors increased quality of care or access to treatment.

In any event, the exclusion of lithotripsy from the definition of inpatient and outpatient services would not obviate the need for the physician-owners to structure their rental arrangements to comply with section 1877 of the Act. Whether lithotripsy is a designated health service or not, the rental arrangement itself would create a financial relationship between the physician-owners and the hospital. Unless the financial relationship (that is, the lithotriptor lease) fit into a compensation exception (such as the equipment rental exception), the physicians could not refer any Medicare patients to the hospital for any inpatient or outpatient services. In short, the relief sought by these commenters would be illusory.

We believe that the changes we have made in Sec. 411.354(d) of these regulations to the volume or value standard (discussed in section V of this preamble) will enable hospitals and urologists to protect bona fide arrangements either under an equipment lease or a personal service arrangements exception or under the fair market value exception. Most importantly, Phase I of this rulemaking clarifies that "per service" or "per use" rental or services payments are permitted, even for services performed on patients referred by the urologist-owner, provided the rental or services payment is fair market value and does not take into account any Federal or private pay business generated between the urologist and the hospital (and provided all other conditions of an exception are met). Because the prevalence of physician ownership of lithotriptors may distort pricing in the marketplace, we believe valuation methods that look to the prices charged by persons not in a position to refer to the hospital or that consider acquisition cost and rate of return are especially appropriate. We also are aware that some manufacturers of lithotriptors lease the machines to urologists on a "per use" basis with the urologists, in turn, leasing the lithotriptors to hospitals on a "per use" basis. In these circumstances, any disparity in the "per use" fee charged by the manufacturer to the urologists and the "per use" fee charged in turn by urologists to the hospital would call into question whether both sets of fees could be fair market value.

Comment: Several commenters suggested that section 1877 of the Act was only intended to address diagnostic procedures. Accordingly, they asked that we exclude therapeutic treatments such as lithotripsy from the definition of inpatient or outpatient hospital services in cases in which the referring urologist or a member of his practice actually treats the referred patient.

Response: The list of DHS in section 1877(h)(6) of the Act contains both therapeutic and diagnostic types of service (for example, physical therapy services are therapeutic and clinical laboratory services are diagnostic). This indicates that the Congress believed that both types of services could be subject to abuse. We have concluded that when a physician initiates a designated health service and personally performs it him or herself, that action would not constitute a referral of the service to an entity under section 1877 of the Act. However, in the context of inpatient and outpatient hospital services, there would still be a referral of any hospital service, technical component, or facility fee billed by the hospital in connection with the personally performed service. Thus, for example, in the case of an inpatient surgery, there would be a referral of the technical component of the surgical service, even though the referring physician personally performs the service. If the referring physician has a financial relationship with the hospital, that relationship must fit in an exception. Potentially available exceptions, depending on the circumstances, include, for example, the personal service arrangements exception, the employee exception, the space or equipment rental exception, the whole hospital exception, and the fair market value exception.

Comment: Several commenters stated that the only reason extracorporeal shock wave lithotripsy (ESWL) is even subject to the physician self-referral provisions is because Medicare only pays for lithotripsy if it is billed through a hospital, thus forcing the procedure into the realm of inpatient or outpatient hospital services. Many commenters have cited debate language pertaining to adopting the Conference Report for OBRA '93, which language suggests that the sponsor of section 1877 of the Act, Representative Stark, did not intend for ESWL to come under the law.

Response: We believe that lithotripsy was meant to be a "designated health service" under the law, since the law does not exclude any particular hospital services, nor does the legislative history indicate that the Congress meant to exclude them. The House Report for the first version of the physician self-referral law mentioned a specific exception for a facility providing lithotripsy services performed personally by the referring physician. (See H. Rep. No. 101–247, 101st Cong. 1041 (1989).) This exception did not apply to the hospital services at issue, nor was it enacted. In adding hospital services to the list of DHS, the legislative history reveals that the Congress was concerned about increased admissions to hospitals, regardless of the reason for the admission. (We discuss this issue further below, where we address hospital services provided "under arrangements.")

Comment: Another commenter pointed out that we proposed excluding from the definition of inpatient hospital services those services performed by physicians and other providers who bill independently. The commenter asked us to clarify whether physician and individual professional services are excluded from the definition of inpatient hospital services when they are billed by a hospital. Hospitals bill for these services when they are part of a global fee that covers both the technical and professional components of a service or when they bill on an assignment (or reassignment) basis. This commenter argued that if these services are not excluded under section 1877 of the Act, a hospital may not be able to compensate a physician for services performed in, and billed by, the hospital, or to compensate a doctor who supervises a nurse practitioner in a hospital. The commenter also suggested that we clarify that we will treat both inpatient hospital services and outpatient hospital services the same way.

Response: Professional services that Medicare pays independently of an inpatient or outpatient hospital service do not become DHS if they are billed by a hospital under assignment or reassignment; they remain physician services and are not considered hospital services. Any other service for which a hospital bills is a hospital inpatient or outpatient service, even though it may consist of both a technical and professional component. Therefore, these services constitute DHS under section 1877 of the Act. However, if a hospital is paying the physician for his or her professional services under either a personal services contract or an employment agreement, the physician can still refer to the hospital as long as the compensation arrangement meets an exception, such as the exception that applies to personal service arrangements or the exception for employment agreements. These exceptions require, among other things, that the hospital pay the physician an amount that is based on a fair market value standard.

Comment: Several commenters expressed concern with the effect the definitions of inpatient and outpatient hospital services may have when a hospital purchases services "under arrangements" from an entity owned in whole or in part by a referring physician. Commenters fear that if services are deemed to be inpatient or outpatient hospital services for the purposes of 1877 of the Act when furnished by a hospital "under arrangements" with an entity owned by a physician, physicians may be unwilling to invest in equipment using new technologies. One commenter specifically proposed an exception that would apply to any service that would be exempt from the physician self-referral prohibition if the physician referred directly to the entity, outside of the hospital context. According to several commenters, it is the nature of the service itself that should determine whether or not a referral may be made, not the inpatient or outpatient status of the patient. Commenters were concerned that a physician will not be able to refer a patient to a hospital if the hospital has an arrangement with an entity that the physician owns. The commenters believe that, as long as the actual services are compensated at fair market value, there should be no risk of program or patient abuse.

Response: The Congress specifically chose to include inpatient and outpatient services as DHS under section 1877(h)(6)(K) of the Act. Inpatient and outpatient hospital services include any services that a hospital provides to a hospital patient, whether it provides them itself or provides them by purchasing them from another entity under arrangements; any other policy would encourage hospitals to purchase as many services as possible under arrangements in order to avoid the effects of the physician self-referral provision. In light of the description of "volume or value" in Phase I of this rulemaking, we believe that bona fide "under arrangements" relationships can easily be structured to comply with the personal service arrangements exception, or, in some cases, the fair market value exception. We believe this approach is consistent with section 1877(e)(7) of the Act, which provides a limited exception for certain "under arrangements" relationships that were established before 1989 and met several other requirements.

We are concerned that the provision of services "under arrangements" could be used to circumvent the prohibition in section 1877(c)(3) of the Act of physician ownership of parts of hospitals. We understand that some hospitals are leasing hospital space to physician groups, which the groups then use to provide services "under arrangements" that the hospital had previously provided directly. These arrangements, especially when they involve particularly lucrative lines of business, raise significant issues under section 1877 of the Act, as well as the anti-kickback statute.

However, we also recognize that "under arrangements" relationships are pervasive in the hospital industry and that many of the services being provided by physician groups "under arrangements" are services that the physicians provide in physician-owned facilities primarily to their own patients who are hospital inpatients. In these situations, an "under arrangements" relationship can avoid unnecessary duplication of costs and underutilization of expensive equipment.

While we believe section 1877 of the Act could reasonably be interpreted to prohibit "under arrangements" relationships as constituting prohibited ownership interests in a part of a hospital, we decline to do so at this time for several reasons. First, given the sheer number of these arrangements, we think prohibiting these arrangements would seriously disrupt patient care. Second, almost all these arrangements could be restructured to fit into a combination of the personal service arrangements and equipment lease exceptions (or fair market value exception), although this restructuring will in some cases be administratively burdensome. Third, we believe there is precedent in the statute for treating this situation solely as a compensation arrangement. In section 1877(e)(7) of the Act, the Congress created a specific compensation exception for certain hospital services provided by physician groups "under arrangements." Since, by definition, all services protected under section 1877(e)(7) of the Act — and the resources used to produce them — were "owned" by the physician groups, the Congress would not have created a protected compensation relationship unless it had first determined that these arrangements did not create a prohibited ownership or investment interest in the hospitals. Simply stated, the

Congress would not have excepted these relationships from the compensation arrangement restriction, if they were prohibited as an ownership or investment interest.

In sum, for purposes of section 1877 of the Act, we will treat "under arrangements" financial arrangements between hospitals and physician-owned entities as compensation and not ownership relationships. These arrangements can be protected provided they meet an appropriate compensation exception. We will, however, monitor these arrangements and may reconsider our decision if it appears that the arrangements are abused. We also caution physician groups and hospitals that these arrangements remain subject to the Federal anti-kickback statute.

Comment: One commenter requested that we clarify how the physician self-referral law applies in cases in which a financial relationship arises solely because of Medicare requirements. The commenter discussed a situation in which a radiation therapy group and a radiation therapy facility (owned by some or all of the group members) are located in a medical office building across the street from a hospital in a nonrural area. The closest comparable facility is over 35 miles away. Occasionally, the hospital sends an inpatient for radiation therapy to the radiation facility, which provides the services as "arranged for" inpatient hospital services. The hospital pays the facility for use of the radiation equipment from money it receives from Medicare for the inpatient hospital stay. (The group practice bills Medicare for the professional services of the radiation oncologists.) The commenter erroneously asserted that Medicare requires the hospital to pay the radiation facility for the amount that it would have received under Medicare Part B if the radiation therapy had been provided as an outpatient service. The commenter believes that the payment by the hospital to the radiation therapy facility creates a compensation arrangement with the facility and, in turn, the physicians.

Often, a radiation oncologist will refer a patient of the radiation facility to the hospital for certain tests and other services. The radiation oncologist receives no economic benefit for referring patients to the hospital and refers there for the patient's convenience, not because there is any requirement to do so. The commenter believes that, under our proposed rule, the "under arrangements" compensation arrangement would trigger the physician self-referral law, preventing the radiation oncologists from referring Medicare patients to the hospital for services, even though this financial relationship is not voluntary and not subject to abuse.

The commenter requested clarification whether the proposed Sec. 411.355(d)(2), covering services furnished under composite types of payment rates that the Secretary determines provide no financial incentive for underutilization or overutilization, or any other risk of program or patient abuse, would apply. The commenter also wished to know whether we could include an additional described compensation arrangement exception under Sec. 411.357(d) (the personal service arrangements exception) or clarify Sec. 411.357(g) (the exception for remuneration from a hospital to a physician if the remuneration does not relate to the furnishing of DHS) to include the arrangements the commenter mentioned, or create some variation in the fair market value exception in Sec. 411.357(l)(3) that would allow compensation determined on the basis of the volume of services (that is, fee-for-service payments as covered under Medicare Part B) in the type of situation the commenter described.

Response: As discussed above in section VIII.A of this preamble, we have determined not to include the proposed Sec. 411.355(d)(2) in Phase I of this rulemaking for DHS other than clinical laboratory services. However, as discussed in the preceding response, the arrangement described by the commenter would be a compensation arrangement that could be structured to fit in one of the compensation exceptions, such as the equipment rental, personal service arrangements, or the new fair market value exceptions.

N. Other Definitions

1. Consultation

The definition of "consultation" is addressed in section III.B.2 of this preamble and in the regulations in Sec. 411.351.

2. Entity

In Sec. 411.351 of the August 1995 final rule covering referrals for clinical laboratory services, we defined the term "entity" broadly to cover a sole proprietorship, trust, corporation, partnership, foundation, not-for-profit corporation, or unincorporated association. We revised this definition in the January 1998 proposed rule to make it clear that the definition covers a physician's sole practice or a practice of multiple physicians that provides for the furnishing of DHS, or any other sole proprietorship, trust, corporation, partnership, foundation, not-for-profit corporation, or unincorporated association. We explained in the preamble to the January 1998 proposed rule at 63 FR 1706 that we regard an "entity" for purposes of the referral prohibition as the business organization, or other association that actually furnishes, or provides for the furnishing of, a service to a Medicare or Medicaid patient and bills for that service (or receives payment for the service from the billing entity as part of an "under arrangements" or similar agreement). We explained that we meant that the referral prohibition applies to a physician's referrals to any entity that directly furnishes services to program patients, or to any entity that arranges for the furnishing of these services under arrangements. We are clarifying in Phase I of this rulemaking that, for purposes of section 1877 of the Act, a person or entity is considered to be furnishing DHS if it is the person or entity to which we make payment for the DHS, directly or upon assignment on the patient's behalf, except that if the person or entity has reassigned its right to payment to (i) an employer pursuant to Sec. 424.80(b)(1); (ii) a facility pursuant to Sec. 424.80(b)(2); or (iii) a health care delivery system, including clinics, pursuant to Sec. 424.80(b)(3) (other than a health care delivery system that is a health plan (as defined in Sec. 1000.952(l)), and other than any MCO, PSO, or IPA with which a health plan contracts for services provided to plan enrollees), the person or entity furnishing DHS is the person or entity to which payment has been reassigned. Provided further, that a health plan, MCO, PSO, or IPA that employs a supplier or operates a facility that could accept reassignment from a supplier pursuant to Secs. 424.80(b)(1) and (b)(2) is the entity furnishing DHS for any services provided by such supplier.

A number of commenters pointed out, in various contexts, that they did not believe a physician could make a "referral" to himself or herself. We agree and discuss this issue in section III.B of this preamble, which covers the definition of a referral. In our analysis of this issue, we also concluded that when a physician is referring to himself or herself, that act is not a referral to an "entity," as we have defined it in Sec. 411.351. However, when the physician requests a service from another member of his or her group practice or from the practice's staff, that would be a referral to the practice for purposes of the physician self-referral law. These concepts are discussed in more detail in our responses to specific comments on the definition of a "referral" and on some of the DHS.

In the preamble to the January 1998 proposed regulation (63 FR 1710), we addressed the question of when the owner of a DHS provider is considered to be equivalent to the entity providing DHS. We had proposed to equate a referring physician with the entity when the physician (or a family member) has a significant ownership or controlling interest that allows the physician to determine how the entity conducts its business and with whom. We used two examples to illustrate this concept. Commenters found both our analysis and those examples to be confusing. As a result, we have abandoned this analysis and will simply apply the rules related to indirect financial relationships and indirect referrals as described in detail in section III of this preamble, which covers the general referral prohibition under section 1877(a) of the Act. Section III.A of this preamble includes a discussion about when there is a financial relationship between a physician and an entity.

Comment: A commenter suggested that we clarify in both the preamble and regulations text that a medical device manufacturing company is not an "entity" for the purposes of section 1877 of the Act, and that the manufacturer does not receive payments from billings "under arrangements." Another commenter requested that we clarify that drug manufacturers are not "entities" for purposes of section 1877 of the Act, and that a referral for outpatient prescription drugs only occurs when a physician sends a patient to a particular entity that actively furnishes drugs, such as a pharmacy.

Response: We generally do not regard manufacturers as entities that furnish items or services directly to patients, or as entities that furnish services "under arrangements." Thus, the commenters are correct in stating that a medical device manufacturer or a drug manufacturer is unlikely to be an entity furnishing DHS for purposes of section 1877 of the Act, while a pharmacy, which delivers outpatient prescription drugs directly to patients, would be one. (We discuss this issue in more detail in section VIII.B of this preamble.) A person or entity is considered to be furnishing DHS if it is the person or entity to which we make payment for the DHS, directly or upon assignment on the patient's behalf, except that if the person or entity has reassigned its right to payment to (i) an employer pursuant to Sec. 424.80(b)(1); (ii) a facility pursuant to Sec. 424.80(b)(2); or (iii) a health care delivery system, including clinics, pursuant to Sec. 424.80(b)(3) (other than a health care delivery system that is a health plan (as defined in Sec. 1000.952(l)), and other than any MCO, PSO, or IPA with which a health plan contracts for services provided to plan enrollees), the person or entity furnishing DHS is the person or entity to which payment has been reassigned. Provided further, that a health plan, MCO, PSO, or IPA that employs a supplier or operates a facility that could accept reassignment from a supplier pursuant to Secs. 424.80(b)(1) and (b)(2) is the entity furnishing DHS for any services provided by such supplier.

Comment: A commenter asked us to clarify that State governments and their instrumentalities are not "entities" for purposes of section 1877 of the Act. The commenter noted that many State and local governments create integrated delivery systems and payment arrangements in order to increase access to and decrease the cost of publicly provided care. If the governments or their instrumentalities were to be considered "entities," the commenter argued that State-sponsored clinics and programs may cease to exist, thus restricting access to, and raising the costs of, public programs.

Response: The referral prohibition applies whenever a physician has an unexcepted financial relationship with "an entity" that furnishes DHS. The statute makes no distinction between private and governmental entities, nor do we believe that we have the authority to make such a distinction. We have no basis for concluding that referrals to governmental entities are always free from potential patient or program abuse, so we see no grounds for creating an additional exception under section 1877(b)(4) of the Act. However, we would assume that many governmental entities have compensation arrangements with physicians, rather than being owned in any way by physicians. If this is the case, there are a number of compensation related exceptions in the statute and regulations that are designed to allow physicians who receive fair compensation to continue making referrals.

3. Fair Market Value

The term "fair market value" appears in most of the compensation related exceptions. These exceptions, among other things, require that compensation between physicians (or family members) and entities be based on the fair market value of the particular items or services that these parties are exchanging. We defined this term in the August 1995 final rule covering referrals for clinical laboratory services by using the definition that appears in section 1877(h)(3) of the Act. This provision defines fair market value as the value in arm's-length transactions, consistent with the general market value, with other specific terms for rentals or leases.

In the January 1998 proposed rule, we discussed what constitutes a value that is "consistent with the general market value." We drafted the definition as follows so that it applies to any arrangements involving items or services, including, but not limited to, employment relationships, personal service arrangements, and rental agreements:

"General market value" is the price that an asset would bring, as the result of bona fide bargaining between well-informed buyers and sellers, or the compensation that would be included in a service agreement, as the result of bona fide bargaining between well-informed parties to the agreement, on the date of acquisition of the asset or at the time of the service agreement. Usually the fair market price is the price at which bona fide sales have been consummated for assets of like type, quality, and quantity in a particular market at the time of acquisition, or the compensation that has been included in bona fide service agreements with comparable terms at the time of the agreement.

The definition of "fair market value" in the proposed rule continued to include the additional requirements in section 1877(h)(3) of the Act for rentals or leases. Among other things, the statute defines the fair market value of rental property as its value for general commercial purposes, not taking into account its intended use. Most of the comments we received addressed the question of how to establish the fair market value of an asset or agreement and how to value rental property "for general commercial purposes." We have tried to clarify these concepts in our responses.

Comment: Several commenters asked that we clarify the documentation that will sufficiently establish a transaction as consistent with fair market value (and general market value) for the exceptions that apply to compensation arrangements. The proposed definition of fair market value states that "usually the fair market price is the price at which bona fide sales have been consummated for assets of like type, quality, and quantity in a particular market at the time of acquisition or the compensation that has been included in bona fide service agreements with comparable terms at the time of the agreement." One commenter stated that using the word "usually" may create ambiguities and suggested making clear in the definition of fair market value that the standard of comparable transactions is only one potential means of establishing fair market value.

Another commenter stated that the January 1998 proposed rule is unclear about the steps that must be taken to confirm fair market value. The commenter asked that we adopt the position that a valuation from an independent person experienced in the valuation of health care operations is sufficient as one approach (but not the only approach) to establishing fair market value. However, the commenter further stated that, because sales of medical practices are private and not reported to any central data base, and because there is often a lack of a representative pool upon which to draw comparisons, we should adopt the position that confirmation of fair market value does not necessarily require the finding of comparable entities for comparison. Another commenter stated that the Internal Revenue Service (IRS) guidelines for determining fair market value with respect to tax exempt organizations are too restrictive and are inappropriate for application to for-profit entities.

Response: To establish the fair market value (and general market value) of a transaction that involves compensation paid for assets or services, we intend to accept any method that is commercially reasonable and provides us with evidence that the compensation is comparable to what is ordinarily paid for an item or service in the location at issue, by parties in arm's-length transactions who are not in a position to refer to one another. (As discussed in section V of this preamble, in most instances the fair market value standard is further modified by language that precludes taking into account the "volume or value" of referrals, and, in some cases, other business generated by the referring physician. Depending on the circumstances, the "volume or value" restriction will preclude reliance on comparables that involve entities and physicians in a position to refer or generate business.) The amount of documentation that will be sufficient to confirm fair market value (and general market value) will vary depending on the circumstances in any given case; that is, there is no rule of thumb that will suffice for all situations. The burden of establishing the "fairness" of an agreement rests with the parties involved in the agreement. Depending on the circumstances, parties may want to consider obtaining good faith, written assurances as to fair market value from the party paying or receiving the compensation, although such written assurances are not determinative.

For example, a commercially reasonable method of establishing fair market value (and general market value) for the rental of office space can include providing us with a list of comparables. We would also find acceptable an appraisal that the parties have received from a qualified independent expert. Although some transactions are not subject to public scrutiny, we believe generally that there should be sufficient documentation of similar public transactions that the parties can use as a basis of comparison. In regions with inadequate direct comparables, such as rural areas, a reasonable alternative may involve comparing institutions or entities located in different, but similar, areas where property is zoned for similar use. For example, a hospital affiliated with a university in one part of the country could be comparable to other hospitals affiliated with universities that are located in similar types of communities. In other cases, all the comparables or market values may involve transactions between entities that are in a position to refer or generate other business. For example, in some markets, physician-owned equipment lessors have driven out competitive third-party lessors of similar equipment. In such situations, we would look to alternative valuation methodologies, including, but not limited to, cost plus reasonable rate of return on investment on leases of comparable medical equipment from disinterested lessors.

In contrast, there may be cases in which finding a commercially reasonable representation of fair market value (or general market value) could be as simple as consulting a price list. As for using the IRS guidelines for determining fair market value that applies to tax exempt organizations, we recognize that in some cases they may not be appropriate for for-profit entities. Nonetheless, it is our view that some elements of the IRS guidelines could be applied under certain circumstances, depending upon the specifics of any particular agreement. We do not wish to either mandate their use or rule them out if they can be appropriately used to demonstrate fair market value.

Comment: One commenter noted that, as part of our definition of "fair market value," we include the term "general market value," which applies to any arrangement involving items and services, including employment relationships, personal service arrangements, and rental agreements. The commenter pointed out that in the January 1998 proposed rule we do not address the specific documentation requirements necessary to verify and document that the price of an asset or the compensation for certain services actually reflects the market rate. The commenter requested that we confirm that internally generated surveys are sufficient for establishing the market rate, and that there is no requirement to use an independent valuation consultant.

Response: We agree that there is no requirement that parties use an independent valuation consultant for any given arrangement when other appropriate valuation methods are available. However, while internally generated surveys can be appropriate as a method of establishing fair market value in some circumstances, due to their susceptibility to manipulation and absent independent verification, such surveys do not have strong evidentiary value and, therefore, may be subject to more intensive scrutiny than an independent survey.

Special Rule for Rental Property. Under section 1877(h)(3) of the Act, fair market value means the value of rental property for general commercial purposes (not taking into account its intended use). In the case of a lease of space, this value may not be adjusted to reflect the additional value the prospective lessee or lessor would attribute to the proximity or convenience to the lessor where the lessor is a potential source of patient referrals to the lessee. We incorporated this provision into the August 1995 final rule covering referrals for clinical laboratory services and into the January 1998 proposed rule at Sec. 411.351. Commenters raised questions about the meaning of the statutory provision.

Comment: With respect to the rental of property, commenters questioned our definition of fair market value as "the value of rental property for general commercial purposes (not taking into account its intended use)." The commenters believe this language is problematic for appraising a medical office building because it requires the appraiser to compare the property to the broad category of properties that are "used for general commercial purposes." This latter category can include properties that are highly dissimilar in character and value. For example, the appraisal for medical office property could include retail or industrial rates. Such an approach conflicts with the fundamental principle that appraisals should be based on comparing properties with similar attributes.

Response: We believe that a rental property meets the requirement that a payment reflect the "value of property for general commercial purposes, not taking into account its intended use" when the payment takes into account any costs that were incurred by the lessor in developing or upgrading the property, or maintaining the property or its improvements, regardless of why the improvements were added. That is, the rental payment can reflect the value of any similar commercial property with improvements or amenities of a similar value, regardless of why the property was improved. On the other hand, we also believe that rental payments would specifically take into account the intended use of the property if the lessee paid inflated amounts solely to enhance his or her medical practice. For example, rental payments by a physical therapist would not be fair market value for purposes of section 1877 of the Act if the physical therapist agreed to pay an inflated rate that was not justified by improvements or other amenities and was higher than the rate paid by other, similarly situated medical practitioners in the same building just because the building was occupied by several orthopedic practices.

A rental payment cannot be adjusted to reflect the additional value the prospective lessee or lessor would attribute to the proximity or convenience to the lessor where the lessor is a physician and a potential source of patient referrals to the lessee. We interpret this requirement to allow rental payments that reflect the fair market value of the area in which the property is located, even if a lease is for medical property in a "medical community." To qualify, the payments should not reflect any additional value, such as an amount that is above that paid by other medical practitioners in the same building or in the same or in a similar location, just because the lessor is a potential source of referrals to the lessee. That is, the rental payments should be roughly equivalent to those charged to similarly situated parties in arrangements in which referrals are not an issue.

Also, the statute requires that the rental payments not reflect the additional value either party attributes to the proximity or convenience to the lessor where the lessor is a potential source of patient referrals to the lessee. The definition of a "referral" by a "referring physician" in section 1877(h)(5) of the Act focuses only on actions and requests for services that are initiated by physicians; it does not include any requests for services initiated by entities or other providers or suppliers, nor does the referral prohibition itself apply to anything but physician referrals. Thus, we believe that it is fair to interpret the limitation in the fair market value definition as confined to situations in which a physician is the lessor and a potential source of referrals to an entity lessee. That limitation does not appear to us to apply when an entity, such as a hospital, is the lessor that rents space to physicians, even if the hospital is in a position to refer to the physicians. As a result, we believe a hospital should factor in the value of proximity when charging rent to lessee physicians.

4. Group Practice

The definition of a group practice under section 1877(h)(4) of the Act is addressed in this preamble at section VI.C and in the regulations at Sec. 411.352.

5. Health Professional Shortage Areas

The existing regulations covering referrals for clinical laboratory services define a health professional shortage area (HPSA) for purposes of section 1877 of the Act as "an area designated as a health professional shortage area under section 332(a)(1)(A) of the Public Health Service Act for primary medical care professionals (in accordance with the criteria specified in 42 CFR part 5, appendix A, part I — Geographic Areas)" and, in addition, "an area designated as a health professional shortage area under section 332(a)(1)(A) of the Public Health Service Act for dental professionals, mental health professionals, vision care professionals, podiatric professionals, and pharmacy professionals. We proposed no changes to the existing rule.

The definition of a HPSA for purposes of Phase I of this rulemaking is intended to track the definition of a HPSA as promulgated by the Health Resources Services Administration (HRSA), which administers the HPSA designation process. HRSA has proposed revising the existing HPSA regulations. (See 63 FR 46538; 64 FR 29831.) We have modified the definition of a HPSA in these regulations to track current HRSA interpretations of the HPSA regulations and to make clear that the definition incorporates any future changes or amendments to HRSA's definition of a HPSA, which is codified in 42 CFR part 5.

6. Employee

We defined an "employee" in the existing regulation and in the January 1998 proposed regulation in Sec. 411.351 by reiterating the statute. Section 1877(h)(2) of the Act specifically defines an "employee" of an entity as an individual who would be considered to be an employee under the usual common law rules that apply in determining the employer-employee relationship, as applied for purposes of section 3121(d)(2) of the Internal Revenue Code of 1986.

Comment: Two commenters recommended an expansion of the proposed definition of "employee" to include "leased employees" to better reflect the realities of the market place. The current definition, which references income tax law, limits an employee to an individual who meets the definition of a "common law" employee. But the definition of a common law employee does not include leased employees, who are defined by State law and have a quasi-common law status.

Response: We do not believe we have the authority to expand the definition of employee that appears in the law. It is our understanding that leased employees are essentially regarded by the courts, the IRS, and Federal legislators as "contingent employees." Contingent workers are generally described as workers who are not part of the employer's regular work force, but are hired to meet certain needs. These workers are technically employed by an entity other than the one for whom the services are performed. Other types of contingent workers include independent contractors and consultants.

A leased employee is defined in section 414(n) of the Internal Revenue Service Code as an individual who performs services under an agreement between the service recipient and a leasing/staffing organization; performs services under the primary direction or control of the service recipient; and performs services for the service recipient on a substantially full-time basis for a 12-month period. The labeling of a worker as a leased employee under a leasing/staffing arrangement does not mean that the worker will be defined as a "leased employee" under section 414(n) of the Internal Revenue Code for employee benefit plan purposes. The IRS determines the common law employment relationship between a worker and an organization by analyzing the facts and circumstances of each particular situation. The IRS uses guidelines, in the form of a list of factors, for classifying workers as either employees or independent contractors, in order to determine whether there is actually an employer/employee relationship. We would regard any leased employee that qualifies as an "employee" under the IRS test as an employee for purposes of section 1877 of the Act.

7. Immediate Family Members

The referral prohibition in section 1877(a) of the Act states that if a physician, or immediate family member, has a financial relationship with an entity, the physician cannot refer a Medicare patient to that entity for the furnishing of DHS, unless an exception applies. In the August 1995 final rule, we listed in Sec. 411.351 the individuals who qualify as a physician's "immediate" family members. These individuals include a husband or wife; natural or adoptive parent, child, or sibling; stepparent, stepchild, stepbrother, or stepsister; father-in-law, mother-in-law, son-in-law, daughter-in-law, brother-in-law, or sister-in-law; grandparent or grandchild; and spouse of a grandparent or grandchild. We adopted this definition without any changes in the January 1998 proposed rule.

We did not receive any comments on this definition. We did receive comments that relate to whether physicians should be precluded from referring to people who qualify as members of their immediate family. We have addressed these comments in section VI.B of this preamble. To conform to common usage, we have amended the definition to substitute the term "birth" for "natural" parent.

8. Referral

The definition of "referral" is addressed in this preamble in section III and in Sec. 411.351 of the regulations.

9. Remuneration and the Exceptions in Section 1877(h)(1)(C) of the Act

The definition of "remuneration" in section 1877(h)(1)(B) of the Act is drafted broadly to include "any remuneration, directly or indirectly, in cash or in kind." However, a "compensation arrangement" is defined in paragraph (h)(1)(A) of section 1877 of the Act to specifically exclude various kinds of remuneration that are listed in paragraph (h)(1)(C) of section 1877 of the Act. These are arrangements involving only the following remuneration:

(i) the forgiveness of amounts owed for inaccurate tests or procedures, mistakenly performed tests or procedures, or the correction of minor billing errors;

(ii) the provision of items, devices, or supplies that are used solely to—

(I) collect, transport, process, or store specimens for the entity furnishing the item, device, or supply, or

(II) to order or communicate the results of tests or procedures for such entity.

(iii) a payment made by an insurer or a self-insured plan to a physician to satisfy a claim, submitted on a fee for service basis, for the furnishing of health services by that physician to an individual who is covered by a policy with the insurer or by the self-insured plan, if—

(I) the health services are not furnished, and the payment is not made under a contract or other arrangement between the insurer or the plan and the physician,

(II) the payment is made to the physician on behalf of the covered individual and would otherwise be made directly to the individual,

(III) the amount of the payment is set in advance, does not exceed fair market value, and is not determined in a manner that takes into account directly or indirectly the volume or value of any referrals, and

(IV) the payment meets such other requirements as the Secretary may impose by regulation as needed to protect against program or patient abuse.

We incorporated these exclusions from the definition of "remuneration" into the August 1995 final rule and into the January 1998 proposed rule in Sec. 411.351. We interpreted the exclusions in the January 1998 proposed rule at 63 FR 1693 through 1694 to mean that the portion of any business arrangement that consists of the remuneration listed in paragraph (h)(1)(C) of section 1877 of the Act alone does not constitute a compensation arrangement. The final regulation adopts our proposed regulations text and incorporates expressly the interpretation applicable to arrangements that include portions of remuneration that meet the exclusions in section 1877 (h)(1)(C) of the Act.

a. Minor Billing Errors.

Comment: One commenter, in referring to the exclusion from remuneration of forgiveness for amounts due to corrections of minor billing errors, stated that even a "minor" billing error might have large dollar consequences, particularly if the same minor mistake were repeated on numerous bills. This could easily happen because virtually all bills are now computer-generated. The commenter stated that the term "minor" should refer to the type of error, rather than the sum of money that may be involved.

Response: We agree with the commenter's suggestion that a "minor" billing error could have large dollar consequences, particularly in situations in which bills are computer generated. We also agree that the term "minor" should refer to the kind of billing error rather than the sum of money involved. Therefore, we are interpreting "minor billing errors" to cover isolated or infrequent instances in which an administrative error, such as a typographic, keying, or other transcribing error, results in an incorrect charge or bill. On the other hand, a pattern of similar or consistent billing error "corrections" may suggest improper remuneration and subject the business arrangement to scrutiny.

b. Medicare as an Insurer.

Section 1877(h)(1)(C)(iii) of the Act "excepts" from the definition of a compensation arrangement situations involving payments made by an insurer or self-insured plan to a physician. The payments must satisfy a physician's fee-for-service claim for furnishing health services to an individual who is covered by a policy with the insurer or the self-insured plan.

Comment: One commenter asked whether the term "insurer" includes the Medicare program. The commenter believes that Medicare is included within the meaning of the term "insurer," and cited for support references in the preamble, as well as the designation of Medicare in the Act as "Health Insurance for the Aged and Disabled."

Response: In the preamble to the January 1998 proposed rule at 63 FR 1694, we pointed out that we believed this provision was designed for situations in which an insurer is also involved in the delivery of health care services. If the insurer owns a health care facility, a physician might otherwise be precluded from referring to that facility just because the physician receives compensation from the insurer in the form of payments that satisfy the physician's claims.

The Medicare program is not directly involved in the delivery of services, but is simply a payer of services; that is, Medicare never actually furnishes services to program patients but pays for claims from providers and suppliers or makes payments to managed care organizations. The physician self-referral law is only implicated if a physician refers a patient to an entity for DHS and the physician has an ownership or investment interest in the entity or receives direct or indirect remuneration from the entity. Since a physician would never refer a patient to the Medicare program to receive a designated health service, these payments from Medicare to a physician are totally irrelevant under this law.

c. Items, Devices, or Supplies Used Solely To Collect Specimens.

Comment: One commenter thought there was a possible inconsistency in the preamble to the January 1998 proposed rule in the section discussing whether biopsy needles are excluded from the definition of remuneration under section 1877(h)(1)(C)(ii) of the Act. Section 1877(h)(1)(C)(ii) of the Act covers items, devices, or supplies that are used solely to collect, transport, process, or store specimens for the entity providing the items, devices, or supplies. First, the commenter noted our conclusion at 63 FR 1693 through 1694 that biopsy needles do not function solely as specimen collection devices and therefore are categorically excluded from "items, devices, or supplies that are used solely" for specimen collection purposes. In other words, biopsy needles may constitute remuneration under section 1877 of the Act. This discussion is followed in the preamble by a statement that any items, supplies, or devices provided to a physician must be used solely in connection with specimens sent by the physician to the entity that supplied the items, devices, or supplies. Accordingly, the preamble indicates that the number of items, supplies, or devices furnished should not exceed the number of specimens sent to the laboratory for processing. The commenter suggested that the proximity and sequence of these discussions in the preamble has caused confusion in the industry; some have concluded that, regardless of the first discussion and conclusion, biopsy needles might not constitute remuneration if the number of biopsy needles provided by a laboratory were to correlate to the number of biopsy specimens sent to the laboratory.

The commenter urged us to adopt the view that biopsy needles are surgical or medical devices, rather than items, devices, or supplies solely used for specimen collection purposes in all cases. The commenter noted that this interpretation would be consistent with statements made by the OIG that the free provision of biopsy needles from a laboratory to a physician would be suspect under the anti-kickback statute because the needles have independent value to the physician as a surgical device used in surgical procedures. (See the letter dated August 4, 1997, available on the OIG website at http://www.dhhs.oig/gov.) A second commenter concurred with this conclusion, and suggested that the same analysis should apply to other surgical or medical devices that may be used during a procedure to collect specimens, but have independent value to physicians, such as snares and reusable aspiration and injection needles.

Response: We agree with the first commenter that the proximity and sequence of our discussion of this topic in the preamble might have been confusing. We wish to clarify our views on the "items, devices, and supplies" provision here. First, in enacting section 1877(h)(1)(C)(ii) of the Act, we believe that the Congress did not intend to allow laboratories to supply physicians with surgical instruments for free or below fair market value prices. Rather, we believe the Congress intended to include in this section items, supplies, and devices of low value, such as single use needles, vials, and specimen cups, that are primarily provided by laboratories to physicians to ensure proper collection of specimens for processing at the laboratory and that have little, if any, independent economic value to the physicians who receive them. In many cases, the cost of these items may already be included in the practice expense portion of the Medicare payment made to the physician. In addition, to the extent the items are reusable, they may have value unrelated to the collection of specimens for processing by the laboratory providing the items. The provision of such items for free or below fair market value poses a risk that the items may constitute compensation from the laboratories for the physician's referrals and increase the risk of overutilization. Accordingly, biopsy needles and like devices, such as snares and reusable aspiration and injection needles, are categorically excluded from the items, devices, and supplies covered by section 1877(h)(1)(C)(ii) of the Act, although arrangements for providing such items may be structured to fit into the exception for payments by a physician for items and services to an entity if the items or services are furnished at a price that is consistent with fair market value. (See section 1877(e)(7) of the Act and Sec. 411.357(i).) This view is consistent with the guidance published by the OIG noted in the preceding comment.

The discussion of the correlation of the number of supplies to the number of specimens sent to the laboratory has no application to biopsy needles and other devices that fall outside section 1877(h)(1)(C)(ii) of the Act. As to those single use, low value items, devices, and supplies that come within the scope of section 1877(h)(1)(C)(ii) of the Act, the fact that the number of supplies provided to a physician approximates the number of specimens sent by the physician to the laboratory providing the supplies is merely one indicator that the supplies have been provided in connection with specimen collection for the entity providing the supplies. The numerical correlation is not a statutory or regulatory requirement. However, the provision of an excessive number of supplies creates an inference that the supplies are not provided solely to collect, transport, process, or store specimens for the entity providing them.

Comment: A commenter noted that certain supplies that are used in connection with the collection of specimens, such as gloves, can also be used by a physician for other purposes. Since the laboratory cannot guarantee that the gloves it supplies are used by the physician only for collecting specimens, the commenter recommended that the laboratory monitor the volume of the items supplied. The commenter asserted that if the number of gloves supplied equals, or is close to, the number needed for the collection of specimens by this physician, we should consider the conditions in the exception in section 1877(h)(1)(C)(ii) of the Act to have been met.

Response: While we recognize that sterile gloves are essential to the proper collection of specimens, we believe they are not items, devices, or supplies used solely to collect, transport, process, or store specimens. To be sure, sterile gloves are essential to the specimen collection process, but their main function is to prevent infection or contamination. Also, sterile gloves are fungible, general purpose supplies typically found in a physician's office and used for a wide range of examinations and procedures. We believe it would be impractical for physicians' offices to monitor and regulate the use of gloves so as to limit their use to the collection of specimens for the laboratory that provided them. Accordingly, we believe the provision of free gloves is remuneration subject to the general prohibition of section 1877 of the Act, in the absence of an applicable exception.

Comment: A commenter questioned how a laboratory should measure the volume of specimen collection supplies it provides to a new physician or group client with whom it has no experience. In such a situation, the commenter believes the laboratory should be allowed to rely on the anticipated volume of services, until an actual pattern of referral can be established, to meet the requirement that items furnished by the laboratory be consistent with the number of tests referred to the laboratory.

Response: As noted above, there is no explicit requirement in the statute that the volume of supplies provided by a laboratory correlate with the volume of specimens sent to the laboratory for processing. Rather, a correlation is one indicator that the provision of the supplies meets the requirement that they be used to collect, transport, process, or store specimens for the laboratory that provided them and that the supplies are not for the physician's general office use. We understand that a laboratory may not have a pattern of referrals on which to base the provision of items, devices, and supplies to a new physician or group practice client. In these instances, the laboratory may elect to provide supplies based on the number of tests typically ordered by physicians or group practices of like type and size in that community until the physician or group practice establishes a pattern of referrals with the laboratory sufficient to determine the appropriate number of supplies. The laboratory or physician should be prepared to demonstrate that the items, devices, or supplies were furnished based on a community standard and to describe the standard.

Comment: One commenter asked that we clarify how section 1877 of the Act applies to a clinical laboratory's provision of a phlebotomist to a physician, group practice, or ESRD facility without charge to the physician, group, or ESRD facility.

Response: Under section 1877(h)(1)(B) of the Act, remuneration includes "any remuneration, directly or indirectly, overtly or covertly, in cash or in kind," with the exception of certain items of potential value listed in section 1877(h)(1)(C) of the Act. The provision of personnel, such as a phlebotomist, does not fit in any category listed in section 1877(h)(1)(C). Thus, the provision of a phlebotomist, as described by the commenter, may constitute remuneration, and therefore create a compensation arrangement, for purposes of section 1877 of the Act. Whether a particular phlebotomist arrangement confers a benefit on a physician or group practice depends on the specific facts and circumstances. (The provision of a phlebotomist to an ESRD facility would not implicate section 1877 of the Act, unless the arrangement conferred a direct or indirect benefit on a physician or physician group; such laboratory-ESRD facility arrangements may implicate the anti-kickback statute.)

The OIG has issued a special fraud alert addressing the provision of free goods and services to physicians under the anti-kickback statute, 59 FR 242 (December 9, 1994). We believe the fraud alert is instructive here. Discussing the issue of laboratory phlebotomists placed in physicians' offices, it observes:

When permitted by State law, a laboratory may make available to a physician's office a phlebotomist who collects specimens from patients for testing by the outside laboratory. While the mere placement of a laboratory employee in the physician's office would not necessarily serve as an inducement prohibited by the anti-kickback statute, the statute is implicated when the phlebotomist performs additional tasks that are normally the responsibility of the physician's office staff. These tasks can include taking vital signs or other nursing functions, testing for the physician's office laboratory, or performing clerical services. Where the phlebotomist performs clerical or medical functions not directly related to the collection or processing of laboratory specimens, a strong inference arises that he or she is providing a benefit in return for the physician's referrals to the laboratory. In such a case, the physician, the phlebotomist, and the laboratory may have exposure under the anti-kickback statute. This analysis applies equally to the placement of phlebotomists in other health care settings, including nursing homes, clinics and hospitals. Furthermore, the mere existence of a contract between the laboratory and the health care provider that prohibits the phlebotomist from performing services unrelated to specimen collection does not eliminate the OIG's concern, where the phlebotomist is not closely monitored by his [or her] employer or where the contractual prohibition is not rigorously enforced.

Like the OIG, we believe that if the phlebotomist is purely performing laboratory functions for the laboratory that places the phlebotomist, then there would be no remuneration to the physician or group practice (that is, no compensation arrangement). Put another way, there would be no services to the physician or group for which they should pay. However, if the phlebotomist performs services that are not directly related to the collection or processing of laboratory specimens for the laboratory that has provided the phlebotomist, he or she may be providing a benefit to the physician or group practice, thus creating a compensation arrangement between the physician and the clinical laboratory that furnished the phlebotomist. Such arrangements may be structured to fit in an exception to section 1877 of the Act, such as the personal service arrangements exception, the fair market value exception, or the exception for payments by physicians for items or services.

Comment: Another commenter asked that we establish a clear standard governing the use by ESRD facilities of personnel from a clinical laboratory. The commenter recommended that employees of clinical laboratories only be allowed to perform duties directly associated with collecting and preparing specimens, and making test results available to the ESRD facility. Activities involved in ESRD facility administration, patient care, or handling of specimens or data from other laboratories would not be allowed.

Response: As noted above, the provision of a phlebotomist to an ESRD facility would not implicate section 1877 of the Act unless the arrangement benefits a physician or physician group.

Comment: One commenter inquired whether a laboratory may provide medical waste disposal supplies and services to physicians free of charge. The commenter asserted that the services would be provided only for medical waste generated in connection with the collection, transportation, processing, or storage of specimens.

Response: Section 1877(h)(1)(C)(ii) of the Act excludes from the definition of a compensation arrangement remuneration that consists of "the provision of items, devices, or supplies that are used solely to—(I) collect, transport, process, or store specimens for the entity providing the item, device, or supply * * *. " The provision does not specifically allow laboratories to furnish physicians and group practices with medical waste disposal supplies and services at no charge. However, we believe that supplies and the disposal of items used solely in connection with the collection of specimens for this clinical laboratory are part of the process the laboratory engages in when it collects, transports, and processes specimens. If a laboratory can provide a needle for collection and it can take away the specimen, we believe that the laboratory can also take away the needle and other items that are used in the process. However, we do not believe this exception covers the disposal of needles or other waste items that have been used by the physician practice for other purposes.

IX. Collection of Information Requirements

Under the Paperwork Reduction Act of 1995 (PRA), agencies are required to provide a 30-day notice in the **Federal Register** and solicit public comment when a collection of information requirement is submitted to the Office of Management and Budget (OMB) for review and approval. To fairly evaluate whether an information collection should be approved by OMB, section 3506(c)(2)(A) of the PRA requires that we solicit comments on the following issues:

Whether the information collection is necessary and useful to carry out the proper functions of the agency;

The accuracy of the agency's estimate of the information collection burden;

The quality, utility, and clarity of the information to be collected; and

Recommendations to minimize the information collection burden on the affected public, including automated collection techniques. Therefore, we are soliciting public comment on each of these issues for the information collection requirements discussed below.

Section 411.352 Group Practice

Paragraph (d) requires that, except as provided in paragraphs (d)(2) and (d)(3) of this section, substantially all of the patient care services of the physicians who are members of the group (that is, at least 75 percent of the total patient care services of the group practice members) must be furnished through the group and billed under a billing number assigned to the group; the amounts received must be treated as receipts of the group; and "patient care services" must be measured and documented by any reasonable means (including, but not limited to, time cards, appointment schedules, or personal diaries) or any alternative measure that is reasonable, fixed in advance of the performance of the services being measured, uniformly applied over time, verifiable, and documented.

While this requirement is subject to the PRA, the burden associated with it is exempt from the PRA because it meets the requirements set forth in 5 CFR 1320.3(b)(2) and/or (b)(3) and 5 CFR 1320.4(a).

Paragraph (i) requires that supporting documentation verifying the method used to calculate the profit shares or productivity bonus under paragraphs (i)(2) and (i)(3) of this section, and the resulting amount of compensation, must be made available to the Secretary upon request.

While this requirement is subject to the PRA, the burden associated with it is exempt from the PRA because it meets the requirements set forth in 5 CFR 1320.3(b)(2) and/or (b)(3) and 5 CFR 1320.4(a).

Section 411.354 Financial Relationship, Compensation, and Ownership or Investment Interest

Paragraph (d) requires that, when special rules are applied to compensation under section 1877 of the Act and under these regulations in subpart J of this part, the compensation will be considered "set in advance" if the aggregate compensation or a time-based or per unit of service-based (whether per-use or per-service) amount is set in advance in the initial agreement, in writing, between the parties in sufficient detail so that it can be objectively verified, and meets the terms and conditions of this section.

While this requirement is subject to the PRA, the burden associated with it is exempt from the PRA because it meets the requirements set forth in 5 CFR 1320.3(b)(2) and/or (b)(3) and 5 CFR 1320.4(a).

Section 411.355 General Exceptions to the Referral Prohibition Related to Both Ownership/Investment and Compensation

Paragraph (e) requires that the relationship of the components of the academic medical center must be set forth in a written agreement that has been adopted by the governing body of each component.

While this requirement is subject to the PRA, the burden associated with it is exempt from the PRA because it meets the requirements set forth in 5 CFR 1320.3(b)(2) and/or (b)(3) and 5 CFR 1320.4(a).

Section 411.357 Exceptions to the Referral Prohibition Related to Compensation Arrangements

Paragraph (l) requires that compensation resulting from an arrangement between an entity and a physician (or an immediate family member) or any group of physicians (regardless of whether the group meets the definition of a group practice set forth in Sec. 411.351) for the provision of items or services by the physician (or an immediate family member) or group practice to the entity, must be set forth in an agreement, be in writing, and meet the conditions of the section.

While this requirement is subject to the PRA, the burden associated with it is exempt from the PRA because it meets the requirements set forth in 5 CFR 1320.3(b)(2) and/or (b)(3) and 5 CFR 1320.4(a).

Paragraph (p) requires that, for indirect compensation arrangements, as defined in Sec. 411.354(c)(2), the compensation described in Sec. 411.354(c)(2)(ii) is part of an arrangement that is set out in writing and meets all of the conditions and requirements set forth in this section.

While this requirement is subject to the PRA, the burden associated with it is exempt from the PRA because it meets the requirements set forth in 5 CFR 1320.3(b)(2) and/or (b)(3) and 5 CFR 1320.4(a).

We have submitted a copy of this final rule to OMB for its review of the information collection requirements in Secs. 411.352, 411.354, 411.355, and 411.357. These requirements are not effective until they have been approved by OMB.

If you have any comments on any of these information collection and record keeping requirements, please mail the original and 3 copies within 30 days of this publication date directly to the following:

Office of Information and Regulatory Affairs, Office of Management and Budget, Room 10235, New Executive Office Building, Washington, DC 20503, Attn: Allison Heron Eydt, HCFA Desk Officer; and

Health Care Financing Administration, Office of Information Services, Information Technology Investment Management Group, Division of HCFA Enterprise Standards, Room N2–14–26, 7500 Security Boulevard, Baltimore, MD 21244–1850, Attn: John Burke HCFA-1809.

X. Regulatory Impact Statement

A. Overall Impact

We have examined the impacts of Phase I of this rulemaking as required by Executive Order 12866 (September 1993, Regulatory Planning and Review) and the Regulatory Flexibility Act (RFA) (Pub. L. 96–354, enacted September 19, 1980). Executive Order 12866 directs agencies to assess all costs and benefits of available regulatory alternatives and, if regulation is necessary, to select regulatory approaches that maximize net benefits (including potential economic, environmental, public health and safety effects, distributive impacts, and equity). A regulatory impact analysis (RIA) must be prepared for major rules with economically significant effects ($100 million or more annually). We do not believe that Phase I of this rulemaking is a major rule that will have an economically significant effect. We have no way of determining with any certainty the aggregate amount of savings or costs Phase I of this rulemaking will impose, but do not believe it will approach $100 million or more annually.

The RFA requires agencies to analyze options for regulatory relief of small businesses. For purposes of the RFA, small entities include small businesses, nonprofit organizations and government agencies. Most hospitals and most other providers and suppliers are small entities, either by nonprofit status or by having revenues of $5 million or less annually. For purposes of the RFA, most physician practices are considered to be small entities. Individuals and States are not included in the definition of a small entity.

In addition, section 1102(b) of the Act requires us to prepare an RIA if a rule may have a significant impact on the operations of a substantial number of small rural hospitals. This analysis must conform to the provisions of section 604 of the RFA. For purposes of section 1102(b) of the Act, we define a small rural hospital as a hospital that is located outside of a Metropolitan Statistical Area and has fewer than 50 beds. We do not believe Phase I of this rulemaking will have a significant impact on the operations of a substantial number of small rural hospitals.

Section 202 of the Unfunded Mandates Reform Act of 1995 also requires that agencies assess anticipated costs and benefits before issuing any rule that may result in an expenditure in any 1 year by State, local, or tribal governments, in the aggregate, or by the private sector, of $100 million. Phase I of this rulemaking will not have such an effect on the governments mentioned, and we do not believe the private sector costs will meet the $100 million threshold.

Executive Order 13132 establishes certain requirements that an agency must meet when it promulgates a proposed rule (and subsequent final rule) that imposes substantial direct requirement costs on State and local governments, preempts State law, or otherwise has Federalism implications. We do not anticipate that Phase I of this rulemaking will have a substantial effect on State or local governments.

B. Anticipated Effects

We stated in the impact analysis in the January 1998 proposed rule that any estimate of the individual or aggregate economic impact of the provisions of the final rule would be purely speculative. We explained that we could not gauge with any certainty the number of physicians and entities that would be affected, or the extent of any changes they would have to make to comply with the rule. As we noted in the January 1998 proposed rule at 63 FR 1716, various studies have indicated that the degree of conflict of interest presented by a physician's investment in entities to which he or she refers patients is unknown. We pointed out that ownership information or information on the compensation arrangements between physicians and all of their immediate family members and the entities that furnish any of 11 DHS constitutes an enormous amount of data that is continually subject to change. We also expected that the American Medical Association's declaration that self-referrals are unethical outside of a physician's practice, in conjunction with State laws restricting or qualifying self-referrals and the referral prohibition under section 1877 of the Act itself, have already led to a decline in self-referral activity and financial relationships between physicians and entities. However, we lack the data necessary to either confirm or refute this supposition. We also lack data that would tell us how many of the financial relationships that physicians have with a furnishing entity would already be exempted under the statute.

We stated that, although the provisions in the rule do not lend themselves to a quantitative impact estimate, we did not anticipate that they would have a significant economic impact on a substantial number of small entities. We based this assessment on the many exceptions in the rule (including a broad exception for ownership in rural entities), as well as the actions parties can take to revise their business arrangements to avoid the referral prohibition. We still believe this to be the case. In fact, we expect that Phase I of this rulemaking will have a much smaller impact than the provisions that we proposed. However, because Phase I of this rulemaking may have significant effects on some health care practitioners, or be viewed as controversial, we wish to inform the public of what we regard as the possible major effects of Phase I of this rulemaking.

We stated in the January 1998 proposed rule that we expected that physicians who refer Medicare patients for DHS and entities that furnish DHS, including hospitals, would be the parties that are primarily affected by this rule. In response to comments on the January 1998 proposed rule, we have liberalized a wide variety of the provisions that could affect these parties. We have tried to create a more manageable regulation that includes "bright line" rules to help the health care community determine more easily when a physician's referrals are in compliance with the law. We have made numerous changes to the rule to try to mold it around existing business practices, and have attempted to reinterpret the law so that it has a more practical and realistic effect on physicians and the entities that provide DHS. The result, we believe, is an overall approach that should have far less impact on the business relationships of individuals and entities than the provisions of the January 1998 proposed rule. We discuss below some of the major issues affecting physicians and furnishing entities. We also briefly discuss the effects of the rule on Medicare beneficiaries.

1. Effects on Physicians

A physician can be financially related to an entity either through an ownership or investment interest in the entity, or through a compensation arrangement with the entity. A physician who has (or whose immediate family member has) a financial relationship with an entity that does not qualify for an exception is prohibited from referring Medicare patients to that entity for the provision of DHS. Also, when a physician with such a relationship makes a prohibited referral, there is a risk that the entity will receive no Medicare payment for those DHS. These provisions can have a significant effect on the business arrangements in which a physician will participate and the manner in which the physician will structure his or her practice.

The potential impact of the regulation on physicians and other individual parties was revealed to us by the voluminous comments from the public and health care community we received in response to the January 1998 proposed rule. In addition to specific complaints and objections, the commenters expressed a number of general concerns, including that the proposed regulation inappropriately intruded into the organization and delivery of medical care within physicians' offices; that the regulation in many respects was counter to our other longstanding policies on coverage and similar issues; that the rule was unclear in many areas and that in light of the severe penalty (that is, payment denial), "bright line" rules were essential; and that some aspects of the proposed rule, such as its treatment of indirect financial relationships, were administratively impractical or would have been prohibitively costly in terms of monitoring compliance.

We believe Phase I of this rulemaking substantially addresses the concerns raised by the commenters and yet is consistent with the statute. Phase I of this rulemaking clarifies the definitions of DHS; substantially broadens the in-office ancillary services exception (which allows physicians to refer within their own practices) by easing the criteria for qualifying as a group practice and conforming the supervision requirements to our coverage and other payment policies; permits shared facilities in the same building where physicians routinely provide services that are neither Federal nor private pay DHS; excludes from the definition of "referral" services personally performed by the referring physician; expands the in-office ancillary services exception to cover certain DME provided to patients in physicians' offices; creates a new exception for compensation of faculty in academic medical centers; and clarifies when a managed care organization (MCO) is an entity furnishing DHS. All of these issues are described in greater detail elsewhere in the preamble, along with a number of lesser issues that could affect physicians.

2. Effects on Other Providers

As we stated above, Phase I of this rulemaking affects entities that furnish DHS by preventing them from receiving payment for services that they furnish as the result of a physician's prohibited referral. Entities can also be subject to various other sanctions, including fines and exclusion from Federal health care programs if they knowingly submit a claim in violation of the prohibition. We lack the data to determine the number of entities that could be affected by Phase I of this rulemaking. However, we believe they will be fewer in number than we had anticipated in the January 1998 proposed rule because, as we described above, physicians will have far more leeway to refer.

3. Effects on the Medicare and Medicaid Programs

Section 1877 of the Act was enacted primarily to address overutilization of health care services covered by Medicare. We have tried to focus Phase I of this rulemaking on financial relationships that may result in overutilization. We expect that Phase I of this rulemaking will result in savings to the program by providing physicians and entities with "bright line" rules on how to avoid the prohibited referrals that can result in overutilization of covered services. We cannot gauge with any certainty the extent of these savings to the program at this time. (We will discuss the effects on the Medicaid program in Phase II of this rulemaking.)

4. Effects on Beneficiaries

Some commenters thought the January 1998 proposed regulations exceeded our statutory authority and imposed unnecessary and costly burdens on physicians that would harm patient access to health care facilities and services. In Phase I of this rulemaking, we have tried to ensure that the rule will not adversely impact the medical care of Federal health care beneficiaries or other patients. Where we have determined that Phase I of this rulemaking may impact current arrangements under which patients are receiving medical care, we have attempted to verify that there are other ways available to structure the arrangement, so that patients could continue to receive the care in the same location. In almost all cases, we believe Phase I of this rulemaking should not require substantial changes in delivery arrangements, although it may affect the referring physician's or group practice's ability to bill for the care.

In addition, we have significantly expanded the scope of services potentially included in the in-office ancillary services exception and thus readily available to a referring physician's patients by: (1) Making clear that outpatient prescription drugs may be "furnished" in the office, even if they are used by the patient at home; (2) explicitly permitting external ambulatory infusion pumps that are DME to be provided under the in-office ancillary services exception; (3) making clear that chemotherapy infusion drugs may be provided under the in-office ancillary services exception through the administration or dispensing of the drugs to patients in the physician's office; and (4) creating a new exception for certain items of DME furnished in a physician's office for the convenience of the physician's patients.

C. Alternatives Considered

In drafting the January 1998 proposed rule covering a physician's referrals for DHS, we attempted to interpret the statute strictly and literally. After reviewing the voluminous number of comments we received, we have considered many alternative ways to interpret the statute to accommodate the practical problems that commenters raised, while still fulfilling the intent of the law. For example, we revised the "same building" requirements in the in-office ancillary services exception to address commenters' concerns. Under section 1877(b)(2)(A)(ii)(I) of the Act, services qualify for the in-office ancillary services exception if they are furnished "in a building in which the referring physician (or another physician who is a member of the same group practice) furnishes physician services unrelated to the furnishing of designated health services." In the January 1998 proposed rule, we made it clear that we regarded the building requirement of the in-office ancillary services exception, in combination with the supervision and billing requirements, as the Congress's attempt to circumscribe the exception so that it applies only to services provided within the referring physician's actual sphere of practice. Without these requirements, physicians could refer to, and profit from, almost any entity, with the claim that somehow the referred services are "in-office" services that are being supervised from some remote place.

Notwithstanding, we now realize that our proposed definition of a "building" that attempted to define a building in architectural terms could cause practical problems for some physicians and that a clearer, "bright line" rule would be preferable. Accordingly, having considered the various alternatives suggested by the commenters, we concluded that for purposes of Phase I of this rulemaking, we would define a "building" as a structure with, or combination of structures that share, a single street address as assigned by the U.S. Postal Service. A building would be considered as one building for all suites or room numbers located inside that are required by the U.S. Postal Service to use the same street address, regardless of the suite number. Under Phase I of this rulemaking, suites used by the same group practice or solo physician in buildings with separate street addresses will be treated as separate buildings for the purposes of the in-office ancillary services exception. While we recognize that this mailing address rule may result in an occasional anomaly, we are persuaded that it creates a "bright line" rule that will be easy to apply and will produce fair results in the vast majority of cases.

We have also responded to the commenters' numerous concerns that the space in the building in which the DHS are provided must be adjacent to the space in which services that are not DHS are provided. We have revised the regulation so that an adjacent space is no longer necessary (subject to the dictates of any Medicare or Medicaid payment or coverage supervision rules). Shared facilities in the same building are now permitted to the extent they comply with the supervision, location, and billing requirements of the in-office ancillary services exception. However, because of the increased risk of abuse in this expansion, we felt that we could not protect DHS provided by mobile vans or other mobile facilities under the in-office ancillary services exception, except in very limited circumstances.

As these examples demonstrate, our approach in Phase I of this rulemaking was to address as many of the industry's concerns as possible. We considered a variety of suggestions and alternatives, selecting only those that were consistent with the statute's goals and directives, and that would protect Federal health care program beneficiaries' access to services.

D. Conclusion

For the reasons stated above, we are not preparing analyses for either the RFA or section 1102(b) of the Act because we have determined, and we certify, that Phase I of this rulemaking will not have a significant economic impact on a substantial number of small entities or a significant impact on the operations of a substantial number of small rural hospitals.

In accordance with the provisions of Executive Order 12866, Phase I of this rulemaking was reviewed by the Office of Management and Budget.

List of Subjects

42 CFR Part 411

Kidney diseases, Medicare, Physician referral, Reporting and recordkeeping requirements.

42 CFR Part 424

Emergency medical services, Health facilities, Health professions, Medicare.

For the reasons set forth in the preamble, HCFA amends 42 CFR chapter IV as set forth below:

PART 411 — EXCLUSIONS FROM MEDICARE AND LIMITATIONS ON MEDICARE PAYMENT

A. Part 411 is amended as follows:

1. The authority citation for part 411 continues to read as follows:

Authority: Secs. 1102 and 1871 of the Social Security Act (42 U.S.C. 1302 and 1395hh).

Subpart A — General Exclusions and Exclusions of Particular Services

2. In Sec. 411.1, paragraph (a) is revised to read as follows:

Sec. 411.1 Basis and scope.

(a) Statutory basis. Sections 1814(a) and 1835(a) of the Act require that a physician certify or recertify a patient's need for home health services but, in general, prohibit a physician from certifying or recertifying the need for services if the services will be furnished by an HHA in which the physician has a significant ownership interest, or with which the physician has a significant financial or contractual relationship. Sections 1814(c), 1835(d), and 1862 of the Act exclude from Medicare payment certain specified services. The Act provides special rules for payment of services furnished by the following: Federal providers or agencies (sections 1814(c) and 1835(d)); hospitals and physicians outside of the U.S. (sections 1814(f) and

1862(a)(4)); and hospitals and SNFs of the Indian Health Service (section 1880 of the Act). Section 1877 of the Act sets forth limitations on referrals and payment for designated health services furnished by entities with which the referring physician (or an immediate family member of the referring physician) has a financial relationship.

* * * * *

Subpart J — Physician Ownership of, and Referral of Patients or Laboratory Specimens to, Entities Furnishing Clinical Laboratory or Other Health Services

3. Section 411.350 is revised to read as follows:

Sec. 411.350 Scope of subpart.

(a) This subpart implements section 1877 of the Act, which generally prohibits a physician from making a referral under Medicare for designated health services to an entity with which the physician or a member of the physician's immediate family has a financial relationship.

(b) This subpart does not provide for exceptions or immunity from civil or criminal prosecution or other sanctions applicable under any State laws or under Federal law other than section 1877 of the Act. For example, although a particular arrangement involving a physician's financial relationship with an entity may not prohibit the physician from making referrals to the entity under this subpart, the arrangement may nevertheless violate another provision of the Act or other laws administered by HHS, the Federal Trade Commission, the Securities and Exchange Commission, the Internal Revenue Service, or any other Federal or State agency.

(c) This subpart requires, with some exceptions, that certain entities furnishing covered services under Medicare Part A or Part B report information concerning their ownership, investment, or compensation arrangements in the form, manner, and at the times specified by HCFA.

4. Section 411.351 is revised to read as follows:

Sec. 411.351 Definitions.

As used in this subpart, unless the context indicates otherwise:

Centralized building means all or part of a building, including, for purposes of this definition only, a mobile vehicle, van, or trailer that is owned or leased on a full-time basis (that is, 24 hours per day, 7 days per week, for a term of not less than 6 months) by a group practice and that is used exclusively by the group practice. Space in a building or a mobile vehicle, van, or trailer that is shared by more than one group practice, by a group practice and one or more solo practitioners, or by a group practice and another provider (for example, a diagnostic imaging facility) is not a centralized building for purposes of this rule. This provision does not preclude a group practice from providing services to other providers (for example, purchased diagnostic tests) in the group practice's centralized building. A group practice may have more than one centralized building.

Clinical laboratory services means the biological, microbiological, serological, chemical, immunohematological, hematological, biophysical, cytological, pathological, or other examination of materials derived from the human body for the purpose of providing information for the diagnosis, prevention, or treatment of any disease or impairment of, or the assessment of the health of, human beings, including procedures to determine, measure, or otherwise describe the presence or absence of various substances or organisms in the body, as specifically identified by the CPT and HCPCS codes posted on the HCFA web site, http://www.hcfa.gov, (and in annual updates published in the **Federal Register** and posted on the HCFA web site), except as specifically excluded on the HCFA web site and in annual updates. All services identified on the HCFA web site and in annual updates are clinical laboratory services for purposes of these regulations. Any service not specifically identified on the HCFA web site, as amended from time to time and published in the **Federal Register**, is not a clinical laboratory service for purposes of these regulations.

Consultation means a professional service furnished to a patient by a physician if the following conditions are satisfied:

(1) The physician's opinion or advice regarding evaluation and/or management of a specific medical problem is requested by another physician.

(2) The request and need for the consultation are documented in the patient's medical record.

(3) After the consultation is provided, the physician prepares a written report of his or her findings, which is provided to the physician who requested the consultation.

(4) With respect to radiation therapy services provided by a radiation oncologist, a course of radiation treatments over a period of time will be considered to be pursuant to a consultation, provided the radiation oncologist communicates with the referring physician on a regular basis about the patient's course of treatment and progress.

Designated health services (DHS) means any of the following services (other than those provided as emergency physician services furnished outside of the U.S.), as they are defined in this section:

(1) Clinical laboratory services.
(2) Physical therapy, occupational therapy, and speech-language pathology services.
(3) Radiology and certain other imaging services.
(4) Radiation therapy services and supplies.
(5) Durable medical equipment and supplies.
(6) Parenteral and enteral nutrients, equipment, and supplies.
(7) Prosthetics, orthotics, and prosthetic devices and supplies.
(8) Home health services.
(9) Outpatient prescription drugs.
(10) Inpatient and outpatient hospital services.

Except as otherwise noted in these regulations, the term "designated health services (DHS)" means only DHS payable, in whole or in part, by Medicare. DHS do not include services that are reimbursed by Medicare as part of a composite rate (for example, ambulatory surgical center services or SNF Part A payments), except to the extent the services listed in paragraphs (1) through (10) of this definition are themselves payable through a composite rate (that is, all services provided as home health services or inpatient and outpatient hospital services are DHS).

Durable medical equipment (DME) and supplies has the meaning given in section 1861(n) of the Act and Sec. 414.202 of this chapter.

Employee means any individual who, under the common law rules that apply in determining the employer-employee relationship (as applied for purposes of section 3121(d)(2) of the Internal Revenue Code of 1986), is considered to be employed by, or an employee of, an entity. (Application of these common law rules is discussed in 20 CFR 404.1007 and 26 CFR 31.3121(d)-1(c).)

Entity means a physician's sole practice or a practice of multiple physicians or any other person, sole proprietorship, public or private agency or trust, corporation, partnership, limited liability company, foundation, not-for-profit corporation, or unincorporated association that furnishes DHS. For purposes of this definition, an entity does not include the referring physician himself or herself, but does include his or her medical practice. A person or entity is considered to be furnishing DHS if it is the person or entity to which HCFA makes payment for the DHS, directly or upon assignment on the patient's behalf, except that if the person or entity has reassigned its right to payment to an employer pursuant to Sec. 424.80(b)(1) of this chapter; a facility pursuant to Sec. 424.80(b)(2) of this chapter; or a health care delivery system, including clinics, pursuant to Sec. 424.80(b)(3) of this chapter (other than a health care delivery system that is a health plan (as defined in Sec. 1000.952(l) of this title), and other than any managed care organization (MCO), provider-sponsored organization (PSO), or independent practice association (IPA) with which a health plan contracts for services provided to plan enrollees), the person or entity furnishing DHS is the person or entity to which payment has been reassigned. Provided further, that a health plan, MCO, PSO, or IPA that employs a supplier or operates a facility that could accept reassignment from a supplier pursuant to Secs. 424.80(b)(1) and (b)(2) of this chapter is the entity furnishing DHS for any services provided by such supplier.

Fair market value means the value in arm's-length transactions, consistent with the general market value. "General market value" means the price that an asset would bring, as the result of bona fide bargaining between well-informed buyers and sellers who are not otherwise in a position to generate business for the other party; or the compensation that would be included in a service agreement, as the result of bona fide bargaining between well-informed parties to the agreement who are not otherwise in a position to generate business for the other party, on the date of acquisition of the asset or at the time of the service agreement. Usually, the fair market price is the price at which bona fide sales have been consummated for assets of like type, quality, and quantity in a particular market at the time of acquisition, or the compensation that has been included in bona fide service agreements with comparable terms at the time of the agreement. With respect to the rentals and leases described in Sec. 411.357(a) and (b), "fair market value" means the value of rental property for general commercial purposes (not taking into account its intended use). In the case of a lease of space, this value may not be adjusted to reflect the additional value the prospective lessee or lessor would attribute to the proximity or convenience to the lessor when the lessor is a potential source of patient referrals to the lessee. For purposes of this section, a rental payment does not take into account intended use if it takes into account costs incurred by the lessor in developing or upgrading the property or maintaining the property or its improvements.

Home health services means the services described in section 1861(m) of the Act and part 409, subpart E of this chapter.

Hospital means any entity that qualifies as a "hospital" under section 1861(e) of the Act, as a "psychiatric hospital" under section 1861(f) of the Act, or as a "rural primary care hospital" under section 1861(mm)(1) of the Act, and refers to any separate legally organized operating entity plus any subsidiary, related entity, or other entities that perform services for the hospital's patients and for which the hospital bills. However, a "hospital" does not include entities that perform services for hospital patients "under arrangements" with the hospital.

HPSA means, for purposes of this subpart, an area designated as a health professional shortage area under section 332(a)(1)(A) of the Public Health Service Act for primary medical care professionals (in accordance with the criteria specified in part 5 of this title).

Immediate family member or member of a physician's immediate family means husband or wife; birth or adoptive parent, child, or sibling; stepparent, stepchild, stepbrother, or stepsister; father-in-law, mother-in-law, son-in-law, daughter-in-law, brother-in-law, or sister-in-law; grandparent or grandchild; and spouse of a grandparent or grandchild.

"Incident to" services means those services that meet the requirements of section 1861(s)(2)(A) of the Act and section 2050 of the Medicare Carriers Manual (HCFA Pub. 14–3), Part 3 — Claims Process. (Those wishing to subscribe to program manuals should contact either the Government Printing Office (GPO) or the National Technical Information Service (NTIS) at the following addresses: Superintendent of Documents, Government Printing Office, ATTN: New Orders, P.O. Box 371954, Pittsburgh, PA 15250–7954, Telephone (202) 512–1800, Fax number (202) 512–2250 (for credit card orders); or National Technical Information Service, Department of Commerce, 5825 Port Royal Road, Springfield, VA 22161, Telephone (703) 487–4630. In addition, individual manual transmittals and Program Memoranda can be purchased from NTIS. Interested parties should identify the transmittal(s) they want. GPO or NTIS can give complete details on how to obtain the publications they sell.

Additionally, all manuals are available at the following Internet address: http://www.hcfa.gov/pubforms/progman.htm.)

Inpatient hospital services means those services as defined in section 1861(b) of the Act and Sec. 409.10(a) and (b) of this chapter and includes inpatient psychiatric hospital services listed in section 1861(c) of the Act and inpatient rural primary care hospital services, as defined in section 1861(mm)(2) of the Act. "Inpatient hospital services" do not include emergency inpatient services provided by a hospital located outside of the U.S. and covered under the authority in section 1814(f)(2) of the Act and part 424, subpart H of this chapter, or emergency inpatient services provided by a nonparticipating hospital within the U.S., as authorized by section 1814(d) of the Act and described in part 424, subpart G of this chapter. These services also do not include dialysis furnished by a hospital that is not certified to provide end-stage renal dialysis (ESRD) services under subpart U of part 405 of this chapter. Inpatient hospital services include services that a hospital provides for its patients that are furnished either by the hospital or by others under arrangements with the hospital. "Inpatient hospital services" do not include professional services performed by physicians, physician assistants, nurse practitioners, clinical nurse specialists, certified nurse midwives, and certified registered nurse anesthetists and qualified psychologists if Medicare reimburses the services independently and not as part of the inpatient hospital service (even if they are billed by a hospital under an assignment or reassignment).

Laboratory means an entity furnishing biological, microbiological, serological, chemical, immunohematological, hematological, biophysical, cytological, pathological, or other examination of materials derived from the human body for the purpose of providing information for the diagnosis, prevention, or treatment of any disease or impairment of, or the assessment of the health of, human beings. These examinations also include procedures to determine, measure, or otherwise describe the presence or absence of various substances or organisms in the body. Entities only collecting or preparing specimens (or both) or only serving as a mailing service and not performing testing are not considered laboratories.

List of CPT/HCPCS Codes Used to Describe Certain Designated Health Services Under the Physician Referral Provisions (Section 1877 of the Social Security Act) means the list of certain designated health services under section 1877 of the Act initially posted on the

HCFA web site and updated annually thereafter in an addendum to the physician fee schedule final rule and on the HCFA web site.

Member of the group means, for purposes of this rule, a direct or indirect physician owner of a group practice (including a physician whose interest is held by his or her individual professional corporation or by another entity), a physician employee of the group practice (including a physician employed by his or her individual professional corporation that has an equity interest in the group practice), a locum tenens physician (as defined in this section), or an on-call physician while the physician is providing on-call services for members of the group practice. A physician is a member of the group during the time he or she furnishes "patient care services" to the group as defined in this section. An independent contractor or a leased employee is not a member of the group. "Locum tenens physician" means a physician who substitutes (that is, "stands in the shoes") in exigent circumstances for a regular physician who is a member of the group, in accordance with applicable reassignment rules and regulations, including section 3060.7 of the Medicare Carriers Manual (HCFA Pub. 14–3), Part 3 — Claims Process.

Outpatient hospital services means the therapeutic, diagnostic, and partial hospitalization services listed under sections 1861(s)(2)(B) and (C) of the Act; outpatient services furnished by a psychiatric hospital, as defined in section 1861(f) of the Act; and outpatient rural primary care hospital services, as defined in section 1861(mm)(3) of the Act. Emergency services covered in nonparticipating hospitals are excluded under the conditions described in section 1835(b) of the Act and subpart G of part 424 of this chapter. "Outpatient hospital services" includes services that a hospital provides for its patients that are furnished either by the hospital or by others under arrangements with the hospital. "Outpatient hospital services" do not include professional services performed by physicians, physician assistants, nurse practitioners, clinical nurse specialists, certified nurse midwives, certified registered nurse anesthetists, and qualified psychologists if Medicare reimburses the services independently and not as part of the outpatient hospital service (even if they are billed by a hospital under an assignment or reassignment).

Outpatient prescription drugs means all prescription drugs covered by Medicare Part B.

Parenteral and enteral nutrients, equipment, and supplies means the following services (including all HCPCS level 2 codes for these services):

(1) Parenteral nutrients, equipment, and supplies, meaning those items and supplies needed to provide nutriment to a patient with permanent, severe pathology of the alimentary tract that does not allow absorption of sufficient nutrients to maintain strength commensurate with the patient's general condition, as described in section 65–10 of the Medicare Coverage Issues Manual (HCFA Pub. 6); and

(2) Enteral nutrients, equipment, and supplies, meaning items and supplies needed to provide enteral nutrition to a patient with a functioning gastrointestinal tract who, due to pathology to or nonfunction of the structures that normally permit food to reach the digestive tract, cannot maintain weight and strength commensurate with his or her general condition, as described in section 65–10 of the Medicare Coverage Issues Manual (HCFA Pub. 6).

Patient care services means any tasks performed by a physician in the group practice that address the medical needs of specific patients or patients in general, regardless of whether they involve direct patient encounters; or generally benefit a particular practice. Patient care services can include, for example, the services of physicians who do not directly treat patients, such as time spent by a physician consulting with other physicians or reviewing laboratory tests, or time spent training staff members, arranging for equipment, or performing administrative or management tasks.

Physical therapy, occupational therapy, and speech-language pathology services means those particular services identified by the CPT and HCPCS codes on the HCFA web site (and in annual updates published in the **Federal Register**). All services identified on the HCFA web site and in annual updates are physical therapy, occupational therapy, and speech-language pathology services for purposes of these regulations. Any service not specifically identified on the HCFA web site, as amended from time to time and published in the **Federal Register**, is not a physical therapy, occupational therapy, or speech-language pathology service for purposes of these regulations. The list of codes identifying physical therapy, occupational therapy, and speech-language pathology services for purposes of these regulations includes the following:

(1) Physical therapy services, meaning those outpatient physical therapy services (including speech-language pathology services)

described at section 1861(p) of the Act that are covered under Medicare Part A or Part B, regardless of who provides them, if the services include —

(i) Assessments, function tests and measurements of strength, balance, endurance, range of motion, and activities of daily living;

(ii) Therapeutic exercises, massage, and use of physical medicine modalities, assistive devices, and adaptive equipment;

(iii) Establishment of a maintenance therapy program for an individual whose restoration potential has been reached; however, maintenance therapy itself is not covered as part of these services; or

(iv) Speech-language pathology services that are for the diagnosis and treatment of speech, language, and cognitive disorders that include swallowing and other oral-motor dysfunctions.

(2) Occupational therapy services, meaning those services described at section 1861(g) of the Act that are covered under Medicare Part A or Part B, regardless of who provides them, if the services include —

(i) Teaching of compensatory techniques to permit an individual with a physical or cognitive impairment or limitation to engage in daily activities;

(ii) Evaluation of an individual's level of independent functioning;

(iii) Selection and teaching of task-oriented therapeutic activities to restore sensory-integrative function; or

(iv) Assessment of an individual's vocational potential, except when the assessment is related solely to vocational rehabilitation.

Physician means a doctor of medicine or osteopathy, a doctor of dental surgery or dental medicine, a doctor of podiatric medicine, a doctor of optometry, or a chiropractor, as defined in section 1861(r) of the Act.

Physician in the group practice means a member of the group practice, as well as an independent contractor physician, during the time the independent contractor is furnishing patient care services (as defined in this section) to the group practice under a contractual arrangement with the group practice to provide services to the group practice's patients in the group practice's facilities. The contract must contain the same restrictions on compensation that apply to members of the group practice under Sec. 411.352(g) (or the contract fits in the personal services exception in Sec. 411.357(d)), and the independent contractor's arrangement with the group practice must comply with the reassignment rules at Sec. 424.80(b)(3) of this chapter (see also section 3060.3 of the Medicare Carriers Manual (HCFA

Pub. 14–3), Part 3 — Claims Process). Referrals from an independent contractor who is a physician in the group are subject to the prohibition on referrals in Sec. 411.353(a), and the group practice is subject to the limitation on billing for those referrals in Sec. 411.353(b).

Physician incentive plan means any compensation arrangement between an entity and a physician or physician group that may directly or indirectly have the effect of reducing or limiting services furnished with respect to individuals enrolled with the entity.

Plan of care means the establishment by a physician of a course of diagnosis or treatment (or both) for a particular patient, including the ordering of services.

Prosthetics, Orthotics, and Prosthetic Devices and Supplies means the following services (including all HCPCS level 2 codes for these services that are covered by Medicare):

(1) Orthotics, meaning leg, arm, back, and neck braces, as listed in section 1861(s)(9) of the Act.

(2) Prosthetics, meaning artificial legs, arms, and eyes, as described in section 1861(s)(9) of the Act.

(3) Prosthetic devices, meaning devices (other than a dental device) listed in section 1861(s)(8) of the Act that replace all or part of an internal body organ, including colostomy bags, and one pair of conventional eyeglasses or contact lenses furnished subsequent to each cataract surgery with insertion of an intraocular lens.

(4) Prosthetic supplies, meaning supplies that are necessary for the effective use of a prosthetic device (including supplies directly related to colostomy care).

Radiation therapy services and supplies means those particular services and supplies identified by the CPT and HCPCS codes on the HCFA web site and in annual updates published in the **Federal Register**. All services identified on the HCFA web site and in annual updates are radiation therapy services and supplies for purposes of these regulations. Any service not specifically identified on the HCFA web site, as amended from time to time and published in the **Federal Register**, is not a radiation therapy service or supply for purposes of these regulations. The list of codes for radiation therapy services and supplies identified on the HCFA web site and in annual updates is based on section 1861(s)(4) of the Act and Sec. 410.35 of this chapter but does not include nuclear medicine procedures.

Radiology and certain other imaging services means those particular services identified by the CPT and HCPCS codes on the HCFA web site and in annual updates published in the **Federal Register** (except as otherwise specifically excluded on the HCFA web site and in annual updates). All services identified on the HCFA web site and in annual updates are radiology and certain other imaging services for purposes of these regulations. Any service not specifically identified on the HCFA web site, as amended from time to time and published in the **Federal Register**, is not a radiology or certain other imaging service for purposes of these regulations. The list of radiology and certain other imaging services set forth on the HCFA web site and in annual updates includes the professional and technical components of any diagnostic test or procedure using x-rays, ultrasound, or other imaging services, computerized axial tomography, or magnetic resonance imaging, as covered under section 1861(s)(3) of the Act and Secs. 410.32 and 410.34 of this chapter but does not include —

(1) X-ray, fluoroscopy, or ultrasonic procedures that require the insertion of a needle, catheter, tube, or probe through the skin or into a body orifice;

(2) Radiology procedures that are integral to the performance of, and performed during, nonradiological medical procedures; and

(3) Nuclear medicine procedures.

Referral —

(1) Means either of the following:

(i) Except as provided in paragraph (2) of this definition, the request by a physician for, or ordering of, or the certifying or recertifying of the need for, any designated health service for which payment may be made under Medicare Part B, including a request for a consultation with another physician and any test or procedure ordered by or to be performed by (or under the supervision of) that other physician, but not including any designated health service personally performed or provided by the referring physician. A designated health service is not personally performed or provided by the referring physician if it is performed or provided by any other person, including, but not limited to, the referring physician's employees, independent contractors, or group practice members.

(ii) Except as provided in paragraph (2) of this definition, a request by a physician that includes the provision of any designated health service for which payment may be made under Medicare, the establishment of a plan of care by a physician that includes the provision of such a designated health service, or the certifying or recertifying of the need for such a designated health service, but not including any designated health service personally performed or provided by the referring physician. A designated health service is not personally performed or provided by the referring physician if it is performed or provided by any other person including, but not limited to, the referring physician's employees, independent contractors, or group practice members.

(2) Does not include a request by a pathologist for clinical diagnostic laboratory tests and pathological examination services, by a radiologist for diagnostic radiology services, and by a radiation oncologist for radiation therapy, if—

(i) The request results from a consultation initiated by another physician (whether the request for a consultation was made to a particular physician or to an entity with which the physician is affiliated); and

(ii) The tests or services are furnished by or under the supervision of the pathologist, radiologist, or radiation oncologist.

(3) Can be in any form, including, but not limited to, written, oral, or electronic.

Referring physician means a physician who makes a referral as defined in this section or who directs another person or entity to make a referral or who controls referrals made by another person or entity.

Remuneration means any payment or other benefit made directly or indirectly, overtly or covertly, in cash or in kind, except that the following are not considered remuneration for purposes of this section:

(1) The forgiveness of amounts owed for inaccurate tests or procedures, mistakenly performed tests or procedures, or the correction of minor billing errors.

(2) The furnishing of items, devices, or supplies (not including surgical items, devices, or supplies) that are used solely to collect, transport, process, or store specimens for the entity furnishing the items, devices, or supplies or are used solely to order or communicate the results of tests or procedures for the entity.

(3) A payment made by an insurer or a self-insured plan to a physician to satisfy a claim, submitted on a fee-for-service basis, for the furnishing of health services by that physician to an individual who is covered by a policy with the insurer or by the self-insured plan, if—

(i) The health services are not furnished, and the payment is not made, under a contract or other arrangement between the insurer or the plan and the physician;

(ii) The payment is made to the physician on behalf of the covered individual and would otherwise be made directly to the individual; and

(iii) The amount of the payment is set in advance, does not exceed fair market value, and is not determined in a manner that takes into account directly or indirectly the volume or value of any referrals.

Same building means a structure with, or combination of structures that share, a single street address as assigned by the U.S. Postal Service, excluding all exterior spaces (for example, lawns, courtyards, driveways, parking lots) and interior parking garages. For purposes of this rule, the "same building" does not include a mobile vehicle, van, or trailer.

5. Section 411.352 is added to read as follows:

Sec. 411.352 Group practice.

For purposes of this subpart, a group practice is a physician practice that meets the following conditions:

(a) Single legal entity. The group practice must consist of a single legal entity formed primarily for the purpose of being a physician group practice in any organizational form recognized by the State in which the group practice achieves its legal status, including, but not limited to, a partnership, professional corporation, limited liability company, foundation, not-for-profit corporation, faculty practice plan, or similar association. The single legal entity may be organized by any party or parties, including, but not limited to, physicians, health care facilities, or other persons or entities (including, but not limited to, physicians individually incorporated as professional corporations). The single legal entity may not be organized or owned (in whole or in part) by another medical practice that is an operating physician practice (regardless of whether the medical practice meets the conditions for a group practice under this section). For purposes of this rule, a single legal entity does not include informal affiliations of physicians formed substantially to share profits from referrals, or separate group practices under common ownership or control through a physician practice management company, hospital, health system, or other entity or organization. A group practice that is otherwise a single legal entity may itself own subsidiary entities.

(b) Physicians. The group practice must have at least two physicians who are members of the group (whether employees or direct or indirect owners), as defined in this section.

(c) Range of care. Each physician who is a member of the group, as defined in Sec. 411.351, must furnish substantially the full range of patient care services that the physician routinely furnishes, including medical care, consultation, diagnosis, and treatment, through the joint use of shared office space, facilities, equipment, and personnel.

(d) Services furnished by group practice members. (1) Except as provided in paragraphs (d)(2) and (d)(3) of this section, substantially all of the patient care services of the physicians who are members of the group (that is, at least 75 percent of the total patient care services of the group practice members) must be furnished through the group and billed under a billing number assigned to the group, and the amounts received must be treated as receipts of the group. "Patient care services" must be measured by one of the following:

(i) The total time each member spends on patient care services documented by any reasonable means (including, but not limited to, time cards, appointment schedules, or personal diaries). (For example, if a physician practices 40 hours a week and spends 30 hours on patient care services for a group practice, the physician has spent 75 percent of his or her time providing patient care services for the group.)

(ii) Any alternative measure that is reasonable, fixed in advance of the performance of the services being measured, uniformly applied over time, verifiable, and documented.

(2) The data used to calculate compliance with this "substantially all test" and related supportive documentation must be made available to the Secretary upon request.

(3) The "substantially all test" does not apply to any group practice that is located solely in an HPSA, as defined in Sec. 411.351.

(4) For a group practice located outside of an HPSA (as defined in Sec. 411.351), any time spent by a group practice member providing services in an HPSA should not be used to calculate whether the group practice has met the "substantially all test," regardless of whether the member's time in the HPSA is spent in a group practice, clinic, or office setting.

(5) During the "start up" period (not to exceed 12 months) that begins on the date of the initial formation of a new group practice, a group practice must make a reasonable, good faith effort to ensure

that the group practice complies with the requirement set forth in paragraph (d)(1) of this section as soon as practicable, but no later than 12 months from the date of the initial formation of the group practice. This paragraph (d)(5) does not apply when an existing group practice admits a new member or when an existing group practice reorganizes.

(e) Distribution of expenses and income. The overhead expenses of, and income from, the practice must be distributed according to methods that are determined before the receipt of payment for the services giving rise to the overhead expense or producing the income. Nothing in this rule prevents a group practice from adjusting its compensation methodology prospectively, subject to restrictions on the distribution of revenue from DHS under paragraph (i) of this section.

(f) Unified business. (1) The group practice must be a unified business having at least the following features:

(i) Centralized decision-making by a body representative of the group practice that maintains effective control over the group's assets and liabilities (including, but not limited to, budgets, compensation, and salaries).

(ii) Consolidated billing, accounting, and financial reporting.

(iii) Centralized utilization review.

(2) Location and specialty-based compensation practices are permitted with respect to revenues derived from services that are not DHS and may be permitted with respect to revenues derived from DHS under paragraph (i) of this section.

(g) Volume or value of referrals. No physician who is a member of the group practice directly or indirectly receives compensation based on the volume or value of referrals by the physician, except as provided in paragraph (i) of this section.

(h) Physician-patient encounters. Members of the group must personally conduct no less than 75 percent of the physician-patient encounters of the group practice.

(i) Special rule for productivity bonuses and profit shares. (1) A physician in a group practice may be paid a share of overall profits of the group, or a productivity bonus based on services that he or she has personally performed (including services "incident to" those personally performed services as defined in Sec. 411.351), provided that the share or bonus is not determined in any manner that is directly related to the volume or value of referrals of DHS by the physician.

(2) "Overall profits" means the group's entire profits derived from DHS payable by Medicare or Medicaid or the profits derived from DHS payable by Medicare or Medicaid of any component of the group practice that consists of at least five physicians. The share of overall profits will be deemed not to relate directly to the volume or value of referrals if one of the following conditions is met:

(i) The group's profits are divided per capita (for example, per member of the group or per physician in the group).

(ii) Revenues derived from DHS are distributed based on the distribution of the group practice's revenues attributed to services that are not DHS payable by any Federal health care program or private payer.

(iii) Revenues derived from DHS constitute less than 5 percent of the group practice's total revenues, and the allocated portion of those revenues to each physician in the group practice constitutes 5 percent or less of his or her total compensation from the group.

(iv) Overall profits are divided in a reasonable and verifiable manner that is not directly related to the volume or value of the physician's referrals of DHS.

(3) A productivity bonus for personally performed services (including services "incident to" those personally performed services as defined in Sec. 411.351) will be deemed not to relate directly to the volume or value of referrals of DHS if one of the following conditions is met:

(i) The bonus is based on the physician's total patient encounters or relative value units (RVUs). The methodology for establishing RVUs is set forth in Sec. 414.22 of this chapter.

(ii) The bonus is based on the allocation of the physician's compensation attributable to services that are not DHS payable by any Federal health care program or private payer.

(iii) Revenues derived from DHS are less than 5 percent of the group practice's total revenues, and the allocated portion of those revenues to each physician in the group practice constitutes 5 percent or less of his or her total compensation from the group practice.

(iv) The bonus is calculated in a reasonable and verifiable manner that is not directly related to the volume or value of the physician's referrals of DHS.

(4) Supporting documentation verifying the method used to calculate the profit shares or productivity bonus under paragraphs (i)(2) and (i)(3) of this section, and the resulting amount of compensation, must be made available to the Secretary upon request.

6. Section 411.353 is revised to read as follows:

Sec. 411.353 Prohibition on certain referrals by physicians and limitations on billing.

(a) Prohibition on referrals. Except as provided in this subpart, a physician who has a direct or indirect financial relationship with an entity, or who has an immediate family member who has a direct or indirect financial relationship with the entity, may not make a referral to that entity for the furnishing of DHS for which payment otherwise may be made under Medicare. A physician's prohibited financial relationship with an entity that furnishes DHS is not imputed to his or her group practice or its members or its staff; however, a referral made by a physician's group practice, its members, or its staff may be imputed to the physician, if the physician directs the group practice, its members, or its staff to make the referral or if the physician controls referrals made by his or her group practice, its members, or its staff.

(b) Limitations on billing. An entity that furnishes DHS pursuant to a referral that is prohibited by paragraph (a) of this section may not present or cause to be presented a claim or bill to the Medicare program or to any individual, third party payer, or other entity for the DHS performed pursuant to the prohibited referral.

(c) Denial of payment. Except as provided in paragraph (e) of this section, no Medicare payment may be made for a designated health service that is furnished pursuant to a prohibited referral.

(d) Refunds. An entity that collects payment for a designated health service that was performed under a prohibited referral must refund all collected amounts on a timely basis, as defined in Sec. 1003.101 of this title.

(e) Exception for certain entities. Payment may be made to an entity that submits a claim for a designated health service if—

(1) The entity did not have actual knowledge of, and did not act in reckless disregard or deliberate ignorance of, the identity of the physician who made the referral of the designated health service to the entity; and

(2) The claim otherwise complies with all applicable Federal laws, rules, and regulations.

7. Section 411.354 is added to read as follows:

Sec. 411.354 Financial relationship, compensation, and ownership or investment interest.

(a) Financial relationships. (1) Financial relationship means —

(i) A direct or indirect ownership or investment interest (as defined in paragraph (b) of this section) in any entity that furnishes DHS; or

(ii) A direct or indirect compensation arrangement (as defined in paragraph (c) of this section) with an entity that furnishes DHS.

(2) A direct financial relationship exists if remuneration passes between the referring physician (or a member of his or her immediate family) and the entity furnishing DHS without any intervening persons or entities (not including an agent of the physician, the immediate family member, or the entity furnishing DHS).

(3) An indirect financial relationship exists under the conditions described in paragraphs (b)(5) and (c)(2) of this section.

(b) Ownership or investment interest. An ownership or investment interest may be through equity, debt, or other means, and includes an interest in an entity that holds an ownership or investment interest in any entity that furnishes DHS.

(1) An ownership or investment interest includes, but is not limited to, stock, partnership shares, limited liability company memberships, as well as loans, bonds, or other financial instruments that are secured with an entity's property or revenue or a portion of that property or revenue.

(2) An ownership or investment interest in a subsidiary company is neither an ownership or investment interest in the parent company, nor in any other subsidiary of the parent, unless the subsidiary company itself has an ownership or investment interest in the parent or such other subsidiaries. It may, however, be part of an indirect financial relationship.

(3) Ownership and investment interests do not include, among other things —

(i) An interest in a retirement plan;

(ii) Stock options and convertible securities until the stock options are exercised or the convertible securities are converted to equity (before this time they are compensation arrangements as defined in paragraph (c) of this section);

(iii) An unsecured loan subordinated to a credit facility (which is a compensation arrangement as defined in paragraph (c) of this section); or

(iv) An "under arrangements" contract between a hospital and an entity owned by one or more physicians (or a group of physicians) providing DHS "under arrangements" to the hospital.

(4) An ownership or investment interest that meets an exception set forth in Secs. 411.355 or 411.356 need not also meet an exception for compensation arrangements set forth in Sec. 411.357 with respect to profit distributions, dividends, interest payments on secured obligations, or the like.

(5) Indirect ownership or investment interest. (i) An indirect ownership or investment interest exists if—

(A) Between the referring physician (or immediate family member) and the entity furnishing DHS there exists an unbroken chain of any number (but no fewer than one) of persons or entities having ownership or investment interests between them; and

(B) The entity furnishing DHS has actual knowledge of, or acts in reckless disregard or deliberate ignorance of, the fact that the referring physician (or immediate family member) has some ownership or investment interest (through any number of intermediary ownership or investment interests) in the entity furnishing the DHS.

(ii) The entity furnishing DHS need not know, or act in reckless disregard or deliberate ignorance of, the precise composition of the unbroken chain or the specific terms of the ownership or investment interests that form the links in the chain.

(c) Compensation arrangement. A compensation arrangement can be any arrangement involving remuneration, direct or indirect, between a physician (or a member of a physician's immediate family) and an entity. An "under arrangements" contract between a hospital and an entity providing DHS "under arrangements" to the hospital creates a compensation arrangement for purposes of these regulations.

(1) A compensation arrangement does not include any of the following:

(i) The portion of any business arrangement that consists solely of the remuneration described in section 1877(h)(1)(C) of the Act and in paragraphs (1) through (3) of the definition of the term "remuneration" in Sec. 411.351. (However, any other portion of the arrangement may still constitute a compensation arrangement.)

(ii) Payments made by a consultant to a referring physician under Sec. 414.65(e) of this chapter.

(2) Indirect compensation arrangement. An indirect compensation arrangement exists if—

(i) Between the referring physician (or a member of his or her immediate family) and the entity furnishing DHS there exists an unbroken chain of any number (but not fewer than one) of persons or entities that have financial relationships (as defined in paragraph (a) of this section) between them (that is, each link in the chain has either an ownership or investment interest or a compensation arrangement with the preceding link);

(ii) The referring physician (or immediate family member) receives aggregate compensation from the person or entity in the chain with which the physician (or immediate family member) has a direct financial relationship that varies with, or otherwise reflects, the volume or value of referrals or other business generated by the referring physician for the entity furnishing the DHS. If the financial relationship between the physician (or immediate family member) and the person or entity in the chain with which the referring physician (or immediate family member) has a direct financial relationship is an ownership or investment interest, the determination whether the aggregate compensation varies with, or otherwise reflects, the volume or value of referrals or other business generated by the referring physician for the entity furnishing the DHS will be measured by the nonownership or noninvestment interest closest to the referring physician (or immediate family member). (For example, if a referring physician has an ownership interest in company A, which owns company B, which has a compensation arrangement with company C, which has a compensation arrangement with entity D that furnishes DHS, we would look to the aggregate compensation between company B and company C for purposes of this paragraph (c)(2)(ii)); and

(iii) The entity furnishing DHS has actual knowledge of, or acts in reckless disregard or deliberate ignorance of, the fact that the referring physician (or immediate family member) receives aggregate compensation that varies with, or otherwise reflects, the value or volume of referrals or other business generated by the referring physician for the entity furnishing the DHS.

(d) Special rules on compensation. The following special rules apply only to compensation under section 1877 of the Act and these regulations in subpart J of this part.

(1) Compensation will be considered "set in advance" if the aggregate compensation or a time-based or per unit of service-based (whether per-use or per-service) amount is set in advance in the initial agreement between the parties in sufficient detail so that it can be objectively verified. The payment amount must be fair market value compensation for services or items actually provided, not taking into account the volume or value of referrals or other business generated by the referring physician at the time of the initial agreement or during the term of the agreement. Percentage compensation arrangements do not constitute compensation that is "set in advance" in which the percentage compensation is based on fluctuating or indeterminate measures or in which the arrangement results in the seller receiving different payment amounts for the same service from the same purchaser.

(2) Compensation (including time-based or per unit of service-based compensation) will be deemed not to take into account "the volume or value of referrals" if the compensation is fair market value for services or items actually provided and does not vary during the course of the compensation agreement in any manner that takes into account referrals of DHS.

(3) Compensation (including time-based or per unit of service-based compensation) will be deemed to not take into account "other business generated between the parties" so long as the compensation is fair market value and does not vary during the term of the agreement in any manner that takes into account referrals or other business generated by the referring physician, including private pay health care business.

(4) A physician's compensation may be conditioned on the physician's referrals to a particular provider, practitioner, or supplier, so long as the compensation arrangement —

(i) Is fixed in advance for the term of the agreement;

(ii) Is consistent with fair market value for services performed (that is, the payment does not take into account the volume or value of anticipated or required referrals);

(iii) Complies with an applicable exception under Secs. 411.355 or 411.357; and

(iv) Complies with the following conditions:

(A) The requirement to make referrals to a particular provider, practitioner, or supplier is set forth in a written agreement signed by the parties.

(B) The requirement to make referrals to a particular provider, practitioner, or supplier does not apply if the patient expresses a preference for a different provider, practitioner, or supplier; the patient's insurer determines the provider, practitioner, or supplier; or the referral is not in the patient's best medical interests in the physician's judgement.

8. Section 411.355 is revised to read as follows:

Sec. 411.355 General exceptions to the referral prohibition related to both ownership/investment and compensation.

The prohibition on referrals set forth in Sec. 411.353 does not apply to the following types of services:

(a) Physician services. (1) Physician services as defined in Sec. 410.20(a) of this chapter that are furnished—

(i) Personally by another physician who is a member of the referring physician's group practice or is a physician in the same group practice (as defined in Sec. 411.351) as the referring physician; or

(ii) Under the supervision of another physician who is a member of the referring physician's group practice or is a physician in the same group practice (as defined at Sec. 411.351) as the referring physician, provided that the supervision complies with all other applicable Medicare payment and coverage rules for the physician services.

(2) For purposes of paragraph (a) of this section, "physician services" includes only those "incident to" services (as defined in Sec. 411.351) that are physician services under Sec. 410.20(a) of this chapter.

(3) All other "incident to" services (for example, diagnostic tests, physical therapy) are outside the scope of paragraph (a) of this section.

(b) In-office ancillary services. Services (including certain items of durable medical equipment (DME), as defined in paragraph (b)(4) of this section, and infusion pumps that are DME (including external ambulatory infusion pumps), but excluding all other DME and parenteral and enteral nutrients, equipment, and supplies (such as infusion pumps used for PEN), that meet the following conditions:

(1) They are furnished personally by one of the following individuals:

(i) The referring physician.

(ii) A physician who is a member of the same group practice as the referring physician.

(iii) An individual who is supervised by the referring physician or by another physician in the group practice, provided the supervision complies with all other applicable Medicare payment and coverage rules for the services.

(2) They are furnished in one of the following locations:

(i) The same building (as defined in Sec. 411.351), but not necessarily in the same space or part of the building, in which —

(A) The referring physician (or another physician who is a member of the same group practice) furnishes substantial physician services that are unrelated to the furnishing of DHS payable by Medicare, any other Federal health care payer, or a private payer, even though the unrelated services may lead to the ordering of DHS;

(B) The physician services that are unrelated to the furnishing of DHS in paragraph (b)(2)(i)(A) of this section must represent substantially the full range of physician services unrelated to the furnishing of DHS that the referring physician routinely provides (or, in the case of a referring physician who is a member of a group practice, the full range of physician services that the physician routinely provides for the group practice); and

(C) The receipt of DHS (whether payable by a Federal health care program or a private payer) is not the primary reason the patient comes in contact with the referring physician or his or her group practice.

(ii) A centralized building (as defined in Sec. 411.351) that is used by the group practice for the provision of some or all of the group practice's clinical laboratory services.

(iii) A centralized building (as defined in Sec. 411.351) that is used by the group practice for the provision of some or all of the group practice's DHS (other than clinical laboratory services).

(3) They must be billed by one of the following:

(i) The physician performing or supervising the service.

(ii) The group practice of which the performing or supervising physician is a member under a billing number assigned to the group practice.

(iii) The group practice if the supervising physician is a "physician in the group" (as defined at Sec. 411.351) under a billing number assigned to the group practice.

(iv) An entity that is wholly owned by the performing or supervising physician or by that physician's group practice under the entity's own billing number or under a billing number assigned to the physician or group practice.

(v) An independent third party billing company acting as an agent of the physician, group practice, or entity specified in paragraphs (b)(3)(i) through (b)(3)(iv) of this section under a billing number assigned to the physician, group practice, or entity, provided the billing arrangement meets the requirements of Sec. 424.80(b)(6) of this chapter. For purposes of this paragraph (b)(3), a group practice may have, and bill under, more than one Medicare billing number, subject to any applicable Medicare program restrictions.

(4) For purposes of paragraph (b) of this section, DME covered by the in-office ancillary services exception means canes, crutches, walkers and folding manual wheelchairs, and blood glucose monitors, that meet the following conditions:

(i) The item is one that a patient requires for the purposes of ambulating, uses in order to depart from the physician's office, or is a blood glucose monitor (including one starter set of test strips and lancets, consisting of no more than 100 of each). A blood glucose monitor may be furnished only by a physician or employee of a physician or group practice that also furnishes outpatient diabetes self-management training to the patient.

(ii) The item is furnished in a building that meets the "same building" requirements in the in-office ancillary services exception as part of the treatment for the specific condition for which the patient-physician encounter occurred.

(iii) The item is furnished personally by the physician who ordered the DME, by another physician in the group practice, or by an employee of the physician or the group practice.

(iv) A physician or group practice that furnishes the DME meets all DME supplier standards located in Sec. 424.57(c) of this chapter.

(v) The arrangement does not violate the anti-kickback statute, section 1128B(b) of the Act, or any law or regulation governing billing or claims submission.

(vi) All other requirements of the in-office ancillary services exception in paragraph (b) of this section are met.

(5) A designated health service is "furnished" for purposes of paragraph (b) of this section in the location where the service is actually performed upon a patient or where an item is dispensed to a patient in a manner that is sufficient to meet the applicable Medicare payment and coverage rules.

(6) Special rule for home care physicians. In the case of a referring physician whose principal medical practice consists of treating patients in their private homes, the "same building" requirements of

paragraph (b)(2)(i) of this section are met if the referring physician (or a qualified person accompanying the physician, such as a nurse or technician) provides the DHS contemporaneously with a physician service that is not a designated health service provided by the referring physician to the patient in the patient's private home. For purposes of paragraph (b)(5) of this section, a private home does not include a nursing, long-term care, or other facility or institution.

(c) Services furnished by an organization (or its contractors or subcontractors) to enrollees. Services furnished by an organization (or its contractors or subcontractors) to enrollees of one of the following prepaid health plans (not including services provided to enrollees in any other plan or line of business offered or administered by the same organization):

(1) An HMO or a CMP in accordance with a contract with HCFA under section 1876 of the Act and part 417, subparts J through M of this chapter, which set forth qualifying conditions for Medicare contracts; enrollment, entitlement, and disenrollment under Medicare contracts; Medicare contract requirements; and change of ownership and leasing of facilities: effect on Medicare contracts.

(2) A health care prepayment plan in accordance with an agreement with HCFA under section 1833(a)(1)(A) of the Act and part 417, subpart U of this chapter.

(3) An organization that is receiving payments on a prepaid basis for Medicare enrollees through a demonstration project under section 402(a) of the Social Security Amendments of 1967 (42 U.S.C. 1395b-1) or under section 222(a) of the Social Security Amendments of 1972 (42 U.S.C. 1395b — 1 note).

(4) A qualified HMO (within the meaning of section 1310(d) of the Public Health Service Act).

(5) A coordinated care plan (within the meaning of section 1851(a)(2)(A) of the Act) offered by an organization in accordance with a contract with HCFA under section 1857 of the Act and part 422 of this chapter.

(d) Clinical laboratory services furnished in an ambulatory surgical center (ASC) or end-stage renal disease (ESRD) facility, or by a hospice if payment for those services is included in the ASC rate, the ESRD composite rate, or as part of the per diem hospice charge, respectively.

(e) Academic medical centers. (1) Services provided by an academic medical center if all of the following conditions are met:

(i) The referring physician —

(A) Is a bona fide employee of a component of the academic medical center on a full-time or substantial part-time basis. ("Components" of an academic medical center means an affiliated medical school, faculty practice plan, hospital, teaching facility, institution of higher education, or departmental professional corporation.);

(B) Is licensed to practice medicine in the State;

(C) Has a bona fide faculty appointment at the affiliated medical school; and

(D) Provides either substantial academic or substantial clinical teaching services for which the faculty member receives compensation as part of his or her employment relationship with the academic medical center.

(ii) The total compensation paid for the previous 12-month period (or fiscal year or calendar year) from all academic medical center components to the referring physician is set in advance and, in the aggregate, does not exceed fair market value for the services provided, and is not determined in a manner that takes into account the volume or value of any referrals or other business generated by the referring physician within the academic medical center.

(iii) The academic medical center must meet all of the following conditions:

(A) All transfers of money between components of the academic medical center must directly or indirectly support the missions of teaching, indigent care, research, or community service.

(B) The relationship of the components of the academic medical center must be set forth in a written agreement that has been adopted by the governing body of each component.

(C) All money paid to a referring physician for research must be used solely to support bona fide research.

(iv) The referring physician's compensation arrangement does not violate the anti-kickback statute, section 1128B(b) of the Act.

(2) The "academic medical center" for purposes of this section consists of—

(i) An accredited medical school (including a university, when appropriate);

(ii) An affiliated faculty practice plan that is a 501(c)(3) or (c)(4) of the Internal Revenue Code nonprofit, tax-exempt organization under IRS regulations (or is a part of such an organization under an umbrella designation); and

(iii) One or more affiliated hospital(s) in which a majority of the hospital medical staff consists of physicians who are faculty members and a majority of all hospital admissions are made by physicians who are faculty members.

(f) Implants in an ASC. Implants, including, but not limited to, cochlear implants, intraocular lenses, and other implanted prosthetics, implanted prosthetic devices and implanted DME that meet the following conditions:

(1) The implant is furnished by the referring physician or a member of the referring physician's group practice in a Medicare-certified ASC (under part 416 of this chapter) with which the referring physician has a financial relationship.

(2) The implant is implanted in the patient during a surgical procedure performed in the same ASC where the implant is furnished.

(3) The arrangement for the furnishing of the implant does not violate the Federal anti-kickback statute, section 1128B(b) of the Act.

(4) Billing and claims submission for the implants complies with all Federal and State laws and regulations.

(5) The exception set forth in this paragraph (f) does not apply to any financial relationships between the referring physician and any entity other than the ASC in which the implant is furnished to and implanted in the patient.

(g) EPO and other dialysis-related outpatient prescription drugs furnished in or by an ESRD facility. EPO and other dialysis-related outpatient prescription drugs that are identified by the CPT and HCPCS codes on the HCFA web site, http://www.hcfa.gov, and in annual updates published in the **Federal Register** and that meet the following conditions:

(1) The EPO and other dialysis-related drugs are furnished in or by an ESRD facility. For purposes of this paragraph, "furnished" means that the EPO or drugs are either administered or dispensed to a patient in or by the ESRD facility, even if the EPO or drugs are furnished to the patient at home. "Dialysis-related drugs" means certain drugs required for the efficacy of dialysis, as identified on the HCFA web site and in annual updates.

(2) The arrangement for the furnishing of the EPO and other dialysis-related drugs does not violate the Federal anti-kickback statute, section 1128B(b) of the Act.

(3) Billing and claims submission for the EPO and other dialysis related drugs complies with all Federal and State laws and regulations.

(4) The exception set forth in this paragraph (g) does not apply to any financial relationships between the referring physician and any entity other than the ESRD facility that furnishes the EPO and other dialysis-related drugs to the patient.

(h) Preventive screening tests, immunizations, and vaccines. Preventive screening tests, immunizations, and vaccines that are covered by Medicare and identified by the CPT and HCPCS codes included on the HCFA web site and in annual updates published in the **Federal Register** and that meet the following conditions:

(1) The preventive screening tests, immunizations, and vaccines are subject to HCFA-mandated frequency limits.

(2) The preventive screening tests, immunizations, and vaccines are reimbursed by Medicare based on a fee schedule.

(3) The arrangement for the provision of the preventive screening tests, immunizations, and vaccines does not violate the Federal anti-kickback statute, section 1128B(b) of the Act.

(4) Billing and claims submission for the preventive screening tests, immunizations, and vaccines complies with all Federal and State laws and regulations.

(5) To qualify under this exception, the preventive screening tests, immunizations, and vaccines must be covered by Medicare and must be listed on the HCFA web site and in annual updates.

(i) Eyeglasses and contact lenses following cataract surgery. Eyeglasses and contact lenses that are covered by Medicare when furnished to patients following cataract surgery that meet the following conditions:

(1) The eyeglasses or contact lenses are provided in accordance with the coverage and payment provisions set forth in Sec. 410.36(a)(2)(ii) and Sec. 414.228 of this chapter, respectively.

(2) The arrangement for the furnishing of the eyeglasses or contact lenses does not violate the Federal anti-kickback statute, section 1128B(b) of the Act.

(3) Billing and claims submission for the eyeglasses or contact lenses complies with all Federal and State laws and regulations.

9. In Sec. 411.357, paragraph (j) is added and reserved, and paragraphs (k), (l), (m), (n), (o), and (p) are added to read as follows:

Sec. 411.357 Exceptions to the referral prohibition related to compensation arrangements.

* * * * *

(j) [Reserved]

(k) Non-monetary compensation up to $300. Compensation from an entity in the form of items or services (not including cash or cash equivalents) that does not exceed an aggregate of $300 per year, if all of the following conditions are satisfied:

(1) The compensation is not determined in any manner that takes into account the volume or value of referrals or other business generated by the referring physician.

(2) The compensation may not be solicited by the physician or the physician's practice (including employees and staff members).

(3) The compensation arrangement does not violate the Federal anti-kickback statute, section 1128B(b) of the Act.

(l) Fair market value compensation. Compensation resulting from an arrangement between an entity and a physician (or an immediate family member) or any group of physicians (regardless of whether the group meets the definition of a group practice set forth in Sec. 411.351) for the provision of items or services by the physician (or an immediate family member) or group practice to the entity, if the arrangement is set forth in an agreement that meets the following conditions:

(1) It is in writing, signed by the parties, and covers only identifiable items or services, all of which are specified in the agreement.

(2) It specifies the timeframe for the arrangement, which can be for any period of time and contain a termination clause, provided the parties enter into only one arrangement for the same items or services during the course of a year. An arrangement made for less than 1 year may be renewed any number of times if the terms of the arrangement and the compensation for the same items or services do not change.

(3) It specifies the compensation that will be provided under the arrangement. The compensation must be set in advance, be consistent with fair market value, and not be determined in a manner that takes into account the volume or value of any referrals or any other business generated by the referring physician.

(4) It involves a transaction that is commercially reasonable (taking into account the nature and scope of the transaction) and furthers the legitimate business purposes of the parties.

(5) It meets a safe harbor under the anti-kickback statute in Sec. 1001.952 of this title, has been approved by the OIG under a favorable advisory opinion issued in accordance with part 1008 of this title, or does not violate the anti-kickback provisions in section 1128B(b) of the Act.

(6) The services to be performed under the arrangement do not involve the counseling or promotion of a business arrangement or other activity that violates a State or Federal law.

(m) Medical staff incidental benefits. Compensation in the form of items or services (not including cash or cash equivalents) from a hospital to a member of its medical staff when the item or service is used on the hospital's campus, if all of the following conditions are met:

(1) The compensation is offered to all members of the medical staff without regard to the volume or value of referrals or other business generated between the parties.

(2) The compensation is offered only during periods when the medical staff members are making rounds or performing other duties that benefit the hospital or its patients.

(3) The compensation is provided by the hospital and used by the medical staff members only on the hospital's campus.

(4) The compensation is reasonably related to the provision of, or designed to facilitate directly or indirectly the delivery of, medical services at the hospital.

(5) The compensation is consistent with the types of benefits offered to medical staff members —

(i) By other hospitals within the same local region; or

(ii) If no such hospitals exist within the same local region, by comparable hospitals in comparable regions.

(6) The compensation is of low value (that is, less than $25) with respect to each occurrence of the benefit (for example, each meal given to a physician while he or she is serving patients who are hospitalized must be of low value).

(7) The compensation is not determined in any manner that takes into account the volume or value of referrals or other business generated between the parties.

(8) The compensation arrangement does not violate the Federal anti-kickback provisions in section 1128B(b) of the Act.

(n) Risk sharing arrangements. Compensation pursuant to a risk-sharing arrangement (including, but not limited to, withholds, bonuses, and risk pools) between a managed care organization or an independent physicians association and a physician (either directly or indirectly through a subcontractor) for services provided to enrollees of a health plan, provided that the arrangement does not violate the Federal anti-kickback statute, section 1128B(b) of the Act, or any law or regulation governing billing or claims submission. For purposes of this paragraph (n), "health plan" and "enrollees" have the meanings ascribed to those terms in Sec. 1001.952(l) of this title.

(o) Compliance training. Compliance training provided by a hospital to a physician (or the physician's immediate family member) who practices in the hospital's local community or service area, provided the training is held in the local community or service area. For purposes of this paragraph (o), "compliance training" means training regarding the basic elements of a compliance program (for example, establishing policies and procedures, training of staff, internal monitoring, reporting) or specific training regarding the requirements of Federal health care programs (for example, billing, coding, reasonable and necessary services, documentation, unlawful referral arrangements).

(p) Indirect compensation arrangements. Indirect compensation arrangements, as defined in Sec. 411.354(c)(2), if all of the following conditions are satisfied:

(1) The compensation received by the referring physician (or immediate family member) described in Sec. 411.354(c)(2)(ii) is fair market value for services and items actually provided not taking into account the value or volume of referrals or other business generated by the referring physician for the entity furnishing DHS.

(2) The compensation arrangement described in Sec. 411.354(c)(2)(ii) is set out in writing, signed by the parties, and specifies the services covered by the arrangement, except in the case of a bona fide employment relationship between an employer and an employee, in which case the arrangement need not be set out in a written contract, but must be for identifiable services and be commercially reasonable even if no referrals are made to the employer.

(3) The compensation arrangement does not violate the anti-kickback statute or any laws or regulations governing billing or claims submission.

PART 424 — CONDITIONS FOR MEDICARE PAYMENT

B. Part 424 is amended as follows:

1. The authority citation for part 424 continues to read as follows:

Authority: Secs. 1102 and 1871 of the Social Security Act (42 U.S.C. 1302 and 1395hh).

Subpart B — Certification and Plan of Treatment Requirements

2. In Sec. 424.22, paragraph (d) is revised to read as set forth below, and paragraphs (e), (f), and (g) are removed.

Sec. 424.22 Requirements for home health services.

* * * * *

(d) Limitation on the performance of certification and plan of treatment functions. The need for home health services to be provided by an HHA may not be certified or recertified, and a plan of treatment may not be established and reviewed, by any physician who has a financial relationship, as defined in Sec. 411.351 of this chapter, with that HHA, unless the physician's relationship meets one of the exceptions in section 1877 of the Act, which sets forth general exceptions to the referral prohibition related to both ownership/investment and compensation; exceptions to the referral prohibition related to ownership or investment interests; and exceptions to the referral prohibition related to compensation arrangements.

(Catalog of Federal Domestic Assistance Program No. 93.773, Medicare-Hospital Insurance; Program No. 93.774, Medicare-Supplementary Medical Insurance Program; and Program No. 93.778, Medical Assistance Program)

Dated: October 6, 2000.

Michael M. Hash,

Acting Administrator, Health Care Financing Administration.

Dated: October 16, 2000.

Donna E. Shalala,

Secretary.

Note: The following attachment will not appear in the Code of Federal Regulations.

Attachment

List of CPT[1] /HCPCS Codes Used To Describe Certain Designated Health Services Under the Physician Referral Provisions (Section 1877 of the Social Security Act)

Clinical Laboratory Services

Include CPT codes for all clinical laboratory services in the 80000 series, except Exclude CPT codes for the following blood component collection services:

86890 Autologous blood process
86891 Autologous blood, op salvage
86915 Bone marrow/stem cell prep
86927 Plasma, fresh frozen
86930 Frozen blood prep
86931 Frozen blood thaw
86932 Frozen blood freeze/thaw
86945 Blood product/irradiation
86950 Leukacyte transfusion
86965 Pooling blood platelets
86985 Split blood or products

Include HCPCS level 2 codes for other clinical laboratory services:

G0001 Drawing blood for specimen
G0026 Fecal leukocyte examination
G0027 Semen analysis
G0103 Psa, total screening
G0107 CA screen; fecal blood test
G0123 Screen cerv/vag thin layer
G0124 Screen c/v thin layer by MD
G0141 Scr c/v cyto,autosys and md
G0143-G0145 Scr c/v cyto, thinlayer, rescr
G0147 Scr c/v cyto, automated sys
G0148 Scr c/v cyto, autosys, rescr
P2028 Cephalin floculation test
P2029 Congo red blood test
P2031 Hair analysis
P2033 Blood thymol turbidity

---

[1] CPT codes, descriptions and other data only are copyright 2000 American Medical Association. All Rights Reserved. Applicable FARS/DFARS Clauses Apply.

P2038 Blood mucoprotein
P3000 Screen pap by tech w md supv
P3001 Screening pap smear by phys
P7001 Culture bacterial urine
P9612 Catheterize for urine spec
P9615 Urine specimen collect mult
Q0111 Wet mounts/w preparations
Q0112 Potassium hydroxide preps
Q0113 Pinworm examinations
Q0114 Fern test
Q0115 Post-coital mucous exam

Physical Therapy/Occupational Therapy/Speech-Language Pathology

Include the following CPT codes for the physical therapy/occupational therapy/speech-language pathology services in the 97000 series:

97001 Pt evaluation
97002 Pt re-evaluation
97003 Ot evaluation
97004 Ot re-evaluation
97010 Hot or cold packs therapy
97012 Mechanical traction therapy
97014 Electric stimulation therapy
97016 Vasopneumatic device therapy
97018 Paraffin bath therapy
97020 Microwave therapy
97022 Whirlpool therapy
97024 Diathermy treatment
97026 Infrared therapy
97028 Ultraviolet therapy
97032 Electrical stimulation
97033 Electric current therapy
97034 Contrast bath therapy
97035 Ultrasound therapy
97036 Hydrotherapy
97039 Physical therapy treatment
97110 Therapeutic exercises
97112 Neuromuscular reeducation
97113 Aquatic therapy/exercises
97116 Gait training therapy

97124 Massage therapy
97139 Physical medicine procedure
97140 Manual therapy
97150 Group therapeutic procedures
97504 Orthotic training
97520 Prosthetic training
97530 Therapeutic activities
97532 Cognitive skills development
97533 Sensory integration
97535 Self care mngment training
97537 Community/work reintegration
97542 Wheelchair mngment training
97545 Work hardening
97546 Work hardening add-on
97703 Prosthetic checkout
97750 Physical performance test
97799 Physical medicine procedure

Include CPT codes for physical therapy/occupational therapy/speech-language pathology services not in the 97000 series:

64550 Apply neurostimulator
90901 Biofeedback train, any meth
90911 Biofeedback peri/uro/rectal
92506 Speech/hearing evaluation
92507–92508 Speech/hearing therapy
92510 Rehab for ear implant
92526 Oral function therapy
93797 Cardiac rehab
93798 Cardiac rehab/monitor
94667–94668 Chest wall manipulation
94762 Measure blood oxygen level
95831 Limb muscle testing, manual
95832 Hand muscle testing, manual
95833–95834 Body muscle testing, manual
95851–95852 Range of motion measurements
96105 Assessment of aphasia
96110 Developmental test, lim
96111 Developmental test, extend
96115 Neurobehavior status exam

Include HCPCS level 2 codes for the following physical therapy/occupational therapy/speech-language pathology services:

G0193 Endoscopic study swallow functn
G0194 Sensory testing endoscopic stud
G0195 Clinical eval swallowing funct
G0196 Eval of swallowing with radioopa
G0197 Eval of pt for prescip speech devi
G0198 Patient adapation & train for spe
G0199 Reevaluation of patient use spec
G0200 Eval of patient prescip of voice p
G0201 Modi for training in use voice pro
Q0086 Physical therapy evaluation

Radiology

Include the following radiology and certain other imaging services in the CPT 70000 series:

70100–70110 X-ray exam of jaw
70120–70130 X-ray exam of mastoids
70134 X-ray exam of middle ear
70140–70150 X-ray exam of facial bones
70160 X-ray exam of nasal bones
70190–70200 X-ray exam of eye sockets
70210–70220 X-ray exam of sinuses
70240 X-ray exam, pituitary saddle
70250–70260 X-ray exam of skull
70300–70310 X-ray exam of teeth
70320 Full mouth x-ray of teeth
70328 X-ray exam of jaw joint
70330 X-ray exam of jaw joints
70336 Magnetic image, jaw joint
70350 X-ray head for orthodontia
70355 Panoramic x-ray of jaws
70360 X-ray exam of neck
70370 Throat x-ray & fluoroscopy
70371 Speech evaluation, complex
70380 X-ray exam of salivary gland
70450 CT head/brain w/o dye
70460 CT head/brain w/dye
70470 CT head/brain w/o&w dye
70480 CT orbit/ear/fossa w/o dye
70481 CT orbit/ear/fossa w/dye

70482 CT orbit/ear/fossa w/o&w dye
70486 CT maxillofacial w/o dye
70487 CT maxillofacial w/dye
70488 CT maxillofacial w/o&w dye
70490 CT soft tissue neck w/o dye
70491 CT soft tissue neck w/dye
70492 CT sft tsue nck w/o & w/dye
70496 CT angiography, head
70498 CT angiography, neck
70540 MRI orbit/face/neck w/o dye
70542 MRI orbit/face/neck w/dye
70543 MRI orbt/fac/nck w/o&w dye
70544 MR angiography head w/o dye
70545 MR angiography head w/dye
70546 MR angiograph head w/o&w dye
70547 MR angiography neck w/o dye
70548 MR angiography neck w/dye
70549 MR angiograph neck w/o&w dye
70551 MRI brain w/o dye
70552 MRI brain w/dye
70553 MRI brain w/o&w dye
71010–71022 Chest x-ray
71023 Chest x-ray and fluoroscopy
71030 Chest x-ray
71034 Chest x-ray and fluoroscopy
71035 Chest x-ray
71100 X-ray exam of ribs
71101 X-ray exam of ribs/chest
71110 X-ray exam of ribs
71111 X-ray exam of ribs/chest
71120–71130 X-ray exam of breastbone
71250 CT thorax w/o dye
71260 CT thorax w/dye
71270 CT thorax w/o&w dye
71275 CT angiography, chest
71550 MRI chest w/o dye
71551 MRI chest w/dye
71552 MRI chest w/o&w dye
71555 MRI angio chest w or w/o dye
72010–72020 X-ray exam of spine
72040–72052 X-ray exam of neck spine

72069 X-ray exam of trunk spine
72070–72074 X-ray exam of thoracic spine
72080–72090 X-ray exam of trunk spine
72100–72120 X-ray exam of lower spine
72125 CT neck spine w/o dye
72126 CT neck spine w/dye
72127 CT neck spine w/o&w dye
72128 CT chest spine w/o dye
72129 CT chest spine w/dye
72130 CT chest spine w/o&w dye
72131 CT lumbar spine w/o dye
72132 CT lumbar spine w/dye
72133 CT lumbar spine w/o&w dye
72141 MRI neck spine w/o dye
72142 MRI neck spine w/dye
72146 MRI chest spine w/o dye
72147 MRI chest spine w/dye
72148 MRI lumbar spine w/o dye
72149 MRI lumbar spine w/dye
72156 MRI neck spine w/o&w dye
72157 MRI chest spine w/o&w dye
72158 MRI lumbar spine w/o&w dye
72170–72190 X-ray exam of pelvis
72191 CT angiograph pelv w/o&w dye
72192 CT pelvis w/o dye
72193 CT pelvis w/dye
72194 CT pelvis w/o&w dye
72195 MRI pelvis w/o dye
72196 MRI pelvis w/dye
72197 MRI pelvis w/o&w dye
72200–72202 X-ray exam sacroiliac joints
72220 X-ray exam of tailbone
73000 X-ray exam of collar bone
73010 X-ray exam of shoulder blade
73020–73030 X-ray exam of shoulder
73050 X-ray exam of shoulders
73060 X-ray exam of humerus
73070–73080 X-ray exam of elbow
73090 X-ray exam of forearm
73092 X-ray exam of arm, infant
73100–73110 X-ray exam of wrist

73120–73130 X-ray exam of hand
73140 X-ray exam of finger(s)
73200 CT upper extremity w/o dye
73201 CT upper extremity w/dye
73202 CT uppr extremity w/o&w dye
73206 CT angio upr extrm w/o&w dye
73218 MRI upper extremity w/o dye
73219 MRI upper extremity w/dye
73220 MRI uppr extremity w/o&w dye
73221 MRI joint upr extrem w/o dye
73222 MRI joint upr extrem w/ dye
73223 MRI joint upr extr w/o&w dye
73500–73510 X-ray exam of hip
73520 X-ray exam of hips
73540 X-ray exam of pelvis & hips
73550 X-ray exam of thigh
73560 X-ray exam of knee, 1 or 2
73562 X-ray exam of knee, 3
73564 X-ray exam, knee, 4 or more
73565 X-ray exam of knees
73590 X-ray exam of lower leg
73592 X-ray exam of leg, infant
73600–73610 X-ray exam of ankle
73620–73630 X-ray exam of foot
73650 X-ray exam of heel
73660 X-ray exam of toe(s)
73700 CT lower extremity w/o dye
73701 CT lower extremity w/dye
73702 CT lwr extremity w/o&w dye
73706 CT angio lwr extr w/o&w dye
73718 MRI lower extremity w/o dye
73719 MRI lower extremity w/dye
73720 MRI lwr extremity w/o&w dye
73721 MRI joint of lwr extre w/o d
73722 MRI joint of lwr extr w/dye
73723 MRI joint lwr extr w/o&w dye
73725 MR ang lwr ext w or w/o dye
74000–74020 X-ray exam of abdomen
74022 X-ray exam series, abdomen
74150 CT abdomen w/o dye
74160 CT abdomen w/dye

74170 CT abdomen w/o&w dye
74175 CT angio abdom w/o&w dye
74181 MRI abdomen w/o dye
74182 MRI abdomen w/dye
74183 MRI abdomen w/o&w dye
74185 MRI angio, abdom w or w/o dy
74210 Contrst x-ray exam of throat
74220 Contrast x-ray, esophagus
74230 Cinema x-ray, throat/esoph
74240–74245 X-ray exam, upper gi tract
74246–74249 Contrst x-ray uppr gi tract
74250 X-ray exam of small bowel
74290 Contrast x-ray, gallbladder
74291 Contrast x-rays, gallbladder
74710 X-ray measurement of pelvis
75552 Heart MRI for morph w/o dye
75553 Heart MRI for morph w/dye
75554 Cardiac MRI/function
75555 Cardiac MRI/limited study
75635 CT angio abdominal arteries
76000 Fluoroscope examination
76006 X-ray stress view
76010 X-ray, nose to rectum
76020 X-rays for bone age
76040 X-rays, bone evaluation
76061–76062 X-rays, bone survey
76065 X-rays, bone evaluation
76066 Joint(s) survey, single film
76090 Mammogram, one breast
76091 Mammogram, both breasts
76092 Mammogram, screening
76093 Magnetic image, breast
76094 Magnetic image, both breasts
76100 X-ray exam of body section
76101 Complex body section x-ray
76102 Complex body section x-rays
76120 Cinematic x-rays
76125 Cinematic x-rays add-on
76150 X-ray exam, dry process
76370 CAT scan for therapy guide
76375 3d/holograph reconstr add-on

76380 CAT scan follow-up study
76390 Mr spectroscopy
76400 Magnetic image, bone marrow
76499 Radiographic procedure
76506 Echo exam of head
76511–76512 Echo exam of eye
76513 Echo exam of eye, water bath
76516–76519 Echo exam of eye
76536 Echo exam of head and neck
76604 Echo exam of chest
76645 Echo exam of breast(s)
76700–76705 Echo exam of abdomen
76770–76775 Echo exam abdomen back wall
76778 Echo exam kidney transplant
76800 Echo exam spinal canal
76805–76815 Echo exam of pregnant uterus
76816 Echo exam follow-up/repeat
76818 Fetl biophys profil w/stress
76819 Fetl biophys profil w/o strs
76825–76828 Echo exam of fetal heart
76830 Echo exam, transvaginal
76831 Echo exam, uterus
76856–76857 Echo exam of pelvis
76870 Echo exam of scrotum
76872 Echo exam, transrectal
76873 Echograp trans r, pros study
76880 Echo exam of extremity
76885–76886 Echo exam, infant hips
76970 Ultrasound exam follow-up
76977 Us bone density measure
76999 Echo examination procedure

Include the following CPT codes for echocardiography and vascular ultrasound:

93303–93304 Echo transthoracic
93307–93308 Echo exam of heart
93320–93321 Doppler echo exam, heart, if used in conjunction with 93303–93308
93325 Doppler color flow add-on, if used in conjunction with 93303–93308

93875–93882 Extracranial study
93886–93888 Intracranial study
93922–93924 Extremity study
93925–93926 Lower extremity study
93930–93931 Upper extremity study
93965–93971 Extremity study
93975–93979 Vascular study
93980–93981 Penile vascular study
93990 Doppler flow testing

Include miscellaneous other HCPCS level 2 codes for radiology and certain other imaging services:

G0050 Residual urine by ultrasound
G0131–132 CT scan, bone density study
G0188 Xray lwr extrmty-full lngth
R0070 Transport portable x-ray
R0075 Transport port x-ray multipl
Radiation Therapy Services and Supplies

Include CPT codes for all radiation therapy services and supplies in the CPT 70000 series:

77261–77263 Radiation therapy planning
77280–77295 Set radiation therapy field
77299 Radiation therapy planning
77300–77315 Radiation therapy dose plan
77321 Radiation therapy port plan
77326–77328 Radiation therapy dose plan
77331 Special radiation dosimetry
77332–77334 Radiation treatment aid(s)
77336–77370 Radiation physics consult
77399 External radiation dosimetry
77401–77416 Radiation treatment delivery
77417 Radiology port film(s)
77427 Radiation tx management, x5
77431 Radiation therapy management
77432 Stereotactic radiation trmt
77470 Special radiation treatment
77499 Radiation therapy management
77520 Proton trmt, simple w/o comp
77522 Proton trmt, simple w/comp
77523 Proton trmt, intermediate

77525 Proton treatment, complex
77600–77620 Hyperthermia treatment
77750 Infuse radioactive materials
77761 Apply intrcav radiat simple
77762 Apply intrcav radiat interm
77763 Apply intrcav radiat compl
77776 Apply interstit radiat simpl
77777 Apply interstit radiat inter
77778 Apply iterstit radiat compl
77781–77784 High intensity brachytherapy
77789 Apply surface radiation
77790 Radiation handling
77799 Radium/radioisotope therapy

Include CPT codes for radiation therapy classified elsewhere:

31643 Diag bronchoscope/catheter
50559 Renal endoscopy/radiotracer
55859 Percut/needle insert, pros
61770 Incise skull for treatment
61793 Focus radiation beam

Preventive Screening Tests, Immunizations and Vaccines

The following CPT and HCPCS codes are excluded under Sec. 411.355(h) as screening tests:

76092 Mammogram, screening
76977 Us bone density measure
G0103 Psa, total screening
G0107 CA screen; fecal blood test
G0123 Screen cerv/vag thin layer
G0124 Screen c/v thin layer by MD
G0141 Scr c/v cyto,autosys and md
G0143-G0145 Scr c/v cyto, thin layer, rescr
G0147 Scr c/v cyto, automated sys
G0148 Scr c/v cyto, autosys, rescr
P3000 Screen pap by tech w md supv
P3001 Screening pap smear by phys

The following CPT codes are excluded under Sec. 411.355(h) as vaccines:

90657 Flu vaccine, 6–35 mo, im

90658 Flu vaccine, 3 yrs, im
90659 Flu vacine, whole, im
90732 Pneumococcal vacc, adult/ill
90744 Hepb vacc ped/adol 3 dose im
90746 Hep b vaccine, adult, im
90747 Hepb vacc, ill pat 4 dose im
90748 Hep b/hib vaccine, im

Drugs Used by Patients Undergoing Dialysis

The following HCPCS codes are excluded under Sec. 411.355(g) as EPO and other dialysis related outpatient prescription drugs furnished in or by an ESRD facility:

J0635 Calcitriol injection
J0895 Deferoxamine meslyate inj
J1750 Iron dextran
J2915 NA Ferric Gluconate Complex
J2997 Alteplase recombinant
Q9920 Epoetin with hct =20
Q9921 Epoetin with hct = 21
Q9922 Epoetin with hct = 22
Q9923 Epoetin with hct = 23
Q9924 Epoetin with hct = 24
Q9925 Epoetin with hct = 25
Q9926 Epoetin with hct = 26
Q9927 Epoetin with hct = 27
Q9928 Epoetin with hct = 28
Q9929 Epoetin with hct = 29
Q9930 Epoetin with hct = 30
Q9931 Epoetin with hct = 31
Q9932 Epoetin with hct = 32
Q9933 Epoetin with hct = 33
Q9934 Epoetin with hct = 34
Q9935 Epoetin with hct = 35
Q9936 Epoetin with hct = 36
Q9937 Epoetin with hct = 37
Q9938 Epoetin with hct = 38
Q9939 Epoetin with hct = 39
Q9940 Epoetin with hct >= 40

[FR Doc. 01–4 Filed 1–3-01; 8:45 am]

BILLING CODE 4120–03-P

Health Care Fraud and Abuse: A Guide to Federal Sanctions

Volume 3

The West Group Health Law Library

Health Care & Antitrust Law: Principles and Practice
by John J. Miles

Health Care Financial Transactions Manual
by Thomas C. Fox, Carol Colborn Loepere, and Joseph W. Metro

Health Care Fraud and Abuse: A Guide to Federal Sanctions
by Paul P. Cacioppo

Patient Care Decision-Making: A Legal Guide for Providers
by Claire C. Obade

Health Law Handbook
edited by Alice G. Gosfield

Health Law Practice Guide
by the National Health Lawyers Association/American Academy of Healthcare Attorneys

Related Titles from West Group

Advance Medical Directives
by Alan D. Lieberson

Attorneys Medical Deskbook
by Dan J. Tennenhouse

Medical Malpractice Digest
by Dean E. Snyder

Medical Information Systems for Lawyers
by J. Stanley McQuade

Medico-Legal Implications of Death and Dying
by David W. Meyers

Medico-Legal Watch
edited by Gary Freed, M.D.

The Law of Medical Practice in Illinois
by Theodore R. LeBlang, W. Eugene Basanta and Robert John Kane

The Law of Medical Practice in Ohio
by Gregory G. Binford and Janet K. Feldcamp

The Law of Medical Practice in Pennsylvania and New Jersey
by Barton L. Post, Brian M. Peters, and Stanley P. Stahl

Health Care Fraud and Abuse:

A Guide to Federal Sanctions

Paul P. Cacioppo

Volume 3

WEST GROUP
A THOMSON COMPANY

(Release #17, 12/2001)

Note: In this work, every effort has been made to use gender neutral language. Where clarity requires, however, the masculine pronoun has been used. The reader should note that it refers to persons of either gender.

Library of Congress Cataloging-in-Publication Data

Cacioppo, Paul P.
Health care fraud and abuse: a guide to federal sanctions/by Paul P. Cacioppo.
p. cm.
ISBN 0–87632–806–0
1. Medicare fraud. 2. Medicaid fraud. 3. Sanctions, Administrative–United States. I. Title. KF3608.A4C33 1991
345.73'0263—dc20
[347.305263]

90-23174
CIP

Table of Contents

Volume 3

Part III APPENDIXES (Continued)

Appendix Guide

This Guide is provided as a supplement to the Table of Contents to aid the reader in identifying and locating *Health Care Fraud and Abuse* appendix material.

Regulatory Provisions Governing Medicare Safe Harbors

Office of Inspector General Advisory Opinions— Section 1128D Of the Social Security Act, 42 U.S.C. 1320a-7(d)

1997

Whether it is permissible for a charitable organization partly funded by kidney dialysis providers to pay Medicare Part B, Medigap and other health insurance premiums for end-stage renal disease patients who are financially needy.

Whether a state-funded program that pays for insurance premiums for financially needy Medicare beneficiaries with end-stage renal disease would constitute grounds for the imposition of a civil monetary penalty under Section 231(h) of [HIPAA].

Whether Mrs. P's transfer of assets to her nephew, Mr. S, and subsequent application for Medicaid benefits, subjects her to sanction under 42 U.S.C. 1320a-7b(a)(6), which prohibits certain dispositions of assets for the purpose of qualifying for Medicaid.

Whether declining to pursue collection of copayments from certain patients who have employer-sponsored Medicare complementary coverage constitutes grounds for imposition of sanctions under Section 231(h) of [HIPAA] . . . or under Sections 1128B(b) (the anti-kickback statute) or 1128A(7) (relating to payment of kickbacks) of the Social Security Act.

Whether an outpatient radiology imaging center joint venture owned by a medical group specializing in radiology and a hospital care provider (i) generates prohibited remuneration within the meaning of the anti-kickback statute, Section 1128B of the Social Security Act; (ii) constitutes grounds for the imposition of an exclusion under Section 1128(b)(7) of the Act (as it applies to kickbacks); (iii) constitutes grounds for criminal sanctions under Section 1128B(b) of the Act; and/or (iv) satisfies the criteria set out in Section 1128B(b)(3) of the Act or associated regulations.

Advisory Opinion 97-6, October 8, 1997 Appendix F14

Whether a proposed arrangement for restocking ambulance supplies and medications (the "Proposed Arrangement") would constitute illegal remuneration as defined in the anti-kickback statute.

1998

Advisory Opinion 98-1, March 19, 1998 Appendix F17

Whether a contractual arrangement for distribution and billing services between Company A and Company B ... constitutes grounds for sanction under the anti-kickback statute.

Advisory Opinion 98-2, April 8, 1998 Appendix F17.1

Whether certain pharmaceutical discount pricing arrangements that are limited to arrangements between a manufacturer and wholesalers . . . will subject you to sanction under the anti-kickback statute.

Advisory Opinion 98-3, April 8, 1998 Appendix F17.2

Whether a hospital system's provision of an ambulance to a municipal fire department as described in your request . . .

Advisory Opinion 98-4, April 14, 1998 Appendix F17.3

Whether a proposed management services contract between a medical practice management company and a physician practice, which provides that the management company will be reimbursed for its costs and paid a percentage of net practice revenues...

Advisory Opinion 98-5, April 24, 1998 Appendix F17.4

. . .Which seeks our opinion regarding the "coordination of benefits" ("COB") provisions of a provider agreement between Nursing Home A . . . and a health care plan.

Advisory Opinion 98-6, April 24, 1998 Appendix F17.5

Whether waiving coinsurance obligations for participants in a clinical study sponsored by the Health Care Financing Administration and the National Heart, Lung, and Blood Institute...

Advisory Opinion 98-7, June 11, 1998 — Appendix F17.6

Whether an ambulance restocking and continuing education arrangement . . . constitutes prohibited remuneration under the anti-kickback statute.

Advisory Opinion 98-8, July 6, 1998 — Appendix F18

Whether Company A . . ., a wholly-owned subsidiary of Company B . . . would be subject to exclusion from Federal health care programs pursuant to 42 U.S.C. § 1320a-7(b) . . .

Advisory Opinion 98-9, July 13, 1998 — Appendix F19

Whether a compensation arrangement for registered nurses and certain other employees pursuant to a collective bargaining agreement with the nurses' union...

Advisory Opinion 98-10, August 31, 1998 — Appendix F23

Whether the payment of a sales commission to an independent manufacturers' representative . . . constitutes grounds for sanctions under the anti-kickback statute.

Advisory Opinion 98-11, September 14, 1998 — Appendix F24

Whether a proposed purchasing arrangement involving a trade association, its nursing home members, and an electrical utility consultant . . . constitutes prohibited remuneration under the anti-kickback statute.

Advisory Opinion 98-12, September 16, 1998 — Appendix F25

Whether a proposed joint venture among several orthopedic surgeons and anesthesiologists specializing in pain management to establish an ambulatory surgical center, as described in your request letter and supplemental submissions . . ., would generate prohibited remuneration . . .

Advisory Opinion 98-13, September 23, 1998 — Appendix F26

Whether an ambulance restocking program, coordinated through a local emergency medical services council ..., constitutes prohibited remuneration under the anti-kickback statute...and, if so, whether the Program constitutes grounds for the imposition of sanctions under the anti-kickback statute.

Advisory Opinion 98-14, October 21, 1998 — Appendix F27

Whether an existing pharmaceutical restocking program ... and a proposed medical supplies restocking program . . . constitute prohibited remuneration under the anti-kickback statute.

Advisory Opinion 98-15, November 2, 1998 — Appendix F28

Whether an arrangement for contracted pharmacy services between University A and Pharmacy Company B to facilitate an outpatient pharmacy program for the University's hemophilia center pursuant to section

340B of the Public Health Service Act ...would constitute grounds for sanctions under the anti-kickback statute.

Advisory Opinion 98-16, November 3, 1998 Appendix F29

Whether a proposed arrangement under which [Name redacted] would assign an employee pharmacist to work in designated hospital transplant centers for the purpose of providing pharmacy-related products and services . . . would constitute prohibited remuneration under the anti-kickback statute.

Advisory Opinion 98-17, November 6, 1998 Appendix F30

Whether donations by Company X . . . to Organization A . . . (an independent, 501(c)(3) charitable organization) for the purpose of funding a program to pay for Supplementary Medical Insurance . . . or Medicare Supplementary Health Insurance . . . premiums for financially needy Medicare beneficiaries with end-stage renal disease . . .

Advisory Opinion 98-18, November 25, 1998 Appendix F31

Whether an ophthalmologist's proposed sublease to an optometrist of certain imaging equipment . . . would meet the criteria of the equipment rental safe harbor.

Advisory Opinion 98-19, December 14, 1998 Appendix F32

Whether an arrangement whereby an independent physician association would acquire an equity interest in a managed care organization would constitute grounds for the imposition of sanctions under the anti-kickback statute.

1999

Advisory Opinion 99-1, January 20, 1999 Appendix F33

Whether the Arrangement [for the provision of back-up emergency ambulance services that involves waivers of copayments and deductible amounts] constitutes prohibited remuneration within the meaning of the anti-kickback statute.

Advisory Opinion 99-2, February 26, 1999 Appendix F34

Whether certain arrangements for discounted ambulance services provided to residents of Medicare skilled nursing facilities would result in prohibited remuneration and sanctions under the anti-kickback statute.

Advisory Opinion 99-3, March 16, 1999 Appendix F35

Whether a proposed pricing arrangement for a package of therapeutic mattresses for SNF patients to be marketed by a company, and certain commissioned agents, would result in prohibited remuneration under the anti-kickback statute.

Advisory Opinion 99-4, March 31, 1999 Appendix F36

Whether a proposed agreement . . . pursuant to which Hospital District No.1 . . . would locate a medical clinic within the geographic boundaries of Hospital District No. 2 . . . would constitute grounds for sanctions under the anti-kickback statute.

Advisory Opinion 99-5, April 1, 1999 Appendix F37

Whether an annual fee imposed by city ordinance on ambulance companies wishing to provide ambulance services in the city . . . constitutes prohibited remuneration under the anti-kickback statute, . . . and, if so, whether the Ambulance Fee assessment constitutes grounds for the imposition of sanctions.

Advisory Opinion 99-6, April 7, 1999 Appendix F38

Whether the longstanding policy of a hospital, specializing in pediatric oncology research, of not billing its patients for any amounts associated with their treatment, including copayment amounts...

Advisory Opinion 99-7, June 30, 1999 Appendix F39

Whether an across-the-board waiver of any out-of-pocket beneficiary copayments for medical services covered by the national Eye Care Project constitutes grounds for the imposition of a sanction under section 1128A(a)(5) of the Act.

Advisory Opinion 99-8, July 6, 1999 Appendix F40

Whether an arrangement to provide for personal appearances by podiatrists to certain retail stores constitutes grounds for sanctions under the anti-kickback statute.

Advisory Opinion 99-9, September 30, 1999 Appendix F41

Regarding a proposed contractual arrangement between a self-insured employer health plan and a single-specialty managed care organization to provide managed podiatry benefits for the employer's retirees.

Advisory Opinion 99-10, October 25, 1999 Appendix F42

Whether a corporate sponsorship program between Drug Company A and Charity B . . . constitutes grounds for sanctions under the anti-kickback statute.

Advisory Opinion 99-11, October 25, 1999 Appendix F43

Concerning an arrangement sponsored by Coalition A to provide psychotherapy services at free or reduced prices using residents from local teaching facilities as clinicians.

Advisory Opinion 99-12, November 23, 1999 Appendix F44

About a proposed marketing program involving the use of physician practices and health care clinics to distribute coupons redeemable by certain retailers . . . for discounts on items or services that are not reimbursable by any Federal health care program.

2000

Advisory Opinion No. 00-9, December 8, 2000 Appendix F55

Whether a proposed ambulance restocking arrangement constitutes prohibited remuneration.

Advisory Opinion No. 00-10, December 28, 2000 Appendix F56

Regarding a program designed to promote an expensive new drug used to prevent certain respiratory infections ... in pediatric patients.

Advisory Opinion No. 00-11, December 28, 2000 Appendix F57

Regarding a proposed charitable donation of up to $5,000 from Association A to EMS Service B... for the purchase of equipment and payment of paramedic training expenses.

2001

Advisory Opinion No. 01-1, January 11, 2001 Appendix F58

Concerning a proposed arrangement in which a hospital will share with a group of cardiac surgeons a percentage of the hospital's cost savings arising from the surgeons' implementation of a number of cost reduction measures in certain surgical procedures.

Advisory Opinion No. 01-2, March 17, 2001 Appendix F59

Concerning an annual charity golf tournament for which some of its vendors and suppliers pay money as sponsors and tournament participants.

Advisory Opinion No. 01-3, May —, 2001 Appendix F60

Concerning whether proposed contracts for discounted services between a Federally-recognized Indian tribe and local hospitals would constitute grounds for the imposition of exclusions under section1128(7) of the Act or civil money penalties under section 1128A(a)(7) of the Act.

Advisory Opinion No. 01-4, May 10, 2001 Appendix F61

Concerning a proposed arrangement between a hospital and a new physician whom the hospital would like to recruit to practice within its service area.

Advisory Opinion No. 01-5, May 24, 2001 Appendix F62

Concerning a proposed lease of cardiac diagnostic equipment to emergency medical services providers for a nominal charge.

Advisory Opinion No. 01-6, May 29, 2001 Appendix F63

Concerning pyments by vendors to a group purchasing organization (GPO) owned by entities affiliated with health care providers that purchase items covered by the GPO's vendor contracts.

The Office of Inspector General (OIG) was established at the Department of Health and Human Services by Congress in 1976 to identify and eliminate fraud, abuse, and waste in the Department's programs, including the Medicare and Medicaid programs, and to promote efficiency, economy, and effectiveness in departmental operations.

Office of Inspector General Advisory Opinions Under the Stark Bill—Section 1877 of the Social Security Act

Concerning whether a physician's referrals for certain services are prohibited under section 1877 of the Social Security Act

Whether the partners and physician employees of a proposed partnership may, under the "in-office ancillary services" exception defined in section 1877(b)(2) of the Social Security Act, refer Medicare and/or Medicaid patients to the partnership for eyeglass prescriptions filled subsequent to cataract surgery with the insertion of an intraocular lens.

Office of Inspector General Special Fraud Alerts

Office of Inspector General Medicare Advisory Bulletins

Office of Inspector General Special Advisory Bulletins

Office of Inspector General Compliance Program Guides

Other Civil and Criminal Statutes Pertinent to Health Care Fraud and Abuse

Recent Regulatory Provisions Applicable to Civil Money Penalties, Exclusions and Other Remedies

APPENDIX F17

Advisory Opinion No. 98–1

Posted: March 25, 1998

[March 19, 1998]

[name and address redacted]

Re: Advisory Opinion No. 98–1

Ladies and Gentlemen:

We are writing in response to your request for an advisory opinion, in which you asked whether a contractual arrangement for distribution and billing services between Company A and Company B (the "Arrangement") constitutes grounds for sanction under the anti-kickback statute, section 1128B(b) of the Social Security Act (the "Act"), for exclusion under sections 1128(b)(6) [claims substantially in excess of usual charges] and 1128(b)(7) [fraud, kickbacks, and other prohibited activities] of the Act, or for civil monetary penalties under sections 1128A(a)(1)(A) [items or services not provided as claimed], 1128A(a)(1)(B) [false claims], or 1128A(a)(7) [kickbacks] of the Act.

You have certified that all of the information you provided in your request, including all supplementary letters, is true and correct, and constitutes a complete description of the facts and agreements among the parties regarding the Arrangement.

In issuing this opinion, we have relied solely on the facts and information you presented to us. We have not undertaken any independent investigation of such information. This opinion is limited to the facts presented.

Based on the information you have provided, we conclude that payments under the Arrangement potentially constitute prohibited remuneration under the anti-kickback statute and may subject the parties to sanction under sections 1128B(b), 1128(b)(7), and 1128A(a)(7) of the Act. As further explained below, because we lack sufficient information to render an opinion, we reach no conclusion regarding the applicablility of sections 1128(b)(6), 1128A(a)(1)(A), or 1128A(a)(1)(B) of the Act. We note, however, that the Arrangement contains features that suggest that some or all of these authorities may be implicated.

I. FACTUAL BACKGROUND

A. The Parties

Company A is a manufacturer of, among other things, orthopedic "soft goods" products, including splints, cervical collars, supports, joint immobilizers, neoprene products, cast shoes, walkers, post-op shoes, traction products, anti-embolism stockings, cold packs, and elastic bandages. Company A sells its soft goods products directly to orthopedic physicians, among other customers. Typically, these physicians purchase a supply of orthopedic products for their offices sufficient to meet the anticipated needs of their patients. They prescribe the products where medically indicated and dispense them incident to the medical treatment provided to the patient. The physicians submit claims to third-party payers, including Federal and state health care programs.

Company B is a State X-based corporation engaged in the business of providing marketing consulting and medical billing in connection with home medical equipment.

2. The Arrangement

On July 1, 1997, Company A entered into an agreement with Company B pursuant to a contract entitled "Independent Contractor Agreement (Third Party Billing)" for certain distribution, marketing, and billing services.[1] Under the Arrangement, Company A will consign soft goods products to Company B, which will, in turn, consign them to physicians, except as otherwise noted in the discussion of the "Company B Loaner Program" below. Because they will be supplied to Company B and subsequently to physicians on a consignment basis, the products will remain Company A's property until they are sold to a patient. Company A personnel will provide Com-

---

[1] Company A has represented that the contract has been executed, but not implemented. Payments under the contract have not been made, except for one payment to Company B for consulting services not yet performed. Company A has represented that it will discontinue further implementation of the agreement if this Office concludes that the Arrangement could result in sanctions.

pany B with initial introductions to current customer accounts. Company B will assume responsibility for marketing to and servicing those accounts, as well as for developing new ones under a program it calls the "Company B Program."

Under the Arrangement, Company B will bill, submitting claims to contracted insurance carriers, including the Medicare and Medicaid programs. Company B will accept assignment and bill Medicare and Medicaid under its own supplier numbers. On a regular basis, Company B will forward reimbursements to Company A, less Company B's fee, which ranges from 20 – 25% of collected revenues, depending on the dollar value of business generated in a calendar year.[2]

Company B will contract with payers and bill for Company A's products according to a fee schedule devised by Company B (the "Company B Contract Price List"). The Company B Contract Price List reflects, among other things, the Medicare fee schedule ceiling for each item under a column designated "Medicare Price". In nearly all cases, the "Medicare Price" listed exceeds the price at which Company A currently sells the identical product to any other purchaser (the "Company A List Price"). In many cases, the Company B "Medicare Price" exceeds the Company A List Price by 4–5 times, and in one case by over 13 times. The Company B Contract Price List price to private paying patients is lower than the Medicare Price in almost all cases.

The contract also provides that Company B will provide 100 person-days of consulting services to train Company A employees about sales and reimbursement issues. Company A will pay Company B $1,000 per day plus travel expenses for these services. The contract provides that the specific training requirements and outcomes to be achieved will be determined in advance of any training activities.

A further element of the Arrangement is an "Company B Loaner Program" applicable to Company A products supplied to Medicare patients. This program was developed in response to an interpretation of the supplier standards under 42 C.F.R. § 424.57(c) issued by the Durable Medical Equipment Regional Carrier (DMERC) for Region D. Under the DMERC interpretation, payment can only be

---

[2] To ensure collections, Company B plans to charge patients' credit cards directly where their insurance carriers do not pay outstanding claims for over 90 days. We express no opinion on the legality of this procedure here; however, charging patients in this manner raises legal concerns in connection with assignment agreements under the Medicare program.

made to a supplier when the supplier provides a product directly to the patient. This interpretation prohibits suppliers from leaving equipment in a physician's office for dispensing by the physician to a beneficiary for home use. Under the Company B Loaner Program, physicians generally will order Company A orthotic supplies for Medicare patients from Company B, which will arrange for Company A to ship the products directly to the patients' homes. Company B will telephone patients first to alert them to the forthcoming deliveries.[3] The products shipped by Company A will be treated as a consignment of goods to Company B. In a substantial number of cases, the patient will need to have a product dispensed immediately in the physician's office from the physician's consignment inventory. Such products dispensed in the physician's office for immediate use will be treated as "loaned" to the patient until the patient receives an identical replacement product by mail. Upon receipt of the replacement product, the patient will be asked to return it to the physician to restock the physician's inventory. Because the "loaned" product will not typically be reusable, in most instances the patient will continue to use the "loaned" product and will return the new, unused product to the physician. Patients who fail to return a product to the physician will be charged "rent" for the use of the product.[4]

II. LEGAL ANALYSIS

1. Anti-kickback Law and Prior Guidance

The anti-kickback statute makes it a criminal offense knowingly and willfully to offer, pay, solicit, or receive any remuneration to induce referrals of items or services reimbursable by the Federal health care programs. 42 U.S.C. § 1320a-7b(b). Where remuneration is paid purposefully to induce referrals of items or services paid for by a Federal health care program, the anti-kickback statute is violated. By its terms, the statute ascribes criminal liability to parties on both sides of an impermissible "kickback" transaction. For purposes of the anti-kickback statute, "remuneration" includes the transfer of anything of value, in cash or in-kind, directly or indi-

[3] In addition, under the Medicare supplier rules, a supplier must, among other things, respond to beneficiary questions or complaints and disclose certain consumer information to beneficiaries. See 42 C.F.R. § 424.57(c) and (f).

[4] The processing of the paperwork related to the Company B Loaner Program will be handled by a Company B affiliate called Company C.

rectly, covertly or overtly. Under the statute, referrals include, but are not limited to, arranging for or recommending purchasing, leasing, or ordering any good, facility, service, or item for which payment may be made by a Federal health care program.

The statute has been interpreted to cover any arrangement where one purpose of the remuneration is to obtain money for the referral of services or to induce further referrals. *United States v. Kats,* 871 F.2d 105 (9 th Cir. 1989); *United States v. Greber,* 760 F.2d 68 (3d Cir.), *cert. denied,* 476 U.S. 988 (1985). Violation of the statute constitutes a felony punishable by a maximum fine of $25,000, imprisonment up to five years or both. Conviction will also lead to automatic exclusion from Federal health care programs, including Medicare and Medicaid. This Office may also initiate administrative proceedings to exclude persons from the Federal and State health care programs or to impose civil monetary penalties for fraud, kickbacks, and other prohibited activities under sections 1128(b)(7) and 1128A(a)(7) of the Act.[5]

A number of statutory and regulatory "safe harbors" protect certain arrangements that might otherwise technically violate the anti-kickback statute from prosecution. *See* 42 U.S.C. § 1320a-7b(b)(3); 42 C.F.R. § 1001.952. Pertinent here is a regulatory safe harbor that protects certain personal services and management contracts that, among other conditions, (i) fix in advance the aggregate compensation to be paid under the contract; (ii) base the compensation on fair market value; and (iii) do not determine compensation in a manner that takes into account the volume or value of any referrals or business otherwise generated between the parties for which payment may be made by Medicare or a state health care program. For part-time, periodic, or sporadic services, the safe harbor requires that the schedule and precise length of the intervals for the performance of services be set forth in the contract. *See* 42 C.F.R. § 1001.952 (d).

This Office has long been concerned about potentially abusive marketing arrangements involving health care goods and services paid for in whole or in part by Federal health care programs. In our preamble to the 1991 final safe harbor rules, 56 Fed. Reg. 35952 (July 29, 1991), we explained that the anti-kickback statute "on its

---

[5] Because both the criminal and administrative sanctions related to the anti-kickback implications of the Arrangement are based on violations of the anti-kickback statute, the analysis for purposes of this advisory opinion is the same under all three provisions.

face prohibits offering or acceptance of remuneration, inter alia, for the purposes of 'arranging for or recommending purchasing, leasing, or ordering any . . . service or item payable under Medicare or Medicaid.' Thus, we believe that many marketing and advertising activities may involve at least technical violations of the statute." 56 Fed. Reg. at 35974. Since publication of the 1991 rule, we have continued to learn of abusive relationships involving marketing activities that adversely affect the Federal health care programs and their beneficiaries.

(i) Percentage Compensation

As a threshold matter, the Arrangement does not qualify for safe harbor protection under the personal services and management contracts safe harbor, since the majority of the compensation to be paid by Company A to Company B is calculated based on a percentage of reimbursements collected by Company B for its sales of Company A products. Thus, the amount of compensation to be paid to Company B under the contract is not fixed in advance and is determined in a manner that takes into account the value or volume of business generated between the parties, including Federal health care program business. *See*42 C.F.R. § 1001.952(d).

Because compliance with a safe harbor is not mandatory, the fact that the Arrangement does not fit within a safe harbor does not mean that the Arrangement is unlawful. Percentage compensation arrangements are potentially abusive, however, because they provide financial incentives that may encourage overutilization of items and services and may increase program costs. Here, the percentage compensation arrangement is problematic for the following reasons:

- *The Arrangement includes significant financial incentives that increase the risk of abusive marketing and billing practices.* The percentage amount of Company B's compensation is a factor in evaluating the Arrangement's financial incentives. Moreover, the compensation is based on a percentage of the volume or value of business generated between the parties. Whereas Company A is not a Medicare supplier, Company B will be a supplier and will actually bill the Federal health care programs. The "Medicare Prices" shown on the Company B Contract Price List are in many cases substantially in excess of Company A's list prices. To the extent that revenues under the Arrangement exceed — in some instances by substantial amounts — the revenues derived from prices currently charged by Company A to its list price purchasers, both Company A and Company B stand to profit substantially.

- *Company B will have opportunities to unduly influence referral sources and patients.* The Arrangement involves active marketing, including direct contacts, by Company B and Company A to physicians who order and dispense orthotic products. In addition, the Arrangement provides Company B with opportunities to market directly to Medicare patients.
- *The Arrangement contains no safeguards against fraud and abuse.* The Arrangement is particularly susceptible to abusive practices because the orthotic products at issue are paid for by third-party payers and patients, including the government, instead of by the physicians who order and dispense them.[6] A recent OIG study confirmed that orthotics are subject to significant abuse. *See* Medicare Orthotics (OEI-02–95–00380, 10/97).

These reasons are sufficient to persuade us that the Arrangement poses an unacceptable risk of fraud and abuse so as to preclude a favorable advisory opinion; however, the determination of an actual anti-kickback violation in any given case depends on the totality of the facts and circumstances, and no one fact or aspect of the Arrangement is necessarily determinative.[7]

(ii) Training Services

Company A has also requested our opinion with regard to whether the training fees to be paid by Company A to Company B violate the anti-kickback statute. As a threshold matter, the training fee portion of the contract does not satisfy the safe harbor requirement that

[6] Although we have received no information indicating that the Arrangement involves any improper payments from Company B to physicians to induce them to order Company A products, we note that the Arrangement contains no apparent safeguards against such payments.

[7] We have adopted for purposes of this opinion Company A's characterization of the Arrangement as one in which Company B is paid a fee for marketing and billing services. We note that there are two other plausible interpretations of the Arrangement. The Arrangement may be viewed as one in which Company B pays remuneration to Company A in the form of a percentage of collections on Company A's products. Alternatively, the Arrangement could be viewed as a joint venture between Company A and Company B. In both scenarios, amounts paid to Company A could be construed as payment for referrals of existing physician customers and their patients.

for periodic, sporadic, or part-time services, the schedule and precise length of the intervals for the performance of the services be set in advance. However, as noted above, compliance with a safe harbor is not required.

Again, the initial inquiry is whether there is remuneration being offered, paid, solicited, or received to induce the referral of Federal program business. In this case, the issue is whether the contractual amount of $100,000 represents fair market value for the training services. Pursuant to 42 U.S.C. § 1320a-7d(b)(3), we are unable to make that determination. However, given that Company B's own staff will assume primary responsibility for marketing and distributing Company A's orthotic products under the Company B Program, the need for training of Company A's employees by Company B is unclear. It is possible that the training fees may represent disguised compensation for Company B's activities that generate business, including Federal program business.

2. Claims Issues and the Loaner Program

As indicated above, Company A has further inquired about the applicability to the Arrangement of certain permissive exclusion and civil monetary penalty provisions involving Federal program claims filing and reimbursement. However, no claims have actually been filed for Federal program reimbursement under the Arrangement, and we have no certified information regarding how, for example, Company B plans to report charges on its claims or code its claims. Accordingly, we make no determination with respect to these issues. We wish to make clear, however, that aspects of the Arrangement described in the materials submitted by Company A, including the Company B Contract Price List and the Company B Loaner Program, raise substantial questions with respect to claims filing and coding under the Arrangement. These questions further support our view the Arrangement may pose more than a minimal risk of fraud or abuse.

3. Conclusion

The advisory opinion process permits this Office to protect specific arrangements that "contain[] limitations, requirements, or controls that give adequate assurance that Federal health care programs cannot be abused." *See* Preamble to the 1991 final rule for safe harbors, 62 Fed. Reg. 7350, 7351 (February 19, 1997). The Arrangement contains no such limitations, requirements, or controls. To the contrary, the Arrangement provides multiple opportunities and financial incentives for marketing and billing activities that may lead, individually or collectively, to more than a minimal risk of Federal health care program abuse.[8]

Therefore, for the above-stated reasons, we conclude that the Arrangement may involve prohibited remuneration under the anti-kickback statute and thus potentially be subject to sanction under section 1128B(b) of the Act, to exclusion under section 1128(b)(7) of the Act, and civil monetary penalties under section 1128A(a)(7). Any definitive conclusion regarding the existence of an anti-kickback violation requires a determination of the parties' intent, which determination is beyond the scope of the advisory opinion process. In addition, although we have insufficient information to make a determination, we are concerned that the Arrangement may potentially involve activities that would subject the parties to exclusion under section 1128(b)(6) or civil monetary penalties under section 1128A(a)(1)(A) or 1128A(a)(1)(B).

III. LIMITATIONS

The limitations applicable to this opinion include the following:

- This advisory opinion is applicable only to the statutory provisions specifically noted in the first paragraph of this advisory opinion. No opinion is herein expressed or implied with respect to the application of any other Federal, state, or local statute, rule, regulation, ordinance, or other law that may be applicable to the Arrangement.
- This advisory opinion will not bind or obligate any agency other than the U.S. Department of Health and Human Services.

This opinion is also subject to any additional limitations set forth at 42 C.F.R. Part 1008.

The OIG reserves the right to reconsider the questions and issues raised in this advisory opinion and, where the public interest requires, modify or terminate this opinion.

---

[8] Our conclusion regarding the risk of abuse in relation to the anti-kickback statute should not be construed to mean that a finding of abuse is an implied element necessary to establish a violation of the statute.

Sincerely,

D. McCarty Thornton
Chief Counsel to the Inspector General

APPENDIX F17.1

Advisory Opinion No. 98–2

Posted: April 8, 1998

[name and address redacted]

Re: Advisory Opinion No. 98–2

Dear [name redacted]

We are writing in response to your request for an advisory opinion, in which you ask whether certain pharmaceutical discount pricing arrangements that are limited to arrangements between a manufacturer and wholesalers (the "Proposed Arrangement") will subject you to sanction under the anti-kickback statute, section 1128B(b) of the Social Security Act (the "Act"), the exclusion authority related to kickbacks, section 1128(b)(7) of the Act, or the civil monetary penalty provision for kickbacks, section 1128A(a)(7) of the Act.

You have certified that all of the information you provided in your request, including all supplementary letters, is true and correct, and constitutes a complete description of the material facts regarding the Proposed Arrangement. In issuing this opinion, we have relied solely on the facts and information you presented to us. We have not undertaken any independent investigation of such information. This opinion is limited to the facts presented. If material facts have not been disclosed, this opinion is without force and effect.

Based on the information provided and subject to certain conditions described below, we conclude that the Proposed Arrangement (as further defined below) would not constitute prohibited remuneration under the anti-kickback statute, section 1128B(b) of the Act, and would not constitute grounds for sanctions under sections 1128 (b)(7) or 1128A(a)(7) of the Act. This opinion may not be relied on by any person other than the addressee and is further qualified as set out in Part III below and in 42 C.F.R. Part 1008.

I. FACTUAL BACKGROUND

Company A proposes to enter into contracts with pharmaceutical wholesalers for the purchase of certain multi-source generic pharmaceuticals at a fixed percentage price reduction (the "Proposed Arrangement"). As part of the contractual arrangement, the wholesalers will provide limited promotional support for the purchased pharmaceuticals. The pharmaceutical wholesalers' customers include retail pharmacies, hospitals, and other health care providers that dispense the pharmaceuticals to patients pursuant to physician prescriptions. Some of these patients will be Federal program beneficiaries. [1] The Proposed Arrangement would generally be available to all pharmaceutical wholesalers willing to accept the terms offered by Company A. The wholesalers will not bill any Federal health care program. Rather, they will sell products to retail pharmacies, hospitals, and other health care providers that may, in turn, submit claims for program reimbursement.

The Proposed Arrangement pertains only to bioequivalent generic products that are available from more than one manufacturer, i.e. "multi-source generic products." Under the Proposed Arrangement, Company A would offer a wholesaler discount pricing on multi-source generic products that the wholesaler agrees to make its "preferred generic" for a given product line. The contracts between Company A and the wholesalers will specify the particular generic products that are "preferred generics" eligible for the price reduction to the wholesalers (the "Contracted Products").

Under the Proposed Arrangement, the amount of the price reduction, which would be paid in the form of quarterly rebates, would be calculated by taking the wholesaler's contracted product purchases, subtracting returns of Contracted Products, invoice adjustments, [2]

---

[1] The Medicare program generally does not cover self-administered outpatient prescription drugs, such as those sold by Company A. However, such drugs are typically covered by Medicaid, and may be covered by other Federal health care programs. Medicaid payments for covered drugs are usually made directly to the pharmacy, hospital, or other provider, although in some circumstances program reimbursement may be made to the patient. In addition, prescription drugs may be covered for Medicare beneficiaries enrolled in Medicare HMOs.

[2] Adjustments include invoices priced incorrectly, discounts for prompt payment, and credits for inventory that may have decreased in price since the original purchase, i.e. floor stock adjustments.

and chargebacks,[3] and multiplying the resulting amount by a fixed 2 3 percentage. All purchases, returns, adjustments (if applicable), and chargebacks would occur within a single calendar quarter. The applicable fixed percentage would be set in advance pursuant to a written agreement with the wholesaler.[4]

A portion of the price reduction offered to certain wholesalers may be conditioned on the wholesalers' agreement to provide certain promotional support for the Contracted Products. These promotional activities are limited to the following:

- making informational phone calls to the wholesalers' retail customers regarding Contracted Products and special pricing on Contracted Products that may be available through the wholesaler;
- including Company A advertising materials relating to the Contracted Products in the wholesalers' mailings and deliveries to its customers;
- featuring advertisements for Contracted Products in the wholesalers' catalogs or other sales materials; and
- featuring the Contracted Products in the wholesalers' generic source catalog and trade show promotions.

In all cases, the promotional support contemplated by the Proposed Arrangement will relate exclusively to Contracted Products.

Company A has represented that it will comply with all reporting requirements for pharmaceutical manufacturers under all Federal and state health care programs.[5] In particular, Company A will include any rebates paid under the Proposed Arrangement in its calculations of "average manufacturer price" or "best price" under the Medicaid drug rebate program. *See* 42 U.S.C. § 1396r-8. Under

[3] A chargeback is a sale to a Company A retail customer and is not considered a sale generated through the wholesaler's source program.

[4] The percentages for the Proposed Arrangement are disclosed in Company A's request for an advisory opinion. Because these numbers are potentially proprietary business information of Company A, we are not disclosing them here. We have, however, considered them in rendering our opinion. The portion of the price reduction attributable to wholesaler promotional activities will be no more than 25% of the total price reduction under the Proposed Arrangement.

[5] This opinion is without force and effect if Company A fails to comply with all reporting requirements for pharmaceutical manufacturers under all Federal and state health care programs. We express no opinion about the manner or methods used by Company A to meet these reporting requirements.

the Medicaid drug rebate program, in order for Medicaid payment to be available to states for a manufacturer's covered outpatient drugs, the manufacturer generally must have entered into and have in effect a rebate agreement with the Secretary, on behalf of the states, or with states directly, to the extent authorized by the Secretary. *See* 42 U.S.C. § 1396r-8a. Pursuant to these rebate agreements, a manufacturer must report its "average manufacturer price" and "best price", as defined in the statute. See 42 U.S.C. § 1396r-8b.

In addition, Company A has represented that:

- the Proposed Arrangement is not dependent on and does not operate in conjunction with (either explicitly or implicitly) any other arrangement or agreement between or among Company A, the wholesalers, any retail customers or providers, or any other party with respect to the Contracted Products.[6]
- Company A will (1) fully and accurately report the existence of the discount on the invoices, coupons, or statements submitted to the wholesalers; (2) inform the wholesalers in an effective manner that they may have obligations to report the discount; and (3) refrain from doing anything that would impede the wholesalers or the wholesalers' customers from meeting any obligations to report the discount. Contracts under the Proposed Arrangement between Company A and the wholesalers will contain a statement advising the wholesalers that they may have obligations to report discounts accurately, including quarterly rebates, to appropriate Federal and state payors.

II. LEGAL ANALYSIS

A. Law

The anti-kickback statute, 42 U.S.C. § 1320a-7b(b), makes it a criminal offense knowingly and willfully to offer, pay, solicit, or receive any remuneration to induce the referral of business covered by a Federal health care program. Specifically, the statute provides that:

[6] The Proposed Arrangement is the complete and entire arrangement that is the subject of this advisory opinion. The Proposed Arrangement may become illegal when considered in the context of other related conduct or arrangements. In such circumstances, this advisory opinion is without force and effect.

> Whoever knowingly and willfully offers or pays [or solicits or receives] any remuneration (including any kickback, bribe, or rebate) directly or indirectly, overtly or covertly, in cash or in kind to any person to induce such person — to refer an individual to a person for the furnishing or arranging for the furnishing of any item or service for which payment may be made in whole or in part under a Federal health care program, or to purchase, lease, order, or arrange for or recommend purchasing, leasing, or ordering any good, facility, service, or item for which payment may be made in whole or in part under a Federal health care program, shall be guilty of a felony.

42 U.S.C. § 1320a-7b(b). In other words, the statute prohibits payments made purposefully to induce referrals of business payable by a Federal health care program. The statute ascribes liability to both sides of an impermissible "kickback" transaction. The statute has been interpreted to cover any arrangement where one purpose of the remuneration was to obtain money for the referral of services or to induce further referrals. *United States v. Kats,* 871 F.2d 105 (9th Cir. 1989); *United States v. Greber,* 760 F.2d 68 (3d Cir.), *cert. denied,* 474 U.S. 988 (1985). "Remuneration" for purposes of the anti-kickback statute includes the transfer of anything of value, in cash or in kind, directly or indirectly, covertly or overtly.

The anti-kickback statute contains a statutory exception for "a discount or other reduction in price obtained by a provider of services or other entity under a Federal health care program if the reduction in price is properly disclosed and appropriately reflected in the costs claimed or charges made by the provider or entity under a Federal health care program." 42 U.S.C. § 1320a-7b(b)(3)(A). Regulations implementing this discount "safe harbor" exception define the term "discount", in relevant part, as:

> a reduction in the amount a seller charges a buyer (who buys either directly or through a wholesaler or group purchasing organization) for a good or service based on an arms-length transaction. The term discount may include a rebate check, credit or coupon directly redeemable from the seller only to the extent that such reductions in price are attributable to the original good or service that was purchased or furnished.

42 C.F.R. § 1001.952(h)(3). The regulation further provides that the definition of discount does not include "services provided in accordance with a personal or management services contract."*Id.*

The discount safe harbor regulations provide, in relevant part, that prohibited remuneration does not include a discount, as defined above, on a good or service received by a buyer "which submits a claim or request for payment for the good or service for which payment may be made in whole or in part under Medicare or a State health care program," provided certain other conditions described in the regulations are satisfied.[7] See 42 C.F.R. § 1001.952(h). These additional requirements, imposed on both sellers and buyers, vary depending on how the buyers are reimbursed by the Medicare and Medicaid programs. Included among them are requirements that a discount be fully and accurately disclosed so that the benefit of the discount can inure to the Medicare and Medicaid programs, that a discount be for the specific good or service being purchased, and that discounts be earned in the same fiscal year as the purchase of the applicable good or service.

In 1994, we published certain proposed clarifications to the discount safe harbor. These clarifications included a proposal to define "rebate" for purposes of the regulations as "any discount which is not given at the time of sale." Accordingly, rebates would be covered by the safe harbor if offered to cost report buyers and capitated health plans under section 1876 of the Act, but would not be covered if offered to "other" buyers, because protected discounts to those buyers must be given at the time of the sale. The proposed clarifications also would make clear that a seller could receive safe harbor protection even if the buyer does not meet its obligations under the safe harbor, provided that the seller has acted in good faith and has not done anything that would impede the buyer from meeting its obligations.

A further safe harbor regulation exists for personal services and management contracts. That safe harbor provides protection for written personal services contracts of at least one year's duration where (i) the services to be performed and, in certain circumstances, the schedule for performance are specified in the contract, and (ii) the aggregate amount of compensation is fixed in advance, based on fair market value in an arms-length transaction, and not determined in a manner that takes into account the volume or value of any referrals or business otherwise generated between the parties for which payment may be made by Medicare or a state health care program. *See* 42 C.F.R. § 1001.952(d).

---

[7] See 42 C.F.R. § 1001.952(h)(1)-(3). In the preamble to the regulation, we explained that the statutory discount safe harbor "applies only to discounts obtained by health care providers who submit claims to the Medicare and Medicaid programs." 56 Fed. Reg. 35952, 35977 (July 29, 1991).

B. Analysis

For the reasons set out below, we conclude as follows:

- the Proposed Arrangement potentially is subject to the anti-kickback statute;
- the Proposed Arrangement does not qualify for either the discount or personal services contract "safe harbor"; but
- the Proposed Arrangement does not constitute prohibited remuneration for purposes of the anti-kickback statute.

First, the Proposed Arrangement is potentially implicated under the plain language of the anti-kickback statute, which prohibits the knowing and willful offer, payment, solicitation, or receipt of remuneration to induce a person to "arrange for or recommend purchasing, leasing, or ordering any good . . . or item for which payment may be made in whole or in part under a Federal health care program." 42 U.S.C. § 1320a-7b(b)(2). Here, the wholesalers will be offered remuneration in the form of a price reduction to induce them to purchase Contracted Products and to induce them to recommend or arrange for their customers to purchase such products from the wholesalers. Some of these customers may receive reimbursement under a Federal health care program.

Second, the Proposed Arrangement cannot fit into the discount "safe harbor". Strict compliance with all components of a safe harbor is necessary in order for a transaction to be protected by the safe harbor. In this case, the discount safe harbor only protects remuneration on a good or service received by a buyer that "submits a claim or request for payment for the good or service for which payment may be made in whole or in part under Medicare or a State health care program." 42 C.F.R. § 1001.952(h). Since Company A has represented that its wholesale customers will not submit claims or requests for payment to Medicare or Medicaid, the arrangement cannot qualify for the safe harbor.

Third, notwithstanding the unavailability of the safe harbor, the Proposed Arrangement does not constitute prohibited remuneration for purposes of the anti-kickback statute. We have previously observed that the discount exception to the anti-kickback statute manifests congressional intent to encourage price competition that benefits the Medicare and Medicaid programs. *See* 54 Fed. Reg. 3092 (January 23, 1989). Based on our review, the Proposed Arrangement furthers this legislative intent without otherwise posing a risk of program abuse.

As a threshold matter, the Proposed Arrangement is substantially similar to the arrangements protected by the current discount safe harbor. The discount under the Proposed Arrangement is applicable to specific transactions for specific products. Although the amount of the rebate to the wholesaler will not be known at the time of sale, the rebate will be available and accounted for by Company A in calculating its quarterly "average manufacturer price" or "best price" (depending on the product) for purposes of determining its Medicaid rebate. In sum, even though the wholesalers do not submit claims to Medicare or Medicaid for these purchases, [8] Company A's disclosures will ensure that the discounts are properly reported and reflected in the Medicaid rebate.

Under the Proposed Arrangement, the wholesaler may receive an additional price reduction on its purchases of Contracted Products for certain marketing activities directed at its retail customers. Historically, this Office has expressed concern about compensation for marketing activities based on a percentage of product sold; such arrangements can, in some circumstances, encourage overutilization or the inappropriate steering of Federal health care program business. We recognize that the portion of the price reduction conditioned on wholesaler marketing activities does not come within the personal services safe harbor, as the amount of compensation payable for those activities is neither fixed in advance nor unrelated to the volume or value of business generated for which payment may be made indirectly by a Federal health care program.

The Proposed Arrangement involves a discount on multi-source generic pharmaceutical products purchased by the wholesaler for its own account; in other words, the discount is not a commission. Implicit in any manufacturer's discount to a wholesale purchaser is a financial incentive to the wholesale purchaser to increase its retail sales of the discounted product. That financial incentive does not change simply because the Proposed Arrangement conditions the discount on the performance of certain limited activities that directly support the resale of the Contracted Products. In such circumstances

[8] Company A has represented that it will inform its wholesale customers that they may be required to report the discounts. Although there currently appear to be no reporting requirements for wholesale purchasers of pharmaceutical supplies that do not submit claims or requests for payment, Company A has represented that the prices charged for specific items under the Proposed Arrangement could be measured and fully reported to the appropriate Federal authorities, if such reporting were to be required.

and in the context of generic drugs, there is little reason for disparate treatment between the Proposed Arrangement and a straightforward price reduction.[9]

C. Conclusion

For the above-stated reasons, we conclude that the Proposed Arrangement would not constitute prohibited remuneration under 42 U.S.C. § 1320a-7b(b).

We wish to make clear that the specific arrangement as approved in this advisory opinion may become illegal when considered in the context of other related conduct or arrangements. Moreover, this opinion letter is without force and effect if (1) any contract entered into under the Proposed Arrangement is dependent on or operates in conjunction with (either explicitly or implicitly) any other arrangement or agreement between Company A and the wholesaler with respect to Contracted Products; or (2) any contract entered into under the arrangement is dependent on or operates in conjunction with (either explicitly or implicitly) any other arrangement or agreement involving third parties (i.e. parties other than Company A or the wholesaler) with respect to Contracted Products.

III. LIMITATIONS

The limitations applicable to this opinion include the following:

- This advisory opinion is issued only to Company A, which is the Requestor of this opinion. This advisory opinion has no application, and cannot be relied upon, by any other individual or entity.
- This advisory opinion may not be introduced into evidence in any matter involving an entity or individual that is not a Requestor to this opinion.
- This advisory opinion is applicable only to the statutory provisions specifically noted above. No opinion is herein expressed or implied with respect to the application of any other Federal, state, or local statute, rule, regulation, ordinance, or other law that may be applicable to the Proposed Arrangement.

---

[9] Nothing in this advisory opinion should be construed as suggesting that the same result would pertain for marketing services arrangements where the marketing agent is compensated by a commission based on a percentage of sales.

- This advisory opinion will not bind or obligate any agency other than the U.S. Department of Health and Human Services.
- This advisory opinion is limited in scope to the specific arrangement described in this letter and has no applicability to other arrangements, even those which appear similar in nature or scope.

This opinion is also subject to any additional limitations set forth at 42 C.F.R. Part 1008.

The OIG will not proceed against the Requestor with respect to any action that is part of the Proposed Arrangement taken in good faith reliance upon this advisory opinion as long as all of the material facts have been fully, completely, and accurately presented, and the arrangement in practice comports with the information provided. The OIG reserves the right to reconsider the questions and issues raised in this advisory opinion and, where the public interest requires, modify or terminate this opinion. In the event that this advisory opinion is modified or terminated, the OIG will not proceed against the Requestor with respect to any action taken in good faith reliance upon this advisory opinion, where all of the relevant facts were fully, completely, and accurately presented and where such action was promptly discontinued upon notification of the modification or termination of this advisory opinion.

Sincerely,

D. McCarty Thornton
Chief Counsel to the Inspector General

APPENDIX F17.2

Advisory Opinion No. 98–3

Posted: 4–14–98

[April 6, 1998]

[name redacted]

Re: Advisory Opinion 98–3

Dear [name redacted]:

We are writing in response to your request for an advisory opinion on behalf of Company A ("Company A") regarding whether a hospital system's provision of an ambulance to a municipal fire department as described in your request letter and supplemental submissions (the "Proposed Arrangement"): (i) constitutes grounds for the imposition of criminal sanctions under § 1128B(b) of the Social Security Act (the "Act"), 42 U.S.C. § 1320a-7b(b); (ii) constitutes grounds for the imposition of an exclusion under § 1128(b)(7) of the Act, 42 U.S.C. § 1320a-7(b)(7) (as it applies to kickbacks); or (iii) constitutes grounds for the imposition of civil monetary penalties within the meaning of § 1128A(a)(7) of the Act, 42 U.S.C. § 1320a-7a(a)(7).

Company A has certified that all of the information provided in the request, including all supplementary letters, is true and correct, and constitutes a complete description of the relevant facts and agreements among the parties. Company A has also certified that upon our approval, it will undertake to effectuate the Proposed Arrangement.

In issuing this opinion, we have relied solely on the facts and information presented to us. We have not undertaken an independent investigation of such information. This opinion is limited to the facts presented. If material facts have not been disclosed, this opinion is without force and effect.

Based on the information provided and subject to certain conditions described below, we have determined that the Proposed Arrangement may potentially generate prohibited remuneration within the meaning of the anti-kickback statute, but, for the reasons set out herein, would not constitute grounds for the imposition of criminal sanctions under § 1128B(b) of the Act, an exclusion under § 1128(b)(7) of the Act (as it applies to kickbacks), or civil monetary penalties under § 1128A(a)(7) of the Act.

This opinion may not be relied on by any person or entity other than the addressee and is further qualified as set out in Part III below and in 42 C.F.R. Part 1008.

I. FACTUAL BACKGROUND

Company A has made the following representations with respect to the Proposed Arrangement.

Company A Health System, a State W corporation, provides health care services to patients in County Y, including City X ("the City" or "City X"). Approximately 67,000 of the approximately 450,000 residents of City X are members of managed care plans that list Company A facilities as preferred providers. A portion of these 67,000 patients are enrolled in managed care plans for which Company A facilities are exclusive providers.

Prior to February 1997, Company A operated four hospitals, three of which were located in City X. In February 1997, Company A opened Health Facility B ("Health Facility B"), a new comprehensive health care facility with emergency room services in City of Z, located in County Y, approximately ten miles from City X. Subsequent to the opening of Health Facility B, Company A continued to operate two inpatient facilities in City X, each with an emergency room. As of January 31, 1998, Company A consolidated all of its inpatient operations at Health Facility B, in the process closing its two remaining inpatient facilities in City X. Company A currently maintains two free-standing outpatient surgical facilities in City X, which are permitted to provide some, but not all, emergency services.[1]

Although Health Facility B is located within County Y, it is significantly farther from City X than the only other two hospitals with emergency rooms in the county, which are located in City X. These

[1] The free-standing outpatient surgical facilities may not receive patients via 1 ambulance with certain severe conditions, including, but not limited to, multi-system trauma, blunt torso trauma, penetrating torso trauma, active labor, or high risk obstetrical conditions.

two hospitals are not affiliated with Company A.[2]

Pursuant to § [redacted] of the State W Public Health Code ([cite redacted]), the State W Department of Public Health (now known as the State W Department of Community Health) designated the County Y Medical Control Authority ("MCA") as the responsible authority for developing protocols for providing emergency services in County Y (the "MCA Protocol Guidelines"). Under the statute, the Chief of the City Fire Department and every hospital in County Y are members of the MCA and are required to abide by the protocols adopted by the MCA. The MCA Protocol Guidelines adopted by the MCA apply to all providers of emergency services in County Y.

The MCA Protocol Guidelines provide that a patient needing pre-hospital care ambulance services must be transported to any facility in County Y of the patient's choice, unless the patient is medically unstable and the choice would endanger the patient's health. Emergency medical technicians are required to consider whether the patient's choice of facility would jeopardize the patient's health due to: (i) the facility's distance; (ii) the inadequacy of the facility with respect to the patient's condition; or (iii) the facility being overburdened.

In correspondence submitted by Company A in support of its advisory opinion request, the City, through its Director of Finance, acknowledged its obligations under the MCA Protocol Guidelines, but represented to Company A and its counsel that the City lacks adequate ambulance resources to comply fully. The City also stated that it cannot purchase an additional ambulance because of severe budget constraints. According to facts certified by Company A, the City believes that because of the distance to Health Facility B, ambulances going there would be out of commission for lengthy periods of time, which would decrease the Fire Department's capacity to provide adequate EMS and advanced life support to the citizens of City X, the constituency the City must serve.[3]

---

[2] The two hospitals are Hospital C, owned and operated by the City X, and 2 Hospital D, which is privately owned. This opinion may not be relied on by any person or entity other than the addressee and is further qualified as set out in Part III below and in 42 C.F.R. Part 1008.

[3] The MCA Protocol Guidelines permit an emergency medical or advanced life support system to obtain approval of the central medical control physician to override the patient's decision when the facility is an "extreme distance away, [thereby] removing the EMS vehicle from availability for an extensive period of time." However, the MCA Protocol Guidelines specifi-

Notwithstanding the MCA Protocol Guidelines, from the opening of Health Facility B until February 1, 1998, the Fire Department declined to transport patients directly to Health Facility B, even upon a patient's request. Patients requesting transport to Health Facility B were taken either to one of Company A's two inpatient facilities in City X or provided initial treatment by the Fire Department and then transferred to another ambulance company which would transport the patient to Health Facility B. Initially, the City represented to Company A that it would not transport any patients to Health Facility B after January 31, 1998. However, since February 1, 1998, the City has transported some patients to Health Facility B, to the extent it has deemed its resources adequate.

Under the Proposed Arrangement, Company A will donate an ambulance furnished with such equipment as is necessary to provide advanced life support services (a donation worth approximately $150,000) to City X.[4] Title will pass free and clear to the City with no conditions on the use of the ambulance. After the initial donation, Company A will not provide or furnish any personnel, supplies, equipment, salaries, or repairs for the donated ambulance. Nor will it make donations of any kind to the Fire Department for a five-year period commencing on the date of the ambulance donation, except for donations exclusively in connection with civic or community events that are funded by donations solicited from and submitted by individuals or entities in the community generally (e.g., a City-wide "Fun Run").

II. LEGAL ANALYSIS

The anti-kickback statute makes it a criminal offense knowingly and willfully to offer, pay, solicit or receive any remuneration to induce referrals of items or services reimbursable by the Federal health care programs. *See* 42 U.S.C. § 1320a-7b(b). Where remuneration is paid purposefully to induce referrals of items or services for which payment may be made by a Federal health care program, the

---

cally state that "extreme distance away" means "out of [County Y]." Paragraph 5, MCA Protocol Guidelines.

[4] Company A has suggested that it may be interested in donating a "cash 4 equivalent" instead of an actual ambulance. This alternative was not raised in the original advisory opinion request, and is not addressed here. This opinion is without force and effect with respect to any "cash equivalent" donation. We note that we might reach a different conclusion if the donation were a "cash equivalent".

anti-kickback statute is violated. By its terms, the statute ascribes criminal liability to parties on both sides of an impermissible "kick-back" transaction. For purposes of the anti-kickback statute, "remuneration" includes the transfer of any thing of value, in cash or in-kind, directly or indirectly, covertly or overtly.

The statute has been interpreted to cover any arrangement where one purpose of the remuneration is to obtain money for the referral of services or to induce further referrals. *United States v. Kats,* 871 F.2d 105 (9th Cir. 1989); United States v. Greber, 760 F.2d 68 th (3d Cir.), *cert. denied,* 476 U.S. 988 (1985). Violation of the statute constitutes a felony punishable by a maximum fine of $25,000, imprisonment up to five years or both. Conviction will also lead to automatic exclusion from Federal health care programs, including Medicare and Medicaid. This Office may also initiate administrative proceedings to exclude persons from the Federal and State health care programs or to impose civil monetary penalties for fraud, kick-backs, and other prohibited activities under sections 1128(b)(7) and 1128A(a)(7) of the Act.[5]

A. The Proposed Arrangement May Be Prohibited Remuneration

This Office's concern with the provision of goods and services for free or at below-market rates to potential referral sources is long-standing and clear: such arrangements are suspect. The provision of free goods to any referral source may violate the anti-kickback statute if one purpose of the gift is to induce referrals of Federal program business. In general, the provision of free goods to referral sources gives rise to an inference that one purpose of the gift is to induce referrals. However, the strength of that inference may vary with the circumstances.

Because the Fire Department is a major provider of EMS services in City X and the sole provider of advanced life support services, the Fire Department has some ability to affect the transport of patients from City X to Health Facility B. To the extent that the donation of the ambulance will provide additional resources to the Fire Department, the gift will make it easier for the Fire Department to take patients directly to Health Facility B, potentially increasing the

[5] Because both the criminal and administrative sanctions related to the Proposed Arrangement are based on violations of the anti-kickback statute, the analysis for purposes of this advisory opinion is the same under all three provisions.

number of transports to Health Facility B. In other words, Company A will be giving something of value to the Fire Department, which potentially will increase the number of patients, including Medicare and Medicaid patients, that the Fire Department transports to Health Facility B.

In our preamble to the Interim Final Rule on the advisory opinion process, we stated that an advisory opinion is a "means of relating the anti-kickback statute to the particular facts of a specific arrangement." 62 Fed. Reg. 7350, 7351 (February 19, 1997). We went on to say that "[t]here are likely to be factors that make some specific arrangements appropriate for a favorable advisory opinion, even in subject matter areas where a generalized safe harbor may be impractical." *Id.* Thus, while the Proposed Arrangement could potentially involve a payment of remuneration to induce the referral of Federal health care program business, the advisory opinion process permits this Office to protect specific arrangements that "contain[] limitations, requirements, or controls that give adequate assurance that Federal health care programs cannot be abused." Id.

B. The Proposed Arrangement Presents Minimal Risk of Abuse of Federal Health Care Programs

In the specific factual context presented, we believe the Proposed Arrangement presents a minimal risk of abuse of Federal health care programs, while providing significant benefits to the City X community. For the reasons set out below, we think the Proposed Arrangement would not constitute grounds for sanction under the anti-kickback statute.

In assessing the potential risk of abuse from the Proposed Arrangement, our concerns are fourfold: increased risk of overutilization, increased program costs, patient freedom of choice, and unfair competition. In this case, the Proposed Arrangement presents little risk of overutilization or increased costs [6] to any Federal health care program. Simply put, the number of patients requiring emergency transport is unrelated to whether the Fire Department receives a new ambulance. Nor should the quantity or cost of services rendered to these patients be affected; the patients will still be treated by some health facility. Accordingly, our focus is on: (i) the Arrangement's potential impact on patient freedom of choice; and (ii)

[6] There may be some additional mileage charges depending on the ambulance reimbursement methodology used by the regional carrier.

whether the Arrangement is likely to give Health Facility B an unfair competitive advantage because of possible inappropriate "steering" of patients by the Fire Department.

With respect to the effect on patient freedom of choice, we conclude that the Proposed Arrangement is likely to improve freedom of choice for patients who wish to go to Health Facility B. Currently, a significant number of those patients may endure unnecessary delays and vehicular transfers in order to secure transport. To the extent that some patients go elsewhere for care that they would prefer to receive at Health Facility B, such patients are being denied access to their hospital of choice. Thus, the Proposed Arrangement may have a demonstrable and positive impact on patient freedom of choice in County Y.

For the same reasons, we conclude that the Proposed Arrangement is likely to result in fairer competition among the hospitals serving the City X area. The keystone of our analysis is the recognition that continuation of the status quo places Health Facility B at an unfair competitive disadvantage. Under the MCA Protocol Guidelines, patients who wish to go to Health Facility B should receive the same treatment as patients wishing to go to any other County facility. However, depending on the Fire Department's assessment of its resources at a given moment in time, such patients may be: (1) transported directly to Health Facility B; (2) stabilized by the Fire Department and then transferred to another ambulance company for transport to Health Facility B; or (3) transported to Company A's City X emergency room for transport to be arranged by Health Facility B.[7] Thus, the Proposed Arrangement will both increase patient freedom of choice and promote fairer competition among the area hospitals.

Notwithstanding the potential community benefits, the Proposed Arrangement could potentially induce the Fire Department to steer patients who do not have a preferred destination facility to Health Facility B. In assessing that risk, we must first evaluate the Department's ability to determine patients' choice of hospital. Under the MCA Protocol, the Fire Department must take any patient in exigent circumstances to the nearest hospital. Of the three hospitals in the area, Health Facility B is the furthest hospital from City X. The

[7] Pursuant to representations from the City, the City Fire Department's inability to 7 fulfill its obligations under the MCA Protocol Guidelines is due in large part to its limited financial resources. City X has severe budgetary constraints resulting in part from several major plant closings.

Fire Department only picks up patients in the City. With respect to non-exigent patients, the Protocol requires the Fire Department to take the patients to their hospital of choice. In some cases, a patient's insurance plan will dictate the choice of hospital; other patients will have a preferred choice based on past experience or other reasons. In other words, the MCA Protocol Guidelines limit the number of patients that the Fire Department could potentially "steer" to Health Facility B.

Finally, the Proposed Arrangement is not structured to provide any financial incentive or reward to the Fire Department for referrals to Health Facility B.[8] Unlike many suspect 8 arrangements, the amount of remuneration is fixed and will not vary in any way based on the volume or value of referrals. Indeed, Health Facility B's location outside the City may be a disincentive for the Fire Department to transport patients to Health Facility B, because traveling the extended distance would drain City resources through higher operational costs (*e.g.,* gasoline, maintenance, time expended). Finally, Company A has agreed that Company A will not make donations of any kind to the Fire Department for the next five years, except for donations exclusively in connection with civic or community events that are funded by donations solicited from and submitted by individuals or entities in the community generally (e.g., a City-wide "Fun Run").[9]

C. Conclusion

Given the specific circumstances of the Proposed Arrangement, we are persuaded that the Proposed Arrangement does not pose a significant risk of fraud or abuse to the Federal health care programs. Therefore, for the reasons set forth above, we conclude that the Proposed Arrangement does not constitute grounds for the imposition of criminal sanctions under section 1128B(b) of the Act, an

---

[8] In advisory opinion 97–6, we stated that a protocol similar to the MCA Protocol Guidelines was not sufficient to deter abuses addressed by the anti-kickback statute where the payments offered to the ambulance service related directly to the delivery of individual patients.

[9] While we note that the donation of the ambulance is unconditional and the City 9 retains absolute discretion over use of the ambulance, we place little weight on potentially self-serving contractual provisions. Many abusive schemes contain no written obligations to make referrals. Similarly, written agreements that preclude payments for referrals are not determinative of non-abusive relationships.

exclusion under section 1128(b)(7) of the Act (as it applies to kickbacks), or civil monetary penalties under section 1128A(a)(7) of the Act.

III. LIMITATIONS

The limitations applicable to this opinion include the following:

- This advisory opinion is issued only to Company A, which is the Requestor of this opinion. This advisory opinion has no application, and cannot be relied upon, by any other individual or entity.
- This advisory opinion may not be introduced into evidence in any matter involving an entity or individual that is not a Requestor to this opinion.
- This advisory opinion is applicable only to the statutory provisions specifically noted in the first paragraph of this advisory opinion. No opinion is herein expressed or implied with respect to the application of any other Federal, state, or local statute, rule, regulation, ordinance, or other law that may be applicable to the Proposed Arrangement.
- This advisory opinion will not bind or obligate any agency other than the U.S. Department of Health and Human Services.
- This advisory opinion is limited in scope to the specific arrangement described in this letter and has no applicability to other arrangements, even those which appear similar in nature or scope.

This opinion is also subject to any additional limitations set forth at 42 C.F.R. Part 1008

The OIG will not proceed against the Requestor with respect to any action that is part of the Proposed Arrangement taken in good faith reliance upon this advisory opinion as long as all of the material facts have been fully, completely, and accurately presented, and the arrangement in practice comports with the information provided. The OIG reserves the right to reconsider the questions and issues raised in this advisory opinion and, where the public interest requires, modify or terminate this opinion. In the event that this advisory opinion is modified or terminated, the OIG will not proceed against the requestor with respect to any action taken in good faith reliance upon this advisory opinion, where all of the relevant facts were fully, completely, and accurately presented and where such

action was promptly discontinued upon notification of the modification or termination of this advisory opinion.

Sincerely,

D. McCarty Thornton
Chief Counsel to the Inspector General

APPENDIX F17.3

Advisory Opinion No. 98–4

[April 15, 1998]

[Name Redacted]

Re: Advisory Opinion No. 98–4

Dear [Name Redacted]:

We are writing in response to your request for an advisory opinion, in which you ask whether a proposed management services contract between a medical practice management company and a physician practice, which provides that the management company will be reimbursed for its costs and paid a percentage of net practice revenues (the "Proposed Arrangement"), would constitute illegal remuneration as defined in the anti-kickback statute, § 1128B(b) of the Social Security Act (the "Act").

You have certified that all of the information you provided in your request, including all supplementary letters, is true and correct, and constitutes a complete description of the material facts regarding the Proposed Arrangement. In issuing this opinion, we have relied solely on the facts and information you presented to us. We have not undertaken any independent investigation of such information.

Based on the information provided, we conclude that the Proposed Arrangement may constitute prohibited remuneration under § 1128B(b) of the Act.

I. FACTUAL BACKGROUND

A. The Parties

Dr. X is a family practice physician who has incorporated as, and practices under the name of, Company A ("Company A"). Company A is proposing to enter into an agreement to establish a family practice and walk-in clinic with a corporation, Company B ("Company B"). Dr. X is the sole Requestor of this advisory opinion.

B. The Arrangement

Under the Proposed Arrangement, Company A will provide all physician services at the clinic. Company A may hire additional physicians and other medical personnel with the mutual agreement of Company B. Company A will pay all physician compensation and fringe benefits, including but not limited to, licensing fees, continuing education, and malpractice premiums.

Company B will find a suitable location for the clinic and furnish the initial capital for the office, furniture, and operating expenses. Once operational, Company B will provide or arrange for all operating services for the clinic, including accounting, billing, purchasing, direct marketing, and hiring of non-medical personnel and outside vendors.

Company B will also provide Company A with management and marketing services for the clinic, including the negotiation and oversight of health care contracts with various payors, including indemnity plans, managed care plans, and Federal health care programs.

In addition to Company B's activities on behalf of Company A, Company B will set up provider networks. These networks may include Company A and, if required by Company B, Company A has agreed that it will refer its patients to the providers in such networks.

In return for its services, Company B's payment will have three components. Company A will be required to make a capital payment equal to a percentage of the initial cost of each capital asset purchased for Company A per year for six years. Company B will also receive a fair market value payment for the operating services it provides and an at-cost payment for any operating services for which it contracts. Company B will receive a percentage of Company A's monthly net revenues for its management services.

If the percentage payment described above is not permitted by law, then the parties will establish a management fee reflecting the contemplated financial results of the arrangement or, if the parties cannot agree to a fixed amount, the parties will hire an accounting firm to determine an appropriate fixed fee (the "Alternative Proposed Arrangement").

II. LEGAL ANALYSIS

A. Anti-kickback Statute

The anti-kickback statute, § 1128B(b) of the Act, makes it a criminal offense knowingly and willfully to offer, pay, solicit, or receive any remuneration to induce the referral of business covered by a Federal health care program. Specifically, the statute provides that:

> Whoever knowingly and willfully offers or pays [or solicits or receives] any remuneration (including any kickback, bribe, or rebate) directly or indirectly, overtly or covertly, in cash or in kind to any person to induce such person — to refer an individual to a person for the furnishing or arranging for the furnishing of any item or service for which payment may be made in whole or in part under a Federal health care program, or to purchase, lease, order, or arrange for or recommend purchasing, leasing, or ordering any good, facility, service, or item for which payment may be made in whole or in part under a Federal health care program, shall be guilty of a felony.

§ 1128B(b) of the Act. In other words, the statute prohibits payments made purposefully to induce referrals of business payable by a Federal health care program. The statute ascribes liability to both sides of an impermissible "kickback" transaction. The statute has been interpreted to cover any arrangement where one purpose of the remuneration was to obtain money for the referral of services or to induce further referrals. *United States v. Kats,* 871 F.2d 105 (9th Cir. 1989); United States v. Greber, 760 F.2d 68 (3d Cir.), *cert. denied,* 474 U.S. 988 (1985).

Violation of the statute constitutes a felony punishable by a maximum fine of $25,000, imprisonment up to five years or both. Conviction will also lead to automatic exclusion from Federal health care programs, including Medicare and Medicaid.

This Office may also initiate administrative proceedings to exclude persons from Federal and State health care programs or to impose civil monetary penalties for fraud, kickbacks, and other prohibited activities. See §§ 1128(b)(7), 1128A(a)(7) of the Act. [1]

---

[1] Because both the criminal and administrative sanctions related to the anti- 1 kickback implications of the Proposed Arrangement are based on violations of the anti-kickback statute, the analysis for the purposes of this advisory opinion is the same under both.

B. Safe Harbor Regulations

In 1991, the Department of Health and Human Services (the "Department") published safe harbor regulations that define practices that are not subject to the anti-kickback statute because such practices would be unlikely to result in fraud or abuse. Failure to comply with a safe harbor provision does not make an arrangement *per se* illegal. For this Proposed Arrangement, the only safe harbor regulation potentially available is the personal services and management contracts safe harbor. *See* 42 C.F.R. § 1001.952(d).

The personal services and management contracts safe harbor provides protection for personal services contracts if all of the following six standards are met: (i) the agreement is set out in writing and signed by the parties; (ii) the agreement specifies the services to be performed; (iii) if the services are to be performed on a part-time basis, the schedule for performance is specified in the contract; (iv) the agreement is for not less than one year; (v) the aggregate amount of compensation is fixed in advance, based on fair market value in an arms-length transaction, and not determined in a manner that takes into account the volume or value of any referrals or business otherwise generated between the parties for which payment may be made by Medicare or a State health care program; and (vi) the services performed under the agreement do not involve the promotion of business that violates any Federal or State law.

We conclude that the Proposed Arrangement does not qualify for this safe harbor. In order for an agreement to be protected by this safe harbor, strict compliance with all six standards is necessary. In this case, the compensation is not an aggregate amount, fixed in advance, as the safe harbor requires. Accordingly, the safe harbor standards are not satisfied.

C. Percentage Compensation Arrangement

Because compliance with a safe harbor is not mandatory, the fact that the Proposed Arrangement does not fit within a safe harbor does not mean that the Proposed Arrangement is necessarily unlawful. Rather, we must analyze this Proposed Arrangement on a case-by-case basis.

Percentage compensation arrangements for marketing services may implicate the anti-kickback statute. In our preamble to the 1991 final safe harbor rules, 56 Fed. Reg. 35952 (July 29, 1991), we explained that the anti-kickback statute "on its face prohibits offering or acceptance of remuneration, *inter alia*, for the purposes of 'arranging for or recommending purchasing, leasing, or ordering any . . . service or item' payable under Medicare or Medicaid. Thus, we believe that many marketing and advertising activities may involve at least technical violations of the statute." 56 Fed. Reg. at 35974.

This Proposed Arrangement is problematic for the following reasons.

- **The Proposed Arrangement may include financial incentives to increase patient referrals.** The compensation that Company B receives for its management services is a percentage of Company A's net revenue, including revenue from business derived from managed care contracts arranged by Company B. Such activities may potentially implicate the anti-kickback statute, because the compensation Company B will receive will be in part for marketing services. Where such compensation is based on a percentage, there is at least a potential technical violation of the anti-kickback statute. In addition, Company B will be establishing networks of specialist physicians to whom Company A may be required to refer in some circumstances. Further, Company B will presumably receive some compensation for its efforts in connection with the development and operation of these specialist networks. In these circumstances, any evaluation of the Proposed Arrangement requires information about the relevant financial relationships. However, Company B is not a requestor for this advisory opinion, and Company A does not have information regarding Company B's related business arrangements.

  Accordingly, we have insufficient information to ascertain the level of risk of fraud or abuse presented by the Proposed Arrangement. [2]
- **The Proposed Arrangement contains no safeguards against overutilization.** In light of the proposed establishment of provider networks with required referral arrangements, there is a risk of potential overutilization. Under the Proposed Arrangement, we are unable to determine what, if any, controls will be implemented under managed care

[2] We are also precluded from reaching a conclusion about the Alternative Proposed Arrangement. Such a determination would require us to evaluate whether the agreed upon fee is fixed at fair market value. We are prevented from making that determination by § 1128D(b)(3)(A) of the Act, which prohibits our opining on fair market value in an advisory opinion.

contracts negotiated for Company A by Company B. Without such controls, we can not be assured that items and services paid for by Federal health care programs will not be overutilized.

- **The Proposed Arrangement may include financial incentives that increase the risk of abusive billing practices.** Since Company B receives a percentage of Company A's revenue and will arrange for Company A's billing, Company B has an incentive to maximize Company A's revenue. This Office has a longstanding concern that percentage billing arrangements may increase the risk of upcoding and similar abusive billing practices.

III. CONCLUSION

The advisory opinion process permits the OIG to protect specific arrangements that "contain[ ] limitations, requirements, or controls, that give adequate assurances that Federal health care programs cannot be abused." *See*62 Fed. Reg. 7350, 7351 (February 19, 1997). Based on the facts we have been presented, the Proposed Arrangement appears to contain no limitations, requirements, or controls that would minimize any fraud or abuse.

Therefore, since we cannot be confident that there is no more than a minimal risk of fraud or abuse, we must conclude that the Proposed Arrangement may involve prohibited remuneration under the anti-kickback statute and thus potentially be subject to sanction under the anti-kickback statute, § 1128B(b) of the Act. Any definitive conclusion regarding the existence of an anti-kickback violation requires a determination of the parties' intent, which determination is beyond the scope of the advisory opinion process. [3]

IV. LIMITATIONS

The limitations applicable to this opinion include the following:

- This advisory opinion is issued only to Dr. X, who is the Requestor of this opinion. This advisory opinion has no application, and cannot be relied upon, by any other individual or entity.

---

[3] Our conclusion regarding the risk of fraud or abuse in relation to the anti-kickback 3 statute should not be construed to mean that a finding of fraud or abuse is an implied element necessary to establish a violation of the statute.

- This advisory opinion is applicable only to the statutory provision specifically noted above. No opinion is herein expressed or implied with respect to the application of any other Federal, state, or local statute, rule, regulation, ordinance, or other law that may be applicable to the Proposed Arrangement.
- This advisory opinion will not bind or obligate any agency other than the U.S. Department of Health and Human Services.

This opinion is also subject to any additional limitations set forth at 42 C.F.R. Part 1008.

Sincerely,

D. McCarty Thornton
Chief Counsel to the Inspector General

APPENDIX F17.4

Advisory Opinion No. 98–5

Posted on 4/24/98

[date]

[name and address redacted]

Re: [name redacted] Advisory Opinion No. 98–5

Dear [name redacted]:

We are writing in response to your request for an advisory opinion, which seeks our opinion regarding the "coordination of benefits" ("COB") provisions of a provider agreement between Nursing Home A (the "Nursing Home") and a health care plan. In particular, your request asks whether the health care plan's method of coordinating insurance benefits (the "Arrangement"), which effectively requires Nursing Home A to forgo certain Medicare cost-sharing amounts, involves prohibited remuneration under the anti-kickback statute, § 1128B(b) of the Social Security Act (the "Act") or would be grounds for sanction under § 1128B(b) of the Act, exclusion under § 1128(b)(7) of the Act [fraud, kickbacks, and other prohibited activities], or civil monetary penalties under § 1128A(a)(7) of the Act [to the extent it relates to kickbacks].

You have certified that all of the information you provided in your request, including all supplementary letters, is true and correct, and constitutes a complete description of the facts and agreements among the parties regarding the Arrangement. In issuing this opinion, we have relied solely on the facts and information you presented to us. This opinion is limited to the facts presented. We have not undertaken any independent investigation of such information.

Based on the information you have provided, we conclude that the Arrangement may involve prohibited remuneration under the anti-kickback statute and may subject the parties to sanction under sections 1128B(b), 1128(b)(7), and 1128A(a)(7) of the Act.

I. FACTUAL BACKGROUND

A. The Parties

Nursing Home A is a State X not-for-profit corporation licensed as a residential health care center by the State X Department of Health. The Nursing Home provides long and short term skilled nursing, subacute, and rehabilitative services to approximately xxx residents. The Nursing Home is a Medicare provider and participates in the Medicare RUGs III Demonstration Project.[1]

Health Plan B (the "Plan") is a State X, not-for-profit corporation licensed as a health maintenance organization under [citation redacted] of the State X Public Health Law. Health Plan B and its affiliated companies offer multiple health care products, including a health maintenance organization (the "HMO"), a point of service plan, a Medicare managed care plan, and customized coverage for self-funded benefit programs.

B. The Arrangement

Since 1985, the Nursing Home has provided short term subacute and rehabilitative services to the Plan's HMO members, including members who are eligible for Medicare Part A and are not enrolled in the Plan's Medicare managed care plan, pursuant to various oral and written agreements. In 1997, the Nursing Home entered into a provider agreement with the Plan that contained a fee schedule for services provided by the Nursing Home to Plan members (the "Plan Fee Schedule") and certain coordination of benefits provisions that (i) release the Plan from any obligation to pay benefits where the Nursing Home has already received payment from the patient's primary insurer in an amount equal to or exceeding the Plan Fee Schedule amount and (ii) require the Nursing Home to hold Plan members harmless from any charges, including copayments and deductibles (the "Coordination of Benefits" or "COB" provisions). Specifically, § 6.2 of the provider agreement provides:

> When Health Care Plan C is a secondary or later plan (not primary plan as defined in [statutory citation redacted], it shall only pay when the Health Plan C allowed amount listed on Schedule B has

[1] The RUGs III Demonstration Project tests a case-mix adjusted payment system pursuant to which a SNF's per diem payment is tied to the intensity of care and services required for each patient. The demonstration involves forty-four Resource Utilization Groups (RUGs).

not been paid to Participating Provider by the primary plan. If the Health Plan C allowed amount listed in Schedule B has been paid to Participating Provider by the primary plan, then Participating Provider shall hold the Member harmless from an against any and all charges including charges for copayments and deductibles. For purposes of this Agreement, primary plan may include hospital service corporations, indemnity corporations, commercial carriers, self-insured or self-funded plans and Medicare. [2]

The Nursing Home has asked whether the provider agreement's COB provisions violate the anti-kickback statute when applied to reimbursement for Nursing Home services to Plan members who have primary coverage under Medicare Part A and are not members of the Plan's Medicare managed care plan. These members typically receive Plan coverage as retirees through various employer group health plans purchased from the Plan by their former employers. For purposes of coordinating benefits, the Plan has determined that Medicare is primary payer for these beneficiaries. [3]

II. LEGAL ANALYSIS

The anti-kickback statute makes it a criminal offense knowingly and willfully to offer, pay, solicit, or receive any remuneration to induce referrals of items or services reimbursable by the Federal health care programs. *See* § 1128B(b) of the Act. Where remuneration is paid purposefully to induce referrals of items or services for which payment may be made by a Federal health care program, the anti-kickback statute is violated. By its terms, the statute ascribes criminal liability to parties on both sides of an impermissible "kickback" transaction. For purposes of the anti-kickback statute,

[2] A second provision, § 5.2 of the contract, expressly prohibits direct billing of Plan members: "Participating Provider hereby agrees that in no event . . . shall Participating Provider bill, charge, collect a deposit from, seek compensation, remuneration or reimbursement from, or have any recourse against Health Care Plan C Members. . . ."

[3] We assume, for purposes of this advisory opinion, that the provider agreement's COB provisions are enforceable. However, we believe the enforceability of these provisions is questionable. *Cf. Pennsylvania Medical Society v. Snider,* 29 F.3d 886 (3d Cir. 1994); *Rehabilitation Association of Virginia, Inc. v. Kozlowski,* 42 F.3d 1444 (4 th Cir. 1994); *New York City Health and Hospitals v. Perales*, 954 F.2d 854 (2d Cir. 1992) (holding that for Qualified Medicare Beneficiaries, states could not limit cost-sharing payments to Medicare Part B providers to ensure that total payments to the providers, including Medicare reimbursement, did not exceed the states' Medicaid reimbursement levels for the same items and services).

"remuneration" includes the transfer of anything of value, in cash or in-kind, directly or indirectly, covertly or overtly.

The statute has been interpreted to cover any arrangement where one purpose of the remuneration is to obtain money for the referral of services or to induce further referrals. *United States v. Kats,* 871 F.2d 105 (9 Cir. 1989); United States v. Greber, 760 F.2d 68 th (3d Cir.), *cert. denied,* 476 U.S. 988 (1985). Violation of the statute constitutes a felony punishable by a maximum fine of $25,000, imprisonment up to five years or both. Conviction will also lead to automatic exclusion from Federal health care programs, including Medicare and Medicaid. This Office may also initiate administrative proceedings to exclude persons from the Federal and State health care programs or to impose civil monetary penalties for fraud, kickbacks, and other prohibited activities under §§ 1128(b)(7) and 1128A (a)(7) of the Act.[4]

A number of statutory and regulatory "safe harbors" protect certain arrangements that might otherwise technically violate the anti-kickback statute from prosecution. *See* § 1128B(b)(3) of the Act; 42 C.F.R. § 1001.952. The safe harbors for the following payment practices are potentially relevant here: (1) certain price reductions to health plans, 42 C.F.R. § 1001.952(m); (2) certain discounts to purchasers of health care items and services, 42 C.F.R. § 1001.952(h); and (3) certain waivers of beneficiary copayments and deductible amounts for inpatient hospital services, 42 C.F.R. § 1001.952(k). Safe harbor protection is afforded only to those arrangements that precisely meet all of the conditions set forth in the safe harbor. Arrangements that do not fit squarely in a safe harbor are not necessarily illegal and must be evaluated on a case-by-case basis.

A. The Arrangement May Involve Prohibited Remuneration

As a preliminary matter, many Medicare beneficiaries have additional health insurance coverage that supplements their Medicare coverage, such as retiree health benefits. Generally, if supplemental coverage exists for Medicare beneficiaries, claims for Medicare covered health services for such beneficiaries are first submitted to

[4] Because both the criminal and administrative sanctions related to the anti-kickback implications of the Arrangement are based on violations of the anti-kickback statute, the analysis for purposes of this advisory opinion is the same under all three provisions.

Medicare (the "primary insurer") and the amounts not paid by Medicare are then submitted to the supplemental or "secondary" insurer. [5]

In evaluating the provider agreement's COB provisions, we begin with the applicable reimbursement principles for skilled nursing facilities ("SNFs"). Under Medicare Part A, Medicare pays the full amount of the facility's applicable SNF per diem rate, (in this case, the applicable rate under the RUGs III Demonstration Project), for the first 20 days of a beneficiary's stay; however, for days 21 through 100, the facility's payment from Medicare is reduced by an amount equal to one-eighth of the hospital inpatient deductible. [6]*See* 42 U.S.C. § 1395e; 42 C.F.R. § 409.85. Under the Act and 6 implementing regulations, this cost-sharing amount is a beneficiary obligation. *See, e.g.,* 42 C.F.R. § 409.85; 42 C.F.R. § 409.61(b).

The COB provisions contained in the Nursing Home's provider agreement with the Plan, in conjunction with the Plan Fee Schedule, result in a full or partial waiver of this Medicare cost-sharing amount when Medicare is the primary payer and the applicable Medicare reimbursement is higher than the Plan Fee Schedule amount. The following hypothetical example provided by the Nursing Home is illustrative:

> For purposes of this example, the Nursing Home's Medicare RUGs rate is $300/day. The Medicare copayment is $95/day for days 21–100. The Plan Fee Schedule rate is $225/day.
>
> A patient is admitted to the Nursing Home for a 31 day stay. A Medicare copayment of $950 ($95 x 10 days) applies to the last 10 days. For those days, the Nursing Home is entitled to Medicare reimbursement of $3,000 ($300 x 10 days). Medicare pays the Nursing Home $2,050 ($3,000 — $950 copayment). The Nursing Home bills the Plan for the $950 copayment.
>
> The Plan, applying its COB provisions, limits the Nursing Home's reimbursement to $2,250 ($225 x 10 days). The Plan pays the Nursing Home $200 ($2,250 – $2,050 Medicare payment). The Nursing Home still has a balance owing of $750 for the Medicare copayment. Under its agreement with the Plan, the Nursing Home is prohibited from billing the patient for the balance of the copayment.

---

[5] In some situations not relevant here, employer plans are primary to Medicare under section 1862(b)(2) of the Act.

[6] In some circumstances, the applicable copayment may be a lesser amount if a facility's actual charge is less than one-eighth of the hospital inpatient deductible. In such cases, the daily coinsurance is the amount of the actual charge per day. *See* 42 C.F.R. § 409.85.

In this example, the balance of the Medicare copayment owed to the Nursing Home is effectively waived. This waiver potentially implicates the anti-kickback statute, because it represents a financial benefit from the Nursing Home to the Plan (i.e. forgiveness of the obligation to pay the remaining coinsurance amount) that may be for the purpose of inducing the Plan's referral of Plan members, including Medicare beneficiaries, to the Nursing Home.[7]

B. The Arrangement Does Not Fit Any Safe Harbor

The Arrangement does not fit within any available safe harbor to the anti-kickback statute. First, the Arrangement does not fit within the safe harbor for price reductions offered by contracted providers to health care plans. That safe harbor has six elements, one of which prohibits a provider that submits claims or requests for payment to Medicare for items or services furnished in accordance with a contract between the provider and a plan from claiming or requesting payment for amounts in excess of the contract's fee schedule. See 42 C.F.R. § 1001.952(m). The Arrangement fails to satisfy this requirement because the Nursing Home submits its claims to Medicare for services to Medicare beneficiaries using the full Medicare reimbursement under the RUGs III Demonstration Project.[8]

Second, the Arrangement does not qualify under the waiver of coinsurance safe harbor, because that safe harbor is limited to certain waivers of coinsurance by hospitals for inpatient hospital services. The safe harbor specifically provides that protected waivers do not include waivers that are part of cost reduction agreements

[7] its The parties' agreement that the Nursing Home will not collect cost-sharing amounts from beneficiaries in effect shifts the Medicare copayment obligation from the Plan's members to the Plan.

[8] Although we do not decide the issue here, we note that the Arrangement might fit in the price reduction safe harbor if the Nursing Home were able to bill Medicare in a manner that satisfies the following requirements: (i) Medicare is billed an amount less than or equal to the Plan Fee Schedule amount; (ii) the billing methodology results in the Plan paying the full amount of the applicable Medicare copayment; and (iii) the billing methodology is acceptable to the Nursing Home's fiscal intermediary. It is not clear that a satisfactory reimbursement methodology could be developed for Part A reimbursement. We note that for similarly situated plans and providers contracting for Part B services, agreements that require providers to bill Medicare no more than the contracted fee schedule amount may qualify for safe harbor protection, provided they meet all other applicable conditions.

between hospitals and plans, other than Medicare SELECT plans. *See* 42 C.F.R. § 1001.952(k).

Third, the discount safe harbor is not applicable. The discount safe harbor applies only to discounts obtained by the party submitting claims to the Medicare program. *See* 42 C.F.R. § 1001.952(h). In the Arrangement, the Nursing Home, which submits claims to Medicare, is the party that provides the discount, rather than the party that receives it. Accordingly, the Arrangement does not satisfy the safe harbor conditions. *See*61 Fed. Reg. 2122, 2124 (January 25, 1996). Moreover, the safe harbor requires that the discount be offered to Medicare and Medicaid. This is not the case here.

C. The Arrangement Poses a Potential Risk of Program Fraud and Abuse

The potential for fraud and abuse from the routine waiver of Medicare cost-sharing amounts by providers has been a longstanding concern of this Office. *See* Preamble to Final Rule, 61 Fed. Reg. 2122 (January 25, 1996); *cf.* Special Fraud Alert, 59 Fed. Reg. 242 (1994). Most recently, in OIG Advisory Opinion 97–4, we addressed a provider's proposal to forgo collecting copayments from Medicare beneficiaries where a health plan providing secondary coverage was refusing to pay the Medicare copayments. In that case, the provider did not have an agreement with the health care plan and was not contractually prohibited from billing Medicare beneficiaries for copayment amounts. In those circumstances, we concluded that the provider's failure to undertake reasonable collection efforts, including seeking collection from beneficiaries, could constitute a violation of the anti-kickback statute.

We have also previously articulated our concern that agreements between providers and health plans to forgo deductible or coinsurance amounts may result in kickbacks from providers to health care plans in exchange for Federal program business. For example, we stated in our preamble to the 1996 Final Rule establishing certain managed care safe harbors that:

> The [anti-kickback] statute prohibits any remuneration which is in return for, or which is designed to induce, the flow of Medicare and Medicaid program-related business. Therefore, it could cover a hospital's agreement to forego or reduce coinsurance or deductibles in exchange for increased program-related business. It does not matter that the payment is made to a third party rather than the beneficiary.

61 Fed. Reg. 2122, 2124 (January 25, 1996). Arrangements that release both the beneficiaries and the secondary insurer from the obligation to pay Medicare cost-sharing amounts pose a risk of overutilization and increased program costs. Thus, under the Arrangement, the Nursing Home may have an incentive to prolong Medicare patient stays in order to recoup forgone copayments, while the Plan has no incentive to control costs associated with Medicare fee-for-service beneficiaries for whom it pays little or nothing.[9] Moreover, to the extent that the Nursing Home receives less than the applicable RUGs III reimbursement rate (including copayments and deductibles), the Nursing Home may have an increased incentive to shortchange Medicare beneficiaries by stinting on services. Finally, the Arrangement may lead to unfair competition for competing health plans that meet their insureds' Medicare copayment obligations and refuse to participate in comparable schemes.[10] Given these risks, we cannot conclude that the Arrangement poses little or no risk of Federal program fraud or abuse.[11]

D. Conclusion

For the above-stated reasons, we conclude that the Arrangement may involve prohibited remuneration under the anti-kickback statute and thus potentially be subject to sanction under section 1128B (b) of the Act, to exclusion under section 1128(b)(7) of the Act, and civil monetary penalties under 1128A(a)(7).[12] This conclusion is consistent with our prior guidance on waivers of copayments generally and on waivers negotiated between providers and health plans spe-

---

[9] In addition, arrangements such as the one at issue here may, in some 9 circumstances, provide an incentive for providers to offer lower rates to health care plans for non-Medicare "managed care" patients in exchange for access to Medicare beneficiaries for whom the providers can bill Medicare on a fee-for-service basis.

[10] We note further that the Arrangement may violate other fraud laws in connection with representations that the Plan may have made to Plan members and the Plan's collection of premiums, if any, from beneficiaries. In addition, the Arrangement may violate other state insurance or consumer protection statutes.

[11] Our conclusion regarding the risk of abuse in relation to the anti-kickback statute should not be construed to mean that a finding of abuse is an implied element necessary to establish a violation of the statute.

[12] Any definitive conclusion regarding the existence of an anti-kickback violation requires a determination of the parties' intent, which determination is beyond the scope of the advisory opinion process.

cifically. It is also consistent with the legal principle that a private contractual arrangement cannot override a requirement of Federal law (cf. note 2 above).

III. LIMITATIONS

The limitations applicable to this opinion include the following:

- This advisory opinion is applicable only to the statutory provisions specifically noted in the first paragraph of this advisory opinion. No opinion is herein expressed or implied with respect to the application of any other Federal, state, or local statute, rule, regulation, ordinance, or other law that may be applicable to the Arrangement.
- This advisory opinion will not bind or obligate any agency other than the U.S. Department of Health and Human Services.

This opinion is also subject to any additional limitations set forth at 42 C.F.R. Part 1008.

The OIG reserves the right to reconsider the questions and issues raised in this advisory opinion and, where the public interest requires, modify or terminate this opinion.

Sincerely,

D. McCarty Thornton
Chief Counsel to the Inspector General

APPENDIX F17.5

Advisory Opinion No. 98–6

Posted: May 1, 1998

To: **ATTACHED DISTRIBUTION LIST [redacted]**

Re: National Emphysema Treatment Trial (NETT)
Advisory Opinion No. 98–6

Ladies and Gentlemen:

We are writing in response to your request for an advisory opinion, in which you ask whether waiving coinsurance obligations for participants in a clinical study sponsored by the Health Care Financing Administration and the National Heart, Lung, and Blood Institute (the "Proposed Arrangement") will subject you to sanction under section 1128A(a)(5) of the Social Security Act (the "Act") [42 U.S.C. § 1320a-7a(a)(5)] or under the anti-kickback statute, section 1128B (b) of the Act [42 U.S.C. § 1320a-7b(b)].

You have certified that all of the information you provided in your request, including all supplementary letters, is true and correct, and constitutes a complete description of the material facts regarding the Proposed Arrangement. In issuing this opinion, we have relied solely on the facts and information you presented to us. We have not undertaken any independent investigation of such information. This opinion is limited to the facts presented. If material facts have not been disclosed, this opinion is without force and effect.

Based on the information provided and subject to certain conditions described below, we conclude that the Proposed Arrangement would not constitute grounds for the imposition of sanctions under sections 1128A(a)(5) or 1128B(b) of the Act. This opinion may not be relied on by any person other than the individuals and entities listed on the attached Distribution List [redacted] and is further qualified as set out in Part III below and in 42 C.F.R. Part 1008.

I. FACTUAL BACKGROUND

A. NETT

1. Parties to NETT

The National Emphysema Treatment Trial ("NETT") is a multicenter, randomized clinical trial of medical therapy alone versus medical therapy plus Lung Volume Reduction Surgery ("LVRS") for treatment of moderate to severe emphysema. The primary purpose of NETT is to determine whether the addition of LVRS results in improved survival of emphysema patients. In addition, NETT will be used to evaluate the relative benefits and risks of surgical versus medical therapy, including health care utilization and costs.

NETT is a collaborative effort between the Health Care Financing Administration ("HCFA") and the National Heart, Lung, and Blood Institute ("NHLBI") of the National Institutes of Health. Pursuant to a Memorandum of Understanding (the "MOU") between HCFA and NHLBI executed in June 1996, HCFA has agreed to pay for Medicare allowable patient care services, including LVRS, covered by the NETT protocol (*see* section B.1 below). NHLBI has agreed to be responsible for all activities relating to negotiating, awarding, directing, and terminating contracts with participating health care facilities and for monitoring and evaluating program progress. HCFA hopes to use the results of NETT to determine whether and under what circumstances LVRS should be considered a reasonable and necessary treatment and hence whether and under what circumstances it should be a Medicare covered service.

NHLBI has contracted with Johns Hopkins Center for Clinical Trials to be the coordinating center for the trial and with certain clinical centers around the country to be NETT participating clinics. In addition, some contracting centers have subcontracted with rehabilitation facilities to provide services covered by the NETT protocol.[1] Pursuant to these contracts, investigators from these cen-

[1] Johns Hopkins Center for Clinical Trials, and those clinical centers, rehabilitation 1 facilities, and individual providers listed on the attached Distribution List [redacted] are collectively the "Requesters" of this opinion. Only those entities and individuals specifically named on the attached Distribution list [redacted] are "Requesters" for purposes of this opinion. NHLBI anticipates that the identities of the NETT participating facilities and individuals may change from time to time during the course of the trial. This opinion is not binding on facilities or individuals that are not Requesters for purposes of this opinion.

ters will conduct the randomized clinical trial and establish an associated registry of patients. The trial will consist of a main protocol, performed by all participating centers and involving all enrolled patients, and several sub-studies, performed by selected centers and involving only patients enrolled at those centers.

2. Treatment Protocol

NETT will be conducted over a fifty-four month period and will involve 4,700 patients, post-randomization.[2] Patients will be referred to NETT contracting centers by their private physicians, who will provide NETT investigators with certain background information and test results.[3] Participating patients must be Medicare beneficiaries or have other insurance to cover the costs of participation in NETT. Eligible patients will be asked to consent to enrollment in a pulmonary rehabilitation program and to randomization, which will occur after six to ten weeks of pulmonary rehabilitation, further eligibility determinations, and pre-randomization assessments.

The NETT randomized study is essentially divides patients into two groups pursuant to the Protocol. One group will receive medical therapy, which consists of two parts: medical management and pulmonary rehabilitation. The overall responsibility for medical management of NETT patients will remain with the patient's regular primary care physician. However, NETT patients will be evaluated by a NETT physician to insure that NETT treatment standards are met. The NETT physicians will make recommendations for medical management to the primary care physicians. The pulmonary rehabilitation program, which is divided into three phases, spans the duration of the NETT trial (approximately fifty-four months). Certain portions of the pulmonary rehabilitation program must take place at NETT centers; to accommodate patients who may not live near a NETT center, other portions may occur at "satellite" rehabilitation centers certified for participation in NETT.

The second group will receive the surgical treatment. LVRS will be performed by NETT center surgeons at a NETT center. LVRS

---

[2] "Randomization" is the process of randomly assigning patients to the surgical and non-surgical study groups. An undetermined number of patients not ultimately selected for randomization will participate in NETT for screening and evaluation purposes.

[3] To be eligible for the NETT study, patients must satisfy specific selection and exclusion criteria set forth in the Protocol.

patients will be managed post-operatively in a manner similar to other patients undergoing major thoracic surgery. The Protocol describes in detail required post-operative care procedures and management of complications.

All NETT patients will be seen at NETT clinics for follow-up visits and data collection at six month intervals for two years after randomization and annually thereafter. These follow-up visits are expected to last one to two days, depending on the patient's condition and the procedures scheduled. Patients will also be required to complete questionnaires at home. NETT centers will maintain telephone contact with patients in accordance with a schedule set forth in the Protocol.

B. The Proposed Arrangement

1. HCFA Reimbursement for NETT Items and Services

Currently, LVRS is not a Medicare covered service, unless it is performed as part of the NETT study.[4] See Coverage Issues Manual ("CIM") (HCFA-Pub 6) at 35–93. [5]HCFA has agreed to provide reimbursement directly to NETT clinical center contractors and other designated providers for patient care services, including inpatient hospital services, physician and other professional services, and laboratory, diagnostic, and other therapeutic services for Medicare beneficiaries participating in NETT. HCFA will cover these services if NHLBI certifies that the provider is in compliance with the Proto-

---

[4] HCFA adopted a nonreimbursement policy for LVRS in 1995 because of the dearth of medical evidence supporting the surgery's effectiveness and the potential for high morbidity and mortality among Medicare beneficiaries who might receive LVRS. That same year, HCFA requested a technology assessment of LVRS by the Center for Health Care Technology (CHCT) within the Agency for Health Care Policy Research. The resulting CHCT report concluded that the objective data available did not permit a logical and scientifically defensible conclusion about the risks and benefits of LVRS. The report further concluded that some proportion of patients may have realized some benefits from the procedure and that a prospective trial of LVRS was both ethically and scientifically essential. Based on the CHCT assessment, HCFA approached NHLBI about collaborating on the evaluation of LVRS.

[5] CIM § 35–93 states, "HCFA has determined that LVRS is reasonable and necessary when it is provided under the conditions detailed by the protocol of the HCFA/NHLBI clinical study. Therefore, Medicare will cover LVRS in those limited circumstances when it is provided to a Medicare beneficiary under the protocols established for the study."

col and the NETT manual of operations. NETT providers will not be reimbursed for items and services not allowable under Medicare, such as oral prescriptions. HCFA will continue to pay for services for Medicare beneficiaries recruited into NETT until the contracts with the NETT centers expire or are terminated by NHLBI or until a patient is no longer eligible to participate in NETT. HCFA may withhold payments if documentation is missing, incomplete, or inaccurate. NHLBI will be required to provide HCFA with lists of participating NETT patients and providers. Claims will be processed using normal Medicare reimbursement procedures. However, claims for NETT items and services will indicate, through special codes, whether the patient is a NETT patient, whether the provider is a NETT provider, and whether the patient has been randomized into the surgical group.

2. Proposal to Waive Copayments and Deductibles

Under section 1833 of the Social Security Act and implementing regulations, Medicare beneficiaries are obligated to pay certain coinsurance and deductible amounts for Medicare Part B covered services. *See, e.g.,* 42 U.S.C. § 1395; 42 C.F.R. Part 410. The Requestors seek to waive these copayments and deductibles for items and services within the scope of the NETT Protocol and covered under Medicare Part B. The Requestors assert that waiving these copayment amounts will enhance the reliability of the study and the validity of its results by promoting patient compliance with the NETT Protocol, including patient cooperation in follow-up data collection efforts. The Requestors further assert that requiring payment of Part B copayments and deductibles may cause an undue hardship on economically disadvantaged patients that would undermine their participation in the NETT study and compromise its integrity. The Requesters assert that patients typically do not pay to participate in research projects.

II. LEGAL ANALYSIS

A. Law

The anti-kickback statute, 42 U.S.C. § 1320a-7b(b), makes it a criminal offense knowingly and willfully to offer, pay, solicit, or receive any remuneration to induce the referral of business covered by a Federal health care program. Specifically, the statute provides that:

> Whoever knowingly and willfully offers or pays [or solicits or receives] any remuneration (including any kickback, bribe, or rebate) directly or indirectly, overtly or covertly, in cash or in kind to any person to induce such person — to refer an individual to a person for the furnishing or arranging for the furnishing of any item or service for which payment may be made in whole or in part under a Federal health care program, or to purchase, lease, order, or arrange for or recommend purchasing, leasing, or ordering any good, facility, service, or item for which payment may be made in whole or in part under a Federal health care program, shall be guilty of a felony.

42 U.S.C. § 1320a-7b(b). In other words, the statute prohibits payments made purposefully to induce referrals of business for which payment may be made by a Federal health care program. The statute ascribes liability to both sides of an impermissible "kickback" transaction. The statute has been interpreted to cover any arrangement where one purpose of the remuneration is to obtain money for the referral of services or to induce further referrals. *United States v. Kats,* 871 F.2d 105 (9th Cir. 1989); *United States v. Greber,* 760 F.2d 68 (3d Cir.), *cert. denied,* 474 U.S. 988 (1985). "Remuneration" for purposes of the anti-kickback statute includes the transfer of any thing of value, in cash or in-kind, directly or indirectly, covertly or overtly.

Violation of the anti-kickback statute constitutes a felony punishable by a maximum fine of $25,000, imprisonment up to five years, or both. Conviction will also lead to automatic exclusion from Federal health care programs, including Medicare and Medicaid. This Office may also initiate administrative proceedings to exclude persons from the Federal and State health care programs or to impose civil monetary penalties for fraud, kickbacks, and other prohibited activities under sections 1128(b)(7) and 1128A(a)(7) of the Act.[6]

Section 231(h) of the Health Insurance Portability and Accountability Act of 1996 ("HIPAA"), section 1128A(a)(5) of the Act, provides for the imposition of civil monetary penalties against any person who:

> offers or transfers remuneration to any individual eligible for benefits under [Federal health care programs (including Medicare or

---

[6] Because both the criminal and administrative sanctions related to the anti- 6 kickback implications of the Proposed Arrangement are based on violations of the anti-kickback statute, the analysis for purposes of this advisory opinion is the same under both.

Medicaid)] that such person knows or should know is likely to influence such individual to order or receive from a particular provider, practitioner, or supplier any item or service for which payment may be made, in whole or in part, [by a Federal health care program].

Section 231(h) defines "remuneration" as including, *inter alia,* the waiver of coinsurance and deductible amounts (or any part thereof).[7]

We have said previously in a Special Fraud Alert that providers who routinely waive Medicare copayments and deductibles may be held liable under the anti-kickback statute. *See* OIG Special Fraud Alert, 59 Fed. Reg. 242 (1994).[8] We explained that when providers forgive financial obligations for reasons other than genuine financial hardship of the particular patient, they may be unlawfully inducing the patient to purchase items or services in violation of the anti-kickback statute's proscription against offering or paying something of value as an inducement to generate business payable by Medicare. We further stated that except in cases of financial hardship, a good faith effort to collect deductibles and copayments must be made. Finally, we noted in our Special Fraud Alert that one indicator of a potentially prohibited waiver is the failure to collect copayments or deductibles for a specific group of Medicare patients for reasons unrelated to indigency.

B. Analysis

The Proposed Arrangement, which would waive deductible and coinsurance amounts routinely and without regard to financial hardship,[9] implicates the anti-kickback statute's proscription against

[7] The statute contains certain exceptions to the definition of remuneration for certain waivers of copayments that are not advertised, that are not routine, and that are granted to financially needy patients or for which reasonable collection efforts have been made. The statute contains further exceptions for certain differentials in coinsurance and deductible amounts as part of a benefit plan and for certain incentives to individuals to promote the delivery of preventive care. Because we find that the Proposed Arrangement would not be subject to sanction under the statutory prohibition, we do not reach the issue of whether any of the statutory exceptions would apply.

[8] Although the Special Fraud Alert primarily addressed charge-based providers, we expressly stated that the Special Fraud Alert should not be interpreted to legitimize routine waiver of copayments and deductibles with respect to providers paid under prospective payment or cost-based systems.

[9] With respect to NETT's economically disadvantaged patients, individualized determinations of indigency might suffice to exempt NETT providers from their obligation to collect copayments for those specific patients.

offering or paying something of value as an inducement to generate business payable by a Federal health care program. Nevertheless, for the reasons elaborated below, we conclude that in the particular circumstances presented here, the Proposed Arrangement would not be subject to sanction under the anti-kickback statute. We further conclude that the Proposed Arrangement would not constitute grounds for the imposition of civil monetary penalties under section 231(h) of HIPAA, which prohibits giving something of value to a beneficiary that the donor knows or should know is likely to influence the beneficiary's choice of a particular provider.

Based on the facts presented, we find that the following factors adequately protect the Proposed Arrangement against the risk of fraud or abuse:

- *The Proposed Arrangement is unlikely to influence beneficiaries to obtain Medicare covered services from NETT providers.* Where remuneration is paid by a provider to a beneficiary, the inquiry under the anti-kickback statute is whether such remuneration is paid to induce Federal health program business, whereas under section 231(h) of HIPAA, the test for a violation is whether such remuneration is something that the donor knows or should know is likely to induce the beneficiary's selection of a provider of Federal program services. The Proposed Arrangement is unlikely to have either of these prohibited effects. Simply put, Medicare patients will enroll in NETT because enrollment in NETT is the only means of obtaining Medicare coverage of LVRS, not because copayments are waived. As a practical matter, Medicare beneficiaries have no choice of LVRS providers outside of NETT. Nor is the Proposed Arrangement likely to influence the choice of providers within NETT; NETT anticipates that all providers will waive deductibles and copayments. In short, the purpose of the waivers of NETT cost-sharing amounts is to induce participation in a scientific study, not to induce utilization of Medicare covered services.
- *The Proposed Arrangement will not increase the risk of overutilization of Medicare covered services.* One adverse consequence of routine waivers of coinsurance obligations is the increased risk of overutilization of services payable by Medicare. Here, the Protocol controls utilization of services. The Proposed Arrangement would not apply to health care services

that are not included in the Protocol. Nor would it apply for any period of time during which a Medicare beneficiary ceases to be a NETT patient.[10] Thus, the Proposed Arrangement is unlikely to result in an increased risk of overutilization of Medicare covered services.[11] In addition, the risk of increased overutilization is minimized because the number of Medicare patients participating in the full NETT study will be limited to 4,700 over a fifty-four month period.[12] This number may be even smaller, because some NETT patients may be privately insured.

- *The Proposed Arrangement is a reasonable means of enhancing the likelihood of success of the NETT study.* Patient compliance with all aspects of the study, including visits to NETT clinics when required and cooperation with follow-up data collection efforts, is essential to producing valid study results. HCFA has determined that it needs a thorough and accurate study of LVRS in order to evaluate the surgery's efficacy and cost-effectiveness for the purpose of deciding whether to cover LVRS as a "reasonable and necessary" service under the Medicare program. Patients may be disinclined to participate fully for the duration of the study if they are required to pay to participate. This may be particularly true for patients who are not randomized into the surgical group or who are not satisfied with the outcome of their surgery. In these circumstances, waiving copayments is a reasonable means of enhancing patient compliance with study requirements and retaining patients for the entire study period. Waiving copayments will

---

[10] It is anticipated that some people may begin the initial screening process, be found ineligible for the study, but later reapply and be admitted to the study. HCFA would not consider these patients NETT patients for the period between the ineligibility determination and the reapplication.

[11] Nothing in this advisory opinion should be construed as indicating that a showing of actual, or increased risk of, overutilization is a required element of an anti-kickback statute violation. A risk of overutilization is merely one potential indicator of potential fraud or abuse.

[12] We recognize that an indeterminate number of patients who do not ultimately qualify for NETT may obtain some copayment waivers during the screening process. The numbers of these patients will be limited by the initial screening criteria. HCFA has agreed to reimburse NETT providers for services performed during the screening process in order to ensure that the NETT study can serve the purposes for which it is intended. We do not think that these limited waivers will lead to an increased risk of abuse of the Medicare program.

also ensure that economically disadvantaged patients are not precluded from the study.

In sum, the Proposed Arrangement reasonably accommodates the needs of an important, government-sponsored scientific study, without posing a significant risk of fraud and abuse of the Medicare program.

C. Conclusion

For the above-stated reasons, and based on the information provided by the Requesters and subject to certain conditions described below, we conclude that the Proposed Arrangement would not constitute grounds for the imposition of sanctions under 42 U.S.C. §§ 1320a-7a(a)(5) or 1320a-7b(b).

III. LIMITATIONS

The limitations applicable to this opinion include the following:

- This advisory opinion is issued only to the individuals and entities listed on the attached Distribution List [redacted], which are the Requesters of this opinion. This advisory opinion has no application, and cannot be relied upon, by any other individual or entity.
- This advisory opinion may not be introduced into evidence in any matter involving an entity or individual that is not a Requestor to this opinion.
- This advisory opinion is applicable only to the statutory provisions specifically noted above. No opinion is herein expressed or implied with respect to the application of any other Federal, state, or local statute, rule, regulation, ordinance, or other law that may be applicable to the Proposed Arrangement.
- This advisory opinion will not bind or obligate any agency other than the U.S. Department of Health and Human Services.
- This advisory opinion is limited in scope to the specific arrangement described in this letter and has no applicability to other arrangements, even those which appear similar in nature or scope.

This opinion is also subject to any additional limitations set forth at 42 C.F.R. Part 1008.

The OIG will not proceed against the Requesters with respect to any action that is part of the Proposed Arrangement taken in good faith reliance upon this advisory opinion as long as all of the material facts have been fully, completely, and accurately presented, and the arrangement in practice comports with the information provided.

The OIG reserves the right to reconsider the questions and issues raised in this advisory opinion and, where the public interest requires, modify or terminate this opinion. In the event that this advisory opinion is modified or terminated, the OIG will not proceed against the requesters with respect to any action taken in good faith reliance upon this advisory opinion, where all of the relevant facts were fully, completely, and accurately presented and where such action was promptly discontinued upon notification of the modification or termination of this advisory opinion.

Sincerely,

D. McCarty Thornton
Chief Counsel to the Inspector General

APPENDIX F17.6

Advisory Opinion No. 98–7

Posted: June 16, 1998

[June 11, 1998]

To: The Attached Distribution List

Re: Advisory Opinion No. 98–7

Ladies and Gentlemen:

We are writing in response to your request for an advisory opinion, in which you ask whether an ambulance restocking and continuing education arrangement (the "Arrangement"[1]) constitutes prohibited remuneration under the anti-kickback statute, section 1128B(b) of the Social Security Act (the "Act") and, if so, whether the Arrangement constitutes grounds for the imposition of sanctions under the anti-kickback statute, section 1128B(b) of the Act, the exclusion authority related to kickbacks, section 1128(b)(7) of the Act, or the civil monetary penalty provision for kickbacks, section 1128A(a)(7) of the Act.

You have certified that all of the information you provided in your request, including all supplementary letters, is true and correct, and constitutes a complete description of the material facts regarding the Arrangement. In issuing this opinion, we have relied solely on the facts and information you presented to us. We have not undertaken any independent investigation of such information. This opinion is limited to the facts presented. If material facts have not been disclosed, this opinion is without force and effect.

Based on the facts certified in your request for an advisory opinion, we conclude that the Arrangement could constitute prohibited remuneration under the anti-kickback statute if the requisite intent to

[1] Specifically, the Arrangement includes (1) a "drug box" exchange program; (2) a linens and medical supply exchange program; (3) a "pedi bag" exchange program for pediatric supplies; and (4) a continuing emergency medical services education program.

induce referrals were present, but that the OIG will not subject the Arrangement, as described in the request and supplemental submissions, to sanctions arising under the anti-kickback statute pursuant to sections 1128B(b), 1128(b)(7), or 1128A(a)(7) of the Act.

This opinion may not be relied on by any persons other than the addressees and is further qualified as set out in Part III below and in 42 C.F.R. Part 1008.

I. FACTUAL BACKGROUND

The requesters of this advisory opinion are twenty non-profit hospitals located in ten counties in the City A area of State B (the "Hospitals") and the City A Hospital Association (the "Association"), a non-profit corporation exempt from federal income tax pursuant to section 501(c)(6) of the Internal Revenue Code.[2] The Hospitals represent all of the hospitals in the City A area.

The Hospitals and the Association are dues paying members of the Region C Emergency Medical Services Council, Inc. (the "Council"), a State B nonprofit and tax exempt corporation founded in 1972, whose membership also includes all private and public ambulance providers in the area, local educational institutions, physicians, and at-large community members. The Council's mission is to coordinate the efforts of public and private ambulance service pre-hospital care providers, hospital emergency department staff, and consumers to ensure the best possible pre-hospital medical care for the victims of sudden illness or injury. The Council develops protocols for, and conducts ongoing evaluation and improvement of, the local emergency medical services ("EMS") delivery system, performs EMS quality assurance audits, distributes drug boxes to the local ambulances, provides continuing education to EMS personnel, sponsors education programs related to EMS for the general public, acts as an information clearinghouse for EMS activities, and otherwise seeks to promote high quality EMS care for the region.

Under the Council's auspices and pursuant to Council-developed protocols, the Hospitals and EMS organizations in the City A area

---

[2] The Hospitals are all members of the Association. The Association has presented itself as an additional requestor on the ground that it facilitates the uniform participation of the Hospitals in the Arrangement. Although trade associations are not typically appropriate requesters on behalf of their members, see 42 C.F.R. § 1008.11, a trade association may be a proper requestor if it is itself a party to an arrangement that is the subject of a request for an advisory opinion.

have engaged in various drug and medical supply exchange programs in connection with emergency medical transports since approximately 1973. Typically under these exchange programs, a receiving hospital restocks an ambulance with medications and supplies used in connection with emergency medical pre-hospital services provided to the transported patient. The ambulance providers are not charged, and do not pay, for the restocked items. Drugs are exchanged through a "drug box" program, pursuant to which EMS squads exchange depleted drug boxes used during a patient run for fully-stocked boxes provided by the receiving hospital. Hospital pharmacists review the used drug boxes, replenishing used, outdated, or improperly sealed items, and return them to inventory for future exchange.[3]

Under the linens and medical supplies exchange program, receiving hospitals restock ambulances with linens and medical supplies used on patients during emergency pre-hospital services. The program enables ambulances to be fully stocked at all times and ensures standardization of supplies, so that, for example, tubing used by EMS units can be connected to hospital systems without interruption.

The continuing education programs in which the Hospitals participate serve to update EMS personnel on the latest techniques in patient care. These programs also enable EMS personnel to remain current with emergency room protocols in the Hospitals. Hospital personnel also visit EMS squads to test the skills of EMS personnel, as required by regional standing orders pertaining to EMS certification.

Also under the Arrangement, Hospital Z in City A, the area's children's specialty hospital and a requestor of this opinion, distributes "pedi bags" to EMS providers to ensure that EMS units carry a variety of pediatric-sized airway tubes and related equipment for use with children. These bags have been distributed to all EMS squads in the City A area. Private EMS squads pay a nominal

[3] The drug box exchange program has been approved by the State B Board of Pharmacy and complies with [code section redacted], which provides a mechanism for EMS units to obtain drug stocks legally "on a replacement basis" from hospitals to which patients are delivered. We have previously stated our belief that ambulance restocking performed pursuant to a state law mandate would not violate the anti-kickback statute. However, because [code section redacted] permits, but does not require, drug restocking by hospitals, the statute is insufficient by itself to foreclose the possibility of improper intent to induce referrals.

start-up fee of $100 per bag. Hospital Z provides the bags to community and volunteer EMS squads at no charge. As with the other exchange programs, the supplies within the bags are restocked on an exchange basis, and all adult hospitals in the area keep on hand a small supply of these children's items.

II. LEGAL ANALYSIS

A. Law

The anti-kickback statute makes it a criminal offense knowingly and willfully to offer, pay, solicit, or receive any remuneration to induce referrals of items or services reimbursable by any Federal health care program. *See* 42 U.S.C. § 1320a-7b(b). Where remuneration is paid purposefully to induce referrals of items or services for which payment may be made by a Federal health care program, the anti-kickback statute is violated. By its terms, the statute ascribes criminal liability to parties on both sides of an impermissible "kickback" transaction.

The statute has been interpreted to cover any arrangement where one purpose of the remuneration was to obtain money for the referral of services or to induce further referrals. *United States v. Kats,* 871 F.2d 105 (9th Cir. 1989); *United States v. Greber,* 760 F.2d 68 (3d Cir.), *cert. denied,* 474 U.S. 988 (1985). "Remuneration" for purposes of the anti-kickback statute includes the transfer of anything of value, in cash or in kind, directly or indirectly, covertly or overtly. Violation of the statute constitutes a felony punishable by a maximum fine of $25,000, imprisonment up to five years, or both. Conviction will also lead to automatic exclusion from Federal health care programs, including Medicare and Medicaid. This Office may also initiate administrative proceedings to exclude persons from Federal and state health care programs or to impose civil monetary penalties for fraud, kickbacks, and other prohibited activities under sections 1128(b)(7) and 1128A(a)(7) of the Act.[4]

This Office's concern with the provision of goods and services for free or at below-market rates to potential referral sources is longstanding and clear: such arrangements are suspect under the anti-kickback statute. The provision of free or below-market rate

[4] Because both the criminal and administrative sanctions related to the anti-kickback implications of the Arrangement are based on violations of the anti-kickback statute, the analysis for purposes of this advisory opinion is the same under both.

goods or services to a referral source may violate the anti-kickback statute if one purpose of the gift is to induce referrals of Federal health care program business.

The provision by a hospital of free supplies, medications, and services to an ambulance service fits squarely within the meaning of remuneration for purposes of the anti-kickback statute. An inference may be drawn that one purpose of such remuneration is to induce the ambulance company to bring patients to the hospital. However, the strength of that inference may vary with the circumstances of the specific arrangement.

In assessing the potential risk of fraud or abuse under the anti-kickback statute, our concerns are principally fourfold: increased risk of overutilization, increased program costs, patient freedom of choice, and unfair competition. Because it is limited to emergency medical services, the Arrangement does not increase the risk of overutilization and is unlikely to lead to increased costs to Federal health care programs. Neither the number of Federal program beneficiaries requiring emergency transport in the City A area, nor the treatment these patients will require or receive at the Hospitals, is related to the existence or operation of the Arrangement. [5]

With respect to freedom of choice and unfair competition, under the Arrangement it appears that emergency ambulance crews have relatively limited opportunities to steer patients to particular hospitals. In life threatening cases, the selection of a receiving hospital will be dictated by the patient's condition. In other circumstances, the choice of receiving hospital will frequently be dictated by the patient, the patient's physician, or the patient's insurer. Notwithstanding, there will inevitably be situations in which ambulance company personnel would be able to steer patients who do not have a preference to a particular facility. In the circumstances presented here, however, there would appear to be no financial reason arising from the Arrangement for ambulance personnel to steer patients to a particular hospital, since all area hospitals participate in the Arrangement.

However, the mere fact that all hospitals may be restocking ambulances without charge does not immunize conduct that might

[5] This advisory opinion only relates to drugs, supplies, and educational programs provided by the Hospitals that directly relate to the provision of emergency pre-hospital services in the City A area. Restocking of drugs or supplies used in the course of non-emergency services and educational programs not directly related to emergency medical services are outside the scope of this opinion.

otherwise violate the anti-kickback statute. Some institutions may well participate in the restocking because of fear of adverse competitive consequences if they do not. In short, remuneration that is given to retain or maintain existing referrals may violate the anti-kickback statute.

We previously addressed the application of the anti-kickback statute to an ambulance restocking arrangement in OIG Advisory Opinion 97–6 (October 8, 1997). Based on the specific facts presented by the hospital requestor, we found that, notwithstanding a state administrative regulation that required ambulances to transport patients to the facility of the patient's choice except in exigent circumstances, the hospital's proposed arrangement for free restocking of supplies and medications posed a risk of improper steering and unfair competition. Accordingly, we concluded that the arrangement could potentially violate the anti-kickback statute if the requisite intent to induce referrals were present.

The facts presented here differ in material respects from those presented in OIG Advisory Opinion 97–6. *First,* the Arrangement is not a unilateral arrangement; rather, it was developed and implemented pursuant to an ongoing effort by the Council and its members to maintain and improve a regional emergency medical system through a comprehensive program that coordinates all EMS components. The Council, a non-profit corporation founded in 1972, is open to all hospitals and emergency ambulance providers in the area, as well as local educational institutions, physicians, and other community members. Regional EMS councils, like the one at issue here, were formed in the early 1970s in response to a growing recognition of the inadequacy of then existing emergency medical care and the high cost in human lives and physical disabilities due to accidents and sudden illness and injury.[6] EMS councils were established to coordinate emergency care among all levels of a region's EMS system, including public safety organizations, private and hospital-based ambulance services, hospitals and other critical care facilities, and local physicians and community groups.

Second, the restocking aspects of the Arrangement are not free-standing; the Arrangement is part and parcel of a comprehensive and coordinated regional effort to integrate and improve all

[6] *See, e.g. Accidental Death and Disability: The Neglected Disease of Modern Society*, National Academy of Sciences and National Research Council (September 1966).

aspects of the emergency medical care system. In addition to the drug and supply exchange programs, the Council establishes protocols addressing various aspects of the emergency medical system and otherwise administers the exchange and educational programs.[7] It also conducts ongoing evaluation and improvement of the local 7 EMS delivery system, performs EMS quality assurance audits, sponsors educational programs related to EMS for the general public, acts as an information clearinghouse for EMS activities, and otherwise seeks to promote high quality EMS care for the region.

Third, regional and local programs to improve and coordinate the delivery of quality emergency medical services have been actively encouraged and promoted by the Federal government over the past twenty-five years. In 1973 — the year the first exchange program began in the City A area — the Federal government enacted the Emergency Medical Services Systems Act of 1973 ("EMSSA"), Pub L. 93–154, 87 Stat. 594 (1973), which provided federal funding for the development of regional EMS systems at the state, regional, and local levels.[8] These regional systems were to develop comprehensive programs to improve such areas as communications (including "911" systems); transportation; provision and training of emergency personnel; facilities; critical care units; use of public safety agencies; accessibility to care; consumer participation, education, and information; transfer of patients; standard medical record keeping; independent review and evaluation of EMS; disaster linkage; and mutual aid agreements among communities. EMSSA was one of several Federal legislative efforts to promote EMS delivery systems, including the Highway Safety Act of 1966, Pub. L. 89–594, 80 Stat. 731 (1966), which established an EMS program in the Department of Transportation; the Emergency Medical Services for Children Program, under the Public Health Act, Pub. L. 98–555, 99 Stat. 2854 (1984), which provided funds for enhancing pediatric EMS; and the

---

[7] The "pedi bag" program is administered by the local children's medical center, but is part of the comprehensive regional EMS system and is included in the Arrangement for purposes of this advisory opinion.

[8] EMSSA defined "emergency medical services system" as "a system which provides for the arrangement of personnel, facilities, and equipment for the effective and coordinated delivery in an appropriate geographical area of health care services under emergency conditions . . . and which is administered by a public or nonprofit private entity which has the authority and the resources to provide effective administration of the system." 87 Stat. at 595.

Trauma Care Systems Planning and Development Act of 1990, Pub. L. 101–590, 104 Stat. 2915 (1990).

Finally — and importantly — the Arrangement is likely to have a positive impact on the quality of patient care. By providing a mechanism to ensure that ambulances are fully stocked with current medications and appropriate supplies compatible with all local hospital emergency rooms and that EMS personnel are adequately trained, the Arrangement is likely to foster fast, efficient, and effective pre-hospital emergency care for the City A area community. This significant community benefit, coupled with the conditions, requirements, and limitations outlined above, persuade us that the Arrangement poses minimal risk of fraud and abuse under the anti-kickback statute, and therefore the OIG would not subject it to sanction.

III. CONCLUSION

The advisory opinion process is a "means of relating the anti-kickback statute to the particular facts of a specific arrangement." 62 Fed. Reg. 7350, 7351 (February 19, 1997). The advisory opinion process permits this Office to protect specific arrangements that "contain[] limitations, requirements, or controls that give adequate assurance that Federal health care programs cannot be abused." *Id.* In evaluating an arrangement's potential to lead to fraud or abuse of Federal health care programs, no one fact or element is necessarily dispositive. Here, we are persuaded that the Arrangement is likely to result in substantial community benefit consistent with longstanding national policy objectives. We are further persuaded that, taken as a whole, the aspects of the Arrangement described above — including, but not limited to, the Arrangement's relationship to a coordinated regional EMS system, the role of the regional Council, the Arrangement's limitation to emergency medical services, and the uniformity of the Arrangement across providers — create sufficient limitations, requirements, or controls so as to give adequate assurance that the Arrangement will not lead to program abuse under the anti-kickback statute.[9]

[9] We express no opinion regarding liability of the requesters under the False Claims Act or other legal authorities in connection with any improper billing or claims submission directly or indirectly related to, or arising from, the Arrangement.

Accordingly, we conclude that while the Arrangement might technically violate the anti-kickback statute if the requisite intent to induce referrals were present, the OIG will not impose sanctions on the requesters under sections 1128(b)(7) (as it relates to kickbacks) or 1128A(a)(7) of the Act, based on the facts certified in the requesters' request for an advisory opinion.

IV. LIMITATIONS

The limitations applicable to this opinion include the following:

- This advisory opinion is issued only to the requesters listed on the Attached Distribution List, which are the requesters of this opinion. This advisory opinion has no application, and cannot be relied upon, by any other individual or entity.
- This advisory opinion may not be introduced into evidence in any matter involving an entity or individual that is not a Requestor to this opinion.
- This advisory opinion is applicable only to the statutory provisions specifically noted in the first paragraph of this advisory opinion. No opinion is herein expressed or implied with respect to the application of any other Federal, state, or local statute, rule, regulation, ordinance, or other law that may be applicable to the Arrangement.
- This advisory opinion will not bind or obligate any agency other than the U.S. Department of Health and Human Services.
- This advisory opinion is limited in scope to the specific arrangement described in this letter and has no applicability to other arrangements, even those which appear similar in nature or scope.

This opinion is also subject to any additional limitations set forth at 42 C.F.R. Part 1008.

The OIG will not proceed against the requesters with respect to any action that is part of the Arrangement taken in good faith reliance upon this advisory opinion as long as all of the material facts have been fully, completely, and accurately presented, and the Arrangement in practice comports with the information provided. The OIG reserves the right to reconsider the questions and issues raised in this advisory opinion and, where the public interest requires, modify or terminate this opinion. In the event that this advisory opinion is modified or terminated, the OIG will not proceed against any requestor with respect to any action taken in good faith reliance upon this advisory opinion, where all of the relevant facts were fully, completely, and accurately presented and where such action was promptly discontinued upon notification of the modification or termination of this advisory opinion.

Sincerely,

D. McCarty Thornton
Chief Counsel to the Inspector General

APPENDIX F18

Advisory Opinion No. 98–8

[Name Redacted]

Re: Advisory Opinion No. 98–8

Dear [Name Redacted]:

We are writing in response to your request for an advisory opinion concerning whether Company A ("Company A"), a wholly-owned subsidiary of Company B ("Company B") (collectively referred to as "Company AB") would be subject to exclusion from Federal health care programs pursuant to 42 U.S.C. § 1320a-7(b)(6) for the submission of claims for durable medical equipment ("DME") substantially in excess of its usual charges, if it charges Medicare 21–32% (based on five sample charges) more than it charges "cash and carry" retail customers for the identical DME products ("Proposed Arrangement").

In issuing this opinion, we have relied solely on the facts and information presented to us. We have not undertaken an independent investigation of such information. This opinion is limited to the facts presented. If material facts have not been disclosed, this opinion is without force and effect.

This opinion may not be relied on by any person other than the addressee and is further qualified as set out in Part III below and in 42 C.F.R. Part 1008.

I. FACTUAL BACKGROUND

Company AB develops and operates, either by franchisees or through wholly-owned subsidiaries, a number of "superstores" that sell a wide selection of medical and health related products to customers for use in their homes. Company A, a wholly-owned subsidiary of Company B, operates a store occupying 5,000 square feet of retail space and offering a selection of over 3,000 different products. Product lines carried by Company AB include, but are not limited to, nutrition, back care, sports therapy, foot care, wound care, bathroom safety, personal care, oncology, and mobility and accessibility items.

Approximately 300 of the 3,000 products that Company AB sells are reimbursable under the Medicare program as DME, including urological, ostomy, orthotic, and wound care products. In order to participate in the Medicare program, a DME supplier must meet certain supplier standards. See 42 C.F.R. § 424.57. Medicare regulations allow a supplier to bill Medicare the lesser of (i) its actual charge to the patient for the equipment or (ii) an amount calculated in accordance with a specific Medicare payment methodology, reduced by the applicable Part B deductible and coinsurance payments. See 42 U.S.C. § 1395m(a)(1)(B).

While Company AB does not currently participate in the Medicare program, Company A intends to apply to become a Medicare-approved supplier. Company AB proposes to charge Medicare an amount equal to the maximum reimbursement amount allowable under Medicare's payment regulations. According to Company AB, its proposed charges to Medicare will generally be higher than its charges to its "cash and carry" customers.

Company AB has determined that providing DME to Medicare beneficiaries will result in significant additional costs as compared to its "cash and carry" trade. Company AB has identified several areas where the Medicare supplier standards will create additional costs associated with serving Medicare beneficiaries.

- **Documentation Requirements** — The procedures necessary to obtain required physician prescriptions and certificates of medical necessity will increase costs due to the need to train staff and the time demands that will be placed upon that staff in assuring the completeness and accuracy of that documentation.
- **Claims Processing** — Rather than simply receiving cash in return for providing an item, Company AB will need to complete and submit claims for payment, requiring additional staff and upgrades for its computer system, in order to conduct intake for Medicare beneficiaries and process and track claims.
- **Delivery and Distribution** — Company AB will be required to deliver Medicare covered items upon request. Company AB will also need to rent or purchase warehouse space to operate a repair center and to store rental DME and returns.
- **Surety Bond** — The Health Care Financing Administration ("HCFA") has proposed a rule requiring DME suppliers to

obtain a surety bond in favor of HCFA in an amount of not less than $50,000. See 63 Fed. Reg. 2926, 2930 (Jan. 20, 1998).

Company AB asserts that additional costs will also be incurred in connection with Medicare requirements related to equipment leasing, product returns, and delays and denials in payment.

II. APPLICABLE LAWS AND ANALYSIS

Reimbursement to DME suppliers is determined according to the Medicare statute and regulations. With respect to a covered item of DME, the payment basis is the lesser of the actual charge for the item or the particular DME payment formula applicable to such item. See 42 U.S.C. § 1395m(a)(1). In general, most DME suppliers receive payment in the amount determined by the DME payment formula.

Under 42 U.S.C. § 1320a-7(b)(6), the Office of Inspector General has the authority to exclude individuals and entities from participation in the Federal health care programs (including Medicare) when it determines that an individual or entity has:

> submitted or caused to be submitted bills or requests for payment (where such bills or requests are based on charges or cost) under subchapter VIII of this chapter . . . for items or services furnished substantially in excess of such individual's or entity's usual charges . . . for such items or services, unless the Secretary finds there is good cause for such bills or requests containing such charges or costs.

42 U.S.C. § 1320a-7(b)(6). Any permissive exclusion imposed under this section will be for not less than one year. See 42 U.S.C. § 1320a-7 (c)(3)(F).

The OIG has promulgated regulations implementing this exclusion authority. The regulations state that charges substantially in excess of a supplier's usual charges are permissible when they are "due to unusual circumstances or medical complications requiring additional time, effort, expense or other good cause." 42 C.F.R. § 1007.701(c) (emphasis added).

Applying the statute and regulations, the initial inquiry is whether the proposed charges are substantially in excess of Company AB's usual charge. Currently, Company AB sells virtually all of its products, including the DME products that would be eligible for Medicare reimbursement, to customers on a "cash and carry" basis at posted prices. Accordingly, Company AB's usual charge for an item of DME is its current "cash and carry" price for that product. Because the amount Company AB proposes to charge Medicare is generally 21–32% higher than its "cash and carry" price for any given item, we believe that Company AB's charges to Medicare for some products would be substantially in excess of its usual charges and potentially subject Company AB to exclusion absent "good cause".

We agree that additional costs incurred by Company AB that are solely attributable to complying with Medicare requirements may constitute "good cause" for charging Medicare substantially in excess of Company AB's usual charge for identical items. However, the higher Medicare charge should bear a direct and reasonable relationship to the additional costs incurred by the supplier to comply with Medicare program requirements, after subtracting any costs solely attributable to the "cash and carry" business. These additional costs should be allocated to items provided to Medicare beneficiaries using a reasonable and generally accepted accounting methodology.

A useful benchmark for determining whether the higher Medicare charge would meet the "good cause" exception is to compare the profit margin on the Medicare sale to the margin on the "cash and carry" sale. So long as the profit margin for the Medicare sale is less than or equal to the "cash and carry" sale, we think the "good cause" exception would be satisfied.

On the limited information submitted, we cannot determine whether Company AB's proposed fee structure is sufficiently related to its anticipated additional costs attributable to Medicare participation to constitute "good cause" within the statutory and regulatory exception. In particular, Company AB has acknowledged that it does not yet know the entirety of the additional costs it will incur. Accordingly, we cannot determine whether Company AB's charge for any particular item would meet the "good cause" test, and therefore whether Company AB would be subject to exclusion under 42 U.S.C. 1320a-7(b)(6) for charging substantially in excess of its usual charges.

III. LIMITATIONS

The limitations applicable to this opinion include the following:

- This advisory opinion is issued only to Company A and Company B, which are the Requesters of this opinion. This advisory opinion has no application, and cannot be relied upon, by any other individual or entity.

- This advisory opinion may not be introduced into evidence in any matter involving an entity or individual that is not a Requestor to this opinion.
- This advisory opinion is applicable only to the statutory provisions specifically noted in the first paragraph of this advisory opinion. No opinion is herein expressed or implied with respect to the application of any other Federal, state, or local statute, rule, regulation, ordinance, or other law that may be applicable to the Proposed Arrangement.
- This advisory opinion will not bind or obligate any agency other than the U.S. Department of Health and Human Services.
- This advisory opinion is limited in scope to the specific arrangement described in this letter and has no applicability to other arrangements, even those which appear similar in nature or scope.

This opinion is also subject to any additional limitations set forth at 42 C.F.R. Part 1008.

The OIG reserves the right to reconsider the questions and issues raised in this advisory opinion and, where the public interest requires, modify or terminate this opinion.

Sincerely, D. McCarty Thornton

Chief Counsel to the Inspector General

APPENDIX F19

Advisory Opinion No. 98–9

POSTED: July 21, 1998

[Issued July 13, 1998]

[name and address redacted]

Re: Advisory Opinion No. 98–9

Dear [name redacted]

We are writing in response to your request for an advisory opinion, in which you ask: (1) whether a compensation arrangement for registered nurses and certain other employees pursuant to a collective bargaining agreement with the nurses' union (the "Proposed Arrangement") constitutes prohibited remuneration under the anti-kickback statute, section 1128B(b) of the Social Security Act (the "Act");

(2) whether the Proposed Arrangement satisfies the criteria set forth in section 1128B(b)(3)(B) of the Act and 42 C.F.R. § 1001.952(i) (the employee exception and "safe harbor" regulation); and

(3) whether the Proposed Arrangement constitutes grounds for the imposition of sanctions under the anti-kickback statute, section 1128B(b) of the Act; the exclusion authority related to kickbacks, section 1128(b)(7) of the Act; the civil monetary penalty provision for kickbacks, section 1128A(a)(7) of the Act; or the civil monetary penalty provision for inducements to beneficiaries, section 1128A(a)(5) of the Act.

You have certified that all of the information you provided in your request, including all supplementary letters, is true and correct, and constitutes a complete description of the material facts regarding the Proposed Arrangement. In issuing this opinion, we have relied solely on the facts and information you presented to us. We have not undertaken any independent investigation of such information. This opinion is limited to the facts presented. If material facts have not been disclosed, this opinion is without force and effect.

Based on the information provided and circumstances described, we conclude that the Proposed Arrangement satisfies the criteria set forth in section 1128B(b)(3)(B) of the Act and 42 C.F.R. § 1001.952(i) (the employee exception and safe harbor regulation) and therefore does not constitute prohibited remuneration under the anti-kickback statute, section 1128B(b) of the Act. Accordingly, the Proposed Arrangement would not constitute grounds for the imposition of sanctions under section 1128B(b) of the Act, section 1128(b)(7) of the Act (as it relates to kickbacks), or section 1128A(a)(7) of the Act. Moreover, we conclude that the OIG would not impose a civil monetary penalty on the requestor in connection with the Proposed Arrangement under section 1128A(a)(5) of the Act. This opinion may not be relied on by any person other than the addressee and is further qualified as set out in Part III below and in 42 C.F.R. Part 1008.

I. FACTUAL BACKGROUND

A. The Parties

Hospital A, a Delaware corporation, owns and operates an inpatient hospital facility located in City X, State Y (the "Hospital").

Union B ("Union") is a labor organization, organized pursuant to the National Labor Relations Act. The Union currently is the collective bargaining representative for certain nurses and non-professional Hospital employees, including service employees, health care aides ("HCAs"), and patient care aides ("PCAs") (collectively the "Union Employees"). None of the Union Employees is a physician. The Union also represents skilled laborers and construction workers not employed by the Hospital, but who may work for contractors who provide services to the Hospital from time to time. The Hospitals' Union Employees constitute approximately one-third of the total Union membership. The Union does not represent nurses, service workers, HCA, or PCAs who are employed by other hospitals in the area.

The Union is part of a coalition of six unions (the "Coalition"). The Coalition facilitates access to certain health plans for its unions' members and their dependents. Coalition union members and dependents who are covered by these health plans are "Covered Coalition Members" for purposes of this opinion. There are approximately 7,900 Covered Coalition Members, of which approximately nineteen percent, or 1,500, are also eligible for Medicare.

B. Proposed Compensation Adjustment Program

The Hospital and the Union are currently negotiating a collective bargaining agreement for registered nurses, HCAs, PCAs, and certain Hospital service workers. As part of the agreement, the Hospital proposes paying the nurses an additional amount as part of their hourly wage based on the number of Covered Coalition Members who are admitted as Hospital inpatients during defined six-month periods.

Specifically, the proposed compensation adjustment program would work as follows. The Hospital will track the total number of Hospital admissions of Covered Coalition Members. At six-month intervals, the Hospital will provide extra compensation to its Union Employees (and possibly to some non-union employees)(1) based on the previous six-months' inpatient admissions of Covered Coalition Members (the "Admissions Adjustment"). The collective bargaining agreement will include a fixed formula for calculation of the Admissions Adjustment based on the total number of admissions above a baseline of zero. The formula will provide for incremental additional compensation of one percent of the base wage rate for all Union Employees as certain threshold levels of increases in Hospital admissions of Covered Coalition Members are met over a six-month period, as follows: X% extra compensation for an increase of over X admissions,X% for an increase of over X admissions, X% for an increase of overX admissions, andX% for an increase of over X admissions. The amount of the Admissions Adjustment is capped at 4% of the base wage rate. At the end of every six-month period, the baseline for Hospital admissions for Covered Coalition Members will be reset at zero.

The Admissions Adjustment available to Union Employees is tied to aggregate admissions and not to specific admissions or services. No person in a position to refer patients to the Hospital will be eligible for the Admissions Adjustment.(2) Based on the current average wage rate for Union Employees at the Hospital, the maximum additional compensation would be $.X/hour for nurses, $0.X/hour for service workers, and $0.X/hour for HCA and PCAs.

II. LEGAL ANALYSIS

A. The Proposed Arrangement Satisfies the Criteria of the Statutory Exception and Regulatory Safe Harbor for Employee Compensation.

The anti-kickback statute makes it a criminal offense knowingly and willfully to offer, pay, solicit, or receive any remuneration to induce the referral of business for which payment may be made by a Federal health care program. Specifically, the statute provides that:

> Whoever knowingly and willfully offers or pays [or solicits or receives] any remuneration (including any kickback, bribe, or rebate) directly or indirectly, overtly or covertly, in cash or in kind to any person to induce such person — to refer an individual to a person for the furnishing or arranging for the furnishing of any item or service for which payment may be made in whole or in part under a Federal health care program, or to purchase, lease, order, or arrange for or recommend purchasing, leasing, or ordering any good, facility, service, or item for which payment may be made in whole or in part under a Federal health care program, shall be guilty of a felony.

Section 1128B(b) of the Act. In other words, the statute prohibits payments made purposefully to induce referrals of business payable by a Federal health care program. The statute ascribes liability to both sides of an impermissible "kickback" transaction. The statute has been interpreted to cover any arrangement where one purpose of the remuneration was to obtain money for the referral of services or to induce further referrals. *United States v. Kats,* 871 F.2d 105 (9th Cir. 1989); *United States v. Greber,* 760 F.2d 68 (3d Cir.), *cert. denied,* 474 U.S. 988 (1985). "Remuneration" for purposes of the anti-kickback statute includes the transfer of anything of value, in cash or in kind, directly or indirectly, covertly or overtly.

Violation of the statute constitutes a felony punishable by a maximum fine of $25,000, imprisonment for up to five years or both. Conviction will also lead to automatic exclusion from Federal health care programs, including Medicare and Medicaid. This Office may also initiate administrative proceedings to exclude persons from the Federal and State health care programs or to impose civil monetary penalties for fraud, kickbacks, and other prohibited activities under sections 1128(b)(7) and 1128A(a)(7) of the Act.[3]

The anti-kickback statute excepts from its reach "any amount paid by an employer to an employee (who has a *bona fide* employment relationship with such employer) for employment in the provision of covered items or services." Section 1128B(b)(3)(B) of the Act. The OIG safe harbor regulations provide that the term "remuneration", as used in the anti-kickback statute, does not include:

> [A]ny amount paid by an employer to an employee, who has a *bona fide* employment relationship with the employer, for employment in the furnishing of any item or service for which payment may be made in whole or in part under Medicare or a State health care program. For purposes of paragraph (i) of this section, the term *employee* has the same meaning as it does for purposes of 26 U.S.C. 3121(d)(2).

42 C.F.R. § 1001.952(i).

Whether an employee is a *bona fide* employee for purposes of the employee exception to the anti-kickback statute is a matter that is outside the scope of the advisory opinion process. See section 1128D (b)(3)(B) of the Act. Thus, for purposes of rendering this advisory opinion, we assume that the Hospital's Union Employees who will receive the Admissions Adjustment under the Proposed Arrangement are *bona fide* employees in accordance with the Internal Revenue Service's ("IRS's") definition of the term set forth at 26 U.S.C. § 3121(d)(2) and IRS interpretations of that provision as codified in its regulations and other interpretive sources. If the Union Employees are not *bona fide* employees under the IRS definition, this advisory opinion is without force and effect.

Based on the facts presented, including, but not limited to, the fact that the Union Employees must perform nursing and other health care related services to be eligible for the Admissions Adjustment, and our assumption that the employees are *bona fide* employees, we conclude that the Proposed Arrangement falls within the plain language of the statutory exception and regulatory safe harbor for employee compensation. The Admissions Adjustment is paid to the Union Employees pursuant to a collective bargaining agreement as compensation for their employment in the furnishing of services payable by a Federal health care program.

Accordingly, the adjusted compensation under the Proposed Arrangement does not constitute prohibited remuneration under the anti-kickback statute, section 1128B(b) of the Act.

B. The Proposed Arrangement Does Not Violate Section 1128A(a)(5) of the Act.

Section 1128A(a)(5) of the Act provides for the imposition of civil monetary penalties against any person who:

> offers or transfers remuneration to any individual eligible for benefits under [Federal health care programs (including Medicare or Medicaid)] that such person knows or should know is likely to influence such individual to order or receive from a particular provider, practitioner, or supplier any item or service for which payment may be made, in whole or in part, [by a Federal health care program].

Section 1128A(i)(6) defines "remuneration" for purposes of section 1128A(a)(5) of the Act as including "the waiver of coinsurance and deductible amounts (or any part thereof), and transfers of items or services for free or for other than fair market value." Unlike the anti-kickback statute, section 1128A(a)(5) is solely concerned with remuneration offered or transferred to Federal health care program beneficiaries.

The Admissions Adjustment may be paid to some Union Employees who are Medicare beneficiaries and who themselves may become inpatients at the Hospital. Thus, the Hospital has inquired whether the adjusted compensation runs afoul of section 1128A(a)(5) of the Act.

We think that section 1128A(a)(5) was not intended to apply to the Proposed Arrangement. The gravamen of section 1128A(a)(5) is a prohibition on offering remuneration to beneficiaries that is likely to induce such beneficiaries to select a particular health care provider. However, Congress did not intend for the penalty to apply to remuneration of nominal value. See, e.g., 63 Fed. Reg. 14393, 14395–96 (March 25, 1998) (discussion of Congressional intent in preamble to proposed civil monetary penalties rule). Because payment of an Admissions Adjustment is contingent on significant factors beyond any individual employee's control, such payment is so speculative as to be, at best, nominal remuneration not subject to the statutory proscription.

Accordingly, the OIG will not impose sanctions on the Hospital under section 1128A(a)(5) of the Act in connection with the Admissions Adjustment in the Proposed Arrangement, based on the certified facts submitted by the Hospital in connection with this advisory opinion.

III. LIMITATIONS

The limitations applicable to this opinion include the following:

This advisory opinion is issued only to Hospital A, doing business as Hosptial A Center, which is the Requestor of this opinion. This advisory opinion has no application, and cannot be relied upon, by any other individual or entity.

This advisory opinion may not be introduced into evidence in any matter involving an entity or individual that is not a Requestor to this opinion.

This advisory opinion is applicable only to the statutory provisions specifically noted in the first paragraph of this advisory opinion. No opinion is herein expressed or implied with respect to the application of any other Federal, state, or local statute, rule, regulation, ordinance, or other law that may be applicable to the Proposed Arrangement.

This advisory opinion will not bind or obligate any agency other than the U.S. Department of Health and Human Services.

This advisory opinion is limited in scope to the specific arrangement described in this letter and has no applicability to other arrangements, even those which appear similar in nature or scope.

This opinion is also subject to any additional limitations set forth at 42 C.F.R. Part 1008.

The OIG will not proceed against the requester with respect to any action that is part of the Proposed Arrangement taken in good faith reliance upon this advisory opinion as long as all of the material facts have been fully, completely, and accurately presented, and the Proposed Arrangement in practice comports with the information provided. The OIG reserves the right to reconsider the questions and issues raised in this advisory opinion and, where the public interest requires, modify or terminate this opinion. In the event that this advisory opinion is modified or terminated, the OIG will not proceed against the requestor with respect to any action taken in good faith reliance upon this advisory opinion, where all of the relevant facts were fully, completely, and accurately presented and where such action was promptly discontinued upon notification of the modification or termination of this advisory opinion.

Sincerely,

/s/
D. McCarty Thornton

Chief Counsel to the Inspector General

1. Payments to non-union employees are not the subject of this advisory opinion, and we express no opinion with respect to any such payments.

2. As part of the collective bargaining agreement, the Union and the Union Employees will agree to comply with certain guidelines that restrain Union Employees from providing remuneration to Covered Coalition Members to induce them to select the Hospital for inpatient services and that promote the dissemination of full and truthful information to Covered Coalition Members. The proposed guidelines may help reduce the risk that Union Employees will improperly influence Covered Coalition Members to select the Hospital for inpatient services by providing the Covered Coalition Members with improper remunerative inducements or false or misleading information.

Accordingly, the guidelines may describe prudent business practices. However, they are not sufficient in and of themselves to safeguard against fraud and abuse.

3. Because both the criminal and administrative sanctions related to the anti-kickback implications of the Arrangement are based on violations of the anti-kickback statute, the analysis for purposes of this advisory opinion is the same under both.

APPENDIX F20

OIG Final Rule: Medicare and State Health Programs: Fraud and Abuse; Issuance of Advisory Opinions by the OIG

Office of Inspector General

42 CFR Part 1008

RIN 0991-AA85

Medicare and State Health Care Programs: Fraud and Abuse; Issuance of Advisory Opinions by the OIG

AGENCY: Office of Inspector General (OIG), HHS.

ACTION: Final rule.

SUMMARY: In accordance with section 205 of the Health Insurance Portability and Accountability Act of 1996, this final rule sets forth the specific procedures by which the Department, through the Office of Inspector General (OIG), in consultation with the Department of Justice (DoJ), will issue advisory opinions to outside parties regarding the interpretation and applicability of certain statutes relating to the Federal and State health care programs. The procedures for submitting a request and obtaining an advisory opinion from the OIG were established through interim final regulations published in the Federal Register on February 19, 1997. In response to public comments received on these interim final regulations, this final rule revises and clarifies various aspects of the earlier rulemaking.

EFFECTIVE DATE: This rule is effective on July 16, 1998.

FOR FURTHER INFORMATION CONTACT: Joel Schaer, (202) 619–0089, OIG Regulations Officer.

SUPPLEMENTARY INFORMATION:

I. Background

A. Section 205 of Public Law 104–191

The Health Insurance Portability and Accountability Act of 1996 (HIPAA), Public Law 104–191, specifically required the Department to provide a formal guidance process to requesting individuals and entities regarding the application of the anti-kickback statute, the safe harbor provisions, and other OIG health care fraud and abuse sanctions. In accordance with section 205 of HIPAA, the Department, in consultation with the DoJ, issues written advisory opinions to parties with regard to: (1) what constitutes prohibited remuneration under the anti-kickback statute; (2) whether an arrangement or proposed arrangement satisfies the criteria in section 1128B(b)(3) of the Social Security Act (the Act), or established by regulation, for activities which do not result in prohibited remuneration; (3) what constitutes an inducement to reduce or limit services to Medicare or Medicaid program beneficiaries under section 1128A(b) of the Act[1]; and (4) whether an activity or proposed activity constitutes grounds for the imposition of civil or criminal sanctions under sections 1128, 1128A, or 1128B of the Act. Thus, advisory opinions may be issued with regard to the criminal provisions of section 1128B of the Act, which includes the anti-kickback statute, as well as the provisions of section 1128 of the Act, which authorizes the Department to exclude individuals and entities from participation in Federal and State health care programs. Exclusions are authorized in a wide variety of circumstances, including, for example, conviction of health care related offenses, State licensure action, and submission of claims in excess of usual charges or for services that fail to meet professionally recognized standards of health care. In addition, advisory opinions are available regarding the civil money penalty provisions of section 1128A of the Act, which authorizes penalties for a variety of acts, including, among others, presentation of a false or fraudulent Medicare or Medicaid claim and hospital payments to physicians to induce them to reduce or limit care to any Medicare or Medicaid beneficiary under their direct care.

[1] Public Law 104–191 erroneously cited this provision as section 1128B(b) of the Act. Section 4331(a) of the Balanced Budget Act of 1997, Public Law 105–33, corrected this citation to section 1128A(b) of the Act.

B. OIG Interim Final Regulations

Because HIPAA required that specific procedures and final regulations on the advisory opinion process be in place by February 21, 1997, the Secretary determined that it was both impracticable and contrary to the public interest to first issue regulations in proposed rulemaking form. As a result, on February 19, 1997, the OIG published interim final regulations (62 FR 7350) establishing a new part 1008 in 42 CFR chapter V addressing the various procedural issues and aspects of the advisory opinion process. Specifically, the interim final rule set forth (1) the procedures to be followed by parties applying for advisory opinions and by the OIG in responding to these requests; (2) the time frames pursuant to which the OIG will receive and respond to requests; (3) the type and amount of fees to be charged to requesting parties; and (4) the manner in which the public will be informed of the issuance of any advisory opinions.

The interim final rule also set forth a 60-day public comment period for specific comments and recommendations for refining the advisory opinion process.

C. Summary of the Interim Final Rule

The establishment of a new part 1008 in 42 CFR chapter V specifically addressed, among other provisions, the following procedural aspects of the advisory opinion process:

1. Responsibilities of Outside Parties

Section 1008.15 of the interim final rule indicated that any individual or entity may submit a request for an advisory opinion, but that the arrangement in question must, at the time of the request for an opinion, either be in existence or be an arrangement into which the parties have a good faith intention to enter in the future.[2] Section 1008.15(b) stated that requests presenting general questions of interpretation, posing hypothetical situations, or seeking an opinion about the activities of third parties would not qualify for advisory opinions. Section 1008.11 stated that the OIG would not provide advisory opinions to persons not involved directly in the arrange-

[2] Any individual or entity may submit a request for an advisory opinion. However, we anticipate that most requests will apply to health care business arrangements. Therefore, for purposes of this discussion, we will generally use the term "arrangement" to refer to the factual circumstances about which an advisory opinion is requested, even though we realize that some requests will involve facts not related to a business arrangement.

ment. In addition, Secs. 1008.53 and 1008.55(b) of the rule stated that an advisory opinion would be legally binding on the Department and the requesting party only with respect to the specific conduct of the requesting party; it would not be legally binding with respect to third party conduct, even if such conduct appears similar to the conduct of the initial requestor.

Section 1008.36 of the interim final rule indicated that a request for an advisory opinion must be submitted to the OIG in written form and must present all facts relevant to the subject matter for which the opinion is being requested. Section 1008.37 provided that all parties and potential parties to the arrangement must be Section 1008.38 of the regulations required the requesting party to certify to the truth, correctness, and completeness of all information submitted to the OIG, to the requestor's best knowledge. It also required a requesting party seeking an advisory opinion about a proposed arrangement to certify its good faith intent to enter into the arrangement upon receipt of a favorable advisory opinion.

Section 1008.18 of the interim final rule provided that requestors may contact the OIG directly to inquire about the type and scope of information needed to process their requests, and that the OIG could provide requestors with a list of suggested preliminary questions to aid in formulating their requests. As set forth in § 1008.39, at any time after the preliminary request for an advisory opinion, the OIG may request additional information that the OIG deems necessary to address the advisory opinion request.

2. Fees To Be Charged

In accordance with HIPAA, subpart C of 42 CFR part 1008 of the regulations addressed fees for the cost of advisory opinions. Specifically, § 1008.31 of the regulations stated that the OIG will charge a fee to the requestor (payable to the U.S. Treasury) equal to the costs incurred by the Department in responding to the request. The regulations stated that the fees will factor in the salary, benefits, and overhead costs of attorneys and others who work on analyzing the request and writing the advisory opinion. Because processing fees will vary according to the complexity of the request and the time needed to prepare the response, the rule did not establish specific processing costs in advance. The interim final rule's preamble discussion, however, contains broad estimates of costs and staff time to aid prospective requestors.

3. Responding to the Advisory Opinion Request

Subpart E of the interim final rule addressed the obligations and responsibilities of the OIG in accepting and issuing formal advisory opinions. Section 1008.41 specifically indicated that the OIG would promptly examine the request for an advisory opinion upon receipt and determine whether additional information would be required. The regulations established that within ten (10) working days of receiving the request, the OIG would notify the requestor in writing that (i) it was formally accepting the request, (ii) it was declining to accept the request, or (iii) it needed additional information to process the request.

In accordance with § 1008.43(c) of the rule, once sufficient information is provided to the OIG, the OIG will consult with DoJ and issue an advisory opinion within sixty (60) days after formally accepting the advisory opinion request. Section 1008.45 of the regulations addresses the OIG's right to rescind an advisory opinion after its issuance in limited circumstances.

4. Dissemination of Advisory Opinions

Section 1008.47 of the interim final rule addressed the circumstances under which the OIG may disclose information submitted by requestors, including making copies of issued opinions available for public inspection and on the OIG's Internet web site.[3]

II. Response to Comments and Summary of Revisions

As indicated above, the interim final rule established a 60 day comment period for soliciting relevant public comments on the scope and applicability of the provisions set forth in 42 CFR part 1008. We received a total of twenty (20) timely-filed public comments from various health care associations and organizations and from several State and professional medical societies. The comments included both broad concerns about the issuance of advisory opinions in general and more detailed comments on specific aspects of the advisory opinion process. In addition, based on informal discussions with potential requestors and experience gained in reviewing and processing advisory opinion requests since issuance of the interim final rule, the OIG is using this opportunity to clarify portions of the regulations consistent with the statute and the intent of this procedural rulemaking. Set forth below is a synopsis of the various

[3] http://www.dhhs.gov/progorg/oig

comments received and a summary of the specific revisions and clarifications being made to the regulations in 42 CFR part 1008.

A. General Comments

Comment: Many commenters welcomed the prospect of advisory opinions and expressed general support for the advisory opinion process established by the interim final rule. One commenter indicated that the interim final rule is an attempt "to develop an effective advisory opinion process as a method of bringing clarity to the current Federal fraud and abuse statutory and regulatory system." Another commenter stated that the interim final rule was a "positive step in the right direction." A third commenter, reflecting the view of several, stated that "the best deterrent to fraud and abuse in the health care industry is clear guidance from the Government concerning its view of the applicable requirements."

The general support of these remarks notwithstanding, these commenters and others expressed concerns about the advisory opinion process. Several commenters viewed the regulations as overly restrictive and complex. Commenters stated that the requirements for submitting substantial amounts of supporting information would dissuade parties from seeking advisory opinions. One commenter stated that other agencies rendering advisory opinions have less onerous requirements, citing the DoJ Antitrust Division Procedures for Business Review Letters, 28 CFR 50.6, and the Federal Trade Commission (FTC) Advisory Opinion Procedures, 16 CFR 1.1 through 1.4. This commenter and others believed that the OIG advisory opinion process could be simplified without compromising the OIG's position. One commenter suggested that the requirements, which it perceived as burdensome, reflect the OIG's opposition to issuing advisory opinions during the legislative process.

Response: The OIG intends to carry out Congress' mandate in good faith and to the best of our ability. We are hopeful that an effective advisory opinion program will further the OIG's fraud-fighting mission by aiding requestors in complying with the fraud and abuse laws. Deterring fraud and abuse in the Federal health care programs continues to be an integral part of that mission. For example, the OIG special fraud alerts and model compliance plans are specifically targeted at deterring fraudulent and abusive activities. Consistent with the OIG mission, we endeavored to develop an advisory opinion process that balances the industry's desire for a process that is not overly burdensome with the OIG's need for full and complete disclosure of facts pertaining to the arrangements under review.

Our goal is to render meaningful and informed opinions based on a complete and comprehensive understanding of the relevant facts and circumstances of a given arrangement, protecting in the process only those arrangements that pose little or no risk of fraud or abuse to the Federal health care programs. For complex arrangements, this may require relatively extensive submissions by a requestor. We believe that it is difficult to develop bright line rules for the submission of information uniformly applicable to the wide array of arrangements and sanction authorities that may be the subject of advisory opinions.

The Department is in a unique position among agencies of being compelled by statute to provide advisory opinions that bind the Department and the requestors in criminal, as well as civil, matters. The Department must issue these opinions within a sixty (60) day period, regardless of the complexity of the arrangement in question. Accordingly, the OIG has a heightened need to scrutinize arrangements closely to assure that fraudulent or abusive arrangements are not inappropriately granted protection from sanction.

As we gain experience in issuing advisory opinions, we will continue to look for ways to simplify the process. Presently, we are revising these regulations to provide increased flexibility to respond to the circumstances of individual situations. As described in greater detail below, these changes include, among others, expressly permitting submission of requests by counsel; allowing submission of drafts, models, or narrative descriptions of operative documents for proposed arrangements; providing for informal consultation with requestors to aid the OIG's deliberative process; and providing for notice, an opportunity to respond, and a reasonable unwinding period in the unlikely event of termination of a favorable advisory opinion. In addition, these regulations add a procedure for obtaining initial non-binding fee estimates.

Comment: One commenter recommended that the OIG publish generic standards and criteria by which the "case specific" safe harbors afforded by advisory opinions would be granted. The commenter believed that without the promulgation of such standards and criteria, the advisory opinion process could be viewed as arbitrary and capricious.

Response: These regulations are designed to establish procedures for obtaining advisory opinions that will provide the public with meaningful advice regarding the anti-kickback statutes and other OIG sanction authorities as applied to specific factual situations. The statutory and regulatory safe harbors to the anti-kickback statute describe generalized, hypothetical arrangements that are protected. In contrast, an advisory opinion is a means of relating the anti-kickback statute, as well as other OIG sanction authorities, to the facts of a particular arrangement. There are likely to be factors that make some specific arrangements appropriate for a favorable advisory opinion, even in subject matter areas where a generalized safe harbor may be impractical. Thus, we believe that particularized or "case specific" safe harbor treatment is appropriate where the specific arrangement contains limitations, requirements, or controls that give adequate assurance that Federal health care programs cannot be abused. Our use of the phrase "particularized" or "case specific" safe harbors refers simply to a determination by the OIG, in the exercise of prosecutorial discretion, not to impose sanctions for specific arrangements that may constitute technical violations of OIG authorities.

B. Specific Comments on the Advisory Opinion Process

Section 1008.1, Basis and Purpose

Comment: A number of commenters suggested that requiring a requestor to be a party to the arrangement, or proposed arrangement, that is the subject of a request appears to prevent an attorney from requesting an advisory opinion on behalf of a client.

Response: We recognize that many requesting parties will employ attorneys to assist them in preparing advisory opinion requests. We believe that it is appropriate for an attorney, acting as counsel, to submit an advisory opinion request on behalf of a client, provided that the client is a proper requesting party in all respects under these regulations. This means that the client itself must comply with all requirements for being a proper requesting party under these regulations, including, but not limited to, the requirements under § 1008.36 that the requesting party be specifically identified, and under § 1008.38 that the requesting party provide certain certifications (these certifications must be signed by the client, not by the attorney). Section 1008.1 is being clarified accordingly.

Section 1008.5, Matters Subject to Advisory Opinions

Comment: One commenter requested that we clarify the meaning of the term "authority" as we used it in our preamble to the interim final rule at page 7352. Specifically, the preamble stated:

> "To the extent that the subject matter of the request is the requestor's potential liability under one sanction authority, we believe the request should provide a complete description of the facts addressing the elements of that authority. Under these interim final regulations, if the request asks the OIG to advise on whether an arrangement is subject to sanction under more than one legal authority, we believe the submission should include a complete description of the facts regarding the different sanction authorities in those statutes."

Response: We agree with the commenter that clarification of our use of the term "authority" would be helpful. "Authority," as used in the interim final rule preamble cited above, refers to each separate sanction authority enumerated in sections 1128, 1128A, 1128B of the Act, i.e., each potential ground for exclusion, civil money penalty, or criminal penalty. The section 1128, 1128A, and 1128B sanction authorities cover a wide range of conduct, from kickbacks to false claims to doing business with sanctioned persons. It is unlikely that any one arrangement that is the subject of an advisory opinion would implicate all of the section 1128, 1128A, and 1128B sanction authorities. Because it is most familiar with the circumstances of its arrangement, a requesting party is in the best position, as an initial matter, to identify those authorities that may be implicated in its arrangement and thus expedite processing of its advisory opinion request. Accordingly, when submitting advisory opinion requests, requestors should identify the specific sanction authority or authorities within sections 1128, 1128A, and 1128B of the Act about which they seek an advisory opinion and should describe the facts relevant to each identified authority. Requesting parties may seek an advisory opinion on all sanction authorities they believe may be implicated by their arrangements. However, a blanket designation that a party seeks an advisory opinion on sections 1128, 1128A, and 1128B of the Act, without more specificity, is likely to elicit an OIG request for substantial additional information and delay processing of the advisory opinion. For these same reasons, requestors seeking opinions on compliance with the anti-kickback safe harbors should specify those safe harbors they believe may apply to their arrangements. We have revised the regulations to require designation of the specific sanction authorities about which an advisory opinion has been requested.

Comment: In HIPAA, Congress enacted a new statutory safe harbor to the anti-kickback statute for certain shared-risk arrangements (section 1128B(b)(3)(F) of the Act). This safe harbor is the subject of an on-going negotiated rulemaking process mandated by HIPAA and being conducted under the auspices of the OIG. The goal of the negotiated rulemaking is the promulgation of regulations governing the safe harbor. One commenter expressed the view that the OIG should not withhold advisory opinions on the shared-risk exception pending the outcome of the negotiated rulemaking.

Response: We discern nothing in HIPAA that permits us to decline to give advisory opinions on the shared-risk safe harbor pending the outcome of the negotiated rulemaking and promulgation of applicable regulations. Accordingly, we will opine on the statute as written. Any advisory opinion issued will be binding on the Department and the requesting parties as provided in these regulations. However, favorable and unfavorable advisory opinions issued before the outcome of the rulemaking process may be subject to modification or termination based on the rule eventually promulgated.

Comment: Two commenters believed that the OIG advisory opinions should address the application of the "Stark amendment" under section 1877 of the Act.

Response: Section 4314 of the Balanced Budget Act of 1997, Public Law 105–33, includes a new requirement that the Department issue advisory opinions on the "Stark" provisions. These opinions will be issued by the Health Care Financing Administration (HCFA) in accordance with regulations issued by the Department. To aid in coordinating both advisory opinion processes, we are modifying our regulations to require requesting parties to notify the OIG if they apply to HCFA for a "Stark" opinion on the same arrangement for which they are seeking an OIG advisory opinion.

Section 1008.15, Facts Subject to Advisory Opinions

Comment: Several commenters suggested that trade associations should be permitted to seek advisory opinions on behalf of their members. These commenters assert that such requests would benefit association members who may not have sufficient resources to obtain an advisory opinion independently. One commenter noted that trade association opinions would be particularly valuable for arrangements involving "national issues." Several commenters also suggested that we issue advisory opinions about "model" arrangements that might be duplicated by many individual entities and that we issue non-binding opinions or business guidance to individual parties and trade associations similar to advice provided by the FTC and DoJ on antitrust matters.

Response: Section 205 of HIPAA contemplates advisory opinions regarding arrangements currently existing or proposed by specific, identified requestors. This follows from HIPAA's mandate that advisory opinions be binding on the parties, as well as the Department. It is difficult to discern how an advisory opinion issued to a trade association could be made binding for association members or others who later implement an arrangement described in a trade association request. The same difficulty would arise with respect to parties attempting to duplicate protected "model" arrangements. HIPAA's requirements notwithstanding, it is unlikely that a party could precisely duplicate an approved arrangement; invariably, there would be differences, some of which might be significant. Sanction authorities impose liability based on acts by specific people in particular factual circumstances. Thus, a particular arrangement may be legal with respect to one party, but not with respect to another. We believe that it is impossible to identify all hypothetical factors that might lead to different results.

We will continue, however, to offer other industry guidance in the form of safe harbor regulations and special fraud alerts. As part of the OIG's expanded fraud-fighting efforts, we are actively working to finalize the existing proposed safe harbors, to issue new special fraud alerts, and to consider new safe harbors proposed by the public. In accordance with HIPAA, we will formally solicit public comments annually regarding new proposals for safe harbors and special fraud alerts. However, we welcome written comments from the public at any time regarding these topics or other fraud and abuse concerns.

Section 1008.31, Oig Fees for the Cost of Advisory Opinions

Comment: We received several comments regarding the fee provisions of the regulations. A number of commenters objected to the OIG charging a fee for processing an advisory opinion. These commenters believed that a fee would deter some requesting parties and would impose an undue burden on small companies.

Response: Under section 205 of HIPAA Congress directed that the Department charge a fee equal to the costs incurred by the Department in processing an advisory opinion (42 U.S.C. 1320a-7d(b)(5)(B)(ii)).

Comment: Many commenters believed that the amount of the fee charged for an advisory opinion should be limited. These commenters contend that uncertainty about the ultimate fee to be charged for an opinion will be especially problematic for individuals and small entities. Several commenters suggested that the "triggering dollar amount" provided for in the interim final rule, permitting requestors to designate the maximum fee they are willing to incur, does not adequately address the problem of unlimited fees, although some commenters generally supported the concept and advocated its retention. One commenter observed that once the triggering dollar amount is reached, a requesting party "is faced with the untenable decision of paying the triggering dollar amount and receiving nothing to show for its money, or authorizing the OIG to proceed to process the request regardless of the cost." Many commenters suggested that the solution to this dilemma would be for the OIG to provide a fee estimate based on an initial review of the request. Commenters essentially proposed two types of estimates: (1) an initial estimate, with a cap on the final fee equal to a certain percentage above the original estimate (for example, 110% of the original estimate), or (2) a non-binding estimate combined with continued use of the triggering dollar amount designation, which designation could be amended based on the non-binding estimate. Additionally, four commenters suggested that the OIG adopt a fixed fee schedule similar to the one used by the Internal Revenue Service (IRS) for processing private letter rulings.

Response: In light of our limited experience with the advisory opinion process, at this time we believe that a binding estimate with a percentage cap would be contrary to section 205 of HIPAA, which requires recovery of actual costs incurred. We do not have enough experience to estimate actual costs with sufficient reliability to make such estimates binding. Similarly, it is not possible at this time to develop fee schedules that would reflect actual costs. As the OIG gains experience, we may be able to provide binding estimates or fee schedules; nothing in these regulations precludes us from revising these proposals at a later date if circumstances warrant.

Until such time, we believe that providing an initial, non-binding estimate is reasonable and feasible. Accordingly, we are revising the regulations to provide for a non-binding, good faith estimate, if requested, based on an initial review of an opinion request. This initial estimate will be provided at the time an advisory opinion is accepted. However, we will toll processing of the advisory opinion request from the date of acceptance of the request until the requesting party authorizes us in writing to continue the processing. This tolling will enable requesting parties who find that the estimated fee is more than they wish to spend to withdraw their requests before incurring additional costs. We are retaining the triggering dollar amount designation procedures and providing for revised designations in response to our non-binding fee estimates. We note that fees for advisory opinions issued to date generally have been in the range of $1,500 to $3,000, with several costing considerably less.

Comment: Some commenters believed that not all requestors may be able to afford advisory opinions. One commenter suggested that the OIG use a sliding fee schedule based on after-tax net profits of the requestor. Further, one commenter believed that the $250 deposit was excessive for individuals and small entities making simple requests for which the costs might not total $250, i.e., requesting confirmation of the applicability of an existing opinion to a new participant in the arrangement. Another commenter urged the OIG to notify the requestor prior to processing an advisor opinion if the processing costs are likely to exceed the designated triggering dollar amount to permit requestors who do not wish to pay more than the designated amount to withdraw their requests before incurring costs.

Response: Section 205 of HIPAA contains no financial hardship exception to the mandate that the Department collect a fee equal to the costs incurred by the Department. Even if there were such an exception, the proposal for a sliding scale based on a requestor's after-tax net profits strikes us as impractical to calculate and administer. It is unclear how such a system would apply to individual requestors or non-profit organizations. The $250 initial deposit represents the OIG's reasonable assessment of the minimum processing costs for advisory opinion requests. Every request for an advisory opinion takes time to read and analyze to ensure that the OIG has an accurate understanding of the facts submitted and the application of the fraud statutes to those facts. The OIG must then consult with DoJ and write the actual advisory opinion. Our experience thus far demonstrates that it is unlikely that even the simplest advisory opinions will cost the agency less than $250. Where possible, we will try to notify requestors informally if, as an initial matter, we believe that their designated triggering dollar amounts are likely to be exceeded.

Comment: One commenter suggested that the OIG notify requestors if experts for which costs will be incurred will be required.

Response: Section 1008.33 of the interim final rule provided for notice to requestors, with an estimate of costs, if expert opinions are required. For purposes of clarity, that provision is being moved to § 1008.31(e). We are further revising the rule to clarify that requestors will be responsible for payment of the actual costs of expert opinions and that the expert's work and opinion will be subject to the sole direction of the OIG regardless of the source of payment.

Section 1008.33, Expert Opinions From Outside Sources

Comment: One commenter suggested that requestors should be permitted to review and comment on expert opinions from outside sources, and should be given an opportunity to provide their own expert opinions.

Response: Nothing in the regulations precludes a requestor from submitting an expert opinion if they so desire. In addition, the OIG can solicit a requestor's views on expert opinions if the OIG believes such input would aid its deliberative process. However, we do not believe that it is necessary or cost-efficient to require the OIG to consult with requestors regarding expert opinions in all cases.

Subpart D, Submission of a Formal Request for an Advisory Opinion

Comment: Subpart D of these regulations enumerates the information requestors must submit with their advisory opinion requests. A number of commenters found the requirements of this subpart overly burdensome and likely to dissuade parties from seeking advisory opinions. These commenters expressed the view that the advisory opinion process was not intended as a preliminary enforcement tool by which the OIG could collect large quantities of information about providers and other health care entities.

Response: The procedural requirements set forth in this subpart are intended to ensure that the OIG has a complete record on which to base its advisory opinion, which will bind the Department and the parties. An advisory opinion serves as an individualized safe harbor against criminal and civil penalties; therefore, it is incumbent upon the OIG to conduct a thorough review.

Section 1008.36, Submission of a Request

Comment: Several commenters stated that requesting parties should not be required to provide extensive information about potential participants in an arrangement who are not actual requestors. One commenter expressed the view that the focus of an advisory opinion should be on the factual circumstances of an arrangement, not on the identities of the parties. Additionally, several commenters believed that sometimes it would be impossible or highly impractical to identify all potential participants to an arrangement. According to their concerns, some arrangements might involve hundreds or even thousands of parties. One commenter cited as an example a request involving all network providers in a managed care plan. The commenter explained that there might be practical difficulties in identifying all such providers; moreover, the problem could be further complicated if the roster of providers were subject to change as a direct result of implementation of the arrangement.

Response: We believe that the identity of parties is sometimes important to rendering an informed decision about an arrangement. There may be different implications under the sanction authorities for different parties in similar factual circumstances. For example, the analysis of a proposed joint venture arrangement under the anti-kickback statute may depend on whether or not the proposed investors are potential referral sources or have other business relationships. Furthermore, identification of parties helps the OIG to determine if the arrangement in question or a similar arrangement is the subject of any ongoing investigation or is, or has been, the subject of a governmental proceeding. As stated in § 1008.15 of these regulations, the OIG will not opine on any matters under investigation.

Section 1008.36(b)(1) requires disclosure of participants to the extent known to the requestor. We agree that there may be situations in which it is not possible or practical to identify all potential participants in an arrangement. In many of these select cases, the OIG may be able to render an informed opinion without knowing the identities of all participants. The managed care network described above might be one such case. Another example might be a proposed pricing arrangement affecting hundreds or thousands of potential customers. In these types of circumstances, requesting parties should make clear in their requests the reasons why the identities of all potential participants cannot be provided. If it appears to the OIG that the identities of potential participants are reasonably available, the OIG may decline to process the request or may accept the request subject to the subsequent receipt of the identities of potential participants. An advisory opinion issued in such circumstances will be binding only on the requesting party. The requesting party may not be protected by an advisory opinion if the material facts about the unidentified parties differ from the material facts described in the request. For example, if a requestor seeking an advisory opinion about a pricing arrangement describes potential customers as hospitals and the character of the customers is material, a favorable advisory opinion would not be binding on sales to non-hospital customers. Parties joining an arrangement after issuance of an advisory opinion may seek a separate advisory opinion in their own right.

Comment: Several commenters recommended that requestors be permitted to submit anonymous requests, identifying themselves only when it appeared that the OIG would issue a favorable opinion.

Response: Early identification of requestors helps the OIG determine whether the party making the request is under investigation or is involved in proceedings involving the Department or other governmental agencies that would preclude issuance of an advisory opinion under § 1008.15. By making this determination as early in the process as practicable, the OIG can minimize processing fees incurred by requestors.

Comment: Several commenters objected to the required disclosure of the identities of non-requesting parties. Commenters were concerned that such disclosures could undermine the business and competitive interests of all parties to an arrangement. One commenter explained that non-requesting parties may not want to identify themselves in the early planning stages of a transaction, before they are assured that the proposed transaction passes fraud and abuse muster. This is especially true, according to some commenters, because the anti-kickback statute reaches mere offers of prohibited remuneration. Further, they believe there may also be proprietary business reasons for non-requesting parties to withhold their identities. For example, they may be engaged in preliminary discussions and not want to risk being disadvantaged by competitors who may discover their identity. For these reasons, some commenters believed that the OIG should permit generic descriptions of non-requesting parties to the transaction.

Response: For reasons previously stated, we believe that the identities of parties can be essential to rendering an informed opinion about an arrangement. We recognize that some proposed arrangements may be presented to us at an early stage before all parties are fully committed to participate in the arrangement. For example, a group of surgeons planning an ambulatory surgical center may not have commitments from all prospective investors. Requestors in such circumstances run the risk that the OIG response may be rendered meaningless by subsequent changes in the identities of the parties, i.e., a non-referral source party is replaced in an arrangement by a potential referral source. As set forth in § 1008.53, advisory opinions are operative and binding only for requestors. If parties desire protection, they must be identified as requestors. Non-requesting parties seeking protection after the advisory opinion is issued would need to submit a new request for an advisory opinion.

We are mindful that the risk of disclosures of proprietary information may be troublesome from a business perspective. The OIG is subject to the Freedom of Information Act (FOIA), 5 U.S.C. 552, and the Department's FOIA regulations set forth in 45 CFR part 5. The OIG will endeavor to protect submissions of proprietary information to the extent and in the manner permitted by these authorities.

Comment: Several commenters suggested that the OIG not require requestors to provide complete copies of all operative documents. Instead, these commenters advocated permitting detailed descriptions of such documents. In addition, some commenters noted that operative documents may not be available for proposed arrangements and that requiring their preparation would impose significant costs for arrangements that might never be implemented. Commenters also expressed concerns regarding the potential for disclosure of operative documents under FOIA. One commenter asked that the OIG clarify the meaning of the term "operative documents."

Response: As used in these regulations, "operative documents" broadly encompasses all written documents relevant to the organization or operation of the arrangement in question. These may include, but are not limited to, contracts, leases, lease guarantees, deeds, loan documents (promissory notes, loan agreements, guarantees, mortgages, etc.), employment agreements, court documents and records, settlement agreements, licenses, permits, corporate and partnership organizational documents (articles of incorporation, bylaws, partnership agreements, operating agreements, etc.), and any documents related to these documents. The specific documents required for review of a particular arrangement will depend on the nature of the arrangement.

We are clarifying the regulations to provide that for proposed arrangements, draft or model documents or detailed descriptions of material terms to be contained in such documents may be provided in lieu of operative documents. We caution requestors that material differences between the drafts, models, or descriptions provided and the final operative documents, including changes or omissions, may affect the enforceability of their options. Accordingly, requestors are encouraged to provide full, complete, and accurate information regarding material terms of operative documents for proposed arrangements.

We are further revising these regulations to permit parties to submit initially only those portions of documents relevant to the arrangement at issue. Parties submitting partial documents must clearly identify and describe in general terms those portions that have been withheld. For example, a diversified corporation may elect to submit only those portions of its business plan relating to health care items or services that are the subject of the request. Nothing in these regulations precludes the OIG from subsequently requesting copies of the withheld portions (and from tolling the processing time in accordance with § 1008.39 pending receipt), if the OIG deems those portions necessary in order to render an informed opinion. The ultimate determination of the relevancy of operative documents, or portions thereof, rests in the sole discretion of the OIG.

Comment: One commenter proposed eliminating the requirement that requesting parties provide Medicare and Medicaid provider numbers.

Response: We agree that provider numbers are not necessary in every case. We are eliminating the requirement for submitting these numbers, but reserve the right to request provider numbers, or other identifying information, if we determine that they are necessary in particular circumstances. We have determined, however, that the Debt Collection Improvement Act of 1996 (section 31001 of Public Law 104–134) requires agencies to collect the Taxpayer Identification Number (TIN) from all persons or business entities "doing business with a Federal agency" (see 31 U.S.C. 7701(c)). We believe that requesting, receiving and paying for the OIG's work on an advisory opinion fits into the category of "doing business with a Federal agency." Therefore, a request for an advisory opinion must include the requestor's TIN. The TIN will be used for purposes of collecting and reporting on any delinquent amounts arising out of the requestor's failure to render proper payment for the advisory opinion.

Comment: Five commenters stated that requiring requestors to provide detailed and highly specific information regarding existing or prospective arrangements raises questions about the requesting and non-requesting parties' exposure to sanction in the event of an unfavorable opinion. These commenters considered this potential exposure to be a disincentive to using the advisory opinion process. One commenter explained, for example, that if the OIG determines that an arrangement violates the anti-kickback statute, the requester will have given the OIG much, if not all, of the information necessary to prosecute. This commenter suggested that the OIG adopt a "grace" period to allow parties found to be in violation to terminate or restrict an arrangement without risk of prosecution.

Response: There is an unavoidable risk in submitting a request for an advisory opinion regarding the potential applicability of a criminal statute to an existing arrangement. A thorough and detailed understanding of arrangements about which advisory opinions are sought is necessary for the OIG to render an informed opinion. to the extent the arrangement does not qualify for a "safe harbor" or a favorable advisory opinion, it is subject to scrutiny and potential investigation. Otherwise, we believe unscrupulous parties could use the advisory opinion process to immunize themselves from prosecution. In most instances, however, we believe the risk to be minimal. First, most requests will be about arrangements that are not yet operative. Second, in seeking an advisory opinion, most requesting parties presumably will have reviewed the arrangement and determined that it poses little risk of fraud and abuse to Federal health care programs. Third, the failure to obtain a favorable advisory opinion does not mean that an arrangement is illegal; it means only that the arrangement may pose some risk of fraud and abuse.

As we have observed in the past, the fact that an arrangement does not qualify for a safe harbor or for a favorable advisory opinion does not mean that the anti-kickback statute has been violated or that an enforcement action is appropriate. For example, in an enforcement proceeding, whether an arrangement in fact constitutes a violation of the anti-kickback statute would depend on a showing of requisite intent to solicit, receive, offer, or pay remuneration to induce referrals or business covered by a Federal health care program.

Comment: We indicated in the preamble to the interim final rule that because of the wide diversity of arrangements about which the OIG might be asked to opine, we could not detail in the regulations all of the information a particular requestor would need to submit. Instead, we provided for the use of suggested preliminary questions, which we would provide, and permitted potential requestors to contact us for further guidance about what information to submit. We specifically solicited comments regarding this approach. One commenter agreed that the information necessary to issue an advisory opinion depends on the nature of the request, and that it is not feasible to set hard and fast rules regarding the specific types of information required to issue an advisory opinion.

Response: We are leaving in place the provision regarding the use of the preliminary questions. Moreover, we will continue to permit potential requestors to contact us in writing for guidance on the specific types of information that might be needed for their particular requests.

Section 1008.37, Disclosure of Ownership and Related Information

Comment: One commenter opposed the requirement that requesting parties disclose ownership and related information on the ground that such requirement is burdensome.

Response: We are not persuaded that this requirement is burdensome. The majority of requestors will likely already be providing this information to HCFA through required filings of HCFA form 1513. A copy of a requestor's current HCFA form 1513 will satisfy this requirement.

Section 1008.38, Signed Certifications by the Requestor

Comment: We solicited comments regarding the certification process outlined in the interim final rule. This process requires requesting parties to certify to the truthfulness of their submissions, including their good faith intent to enter into proposed arrangements. Several commenters viewed the certification requirement as an unnecessary and burdensome requirement not contemplated by section 205 of HIPAA. These commenters stated that the certification requirement is unnecessary because the OIG is not bound by an advisory opinion if it later discovers that a requestor did not fully and accurately disclose information. One commenter suggested that we replace the certification requirement with a provision stating that the protection afforded by an advisory opinion would be applicable only to the arrangement as described in the request and only to the extent implemented by the requestor in accordance with the facts represented in the request. Another commenter believed that certifications were unnecessary, because the advisory opinion process itself is a complicated and costly procedure adequate to deter providers from seeking advisory opinions on arrangements that are hypothetical or not under serious consideration.

Response: The required certifications help ensure that the OIG's time and resources are spent addressing real concerns of legitimate requestors. In particular, the requirement that requestors seeking advisory opinions about proposed arrangements certify to a good faith intent to enter into the proposed arrangement safeguards against abuse of the advisory opinion process by requestors seeking opinions about competitor's practices or hypothetical questions. We are not persuaded that our ability to invalidate an opinion upon later discovery of discrepancies in the facts or implementation is a sufficient or efficient means of protecting against improper or inappropriate requests. In addition, we are not convinced that the advisory opinion process is so costly or complex as to thwart misuse of the process.

As a practical matter, our experience suggests that the certification requirement benefits requesting parties as well. The requirement serves as an incentive to requestors to focus on the completeness and accuracy of their presentations and to research thoroughly and document their arrangements before submitting their requests or submitting additional information. We believe that this keeps costs down and expedites issuance of opinions by reducing our need to request clarifications and additional information. Additionally, enhanced diligence should reduce the need for ancillary opinions after issuance of the original advisory opinion when new facts or understandings surface that were not fully investigated or considered by the requestor at the time of the initial request. Consequently, we believe that certifications will help ensure more meaningful and informed opinions.

We are clarifying the certification requirements in § 1008.38 in two ways. First, we are adding a provision, inadvertently omitted from the interim final rule, designating the appropriate signatory on behalf of requestors that are limited liability companies. Second, we are clarifying that each requesting party must provide the required certification. These certifications must be signed by the requesting party, not by its attorney.

Comment: Several commenters objected to the requirement for certification of a good faith intent to enter into an arrangement upon receipt of a favorably advisory opinion. These commenters argue that there may be legitimate business reasons, unrelated to the fraud and abuse determination, that an arrangement is not consummated. For example, seeking an advisory opinion may be part of the parties' initial feasibility determinations. Commenters explained that in the fluid and changing health care marketplace, many legitimate business factors may arise between the time a request is filed and the advisory opinion is issued would cause the parties to abandon their proposed arrangements. One commenter questioned what action the OIG would or could take if an arrangement described in a favorable advisory opinion is not implemented. Several commenters urged that failure to implement an approved arrangement should not subject a requestor to any adverse action or inference.

Response: We continue to believe that requiring a good faith intent to enter into a transaction is a reasonable safeguard against misuse of an advisory opinion process. The certification requirement as set forth in these regulations does not preclude abandonment of a proposed arrangement for legitimate business reasons (i.e., an investor withdraws, financing becomes unavailable) that were not reasonably foreseeable at the time the certification was signed.

Comment: One commentor requested that we revise § 1008.38 to accommodate a change in the individual signing additional certifications if, for example, the requestor hires a new chief executive officer while the advisory opinion is pending.

Response: The person signing certifications on behalf of a requestor should be the person occupying the position listed in § 1008.38(c). We are clarifying this section to make clear that changes of the type described by this commentor are allowed.

Section 1008.40, Withdrawal

Comment: Three commenters suggested that all documents submitted in support of a withdrawal request should be returned to the requestor.

Response: We do not believe that requesting parties have a right to the return of documents voluntarily submitted to the Government.

In particular, there is no right to the return of potential evidence of a violation of law, and the Government would be remiss in returning such information. In addition, it may be necessary to retain submitted materials to document the workings of the advisory opinion process. Nevertheless, although the OIG reserves the right to retain documents submitted by requestors, nothing in these regulations precludes the OIG from returning documents in its discretion to the extent allowed by law. Parties should note that as part of OIG's required consultation with DoJ, copies of requests and related documents may be sent to DoJ. The OIG can make no representation as to return of such documents to DoJ.

Section 1008.41, Oig Acceptance of the Request

Comment: We requested comments on the process for screening requests for advisory opinions. One commenter suggested that instead of screening and rejecting incomplete requests, such requests should be accepted contingent on receipt of the missing information, and the processing time should be tolled until the missing information is submitted. This commenter explained that in the dynamic health care marketplace, all information may not be available at the time of the request. Another commenter maintained that § 1008.41(b)(3), which provides for formally declining a request, is unnecessary and should be deleted.

Response: We disagree that § 1008.41(b)(3) is unnecessary. There may be circumstances in which a request must be declined in accordance with section 205 of HIPAA, for example, where it seeks a determination of fair market value or asks whether a physician is an employee of a hospital for purposes of qualifying for the employee safe harbor to the anti-kickback statute. However, nothing in these regulations precludes the OIG, in appropriate circumstances, from accepting incomplete requests conditionally, and we have done so in practice.

Comment: One commenter suggested that the OIG should provide a written statement of reasons for declining a request.

Response: In order to make the advisory opinion program meaningful, it has generally been our practice to inform requestors of the bases for declining to issue a requested advisory opinion, particularly in situations where the requestor may be able to correct or modify a request so as to make it acceptable. Section 1008.15 sets forth certain circumstances under which advisory opinions will not be issued. We are taking this opportunity to clarify in the rule that the circumstances set forth in § 1008.15 preclude both acceptance and issuance of advisory opinions. In addition, requests will not be accepted if they fall outside the scope of the advisory opinion process, as set forth in § 1008.5, or otherwise fail to satisfy the technical requirements of these regulations.

Section 1008.43, Issuance of a Formal Advisory Opinion

Comment: Several commenters suggested that requestors be given an opportunity to meet with the OIG during processing of requests to answer questions and address any concerns the OIG might have about their arrangements. Commenters proposed that the OIG provide prior notice to requestors if the OIG determines that it is going to issue an unfavorable opinion, thus permitting requestors to withdraw their requests or make changes to their proposed arrangements to address OIG objections.

Response: Our experience with advisory opinions has demonstrated that informal oral consultation with requestors often aids our understanding of the arrangements at issue and better enables us to render meaningful and informed opinions. However, requiring consultation for every request would impose an unwarranted burden on the OIG and, in many cases, serve only to increase costs to requesting parties with no significant benefit to the process. Nothing in these regulations precludes informal consultation, and we intend to continue working with requestors in appropriate circumstances to facilitate the advisory opinion process. During these informal consultations, we may identify concerns that, if not adequately addressed by the requestor before the advisory opinion is issued, may lead us to render an unfavorable opinion. However, it is not our role to structure business arrangements. We believe that parties needing such assistance should seek private business and legal guidance.

We are aware that some requestors may want an opportunity to address the OIG's concerns about their arrangements in a manner that would enable them to structure acceptable arrangements and avoid, where possible, an unfavorable outcome. A formal notification requirement, however, could permit unscrupulous parties to misuse the advisory opinion process to "test" hypothetical arrangements, as well as lead to inefficient use of the OIG's resources. We believe that the informal consultation process described above is a better approach and will more effectively address the concerns of requestors who may want an opportunity to modify their arrangements in response to the OIG's concerns.

While requestors may request informal consultations, we anticipate that we will initiate most consultations when we determine that the requestor's input would be helpful. If there are facts or issues that a requestor wants us to consider, the requestor should bring those facts or issues to our attention (and provide any desired explanation) either in its request for an advisory opinion or, if the facts or issues arise after the initial request, in a supplemental submission of additional information.

Additional material information provided in the course of oral consultations will need to be submitted in writing and certified in accordance with Secs. 1008.38 and 1008.39. For purposes of calculating the time for issuing the opinion, if the additional information substantially changes the arrangement under consideration, the original request will be treated as having been withdrawn and a new request as having been resubmitted as of the date the OIG receives the additional information in writing.

Comment: Several commenters proposed that the OIG be required to explain its analysis and bases for decision in the written advisory opinion, since the analysis and reasoning will serve as useful guidance to the requestors, the Department and the health care industry.

Response: As indicated in the preamble to the interim final rule, advisory opinions will restate the material facts known to the OIG and will discuss the OIG's analysis and conclusions regarding the legal questions to be applied to the facts presented. We believe that § 1008.43, as written, reflects this intent. We iterate that opinions are only binding upon the specific parties to whom they are issued.

Comment: One commenter suggested that changes made to an arrangement to correct aspects deemed objectionable by the OIG in an unfavorable advisory opinion should not require an additional advisory opinion in order to be protected.

Response: We are not persuaded that this suggestion is workable in practice. We are unwilling to rely on a determination by the parties that modifications or changes they have made to their arrangements correct in all respects those aspects to which we objected. Moreover, we could not be certain, without further review, that modifications or changes made to one aspect of an arrangement would not adversely impact some other aspect of the arrangement. We are mindful, however, that requestors want to minimize costs associated with requesting a second opinion. We will make a good faith effort to control costs of a subsequent advisory opinion by avoiding duplication of effort expended on the first advisory opinion to the extent possible. Section 1008.45, Rescission

Comment: The OIG received many responses to its solicitation of comments regarding whether § 1008.45 reasonably balances the Government's need to ensure that advisory opinions are legally correct and the requestor's interest in finality of advisory opinions. Most commenters were concerned that the OIG's authority to rescind advisory opinions defeats the main purpose of obtaining an opinion, which is to ensure that an arrangement will not be subject to sanction under the fraud and abuse statutes. Several commenters urged the OIG to identify a narrower standard to be applied in deciding to rescind an advisory opinion than "in the public interest". These commenters indicated that rescission should be limited to changes in law or material facts. Some commenters objected to using good faith reliance on the request as the standard for enforcement proceedings, suggesting instead that the OIG not proceed against a requestor unless the requestor failed to disclose materially adverse facts. One commenter thought that the OIG should not require parties to unwind transactions unless the OIG had not been provided with all relevant information or the information provided was misleading or inaccurate. If unwinding were to be required, several commenters urged the OIG to permit a reasonable unwinding period during which a requestor would not be subject to sanction. Further, several commenters noted the significant investment of time and money involved in arrangements operating under the protection of advisory opinions. It was suggested that the OIG limit the use of rescinded opinions to putting parties on notice that the OIG has changed its analysis for the future. Another commenter recommended that the OIG's right to rescind an advisory opinion should be limited to one year from the date of the opinion.

Response: In crafting these regulations, we have been mindful of a requestor's significant interest in the finality of an advisory opinion and have endeavored to balance that interest against the government's compelling interest in protecting the integrity of the Federal agencies, including the Federal Trade Commission, the International Trade Commission, the Food and Drug Administration, and the Internal Revenue Service (See, for example, 16 CFR 1.1.3, 19 CFR 211.54(b), 21 CFR 108.5, and 26 CFR 601.201(1).)

Our use of the words "rescind" and "revoke" in § 1008.45 may have led some members of the public to misconstrue the intent of this section. If a requestor has fully and accurately provided all material information regarding an arrangement in its submission to the OIG, its advisory opinion will bind the Department and the parties during the period it is in effect, that is, until it is terminated, if ever. If, on the other hand, the OIG determines that a requestor's submissions did not fully and accurately provide all material information regarding an arrangement, the OIG may rescind the advisory opinion retroactively to the date of issuance. For purposes of clarity, we are substituting the word "terminate" for "revoke" where appropriate in this section, to more clearly distinguish these two concepts. In addition, as discussed below, we are amending § 1008.45 to make clear that in appropriate cases there is a third, intermediate possibility which is modification of an advisory opinion.

Accordingly, for the purposes of part 1008 we are adding definitions in § 1008.45 for the terms "rescind," "terminate," and "modify." To "rescind" an advisory opinion will mean that the advisory opinion is revoked retroactively to the original date of issuance with the result that the advisory opinion will be deemed to have been without force and effect from the original date of issuance. Rescission will be reserved for those situations where a requestor has not fully, completely and accurately disclosed facts to the OIG that it knew, or should have known, were relevant and material to the subject matter of the advisory opinion. (The OIG will make the determination of whether the requestor had this state of mind following an opportunity for the requestor to comment on this issue.)

To "terminate" an advisory opinion will mean that the advisory opinion is revoked as of the termination date and is no longer in force and effect after the termination date. However, the opinion will have been in effect as originally issued from the date of issuance until the date of termination.

To "modify" an advisory opinion will mean that the advisory opinion is amended, altered or limited, and that the advisory opinion continues in full force and effect in modified form thereafter. However, the opinion will have been in effect as originally issued from the date of issuance until the date of modification.

The regulations reserve the right of the OIG to rescind, terminate, or modify an advisory opinion after its issuance solely in circumstances "where the public interest requires." We expect that rescissions, terminations, and modifications of advisory opinions will be rare, occurring only in limited circumstances, such as when the OIG learns after the issuance of the opinion that the arrangement in question may lead to fraud or abuse, and the potential for such fraud or abuse was not foreseeable at the time the advisory opinion was issued. Situations that might lead to termination or modification of an advisory opinion may include the following circumstances—

- changes in the law or the business operations of the health care industry that make it possible for an arrangement that previously carried little risk of fraud or abuse to result in fraud or abuse in the future;
- changes in medical science or technology that render an arrangement subject to the risk of fraud or abuse;
- material changes in the arrangement during the course of its implementation; or,
- the operation of the arrangement in practice differs from what the OIG anticipated based on the advisory opinion request.

The latter two examples reflect the fact that proposed business arrangements sometimes change in unexpected ways during and after their implementation.

Prior to any rescission, termination or modification, the OIG will notify the requesting party that it intends to rescind, terminate, or modify the advisory opinion and afford the requesting party a reasonable opportunity to comment in response. An advisory opinion will only be rescinded, terminated, or modified after appropriate consultation with the requesting party. With respect to modifications, if the party does not agree to modifications proposed by the OIG, or does not itself suggest modifications that satisfy the OIG's concerns, the OIG may instead terminate the advisory opinion under this section. In the event of a determination to rescind, terminate, or modify an advisory opinion under § 1008.45, the OIG will notify the requestor and make such final notice available to the same extent as an advisory opinion.

Except as discussed below, the requestor will not be subject to OIG sanction for actions it took prior to the final notice of termination or modification if the requestor (1) acted in good faith reliance on the advisory opinion, and (2) promptly discontinues such actions upon notification of a termination or promptly modifies such actions upon notification of a modification, as the case may be. We recognize that it may be impracticable to discontinue immediately certain complex business arrangements. Accordingly, except in exceptional circumstances or as otherwise described below, a requestor will be afforded a reasonable opportunity to unwind or otherwise disengage from arrangements subject to terminated advisory opinions, provided that the requestor pursues such unwinding or disengagement promptly, diligently and in good faith. A requestor will be afforded a similar reasonable opportunity to implement modifications to an arrangement that is subject to a modified advisory opinion. During any unwinding period, the protection afforded by the advisory opinion will continue in effect.

We are revising § 1008.45 to provide for a reasonable unwinding period set at the discretion of OIG, after consultation with the requestor, based on the facts and circumstances of the arrangement. For example, the unwinding period for a complex business structure may be a period of years, whereas it may be a much shorter period for a simple compensation arrangement. In determining the duration of the reasonable unwinding or modification period, the OIG will take into account the complexity of the arrangements involved and the impact of unwinding or modification of Federal program beneficiaries. If the OIG determines, however, that the requestor failed to provide material information or provided untruthful information in its submissions to the OIG, the advisory opinion will be deemed to have been without effect from the time is was issued and no unwinding period will be recognized.

Comment: One commenter requested that the OIG return documents submitted in connection with rescinded opinions. This commenter argued that such documents should be exempted from FOIA as pre-decisional documents.

Response: As indicated in our discussion of § 1008.40, we do not believe that requesting parties have a right to the return of documents voluntarily submitted to the Government, especially where those documents are potential evidence of a violation of law. In addition, retention of submitted materials may be necessary to document the workings of the advisory opinion process. However, the OIG may return such documents at its discretion to the extent allowed by law. While certain documents may have been provided to DoJ in the course of our consultations, the OIG has no authority over the return of such documents by DoJ. The OIG is subject to FOIA and intends to release documents if required by FOIA, in accordance with procedures set forth in 45 CFR part 5.

Section 1008.47, Disclosure

Comment: Several commenters stated that the disclosure provisions of § 1008.47 do not comport with congressional intent in enacting the advisory opinion program. Several commenters expressed concern about our statement that we could use information submitted by requestors for "any governmental purpose." One commenter specifically stated that if "any governmental purpose" means that the OIG can use information submitted with requests as a basis for investigation, the OIG should expressly say so and put parties on notice to that effect. These commenters indicated that the risk of information being used for any governmental purpose would inhibit the industry from seeking guidance, and considered the risk of public disclosure of a requestor's identity and of the result of its advisory opinion as a further deterrent. One commenter believed that such disclosure could adversely impact a requestor's stock prices or general competitiveness. Response: Our primary purpose under these regulations is to gather and assess information in order to render informed advisory opinions. However, the anti-kickback statute is a criminal statute, and therefore review of arrangements that potentially implicate the statute requires heightened scrutiny. As a law enforcement agency, the OIG cannot ignore information lawfully obtained to further legitimate governmental purposes.

Comment: Several commenters recommended that the OIG redact names and identifying information from published advisory opinions, as the IRS does with its private letter rulings.

Response: Our current practice is to limit public disclosure of names and identifying information, subject to the requirements of FOIA. Unlike the OIG, the IRS has a specific statutory exception (26 U.S.C. 6110) to FOIA that affords it greater latitude in protecting information from disclosure.

Comment: One commenter requested that the OIG not disclose information without first notifying the requestor and obtaining its consent.

Response: The OIG is subject to FOIA and the Department's FOIA regulations set forth at 45 CFR part 5. These regulations provide that the Department will make reasonable efforts to notify submitters — in this case, the requestors — if the Department determines that material that submitters have designated as exempt from disclosure under exemption 4 to FOIA (trade secrets and confidential commercial or financial information) may have to be disclosed in response to a FOIA request. The regulations at 45 CFR 5.65 provide that submitters of records may designate in writing that all or part of the information contained in such records is exempt from disclosure under exemption 4 at the time they submit such records or within a reasonable time thereafter. Under the Department's FOIA regulations, requestors have an opportunity to respond and, if desired, file a court action to prevent disclosure of exempt records. Requesting parties must specifically identify in their requests for advisory opinions any information they reasonably believe is exempt from disclosure under exemption 4.

These advisory opinion regulations have been amended to incorporate more clearly the requirement for designating trade secrets and confidential commercial or financial information with specificity. Information should be designated in the manner described in 45 CFR 5.65(c) and (d). Parties are encouraged to refrain from designating more information than arguably may be classified as trade secrets or confidential commercial or financial information. Wholesale designations of entire request letters are counterproductive and may make it more difficult for legitimately exempt information to be protected under FOIA. The requestor's assertions about the nature of the information it has submitted are not controlling. Consistent with the OIG's law enforcement responsibilities, we reserve the right to make disclosures other than in response to FOIA requests where the public interest requires, to the extent authorized by law. Unauthorized releases of confidential information would be a criminal violation of 18 U.S.C. 1905 (the Trade Secrets Act).

In addition, although a document may be exempt from disclosure under FOIA, facts reflected in that document may become part of the advisory opinion that the OIG will provide to the public. We will describe the material facts of the arrangement in question in the body of each advisory opinion, which will be made available to the public. To the extent that it may be necessary to reveal specific facts that could be regarded as confidential information, we believe we have the authority to do so under sections 1106(a) and 1128D(b) of the Act. Nevertheless, we do not intend to incorporate any such facts into the body of an advisory opinion unless we believe incorporating such information is necessary in order to render an informed opinion. Moreover, where we intend to incorporate into an advisory opinion information designated by the requesting party as confidential proprietary information, we will endeavor to provide the requesting party with reasonable notice and a reasonable opportunity to respond or withdraw its request.

Section 1008.53, Affected Parties

Comment: One commenter suggested that all parties should be required to consent to a request for an advisory opinion and that the requestor should be required to certify that such consent has been obtained.

Response: The crux of this comment appears to center around a concern that one party to an arrangement may submit information to the OIG without the knowledge or consent of another party who may not want such information disclosed. We believe that this is a matter best handled and resolved between the parties. In addition, for reasons set forth above, we believe that it may be impractical, if not impossible, to obtain consent from all potential parties to certain types of arrangements.

Section 1008.55, Admissibility of Evidence

Comment: While several commenters commended the OIG for prohibiting adverse inferences to be drawn from a party's failure to obtain an advisory opinion, other commenters suggested that we delete or clarify § 1008.55(b), which they found confusing with regard to the prohibition on the use of advisory opinions by third parties. One commenter objected to paragraph (b) of this section because an advisory opinion may be probative evidence as to why someone structured an arrangement in a particular way. The commenter questioned whether the OIG has the power to create evidentiary rules that would be binding on courts or administrative law judges.

Response: We agree that § 1008.55(b) was confusing as originally written. Consistent with our original intent to preclude legal reliance by non-requestors, this section is being revised to read as follows: "An advisory opinion may not be introduced into evidence by a person or entity that was not the requester of the advisory opinion to prove that the person or entity did not violate the provisions of sections 1128, 1128A, or 1128B of the Act or any other law." The Department has the authority to create procedural rules applicable in its tribunals (42 CFR 1005, for example). With respect to other tribunals, the OIG believes it is proper to limit the use of documents created by the OIG for a specific purpose. Consistent with HIPAACs statutory directive that advisory opinions bind only requesting parties and the Department, it is our intention to preclude legal reliance by non-requestors; it follows necessarily that an advisory opinion may not be introduced into evidence by such non-requestors in any tribunal.

Section 1008.59, Range of Advisory Opinion

Comment: One commenter stated that advisory opinions should be binding on DoJ as well. The commenter believed that it would be unfair if DoJ, which must be consulted during the advisory opinion process, could still instigate enforcement proceedings against a requestor that has a favorable advisory opinion from the Department.

Response: Section 205 of HIPAA requires only that advisory opinions be binding on this Department. The Department lacks the authority to bind DoJ through the Department's rulemaking.

III. Additional Technical Changes

- In § 1008.5(b)(1), the phrase "what the" is being changed to "whether" to correct a technical error, and the word "and" is being changed to "or" to be consistent with the statutory directive and our intent that we will not opine on questions of fair market value or bona fide employee status.
- In § 1008.31(c), the phrase "to be" in the first sentence is being deleted to be consistent with the intent of the regulation that the OIG will calculate the actual costs incurred by the Department in responding to an advisory opinion request.
- The phrase "from the time the OIG notifies the requestor" is being added in § 1008.31(d)(4) to be consistent with our original intention that the time period in question commences upon the OIG's notice.
- In § 1008.37, the phrase "will" in the first sentence is being replaced by "must" to be consistent with the mandatory nature of the requirement, and the phrase "or entity" is being inserted to be consistent with the usage of the same term at the beginning of the sentence.
- In § 1008.38(c), the phrase "will" is being replaced by "must" to be consistent with the mandatory nature of the requirement.
- In § 1008.43(a), the word "when" is being replaced by "and" to clarify, consistent with our original intent and practice, that an

advisory opinion is issued when payment is received and the opinion is dated, numbered, and signed.

- In § 1008.43(b) is being revised to provide internal consistency within the section and to be consistent with our intent that advisory opinions will be based on the information provided by requestors.
- The word "next" appearing in § 1008.43(c)(2) has been repositioned to correct a technical error. In § 1008.47(c), the word "in" is being replaced by the word "by" to correct a technical error.
- Section 1008.59 has been revised to reflect more clearly our intent that the OIG will not provide legal opinions on questions or issues regarding authorities vested in other Federal, State, or local government agencies.

IV. Regulatory Impact Analysis

Executive Order 12866

The Office of Management and Budget (OMB) has reviewed this final rule in accordance with the provisions of Executive Order 12866. Executive Order 12866 directs agencies to assess all costs and benefits of available regulatory alternatives and, when rulemaking is necessary, to select regulatory approaches that maximize net benefits (including potential economic, environmental, public health, safety, distributive, and equity effects).

As indicated in our preamble discussions, this rule addresses procedural issues involved in processing requests for advisory opinions submitted to the OIG. It sets up the procedures, as required by Public Law 104–191, for obtaining an advisory opinion on whether or not certain activities violate designated fraud and abuse authorities. This rule does not address the substance of the anti-kickback or other sanction statutes. Nor does it address the substance or content of advisory opinions which may be issued in the future. To the extent that advisory opinions affect the behavior of health care providers, that effect is the product of the substantive content of the sanction statutes themselves and the substantive content of the advisory opinions which will be issued on a case-by-case basis in the future. The effect of advisory opinions on health care providers is not a function of the process for requesting an advisory opinion.

In addition, the extent to which advisory opinions will result in alteration of future business practices, if any, is impossible to analyze without experience. It would be completely speculative to try to divine to what degree business deals may or may not occur as a result of the substance of advisory opinions issued in the future.

Moreover, we have no way of knowing in advance what the volume of requests for advisory opinions will be. However, we estimate that we will receive approximately 100 requests per year that will generally require between 3 and 60 hours each to process. Accordingly, it would likely cost in the range of $30,000 to $600,000 per year to issue advisory opinions.

Regulatory Flexibility Act

Under the Regulatory Flexibility Act (5 U.S.C. 601–612), if a rule has a significant economic effect on a substantial number of small businesses the Secretary must specifically consider the effects of the rule on small business entities and analyze regulatory options that could lessen the impact of the rule. As stated above, this rule does not address the substance of the fraud and abuse statutes or the substance of advisory opinions which may be issued in the future. It describes the process by which an individual or entity may receive an opinion about the application of these statutes to particular business practices. The aggregate economic impact of this rulemaking on small business entities should, therefore, be minimal. There will, however, be costs involved in filing requests for opinions by OIG. Those costs will vary depending on the complexity of the request. Compared to the costs of seeking private legal advice, it would appear that fees charged for the OIG's review will not be substantial. Furthermore, the requirement that applicants pay cost-based fees for advisory opinions is not a product of this rulemaking; it is prescribed by statute. This rule merely lays out the procedures for such costs to be paid. Thus, we have concluded, and the Secretary certifies, that this final rule will not have a significant economic impact on a substantial number of small business entities, and that a regulatory flexibility analysis is not required for this rulemaking.

V. Paperwork Reduction Act

A. Introduction

In order to provide appropriate advisory opinions, the OIG has specified certain information from the parties who request advisory opinions. Under section 3506(c)(2)(A) of the Paperwork Reduction Act of 1995, we are required to solicit public comments and secure final approval from OMB on these information collection requirements. In the interim final regulations published on February 19, 1997, we indicated that Secs. 1008.18, 1008.36(b) and 1008.37 through 1008.40, along with a listing of voluntary preliminary questions, specifically contained information collection requirements that required approval by OMB. As a result, the OIG published a Federal Register notice on March 21, 1997 (62 FR 13621) specifically requesting comments on these information collection activities. The information collection requirements set forth in the interim final rule were subsequently approved by OMB in September, 1997 under control number 0990–0213. OMB also approved a set of preliminary questions which provide guidance as toe what should be included in a request for an advisory opinion.

B. Discussion of Revised Information Collection Requirements

This final rulemaking is now easing or streamlining a number of these information collection activities in response to public comments received on the interim final regulations. Specifically, as indicated in this preamble, we are revising § 1008.36(b), with respect to the submission of a request, to permit parties to submit only those portions of documents relevant to the arrangement at issue, and describe in general terms those portions of the documents that have been withheld. In addition, to avoid a blanket designation when a party seeks an advisory opinion, we have revised § 1008.36(b)(3) to indicate that requestors must give explicit designation of the specific sanction authorities about which an advisory opinion has been requested. Also in § 1008.36, we are eliminating the requirement that requesting parties submit their Medicare and Medicaid provider numbers. We are, however, adding a new paragraph (b)(8) to this section to require, in accordance with the Debt Collection Improvement Act of 1996, that requesting parties include their Taxpayer Identification Number when requesting an advisory opinion.

Further, new Secs. 1008.36(b)(7) and 1008.39(e) are also being added to require requesting parties to notify the OIG if they apply to HCFA for an advisory opinion in accordance with 42 CFR part 411 on the same arrangement for which they are seeking an OIG advisory opinion. We believe that this change will better aid efforts to address and coordinate both the OIG and the HCFA advisory opinion processes.

Finally, we are revising or clarifying certain requirements in § 1008.38(c) concerning who may sign original (and additional) certifications submitted by requestors. Specifically, this revised section now clearly designates the appropriate signatory on behalf of requestors that are limited liability companies, and clarifies that each requesting party, and not its attorney, must provide the required certifications.

C. Proposed Information Collection Activities

The proposed information collection requirement described below will be submitted to the OMB for review and approval, as required by the Paperwork Reduction Act. In accordance with the Paperwork Reduction Act, we are soliciting public comment on the collection of the information in conjunction with section 205 of HIPAA that are contained in this revised final. Interested persons are invited to send comments regarding burden estimates or any aspect of the collection of information, including (1) whether the proposed collection of information is necessary for the proper performance of the functions of the agency, including whether the information will have practical utility; (2) the accuracy of the agency's estimate of the burden of the proposed collection of information; (3) ways to enhance the quality, utility and clarity of the information to be collected; and (4) ways to minimize the burden of the collection of information on respondents, including through the use of automated collection techniques or other forms of information technology.

Type of information collection request: OIG Advisory Opinion Procedures in 42 CFR Part 1008. Section 205 of HIPAA, Public Law 104-191, requires the Department to provide advisory opinions to the public regarding several categories of subject matter, including the requestor's potential liability under sections 1128, 1128A and 1128B of the Social Security Act (the Act). The OIG published interim final regulations in the Federal Register on February 19, 1997 (62 FR 7350), setting forth the procedures under which members of the public may request advisory opinions from the OIG, and a Federal Register notice on March 21, 1997 (62 FR 13621) that contained a more thorough discussion of the information collection activities associated with the advisory opinion process. In order to aid potential requestors and the OIG in providing opinions under this process, a series of preliminary questions that may be answered in an advisory opinion request was developed by the OIG. These preliminary questions remain voluntary. The information collection requirements in the interim final rule and the preliminary questions were approved by OMB under control number 0990-0213.

The aggregate information burden for the information collection requirements contained in these revised final regulations is set forth below.

Respondents: The "respondents" for the collection of information described in the OIG rulemaking will be self-selected individuals and entities that choose to submit request for advisory opinions to the OIG. We anticipate that the respondents will include many types of health care providers, from sole practitioner physicians to large diversified publicly-traded corporations.

Estimated number of respondents: 500. Most individuals and entities that provide medical services that may be paid for by Medicare, Medicaid or Federal health care programs could potentially have questions regarding one of the subject matters about which the OIG will issue advisory opinions. In reality, we believe that the number of requestors will be a small fraction of such providers.

Over the past several years, the Office of the General Counsel, Inspector General Division has answered telephone inquires from individuals and entities seeking informal guidance with respect to the Medicare and State health care programs' anti-kickback statute and other sanction authorities. Many of the inquires related to authorities outside the scope of the advisory opinion process, such as the self-referral provisions of section 1877 of the Act. In addition, we believe that most of the inquiries received have been of a nature that the caller or requestor would be unlikely to request a formal written advisory opinion on the subject matter. Many inquiries related to rather simple and straight-forward matters that could have been researched by private counsel at relatively minor expense. Nevertheless, the rate of telephone inquiries form a starting point for estimating point for estimating the potential number of advisory opinion requests.

We estimate that the OIG received an average of six related telephone inquiries per day over the past several years. Using that history as a general guide and benchmark, we estimate an annual number of 500 respondents. Obviously, the actual number of requests could be larger since, for the first time, formal written opinions are available. Conversely, the number of inquiries could be less based on combination of several unquantifiable reasons, including the desire not to have one's arrangement be subject to scrutiny by the OIG (following issuance of the opinion) and the general public.

Estimated number of responses per respondent: One.

Estimated total annual (hour) burden on respondents: 5,000 hours. We believe that the burden of preparing requests for advisory opinions will vary widely depending upon the differences in the size of the entity making the request and the complexity of the advice sought. We estimate that the average burden for each submitted request for an advisory opinion will be in the range of 2 to 40 hours. We further believe that the burden for most request will be closer to the lower end of this range, with an average burden of approximately 10 hours per respondent.

The OIG is requiring requests for advisory opinions to involve actual or intended fact scenarios. We anticipate that most requests will involve business arrangements into which the requesting party intends to enter. Because the facts will relate to business plans, the requesting party will have collected and analyzed all, or almost all, of the information we will need to collect to review the request. Therefore, in order to request an advisory opinion, in many instances the requestor will simply have need to compile already collected information for our examination. In some cases, the requestor may need to expend a more significant amount of time and cost in preparing a submission related to more complex arrangements that involve a large number of parties or participants.

Estimated annual cost burden on respondents (in addition to the hour burden): $1,000,000. In addition to the hour burden on respondents discussed above, some respondents may incur additional information collection costs related to the purchase of outside professional services, such as attorneys or consultants. We believe that the cost burden related to such outside assistance will vary from zero to 40 hours per request, with an average of 10 hours. At the rate of $200 per hour, this total burden would amount to $1,000,000.

Authority: Section 3506 of the Paperwork Reduction Act of 1995, 44 U.S.C. Chapter 35, as amended.

Interested persons are invited to submit comments regarding this collection of information. Comments on this information collection should refer to the document identifier code OIG-10-F, and should be sent both to: Cynthia Agens Bauer, OS Reports Clearance Officer, Room 503H, Humphrey Building, 200 Independence Avenue, S.W., Washington, D.C. 20201, FAX: (202) 690–6352; and Allison Herron Eydt, OIG Desk Officer, Office of Management and Budget, Room 10235, New Executive Office Building, 725 17th Street, N.W., Washington, D.C. 20053, FAX: (202) 395–6974.

To request more information on the project or to obtain a copy of the information collection plans, please contact the OS Reports Clearance Officer, (202) 690–6207. Written comments should be received by [60 days from date of publication in the Federal Register], but in order to expedite full consideration of any concerns we recommend that comments be submitted as soon as possible within the first 30 days. After due consideration of all timely-filed public comments on these revised information collection activities, we will re-submit these sections to OMB for their approval under the Paperwork Reduction Act. These sections will not become effective until cleared by OMB. In the interim, requestors should rely on the preliminary questions issued by the OIG on which OMB has already granted approval.

List of Subjects in 42 CFR Part 1008

Administrative practice and procedures, Fraud, Grant programs — health, Health facilities, Health professions, Medicaid, Medicare, Penalties.

Accordingly, the interim final rule adding 42 CFR part 1008, which was published at 62 FR 7350 on February 19, 1997, is adopted as a final rule with the following changes:

PART 1008 — [AMENDED]

1. The authority citation for part 1008 continues to read as follows:

Authority: 42 U.S.C. 1320a-7d(b).

2. Section 1008.1 is amended by revising paragraphs (a) and (b) to read as follows:

§ 1008.1 Basis and purpose.

(a) This part contains the specific procedures for the submission of requests by an individual or entity for advisory opinions to, and the issuance of advisory opinions by, the OIG, in consultation with the Department of Justice (DoJ), in accordance with section 1128D(b) of the Social Security Act (Act), 42 U.S.C. 1320a-7d(b). The OIG will issue such advisory opinions based on actual or proposed factual circumstances submitted by the requesting individual or entity, or by counsel on behalf of the requesting individual or entity, provided all other requirements of this part are satisfied (including the requirement that the requesting individual or entity provide the certifications required in accordance with § 1008.38 of this part).

(b) An individual or entity may request an advisory opinion from the OIG regarding any of five specific subject matters described in § 1008.5 of this part.

* * * * *

3. Section 1008.5 is amended by republishing introductory paragraph (b) and by revising paragraph (b)(1) to read as follows:

§ 1008.5 Matters subject to advisory opinions.

* * * * *

(b) Exceptions. The OIG will not address through the advisory opinion process —

(1) What the fair market value will be, or whether fair market value was paid or received, for any goods, services or property; or

* * * * *

4. Section 1008.15 is amended by revising introductory paragraph (c) and paragraph (c)(3) to read as follows:

§ 1008.15 Facts subject to advisory opinions.

* * * * *

(c) Advisory opinion request will not be accepted, and/or opinions will not be issued when —

* * * * *

(3) An informed opinion cannot be made, or could be made only after extensive investigation, clinical study, testing, or collateral inquiry.

5. Section 1008.18 is amended by revising paragraph (b) to read as follows:

§ 1008.18 Preliminary questions suggested for the requesting party.

* * * * *

(b) Questions the OIG suggests that the requestor address may be obtained from the OIG. Requests should be made in writing, specify the subject matter, and be sent to the headquarter offices of the OIG.

* * * * *

6. Section 1008.31 is amended by revising paragraphs (c), (d)(1), (d)(2), (d)(3), and (e)(2); by redesignating paragraphs (d)(2) through (d)(5) as paragraphs (d)(3) through (d)(6) respectively; and by adding a new paragraph (d)(2) to read as follows:

§ 1008.31 OIG fees for the cost of advisory opinions.

* * * * *

(c) Calculation of costs: Prior to the issuance of the advisory opinion, the OIG will calculate the costs incurred by the Department in responding to the request. The calculation will include the costs of salaries and benefits payable to attorneys and others who have worked on the request in question, as well as administrative and supervisory support for such person. The OIG has the exclusive authority to determine the cost of responding to a request for an advisory opinion and such determination is not reviewable or waiveable.

(d) Agreement to pay all costs. (1) By submitting the request for an advisory opinion, the requestor agrees, except as indicated in paragraph (d)(4) of this section, to pay all costs incurred by the OIG in responding to the request for an advisory opinion.

(2) In its request for an advisory opinion, the requestor may request a written estimate of the cost involved in processing the advisory opinion. Within 10 business days of receipt of the request, the OIG will notify in writing of such estimate. Such estimate will not be binding on the Department, and the actual cost to be paid may be higher or lower than estimated. The time period for issuing the advisory opinion will be tolled from the time the OIG notifies the requestor of the estimate until the OIG receives written confirmation from the requestor that the requestor wants the OIG to continue processing the request. Such notice may include a new or revised

triggering dollar amount, as set forth in paragraph (d)(3) of this section.

(3) In its request for an advisory opinion, the requestor may designate a triggering dollar amount. If the OIG estimates that the costs of processing the advisory opinion request have reached, or are likely to exceed, the designated triggering dollar amount, the OIG will notify the requestor. The requestor may revise its designated triggering dollar amount in writing in its response to notification of a cost estimate in accordance with paragraph (d)(2) of this section.

* * * * *

(e) Fees for outside experts. * * *

(2) If the OIG determines that it is necessary to obtain expert advice to issue a requested advisory opinion, the OIG will notify the requestor of that fact and provide the identity of the appropriate expert and an estimate of the costs of the expert advice.

7. Section 1008.33 is amended by revising paragraphs (b) and (c) to read as follows:

§ 1008.33 Expert opinions from outside sources.

* * * * *

(b) The time period for issuing an advisory opinion will be tolled from the time that the OIG notifies the requestor of the need for an outside expert opinion until the time the OIG receives the necessary expert opinion.

(c) Once payment is made for the cost of the expert opinion, as set forth in § 1008.31(e) of this part, either directly to the expert or otherwise, the OIG will arrange for a prompt expert review of the issue or issues in question. Regardless of the manner of payment, the expert's work and opinion will be subject to the sole direction of the OIG.

8. Section 1008.36 is amended by republishing introductory paragraph (b); by revising paragraphs (b)(1), (b)(3), and (b)(4); by deleting existing paragraph (b)(5); by redesignating (b)(6) and (b)(7) as (b)(5) and (b)(6) respectively and revising them; and by adding new paragraphs (b)(7) and (b)(8) to read as follows:

§ 1008.36 Submission of a request.

* * * * *

(b) Each request for an advisory opinion must include —

(1) To the extent known to the requestor, the identities, including the names and addresses, of the requestor and of all other actual and potential parties to the arrangement, that are the subject of the request for an advisory opinion;

* * * * *

(3) A declaration of the subject category or categories as described in § 1008.5 of this part for which the advisory opinion is requested. To the extent an individual or entity requests an advisory opinion in accordance with Secs. 1008.5(a)(3) or (a)(5) of this part, the requesting individual or entity should identify the specific subsections of sections 1128, 1128A or 1128B of the Act or the specific provision of § 1001.952 of this chapter about which an advisory opinion is sought:

(4) A complete and specific description of all relevant information bearing on the arrangement for which an advisory opinion is requested and on the circumstances of the conduct,[1] including —

(i) Background information,

(ii) For existing arrangements, complete copies of all operative documents,

(iii) For proposed arrangements, complete copies of all operative documents, if possible, and otherwise descriptions of proposed terms, drafts, or models of documents sufficient to permit the OIG to render an informed opinion,

(iv) Detailed statements of all collateral or oral understandings, if any, and

(v) If applicable, a designation of trade secrets or confidential commercial or financial information in the manner described in 45 CFR 5.65;

(5) Signed certifications by the requestor(s), as described in § 1008.37 of this part;

(6) A check or money order payable to the Treasury of the United States in the amount of $250, as discussed in § 1008.31(b) of this part;

[1] The requestor is under an affirmative obligation to make full and true disclosure with respect to the facts regarding the advisory opinion being requested.

(7) A declaration regarding whether an advisory opinion in accordance with part 411 of this title has been or will be requested from HCFA about the arrangement that is the subject of the advisory opinion request; and

(8) Each requesting party's Taxpayer Identification Number. (Approved by the Office of Management and Budget under control number 0990–0213)

9. Section 1008.37 is revised to read as follows:

§ 1008.37 Disclosure of ownership and related information.

Each individual or entity requesting an advisory opinion must supply full and complete information as to the identity of each entity owned or controlled by the individual or entity, and of each person with an ownership or control interest in the entity, as defined in section 1124(a)(1) of the Social Security Act (42 U.S.C. 1302a-3(a)(1)) and part 420 of this chapter. (Approved by the Office of Management and Budget under control #0990–0213)

10. Section 1008.38 is amended by revising paragraphs (a) and (b), introductory paragraph (c), paragraphs (c)(2) and (c)(3); and by adding a new paragraph (c)(4) to read as follows:

§ 1008.38 Signed certifications by the requestor.

(a) Every request must include the following signed certification from all requestors: "With knowledge of the penalties for false statements provided by 18 U.S.C. 1001 and with knowledge that this request for an advisory opinion is being submitted to the Department of Health and Human Services, I certify that all of the information provided is true and correct, and constitutes a complete description of the facts regarding which an advisory opinion is sought, to the best of my knowledge and belief."

(b) If the advisory opinion relates to a proposed arrangement, the request must also include the following signed certification from all requestors: "The arrangement described in this request for an advisory opinion is one that [the requestor(s)] in good faith plan(s) to undertake." This statement may be made contingent on a favorable OIG advisory opinion, in which case, the phrase "if the OIG issues a favorable advisory opinion" should be added to the certification.

(c) The certification(s) must be signed by—

* * * * *

(2) The chief executive officer, or comparable officer, of the requestor, if the requestor is a corporation;

(3) The managing partner of the requestor, if the requestor is a partnership; or

(4) The managing member, or comparable person, if the requestor is a limited liability company.

11. Section 1008.39 is amended by revising paragraph (c) and by adding new paragraphs (e) and (f) to read as follows:

§ 1008.38 Additional information.

* * * * *

(c) Additional information should be provided in writing and certified to be a true, correct and complete disclosure of the requested information in a manner equivalent to that described in § 1008.38 of this part.

* * * * *

(e) Requesting parties are required to notify the OIG if they request an advisory opinion in accordance with part 411 of this title from HCFA about the arrangement that is the subject of their advisory opinion request.

(f) Where appropriate, after receipt of an advisory opinion request, the OIG may consult with the requesting parties to the extent the OIG deems necessary.

12. Section 1008.41 is amended by revising paragraph (a); and by republishing introductory paragraph (b) and revising paragraph (b) (3) to read as follows:

§ 1008.41 OIG acceptance of the request.

(a) Upon receipt of a request for an advisory opinion, the OIG will promptly make an initial determination whether the submission includes all of the information the OIG will require to process the request.

(b) Within 10 working days of receipt of the request, the OIG will—

* * * * *

(3) Formally decline to accept the request.

* * * * *

13. Section 1008.43 is amended by revising paragraphs (a), (b) and (c)(2); and by republishing introductory paragraph (c)(3) and revising paragraph (c)(3)(i) to read as follows:

§ 1008.43 Issuance of a formal advisory opinion.

(a) An advisory opinion will be considered issued once payment is received and it is dated, numbered, and signed by an authorized official of the OIG.

(b) An advisory opinion will contain a description of the material facts provided to the OIG with regard to the arrangement for which an advisory opinion has been requested. The advisory opinion will state the OIG's opinion regarding the subject matter of the request based on the facts provided to the OIG. If necessary, to fully describe the arrangement, the OIG is authorized to include in the advisory opinion the material facts of the arrangement, notwithstanding that some of these facts could be considered confidential information or trade secrets within the meaning of 18 U.S.C. 1905.

(c) * * * * *

(2) If the 60th day falls on a Saturday, Sunday, or Federal holiday, the time period will end at the close of the next business day following the weekend or holiday;

(3) The 60 day period will be tolled from the time the OIG —

(i) Notifies the requestor that the costs have reached, or are likely to exceed, the triggering amount until the time when the OIG receives written notice from the requestor to continue processing the request;

* * * * *

14. Section 1008.45 is revised to read as follows:

§ 1008.45 Rescission, termination or modification.

(a) Any advisory opinion given by the OIG is without prejudice to the right of the OIG to reconsider the questions involved and, where the public interest requires, to rescind, terminate or modify the advisory opinion. Requestors will be given a preliminary notice of the OIG's intent to rescind, terminate or modify the opinion, and will be provided a reasonable opportunity to respond. A final notice of rescission, termination or modification will be given to the requestor so that the individual or entity may discontinue or modify, as the case may be, the course of action taken in accordance with the OIG advisory opinion.

(b) For purposes of this part—

(1) To rescind an advisory opinion means that the advisory opinion is revoked retroactively to the original date of issuance with the result that the advisory opinion will be deemed to have been without force and effect from the original date of issuance. Recission may occur only where relevant and material facts were not fully, completely and accurately disclosed to the OIG.

(2) To terminate an advisory opinion means that the advisory opinion is revoked as of the termination date and is no longer in force and effect after the termination date. The OIG will not proceed against the requestor under this part if such action was promptly, diligently, and in good faith discontinued in accordance with reasonable time frames established by the OIG after consultation with the requestor.

(3) To modify an advisory opinion means that the advisory opinion is amended, altered, or limited, and that the advisory opinion continues in full force and effect in modified form thereafter. The OIG will not proceed against the requestor under this part if such action was promptly, diligently, and in good faith modified in accordance with reasonable time frames established by the OIG after consultation with the requestor.

15. Section 1008.47 is amended by revising paragraphs (c) and (d) to read as follows:

§ 1008.47 Disclosure.

* * * * *

(c) Any pre-decisional document, or part of such pre-decisional document, that is prepared by the OIG, DoJ, or any other Department or agency of the United States in connection with an advisory opinion request under the procedures set forth in this part generally will be exempt from disclosure under 5 U.S.C. 552, and will not be made publicly available.

(d) Documents submitted by the requestor to the OIG in connection with a request for an advisory opinion may be available to the public in accordance with 5 U.S.C. 552 through procedures set forth in 45 CFR part 5.

* * * * *

16. Section 1008.55 is amended by revising paragraph (b) to read as follows:

§ 1008.55 Admissibility of evidence.

* * * * *

(b) An advisory opinion may not be introduced into evidence by a person or entity that was not the requestor of the advisory opinion to prove that the person or entity did not violate the provisions of sections 1128, 1128A or 1128B of the Act or any other law.

17. Section 1008.59 is amended by revising paragraph (a) to read as follows:

§ 1008.59 Range of the advisory opinion.

(a) An advisory opinion will state only the OIG's opinion regarding the subject matter of the request. If the arrangement for which an advisory opinion is requested is subject to approval or regulation by any other Federal, State or local government agency, such advisory opinion may not be taken to indicate the OIG's views on the legal or factual issues that may be raised before that agency. The OIG will not provide any legal opinion on questions or issues regarding an authority which is vested in other Federal, State or local government agencies.

* * * * *

Dated: February 6, 1998.

June Gibbs Brown,

Inspector General, Department of Health and Human Services.

Approved: March 24, 1998.

Donna E. Shalala,

Secretary.

[FR Doc. 98–18874 Filed 7–15–98; 8:45 am]

BILLING CODE 4150–04-M

APPENDIX F21

HCFA Proposed Rule: Medicare Program; Medicare Integrity Program, Intermediary and Carrier Functions, and Conflict of Interest Requirements

DEPARTMENT OF HEALTH AND HUMAN SERVICES

Health Care Financing Administration

42 CFR Parts 400 and 421

[HCFA-7020-P]

RIN 0938-AI09

Medicare Program; Medicare Integrity Program, Intermediary and Carrier Functions, and Conflict of Interest Requirements

AGENCY: Health Care Financing Administration (HCFA), HHS.

ACTION: Proposed rule.

SUMMARY: This proposed rule would implement section 1893 of the Social Security Act (the Act) by establishing the Medicare integrity program (MIP) to carry out Medicare program integrity activities that are funded from the Medicare Trust Funds. Section 1893 expands our contracting authority to allow us to contract with "eligible entities" to perform Medicare program integrity activities. These activities include review of provider and supplier activities, including medical, fraud, and utilization review; cost report audits; Medicare secondary payer determinations; education of providers, suppliers, beneficiaries, and other persons regarding payment integrity and benefit quality assurance issues; and developing and updating a list of durable medical equipment items that are subject to prior authorization. This proposed rule would set forth the definition of eligible entities, services to be procured, competitive requirements based on Federal acquisition regulations and exceptions (guidelines for automatic renewal), procedures for identification, evaluation, and resolution of conflicts of interest, and limitations on contractor liability.

In addition, this proposed rule would bring certain sections of the Medicare regulations concerning fiscal intermediaries and carriers into conformity with the Act. The rule would distinguish between those functions that the statute requires be included in agreements with intermediaries and those that may be included in the agreements. It would also provide that some or all of the listed functions may be included in carrier contracts. Currently all these functions are mandatory for carrier contracts. These changes would give us the flexibility to transfer functions from one intermediary or carrier to another or to otherwise limit the functions an intermediary or carrier performs if we determine that to do so would result in more effective and efficient program administration.

DATES: Comments will be considered if we receive them at the appropriate address, as provided below, no later than 5 p.m. on May 19, 1998.

ADDRESSES: Mail written comments (1 original and 3 copies) to the following address: Health Care Financing Administration, Department of Health and Human Services, Attention: HCFA-7020-P, P.O. Box 26676, Baltimore, MD 21207–0519.

If you prefer, you may deliver your written comments (1 original and 3 copies) to one of the following addresses:

Room 309-G, Hubert H. Humphrey Building, 200 Independence Avenue, SW., Washington, DC 20201, or

Room C5–09–26, 7500 Security Boulevard, Baltimore, MD 21244–1850.

Because of staffing and resource limitations, we cannot accept comments by facsimile (FAX) transmission. In commenting, please refer to file code HCFA-7020-P. Comments received timely will be available for public inspection as they are received, generally beginning approximately 3 weeks after publication of a document, in Room 309-G of the Department's offices at 200 Independence Avenue, SW., Washington, DC, on Monday through Friday of each week from 8:30 a.m. to 5 p.m. (phone: (202) 690–7890).

FOR FURTHER INFORMATION CONTACT: Brenda Thew (410) 786–4889.

SUPPLEMENTARY INFORMATION:

I. Background

A. Current Medicare Contracting Environment

The current Medicare contracting authorities have been in place since the inception of the Medicare program in 1965. At that time, the health insurance and medical communities raised concerns that the enactment of Medicare could result in a large Federal presence in the provision of health care. In response, under sections 1816(a) and 1842(a) of the Social Security Act (the Act), Congress provided that public or private entities and agencies may participate in the administration of the Medicare program under agreements or contracts entered into with us.

These Medicare contractors are known as intermediaries (section 1816(a) of the Act) and carriers (section 1842(a) of the Act). With certain exceptions, intermediaries perform bill processing and benefit payment functions for Part A of the program (Hospital Insurance) and carriers perform claims processing and benefit payment functions for Part B of the program (Supplementary Medical Insurance).

(For the following discussion, the terms "provider" and "supplier" are used as those terms are defined in 42 CFR 400.202. That is, a provider is a hospital, rural care primary hospital, skilled nursing facility, home health agency, or a hospice that has in effect an agreement to participate in Medicare, or a clinic, a rehabilitation agency, or a public health agency that has a similar agreement to furnish outpatient physical therapy or speech pathology services. Supplier is defined as a physician or other practitioner or an entity other than a "provider," that furnishes health care services under Medicare.)

Section 1842(a) of the Act authorizes us to contract with private entities (carriers) for the purpose of administering the Medicare Part B program. Medicare carriers determine payment amounts and make payments for services (including items) furnished by physicians and other suppliers such as nonphysician practitioners, laboratories, and durable medical equipment suppliers. In addition, carriers perform other functions required for the efficient and effective administration of the Part B program. Section 1842(f) of the Act provides that a carrier must be a "voluntary association, corporation, partnership, or other nongovernmental entity which is lawfully engaged in providing, paying for, or reimbursing the cost of, health services under group insurance policies or contracts, medical or hospital service agreements, membership or subscription contracts, or similar group arrangements, in consideration of premiums or other periodic charges payable to the carrier, including a health benefits plan duly sponsored or underwritten by an employee entity." No entity may be considered for carrier contracts unless it can demonstrate that it meets this definition of carrier.

Section 1842(b) provides us with the discretion to enter into carrier contracts without regard to any provision of the law requiring competitive bidding. Other provisions of generally applicable Federal contract law and regulations, as well as HHS procurement regulations, remain in effect for carrier contracts.

Section 1816(a) of the Act authorizes us to enter into agreements with private agencies or entities (intermediaries) for the purpose of administering Medicare Part A. These entities are responsible for determining the amount of payment due to providers in consideration of services provided to beneficiaries and for making these payments. We may enter into an agreement with an entity to serve as an intermediary if the entity has first been "nominated" by a group or association of providers to make Medicare payments to it. Other portions of section 1816 of the Act provide further details concerning the "nomination process" and assignment and reassignment of providers to intermediaries.

Our regulations at § 421.100 require that the agreement between us and an intermediary specify the functions the intermediary must perform. In addition to requiring any items specified by us in the agreement that are unique to that intermediary, our regulations require that all intermediaries perform activities relating to determining and making payments for covered Medicare services, fiscal management, provider audits, utilization patterns, resolution of cost report disputes, and reconsideration of determinations. Finally, our regulations require that all intermediaries furnish information and reports, perform certain functions with respect to provider-based home health agencies and provider-based hospices, and comply with all applicable laws and regulations and with any other terms and conditions included in their agreements.

Similarly, § 421.200 of our regulations, requires that the contract between us and a Part B carrier specify the functions the carrier must perform. In addition to requiring any items specified by us in the contract that are unique to that carrier, our regulations require that all Part B carriers perform activities relating to determining and making payments (on a cost or charge basis) for covered Medicare services, fiscal management, provider audits, utilization patterns, and Part B beneficiary hearings. In addition, § 421.200

requires that all carriers furnish information and reports, maintain and make available records, and comply with any other terms and conditions included in their contracts.

It is within the above context that Medicare intermediary and carrier contracts are significantly different from standard Federal Government contracts.

Specifically, the Medicare intermediary and carrier contracts are normally renewed automatically from year to year, in contrast to the typical Government contract that is recompeted at the conclusion of the contract term. Congress, in providing for the nomination process under section 1816 of the Act, and authorizing the automatic renewal of the carrier contracts in section 1842(b)(5) of the Act, contemplated a contracting process that would permit us to noncompetitively renew the Medicare contracts from year to year.

For both intermediaries and carriers, § 421.5 states that we have the authority not to renew a Part A agreement or a Part B contract when it expires. Section 421.126 provides for termination of the intermediary agreements in certain circumstances, and, similarly, § 421.205 provides for termination of carrier contracts.

Each year, Congress appropriates funds to support Medicare contractor activities. These funds are distributed to the contractors through an annual Budget Performance Requirements process, which allocates funds by program activity to each of the current 69 Medicare contractors. Historically, approximately one-half of the funds have been for payment for the processing of claims; one-quarter of the funds have been for "payment safeguard" activities to fund activities such as conducting medical review of claims to determine whether services are medically necessary and constitute an appropriate level of care, deterring and detecting Medicare fraud, auditing provider cost reports, and ensuring that Medicare acts as a secondary payer when a beneficiary has primary coverage through other insurance. The remainder of the funds have been allocated for beneficiary and provider/supplier services and for various productivity investments.

B. The Medicare Integrity Program

The Health Insurance Portability and Accountability Act of 1996 (Public Law 104–191) was enacted on August 21, 1996. Section 202 of Public Law 104–191 adds a new section 1893 to the Act establishing the Medicare integrity program (MIP). This program is funded from the Medicare Hospital Insurance Trust Fund for activities related to both Part A and Part B of Medicare. Specifically, section 1893 of the Act expands our contracting authority to allow us to contract with eligible entities to perform Medicare program integrity activities performed currently by intermediaries and carriers. These activities include medical, fraud, and utilization review; cost report audits; Medicare secondary payer determinations; overpayment recovery; education of providers, suppliers, beneficiaries, and other persons regarding payment integrity and benefit quality assurance issues; and developing and updating a list of durable medical equipment items that, under section 1834(a)(15) of the Act, are subject to prior authorization.

Section 1893(d) of the Act requires us to set forth, through regulations, procedures for entering into contracts for the performance of specific Medicare program integrity activities. These procedures are to include the following:

1. A process for identifying, evaluating, and resolving organizational conflicts of interest that are generally applicable to Federal acquisition and procurement.
2. Competitive procedures for entering into new contracts under section 1893 of the Act, a process for entering into contracts that may result in the elimination of responsibilities of an individual intermediary or carrier, and other procedures we deem appropriate.
3. A process for renewing contracts entered into under section 1893 of the Act.

Section 1893(d) also provides that we may enter into these contracts without publication of final rules.

In addition, section 1893(e) of the Act requires us to set forth, through regulations, the limitation of a contractor's liability for actions taken to carry out a contract.

Congress established section 1893 of the Act to strengthen our ability to deter fraud and abuse in the Medicare program in a number of ways. First, it provides a separate and stable long-term funding mechanism for MIP activities. Historically, Medicare contractor budgets had been subject to wide fluctuations in funding levels from year to year. The variations in funding did not have anything to do with the underlying requirements for program integrity activities. This instability made it difficult for us to invest in innovative strategies to control fraud and abuse. Our contractors also found it difficult to attract, train, and retain qualified professional staff, including auditors and fraud investigators. A dependable funding source allows us the flexibility to invest in innovative strategies to combat fraud and abuse. It will help us shift emphasis from post-payment recoveries on fraudulent claims to prepayment strategies designed to ensure that more claims are paid correctly the first time.

Second, to allow us to more aggressively carry out the MIP functions and to require us to use procedures and technologies that exceed those currently being used, section 1893 greatly expands our contracting authority. Previously, we had a limited pool of entities with whom to contract. This limited our ability to maximize efforts to effectively carry out the MIP functions. Section 1893 now permits us to attract a variety of offerors with potentially new and different skill sets and will allow those offerors to propose innovative approaches to implement MIP to deter fraud and abuse. By using competitive procedures, as established in the FAR, our ability to manage the MIP activities is greatly enhanced, and the Government can seek to obtain the best value for its contracted services.

Third, section 1893 requires us to address potential conflicts of interest among potential MIP contractors before entering into any contracting arrangements with them. By requiring offerors/contractors to report situations that may constitute conflicts of interest, we can minimize the number of situations where there is either an actual or an apparent conflict of interest. This is a concern particularly when intermediaries and carriers processing Medicare claims are also private health insurance companies.

From the inception of the Medicare program, intermediary and carrier contracts have contained provisions that have precluded contractors from using their Medicare contract to benefit their private lines of business. These conflicts of interest were rarely a problem in the early years of Medicare because these companies did only health insurance business within prescribed market areas. In recent years, however, Medicare intermediaries and carriers, like most health insuring organizations, have expanded their businesses and product lines to become large integrated health care delivery systems. Some organizations have diversified into corporations with many subsidiaries and a variety of arrangements. These range from overlapping ownership of other insurers, third party administrators, providers, and managed care entities to the marketing of management services and software products. This creates a conflict of interest when the contractor reviews claims, identifies Medicare secondary payer instances, and performs other payment safeguard activities for its own providers and suppliers as well as for its provider's and supplier's competitors.

We have been criticized for the lack of effective mechanisms to mitigate these conflicts of interest. Even when we are assured that proper mechanisms are in place, the appearance of a conflict remains in the eyes of competitors. An even more difficult problem arises with respect to program integrity activities. Medicare contractors exercise considerable discretion in their audit functions, the use of prepayment screens, the conduct of fraud investigations, and referrals to law enforcement agencies regarding incidences of fraud and abuse. These activities depend upon the ability of the contractor to conduct independent reviews, negotiate disputes, and to manipulate data with great sophistication to discover situations where providers and suppliers are engaged in fraudulent activity. These activities would be largely ineffective if contractor-owned providers and suppliers benefit from bias or forewarning.

When a Medicare contractor owns a provider or supplier, it necessarily finds itself in a situation in which potential conflicts of interest could arise. On the one hand, it has a fiduciary duty to its stockholders to use its best efforts to capture market share and to maximize profits. On the other hand, it has an obligation to Medicare and to the public not to take advantage of its position as a Medicare contractor. For example, the Medicare contractor —

- Has access to information about beneficiaries, providers, and suppliers that would be enormously useful in marketing and other business decisions, including provider/supplier information that is considered "proprietary."
- As the claims administrator for an area, it has extraordinary leverage over providers and suppliers. That leverage could be used, implicitly or explicitly, to persuade providers and suppliers to join a network or to agree to business arrangements that are favorable to the Medicare contractor.
- Has knowledge and experience as a Medicare claims administrator that would give it a competitive advantage in knowing how to submit claims to avoid payment screens and in having other information that is not available to other providers/suppliers that could assist in maximizing payments to its own providers/suppliers.

- May also offer other health insurance coverage that is primary or supplemental to Medicare. In this situation, there is always the temptation to let Medicare pay first, knowing that even if the mistaken Medicare payment is later discovered and reimbursed, the contractor has received a temporary interest free loan from the Government.

The MIP, however, allows us to separate payment safeguard functions from all of the functions now being performed by current intermediaries and carriers. This allows current contractors that are performing important functions such as beneficiary and provider/supplier services well to continue to do so, or possibly to review claims from providers/ suppliers with which they have no financial relationship.

Conflict of interest situations can also occur when Medicare contractors own managed care entities, for example health maintenance organizations (HMOs). The mere ownership of an HMO by a Medicare contractor would seem to create no conflict of interest concerns since the HMO would be dealing directly with the Government. However, in the situation in which a physician both works for a contractor-owned HMO and maintains a fee-for-service practice, the contractor could give the physician a "bonus" by doing a less thorough review of his or her claims. Additionally, the contractor-owned HMO could use its Medicare beneficiary database to perform health screening of beneficiaries, or its utilization data, marketing information, etc. for its commercial benefit. It could also influence the HMO market by promoting itself as the local intermediary or carrier.

Medicare contractors also provide management services and develop software to facilitate the filing of claims and compliance with Medicare requirements. Since Medicare contractors have an intimate knowledge of Medicare claims systems and administration, they may derive an unfair competitive advantage if they were to sell information that is not generally available to the public. They may also shift development and training costs to Medicare for services they market to the public.

For all these reasons this legislation is providing us an opportunity to increase our ability to protect the Medicare program from instances of fraud and abuse by establishing procedures for identifying, evaluating, and resolving organizational conflicts of interest.

II. Provisions of the Proposed Rule

This regulation is part of our overall contracting strategy, which is designed to build on the strengths of the marketplace. We intend to implement the MIP incrementally in a manner that will provide a way to test alternatives and to transition integrity activities to MIP contractors. We are committed to conducting procurements using full and open competition that will provide opportunities for a wide range of contractors to participate in the program. We will continue to encourage new and innovative approaches in the marketplace to protect the Medicare Trust Funds.

A. The Medicare Integrity Program

1. Basis, Scope, and Applicability

In accordance with section 1893 of the Act, this proposed rule would amend part 421 by adding a new subpart D entitled, "Medicare Integrity Program Contractors". This subpart would define the types of entities eligible to become MIP contractors; identify the program integrity functions a MIP contractor may perform; describe procedures for awarding and renewing contracts; establish procedures for identifying, evaluating, and resolving organizational conflicts of interest; prescribe responsibilities; and set forth limitations on MIP contractor liability. The provisions of this subpart supplement the Federal acquisition regulations set forth at 48 CFR chapter 1 and the Department's acquisition regulations at 48 CFR chapter 3. Subpart D would be applicable to entities that seek to compete for or receive award of a contract under section 1893 of the Act including entities that perform functions under this subpart emanating from the processing of claims for individuals entitled to benefits as qualified railroad retirement beneficiaries. We would set forth the basis, scope, and applicability of subpart D in § 421.300.

2. Definition of Eligible Entities

As discussed earlier, under sections 1816(a) and 1842(a) of the Act, public or private entities and agencies (Medicare intermediaries and carriers) participate in the administration of the Medicare program under agreements or contracts entered into with us (on the Secretary's behalf). Basically, the carrier must be a voluntary association, corporation, partnership, or other nongovernmental entity lawfully engaged in providing or paying for health services under group insurance policies or contracts, medical or hospital service agreements, membership or subscription contracts, or similar group arrangements. In general, the intermediary must be an entity that has an agreement with us and has been nominated by a provider to determine and make Medicare Part A payments and to perform other related functions. Current regulations at §§ 421.110 and 421.202 specify the eligibility requirements current Medicare contractors must meet before entering into or renewing an agreement or contract.

In accordance with section 1893(c) of the Act, proposed § 421.302 would provide that an entity is eligible to enter into a MIP contract if, in general, it demonstrates the capability to perform MIP contractor functions; it agrees to cooperate with the Office of Inspector General (OIG), the Attorney General, and other law enforcement agencies in the investigation and deterrence of fraud and abuse of the Medicare program, including making referrals; it complies with the conflict of interest standards in 48 CFR Chapters 1 and 3 and is not excluded under the conflict of interest provisions established by this rule; and it meets other requirements that we may impose. Also, in accordance with the undesignated paragraph following section 1893(c)(4) of the Act, we would specify that Medicare carriers are deemed to be eligible to perform the activity of developing and periodically updating a list of durable medical equipment items that are subject to prior authorization.

Note that, in accordance with section 1893(d) of the Act, we may continue to contract, for the performance of MIP activities, with intermediaries and carriers that had a contract with us on August 21, 1996 (the effective date of enactment of Public Law 104–191). However, in accordance with section 1816(l) or section 1842(c)(6) of the Act (both added by Public Law 104–191), they may not duplicate activities under both an intermediary agreement or carrier contract and a MIP contract, with one excepted activity. The exception permits a carrier to develop and update a list of items of durable medical equipment that are subject to prior authorization both under the MIP contract and its contract under section 1842 of the Act.

3. Definition of MIP Contractor

We propose to define "Medicare integrity program contractor," at § 400.202 (Definitions specific to Medicare), as an entity that has a contract with us under section 1893 of the Act to perform program integrity activities.

4. Services to be Procured

A MIP contractor may perform some or all of the MIP activities performed currently by intermediaries and carriers. Section 421.304 would state that the contract between HCFA and a MIP contractor specifies the functions the contractor performs. In accordance with section 1893(b) of the Act, proposed § 421.304 identifies the following as MIP activities.

a. Medical, utilization, and fraud review. Medical and utilization review includes the processes necessary to ensure both the appropriate utilization of services and that services meet the professionally recognized standards of care. These processes include review of claims, medical records, and medical necessity documentation and analysis of patterns of utilization to identify inappropriate utilization of services. This would include reviewing the activities of providers/suppliers and other individuals and entities (including health maintenance organizations, competitive medical plans, and health care prepayment plans). This function results in the identification of overpayments, prepayment denials, recommendations for changes in national coverage policy, changes in local medical review policies and payment screens, referrals for fraud and abuse, and the identification of the education needs of beneficiaries, providers, and suppliers.

Fraud review includes fraud prevention initiatives, responding to external customer complaints of alleged fraud, the development of strategies to detect potentially fraudulent activities that may result in improper Medicare payment, and the identification and development of fraud cases for referral to law enforcement. Each solicitation will specify when cases should be referred to the OIG. In general, however, identified overpayments exceeding a threshold amount set by the OIG, recurring acts of improper billing, and substantiated allegations of fraudulent activity will be promptly referred to a Regional Office of Investigation.

b. Cost report audits. Providers and managed care plans receiving Medicare payments are subject to audit for all payments applicable to services furnished to beneficiaries. The audit ensures that proper payments are made for covered services, provides verified financial information for making a final determination of allowable costs, identifies potential instances of fraud and abuse, and ensures the completion of special projects.

This functional area includes the receipt, processing, and settlement of cost reports based on reasonable costs, prospective payment, or any other basis, and the establishment or adjustment of the interim payment rate using cost report or other information.

c. Medicare secondary payer activities. The Medicare secondary payer function is a process developed as a payment safeguard to protect the Medicare program against mistaken primary payments. The focus of this process is to ensure that the Medicare program pays only to the extent required by statute. Entities under a MIP contract that includes Medicare secondary payer functions would be responsible for identifying Medicare secondary payer situations and/or pursuing recovery of mistaken payments from the appropriate entity or individual, depending on the specifics of the contract.

This functional area includes the processes performed to identify beneficiaries for whom there is coverage which is primary to Medicare. Through these processes, information may be acquired for subsequent use in beneficiary claims adjudication, recovery, and litigation.

d. Education. This functional area includes educating beneficiaries, providers, suppliers, and other individuals regarding payment integrity and benefit quality assurance issues.

e. Developing prior authorization lists. This functional area includes developing and periodically updating a list of durable medical equipment items that, in accordance with section 1834(a)(15) of the Act, are subject to prior authorization. Section 1834(a)(15) requires prior authorization to be performed on the following items of durable medical equipment: Items identified as subject to unnecessary utilization; items supplied by suppliers that have had a substantial number of claims denied under section 1862(a)(1) of the Act as not reasonable or necessary or for whom a pattern of overutilization has been identified; or a customized item if the beneficiary or supplier has requested an advance determination. Prior authorization is a determination that an item of durable medical equipment is covered prior to when the equipment is delivered to the Medicare beneficiary.

Application of MIP — It should be noted that the MIP functions are not limited to services furnished under fee-for-service payment methodologies. MIP functions are applicable to all types of claims. They are also applicable to all types of payment systems including, but not limited to, managed care and demonstration projects. 5. Competitive Requirements

We would specify, in § 421.306(a), that MIP contracts will be awarded in accordance with 48 CFR chapters 1 and 3, 42 CFR part 421 subpart D, and all other applicable laws and regulations. Further, in accordance with section 1893(d)(2) of the Act, we would specify that the procedures set forth in these authorities will be used: (1) When entering into new contracts; (2) when entering into contracts that may result in the elimination of responsibilities of an individual intermediary or carrier; and (3) at any other time we consider appropriate.

In proposed section 421.306(b), we would establish an exception to competition which allows a successor in interest to an intermediary agreement or carrier contract to be awarded a contract for MIP functions without competition, if its predecessor performed program integrity functions under the transferred agreement or contract and the resources, including personnel, which were involved in performing those functions, were transferred to the successor.

This proposal is made in anticipation that some intermediaries and carriers may engage in transactions under which the recognition of a successor in interest by means of a novation agreement may be appropriate, and the resources involved in the intermediary's or carrier's MIP activities are transferred along with its other Medicare-related resources to the successor in interest. For example, the intermediary or carrier may undergo a corporate reorganization under which the corporation's Medicare business is transferred entirely to a new subsidiary corporation. When all of a contractor's resources or the entire portion of the resources involved in performing a contract are transferred to a third party, HCFA may recognize the third party as the successor in interest to the contract through approval of a novation agreement. See 48 CFR 42.12.

If the intermediary or carrier were performing MIP activities under its contract on August 21, 1996, the date of the enactment of the MIP legislation, the statute permits HCFA to continue to contract with the intermediary or carrier for the performance of those activities without using competitive procedures. In the context of a corporate reorganization, under which all of the resources involved in performing the contract, including those involved in performing MIP activities, are transferred to a successor in interest, HCFA may determine that breaking out the MIP activities and competing them separately would not be in the best interest of the government.

Inherent in the requirement of section 1893(d) of the Act that the Secretary establish competitive procedures to be used when entering into contracts for MIP functions is the authority to establish exceptions to those procedures. See 48 CFR 6.3. Moreover, intermediary agreements and carrier contracts have, by statute, been noncompetitively awarded under sections 1816(a) and 1842(b)(1) of the Act. Furthermore, those agreements and contracts have in recent years prior to the enactment of the MIP legislation included program integrity activities, a fact that the Congress acknowledged in section 1893(d)(2) of the Act. We believe that creating an exception to the use of competition for cases in which the same resources, including the same personnel, continue to be used by a third party as successor in interest to an intermediary agreement or carrier contract is consistent with Congress' authorization to forgo competition when the contracting entity was carrying out the MIP functions on the date of enactment of the MIP legislation. Section 421.306(b) would provide an interim solution to permit continuity in the performance of the MIP functions until such time as we are prepared to procure MIP functions on the basis of full and open competition.

We would further specify, in § 421.306(c), that an entity must meet the eligibility requirements established in proposed § 421.302 to be eligible to be awarded a MIP contract.

We would state, in § 421.308(a), that we specify an initial contract term in the MIP contract and that contracts may contain renewal clauses. Contract renewal provides a mutual benefit to both parties. Renewing a contract, when appropriate, results in continuity both for us and the contractor and is in the best interest of the Medicare program. The benefits are realized through early communication of our intention whether to renew a contract, which permits both parties to plan for any necessary changes in the event of nonrenewal. Furthermore, as a prudent administrator of the Medicare program, we must ensure that we have sufficient time to transfer the MIP functions should a reassignment of the functions be necessary (either because the contractor has given notice of its intent to nonrenew or because we have determined that reassignment is in the best interest of the Medicare program). Therefore, in § 421.308 (a), we would specify that we may renew a MIP contract, as we determine appropriate, by giving the contractor notice, within timeframes specified in the contract, of our intention to do so. (The solicitation document that resulted in the contract will contain further details regarding this provision.)

Based on section 1893(d)(3) of the Act, we would specify, in paragraph (b) of § 421.308, that we may renew a MIP contract without competition if the contractor continues to meet all the requirements of proposed subpart D of part 421, the contractor meets or exceeds all performance standards and requirements in the contract, and it is in the best interest of the Government.

We would provide, at § 421.308(c), that, if we do not renew the contract, the contract will end in accordance with its terms, and the contractor does not have a right to a hearing or judicial review regarding the nonrenewal. This is consistent with our longstanding policy with regard to intermediary and carrier contracts. 6. Conflict of Interest Rules

This proposed rule would establish the process for identifying, evaluating, and resolving conflicts of interest as required by section 1893(d)(1) of the Act. The process has been designed to ensure that the more diversified business arrangements of potential contractors do not inhibit competition between providers/suppliers or in other types of businesses related to the insurance industry or have the potential for harming Government interests.

On December 6, 1996, we held an open forum discussion with certain organizations and groups that may, or whose members may, be directly affected by contracts awarded to perform functions under the MIP. During the forum, participants discussed whether certain examples were conflicts of interest and how the conflicts, when present, could be mitigated. In addition, the conflict of interest situations were made available for public review on our Internet home page.

In general, some of the participants had concerns that a MIP contractor could not perform audit or review functions on itself, its subsidiaries, its direct competitors, or its private sector clients without the presence of a potential conflict of interest. The conflicts of interest described could make it impossible for contractor personnel to be objective in performing contract work or to provide impartial assistance or advice to the Government or could give the contractor an unfair competitive advantage.

Some of the participants recommended that the conflict of interest standards we establish restrict a MIP contractor from having an ownership interest or contractual relationship with any provider it will be auditing or reviewing. Also, the participants generally agreed that requirements dictating disclosure of a contractor's financial interests would help mitigate conflicts of interest and that each contractor's situation should be considered on a case-by-case basis.

In developing the conflict of interest requirements, we had several options. We could refuse to contract with any entity if a conflict of interest situation either exists or is perceived to exist, or we could choose not to contract with any health-care related entities. We could try to develop a list of all potential situations where a conflict of interest could possibly arise.

We rejected all of these options and adopted a "process approach." While the process described below employs a greater test than generally prescribed in the Federal acquisition regulations for conflict of interest situations, we believe that the sensitive nature of the work to be performed under the contract, the need to preserve the public trust, and the history of fraud and abuse in the Medicare program merits these further requirements. The emphasis on process requires —

- Disclosure by the offeror or contractor via an Organizational Conflicts of Interest Certificate;
- The offeror or contractor to submit a plan to mitigate situations that could be considered potential conflicts of interest;
- The offeror to describe a program that it will establish, if awarded the contract, to monitor its compliance with any plans approved by us to resolve conflicts of interest; and
- The offeror to describe plans to have a compliance audit completed by an independent auditor.

Specifically, in § 421.310(b), we would state the general rule that, except as provided in § 421.310(d), we do not enter into a MIP contract with an offeror or contractor that we have determined has, or has the potential for, an unresolved organizational conflict of interest. Paragraph (d) of § 421.310 would provide that we may contract with an offeror or contractor that has an unresolved conflict if we determine that it is in the best interest of the Government to do so. We would define "organizational conflict of interest," at § 421.310(a), basing our definition on the definition of that term contained in the FAR at 48 CFR 9.501(d). That definition states that organizational conflict of interest means "that because of other activities or relationships with other persons, a person is unable or potentially unable to render impartial assistance or advice to the Government, or the person's objectivity in performing the contract work is or might be otherwise impaired, or a person has an unfair competitive advantage." To clarify how this definition would apply to the MIP contract, we would add that, for purposes of the MIP contract, the activities and relationships described include those of the offeror or contractor itself and other business related to it and those of its officers, directors (including medical directors), managers, and subcontractors.

In paragraph (c) of § 421.310, we would state that we determine that an offeror or contractor has an organizational conflict of interest, or a potential for the conflict exists, if the offeror or contractor either is, or has a present, or known future, direct or indirect financial relationship with, an entity we describe in § 421.310(c)(3), which is discussed later in this preamble. In paragraph (a) of § 421.310, we would define "financial relationship" as (1) a direct or indirect ownership or investment interest (including an option or nonvested interest) in any entity that exists through equity, debt, or other means and includes any indirect ownership or investment interest no matter how many levels removed from a direct interest, or (2) a compensation arrangement with an entity. This definition is similar to the definition at § 411.351, which is used for purposes of the provision which generally prohibits physicians from making referrals for Medicare services to entities with which the physician or a member of the physician's immediate family has a financial relationship. The definition at § 411.351 was based on section 1877(a)(2) of the Act as it read before January 1, 1995. To reflect the current reading of section 1877(a)(2), we have added, in our proposed definition, that an indirect interest can exist through multiple levels.

In paragraph (c)(2) of § 421.310, we would specify that a financial relationship may exist either through an offeror's or contractor's parent companies, subsidiaries, affiliates, subcontractors, or current clients. We would also specify that a financial relationship may exist from the activities and relationships of the officers, directors (including medical directors), or managers of the offeror or contractor and may be either direct or indirect. We would define an indirect financial relationship as an ownership or investment interest that is held in the name of another but provides benefits to the officer, director, or manager.

In § 421.310(c)(3), we would provide that an offeror or contractor has a conflict of interest, or a potential conflict of interest, if it is, or has a present or known future financial relationship with, an entity that—

- Provides, insures, or pays for health benefits, with the exception of health plans provided as the entity's employee fringe benefit;

- Conducts audits of health benefit payments or cost reports;
- Conducts statistical analysis of health benefit utilization;
- Would review or does review, under the contract, Medicare services furnished by a provider or supplier that is a direct competitor of the offeror or contractor;
- Prepared work or is under contract to prepare work that would be reviewed under the MIP contract; or
- Is affiliated, as that term is explained in 48 CFR 19.101, with a provider or supplier to be reviewed under the MIP contract. (Section 19.101 of 48 CFR states that—

> * * * business concerns are affiliates of each other if, directly or indirectly, either one controls or has the power to control the other, or another concern controls or has the power to control both. In determining whether affiliation exists, consideration is given to all appropriate factors including common ownership, common management, and contractual relationships; provided, that restraints imposed by a franchise agreement are not considered in determining whether the franchisor controls or has the power to control the franchisee, if the franchisee has the right to profit from its effort, commensurate with ownership, and bears the risk of loss of failure. Any business entity may be found to be an affiliate, whether or not it is organized for profit or located inside the United States.

Section 19.101 explains that control may exist through stock ownership, stock options, convertible debentures, voting trusts, common management, and contractual relationships.)

We would be interested in receiving comments as to how we might better identify those situations that create a conflict of interest. For example, we had originally considered including all entities that provide, insure, or pay for health benefits. We have, however, identified the situation in which an offeror or contractor provides health benefits as an employee fringe benefit as being one where the likelihood of a conflict would not exist. We would be interested in receiving comments as to whether it would be appropriate to create other exceptions.

In § 421.310(c)(4), we would specify that we may determine that an offeror or contractor has an organizational conflict of interest, or the potential for one exists, based on apparent organizational conflicts of interest or on other contracts and grants with the Federal Government. We would provide that an apparent conflict of interest exists if a prudent business person has cause to believe that the offeror or contractor would have a conflict of interest in performing the requirements of the MIP contract. We would further provide that no inappropriate action by the offeror or contractor is necessary for an apparent conflict to exist. We believe it is necessary to consider the offeror's or contractor's other contracts and grants with the Federal Government to determine whether the offeror's or contractor's financial dependence upon the Government could influence the likelihood that it would provide unbiased opinions, conclusions, and work products.

In paragraph (e) of § 421.310, we would specify that an offeror or contractor is responsible for determining whether an organizational conflict of interest exists in any of its proposed or actual subcontractors and consultants at any tier. We also would specify that the offeror or contractor is responsible for ensuring that its subcontractors and consultants have mitigated any conflicts or potential conflicts.

In paragraph (f) of § 421.310, we would state that we consider that a conflict of interest has occurred if, during the term of the contract, the contractor received any fee, compensation, gift, payment of expenses, or any other thing of value from an entity that is reviewed, audited, investigated, or contacted during the normal course of performing activities under the MIP contract. We have considered creating an exception for those compensations, fees, gifts, and other things of value that are in an amount that would not affect a contractor's impartiality or objectivity in carrying out its responsibilities under the MIP contract. We would be interested in receiving comments suggesting how we might determine an appropriate dollar amount for such an exception.

We would also specify in paragraph (f) of § 421.310 that a conflict of interest has occurred during the term of the contract if we determine that the contractor's activities are creating a conflict. In addition, we would specify that, if we determine that a conflict of interest exists, among other actions, we may, as we deem appropriate—

- Not renew the contract for an additional term;
- Modify the contract; or
- Terminate the contract.

In § 421.312(a), we would specify that offerors and MIP contractors must submit an Organizational Conflicts of Interest Certificate that contains the following information unless it has otherwise been provided in the proposal, in which case it must be referenced:

- A description of all business or contractual relationships or activities that may be viewed by a prudent business person as a conflict of interest.
- A description of the methods the offeror or contractor will apply to mitigate any situation listed in the Certificate that could be identified as a conflict of interest.
- A description of the offeror' s or contractor's program to monitor its compliance and the compliance of its proposed and actual subcontractors and consultants with the conflict of interest requirements as identified in the relevant solicitation.
- A description of the offeror' s or contractor's plans to contract for a compliance audit to be conducted by an independent auditor would be required for all MIP contractor procurements.
- An affirmation, using language that we may prescribe, signed by an official authorized to bind the offeror or contractor, that the offeror or contractor understands that we may consider any deception or omission in the Certificate grounds for nonconsideration for contract award in the procurement process, termination of the contract, or other contract action.
- Corporate and organizational structure.
- Financial interests in other entities, including the following:
  + Percentage of ownership in any other entity.
  + Income generated from other sources.
  + A list of current or known future contracts or arrangements, regardless of size, with any insurance organization; subcontractor of an insurance organization; or providers or suppliers furnishing services for which payment may be made under the Medicare program. This information is to include the dollar amount of the contracts or arrangements, the type of work performed, and the period of performance.
- Information regarding potential conflicts of interest and financial information regarding certain contracts for all of the offeror's or contractor's officers, directors (including medical directors), and managers who would be or are involved in the performance of the MIP contract. We may also require officers, directors (including medical directors) and managers to provide financial information regarding their ownership in other entities and their income from other sources.

We would also specify that the solicitation may require more detailed information than identified above. Our proposed provisions do not describe all of the information that may be required, or the level of detail that would be required, because we wish to have the flexibility to tailor the disclosure requirements to each specific procurement.

With regard to ownership, we invite public comments to establish the level of financial interest that could be considered a material interest in different situations. While we would not establish this level in the final rule, it may be included in solicitations for specific contract situations.

We intend to reduce the reporting and recordkeeping requirements as much as is feasible, while taking into consideration our need to have assurance that a conflict of interest does not exist in the MIP contractors. By providing documentation of potential conflicts of interest and how the offeror plans to mitigate those conflicts in the Certificate, the offeror gives us enough information to determine on a case-by-case basis if conflicts of interest have been adequately mitigated or should preclude award of MIP contracts. The burden associated with providing the requested information is justified by the large expansion of competition the process allows.

We propose, in § 421.312(b) that the Organizational Conflicts of Interest Certificate be disclosed —

- With the offeror's proposal;
- When the HCFA Contracting Officer requests a revision in the Certificate;
- As part of a compliance audit by the independent auditor; Forty-five days before any change in the information submitted on the Certificate. In this case, only changed information must be submitted.

We would state, in § 421.312(c), that we evaluate organizational conflicts of interest and potential conflicts using the information provided in the Certificate.

Because potential offerors may have questions about whether information submitted in response to a solicitation, including the Organizational Conflicts of Interest Certificate, may be redisclosed under the Freedom of Information Act, we provide the following information.

To the extent that a proposal containing the Organizational Conflicts of Interest Certificate is submitted to us as a requirement of a competitive solicitation under 41 U.S.C. Chapter 4, Subchapter IV, we will withhold the proposal when requested under the Freedom of Information Act. This withholding is based upon 41 U.S.C. § 253b (m). However, there is one exception to this policy. It involves any proposal that is set forth or incorporated by reference in the contract awarded to the proposing bidder. Such a proposal may not receive categorical protection. Rather, we will withhold, under 5 U.S.C. 552 (b)(4), information within the proposal (and Certificate) that is required to be submitted that constitutes trade secrets or commercial or financial information that is privileged or confidential provided the criteria established by National Parks & Conservation Association v. Morton, 498 F.2d 765 (D.C. Cir 1974), as applicable, are met. For any such proposal, we will follow pre-disclosure notification procedures set forth at 45 CFR 5.65(d). In addition, we will protect under 5 U.S.C. 552(b)(6) any information within the Certificate that is of a highly sensitive personal nature.

Any proposal containing the Organizational Conflicts of Interest Certificate submitted to us under an authority other than 41 U.S.C. Chapter 4, Subchapter IV, and any Certificate or information submitted independent of a proposal will be evaluated solely on the criteria established by National Parks & Conservation Association v. Morton and other appropriate authorities to determine if the proposal or Certificate in whole or in part contains trade secrets or commercial or financial information that is privileged or confidential and protected from disclosure under 5 U.S.C. 552(b)(4). Again, for any such proposal or Certificate, we will follow pre-disclosure notification procedures set forth at 45 CFR 5.65(d) and will also invoke 5 U.S.C. 552(b)(6) to protect information that is of a highly sensitive personal nature.

We already protect information we receive in the contracting process. However, to allay any fears potential offerors might have about disclosure, we propose to provide, at § 421.312(d), that we protect disclosed proprietary information as allowed under the Freedom of Information Act and that we require signed statements from our personnel with access to proprietary information that prohibit personal use during the procurement process and term of the contract.

In proposed § 421.314, we describe how conflicts of interest are resolved. We specify that we establish a Conflicts of Interest Review Board to resolve conflicts of interest and that we determine when the Board is convened. We would define resolution of an organizational conflict of interest as a determination that—

- The conflict has been mitigated;
- The conflict precludes award of a contract to the offeror;
- The conflict requires that we modify an existing contract;

- The conflict requires that we terminate an existing contract; or
- It is in the best interest of the Government to contract with the offeror or contractor even though the conflict exists.

Examples of methods an offeror or contractor may use to mitigate organizational conflicts of interest, including those created as a result of the financial relationships of individuals within the organization are shown below. These examples are not intended to be an exhaustive list of all the possible methods to mitigate conflicts of interest nor are we obligated to approve a mitigation method that uses one or more of these examples. An offeror's or contractor's method of mitigating conflicts of interest would be evaluated on a case-by-case basis.

- Divestiture of or reduction in the amount of the financial relationship the organization has in another organization to a level acceptable to us and appropriate for the situation.
- If shared responsibilities create the conflict, a plan, included in the Organizational Conflicts of Interest Certificate and approved by us, to separate lines of business and management or critical staff from work on the MIP contract.
- If the conflict exists because of the amount of financial dependence upon the Federal Government, negotiating a phasing out of other contracts or grants that continue in effect at the start of the MIP contract.
- If the conflict exists because of the financial relationships of individuals within the organization, divestiture of the relationships by the individual involved.
- If the conflict exists because of an individual's indirect interest, divestiture of the interest to levels acceptable to us or removal of the individual from the work under the MIP contract.

In the procurement process, we determine which proposals are in a "competitive range." The competitive range is based on cost or price and other factors that are stated in the solicitation and includes all proposals that have a reasonable chance for contract award. Using the process proposed in this regulation, offerors will not be excluded from the competitive range based solely on conflicts of interest. If we determine that an offeror in the competitive range has a conflict of interest that is not adequately mitigated, we would inform the offeror of the deficiency and give it an opportunity to submit a revised Certificate. At any time during the procurement process, we may convene the Conflict of Interest Review Board to evaluate and resolve conflicts of interest.

By providing a better process for the identification, evaluation, and resolution of conflicts of interest, we not only protect Government interests but help ensure that contractors will not restrict competition in their service areas by using their position as a MIP contractor.

7. Limitation on MIP Contractor Liability and Payment of Legal Expenses

As discussed earlier, contractors who perform activities under the MIP contract will be reviewing activities of providers and suppliers that provide services to Medicare beneficiaries. Their contracts will authorize them to evaluate the performance of providers, suppliers, individuals, and other entities that may subsequently challenge their decisions. To reduce or eliminate a MIP contractor's exposure to possible legal action from those it reviews, section 1893(e) of the Act requires that we, by regulation, limit a MIP contractor's liability for actions taken in carrying out its contract. We must establish, to the extent we find appropriate, standards and other substantive and procedural provisions that are the same as, or comparable to, those contained in section 1157 of the Act.

Section 1157 of the Act limits liability and provides for the payment of legal expenses of an Utilization and Quality Control Peer Review Organization (PRO) that contracts to carry out functions under section 1154(e) of the Act. Specifically, section 1157 provides that PROs, their employees, fiduciaries, and anyone who furnishes professional services to a PRO are protected from civil and criminal liability in performing their duties under the Act or their contract, provided these duties are performed with due care. Following the mandate of section 1893(e), this proposed rule, at § 421.316(a), would protect MIP contractors from liability in the performance of their contracts provided they carry out their contractual duties with care.

In accordance with section 1893(e), we propose to employ the same standards for the payment of legal expenses as are contained in section 1157(d) of the Act. Therefore, § 421.316(b) will provide that we will make payment to MIP contractors, their members, employees, and anyone who provides them legal counsel or services for expenses incurred in the defense of any legal action related to the performance of a MIP contract. We propose that the payment be limited to the reasonable amount of expenses incurred, as determined by us, provided funds are available and that the payment is otherwise allowable under the terms of the contract.

In drafting § 421.316(2), we considered employing a standard for the limitation of liability other than the due care standard. For example, we considered whether it would be appropriate to provide that a contractor would not be criminally or civilly liable by reason of the performance of any duty, function, or activity under its contract provided the contractor was not grossly negligent in that performance. However, section 1893(e) requires that we employ the same or comparable standards and provisions as are contained in section 1157 of the Act. We do not believe that it would be appropriate to expand the scope of immunity to a standard of gross negligence, as it would not be a comparable standard to that set forth in section 1157 (b) of the Act.

We also considered indemnifying MIP contractors employing provisions similar to those contained in the current Medicare intermediary agreements and carrier contracts. Generally, intermediaries and carriers are indemnified for any liability arising from the performance of contract functions provided the intermediary's or carrier's conduct was not grossly negligent, fraudulent, or criminal. However, we may indemnify a MIP contractor only to the extent we have specific statutory authority to do so. Section 1893(e) does not provide that authority. In addition, § 421.316(a) provides for immunity from liability in connection with the performance of a MIP contract provided the contractor exercised due care. Indemnification is not necessary since the MIP contractors will have immunity from liability under § 421.316(a).

B. Intermediary and Carrier Functions

Section 1816(a) of the Act, which provides that providers may nominate an intermediary, requires only that nominated intermediaries perform the functions of determining payment amounts and making payment, and section 1842(a) of the Act requires only that carriers perform "some or all" of the functions cited in that section. Our requirements at §§ 421.100 and 421.200 concerning functions to be included in intermediary agreements and carrier contracts far exceed those of the statute. Therefore, on February 22, 1994, we published a proposed rule (59 FR 8446) that would distinguish between those functions that the statute requires be included in agreements with intermediaries and those functions, which although not required to be performed by intermediaries, may be included in intermediary agreements at our discretion. We also proposed that any functions included in carrier contracts would be included at our discretion. In addition, we proposed to add payment on a fee schedule basis as a new function that may be performed by carriers.

In light of the expansion of our contracting authority by section 1893 of the Act to allow us to contract with eligible entities to perform Medicare program integrity activities performed currently by intermediaries and carriers, we have decided not to finalize the February 1994 proposed rule. Instead, in this proposed rule we are setting forth a new proposal to bring those sections of the regulations that concern the functions Medicare intermediaries and carriers perform into conformity with the provisions of sections 1816(a), 1842 (a), and 1893(b) of the Act.

As noted in section I.A. of this preamble, our regulations at § 421.100 specify a list of functions that must, at a minimum, be included in all intermediary agreements. Similarly, § 421.200 specifies a list of functions that must, at a minimum, be included in all carrier contracts. These requirements far exceed those of the statute.

Section 1816(a) of the Act requires only that an intermediary agreement provide for determination of the amount of payments to be made to providers and for the making of the payments. Section 1816(a) permits, but does not require, an intermediary agreement to include provisions for the intermediary to provide consultative services to providers to enable them to establish and maintain fiscal records or to otherwise qualify as providers. It also provides that, for those providers to which the intermediary makes payments, the intermediary may serve as a channel of communications between us and the providers, may make audits of the records of the providers, and may perform other functions as are necessary.

We believe that section 1816(a) mandates only that an intermediary make payment determinations and make payments and that, because of the nomination provision of section 1816(a), these functions must remain with intermediaries. We believe that section 1816 (a) does not require that the other functions set forth at § 421.100 (c) through (i) be included in all intermediary agreements. Further, section 1893 of the Act permits the performance of functions related to Medicare program integrity by other entities. Thus, § 421.100 needs to be revised to be consistent with section 1893 and the implementing regulation. We also believe that mandatory inclusion of all functions in all agreements limits our ability to efficiently and effectively administer the Medicare program. For example, if an otherwise competent intermediary performs a single function poorly, it would be efficient and effective to have that function transferred to another contractor that could carry it out in a satisfactory manner. The alternative is to not renew or to terminate the agreement of that intermediary and to transfer all functions to a new contractor that may not have had an ongoing relationship with the local provider community. Therefore, we would revise § 421.100 to specify that an agreement between us and an intermediary specifies the functions to be performed by the intermediary and that these must include determining the amount of payments to be made to providers for covered services furnished to Medicare beneficiaries and making the payments and may include any or all of the following functions:

- Any or all of the MIP functions identified in proposed § 421.304, provided that they are continuing to be performed under an agreement entered into under section 1816 of the Act that was in effect on August 21, 1996, and they do not duplicate work being performed under a MIP contract.
- Undertaking to adjust overpayments and underpayments and to recover overpayments when it has been determined that an overpayment has been made.
- Furnishing to us timely information and reports that we request in order to carry out our responsibilities in the administration of the Medicare program.
- Establishing and maintaining procedures that we approve for the review and reconsideration of payment determinations.
- Maintaining records and making available to us the records necessary for verification of payments and for other related purposes
- Upon inquiry, assisting individuals with respect to matters pertaining to an intermediary contract.
- Serving as a channel of communication to and from us of information, instructions, and other material as necessary for the effective and efficient performance of an intermediary contract.
- Undertaking other functions as mutually agreed to by us and the intermediary.

In § 421.100(c), we would specify that, with respect to the responsibility for services to a provider-based HHA or a provider-based hospice, when different intermediaries serve the HHA or hospice and its parent provider under § 421.117, the designated regional intermediary determines the amount of payment and makes payments to the HHA or hospice. The intermediary and/or MIP contractor serving the parent provider performs fiscal functions, including audits and settlement of the Medicare cost reports and the HHA and hospice supplement worksheets.

Section 1842(a), which pertains to carrier contracts, requires that the contract provide for some or all of the functions listed in that paragraph, but does not specify any functions that must be included in a carrier contract. As in the case of intermediary agreements, our experience has been that mandatory inclusion of a long list of functions in all contracts restricts our ability to administer the carrier contracts with optimum efficiency and effectiveness. We believe that the requirements of the regulations for both intermediaries and carriers should be brought into conformity with the statutory requirements. Therefore, we would revise existing § 421.200, "Carrier functions," to make it consistent with section 1893 of the Act and the implementing regulations. We would provide that a contract between HCFA and a carrier specifies the functions to be performed by the carrier, which may include the following:

- Any or all of the MIP functions described in § 421.304 if the following conditions are met: (1) The carrier is continuing those functions under a contract entered into under section 1842 of the Act that was in effect on August 21, 1996; and (2) they do not duplicate work being performed under a MIP contract, except that the function related to developing and maintaining a list of durable medical equipment may be performed under both a carrier contract and a MIP contract.
- Receiving, disbursing, and accounting for funds in making payments for services furnished to eligible individuals within the jurisdiction of the carrier.
- Determining the amount of payment for services furnished to an eligible individual.
- Undertaking to adjust incorrect payments and recover overpayments when it has been determined that an overpayment has been made.
- Furnishing to us timely information and reports that we request in order to carry out our responsibilities in the administration of the Medicare program.

- Maintaining records and making available to us the records necessary for verification of payments and for other related purposes.
- Establishing and maintaining procedures under which an individual enrolled under Part B will be granted an opportunity for a fair hearing.
- Upon inquiry, assisting individuals with matters pertaining to a carrier contract.
- Serving as a channel of communication to and from us of information, instructions, and other material as necessary for the effective and efficient performance of a carrier contract.
- Undertaking other functions as mutually agreed to by us and the carrier.

C. Technical and Editorial Changes

Because we propose to add a new subpart D to part 421 that would apply to MIP contractors, we propose to change the title of part 421 from "Intermediaries and Carriers" to "Medicare Contracting". We also propose to revise § 421.1, which sets forth the basis, scope, and applicability of part 421. We would revise this section to add section 1893 of the Act to the list of provisions upon which the part is based. We would also make editorial and other changes (such as reorganizing the contents of the section and providing headings) that improve the readability of the section without affecting its substance.

In addition, numerous sections of our regulations specifically refer to an action being taken by an intermediary or a carrier. If the action being described may now be performed by a MIP contractor that is not an intermediary or a carrier, we would revise those sections to indicate that this is the case. As an example, § 424.11, which sets forth the responsibilities of a provider, specifies, in paragraph (a)(2), that the provider must keep certification and recertification statements on file for verification by the intermediary. A MIP contractor now may also perform the verification. Therefore, we would revise § 424.11(a)(2) to specify that the provider must keep certification and recertification statements on file for verification by the intermediary or MIP contractor. Because our regulations are continuously being revised and sections redesignated, we have not identified all such sections that will have technical changes in this rule, but we will do so in the final rule. If we determine that substantive changes to our regulations are necessary, we will make those changes through separate rulemaking.

III. Response to Comments

Because of the large number of items of correspondence we normally receive on Federal Register documents published for comment, we are not able to acknowledge or respond to them individually. We will consider all comments we receive by the date and time specified in the DATES section of this preamble, and, if we proceed with a subsequent document, we will respond to the comments in the preamble to that document.

IV. Collection of Information Requirements

Under the Paperwork Reduction Act of 1995, we are required to provide 60-day notice in the Federal Register and solicit public comment before a collection of information requirement is submitted to the Office of Management and Budget (OMB) for review and approval. In order to fairly evaluate whether an information collection should be approved by OMB, section 3506(c)(2)(A) of the Paperwork Reduction Act of 1995 requires that we solicit comment on the following issues:

- The need for the information collection and its usefulness in carrying out the proper functions of our agency.
- The accuracy of our estimate of the information collection burden.
- The quality, utility, and clarity of the information to be collected.
- Recommendations to minimize the information collection burden on the affected public, including automated collection techniques.

We are soliciting public comment on each of the issues for sections §§ 421.310 and 421.312 of this document, which contain information collection requirements.

Section 421.310 Conflict of Interest Identification

Section 421.310(e) requires offerors to determine if an organizational conflict of interest exists in any of its proposed or actual subcontractors at any tier and to ensure that the subcontractors have mitigated any conflict of interest or potential conflict of interest. As discussed below, the information collection requirements for § 421.312 also require an offeror to list in an Organizational Conflicts of Interest Certificate situations that could be identified as conflicts of interest and to describe methods it would apply to mitigate those situations. Based on our best estimate, we believe that the requirement will impose a burden of 80 hours on each offeror with respect to information it provides for its own organization. It is assumed that offerors will impose the same or similar disclosure requirements on their proposed or actual subcontractors as imposed by us on offerors, with the understanding that we would not expect them to require that independent auditors perform compliance audits on subcontractors. Based on this assumption, an offeror's burden with respect to its subcontractors is estimated to be one-half the burden imposed on an offeror with respect to its own organization.

We expect 15 offerors for each type of MIP contract. We estimate that the requirement of this provision will impose a burden of 40 hours per subcontractor on each offeror to identify and mitigate any organizational conflicts of interest for its subcontractors at any tier. We believe that, on average, each offeror will need to evaluate three subcontractors. The total burden referenced in § 421.310(e) with respect to an offeror's subcontractors is 1,800 burden hours.

Section 421.312 Conflict of Interest Evaluation

Section 421.312 requires offerors that wish to be eligible for the award of a contract under this subpart and MIP contractors to submit an Organizational Conflicts of Interest Certificate for pre-and post-award purposes.

Based on comments provided by the public on possible methods we could use to identify, evaluate, and resolve potential conflicts of interest, we found that only by imposing the information collection requirements referenced in this section could competition remain open to all interested parties regardless of their current lines of business and, at the same time provide us with enough information to determine on a case-by-case basis if conflicts of interest have been properly identified and adequately mitigated. Only by imposing these information collection requirements can we determine whether an offeror should be awarded a MIP contract.

Below is a summary of the proposed Organizational Conflict of Interest Certificate disclosure requirements and related burden required with the offeror's proposal. The items of information described below will be required for all MIP contractor procurements, unless the information is otherwise provided in the proposal, in which case it must be referenced. The last item identifies some information that officers, directors, and managers will be required to provide in all MIP procurements and some information that they may be required to provide in a MIP procurement.

• *A description of all business or contractual relationships or activities that a prudent business person may view as a conflict of interest.*

We have received comments from the insurance industry and affiliated sources that some situations that we may not readily identify as conflicts nonetheless appear to create conflicts of interest. If a prudent business person could believe a conflict of interest exists in a situation, the entity is required to report the situation even if we have not created a "classification" for the situation. We would use this information to evaluate the situation and to determine if it is adequately mitigated or requires no mitigation. In addition, we would use this information to adapt to changing environments and to modify the conflict of interest requirements.

• *A description of the methods the offeror/contractor will apply to mitigate any situations listed in the Certification that could be identified as conflicts of interest.*

We would use the description of the methods the offeror/contractor will apply to mitigate any situations listed in the Certification that could be identified as conflicts of interest to determine if conflicts would be neutralized effectively by the methods described. Generally, we consider a conflict of interest to exist when a contractor's ability to make impartial decisions or perform its work under its contract objectively has been or may be compromised. The offeror/contractor could propose to mitigate a conflict of interest by using methods such as divestiture or reduction of a conflicting financial interest, reassignment of work responsibilities to exclude individuals with conflicting interests from performing work under the contract, or separating lines of business. We would assess the effectiveness of the mitigation method using the information disclosed regarding an offeror's/contractor's organizational structure, financial interests, or other relationships as may be required in a solicitation as discussed below.

• *A description of the offeror's/contractor's program to monitor its compliance and the compliance of its proposed and actual subcontractors with the conflict of interest requirements as identified in the relevant solicitation.*

We would evaluate the proposed compliance program to determine if the program would enable an offeror/contractor to effectively monitor its compliance and its subcontractors' compliance with conflict of interest requirements specific to the contract. This requirement is integrally connected with an entity's description of its method to mitigate conflicts. Once conflicts are mitigated at the inception of a contract, an entity must be vigilant to ensure that the methods are followed and that new conflicts of interest that arise during the term of the contract are identified and mitigated. We would use the compliance program to ensure we award contracts only to offerors that will follow proposed methods for mitigation of conflicts and that offerors establish an administrative mechanism for disclosure of changing situations that may require contract modifications.

• *An affirmation, using language that we may prescribe, that the offeror/contractor understands that we may consider any deception or omission in the Certificate grounds for nonconsideration in the procurement process, termination of the contract, or other contract action.*

The affirmation places a higher degree of accountability on the entity for the accuracy of the information disclosed than would otherwise be afforded. By signing the affirmation, the offeror/ contractor will be put on notice of the consequences for any false statement or omission of information regarding conflicts of interest. The person signing the affirmation will be put on notice of the offeror's/contractor's responsibility for ensuring the veracity of the information disclosed. We would consider the provision of false or deceptive information in the affirmation as possible grounds for elimination of an offeror from consideration in the procurement process or taking other appropriate contract or legal action.

• *A description of the offeror's/contractor's plans to contract with an independent auditor to conduct a compliance audit.*

We would use this information to ensure that the offeror has an arrangement with an independent source that will verify compliance with conflict of interest requirements.

• *Corporate and organizational structure.*

We would require this information to determine if legal entities are connected through partnerships, joint ventures, or other legal arrangements. We would assess the types of relationships, evaluate an offeror's/contractor's mitigation methods, and determine if the conflicts of interest based on an offeror's/contractor's relationships have been resolved as part of the procurement process. This information would also be used during the term of the contract to evaluate the mitigation of conflicts when structures change.

• *Financial interests in other entities, including the following:*

+ Percentage of ownership in any other entity. We would use the percentage of ownership interest and the dollar value of financial interests to evaluate reported conflicts of interest and the adequacy of an offeror's/contractor's mitigation methods. Both these measures were suggested by the participants in the 1996 open forum discussion as appropriate considerations in evaluating conflicts of interest. We would perform the evaluation on a case-by-case basis.

• *Income generated from other sources.*

We would use this information to determine if the offeror/contractor could be unduly influenced by other financial relationships it may have with possible customers, competitors, or other parties interested in influencing the performance of the MIP contractor. Income can be generated in a variety of ways, for example, as fees, salaries, reimbursements, or stock options. This information would enable us to evaluate the adequacy of an offeror's/contractor's proposed mitigation methods for conflicts of interest that arise from financial dependence on other entities.

• *A list of current or known future contracts or arrangements, regardless of size, with any insurance organization; subcontractor of an insurance organization; or provider or supplier furnishing services for which payment may be made under the Medicare program. This information is to include the dollar amount of the contracts or arrangements, the type of work performed, and the period of performance*

We would use this information to evaluate an offeror's/contractor's conflicts that are based on contractual arrangements and to assess the adequacy of its mitigation method. The offeror/contractor would be required to disclose future contracts so that we can assess whether mitigation methods address conflicts that will develop during the procurement process or during the term of the contract.

• *Information regarding potential conflicts of interest and financial information regarding certain contracts for all of the offeror's / contractor's officers, directors (including medical directors), and managers who would be or are involved in the performance of the MIP contract*

We would evaluate this information to determine if individuals who can control the outcome of work performed under a MIP contract may be unduly influenced by their own or their close relatives' business relationships or contracts. We need the information to protect the monies disbursed for both program and administrative services and to ensure that an offeror's/contractor's mitigation methods adequately eliminate any conflicts that exist due to relationships of an offeror's/contractor's officers, directors, or managers.

Private sector participants at the December 6, 1996 open forum discussion expressed the opinion that full disclosure of all of an offeror's/contractor's relationships would ameliorate conflicts of interest. We considered that, while this might be appropriate in some MIP contractor procurements, it would be unduly burdensome and unnecessary as a blanket requirement in all MIP procurements. Instead, we identified information, described above, that we believe to be essential to the process and require this information to be disclosed in MIP procurements.

The amount of burden associated with these requirements will generally decrease as the size of the offeror/contractor decreases. Smaller offerors/contractors and those not involved in the insurance industry may have no potential conflicts of interest to report if they do not participate in other lines of business and/or if they do not participate in lines of business related to the insurance, health, and health management and consulting industries that are likely to have potential conflicts of interest.

Therefore, based on comments provided by the public and our prior experience, we expect the Certificate and supporting materials will take approximately 80 hours to prepare by each offeror/contractor for its own organization. This estimate is based on the fact that the majority of these disclosure requirements will be compiled using existing data, which an offeror/contractor uses to satisfy other business needs, and the assumption that approximately one-third of the offerors will not have any potential conflicts of interest to report. We expect 15 offerors for each MIP contract. The total burden referenced in this section is 1,200 burden hours.

As required by section 3504(h) of the Paperwork Reduction Act of 1995, we have submitted a copy of this document to the Office of Management and Budget (OMB) for its review of these information collection requirements.

If you comment on these information collection and recordkeeping requirements, please mail copies directly to the following:

Health Care Financing Administration, Office of Financial and Human Resources, Management Planning and Analysis Staff, Attn: John Burke, Attn: HCFA-7020-P, Room C2–26–17, 7500 Security Boulevard, Baltimore, MD 21244–1850 Office of Information and Regulatory Affairs, Office of Management and Budget, Room 10235,

New Executive Office Building, Washington, DC 20503, Attn: Allison Herron Eydt, HCFA Desk Officer

V. Regulatory Impact Statement

A. Introduction

We have examined the impacts of this proposed rule as required by Executive Order 12866 and the Regulatory Flexibility Act (RFA) (Public Law 96–354). Executive Order 12866 directs agencies to assess all costs and benefits of available regulatory alternatives and, when regulation is necessary, to select regulatory approaches that maximize net benefits (including potential economic, environmental, public health and safety effects, distributive impacts, and equity). The RFA requires agencies to analyze options for regulatory relief of small businesses. For purposes of the RFA, small entities include small businesses, non-profit organizations and governmental agencies. Most hospitals and most other providers and suppliers are small entities, either by nonprofit status or by having revenues of $5 million or less annually. Intermediaries and carriers are not considered to be small entities.

Section 1102(b) of the Social Security Act requires us to prepare a regulatory impact analysis for any proposed rule that may have a significant impact on the operations of a substantial number of small rural hospitals. This analysis must conform to the provisions of section 603 of the RFA. For purposes of section 1102(b) of the Act, we define a small rural hospital as a hospital that is located outside a Metropolitan Statistical Area and has fewer than 50 beds.

B. Summary of the Proposed Rule

As discussed in detail above, this rule implements section 1893 of the Act, which encourages proactive measures to combat waste, fraud, and abuse and to protect the integrity of the Medicare program. The objective of the proposed regulation is to provide a procurement procedure to supplement the requirements of the FAR and specifically address contracts to perform MIP functions identified in the law.

As part of their existing contractual duties, both intermediaries and carriers must perform certain program integrity activities or payment safeguard activities. These activities include, but are not limited to, conducting review of claims to determine whether services were reasonable and necessary, deterring and detecting

Medicare fraud, auditing provider cost reports, and ensuring that Medicare pays the appropriate amount when a beneficiary has other health insurance. This rule provides that these functions, as specified below, will be performed under new MIP contracts:

- Review of provider activities such as medical review, utilization review, and fraud review.
- Audit of cost reports.
- Medicare secondary payer review and payment recovery.
- Provider and beneficiary education on payment integrity and benefit quality assurance issues.
- Developing and updating lists of durable medical equipment items that are to be subject to prior approval provisions.

C. Discussion of Impact

We expect that this rule will have a positive impact on the Medicare program, Medicare beneficiaries, providers, suppliers, and entities that have not previously contracted with us. It is possible that some providers and suppliers may experience a slight increase in administrative costs as their claims are subjected to closer review. Current intermediaries and carriers that seek award of MIP contracts may incur costs in complying with new requirements set forth in the rule, but the effect is not expected to be material. To the extent that small entities could be affected by the rule, and because the rule raises certain policy issues with respect to conflict of interest standards, we provide an impact analysis for those entities we believe will be most heavily affected by the rule.

We believe that this rule will have an impact, although not a significant one, in five general areas. The Medicare program and Health Insurance Trust Funds, Medicare beneficiaries and taxpayers, entities that have not previously contracted with us, and Medicare providers and suppliers would benefit from the rule. Current intermediaries and carriers may experience a somewhat negative impact, although the effect on these organization should be tempered by the benefits the new rule will confer.

1. The Medicare Program and Health Insurance Trust Funds

In recent years, sizable cuts in intermediaries' and carriers' budgets for program safeguards have diminished efforts to thwart improper billing practices. The Health Insurance Portability and Accountability Act provides for a direct apportionment from the

Health Insurance Trust Funds for carrying out the MIP. Appropriations totaled $440 million for FY 1998 and $500 million for FY 1998. By FY 2003, appropriations are expected to grow to $720 million.

Creating a separate and dependable long-term funding source for MIP will allow us the flexibility to invest in innovative strategies to combat the fraud and abuse drain on the Trust Funds. By shifting emphasis from post-payment recoveries on incorrectly paid claims to pre-payment strategies, most claims will be paid correctly the first time.

Improper billing and health care fraud are difficult to quantify because of their hidden nature. However, a General Accounting Office (GAO) report on Medicare (GAO/HR-91–10, February 1997) suggests that by reducing unnecessary or inappropriate payments, the Federal Government would realize large savings and help slow the growth in Medicare costs. In this report, the GAO states that estimates of "the costs of fraud and abuse ranging from 3 to 10 percent have been cited for health expenditures nationwide, so applying this range to Medicare suggests that such losses in fiscal year 1996 could have been from $6 billion to as much as $20 billion."

The savings realized from our payment safeguard activities for FYs 1988–1996 were as follows:

Year	Total cost*	Total savings*	Return on investment
FY1988	$313.6	$3,654.1	12:1
FY1989	376.3	3,961.6	11:1
FY1990	348.7	5,234.4	15:1
FY1991	360.7	5,703.4	16:1
FY1992	350.7	5,153.2	15:1
FY1993	406.3	6,506.6	16:1
FY1994	412.4	5,412.7	13:1
FY1995	428.3	6,314.9	15:1
FY1996	441.1	6,190.4	14:1

In our Justification of Estimates for Appropriations Committees for fiscal year 1998, we projected the return on investment for various payment safeguard activities under MIP. Overall, we expect that every dollar expended in fiscal year 1998 to perform integrity functions will save $12 for the Medicare program. We estimate that medical review and utilization review performed under MIP will

* Dollars in millions.

produce a return on investment of 8:1 for Part A claims and 14:1 for Part B claims. Every dollar spent on audit functions under MIP is expected to save $6 for the Medicare program. For Medicare secondary payer functions, we project a 50:1 return on investment for Part A claims and a 9:1 return for Part B claims. The overall return for Medicare secondary payer functions performed under MIP is estimated to be 26:1.

In addition to these economic advantages, the Medicare program will benefit in a qualitative way. MIP, as this proposed rule would implement it, gives us a tool to better administer the Medicare program and accomplish our mission of providing access to quality health care for Medicare beneficiaries. Under this rule, program integrity activities will be performed under specialized contracts that are subject to more stringent conflict of interest standards than were previously employed. In addition, for the first time we will be able to use competitive procedures to separately contract for the performance of integrity functions. In general, economic theory postulates that competition results in a better price for the consumer who, in this instance, is HCFA on behalf of Medicare beneficiaries and taxpayers. Competition should also encourage the use of innovative techniques to perform integrity functions that will, in turn, result in more efficient and effective safeguards for the Trust Funds.

2. Medicare Beneficiaries and Taxpayers

We expect that overall this rule would have a positive effect on Medicare beneficiaries and taxpayers. Beneficiaries pay deductibles and Part B Medicare premiums. Taxpayers, including those who are not yet eligible for Medicare, contribute part of their earnings to the Part A Trust Fund. Taxpayers and beneficiaries contribute indirectly to the Part B Trust Funds because it is funded, in part, from general tax revenues. Consistent performance of program integrity activities will ensure that less money is wasted on inappropriate treatment or unnecessary services. As a result, current and future beneficiaries will obtain more value for every Medicare dollar spent.

Medicare contractors estimate that of the 130,000 calls they receive yearly concerning potential fraud and abuse, 94,000 are from beneficiaries, many of whom call to question the propriety of claims made on their behalf. Beneficiary education monies, especially when used to provide more Medicare "scam alerts," will enhance a beneficiary's attention to detail and increase savings.

Beneficiaries may experience higher denial rates due to the more stringent claims review. It is expected, however, that most of the potential increase in denials will result from a determination that the services provided were not reasonable and necessary under Medicare authorities and guidelines. There are established limitations on beneficiary liability when claims are denied on this basis; thus the impact on beneficiaries will be minimized.

3. Current Intermediaries and Carriers

Although intermediaries and carriers are not considered small entities for purposes of the RFA, we are providing the following analysis. There are currently 43 Medicare intermediaries and 27 Medicare carriers plus 4 durable medical equipment regional contractors. All but 13 of these contractors are Blue Cross/Blue Shield plans. Presently, all contractors perform payment safeguard activities, and, in FY 1996, approximately 28 percent of the total contractor budget was dedicated to program integrity.

We considered prohibiting current intermediaries and carriers from entering into MIP contracts. We also considered entering into contracts with new organizations to perform all functions while simultaneously removing all payment safeguard functions from current contractors. Neither of these options appeared viable because the effect on the Medicare program would have been unduly disruptive. We do, however, expect to reduce the number of contractors when we shift and consolidate the integrity functions to MIP contractors, but the exact number cannot be determined until we begin implementing the program. The reduction in the number of contractors performing integrity functions does not mean that local contractor presence will be eliminated. Medical directors would continue to play an important role in benefit integrity activities, and we intend to retain locally-based medical directors to continue our relationship with local physicians by using groups like Carrier Advisory Committees. Locally-based fraud investigators and auditors are also likely to be used. Review policies will be coordinated across contractors to ensure consistency, but local practice will be incorporated where appropriate.

This rule may have a negative impact on current intermediaries and carriers in some respects. Current contractors will lose a portion of their Medicare business as payment safeguard functions are transferred to MIP contractors. Although their workload will be reduced, the effect on current contractors will be gradual because we have a long-term strategy for the implementation of MIP. As discussed above, we believe that it would be too disruptive to the Medicare program to make a sudden, across-the-board change in contractors. The change will be made over time, in an incremental fashion, as MIP contracts are awarded; therefore, we cannot quantify the effect.

On the other hand, current contractors would benefit from this proposed rule because, under its provisions, they are eligible to compete for MIP contracts as long as they comply with all conflict of interest and other requirements. (Current contractors may not receive payment for performing the same program integrity activities under both a MIP contract and their existing contract.) We considered proposing rules that identified specific conflict of interest situations that would prohibit the award of a MIP contract. We also considered prohibiting a MIP contractor whose contract was completed or terminated from competing for another MIP contract for a certain period. Instead, the proposed rule would establish a process for evaluating, on a case-by-case basis, situations that may constitute conflicts of interest. It permits current contractors to position themselves to be eligible for a MIP contract by mitigating any conflicts of interest they may have in order to compete. The economic impact on intermediaries and carriers is lessened by the proposed approach when compared to the alternatives we considered.

The current contractors who are awarded MIP contracts will also benefit from the consistent funding provided by the law for program integrity activities. This stable, long-term funding mechanism will allow Medicare contractors to attract, train, and retain qualified professional staff to perform claims review and audit, to identify and refer fraud cases to law enforcement agencies and to support the ongoing development of these cases for prosecution by the Department of Justice.

There will be an economic impact on current contractors that propose to perform MIP contracts using subcontractors. MIP contractors would be required to determine if any of their subcontractors, at any tier, have conflicts of interest and to ensure that any conflicts are mitigated. A MIP contractor would apply to its subcontractors the same conflict of interest standard to which it must adhere. It is impossible to assess the precise economic impact of this portion of the proposed rule because a MIP contractor is free to contract with any subcontractor. A MIP contractor may seek out subcontractors that are conflict free, which would reduce or eliminate the time expended monitoring conflict of interest situations.

4. New Contracting Entities

Entities that have not previously performed Medicare payment safeguard activities will experience a positive effect from this rule. Integrity functions such as audit, medical review, and fraud investigation may be consolidated in a MIP contract to allow suspect claims to be identified and investigated from all angles. Contractors may subcontract for these specific integrity functions, thus creating new markets and opportunities for small, small disadvantaged, and woman-owned businesses.

Use of full and open competition to award MIP contracts may encourage innovation and the creation of new technology. Historically, cutting edge technologies and analytical methodologies created for the Medicare program have benefitted the private insurance arena.

This proposed rule, however, could also have an adverse economic impact on newly-contracting entities. They, like existing contractors, will be required to absorb the cost of mitigating conflicts of interest and complying with conflict of interest requirements.

5. Providers and Suppliers

There could be some burden imposed on providers and suppliers that are small businesses or not-for-profit organizations by the need to deal with a new set of contractors. There are approximately 1 million health care providers and suppliers (depending on how group practices and multiple locations are counted) that bill independently. The proposed rule does not necessarily impose any action on the part of these providers and suppliers. It is possible that some of them would have to devote more effort in responding to MIP contractors' inquiries generated by more stringent claims review and that they could incur a modest increase in administrative costs. In our analysis of possible administrative costs to providers and suppliers, we assumed that a contractor would make two follow-up inquiries to a provider or supplier for each potential recovery of an incorrect payment. Assuming that the response to each inquiry would require a provider or supplier to expend 30 minutes of clerical time, at $10 per hour, and 15 minutes of professional time, at $100 per hour, we estimate that the average response to an inquiry would cost $30. The resulting added cost to providers and suppliers would be under $10 million annually.

Most Medicare contractors do not maintain toll-free lines for providers or suppliers. A provider's or supplier's telephone bill could increase if it must contact a MIP contractor that is out of its calling area. However, it is possible that a provider's or supplier's intermediary or carrier may also be its MIP contractor. We believe that the centralization of certain functions would result in more consistent policy and lessen the need for a provider or supplier to communicate with its contractor. Since we plan to phase-in the transfer of the MIP activities, we do not anticipate a significant annual impact on telephone bills.

Overall, we expect that providers and suppliers will benefit qualitatively from this proposed rule. Many providers and suppliers perceive that their reputations are tarnished by the few dishonest providers and suppliers that take advantage of the Medicare program. The media often focus on the most egregious cases of Medicare fraud and abuse, leaving the public with the perception that physicians and other health care practitioners routinely make improper claims. This rule would allow us to take a more effective and wider ranging approach to identifying, stopping, and recovering from unscrupulous providers and suppliers. As the number of dishonest providers and suppliers and improper claims diminishes, ethical providers and suppliers will benefit.

This proposed rule could be considered to have a negative impact on any provider or supplier that routinely submits questionable claims and would impact those that have been receiving inappropriate payments. Since the objective of this proposed rule is to eliminate improper payments, we will not analyze the effect the rule may have on unscrupulous providers or suppliers. We do not believe that this rule will reduce a provider's or supplier's legitimate income from Medicare. As claims are more closely and systematically reviewed, providers and suppliers may experience an increase in the number of claims denied. This slight negative impact should decrease as providers become more knowledgeable regarding what claims are appropriate.

D. Conclusion

We conclude that money would be saved and the solvency of the Trust Funds extended as a result of this proposed rule. The dynamic nature of fraud and abuse is illustrated by the fact that wrongdoers continue to find ways to evade safeguards. This supports the need for constant vigilance and increasingly sophisticated ways to protect against "gaming" of the system. We solicit public comments as well as data on the extent to which any of the affected entities would be significantly economically affected by this proposed rule. However, based on the above analysis, we have determined, and certify, that this proposed rule would not have a significant economic impact on a substantial number of small entities. We also have determined, and certify, that this proposed rule would not have a significant impact on the operations of a substantial number of small rural hospitals. In accordance with the provisions of Executive Order 12866, this proposed rule was reviewed by the Office of Management and Budget.

List of Subjects

42 CFR Part 400

Grant programs — health, Health facilities, Health maintenance organizations (HMO), Medicaid, Medicare, Reporting and recordkeeping requirements.

42 CFR Part 421

Administrative practice and procedure, Health facilities, Health professions, Medicare, Reporting and recordkeeping requirements.

42 CFR chapter IV would be amended as follows:

A. Part 400

PART 400 — INTRODUCTION; DEFINITIONS

1. The authority citation for part 400 continues to read as follows:

Authority: §§ 1102 and 1871 of the Social Security Act (42 U.S.C. 1302 and 1395hh) and 44 U.S.C. Chapter 35.

2. Section 400.202 is amended by adding the following definition in alphabetical order, to read as follows:

§ 400.202 Definitions specific to Medicare.

* * * * *

Medicare integrity program contractor means an entity that has a contract with HCFA under section 1893 of the Act to perform program integrity activities.

* * * * *

B. Part 421

PART 421 — MEDICARE CONTRACTING

1. The part heading is revised to read as set forth above.
2. The authority citation for part 421 continues to read as follows:

Authority: §§ 1102 and 1871 of the Social Security Act (42 U.S.C. 1302 and 1395hh).

3. Section 421.1 is revised to read as follows:

§ 421.1 Basis, applicability, and scope.

(a) Basis. This part is based on the indicated provisions of the following sections of the Act:

1124 — Requirements for disclosure of certain information.

1816 and 1842 — Use of organizations and agencies in making Medicare payments to providers and suppliers of services.

1893 — Requirements for protecting the integrity of the Medicare program.

(b) Additional basis. Section 421.118 is also based on 42 U.S.C. 1395(b)-1(a)(1)(F), which authorizes demonstration projects involving intermediary agreements and carrier contracts.

(c) Applicability. The provisions of this part apply to agreements with Part A (Hospital Insurance) intermediaries, contracts with Part B (Supplementary Medical Insurance) carriers, and contracts with Medicare integrity program contractors that perform program integrity functions.

(d) Scope. The provisions of this part state that HCFA may perform certain functions directly or by contract. They specify criteria and standards HCFA uses in selecting intermediaries and evaluating their performance, in assigning or reassigning a provider or providers to particular intermediaries, and in designating regional or national intermediaries for certain classes of providers. The provisions provide the opportunity for a hearing for intermediaries and carriers affected by certain adverse actions. They also provide adversely affected intermediaries an opportunity for judicial review of certain hearing decisions. They also set forth requirements related to contracts with Medicare integrity program contractors.

4. Section 421.100 is revised to read as follows:

§ 421.100 Intermediary functions.

An agreement between HCFA and an intermediary specifies the functions to be performed by the intermediary.

(a) Mandatory functions. The contract must include the following functions:

(1) Determining the amount of payments to be made to providers for covered services furnished to Medicare beneficiaries.

(2) Making the payments.

(b) Additional functions. The contract may include any or all of the following functions:

(1) Any or all of the program integrity functions described in § 421.304, provided the intermediary is continuing those functions under an agreement entered into under section 1816 of the Act that was in effect on August 21, 1996, and they do not duplicate work being performed under a Medicare integrity program contract.

(2) Undertaking to adjust incorrect payments and recover overpayments when it has been determined that an overpayment has been made.

(3) Furnishing to HCFA timely information and reports that HCFA requests in order to carry out its responsibilities in the administration of the Medicare program.

(4) Establishing and maintaining procedures as approved by HCFA for the review and reconsideration of payment determinations.

(5) Maintaining records and making available to HCFA the records necessary for verification of payments and for other related purposes.

(6) Upon inquiry, assisting individuals with respect to matters pertaining to an intermediary contract.

(7) Serving as a channel of communication to and from HCFA of information, instructions, and other material as necessary for the effective and efficient performance of an intermediary agreement.

(8) Undertaking other functions as mutually agreed to by HCFA and the intermediary.

(c) Dual intermediary responsibilities. With respect to the responsibility for services to a provider-based HHA or a provider-based hospice, when different intermediaries serve the HHA or hospice and its parent provider under § 421.117, the designated regional intermediary determines the amount of payment and makes payments to the HHA or hospice. The intermediary and/or Medicare integrity program contractor serving the parent provider performs fiscal functions, including audits and settlement of the Medicare cost reports and the HHA and hospice supplement worksheets.

5. Section 421.200 is revised to read as follows:

§ 421.200 Carrier functions.

A contract between HCFA and a carrier specifies the functions to be performed by the carrier. The contract may include any or all of the following functions:

(a) Any or all of the program integrity functions described in § 421.304 provided—

(1) The carrier is continuing those functions under a contract entered into under section 1842 of the Act that was in effect on August 21, 1996; and

(2) The functions do not duplicate work being performed under a Medicare integrity program contract, except that the function related to developing and maintaining a list of durable medical equipment may be performed under both a carrier contract and a Medicare integrity program contract.

(b) Receiving, disbursing, and accounting for funds in making payments for services furnished to eligible individuals within the jurisdiction of the carrier.

(c) Determining the amount of payment for services furnished to an eligible individual.

(d) Undertaking to adjust incorrect payments and recover overpayments when it has been determined that an overpayment has been made.

(e) Furnishing to HCFA timely information and reports that HCFA requests in order to carry out its responsibilities in the administration of the Medicare program.

(f) Maintaining records and making available to HCFA the records necessary for verification of payments and for other related purposes.

(g) Establishing and maintaining procedures under which an individual enrolled under Part B will be granted an opportunity for a fair hearing.

(h) Upon inquiry, assisting individuals with matters pertaining to a carrier contract.

(i) Serving as a channel of communication to and from HCFA of information, instructions, and other material as necessary for the effective and efficient performance of a carrier contract.

(j) Undertaking other functions as mutually agreed to by HCFA and the carrier.

6. A new subpart D is added to part 421 to read as follows:

Subpart D —Medicare Integrity Program Contractors

Sec.

Subpart D —Medicare Integrity Program Contractors

§ 421.300 Basis, applicability, and scope.

(a) Basis. This subpart implements section 1893 of the Act, which requires HCFA to protect the integrity of the Medicare program by entering into contracts with eligible entities to carry out Medicare integrity program functions.

(b) Applicability. This subpart applies to entities that seek to compete or receive award of a contract under section 1893 of the Act including entities that perform functions under this subpart emanating from the processing of claims for individuals entitled to benefits as qualified railroad retirement beneficiaries.

(c) Scope. This subpart defines the types of entities eligible to become Medicare integrity program contractors; identifies the program integrity functions a Medicare integrity program contractor performs; describes procedures for awarding and renewing contracts; establishes procedures for identifying, evaluating, and resolving organizational conflicts of interest; prescribes responsibilities; and sets forth limitations on contractor liability. The provisions of this subpart are based on the acquisition regulations set forth at 48 CFR Chapters 1 and 3.

§ 421.302 Eligibility requirements for Medicare integrity program contractors.

If an entity meets the following conditions, HCFA may enter into a contract with it to perform the functions described in § 421.304:

(a) Demonstrates the ability to perform the Medicare integrity program contractor functions described in § 421.304. For purposes of developing and periodically updating a list of DME under § 421.304 (e), an entity is deemed to be eligible to enter into a contract under the Medicare integrity program to perform the function if the entity is a carrier with a contract in effect under section 1842 of the Act.

(b) Agrees to cooperate with the OIG, the Attorney General, and other law enforcement agencies, as appropriate, including making referrals, in the investigation and deterrence of fraud and abuse of the Medicare program.

(c) Complies with conflict of interest provisions in 48 CFR Chapters 1 and 3 and is not excluded under the conflict of interest provision at § 421.310.

(d) Meets other requirements that HCFA establishes.

§ 421.304 Medicare integrity program contractor functions.

The contract between HCFA and a Medicare integrity program contractor specifies the functions the contractor performs. The contract may include any or all of the following functions:

(a) Conducting medical reviews, utilization reviews, and fraud reviews related to the activities of providers of services and other individuals and entities (including entities contracting with HCFA under part 417 of this chapter) furnishing services for Medicare payment. These reviews include medical, utilization, and fraud reviews.

(b) Auditing cost reports of providers of services, or other individuals or entities (including entities contracting with HCFA under part 417 of this chapter), as necessary to ensure proper Medicare payment.

(c) Determining appropriate Medicare payment to be made for services, as specified in section 1862(b) of the Act, and taking action to recover inappropriate payments.

(d) Educating providers, suppliers, beneficiaries, and other persons regarding payment integrity and benefit quality assurance issues.

(e) Developing, and periodically updating, a list of items of durable medical equipment that are frequently subject to unnecessary utilization throughout the contractor's entire service area or a portion of the area, in accordance with section 1834(a)(15)(A) of the Act.

§ 421.306 Awarding of a contract.

(a) HCFA awards Medicare integrity program contracts in accordance with acquisition regulations set forth at 48 CFR chapters 1 and 3, this subpart, and all other applicable laws and regulations. These requirements for awarding Medicare integrity program contracts are used—

(1) When entering into new contracts;

(2) When entering into contracts that may result in the elimination of responsibilities of an individual intermediary or carrier under section 1816(l) or section 1842(c) of the Act, respectively; and

(3) At any other time HCFA considers appropriate.

(b) HCFA may award an entity a Medicare integrity program contract without competition if—

(1) Through approval of a novation agreement, HCFA recognizes the entity as the successor in interest to an intermediary agreement or carrier contract under which the intermediary or carrier was performing activities described in section 1893(b) of the Act on August 21, 1996;

(2) The intermediary or carrier has transferred to the entity all of the resources, including personnel, that were involved in performance under the intermediary agreement or carrier contract and performance of Medicare integrity program activities; and

(3) The intermediary or carrier continued to perform Medicare integrity program activities until transferring the resources to the entity.

(c) An entity is eligible to be awarded a Medicare integrity program contract only if it meets the eligibility requirements established in § 421.302.

§ 421.308 Renewal of a contract.

(a) HCFA specifies an initial contract term in the Medicare integrity program contract. Contracts under this subpart may contain renewal clauses. HCFA may renew the Medicare integrity program contract, without regard to any provision of law requiring competition, as it determines to be appropriate, by giving the contractor notice, within timeframes specified in the contract, of its intent to do so.

(b) HCFA may renew a Medicare integrity program contract without competition if—

(1) The Medicare integrity program contractor continues to meet the requirements established in this subpart;

(2) The Medicare integrity program contractor meets or exceeds all of the performance requirements established in its current contract; and

(3) It is in the best interest of the Government.

(c) If HCFA does not renew a contract, the contract will end in accordance with its terms, and the contractor does not have the right to a hearing or judicial review of the nonrenewal decision.

§ 421.310 Conflict of interest identification.

(a) Definitions. As used in this subpart, the following definitions apply:

Financial relationship means —

(1) A direct or indirect ownership or investment interest (including an option or nonvested interest) in any entity that exists through equity, debt, or other means and includes any indirect ownership or investment interest no matter how many levels removed from a direct interest; or

(2) A compensation arrangement with an entity.

Organizational conflict of interest has the meaning given at 48 CFR 9.501, except that, for purposes of this subpart, the activities and relationships described include those of the offeror or contractor itself and other business related to it and those of its officers, directors (including medical directors), managers, and subcontractors.

(b) General. Except as provided in paragraph (d) of this section, HCFA does not enter into a contract under this subpart with an offeror or contractor that HCFA determines has, or has the potential for, an unresolved organizational conflict of interest.

(c) Identification of conflict. (1) HCFA determines that an offeror or contractor has an organizational conflict of interest, or the potential for the conflict exists, if—

(i) The offeror or contractor is an entity described in paragraph (c)(3) of this section; or

(ii) The offeror or contractor has a present, or known future, direct or indirect financial relationship with an entity described in paragraph (c)(3) of this section.

(2) A financial relationship may exist either—

(i) Through an offeror's or contractor's parent companies, subsidiaries, affiliates, subcontractors, or current clients; or

(ii) From the activities and relationships of the officers, directors (including medical directors), or managers of the offeror or contractor and may be either direct or indirect. An officer, director, or manager has an indirect financial relationship if an ownership or investment interest is held in the name of another but provides benefits to the officer, director, or manager. Examples of indirect financial relationships are holdings in the name of a spouse or dependent child of the officer, director, or manager and holdings of other relatives who reside with the officer, director, or manager.

(3) For purposes of paragraphs (c)(1)(i) and (c)(1)(ii) of this section, the entity is one that—

(i) Provides, insures, or pays for health benefits, with the exception of health plans provided as the entity's employee fringe benefit;

(ii) Conducts audits of health benefit payments or cost reports;

(iii) Conducts statistical analysis of health benefit utilization;

(iv) Would review or does review, under the contract, Medicare services furnished by a provider or supplier that is a direct competitor of the offeror or contractor;

(v) Prepared work or is under contract to prepare work that would be reviewed under the Medicare program integrity contract;

(vi) Is affiliated, as that term is explained in 48 CFR 19.101, with a provider or supplier to be reviewed under the contract.

(4) HCFA may determine that an offeror or contractor has an organizational conflict of interest, or the potential for a conflict exists, based on the following:

(i) Apparent organizational conflicts of interest. An apparent organizational conflict of interest exists if a prudent business person has cause to believe that the offeror or contractor would have a conflict of interest in performing the requirements of a contract under this subpart. No inappropriate action by the offeror or contractor is necessary for an apparent organizational conflict of interest to exist.

(ii) Other contracts and grants with the Federal Government.

(d) Exception. HCFA may contract with an offeror or contractor that has an unresolved conflict of interest if HCFA determines that it is in the best interest of the Government to do so.

(e) Offeror's or contractor's responsibility with regard to subcontractors. An offeror or contractor is responsible for determining whether an organizational conflict of interest exists in any of its proposed or actual subcontractors at any tier and is responsible for ensuring that the subcontractors have mitigated any conflict of interest or potential conflict of interest.

(f) Post-award conflicts of interest. (1) In addition to the conflicts identified in paragraph (c) of this section, HCFA considers that a conflict of interest has occurred if during the term of the contract —

(i) The contractor receives any fee, compensation, gift, payment of expenses, or any other thing of value from any entity that is reviewed, audited, investigated, or contacted during the normal course of performing activities under the Medicare integrity program contract; or

(ii) HCFA determines that the contractor's activities are creating a conflict of interest.

(2) In the event HCFA determines that a conflict of interest exists during the term of the contract, among other actions, it may, as it deems appropriate —

(i) Not renew the contract for an additional term;

(ii) Modify the contract; or

(iii) Terminate the contract.

§ 421.312 Conflict of interest evaluation.

(a) Disclosure. Offerors that wish to be eligible for the award of a contract under this subpart and Medicare integrity program contractors must submit, at times specified in paragraph (b) of this section, an Organizational Conflicts of Interest Certificate. The Certificate must contain the information specified in paragraphs (a)(1) through (a)(8) of this section, unless the information has otherwise been provided in the proposal, in which case it must be referenced. Each solicitation issued for a contract under this subpart contains the requirements for disclosure for pre- and post-award purposes.

The solicitation may require more detailed information than identified in this section.

(1) A description of all business or contractual relationships or activities that may be viewed by a prudent business person as a conflict of interest.

(2) A description of the methods the offeror or contractor will apply to mitigate any situations listed in the Certificate that could be identified as a conflict of interest.

(3) A description of the offeror's or contractor's program to monitor its compliance and the compliance of its proposed and actual subcontractors with the conflict of interest requirements as identified in the relevant solicitation.

(4) A description of the offeror's or contractor's plans to contract with an independent auditor to conduct a compliance audit.

(5) An affirmation, using language that HCFA may prescribe, signed by an official authorized to bind the contractor, that the offeror or contractor understands that HCFA may consider any deception or omission in the Certificate grounds for nonconsideration for contract award in the procurement process, termination of the contract, or other contract or legal action.

(6) Corporate and organizational structure.

(7) Financial interests in other entities, including the following:

(i) Percentage of ownership in any other entity.

(ii) Income generated from other sources.

(iii) A list of current or known future contracts or arrangements, regardless of size, with any—

(A) Insurance organization or subcontractor of an insurance organization; or

(B) Providers or suppliers furnishing health services for which payment may be made under the Medicare program.

(iv) In the case of contracts or arrangements identified in accordance with paragraph (a)(7)(iii) of this section, the dollar amount of the contracts or arrangements, the type of work performed, and the period of performance.

(8) The following information for all of the offeror's or contractor's officers, directors (including medical directors), and managers who would be or are involved with the performance of the Medicare integrity program contract:

(i) The information required under paragraphs (a)(1), (a)(7)(iii), and (a)(7)(iv) of this section.

(ii) If required by the solicitation, the information specified in paragraphs (a)(7)(i) and (a)(7)(ii) of this section.

(b) When disclosure is made. The Organizational Conflicts of Interest Certificate is submitted—

(1) With the offeror's proposal;

(2) When the HCFA Contracting Officer requests a revision in the Certificate;

(3) As part of a compliance audit by an independent auditor; and

(4) 45 days before any change in the information submitted in accordance with paragraph (a) or paragraph (b) of this section. Only changed information must be submitted.

(c) Evaluation. HCFA evaluates organizational conflicts of interest and potential conflicts, using the information provided in the Organizational Conflicts of Interest Certificate, in order to promote the effective and efficient administration of the Medicare program.

(d) Protection of proprietary information disclosed. (1) HCFA protects disclosed proprietary information as allowed under the Freedom of Information Act (5 U.S.C. 552).

(2) HCFA requires signed statements from HCFA personnel with access to proprietary information that prohibit personal use during the procurement process and term of the contract.

§ 421.314 Conflict of interest resolution.

(a) Review Board. HCFA establishes a Conflicts of Interest Review Board to resolve organizational conflicts of interest and determines when the Board is convened.

(b) Resolution. Resolution of an organizational conflict of interest is a determination that—

(1) The conflict has been mitigated;

(2) The conflict precludes award of a contract to the offeror;

(3) The conflict requires that HCFA modify an existing contract;

(4) The conflict requires that HCFA terminate an existing contract; or

(5) It is in the best interest of the Government to contract with the offeror or contractor even though the conflict exists.

§ 421.316 Limitation on Medicare integrity program contractor liability.

(a) None of the following will be held by reason of the performance of any duty, function, or activity required or authorized under this subpart or under a valid contract entered into under this subpart to have violated any criminal law or to be civilly liable under any law of the United States or of any State (or political subdivision thereof) provided due care was exercised in that performance:

(1) An entity having a contract with HCFA under this subpart (that is, a contractor under this subpart).

(2) A person employed by or who has a fiduciary relationship with or who furnishes professional services to a contractor under this subpart.

(b) HCFA makes payment, to a contractor under this subpart, or to a member or employee of the contractor, or to any person who furnishes legal counsel or services to the contractor, of an amount equal to the reasonable amount of the expenses incurred in connection with the defense of a suit, action, or proceeding, as determined by HCFA, if—

(1) The suit, action, or proceeding was brought against the contractor, or a member or employee of the contractor, by a third party and relates to the performance by the contractor, member, or employee of any duty, function, or activity under a contract entered into with HCFA under this subpart;

(2) The funds are available; and

(3) The expenses are otherwise allowable under the terms of the contract.

(Catalog of Federal Domestic Assistance Program No. 93.773, Medicare—Hospital Insurance; and Program No. 93.774, Medicare— Supplementary Medical Insurance Program)

Dated: March 5, 1998.

Nancy-Ann Min DeParle,

Administrator, Health Care Financing Administration.

Approved: March 16, 1998.

Donna E. Shalala,

Secretary.

[FR Doc. 98–7190 Filed 3–16–98; 5:00 pm]

BILLING CODE 4120–01-P

APPENDIX F22

HCFA Final Rule: Medicare Programs; Incentive Programs — Fraud and Abuse

DEPARTMENT OF HEALTH AND HUMAN SERVICES

Health Care Financing Administration

42 CFR Parts 420

[HCFA-6144-FC]

RIN 0938-AH86

Medicare Program; Incentive Programs-Fraud and Abuse

AGENCY: Health Care Financing Administration (HCFA), HHS.

ACTION: Final rule with comment period.

SUMMARY: This final rule with comment period establishes a program for payment to individuals who provide information on Medicare fraud and abuse or other sanctionable activities. This final rule implements section 203(b) of the Health Insurance Portability and Accountability Act of 1996.

DATES: Effective date: This final rule is effective July 8, 1998. Comment period: Comments will be considered if we receive them at the appropriate address, as provided below, no later than 5 p.m. on August 7. 1998.

ADDRESSES: Mail written comments (1 original and 3 copies) to the following address: Health Care Financing Administration, Department of Health and Human Services, Attention: HCFA-6144-FC, P.O. Box 26688, Baltimore, MD 21207–0488.

If you prefer, you may deliver your written comments (1 original and 3 copies) to one of the following addresses:

Room 309-G, Hubert H. Humphrey Building, 7500 Independence Avenue, SW., Washington, DC 20201, or Room C5–09–26, 7500 Security Boulevard, Baltimore, MD 21244–1850.

FOR FURTHER INFORMATION CONTACT: Delilah Schmitt, (410) 786–4300.

SUPPLEMENTARY INFORMATION: Comments may also be submitted electronically to the following e-mail address: hcfa6144fc@hcfa.gov. E-mail comments must include the full name and address of the sender and must be submitted to the referenced address to be considered. All comments must be incorporated in the e-mail message because we may not be able to access attachments. Electronically submitted comments will be available for public inspection at the Independence Avenue address below.

Because of staffing and resource limitations, we cannot accept comments by facsimile (FAX) transmission. In commenting, please refer to file code HCFA-6144-FC. Comments received timely will be available for public inspection as they are received, generally beginning approximately 3 weeks after publication of a document, in Room 309-G of the Department's offices at 200 Independence Avenue, SW., Washington, DC, on Monday through Friday of each week from 8:30 a.m. to 5 p.m. (phone: (202) 690–7890).

I. Rewards for Information Relating to Medicare Fraud and Abuse

A. Background

Section 203(b)(1) of the Health Insurance Portability and Accountability Act of 1996 (Public Law 104–191) instructs the Secretary to establish a program to encourage individuals to report information on individuals and entities that are engaged in or have engaged in acts or omissions that constitute grounds for the imposition of a sanction under section 1128, 1128A, or 1128B of the Social Security Act (the Act) or who have otherwise engaged in sanctionable fraud and abuse against the Medicare program under title XVIII of the Act. By increasing the incentives for concerned citizens to report evidence of suspected fraudulent behavior, Congress hopes to protect beneficiaries and the Medicare Trust Funds.

Section 203(b)(2) of Public Law 104–191 authorizes the Secretary to pay a reward to individuals who provide information under the program established under section 203(b)(1) if the information leads to the recovery of at least $100 (excluding penalties under section 1128B of the Act) by the Secretary or the Attorney General of the United States. Public Law 104–191 requires the reward to come from the amounts collected. The Statute also addresses a suggestion program. We are still analyzing the most effective methods for implementing this requirement and will address it in subsequent rulemaking.

B. Provisions of this Final Rule

This rule adds a new Subpart E, consisting of §§ 420.400 through 420.405, to 42 CFR part 420 ("Program Integrity: Medicare). New Subpart E includes provisions to implement section 203(b) of Public Law 104–191 and is entitled as "Rewards for Information Relating to Medicare Fraud and Abuse".

Section § 420.400 sets forth the statutory basis and scope of Subpart E.

Section § 420.405 sets forth our policies regarding, and procedures for, rewarding individuals for furnishing information relating to Medicare fraud and abuse. The statute contains no provisions limiting or restricting our discretion in determining the rewards to be granted under the program established under section 203(b). Therefore, in paragraph (a) of § 420.405, we specify that when HCFA exercises its discretion in determining that someone is eligible for a reward and the reward amount, the reward will be granted and the individual notified according to the procedures in § 420.405(d). Further, we specify that we may make a monetary reward only for information that leads to a minimum recovery of $100 of Medicare funds from individuals and entities that are engaging in, or have engaged in, acts or omissions that constitute grounds for the imposition of a sanction under section 1128, section 1128A, or section 1128B of the Act or that have otherwise engaged in fraud and abuse against the Medicare program under title XVIII of the Act and for which there is a sanction provided under law. This provision, which is specifically mandated in the authorizing statute, ensures that a reward is paid only if Medicare funds are recovered because of the commission of certain specifically sanctionable offenses. These include the defrauding of the Medicare program or the offering of or solicitation of kickbacks for services payable by Medicare. Individuals who furnish information concerning actions or omissions for which there are no sanctions at law are not eligible to receive a reward under this program even if the information leads to the recovery of Medicare payments.

Finally, in order to ensure that the program does not duplicate other Government incentive programs, we also specify, in paragraph (a), that we may pay rewards only in instances in which a reward is not otherwise provided at law. That is, if the information furnished qualifies the participant for a reward under another Government program, the individual is not entitled to a reward under this program.

Paragraph (b) of § 420.405 specifies the information that would be required in order for a participant to be eligible to receive a reward. Section 203(b)(1) of Public Law 104–191 requires that the reward program discourage the submission of information that is frivolous or otherwise not relevant or material to the imposition of a sanction. Such information will not be considered by the Secretary. Therefore, we have developed criteria to ensure that only individuals who provide information that directly contributes to the recovery of Medicare funds from a fraudulent provider or supplier are considered for a reward. Those criteria are discussed below.

Paragraph (b)(1) of § 420.405 specifies that, in order for an individual to qualify for a reward, the information furnished by that individual must relate to a specific situation, individual, or entity, and must specify the time period of the alleged activities. This provision is intended to discourage individuals from furnishing information of a general nature and to ensure that information submitted be of assistance in the investigation of a specific sanctionable offense. To be of assistance in the development of an investigation, information must relate to specific actions by a specific individual or entity. Any information that is too general in nature (for example, "Medicare should look into home health agencies in Smith County") is of little or no use in targeting scarce investigation resources and does not show that the individual has any specific knowledge of wrongdoing on the part of a certain individual or entity. An example of the kind of information that would meet the requirements of this provision would be that a particular home health agency is billing Medicare for visits not actually furnished.

Paragraph (b)(2) of § 420.405 specifies that we do not give a reward for the submission of information relating to sanctionable activities already known or suspected by the Government, its contractors, or State or local law enforcement agencies. Accordingly, information relating to an individual or entity that, at the time the information is provided, is already the subject of a review or investigation by us, our contractors, or the Office of Inspector General (OIG), the Department of Justice, the Federal Bureau of Investigation, or any other Federal, State, or local law enforcement agency would not serve as the "basis for the collection" and could not be compensated. Paragraph (c) of § 420.405 sets forth the criteria that an individual must meet in order to be eligible for a reward. Paragraph (c)(1) provides that any person, other than one excluded under paragraph (c)(2), is eligible to receive a reward under the reward program if he or she submits the information in the prescribed manner (discussed later in this preamble). Accordingly, Medicare beneficiaries, Medicare providers, and any other individuals may be eligible to receive awards under this reward program.

Paragraph (c)(2) specifies who is ineligible to receive a reward under the reward program. Specifically, paragraph (c)(2)(i) provides that an individual who was or is an immediate family member of an officer or employee of the Department of Health and Human Services (HHS) or its contractors, the Social Security Administration, a State Medicaid agency, the OIG, or the Department of Justice, the Federal Bureau of Investigation, or any other Federal, State, or local law enforcement agency at the time he or she came into possession of or reported information leading to a recovery of Medicare funds is not eligible to receive a reward. Paragraph (c)(2)(ii) specifies that any other Federal or State employee or contractor or HHS grantee is not eligible for a reward if he or she acquired the submitted information in the course of his or her official duties.

The purpose of the exclusion is to prevent Government employees, contractors, or grantees from personally profiting from information gained while doing public business. These individuals may, in the course of performing their official duties, obtain information relating to sanctionable offenses by individuals or entities providing services under the Medicare program. As a responsibility of their position, however, these individuals are obligated to take the necessary steps to ensure that this information is reported to the appropriate authorities. This exclusion also applies to former employees of the specified organizations if the information in question was obtained during their employment. Similarly, any other Federal, State, or local government employee or contractor or HHS grantee is excluded from receiving a reward under this reward program if the information was obtained in the course of his or her official duties. As with the previous exclusion, this exclusion is intended to prevent individuals from personally profiting from information gained in the course of conducting public business.

Paragraph (c)(2)(iii) excludes any individual who illegally obtained the information he or she submitted from receiving a reward under this program. Paragraph (c)(2)(iv) excludes any participants in the alleged sanctionable offense with respect to which payment would be made from receiving a reward under this program. These exclusions are intended to prevent those who have violated the law from profiting from their actions at the expense of this program.

Paragraph (d) of § 420.405 sets forth reward notification procedures. Paragraph (d)(1) specifies that, as a general rule, we notify an individual of his or her eligibility to receive a reward, by letter sent to the individual's last known address. Paragraph (d)(1) further specifies that the notification is sent after Medicare funds have been recovered and a participant has been determined eligible to receive a reward. We add that it is the individual's responsibility to provide all relevant information and to ensure that the reward program is notified of any changes in that information.

Paragraph (d)(2) provides that an individual has up to 1 year from the date on the notification letter to claim his or her reward. This paragraph also specifies that no interest is paid on rewards that are not immediately claimed.

Paragraph (d)(2) also specifies that, if the participant has become incapacitated or died, an executor, administrator, or other legal representative may claim the reward on behalf of the participant or participant's estate. In order to protect participants from being defrauded by individuals falsely claiming to be their legal representatives, we add that the claimant must submit certified copies of letters testamentary, letters of administration, or other similar evidence to show his or her authority to claim the reward. Here, again, we specify that the reward must be claimed within 1 year from the date on which we mailed notification to the participant.

We have set these 1-year limitations to minimize the administrative burden associated with the reward program. We believe 1 year is a reasonable period of time during which an individual may claim his or her reward. In addition, the 1-year limitation protects the Government from the administrative and fiscal burden that would be associated with maintaining claims for a longer or indefinite period. Rewards not claimed within 1 year from the date of the notification letter will not be awarded.

In paragraph (e) of § 420.405, we establish the limits on rewards and set forth the processes by which we determine whether we will pay a reward and, if a reward is to be paid, the amount of the reward. Paragraph (e)(1) specifies that, in determining whether we will pay a reward, and the amount of the reward, we take into consideration all relevant factors, including the significance of the information furnished in relation to the ultimate resolution of the case and the recovery of Medicare funds.

To give participants a realistic expectation of potential reward amounts, we establish general guidelines for the calculation of the amount of any reward and a maximum potential reward amount. Since the primary goal of this program is to preserve and protect the Medicare Trust Funds, and because the funds used for rewards under the program will come from recovered trust fund monies, it would be inappropriate to grant excessive or overly-generous rewards. Therefore, § 420.405(e)(2) specifies that the amount of a reward represents what we consider to be adequate compensation in the particular case, not to exceed 10 percent of the overpayments recovered in the case, or $1,000, whichever is less. We believe this approach provides adequate compensation and notification to those individuals who provide important information on sanctionable activities, while also establishing an objective limit on Trust Fund disbursements.

We anticipate that some commenters will object to this limit as being too low. In response, we point out that persons with information on individuals or entities purportedly defrauding the Medicare program also have the option of initiating a "qui tam" action against the fraudulent individual or entity in cooperation with the Government. (A qui tam action is an action brought by a private individual, under a statute that establishes a penalty for the commission or omission of a certain act that is recoverable in a civil action. In a qui tam action, an individual brings the civil action on behalf of him or herself and the Government, State, or other entity. Part of any collected penalty goes to the person who brings the civil action.)

We determine reward amounts on a case by case basis. Section 420.405(e)(3) specifies that, if more than one participant provides information that leads to the recovery of Medicare funds, we allocate the overall reward (not to exceed 10 percent of the overpayments recovered in that case or $1,000, whichever is less) among the total number of participants. Again, this provision is intended to protect the Medicare Trust Funds to the greatest possible extent.

In accordance with section 203(b)(2) of Public Law 104–191, § 420.405(e)(4) specifies that rewards are based solely on recovered Medicare payments and not on amounts collected as penalties or fines. Section 420.405(e)(5) specifies that rewards are awarded only after all overpayments, fines, and penalties have been collected. It is important for participants to understand that the investigation, development, and prosecution or settlement of a fraud case is a complicated and lengthy process. Given the material and human resource constraints, it is not unusual for 3 to 5 years to elapse before fraudulently-obtained Medicare funds are recovered and any applicable fines or penalties collected. This means that, on average, a participant who provides information that leads to a Medicare recovery from an individual or entity that committed a sanctionable offense would have to wait several years before receiving a reward under this program.

Section 420.405(e)(6) specifies that no person may make any offer or promise or otherwise bind us or HHS with respect to the payment of any reward or the amount of the reward.

Paragraph (f) of § 420.405 describes the procedure individuals must follow when submitting information in order to be eligible to receive a reward under this program. Paragraph (f)(1) provides that an individual may submit information to us on individuals and/or entities allegedly engaging in, or that have allegedly engaged in, fraud and abuse against the Medicare program by calling the Office of Inspector General or the Medicare intermediary or carrier that has jurisdiction over the suspected fraudulent provider or supplier.

Paragraph (f)(2) of § 420.405 adds that an individual interested in receiving a reward must provide his or her name, address, telephone number, and any other requested identifying information so that he or she may be contacted, if necessary, for additional information and, when applicable, for the payment of a reward upon resolution of the case. An individual may elect to furnish information to the Office of the Inspector General, or to the intermediary or carrier anonymously. However, if an individual elects to do so, he or she would not be eligible to receive a reward under this program.

Section 420.405(g) specifies that we do not disclose the participant's identity to any persons except as required by law. Finally, § 420.405(h) specifies that, if, after an award had been accepted, the awardee is determined ineligible to receive a reward under this program, the Government is not liable for the reward and the awardee must refund all monies received. This provision is intended to protect the Government from paying rewards to individuals it later finds were not eligible to participate in the program. For example, the Government would recover a reward granted to a participant who was later found to have participated in the sanctionable offense with respect to which payment was made.

II. Response to Comments

Because of the large number of items of correspondence we normally receive on Federal Register documents published for comment, we are not able to acknowledge or respond to them individually. We will consider all comments we receive by the date and time specified in the DATES section of this preamble, and, if we proceed with a subsequent document, we will respond to the comments in the preamble to that document.

III. Regulatory Impact Analysis

A. Introduction

We have examined the impact of this rule as required by Executive Order 12866 and the Regulatory Flexibility Act (RFA) (Public Law 96-354). Executive Order 12866 directs agencies to assess all costs and benefits of available regulatory alternatives and, when regulation is necessary, to select regulatory approaches that maximize net benefits (including potential economic, environmental, public health and safety effects, distributive impacts, and equity). The RFA requires agencies to analyze options for regulatory relief of small businesses. For purposes of the RFA, small entities include small businesses, nonprofit organizations, and governmental agencies. Most hospitals and most other providers and suppliers are small entities, either by nonprofit status or by having revenues of $5 million or less annually. Individuals are not considered to be small entities.

Section 1102(b) of the Social Security Act requires us to prepare a regulatory impact analysis for any rule that may have a significant impact on the operations of a substantial number of small rural hospitals. This analysis must conform to the provisions of section 603 of the RFA. For purposes of section 1102(b), we define a small rural hospital as a hospital that is located outside a Metropolitan Statistical Area and has fewer than 50 beds.

B. Summary of This Rule

This rule establishes a payment system as a means of encouraging individuals to report instances of suspected fraud and abuse or other sanctionable activities under the Medicare program. The rule delineates program parameters, information requirements, eligibility criteria, establishes an upper limit for payments, defines proportionate distribution in cases of multiple informants, and outlines the process and time limitations for obtaining a reward.

C. Discussion of Impact

This rule is expected to affect beneficiaries, their personal representatives, providers, physicians, other suppliers, and managed care plans. (We have separate authority to impose intermediate sanctions against managed care plans participating in the Medicare program. The law also permits the Office of Inspector General to impose civil money penalties on the health maintenance organization or competitive medical plan as set forth in 42 CFR part 1003.) Taxpayers and the trust fund could also be impacted by this rule.

Beneficiaries as a group are expected to be impacted by this regulation in a variety of ways. First, beneficiaries are often the first to recognize and question provider practices. This regulation encourages these individuals to share such information with the agency by (1) providing a clearly defined process for submitting information to the appropriate source and (2) offering a monetary incentive to support the effort. Secondly, this group would benefit from fraud reduction through greater confidence in the program and its continued financial viability. Some beneficiaries may or may not be motivated by a reward system to report fraudulent provider activity because of a perceived potential for breaching the provider/patient relationship.

Notwithstanding some minimal hesitancy in reporting fraud, beneficiaries are already one of our strongest allies in quickly detecting and providing us with a great many leads about instances of fraud and abuse in the Medicare program. Beneficiaries are asked to review the Explanation of Medicare Benefits form, which lists services and charges and is sent to each beneficiary when a service is furnished, and report any discrepancies concerning those services to the Medicare contractor serving their area. Medicare contractors estimate that of the 130,000 calls they receive yearly concerning potential fraud and abuse, 94,000 are from beneficiaries, many of whom call to question the propriety of claims made on their behalf. We estimate that there will be a 5 or 10 percent increase in the volume of calls received as a result of this monetary reward incentive program. We support this activity by regularly advising beneficiaries and their representatives about opportunities to preserve trust fund dollars and how they can help combat fraud and abuse.

Fraud, waste, and abuse in medical care encompass a wide range of practices, limited only by the scope of human imagination. To the fraudulent provider of health care services, fee-for-service reimbursement provides the opportunity for: (1) Billing for services not provided; (2) billing for a more expensive service than was actually provided; (3) providing and billing for unnecessary services; (4) paying kickbacks for referrals, including self-referrals; and (5) duplicate billing. Two fraudulent schemes involving falsifying records and overcharging include "upcoding" and "unbundling.' ' Upcoding involves switching primary and secondary diagnoses to substitute more costly procedures and services than were actually administered to the patient. Unbundling involves improperly separately billing for procedures that should be billed for under one code.

Under managed care, fraudulent and abusive practices may include: (1) Enrolling beneficiaries without their active consent; (2) engaging in deceptive marketing practices to entice enrollment; (3) denying medically necessary services; and (4) failure to disclose appeal rights.

We believe the exact amount of improper billing and health care fraud are difficult to quantify because of their hidden nature. However, a Government Accounting Office (GAO) report on Medicare (GAO/ HR-91–10, February 1997) suggests that by reducing unnecessary or inappropriate payments, the Federal Government would realize large savings and help dampen the growth in Medicare costs. In this report, the GAO states that estimates of the costs of fraud and abuse, ranging from 3 to 10 percent, have been cited for health expenditures nationwide, "so applying this range to Medicare suggests that such losses in fiscal year 1996 could range from $6 billion to as much as $20 billion." Program savings would be offset by the amount of incentives awarded under this rule. The total amount of awards made in any year is unknown but is expected to be nominal.

Overall, we expect that providers and suppliers will benefit qualitatively from this rule. Not only do many providers and suppliers perceive that their reputations are tarnished by the few dishonest providers and suppliers that take advantage of the Medicare program, but some providers may have ideas that could minimize the impact of this adverse behavior. The media often focus on the most egregious cases of Medicare fraud and abuse, leaving the public with the misperception that physicians and other health care practitioners routinely make improper claims. This rule encourages individuals to report instances of suspected fraud and abuse. As the number of dishonest providers and suppliers and improper claims diminishes, ethical providers and suppliers will benefit.

This rule could be considered to have a negative impact on any provider or supplier that routinely submits questionable claims and those that have been receiving inappropriate payments, including managed care plans. Since one objective of this rule is to eliminate improper payments, we will not analyze the effect the rule may have on unscrupulous providers or suppliers. We do not believe that this rule will reduce a provider's or supplier's legitimate income from Medicare.

The reporting of instances of suspected fraud and abuse or other sanctionable activities is not expected to impose a paperwork burden on individuals participating in this award program. Beneficiaries and other participating entities are expected to rely upon existing record collection, record keeping, review and reporting processes similar to those already in use.

D. Conclusion

We conclude that money would be saved, and the solvency of the Trust Funds extended as a result of this rule. The growing complexity of the Medicare program easily lends itself to objective critiques by those who are most affected by the myriad of Medicare statutes, provisions, and guidelines. In addition, the dynamic nature of fraud and abuse, as illustrated by the fact that wrongdoers continue to find ways to evade safeguards, supports the need for constant vigilance and increasingly sophisticated ways to protect against "gaming" of the system.

Based on the above analysis, we have determined, and certify, that this rule will not have a significant economic impact on a substantial number of small entities. We also have determined, and certify, that this rule will not have a significant impact on the operations of a substantial number of small rural hospitals. In accordance with the provisions of Executive Order 12866, this rule was not reviewed by the Office of Management and Budget.

E. Waiver of Proposed Rulemaking

We ordinarily publish a notice of proposed rulemaking in the Federal Register and invite public comment on the proposed rule. The notice of proposed rulemaking includes a reference to the legal authority under which the rule is proposed, and the terms and substances of the proposed rule or a description of the subjects and issues involved. This procedure can be waived, however, if an agency finds good cause that a notice-and-comment procedure is impracticable, unnecessary, or contrary to the public interest and incorporates a statement of the finding and its reasons in the rule issued.

Publishing this rule expeditiously to supplement activities that identify and curtail fraud and abuse activities that reduce the monetary drain on the Medicare trust fund is in the public interest. Specifically, we anticipate that the implementation of this rule will encourage individuals to report potentially fraudulent and abusive activities and we anticipate that such reports will facilitate expeditious recovery of money owed to the Medicare trust funds. Further delaying implementation of this program in order to give the public an opportunity to comment would deprive individuals of the financial incentives that Congress intended to provide to individuals who come forward with relevant information. Additional delay following the publication of a proposed rule may cause some individuals to withhold information necessary to support the Government's efforts until final rules are effective. Because the delay may make it more difficult to successfully complete investigation of those cases, waiving notice and comment clearly is within the public interest.

Therefore, we find good cause to waive the notice of proposed rulemaking and to issue this final rule with comment period. We are providing a 60-day comment period for public comment.

List of Subjects in 42 CFR Part 420

Fraud, Health facilities, Health professions, Incentive programs, Medicare.

For the reasons set forth in the preamble, 42 CFR part 420 is amended as set forth below:

PART 420 — PROGRAM INTEGRITY: MEDICARE

1. The authority citation for part 420 continues to read as follows:

Authority: §§ 1102 and 1871 of the Social Security Act (42 U.S.C. 1302 and 1395hh).

2. A new subpart E is added to part 420 to read as follows:

Subpart E — Rewards for Information Relating to Medicare Fraud and Abuse

Subpart E — Rewards for Information Relating to Medicare Fraud and Abuse

§ 420.400 Basis and scope.

This subpart implements section 203 (b) of Public Law 104–191, which requires the establishment of a program to encourage individuals to report suspected cases of fraud and abuse. Sections 203 (b) of Public Law 104–191 also provides the authority for HCFA to reward individuals for reporting fraud and abuse. This subpart sets forth procedures for rewarding individuals.

§ 420.405 Rewards for information relating to Medicare fraud and abuse.

(a) General rule. HCFA pays a monetary reward for information that leads to the recovery of at least $100 of Medicare funds from individuals and entities that are engaging in, or have engaged in, acts or omissions that constitute grounds for the imposition of a sanction under section 1128, section 1128A, or section 1128B of the Act or that have otherwise engaged in sanctionable fraud and abuse against the Medicare program. The determination of whether an individual meets the criteria for an award, and the amount of the award, is at the discretion of HCFA. HCFA pays rewards only if a reward is not otherwise provided for by law. When HCFA applies the criteria specified in paragraphs (b), (c), and (e) of this section to determine the eligibility and the amount of the reward, it notifies the recipient as specified in paragraph (d) of this section.

(b) Information eligible for reward. (1) In order for an individual to be eligible to receive a reward, the information he or she supplied must relate to the activities of a specific individual or entity and must specify the time period of the alleged activities.

(2) HCFA does not give a reward for information relating to an individual or entity that, at the time the information is provided, is already the subject of a review or investigation by HCFA or its

contractors, or the OIG, the Department of Justice, the Federal Bureau of Investigation, or any other Federal, State, or local law enforcement agency.

(c) Persons eligible to receive a reward— (1) General rule. Any person (other than one excluded under paragraph (c)(2) of this section) is eligible to receive a reward under this section if the person submits the information in the manner set forth in paragraph (f) of this section.

(2) Excluded individuals. (i) An individual who was, or is an immediate family member of, an officer or employee of HHS or its contractors, the SSA, the OIG, a State Medicaid Agency, or the Department of Justice, the Federal Bureau of Investigation, or any other Federal, State, or local law enforcement agency at the time he or she came into possession of, or divulged, information leading to a recovery of Medicare funds is not eligible to receive a reward under this section.

(ii) Any other Federal or State employee or contractor or an HHS grantee is not eligible for a reward under this section if the information submitted came to his or her knowledge in the course of his or her official duties.

(iii) An individual who illegally obtained the information he or she submitted is excluded from receiving a reward under this section.

(iv) An individual who participated in the sanctionable offense with respect to which payment would be made is excluded from receiving a reward under this section.

(d) Notification of eligibility—(1) General rule. After all Medicare funds have been recovered and HCFA has determined a participant eligible to receive a reward under the provisions of this section, it notifies the informant of his or her eligibility, by mail, at the most recent address supplied by the individual. It is the individual's responsibility to ensure that the reward program has been notified of any change in his or her address or other relevant personal information (for example, change of name, phone number).

(2) Special circumstances. (i) If the individual has relocated to an unknown address, the individual or his or her legal representative may claim the reward by contacting HCFA within 1 year from the date on which HCFA first attempted to notify the individual about a reward. HCFA does not consider the individual or his or her legal representative eligible for a reward more than 1 year after the date on which it first attempted to give notice. HCFA does not pay interest on rewards that are not immediately claimed.

(ii) If the individual has become incapacitated or has died, an executor, administrator, or other legal representative may claim the reward on behalf of the individual or the individual's estate. The claimant must submit certified copies of the letters testamentary, letters of administration, or other similar evidence to show his or her authority to claim the reward. The claim must be filed within 1 year from the date on which HCFA first gave or attempted to give notice of the reward.

(e) Amount and payment of reward. (1) In determining whether it will pay a reward and, if so, the amount of the reward, HCFA takes into account all relevant factors, including the significance of the information furnished in relation to the ultimate resolution of the case and the recovery of Medicare funds.

(2) The amount of a reward represents what HCFA considers to be adequate compensation in the particular case, not to exceed 10 percent of the overpayments recovered in the case or $1,000, whichever is less.

(3) If more than one person is eligible to receive a reward in a particular case, HCFA allocates the total reward amount (not to exceed 10 percent of the overpayments recovered in that case or $1,000, whichever is less) among the participants.

(4) HCFA bases rewards only on recovered Medicare payments and not on amounts collected as penalties or fines.

(5) HCFA makes payments as promptly as the circumstances of the case permit, but not until it has collected all Medicare overpayments, fines, and penalties.

(6) No person may make any offer or promise or otherwise bind HCFA or HHS with respect to the payment of any reward under this section or the amount of the reward.

(f) Submission of information. (1) An individual may submit information on persons or entities engaging in, or that have engaged in, fraud and abuse against the Medicare program to the Office of the Inspector General, or to the Medicare intermediary or carrier that has jurisdiction over the suspected fraudulent provider or supplier.

(2) A participant interested in receiving a reward must provide his or her name, address, telephone number, and any other requested identifying information so that he or she may be contacted, if necessary, for additional information and, when applicable, for the payment of a reward upon resolution of the case.

(g) Confidentiality. HCFA does not reveal a participant's identity to any person, except as required by law.

(h) Finding of ineligibility after reward is accepted. If, after a reward is accepted, HCFA finds that the awardee was ineligible to receive the reward, the Government is not liable for the reward and the awardee must refund all monies received.

(Catalog of Federal Domestic Assistance Program No. 93.774, Medicare — Supplementary Medical Insurance Program)

Dated: April 4, 1998.

Nancy-Ann Min DeParle,

Administrator, Health Care Financing Administration.

Dated: June 2, 1998.

Donna E. Shalala,

Secretary.

[FR Doc. 98–15155 Filed 6–3–98; 1:19 pm]

BILLING CODE 4120–01-P

APPENDIX F23

Advisory Opinion No. 98-10

POSTED ON: September 8, 1998

[Issued August 31, 1998]

[name and address redacted]

Re: Advisory Request No. 98–10

Dear [name redacted]:

We are writing in response to your request for an advisory opinion, in which you asked whether the payment of a sales commission to an independent manufacturers' representative (the "Arrangement") constitutes grounds for sanctions under the anti-kickback statute, section 1128B(b) of the Social Security Act (the "Act"), the exclusion authority for kickbacks, section 1128(b)(7) of the Act, or the civil monetary penalty provision for kickbacks, section 1128A(a)(7) of the Act.

You have certified that all of the information you provided in your request, including all supplementary letters, is true and correct and constitutes a complete description of the material facts regarding the Arrangement. In issuing this opinion, we have relied solely on the facts and information you presented to us. We have not undertaken any independent investigation of such information.

Based on the facts certified in your request for an advisory opinion, we conclude that the Arrangement could constitute prohibited remuneration under the anti-kickback statute if the requisite intent to induce referrals were present, but that the OIG will not subject the Arrangement, as described in the request and supplemental submissions, to sanctions arising under the anti-kickback statute pursuant to sections 1128(b)(7) or 1128A(a)(7) of the Act.

This opinion may not be relied on by any person other than the requestor and is further qualified as set out in Part IV below and in 42 C.F.R. § 1008.

I. Factual Background

A. The Parties

Requestor is the sole shareholder and employee of Sales Agent A ("Sales Agent A"), an independent manufacturers' representative. Sales Agent A markets itself as a service providing "negotiation of national hospital agreements." Manufacturer B ("Manufacturer B") is a manufacturer of, among other things, disposable medical supplies.

B. The Arrangement

In April 1997, Sales Agent A entered into a sales agency contract (the "Contract") with Manufacturer B.[1] Under the Contract, Sales Agent A agreed to submit bids and negotiate contracts on behalf of Manufacturer B for the sale and distribution of disposable medical supplies, including adult diapers and disposable underpads, to six potential purchasers (the "Purchasers").[2] Each Purchaser was either a multi-hospital health care system or a group purchasing organization representing primarily hospitals and hospital systems. As compensation for Sales Agent A's efforts, Manufacturer B agreed to pay Sales Agent A a monthly commission of between 1% and 1.25% of invoiced amounts, the specific percentage being set in advance for each Purchaser.[3] Sales Agent A has certified that this compensation represents fair market value. Sales Agent A performed services under the Contract for which it has not yet been paid. The Contract was subsequently canceled as to future Sales Agent A services.

The Contract was the only financial arrangement between Sales Agent A and Manufacturer B, and Sales Agent A had no arrangements with any of the Purchasers for or involving Manufacturer B products. To Sales Agent A's knowledge, Manufacturer B had no financial arrangements with any of the Purchasers involving Manufacturer B products covered by the Contract, other than those arrangements set forth in the contracts negotiated by Sales Agent A.

[1] Specifically, the Contract is between Sales Agent A and Subsidiary B, a division of Manufacturer B.

[2] Sales Agent A successfully negotiated contracts with three of the six potential purchasers identified in the Contract.

[3] In 1997, Sales Agent A's sales commission from Subsidiary B was renegotiated and reduced, in part because Sales Agent A's customers were demanding price reductions.

Sales Agent A has certified that the group purchasing organization fees paid by Manufacturer B to the Purchasers that are group purchasing organizations were 2% or less of sales volume, and that, to Sales Agent A's knowledge, rebates offered to multi-hospital systems were allocated down to each purchasing hospital and properly disclosed to the Federal health care programs. Neither Sales Agent A nor Manufacturer B billed or received any payment from a Federal health care program for the goods sold under the contracts Sales Agent A negotiated.

Sales Agent A's representation of Manufacturer B was limited to submitting bids to and negotiating contracts with the Purchasers and making routine follow-up calls to the Purchasers to resolve questions and to report and reconcile group purchasing organization fees and discounts[4] earned by the Purchasers. Specific orders for goods under the Purchasers' contracts were placed by the Purchasers' purchasing agents directly with Manufacturer B or one of its authorized distributors. Sales Agent A interacted exclusively with centralized purchasing departments of multi-hospital systems and group purchasing organizations; it had no contact with individual hospitals, physicians, or beneficiaries and did not contact or market to anyone in a professional position to make referrals or order goods or services on behalf of individual patients.

II. Legal Analysis

The anti-kickback statute makes it a criminal offense knowingly and wilfully to offer, pay, solicit, or receive any remuneration to induce referrals of items or services reimbursable by Federal health care programs. *See* section 1128B(b) of the Act. Where remuneration is paid purposefully to induce referrals of items or services paid for by a Federal health care program, the anti-kickback statute is violated. By its terms, the statute ascribes liability to parties on both sides of an impermissible "kickback" transaction. For purposes of the anti-kickback statute, "remuneration" includes the transfer of anything of value, in cash or in-kind, directly or indirectly, covertly or overtly.

The statute has been interpreted to cover any arrangement where *one* purpose of the remuneration is to obtain money for referral of services or to induce further referrals. *United States v. Kats,* 871 F.

---

[4] Manufacturer B gave hospital systems discounts in the form of rebates based on sales volume. Nothing in this advisory opinion should be construed as expressing an opinion as to the legality of such rebates.

2d 105 (9th Cir. 1989); *United States v. Greber,* 760 F. 2d 68 (3rd Cir.), *cert. denied,* 476 U.S. 988 (1985). Violation of the statute constitutes a felony punishable by a maximum fine of $25,000, imprisonment up to five years or both. Conviction will also lead to automatic exclusion from Federal health care programs, including Medicare and Medicaid. This Office may also initiate administrative proceedings to exclude persons from Federal health care programs or to impose civil monetary penalties for fraud, kickbacks, and other prohibited activities under sections 1128(b)(7) and 1128A(a)(7) of the Act.[5]

Sales agents are in the business of recommending or arranging for the purchase of the items or services they offer for sale on behalf of their principals, typically manufacturers, or other sellers (collectively, "Sellers"). Accordingly, any compensation arrangement between a Seller and an independent sales agent for the purpose of selling health care items or services that are directly or indirectly reimbursable by a Federal health care program potentially implicates the anti-kickback statute, irrespective of the methodology used to compensate the agent. Moreover, because such agents are independent contractors, they are less accountable to the Seller than an employee. *See* 56 Fed. Reg. 35952, 35981 (July 29, 1991); 54 Fed. Reg. 3088, 3093 (Jan. 23, 1989). For these reasons, this Office has a longstanding concern with independent sales agency arrangements.

In some circumstances, our concerns can be addressed by structuring a sales agency arrangement to fit in a safe harbor. *See, e.g.,* 56 Fed. Reg. at 35974. The Department of Health and Human Services has published safe harbor regulations that protect certain arrangements that might otherwise technically violate the anti-kickback statute from prosecution. *See* section 1128B(b)(3) of the Act; 42 C.F.R. § 1001.952. The safe harbors set forth specific conditions that, if met, assure entities involved of not being prosecuted or sanctioned for the arrangement qualifying for the safe harbor. However, safe harbor protection is only afforded to those arrangements that precisely meet all of the conditions set forth in the safe harbor. The regulatory safe harbor potentially applicable to the Arrangement is the personal services and management contracts safe harbor. *See* 42 C.F.R. § 1001.952(d). The Arrangement could not qualify under this

[5] Because both the criminal and administrative sanctions related to the anti-kickback implications of the Arrangement are based on violations of the anti-kickback statute, the analysis for the purposes of this advisory opinion is the same under both.

safe harbor, however, since the nature of the services provided under the Contract precluded an exact specification of the schedule for the performance of Sales Agent A's services and a determination of Sales Agent A's total aggregate compensation in advance, as required by the regulation.

In reviewing sales arrangements that do not fit in the personal services and management contracts safe harbor, this Office has identified several characteristics of arrangements among Sellers, sales agents, and purchasers that appear to be associated with an increased potential for program abuse, particularly overutilization and excessive program costs. These suspect characteristics include, but are not limited to:

- compensation based on percentage of sales;
- direct billing of a Federal health care program by the Seller for the item or service sold by the sales agent;
- direct contact between the sales agent and physicians in a position to order items or services that are then paid for by a Federal health care program;
- direct contact between the sales agent and Federal health care program beneficiaries;
- use of sales agents who are health care professionals or persons in a similar position to exert undue influence on purchasers or patients; or
- marketing of items or services that are separately reimbursable by a Federal health care program (e.g., items or services not bundled with other items or services covered by a DRG payment), whether on the basis of charges or costs.

This list is illustrative, not exhaustive, and the absence of any of these factors certainly does not mean that a sales arrangement is permissible under the anti-kickback statute. However, the more factors that are present, the greater the scrutiny we ordinarily will give an arrangement. Of course, in all cases the statute is not violated unless the parties have the requisite intent to induce referrals.

While Sales Agent A's compensation was established as a percentage of the sales made to specified accounts, none of the other factors triggering increased scrutiny was present. Neither Manufacturer B nor Subsidiary B billed any payer for the items being sold. There was no contact between Sales Agent A and patients or physicians. Sales Agent A was not in a position to exert undue influence on medical decision-making. Sales Agent A's direct contacts were with sophisticated purchasers, either group purchasing organizations or the purchasing units of multi-hospital systems, none of whom were in a position to order specific products for individual patients. Disposable medical supplies, including adult diapers and disposable underpads, are not, as a general matter, separately reimbursed to hospitals by Federal health care programs.

Sales Agent A has certified that most of the ultimate purchasers of the products were acute care hospitals. Because the particular products being sold, i.e., adult diapers and disposable underpads, are generally not separately reimbursable by Federal health care programs, the cost of the items furnished to inpatients represents an expense to the hospitals that must be covered by the fixed DRG payment. Such costs necessarily reduce the amount of profit for the hospital; thus, there is little, if any, incentive to overutilize the products or to pay more than necessary for the items, unless there are side agreements that confer additional benefits on the hospitals.[6] This conclusion is consistent with Sales Agent A's certification that in 1997 its sales commission from Subsidiary B was renegotiated and reduced in part because Sales Agent A's customers were demanding price reductions. In such circumstances, the risk of overutilization and excessive costs is largely offset by the inability of the purchaser to pass on the costs of the items purchased to the Federal health care programs.[7]

Finally, this opinion is premised on Sales Agent A's certifications that: (i) Sales Agent A had no commission-splitting or other arrangements with any Purchaser; (ii) Sales Agent A had no arrangement with Manufacturer B other than the Contract; (iii) to Sales Agent A's knowledge, Manufacturer B had no arrangements with the Purchasers with respect to the products sold in connection with the Contract, other than the rebates and group purchasing fees disclosed in the request for an advisory opinion; (iv) the group purchasing fees paid by Manufacturer B were 2% or less of sales volume; and (v) to Sales

---

[6] The fact that some small number of ultimate purchasers may have been skilled nursing facilities or other providers receiving cost-based reimbursement would not have reduced the incentive of the group purchasing organization or hospital system that negotiated with Sales Agent A to obtain the best deal and lowest prices for their clients as a whole.

[7] We express no opinion regarding the liability of the Purchasers or any other party under the False Claims Act or other legal authorities for any improper billing, claims submission, or other conduct in connection with products purchased pursuant to the Arrangement.

Agent A's knowledge, discounts from Manufacturer B to the Purchasers for products sold in connection with the Contract were allocated down to the purchasing hospital and properly disclosed to the Federal health care programs.

III. Conclusion

For the above reasons, we conclude that, although the Arrangement would technically fall within the prohibition of the anti-kickback statute if the requisite intent were present, we would not seek to impose sanctions under sections 1128(b)(7) (as it relates to kickbacks) or 1128A(a)(7) of the Act for payments made under the Contract, provided the compensation is fair market value as Sales Agent A has certified.[8]

IV. Limitations

The limitations applicable to this opinion include the following:

- This advisory opinion is issued only to Sales Agent A, the requestor of this opinion. This advisory opinion has no application, and cannot be relied upon, by any other individual or entity.
- This advisory opinion may not be introduced into evidence in any matter involving an entity or individual that is not a requestor to this opinion.
- This advisory opinion is applicable only to the statutory provisions specifically noted above. No opinion is herein expressed or implied with respect to the application of any other Federal, state, or local statute, rule, regulation, ordinance, or other law that may be applicable to the Arrangement.
- This advisory opinion will not bind or obligate any agency other than the U.S. Department of Health and Human Services.
- This advisory opinion is limited in scope to the specific arrangement described in this letter and has no applicability to other arrangements, even those that appear similar in nature or scope.

---

[8] While we are not authorized to opine on "fair market value," *see* section 1128D(b)(3) of the Act, we note that Sales Agent A's percentage commission under the Contract was less than one-half of the 3% amount established in the safe harbor for group purchasing organizations, *see* 42 C.F.R. § 1001.952 (j), and that the amount of the sales price paid as a commission to Sales Agent A and the group purchasing organizations together either equaled or only slightly exceeded the 3% amount.

This opinion is also subject to any additional limitations set forth at 42 C.F.R. Part 1008.

The OIG will not proceed against the requester with respect to any action that is part of the Arrangement taken in good faith reliance upon this advisory opinion as long as all of the material facts have been fully, completely, and accurately presented, the compensation under the Contract represented fair market value, and the Arrangement in practice comports with the information provided. The OIG reserves the right to reconsider the questions and issues raised in this advisory opinion and, where the public interest requires, rescind, modify, or terminate this opinion. In the event that this advisory opinion is modified or terminated, the OIG will not proceed against the requestor with respect to any action taken in good faith reliance upon this advisory opinion, where all of the relevant facts were fully, completely, and accurately presented, where the compensation under the Contract represented fair market value, and where such action was promptly discontinued upon notification of the modification or termination of this advisory opinion. An advisory opinion may be rescinded only if the relevant and material facts have not been fully, completely, and accurately disclosed to the OIG.

Sincerely,

/s/

D. McCarty Thornton

Chief Counsel to the Inspector General

APPENDIX F24

Advisory Opinion No. 98-11

[Issued: September 14, 1998]

[Posted on the OIG Web Site: September 21, 1998]

[Names and addresses redacted]

Re: [Names redacted]

Advisory Opinion No. 98–11

Dear Sirs: We are writing in response to your request for an advisory opinion, in which you ask whether a proposed purchasing arrangement involving a trade association, its nursing home members, and an electrical utility consultant (the "Proposed Arrangement") constitutes prohibited remuneration under the anti-kickback statute, section 1128B(b) of the Social Security Act (the "Act"), and if so, whether the Proposed Arrangement constitutes grounds for the imposition of sanctions under the anti-kickback statute, section 1128B(b) of the Act; the civil monetary penalty provision for kickbacks, section 1128A(a)(7) of the Act; or the exclusion authority related to kickbacks, section 1128(b)(7) of the Act.

You have certified that all of the information you provided in your request is true and correct and constitutes a complete description of the material facts regarding the Proposed Arrangement. In issuing this opinion, we have relied solely on the facts and information you presented to us. We have not undertaken any independent investigation of such information. This opinion is limited to the facts presented. If material facts have not been disclosed, this opinion is without force and effect.

I. FACTUAL BACKGROUND

A. The Parties

The Trade Association is a not-for-profit trade association representing nursing homes and assisted living facilities (the "Nursing

Homes"). The Utility Consultant is an electricity consultant licensed by State X.[1] Many of the individual Nursing Homes are certified Medicare and Medicaid providers; the Trade Association and the Utility Consultant are not.

B. The Proposed Arrangement

In 1997, State X enacted legislation deregulating the electric utility industry. Effective March 1, 1998, certain reductions in electricity charges were mandated, including a "standard offer service" and a "default service," which are expected to reduce overall electricity charges for users. To help users obtain even greater savings, State X is licensing competitive power suppliers to sell electricity in the State. Consistent with the purposes of this competitive market, licensed brokers and others are permitted to seek out lower cost suppliers of electricity and to arrange for the sale of this lower cost electricity to customers.

To make such brokerage services available to its members at the best possible price, the Trade Association proposes to enter into a contract with the Utility Consultant, pursuant to which the Utility Consultant will agree to provide electricity brokerage and consulting services to Trade Association members for a fee equal to seventeen percent of the cost savings achieved by the Utility Consultant for each Nursing Home.[2] Cost savings will be measured by comparing a Nursing Home's actual cost of electricity, as negotiated by the Utility Consultant, with the amount that the Nursing Home would have paid for "standard offer service," if available, or the "default service." Pursuant to the contract, the Trade Association will make its member list available to the Utility Consultant and will permit the Utility Consultant to use the Trade Association's name for marketing purposes. The Trade Association will receive a fee equal to eleven percent of the fees the Utility Consultant receives from the Nursing Homes.

Each Nursing Home that elects to use the Utility Consultant's consulting and brokerage services will enter into a separate contract

---

[1] The Trade Association and the Utility Consultant are joint "Requestors" of this advisory opinion.

[2] The Requestors have represented that the payment terms between the Nursing Homes and the Utility Consultant may be modified in the future by agreement of the parties. We express no opinion about any different compensation terms. This opinion is limited to the compensation terms described here.

with the Utility Consultant. No Nursing Home will be obligated to use the Utility Consultant's services. Nursing Homes will have an opportunity to compare electricity prices with other consultants or utility providers before accepting the price negotiated by the Utility Consultant. Each contract between the Utility Consultant and an individual Nursing Home will have a term of three years, but if no reduction in electricity costs is obtained, the Nursing Home will be permitted to cancel the contract after one year.

Pursuant to a letter agreement between the Trade Association and each Nursing Home, the Nursing Home will authorize the Trade Association to act as its purchasing agent for electricity brokerage services, and the Trade Association will disclose the amount of its fee from the Utility Consultant. The Trade Association will also report to each Nursing Home annually, and to the Department of Health and Human Services ("HHS") upon request, the share of the Trade Association's fee attributable to each Nursing Home.

II. LEGAL ANALYSIS

The anti-kickback statute makes it a criminal offense knowingly and willfully to offer, pay, solicit, or receive any remuneration to induce the referral of business covered by a Federal health care program. Specifically, the statute provides that:

Whoever knowingly and willfully offers or pays [or solicits or receives] any remuneration (including any kickback, bribe, or rebate) directly or indirectly, overtly or covertly, in cash or in kind to any person to induce such person — to refer an individual to a person for the furnishing or arranging for the furnishing of any item or service for which payment may be made in whole or in part under a Federal health care program, or to purchase, lease, order, or arrange for or recommend purchasing, leasing, or ordering any good, facility, service, or item for which payment may be made in whole or in part under a Federal health care program, shall be guilty of a felony.

Section 1128B(b) of the Act. In other words, the statute prohibits payments made purposefully to induce referrals of business payable by a Federal health care program. The statute ascribes liability to both sides of an impermissible "kickback" transaction. The statute has been interpreted to cover any arrangement where *one* purpose of the remuneration was to obtain money for the referral of services or to induce further referrals. *United States v. Kats*, 871 F.2d 105 (9th Cir. 1989); *United States v. Greber*, 760 F.2d 68 (3d Cir.), *cert. denied*, 474 U.S. 988 (1985). "Remuneration" for purposes of the anti-kickback statute includes the transfer of anything of value, in cash or in kind, directly or indirectly, covertly or overtly. Violation of the statute constitutes a felony punishable by a maximum fine of $25,000, imprisonment up to five years or both. Conviction will also lead to automatic exclusion from Federal health care programs, including Medicare and Medicaid. This Office may also initiate administrative proceedings to exclude persons from the Federal and State health care programs or to impose civil monetary penalties for fraud, kickbacks, and other prohibited activities under sections 1128 (b)(7) and 1128A(a)(7) of the Act.[3]

A number of statutory and regulatory "safe harbors" protect certain arrangements that might otherwise technically violate the anti-kickback statute from prosecution. *See* section 1128B(b)(3) of the Act; 42 C.F.R. § 1001.952. Safe harbor protection is afforded only to those arrangements that precisely meet all of the conditions set forth in the safe harbor. The relevant safe harbor here is the group purchasing organizations ("GPO") safe harbor. *See* 42 C.R.F. § 1001.952(j).

The GPO safe harbor provides protection for payments by a vendor of goods or services to a GPO (the "GPO fee"). For purposes of this safe harbor, a GPO is defined as an entity authorized to act as a purchasing agent for a group of individuals or entities who (i) are furnishing services for which payment may be made in whole or in part under Medicare or a State health care program and (ii) are neither wholly owned by the GPO nor subsidiaries of a parent corporation that wholly owns the GPO (either directly or through another wholly-owned entity). The GPO fee must be paid as part of an agreement to furnish goods or services to the group of individuals or entities for which the GPO is the authorized agent.

The GPO must have a written agreement with each individual or entity that will purchase items or services from the vendor. The agreement must accurately reflect the amount of the GPO fee by satisfying one of the following two conditions. First, the agreement may state that the GPO fee will be three percent or less of the purchase price of the goods or services sold by the vendor to the individual or entity. Second, if the GPO fee is greater than three percent, the agreement must state the specific amount of the fee,

[3] Because both the criminal and administrative sanctions related to the anti-kickback implications of the Proposed Arrangement are based on violations of the anti-kickback statute, the analysis for purposes of this advisory opinion is the same under both.

expressed either as a fixed sum or as a fixed percentage of the value of the purchases made from the vendor by the members of the group under the contract between the vendor and the GPO. If the amount of the GPO fee is not known at the time the agreement is signed, the agreement must state the maximum amount to be paid to the GPO by the vendor. In addition, where the entity that receives the goods or services from the vendor is a health care provider of services, the GPO must disclose in writing to the entity at least annually, and to the Secretary upon request, the amount received from each vendor with respect to purchases made by or on behalf of the entity. *See* 42 C.F.R. § 1001.952(j).

In the circumstances presented here, the fee paid by the Utility Consultant to the Trade Association will fit squarely within the GPO safe harbor. The Utility Consultant is a vendor of electricity brokerage services. The Trade Association will be authorized by its Nursing Home members pursuant to the letter agreements to act as a purchasing agent for electricity brokerage services. The Trade Association will negotiate the terms upon which the Nursing Homes will enter into contracts with the Utility Consultant for its services, including payment terms. Each Nursing Home's payment will be based on its cost savings. The Nursing Homes furnish items and services that are reimbursable by the Federal health care programs and will appropriately reflect the cost savings on their cost reports. The Trade Association will accept as payment from the Utility Consultant a quarterly sum equal to eleven percent of the Utility Consultant's fee from the Nursing Homes and will disclose this fee to the Nursing Homes. The Trade Association will also provide an annual report to each Nursing Home disclosing that Nursing Home's proportionate share of the Trade Association's fee from the Utility Consultant. None of the Nursing Homes are wholly owned by the Trade Association nor are they subsidiaries of a parent corporation that wholly owns the Trade Association.

The GPO safe harbor protects only the fee from the vendor to the GPO. Potential remuneration between the vendor and the GPO members must be separately analyzed. Here, there is minimal risk of fraud or abuse between the Nursing Homes and the Utility Consultant. First, neither party is likely to be a referral source for the other. Moreover, the Utility Consultant's fee is based solely on electricity cost savings recognized by the Nursing Homes through arrangements fostered by the Utility Consultant. The net cost of electricity used by the Nursing Homes will be accurately reflected on the Nursing Homes' cost reports, and thus any cost savings achieved through the Proposed Arrangement will benefit the Federal health care programs.

III. CONCLUSION

Based on the facts presented, we conclude that the fee to be paid by the Utility Consultant to the Trade Association falls within the plain language of the GPO safe harbor. We further conclude, based on the certified facts in the Requestors' request for an advisory opinion (including the fact that the Nursing Homes will accurately reflect electricity costs on their cost reports), that the Requestors will not be subject to OIG sanctions under sections 1128(b)(7)(as it relates to kickbacks) or 1128A(a)(7) of the Act for payment of the Utility Consultant's fee by the Nursing Homes.

IV. LIMITATIONS

The limitations applicable to this opinion include the following:

- This advisory opinion is issued only to the Requestors of this opinion. This advisory opinion has no application, and cannot be relied upon, by any other individual or entity.
- This advisory opinion may not be introduced into evidence in any matter involving an entity or individual that is not a Requestor to this opinion.
- This advisory opinion is applicable only to the statutory provisions specifically noted in the first paragraph of this advisory opinion. No opinion is herein expressed or implied with respect to the application of any other Federal, state, or local statute, rule, regulation, ordinance, or other law that may be applicable to the Proposed Arrangement.
- This advisory opinion will not bind or obligate any agency other than the U.S. Department of Health and Human Services.
- This advisory opinion is limited in scope to the specific arrangement described in this letter and has no applicability to other arrangements, even those which appear similar in nature or scope.

This opinion is also subject to any additional limitations set forth at 42 C.F.R. Part 1008.

The OIG will not proceed against the requestors with respect to any action that is part of the Proposed Arrangement taken in good faith reliance upon this advisory opinion as long as all of the material facts have been fully, completely, and accurately presented, and the Proposed Arrangement in practice comports with the information provided. The OIG reserves the right to reconsider the questions and issues raised in this advisory opinion and, where the public interest requires, rescind, modify, or terminate this opinion. In the event that this advisory opinion is modified or terminated, the OIG will not proceed against the requestors with respect to any action taken in good faith reliance upon this advisory opinion, where all of the relevant facts were fully, completely, and accurately presented and where such action was promptly discontinued upon notification of the modification or termination of this advisory opinion. An advisory opinion may be rescinded only if the relevant and material facts have not been fully, completely, and accurately disclosed to the OIG.

Sincerely,

/s/

D. McCarty Thornton

Chief Counsel to the Inspector General

APPENDIX F25

Advisory Opinion No. 98-12

[Posted September 23, 1998]

[Issued September 16, 1998]

To: The Attached Distribution List [redacted]

Re: Advisory Opinion 98–12

Gentlemen:

We are writing in response to your request for an advisory opinion regarding whether a proposed joint venture among several orthopedic surgeons and anesthesiologists specializing in pain management to establish an ambulatory surgical center, as described in your request letter and supplemental submissions (the "Proposed Arrangement"), would generate prohibited remuneration within the meaning of the anti-kickback statute pursuant to section 1128B(b) of the Social Security Act.

Dr. A, Dr. B, Dr. C, Dr. D, and Dr. E (collectively, the "Requestors") have certified that all of the information provided in the request, including all supplementary letters, is true and correct and constitutes a complete description of the relevant facts and agreements among the parties. The Requestors have also certified that, upon our approval, they will undertake to effectuate the Proposed Arrangement.

In issuing this opinion, we have relied solely on the facts and information presented to us. We have not undertaken an independent investigation of such information. This opinion is limited to the facts presented. If material facts have not been disclosed, this opinion is without force and effect.

Based on the facts certified in your request for an advisory opinion, we conclude that the Proposed Arrangement could potentially generate prohibited remuneration under the anti-kickback statute if the requisite intent to induce referrals were present, but that the OIG will not subject the Proposed Arrangement, as described in the request letter and supplemental submissions, to sanctions arising under the anti-kickback statute.

This opinion may not be relied on by any persons other than the Requestors and is further qualified as set out in Part IV below and in 42 C.F.R. Part 1008.

I. FACTUAL BACKGROUND

The requesting physicians, Drs. A, B, C, D, and E (the "Physician-Investors"), propose establishing an ambulatory surgical center (the "ASC") designed primarily for the treatment of musculoskeletal conditions resulting from work and sports-related injuries. Two of the Physician-Investors are anesthesiologists specializing in pain management;[1] three are orthopedic surgeons specializing in work and/or sports-related injuries.

The ASC will be formed either as a State M corporation or a State M limited liability company. The Physician-Investors have represented that the ASC will be a certified ambulatory surgical center under 42 C.F.R. Part 416. The ASC will consist of two operating rooms and will offer a full range of state-of-the-art surgical equipment, including arthroscopy units, carbon-fiber tables, a fluoroscope, orthopedic surgical instrumentation, and other mechanical and implantable devices used in arthroscopic and pain management procedures. The ASC will employ a facility administrator to manage and administer services for the ASC, as well as nurses, surgical technicians, janitorial staff, and other administrative personnel.

The Physician-Investors will be the shareholders of the corporation, or the owner-members of the limited liability company, and will make substantial capital contributions to the ASC. The total capital contribution to establish the ASC will be approximately $X. The capital contributions will vary, but each Physician-Investor will contribute at least $Y. The Physician-Investors have certified that the amount of their capital contributions will not be based on any

[1] The anesthesiologists will exclusively practice pain medicine at the ASC, except in emergency circumstances. Pain medicine involves treating those patients who suffer from disorders that result in pain emanating from a discrete cause, e.g., postoperative pain or pain associated with malignancy, or from a syndrome in which pain constitutes the primary problem, e.g., neuropathic pains or headaches. Treatments include central and peripheral neural blockade and monitored drug infusions. *See* Definition of "Pain Medicine" adopted by the Board of Directors of the American Academy of Pain Medicine (October 1997).

expected volume of referrals to the other Physician-Investors. The Physician-Investors will receive voting and distribution rights proportional to their investments. In addition to their capital contributions, the Physician-Investors will personally guarantee payment under the lease for the ASC's premises.

The Physician-Investors expect to utilize the ASC as their preferred ambulatory surgical center for procedures for which it is appropriately equipped. The Physician-Investors have represented that each Physician-Investor will perform the majority of his ambulatory surgical center procedures at the ASC. For purposes of this opinion, ambulatory surgical center procedures are Medicare-covered surgical and other medical procedures included on the applicable list of ambulatory surgical center covered procedures published by the Health Care Financing Administration (HCFA) in the *Federal Register* ("ASC Procedures"). *See* 42 C.F.R. § 416.65(c).[2] ASC Procedures currently include certain pain management procedures performed by the Physician-Investors who are anesthesiologists.[3] Although the ASC will be available for use by non-investor physicians, the Physician-Investors will be given priority scheduling and have represented that they will perform over 80% of the total procedures performed at the ASC. All ancillary services performed at or by the ASC will be integrally related to the primary procedure a Physician-Investor is performing at the ASC. The Physician-Investors have certified that Medicare reimbursement will account for approximately five percent of the ASC annual revenue.

---

[2] Section 416.65 establishes standards that surgical and other medical procedures must meet to be included on the HCFA list of procedures eligible for facility fee reimbursement when performed in an ambulatory surgical center. Eligible procedures include procedures that are commonly performed on an inpatient basis in hospitals, but that may be safely performed in ambulatory surgical centers; they do not include procedures that are not of a type commonly performed, or that may be safely performed, in physicians' offices. Additional standards address post-operative recovery, operating and recovery room space, the duration of procedures, and the use of anesthesia.

[3] HCFA has proposed altering its list of ASC Procedures, eliminating Medicare ambulatory surgical center facility fee reimbursement for many, if not most, of the pain management procedures currently performed by the Physician-Investors. *See* Update of Ratesetting Methodology, Payment Rates, Payment Policies, and the List of Covered Surgical Procedures for Ambulatory Surgical Centers Effective October 1, 1998, 63 Fed. Reg. 32290 (1998) (to be codified at 42 C.F.R. Pts. 416, 488) (proposed June 12, 1998).

The practice of procedures in ambulatory surgical centers is an integral and major part of each Physician-Investor's medical practice. For the period from January 1, 1998, through May 31, 1998, at least 40% of each Physician-Investor's total medical practice income was generated from performing ASC Procedures. The Physician-Investors anticipate continuing to derive this percentage of medical practice income from such procedures.[4]

Each of the Physician-Investors will directly bill his patients and related third-party payers, including Medicare and Medicaid, for the professional component of the ASC Procedures he performs. The ASC will separately bill the facility fee and any technical component to such patients and third-party payers. The Physician-Investors will provide their patients with a written disclosure of their ownership in the ASC, explaining that they are referring patients to the ASC.

II. LEGAL ANALYSIS

A. The Anti-Kickback Statute

The anti-kickback statute makes it a criminal offense knowingly and willfully to offer, pay, solicit or receive any remuneration to induce referrals of items or services reimbursable by the Federal health care programs. 42 U.S.C. § 1320a-7b(b). Where remuneration is paid purposefully to induce referrals of items or services paid for by a Federal health care program, the anti-kickback statute is violated. By its terms, the statute ascribes criminal liability to parties on both sides of an impermissible "kickback" transaction. For purposes of the anti-kickback statute, "remuneration" includes the transfer of anything of value, in cash or in-kind, directly or indirectly, covertly or overtly.

The statute has been interpreted to cover any arrangement where *one* purpose of the remuneration is to obtain money for the referral of services or to induce further referrals. *United States v. Kats*, 871 F.2d 105 (9th Cir. 1989); *United States v. Greber*, 760 F.2d 68 (3d Cir.), *cert. denied*, 476 U.S. 988 (1985). Violations of the statute constitute a felony punishable by a maximum fine of $25,000, imprisonment up to five years or both. Conviction will also lead to

[4] If the percentage of each Physician-Investor's total medical practice income generated from performing ASC Procedures drops below 33.3% for any reason, including publication of a new HCFA list of ASC Procedures, then this advisory opinion will be without force and effect.

automatic exclusion from Federal health care programs, including Medicare and Medicaid. This Office may also initiate administrative proceedings to exclude persons from the Federal and State health care programs or to impose civil monetary penalties for fraud, kickbacks, and other prohibited activities under sections 1128(b)(7) and 1128A(a)(5) of the Act.[5]

B. Joint Ventures

This Office has long been concerned with the risk of abuse posed by health care joint ventures in which investors are also sources of referrals or suppliers of items or services to the joint venture. In 1989, the Office of Inspector General issued a "Special Fraud Alert" specifically addressing joint venture arrangements.[6] The Special Fraud Alert distinguishes between those joint ventures that are clearly legitimate and those that are suspect under the anti-kickback statute. A joint venture may be suspect when physicians are both investors in the joint venture and are in a position to refer to the joint venture. Under these circumstances, remuneration paid to the physicians in exchange for referrals may be disguised as profit distributions. Such suspect joint ventures:

> . . . may be intended not so much to raise investment capital legitimately to start a business, but to lock up a stream of referrals from the physician investors and to compensate them indirectly for these referrals. Because physician investors can benefit financially from their referrals, unnecessary procedures and tests may be ordered or performed, resulting in unnecessary program expenditures.

59 Fed. Reg. 65373–74 (Dec. 19, 1994). Substantial ownership by investors who are in a position to refer patients to the joint venture ("Interested Investors") is an indicator of a suspect joint venture because such ownership increases the likelihood that the joint venture's primary purpose is to control a stream of referrals. *See* 56 Fed. Reg. 35969 (July 29, 1991). Other factors that could indicate potentially unlawful activity include the Interested Investors' receiving a disproportionate return on their investments, and the joint venture

[5] Because both the criminal and administrative sanctions related to the Proposed Arrangement are based on violations of the anti-kickback statute, the analysis for purposes of this advisory opinion is the same for both.

[6] *See* Special Fraud Alert, "Joint Venture Arrangements" (OIG-89–4), *reprinted in* 59 Fed. Reg. 65373 (December 19, 1994).

being structured as a "shell" for use by on-going entities already engaged in a particular line of business.

Nevertheless, we recognize that some joint venture arrangements do not pose a risk of fraud and abuse under the anti-kickback statute. We have promulgated two safe harbors that describe joint ventures involving Interested Investors that do not violate the statute: the investment interests in large publicly traded entities safe harbor and the investment interests in small entities safe harbor. 42 C.F.R. § 1001.952(a)(1) & (2) . An important common element in both safe harbors is evidence of a significant business operation independent of any "tainted referrals." The requirements of the safe harbor for investments in large publicly traded entities ensure that referring investors will own such a small share of the total stock issuance that the return on investment is, at most, tangentially related to any referrals. *See* 54 Fed. Reg. 3090 (Jan. 23, 1989). Similarly, the small entities safe harbor places substantial limitations both on the amount of investment in the business by referring investors and on the amount of business revenue generated by any "tainted" referrals.

In sum, the current safe harbors protect against possible illegal remuneration by ensuring that Interested Investors are not in a position to dominate the joint venture's business, thereby increasing the likelihood that the joint venture has an independent and legitimate business purpose, and that any return on investment derives predominantly from such business.

C. The Proposed Arrangement

The Proposed Arrangement is the antithesis of the small entity investment safe harbor business structure. All of the investors will be referral sources to the ASC, and virtually all such business of the ASC will be from investor referrals. Nevertheless, for the reasons and in the circumstances set out below, we conclude that although the Proposed Arrangement may potentially violate the anti-kickback statute, we would not impose sanctions.

At the outset, we note that the Health Care Financing Administration promotes ambulatory surgical centers as a cost-effective alternative to higher cost settings, such as hospital inpatient surgery facilities. Many patients prefer treatment in less intensive settings, such as ambulatory surgical centers. Thus, ambulatory surgical centers benefit both the Medicare program and its beneficiaries.

This Office has proposed a safe harbor to protect surgeons who, as an extension of their personal office practice, routinely perform procedures in ambulatory surgical centers in which they have investment interests. *See* 58 Fed. Reg. 49013 (Sept. 21, 1993). There are obvious and legitimate business and professional reasons for surgeons to want to own an ambulatory surgical center in which they will personally perform services on a routine basis. These reasons include personal and patient convenience, professional autonomy, accountability, and quality control. Moreover, any risk of overutilization or unnecessary surgery is already present by reason of the opportunity for a surgeon to generate his professional fee; the additional financial return from the ambulatory surgical center investment is not likely to increase the risk of overutilization substantially.

Notwithstanding, this Office is concerned about the potential for investments in ambulatory surgical centers to serve as vehicles to reward referring physicians indirectly. For example, a primary care physician, who performs little or no services in an ambulatory surgical center in which he has an ownership interest, may refer to surgeons utilizing the ambulatory surgical center, thereby receiving indirect remuneration for the referral through the ambulatory surgical center's profit distribution. Similarly, an investment by orthopedic surgeons in an ambulatory surgical center that is not equipped for orthopedic surgical procedures, or that is exclusively used by anesthesiologists performing pain management procedures on patients referred by the orthopedic surgeons, would be suspect.

The situation presented here is very different. First, all Physician-Investors will be making substantial financial investments in the ASC and incurring financial exposure for the ASC's lease. Second, although not all Physician-Investors are surgeons, each Physician-Investor has certified that he currently derives, and anticipates continuing to derive, at least 40% of his aggregate medical practice income from ASC Procedures. In addition, each Physician-Investor has certified that he will perform the majority of his ASC Procedures in the ASC. Third, given that the revenue from procedures on Medicare beneficiaries is estimated to be only 5% of the ASC's total revenues, any income from procedures performed on referred Medicare patients will be insubstantial compared to the income from procedures performed on the Physician-Investors' own patients. Fourth, any return on investment to the Physician-Investors will be proportional to their capital investments, and not based on referrals. In these circumstances, the Proposed Arrangement is substantively equivalent to an "all surgeon" ambulatory surgical center and presents a minimal risk that the return on investment would be a disguised payment for referrals.

Finally, the Physician-Investors will provide their patients with a written disclosure of their ownership in the ASC, explaining that they are referring patients to the ASC. This written disclosure is required by State M law. [State M Statutory Compilation.] While we do not believe that disclosure to patients offers sufficient protection from program abuse, effective and meaningful disclosure offers some protection against possible abuses of patient trust.

III. Conclusion

Based on the facts certified in the Physician-Investors' request for an advisory opinion and supplemental submissions, we conclude that while the Proposed Arrangement might technically violate the anti-kickback statute if the requisite intent to induce referrals were present, the OIG will not impose sanctions on the Physician-Investors under sections 1128(b)(7) (as it relates to kickbacks) or 1128A(a)(7) of the Act.

IV. Limitations

The limitations applicable to this opinion include the following:

- This advisory opinion is issued only to Dr. A, Dr. B, Dr. C, Dr. D, and Dr. E, who are the Requesters of this opinion. This advisory opinion has no application, and cannot be relied upon, by any other individual or entity.
- This advisory opinion may not be introduced into evidence in any matter involving an entity or individual that is not a Requestor to this opinion.
- This advisory opinion is applicable only to the statutory provisions specifically noted above. No opinion is herein expressed or implied with respect to the application of any other Federal, state, or local statute, rule, regulation, ordinance, or other law that may be applicable to the Proposed Arrangement.
- This advisory opinion will not bind or obligate any agency other than the U.S. Department of Health and Human Services.

- This advisory opinion is limited in scope to the specific arrangement described in this letter and has no applicability to other arrangements, even those which appear similar in nature or scope.

This opinion is also subject to any additional limitations set forth at 42 C.F.R. Part 1008.

The OIG will not proceed against the Physician-Investors with respect to any action that is part of the Proposed Arrangement taken in good faith reliance upon this advisory opinion as long as all of the material facts have been fully, completely, and accurately presented, and the Proposed Arrangement in practice comports with the information provided. The OIG reserves the right to reconsider the questions and issues raised in this advisory opinion and, where the public interest requires, rescind, modify or terminate this opinion. In the event that this advisory opinion is modified or terminated, the OIG will not proceed against the Physician-Investors with respect to any action taken in good faith reliance upon this advisory opinion, where all of the relevant facts were fully, completely, and accurately presented and where such action was promptly discontinued upon notification of the modification or termination of this advisory opinion. An advisory opinion may be rescinded only if the relevant and material facts have not been fully, completely and accurately disclosed to the OIG.

Sincerely,
/s/
D. McCarty Thornton
Chief Counsel to the Inspector General

APPENDIX F26

Advisory Opinion No. 98-13

[Issued September 23, 1998]

[Posted on the OIG Web Site September 30, 1998]

To: The Attached Distribution List [redacted]

Re: [Name redacted]

Advisory Opinion No. 98-13

Ladies and Gentlemen:

We are writing in response to your request for an advisory opinion, in which you ask whether an ambulance restocking program, coordinated through a local emergency medical services council (the "Program"), constitutes prohibited remuneration under the anti-kickback statute, section 1128B(b) of the Social Security Act (the "Act"), and, if so, whether the Program constitutes grounds for the imposition of sanctions under the anti-kickback statute, section 1128B(b) of the Act, the exclusion authority related to kickbacks, section 1128(b)(7) of the Act, or the civil monetary penalty provision for kickbacks, section 1128A(a)(7) of the Act.

You have certified that all of the information you provided in your request, including all supplementary information, is true and correct, and constitutes a complete description of the material facts regarding the Program. In issuing this opinion, we have relied solely on the facts and information you presented to us. We have not undertaken any independent investigation of such information. This opinion is limited to the facts presented. If material facts have not been disclosed, this opinion is without force and effect.

Based on the facts certified in your request for an advisory opinion, we conclude that the Program could constitute prohibited remuneration under the anti-kickback statute if the requisite intent to induce referrals were present, but that the OIG will not subject the Program, as described in the request and supplemental submissions, to sanctions arising under the anti-kickback statute pursuant to sections 1128B(b), 1128(b)(7), or 1128A(a)(7) of the Act.

This opinion may not be relied on by any persons other than the addressees and is further qualified as set out in Part IV below and in 42 C.F.R. Part 1008.

I. FACTUAL BACKGROUND

The requesters of this advisory opinion are eight fire departments (listed on the attached distribution list) and The County X Ambulance District located in County X, State Y. All of the fire departments and the ambulance district are owned and operated by municipal governments and provide emergency medical services ("EMS").

The requesters are members of the County X Emergency Medical Services Council (the "Council"), a non-profit association founded in 1980. The Council is an advisory and coordinating organization whose mission is to promote and advance EMS throughout County X. Membership on the Council includes those who are providing EMS and those who are interested in furthering the goals of the Council. The Council's current membership includes public and private ambulance providers, hospitals, medical directors, and local educational facilities. The Council's goals include: standardization of EMS practices and equipment; provision of education and training for EMS providers; and improvement of EMS capabilities in the Council's service area. Through its Executive Committee, the Council may appoint working committees to accomplish its goals. One such committee is a practice committee.

The practice committee has oversight of the restocking Program and is responsible for standardizing the Program within the local EMS community, educating Council members regarding the Program, and disseminating information about the Program. The Program has been in operation in County X for eighteen years. The Program provides for the free exchange of drugs and medical supplies used by EMS providers when they bring an individual to a hospital for emergency treatment. Currently, all hospitals and EMS providers in the County X service area participate in the Program. Under the Program protocol, the hospital that receives the patient restocks the ambulance with the medications and supplies used in connection with the patient's emergency medical treatment. Both an EMS provider and a representative of the receiving hospital fill out and sign an emergency medical response for each patient (the "Report"). One copy of the Report is placed in the patient's record and one copy of the Report is used for inventory documentation of the expended drugs and medical supplies. The ambulance providers are not charged, and do not pay, for restocked items. The cost of the drugs and medical supplies is charged to the patient by the receiving hospital in the manner of other billing for the services to the patient.

II. LEGAL ANALYSIS

The anti-kickback statute makes it a criminal offense knowingly and willfully to offer, pay, solicit, or receive any remuneration to induce referrals of items or services reimbursable by any Federal health care program. *See* section 1128B(b) of the Act. Where remuneration is paid purposefully to induce referrals of items or services for which payment may be made by a Federal health care program, the anti-kickback statute is violated. By its terms, the statute ascribes criminal liability to parties on both sides of an impermissible "kickback" transaction. For purposes of the anti-kickback statute, "remuneration" includes the transfer of anything of value, in cash or in-kind, directly or indirectly, covertly or overtly.

The statute has been interpreted to cover any arrangement where *one* purpose of the remuneration was to obtain money for the referral of services or to induce further referrals. *United States v. Kats*, 871 F.2d 105 (9th Cir. 1989); *United States v. Greber*, 760 F.2d 68 (3d Cir.), *cert. denied*, 474 U.S. 988 (1985). Violation of the statute constitutes a felony punishable by a maximum fine of $25,000, imprisonment up to five years, or both. Conviction will also lead to automatic exclusion from Federal health care programs, including Medicare and Medicaid. This Office may also initiate administrative proceedings to exclude persons from Federal and state health care programs or to impose civil monetary penalties for fraud, kickbacks, and other prohibited activities under sections 1128(b)(7) and 1128A (a)(7) of the Act.[1]

This Office's concern with the provision of goods and services for free or at below-market rates to potential referral sources is longstanding and clear: such arrangements are suspect under the anti-kickback statute. The provision of free or below-market rate

---

[1] Because both the criminal and administrative sanctions related to the anti-kickback implications of the Program are based on violations of the anti-kickback statute, the analysis for purposes of this advisory opinion is the same under both.

goods or services to a referral source may violate the anti-kickback statute if one purpose of the gift is to induce referrals of Federal health care program business.

The provision by a hospital of free supplies and medications to an ambulance provider fits squarely within the meaning of remuneration for purposes of the anti-kickback statute. An inference may be drawn that one purpose of such remuneration is to induce the ambulance provider to bring patients to the hospital. However, the strength of that inference may vary with the circumstances of the specific arrangement.

In assessing the potential risk of fraud or abuse under the anti-kickback statute, our concerns are principally fourfold: increased risk of overutilization, increased program costs, patient freedom of choice, and unfair competition. Because it is limited to emergency medical services, the Program does not increase the risk of overutilization and is unlikely to lead to increased costs to Federal health care programs. Neither the number of Federal program beneficiaries requiring emergency transport in County X, nor the treatment these patients will require or receive at a hospital, is related to the existence or operation of the Program.[2]

With respect to freedom of choice and unfair competition, emergency ambulance crews have relatively limited opportunities to steer patients to particular hospitals. In life threatening cases, the selection of a receiving hospital will be dictated by the patient's condition. In other circumstances, the choice of receiving hospital will frequently be dictated by the patient, the patient's physician, or the patient's insurer. Notwithstanding, there will inevitably be situations in which ambulance provider personnel would be able to steer patients who do not have a preference to a particular facility. In the circumstances presented here, however, there would appear to be no financial reason arising from the Program for ambulance personnel to steer patients to a particular hospital, since all area hospitals participate in the Program.

However, the mere fact that all hospitals may be restocking ambulances without charge does not immunize conduct that might otherwise violate the anti-kickback statute. Some institutions may well participate in the restocking because of fear of adverse competi-

[2] This advisory opinion only relates to drugs and supplies directly related to the provision of emergency pre-hospital services in the Program's service area. Restocking of drugs or supplies used in connection with non-emergency services is outside the scope of this opinion.

tive consequences if they do not. In short, remuneration that is given to retain or maintain existing referrals may violate the anti-kickback statute.

We previously addressed an ambulance restocking arrangement that raised concerns under the anti-kickback statute in OIG Advisory Opinion 97-6 (October 8, 1997). Based on the specific facts presented by the hospital requester, we found that, notwithstanding a state administrative regulation that required ambulances to transport patients to the facility of the patient's choice except in exigent circumstances, the hospital's proposed arrangement for free restocking of supplies and medications posed a risk of improper steering and unfair competition. Accordingly, we concluded that the arrangement could potentially violate the anti-kickback statute if the requisite intent to induce referrals were present.

The facts presented here differ in material respects from those presented in OIG Advisory Opinion 97-6 for the following reasons:[3]

First, the Program is not a unilateral arrangement; rather, it is part of an ongoing effort by the Council and its members to maintain and improve EMS throughout the County X service area. The Council, a non-profit association founded in 1980, is open to all hospitals and emergency ambulance providers in the area, as well as local educational institutions, physicians, and other community members. Regional EMS councils, like the one at issue here, were formed in the early 1970s in response to a growing recognition of the inadequacy of then existing emergency medical care and the high cost in human lives and physical disabilities due to accidents and sudden illness and injury.[4] EMS councils were established to coordinate emergency care among all levels of a region's EMS system, including public safety organizations, private and hospital-based ambulance providers, hospitals and other critical care facilities, and local physicians and community groups.

Second, the restocking aspects of the Program are not free-standing; the Program is part and parcel of a coordinated regional effort to integrate and improve the emergency medical care system. In addition to the drug and supply exchange programs, the

---

[3] We note that may aspects of the Program are similar to aspects of the proposed arrangement in OIG Advisory Opinion 98-7, which addressed an ambulance restocking arrangement that we concluded would not be subject to OIG sanction.

[4] *See, e.g. Accidental Death and Disability: The Neglected Disease of Modern Society*, National Academy of Sciences and National Research Council (September 1966).

Council promotes the standardization of practices and equipment within the emergency medical system and provides education and training for EMS providers. It also evaluates and supports requests for improvements to the local EMS delivery system, sponsors educational programs related to EMS, and otherwise seeks to promote high quality EMS care for the region.

Third, regional and local programs to improve and coordinate the delivery of quality EMS have been actively encouraged and promoted by the Federal government over the past twenty-five years. In 1973 the Federal government enacted the Emergency Medical Services Systems Act of 1973 ("EMSSA"), Pub L. 93-154, 87 Stat. 594 (1973), which provided federal funding for the development of regional EMS systems at the state, regional, and local levels.[5] These regional systems were to develop comprehensive programs to improve such areas as communications (including "911" systems); transportation; provision and training of emergency personnel; facilities; critical care units; use of public safety agencies; accessibility to care; consumer participation, education, and information; transfer of patients; standard medical record keeping; independent review and evaluation of EMS; disaster linkage; and mutual aid agreements among communities. EMSSA was one of several Federal legislative efforts to promote EMS delivery systems, including the Highway Safety Act of 1966, Pub. L. 89-594, 80 Stat. 731 (1966), which established an EMS program in the Department of Transportation; the Emergency Medical Services for Children Program, under the Public Health Act, Pub. L. 98-555, 99 Stat. 2854 (1984), which provided funds for enhancing pediatric EMS; and the Trauma Care Systems Planning and Development Act of 1990, Pub. L. 101-590, 104 Stat. 2915 (1990).

Finally — and importantly — the Program is likely to have a positive impact on the quality of patient care. By providing a mechanism to ensure that ambulances are fully stocked with current medications and appropriate supplies, the Program is likely to foster fast, efficient, and effective pre-hospital emergency care for the County X

---

[5] EMSSA defined "emergency medical services system" as "a system which provides for the arrangement of personnel, facilities, and equipment for the effective and coordinated delivery in an appropriate geographical area of health care services under emergency conditions . . . and which is administered by a public or nonprofit private entity which has the authority and the resources to provide effective administration of the system." 87 Stat. at 595.

service area. These significant community benefits, coupled with the conditions, requirements, and limitations outlined above, persuade us that the Program poses minimal risk of fraud and abuse under the anti-kickback statute, and therefore the OIG would not subject it to sanction.

III. CONCLUSION

The advisory opinion process is a "means of relating the anti-kickback statute to the particular facts of a specific arrangement." 62 Fed. Reg. 7350, 7351 (February 19, 1997). The advisory opinion process permits this Office to protect specific arrangements that "contain[] limitations, requirements, or controls that give adequate assurance that Federal health care programs cannot be abused." *Id.* In evaluating an arrangement's potential to lead to fraud or abuse of Federal health care programs, no one fact or element is necessarily dispositive. Here, we are persuaded that the Program is likely to result in substantial community benefit consistent with longstanding national policy objectives. We are further persuaded that, taken as a whole, the aspects of the Program described above — including, but not limited to, the Program's relationship to a coordinated regional EMS system, the role of the regional Council, the Program's limitation to emergency medical services, and the uniformity of the Program across providers — create sufficient limitations, requirements, or controls so as to give adequate assurance that the Program will not lead to program abuse under the anti-kickback statute. [6]

Accordingly, we conclude that while the Program might technically violate the anti-kickback statute if the requisite intent to induce referrals were present, the OIG will not impose sanctions on the requesters under sections 1128(b)(7) (as it relates to kickbacks) or 1128A(a)(7) of the Act, based on the facts certified in the requesters' request for an advisory opinion.

IV. LIMITATIONS

The limitations applicable to this opinion include the following:

---

[6] We express no opinion regarding liability of the requesters under the False Claims Act or other legal authorities in connection with any improper billing or claims submission directly or indirectly related to, or arising from, the Program.

- This advisory opinion is issued only to the requesters listed on the Attached Distribution List, which are the requesters of this opinion. This advisory opinion has no application, and cannot be relied upon, by any other individual or entity. This advisory opinion may not be introduced into evidence in any matter involving an entity or individual that is not a requester to this opinion.
- This advisory opinion is applicable only to the statutory provisions specifically noted in the first paragraph of this advisory opinion. No opinion is herein expressed or implied with respect to the application of any other Federal, state, or local statute, rule, regulation, ordinance, or other law that may be applicable to the Program.
- This advisory opinion will not bind or obligate any agency other than the U.S. Department of Health and Human Services.
- This advisory opinion is limited in scope to the specific arrangement described in this letter and has no applicability to other arrangements, even those which appear similar in nature or scope.

This opinion is also subject to any additional limitations set forth at 42 C.F.R. Part 1008.

The OIG will not proceed against the requesters with respect to any action that is part of the Program taken in good faith reliance upon this advisory opinion as long as all of the material facts have been fully, completely, and accurately presented, and the Program in practice comports with the information provided. The OIG reserves the right to reconsider the questions and issues raised in this advisory opinion and, where the public interest requires, rescind, modify or terminate this opinion. In the event that this advisory opinion is modified or terminated, the OIG will not proceed against any requester with respect to any action taken in good faith reliance upon this advisory opinion, where all of the relevant facts were fully, completely, and accurately presented and where such action was promptly discontinued upon notification of the modification or termination of this advisory opinion. An advisory opinion may be rescinded only if the relevant and material facts have not been fully, completely, and accurately disclosed to the OIG.

Sincerely,

/s/

D. McCarty Thornton

Chief Counsel to the Inspector General
[Attached Distribution List Redacted]

APPENDIX F27

Advisory Opinion No. 98-14

[Posted October 28, 1998]

[Issued October 21, 1998]

To: The Attached Distribution List [redacted]

Re: [Name redacted]

Advisory Opinion No. 98–14

Ladies and Gentlemen:

We are writing in response to your request for an advisory opinion, in which you ask whether an existing pharmaceutical restocking program (the "Drug Program") and a proposed medical supplies restocking program (the "Supply Program) (collectively, the "Arrangements") constitute prohibited remuneration under the anti-kickback statute, section 1128B(b) of the Social Security Act (the "Act"), and, if so, whether the Arrangements constitute grounds for the imposition of sanctions under the anti-kickback statute, section 1128B(b) of the Act, the exclusion authority related to kickbacks, section 1128(b)(7) of the Act, or the civil monetary penalty provision for kickbacks, section 1128A(a)(7) of the Act.

You have certified that all of the information you provided in your request, including all supplementary information, is true and correct, and constitutes a complete description of the material facts regarding the Arrangements. In issuing this opinion, we have relied solely on the facts and information you presented to us. We have not undertaken any independent investigation of such information. This opinion is limited to the facts presented. If material facts have not been disclosed, this opinion is without force and effect.

Based on the facts certified in your request for an advisory opinion, we conclude that the Arrangements described in your advisory opinion request and supplemental submissions *could* constitute prohibited remuneration under the anti-kickback statute, *if* the requisite intent to induce referrals of Federal health care program business were present, but that the OIG will not subject the Drug Program, as described in the request and supplemental submissions, to sanctions arising under the anti-kickback statute pursuant to sections 1128B(b), 1128(b)(7), or 1128A(a)(7) of the Act.

This opinion may not be relied on by any persons other than the addressees and is further qualified as set out in Part IV below and in 42 C.F.R. Part 1008.

I. FACTUAL BACKGROUND

The requesters of this advisory opinion are four hospital providers located in four counties in the northeast of State X (the "Hospitals"). The first requester is Hospital One ("Hospital One"), which operates one hospital in County A, State X, and three hospitals in County B, State X. The second requester is Hospital Two ("Hospital Two"), which operates one hospital in County A, State X, one hospital in County B, State X, and one free-standing emergency facility in County C, State X. The third requester is Hospital Three ("Hospital Three") located in County D, State X. The final requester is Hospital Four ("Hospital Four") located in County B, State X. These Hospitals represent all of the hospital providers in the greater [four county] metropolitan emergency medical services area (the "Four County EMS Area").[1]

Each Hospital is a member of at least one of the three emergency medical services ("EMS") councils operating in the four-county area (the "EMS Councils"). The first EMS council is Council F ("Council F"), which operates in County A. Council F's mission is, among other things, to coordinate the various levels of EMS, educational programs, and interaction between pre-hospital care providers and other health care providers in the county and to encourage the implementation of EMS standards and criteria pursuant to local, state, and national guidelines. Hospital One and Hospital Two are members of Council F. The second EMS council is Council G ("Council G"), which operates in Counties B and D. Council G's mission includes upgrading emergency medical care in the region; serving as a central coordinating body; and implementing and monitoring systems of quality assurance for EMS in the region. Hospitals One, Two, Three, and Four are all members of Council G. The third EMS

[1] There are other hospitals in the four-county area that are geographically distant from the Hospitals and therefore not part of the Four County EMS Area.

council is Council H ("Council H"). Council H was formed to oversee pre-hospital emergency medical care in the county, including promulgating standard, community-wide pre-hospital EMS operating protocols. Hospital Two is a member of Council H. Each EMS Council has diverse membership, including, among others, local physicians, hospital representatives, paramedics, EMS technicians, consumer representatives, EMS education providers, and local officials.

The Hospitals participate in a pharmaceutical restocking program (the "Drug Program") with area ambulance providers in connection with emergency medical transports. Typically under the Drug Program, a receiving hospital restocks an ambulance with the medications used in connection with emergency pre-hospital services provided by the ambulance provider to the transported patient. The EMS units are not charged, and do not pay, for restocked items. As part of the exchange, the EMS unit must provide documentation of the drugs used during the ambulance run. All hospitals in the Four County EMS Area participate in the Drug Program; any other hospital located within the four- county area may participate. The restocked pharmaceuticals are provided to any ambulance provider that transports an emergency patient to the hospital.

Council F, Council G, and Council H have facilitated the Drug Program within the four-county area in various ways. The EMS Councils' activities have included, for example: initiating drug exchange programs; approving policies and protocols that govern drug exchange programs; creating and implementing protocols for the administration of drugs used during patient transport; and coordinating efforts between public and private pre-hospital providers, hospital emergency staff, and consumers to promote the highest quality medical care for victims of sudden illness or injury.

The Hospitals also propose a limited medical supplies restocking program (the "Supply Program"), pursuant to which the Hospitals would restock certain supplies used by ambulance providers during emergency pre-hospital transportation. To initiate, coordinate, and monitor the Supply Program, the Hospitals have established a joint committee, comprised of the EMS coordinator or a higher level employee from each Hospital. Any hospital located within the four-county area may participate. The restocked medical supplies will be provided to any ambulance provider that transports an emergency patient to a participating hospital.

The Hospitals want to establish a limited supply exchange program targeting specific supplies that they believe will enhance efficient coordination and integration between their emergency rooms and emergency pre-hospital care providers. To this end, the joint committee developed the following list of medical supplies to be restocked under the auspices of the Supply Program: intravenous solutions; intravenous tubing; intravenous catheters and needles; oxygen cannulas and oxygen masks; endotracheal tubes; tuberculin, intramuscular and 10 cc syringes; blood collection tubes; and linens.[2]

The Supply Program will allow ambulances to be fully stocked with a standard complement of these supplies, making it easier, for example, for patients arriving by emergency ambulance to be connected to Hospital emergency room systems without interruption.

II. LEGAL ANALYSIS

The anti-kickback statute makes it a criminal offense knowingly and willfully to offer, pay, solicit, or receive any remuneration to induce referrals of items or services reimbursable by any Federal health care program. *See* section 1128B(b) of the Act. Where remuneration is paid purposefully to induce referrals of items or services for which payment may be made by a Federal health care program, the anti-kickback statute is violated. By its terms, the statute ascribes criminal liability to parties on both sides of an impermissible "kickback" transaction. For purposes of the anti-kickback statute, "remuneration" includes the transfer of anything of value, in cash or in kind, directly or indirectly, covertly or overtly.

The statute has been interpreted to cover any arrangement where *one* purpose of the remuneration was to obtain money for the referral of services or to induce further referrals. *United States v. Kats*, 871 F.2d 105 (9th Cir. 1989); *United States v. Greber*, 760 F.2d 68 (3d Cir.), *cert. denied*, 474 U.S. 988 (1985). Violation of the statute constitutes a felony punishable by a maximum fine of $25,000, imprisonment up to five years, or both. Conviction will also lead to automatic exclusion from Federal health care programs, including Medicare and Medicaid. This Office may also initiate administrative proceedings to exclude persons from Federal and state health care

[2] Linens are included to ensure appropriate compliance with sanitization requirements for laundering linens used by hospital and ambulance patients.

programs or to impose civil monetary penalties for fraud, kickbacks, and other prohibited activities under sections 1128(b)(7) and 1128A (a)(7) of the Act.[3]

This Office's concern with the provision of goods and services for free or at below-market rates to potential referral sources is long-standing and clear: such arrangements are suspect and may violate the anti-kickback statute if one purpose is to induce referrals of Federal health care program business.

The provision by a hospital of free supplies and medications to an ambulance provider fits squarely within the meaning of remuneration for purposes of the anti-kickback statute. An inference may be drawn that one purpose of such remuneration is to induce the ambulance provider to bring patients to the hospital. However, the strength of that inference may vary with the circumstances of the specific arrangement.

With respect to the Drug Program, the factual circumstances presented here are substantially similar to those present in the factual circumstances addressed by OIG Advisory Opinions 98–7 and 98–13. Thus, for the reasons stated in those opinions, we conclude that the OIG would not subject the Drug Program, as described in the request letter and supplemental submissions, to sanctions under section 1128B(b), 1128(b)(7), or 1128A(a)(7) of the Act.[4] As in those opinions, the involvement of the entire EMS community in the Drug Program, including hospitals, EMS physicians, ambulance providers, paramedics, EMS education providers, consumer representatives, and local officials, provides adequate assurance that the plan is designed to improve and enhance the delivery of EMS in the Four County EMS Area for the benefit of the entire community.

While we recognize that the Supply Program may also provide a community benefit, we are unable to reach a similar conclusion with respect to the application of the anti-kickback statute to that program. The Supply Program would be implemented under the auspices of a committee formed exclusively of Hospital representatives, rather than an EMS council or similar group more broadly

---

[3] Because both the criminal and administrative sanctions related to the anti-kickback implications of the Arrangements are based on violations of the anti-kickback statute, the analysis for purposes of this advisory opinion is the same under both.

[4] This advisory opinion only relates to the restocking of drugs and supplies directly related to the provision of emergency pre-hospital services. Restocking of drugs or supplies used in connection with non-emergency services are outside the scope of this opinion.

representative of the EMS community at large. The involvement of a broad range of representatives of the EMS community provides substantial assurance that an ambulance restocking program will operate for the benefit of the local community and will not be undertaken solely for the benefit of a single provider or group of providers.

We wish to make clear that this opinion does not mean that the Supply Program (or similar ambulance restocking programs) would violate the anti-kickback statute. Rather, because it involves the provision of free goods to potential referral sources, the Supply Program *might* violate the statute *if* one purpose of the Program is to induce Federal health care program business. Thus, whether the proposed Supply Program would, in fact, be unlawful requires a case-by-case determination of the actual intent of the parties based on all relevant facts and circumstances. We cannot determine intent based solely on documentary submissions; accordingly, a determination of intent is beyond the scope of the advisory opinion process. *See* 62 Fed. Reg. 7351 (Feb. 19, 1997).

III. CONCLUSION

The advisory opinion process is a "means of relating the anti-kickback statute to the particular facts of a specific arrangement." 62 Fed. Reg. 7350, 7351 (Feb. 19, 1997). The advisory opinion process permits this Office to protect specific arrangements that "contain[] limitations, requirements, or controls that give adequate assurance that Federal health care programs cannot be abused." *Id.* In evaluating an arrangement's potential to lead to fraud or abuse of Federal health care programs, no one fact or element is necessarily dispositive. We are further persuaded that, taken as a whole, the aspects of the Drug Program described above — including, but not limited to, the Hospitals' relationships with coordinated regional EMS systems, the role of the regional EMS councils, and the Program's limitation to emergency medical services — create sufficient limitations, requirements, or controls so as to give adequate assurance that the Drug Program will not lead to program abuse under the anti-kickback statute.[5] The Supply program does not contain similar safeguards.

---

[5] We express no opinion regarding liability of the requesters under the False Claims Act or other legal authorities in connection with any improper billing or claims submission directly or indirectly related to, or arising from, the Arrangements.

Accordingly, we conclude that while the Arrangements might technically violate the anti-kickback statute, if the requisite intent to induce referrals were present, the OIG will not impose sanctions on the requesters in connection with the Drug Program under sections 1128(b)(7) (as it relates to kickbacks) or 1128A(a)(7) of the Act, based on the facts certified in the requesters' request for an advisory opinion. The OIG cannot give a similar assurance that the Supply Program would not be subject to sanction if the parties were to have the requisite intent to induce referrals of Federal health care program business.

IV. LIMITATIONS

The limitations applicable to this opinion include the following:

- This advisory opinion is issued only to the Hospitals listed on the Attached Distribution List, which are the requesters of this opinion. This advisory opinion has no application, and cannot be relied upon, by any other individual or entity.
- This advisory opinion may not be introduced into evidence in any matter involving an entity or individual that is not a requester to this opinion.
- This advisory opinion is applicable only to the statutory provisions specifically noted in the first paragraph of this advisory opinion. No opinion is herein expressed or implied with respect to the application of any other Federal, state, or local statute, rule, regulation, ordinance, or other law that may be applicable to the Arrangements.
- This advisory opinion will not bind or obligate any agency other than the U.S. Department of Health and Human Services.
- This advisory opinion is limited in scope to the specific arrangements described in this letter and has no applicability to other arrangements, even those which appear similar in nature or scope.

This opinion is also subject to any additional limitations set forth at 42 C.F.R. Part 1008.

The Office of Inspector General ("OIG") will not proceed against the requesters with respect to any action that is part of the Arrangements taken in good faith reliance upon this advisory opinion as long as all of the material facts have been fully, completely, and accurately presented, and the Arrangements in practice comport with the information provided. The OIG reserves the right to reconsider the questions and issues raised in this advisory opinion and, where the public interest requires, rescind, modify or terminate this opinion. In the event that this advisory opinion is modified or terminated, the OIG will not proceed against any requester with respect to any action taken in good faith reliance upon this advisory opinion, where all of the relevant facts were fully, completely, and accurately presented and where such action was promptly discontinued upon notification of the modification or termination of this advisory opinion. An advisory opinion may be rescinded only if the relevant and material facts have not been fully, completely, and accurately disclosed to the OIG.

Sincerely,

/s/

D. McCarty Thornton

Chief Counsel to the Inspector General

[Attached Distribution List Redacted]

APPENDIX F28

Advisory Opinion No. 98-15

[Posted: November 10, 1998]

Dated: November 2, 1998

[names and addresses redacted]

Re: [names redacted]

Advisory Request No. 98–15

Ladies and Gentlemen:

We are writing in response to your request for an advisory opinion, in which you asked whether an arrangement for contracted pharmacy services between University A and Pharmacy Company B to facilitate an outpatient pharmacy program for the University's hemophilia center pursuant to section 340B of the Public Health Service Act (the "Proposed Arrangement") would constitute grounds for sanctions under the anti-kickback statute, section 1128B(b) of the Social Security Act (the "Act"), the exclusion authority for kickbacks, section 1128(b)(7) of the Act, or the civil monetary penalty provision for kickbacks, section 1128A(a)(7) of the Act.

You have certified that all of the information you provided in your request, including all supplementary letters, is true and correct and constitutes a complete description of the material facts regarding the Proposed Arrangement. In issuing this opinion, we have relied solely on the facts and information you presented to us. We have not undertaken any independent investigation of such information.

Based on the facts certified in your request for an advisory opinion, we conclude that the Office of Inspector General ("OIG") will not subject the Proposed Arrangement, as described in the request and supplemental submissions, to sanctions arising under the anti-kickback statute pursuant to sections 1128(b)(7) or 1128A(a)(7) of the Act, provided that the compensation is fair market value as certified by the requesters.

This opinion may not be relied on by any persons other than the requesters of this advisory opinion and is further qualified as set out in Part IV below and in 42 C.F.R. Part 1008.

I. FACTUAL BACKGROUND

A. The Parties

Pharmacy Company B ("Company B") is a State X corporation in the business of providing home infusion therapies for a number of conditions, including hemophilia. In addition, Company B provides a range of related pharmaceutical services.

University A (the "University"), a State X not-for-profit corporation, operates a comprehensive hemophilia treatment center, for which it receives funding through the Maternal and Child Health Services Block Grant ("MCHB") program. The University provides care to residents of States X, Y, and Z. The University does not have a pharmacy license and does not operate an in-house pharmacy.

B. The Section 340B Drug Discounting Program

Section 340B of the Public Health Service Act was enacted as part of the Veterans Health Care Act of 1992. Section 340B enables certain entities that typically serve a disproportionate number of uninsured and underinsured people to purchase certain drugs for outpatient treatment from drug manufacturers at greatly reduced prices. The entities that are eligible for the reduced prices — defined in the statute as "covered entities" — include comprehensive hemophilia diagnostic treatment centers receiving a grant under the MCHB program. Covered entities may only sell the drugs purchased under section 340B pricing to certain of their patients as defined in program guidance published in the *Federal Register*, 61 Fed. Reg. 55156 (Oct. 24, 1996). In response to a comment in a *Federal Register* notice regarding contracted pharmacy services guidelines, the Department of Health and Human Services (the "Department") noted that a modest drug markup does not appear inconsistent with the 340B program, if the savings resulting from the 340B discounts are used for purposes of the Federal program. *See* 61 Fed. Reg. 43548 (Aug. 23, 1996).

The discounted price under section 340B is calculated based on a formula that takes into account the Medicaid drug rebate manufacturers are required to pay to the states as a condition for payment under the Medicaid program. *See* 42 U.S.C. § 1396r-8.[1] Section 340B requires manufacturers of covered drugs to enter into pricing agreements with the Secretary of the Department. Covered entities enter into agreements with drug manufacturers to purchase covered drugs at or below the ceiling price established in the manufacturer's agreement with the Secretary and in section 340B(2).

Many covered entities do not operate an in-house pharmacy from which to dispense the drugs. To facilitate greater covered entity participation in the 340B program, the Health Resources and Services Administration ("HRSA") published guidelines and model contract terms for contracts between covered entities and pharmacy companies for pharmacy services agreements. *See* 61 Fed. Reg. 43549 (Aug. 23, 1996) (the "Guidelines"). The Guidelines provide a suggested format for such agreements, including the following terms:

(i) the covered entity will purchase the drug and assume responsibility for establishing its price;
(ii) a "ship to/bill to" procedure may be used in which the covered entity purchases the drug, and the manufacturer bills the entity for the drug, but ships the drug to the contract pharmacy;
(iii) the contract pharmacy will provide all pharmacy services (e.g., dispensing, record keeping, utilization review, patient profiling, counseling) and may provide other services (e.g., home care, reimbursement services);
(iv) the covered entity must inform its patients of their freedom to choose a pharmacy provider;
(v) section 340B prices are restricted to patients of the covered entity;
(vi) the contract pharmacy and the covered entity will adhere to all Federal, state, and local laws and requirements;
(vii) the contractor, with the assistance of the covered entity, will establish and maintain a tracking system suitable to prevent diversion of section 340B discounted drugs to individuals who are not patients;
(viii) the parties will not use drugs purchased under section 340B to dispense Medicaid prescriptions, unless the contract

---

[1] The price may not exceed the average manufacturers price for the drug reduced by a rebate percentage equal to the average total Medicaid drug rebate required under section 1927(c) of the Social Security Act divided by the average manufacturers price.

pharmacy and the state Medicaid agency have established an arrangement to prevent duplicate discounting (see further discussion below); and

(ix) the parties understand that they are subject to audits by the Department and the participating manufacturers.

Because covered entities typically have patients who are Medicaid beneficiaries, the section 340B drug discounting program potentially subjects drug manufacturers to a risk of double discounting if the manufacturer pays a Medicaid drug rebate on a drug sold under 340B pricing. For example, if a drug purchased pursuant to section 340B were to be sold to a Medicaid patient and billed to a Medicaid program, the manufacturer could end up providing two discounts: (1) a discount at the time of sale due to the 340B price limits and (2) a discount in the form of the quarterly Medicaid rebate required of manufacturers under the Medicaid program. To prevent this result, section 340B provides that the dispensing of drugs purchased with a 340B discount must not result in the generation of a Medicaid rebate. Assuming this requirement is satisfied, covered entities may bill Medicaid for drugs purchased under section 340B pricing, although the amount charged to Medicaid may not exceed the 340B price plus a reasonable dispensing fee. *See* 58 Fed. Reg. 27293 (May 7, 1993), 58 Fed. Reg. 34058 (June 23, 1993). However, the Guidelines suggest that Medicaid prescriptions should not be filled with drugs purchased at 340B pricing, unless the contract pharmacy and the state Medicaid agency have established an arrangement to prevent duplicate discounting.[2]

In addition, covered entities that use a contract pharmacy may not be able to bill Medicaid for drugs purchased under the 340B drug discounting program because of the Medicaid prohibition on reassignment. Pursuant to the prohibition on reassignment, the entity that dispenses the drugs and provides related administrative services (i.e., the contract pharmacy) must be the entity that bills Medicaid.

C. The Proposed Arrangement

The complexities of section 340B drug discounting notwithstanding, the Proposed Arrangement itself is straightforward. The University, which the parties have represented is a covered entity

[2] The requesters have represented that they are aware of no such state arrangement to date.

for purposes of section 340B, desires to enter into a pharmacy services contract (the "Agreement") with Company B (i) to dispense anti-hemophilia factor (a covered outpatient drug) and other outpatient drugs prescribed by the University's hemophilia center for certain of its patients and (ii) to provide outpatient pharmacy services in connection with the 340B program for those patients, including, but not limited to, inventory management, billings, collections, and educational support. Company B's services will be available on an as-needed basis. The University selected Company B through a competitive procurement process. The Agreement is, and will be for its term, the only financial arrangement between the parties. In all respects material here, the Agreement complies with the Guidance issued by HRSA described above.[3] The compensation to be paid to Company B will be calculated in accordance with a fee schedule attached to the Agreement. The fee schedule provides for Company B to be paid a fixed amount per unit of anti-hemophilia factor dispensed. The amount per unit drops if the volume dispensed exceeds a certain monthly threshold. The compensation may be renegotiated annually. The parties have represented that at all times the compensation will represent fair market value in an arms-length transaction for the services rendered.

To prevent duplicate discounting and to comply with the Medicaid prohibition on reassignment, the Agreement has been structured to exclude Medicaid fee-for-service patients from receiving drugs through the University's outpatient drug program.[4] Medicaid fee-for-service patients will be notified of this limitation in advance and will be informed that they must seek pharmaceutical services elsewhere. These patients may choose to seek such services directly from Company B or from another provider. All University patients (Medicaid and non-Medicaid) will be required to complete a patient

[3] Although the parties have represented that the Agreement incorporates all of the suggestions contained in the Guidelines, we note that there appear to be some differences between the two. The differences are not material for purposes of analyzing the Agreement under the anti-kickback statute; we express no opinion regarding the Agreement's terms for any other purposes. For purposes of this opinion, we have assumed, based on the requesters' certifications, that the Proposed Arrangement will comply with the requirements of the 340B program.

[4] Medicaid managed care patients are not excluded, because drugs purchased under capitated Medicaid managed care arrangements are not subject to the requirements of the Medicaid drug rebate program, and therefore there is no risk of duplicate discounting.

choice form that lists alternate pharmacy services providers. The form states that the University and Company B have a financial relationship and requires the patient to acknowledge that he or she has selected a provider freely. Company B will segregate section 340B drugs purchased by the University from other pharmaceuticals and will maintain a tracking system capable of locating them.

II. LEGAL ANALYSIS

The anti-kickback statute makes it a criminal offense knowingly and wilfully to offer, pay, solicit, or receive any remuneration to induce referrals of items or services reimbursable by Federal health care programs. *See* section 1128B(b) of the Act. Where remuneration is paid purposefully to induce referrals of items or services paid for by a Federal health care program, the anti-kickback statute is violated. By its terms, the statute ascribes liability to parties on both sides of an impermissible "kickback" transaction. For purposes of the anti-kickback statute, "remuneration" includes the transfer of anything of value, in cash or in-kind, directly or indirectly, covertly or overtly.

The statute has been interpreted to cover any arrangement where *one* purpose of the remuneration is to obtain money for referral of services or to induce further referrals. *United States v. Kats*, 871 F. 2d 105 (9th Cir. 1989); *United States v. Greber*, 760 F. 2d 68 (3rd Cir.), *cert. denied*, 476 U.S. 988 (1985). Violation of the statute constitutes a felony punishable by a maximum fine of $25,000, imprisonment up to five years, or both. Conviction will also lead to automatic exclusion from Federal health care programs, including Medicare and Medicaid. This Office may also initiate administrative proceedings to exclude persons from Federal health care programs or to impose civil monetary penalties for fraud, kickbacks, and other prohibited activities under sections 1128(b)(7) and 1128A(a)(7) of the Act.[5]

The Department has published safe harbor regulations that protect certain arrangements that might otherwise technically violate the anti-kickback statute from prosecution. *See* 42 C.F.R. § 1001.952. The safe harbors set forth specific conditions that, if met,

---

[5] Because both the criminal and administrative sanctions related to the anti-kickback implications of the Arrangement are based on violations of the anti-kickback statute, the analysis for the purposes of this advisory opinion is the same under both.

assure entities involved of not being prosecuted or sanctioned for the arrangement qualifying for the safe harbor. However, safe harbor protection is only afforded to those arrangements that precisely meet all of the conditions set forth in the safe harbor. The regulatory safe harbor potentially applicable to the Proposed Arrangement is the personal services and management contracts safe harbor. *See* 42 C.F.R. § 1001.952(d). The Proposed Arrangement cannot qualify under this safe harbor, however, since, among other things, the nature of the services provided under the Agreement preclude an exact specification of the schedule for their performance and the aggregate amount of compensation is not set in advance, as required by the regulation.

Nevertheless, arrangements that do not fit squarely within a safe harbor do not necessarily violate the anti-kickback statute. *See, e.g.*, 56 Fed. Reg. 35952, 35954 (July 29, 1991). Such arrangements must be evaluated on a case-by-case basis. For the following reasons, we conclude that the Proposed Arrangement poses a minimal risk of fraud or abuse and would not be subject to OIG sanctions:

- *The Proposed Arrangement implements the congressional intent embodied in section 340B and the HRSA Guidelines.* The Proposed Arrangement enables the University's hemophilia center, which does not have access to an in-house pharmacy, to receive the benefits of the discounted drugs available under section 340B to hemophilia centers funded through the MCHB program. The Agreement comports in all aspects material to an inquiry under the anti-kickback statute with the Guidelines published by HRSA for entities seeking to comply with section 340B. The Guidelines make clear that the parties are responsible for complying with all Federal, state, and local laws and requirements, including the anti-kickback statute. The Guidelines also provide that the parties will be subject to governmental reporting and auditing requirements.
- *Company B will be paid fair market value for services rendered.* The only compensation Company B will receive under the Proposed Arrangement is for pharmacy services rendered, which services do not include marketing. Company B will not receive payment for the drugs themselves, which will be purchased by the University from drug manufacturers. The compensation will be based on a fixed amount per unit of anti-hemophilia factor dispensed; Company B has no control over the number of units dispensed. The parties have represented that Company

B's compensation will represent fair market value in an arms-length transaction for the services rendered. Company B will be paid by the University, and not by patients or insurers, for services provided under the Agreement to patients participating in the University's outpatient pharmacy program.[6]

- *Company B is not paying for referrals of Medicaid fee-for-service patients*. Typically, contractual provisions that attempt to exclude Federal health care program business from an arrangement that might otherwise violate the anti-kickback statute are suspect, because often in practice the Federal health care program business is improperly affected by the tainted referral arrangement despite the purported "carve-out". Moreover, parallel arrangements that bifurcate services between Federal and private pay business may create a risk that parties will "swap" discounted private pay business for referrals of higher paying Federal business. The Proposed Arrangement contains several safeguards to minimize the risk of "swapping". First, under the Agreement Company B will not control the price charged for drugs for non-Medicaid patients and will not file claims for such drugs in its own right. Second, assuming Company B's compensation under the Agreement will be fair market value for the term of the Agreement, and based on the parties' representation that the Agreement is and will be the only financial arrangement between the parties, there will be no remuneration from Company B to the University through the provision of free or below-market services. Hence, no inference arises that Company B is paying for referrals. Third, the exclusion of Medicaid fee-for-service patients contemplated by the Agreement is consistent with the section 340B bar on duplicate discounting and the Medicaid prohibition against reassignment.
- *The Proposed Arrangement preserves patient freedom of choice*. The Proposed Arrangement preserves freedom of choice for Medicaid fee-for-service patients by affording them the opportunity to use Company B as their pharmacy provider. In

[6] We express no opinion regarding the liability of any party under the False Claims Act or other legal authorities for any improper billing, claims submission, or other related conduct. We note, however, that Company B's compensation under the Agreement is not tied to the University's revenue, and therefore Company B does not appear to have any added incentive to upcode or otherwise bill in a manner that maximizes the University's reimbursement.

addition, all patients will be provided with (and will be required to acknowledge in writing) patient freedom of choice forms listing alternate pharmacy providers and disclosing the financial relationship between the University and Company B. Although such disclosures are not sufficient in and of themselves to mitigate the risk of fraud, they serve an important function by promoting informed patient decision-making.

III. CONCLUSION

For the above reasons and based on the facts as certified by the requesters, we conclude that, although the Proposed Arrangement might technically fall within the prohibition of the anti-kickback statute if the requisite intent were present, the OIG would not seek to impose sanctions under section 1128(b)(7) of the Act (as it relates to kickbacks) or section 1128A(a)(7) of the Act for payments made under the Agreement, provided the compensation is fair market value as certified by the requesters.[7]

IV. LIMITATIONS

The limitations applicable to this opinion include the following:

- This advisory opinion is issued only to Company B and University A, the requesters of this opinion. This advisory opinion has no application, and cannot be relied upon, by any other individual or entity.
- This advisory opinion may not be introduced into evidence in any matter involving an entity or individual that is not a requestor to this opinion.
- This advisory opinion is applicable only to the statutory provisions specifically noted above. No opinion is herein expressed or implied with respect to the application of any other Federal, state, or local statute, rule, regulation, ordinance, or other law that may be applicable to the Arrangement, nor is any opinion expressed regarding the parties' compliance with the 340B drug program.
- This advisory opinion will not bind or obligate any agency other than the U.S. Department of Health and Human Services.

[7] We are not authorized to opine on "fair market value." *See* section 1128D (b)(3) of the Act. Therefore, for purposes of this opinion, we have assumed fair market value compensation based on the requesters' certifications. If the compensation under the Agreement is not at fair market value, this opinion will be without force and effect.

- This advisory opinion is limited in scope to the specific arrangement described in this letter and has no applicability to other arrangements, even those that appear similar in nature or scope.

This opinion is also subject to any additional limitations set forth at 42 C.F.R. Part 1008.

The Office of Inspector General ("OIG") will not proceed against the requesters with respect to any action that is part of the Proposed Arrangement taken in good faith reliance upon this advisory opinion as long as all of the material facts have been fully, completely, and accurately presented, the compensation under the Agreement represents fair market value, and the Proposed Arrangement in practice comports with the information provided. The OIG reserves the right to reconsider the questions and issues raised in this advisory opinion and, where the public interest requires, rescind, modify, or terminate this opinion. In the event that this advisory opinion is modified or terminated, the OIG will not proceed against the requesters with respect to any action taken in good faith reliance upon this advisory opinion, where all of the relevant facts were fully, completely, and accurately presented, where the compensation under the Agreement represents fair market value, and where such action was promptly discontinued upon notification of the modification or termination of this advisory opinion. An advisory opinion may be rescinded only if the relevant and material facts have not been fully, completely, and accurately disclosed to the OIG.

Sincerely,

/s/

D. McCarty Thornton
Chief Counsel to the Inspector General

APPENDIX F29

Advisory Opinion No. 98-16

[Posted November 10, 1998]

[Issued November 3, 1998]

[Name and address redacted]

Re: Advisory Opinion No. 98–16

Dear [Name redacted]:

We are writing in response to your request for an advisory opinion, in which you ask whether a proposed arrangement under which [Name redacted] would assign an employee pharmacist to work in designated hospital transplant centers for the purpose of providing pharmacy-related products and services (the "Proposed Arrangement") would constitute prohibited remuneration under the anti-kickback statute, section 1128B(b) of the Social Security Act (the "Act"), and, if so, whether the Proposed Arrangement would constitute grounds for the imposition of sanctions under the anti-kickback statute, section 1128B(b) of the Act, the exclusion authority related to kickbacks, section 1128(b)(7) of the Act, or the civil monetary penalty provision for kickbacks, section 1128A(a)(7) of the Act.

You have certified that all of the information you provided in your request, including all supplementary information, is true and correct and constitutes a complete description of the material facts regarding the Proposed Arrangement. In issuing this opinion, we have relied solely on the facts and information you presented to us. We have not undertaken any independent investigation of such information.

Based on the facts certified in your request for an advisory opinion, we conclude that the Proposed Arrangement may constitute prohibited remuneration under section 1128B(b) of the Act.

I. FACTUAL BACKGROUND

A. The Requestor

[Name redacted] (the "Pharmacy"), is a mail-order pharmacy, wholly owned by [Name redacted]. The Pharmacy specializes in supplying medications and pharmaceuticals to organ transplant recipients. The Pharmacy offers a number of services, including express medication delivery, medication counseling, and direct insurance billing.

B. Organ Transplantation

Organ transplantation involves the surgical replacement of a failed organ. In order to prevent rejection of the organ, transplant patients require life-long immunosuppressive drug therapy. The drug therapy begins immediately after transplantation and involves a plan of treatment developed by a team of clinicians, including a pharmacist. Federal health care programs provide drug coverage for this immunosuppressive therapy. Medicare provides a maximum of thirty-six months of coverage for immunosuppressive therapy after a transplant (*see* 42 U.S.C. § 1395x(s)(2)(J)), and state Medicaid programs cover immunosuppressive drug therapy under their outpatient drug benefits (*see* 42 U.S.C. § 1396d).

Approximately 275 hospitals perform organ transplantation in this country. In order to be eligible for Medicare reimbursement, these hospitals are required to meet conditions of Medicare participation. Relevant to this opinion are the conditions applicable to pharmacy management (42 C.F.R. § 482.25) and discharge planning (42 C.F.R. § 482.43). These regulatory standards require hospitals to provide or furnish qualified personnel and quality pharmaceutical services, either directly or through contractual arrangements, and to have in effect a discharge planning process that applies to all patients.

C. The Proposed Arrangement

Through employee services agreements, the Pharmacy proposes placing a licensed pharmacist in hospital transplant centers (the "Centers") interested in the Pharmacy's services. The Pharmacy would employ the pharmacist and would be responsible for all employee costs, such as wages, benefits, and taxes. To fill the pharmacist position, the Pharmacy may offer the position to current or former employees or independent contractors of a Center.

The pharmacist's duties would include: working with transplant teams to facilitate the patient's post-transplant care; preparing pharmaceutical care plans; overseeing patient compliance with pharmaceutical care plans after discharge; securing the patient's insurance coverage for pharmaceuticals and services provided by the Pharmacy; and processing prescriptions through the Pharmacy's pharmaceutical distribution center. The pharmacist would also perform all billing and collections for Pharmacy services. These items and services may be paid in whole or in part by a Federal health care program.

The Centers would incur no cost under the Proposed Arrangement, but would be responsible for providing the pharmacists with a work area and access to their patients. The Centers could submit recommendations for the on-site pharmacist position and could rehire any former employee hired and subsequently terminated by the Pharmacy.

II. LEGAL ANALYSIS

A. Law

The anti-kickback statute makes it a criminal offense knowingly and willfully to offer, pay, solicit, or receive any remuneration to induce referrals of items or services reimbursable by any Federal health care program. *See* section 1128B(b) of the Act. Where remuneration is paid purposefully to induce referrals of items or services for which payment may be made by a Federal health care program, the anti-kickback statute is violated. By its terms, the statute ascribes criminal liability to parties on both sides of an impermissible "kickback" transaction. For purposes of the anti-kickback statute, "remuneration" includes the transfer of anything of value, in cash or in-kind, directly or indirectly, covertly or overtly.

The statute has been interpreted to cover any arrangement where *one* purpose of the remuneration was to obtain money for the referral of services or to induce further referrals. *United States v. Kats*, 871 F.2d 105 (9th Cir. 1989); *United States v. Greber*, 760 F.2d 68 (3d Cir.), *cert. denied*, 474 U.S. 988 (1985). Violation of the statute constitutes a felony punishable by a maximum fine of $25,000, imprisonment up to five years, or both. Conviction will also lead to automatic exclusion from Federal health care programs, including

Medicare and Medicaid. This Office may also initiate administrative proceedings to exclude persons from Federal and state health care programs or to impose civil monetary penalties for fraud, kickbacks, and other prohibited activities under sections 1128(b)(7) and 1128A (a)(7) of the Act.[1]

The Department of Health and Human Services has published safe harbor regulations that define practices that are not subject to the anti-kickback statute because such practices would unlikely result in fraud or abuse. *See* 42 C.F.R. § 1001.952. The safe harbors set forth specific conditions that, if met, assure entities involved of not being prosecuted or sanctioned for the arrangement qualifying for the safe harbor. However, safe harbor protection is only afforded to those arrangements that precisely meet all of the conditions set forth in the safe harbor. The regulatory safe harbor potentially applicable to the Proposed Arrangement is the personal services and management contracts safe harbor. *See* 42 C.F.R. § 1001.952(d). The Proposed Arrangement does not qualify under this safe harbor, however, since there is no compensation paid by the Centers to the Pharmacy, despite the fact that at least some of the services will have value to the Centers, which are obligated to provide them in accordance with the Health Care Financing Administration's ("HCFA") conditions of participation. The personal services safe harbor requires that the compensation paid for services be set at fair market value in arms-length transactions. *See* 42 C.F.R. § 1001.952 (d)(5).

B. Prior Guidance

The OIG has stated on numerous occasions its view that the provision of free goods or services to an actual or potential referral source may violate the anti-kickback statute, depending on the circumstances. For example, in the preamble to the 1991 safe harbor regulations, we stated that giving free goods that have an independent value to a physician may violate the anti-kickback statute. *See* 56 Fed. Reg. 35978 (July 29, 1991). The OIG has also issued a Special Fraud Alert relating to the provision of free services by a clinical laboratory phlebotomist placed in a physician's office:

---

[1] Because both the criminal and administrative sanctions related to the anti-kickback implications of the Proposed Arrangement are based on violations of the anti-kickback statute, the analysis for purposes of this advisory opinion is the same under both.

"While the mere placement of a laboratory employee in the physician's office would not necessarily serve as an inducement prohibited by the anti-kickback statute, the statute is implicated when the phlebotomist performs additional tasks that are not normally the responsibility of the physician's office staff. These tasks can include taking vital signs or other nursing functions, testing for the physician's office laboratory, or performing clerical services.

Where the phlebotomist performs clerical or medical functions not directly related to the collection or processing of laboratory specimens, a strong inference arises that he or she is providing a benefit in return for the physician's referrals to the laboratory. In such a case, the physician, the phlebotomist, and the laboratory may have exposure under the anti-kickback statute. This analysis applies equally to the placement of phlebotomists in other health care settings, including nursing homes, clinics, and hospitals."

59 Fed. Reg. 65372, 65377 (Dec. 19, 1994). This analysis generally applies to the provision of any free or below market rate goods or services to actual or potential referral sources. If the intent of providing free goods or services is to induce or reward referrals of Federal health care program business, the anti-kickback statute would be violated.

C. Analysis of the Proposed Arrangement

Our concern under the anti-kickback statute is whether the Pharmacy would be giving a Center something of value in order to induce referrals of business reimbursed by a Federal health care program. This Office has a longstanding antipathy to arrangements where a party gives an existing or potential referral source valuable services or goods for free or below fair market value. In such cases, an inference arises that one purpose of the arrangement is to induce or reward referrals. The Proposed Arrangement has all the hallmarks of such disfavored arrangements.

First, the provision of a transplant pharmacist to a Center at no cost is a tangible benefit to the Center. Prior to entering into the Proposed Arrangement, a Center will have been providing at least some of the same pharmacy and discharge planning services to its transplant patients, including outpatients; such services are required as conditions of participation for hospitals in the Medicare program. It is likely that some services provided by the Pharmacy's pharmacist will substitute for services currently provided by a Center at its expense and for which it will be receiving indirect reimbursement through its DRG payments. In such circumstances, there would be a financial benefit to the Center.

This conclusion is supported by materials submitted by the Pharmacy. First, an advertisement for a similar arrangement promoted by a pharmacy competitor promises Centers savings in costly staff positions and relief of burdens imposed on existing staff. Second, the contract for the Proposed Arrangement specifically permits: (i) the Centers to submit recommendations for the on-site pharmacist position to the Pharmacy; (ii) the Pharmacy to offer employment to current or former employees or independent contractors of the Center; and (iii) the Centers to rehire any former employee terminated by the Pharmacy. In effect, the Proposed Arrangement offers Centers the opportunity to shift payroll or contractual costs to the Pharmacy.

Second, we infer that one purpose of the free services is to induce referrals. Such inference is appropriate with respect to the Proposed Arrangement for the following reasons:

- The services will be offered to a party that is in a position to influence substantially the initial recommendation of a pharmacy to patients.
- Transplant patients need lifetime pharmacy services.
- The services required by the patients are extremely expensive and will generate significant revenue for the Pharmacy. The cost of anti-rejection drugs and other medications can easily exceed $10,000 per year.
- Immunosuppresive therapy is critical to the success of a transplant. Depending on risk factors and therapy, a significant number of transplant recipients undergo one or more episodes of rejection during the year immediately following transplantation. Common sense suggests that a Center's recommendation of a preferred outpatient pharmacy to a patient will be given great weight.

In short, the Centers will exercise substantial influence over a significant source of revenue for the Pharmacy.

One purpose of the anti-kickback statute is to protect patients from inappropriate medical referrals by providers who may be unduly influenced by financial incentives. The statute seeks to ensure that referrals will be based on sound medical judgment and that providers will compete for business based on quality and convenience, instead of paying for it. Given the significance of the outpatient pharmacy to the transplant patient, any arrangement that might influence medical judgment in recommending a particular pharmacy provider is problematic and must be closely scrutinized. The Proposed Arrangement contains no safeguards, conditions, or controls that mitigate the risk of improper patient steering by Centers improperly influenced by the provision of free services.[2]

We recognize that close coordination between a transplant center and outpatient pharmacies is desirable and may significantly benefit patients, their families, and their caretakers by improving quality of care and by facilitating patient access to appropriate pharmaceutical supervision in a highly specialized area. HCFA has recognized the value of such services and has made providing them conditions of participation for purposes of Medicare reimbursement. *See, e.g.*, 42 C.F.R. §§ 482.25, .43. A transplant center may provide these services for patients in collaboration with pharmacies or others; however, they may not do so in a manner that provides financial incentives for referrals.

III. CONCLUSION

Based on the facts presented, we conclude that the Proposed Arrangement might constitute prohibited remuneration under the anti-kickback statute, if the requisite intent to induce referrals were present, and thus the Pharmacy may potentially be subject to sanction under sections 1128B(b), 1128(b)(7), and 1128A(a)(7) of the Act.[3]

IV. LIMITATIONS

The limitations applicable to this opinion include the following:

- This advisory opinion is issued only to [Name redacted], which is the requester of this opinion. This advisory opinion has no application, and cannot be relied upon, by any other individual or entity.

---

[2] Some transplant pharmacies may have special arrangements with particular drug manufacturers or even be affiliated with a drug manufacturer that has products in the immunosuppression market. We would have significant additional concerns with such arrangements.

[3] We express no opinion regarding the liability of the requester or any other party under the False Claims Act or other legal authorities for any improper billing, claims submission, or other conduct in connection with the services and products provided under the Proposed Arrangement.

- This advisory opinion will not bind or obligate any agency other than the U.S. Department of Health and Human Services.
- This advisory opinion is applicable only to the statutory provisions specifically noted in the first paragraph of this advisory opinion. No opinion is herein expressed or implied with respect to the application of any other Federal, state, or local statute, rule, regulation, ordinance, or other law that may be applicable to the Program.
- No opinion is expressed herein regarding the liability of any party under the False Claims Act or other legal authorities for any improper billing, claims submission, cost reporting, or related conduct.

This opinion is also subject to any additional limitations set forth at 42 C.F.R. Part 1008.

The Office of Inspector General reserves the right to reconsider the questions and issues raised in this advisory opinion and, where the public interest requires, rescind, modify or terminate this opinion.

Sincerely,

/s/

D. McCarty Thornton

Chief Counsel to the Inspector General

APPENDIX F30

Advisory Opinion No. 98-17

[Posted November 13, 1998]

[Issued November 6, 1998]

[Names and addresses redacted]

Re: Advisory Opinion No. 98–17

Dear [Names redacted]:

We are writing in response to your request for an advisory opinion, in which you ask whether donations by Company X ("Company X") to Organization A ("Organization A") (an independent, 501(c)(3) charitable organization) for the purpose of funding a program to pay for Supplementary Medical Insurance ("Medicare Part B") or Medicare Supplementary Health Insurance ("Medigap") premiums for financially needy Medicare beneficiaries with end-stage renal disease, where some or all of the beneficiaries may be receiving treatment from Company X (the "Proposed Arrangement"), would constitute grounds for the imposition of civil monetary penalties under section 1128A(a)(5) of the Social Security Act (the "Act").

You have certified that all of the information you provided in your request, including all supplementary letters, is true and correct and constitutes a complete description of the material facts and agreements among the parties regarding the Proposed Arrangement. In issuing this opinion, we have relied solely on the facts and information you presented to us. We have not undertaken any independent investigation of such information. This opinion is limited to the facts presented. If material facts have not been disclosed, this opinion is without force and effect.

Based on the facts certified in your request for an advisory opinion and subject to the conditions described below, we conclude that the Proposed Arrangement would not constitute grounds for the imposition of civil monetary penalties under section 1128A(a)(5) of the Act.

This opinion may not be relied on by any person other than the requesters and is further qualified as set out in Part IV below and in 42 C.F.R. Part 1008.

I. FACTUAL BACKGROUND

A. End-Stage Renal Disease and Medicare's Dialysis Benefit

End-stage renal disease ("ESRD") is a chronic disease that requires routine dialysis, as well as regular monitoring of laboratory values, diet, and medication. In addition to chronic renal failure, ESRD patients commonly suffer from certain co-morbid conditions, such as diabetes, anemia, hypertension, and congestive heart failure.

In 1972, Congress created a special Medicare benefit for all individuals with ESRD who are eligible for Social Security benefits (or are dependents of those who are eligible). Eligible persons are entitled to benefits under Medicare Part A and are eligible to enroll in Medicare Part B. Medicare Part B payments generally cover eighty percent of the composite rate for Medicare-covered maintenance dialysis services, as well as eighty percent of physician services and certain ancillary services, with the patient responsible for the remaining twenty percent.[1] Medigap insurance can be purchased to cover a patient's annual Medicare coinsurance obligations for Medicare-covered services.

B. The Parties

Company X owns twelve renal dialysis facilities in State Z and is a wholly-owned, direct subsidiary of Company Y. Organization A is an independent, 501(c)(3) charitable organization providing financial support to needy persons in State Z with ESRD for items such as transportation, medication, and other living expenses. Organization A is governed by a board of directors comprised of health professionals, community volunteers, and persons with kidney disease. No employee or affiliate of Company X or Company Y, serves on the Organization A board. The Organization A board is not directly or indirectly controlled by Company X, Company Y, or any of its subsid-

[1] The composite rate is a prospective payment system for outpatient maintenance dialysis services to Medicare beneficiaries. We note that Medicare reimbursement for some medical services provided to ESRD patients, such as certain lab services, are not covered under the composite rate.

iaries or affiliates. It has been the policy of the Organization A board not to have any employees of dialysis programs serve on the board.

Organization A provides financial support to financially needy ESRD patients through a general fund and an emergency fund. Grants from the general fund require a patient to fill out an application providing detailed financial information for the applicant's entire household. [2] Eligibility for the general fund is based on guidelines measuring monthly income and family size and a demonstration that the applicant is unable to pay his or her monthly expenses. Individuals who meet the guidelines are eligible to receive $500 per calender year from the general fund. A social worker submits the applications to the Organization A board, which gives approval and distributes the funds. Individuals receiving assistance from the emergency fund must show a demonstrated need and receive approval by a social worker. Emergency funds do not require an individual to fill out a financial application. Requests from the emergency fund are limited to $35, four times a year, or a maximum of $140 per year per individual.

C. The Proposed Arrangement

Organization A wishes to extend the general fund assistance program to include financial assistance to financially needy ESRD patients for the costs of health insurance premiums, including Medicare Part B and Medigap premiums. Social workers will assist patients in identifying all available sources of assistance for which they qualify, including assistance for health insurance premiums and, if appropriate, will refer financially needy patients to Organization A for such assistance. Although most, if not all, patient contact with Organization A is through a provider's social worker, if a patient who does not already have a provider contacts Organization A to inquire about dialysis facilities, Organization A will provide the patient with a complete list of all dialysis facilities in the area and will not express any preference among facilities.

Organization A will continue to use its current financial assistance application in assessing the financial need and eligibility of all patients, whether self-referred, referred by Company X, or referred

[2] The information required includes: assets held in checking, savings, and CD accounts; monthly income (which is made up of the take-home pay of the patient and spouse, social security, retirement income, etc.); and monthly expenses for rent, mortgage, food, utilities, transportation, medical expenses, insurance, charge accounts, and loans.

by other non-donor dialysis providers. In most cases, an ESRD social worker, employed by the dialysis provider, will submit a completed application to Organization A. Approval of the health insurance premium application will be made by the Organization A board's executive committee comprised of the president, vice president, secretary, treasurer, and two "at-large" board members. Determinations will be based solely on Organization A's good faith assessment of a patient's financial need. Organization A will not take the identity of the referring facility or the amount of any provider's donation into consideration when assessing patient applications or making grant determinations. Any qualified person will be free, and encouraged, to apply for grants under the expanded program. The patient can re-apply at any time his or her financial or family situation changes. All grants will be reviewed on an annual basis for eligibility. Organization A will send all premium payments directly to the insurance company.

Under the Proposed Arrangement, funding for the expanded program will be primarily donated by Company X. Company X will make contributions to Organization A without any restrictions or conditions placed on the donation. Company X has acknowledged that "contributions . . . will be gifts without any guarantee or promise on the part of Organization A that patients referred to Organization A for possible financial assistance with their insurance premiums will receive such assistance. Organization A's discretion as to the uses of contributions will be absolute, independent, and autonomous."

Company X will not track the amount that Organization A pays on behalf of patients dialyzing at its facilities in order to calculate future contributions. However, in calculating its contributions to Organization A, Company X has indicated that it may consider what it would have otherwise paid on behalf of financially needy patients. Company X will not advertise the availability of possible financial assistance to the public and will not disclose directly or indirectly to individual patients it refers to Organization A that Company X has donated to Organization A.

II. LEGAL ANALYSIS

Section 1128A(a)(5) of the Act provides for the imposition of civil monetary penalties against any person who:

> "offers to or transfers remuneration to any individual eligible for benefits under subchapter XVIII of this chapter, or under a State health care program (as defined in section [1128(h) of the Act]) that such person knows or should know is likely to influence such individual to order or receive from a particular provider, practitioner, or supplier any item or service for which payment may be made, in whole or in part, under subchapter XVIII of this chapter, or a State health care program (as so defined)."

Section 1128A(i)(6) defines "remuneration", in relevant part, as "transfers of items or services for free or for other than fair market value."[3]

A. Donations by Company X Do Not Constitute Remuneration to an Eligible Beneficiary

Company X's contributions to Organization A would not constitute grounds for the imposition of civil monetary penalties under section 1128A(a)(5) of the Act, because the contributions are not made to, or on behalf of, an individual eligible for Medicare or State health care program benefits. Organization A is an independent, 501(c)(3) charitable organization whose charitable purposes include aiding ESRD patients and their families and is not subject to control, directly or indirectly, by Company X, Company Y, or any of its subsidiaries or affiliates. Under the Proposed Arrangement, Organization A will have absolute discretion regarding the use of provider contributions made to Organization A.

In addition, eligibility for Organization A's health insurance premium assistance is available to any financially needy ESRD patient regardless of the provider; it is not limited to patients of Company X. Organization A will make all health insurance premium eligibility determinations using its own criteria, and Organization A will not take into account the identity of the referring provider or the amount of the provider's donation to Organization A.

As an additional safeguard, Company X has represented that it will not track the amounts that Organization A pays on behalf of patients dialyzing at its facilities in order to calculate amounts of future contributions, although donations may take into account the amounts that Company X would have otherwise expended on financially needy patients. Contributions will not be earmarked for the use of particular beneficiaries or groups of beneficiaries. Company X

[3] This definition of remuneration also provides an exception, not applicable here, for certain waivers of coinsurance and deductible amounts.

may change the amount of its contributions or discontinue contributing to Organization A at any time. Company X has represented that it will determine the amount of its contributions without consulting any other dialysis providers.

In sum, Organization A's status as an independent, 501(c)(3) charitable organization and its administration of the Proposed Arrangement provides sufficient insulation so that the premium payments should not be attributed to Company X. Company X's contributions to Organization A will not assure that the amount of health insurance premium assistance its patients receive bears any relationship to the amount of its donations. Indeed, Company X is not guaranteed that beneficiaries it refers to Organization A will receive any assistance at all. In these circumstances, we do not believe that the donations by Company X to Organization A can reasonably be construed as payments to eligible beneficiaries of Medicare or a State health care program.

B. Organization A's Purchase of Premiums Is Not Likely to Influence a Beneficiary's Choice of a Particular Provider

Section 1128A(a)(5) of the Act prohibits payments to, or on behalf of, Medicare or State health care program beneficiaries only if the payments are likely to influence such beneficiaries to use a particular provider. In the circumstances presented by the Proposed Arrangement, we believe that Organization A's payments of premiums on behalf of financially needy beneficiaries are not likely to influence a beneficiary's selection of a particular provider.

As part of the application process for health insurance premium assistance, Organization A requires certain financial information from the applicant, as well as additional information from the social worker. While patients may apply directly to Organization A, more commonly the dialysis provider's social worker refers the application to Organization A on the patient's behalf. Thus, a patient will often have selected a provider prior to submitting his or her application for assistance or prior to the initial Organization A premium payment. Moreover, Company X will not publicly advertise the availability of possible financial assistance. This should reduce the probability that a beneficiary would select a Company X facility based on its participation in the health insurance premium program. Most importantly, once in possession of Medicare Part B or Medigap coverage, a beneficiary will be able to select any provider of his or her choice. Simply put, Organization A's payment of premiums will expand, rather than limit, beneficiaries' freedom of choice of providers.

III. CONCLUSION

We conclude that the Proposed Arrangement would not constitute grounds for the imposition of civil monetary penalties under section 1128A(a)(5) of the Act. A violation of section 1128A(a)(5) of the Act requires that something of value be given to a beneficiary, either directly or on his or her behalf. The contributions to Organization A by Company X are not made to or on behalf of beneficiaries.[4] Moreover, while the premium payments by Organization A may constitute remuneration to beneficiaries, they are not likely to influence patients to order or receive services from particular providers. To the contrary, the insurance coverage purchased by Organization A will follow a patient regardless of which provider the patient selects, thereby enhancing patient freedom of choice in health care providers.

IV. LIMITATIONS

The limitations applicable to this opinion include the following:

- This advisory opinion is issued only to Organization A and Company X, the requesters of this opinion. This advisory opinion has no application, and cannot be relied upon, by any other individual or entity.
- This advisory opinion may not be introduced into evidence in any matter involving an entity or individual that is not a requester to this opinion.
- This advisory opinion does not address any other current or past arrangement for the payment of Part B or Medigap premiums by any dialysis provider or any other charitable or non-profit organization. The U.S. Department of Health and Human Services does not accept or acquiesce in any characterizations of the propriety of such arrangements in the materials submitted by the requesters.
- This advisory opinion is applicable only to the statutory provision specifically noted above. No opinion is herein expressed or

[4] The Proposed Arrangement differs from an arrangement where a renal dialysis provider directly pays premiums for beneficiaries, thus potentially influencing them to continue to use that particular dialysis provider in order to ensure continuing payment of premiums.

implied with respect to the application of any other Federal, state, or local statute, rule, regulation, ordinance, or other law that may be applicable to the Proposed Arrangement.

- This advisory opinion will not bind or obligate any agency other than the U.S. Department of Health and Human Services.
- This advisory opinion is limited in scope to the specific arrangement described in this letter and has no applicability to other arrangements, even those that appear similar in nature or scope.
- No opinion is expressed herein regarding the liability of any party under the False Claims Act or other legal authorities for any improper billing, claims submission, cost reporting, or related conduct.

The Office of Inspector General ("OIG") will not proceed against the requesters with respect to any action that is part of the Proposed Arrangement taken in good faith reliance upon this advisory opinion as long as all of the material facts have been fully, completely, and accurately presented, and the Proposed Arrangement in practice comports with the information provided. The OIG reserves the right to reconsider the questions and issues raised in this advisory opinion and, where the public interest requires, rescind, modify, or terminate this opinion. In the event that this advisory opinion is modified or terminated, the OIG will not proceed against the requesters with respect to any action taken in good faith reliance upon this advisory opinion, where all of the relevant facts were fully, completely, and accurately presented and where such action was promptly discontinued upon notification of the modification or termination of this advisory opinion. An advisory opinion may be rescinded only if the relevant and material facts have not been fully, completely, and accurately disclosed to the OIG.

Sincerely,

/s/

D. McCarty Thornton

Chief Counsel to the Inspector General

APPENDIX F31

Advisory Opinion No. 98-18

[Posted December 3, 1998]

[Issued November 25, 1998]

[Name and address redacted]

Re: Advisory Opinion No. 98–18

Dear [Name redacted]:

We are writing in response to your request for an advisory opinion regarding whether an ophthalmologist's proposed sublease to an optometrist of certain imaging equipment (the "Sublease") would meet the criteria of the equipment rental safe harbor, 42 C.F.R. § 1001.952(c). The imaging equipment may be used by the ophthalmologist to conduct telemedicine consultations relating to the optometrist's patients. The Sublease and the telemedicine consultation arrangement are referred to in this opinion letter collectively as the "Proposed Arrangement".

You have certified that all of the information provided in the request letter, including all supplementary submissions, is true and correct and constitutes a complete description of the relevant facts and agreements among the parties. You have also certified that, upon our approval, you will undertake to effectuate the Proposed Arrangement.

In issuing this opinion, we have relied solely on the facts and information presented to us. We have not undertaken an independent investigation of such information. This opinion is limited to the facts presented. If material facts have not been disclosed, this opinion is without force and effect.

Based on the facts certified in the request for an advisory opinion (including the certification of fair market value), we conclude that the Sublease satisfies the criteria of the equipment rental safe harbor, 42 C.F.R. § 1001.952(c). We further conclude that the arrangement for the provision of telemedicine consultations may involve prohibited remuneration if the requisite intent to induce referrals is present, but would not be subject to Office of Inspector General ("OIG") sanctions arising under the anti-kickback statute, 42 U.S.C. § 1320a-7b(b), based on the facts presented.

This opinion may not be relied on by any persons other than the requestor and is further qualified as set out in Part IV below and in 42 C.F.R. § 1008.

I. FACTUAL BACKGROUND

A. The Parties

Dr. Y (the "Requestor") is an ophthalmologist licensed to practice medicine in State A. He is a participating provider in the Medicare and Medicaid programs. Dr. X is an optometrist licensed to practice optometry in State A. Dr. X is a Medicare provider who performs Medicare-covered services. She has several office locations. The office location relevant to the Proposed Arrangement is located approximately twenty miles from Dr. Y's office.

B. The Proposed Arrangement

Dr. Y wishes to conduct telemedicine consultations for patients in remote locations. To this end, Dr. Y intends to lease from a third-party equipment leasing company (the "Lessor") certain telemedicine equipment (the "Leased Equipment") that will enable him to view images of a patient's eye transmitted from such locations. Dr. Y proposes to enter into an arrangement with Dr. X to locate in Dr. X's office the components of the Leased Equipment that transmit the images to Dr. Y's office. These components can also be used by Dr. X as a fundus photography system to document a patient's ocular disease. Dr. Y will retain in his office the components of the Leased Equipment that allow him to view the transmitted images. This arrangement will enable Dr. Y to consult with Dr. X in connection with those of her patients who may require ophthalmologist services beyond the scope of her optometry practice. If, after such consultation, Dr. Y determines that a patient requires services beyond the scope of Dr. X's practice, Dr. X may refer the patient to Dr. Y, although the patient will be free to select any ophthalmologist. Neither Dr. Y nor Dr. X will bill the patient or any insurer for the telemedicine consultation.

Dr. Y proposes subleasing the equipment to Dr. X pursuant to a written sublease ("Sublease"). The Sublease will describe the subleased equipment with specificity and will cover all of the equipment leased between Dr. Y and Dr. X for the twelve-month term of the Sublease. The Sublease will provide for monthly rent of $[redacted], an amount determined by multiplying the cost associated with purchasing a fundus photography unit from the Lessor by a rental factor of [redacted]. This rental factor is ordinarily applied by the Lessor to equipment leases of the length involved here for the equipment. The rent to Dr. X amounts to a direct "pass through" of the rent being paid by Dr. Y to the Lessor for the same equipment. Dr. Y has certified that the rental amount under the Sublease constitutes fair market rent for the subleased equipment. The Sublease will prohibit Dr. X from advertising or marketing in any respect her ability to provide telemedicine consultation services. The only arrangement between Dr. Y and Dr. X is the Sublease and there are, and will be, no oral or written collateral agreements or understandings between them, including agreements or understandings regarding the referral of patients from either party to the other.

II. LEGAL ANALYSIS

A. The Anti-Kickback Statute

The anti-kickback statute makes it a criminal offense knowingly and willfully to offer, pay, solicit or receive any remuneration to induce referrals of items or services reimbursable by any Federal health care program. *See* 42 U.S.C. § 1320a-7b(b). Where remuneration is paid purposefully to induce referrals of items or services paid for by a Federal health care program, the anti-kickback statute is violated. By its terms, the statute ascribes criminal liability to parties on both sides of an impermissible "kickback" transaction. For purposes of the anti-kickback statute, "remuneration" includes the transfer of anything of value, in cash or in-kind, directly or indirectly, covertly or overtly.

The statute has been interpreted to cover any arrangement where *one* purpose of the remuneration is to obtain money for the referral of services or to induce further referrals. *United States v. Kats*, 871 F.2d 105 (9th Cir. 1989); *United States v. Greber*, 760 F.2d 68 (3d Cir.), *cert. denied*, 476 U.S. 988 (1985). Violations of the statute constitute a felony punishable by a maximum fine of $25,000, imprisonment up to five years or both. Conviction will also lead to automatic exclusion from Federal health care programs, including Medicare and Medicaid. This Office may also initiate administrative proceedings to exclude persons from the Federal and State health care programs or to impose civil monetary penalties for fraud, kickbacks, and other prohibited activities under 42 U.S.C. §§ 1320a-7(b)(7), 1320a-7a(a)(7).[1]

We have previously stated our view that a gift to an existing or potential referral source that has independent value to such source implicates the anti-kickback statute and may be unlawful if the donor of the gift has the requisite intent to induce Federal health care program referrals. For example, in the preamble to the 1991 safe harbor regulations, we stated that giving a physician who is a referral source a free computer that has independent value to the physician may violate the statute. *See* 56 Fed. Reg. 35978 (July 1991); *see also, e.g.*, OIG Special Fraud Alert, 56 Fed. Reg. 65377 (Oct. 1994) (explaining that the anti-kickback statute is implicated where a clinical laboratory provides a phlebotomist to a physician to perform tasks normally the responsibility of the physician's office staff).

A number of statutory and regulatory "safe harbors" protect certain arrangements that might otherwise technically violate the anti-kickback statute from prosecution. *See* 42 U.S.C. § 1320a-7b(b)(3); 42 C.F.R. § 1001.952. The safe harbor potentially applicable to the Sublease is the equipment rental safe harbor at 42 C.F.R. § 1001.952(c). This safe harbor protects equipment rental payments if:

- there is a written lease signed by the parties;
- the lease specifies the equipment covered by the lease;
- where the lease is intended to provide the lessee with the use of the equipment for periodic intervals, rather than full-time for the term of the lease, the lease specifies the exact schedule, length, and rent for the intervals;
- the term of the lease is for at least one year; and
- the aggregate rental charge is set in advance, consistent with fair market value in an arms-length transaction, and is not determined in a manner that takes into account the volume or value of any referrals or business otherwise generated between the parties for which payment may be made in whole or in part under Medicare or a State health care program.

---

[1] Because both the criminal and administrative sanctions related to the Proposed Arrangement are based on violations of the anti-kickback statute, the analysis for purposes of this advisory opinion is the same for both.

42 C.F.R. § 1001.952(c). For purposes of the equipment rental safe harbor, "fair market value" means the value of the equipment when obtained from a manufacturer or professional distributor, provided that the value is not adjusted to reflect any additional value one party would attribute to the equipment as a result of its proximity or convenience to sources of referrals or business otherwise generated for which payment may be made in whole or in part under Medicare or a State health care program. Strict compliance with all safe harbor elements is required in order to receive safe harbor protection. *See* 56 Fed. Reg. 35952, 35954 (July 29, 1991).

B. The Proposed Arrangement

Dr. Y and Dr. X are potential sources of referrals of Federal health care program business for one another and therefore anything of value exchanged between them potentially implicates the anti-kickback statute. In this regard, there are two aspects of the Proposed Arrangement to be analyzed: the Sublease for the fundus photography equipment and the arrangement for free telemedicine consultations.

1. The Sublease

The Sublease will be in writing and will specify the exact equipment subleased. The Sublease will cover all of the equipment subleased between Dr. Y and Dr. X for its twelve-month term.[2] The Sublease will provide for a fixed rental payment of $[redacted] per month, resulting in an annual aggregate rental payment fixed in advance of $[redacted]. The rent to be paid under the Sublease, presumed to be fair market value for purposes of this advisory opinion,[3] is based on the equipment's value to Dr. X as a fundus photography unit. The rental charge has been determined by multiplying the supplier's purchase price for a fundus photography unit by a rental factor ordinarily applied by the supplier for leases of the

[2] The Sublease agreement provides for early "for cause" termination by Dr. Y, if Dr. X fails to perform any conditions or covenants of the Sublease or removes, or attempts to remove, the subleased equipment from her office without Dr. Y's consent. For purposes of this advisory opinion, termination of the Sublease prior to the end of the initial one-year term would be deemed to be a material change in the facts presented and result in this advisory opinion being without force and effect.

[3] We are precluded by statute from opining on whether fair market value shall be or was paid for goods, services, or property. *See* 42 U.S.C. § 1320a-7d (b)(3)(A).

duration of the Sublease. Thus, the rental charge will not be determined in a manner that takes into account the volume or value of any referrals or business generated between the parties. In sum, because all safe harbor elements are satisfied (assuming fair market value), the rent paid under the Sublease would not constitute prohibited remuneration under the anti-kickback statute.

2. The Telemedicine Consultations

The Sublease will only cover the rental of a fundus photography system to be used for producing images of the eye in Dr. X's office. However, the arrangement for telemedicine consultations itself may have value to Dr. X. When connected to the receiving components retained by Dr. Y (for which Dr. X will not be paying under the Sublease), the subleased equipment will enable Dr. X to access telemedicine consultations with Dr. Y. This may enable Dr. X to expand her business or to earn additional fees associated with her role in performing the consultations. However, based on the facts submitted by Dr. Y, Dr. X will not advertise or market her access to telemedicine consultations and will not charge a fee in connection with such consultations. Therefore, the telemedicine consultations will have minimal, if any, value to Dr. X.

Conversely, the arrangement for telemedicine consultations may have value to Dr. Y. Dr. X's referral of a patient to Dr. Y in conjunction with a telemedicine consultation will provide Dr. Y the opportunity to generate Federal health care program business. However, the Proposed Arrangement permits Dr. X's patients the freedom to choose any ophthalmologist. In addition, Dr. Y has certified that the only arrangement between Dr. Y and Dr. X is the Sublease and that there are, and will be, no oral or written collateral agreements or understandings between them, including agreements or understandings regarding the referral of patients from either party to the other. Based on these representations, any opportunity for Dr. Y to generate business from telemedicine consultations will not be an inducement for Dr. Y to refer patients to Dr. X.

Accordingly, although the telemedicine consultation arrangement may constitute prohibited remuneration under the anti-kickback statute if the requisite intent is present, the OIG will not subject it to sanctions arising under the anti-kickback statute.[4]

III. CONCLUSION

Based on the facts as certified by Dr. Y (including Dr. Y's certification that the rental amount to be paid under the Sublease constitutes fair market value in an arms-length transaction) and subject to the conditions stated in this opinion letter, we conclude that the Sublease would meet the criteria of the equipment rental safe harbor at 42 C.F.R. § 1001.952(c). We further conclude that the arrangement for the provision of telemedicine consultations may involve prohibited remuneration if the requisite intent to induce referrals is present, but would not be subject to OIG sanctions under 42 U.S.C. §§ 1320a-7(b)(7) & 1320a-7a(a)(7), based on the facts presented.

IV. LIMITATIONS

The limitations applicable to this opinion include the following:

- This advisory opinion is issued only to Dr. Y, the Requestor of this opinion. This advisory opinion has no application, and cannot be relied upon, by any other individual or entity.
- This advisory opinion may not be introduced into evidence in any matter involving an entity or individual that is not a requestor to this opinion.
- This advisory opinion is applicable only to the statutory provisions specifically noted above. No opinion is herein expressed or implied with respect to the application of any other Federal, state, or local statute, rule, regulation, ordinance, or other law that may be applicable to the Proposed Arrangement.
- This advisory opinion will not bind or obligate any agency other than the U.S. Department of Health and Human Services.
- This advisory opinion is limited in scope to the specific arrangement described in this letter and has no applicability to other arrangements, even those that appear similar in nature or scope.
- No opinion is expressed herein regarding the liability of any party under the False Claims Act or other legal authorities for

[4] This advisory opinion will be without force and effect if Dr. X charges a fee for the telemedicine consultations or does not comply fully with the prohibition on marketing her access to telemedicine consultations.

any improper billing, claims submission, cost reporting, or related conduct.

This opinion is also subject to any additional limitations set forth at 42 C.F.R. Part 1008.

The OIG will not proceed against the Requestor with respect to any action that is part of the Proposed Arrangement taken in good faith reliance upon this advisory opinion as long as all of the material facts have been fully, completely, and accurately presented, the compensation under the Sublease represents fair market value in accordance with the requirements of 42 C.F.R.

§ 1001.952(c), and the Proposed Arrangement in practice comports with the information provided. The OIG reserves the right to reconsider the questions and issues raised in this advisory opinion and, where the public interest requires, rescind, modify, or terminate this opinion. In the event that this advisory opinion is modified or terminated, the OIG will not proceed against the Requestor with respect to any action taken in good faith reliance upon this advisory opinion, where all of the relevant facts were fully, completely, and accurately presented, where the compensation under the Sublease represents fair market value pursuant to 42 C.F.R.

§ 1001.952(c), and where such action was promptly discontinued upon notification of the modification or termination of this advisory opinion. An advisory opinion may be rescinded only if the relevant and material facts have not been fully, completely, and accurately disclosed to the OIG.

Sincerely,

/s/

D. McCarty Thornton

Chief Counsel to the Inspector General

APPENDIX F32

Advisory Opinion No. 98-19

[Posted December 21, 1998]

[Issued December 14, 1998]

[names redacted]

Re: [names redacted]

OIG Advisory Opinion No. 98–19

Gentlemen:

We are writing in response to your request for an advisory opinion, in which you asked whether an arrangement whereby an independent physician association would acquire an equity interest in a managed care organization would constitute grounds for the imposition of sanctions under the anti-kickback statute, section 1128B(b) of the Social Security Act (the "Act"), the exclusion authority for kickbacks, section 1128(b)(7) of the Act, or the civil monetary penalty provision for kickbacks, section 1128A(a)(7) of the Act.

In accordance with our regulations at 42 C.F.R. Part 1008, your request for an advisory opinion disclosed a number of additional arrangements involving Company A ("Company A"), about which no opinion has been sought. For purposes of this advisory opinion, the term "Proposed Arrangement" collectively includes only the following arrangements described in your request for an advisory opinion and supplemental submissions (as described in greater detail below): the acquisition by Company B (the "IPA") of a [less than 15 percent] equity interest in Company A and the consequent return on the equity investment; the assignment of physician services agreements as consideration for Company A's equity investment; the Network Service Agreement; the Administrative Service Agreement; and the Incentive Stock Plan.

You have certified that all of the information provided in your request, including all supplementary materials, is true and correct and constitutes a complete description of the material facts regarding the Proposed Arrangement. In issuing this opinion, we have relied solely on the facts and information you presented to us. We have not undertaken any independent investigation of such information.

Based on the facts certified in your request for an advisory opinion and supplemental submissions, we conclude that the Office of Inspector General ("OIG") will not subject the Proposed Arrangement to sanctions arising under the anti-kickback statute pursuant to sections 1128(b)(7) or 1128A(a)(7) of the Act, provided that all compensation in connection with the Proposed Arrangement is fair market value as you have certified. We express no opinion about the Medical Management Program Agreement (or any agreement entered into in accordance with its terms) or about any arrangement disclosed or referenced in your request letter or supplemental submissions other than the Proposed Arrangement.

This opinion may not be relied on by any persons other than the Requesters[1] of this advisory opinion and is further qualified as set out in Part IV below and in 42 C.F.R. Part 1008.

I. FACTUAL BACKGROUND

A. The Parties

1. The Managed Care Organization

Company A is a managed care organization organized pursuant to the laws of the state of Y. Company A traces its corporate roots to the early 1980s, when a group of local hospitals formed a preferred provider organization ("PPO"). Several years ago, the preferred provider organization merged with a licensed health maintenance organization ("HMO") in an effort to develop HMO capabilities. Company A was formed as the holding company for the PPO and HMO as part of the merger transaction.

Company A currently has eight shareholders, each of which is either a hospital, the owner of a hospital facility, or a related entity of a hospital located in the City X metropolitan area (collectively, the "Shareholder Hospitals"). Company A is the parent company of four wholly-owned subsidiaries. The two subsidiaries relevant to the Proposed Arrangement are Company C, a preferred provider organization ("Company C" or the "P.O.") incorporated in State Y,

[1] For purposes of this advisory opinion, Company A and the IPA are the "Requesters."

and Company D, a health maintenance organization domiciled in the State of Y and authorized to do business in State Y and State Z ("Company D" or the "HMO").[2]

As a preferred provider organization, the P.O. contracts with various physicians and hospitals in the City X metropolitan area in order to form a network of providers that may be utilized by various third-party payers in offering covered health care services to their subscribers. For its services in establishing and maintaining the network, the P.O. receives a fee from each of its network hospitals, including the Shareholder Hospitals;[3] the fee varies in direct proportion to the amount of revenue each hospital earns as a result of its participation in the P.O.'s P.O. network.[4]

The P.O. contracts with third-party payers (typically employers or other entities in the commercial group health insurance market), who pay a negotiated fee to the P.O. for access to the PPO network. As part of its services, the P.O. assists the third-party payers in establishing the discounted rates they will pay network providers for covered health care services. The third-party payers set and collect their own subscriber premiums. There are no Medicaid enrollees in the P.O.'s P.O. product lines, but there may be some Medicare enrollees. The PPO lines of business currently constitute approximately []% of Company A's business.

The HMO — Company A's HMO subsidiary — offers its own plans directly to subscribers in the City X metropolitan area. These plans include non-governmental sponsored plans and a Medicare risk contract. The HMO also participates in the State Y and State Z Medicaid managed care programs. Unlike the P.O., the HMO receives no access fees from its network providers or from third-party payers. The HMO charges and receives premiums directly from contracting subscribers or receives capitation payments from Medicare or Medicaid.

---

[2] In addition, Company A is the parent of an offshore reinsurance company and a management services organization, which are not involved in the Proposed Arrangement. The management services organization has no employees or current business, and Company A has no plans to develop business for the management company and is considering selling its name to a third party.

[3] The PPO network presently is comprised of approximately 42 area hospitals.

[4] We express no opinion regarding any access fees paid by these hospitals to the P.O.

The HMO pays its network hospitals and physicians in accordance with negotiated provider contracts. Some hospitals are paid on a per diem basis, while others are paid under a full or modified risk arrangement. Primary care physicians are generally paid a capitated amount per subscriber who selects the physician, while specialists are paid on a discounted fee-for-service basis. The amount to be paid to a physician for services, whether a capitation or fee-for-service amount, will be fixed by the HMO in advance.

The substantial majority of the P.O. and the HMO business is derived from the commercial group health insurance market, including virtually all of the PPO business.

2. The Independent Physician Association

The IPA ("Company B" or the "IPA") is a State Y corporation established in 1984 and organized as an independent physician association. Its approximately 2200 shareholders are primary care and specialty care physicians, all of whom practice in the City X metropolitan area. Profit distributions are made to the IPA's shareholders based on their IPA share ownership, which has no relationship to any past, present, or future referrals to Company A. Currently, each physician-shareholder has a single share in the IPA; pursuant to the proposed Incentive Stock Plan described below, future shareholdings will be based, in part, on physician performance on a number of pre-set quality indicators and performance standards.

The IPA enters into physician service agreements ("PSAs")[5] with its shareholder physicians and with non-shareholder physicians and contracts with health plans on behalf of its physician panel. The IPA physicians, along with other physicians in outlying areas, serve as network providers for Company A health plans, as well as for competing health plans. The IPA physicians admit patients to hospitals in the Company A health plan networks, including the Shareholder Hospitals.

B. The Proposed Arrangement

Company A seeks to expand its HMO business in the City X metropolitan area. To facilitate this expansion, Company A desires to ensure a stable and sufficient network of physicians for the additional HMO business. Accordingly, Company A proposes selling a

---

[5] We express no opinion with respect to the legality of any existing or proposed PSA.

[less than 15 percent] interest in Company A to the IPA and entering into certain ancillary agreements with the IPA, as described below.

1. The Stock Purchase and the Assignment Agreement

Pursuant to a subscription agreement and a shareholder agreement, the IPA will purchase shares of Company A stock equal to a [less than 15 percent] equity interest. The shares would constitute a separate class of non-voting stock (Class B shares) with the right to elect no less than one Company A board member. Both the Shareholder Hospitals and the IPA will have made substantial investments in Company A, and the distribution of profits will be in direct proportion to the fair market value of such investments.

As consideration for the stock, the IPA will assign to Company A the IPA's contract rights under certain long-term PSAs with its shareholder (and potentially some non-shareholder) physicians. Specifically, the IPA will assign PSAs for no less than [ ]% of its existing primary care physicians and [ ]% of its specialty physicians. The exact percentages of assigned PSAs will be fixed prior to the stock transfer. The Requesters have certified that the Proposed Arrangement will not be consummated unless the aggregate value of the assigned PSA contract rights is fair market value for the Company A stock based on an arms-length transaction and not based on the volume or value of referrals or business otherwise generated between the parties.

In connection with the stock transfer, the IPA will become the exclusive physician provider panel for all managed care arrangements in which Company A participates (including the P.O. and the HMO plans) and will agree not to serve as a provider panel for any other health care entity. Individual IPA physicians, however, will be permitted to serve on panels for other health plans, subject to certain limitations applicable to physicians with significant ownership or control interests in a competing health care plan.

The Requesters have certified that there will be no financial arrangements or intentional efforts by Company A or any of its health care plans to have IPA physicians enroll persons in any of the Company A health care plans or to have IPA physicians encourage persons to enroll in any of the Company A plans.

2. The Ancillary Agreements

The Proposed Arrangement includes three ancillary personal services agreements between the IPA and Company A: a Network

Service Agreement, a Medical Management Program Agreement, and an Administrative Services Agreement.

The **Network Service Agreement** is intended to ensure that Company A health plans have sufficiently large panels of available physicians to meet subscriber demand. Pursuant to the Network Service Agreement, the IPA will be responsible for developing and maintaining the provider network for the Company A plans for a term of ten years. It will fulfill these obligations by entering into PSAs with primary and specialty care physicians. Company A will pay the IPA an annual fee for access to the IPA's network of physicians and for maintenance of the network. The fee will be set at $[ ] per covered employee in the PPO health plans per year, with a minimum payment of $[ ] per year and a maximum of $[ ] per year for the first five years. The Requesters have certified that compensation to be paid under the Network Service Agreement will be consistent with fair market value in arms-length transactions and will not be determined in a manner that takes into account the volume or value of any referrals or business otherwise generated between the parties.

The IPA and Company A will also enter into a ten-year **Medical Management Program Agreement**, pursuant to which the IPA shareholder physicians will develop and implement various programs for Company A health plans, including, but not limited to, programs in the areas of credentialing, utilization management, quality improvement, and case management. The IPA and Company A will negotiate separately the scope of services and specific compensation for each medical program developed under the Medical Management Program Agreement.

The Medical Management Program Agreement is, in essence, an agreement to enter into an undetermined number of future consulting contracts. Pursuant to the Medical Management Program Agreement, each of these future contracts will provide for "fair and reasonable" compensation in accordance with pre-set guidelines that establish the following principles:

- the nature, scope, and duration of services shall be agreed upon before the amount of compensation is established;
- the compensation shall be established at fair market value rates based upon the level of experience, education, or professional qualifications deemed necessary to carry out the services;

- the services will not exceed the level of services necessary and reasonable to fulfill the business purpose of the arrangement;
- the compensation, duties, and obligations of the parties shall be set forth in writing;
- the compensation shall be established for no less than one year and shall not be based upon, or related to, the value or volume of any referrals to any physicians being compensated by the IPA to participate in any medical management program established pursuant to the Medical Management Program Agreement, or based on any other business relationship between the IPA and Company A; and
- the compensation and services shall not involve the counseling or promotion of a business arrangement or other activity that violates any state or Federal law.

The Requesters have certified that all compensation to be paid under the future contracts will be consistent with fair market value in arms-length transactions and will not be determined in a manner that takes into account the volume or value of any referrals or business otherwise generated between the parties.

Finally, the IPA and Company A will enter into a ten-year **Administrative Services Agreement**, pursuant to which Company A will provide the IPA with certain administrative services, such as credentialing, accounting and auditing, utilization and quality management, and office administration. The IPA will pay Company A a predetermined rate, which will initially be an annual fee of $[ ] per physician with an executed PSA. The Requesters have certified that compensation to be paid under the Administrative Services Agreement will be consistent with fair market value in arms-length transactions and will not be determined in a manner that takes into account the volume or value of any referrals or business otherwise generated between the parties.

3. The IPA Incentive Stock Plan

In accordance with its proposed shareholder agreement with Company A and to provide its shareholder physicians with a personal investment in the success of Company A, the IPA will offer additional shares of stock to those of its shareholder physicians who agree to assume certain levels of financial risk (the "Incentive Stock Plan"). Benefits under the Incentive Stock Plan are tied to physician acceptance of risk, HMO participation, and quality of service, and will vary depending on the degree of a physician's participation in systems of care that have assumed financial risk and responsibility for provision of medical services to the HMO subscribers. The Requesters estimate that approximately 90% of the IPA physicians will be eligible to participate in the Incentive Stock Plan.

Shareholder physicians who choose to participate in the Incentive Stock Plan will be required to have entered into a PSA with for a term of at least five years.[6] These PSAs will establish certain rights and restrictions, including the following: (i) the physician will be permitted to contract with any other payer and/or health system; (ii) the physician will be required to have active medical staff privileges at a Company A affiliated hospital; (iii) the physician will not be permitted to be employed by, or have "prohibited affiliations"[7] with, a medical group that is owned by a health system or managed care plan that competes with Company A or the Company A health plans; (iv) subject to Company A approval based on product or plan needs, the physician will be required to participate in all Company A health plans; and (v) the physician's ability to transfer shares in the IPA will be restricted.[8] The PSAs will require physicians to comply with the health plans' quality improvement and utilization management programs.

4. Payments for Provider Services

The IPA physician shareholders and the Shareholder Hospitals will receive reimbursement from the HMO and from the PPO third-party payers for health care services they provide. The Requesters have certified that the remuneration paid to physicians and hospitals for services provided to the PPO or the HMO subscribers

[6] As described above, these PSAs will be assigned to Company A as part of the stock purchase transaction.

[7] For purposes of the Network Service Agreement, a prohibited affiliation generally means employment of a provider by a competing managed care entity or a provider's ownership interest in a competing health care entity, unless such ownership interest is no more than [ ]% of a publicly traded competing managed care entity's total outstanding equity.

[8] Physicians who are not eligible to participate in the Incentive Stock Plan will enter into one-year PSAs with the IPA (renewable at Company A's discretion) and, among other things, will be required (i) to have active medical staff privileges at a Company A-affiliated hospital; (ii) to meet a specific market area or practice area business need, as determined by Company A, the PPO, or the HMO; and (iii) to participate in all Company A health plans, subject to Company A, PPO, or HMO approval based on specific plan needs.

will represent fair market value in an arms-length transaction for the services the physicians or hospitals provide and will not take into account the volume or value of referrals or other business generated between the parties.

II. LEGAL ANALYSIS

A. The Law

The anti-kickback statute makes it a criminal offense knowingly and wilfully to offer, pay, solicit, or receive any remuneration to induce referrals of items or services reimbursable by Federal health care programs. *See* section 1128B(b) of the Act. Where remuneration is paid purposefully to induce referrals of items or services paid for by a Federal health care program, the anti-kickback statute is violated. By its terms, the statute ascribes liability to parties on both sides of an impermissible "kickback" transaction. For purposes of the anti-kickback statute, "remuneration" includes the transfer of anything of value, in cash or in kind, directly or indirectly, covertly or overtly.

The statute has been interpreted to cover any arrangement where *one* purpose of the remuneration is to obtain money for referral of services or to induce further referrals. *United States v. Kats*, 871 F. 2d 105 (9th Cir. 1989); *United States v. Greber*, 760 F. 2d 68 (3rd Cir.), *cert. denied*, 476 U.S. 988 (1985). Violation of the statute constitutes a felony punishable by a maximum fine of $25,000, imprisonment up to five years, or both. Conviction will also lead to automatic exclusion from Federal health care programs, including Medicare and Medicaid. This Office may also initiate administrative proceedings to exclude persons from Federal health care programs or to impose civil monetary penalties for fraud, kickbacks, and other prohibited activities under sections 1128(b)(7) and 1128A(a)(7) of the Act.[9]

The Department has published safe harbor regulations that protect certain arrangements that might otherwise technically violate the anti-kickback statute from prosecution. *See* 42 C.F.R. § 1001.952. The safe harbors set forth specific conditions that, if met, assure entities involved of not being prosecuted or sanctioned for the

[9] Because both the criminal and administrative sanctions related to the anti-kickback implications of the Proposed Arrangement are based on violations of the anti-kickback statute, the analysis for the purposes of this advisory opinion is the same under both.

arrangement qualifying for the safe harbor. However, safe harbor protection is only afforded to those arrangements that precisely meet all of the conditions set forth in the safe harbor. Notwithstanding, arrangements that do not fit squarely within a safe harbor do not necessarily violate the anti-kickback statute. *See, e.g.*, 56 Fed. Reg. 35952, 35954 (July 29, 1991).

B. The Proposed Arrangement

1. The Stock Purchase and Assignment Agreements

Although the Proposed Arrangement involves a complex web of contracts, the basic business transaction is straightforward: the IPA is purchasing an equity interest in Company A in exchange for its physicians' long term commitment to serve as the exclusive provider panel and provide medical management services for the Company A health plans. In other words, the Shareholder Hospitals and the IPA are joint venturing in a managed care organization. Accordingly, we start by applying a joint venture analysis to the Proposed Arrangement.

Health care joint ventures in which investors are also sources of referrals or suppliers of items or services to the joint venture raise many questions under the anti-kickback statute. In 1989, the OIG issued a Special Fraud Alert specifically discussing joint venture arrangements that may violate the anti-kickback statute. In general, joint ventures between physicians and hospitals in which they practice may be suspect, because distributions from the joint ventures may be disguised remuneration paid in return for referrals. Like any kickback scheme, these arrangements can lead to overutilization of services, increased costs for Federal health care programs, corruption of professional judgment, and unfair competition.

a. The Proposed Arrangement Does Not Fit the Safe Harbor for Investment Interests in Small Entities

The safe harbor for investments in small entities, 42 C.F.R. § 1001.952(a)(2), has eight elements, each of which must be satisfied in order for an arrangement to qualify for the exception. The eight elements address three areas of concern in abusive joint ventures: (i) how investors are selected and retained; (ii) the nature of the business structure; and (iii) the financing and profit distributions. Although the Requesters have certified that the IPA's assignment of the PSAs will represent fair market value for the equity interest, the stock purchase arrangement fails to meet several of the elements of the safe harbor; in particular, all of the proposed investors will be furnishing items or services to Company A health plans, and the investment opportunity is only being offered to the IPA shareholders.

b. The Proposed Arrangement Potentially Violates the Anti-Kickback Statute

The initial question to be addressed is whether equity ownership in a managed care organization by an independent physician association may provide physicians with remuneration for referrals of their patients to the managed care organization. This Office has recognized that Congress did not intend the anti-kickback statute to bar all forms of investment or ownership in health care providers by referral sources. *See, e.g.*, 54 Fed. Reg. 3090 (Jan. 1, 1989). Recent legislation permitting provider-sponsored organizations to enter into Medicare + Choice contracts reflects an implicit determination by Congress that physician-hospital ownership of managed care organizations is acceptable, provided such organizations comply with all relevant statutory and regulatory authorities, including the anti-kickback statute. The literal language of the anti-kickback statute encompasses any knowing or willful payment to a physician to induce the physician to recommend a health plan pursuant to which services are reimbursed by a Federal health care program. For example, payments to physicians by a health plan for marketing the plan clearly implicate the statute.

With respect to joint ventures, the major concern is that the profit distributions to investors in the joint venture that are also referral sources to the joint venture may potentially represent remuneration for those referrals. A related concern is that, where the investing parties have a referral relationship wholly apart from the joint venture, distributions from the joint venture could potentially represent remuneration to one party for referrals to the other party based on those independent relationships. In either case, the remuneration could result in increased utilization of services or increased costs to Federal health care programs. Accordingly, all aspects of all relationships between the parties must be examined.

c. Distributions from Company A to the IPA Are Unlikely to Constitute Remuneration for Referrals to Company A

Our initial inquiry is whether the distributions from the joint venture may be "disguised" remuneration to the IPA physician-shareholders for referrals of their patients to the joint venture. In other words, do the IPA's physician-shareholders refer patients to Company A's health plans and, if so, do the physicians receive remuneration for those referrals either directly or indirectly? For purposes of this opinion, we are addressing only the potential return on the IPA's equity investment in Company A, in the absence, as certified by the Requesters, of any financial arrangement or intentional effort by Company A or any of the Company A health care plans to have physicians enroll persons in the Company A plans or to have physicians encourage persons to enroll in the Company A plans.

On the threshhold issue of whether a physician's recommendation of a particular health plan to a patient would potential implicate the anti-kickback statute, we recognize that in many instances a physician's ability to influence a patient's enrollment in Company A's HMO or PPO products may be limited. Unlike the referrals in many illegal joint venture arrangements, in which a physician's order almost always results in the delivery of the item or service ordered, a physician's recommendation of a health plan is only one of many factors that may influence a person's choice of an insurance plan. For example, other considerations may include (i) whether a plan is available under a patient's employer plan; (ii) the benefit package in light of the patient and other family member needs; (iii) premium and other costs; (iv) recommendations from other family members' physicians; and (v) other health plans in which the physician participates.[10]

With respect to Company A, most of its business is in the group health insurance market, including virtually all of its PPO business. In the group market, employers or other sponsors select the plans, and price is usually the most important consideration. With respect to such group business, a physician's ability to influence signifi-

[10] The IPA physicians participate in a number of health care delivery systems that compete with Company A plans. Thus, a patient will sometimes have a choice of plans that include his or her preferred physician. In addition, factors other than ownership in a particular plan, such as payment levels, could inform a physician's recommendation of one or another plan in which he or she participates.

cantly plan revenues through enrollment recommendations is marginal. Accordingly, in the absence of any specific marketing efforts by the IPA's physician-shareholders to promote enrollment in Company A's group HMO and PPO plans, we do not think it likely that their recommendations, if any, would result in appreciable revenues to Company A.

With respect to individual enrollment in Company A's Medicare and Medicaid risk contracts, we believe a physician's recommendation may carry more weight. Accordingly, the second focus of our inquiry is to determine whether, assuming that a physician successfully recommends a Company D HMO to a patient, the possible return on the IPA's investment in Company A would constitute direct or indirect remuneration to the referring physician. Historically in most suspect joint ventures, there are relatively direct connections between the referral, the generation of a fee, the consequent profit to the joint venture, and the return to the referral source as dividends or otherwise. By contrast, HMOs assume significant financial risk by agreeing to provide comprehensive coverage to enrollees for a fixed price over a fixed period of time. Profitability depends on successful management of the risk and not simply on the delivery of medical services. In managed care, physician or provider support, or even high enrollment, is not sufficient to guarantee success, as demonstrated by the recent failures of a number of provider-owned managed care entities.

Certain characteristics of the IPA provide further assurance that any distributions to the IPA's shareholder-physicians are unlikely to constitute prohibited remuneration for referrals. The IPA is a pre-existing and functioning entity that has not been formed for the purpose of entering into the Proposed Arrangement. Moreover, ownership in the IPA presently is based on a *per capita* share distribution; under the Incentive Stock Plan, future shareholdings will be based, in part, on physician assumption of risk and performance on a number of pre-set quality and performance standards, but not on referrals to Company A plans. Given these factors, the interposition of the IPA as the equity owner in Company A will further dilute any potential financial nexus between a physician's recommendation to a patient of a Company A plan and his or her return on the Company A investment. Simply put, any distribution from Company A will go to the IPA, not the physician, and will be proportional to the IPA's share of the total investment in Company A. To the extent the IPA's board distributes any monies received from Company A to the IPA's shareholders, that distribution will be based on the shareholders' share ownership in the IPA, which has no relationship to any past, present, or future referrals to Company A.

Finally, assuming that physicians can influence the selection of an HMO, the Proposed Arrangement is unlikely to result in increased costs to Federal health care programs or overutilization of services, since the Company D HMO plans provide services on a capitated basis, discouraging unnecessary services.

In sum, in the circumstances presented here, these factors — the limited ability of physician-shareholders in the IPA to influence referrals to Company A health plans or to generate revenues through recommending Company A health plans, the interposition of an investor that is a pre-existing and functioning entity with a stock distribution structure unrelated to referrals to the investment entity, and the minimal risk of increased program costs — significantly reduce the likelihood that the Proposed Arrangement will result in unlawful remuneration for referrals.

d. Prohibited Remuneration for Referrals Outside of Joint Venture Is Unlikely

The Shareholder Hospitals may derive a substantial amount of revenue from patients referred to them by the IPA physicians wholly apart from any Company A-related business. This raises the possibility that the joint venture may be a vehicle by which the hospitals may indirectly reward the physicians for revenues the hospitals receive as a result of the physicians' referrals of fee-for-service patients to the hospitals.

In determining whether the joint venture may be a vehicle for illegally remunerating one investor for referrals to another investor, we examine initially whether the party making the referrals receives a disproportionate return on its investment compared to the return on the investment of the party receiving the referrals. Any excess or disproportionate return on the investment may be remuneration for referrals. Based on the facts and circumstances as represented by the Requesters, all equity owners in Company A will have made substantial investments in the venture and distribution of profits will be in direct proportion to the fair market value of such investments. Thus, all investors' returns on investment will be commensurate with their undertakings; the IPA's return will not include any "unearned" remuneration to the IPA or its physician-shareholders attributable to their referrals to the Shareholder Hospitals. Accordingly, any profit distributions from Company A would not represent compensation to physicians for their referrals to the hospitals.

However, even in situations where each party's return is proportionate with its investment, the mere opportunity to invest (and consequently receive profit distributions) may in certain circumstances constitute illegal remuneration if offered in exchange for past or future referrals. Such situations may include arrangements where one or several investors in a joint venture control a sufficiently large stream of referrals to make the venture's financial success highly likely, or where one investor has an established track record with similar ventures or the financial investment required is so small that the investors have little or no real risk. By contrast, here there are no such indicia that the Proposed Arrangement will generate any profits for its investors, since the managed care industry is highly competitive. Nor are there any indicia that the physicians control a stream of referrals to the managed care joint venture. In light of the substantial financial investment being made by the IPA, the mere opportunity to participate as an investor in Company A is unlikely to constitute remuneration for referrals from the IPA or the IPA's physicians to the Shareholder Hospitals.

2. The Ancillary Contractual Arrangements

In addition to the stock purchase and assignment agreements that effectuate the joint venture, there will be a number of ancillary agreements that obligate the parties in connection with the joint venture and therefore must be considered.

a. The Network Service Agreement

The first ancillary agreement is the ten-year Network Service Agreement, pursuant to which the IPA will become the exclusive provider of professional health care services for all managed care arrangements in which Company A participates and will develop and maintain Company A's provider networks during the term of the agreement. As consideration for the IPA's services, Company A will pay the IPA an annual fee of $[ ] per covered employee in Company A's preferred provider programs. For the first five years, the fee will be no less than$[ ] and no more than$[ ]. The Network Service Agreement will be a full-time agreement.

The safe harbor potentially relevant to the Network Service Agreement is the personal services and management contracts safe harbor, 42 C.F.R. § 1001.952(d), which protects certain arrangements that comply with the following conditions:

- the agreement is in writing and signed by the parties;
- the agreement specifies the services to be provided;
- if the agreement is intended to be for services on a periodic, sporadic, or part-time basis, rather than on a full-time basis for the term of the agreement, the agreement specifies exactly the schedule of such intervals, their precise length, and the exact charge for such intervals;
- the term of the agreement is for not less than one year;
- the aggregate compensation paid over the term of the agreement is set in advance, is consistent with fair market value in arms-length transactions and is not determined in a manner that takes into account the volume or value of any referrals or business generated between the parties for which payment may be made in whole or in part under Medicare or a State health care program; and
- the services performed under the agreement do not involve the counseling or promotion of a business arrangement or other activity that violates any State or Federal law.

42 C.F.R. § 1001.952(d).

The Network Service Agreement does not fit into the personal services safe harbor because the aggregate compensation to be paid over the term of the agreement is not set out in advance, as required by the regulation. However, the Requesters have certified that the IPA's compensation will represent fair market value in an arms-length transaction for the services to be rendered by the IPA and will not be determined in a manner that takes into account the volume or value of business generated between the parties. Moreover, the methodology to be used to determine the amount of the compensation — $[ ] per covered PPO employee — will be established in advance for the term of the contract and will not take into account the volume or value of business generated between the parties. Finally, for the reasons discussed above at section II.B.1.c, payments under the Network Service Agreement are not likely to be disguised payments for referrals from Company A to the IPA.

b. The Medical Management Program Agreement

The second ancillary contract is the Medical Management Program Agreement, pursuant to which the IPA would agree to arrange for its shareholder physicians to participate in the development of credentialing, utilization review, quality improvement, and case management programs and treatment protocols for Company A's managed care products. The IPA and Company A would negotiate separately the specific compensation for each medical program to be developed. As described above, the agreement would establish a detailed set of guidelines for determining the compensation for each program. These guidelines generally reflect the requirements of our personal services and management contracts safe harbor, 42 C.F.R. § 1001.952(d), and expressly provide that services to be rendered will not exceed the level of services necessary and reasonable to fulfill the business purposes of the arrangement.

The Medical Management Program Agreement lacks sufficient specificity to enable us to make a determination regarding its propriety under the anti-kickback statute. For practical purposes, it represents an agreement to agree to enter into unspecified future personal services contracts. Because physician consulting arrangements generally represent an area of significant abuse, personal services contracts for consulting services must be subject to careful, individualized scrutiny. In examining such contracts, we need to know, at a minimum, specific information about the compensation, the nature of the services to be performed, the identity of the particular physicians providing the services, and the existence of any other relationships between the parties. This information is not presently available for contracts that may be entered into pursuant to the Medical Management Program Agreement. Accordingly, we express no opinion with respect to the Medical Management Program Agreement; agreements entered into in accordance with its terms may be subject to sanction if they violate the anti-kickback statute. However, such agreements may be protected to the extent they comply with the personal services and management contracts safe harbor.

c. The Administrative Services Agreement

The third ancillary contract is the Administrative Services Agreement. Under this agreement, the IPA will pay Company A $[ ] annually per network physician with an executed PSA for performing certain designated services specified in the Agreement, such as credentialing and office administration, for the IPA and its physicians. The term of the contract will be ten years.

The analysis of the Administrative Services Agreement is the same as the Network Service Agreement described above. The contract does not meet the personal services safe harbor because the aggregate compensation to be paid for the term of the agreement is not set out in advance; rather, the compensation will vary over time based on the number of the IPA physicians in the network. Nevertheless, the Requesters have certified that the compensation to be paid under the Agreement will represent fair market value and will not take into account the value or volume of business generated between the parties, and the methodology to be used to determine the amount of the compensation — $[ ] per network physician — will be established in advance and will not take into account the value or volume of business generated between the parties.Also for reasons discussed above, the payments are not likely to be disguised remuneration for referrals.

d. The IPA Incentive Stock Plan

Integral to the joint venture arrangement is the Incentive Stock Plan to be offered by the IPA to its shareholder physicians. Under the Plan, the IPA will grant additional shares of the IPA stock to shareholder physicians who have executed a PSA with the IPA and who meet specified performance goals related to quality of HMO services, acceptance of HMO risk arrangements, and total number of HMO patients. The goal of the Plan is to create incentives for physician shareholders to act in a manner that will contribute to the success of Company A, thereby benefitting the IPA.

The Incentive Stock Plan will not implicate the anti-kickback statute, since the physicians receiving the stock are not in a position to refer business to the IPA, an IPA that does not provide items or services reimbursable by a Federal health care program. Nor could the receipt of such stock be construed as indirect remuneration from Company A in exchange for referrals; eligibility for additional the IPA stock is tied not to referrals to the managed care organization, but to the assumption of risk by physicians and to measures of enrollee satisfaction.

e. Provider Reimbursement for Services to Company A Plans' Enrollees

The Requesters have certified that all payments to physicians and hospitals providing health care services to enrollees of the various Company A plans will be at fair market value based on arms-length transactions and will not take into account the volume or value of referrals to, or other business with, Company A or with any of its participating hospitals or physicians. Accordingly, we need not address the possibility that physicians might provide services for some Company A products at below market prices in exchange for the opportunity to obtain more remunerative business reimbursable by a Federal health care program. Similarly, we need not address whether the Shareholder Hospitals may cause Company A to pay physicians above fair market rates for services to plan enrollees in order to induce the physicians to refer their fee-for-service Medicare or other Federal health care program business to the Shareholder Hospitals.

III. CONCLUSION

In sum, for the reasons stated above, we conclude that the Proposed Arrangement, considered in its totality, poses no more than a minimal risk of fraud and abuse. Accordingly, based on the facts certified in your request for an advisory opinion and supplemental submissions, we conclude that the OIG will not subject the Proposed Arrangement to sanctions arising under the anti-kickback statute pursuant to sections 1128(b)(7) or 1128A(a)(7) of the Act, provided that all compensation in connection with the Proposed Arrangement is fair market value as certified by the Requesters. [11] We express no opinion about the Medical Management Services Agreement (or any agreement entered into in accordance with its terms) or about any arrangement disclosed in the Requesters' request letter other than the Proposed Arrangement.

IV. LIMITATIONS

The limitations applicable to this opinion include the following:

---

[11] We are not authorized to opine on "fair market value." *See* section 1128D(b)(3) of the Act. Therefore, for purposes of this opinion, we have assumed fair market value compensation based on the Requesters' certifications. If the compensation under the Proposed Arrangement is not at fair market value, this opinion will be without force and effect.

- This advisory opinion is issued only to Company A and Company B, the Requesters of this opinion.
- This advisory opinion has no application, and cannot be relied upon, by any other individual or entity.
- This advisory opinion may not be introduced into evidence in any matter involving an entity or individual that is not a Requester to this opinion.
- This advisory opinion is applicable only to the statutory provisions specifically noted above and to their application to those arrangements specifically included in the definitions of the Proposed Arrangement contained in this advisory opinion. No opinion is herein expressed or implied with respect to the application of any other Federal, state, or local statute, rule, regulation, ordinance, or other law that may be applicable to the Proposed Arrangement.
- This advisory opinion will not bind or obligate any agency other than the U.S. Department of Health and Human Services.
- This advisory opinion is limited in scope to the specific arrangement described in this letter and has no applicability to other arrangements, even those that appear similar in nature or scope.
- No opinion is expressed herein regarding the liability of any party under the False Claims Act or other legal authorities for any improper billing, claims submission, cost reporting, or related conduct.

This opinion is also subject to any additional limitations set forth at 42 C.F.R. Part 1008.

The OIG will not proceed against the Requesters with respect to any action that is part of the Proposed Arrangement taken in good faith reliance upon this advisory opinion as long as all of the material facts have been fully, completely, and accurately presented, all compensation under the Proposed Arrangement is consistent with fair market value, and the Proposed Arrangement in practice comports with the information provided. The OIG reserves the right to reconsider the questions and issues raised in this advisory opinion and, where the public interest requires, rescind, modify, or terminate this opinion. In the event that this advisory opinion is modified or terminated, the OIG will not proceed against the Requesters with respect to any action taken in good faith reliance upon this advisory opinion, where all of the relevant facts were fully, completely, and accurately presented, where all compensation under the Proposed Arrangement constitutes fair market value, and where such action was promptly discontinued upon notification of the modification or termination of this advisory opinion. An advisory opinion may be rescinded only if the relevant and material facts have not been fully, completely, and accurately disclosed to the OIG.

Sincerely,
/s/
D. McCarty Thornton
Chief Counsel to the Inspector General

APPENDIX F33

Advisory Opinion No. 99-1, January 20, 1999

Whether an arrangement for the provision of back-up emergency ambulance services that involves waivers of copayments and deductible amounts constitutes prohibited remuneration within the meaning of the anti-kickback statute.

[*We have redacted specific information regarding the requestor and certain privileged, confidential or financial information associated with the individual or entity, unless otherwise specified by the requestor.*]

[Posted: 1/27/99]

[Dated: 1/20/99]

[Name and Address Redacted]

Re: [Name Redacted]

OIG Advisory Opinion 99–1

Dear [Name Redacted]:

We are writing in response to your request for an advisory opinion regarding an arrangement for the provision of back-up emergency ambulance services that involves waivers of copayments and deductible amounts (the "Arrangement"). You have asked whether the Arrangement constitutes prohibited remuneration within the meaning of the anti-kickback statute, section 1128B(b) of the Social Security Act (the "Act").

You have certified that all of the information provided in the request, including all supplementary letters, is true and correct and constitutes a complete description of the relevant facts and agreements among the parties.

In issuing this opinion, we have relied solely on the facts and information presented to us. We have not undertaken an indepen-

dent investigation of such information. This opinion is limited to the facts presented. If material facts have not been disclosed, this opinion is without force and effect.

Based on the facts certified in your request for an advisory opinion, we conclude that the Arrangement could potentially violate the anti-kickback statute if the requisite intent to induce referrals were present, but that the Office of Inspector General ("OIG") will not subject the Arrangement, as described in the request letter and supplemental submissions, to sanctions arising under the anti-kickback statute, section 1128B(b) of the Act.

This opinion may not be relied on by any persons other than the requestor and is further qualified as set out in Part IV below and in 42 C.F.R. Part 1008.

I. FACTUAL BACKGROUND

The State A Emergency Medical Response System & Company X

In State A, there are two types of emergency medical response services. The first is basic ambulance service, which involves transportation only ("Emergency BAS").[1] More than seventy-three basic ambulance service providers operate in the service area relevant to the Arrangement (County B and County C). Approximately 95% of these providers are volunteer first aid squads.

The second type of service is paramedic service, which requires a State A certificate of need. In general, paramedic service providers do not transport patients. Thus, if paramedic services are needed at the scene of an emergency injury or illness, both a paramedic unit and a volunteer first aid squad (or other transport service) are called.[2] Patients receive paramedic treatment at the scene from the paramedic service and are transported to the hospital by the local volunteer first aid squad, accompanied by paramedics from the paramedic service, if appropriate.

---

[1] According to the request for an advisory opinion and supplemental submissions, State A's two types of emergency transportation services are known as basic life support ("BLS") and advanced life support ("ALS"). To avoid confusion with the use of the terms BLS and ALS for purposes of Medicare reimbursement, this advisory opinion uses the terms "basic ambulance service" and "paramedic service" to describe the two State A services.

[2] In rare circumstances, Emergency BAS may be provided by providers other than volunteer first aid squads.

Requests for "911" emergency ambulance transportation are received by public safety answering points ("PSAPs"), which determine the appropriate level of ambulance service to send in response. The PSAPs have sole discretion in determining how to direct responses. They are operated by municipal law enforcement agencies supported by city and county taxes.

Company X ("Company X" or the "Requestor") is a non-profit 501 (c)(3) corporation owned in equal shares by nine acute care hospitals in Counties B and C, State A. Company X provides various shared services on behalf of its owner-member hospitals, among them basic ambulance and paramedic services. Company X operates a number of paramedic units in its service area.[3]

Because Company X is the sole certificate of need holder providing paramedic services within its response area, all requests for paramedic services are referred to Company X. Company X is prohibited, pursuant to its certificate of need, from transporting patients in conjunction with its paramedic services, except in exigent circumstances.[4]

The Arrangement

Volunteer first aid squads are sometimes unable to respond to Emergency BAS requests in a timely manner. In these circumstances, Company X is willing to provide back-up transportation services. These back-up services are offered on an occasional basis as a community service and are not part of any formal arrangement or agreement between Company X and any PSAP or municipal or county government or agency. Providing the back-up service is not a condition of any contract or referral arrangement, and Company X may decline to provide the back-up service at any time.

Company X offers back-up Emergency BAS in two circumstances: (1) when Company X responds to a paramedic service request and a volunteer first aid squad fails to arrive at the scene to transport the patient to a hospital ("Emergency BAS incidental to paramedic service"); and (2) when a PSAP receives a "911" request for Emergency BAS, but a volunteer first aid squad is not available to respond

---

[3] As required by state regulation, Company X operates a minimum of 7.5 full time equivalent paramedic units in its service area.

[4] Company X provides non-Emergency BAS and paramedic services under contractual arrangements not relevant here. This opinion is limited to emergency transport services only. No opinion is expressed with respect to any non-emergency services.

("Back-up Emergency BAS"). Unless the circumstances are exigent, Company X usually waits approximately thirty minutes for a volunteer squad to arrive before transporting a patient to a hospital.[5]

The volunteer first aid squads in Company X's service area bill neither Federal programs, private payors, nor patients for their services. Thus, typically basic ambulance service to a hospital is provided without cost to insurers and to patients. By contrast, Company X bills for its services in three ways. First, Company X bills insurers when Company X provides paramedic services. These paramedic services are provided under arrangement with hospitals, and, in the case of Medicare, are paid under Part A. Second, when Company X provides Emergency BAS incidental to paramedic ambulance service, the paramedic services are billed, but no payor or patient is billed for the basic ambulance service. Third, when Company X provides Back-up Emergency BAS only (i.e., without any paramedic services), Company X bills insurers, including Medicare, for transportation. Specifically, it bills Medicare Part B under Method 4.[6] Company X's charges for its Back-up Emergency BAS do not vary based on the payor.

It is the third billing situation that gives rise to the Arrangement. Because the patients in Company X's service area do not typically pay fees for basic ambulance service and because collection of such fees would tend to cast the volunteer basic ambulance service system in a poor light, Company X waives patient copayments and deductibles when it provides Back-up Emergency BAS for volunteer first aid squads.[7] Company X does not advertise this practice. Except in these circumstances, Company X collects applicable coinsurance whenever it bills an insurer.

Pursuant to the Arrangement, Company X waives copayments and deductibles for only a small number of its patients. For the

---

[5] Usually Company X provides basic ambulance service only within its service area; however, under exigent circumstances it will receive and respond to requests for basic ambulance service from outside its service area.

[6] Under Method 4, providers bill separate charges for services, mileage, and supplies.

[7] Company X waives copayments and deductibles only in connection with its provision of Back-up Emergency BAS for volunteer first aid squads. Except for waivers of copayments and deductibles in connection with Back-up Emergency BAS for volunteer first aid squads, this opinion is without force and effect for waivers of a Federal health care program coinsurance amount.

period from August 25, 1997, to August 25, 1998, Company X waived copayments and deductibles for [] patients. These [] patients constituted [less than one percent] of Company X's total patients and [less than three percent] of its Medicare Part B patients. Company X waived Medicare Part B copayments and deductibles in the amount of $[], representing [less than one percent] of Company X's $[] in total Medicare Part B program payments, including copayments and deductibles. During this period, Company X collected $[] in payments from private insurers, including applicable copayments and deductibles.

The only patients who receive Company X's Back-up Emergency BAS are those who have dialed "911" to request basic ambulance service in an emergency. Routine scheduled transportation services (i.e., home to physician's office, home to diagnostic testing, home to dialysis center, Emergency Department discharge to home, etc.) are not provided under any circumstances as part of the Arrangement.

II. LEGAL ANALYSIS

The anti-kickback statute makes it a criminal offense knowingly and willfully to offer, pay, solicit or receive any remuneration to induce referrals of items or services reimbursable by the Federal health care programs. Section 1128B(b) of the Act. Where remuneration is paid purposefully to induce referrals of items or services paid for by a Federal health care program, the anti-kickback statute is violated. By its terms, the statute ascribes criminal liability to parties on both sides of an impermissible "kickback" transaction. For purposes of the anti-kickback statute, "remuneration" includes the transfer of anything of value, in cash or in-kind, directly or indirectly, covertly or overtly.

The statute has been interpreted to cover any arrangement where *one* purpose of the remuneration is to obtain money for the referral of services or to induce further referrals. *United States v. Kats*, 871 F.2d 105 (9th Cir. 1989); *United States v. Greber*, 760 F.2d 68 (3d Cir.), *cert. denied*, 476 U.S. 988 (1985). Violations of the statute constitute a felony punishable by a maximum fine of $25,000, imprisonment up to five years, or both. Conviction will also lead to automatic exclusion from Federal health care programs, including Medicare and Medicaid. This Office may also initiate administrative proceedings to exclude persons from the Federal and state health care programs or to impose civil monetary penalties for fraud, kickbacks, and other prohibited activities under sections 1128(b)(7) and

1128A(a)(7) of the Act.[8]

We have a clear and long-standing concern about potentially abusive waivers of Medicare copayments and deductibles. For example, we have previously stated that providers who routinely waive Medicare copayments or deductibles may be held liable under the anti-kickback statute. *See, e.g.*, Special Fraud Alert, 59 Fed. Reg. 65374 (Dec. 19, 1994); Advisory Opinion 98–6 (April 20, 1998); Advisory Opinion 97–4 (Sept. 25, 1997). One indicator of a potentially prohibited waiver is the failure to collect copayments or deductibles for a specific group of Medicare patients for reasons unrelated to individualized, good faith assessments of financial hardship.

Waivers of copayments and deductibles offered to Federal health care program beneficiaries may constitute prohibited remuneration to induce self-referrals under the anti-kickback statute. In the circumstances presented here, however, the risk of such prohibited remuneration is minimal. Critical to this determination is a recognition that in areas where Company X provides Back-up Emergency BAS for volunteer first aid squads, there is no expectation on the part of an emergency patient that there will be a charge — much less a copayment — for Emergency BAS. In light of that fact, Company X's failure to collect a copayment for the isolated instances in which it provides Back-up Emergency BAS can hardly be described as an inducement to use the service. Moreover, even if Company X were trying to induce referrals, the certificate of need requirements preclude it from expanding its provision of such services substantially.

III. CONCLUSION

Based on the facts certified by Company X, we conclude that, although the Arrangement technically would fall within the prohibition of the anti-kickback statute if the requisite intent were present, we will not seek to impose sanctions under sections 1128(b)(7) (as it relates to kickbacks) or 1128A(a)(7) of the Act for waivers of copayments and deductibles made under the Arrangement.

IV. LIMITATIONS

The limitations applicable to this opinion include the following:

---

[8] Because both the criminal and administrative sanctions related to the Arrangement are based on violations of the anti-kickback statute, the analysis for purposes of this advisory opinion is the same for both.

- This advisory opinion is issued only to Company X, the Requestor of this opinion. This advisory opinion has no application, and cannot be relied upon, by any other individual or entity.
- This advisory opinion may not be introduced into evidence in any matter involving an entity or individual that is not a requestor to this opinion.
- This advisory opinion is applicable only to the statutory provisions specifically noted above. No opinion is herein expressed or implied with respect to the application of any other Federal, state, or local statute, rule, regulation, ordinance, or other law that may be applicable to the Arrangement. We express no opinion with respect to State A law.
- No opinion is herein expressed or implied regarding the liability of any party under the False Claims Act or other legal authorities for any improper billing, claims submission, cost reporting, or related conduct.
- This advisory opinion will not bind or obligate any agency other than the U.S. Department of Health and Human Services.
- This advisory opinion is limited in scope to the specific arrangement described in this letter and has no applicability to other arrangements, even those which appear similar in nature or scope.

This opinion is also subject to any additional limitations set forth at 42 C.F.R. Part 1008.

The OIG will not proceed against the Requestor with respect to any action that is part of the Arrangement taken in good faith reliance upon this advisory opinion as long as all of the material facts have been fully, completely, and accurately presented, and the Arrangement in practice comports with the information provided. The OIG reserves the right to reconsider the questions and issues raised in this advisory opinion and, where the public interest requires, rescind, modify or terminate this opinion. In the event that this advisory opinion is modified or terminated, the OIG will not proceed against the Requestor with respect to any action taken in good faith reliance upon this advisory opinion, where all of the relevant facts were fully, completely, and accurately presented and where such action was promptly discontinued upon notification of the modification or termination of this advisory opinion. An advisory opinion may be rescinded only if the relevant and material facts have not been fully, completely and accurately disclosed to the OIG.

Sincerely,

/s/
D. McCarty Thornton
Chief Counsel to the Inspector General

APPENDIX F34

Advisory Opinion No. 99-2, February 26, 1999

Whether certain arrangements for discounted ambulance services provided to residents of Medicare skilled nursing facilities would result in prohibited remuneration and sanctions under the anti-kickback statute.

[*We have redacted specific information regarding the requestor and certain potentially privileged, confidential or financial information associated with the individual or entity, unless otherwise specified by the requestor.*]

Posted: March 4, 1999

Issued: February 26, 1999

[Name and Address Redacted]

Re: [Company Name Redacted]

OIG Advisory Opinion No. 99–2

Dear [Name Redacted]:

We are writing in response to your request for an advisory opinion regarding certain arrangements for discounted ambulance services provided to residents of Medicare skilled nursing facilities (collectively, the "Arrangement"). You have asked whether the Arrangement would result in prohibited remuneration under the anti-kickback statute, section 1128B(b) of the Social Security Act (the "Act") or would constitute grounds for the imposition of sanctions under the anti-kickback statute, section 1128B(b) of the Act, the exclusion authority related to kickbacks, section 1128(b)(7) of the Act, or the civil monetary penalty provision for kickbacks, section 1128A(a)(7) of the Act.

In issuing this opinion, we have relied solely on the facts and information presented to us. We have not undertaken an indepen-

dent investigation of such information. This opinion is limited to the facts presented. If material facts have not been disclosed, this opinion is without force and effect.

Based on the facts certified in your request for an advisory opinion, we conclude that the Arrangement might constitute prohibited remuneration under the anti-kickback statute if the requisite intent to induce referrals of Federal health care program business were present and might be subject to sanctions arising under sections 1128B(b), 1128(b)(7), and 1128A(a)(7) of the Act, as well as section 1128(b)(6)(A) of the Act.

This opinion may not be relied on by any person other than the addressee and is further qualified as set out in Part III below and in 42 C.F.R. Part 1008.

I. FACTUAL BACKGROUND

Ambulance Reimbursement Under the SNF Prospective Payment System

The genesis of the Arrangement is Medicare's new prospective payment system for Medicare-certified skilled nursing facilities ("SNFs"). In 1997, Congress significantly changed the way SNFs are reimbursed for services to patients covered under Medicare Part A, the hospital benefit.[1] Specifically, the Balanced Budget Act of 1997 enacted a prospective payment system ("PPS") for SNFs covering all costs (routine, ancillary, and capital) related to services furnished to beneficiaries covered under Part A, including certain Part B services.[2] Other Part B services will continue to be reimbursed separately to the providers of such services pending implementation of a new consolidated billing system.[3]

---

[1] Medicare Part A covers up to 100 days of post-hospital SNF charges. *See* 42 U.S.C. § 1395d. In addition, Medicare Part B, the supplementary benefit, covers certain ancillary services provided to SNF patients, both during a covered Part A stay and afterwards.

[2] *See* Section 4432 of the Balanced Budget Act of 1997, Pub. Law 105-33. The PPS system for SNFs is being implemented for cost reporting periods beginning after July 1, 1998. There is a transition phase during the first three cost reporting years, during which SNFs will receive a blend of a new Federal case mix adjusted rate and a facility specific rate based on the facility's allowable costs for SNF services for the fiscal 1995 cost reporting period.

[3] Section 4432(b) of the Balanced Budget Act of 1997 amended the Social Security Act to establish a requirement for SNF consolidated billing, effec-

The basic PPS methodology is a prospectively fixed per diem payment adjusted to reflect the patient's health status and needs and the regional wage rate (the "Federal case mix adjusted rate"). Under PPS, the SNF per diem payment will include payment for certain ancillary Part B services previously reimbursed by Medicare directly to the providers of such services. This new payment scheme shifts risk to the SNFs, giving them a significant financial incentive to reduce costs, and may indirectly result in lower payments to suppliers and providers of items and services covered by the PPS payment.

Among the Part B services affected by the change in SNF reimbursement are ambulance services. Traditionally, ambulance services rendered to Medicare patients residing in SNFs have been covered by Medicare Part B and reimbursed on a reasonable charge basis. Under PPS, ambulance services that are within the normal scope of the patient's plan of care ("Plan of Care Ambulance Services") are included in the fixed PPS per diem payment. SNFs must provide the Plan of Care Ambulance Services directly or "under arrangement" with an ambulance company.[4] Plan of Care Ambulance Services comprise a relatively small portion of the ambulance services required by most SNF Part A patients, and an even smaller portion of the total ambulance services required by SNF patients generally.[5] Pending full implementation of consolidated billing, Medicare will continue to reimburse ambulance providers for non-PPS covered ambulance services for Part A patients and for

---

tive for items and services furnished on or after July 1, 1998. The SNF consolidated billing is a comprehensive billing requirement pursuant to which the SNF itself is responsible for billing Medicare for virtually all of the services that its residents receive. *See* 63 Fed. Reg. 26294 (May 12, 1998). Full implementation of SNF consolidated billing has been postponed indefinitely. *See* HCFA Program Memorandum Transmittal no. AB-98-35.60 (July 1998).

[4] *See* 63 Fed. Reg. 26252 (May 12, 1998).

[5] The following types of ambulance services are expressly excluded from the PPS payment by regulation: ambulance trips that initially convey an individual to the SNF to be admitted as a resident; trips that convey the individual to a hospital to be admitted as an inpatient; trips that convey an individual in connection with the receipt of services from a Medicare-participating home health agency under a plan of care; trips that convey an individual to a hospital in connection with the receipt of outpatient services that are not furnished pursuant to the individual's comprehensive care plan; and trips that convey an individual from a SNF after formal discharge, unless the individual is readmitted or returns within a specified period of time. *Id.* These excluded services constitute a significant part of the ambulance services provided to SNF patients.

services for Medicare patients whose stays are not covered under Part A,[6] based on reasonable charges for services provided until January 1, 2000, and on a fee schedule thereafter.[7]

In sum, pursuant to SNF PPS, Medicare will pay SNFs a fixed per diem amount for patients during a covered Part A stay, and the SNFs will be responsible for paying for virtually all patient care services -- including Plan of Care Ambulance Services --out of that fixed payment. These PPS-covered ambulance services are the subject of the Arrangement at issue here.

The Arrangement

The Arrangement involves an agreement for PPS-covered ambulance services between Ambulance Company X ("Ambulance Company X") and Nursing Home Y (the "Nursing Home"). Ambulance Company X is a Medicare-certified ambulance supplier operating in the State A market. The Nursing Home is a Medicare-certified SNF paid under PPS for patients covered by Medicare Part A. With the advent of PPS, the Nursing Home has arranged for Ambulance Company X to provide Plan of Care Ambulance Services for its PPS-covered patients "under arrangement". In addition to its PPS-covered patients, the Nursing Home has patients who require ambulance services that are not covered by a PPS payment and that are reimbursed to the ambulance services provider by Medicare under Part B or by other payers.

Ambulance Company X and the Nursing Home have entered into a Medical Transportation Services Agreement (the "Agreement") for the provision of Plan of Care Ambulance Services and chair car services to Nursing Home residents who are covered under the PPS system. The Agreement also applies to Nursing Home residents for whom the Nursing Home is reimbursed by other public or private reimbursement systems under a capitated, per-diem, or other all-inclusive payment that includes ambulance services and residents for whom the Nursing Home otherwise agrees to be financially responsible. In other words, the Agreement applies when the Nursing Home bears the risk for providing ambulance services.

Pursuant to the Agreement, Ambulance Company X will charge the Nursing Home fixed per-transport rates for basic life support

---

[6] Room and board for these patients is typically covered by Medicaid or through private funds or insurance.

[7] *See* Section 4531 of the Balanced Budget Act of 1997, Pub. Law 105-33.

("BLS"), advanced life support ("ALS"), and chair car services. The contractual rates for BLS and ALS services represent discounts of up to 50% of the "reasonable charge" established by Medicare for Ambulance Company X's services in the State A area.[8] Ambulance Company X will charge Medicare its full usual and customary amount for transporting Nursing Home residents for whom ambulance services are covered under Medicare Part B.

With respect to the amount of the discount, Ambulance Company X has represented that part of the proposed discount would be directly attributable to cost savings Ambulance Company X can achieve when providing services for PPS residents. For example, Ambulance Company X has certified that its billing costs should be substantially less for services for PPS-covered residents because Ambulance Company X will submit a single, consolidated bill to each SNF at the end of each month and because Ambulance Company X will not need to bill residents for copayments or deductibles. Ambulance Company X also believes its collection rate will generally be higher for PPS residents. Ambulance Company X estimates that these factors can reasonably be expected to result in savings equal to approximately 10% of the Medicare reasonable charge for each transport rendered to a PPS resident, depending on the circumstances. Nonetheless, in light of the competitive market, Ambulance Company X is offering discounts in excess of anticipated savings attributable substantially to SNF PPS.

Ambulance Company X proposes entering into similar discount arrangements with other SNFs in its service area. Like Ambulance Company X's arrangement with the Nursing Home, these proposed discount arrangements would be with SNFs that are being reimbursed for Medicare Part A services under PPS and would apply to ambulance transports provided to the Medicare residents during a covered Part A stay. The discounts would not apply to Part B services. The discount arrangement between Ambulance Company X and the Nursing Home and the proposed discount arrangements between Ambulance Company X and other SNFs described in the request letter are collectively referred to in this opinion letter as the "Arrangement".

---

[8] Chair car services will be provided at the applicable State Medicaid rates. Chair car services are not covered by Medicare.

II. LEGAL ANALYSIS

The Anti-Kickback Statute

The anti-kickback statute makes it a criminal offense knowingly and wilfully to offer, pay, solicit, or receive any remuneration to induce referrals of items or services reimbursable by Federal health care programs. *See* section 1128B(b) of the Act. Where remuneration is paid purposefully to induce referrals of items or services paid for by a Federal health care program, the anti-kickback statute is violated. By its terms, the statute ascribes liability to parties on both sides of an impermissible "kickback" transaction. For purposes of the anti-kickback statute, "remuneration" includes the transfer of anything of value, in cash or in-kind, directly or indirectly, covertly or overtly.

The statute has been interpreted to cover any arrangement where *one* purpose of the remuneration is to obtain money for referral of services or to induce further referrals. *United States v. Kats,* 871 F. 2d 105 (9th Cir. 1989); *United States v. Greber,* 760 F. 2d 68 (3rd Cir.), *cert. denied,* 476 U.S. 988 (1985). Violation of the statute constitutes a felony punishable by a maximum fine of $25,000, imprisonment up to five years or both. Conviction will also lead to automatic exclusion from Federal health care programs, including Medicare and Medicaid. This Office may also initiate administrative proceedings to exclude persons from Federal health care programs or to impose civil monetary penalties for fraud, kickbacks, and other prohibited activities under sections 1128(b)(7) and 1128A(a)(7) of the Act.[9]

The anti-kickback statute contains a statutory exception for "a discount or other reduction in price obtained by a provider of services or other entity under a Federal health care program if the reduction in price is properly disclosed and appropriately reflected in the costs claimed or charges made by the provider or entity under a Federal health care program." 42 U.S.C. § 1320a-7b(b)(3)(A). This discount exception reflects the intent of Congress to encourage price competition that benefits the Medicare and Medicaid programs. The Department of Health and Human Services has published regula-

[9] Because both the criminal and administrative sanctions related to the anti-kickback implications of the Arrangement are based on violations of the anti-kickback statute, the analysis for the purposes of this advisory opinion is the same under both.

tions implementing this discount "safe harbor" exception. *See* 42 C.F.R. § 1001.952(h).

The Discount Pricing Arrangement

Our initial inquiry is whether the Arrangement fits within the discount safe harbor. We conclude it does not. The statutory exception for discounts, as implemented by the regulatory safe harbor, does not protect price reductions -- like those at issue here -- offered to one payer but not offered to Medicare or Medicaid. In the preamble to the discount safe harbor, we illustrated the potential problem with such price reductions:

> [W]e are aware of cases where laboratories offer a discount to physicians who then bill the patient, but do not offer the same discount to the Medicare program. In some of these cases, the discount offered to the physician is explicitly conditioned on the physician's referral of all of his or her laboratory business. Such a "discount" does not benefit Medicare, and is therefore inconsistent with the statutory intent for discounts to be reported to the programs with costs and charges reduced appropriately to reflect the discounts.

56 Fed. Reg. 35977 (July 29, 1991). In essence, such price reductions create a risk that a supplier may be offering remuneration in the form of discounts on business for which the purchaser pays the supplier, in exchange for the opportunity to service and bill for higher paying Federal health care program business reimbursed directly by the program to the supplier. In such circumstances, neither Medicare nor Medicaid benefits from the discount; to the contrary, Medicare and Medicaid may, in effect, subsidize the other payer's discounted rates.[10] Moreover, suppliers may have an incentive to inappropriately increase utilization or engage in abusive billing practices to recoup losses on the discounted business. Accordingly, the discount safe harbor specifically excludes "[a] reduction in price applicable to one payor but not to Medicare or a State health care program." *See* 42 C.F.R. § 1001.952(h)(3)(iii).

Having concluded that the Arrangement does not fit in the safe harbor, we must consider whether the discount arrangement between Ambulance Company X and the Nursing Home and similar arrangements with other SNFs may involve illegal remuneration for

[10] This is particularly problematic when the contracting payor is a PPS SNF, because Medicare Part B payments essentially may subsidize Part A PPS payments that the government has determined are appropriate and adequate to cover the SNF's costs.

the SNFs' referrals of ambulance business not covered by the PPS payment and not subject to the discount. We conclude that they may.

The circumstances surrounding the Arrangement suggest that a nexus may exist between the discount to the SNFs for PPS-covered transports and referrals of other Federal health care program business.[11] *First,* the SNFs are in a position to direct a significant amount of business to Ambulance Company X that is not covered by the PPS payment. *Second,* both parties have obvious motives for agreeing to trade discounts on PPS business for referrals of non-PPS business: the SNFs to minimize risk of losses under the PPS system and Ambulance Company X to secure business in a highly competitive market. *Third,* Ambulance Company X's request for an advisory opinion comes amidst a considerable number of informal inquiries and anecdotal reports regarding discounts to SNFs that this Office has received since enactment of SNF PPS. These inquiries and reports suggest that suppliers of a wide range of SNF services are giving SNFs discounts for PPS-covered business that are linked, directly or indirectly, to referrals of Part B business.

In evaluating whether an improper nexus exists between a discount and referrals of Federal business in a particular arrangement, we look for indicia that the discount is not commercially reasonable in the absence of other, non-discounted business. In this regard, discounts on SNF PPS business that are particularly suspect include, but are not limited to:

- discounted prices that are below the supplier's cost,[12] and
- discounted prices that are lower than the prices that the supplier offers to a buyer that (i) generates a volume of business for the supplier that is the same or greater than the volume of Part A business generated by the PPS SNF, but (ii) does not have any potentially available Part B or other Federal health care program business.

---

[11] We note that the Agreement contains statements to the effect that remuneration provided under the Agreement is not intended to induce referrals of other business. We find these statements self-serving and not persuasive.

[12] In this regard, we do not think it sufficient to consider only a supplier's marginal costs. Rather, in determining whether a discount is below cost, we look, for example, at the total of all costs divided by the total number of ambulance trips.

This is an illustrative, not exhaustive, list of suspect discounts; other arrangements may be equally suspect. Each of the above pricing arrangements independently gives rise to an inference that the supplier and the SNF may be "swapping" discounts on Part A business in exchange for profitable non-discounted Part B business, from which the supplier can recoup losses incurred on the discounted business, potentially through overutilization or abusive billing practices. *In connection with items or services provided to PPS SNFs, the presence of **either** of these discount arrangements is particularly suspect under the anti-kickback statute.* Other indicators of suspect discounts include (i) discounts on PPS-covered business that are coupled with exclusive supplier agreements and (ii) discounts on Medicare PPS or other capitated or prospective payment business made in conjunction with explicit or implicit agreements to refer other facility business to the supplier, including Part B or other Federal health care program business.

Based on the limited facts presented here, we are unable to exclude the possibility that Ambulance Company X may be offering improper discounts to the Nursing Home and other SNFs for their PPS-covered Part A business with the intent to induce referrals of more lucrative Part B business. Nor are we able to exclude the possibility that the Nursing Home or other SNFs may be soliciting improper discounts on business for which they bear risk in exchange for referrals of business for which they bear no risk. Indeed, the Arrangement poses a significant risk of such improper "swapping" of business, especially in light of Ambulance Company X's representation that many of its competitors are agreeing to such discounts. These competitor discount arrangements may similarly run afoul of the anti-kickback statute. The risk of improper "swapping" is compounded by the likelihood that SNFs will refer non-PPS business to their contracted PPS provider, both as a matter of practical convenience and because SNF personnel may not always know which patients or transports will be covered by PPS when the services are ordered. In these latter circumstances, the simplest way for a SNF to ensure that it is using its contracted provider for its PPS patients -- and therefore securing the Part A discounts -- is for the SNF to refer most patients to that provider.

Price reductions offered to SNFs that are not offered to Medicare or Medicaid patients residing in the same facility raise additional issues under section 1128(b)(6)(A) of the Act, which provides for permissive exclusion from the Federal health care programs of individuals or entities that submit or cause to be submitted bills or requests for payment (based on charges or costs) under Medicare or Medicaid that are substantially in excess of such individual's or entity's usual charges or costs, unless the Secretary finds good cause for such bills or requests. In determining an individual's or entity's "usual" charges, we will look at the amounts charged to non-Federal payers, including SNFs. If the charge to Medicare substantially exceeds the amount the supplier most frequently expects to receive from non-Federal payers, the supplier may be subject to exclusion under section 1128(b)(6)(A) of the Act.

The limited information submitted by Ambulance Company X is insufficient to make a determination whether the Arrangement may run afoul of section 1128(b)(6)(A). However, Ambulance Company X estimates that its costs for services under Medicare Part B are approximately 11% higher than its costs for services under Part A PPS. Yet Ambulance Company X intends to charge SNFs as much as 50% less than it charges Medicare for Part B services. At the very least, these facts give rise to an inference that Ambulance Company X might be charging Medicare amounts substantially in excess of its usual charges.

III. CONCLUSION

Based on the facts certified in the request for an advisory opinion and supplemental submissions, we conclude that the Arrangement -- like many similar arrangements with PPS SNFs -- might constitute prohibited remuneration under the anti-kickback statute if the requisite intent to induce referrals of Federal health care program business were present and might be subject to sanctions arising under the anti-kickback statute pursuant to sections 1128(b)(6) and (7), 1128A(a)(7), or 1128B(b) of the Act.

IV. LIMITATIONS

The limitations applicable to this opinion include the following:

- This advisory opinion is issued only to Ambulance Company X, the requester of this opinion. This advisory opinion has no application, and cannot be relied upon, by any other individual or entity.
- This advisory opinion may not be introduced into evidence in any matter involving an entity or individual that is not a requester to this opinion.

- This advisory opinion is applicable only to the statutory provisions specifically noted above. No opinion is herein expressed or implied with respect to the application of any other Federal, state, or local statute, rule, regulation, ordinance, or other law that may be applicable to the Arrangement.
- This advisory opinion will not bind or obligate any agency other than the U.S. Department of Health and Human Services.
- This advisory opinion is limited in scope to the specific arrangement described in this letter and has no applicability to other arrangements, even those that appear similar in nature or scope.
- No opinion is expressed herein regarding the liability of any party under the False Claims Act or other legal authorities for any improper billing, claims submission, cost reporting, or related conduct.

This opinion is also subject to any additional limitations set forth at 42 C.F.R. Part 1008.

The Office of Inspector General reserves the right to reconsider the questions and issues raised in this advisory opinion and, where the public interest requires, rescind, modify, or terminate this opinion.

Sincerely,

/s/

D. McCarty Thornton

Chief Counsel to the Inspector General

APPENDIX F35

Advisory Opinion No. 99-3, March 16, 1999

Whether a proposed pricing arrangement for a package of therapeutic mattresses for SNF patients to be marketed by a company, and certain commissioned agents, would result in prohibited remuneration under the anti-kickback statute.

[*We have redacted specific information regarding the requestor and certain potentially privileged, confidential or financial information associated with the individual or entity, unless otherwise specified by the requestor.*]

Dated: March 16, 1999

Posted: March 23, 1999

[Name and Address Redacted]

Re: [Name Redacted]

OIG Advisory Opinion 99–3

Dear [Name Redacted]:

We are writing in response to your request on behalf of Company A, for an advisory opinion concerning whether a proposed pricing arrangement for a package of therapeutic mattresses for skilled nursing facility patients to be marketed by Company A, and certain commissioned agents (the "Proposed Arrangement") would result in prohibited remuneration under the anti-kickback statute, section 1128B(b) of the Social Security Act (the "Act") or would constitute grounds for the imposition of sanctions under the anti-kickback statute, section 1128B(b) of the Act, the exclusion authority related to kickbacks, section 1128(b)(7) of the Act, or the civil monetary penalty provision for kickbacks, section 1128A(a)(7) of the Act.

In issuing this opinion, we have relied solely on the facts and information presented to us. We have not undertaken an indepen-

dent investigation of such information. This opinion is limited to the facts presented. If material facts have not been disclosed, this opinion is without force and effect.

Based on the facts certified in your request for an advisory opinion, we conclude that the Proposed Arrangement, as described in your advisory opinion request and supplemental submissions, might constitute prohibited remuneration under the anti-kickback statute, if the requisite intent to induce referrals of Federal health care program business were present, but that the Office of Inspector General ("OIG") will not subject it to sanctions arising under the anti-kickback statute pursuant to sections 1128(b)(7) or 1128A(a)(7) of the Act.

This opinion may not be relied on by any person other than the addressee and is further qualified as set out in Part III below and in 42 C.F.R. Part 1008.

I. FACTUAL BACKGROUND

Company A ("Company A"), a wholly-owned subsidiary of Company B, is a distributor of therapeutic mattresses used for the treatment and prevention of pressure ulcers. The Proposed Arrangement involves two types of mattresses (also known as support surfaces): (i) a powered support surface, the Company A therapeutic mattress system; and (ii) a non-powered support surface, the Company A pressure relieving mattress. Typically, a powered mattress is used as part of a treatment protocol for aggressive wound healing, while a non-powered mattress may be used to complete the course of treatment by facilitating continued healing and preventing the recurrence of pressure ulcers. Company A has certified that the Company A powered mattress has a fair market rental value of $x per month.[1] Company A has certified that $y is the fair market value of a single non-powered mattress purchased by an institution.

Company A proposes offering Medicare-certified skilled nursing facilities ("SNFs") special pricing for these therapeutic mattresses

[1] Company A has not previously rented the power mattress and has based its fair market rental rate on rates for comparable products rented by other distributors; we are not authorized to opine on "fair market value" (*see* section 1128D(b)(3) of the Act) and therefore assume the truth of Company A's fair market value certifications for purposes of this opinion. We express no opinion as to whether the rental rates selected by Company A are, in fact, fair market value. If they are not fair market value, this opinion is without force and effect.

for patients undergoing treatment for pressure ulcers. Under the Proposed Arrangement, Company A will rent a SNF a powered mattress for thirty days for a fixed amount ($x) set in advance by Company A and applicable to all similarly-situated SNF customers. The rental price includes the provision of a non-powered mattress at no additional charge, to be used when the patient's condition improves such that he or she no longer requires the powered mattress. If the patient continues to require a powered mattress after the initial thirty days, Company A will provide the powered mattress for additional thirty-day periods at half of the original thirty day rental amount ($(1/2)(x)/month). The total amount charged for the powered/non-powered mattress combination ($x) will be substantially lower than the price Company A currently charges for these mattresses when rented and sold separately ($x+$y = $(x+y)). The price charged for successive months' rental of the powered mattress will also be lower than the price charged for the same number of months rented separately. For example, a package of two months' rental of the powered mattress will cost $(x+1/2x), whereas two months rented separately costs $2x [($x+$x)].

While Company A will market the Proposed Arrangement directly to its major customers, it will also contract with durable medical equipment ("DME") suppliers to serve as sales agents to market the Proposed Arrangement to some SNFs. As compensation, the DME sales agents will receive 20% of collections from any Proposed Arrangements for which they are responsible.[2] The compensation covers the cost of selling activities, delivery, follow-up, and assistance in the collections process when necessary. Company A has certified that the compensation represents fair market value in an arms-length transaction.[3] Payment for the mattresses will be made by the SNF customers directly to Company A. The contracted sales agents may market to SNFs products of other manufacturers and suppliers that are reimbursable under either Part A or Part B of the Medicare program.

---

[2] Company A has certified that the compensation rate is tentatively set at 20% and that it reserves the right to adjust the amount of compensation as necessary. This opinion is limited to the compensation terms described in this advisory opinion. We express no opinion about any different compensation terms.

[3] As we are not authorized to opine on "fair market value" (*see* section 1128D(b)(3) of the Act), we assume the truth of Company A's fair market value certification for purposes of this opinion. If the certification is not true, this opinion is without force and effect.

Company A will require each DME supplier to provide Company A with an ownership statement and to agree not to market Company A's therapeutic mattresses to SNFs with which the DME supplier has a financial relationship. Company A has certified that it will monitor the DME supplier's compliance with these conditions. In addition, Company A will require the DME sales agents to disclose the special mattress pricing to their SNF customers in writing and to inform the customers of their obligation to report discounted prices accurately as required by any Federal or state agency, in a manner consistent with the requirements of 42 C.F.R. § 1001.952(h)(2)(ii).

All ordering and billing for the Proposed Arrangement will be done by Company A, regardless of whether the order is generated by Company A or by a contracting DME supplier. Company A's invoices for mattress packages purchased pursuant to the Proposed Arrangement will fully, accurately, and clearly reflect the discounted price of the package. For powered/non-powered mattress packages, Company A will apportion the discount between the two products in proportion to their fair market values. For one package, it will calculate the rental rate net of discount for the powered mattress by multiplying the ratio of the undiscounted rental rate for the powered mattress ($x) to the undiscounted bundled or combined price ($x+y) by the discounted combined price ($x). It will thus report a net rental rate of $z [where z = (x)(x/(x+y))] for the powered mattress on the invoice. Using the same methodology, it will report a net sales price for the non-powered mattress of $w [where w = (x)(y/(x+y))]. For additional consecutive months' rental of the powered mattress, Company A will report the total price on the invoice ($(1/2x)/month). The invoice will clearly state that the buyer has an obligation to report the discounted price on any cost reports or other reports required by any Federal or state agency, in a manner consistent with the requirements of 42 C.F.R. § 1001.952(h)(2)(ii).

Company A states that the market for the Proposed Arrangement will primarily be SNFs that are being reimbursed for Medicare Part A services using the new prospective payment system. The Balanced Budget Act of 1997, Public Law 105-33, required the implementation of a prospective payment system ("PPS") covering all costs (routine, ancillary, and capital) related to SNF services furnished to beneficiaries under Part A of the Medicare program. The PPS for SNFs is being implemented for the cost reporting period beginning after July 1, 1998. The basic methodology is a prospectively fixed per diem payment adjusted to reflect the resident's health status and needs and regional wage rate (the "Federal case mix adjusted rate"). The per diem payment is based on classifications of patients according to the amount and type of resources they use (resource utilization groups, or "RUGs"). There is a transition phase during the first three cost reporting years, during which SNFs will receive a blend of the Federal case mix adjusted rate and a facility specific rate based on the facility's allowable costs for SNF services for the fiscal 1995 cost reporting period.

One purpose of the Proposed Arrangement is to encourage SNFs to use the non-powered mattress as a routine step-down treatment and to demonstrate that such use can help prevent recurrences of ulcers, thereby saving costs and minimizing the SNFs' risk under the new PPS system.

Company A has certified that the Company A powered mattress and the non-powered Company A pressure relieving mattress included in the Proposed Arrangement are the only items marketed or provided by Company A that are covered by Medicare Part A. Moreover, Company A has certified that neither mattress is reimbursable under Part B of the Medicare program for patients in nursing facilities. In addition, Company A does not market or provide other items or services to potential SNF customers that are reimbursable under Part B of the Medicare program. Company A has also certified that, to its knowledge, only three State health care programs (New York, Ohio, and California) may, in infrequent circumstances, provide separate reimbursement for support surfaces used in long-term care facilities.

Company A has further certified that (i) Company A will have no financial arrangements with any SNF that participates in the Proposed Arrangement apart from the Proposed Arrangement; and (ii) Company A will have no commission-splitting or other financial arrangements with any of the DME suppliers that will market the Proposed Arrangement, except as disclosed in the request for an advisory opinion.

II. LEGAL ANALYSIS

The Anti-Kickback Statute

The anti-kickback statute makes it a criminal offense knowingly and wilfully to offer, pay, solicit, or receive any remuneration to induce referrals of items or services reimbursable by the Federal health care programs. *See* section 1128B(b) of the Act. Where remuneration is paid purposefully to induce referrals of items or services paid for by a Federal health care program, the anti-kickback statute is violated. By its terms, the statute ascribes liability to parties on both sides of an impermissible "kickback" transaction. For purposes of the anti-kickback statute, "remuneration" includes the transfer of anything of value, in cash or in-kind, directly or indirectly, covertly or overtly.

The statute has been interpreted to cover any arrangement where one purpose of the remuneration is to obtain money for referral of services or to induce further referrals. *United States v. Kats*, 871 F. 2d 105 (9th Cir. 1989); *United States v. Greber*, 760 F. 2d 68 (3rd Cir.), *cert. denied*, 476 U.S. 988 (1985). Violation of the statute constitutes a felony punishable by a maximum fine of $25,000, imprisonment up to five years or both. Conviction will also lead to automatic exclusion from Federal health care programs, including Medicare and Medicaid. This Office may also initiate administrative proceedings to exclude persons from Federal health care programs or to impose civil monetary penalties for fraud, kickbacks, and other prohibited activities under sections 1128(b)(7) and 1128A(a)(7) of the Act.[4]

The anti-kickback statute contains a statutory exception for "a discount or other reduction in price obtained by a provider of services or other entity under a Federal health care program if the reduction in price is properly disclosed and appropriately reflected in the costs claimed or charges made by the provider or entity under a Federal health care program." 42 U.S.C. § 1320a-7b(b)(3)(A). The Department of Health and Human Services has published regulations implementing this discount "safe harbor" exception. *See* 42 C.F.R. § 1001.952(h).

The Bundled Pricing

The statutory discount exception, as implemented by the regulatory safe harbor, does not protect "the practice of a seller giving away, or reducing the price of, one good in connection with the purchase of a different good." *See* 56 Fed. Reg. 35952, 35978 (July 29, 1991). One of our major concerns with such arrangements is the

---

[4] Because both the criminal and administrative sanctions related to the anti-kickback implications of the Arrangement are based on violations of the anti-kickback statute, the analysis for the purposes of this advisory opinion is the same under both.

difficulty in ensuring that the monetary value of the discount is appropriately apportioned and fully reported to the Federal health care programs. *Id.* In other words, such "discounts" may shift costs among reimbursement systems or distort the true costs of the items, making it difficult for the Federal health care programs to determine appropriate reimbursement levels. Accordingly, the final discount safe harbor specifically excludes from the definition of discounts "furnishing one good or service without charge or at a reduced charge in exchange for any agreement to buy a different good or service." *See* 42 C.F.R. § 1001.952(h)(3)(ii).

The Proposed Arrangement involves a bundled therapeutic mattress package consisting of an initial thirty day powered mattress rental, which includes a non-powered mattress, and, if needed, additional thirty day rental periods at half price. Where items are bundled, we will examine the circumstances to determine the desirability of prosecuting such arrangements. The factors that we will look at may include: (1) the amount of the benefit that is reported and passed along to the programs, (2) whether the items are separately reimbursable, and (3) the intent behind the arrangement. *See* 56 Fed. Reg. at 35978.

The Proposed Arrangement, as described and certified by Company A, poses a minimal risk of kickback violations, and accordingly we would not subject it to sanctions under the anti-kickback statute. The methodology used by Company A to apportion the discount between the powered and non-powered mattresses is reasonable and, assuming proper reporting by the SNF purchasers,[5] will assure that the price reported to any Federal health care program for each product will fairly reflect the value of the discount. Moreover, the mattresses that are the subject of the Proposed Arrangement will be used primarily in SNFs that will be reimbursed a fixed prospectively determined amount for Part A beneficiaries. Because the SNFs receive fixed per diem payments based on the patient's RUG classification, regardless of the costs of the services provided to the patient, the SNFs have an incentive to be prudent purchasers, i.e. to seek the lowest price for mattresses and not to pay for any mattresses unless absolutely necessary. In sum, so long as the discounted price for the package of mattresses is reflected properly on the SNFs' cost reports,

[5] The OIG will not hold Company A liable for omissions of the SNFs in connection with their claims filing and reporting obligations, provided that Company A does everything it reasonably can to ensure that the SNFs understand their obligations to report the discount accurately.

there is minimal risk of program fraud or abuse from the Proposed Arrangement.

In addition, the Proposed Arrangement poses a minimal risk that discounts on Part A items and services will be "swapped" for referrals of Part B business. Many items that are included in the Part A SNF PPS payment may be separately reimbursable on a charge or fee schedule basis under Part B when provided to Medicare beneficiaries who are not eligible for skilled nursing care under Part A, but who reside in a nursing facility with a SNF unit. In such situations, there is a significant risk that suppliers might offer the SNF an excessively low price for items or services provided to SNF Part A patients reimbursed under the PPS methodology in return for the opportunity to service and bill nursing facility patients with Part B coverage. Such arrangements are highly suspect under the anti-kickback statute. In this case, however, Company A has certified that neither the powered nor the non-powered mattress is separately reimbursable by Medicare under Part B of the Medicare program for patients in Medicare and Medicaid certified nursing facilities. Moreover, Company A does not market or provide any items or services that are reimbursable under Part B to potential SNF customers. Thus, Company A has no incentive to offer SNFs a discounted price for mattresses to induce orders for Part B covered items or services.

Finally, some SNFs may also utilize the powered or non-powered mattresses for their residents receiving care pursuant to a State health care program. While reimbursement methodologies vary widely among states, Company A has certified that, to its knowledge, only three State health care programs (New York, Ohio, and California) may, in infrequent circumstances, provide separate reimbursement for support surfaces used in long-term care facilities. Except in these three states, the cost of the mattresses would typically be included in the facility's daily room and board rate. In a small number of states, the rate may be adjusted based on a RUGS-type assessment. In any case, Company A's method of allocating the discount between the two mattresses on the invoice will permit apportionment among payors, including State health care programs, according to the appropriate cost reporting principles in the same manner as other items and services used for patients in such programs.

The Use of DME Sales Agents

The proposed use of independent DME sales agents to provide sales and service support to some customers raises different issues. Sales agents are in the business of recommending or arranging for the purchase of the items or services they offer for sale on behalf of their principals, typically manufacturers, or other sellers (collectively, "Sellers"). Accordingly, any compensation arrangement between a Seller and an independent sales agent for the purpose of selling health care items or services that are directly or indirectly reimbursable by a Federal health care program potentially implicates the anti-kickback statute, irrespective of the methodology used to compensate the agent. Moreover, because such agents are independent contractors, they are less accountable to the Seller than an employee. *See* 56 Fed. Reg. 35952, 35981 (July 29, 1991); 54 Fed. Reg. 3088, 3093 (Jan. 23, 1989). For these reasons, this Office has a longstanding concern with independent sales agency arrangements.

In some circumstances, our concerns can be addressed by structuring a sales agency arrangement to fit in a safe harbor. *See, e.g.*, 56 Fed. Reg. at 35974. The Department of Health and Human Services has published safe harbor regulations that protect certain arrangements that might otherwise technically violate the anti-kickback statute from prosecution. *See* section 1128B(b)(3) of the Act; 42 C.F.R. § 1001.952. The regulatory safe harbor potentially applicable to the Proposed Arrangement is the personal services and management contracts safe harbor. *See* 42 C.F.R. § 1001.952(d). The Proposed Arrangement cannot qualify under this safe harbor, however, since the nature of the services to be provided by the DME sales agents precludes an exact specification of the schedule for performance of services and a determination of the total aggregate compensation in advance, as required by the safe harbor regulation.

In reviewing sales arrangements that do not fit in the personal services and management contracts safe harbor, this Office has identified several characteristics of arrangements among Sellers, sales agents, and purchasers that appear to be associated with an increased potential for program abuse, particularly overutilization and excessive program costs. These suspect characteristics include, but are not limited to:

- — compensation based on percentage of sales;
- — direct billing of a Federal health care program by the Seller for the item or service sold by the sales agent;

- — direct contact between the sales agent and physicians in a position to order items or services that are then paid for by a Federal health care program;
- — direct contact between the sales agent and Federal health care program beneficiaries;
- — use of sales agents who are health care professionals or persons in a similar position to exert undue influence on purchasers or patients; and
- — marketing of items or services that are separately reimbursable by a Federal health care program (e.g., items or services not included in the SNF PPS payment), whether on the basis of charges or costs.

This list is illustrative, not exhaustive, and the absence of any of these factors certainly does not mean that a sales arrangement is permissible under the anti-kickback statute. However, the more factors that are present, the greater the scrutiny we ordinarily will give an arrangement. Of course, in all cases the statute is not violated unless the parties have the requisite intent to induce referrals.

In this case, while the sales agent compensation will be based on a percentage of collections attributable to the Proposed Arrangement and may involve contact between the sales agent and persons in a position to order the services, the particular products being sold and rented, i.e., powered and non-powered mattresses, are not separately reimbursable for patients in Medicare and Medicaid certified nursing facilities and are used almost exclusively for SNF patients. To the extent that the purchasers of the mattresses will be SNFs reimbursed under the new Part A PPS, the cost of the mattresses will represent an expense to the SNFs that must be covered by the fixed PPS payment and will necessarily reduce the amount of profit for the SNF. Accordingly, the risk of overutilization and excessive program costs will largely be offset by the inability of the SNFs to pass on the costs of the items purchased to the Federal health care programs. In addition, the percentage compensation to be paid to the DME sales agents is a fixed percentage, which Company A has represented will be fair market value in an arms-length transaction.[6]

---

[6] As noted above, we are not authorized to opine on "fair market value" in an advisory opinion. *See* section 1128D(b)(3) of the Act. Therefore, for purposes of this opinion, we have assumed fair market value compensation based on Company A's certification. If the compensation paid to DME sales

In the circumstances of the Proposed Arrangement, the fact that the sales agents may be marketing other products should not affect this conclusion. Because the price for the therapeutic mattress package is fixed and collected by Company A, there is no financial benefit to be gained by the DME sales agents from "swapping" the Part A mattress arrangement for other Part B business or Part B business for the Part A mattress business.

Finally, this opinion is premised on Company A's certifications that: (i) Company A will have no financial arrangements with any SNF that participates in the Proposed Arrangement apart from the Proposed Arrangement; and (ii) Company A will have no commission-splitting or other financial arrangements with any of the DME suppliers that will market the Proposed Arrangement, except as specifically disclosed in the request for an advisory opinion.

III. CONCLUSION

Based on the facts certified in the request for an advisory opinion, we conclude that the Proposed Arrangement, as described in the advisory opinion request and supplemental submissions, might constitute prohibited remuneration under the anti-kickback statute, if the requisite intent to induce referrals of Federal health care program business were present, but that the OIG will not subject Company A to sanctions in connection with the Proposed Arrangement arising under the anti-kickback statute pursuant to sections 1128(b)(7) or 1128A(a)(7) of the Act.

IV. LIMITATIONS

The limitations applicable to this opinion include the following:

- This advisory opinion is issued only to Company A, the requester of this opinion. This advisory opinion has no application, and cannot be relied upon, by any other individual or entity.
- This advisory opinion may not be introduced into evidence in any matter involving an entity or individual that is not a requester to this opinion.
- This advisory opinion is applicable only to the statutory provisions specifically noted above. No opinion is herein expressed or implied with respect to the application of any other Federal,

agents under the Proposed Arrangement is not fair market value, this opinion will be without force and effect.

state, or local statute, rule, regulation, ordinance, or other law that may be applicable to the Proposed Arrangement.

- This advisory opinion will not bind or obligate any agency other than the U.S. Department of Health and Human Services.
- This advisory opinion is limited in scope to the specific arrangement described in this letter and has no applicability to other arrangements, even those that appear similar in nature or scope.
- No opinion is expressed herein regarding the liability of any party under the False Claims Act or other legal authorities for any improper billing, claims submission, cost reporting, or related conduct.

This opinion is also subject to any additional limitations set forth at 42 C.F.R. Part 1008.

The OIG will not proceed against the requester with respect to any action that is part of the Proposed Arrangement taken in good faith reliance upon this advisory opinion as long as (i) all of the material facts have been fully, completely, and accurately presented, (ii) the certified values of the mattresses reflect fair market rental rates and sales prices, (iii) the compensation paid to sales agents represents fair market value in an arms-length transaction, and (iv) the Proposed Arrangement in practice comports with the information provided. The OIG reserves the right to reconsider the questions and issues raised in this advisory opinion and, where the public interest requires, rescind, modify, or terminate this opinion. In the event that this advisory opinion is modified or terminated, the OIG will not proceed against the requester with respect to any action taken in good faith reliance upon this advisory opinion, where (i) all of the relevant facts were fully, completely, and accurately presented, (ii) the certified values of the mattresses reflect fair market rental rates and sales prices, (iii) the compensation to sales agents represents fair market value in an arms-length transaction, and (iv) such action was promptly discontinued upon notification of the modification or termination of this advisory opinion. An advisory opinion may be rescinded only if the relevant and material facts have not been fully, completely, and accurately disclosed to the OIG.

Sincerely,

/s/

D. McCarty Thornton

Chief Counsel to the Inspector General

APPENDIX F36

Advisory Opinion No. 99-4, March 31, 1999

Whether a proposed agreement, pursuant to which Hospital District No.1 would locate a medical clinic within the geographic boundaries of Hospital District No. 2, would constitute grounds for sanctions under the anti-kickback statute.

[*We have redacted specific information regarding the requestor and certain potentially privileged, confidential or financial information associated with the individual or entity, unless otherwise specified by the requestor.*]

[Posted April 8, 1999]

[Issued March 31, 1999]

[Name and Address Redacted]

Re: Advisory Opinion No. 99–4

Dear [Name Redacted]:

We are writing in response to your request for an advisory opinion, in which you ask whether a proposed agreement (the "Proposed Agreement"), pursuant to which Hospital District No.1 ("District One" or the "Requestor") would locate a medical clinic within the geographic boundaries of Hospital District No. 2 ("District Two"), would constitute grounds for sanctions under the anti-kickback statute, section 1128B(b) of the Social Security Act (the "Act"), the exclusion authority for kickbacks, section 1128(b)(7) of the Act, or the civil monetary penalty provisions for kickbacks, section 1128A(a)(7) of the Act.

You have certified that all of the information you provided in your request, including all supplementary information, is true and correct, and constitutes a complete description of the material facts regarding the Proposed Agreement. In issuing this opinion, we have relied solely on the facts and information you presented to us. We have not undertaken any independent investigation of such information.

Based on the facts certified in your request for an advisory opinion and supplemental submissions, we conclude that the Office of Inspector General ("OIG") will not subject the Requestor to sanctions arising under the anti-kickback statute pursuant to sections 1128(b)(7) or 1128A(a)(7) of the Act in connection with the Proposed Agreement between District One and District Two.

This opinion may not be relied on by any persons other than the Requestor and is further qualified as set out in Part III below and in 42 C.F.R. Part 1008.

I. FACTUAL BACKGROUND

Under State A law, hospital districts may be organized within a county boundary to provide health care services to the general public. *See* State A Code § []. District One and District Two are hospital districts located in County B, State A. District One owns and operates a public hospital and clinic in City C, State A. District Two owns and previously operated a hospital and clinic located in City D and City E, State A. District Two ceased operation of its health care facilities on September 30, 1998. District Two does not currently operate any health care facilities or provide any health care services.[1]

District One and District Two propose entering the Proposed Agreement (entitled "Mutual Interagency Agreement For Physician Services") whereby District One will locate a medical clinic (the "District One Clinic") within District Two's hospital district.[2] The Proposed Agreement is subject to revocation at any time, with or without cause, on one year's notice from District Two. District One will obtain office space for and staff the District One Clinic without any financial support or participation from District Two. District Two will not exercise operational control over the District One Clinic, nor will District Two be entitled to any revenues from the District One Clinic. Under the Proposed Agreement, no payments or

---

[1] This opinion is premised on the facts that District Two does not operate any health care facilities and District Two does not provide any health care services. If either of these facts change, this opinion is without force and effect.

[2] Under State A law, a public agency may contract with another public agency to perform services the first public agency is authorized by law to perform. *See* State A Code § [__].

other remuneration will be made or exchanged between District One and District Two (other than District Two authorizing District One to locate a clinic in District Two's hospital district). District One has represented that there are no oral or other collateral agreements or understandings between District One and District Two.

II. LEGAL ANALYSIS

The anti-kickback statute makes it a criminal offense knowingly and willfully to offer, pay, solicit, or receive any remuneration to induce referrals of items or services reimbursable by any Federal health care program. *See* section 1128B(b) of the Act.

Where remuneration is paid purposefully to induce referrals of items or services for which payment may be made by a Federal health care program, the anti-kickback statute is violated. By its terms, the statute ascribes criminal liability to parties on both sides of an impermissible "kickback" transaction. For purposes of the anti-kickback statute, "remuneration" includes the transfer of anything of value, in cash or in-kind, directly or indirectly, covertly or overtly.

The statute has been interpreted to cover any arrangement where one purpose of the remuneration was to obtain money for the referral of services or to induce further referrals. *United States v. Kats,* 871 F.2d 105 (9th Cir. 1989); *United States v. Greber,* 760 F.2d 68 (3d Cir.), *cert. denied,* 474 U.S. 988 (1985). Violation of the statute constitutes a felony punishable by a maximum fine of $25,000, imprisonment up to five years, or both. Conviction will also lead to automatic exclusion from Federal health care programs, including Medicare and Medicaid. This Office may also initiate administrative proceedings to exclude persons from Federal and state health care programs or to impose civil monetary penalties for fraud, kickbacks, and other prohibited activities under sections 1128(b)(7) and 1128A (a)(7) of the Act.

By granting District One an opportunity to locate its clinic in District Two's district, District Two may be bestowing on District One something of value, that is, an opportunity to generate business in District Two. Notwithstanding, it is axiomatic that there can be no violation of the anti-kickback statute absent a prohibited referral. On the facts stated, District One cannot refer any health care business to District Two, because District Two does not operate any health care facilities or provide any health care services.

Based on the facts certified in the request for an advisory opinion and supplemental submissions, we conclude that the OIG will not subject the Requestor to sanctions arising under the anti-kickback statute pursuant to sections 1128(b)(7) or 1128A(a)(7) of the Act in connection with the Proposed Agreement between District One and Two. [3]

III. LIMITATIONS

The limitations applicable to this opinion include the following:

- This advisory opinion is issued only to Hospital District No.1, the Requestor of this opinion. This advisory opinion has no application, and cannot be relied upon, by any other individual or entity.
- This advisory opinion will not bind or obligate any agency other than the U.S. Department of Health and Human Services.
- This advisory opinion is applicable only to the statutory provisions specifically noted in the first paragraph of this advisory opinion. No opinion is herein expressed or implied with respect to the application of any other Federal, state, or local statute, rule, regulation, ordinance, or other law that may be applicable to the Proposed Agreement. We express no opinion with respect to State A law.
- This advisory opinion is limited in scope to the specific arrangements described in this letter and has no applicability to other arrangements, even those which appear similar in nature or scope.
- No opinion is expressed herein regarding the liability of any party under the False Claims Act or other legal authorities for any improper billing, claims submission, cost reporting, or related conduct.

This opinion is also subject to any additional limitations set forth at 42 C.F.R. Part 1008.

The OIG will not proceed against the Requestor with respect to any action that is part of the Proposed Agreement taken in good faith reliance upon this advisory opinion as long as all of the material facts have been fully, completely, and accurately presented, and the Pro-

[3] This advisory opinion only relates to the agreement to locate the District One Clinic within District Two's hospital district. We express no opinion with regard to any relationship between District One and its employees or independent contractors.

posed Agreement in practice comports with the information provided. The OIG reserves the right to reconsider the questions and issues raised in this advisory opinion and, where the public interest requires, rescind, modify or terminate this opinion. In the event that this advisory opinion is modified or terminated, the OIG will not proceed against the Requestor with respect to any action taken in good faith reliance upon this advisory opinion, where all of the relevant facts were fully, completely, and accurately presented and where such action was promptly discontinued upon notification of the modification or termination of this advisory opinion. An advisory opinion may be rescinded only if the relevant and material facts have not been fully, completely, and accurately disclosed to the OIG.

Sincerely,

/s/

D. McCarty Thornton

Chief Counsel to the Inspector General

APPENDIX F37

Advisory Opinion No. 99-5, April 1, 1999

Whether an annual fee imposed by city ordinance on ambulance companies wishing to provide ambulance services in the city constitutes prohibited remuneration under the anti-kickback statute, ... and, if so, whether the Ambulance Fee assessment constitutes grounds for the imposition of sanctions.

[*We have redacted specific information regarding the requestor and certain potentially privileged, confidential or financial information associated with the individual or entity, unless otherwise specified by the requestor.*]

Dated: April 1, 1999

Posted: April 8, 1999

[Name and Address Redacted]

Re: [Name Redacted]

Advisory Opinion 99–5

Dear [Name Redacted]:

We are writing in response to your request for an advisory opinion, in which you ask whether an annual fee imposed by city ordinance on ambulance companies wishing to provide ambulance services in the city (the "Ambulance Fee") constitutes prohibited remuneration under the anti-kickback statute, section 1128B(b) of the Social Security Act (the "Act"), and, if so, whether the Ambulance Fee assessment constitutes grounds for the imposition of sanctions under the anti-kickback statute, section 1128B(b) of the Act, the exclusion authority related to kickbacks, section 1128(b)(7) of the Act, or the civil monetary penalty provision for kickbacks, section 1128A(a)(7) of the Act.

You have certified that all of the information you provided in your request, including all supplementary information, is true and correct, and constitutes a complete description of the material facts regarding the assessment of the Ambulance Fee. In issuing this opinion, we have relied solely on the facts and information you presented to us. We have not undertaken any independent investigation of such information. This opinion is limited to the facts presented. If material facts have not been disclosed, this opinion is without force and effect.

Based on the facts certified in your request for an advisory opinion, we conclude that the Ambulance Fee could constitute prohibited remuneration under the anti-kickback statute if the requisite intent to induce referrals were present, but that the Office of Inspector General ("OIG") will not subject the Ambulance Fee, as described in the request and supplemental submissions, to sanctions arising under the anti-kickback statute pursuant to sections 1128(b)(7) or 1128A(a)(7) of the Act. This opinion may not be relied on by any persons other than the addressee and is further qualified as set out in Part IV below and in 42 C.F.R. Part 1008.

I. FACTUAL BACKGROUND

The requester of this advisory opinion is the City of [name redacted] (the "City"). By city ordinance, the City established the Ambulance Fee ($50,000 per year) for ambulance companies wishing to provide ambulance services in the City. The City intends that the collected Ambulance Fees will partially offset the costs of the City's 911 dispatch system. The factual background is as follows.

In addition to fire fighting, the City's fire department operates the City's emergency "911" dispatch service, as well as its Basic Life Support First Responder service (the "First Responder" service). The 911 system receives and dispatches calls for assistance from police, fire, and emergency medical services ("EMS"). In the event of a medical emergency, the 911 dispatcher will dispatch both a fire department vehicle to provide First Responder service and a City-licensed ambulance company vehicle. In 1998, the 911 dispatch service received 4,886 calls, of which 3,232 (approximately 66%) required the dispatching of an ambulance. The costs of providing the fire department's 911 dispatch service and the First Responder service are not reimbursed by any Federal health care program.

Until recently, the City was served by one ambulance company. On August 11, 1998, the City Council adopted Ordinance No. 98-49 (the "Ordinance"). The Ordinance amended the City's existing ambulance regulations to allow the City to enter into ambulance agreements with any ambulance company that pays the requisite fees and meets specified regulatory requirements, such as minimum levels of equipment, staffing and insurance. Under the Ordinance, companies that desire to operate an ambulance in the City must file a sworn application with a non-refundable application fee of $1,000. If the City approves the application, the company may enter into a three-year ambulance agreement with the City and pay the City an annual fee of $50,000. There is no other remuneration from the ambulance company to the City.[1]

If the new arrangement created by the Ordinance leads to more than one ambulance company operating in the City, then the referral of emergency 911 calls shall rotate among the participating ambulance companies on a weekly basis. Each ambulance company shall be responsible for responding to all emergency 911 calls during the one-week "shift" assigned to it. When each participating ambulance company has served its one-week shift, the rotation shall repeat in the same order. To date, two ambulance companies have paid the $50,000 annual fee to participate in the ambulance arrangement created by the Ordinance.

The City Council determined $50,000 to be a reasonable amount for the Ambulance Fee after reviewing the cost and scope of the City fire department's involvement in the provision of EMS in the City. This process included the formation of a committee[2] (the "Ambulance Committee") to review the proposed ambulance arrangement later adopted by the Ordinance. The Ambulance Committee considered the City's FY 1998 budget, as well as the fact that the majority of calls to which the fire department responded in 1997 involved emergencies requiring both ambulance and First Responder services.

---

[1] The City has certified that ambulance companies operating in the City have restocked medical supplies used by the fire department when assisting the ambulance companies with First Responder services. The Ambulance Fee arrangement is the complete and entire arrangement that is the subject of this advisory opinion. No opinion is expressed with respect to the fire department restocking.

[2] The Committee was comprised of the City's Mayor, City Manager, City Attorney, Fire Chief, Police Chief, and two City Council members.

The City has certified that the cost to the City of its 911 system for dispatching EMS calls is approximately $150,000 per year (including salaries, benefits and overhead).[3] This amount represents the proportion of the total cost of the 911 system attributable to ambulance dispatching services.

The City Attorney has certified that the Ordinance was duly noticed as required by the State's Open Meetings Act, that the Ordinance and Ambulance Fee fall within the City's authority under the State's Health and Safety Code to regulate EMS, and that the Ordinance's enactment was in accordance with local and state law.

II. LEGAL ANALYSIS

The anti-kickback statute makes it a criminal offense knowingly and willfully to offer, pay, solicit, or receive any remuneration to induce referrals of items or services reimbursable by any Federal health care program. *See* section 1128B(b) of the Act. Where remuneration is paid purposefully to induce referrals of items or services for which payment may be made by a Federal health care program, the anti-kickback statute is violated. By its terms, the statute ascribes criminal liability to parties on both sides of an impermissible "kickback" transaction. For purposes of the anti-kickback statute, "remuneration" includes the transfer of anything of value, in cash or in-kind, directly or indirectly, covertly or overtly.

The statute has been interpreted to cover any arrangement where one purpose of the remuneration was to obtain money for the referral of services or to induce further referrals. *United States v. Kats,* 871 F.2d 105 (9th Cir. 1989); *United States v. Greber,* 760 F.2d 68 (3d Cir.), *cert. denied,* 474 U.S. 988 (1985). Violation of the statute constitutes a felony punishable by a maximum fine of $25,000, imprisonment up to five years, or both. Conviction will also lead to automatic exclusion from Federal health care programs, including Medicare and Medicaid. This Office may also initiate administrative proceedings to exclude persons from Federal and state health care programs or to impose civil monetary penalties for fraud, kickbacks, and other prohibited activities under sections 1128(b)(7) and 1128A

---

[3] While the OIG does not make independent assessments of the fair market value of given services (*see* section 1128D(b)(3) of the Act), we note that the City justified its figure for the cost of its 911 system by delineating the cost of each item of overhead and then apportioning those costs in accordance with the ratio of ambulance calls to total 911 calls.

(a)(7) of the Act.[4]

"Pay to play" arrangements, like the proposed arrangement between the ambulance companies and the City enacted by the Ordinance, clearly implicate the anti-kickback statute. The payment of the Ambulance Fee to the City for the opportunity to provide EMS fits squarely within the language of the anti-kickback statute. Depending on the intent of the parties, the proposed arrangement could violate the statute.

However, for the following reasons and based on the facts certified in your request for an advisory opinion and in subsequent submissions, the OIG will not subject the Ambulance Fee to sanctions arising under the anti-kickback statute pursuant to sections 1128(b)(7) or 1128A(a)(7) of the Act. *First,* the Ambulance Fee is only one part of a comprehensive regulatory scheme by the City to provide oversight and fiscal management to the delivery of EMS. The Ambulance Fee was established by a valid governmental entity legally empowered to regulate the provision of EMS in the City.

Second, the Ambulance Fee is reasonably related to the costs of the operation of the City's 911 system attributable to dispatching ambulances. The City has certified that its annual cost of dispatching ambulances is approximately $150,000. So long as the aggregate collected Ambulance Fees do not exceed the City's cost of dispatching ambulances, then the Fee is a reasonable charge to participating ambulance companies. To date, only two ambulance companies have paid Ambulance Fees, the aggregate of which ($102,000[5]) falls far short of the City's cost of dispatching ambulances.

Third, the Ambulance Fee is not tied directly or indirectly to the volume or value of referrals. The amount of the Ambulance Fee is the same regardless of the volume of business that accrues to the ambulance company that pays it. The City's 911 system employs a fixed rotation system for distributing calls. There is no guarantee as to the volume of business that will accrue to any single ambulance company. Indeed, there is no guarantee against a decrease in business volume resulting from an additional ambulance company contracting with the City for a place in the rotation.

---

[4] Because both the criminal and administrative sanctions related to the anti-kickback implications of the Ambulance Fee are based on violations of the anti-kickback statute, the analysis for purposes of this advisory opinion is the same under both.

[5] This figure includes a $1,000 application fee per ambulance company.

Fourth, the Ambulance Fee assessment should not increase the risk of overutilization or costs to Federal health care programs. Neither the number of Federal program beneficiaries requiring emergency transport in the City, nor the treatment these patients will require or receive at a hospital, is related to the existence or use of the Ambulance Fee. In light of the specific circumstances presented, we would not impose sanctions arising under the anti-kickback statute in connection with the Ambulance Fee.

III. CONCLUSION

The advisory opinion process is a "means of relating the anti-kickback statute to the particular facts of a specific arrangement." 62 Fed. Reg. 7350, 7351 (Feb. 19, 1997). The advisory opinion process permits the OIG to protect specific arrangements that "contain[] limitations, requirements, or controls that give adequate assurance that Federal health care programs cannot be abused." Id. In evaluating an arrangement's potential to lead to fraud or abuse of the Federal health care programs, no one fact or element is necessarily dispositive. We are persuaded that, taken as a whole, the aspects of the Ambulance Fee described above -- including, but not limited to, its reasonable relationship to the costs of the 911 system, its existence within a municipal regulatory scheme and legislative-representative context, and its uniformity across providers -- create sufficient limitations, requirements, or controls so as to give adequate assurance that the Ambulance Fee will not lead to program abuse under the anti-kickback statute.

Accordingly, we conclude that while the Ambulance Fee might technically violate the anti-kickback statute if the requisite intent to induce referrals were present, the OIG will not impose sanctions on the requesters under sections 1128(b)(7) (as it relates to kickbacks) or 1128A(a)(7) of the Act, based on the facts certified in the requester's request for an advisory opinion.

IV. LIMITATIONS

The limitations applicable to this opinion include the following:

- This advisory opinion is issued only to the City of [name redacted], the requester of this opinion. This advisory opinion has no application, and cannot be relied upon, by any other individual or entity.

- This advisory opinion may not be introduced into evidence in any matter involving an entity or individual that is not a requester to this opinion.
- This advisory opinion is applicable only to the statutory provisions specifically noted in the first paragraph of this advisory opinion. No opinion is herein expressed or implied with respect to the application of any other Federal, state, or local statute, rule, regulation, ordinance, or other law that may be applicable to the Ambulance Fee or the Ordinance.
- This advisory opinion will not bind or obligate any agency other than the U.S. Department of Health and Human Services.
- This advisory opinion is limited in scope to the specific arrangement described in this letter and has no applicability to other arrangements, even those which appear similar in nature or scope.
- No opinion is expressed herein regarding the liability of any party under the False Claims Act or other legal authorities for any improper billing, claims submission, cost reporting, or related conduct.

This opinion is also subject to any additional limitations set forth at 42 C.F.R. Part 1008.

The OIG will not proceed against the requester with respect to any action regarding the Ambulance Fee taken in good faith reliance upon this advisory opinion as long as all of the material facts have been fully, completely, and accurately presented, and the administration of the Ambulance Fee in practice comports with the information provided. The OIG reserves the right to reconsider the questions and issues raised in this advisory opinion and, where the public interest requires, rescind, modify or terminate this opinion. In the event that this advisory opinion is modified or terminated, the OIG will not proceed against any requester with respect to any action taken in good faith reliance upon this advisory opinion, where all of the relevant facts were fully, completely, and accurately presented and where such action was promptly discontinued upon notification of the modification or termination of this advisory opinion. An advisory opinion may be rescinded only if the relevant and material facts have not been fully, completely, and accurately disclosed to the OIG.

Sincerely,

/s/

D. McCarty Thornton

Chief Counsel to the Inspector General

APPENDIX F38

Advisory Opinion No. 99-6, April 7, 1999

Whether the longstanding policy of a hospital, specializing in pediatric oncology research, of not billing its patients for any amounts associated with their treatment, including copayment amounts.

[*We have redacted specific information regarding the requestor and certain potentially privileged, confidential or financial information associated with the individual or entity, unless otherwise specified by the requestor.*]

Date Issued: April 7, 1999

Date Posted: April 14, 1999

John D. Nash

Executive Vice President/Chief Operating Officer
St. Jude Children's Research Hospital
332 N. Lauderdale Street.
Memphis, TN. 38105-2794

[Name and Address Redacted]

[Name and Address Redacted]

Re: OIG Advisory Opinion 99–6

Ladies and Gentlemen:

We are writing in response to your request for an advisory opinion concerning the practice of St. Jude Children's Research Hospital ("St. Jude") of not billing pediatric oncology patients for coinsurance and deductible amounts and the extension of a variation of that practice to Hospital A and Hospital B (collectively, the "Affiliates") pursuant to certain affiliation agreements with St. Jude (as described in more detail in Part I below). Specifically, you have inquired whether these practices (collectively, the "Billing Policy") constitute grounds for sanctions under the anti-kickback statute, section 1128B(b) of the Social Security Act (the "Act"), or under section 1128A(a)(5) of the Act (civil money penalties for illegal remuneration to beneficiaries) in the circumstances presented.

In issuing this opinion, we have relied solely on the facts and information presented to us. We have not undertaken an independent investigation of such information. This opinion is limited to the facts presented. If material facts have not been disclosed, this opinion is without force and effect.

Based on the information provided and subject to certain conditions described below, we conclude: (i) that the Billing Policy could potentially generate prohibited remuneration under the anti-kickback statute, if the requisite intent to induce referrals were present, but that the Office of Inspector General ("OIG") will not subject the Billing Policy as practiced by St. Jude or the Affiliates (as described in the request letter and supplemental submissions) to sanctions arising under the anti-kickback statute pursuant to sections 1128(b)(7) or 1128A(a)(7) of the Act; and (ii) that the OIG will not subject St. Jude or the Affiliates to sanctions under section 1128A(a)(5) of the Act in connection with the Billing Policy.

This opinion may not be relied on by any persons other than the Requesters[1] and is further qualified as set out in Part III below and in 42 C.F.R. Part 1008.

I. FACTUAL BACKGROUND

A. St. Jude

Founded by actor Danny Thomas in 1962, St. Jude is a nationally-known, not-for-profit pediatric facility dedicated to finding cures for children with catastrophic illnesses through research and treatment. St. Jude specializes in research involving pediatric cancers, acquired and inherited immuno-deficiencies, and genetic disorders.

Children come to St. Jude from across the nation and around the world. To be eligible for services at St. Jude, children must be referred by a physician, usually a community-based pediatrician.

[1] For purposes of this advisory opinion, St. Jude Children's Research Hospital, Hospital A, and Hospital B are, collectively, the "Requesters".

Typically, children are accepted for treatment at St. Jude based solely on their eligibility and willingness to participate in various research protocols developed by St. Jude, the Children's Cancer Group ("CCG"), or the Pediatric Oncology Group ("POG").[2] Children are eligible if there is an open research protocol and if they have not received prior treatment for their illness.[3]

Generally, physicians who treat patients at St. Jude are full-time, salaried faculty members of St. Jude.[4] Salaries for these physicians are fixed annually and do not vary based on the volume or value of services the physicians provide or order. In addition to treating patients, the physicians conduct laboratory-based research and develop clinical research treatment protocols directed toward improving patient outcomes. None of the employed physicians is permitted to have an outside medical practice.

St. Jude treats approximately 600 children each year, of whom approximately 400 have cancer and the rest have other catastrophic illnesses. Many of these children experience extended and/or repeated hospital stays. While new developments in treatment methods have enabled an increasing number of children to be treated on an outpatient ambulatory basis, many patients are still required to travel to, and stay in, Memphis for St. Jude's diagnostic studies and treatment. To defray costs for families during the course

---

[2] CCG is a national cooperative research organization founded in 1995 that is funded primarily by the National Institutes of Health and the National Childhood Cancer Foundation. POG, founded in 1980, is a National Cancer Institute-sponsored clinical trial cooperative.

[3] Open research protocols exist for most common forms of childhood cancer. Children enrolled at St. Jude in the absence of a protocol fall into two categories: children in St. Jude's Memphis service area with rare forms of cancer that are not the subject of any on-going protocol and children outside the service area with similar rare cancers that also are not the subject of open protocols and whose cancers cannot be treated elsewhere. For these children, treatment is dictated by a management plan or multi-disciplinary group plan established at the time the child is accepted for treatment. These children participate in St. Jude's research through contributions of tumor tissue, normal tissue, and blood for laboratory research into the causes and biological characteristics of childhood cancer.

[4] St. Jude contracts with a small number of specialists to provide services to St. Jude patients on an as-needed basis in areas, such as urology, where St. Jude generally has a limited need. These physicians provide only approximately 1% of the services furnished to children at St. Jude. All services are provided "under arrangement" pursuant to written contracts that provide for compensation that is fixed in advance. The specialists assign their rights to third-party reimbursement to St. Jude.

of treatment, St. Jude sponsors a comprehensive domiciliary care program funded entirely by philanthropic sources to provide meals, housing, and transportation for children and families.

St. Jude receives more than half of its total operating revenues (totaling approximately $167 million in 1998) from volunteer contributions raised by the American Lebanese Syrian Associated Charities ("ALSAC"), a not-for-profit foundation established in 1957 that operates in support of St. Jude. For the six year period from 1994 through 1998, for example, approximately 55% of St. Jude's operating expenses (excluding depreciation) were covered through ALSAC's philanthropic support. The remainder of its operating funds comes from third party payers (including Medicaid and CHAMPUS[5]), research grants (including grants from the National Institutes of Health), and investments or other miscellaneous sources. For example, for fiscal year 1998, the revenue mix was as follows: philanthropy (51.4%), third party payers (28.3%), research grants (16.2%), and investments/other (4.1%). In general, third-party payments -- both public and private -- are insufficient to cover the patient care costs incurred by St. Jude for insured children. With respect to Federal program beneficiaries, for example, St. Jude expected to recover in fiscal year 1998 only about 25 cents for every dollar it incurred in patient care costs.

St. Jude also provides a significant amount of charity care for uninsured children, who comprise approximately 20% of its patient population. In fiscal year 1998, St. Jude provided the equivalent of approximately $20 million in medical care to these children, or roughly 12% of its total operating revenues. In addition, consistent with its research mission, St. Jude provides substantial experimental and investigational care that generally is not covered by Federal or private health insurance programs.

B. St. Jude's Billing Policy

Since its inception, St. Jude has never billed children or their families for any part of the cost of their medical care. This policy provides financial relief to families of children with chronic and severe diseases for whom the costs of care might otherwise be prohib-

[5] The Department of Defense CHAMPUS program has been renamed Tricare. For purposes of this advisory opinion, we will refer to the program as CHAMPUS.

itive and enhances participation in, and compliance with, St. Jude's research protocols.

Because its patient population is limited to children, very few of whom are eligible for Medicare coverage, St. Jude does not participate in the Medicare program. However, it bills Medicaid, which imposes no cost-sharing amounts on children under age eighteen,[6] and CHAMPUS. In total, for fiscal year 1998, St. Jude waived less than $20,000 in Medicaid and CHAMPUS deductibles and coinsurance amounts ($[x] for Medicaid and $[y] for CHAMPUS). These copayment amounts were owed in connection with approximately $6.3 million in Medicaid and CHAMPUS receipts (approximately $6.2 million from Medicaid and $115,000 from CHAMPUS). The costs for delivering services to this Federal patient population were almost $25.1 million, necessitating an infusion of significant philanthropic resources from ALSAC for these children.

St. Jude neither advertises nor markets the Billing Policy to prospective patients, their families, or referring physicians. Nor is the Billing Policy part of a price reduction agreement between St. Jude and any third-party payer. The Billing Policy applies to all patients, without regard to the reason for the patient's inpatient or outpatient visit, the length of the patient's hospital stay, or the patient's Diagnosis Related Group ("DRG") code or outpatient procedure. St. Jude does not claim amounts attributable to unbilled coinsurance as bad debt on its Federal program cost reports, and it does not shift these costs to other third-party payers in the form of higher rates or charges.

C. The St. Jude Affiliated Hospitals

Historically, to avail themselves of St. Jude's cutting edge research and treatment, children and their families have had to be at St. Jude. In many cases, this has meant that children and families have had to relocate temporarily to Memphis, sometimes on multiple

---

[6] The Act generally permits states to impose "nominal" cost-sharing requirements on Medicaid beneficiaries; however, no cost-sharing amounts are allowed for individuals under age 18. *See* 42 U.S.C. § 1396o; 42 C.F.R. § 447.53(b)(1) (1998). St. Jude treats a limited number of patients above age 18, primarily young people undergoing extended treatments. The Medicaid statute permits states to exercise several options concerning coinsurance and deductibles. In some states, the restriction on cost-sharing could extend to age 21. *See id.* The relevant rules are contained in the Medicaid state plan for the state in which the Medicaid recipient resides. *See* 42 C.F.R. § 435.403.

occasions, resulting in a significant financial burden (sometimes including lost jobs for parents needing extended leave) and disruption to family life, including separation of sick children from parents and siblings.

To expand the number of children receiving St. Jude services and to ease the financial and other burdens associated with participating in St. Jude-sponsored research, St. Jude has entered into affiliation arrangements with several providers in the Mid-South region of the country. Pursuant to these affiliations, St. Jude clinics are established at the affiliated facility; eligible children can participate in St. Jude's research program and receive treatment and monitoring through the clinics. In some cases, children will receive all of their medical care at the local facility; in other cases, children will receive some care at the local facility, but will also travel to St. Jude in Memphis to receive specialized care not available locally, such as molecular diagnosis, bone marrow transplants, and limb salvage procedures.

Application of the Billing Policy by two affiliates is also the subject of this advisory opinion. The requesting affiliates are Hospital A ("Hospital A"), a not-for-profit children's hospital in City A, State A, and Hospital B ("Hospital B"), a not-for-profit acute care facility in City B, State B. Hospital A and Hospital B are collectively the "Affiliates" for purposes of this opinion.

Each Affiliate has entered into one or more agreements with St. Jude to provide pediatric oncology services locally under the auspices of St. Jude.[7] The two Affiliate arrangements have common elements. Both involve the establishment of a distinct pediatric oncology clinic for "St. Jude Patients" being treated at the Affiliate. "St. Jude Patients" are patients who have been accepted at the St. Jude-affiliated clinic based on the same criteria that apply to patients enrolled and treated at St. Jude. In 1998, each Affiliate admitted approximately 50 St. Jude Patients. Like children treated

[7] In general, the Affiliate arrangements involve various services, management, and rental agreements. St. Jude and the Affiliates have certified that all compensation under these agreements represents, and will continue to represent, fair market value in an arms-length transaction and is not and will not be based on the volume or value of business generated between the parties. The Billing Policy is the sole subject of this advisory opinion; we express no opinion about any other agreements between or among the Requesters or any other parties, including, but not limited to, agreements with physicians affiliated with any of the Requesters.

at St. Jude, most St. Jude Patients will be enrolled on a St. Jude, CCG, or POG protocol, although some children for whom these protocols are not appropriate may be treated under pre-established treatment plans.

St. Jude will review and monitor all treatment provided at the Affiliates' clinics and ensure compliance with eligibility criteria and protocol requirements. Each Affiliate clinic will be staffed by a salaried physician who will act as a "gatekeeper" for all items and services provided to St. Jude Patients, reviewing and signing all orders and prescriptions for St. Jude Patients. At Hospital B, the gatekeeper physician will be employed by St. Jude. The gatekeeper physician at Hospital A will be a Hospital A employee. In both instances, the gatekeeper physicians' salaries will be set in advance annually and will not vary directly or indirectly based on the volume or value of items or services provided or ordered for St. Jude patients.[8]

D. The Billing Policy as Applied to the Affiliates

Pursuant to their agreements with St. Jude, the Affiliates follow St. Jude's Billing Policy and do not bill St. Jude Patients or their families. As with St. Jude, the Billing Policy is not advertised or marketed by the Affiliates to prospective patients or referring physicians. Nor is the Billing Policy part of a price reduction agreement between the Affiliates and any third-party payer. The Billing Policy applies to all St. Jude patients, regardless of the reason for the patient's inpatient or outpatient visit, the length of the patient's hospital stay, or the patient's DRG code or outpatient procedure. The Affiliates have certified that they do not claim amounts attributable to unbilled coinsurance as bad debt on their Medicare or Medicaid cost reports, and they do not shift these costs to other third-party payers through higher rates or charges. The Billing Policy will be disclosed to all third-party payers.[9]

[8] To ensure that this condition is satisfied, St. Jude has certified that it will obtain an annual certification from the Affiliates that will include a summary analysis of the annual compensation received by the gatekeeper physicians and that it will audit the operations of the Affiliates at two year intervals to confirm compliance with the compensation restrictions.

[9] Third-party payers will be informed of the Billing Policy. We express no opinion regarding the liability of any party under the False Claims Act or other legal authorities for any improper billing, claims submission, or other related conduct.

The Affiliates participate in the Medicare, Medicaid, and CHAMPUS programs. However, virtually all Federal health care program coinsurance amounts waived pursuant to the Billing Policy arise under Medicaid.[10] For example, for fiscal year 1998, Hospital A waived a total of [less than $600] in Medicaid copayments and no CHAMPUS copayments. Hospital B waived no Federal coinsurance amounts for any St. Jude Patients for the period from July 1997 through December 1998.[11]

ALSAC has agreed to pay all deductible and coinsurance amounts for St. Jude Patients enrolled at the Affiliates.[12] ALSAC anticipates that its copayment obligations, mostly on behalf of private pay patients, will equal approximately two percent of the Affiliates' gross revenues. The Affiliates will submit an itemized bill for such copayments to ALSAC on a quarterly basis, and ALSAC will pay such copayments in a timely manner. In connection with its coinsurance payment obligation and pursuant to the affiliation agreements, ALSAC and St. Jude will audit and monitor the Affiliates' utilization of services for St. Jude Patients.

II. ST. JUDE'S WAIVER POLICY IMPLICATES THE ANTI-KICKBACK STATUTE, BUT WILL NOT BE SUBJECT TO OIG SANCTIONS

A. Applicable Law and Guidance

The anti-kickback statute makes it a criminal offense knowingly and wilfully to offer, pay, solicit, or receive any remuneration to induce referrals of items or services reimbursable by Federal health

---

[10] For fiscal year 1998, Hospital A has reported a singular case of a Medicare disability beneficiary being treated for a malignant tumor for whom copayments were waived in the amount of [less than $3,000]. The patient was originally treated at St. Jude.

[11] Hospital B reported no Medicare or CHAMPUS patients for that period. It identified approximately 400 inpatient and outpatient occasions of service related to Medicaid patients. However, the Louisiana Medicaid program does not impose any deductible or coinsurance obligations. Hospital B reported having no out-of-state pediatric cancer patients who might be subject to coinsurance obligations.

[12] ALSAC will not cover other losses incurred by the Affiliates in connection with uninsured patients or patients obtaining procedures not covered by the patient's insurance. These patients will be treated in accordance with the Affiliates' existing charity care policies or they may be referred to St. Jude for treatment.

care programs. See section 1128B(b) of the Act. Where remuneration is paid purposefully to induce referrals of items or services paid for by a Federal health care program, the anti-kickback statute is violated. By its terms, the statute ascribes liability to parties on both sides of an impermissible "kickback" transaction. For purposes of the anti-kickback statute, "remuneration" includes the transfer of anything of value, in cash or in-kind, directly or indirectly, covertly or overtly.

The statute has been interpreted to cover any arrangement where one purpose of the remuneration is to obtain money for referral of services or to induce further referrals. *United States v. Kats,* 871 F. 2d 105 (9th Cir. 1989); *United States v. Greber,* 760 F. 2d 68 (3rd Cir.), *cert. denied,* 476 U.S. 988 (1985). Violation of the statute constitutes a felony punishable by a maximum fine of $25,000, imprisonment up to five years or both. Conviction will also lead to automatic exclusion from Federal health care programs, including Medicare and Medicaid. This Office may also initiate administrative proceedings to exclude persons from Federal health care programs or to impose civil monetary penalties for fraud, kickbacks, and other prohibited activities under sections 1128(b)(7) and 1128A(a)(7) of the Act.[13]

Waivers of Federal health care program coinsurance and deductible amounts implicate the anti-kickback statute because such waivers may constitute an inducement to beneficiaries to use services in exchange for something of value, i.e., the forgiveness of a financial obligation.

The Department of Health and Human Services has published "safe harbor" regulations that define practices that are not subject to the anti-kickback statute because such practices would unlikely result in fraud or abuse. *See* section 1128B(b)(3) of the Act; 42 C.F.R. § 1001.952. The safe harbors set forth specific conditions that, if met, assure entities involved of not being prosecuted or sanctioned for the arrangement qualifying for the safe harbor. However, safe harbor protection is only afforded to those arrangements that precisely meet all of the conditions set forth in the safe harbor. Potentially applicable here is the safe harbor for waivers of inpatient Part A coinsurance and deductibles where the Medicare program

---

[13] Because both the criminal and administrative sanctions related to the anti-kickback implications of the Arrangement are based on violations of the anti-kickback statute, the analysis for the purposes of this advisory opinion is the same under both.

pays a hospital under the prospective payment system. See 42 C.F.R. § 1001.952(k).

In a Special Fraud Alert issued in May 1991, we stated that providers who routinely waive Medicare Part B coinsurance and deductibles may be held liable under the anti-kickback statute. *See* Special Fraud Alert, 59 Fed. Reg. 242 (published in the *Federal Register* in 1994).[14] When providers forgive financial obligations for reasons other than genuine financial hardship of the particular patient, they may be unlawfully inducing the patient to purchase items or services in violation of the anti-kickback statute's proscription against offering or paying something of value as an inducement to generate business payable by a Federal health care program. We noted that waivers of coinsurance and deductibles may make beneficiaries less conscientious health care consumers, selecting services simply because they are free, rather than because they are medically necessary. Thus, routine waivers of Medicare Part B coinsurance and deductibles are suspect under the anti-kickback statute.

B. Analysis

1. The Billing Policy with Respect to Part A Inpatient Coinsurance Does Not Meet the Safe Harbor Requirements.

The safe harbor for routine Part A coinsurance waivers applies where a hospital is paid by Medicare on a prospective payment basis, and the hospital satisfies three standards enumerated in the regulation at 42 C.F.R. § 1001.952(k). By its terms, the safe harbor does not apply to waivers of Medicaid or CHAMPUS coinsurance amounts. Therefore, the safe harbor does not protect the Billing Policy.

2. The Billing Policy as Practiced by St. Jude Will Not Result in OIG Sanctions Under the Anti-Kickback Statute.

Although the Billing Policy as practiced by St. Jude might violate the anti-kickback statute if the requisite intent were present, we conclude that we will not seek to impose sanctions on St. Jude arising under the anti-kickback statute in the particular circumstances presented here.

---

[14] The Special Fraud Alert specifically addressed charge-based providers; however, the Fraud Alert notes that it should not be construed as endorsing, by omission, routine waivers of Medicare copayments by providers paid under prospective payment or cost-based systems.

This conclusion rests in the first instance on a recognition that St. Jude's Billing Policy is a singular vestige of St. Jude's founding and continuing charitable research mission. The Billing Policy predates the Medicare and Medicaid programs and has been consistently applied to all patients. Moreover, the Billing Policy is an integral component of St. Jude's extra-ordinary commitment to charitable care and medical research. This institutional history merits a deference to the Billing Policy that would be inappropriate for an identical policy implemented today.

Standing alone, an institutional history will not protect an otherwise improper practice from sanctions under the anti-kickback statute. In this case, however, that history is conjoined with certain aspects of St. Jude's organization that, taken together, reduce the risk that the Billing Policy will result in overutilization or unnecessary services. Most significantly, 99% of physician care at St. Jude is provided by salaried physicians whose compensation does not vary directly or indirectly based on the volume or value of items or services they order or perform and who do not have outside medical practices; the remaining 1% of services are provided by contracted specialists whose compensation is fixed in advance. This compensation arrangement significantly reduces any personal financial incentive to provide unnecessary services to patients. In addition, the highly specialized services provided by St. Jude reduce the likelihood of self-referral to the hospital or its physicians.[15]

Finally, the fact that St. Jude's primary mission is the research of childhood diseases presents the following special considerations:

- Because much of the children's treatment is dictated by peer-reviewed clinical protocols, there is some protection against overutilization of services.
- Given the significant additional burdens on patients of participating in St. Jude's research, waiving copayments is a reasonable means of inducing participation and on-going compliance with protocol requirements.
- St. Jude's research results in a substantial public benefit.
- The Billing Policy, which is uniformly applied to all patients, affects very few Federal health care program beneficiaries, and

[15] St. Jude has certified that the Billing Policy is not advertised or marketed to patients or physicians. However, it is likely that many pediatricians and oncologists practicing in areas from which St. Jude draws patients may be aware of St. Jude's Billing Policy, either from experience with St. Jude or as a result of ALSAC activities on behalf of St. Jude.

the amounts of Federal copayments waived are relatively insubstantial.

Based on the totality of these factors, including the potential benefits of the Billing Policy and the safeguards described in the preceding three paragraphs, we conclude that we will not subject St. Jude to sanctions arising under the anti-kickback statute in connection with the Billing Policy.[16]

2. The Billing Policy as Practiced by the Affiliates Will Not Result in OIG Sanctions Under the Anti-Kickback Statute.

The Billing Policy as applied by the Affiliates requires a somewhat different analysis. As a technical matter, there is no waiver of copayments by the Affiliates, since ALSAC is accepting responsibility to pay for any applicable copayments.[17] Nonetheless, the Billing Policy could implicate the anti-kickback statute, because it provides a financial benefit to St. Jude Patients being treated at the Affiliates and could be an inducement to self-refer. In addition, the Billing Policy, including the payment of copayments by ALSAC, could potentially induce referrals by the Affiliates to St. Jude.

Turning to the first of our concerns -- whether the Billing Policy is an inducement to patients to self-refer -- our analysis is essentially the same as for the Billing Policy at St. Jude. Safeguards at the Affiliates are comparable to those at St. Jude, including the fact that patients can only be seen if referred by a community physician; that they must meet St. Jude's medical eligibility criteria, including protocol requirements; and that the scope of services is generally governed by protocols. As at St. Jude, the number of St. Jude Patients for whom copayments are waived is small in comparison to the total number of St. Jude Patients, and there is a strong public benefit from the research promoted by the affiliation arrangements,

---

[16] We note that 11 U.S.C. § 1079 appears to permit waivers of CHAMPUS copayments in situations similar to those present here. Given our conclusion, we need not consider whether that statute applies to the Billing Policy as practiced by St. Jude.

[17] ALSAC is a 501(c)(3) charitable entity unrelated to the Affiliates. We note that a similar payment arrangement between ALSAC and St. Jude, which are related, would be analyzed as a routine waiver of coinsurance, as it would have the practical effect of simply moving money from one pocket to another. Such payments would provide no meaningful check on potential overutilization.

including faster research results due to enrollment of more patients in St. Jude's research program.

Our second concern is with potential inducements to the Affiliates to refer patients to St. Jude. By arranging for ALSAC to cover patients' coinsurance obligations, St. Jude confers a benefit on the Affiliates that, if done with the intent to induce referrals, could potentially violate the anti-kickback statute. By way of example, an arrangement between a hospital and a physician whereby the hospital pays the physician's patients' copayments to induce referrals from the physician (who could, in turn, advertise the arrangement to attract patients or simply avoid collection costs, including bad debt) would implicate the anti-kickback statute.

Three factors suggest that the Billing Policy, although potentially remuneration to the Affiliates, poses a minimal risk of Federal health care program fraud or abuse in the circumstances presented. *First,* the benefit, if any, to the Affiliates of ALSAC's assumption of the copayment obligation is minimal, since it merely puts the Affiliates in the same position they would have been in absent the affiliation with St. Jude, i.e., able to collect copayments for services rendered to pediatric cancer patients. While the arrangement may result in some avoided costs for the Affiliates (e.g., bad debt, costs of collection), such amounts are likely to be relatively small and speculative. This benefit, if any, is likely to be far less significant to the Affiliates than the mere affiliation with St. Jude itself, which enables Affiliates to make St. Jude's treatment and research available locally. Such benefit is separate and apart from the Billing Policy.

Second, while we cannot determine a party's intent, we think it is implausible that St. Jude would arrange for ALSAC to pay copayments in order to generate referrals of Federal program business from the Affiliates. Simply put, if St. Jude wanted referrals of children from the Affiliates it would not have entered into the affiliations in the first place. In fact, the affiliation arrangements are designed to *minimize* referrals to St. Jude, making St. Jude's research more economical by reducing costs associated with patient care and expanding participation in research studies through a more convenient and less burdensome arrangement for patients.

Third, there is little risk that referrals from the Affiliates, if any, would result in inappropriate utilization or increased program costs at St. Jude, since the Affiliates have no interest in referring children to St. Jude unless they cannot provide the services themselves, and virtually all children referred to St. Jude will be subject to research protocols. Of the children who are referred, the majority typically will need experimental and investigational procedures not generally covered by Federal or private insurance. Moreover, St. Jude and ALSAC have a significant financial incentive to monitor utilization for St. Jude Patients so as to keep ALSAC's copayments to a minimum.

For all of these reasons and because there is a substantial public benefit from expanded research into childhood cancer, we conclude that the OIG will not subject the Affiliates to sanctions arising under the anti-kickback statute in connection with the Billing Policy.

III. NEITHER ST. JUDE NOR THE AFFILIATES WILL BE SUBJECT TO CIVIL MONETARY PENALTIES UNDER SECTION 1128A(a)(5) OF THE ACT

Section 1128A(a)(5) of the Act prohibits a person from offering or transferring remuneration to a beneficiary that such person knows or should know is likely to influence the beneficiary to order items or services from a particular provider or supplier for which payment may be made under the Medicare and Medicaid programs. "Remuneration" is defined as including the waiver of coinsurance and deductible amounts, with exceptions for certain financial hardship waivers, which are not prohibited. The Billing Policy as practiced by both St. Jude and the Affiliates could potentially influence Medicaid beneficiaries to seek treatment at St. Jude or an Affiliate and thus potentially implicates section 1128A(a)(5). However, for the reasons stated above in Section II(B), the OIG will not subject St. Jude or the Affiliates to sanctions under section 1128A(a)(5) of the Act in connection with the Billing Policy.

IV. CONCLUSION

For the above reasons and based on the facts as certified in the request letter and supplemental submissions, we conclude: (i) that the Billing Policy could potentially generate prohibited remuneration under the anti-kickback statute, if the requisite intent to induce referrals were present, but that the OIG will not subject the Billing Policy as practiced by St. Jude or the Affiliates (as described in the request letter and supplemental submissions) to sanctions arising under the anti-kickback statute pursuant to sections 1128(b)(7) or 1128A(a)(7) of the Act; and (ii) that the OIG will not subject St. Jude or the Affiliates to sanctions under section 1128A(a)(5) of the Act in connection with the Billing Policy.

V. LIMITATIONS

The limitations applicable to this opinion include the following:

- This advisory opinion is issued only to St. Jude Children's Research Hospital, Hospital A, and Hospital B, the requesters of this opinion. This advisory opinion has no application, and cannot be relied upon, by any other individual or entity.
- This advisory opinion may not be introduced into evidence in any matter involving an entity or individual that is not a Requester to this opinion.
- This advisory opinion is applicable only to the statutory provisions specifically noted above. No opinion is herein expressed or implied with respect to the application of any other Federal, state, or local statute, rule, regulation, ordinance, or other law that may be applicable to the Billing Policy.
- This advisory opinion will not bind or obligate any agency other than the U.S. Department of Health and Human Services.
- This advisory opinion is limited in scope to the specific arrangement described in this letter and has no applicability to other arrangements, even those that appear similar in nature or scope.
- No opinion is expressed herein regarding the liability of any party under the False Claims Act or other legal authorities for any improper billing, claims submission, cost reporting, or related conduct.

This opinion is also subject to any additional limitations set forth at 42 C.F.R. Part 1008.

The OIG will not proceed against the Requesters with respect to any action that is part of the Billing Policy taken in good faith reliance upon this advisory opinion as long as all of the material facts have been fully, completely, and accurately presented and the Billing Policy in practice comports with the information provided. The OIG reserves the right to reconsider the questions and issues raised in this advisory opinion and, where the public interest requires, rescind, modify, or terminate this opinion. In the event that this advisory opinion is modified or terminated, the OIG will not proceed against the Requesters with respect to any action taken in good faith reliance upon this advisory opinion, where all of the relevant facts were fully, completely, and accurately presented and where such action was promptly discontinued upon notification of the modification or termination of this advisory opinion. An advisory opinion may be rescinded only if the relevant and material facts have not been fully, completely, and accurately disclosed to the OIG.

Sincerely,

/s/

D. McCarty Thornton

Chief Counsel to the Inspector General

APPENDIX F39

Advisory Opinion No. 99-7, July 9, 1999

Whether an across-the-board waiver of any out-of-pocket beneficiary copayments for medical services covered by the National Eye Care Project constitutes grounds for the imposition of a sanction under section 1128A(a)(5) of the Act.

[*We have redacted specific information regarding the requestor and certain potentially privileged, confidential or financial information associated with the individual or entity, unless otherwise specified by the requestor.*]

Date Issued: June 30, 1999

Date Posted: July 9, 1999

[Name and Address Redacted]

Re: [Name and Title Redacted]
National Eye Care Project
P.O. Box 429098
San Francisco, CA 94142

Re: OIG Advisory Opinion 99–7

Dear [Name Redacted] and [Name Redacted]:

We are writing in response to your request for an advisory opinion concerning the National Eye Care Project ("NECP") and Dr. A's participation in the NECP. A key component of the NECP involves an insurance only billing policy (i.e., an across-the-board waiver of any out-of-pocket beneficiary copayments) for medical services covered by the NECP. Specifically, you have requested confirmation that this policy does not constitute grounds for the imposition of a sanction under section 1128A(a)(5) of the Social Security Act (the "Act"), which prohibits the offering of inducements to beneficiaries in order to influence their selection of a provider for Medicare or Medicaid covered services.

In issuing this opinion, we have relied solely on the facts and information presented to us. We have not undertaken an independent investigation of such information. This opinion is limited to the facts presented. If material facts have not been disclosed or have been misrepresented, this opinion is without force and effect.

Based on the information provided, the insurance only billing practice (to the extent it results in waivers of coinsurance obligations for eligible Medicare or Medicaid patients referred by the NECP) constitutes prohibited remuneration within the meaning of section 1128A(a)(5). Notwithstanding, for the reasons set forth below and subject to certain conditions described below, in the particular circumstances presented, the OIG will not subject the NECP or Dr. A (as a participating NECP ophthalmologist) to sanctions under section 1128A(a)(5).[1]

This opinion may not be relied on by any person other than the addressees and is further qualified as set out in Part IV below and in 42 C.F.R. Part 1008.

I. FACTUAL BACKGROUND

The National Eye Care Project is a public outreach program that provides medical eye care for eligible senior citizens. The program began in 1983 and is cosponsored by the Foundation of the American Academy of Ophthalmology ("Foundation") and the Knights Templar Eye Foundation, Inc. Dr. A is the [title redacted] and is one of the participating ophthalmologists.

The NECP encourages elderly citizens to protect their eyesight by having a comprehensive eye exam and any needed treatment. The Foundation has set up a referral network of ophthalmologists who agree to provide a comprehensive medical eye examination and up to twelve months of follow-up care for any condition diagnosed at the initial visit without any out-of-pocket cost to the NECP patients. The NECP does not cover eyeglasses, prescription drugs, hospital services, or services of other medical professionals.[2]

[1] We express no opinion regarding the liability of any party under the False Claims Act or other legal authorities for any improper billing, claims submission, or other related conduct.

[2] If hospital care is needed, the participating ophthalmologist requests that the hospital provide the services without charge. We express no opinion with respect to this practice.

Participating ophthalmologists agree to accept insurance reimbursement as payment in full for care rendered to the NECP patients; no copayments or deductibles (collectively referred to as "coinsurance") are collected from any patient for the treatment of any condition diagnosed at the initial visit. If the treatment continues for more than one year after the initial diagnosis, a participating ophthalmologist may waive the coinsurance only if he or she determines that the patient is in financial need according to an individualized need determination performed by the ophthalmologist. If a patient has no insurance coverage, the participating ophthalmologist will render eye care without charge.

The NECP is promoted through public service announcements by the Foundation. Individual ophthalmologists do not refer patients to, or advertise their participation in, the NECP. The advertisements encourage the elderly to call an 800 number maintained by the Foundation, either for free eye care information or for referral to a participating ophthalmologist. A caller to the Foundation's 800 number who wishes to see an ophthalmologist is screened for eligibility. Individuals are eligible if they are U.S. citizens or legal residents, age 65 and older, who have not seen an ophthalmologist in the past three years.[3] In most cases, the NECP will only refer a caller once.

Once a person is determined to be eligible, he or she is assigned to a participating ophthalmologist by a computer program that uses zip codes and geographic proximity to match the person with a nearby participating ophthalmologist. Computer assignments are made on a rotating basis; a physician only receives a second patient after all other participating ophthalmologists in that area have been assigned a first patient. In addition, participating ophthalmologists cannot examine or treat more than fifteen new NECP patients in any one calendar year. The only exception to this limit is for participating ophthalmologists practicing in health professional shortage areas or medically underserved areas. Consequently, the number of NECP patients any participating ophthalmologist sees is unlikely to constitute a significant proportion of his or her practice.

The NECP has received national recognition during its sixteen year history, including the President's Citation for Private Sector Initiative in 1986 and 1988, the American Medical Association's

---

[3] Individuals enrolled in prepaid health care plans or who receive care through the armed forces or Veterans Administration hospitals are not eligible.

President's Citation for Service to the Public, the American Association of Retired Persons Award for Public Service, and more than thirty other citations and commendations from government agencies.

Prior to the initial implementation of the NECP, the Foundation consulted with the OIG to assure that the program would not violate the anti-kickback statute. In a letter dated October 30, 1984, then Inspector General Richard P. Kusserow approved the NECP as long as: (i) all ophthalmologists are free to participate; (ii) the ophthalmologists who participate are aware of Medicare reimbursement policy for ophthalmological services; (iii) referrals by the project to ophthalmologists are made on a rotating basis; and (iv) the number of beneficiaries for whom coinsurance is waived does not constitute a significant proportion of any one ophthalmologist's practice. The NECP has certified that it is in compliance with these requirements.

Prior to enactment of the Health Insurance Portability and Accountability Act of 1996 ("HIPAA"), the NECP requested that participating ophthalmologists waive the coinsurance for eligible patients referred to them by the NECP without performing any financial need determination. However, as of January 1, 1997, when HIPAA took effect, the NECP modified its program to comply with section 231(h) of HIPAA, now section 1128A(a)(5) of the Act (described below), and narrowed the focus of its advertising and outreach efforts to target only seniors who would meet financial need criteria. Information sheets were modified to read: "For seniors *without the means to pay,* the fees for the examination and treatment are waived." (emphasis added). When potential patients telephone the NECP, operators now perform a financial need analysis before the patients are referred to a participating physician. As a result of this and other factors (such as a decrease in advertising by the NECP), the number of callers dropped from 5,698 in 1996 to 1,913 in 1997.

The NECP has requested an opinion as to whether its former practice of insurance only billing for all patients irrespective of financial need would run afoul of section 1128A(a)(5) of the Act.

II. THE NECP'S WAIVER OF COINSURANCE IMPLICATES THE CIVIL MONETARY PENALTY PROHIBITING INDUCEMENTS TO BENEFICIARIES

Applicable Law

Section 1128A(a)(5) of the Act prohibits a person from offering or transferring remuneration to any individual eligible for benefits under Medicare or Medicaid that such person knows or should know is likely to influence such individual to order or receive from a particular provider, practitioner, or supplier any item or service for which payment may be made, in whole or in part, under Medicare or Medicaid. For purposes of this section, "remuneration" is defined as including the waiver of coinsurance amounts, except in certain narrowly defined circumstances, such as copayment waivers that are not advertised, not routine, and made after a good faith financial determination. The definition of remuneration also includes an exception for certain incentives given to individuals to promote the delivery of preventive care. *See* Section 1128A(i)(6)(D) of the Act.[4]

Analysis

The NECP clearly falls within the activities proscribed by section 1128A(a)(5) of the Act. Congress specifically included waivers of coinsurance in its statutory definition of "remuneration." However laudatory the goal, the NECP uses the promise of free care to motivate otherwise reluctant patients to undergo eye examination and treatment (if needed). In short, the patient visits the *particular* ophthalmologist identified by the NECP because the patient is told that the ophthalmologist will waive any out-of-pocket costs associated with the treatment.

The statutory proscription in section 1128A(a)(5) of the Act reflects serious programmatic concerns with waivers of coinsurance. We published a Special Fraud Alert ("Fraud Alert") in May 1991, which stated that providers who routinely waive Medicare Part B coinsurance may be held liable under the anti-kickback statute. *See* Special Fraud Alert, *reprinted in* 59 Fed. Reg. 242 (1994). Although the Fraud Alert pre-dates the passage of section 1128A(a)(5) and

---

[4] The other permissible exceptions to the civil money penalty are: (i) failure to collect after reasonable collection efforts; (ii) differentials in coinsurance as a part of a benefit plan design; and (iii) payment practices safe harbored under section 1128B(b)(3) of the Act or in regulations under section 42 C.F.R. § 1001.952.

therefore addresses only the potential problems under the anti-kickback and false claims statutes, the programmatic concerns are identical. When providers forgive financial obligations for reasons other than genuine financial hardship of the particular patient, they may be inducing the patient to use items or services that are unnecessary, simply because they are free. Thus, except in those special cases specifically excepted from section 1128A(a)(5), Medicare Part B waivers of coinsurance are highly problematic.

However, for the reasons set forth below, we conclude that we will not impose sanctions on the NECP under section 1128A(a)(5) of the Act in the particular circumstances presented here. We stress that, standing alone, none of the factors below would assure us that the NECP program is not prone to fraud and abuse, nor would we necessarily reach the same conclusion if we were reviewing the NECP for the first time. However, because of the NECP's reliance on prior written approval from the Inspector General, coupled with the unique nature of the program and the safeguards the NECP has put in place, we will not impose sanctions.

First, our determination is based on our recognition that the NECP program was created nearly fifteen years ago in reliance on explicit approval from this Office. When the NECP was first developed, its counsel consulted the OIG and, on October 30, 1984, then Inspector General Kusserow issued a letter to the NECP that approved the project, as long as (i) all ophthalmologists are free to participate; (ii) the ophthalmologists who participate are aware of Medicare reimbursement policy for ophthalmological services; (iii) referrals by the project to ophthalmologists are made on a rotating basis; and (iv) the number of beneficiaries for whom coinsurance is waived does not constitute a significant proportion of any one ophthalmologist's practice. The NECP has operated its program in reliance on this approval.

Second, we are not aware of any documented overutilization by participating ophthalmologists or any other documented abuses associated with the NECP during its fifteen years of operation. While no demonstration of harm is required by section 1128A(a)(5) or many of the other health care fraud and abuse authorities, in this particular instance -- where the NECP sought and received official written approval in advance of operation and has complied with the terms of that approval -- it is reasonable to take the absence of any evidence of abuse into consideration.

Third, while the NECP is over-inclusive in that the waiver of coinsurance is not limited to the financially needy, the NECP has nevertheless provided a significant benefit to financially needy individuals who may not otherwise have sought or received care. The NECP has been recognized by, and received awards from, the public and private sectors for its benefits to public welfare including recognition by several United States Presidents and the American Medical Association. Congressional recognition of the value of the NECP and of the inadvertent impact of section 1128A(a)(5) on the NECP was a major impetus in the recent amendment specifically confirming the Secretary's discretion under section 1128D(b)(2)(E) of the Act to exempt certain practices that would otherwise be prohibited under section 1128A(a)(5). *See* Pub. L. No. 105-277 (1998); 144 Cong. Rec. H10243, 10253 & 10258 (1998) ("HHS is authorized to issue an advisory opinion permitting waiver of [the coinsurance and deductibles] requirements with regard to [services provided by the NECP].") (statement of Rep. Stearns).

Fourth, at least some parts of the comprehensive eye examination given to the NECP patients on their initial visit constitute preventive care services and would be exempt from the definition of remuneration in any event. *See* Section 1128A(i)(6)(D) of the Act.

Finally, the benefit to any one ophthalmologist is limited. The rotating basis upon which the NECP pairs eligible patients with ophthalmologists greatly reduces the risk that an ophthalmologist participating in the NECP could benefit in any significant way from the NECP referrals, thus minimizing any risk of fraud and abuse. Participating ophthalmologists do not advertise that they participate in the NECP and cannot refer patients to themselves through the NECP. A computer assigns the eligible patients on a rotating basis. Each participating ophthalmologist in a location (defined by zip code and geographic proximity) receives one patient before any other participating ophthalmologist in that area receives a second patient.

Moreover, ophthalmologists cannot examine or treat more than fifteen new NECP patients in any one calendar year.[5] The only exceptions to this policy are for ophthalmologists practicing in health professional shortage areas or medically underserved areas.

---

[5] We do not intend the fifteen patient cap to create a *de minimis* exception to the prohibition on waivers of coinsurance under section 1128A(a)(5) of the Act. We reiterate that this factor must be read in conjunction with all of the reasons set forth in this opinion.

Consequently, the number of NECP patients is not likely to constitute a significant percentage of any participating ophthalmologist's practice

III. CONCLUSION

For the above reasons and based on the facts as certified in the request letter and supplemental submissions, we conclude that the insurance only billing practice (to the extent it results in waivers of coinsurance obligations for eligible Medicare or Medicaid patients referred by the NECP) constitutes prohibited remuneration within the meaning of section 1128A(a)(5). Notwithstanding, for the reasons and subject to the conditions set forth above, in the particular circumstances presented, the OIG will not subject the NECP or Dr. A (as a participating NECP ophthalmologist) to sanctions under section 1128A(a)(5) of the Act.

IV. LIMITATIONS

The limitations applicable to this opinion include the following:

- This advisory opinion is issued only to Dr. A, and the National Eye Care Project, the requesters of this opinion. This advisory opinion has no application to, and cannot be relied upon by, any other individual or entity.
- This advisory opinion may not be introduced into evidence in any matter involving an entity or individual that is not a requester to this opinion.
- This advisory opinion is applicable only to the statutory provisions specifically noted above. No opinion is herein expressed or implied with respect to the application of any other Federal, state, or local statute, rule, regulation, ordinance, or other law that may be applicable to the NECP or Dr. A.
- This advisory opinion will not bind or obligate any agency other than the U.S. Department of Health and Human Services.
- This advisory opinion is limited in scope to the specific arrangement described in this letter and has no applicability to other arrangements, even those that appear similar in nature or scope.
- No opinion is expressed herein regarding the liability of any party under the False Claims Act or other legal authorities for any improper billing, claims submission, cost reporting, or related conduct.

This opinion is also subject to any additional limitations set forth at 42 C.F.R. Part 1008.

The OIG will not proceed against the requesters with respect to any action that is part of the NECP taken in good faith reliance upon this advisory opinion as long as all of the material facts have been fully, completely, and accurately presented, and the NECP and Dr. A comply with the certifications provided. The OIG reserves the right to reconsider the questions and issues raised in this advisory opinion and, where the public interest requires, rescind, modify, or terminate this opinion. In the event that this advisory opinion is modified or terminated, the OIG will not proceed against the requesters with respect to any action taken in good faith reliance upon this advisory opinion, where all of the relevant facts were fully, completely, and accurately presented and where such action was promptly discontinued upon notification of the modification or termination of this advisory opinion. An advisory opinion may be rescinded only if the relevant and material facts have not been fully, completely, and accurately disclosed to the OIG.

Sincerely,

/s/

D. McCarty Thornton

Chief Counsel to the Inspector General

APPENDIX F40

Advisory Opinion No. 99-8, July 6, 1999

Whether an arrangement to provide for personal appearances by podiatrists to certain retail stores constitutes grounds for sanctions under the anti-kickback statute.

[*We have redacted specific information regarding the requestor and certain potentially privileged, confidential or financial information associated with the individual or entity, unless otherwise specified by the requestor.*]

Issued: July 6, 1999

Posted: July 13, 1999

[Name and Address Redacted]

Re: OIG Advisory Opinion 99–8

Dear [Name Redacted]:

We are writing in response to your request for an advisory opinion concerning Company A's arrangements with Company B, to facilitate a program of professional training for Company B's shoe sales associates and to arrange for personal appearances by podiatrists at Company B's shoe departments (collectively, the "Arrangement"). Specifically, you have inquired whether the Arrangement constitutes grounds for sanctions under the anti-kickback statute, section 1128B(b) of the Social Security Act (the "Act"), in the circumstances presented.

In issuing this opinion, we have relied solely on the facts and information presented to us. We have not undertaken an independent investigation of such information. This opinion is limited to the facts presented. If material facts have not been disclosed or have been misrepresented, this opinion is without force and effect.

Based on the information provided, we conclude that the Arrangement would potentially generate prohibited remuneration under the anti-kickback statute, if the requisite intent to induce referrals were present, but that, based on the totality of the facts and the safeguards present in the Arrangement, the Office of Inspector General ("OIG") will not subject Company A to sanctions for violations of the anti-kickback statute pursuant to sections 1128(b)(7) or 1128A(a)(7) of the Act in connection with the Arrangement, as described and certified in your request letter and supplemental submissions.

This opinion may not be relied on by any persons other than Company A, the requester of this opinion, and is further qualified as set out in Part V below and in 42 C.F.R. Part 1008.

I. FACTUAL BACKGROUND

A. The Parties

Company A ("Company A") is a State D corporation engaged in the business of professional training and publishing. Company A is a wholly-owned subsidiary of Company C, another State D corporation. Company A is not related to any other party to, or participant in, the Arrangement.

Company B, ("Company B") is a major discount retailer and retailer of shoes. [Further identifying information redacted.]

B. The Arrangement

The Arrangement consists of two parts, each more fully described below. The first part, the "X Program", is a professional training program for Company B's shoe sales managers and associates. The second part, the "Y Network", is a program related to the X Program through which Company A assembles a network of podiatrists across the country to make scheduled appearances at Company B's shoe departments to advise and consult with Company B's customers and shoe sales associates.

1. The X Program

In May 1997, Company A entered into a pilot agreement (the "Initial Agreement") with Company B to test the X Program in selected stores. Under the Initial Agreement, Company A agreed, among other things, to do the following:

- License the trademark "X" to Company B on an exclusive basis.

- Develop "learning criteria" for shoe sales managers and associates in the areas of human anatomy of the foot and shoe design function.
- Create computer-based training modules for Company B's shoe sales managers and associates and develop achievement tests for persons who complete the training.
- Design lapel pins and certificates of merit to be manufactured or purchased by Company B and distributed to successfully trained employees.
- Arrange for certification of the training program by a nationally recognized podiatric organization.
- Design in-store posters to promote the program to customers and employees, to be printed, distributed, and placed by Company B.

For its part, Company B agreed to pay Company A certain fees for its services based upon the achievement of certain benchmarks in the development of the X Program and the number of stores participating. In addition, Company B committed to support the program through public relations and in-store awareness campaigns for both its employees and customers.

According to materials submitted by Company A, Company B anticipated that the X Program would better train shoe department sales associates, reduce sales associate turnover rates through greater employee job satisfaction, improve customer service, build consumer confidence, create consumer awareness, familiarize participating podiatrists with Company B's shoes, and ultimately increase shoe sales and profits.

The pilot program proved successful, with improved retention of shoe department sales associates and positive customer feedback. In July 1998, Company B and Company A entered into a second agreement (the "Implementing Agreement") to continue and expand the X Program at Company B stores on an exclusive basis for two years. In addition to its existing obligations under the Initial Agreement, Company A agreed to assist Company B with periodic upgrades of its computer training modules and, with Company B's "reasonable assistance", to create a "referral service" of podiatrists located near the participating Company B stores (the Y Network, described below).[1]

---

[1] The concept of a podiatrist "referral service" first appeared in the Initial Agreement, but no such referral service was created pursuant to that agreement.

Under the Implementing Agreement, Company B agreed to pay Company A an exclusive licensing fee of $[redacted] per year and a program fee of $[redacted] per year, subject to certain adjustments tied to reductions in turnover of sales associates. Company A has represented that all fees paid, or to be paid, by Company B under the Initial and Implementing Agreements represent fair market value for the services rendered or to be rendered by Company A.[2]

1. The Y Network

The Y Network ("Y Network") is a program designed to create a pool of participating podiatrists to make scheduled appearances in Company B's shoe departments, as contemplated in the Implementing Agreement for the X Program. Participating podiatrists enter into one-year agreements with Company A pursuant to which they agree to provide one four-hour appearance each month at an assigned Company B location.[3] The monthly in-store appearances are publicized by a plaque or posters in the store identifying the podiatrist and the date and time of his or her next appearance. In addition to the monthly in-store appearances, the podiatrist may participate from time to time in special events, including product knowledge demonstrations. During the scheduled appearances, the podiatrist answers questions from Company B's customers and employees regarding foot care and foot problems and conducts brief "foot screenings" in conjunction with answering questions.[4] As an additional service, some podiatrists provide free blood pressure screenings to Company B's customers.[5]

If a customer or employee asks a podiatrist about his or her private practice, the podiatrist is required to provide a written notice with

---

[2] We are precluded by statute from opining on whether fair market value shall be or was paid for goods, services, or property. *See* 42 U.S.C. § 1320a-7d(b)(3)(A). For purposes of this advisory opinion, we rely on the requesting party's certification of fair market value. If the fees paid are not fair market value, this opinion is without force and effect.

[3] When first entering the Y Network, podiatrists enroll for an initial six month trial period, followed by an additional six month period. The trial period allows the podiatrists to test the program and permits Company A to comply with certain franchising regulations.

[4] According to Company A, a "foot screening" is understood by the podiatric medical community as a brief look at the feet, not an examination to evaluate a patient's need for medical treatment.

[5] Company A has certified that these blood pressure screenings are the only additional services provided by the podiatrists.

explicit statements that Company B does not endorse the services of any individual participating podiatrist; that the podiatrist has an active license in good standing and has paid to participate in the Y Network; and that Company B's customers and employees are free to choose any provider of podiatric services. Participating podiatrists are not permitted to make on-the-spot appointments for their private practices, nor write prescriptions while on Company B's premises.

Podiatrists are not compensated for the in-store appearances. Materials marketing the Y Network to podiatrists promise the podiatrists high visibility, exposure to a large volume of customers, and the opportunity to be the exclusive, local foot care specialist at their Company B stores.

To participate in the Y Network, a podiatrist pays Company A a fixed annual fee, regardless of the size or volume of business of the store to which he or she is assigned.[6] Company A has certified that this fee represents fair market value for the costs of operating the Y Network, including the costs of enrolling podiatrists, credentialing them, and assigning them to particular stores. To enroll as a Y Network podiatrist, a podiatrist must have an active license in good standing to practice podiatric medicine in the state in which the podiatrist practices and he or she must maintain professional malpractice insurance. Pursuant to the Implementing Agreement, Company B retained the right to disapprove any participating podiatrist for any lawful reason. The Implementing Agreement also provides that participating podiatrists must comply with written standards of conduct promulgated by Company B. In addition, podiatrists must also comply with the standards of conduct of the relevant state podiatric boards.

Podiatrists are assigned to Company B stores on a "first-come, first-served" basis. A second podiatrist may be assigned to a particular Company B store only with the consent of the first assigned podiatrist. Company A maintains a waiting list of podiatrists for whom there is currently no store available. Groups of podiatrists may share Company B locations for convenience, to spread the cost of the Y Network fee among several practitioners, and to ensure that

---

[6] Podiatrists pay $[redacted] for an initial six month trial period. For purposes of this advisory opinion, we rely on Company A's certification that the fees charged to podiatrists represent fair market value for services provided. If the fees paid are not fair market value, this opinion is without force and effect.

a podiatrist is always available for the required in-store appearances.

In sum, the Arrangement consists of conjoined programs -- the X Program and the Y Network -- through which Company A provides Company B with professional training and in-store podiatrists and provides participating podiatrists with access to Company B's customers.

C. Federal Health Care Program Reimbursement

Some professional services provided by the podiatrists in their private practices are potentially reimbursable by Medicare, Medicaid, or other Federal health care programs.[7] Additionally, some orthotics and other podiatric supplies and devices, as well as some drugs prescribed by podiatrists, may be available through Company B's pharmacy operations and may be reimbursable under Medicare, Medicaid, or other Federal health care program. Company A has certified that none of the services the podiatrists perform while at the Company B stores is reimbursable by any Federal health care program, and the podiatrists will not bill any Federal program for such services. Company A has further certified that neither Company B's pharmacies nor its pharmacy employees, contractors, vendors, or suppliers will promote, or participate in, the Arrangement and that there will be no direct or indirect connection between the Arrangement and Company B's pharmacy operations. Company A has also certified that none of the shoes or shoe products sold in the shoe departments of Company B's retail stores are reimbursable under any Federal health care program.

II. LAW

The anti-kickback statute makes it a criminal offense knowingly and willfully to offer, pay, solicit, or receive any remuneration to induce referrals of items or services reimbursable by any Federal health care program. See section 1128B(b) of the Act. Specifically, the statute provides that:

> "Whoever knowingly and willfully offers or pays [or solicits or receives] any remuneration (including any kickback, bribe, or rebate) directly or indirectly, overtly or covertly, in cash or in kind to

[7] Routine foot care services are generally excluded from coverage under Part A and Part B of Medicare, as are most orthopedic shoes and other supportive devices. *See* 42 U.S.C. § § 1395y(a)(8) & (13).

> any person to induce such person -- to refer an individual to a person for the furnishing or arranging for the furnishing of any item or service for which payment may be made in whole or in part under a Federal health care program, or to purchase, lease, order, or arrange for or recommend purchasing, leasing, or ordering any good, facility, service, or item for which payment may be made in whole or in part under a Federal health care program, shall be guilty of a felony."

Id. Thus, where remuneration is paid purposefully to induce referrals of items or services for which payment may be made by a Federal health care program, the anti-kickback statute is violated. By its terms, the statute ascribes criminal liability to parties on both sides of an impermissible "kickback" transaction. For purposes of the anti-kickback statute, "remuneration" includes the transfer of anything of value, in cash or in-kind, directly or indirectly, covertly or overtly.

The statute has been interpreted to cover any arrangement where *one* purpose of the remuneration was to obtain money for the referral of services or to induce further referrals. *United States v. Kats,* 871 F.2d 105 (9th Cir. 1989); *United States v. Greber,* 760 F.2d 68 (3d Cir.), *cert. denied,* 474 U.S. 988 (1985). Violation of the statute constitutes a felony punishable by a maximum fine of $25,000, imprisonment up to five years, or both. Conviction will also lead to automatic exclusion from Federal health care programs, including Medicare and Medicaid. This Office may also initiate administrative proceedings to exclude persons from Federal and state health care programs or to impose civil monetary penalties for fraud, kickbacks, and other prohibited activities under sections 1128(b)(7) and 1128A (a)(7) of the Act.[8]

The Department of Health and Human Services has promulgated safe harbor regulations that define practices that are not subject to the anti-kickback statute because such practices would be unlikely to result in fraud or abuse. *See* 42 C.F.R. § 1001.952. The safe harbors set forth specific conditions that, if met, assure entities involved of not being prosecuted or sanctioned for the arrangement qualifying for the safe harbor. However, safe harbor protection is afforded only to those arrangements that precisely meet all of the conditions set forth in the safe harbor. The regulatory safe harbors

[8] Because both the criminal and administrative sanctions related to the anti-kickback implications of the Proposed Arrangement are based on violations of the anti-kickback statute, the analysis for purposes of this advisory opinion is the same under both.

potentially applicable to the Arrangement are the personal services and management contracts safe harbor, 42 C.F.R. § 1001.952(d), and the referral services safe harbor, 42 C.F.R. § 1001.952(f). In relevant part for purposes of this advisory opinion, the personal services safe harbor requires that the compensation paid for services be set at fair market value in an arms-length transaction, 42 C.F.R. § 1001.952(d)(5); the referral services safe harbor requires that the referral service be open to anyone who meets the qualifications for participation and that payments made by participants be based only on the costs of operating the referral service, 42 C.F.R. § § 1001.952 (f)(1) & (2).

III. ANALYSIS

The threshold inquiry under the anti-kickback statute is whether the Arrangement involves any transfer of remuneration to a person or entity who refers Federal health care program business or arranges for or recommends the purchase, lease, or ordering of items or services reimbursable by a Federal health care program. Company A claims that the promotional activities contemplated under the Arrangement do not involve "arranging for or recommending" within the meaning of the statute, and that, in any event, no economic benefit flows from the podiatrists to Company B for any referrals as a result of the interposition of Company A as an unrelated third-party intermediary. For the reasons set forth below, we disagree.

The promotional activities conducted by Company A and Company B come within the plain language of the statute, which prohibits payments to a person to "arrange for or recommend" the purchasing or ordering of a good or service payable by a Federal health care program. Not only are Company A and Company B providing in-store posters and "awareness" campaigns, they are also orchestrating an opportunity for the podiatrists to market their services personally -- and exclusively -- to potential patients. The in-store signs, special promotions, and authorized presence of the podiatrists in Company B's shoe departments, coupled with Company B's retained right to disapprove any participating podiatrist, amount to an implied recommendation of the podiatrists by Company B, notwithstanding the written disclaimers the podiatrists are required to distribute to customers. Some of those customers will be Federal health care program beneficiaries, and some of the services subsequently provided by the podiatrists to those customers in the podiatrists' private practice may be reimbursable under a Federal health care program.

Having established an implied recommendation, we also think that both Company A and Company B receive an economic benefit (or "remuneration") in exchange for these promotional activities, since the podiatrists receive no monetary compensation for their in-store appearances each month.[9] These free services benefit both Company A, which otherwise has a contractual obligation to Company B to provide the podiatrists, and Company B, which desires the podiatrists' monthly in-store appearances for its own purposes. The OIG's position on the provision of free or below market value goods or services to potential referral sources is longstanding and clear: the provision of free goods or services to an actual or potential referral source may violate the anti-kickback statute, depending on the circumstances. For example, the preamble to the 1991 safe harbor regulations explains that giving free goods that have an independent value to a physician may violate the anti-kickback statute. *See* 56 Fed. Reg. 35978 (July 29, 1991); *see also* Special Fraud Alert, 59 Fed. Reg. 65372, 65377 (Dec. 19, 1994); OIG Advisory Opinion 98-16. This analysis generally applies to the provision of any free or below market value goods or services to actual or potential referral sources. If the requisite intent to induce or reward referrals of Federal health care program business is present, the anti-kickback statute is violated.

The interposition of Company A as an intermediary between Company B and the podiatrists does not vitiate our anti-kickback concerns. Through its contractual arrangements with Company B and the participating podiatrists, Company A is in a position to channel "recommendations" from Company B to the podiatrists and "remuneration" from the podiatrists to Company B. Moreover, in some circumstances this type of arrangement could pose a risk that the intermediary would be buying one party's recommendations and reselling them to another party. For example, Company A could accomplish this result if it were to "purchase" Company B's recommendations by selling its X Program services to Company B for less than fair market value (i.e., giving "remuneration") and then "sell"

[9] In addition, Company A collects fees from the podiatrists to participate in the Y Network. Company A has certified that these fees are fair market value for services rendered by Company A. However, this certification does not account for the value of the podiatrists' free services.

the recommendations to the participating podiatrists by providing its Y Network services at more than fair market value (i.e., receiving "remuneration"). However, as noted above, Company A has certified that its fees from both Company B and the podiatrists are at fair market value.

Neither of the potentially applicable safe harbors protects the Arrangement. The personal services contracts safe harbor does not apply, because the podiatrists are not compensated for the free services they render, apart from the opportunity to generate business. *See* 42 C.F.R. § 1001.952(d)(5). The referral services safe harbor is also inapplicable, because the exclusive location feature of the Y Network excludes some podiatrists from participating and because Company A intends to operate the Y Network at a profit. *See* 42 C.F.R. § § 1001.952(f)(1) & (2).

In these circumstances, we conclude that the Arrangement potentially violates the anti-kickback statute insofar as the podiatrists may be giving something of value to Company B and Company A in exchange for promotional activities that rise to the level of "arranging for or recommending" within the meaning of the statute.

Notwithstanding, in the particular factual circumstances presented and based on the totality of the following factors, we conclude that for purposes of the anti-kickback statute the Arrangement poses a low risk of fraud and abuse and contains safeguards that further reduce that risk for the reasons set forth below.

The risk of program or patient abuse from the Arrangement is relatively low, since Company B and Company A have a limited ability to influence a significant flow of Federal health care program business to the podiatrists. In evaluating the risks posed by arrangements involving direct or indirect promotional or marketing activity involving potential patients, like Company B's constructive endorsement of the participating podiatrists, we look to a number of factors, including, but not limited to, the following:

- **The identity of the party engaged in the marketing or promotional activity and the party's relationship with its audience.** For example, relevant inquiries may include whether the party is involved in the delivery of health care (e.g., a doctor, a nurse, a home health aide, or the like) and whether the party is otherwise in a position to exert undue influence on potential purchasers or patients.

- **The nature of the marketing or promotional activity.** One relevant factor is whether and to what degree the activity may be coercive, or perceived to be coercive, by the party to whom the activity is directed. For example, door-to-door marketing, telephone solicitations, and direct mailings are more intrusive, and typically pose a greater potential for abuse, than truthful passive advertising in general circulation newspapers or on television.
- **The item or service being promoted or marketed.** Pertinent here, for example, is whether the marketing or promotion identifies specific items or services or whether it consists of more general descriptions of providers or suppliers (e.g., "image" advertising). Another consideration is whether the item or service marketed or promoted is one for which there is a likelihood of overutilization based on the historical experience of the Federal health care programs, reimbursement methodology, or other reason.
- **The target audience.** Relevant aspects include whether the activity is specifically directed at senior citizens, Medicaid beneficiaries, or other particularly vulnerable populations. The more focused the marketing or promotional activity is on persons likely to be Federal health care program beneficiaries, the greater the risk to the Federal health care programs and their beneficiaries.

We emphasize that these factors are not indicative or necessarily probative of whether a practice, in fact, actually violates the anti-kickback statute. Rather, we weigh these factors, as well as other relevant concerns, in assessing the level of risk presented by promotional and marketing activity. These factors are not exclusive and the presence or absence of any one factor is not determinative of whether, in our discretion, we would subject parties engaged in marketing or promotional activity to sanctions for violating the anti-kickback statute.

In the instant case, consideration of these factors, coupled with the safeguards described below, suggests that the risk posed by the Arrangement is low. Neither Company B's shoe departments[10] nor Company A is involved in the delivery of health care. Company B's shoe departments sell no products and provide no services reimburs-

---

[10] Company B's pharmacy operations are specifically excluded from any involvement in the Arrangement.

able by any Federal health care program. Neither Company B, a diversified discount retailer serving a broad spectrum of the general public, nor Company A, a professional training and publishing company, has any special health care relationship with Company B's shoe department customers.[11] While participating podiatrists may benefit from the halo effect attributable to their association with Company B, the Arrangement involves no explicit arranging for or recommending of any good, facility, service, or item payable by a Federal health care program by either Company B or Company A. No specific podiatric services are promoted or marketed. Finally, while it involves direct patient contact, the Arrangement is not targeted at Federal health care program beneficiaries, and neither Company B nor Company A has control over the prospective patient mix of the shoe department customers.

Three safeguards provide additional protection against fraud and abuse. *First,* the fees paid by the podiatrists to Company A do not vary based on the actual or anticipated volume or value of referrals. Podiatrists each pay the same fixed fee regardless of the size or volume of business of the stores to which they are assigned. After an initial six-month trial period, podiatrists must commit to a second six-month term and then to one-year terms thereafter, during which terms they are obligated to provide in-store appearances, even if no referrals result.

Second, the podiatrists provide Company B's customers and employees who inquire about their private practices with written disclosures indicating that Company B does not endorse the in-store podiatrist and informing them of their freedom of choice. While we do not believe that such disclosures offer sufficient protection from program abuse, effective and meaningful disclosure offers some protection against possible abuses of patient trust.

Third, the risk of cross-referrals to Company B's pharmacy is minimal. Neither Company B's pharmacies nor its pharmacy employees, contractors, vendors, or suppliers will promote, or participate in, the Arrangement, and there will be no direct or indirect connection between the Arrangement and Company B's pharmacy operations. The participating podiatrists are barred from writing prescriptions while on Company B's premises.

---

[11] Unless, of course, the shoe department customers are also customers of the pharmacy or other department selling health care or personal care items or services.

As indicated above, our determination not to impose sanctions in these circumstances is attributable to the entirety of the facts of the Arrangement, including, but not limited to, the identities of the parties and the level of promotional activities. We would likely reach a different conclusion if the Arrangement involved a different setting or different parties, for example, if the participating podiatrists were providing free services (whether directly or facilitated by an intermediary) to nursing homes, assisted living facilities, senior centers, community clinics, physicians' offices, hospitals, home health agencies, or other more traditional sources of referrals of Federal health care business or places where Federal health care program beneficiaries typically seek health care or personal care services. Likewise, we would find suspect a similar arrangement involving Company B's pharmacy departments and physician in-store appearances or one involving an express Company B endorsement of a health care provider.

IV. CONCLUSION

Based on the information provided, we conclude that the Arrangement would potentially generate prohibited remuneration under the anti-kickback statute, if the requisite intent to induce referrals were present, but that, based on the totality of the facts and the safeguards present in the Arrangement, the OIG will not subject Company A to sanctions for violations of the anti-kickback statute pursuant to sections 1128(b)(7) or 1128A(a)(7) of the Act in connection with the Arrangement, as described and certified in the request letter and supplemental submissions.

V. LIMITATIONS

The limitations applicable to this opinion include the following:

- This advisory opinion is issued only to Company A, the requester of this opinion. This advisory opinion has no application to, and cannot be relied upon by, any other individual or entity.
- This advisory opinion may not be introduced into evidence in any matter involving an entity or individual that is not a requester to this opinion.
- This advisory opinion is applicable only to the statutory provisions specifically noted above. No opinion is herein expressed or implied with respect to the application of any other Federal,

state, or local statute, rule, regulation, ordinance, or other law that may be applicable to the Arrangement.

- This advisory opinion will not bind or obligate any agency other than the U.S. Department of Health and Human Services.
- This advisory opinion is limited in scope to the specific arrangement described in this letter and has no applicability to other arrangements, even those that appear similar in nature or scope.
- No opinion is expressed herein regarding the liability of any party under the False Claims Act or other legal authorities for any improper billing, claims submission, cost reporting, or related conduct.

This opinion is also subject to any additional limitations set forth at 42 C.F.R. Part 1008.

The OIG will not proceed against the requester with respect to any action that is part of the Arrangement taken in good faith reliance upon this advisory opinion as long as all of the material facts have been fully, completely, and accurately presented, the fees paid under the Arrangement are fair market value, and the Arrangement in practice comports with the information provided. The OIG reserves the right to reconsider the questions and issues raised in this advisory opinion and, where the public interest requires, rescind, modify, or terminate this opinion. In the event that this advisory opinion is modified or terminated, the OIG will not proceed against the requester with respect to any action taken in good faith reliance upon this advisory opinion, where all of the relevant facts were fully, completely, and accurately presented, where the fees paid under the Arrangement were at fair market value, and where such action was promptly discontinued upon notification of the modification or termination of this advisory opinion. An advisory opinion may be rescinded only if the relevant and material facts have not been fully, completely, and accurately disclosed to the OIG.

Sincerely,

/s/

D. McCarty Thornton

Chief Counsel to the Inspector General

APPENDIX F41

Advisory Opinion No. 99–9, September 30, 1999

Regarding a proposed contractual arrangement between a self-insured employer health plan and a single-specialty managed care organization to provide managed podiatry benefits for the employer's retirees.

Issued: September 30, 1999

[Name & Address Redacted]

Re: OIG Advisory Opinion No. 99–9

Dear [Name Redacted]:

We are writing in response to your request for an advisory opinion about a proposed contractual arrangement between a self-insured employer health plan and a single-specialty managed care organization to provide managed podiatry benefits for the employer's retirees (the "Proposed Arrangement"). Specifically, you have inquired whether the Proposed Arrangement would constitute grounds for sanctions under the anti-kickback statute, section 1128B(b) of the Social Security Act (the "Act"), or under the civil money penalty provision for inducements to beneficiaries, section 1128A(a)(5) of the Act, in the circumstances presented.

In issuing this opinion, we have relied solely on the facts and information presented to us. We have not undertaken an independent investigation of such information. This opinion is limited to the facts presented. If material facts have not been disclosed or have been misrepresented, this opinion is without force and effect.

Based on the information provided and subject to certain conditions described below, we conclude that (i) the Proposed Arrangement could involve prohibited remuneration under section 1128B(b) of the Act, if the requisite intent to induce referrals were present, but that the Office of Inspector General ("OIG") will not impose sanctions on Corporation A, pursuant to the anti-kickback statute under sections 1128(b)(7) or 1128A(a)(7) of the Act in connection with the Proposed Arrangement; and (ii) the OIG will not subject Corporation A to sanctions under section 1128A(a)(5) of the Act in connection with the Proposed Arrangement.

This opinion may not be relied on by any persons other than Corporation A, the requester of this opinion, and is further qualified as set out in Part V below and in 42 C.F.R. Part 1008.

I. BACKGROUND

A. Corporation A

Corporation A, (the "Plan") is a State X corporation in the business since [year redacted] of providing specialized management of podiatry benefits for self-insured employer plans. The Plan is licensed in State X as a health care alternative financing and delivery system. As such, its operations are subject to regulation under the State X HMO Act by the State X Insurance Bureau and the State X Department of Community Health. The Plan is not owned or controlled by podiatrists or any organization affiliated with podiatrists, nor are there podiatrists on the Plan's Board of Directors. The Plan employs podiatrists as medical directors.

The Plan has provided Corporation B (now known as [name redacted]) (the "Employer") with managed podiatry benefits for its employees for over sixteen years (the "Employee Program").[1] As a result of the Employee Program, the Employer has experienced significant cost savings and reductions in abuses related to podiatry benefits, including overutilization and inappropriate treatment. For example, the Employer has represented that it saved $3.4 million in health care benefits related to foot care in one state during the first two years of the Employee Program and that it also experienced significant reductions in disability and sick leave expenditures related to foot care.

B. The Proposed Arrangement

The Plan proposes entering into a new arrangement with the Employer to provide similar managed podiatry benefits for the Employer's retirees (the "Retiree Program" or the "Proposed Arrangement"). Most retirees covered by the Employer's health plan are Medicare fee-for-service beneficiaries for whom the Employer acts as a supplemental insurer, paying their Medicare deductibles and copayments (collectively, "Medicare cost-sharing") on a per-claim basis. The Employer engages in little or no utilization review of such cost-sharing claims. Through the Retiree Program,

---

[1] The Employer sponsors health plans for its employees and retirees pursuant to collective bargaining agreements with Union Y (the "Union").

the Employer anticipates reducing its expenditures on Medicare cost-sharing for podiatry services, while simultaneously offering retirees more covered podiatry benefits. The Retiree Program will be identical to the Employee Program in all material respects, including the scope of covered benefits and controls on utilization of services with the exception of the Retiree Program's interplay with the Medicare Program (for which there is no Employee Program counterpart) and the enhancement of the utilization review program as discussed elsewhere in this letter. The Union has been, and remains, involved in the decision to adopt the Retiree Program and in the related approval process.

Under the Proposed Arrangement, the Employer will pay the Plan annually a fixed, capitated fee. The fee will reflect the Employer's historic annual expenditures for Medicare cost-sharing, discounted by an amount estimated to reflect the projected reduction in utilization of foot care services under the Retiree Program.

In exchange for this fee, the Plan will assume full financial risk for all Medicare cost-sharing and all administrative costs in connection with the provision of all medically necessary foot care services for the Employer's retirees, except for inpatient facility services and services within the first seventy-two hours related to accidental injuries (including fractures and sprains), which will continue to be covered under the Employer's regular health insurance benefit. In essence, the Plan will assume the Employer's role of supplemental insurer for the retirees, thus taking on the obligation to pay Medicare cost-sharing amounts to individual providers.

The Plan contracts with a network of approximately 3,300 credentialed podiatrists and other physicians and providers nationwide (the "Network Providers"), most of whom will be required to participate in both the Employee and Retiree Programs.[2] The Network Providers will participate in the Retiree Program pursuant to one-year written contracts. In establishing the financial terms of the Retiree Program, neither the Plan nor the Network Providers have given or received, or will give or receive, a discount on the Employee Program's financial terms.

The Plan will pay the Medicare cost-sharing amounts on a per-claim basis for all non-routine professional services, and all out-

---

[2] There are limited exceptions for certain providers who do not wish to participate in the Retiree Program, but who are needed to provide adequate coverage under the Employee Program in areas with few alternative providers.

patient facility services, treatment by subspecialists, anesthesiology, and other specialized or supplemental services, bone scans, and other diagnostic tests (except x-rays) (the "Retained-Risk" services) to the extent they are covered by Medicare.[3] The Plan will also pay Network Providers a capitated amount per enrollee that will cover any Medicare cost-sharing for routine professional podiatric services (i.e., Medicare reimbursable podiatric services other than the Retained-Risk services), as well as additional services which are not typically covered by Medicare. These additional services include routine office visits, preventive care, and orthotics (the "Additional Services"). With respect to Medicare-reimbursable services covered by the capitated amount, the Network Providers will bill Medicare on a fee-for-service basis and accept the capitation in lieu of collecting Medicare cost-sharing amounts from the Employer or the retirees. The Network Providers will be required to submit to the Plan's utilization control mechanisms for services payable by the Medicare program. The Plan will assign retirees to Network Providers on a geographical basis, allocating them among Network Providers within zip code areas. A retiree will be able to obtain services from a provider other than his or her assigned Network Provider, including providers outside the network, but would then be responsible for paying Medicare cost-sharing amounts up to an out-of-pocket maximum.[4] The Plan will pay Medicare cost-sharing amounts over the out-of-pocket maximum in full. Retirees who reside more than twenty-five miles from the nearest Network Provider will be allowed to obtain services out-of-network at no cost to the retiree.

C. The Proposed Arrangement's UR/QA Program

The Plan's extensive utilization review and quality assurance programs for the Employee Program (collectively, the "UR/QA program") will be expanded to apply equally to the Retiree Program. The UR/QA program consists of two parts: a pre-certification requirement applicable to surgeries and referrals to hospitals or

---

[3] The Retained-Risk services include most of the procedures described in the top twenty Medicare procedure codes shown on the State X Medicare Part B Procedure Code Analysis by Speciality (#48-Podiatry) published by the Health Care Service Corporation and submitted by the Plan, accounting for approximately 74% of Medicare's dollar volume relating to procedures that may be performed by podiatrists.

[4] The amount of the out-of-pocket maximum will be subject to the Union's concurrence.

outpatient surgery centers and an "adjudication system" for routine office visits and preventive care services.

The pre-certification procedure for surgeries and referrals to hospitals or outpatient surgery centers uses medical necessity guidelines developed by the Plan. If a provider or patient disagrees with a pre-certification determination, a peer review procedure is in place that includes review by a panel of independent physicians and podiatrists, whose determination is honored. Under the Retiree Program, Network Providers will not be allowed to bill Medicare for any covered foot care service for which pre-certification is required but not obtained.[5] Network Providers must also participate in certain other quality of care and educational programs designed to detect and correct patterns of overutilization or other inappropriate practices. In addition, the Plan is considering establishing a funds withholding and risk pool arrangement as an additional incentive to Network Providers to cooperate with the pre-certification requirements and the restrictions on billing Medicare. The second component of the UR/QA program — the "adjudication system" — applies to services that are not subject to pre-certification, primarily services provided during routine office visits. Under the adjudication system, Network Providers submit monthly encounter data reports, which are reviewed by the Plan's management, including its medical director. The utilization reports identify utilization rates for all procedures, including those for which the Network Providers are at risk under the capitation. The Plan uses the encounter data to identify Network Providers whose use of a procedure is significantly above or below the median utilization of the procedure by all Network Providers, using statistically valid methods and taking into account geographical considerations and recognized medical standards.

---

5 The Plan currently has pre-certification requirements and guidelines in place for approximately 325 of the 500 procedure codes for which Medicare will pay podiatrists, or approximately 65% of the total number of applicable Medicare codes. The remaining codes are primarily for routine care, office visits, and preventive care, many of which are not covered by Medicare. Using existing guidelines, the Plan will control and pre-certify most of the procedures described in the top twenty Medicare podiatry procedure codes, accounting for approximately 74% of Medicare's dollar volume relating to procedures that may be performed by podiatrists. The guidelines will be expanded over the next two years to cover all of the top twenty codes and substantially all of the top fifty (which account for 91.6% of total Medicare dollars paid for podiatry services). See State X Medicare Part B Procedure Code Analysis by Speciality (#48-Podiatry).

The Plan employs a system of random audits and surveys to verify compliance with the UR/QA program. In addition, the Plan randomly selects 100 claims each month for review of clerical accuracy, CPT code accuracy, medical necessity, and appropriateness of care. The Plan will make available to the Health Care Financing Administration, upon request, all records relating to these audits and surveys, as well as other utilization and quality control information in connection with the Retiree Program.

Network Providers identified by the Plan as significantly under- or overutilizing a procedure are subject to counseling, corrective action, or dismissal from the network. The enforcement process consists of education and counseling, a probationary period during which the Network Provider's data is monitored, and, if the Network Provider fails to adhere to reasonable norms, termination of his or her contract. For the period from January 1997 until April 1999, the Plan counseled a total of eighty-eight Network Providers and terminated twenty-one for overutilization. In particular, four Network Providers were terminated for overutilization of services covered solely by the Plan's capitated payment, even though the Plan incurred no financial loss. In combination, the pre-certification and adjudication systems will subject virtually all Medicare-covered services to utilization review. To ensure effective review of Medicare-covered services, the UR/QA program will be applied identically in the Employee and Retiree Programs and "blinded" so that reviewing personnel will not know whether the patient is an employee — for whom the Employer pays under the Employee Program — or a retiree — for whom Medicare is primarily at risk.

To further protect the Medicare program from provider attempts to circumvent the UR/QA program, the Plan will obtain information from fiscal intermediaries about procedures performed by Network Providers and billed to Medicare. The Plan will conduct random utilization management audits of the information to identify any Network Providers who are not submitting encounter reports for all procedures performed on Medicare enrollees or who are not cooperating with the pre-certification requirements. The information will also be used to identify charts to be pulled in random audits. The confidentiality of patient records will be protected.

Finally, the Plan plans to develop guidelines applicable to procedures for which pre-certification will not be required under the Retiree Program, but that are subject to abuse or should be monitored for other reasons. For example, independent of the Proposed

Arrangement, the Plan is developing a guideline for conservative treatment of mycotic toenails, an area the Plan has identified as problematic in the Employee Program and an area that has led to abuses in the Medicare program.

D. Medicare Reimbursement

Medically necessary foot care services are covered under Part A and Part B of Medicare; however, routine foot care services are generally excluded from coverage, as are most orthopedic shoes and other supportive devices. See 42 U.S.C. § § 1395y(a)(8) & (13). Limited orthotics are covered for some diabetic patients. In addition, Medicare covers a limited number of routine services, such as treatment of mycotic toenails, which are only covered when a patient has a systemic disease of sufficient severity that unskilled performance of such a procedure would be hazardous. See, e.g., Medicare Carriers Manual § 4120.1.

II. ALTHOUGH THE PROPOSED ARRANGEMENT POTENTIALLY IMPLICATES THE ANTI-KICKBACK STATUTE, THE OIG WILL NOT IMPOSE SANCTIONS.

A. Law

The anti-kickback statute makes it a criminal offense knowingly and wilfully to offer, pay, solicit, or receive any remuneration to induce referrals of items or services reimbursable by the Federal health care programs. See section 1128B(b) of the Act. Where remuneration is paid purposefully to induce referrals of items or services paid for by a Federal health care program, the anti-kickback statute is violated. By its terms, the statute ascribes liability to parties on both sides of an impermissible "kickback" transaction. For purposes of the anti-kickback statute, "remuneration" includes the transfer of anything of value, in cash or in-kind, directly or indirectly, covertly or overtly. The statute has been interpreted to cover any arrangement where one purpose of the remuneration is to obtain money for referral of services or to induce further referrals. United States v. Kats, 871 F. 2d 105 (9th Cir. 1989); United States v. Greber, 760 F. 2d 68 (3rd Cir.), cert. denied, 474 U.S. 988 (1985). Violation of the statute constitutes a felony punishable by a maximum fine of $25,000, imprisonment up to five years or both. Conviction will also lead to automatic exclusion from Federal health care programs, including Medicare and Medicaid. This Office may also initiate administrative proceedings to exclude persons from Federal health care programs or to impose civil monetary penalties for fraud, kickbacks, and other prohibited activities under sections 1128(b)(7) and

1128A(a)(7) of the Act.[6]

There are several statutory exceptions and regulatory "safe harbors" under the anti-kickback statute. As a threshold matter, the Proposed Arrangement is not protected by the exception to the anti-kickback statute for certain risk-sharing arrangements, section 1128B(b)(3)(F) of the Act. Although similar in some respects to managed care arrangements addressed by that exception, the Proposed Arrangement will not be implemented pursuant to a contract with Medicare or a State health care program, nor will the Plan or its providers be put at substantial financial risk for the cost or utilization of items or services provided to Federal health care program beneficiaries. Similarly, the Proposed Arrangement does not come within the definition of a protected health plan under the existing regulatory safe harbor for increased coverage, reduced cost-sharing amounts, or reduced premium amounts offered by health plans, 42 C.F.R. § 1001.952(l), which requires that a protected health plan have a contract with the Health Care Financing Administration.

The OIG's concern about the potential for fraud and abuse arising from the routine waiver of Medicare cost-sharing amounts is longstanding. See, e.g., Preamble to Final Rule on Safe Harbors for Protecting Health Plans, 61 Fed. Reg. 2122, 2124 (Jan. 25, 1996); Special Fraud Alert: Routine Waiver of Copayments or Deductibles Under Medicare Part B, 59 Fed. Reg. 35373, 35374 (Dec. 19, 1994). Such waivers undermine the important utilization and cost control functions of the cost-sharing requirement.

We have also previously articulated our concern that agreements between providers and health plans to forgo cost-sharing amounts may result in kickbacks from providers to health care plans in exchange for referrals of Federal program business. For example, the preamble to the 1996 Final Rule establishing certain managed care safe harbors explained that:

"[t]he [anti-kickback] statute prohibits any remuneration which is in return for, or which is designed to induce, the flow of Medicare and Medicaid program-related business. Therefore, it could cover a hospital's agreement to forego or reduce coinsurance or deductibles in exchange for increased program-related business. It does not matter

---

[6] Because both the criminal and administrative sanctions related to the anti-kickback implications of the Arrangement are based on violations of the anti-kickback statute, the analysis for the purposes of this advisory opinion is the same under both.

that the payment is made to a third party rather than the beneficiary." 61 Fed. Reg. 2124; see also OIG Advisory Opinion 98–5 (Apr. 17, 1998).

B. Analysis

The principal issue raised by the Proposed Arrangement is whether, in exchange for the Employer's retiree business, the Plan and its Network Providers will be giving the Employer a discount on the Medicare copayment obligation the Employer would otherwise have to satisfy on behalf of its Medicare-eligible retirees. Since a reduction in an amount legally owed confers a financial benefit on the party receiving the reduction, full or partial waivers of Medicare copayment obligations used to attract business have long been suspect under the anti-kickback statute.

The Proposed Arrangement is similar in some respects to the arrangement that raised substantial concerns under the anti-kickback statute in OIG Advisory Opinion 98–5. In that arrangement, a nursing home entered into an agreement with a health care plan to accept the health care plan's per diem amount as payment in full for services rendered to all plan members, including retirees for whom Medicare was the primary payer and the plan was only secondarily liable. For those plan members who were Medicare beneficiaries, the contractual arrangement effectively required the nursing home to forgo certain Medicare cost-sharing amounts that the health care plan would otherwise have had to pay on behalf of its retiree beneficiaries. We concluded that the arrangement potentially violated the anti-kickback statute.

One of our concerns about the arrangement in OIG Advisory Opinion 98–5 was that the nursing home's willingness to forgo cost-sharing revenue was, in essence, a price concession offered to the health plan in exchange for the opportunity to treat the health plan's Medicare population. By releasing the health plan from its obligation to pay the Medicare copayment, the arrangement posed an increased risk of overutilization and increased program costs by eliminating the health plan's financial incentive to control the level and intensity of health care services provided to Medicare beneficiaries. In effect, the nursing home agreed to provide care to plan members paid for by the plan at a low price (including savings on copayments) in exchange for referrals of Medicare beneficiaries paid for by Medicare. See also OIG Advisory Opinion 99–2 (Feb. 26, 1999).

The Proposed Arrangement is different from the suspect arrangement in OIG Advisory Opinion 98–5. Most importantly, the

Employer will pay the full amount of its projected copayment obligation for podiatry services for its retirees. Similarly, the contracted Network Providers, in the aggregate, will receive their full anticipated copayment amounts minus only an amount to fund the Plan's operating expenses. In other words, there may be no waiver of any Employer copayment obligation.

A key to determining the adequacy of the Employer's payment is an assessment of the effectiveness of the Plan's management of the podiatric network and services. Many utilization review and quality assurance activities are of questionable benefit in controlling unnecessary utilization and containing health care costs. For example, many programs are of the "pay-and-chase" variety, reviewing utilization either retrospectively or concurrently (rather than prospectively). Moreover, most utilization programs rely primarily on identifying providers with aberrant utilization patterns (i.e., extreme outliers compared to other providers); these programs do not address the situation of a physician or physicians routinely providing medically unnecessary care without exceeding the "aberrant" threshold. For these and other reasons, utilization review programs have limited effectiveness as fraud and abuse controls. There is substantial evidence, however, that the Proposed Arrangement's UR/QA program offers meaningful review. For example:

- The identical program (i.e., the Employee Program) has been in effect for over sixteen years and has been effective in reducing utilization among the Employer's active workers. Accordingly, the Employer has a reasonable historical experience with virtually the identical program upon which to assess anticipated utilization and corresponding copayment obligations. The review process will be blinded so that services provided to Medicare retirees will be reviewed in the same manner and subject to the same standards as services provided to employees for whom the Employer is fully liable under the Employee Program.
- Virtually all of the Retained-Risk services billed to Medicare (accounting for approximately 70% of Medicare's dollar volume for podiatry services) will be subject to pre-certification. In other words, the medical necessity of these services will be evaluated prospectively based on the particular circumstances of each case.

- The program has an established record in tracking, monitoring, and disciplining podiatrists who fail to adhere to the UR/QA program guidelines and protocols, even in circumstances where the Plan has not been at-risk for the cost of the services.
- Because the Plan is not a provider-sponsored or controlled organization, it has an arms-length relationship with its Network Providers and no incentive to manipulate the UR/QA system to benefit them.
- The pre-certification protocols and the additional guideline for mycotic toenails have been reviewed and approved for appropriateness by an outside expert pursuant to the provisions of 42 C.F.R. § 1008.33.[7]

In light of these characteristics, it is reasonable to conclude that (i) the Proposed Arrangement is likely to result in a reduction in unnecessary podiatry services and (ii) the Employer payment to the Plan will substantially approximate its applicable copayment obligation in the aggregate.

Moreover, even if some part of the copayment obligation would be waived, we would not impose sanctions on the Plan in connection with such waiver in light of the overall structure of the UR/QA program, the fact that the Proposed Arrangement is very likely to result in a reduction in Federal health care expenditures, and the potential for increased benefits to Medicare beneficiaries.

Simply put, for every dollar that the Employer saves in Medicare copayments through elimination of unnecessary foot care for retirees, the Federal government saves four dollars. Thus, even if the copayment match is only roughly approximate, the Proposed Arrangement is likely to confer a substantial financial benefit on the Federal fisc as the primary beneficiary of the Plan's management of the foot care benefit.

In addition, the Proposed Arrangement is likely to benefit Federal beneficiaries through access to expanded insurance coverage for the Additional Services. The Proposed Arrangement preserves freedom of choice for Medicare beneficiaries through the out-of-network alternative, which permits retirees to select any provider. Retiree

---

[7] In reviewing the Plan's UR/QA program for purposes of this advisory opinion, we looked at whether the program was likely to be effective in reducing utilization and whether it would be likely to result in denials of medically necessary care. Determinations made by the Plan or the UR/QA program with respect to a Network Provider's utilization are not, and will not be, binding on the OIG in any enforcement action.

interests are further protected through the participation of the Union as a collective bargaining agent.

Finally, the Proposed Arrangement preserves the primary purpose of Medicare copayments as a check on unnecessary utilization. Copayments encourage responsible use of health care services by giving beneficiaries a financial stake in their health care. This function is undermined when beneficiaries obtain supplemental insurance coverage for cost-sharing amounts through employer plans or Medigap policies, since those beneficiaries have no financial incentive to reduce utilization. Like the Employer under its current practice, most employer plans and Medigap insurers engage in little or no utilization review of Medicare copayment claims since such review is not cost effective given the plans' relatively limited financial exposure for any given service. By establishing a Retiree Program comparable to its existing Employee Program, the Employer will be using its cost-sharing dollars for their intended purpose: to encourage efficient and judicious use of foot care services paid for by Medicare.

We recognize that, despite the safeguards incorporated into the Proposed Arrangement, there may be "rogue" providers who bill for medically unnecessary services, upcode claims, bill for services not provided, or engage in similar illegal activities. Nothing in this advisory opinion protects such providers or activities or limits the OIG's ability to enforce the Federal anti-fraud and abuse authorities against such unscrupulous providers.

III. THE OIG WILL NOT SUBJECT THE PLAN TO CIVIL MONEY PENALTIES UNDER SECTION 1128A(a)(5) OF THE ACT IN CONNECTION WITH THE PROPOSED ARRANGEMENT.

A further question arises as to whether the Additional Services provided to Medicare beneficiaries violate section 1128A(a)(5) of the Act, which prohibits a person from offering or transferring remuneration to a beneficiary that such person knows or should know is likely to influence the beneficiary to order items or services from a particular provider or supplier for which payment may be made under the Medicare and Medicaid programs. The Plan will offer the Additional Services to retirees to induce them to use the managed services network generally. All Network Providers will offer the Additional Services, and thus the services will not be an incentive to choose a particular provider within the network. For these reasons, the OIG will not subject the Plan to sanctions under section 1128A(a)(5) of the Act in connection with the Proposed Arrangement.

IV. CONCLUSION

For the above-stated reasons and based on the facts as certified in the request letter and supplemental submissions, we conclude that (i) the Proposed Arrangement could involve prohibited remuneration under section 1128B(b) of the Act, if the requisite intent to induce referrals were present, but that the OIG will not impose sanctions on the requester pursuant to the anti-kickback statute under sections 1128(b)(7) and 1128A(a)(7) of the Act in connection with the Proposed Arrangement; and (ii) the OIG will not subject the Plan to sanctions under section 1128A(a)(5) of the Act in connection with the Proposed Arrangement.

V. LIMITATIONS

The limitations applicable to this opinion include the following:

- This advisory opinion is issued only to the Plan, the requester of this opinion. This advisory opinion has no application to, and cannot be relied upon by, any other individual or entity.
- This advisory opinion may not be introduced into evidence in any matter involving an entity or individual that is not a requester to this opinion.
- This advisory opinion is applicable only to the statutory provisions specifically noted above. No opinion is herein expressed or implied with respect to the application of any other Federal, state, or local statute, rule, regulation, ordinance, or other law that may be applicable to the Plan or any other party involved in the Proposed Arrangement.
- This advisory opinion will not bind or obligate any agency other than the U.S. Department of Health and Human Services.
- This advisory opinion is limited in scope to the specific arrangement described in this letter and has no applicability to other arrangements, even those that appear similar in nature or scope.
- No opinion is expressed herein regarding the liability of any party under the False Claims Act or other legal authorities for any improper billing, claims submission, cost reporting, or related conduct.

This opinion is also subject to any additional limitations set forth at 42 C.F.R. Part 1008.

The OIG will not proceed against the requester with respect to any action that is part of the Proposed Arrangement taken in good faith reliance upon this advisory opinion as long as all of the material facts have been fully, completely, and accurately presented and the Proposed Arrangement in practice comports with the information provided. The OIG reserves the right to reconsider the questions and issues raised in this advisory opinion and, where the public interest requires, rescind, modify, or terminate this opinion. In the event that this advisory opinion is modified or terminated, the OIG will not proceed against the requester with respect to any action taken in good faith reliance upon this advisory opinion, where all of the relevant facts were fully, completely, and accurately presented and the Proposed Arrangement in practice comported with the information provided and where such action was promptly discontinued upon notification of the modification or termination of this advisory opinion. An advisory opinion may be rescinded only if the relevant and material facts have not been fully, completely, and accurately disclosed to the OIG.

Sincerely,

/s/

D. McCarty Thornton Chief Counsel to the Inspector General

APPENDIX F42

Advisory Opinion No. 99–10, October 25, 1999

Whether a corporate sponsorship program between Drug Company A and Charity B . . . constitutes grounds for sanctions under the anti-kickback statute,

Issued: October 25, 1999

[Names and Addresses redacted]

Re: OIG Advisory Opinion No. 99–10 Ladies and Gentlemen: We are writing in response to your request for an advisory opinion concerning a corporate sponsorship program between Drug Company A ("Company A") and Charity B ("Charity B") (the "Proposed Arrangement"). Specifically, you have inquired whether the Proposed Arrangement constitutes grounds for sanctions under the anti-kickback statute, section 1128B(b) of the Social Security Act (the "Act"), or under the civil monetary penalty provision for inducements to beneficiaries, section 1128A(a)(5) of the Act, in the circumstances presented.

In issuing this opinion, we have relied solely on the facts and information presented to us. We have not undertaken an independent investigation of such information. This opinion is limited to the facts presented. If material facts have not been disclosed or have been misrepresented, this opinion is without force and effect.

Based on the information provided, we conclude that (i) the Proposed Arrangement would potentially generate prohibited remuneration under the anti-kickback statute, if the requisite intent to induce referrals were present, but that the Office of Inspector General ("OIG") will not subject Company A or Charity B to sanctions arising under the anti-kickback statute pursuant to sections 1128(b)(7) or 1128A(a)(7) of the Act in connection with the Proposed Arrangement, as described and certified in the request letter and supplemental submissions; and (ii) the OIG will not subject Company A or Charity B to sanctions under section 1128A(a)(5) of the Act in connection with the Proposed Arrangement.

This opinion may not be relied on by any persons other than Company A and Charity B, the requesters of this opinion, and it is further qualified as set out in Part VI below and in 42 C.F.R. Part 1008. I. FACTUAL BACKGROUND

A. The Parties

Company A is a licensed pharmacy that dispenses respiratory drugs via mail order to patients in State X and other states. Respiratory drugs, and the nebulizers used to inhale them, are provided pursuant to a prescription from a patient's physician. Patients usually obtain the drugs from a pharmacy and the nebulizer from a durable medical equipment ("DME") supplier. Company A's business typically comes from referrals from physicians and DME suppliers. Many customers are covered by Medicare, Medicaid, or other Federal health care program. Charity B is a 501(c)(3) charitable organization in State X formed to conduct educational and public awareness campaigns about lung diseases and the hazards of smoking and to promote activities that lead to healthy lungs. Charity B is a state constituent of the American Lung Association. Charity B does not provide any DME or prescribe any drugs, make any referrals to particular providers of health care services (including pharmacies), or express any preferences regarding any providers. Charity B receives financial support from individuals and corporations. Aggregate annual donations typically fluctuate between $[x] and $[y] million. No shareholders, officers, directors, or employees of Company A serve on Charity B's board of directors or on any other Charity B decision-making body.

B. The Proposed Arrangement

Company A and Charity B wish to enter into an arrangement pursuant to which Company A will make charitable donations to Charity B, and Charity B will allow Company A to use its name, logo, and other proprietary symbols and phrases (collectively, for purposes of this opinion, "Charity B's marks") for certain limited promotional activities (the "Proposed Arrangement"). There will be no other business arrangements between Company A and Charity B. Company A will not offer patients rebates or discounts on nebulizer drugs in connection with the Proposed Arrangement.

Under the Proposed Arrangement, Company A would donate a fixed sum to Charity B for each nebulizer drug prescription Company A fills for patients residing in State X. The sum would not exceed ten dollars per prescription shipment. In order to calculate the aggregate donation, Company A would track prescriptions by the state in which the patient resides, but not by referral source or patient name. The Proposed Arrangement would be an exclusive arrangement; neither Company A nor Charity B would enter into a similar arrangement with any other party.

Charity B will permit Company A to use Charity B's marks solely in advertising and promotional materials that generally identify, describe, or portray the Proposed Arrangement or Charity B's charitable activities. The thrust of any advertising will be the promotion of Charity B's charitable activities and Company A's financial support of those activities. For example, promotional material may describe Charity B's children's programs and may indicate that Company A is providing financial support for those activities. [1] Promotional material under the Proposed Arrangement will not refer to Company A's products or services, and Charity B's marks will not be used in, or in connection with, any advertising for Company A's products or services. Advertisements will not be placed or distributed so as to suggest Charity B's endorsement of any specific Company A product or service (e.g., advertisements about the Proposed Arrangement will not be placed alongside or in the vicinity of Company A product advertisements; brochures about the Proposed Arrangement will not be accompanied by advertisements for specific Company A products or services).

The majority of Company A advertising of the Proposed Arrangement will be placed in regional trade publications directed at DME companies, physicians, respiratory therapists, and other health care professionals who have direct contact with patients using nebulizer drugs. None of these health care professionals will receive any financial incentive to induce referrals as a result of the Proposed

[1] A prototype advertisement submitted with the advisory opinion request shows a photograph of children at summer camp with a caption stating that Company A is teaming up with Charity B to help asthmatic children attend Charity B's special summer camp and that a portion of the proceeds from the purchase of nebulizer drugs will be donated to Charity B to support the summer camp. The advertisement incorporates both Company A's and Charity B's logos. A preliminary version of the prototype included an instruction to readers (presumably physicians, DME suppliers, and respiratory therapists) to call Company A at a 1–800 number and "mention this offer." This element was subsequently deleted. Company A and Charity B have certified that advertisements under the Proposed Arrangement will not include any instructions to contact Company A or any suggestion that readers may receive a benefit if they contact Company A or if they recommend or purchase Company A's products or services. Advertisements may include instructions for contacting Charity B about Charity B's programs.

Arrangement.[2] Company A may also send brochures explaining the Proposed Arrangement to its existing patient customers, as well as DME suppliers, physicians, respiratory therapists, and other appropriate health care professionals. Company A will not send brochures or other marketing materials to prospective patient customers. .

All advertising or other materials that use Charity B's marks will be subject to Charity B's review and approval. Charity B has represented that it will not permit Company A to use Charity B's marks in any way that would constitute an endorsement of Company A's products or services. Charity B may itself promote the Proposed Arrangement through its newsletter or in a separate letter from Charity B's president to its membership. Neither the newsletter nor the president's letter will describe, recommend, or endorse any particular Company A product or service

Company A and Charity B have certified that all advertising and promotional activity under the Proposed Arrangement will comply with all applicable Federal and state laws and regulations, including, but not limited to, compliance with consumer laws prohibiting false advertising, unfair and/or deceptive advertising, and consumer fraud.[3]

Charity B would treat Company A's donations as unrestricted general corporate donations. The proceeds would go into Charity B's general fund to be used at the sole discretion of Charity B's board of directors. Although the funds are unrestricted and may be used as the board sees fit, the parties anticipate that Company A's funds would be used for three Charity B projects that serve children with asthma: a free summer camp with special asthma-related activities, an asthma screening program to identify children at risk for asthma, and a school-based educational program to teach children to manage their asthma. The funding and operation of these programs, including the selection of participating children, is wholly the

[2] The requesters point out that some providers may benefit incidentally and indirectly if their pediatric patients partake of Charity B's asthma-related services supported by Company A and thus become better able to comply with their treatment plans.

[3] Endorsements of commercial products by charitable organizations raise significant issues, not addressed here, of consumer and business law. This advisory opinion is limited to consideration of potential implications of the Proposed Arrangement under the anti-kickback statute and the section 1128A(a)(5) prohibition against inducements to beneficiaries. We express no opinion about the legality of the Proposed Arrangement under other laws.

responsibility of Charity B, without any participation by Company A. Company A is not informed of the identity of program participants. While the scope and intensity of program services will be enhanced by Company A's donations, none of the Charity B programs will be dependent on them. At ten dollars per prescription shipment, Company A estimates that its annual donations to Charity B will be in the range of $[c] to [d], amounting to approximately [less than 9%] of Charity B's total revenue from grants and donations.

C. Federal Reimbursement

Because they are considered supplies necessary for the proper use of a nebulizer, respiratory drugs are covered by Medicare Part B's DME, prosthetics, orthotics, and supplies ("DMEPOS") benefit. For covered nebulizer drugs, Medicare pays the dispensing pharmacy 80% of the lesser of (i) the actual charge or (ii) the allowable 95% of the average wholesale price. See sections 1833(a)(1) and 1842(o) of the Act. The beneficiary is responsible for paying the dispensing pharmacy the remaining 20% of the actual charge or 20% of the allowable 95% of the average wholesale price as a Medicare copayment.[4] Company A has represented that the Medicare fee schedule is approximately eighty percent of Company A's usual and customary prices for respiratory drugs. Medicaid reimburses nebulizer drugs as a prescription drug benefit in accordance with the upper limits established by the Health Care Financing Administration. See 42 C.F.R. § § 447.331-.334. Company A has certified that it will not seek to pass the costs of its donations through to any Federal health care program or beneficiary.

II. LAW

The anti-kickback statute makes it a criminal offense knowingly and willfully to offer, pay, solicit, or receive any remuneration to induce referrals of items or services reimbursable by any Federal health care program. See section 1128B(b) of the Act. Specifically, the statute provides that:

"Whoever knowingly and willfully offers or pays [or solicits or receives] any remuneration (including any kickback, bribe, or rebate) directly or indirectly, overtly or covertly, in cash or in kind to any person to induce such person — to refer an individual to a

[4] If the provider does not accept assignment, there is no limiting charge; thus, beneficiaries may be charged amounts in excess of the Medicare allowable amount. Company A has certified that it will not require beneficiaries to pay more than 20% of the Medicare allowable amount.

person for the furnishing or arranging for the furnishing of any item or service for which payment may be made in whole or in part under a Federal health care program, or to purchase, lease, order, or arrange for or recommend purchasing, leasing, or ordering any good, facility, service, or item for which payment may be made in whole or in part under a Federal health care program, shall be guilty of a felony."

Id. Thus, where remuneration is paid purposefully to induce referrals of items or services for which payment may be made by a Federal health care program, the anti-kickback statute is violated. By its terms, the statute ascribes criminal liability to parties on both sides of an impermissible "kickback" transaction. For purposes of the anti-kickback statute, "remuneration" includes the transfer of anything of value, in cash or in-kind, directly or indirectly, covertly or overtly.

The statute has been interpreted to cover any arrangement where one purpose of the remuneration was to obtain money for the referral of services or to induce further referrals. United States v. Kats, 871 F.2d 105 (9th Cir. 1989); United States v. Greber, 760 F.2d 68 (3d Cir.), cert. denied, 474 U.S. 988 (1985). Violation of the statute constitutes a felony punishable by a maximum fine of $25,000, imprisonment up to five years, or both. Conviction will also lead to automatic exclusion from Federal health care programs, including Medicare and Medicaid. This Office may also initiate administrative proceedings to exclude persons from Federal and state health care programs or to impose civil monetary penalties for fraud, kickbacks, and other prohibited activities under sections 1128(b)(7) and 1128A (a)(7) of the Act. [5]

III. THE OIG WILL NOT SUBJECT THE REQUESTERS TO SANCTIONS UNDER SECTION 1128B(B) OF THE ACT

The threshold inquiry under the anti-kickback statute is whether the Proposed Arrangement involves any transfer of remuneration to a potential referral source, that is, to a person or entity that refers Federal health care program business or arranges for or recommends the purchase, lease, or ordering of items or services reimbursable by a Federal health care program. Payments by a health care entity to a charitable organization — particularly one

[5] Because both the criminal and administrative sanctions related to the anti-kickback implications of the Proposed Arrangement are based on violations of the anti-kickback statute, the analysis for purposes of this advisory opinion is the same under both.

with a health care mission — in exchange for the exclusive use of the charitable organization's name, logo, and other proprietary symbols and phrases for promotional purposes potentially implicate the plain language of the statute. Depending on the circumstances, the use of the name, logo, and other propriety material in promotional materials may amount to an express or implied recommendation by the charitable organization of the entity's products or services. To the extent such products or services are covered by the Federal health care programs, the statute may be implicated. We have said previously that in evaluating the risks posed by arrangements involving direct or indirect promotional or marketing activity, we look at a number of factors, including, but not limited to, the following:

- The identity of the party engaged in the marketing or promotional activity and the party's relationship with its audience.
- The item or service being promoted or marketed.
- The nature of the marketing or promotional activity.
- The target audience.[6]

These factors are not indicative or necessarily probative of whether a practice, in fact, violates the anti-kickback statute. Rather, we weigh these factors, as well as other relevant concerns, in assessing the level of risk presented by promotional and marketing activity. These factors are not exclusive and the presence or absence of any one factor is not determinative of whether, in our discretion, we would subject parties engaged in marketing or promotional activity to sanctions for violating the anti-kickback statute.

In the instant case, consideration of these factors, coupled with other factors described below, suggests that the risk of unlawful kickbacks posed by the Proposed Arrangement is low.

We begin by recognizing that Charity B, like many nonprofit organizations, likely enjoys a high level of public recognition and trust, particularly among those in State X affected by respiratory diseases. Thus, a recommendation or endorsement by Charity B of Company A's products or services would probably carry great weight. However, where, as here, there is no recommendation or endorsement of any Company A product or service, Charity B's ability to influence referrals is more limited. In this regard, Company A and Charity B have certified that:

[6] See OIG Advisory Opinion 99–8 (July 6, 1999).

- Promotional activities will be limited to identifying, describing, or portraying generally the Proposed Arrangement and/or Charity B's charitable activities, without reference to any of Company A's products or services;
- Charity B's marks will not be used in, or in connection with, any Company A product or service advertising; and
- Advertisements will not be placed or distributed in such a way as to suggest Charity B's endorsement of any Company A product or service (e.g., advertisements about the Proposed Arrangement will not be placed alongside or in the vicinity of any Company A product advertisements; customer brochures about the Proposed Arrangement will not be accompanied by advertisements for specific Company A products or services).

Moreover, the promotional activities primarily involve print advertisements in trade publications aimed, not at prospective patient customers, but at a less vulnerable audience (i.e., health care professionals, such as DME suppliers, physicians, and respiratory therapists). There will be no direct contact with prospective Company A patient customers. Direct contact with existing customers will be limited to brochures generally describing the Proposed Arrangement, without reference to specific Company A products or services.

Other aspects of the arrangement provide additional protection against fraud and abuse. No physician, DME supplier, respiratory therapist, or other health care professional in a position to refer patients to Company A will receive any remuneration under the Proposed Arrangement. Moreover, there is no risk that Company A will pass the costs of its donations on to Medicare through increased billings, as Company A's usual and customary charge is already substantially higher than the Medicare fee schedule.[7] Nor will it pass those costs on to Medicaid, which pays under a fee schedule. In addition, Company A has certified that it will not seek to pass the costs of donations on to Federal beneficiaries by charging them in excess of the Federal program allowable amount.

---

[7] It would be inappropriate for Company A to offset its donations through higher billings to Medicare or other Federal programs. Thus, for example, if Company A's actual charges were lower than the Medicare fee schedule, Company A would be expected to bill Medicare the lower amount, without passing the cost of the donation to Charity B through to Medicare.

Finally, we recognize that the Proposed Arrangement's fund-raising potential may significantly benefit children with asthma and others affected by respiratory diseases. In addition, the Proposed Arrangement may help Charity B publicize its programs to physicians and others in a position to refer children for Charity B services, while conserving scarce Charity B resources that might otherwise be spent on outreach efforts. Assuming that promotional activity under the Proposed Arrangement is truthful, non-deceptive, and not misleading, we think the Proposed Arrangement will generally benefit the public.

In sum, for the totality of the above reasons, we would not subject Company A or Charity B to sanctions arising under the anti-kickback statute in connection with the Proposed Arrangement.

IV. THE OIG WILL NOT SUBJECT THE REQUESTERS TO CIVIL MONETARY PENALTIES UNDER SECTION 1128A(a)(5) OF THE ACT

Section 1128A(a)(5) of the Act prohibits a person from offering or transferring remuneration to a beneficiary that such person knows or should know is likely to influence the beneficiary to order items or services from a particular provider or supplier for which payment may be made under the Medicare and Medicaid programs.

Company A and Charity B are concerned that the Proposed Arrangement may implicate section 1128A(a)(5), insofar as some beneficiaries might believe they stand a better chance of being able to participate in free Charity B programs (which are sometimes oversubscribed) if they purchase Company A's products. Even if this were likely, on the facts presented we do not believe the statute would be implicated. Any connection between participation in a Charity B program and the purchase of Company A's products would be wholly speculative. Thus, for the reasons stated here and above in Section III, the OIG will not subject Company A or Charity B to sanctions under section 1128A(a)(5) of the Act in connection with the Proposed Arrangement.

V. CONCLUSION

Based on the information provided, we conclude that (i) the Proposed Arrangement would potentially generate prohibited remuneration under the anti-kickback statute, if the requisite intent to induce referrals were present, but that the OIG will not subject Company A or Charity B to sanctions arising under the anti-kickback statute pursuant to sections 1128(b)(7) or 1128A(a)(7) of the Act in connection with the Proposed Arrangement, as described and certified in the request letter and supplemental submissions; and (ii) the OIG will not subject Company A or Charity B to sanctions under section 1128A(a)(5) of the Act in connection with the Proposed Arrangement.

VI. LIMITATIONS

The limitations applicable to this opinion include the following:

- This advisory opinion is issued only to Company A, and Charity B, the requesters of this opinion. This advisory opinion has no application to, and cannot be relied upon by, any other individual or entity.
- This advisory opinion may not be introduced into evidence in any matter involving an entity or individual that is not a requester to this opinion.
- This advisory opinion is applicable only to the statutory provisions specifically noted above in the first paragraph of this opinion. No opinion is herein expressed or implied with respect to the application of any other Federal, state, or local statute, rule, regulation, ordinance, or other law that may be applicable to the Proposed Arrangement.
- This advisory opinion will not bind or obligate any agency other than the U.S. Department of Health and Human Services.
- This advisory opinion is limited in scope to the specific arrangement described in this letter and has no applicability to other arrangements, even those that appear similar in nature or scope.
- No opinion is expressed herein regarding the liability of any party under the False Claims Act or other legal authorities for any improper billing, claims submission, cost reporting, or related conduct.

This opinion is also subject to any additional limitations set forth at 42 C.F.R. Part 1008.

The OIG will not proceed against the requesters with respect to any action that is part of the Proposed Arrangement taken in good faith reliance upon this advisory opinion as long as all of the material facts have been fully, completely, and accurately presented, and the Proposed Arrangement in practice comports with the information provided. The OIG reserves the right to reconsider the questions and issues raised in this advisory opinion and, where the public interest requires, rescind, modify, or terminate this opinion. In the event that this advisory opinion is modified or terminated, the OIG will not proceed against the requesters with respect to any action taken in good faith reliance upon this advisory opinion, where all of the relevant facts were fully, completely, and accurately presented, and where such action was promptly discontinued upon notification of the modification or termination of this advisory opinion. An advisory opinion may be rescinded only if the relevant and material facts have not been fully, completely, and accurately disclosed to the OIG.

Sincerely,

/s/

D. McCarty Thornton Chief Counsel to the Inspector General

APPENDIX F43

Advisory Opinion No. 99–11, October 25, 1999

Concerning an arrangement sponsored by Coalition A to provide psychotherapy services at free or reduced prices using residents from local teaching facilities as clinicians.

Issued: October 25, 1999

[Name & Address Redacted]

Re: OIG Advisory Opinion No. 99–11 Dear [Name Redacted]: We are writing in response to your request for an advisory opinion concerning an arrangement sponsored by Coalition A (the "Coalition") to provide psychotherapy services at free or reduced prices using residents from local teaching facilities as clinicians (the "Arrangement"). Specifically, you have inquired whether the Arrangement constitutes grounds for sanctions under the anti-kickback statute, section 1128B(b) of the Social Security Act (the "Act"), or under section 1128A(a)(5) of the Act, which prohibits the offering of inducements to beneficiaries in order to influence their selection of a provider for Medicare or Medicaid covered services.

In issuing this opinion, we have relied solely on the facts and information presented to us. We have not undertaken an independent investigation of such information. This opinion is limited to the facts presented. If material facts have not been disclosed or have been misrepresented, this opinion is without force and effect.

Based on the information provided, we conclude (i) that the Arrangement would potentially generate prohibited remuneration under the anti-kickback statute, if the requisite intent to induce referrals were present, but that, based on the totality of the facts present in the Arrangement as described and certified in your request letter and supplemental submissions, the Office of Inspector General ("OIG") will not subject the Coalition to sanctions for violations of the anti-kickback statute under sections 1128(b)(7) or 1128A (a)(7) of the Act; and (ii) that the OIG will not subject the Coalition to sanctions under section 1128A(a)(5) of the Act in connection with the

Arrangement as described and certified in your request letter and supplemental submissions.

This opinion may not be relied on by any persons other than the Coalition, the requester of this opinion, and is further qualified as set out in Part IV below and in 42 C.F.R. Part 1008.

I. FACTUAL BACKGROUND

The Coalition is a State X nonprofit organization formed by Foundation B, a 501(c)(3) charitable organization that operates for the benefit and in support of the Coalition; Entity C; and Entity D. Pursuant to the Arrangement, the Coalition provides psychodynamically-oriented psychotherapy at free or reduced prices to individuals who meet financial and clinical criteria. The therapy is typically provided by advanced psychiatric residents from local teaching facilities. [1] The residents donate their time and services to the Coalition, as do members of the teaching faculties who provide clinical training and supervision.

The teaching facilities involved in the Arrangement are Hospital E, Hospital F, and Hospital G (collectively, the "Participating Institutions"). The Arrangement enables the Participating Institutions to provide training to their residents in psychodynamically-oriented psychotherapy (a less time-intensive and less costly form of talk therapy than psychoanalysis) which they are not currently providing. A total of 45 to 50 residents provide services under the Arrangement. Prior to the Arrangement, these residents had to arrange and pay for supervised training in this form of therapy outside their residency programs.

The Coalition handles all billing and collections; neither the clinicians, nor their supervisors, bill for services provided under the Arrangement. Although some services that the Coalition provides may be covered by insurance, including Medicare or Medicaid, the Coalition does not bill Medicare, Medicaid, or any other third party insurer. In addition, the Coalition notifies patients that they are ineligible for Coalition services if they seek third-party reimbursement.

The Coalition screens prospective patients based on financial and clinical criteria. Most of the Coalition's patients self-pay for the therapy sessions on a sliding fee schedule based on income and family size. However, the Coalition does not charge Medicare benefi-

[1] Any qualified psychiatrist may participate in the Arrangement, although most clinicians are expected to be psychiatric residents.

ciaries for any Medicare-covered services. The Coalition anticipates that no more than ten percent of its total patient population will be Medicare beneficiaries.

If a clinician determines that a patient is not suitable for long-term psychoanalytic treatment after a four to six session evaluation (e.g., the patient needs hospitalization or treatment for drug or alcohol addiction), the Coalition suggests that the patient obtain services from an alternative treatment resource. The Coalition provides the patient with a list of such resources, but does not take further steps to refer the patient (the Coalition does make a follow-up phone call to the patient to try to ensure that the patient contacts an alternative treatment provider). The top resource on the list is the community mental health clinic for the catchment area in which the patient resides. The list does not include any Participating Institutions, unless the patient was originally referred to the Coalition from a Participating Institution, in which case the list may include the Participating Institution.[2]

The Coalition anticipates making an average of two alternative treatment referrals each year, even if the patient enrollment in the Arrangement is at capacity.[3] The alternative treatment services are provided outside the scope of the Arrangement, and providers of such services may bill third-party insurers, including Medicare and Medicaid.

Currently, there are no more than twenty patients enrolled on an on-going basis. The Coalition estimates that it will serve approximately forty to fifty patients each year.[4] The Coalition publicizes the availability of the Arrangement (primarily through word-of-mouth) to prospective patients and to other programs that may be interested in the Arrangement, such as university counseling centers, research

---

[2] The Coalition discloses to patients the Participating Institutions' affiliation with the Arrangement and makes the five disclosures to patients enumerated in 42 C.F.R. § 1001.952(f)(4). Although disclosures of this type are insufficient to guard against Federal health care program abuses, effective disclosures offer some protection against possible abuses of patient trust.

[3] Any substantial increase in the number of referrals, particularly referrals to the Participating Institutions, could constitute a material change of fact and render this advisory opinion without force and effect.

[4] If the Coalition perceives that the community's needs exceed its twenty-patient capacity, the Coalition may consider expanding the Arrangement. Any substantial increase in enrollment could constitute a material change of fact and render this advisory opinion without force and effect.

programs, and employee assistance programs. Services are provided to patients at the clinicians' own offices.

The Coalition's costs of administering the Arrangement are funded through a mix of patient fee payments, various grant sources, and funding from its supporting foundation. Even at full capacity, the Coalition projects an operating loss for the Arrangement of approximately $[Y] per month.

II. LEGAL ANALYSIS

The anti-kickback statute makes it a criminal offense knowingly and willfully to offer, pay, solicit, or receive any remuneration to induce referrals of items or services reimbursable by any Federal health care program. See section 1128B(b) of the Act. Specifically, the statute provides that:

"Whoever knowingly and willfully offers or pays [or solicits or receives] any remuneration (including any kickback, bribe, or rebate) directly or indirectly, overtly or covertly, in cash or in kind to any person to induce such person — to refer an individual to a person for the furnishing or arranging for the furnishing of any item or service for which payment may be made in whole or in part under a Federal health care program, or to purchase, lease, order, or arrange for or recommend purchasing, leasing, or ordering any good, facility, service, or item for which payment may be made in whole or in part under a Federal health care program, shall be guilty of a felony."

Id. Thus, where remuneration is paid purposefully to induce referrals of items or services for which payment may be made by a Federal health care program, the anti-kickback statute is violated. By its terms, the statute ascribes criminal liability to parties on both sides of an impermissible "kickback" transaction. For purposes of the anti-kickback statute, "remuneration" includes the transfer of anything of value, in cash or in-kind, directly or indirectly, covertly or overtly. The statute has been interpreted to cover any arrangement where one purpose of the remuneration was to obtain money for the referral of services or to induce further referrals. United States v. Kats, 871 F.2d 105 (9th Cir. 1989); United States v. Greber, 760 F.2d 68 (3d Cir.), cert. denied, 474 U.S. 988 (1985). Violation of the statute constitutes a felony punishable by a maximum fine of $25,000, imprisonment up to five years, or both. Conviction will also lead to automatic exclusion from Federal health care programs, including Medicare and Medicaid. The OIG may also initiate administrative proceedings to exclude persons from Federal and State health care programs or to impose civil monetary penalties for fraud, kickbacks, and other prohibited activities under sections 1128(b)(7) and 1128A(a)(7) of the Act.[5]

The Department of Health and Human Services has promulgated safe harbor regulations that define practices that are not subject to the anti-kickback statute because such practices would be unlikely to result in fraud or abuse. See 42 C.F.R. § 1001.952. The safe harbors set forth specific conditions that, if met, assure entities involved of not being prosecuted or sanctioned for the arrangement qualifying for the safe harbor. However, safe harbor protection is afforded only to those arrangements that precisely meet all of the conditions set forth in the safe harbor. The regulatory safe harbor potentially applicable to the Arrangement protects certain referral services, 42 C.F.R. § 1001.952(f). However, based on the facts presented, the Arrangement is not a referral service; rather, through the Arrangement, the Coalition provides clinical services for which it collects fees from patients.

The Arrangement raises concerns under the anti-kickback statute to the extent that the Participating Institutions may be providing free clinical services to the Coalition as a means of generating referrals of alternative treatment mental health business that they can bill to a Federal health care program. The OIG's position on the provision of free or below market value goods or services to potential referral sources is longstanding and clear: the provision of free goods or services to an actual or potential referral source may violate the anti-kickback statute, depending on the circumstances. For example, the preamble to the 1991 safe harbor regulations explains that giving free goods that have an independent value to a physician may violate the anti-kickback statute. See 56 Fed. Reg. 35978 (July 29, 1991); see also Special Fraud Alert, 59 Fed. Reg. 65372, 65377 (Dec. 19, 1994); OIG Advisory Opinion 98–16. This analysis generally applies to the provision of any free or below market value goods or services to actual or potential referral sources. If the requisite intent to induce or reward referrals of Federal health care program business is present, the anti-kickback statute is violated.

In addition, we generally have heightened concerns about abuses in the area of mental health services, where medical necessity deter-

---

[5] Because both the criminal and administrative sanctions related to the anti-kickback implications of the Arrangement are based on violations of the anti-kickback statute, the analysis for purposes of this advisory opinion is the same under both.

minations are often subjective and the risk of overutilization is substantial. See, e.g., Review of Partial Hospitalization Services Provided Through Community Mental Health Centers (A-04–98–02146; 10/98).

Notwithstanding, based on the totality of the facts presented, we conclude that the Arrangement poses a minimal risk of Federal health care program or patient fraud or abuse given the small number of patients enrolled at any given time, the limited number of anticipated alternative treatment source referrals, and the fact that no Federal health care programs are billed for services provided under the Arrangement. Moreover, the Participating Institutions have a legitimate business purpose for participating in the Arrangement, namely that the Arrangement affords them additional training opportunities for their advanced psychiatric residents. Finally, the Arrangement potentially offers a significant community benefit through increased access to mental health services for lower income community residents.

For these reasons, we would not impose sanctions on the Coalition for violations of the anti-kickback statute in connection with the Arrangement. In addition, we would not impose sanctions arising under section 1128A(a)(5) of the Act (the civil money penalty provision prohibiting inducements to beneficiaries to influence their selection of providers of Medicare or Medicaid covered services), because the Coalition does not provide any services for which it — or anyone else — bills Medicare or Medicaid.

III. CONCLUSION

Based on the information provided, we conclude (i) that the Arrangement would potentially generate prohibited remuneration under the anti-kickback statute, if the requisite intent to induce referrals were present, but that, based on the totality of the facts present in the Arrangement as described and certified in the request letter and supplemental submissions, the OIG will not subject the Coalition to sanctions for violations of the anti-kickback statute under sections 1128(b)(7) or 1128A(a)(7) of the Act; and (ii) that the OIG will not subject the Coalition to sanctions under section 1128A (a)(5) of the Act in connection with the Arrangement as described and certified in the request letter and supplemental submissions.

IV. LIMITATIONS

The limitations applicable to this opinion include the following:

- This advisory opinion is issued only to the Coalition, the requester of this opinion.
- This advisory opinion has no application to, and cannot be relied upon by, any other individual or entity.
- This advisory opinion may not be introduced into evidence in any matter involving an entity or individual that is not a requester to this opinion.
- This advisory opinion is applicable only to the statutory provisions specifically noted above in the first paragraph of this opinion.
- No opinion is herein expressed or implied with respect to the application of any other Federal, state, or local statute, rule, regulation, ordinance, or other law that may be applicable to the Arrangement.
- This advisory opinion will not bind or obligate any agency other than the U.S. Department of Health and Human Services.

This advisory opinion is limited in scope to the specific arrangement described in this letter and has no applicability to other arrangements, even those that appear similar in nature or scope.

No opinion is expressed herein regarding the liability of any party under the False Claims Act or other legal authorities for any improper billing, claims submission, cost reporting, or related conduct. This opinion is also subject to any additional limitations set forth at 42 C.F.R. Part 1008. The OIG will not proceed against the requester with respect to any action that is part of the Arrangement taken in good faith reliance upon this advisory opinion as long as all of the material facts have been fully, completely, and accurately presented, and the Arrangement in practice comports with the information provided. The OIG reserves the right to reconsider the questions and issues raised in this advisory opinion and, where the public interest requires, rescind, modify, or terminate this opinion. In the event that this advisory opinion is modified or terminated, the OIG will not proceed against the requester with respect to any action taken in good faith reliance upon this advisory opinion, where all of the relevant facts were fully, completely, and accurately presented, and where such action was promptly discontinued upon notification of the modification or termination of this advisory opinion. An advisory opinion may be rescinded only if the relevant and material facts have not been fully, completely, and accurately disclosed to the OIG.

Sincerely,

/s/

D. McCarty Thornton
Chief Counsel to the Inspector General

APPENDIX F44

Advisory Opinion No. 99–12, November 23, 1999

About a proposed marketing program involving the use of physician practices and health care clinics to distribute coupons redeemable by certain retailers . . . for discounts on items or services that are not reimbursable by any Federal health care program.

Issued: November 23, 1999

[name and address redacted]

Re: OIG Advisory Opinion No. 99–12

Dear [name redacted]:

We are writing in response to your request for an advisory opinion about a proposed marketing program involving the use of physician practices and health care clinics to distribute coupons redeemable by certain retailers (including grocery stores, pharmacies, and internet companies) for discounts on items or services that are not reimbursable by any Federal health care program (the "Proposed Arrangement"). Specifically, the question raised by your request is whether the Proposed Arrangement constitutes grounds for sanctions under the anti-kickback statute, section 1128B(b) of the Social Security Act (the "Act"), or under the civil monetary penalty for inducements to beneficiaries, section 1128A(a)(5) of the Act, in the circumstances presented.

In issuing this opinion, we have relied solely on the facts and information presented to us. We have not undertaken an independent investigation of such information. This opinion is limited to the facts presented. If material facts have not been disclosed or have been misrepresented, this opinion is without force and effect.

Based on the information provided, we conclude that, based on the totality of the facts of the Proposed Arrangement (as described and certified in the request letter and supplemental submissions), the Proposed Arrangement does not implicate the anti-kickback statute and that the Office of Inspector General ("OIG") will not subject Company A to sanctions for violations of the anti-kickback statute pursuant to sections 1128(b)(7) or 1128A(a)(7) of the Act in connection with the Proposed Arrangement, nor will the OIG impose civil monetary penalties on Company A in connection with the Proposed Arrangement for violations of the prohibition against inducements to beneficiaries under section 1128A(a)(5) of the Act.

This opinion may not be relied on by any persons other than Company A, the requester of this opinion, and is further qualified as set out in Part V below and in 42 C.F.R. Part 1008.

I. FACTUAL BACKGROUND

Company A ("Company A") is a closely-held State X corporation formed for the purpose of marketing products related and unrelated to the delivery of health care. Company A is not owned by, or affiliated with, any entity or person involved in the health care business. Company A has developed the Proposed Arrangement, a marketing program designed to increase customer traffic for participating retailers through the distribution of discount coupons by physicians and health care clinics.

Under the Proposed Arrangement, Company A will contract with retailers, including retail grocery stores, pharmacies, and internet companies (collectively, the "contracting retailers") to coordinate the printing and distribution of coupons redeemable for discounts at the retailers. Some of these contracting retailers will be involved in the delivery of health care items or services, and some people who receive the coupons will be Federal health care program beneficiaries who may purchase or order products or services from the contracting retailer that are reimbursable under a Federal health care program (e.g., prescription drugs payable by Medicaid). However, the coupons will not be valid for discounts on any items or services reimbursable by a Federal health care program, nor will their redemption be conditioned in any fashion on the purchase of any items or services reimbursable by a Federal health care program; rather, the coupons will offer discounts on non-prescription, over-the-counter products. The coupons will be given to all individuals as they exit a clinic or physician's office, irrespective of their insurance coverage or whether they are likely to require covered items or services that the contracting retailer provides. Coupon recipients will be free to use or discard the coupon. The coupons are typically expected to be worth approximately $[x] and will not exceed $[y].

Company A has represented that the fee for its marketing services will be a fixed amount set in arms-length negotiations between Company A and each contracting retailer, will represent fair market value for Company A's marketing services,[1] and will not be determined in a manner that takes into account the volume or value of any Federally-reimbursable business generated (directly or indirectly) by the Proposed Arrangement. The fee paid by each contracting retailer will cover all of Company A's costs associated with performance of the contract to which the fee applies, including all costs associated with engaging physicians and health care clinics to distribute the coupons. Accordingly, Company A has a significant economic incentive to contain costs.

Taking into account the retailers' preferences as to markets and geographic location for the coupon distribution, Company A will enter into contracts with health care clinics and physician groups in the relevant locations to distribute the coupons. The length of the contracts will vary depending on the volume of coupons to be distributed by the particular clinic or physician group (in some cases the volume of coupons could be in the many thousands).

Company A has represented that the fee to be paid to the physicians and clinics will be fixed in arms-length transactions between Company A and the physicians and clinics, will be a few cents per coupon (usually less than [z] cents), will be set in advance (typically a fixed amount per coupon distributed), will represent fair market value for the distribution services, and will not be determined in a manner that takes into account the volume or value of any Federally-reimbursable business generated (directly or indirectly) by the Proposed Arrangement.

II. THE ANTI-KICKBACK STATUTE

The anti-kickback statute makes it a criminal offense knowingly and wilfully to offer, pay, solicit, or receive any remuneration to induce referrals of items or services reimbursable by the Federal health care programs. See section 1128B(b) of the Act. In relevant part for purposes of this advisory opinion, the statute prohibits the purposeful transfer of remuneration to a person or entity to induce the person or entity to arrange for or recommend the purchasing or ordering of a good or service payable by a Federal health care program. By its terms, the statute ascribes liability to parties on both sides of an impermissible "kickback" transaction. For purposes of

[1] We are not authorized to opine on "fair market value." See section 1128D(b)(3) of the Act. Therefore, for purposes of this opinion, we have assumed fair market value compensation based on Company A's certifications. If the compensation under the Proposed Arrangement is not at fair market value, this opinion will be without force and effect.

the anti-kickback statute, "remuneration" includes the transfer of anything of value, in cash or in-kind, directly or indirectly, covertly or overtly.[2]

The statute has been interpreted to cover any arrangement where one purpose of the remuneration was to obtain money for the referral of services or to induce further referrals. United States v. Kats, 871 F.2d 105 (9th Cir. 1989); United States v. Greber, 760 F.2d 68 (3d Cir.), cert. denied, 474 U.S. 988 (1985). Violation of the statute constitutes a felony punishable by a maximum fine of $25,000, imprisonment up to five years, or both. Conviction will also lead to automatic exclusion from Federal health care programs, including Medicare and Medicaid. The OIG may also initiate administrative proceedings to exclude persons from Federal and State health care programs or to impose civil monetary penalties for fraud, kickbacks, and other prohibited activities under sections 1128(b)(7) and 1128A (a)(7) of the Act.[3]

A. Analysis

Marketing by physicians or other health care professionals — sometimes referred to as "white coat" marketing — is closely scrutinized under the anti-kickback statute. Such parties are in an exceptional position of public trust and thus may exert undue influence when recommending health care-related items or services, especially when marketing to their patients. See, e.g., 56 Fed. Reg. 35974. Given the nature of the physician-patient relationship, when physicians market items and services to their patients, patients may have difficulty distinguishing between the physician's professional medical advice on the one hand and a commercial sales pitch on the other.

Notwithstanding, we conclude that, on the facts presented, the Proposed Arrangement does not fall within the ambit of the anti-kickback statute, and even if it did, we would not subject Com-

---

[2] Although the Department of Health and Human Services has promulgated safe harbor regulations that define practices that are not subject to the anti-kickback statute, 42 C.F.R. § 1001.952, no safe harbor protects the Proposed Arrangement. The requirements of the personal services and management contracts safe harbor, § 1001.952(d), will not be met here in every case.

[3] Because both the criminal and administrative sanctions related to the anti-kickback implications of the Proposed Arrangement are based on violations of the anti-kickback statute, the analysis for purposes of this advisory opinion is the same under both.

pany A to OIG sanctions for violation of the anti-kickback statute. Simply put, on the facts presented, neither the contracting retailers nor Company A is paying the physicians and health care clinics to arrange for or recommend the purchase or order of items or services reimbursable by a Federal health care program.

Under the Proposed Arrangement, the physicians and clinics will be paid to distribute coupons that will entitle the holders to discounts on purchases of certain items that are not reimbursable by any Federal health care program at select retail stores.[4] The coupons will not be tied directly or indirectly to the purchase or order of any items or services covered by a Federal health care program. The physicians and clinics will be required to distribute the coupons to all of their patients, without regard to their insurance coverage or the likelihood that they will require Federally-covered items or services provided by the retailer, or indeed will patronize the retailer at all. The contracting retailers will be businesses offering a wide variety of medical and non-medical items and services; none will be businesses specializing in Federally-reimbursable items or services (e.g., storefront medical equipment shops). Given the totality of the circumstances, the conduct of the physicians and health clinics under the Proposed Arrangement cannot reasonably be construed as recommending or arranging for the purchase or order of Federally-reimbursable items or services.

Our conclusion that the Proposed Arrangement does not implicate the anti-kickback statute derives from the particular facts presented. In the instant case, we might have reached a different conclusion if, by way of example only, any of the following factors had been present:

---

[4] Company A has certified that the physicians' and clinics' compensation for distributing the coupons will be consistent with fair market value and fixed in arms-length negotiations. See supra note 1. "Per click", "per patient", "per order", and similar payment arrangements are highly disfavored under the anti-kickback statute. Here, compensation under the Proposed Arrangement will not be based directly or indirectly on the volume or value of business — Federal or otherwise — that the coupons generate (as might be the case, for example, if the physicians and clinics were paid based on the number of coupons redeemed by, or the value of retail sales made to, their patients). While it is possible that some physicians and clinics may realize an intangible "good will" benefit from distributing retail coupons to patients, the value of any such benefit is likely to be small in these particular circumstances and, given the economic structure of the Proposed Arrangement, accounted for in the arms-length negotiations between Company A and the physicians and clinics.

- Coupons tied directly or indirectly to the order or purchase of an item or service covered by a Federal health care program (e.g., coupon redemption conditioned directly or indirectly on the purchase of a reimbursable item or service, such as a covered prescription drug or device; or coupons with values that vary based on the purchase of a Federally-reimbursable item or service);
- Distribution of coupons targeted at Federal health care program beneficiaries (e.g., distributed primarily to Federal health care program beneficiaries); or
- Coupons with exceptionally large values.

Any one of these or other factors may have resulted in a different outcome in this opinion.

III. SECTION 1128A(a)(5) OF THE ACT

A further question arises as to whether the Proposed Arrangement violates section 1128A(a)(5) of the Act, which prohibits a person from offering or transferring remuneration to a beneficiary that such person knows or should know is likely to influence the beneficiary to order items or services from a particular provider, practitioner, or supplier for which payment may be made by Medicare or a State health care program. For purposes of section 1128A (a)(5), "remuneration" includes transfers of items or services for free or for other than fair market value. See section 1128A(a)(6) of the Act.

Under the Proposed Arrangement, the relationship between the coupon distribution and any inducement to a Medicare or Medicaid beneficiary to choose a particular provider for a covered item or service will be attenuated, at best. As noted above, the coupons are not tied (directly or indirectly) to the purchase of any items or services covered by Medicare or Medicaid, nor is the distribution targeted at patients who are likely to purchase or order items or services for which Medicare or Medicaid will reimburse the retailer offering the discount (e.g., the coupons are not distributed only to patients who leave their physician's office with a prescription in hand). The coupons may not be applied to any Medicare- or Medicaid-covered item or service. The Proposed Arrangement is unlikely to give the clinics or physicians that distribute the coupons a significant competitive advantage in the marketplace. For these reasons, in the particular circumstances of the Proposed Arrangement, the

OIG will not subject Company A to sanctions under section 1128A(a)(5) of the Act in connection with the Proposed Arrangement.

IV. CONCLUSION

Based on the information provided, we conclude that, based on the totality of the facts of the Proposed Arrangement (as described and certified in the request letter and supplemental submissions), the Proposed Arrangement does not implicate the anti-kickback statute and that the OIG will not subject Company A to sanctions for violations of the anti-kickback statute pursuant to sections 1128(b)(7) or 1128A(a)(7) of the Act in connection with the Proposed Arrangement, nor will the OIG impose civil monetary penalties on Company A, in connection with the Proposed Arrangement for violations of the prohibition against inducements to beneficiaries under section 1128A(a)(5) of the Act.

V. LIMITATIONS

The limitations applicable to this opinion include the following:

- This advisory opinion is issued only to Company A, the requester of this opinion. This advisory opinion has no application to, and cannot be relied upon by, any other individual or entity.
- This advisory opinion may not be introduced into evidence in any matter involving an entity or individual that is not a requester to this opinion.
- This advisory opinion is applicable only to the statutory provisions specifically noted above. No opinion is herein expressed or implied with respect to the application of any other Federal, state, or local statute, rule, regulation, ordinance, or other law that may be applicable to the Proposed Arrangement.
- This advisory opinion will not bind or obligate any agency other than the U.S. Department of Health and Human Services.
- This advisory opinion is limited in scope to the specific arrangement described in this letter and has no applicability to other arrangements, even those that appear similar in nature or scope.
- No opinion is expressed herein regarding the liability of any party under the False Claims Act or other legal authorities for any improper billing, claims submission, cost reporting, or related conduct. This opinion is also subject to any additional limitations set forth at 42 C.F.R. Part 1008.

The OIG will not proceed against the requester with respect to any action that is part of the Proposed Arrangement taken in good faith reliance upon this advisory opinion as long as all of the material facts have been fully, completely, and accurately presented, the fees paid under the Proposed Arrangement are fair market value, and the Proposed Arrangement in practice comports with the information provided. The OIG reserves the right to reconsider the questions and issues raised in this advisory opinion and, where the public interest requires, rescind, modify, or terminate this opinion. In the event that this advisory opinion is modified or terminated, the OIG will not proceed against the requester with respect to any action taken in good faith reliance upon this advisory opinion, where all of the relevant facts were fully, completely, and accurately presented, where the fees paid under the Proposed Arrangement were at fair market value, and where such action was promptly discontinued upon notification of the modification or termination of this advisory opinion. An advisory opinion may be rescinded only if the relevant and material facts have not been fully, completely, and accurately disclosed to the OIG.

Sincerely,
D. McCarty Thornton
Chief Counsel to the Inspector General

APPENDIX F45

Advisory Opinion No. 99–13, November 30, 1999

Regarding certain arrangements for discounted pathology services provided to physicians.

Issued: November 30, 1999

[name and address redacted]

Re: OIG Advisory Opinion No. 99–13 Dear [name redacted]:

We are writing in response to your request for an advisory opinion regarding certain arrangements for discounted pathology services provided to physicians (the "Proposed Arrangement"). You have asked whether the Proposed Arrangement would result in prohibited remuneration under the anti-kickback statute, section 1128B(b) of the Social Security Act (the "Act") or would constitute grounds for the imposition of sanctions under the anti-kickback statute, section 1128B(b) of the Act, the exclusion authority related to kickbacks, section 1128(b)(7) of the Act, or the civil monetary penalty provision for kickbacks, section 1128A(a)(7) of the Act. In addition, you have asked whether the Proposed Arrangement would constitute grounds for a permissive exclusion for charging Medicare or Medicaid substantially in excess of the usual charges, section 1128(b)(6)(A) of the Act.

In issuing this opinion, we have relied solely on the facts and information presented to us. We have not undertaken an independent investigation of such information. This opinion is limited to the facts presented. If material facts have not been disclosed or have been misrepresented, this opinion is without force and effect.

Based on the facts certified in your request for an advisory opinion, we conclude that the Proposed Arrangement might constitute prohibited remuneration under the anti-kickback statute if the requisite intent to induce referrals of Federal health care program business were present and might be subject to sanctions arising under sections 1128B(b), 1128(b)(7), and 1128A(a)(7) of the Act, as well as grounds for a permissive exclusion under section 1128(b)(6)(A) of the Act.

This opinion may not be relied on by any person other than the addressee and is further qualified as set out in Part IV below and in 42 C.F.R. Part 1008.

I. FACTUAL BACKGROUND

A. [Company A]

Company A is a State X professional corporation with three shareholders, all of whom are specialists in pathology and are licensed to practice medicine in State X. Company A employs five pathologists and fourteen technicians. It provides pathology services (including clinical and anatomic pathology services)[1] to five hospitals, as well as to the patients of physicians in private practice.

B. Billing Procedures

Company A has several billing methodologies depending upon the payor. For Federal health care program patients, Company A bills its charges to the government payor and bills the patients for any applicable copayments or deductibles.

For non-Federal health care program patients, referring physicians have two payment options. One option is for Company A to bill its charges directly to the applicable third-party payor, and bill the patients for any copayments or deductibles. The alternative is for Company A to bill the physicians for the pathology services and accept that payment as payment in full. The physicians then bill the third-party payors and patients for the purchased pathology services. This option is commonly referred to as "account billing".

Under its account billing arrangements, Company A has traditionally offered physicians a discount off its usual charges which reflects the cost savings it realizes. Company A generates a single monthly statement to the referring physician who is required to pay on a prompt basis. Company A has represented that an account billing arrangement saves time and expense because: (i) claims are not submitted to a wide range of payors; (ii) Company A need not consider the claims submission criteria of the various payors; and (iii) Company A is not responsible for determining and collecting applicable copayments and deductibles owed by the patients. In addition, Company A realizes a better collection rate under account billing. Most physicians who have an account billing arrangement with Company A refer virtually all of their patients to Company A, whether the patients' specimens are covered under the account bill-

[1] Throughout this opinion, the term pathology services is synonymous with laboratory services.

ing arrangement or are directly billed to the Federal health care programs.[2]

C. The Proposed Arrangement

Under the Proposed Arrangement, Company A will offer its account billing customers discounts that are greater than its cost savings, in order to match the prices of its competitors. Some of the discounted charges will be below the actual cost of providing the pathology services. In addition, Company A's profit margin for the non-Federal health care program business under the Proposed Arrangement would be less than the profit margin on the services that it bills directly to Federal health care programs. The discount will not be conditioned upon the physicians sending Company A its Federal health care program business. However, Company A has assumed that the physicians receiving discounts under the Proposed Arrangement will send virtually all of their patients to Company A. If Company A does not match the discounts of its competitors, Company A has represented that it will lose both the account billing business and the Federal health care program business of those clients.

II. LEGAL ANALYSIS

A. The Anti-Kickback Statute

The anti-kickback statute makes it a criminal offense knowingly and wilfully to offer, pay, solicit, or receive any remuneration to induce referrals of items or services reimbursable by Federal health care programs. See section 1128B(b) of the Act. Where remuneration is paid purposefully to induce referrals of items or services paid for by a Federal health care program, the anti-kickback statute is violated. By its terms, the statute ascribes liability to parties on both sides of an impermissible "kickback" transaction. For purposes of the anti-kickback statute, "remuneration" includes the transfer of anything of value, in cash or in-kind, directly or indirectly, covertly or overtly. The statute has been interpreted to cover any arrangement where one purpose of the remuneration is to obtain money for referral of services or to induce further referrals. United States v. Kats, 871 F.2d 105 (9th Cir. 1989); United States v. Greber, 760 F.2d 68 (3d Cir.), cert. denied, 474 U.S. 988 (1985). Violation of the statute constitutes a felony punishable by a maximum fine of $25,000, imprisonment up to five years or both. Conviction will also lead to

---

[2] We express no opinion regarding the legality of their existing account billing arrangement under the anti-kickback statute, permissive exclusion, or any other legal authority.

automatic exclusion from Federal health care programs, including Medicare and Medicaid. This Office may also initiate administrative proceedings to exclude persons from Federal health care programs or to impose civil monetary penalties for fraud, kickbacks, and other prohibited activities under sections 1128(b)(7) and 1128A(a)(7) of the Act.[3]

1. Special Fraud Alert Relating to Arrangements for the Provision of Clinical Laboratory Services

In 1994, we issued a Special Fraud Alert describing certain laboratory practices that implicated the anti-kickback statute. The Special Fraud Alert set forth our analysis that when a laboratory offers or gives to a referral source anything of value for less than fair market value, an inference may be made that the thing of value is offered to induce the referral of business. Specifically, we gave the example of laboratories waiving charges for laboratory tests to physicians for managed care patients, in order to retain the high-paying non-managed care business. In that example, the free laboratory services for managed care patients could be a kickback between the laboratory and the physician for the fee-for-service patients.

2. The Discount Exception and Safe Harbor

The anti-kickback statute contains a statutory exception for "a discount or other reduction in price obtained by a provider of services or other entity under a Federal health care program if the reduction in price is properly disclosed and appropriately reflected in the costs claimed or charges made by the provider or entity under a Federal health care program." Section 1128B(b)(3)(A) of the Act. This discount exception reflects the intent of Congress to encourage price competition that benefits the Medicare and Medicaid programs. The Department of Health and Human Services has published regulations implementing this discount "safe harbor" exception. See 42 C.F.R. § 1001.952(h).

To determine whether Company A's proposed discount practice implicates the anti-kickback statute, we must determine whether the Proposed Arrangement fits within the discount safe harbor. We conclude that the Proposed Arrangement does not fit within the safe harbor. The statutory exception for discounts, as implemented by the regulatory safe harbor, does not protect price reductions — like

[3] Because both the criminal and administrative sanctions related to the Proposed Arrangement are based on violations of the anti-kickback statute, the analysis for purposes of this advisory opinion is the same for both.

those at issue here — offered to one payor but not offered to Medicare or Medicaid. See 42 C.F.R. § 1001.952(h)(3)(iii).

Specifically, the preamble to the discount safe harbor illustrated the potential problem with laboratory price reductions:

> [W]e are aware of cases where laboratories offer a discount to physicians who then bill the patient, but do not offer the same discount to the Medicare program. In some of these cases, the discount offered to the physician is explicitly conditioned on the physician's referral of all of his or her laboratory business. Such a "discount" does not benefit Medicare, and is therefore inconsistent with the statutory intent for discounts to be reported to the programs with costs and charges reduced appropriately to reflect the discounts. 56 Fed. Reg. 35977 (July 29, 1991). Such price reductions create a risk that a laboratory may be offering remuneration in the form of discounts on business for which the purchaser pays the laboratory, in exchange for the opportunity to service and bill for higher paying Federal health care program business reimbursed directly by the program to the laboratory. In such circumstances, neither Medicare nor Medicaid benefits from the discount; to the contrary, Medicare and Medicaid may, in effect, subsidize the other payor's discounted rates. Moreover, laboratories may have an incentive to engage in abusive billing practices to recoup losses on the discounted business. Accordingly, the Proposed Arrangement does not fit in the discount safe harbor.

Having concluded that the Proposed Arrangement does not fit in the safe harbor, we must consider whether the discount arrangement between Company A and physicians utilizing account billing under the Proposed Arrangement may involve illegal remuneration to the physicians for their referrals of Federal health care program business not covered by the account billing arrangement and not subject to the discount. We conclude that it may.

The circumstances surrounding the Proposed Arrangement suggest that a nexus may exist between the discount to the physicians for non-Federal health care program business and referrals of Federal health care program business. First, the physicians are in a position to direct a significant amount of Federal health care program business to Company A that is not covered by the account billing component of the Proposed Arrangement. Second, both parties have obvious motives for agreeing to trade business: the physicians have the opportunity to make a larger profit on the non-Federal health care program business, and Company A is able to secure profitable Federal health care program business in a highly competitive market. Third, Company A has represented that it is likely that physicians who have account billing arrangements with Company A will refer Federal health care program business to Company A as a matter of practical convenience.

In evaluating whether an improper nexus exists between a discount and referrals of Federal business in a particular arrangement, neither the size nor structure of the discount is determinative of an anti-kickback violation. Rather, the appropriate question to ask is whether the discount — regardless of its size or structure — is tied or linked directly or indirectly to referrals of other Federal health care program business. Evidence that the discount is not commercially reasonable in the absence of other, non-discounted business is highly probative. In this regard, discounts on account billing business that are particularly suspect include, but are not limited to:

- discounted prices that are below the laboratory's cost, [4] and
- discounted prices that are lower than the prices that the laboratory offers to a buyer that (i) generates a volume of business for the supplier that is the same or greater than the volume of account billing business generated by the physician, but (ii) does not have any potentially available Federal health care program business. This is an illustrative, not exhaustive, list of suspect discounts; other arrangements may be equally suspect. Each of the above pricing arrangements independently gives rise to an inference that the laboratory and the physicians may be "swapping" discounts on account billing business in exchange for profitable non-discounted Federal health care program business.

Based on the facts presented here, we are unable to exclude the possibility that Company A may be offering improper discounts under the Proposed Arrangement with the intent to induce referrals of more lucrative Federal health care program business. Nor are we able to exclude the possibility that the physicians may be soliciting improper discounts on business for which they have the opportunity to earn money in exchange for referrals of business for which they have no opportunity, but for which the laboratories can receive additional revenue. Indeed, the Proposed Arrangement poses a significant risk of such improper "swapping" of business, especially in light of Company A's representation that many of its competitors

[4] In determining whether a discount is below cost, we look, for example, at the total of all costs (including labor, overhead, equipment, etc.) divided by the total number of laboratory tests.

are agreeing to such discounts. These competitor discount arrangements may similarly run afoul of the anti-kickback statute. The risk of improper "swapping" is compounded by the likelihood that physicians will refer Federal health care program business to their account billing laboratory as a matter of practical convenience.

B. Permissive Exclusion for Billing Medicare Substantially in Excess of Usual Charges

Price reductions offered to physicians that are not offered to Medicare or Medicaid raise additional issues under section 1128(b)(6)(A) of the Act, which provides for permissive exclusion from the Federal health care programs of individuals or entities that submit or cause to be submitted bills or requests for payment (based on charges or costs) under Medicare or Medicaid that are substantially in excess of such individual's or entity's usual charges or costs, unless the Secretary finds good cause for such bills or requests. In determining an individual's or entity's "usual" charges, we will look at the amounts charged to non-Federal payors, including physicians. If the charge to Medicare or Medicaid substantially exceeds the amount the laboratory most frequently charges or has contractually agreed to accept from non-Federal payors, the laboratory may be subject to exclusion under section 1128(b)(6)(A) of the Act.

The limited information submitted by Company A is insufficient to make a determination as to whether the Proposed Arrangement may run afoul of section 1128(b)(6)(A).[5]

III. CONCLUSION

Based on the facts certified in the request for an advisory opinion and supplemental submissions, we conclude that the Proposed Arrangement might constitute prohibited remuneration under the anti-kickback statute, if the requisite intent to induce referrals of Federal health care program business were present, and might be subject to sanctions arising under the anti-kickback statute pursuant to sections 1128(b)(7), 1128A(a)(7), or 1128B(b) of the Act, and the permissive exclusion provision under section 1128(b)(6)(A).

IV. LIMITATIONS

The limitations applicable to this opinion include the following:

- This advisory opinion is issued only to Company A, the requester of this opinion. This advisory opinion has no applica-

[5] We express no opinion regarding the legality of the current account billing arrangement under the permissive exclusion or any other legal authority.

tion to, and cannot be relied upon by, any other individual or entity.

- This advisory opinion may not be introduced into evidence in any matter involving an entity or individual that is not a requester to this opinion.
- This advisory opinion is applicable only to the statutory provisions specifically noted above. No opinion is herein expressed or implied with respect to the application of any other Federal, state, or local statute, rule, regulation, ordinance, or other law that may be applicable to the Proposed Arrangement.
- This advisory opinion will not bind or obligate any agency other than the U.S. Department of Health and Human Services.
- This advisory opinion is limited in scope to the specific arrangement described in this letter and has no applicability to other arrangements, even those that appear similar in nature or scope.
- No opinion is expressed herein regarding the liability of any party under the False Claims Act or other legal authorities for any improper billing, claims submission, cost reporting, or related conduct.

This opinion is also subject to any additional limitations set forth at 42 C.F.R. Part 1008.

The Office of Inspector General reserves the right to reconsider the questions and issues raised in this advisory opinion and, where the public interest requires, rescind, modify, or terminate this opinion.

Sincerely,

/s/

D. McCarty Thornton

Chief Counsel to the Inspector General

APPENDIX F46

Advisory Opinion No. 99–14, December 28, 1999

About a rural telemedicine network arrangement implemented and operated pursuant to Federal grants.

Issued: December 28, 1999

[Name and address redacted]

Re: OIG Advisory Opinion No. 99–14

Ladies and Gentlemen:

We are writing in response to your request for an advisory opinion about a rural telemedicine network arrangement implemented and operated pursuant to Federal grants from the Office of Rural Health Policy ("ORHP") and the Office for the Advancement of Telehealth ("OAT"), divisions of the Health Resources Services Administration ("HRSA"). Specifically, you have inquired whether the use of Federal grant funds and the continued operation of the telemedicine network after the expiration of the grant period would, in the circumstances presented, constitute grounds for the imposition of sanctions for violations of the anti-kickback statute, section 1128B(b) of the Social Security Act (the "Act"), pursuant to sections 1128(b)(7) and 1128A (a)(7) of the Act.

In issuing this opinion, we have relied solely on the facts and information presented to us. We have not undertaken an independent investigation of such information. This opinion is limited to the facts presented. If material facts have not been disclosed or have been misrepresented, this opinion is without force and effect.

Based on the information provided, we conclude that the Arrangement (as defined in the next sentence) could potentially involve prohibited remuneration under section 1128B(b) of the Act, if the requisite intent to induce referrals were present; however, the Office of Inspector General ("OIG") will not impose sanctions on Health System A ("Health System A") for violations of the anti-kickback statute arising under sections 1128(b)(7) or 1128A(a)(7) of the Act in connection with the Arrangement (limited as set forth in the next sentence), as described and certified in the request letter and supplemental submissions. For purposes of this advisory opinion, the "Arrangement" means, collectively, Health System A's (i) use of Federal grant funds under the terms of the ORHP/OAT grants; (ii) continued provision of telemedicine consultations within the Telemedicine Network ("Telemedicine Network") after the end of the grant period; (iii) continued payment of transmission line charges related to the Telemedicine Network (whether by Health System A or third party sources arranged for by Health System A) after the end of the grant period; (iv) continued payments after the end of the grant period to an unrelated third-party vendor to maintain the existing telemedicine equipment owned by Health System A until January 2003; (v) lease of telemedicine equipment to members of the Telemedicine Network pursuant to leases that satisfy the equipment rental safe harbor at 42 C.F.R. § 1001.952(d) after the end of the grant period; and (vi) participation in the administration of the Telemedicine Network for telemedicine purposes after the end of the grant period.[1]

This opinion may not be relied on by any persons other than Health System A and is further qualified as set out in Part IV below and in 42 C.F.R. Part 1008.

I. BACKGROUND

A. The Rural Telemedicine Grant Program

We begin with a discussion of the relevant Federal telemedicine grant programs. For purposes of this advisory opinion, the two grant programs described below will be collectively referred to as the "Telemedicine Grant Program" or "TGP".

Congress established the Rural Telemedicine Grant Program through the Department of Health and Human Services Appropriations Act of FY 1994 (Pub. L. 103–112) to demonstrate and collect information on the feasibility, cost, appropriateness, and acceptability (to practitioners and patients) of telemedicine consultations for improving access to health care services for rural residents and for reducing the isolation of rural practitioners. The program, adminis-

[1] No opinion is expressed or implied with respect to any other relationship between or among the Telemedicine Network members or any other party. Except as it relates to the relationship between Health System A and the Telemedicine Network members, no opinion is expressed or implied with respect to the legality of the maintenance contract between Health System A and the vendor.

tered by ORHP (later OAT[2]), was designed to demonstrate how telemedicine could be used as an effective tool in the development of integrated systems of health care for rural residents. See 1994 TGP Program Guide at 1.

For purposes of the TGP, ORHP defined telemedicine as the use of telecommunications for medical diagnosis and patient care, including patient counseling and clinical training of residents and health professions students when such training is a by-product of direct patient care. See Id. at 1. Under the 1994 grant program, telemedicine consultations could be performed with or without the patient present, as appropriate. See id. at 2.

The 1994 grant program required recipients to participate in a telemedicine network composed of (i) a "hub" multi-speciality entity capable of providing 24-hour a day specialty consultations for all specialty services offered through the network[3] and (ii) at least one small rural hospital (fewer than 100 beds) and one rural primary care practitioner office or clinic (the "spokes"). Other rural sites could also participate, including long-term care facilities, mental health clinics, school-based clinics, emergency services providers, home health providers, and health professions schools. See id. at 1–2.

To be eligible for grant purposes, a telemedicine network had to consist of a partnership (whether a consortium of independent entities or other more formal affiliation)[4] evidenced by:

- a resource contribution from each member (in cash or in kind);
- a specified role for each member;
- active participation of each member in the planning and implementation of the telemedicine project;
- a clearly articulated relationship evidenced by a signed and dated memorandum of agreement delineating the roles and resource contributions of each member; and

---

[2] The Office of Rural Health Policy ("ORHP") preceded the Office for the Advancement of Telehealth ("OAT"). For purposes of this advisory opinion, references to the ORHP should be considered synonymous with the present OAT.

[3] Pursuant to the 1994 Program Guide, an entity was capable of providing 24-hour consultations if it had relevant specialists on-call. See 1994 TGP Program Guide at 3.

[4] Grant applicants had to agree to obtain prior approval from ORHP before altering the network's membership.

- a long-term commitment by each member to continue working together beyond the funding period of the grant program.

See id. Grant recipients had to provide teleconsultation services in a minimum of eight core areas: teleradiology, cardiology, dermatology, mental health and/or substance abuse, obstetrics and gynecology, orthopedics, subspecialities of pediatrics, and resuscitation of trauma patients. See id. at 3. TGP grants were typically awarded to the "hub" entities or to the network itself (if the network were a legal entity capable of receiving grant funds).

In 1996, Congress passed the Health Centers Consolidation Act of 1996 ("HCCA"), which established, inter alia, the Rural Health Outreach, Network Development, and Telemedicine Grant Program under section 330A of the Public Health Service Act (42 U.S.C. § 254c) and specifically authorized the Director of ORHP to award grants "to expand access to, coordinate, restrain the cost of, and improve the quality of essential health care services, including preventive and emergency services, through the development of integrated health care delivery systems or networks in rural areas and regions." 42 U.S.C. § 254c(b). Under HCCA, telemedicine grants could be used within specified limits to:

- demonstrate the use of telemedicine in facilitating the development of rural health care networks and improving the access to health care services for rural citizens;
- provide a baseline of information for a systematic evaluation of telemedicine systems serving rural areas;
- purchase or lease and install telemedicine equipment; and
- operate and evaluate the telemedicine system.

42 U.S.C. § 254c(e)(3)(A).

In 1997, the TGP grant application procedure and requirements were largely the same as in 1994, except that ORHP additionally required all applicants to document current referral patterns, including both referral patterns among network members and referral patterns that extended beyond network members. See 1997 TGP Program Guide. In addition, ORHP allowed grant funds to be used to make clinician incentive payments to consulting specialists of up to $60 per consultation, so long as there were no third-party payers, including Medicare and Medicaid, that could be billed for such consultations (regardless of whether they were in fact billed). See id. at 3. The 1997 grant required applicants to provide at least seven clinical telemedicine services, specifically including the stabilization of patients in emergency situations and at least two consultative services provided by physician specialists. The grant recipients could select the other six services based on community need (e.g., services not available locally or services rural residents might forgo if they had to travel far or often to receive them). See id. at 18.

B. The Arrangement

The Arrangement is a telemedicine network organized by Health System A and ten outlying rural facilities and funded in part through two TGP grants.

Health System A is a [# redacted]-bed regional health care center located in City W, State X, serving over [# redacted] persons spread over [# redacted] square miles in [geographical designation redacted] State X and [geographical designation redacted] State Y. Health System A is a 501(c)(3) tax-exempt charitable institution consisting of the following subsidiaries: Health System A Hospital (a [# redacted]-bed general acute care hospital and U.S. Designated Regional Referral Center), Hospital B (an [# redacted]-bed psychiatric and chemical dependency facility), [names of subsidiaries redacted], and Health System A Hospital Foundation, a 501(c)(3) tax-exempt charitable institution whose mission is to support the health care services, research, and educational mission of Health System A. Health System A belongs to Network C, a national health care network. Health System A also participates in a physician-hospital organization with its medical staff and is developing a health maintenance organization to provide services in its service area.

In 1994, Health System A formed the Telemedicine Network[5] with the stated goal of using telemedicine to provide better access to health care services for rural citizens at remote locations without the inconvenience or risks normally associated with travel or delays in treatment. Telemedicine Network's service area includes approximately [# redacted] residents in an area of approximately [# redacted] square miles. Telemedicine Network currently consists of Health System A (the "hub") and [# redacted] outlying rural health care facilities (the "spokes"), including [# redacted] hospitals and [#

[5] Telemedicine Network is a consortium of hospitals and clinics, but not a separately incorporated legal entity. The members of Telemedicine Network or their affiliates may be engaged in, or contemplating, other joint business relationships. Those relationships are outside the scope of this advisory opinion.

redacted] rural health clinics.[6]

Each outlying "spoke" facility has a written telemedicine network provider agreement with Health System A. Under these agreements, Health System A agrees to provide the "spoke" facilities with technical communications capability, telemedicine equipment (which remains the property of Health System A), and technical assistance and training. In addition, Health System A agrees to coordinate the Telemedicine Network telemedicine program and assume responsibility for paying transmission line charges during the period it receives grant funds under the TGP. In turn, the "spokes" agree to provide space and a consultation room for the telemedicine equipment (including any remodeling necessary to accommodate the equipment), site facilitators, local data collection and documentation assistance, additional equipment such as video cassette recorders and video tapes, and security for the telemedicine equipment. The "spokes" also agree to promote the use of the Telemedicine Network for medical consultations to their medical staffs and to encourage and train their physicians in the implementation of the telemedicine program.

In 1994 and again in 1997, Health System A Hospital Foundation applied for, and was awarded, TGP grants to support the Telemedicine Network in the amounts of $[x] and $[y], respectively.[7] Each grant had a three-year term. The grant funds were designated in part for the purchase of telemedicine equipment and its placement in the outlying "spoke" facilities and for payment of necessary line costs so that patients, physicians, and other health care professionals could receive professional consultations from physicians at Health System A's tertiary care facilities: Health System A Hospital and Hospital B.[8] The 1997 grant funds were further designated to pay fees to the physicians providing the consultations.

Health System A has certified that its use of the TGP grant funds has been, and will continue to be, consistent with the statutory and

---

[6] The facilities are: [names and locations redacted]

[7] Because it is not a legal entity, the Telemedicine Network was ineligible to serve as a grant recipient. Nor could any of the "spokes" qualify as grant recipients, because none provided the required multi-specialty, 24-hour consultations.

[8] The telemedicine equipment may also be used, and is used, by health care professionals at the "spoke" facilities to communicate and consult with one another and with practitioners not affiliated with Telemedicine Network.

regulatory TGP grant guidelines and conditions, which include, without limitation, the following:

- Funds may be used to support the operating costs of the telemedicine system, including compensation for specialists and referring practitioners.
- No more than 40% of the total grant award may be used to purchase or lease telemedicine equipment. No grant funds may be used for the costs of purchasing and installing transmission equipment, such as laying cable or telephone lines, microwave towers, digital switching equipment, amplifiers, and the like. Grant funds may be used to pay transmission costs, such as the cost of satellite time or use of phone lines.
- Grant funds may not be used for construction, except minor renovations to accommodate the installation of the telemedicine equipment. Grant dollars may not be used to acquire or build real property.
- No more than 20% of the grant funds may be used to cover indirect costs associated with the network.
- All grant funds must be used for services provided to or in rural communities and a majority of grant dollars must actually be spent in rural communities for direct services to those communities, including salaries, maintenance of equipment, and transmission costs.
- Grant funds may be used for clinician incentive payments of up to $60 per physician, per consultation, only if no third-party payer could be billed for such consultation [added by OAT in 1997].
- Grant dollars may be used to support the development of a business plan as part of the network's required continuation proposal. As a condition on Health System A's receiving grant funding throughout the term of the grant, ORHP must approve the business plan (submitted in year two of the grant) to continue the network after the grant term expires [added by OAT in 1997].

Currently, the Telemedicine Network offers interactive and asynchronous telemedicine consultations in thirty-five medical specialties. Health System A has agreements with approximately [over one hundred] physicians to provide telemedicine consultations through the network. Of these physicians, approximately 10% are employed by Health System A; the remainder are on the Health

System A hospital medical staff. The greatest number of consultations are provided in the area of mental health, followed by teleradiology and speech pathology.[9] The network is also used to provide educational and in-service training programs. The Telemedicine Network is overseen by a project manager and a Telemedicine Advisory Committee consisting of representatives of Health System A and the "spoke" facilities.

In its 1997 grant application, Health System A estimated that it would receive one inpatient admission for every twenty-five telemedicine consultation services it provides to the network. Health System A has represented that apart from the telemedicine equipment funded by the TGP grants and its own payment of line and some maintenance costs, Health System A has not made (and will not make) any payments to, and has not financially supported (and will not financially support), directly or indirectly, telemedicine related services of the other members of the Telemedicine Network or any of their affiliated physicians or health care professionals.

Health System A is currently preparing its business plan for the continuation and expansion of the Telemedicine Network after the grant period expires on August 31, 2000. In general, the network will operate for the same purpose and in the same manner as under the TGP grants. Health System A plans to continue paying for all or part of the transmission line charges related to Telemedicine Network services, with the assistance of third party sources as available.[10] In addition, until no later than January 2003, Health System A will continue to pay for maintenance of the telemedicine equipment

[9] In the initial years, teleradiology played a small role in the Telemedicine Network, although it was a core required service for the 1994 grant. Of the original [# redacted] physicians who agreed to provide consultations, only [# redacted] were radiologists, and the Telemedicine Network didn't begin teleradiology services until April 1998. Because of certain limitations of available technology (e.g., resolution of transmissions), grant-funded teleradiology equipment has been installed in only one spoke facility. However, Telemedicine Network may expand its teleradiology capabilities using TGP grant funds to purchase and place teleradiology equipment in the "spoke" facilities.

[10] Health System A expects that the Telemedicine Network's transmission line charges may be reduced by as much as 60% as a result of the Universal Service Fund ("USF") provisions of the Telecommunications Act of 1996 and recent Federal Communications Commission rulings addressing rural telecommunications rates. Telemedicine Network's application for USF funding has been approved.

owned by Health System A and placed at the "spoke" facilities during the grant period.[11] Except as provided in the previous sentence, the rural "spoke" facilities will provide their own staffing, space, and maintenance for telemedicine equipment. Existing and new "spoke" facilities will be responsible for the costs of purchasing new or replacement equipment for their respective sites. In some cases, Health System A may purchase telemedicine equipment centrally and lease it to the "spoke" facilities at fair market rental rates pursuant to rental agreements that meet the requirements of the equipment rental safe harbor at 42 C.F.R. § 1001.952(c). Health System A has not paid, and does not intend to pay, any cash or cash equivalent to any "spoke" facility with respect to telemedicine.

C. Federal Reimbursement for Telemedicine Services

A key component of the operation and continuation of the Telemedicine Network is the evolving system of reimbursement for telemedicine services.

Historically, Medicare has reimbursed only those telemedicine applications where, under conventional health care delivery methods, the medical services do not require face-to-face, "hands on" contact between patient and physician. For example, Medicare has covered teleradiology, the most widely used and reimbursed form of telemedicine, as well as physician interpretation of electrocardiogram and electroencephalogram readings that are transmitted electronically. By contrast, Medicare has not, until recently, covered other physician services delivered through telecommunications systems because under the conventional delivery of medicine, those services are furnished in person. See generally Medicare Program Payment for Teleconsultations in Rural Health Professional Shortage Areas (Proposed Rule), 63 Fed. Reg. 33,882 (June 22, 1998); 63 Fed. Reg. 58,879 (Nov. 2, 1998) (Final Rule).

Under section 4206 of the Balanced Budget Act of 1997 ("BBA") (Pub. L. 105–33), Congress required Medicare Part B, as of January 1, 1999, to begin paying for certain professional consultations via telecommunications systems for beneficiaries residing in rural areas designated as health professional shortage areas ("HPSAs"). Congress further required, among other things, that the payment be

[11] Specifically, Health System A will pay a fixed fee to an unrelated, third party vendor for maintenance services. This vendor is the only vendor in the area that services the specific telemedicine equipment, and Health System A expects that the vendor will cease providing parts and servicing for the equipment by January 2003.

shared between the referring practitioner and the consulting practitioner; that the amount of the payment not exceed the current fee schedule amount that would be paid to the consulting practitioner; that the payment not include any reimbursement for telephone line charges or facility fees; and that beneficiaries not be billed for any transmission line charges or facility fees (although beneficiaries remain obligated for applicable Medicare copayments and deductibles).

The Health Care Financing Administration ("HCFA") has promulgated regulations implementing section 4206. See 63 Fed. Reg. 58,879, 58,909 (1998) (to be codified at 42 C.F.R. § 410.78). HCFA interprets section 4206 as applying only to interactive patient encounters where the patient is present and the telecommunications technology allows the consulting practitioner to control the interactive medical examination of the patient. Id. at 58,909–10. "Store-and-forward" technologies, like those used in teleradiology, typically do not meet this requirement (although HCFA allows for payment when such technologies are used for interactive patient encounters that meet the teleconsultation requirements). Under the regulations, the practitioner who provides the consultation is paid the applicable physician fee schedule amount and is required to pay 25% of that amount to the referring (e.g., the "spoke") practitioner. The regulations do not provide for any payment of facility fees or technical components to hospitals or other facilities.

Health System A currently receives no reimbursement from any Federal health care program for teleconsultations provided through the network. Given the limitations of section 4206 of BBA and the HCFA regulations (in particular, the requirements that patients reside in HPSAs and that no hospital or facility technical fees are paid), Health System A anticipates receiving limited Medicare reimbursement related to the Telemedicine Network in the future. Health System A may receive some technical fees related to teleradiology services reimbursed under the conventional (i.e., "hands-on" services) rules.

Network practitioners, however, may be paid for telemedicine services in several ways:

- consulting practitioners may receive Medicare payments for interactive consultations under section 4206 of the BBA and the corresponding regulations; the consulting practitioners are required to remit 25% of the fee to the referring practitioners;

- consulting radiologists whose services are not interactive will continue to bill and be reimbursed as they always have for teleradiology services (see generally Medicare Carriers Manual § 2020A); however, referring practitioners receive no Medicare reimbursement related to an interpretation of an x-ray via telecommunications (i.e., the 25% split does not apply);
- as of July 1, 2000, consulting and referring practitioners may be eligible for Medicaid payments pursuant to recently enacted legislation in State X; and
- to the extent no Federal or other third-party payments are available, consulting practitioners may be paid the $60 clinician incentive fee from the 1997 grant funds until the expiration of the grant term in 2000.

II. LAW AND ANALYSIS

The anti-kickback statute makes it a criminal offense knowingly and wilfully to offer, pay, solicit, or receive any remuneration to induce referrals of items or services reimbursable by the Federal health care programs. See section 1128B(b) of the Act. Where remuneration is paid purposefully to induce referrals of items or services paid for by a Federal health care program, the anti-kickback statute is violated. By its terms, the statute ascribes liability to parties on both sides of an impermissible "kickback" transaction. For purposes of the anti-kickback statute, "remuneration" includes the transfer of anything of value, in cash or in-kind, directly or indirectly, covertly or overtly. The statute has been interpreted to cover any arrangement where one purpose of the remuneration is to obtain money for referral of services or to induce further referrals. United States v. Kats, 871 F. 2d 105 (9th Cir. 1989); United States v. Greber, 760 F.2d 68 (3d Cir.), cert. denied, 474 U.S. 988 (1985). Violation of the statute constitutes a felony punishable by a maximum fine of $25,000, imprisonment up to five years or both. Conviction will also lead to automatic exclusion from Federal health care programs, including Medicare and Medicaid. The OIG may also initiate administrative proceedings to exclude persons from Federal health care programs or to impose civil monetary penalties for fraud, kickbacks, and other prohibited activities under sections 1128(b)(7) and 1128A(a)(7) of the Act.[12]

---

[12] Because both the criminal and administrative sanctions related to the anti-kickback implications of the Arrangement are based on violations of the anti-kickback statute, the analysis for the purposes of this advisory opinion is the same under both.

We have stated often our view that a gift to an existing or potential referral source that has independent value to such source implicates the anti-kickback statute and may be unlawful if the donor of the gift has the requisite intent to induce Federal health care program referrals. For example, in the preamble to the 1991 safe harbor regulations, we stated that giving a physician who is a referral source a free computer that has independent value to the physician may violate the statute. See 56 Fed. Reg. 35,978 (July 29, 1991); see also, e.g., OIG Advisory Opinion 98–16 (Nov. 3, 1998) (concluding that the provision of free transplant pharmacy services to a transplant center may violate the anti-kickback statute); OIG Special Fraud Alert, 59 Fed. Reg. 65373 (Dec. 19, 1994) (explaining that the anti-kickback statute is implicated if a clinical laboratory provides a phlebotomist to a physician to perform tasks normally the responsibility of the physician's office staff).

With these concerns in mind, in OIG Advisory Opinion 98–18 (Nov. 25, 1998), we concluded that we would not impose sanctions on an arrangement for the provision of telemedicine equipment between an ophthalmologist and an optometrist where the optometrist would pay fair market value (as certified by the requesting party), and the lease would fit in the equipment rental safe harbor. As noted in 98–18, our concern about possible anti-kickback implications extended beyond the value of the equipment itself to the value of the resulting teleconsultations to both the referring and consulting practitioners. In 98–18, these concerns were addressed through certifications that (i) the arrangement would have no independent value to the optometrist, because she would neither use the arrangement for marketing purposes, nor collect a fee for the teleconsultation services, and (ii) the parties had no oral or written collateral agreements or understandings between them, including agreements or understandings regarding the referral of patients from either party to the other.

Despite factual differences, the Arrangement here presents similar kickback concerns. By developing, operating, administering, and funding the Telemedicine Network's telemedicine network (in whole or in part), Health System A confers a benefit on two potential referral sources: (i) the rural "spokes" (and, by extension, the referring health care professionals), which obtain free equipment and subsidized line charges, and (ii) the "hub" consulting practitioners, who receive additional opportunities to earn fees. If one purpose of this remuneration is to induce referrals to a Health System A facility or practitioner, the anti-kickback statute would be implicated.

Notwithstanding, the Telemedicine Network presently operates under the auspices of the TGP, pursuant to a clearly expressed congressional directive to promote telemedicine networks in rural areas, subject to certain statutory limitations and oversight by ORHP/OAT. So long as Health System A is a grant recipient in good standing, and Health System A and the Telemedicine Network satisfy all statutory, regulatory, and administrative grant requirements (including, but not limited to, the expenditure of grant funds and the 24-hour provision of specialty consultations), we do not believe, on the facts presented, that the Arrangement (limited to those aspects described in Part III below) falls into the category of payment practices Congress intended to outlaw under the anti-kickback statute.[13]

The continued operation of the Telemedicine Network beyond the grant-funded period is also consistent with congressional intent and the TGP program. However, the absence of applicable grant restrictions and OAT oversight in the post-grant period increases the risk that improper payments for referrals could be masked as payments for telemedicine network purposes. This is especially true where, as here, some parties to the telemedicine network are engaged in, or contemplating, other joint business relationships.

Under the Arrangement in the post-grant period, payments from Health System A to the "spoke" facilities will be limited to supplemental funding of (i) all or part of the transmission line charges related to the teleconsultation services provided through the Telemedicine Network and (ii) until January 2003, continued maintenance of existing telemedicine equipment owned by Health System A. For everything else, the "spokes" pay their own way, with financial responsibility for all of their own staffing, operational, and maintenance costs, as well as the costs of new or replacement equipment. The "spokes" will remain free (though not necessarily encouraged) to use teleconsultants who are not part of the Telemedicine Network. The Advisory Board will continue to operate in its same capacity.

---

[13] This opinion is limited to the facts presented. Circumstances may exist in which parties use Federal grant programs or funds to further fraudulent or abusive schemes. This opinion should not be construed as standing for the proposition that the use of Federal grant programs or funds immunizes a party from sanction under the anti-kickback statute.

By subsidizing the Telemedicine Network's transmission line charges and equipment maintenance beyond the grant-funded period, Health System A may in some cases subsidize the private practice incomes of its "hub" consulting practitioners and the referring "spoke" practitioners, many of whom are potential referral sources for Health System A's facilities and providers. Typically these consulting and referring practitioners are not performing a hospital service when they participate in a telemedicine consultation through the Telemedicine Network; rather, they are engaged in their own private medical practices. Absent changes to HCFA's reimbursement rules (under which hospitals are not reimbursed for telemedicine services), if such practitioners are permitted to participate in the network without bearing a "fair share" of its costs, they stand to reap future financial rewards while Health System A bears the corresponding financial burdens. However, we would expect that, at such time as telemedicine becomes financially viable, the practitioners who benefit economically from the Telemedicine Network will also pay their share of its costs.

Finally and importantly, the Arrangement presents an opportunity for significant community benefit through the study and development of telemedicine as a mechanism to (i) improve access to essential health care services (including preventive and emergency services) for rural patients who may otherwise forgo care; (ii) constrain health care costs in rural areas; and (iii) reduce the isolation of rural health care professionals.

Given all of the facts and circumstances, including, without limitation, (i) the clear congressional policy favoring the study and development of rural telemedicine networks, (ii) the oversight of the Telemedicine Network by ORHP/OAT during the grant period, (iii) Health System A's representation that it has complied fully (and will continue to comply fully) with the terms of its TGP grants, (iv) the comprehensive range of telemedicine services provided through the network, (v) the limited remuneration during the post-grant period, and (vi) the significant potential community benefit to rural citizens through increased access to health care, we conclude that we would not impose sanctions on Health System A for violations of the anti-kickback statute arising from the Arrangement.

III. CONCLUSION

Based on the information provided, we conclude that the Arrangement (as defined in the next sentence) could potentially involve prohibited remuneration under section 1128B(b) of the Act, if the requisite intent to induce referrals were present; however, the Office of Inspector General ("OIG") will not impose sanctions on Health System A for violations of the anti-kickback statute arising under sections 1128(b)(7) or 1128A(a)(7) of the Act in connection with the Arrangement (limited as set forth in the next sentence), as described and certified in the request letter and supplemental submissions. For purposes of this paragraph, the "Arrangement" means, collectively, Health System A's (i) use of Federal grant funds under the terms of the ORHP/OAT grants; (ii) continued provision of telemedicine consultations within the Telemedicine Network after the end of the grant period; (iii) continued payment of transmission line charges related to the Telemedicine Network (whether by Health System A or third party sources arranged for by Health System A) after the end of the grant period; (iv) continued payments after the end of the grant period to an unrelated third-party vendor to maintain the existing telemedicine equipment owned by Health System A until January 2003; (v) lease of telemedicine equipment to members of the Telemedicine Network pursuant to leases that satisfy the equipment rental safe harbor at 42 C.F.R. § 1001.952(d) after the end of the grant period; and (vi) participation in the administration of the Telemedicine Network for telemedicine purposes after the end of the grant period.

IV. LIMITATIONS

The limitations applicable to this opinion include the following:

- This advisory opinion is issued only to the Health System A, the requester of this opinion. This advisory opinion has no application to, and cannot be relied upon by, any other individual or entity.
- This advisory opinion may not be introduced into evidence in any matter involving an entity or individual that is not a requester to this opinion.
- This advisory opinion is applicable only to the statutory provisions specifically noted above. No opinion is herein expressed or implied with respect to the application of any other Federal, state, or local statute, rule, regulation, ordinance, or other law that may be applicable to Health System A or any other party involved in the Arrangement.
- This advisory opinion will not bind or obligate any agency other than the U.S. Department of Health and Human Services.
- This advisory opinion is limited in scope to the specific arrangement described in this letter and has no applicability to other

arrangements, even those that appear similar in nature or scope.

- No opinion is expressed herein regarding the liability of any party under the False Claims Act or other legal authorities for any improper billing, claims submission, cost reporting, or related conduct.

This opinion is also subject to any additional limitations set forth at 42 C.F.R. Part 1008.

The OIG will not proceed against the requester with respect to any action that is part of the Arrangement taken in good faith reliance upon this advisory opinion as long as all of the material facts have been fully, completely, and accurately presented and the Arrangement in practice comports with the information provided. The OIG reserves the right to reconsider the questions and issues raised in this advisory opinion and, where the public interest requires, rescind, modify, or terminate this opinion. In the event that this advisory opinion is modified or terminated, the OIG will not proceed against the requester with respect to any action taken in good faith reliance upon this advisory opinion, where all of the relevant facts were fully, completely, and accurately presented and the Arrangement in practice comported with the information provided and where such action was promptly discontinued upon notification of the modification or termination of this advisory opinion. An advisory opinion may be rescinded only if the relevant and material facts have not been fully, completely, and accurately disclosed to the OIG.

Sincerely,

/s/

D. McCarty Thornton

Chief Counsel to the Inspector General

APPENDIX F47

Advisory Opinion No. 00–1, March 9, 2000

Concerning a consulting firm's contractual payment arrangements for the performance of auditing services to identify hospital undercharges and overcharges associated with private payors.

Issued: March 9, 2000

[Name & Address of Requestor]

Re: OIG Advisory Opinion No. 00–1

Dear [Name Redacted]:

We are writing in response to your request for an advisory opinion concerning a consulting firm's contractual payment arrangements for the performance of auditing services to identify hospital undercharges and overcharges associated with private payors (the "Arrangement"). Specifically, you have inquired whether the Arrangement constitutes grounds for sanctions under the anti-kickback statute, section 1128B(b) of the Social Security Act (the "Act").

In issuing this opinion, we have relied solely on the facts and information presented to us. We have not undertaken an independent investigation of such information. This opinion is limited to the facts presented. If material facts have not been disclosed or have been misrepresented, this opinion is without force and effect.

Based on the totality of the facts present in the Arrangement, as described and certified in your request letter and supplemental submissions, the Office of Inspector General ("OIG") will not subject Company A, the requestor of this opinion, to sanctions for violations of the anti-kickback statute under sections 1128(b)(7) or 1128A(a)(7) of the Act in connection with the Arrangement.

This opinion may not be relied on by any persons other than Company A and is further qualified as set out in Part IV below and in 42 C.F.R. Part 1008.

I. FACTUAL BACKGROUND

Company A is a consulting organization that enters into contracts with hospitals to audit hospital bills for undercharges (hospitals claiming too little) and overcharges (hospitals claiming too much) to private insurers paying on a charge basis.[1] Company A audits only cases in the following three hospital service areas: labor and delivery, endoscopies (gastrointestinal), and surgeries.[2] Company A does not audit or review any charges for services provided by ancillary departments (e.g., lab tests and x-rays).

Company A provides services in three phases: (i) Company A audits hospital records for undercharges and overcharges on bills issued during the twelve-month period before the effective date of the contract between Company A and the hospital and on bills issued during the audit, and works with payors to reconcile incorrect bills ("Phase I"); (ii) Company A holds a post-audit session during which it presents the Phase I audit report findings to hospital nursing directors of the service areas covered by the audit to prevent undercharges and overcharges in the future ("Phase II"); and (iii) Company A conducts a six-month follow-up audit to monitor hospital improvement using the same procedures applied in Phase I ("Phase III").

Hospitals compensate Company A by paying Company A [x]% of the amount that the hospitals recover through Phase I. Company A audits only those items or services billed on a charge-basis. Company A does not audit amounts paid on the basis of diagnosis or procedure related groups or codes.

Company A does not audit bills reimbursed by the Federal or State health care programs, whether as primary or secondary payors. The Arrangement — including Phases II and III — does not involve any Federal or State health care program business, directly or indirectly. Company A has instituted the following procedure for excluding

[1] Company A also offers managed care payment review services to hospitals. Such services are outside the scope of this advisory opinion.

[2] In its advisory opinion request and supplemental submissions, Company A specified in detail its procedures for identifying undercharges and overcharges contained in hospital bills. For purposes of this advisory opinion, it is sufficient to note that the auditors search for errors in a hospital's charging and billing by comparing the patients' medical records to their billing records. In performing its audits, Company A uses the charge protocols that existed at the time the hospital originally determined the charges for a given procedure.

Federal and State health care program business. Company A first eliminates any bills for patients who are 65 years of age or older. For the remaining hospital bills, Company A identifies a patient's primary and secondary insurers from the UB-92 form (which is the same as the HCFA-1450 form, also used by other Federal and State health care programs). The Federal and State health care programs will not pay a claim without a designation on the UB-92 form stating that they are primary or secondary payors. If the UB-92 form reflects that a Federal or State health care program (including CHAMPUS and the Title XXI children's health insurance program) is a primary or secondary payor, Company A will not review that patient's charges.

II. LEGAL ANALYSIS

The anti-kickback statute makes it a criminal offense knowingly and willfully to offer, pay, solicit, or receive any remuneration to induce referrals of items or services reimbursable by any Federal health care program. See section 1128B(b) of the Act. Specifically, the statute provides that:

Whoever knowingly and willfully offers or pays [or solicits or receives] any remuneration (including any kickback, bribe, or rebate) directly or indirectly, overtly or covertly, in cash or in kind to any person to induce such person — to refer an individual to a person for the furnishing or arranging for the furnishing of any item or service for which payment may be made in whole or in part under a Federal health care program, or to purchase, lease, order, or arrange for or recommend purchasing, leasing, or ordering any good, facility, service, or item for which payment may be made in whole or in part under a Federal health care program, shall be guilty of a felony.

Id. Thus, where remuneration is paid purposefully to induce referrals of items or services for which payment may be made by a Federal health care program, the anti-kickback statute is violated. By its terms, the statute ascribes criminal liability to parties on both sides of an impermissible "kickback" transaction. For purposes of the anti-kickback statute, "remuneration" includes the transfer of anything of value, in cash or in-kind, directly or indirectly, covertly or overtly.

The statute has been interpreted to cover any arrangement where one purpose of the remuneration was to obtain money for the referral of services or to induce further referrals. United States v. Kats, 871

F.2d 105 (9th Cir. 1989); United States v. Greber, 760 F.2d 68 (3d Cir.), cert. denied, 474 U.S. 988 (1985). Violation of the statute constitutes a felony punishable by a maximum fine of $25,000, imprisonment up to five years, or both. Conviction will also lead to automatic exclusion from Federal health care programs, including Medicare and Medicaid. The OIG may also initiate administrative proceedings to exclude persons from Federal and State health care programs or to impose civil monetary penalties for fraud, kickbacks, and other prohibited activities under sections 1128(b)(7) and 1128A (a)(7) of the Act.[3]

As a threshold matter, we recognize that the Arrangement only applies to non-Federal health care program billing practices and would appear not to implicate the anti-kickback statute. The mere "carve-out" of Federal health care program billing, however, does not end our inquiry, since such arrangements could have a "spillover" effect on billing or coding for Federal health care program items or services. Where such effect occurs and is intended by one or both parties, the statute may be implicated.

In this case, the Arrangement poses a limited risk of fraud or abuse under the anti-kickback statute. First, Company A has certified that the Arrangement does not involve Federal health care program business, directly or indirectly. Second, the principal activity under the Arrangement is a one-time, wholly retrospective billing audit. Such audits raise few questions under the anti-kickback statute because where items or services have been entirely ordered, provided, and claimed prior to the audit, there is little risk that the audit will involve an improper referral under the anti-kickback statute.[4] Third, the prospective portions of the Arrangement, Phases II and III, are limited in nature and present few, if any, opportunities for spillover effects on Federal health care program billing or

---

[3] Because both the criminal and administrative sanctions related to the anti-kickback implications of the Arrangement are based on violations of the anti-kickback statute, the analysis for purposes of this advisory opinion is the same under both.

[4] We have identified a number of risk areas, including false claims liability, with respect to the operation of third party billing companies. See The Office of Inspector General's Compliance Program Guidance for Third-Party Medical Billing Companies (Nov. 24, 1998), reprinted in 63 Fed. Reg. 70,138 (Dec. 18, 1998). Institutions and individuals are legally responsible for the appropriateness of claims submitted by third party billing companies to Federal or State health care programs on their behalf.

coding.[5]

Accordingly, based on the totality of the facts present in the Arrangement, we conclude there is a minimal risk that the Arrangement will have an adverse effect on Federal health care program business.

For the above reasons, including, without limitation, Company A's representation that the Arrangement will not involve Federal health care program business in any respect, we will not subject Company A to sanctions arising under the anti-kickback statute in connection with the Arrangement. No opinion is herein expressed or implied regarding the liability of any party under the False Claims Act or other legal authorities for any improper billing, claims submission, cost reporting, or related conduct directly or indirectly related to the Arrangement.

III. CONCLUSION

Based on the totality of the facts present in the Arrangement as described and certified in the request letter and supplemental submissions, the OIG will not subject Company A to sanctions for violations of the anti-kickback statute under sections 1128(b)(7) or 1128A(a)(7) of the Act in connection with the Arrangement.

IV. LIMITATIONS

The limitations applicable to this opinion include the following:

- This advisory opinion is issued only to Company A, the requestor of this opinion. This advisory opinion has no application to, and cannot be relied upon by, any other individual or entity.
- This advisory opinion may not be introduced into evidence in any matter involving an entity or individual that is not a requestor to this opinion.
- This advisory opinion is applicable only to the statutory provisions specifically noted above in the first paragraph of this opinion. No opinion is herein expressed or implied with respect

[5] Our determination not to impose sanctions in these circumstances is attributable to the entirety of the facts of the Arrangement. In other circumstances, prospective advice and training programs could implicate the anti-kickback statute, False Claims Act, and other legal authorities. By way of example only, such statutes may be violated if a hospital pays a consultant based on a percentage of collections to train the hospital's coders to characterize services in ways that may result in upcoding of the services being ordered.

to the application of any other Federal, state, or local statute, rule, regulation, ordinance, or other law that may be applicable to the Arrangement.

- This advisory opinion will not bind or obligate any agency other than the U.S. Department of Health and Human Services.
- This advisory opinion is limited in scope to the specific arrangement described in this letter and has no applicability to other arrangements, even those that appear similar in nature or scope.
- No opinion is expressed herein regarding the liability of any party under the False Claims Act or other legal authorities for any improper billing, claims submission, cost reporting, or related conduct.

This opinion is also subject to any additional limitations set forth at 42 C.F.R. Part 1008.

The OIG will not proceed against the requestor with respect to any action that is part of the Arrangement taken in good faith reliance upon this advisory opinion as long as all of the material facts have been fully, completely, and accurately presented, and the Arrangement in practice comports with the information provided. The OIG reserves the right to reconsider the questions and issues raised in this advisory opinion and, where the public interest requires, rescind, modify, or terminate this opinion. In the event that this advisory opinion is modified or terminated, the OIG will not proceed against the requestor with respect to any action taken in good faith reliance upon this advisory opinion, where all of the relevant facts were fully, completely, and accurately presented, and where such action was promptly discontinued upon notification of the modification or termination of this advisory opinion. An advisory opinion may be rescinded only if the relevant and material facts have not been fully, completely, and accurately disclosed to the OIG.

Sincerely,

/s/

D. McCarty Thornton

Chief Counsel to the Inspector General

APPENDIX F48

Advisory Opinion No. 00–2, April 4, 2000

About a proposed cost-savings program pursuant to which (the "Hospital") would reward its non-physician employees for submitting cost-savings suggestions.

Issued: April 4, 2000

[name and address redacted]

Re: OIG Advisory Opinion No. 00–02

Dear [name redacted]:

We are writing in response to your request for an advisory opinion about a proposed cost- savings program pursuant to which [name of hospital redacted] (the "Hospital") would reward its non-physician employees for submitting cost-savings suggestions that the Hospital elects to implement (the "Proposed Arrangement"). Specifically, the question raised by your request is whether the Proposed Arrangement would constitute grounds for sanctions under the civil monetary penalty for financial incentives to reduce or limit items or services, section 1128A(b)(1) of the Social Security Act (the "Act"), or under the anti-kickback statute, section 1128B(b) of the Act, in the circumstances presented.

In issuing this opinion, we have relied solely on the facts and information presented to us. We have not undertaken an independent investigation of such information. This opinion is limited to the facts presented. If material facts have not been disclosed or have been misrepresented, this opinion is without force and effect.

Based on the information provided, we conclude that the Proposed Arrangement, as described and certified in your request letter and supplemental submissions: (i) would not constitute a prohibited inducement to reduce or limit items or services under section 1128A (b)(1) of the Act, and (ii) could potentially generate prohibited remuneration under the anti-kickback statute, if the requisite intent to induce referrals were present, but that the OIG will not subject the Hospital to sanctions arising under the anti-kickback statute pursuant to sections 1128(b)(7) or 1128A(a)(7) of the Act in connection with the establishment of the Proposed Arrangement itself; provided, however, that our conclusion does not apply to specific payments made by the Hospital for specific suggestions.

This opinion may not be relied on by any persons other than the Hospital, the requestor of this opinion, and is further qualified as set out in Part V below and in 42 C.F.R. Part 1008.

I. FACTUAL BACKGROUND

The Hospital, a State X not-for-profit corporation, operates an acute care hospital that has a high percentage of Medicare and Medicaid patients. The Hospital would like to implement an employee cost-savings program. Participation in the program will be limited to non-physician employees of the Hospital,[1] although some of the participating employees may be in a position to make referrals for, or arrange for the referral or provision of, items or services reimbursable by Federal health care programs.

Under the Proposed Arrangement, non-physician employees will be permitted to submit written cost-savings suggestions to the Human Resource Department of the Hospital. If the Hospital determines that a suggestion has merit and is feasible, it will pay the employee a percentage of the cost savings generated by the suggestion. For suggestions resulting in quantifiable and measurable financial savings, the Hospital will pay the employee an amount equal to [Y] percent of the cost savings derived during the first year the suggestion is implemented. For cost-savings suggestions that cannot be measured or quantified, the Hospital will estimate its savings and pay the employee an amount based upon a predetermined, sliding scale, subject to a maximum reward of [amount redacted].[2]

The Hospital has certified that:

---

[1] Eligible non-physician employees include, but are not limited to, nurses, nurses' aides, pharmacists, phlebotomists, respiratory technicians, x-ray technicians, physical therapists, maintenance workers, cafeteria workers, secretaries, medical records personnel, and custodians.

[2] In special circumstances, the Hospital's Board of Directors may authorize a payment in excess of the stated maximum reward, if the suggestion has significantly improved Hospital operations and increased patient, employee, or physician satisfaction.

- no payments will be made directly or indirectly to physicians under the Proposed Arrangement;
- the Proposed Arrangement will not reward or implement suggestions that would reduce or limit health care services provided to its patients or impair the quality of care delivered to its patients;
- the Proposed Arrangement will not reward suggestions that identify specific vendors, directly or indirectly; and
- the Proposed Arrangement will not reward or implement suggestions that shift costs to any Federal health care program.

II. SECTION 1128A(b)(1) OF THE ACT

Our first inquiry is whether the Proposed Arrangement would violate section 1128A(b)(1) of the Act, which prohibits a hospital from making a payment, directly or indirectly, to induce a physician to reduce or limit services to Federal health care beneficiaries under the physician's direct care. A hospital that makes, and any physician who accepts, such payments is subject to civil money penalties of up to $2,000 for each patient covered by the improper payments. See sections 1128A(b)(1) & (2) of the Act.

Section 1128A(b)(1) only applies to arrangements between hospitals and physicians. Since physicians are prohibited from participating, directly or indirectly, in the Proposed Arrangement, the Proposed Arrangement does not implicate section 1128A(b)(1) of the Act.

III. THE ANTI-KICKBACK STATUTE

A. Law

A further question arises as to whether the Proposed Arrangement would violate the anti-kickback statute. The anti-kickback statute makes it a criminal offense knowingly and willfully to offer, pay, solicit, or receive any remuneration to induce referrals of items or services reimbursable by any Federal health care program. See section 1128B(b) of the Act. Specifically, the statute provides that:

Whoever knowingly and willfully offers or pays [or solicits or receives] any remuneration (including any kickback, bribe, or rebate) directly or indirectly, overtly or covertly, in cash or in kind to any person to induce such person — to refer an individual to a person for the furnishing or arranging for the furnishing of any item or service for which payment may be made in whole or in part under a Federal health care program, or to purchase, lease, order, or arrange for or recommend purchasing, leasing, or ordering any good, facility, service, or item for which payment may be made in whole or in part under a Federal health care program, shall be guilty of a felony.

Id. Thus, where remuneration is paid purposefully to induce referrals of items or services for which payment may be made by a Federal health care program, the anti-kickback statute is violated. By its terms, the statute ascribes criminal liability to parties on both sides of an impermissible "kickback" transaction. For purposes of the anti-kickback statute, "remuneration" includes the transfer of anything of value, in cash or in-kind, directly or indirectly, covertly or overtly.

The statute has been interpreted to cover any arrangement where one purpose of the remuneration was to obtain money for the referral of services or to induce further referrals. United States v. Kats, 871 F.2d 105 (9th Cir. 1989); United States v. Greber, 760 F.2d 68 (3d Cir.), cert. denied, 474 U.S. 988 (1985). Violation of the statute constitutes a felony punishable by a maximum fine of $25,000, imprisonment up to five years, or both. Conviction will also lead to automatic exclusion from Federal health care programs, including Medicare and Medicaid. The Office of Inspector General ("OIG") may also initiate administrative proceedings to exclude persons from Federal and State health care programs or to impose civil monetary penalties for fraud, kickbacks, and other prohibited activities under sections 1128(b)(7) and 1128A(a)(7) of the Act.[3]

The anti-kickback statute excepts from its reach "any amount paid by an employer to an employee (who has a bona fide employment relationship with such employer) for employment in the provision of covered items or services." Section 1128B(b)(3)(B) of the Act. The OIG safe harbor regulations provide that the term "remuneration", as used in the anti-kickback statute, does not include:

> [A]ny amount paid by an employer to an employee, who has a bona fide employment relationship with the employer, for employment in the furnishing of any item or service for which payment may be made in whole or in part under Medicare or a State health care

[3] Because both the criminal and administrative sanctions related to the anti-kickback implications of the Proposed Arrangement are based on violations of the anti-kickback statute, the analysis for purposes of this advisory opinion is the same under both.

program. For purposes of paragraph (i) of this section, the term employee has the same meaning as it does for purposes of 26 U.S.C. 3121(d)(2).

42 C.F.R. § 1001.952(i).

Whether an individual is a bona fide employee for purposes of the employee exception to the anti-kickback statute is a matter that is outside the scope of the advisory opinion process. See section 1128D (b)(3)(B) of the Act. Thus, for purposes of rendering this advisory opinion, we rely on the Hospital's certification that individuals who will receive payments under the Proposed Arrangement are bona fide employees in accordance with the Internal Revenue Service's ("IRS's") definition of the term set forth at 26 U.S.C. § 3121(d)(2) and IRS interpretations of that provision as codified in its regulations and other interpretive sources. If the individuals are not bona fide employees, this opinion is without force and effect.

B. Analysis

Based upon the facts presented, we believe that most of the suggestions and payments that would be made pursuant to the Proposed Arrangement are unlikely to implicate the anti-kickback statute.[4] First, even if a proposed suggestion involves the purchase or use of a particular item or service that is ultimately reimbursable in whole or in part, directly or indirectly, by a Federal health care program, in most cases, the non-physician employee who would receive the payment under the Proposed Arrangement would not have the decision-making authority necessary to implement the suggestion. Second, the Proposed Arrangement will not reward suggestions that specify, directly or indirectly, a particular vendor. Therefore, although some non-physician employees could be in a position to make referrals for, or recommend, items or services within the meaning of the statute, the Proposed Arrangement does not create an inducement for such non-physician employees to steer patients to one provider over another. Third, the risk that a proposed suggestion could result in increased costs for, or overutilization of items or services reimbursable by, Federal health care programs is minimized because the Proposed Arrangement (a) will only reward suggestions that increase efficiency or reduce costs, and (b) will not

[4] However, even if the anti-kickback statute were implicated, payments made to Hospital employees under the Proposed Arrangement may fit within the employee exception, depending on the specific suggestion.

reward or implement suggestions that shift costs to any Federal health care program.

Notwithstanding, we are not in a position to pre-approve every possible payment under the Proposed Arrangement. We do not know the amount of the potential payment, the person to whom the payment will be made, or the action or activity that will be proposed. Simply put, a blanket determination as to the propriety of all payments that might be made under the Proposed Arrangement is hypothetical and not a proper subject for an advisory opinion. See, 42 C.F.R. § 1008.15(b).

Nevertheless, we conclude that, although some payments that would be made under the Proposed Arrangement might implicate the anti-kickback statute if the requisite intent to induce referrals were present, the OIG will not subject the Hospital to sanctions arising under the anti-kickback statute pursuant to sections 1128(b)(7) or 1128A(a)(7) of the Act in connection with the establishment of the Proposed Arrangement itself. We caution, however, that our conclusion applies only to the establishment of the Proposed Arrangement, not to specific payments for specific suggestions.

IV. CONCLUSION

Based on the facts of the Proposed Arrangement (as described and certified in the request letter and supplemental submissions), we conclude that the Proposed Arrangement: (i) would not violate section 1128A(b)(1) of the Act, which prohibits financial incentives to reduce or limit items or services, and (ii) could potentially generate prohibited remuneration under the anti-kickback statute, if the requisite intent to induce referrals were present, but that the OIG will not subject the Hospital to sanctions arising under the anti-kickback statute pursuant to sections 1128(b)(7) or 1128A(a)(7) of the Act in connection with the establishment of the Proposed Arrangement itself; provided, however, that our conclusion does not apply to specific payments made by the Hospital for specific suggestions.

V. LIMITATIONS

The limitations applicable to this opinion include the following:

- This advisory opinion is issued only to the Hospital, the requestor of this opinion. This advisory opinion has no application to, and cannot be relied upon by, any other individual or entity.

- This advisory opinion may not be introduced into evidence in any matter involving an entity or individual that is not a requestor to this opinion.
- This advisory opinion is applicable only to the statutory provisions specifically noted above. No opinion is herein expressed or implied with respect to the application of any other Federal, state, or local statute, rule, regulation, ordinance, or other law that may be applicable to the Proposed Arrangement.
- This advisory opinion will not bind or obligate any agency other than the U.S. Department of Health and Human Services.
- This advisory opinion is limited in scope to the specific arrangement described in this letter and has no applicability to other arrangements, even those that appear similar in nature or scope.
- No opinion is expressed herein regarding the liability of any party under the False Claims Act or other legal authorities for any improper billing, claims submission, cost reporting, or related conduct.

This opinion is also subject to any additional limitations set forth at 42 C.F.R. Part 1008.

The OIG will not proceed against the requestor with respect to any action that is part of the Proposed Arrangement taken in good faith reliance upon this advisory opinion as long as all of the material facts have been fully, completely, and accurately presented, all individuals who will receive payments under the Proposed Arrangement are bona fide employees in accordance with the Internal Revenue Service's ("IRS's") definition of the term set forth at 26 U.S.C. § 3121(d)(2) and IRS interpretations of that provision as codified in its regulations and other interpretive sources, and the Proposed Arrangement in practice comports with the information provided. Notwithstanding, this advisory opinion is limited in scope to the establishment of the Proposed Arrangement, and no opinion is expressed herein regarding the application of the anti-kickback statute or any other Federal, state, or local statute, rule, regulation, ordinance, or other law to a specific payment made by the Hospital under the Proposed Arrangement for a specific suggestion. The OIG reserves the right to reconsider the questions and issues raised in this advisory opinion and, where the public interest requires, rescind, modify, or terminate this opinion. In the event that this advisory opinion is modified or terminated, the OIG will not proceed against the requestor with respect to any action taken in good faith reliance upon this advisory opinion, where all of the relevant facts were fully, completely, and accurately presented, and where such action was promptly discontinued upon notification of the modification or termination of this advisory opinion. An advisory opinion may be rescinded only if the relevant and material facts have not been fully, completely, and accurately disclosed to the OIG.

Sincerely,
/s/
D. McCarty Thornton
Chief Counsel to the Inspector General

APPENDIX F49

Advisory Opinion No. 00–3, April 7, 2000

Concerning an arrangement to provide various services free of charge to patients with terminal illnesses.

[Issued: April 7, 2000]

[Name Redacted]

President
The Hospice of Martin & St. Lucie, Inc.
The Hospice Foundation of Martin & St. Lucie, Inc.
2030 S.E. Ocean Blvd.
Stuart, FL 34996

Re: OIG Advisory Opinion No. 00–3

Dear [Name Redacted]:

We are writing in response to your request for an advisory opinion concerning an arrangement to provide various services free of charge to patients with terminal illnesses who have a prognosis of one year or less to live (the "Program"). Specifically, you have inquired whether the Program constitutes grounds for sanctions under the anti-kickback statute, section 1128B(b) of the Social Security Act (the "Act"), or under section 1128A(a)(5) of the Act, which prohibits the offering of inducements to beneficiaries in order to influence their selection of a provider for Medicare or Medicaid covered services.

In issuing this opinion, we have relied solely on the facts and information presented to us. We have not undertaken an independent investigation of such information. This opinion is limited to the facts presented. If material facts have not been disclosed or have been misrepresented, this opinion is without force and effect.

Based on the information provided, we conclude that: (i) the Program would potentially generate prohibited remuneration under the anti-kickback statute, if the requisite intent to induce referrals were present, but that, based on the totality of the facts as described and certified in your request letter and supplemental submissions, the Office of Inspector General ("OIG") will not subject the Hospice of Martin & St. Lucie, Inc., and the Hospice Foundation of Martin & St. Lucie, Inc., (collectively referred to as the "Hospice") to sanctions for violations of the anti-kickback statute under sections 1128(b)(7) or 1128A(a)(7) of the Act in connection with the Program; and (ii) the OIG will not subject the Hospice to sanctions under section 1128A(a)(5) of the Act in connection with the Program as described and certified in your request letter and supplemental submissions.

This opinion may not be relied on by any persons other than the Hospice, and is further qualified as set out in Part IV below and in 42 C.F.R. Part 1008.

I. FACTUAL BACKGROUND

A. The Parties

The Hospice Foundation of Martin & St. Lucie, Inc., is a Florida nonprofit organization that acts as the supporting foundation for the Hospice of Martin & St. Lucie, Inc., a nonprofit organization that provides various "end of life" services. The Hospice Foundation of Martin & St. Lucie, Inc., establishes and maintains programs to assist the Hospice of Martin & St. Lucie, Inc., in achieving its mission. For purposes of our analysis in this advisory opinion, we will consider the Hospice Foundation of Martin & St. Lucie, Inc., and the Hospice of Martin & St. Lucie, Inc., as a single entity in light of their close relationship, collectively referred to as the "Hospice".

The Hospice offers hospice services to patients and offers bereavement programs, community-wide support programs, and educational programs to the patients' families, friends, co-workers, caregivers, and the community-at-large. The Hospice's eligibility requirements for hospice services are consistent with those for the Medicare hospice benefit: patients must be diagnosed with a terminal illness and a prognosis of no more than six months to live if the illness runs its normal course. The Hospice provides hospice care to eligible patients, regardless of their ability to pay; however, the hospice care services are funded largely through Medicare, Medicaid, and private insurance. Donations are the primary source of funding for the bereavement, community-wide support, and educational programs. The Hospice has certified that its contracts with nursing homes to provide hospice services to their patients contain provisions for payment that are consistent with fair market value in arms-length transactions.

B. The Program

The Program is a community service program sponsored by a non-profit hospice that uses unpaid volunteers to provide assistance, companionship, and other complimentary services (i.e., without charge) to the terminally ill who have a prognosis of one year or less to live, if the illness runs its normal course. [1] Most of the patients receiving the services are not eligible for the Hospice's hospice services (because they have a life expectancy of over six months) or, although eligible, have elected to continue curative treatment.

The Program's services vary depending on whether the patient lives in his or her private residence or in a nursing home. If a patient lives in his or her private residence, the Hospice sends a "home service volunteer," who offers the following services:

(i) friendship and visitation;
(ii) transportation; [2]
(iii) assistance with writing and reading correspondence;
(iv) running errands;
(v) food preparation; and
(vi) respite "breaks" for the family or caregiver.

If the patient lives in a nursing home, the Hospice sends a "nursing home volunteer" who offers a more limited range of services. The nursing home volunteer offers only the services listed in (i) through (iii) above.

Under the Program, the Hospice does not offer any services to nursing home patients that duplicate services the nursing homes are obligated to provide, such as food preparation and respite care or

[1] Transitions Prehospice, Inc. ("TPI"), a consulting organization that trains hospices and other organizations in how to establish programs for patients diagnosed as terminally ill with a life expectancy of one year or less, assisted the Hospice in setting up the Program. Under the contract between TPI and the Hospice, TPI provided the Hospice: (i) a training manual; (ii) two days of on-site training; (iii) the right to use TPI's trademarked name, subject to certain limitations; and (iv) eight hours of follow-up consultation. We express no opinion regarding the contract between the Hospice and TPI.

[2] The transportation services for both at-home and nursing home patients may include driving a patient to medical appointments and driving a patient's relatives to visit the patient. All transportation under the Program is provided in the volunteers' private automobiles.

that are covered by the Florida Medicaid nursing facility per diem.[3] Regardless of the setting, complimentary services do not include any nursing services, home health aide services, medical social work services, measuring and/or administering of medications, or rendering of professional care or advice.

Once a patient begins receiving services under the Program, the Hospice informs the patient of the various organizations in the community that provide continuing care services, which may include home health care or hospice care (including the Hospice). In addition, the Hospice will provide a similar list to the nursing homes in which it offers the Program's services.

The Hospice has been operating the Program since August 1999. The costs of employing a manager of the Program, training the volunteers, and other expenses related to the Program are funded by the Hospice from charitable donations. At present, the Hospice has seven patients enrolled under the Program, all of whom are home-based. Although the Hospice currently does not have any nursing home-based patients who receive services under the Program, the Hospice anticipates that in the future some of the Program's patients will live in nursing homes. The Hospice disseminates information about the Program by communicating not only with nursing homes, but also with physicians, discharge planners, churches, synagogues, and aging and disability advocacy groups. The Hospice provides the Program services only to patients in the state of Florida.

C. Federal Health Care Program Reimbursement

Medicare's hospice benefit provides palliative care to individuals who are terminally ill. Palliative care focuses on pain control, symptom management, and counseling for both the patient and family. In order to elect the hospice benefit, a Medicare beneficiary must be entitled to Medicare Part A services and certified as terminally ill, which is defined (for Medicare purposes) as a medical prognosis of six months or less to live, if the illness runs its normal course. A beneficiary who elects to enroll in a hospice program waives all his or her rights to Medicare payments for curative care related to his or her terminal illness during the period of election of hospice care.

[3] If a nursing home were required to provide Program services as a condition of participation in a Federal health care program, such a requirement would constitute a material change in fact that would render this advisory opinion without force and effect as to the operation of the Program in that nursing home.

However, Medicare will continue to pay for services furnished by the patient's non-hospice attending physician and for the treatment of conditions unrelated to the terminal illness.

Because hospice services are typically provided to patients in their homes, the routine home care hospice rate does not include any payment for room or board. For services provided to patients in nursing homes, Medicare pays hospices the Medicare routine home care rate, which is a fixed amount per day for the services provided by the hospice, regardless of the volume or intensity of the services provided. Accordingly, if the hospice patient resides in a nursing home, the patient remains responsible for payment of the nursing home's room and board charges.

If, however, a patient receiving Medicare hospice benefits in a nursing home is also eligible for Medicaid, Medicaid will pay the hospice at least 95 percent of the state's daily nursing home rate, and the hospice is then responsible for paying the nursing home for the beneficiary's room and board. The specific services included in the daily rate payment are determined by a state's Medicaid program and may vary from state to state. In addition to the room and board payment, a hospice may contract with the nursing home for the nursing home to provide non-core hospice services (i.e., those services the hospice is not required by law to provide itself) to its hospice patients.

II. LEGAL ANALYSIS

The provision of free services to potential hospice patients may implicate two statutes: (i) the civil monetary penalty prohibiting the offer or transfer of remuneration to beneficiaries as inducements to use a particular provider, practitioner or supplier, section 1128A(a)(5) of the Act; and (ii) the anti-kickback statute, section 1128B(b) of the Act. Moreover, the provision of these free services to patients of nursing homes raises the possibility of illegal kickbacks in the Program between the Hospice and the nursing homes.

A. Law

Section 1128A(a)(5) of the Act prohibits a person from offering or transferring remuneration to a beneficiary that such person knows or should know is likely to influence the beneficiary to order items or services from a particular provider, practitioner, or supplier for which payment may be made by Medicare or a State health care program. For purposes of section 1128A(a)(5), "remuneration" includes transfers of items or services for free or for other than fair market value. See section 1128A(i)(6) of the Act.

The anti-kickback statute makes it a criminal offense knowingly and willfully to offer, pay, solicit, or receive any remuneration to induce referrals of items or services reimbursable by any Federal health care program. See section 1128B(b) of the Act. Specifically, the statute provides that:

> Whoever knowingly and willfully offers or pays [or solicits or receives] any remuneration (including any kickback, bribe, or rebate) directly or indirectly, overtly or covertly, in cash or in kind to any person to induce such person — to refer an individual to a person for the furnishing or arranging for the furnishing of any item or service for which payment may be made in whole or in part under a Federal health care program, or to purchase, lease, order, or arrange for or recommend purchasing, leasing, or ordering any good, facility, service, or item for which payment may be made in whole or in part under a Federal health care program, shall be guilty of a felony.

Id. Thus, where remuneration is paid purposefully to induce referrals of items or services for which payment may be made by a Federal health care program, the anti-kickback statute is violated. By its terms, the statute ascribes criminal liability to parties on both sides of an impermissible "kickback" transaction. For purposes of the anti-kickback statute, "remuneration" includes the transfer of anything of value, in cash or in-kind, directly or indirectly, covertly or overtly.

The statute has been interpreted to cover any arrangement where one purpose of the remuneration was to obtain money for the referral of services or to induce further referrals. United States v. Kats, 871 F.2d 105 (9th Cir. 1989); United States v. Greber, 760 F.2d 68 (3d Cir.), cert. denied, 474 U.S. 988 (1985). Violation of the statute constitutes a felony punishable by a maximum fine of $25,000, imprisonment up to five years, or both. Conviction will also lead to automatic exclusion from Federal health care programs, including Medicare and Medicaid. The OIG may also initiate administrative proceedings to exclude persons from Federal and State health care programs or to impose civil monetary penalties for fraud, kickbacks, and other prohibited activities under sections 1128(b)(7) and 1128A (a)(7) of the Act.[4]

We have issued a special fraud alert detailing problematic arrangements between nursing homes and hospices. See Special Fraud Alert, "Fraud and Abuse in Nursing Home Programs with Hospices," 63 Fed. Reg. 20415 (Apr. 24, 1998). Among the arrangements identified as suspect in the special fraud alert were: a hospice's offer of free care to nursing home patients for whom the nursing home is receiving Medicare payment under the skilled nursing facility benefit, with the expectation that after the patient exhausts the skilled nursing facility benefit, the patient will receive hospice services from that hospice; and a hospice's payments to the nursing home for "additional" services that the State's Medicaid program considers to be included in its room and board payment to the hospice. *Id.*

B. Analysis

The Program raises three principal issues under the two statutes discussed above: (i) whether the Hospice knows or should know that its provision of free services to potential hospice patients will be likely to influence the patients' choice of hospice provider; (ii) whether one purpose of the Hospice's provision of complimentary services to the patients under the Program is to induce them to use the Hospice's hospice services; and (iii) whether the provision of services to the patients who live in nursing homes may be remuneration to the nursing homes for permitting the Hospice access to their patients.

With respect to the first two issues, we think that at least some of the services being provided may have value and constitute remuneration within the meaning of both statutes. Moreover, we think it likely that the benefits are provided at least in part to induce the patients to obtain hospice care from the Hospice at the appropriate time. Notwithstanding, we would not subject the Program to sanction under section 1128A(a)(5) of the Act and the anti-kickback statute for the following reasons in combination:

- First, the services are provided by unpaid volunteers;
- Second, the benefits of the Program are primarily intangible and psychic in the sense that the services are designed to help

[4] Because both the criminal and administrative sanctions related to the anti-kickback implications of the Program are based on violations of the anti-kickback statute, the analysis for purposes of this advisory opinion is the same under both.

the patients adjust to their illnesses by helping them and their friends and families to cope with the day to day burdens of life;

- Third, the Program provides a substantial benefit to a vulnerable patient group; and
- Fourth, there are substantial barriers to a beneficiary's election of hospice care, including the requirement that he or she renounce coverage for curative medical treatment for the terminal condition.

In these circumstances, we would not subject the Hospice to sanction under sections 1128A(a)(5), 1128(b)(7), or 1128A(a)(7) of the Act in connection with the Program in the absence of other inculpatory activity. In particular, our recognition that there are substantial barriers to a beneficiary's election of hospice care does not mean that hospice providers can offer inducements to patients to elect hospice. We mean only that in the particular circumstances here, i.e., services of relatively small monetary value provided by unpaid volunteers, the requirement that hospice patients forgo curative care for their underlying terminal illnesses provides a safeguard against the overutilization often associated with such inducements.

We have additional concerns, however, with the provision of these services to patients in nursing homes. In particular, we are concerned that the services provided by the Hospice could substitute for services the nursing home would otherwise have to provide, thereby resulting in the Hospice providing free services to the nursing home. As we stated in the special fraud alert, there is a substantial overlap in hospice and nursing home services and the substitution of hospice services for nursing home services may be disguised remuneration from the hospice for access to the nursing home's patients. In this case, the complimentary services provided pursuant to the Program have been carefully delineated and, pursuant to the Hospice's certification, do not duplicate any nursing home services. Moreover, the fact that the services are provided by unpaid volunteers, most of whom are not health care professionals or workers, makes it unlikely that the services being provided will substitute for services required to be provided by the nursing homes.

We continue to have serious concerns regarding the provision of free or below market value goods to actual or potential referral sources. Such practices may constitute violations of the anti-kickback statute, depending on the circumstances. However, with respect to this Program, where the free services (i) are provided by unpaid volunteers, (ii) result in benefits that are primarily intangible and psychic, and (iii) support a vulnerable patient population, we would not impose sanctions arising under the anti-kickback statute. Nothing in this opinion should be taken to permit or protect any other relationships between the Hospice and any nursing facilities.

For these reasons, we would not impose sanctions on the Hospice arising under either the anti-kickback statute, section 1128B(b), or under section 1128A(a)(5) of the Act in connection with the Program.

III. CONCLUSION

Based on the information provided, we conclude (i) that the Program would potentially generate prohibited remuneration under the anti-kickback statute, if the requisite intent to induce referrals were present, but that, based on the totality of the facts present in the Program as described and certified in the request letter and supplemental submissions, the OIG will not subject the Hospice to sanctions for violations of the anti-kickback statute under sections 1128(b)(7) or 1128A(a)(7) of the Act in connection with the Program; and (ii) that the OIG will not subject the Hospice to sanctions under section 1128A(a)(5) of the Act in connection with the Program as described and certified in the request letter and supplemental submissions.

IV. LIMITATIONS

The limitations applicable to this opinion include the following:

- This advisory opinion is issued only to the Hospice of Martin & St. Lucie, Inc., and the Hospice Foundation of Martin & St. Lucie, Inc., the requestors of this opinion. This advisory opinion has no application to, and cannot be relied upon by, any other individual or entity.
- This advisory opinion may not be introduced into evidence in any matter involving an entity or individual that is not a requestor to this opinion.
- This advisory opinion is applicable only to the statutory provisions specifically noted above. No opinion is herein expressed or implied with respect to the application of any other Federal, state, or local statute, rule, regulation, ordinance, or other law that may be applicable to the Program.
- This advisory opinion will not bind or obligate any agency other than the U.S. Department of Health and Human Services.

- This advisory opinion is limited in scope to the specific arrangement described in this letter and has no applicability to other arrangements, even those that appear similar in nature or scope.
- No opinion is expressed herein regarding the liability of any party under the False Claims Act or other legal authorities for any improper billing, claims submission, cost reporting, or related conduct.

This opinion is also subject to any additional limitations set forth at 42 C.F.R. Part 1008.

The OIG will not proceed against the requestors with respect to any action that is part of the Program taken in good faith reliance upon this advisory opinion as long as all of the material facts have been fully, completely, and accurately presented, and the Program in practice comports with the information provided. The OIG reserves the right to reconsider the questions and issues raised in this advisory opinion and, where the public interest requires, rescind, modify, or terminate this opinion. In the event that this advisory opinion is modified or terminated, the OIG will not proceed against the requestors with respect to any action taken in good faith reliance upon this advisory opinion, where all of the relevant facts were fully, completely, and accurately presented, and where such action was promptly discontinued upon notification of the modification or termination of this advisory opinion. An advisory opinion may be rescinded only if the relevant and material facts have not been fully, completely, and accurately disclosed to the OIG.

Sincerely,

/s/

D. McCarty Thornton

Chief Counsel to the Inspector General

APPENDIX F50

Advisory Opinion No. 00–4, June 20, 2000

Concerning a lifestyle modification program for individuals with chronic disease that uses physicians to monitor and evaluate the program's participants.

[Issued: June 20, 2000]

Dr. Neil F. Gordon
INTERxVENTUSA, Inc.
340 Eisenhower Drive
1400 Central Park, Suite 17
Savannah, GA 31406

Re: OIG Advisory Opinion No. 00–4

Dear Dr. Gordon:

We are writing in response to your request for an advisory opinion concerning a lifestyle modification program for individuals with chronic disease that uses physicians to monitor and evaluate the program's participants (the "Proposed Arrangement" or the "Program"). Specifically, you have inquired whether the Proposed Arrangement constitutes grounds for sanctions under the anti-kickback statute, section 1128B(b) of the Social Security Act (the "Act").

In issuing this opinion, we have relied solely on the facts and information presented to us. We have not undertaken an independent investigation of such information. This opinion is limited to the facts presented. If material facts have not been disclosed or have been misrepresented, this opinion is without force and effect.

Based on the information provided, we conclude that the Proposed Arrangement would potentially generate prohibited remuneration under the anti-kickback statute, if the requisite intent to induce referrals were present, but that, based on the totality of the facts as described and certified in your request letter and supplemental submissions, the Office of Inspector General ("OIG") will not subject

INTERxVENTUSA, Inc., to sanctions for violations of the anti-kickback statute under sections 1128(b)(7) or 1128A(a)(7) of the Act in connection with the Proposed Arrangement.

This opinion may not be relied on by any persons other than INTERxVENTUSA, Inc., and is further qualified as set out in Part IV below and in 42 C.F.R. Part 1008.

I. FACTUAL BACKGROUND

INTERxVENTUSA, Inc. ("INTERxVENT" or the "Requestor"), has created the Program, a coordinated lifestyle and behavior modification program that focuses on nutrition, exercise, smoking cessation, and stress management for individuals with, or at risk for, certain chronic diseases (the "Participants"). Most Participants have, or are at risk for, cardiovascular disease or stroke. In essence, the Proposed Arrangement is a preventive health program for chronic disease patients.

The following aspects of the Program are described below: (i) the Program's services; (ii) the Program's physician network; and (iii) payment for the Program's services.

A. The Program's Services

The core of the Program's services is an individualized "risk reduction" program. INTERxVENT has created a computer program that will generate a set of "risk reduction goals" and a "personal action plan" for each Participant, based on guidelines set by the American Heart Association, the American College of Cardiology, the U.S. Public Health Service Preventive Services Task Force, and other national organizations. The INTERxVENT computer program uses information from questionnaires that each Participant must complete on his or her medical history and health habits, in addition to certain other data, such as the Participant's weight and blood pressure. The Program reinforces the lifestyle changes specified in the personal action plans by requiring the Participants' attendance at regular meetings with non-physician health care professionals ("Mentors"), such as nurses, physical therapists, exercise physiologists, and dietitians. Mentors counsel the Participants on how to alter their nutrition, exercise, and other lifestyle habits, and thereby improve their health.

Using the risk reduction goals and the personal action plan as a guide, each Participant visits a Mentor approximately twenty times during the first year of enrollment in the Program. After the first year, the Participants visit their Mentors approximately twelve times per year (once per month). During each visit, the Mentor works with the Participant using various behavior modification techniques. Participants are required to keep diet and exercise diaries that the Mentors check during each visit. The Program uses a computerized system to manage and track the Participants' compliance with the action plan.

Occasionally, where clinical intervention is indicated based on medical guidelines, the Mentors may refer Participants to physicians to help the Participants meet their risk reduction goals. A Participant may be referred to a physician to consider testing (e.g., a blood test for cholesterol and triglyceride levels) and drug therapy (e.g., prescribing cholesterol lowering drugs, anti-hypertensive agents, oral hypoglycemic agents, hormone replacement therapy, etc.). Generally, these referrals will be to the Participant's own personal physician. However, if a Participant does not have a personal physician, the Participant may choose a physician from a list of physicians in INTERxVENT's physician network ("Network Physicians"), as described below. For Participants who would like INTERxVENT to recommend a specific physician, one will be chosen from the list based on geographic proximity, on a rotating basis.

An integral part of the Program is INTERxVENT's ongoing research study, in which Participants are required to participate. An objective of the study is to follow patients with, or at risk for, chronic disease treated in community-based physician practices, tracking the effect of changes in nutrition, exercise, and other lifestyle habits on their conditions.

B. The Physician Network

Participants may access the Program's services in one of three ways: (i) through an institution (e.g., an employer or a managed care plan); (ii) through self-referral to the Program; or (iii) through Network Physicians.[1] Relevant to this opinion are only the Program's aspects that involve the Network Physicians.

Network Physicians are usually cardiologists, primary care physicians, and internal medicine physicians to whom INTERxVENT has

[1] In rare cases, a physician group may obtain a license from INTERxVENT to run its own Program. However, in such cases, the individual physicians in the group are not Network Physicians and receive no money from INTERxVENT.

marketed the Program as a low cost, high benefit behavior modification program that physicians can offer to their patients with, or at risk for, chronic disease as an adjunct to their medical care. In most cases, the Network Physicians will be referring their own patients to participate in the Program, rather than receiving new referrals from the Program. New referrals of patients from the Program will be rare because under the Program, if a Participant needs a referral to a physician, Participants are referred first to their personal physician. Thus, most of the referrals from the Program to the Network Physicians will be their own patients returning for check-ups or for possible testing or changes to their medication in accordance with national medical guidelines.

The Network Physicians periodically will evaluate the Participants that they refer to the Program. In most cases, the INTERxVENT Mentor will guide the Participants through the questionnaires and will take the various measurements needed to evaluate the Participants' progress and generate reports. However, the Network Physicians will review and sign the action plans, risk reduction goals, and progress reports that are generated, and will modify them as needed. The Program will pay the physicians $[ ] for the initial evaluation report and $[] for each subsequent re-evaluation report.

Each Network Physician will pay INTERxVENT a participation fee of $[ ] initially and thereafter will pay a $[ ] annual fee. Occasionally, these fees may be discounted or waived based on sponsorship of the physician or physician group by a JCAHO accredited health system, the number of their patients who participate in the program, and the number of patients who meet their goals. The fee will cover the costs of Program materials, computer software, and free or discounted participation in the Program for the Network Physician's employees (as described below).

C. Payment for the Program's Services

In general, a Participant pays out of pocket for the Program's services; however, if the Participant is enrolled through an institution, such as an employer or a managed care plan, then the institution may pay on the Participant's behalf. In either situation, a key to the Program is keeping the costs of participation low.

In general, Participants pay $[ ] per year to enroll in the Program, subject to the following discounts. First, all employees of Network

Physicians may attend the Program's orientation session and initial evaluation session free of charge. In addition, up to five of a Network Physician's employees may enroll in the Program free of charge; any additional employees may participate in the Program at a discounted rate of $[ ] per Participant per year.

Second, if the Participant enrolls in the Program through an institution, the Program currently charges the institution at a rate of $X per Participant per year, or $Y per identified high risk covered person per year. The $Y fee is collected regardless of whether the Program is actually used. Such institutions may include Medicare Plus Choice organizations, with which INTERxVENT may contract to provide the Program's services to the plans' at risk chronic disease patient population.[2] At present, INTERxVENT does not have any contracts with Medicare Plus Choice organizations.

II. LEGAL ANALYSIS

A. Law

The anti-kickback statute makes it a criminal offense knowingly and willfully to offer, pay, solicit, or receive any remuneration to induce referrals of items or services reimbursable by any Federal health care program. See section 1128B(b) of the Act. Specifically, the statute provides that: Whoever knowingly and willfully offers or pays [or solicits or receives] any remuneration (including any kickback, bribe, or rebate) directly or indirectly, overtly or covertly, in cash or in kind to any person to induce such person — to refer an individual to a person for the furnishing or arranging for the furnishing of any item or service for which payment may be made in whole or in part under a Federal health care program, or to purchase, lease, order, or arrange for or recommend purchasing, leasing, or ordering any good, facility, service, or item for which payment may be made in whole or in part under a Federal health care program, shall be guilty of a felony.

Id. Thus, where remuneration is paid purposefully to induce referrals of items or services for which payment may be made by a Federal health care program, the anti-kickback statute is violated. By its terms, the statute ascribes criminal liability to parties on both sides of an impermissible "kickback" transaction. For purposes of the anti-kickback statute, "remuneration" includes the transfer of

---

[2] The Medicare Plus Choice Plan may provide the Program's services through, for example, a cardiac rehabilitation provider.

anything of value, in cash or in-kind, directly or indirectly, covertly or overtly.

The statute has been interpreted to cover any arrangement where one purpose of the remuneration was to obtain money for the referral of services or to induce further referrals. United States v. Kats, 871 F.2d 105 (9th Cir. 1989); United States v. Greber, 760 F.2d 68 (3d Cir.), cert. denied, 474 U.S. 988 (1985). Violation of the statute constitutes a felony punishable by a maximum fine of $25,000, imprisonment up to five years, or both. Conviction will also lead to automatic exclusion from Federal health care programs, including Medicare and Medicaid. The OIG may also initiate administrative proceedings to exclude persons from Federal and State health care programs or to impose civil monetary penalties for fraud, kickbacks, and other prohibited activities under sections 1128(b)(7) and 1128A (a)(7) of the Act.[3]

B. Analysis

The Proposed Arrangement raises the following two issues under the anti-kickback statute: (i) whether the Network Physicians will pay participation fees to INTERxVENT in exchange for INTERxVENT's referrals of patients to the Network Physicians for Federal health care program-covered services; and (ii) whether INTERxVENT will pay the Network Physicians fees in exchange for the Network Physicians' referrals of patients whose Program services may be paid for by the Federal health care programs.

The Proposed Arrangement poses a minimal risk of fraud or abuse for the following reasons:

- The Network Physicians pay INTERxVENT's initial and annual participation fee payments to offer their patients access to the Program and to offer their employees the benefit of free or discounted Program services. The Network Physicians only occasionally will receive referrals from INTERxVENT. Moreover, when a Network Physician receives a referral, in most cases the referral will be of a Participant who was originally the Network Physician's own patient. The Network Physician would perform services on these patients that generally would be performed at a regular check-up. A very

[3] Because both the criminal and administrative sanctions related to the anti-kickback implications of the Program are based on violations of the anti-kickback statute, the analysis for purposes of this advisory opinion is the same under both.

small number of referrals from INTERxVENT to the Network Physicians will be new patients.

• The Program will not increase Federal health care program costs. The vast majority of Participants will pay for the Program's services out of their own pockets or will have employers who will pay for them. Although currently INTERxVENT does not have any agreements negotiated with Medicare Plus Choice organizations for coverage of the Participants' enrollment fees, in the future, some Participants may have the Program's enrollment fees covered by their Medicare Plus Choice plans. However, because the Federal health care programs pay Medicare Plus Choice plans a capitated rate, a plan's decision to cover enrollment fees will not increase Federal health care program costs. [4]

As a result, the Program poses a minimal risk of fraud or abuse. Furthermore, the Program potentially offers significant benefits to individuals with chronic disease. The Program is designed to improve patient compliance with risk reduction programs, thereby potentially improving their health and reducing Federal health care program costs. In addition, the Program will enable INTERxVENT to conduct independent research on the effect of preventive measures on patients whose chronic diseases are being managed clinically in individual community-based physician practices.

For these reasons, we would not impose sanctions on the Requestor arising under the anti-kickback statute, section 1128B(b) of the Act.

III. CONCLUSION

Based on the information provided, we conclude that the Proposed Arrangement would potentially generate prohibited remuneration under the anti-kickback statute, if the requisite intent to induce referrals were present, but that, based on the totality of the facts present in the Proposed Arrangement as described and certified in the request letter and supplemental submissions, the OIG will not subject the Requestor to sanctions for violations of the anti-kickback

[4] The safe harbor for price reductions offered to eligible managed care organizations, 42 C.F.R. § 1001.952(t)(i), may apply to arrangements between INTERxVENT and Medicare Plus Choice organizations. However, because INTERxVENT is not proposing to enter into any arrangements with specific Medicare Plus Choice organizations, we will not opine on whether such an arrangement would meet the safe harbor's requirements.

statute under sections 1128(b)(7) or 1128A(a)(7) of the Act in connection with the Proposed Arrangement.

IV. LIMITATIONS

The limitations applicable to this opinion include the following:

- This advisory opinion is issued only to INTERxVENTUSA, Inc., the requestor of this opinion. This advisory opinion has no application to, and cannot be relied upon by, any other individual or entity.
- This advisory opinion may not be introduced into evidence in any matter involving an entity or individual that is not a requestor to this opinion.
- This advisory opinion is applicable only to the statutory provisions specifically noted above. No opinion is herein expressed or implied with respect to the application of any other Federal, state, or local statute, rule, regulation, ordinance, or other law that may be applicable to the Proposed Arrangement.
- This advisory opinion will not bind or obligate any agency other than the U.S. Department of Health and Human Services.
- This advisory opinion is limited in scope to the specific arrangement described in this letter and has no applicability to other arrangements, even those that appear similar in nature or scope.
- No opinion is expressed herein regarding the liability of any party under the False Claims Act or other legal authorities for any improper billing, claims submission, cost reporting, or related conduct.

This opinion is also subject to any additional limitations set forth at 42 C.F.R. Part 1008.

The OIG will not proceed against the requestor with respect to any action that is part of the Proposed Arrangement taken in good faith reliance upon this advisory opinion as long as all of the material facts have been fully, completely, and accurately presented, and the Proposed Arrangement in practice comports with the information provided. The OIG reserves the right to reconsider the questions and issues raised in this advisory opinion and, where the public interest requires, rescind, modify, or terminate this opinion. In the event that this advisory opinion is modified or terminated, the OIG will not proceed against the requestors with respect to any action taken in good faith reliance upon this advisory opinion, where all of the relevant facts were fully, completely, and accurately presented, and where such action was promptly discontinued upon notification of the modification or termination of this advisory opinion. An advisory opinion may be rescinded only if the relevant and material facts have not been fully, completely, and accurately disclosed to the OIG.

Sincerely,

/s/

D. McCarty Thornton

Chief Counsel to the Inspector General

APPENDIX F51

Advisory Opinion No. 00–5, June 30, 2000

Whether waiving Medicare Part A and Part B copayment and deductible obligations for participants in a clinical study sponsored by the Health Care Financing Administration and the National Heart, Lung, and Blood Institute. . .

Issued: June 30, 2000

To: ATTACHED DISTRIBUTION LIST [redacted]

Re: National Emphysema Treatment Trial (NETT) Advisory Opinion No. 00–5

Ladies and Gentlemen:

We are writing in response to your request for an advisory opinion, in which you ask whether waiving Medicare Part A and Part B copayment and deductible obligations for participants in a clinical study sponsored by the Health Care Financing Administration and the National Heart, Lung, and Blood Institute (the "Proposed Arrangement") will subject you to sanction under section 1128A(a)(5) of the Social Security Act (the "Act"), or under the anti-kickback statute, section 1128B(b) of the Act.

You have certified that all of the information you provided in your request, including all supplementary letters, is true and correct, and constitutes a complete description of the material facts regarding the Proposed Arrangement. In issuing this opinion, we have relied solely on the facts and information presented to us. We have not undertaken an independent investigation of such information. This opinion is limited to the facts presented. If material facts have not been disclosed or have been misrepresented, this opinion is without force and effect.

Based on the information provided, we conclude that: (i) the Proposed Arrangement would potentially generate prohibited remuneration under the anti-kickback statute, if the requisite intent to induce referrals were present, but that, based on the totality of the facts as described and certified in your request letter and supplemental submissions, the Office of Inspector General ("OIG") will not subject the individuals and entities listed on the attached Distribution List (the "Requestors") to sanctions for violations of the anti-kickback statute under sections 1128(b)(7) or 1128A(a)(7) of the Act in connection with the Proposed Arrangement; and (ii) the OIG will not subject the Requestors to sanctions under section 1128A(a)(5) of the Act in connection with the Proposed Arrangement as described and certified in your request letter and supplemental submissions.[1] This advisory opinion may not be relied on by any person other than the individuals and entities listed on the attached Distribution List and is further qualified as set out in Part IV below and in 42 C.F.R. Part 1008.

I. FACTUAL BACKGROUND

A. Procedural History

This opinion reflects a second request for an advisory opinion in connection with the National Emphysema Treatment Trial (the "NETT"), a clinical trial sponsored by the Health Care Financing Administration ("HCFA") and the National Heart, Lung, and Blood Institute ("NHLBI") of the National Institutes of Health. The first request was filed in 1997 by a number of clinics and physicians participating in the NETT ("NETT Request I"). NETT Request I sought an opinion about whether the practice of waiving copayments and deductibles for items and services covered by Medicare Part B and within the scope of the clinical protocol that governs the NETT (the "NETT Protocol") would be subject to sanction under sections 1128A(a)(5) and 1128B(b) of the Act. In response, the OIG issued OIG Advisory Opinion 98–6 on April 20, 1998. The opinion held that in the specific circumstances presented, the OIG would not subject the requestors of NETT Request I to sanctions arising under sections 1128A(a)(5) and 1128B(b) of the Act for their waivers of Part B copayments and deductibles for services within the scope of the NETT Protocol. As is the case with all OIG advisory opinions, Advi-

[1] The legal effect of this conclusion is the same as that reached in OIG Advisory Opinion 98–6 (April 20, 1998), in that the OIG would not impose sanctions under sections 1128B(b) and 1128A(a)(5) of the Act on the advisory opinion's requestors, in connection with each respective advisory opinion request.

sory Opinion 98–6 is binding only on the NETT clinics and physicians that signed on as requestors.

The second NETT advisory opinion request ("NETT Request II") gives rise to the present advisory opinion. NETT Request II was submitted by the NETT clinics and physicians, some of whom were requestors of NETT Request I (the "Original Requesting Parties"),[2] and some of whom were not (the "New Requesting Parties"). NETT Request II seeks (i) an opinion as to the same conduct raised in NETT Request I for the New Requesting Parties (i.e., waivers of Medicare Part B copayments and deductibles), and (ii) an opinion for both the New Requesting Parties and the Original Requesting Parties regarding waivers of Medicare Part A copayments and deductibles attributable to services provided under the NETT Protocol. Thus, the core difference between NETT Request II and NETT Request I is that NETT Request II deals with waivers of copayments and deductibles for the NETT Protocol services covered by both Medicare Parts A and B. The NETT seeks the expanded waiver authority in light of its continuing difficulties in securing adequate participation in the NETT clinical study (as further described below).

B. The Proposed Arrangement

The Proposed Arrangement at issue in NETT Request II is substantially the same as the program described in NETT Request I. Accordingly, the facts as described in Advisory Opinion 98–6 are incorporated into this opinion by reference.

As described in Advisory Opinion 98–6, the NETT is a multicenter, randomized clinical trial to study the effectiveness of lung volume reduction surgery ("LVRS") to treat moderate to severe emphysema. The trial is a collaboration between HCFA and the NHLBI. The NETT Protocol was independently peer reviewed by a panel comprised of individuals with appropriate expertise in a number of areas, including relevant areas of medicine and public health. HCFA has agreed to pay for Medicare allowable patient care services, including LVRS, covered by the NETT Protocol and hopes to use the trial's results to determine if LVRS should be covered by Medicare as a reasonable and necessary treatment.

---

[2] For purposes of this advisory opinion, "Original Requesting Parties" includes only those requesting parties from NETT Request I who have signed on as requestors of NETT Request II.

NHLBI has contracted with numerous clinical centers around the country to be the NETT participating clinics that will provide services covered by the NETT Protocol. The trial will be conducted over a fifty-four month period and will involve 2,500 patients.[3] The NETT patients, who must meet the study's selection criteria, will be referred to the NETT contracting centers by their private physicians. The NETT patients must be Medicare beneficiaries or have other insurance to cover the cost of the NETT services. Eligible patients will be asked to consent to: (i) enrollment in a pulmonary rehabilitation program; and (ii) random assignment into one of two study groups, only one of which will receive LVRS.

Although overall responsibility for medical management of the NETT patients will remain with each patient's regular primary care physician, the NETT patients will be evaluated by the NETT physicians to ensure that the NETT treatment standards are met. Patients in the LVRS group will be managed pursuant to post-operative care and complication management procedures described in the NETT Protocol.

All of the NETT patients will be seen at the NETT participating clinics for follow-up visits, which are expected to last one to two days per visit, and for data collection at six-month intervals for two years after randomization and annually thereafter. In addition, the patients will be required to complete questionnaires at home and will be contacted by telephone according to a schedule set forth in the NETT Protocol.

Under sections 1813 and 1833 of the Act and implementing regulations, Medicare beneficiaries are obligated to pay certain copayment and deductible amounts for Medicare Part A and Part B covered services. See, e.g., 42 U.S.C. §§ 1395e & 1395l; 42 C.F.R. Parts 409 & 410. The Requestors seek to waive these copayments and deductibles for items and services that are (i) within the scope of the NETT Protocol and (ii) covered under Medicare Parts A and B, without regard to the patient's ability to pay. The following Medicare Part A covered services would be subject to the waiver when provided to the NETT patients within the scope of the NETT Protocol: (i) inpatient hospital services; (ii) skilled nursing facility services; and (iii) long-term care and rehabilitation hospital services. The Requestors

[3] Since the issuance of Advisory Opinion 98–6, the expected patient sample size for the study has dropped from 4,700 to 2,500 due to revisions in the study's assumptions and the difficulties that the NETT participating clinics have encountered in recruiting patients for the study.

have certified that they will not claim the waived Part A and Part B copayment and deductible amounts as bad debt on any Federal or state cost reports. Copayment and deductible waivers for Part A and Part B services provided outside the scope of the NETT Protocol are not included in the Proposed Arrangement.

The Requestors assert that waiving copayment and deductible amounts for the NETT patients will enhance the reliability of the study and the validity of its results by promoting patient compliance with the NETT Protocol, including patient cooperation in follow-up data collection efforts. As noted in footnote 1, the NETT has experienced unexpected difficulties in recruiting sufficient eligible patients for the clinical trial. They anticipate that theaddition of Part A copayment and deductible waivers within the limited scope of the NETT Protocol may persuade more patients to enroll in the study. The Requestors are also concerned that requiring payment of Part A and Part B copayments and deductibles may cause an undue hardship on economically disadvantaged patients that would undermine their participation in the NETT study and compromise its integrity.

II. LEGAL ANALYSIS

A. Law

The anti-kickback statute, section 1128B(b) of the Act, makes it a criminal offense knowingly and willfully to offer, pay, solicit, or receive any remuneration to induce the referral of business covered by a Federal health care program. Specifically, the statute provides that:

> "Whoever knowingly and willfully offers or pays [or solicits or receives] any remuneration (including any kickback, bribe, or rebate) directly or indirectly, overtly or covertly, in cash or in kind to any person to induce such person — to refer an individual to a person for the furnishing or arranging for the furnishing of any item or service for which payment may be made in whole or in part under a Federal health care program, or to purchase, lease, order, or arrange for or recommend purchasing, leasing, or ordering any good, facility, service, or item for which payment may be made in whole or in part under a Federal health care program, shall be guilty of a felony."

Section 1128B(b) of the Act. In other words, the statute prohibits payments made purposefully to induce referrals of business for which payment may be made by a Federal health care program. The statute ascribes liability to both sides of an impermissible "kickback" transaction. The statute has been interpreted to cover any arrangement where one purpose of the remuneration is to obtain money for the referral of services or to induce further referrals. United States v. Kats, 871 F.2d 105 (9th Cir. 1989); United States v. Greber, 760 F.2d 68 (3d Cir.), cert. denied, 474 U.S. 988 (1985). "Remuneration" for purposes of the anti-kickback statute includes the transfer of any thing of value, in cash or in-kind, directly or indirectly, covertly or overtly.

Violation of the anti-kickback statute constitutes a felony punishable by a maximum fine of $25,000, imprisonment up to five years, or both. Conviction will also lead to automatic exclusion from Federal health care programs, including Medicare and Medicaid. This Office may also initiate administrative proceedings to exclude persons from the Federal and State health care programs or to impose civil monetary penalties for fraud, kickbacks, and other prohibited activities under sections 1128(b)(7) and 1128A(a)(7) of the Act.[4] Section 231(h) of the Health Insurance Portability and Accountability Act of 1996 ("HIPAA"), section 1128A(a)(5) of the Act, provides for the imposition of civil monetary penalties against any person who:

> "offers or transfers remuneration to any individual eligible for benefits under [Federal health care programs (including Medicare or Medicaid)] that such person knows or should know is likely to influence such individual to order or receive from a particular provider, practitioner, or supplier any item or service for which payment may be made, in whole or in part, [by a Federal health care program]."

Section 231(h) defines "remuneration" as including, inter alia, the waiver of copayment and deductible amounts (or any part thereof). The statute contains certain exceptions to the definition of remuneration for certain waivers of copayments that are not advertised, that are not routine, and that are granted to financially needy patients or for which reasonable collection efforts have been made.

---

[4] Because both the criminal and administrative sanctions related to the anti-kickback implications of the Proposed Arrangement are based on violations of the anti-kickback statute, the analysis for purposes of this advisory opinion is the same under both.

B. Analysis

As was the case in OIG Advisory Opinion 98–6, under the Proposed Arrangement, the NETT participating clinics and providers would waive deductible and copayment amounts routinely and without regard to financial hardship. [5] Thus, the Proposed Arrangement implicates the anti-kickback statute's proscription against offering or paying something of value as an inducement to generate business payable by a Federal health care program. Nevertheless, for the reasons articulated in OIG Advisory Opinion 98–6 and summarized below, we conclude that in the particular circumstances presented here, we would not impose sanctions arising under the anti-kickback statute on the Requestors in connection with the Proposed Arrangement (including the waiver of both Medicare Part A and Part B copayment and deductible amounts). We further conclude that we would not impose sanctions under section 1128A(a)(5) of the Act, which prohibits giving something of value to a beneficiary that the donor knows or should know is likely to influence the beneficiary's choice of a particular provider, in connection with the Proposed Arrangement.

Based on the facts presented, we find that the following factors adequately protect the Proposed Arrangement against the risk of fraud or abuse:

- The Proposed Arrangement is unlikely to influence beneficiaries to obtain Medicare covered services from the NETT providers. Medicare patients will enroll in the NETT because enrollment in the NETT is the only means of obtaining Medicare coverage of LVRS, not because copayments and deductibles are waived. As a practical matter, Medicare beneficiaries have no choice of LVRS providers outside of the NETT. Nor is the Proposed Arrangement likely to influence the choice of providers within the NETT because all providers will waive deductibles and copayments. In short, the purpose of the waivers of the NETT cost-sharing amounts is to induce participation in a HCFA-sponsored scientific study, not to induce utilization of Medicare covered services.
- The Proposed Arrangement will not increase the risk of overutilization of Medicare covered services. The NETT Protocol controls utilization of services, and the Proposed Arrangement would not

[5] With respect to the NETT's economically disadvantaged patients, individualized determinations of indigency might suffice to exempt the NETT providers from their obligation to collect copayments and deductibles for those specific patients.

apply to health care services that are not included in the NETT Protocol. Nor would it apply for any period of time during which a Medicare beneficiary ceases to be a NETT patient.[6] Thus, the Proposed Arrangement is unlikely to result in an increased risk of overutilization of Medicare covered services.[7] In addition, the risk of increased overutilization is minimized because the number of Medicare patients participating in the full NETT study will be limited to 2,500 over a fifty-four month period.[8] This number may be even smaller, because some of the NETT patients may be privately insured.

- The Proposed Arrangement is a reasonable means of enhancing the likelihood of success of the HCFA-sponsored NETT study. Patient compliance with all aspects of the study, including visits to the NETT participating clinics when required and cooperation with follow-up data collection efforts, is essential to producing valid study results. Patients may be disinclined to participate fully for the duration of the study if they are required to pay to participate. This may be particularly true for patients who are not randomized into the surgical group or who are not satisfied with the outcome of their surgery. The NETT reports that it is experiencing difficulties enrolling sufficient numbers of eligible patients. In these circumstances, waiving copayments and deductibles is a reasonable means of enhancing patient compliance with study requirements and retaining patients for the entire study period. Waiving copayments and deductibles will also ensure that economically disadvantaged patients are not precluded from participating in the study.

---

[6] It is anticipated that some people may begin the initial screening process, be found ineligible for the study, but later reapply and be admitted to the study. HCFA would not consider these patients NETT patients for the period between the ineligibility determination and the reapplication.

[7] Nothing in this advisory opinion should be construed as indicating that a showing of actual, or increased risk of, overutilization is a required element of an anti-kickback statute violation. A risk of overutilization is merely one potential indicator of potential fraud or abuse.

[8] We recognize that an indeterminate number of patients who do not ultimately qualify for the NETT may obtain some copayment and deductible waivers during the screening process. The number of these patients will be limited by the initial screening criteria. HCFA has agreed to reimburse the NETT providers for services performed during the screening process in order to ensure that the NETT study can serve the purposes for which it is intended. We do not think that these limited waivers will lead to an increased risk of abuse of the Medicare program.

In sum, the Proposed Arrangement reasonably accommodates the needs of an important, HCFA-sponsored scientific study, without posing a significant risk of fraud and abuse of the Medicare program.

Nothing in this opinion should be taken to permit or protect waivers of Part A or Part B copayments and deductibles provided in the context of clinical studies generally. The Proposed Arrangement presents unique circumstances not found in the context of many other research programs, chief among them HCFA sponsorship of the NETT.

III. CONCLUSION

For the above-stated reasons, and based on the information provided, we conclude that: (i) the Proposed Arrangement would potentially generate prohibited remuneration under the anti-kickback statute, if the requisite intent to induce referrals were present, but that, based on the totality of the facts as described and certified in your request letter and supplemental submissions, the OIG will not subject the Requestors to sanctions for violations of the anti-kickback statute under sections 1128(b)(7) or 1128A(a)(7) of the Act in connection with the Proposed Arrangement; and (ii) the OIG will not subject the Requestors to sanctions under section 1128A(a)(5) of the Act in connection with the Proposed Arrangement as described and certified in your request letter and supplemental submissions.

IV. LIMITATIONS

The limitations applicable to this opinion include the following:

- This advisory opinion is issued only to the individuals and entities listed on the attached Distribution List, which are the requestors of this opinion. This advisory opinion has no application, and cannot be relied upon, by any other individual or entity.
- This advisory opinion may not be introduced into evidence in any matter involving an entity or individual that is not a requestor to this opinion.
- This advisory opinion is applicable only to the statutory provisions specifically noted above. No opinion is herein expressed or implied with respect to the application of any other Federal, state, or local statute, rule, regulation, ordinance, or other law that may be applicable to the Proposed Arrangement.

- This advisory opinion will not bind or obligate any agency other than the U.S. Department of Health and Human Services.
- This advisory opinion is limited in scope to the specific arrangement described in this letter and has no applicability to other arrangements, even those which appear similar in nature or scope.
- No opinion is expressed herein regarding the liability of any party under the False Claims Act or other legal authorities for any improper billing, claims submission, cost reporting, or related conduct.

This opinion is also subject to any additional limitations set forth at 42 C.F.R. Part 1008.

The OIG will not proceed against the Requestors with respect to any action that is part of the Proposed Arrangement taken in good faith reliance upon this advisory opinion as long as all of the material facts have been fully, completely, and accurately presented, and the arrangement in practice comports with the information provided. The OIG reserves the right to reconsider the questions and issues raised in this advisory opinion and, where the public interest requires, modify or terminate this opinion. In the event that this advisory opinion is modified or terminated, the OIG will not proceed against the Requestors with respect to any action taken in good faith reliance upon this advisory opinion, where all of the relevant facts were fully, completely, and accurately presented and where such action was promptly discontinued upon notification of the modification or termination of this advisory opinion. An advisory opinion may be rescinded only if the relevant and material facts have not been fully, completely, and accurately disclosed to the OIG.

Sincerely,

/s/

D. McCarty Thornton

Chief Counsel to the Inspector General

[Attached Distribution List Redacted]

APPENDIX F52

Advisory Opinion No. 00–6, September 29, 2000

Regarding Hospital X's proposed donation of its ownership interest in a portion of a medical office building to an agency of the State for use by the Medical School.

Issued: September 29, 2000
[Names and Addresses Redacted]

Re: OIG Advisory Opinion No. 00–6

Dear [Names Redacted]:

We are writing in response to your request for an advisory opinion regarding Hospital X's proposed donation of its ownership interest in a portion of a medical office building to an agency of the State of [name redacted] (the "State") for use by the Medical School (the "Proposed Donation"). Specifically, the question raised by your request is whether the Proposed Donation would constitute grounds for sanctions under the anti-kickback statute, section 1128B(b) of the Social Security Act (the "Act"), in the circumstances presented.

You have certified that all of the information provided in your request, including all supplementary letters, is true and correct and constitutes a complete description of the relevant facts and agreements among the parties. You have also certified that, upon our approval, you will undertake to effectuate the Proposed Donation. In issuing this opinion, we have relied solely on the facts and information presented to us. We have not undertaken an independent investigation of such information. This opinion is limited to the facts presented. If material facts have not been disclosed or have been misrepresented, this opinion is without force and effect. Based on the information provided, we conclude that the Proposed Donation could potentially generate prohibited remuneration under the anti-kickback statute if the requisite intent to induce referrals were present, but that the Office of Inspector General ("OIG") will not subject the Medical School or Hospital X (the "Requestors") to sanctions for violations of the anti-kickback statute under sections 1128(b)(7) or 1128A(a)(7) of the Act in connection with the Proposed Donation, as described and certified in the request letter and supplemental submissions. In accordance with our regulations at 42 C.F.R. Part 1008, your advisory opinion request disclosed a number of additional arrangements which directly or indirectly involve the Requestors, and about which no opinion is being sought. This opinion is limited to the Proposed Donation, and we express no opinion about any other agreements or arrangements disclosed or referenced in your request letter or supplemental submissions. This opinion may not be relied on by any persons other than the Requestors, and is further qualified as set out in Part V below and in 42 C.F.R. Part 1008.

I. FACTUAL BACKGROUND

A. Parties

The State Agency is an agency of the State that oversees facilities, programs, and policies related to students, staff, and faculty at institutions within the State Agency. University Y is the division of the State Agency that operates the Medical School in [city redacted] (the "City"), State. University Y's faculty practice plan is operated by the Faculty Practice Plan, a tax-exempt, nonprofit corporation.

For purposes relevant to our analysis, we consider the State Agency, University Y, the Medical School, and the Faculty Practice Plan to be sufficiently related to be treated as a single entity. Therefore, for purposes of this advisory opinion, each of the foregoing, as well as all entities that are owned or controlled, in whole or in part, directly or indirectly, by any of the foregoing and related, directly or indirectly, to the operation of University Y (including, without limitation, [names redacted]) will be referred to collectively as "Entity Y."[1] Physicians employed by, or affiliated with, University Y, the Medical School, the Faculty Practice Plan, or [names redacted] (including, without limitation, the Teaching Physicians, as hereinafter defined) will be referred to for purposes of this advisory opinion collectively as "Entity Y Physicians."

Entity Y's medical education programs include a clinical component and an academic component, both of which are administered by

[1] Notwithstanding, as more fully set forth in Part V below and in 42 C.F.R. Part 1008, this opinion is issued only to, and can only be relied upon by, the Requestors.

certain Entity Y Physicians. These physicians (the "Teaching Physicians") are employed by the Faculty Practice Plan for their clinical services, and, with a few minor exceptions, by the Medical School for their academic services. Entity Y pays its Teaching Physicians (i) a fixed annual salary for academic services provided on behalf of the Medical School, and (ii) a fixed annual salary, together with a productivity bonus, for clinical services provided through the Faculty Practice Plan. Teaching Physicians, as well as other Entity Y Physicians, refer patients to Hospital X and other area hospitals for the provision of various hospital and ancillary services, some of which are reimbursable by Federal health care programs. However, neither the fixed annual salaries nor the bonuses paid to Teaching Physicians are related to the volume or value of referrals to Hospital X or any other institution.

Much of the State is medically underserved, and many of the medically underserved areas are rural. The Medical School was created to alleviate the inadequate number of physicians available to provide services in underserved areas and to underserved populations. Thus, the Medical School provides medical education and residency training programs with an emphasis on primary care and rural health issues.

Hospital X is a tax-exempt, nonprofit, academic medical center located in City, State. Hospital X was originally organized as a public, city-county community hospital known as [Hospital X's predecessor]. In 1987, the City and [county redacted] county (the "County"), State, entered into a restructuring agreement pursuant to which they permitted the transfer of the hospital's assets and operations to the private, non-profit corporation currently known as Hospital X.

In structuring the transfer, Hospital X's continued support for the Medical School and medical training was a matter of significant concern to both the City and the County. The transfer was subject, in part, to the general condition that Hospital X "continue the training and educational programs for health care personnel similar to those heretofore conducted by [Hospital X's predecessor]." Moreover, Hospital X and its predecessor concluded that "the facilities presently housing the office practices of its medical staff physicians . . . [were] inadequate to meet the needs of such physicians and fail[ed] to respond to the requirements of the Medical School relating to the provision of ambulatory care." Therefore, the transfer was subject to Hospital X making a [amount redacted] grant to Entity Y (the

"Grant") designated for the purpose of "acquiring, by purchase, lease or otherwise, constructing, furnishing, and equipping a medical diagnostic clinic and office practice center for physician employees and staff members of [the Medical School]." Pursuant to the Grant, the location of the building was to be "within [the City] at such location as may be selected by the President of [University Y] with the concurrence of the [University Y] Advisory Board."

B. The Medical Center

The Medical Center is a six story building consisting of clearly defined areas devoted solely to clinical endeavors (the "Clinical Areas") and clearly defined areas devoted solely to academic endeavors (the "Academic Areas"). The Academic Areas are owned in undivided interests by Hospital X ([n%]) and Entity Y ([(100-n)%]). As a result of Entity Y's recent and partial exercise of its purchase option (as more fully described below), Entity Y is currently the sole owner of the Clinical Areas.

The Academic Areas are located in the outer rim of all six floors of the Medical Center, and the Clinical Areas are located within the inner portions of each floor. The Academic Areas are not designed for the performance of any clinical activity, and are used for faculty office space, medical school classrooms, and other medical education purposes related to the graduate and postgraduate medical education programs that Entity Y operates in cooperation with Hospital X. The Clinical Areas are used for the provision of clinical services.

In 1992, Entity Y selected Hospital X's campus as the location for the Medical Center and, together with Hospital X, undertook construction of the Medical Center. The Requestors have certified that, at the time of site selection and at the commencement of construction, there was a common understanding that each party would bear its respective share of the financial burden. Upon completion of construction in 1998, both the Academic Areas and the Clinical Areas of the Medical Center were owned in undivided interests as follows: [n%] by Hospital X and [(100-n)%] by Entity Y.

Entity Y's participation in the construction was based, in part, on initial pre-construction analyses conducted in 1995. As initially conceived (the "Original Model"), the building was to house two distinct components: (i) a provider-based outpatient clinic that would have been wholly-owned by Hospital X and staffed by Teaching Physicians, and (ii) academic office space for the Medical School's faculty members (i.e., the Teaching Physicians) that would have been wholly-owned by Entity Y. Because Hospital X and Entity Y would have owned their respective portions of the building, neither would have incurred rental charges under the Original Model.

Subsequent regulatory and statutory developments substantially altered the assumptions upon which the initial financing projections were based, and the design of the Original Model was changed significantly. In particular, under the revised model (the "Revised Model"), the clinical space was changed from a provider-based outpatient clinic to free-standing physician offices. Moreover, it was determined that Entity Y and Hospital X would be given their respective percentage ownership interests as undivided interests in the whole building. Notwithstanding the design change, the end result (i.e., creation of a modern facility in which Teaching Physicians would provide both academic and clinical services) remained the same.

Once the Medical Center was ready for occupancy, Hospital X and Entity Y, as owners and lessors of both the Academic Areas and Clinical Areas of the Medical Center, entered into two written leases with Entity Y, as lessee: one for the Academic Areas and one for the Clinical Areas. The lease for the Academic Areas permits Entity Y, in its capacity as lessee, to defer rental payments until September 30, 2000, and Entity Y has elected deferment.[2] In addition, the lease for the Academic Areas granted Entity Y an option (the "Option") to purchase Hospital X's ownership interest in the Medical Center. Recently, Entity Y exercised its Option with respect to the Clinical Areas only.[3] As a result, Entity Y is currently the sole owner of the Clinical Areas.[4] Entity Y did not exercise its Option with respect to the Academic Areas. Therefore, Hospital X still owns [n%] of the Academic Areas and Entity Y still owns the remaining [(100-n)%] of the Academic Areas.

Under the Revised Model, Entity Y incurs rental charges, and will make rental payments, for the same academic space that it would have had access to, under the Original Model, without incurring any rental charges. The Requestors have certified that payment of these

---

[2] Deferred rental payments accrue interest and must be secured.

[3] Entity Y financed its purchase of the Clinical Areas through the issuance of tax-exempt revenue bonds.

[4] The lease for the Clinical Areas formerly existing between Hospital X and Entity Y, as owners and lessors of the Clinical Areas, and Entity Y, as lessee, was terminated, and a new lease for the Clinical Areas was executed with the State Agency, as lessor, and the Faculty Practice Plan, as lessee. The State Agency will use the rental payments it receives under this new lease to retire the bonds described supra note 3.

rental charges would severely strain Entity Y's financial resources and jeopardize other services.

C. The Proposed Donation

Hospital X proposes to donate its existing [n%] interest in the Academic Areas of the Medical Center to Entity Y. The Proposed Donation would be retroactive to Entity Y's initial occupancy of the Academic Areas, and the only condition would be that the Academic Areas must be used for medical academic purposes. After the Proposed Donation, the Academic Areas would continue to be used by Entity Y just as they are currently.

The Proposed Donation would not be subject to any explicit or implicit requirements as to the use of the Clinical Areas or referrals to Hospital X. In addition, Entity Y has certified as follows:

- Entity Y will not require or encourage Entity Y Physicians to refer patients to Hospital X or any other institution. [5]
- Entity Y will not track referrals made by Entity Y Physicians to Hospital X or any other institution. [6]
- Compensation paid to Entity Y Physicians (including, without limitation, base salaries paid for Teaching Physicians' clinical or academic services and variable bonuses paid for their clinical services) will not be related to the volume or value of referrals by such physicians to Hospital X or any other institution. Such compensation will be consistent with fair market value in arm's-length transactions.
- On an annual basis, Entity Y will provide written notice of the limitations described in each of the three foregoing paragraphs to all Entity Y Physicians.

Hospital X has certified that it has not, and will not, provide to Entity Y any free or below market value goods or services that are directly or indirectly related to the Academic Areas, including, with-

---

[5] Consistent with its responsibilities as a teaching institution, the Medical School requires Teaching Physicians to admit patients only to facilities that have an academic affiliation with the Medical School. All hospitals within the City or the County have such an affiliation with the Medical School.

[6] Consistent with accreditation and similar requirements, for purposes of medical student and resident teaching and supervision, the Medical School keeps records of where Teaching Physicians perform procedures, but the Medical School has certified that it does not use those records for any purpose relating to setting physician compensation or influencing choice of hospital.

out limitation, all utilities (e.g., sewer charges, water, gas, electricity, telephone and every other service supplied to Entity Y or used upon, or in connection with, the Academic Areas), expenses, real estate taxes and all other taxes associated with or assessed against the Academic Areas.

II. THE ANTI-KICKBACK STATUTE

The anti-kickback statute makes it a criminal offense knowingly and willfully to offer, pay, solicit, or receive any remuneration to induce referrals of items or services reimbursable by any Federal health care program. See section 1128B(b) of the Act. Specifically, the statute provides that:

> Whoever knowingly and willfully offers or pays [or solicits or receives] any remuneration (including any kickback, bribe, or rebate) directly or indirectly, overtly or covertly, in cash or in kind to any person to induce such person — to refer an individual to a person for the furnishing or arranging for the furnishing of any item or service for which payment may be made in whole or in part under a Federal health care program, or to purchase, lease, order, or arrange for or recommend purchasing, leasing, or ordering any good, facility, service, or item for which payment may be made in whole or in part under a Federal health care program, shall be guilty of a felony.

Id. Thus, where remuneration is paid purposefully to induce referrals of items or services for which payment may be made by a Federal health care program, the anti-kickback statute is violated. By its terms, the statute ascribes criminal liability to parties on both sides of an impermissible "kickback" transaction. For purposes of the anti-kickback statute, "remuneration" includes the transfer of anything of value, in cash or in-kind, directly or indirectly, covertly or overtly.

The statute has been interpreted to cover any arrangement where one purpose of the remuneration was to obtain money for the referral of services or to induce further referrals. United States v. Kats, 871 F.2d 105 (9th Cir. 1989); United States v. Greber, 760 F.2d 68 (3d Cir.), cert. denied, 474 U.S. 988 (1985). Violation of the statute constitutes a felony punishable by a maximum fine of $25,000, imprisonment up to five years, or both. Conviction will also lead to automatic exclusion from Federal health care programs, including Medicare and Medicaid. The OIG may also initiate administrative proceedings to exclude persons from Federal and State health care programs or to impose civil monetary penalties for fraud, kickbacks, and other prohibited activities under sections 1128(b)(7) and 1128A (a)(7) of the Act.[7]

III. ANALYSIS

The OIG's position on the provision of free or below market value goods or services to referral sources is longstanding and clear: such arrangements are suspect. That is, the provision of free goods or services to any referral source may violate the anti-kickback statute if one purpose of the gift is to induce or reward referrals of Federal program business. In general, such arrangements give rise to an inference that one purpose of the gift is to induce referrals. The Proposed Donation is as straightforward as it is problematic: a substantial one-time donation by a hospital to a major referral source. (Since Entity Y employs, and is affiliated with, physicians who make referrals to Hospital X, Entity Y is a referral source for Hospital X.) Accordingly, the Proposed Donation implicates the Federal anti-kickback statute.

However, for the following reasons, we would not impose sanctions in connection with the Proposed Donation. First, the transaction is between components of an academic medical center that historically have shared both a common mission in training physicians for, and providing quality medical care to, the people of the State and a common heritage as public institutions. We recognize that the relationships among components of academic medical centers are often organizationally and financially complex. The Requestors have certified that, at the time of site selection and at the commencement of construction, there was a common understanding that each party would bear its respective share of the financial burden. Given the Requestors' shared history, mission, and public provenance, the Proposed Donation appears to be a reasonable accommodation to changed financial circumstances and consistent with the Requestors' shared charitable mission.

Second, Entity Y has certified that it will take a number of steps to insulate physician judgment and income from pressure to refer to Hospital X, including the following:

---

[7] Because both the criminal and administrative sanctions related to the anti-kickback implications of the Proposed Donation are based on violations of the anti-kickback statute, the analysis for purposes of this advisory opinion is the same under both.

Entity Y will not require or encourage Entity Y Physicians to refer patients to Hospital X or any other institution.[8]

Entity Y will not track referrals made by Entity Y Physicians to Hospital X or any other institution.[9]

Compensation paid to Entity Y Physicians (including, without limitation, base salaries paid for Teaching Physicians' clinical or academic services and variable bonuses paid for their clinical services) will not be related to the volume or value of referrals by such physicians to Hospital X or any other institution. Such compensation will be consistent with fair market value in arm's-length transactions.

On an annual basis, Entity Y will provide written notice of the limitations described in each of the three foregoing paragraphs to all Entity Y Physicians.

Thus, Entity Y's ability to direct the referrals of Entity Y Physicians will be significantly constrained.

Third, the Proposed Donation will confer a community benefit on the residents of the City and the State. The State continues to have many medically underserved areas, many of which are rural. As part of the State's effort to alleviate the inadequate number of physicians providing services in underserved areas and to underserved populations, the Medical School specializes in rural health issues and training of primary care physicians.

IV. CONCLUSION

For all of the above reasons, and based on the information provided, we conclude that the Proposed Donation could potentially generate prohibited remuneration under the anti-kickback statute if the requisite intent to induce referrals were present, but that the OIG will not subject the Medical School or Hospital X to sanctions for violations of the anti-kickback statute under sections 1128(b)(7) or 1128A(a)(7) of the Act in connection with the Proposed Donation, as described and certified in the request letter and supplemental submissions. This opinion is limited to the Proposed Donation and, therefore, we express no opinion about any other agreements or arrangements disclosed or referenced in your request letter or supplemental submissions.

---

[8] See supra note 5.

[9] See supra note 6.

V. LIMITATIONS

The limitations applicable to this opinion include the following:

- This advisory opinion is issued only to the Medical School and Hospital X, who are the requestors of this opinion. This advisory opinion has no application, and cannot be relied upon, by any other individual or entity.
- This advisory opinion may not be introduced into evidence in any matter involving an entity or individual that is not a requestor to this opinion.
- This advisory opinion is applicable only to the statutory provisions specifically noted above.
- No opinion is herein expressed or implied with respect to the application of any other Federal, state, or local statute, rule, regulation, ordinance, or other law that may be applicable to the Proposed Donation.
- This advisory opinion will not bind or obligate any agency other than the U.S. Department of Health and Human Services.
- This advisory opinion is limited in scope to the specific arrangement described in this letter and has no applicability to other arrangements, even those which appear similar in nature or scope.
- No opinion is expressed herein regarding the liability of any party under the False Claims Act or other legal authorities for any improper billing, claims submission, cost reporting, or related conduct.

This opinion is also subject to any additional limitations set forth at 42 C.F.R. Part 1008.

The OIG will not proceed against the Requestors with respect to any action that is part of the Proposed Donation taken in good faith reliance upon this advisory opinion as long as all of the material facts have been fully, completely, and accurately presented, and the Proposed Donation in practice comports with the information provided. The OIG reserves the right to reconsider the questions and issues raised in this advisory opinion and, where the public interest requires, rescind, modify or terminate this opinion. In the event that this advisory opinion is modified or terminated, the OIG will not proceed against the Requestors with respect to any action taken in good faith reliance upon this advisory opinion, where all of the relevant facts were fully, completely, and accurately presented and where such action was promptly discontinued upon notification of the modification or termination of this advisory opinion. An advisory opinion may be rescinded only if the relevant and material facts have not been fully, completely and accurately disclosed to the OIG.

Sincerely,

/s/

D. McCarty Thornton

Chief Counsel to the Inspector General

APPENDIX F53

Advisory Opinion No. 00–7, November 17, 2000

Regarding free transportation services that Hospital X offers to certain patients who have been referred to Hospital X for extended courses of treatment.

Issued: November 17, 2000
[Name and Address Redacted]

Re: OIG Advisory Opinion No. 00–7

Dear [Name Redacted]:

We are writing in response to your request for an advisory opinion regarding free transportation services that Hospital X ("Hospital X" or the "Requestor") offers to certain patients who have been referred to Hospital X for extended courses of treatment involving chemotherapy, dialysis, radiation therapy, cardio/pulmonary rehabilitation treatment, or certain similar services (the "Arrangement"). Specifically, the question raised by your request is whether the Arrangement constitutes grounds for sanctions under the civil monetary penalty provision prohibiting inducements to beneficiaries, section 1128A(a)(5) of the Social Security Act (the "Act"), or the anti-kickback statute, section 1128B(b) of the Act, in the circumstances presented.

You have certified that all of the information provided in your request, including all supplementary letters, is true and correct and constitutes a complete description of the relevant facts and agreements among the parties.

In issuing this opinion, we have relied solely on the facts and information presented to us. We have not undertaken an independent investigation of such information. This opinion is limited to the facts presented. If material facts have not been disclosed or have been misrepresented, this opinion is without force and effect.

Based on the information provided, we conclude that: (i) the Office of Inspector General ("OIG") will not impose a civil monetary penalty under section 1128A(a)(5) of the Act on Hospital X in connection with the Arrangement, as described and certified in your request letter and supplemental submissions; and (ii) the Arrangement could potentially generate prohibited remuneration under the anti-kickback statute if the requisite intent were present, but that the OIG will not subject Hospital X to sanctions for violations of the anti-kickback statute under sections 1128(b)(7) or 1128A(a)(7) of the Act in connection with the Arrangement, as described and certified in your request letter and supplemental submissions.

This opinion may not be relied on by any persons other than Hospital X, and is further qualified as set out in Part IV below and in 42 C.F.R. Part 1008.

I. FACTUAL BACKGROUND

Hospital X is a not-for-profit health care system located in City A, State B. Hospital X has three City A locations at which medical services are provided:

> the West Campus, where acute care services, emergency services, cancer care, cardiac care, cardiac and pulmonary rehabilitation services, diagnostic services, and other services are provided. Hospital X's [number redacted]-bed acute care hospital, the only acute care hospital in City A, and its [name redacted] Cancer Center are located on this campus; the East Campus, where outpatient clinic services and medical rehabilitation services are provided for patients who suffer from spinal cord injury, stroke, amputation, brain trauma, and musculoskeletal diseases; and the [name redacted] Dialysis Center.

Hospital X's primary service area encompasses not only City A, but a ten-county rural area in [area redacted] State B covering [over 8,000] square miles. Many of the counties within Hospital X's primary service area are rural or contain medically underserved areas and populations. Hospital X is the only provider of radiation oncology within its primary service area. Moreover, within Hospital X's primary service area, there is only one other provider of dialysis services, and there are only two other providers of cardiac rehabilitation services.

Public transportation within Hospital X's primary service area is very limited. Within the City A city limits, there is one taxi service, which has five or fewer vehicles, and a single "Handibus," which runs on a set schedule and provides transportation to handicapped individuals. No public transportation is available outside the City A city limits.

The Arrangement is set forth in a written policy which describes in detail Hospital X's free transportation policy and procedures. Under the Arrangement, Hospital X uses two of its own vehicles to provide free one-way or round-trip general transportation services between Hospital X and each eligible patient's residence. Transportation is only provided to patients who reside within Hospital X's primary service area or for whom Hospital X is the nearest provider of the prescribed treatments. The transportation services are not ambulance-level services, and no state license is required. Notwithstanding, most drivers have a current state emergency medical technician ("EMT") license, which allows them to respond appropriately if a medical emergency arises en route. To be eligible for the free transportation services, a patient must: (i) have been referred to Hospital X for an extended course of treatment involving chemotherapy, dialysis, radiation therapy, cardio/pulmonary rehabilitation treatment, or certain similar services; (ii) be unable to provide his or her own transportation and have no other regular and reliable means of transportation (public or private); and (iii) be at significant medical risk if treatment is not provided.

Hospital X does not charge the patient or any third party payor for the transportation services. General transportation, such as the type offered by Hospital X under the Arrangement, is not reimbursable under any Federal health care program. Hospital X has certified that the costs of the free transportation services will not be claimed directly or indirectly on any Federal health care program cost report or claim or otherwise shifted to any Federal health care program.

Hospital X has not, and will not, market or advertise the availability of its free transportation services. Under the Arrangement, Hospital X's hospital staff are instructed that, in the course of arranging for extended courses of treatment, they should be alert for those patients who indicate an inability to obtain regular and reliable transportation to and from Hospital X, obtain information from the patients about their particular circumstances, and recommend such patients to the appropriate department director for review. If the department director determines that the patient meets the eligibility requirements described above, the department director offers free transportation services to the patient, and upon acceptance of the offer, refers the patient to the Patient Transportation Department. The Patient Transportation Department prioritizes the referred patients' requests based upon medical need, travel distance, the number of other patients needing transportation, and the time of treatment. Hospital X has certified that neither referrals made by Hospital X's hospital staff, decisions made by department directors, nor decisions made by the Patient Transportation Department will be based, directly or indirectly, upon the patient's ability to pay for the underlying medical services or the existence, nature, or extent of the patient's insurance coverage.

Historically, Hospital X has offered free transportation services to a limited number of patients, averaging approximately 6% of all radiation oncology, dialysis, and cardio/pulmonary patients. The average age of individuals receiving transportation under the Arrangement is sixty-six, and the average distance of the transportation is twenty-eight miles.

II. LEGAL ANALYSIS

A. Fraud and Abuse Implications of Free Transportation Services

Health care providers that offer free goods or services, such as free transportation services, to Federal health care beneficiaries may be subject to civil monetary penalties. In section 1128A(a)(5) of the Act, Congress specifically addressed the issue of providers offering remuneration to Medicare and Medicaid beneficiaries in order to influence their selection of a particular provider by authorizing the imposition of civil monetary penalties against such providers. Moreover, free transportation services may implicate the criminal anti-kickback statute which prohibits offering anything of value to any "person" (including a Federal health care beneficiary) to reward or induce referrals (including self-referrals) for items or services reimbursable under any Federal health care program.[1] Given the overlap between the two statutes, we will begin with some general observations about free transportation services.[2]

First, we recognize that many arrangements involving free transportation have important and beneficial effects on patient care,

[1] Because both the criminal and administrative sanctions related to the anti-kickback implications of the Arrangement are based on violations of the anti-kickback statute, the analysis for purposes of this advisory opinion is the same under both.

[2] Providers offering transportation services to beneficiaries at a price that is below fair market value would be subject to the same concerns, analysis, and, if applicable, sanctions as offerors of free transportation services.

especially where such arrangements are narrowly tailored to address issues of financial need, limited transportation resources, treatment compliance, or safety.

Second, we also recognize that free transportation services are sometimes an integral part of fraudulent or abusive schemes which lead to inappropriate steering of patients, overutilization, and the provision of medically unnecessary services. Examples of abusive arrangements involving free transportation services include:

- Psychiatric facilities offering out-of-state patients free round-trip airline tickets to Florida in order to receive services at their facilities;
- Van drivers soliciting, and offering free transportation services to, Medicaid patients for health care providers who compensate the drivers on a per patient or per service basis;
- Unscrupulous health care providers offering residents of nursing facilities and other congregate care facilities free transportation services to and from their offices for services that are frequently of questionable necessity;
- Hospitals offering patients free limousine services; and Hospitals offering patients free ambulance services without making individual determinations of financial need.

Third, given their potential for abuse, we evaluate arrangements involving free transportation services on a case-by-case basis. We have identified several risk factors including, but not limited to, the following:

- The population to whom free transportation services are offered. While free transportation services offered to "all comers" can implicate section 1128A(a)(5) of the Act and the anti-kickback statute, so can free transportation services offered to select patients or populations. To the extent the services are offered selectively, we evaluate the basis on which the selection is made. For example, an offeror of free transportation services might select individuals based upon one or more of the following criteria: relationship with the offeror (including physician-patient relationships); relationship with other providers (including nursing facility-resident relationships); diagnosis; insurance coverage; geographic location; financial need; or concerns regarding safety or treatment compliance.

- The nature or type of free transportation services offered. Expensive transportation services such as limousines, airline tickets, or ambulance transports raise greater concerns.
- The geographic area in which free transportation services are offered. Services offered within a provider's historic service area are less suspect than services offered outside its historic service area.
- The availability and affordability of alternate means of transportation. Whether free transportation services are marketed or advertised and, if so, how.
- The type of provider offering the free transportation services. Free transportation services offered by individual or small groups of providers, including physicians, or by freestanding clinics are subject to greater scrutiny. Historically, unscrupulous providers and clinics have offered free transportation services in conjunction with Medicare and Medicaid mills. Whether the costs of the free transportation services will be claimed directly or indirectly on any Federal health care program cost report or claim or otherwise shifted to any Federal health care program.

These factors are not exclusive, and the presence or absence of any one factor is not determinative of whether the OIG would subject parties to sanctions for providing free transportation services to patients.

Fourth, we weigh these factors, as well as other relevant concerns, in assessing the level of risk presented by an arrangement. They are not necessarily determinative or probative of whether an arrangement violates the applicable statutes. The elements required for a violation of the statutes are discussed below.

B. Application of Section 1128A(a)(5) of the Act

Section 1128A(a)(5) of the Act provides for the imposition of civil monetary penalties against any person who:

> offers or transfers remuneration to any individual eligible for benefits under [Medicare or a State health care program] that such person knows or should know is likely to influence such individual to order or receive from a particular provider, practitioner, or supplier any item or service for which payment may be made, in whole or in part, under [Medicare or a State health care program].

See also 65 Fed. Reg. 24400, 24416 (April 26, 2000) (to be codified at 42 C.F.R. § 1003.102(b)(13)). Section 1128A(i)(6) of the Act defines "remuneration" for purposes of section 1128A(a)(5) of the Act as including, among other things, "transfers of items or services for free or for other than fair market value." Unlike the anti-kickback statute, section 1128A(a)(5) of the Act is solely concerned with remuneration offered or transferred to Medicare or State health care program beneficiaries.

Although free transportation services clearly fall within the ambit of the prohibition, legislative history indicates that, in enacting section 1128A(a)(5), Congress did not intend to impose civil monetary penalties against persons offering complimentary local transportation of nominal value. H.R. Conf. Rep. No. 104–736, at 255 (1996). In the preamble to 42 C.F.R. § 1003.102(b)(13), the final rule addressing section 1128A(a)(5) of the Act, we interpreted nominal value for purposes of section 1128A(a)(5) to be no more than $10 per item, or $50 in the aggregate on an annual basis. 65 Fed. Reg. 24400, 24411 (April 26, 2000). Moreover, we theorized that "frequent rendering of items or services to any individual may preclude such items and services from being classified as nominal in value." Id. at 24407. However, many free transports, including many of those provided under the Arrangement, exceed the nominal value and local service limits.

Notwithstanding, for all of the following reasons, we will not subject Hospital X to civil monetary penalties under section 1128A(a)(5) of the Act in connection with the Arrangement:

- There is either limited or no economical means of public transportation in the geographic area where Hospital X provides the free transportation services.
- The free transportation services are not advertised and are available only to individuals who have already been referred to, or are being treated at, Hospital X.
- The free transportation services are available only if there has been an individualized determination of need (i.e., the patient has no other regular and reliable means of transportation).
- The free transportation services are available to all qualified patients who require a course of multiple treatments, subject to available resources. The Arrangement is not limited to, or targeted at, particular profitable treatments or patient populations.
- The costs of the free transportation services will not be claimed directly or indirectly on any Federal health care program cost

report or claim or otherwise shifted to any Federal health care program.

- The geographic area within which the free transportation services are offered is limited to Hospital X's historic primary service area, the size of which is determined in part by its rural location, and other areas that include patients for whom Hospital X is the nearest provider of the prescribed treatments.
- Consistent with Hospital X's not-for-profit mission, the Arrangement provides a benefit to the community by giving elderly and low-income Hospital X patients access to medically necessary, life-prolonging treatments that they may otherwise forego, in whole or in part, because of inadequate transportation.

C. Application of the Anti-Kickback Statute

The anti-kickback statute makes it a criminal offense knowingly and willfully to offer, pay, solicit, or receive any remuneration to induce referrals of items or services reimbursable by any Federal health care program. See section 1128B(b) of the Act. Specifically, the statute provides that:

> Whoever knowingly and willfully offers or pays [or solicits or receives] any remuneration (including any kickback, bribe, or rebate) directly or indirectly, overtly or covertly, in cash or in kind to any person to induce such person — to refer an individual to a person for the furnishing or arranging for the furnishing of any item or service for which payment may be made in whole or in part under a Federal health care program, or to purchase, lease, order, or arrange for or recommend purchasing, leasing, or ordering any good, facility, service, or item for which payment may be made in whole or in part under a Federal health care program, shall be guilty of a felony.

Id. Thus, where remuneration is paid purposefully to induce referrals of items or services for which payment may be made by a Federal health care program, the anti-kickback statute is violated. By its terms, the statute ascribes criminal liability to parties on both sides of an impermissible "kickback" transaction. For purposes of the anti-kickback statute, "remuneration" includes the transfer of anything of value, in cash or in-kind, directly or indirectly, covertly or overtly.

The statute has been interpreted to cover any arrangement where one purpose of the remuneration was to obtain money for the referral of services or to induce further referrals. United States v. Kats, 871 F.2d 105 (9th Cir. 1989); United States v. Greber, 760 F.2d 68 (3d Cir.), cert. denied, 474 U.S. 988 (1985). Violation of the statute constitutes a felony punishable by a maximum fine of $25,000, imprisonment up to five years, or both. Conviction will also lead to automatic exclusion from Federal health care programs, including Medicare and Medicaid. The OIG may also initiate administrative proceedings to exclude persons from Federal and State health care programs or to impose civil monetary penalties for fraud, kickbacks, and other prohibited activities under sections 1128(b)(7) and 1128A (a)(7) of the Act.

Remuneration from a hospital to a patient that is intended to induce the patient to obtain hospital services implicates the anti-kickback statute. For example, the routine waiver of Medicare Part B coinsurance — a payment obligation required by Federal law — implicates the anti-kickback statute, as would offers of cash or other valuable gifts that are intended to induce patients to order services paid for in whole or in part by a Federal health care program. Free transportation services offered by a hospital to Federal health care program beneficiaries may have monetary value and implicate the anti-kickback statute, if the requisite intent to induce self-referrals is present. Notwithstanding, in the instant case, for all of the reasons set forth above in the analysis of section 1128A(a)(5) of the Act, we will not subject Hospital X to sanctions for violations arising under the Federal anti-kickback statute in connection with the Arrangement.

III. CONCLUSION

For all of the above reasons, and based on the information provided, we conclude that: (i) the OIG will not impose a civil monetary penalty under section 1128A(a)(5) of the Act on Hospital X in connection with the Arrangement, as described and certified in your request letter and supplemental submissions; and (ii) the Arrangement could potentially generate prohibited remuneration under the anti-kickback statute if the requisite intent were present, but that the OIG will not subject Hospital X to sanctions for violations of the anti-kickback statute under sections 1128(b)(7) or 1128A(a)(7) of the Act in connection with the Arrangement, as described and certified in your request letter and supplemental submissions.

IV. LIMITATIONS

The limitations applicable to this opinion include the following:

- This advisory opinion is issued only to Hospital X, who is the requestor of this opinion. This advisory opinion has no application, and cannot be relied upon, by any other individual or entity.
- This advisory opinion may not be introduced into evidence in any matter involving an entity or individual that is not a requestor to this opinion.
- This advisory opinion is applicable only to the statutory provisions specifically noted above. No opinion is herein expressed or implied with respect to the application of any other Federal, state, or local statute, rule, regulation, ordinance, or other law that may be applicable to the Arrangement.
- This advisory opinion will not bind or obligate any agency other than the U.S. Department of Health and Human Services.
- This advisory opinion is limited in scope to the specific arrangement described in this letter and has no applicability to other arrangements, even those which appear similar in nature or scope.
- No opinion is expressed herein regarding the liability of any party under the False Claims Act or other legal authorities for any improper billing, claims submission, cost reporting, or related conduct.

This opinion is also subject to any additional limitations set forth at 42 C.F.R. Part 1008. The OIG will not proceed against the Requestor with respect to any action that is part of the Arrangement taken in good faith reliance upon this advisory opinion as long as all of the material facts have been fully, completely, and accurately presented, and the Arrangement in practice comports with the information provided. The OIG reserves the right to reconsider the questions and issues raised in this advisory opinion and, where the public interest requires, rescind, modify or terminate this opinion. In the event that this advisory opinion is modified or terminated, the OIG will not proceed against the Requestor with respect to any action taken in good faith reliance upon this advisory opinion, where all of the relevant facts were fully, completely, and accurately presented and where such action was promptly discontinued upon notification of the modification or termination of this advisory opinion. An advisory opinion may be rescinded only if the relevant and material facts have not been fully, completely and accurately disclosed to the OIG.

Sincerely,

/s/

D. McCarty Thornton

Chief Counsel to the Inspector General

APPENDIX F54

Advisory Opinion No. 00–8, December 5, 2000

Whether operating a housing referral service for the elderly is subject to sanction.

[*We redact certain identifying information and certain potentially privileged, confidential, or proprietary information associated with the individual or entity, unless otherwise approved by the requestor.*]

DEPARTMENT OF HEALTH & HUMAN SERVICES
Office of Inspector General
Washington, D.C. 20201

Issued: December 5, 2000

Posted: December 12, 2000

Ms. Ann Sweeney
Director
Housing Referrals of Maine
P.O. Box 2347
Augusta, ME 04338–2347

Re: Spectrum Housing, d/b/a Housing Referrals of Maine

OIG Advisory Opinion No. 00-8

Dear Ms. Sweeney:

We are writing in response to your request for an advisory opinion, in which you ask whether operating a housing referral service for the elderly (the "Service") will subject you to sanction under the anti-kickback statute, section 1128B(b) of the Social Security Act (the "Act").

You have certified that all of the information you provided in your request, including all supplementary letters, is true and correct, and constitutes a complete description of the material facts regarding the Service. In issuing this opinion, we have relied solely on the facts and information presented to us. We have not undertaken an independent investigation of such information. This opinion is limited to the facts presented. If material facts have not been disclosed or have been misrepresented, this opinion is without force and effect.

Based on the information provided, we conclude that the Service would potentially generate prohibited remuneration under the anti-kickback statute, if the requisite intent to induce referrals were present, but that, based on the totality of the facts as described and certified in your request letter and supplemental submissions, the Office of Inspector General ("OIG") will not subject Spectrum Housing, d/b/a Housing Referrals of Maine (the "Requestor"), to sanctions for violations of the anti-kickback statute under sections 1128(b)(7) or 1128A(a)(7) of the Act in connection with the Service. This advisory opinion may not be relied on by any person other than the Requestor and is further qualified as set out in Part IV below and in 42 C.F.R. Part 1008.

I. FACTUAL BACKGROUND

The Requestor is a non-profit agency operating a housing referral service (the "Service") that places the elderly (the "Prospective Tenants" or "Tenants") in various types of housing facilities located within the state of Maine (the "State"). The Requestor has referral service contracts with facilities (the "Facilities") that include nursing homes, senior apartment complexes, retirement communities, and assisted living facilities.

Facilities must meet certain "qualifications for participation" to register with the Service. The Requestor determines whether a facility is qualified to participate by inspecting each facility to ensure that it is State licensed and performing services in compliance with State laws. The Requestor also uses the site inspection to determine what services are provided by the Facility. The Requestor does not exclude from the Service any facilities that meet the qualifications for participation. The Requestor imposes no requirements on the manner in which a Facility provides services, except that the Requestor requires that the Facilities charge the Prospective Tenants referred through the Service the same rate that it charges other individuals.

In addition, each Facility pays a fee to the Requestor to register with the Service. The Facilities pay the Requestor in one of the following ways: (i) if a Facility accepts any Federal health care program payment (rendering it a "Federal Payment Facility"), then the Requestor charges the Facility a set rate for a period of one year; (ii) if a Facility does not accept any Federal health care program payment, i.e., private payment only (a "Private Payment Facility"), then the Requestor charges the Facility [X]% of each placed Tenant's first month's charges for rent and personal care services, provided the Tenant resides in the Facility for more than one month.[1] The Requestor has certified that the charges to the Federal Payment Facilities are less than or equal to the cost of the Requestor's provision of the services to the Federal Payment Facilities. At present, all of the Federal Payment Facilities are nursing homes.

Prospective Tenants contact the Requestor to find housing in Facilities that suit their needs. Upon a Prospective Tenant's initial contact with the Requestor, the Requestor describes to the Prospective Tenant the services provided through the Service and the various housing and care options available. The Requestor then interviews the Prospective Tenant to determine the Prospective Tenant's medical, financial, and geographical needs. Using the information gathered, the Requestor selects a number of Facilities for the Prospective Tenant. Prospective Tenants are only referred to Facilities with whom the Requestor has a referral service contract. The Requestor does not charge the Prospective Tenants for using the referral services.

The Requestor makes the following five disclosures in writing to each Prospective Tenant:

- That the Requestor selects the Facilities to which it refers, in the manner described above;
- That the Facility has paid a fee to the Requestor to register with the Service;
- That the Requestor selects one or more Facilities for the Prospective Tenant according to information regarding the Prospective Tenant's medical, financial, and geographical needs;
- That the only relationship between the Requestor and the Facilities to whom it makes referrals is the relationship through the Service; and
- That a Facility would be excluded from continuing to participate in the Service if the Facility ceases to meet the

[1] If a Tenant resides in a Private Payment Facility for less than one month, the Requestor charges the Facility progressively smaller percentages of the first month's charges, depending on the Tenant's length of stay.

qualifications for participation, or if a Facility represents that it will provide a service but fails to do so.

The Requestor requires each Prospective Tenant to sign a confirmation certifying that the Prospective Tenant has read these disclosures.

II. LEGAL ANALYSIS

A. Law

The anti-kickback statute, section 1128B(b) of the Act, makes it a criminal offense knowingly and willfully to offer, pay, solicit, or receive any remuneration to induce the referral of business covered by a Federal health care program. Specifically, the statute provides that:

> Whoever knowingly and willfully offers or pays [or solicits or receives] any remuneration (including any kickback, bribe, or rebate) directly or indirectly, overtly or covertly, in cash or in kind to any person to induce such person — to refer an individual to a person for the furnishing or arranging for the furnishing of any item or service for which payment may be made in whole or in part under a Federal health care program, or to purchase, lease, order, or arrange for or recommend purchasing, leasing, or ordering any good, facility, service, or item for which payment may be made in whole or in part under a Federal health care program, shall be guilty of a felony.

Section 1128B(b) of the Act. In other words, the statute prohibits payments made purposefully to induce referrals of business for which payment may be made by a Federal health care program. The statute ascribes liability to both sides of an impermissible "kickback" transaction. The statute has been interpreted to cover any arrangement where one purpose of the remuneration is to obtain money for the referral of services or to induce further referrals. United States v. Kats, 871 F.2d 105 (9th Cir. 1989); United States v. Greber, 760 F.2d 68 (3d Cir.), cert. denied, 474 U.S. 988 (1985). "Remuneration" for purposes of the anti-kickback statute includes the transfer of any thing of value, in cash or in-kind, directly or indirectly, covertly or overtly.

Violation of the anti-kickback statute constitutes a felony punishable by a maximum fine of $25,000, imprisonment up to five years, or both. Conviction will also lead to automatic exclusion from Federal health care programs, including Medicare and Medicaid. This Office may also initiate administrative proceedings to exclude persons from the Federal and State health care programs or to impose civil monetary penalties for fraud, kickbacks, and other prohibited activities under sections 1128(b)(7) and 1128A(a)(7) of the Act.[2]

A number of statutory and regulatory "safe harbors" protect certain arrangements that might otherwise violate the anti-kickback statute. See 42 U.S.C. § 1320a-7b(b)(3); 42 C.F.R. § 1001.952. The safe harbor potentially applicable to the Service is the referral services safe harbor at 42 C.F.R. § 1001.952(f). This safe harbor protects referral service payments between an individual or entity (a "participant") and another entity serving as a referral service (a "referral service"), provided certain conditions described in the regulation are satisfied. Among the conditions to be satisfied under the safe harbor are that payments made by participants to the referral service are assessed equally against and collected equally from all participants, and are based only on the cost of operating the referral service, rather than the volume or value of referrals to or business generated by either party for the other party for which payment may be made in whole or in part under Medicare or a State health care program. In addition, the safe harbor requires that the referral service make specific disclosures to each person seeking a referral. 42 C.F.R. § 1001.952(f). Strict compliance with all safe harbor elements is required in order to receive safe harbor protection. See 56 Fed. Reg. 35952, 35954 (July 29, 1991).

B. Analysis

Referral services, such as the Service, clearly implicate the anti-kickback statute to the extent that individuals or entities make payments to the referral services in exchange for referrals or business for which payment may be made by a Federal health care program. In this instance, the Service meets all of the requirements of the safe harbor, except for the requirement that fees be assessed equally against all participants in the referral service.

There are no financial relationships between the Requestor and the Facilities other than the referral service relationship. The Service is open to all facilities that meet the qualifications for participation and the participation fees charged to the Federal Payment Facilities are less than the Requestor's cost of operating the

[2] Because both the criminal and administrative sanctions related to the anti-kickback implications of the Service are based on violations of the anti-kickback statute, the analysis for purposes of this advisory opinion is the same under both.

Service. The Requestor imposes no requirements on the manner in which a Facility provides services, except that the Requestor requires that the Facilities charge the prospective Tenants referred through the Service at the same rate as it charges other individuals. The Requestor makes the five disclosures, as described in the referral services safe harbor, in the manner prescribed by the safe harbor. 42 C.F.R. § 1001.952(f)(4).

Notwithstanding these similarities, the payment methodology "carves out" Federal Payment Facilities from the other Facilities. Such differential payment arrangements do not meet the safe harbor requirement that any payment made by a participant to a referral service be assessed equally against and collected equally from all participants. See 42 C.F.R. § 1001.952(f)(4). We want to reiterate our longstanding antipathy to attempts by referring parties to "carve out" referrals of Federal health care beneficiaries or business generated by Federal healthcare programs from otherwise questionable financial arrangements. Such arrangements may violate the anti-kickback statute by disguising remuneration for Federal referrals through offers or payments of inflated amounts for non-Federal business or simply by offering or paying remuneration for non-Federal referrals to "pull through" the Federal business. In the nursing home context, for example, even if payment to the referral service is based only on referrals of private pay beneficiaries, we are mindful that a substantial portion of those private pay beneficiaries ultimately will "spend down" their assets and qualify for Medicaid. The referral fee is for the patients' entire stream of funding, including the Federal health care program payment.

Under the proposed arrangement, however, the Service receives a fixed, annual payment from participating Facilities that receive any reimbursement or payment from a Federal health care program, regardless of whether the patients referred by the Service are covered by a Federal health care program or commercial insurance. These Federal Payment Facilities do not pay the Service based on the volume or value of referrals. As a practical matter, the Service's payment methodology as applied to Federal Payment Facilities is effectively equivalent to the safe harbor requirement that fees be assessed against and collected equally from all participants; all referrals to any Federal Payment Facility for any beneficiary will be covered by the fixed annual fee, eliminating the risk that the commercial fee will be manipulated to reward referrals of Federal business.

In light of the minimal risk of Federal health care program fraud or abuse posed by the Service, we consider the benefits that result from the Service. The Service provides some benefit to the elderly by helping them to find housing that will meet their needs efficiently. For all of these reasons, we vi11 not subject the Requestor to sanctions under sections 1128(b)(7) or 1128A(a)(7) of the Act in connection with the Service.

III. CONCLUSION

For the above-stated reasons, and based on the information provided, we conclude that the Service would potentially generate prohibited remuneration under the anti-kickback statute, if the requisite intent to induce referrals were present, but that, based on the totality of the facts as described and certified in your request letter and supplemental submissions, the OIG will not subject the Requestor to sanctions for violations of the anti-kickback statute under sections 1128(b)(7) or 1128A(a)(7) of the Act in connection with the Service.

IV. LIMITATIONS

The limitations applicable to this opinion include the following:

- This advisory opinion is issued only to Spectrum Housing, d/b/a Housing Referrals of Maine, the Requestor of this opinion. This advisory opinion has no application, and cannot be relied upon, by any other individual or entity.
- This advisory opinion may not be introduced into evidence in any matter involving an entity or individual that is not a Requestor to this opinion.
- This advisory opinion is applicable only to the statutory provisions specifically noted above. No opinion is herein expressed or implied with respect to the application of any other Federal, state, or local statute, rule, regulation, ordinance, or other law that may be applicable to the Service.
- This advisory opinion will not bind or obligate any agency other than the U.S. Department of Health and Human Services.
- This advisory opinion is limited in scope to the specific arrangement described in this letter and has no applicability to other arrangements, even those which appear similar in nature or scope.

- No opinion is expressed herein regarding the liability of any party under the False Claims Act or other legal authorities for any improper billing, claims submission, cost reporting, or related conduct.

This opinion is also subject to any additional limitations set forth at 42 C.F.R. Part 1008.

The OIG will not proceed against the Requestor with respect to any action that is part of the Service taken in good faith reliance upon this advisory opinion as long as all of the material facts have been fully, completely, and accurately presented, and the arrangement in practice comports with the information provided. The OIG reserves the right to reconsider the questions and issues raised in this advisory opinion and, where the public interest requires, modify or terminate this opinion. In the event that this advisory opinion is modified or terminated, the OIG will not proceed against the Requestor with respect to any action taken in good faith reliance upon this advisory opinion, where all of the relevant facts were fully, completely, and accurately presented and where such action was promptly discontinued upon notification of the modification or termination of this advisory opinion. An advisory opinion may be rescinded only if the relevant and material facts have not been fully, completely, and accurately disclosed to the OIG.

Sincerely,

/s/

D. McCarty Thornton

Chief Counsel to the Inspector General

APPENDIX F55

Advisory Opinion No. 00–9, December 8, 2000

Whether a proposed ambulance restocking arrangement constitutes prohibited remuneration.

[*We redact certain identifying information and certain potentially privileged, confidential, or proprietary information associated with the individual or entity, unless otherwise approved by the requestor.*]

Date Issued: December 8, 2000

Date Posted: December 21, 2000

[Name and Address Redacted]

Re: [name redacted]

Advisory Opinion No. 00–9

Dear [Name Redacted]:

We are writing in response to your request for an advisory opinion, in which you ask whether a proposed ambulance restocking arrangement (the "Proposed Arrangement") constitutes prohibited remuneration under the anti-kickback statute, section 1128B(b) of the Social Security Act (the "Act"), and, if so, whether the Proposed Arrangement would constitute grounds for the imposition of sanctions arising under the anti-kickback statute.

You have certified that all of the information provided in your request letter, including all supplementary information, is true and correct, and constitutes a complete description of the material facts regarding the Proposed Arrangement. You have also certified that, upon our approval, you will undertake to effectuate the Proposed Arrangement.

In issuing this opinion, we have relied solely on the facts and information presented to us. We have not undertaken any independent investigation of such information. This opinion is limited to the

facts presented. If material facts have not been disclosed or have been misrepresented, this opinion is without force and effect.

Based on the facts certified in your request for an advisory opinion, we conclude that the Proposed Arrangement described in your advisory opinion request and supplemental submissions could constitute prohibited remuneration under the anti-kickback statute, if the requisite intent to induce referrals of Federal health care program business were present, but that the Office of Inspector General ("OIG") will not subject Hospital A to sanctions in connection with the Proposed Arrangement, as described and certified in the request letter and supplemental submissions, arising under the anti-kickback statute pursuant to sections 1128(b)(7) or 1128A(a)(7) of the Act.

This opinion may not be relied on by any persons other than Hospital A and is further qualified as set out in Part IV below and in 42 C.F.R. Part 1008.

I. FACTUAL BACKGROUND

Hospital A (the "Hospital") is a non-profit, tax-exempt corporation organized under the laws of the State of Y. The Hospital is located in City X, State Y, and is the only hospital in the greater City X area. Emergency medical services ("EMS") ambulances in the greater City X area transport the majority of their patients – in excess of 85% – to the Hospital due to the Hospital's proximity to area towns.

In State Y, the Department of Public Health oversees regional EMS councils throughout the state. These councils plan, coordinate, and administer local emergency medical services. The greater State Y area is located within the jurisdiction covered by the Z Emergency Medical Services Regional Council (the "EMS Council"). The Z Region is the largest in the State, covering forty-three towns and six hospitals. The EMS Council's mission is, among other things, to coordinate the various levels of EMS, educational programs, and interaction between pre-hospital care providers and other health care providers in the region and to encourage the implementation of EMS standards and criteria pursuant to local, state, and national guidelines. The EMS Council is composed of representatives from EMS providers, health care entities, and consumers and has oversight responsibilities for the provision of EMS in the region. As part of its oversight responsibilities, the EMS Council reviews protocols for EMS developed by each hospital in the region. The EMS Council has established a Medical Advisory Committee with representatives from each hospital in the region, including the Hospital. In addition, the Hospital serves as the "sponsor hospital" for twelve area EMS services pursuant to an agreement with the State Y. In this capacity, the Hospital provides medical control for the EMS providers and helps to ensure a well-structured EMS system in the greater City X area.

To further its mission to promote quality EMS, the EMS Council is working to coordinate a region-wide ambulance restocking program to ensure timely and appropriate restocking throughout its jurisdiction.

Four of the eleven EMS transport services that convey patients to the Hospital are volunteer ambulance services that do not charge insurers or patients for transport services (the "Non-Billing Volunteer Services").[1] Under the Proposed Arrangement, the Hospital 1 will restock the Non-Billing Volunteer Services' ambulances with certain medical supplies[2] and pharmaceuticals used in connection with emergency pre-hospital services provided by the Non-Billing Volunteer Services. The Non-Billing Volunteer Services will not be charged, and will not pay, for the restocked items, and neither the Non-Billing Volunteer Services nor the Hospital will bill or otherwise seek reimbursement, directly or indirectly, from any Federal health care program or other party for restocked items. To qualify for exchanges of pharmaceuticals, the Non-Billing Volunteer Services must provide documentation of the drugs used during emergency ambulance runs. Restocked supplies will also be documented. The Proposed Arrangement seeks to ensure that the Non-Billing Volunteer Services' ambulances are fully stocked with a standard complement of the supplies and drugs covered by the Proposed Arrangement. This will make it easier, for example, for patients arriving by emergency ambulance to be connected to the Hospital's emergency room systems without interruption. The Proposed Arrangement will be consistent with the restocking practices promoted by the EMS Council.

---

[1] The other emergency ambulance services will not participate in the Proposed Arrangement. They consist of volunteer companies that charge for their services and a private ambulance company managed through a subsidiary of the Hospital.

[2] The medical supplies covered by the Proposed Arrangement are intravenous solutions, intravenous tubing, intravenous catheters and needles, oxygen cannulas and oxygen masks, endotracheal tubing, tuberculin, intramuscular syringes, blood collection tubes, sterile gauzes, and linen.

The Hospital restocks, and will continue to restock, other ambulance services with supplies and medications used during emergency pre-hospital transports, but those ambulance services must pay fair market value for the restocked items.

II. LEGAL ANALYSIS.

The anti-kickback statute makes it a criminal offense knowingly and willfully to offer, pay, solicit, or receive any remuneration to induce referrals of items or services reimbursable by any Federal health care program. See section 1128B(b) of the Act. Where remuneration is paid purposefully to induce referrals of items or services for which payment may be made by a Federal health care program, the anti-kickback statute is violated. By its terms, the statute ascribes criminal liability to parties on both sides of an impermissible "kickback" transaction. For purposes of the anti-kickback statute, "remuneration" includes the transfer of anything of value, in cash or in kind, directly or indirectly, covertly or overtly.

The statute has been interpreted to cover any arrangement where one purpose of the remuneration was to obtain money for the referral of services or to induce further referrals. United States v. Kats, 871 F.2d 105 (9th Cir. 1989); United States v. Greber, 760 F.2d 68 (3d Cir.), cert. denied, 474 U.S. 988 (1985). Violation of the statute constitutes a felony punishable by a maximum fine of $25,000, imprisonment up to five years, or both. Conviction will also lead to automatic exclusion from Federal health care programs, including Medicare and Medicaid. This Office may also initiate administrative proceedings to exclude persons from Federal and state health care programs or to impose civil monetary penalties for fraud, kickbacks, and other prohibited activities under sections 1128(b)(7) and 1128A (a)(7) of the Act.[3]

This Office's concern with the provision of goods and services for free or at below-market rates to actual or potential referral sources is longstanding and clear: such arrangements are suspect and may violate the anti-kickback statute if one purpose is to induce or reward referrals of Federal health care program business.

---

[3] Because both the criminal and administrative sanctions related to the anti-kickback implications of the Proposed Arrangement are based on violations of the anti-kickback statute, the analysis for purposes of this advisory opinion is the same under both.

The provision by a hospital of free supplies and medications to an ambulance provider fits squarely within the meaning of remuneration for purposes of the anti-kickback statute.[4] Under certain circumstances, an inference may be drawn that one purpose of such remuneration is to induce the ambulance provider to bring patients to that particular hospital. However, the strength of that inference may vary with the circumstances of the specific arrangement.

Based on the totality of facts and circumstances presented, we conclude that the OIG would not subject the Hospital to sanctions in connection with the Proposed Arrangement under sections 1128(b)(7) or 1128A(a)(7) of the Act. The relationship of the Proposed Arrangement to the overall EMS system in the community provides adequate assurance that the Proposed Arrangement is designed to improve and enhance the delivery of EMS for the benefit of the entire community and will not be undertaken solely for the benefit of a single provider or group of providers. Regional and local programs to improve and coordinate the delivery of quality EMS are consistent with longstanding Federal policy. The Proposed Arrangement will be limited to free restocking of supplies and drugs related to emergency transports.

In the circumstances presented, the fact that the Hospital offers free restocking *only* to volunteer emergency ambulance companies that do not bill for their services does not change our analysis. The Hospital has a legitimate interest in containing the cost of its ambulance restocking program. Limiting the scope of free restocking to the Non-Billing Volunteer Services represents a reasonable distinction drawn by the Hospital that is not related to the volume or value of referrals or other business generated for the Hospital.

III. CONCLUSION

The advisory opinion process is a "means of relating the anti-kickback statute to the particular facts of a specific arrangement." 62 Fed. Reg. 7350, 7351 (Feb. 19, 1997). The issuance of an advisory opinion is not necessarily indicative of a government enforcement priority, nor does it mean that we consider the subject matter of the opinion to represent a significant area of fraud and

---

[4] Pursuant to the Secretary's authority under section 1128B(b)(3)(E) of the Act, we have published a notice of proposed rulemaking for a "safe harbor" for certain ambulance restocking arrangements that pose a minimal risk of fraud or abuse. See 65 Federal Register 32060 (May 22, 2000). The final rule is pending.

abuse. In evaluating an arrangement's potential to lead to fraud or abuse of Federal health care programs, no one fact or element is necessarily dispositive. We are persuaded that, taken as a whole, the aspects of the Proposed Arrangement described above — including, but not limited to, the Hospital's relationship with a coordinated regional EMS system, the role of the regional EMS council, and the fact that free restocking will be offered only for emergency transports — create sufficient limitations, requirements, or controls so as to give adequate assurance that the Proposed Arrangement will not lead to program abuse under the anti-kickback statute.[5] Accordingly, we conclude that while the Proposed Arrangement might technically violate the anti-kickback statute if the requisite intent to induce referrals were present, the OIG will not impose sanctions on the Hospital in connection with the Proposed Arrangement under sections 1128(b)(7) (as it relates to kickbacks) or 1128A(a)(7) of the Act, based on the facts certified in the Hospital's request for an advisory opinion and supplemental submissions.

IV. LIMITATIONS

The limitations applicable to this opinion include the following:

- This advisory opinion is issued only to Hospital A, the requester of this advisory opinion. This advisory opinion has no application to, and cannot be relied upon by, any other individual or entity.
- This advisory opinion may not be introduced into evidence in any matter involving an entity or individual that is not a requester of this opinion.
- This advisory opinion is applicable only to the statutory provisions specifically noted in the first paragraph of this advisory opinion. No opinion is herein expressed or implied with respect to the application of any other Federal, state, or local statute, rule, regulation, ordinance, or other law that may be applicable to the Proposed Arrangement.

---

[5] This advisory opinion only applies to the restocking of drugs and supplies directly related to the provision of emergency pre-hospital services. Restocking of drugs or supplies used in connection with non-emergency services are outside the scope of this hospital. opinion. We express no opinion regarding liability of the Hospital under the False Claims Act or other legal authorities in connection with any improper billing or claims submission directly or indirectly related to, or arising from, the Proposed Arrangement.

- This advisory opinion will not bind or obligate any agency other than the U.S. Department of Health and Human Services.
- This advisory opinion is limited in scope to the specific arrangements described in this letter and has no applicability to other arrangements, even those which appear similar in nature or scope.

This opinion is also subject to any additional limitations set forth at 42 C.F.R. Part 1008. The OIG will not proceed against the requester with respect to any action that is part of the Proposed Arrangement taken in good faith reliance upon this advisory opinion as long as all of the material facts have been fully, completely, and accurately presented, and the Proposed Arrangement in practice comports with the information provided. The OIG reserves the right to reconsider the questions and issues raised in this advisory opinion and, where the public interest requires, rescind, modify or terminate this opinion. In the event that this advisory opinion is modified or terminated, the OIG will not proceed against the requester with respect to any action taken in good faith reliance upon this advisory opinion, where all of the relevant facts were fully, completely, and accurately presented and where such action was promptly discontinued upon notification of the modification or termination of this advisory opinion. An advisory opinion may be rescinded only if the relevant and material facts have not been fully, completely, and accurately disclosed to the OIG.

Sincerely,
/s/
D. McCarty Thornton
Chief Counsel to the Inspector General

APPENDIX F56

Advisory Opinion No. 00–10, December 15, 2000

Regarding a program designed to promote an expensive new drug used to prevent certain respiratory infections . . . in pediatric patients.

[*We redact certain identifying information and certain potentially privileged, confidential, or proprietary information associated with the individual or entity, unless otherwise approved by the requestor.*]

Issued: December 15, 2000
Posted: December 28, 2000
[Name and Address Redacted]

Re: OIG Advisory Opinion No. 00–10

Dear [Name Redacted]:

We are writing in response to your request for an advisory opinion regarding the [program name redacted] (the "Program"), a program designed to promote [drug name redacted] (the "Drug"), an expensive new drug used to prevent certain respiratory infections caused by [condition X] disease in pediatric patients. Specifically, the question raised by your request is whether the Program constitutes grounds for sanctions under the anti-kickback statute, section 1128B(b) of the Social Security Act (the "Act"), or the civil monetary penalty provision prohibiting inducements to beneficiaries, section 1128A(a)(5) of the Act, in the circumstances presented.

You have certified that all of the information provided in your request, including all supplementary letters, is true and correct and constitutes a complete description of the relevant facts and agreements among the parties.

In issuing this opinion, we have relied solely on the facts and information presented to us. We have not undertaken an independent investigation of such information. This opinion is limited to the facts presented. If material facts have not been disclosed or have been misrepresented, this opinion is without force and effect.

Based on the information provided, we conclude that: (i) the Program could potentially generate prohibited remuneration under the anti-kickback statute if the requisite intent to induce referrals were present, but that the Office of Inspector General ("OIG") will not subject [Company A] to sanctions for violations of the anti-kickback statute under sections 1128(b)(7) or 1128A(a)(7) of the Act in connection with the Program, as described and certified in your request letter and supplemental submissions; and (ii) the OIG will not impose a civil monetary penalty under section 1128A(a)(5) of the Act on [Company A] in connection with the Program, as described and certified in your request letter and supplemental submissions.

This opinion may not be relied on by any persons other than [Company A], the requestor of this opinion, and is further qualified as set out in Part V below and in 42 C.F.R. Part 1008.

I. FACTUAL BACKGROUND

A. The Drug and Its History

[Company A] (the "Company") is a publicly-traded corporation engaged in the development, manufacture, and sale of pharmaceuticals, including the Drug. The Drug is used in the prevention of serious lower respiratory tract infections caused by [condition X] disease in high-risk pediatric patients.

According to the Company, [condition X] disease is the most common cause of pneumonia and bronchiolitis in infants and children and is responsible for as many as 126,000 hospitalizations annually. The fatality rate associated with [condition X] infections is approximately two percent in hospitalized high-risk infants and five percent in infants with chronic lung disease ("CLD"). Infants at risk for [condition X] infections include certain infants who were born prematurely and certain infants with CLD.

The American Academy of Pediatrics (the "Academy") has issued guidelines recommending that physicians consider preventive treatment for infants and toddlers at high risk for [condition X] disease.[1]

---

[1] Pursuant to Academy guidelines, only the following infants and children should be considered for [condition X] prophylaxis: (i) infants and children who are younger than two years of age with CLD who have required medical therapy for their CLD within six months before the anticipated [condition X] season; (ii) infants who are born at thirty-two weeks of gestation or earlier; and (iii) infants who are born between thirty-two to thirty-five weeks of gestation and who have additional risk factors, including other underlying conditions that predispose them to respiratory complications (e.g., neuro-

[Citation redacted.] Currently, there are only two drugs approved by the Food and Drug Administration for the prevention of respiratory infections caused by [condition X] disease, both of which are made by the Company. The other drug has not been widely used, especially among infant populations, in part because it can only be administered through an intravenous line using a constant infusion pump. According to the Academy, the Drug is the preferred treatment for most children at high risk for [condition X] disease "because of ease of administration (intramuscular), lack of interference with measles-mumps-rubella vaccine and varicella vaccine, and lack of complications associated with intravenous administration of human immune globulin products." Id.

Treatment with the Drug is expensive. Since the Drug is currently available only through intramuscular injection, it must be administered by a physician or some other health care professional. The Drug is administered once a month during the [condition X] season, which varies regionally and annually, but typically runs from October through April. A course of treatment consists of a series of five or six intramuscular injections at a total cost to physicians of approximately $5,000 to $6,000 (or about $1,000 per injection).

The Drug is potentially reimbursable by various State health care programs (collectively, "Medicaid") and other Federal health care programs. Most third party payors, including most Medicaid programs, limit coverage to patients at high risk of [condition X] disease, and many payors follow the Academy's guidelines in determining medical necessity.

B. The Program

The Program, which is generally open to all physicians, comprises several components, [2]

including pre-qualification of patients for third party coverage and reimbursement, extended payment terms for participating physicians, and credits for denied claims. Services provided under the Program are in addition to the general reimbursement support services (e.g., advice regarding payor coverage and benefits, coding, and

---

logic disease in very low birth weight infants), exposure to young siblings, child care center attendance, exposure to tobacco smoke in the home, anticipated cardiac surgery, and distance to and availability of hospital care for severe respiratory illness.

[2] Physicians practicing in group practices that are fully-capitated for products such as the Drug or group practices that account for such products as part of their negotiated rates, with the practice assuming full risk (e.g., staff model HMOs), cannot participate in the Program.

claims processing requirements) that the Company makes available to any provider seeking advice about the Drug. To participate in the Program, a physician must (i) plan to administer the Drug in the office setting, and (ii) sign a Physician Agreement. For each[3] physician, participation in the Program is limited to a maximum of three years, which must run consecutively.

A detailed description of the Program is set forth below. While the Company has contracted with another company for the administration of the Program, for purposes of our analysis, we will attribute all such activities to the Company.

- Patient Insurance Pre-Qualification. Participating physicians submit a Patient Enrollment Form and a Patient Consent Form to the Company. Prior to enrolling a patient of a participating physician in the Program, the Company verifies that the patient (i) has insurance coverage,[4] and (ii) is a medically appropriate candidate for [condition X] prophylaxis with the Drug.[5] Once the patient is enrolled, the Drug is shipped directly to the physician by a participating distributor. The Company continues to monitor the shipments of the Drug, the patients' Drug treatment schedules, and the status of insurance claims filed by physicians.
- Prompt Payment Discount and Extended Payment Terms. Under the Program, the distributors' markup to physicians cannot exceed 6% of the wholesale acquisition cost, and the distributors must give physicians a prompt payment discount, if the distributors are paid within sixty days of shipment. In

[3] Under the Physician Agreement, the physician agrees to file each insurance claim within ten days of administering the Drug, provide a copy of each filed claim to the Company, and pay the distributor of the Drug within fifteen days after receiving insurance reimbursement.

[4] Candidates who have no private or public health insurance and who do not have the financial resources to pay for the Drug may be eligible to receive the Drug without charge under a separate, independent program sponsored by the Company (the "Assistance Program"). Last year, the Company provided 256 free vials of the Drug to 86 patients under the Assistance Program.

[5] In verifying that the patient is a medically appropriate candidate for the Drug, the Company does not make an independent assessment of medical necessity. Instead, the Company merely determines whether the treatment would be covered by the applicable third party payor based upon coverage guidelines provided by the payor and patient information provided by the physician.

addition, distributors must give physicians up to 180 days after the Drug is shipped to pay for the Drug. To reimburse distributors for the carrying costs associated with the extended payment terms, the Company gives distributors a credit of 0.5% of the cost of the Drug once every thirty days, beginning on the 61 day and ending on the earlier of the st date that payment is received or 211 days after shipment (i.e., thirty days after the 180-day extended payment period ends).

- Invoice Credit for Denied Claims. If the claim is denied, notwithstanding the Company's prior verification of insurance coverage, or if the physician does not receive reimbursement from the third party payor within 180 days, the Company makes the distributor whole and the distributor in turn makes the physician whole. If the physician has not paid the distributor, the distributor provides an invoice credit to the physician for the amount the distributor charged for the Drug, and the Company provides a replacement vial of the Drug to the distributor. If the physician has paid the distributor, the distributor provides a replacement vial of the Drug to the physician, instead of an invoice credit, and the Company provides a replacement vial of the Drug to the distributor. If the physician is reimbursed by the third party payor after receiving the invoice credit or replacement vial of the Drug, the physician is required to pay the distributor for the Drug, and the Company charges the distributor for the replacement vial of the Drug.

Under the Program, physicians are required to collect and manage patients' deductibles and copayments in accordance with their routine business practices and the requirements of their patients' health plans. A participating physician is not permitted to receive an invoice credit or replacement vial of the Drug through the Program in connection with an enrolled patient's insurance claim if (i) the patient makes a full payment or percentage-based copayment (e.g., 20% of the charge) for the Drug,[6]

or (ii) the physician receives any reimbursement from the third party payor for the claim. The Program does not reimburse physicians for the difference between the amount billed to the third party payor and the amount received therefrom.

---

[6] No such proscription exists in connection with claims for which the patient has paid a fixed copayment designated by the patient's insurer (e.g., $10 per visit).

Pursuant to current data from the 1999/2000 [condition X] season, 2,078 claims have been filed in connection with the Program, of which less than 2% were initially denied by third party payors and less than 7% took more than 180 days for third party payors to process.[7]

To date, approximately 35% to 40% of the patients enrolled in the Program have been Medicaid beneficiaries.

II. THE ANTI-KICKBACK STATUTE

A. Law

The anti-kickback statute makes it a criminal offense knowingly and willfully to offer, pay, solicit, or receive any remuneration to induce referrals of items or services reimbursable by any Federal health care program. See section 1128B(b) of the Act. Specifically, the statute provides that:

> Whoever knowingly and willfully offers or pays [or solicits or receives] any remuneration (including any kickback, bribe, or rebate) directly or indirectly, overtly or covertly, in cash or in kind to any person to induce such person — to refer an individual to a person for the furnishing or arranging for the furnishing of any item or service for which payment may be made in whole or in part under a Federal health care program, or to purchase, lease, order, or arrange for or recommend purchasing, leasing, or ordering any good, facility, service, or item for which payment may be made in whole or in part under a Federal health care program, shall be guilty of a felony.

Id. Thus, where remuneration is paid purposefully to induce referrals of items or services for which payment may be made by a Federal health care program, the anti-kickback statute is violated. By its terms, the statute ascribes criminal liability to parties on both sides of an impermissible "kickback" transaction. For purposes of the anti-kickback statute, "remuneration" includes the transfer of anything of value, in cash or in-kind, directly or indirectly, covertly or overtly.

The statute has been interpreted to cover any arrangement where one purpose of the remuneration was to obtain money for the referral of services or to induce further referrals. United States v. Kats, 871 F.2d 105 (9th Cir. 1989); United States v. Greber, 760 F.2d 68 (3d Cir.), cert. denied, 474 U.S. 988 (1985). Violation of the statute con-

[7] Appeals are pending on all of the denied claims.

stitutes a felony punishable by a maximum fine of $25,000, imprisonment up to five years, or both. Conviction will also lead to automatic exclusion from Federal health care programs, including Medicare and Medicaid. The OIG may also initiate administrative proceedings to exclude persons from Federal and State health care programs or to impose civil monetary penalties for fraud, kickbacks, and other prohibited activities under sections 1128(b)(7) and 1128A (a)(7) of the Act.[8]

B. Analysis

Drug manufacturers often offer free assistance to physicians and other providers by serving as a clearinghouse for information regarding insurance coverage criteria and reimbursement levels for their products. Since these services have no independent value to providers apart from the products, they are properly considered part of the products purchased and their cost is already included in the products' price. Therefore, standing alone, these services have no substantial independent value and do not implicate the Federal anti-kickback statute.[9]

However, the Federal anti-kickback statute may be implicated when drug manufacturers combine these types of reimbursement support services with other services or programs which do confer an independent financial benefit upon referring providers. For example, coupling a reimbursement support service with a program either requiring payment for ordered products only if the referring provider is paid or guaranteeing a minimum "spread" between the purchase price and third party reimbursement levels would implicate the anti-kickback statute. Such programs eliminate the normal financial risks facing providers, potentially raising the risk of overutilization and increased Federal health care program costs.

The Program falls into this latter category and, therefore, implicates the Federal anti-kickback statute. Under the Program, the Company couples reimbursement support services with extended payment terms and, if necessary, an invoice credit or replacement vial of the Drug. These additional elements confer an independent

---

[8] Because both the criminal and administrative sanctions related to the anti- kickback implications of the Program are based on violations of the anti-kickback statute, the analysis for purposes of this advisory opinion is the same under both.

[9] We express no opinion regarding liability of the Company under the False Claims Act or other legal authorities in connection with any improper billing or claims submission directly or indirectly related to, or arising from, the reimbursement support services or the Program.

financial benefit upon referring physicians by shifting the financial risk of unanticipated delays and denials associated with obtaining third party payor reimbursement from the prescribing physicians to the Company.

Notwithstanding, we will not subject the Company to sanctions under the anti-kickback statute in connection with the Program for the reasons set forth below. First, the Program is narrowly-tailored to address the unique access problems caused by the cumulative effect of certain verifiable characteristics of the Drug, including its cost, target population, and preventive nature. Specifically, the Program is limited to one product – a new, expensive, prophylactic drug. Moreover, a substantial portion of the patients, who are at high risk for [condition X] disease and would benefit from prophylaxis with the Drug, are members of low-income families that typically do not have the financial resources necessary to prepay, or personally guarantee payment, for the Drug. Thus, for these low-income families and their physicians, the cost of the Drug, coupled with the possibility of unanticipated reimbursement delays and denials and the lack of urgency often associated with curative treatments, can create a formidable hurdle to obtaining a recommended preventive treatment.

Second, based on historical experience, the remuneration actually provided to physicians is minimal. Pursuant to current data from the 1999/2000 [condition X] season, less than 2% of the claims filed in connection with the Program were initially denied by third party payors and less than 7% of the claims took more than 180 days for third party payors to process. In this case, it appears that the Program provides as much psychological support as financial support. In addition, physician participation in the Program is limited to three years, further limiting the potential remuneration. While the amount of the remuneration is not determinative of whether an arrangement violates the anti-kickback statute, it is one factor that we consider in determining whether to exercise our sanction authority.

Third, the structure of the Program should not result in overutilization. Prior to enrolling a patient of a physician in the Program, the Company verifies that the patient meets the medical coverage guidelines established by the patient's third party payor. Given the cost of the Drug, most third party payors, including most Medicaid programs, limit coverage to patients at high risk of [condition X] disease, and many payors follow the Academy's guidelines.

In light of all of the foregoing, we would not subject the Company to sanctions under the anti-kickback statute in connection with the Program.

III. SECTION 1128A(a)(5) OF THE ACT

A. Law

Section 1128A(a)(5) of the Act provides for the imposition of civil monetary penalties against any person who:

> offers or transfers remuneration to any individual eligible for benefits under [Medicare or a State health care program] that such person knows or should know is likely to influence such individual to order or receive from a particular provider, practitioner, or supplier any item or service for which payment may be made, in whole or in part, under [Medicare or a State health care program].

See also 42 C.F.R. § 1003.102(b)(13). Unlike the anti-kickback statute, section 1128A(a)(5) of the Act is solely concerned with remuneration offered or transferred to Medicare or State health care program beneficiaries.

Section 1128A(i)(6) of the Act defines "remuneration" for purposes of section 1128A(a)(5) of the Act as including, among other things, "transfers of items or services for free or for other than fair market value" and as excluding, among other things, "incentives given to individuals to promote the delivery of preventive care as determined by the Secretary in regulations so promulgated." In 42 C.F.R. § 1003.101, the new final rule addressing section 1128A(a)(5) of the Act, we defined "preventive care" to mean any service that "(1) [i]s a prenatal service or post-natal well-baby visit or is a specific clinical service described in the current U.S. Preventive Services Task Force's Guide to Clinical Preventive Services, and (2) is reimbursable in whole or in part by Medicare or an applicable State health care program." 65 Fed. Reg. 24400, 24415 (April 26, 2000).

B. Analysis

The Program potentially implicates section 1128A(a)(5) of the Act. A low-income Medicaid beneficiary who receives prophylaxis with the Drug and whose Medicaid claims are subsequently denied will incur a financial obligation totaling approximately $5,000 to $6,000. However, under the Program, if Medicaid denies a physician's claim after the Company has verified coverage, the Company (indirectly through a participating distributor) provides an invoice credit or replacement vial of the Drug to the physician, thereby relieving the patient of his or her obligation to pay for the denied Medicaid claims.

Fulfilling a financial obligation owed by a patient constitutes remuneration to the patient which may influence the patient's choice of provider.

Notwithstanding, we will not subject the Company to sanctions under section 1128A(a)(5) of the Act in connection with the Program. First, although the Drug is not listed in the current U.S. Preventive Services Task Force's Guide to Clinical Preventive Services and, therefore, does not qualify for the preventive care exemption, it is very similar to services listed therein. Second, the financial benefit to the beneficiary is more theoretical than real, since few Medicaid beneficiaries will be in a position to discharge a $5,000 obligation. The more tangible benefit accrues to the physician who will not have to write off the cost of the Drug. Since we have already decided not to seek sanctions for benefits accruing to physicians under the Program for the reasons set out in the prior section, we will not seek sanctions for the resulting incidental benefits accruing to beneficiaries.

IV. CONCLUSION

Based on the information provided, we conclude that: (i) the Program could potentially generate prohibited remuneration under the anti-kickback statute if the requisite intent to induce referrals were present, but that the OIG will not subject the Company to sanctions for violations of the anti-kickback statute under sections 1128(b)(7) or 1128A(a)(7) of the Act in connection with the Program, as described and certified in your request letter and supplemental submissions; and (ii) the OIG will not impose a civil monetary penalty under section 1128A(a)(5) of the Act on the Company in connection with the Program, as described and certified in your request letter and supplemental submissions.

V. LIMITATIONS

The limitations applicable to this opinion include the following:

- This advisory opinion is issued only to [company name redacted], who is the requestor of this opinion. This advisory opinion has no application, and cannot be relied upon, by any other individual or entity.
- This advisory opinion may not be introduced into evidence in any matter involving an entity or individual that is not a requestor to this opinion.

- This advisory opinion is applicable only to the statutory provisions specifically noted above. No opinion is herein expressed or implied with respect to the application of any other Federal, state, or local statute, rule, regulation, ordinance, or other law that may be applicable to the Program.
- This advisory opinion will not bind or obligate any agency other than the U.S. Department of Health and Human Services.
- This advisory opinion is limited in scope to the specific arrangement described in this letter and has no applicability to other arrangements, even those which appear similar in nature or scope.

No opinion is expressed herein regarding the liability of any party under the False Claims Act or other legal authorities for any improper billing, claims submission, cost reporting, or related conduct.

This opinion is also subject to any additional limitations set forth at 42 C.F.R. Part 1008. The OIG will not proceed against the Company with respect to any action that is part of the Program taken in good faith reliance upon this advisory opinion as long as all of the material facts have been fully, completely, and accurately presented, and the Program in practice comports with the information provided. The OIG reserves the right to reconsider the questions and issues raised in this advisory opinion and, where the public interest requires, rescind, modify or terminate this opinion. In the event that this advisory opinion is modified or terminated, the OIG will not proceed against the Company with respect to any action taken in good faith reliance upon this advisory opinion, where all of the relevant facts were fully, completely, and accurately presented and where such action was promptly discontinued upon notification of the modification or termination of this advisory opinion. An advisory opinion may be rescinded only if the relevant and material facts have not been fully, completely and accurately disclosed to the OIG.

Sincerely,

/s/

D. McCarty Thornton

Chief Counsel to the Inspector General

APPENDIX F57

Advisory Opinion No. 00–11, December 19, 2000

Regarding a proposed charitable donation of up to $5,000 from Association A to EMS Service B. . . for the purchase of equipment and payment of paramedic training expenses.

[*We redact certain identifying information and certain potentially privileged, confidential, or proprietary information associated with the individual or entity, unless otherwise approved by the requester.*]

Date Issued: December 19, 2000

Date Posted: December 28, 2000

[Name and Address redacted]

Re: OIG Advisory Opinion No. 00–11

Dear [name redacted]:

We are writing in response to your request for an advisory opinion regarding a proposed charitable donation of up to $5,000 from Association A (the "Requester") to EMS Service B ("EMS Service B"), a tax-exempt entity, to be used for the purchase of equipment and payment of paramedic training expenses (the "Proposed Donation"). Specifically, the question raised by your request is whether the Proposed Donation would constitute grounds for the imposition of sanctions under the anti-kickback statute, section 1128B(b) of the Social Security Act (the "Act"), in the circumstances presented.

You have certified that all of the information provided in your request, including all supplementary letters, is true and correct and constitutes a complete description of the relevant facts and agreements among the parties.

In issuing this opinion, we have relied solely on the facts and information presented to us. We have not undertaken an independent investigation of such information. This opinion is limited to the

facts presented. If material facts have not been disclosed or have been misrepresented, this opinion is without force and effect.

Based on the facts provided, we conclude that the Proposed Donation might constitute prohibited remuneration under the anti-kickback statute, if the requisite intent to induce referrals of Federal health care program business were present, but that the Office of Inspector General ("OIG") would not subject the Requester to sanctions arising under the anti-kickback statute in connection with the Proposed Donation. We express no opinion with respect to additional payments the Requester may make in the future.

This opinion may not be relied on by any persons other than the Requester, and is further qualified as set out in Part V below and in 42 C.F.R. Part 1008.

I. FACTUAL BACKGROUND

The Requester operates Hospital C (the "Hospital"), a 113-bed acute care facility in City D, State E. In 1963, voters in City D, Township E, and Township F (which includes the City of G) created the [name redacted] Joint Township District to construct the Hospital to replace City D Municipal Hospital. The Hospital's Board of Trustees consists of five members appointed by the participating governments, six members elected from the Association A membership, which is open to any adult residing within the Hospital's district, and three physicians from the Hospital's medical staff. The Hospital is tax-exempt under Federal and state law. The Hospital maintains a Level III emergency department.

EMS Service B is an all-volunteer, tax-supported emergency medical services entity serving City G, approximately five miles from the Hospital. In 1999, EMS Service B brought approximately 73% of its transports to the Hospital.

The city manager of City G has asked the Hospital to provide financial assistance to EMS Service B. The Requester proposes to provide EMS Service B with up to $5,000, depending on the availability of Hospital funds, in a one-time payment to assist EMS Service B with equipment purchases, paramedic training, or other educational expenses. The Requester has not previously donated funds to EMS Service B. The Requester has certified that neither its decision to make the donation, nor the amount of the donation, would be influenced by, or conditioned on, the number or type of patients taken by EMS Service B to the Hospital or by any other business between the parties.[1]

II. THE ANTI-KICKBACK STATUTE

The anti-kickback statute makes it a criminal offense knowingly and willfully to offer, pay, solicit, or receive any remuneration to induce referrals of items or services reimbursable by any Federal health care program. See section 1128B(b) of the Act. Specifically, the statute provides that:

> Whoever knowingly and willfully offers or pays [or solicits or receives] any remuneration (including any kickback, bribe, or rebate) directly or indirectly, overtly or covertly, in cash or in kind to any person to induce such person — to refer an individual to a person for the furnishing or arranging for the furnishing of any item or service for which payment may be made in whole or in part under a Federal health care program, or to purchase, lease, order, or arrange for or recommend purchasing, leasing, or ordering any good, facility, service, or item for which payment may be made in whole or in part under a Federal health care program, shall be guilty of a felony.

Id. Thus, where remuneration is paid purposefully to induce referrals of items or services for which payment may be made by a Federal health care program, the anti-kickback statute is violated. By its terms, the statute ascribes criminal liability to parties on both sides of an impermissible "kickback" transaction. For purposes of the anti-kickback statute, "remuneration" includes the transfer of anything of value, in cash or in kind, directly or indirectly, covertly or overtly.

The statute has been interpreted to cover any arrangement where one purpose of the remuneration was to obtain money for the referral of services or to induce further referrals. United States v. Kats, 871 F.2d 105 (9th Cir. 1989); United States v. Greber, 760 F.2d 68 (3d Cir.), cert. denied, 474 U.S. 988 (1985). Violation of the statute constitutes a felony punishable by a maximum fine of $25,000, imprisonment up to five years, or both. Conviction will also lead to automatic exclusion from Federal health care programs, including

[1] The Requester has indicated in its request letter that it will consider making additional contributions to EMS Service B of up to $5,000 annually. We are unable to opine at this time about the propriety of possible future donations; such possible donations and the facts and circumstances surrounding them are hypothetical and not a proper subject for an advisory opinion. See 42 C.F.R. § 1008.15(b).

Medicare and Medicaid. The OIG may also initiate administrative proceedings to exclude persons from Federal and State health care programs or to impose civil monetary penalties for fraud, kickbacks, and other prohibited activities under sections 1128(b)(7) and 1128A (a)(7) of the Act. [2]

This Office's concern with the provision of free goods and services to actual or potential referral sources is longstanding and clear: such arrangements are suspect and may violate the anti-kickback statute if one purpose is to induce or reward referrals of Federal health care program business. Those concerns necessarily extend to donations of goods, services, or money to actual or potential referral sources.

III. ANALYSIS

A monetary donation by a hospital to a local ambulance company fits within the meaning of remuneration for purposes of the anti-kickback statute, if an intent to induce referrals of services or other business for which payment may be made under a Federal health care program is present. Stated another way, a monetary donation by a hospital to a local ambulance company is permissible if the parties have no intention to induce Federal health care program referrals or to generate Federal health care program business.

We believe that the majority of donors who make contributions to tax-exempt organizations, including donors with ongoing business relationships with the donees, are motivated by *bona fide* charitable purposes and a desire to help their communities. Substantial numbers of health care providers are not-for-profit organizations, many of which are religious or public charities, and depend on tax-deductible charitable donations to fund all or part of their operations. We recognize that soliciting donations is vital to these providers' viability and that the potential donor pool will include many persons and entities in the local community with which the soliciting entity has past, present, or potential business relationships. Invariably, some of the persons or entities solicited will be in a position to influence referrals to, or otherwise generate business for, the soliciting provider; other solicited parties will be in a position to receive referrals or business from the soliciting provider. Such busi-

---

[2] Because both the criminal and administrative sanctions related to the anti- kickback implications of the Proposed Donation are based on violations of the anti-kickback statute, the analysis for purposes of this advisory opinion is the same under both.

ness relationships do not make a tax-deductible donation automatically suspect under the anti-kickback statute.

Notwithstanding our favorable predisposition towards *bona fide* charitable donations, we caution that the substance of an arrangement – and not its characterization – ultimately determines its propriety under the anti-kickback statute. Unfortunately, in some circumstances, payments characterized as "donations" or "grants" are nothing more than disguised kickbacks intended in part to induce or reward referrals, directly or indirectly. However, in order to avoid chilling *bona fide* charitable activities, the OIG recognizes the need for us to exercise caution in undertaking any enforcement action in this area.

In the present case, the Proposed Donation presents a minimal risk of Federal health care program abuse, while providing significant benefits to the community. First, the Proposed Donation presents little risk of overutilization or increased costs to any Federal health care program. Simply put, the number of patients requiring emergency transport is unrelated to the Proposed Donation. Second, the Proposed Donation will be a relatively modest, one-time payment, and the aggregate amount will be fixed at the time it is made and will not be conditioned or vary in any way based on the volume or value of referrals. Third, the parties to the Proposed Donation are both charitable entities that share a common mission in promoting effective, efficient, high quality emergency medical services in their community. The uses to which the donated sum will be put – EMS equipment, paramedic training, education — clearly further this mission. In sum, based on the totality of the facts and circumstances, the Proposed Donation appears to be a *bona fide* charitable donation.

IV. CONCLUSION

Based on the facts certified in the request for an advisory opinion and supplemental submissions, we conclude that the Proposed Donation might constitute prohibited remuneration under the anti-kickback statute, if the requisite intent to induce referrals of Federal health care program business were present, but that the OIG would not subject the Requester to sanctions arising under the anti-kickback statute under sections 1128(b)(7) or 1128A(a)(7) in connection with the Proposed Donation. We express no opinion with respect to additional payments the Requester may make in the future.

V. LIMITATIONS

The limitations applicable to this opinion include the following:

- This advisory opinion is issued only to Association A, the requester of this opinion.
- This advisory opinion has no application to, and cannot be relied upon by, any other individual or entity.
- This advisory opinion may not be introduced into evidence in any matter involving an entity or individual that is not a requester to this opinion.
- This advisory opinion is applicable only to the statutory provisions specifically noted above. No opinion is herein expressed or implied with respect to the application of any other Federal, state, or local statute, rule, regulation, ordinance, or other law that may be applicable to the Proposed Donation.
- This advisory opinion will not bind or obligate any agency other than the U.S. Department of Health and Human Services.
- This advisory opinion is limited in scope to the specific arrangement described in this letter and has no applicability to other arrangements, even those that appear similar in nature or scope. No opinion is expressed herein regarding the liability of any party under the False Claims Act or other legal authorities for any improper billing, claims submission, cost reporting, or related conduct.

This opinion is also subject to any additional limitations set forth at 42 C.F.R. Part 1008.

The OIG will not proceed against the Requester with respect to any action that is part of the Proposed Donation taken in good faith reliance upon this advisory opinion as long as all of the material facts have been fully, completely, and accurately presented, and the Proposed Donation in practice comports with the information provided. The OIG reserves the right to reconsider the questions and issues raised in this advisory opinion and, where the public interest requires, rescind, modify, or terminate this opinion. In the event that this advisory opinion is modified or terminated, the OIG will not proceed against the Requester with respect to any action taken in good faith reliance upon this advisory opinion, where all of the relevant facts were fully, completely, and accurately presented, and where such action was promptly discontinued upon notification of the modification or termination of this advisory opinion. An advisory opinion may be rescinded only if the relevant and material facts have not been fully, completely, and accurately disclosed to the OIG.

Sincerely,

/s/

D. McCarty Thornton

Chief Counsel to the Inspector General

APPENDIX F58

Advisory Opinion No. 01–1, January 11, 2001

Concerning a proposed arrangement in which a hospital will share with a group of cardiac surgeons a percentage of the hospital's cost savings arising from the surgeons' implementation of a number of cost reduction measures in certain surgical procedures.

[*We redact certain identifying information and certain potentially privileged, confidential, or proprietary information associated with the individual or entity, unless otherwise approved by the requester.*]

Date Issued: January 11, 2001
Date Posted: January 18, 2001
[Names and Addresses Redacted]

Re: OIG Advisory Opinion No. 01–1

Ladies & Gentlemen:

We are writing in response to your request for an advisory opinion concerning a proposed arrangement in which a hospital will share with a group of cardiac surgeons a percentage of the hospital's cost savings arising from the surgeons' implementation of a number of cost reduction measures in certain surgical procedures (the "Proposed Arrangement"). The cost savings will be measured based on the surgeons' use of specific supplies and medications during designated cardiac surgery procedures. You have inquired whether the Proposed Arrangement would constitute grounds for sanctions arising under (i) the civil monetary penalty for a hospital's payment to a physician to induce reductions or limitations of services to Medicare or Medicaid beneficiaries under the physician's direct care, section 1128A(b)(1)-(2) of the Social Security Act (the "Act"), or (ii) the anti-kickback statute, section 1128B(b) of the Act.

In issuing this opinion, we have relied solely on the facts and information presented to us. We have not undertaken an independent investigation of such information. This opinion is limited to the

facts presented. If material facts have not been disclosed or have been misrepresented, this opinion is without force and effect.

Based on the information provided and the totality of the facts as described and certified in your request letter and supplemental submissions, we conclude that: (i) the Proposed Arrangement would constitute an improper payment to induce reduction or limitation of services pursuant to section 1128A(b)(1)-(2) of the Act, but that the Office of Inspector General ("OIG") will not impose sanctions on the requestors of this advisory opinion, [names redacted] (the "Requestors"), in connection with the Proposed Arrangement; and (ii) the Proposed Arrangement would potentially generate prohibited remuneration under the anti-kickback statute, if the requisite intent to induce referrals were present, but that the OIG will not subject the Requestors to sanctions for violations of the anti-kickback statute under sections 1128(b)(7) or 1128A(a)(7) of the Act in connection with the Proposed Arrangement.

This opinion may not be relied on by any persons other than the Requestors and is further qualified as set out in Part IV below and in 42 C.F.R. Part 1008.

I. FACTUAL BACKGROUND

A. Parties

The Hospital. [Name redacted] (the "Hospital"), is an acute care, not-for-profit hospital in [City X], [State Y], that offers a broad range of inpatient and outpatient hospital services, including cardiac surgery services. The Hospital is a participating provider in the Medicare and Medicaid programs.

The Surgeon Group. [Name redacted] (the "Surgeon Group"), is a professional association composed exclusively of cardiac surgeons who are licensed in [State Y] and have active medical staff privileges at the Hospital. The cardiac surgeons refer patients to the Hospital for inpatient and outpatient hospital services. The Surgeon Group is the dominant group of cardiac surgeons that practices at the Hospital.[1] Surgeons in the Surgeon Group also practice at several other

[1] Surgeons in the Surgeon Group perform 85% of the Hospital's cardiac surgery. Several cardiac surgeons who are not members of the Surgeon Group have active medical staff privileges at the Hospital. These cardiac surgeons will not participate in the Proposed Arrangement; however, the Hospital expects to include them in future cost savings sharing arrangements on terms and conditions substantially comparable to those under which it offers cost savings sharing to the Surgeon Group.

hospitals in the [City X] area.

The Program Administrator. The Hospital has engaged [name redacted] (the "Program Administrator") to administer the Proposed Arrangement. The Program Administrator will collect data and analyze and manage the Proposed Arrangement. The Hospital will pay the Program Administrator a monthly fixed fee certified by the Requestors to be fair market value in an arms-length transaction for services to be provided by the Program Administrator under the Proposed Arrangement. The fee will not be tied to cost savings or the Surgeon Group's compensation under the Proposed Arrangement.

B. The Proposed Arrangement

Under the Proposed Arrangement, the Hospital will pay the Surgeon Group a share of the first year cost savings directly attributable to specific changes in the Surgeon Group's operating room practices. The Program Administrator conducted a study of the historic practices at the Hospital's cardiac surgery department and identified nineteen specific cost-savings opportunities. The results of the Program Administrator's study of the Surgeon Group and the specific cost-savings opportunities are summarized in a "Practice Patterns Report".[2] The Hospital and the Surgeon Group have reviewed the Practice Patterns Report for medical appropriateness and each has adopted its recommendations and conclusions.

In general, the Practice Patterns Report recommends that the Surgeon Group change its current operating room practices to curb the inappropriate use or waste of medical supplies. The nineteen specific recommendations can be roughly grouped into three categories. The first category consists of fourteen recommendations that involve opening packaged items only as needed during a procedure. Most of these "open as needed" items are surgical tray or comparable supplies. These items will be readily available, albeit unopened, in the operating room. One "open as needed" recommendation involves not opening disposable components of the cell saver unit until a patient experiences excessive bleeding. The Requestors have certified that the resulting delay in cell saver readiness should not exceed two to five minutes and will not adversely affect patient care. The second category, involving four recommendations, consists of the substitution, in whole or in part, of less costly items for the items currently being used by the surgeons. The final category consists of a recommendation to limit use of Aprotinin – a medication currently

---

[2] The Practice Patterns Report for the Surgeon Group, dated April 4, 2000, is attached to this advisory opinion as Appendix A.

given to many surgical patients pre-operatively to prevent hemorrhaging – to patients that are at higher risk of perioperative hemorrhage as indicated by objective clinical standards.

The Proposed Arrangement contains several safeguards intended to protect against inappropriate reductions in services. With respect to the cell saver and the substitution recommendations, the Proposed Arrangement would utilize objective historical and clinical measures reasonably related to the practices and the patient population at the Hospital to establish a "floor" below which no savings would accrue to the Surgeon Group. For example, the cell saver is currently used in approximately [A]% of the cardiac procedures specified under the Proposed Arrangement. Accordingly, the Surgeon Group will receive no share of any savings resulting from any reductions in cell saver use for cases below the [A]% floor. Similarly, for each of the proposed substitution recommendations, the Program Administrator has identified historic patterns of use at the Hospital or at hospitals with comparable practices and patient populations and has established thresholds below which no cost savings will be credited. For example, the Practice Patterns Report indicates that certain less expensive forms of sutures could be used in [B] % of the cases without having an adverse impact on patient care.[3] Accordingly, any savings from using less expensive sutures in more than [B]% of the cases will not be credited to the Surgeon Group.

With respect to Aprotinin, the Proposed Arrangement uses specific, objective, generally-accepted clinical indicators reasonably related to the practices of the Hospital and its patient population to determine medical appropriateness.[4] Currently, approximately [C]% of patients to whom Aprotinin is administered by the Surgeon Group at the Hospital meet these objective clinical indicators. Under the Proposed Arrangement, savings from reduced use of Aprotinin will not be credited to the Surgeon Group if the savings result from utilization of Aprotinin in less than [C]% of cases or if the savings result from failure to use Aprotinin in a case that meets the clinical indicators. All surgical cases – including cases in which Aprotinin is not administered – will be reviewed by the Program Administrator

---

[3] We note that the Practice Patterns Report identifies with specificity the kinds of sutures at issue.

[4] The objective clinical indicators used in the Proposed Arrangement to determine when Aprotinin is administered appropriately are cited in medical literature. Lemmer et al., ATS 62: 1659–68 (1996).

to determine if the surgeons followed the objective clinical indicators for determining whether Aprotinin was used appropriately.

According to the Program Administrator, if implemented in accordance with the Practice Patterns Report's specifications, the nineteen recommendations would present substantial cost savings opportunities for the Hospital without adversely impacting the quality of patient care. Seventy-five percent of the potential cost savings would come from the proposed reduction in routine use of Aprotinin and another ten percent from the proposed delay in setting up the cell saver.

The Hospital will pay the Surgeon Group 50% of the cost savings achieved by implementing the nineteen recommendations in the Practice Patterns Report for a period of one year. At the end of the year, cost savings will be calculated separately for each of the nineteen recommendations; this will preclude shifting of cost savings and ensure that savings generated by utilization below the set targets will not be credited to the Surgeon Group. This payment will constitute the entire compensation paid to the Surgeon Group for services performed under the contract memorializing the Proposed Arrangement between the Surgeon Group and the Hospital. The payment to the Surgeon Group will be calculated by subtracting the actual costs incurred for the items specified in the nineteen recommendations when used by surgeons in the Surgeon Group during the specified surgical procedures (the "current year costs"[5]) from the historic costs for the same items when used during comparable surgical procedures in the base year (the "base year costs"[6]). The current year costs will be adjusted to account for any inappropriate reductions in use of items below the targets set in the Practice Patterns Report. The Surgeon Group will be paid 50% of the difference between the adjusted current year costs and base year costs, if any.

The Hospital will make an aggregate payment to the Surgeon Group, which distributes its profits to each of its members on a per

---

[5] The current year will be the twelve month term of the contract for which the Surgeon Group will be compensated under the Proposed Arrangement.

[6] The "base year" will be the twelve months preceding the effective date of the contract. For purposes of this opinion, the Proposed Arrangement is limited to the one year term of the contract; accordingly, this opinion is without force and effect with respect to any future renewal or extension of the Proposed Arrangement. Notwithstanding, we note that any renewal or extension of the Proposed Arrangement should incorporate updated base year costs.

capita basis. Payments to the Surgeon Group will also be subject to the following limitations:

- If the volume of procedures payable by a Federal health care program in the current year exceeds the volume of like procedures payable by a Federal health care program performed in the base year, there will be no sharing of cost savings for the additional procedures.
- To minimize the surgeons' financial incentive to steer more costly patients to other hospitals, the case severity, ages, and payors of the patient population treated under the Proposed Arrangement will be monitored by a committee composed of representatives of the Requestors, using generally-accepted standards. If there are significant changes from historical measures, the surgeon at issue will be terminated from participation in the Proposed Arrangement.
- The aggregate payment to the Surgeon Group will not exceed 50% of the projected cost savings identified in the Practice Patterns Report.

The Requestors have certified that this payment methodology will generate payments to the Surgeon Group that will be consistent with fair market value for services rendered to the Hospital in arms-length transactions.

The Hospital and the Surgeon Group will document the activities and the payment methodology under the Proposed Arrangement and will make the documentation available to the Secretary of the U.S. Department of Health and Human Services (the "Department"), upon request. In addition, the Hospital and the Surgeon Group will disclose the Proposed Arrangement to the patient, including the fact that the Surgeon Group's compensation is based on a percentage of the Hospital's cost savings. The disclosure will be made to the patient before the patient is admitted to the Hospital for a procedure covered by the Proposed Arrangement; if pre-admission disclosure is impracticable (e.g., the patient is admitted for an unscheduled procedure or the need for the procedure is determined after admission), the disclosure will be made before the patient consents to the surgery. The disclosures will be in writing, and patients will have an opportunity, if desired, to review details of the Proposed Arrangement, including the specific cost savings measures applicable to the patient's surgery.

II. LEGAL ANALYSIS

Arrangements like the Proposed Arrangement are designed to align incentives by offering physicians a portion of a hospital's cost savings in exchange for implementing cost saving strategies. Under the current reimbursement system, the burden of these costs falls on hospitals, not physicians. Payments based on cost savings to physicians may be intended to motivate them to reduce hospital costs associated with procedures performed by physicians at the hospitals.

Properly structured, cost sharing arrangements can serve legitimate business and medical purposes. Specifically, properly structured arrangements may increase efficiency and reduce waste, thereby potentially increasing a hospital's profitability. However, such arrangements can potentially influence physician judgment to the detriment of patient care. Our concerns include, but are not limited to, the following: (i) stinting on patient care; (ii) "cherry picking" healthy patients and steering sicker (and more costly) patients to hospitals that do not offer such arrangements; (iii) payments in exchange for patient referrals; and (iv) unfair competition (a "race to the bottom") among hospitals offering cost sharing programs to foster physician loyalty and to attract more referrals.

Hospital cost savings programs in general, and the Proposed Arrangement in particular, may implicate at least three legal authorities: (i) the civil monetary penalty for reductions or limitations of direct patient care services provided to Federal health care program beneficiaries, section 1128A(b)(1)-(2) of the Act; (ii) the anti-kickback statute, section 1128B(b) of the Act; and (iii) the physician self-referral law, section 1877 of the Act.[7]

We address the first two of these authorities; section 1877 of the Act falls outside the scope of the OIG's advisory opinion authority. We express no opinion on the application of section 1877 to the Proposed Arrangement.

A. The Civil Monetary Penalty, Section 1128A(b)(1)-(2) of the Act

Section 1128A(b)(1)-(2) of the Act establishes a civil monetary penalty ("CMP") against any hospital or critical access hospital that knowingly makes a payment directly or indirectly to a physician (and any physician that receives such a payment) as an inducement

---

[7] In addition, non-profit hospital arrangements raise issues of private inurement and private benefit under the Internal Revenue Service's income tax regulations in connection with section 501(c)(3) of the Internal Revenue Code. See Rev. Rul. 69–383, 1969–2 C.B. 113.

to reduce or limit items or services to Medicare or Medicaid beneficiaries under the physician's direct care. Hospitals that make (and physicians that receive) such payments are liable for CMPs of up to $2,000 per patient covered by the payments (section 1128A(b)(1) & (2) of the Act). There is no requirement that the prohibited payment be tied to a specific patient or to a reduction in medically necessary care. The CMP applies only to reductions or limitations of items or services provided to Medicare and Medicaid fee-for-service beneficiaries.[8]

The CMP prohibits payments by hospitals to physicians that may induce physicians to reduce or limit items or services furnished to their Medicare and Medicaid patients. A threshold inquiry is whether the Proposed Arrangement will induce physicians to reduce or limit items or services. Given the specificity of the Proposed Arrangement, it is possible to review the proposed opportunities for savings individually and evaluate their potential impact on patient care.

Having reviewed the nineteen individual recommendations, we conclude that, except for the unopened surgical tray items (discussed in more detail below), the recommendations implicate the CMP. Simply put, with respect to the recommendations regarding the disposable cell saver components, Aprotinin, and the substitution of less costly items, the Proposed Arrangement constitutes an inducement to reduce or limit the current medical practice at the Hospital. We recognize that the current medical practice may involve care that exceeds the requirements of medical necessity. However, whether the current medical practice reflects necessity or prudence is irrelevant for purposes of the CMP.

With respect to the recommendations regarding "open as needed" surgical tray items, we reach a different conclusion. To the extent that the sole delay in providing items or services is the insubstantial

---

[8] Physician incentive arrangements related to Medicare risk-based managed care contracts, similar Medicaid contracts, and Medicare+Choice plans are subject to regulation by the Secretary pursuant to sections 1876(i)(8), 1903(m)(2)(A)(x), and 1852(j)(4) of the Act (respectively), in lieu of being subject to sections 1128A(b)(1) and (2). See OIG letter regarding hospital-physician incentive plans for Medicare and Medicaid beneficiaries enrolled in managed care plans (dated August 19, 1999), available at http://oig.hhs.gov/frdalrt/gsletter.htm; see also 42 C.F.R. § 417.479(i); 61 Fed. Reg. 13430, 13439 (Mar. 27, 1996); 42 C.F.R. § 434.70 (comparable regulations for physician incentive plans associated with Medicaid managed care organizations).

time it takes to open a package of supplies readily available in the operating room, we believe there will be no perceptible reduction or limitation in the provision of items or services to patients sufficient to trigger the CMP. However, this conclusion does not apply to the disposable cell saver components. Because the components must be attached to the machine and the machine must be started up, there will be an additional delay in the cell saver's availability beyond merely opening the disposable components. Therefore, there is a greater potential for harm. Accordingly, we conclude that the cell saver incentive is subject to the statutory proscription of the CMP.

In sum, while the recommendations for the "open as needed" surgical tray items do not run afoul of the CMP, we find that the CMP would apply to the remaining recommendations involving the cell saver components, Aprotinin, and the various substitutions. Notwithstanding, the Proposed Arrangement has several features that, in combination, provide sufficient safeguards so that we would not seek sanctions against the Requestors under section 1128A(b)(1) and (2) of the Act.

First, the specific cost-saving actions and resulting savings are clearly and separately identified. The transparency of the Proposed Arrangement will allow for public scrutiny and individual physician accountability for any adverse effects of the Proposed Arrangement, including any difference in treatment among patients based on non-clinical indicators. The transparency of the incentives for specific actions and specific procedures will also facilitate accountability through the medical-legal professional liability system.

Second, the Requestors have proffered credible medical support for the position that implementation of the recommendations, including the reduction in routine use of Aprotinin, will not adversely affect patient care. The Proposed Arrangement will be periodically reviewed to confirm that the Proposed Arrangement is not having an adverse impact on clinical care.[9]

Third, the payments under the Proposed Arrangement are based on all surgeries regardless of the patients' insurance coverage, sub-

---

[9] We have had the Proposed Arrangement reviewed by an independent medical expert, as well as a government medical expert. Both have concluded that the proposed cost savings measures, as described in the advisory opinion request and supplemental submissions, should not adversely affect patient care. For purposes of this opinion, however, we rely solely on the Requestors' certifications and nothing in this advisory opinion should be construed as an endorsement or conclusion as to the medical propriety of the specific activities being undertaken as part of the Proposed Arrangement.

ject to the cap on payment for Federal health care program procedures. Moreover, the surgical procedures to which the Proposed Arrangement applies are not disproportionately performed on Federal health care program beneficiaries. Additionally, the cost savings are calculated on the Hospital's actual out-of-pocket acquisition costs, not an accounting convention.

Fourth, the Proposed Arrangement protects against inappropriate reductions in services by utilizing objective historical and clinical measures to establish baseline thresholds below which no savings accrue to the Surgeon Group. The Requestors have certified that these baseline measures are reasonably related to the Hospital's or comparable hospitals' practices and patient populations. These safeguards are action-specific and not simply based on isolated patient outcome data unrelated to the specific changes in operating room practices.

Fifth, the Hospital and the Surgeon Group will provide written disclosures of their involvement in the Proposed Arrangement to patients whose care may be affected by the Proposed Arrangement and will provide patients an opportunity to review the cost savings recommendations prior to admission to the Hospital (or, where pre-admission consent is impracticable, prior to consenting to surgery). While we do not believe that, standing alone, such disclosures offer sufficient protection from program or patient abuse, effective and meaningful disclosure offers some protection against possible abuses of patient trust. [10]

Sixth, the financial incentives under the Proposed Arrangement are reasonably limited in duration and amount.

Seventh, because the Surgeon Group's profits are distributed to its members on a per capita basis, any incentive for an individual surgeon to generate disproportionate cost savings is mitigated.

Our decision not to impose sanctions on the Requestors in connection with the Proposed Arrangement is an exercise of our discretion and is consistent with our Special Advisory Bulletin on "Gainsharing Arrangements and CMPs for Hospital Payments to Physicians to Reduce or Limit Services to Beneficiaries" (July 1999) (the "Special Advisory Bulletin"). We reiterate that the CMP applies to any pay-

---

[10] Ordinarily, we would expect patient disclosures to be coupled with patient satisfaction surveys that closely monitor patient perceptions of their care. However, in the context of the Proposed Arrangement, which focuses on items and medications used in operating rooms, we believe that patient satisfaction surveys would not be effective.

ment by a hospital to a physician that is intended to induce the reduction or limitation of items or services to Medicare or Medicaid patients under the physician's direct clinical care. The Proposed Arrangement is markedly different from many "gainsharing" plans, particularly those that purport to pay physicians a percentage of generalized cost savings not tied to specific, identifiable cost-lowering activities. Importantly, the Proposed Arrangement sets out the specific actions to be taken and ties the remuneration to the actual, verifiable cost savings attributable to those actions. This transparency allows an assessment of the likely effect of the Proposed Arrangement on quality of care and ensures that the identified actions will be the cause of the savings.

By contrast, many gainsharing plans contain features that heighten the risk that payments will lead to inappropriate reductions or limitations of services. These features include, but are not limited to, the following:

- There is no demonstrable direct connection between individual actions and any reduction in the hospital's out-of-pocket costs (and any corresponding "gainsharing" payment).
- The individual actions that would give rise to the savings are not identified with specificity.
- There are insufficient safeguards against the risk that the other, unidentified actions, such as premature hospital discharges, might actually account for any "savings."
- The quality of care indicators are of questionable validity and statistical significance.
- There is no independent verification of cost savings, quality of care indicators, or other essential aspects of the arrangement.

Simply put, many "gainsharing" plans present substantial risks for both patient and program abuse – risks that are not present in the Proposed Arrangement. Given the limited duration and scope of the Proposed Arrangement, the safeguards provide sufficient protections against patient and program abuse. Other arrangements, including those that are longer in duration or more expansive in scope than the Proposed Arrangement, are likely to require additional or different safeguards.

B. The Anti-Kickback Statute

The anti-kickback statute makes it a criminal offense knowingly and willfully to offer, pay, solicit, or receive any remuneration to induce referrals of items or services reimbursable by any Federal health care program. See section 1128B(b) of the Act. Specifically, the statute provides that:

> Whoever knowingly and willfully offers or pays [or solicits or receives] any remuneration (including any kickback, bribe, or rebate) directly or indirectly, overtly or covertly, in cash or in kind to any person to induce such person — to refer an individual to a person for the furnishing or arranging for the furnishing of any item or service for which payment may be made in whole or in part under a Federal health care program, or to purchase, lease, order, or arrange for or recommend purchasing, leasing, or ordering any good, facility, service, or item for which payment may be made in whole or in part under a Federal health care program, shall be guilty of a felony.

Id. Thus, where remuneration is paid purposefully to induce referrals of items or services for which payment may be made by a Federal health care program, the anti-kickback statute is violated. By its terms, the statute ascribes criminal liability to parties on both sides of an impermissible "kickback" transaction. For purposes of the anti-kickback statute, "remuneration" includes the transfer of anything of value, in cash or in-kind, directly or indirectly, covertly or overtly.

The statute has been interpreted to cover any arrangement where one purpose of the remuneration was to obtain money for the referral of services or to induce further referrals. United States v. Kats, 871 F.2d 105 (9th Cir. 1989); United States v. Greber, 760 F.2d 68 (3d Cir.), cert. denied, 474 U.S. 988 (1985). Violation of the statute constitutes a felony punishable by a maximum fine of $25,000, imprisonment up to five years, or both. Conviction will also lead to automatic exclusion from Federal health care programs, including Medicare and Medicaid. The OIG may also initiate administrative proceedings to exclude persons from Federal and State health care programs or to impose civil monetary penalties for fraud, kickbacks, and other prohibited activities under sections 1128(b)(7) and 1128A (a)(7) of the Act.[11]

The Department of Health and Human Services has promulgated safe harbor regulations that define practices that are not subject to the anti-kickback statute because such practices would be unlikely

---

[11] Because both the criminal and administrative sanctions related to the anti- kickback implications of the Arrangement are based on violations of the anti-kickback statute, the analysis for purposes of this advisory opinion is the same under both.

to result in fraud or abuse. See 42 C.F.R. § 1001.952. The safe harbors set forth specific conditions that, if met, assure entities involved of not being prosecuted or sanctioned for the arrangement qualifying for the safe harbor. However, safe harbor protection is afforded only to those arrangements that precisely meet all of the conditions set forth in the safe harbor. The regulatory safe harbor potentially applicable to the Proposed Arrangement is the personal services and management contracts safe harbor, 42 C.F.R. § 1001.952(d). In relevant part for purposes of this advisory opinion, the personal services safe harbor requires that the aggregate compensation paid for the services be set in advance and consistent with fair market value in an arms-length transactions, 42 C.F.R. § 1001.952(d)(5). The Proposed Arrangement would not fit in the safe harbor because the Surgeon Group will be paid on a percentage basis, and thus the compensation would not be set in advance. However, the absence of safe harbor protection is not fatal. Instead, the Proposed Arrangement must be subject to case-by-case evaluation.

Like any compensation arrangement between a hospital and a physician who admits or refers patients to such hospital, we are concerned that the Proposed Arrangement could be used to disguise remuneration from the Hospital to reward or induce referrals by the Surgeon Group. Specifically, the Proposed Arrangement could encourage the surgeons to admit Federal health care program patients to the Hospital, since the surgeons would receive not only their Medicare Part B professional fee, but also, indirectly, a share of the Hospital's payment, depending on cost savings. In other words, the more procedures a surgeon performs at the Hospital, the more money he or she is likely to receive under the Proposed Arrangement.

While we believe the Proposed Arrangement could result in illegal remuneration if the requisite intent to induce referrals were present, we would not impose sanctions in the particular circumstances presented here. First, the circumstances and safeguards of the Proposed Arrangement reduce the likelihood that the arrangement will be used to attract referring physicians or to increase referrals from existing physicians. Specifically, participation in the Proposed Arrangement will be limited to surgeons already on the medical staff, thus limiting the Proposed Arrangement's effectiveness in attracting other surgeons. Only surgeons in the Surgeon Group will participate; however, based on the Requestors' certifications, we expect that if the Proposed Arrangement is renewed or continued beyond the one year term, the Hospital and the Program Administrator will offer a substantially comparable cost savings program to other cardiac surgeons on the medical staff. In addition, the potential savings derived from procedures for Federal health care program beneficiaries will be capped based on the prior year's admissions of Federal health care program beneficiaries. Finally, the contract term will be limited to one year, reducing any incentive to switch facilities, and admissions will be monitored for changes in severity, age, or payer. Thus, while the incentive to refer will not necessarily be eliminated, it will be substantially reduced.

Second, the structure of the Proposed Arrangement eliminates the risk that the Proposed Arrangement will be used to reward cardiologists or other physicians who refer patients to the Surgeon Group or its surgeons. The Surgeon Group is the sole participant in the Proposed Arrangement and is composed entirely of cardiac surgeons; no cardiologists or other physicians are members of the Surgeon Group or share in its profit distributions. Within the Surgeon Group, profits are distributed to its members on a per capita basis, mitigating any incentive for an individual surgeon to generate disproportionate cost savings.

Third, the Proposed Arrangement sets out with specificity the particular actions that will generate the cost savings on which the payments are based. While many of the recommendations in the Practice Patterns Report are simple common sense, they do represent a change in operating room practice for which the surgeon is responsible and will have liability exposure. While most of the recommendations would appear to present minimal risk, the preparation of the cell saver and the administration of Aprotinin both carry some increased liability risk for the physicians. It is not unreasonable for the surgeon to receive compensation for the increased risk from the proposed change in practice. Moreover, the payments will represent a portion of one year's worth of cost savings and will be limited in amount (i.e., the aggregate cap), duration (i.e., the limited contract term), and scope (i.e., the total savings that can be achieved from the implementation of any one recommendation are limited by appropriate utilization levels). While we are precluded from opining on whether a payment is fair market value,[12] the payments under

---

[12] We are precluded by statute from opining on whether fair market value shall be or was paid for goods, services, or property. See 42 U.S.C. § 1320a-7d (b)(3)(A).

the Proposed Arrangement do not appear unreasonable, given, among other things, the nature of the nineteen recommended actions, the specificity of the payment formula, and the cap on total remuneration to the Surgeon Group. We caution that payments of 50% of cost savings in other arrangements, including multi-year arrangements or arrangements with generalized cost savings formulae, could well lead to a different result.

In light of these circumstances and safeguards, the Proposed Arrangement poses a low risk of fraud or abuse under the anti-kickback statute.

III. CONCLUSION

Notwithstanding the foregoing, we reiterate our concerns regarding many arrangements between hospitals and physicians to share cost savings. Improperly designed or implemented arrangements risk adversely affecting patient care and could be vehicles to disguise payments for referrals. For example, an arrangement that cannot be adequately and accurately measured for quality of care would pose a high risk of fraud or abuse, as would one that rewards physicians based on overall cost savings without accountability for specific cost reduction measures. Moreover, arrangements structured so as to pose a heightened potential for patient steering and unfair competition would be considered suspect. In short, this opinion is predicated on the specific arrangement posed by the Requestors and is limited to that specific arrangement. Other apparently similar arrangements could raise different concerns and lead to a different result.

Based on the information provided, we conclude: (i) the Proposed Arrangement would constitute an improper payment to induce reduction or limitation of services pursuant to section 1128A(b)(1)-(2) of the Act, but that the OIG will not impose sanctions under section 1128A(b)(1)-(2) on the Requestors in connection with the Proposed Arrangement; and (ii) the Proposed Arrangement would potentially generate prohibited remuneration under the anti-kickback statute, if the requisite intent to induce referrals were present, but that, based on the totality of the facts present in the Proposed Arrangement as described and certified in the request letter and supplemental submissions, the OIG will not subject the Requestors to sanctions for violations of the anti-kickback statute under sections 1128(b)(7) or 1128A(a)(7) of the Act.

IV. LIMITATIONS

The limitations applicable to this opinion include the following:

- This advisory opinion is issued only to [names redacted], the requestors of this opinion. This advisory opinion has no application to, and cannot be relied upon by, any other individual or entity.
- This advisory opinion may not be introduced into evidence in any matter involving an entity or individual that is not a requestor to this opinion.
- This advisory opinion is applicable only to the statutory provisions specifically noted above in the first paragraph of this opinion. No opinion is herein expressed or implied with respect to the application of any other Federal, state, or local statute, rule, regulation, ordinance, or other law that may be applicable to the Proposed Arrangement.
- This advisory opinion will not bind or obligate any agency other than the U.S. Department of Health and Human Services.
- This advisory opinion is limited in scope to the specific arrangement described in this letter and has no applicability to other arrangements, even those that appear similar in nature or scope.
- No opinion is expressed herein regarding the liability of any party under the False Claims Act or other legal authorities for any improper billing, claims submission, cost reporting, or related conduct.

This opinion is also subject to any additional limitations set forth at 42 C.F.R. Part 1008.

The OIG will not proceed against the Requestors with respect to any action that is part of the Proposed Arrangement taken in good faith reliance upon this advisory opinion as long as all of the material facts have been fully, completely, and accurately presented, and the Proposed Arrangement in practice comports with the information provided. The OIG reserves the right to reconsider the questions and issues raised in this advisory opinion and, where the public interest requires, rescind, modify, or terminate this opinion. In the event that this advisory opinion is modified or terminated, the OIG will not proceed against the Requestors with respect to any action taken in good faith reliance upon this advisory opinion, where all of the relevant facts were fully, completely, and accurately presented, and where such action was promptly discontinued upon notification of the modification or termination of this advisory opinion. An advisory opinion may be rescinded only if the relevant and material facts have not been fully, completely, and accurately disclosed to the OIG.

Sincerely,

/s/

D. McCarty Thornton

Chief Counsel to the Inspector General

[Appendix A redacted]

APPENDIX F59

Advisory Opinion No. 01–2, March 27, 2001

Concerning an annual charity golf tournament for which some of its vendors and suppliers pay money as sponsors and tournament participants.

[*We redact certain identifying information and certain potentially privileged, confidential, or proprietary information associated with the individual or entity, unless otherwise approved by the requester.*]

Date Issued: March 20, 2001
Date Posted: March 27, 2001
[Names and Addresses Redacted]

Re: OIG Advisory Opinion No. 01–2

Dear [name redacted]:

We are writing in response to your request for an advisory opinion regarding the solicitation and acceptance by [name redacted] (the "Health Center" or the "Requester") of proceeds from a charitable fund–raising event — a golf tournament to be held on its behalf in July 2001 — in which some of the Health Center's vendors and suppliers participate as sponsors and registrants (the "Proposed Arrangement"). Specifically, the question raised by your request is whether the Proposed Arrangement would constitute grounds for the imposition of sanctions under the exclusion authority at section 1128(b)(7) of the Social Security Act (the "Act") or the civil monetary penalty provision at section 1128A(a)(7) of the Act, as those sections relate to the commission of acts described in section 1128B(b) of the Act.

You have certified that all of the information provided in your request, including all supplementary letters, is true and correct and constitutes a complete description of the relevant facts and agreements among the parties. In issuing this opinion, we have relied solely on the facts and information presented to us. We have not undertaken an independent investigation of such information. This opinion is limited to the facts presented. If material facts have not been disclosed or have been misrepresented, this opinion is without force and effect.

Based on the facts certified in your request for an advisory opinion and supplemental submissions, we conclude that the Proposed Arrangement would potentially generate prohibited remuneration under the anti–kickback statute, if the requisite intent to induce or reward referrals of Federal health care program business were present, but that the Office of Inspector General ("OIG") would not impose administrative sanctions on the Requester under sections 1128(b)(7) or 1128A(a)(7) of the Act (as those sections relate to the commission of acts described in section 1128B(b) of the Act) in connection with the Proposed Arrangement. We express no opinion with respect to donations outside the Proposed Arrangement or the proceeds from other charitable events to benefit the Requester. [1]

This opinion may not be relied on by any persons other than the Requester, and is further qualified as set out in Part V below and in 42 C.F.R. Part 1008.

I. Factual Background

The Requester is a not–for–profit, multi–site community health center that is tax–exempt under Federal and state law. The Health Center was created to serve the Hispanic community with an emphasis on underserved and uninsured populations. It operates a skilled nursing facility, a vocational counseling center, a childcare center, a home health division, a family practice residency program, substance abuse residential treatment centers, and medical, dental, and mental health clinics, some of which are satellite clinics that serve migrant and seasonal farm workers and the homeless in rural settings. The Health Center participates in Medicare and State health care programs and receives Federal grants to deliver health care services as a Federally qualified community health center.

[1] We are unable to opine at this time about the propriety of donations other than the tournament registration fee and the three levels of sponsorship (described in Part I of this opinion) for the golf tournament scheduled for July 2001, or about sponsorship of charitable events other than the golf tournament scheduled for July 2001. Such possible donations and tournaments and the facts and circumstances surrounding them are hypothetical or have not been presented for our consideration and, therefore, are not a proper subject for an advisory opinion. See 42 C.F.R. § 1008.15(b).

Some years ago, community members and business people who support the Requester organized the [name redacted] Golf Committee (the "Golf Committee") to hold an annual golf tournament to raise funds to support the Requester's mission. The tournament as been held for several consecutive years.

The Golf Committee is an unincorporated association whose members are business and civic leaders drawn from the community–at–large, including state legislators, local officials, and members of the academic community from the local university. While the Requester's Chief Executive Officer and some persons who do business with the Requester may serve on the Golf Committee, a majority of the Golf Committee members have no business or employment relationship with the Requester. The Requester does provide support to the Golf Committee, including an employee of the Requester who serves as the tournament director (mostly on his own time) and other staff who voluntarily provide assistance for the event itself, such as assistance with tournament registration.

The Golf Committee organizes and promotes the annual golf tournament and solicits sponsorships, registrations, and donated items from businesses and individuals. The sponsorship levels range from $2,500 to $15,000.[2] Each level entitles the sponsor to registration of multiple players, tickets to the banquet, and some advertising on tournament materials. The Committee solicits sponsors and participants broadly from the local community. Recent sponsors include architects, construction companies, shipping companies, the local port authority, and other local business people. Non–sponsors may compete in the golf tournament at a cost of $1,000 per foursome.[3] Participating players in past tournaments have also broadly represented the local community. In sum, while some sponsors and participants have been vendors that do business with the Requester, including providers of items or services to the Requester that are reimbursed in whole or in part by the Federal health care programs, both the solicitation for, and actual participation in, the event are part of a much broader community–wide effort. The Requester has certified that it does not take tournament participation into account

---

[2] Most of each sponsorship donation is tax–deductible, as follows: $1,703.50 of the $2,500 donation; $4,191 of the $5,000 donation; $12,598 of the $15,000 donation.

[3] The tax–deductible portion of the $1,000 foursome registration fee is $216.00.

when awarding or renewing contracts or purchasing items or services.

In the prior two years, the Golf Committee has grossed in excess of $90,000 per year from the tournament, generating in excess of $50,000 in net proceeds for the Requester. In past years, the proceeds have been used for scholarship awards, holiday gifts to low–income families, the Requester's homeless programs, and the Requester's senior programs. The Requester anticipates that the proceeds from the July 2001 tournament will be put to the same or similar uses.

II. THE ANTI–KICKBACK STATUTE

The anti–kickback statute makes it a criminal offense knowingly and willfully to offer, pay, solicit, or receive any remuneration to induce referrals of items or services reimbursable by Federal health care programs. See section 1128B(b) of the Act. Where remuneration is paid purposefully to induce referrals of items or services paid for by a Federal health care program, the anti–kickback statute is violated. By its terms, the statute ascribes criminal liability to parties on both sides of an impermissible "kickback" transaction. For purposes of the anti–kickback statute, "remuneration" includes the transfer of anything of value, in cash or in–kind, directly or indirectly, covertly or overtly.

The statute has been interpreted to cover any arrangement where one purpose of the remuneration was to obtain money for the referral of services or to induce further referrals. United States v. Kats, 871 F.2d 105 (9th Cir. 1989); United States v. Greber, 760 F.2d 68 (3rd Cir.), cert. denied, 474 U.S. 988 (1985). Violation of the statute constitutes a felony punishable by a maximum fine of $25,000, imprisonment up to five years, or both. Conviction will also lead to automatic exclusion from Federal health care programs, including Medicare and Medicaid. Where a party commits an act described in section 1128B(b) of the Act, the OIG may initiate administrative proceedings to impose civil monetary penalties on such party under section 1128A(a)(7) of the act. The OIG may also initiate administrative proceedings to exclude such party from the Federal health care programs under section 1128(b)(7) of the Act.

This Office's concern with the provision of monetary donations to actual or potential referral sources is longstanding and clear: such arrangements are suspect and may violate the anti–kickback statute if one purpose is to induce or reward referrals of Federal health care program business. Those concerns are not necessarily ameliorated when the donation is in the form of sponsorships or participation in a charity golf tournament that would benefit the Requester, an actual or potential source of Federal health care program business for some sponsors and participants.

III. ANALYSIS

We accept that the majority of donors who make contributions to tax–exempt organizations, including donors with ongoing business relationships with the donees, are motivated by bona fide charitable purposes and a desire to help their communities. Substantial numbers of health care providers are not–for–profit organizations, many of which are community–based service providers, and depend on tax–deductible charitable donations to fund all or part of their operations. We recognize that soliciting donations is vital to these providers' viability and that the potential donor pool will include many persons and entities in the local community with which the soliciting entity has past, present, or potential business relationships. Invariably, some of the persons or entities solicited will be in a position to receive referrals or business from the soliciting provider. This business relationship does not make a tax–deductible donation automatically suspect under the anti–kickback statute.

For the following reasons, the Proposed Arrangement presents a minimal risk of abuse of Federal health care programs, while providing significant community benefits. First, the golf tournament appears to be a bona fide charitable event intended to provide benefits to the community, in particular, to the local Hispanic community with an emphasis on underserved and uninsured populations. The purposes to which the Requester expects to put the donated sums —social service programs, scholarships, and holiday gift giving to low–income families — clearly further that mission. Second, the participation of the Requester's vendors is incidental to the broad community solicitation and broad participation by non–vendors. The Golf Committee's members and tournament sponsors and participants are drawn from a broad pool of civic leaders and business sources, many of whom have little or no nexus to the health care industry or to the Requester's business with the Federal health care programs. The tournament's promotional materials are widely disseminated and emphasize the community service provided by the Requester and the tournament's charitable goals. Third, the

Requester has certified that it does not take tournament participation or sponsorship into account when awarding or renewing contracts or purchasing items or services. Overall, the Proposed Arrangement provides significant community benefits without presenting a significant risk of abuse of Federal health care programs.

IV. CONCLUSION

Based on the facts certified in your request for an advisory opinion and supplemental submissions, we conclude that the Proposed Arrangement would potentially generate prohibited remuneration under the anti–kickback statute, if the requisite intent to induce or reward referrals of Federal health care program business were present, but that the OIG would not impose administrative sanctions on the Requester under sections 1128(b)(7) or 1128A(a)(7) of the Act (as those sections relate to the commission of acts described in section 1128B(b) of the Act) in connection with the Proposed Arrangement. We express no opinion with respect to other donations or payments.

V. LIMITATIONS

The limitations applicable to this opinion include the following:

- This advisory opinion is issued only to [name redacted] Community Health Centers, the requester of this opinion.
- This advisory opinion has no application to, and cannot be relied upon by, any other individual or entity.
- This advisory opinion may not be introduced into evidence in any matter involving an entity or individual that is not a requester to this opinion.
- This advisory opinion is applicable only to the statutory provisions specifically noted above. No opinion is herein expressed or implied with respect to the application of any other Federal, state, or local statute, rule, regulation, ordinance, or other law that may be applicable to the Proposed Arrangement.
- This advisory opinion will not bind or obligate any agency other than the U.S. Department of Health and Human Services.
- This advisory opinion is limited in scope to the specific Proposed Arrangement described in this letter and has no applicability to other arrangements or proposed arrangements, even those that appear similar in nature or scope. No opinion is expressed herein regarding the liability of any party under the False

Claims Act or other legal authorities for any improper billing, claims submissions, cost reporting, or related conduct.
- This opinion is also subject to any additional limitations set forth at 42 C.F.R. Part 1008.

The OIG will not proceed against the Requester with respect to any action that is part of the Proposed Arrangement taken in good faith reliance upon this advisory opinion as long as all of the material facts have been fully, completely, and accurately presented, and the Proposed Arrangement in practice comports with the information provided. The OIG reserves the right to reconsider the questions and issues raised in this advisory opinion and, where the public interest requires, rescind, modify or terminate this opinion. In the event that this advisory opinion is modified or terminated, the OIG will not proceed against the Requester with respect to any action taken in good faith reliance upon this advisory opinion, where all of the relevant facts were fully, completely, and accurately presented and where such action was promptly discontinued upon notification of the modification or termination of this advisory opinion. An advisory opinion may be rescinded only if the relevant and material facts have not been fully, completely, and accurately disclosed to the OIG.

Sincerely,
/S/
D. McCarty Thornton
Chief Counsel to the Inspector General

APPENDIX F60

Advisory Opinion No. 01–03, May —, 2001

Concerning whether proposed contracts for discounted services between a Federally–recognized Indian tribe and local hospitals would constitute grounds for the imposition of exclusions under section 1128(b)(7) of the Act or civil money penalties under section 1128A(a)(7) of the Act.

[*We redact certain identifying information and certain potentially privileged, confidential, or proprietary information associated with the individual or entity, unless otherwise approved by the requester.*]

Date Issued: May 3, 2001
Date Posted: May —, 2001
[Name and Address Redacted]

Re: OIG Advisory Opinion No. 01–03

Dear [name redacted]:

We are writing in response to your request for an advisory opinion as to whether proposed contracts for discounted services between the [name redacted], a Federally–recognized Indian tribe, and local hospitals (the "Proposed Arrangement") would constitute grounds for the imposition of sanctions under the exclusion authority at section 1128(b)(7) of the Social Security Act (the "Act") or the civil monetary penalty provision at section 1128A(a)(7) of the Act, as those sections relate to the commission of acts described in section 1128B(b) of the Act.

In issuing this opinion, we have relied solely on the facts and information presented to us. We have not undertaken an independent investigation of such information. This opinion is limited to the facts presented. If material facts have not been disclosed or have been misrepresented, this opinion is without force and effect.

Based on the facts certified in your request for an advisory opinion and supplemental submissions, we conclude that the Proposed Arrangement would potentially generate prohibited remuneration under the anti–kickback statute, if the requisite intent to induce or reward referrals of Federal health care program business were present, but that the Office of Inspector General ("OIG") would not impose administrative sanctions on the [name of tribe redacted], under sections 1128(b)(7) or 1128A(a)(7) of the Act (as those sections relate to the commission of acts described in section 1128B(b) of the Act) in connection with the Proposed Arrangement.

This opinion may not be relied on by any persons other than the [name of tribe redacted], and is further qualified as set out in Part IV below and in 42 C.F.R. Part 1008.

I. FACTUAL BACKGROUND

The [name of tribe redacted], also known as [name redacted] (the "Tribe"), is a Federally–recognized Indian tribe located in [city, country, state redacted]. The Tribe is a sovereign Indian nation retaining the right of self–government over its members and territory, subject to the authority of Congress. The Tribe has been designated as a Federally–recognized Health Professional Shortage Area, and [name of town], in [name of country], has been designated as a medically underserved area.

Pursuant to the Indian Self–Determination and Education Assistance Act of 1975, Pub. L. No. 93–638 (the "Self–Determination Act"), the Tribe has entered into a self–determination agreement with the Indian Health Service ("IHS")[1] under which the Tribe receives Federal funds from the IHS to provide Tribe members with health care services that would otherwise be provided by IHS.[2]

The Tribe owns and operates the [name of tribe redacted] Health Center (the "Health Center"), where it provides primary health care

[1] IHS is an agency of the Public Health Service within the Department of Health and Human Services tasked with assuring that basic health care is available to Indian people. Persons eligible for IHS services include members of Federally–recognized Indian tribes; certain individuals under the age of nineteen who are natural or adopted children, step–children, foster children, legal wards, or orphans of an eligible Indian; and certain non–Indian spouses of Indians. 25 U.S.C. § 1680(c).

[2] The Self–Determination Act requires IHS to provide funds for health care programs and facilities operated by tribes and tribal organizations under self–determination contracts on the same basis as such funds are provided to programs and facilities operated directly by IHS. 25 U.S.C. § 1680(a).

services to approximately 1500 Tribe members and dependents,[3] as well as approximately 540 Tribe employees.[4] The Health Center is funded through IHS funds (approximately 43%), third party insurance reimbursements, including Medicare and Medicaid (approximately 43%), other tribal sources (approximately 11%), and the "[name redacted]" program, a state assistance program (approximately 3%).

For necessary services for eligible Tribe members and dependents not provided directly by the Health Center, such as specialty and hospital services, the IHS appropriates to the Tribe an annual, fixed sum pursuant to the IHS Contract Health Services program (the "CHS program"). CHS funds may be used to pay third parties to provide such services. The Tribe has experienced shortfalls of CHS funds for medically necessary specialty and hospital services in recent years. When CHS funds are not available, the Health Center applies for emergency funding from other sources, including the Federal Catastrophic Health Emergency Fund ("CHEF"), uses other funds, if available, or requires that the patient seek admission as a charity care patient.[5] To conserve CHS dollars, the IHS encourages tribes to be prudent purchasers of CHS–funded services through the negotiation of discounted rates with third party providers.

The CHS program serves as a supplemental payer for Tribe members and dependents who have other health insurance, such as employer–sponsored insurance or Medicare. See 42 C.F.R. § 36.61. Thus, for virtually all Tribe members and dependents who are Medicare beneficiaries, Medicare is the Primary payer.[6] In addition, the law expressly exempts individuals eligible for CHS–funded services

[3] Of these 1500 patients, 121 were Medicare beneficiaries (8%) and 227 were Medicaid beneficiaries (15%) in the most recent fiscal year.

[4] The employees are insured under the Tribe's self–funded employee group health plan. No IHS funds are used for benefits under the employee group health plan. Of the 540 employees, fewer than seventeen are Medicare beneficiaries for whom the Tribe is secondary insurer.

[5] An OIG audit report concluded that in recent years, CHS funding has failed to keep pace with inflation, resulting in curtailed services to IHS beneficiaries. See "Review of the Indian Health Service's Contract Health Services Program," Office of Inspector General (A–15–97–50001). The audit report noted that in fiscal year 1995, the CHS program was unable to provide over 90,000 recommended or requested services; on occasion, medical care of the highest priority level was denied or deferred due to the shortage of funds.

[6] The exception may be certain employees for whom the Tribe's employer plan is primary and Medicare is secondary.

from any liability for charges or costs associated with such services, including applicable Medicare copayments and deductibles. See 25 U.S.C. § 1621(u). In this regard, HCFA policy provides that "in the case of contract health services to Indians and their dependents entitled under the IHS program, Medicare will be the primary payer and the IHS the secondary payer." See Hospital Manual § 260.3B. Thus, the IHS or tribes operating under self–determination agreements act as the secondary payer for CHS–funded services.[7]

Under the Proposed Arrangement, the Tribe will enter into agreements with any willing local hospital pursuant to which the hospital will reduce by 10% its normal charges to the Tribe for hospital services provided to Health Center patients. For Medicare beneficiaries — for whom the Tribe's financial responsibility is limited to paying the Medicare copayment and deductible amounts — the hospital will reduce its copayment and deductible charges (hereafter, the "copayment") by 10% of the hospital's actual charge for the patient, resulting, in most cases, in a reduction of approximately 50% of the copayment amount.[8] The hospital will bill Medicare as the primary insurer according to its normal billing procedures and later bill the Tribe for any copayment amount.[9] The Tribe will not submit any claims to Medicare for hospital services provided under the Proposed Arrangement. Under the Proposed Arrangement, the hospital will not claim the waived portion of the copayment amounts as bad debt or otherwise shift the burden of nonpayment to other payers.

The Proposed Arrangement, in conjunction with applicable Federal laws and regulations, contains a number of safeguards against overutilization of CHS–funded services and increased Medicare program costs:

---

[7] Ordinarily, Medicare payment may not be made for items or services that neither the beneficiary nor any other person or organization has a legal obligation to pay. Nor is Medicare payment ordinarily made for items or services that a provider is obligated to furnish at public expense pursuant to an authorization issued by a Federal agency.

[8] Some Tribe members and dependents are eligible for Medicaid. Where Medicaid is the primary insurer, there are typically few, if any, copayment requirements. Under the Proposed Arrangement, for services provided to Medicaid–eligible beneficiaries, the hospitals will bill Medicaid in accordance with their customary billing procedures. The Tribe will not bill Medicaid for any hospital services under the Proposed Arrangement.

[9] We express no opinion as to the propriety of the billing by the hospitals.

- Under the CHS program, tribes must allocate scarce CHS funds according to a medical priority system that targets urgent or emergent care. See 42 C.F.R. § 36.23(e). The CHS program further requires Tribe members to seek services from the Health Center, rather than an outside provider, whenever possible.
- The Health Center has established internal procedures to control utilization of CHS–funded services. Patients may not obtain CHS–funded services without a signed referral from, or approved by, a full–time Health Center physician. [10] A separate referral form is required for each patient visit. [11]
- Neither of the Health Center's two full–time physicians has any financial relationship with any local hospitals, although one has staff privileges at one local hospital.
- Under the Proposed Arrangement, the contracting hospitals will not perform any non–emergent covered services for Health Center patients unless specifically authorized by a referral from the Health Center.

Patients may, but are not required to, obtain services from the contracting hospitals. They are free to obtain a referral to a hospital that is not a party to the Proposed Arrangement (subject to the rules governing pre–approval and prioritization of CHS funds).

II. LEGAL ANALYSIS

The anti–kickback statute make it a criminal offense knowingly and wilfully to offer, pay, solicit, or receive any remuneration to induce referrals of items or services reimbursable by Federal health care programs. See section 1128B(b) of the Act. Where remuneration is paid purposefully to induce referrals of items or services paid for by a Federal health care program, the anti–kickback statute is violated. By its terms, the statute ascribes liability to parties on both sides of an impermissible "kickback" transaction. For purposes of the anti–kickback statute, "remuneration" includes the transfer of

[10] The Health Center has two full–time staff physicians and employs a part–time physician approximately one day per week. Referrals for CHS–funded services made by the part–time physician must be approved by a full–time Health Center physician.

[11] The patient submits a referral form to the CHS provider, who is thereby advised about the potential availability of CHS funds to pay for the services and the CHS rules for collection. In the absence of available CHS funds, the provider has no assurance of payment.

anything of value, in cash or in–kind, directly or indirectly, covertly or overtly.

The statute has been interpreted to cover any arrangement where one purpose of the remuneration is to obtain money for referral of services or to induce further referrals. United States v. Kats, 871 F. 2d 105 (9th Cir. 1989); United States v. Greber, 760 F. 2d 68 (3rd Cir.), cert. denied, 476 U.S. 988 (1985). Violation of the statute constitutes a felony punishable by a maximum fine of $25,000, imprisonment up to five years or both. Conviction will also lead to automatic exclusion from Federal health care programs, including Medicare and Medicaid. Where a party commits an act described in section 1128B(b) of the Act, the OIG may initiate administrative proceedings to impose civil monetary penalties on such party under section 1128A(a)(7) of the Act. The OIG may also initiate administrative proceedings to exclude such part from the Federal health care program under section 1128b(7) of the Act.

Although styled as a "discount," the Proposed Arrangement, as applied to Medicare services, is a routine waiver of part of the Medicare copayment. The routine waiver of all or a portion of the Medicare copayment is suspect under the anti–kickback statute.[12]

Notwithstanding, in the circumstances presented here, the OIG would not seek to impose administrative sanctions related to the anti–kickback statute for acts in connection with the Proposed Arrangement. First, the Federal government receives the full benefit of the discount under the Proposed Arrangement. Unlike the usual situation in which the copayment obligation is owed by either the beneficiary or the beneficiary's insurer, the Federal government through the IHS (or the Tribe on IHS's behalf) is responsible for copayments for the Tribe's Medicare beneficiaries. Because Medicare reimburses both Part A inpatient and Part B outpatient hospital services at fixed prices, there is no opportunity for Medicare to capture any part of the 10% discount offered to the Tribe under the

[12] See, e.g., Special Fraud Alert, 59 Reg. 65,372, 65,374 (published in the Federal Register on Dec. 19, 1994). Copayment waivers also potentially implicate section 1128A(a)(5) of the Act, the prohibition on inducements offered to Medicare and Medicaid beneficiaries. Because Tribe members have no statutory liability for Medicare or Medicaid copayments for CHS–funded services, section 1128A(a)(5) is not implicated here. Simply put, in these circumstances, the partial copayment waiver is not an inducement to the beneficiaries who have no obligation to pay it.

Proposed Arrangement.[13] However, by applying the discount to the remaining copayment, which is also paid substantially with Federal funds, the Federal government's aggregate payment for the service is reduced by 10% — the same discount received by the Tribe for its non–Medicare patients. In short, although Medicare may not receive the benefit of the discount, the Federal fisc does.

Second, the Proposed Arrangement will not result in unfair competition. The Tribe is willing, even eager, to enter into the Proposed Arrangement with any willing hospital provider. The fact that some hospitals may not wish to provide services for the discounted amount does not mean that the pricing arrangement is illegal or improper. Public policy favors open and legitimate price competition in the Medicare program so long as the savings are shared with the Federal government. See 1128B(b)(A) of the Act (exception for price reductions).

Third, there appears to be no substantial risk of "swapping." We have previously articulated our concern about discounts offered on non–Medicare business that are tied to, or conditioned on, referrals of Medicare patients for whom Medicare pays a higher, non–discounted rate. (See, e.g., OIG Advisory Opinions 99–2 and 99–13). Here, the number of Medicare beneficiaries among the Health Center's patients is relatively small in comparison to the total number of patients (approximately 138 out of 2040, or approximately 7%). Medicaid patients comprise an additional 15% of the patient pool. In the circumstances presented, there is little likelihood that a hospital will agree to discount approximately 75% of its business in order to secure these Medicare and Medicaid referrals. This is especially true where, as here, Medicare and Medicaid payment rates are in many cases lower than the Tribe's negotiated rate for a comparable service for a non–Federal patient.

Fourth, the Proposed Arrangement should not appreciably increase the risk of overutilization of services. Patients are only permitted to seek CHS–funded services at a hospital if such services are not available at the Health Center. Moreover, all non–emergent CHS–funded hospital services are subject to pre–authorization by a Health Center physician. Given the scarcity of CHS and other funds

[13] This would not be the case if the discount arrangement involved Part B services, such as physician services, that are reimbursed on the basis of the lower of the provider's actual charges or a Medicare fee schedule amount. In such case, the discount could be allocated to the government's portion of the payment.

and the large number of Tribe patients with no outside insurance, the Tribe has significant financial incentives to control utilization of CHS services provided to Medicare patients.

Finally, the Proposed Arrangement arises in the context of the unique and historic relationship between the Federal government and the sovereign Indian nations, pursuant to which Congress has promulgated certain health care programs for the benefit of Indian people. As part of that relationship, Congress created the CHS program, deemed Medicare the primary payer for CHS–covered services for eligible Medicare beneficiaries, and exempted those beneficiaries from copayment liability. Instead, the IHS or the Indian tribes assume responsibility for paying the Medicare copayment amounts. The Proposed Arrangement is fully consistent with IHS policy encouraging tribes to be prudent purchasers of CHS–covered services.

III. CONCLUSION

Based on the facts certified in your request for an advisory opinion and supplemental submissions, we conclude that the Proposed Arrangement would potentially generate prohibited remuneration under the anti–kickback statute, if the requisite intent to induce or reward referrals of Federal health care program business were present, but that the OIG would not impose administrative sanctions on the [name of tribe redacted] under sections 1128(b)(7) or 1128A(a)(7) of the Act (as those sections relate to the commission of acts described in section 1128B(b) of the Act) in connection with the Proposed Arrangement.

IV. LIMITATIONS

The limitations applicable to this opinion include the following:

- This advisory opinion is issued only to the [name of tribe redacted], the requester of this opinion. This advisory opinion has no application to, and cannot be relied upon by, any other individual or entity.
- This advisory opinion may not be introduced into evidence in any other matter involving an entity or individual that is not a requester to this opinion.
- This advisory opinion is applicable only to the statutory provisions specifically noted above in the first paragraph of this opinion. No opinion is herein expressed or implied with respect

to the application of any other Federal, state, or local statute, rule, regulation, ordinance, or other law that may be applicable to Proposed Arrangement.

- This advisory opinion will not bind or obligate any agency other than the U.S. Department of Health and Human Services.
- This advisory opinion is limited in scope to the specific arrangement described in this letter and has no applicability to other arrangements, even those that appear similar in nature or scope.
- No opinion is expressed herein regarding the liability of any party under the False Claims Act or other legal authorities for any improper billing, claims submission, cost reporting, or related conduct.

This opinion is also subject to any additional limitations set forth at 42 C.F.R. Part 1008.

The OIG will not proceed against the requester with respect to any action that is part of the Proposed Arrangement taken in good faith reliance upon this advisory opinion as long as all of the material facts have been fully, completely, and accurately presented, and the Proposed Arrangement in practice comports with the information provided. The OIG reserves the right to reconsider the questions and issues raised in this advisory opinion and, where the public interest requires, rescind, modify, or terminate this opinion. In the event that this advisory opinion is modified or terminated, the OIG will not proceed against the requester with respect to any action taken in good faith reliance upon this advisory opinion, where all of the relevant facts were fully, completely, and accurately presented, and where such action was promptly discontinued upon notification of the modification or termination of this advisory opinion. An advisory opinion may be rescinded only if the relevant and material facts have not been fully, completely, and accurately disclosed to the OIG.

Sincerely,

/s/

D. McCarty Thornton

Chief Counsel to the Inspector General

APPENDIX F61

Advisory Opinion No. 01–4, May 10, 2001

Concerning a proposed arrangement between a hospital and a new physician whom the hospital would like to recruit to practice within its service area.

[*We redact certain identifying information and certain potentially privileged, confidential, or proprietary information associated with the individual or entity, unless otherwise approved by the requester.*]

Date Issued: May 3, 2001
Date Posted: May 10, 2001
[Name and Address Redacted]

Re: OIG Advisory Opinion No. 01–4

Dear [name redacted]:

We are writing in response to your request for an advisory opinion regarding a proposed arrangement between [name of hospital redacted] (the "Hospital") and a new physician whom the Hospital would like to recruit to practice within its service area (the "Proposed Arrangement"). Specifically, the question raised by your request is whether the Proposed Arrangement would constitute grounds for the imposition of sanctions under the exclusion authority at section 1128(b)(7) of the Social Security Act (the "Act") or the civil monetary penalty provision at section 1128(a)(7) of the Act, as those sections relate to the commission of acts described in 1128(b) of the Act.

You have certified that all of the information provided in the request, including all supplementary letters, is true and correct and constitutes a complete description of the relevant facts and agreements among the parties. You have also certified that, upon our approval, you will undertake to effectuate the Proposed Agreement.

In issuing this opinion, we have relied solely on the facts and information presented to us. We have not undertaken an independent investigation of such information. This opinion is limited to the

facts presented. If material facts have not been disclosed or have been misrepresented, this opinion is without force and effect.

Based on the facts certified in your request for an advisory opinion and supplemental submissions, we conclude that the Proposed Arrangement would potentially generate prohibited remuneration under the anti–kickback statute, if the requisite intent to induce or reward referrals of Federal health care program business were present, but that the Office of the Inspector General ("OIG") would not impose administrative sanctions on the Hospital under sections 1128(b)(7) or 1128(a)(7) of the Act (as those sections relate to the commission of acts described in section 1128B(b) of the Act) in connection with the Proposed Arrangement.

This opinion may not be relied on by any persons other than the Hospital, the requestor of this opinion, and is further qualified as set out in Part IV below and in 42 C.F.R. Part 1008.

I. Factual Background

The Hospital is a tax–exempt organization under section 501(c)(3) of the Internal Revenue Code. It operates an acute care hospital in the city of [city redacted] (the "City") which is located in rural eastern [state redacted]. A large percentage of the Hospital's revenues is derived from Federal health care program business. The Hospital's service area includes [county redacted] County (the "County") and several other surrounding counties. The County is not designated as a health professional shortage area ("HPSA"), as defined in regulations issued by the Department of Health and Human Services (the "Department"), for any medical specialty. However, the Hospital has certified that the County and all other counties within the Hospital's service area are currently designated as medically underserved areas ("MUAs"), as defined in regulations issued by the Department, and that, based upon a *bona fide* needs analysis that the Hospital conducted using objective criteria, there is a shortage of otolaryngologists and head and neck surgeons within its service area.[1]

The Hospital would like to recruit [name redacted] (the "Physician"), a recent medical school graduate who has agreed to relocate to the City upon completion of a five–year residency program for

[1] The Hospital has presented a copy of its needs analysis to the OIG. We express no opinion regarding whether the Internal Revenue Service ("IRS") would deem the Hospital's needs analysis to be "objective evidence of a demonstrable community need" for purposes of determining whether the Proposed Arrangement would jeopardize the Hospital's tax–exempt status.

otolaryngology and head and neck surgery (collectively, the "Specialties"). The Physician's residency program, which began on July 1, 2000, is at an unaffiliated institution located more than 100 miles from the Hospital. The Hospital has certified that it expects that the shortage of otolaryngologists and head and neck surgeons within its service area will not be alleviated prior to the Physician's completion of his five–year residency program. [2]

Under the Proposed Arrangement, the Hospital would loan the Physician [amount redacted] dollars ($[X]) annually during the five years of his residency training, for an aggregate principal amount of [amount redacted] dollars ($[5X]). The Hospital has certified that the loan amount is equal to the aggregate monthly payments (i.e., $[M] per month for 60 months) that the Physician is required to make on his medical school loans during his residency program, plus an additional $[N] per year during each year of his residency program to be used for any other educational expenses. Interest on the loan would accrue from the date of each annual disbursement and would continue to accrue on the outstanding loan balance until paid or forgiven in the manner described below. The interest rate applicable to the loan would be the prime rate, as determined by a designated local bank, plus one percent (1%), with the rate being adjusted semi–annually.

The Physician's obligations under the Proposed Arrangement would begin upon completion of his residency training, but not later than August 1, 2005, and continue for three consecutive years. These obligations include: (i) establishing and maintaining a full–time private practice of the Specialties within a three–mile radius of the City; (ii) acquiring and maintaining active professional staff privileges in the Specialties at the Hospital; (iii) accepting patients referred by the Hospital's emergency room while on–call, regardless of the patients' ability to pay; (iv) assisting the Hospital in its educational programs; (v) upon request, assisting the Hospital in fund–raising efforts in order to promote the charitable and educational purposes of the Hospital; (vi) providing reasonable assistance to the Hospital in it physician recruitment programs; and (vii) agreeing to treat patients receiving medical benefits or assistance under any Federal health care program in a nondiscriminatory manner. In

[2] The Hospital's certfication is based upon several factors, including difficulties associated with recruiting physicians to the City and the announced plan of one of the otolaryngologists currently practicing at the Hospital to retire upon the Physician's arrival.

no event will the number of hours that the Physician spends fulfilling the obligations listed under subsections (iv), (v), and (vi) above exceed twenty hours per month.

The Physician would agree to repay the loan, together with accrued interest, in three equal annual payments, with the first installment becoming due on August 1, 2006. However, the Hospital would incrementally forgive the Physician's obligation to make installment payments by forgiving one–third of his payment obligations for each year that the Physician fulfills the obligations listed above. If the Physician were to default on any of his obligations, the outstanding balance (i.e., the principal and accrued interest minus all amounts forgiven in the manner described above, if any) would become immediately due and payable. For example, if the Physician were to cease his practice within the City after one year of his three–year commitment, he would repay the entire outstanding balance which would be approximately equal to two–thirds of the original principal together with the accrued interest.

The Hospital has agreed as follows:

- The Proposed Arrangement would not be renegotiated in any substantial aspect during its term;
- The Proposed Arrangement would not be conditioned upon the Physician making referrals to, or being in a position to make or influence referrals to, or otherwise generating business for the Hospital;
- The Physician would not be restricted from establishing staff privileges at, referring any service to, or otherwise generating any business for any other entity or his choosing;
- The amount or value of the remuneration provided under the Proposed Arrangement would not vary (or be adjusted or renegotiated) in any manner based on the volume or value of any expected referrals to, or business otherwise generated for, the Hospital by the Physician for which payment may be made in whole or in part under any Federal health care program;
- At least seventy–five percent (75%) of the revenues of the Physician's new practice will be generated from patients residing in a HPSA or a MUA or who are part of a Medically Underserved Population ("MUP"), as defined in regulations issued by the Department; and
- The Proposed Arrangement would not directly or indirectly benefit any person (other than the Physician and his patients)

or entity in a position to make or influence referrals to the Hospital of items or services payable by a Federal health care program.

II. The Anti–Kickback Statute

A. Law

The anti–kickback statute makes it a criminal offense knowingly and willfully to offer, pay, solicit, or receive any remuneration to induce referrals of items or services reimbursable by Federal health care programs. See section 1128(b) of the Act. Where remuneration is paid purposefully to induce referrals of items or services paid for by a Federal health care program, the anti–kickback statute is violated. By its terms, the statute ascribes criminal liability to parties on both sides of an impermissible "kickback" transaction. For purposes of the anti–kickback statute, "remuneration" includes the transfer of anything of value, in cash or in–kind, directly or indirectly, covertly or overtly.

The statute has been interpreted to cover any arrangement where one purpose of the remuneration was to obtain money for the referral of services or to induce further referrals. United States v. Kats, 871 F.2d 105 (9th Cir. 1989); United States v. Greber, 760 F.2d 68 (3d Cir.), cert. denied, 474 U.S. 988 (1985). Violation of the statute constitutes a felony punishable by a maximum fine of $25,000, imprisonment up to five years, or both. Conviction will also lead to automatic exclusion from Federal health care programs, including Medicare and Medicaid. Where a party commits an act described in section 1128(b) of the Act, the OIG may initiate administrative proceedings to impose civil monetary penalties on such party under section 1128(a)(7) of the Act. The OIG may also initiate administrative proceedings to exclude such party from the Federal health care programs under section 1128(b)(7) of the Act.

The Department has promulgated safe harbor regulations that define arrangements that are not subject to the anti–kickback statute because such arrangements would be unlikely to result in fraud or abuse. See 42 C.F.R. § 1001.952. The safe harbors set forth specific conditions that, if met, assure entities involved of not being prosecuted or sanctioned for the arrangement qualifying for the safe harbor. However, safe harbor protection is afforded only to those arrangements that precisely meet all of the conditions set forth in the safe harbor.

The OIG promulgated a new safe harbor for certain payments or benefits offered by hospitals and other entities to attract physicians and other practitioners to HPSAs. See 42 C.F.R. § 1001.952(n). The safe harbor is designed to facilitate recruitment of needed health care professionals to rural and urban undeserved areas, without protecting "recruitment" payments that are really camouflaged kickbacks for referrals of Federal health care program business to recruiting hospitals and entities. The safe harbor protects newly–minted practitioners, as well as practitioners relocating to underserved geographic areas and starting new practices. The safe harbor does not protect recruitment arrangements in areas that are not HPSAs.

To achieve safe harbor protection, a recruitment arrangement must satisfy nine express conditions enumerated in the safe harbor regulation. More specifically, the practitioner recruitment safe harbor protects any payment or exchange of anything of value by an entity in order to induce a practitioner who has been practicing within his or her current specialty for less than one year to locate, or to induce any other practitioner to relocate, his or her primary place of practice to a HPSA for his or her specialty area, as long as all of the following nine standards are met:

- the arrangement is set forth in a written agreement signed by the parties that specifies the benefits provided by the entity, the terms under which the benefits are to be provided, and the obligations of each party;
- if the practitioner is leaving an established practice, at least seventy–five percent (75%) of the revenues of the new practice must be generated from new patients not previously seen by the practitioner at his or her former practice;
- the benefits are provided by the entity for a period not in excess of three years, and the terms of the agreement are not renegotiated during that three–year period in any substantial aspect;
- there is no requirement that the practitioner make referrals to, be in a position to make or influence referrals to, or otherwise generate business for the entity as a condition for receiving benefits; provided, however, that for purposes of this paragraph, the entity may require as a condition for receiving benefits that the practitioner maintain staff privileges at the entity;

- the practitioner is not restricted from establishing staff privileges at, referring any service to, or otherwise generating any business for any other entity of his or her choosing;
- the amount or value of the benefits provided by the entity may not vary (or be adjusted or renegotiated) in any manner based on the volume or value of any expected referrals to or business otherwise generated for the entity by the practitioner for which payment may be made in whole or in part under any Federal health care program;
- the practitioner agrees to treat patients receiving medical benefits or assistance under any Federal health care program in a nondiscriminatory manner;
- at least seventy–five percent (75%) of the revenues of the new practice must be generated from patients residing in a HPSA or a MUA or who are part of a MUP; and
- the payment or exchange or anything of value may not directly or indirectly benefit any person (other than the practitioner being recruited) or entity in a position to make or influence referrals to the entity providing the recruitment payments or benefits of items or services payable by a Federal health care program.

See 42 C.F.R. § 1001.952(n). These conditions are designed to ensure that the payments are genuine recruitment payments, rather than retention payments or payments to lock up existing streams of referrals, and that the payments further the primary goal of the safe harbor: improving access to needed health care services for underserved patients.

B. General Observations About Practitioner Recruitment Arrangements

It is not uncommon for a rural tax–exempt hospital to provide incentives to recruit a physician to join its medical staff and provide medical services to the surrounding community, but not necessarily for, or on behalf of, the hospital. Pursuant to the IRS's Revenue Ruling 97–21, such recruitment activities would not jeopardize the hospital's status as a tax–exempt organization, if there is objective evidence demonstrating a need for the physician's medical services within the hospital's service area and if certain other conditions are met. See Rev. Rul. 97–21, 1997–1 C.B. 121.

Notwithstanding, such arrangements may be unlawful under the anti–kickback statute. When a hospital provides remuneration to a physician in exchange for relocating or establishing his or her medical practice within the hospital's service area, an inference may be drawn that one purpose of the remuneration is to generate referrals for the hospital, including referrals of Federal health care program beneficiaries.

While practitioner recruitment is an area that is subject to abusive practices, the OIG recognizes that: (i) many rural and urban underserved communities have difficulty attracting medical professionals, and may need to offer additional financial incentives to acquire needed staff; and (ii) when payments are made to new or relocating physicians who do not have an established patient base in the new area, the risk of kickbacks is more attenuated. However, even if an arrangement is crafted under the foregoing circumstances, it may not qualify for safe harbor protection.

Practitioner recruitment arrangements that implicate the anti–kickback statute, but do not qualify for the practitioner recruitment safe harbor, must be evaluated on a case–by–case basis. In evaluating the risks posed by a specific arrangement, the OIG looks to a number of factors, including, but not limited to, the following:

- **Whether there is documented evidence of an objective need for the practitioner's services.** Generally, recruitment activities based upon documented evidence of an objective need for the practitioner's services are less suspect than recruitment activities used to attract a practitioner to an area which has no practitioner shortages for his specialty. For purposes of our analysis, the fact that the area to which a practitioner is recruited is a HPSA for the practitioner's particular specialty will, in most cases, represent documented evidence of an objective need for the practitioner's services. We recognize, however, that even when an area is not designated as a HPSA, the area may be deficient with respect to a particular specialty. [3] In such cases, we would consider the validity of other documented evidence of an objective need on a case–by–case basis.
- **Whether the practitioner has an existing stream of referrals within the recruiting entity's service area.** The risk of

[3] In fact, an area can only be designated as a HPSA for one or more of seven health professional types (i.e., primary medical care, dental, mental health, vision care, podiatric, pharmacy, and veterinary). See 42 C.F.R. pt. 5. Moreover, the definition of primary medical care is limited to doctors of medicine or osteopathy who practice primarily in one of four primary care specialties — general or family practice, general internal medicine, pediatrics, and obstetrics and gynecology. See 42 C.F.R. pt. 5 app. A.

kickbacks is mitigated when payments are made to new or relocating practitioners who do not have established referral streams that can be locked up through inappropriate incentives and loyalties. Practitioners in urban areas who relocate their offices short distances to underserved areas could still have an existing stream of referrals, and therefore inducements offered to such practitioners could be suspect if patients residing in the nearby urban area continue to represent a large percentage of the practitioner's practice.

- **Whether the benefit is narrowly tailored so that it does not exceed that which is reasonably necessary to recruit a practitioner.** Whether the value or duration of a benefit is indicative of abusive practices varies based upon a number of factors including, for example, whether there is a reasonable and documented basis for the benefit's value and duration. Generally, benefits of greater value and benefits provided over longer durations (i.e., more than three years) are more suspect.[4]
- **Whether the remuneration directly or indirectly benefits other referral sources.** Remuneration is more suspect if it directly or indirectly benefits actual or potential referral sources, other than the recruited practitioner, or if it is directly or indirectly related to broader arrangements that the entity has with the recruited practitioner or other actual or potential referral sources. For example, we are aware of many joint recruitment arrangements between hospitals and other referral sources (e.g., solo practitioners, group practices, or managed care organizations) pursuant to which the hospital makes payments directly or indirectly to the other referral source to assist the referral source in recruiting a new practitioner. Such arrangements are subject to a higher degree of scrutiny to ensure that the remuneration is not a disguised payment for past or future referrals.

We emphasize that these factors are not indicative or necessarily probative of whether a practice, in fact, actually violates the anti–kickback statute. Rather, we weigh these factors, as well as other relevant concerns, in assessing the level of risk presented by a

[4] Generally, the three–year period begins on the earlier of (i) the date of the first payment or transfer of anything of value to the recruited practitioner or (ii) the date that the practitioner begins his or her new practice in, or relocates his or her practice to, the area.

practitioner recruitment arrangement. These factors are not exhaustive, and the presence or absence of any one factor is not determinative of whether, in our discretion, the OIG would subject the parties involved in a practitioner recruitment arrangement to administrative sanctions for violating the anti–kickback statute.

C. Application of the Anti–Kickback Statute

In the instant case, the Hospital would provide remuneration (i.e., a loan subject to favorable terms, together with conditional loan forgiveness) to the Physician, a potential referral source, to relocate to, and practice medicine within, the Hospital's service area.[5] Since such an arrangement gives rise to an inference that one purpose of the remuneration is to induce or reward referrals of Federal health care program business, the anti–kickback statute is implicated. Moreover, the Proposed Arrangement does not qualify for safe harbor protection because it fails to satisfy two of the requirements of the practitioner recruitment safe harbor (i.e., the Physician is not relocating to a HPSA and the benefit is not limited to three years).[6]

Notwithstanding, we would not subject the Hospital to administrative sanctions for violations of the Federal anti–kickback statute in connection with the Proposed Arrangement for the following reasons. First, consideration of the factors listed above suggests that the Proposed Arrangement would pose a minimal risk of Federal health care program fraud and abuse. Specifically, in addition to servicing a rural area which has a documented shortage of health care services generally,[7] the Hospital has certified that its service area has a specific, documented shortage of physicians practicing the Specialties. Moreover, upon relocation, the Physician would not have a

[5] In the instant case, the limited additional services that the Physician would provide to the Hospital (e.g., assisting the Hospital in its educational programs) do not materially impact our analysis.

[6] We recognize that even if there were a dire shortage of physicians practicing the Specialties within the County, the County could not be designated as a HPSA for the Specialties, because HPSA designations are only available for certain limited primary care specialties. See supra note 3.

[7] The fact that the Hospital's service area consists exclusively of areas designated as MUAs is not determinative and is only one of many factors that we consider. In fact, in revising the practitioner recruitment safe harbor, we considered whether we should protect arrangements where practitioners relocate to a MUA, but we rejected the use of MUAs, because unlike HPSAs, which target practitioner shortages, MUAs only measure shortages of health care services generally. See 64 Fed. Reg. 63,518, 63,542 (Nov. 19, 1999).

ready stream of referrals. Although the duration of the Proposed Arrangement (i.e., eight years) would exceed the three–year threshold, the repayment period, the only period of the Proposed Arrangement during which the Physician could make referrals to the Hospital, is limited to three years. In addition, there is a reasonable, documented basis for both the monetary value of the original loan amount and the duration over which it is paid. Moreover, the Hospital has certified that the benefit would be provided directly to the Physician and it would not directly or indirectly benefit any other potential or actual referral source.

Second, the Proposed Arrangement would contain the following safeguards that would further reduce the risk of fraud and abuse:

- The Proposed Arrangement would not be renegotiated in any substantial aspect during its term;
- The Proposed Arrangement would not be conditioned upon the Physician making referrals to, or being in a position to make or influence referrals to, or otherwise generating business for the Hospital;
- The Physician would not be restricted from establishing staff privileges at, referring any service to, or otherwise generating any business for any other entity of his choosing; and
- The amount or value of the remuneration provided under the Proposed Arrangement would not vary (or be adjusted or renegotiated) in any manner based on the volume or value of any expected referrals to, or business otherwise generated for, the Hospital by the Physician for which payment may be made in whole or in part under any Federal health care program.

In light of the foregoing, the Physician would be free to make referrals based upon clinical judgment without fear of reproach from the Hospital.

Third, because all of the counties in the Hospital's service area have been designated as MUAs by the Department, the Proposed Arrangement will benefit the public by increasing access to health care services in medically underserved areas.

III. Conclusion

Based on the facts certified in your request for an advisory opinion and supplemental submissions, we conclude that the Proposed Arrangement would potentially generate prohibited remuneration under the anti–kickback statute, if the requisite intent to induce or reward referrals of Federal health care program business were present, but that the OIG would not impose administrative sanctions on the Hospital under sections 1128(b)(7) or 1128A(a)(7) of the act (as those sections relate to the commission of acts described in section 1128B(b) of the Act) in connection with the Proposed Arrangement.

IV. Limitations

The limitations applicable to this opinion include the following:

- This advisory opinion is issued only to [name of hospital redacted], who is the requestor of this opinion. This advisory opinion has no application, and cannot be relied upon, by any other individual or entity.
- This advisory opinion may not be introduced into evidence in any matter involving an entity or individual that is not a requestor to this opinion.
- This advisory opinion is applicable only to the statutory provisions specifically noted above. No opinion is herein expressed or implied with respect to the application of any other Federal, state, or local statute, rule, regulation, ordinance, or other law that may be applicable to the Proposed Arrangement.
- This advisory opinion will not bind or obligate any agency other than the U.S. Department of Health and Human Services.
- This advisory opinion is limited in scope to the specific arrangement described in this letter and has no applicability to other arrangements, even those which appear similar in nature or scope.
- No opinion is expressed herein regarding the liability of any party under the False Claims Act or other legal authorities for any improper billing, claims submission, cost reporting, or related conduct.

This opinion is also subject to any additional limitations set forth at 42 C.F.R. Part 1008.

The OIG will not proceed against the Hospital with respect to any action that is part of the Proposed Arrangement taken in good faith reliance upon this advisory opinion as long as all of the material facts have been fully, completely, and accurately presented, and the Proposed Arrangement in practice comports with the information provided. The OIG reserves the right to reconsider the questions and issues raised in this advisory opinion and, where the public interest requires, rescind, modify or terminate this opinion. In the event that this advisory opinion is modified or terminated, the OIG will not proceed against the Hospital with respect to any action taken in good faith reliance upon this advisory opinion, where all of the relevant facts were fully, completely, and accurately presented and where such action was promptly discontinued upon notification of the modification or termination of this advisory opinion. An advisory opinion may be rescinded only if the relevant and material facts have not been fully, completely and accurately disclosed to the OIG.

Sincerely,

/s/

D. McCarty Thornton

Chief Counsel to the Inspector General

APPENDIX F62

Advisory Opinion No. 01–5, May 24, 2001

Concerning a proposed lease of cardiac diagnostic equipment to emergency medical services providers for a nominal charge.

[*We redact certain identifying information and certain potentially privileged, confidential, or proprietary information associated with the individual or entity, unless otherwise approved by the requester.*]

Date Issued: May 18, 2001
Date Posted: May 24, 2001
[Name and Address redacted]

Re: OIG Advisory Opinion No. 01–5

Dear [name redacted]:

We are writing in response to your request for an advisory opinion on behalf of [name redacted] (the "Foundation") and [name redacted] ("Hospital A") (collectively, the "Requesters"), in which you ask whether a proposed lease of cardiac diagnostic equipment to emergency medical services ("EMS") providers for a nominal charge (the "Proposed Arrangement") would constitute grounds for the imposition of sanctions under the exclusion authority at section 1128(b)(7) of the Social Security Act (the "Act") or the civil monetary penalty provision at section 1128A(a)(7) of the Act, as those sections relate to the commission of acts described in section 1128B(b) of the Act.

You have certified that all of the information provided in your request letter, including all supplementary information, is true and correct, and constitutes a complete description of the material facts regarding the Proposed Arrangement. You have also certified that, upon our approval, you will undertake to effectuate the Proposed Arrangement.

In issuing this opinion, we have relied solely on the facts and information presented to us. We have not undertaken any independent investigation of such information. This opinion is limited to the

facts presented. If material facts have not been disclosed or have been misrepresented, this opinion is without force and effect.

Based on the facts certified in your request for an advisory opinion and supplemental submissions, we conclude that the Proposed Arrangement would potentially generate prohibited remuneration under the kick–back statute, if the requisite intent to induce or reward referrals of Federal health care program business were present, but that the Office of Inspector General ("OIG") would not impose administrative sanctions on the Requestors under sections 1128(b)(7) or 1128A(a)(7) of the Act (as those sections relate to the commission of acts described in section 1128B(b) of the Act) in connection with the Proposed Arrangement.

This opinion may not be relied on by any persons other than the Requesters and is further qualified as set out in Part IV below and in 42 C.F.R. Part 1008.

I. FACTUAL BACKGROUND

The Requesters have asked whether a proposed lease of cardiac diagnostic equipment to EMS providers for a nominal amount would constitute grounds for the imposition of sanctions under the Social Security Act's exclusion and civil monetary penalty authorities related to kickbacks.

A. The Parties

The Foundation is a non–profit, tax–exempt corporation organized under the laws of the State of [name redacted] (the "State"). The Foundation is a supporting Foundation of Hospital A, an acute care hospital organized as a non–profit, tax exempt corporation. The Foundation and Hospital A share the same board of directors. For purposes of this analysis, given the close relationship between the Foundation and Hospital A, we will consider the Foundation and Hospital A to be one entity.

Hospital A is located in City B, State C, and with its affiliates provides approximately 400,000 patient care visits annually, including 55,000 emergency department visits. Hospital A is [name redacted] County's only Level I trauma center and the State's only burn center with dedicated aftercare and wound service beds. Hospital A is one of only seven open–heart surgery and invasive cardiology centers in the State.

The other parties to the Proposed Arrangement comprise the four EMS providers that provide advanced life support ("ALS") in the area surrounding City B, State C (hereinafter, the "Greater [name redacted] Area" or the "[GXA]"). Two of these are for–profit corporations ([name redacted], and [name redacted], d/b/a/ [name redacted]), and the remaining two are non-profit volunteer EMS providers ([name redacted] and [name redacted]).

In the State, the Department of Public Health is responsible for the licensure and certification of ambulance operations and related emergency services in the State and oversees regional EMS councils which are responsible for planning, coordinating, and administering the emergency medical services in their respective regions. Regions are further subdivided into areas, each of which has a "Sponsor Hospital" responsible for the provision of medical oversight to local EMS providers. The Sponsor Hospital for the GXA is known as the [name redacted] (the "[ABCD]"), which is actually an unincorporated joint venture of two hospitals —Hospital A and [name redacted] ("Hospital B").[1] For any particular ambulance run, the emergency receiving hospital to whom the patient is to be delivered provides active medical direction, which is usually the hospital that is geographically closest to the patient.[2]

The Department of Public Health assigns an EMS provider a primary service area in which it may provide licensed services. The EMS providers that would participate in the Proposed Arrangement comprise all ALS providers in the GXA, all of whom regularly transport patients to Hospital A from their respective primary service areas. The primary service area assignment to an EMS provider is governed, in part, by an EMS Policy and Procedures Manual (the "EMS Manual"). Under State law, transport destination is governed first and foremost by medical need. In most cases, EMS providers are required to transport patients to the closest emergency receiving hospital. See EMS manual § I.

B. The Proposed Arrangement

The Foundation proposes to lease electrocardiogram equipment ("Life Pack Units") to EMS providers for use in ambulances providing ALS in the GXA. The Life Pack Units would enable the parties to obtain an electrocardiogram prior to arrival at the hospital, reducing the time in which a patient with a cardiac condition could be diag-

---

[1] Although [State] law requires that each EMS provider be assigned one Sponsor Hospital, The EMS providers in the GXA actually have two as a result of the ABCD's designation as a Sponsor Hospital.

[2] There are four emergency receiving hospitals in the GXA. These are Hospital A, Hospital B, [name redacted], and [name redacted].

nosed and treated. For example, if a myocardial infraction is diagnosed during transport, the receiving hospital could begin preparations for a potentially lifesaving thrombolytic therapy or primary angioplasty prior to the patient's arrival. By two–way radio, the paramedic would operate the Life Pack Unit under the medical direction of medical staff at the receiving hospital. If the receiving hospital has its own electrocardiogram receiving unit (functionally similar to a facsimile machine), it would be able to receive and print its own electrocardiogram reading. Hospital A intends to purchase a receiving unit if the Proposed Arrangement is consummated and the other emergency receiving hospitals in the GXA could purchase their own without great expense. [3] The EMS Council has provided the OIG with its written opinion that the Proposed Arrangement would enhance the quality of care for cardiac patients in the GXA. [4]

In order to equip all ALS providers in the GXA, fourteen (14) Life Pack Units are needed. The EMS providers have determined that they are unable to incur the expense of purchasing all fourteen of the Life Pack Units on their own. Under the Proposed Arrangement, each participating EMS provider would agree to purchase half of the number of Life Pack Units needed to provide electrocardiogram service in its own primary service area.

The Foundation would purchase seven (7) Life Pack Units for $80,000, and would lease each of them (under separate leases) to the individual EMS providers for one dollar ($1.00) per year. The leases would be terminable by the Foundation at any time if the equipment is taken out of use in the GXA; or if it is not maintained by the EMS provider consistent with the manufacturer's specifications; or if it is not used in a fashion consistent with the manufacturer's specifications; or if the Foundation, in consultation with the EMS Council, determines that the EMS provider improperly directed patient transports to any hospital, including Hospital A. There would be no

---

[3] The Requesters have certified that a hospital's cost of acquiring a receiving unit is approximately $300. Although the Life Pack Unit is capable of printing its own electrocardiogram reading, it only has one lead, making it considerably less precise and useful than a twelve lead reading by a receiving unit.

[4] The EMS Council's opinion also states that the Proposed Arrangement would have minimal influence, if any, on which hospital receives EMS providers' transports, because EMS providers have little discretion in determining patient destination and the other hospital in City B (Hospital B) could retain a receiving unit as well.

other grounds for early termination of the lease. Each lease would run for a five–year term, renewable upon the consent of the Foundation, in consultation with the EMS Council.

Under the terms of each lease, oversight of quality assurance regarding the use of the Life Pack Units would be the responsibility of the ABCD, in consultation with the EMS Council. For example, EMS providers would be required to submit annual maintenance reports regarding their respective Life Pack Units to the ABCD, as well as annual reports describing the utilization of the equipment.

II. LEGAL ANALYSIS

The anti–kickback statute makes it a criminal offense knowingly and willfully to offer, pay, solicit, or receive any remuneration to induce referrals of items or services reimbursable by Federal health care programs. See section 1128B(b) of the Act. Where remuneration is paid purposefully to induce referrals of items or services paid for by a Federal health care program, the anti–kickback statue is violated. By its terms, the statue ascribes criminal liability to parties on both sides of an impermissible "kickback" transaction. For purposes of the anti–kickback statute, "remuneration" includes the transfer of anything of value, in cash or in–kind, directly or indirectly, covertly or overtly.

The statute has been interpreted to cover any arrangement where one purpose of the remuneration was to obtain money for the referral of services or to induce further referrals. United States v. Kats, 871 F.2d 105 (9th Cir. 1989); United States v. Greber, 760 F.2d 68 (3rd Cir.), cert. denied, 474 U.S. 988 (1985). Violation of the statute constitutes a felony punishable by a maximum fine of $25,000, imprisonment up to five years, or both. Conviction will lead to automatic exclusion from Federal health care programs, including Medicare or Medicaid. Where a party commits an act described in section 1128B(b) of the Act, the OIG may initiate administrative proceedings to impose civil monetary penalties on such party under section 1128A(a)(7) of the Act. The OIG may also initiate administrative proceedings to exclude such party from the Federal health care programs under section 1128(b)(7) of the Act.

This Office's concern with the provision of goods and services for nominal or at below–market rates to actual or potential referral sources is longstanding and clear: such arrangements are suspect and may violate the anti–kickback statute if one purpose is to induce or reward referrals of Federal health care program business.

The Proposed Arrangement raised issues under the anti–kickback statute because equipment will be leased for a nominal amount to EMS providers that are current and future referral sources. The provision of cardiac equipment by a hospital at a nominal, below–market rate fits within the meaning of remuneration for purposes of the anti–kickback statute.

In the present case, the Proposed Arrangement presents a minimal risk of Federal health care program abuse, while providing significant benefits to the community. First, because it relates to emergency medical services only, the Proposed Arrangement presents little risk of overutilization or increased costs to any Federal health care program. The number of Federal program beneficiaries requiring emergency transport in the GXA is not related to the existence or operation of the Proposed Arrangement. Also, the provision of Life Pack Units does not generate additional ambulance runs for EMS providers. Rather, the Life Pack Units enable them to provide an enhancement (pre–hospital electrocardiograms) to a service that would be provided even in the absence of Life Pack Units.

Second, the Proposed Arrangement should not result in the steering of patients to Hospital A. The referral pattern between the EMS providers and the hospitals in the GXA, including Hospital A, is pre–existing and governed by extensive State and local regulatory protocols and procedures. Also, the EMS providers could employ Life Pack Units in conjunction with any emergency–receiving hospital that operates a receiving unit. Conversely, all of the EMS providers that provide ALS in the GXA are parties to the Proposed Arrangement. The Foundation has not favored any ALS–EMS provider to the exclusion of another. Finally, as Hospital A's co–Sponsor Hospital and co–member of the ABCD and EMS Council, Hospital B is in a unique position to raise any issues of perceived steering of emergency patients to Hospital A, which is its competitor in the GXA.

Third, the Proposed Arrangement is consistent with a local EMS system that seeks to regulate, improve, and safeguard the provision of EMS in the GXA. In addition to Hospital B oversight (as described above), Hospital A's interaction with EMS providers is overseen by the EMS Council and, ultimately, the Department of Public Health. For example, under the terms of each lease, oversight of quality assurance in the use of the Life Pack Units would be the responsibility of the ABCD, in consultation with the EMS Council. EMS providers would be required to submit annual maintenance reports regarding their respective Life Pack Units to the ABCD, as well as annual reports describing utilization of the equipment. Furthermore, the leases could be renewed only upon consultation with the EMS Council. Thus, the Proposed Arrangement would function in the context of a pre–existing, coordinated effort to integrate and improve the EMS system in the GXA.

Fourth, the Proposed Arrangement is likely to have a positive impact on the quality of patient care. By permitting earlier and more accurate pre–hospital screening, the Proposed Arrangement could reduce the time in which patients having myocardial infarctions or other cardiac conditions receive lifesaving treatment. This significant community benefit, coupled with the conditions, requirements, and limitations outlined above, persuade us the Proposed Arrangement poses a minimal risk of fraud and abuse under the anti–kickback statute, and therefore the OIG would not subject it to administrative sanction.

III. CONCLUSION

Based on the facts certified in your request for an advisory opinion and supplemental submissions, we conclude that the Proposed Arrangement would potentially generate prohibited remuneration under the anti–kickback statute, if the requisite intent to induce or reward referrals of Federal health care program business were present, but that the OIG would not impose administrative sanctions on the Requesters under sections 1128(b)(7) or 1128A(a)(7) of the Act (as those sections relate to the commission of acts described in section 1128B(b) of the Act) in connection with the Proposed Arrangement.

IV. LIMITATIONS

The limitations applicable to this opinion include the following:

- This advisory opinion is issued only to [name redacted] Foundation, Inc., and to [name redacted] Hospital, the requesters of this opinion.
- This advisory opinion has no application to, and cannot be relied upon by, any other individual or entity.
- This advisory opinion may not be introduced into evidence in any matter involving an entity or individual that is not a requester of this opinion.

- This advisory opinion is applicable only to the statutory provisions specifically noted above. No opinion is herein expressed or implied with respect to the application of any other Federal, State, or local statute, rule, regulation, ordinance, or other law that may be applicable to the Proposed Arrangement.
- This advisory opinion will not bind or obligate any agency other than the U.S. Department of Health and Human Services.
- This advisory opinion is limited in scope to the specific Proposed Arrangement described in this letter and has no applicability to other arrangements or proposed arrangements, even those that appear similar in nature or scope. No opinion is expressed herein regarding the liability of any party under the False Claims Act or other legal authorities for any improper billing, claims submission, cost reporting, or related conduct.
- This opinion is also subject to any additional limitations set forth at 42 C.F.R. Part 1008.

The OIG will not proceed against the Requesters with respect to any action that is part of the Proposed Arrangement taken in good faith reliance upon this advisory opinion as long as all of the material facts have been fully, completely, and accurately presented, and the Proposed Arrangement in practice comports with the information provided. The OIG reserves the right to reconsider the questions and issues raised in this advisory opinion and, where public interest requires, rescind, modify, or terminate this opinion. In the event that this advisory opinion is modified or terminated, the OIG will not proceed against the Requesters with respect to any action taken in good faith reliance upon this advisory opinion, where all of the relevant facts were fully, completely, and accurately presented and where such action was promptly discontinued upon notification of modification or termination of this advisory opinion. An advisory opinion may be rescinded only if the relevant and material facts have not been fully, completely, and accurately disclosed to the OIG.

Sincerely,

D. McCarty Thornton

Chief Counsel to the Inspector General

APPENDIX F63

Advisory Opinion No. 01–6, May 29, 2001

Concerning payments by vendors to a group purchasing organization (GPO) owned by entities affiliated with health care providers that purchase items covered by the GPO's vendor contracts.

[*We redact certain identifying information and certain potentially privileged, confidential, or proprietary information associated with the individual or entity, unless otherwise approved by the requester.*]

Date Issued: May 22, 2001
Date Posted: May 29, 2001
[Name and address redacted]

Re: OIG Advisory Opinion No. 01–6

Dear [Name redacted]:

We are writing in response to your request for an advisory opinion regarding payments by vendors to a group purchasing organization ("GPO") owned by entities affiliated with various health care providers that purchase items covered by the GPO's vendor contracts (the "Arrangement"). In particular, you ask whether the Arrangement would constitute grounds for the imposition of sanctions under the exclusion authority at section 1128(b)(7) of the Social Security Act (the "Act") or the civil monetary penalty provision at section 1128A (a)(7) of the Act, as those sections relate to the commission of acts described in section 1128B(b) of the Act.

You have certified that all of the information provided in your request, including all supplementary letters, is true and correct, and constitutes a complete description of the facts and agreements among the parties regarding the Arrangement. In issuing this opinion, we have relied solely on the facts and information you presented us. This opinion is limited to the facts presented. We have not undertaken any independent investigation of such information.

Based on the facts certified in your request for an advisory opinion and supplemental submissions, we conclude that the Arrangement satisfies the criteria of the group purchasing organizations safe harbor, section 1128B(b)(3)(C) of the Act (and 42 C.F.R. § 1001.952(j)), and thus the Office of the Inspector General ("OIG") would not impose administrative sanctions on [name of requester redacted], under section 1128(b)(7) or 1128A(a)(7) of the Act (as those sections relate to the commission of acts described in section 1128B(b) of the Act) in connection with the Arrangement.

This opinion may not be relied on by any person other than [name of requester redacted], and is further qualified as set out in Part IV below and in 42 C.F.R. Part 1008.

I. FACTUAL BACKGROUND

[Name of requester redacted] ("Purchasing Group A"), is a group purchasing organization that negotiates with vendors of health care products (the "Vendors") for discounted prices on behalf of contracting health care providers (the "Purchasers") that furnish items and services reimbursable, in whole or in part, by a Federal health care program.

Purchasing Group A itself is a limited partnership consisting of a general partner and four limited partners, each of which is affiliated with a health care system that purchases substantial quantities of items through Purchasing Group A (the "Affiliated Purchasers"). The general partner and one of the limited partners are wholly–owned by [name of health system redacted] (the "Health System"), which also wholly owns one of the Purchasers. [1] Two of the other limited partners are affiliated with health care systems that are former subsidiaries of the Health System. The fourth limited partner in Purchasing Group A is an entity that has no current or former affiliations with the Health System or any of the other Purchasing Group A partners.

In addition to the Affiliated Purchasers, there are several other health care providers that have contracted with Purchasing Group A to purchase health care products and services from Vendors under

[1] The Purchaser that is wholly–owned by the Health System has a "Management Services Agreement" with Purchasing Group A to provide advisory and consulting services, space, and personnel to Purchasing Group A, and negotiates and enters into Purchasing Group A's vendor agreements on Purchasing Group A's behalf. The Management Services Agreement is outside the scope of this advisory opinion.

terms negotiated by Purchasing Group A (the "Non–Affiliated Purchasers"). The Non–Affiliated Purchasers account for approximately [X]% of total purchases and [Y]% of Purchasing Group A revenue.

Each of the Purchasers has entered into a written agreement with Purchasing Group A (the "Participation Agreement") to permit Purchasing Group A to act as its purchasing agent. For purposes of this advisory opinion, the Arrangement covers the period beginning in calendar year 2000. under the Participation Agreements, the Purchasers acknowledge that Purchasing Group A will receive group purchasing organization fees quarterly from the Vendors in connection with the Purchasers' purchases. The Participation Agreements specify: (i) the Vendors who pay a fee to Purchasing Group A of three percent or less of the purchase price of the health care products and services provided by those Vendors, without specifying the exact percentage paid; and (ii) the Vendors who pay a fee to Purchasing Group A of more than three percent, specifying the exact percentage paid by each Vendor.

Purchasing Group A discloses in writing to the Purchasers on an annual basis, and to the Secretary of the U.S. Department of Health & Human Services upon request, the amount received from each Vendor with respect to purchases attributable to each Purchaser.

None of the Purchasers is wholly–owned by Purchasing Group A or is a subsidiary of a parent corporation that wholly owns Purchasing Group A (either directory or through another wholly–owned entity). [2]

Purchasing Group A has certified that it will promptly advise the Affiliated Purchasers by letter that the provisions of 42 C.F.R. § 413.17 (Cost to related organizations) may apply to their organizations.

---

[2] Purchasing Group A has an "Access Agreement" with [name of other GPO redacted] ("Purchasing Group B"), a group purchasing organization for pharmaceutical and biological products. The Access Agreement permits health care providers participating in either Purchasing Group A or Purchasing Group B to enter into Participation Agreements with either Purchasing Group A or Purchasing Group B and have access to either GPO's vendor agreements. None of the entities that have Participation Agreements with Purchasing Group A through the Access Agreement is wholly–owned by Purchasing Group A. Any relationship between Purchasing Group A and Purchasing Group B, including the arrangement described in the Access Agreement, is not within the scope of this advisory opinion.

II. LEGAL ANALYSIS

The anti–kickback statute makes it a criminal offense knowingly and wilfully to offer, pay, solicit, or receive any remuneration to induce referrals of items or services reimbursable by Federal health care programs. See section 1128B(b) of the Act. Where remuneration is paid purposefully to induce referrals of items or services paid for by a Federal health care program, the anti–kickback statute is violated. By its terms, the statute ascribes criminal liability to parties on both sides of an impermissible "kickback" transaction. For purposes of the anti–kickback statute, "remuneration" includes the transfer of anything of value, in cash or in–kind, directly or indirectly, covertly of overtly.

The statute has been interpreted to cover any arrangement where one purpose of the remuneration was to obtain money for the referral of services or to induce further referrals. United States v. Kats, 871 F.2d 105 (9th Cir. 1989); United States v. Greber, 760 F.2d 68 (3d. Cir.) cert. denied, 474 U.S. 988 (1985). Violation of the statute constitutes a felony punishable by a maximum fine of $25,000, imprisonment up to five years, or both. Conviction will also lead to automatic exclusion from Federal health care programs, including Medicare and Medicaid. Where a party commits an act described in section 1128B(b) of the Act, the OIG may initiate administrative proceedings to impose civil monetary penalties on such party under section 1128A(a)(7) of the Act. The OIG may also initiate administrative proceedings to exclude such party from the Federal health care programs under section 1128(b)(7) of the Act.

A number of statutory and regulatory "safe harbors" protect certain arrangements that might otherwise technically violate the anti–kickback statute from prosecution. See section 1128B(b)(3) of the Act; 42 C.F.R. § 1001.952. Safe harbor protection is afforded only to those arrangements that precisely meet all of the conditions set forth in the safe harbor. The relevant safe harbor here is the group purchasing organizations safe harbor. See section 1128B(b)(3)(C) of the Act; 42 C.F.R. § 1001.952(j).

The GPO safe harbor provides protection for payments by a vendor of goods or services to a GPO (the "GPO fee"). The GPO safe harbor contains the following requirements.

- The GPO must be an entity authorized to act as a purchasing agent for a group of individuals or entities who (i) are furnishing services for which payment may be made in whole or in part under Medicare or a State health care program and (ii) are neither wholly–owned by the GPO nor subsidiaries of a parent corporation that wholly owns the GPO (either directly or through another wholly–owned entity).

- The GPO fee must be paid as part of an agreement to furnish goods or services to the group of individuals or entities for which the GPO is the authorized agent.
- The GPO must have a written agreement with each individual or entity that will purchase items or services from the vendor.
- The agreement must accurately reflect the amount of the GPO fee by satisfying one of the following two conditions:
- First, the agreement may state that the GPO fee will be three percent of less of the purchase price of the goods or services sold by the vendor to the individual or entity.
- Where the entity that receives the goods or services from the vendor is a health care provider of services, the GPO must disclose in writing to the entity at least annually, and to the Secretary upon request, the amount received from each vendor with respect to purchases made by or on behalf of the entity.
- Second, if the GPO fee is greater than the three percent, the agreement must state the specific amount of the fee, expressed either as a fixed sum or as a fixed percentage of the value of the purchases made from the vendor by the members of the group under the contract between the vendor and the GPO. If the amount of the GPO fee is not known at the time the agreement is signed, the agreement must state the maximum amount to be paid to the GPO by the vendor.

See 42 C.F.R. § 1001.952(j).

In the circumstances presented and certified by Purchasing Group A, the fee paid by the Vendors to Purchasing Group A will fit squarely within the GPO safe harbor. Because all of the GPO safe harbor elements are satisfied, the GPO fees paid by the Vendors to Purchasing Group A would not constitute prohibited remuneration under the anti–kickback statute.

This advisory opinion relates only to the GPO fees paid by the Vendors to Purchasing Group A. We express no opinion regarding any other arrangements or remuneration, direct or indirect, between the Vendors and Purchasing Group A or the Purchasers. In addition, given the relationships between Purchasing Group A's limited partners and the Affiliated Purchasers, we express no opinion as to whether, or to what extent, the amounts paid to the GPO must be accounted for on cost reports filed by the Affiliated Purchasers under applicable cost reporting rules and principles, including, but not limited to, 42 C.F.R. § 413.17.

III. CONCLUSION

Based on the facts certified in your request for an advisory opinion and supplemental submissions, we conclude that the Arrangement satisfies the criteria of the group purchasing organizations safe harbor, section 1128B(b)(3)(C) of the Act (and 42 C.F.R. § 1001.952(j)), and thus the OIG would not impose administrative sanctions on [name of requester redacted] under section 1128(b)(7) or 1128A(a)(7) of the Act (as those sections relate to the commission of acts described in section 1128B(b) of the Act) in connection with the Arrangement.

IV. LIMITATIONS

The limitations applicable to this opinion include the following:

- This advisory opinion is issued on to [name of the requester redacted], the requester of this opinion.
- This advisory opinion has no application to, and cannot be relied upon by, any other individual or entity.
- This advisory opinion may not be introduced into evidence in any matter involving an entity or individual that is not a requester to this opinion.
- This advisory opinion is applicable only to the statutory provisions specifically noted above. No opinion is herein expressed or implied with respect to the application of any other Federal, state, or local statute, rule, regulation, ordinance, or other law that may be applicable to the Arrangement.
- This advisory opinion will not bind or obligate any agency other than the U.S. Department of Health and Human Services.
- This advisory opinion is limited in scope to the specific Arrangement described in this letter and has no applicability to other arrangements or proposed arrangements, even those that appear similar in nature or scope. No opinion is expressed herein regarding the liability of any party under the False Claims Act or other legal authorities for any improper billing, claims submission, cost reporting, or related conduct.
- This opinion is also subject to any additional limitations set forth at 42 C.F.R. Part 1008.

The OIG will not proceed against the requester with respect to any action that is part of the Arrangement taken in good faith reliance upon this advisory opinion as long as all of the material facts have been fully, completely, and accurately presented, and the Arrangement in practice comports with the information provided. The OIG reserves the right to reconsider the questions and issues raised in this advisory opinion and, where the public interest requires, rescind, modify or terminate this opinion. In the event that this advisory opinion is modified or terminated, the OIG will not proceed against the requester with respect to any action taken in good faith reliance upon this advisory opinion, where all of the relevant facts were fully, completely, and accurately presented and where such action was promptly discontinued upon notification of the modification or termination of this advisory opinion. An advisory opinion may be rescinded only if the relevant and material facts have not been fully, completely, and accurately disclosed to the OIG.

Sincerely,

/s/

D. McCarty Thornton

Chief Counsel to the Inspector General

APPENDIX F64

OFFICE OF INSPECTOR GENERAL

SPECIAL ADVISORY BULLETIN
Practices of Business Consultants
June 2001
INTRODUCTION

The Office of Inspector General (OIG) was established at the Department of Health and Human Services by Congress in 1976 to identify and eliminate fraud, abuse, and waste in the Department's programs, including the Medicare and Medicaid programs, and to promote efficiency, economy, and effectiveness in departmental operations. Historically, the OIG has primarily carried out this mission through a nationwide program of audits, investigations, and inspections. More recently, the OIG has augmented its efforts to detect fraud, abuse, and waste with increased efforts to promote prevention through the issuance of guidance to the health care industry.

Providers, suppliers, and others[1] involved in the health care industry not only serve the health care needs of Federal program beneficiaries, but they also play an essential role in safeguarding the integrity of the Federal programs. As part of our commitment to working with industry, we want to alert providers to certain marketing and other practices used by some independent consultants that should concern providers and that may put the Medicare and Medicaid programs at increased risk of abuse. While some of the practices described in this bulletin may not themselves rise to the level of fraud and may not be illegal in all cases, all of the practices increase the risk of abuse of the Medicare and Medicaid programs. We encourage providers to recognize and protect themselves and the Federal programs against these questionable practices.

Providers use the legitimate services of consultants, such as accountants, attorneys, business advisors, and reimbursement spe-

---

[1] For purposes of simplicity, the term "providers" as used in this bulletin refers to providers, suppliers, and practitioners that provide items or services payable in whole or in part by a Federal health care program.

cialists, for many *bona fide* reasons, including, for example, improving the efficiency and effectiveness of the provider's operations (including its coding and billing systems), enhancing the accuracy of the provider's claims, conserving resources through outsourcing, and ensuring compliance with applicable laws, regulations, and rules. Responsible consultants play an integral role in developing and maintaining practices that enhance a client s business objectives, as well as in improving the overall integrity of the health care system.

We believe that most consultants, like most providers, are honest and that the vast majority of relationships between providers and consultants are legitimate business activities. Unfortunately, a small minority of unscrupulous consultants engage in improper practices or encourage abuse of the Medicare and Medicaid programs. Depending on the circumstances, these practices may expose both the consultants and their clients to potential legal liability.[2] Hiring a consultant does not relieve a provider of responsibility for ensuring the integrity of its dealings with the Federal health care programs.

QUESTIONABLE PRACTICES

To safeguard themselves, providers engaging the services of consultants should be alert to the following questionable practices:

> **Illegal or Misleading Representations**. Consultants may make illegal or misleading statements or representations about their relationship with the Medicare program, the Centers for Medicare and Medicaid Services (CMS),[3] or the OIG. For example, consultants may misrepresent that they have "inside" or "special" access to the OIG or to OIG materials. In other

---

[2] The practices described in this bulletin are illustrative, and this bulletin does not purport to identify every potentially improper practice arising from the relationship between a provider and a consultant, nor does it purport to identify every potential violation of the criminal or civil statutes. In particular, this bulletin is not intended to identify every potential violation of the False Claims Act or the Anti–Kickback Statute, although some of the practices described may contribute to, or increase the risk of, violations of these provisions. This bulletin does not address the many fraud and abuse concerns that arise from sham consulting arrangements.

[3] The Health Care Financing Administration (HCFA) is being renamed the Centers for Medicare and Medicaid Services; misuse of the either the new or former name would be equally deceptive.

cases, consultants may misrepresent that their services or products are approved, certified, or recommended by Medicare, CMS, the Department of Health or Human Services, or the OIG. Such claims are misleading and potentially harmful to well–meaning providers. Illegal or misleading statements or representations include, for example:

- An educational consultant misrepresenting that its Medicare reimbursement seminars are mandatory for obtaining or maintaining a Medicare provider number. Although such training may be valuable, the Medicare program does not require a provider to attend training courses in order to participate in the Medicare program.
- A consultant misrepresenting that a provider that fails to attend its "Medicare–sanctioned" seminars will be subject to government penalties. In truth, the government does not penalize providers for such conduct.
- A consultant improperly using Federal program logos or symbols on its marketing materials.[4]
- A consultant claiming that it is recommended by the OIG. The OIG does not recommend or endorse particular consultants or particular consultants' services.
- A compliance consultant falsely asserting or implying that it offers recognized accreditation or certification for compliance programs or compliance officers.

Promises and Guarantees. Consultants may explicitly or implicitly promise or guarantee specific results that are unreasonable or improbable. In some cases, consultants may resort to improper means to effectuate these promises or guarantees, such as submitting false claims or preparing false cost reports on behalf of a client. This misconduct potentially subjects both the consultant and the provider to liability under the False Claims Act.[5] Problematic promises would include, for

---

[4] Section 1140 of the Social Security Act prohibits the improper use of the words "Medicare", "Medicaid", "Health Care Financing Administration", "HCFA", "Department of Health and Human Services", "DHHS", "Health and Human Services", "HHS", "Social Security", "Social Security Account", "Social Security System", "Social Security Administration", "Supplemental Security Income Program", "SSI", and "SSA", and any variation on these words, as well as the symbols or emblems for the SSA, HCFA and HHS. Violations are punishable by civil money penalties of $5,000 per violation (in the case of mail solicitation or advertisement, each piece of mail constitutes a separate violation) or $ 25,000 in the case of a broadcast or telecast. The OIG enforces this authority.

[5] The False Claims Act ascribes liability only where the party knows or acts with reckless disregard or deliberate ignorance of the falsity of the claim.

example:

- A valuation consultant promising or assuring a client that its appraisal of a physician's practice will yield a "fair market value" that satisfies the client's need for a particular valuation, regardless of the actual value of the practice.
- A billing consultant promising a prospective client that its advice or services will produce a specific dollar or percentage increase in the client's Medicare reimbursements. The consultant's fee is often based on a percentage of this increased reimbursement.

Encouraging Abusive Practices. Some consultants may knowingly encourage abuse of the Medicare or Medicaid programs. In some cases, reimbursement specialists or other consultants advocate that their clients engage in aggressive billing schemes or unreasonable practices that are fraudulent or abusive of the Medicare or Medicaid programs. This conduct potentially subjects both the consultant and the client to liability under the False Claims Act. For example:

- A reimbursement specialist may suggest that a client use inappropriate billing codes in order to elevate reimbursement and may describe methods to avoid detection.
- A consultant may encourage a client to modify or customize a routine medical supply in an insignificant manner to justify billing the supply as a device that generates higher reimbursement.
- A reimbursement specialist may advise a client to bill for an expensive item or service with a high reimbursement rate when a less expensive item or service with a lower reimbursement rate was actually provided to the patient.
- A consultant may advise a client to adopt a patently unreasonable interpretation of a reimbursement law, regulation, or rule to justify substantially greater reimbursement.
- A consultant may promise to increase Medicare revenues for laboratory services by showing its clients how to disguise double billings and claims for medically unnecessary services.
- A consultant may suggest the creation of deceptive documentation in order to mislead potential reviewers.

Discouraging Compliance Efforts. Some consultants may make absolute or blanket statements that a client should not undertake certain compliance efforts (such as retrospective billing reviews) or cooperate with payor audits, regardless of the client's circumstances. As reflected in the OIG's compliance guidances,[6] the OIG believes that voluntary compliance efforts, such as internal auditing and self–review, are important tools for doing business with the Federal health care programs. Left undetected and, therefore, unchecked and uncorrected, improper billing or other conduct may exacerbate fraud and abuse problems for a provider in the future.

CONCLUSION

Consultants who abuse their position of trust pose a risk to their provider clients, to the Federal health care programs, and to themselves. While most consultants are honest and provide valuable services to their clients, a small minority engage in questionable practices or promote abuse of the Federal health care programs. In general, if a consultant's advice seems too good to be true, it probably is. We urge providers to be vigilant and to exercise judgment when selecting and relying on consultants.

[6] The OIG's compliance guidances are available on our webpage at http://www.hhs.gov/oig.

APPENDIX G

FRAUD ALERTS, MEDICARE ADVISORY BULLETINS AND SPECIAL ADVISORY BULLETINS

APPENDIX G1

PUBLICATION OF OIG SPECIAL FRAUD ALERTS, DECEMBER 19, 1994

appg_1

Publication of OIG Special Fraud Alerts

AGENCY: Office of Inspector General, HHS.

ACTION: Notice.

SUMMARY: This Federal Register notice sets forth the 5 previously-developed Special Fraud Alerts issued directly to the health care provider community by the HHS Office of Inspector General (OIG). In keeping with the OIG's goal and intent of publicizing its concern about possible widespread and abusive health care industry practices, and seeking wider dissemination of this information to the general public, we are republishing the main content of these Special Fraud Alerts in the Federal Register. This notice also serves to alert the general public of our intention to publish all future OIG Special Fraud Alerts in this same manner, in addition to the current method used to distribute this material to Medicare and State health care program providers.

FOR FURTHER INFORMATION CONTACT: Joel J. Schaer, Legislation, Regulations and Public Affairs Staff, (202) 619–0089.

SUPPLEMENTARY INFORMATION:

I. Background

The Use of Fraud Alerts by the OIG

Over the years, the OIG has used fraud alerts as a vehicle to identify fraudulent and abusive practices within the health care industry. The majority of these fraud alerts are disseminated internally to the OIG's Office of Investigations and other agencies within the Department. However, the OIG has also developed and issued Special Fraud Alerts intended for extensive distribution directly to the health care provider community.

Special Fraud Alerts

Since 1988, the OIG has issued 5 "Special Fraud Alerts" addressing specific trends of health care fraud and certain practices of an industry-wide character. Specifically, the OIG Special Fraud Alerts have served to provide general guidance to the health care industry on violations of Federal law (including various aspects of the anti-kickback statute), as well as to provide additional insight to the Medicare carrier fraud units in identifying health care fraud schemes.

In developing these Special Fraud Alerts, the OIG relies on a number of sources, such as studies or management and program evaluations conducted by the OIG's Office of Evaluation and Inspections. In addition, the OIG may consult with experts in the subject field, including those within the OIG, other agencies of the Department, other Federal and State agencies, and from those in the health care industry.

The Nature of Past Special Fraud Alerts

For the most part, the OIG Special Fraud Alerts have been reserved for national trends in health care fraud and have addressed potential violations of the Medicare and State health care programs' anti-kickback statute. The Special Fraud Alerts have addressed the following topic areas that could violate the anti-kickback statute:

- Joint venture arrangements;
- Routine waiver of Medicare Part B copayments and deductibles;
- Hospital incentives to referring physicians;
- Prescription drug marketing practices;
- Arrangements for the provision of clinical laboratory services.

II. Federal Register Publication of Special Fraud Alerts

In the past, the OIG has always printed and distributed copies of these Special Fraud Alerts directly to all Medicare program providers. While the OIG Special Fraud Alerts have been designed to be available to all affected program providers, we believe it is useful to publicize these various issues and concerns involving potential abusive health care industry practices to a more widespread audience. For this reason, we are using this **Federal Register** notice as a vehicle to reprint the substance of the 5 previously-issued Special Fraud Alerts cited above. It is our intention to use this same **Federal Register** form for publishing future Special Fraud Alerts developed by the OIG.

Because each of the previously-developed Special Fraud Alerts contained a similar brief narrative as to the nature of the OIG and a description of the Medicare and Medicaid anti-kickback statute, we will first summarize and set out this material in one section, as it is germane to all 5 subject issuances. Following that will be the main body and content of each of the Special Fraud Alerts. Lastly, we have provided the general information set forth in each of these Special Fraud Alerts addressing information on how to report information on suspected violations.

The OIG Special Fraud Alerts

A. General Background

The Office of Inspector General was established at the Department of Health and Human Services by Congress in 1976 to identify and eliminate fraud, abuse and waste in Health and Human Services programs and to promote efficiency and economy in departmental operations. The OIG carries out this mission through a nationwide program of audits, investigations and inspections. To help reduce fraud in the Medicare and Medicaid programs, the OIG is actively investigating violations of the Medicare and Medicaid anti-kickback statute, 42 U.S.C. Section 1320a-7b(b).

What Is the Medicare and Medicaid Anti-Kickback Law?

Among its provisions, the anti-kickback statute penalizes anyone who knowingly and willfully solicits, receives, offers or pays remuneration in cash or in kind to induce, or in return for:

A. Referring an individual to a person for the furnishing, or arranging for the furnishing, of any item or service payable under the Medicare or Medicaid program; or

B. Purchasing, leasing or ordering, or arranging for or recommending purchasing, leasing or ordering, any goods, facility, service or item payable under the Medicare or Medicaid program.

Violators are subject to criminal penalties, or exclusion from participation in the Medicare and Medicaid programs, or both. In 1987, section 14 of the Medicare and Medicaid Patient and Program Protection Act, PL 100–93, directed this Department to promulgate "safe harbor" regulations, in order to provide health care providers a mechanism to assure them that they will not be prosecuted under the anti-kickback statute for engaging in particular practices. The Department published 11 final "safe harbor" regulations on July 29, 1991 (42 CFR 1001.952, 56 FR 35952), and two more on November 5, 1992 (42 CFR 1001.952, 57 FR 52723). The scope of the anti-kickback statute is not expanded by the "safe harbor" regulations; these regulations give those in good faith compliance with a "safe harbor" the assurance that they will not be prosecuted under the anti-kickback statute.

B. Special Fraud Alert: Joint Venture Arrangements

(Issued August 1989)

The Office of Inspector General has become aware of a proliferation of arrangements between those in a position to refer business, such as physicians, and those providing items or services for which Medicare or Medicaid pays. Some examples of the items or services provided in these arrangements include clinical diagnostic laboratory services, durable medical equipment (DME), and other diagnostic services. Sometimes these deals are called "joint ventures." A joint venture may take a variety of forms: it may be a contractual arrangement between two or more parties to cooperate in providing services, or it may involve the creation of a new legal entity by the parties, such as a limited partnership or closely held corporation, to provide such services. Of course, there may be legitimate reasons to form a joint venture, such as raising necessary investment capital. However, the Office of Inspector General believes that some of these joint ventures may violate the Medicare and Medicaid anti-kickback statute.

Under these suspect joint ventures, physicians may become investors in a newly formed joint venture entity. The investors refer their patients to this new entity, and are paid by the entity in the form of "profit distributions." These subject joint ventures may be intended not so much to raise investment capital legitimately to start a business, but to lock up a stream of referrals from the physician investors and to compensate them indirectly for these referrals. Because physician investors can benefit financially from their referrals, unnecessary procedures and tests may be ordered or performed, resulting in unnecessary program expenditures.

The questionable features of these suspect joint ventures may be reflected in three areas:

(1) The manner in which investors are selected and retained;

(2) The nature of the business structure of the joint venture; and

(3) The financing and profit distributions.

Suspect Joint Ventures: What To Look For

To help you identify these suspect joint ventures, the following are examples of questionable features, which separately or taken together may result in a business arrangement that violates the anti-kickback statute. Please note that this is not intended as an exhaustive list, but rather gives examples of indicators of potentially unlawful activity.

Investor

- Investors are chosen because they are in a position to make referrals.
- Physicians who are expected to make a large number of referrals may be offered a greater investment opportunity in the joint venture than those anticipated to make fewer referrals.
- Physician investors may be actively encouraged to make referrals to the joint venture, and may be encouraged to divest their ownership interest if they fail to sustain an "acceptable" level of referrals.
- The joint venture tracks its sources of referrals, and distributes this information to the investors.
- Investors may be required to divest their ownership interest if they cease to practice in the service area, for example, if they move, become disabled or retire.
- Investment interests may be nontransferable.

Business Structure

- The structure of some joint ventures may be suspect. For example, one of the parties may be an ongoing entity already engaged in a particular line of business. That party may act as the reference laboratory or DME supplier for the joint venture. In some of these cases, the joint venture can be best characterized as a "shell."
- In the case of a shell laboratory joint venture, for example:

—It conducts very little testing on the premises, even though it is Medicare certified.

—The reference laboratory may do the vast bulk of the testing at its central processing laboratory, even though it also serves as the "manager" of the shell laboratory.

—Despite the location of the actual testing, the local "shell" laboratory bills Medicare directly for these tests.

- In the case of a shell DME joint venture, for example:

—It owns very little of the DME or other capital equipment; rather the ongoing entity owns them.

—The ongoing entity is responsible for all day-to-day operations of the joint venture, such as delivery of the DME and billing.

Financing and Profit Distribution

- The amount of capital invested by the physician may be disproportionately small and the returns on investment may be disproportionately large when compared to a typical investment in a new business enterprise.
- Physician investors may invest only a nominal amount, such as $500 to $1500.
- Physician investors may be permitted to "borrow" the amount of the "investment" from the entity, and pay it back through deductions from profit distributions, thus eliminating even the need to contribute cash to the partnership.
- Investors may be paid extraordinary returns on the investment in comparison with the risk involved, often well over 50 to 100 percent per year.

C. Special Fraud Alert: Routine Waiver of Copayments or Deductibles Under Medicare Part B

(Issued May 1991)

To help reduce fraud in the Medicare program, the Office of Inspector General is actively investigating health care providers, practitioners and suppliers of health care items and services who (1) are paid on the basis of charges[1] and (2) routinely waive (do not bill) Medicare deductible and copayment charges to beneficiaries for items and services covered by the Medicare program.

What Are Medicare Deductible and Copayment Charges?

The Medicare "deductible" is the amount that must be paid by a Medicare beneficiary before Medicare will pay for any items or services for that individual. Currently, the Medicare Part B deductible is $100 per year.

"Copayment" ("coinsurance") is the portion of the cost of an item or service which the Medicare beneficiary must pay. Currently, the Medicare Part B coinsurance is generally 20 percent of the reasonable charge for the item or service. Typically, if the Medicare reasonable charge for a Part B item or service is $100, the Medicare beneficiary (who has met his [or her] deductible) must pay $20 of the physician's bill, and Medicare will pay $80.

Why Is it Illegal for "Charged-Based" Providers, Practitioners and Suppliers to Routinely Waive Medicare Copayment and Deductibles?

Routine waiver of deductibles and copayments by charge-based providers, practitioners or suppliers is unlawful because it results in (1) false claims, (2) violations of the anti-kickback statute, and (3) excessive utilization of items and services paid for by Medicare.

A "charge-based" provider, practitioner or supplier is one who is paid by Medicare on the basis of the "reasonable charge" for the item or service provided. 42 U.S.C. 1395u(b)(3), 42 CFR 405.501. Medicare typically pays 80 percent of the reasonable charge. 42 U.S.C. 1395l(a)(1). The criteria for determining what charges are reasonable are contained in regulations, and include an examination of (1) the actual charge for the item or service, (2) the customary charge for the item or service, (3) the prevailing charge in the same locality for similar items or services. The Medicare reasonable charge cannot exceed the actual charge for the item or service, and may generally not exceed the customary charge or the highest prevailing charge for the item or service. In some cases, the provider, practitioner or supplier will be paid the lesser of his [or her] actual charge or an amount established by a fee schedule.

A provider, practitioner or supplier who routinely waives Medicare copayments or deductibles is misstating

[1] This fraud alert is not intended to address the routine waiver of copayments and deductibles by providers, practitioners or suppliers who are paid on the basis of costs or diagnostic related groups. The fact that these types of services are not discussed in this fraud alert should not be interpreted to legitimize routine waiver of deductibles and copayments with respect to these payment methods. Also, it does not apply to a waiver of any copayment by a Federally qualified health care center with respect to an individual who qualifies for subsidized services under a provision of the Public Health Service Act.

its actual charge. For example, if a supplier claims that its charge for a piece of equipment is $100, but routinely waives the copayment, the actual charge is $80. Medicare should be paying 80 percent of $80 (or $64), rather than 80 percent of $100 (or $80). As a result of the supplier's misrepresentation, the Medicare program is paying $16 more than it should for this item.

In certain cases, a provider, practitioner or supplier who routinely waives Medicare copayments or deductibles also could be held liable under the Medicare and Medicaid anti-kickback statute. 42 U.S.C. 1320a–7b(b). The statute makes it illegal to offer, pay, solicit or receive anything of value as an inducement to generate business payable by Medicare or Medicaid. When providers, practitioners or suppliers forgive financial obligations for reasons other than genuine financial hardship of the particular patient, they may be unlawfully inducing that patient to purchase items or services from them.

At first glance, it may appear that routine waiver of copayments and deductibles helps Medicare beneficiaries. By waiving Medicare copayments and deductibles, the provider of services may claim that the beneficiary incurs no costs. In fact, this is not true. Studies have shown that if patients are required to pay even a small portion of their care, they will be better health care consumers, and select items or services because they are medically needed, rather than simply because they are free. Ultimately, if Medicare pays more for an item or service than it should, or if it pays for unnecessary items or services, there are less Medicare funds available to pay for truly needed services.

One important exception to the prohibition against waiving copayments and deductibles is that providers, practitioners or suppliers may forgive the copayment in consideration of a particular patient's financial hardship. This hardship exception, however, must not be used routinely; it should be used occasionally to address the special financial needs of a particular patient. Except in such special cases, a good faith effort to collect deductibles and copayments must be made. Otherwise, claims submitted to Medicare mat violate the statutes discussed above and other provisions of the law.

What Penalties Can Someone Be Subject to for Routinely Waiving Medicare Copayments or Deductibles?

Whoever submits a false claim to the Medicare program (for example, a claim misrepresents an actual charge) may be subject to criminal, civil or administrative liability for making false statements and/or submitting false claims to the Government. 18 U.S.C. 287 and 1001; 31 U.S.C. 3729; 42 CFR 1320a–7a]. Penalties can include imprisonment, criminal fines, civil damages and forfeitures, civil monetary penalties and exclusion from Medicare and the State health care programs.

In addition, anyone who routinely waives copayments or deductibles can be criminally prosecuted under 42 U.S.C. 1320a–7b(b), and excluded from participating in Medicare and the State health care programs under the anti-kickback statute. 42 U.S.C. 1320a–7(b)(7).

Finally, anyone who furnishes items or services to patient substantially in excess of the needs of such patients can be excluded from Medicare and the State health care programs. 42 U.S.C. 1320a–7(b)(6)(B).

Indications of Improper Waiver of Deductibles and Copayments

To help you identify charge-based providers, practitioners or suppliers who routinely waive Medicare deductibles and copayments, listed below are some suspect marketing practices. Please note that this list is not intended to be exhaustive but, rather, to highlight some indicators of potentially unlawful activity.

- Advertisements which state: "Medicare Accepted As Payment in Full," "Insurance Accepted As Payment in Full," or "No Out-Of-Pocket Expense."
- Advertisements which promise that "discounts" will be given to Medicare beneficiaries.
- Routine use of "Financial hardship" forms which state that the beneficiary is unable to pay the coinsurance/deductible (i.e., there is no good faith attempt to determine the beneficiary's actual financial condition).
- Collection of copayments and deductibles only where the beneficiary has Medicare supplemental insurance ("Medigap") coverage (i.e., the items or services are "free" to the beneficiary).
- Charges to Medicare beneficiaries which are higher than those made to other persons for similar services and items (the higher charges offset the waiver of coinsurance.)
- Failure to collect copayments or deductibles for a specific group of Medicare patients for reasons unrelated to indigency (e.g., a supplier waives coinsurance or deductible for all patients from a particular hospital, in order to get referrals).
- "Insurance programs" which cover copayments or deductibles only for items or services provided by the entity offering the insurance. The "insurance premium" paid by the beneficiary is insignificant and can be as low as $1 a month or even $1 a year. These premiums are not based upon actuarial risks, but instead are a sham used to disguise the routine waiver of copayments and deductibles.

D. Special Fraud Alert: Hospital Incentives to Physicians

(Issued May 1992)

Why Do Hospitals Provide Economic Incentives to Physicians?

As many hospitals have become more aggressive in their attempts to recruit and retain physicians and increase patient referrals, physician incentives (sometimes referred to as "practice enhancements") are becoming increasingly common. Some physicians actively solicit such incentives. These incentives may result in reductions in the physician's professional expenses or an increase in his or her revenues. In exchange, the physician is aware that he or she is often expected to refer the majority, if not all, of his or her patients to the hospital providing the incentives.

Why Is it Illegal for Hospitals to Provide Financial Incentives to Physicians for Their Referrals?

The Office of Inspector General has become aware of a variety of hospital incentive programs used to compensate physicians (directly or indirectly) for referring patients to the hospital. These arrangements are implicated by the anti-kickback statute because they can constitute remuneration offered to induce, or in return for, the referral of business paid for by Medicare or Medicaid. In addition, they are not protected under the existing "safe harbor" regulations.

These incentive programs can interfere with the physician's judgment of what is the most appropriate care for a patient. They can inflate costs to the Medicare program by causing physicians to overuse inappropriately the services of a particular hospital. The incentives may result in the delivery of inappropriate care to Medicare beneficiaries and Medicaid recipients by inducing the physician to refer patients to the hospital providing financial incentives rather than to another hospital (or non-acute care facility) offering the best or most appropriate care for that patient.

Suspect Hospital Incentive Arrangements—What To Look For

To help identify suspect incentive arrangements, examples of practices which are often questionable are listed [below]. Please note that this list is not intended to be exhaustive but, rather, to suggest some indicators of potentially unlawful activity.

- Payment of any sort of incentive by the hospital each time a physician refers a patient to the hospital.
- The use of free or significantly discounted office space or equipment (in facilities usually located close to the hospital).
- Provision of free or significantly discounted billing, nursing or other staff services.
- Free training for a physician's office staff in such areas as management techniques, CPT coding and laboratory techniques.
- Guarantees which provide that, if the physician's income fails to reach a predetermined level, the hospital will supplement the remainder up to a certain amount.
- Low-interest or interest-free loans, or loans which may be "forgiven" if a physician refers patients (or some number of patients) to the hospital.
- Payment of the cost of a physician's travel and expenses for conferences.
- Payment for a physician's continuing education courses.
- Coverage on hospitals' group health insurance plans at an inappropriately low cost to the physician.
- Payment for services (which may include consultations at the hospital) which require few, if any, substantive duties by the physician, or payment for services in excess of the fair market value of services rendered.

Financial incentive packages which incorporate these or similar features may be subject to prosecution under the Medicare and Medicaid anti-kickback statute, if one of the purposes of the incentive is to influence the physician's medical decision as to where to refer his or her patients for treatment.

E. Special Fraud Alert: Prescription Drug Marketing Schemes

(Issued August 1994)

How Does the Anti-Kickback Law Relate to Prescription Drug Marketing Schemes?

In recent years, prescription drug companies in the United States have increased their marketing activities among providers, patients and suppliers such as pharmacies. Many prescription drug marketing activities go far beyond traditional advertising and educational contacts. Physicians, suppliers and, increasingly, patients are being offered valuable, non-medical benefits in exchange for selecting specific prescription drug brands. Traditionally, physicians and pharmacists have been trusted to provide treatments and recommend products in the best interest of the patient. In an era of aggressive drug marketing, however, patients may now be using prescription drug items, unaware that their physician or pharmacist is being compensated for promoting the selection of a specific product. Prescription drugs supplied under one of these programs are often reimbursed under Medicaid. Among the specific activities, which the OIG has identified, are the following actual cases:

- A "product conversion" program which resulted in 96,000 brand-name conversions. In this scenario, for instance, Drug Company A offered a cash award to pharmacies for each time a drug prescription was changed from Drug Company B's product to Drug Company A's product. The pharmacies were induced to help persuade physicians, who were unaware of the pharmacies' financial interest, to change prescription.
- A "frequent flier" campaign in which physicians were given credit toward airline frequent flier mileage each time the physician completed a questionnaire for a new patient placed on the drug company's product.
- A "research grant" program in which physicians were given substantial payments for de minimis recordkeeping tasks. The physician administered the drug manufacturer's product to the patient and made brief notes, sometimes a single word, about the treatment outcome. Upon completion of a limited number of such "studies," the physician received payment from the manufacturer.

If one purpose of any of these marketing schemes is to induce the provision of a prescription drug item reimbursable by Medicaid, then the criminal anti-kickback statute is implicated. There is no statutory exception or "safe harbor" to protect such activities. Thus a physician, pharmacy or other practitioner or supplier receiving payment under these activities may be subject to criminal prosecution and exclusion from participation in the Medicare and Medicaid programs.

A marketing program that is illegal under the anti-kickback statute may pose a danger to patients because the offering or payment of remuneration may interfere with a physician's judgment in determining the most appropriate treatment for a patient. Further, where the patient is a Medicaid beneficiary, these drug marketing practices may increase the Federal government's costs of reimbursing suppliers for the products. The OIG is investigating various drug marketing schemes, and enforcing the anti-kickback laws where these practices affect the Federal health care programs.

What To Look For

Generally, a payment or gift may be considered improper under 42 U.S.C. 1320a–7b(b) if it is:

- Made to a person in a position to generate business for the paying party;
- Related to the volume of business generated; and
- More than nominal in value and/or exceeds fair market value of any legitimate service rendered to the payer, or is unrelated to any service at all other than referral of patients.

OIG investigation may be warranted where one or more of the following features is present in prescription drug marketing activities:

- Any prize, gift or cash payment, coupon or bonus (e.g., airline discounts and related travel premiums), offered to physicians and/or suppliers (including pharmacies, mail order prescription drug companies and managed care organizations) in exchange for, or based on, prescribing or providing specific prescription products. These items are particularly suspect if based on value or volume of business generated for the drug company.
- Materials which offer cash or other benefits to pharmacists (or others in a position to recommend prescription drug products) in exchange for performing marketing tasks in the course of pharmacy practice related to Medicare or Medicaid. The marketing tasks may include sales-oriented "educational" or "counseling" contacts, or physician and/or patient outreach, etc.
- Grants to physicians and clinicians for studies of prescription products when the studies are of questionable scientific value and require little or no actual scientific pursuit. The grants may nonetheless offer substantial benefits based on, or related to, use of the product.
- Any payment, including cash or other benefit, given to a patient, provider or supplier for changing a prescription, or recommending or requesting such a change, from one product to another, unless the payment is made fully consistent with a "safe harbor" regulation, 42 CFR 1001.952, or other Federal provision governing the reporting of prescription drug prices.

F. Special Fraud Alert: Arrangements for the Provision of Clinical Lab Services

(Issued October 1994)

How Does the Anti-Kickback Statute Relate to Arrangements for the Provision of Clinical Lab Services?

Many physicians and other health care providers rely on the services of outside clinical laboratories to which they may refer high volumes of patient specimens every day. The quality, timeliness and cost of these services are of obvious concern to Medicare and Medicaid patients and to the programs that finance their health care services. Since the physician, not the patient, generally selects the clinical laboratory, it is essential that the physician's decision regarding where to refer specimens is based only on the best interests of the patient.

Whenever a laboratory offers or gives to a source of referrals anything of value not paid for at fair market value, the inference may be made that the thing of value is offered to induce the referral of business. The same is true whenever a referral source solicits or receives anything of value from the laboratory By "fair market value" we mean value for general commercial purposes. However, "fair market value" must reflect an arms length transaction which has not been adjusted to include the additional value which one or both of the parties has attributed to the referral of business between them.

The office of Inspector General has become aware of a number of practices engaged in by clinical laboratories and health care providers that implicate the anti-kickback statute in this manner Below are some examples of lab services arrangements that may violate the anti-kickback statute.

Provision of Phlebotomy Services to Physicians

When permitted by State law, a laboratory may make available to a physician's office a phlebotomist who collects specimens from patients for testing by the outside laboratory. While the mere placement of a laboratory employee in the physician's office would not necessarily serve as an inducement prohibited by the anti-kickback statute, the statute is implicated when the phlebotomist performs additional tasks that are normally the responsibility of the physician's office staff. These tasks can include taking vital signs or other nursing functions, testing for the physician's office laboratory, or performing clerical services.

Where the phlebotomist performs clerical or medical functions not directly related to the collection or processing of laboratory specimens, a strong inference arises that he or she is providing a benefit in return for the physician's referrals to the laboratory In such a case, the physician, the phlebotomist, and the laboratory may have exposure under the anti-kickback statute. This analysis applies equally to the placement of phlebotomists in other health care settings, including nursing homes, clinics and hospitals.

Furthermore, the mere existence of a contract between the laboratory and the health care provider that prohibits the phlebotomist from performing services unrelated to specimen collection does not eliminate the OIG's concern, where the phlebotomist is not closely monitored by his [or her] employer or where the contractual prohibition is not rigorously enforced.

Lab Pricing at Renal Dialysis Centers

The Medicare program pays for laboratory tests provided to patients with end stage renal disease (ESRD) in two different ways. Some laboratory testing is considered routine and payment is included in the composite rate paid by Medicare to the ESRD facility which in turn pays the laboratory. Some laboratory testing required by the patient is not included in the composite rate, and these additional tests are billed by the laboratory directly to Medicare and paid at the usual laboratory fee schedule price.

The OIG is aware of cases where a laboratory offers to perform the tests encompassed by the composite rate at a price below fair market value of the tests performed. In order to offset the low charges on the composite rate tests, the ESRD facility agrees to refer all or most of its non-composite rate tests to the laboratory. This arrangement appears to be an offer of something of value (composite rate tests below fair market value) in return for the ordering of additional tests which are billed directly to the Medicare program.

If offered or accepted in return for referral of additional business, the lab's pricing scheme is illegal remuneration under the anti-kickback statute. The statutory exception and "safe harbor" for "discounts" does not apply to immunize parties to this type of transaction, since discounts on the composite rate tests are offered to induce referral of *other* tests. See 42 CFR 1001.952(h)(3)(ii).

Waiver of Charges To Managed Care Patients

Managed care plans may require a physician or other health care provider to use only the laboratory with which the plan has negotiated a fee schedule. In such situations, the plan usually will refuse to pay claims submitted by other laboratories. The provider, however, may use a different laboratory and may wish to continue to use that laboratory for non-managed care patients. In order to retain the provider as a client, the laboratory that does not have the managed care contract may agree to perform the managed care work free of charge.

The status of such agreements under the anti-kickback statute depends in part on the nature of the contractual relationship between the managed care plan and its providers. Under the terms of many managed care contracts, a provider receives a bonus or other payment if utilization of ancillary services, such as laboratory testing, is kept below a particular level. Other managed care plans impose financial penalties if the provider's utilization of services exceeds pre-established levels. When the laboratory agrees to write off charges for the physician's managed care work, the physician may realize a financial benefit from the managed care plan created by the appearance that utilization of tests has been reduced.

In cases where the provision of free services results in a benefit to the provider, the anti-kickback statute is implicated. If offered or accepted in return for the referral of Medicare or State health care plan business, both the laboratory and the physician may be violating the anti-kickback statute. There is no statutory exception or "safe harbor" to immunize any party to such a practice because the Federal programs do not realize the benefit of these "free" services. See 42 CFR 1001.952(h)(3)(iii)

Other Inducements

The following are additional examples of inducements offered by clinical laboratories which may implicate the anti-kickback statute:

- Free pick-up and disposal of bio-hazardous waste products (such as sharps) unrelated to the collection of specimens for the outside laboratory
- Provision of computers or fax machines, unless such equipment is integral to, and exclusively used for, performance of the outside laboratory's work.
- Provision of free laboratory testing for health care providers, their families and their employees.

When one purpose of these arrangements is to induce the referral of program-reimbursed laboratory testing, both the clinical laboratory and the health care provider may be liable under the statute and may be subject to criminal prosecution and exclusion from participation in the Medicare and Medicaid programs.

G. Reporting Information

What To Do If You Have Information About Suspect Activities or Arrangements

If you have information about health care providers, practitioners, entities or other persons engaging in these types of activities or arrangements described above, contact any of the regional offices of the Office of Investigations of the Office of Inspector General, U.S. Department of Health and Human Services, at the following locations:

Regions	States served	Telephone
Boston	MA, VT, NH, ME, RI, CT	617-565-2660
New York	NY, NJ, PR, VI	212-264-1691
Philadelphia	PA, MD, DE, WV, VA	215-596-6796
Atlanta	GA, KY, NC, SC, FL, TN, AL, MS (No. District)	404-331-2131
Chicago	IL, MN, WI, MI, IN, OH, IA, MO	312-353-2740
Dallas	TX, NM, OK, AR, LA, MS (So. District)	214-767-8406
Denver	CO, UT, WY, MT, ND, SD, NE, KS	303-844-5621
Los Angeles	AZ, NV (Clark Co.), So. CA	714-836-2372
San Francisco	No. CA, NV, AZ, HI, OR, ID, WA	415-556-8880
Washington, DC	DC and Metropolitan areas of VA and MD	202-619-1900

Dated: December 2, 1994.
June Gibbs Brown,
Inspector General.
[FR Doc. 94-31157 Filed 12-16-94; 8:45 am]
BILLING CODE 4150-04-P

APPENDIX G2

NEW FRAUD ALERT FOR HOME HEALTH FRAUD, AND FRAUD AND ABUSE IN THE PROVISION OF MEDICAL SUPPLIES TO NURSING FACILITIES, AUGUST 10, 1995

Office of Inspector General

Publication of OIG Special Fraud Alerts: Home Health Fraud, and Fraud and Abuse in the Provision of Medical Supplies to Nursing Facilities

AGENCY: Office of Inspector General (OIG), HHS.

ACTION: Notice.

SUMMARY: This **Federal Register** notice sets forth two recently issued OIG Special Fraud Alerts concerning fraud and abuse practices in the home health industry and in the provision of medical supplies to nursing facilities. For the most part, the OIG Special Fraud Alerts address national trends in health care fraud, including potential violations of the Medicare anti-kickback statute. These two Special Fraud Alerts, issued directly to the health care provider community and now being reprinted in this issue of the **Federal Register**, specifically address fraud and abuse in the provision of (1) home health services and (2) medical supplies to nursing facilities, including the submission of false claims and anti-kickback violations.

FOR FURTHER INFORMATION CONTACT: Joel J. Schaer, Office of Management and Policy, (202) 619–0089.

SUPPLEMENTARY INFORMATION:

I. Background

The Office of Inspector General (OIG) issues Special Fraud Alerts based on information it obtains concerning particular fraudulent and abusive practices within the health care industry. These Special Fraud Alerts provide the OIG with a means of notifying the industry that we have become aware of certain abusive practices which we plan to pursue and prosecute, or bring civil and administrative action, as appropriate. The alerts also serve as a powerful tool to encourage industry compliance by giving providers an opportunity to examine their own practices.

The Special Fraud Alerts are intended for extensive distribution directly to the health care provider community, as well as those charged with administering the Medicare and Medicaid programs. On December 19, 1994, the OIG published in the **Federal Register** the texts of 5 previously-issued Special Fraud Alerts, and announced the intention to publish in the same manner subsequent issuances as a regular part of distribution of these Special Fraud Alerts (59 FR 65372).

The first of these new Special Fraud Alert serves to point out the prevalence of certain types of home health care fraud, including (1) cost report frauds; (2) billing for excessive services or services not rendered; (3) use of unlicensed or untrained staff; (4) falsified plans of care; (5) forged physician signatures on plans of care; and (6) kickbacks that the OIG has uncovered.

The second new Special Fraud Alert, focusing on the provision of medical supplies to nursing facilities, identifies some of the illegal practices that the OIG has recently uncovered. These include (1) the submitting of claims to Part B of Medicare for medical supplies and equipment that are not medically necessary; (2) submitting claims for items that are not provided as claimed; (3) double billings; and (4) paying or receiving kickbacks in exchange for Medicare or Medicaid referrals.

These two issuances are the first in a series of new Special Fraud Alerts being developed by the OIG over the next year to heighten both the public's and industry's awareness of fraudulent health care practices. A reprint of both of those Special Fraud Alerts follows.

II. Special Fraud Alert: Home Health Fraud

(June 1995)

The Office of Inspector General was established at the Department of Health and Human Services by Congress in 1976 to identify and eliminate fraud, abuse and waste in Health and Human Services programs and to promote efficiency and economy in departmental operations. The OIG carries out this mission through a nationwide program of audits, investigations and inspections.

To help reduce fraud and abuse in the Medicare and Medicaid programs, the OIG actively investigates schemes to fraudulently obtain money from these programs and, when appropriate, issues Special Fraud Alerts which identify segments of the health care industry that are particularly vulnerable to abuse. This Special Fraud Alert focuses on the home health industry and identifies some of the illegal practices the OIG has uncovered.

What Is Home Health Care And Who Is Eligible To Receive It?

Medicare's home health benefit allows people with restricted mobility to remain non-institutionalized and receive needed care at home. Home health services and supplies are typically provided by nurses and aides under a physician-certified plan of care.

Medicare will pay for home health services if a beneficiary's physician certifies that he or she:

• is homebound—i.e., confined to the home except for infrequent or short absences or trips for medical care, and

• requires one or more of the following qualifying services: physical therapy, speech-language pathology, or intermittent skilled nursing.

If a homebound patient requires a qualifying service, Medicare also covers services of medical social workers and certain personal care such as bathing, feeding, and assistance with medications. However, a beneficiary who needs only this type of personal or custodial care does not qualify for the home health benefit.

Fraud and Abuse in the Home Health Industry

Home care is consuming a rapidly increasing portion of the federal health budget. This year, Medicare payments for home health will reach close to $16 billion, up from $3.3 billion in 1990—nearly a five fold increase. Home health care is particularly vulnerable to fraud and abuse because:

- Medicare covers an unlimited number of visits per patient;
- Beneficiaries pay no co-payments except on medical equipment;
- Patients don't receive explanations of benefits (EOBs) for bills submitted for home health services; and
- There is limited direct medical supervision of home health services provided by non-medical personnel.

The OIG has learned of several types of fraudulent conduct, outlined below, which have or could result in improper Medicare reimbursement for home health services.

False or Fraudulent Claims Relating to the Provision of Home Health Services

The government may prosecute persons who submit or cause false or fraudulent claims for payment to be submitted to the Medicare or Medicaid programs. Examples of false or fraudulent claims include claims for services that were never provided, duplicate claims submitted for the same service, and claims for services to ineligible patients. A claim for a service that a health care provider knows was not medically necessary may also be a fraudulent claim.

Submitting or causing false claims to be submitted to Medicare or Medicaid may subject a person to criminal prosecution, civil penalties including treble damages, and exclusion from participation in the Medicare and Medicaid programs. OIG has uncovered the following types of fraudulent claims related to the provision of home health services.

Claims For Home Health Visits That Were Never Made And For Visits to Ineligible Beneficiaries

OIG has uncovered instances where home health agencies are submitting false claims for home health visits. These include:

- Claims for visits not made.
- Claims for visits to beneficiaries not homebound.
- Claims for visits to beneficiaries not requiring a qualifying service.
- Claims for visits not authorized by a physician.

One home health agency billed Medicare for 123 home health visits to a patient who never received a single visit, and submitted claims for beneficiaries who were in an acute care hospital during the period the agency claimed to have provided home visits. Another agency provided a home health aide to a beneficiary so mobile that he volunteered at a local hospital several times a week.

A third agency claimed nearly $26 million during one year in visits that were not made, visits to patients that were not homebound, and visits not authorized by a physician. OIG interviews indicated that beneficiary signatures were forged on visit logs and physician signatures were forged on plans of care. This agency had subcontracted with other entities to provide home health care to its patients, and claimed that the subcontractors falsely documented that visits were made and services were provided.

Medicare permits a home health agency to contract with other organizations, including agencies not certified by Medicare, to provide care to its patients. However, the agency remains liable for all billed services provided by its subcontractors. The use of subcontracted care imposes a duty on home health agencies to monitor the care provided by the subcontractor.

Home health agencies, as well as the physicians who order home health services, are responsible for ensuring the medical necessity of claims submitted to Medicare. A physician who orders unnecessary home health care services may be liable for causing false claims to be submitted by the home health agency, even though the physician does not submit the claim. Furthermore, if agency personnel believe that services ordered by a physician are excessive or otherwise inappropriate, the agency cannot avoid liability for filing improper claims simply because a physician has ordered the services.

Fraud in Annual Cost Report Claims

In addition to submitting claims for specific services, home health agencies submit annual cost reports to Medicare for reimbursement of administrative, overhead and other general costs. For these costs to be allowable, Medicare regulations require that they be (1) reasonable, (2) necessary for the maintenance of the health care entity, and (3) related to patient care. However, the OIG has audited cost reports which include costs for entertainment, travel, lobbying, gifts, and other expenses unrelated to patient care such as luxury automobiles and cruises. One home health agency claimed several million dollars in unallowable costs during one cost reporting year. These included utility and maid service payments for the owner's condominium, golf pro shop expenses, lease payments on a luxury car for the owner's son at college, and payment of cable television fees for the owner's mother.

Medicare also requires home health agencies to disclose in their cost reports the identity of related parties with whom they conduct business, in order to adjust costs that are likely to be inflated by health care providers who self-deal (i.e., purchase goods or services from related companies). A related party issue exists when there is common control or common interest between the provider and the organization with whom it is doing business. OIG has investigated home health agencies which failed to disclose ownership or other relationships with entities with whom they contracted for accounting services, management/consulting services, and medical supplies. These agencies billed Medicare unallowable amounts for marked-up supplies and services.

Paying Or Receiving Kickbacks In Exchange For Medicare or Medicaid Referrals

Kickbacks in exchange for the referral of reimbursable home health services is another type of fraud that OIG has observed. The Medicare program guarantees freedom of choice to its beneficiaries in the selection of health care providers. Because kickbacks violate that principle and also increase the cost of care, they are prohibited under the Medicare and Medicaid programs. Under the anti-kickback statute, it is illegal to knowingly and willfully solicit, receive, offer or pay anything of value to induce, or in return for, referring, recommending or arranging for the furnishing of any item or service payable by Medicare or Medicaid.

OIG is aware of home health providers offering kickbacks to physicians, beneficiaries, hospitals, and rest homes in return for referrals. Kickbacks have taken the following forms:

- Payment of a fee to a physician for each plan of care certified by the physician on behalf of the home health agency.
- Disguising referral fees as salaries by paying referring physicians for services not rendered, or in excess of fair market value for services rendered.
- Offering free services to beneficiaries, including transportation and meals, if they agree to switch home health providers.
- Providing hospitals with discharge planners, home care coordinators, or home care liaisons in order to induce referrals.
- Providing free services, such as 24 hour nursing coverage, to retirement homes or adult congregate living facilities in return for home health referrals.
- Subcontracting with retirement homes or adult congregate living facilities for the provision of home

health services, to induce the facility to make referrals to the agency.

Parties that violate the anti-kickback statute may be criminally prosecuted, and also may be subject to exclusion from the Medicare and Medicaid programs.

Marketing Uncovered Or Unneeded Home Care Services to Beneficiaries

OIG has learned of high pressure sales tactics employed by some agencies in the home health community to maximize their patient population and their profits. These agencies target healthy beneficiaries on the street or in their homes and offer non-covered services, such as grocery shopping or housekeeping, in exchange for Medicare identification numbers. Physicians have also reported that some agencies attempt to pressure them to order unnecessary personal care services by informing them that their patients are requesting these services and will find another physician if their demands are not met.

These abusive marketing practices can result in false claims liability on the part of agencies and/or physicians, and may also constitute illegal kickbacks.

III. Special Fraud Alert: Medical Supplies to Nursing Facilities

(August 1995)

The Office of Inspector General was established at the Department of Health and Human Services by Congress in 1976 to identify and eliminate fraud, abuse and waste in Health and Human Services programs and to promote efficiency and economy in departmental operations. The OIG carries out this mission through a nationwide program of audits, investigations and inspections.

To help reduce fraud and abuse in the Medicare and Medicaid programs, the OIG actively investigates schemes to fraudulently obtain money from these programs and, when appropriate, issues Special Fraud Alerts which identify segments of the health care industry that are particularly vulnerable to abuse. This Special Fraud Alert focuses on the provision of medical supplies to nursing facilities and identifies some of the illegal practices that the OIG has uncovered.

How Nursing Facility Benefits are Reimbursed

Many nursing facilities receive reimbursement from Medicare and Medicaid for care and services provided to eligible residents. Under Medicare Part A, skilled nursing facility services are paid on the basis of cost, and compensate the provider for covered nursing stays of a limited length. For Medicaid-eligible residents, extended nursing facility stays may be reimbursed by state-administered programs financed in part by Medicaid. Nursing facility residents may be concurrently eligible for benefits under Medicare Part B. These benefits may include payment for medically necessary equipment, prosthetic devices and supplies.

Nursing facilities and their residents have become common targets for fraudulent schemes involving medical supplies. The OIG has become aware of a number of fraudulent arrangements by which medical suppliers profit from inappropriate business dealings, in the name of unwitting nursing facility residents.

Sometimes, nursing facility management and staff also are involved in these schemes.

False or Fraudulent Claims Relating to the Provision of Medical Supplies

The government may prosecute persons who submit or cause the submission of false or fraudulent claims to the Medicare or Medicaid program. Examples of false or fraudulent claims include claims for items that were never provided or were not provided as claimed, duplicate claims submitted for the same item, and claims for items that the supplier knows are not medically necessary.

Submitting or causing false claims to be submitted to Medicare or Medicaid may subject the individual or entity to criminal prosecution, civil penalties including treble damages, and exclusion from participation in the Medicare and Medicaid programs. The OIG has uncovered the following types of fraudulent transactions related to the provision of medical supplies to nursing facilities.

Claims for Medical Supplies and Equipment That Are Not Medically Necessary

• Many of the supplies and equipment used in the care of nursing facility residents are provided by the nursing facility and should be reflected in the facility's Medicare cost report. The OIG has uncovered numerous instances in which suppliers provide the nursing facility with general medical supplies such as tape, adhesive remover, skin creams and syringes, but rather than bill the facility, the supplier submits claims to Medicare Part B. The claims misrepresent that the items are medically necessary for individual beneficiaries and therefore reimbursable under Part B.

For example, one supplier billed Part B for an "oral/nasal hygiene program" which consisted of supplies, such as saline solution, latex gloves and cotton swabs, marketed as prepackaged kits. Upon investigation, the OIG determined that these items, which were shipped to the facility in bulk quantities, were neither medically necessary, nor used for the care of the residents identified on the claims. In such a case, the supplier may be liable under criminal, civil and administrative laws for submitting fraudulent claims. The nursing facility may also be liable if the OIG determines that the nursing facility knew or should have known that the claims were false and participated in the offense.

Claims for Items That Are Not Provided as Claimed or Double Billed

• Many inappropriate transactions involve marketing of incontinence supplies. In one case, a supplier was found to have delivered adult diapers, which are not covered by Medicare Part B, and improperly billed these items as expensive prosthetic devices called "female external urinary collection devices." In another case, a supplier delivered only incontinence care products, such as lubricants and cleansers. These items are covered only as accessories to medically necessary prosthetic devices such as female external urinary collection devices. Medicare received bills for each accessory, even though the primary item was not provided.

• In some cases, multiple payments are made for particular items shipped to nursing facilities. For instance, a nursing facility ordered and accepted delivery of certain medical supplies for the facility's general use. The nursing facility appropriately claimed the supplies as expenses related to patient care on its Medicare cost report. However, the supplier also submitted separate claims to Medicare Part B on behalf of each resident in the facility. In order to receive Part B reimbursement, the supplier misrepresented its entitlement to payment, as well as the eligibility and coverage of individual beneficiaries. Other payment sources, such as Medicaid or private payers, may also have been billed by the supplier. The supplier may be liable under criminal, civil and administrative provisions if the supplier claimed falsely that the beneficiary met the required eligibility and coverage criteria. The nursing facility may also be liable for falsifying its Part A cost report if it knew or should have known of the duplicate billing and participated in the offense.

Paying or Receiving Kickbacks in Exchange for Medicare or Medicaid Referrals

It is illegal under the anti-kickback statute to knowingly and willfully solicit, receive, offer or pay remuneration in cash or in kind to induce or in return for referring, recommending or arranging for the furnishing of any item or service payable by Medicare or Medicaid.

Violation of the anti-kickback statute may carry criminal penalties, program exclusion, or both. Immunity may be available where otherwise illegal conduct meets the criteria specified in "safe harbor" regulations published by the Secretary of the Department of Health and Human Services. These regulations may be found in 42 CFR part 1001.

- A supplier gives a nursing facility non-covered medical products at no charge, provided the facility assists in the ordering of Medicare-reimbursed products. For instance, incontinence care kits may consist of reimbursable supplies as well as non-reimbursable items, such as disposable underpads or adult diapers. The OIG has identified instances where suppliers have billed the program for providing nursing facilities with thousands of medical supplies contained within incontinence kits which were not medically necessary for the care of the patients. The nursing facilities accepted delivery of the kits, removed the diapers and other items useful in general patient care, and discarded the remainder of the kits. At the same time, the supplier received Medicare reimbursement for shipment of products which were not medically necessary and often not used.

Both the supplier and the nursing facility may be liable for false claims as in the previous examples. However, both parties may also be liable under the anti-kickback statute, if one purpose of providing the free diaper was to induce the nursing facility to arrange for the procurement of items paid for by Medicare or Medicaid.

Other Examples of Fraudulent Practices

The OIG has received many complaints from nursing facility administrators and staff about suppliers that deliver unordered goods which are billed to Medicare. Analysts and investigators also have found that many nursing facilities do not always report such abuses, perhaps because the nursing facilities may gain a benefit from the use of these "free" supplies. In other cases, nursing facilities actively solicit unauthorized deliveries or other items of value, such as cash and in-kind rewards. In exchange, the nursing facility offers the equipment supplier access to patients' medical records and other information needed to bill Medicare.

Note: Under 42 CFR 483.10(e), it is a violation of a resident's rights, and therefore of the facility's conditions of participation, to make unauthorized disclosures from the resident's medical records.

- The OIG has investigated suppliers who supply nursing facilities with low-cost items, but submit Part B claims for high-priced items. For instance, one supplier provided simple restraining devices, but claimed that custom-made orthotic body jackets were provided to specified Part B beneficiaries.
- The OIG also has investigated a case in which a supplier gathered information on the death of nursing facility residents. Immediately thereafter, the supplier back-dated orders of medical supplies in quantities consistent with Medicare's 30-day limitation on after-death shipments.

What To Look For in Nursing Facility Supply Transactions

Suppliers engaged in the fraudulent schemes described above attempt to avoid detection in a variety of ways. Nursing facility administrators and staff aware of supplier fraud may be bribed through the payment of kickbacks and other illegal remuneration. Also, beneficiaries may be kept unaware of fraudulent billings if a supplier routinely "waives," or fails to collect, co-payments from the residents for Part B items. The following factors may also indicate improper supply transactions:

- Excessive volumes of medical supplies delivered to, or solicited by, nursing facilities and kept as inventory for lengthy periods.
- Items provided directly to nursing facility residents that are unordered, unnecessary or unused.
- Unusually active presence in nursing facilities of medical supply sales representatives who are given, or request, unlimited access to patient medical records.
- Questionable documentation for medical necessity of supplies.

IV. Contacting the OIG About Fraud and Abuse

The following common language is set forth in both OIG Special Fraud Alerts:

What To do If You Have Information About Fraud and Abuse Against the Medicare and Medicaid Programs

If you have information about the types of activities described above, contact any of the regional offices of the Office of Investigations of the Office of Inspector General, U.S. Department of Health and Human Services, at the following locations:

Regions	States served	Telephone
Boston	MA, VT, NH, ME, RI, CT	617–565–2660
New York	NY, NJ, PR, VI	212–264–1691
Philadelphia	PA, MD, DE, WV, VA	215–596–6796
Atlanta	GA, KY, NC, SC, FL, TN, AL, MS (No. District)	404–331–2131
Chicago	IL, MN, WI, MI, IN, OH, IA, MO	312–353–2740
Dallas	TX, NM, OK, AR, LA, MS (So. District)	214–767–8406
Denver	CO, UT, WY, MT, ND, SD, NE, KS	303–844–5621
Los Angeles	AZ, NV (Clark Co.), So. CA	714–836–2372
San Francisco	No. CA, NV, AZ, HI, OR, ID, WA	415–556–8880
Washington, D.C.	DC and Metropolitan areas of VA & MD	202–619–1900

To Report Suspected Fraud, Call or Write: 1–800–HHS–TIPS, Department of Health and Human Services, Office of Inspector General, P.O. Box 23489, L'Enfant Plaza Station, Washington, D.C. 20026–3489.

Dated: August 4, 1995.

June Gibbs Brown,

Inspector General.

[FR Doc. 95–19731 Filed 8–9–95; 8:45 am]

BILLING CODE 4150–04–P

APPENDIX G3

INSPECTOR GENERAL PUBLICATION OF THE MEDICARE ADVISORY BULLETIN ON HOSPICE BENEFITS, NOVEMBER 2, 1995

Office of Inspector General

Publication of the Medicare Advisory Bulletin on Hospice Benefits

AGENCY: Office of Inspector General, HHS.

ACTION: Notice.

SUMMARY: This Federal Register notice sets forth a recently issued Advisory Bulletin, in conjunction with Operation Restore Trust, that identifies important eligibility and other information involving the current Medicare hospice benefit. This Advisory Bulletin has been made available to consumers, health care professionals and health care associations, and is now being reprinted in this issue of the Federal Register as a means of ensuring public awareness of the purposes of hospice care and the consequences of electing the Medicare hospice benefit.

FOR FURTHER INFORMATION CONTACT: Joel J. Schaer, Office of Management and Policy, (202) 619–0089.

SUPPLEMENTARY INFORMATION: This Medicare Advisory Bulletin is part of Operation Restore Trust—a joint effort among the Office of Inspector General (OIG), the Health Care Financing Administration (HCFA) and the Administration on Aging within the Department of Health and Human Services to combat fraud, waste and abuse in the Medicare and Medicaid programs. The purpose of this Advisory Bulletin is to inform consumers and health care professionals about certain questionable practices affecting Medicare's hospice program. The issuance calls specific attention to the possible misuse of the hospice benefit, as uncovered through collaborative work undertaken by the OIG and HCFA.

Specifically, the Advisory Bulletin highlights several practices which indicate that some hospice providers may have inappropriately maximized their Medicare reimbursements at beneficiary expense. These practices include:

- Making incorrect determinations of a person's life expectancy for purposes of meeting hospice eligibility criteria;
- Engaging in marketing and sales strategies that offer incomplete or inadequate information about Medicare entitlement under the hospice program to induce beneficiaries to elect hospice and thereby waive aggressive treatment options that Medicare would otherwise cover; and
- Encouraging hospice beneficiaries to temporarily revoke their election of hospice during a period when costly services covered by a plan of care are needed in order for the hospice to avoid the obligation to pay for such services.

A reprint of this Medicare Advisory Bulletin follows.

Medicare Advisory Bulletin—Questionable Practices Affecting the Hospice Benefit October 1995

The Department of Health and Human Services administers the Medicare program for the benefit of 38 million elderly and disabled Americans. In May 1995, the Secretary of Health and Human Services announced Operation Restore Trust, a joint project of the Office of Inspector General, the Health Care Financing Administration and the Administration on Aging. Among its objectives, Operation Restore Trust seeks to identify vulnerabilities in the Medicare program, and pursue ways to reduce Medicare's exposure to fraud, waste and abuse.

This Advisory Bulletin is a product of Operation Restore Trust. The bulletin describes some potentially abusive practices which have been identified through examination of the Medicare hospice benefit.

What Is Medicare's Hospice Program?

The goal of hospice care is to help terminally ill patients continue with their normal activities of daily living as comfortably as possible, while remaining primarily in a home environment. To achieve this goal, the Medicare program shifts the focus of medical attention from curative treatment seeking to reverse an underlying disease or condition to palliative or supportive care, including a wide range of medical, social, and emotional supportive services.

To be eligible for hospice services under Medicare, an individual must be certified as terminally ill by hospice medical staff and the individual's attending physician if he or she has one. Terminal illness is defined as a medical prognosis that the patient's life expectancy is 6 months or less if the terminal illness runs its normal course. The Medicare beneficiary's inclusion in a hospice program is voluntary and can be revoked by the beneficiary at any time.

The decision to elect the hospice benefit has significant consequences because the beneficiary waives the right to receive standard Medicare benefits, related to the terminal illness, including all treatment for the purposes of curing a terminal illness. Hospice coverage is divided into four discrete election periods, during each of which the beneficiary must be certified as terminally ill. The fourth and last election period has an indefinite duration, unless or until the beneficiary no longer meets the eligibility requirement of a prognosis of 6 months or less to live.

What Problems Have Been Identified?

In the course of reviewing trends in Medicare's hospice program, the Office of Inspector General has learned of activities that should be of concern to beneficiaries who are in hospice or who are considering the option of hospice. These questionable practices primarily involve issues of hospice enrollment and are the subject of ongoing analysis by the Medicare program and, in appropriate cases, investigations and audits by the Office of Inspector General. Some hospice providers, in efforts to maximize their Medicare reimbursement, may knowingly engage in one or more of the following activities:

- Making incorrect determinations of a person's life expectancy, for the purposes of meeting hospice eligibility criteria.
- Engaging in marketing/sales strategies that offer incomplete or inadequate information about Medicare entitlement and restrictions under the hospice program, in order to induce beneficiaries to elect hospice and thereby waive other treatment benefits.
- Encouraging hospice beneficiaries or their representatives to temporarily revoke their election of hospice during a period when costly services covered by the hospice plan of care are needed, so that the hospice may avoid the obligation to pay for these services.

Important Features of the Medicare Hospice Benefit

- *The hospice benefit is restricted to patients with a diagnosis of terminal illness and prognosis of 6 months or less to live.*

In several recent medical reviews of beneficiary eligibility for hospice, the Office of Inspector General has found significant inaccuracies in the determinations of terminal illness. These findings have prompted a concern that some hospices may intentionally misrepresent a condition as terminal in order to secure Medicare reimbursement. For instance, investigators have encountered hospices that asked nurse employees to alter notes in patients' records or to otherwise misrepresent patients' medical conditions, in order to falsify the existence of a terminal condition.

There have also been cases where physician certifications of terminal illness have been medically questionable. If a hospice submits claims to Medicare under circumstances where it knows of the absence of a terminal condition, the hospice may be liable for the submission of false claims. Criminal penalties can also be imposed against persons who knowingly and willfully make false representations about a patient's medical condition which are used to determine eligibility for payment of Medicare or Medicaid benefits.

• *A hospice should not refuse to address health care needs relating to a beneficiary's terminal diagnosis.*

Once a Medicare beneficiary elects hospice care, the hospice is responsible for furnishing directly, or arranging for, all supplies and services that relate to the beneficiary's terminal condition, except the services of an attending physician. Hospice beneficiaries have the right to receive covered medical, social and emotional support services from the hospice directly, or through arrangements made by the hospice, and should not be forced to seek or pay for such care from non-hospice providers.

When a beneficiary is receiving hospice care, the hospice is paid a predetermined fee for each day during the length of care, no matter how much care the hospice actually provides. This means that a hospice may have a financial incentive to reduce the number of services provided to each patient, since the hospice will get paid the same amount regardless of the number of services provided.

Medicare has received complaints about hospices neglecting patient needs and ignoring reasonable requests for treatment. One individual reported that his wife's hospice failed on three separate occasions to respond to telephonic requests for emergency services. He was forced to call a non-hospice physician who arranged for hospitalization. His wife's care required a 26-day length of stay. Although the hospital contacted the hospice the day following admission, the hospice did not visit the patient or in any way coordinate her care during the hospital stay.

The Office of Inspector General also has uncovered situations where duplicate claims were submitted by a hospice and other providers (such as skilled nursing homes and hospitals) for services related to the beneficiary's terminal illness. In a nationwide audit of services provided to Medicare beneficiaries enrolled in hospice programs, approximately $21.6 million was improperly paid to hospitals and nursing homes for the treatment of hospice beneficiaries. Hospices are required to make financial arrangements for hospitalization, nursing services and all other health care needs related to the beneficiary's terminal illness and included in the hospice plan of care. The cost of these services should be paid by the hospices.

• *A beneficiary has a right to expect a hospice to provide complete and accurate information about the consequences of hospice election and revocation.*

A hospice is obligated to inform beneficiaries or their representatives that by electing the hospice benefit, they waive all rights to curative treatment or other standard Medicare benefits related to the terminal illness, except for the services of an attending physician. Some hospices inappropriately induce beneficiaries or their representatives to enroll in the hospice program without explaining that hospice election results in forfeiture of curative treatment benefits under Medicare. For instance, some hospices have solicited the beneficiary's neighbors and friends, who in some jurisdictions may act as beneficiary representatives, and who may not be familiar with the beneficiary's medical condition. In these situations, the beneficiary and/or representative may not appreciate that traditional Medicare benefits will be denied once the hospice benefit is elected.

The Office of Inspector General also has learned of hospices which induce beneficiaries to revoke the hospice election if expensive palliative treatment, even for a temporary period, becomes necessary. As a consequence, beneficiaries may then be burdened with substantial co-payments that would not be charged under hospice. It is especially important to note that when a beneficiary revokes the hospice election during the last election period, re-enrollment in the Medicare hospice benefit will be precluded permanently.

You Should Be Alert to the Following Questionable Activities

• Hospice recruiters failing to notify prospective patients or their representatives that they will no longer be entitled to Medicare coverage of curative treatment if they elect the hospice benefit.

• Hospice personnel inducing beneficiaries to revoke their hospice election when more costly treatment is needed.

• A hospice refusing or failing to provide or arrange for needed care;

• Nursing home residents being induced to elect hospice but not receiving the additional benefits of hospice care;

• Non-hospice providers charging Medicare for services to hospice patients that hospices can and should provide, such as counseling or medical equipment.

What To Do With Information About Questionable Practices Involving Hospice

If you have questions about the scope of the hospice benefit or the care you are receiving in hospice, you should first consider discussing these matters with your attending physician or the hospice provider. If you wish to report questionable practices, call or write: 1–800–HHS–TIPS, Department of Health and Human Services, Office of Inspector General, P.O. Box 23489, L'Enfant Plaza Station, Washington, D.C. 20026–3489.

Dated: October 23, 1995.

June Gibbs Brown,

Inspector General.

[FR Doc. 95–27217 Filed 11–1–95; 8:45 am]

BILLING CODE 4150-04-P

APPENDIX G4

INSPECTOR GENERAL PUBLICATION OF OIG SPECIAL FRAUD ALERT: FRAUD AND ABUSE IN THE PROVISION OF SERVICES IN NURSING FACILITIES, JUNE 17, 1996

Federal Register / Vol. 61, No. 117 / Monday, June 17, 1996 / Notices 30623

Office of Inspector General

Publication of OIG Special Fraud Alert: Fraud and Abuse in the Provision of Services in Nursing Facilities

AGENCY: Office of Inspector General (OIG), HHS.

ACTION: Notice.

SUMMARY: This Federal Register notice sets forth a recently issued OIG Special Fraud Alert concerning fraud and abuse practices in the provision of medical and other health services to residents of nursing facilities. For the most part, OIG Special Fraud Alerts address national trends in health care fraud, including potential violations of the Medicare anti-kickback statute. This Special Fraud Alert, issued directly to the health care provider community and now being reprinted in this issue of the Federal Register, specifically identifies and highlights some of the illegal practices that the OIG has uncovered in the provision of nursing facility services.

FOR FURTHER INFORMATION CONTACT: Joel J. Schaer, Office of Management and Policy, (202) 619–0089.

SUPPLEMENTARY INFORMATION:

I. Background

The Office of Inspector General (OIG) issues Special Fraud Alerts based on information it obtains concerning particular fraudulent and abusive practices within the health care industry. These Special Fraud Alerts provide the OIG with a means of notifying the industry that we have become aware of certain abusive practices which we plan to pursue and prosecute, or bring civil and administrative action, as appropriate. The Alerts also serve as a powerful tool to encourage industry compliance by giving providers an opportunity to examine their own practices.

The Special Fraud Alerts are intended for extensive distribution directly to the health care provider community, as well as those charged with administering the Medicare and Medicaid programs. On December 19, 1994, the OIG published in the Federal Register the texts of 5 previously-issued Special Fraud Alerts (59 FR 65372), and indicated our intention of publishing all future Special Fraud Alerts in this same manner as a regular part of our dissemination of this information. Two additional OIG Special Fraud Alerts addressing home health fraud and fraud and abuse provisions of medical supplies in nursing facilities was published in the Federal Register on August 10, 1995 (60 FR 40847).

With regard to the provision of health care services reimbursed by Medicare and Medicaid to nursing facilities, this newly-issued Special Fraud Alert highlights such fraudulent practices as (1) making claims for services not rendered or not provided as claimed, and (2) the submission of claims falsified to circumvent coverage limitations on medical specialties. A reprint of this Special Fraud Alert follows.

II. Special Fraud Alert: Fraud and Abuse in the Provision of Services in Nursing Facilities (May 1996)

The Office of Inspector General (OIG) was established at the Department of Health and Human Services by Congress in 1976 to identify and eliminate fraud, waste and abuse in Health and Human Services programs and to promote efficiency and economy in departmental operations. The OIG carries out this mission through a nationwide program of audits, investigations and inspections.

30624 Federal Register / Vol. 61, No. 117 / Monday, June 17, 1996 / Notices

To help reduce fraud and abuse in the Medicare and Medicaid programs, the OIG actively investigates schemes to fraudulently obtain money from these programs and, when appropriate, issues Special Fraud Alerts which identify segments of the health care industry that are particularly vulnerable to abuse. This Special Fraud Alert focuses on the provision of medical and other health care services to residents of nursing facilities and identifies some of the illegal practices that the OIG has uncovered.

How Nursing Facility Benefits Are Reimbursed

There were 17,000 nursing facilities in the United States, as of June 1995. An OIG study reported that in 1992, Medicare payments to nursing facilities included Part B payments of $2.7 billion and Part A payments of $3.1 billion for covered stays in nursing facilities. When the Federal share of the $24 billion spent by Medicaid is factored in, the Federal cost of nursing care reached a total of approximately $20 billion.

Many nursing facilities receive reimbursement from both Medicare and Medicaid for care and services provided to eligible residents. Under Medicare Part A, skilled nursing facility services are paid on the basis of cost for covered stays of a limited length. Nursing facility residents may be concurrently eligible for benefits under Medicare Part B. For Medicaid-eligible residents, extended nursing facility stays may be reimbursed by state-administered programs financed in part by Medicaid.

Nursing facilities and their residents have become common targets for fraudulent schemes. Nursing facilities represent convenient resident "pools" and make it lucrative for unscrupulous persons to carry out fraudulent schemes. The OIG has become aware of a number of fraudulent arrangements by which health care providers, including medical professionals, inappropriately bill Medicare and Medicaid for the provision of unnecessary services and services which were not provided at all. Sometimes, nursing facility management and staff also are involved in these schemes.

False or Fraudulent Claims Relating to the Provision of Health Care Services

The government may prosecute persons who submit or cause the submission of false or fraudulent claims to the Medicare or Medicaid program. Examples of false or fraudulent claims include claims for items that were never provided or were not provided as claimed, and claims for services which a person knows are not medically necessary.

Submitting or causing false claims to be submitted to Medicare or Medicaid may subject the individual or entity to criminal prosecution, civil penalties including treble damages, and exclusion from participation in the Medicare and Medicaid programs. The OIG has uncovered the following types of fraudulent transactions related to the provision of health care services to residents of nursing facilities reimbursed by Medicare and Medicaid:

Claims for Services Not Rendered or Not Provided as Claimed

Common schemes entail falsifying bills and medical records to misrepresent the services, or extent of services, provided at nursing facilities. Some examples follow:

- One physician improperly billed $350,000 over a 2-year period for comprehensive physical examinations of residents without ever seeing a single resident. The physician went so far as to falsify medical records to indicate that nonexistent services were rendered.
- A psychotherapist working in nursing facilities manipulated Medicare billing codes to charge for 3 hours of therapy for each resident when, in fact, he spent only a few minutes with each resident. In a nursing facility, 3 hours of psychotherapy is highly unusual and often clinically inappropriate.
- An investigation of a speech specialist uncovered documentation showing that he overstated the time spent on each session claimed. Claims analysis showed that the speech specialist actually claimed to spend 20 hours with residents every day, far more time than possible. Further investigation revealed that some residents had never met the specialist, and some were dead at the time when the specialist claimed to have provided speech services to them.
- A company providing mobile X-ray services made visits to nursing facilities, and billed for taking two X-rays when only one was actually taken. The case also presented serious concerns about quality of care when the investigation revealed that company personnel were not certified to take X-rays.

Claims Falsified To Circumvent Coverage Limitations on Medical Specialties

Practitioners of medical specialties have been found to misrepresent the nature of services provided to Medicare and Medicaid beneficiaries because the Federally funded programs have stringent coverage limitations for some specialties, including podiatry, audiology, and optometry. For instance:

- The OIG has learned about podiatrists whose entire practices consisted of visits to nursing facilities. Non-covered routine care is provided, e.g., toenail clipping, but Medicare is billed for covered services which were not provided or needed. In one case, an investigator discovered suspicious billing for foot care when it was reported that a podiatrist was performing an excessive number of toenail removals, a service that is covered but not frequently or routinely needed. This podiatrist billed Medicare as much as $100,000 in 1 year for toenail removals. Investigators discovered one resident for whom bills were submitted claiming a total of 11 toenail removals.
- An optometrist claimed reimbursement for covered eye care consultations when he, in fact, performed routine exams and other non-covered services. His billing history indicated that he claimed to have performed as many as 25 consultations in one day at a nursing home. This is an unreasonably high number, given the nature of a Medicare-covered consultation.
- An audiologist made arrangements with a nursing facility and affiliated physicians to get orders for hearing exams that were not medically necessary. The audiologist used this access to residents exclusively to market hearing aids. In this case, the facility and physicians, in addition to the audiologist, could be held liable for false or fraudulent claims if they acted with knowledge of the claims for unnecessary service.

What To Look For in the Provision of Services to Nursing Facilities

The following situations may suggest fraudulent or abusive activities:

- "Gang visits" by one or more medical professionals where large numbers of residents are seen in a single day. The practitioner may be providing medically unnecessary services, or the level of service provided may not be of a sufficient duration or scope consistent with the service billed to Medicare or Medicaid.
- Frequent and recurring "routine visits" by the same medical professional. Seeing residents too often may indicate that the provider is billing for services that are not medically necessary.
- Unusually active presence in nursing facilities by health care practitioners who are given or request unlimited access to resident medical records. These individuals may be

Federal Register / Vol. 61, No. 117 / Monday, June 17, 1996 / Notices 30625

collecting information used in the submission of false claims.

• Questionable documentation for medical necessity of professional services. Practitioners who are billing inappropriately may also enter, or fail to enter, important information on medical charts.

What To Do if You Have Information About Fraud and Abuse Against the Medicare and Medicaid Programs

If you have information about the types of activities described above, contact any of the field offices of the Office of Investigations of the Office of Inspector General, U.S. Department of Health and Human Services, at the following locations:

Field offices	States served	Telephone
Boston	MA, VT, NH, ME RI, CT	617-565-2660
New York	NY, NJ, PR, VI	212-264-1691
Philadelphia	PA, MD, DE, WV, VA	215-596-6796
Atlanta	GA, KY, NC, SC, FL, TN, AL, MS (No. District)	404-331-2131
Chicago	IL, MN, WI, MI, IN, OH, IA, MO	312-353-2740
Dallas	TX, NM, OK, AR, LA, MS (So. District), CO, UT, WY, MT, ND, SD, NE, KS.	214-767-8406
Los Angeles	AZ, NV (Clark Co.), So. CA	714-246-8302
San Francisco	No. CA, NV, AK, HI, OR, ID, WA	415-437-7960
Washington, DC	DC and Metropolitan areas of VA & MD	202-619-1900

To Report Suspected Fraud, Call or Write

1-800-HHS-TIPS, Department of Health and Human Services, Office of Inspector General, P.O. Box 23489, L'Enfant Plaza Station, Washington, D.C. 20026-3489.

Dated: May 29, 1996.

June Gibbs Brown,

Inspector General.

[FR Doc. 96-15269 Filed 6-14-96; 8:45 am]

BILLING CODE 4150-04-P

APPENDIX G5

INSPECTOR GENERAL PUBLICATION OF OIG NOTICE: PUBLICATION OF THE MEDICARE BENEFICIARY ADVISORY BULLETIN ON HMO ARRANGEMENTS

58568 Federal Register / Vol. 61, No. 222 / Friday, November 15, 1996 / Notices

Office of Inspector General

Publication of the Medicare Beneficiary Advisory Bulletin on HMO Arrangements

AGENCY: Office of Inspector General, HHS.

ACTION: Notice.

SUMMARY: This **Federal Register** notice sets forth a recently issued Medicare Beneficiary Advisory Bulletin, developed in cooperation with the Health Care Financing Administration's Office of Managed Care, that identifies potential fraud and abuse issues related to the enrollment, the provision of services, and the disenrollment of Medicare program beneficiaries in health maintenance organizations (HMOs). This Advisory Bulletin has been made available to many consumer and health care association groups, and is now being reprinted in this issue of the **Federal Register** as a means of ensuring greater public awareness of beneficiary rights regarding HMO participation and services.

FOR FURTHER INFORMATION CONTACT: Joel J. Schaer, Office of Management and Policy, (202) 619–0089.

SUPPLEMENTARY INFORMATION: The Office of Inspector General was established by Congress to find and eliminate fraud, waste and abuse. It periodically issues Special Fraud Alerts and Advisory Bulletins to show Medicare beneficiaries where and how to look for potential problems. The Health Care Financing Administration's Office of Managed Care works to ensure that Medicare beneficiaries are given quality health care in their HMO plans.

This specific bulletin is designed to help beneficiaries identify and report improper practices, and should be helpful to Medicare beneficiaries who are thinking about joining an HMO as well as to those who are already enrolled. Specifically, this bulletin provides information about HMO obligations and beneficiary rights regarding HMO enrollment, including a Medicare beneficiary's rights to enroll in an HMO regardless of age or health status. It also gives detailed information on a beneficiary's rights to medical services, such as emergency and out-of-area care, their rights to disenroll, and provides examples of situations in which beneficiaries have the right to file a complaint or appeal an HMO's decision.

A reprint of this Medicare Beneficiary Advisory Bulletin follows.

MEDICARE BENEFICIARY ADVISORY BULLETIN

What Medicare Beneficiaries Need To Know About Health Maintenance Organization (HMO) Arrangements: Know Your Rights

Introduction

If you are thinking of joining a Medicare contracting health maintenance organization (HMO), or are enrolled in an HMO, this advisory bulletin gives you important information. In addition, this bulletin also tells you how you can get help and where you can make complaints if you believe any of your rights have been violated or the HMO has acted inappropriately.

What Are Medicare Contracting HMOs?

Medicare contracts with HMOs to provide a full range of Medicare benefits to you. Medicare contracting HMOs must give you all the health care services that are covered under the Medicare program, except hospice services (See your Medicare Handbook for specific details). In addition, HMOs may offer additional benefits, either at no charge or for an additional charge.

There are two types of Medicare contracting HMOs - risk HMOs and cost HMOs. Most HMOs are risk HMOs, and this bulletin deals exclusively with risk HMOs [1].

In general, if you enroll in a risk HMO plan, sometimes called a health plan or plan:

• You must get all of your medical care through the plan's doctors, hospitals, skilled nursing facilities, home health agencies, and other health care providers. You are "locked-in" to receive care through your HMO plan. You may, however, get emergency care and unforseen out-of-area urgently needed care when necessary from non-plan providers. Some plans may offer a point-of-service option which allows members to use non-plan providers in certain cases.

• You must select a primary care doctor participating in the plan. This doctor is responsible for coordinating your care. You must obtain a referral from this doctor in order to see a specialist or obtain other services through the plan.

Part I: Enrollment and Disenrollment Rights

Enrollment Rights

When you are considering enrolling in an HMO, the HMO:

• Must provide you with complete and accurate information

• Must enroll you without regard to your health status

• Must not offer you gifts or other financial inducements to encourage you to enroll.

Complete and Accurate Information

Before you decide to enroll in a plan, HMO sales, marketing or other plan representatives must give you complete and accurate information about the benefits and the services their HMO provides.

Make sure the HMO representative tells you whether the HMO offers any additional benefits besides those benefits covered under the Medicare program. If so, there may be limits on how often you can use the benefits or how much the HMO will pay for them.

For example, if you take prescription drugs, you should ask the plan before you enroll if the drugs you take are covered. If the drugs are covered, ask about whether there are limits to the coverage and whether you are required to use certain pharmacies.

[**Note:** Many plans do not cover all prescription drugs. Plans may set a maximum dollar amount on the drugs they cover each quarter or each year.]

In addition, the HMO representative must tell you if the HMO requires copayments for any services, including drugs, and the amount of such copayments.

[**Note:** Additional benefits and copayments may change each year.]

Make sure that sales, marketing or other plan representatives tell you about how their HMO operates and about all HMO providers and facilities that will be available to you in your area. This

[1] You should find out whether the HMO you are considering joining is a risk or cost HMO. If it is a cost HMO, be sure to request additional information about the operation and benefits associated with this type of plan. Some of the issues raised in this bulletin may also apply to cost HMOs.

includes the home health agencies and skilled nursing facilities associated with their HMO. Make sure you understand if there are any limitations on using the HMO-affiliated providers. For example, certain hospitals may only be used for special services such as transplants. Some doctors may only work at certain hospitals or with certain specialists.

Make sure you understand which primary care doctors will accept you as a new patient. Some doctors may not be accepting new patients. Also make sure you understand under what circumstances and how frequently you can change primary care doctors and what happens if any of your doctors leave the plan. In addition, sales, marketing and other plan representatives must tell you that you will be "locked-in" to the HMO and its providers once you enroll and what this will mean to you.

Sales, marketing and other plan representatives must tell you that when you enroll in a risk HMO, you cannot continue to use any of your current doctors or hospitals unless they are affiliated directly with the HMO.

If your current doctor is affiliated with the HMO, you still need to be sure that he or she can accept you as an HMO patient.

If you should choose to go to a doctor or hospital not affiliated with your plan, you will have to pay the entire bill yourself.

Sales, marketing and other plan representatives must clearly and accurately describe, and must not misrepresent, HMO benefits and services.

Medicare law prohibits HMO representatives from enrolling you in an HMO without your permission.

• You are not required to sign any HMO forms unless you are enrolling in an HMO. If a sales representative gives you a form to sign and you are not sure what it is, do not sign it. The plan may not ask you to sign what they say is either a form requesting more information, or an acknowledgement that you heard a sales presentation or received information about the HMO, if the form is really an enrollment form.

• Do not give the HMO your Medicare or Social Security number unless you are enrolling.

• HMO marketing representatives are not allowed to come to your home unless you have given them permission in advance. This restriction applies to any personal residence, including your room in a nursing home, rest home or assisted living arrangement.

If you received false, misleading or incomplete information, then you may have been improperly enrolled in an HMO. If so, you have the right to be retroactively disenrolled and to return to traditional Medicare coverage, or to enroll in another HMO.

[**Note:** Of course, you can disenroll from an HMO at any time. See Disenrollment section. Also, enrolling in a new Medicare HMO automatically disenrolls you from your current HMO.]

Enrollment Without Health Screenings

An HMO must enroll all eligible Medicare beneficiaries who want to enroll, regardless of their age, health status or the amount or cost of the health services needed.

HMOs are not allowed to make you undergo a health screening before you enroll. Pre-enrollment health screening or questions about your health or physical status are against the law. These screenings can be used by the HMO to identify sick beneficiaries and those with chronic conditions, and to discourage them from enrolling.

[**Note:** There are two exceptions to the rule about health screening before enrollment. An HMO can ask you whether you are receiving kidney dialysis or have received a kidney transplant, or whether you are receiving hospice services. If you are receiving these services or have these conditions, you can not enroll in an HMO.]

Before you enroll, sales, marketing or other HMO plan representatives should not ask:

• How often you visit the doctor
• How many doctors you have
• How many times you have been hospitalized in the last year
• Whether you have any conditions for which you take medicine on a regular basis, or
• Whether you exercise regularly.

Also be alert for improper screenings when an HMO requires or offers:

• Free physical exams before enrollment
• Free screening or diagnostic tests at health fairs or at marketing presentations.

In addition, watch for sales, marketing or other HMO plan representatives who tell you that the HMO would not be a good choice for you because (1) referrals to specialists would be limited, (2) you might have to wait for services, or (3) services would be more limited in an HMO.

After you enroll, the HMO may ask you questions, give you questionnaires to fill out, or give you a physical exam to assist them in providing your care.

Enrollment Without Being Offered Free Gifts or Other Inducements

It is illegal for an HMO to offer you free gifts or incentives to get you or anyone else to enroll in an HMO.

HMOs are not allowed to offer you free gifts to encourage you to enroll or as a reward for attending marketing presentations. They are not allowed to offer incentives to get you to recommend them to your friends either. These incentives are not allowed because they could affect your decision to enroll or to recommend that a friend enroll. It's okay for the HMO to offer promotional materials worth less than $10, such as key chains, mugs and calendars, as well as light refreshments at a marketing presentation, as long as these are given to everyone regardless of their decision to enroll.

Disenrollment Rights

Disenrollment Is Your Decision

Once you are enrolled in an HMO, you may wish to disenroll at some point. Whether you stay enrolled in or leave an HMO, it is your decision. Your HMO cannot try to keep you from disenrolling nor can the HMO try to get you to leave.

When You Decide To Leave Your HMO

HMOs must process written requests for disenrollment in a timely manner.

HMOs may not delay, withhold disenrollment information or forms, or otherwise make it hard for you to disenroll from a plan. If you want to disenroll from your HMO because you are unhappy or dissatisfied with services, or for any other reason, your HMO should help you disenroll. You must submit a written request to disenroll, and the HMO should help you complete any necessary paperwork.

[**Note:** Whoever has authority under State law to make health care decisions for you can enroll you in or disenroll you from an HMO.] You may also go to a Social Security office to disenroll from your HMO.

Make sure your HMO tells you the date when your disenrollment is effective. It is usually the first day of the month following receipt of your disenrollment request. If you get services from a non-HMO provider when you are still a member of your HMO, neither your HMO nor Medicare will pay.

[**Note:** If you disenroll from a HMO and have any pre-existing medical conditions, many Medicare supplemental insurance (Medigap) policies will not sell you a policy or will impose a waiting period for those conditions. That means you could be without supplemental insurance coverage for that condition for a period of time unless you enroll in another HMO. Also, some Medigap policies only have open enrollment periods once a year. Remember to look for a policy that will provide coverage for your pre-existing conditions, and will be available when you disenroll.]

If Your HMO Encourages You To Disenroll

The premiums that your HMO gets from the Medicare program are designed to reimburse the plan for all the covered services you need. The HMO is not allowed to try to get you to leave or to delay or deny you services because you need heart surgery, transplants, long term nursing or rehabilitative services or other expensive treatments.

Your HMO must not encourage you to disenroll:

- Because it will be expensive to treat your condition or meet your medical needs.
- By delaying expensive medical care for a long time, or by denying such care.
- By telling you that you can re-enroll in the HMO after you have received the necessary high cost services outside the HMO.

Unless you enroll in another HMO, if you disenroll from the HMO to get a specific service or procedure, you will have to pay any deductibles or coinsurance under the payment rules of the traditional Medicare program.

Part II: Your Rights to Medical Services in an HMO

The next part of this advisory bulletin tells you about your rights to medical services and benefits in a Medicare contracting HMO once you are enrolled.

Your Rights to Services

When you are enrolled in an HMO, you have a right to:

- Medically necessary care in a timely manner.
- Emergency medical care and unforseen out-of-area urgent care.

Your HMO must provide all medically necessary covered services. Covered services include all the benefits provided under the Medicare program and any additional services offered by the HMO.

Your HMO must have enough qualified primary care and specialty care doctors, as well as other health care providers and facilities, to provide you with all medically necessary covered services. If the HMO does not have enough qualified providers, it must arrange for services to be provided to you outside the plan at no extra cost to you.

HMOs must make necessary medical care and services available and accessible to you. The HMO may not:

- Create or permit delays like repeated busy signals when you call to make appointments.
- Make you wait an unreasonably long time for appointments.
- Unreasonably restrict the days or hours that you may be seen by the plan's providers.
- Create or permit unreasonable delays in arranging for surgery, hospitalization or other services by using review or approval mechanisms.
- Inappropriately deny or limit referrals to specialists in or outside the plan.
- Unreasonably limit the amount of nursing home, home health or therapy services.

Getting Emergency and Out-of-Area Care

Your HMO must pay for emergency care and for unforseen urgently needed out-of-area care you get from non-HMO health care providers, including necessary follow-up care.

Emergency Care

Emergencies are situations when you need medical care immediately because of sudden or suddenly worsening illness or injury, and the time needed to reach your plan doctor or hospital appears to you to risk permanent damage to your health.

Your HMO must not:

- Tell you that you can only get emergency care through its doctors and at its facilities.
- Require you to get prior authorization for emergency services.
- Deny your claim for emergency services after you get the services, because what appeared to be an emergency condition turned out not to be an emergency condition.

If you believe you have an emergency, you may seek emergency care outside the plan and the HMO must cover and pay for those emergency services you got from the outside provider. Your HMO must pay for all procedures performed during the evaluation and treatment of your emergency condition, unless those services were completely unrelated to the emergency condition. If possible, you should call (or have someone call) your HMO as soon as possible when receiving emergency care.

[**Note:** You should be aware that hospitals are required by law to provide screening for emergency medical conditions. If necessary, hospitals must provide stabilizing treatment or arrange for an appropriate transfer to another facility, whether or not your HMO authorizes these services. The hospital may not refuse to provide emergency services to you because your HMO will not authorize such services.]

Out-of-Area Urgent Care

Urgent care situations are when you have an unexpected illness or injury while you are temporarily outside the HMO's service area. Your HMO must pay for your urgent care if:

- Your illness or injury is unexpected; and
- You are temporarily away from the HMO service area; and
- Your illness or injury requires medical care which cannot be delayed until you return home.

If possible, you should call (or have someone call) your HMO as soon as possible when receiving out-of-area urgent care.

Transfers From Another Facility

An HMO may not attempt to transfer you back to its own facility from another facility outside its plan before the non-HMO facility decides that your condition is stabilized.

Coverage of Follow-Up Care

Your HMO must cover all medically necessary follow-up care related to your emergency condition, or unforseen out-of-area urgent care, provided outside the plan if that care cannot be delayed without adverse medical effects to you.

Part III: How To Make a Complaint

You should be aware that you and your HMO may disagree about what care is medically necessary.

You have the right to appeal if you believe that medically necessary care has been denied, reduced or terminated inappropriately.

Here are some examples of situations in which you have the right to appeal:

- Your doctor does not prescribe covered treatments or tests, refer you to a specialist, or does not admit you for hospital services you believe you need.
- Your HMO refuses to authorize or provide tests, treatments or referrals recommended by your primary care doctor.
- Your HMO does not authorize a second opinion on the need for surgery. (Second opinions are a Medicare covered benefit.)
- Your HMO or your doctor decides to reduce or terminate services you are already receiving, such as home health care or physical therapy, or decides to discharge you from a nursing home.
- You encounter an unreasonable delay or difficulty in arranging for surgery, hospitalization, tests, doctor visits or any other needed services, and you believe this is a way of denying you care.
- Your HMO will not pay your claims for emergency care or out-of-area urgent care you received from a non-HMO provider.
- A decision is made to discharge you from a hospital before you believe you are ready to be discharged.

[**Note:** When you are in the hospital and your HMO decides that you do not need to be there any longer, you can ask for immediate review by a Peer Review Organization (PRO). If you ask for a immediate review, you can stay in the hospital at no charge during the review. The review usually takes at least 24 hours.]

The Appeals Process

Your HMO is required to notify you when it denies, reduces or terminates services or payment for services. (Whether or not you have written notification, you may appeal.) The HMO must also provide you with written information about your appeal rights and the process you must follow, including time frames for each step.

The appeals process begins with your written request to the HMO asking it to review the denial, reduction or termination. If the HMO does not reverse its decision, the appeal automatically goes next to an independent review organization that contracts with Medicare to review HMO denials. If the review organization does not decide fully in your favor, you may request a hearing from Medicare.

If you need help in deciding whether to appeal, or if you have questions regarding what you must do to appeal, you can contact your local or State Insurance Counselling and Assistance (ICA) Program. Call the Medicare Hotline at 1–800–638–6833 to get the number of the ICA in your area.

Complaints About Quality

If you have complaints about the quality of care you have received by your HMO or any of its providers, including hospitals, skilled nursing facilities and home health agencies, you can complain to your HMO or a Peer Review Organization (PRO). PROs are groups of doctors and health care professionals that monitor the quality of care provided to Medicare beneficiaries. Call the Medicare Hotline or your ICA to get the number of the PRO serving your area (See Part IV: Where to Go For Help). The PRO will investigate your complaint.

Other Complaints

If you have other complaints about the HMO, such as physician demeanor or adequacy of the facilities, contact your HMO directly. Your HMO must have written procedures, including time frames, for investigating these types of complaints (also called grievances). The HMO representatives will review these complaints and notify you in writing of their conclusions.

Part IV: Where To Go for Help

What You Need To Do if You Believe Your HMO Is Not Meeting Its Obligations or May Be Violating Your Rights

- Complain directly to the HMO. You must write to your HMO asking it to reconsider its decision to deny, reduce or terminate care, coverage or payment. Every HMO is required to have a process to handle complaints, and the HMO must give you detailed information on how to file a complaint.
- Contact your local or State Insurance Counselling and Assistance Program (ICA) which has been set up to assist Medicare beneficiaries in resolving problems with, or answering questions about, their Medicare benefits. To obtain the phone number of your ICA, you can call the Medicare toll-free Hotline at 1–800–638–6833 or your local area Agency on Aging office. To obtain the number of your local aging office, you can call 1–800–677–1116 (the Eldercare locator number).
- Contact the HHS Office of Inspector General through its toll-free Hotline at 1–800–HHS–TIPS (1–800–447–8477), or contact the HCFA Medicare toll-free Hotline at 1–800–638–6833. Contacting one of these offices about improper practices will not resolve your individual problem, but may help to stop any improper practices.

Quiz Yourself

There are several important questions you should ask yourself regarding HMO participation.

Do you know:

- What lock-in into an HMO means?
- The role of your primary care doctor?
- How the HMO's referral process works?
- The HMO's rules and responsibilities about paying for emergency and out-of-area urgent care?
- Whether HMO enrollment is a good choice for you if you travel or are out of the HMO service area for long periods of time?
- How to disenroll from an HMO?
- How to complain if you have a problem?

Dated: October 18, 1996.

Michael Mangano,

Principal Deputy Inspector General.

[FR Doc. 96–28377 Filed 11–14–96; 8:45 am]

BILLING CODE: 4150–04–P

APPENDIX G6

OIG Notice of Intent to Develop Regulations: Solicitation of New Safe Harbors and Special Fraud Alerts

Federal Register: December 10, 1997 (Volume 62, Number 237)
Proposed Rules
Pages 65049–65053

DEPARTMENT OF HEALTH AND HUMAN SERVICES

Office of Inspector General

42 CFR Part 1001

Solicitation of New Safe Harbors and Special Fraud Alerts

AGENCY: Office of Inspector General (OIG), HHS.

ACTION: Notice of intent to develop regulations.

SUMMARY: In accordance with section 205 of the Health Insurance Portability and Accountability Act (HIPAA) of 1996, this notice solicits proposals and recommendations for developing new and modifying existing safe harbor provisions under the Federal and State health care programs' anti-kickback statute, as well as developing new OIG Special Fraud Alerts. The purpose of developing these documents is to clarify OIG enforcement policy with regard to program fraud and abuse.

DATES: To assure consideration, public comments must be delivered to the address provided below by no later than 5 p.m. on February 9, 1998.

ADDRESSES: Please mail or deliver your written comments to the following address: Office of Inspector General, Department of Health and Human Services, Attention: OIG-21-N, Room 5246, Cohen Building, 330 Independence Avenue, S.W., Washington, D.C. 20201. We do not accept comments by facsimile (FAX) transmission. In commenting, please refer to file code OIG-21-N. Comments received timely will be available for public inspection as they are received, generally beginning approximately 3 weeks after publication of a document, in Room 5541 of the Office of Inspector General at 330 Independence Avenue, S.W., Washington, D.C., on Monday through Friday of each week from 8:00 a.m. to 4:30 p.m.

FOR FURTHER INFORMATION CONTACT: Joel Schaer, (202) 619–0089, OIG Regulations Officer.

SUPPLEMENTARY INFORMATION:

I. Background

A. The OIG Safe Harbor Provisions

Section 1128B(b) of the Social Security Act (the Act) (42 U.S.C. 1320a-7b(b)) provides criminal penalties for individuals or entities that knowingly and willfully offer, pay, solicit or receive remuneration in order to induce business reimbursed under the Federal or State health care programs. The offense is classified as a felony, and is punishable by fines of up to $25,000 and imprisonment for up to 5 years.

The types of remuneration covered specifically include kickbacks, bribes, and rebates, whether made directly or indirectly, overtly or covertly, or in cash or in kind. In addition, prohibited conduct includes not only remuneration intended to induce referrals of patients, but remuneration intended to induce the purchasing, leasing, ordering, or arranging for any good, facility, service, or item paid for by Federal or State health care programs.

Since the statute on its face is so broad, concern has been expressed for many years that some relatively innocuous commercial arrangements are technically covered by the statute and are, therefore, subject to criminal prosecution. As a response to the above concern, the Medicare and Medicaid Patient and Program Protection Act of 1987, section 14 of Public Law 100–93, specifically required the development and promulgation of regulations, the so-called "safe harbor" provisions, designed to specify various payment and business practices which, although potentially capable of inducing referrals of business under the Federal and State health care programs, would not be treated as criminal offenses under the anti-kickback statute (section 1128B(b) of the Act; 42 U.S.C. 1320a-7b(b)) and would not serve as a basis for a program exclusion under section 1128(b)(7) of the Act; 42 U.S.C. 1320a-7(b)(7). The OIG safe harbor provisions have been developed "to limit the reach of the statute somewhat by permitting certain non-abusive arrangements, while encouraging beneficial and innocuous arrangements" (56 FR 35952, July 29, 1991). Health care providers and others may voluntarily seek to comply with these provisions so that they have the assurance that their business practices are not subject to any enforcement action under the anti-kickback statute or program exclusion authority.

To date, the OIG has developed and codified in 42 CFR 1001.952 a total of 13 final safe harbors that describe practices that are sheltered from liability, and is continuing to finalize 8 additional safe harbor provisions (see the OIG notice of proposed rulemaking at 58 FR 49008, September 21, 1993).

B. OIG Special Fraud Alerts

In addition, the OIG has also periodically issued Special Fraud Alerts to give continuing guidance to health care providers with respect to practices the OIG regards as unlawful. These Special Fraud Alerts serve to notify the health care industry that the OIG has become aware of certain abusive practices that the OIG plans to pursue and prosecute, or to bring civil and administrative action, as appropriate. The Special Fraud Alerts also serve as a tool to encourage industry compliance by giving providers an opportunity to examine their own practices. The OIG Special Fraud Alerts are intended for extensive distribution directly to the health care provider community, as well as those charged with administering the Medicare and Medicaid programs.

In developing these Special Fraud Alerts, the OIG has relied on a number of sources and has consulted directly with experts in the subject field, including those within the OIG, other agencies of the Department, other Federal and State agencies, and those in the health care industry. To date, eight individual Special Fraud Alerts have been issued by the OIG and subsequently reprinted in the Federal Register on December 19, 1994 (59 FR 65372), August 10, 1995 (60 FR 40847) and June 17, 1996 (61 FR 30623).

C. Section 205 of Public Law 104–191

In accordance with the Health Insurance Portability and Accountability Act of 1996 (Public Law 104–191), the Department is now required to provide additional formal guidance regarding the application of the anti-kickback statute and the safe harbor provisions, as well as other OIG health care fraud and abuse sanctions. In addition to accepting and responding to requests for advisory opinions to outside parties regarding the interpretation and applicability of certain statutes relating to the Federal and State health care programs, section 205 of Public Law 104–191 requires the Department to develop and publish an annual notice in the Federal Register formally soliciting proposals for (1) modifying existing safe harbors, and (2) developing new safe harbors and OIG Special Fraud Alerts. After considering such proposals and recommendations, the Department, in consultation with the Department of Justice, will consider the issuance of new or modified safe harbor regulations, as appropriate. In addition, the OIG will consider the issuance of additional Special Fraud Alerts.

On December 31, 1996, the Department published the first of these annual Federal Register notice solicitations (61 FR 69060) addressing proposals and recommendations for developing new and modifying existing safe harbor provisions under the Federal and State health care programs' anti-kickback statute, as well as developing new OIG Special Fraud Alerts. As a result, the OIG received a total of 32 timely-filed public comments from a cross-section of organizations, associations and other outside entities. In response to that solicitation, respondents raised a number of issues and comments on a variety of areas, including general comments concerning application of the existing safe harbor provisions, and specific concerns over the existing safe harbors presently codified in 42 CFR 1001.952 and those proposed in our September 1993 notice of proposed rulemaking. Respondents also recommended new safe harbors for, among other practices and arrangements: (1) physician ownership of hospitals; (2) provider sponsorship or support of continuing education programs for health care practitioners and facilities; (3) provision of cataract surgery-related prosthetic devices; (4) loans between parties in a position to refer or arrange for the referral of Medicare covered items; (5) de minimis gifts to beneficiaries for recommending new patients; (6) intercorporate transfers among entities delivering health care through integrated delivery systems; and (7) payments for purposes of physician retention.

Special Fraud Alerts were also suggested to address such areas as: (1) financial arrangements between hospitals and hospital-based physicians; (2) billing management consultants; (3) hospital discharges and transfers; (4) food vendor "value added" services; and (5) demands for discounts by Medigap insurers.

The array of proposals and recommendations received for new safe harbors and Special Fraud Alerts are summarized below, and are still under review within the OIG. When the OIG has fully assessed the merits of these recommendations, we will consider the promulgation of formal proposed regulations to create new safe harbors for those proposals deemed appropriate.

II. Summary of Previously Submitted Recommendations for New Safe Harbors and OIG Special Fraud Alerts

Set forth below is a summary of the major topics previously submitted for consideration in the OIG development of new safe harbors and Fraud Alerts. This listing serves to outline the major concepts and specific proposals received by this office as a result of the December 1996 solicitation notice. The OIG is currently taking these recommendations under advisement, and is *not seeking* additional public comment on *these* proposals at this time.

A. Proposed New Safe Harbors

Interface With the Stark Law

Commenters indicated that physician groups are closely regulated by both the anti-kickback statute and the physician self-referral laws, i.e., the Stark provisions. Since many existing safe harbors are similar but not identical to the statutory exceptions under the Stark law, commenters indicated that physician groups are forced to analyze much of what they do under two separate bodies of law, and are left with regulatory uncertainty. As a result, they recommended that the OIG conform safe harbors to the statutory and regulatory exceptions applicable under the Stark provisions, thus protecting any payment arrangement that meets an exception under the Stark provisions. We intend specifically to address this issue in the final regulations that are being developed in response to the September 1993 proposed rule.

Physician Ownership of Hospitals

Since physician investment in hospitals is expressly recognized under the Stark provisions, a recommendation was made for a companion safe harbor for physicians and group practices that hold ownership interests in hospitals to which they refer.

ASCs, CORFs and Similar Entities

Commenters recommended expanded safe harbors to cover ambulatory surgical centers (ASCs) owned by a group practice (even if not all members of the group are surgeons), and for ASCs that are owned in part by physicians and in part by hospitals or other non-physician investors, as long as the physician's return on investment is based on the performance of the ASC as a whole. A commenter also requested protection for physician ownership in other facilities where they practice, such as comprehensive outpatient rehabilitation facilities. We expect to address these issues in the final regulations being developed in response to our earlier safe harbor proposed rule.

Services Provided by Federally-Funded Community Health Centers

A safe harbor was suggested to allow Federally-funded community health centers to take advantage of opportunities to improve their services to disadvantaged patients, for example, by arranging for discounted services where the arrangement will produce a substantial benefit to a medically underserved population.

Continuing Education

One commenter recommended a safe harbor delineating the circumstances under which manufacturers, commercial laboratories and other providers can sponsor or provide continuing education programs to health care facilities and practitioners. This commenter believed that many educational opportunities may be foregone by practitioners who, at the request of the provider, may have to notify other local practitioners about the presentation to avoid the appearance of impropriety. The commenter was concerned that the OIG may consider a presentation to a single hospital, for example, as an inducement for Medicare referrals.

Cataract Surgery-Related Prosthetic Devices

A recommendation was made for a safe harbor addressing the referral of patients for eyeglasses, contact lenses and intraocular lenses. A commenter stated that eyeglasses and contact lenses sold by optical stores, regardless of who owns the establishment, are consumer items that are subject to specific controls by the Federal Trade Commission, as well as by State regulation and free market competition. With respect to a safe harbor for the provision of intraocular lenses during cataract surgery, the commenter indicated that patients during an operation are not in a position to shop elsewhere for these items, and the selection of these lenses is based on operative techniques and often cannot be done prior to surgery.

New Managed Care Safe Harbors

A new safe harbor was suggested to apply broadly to all Medicare and Medicaid contracting managed care plans that are in compliance with the applicable requirements under Medicare, and plans that are participating in the Health Care Financing Administration (HCFA) managed care demonstrations. A recommendation was also made to establish comparable safe harbor protection for managed care plans that are licensed or regulated by HCFA or State regulatory bodies, involving non-contracting organizations and their activities involved in providing and arranging care for Medicare beneficiaries. Further, a recommendation for new safe harbors was also received that would protect other managed care financial relationships, such as (i) payment arrangements between managed care organizations and manufacturers that relate to usage of the manufacturer's products by the managed care organization's enrollees and (ii) protection for preferred provider organizations that charge administrative fees to providers.

Intercorporate Transfers

Commenters recommended that a new safe harbor be created for integrated delivery systems that would address payments between related entities, including, among others, parent companies and wholly-owned subsidiaries. This safe harbor would serve to clarify permissible transfers of "remuneration" between and among physicians, hospitals, health plans and others who are delivering health care through integrated delivery systems.

Offering Flat Rates for Outpatient Surgery by Hospitals

With regard to outpatient surgeries, a commenter stated that providers should be able to charge Medicare patients in the same fashion as other patients, without fear of sanctions. As a result, they recommended a new safe harbor for flat fees for outpatient surgeries. The commenter suggested that this would enhance access to health services to the extent that the beneficiary would have a greater comfort level knowing the coinsurance charge at the time a procedure is scheduled rather than dealing with uncertainty of not knowing the precise amount of the coinsurance obligation until after the procedure has been billed.

Physician Retention

A new safe harbor was recommended for all physician retention efforts by hospitals, regardless of a hospital's location. The safe harbor would protect payments or benefits offered by hospitals and other entities to retain physicians and other practitioners in the service area.

Investments by Ambulatory Surgical Center (ASC) Administrators and Family Members

A commenter suggested a safe harbor to protect investment interests by certain non-practitioners who are actively involved with the delivery of health care services at an ASC in an administrative or managerial capacity. Since many ASCs are owned, in part, by facility administrators who have a vested interest in the success of the ASC, it was believed that these individuals should be allowed to invest in ASCs and participate in any profits generated by the facility at which they work with the protection of a safe harbor, much like surgeons would be allowed to invest in the ASC even if passive investors. The commenter also believed that a safe harbor should allow investment interests in ASCs to be held by family members of those individuals whose investment interests are protected by the safe harbor so long as those family members are not able to make or influence referrals to the facility. We expect to address this issue in the OIG's final regulations being developed in response to our earlier safe harbors proposal.

ASCs Located in Underserved Rural Areas

To encourage efficient and less-costly medical care delivery, it was recommended that all investments in an ASC in an area where there was previously no ASC or hospital, regardless of their source, should receive protection as long as the investments meet specific criteria set forth in the proposed safe harbor for investments in entities in rural areas. (Proposed revisions to § 1001.952(a)(4) were set forth in the OIG proposed rulemaking of September 21, 1993 (58 FR 49008).)

Loans

A commenter indicated that loans between a provider and practitioner are often the only available source of necessary capital in a community, and recommended protection for loans between parties who may be in a position to refer, recommend or arrange for the referral or recommendation of Medicare or Medicaid covered items or services.

Investments

Although there is a safe harbor under the anti-kickback statute for investment interests, a commenter believed that it expressly protects only payments in the form of "return paid to investors" on investments that comply with the safe harbor's requirement, but not expressly the investments themselves. They indicated that health care providers and practitioners often enter into legitimate business ventures in which the investors are potential recipients of referrals from the venture in which they are investing. As a result, the commenter recommended a new safe harbor to protect legitimate investments from the anti-kickback statute.

De Minimis Gifts

A commenter suggested a new safe harbor addressing de minimis gifts to beneficiaries for recommending a new customer to the provider. For purposes of this proposal, de minimis gifts would be small tokens of a provider's gratitude given to customers and community members who suggest the provider's services or products to other potential customers, consistent with the Internal Revenue Service's definition on limitation on all allowable business gifts. No safe harbor protection would be afforded where gifts, even if de minimis, were made to physicians and other practitioners in a position to influence patients.

Physician/Provider Sponsored Organizations

Commenters requested that a new safe harbor be created for physician/provider sponsored organizations (PSOs). The proposed safe harbor would protect payments to or by any provider, provider sponsor or provider service network for services to beneficiaries enrolled by an eligible organization under section 1876 of the Act in accordance with a full-risk or partial-risk contract. The commenter suggested that protection for PSOs would increase patient access to health care services and increase the health care options available to program beneficiaries.

B. Proposed New OIG Special Fraud Alerts

Limitation on use of Fraud Alerts

A recommendation was made to limit the use of Special Fraud Alerts to circumstances that raise concerns about serious and clear violations, rather than merely "questionable" practices.

Financial Arrangements Between Hospitals and Hospital-Based Physicians

A commenter stated that an increasing number of hospital-based physician agreements with hospitals compensate physicians for less than the fair market value of management and supervisory services they provide to hospitals, or require physicians to pay more than the fair market value for certain services provided by the hospital as a condition for entering into or renewing contracts. As a result, a Fraud Alert was recommended to discuss financial arrangements between hospitals and hospital-based physicians. A second commenter raised concern about the appropriate compensation for hospital-based physicians and physicians serving as medical directors. They recommended a new OIG Fraud Alert addressing services considered integral and not "incident to" physician services, and the proper use of nonphysician practitioners accompanied by the appropriate billing for their services.

Ambiguity in Billing Practices

A suggestion was made to provide clear direction regarding covered and non-covered services and appropriate billing practices and, in conjunction with section 231 of the HIPAA, define the term "pattern of billing for services" that the provider knew or should have known was not medically necessary. The commenter indicated that any Fraud Alert should specify that no sanctions would be taken for a pattern of billing for services considered to be medically unnecessary until the provider has been given written notice of the problem and an opportunity to desist from the billing practice.

Barring Demands by Medicare Supplemental Carriers for Discounts from Providers

Since Medigap carriers other than Medicare SELECT plans continue to seek discounts or waivers of copayment amounts from providers, it was recommended that the OIG clarify that is improper for Medigap insurers (other than Medicare SELECT in connection with Part A services covered by existing safe harbors) to seek discounts and waivers of Medicare coinsurance or deductible amounts.

Payment Arrangements Between Hospice Providers and Nursing Homes

Concern was voiced over certain compensation arrangements between hospices and nursing facilities, including skilled nursing facilities, that suggested suspect incentive arrangements that disguise referral fees as payments for services to such nursing facilities. A Fraud Alert was suggested to address the fact that when a hospice pays a nursing facility more than 95 percent of the Standard Medicaid Per Diem Reimbursement Rate, such arrangements may violate the anti-kickback statute.

Clinical Laboratory Personnel Within an ESRD Facility

A commenter recommended an amendment to the phlebotomy section of the OIG Special Fraud Alert—"Arrangements for the Provision of Clinical lab Services"—that was issued in October 1994. Under that section, a clinical laboratory's placement of a phlebotomist in a physician's office does not in and of itself serve as an inducement prohibited by the anti-kickback statute. However, the commenter indicated that certain tasks could implicate the statute if those functions that benefit the physician are performed by the phlebotomist. As a result, they proposed that the OIG highlight a similar practice of providing a clinical laboratory employee, or processor, to an ESRD facility on a full-time basis to relieve the facility of these duties.

Laboratory Contracting with Billing Management Consultants

It was suggested that a Fraud Alert be developed outlining the potential issues related to contracting with billing management consultants, the appropriate relationship between the facility and the consultants, and the liability of all parties involved in the contract.

Discounted Copayments and Deductibles

In light of new civil money penalty authority for Medicare providers who offer incentives to induce Medicare referrals, it was recommended that a Fraud Alert be developed addressing situations in which a copayment or deductible can be discounted.

Home Health Issues

With regard to the proper certification of Medicare beneficiaries for home health services, a recommendation was made to develop a Fraud Alert defining what is considered "home bound" and what actions should be taken to ensure that the beneficiary is appropriately certified and is eligible for home health services. The commenter also recommended that a Fraud Alert address home health agency procedures related to contacting patients upon discharge from the hospital, and claims for home health visits that occur prior to physician authorization for the visit.

Medicare as Secondary Payer

A commenter indicated that if primary coverage is not identified, Medicare may be billed inappropriately, thus leading to allegations of fraudulent billing. The commenter recommended a new Fraud Alert setting forth the appropriate process to determine primary coverage, and the level of diligence a facility must use to verify primary coverage.

Hospice Care

A new Fraud Alert was recommended outlining the appropriate method for determining life expectancy to meet hospice eligibility criteria, and the responsibility if a patient is subsequently found ineligible for hospice benefits due to an incorrect determination of life expectancy. It was also suggested that the Fraud Alert address billing issues associated with a hospice patient who is transferred to a hospital, and the instances when a hospital should bill the hospice instead of Medicare to avoid duplicate bills to Medicare for the same patient.

Hospital Issues

It was suggested that problems have occurred with PPS hospitals billing Medicare for discharging a patient when the patient was actually transferred to another PPS hospital or unit, and that the

OIG develop a Fraud Alert outlining instances in which a hospital may bill Medicare for a patient discharge and when the hospital must file a claim as a transfer.

Value Added Services

A new Fraud Alert was recommended to address concerns about vendors in the food service industry offering "value added services" to their institutional customers. The commenter stated that many of these practices, intended to induce the initiation or maintenance of a business relationship between parties, raised concerns under the anti-kickback statute since food service sold to health care institutions is reimbursed in part by Medicare and the State health care programs.

Further public comments on the proposals summarized above are not being solicited at this time.

III. Solicitation of Additional New Recommendations and Proposals

In accordance with the requirements of section 205 of Public Law 104–191, we are seeking additional recommendations from affected provider, practitioner, supplier and beneficiary representatives regarding the development of proposed or modified safe harbor regulations and new Special Fraud Alerts beyond those summarized above.

Criteria for Modifying and Establishing Safe Harbor Provisions

In accordance with the statute, we will consider a number of factors in reviewing proposals for new or modified safe harbor provisions, such as the extent to which the proposals would effect an increase or decrease in—

- Access to health care services;
- The quality of care services;
- Patient freedom of choice among health care providers;
- Competition among health care providers;
- The cost to Federal health care programs;
- The potential overutilization of the health care services; and
- The ability of health care facilities to provide services in medically underserved areas or to medically underserved populations.

In addition, we will also take into consideration the existence (or nonexistence) of any potential financial benefit to health care professionals or providers that may vary based on their decisions of whether to (1) order a health care item or service, or (2) arrange for a referral of health care items or services to a particular practitioner or provider.

Criteria for Developing Special Fraud Alerts

In determining whether to issue additional Special Fraud Alerts, we will also consider whether, and to what extent, those practices that would be identified in new Fraud Alerts may result in any of the consequences set forth above, and the volume and frequency of the conduct that would be identified in these Special Fraud Alerts.

A detailed explanation of justification or empirical data supporting the suggestion, and sent to the address indicated above, would prove helpful in our considering and drafting new or modified safe harbor regulations and Special Fraud Alerts.

Dated: December 1, 1997.

June Gibbs Brown,

Inspector General.

[FR Doc. 97–32150 Filed 12–9–97; 8:45 am]

BILLING CODE 4150–04-P

APPENDIX G7

OIG Notice: Publication of OIG Special Fraud Alert: Fraud and Abuse in Nursing Home Arrangements With Hospices

DEPARTMENT OF HEALTH AND HUMAN SERVICES

Office of Inspector General

Publication of OIG Special Fraud Alert: Fraud and Abuse in Nursing Home Arrangements With Hospices

AGENCY: Office of Inspector General (OIG), HHS.

ACTION: Notice.

SUMMARY: This Federal Register notice sets forth a recently issued OIG Special Fraud Alert concerning fraud and abuse practices involving nursing home arrangements with hospices. For the most part, OIG Special Fraud Alerts address national trends in health care fraud, including potential violations of the Medicare anti-kickback statute. This Special Fraud Alert, issued to the health care provider community and now being reprinted in this issue of the Federal Register, specifically identifies and highlights some vulnerabilities in nursing home arrangements with hospices and instances of potential kickbacks between nursing homes and hospices to influence the referral of patients.

FOR FURTHER INFORMATION CONTACT: Joel J. Schaer, Office of Counsel to the Inspector General, (202) 610–0089.

SUPPLEMENTARY INFORMATION:

I. Background

The Office of Inspector General (OIG) issues Special Fraud Alerts based on information it obtains concerning particular fraudulent and abusive practices within the health care industry. These Special Fraud Alerts provide the OIG with a means of notifying the industry that we have become aware of certain abusive practices which we plan to pursue and prosecute, or bring civil and administrative action, as appropriate. The Special Fraud Alerts also serve as an effective tool to encourage industry compliance by giving providers an opportunity to examine their own practices.

Special Fraud Alerts are intended for extensive distribution to the health care provider community, as well as those charged with administering the Medicare and Medicaid programs. To date, the OIG has published in the **Federal Register** the texts of 8 previously-issued Special Fraud Alerts (December 19, 1994, 59 FR 65372; August 10, 1995, 60 FR 40847; and June 17, 1996, 61 FR 30623), and we have indicated our intention of publishing future Special Fraud Alerts in this same manner as a regular part of our dissemination of such information.

With regard to nursing home arrangements with hospices, this newly-issued Special Fraud Alert discusses (1) the nature of hospice care and who is eligible to receive such care; (2) the reimbursement for hospice care provided by nursing homes; (3) the vulnerabilities in nursing home arrangements with hospices; (4) several suspected kickback arrangements that are designed to induce Medicare or Medicaid referrals. A reprint of this Special Fraud Alert follows.

II. Special Fraud Alert: Fraud and Abuse in Nursing Home Arrangements With Hospices (April 1998)

Office of Inspector General was established at the Department of Health and Human Services by Congress in 1976 to identify and eliminate fraud, abuse and waste in the Department's programs and to promote efficiency and economy in departmental operations. The OIG carries out this mission through a nationwide program of audits, investigations, and inspections.

To reduce fraud and abuse in the Federal health care programs, including Medicare and Medicaid, the OIG actively investigates fraudulent schemes to obtain money from these programs and, when appropriate, issues Special Fraud Alerts that identify segments of the health care industry that are particularly vulnerable to abuse. This Special Fraud Alert focuses on the interrelationship between the hospice and nursing home industries and describes some potentially illegal practices the OIG has identified in arrangements between these providers.

What Is Hospice Care and Who Is Eligible To Receive It?

Medicare's hospice benefit provides palliative care to individuals who are terminally ill. Palliative care focuses on pain control, symptom management, and counseling for both the patient and family. Medicare hospice payments increased from about $958 million for Fiscal Year 1993 to over $1.8 billion for Fiscal Year 1995. Although the hospice benefit is still a relatively small portion of total Medicare Part A expenditures (about 1.5 percent), it has grown considerably over the past several years.

In order to elect the hospice benefit, a Medicare beneficiary must be entitled to Medicare Part A services and certified as terminally ill, which is defined as a medical prognosis of a life expectancy of 6 months or less if the illness runs its normal course. A beneficiary who elects to enroll in a hospice program waives his or her rights to all curative care related to his or her terminal illness. Medicare will continue to pay for services furnished by the patient's non-hospice attending physician and for the treatment of conditions unrelated to the terminal illness.

The hospice must have a written plan of care which covers physician and nursing services; physical, occupational, and speech therapy; medical social services; home health aides and homemakers; short-term inpatient care; counseling; respite care; and medical supplies, including drugs and biologicals. Certain of the hospice services ("core services") must be provided directly to the beneficiary by employees of the hospice, while other non-core hospice services may be provided in accordance with contracts with other providers. However, the hospice must retain professional management for all contracted services.

Reimbursement for Hospice Care Provided in Nursing Homes

Medicare does not have a separate payment rate for routine hospice services provided in a nursing home. Because hospice services are typically provided to patients in their homes, the routine home care hospice rate does not include any payment for room or board. For services provided to patients in nursing homes, hospices receive the Medicare routine home care rate, which is a fixed amount per day for the services provided by the hospice, regardless of the volume or intensity of the services provided. Accordingly, where the hospice patient resides in a nursing home, the patient remains responsible for payment of the nursing home's room and board charges.

If, however, a patient receiving Medicare hospice benefits in a nursing home is also eligible for Medicaid, Medicaid will pay the hospice at least 95 percent of the State's daily nursing home rate, and the hospice is then responsible for paying the nursing home for the beneficiary's room and board. The specific services included in the daily rate payment are determined by a State's Medicaid program and may vary from State to State.

In addition to the room and board payment, a hospice may contract with the nursing home for the nursing home to provide non-core hospice services (i.e., those services which the hospice is not required by law to provide itself) to its hospice patients.

Vulnerabilities in Nursing Home Arrangements With Hospices

Hospice services may be appropriate and beneficial to terminally ill nursing home residents who wish to receive palliative care. However, arrangements between nursing homes and hospices are vulnerable to fraud and abuse because nursing home operators have control over the specific hospice or hospices they will permit to provide hospice services to their residents. An exclusive or semi-exclusive arrangement with a nursing home to provide hospice services to its residents may have substantial monetary value to a hospice. In these circumstances, some nursing home operators and/or hospices may request or offer illegal remuneration to influence a nursing home's decision to do business with a particular hospice.

Hospice patients residing in nursing homes may be particularly desirable from a hospice's financial standpoint. First, a nursing home's population represents a sizeable pool of potential hospice patients. Second, nursing home hospice patients may generate higher gross revenues per patient than patients residing in their own homes because nursing home residents receiving hospice care have, on average, longer lengths of stay than hospice patients in their homes. Also, there may be some overlap in the services that the nursing homes and hospices provide, thereby providing one or the other the opportunity to reduce services and costs. A recent OIG report found that residents of certain nursing homes receive fewer services from their hospice than patients in their own homes. Since hospices receive a fixed daily payment regardless of the number of services provided or the location of the patient, fewer services may result in higher profits per patient.

However, a hospice's access to nursing home patients depends on the nursing home operator. Nursing home operators may restrict residents to one or two hospice providers. While an exclusive or semi-exclusive arrangement can promote efficiency and safety by permitting the nursing home operator to coordinate care, screen hospice caregivers, and maintain control of the premises, it also enhances the value of the nursing home operator's decision. In these circumstances, some nursing home operators or hospices may request or offer illegal inducements to influence the selection of a hospice.

Paying or Receiving Kickbacks in Order to Induce Medicare or Medicaid Referrals

Because kickbacks can distort medical decision making, result in overutilization, and have an adverse effect on the quality of care patients receive, they are prohibited under the Federal health care programs, including Medicare and Medicaid. Under the anti-kickback statute, it is illegal to knowingly and willfully solicit, receive, offer, or pay anything of value to induce referrals of items or services payable by a Federal health care program.

The OIG has observed instances of potential kickbacks between hospices and nursing homes to influence the referral of patients. In general, payments by a hospice to a nursing home for "room and board" provided to a Medicaid hospice patient should not exceed what the nursing home otherwise would have received if the patient had not been enrolled in hospice. Any additional payment must represent the fair market value of additional services actually provided to that patient that are not included in the Medicaid daily rate.

Specific practices which are suspected kickbacks include:

- A hospice offering free goods or goods at below fair market value to induce a nursing home to refer patients to the hospice.
- A hospice paying "room and board" payments to the nursing home in amounts in excess of what the nursing home would have received directly from Medicaid had the patient not been enrolled in hospice.
- A hospice paying amounts to the nursing home for "additional" services that Medicaid considers to be included in its room and board payment to the hospice.
- A hospice paying above fair market value for "additional" non-core services which Medicaid does not consider to be included in its room and board payment to the nursing home.

- A hospice referring its patients to a nursing home to induce the nursing home to refer its patients to the hospice.
- A hospice providing free (or below fair market value) care to nursing home patients, for whom the nursing home is receiving Medicare payment under the skilled nursing facility benefit, with the expectation that after the patient exhausts the skilled nursing facility benefit, the patient will receive hospice services from that hospice.
- A hospice providing staff at its expense to the nursing home to perform duties that otherwise would be performed by the nursing home.

Parties that violate the anti-kickback statute may be criminally prosecuted or subject to civil monetary penalties, and also may be subject to exclusion from the Federal health care programs.

What To Do if You Suspect Fraud Involving Arrangements Between Nursing Homes and Hospices

If you have information about nursing homes and hospices engaging in any of the activities described above, contact any of the regional offices of the Office of Investigations of the Office of Inspector General, U.S. Department of Health and Human Services, at the following locations:

Field offices	States served	Telephone
Boston	MA, VT, NH, ME, RI, CT	617–565–2660
New York	NY, NJ, PR, VI	212–264–1691
Philadelphia	PA, MD. DE, WV, VA, DC	215–861–4586
Atlanta	GA, KY, NC, SC, FL, TN, AL, MS	404–562–7603

Field offices	States served	Telephone
Chicago	IL, MN, WI, MI, IN, OH, IA, MO	312–353–2740
Dallas	TX, NM, OK, AR, LA, CO, UT, WY, MT, ND, SD, NE, KS	214–767–8406
Los Angeles	AZ, NV, So. CA	714–246–8302
San Francisco	No. CA, AK, HI, OR, ID, WA	415–437–7960

To Report Suspected Fraud, Call or Write

1–800-HHS-TIPS (1–800–447–8477), Department of Health and Human Services, Office of Inspector General, P.O. Box 23489, L'Enfant Plaza Station, Washington, D.C. 20026–3489.

Dated: April 15, 1998.

June Gibbs Brown,

Inspector General.

[FR Doc. 98–10907 Filed 4–23–98; 8:45 am]

BILLING CODE 4150–04-P

APPENDIX G8

OIG News Release and Related OIG Provider Self-Disclosure Protocol

OIG NEWS RELEASE

For Immediate Release
Wednesday, October 21, 1998
Contact: Judy Holtz (202) 619–0893
Ben St. John (202) 619–1028

OIG Issues Guidance On Voluntary Disclosure of Health Care Fraud

The Department of Health and Human Services's Office of Inspector General (OIG) today unveiled an expanded and simplified program for health care providers to voluntarily report fraudulent conduct affecting Medicare, Medicaid, and other Federal health care programs.

Called the Provider Self-disclosure Protocol, it replaces a voluntary disclosure program pilot tested by the OIG over a two-year period. The Protocol, which is effective immediately, provides detailed guidance to health care providers that decide voluntarily to disclose irregularities in their dealings with the Federal health care programs. It will be published in the Federal Register and posted on the OIG's Internet site (www.hhs.gov/progorg/oig).

Unlike the pilot program, which was only available to certain health care providers in a few states and had strict eligibility requirements, the new program is open to all providers nationwide under significantly relaxed requirements for participation. While not protected from civil or criminal action under the False Claims Act, providers disclosing fraud are advised in the Protocol that the self-reporting of wrongdoing could be a mitigating factor in OIG's recommendations to prosecuting agencies.

"Major modifications have been made to the voluntary disclosure program in response to the needs of the many honest providers trying to do the right thing," Inspector General June Gibbs Brown said in announcing the revisions. "We have sought to address the concerns of the provider community by removing disincentives to participation while at the same time emphasizing that providers have a legal and ethical duty to identify and correct incidents of non-compliance with program requirements."

The pilot voluntary disclosure program was introduced in 1995 as part of Operation Restore Trust (ORT), a major anti-fraud initiative aimed at dishonest durable medical equipment, home health care, nursing home, and hospice care providers in California, Florida, Illinois, New York and Texas. To be eligible, an applicant had to be a corporate entity doing business in one of the ORT States in one of the provider industries being examined. Moreover, a participant had to disclose a matter that was not already under investigation by or known to a Federal or State law enforcement authority. In addition, the participant was required to sign an agreement to fully cooperate with authorities.

These requirements have been dropped from the Protocol. Now all health care providers doing business with Medicare, Medicaid or other Federal health care programs that want to disclose violations of law are eligible for acceptance into the program. There are no pre-disclosure requirements, applications for admission, or preliminary qualifying characteristics that must be met. If, after an initial assessment, a provider uncovers suspected fraud or other problems involving the Federal health care programs, the provider is urged to report the discovery to the OIG. The provider will have the option of doing a self-audit in conformance with OIG guidance. The Protocol offers a detailed step-by-step explanation of how a provider should proceed in reporting and assessing the extent of wrongdoing and how the OIG will go about verifying irregularities.

Self-reporting offers providers the opportunity to minimize the potential cost and disruption of a full scale audit and investigation, to negotiate a fair monetary settlement, and to avoid an OIG permissive exclusion preventing the entity from doing business with the Federal health care programs. Because a provider's disclosure can involve anything from a simple error to outright fraud, the OIG is not making any commitments as to how a particular disclosure will be resolved or the specific benefit that will enure to the disclosing entity. Providers are simply told that full disclosure and cooperation generally benefits the individual or company, and that OIG will report on the provider's involvement and level of cooperation to the

Department of Justice or other government agency affected by the disclosed matter.

Providers can benefit from using the self-disclosure protocol if resolution of the problem includes the imposition by the OIG of a Corporate Integrity Agreement (CIA). Providers under CIAs must meet government-imposed strictures to better ensure their compliance with program requirements. The OIG reports that there are two distinct benefits which a provider may expect when it enters into a CIA as part of the resolution of a voluntary disclosure:

1. Annual audits of an entity's billing operations that are required in CIAs, may be performed by internal or external auditors. Normally a CIA could require these annual audits to be performed by an inde- pendent review organization, such as a law firm or an accounting firm.
2. To the extent that any obligations required by the CIA replicate provisions that already exist in an entity's own voluntary corporate compliance program, those provisions may be deemed acceptable for the purpose of the entity meeting its obligations under the CIA.

"In establishing this new guidance, we are renewing our commitment to promote an environment of openness and cooperation," Inspector General Brown stated, adding, "we believe that we must continue to encourage the health care industry to conduct voluntary self-evaluations and provide viable opportunities for self-disclosure. The government alone can not successfully win the battle against health care fraud; health care providers must be enlisted in this effort."

As greater numbers of providers voluntarily adopt compliance programs, the OIG believes that the Provider Self-disclosure Protocol will serve as the mechanism for them to alert the government when an internal audit uncovers a systemic billing abuse or a hotline caller reports a fraud scheme.

Several providers contacted the OIG about self-disclosure options after the pilot program was launched, and nearly $8 million was recovered. The most recent settlement, in the amount of $840,000, was reached this week with Deborah Heart and Lung Center, a 161-bed, non-profit hospital in Browns Mills, N.J.

PROVIDER SELF-DISCLOSURE PROTOCOL

OFFICE OF INSPECTOR GENERAL

DEPARTMENT OF HEALTH AND HUMAN SERVICES

I. INTRODUCTION

The Office of Inspector General (OIG) of the United States Department of Health and Human Services (HHS) relies heavily upon the health care industry to help identify and resolve matters that adversely affect the Federal health care programs (as defined in 42 U.S.C. § 1320a-7b(f)). OIG believes that, as participants in the Federal health care programs, health care providers have an ethical and legal duty to ensure the integrity of their dealings with these programs. This duty includes an obligation to take measures, such as instituting a compliance program, to detect and prevent fraudulent, abusive and wasteful activities. It also encompasses the need to implement specific procedures and mechanisms to examine and resolve instances of non-compliance with program requirements. Whether as a result of voluntary self-assessment or in response to external forces, health care providers must be prepared to investigate such instances, assess the potential losses suffered by the Federal health care programs, and make full disclosure to the appropriate authorities. To encourage providers to make voluntary disclosures, OIG issues this Provider Self-disclosure Protocol (Protocol).

The concept of voluntary self-disclosure is not new to OIG. For many years, OIG has worked informally with providers and suppliers that came forward to cooperate with OIG to resolve billing, marketing or quality of care problems. In 1995, as part of the Operation Restore Trust (ORT) initiative, HHS and the Department of Justice (DOJ) announced a pilot voluntary disclosure program, which embraced OIG's longstanding policy favoring voluntary self-disclosure. The demonstration program was developed in coordination with representatives of OIG, DOJ, various United States Attorneys' Offices, the Federal Bureau of Investigation and the Health Care Financing Administration (HCFA). The pilot program was limited to five States (New York, Florida, Illinois, Texas and California) and four different types of providers (home health agencies, skilled nursing facilities, durable medical equipment suppliers, and hospice providers). It gave those qualifying entities a formal mechanism for disclosing and seeking the resolution of matters relating to the Medicare and Medicaid programs. In 1997, the pilot voluntary disclosure program was concluded. While there was limited participation in the pilot, OIG gained valuable insight into the variables influencing the decision to make a disclosure to the Government.

OIG believes it must continue encouraging the health care industry to conduct voluntary self-evaluations and providing viable opportunities for self-disclosure. By establishing this Protocol, OIG renews its commitment to promote an environment of openness and cooperation. The Protocol has no rigid requirements or limitations. Rather, it provides OIG's views on what are the appropriate elements of an effective investigative and audit working plan to address instances of non-compliance. Providers that follow the Protocol expedite OIG's verification process and thus diminish the time it takes before the matter can be formally resolved. Failure to conform to each element of the Protocol is not necessarily fatal to the provider's disclosure, but will likely delay the resolution of the matter.

OIG's principal purpose in producing the Protocol is to provide guidance to health care providers that decide voluntarily to disclose irregularities in their dealings with the Federal health care programs. Because a provider's disclosure can involve anything from a simple error to outright fraud, OIG cannot reasonably make firm commitments as to how a particular disclosure will be resolved or the specific benefit that will enure to the disclosing entity. In our experience, however, opening lines of communication with, and making full disclosure to, the investigative agency at an early stage generally benefits the individual or company. In short, the Protocol can help a health care provider initiate with OIG a dialogue directed at resolving its potential liabilities.

The decision to follow OIG's suggested Protocol rests exclusively with the provider. While OIG can offer only limited guidance on what is inherently a case-specific judgement, there are several considerations that should influence the decision. First, a provider that uncovers an ongoing fraud scheme within its organization immediately should contact OIG, but should not follow the Protocol's suggested steps to investigate or quantify the scope of the problem. If the provider follows the Protocol in this type of situation without prior consultation with OIG, there is a substantial risk that the Government's subsequent investigation will be compromised.

Second, OIG anticipates that a provider will apply the Protocol's suggested steps only after an initial assessment substantiates there is a problem with non-compliance with program requirements. The initial identification of potential risk areas should be less intensive and need not conform to the Protocol's suggested procedures. Similarly, when OIG conducts a national review of a particular billing practice, providers should consider the option of conducting a limited assessment of the practice under OIG review, rather than incur the expense of a comprehensive audit. In such cases, an audit that conforms to the Protocol's guidelines may be appropriate only in instances where a preliminary assessment suggests the provider has in fact engaged in the practices under OIG scrutiny.

II. THE PROVIDER SELF-DISCLOSURE PROTOCOL

Unlike the earlier pilot program, there are no pre-disclosure requirements, applications for admission or preliminary qualifying characteristics that must be met. The Provider Self-disclosure Protocol is open to all health care providers, whether individuals or entities, and is not limited to any particular industry, medical specialty or type of service. While no written agreement setting out the terms of the self-assessment will be required, OIG expects the commitment of the health care provider to disclose specific information and engage in specific self-evaluative steps relating to the disclosed matter. In contrast to the pilot disclosure program, the fact that a disclosing health care provider is already subject to Government inquiry (including investigations, audits or routine oversight activities) will not automatically preclude a disclosure. The disclosure, however, must be made in good faith. OIG will not continue to work with a provider that attempts to circumvent an ongoing inquiry or fails to fully cooperate in the self-disclosure process. In short, OIG will continue its practice of working with providers that are the subject of an investigation or audit, provided that the collaboration does not interfere with the efficient and effective resolution of the inquiry.

The Provider Self-disclosure Protocol is intended to facilitate the resolution of only matters that, in the provider's reasonable assessment, are potentially violative of Federal criminal, civil or administrative laws. Matters exclusively involving overpayments or errors that do not suggest that violations of law have occurred should be brought directly to the attention of the entity (*e.g.,* a contractor such as a carrier or an intermediary) that processes claims and issues payment on behalf of the Government agency responsible for the particular Federal health care program (*e.g.*, HCFA for matters involving Medicare). The program contractors are responsible for processing the refund and will review the circumstances surrounding the initial overpayment. If the contractor concludes that the overpayment raises concerns about the integrity of the provider, the matter may be referred to OIG. Accordingly, the provider's initial decision of where to refer a matter involving non-compliance with program requirements should be made carefully.

OIG is not bound by any findings made by the disclosing provider under the Provider Self-disclosure Protocol and is not obligated to resolve the matter in any particular manner. Nevertheless, OIG will work closely with providers that structure their disclosures in accordance with the Provider Self-disclosure Protocol in an effort to coordinate any investigatory steps or other activities necessary to reach an effective and prompt resolution. It is important to note that, upon review of the provider's disclosure submission and/or reports, OIG may conclude that the disclosed matter warrants a referral to DOJ for consideration under its civil and/or criminal authorities. Alternatively, the provider may request the participation of a representative of DOJ or a local United States Attorney's Office in settlement discussions in order to resolve potential liability under the False Claims Act or other laws. In either case, OIG will report on the provider's involvement and level of cooperation throughout the disclosure process to any other Government agencies affected by the disclosed matter.

III. VOLUNTARY DISCLOSURE SUBMISSION

The disclosing provider will be expected to make a submission as follows:

A. EFFECTIVE DISCLOSURE: The disclosure must be made in writing and must be submitted to the Assistant Inspector General for Investigative Operations, Office of Inspector General, Department of Health and Human Services, 330 Independence Avenue, SW, Cohen Building, Room 5409, Washington, DC 20201. Submissions by telecopier, facsimile or other electronic media will not be accepted.

B. BASIC INFORMATION: The submission should include the following:

1. The name, address, provider identification number(s) and tax identification number(s) of the disclosing health care provider. If the provider is an entity that is owned, controlled or is otherwise part of a system or network, include a description or diagram describing the pertinent relationships and the names and addresses of any related entities, as well as any affected corporate divisions, departments or branches. Additionally, provide the name and address of the disclosing entity's designated representative for purposes of the voluntary disclosure.
2. Indicate whether the provider has knowledge that the matter is under current inquiry by a Government agency or contractor. If the provider has knowledge of a pending inquiry, identify any such Government entity or individual representatives involved. The provider must also disclose whether it is under investigation or other inquiry for any other matters relating to a Federal health care program and provide similar information relating to those other matters.
3. A full description of the nature of the matter being disclosed, including the type of claim, transaction or other conduct giving rise to the matter, the names of entities and individuals believed to be implicated and an explanation of their roles in the matter, and the relevant periods involved.
4. The type of health care provider implicated and any provider billing numbers associated with the matter disclosed. Include the Federal health care programs affected, including Government contractors such as carriers, intermediaries and other third-party payers.
5. The reasons why the disclosing provider believes that a violation of Federal criminal, civil or administrative law may have occurred.
6. A certification by the health care provider or, in the case of an entity, an authorized representative on behalf of the disclosing entity stating that, to the best of the individual's knowledge, the submission contains truthful information and is based on a good faith effort to bring the matter to the Government's attention for the purpose of resolving any potential liabilities to the Government.

C. SUBSTANTIVE INFORMATION: As part of its participation in the disclosure process, the disclosing health care provider will be expected to conduct an internal investigation and a self-assessment, and then report its findings to OIG. The internal review may occur after the initial disclosure of the matter. OIG will generally agree, for a reasonable period of time, to forego an investigation of the matter if the provider agrees that it will conduct the review in accordance with the Internal Investigation Guidelines and the Self-Assessment Guidelines set forth below.

IV. INTERNAL INVESTIGATION GUIDELINES

All disclosures to OIG under the Provider Self-disclosure Protocol should include a report based on an internal investigation conducted by the health care provider. While a provider is free to discuss its preliminary findings with OIG prior to completion of its investigation, the matter cannot be resolved until a comprehensive assessment has been completed pursuant to the following guidelines:

A. NATURE AND EXTENT OF THE IMPROPER OR ILLEGAL PRACTICE: A voluntary disclosure report should demonstrate that a full examination of the practice has been conducted. The report should contain a written narrative that:

1. identifies the potential causes of the incident or practice (*e.g.,* intentional conduct, lack of internal controls, circumvention of corporate procedures or Government regulations);
2. describes the incident or practice in detail, including how the incident or practice arose and continued;
3. identifies the division, departments, branches or related entities involved and/or affected;
4. identifies the impact on, and risks to, health, safety, or quality of care posed by the matter disclosed, with sufficient information to allow OIG to assess the immediacy of the impact and risks, the steps that should be taken to address them, as well as the measures taken by the disclosing entity;
5. delineates the period during which the incident or practice occurred;
6. identifies the corporate officials, employees or agents who knew of, encouraged, or participated in, the incident or

practice and any individuals who may have been involved in detecting the matter;

7. identifies the corporate officials, employees or agents who should have known of, but failed to detect, the incident or practice based on their job responsibilities; and
8. estimates the monetary impact of the incident or practice upon the Federal health care programs, pursuant to the Self-Assessment Guidelines below.

B. DISCOVERY AND RESPONSE TO THE MATTER: The internal investigation report should relate the circumstances under which the disclosed matter was discovered and fully document the measures taken upon discovery to address the problem and prevent future abuses. In this regard, the report should:

1. Describe how the incident or practice was identified, and the origin of the information that led to its discovery.
2. Describe the entity's efforts to investigate and document the incident or practice (*e.g.,* use of internal or external legal, audit or consultative resources).
3. Describe in detail the chronology of the investigative steps taken in connection with the entity's internal inquiry into the disclosed matter including the following:
   a. a list of all individuals interviewed, including each individual's business address and telephone number, and their positions and titles in the relevant entities during both the relevant period and at the time the disclosure is being made. For all individuals interviewed, provide the dates of those interviews and the subject matter of each interview, as well as summaries of the interview. The health care provider will be responsible for advising the individual to be interviewed that the information the individual provides may, in turn, be provided to OIG. Additionally, include a list of those individuals who refused to be interviewed and provide the reasons cited;
   b. a description of files, documents, and records reviewed with sufficient particularity to allow their retrieval, if necessary; and
   c. a summary of auditing activity undertaken and a summary of the documents relied upon in support of the

estimation of losses. These documents and information must accompany the report, unless the calculation of losses is undertaken pursuant to the Self-Assessment Guidelines, which contain specific reporting requirements;

4. Describe the actions by the health care provider to stop the inappropriate conduct.
5. Describe any related health care businesses affected by the inappropriate conduct in which the health care provider is involved, all efforts by the health care provider to prevent a recurrence of the incident or practice in the affected division as well as in any related health care entities (*e.g.,* new accounting or internal control procedures, increased internal audit efforts, increased supervision by higher management or through training).
6. Describe any disciplinary action taken against corporate officials, employees and agents as a result of the disclosed matter.
7. Describe appropriate notices, if applicable, provided to other Government agencies, (*e.g.,* Securities and Exchange Commission and Internal Revenue Service) in connection with the disclosed matter.

C. The internal investigation report must include a certification by the health care provider, or in the case of an entity an authorized representative on behalf of the disclosing health care provider, indicating that, to the best of the individual's knowledge, the internal investigation report contains truthful information and is based on a good faith effort to assist OIG in its inquiry and verification of the disclosed matter.

V. SELF-ASSESSMENT GUIDELINES

To estimate the monetary impact of the disclosed matter, the health care provider also should conduct an internal financial assessment and prepare a report of its findings. This self-assessment may be performed at the same time as the internal investigation, or commenced after the scope of the non-compliance with program requirements has been established. In either case, OIG will verify a provider's calculation of Federal health care program losses and it is strongly recommended that, at a minimum, the review conform to the following guidelines:

A. APPROACH: The self-assessment should consist of a review of either: (1) all of the claims affected by the disclosed matter for the relevant period; or (2) a statistically valid sample of the claims that can be projected to the population of claims affected by the matter for the relevant period. This determination should be based on the size of the population believed to be implicated, the variance of characteristics to be reviewed, the cost of the self-assessment, the available resources, the estimated duration of the review, and other factors as appropriate.

B. BASIC INFORMATION: Regardless of which of these two approaches is used, the disclosing provider should submit to OIG a work plan describing the self-assessment process. OIG will review the proposal and, where appropriate, provide comments on the plan in a timely manner. At its option, OIG may choose to carry out any necessary activities at any stage of the review to verify that the process is undertaken correctly and to validate the review findings. While OIG is not obligated to accept the results of a provider's self-assessment, findings based upon procedures which conform to the Protocol will be given substantial weight in determining any program overpayments. In addition, OIG will use the validated provider self-assessment report in preparing a recommendation to DOJ for resolution of the provider's False Claims Act or other liability. Among the issues that should be addressed in the plan are the following:

1. *Review Objective:* There should be a statement clearly articulating the objective of the review and the review procedure or combination of procedures applied to achieve the objective.
2. *Review Population:* The plan should identify the population, which is the group about which information is needed. In addition, there should be an explanation of the methodology used to develop the population and the basis for this determination.
3. *Sources of Data:* The plan should provide a full description of the source of the information upon which the review will be based, including the legal or other standards to be applied, the sources of payment data and the documents that will be relied upon (*e.g.,* employment contracts, rental agreements, etc.).

4. *Personnel Qualifications:* The plan should identify the names and titles of those individuals involved in any aspect of the self-assessment, including statisticians, accountants, auditors, consultants and medical reviewers, and describe their qualifications.

C. SAMPLE ELEMENTS: If the provider, in consultation with OIG, determines that the financial review will be based upon a sample, the work plan should also include the sampling plan as follows:

1. *Sampling Unit:* The plan should define the sampling unit, which is any of the designated elements that comprise the population of interest.
2. *Sampling Frame:* The plan should identify the sampling frame, which is the totality of the sampling units from which the sample will be selected. In addition, the plan should document how the audit population differs from the sampling frame and what effect this difference has on conclusions reached as a result of the audit.
3. *Sample Size:* The size of the sample must be determined through the use of a probe sample. Accordingly, the plan should include a description of both the probe sample and the full sample. At a minimum, the full sample must be designed to generate an estimate with a ninety (90) percent level of confidence and a precision of twenty-five (25) percent. The probe sample must contain at least thirty (30) sample units and cannot be used as part of the full sample.
4. *Random Numbers:* Both the probe sample and the sample must be selected through random numbers. The source of the random numbers used must be shown in the sampling plans. OIG strongly recommends the use of its Office of Audit Services' Statistical Sampling Software, also known as "RAT-STATS," which is currently available free of charge through the "internet" at "www.hhs.gov/progorg/oas/ratstat.html".
5. *Sample Design:* Unless the disclosing provider demonstrates the need to use a different sample design, the self-assessment should use simple random sampling. If necessitated, the provider may use stratified or multistage sampling. Details about the strata, stages and clusters should be included in the description of the audit plan.

6. *Estimate of Review Time per Sample Item:* The plan should estimate the time expended to locate the sample items and the staff hours expended to review a sample item.
7. *Characteristics Measure by the Sample:* The sampling plan should identify the characteristics used for testing each sample item. For example, in a sample drawn to estimate the value of overpayments due to duplicate payments, the characteristics under consideration are the conditions that must exist for a sample item to be a duplicate. The amount of the duplicate payment is the measurement of the overpayment. The sampling plan must also contain the decision rules for determining whether a sample item entirely meets the criterion for having characteristics or only partially meets the criterion.
8. *Missing Sample Items:* The sampling plan must include a discussion of how missing sample items were handled and the rationale.
9. *Other Evidence:* Although sample results should stand on their own in terms of validity, sample results may be combined with other evidence in arriving at specific conclusions. If appropriate, indicate what other substantiating or corroborating evidence was developed.
10. *Estimation Methodology:* Because the general purpose of the review is to estimate the monetary losses to the Federal health care programs, the methodology to be used must be variables sampling using the difference estimator. To estimate the amount implicated in the disclosed matter, the provider must use the mean point estimate. The statistical estimates must be reported using a ninety (90) percent confidence level. The use of RAT-STATS to calculate the estimates is strongly recommended.
11. *Reporting Results:* The sampling plan should indicate how the results will be reported at the conclusion of the review. In preparing the report, enough details must be provided to clearly indicate what estimates are reported.

D. CERTIFICATION: Upon completion of the self-assessment, the disclosing health care provider, or in the case of an entity its authorized representative, must submit to OIG a certification stating that, to the best of the individual's knowledge, the report contains truthful information and is based on a good faith effort to assist OIG in its inquiry and verification of the disclosed matter.

VI. OIG's VERIFICATION

Upon receipt of a health care provider's disclosure submission, OIG will begin its verification of the disclosure information. The extent of OIG's verification effort will depend, in large part, upon the quality and thoroughness of the internal investigative and self-assessment reports. Matters uncovered during the verification process, which are outside of the scope of the matter disclosed to OIG, may be treated as new matters outside the Provider Self-disclosure Protocol.

To facilitate OIG's verification and validation processes, OIG must have access to all audit work papers and other supporting documents without the assertion of privileges or limitations on the information produced. In the normal course of verification, OIG will not request production of written communications subject to the attorney-client privilege. There may be documents or other materials, however, that may be covered by the work product doctrine, but which OIG believes are critical to resolving the disclosure. OIG is prepared to discuss with provider's counsel ways to gain access to the underlying information without the need to waive the protections provided by an appropriately asserted claim of privilege.

VII. PAYMENTS

Because of the need to verify the information provided by a disclosing health provider, OIG will not accept payments of presumed overpayments determined by the health care provider prior to the completion of OIG's inquiry. However, the provider is encouraged to place the overpayment amount in an interest-bearing escrow account to minimize further losses. While the matter is under OIG inquiry, the disclosing provider must refrain from making payment relating to the disclosed matter to the Federal health care programs or their contractors without OIG's prior consent. If OIG consents, the disclosing provider will be required to agree in writing that the acceptance of the payment does not constitute the Government's agreement as to the amount of losses suffered by the programs as a result of the disclosed matter, and does not affect in any manner the Government's ability to pursue criminal, civil or administrative remedies or to obtain additional fines, damages or penalties for the matters disclosed.

VIII. COOPERATION AND REMOVAL FROM THE PROVIDER SELF-DISCLOSURE PROTOCOL

The disclosing entity's diligent and good faith cooperation throughout the entire process is essential. Accordingly, OIG expects to receive documents and information from the entity that relate to the disclosed matter without the need to resort to compulsory methods. If a provider fails to work in good faith with OIG to resolve the disclosed matter, that lack of cooperation will be considered an aggravating factor when OIG assesses the appropriate resolution of the matter. Similarly, the intentional submission of false or otherwise untruthful information, as well as the intentional omission of relevant information, will be referred to DOJ or other Federal agencies and could, in itself, result in criminal and/or civil sanctions, as well as exclusion from participation in the Federal health care programs.

APPENDIX G9

OIG Notice: Solicitation of Comments on the OIG/HCFA Special Advisory Bulletin on the Patient Anti-Dumping Statute

Federal Register: December 7, 1998 (Volume 63, Number 234) [Notices] [Pages 67486–67489]

DEPARTMENT OF HEALTH AND HUMAN SERVICES

Office of Inspector General and Health Care Financing Administration

Solicitation of Comments on the OIG/HCFA Special Advisory Bulletin on the Patient Anti-Dumping Statute

AGENCY: Office of Inspector General (OIG) and Health Care Financing Administration (HCFA), HHS.

ACTION: Notice of Proposed Special Advisory Bulletin.

SUMMARY: This **Federal Register** notice seeks the input and comments of interested parties on a Special Advisory Bulletin being developed by the OIG and HCFA designed to address requirements of the patient anti- dumping statute and the obligations of hospitals to screen all patients seeking emergency services and provide stabilizing medical treatment to enrollees of managed care plans if their condition warrants it. In developing this proposed issuance and soliciting public comment, it is our goal to provide clear and meaningful advice with regard to the application of the anti-dumping provisions, and ensure greater public awareness of the hospitals' obligations in providing emergency medical services to those individuals insured by managed care plans.

DATES: To assure consideration, comments must be delivered to the address provided below by no later than 5 p.m. on January 6, 1999.

ADDRESSES: Please mail or deliver your written comments and recommendations to the following address: Office of Inspector General, Department of Health and Human Services, Attention: OIG-33-SFA, Room 5246, Cohen Building, 330 Independence Avenue, S.W., Washington, D.C. 20201.

We do not accept comments by facsimile (FAX) transmission. In commenting, please refer to file code OIG-33-SFA. Comments received timely will be available for public inspection as they are received, generally beginning approximately 3 weeks after publication of a document, in Room 5541 of the Office of Inspector General at 330 Independence Avenue, S.W., Washington, D.C., on Monday through Friday of each week from 8:00 a.m. to 4:30 p.m.

FOR FURTHER INFORMATION CONTACT: Joel Schaer, Office of Counsel to the Inspector General, (202) 619–0089.

SUPPLEMENTARY INFORMATION: In an effort to identify and eliminate fraud, waste and abuse in the Department's health care programs, the OIG periodically develops and issues Special Fraud Alerts and, with the cooperation of HCFA, Advisory Bulletins to alert health care providers and program beneficiaries about potential problems. This proposed bulletin is being developed by the OIG and HCFA to address the principal requirements of the patient anti-dumping statute (section 1867 of the Social Security Act) and to discuss how the requirements of that statutory provision apply to individuals insured by managed care plans that require "prior authorization" for emergency services. We have attempted to conform this proposed bulletin with policies set forth in the HCFA State Operations Manual on Provider Certification (Transmittal No. 2, May 1998) which provides guidelines and investigative procedures for reviewing the responsibilities of Medicare participating hospitals.

Section 1867 of the Act imposes specific obligations on Medicare-participating hospitals that offer emergency services with respect to individuals coming to the hospital and seeking treatment of possible emergency medical conditions. Specifically, the draft Special Advisory Bulletin proposes to address: (1) The obligations of these hospitals in providing screening to all patients seeking emergency services and stabilizing emergency treatment to individuals seeking such care; (2) the special concerns in the provision of emergency services to enrollees of managed care plans; (3) the rules governing Medicare and Medicaid managed care plans with respect to prior authorization requirements and payment for emergency services; and (4) what types of practices will serve to promote compliance by hospitals with the patient anti-dumping statute when managed care enrollees seek emergency services. We would appreciate receiving specific comments, recommendations and suggestions on the issues discussed in this proposed bulletin.

Set forth below for comment is the proposed OIG/HCFA Special Advisory Bulletin addressing the patient dumping statute.

OBLIGATIONS OF HOSPITALS TO RENDER EMERGENCY CARE TO ENROLLEES OF MANAGED CARE PLANS

What Are the Obligations of Medicare-Participating Hospitals That Offer Emergency Services to Individuals Seeking Such Services?

• The anti-dumping statute (section 1867 of the Social Security Act; 42 U.S.C. 1395dd) sets forth the Federally-mandated responsibilities of Medicare-participating hospitals to individuals with potential emergency medical conditions.

• Under the anti-dumping statute, a hospital must provide to any person who comes seeking emergency services an appropriate medical screening examination sufficient to determine whether he or she has an emergency medical condition, as defined by statute. When appropriate, ancillary services routinely available at the hospital must be provided as part of the medical screening examination.

• If the person is determined to have an emergency medical condition, the hospital is required to stabilize the medical condition of the individual, within the staff and facilities available at the hospital, prior to discharge or transfer.

• If the patient's medical condition cannot be stabilized before a transfer requested by the patient (or determined to be in the patient's best interest by the responsible medical personnel), the hospital is required to follow very specific statutory requirements designed to facilitate a safe transfer to another facility.

• A hospital may not delay the provision of an appropriate medical screening examination or further medical examination and stabilizing medical treatment in order to inquire about the individual's method of payment or insurance status.

• Regulations implementing these statutory obligations are found at 42 CFR part 489. The anti-dumping statute is enforced jointly by the Health Care Financing Administration (HCFA) and the Office of Inspector General (OIG) of the U.S. Department of Health and Human Services (HHS).

•Sanctions that may be imposed by HHS for violations of the anti-dumping statute include the termination of the hospital's provider agreement, and the imposition of civil money penalties against both the hospital and the physician responsible for examination, treatment, or transfer of an individual. In addition, the anti-dumping statute provides for the exclusion of such physician if the violation is gross and flagrant or repeated.

Why Is There a Special Concern About the Provision of Emergency Services to Enrollees of Managed Care Plans?

Many managed care plans require their members to seek prior authorization for some medical services, including emergency services. As noted above, the anti-dumping statute prohibits a hospital's inquiry about a patient's method of payment or insurance status, or use of such information, from delaying a screening examination or stabilizing medical treatment. It has come to our attention that some hospitals routinely seek prior authorization from a patient's primary care physician or from the plan when a managed care patient requests emergency services, since the failure to obtain authorization may result in the plan refusing to pay for the emergency services. In such circumstances, the patient may be personally liable for the costs.

A reasonable argument can be made that patients (other than those arriving in dire condition) should be informed when they request emergency services of their potential financial liability for services. Some would go further and argue that the hospital itself should seek prior approval from the patient's health plan for emergency services to preserve the patient's right to seek coverage for such services. However, our concern is that, such an inquiry may improperly or unduly influence patients to leave the hospital without receiving an appropriate medical screening examination. This result would be inconsistent with the goals of the anti-dumping statute and could leave the hospital exposed to liability under the statute.

Investigations of allegations of the anti-dumping statute violations across the country have persuaded the OIG and HCFA that managed care patients may be at risk of being discharged or transferred without receiving a medical screening examination, largely because of the problems inherent in seeking "prior authorization." Hospitals sometimes are caught between the legal obligations imposed under the anti-dumping statute and the terms of agreements which they have with managed care plans. For example, some Medicaid managed care contractors, as a condition of contracting with hospitals to provide services to their enrollees, have attempted to require such hospitals to obtain prior authorization from the plan before screening or treating an enrollee in order to be eligible for reimbursement for services provided.

The OIG's and HCFA's view of the legal requirements of the anti-dumping statute in this situation is as follows. Notwithstanding the terms of any managed care agreements between plans and hospitals, the anti-dumping statute continues to govern the obligations of hospitals to screen and provide stabilizing medical treatment to individuals who come to the hospital seeking emergency services regardless of the individual's ability to pay. While managed care plans have a financial interest in controlling the kinds of services for which they will pay, and while they may have a legitimate interest in deterring their enrollees from over-utilizing emergency services, no contract between a hospital and a managed care plan can excuse the hospital from its anti- dumping statute obligations. Once a managed care enrollee comes to a hospital that offers emergency services, the hospital must provide the services required under the anti-dumping statute without regard for the patient's insurance status or any prior authorization requirement of such insurance.[1]

What About Arrangements Between Hospitals and Managed Care Plans for "Dual Staffing" of Emergency Departments?

Some managed care organizations (MCOs) and hospitals have entered into, or are considering entering into, arrangements whereby the hospital permits the MCO to station its own physicians in the hospital's emergency department, separate from the hospital's own emergency physician staff, for the purpose of screening and

[1] Separate and apart from the anti-dumping statute, in accordance with sections 1857(g), 1876(i)(6), 1903(m)(5) and 1932(e) of the Social Security Act, the OIG (acting on behalf of the Secretary) has the authority to impose intermediate sanctions against Medicare and Medicaid contracting managed care plans that fail to provide medically necessary services, including emergency services, to enrollees where the failure adversely affects (or has a substantial likelihood of adversely affecting) the enrollee. Medicare and Medicaid managed care plans that fail to comply with the above provision are subject to civil money penalties of up to $25,000 for each denial of medically necessary services.

treating MCO patients who request emergency services. This kind of arrangement is known as "dual staffing." In a dual staffing setting, two separate groups of physicians would be providing emergency care, perhaps using different policies and protocols, performing different procedures, using different referral practices and drug formularies, relying on different on-call physicians, and having different credentials.

It is believed by some that dual staffing in emergency departments can facilitate the expeditious provision of services to MCO patients by physicians and other practitioners in their own health plans, particularly when patients present in emergency departments in stable condition. However, some hospitals and emergency physicians have raised questions about how the requirements of the patient anti-dumping statute may affect dual staffing arrangements, and we have been considering how to respond. As interpreted by this Department, the statute requires that a hospital and its physicians provide medically adequate screening and stabilization, supported by professionally recognized standards of care, to individuals seeking emergency services. Theoretically, one could construct two equally good emergency service "tracks," each adequately staffed and each with equally good access to all of the medical capabilities of the hospital, such that both MCO and non-MCO patients received equal access to screening and stabilizing medical treatment. This arrangement would seem to satisfy the requirements of the anti-dumping statute.

Absent such equivalency, implementation of dual staffing raises some concerns under the patient anti-dumping statute. For example, what if either the MCO or non-MCO track is understaffed or simply overcrowded, and a patient in a particular track is subjected to a significant delay in screening and stabilizing treatment, even though a physician in the alternative track was available to see the individual? What if the protocols, referral patterns, use of specialists and patient guidelines are substantially different between the MCO and non- MCO tracks such that two different standards of care are provided in performing screenings or stabilizing treatment? How can a hospital be sure that all patients requesting emergency services receive, as required by statute, an appropriate screening examination within the full capabilities of the hospital, and necessary stabilizing treatment within the capability of the staff and facilities of the hospital, if the MCO track operates independently from the hospital's own emergency care system? These are difficult questions, and we have not yet determined how to treat issues related to dual staffing under the patient anti-dumping act. As a result, we are specifically soliciting comments and suggestions from the public on this issue, and we expect to offer some specific guidance in this area in the final version of this Special Advisory Bulletin.

What are the Rules Governing Medicare and Medicaid Managed Care Plans with Respect to Prior Authorization Requirements and Payment for Emergency Services?

There are special requirements for managed care plans that contract with Medicare and Medicaid to provide services to beneficiaries of those programs. Congress has specified that Medicare and Medicaid managed care plans may not require prior authorization for emergency services, and must pay for such services, without regard to whether the hospital providing such services has a contractual relationship with the plan. Under statutory amendments recently enacted in the Balanced Budget Act (BBA) of 1997 (Pub. L. 105- 33),[2] Medicare and Medicaid managed care plans are prohibited from requiring prior authorization for emergency services, including those that "are needed to evaluate or stabilize an emergency medical condition." Moreover, Medicare and Medicaid managed care plans are required to pay for emergency services provided to their enrollees. The obligation to pay for emergency services is based on a "prudent layperson" standard, which means that the need for emergency services should be determined from a reasonable patient's perspective at the time of presentation of the symptoms.[3]

---

[2] See section 4001 of the BBA, which created section 1852(d) of the Act. Section 1852(d) covers emergency services and prior authorization for Medicare enrollees. Also, section 4704(a) of the BBA created section 1932(b) of the Act, which contains Medicaid provisions covering emergency services and prior authorization.

[3] With respect to Medicare, prior authorization requirements were already explicitly prohibited by regulations before the passage of the BBA for emergency services provided outside an HMO or competitive medical plan (42 CFR 417.414(c)(1)), and by implication for services provided within such a plan. Similarly, while the BBA clarified and codified the "prudent layperson" standard, a variation of this standard has always been part of the Medicare policy for managed care plans. However, all of these requirements are new to Medicaid.

What Practices Will Promote Compliance with the Anti-Dumping Statute by Hospitals When Managed Care Enrollees Seek Emergency Services?

The OIG and HCFA are concerned that discussion by hospital personnel with a patient regarding the possible need for prior authorization, or his or her potential financial liability for medical services provided by a hospital that offers emergency services, could influence patients to leave the emergency department without receiving an appropriate medical screening examination. Without also informing the patient of his or her rights to a medical screening examination and to stabilizing medical treatment if the patient's condition warrants it, a discussion about insurance, ability to pay and seeking prior authorization may impede a hospital's compliance with its obligation under the anti-dumping statute. Discussions between a hospital staff member and a patient regarding potential prior authorization requirements and their financial consequences that have the effect of delaying a medical screening are violations of the anti-dumping statute. Moreover, the OIG and HCFA believe that in the absence of an initial screening, the decision of a managed care plan regarding the need for treatment is likely to be ill-informed. Patients are entitled to receive a medical screening examination and stabilizing medical treatment under the anti-dumping statute regardless of a hospital's contract with a health plan that requires prior authorization. Accordingly, the OIG and HCFA suggest the following practices to minimize the likelihood that a hospital will violate the statute:

• *No Prior Authorization Before Screening or Stabilization.* It is not appropriate for a hospital to request or a health plan to require prior authorization before the patient has received a medical screening examination to determine the presence or absence of an emergency medical condition or before the patient's emergency medical condition is stabilized.[4]

• *No Financial Responsibility or Advanced Beneficiary Notification Forms.* Prior to performing an appropriate medical screening examination, the hospital should not ask a patient to complete a financial

---

[4] Of course, this would not preclude an emergency physician from contacting the patient's physician at any time to seek advice regarding the patient's medical history and needs that may be relevant to the medical screening and treatment of the patient. Further, a patient who has not already contacted his or her health plan is free to do so at any time during his or her wait for emergency services.

responsibility form or an advanced beneficiary notification form, and should not ask the patient to provide a co-payment for any services rendered. Such a practice could deter the patient from remaining at the hospital to receive care to which he or she is entitled and which the hospital is obligated to provide regardless of ability to pay, and could cause unnecessary delay.

• *Qualified Medical Personnel Must Perform Medical Screening Examination.* A hospital should ensure that either a physician or other qualified medical personnel (i.e., hospital staff approved by the hospital's governing body to perform certain medical functions) provides an appropriate medical screening examination to all individuals seeking emergency services. Depending upon the individual's presenting symptoms, this screening examination may range from a relatively simple examination to a complex one which requires substantial use of ancillary services available at the hospital and on-call physicians.

• *When a Patient Inquires About Financial Liability for Emergency Services.* If a patient inquires about his or her obligation to pay for emergency services, such an inquiry should be answered by a staff member who has been well trained to provide information regarding potential financial liability. This staff member also should be knowledgeable about the hospital's anti-dumping statute obligations and must clearly inform the patient that, notwithstanding the patient's ability to pay, the hospital stands ready and willing to provide a medical screening examination and stabilizing treatment, if necessary. Hospital staff should encourage any patient who believes that he or she may have an emergency medical condition to remain for the medical screening examination and to defer further discussion of financial responsibility issues until after the medical screening has been performed. If the patient chooses to withdraw his or her request for examination or treatment, a staff member with appropriate medical training must discuss the medical issues related to a "voluntary withdrawal."

• *Voluntary Withdrawal.* If an individual chooses to withdraw his or her request for examination or treatment at the presenting hospital, a hospital must perform the following: (1) offer the individual further medical examination and treatment within the staff and facilities available at the hospital as may be required to identify and stabilize an emergency medical condition; (2) inform the individual of the risks and benefits of such examination and treatment, and of the risks and benefits of withdrawal prior to receiving such examination and treatment; and (3) take all reasonable steps to secure the individual's written informed consent to refuse such examination and treatment. The medical record should contain a description of the examination, treatment, or both, if applicable, that was refused.

In the event that an individual, *e.g.,* nurse, doctor, other emergency room staff member or patient, believes that a hospital may have violated the anti-dumping statute, that individual should report the alleged violation to the HCFA office in the region in which the hospital is located.

Dated: November 24, 1998.

June Gibbs Brown,

Inspector General.

Dated: November 24, 1998.

Nancy-Ann Min DeParle,

Administrator, Health Care Financing Administration.

[FR Doc. 98–32480 Filed 12–4–98; 8:45 am]

BILLING CODE 4150–04-P

APPENDIX G10

OIG Notice: Publication of OIG Special Fraud Alert on Physician Liability for Certification in the Provision of Medical Equipment and Supplies and Home Health Services

[Federal Register: January 12, 1999 (Volume 64, Number 7)]
[Notices] [Pages 1813–1816]

DEPARTMENT OF HEALTH AND HUMAN SERVICES

Office of Inspector General

Publication of OIG Special Fraud Alert on Physician Liability for Certifications in the Provision of Medical Equipment and Supplies and Home Health Services

AGENCY: Office of Inspector General (OIG), HHS.

ACTION: Notice

SUMMARY: This **Federal Register** notice sets forth a recently issued OIG Special Fraud Alert concerning physician liability for certifications in the provision of medical equipment and supplies and home health services. For the most part, OIG Special Fraud Alerts address national trends in health care fraud, including potential violations of the Medicare anti-kickback statute. This Special Fraud Alert, issued to the health care provider community and now being reprinted in this issue of the **Federal Register**, specifically highlights physicians' responsibilities in making certifications for home health services and durable medical equipment, and the legal significance of the certifications.

FOR FURTHER INFORMATION CONTACT: Joel J. Schaer, Office of Counsel to the Inspector General, (202) 619–0089.

SUPPLEMENTARY INFORMATION:

I. Background

The Office of Inspector General (OIG) issues Special Fraud Alerts based on information it obtains concerning particular fraudulent or abusive practices within the health care industry.

Special Fraud Alerts are intended for widespread dissemination to the health care provider community, as well as those charged with administering the Medicare and Medicaid programs. To date, the OIG has published in the **Federal Register** the texts of 9 previously-issued Special Fraud Alerts.[1] It is the OIG's intention to publish future Special Fraud Alerts in this same manner as a regular part of our dissemination of such information.[2]

In an effort to promote voluntary compliance in the health care industry and assist providers in their compliance efforts, the OIG has developed a Special Fraud Alert, set forth below, that addresses potential problem areas with regard to physician certification in the provision of medical equipment and supplies and home health services. Among other things, this newly- issued Special Fraud Alert addresses: (1) the importance of physician certification for Medicare; (2) how improper physician certifications foster fraud; and (3) potential consequences for knowingly signing a false or misleading certification, or signing with reckless disregard for the truth. A reprint of this Special Fraud Alert follows.

II. Special Fraud Alert: Physician Liability for Certifications in the Provision of Medical Equipment and Supplies and Home Health Services (January 1999)

The Office of Inspector General (OIG) was established at the Department of Health and Human Services by Congress in 1976 to identify and eliminate fraud, waste, and abuse in the Department's programs and to promote efficiency and economy in departmental operations. The OIG carries out this mission through a nationwide program of audits, inspections, and investigations.

To reduce fraud and abuse in the Federal health care programs, including Medicare and Medicaid, the OIG actively investigates fraudulent schemes that obtain money from these programs and, when appropriate, issues Special Fraud Alerts that identify seg-

[1] See December 19, 1994 (59 FR 65372); August 10, 1995 (60 FR 40847); June 17, 1996 (61 FR 30623); and April 24, 1998 (63 FR 20415).

[2] All OIG Special Fraud Alerts are also available on the internet at the OIG web site at http://www.dhhs.gov/progorg/OIG/frdalrt/index.htm.

ments of the health care industry that are particularly vulnerable to abuse. Copies of all OIG Special Fraud Alerts are available on the internet at http:/ /www.dhhs.gov/progorg/OIG/frdalrt/index.htm.

We are issuing this Fraud Alert because physicians may not appreciate the legal and programmatic significance of certifications they make in connection with the ordering of certain items and services for their Medicare patients. While the OIG believes that the actual incidence of physicians' intentionally submitting false or misleading certifications of medical necessity for durable medical equipment or home health care is relatively infrequent, physician laxity in reviewing and completing these certifications contributes to fraudulent and abusive practices by unscrupulous suppliers and home health providers. We urge physicians and their staff to report any suspicious activity in connection with the solicitation or completion of certifications to the OIG.

Physicians should also be aware that they are subject to substantial criminal, civil, and administrative penalties if they sign a certification knowing that the information relating to medical necessity is false, or with reckless disregard as to the truth of the information being submitted. While a physician's signature on a false or misleading certification made through mistake, simple negligence, or inadvertence will not result in personal liability, the physician may unwittingly be facilitating the perpetration of fraud on Medicare by suppliers or providers. Accordingly, we urge all physicians to review and familiarize themselves with the information in this Fraud Alert. If a physician has any questions as to the application of these requirements to specific facts, the physician should contact the appropriate Medicare Fiscal Intermediary or Carrier.

The Importance of Physician Certification for Medicare

The Medicare program only pays for health care services that are medically necessary. In determining what services are medically necessary, Medicare primarily relies on the professional judgment of the beneficiary's treating physician, since he or she knows the patient's history and makes critical decisions, such as admitting the patient to the hospital; ordering tests, drugs, and treatments; and determining the length of treatment. In other words, the physician has a key role in determining both the medical need for, and utilization of, many health care services, including those furnished and billed by other providers and suppliers.

Congress has conditioned payment for many Medicare items and services on a certification signed by a physician attesting that the item or service is medically necessary. For example, physicians are routinely required to certify to the medical necessity for any service for which they submit bills to the Medicare program.

Physicians also are involved in attesting to medical necessity when ordering services or supplies that must be billed and provided by an independent supplier or provider. Medicare requires physicians to certify to the medical necessity for many of these items and services through prescriptions, orders, or, in certain specific circumstances, Certificates of Medical Necessity (CMNs). These documentation requirements substantiate that the physician has reviewed the patient's condition and has determined that services or supplies are medically necessary.

Two areas where the documentation of medical necessity by physician certification plays a key role are (i) home health services and (ii) durable medical equipment (DME). Through various OIG audits, we have discovered that physicians sometimes fail to discharge their responsibility to assess their patients' conditions and need for home health care. Similarly, the OIG has found numerous examples of physicians who have ordered DME or signed CMNs for DME without reviewing the medical necessity for the item or even knowing the patient.

Physician Certification for Home Health Services

Medicare will pay a Medicare-certified home health agency for home health care provided under a physician's plan of care to a patient confined to the home. Covered services may include skilled nursing services, home health aide services, physical and occupational therapy and speech language pathology, medical social services, medical supplies (other than drugs and biologicals), and DME.

As a condition for payment, Medicare requires a patient's treating physician to certify initially and recertify at least every 62 days (2 months) that:

- The patient is confined to the home;
- The individual needs or needed

  (i) intermittent skilled nursing care;
  (ii) speech or physical therapy or speech-language pathology services; or

(iii) occupational therapy or a continued need for occupational therapy (payment for occupational therapy will be made only upon an initial certification that includes care under (i) or (ii) or a recertification where the initial certification included care under (i) or (ii));

- A plan of care has been established and periodically reviewed by the physician; and
- The services are (were) furnished while the patient is (was) under the care of a physician.

The physician must order the home health services, either orally or in writing, prior to the services being furnished. The physician certification must be obtained at the time the plan of treatment is established or as soon thereafter as possible. The physician certification must be signed and dated prior to the submission of the claim to Medicare. If a physician has any questions as to the application of these requirements to specific facts, the physician should contact the appropriate Medicare Fiscal Intermediary or Carrier.

Physician Orders and Certificates of Medical Necessity for Durable Medical Equipment, Prosthetics, Orthotics, and Supplies for Home Use

DME is equipment that can withstand repeated use, is primarily used for a medical purpose, and is not generally used in the absence of illness or injury. Examples include hospital beds, wheelchairs, and oxygen delivery systems. Medicare will cover medical supplies that are necessary for the effective use of DME, as well as surgical dressings, catheters, and ostomy bags. However, Medicare will only cover DME and supplies that have been ordered or prescribed by a physician. The order or prescription must be personally signed and dated by the patient's treating physician.

DME suppliers that submit bills to Medicare are required to maintain the physician's original written order or prescription in their files. The order or prescription must include:

- The beneficiary's name and full address;
-
- The physician's signature;
- The date the physician signed the prescription or order;
- A description of the items needed;
- The start date of the order (if appropriate); and

the diagnosis (if required by Medicare program policies) and a realistic estimate of the total length of time the equipment will be needed (in months or years).

For certain items or supplies, including supplies provided on a periodic basis and drugs, additional information may be required. For supplies provided on a periodic basis, appropriate information on the quantity used, the frequency of change, and the duration of need should be included. If drugs are included in the order, the dosage, frequency of administration, and, if applicable, the duration of infusion and concentration should be included.

Medicare further requires claims for payment for certain kinds of DME to be accompanied by a CMN signed by a treating physician (unless the DME is prescribed as part of a plan of care for home health services). When a CMN is required, the provider or supplier must keep the CMN containing the treating physician's original signature and date on file.

Generally, a CMN has four sections:

- Section A contains general information on the patient, supplier, and physician. Section A may be completed by the supplier.
- Section B contains the medical necessity justification for DME. This cannot be filled out by the supplier. Section B must be completed by the physician, a non-physician clinician involved in the care of the patient, or a physician employee. If the physician did not personally complete section B, the name of the person who did complete section B and his or her title and employer must be specified.
- Section C contains a description of the equipment and its cost. Section C is completed by the supplier.
- Section D is the treating physician's attestation and signature, which certifies that the physician has reviewed sections A, B, and C of the CMN and that the information in section B is true, accurate, and complete. Section D must be signed by the treating physician. Signature stamps and date stamps are not acceptable.

By signing the CMN, the physician represents that:

He or she is the patient's treating physician and the information regarding the physician's address and unique physician identification number (UPIN) is correct;

The entire CMN, including the sections filled out by the supplier, was completed prior to the physician's signature; and

The information in section B relating to medical necessity is true, accurate, and complete to the best of the physician's knowledge.

Improper Physician Certifications Foster Fraud

Unscrupulous suppliers and providers may steer physicians into signing or authorizing improper certifications of medical necessity. In some instances, the certification forms or statements are completed by DME suppliers or home health agencies and presented to the physician, who then signs the forms without verifying the actual need for the items or services. In many cases, the physician may obtain no personal benefit when signing these unverified orders and is only accommodating the supplier or provider. While a physician's signature on a false or misleading certification made through mistake, simple negligence, or inadvertence will not result in personal liability, the physician may unwittingly be facilitating the perpetration of fraud on Medicare by suppliers or providers. When the physician knows the information is false or acts with reckless disregard as to the truth of the statement, such physician risks criminal, civil, and administrative penalties.

Sometimes, a physician may receive compensation in exchange for his or her signature. Compensation can take the form of cash payments, free goods, or any other thing of value. Such cases may trigger additional criminal and civil penalties under the anti-kickback statute.

The following are examples of inappropriate certifications uncovered by the OIG in the course of its investigations of fraud in the provision of home health services and medical equipment and supplies:

A physician knowingly signs a number of forms provided by a home health agency that falsely represent that skilled nursing services are medically necessary in order to qualify the patient for home health services.

A physician certifies that a patient is confined to the home and qualifies for home health services, even though the patient tells the physician that her only restrictions are due to arthritis in her hands, and she has no restrictions on her routine activities, such as grocery shopping.

At the prompting of a DME supplier, a physician signs a stack of blank CMNs for transcutaneous electrical nerve stimulators (TENS) units. The CMNs are later completed with false information in support of fraudulent claims for the equipment. The false information purports to show that the physician ordered and certified to the medical necessity for the TENS units for which the supplier has submitted claims.

A physician signs CMNs for respiratory medical equipment falsely representing that the equipment was medically necessary.

A physician signs CMNs for wheelchairs and hospital beds without seeing the patients, then falsifies his medical charts to indicate that he treated them.

A physician accepts anywhere from $50 to $400 from a DME supplier for each prescription he signs for oxygen concentrators and nebulizers.

Potential Consequences for Unlawful Acts

A physician is not personally liable for erroneous claims due to mistakes, inadvertence, or simple negligence. However, knowingly signing a false or misleading certification or signing with reckless disregard for the truth can lead to serious criminal, civil, and administrative penalties including:

Criminal prosecution;

Fines as high as $10,000 per false claim plus treble damages; or

administrative sanctions including: exclusion from participation in Federal health care programs, withholding or recovery of payments, and loss of license or disciplinary actions by state regulatory agencies.

Physicians may violate these laws when, for example:

They sign a certification as a "courtesy" to a patient, service provider, or DME supplier when they have not first made a determination of medical necessity;

They knowingly or recklessly sign a false or misleading certification that causes a false claim to be submitted to a Federal health care program; or

They receive any financial benefit for signing the certification (including free or reduced rent, patient referrals, supplies, equipment, or free labor).

Even if they do not receive any financial or other benefit from providers or suppliers, physicians may be liable for making false or misleading certifications.

What To Do If You Have Information About Fraud and Abuse Against Medicare or Medicaid Programs

If you have information about physicians, home health agencies, or medical equipment and supply companies engaging in any of the activities described above, contact any of the regional offices of the Office of Investigations of the Office of Inspector General, U.S. Department of Health and Human Services, at the following locations:

Field offices	States served	Telephone
Boston	MA, VT, NH, ME, RI, CT	617–565–2664
New York	NY, NJ, PR, VI	212–264–1691
Philadelphia	PA, MD, DE, WV, VA, DC	215–861–4586
Atlanta	GA, KY, NC, SC, FL, TN, AL, MS	404–562–7603
Chicago	IL, MN, WI, MI, IN, OH, IA, MO	312–353–2740
Dallas	TX, NM, OK, AR, LA, CO, UT, WY, MT, ND, SD, NE, KS	214–767–8406
Los Angeles	AZ, NV, So. CA	714–246–8302
San Francisco	No. CA, AK, HI OR, ID, WA	415–437–7961

To Report Suspected Fraud, Call or Write: 1–800-HHS-TIPS (1–800- 447–8477), Department of Health and Human Services, Office of Inspector General, P.O. Box 23489, L'Enfant Plaza Station, Washington, D.C. 20026–3489.

Dated: January 6, 1999.

June Gibbs Brown,

Inspector General.

[FR Doc. 99–631 Filed 1–11–99; 8:45 am]

BILLING CODE 4150–04-P

APPENDIX G11

Special Advisory Bulletin on Gainsharing Arrangements and CMP's for Hospital Payments to Physicians to Reduce or Limit Services to Beneficiaries; 64 FR 37985, July 14, 1999

[Federal Register: July 14, 1999 (Volume 64, Number 134)]
[Notices] [Page 37985-37987]

DEPARTMENT OF HEALTH AND HUMAN SERVICES

Office of Inspector General

Publication of the OIG Special Advisory Bulletin on Gainsharing Arrangements and CMPs for Hospital Payments to Physicians to Reduce or Limit Services to Beneficiaries

AGENCY: Office of Inspector General (OIG), HHS.

ACTION: Notice.

SUMMARY: In its role of identifying and eliminating fraud, waste and abuse in the Department's health care programs, the OIG periodically develops and issues guidance, including Special Fraud Alerts and Advisory Bulletins, to alert and inform health care providers and program beneficiaries about potential problems or areas of special interest. This Federal Register notice sets forth the recently-issued OIG Special Advisory Bulletin addressing the civil money penalty (CMP) for hospital payments to physicians as an inducement to reduce or limit services to Medicare or Medicaid beneficiaries, and its application to "gainsharing" arrangements involving hospitals and physicians.

FOR FURTHER INFORMATION CONTACT: Joel Schaer, Office of Counsel to the Inspector General, (202) 619–1306.

SUPPLEMENTARY INFORMATION:

I. Background

This Special Advisory Bulletin addresses the CMP for hospital payments to physicians to induce reductions or limitations in services to Medicare or Medicaid beneficiaries (section 1128A(b)(1) and (2) of the Social Security Act (the Act)), and its application to "gainsharing" arrangements and potentially to certain other hospital-physician clinical ventures. The OIG has concluded that section 1128A(b)(1) of the Act specifically prohibits any gainsharing arrangements that involve payments by or on behalf of a hospital, directly or indirectly, to induce physicians with clinical care responsibilities to reduce or limit services to Medicare or Medicaid patients.

II. Special Advisory Bulletin: Gainsharing Arrangements and CMPs for Hospital Payments to Physicians to Reduce or Limit Services to Beneficiaries

A. Introduction

The Office of Inspector General (OIG) was established at the Department of Health and Human Services by Congress in 1976 to identify and eliminate fraud, abuse and waste in the Department's programs and to promote efficiency and economy in departmental operations. The OIG carries out this mission through a nationwide program of audits, investigations and inspections.

The Fraud and Abuse Control Program, established by the Health Insurance Portability and Accountability Act of 1996, authorized the OIG to provide guidance to the health care industry to prevent fraud and abuse, and to promote the highest level of ethical and lawful conduct. To further these goals, the OIG issues Special Advisory Bulletins about industry practices or arrangements that potentially implicate the fraud and abuse authorities subject to enforcement by the OIG.

This Special Advisory Bulletin addresses the application of sections 1128A(b)(1) and (2) of the Social Security Act (the Act) to gainsharing arrangements.[1] The civil money penalty (CMP) set forth in section 1128A(b)(1) of the Act prohibits any hospital or critical access hospital from knowingly making a payment directly or

[1] Gainsharing arrangements may also implicate the anti-kickback statute (section 1128B(b) of the Act) and the physician self-referral prohibitions of the Act (section 1876 of the Act).

indirectly to a physician as an inducement to reduce or limit services to Medicare or Medicaid beneficiaries under the physician's care.

While the OIG recognizes that appropriately structured gainsharing arrangements may offer significant benefits where there is no adverse impact on the quality of care received by patients, section 1128A(b)(1) of the Act clearly prohibits such arrangements. Moreover, regulatory relief from the CMP prohibition will require statutory authorization.

Some hospitals and physicians may have already implemented programs that involve Medicare or Medicaid beneficiaries. In exercising its enforcement discretion, and in the absence of any evidence that a gainsharing arrangement has violated any other statutes or adversely affected patient care, the OIG will take into consideration whether a gainsharing arrangement was terminated expeditiously following publication of this Bulletin.

B. Prohibition on Hospital Payments to Physicians to Induce Reduction or Limitation of Services

Under section 1128A(b)(1) of the Act, a hospital is prohibited from making a payment, directly or indirectly, to induce a physician to reduce or limit services to Medicare or Medicaid beneficiaries under the physician's direct care. Hospitals that make (and physicians that receive) such payments are liable for CMPs of up to $2,000 per patient covered by the payments (section 1128A(b)(2) of the Act).

The statutory proscription is very broad. The payment need not be tied to an actual diminution in care, so long as the hospital knows that the payment may influence the physician to reduce or limit services to his or her patients. There is no requirement that the prohibited payment be tied to a specific patient or to a reduction in *medically necessary* care. In short, any hospital incentive plan that encourages physicians through payments to reduce or limit clinical services directly or indirectly violates the statute.

The breadth of the prohibition was intentional. As initially enacted by Congress, section 1128A(b)(1) of the Act prohibited payments by both hospitals and Medicare managed care plans to induce physicians to reduce clinical services. [2] Section 1128A(b)(1) of the Act was subsequently amended to delete the reference to Medicare managed care plans, and to add a new subsection to section 1876 of the Act that permitted Medicare managed care plans to implement phy-

[2] Section 9313(c) of the Omnibus Budget Reconciliation Act (OBRA) of 1986 (P.L. 99–509).

sician incentive plans, provided the managed care plan did not induce the reduction of *medically necessary* care to *individual* patients and did not place the physician at substantial financial risk for services not provided by the physician.[3] Further, Congress explicitly gave the Secretary authority to regulate physician incentive plans offered by Medicare risk managed care plans. Because the resulting two provisions address the same issues and were drafted together, the stark difference in otherwise parallel language reflects a congressional decision to prohibit any payment arrangement between hospitals and physicians that is intended to induce a reduction or limitation in services.

This reading of the statute is also consistent with the legislative history surrounding the enactment of section 1128A(b)(1) of the Act. The prohibition was prompted in part by a General Accounting Office (GAO) report for the Chairman of the Subcommittee on Health of the House Ways and Means Committee regarding the physician incentive plans being implemented by hospitals in response to the then-recently enacted diagnostic related group prospective payment system and their potential detrimental effects on quality of care for Medicare patients.[4] The report analyzed four types of hospital-physician incentive plans, of which at least two bear strong similarities, and contain safeguards comparable, to the gainsharing arrangements currently being marketed by the healthcare consulting industry.[5] While the GAO report discussed several features in these plans that reduced the incentive to give substandard care, it concluded that no combination of features could guarantee that such plans would not be subject to abuse.[6]

Congress concurred. The House Committee Report that accompanied the House provision that became section 1128A(b)(1) of the Act stated that "[t]he Committee believes that such incentive payments may create a conflict of interest that may limit the ability of the physician to exercise independent professional judgment in the best interest of his or her patients."[7] In explaining the inclusion of the prohibition in the final budget reconciliation bill that became OBRA

[3] Sections 4204(a) and 4731 of the Omnibus Budget Reconciliation Act of 1990 (P.L. 101-508) (codified at section 1876(i)(8) of the Act).

[4] U.S. General Accounting Office, *Physician Incentive Payments by Hospitals Could Lead to Abuse,* GAO/HRD-86–103 (July 1986).

[5] *Id.* at 14–21

[6] *Id.* at 23

[7] H.R. Rep. No. 99–727, at 441 (1986).

1986, the Chairman of the Subcommittee on Health of the House Ways and Means Committee, who was also a member of the Conference Committee, stated on the floor of the House that:

"[T]he House held firm in its insistence on outlawing certain physician incentive plans. We must not tolerate hospitals paying physicians to reduce or limit services to the elderly."[8]

In sum, we believe that section 1128A(b)(1) of the Act prohibits any hospital payments that induce physicians to reduce or limit clinical services to the physicians' patients.

C. Gainsharing Arrangements

While there is no fixed definition of a "gainsharing" arrangement, the term typically refers to an arrangement in which a hospital gives physicians a percentage share of any reduction in the hospital's costs for patient care attributable in part to the physicians' efforts. In most arrangements, in order to receive any payment, the clinical care must not have been adversely affected as measured by selected quality and performance measures. In addition, many plans require a determination by an independent consultant that the payment represents "fair market value" for the collective physician efforts. Medicare Part B and Medicaid payments to physicians generally are unaffected by a gainsharing arrangement.

Gainsharing arrangements seek to align physician incentives with those of hospitals by offering physicians a share of the hospital's variable cost savings attributable to Medicare and Medicaid reimbursement. Since the institution of the Medicare Part A DRG system of hospital reimbursement and with the growth of managed care, hospitals have experienced significant financial pressures to reduce costs. However, because physicians are paid separately under Medicare Part B and Medicaid, physicians do not have the same incentive to save hospital costs. Gainsharing arrangements are designed to bridge this gap by offering physicians a portion of the hospital's cost savings in exchange for identifying and implementing cost saving strategies.

The OIG recognizes that hospitals have a legitimate interest in enlisting physicians in their efforts to eliminate unnecessary costs. Savings that do not affect the quality of patient care may be generated in many ways, including substituting lower cost but equally effective medical supplies, items or devices; re-engineering hospital surgical and medical procedures; reducing utilization of medically

[8] 144 Cong. Rec. H11,446 (October 17, 1986).

unnecessary ancillary services; and reducing unnecessary lengths of stay. Achieving these savings may require substantial effort on the part of the participating physicians. Obviously, a reduction in health care costs that does not adversely affect the quality of the health care provided to patients is in the best interest of the nation's health care system. Nonetheless, the plain language of section 1128A(b)(1) of the Act prohibits tying the physicians' compensation for such services to reductions or limitations in items or services provided to patients under the physicians' clinical care.

D. Application of Section 1128A(b)(1) of the Act to Gainsharing Arrangements

Gainsharing arrangements that directly or indirectly provide physicians financial incentives to reduce or limit items or services to patients that are under the physicians' clinical care are precisely the kind of physician incentive plans that Congress prohibited when it enacted section 1128A(b)(1) of the Act. The language of the statute, the language of the companion statute on managed care physician incentive plans, and the legislative history compel the conclusion that section 1128A(b)(1) of the Act prohibits any hospital-physician incentive plan that compensates a physician directly or indirectly based on cost savings on items and services furnished to patients under the physician's clinical care. We can perceive no meaningful difference between the kinds of incentive plans proposed in 1986 at the time of enactment of section 1128A(b)(1) of the Act (as reflected in the GAO report) and the variants being promoted by hospitals and health care consultants today.

Moreover, given the clear statutory prohibition on hospital-physician incentive plans, the OIG cannot provide any regulatory relief absent further authorizing legislation. Where Congress intended the Department to regulate physician incentive plans, such as plans offered by risk-based Medicare managed care plans, it did so explicitly. Congress' omission of comparable regulatory authority for the Secretary over hospital-physician incentive plans represents its considered judgment that such plans are flatly prohibited.

We note, however, that hospitals may align incentives with physicians to achieve cost savings through means that do not violate section 1128A(b)(1) of the Act. For example, hospitals and physicians may enter into personal services contracts where hospitals pay physicians based on a fixed fee that is fair market value for services rendered, rather than a percentage of cost savings. Such contracts must meet the requirements of the anti-kickback statute (section 1128B(b) of the Act).

Notwithstanding the statutory prohibition, the OIG has given extensive consideration to whether it would be appropriate to protect individual gainsharing arrangements from OIG administrative sanctions through the issuance of favorable advisory opinions. Based on our review of a number of requests, we have concluded that they contain common elements that preclude our issuance of any favorable opinion. First, to date, the OIG has exercised its discretion to protect various arrangements from sanction only where such arrangements pose a minimal risk of fraud or abuse. By contrast, gainsharing arrangements pose a high risk of abuse. In order to retain or attract high-referring physicians, hospitals will be under pressure from competitors and physicians to increase the percentage of savings shared with the physicians, manipulate the hospital accounts to generate phantom savings, or otherwise game the arrangement to generate income for referring physicians. Given these pressures and the potential adverse impact on patient care from gainsharing arrangements, the OIG believes that immunizing such arrangements from sanction would be imprudent and inappropriate.

Second, gainsharing arrangements will require ongoing oversight both as to quality of care and fraud that is not available through the advisory opinion process. Apart from the potential for fraud and abuse, a critical inquiry is whether the arrangements have adequate and accurate measures of quality of care that would provide assurance that there is no adverse impact on patient care. Based on discussions with experts both within and without the Federal Government, the OIG has determined that any performance measures would require extensive verification through audits or review by an independent party on a continuing basis. The Office of Counsel to the Inspector General, which issues advisory opinions, has neither the resources nor the expertise to police a multitude of such arrangements on an ongoing basis.

Third, case by case determinations by advisory opinions are an inadequate and inequitable substitute for comprehensive and uniform regulation in this area. Were the OIG to issue a favorable opinion to one provider, that provider would have a significant competitive advantage in recruiting and attracting physicians to admit patients to its facility, since the physicians would have the opportunity to earn significant additional income not available at other institutions. The consequences would be that every hospital in the country would request an advisory opinion for its own program, and many would implement their own programs in the hope that their programs were close enough. Given the potentially serious adverse effects on patient care from improperly designed or implemented gainsharing arrangements, regulation of gainsharing arrangements requires clear, uniform, enforceable and independently verifiable standards applicable to all affected providers and not case by case decision-making.

E. Application to Other Arrangements

We are aware of reports that hospitals and physicians are engaging in a number of clinical joint ventures, including both freestanding specialty hospitals (e.g., heart, orthopedic, or maternity hospitals), and arrangements in which a high revenue generating unit or service (e.g., cardiology or cardiac surgery) of an existing hospital is restructured and legally incorporated as a separate hospital.

Typically marketed only to physicians in a position to refer patients to the venture and structured to take advantage of the exception in the physician self-referral law for physician investments in "whole hospitals", these ventures may induce investor-physicians to reduce services to patients through participation in profits generated by cost savings in clinical care. Accordingly, we believe such arrangements may also violate section 1128A(b)(1) of the Act, in at least some circumstances. In addition, such arrangements may implicate the anti-kickback statute (section 1128B(b) of the Act).

F. Conclusion

Absent legislative relief, section 1128A(b)(1) of the Act prohibits any gainsharing arrangements that involve payments by or on behalf of a hospital to physicians with clinical care responsibilities, directly or indirectly, to induce a reduction or limitation of services to Medicare or Medicaid patients. Parties interested in pursuing gainsharing arrangements that are currently prohibited by section 1128A(b)(1) of the Act should seek legislative relief. In the light of reports that some hospitals may already have such arrangements in place, the OIG will, in the absence of any evidence that an arrangement has violated any other statutes or adversely affected patient care, take into consideration in exercising its enforcement discretion whether a gainsharing arrangement was terminated expeditiously following publication of this Bulletin in the **Federal Register**.

Dated: July 6, 1999.

June Gibbs Brown,

Inspector General.

[FR Doc. 99–17889 Filed 7–13–99; 8:45 am]

BILLING CODE 4150–04-P

APPENDIX G12

Special Advisory Bulletin on the Effect of Exclusion from Participation in Federal Health Care Programs; 64 FR 52791, September 30, 1999

[Federal Register: September 30, 1999 (Volume 64, Number 189)][Notices]
From the Federal Register Online via GPO Access [wais.access.gpo.gov][DOCID:fr30se99–83]

DEPARTMENT OF HEALTH AND HUMAN SERVICES

Office of Inspector General

Publication of the OIG Special Advisory Bulletin on the Effect of Exclusion From Participation in Federal Health Care Programs

AGENCY: Office of Inspector General (OIG), HHS.

ACTION: Notice.

SUMMARY: In its role of identifying and eliminating fraud, waste and abuse in the Department's health care programs, the OIG periodically develops and issues guidance, including Special Fraud Alerts and Advisory Bulletins, to alert and inform health care providers and program beneficiaries about potential problems or areas of special interest. This Federal Register notice sets forth the recently-issued OIG Special Advisory Bulletin addressing the effect of an OIG exclusion on an individual's or entity's participation in the Federal health care programs.

FOR FURTHER INFORMATION CONTACT: Robin Schneider, Office of Counsel to the Inspector General, (202) 619–1306.

SUPPLEMENTARY INFORMATION:

I. Background

This Special Advisory Bulletin is designed to help all affected parties better understand the scope of payment prohibitions that apply to items and services provided to Federal program beneficiaries, and to provide guidance to individuals and entities that have been excluded from the Federal health care programs and to those who employ or contract with an excluded individual or entity to provide such items or services.

II. Special Advisory Bulletin: Gainsharing Arrangements and CMPs for Hospital Payments to Physicians To Reduce or Limit Services to Beneficiaries

A. Introduction

The Office of Inspector General (OIG) was established in the U.S. Department of Health and Human Services to identify and eliminate fraud, waste, and abuse in the Department's programs and to promote efficiency and economy in Departmental operations. The OIG carries out this mission through a nationwide program of audits, inspections, and investigations. In addition, the OIG has been given the authority to exclude from participation in Medicare, Medicaid and other Federal health care programs[1] individuals and entities who have engaged in fraud or abuse, and to impose civil money penalties (CMPs) for certain misconduct related to Federal health care programs (sections 1128 and 1128A of the Social Security Act (the Act)).

Recent statutory enactments have strengthened and expanded the OIG's authority to exclude individuals and entities from the Federal health care programs. These laws also expanded the OIG's authority to assess CMPs against individuals and entities that violate the law. With this expanded authority, the OIG believes that it is important to explain the effect of program exclusions under the current statutory and regulatory provisions.

The Health Insurance Portability and Accountability Act (HIPAA) of 1996, Public Law 104–191, authorized the OIG to provide guidance to the health care industry to prevent fraud and abuse, and to promote high levels of ethical and lawful conduct. To further these goals, the OIG issues Special Advisory Bulletins about industry

---

[1] A Federal health care program is defined as any plan or program that provides health benefits, whether directly, through insurance, or otherwise, which is funded directly, in whole or in part, by the United States Government or a State health care program (with the exception of the Federal Employees Health Benefits Program) (section 1128B(f) of the Act). The most significant Federal health care programs are Medicare, Medicaid, Tricare and the Veterans programs.

practices or arrangements that potentially implicate the fraud and abuse authorities subject to enforcement by the OIG.

In order to assist all affected parties in understanding the breadth of the payment prohibitions that apply to items and services provided to Federal program beneficiaries,[2] this Special Advisory Bulletin provides guidance to individuals and entities that have been excluded from Federal health care programs, as well as to those who might employ or contract with an excluded individual or entity to provide items or services reimbursed by a Federal health care program.

B. Statutory Background

In 1977, in the Medicare-Medicaid Anti-Fraud and Abuse Amendments, Public Law 95–142, Congress first mandated the exclusion of physicians and other practitioners convicted of program-related crimes from participation in Medicare and Medicaid (now codified at section 1128 of the Act). This was followed in 1981 with Congressional enactment of the Civil Monetary Penalties Law (CMPL), Public Law 97–35, to further address health care fraud and abuse (section 1128A of the Act). The CMPL authorizes the Department and the OIG to impose CMPs, assessments and program exclusions against individuals and entities who submit false or fraudulent, or otherwise improper claims for Medicare or Medicaid payment. "Improper claims" include claims submitted by an excluded individual or entity for items or services furnished during a period of program exclusion.

To enhance the OIG's ability to protect the Medicare and Medicaid programs and beneficiaries, the Medicare and Medicaid Patient and Program Protection Act of 1987, Public Law 100–93, expanded and revised the OIG's administrative sanction authorities by, among other things, establishing certain mandatory and discretionary exclusions for various types of misconduct.

The enactment of HIPAA in 1996 and the Balanced Budget Act (BBA) of 1997, Public Law 105–33, further expanded the OIG's sanction authorities. These statutes extended the application and scope of the current CMP and exclusion authorities beyond programs funded by the Department to all "Federal health care programs." BBA also authorized a new CMP authority to be imposed against health care providers or entities that employ or enter into contracts

[2] A Federal program beneficiary is an individual that receives health care benefits that are funded, in whole or in part, by a Federal health care program.

with excluded individuals for the provision of services or items to Federal program beneficiaries.

In the discussion that follows, it should be understood that the prohibitions being described apply to items and services provided, directly or indirectly, to Federal program beneficiaries. The ability of an excluded individual or entity to render items and services to others is not affected by an OIG exclusion.

C. Exclusion From Federal Health Care Programs

The effect of an OIG exclusion from Federal health care programs is that no Federal health care program payment may be made for any items or services (1) furnished by an excluded individual or entity, or (2) directed or prescribed by an excluded physician (42 CFR 1001.1901). This payment ban applies to all methods of Federal program reimbursement, whether payment results from itemized claims, cost reports, fee schedules or a prospective payment system (PPS). Any items and services furnished by an excluded individual or entity are not reimbursable under Federal health care programs. In addition, any items and services furnished at the medical direction or prescription of an excluded physician are not reimbursable when the individual or entity furnishing the services either knows or should know of the exclusion. This prohibition applies even when the Federal payment itself is made to another provider, practitioner or supplier that is not excluded.The prohibition against Federal program payment for items or services furnished by excluded individuals or entities also extends to payment for administrative and management services not directly related to patient care, but that are a necessary component of providing items and services to

Federal program beneficiaries. This prohibition continues to apply to an individual even if he or she changes from one health care profession to another while excluded. [3] In addition, no Federal program payment may be made to cover an excluded individual's salary, expenses or fringe benefits, regardless of whether they provide direct patient care.

Set forth below is a listing of some of the types of items or services that are reimbursed by Federal health care programs which, when provided by excluded parties, violate an OIG exclusion. These examples also demonstrate the kinds of items and services that excluded

[3] For example, the prohibition against Federal program payment for items and services would continue to apply in the situation where an excluded pharmacist completes his or her medical degree and becomes a licensed physician.

parties may be furnishing which will subject their employer or contractor to possible CMP liability.

- Services performed by excluded nurses, technicians or other excluded individuals who work for a hospital, nursing home, home health agency or physician practice, where such services are related to administrative duties, preparation of surgical trays or review of treatment plans if such services are reimbursed directly or indirectly (such as through a PPS or a bundled payment) by a Federal health care program, even if the individuals do not furnish direct care to Federal program beneficiaries;
- Services performed by excluded pharmacists or other excluded individuals who input prescription information for pharmacy billing or who are involved in any way in filling prescriptions for drugs reimbursed, directly or indirectly, by any Federal health care program;
- Services performed by excluded pharmacists or other excluded individuals who input prescription information for pharmacy billing or who are involved in any way in filling prescriptions for drugs reimbursed, directly or indirectly, by any Federal health care program;
- Services performed by excluded ambulance drivers, dispatchers and other employees involved in providing transportation reimbursed by a Federal health care program, to hospital patients or nursing home residents;
- Services performed for program beneficiaries by excluded individuals who sell, deliver or refill orders for medical devices or equipment being reimbursed by a Federal health care program;
- Services performed by excluded social workers who are employed by health care entities to provide services to Federal program beneficiaries, and whose services are reimbursed, directly or indirectly, by a Federal health care program;
- Administrative services, including the processing of claims for payment, performed for a Medicare intermediary or carrier, or a Medicaid fiscal agent, by an excluded individual;
- Services performed by an excluded administrator, billing agent, accountant, claims processor or utilization reviewer that are related to and reimbursed, directly or indirectly, by a Federal health care program;
- Items or services provided to a program beneficiary by an excluded individual who works for an entity that has a contrac-

tual agreement with, and is paid by, a Federal health care program; and

- Items or equipment sold by an excluded manufacturer or supplier, used in the care or treatment of beneficiaries and reimbursed, directly or indirectly, by a Federal health care program.

D. Violation of an OIG Exclusion by an Excluded Individual or Entity

An excluded party is in violation of its exclusion if it furnishes to Federal program beneficiaries items or services for which Federal health care program payment is sought. An excluded individual or entity that submits a claim for reimbursement to a Federal health care program, or causes such a claim to be submitted, may be subject to a CMP of $10,000 for each item or service furnished during the period that the person or entity was excluded (section 1128A(a)(1)(D) of the Act). The individual or entity may also be subject to treble damages for the amount claimed for each item or service. In addition, since reinstatement into the programs is not automatic, the excluded individual may jeopardize future reinstatement into Federal health care programs (42 CFR 1001.3002).

E. Employing an Excluded Individual or Entity

As indicated above, BBA authorizes the imposition of CMPs against health care providers and entities that employ or enter into contracts with excluded individuals or entities to provide items or services to Federal program beneficiaries (section 1128A(a)(6) of the Act; 42 CFR 1003.102(a)(2)). This authority parallels the CMP for health maintenance organizations that employ or contract with excluded individuals (section 1857(g)(1)(G) of the Act). Under the CMP authority, providers such as hospitals, nursing homes, hospices and group medical practices may face CMP exposure if they submit claims to a Federal health care program for health care items or services provided, directly or indirectly, by excluded individuals or entities.Thus, a provider or entity that receives Federal health care funding may only employ an excluded individual in limited situations. Those situations would include instances where the provider is both able to pay the individual exclusively with private funds or from other non-federal funding sources, and where the services furnished by the excluded individual relate solely to non-federal program patients.In many instances, the practical effect of an OIG exclusion is to preclude employment of an excluded individual in any capacity by a health care provider that receives reimbursement, indirectly or directly, from any Federal health care program.

F. CMP Liability for Employing or Contracting With an Excluded Individual or Entity

If a health care provider arranges or contracts (by employment or otherwise) with an individual or entity who is excluded by the OIG from program participation for the provision of items or services reimbursable under such a Federal program, the provider may be subject to CMP liability if they render services reimbursed, directly or indirectly, by such a program. CMPs of up to $10,000 for each item or service furnished by the excluded individual or entity and listed on a claim submitted for Federal program reimbursement, as well as an assessment of up to three times the amount claimed and program exclusion may be imposed. For liability to be imposed, the statute requires that the provider submitting the claims for health care items or services furnished by an excluded individual or entity "knows or should know" that the person was excluded from participation in the Federal health care programs (section 1128A(a)(6) of the Act; 42 CFR 1003.102(a)(2)). Providers and contracting entities have an affirmative duty to check the program exclusion status of individuals and entities prior to entering into employment or contractual relationships, or run the risk of CMP liability if they fail to do so.

G. How to Determine If an Individual or Entity is Excluded

In order to avoid potential CMP liability, the OIG urges health care providers and entities to check the OIG List of Excluded Individuals/Entities on the OIG web site (www.hhs.gov/oig) prior to hiring or contracting with individuals or entities. In addition, if they have not already done so, health care providers should periodically check the OIG web site for determining the participation/exclusion status of current employees and contractors. The web site contains OIG program

exclusion information and is updated in both on-line searchable and downloadable formats. This information is updated on a regular basis. The OIG web site sorts the exclusion of individuals and entities by: (1) The legal basis for the exclusion, (2) the types of individuals and entities that have been excluded, and (3) the State where the excluded individual resided at the time they were excluded or the State where the entity was doing business. In addition, the entire exclusion file may be downloaded for persons who wish to set up their own database. Monthly updates are posted to the downloadable information on the web site.

H. Conclusion

In accordance with the expanded sanction authority provided in HIPAA and BBA, and with limited exceptions,[4] an exclusion from Federal health care programs effectively precludes an excluded individual or entity from being employed by, or under contract with, any practitioner, provider or supplier to provide any items and services reimbursed by a Federal health care program. This broad prohibition applies whether the Federal reimbursement is based on itemized claims, cost reports, fee schedules or PPS. Furthermore, it should be recognized that an exclusion remains in effect until the individual or entity has been reinstated to participate in Federal health care programs in accordance with the procedures set forth at 42 CFR 1001.3001 through 1001.3005. Reinstatement does not occur automatically at the end of a term of exclusion, but rather, an excluded party must apply for reinstatement.

If you are an excluded individual or entity, or are considering hiring or contracting with an excluded individual or entity, and question whether or not the employment arrangement may violate the law, the OIG Advisory Opinion process is available to offer formal binding guidance on whether an employment or contractual arrangement may be in violation of the OIG's exclusion and CMP authorities. The process and procedure for submitting an advisory opinion request can be found at 42 CFR 1008, or on the OIG web site at www.hhs.gov/oig.

Dated: September 21, 1999.

June Gibbs Brown,

Inspector General.

[FR Doc. 99–25427 Filed 9–29–99; 8:45 am]

BILLING CODE 4150–04-P

---

[4] In certain instances, a State health care program may request a waiver of an exclusion if an individual or entity is the sole community physician or the sole source of essential specialized services in a community (42 CFR 1001.1801(b)).

APPENDIX G13

OIG Special Fraud Alert on Rental of Space in Physician Offices by Persons or Entities to Which Physicians Refer; 65 FR 9274, February 24, 2000

[Federal Register: February 24, 2000 (Volume 65, Number 37)]
[Notices]
[Page 9274–9277]

DEPARTMENT OF HEALTH AND HUMAN SERVICES

Office of Inspector General

Publication of OIG Special Fraud Alert on Rental of Space in Physician Offices by Persons or Entities to Which Physicians Refer

AGENCY: Office of Inspector General (OIG), HHS.

ACTION: Notice.

SUMMARY: This Federal Register notice sets forth a recently issued OIG Special Fraud Alert concerning rental of space in physicians' offices by persons or entities that provide health care items or services to patients that are referred, either directly or indirectly, by the physician-landlord. For the most part, OIG Special Fraud Alerts address national trends in health care fraud, including potential violations of the anti-kickback statute for Federal health care programs. This Special Fraud Alert specifically highlights questionable or suspect rental arrangements for space in physicians' and other practitioners' offices, and how the space rental safe harbor can protect legitimate arrangements.

FOR FURTHER INFORMATION CONTACT: Julie Kass, Office of Counsel to the Inspector General, (202) 619–0335.

SUPPLEMENTARY INFORMATION:

I. Background

The Office of Inspector General (OIG) issues Special Fraud Alerts based on information it obtains concerning particular fraudulent or abusive practices within the health care industry. Special Fraud Alerts are intended for widespread dissemination to the health care provider community, as well as those charged with administering the Medicare and Medicaid programs. To date, the OIG has published in the Federal Register the texts of ten previously-issued Special Fraud Alerts.[1] It is the OIG's intention to publish future Special Fraud Alerts in this same manner as a regular part of our dissemination of such information.[2]

In an effort to promote voluntary compliance in the health care industry and assist providers in their compliance efforts, the OIG has developed a Special Fraud Alert, set forth below, that addresses potential problem areas with regard to the rental of space in physicians' offices by persons or entities to which physicians refer patients. Among other things, this Special Fraud Alert addresses suspect rental arrangements for space in physicians' offices with regard to: (1) the appropriateness of rental agreements; (2) the rental amounts; and (3) time and space considerations. A reprint of this Special Fraud Alert follows.

II. Special Fraud Alert: Rental of Space in Physician Offices by Persons or Entities to Which Physicians Refer (February 2000)

The Office of Inspector General (OIG) was established at the Department of Health and Human Services by Congress in 1976 to identify and eliminate fraud, abuse and waste in the Department's programs and to promote efficiency and economy in departmental operations. The OIG carries out this mission through a nationwide program of audits, investigations and inspections.

To reduce fraud and abuse in the Federal health care programs, including Medicare and Medicaid, the OIG actively investigates fraudulent schemes that are used to obtain money from these programs and, when appropriate, issues Special Fraud Alerts that identify practices in the health care industry that are particularly vulnerable to abuse.

---

[1] See December 19, 1994 (59 FR 65372); August 10, 1995 (60 FR 40847); June 17, 1996 (61 FR 30623); April 24, 1998 (63 FR 20415); and January 12, 1999 (64 FR 1813).

[2] All OIG Special Fraud Alerts are also available on the internet at the OIG web site at http://www.dhhs.gov/progorg/oig/frdalrt/index.htm.

This Special Fraud Alert focuses on the rental of space in physicians' offices by persons or entities that provide health care items or services (suppliers)[3] to patients that are referred either directly or indirectly by their physician-landlords. In this Special Fraud Alert, we describe some of the potentially illegal practices the OIG has identified in such rental relationships.

Questionable Rental Arrangements for Space in Physician Offices

A number of suppliers that provide health care items or services rent space in the offices of physicians or other practitioners. Typically, most of the items or services provided in the rented space are for patients, referred or sent, either directly or indirectly, to the supplier by the physician-landlord. In particular, we are aware of rental arrangements between physician-landlords and:

- Comprehensive outpatient rehabilitation facilities (CORFs) that provide physical and occupational therapy and speech-language pathology services in physicians' and other practitioners' offices;
- Mobile diagnostic equipment suppliers that perform diagnostic related tests in physicians' offices; and
- Suppliers of durable medical equipment, prosthetics, orthotics and supplies (DMEPOS) that set up "consignment closets" for their supplies in physicians' offices.

The OIG is concerned that in such arrangements, the rental payments may be disguised kickbacks to the physician-landlords to induce referrals. We have received numerous credible reports that in many cases, suppliers, whose businesses depend on physicians' referrals, offer and pay "rents" — either voluntarily or in response to physicians' requests — that are either unnecessary or in excess of the fair market value for the space to access the physicians' potential referrals.

The Anti-Kickback Law Prohibits Any Payments To Induce Referrals

Kickbacks can distort medical decision-making, cause overutilization, increase costs and result in unfair competition by freezing out competitors who are unwilling to pay kickbacks. Kickbacks can also adversely affect the quality of patient care by encouraging physi-

[3] Persons or entities may be either suppliers or providers. For purposes of this Special Fraud Alert, we will refer to such persons as suppliers.

cians to order services or recommend supplies based on profit rather than the patients' best medical interests.

Section 1128B(b) of the Social Security Act (the Act) prohibits knowingly and willfully soliciting, receiving, offering or paying anything of value to induce referrals of items or services payable by a Federal health care program. Both parties to an impermissible kickback transaction are liable. Violation of the statute constitutes a felony punishable by a maximum fine of $25,000, imprisonment up to five years, or both. The OIG may also initiate administrative proceedings to exclude persons from Federal health care programs or to impose civil money penalties for fraud, kickbacks and other prohibited activities under sections 1128(b)(7) and 1128A(a)(7) of the Act. [4]

Suspect Rental Arrangements for Space in Physician Offices

The questionable features of suspect rental arrangements for space in physicians' offices may be reflected in three areas:

- The appropriateness of rental agreements;
- The rental amounts; and
- Time and space considerations.

Below, we examine these suspect areas, which separately or together may result in an arrangement that violates the anti-kickback statute, in order to help identify questionable rental arrangements between physicians and the suppliers to which they refer patients. This list is not exhaustive, but rather gives examples of indicators of potentially unlawful activity.

Appropriateness of Rental Agreements

The threshold inquiry when examining rental payments is whether payment for rent is appropriate at all. Payments of "rent" for space that traditionally has been provided for free or for a nominal charge as an accommodation between the parties for the benefit of the physicians' patients, such as consignment closets for DMEPOS, may be disguised kickbacks. In general, payments for rent of con-

[4] Some of the arrangements identified as suspect in this Special Fraud Alert may also implicate the Ethics in Patient Referrals Act, also known as the Stark law (section 1877 of the Act). The interpretation of the Stark law is under the jurisdiction of the Health Care Financing Administration (HCFA).

signment closets in physicians' offices are suspect.[5]

Rental Amounts

Rental amounts should be at fair market value, be fixed in advance and not take into account, directly or indirectly, the volume or value of referrals or other business generated between the parties. Fair market value rental payments should not exceed the amount paid for comparable property. Moreover, where a physician rents space, the rate paid by the supplier should not exceed the rate paid by the physicians in the primary lease for their office space, except in rare circumstances. Examples of suspect arrangements include:

- Rental amounts in excess of amounts paid for comparable property rented in arms-length transactions between persons not in a position to refer business;
- Rental amounts for subleases that exceed the rental amounts per square foot in the primary lease;
- Rental amounts that are subject to modification more often than annually;
- Rental amounts that vary with the number of patients or referrals;
- Rental arrangements that set a fixed rental fee per hour, but do not fix the number of hours or the schedule of usage in advance (i.e., "as needed" arrangements);
- Rental amounts that are only paid if there are a certain number of Federal health care program beneficiaries referred each month; and
- Rental amounts that are conditioned upon the supplier's receipt of payments from a Federal health care program.

Time and Space Considerations

Suppliers should only rent premises of a size and for a time that is reasonable and necessary for a commercially reasonable business purpose of the supplier. Rental of space that is in excess of suppliers' needs creates a presumption that the payments may be a pretext for giving money to physicians for their referrals. Examples of suspect arrangements include:

- Rental amounts for space that is unnecessary or not used. For instance, a CORF requires one examination room and rents

[5] This Special Fraud Alert does not address the appropriateness of consignment closet arrangements under HCFA's DMEPOS supplier standards. The interpretation of the DMEPOS supplier standards is a matter under HCFA's jurisdiction.

physician office space one afternoon a week when the physician is not in the office. The CORF calculates its rental payment on the square footage for the entire office, since it is the only occupant during that time, even though the CORF only needs one examination room;

- Rental amounts for time when the rented space is not in use by the supplier. For example, an ultrasound supplier has enough business to support the use of one examination room for four hours each week, but rents the space for an amount equivalent to eight hours per week;
- Non-exclusive occupancy of the rented portion of space. For example, a physical therapist does not rent space in a physician's office, but rather moves from examination room to examination room treating patients after they have been seen by the physician. Since no particular space is rented, we will closely scrutinize the proration of time and space used to calculate the therapist's "rent.".

In addition, rental amount calculations should prorate rent based on the amount of space and duration of time the premises are used. The basis for any proration should be documented and updated as necessary. Depending on the circumstances, the supplier's rent can consist of three components: (1) Exclusive office space; (2) interior office common space; and (3) building common space.

1. Apportionment of exclusive office space. — The supplier's rent should be calculated based on the ratio of the time the space is in use by the supplier to the total amount of time the physician's office is in use. In addition, the rent should be calculated based on the ratio of the amount of space that is used exclusively by the supplier to the total amount of space in the physician's office. For example, where a supplier rents an examination room for four hours one afternoon per week in a physician's office that has four examination rooms of equal size and is open eight hours a day, five days per week, the supplier's prorated annual rent would be calculated as follows:

Physician office rent per day	Percent of physician office space rented by supplier	Percent of each day rented by supplier	No. of days rented by supplier per year		
Annual rent of primary lease ÷ no. of work days per year.	x Sq. ft. exclusively occupied by supplier ÷ total office sq. ft.	x 4 hours ÷ 8 hours.	x 52 days (i.e., ÷ 1 day per week).	=	Supplier's annual rent for exclusive space

2. Apportionment of interior office common space. —When permitted by applicable regulations, rental payments may also cover the interior office common space in physicians' offices that are shared by the physicians and any subtenants, such as waiting rooms. If suppliers use such common areas for their patients, it may be appropriate for the suppliers to pay a prorated portion of the charge for such space. The charge for the common space must be apportioned among all physicians and subtenants that use the interior office common space based on the amount of non-common space they occupy and the duration of such occupation. Payment for the use of office common space should not exceed the supplier's pro rata share of the charge for such space based upon the ratio of the space used exclusively by the supplier to the total amount of space (other than common space) occupied by all persons using such common space.

3. Apportionment of building common space. — Where the physician pays a separate charge for areas of a building that are shared by all tenants, such as building lobbies, it may be appropriate for the supplier to pay a prorated portion of such charge. As with interior office common space, the cost of the building common space must be apportioned among all physicians and subtenants based on the amount of non-common space they occupy and the duration of such occupation. For instance, in the example in number one above, the supplier's share of the additional levy for building common space could not be split 50/50.

The Space Rental Safe Harbor Can Protect Legitimate Arrangements

We strongly recommend that parties to rental agreements between physicians and suppliers to whom the physicians refer or for which physicians otherwise generate business make every effort to comply with the space rental safe harbor to the anti-kickback statute. (See 42 CFR 1001.952(b), as amended by 64 FR 63518 (November 19, 1999)). When an arrangement meets all of the criteria of a safe harbor, the arrangement is immune from prosecution under the anti-kickback statute. The following are the safe harbor criteria, all of which must be met:

- The agreement is set out in writing and signed by the parties.
- The agreement covers all of the premises rented by the parties for the term of the agreement and specifies the premises covered by the agreement.
- If the agreement is intended to provide the lessee with access to the premises for periodic intervals of time rather than on a full-time basis for the term of the rental agreement, the rental agreement specifies exactly the schedule of such intervals, their precise length, and the exact rent for such intervals.
- The term of the rental agreement is for not less than one year.
- The aggregate rental charge is set in advance, is consistent with fair market value in arms-length transactions, and is not determined in a manner that takes into account the volume or value of any referrals or business otherwise generated between the parties for which payment may be made in whole or in part under Medicare or a State health care program.
- The aggregate space rented does not exceed that which is reasonably necessary to accomplish the commercially reasonable business purpose of the rental.

Arrangements for office equipment or personal services of physicians' office staff can also be structured to comply with the equipment rental safe harbor and personal services and management contracts safe harbor. (See 42 CFR 1001.952(c) and (d), as amended by 64 FR 63518 (November 19, 1999)). Specific equipment used should be identified and documented and payment limited to the prorated portion of its use. Similarly, any services provided should be documented and payment should be limited to the time actually spent performing such services.

What To Do If You Have Information About Fraud and Abuse Against Medicare or Medicaid Programs

If you have information about physicians, DMEPOS suppliers, CORFs or other suppliers engaging in any of the activities described above, contact any of the regional offices of the Office of Investigations of the Office of Inspector General, U.S. Department of Health and Human Services, at the following locations:

Field offices	States served	Telephone
Boston	MA, VT, NH, ME, RI, CT	617-565-2664
New York	NY, NJ, PR, VI	212-264-1691
Philadelphia	PA, MD, DE, WV, VA, DC.	215-861-4586
Atlanta	GA, KY, NC, SC, FL, TN, AL, MS	404-562-7603
Chicago	IL, MN, WI, MI, IN, OH, IA	312-353-2740
Dallas	TX, NM, OK, AR, LA, CO, UT, WY, MT, ND, SD, NE, KS, MO	214-767-8406
Los Angeles	AZ, NV, So. CA	714-246-8302
San Francisco	No. CA, AK, HI, OR, ID, WA	415-437-7961

Dated: February 16, 2000.
June Gibbs Brown,
Inspector General.
[FR Doc. 00–4212 Filed 2–22–00; 8:45 am]
BILLING CODE 4150–01-U

APPENDIX H

SUPERSEDED MATERIAL

H-1: Former Chapter II-23-A

Failure by Primary Payers to Comply with Medicare Secondary Payer Requirements

The following summary and statutory provisions pertain to section 1862(b) [42 U.S.C.S. 1395y(b)] prior to revision by section 6202(a)(2), section 6202(b)(1)(A), and section 6202(e)(1) of P.L. 101-239, the Omnibus Budget Reconciliation Act of 1989.

Summary

If a Medicare beneficiary is entitled to medical benefits under the workmen's compensation law or plan of a State or of the United States, or under an automobile or other liability policy, including a self-insured plan, or under no-fault insurance, section 1862(b)(1), 42 U.S.C.S. 1395y(b)(1), requires those laws, plans, and policies to be the primary source for payment. This applies to the extent payment has been made or can reasonably be expected to be made promptly. ("Promptly" is determined by regulations.) In such cases, Medicare is the secondary payer, obligated for any Medicare covered expenses which those primary sources are not legally obligated to pay.

Any payment by Medicare prior to payment under any such law, plan, or policies is statutorily conditioned on reimbursement to the appropriate Medicare Trust Fund when notice or other information is received that payment has been or could be made under such a law, plan or policies.

To recover payment the United States may bring an action against any entity which would be responsible for payment or against any entity (including any physician or provider) which has been paid under any such law, plan, or policies. Alternatively, the United States may join or intervene in any action related to the event which caused the need for medical benefits, such as a tort action arising from an automobile accident or other cause of personal injury. In addition, the United States is statutorily subrogated to any right of an individual or any other entity to payment with respect to any Medicare-paid item or service under any such law, plan, or policies. The Secretary may waive the Medicare claim, however, if he determines the probability of recovery or the amount involved does not warrant collection effort.

With regard to persons entitled to Medicare benefits under Part A or eligible to enroll under Part B solely by reason of section 226A of the Social Security Act, 42 U.S.C.S. 426A, which provides Medicare benefits for persons suffering end stage renal disease, section 1862(b)(2), 42 U.S.C.S. 1395y(b)(2), provides that Medicare will not make any payment to the extent payment has been made or can reasonably be expected to be made under any group health plan (as defined in section 162(i)(2) of the Internal Revenue Code of 1954, 26 U.S.C.S. 162(i)(2)). In such cases, Medicare is the secondary payer, obligated for any Medicare covered expenses which any such group health plan is not legally obligated to pay. Prior payments by Medicare are statutorily conditioned on reimbursement to the appropriate Medicare Trust Fund when notice or other information is received that payment for such item or service has been or could be made under such a group health plan.

To recover payment the United States may bring an action against any entity which would be responsible for payment or against any entity (including any physician or provider) which has been paid under such a group health plan. Alternatively, the United States may join or intervene in any action related to the event which caused the need for medical benefits, such as a tort action arising from an automobile accident or other cause of personal injury resulting in end stage renal disease (or, presumably, in any complications thereof, if the disease existed prior to the event which gave rise to the cause of action). In addition, the United States is statutorily subrogated to any right of an individual or any other entity to payment with respect to any Medicare-paid item or service under any such group health plan. The Secretary may waive the Medicare claim, however, if he determines the probability of recovery or the amount involved does not warrant collection effort.

The provisions of section 1862(b)(2)(A) and (B) apply to an individual only during the twelve-month period which begins either the month in which a regular course of renal dialysis is started or, in the case of an individual who receives a kidney transplant, the first month in which he would be eligible for Medicare benefits had he applied pursuant to section 226A, whichever is earlier. Furthermore, when payment under such a group health plan for such an individual is less than the amount of the charge for covered expenses, the Medicare payment will disregard Medicare deductibles and co-insurance for the remainder of the charge. The total Medicare payment may not exceed the amount Medicare would have paid absent such a group health plan, however, and the Medicare payment, when combined with the amount payable under the plan, may not exceed the combined amount payable under Medicare and the group health plan absent this limitation. Thus, increasing a charge will not obligate Medicare to pay more.

Pursuant to section 1862(b)(3), 42 U.S.C.S. 1395y(b)(3), if a Medicare beneficiary or the spouse thereof is employed at the time an item or service covered by Medicare is furnished to the beneficiary, and if payment therefor has been made or can reasonably be expected to be made under a group health plan (as defined in section 162(i)(2) of the Internal Revenue Code), and if the plan is obligated to pay for the beneficiary's medical expenses because of the employment relationship of the beneficiary or the spouse thereof, that employment-related group health plan must be the primary source for payment. In such cases, Medicare is the secondary payer, obligated for any Medicare covered expenses which such a plan is not legally obligated to pay. Any payment by Medicare prior to payment by such a plan is statutorily conditioned on reimbursement to the appropriate Medicare Trust Fund when notice or other information is received that payment for such item or service has been or could be made under the plan.

To recover payment the United States may bring an action against any entity which would be responsible for payment under such an employment-related group health plan or against any entity (including any physician or provider) which has been paid under such a plan. Alternatively, the United States may join or intervene in any action related to the event which caused the need for medical benefits, such as a tort action arising from an automobile accident or other cause of personal injury. In addition, the United States is statutorily subrogated to any right of an individual or any other entity to payment with respect to any Medicare-paid item or service under any such a plan. The Secretary may waive the Medicare claim, however, if he determines the probability of recovery or the amount involved does not warrant collection effort.

Section 1862(b)(3) applies only for the period beginning with the month an individual covered by such an employment-related group health plan becomes entitled to Medicare benefits under section 226(a) of the Social Security Act, 42 U.S.C.S. 426(a), and does not include any month for which the individual would, upon application, be entitled to benefits under section 226A by reason of end stage renal disease. Furthermore, when payment under such an employment-related group health plan is less than the amount of the charge for covered expenses, the Medicare payment will disregard Medicare deductibles and co-insurance for the remainder of the charge. The total Medicare payment may not exceed the amount Medicare would have paid absent such an employment-related group health plan, however, and the Medicare payment, when combined with the amount payable under such a plan, may not exceed the combined amount payable under Medicare and the plan absent this limitation.

That applies in the case of an item or service payment for which is determined by Medicare on the basis of reasonable cost or other cost-related basis, or under the Prospective Payment System. In addition, however, in the case of an item or service payment for which is authorized by Medicare on some other basis, the Medicare payment may not exceed the amount which would be payable under the employment-related group health plan without regard to its deductibles and co-insurance, or the reasonable charge or other amount payable under Medicare without regard to Medicare deductibles and co-insurance, whichever is greater.

According to section 1862(b)(4), 42 U.S.C.S. 1395y(b)(4), if a Medicare beneficiary is covered for medical expenses by a large group health plan (as defined in section 5000 of the Internal Revenue code of 1986, 26 U.S.C.S. 5000, Medicare will not make any payment to the extent payment has been made or can reasonably be expected to be made under the plan. Furthermore, such large group health plans may not take into account the fact that any of their insureds are eligible for Medicare benefits as a disabled person under section 226(b), 42 U.S.C.S. 426(b), other than an individual who is, or would, upon application be, entitled to benefits under section 226A as a person suffering end stage renal disease. In such cases, Medicare is the secondary payer, obligated for any Medicare covered expenses which such large group health plans are not legally obligated to pay. Any payment by Medicare prior to payment by such a large group health plan is statutorily conditioned on reimbursement to the appropriate Medicare Trust Fund. (No mention is made in this provision for reimbursement on notice to Medicare, as is found in sections 1862(b)(1), (2), and (3).)

To recover payment the United States may bring an action against any entity which is required under section 1862(a) to pay, and may collect double damages against that entity, or against any other entity that has received payment from that entity. Alternatively, the United States may join or intervene in any action related to the event that gave rise to the need for medical benefits, such as a tort action arising from an automobile accident or other cause of personal injury. In addition, the United States is statutorily subrogated to any right of an individual or any other entity to payment with respect to any Medicare-paid item or service under any such large group health plan. The Secretary may waive recovery in such cases, however, if he determines that waiver is in the best interests of Medicare.

The same payment limitations applicable to employment-related group health plans under section 1862(b)(3) apply to large group health plans governed by section 1862(b)(4). Section 1862(b)(4) is effective, however, only for items and services furnished on or after January 1, 1987, and before January 1, 1992.

For more information about the obligations of large group health plans vis-a-vis Medicare, see P.L. 99-509, the Omnibus Budget Reconciliation Act of 1986 (OBRA), 100 Stat. 2010, especially the legislative history found at 5 U.S. Code and Congressional Administrative News, pp. 3965-3966, which states in part:

Present law

TEFRA [the Tax Equity and Fiscal Responsibility Act of 1982, P.L. 98-369] required employers to offer their employees ages 65 through 69 the same group health plans [offered] to employees under age 65. When the employee age 65 to 69 elects such coverage, Medicare becomes the secondary payer. The beneficiary retains the right not to elect such coverage and to be covered only by Medicare. DEFRA [the Deficit Reduction Act of 1984, P.L. 98-369] extended this provision to include beneficiaries covered under a working spouse's employer-based group health insurance plan when the working spouse is under age 65. COBRA [the Consolidated Omnibus Budget Reconciliation Act of 1985, P.L. 99-272] further extended the provision to apply to the working aged and spouses over age 69.

Senate amendment

Recodifies current law with respect to secondary payer provisions and amends the Social Security Act to provide that Medicare would be the secondary payer for all Medicare beneficiaries (including disabled and those who buy into Medicare) who elect to be covered by employment based health insurance as a current employee (or family member of such employee) of a large employer. This provision would explicitly include under the secondary payer provision those persons with group health coverage who are the employer, former employees under age 65, individuals associated with the employer in a business relationship, or members of the families of any such persons.. . .

In addition, a tax is imposed on employers and employee organizations that contribute to plans that do not conform with the secondary payer provisions. The tax is 25 percent of the employer's or employee organization's annual contributions to nonconforming group health plans. [See 26 U.S.C.S. 5000(a)]

Having established all those conditions with respect to primary and secondary liability vis-à-vis Medicare, and having given the United States subrogation rights and the Secretary authority to waive claims which he determines are not worth pursuing, and having authorized the double damages remedy of the United States against large group health plans, Congress, in section 1862(b)(5), 42 U.S.C.S. 1395y(b)(5), went on to provide a private right of action against those who fail to live up to their obligations as primary payers under a workmen's compensation law or plan, an automobile or other liability insurance policy or plan, or a no fault insurance plan, a group health plan, or a large group health plan. In such cases, the remedy is double damages.

Statutory Provisions

Section 1862(b), 42 U.S.C.S. 1395y(b), provides:

> (1) Payment under this title may not be made with respect to any item or service to the extent that payment has been made, or can reasonably be expected to be made promptly (as determined in accordance with regulations), with respect to such item or service, under a workmen's compensation law or plan of the United States or a State or under an automobile or liability insurance policy or plan (including a self-insured plan) or under no fault insurance. Any payment under this title with respect to any item or service shall be conditioned on reimbursement to the appropriate Trust Fund established by this title when notice or other information is received that

payment for such item or service has been or could be made under such a law, policy, plan, or insurance. In order to recover payment made under this title for an item or service, the United States may bring an action against any entity which would be responsible for payment with respect to such item or service (or any portion thereof) under such a law, policy, plan, or insurance, or against any entity (including any physician or provider) which has been paid with respect to such item or service under such law, policy, plan, or insurance, and may join or intervene in any action related to the events that gave rise to the need for such item or service. The United States shall be subrogated (to the extent of payment made under this title for an item or service) to any right of an individual or any other entity to payment with respect to such item or service under such a law, policy, plan, or insurance. The Secretary may waive the provisions of this subsection in the case of an individual claim if he determines that the probability of recovery or amount involved in such claim does not warrant the pursuing of the claim.

(2)(A) In the case of an individual who is entitled to benefits under part A or is eligible to enroll under part B solely by reason of section 226A [42 U.S.C.S. 426A, which is the section of Title II of the Social Security Act which provides Medicare benefits for persons suffering end stage renal disease], payment under this title may not be made, except as provided in subparagraph (B), with respect to any item or service furnished during the period described in subparagraph (C) to the extent that payment with respect to expenses for such item or service (i) has been made under any group health plan (as defined in section 162(i)(2) of the Internal Revenue Code of 1954) [26 U.S.C.S. 162(i)(2)] or (ii) can reasonably be expected to be made under such a plan.

(B) Any payment under this title with respect to any item or service furnished to an individual described in subparagraph (A) during the period described in subparagraph (C) shall be conditioned on reimbursement to the appropriate Trust Fund established by this title when notice or other information is received that payment for such item or service has been or could be made under a plan described in subparagraph (A). In order to recover payment made under this title for an item or service, the United States may bring an action against any entity which would be responsible for payment with respect to such item or service (or any portion thereof) under such a plan, or against any entity (including any physician or provider) which has been paid with respect to such item or service under such plan, and may join or intervene in any action related to the events that gave rise to the need for such item or service. The United States shall be subrogated (to the extent of payment made under this title for an item or service) to any right of an individual or any other entity to payment with respect to such item or service under such a plan. The Secretary may waive the provisions of this subparagraph in the case of an individual claim if he determines that the probability of recovery or amount involved in such claim does not warrant the pursuing of the claim.

(C) The provisions of subparagraphs (A) and (B) shall apply to an individual only during the 12-month period which begins with the earlier of—

(i) the month in which a regular course of renal dialysis is initiated, or

(ii) in the case of an individual who receives a kidney transplant, the first month in which he would be eligible for benefits under this title (if he had filed an application for such benefits) under the provisions of section 226A(b)(1)(B) [42 U.S.C.S. 426-1(b)(1)(B)].

(D) Where payment for an item or service under such plan is less than the amount of the charge for such item or service, payment may be made under this title (without regard to deductibles and coinsurance under this title) for the remainder of such charge, but—

(i) such payment under this title may not exceed an amount which would be payable under this title for such item or service in the absence of such group health plan; and

(ii) such payment under this title, when combined with the amount payable under such plan, may not exceed the combined amount which would have been payable under this title and such plan if this paragraph were not in effect.

(3)(A)(i) Payment under this title, may not be made, except as provided in clause (ii), with respect to any item or service furnished in any month during the period described in clause (iii) to an individual (or to the spouse of such individual) who is employed at the time such item or service is furnished to the extent that payment with respect to expenses for such item or service has been made, or can reasonably by expected to be made, under a group health plan (as defined in clause (iv) under which such individual is covered by reason of such employment.

(ii) Any payment under this title with respect to any item or service during the period described in clause (iii) shall be conditioned on reimbursement to the appropriate Trust Fund established by this title when notice or other information is received that payment for such item or service has been or could be made under a group health plan. In order to recover payment made under this title for an item or service, the United States may bring an action against any entity which would be responsible for payment with respect to such item or service (or any portion thereof) under such a plan, or against any entity (including any physician or provider) which has been paid with respect to such item or service under such plan, and may join or intervene in any action related to the events that gave rise to the need for such item or service. The United States shall be subrogated (to the extent of payment made under this title for an item or service) to any right of an individual or any other entity to payment with respect to such item or service under such a plan. The Secretary may waive the provisions of this clause in the case of an individual claim if he determines that the probability of recovery or amount involved in such claim does not warrant the pursuing of the claim.

(iii) The provisions of clauses (i) and (ii) shall apply to an individual only for the period beginning with the month in which such individual becomes entitled to benefits under this title under section 226(a) [42 U.S.C.S. 426(a), which is the section of Title II of the Social Security Act which establishes entitlement to Part A benefits under Title XVIII] and shall not include any month for which the individual would, upon application, be entitled to benefits under section 226A [42 U.S.C.S. 426-1].

(iv) For purposes of this paragraph, the term "group health plan" has the meaning given to such term in section 162(i)(2) of the Internal Revenue Code of 1954.

(B) Where payment for an item or service under a group health plan is less than the amount of the charge for such item or service, payment may be made under this title (without regard to deductibles and coinsurance under this title) for the remainder of such charge, but—

(i) such payment under this title may not exceed an amount which would be payable under this title for such item or service in the absence of such group health plan; and

(ii) such payment under this title, when combined with the amount payable under such plan, may not exceed—

(I) in the case of an item or service payment for which is determined under this title on the basis of reasonable cost (or other cost-related basis) or under section 1886 [which pertains to the Prospective Payment System for inpatient hospital care], the amount which would be payable under this title on such basis; and

(II) in the case of an item or service for which payment is authorized under this title on another basis, the greater of—

(a) the amount which would be payable under the group health plan (without regard to deductibles and coinsurance under such plan), or

(b) the reasonable charge or other amount which would be payable under this title (without regard to deductibles and coinsurance under this title).

(4)(A)(i) A large group health plan may not take into account that an active individual is eligible for or receives benefits under this title under section 226(b), other than an individual who is, or would upon application be, entitled to benefits under section 226A.

(ii) Payment may not be made under this title, except as provided in clause (iii), with respect to any item or service to the extent that payment has been made, or can reasonably be expected to be made, with respect to the item or service as required under clause (i).

(iii) Any payment under this title with respect to any item or service to which clause (i) applies shall be conditioned on reimbursement to the appropriate Trust Fund established by this title. In order to recover payment made under this title for the item or service, the United States may bring an action against any entity which is required under this subsection (a) to pay with respect to the item or service (and may, in accordance with paragraph (5), collect double damages against that entity), or against any other entity that has received payment from that entity with respect to the item or service, and may join or intervene in any action related to the events that gave rise to the need for the item or service. The United States shall be subrogated (to the extent of payment made under this title for an item or service) to any right under clause (i) of an individual or any other entity to payment with respect to the item or service. The Secretary may waive (in whole or in part) the provisions of this clause in the case of an individual claim if the Secretary determines that the waiver is in the best interests of the program established under this title.

(B) In this paragraph:

(i) The term "large group health plan" has the meaning given such term in subsection (b) of section 5000 of the Internal Revenue Code of 1986 [26 U.S.C.S. 5000(b)] without regard to subsection (d) of such section.

(ii) The term "active individual" means an employee (as may be defined in regulations), the employer, an individual associated with the employer in a business relationship, or a member of the family of any of those persons.

(C) The provisions of subparagraph (B) of paragraph (3) shall apply to coordination of payment under this paragraph in the case of large group health plans in the same manner as they apply to coordination of payment under paragraph (3) in the case of group health plans.

(D) The preceding provisions of this paragraph shall only apply to items and services furnished on or after January 1, 1987, and before January 1, 1992.

Section 1862(b)(5), 42 U.S.C.S. 1395y(b)(5), then provides:

There is hereby created a private cause of action for damages (which shall be in an amount double the amount otherwise provided) in the case of a workmen's compensation law or plan, automobile or liability insurance policy or plan or no fault insurance plan, group health plan, or large group health plan which is made a primary payer under paragraph (1), (2), (3), or (4), respectively, and which fails to provide for primary payment (or appropriate reimbursement) in accordance with such respective paragraphs.

H-2: Former Chapter II-38

Violating Limitations on Physician Referrals And Related Reporting Requirements

The following summary and statutory provisions pertain to section 1877 [42 U.S.C.S. 1395nn], commonly referred to as the Stark Bill, prior to revision by section 13562 of P.L. 103-66, the Omnibus Budget Reconciliation Act of 1993.

Summary

Congress imposed significant restrictions on physician referrals for clinical laboratory services made on or after January 1, 1992. It did so effective December 19, 1989, via section 6204(a) of P.L. 101-239, the Omnibus Budget Reconciliation Act of 1989, which added a new section 1877 to Title XVIII of the Social Security Act.

Section 1877(h)(7) defines referral and referring physician in terms of requests for services. According to subparagraph (A), with regard to a clinical laboratory service required by law to be provided by or under the supervision of a physician, the request by a physician for such a service constitutes a "referral" by a "referring physician." The same is true for a request by a physician for a consultation with another physician, and for any test or procedure ordered by, or to be performed by or under supervision of, that other physician.

According to subparagraph (B), with regard to any other clinical laboratory service, the request or establishment of a plan of care by a physician which includes provision of a clinical laboratory service also constitutes a "referral" by a "referring physician." Subparagraph (C) provides, however, that a request by a pathologist for clinical diagnostic laboratory tests and pathological examination services does not constitute a "referral" by a "referring physician" if such services are furnished by or under supervision of the pathologist pursuant to a consultation requested by another physician.

Given that definition of "referral" and "referring physician", section 1877(a), 42 U.S.C.S. 1395nn(a), sets forth what is prohibited. According to section 1877(a)(1), a physician may not make a referral to an entity for clinical laboratory services to be paid for by Medicare if the physician, or an immediate family member of the physician, has a financial relationship with the entity. Furthermore, the entity itself may not present or cause to be presented a Medicare claim to any individual, third party payor, or other entity for clinical laboratory services furnished as a result of a prohibited physician referral.

Section 1877(a)(2) defines financial relationship as an ownership or investment interest in the entity, whether through equity, debt, or other means. Financial relationship also includes a compensation arrangement. Section 1877(h)(1)(A) defines compensation arrangement as any arrangement involving any remuneration between a physician, or a physician's immediate family member, and an entity. Section 1877(h)(1)(B) defines remuneration to include payments directly or indirectly, overtly or covertly, in cash or in kind.

Section 1877(b) provides exceptions to the prohibitions on ownership and investment interests and compensation arrangements. According to section 1877(b)(1), restrictions on physician referrals do not apply to physician services provided personally by, or under personal supervision of, another physician in the same group practice as the referring physician. For this purpose, physician's services are those defined in section 1861(q), 42 U.S.C.S. 1395x(q). The latter includes in the definition such professional services as surgery, consultation, and home, office, and institutional calls. It excludes services in teaching hospitals.

Section 1877(h)(4) defines group practice for the purpose of this exception as a group of two or more physicians legally organized as a partnership, professional corporation, foundation, not-for-profit corporation, faculty practice plan, or similar association—

1. in which each physician member of the group provides substantially the full range of services routinely provided by the physician through joint use of shared office space, facilities,

equipment, and personnel (that is, medical care, consultation, diagnosis, or treatment);

2. for which substantially all of the services of the physician members of the group are provided through the group and billed in the name of the group and amounts received are treated as receipts of the group;
3. in which overhead expenses of and income from the practice are distributed in accordance with methods previously determined by members of the group;
4. which meets such other standards as the Secretary of Health and Human Services may impose by regulation.

With respect to a faculty practice plan associated with a hospital with an approved medical residency training program, the definition of group practice applies only to services provided within the faculty practice plan. In cases where physician members provide a variety of different specialty services and provide professional services both within and outside the group, as well as perform other tasks such as research, the definition does not apply to services provided outside the plan.

Section 1877(b)(2) provides another exception to the restriction on physician referrals. This one applies with respect to in-office ancillary services. If such services are—

1. furnished personally by the referring physician, or
2. personally by a physician member of the same group practice as the referring physician, or
3. personally by individuals employed by such physician or group practice and personally supervised by the physician or by another physician in the group practice, and, if the services are furnished—
4. in a building in which the referring physician or another physician in the same group practice furnishes physicians' services unrelated to furnishing clinical laboratory services, or
5. in the case of a referring physician member of a group practice, in another building used by the group practice for centralized provision of the group's clinical laboratory services, such services are exempt from the prohibition against referrals.

That exemption applies, however, only if the ancillary services are billed by the physician performing or supervising the services by a group practice of which such physician is a member, or by an entity wholly owned by such physician or such group practice. Furthermore, the Secretary may impose by regulation additional limits pertaining to ownership and investment interests as needed to protect against program or patient abuse.

Also exempted from the prohibition against physician referrals for clinical laboratory services, according to section 1877(b)(3), are services furnished by certain prepaid health care plans to their enrollees. Included are—

1. health maintenance organizations (HMO's) and competitive medical plans (CMP's) with Medicare contracts under section 1877, 42 U.S.C.S. 1395mm;
2. organizations qualifying under section 1833(a)(1)(A), 42 U.S.C.S. 1395l(a)(1)(A), which pertains to pre-paid plans which agree to accept 80 percent of their reasonable cost for covered services in lieu of 80 percent of their reasonable charges, and which agree not to charge beneficiaries more than 20 percent of their reasonable cost plus applicable Medicare deductibles; and
3. organizations receiving payments on a prepaid basis via a demonstration project under section 402(a) of P.L. 90-248, the Social Security Amendments of 1967, or under section 222(a) of P.L. 92-403, the Social Security Amendments of 1972.

Section 1877(b)(4) provides an exemption in the case of a financial relationship with a hospital if the financial relationship does not relate to the provision of clinical laboratory services. In addition, section 1877(b)(5) permits exemption for any other financial relationships which the Secretary determines and specifies in regulations do not pose a risk of program or patient abuse.

Section 1877(c) provides an exception from the prohibition against referrals where ownership or investment by the referring physician involves investment securities, such as shares, bonds, debentures, notes, or other debt instruments purchased on terms generally available to the public. Under this exception, the securities must be those of a corporation listed for trading on the New York Stock Exchange, or on the American Stock Exchange, or they must be national market system securities traded under an automated interdealer quotation system operated by the National Association of Securities Dealers.

In addition, the corporation issuing the securities must have had assets exceeding $100,000,000 in its most recent fiscal year.

Section 1877(d) provides additional exceptions related only to the ownership or investment prohibition against referrals, if not otherwise excepted under section 1877(b). One is for clinical laboratory services provided by hospitals located in Puerto Rico. A second is for clinical laboratory services where the laboratory furnishing the services is in a rural area. In such cases, rural area is defined the same as for section 1886(d)(2)(D), 42 U.S.C.S. 1395ww(d)(2)(D). The latter pertains to the Prospective Payment System for inpatient hospital services, which differentiates reimbursement for urban and rural localities. The third is for clinical laboratory services provided by a hospital not in Puerto Rico if the referring physician is authorized to perform services at the hospital, and if the ownership or investment interest is in the hospital itself and not merely in a subdivision thereof.

Section 1877(e) provides several more exceptions from the limitations on physician referrals. These are related to compensation arrangements other than ownership and investment interests.

Section 1877(e)(1) provides that payments for rental or lease of office space does not constitute a compensation arrangement which triggers the prohibition against a physician referral if there is a written agreement, signed by the parties, for the rental or lease, which—

1. specifies the space covered by the agreement and dedicated for the use of the lessee,
2. provides for a term of rental or lease of at least one year,
3. provides for payment on a periodic basis of an amount consistent with fair market value,
4. provides for an amount of aggregate payments that does not vary, directly or indirectly, based on the volume or value of any referrals of business between the parties, and
5. would be considered commercially reasonable even if no referrals were made between the parties.

According to section 1877(h)(3), fair market value means, generally, the value in arms length transactions, consistent with general market value. In addition, with respect to rentals, it means the value of rental property for general commercial purposes, not taking into account its intended use. With respect to leases, it means fair market value not adjusted to reflect additional value a prospective lessee or lessor would attribute to proximity or convenience to the lessor where the lessor is a potential source of patient referrals to the lessee.

In addition, section 1877(e)(1) provides that, in the case of rental or lease of office space in which a physician who is an interested investor, or an interested investor who is an immediate family member of the physician, has an ownership or investment interest, the office space must be in the same building as the building where the physician, or group practice of which the physician is a member, has a practice.

Section 1877(h)(5) defines "interested investor" as a physician in a position to make or to influence referrals or business to the entity in which the investment is made. The term also includes an immediate family member of such an investor. "Disinterested investor" means any investor other than an "interested investor." Moreover, pursuant to section 4207(e) of P.L. 101-508, the Omnibus Budget Reconciliation Act of 1990 (OBRA 90), effective for referrals on or after January 1, 1992, as if enacted by section 6204 of OBRA 89, the term "investor" means, with respect to an entity, a person with a financial relationship specified in subsection (a)(2) with the entity.

Finally, with respect to the exemption of rental and lease of office space from the definition of compensation arrangement, the arrangement must meet such other requirements as the Secretary may impose by regulation to protect against program or patient abuse.

Section 1877(e)(2) pertains to employment and service arrangements with hospitals. These do not come within the meaning of prohibited compensation arrangements even though they are between a hospital and a physician, or immediate family member of the physician, and even though they are for the employment of the physician, or the immediate family member of the physician, and even when they are for provision of administrative services, provided—

1. the arrangement is for identifiable services;
2. the amount of the remuneration under the arrangement is consistent with the fair market value of the services, and is not based, directly or indirectly, on the volume or value of any referrals by the referring physician;
3. the remuneration is provided pursuant to an agreement which would be commercially reasonable even if no referrals were made to the hospital;

4. the arrangement meets such other requirements as the Secretary may impose by regulation as needed to protect against program or patient abuse.

Section 1877(h)(2) provides that an individual is considered "employed by" or an "employee" of an entity if the relationship meets the usual common law rules applicable to determine employer-employee relationship, which are the same rules applied for Internal Revenue Code purposes. See 3121(d)(2) of the Internal Revenue Code of 1986, 26 U.S.C.S. 3121(d)(2).

With regard to other service arrangements with entities other than hospitals, section 1877(e)(3) exempts the following from prohibited compensation arrangements:

1. arrangements for specific identifiable services as medical director or as a member of a medical advisory board at the entity pursuant to a Medicare requirement;
2. arrangements for specific identifiable physician services to be furnished to an individual receiving hospice care if payment for such services may only be made under Medicare as hospice care;
3. arrangements for specific physicians' services furnished to a nonprofit blood center; and
4. arrangements for specific identifiable administrative services, other than direct patient care services, but only under exceptional circumstances specified by the Secretary in regulations.

As with employment and service arrangements with hospitals, service arrangements with other entities also must be for remuneration which is consistent with fair market value of the services. In addition, that remuneration must not be based, directly or indirectly, on the volume or value of any referrals by the referring physician. Moreover, the remuneration must be pursuant to an agreement which would be commercially reasonable even if no referrals were made to the entity. Finally, the arrangements must meet such other requirements as the Secretary may impose by regulation as needed to protect against program or patient abuse.

Section 1877(e)(4) creates another exemption to deal with physician recruitment. Where a hospital provides remuneration to a physician to induce the physician to relocate to the geographic area served by the hospital to be a member of the hospital's medical staff, that is not a prohibited compensatory arrangement, provided—

1. the physician is not required to refer patients to the hospital;
2. the amount of the remuneration under the arrangement is based, directly or indirectly, on the volume or value of any referrals made by the referring physician; and
3. the arrangement meets such other requirements as the Secretary may impose by regulation as needed to protect against program or patient abuse.

Section 1877(e)(5) authorizes exemptions for "isolated transactions." Isolated financial transactions, such as a one-time sale of property, are not prohibited compensatory arrangements if the remuneration is consistent with the fair market value of the services, and if it is not based, directly or indirectly, on the volume or value of any referrals by the referring physician, and if the remuneration is pursuant to an agreement which would be commercially reasonable even if no referrals were made to the entity. As with other exemptions, isolated financial transactions also must meet such other requirements as the Secretary may impose by regulation as needed to protect against program or patient abuse.

Finally, section 1877(e)(6) exempts from prohibited compensatory arrangements those which involve payment by a group practice of the salary of a physician member of the group practice.

Pursuant to section 1877(f), effective October 1, 1990, each entity providing covered items or services which may be paid for by Medicare must provide information about its ownership arrangements to the Secretary. Required information includes the covered items and services provided by the entity, and the names and unique physician identification numbers of all physicians with an ownership or investment interest in the entity or whose immediate relatives have such an ownership or investment. The information must be provided in such form, manner, and at such times as the Secretary specifies, and shall first be provided not later than October 1, 1991.

NOTE: The requirement of this subsection does not apply to covered items and services provided outside the United States. Nor does it apply to entities which the Secretary determines provide services for which payment may be made under this title very infrequently. Furthermore, the Secretary may waive these requirements, and requirements of 44 U.S.C.S. Chapter 35, which pertains to coordination of Federal information policy, with respect to reporting by entities in a State so long as such reporting occurs in at least 10 States. That does not apply, however, to entities providing clinical laboratory services. Moreover, the Secretary may waive such requirements with respect to providers in a State required to report so long as such requirements are not waived with respect to parenteral and enteral suppliers, end stage renal disease facilities, suppliers of ambulance services, hospitals, entities providing physical therapy services, and entities providing diagnostic imaging services of any type.

According to section 1877(g)(5), any person required to make such a report who fails to do so is subject to a civil money penalty of not more than $10,000 for each day for which reporting is required to have been made. Enforcement procedures for this civil money penalty are governed by section 1128A, 42 U.S.C.S. 1320a-7a, which authorizes civil money penalties for a variety of offenses, and which provides for exclusion from Medicare as part of the same administrative proceeding.

Finally, section 1877(g) sets forth sanctions for illegal physician referrals for clinical laboratory services. First is denial of payment. According to section 1877(g)(1), no payment may be made under Medicare for a clinical laboratory service obtained in violation of 1877(a)(1).

Second is mandatory refund. According to section 1877(g)(2), any person who collects any amounts billed in violation of section 1877(a)(1), is liable to the individual billed and must refund any amounts so collected on a timely basis. This appears to be a statutory private right of action.

Third is a civil money penalty, as well as exclusion from Medicare for improper claims. According to section 1877(g)(3), any person who presents or causes to be presented a bill or a claim for a service that such person knows or should know is for a service for which payment may not be made under section 1877(a)(1) is subject to a civil money penalty not to exceed $15,000 for each such service. Enforcement procedures for this civil money penalty are governed by section 1128A, 42 U.S.C.S. 1320a-7a, which authorizes civil money penalties for a variety of offenses, and which provides for exclusion from Medicare as part of the same administrative proceeding.

The civil money penalty and exclusion sanction of section 1877(g)(3) also applies to persons who fail to make refunds required by section 1877(g)(2).

Fourth is a civil money penalty, as well as exclusion, for schemes designed to circumvent the prohibition on physician referrals for clinical laboratory services. According to section 1877(g)(4), any physician or other entity that enters into an arrangement or scheme, such as a cross-referral arrangement, which the physician or entity knows or should know has a principal purpose of assuring referrals by the physician to a particular entity which, if directly made by the physician to the entity would be a violation, is subject to a civil money penalty not to exceed $100,000 for each such arrangement or scheme. By cross-reference, enforcement proceedings for this civil money penalty are also governed by section 1128A, which, as indicated above permits imposition of civil money penalties and exclusion from Medicare via one administrative proceeding.

NOTE: Previous versions of section 1877, dealing with similar and related matters were in part repealed and in part transferred to section 1909 of the Act. See section 4(c) and section 4(e) of P.L. 100-93, the Medicare and Medicaid Patient and Program Protection Act of 1987. See also section 1128B, 42 U.S.C.S. 1320a-7b, which pertains to criminal penalties for kickbacks, bribes, rebates, and other fraudulent acts.

Statutory Provisions

Section 1877, 42 U.S.C.S. 1395nn, provides:

(a) PROHIBITION OF CERTAIN REFERRALS.—

(1) IN GENERAL.—Except as provided in subsection (b), if a physician (or immediate family member of such physician) has a financial relationship with an entity specified in paragraph (2), then—

(A) the physician may not make a referral to the entity for the furnishing of clinical laboratory services for which payment otherwise may be made under this title, and

(B) the entity may not present or cause to be presented a claim under this title or bill to any individual, third party payor, or other entity for clinical laboratory services furnished pursuant to a referral prohibited under subparagraph (A).

(2) FINANCIAL RELATIONSHIP SPECIFIED.—For purposes of this section, a financial relationship of a physician (or

immediate family member) with an entity specified in this paragraph is—

(A) except as provided in subsections (c) and (d), an ownership or investment interest in the entity; or

(B) except as provided in subsection (e), a compensation arrangement (as defined in subsection (h)(1)(A)) between the physician (or immediate family member) and the entity.

An ownership or investment interest described in subparagraph (A) may be through equity, debt, or other means.

(b) GENERAL EXCEPTIONS TO BOTH OWNERSHIP AND COMPENSATION ARRANGEMENT PROHIBITIONS.—Subsection (a) (1) shall not apply in the following cases:

(1) PHYSICIANS' SERVICES.—In the case of physicians' services (as defined in section 1861(q) [42 U.S.C.S. 1395x(q), which pertains to physicians' professional services, including surgery, consultation, and home, office, and institutional calls, but not including services in teaching hospitals as set forth in section 1861(b)(6), 42 U.S.C.S. 1395x(b)(6)] provided personally by (or under the personal supervision of) another physician in the same group practice (as defined in subsection (h)(4)) as the referring physician.

(2) IN–OFFICE ANCILLARY SERVICES.—In the case of services—

(A) that are furnished—

(i) personally by the referring physician, personally by a physician who is a member of the same group practice as the referring physician, or personally by individuals who are employed by such physician or group practice and who are personally supervised by the physician or by another physician in the group practice, and

(ii)(I) in a building in which the referring physician (or another physician who is a member of the same group practice) furnishes physicians' services unrelated to the furnishing of clinical laboratory services, or

(II) in the case of a referring physician who is a member of a group practice, in another building which is used by the group practice for the centralized provision of the group's clinical laboratory services, and

(B) that are billed by the physician performing or supervising the services, by a group practice of which such physician is a member, or by an entity that is wholly owned by such physician or such group practice, if the ownership or investment interest in such services meets such other requirements as the Secretary may impose by regulation as needed to protect against program or patient abuse.

(3) PREPAID PLANS.—In the case of services furnished—

(A) by an organization with a contract under section 1876 [42 U.S.C.S. 1395mm, which pertains to health maintenance organizations and competitive medical plans] to an individual enrolled with the organization,

(B) by an organization described in section 1833(a)(1)(A) [42 U.S.C.S. 1395l(a)(1)(A), which pertains to the option of organizations which provide medical and other health services, or which arrange for their availability, on a prepayment basis to receive 80 percent of the reasonable cost of covered services in lieu of 80 percent of the reasonable charges for such services, provided such organizations agree not to charge beneficiaries more than 20 percent of the reasonable cost plus applicable deductibles] to an individual enrolled with the organization, or

(C) by an organization receiving payments on a prepaid basis, under a demonstration project under section 402(a) of the Social Security Amendments of 1967 or under section 222(a) of the Social Security Amendments of 1972, to an individual enrolled with the organization [P.L. 90-248 and P.L. 92-603, respectively, which are referred to in section 1814(b), 42 U.S.C.S. 1395f(b)].

(4) HOSPITAL FINANCIAL RELATIONSHIP UNRELATED TO THE PROVISION OF CLINICAL LABORATORY SERVICES.—In the case of a financial relationship with a hospital if the financial relationship does not relate to the provision of clinical laboratory services [This paragraph and renumbering of the following paragraph as (5) added by section 4207(e)(2) of P.L. 101-508, the Omnibus Budget Reconciliation Act of 1990 (OBRA 90), effective with respect to referrals after January 1, 1992, as if enacted by section 6204 of OBRA 89].

(5) OTHER PERMISSIBLE EXCEPTIONS.—In the case of any other financial relationship which the Secretary determines, and specifies in regulations, does not pose a risk of program or patient abuse.

(c) GENERAL EXCEPTION RELATED ONLY TO OWNERSHIP OR INVESTMENT PROHIBITION FOR OWNERSHIP IN PUBLICLY-TRADED SECURITIES.—Ownership of investment securities (including shares or bonds, debentures, notes, or other debt instruments) which were purchased on terms generally available to the public and which are in a corporation that—

(1) is listed for trading on the New York Stock Exchange or on the American Stock Exchange, or is a national market system security traded under an automated interdealer quotation system operated by the National Association of Securities Dealers, and

(2) had, at the end of the corporation's most recent fiscal year, total assets exceeding $100,000,000,

shall not be considered to be an ownership or investment interest described in (a)(2)(A).

(d) ADDITIONAL EXCEPTIONS RELATED ONLY TO OWNERSHIP OR INVESTMENT PROHIBITION.—The following, if not otherwise excepted under subsection (b), shall not be considered to be an ownership or investment interest described in subsection (a)(2)(A):

(1) HOSPITALS IN PUERTO RICO.—In the case of clinical laboratory services provided by a hospital located in Puerto Rico.

(2) RURAL PROVIDER.—In the case of clinical laboratory services if the laboratory furnishing the services is in a rural area (as defined in section 1886(d)(2)(D) [42 U.S.C.S. 1395ww(d)(2)(D), which pertains to computation of the Prospective Payment System reimbursement for inpatient hospital services in urban and rural localities]).

(3) HOSPITAL OWNERSHIP.—In the case of clinical laboratory services provided by a hospital (other than a hospital described in paragraph (1)) if—

(A) the referring physician is authorized to perform services at the hospital, and

(B) the ownership or investment interest is in the hospital itself (and not merely in a subdivision thereof).

(e) EXCEPTIONS RELATING TO OTHER COMPENSATION ARRANGEMENTS.—The following shall not be considered to be a compensation arrangement described in subsection (a)(2)(B):

(1) RENTAL OF OFFICE SPACE.—Payments made for the rental or lease of office space if—

(A) there is a written agreement, signed by the parties, for the rental or lease of the space, which agreement—

(i) specifies the space covered by the agreement and dedicated for the use of the lessee,

(ii) provides for a term of rental or lease of at least one year;

(iii) provides for payment on a periodic basis of an amount that is consistent with fair market value;

(iv) provides for an amount of aggregate payments that does not vary (directly or indirectly) based on the volume or value of any referrals of business between the parties; and

(v) would be considered to be commercially reasonable even if no referrals were made between the parties;

(B) in the case of rental or lease of office space in which a physician who is an interested investor (or an interested investor who is an immediate family member of the physician) has an ownership or investment interest, the office space is in the same building as the building in which the physician (or group practice of which the physician is a member) has a practice; and

(C) the arrangement meets such other requirements as the Secretary may impose by regulation as needed to protect against program or patient abuse.

(2) EMPLOYMENT AND SERVICE ARRANGEMENTS WITH HOSPITALS.—An arrangement between a hospital and a physician (or immediate family member) for the employment of the physician (or family member) or for the provision of administrative services, if—

(A) the arrangement is for identifiable services;

(B) the amount of the remuneration under the arrangement—

(i) is consistent with the fair market value of the services, and

(ii) is not determined in a manner that takes into account (directly or indirectly) the volume or value of any referrals by the referring physician;

(C) the remuneration is provided pursuant to an agreement which would be commercially reasonable even if no referrals were made to the hospital; and

(D) the arrangement meets such other requirements as the Secretary may impose by regulation as needed to protect against program or patient abuse.

(3) OTHER SERVICE ARRANGEMENTS.—Remuneration from an entity (other than a hospital) under an arrangement if—

(A) the arrangement is—

(i) for specific identifiable services as the medical director or as a member of a medical advisory board at the entity pursuant to a requirement of this title,

(ii) for specific identifiable physicians' services to be furnished to an individual receiving hospice care if payment for such services may only be made under this title as hospice care,

(iii) for specific physicians' services furnished to a nonprofit blood center, or

(iv) for specific identifiable administrative services (other than direct patient care services), but only under exceptional circumstances specified by the Secretary in regulations;

(B) the requirements described in subparagraph (B) and (C) of paragraph (2) are met with respect to the entity in the same manner as they apply to a hospital; and

(C) the arrangement meets such other requirements as the Secretary may impose by regulation as needed to protect against program or patient abuse.

(4) PHYSICIAN RECRUITMENT.—In the case of remuneration which is provided by a hospital to a physician to induce the physician to relocate to the geographic area served by the hospital in order to be a member of the medical staff of the hospital, if

(A) the physician is not required to refer patients to the hospital,

(B) the amount of the remuneration under the arrangement is not determined in a manner that takes into account (directly or indirectly) the volume or value of any referrals by the referring physician, and

(C) the arrangement meets such other requirements as the Secretary may impose by regulation as needed to protect against program or patient abuse.

(5) ISOLATED TRANSACTIONS.—In the case of an isolated financial transaction, such as a one-time sale of property, if—

(A) the requirements described in subparagraphs (B) and (C) of paragraph (2) are met with respect to the entity in the same manner as they apply to a hospital, and

(B) the transaction meets such other requirements as the Secretary may impose by regulation as needed to protect against program or patient abuse.

(6) SALARIED PHYSICIANS IN A GROUP PRACTICE.-A compensation arrangement involving payment by a group practice of the salary of a physician member of the group practice.

(f) REPORTING REQUIREMENTS.—Each entity providing covered items or services for which payment may be made under this title shall provide the Secretary with the information concerning the entity's ownership arrangements, including—

(1) the covered items and services provided by the entity, and

(2) the names and unique physician identification numbers of all physicians with an ownership or investment interest (as described in subsection (a)(2)(A)) in the entity, or whose immediate relatives have such an ownership or investment. [Prior to enactment of section 4207(e)(3) of OBRA 90, effective as if enacted by section 6204 of OBRA 89, i.e., October 1, 1990, this paragraph (2) read "the names and all of the medicare provider numbers of the physicians who are interested inves-

tors or who are immediate relatives of interested investors. Also below, "October 1, 1991" replaced "1 year after the date of the enactment of this section" and the balance of the paragraph after that date.

Such information shall be provided in such form, manner, and at such times as the Secretary shall specify. Such information shall first be provided not later than October 1, 1991. The requirement of this subsection shall not apply to covered items and services provided outside the United States or to entities which the Secretary determines provides [sic provide] services for which payment may be made under this title very infrequently. The Secretary may waive the requirements of this subsection (and the requirements of chapter 35 of title 44, United States Code, with respect to information provided under this subsection) with respect to reporting by entities in a State (except for entities providing clinical laboratory services) so long as such reporting occurs in at least 10 States, and the Secretary may waive such requirements with respect to the providers in a State required to report so long as such requirements are not waived with respect to parenteral and enteral suppliers, end stage renal disease facilities, suppliers of ambulance services, hospitals, entities providing physical therapy services, and entities providing diagnostic imaging services of any type.

(g) SANCTIONS.—

(1) DENIAL OF PAYMENT.—No payment may be made under this title for a clinical laboratory service which is provided in violation of subsection (a)(1).

(2) REQUIRING REFUNDS FOR CERTAIN CLAIMS.—If a person collects any amounts that were billed in violation of subsection (a) (1), the person shall be liable to the individual for, and shall refund on a timely basis to the individual, any amounts so collected.

(3) CIVIL MONEY PENALTY AND EXCLUSION FOR IMPROPER CLAIMS.—Any person that presents or causes to be presented a bill or a claim for a service that such person knows or should know is for a service for which payment may not be made under paragraph (1) or for which a refund has not been made under paragraph (2) shall be subject to a civil money penalty of not more than $15,000 for each such service.

The provisions of section 1128A [42 U.S.C.S. 1320a-7a, which authorizes civil money penalties for a variety of offenses] (other than the first sentence of subsection (a) and other than subsection (b) [which pertain to certain offenses]) shall apply to a civil money penalty under the previous sentence in the same manner as such provisions apply to a penalty or proceeding under section 1128A(a).

(4) CIVIL MONEY PENALTY AND EXCLUSION FOR CIRCUMVENTION SCHEMES.—Any physician or other entity that enters into an arrangement or scheme (such as a cross-referral arrangement) which the physician or entity knows or should know has a principal purpose of assuring referrals by the physician to a particular entity which, if the physician directly made referrals to such entity, would be in violation of this section, shall be subject to a civil money penalty of not more than $100,000 for each such arrangement or scheme. The provisions of section 1128A (other than the first sentence of subsection (a) and other than subsection (b)) shall apply to a civil money penalty under the previous sentence in the same manner as such provisions apply to a penalty or proceeding under section 1128A(a).

(5) FAILURE TO REPORT INFORMATION.—Any person who is required, but fails, to meet a reporting requirement of subsection (f) is subject to a civil money penalty of not more than $10,000 for each day for which reporting is required to have been made. The provisions of section 1128A [42 U.S.C.S. 1320a-7a] (other than the first sentence of subsection (a) and other than subsection (b)) shall apply to a civil money penalty under the previous sentence in the same manner as such provisions apply to a penalty or proceeding under section 1128A(a). [The last sentence added by section 4207(k)(2) of OBRA 90, effective November 5, 1990.]

(h) DEFINITIONS.—For purposes of this section:

(1) COMPENSATION ARRANGEMENT; REMUNERATION.—(A) The term "compensation arrangement" means any arrangement involving any remuneration between a physician (or immediate family member) and an entity.

(B) The term "remuneration" includes any remuneration, directly or indirectly, overtly or covertly, in cash or in kind.

(2) EMPLOYEE.—An individual is considered to be "employed by" or an "employee" of an entity if the individual would be considered to be an employee of the entity under the usual common law rules applicable in determining the employer-employee relationship (as applied for purposes of section 3121(d)(2) of the Internal Revenue Code of 1986 [26 U.S.C.S. 3121(d)(2)]).

(3) FAIR MARKET VALUE.—The term "fair market value" means the value in arms length transactions, consistent with the general market value, and, with respect to rentals or leases, the value of rental property for general commercial purposes (not taking into account its intended use) and, in the case of a lease of space, not adjusted to reflect the additional value the prospective lessee or lessor would attribute to the proximity or convenience to the lessor where the lessor is a potential source of patient referrals to the lessee.

(4) GROUP PRACTICE.—The term "group practice" means a group of two or more physicians legally organized as a partnership, professional corporation, foundation, not-for-profit corporation, faculty practice plan, or similar association—

(A) in which each physician who is a member of the group provides substantially the full range of services which the physician routinely provides (including medical care, consultation, diagnosis, or treatment) through the joint use of shared office space, facilities, equipment, and personnel;

(B) for which substantially all of the services of the physicians who are members of the group are provided through the group and are billed in the name of the group and amounts so received are treated as receipts of the group;

(C) in which the overhead expenses of and the income from the practice are distributed in accordance with methods previously determined by members of the group; and

(D) which meets such other standards as the Secretary may impose by regulation.

In the case of a faculty practice plan associated with a hospital with an approved medical residency training program in which physician members may provide a variety of different specialty services and provide professional services both within and outside the group (as well as perform other tasks such as research), the previous sentence shall be applied only with respect to the services provided within the faculty practice plan.

(5) INTERESTED INVESTOR; DISINTERESTED INVESTOR.—The term "interested investor" means, with respect to an entity, an investor who is a physician in a position to make or to influence referrals or business to the entity (or who is an immediate family member of such an investor), and the term "disinterested investor" means an investor other than an interested investor.

(6) INVESTOR.—The term "investor" means, with respect to an entity, a person with a financial relationship specified in subsection (a)(2) with the entity. [This paragraph (6) and redesignation of the following paragraph as (7) added by section 4207(e)(1) of OBRA 90, effective with respect to referrals on or after January 1, 1992, as if included in enactment of section 6204 of OBRA 89.]

(7) REFERRAL; REFERRING PHYSICIAN.—

(A) PHYSICIANS' SERVICES.—Except as provided in subparagraph (C), in the case of an item or service for which payment may be made under part B, the request by a physician for the item or service, including the request by a physician for a consultation with another physician (and any test or procedure ordered by, or to be performed by (or under the supervision of) that other physician), constitutes a "referral" by a "referring physician".

[NOTE: Prior to enactment of section 4207(e)(1) of OBRA 90, effective with respect to referrals on or after January 1, 1992, as if enacted by section 6204 of OBRA 89, this paragraph (A) read: Except as provided in subparagraph (C), in the case of a clinical laboratory service which under law is required to be provided by (or under the supervision of) a physician, the request by a physician for the service, including the request by a physician for a consultation with another physician (and any test or procedure ordered by, or to be performed by (or under the supervision of) that other physician), constitutes a 'referral' by a 'referring physician'. " It also deleted the phrase "in the case of another clinical laboratory service," which previously followed "subparagraph (C)" below in paragraph (B).]

(B) OTHER ITEMS.—Except as provided in subparagraph (C), the request or establishment of a plan of care by a physician which includes the provision of the clinical laboratory service constitutes a "referral" by a "referring physician".

(C) CLARIFICATION RESPECTING CERTAIN SERVICES INTEGRAL TO A CONSULTATION BY CERTAIN SPECIALISTS.—A request by a pathologist for clinical diagnostic laboratory tests and pathological examination services, if such services are furnished by (or under the supervision of) such pathologist pursuant to a consultation requested by another physician does not constitute a "referral" by a "referring physician".

H-3: Former Chapter II-40-A

ISSUING MEDICARE SUPPLEMENTAL HEALTH INSURANCE POLICIES IN VIOLATION OF STATE OR FEDERAL STANDARDS

The following summary and statutory provisions pertain to section 1882(a)(2) [42 U.S.C.S. 1395ss(a)(2)] prior to revision by P.L. 101-508, the Omnibus Budget Reconciliation Act of 1990, effective November 5, 1990.

Summary

In section 1882(a), 42 U.S.C.S. 1395ss(a), Congress authorized the Secretary of Health and Human Services to certify that Medicare supplemental health insurance policies meet established standards for coverage and benefits. It also authorized him to permit approved entities to use a Secretarial emblem of certification in their marketing.

A Medicare supplemental policy, according to section 1882(g)(1), is a health insurance policy or other health benefit plan offered by a private entity to Medicare beneficiaries which provides reimbursement for items not payable by Medicare because of deductibles, coinsurance amounts, or other limitations on payment. Not included in the definition is any such policy or plan of one or more employers or labor organizations, or of trustees of a fund established by one or more employers or labor organizations (or combination thereof) which is for employees or former employees (or combination thereof) or for members or former members (or combination thereof) of the labor organizations.

Section 1882(b) established a Supplemental Health Insurance Panel consisting of the Secretary, who serves as the Chairman, and four State commissioners or superintendents of insurance. The latter are appointed by the Secretary and serve at his pleasure. The Panel is authorized to determine that a Medicare supplemental policy issued in any State which the Panel determines has a sufficiently stringent set of standards and conditions for health insurance policies is deemed to meet the standards of section 1882(c).

Generally, this applied where a State had standards equal to or more stringent than those of the National Association of Insurance Commissioners (NAIC), either as adopted June 6, 1979, or as subsequently amended to comply with P.L. 100-360, the Medicare Catastrophic Coverage Act of 1988 (MCCA). After MCCA was repealed, effective January 1, 1990, by P.L. 101-234, the Medicare Catastrophic Coverage Repeal Act of 1989 (MCCRA), the latter authorized a transition period for insurers either to comply with MCCRA, if the NAIC Model Regulation was revised timely to reflect MCCRA, or to comply with revised Federal model standards, if the NAIC Model Regulation was not revised timely to reflect MCCRA. See sections 1882(m) and 1882(n), which were added by MCCRA.

In addition to the NAIC level of standards, according to section 1882(c), before the Secretary can certify a policy, he must find that for group policies it can be expected to return to policyholders in the form of aggregate benefits at least 75 percent of the aggregate amount of premiums collected, and that for individual policies it can be expected to return at least 60 percent of the aggregate amount of premiums collected. Policies issued as a result of solicitations of individuals through the mails or by mass media advertising, including print and broadcast advertising, are deemed to be individual policies. The Secretary also must find that the policy may be returned for full refund of any premiums paid at any time within 30 days after it is issued.

In addition, with respect to the issuer of the policy, the Secretary must find that it accepts a Medicare notice of benefits as a claim form for benefits under the policy in lieu of any other claim form and that it agrees to make a payment determination on the basis of the information in that Medicare notice; that where such a notice is received, the issuer provides notice to such physician or supplier and the beneficiary of the payment determination under the policy, and provides any payment covered by such policy directly to the participating physician or supplier involved; that the issuer provides each enrollee upon enrollment a card listing the policy name and number and a single mailing address to which to send claim notices under the policy; that it agrees to pay any user fees established under Medicare with respect to information transmitted to the issuer; and that the issuer provides to the Secretary at least annually, for transmittal to Medicare carriers, a single mailing address to which Medicare notices of payment are to be sent.

To put teeth into its enforcement procedures and to educate consumers, Congress, in section 1882(e), obligated the Secretary to provide to all Medicare beneficiaries, and, as much as possible, to those about to become beneficiaries, information to help them evaluate not only Medicare supplemental policies but also their relationship to Medicare benefits. That information must include a listing of addresses and telephone numbers of State and Federal agencies and offices that can provide assistance with respect to selection of Medicare supplemental policies. The Secretary was further obliged to inform them about sanctionable actions under section 1882, including the manner in which they may report such improper actions to him and the availability of a toll-free telephone number for making such reports.

Statutory Provisions

Section 1882(a), 42 U.S.C.S. 1395ss(a), provides:

> The Secretary shall establish a procedure whereby medicare supplemental policies (as defined in subsection (g)(1)) may be certified by the Secretary as meeting minimum standards and requirements set forth in subsection (c). Such procedure shall provide an opportunity for any insurer to submit any such policy, and such additional data as the Secretary finds necessary, to the Secretary for his examination and for his certification thereof as meeting the standards and requirements set forth in subsection (c). Subject to subsections (k)(3) [which prohibits Secretarial certification from being made, being continued, or being deemed unless the Medicare supplemental insurance policy meets or exceeds standards set forth in the NAIC Model Regulation, if amended to comply with P.L. 100-360, the Medicare Catastrophic Coverage Act of 1988, or, if not so amended, meets or exceeds Federal model standards—effective either one year after the date the Association first adopts such amended Model Regulation or one year after the date the Secretary first promul-

gates such standards, as the case may be], (k)(4) [sic (l)(4)?], (m), and (n) [(k)(4), (m), and (n) added, effective January 1, 1990, by section 203 of P.L. 101-234, the Medicare Catastrophic Coverage Repeal Act of 1989, to permit insurers to comply with changes required by enactment and repeal of P.L. 100-360, the Medicare Catastrophic Coverage Act of 1988], such certification shall remain in effect if the insurer files a notarized statement with the Secretary no later than June 30 of each year stating that the policy continues to meet such standards and requirements and if the insurer submits such additional data as the Secretary finds necessary to independently verify the accuracy of such notarized statement. Where the Secretary determines such a policy meets (or continues to meet) such standards and requirements, he shall authorize the insurer to have printed on such policy (but only in accordance with such requirements and conditions as the Secretary may prescribe) an emblem which the Secretary shall cause to be designed for use as an indication that a policy has received the Secretary's certification. The Secretary shall provide each State commissioner or superintendent of insurance with a list of all the policies which have received his certification.

Section 1882(g) provides:

(1) For purposes of this section, a medicare supplemental policy is a health insurance policy or other health benefit plan offered by a private entity to individuals who are entitled to have payment made under this title, which provides reimbursement for expenses incurred for services and items for which payment may be made under this title but which are not reimbursable by reason of the applicability of deductibles, coinsurance amounts, or other limitations imposed pursuant to this title; but does not include any such policy or plan of one or more employers or labor organizations, or of the trustees of a fund established by one or more employers or labor organizations (or combination thereof), for employees or former employees (or combination thereof) or for members or former members (or combination thereof) of the labor organizations. For purposes of this section, the term "policy" includes a certificate issued under such policy.

(2) For purposes of this section:

(A) The term "NAIC Model Standards" means the "NAIC Model Regulation to Implement the Individual Accident and Sickness Insurance Minimum Standards Act", adopted by the National Association of Insurance Commissioners on June 6, 1979, as it applies to medicare supplement [sic supplemental] policies.

(B) The term "State with an approved regulatory program" means a State for which the Panel has made a determination under subsection (b)(1).

(C) The State in which a policy is issued means—

(i) in the case of an individual policy, the State in which the policyholder resides; and

(ii) in the case of a group policy, the State in which the holder of the master policy resides.

Section 1882(b) provides:

(1) Any medicare supplemental policy issued in any State which the Supplemental Health Insurance Panel (established under paragraph (2)) determines has established under State law a regulatory program that—

(A) provides for the application of standards with respect to such policies equal to or more stringent than the NAIC Model Standards (as defined in subsection (g)(2)(A));

(B) includes requirements equal to or more stringent than the requirements described in paragraphs (2) through (4) of subsection (c);

(C) provides that—

(i) information with respect to the actual ratio of benefits provided to premiums collected under such policies will be reported to the State on forms conforming to those developed by the National Association of Insurance Commissioners for such purpose, or

(ii) such ratios will be monitored under the program in an alternative manner approved by the Secretary;

(D) provides for application of the standards and requirements described in subparagraphs (A), (B), and (C) to all medicare supplemental policies (as defined in subsection (g)(1)) issued in such State, and

(E) provides the Secretary periodically (but at least annually) with a list containing the name and address of the issuer of each such policy and the name and number of each such policy (including an indication of policies that have been previously approved, newly approved, or withdrawn from approval since the previous list was provided),

shall be deemed (subject to subsection (k)(3), (k)(4) [sic (l)(4)?], (m), and (n) [(k)(4), (m), and (n) added effective January 1, 1990] for so long as the Panel finds that such State regulatory program continues to meet the standards and requirements of this paragraph) to meet the standards and requirements set forth in subsection (c).

(2)(A) There is hereby established a panel (hereinafter in this section referred to as the "Panel") to be known as the Supplemental Health Insurance Panel. The Panel shall consist of the Secretary, who shall serve as the Chairman, and four State commissioners or superintendents of insurance, who shall be appointed by the Secretary and serve at his pleasure. Such members shall first be appointed not later than December 31, 1980.

(B) A majority of the members of the Panel shall constitute a quorum, but a lesser number may conduct hearings.

(C) The Secretary shall provide such technical, secretarial, clerical and other assistance as the Panel may require.

(D) There are authorized to be appropriated such sums as may be necessary to carry out this paragraph.

(E) Members of the Panel shall be allowed, while away from their homes or regular places of business in the performance of services for the Panel, travel expenses (including per diem in lieu of subsistence) in the same manner as persons employed intermittently in the government service are allowed expenses under section 5703 of title 5, United States Code.

(3) Notwithstanding paragraph (1), a medicare supplemental policy offered in a State shall not be deemed to meet the standards and requirements set forth in subsection (c), with respect to an advertisement (whether through written, radio, or television medium) used (or, at a State's option, to be used) for the policy in the State, unless the entity issuing the policy

provides a copy of each advertisement to the Commissioner of Insurance (or comparable officer identified by the Secretary) of that State for review or approval to the extent it may be required under State law.

Then section 1882(c) spells out the standards as follows:

The Secretary shall certify under this section any medicare supplemental policy, or continue certification of such a policy, only if he finds that such policy (or, with respect to paragraph (3), the issuer of the policy)—

(1) meets or exceeds (either in a single policy or, in the case of nonprofit hospital and medical service associations, in one or more policies issued in conjunction with one another) the NAIC Model Standards,

(2) can be expected (as estimated for the entire period for which rates are computed to provide coverage, on the basis of incurred claims experience and earned premiums for such period and in accordance with accepted actuarial principles and practices to return to policyholders in the form of aggregate benefits provided under the policy, at least 75 percent of the aggregate amount of premiums collected in the case of group policies and at least 60 percent of the aggregate amount of premiums collected in the case of individual policies;

(3)(A) accepts a notice under section 1842(h)(3)(B) [42 U.S.C.S. 1395u(h)(3)(B), which pertains to assignment of Medicare claims and the form of notice of payment determination prepared by the Medicare carrier in assignment cases] as a claim form for benefits under such policy in lieu of any claim form otherwise required and agrees to make a payment determination on the basis of the information contained in such notice;

(B) where such a notice is received—

(i) provides notice to such physician or supplier and the beneficiary of the payment determination under the policy, and

(ii) provides any payment covered by such policy directly to the participating physician or supplier involved;

(C) provides each enrollee at the time of enrollment a card listing the policy name and number and a single mailing address to which notices under section 1842(h)(3)(B) respecting the policy are to be sent;

(D) agrees to pay any user fees established under section 1842(h)(3)(B) with respect to information transmitted to the issuer of the policy; and

(E) provides to the Secretary at least annually, for transmittal to carriers, a single mailing address to which notices under section 1842(h)(3)(B) respecting the policy are to be sent; and

(4) may, during a period of not less than 30 days after the policy is issued, be returned for a full refund of any premiums paid (without regard to the manner in which the purchase of the policy was solicited).

For purposes of paragraph (2), policies issued as a result of solicitations of individuals through the mails or by mass media advertising (including both print and broadcast advertising) shall be deemed to be individual policies.

H-4: Former Chapter IV-14

MISUSE OF FEDERAL GOVERNMENT NAMES, SYMBOLS, AND EMBLEMS Section 1140 [42 U.S.C.S. 1320b-10]

The following summary and statutory provisions reflect section 1140 prior to revision by section 108(b)(12) of the Social Security Independence and Program Improvements Act of 1994, P.L. 103-296, effective March 31, 1995, and by section 312(a)-(j) of the same Act, effective August 15, 1995.

Summary

Section 1140(a), 42 U.S.C.S. 1320b-10(a), prohibits the use of the words "Social Security", "Social Security Account", "Social Security System", "Social Security Administration", "Medicare", "Health Care Financing Administration", the letters "SSA" or "HCFA" in any manner which a person knows, or should know, would convey the false impression that an item is approved, endorsed, or authorized by the Social Security Administration (SSA), the Health Care Financing Administration (HCFA), or the Department of Health and Human Services (HHS), or that such person has some connection with, or authorization from, SSA, HCFA, or HHS.

The statute also prohibits such misuse of a symbol or emblem of SSA, including the design of, or a reasonable facsimile of the design of, the Social Security card, the check used for payment of Social Security benefits, and envelopes or other stationery used by SSA; misuse of a symbol or emblem of HCFA; and misuse of any other combination or variation of such symbols or emblems.

These prohibitions apply to misuse in connection with any item constituting an advertisement, solicitation, circular, book, pamphlet, or other communication, or a play, motion picture, broadcast, telecast, or other production; and they apply whether the names, acronyms, symbols, or emblems are used alone or with other words, letters, symbols, or emblems in any combination or variation.

Section 1140(b) authorizes the Secretary of Health and Human Services to impose a civil money penalty on anyone who violates section 1140(a). The amount of the penalty may not to exceed $5,000 for each violation, unless the violation consists of a broadcast or telecast. For such cases, the Secretary may impose a civil money penalty not to exceed $25,000. Regardless the number of violations in a year, however, total penalties may not exceed $100,000 if the violations involve substantially identical communications or productions.

Section 1140(c)(1) provides that subsections (c),(d), (e), (g), (j), (k), and (l) of section 1128A, 42 U.S.C.S. 1320a-7a, which authorizes civil money penalties for a variety of offenses, apply to this civil money penalty provision as well.

Subsection (c) of section 1128A permits the Secretary to initiate a civil money penalty proceeding only after establishing procedures for such cases in conjunction with the Attorney General of the United States. It also imposes a six-year statute of limitations which commences when the violation occurred. In addition, it requires notice and opportunity for a hearing on the record prior to imposition of the penalty, along with the right to representation by counsel, the right to present witnesses, and the right to cross-examine adverse witnesses. Furthermore, it prevents anyone convicted of a crime charging a false statement or fraud from denying the essential elements of the criminal offense in a proceeding by the Secretary to impose a civil money penalty under section 1140 if the administrative proceeding involves the same transaction as in the criminal action. That applies whether the conviction is based upon a verdict, a plea of guilty, or a plea of nolo contendere.

Subsection (c) also authorizes the official conducting the civil money penalty proceeding to sanction a person, including any party or attorney, for failing to comply with an order or procedure, for failing to defend an action, or for other misconduct which would interfere with the speedy, orderly, or fair conduct of the hearing. Any such sanction must relate to the severity and nature of the failure or misconduct, but options include drawing negative factual inferences or deeming facts or matters established in the case of refusal to provide or permit discovery; prohibiting a party from introducing certain evidence or otherwise supporting a particular claim or defense; striking pleadings, in whole or in part; staying proceedings; dismissing the action; entering a default judgment; ordering the party or attorney to pay attorneys' fees and other costs caused by the failure or misconduct; and refusing to consider any motion or other action not filed in a timely manner.

Subsection (d) requires the Secretary to take into account the nature of the offense and the circumstances, the degree of culpability, any history of prior offenses, the financial condition of the violator, and any other matters which justice may require in determining the amount of a penalty.

Subsection (e) establishes the right to judicial review of the Secretary's determination in the United States Court of Appeals where the violator resides. It also establishes procedures governing appeal, including remand to the Secretary for further development, a substantial evidence review of the administrative record, a prohibition against raising new objections absent extraordinary circumstances, and a time limit to seek judicial review which ends 60 days following the date the Secretary notifies the alleged violator of his final decision.

Subsection (g) makes the Secretary's determination final when the time to appeal has expired, and prohibits the violator from raising any matter which was not, but could have been, raised in a hearing before the Secretary or upon judicial review as a defense in any subsequent action by the United States to collect the penalty.

Subsection (j) makes the provisions of section 205(d) and 205(e), 42 U.S.C.S. 405(d) and (e), applicable to administrative hearings in section 1140 cases. It also permits the Secretary to delegate his authority to issue subpenas for investigative purposes to the Inspector General of the Department of Health and Human Services; and it authorizes the Secretary to seek judicial enforcement of such subpenas.

Subsection (k) permits the Secretary to seek injunctive relief when he believes a person has engaged in, is engaging in, or is about to engage in a violation of section 1140, and to prevent a person from concealing, removing, encumbering, or disposing of assets which may be required to pay a civil money penalty if one were to be imposed under section 1140.

Subsection (l) makes a principal liable for a civil money penalty when the principal's agent acting within the scope of the agency commits the violation.

Finally, section 1140(c)(2) permits the Secretary to compromise a civil money penalty imposed under section 1140, or to seek recovery of the penalty by civil action in the Federal District Court for the district where the violation occurred, or where the violator resides, has a principal office, or may be found. It requires amounts recovered to be deposited as miscellaneous receipts of the Treasure of the United States. And it specifies that any amount to be recovered, whether by compromise or by judgment, may be deducted from any sum then or later owing by the United States to the person against whom the penalty was imposed.

Statutory Provisions

Section 1140(a), 42 U.S.C.S. 1320b-10(a), provides:

> No person may use, in connection with any item constituting an advertisement, solicitation, circular, book, pamphlet, or other communication, or a play, motion picture, broadcast, telecast, or other production, alone or with other words, letters, symbols, or emblems —
>
> (1) the words "Social Security", "Social Security Account", "Social Security System", "Social Security Administration", "Medicare", "Health Care Financing Administration", the letters "SSA" or "HCFA", or any other combination or variation of such words or letters, or
>
> (2) a symbol or emblem of the Social Security Administration (including the design of, or a reasonable facsimile of the design of, the social security card issued pursuant to section 205(c)(2)(E), [42 U.S.C.S. 405(c)(2)(E)], the check used for payment of benefits under title II, or envelopes or other stationery used by the Social Security Administration) or of the Health Care Financing Administration, or any other combination or

variation of such symbols or emblems, in a manner which such person knows or should know would convey the false impression that such item is approved, endorsed, or authorized by the Social Security Administration, the Health Care Financing Administration, or the Department of Health and Human Services or that such person has some connection with, or authorization from, the Social Security Administration, the Health Care Financing Administration, or the Department of Health and Human Services.

Section 1140(b) provides:

(1) Subject to paragraph (2), the Secretary may, pursuant to regulations, impose a civil money penalty not to exceed —

(A) except as provided in subparagraph (B), $5,000, or

(B) in the case of a violation consisting of a broadcast or telecast, $25,000,

against any person for each violation by such person of subsection (a).

(2) The total amount of penalties which may be imposed under paragraph (1) with respect to multiple violations in any one year period consisting of substantially identical communications or productions shall not exceed $100,000.

Section 1140(c) provides:

(1) The provisions of section 1128A [42 U.S.C.S. 1320a-7a, which authorizes civil money penalties for a variety of offenses] (other than subsections (a), (b), (f), (h), and (i)) shall apply to civil money penalties under subsection (b) in the same manner as such provisions apply to a penalty or proceeding under section 1128A(a).

(2) Penalties imposed against a person under subsection (b) may be compromised by the Secretary and may be recovered in a civil action in the name of the United States brought in the district court of the United States for the district in which the violation occurred or where the person resides, has its principal office, or may be found, as determined by the Secretary. Amounts recovered under this section shall be paid to the Secretary and shall be deposited as miscellaneous receipts of the Treasury of the United States. The amount of such penalty when finally determined, or the amount agreed upon

in compromise, may be deducted from any sum then or later owing by the United States to the person against whom the penalty has been imposed.

The provisions of section 1128A, referred to above, provide as follows:

(c)(1) The Secretary may initiate a proceeding to determine whether to impose a civil money penalty, assessment, or exclusion under subsection (a) or (b) only as authorized by the Attorney General pursuant to procedures agreed upon by them. The Secretary may not initiate an action under this section with respect to any claim, request for payment, or other occurrence described in this section later than six years after the date the claim was presented, the request for payment was made, or the occurrence took place. The Secretary may initiate an action under this section by serving notice of the action in any manner authorized by rule 4 of the Federal Rules of Civil Procedure.

(2) The Secretary shall not make a determination adverse to any person under subsection (a) or (b) until the person has been given written notice and an opportunity for the determination to be made on the record after a hearing at which the person is entitled to be represented by counsel, to present witnesses, and to cross-examine witnesses against the person.

(3) In a proceeding under subsection (a) or (b) which —

(A) is against a person who has been convicted (whether upon a verdict after trial or upon a plea of guilty or nolo contendere) of a Federal crime charging fraud or false statements, and

(B) involves the same transaction as in the criminal action, the person is estopped from denying the essential elements of the criminal offense.

(4) The official conducting a hearing under this section may sanction a person, including any party or attorney, for failing to comply with an order or procedure, failing to defend an action, or other misconduct as would interfere with the speedy, orderly, or fair conduct of the hearing. Such sanction shall reasonably relate to the severity and nature of the failure or misconduct. Such sanction may include —

(A) in the case of refusal to provide or permit discovery, drawing negative factual inferences or treating such refusal as an admission by deeming the matter, or certain facts, to be established,

(B) prohibiting a party from introducing certain evidence or otherwise supporting a particular claim or defense,

(C) striking pleadings, in whole or in part,

(D) staying the proceedings,

(E) dismissal of the action,

(F) entering a default judgment,

(G) ordering the party or attorney to pay attorneys' fees and other costs caused by the failure or misconduct, and

(H) refusing to consider any motion or other action which is not filed in a timely manner.

(d) In determining the amount or scope of any penalty, assessment, or exclusion imposed pursuant to subsection (a) or (b), the Secretary shall take into account —

(1) the nature of claims and the circumstances under which they were presented,

(2) the degree of culpability, history of prior offenses, and financial condition of the person presenting the claims, and

(3) such other matters as justice may require.

(e) Any person adversely affected by a determination of the Secretary under this section may obtain a review of such determination in the United States Court of Appeals for the circuit in which the person resides, or in which the claim was presented, by filing in such court (within sixty days following the date the person is notified of the Secretary's determination) a written petition requesting that the determination be modified or set aside. A copy of the petition shall be forthwith transmitted by the clerk of the court to the Secretary, and thereupon the Secretary shall file in the Court the record in the proceeding as provided in section 2112 of title 28, United States Code. Upon such filing, the court shall have jurisdiction of the proceeding and of the question determined therein, and shall have the power to make and enter upon the pleadings, testimony, and proceedings set forth in such record a decree affirming, modifying, remanding for further consideration, or setting aside, in whole or in part, the determination of the Secretary and enforcing the same to the extent that such order is affirmed or modified. No objection that has not been urged before the Secretary shall be considered by the court, unless the failure or neglect to urge such objection shall be excused because of extraordinary circumstances. The findings of the Secretary with respect to questions of fact, if supported by substantial evidence on the record considered as a whole, shall be conclusive. If any party shall apply to the court for leave to adduce additional evidence and shall show to the satisfaction of the court that such additional evidence is material and that there were reasonable grounds for the failure to adduce such evidence in the hearing before the Secretary, the court may order such additional evidence to be taken before the Secretary and to be made a part of the record. The Secretary may modify his findings as to the facts, or make new findings, by reason of additional evidence so taken and filed, and he shall file with the court such modified or new findings, which findings with respect to questions of fact, if supported by substantial evidence on the record considered as a whole, shall be conclusive, and his recommendations, if any, for the modification or setting aside of his original order. Upon the filing of the record with it, the jurisdiction of the court shall be exclusive and its judgment and decree shall be final, except that the same shall be subject to review by the Supreme Court of the United States, as provided in section 1254 of title 28, United States Code.

* * *

(g) A determination by the Secretary to impose a penalty, assessment, or exclusion under subsection (a) or (b) shall be final upon the expiration of the sixty-day period referred to in subsection (e). Matters that were raised or that could have been raised in a hearing before the Secretary or in an appeal pursuant to subsection (e) may not be raised as a defense to a civil action by the United States to collect a penalty, assessment, or exclusion assessed under this section.

* * *

(j) The provisions of subsections (d) and (e) of section 205 [42 U.S.C.S. 405(d) and (e), which pertain, respectively, to issuance of subpenas and punishment for failure to comply with them] shall apply with respect to this section to the same extent as they are applicable with respect to title II [which pertains to retirement, survivor, and disability benefits under the Social Security Act]. The Secretary may delegate the authority granted by section 205(d) (as made applicable to this section) to the Inspector General of the Department of Health and Human Services for purposes of any investigation under this section.

(k) Whenever the Secretary has reason to believe that any person has engaged, is engaging, or is about to engage in any activity which makes the person subject to a civil monetary penalty under this section, the Secretary may bring an action in an appropriate district court of the United States (or, if applicable, a United States court of any territory) to enjoin such activity, or to enjoin the person from concealing, removing, encumbering, or disposing of assets which may be required in order to pay a civil monetary penalty if any such penalty were to be imposed or to seek other appropriate relief.

(l) A principal is liable for penalties, assessments, and an exclusion under this section for the actions of the principal's agent acting within the scope of the agency.

With respect to issuance of subpenas and their enforcement, section 205 of the Social Security Act, 42 U.S.C.S. 405, made applicable to section 1140 civil money penalty actions by cross-reference in section 1140(c)(1) to section 1128A(j), provides in pertinent part as follows:

(d) For the purpose of any hearing, investigation, or other proceeding authorized or directed under this title, or relative to any other matter within his jurisdiction hereunder, the Secretary shall have power to issue subpenas requiring the attendance and testimony of witnesses and the production of any evidence that relates to any matter under investigation or in question before the Secretary. Such attendance of witnesses and production of evidence at the designated place of such hearing, investigation, or other proceeding may be required from any place in the United States or in any Territory or possession thereof. Subpenas of the Secretary shall be served by anyone authorized by him (1) by delivering a copy thereof to the individual named therein, or (2) by registered mail or by certified mail addressed to such individual at his last dwelling place or principal place of business. A verified return by the individual so serving the subpena setting forth the manner of service, or, in the case of service by registered mail or by certified mail, the return post-office receipt therefor signed by the individual so served, shall be proof of service. Witnesses so subpenaed shall be paid the same fees and mileage as are paid witnesses in the district courts of the United States.

(e) In case of contumacy by, or refusal to obey a subpena duly served upon, any person, any district court of the United States for the judicial district in which said person charged with contumacy or refusal to obey is found or resides or transacts business, upon application by the Secretary, shall have jurisdiction to issue an order requiring such person to appear and give testimony, or to appear and produce evidence, or both; any failure to obey such order of the court may be punished by said court as contempt thereof.

APPENDIX I

OIG COMPLIANCE PROGRAM GUIDES

APPENDIX I1

OIG Notice: Publication of OIG Compliance Program Guidance for Clinical Laboratories

Federal Register: August 24, 1998 (Volume 63, Number 163)
Notices
Pages 45076–45087

DEPARTMENT OF HEALTH AND HUMAN SERVICES

Office of Inspector General

Publication of OIG Compliance Program Guidance for Clinical Laboratories

AGENCY: Office of Inspector General (OIG), HHS.
ACTION: Notice.

SUMMARY: This **Federal Register** notice sets forth the OIG's recently-issued Compliance Program Guidance for Clinical Laboratories. The OIG had previously developed and published a model compliance plan for the clinical laboratory industry on March 3, 1997. This Compliance Program Guidance for Clinical Laboratories is intended to be more consistent with compliance program guidances issued by the OIG with respect to the hospital industry and to home health agencies, and serves to clarify various aspects of the original model plan. As with previously-issued compliance program guidances, we believe that the development of this guidance for clinical laboratories will continue as a positive step towards promoting a higher level of ethical and lawful conduct throughout the entire health care community.

FOR FURTHER INFORMATION CONTACT: Christine Saxonis, Office of Counsel to the Inspector General, (202) 619–2078.

SUPPLEMENTARY INFORMATION: As part of a major initiative to engage the private health care community in combating fraud and abuse, the OIG developed and published in the **Federal Register** a model compliance plan for the clinical laboratories (62 FR

9435; March 3, 1997). The compliance plan was intended to provide clear guidance to that aspect of the clinical laboratory industry that was interested in reducing fraud and abuse within their organizations. Since that issuance, the OIG has developed and issued specific compliance program guidance for the hospital industry and for home health agencies.

This compliance program guidance is intended to refine and build on the original model guidance plan for clinical laboratories. In developing an effective compliance program, the OIG has identified 7 fundamental elements. They are:

- Implementing written policies, procedures and standards of conduct;
- Designing a compliance officer and compliance committee;
- Conducting effective training and education;
- Developing effective lines of communication;
- Enforcing standards through well-publicized disciplinary guidelines;
- Conducting internal monitoring and auditing; and
- Responding promptly to detected offenses and developing corrective action.

The development of this new Compliance Program Guidance for Clinical Laboratories has been enhanced based upon changes in Health Care Financing Administration (HCFA) policy, private industry's comments on the original model plan and additional comments submitted by HCFA and the Department of Justice.

While the key components of the original plan are still included, this Compliance Program Guidance sets forth a number of clarifying elements. Specifically, the compliance guidance:

- Focuses on the fact that while physicians can order any tests they believe are appropriate, Medicare will only pay for those tests which are covered, reasonable and necessary;
- Recognizes that individuals other than physicians may be authorized to order tests in some States;
- Recognizes additional claim information, such as requesting the diagnosis information contained in the medical record, can be obtained from an authorized person rather than directly from the physician;

- Notes that physicians are required to submit diagnostic information to the laboratory when ordering manyalthough not all laboratory tests;
- Emphasizes the need for the tests performed in accordance with standing orders to be reasonable and necessary; and
- Clarifies laboratories should not charge physicians a price below fair market value for non-federal health program tests in order to include their Federal health care business.

In addition, while the original model laboratory compliance plan focused on the billing of automated multichannel chemistry tests, the American Medical Association has since deleted these codes from the 1998 CPT coding handbook, and HCFA no longer recognizes these as billable or reimbursable codes. As a result, physicians now must individually order tests that once compromised a chemistry profile. This guidance specifically reflects this policy change.

A reprint of the OIG's Compliance Program Guidance for Clinical Laboratories follows.

OIG Compliance Program Guidance for Clinical Laboratories

Introduction

The Office of Inspector General (OIG) of the Department of Health and Human Services (HHS) continues in its efforts to promote voluntarily developed and implemented compliance programs for the health care industry. The following compliance program guidance is intended to assist clinical laboratories in developing effective internal controls that promote adherence to applicable Federal and State law, and the program requirements of Federal, State, and private health plans.[1]

The adoption and implementation of voluntary compliance programs significantly advance the prevention of fraud, abuse, and waste in the clinical laboratory industry while at the same time further the fundamental mission of all health care providers, which is to provide quality services and care to patients.

[1] This guidance is a republication of the model clinical laboratory compliance plan issued by the OIG on February 27, 1997. This guidance has been amended to reflect HCFA policy changes and to be consistent with the OIG's Compliance Program Guidance for Hospitals. See 63 FR 8987 (February 23, 1998) and the OIG's web site at http://www.dhhs.gov/progorg/oig.

Within this document, the OIG intends to provide first, its general views on the value and fundamental principles of clinical laboratory compliance programs, and second, specific elements that each clinical laboratory should consider when developing and implementing an effective compliance program. While this document presents basic procedural and structural guidance for designing a compliance program, it is not in itself a compliance program. Rather, it is a set of guidelines for consideration by a clinical laboratory interested in implementing a compliance program. The recommendations and guidelines provided in this document must be considered depending upon their applicability to each particular clinical laboratory.

Fundamentally, compliance efforts are designed to establish a culture within a clinical laboratory that promotes prevention, detection and resolution of instances of conduct that do not conform to Federal and State law, and Federal, State and private payor health care program requirements, as well as the clinical laboratory's ethical and business policies. In practice, the compliance program should effectively articulate and demonstrate the organization's commitment to the compliance process. The existence of benchmarks that demonstrate implementation and achievements are essential to any effective compliance program.

Eventually, a compliance program should become part of the fabric of routine clinical laboratory operations.

Specifically, compliance programs guide a clinical laboratory's governing body (e.g., Board of Directors), Chief Executive Officer (CEO), managers, technicians, billing personnel, and other employees in the efficient management and operation of a clinical laboratory. These employees are especially critical as an internal control in the reimbursement and payment areas, where claims and billing operations are often the source of fraud and abuse and, therefore, historically have been the focus of Government regulation, scrutiny and sanctions.

It is incumbent upon a clinical laboratory's corporate officers and managers to provide ethical leadership to the organization and to assure that adequate systems are in place to facilitate ethical and legal conduct. Indeed, many clinical laboratories and clinical laboratory organizations have adopted mission statements articulating their commitment to high ethical standards. A formal compliance program, as an additional element in this process, offers a clinical laboratory a further concrete method that may improve quality of services and reduce waste. Compliance programs also provide a central coordinating mechanism for furnishing and disseminating information and guidance on applicable statutes, regulations and other requirements of Federal, State and private health plans.

Adopting and implementing an effective compliance program requires a substantial commitment of time, energy and resources by senior management and the clinical laboratory's governing body.[2] Programs hastily constructed and implemented without appropriate ongoing monitoring will likely be ineffective. While it may require significant additional resources or reallocation of existing resources to implement an effective compliance program, the OIG believes that the long term benefits of implementing the program outweigh the costs.

A. Benefits of a Compliance Program

In addition to fulfilling its legal duty to ensure that it is not submitting false or incorrect claims to Government and private payors, a clinical laboratory may gain numerous additional benefits by implementing an effective compliance program. Such programs make good business sense in that they help a clinical laboratory fulfill its fundamental mission of providing quality services as well as assisting clinical laboratories in identifying weaknesses in internal systems and management. Other important potential benefits include the ability to:

- Concretely demonstrate to employees and the community at large the clinical laboratory's strong commitment to honest and responsible corporate conduct;
- Provide a more accurate view of employee behavior relating to fraud and abuse;
- Identify and prevent criminal and unethical conduct;
- Improve the quality, efficiency and consistency of services;
- Create a centralized source for distributing information on health care statutes, regulations and other program directives related to fraud and abuse and related issues;
- Develop a methodology that encourages employees to report potential problems;

---

[2] Indeed, recent case law suggests that the failure of a corporate Director to attempt in good faith to institute a compliance program in certain situations may be a breach of a Director's fiduciary obligation. See, e.g., In re Caremark International Inc. Derivative Litigation, 698 A.2d 959 (Ct. Chanc. Del. 1996).

- Develop procedures that allow the prompt, thorough investigation of alleged misconduct by corporate officers, managers and other employees;
- Initiate immediate, appropriate, and decisive corrective action; and
- Through early detection and reporting, minimize the lossto the Government from false claims, and thereby reduce the clinical laboratory's exposure to civil damages and penalties, criminal sanctions, and administrative remedies, such as program exclusion. [3]

Overall, the OIG believes that an effective compliance program is a sound investment on the part of a clinical laboratory.

The OIG recognizes that the implementation of a compliance program may not entirely eliminate fraud, abuse and waste from the clinical laboratory system. However, a sincere effort by clinical laboratories to comply with applicable Federal and State standards, as well as the requirements of private health care programs, through the establishment of an effective compliance program, significantly reduces the risk of unlawful or improper conduct.

B. Application of Compliance Program Guidance

There is no single "best" clinical laboratory compliance program, given the diversity of laboratories within the industry. The OIG understands the variances and complexities within the clinical laboratory industry and is sensitive to the differences among large and small clinical laboratories. However, elements of this guidance can be used by all clinical laboratories, regardless of size, location or corporate structure, to establish an effective compliance program. We recognize that some clinical laboratories may not be able to adopt certain elements to the same comprehensive degree that others with more extensive resources may achieve. This guidance represents the OIG's suggestions on how a clinical laboratory can best establish internal controls and monitoring to correct and prevent fraudulent activities. By no means should the contents of this guidance be

---

[3] The OIG, for example, will consider the existence of an effective compliance program that pre-dated any governmental investigation when addressing the appropriateness of administrative penalties. Further, the False Claims Act, 31 U.S.C. 3729–3733, provides that a person who has violated the Act, but who voluntarily discloses the violation to the Government, in certain circumstances will be subject to not less than double, as opposed to treble,damages. See 31 U.S.C. 3729(a).

viewed as an exclusive discussion of the advisable elements of a compliance program.

In drafting this guidance, we took into consideration the Model Compliance Plan for Clinical Laboratories issued by the OIG in February 1997, the clinical laboratory industry's comments on that plan, changes in HCFA policy and the OIG's Compliance Program Guidance for Hospitals.

As appropriate, this guidance may be further modified and expanded as more information and knowledge is obtained by the OIG, and as changes in the rules, policies and procedures of the Federal, State and private health plans occur. We recognize that clinical laboratories are already accountable for complying with an extensive set of statutory and other legal requirements, far more specific and complex than what we have referenced in this document. We also recognize that the development and implementation of compliance programs in clinical laboratories often raise sensitive and complex legal and managerial issues.[4] However, the OIG wishes to offer what it believes is critical guidance for providers who are sincerely attempting to comply with the relevant health care statutes, regulations and other requirements of Federal, State and private health plans.

Compliance Program Elements

The elements proposed by these guidelines are similar to those of the compliance program guidance for hospitals that was published by the OIG in February 1998 and of our corporate integrity agreements.[5] The elements represent a guidea process that can be used by clinical laboratories, whether an independent national laboratory, a hospital laboratory, or a small, regional laboratory. Moreover, the elements can be incorporated into the managerial structure of the clinical laboratory. As we stated in our compliance program guidance for hospitals, these suggested guidelines can be tailored to fit the needs and financial realities of a particular laboratory. The OIG is cognizant that with regard to compliance programs, one model is

---

[4] Nothing stated herein should be substituted for, or used in lieu of, competent legal advice from counsel.

[5] Corporate integrity agreements are executed as part of a civil settlement agreement between the health care provider and the Government to resolve a case based on allegations of health care fraud or abuse. These OIG-imposed programs are in effect for a period of 3 to 5 years and require many of the elements included in this compliance program guidance.

not suitable to every clinical laboratory. Nonetheless, the OIG believes that every clinical laboratory, regardless of size or structure, can benefit from the principles espoused in this guidance.

The OIG believes that every effective compliance program must begin with a formal commitment by the clinical laboratory's governing body to include all of the applicable elements listed below. These elements are based on the seven steps of the Federal Sentencing Guidelines.[6] We recognize that full implementation of all elements may not be immediately feasible for all clinical laboratories. However, as a first step, a good faith and meaningful commitment on the part of the clinical laboratory will substantially contribute to a program's successful implementation.

At a minimum, comprehensive compliance programs should include the following 7 elements:

1. The development and distribution of written standards of conduct, as well as written policies and procedures that promote the clinical laboratory's commitment to compliance (e.g., by including adherence to compliance as an element in evaluating managers and employees) and that address specific areas of potential fraud, such as marketing schemes, CPT/HCPCs coding issues, improper ICD-9 coding, and improper claims submission;
2. The designation of a chief compliance officer and other appropriate bodies (e.g., a corporate compliance committee) charged with the responsibility of operating and monitoring the compliance program, and who report directly to the CEO and the governing body;
3. The development and implementation of regular, effective education and training programs for all affected employees;
4. The maintenance of a process, such as a hotline, to receive complaints, and the adoption of procedures to protect the anonymity of complainants and to protect whistleblowers from retaliation;
5. The development of a system to respond to allegations of improper/illegal activities and the enforcement of appropriate disciplinary action against employees who have violated internal compliance policies, applicable statutes, regulations or requirements of Federal, State or private health plans;

[6] See United States Sentencing Commission Guidelines, Guidelines Manual, 8A1.2 comment. (n.3(k)).

6. The use of audits and/or other evaluation techniques to monitor compliance and assist in the reduction of identified problem areas; and
7. The investigation and remediation of identified systemic problems and the development of policies addressing the non-employment or retention of sanctioned individuals.

A. Written Procedures and Policies

Laboratory compliance programs should require the development and distribution of written compliance policies. These policies should be developed under the supervision and direction of the chief compliance officer or the equivalent and should, at a minimum, be provided to all individuals who are affected by the specific policy at issue. One convenient method of achieving this goal is to create a three-ring compliance policy notebook. This format permits the filing of new and amended or revised compliance policies and ensures that affected individuals have easy access to the laboratory's written policies. A master index should show when policies are changed.

1. Standards of Conduct

Laboratories should develop standards of conduct for all employees that clearly delineate the policies of the laboratory with regard to fraud, waste and abuse and adherence to all statutes, regulations and other program requirements governing Federal, State and private health benefit plans. These standards should be made available to all employees; translated, interpreted (e.g., may be signed for hard of hearing or deaf employees) or put into Braille as necessary, and regularly updated as the policies and regulations are modified.

When an employee first begins working for the clinical laboratory, and each time new standards of conduct are issued, employees should be asked to sign a statement certifying that they have received, read, and understood the standards of conduct. All employee certifications should be retained by the laboratory.

2. Medical Necessity

Laboratory compliance programs, to be effective, should communicate to physicians that claims submitted for services will only be paid if the service is covered, reasonable, and necessary for the beneficiary, given his or her clinical condition. Laboratories should take all reasonable steps to ensure that it is not submitting claims for services that are not covered, reasonable and necessary.[7] Upon request, a laboratory should be able to produce or obtain from the treating physician (test ordering), authorized person on the physician's staff or other individual authorized by law to order tests the documentation to support the medical necessity of the service the laboratory has provided and billed to a Federal or private health care program. We recognize that laboratories do not and cannot treat patients or make medical necessity determinations. However, there are steps that such facilities can take to assure compliance with the applicable statutes, regulations and the requirements of Federal, State and private health plans.

As a preliminary matter, the OIG recognizes that physicians or other authorized individuals must be able to order any tests that they believe are appropriate for the treatment of their patients. However, we believe that physicians must be made aware by the billing laboratory that Medicare will only pay for tests that meet the Medicare coverage criteria and are reasonable and necessary to treat or diagnose an individual patient. Section 1862(a)(1)(A) of the Social Security Act states, "no payment may be made under Part A or Part B for any expenses incurred for items or services which * * * are not reasonable and necessary for the diagnosis or treatment of an illness or injury or to improve the functioning of a malformed body member." Therefore, Medicare may deny payment for a test that the physician believes is appropriate, but which does not meet the Medicare coverage criteria (e.g., done for screening purposes) or where documentation in the entire patient record, including that maintained in the physician's records, does not support that the tests were reasonable and necessary for a given patient. Laboratories can and should advise their clients that tests submitted for Medicare reimbursement must meet program requirements [8] or the claim may be denied.

---

[7] In limited instances, HCFA does allow laboratories to submit claims when the lab believes the test may be denied. Such instances include, but are not limited to: when the beneficiary has signed an Advance Beneficiary Notice (ABN) (See Medicare Carriers Manual Sec. 7300.5) (Part D in this section further addresses ABN issues) and when the beneficiary requests the provider submit the claim (See Medicare Carriers Manual Sec. 3043). In the first instance the lab should include modifier GA on the claim which indicates the beneficiary has signed an ABN and in the latter instance the lab should note on the claim their belief that the service is noncovered and that it is being submitted at the beneficiary's insistence.

[8] See fn. 7.

Laboratories may implement the following steps through their compliance programs or some other appropriate mechanism to ensure that the claims they submit to Federal or private health care programs meet the appropriate program requirements:

a. Requisition design: While HCFA does not design or approve requisition forms, laboratories should construct the requisition form to capture the correct program information as required by Federal or private health care programs and to promote the conscious ordering of tests by physicians or other authorized individuals. The laboratory should construct the requisition form to ensure that the physician or other authorized individual has made an independent medical necessity decision with regard to each test the laboratory will bill. Laboratories should encourage physicians or other authorized individuals to submit diagnosis information for all tests ordered, as documentation of the medical necessity of the service. The form should contain a statement indicating that Medicare generally does not cover routine screening tests.

b. Notices to physicians: While HCFA does not impose educational requirements upon the laboratories, labs are in a unique position to educate their physician clients. Therefore, laboratories should provide all of their physician clients with annual written notices that set forth: (1) The Medicare national policy and Medicare contractor local medical review policy for lab tests; (2) that organ or disease related panels will only be paid and will only be billed when all components are medically necessary; and (3) the Medicare laboratory fee schedule and a statement informing the physician that the Medicaid reimbursement amount will be equal to or less than the amount of Medicare reimbursement. The notice must also provide the phone number of the clinical consultant. The clinical consultant is required under the Clinical Laboratory Improvement Amendment (CLIA) certification (42 CFR 493.1453).

In addition to the general notices above, laboratories that continue to offer clients the opportunity to request customized profiles should provide annual written notices that: (1) Explain the Medicare reimbursement paid for each component of each such profile; (2) inform physicians that using a customized profile may result in the ordering of tests which are not covered, reasonable or necessary and that tests will not be billed; [9] and (3) inform physicians that the OIG takes the position that an individual who knowingly causes a false claim to be

---

[9] See fn. 7.

submitted may be subject to sanctions or remedies available under civil, criminal and administrative law.

c. Physician acknowledgments: Although HCFA does not require physicians to sign acknowledgments, laboratories should have the physician sign an acknowledgment stating he or she understands the potential implications of ordering customized profiles.

d. Use of Advance Beneficiary Notices: Advance Beneficiary Notices (ABNs) are used when there is a likelihood that an ordered service will not be paid. Before the service is furnished, the beneficiary should be notified, in writing, of the likelihood that the specific service will be denied. After being so informed the beneficiary has the choice to either (1) decide to receive the service and sign the agreement to pay on the ABN or (2) decide not to receive the service and therefore does not sign the ABN. Beneficiaries should not be asked to sign blank ABNs.

As the entity furnishing and billing for services, it is ultimately the laboratory's responsibility to produce the ABN, upon request. In many cases, it is difficult for the laboratories to directly obtain an ABN from the beneficiary. Therefore, laboratories may wish to educate physicians on the appropriate use of ABNs.

The notice must be in writing, must clearly identify a particular service, must state that payment for the particular service likely will be denied and must give the reason(s) for the belief that payment is likely to be denied.

Routine notices to beneficiaries which do no more than state that denial of payment is possible or that they never know whether payment will be denied are not considered acceptable evidence of advance notice. Notices should not be given to beneficiaries unless there is some genuine doubt regarding the likelihood of payment as evidenced by the reasons stated on the ABN. Giving notice for all claims or services is not an acceptable practice.

e. Test utilization monitoring: The OIG believes that laboratories can and should take the steps described in this compliance guidance to help ensure appropriate billing of lab tests. We also believe that there are steps laboratories can take to determine whether physicians or other individuals authorized to order tests are being encouraged to order medically unnecessary tests. More importantly, if the laboratory discovers that it has in some way contributed to the ordering of unnecessary tests, the OIG believes the laboratory has a duty to modify its practices, as well as notify the physician(s) or other authorized individual(s) of its concerns and recommend corrective action.

There are many methods by which a laboratory may determine excessive utilization of laboratory services. One approach to self-monitoring is to hire an outside consultant to analyze the laboratory's patterns of utilization, and investigate any potential problems or aberrancies.

Another approach is to analyze test utilization data by CPT or HCPCS code, for the top 30 tests performed each year. Laboratories could do this by keeping track of the number of tests performed by CPT or HCPCS code or of the number of claims submitted for each test. The laboratories would then compute the percentage growth in the number of tests or claims submitted for each of the top 30 tests from one year to the next. We believe that if a test's utilization grows more than 10 percent, the laboratory should undertake a reasonable inquiry to ascertain the cause of such growth. If the laboratory determines that the increase in test utilization occurred for a benign reason, such as the acquisition of a new laboratory facility, then the laboratory need not take any action. However, if the laboratory determines that the increase in utilization was caused by a misunderstanding or ignorance by the ordering physicians or other authorized individuals regarding the billing consequences of the tests they ordered or an action on the part of the facility, the laboratory should take any steps that it deems reasonably necessary to address the issue and to ensure misconduct is not occurring.

3. Billing

Laboratory compliance policies should ensure that all claims for testing services submitted to Medicare or other Federal health care programs correctly identify the services ordered by the physician or other authorized individual and performed by the laboratory.

a. Selection of CPT or HCPCS Codes: Laboratory compliance policies should ensure that the CPT or HCPCS code that is used to bill, accurately describes the service that was ordered and performed. Laboratories cannot alter the physician's order in any way either increasing or decreasing the number of services performed without the express consent of the ordering physician or other authorized individual. To ensure code accuracy, laboratories should require that individuals with technical expertise in laboratory testing review the appropriateness of the codes before the claims are submitted. Intentional or knowing upcoding (i.e., the selection of a code to maximize reimbursement when such code is not the most appropriate descriptor of the service) could violate the False Claims Act and/or other civil laws, and criminal law.

b. Selection of ICD-9-CM codes: Medicare carriers and fiscal intermediaries have the authority to develop and implement Local Medical Review Policy (LMRP) which specify when, and under what circumstances, a service will be considered covered, reasonable and necessary and what documentation will support the need for the service. In some cases, LMRPs may limit coverage for specified laboratory tests to specific medical diagnoses. Laboratory compliance policies should ensure that the lab can support tests billed to Medicare with documentation obtained from the physician ordering the test, an authorized person on the physician's staff or other individual authorized by law to order tests. Laboratories should not: (1) Use information provided by the physician or other authorized individual from earlier dates of service (other than standing orders, as discussed below at paragraph 4); (2) create diagnosis information that has triggered reimbursement in the past; (3) use computer programs that automatically insert diagnosis codes without receipt of diagnostic information from the ordering physician or other authorized individual; or (4) make up information for claim submission purposes. Laboratories should: (1) Contact the ordering physician, authorized person on the physician's staff or other individual authorized to order tests to obtain information in the event that such information was not provided; and (2) accurately translate narrative diagnoses obtained from the physician or other authorized individual to ICD-9-CM codes. Where medical documentation is obtained from a physician or other authorized individual after receipt of the specimen and the requisition form, it should be maintained.

c. Tests covered by claims for reimbursement: Only those tests that are ordered by an authorized individual or physician, are performed and meet Medicare's conditions of coverage are reimbursable by Medicare. If a laboratory receives a specimen without a valid test order or with a test order which is ambiguous, the laboratory must verify the tests which the physician wants and perform them before submitting a claim for reimbursement to Medicare. In this way, if the physician or other authorized individual did not order the test, the laboratory will not erroneously bill for it.

Similarly, if a laboratory did not perform an ordered test due to, for example, a laboratory accident or insufficient quantities of specimen, the laboratory should not submit a claim to Medicare. Medicare payment is made for tests that are ordered, performed, and covered. The submission of a claim for tests that were either not ordered or were not performed could subject a provider to sanctions under administrative, civil or criminal law.

d. Billing of calculations: Consistent with Medicare coverage rules, laboratory compliance policies should ensure that the laboratory does not bill both for calculations (e.g., calculated LDLs, T7s, and indices) and the tests that are performed to derive such calculations. In many situations, physicians are not offered a choice about whether to receive such calculations, nor are they aware of the practice of some laboratories to bill Medicare for such calculations in addition to the underlying tests. The fact that a separate CPT code exists does not mean that Medicare separately reimburses for the service assigned to the code. Billing both for the calculations and the underlying tests constitutes double billing, which may subject a laboratory to sanctions and other remedies available under civil, criminal, and administrative law.

e. Reflex testing: Reflex testing occurs when initial test results are positive or outside normal parameters and indicate that a second related test is medically appropriate. In order to avoid performing unnecessary reflex tests, labs may want to design their requisition form in such a way which would only allow for the reflex test when necessary. Therefore, the condition under which the reflex test will be performed should be clearly indicated on the requisition form. Laboratories may wish to adopt a similar policy for confirmationtesting which may be mandatory. 4. Reliance on Standing Orders

Although standing orders are not prohibited in connection with an extended course of treatment, too often they have led to abusive practices. Standing orders in and of themselves are not usually acceptable documentation that tests are reasonable and necessary. Accordingly, the insurer may reject standing orders as evidence that a test is reasonable and necessary. Medicare contractors can and may require additional documentation to support the medical necessity of the test. As a result of the potential problems standing orders may cause, the use of standing orders is discouraged.

Thus, while laboratory compliance programs may permit the use of standing orders executed in connection with an extended course of treatment, the compliance program should require the laboratory to periodically monitor standing orders. Standing orders should have a fixed term of validity and must be renewed at their expiration. We suggest that, consistent with State law requirements, a laboratory should contact all nursing homes from which the laboratory has received such standing orders and request that they confirm in writing the validity of all current standing orders. In addition, in accordance with State law, laboratories should verify standing orders relied upon at draw stations with the physician, authorized person on the physician's staff, or other authorized individual who has provided the standing orders to the laboratory. With respect to patients with End Stage Renal Disease (ESRD), at least once annually laboratories should contact each ESRD facility or unit to request confirmation in writing of the continued validity of all existing standing orders. 5. Compliance With Applicable HHS Fraud Alerts

The OIG and HCFA periodically issue fraud alerts [10] setting forth activities believed to raise legal and enforcement issues. Laboratory compliance programs should require that any and all fraud alerts issued by OIG and HCFA are carefully considered by the legal staff, chief compliance officer, or other appropriate personnel. Moreover, the compliance programs should require that a laboratory cease and correct any conduct criticized in such a fraud alert, if applicable to laboratories, and take reasonable action to prevent such conduct from reoccurring in the future. If appropriate, a laboratory should take the steps described in Section G regarding investigations, reporting and correction of identified problems.

6. Marketing

Laboratory compliance programs should require honest, straightforward, fully informative and non-deceptive marketing. It is in the best interests of patients, physicians, laboratories, the Government and private health plans that physicians and other individuals authorized to order tests fully understand the services offered by the laboratory, the services that will be provided when tests are ordered, and the financial consequences for Medicare, as well as other payors, when tests are billed. Accordingly, laboratories that market their services should ensure that their marketing information is clear, correct, non-deceptive and fully informative.

---

[10] Both OIG and HCFA fraud alerts can be located on the internet. The OIG web site address is: http://www.dhhs.gov/progorg/ oig. The HCFA web site address is: http://www.hcfa.gov.

7. Prices Charged to Physicians

Laboratories are paid for their services by a variety of payors in addition to Medicare and other Federal health care programs. Such payors often include private health insurers, other health care providers, and physicians. We believe it is essential that the physician take into account the patient's best interest when deciding where to refer the patient's specimen.

The prices that laboratories charge physicians for certain laboratory services raise issues that should be addressed in a laboratory's written compliance policies. These policies should ensure that laboratories are not providing any inducements to gain a physician's business,[11] including charging physicians a price below fair market value for their non-Federal health care program tests. Laboratories that charge physicians a price below fair market value to induce them to refer their Federal health care program business may be risking anti-kickback enforcement and false claims actions.

8. Retention of Records

Compliance programs should ensure that all records required either by Federal or State law or by the compliance program are created and maintained. Adequate documentation of compliance efforts are essential in the event that a laboratory comes under Government scrutiny. 9. Compliance as an Element of a Performance Plan

Clinical laboratories should make the promotion of and adherence to compliance an element in evaluating the performance of managers, supervisors and all other employees. They, along with other employees, should be periodically trained in new compliance policies and procedures. In addition, all managers and supervisors involved in the sale, marketing, or billing of laboratory services, and those who oversee phlebotomists should (1) discuss with all supervised employees the compliance policies and legal requirements applicable to their function; (2) inform all supervised personnel that strict compliance with these policies and requirements is a condition of employment; and (3) disclose to all supervised personnel that the laboratory will take disciplinary action up to and including termina-

---

[11] The OIG has published "Special Fraud Alert: Arrangements for the Provision of Clinical Lab Services" that addresses how the anti-kickback statute relates to arrangements for the provision of clinical lab services. See 59 FR 65377 (December 19, 1994); OIG's web site at http://www.dhhs.gov/progorg/oig.

tion for violation of these policies or requirements. In addition to making performance of these duties an element in evaluations, the compliance officer or laboratory management may also choose to include in the laboratory's compliance program a policy that managers and supervisors may be sanctioned for failure to adequately instruct their subordinates or for failing to detect non-compliance with applicable policies and legal requirements, where reasonable diligence on the part of the manager or supervisor would have led to the discovery of any problems or violations and given the laboratory the opportunity to correct them earlier.

B. Designation of a Compliance Officer and a Compliance Committee

1. Compliance Officer

Every clinical laboratory should designate a compliance officer to serve as the focal point for compliance activities. This responsibility may be the individual's sole duty or added to other management responsibilities, depending upon the size and resources of the clinical laboratory and the complexity of the task. Designating a compliance officer with the appropriate authority is critical to the success of the program, necessitating the appointment of a high-level official in the organization with direct access to the governing body and the CEO.[12] The officer should have sufficient funding and staff to perform his or her responsibilities fully. Coordination and communication are the key functions of the compliance officer with regard to planning, implementing, and monitoring the compliance program.

The compliance officer's primary responsibilities should include:

---

[12] The OIG believes that it is not advisable for the compliance function to be subordinate to the clinical laboratory's general counsel, or comptroller or similar officer. Free standing compliance functions help to ensure independent and objective legal reviews and financial analyses of the institution's compliance efforts and activities. By separating the compliance function from the key management positions of general counsel or chief financial officer (where the size and structure of the clinical laboratory make this a feasible option), a system of checks and balances is established to more effectively achieve the goals of the compliance program.

- Overseeing and monitoring the implementation of the compliance program; [13]
- Reporting on a regular basis to the clinical laboratory's governing body, CEO and compliance committee on the progress of implementation, and assisting these components in establishing methods to improve the clinical laboratory's efficiency and quality of services, and to reduce the clinical laboratory's vulnerability to fraud, abuse and waste;
- Developing and distributing to all affected employees all written compliance policies and procedures. These policies and procedures should be readily understandable by all employees (e.g., translated into other languages, interpreted in sign language, and/or put into Braille as necessary);
- Periodically revising the program in light of changes in the needs of the organization, and in the law, policies and procedures of Government and private payor health plans;
- Developing, coordinating, and participating in a multifaceted educational and training program that focuses on the elements of the compliance program, and seeks to ensure that allappropriate employees and management are knowledgeable of, and comply with, pertinent Federal, State and private payor standards;
- Ensuring that physicians who order services from the clinical laboratory are informed of the clinical laboratory's compliance program standards with respect to coding, billing, and marketing, among other things;
- Assisting the clinical laboratory's financial management in coordinating internal compliance review and monitoring activities, including annual or periodic reviews of policies;
- Independently investigating and acting on matters related to compliance, including the flexibility to design and coordinate internal investigations (e.g., responding to reports of problems or suspected violations) and any resulting corrective action; and
- Developing policies and programs that encourage managers and employees to report suspected fraud and other improprieties without fear of retaliation.

---

[13] For clinical laboratory chains, the OIG encourages coordination with each affiliate owned by the company through the use of a headquarter's compliance officer, communicating with the designated compliance officers in each facility, or regional office, as appropriate.

The compliance officer must have the authority to review all documents and other information that are relevant to compliance activities, including, but not limited to, requisition forms, billing information, claim information, and records concerning the marketing efforts of the clinical laboratory and its arrangements with its clients. This policy enables the compliance officer to review contracts and obligations (seeking the advice of legal counsel, where appropriate) that may contain referral and payment issues that could violate the anti-kickback statute, as well as the physician self-referral prohibition and other legal or regulatory requirements.

2. Compliance Committee

The OIG recommends that a compliance committee be established to advise the compliance officer and assist in the implementation of the compliance program.[14] The committee's functions should include:

- Analyzing the organization's regulatory environment, the legal requirements with which it must comply, and specific risk areas;
- Assessing existing policies and procedures that address these areas for possible incorporation into the compliance program;
- Working within the clinical laboratory to develop standards of conduct and policies and procedures to promote compliance;
- Recommending and monitoring the development of internal systems and controls to implement the clinical laboratory's standards, policies and procedures as part of its daily operations;
- Determining the appropriate strategy/approach to promote compliance with the program and detection of any potential violations, such as through hotlines and other fraud reporting mechanisms; and
- Developing a system to solicit, evaluate and respond to complaints and problems.

The committee may also assume other functions as the compliance concept becomes part of the overall clinical laboratory operating structure and daily routine.

---

[14] The OIG recommends the compliance committee consist of individuals with varying perspectives and responsibilities in the organization.

C. Conducting Effective Training and Education

The proper education, training and retraining of corporate officers, managers, and all other employees are significant elements of an effective compliance program. As part of its compliance program, a clinical laboratory should require all affected employees to attend specific training when they are first hired and on a periodic basis thereafter, including appropriate training in Federal and State statutes, regulations, program requirements, the policies of private payors, and corporate ethics. The training should emphasize the organization's commitment to compliance with these legal requirements and policies.

These training programs should include sessions highlighting the organization's compliance program, summarizing fraud and abuse laws, and discussing coding requirements, claim development and claim submission process and marketing practices that reflect current legal and program standards. The clinical laboratory must take steps to communicate effectively its standards and procedures to all affected employees (e.g., by requiring participation in training programs and disseminating publications that explain in a practical manner specific requirements).[15] Managers of specific departments can assist in identifying areas that require training and in carrying out such training. Training instructors may come from outside or inside the organization. New employees should be targeted for training early in their employment.[16] The compliance officer should document the attendees, the subjects covered, and the material distributed at the training sessions sponsored by the clinical laboratory as part of the compliance program.

A variety of teaching methods, such as interactive training, and training in several different languages, particularly where a clinical laboratory has a culturally diverse staff, should be implemented so that all affected employees are knowledgeable of the clinical laboratory's standards of conduct and procedures for alerting senior

---

[15] Some publications, such as the OIG's Special Fraud Alerts, audit and inspection reports, and advisory opinions are readily available from the OIG and could be the basis for standards and educational courses for appropriate clinical laboratory employees. These documents can be found on the OIG's web site at http:// www.dhhs.gov/progorg/oig.

[16] Certain positions, such as those involving the coding of medical services, create a greater organizational legal exposure, and therefore require specialized training. One recommendation would be for a clinical laboratory to attempt to fill such positions with individuals who have the appropriate educational background and training.

management to problems and concerns. Targeted training should be provided to corporate officers, managers and other employees whose actions affect the accuracy of the claims submitted to Government and private payors, such as employees involved in the coding, billing, and marketing processes. For example, for certain employees involved in the billing and coding functions, periodic training in proper CPT/HCPCs and ICD-9 coding and documentation should be required. In addition to specific training in the areas identified in section II.A, above, basic training for appropriate corporate officers, managers and other employees should include such topics as:

- Government and private payor reimbursement principles;
- General prohibitions on paying or receiving remuneration to induce referrals;
- Proper translation of narrative diagnoses;
- Only billing for services ordered, performed and reported;
- Physician approved amendments to requisition forms;
- Proper documentation or confirmation of services rendered; and
- Duty to report misconduct.

Clarifying and emphasizing these areas of concern through training and educational programs are particularly relevant to a clinical laboratory's marketing representatives, in that the pressure to meet business goals may render these employees vulnerable to engaging in prohibited practices.

The OIG suggests that all affected employees be made part of the clinical laboratory's various educational and training programs. Employees should be required to have a minimum number of educational hours per year, as appropriate, as part of their employment responsibilities.[17] In departments with high employee turnover, periodic training updates are critical.

The OIG recommends that attendance and participation in training programs be made a condition of continued employment and that failure to comply with training requirements should result in disciplinary action, including possible termination, when such failure is serious. Adherence to the provisions of the compliance program, such as training requirements, should be a factor in the annual evaluation of each employee. The clinical laboratory should retain

[17] In its corporate integrity agreements, the OIG usually requires a minimum number of hours annually for basic training in compliance areas. More hours are required for specialty fields such as billing and coding.

adequate records of its training of employees, including attendance logs and material distributed at training sessions.

D. Developing Effective Lines of Communications

1. Access to the Compliance Officer

An open line of communication between the compliance officer and clinical laboratory employees is equally important to the successful implementation of a compliance program and the reduction of any potential for fraud, abuse and waste. Written confidentiality and non-retaliation policies should be developed and distributed to all employees to encourage communication and the reporting of incidents of potential misconduct. [18] The compliance committee should also develop several independent reporting paths for an employee to report fraud, waste or abuse so that such reports cannot be diverted by supervisors or other personnel.

The OIG encourages the establishment of a procedure so that clinical laboratory employees may seek clarification from the compliance officer or members of the compliance committee in the event of any confusion or question with regard to a laboratory policy or procedure. Questions and responses should be documented and dated and, if appropriate, shared with other staff so that standards, policies and procedures can be updated and improved to reflect any necessary changes or clarifications. The compliance officer may want to solicit employee input in developing these communication and reporting systems.

2. Hotlines and Other Forms of Communication

The OIG encourages the use of hotlines (including anonymous hotlines), e-mails, written memoranda, newsletters, and other forms of information exchange to maintain these open lines of communication. If the clinical laboratory establishes a hotline, the telephone number should be made readily available to all employees possibly by conspicuously posting the telephone number in common work

[18] The OIG believes that whistleblowers should be protected against retaliation, a concept embodied in the provisions of the False Claims Act. In many cases, employees sue their employers under the False Claims Act's qui tam provisions out of frustration because of the company's failure to take action when a questionable, fraudulent or abusive situation was brought to the attention of senior corporate officials.

areas.[19] Employees should be permitted to report matters on an anonymous basis. Matters reported through the hotline or other communication sources that suggest substantial violations of compliance policies, regulations, statutes or program requirements of Federal, State and private insurers should be documented and investigated promptly to determine their veracity. A log should be maintained by the compliance officer that records such calls, including the nature of any investigation and its results. Such information should be included in reports to the governing body, the CEO and compliance committee. Further, while the clinical laboratory should always strive to maintain the confidentiality of an employee's identity, it should also explicitly communicate that there may be a point where the individual's identity may become known or may have to be revealed in certain instances when governmental authorities become involved.

The OIG recognizes that assertions of fraud and abuse by employees who may have participated in illegal conduct or committed other malfeasance raise numerous complex legal and management issues that should be examined on a case-by-case basis. The compliance officer should work closely with legal counsel, who can provide guidance regarding such issues.

E. Enforcing Standards Through Well-Publicized Disciplinary Guidelines

1. Discipline Policy and Actions

An effective compliance program should include guidance regarding disciplinary action for corporate officers, managers, and other employees who have failed to comply with the clinical laboratory's standards of conduct, policies and procedures, or Federal and State laws, or those who have otherwise engaged in wrongdoing, which have the potential to impair the clinical laboratory's status as a reliable, honest and trustworthy health care provider.

The OIG believes that the compliance program should include a written policy statement setting forth the degrees of disciplinary actions that may be imposed upon corporate officers, managers, and other employees for failing to comply with the clinical laboratory's standards and policies and applicable statutes and regulations.

---

[19] Clinical laboratories should also post in a prominent, available area the HHS-OIG Hotline telephone number, 1–800-HHS-TIPS (447–8477), in addition to any company hotline number that may be posted.

Intentional or reckless noncompliance should subject transgressors to significant sanctions. Such sanctions could range from oral warnings to suspension or termination. The written standards of conduct should elaborate on the procedures for handling disciplinary problems and those who will be responsible for taking appropriate action. Some disciplinary actions can be handled by department managers, while others may have to be resolved by a senior manager. Disciplinary action may be appropriate where a responsible employee's failure to detect a violation is attributable to his or her negligence or reckless conduct. Employees should be advised by the clinical laboratory that disciplinary action will be taken on a fair and equitable basis. Managers and supervisors should be made aware that they have a responsibility to discipline employees in an appropriate and consistent manner.

It is vital to publish and disseminate the range of disciplinary standards for improper conduct and to educate corporate officers, managers and other employees regarding these standards. The consequences of noncompliance should be consistently applied and enforced, in order for the disciplinary policy to have the required deterrent effect. All levels of employees should be subject to the same disciplinary action for the commission of similar offenses. The commitment to compliance applies to all personnel levels within a clinical laboratory. The OIG believes that corporate officers, managers, and other employees should be held accountable for failing to comply with, or for the foreseeable failure of their subordinates to adhere to, the applicable standards, laws, and procedures.

2. New Employee Policy

For all new employees who have discretionary authority to make decisions that may involve compliance with the law or compliance oversight, clinical laboratories should conduct a reasonable and prudent background investigation, including a reference check, as part of every such employment application.[20] The application should specifically require the applicant to disclose any criminal conviction, as

[20] The Cumulative Sanction Report is an OIG-produced report available on the Internet at http://www.dhhs.gov/progorg/oig. It is updated on a regular basis to reflect the status of health care providers who have been excluded from participation in the Medicare and Medicaid programs. In addition, the General Services Administration maintains a monthly listing of debarred contractors on the Internet at http://www.arnet.gov/epls. Also, once the data base established by the Health Care Fraud and Abuse Data Collection Act of 1996 is fully operational, the hospital should regularly

defined by 42 U.S.C. 1320a-7(i), or exclusion action. Pursuant to the compliance program, clinical laboratory policies should prohibit the employment of individuals who have been recently convicted of a criminal offense related to health care or who are listed as debarred, excluded or otherwise ineligible for participation in Federal health care programs (as defined in 42 U.S.C. 1320a–7b(f)).[21] In addition, pending the resolution of any criminal charges or proposed debarment or exclusion, the OIG recommends that such individuals should be removed from direct responsibility for or involvement in any Federal health care program.[22] With regard to current employees, physicians or other individuals authorized to order tests, if resolution of the matter results in conviction, debarment or exclusion, the clinical laboratory should terminate its employment or other contract arrangement with the individual or physician.

F. Auditing and Monitoring

An ongoing evaluation process involving thorough monitoring and regular reporting to the clinical laboratory's corporate officers is critical to a successful compliance program. Compliance reports created by this ongoing monitoring, including reports of suspected noncompliance, should be maintained by the compliance officer and shared with the clinical laboratory's corporate officers and the compliance committee.

Although many monitoring techniques are available, one effective tool to promote and ensure compliance is the performance of regular compliance audits by internal or external auditors who have expertise in Federal and State health care statutes, regulations and the program requirements of Federal, State and private insurers. At a minimum, these audits should be designed to address the clinical laboratory's compliance with laws governing kickback arrange-

request information from this data bank as part of its employee screening process.

[21] Likewise, clinical laboratory compliance programs should establish standards prohibiting the execution of contracts with physicians or other individual authorized to order tests that have been recently convicted of a criminal offense related to health care or that are listed by a Federal agency as debarred, excluded, or otherwise ineligible for participation in Federal health care programs.

[22] Prospective employees who have been officially reinstated into the Medicare and Medicaid programs by the OIG may be considered for employment upon proof of such reinstatement.

ments, the physician self-referral prohibition, CPT/HCPCS coding and billing, ICD-9 coding, claim development and submission, reimbursement, marketing, reporting and record keeping. In addition, the audits and reviews should inquire into the clinical laboratory's compliance with specific rules and policies that have been the focus of particular attention on the part of the Medicare fiscal intermediaries or carriers, and law enforcement, as evidenced by OIG Special Fraud Alerts, OIG audits and evaluations, and publically announced law enforcement initiatives and also should focus on any areas of concern that have been identified by any entity, (i.e., Federal, State, or internally) specific to the individual clinical laboratory.

Monitoring techniques may include sampling protocols that permit the compliance officer to identify and review variations from an established baseline.[23] Significant variations from the baseline should trigger a reasonable inquiry to determine the cause of the deviation. If the inquiry determines that the deviation occurred for legitimate, explainable reasons, the compliance officer, corporate officer or manager may want to limit any corrective action or take no action. If it is determined that the deviation was caused by improper procedures, misunderstanding of rules, including fraud and systemic problems, the clinical laboratory should take prompt steps to correct the problem. If potential fraud or violations of the False Claims Act are involved, the laboratory should report the potential violation to the OIG or the Department of Justice (see discussion in Section G.2, below). Any repayment of an overpayment which results from such a violation should be made as part of the discussion with law enforcement.

When making any overpayment, the clinical laboratory should inform the payor of the following information (1) the refund is being made pursuant to a voluntary compliance program; (2) a description

[23] The OIG recommends that when a compliance program is established in a clinical laboratory, the compliance officer, with the assistance of corporate officers, should take a "snapshot" of their operations from a compliance perspective. This assessment can be undertaken by outside consultants, law or accounting firms, or internal staff, with authoritative knowledge of health care compliance requirements. This "snapshot," often used as part of benchmarking analyses, becomes a baseline for the compliance officer and other corporate officers to judge the clinical laboratory's progress in reducing or eliminating potential areas of vulnerability. For example, it has been suggested that a baseline level include the frequency and percentile levels of each CPT code in relation to the clinical laboratory's overall billing.

of the complete circumstances surrounding the overpayment; (3) the methodology by which the overpayment was determined; (4) any claim-specific information used to determine the overpayment and; (5) the amount of the overpayment.

The OIG believes that the compliance officer needs to be made aware of these overpayment patterns, violations or deviations and look fortrends that may demonstrate a systemic problem.

An effective compliance program should also incorporate periodic (at least annual) reviews of whether the program's compliance elements have been satisfied, e.g., whether there has been appropriate; (1) dissemination of the program's standards; (2) training; (3) ongoing educational programs; and (4) disciplinary actions, among others. This process will verify actual conformance with the compliance program. The review also should look into whether appropriate records have been created and maintained to document the implementation of an effective program. However, when monitoring discloses that deviations were not detected in a timely manner due to program deficiencies, appropriate modifications must be implemented. Such evaluations, when developed with the support of management, can help ensure compliance with the clinical laboratory's policies and procedures.

As part of the review process, the compliance officer or reviewers should consider techniques such as:

- On-site visits;
- Interviews with personnel involved in management, marketing/sales, operations, coding/billing, claim development and submission, and other related activities;
- Questionnaires developed to solicit impressions of a broad cross-section of the clinical laboratory's employees and referring clients;
- Review of requisition forms and other documents that support claims for reimbursement;
- Review of written materials and documentation produced by the laboratory and used by physicians and other individuals authorized to order tests; and
- Trend analyses, or longitudinal studies, that seek deviations in billing or ordering patterns over a given period.

The reviewers should:

- Be independent of line management;

- Have access to existing audit resources, relevant personnel and all relevant areas of operation;
- Present written evaluative reports on compliance activities to the CEO, governing body and members of the compliance committee on a regular basis, but no less than annually; and
- Specifically identify areas where corrective actions are needed.

With these reports, the clinical laboratory management can take whatever steps are necessary to correct past problems and prevent them from recurring. In certain cases, subsequent reviews or studies would be advisable to ensure that the recommended corrective actions have been implemented successfully.

The clinical laboratory should document its efforts to comply with applicable statutes, regulations and the program requirements of Federal, State and private payors. For example, where a clinical laboratory, in its efforts to comply with a particular statute, regulation or program requirement, requests advice from a Government agency (including a Medicare fiscal intermediary or carrier) charged with administering a Federal health care program, the clinical laboratory should document and retain a record of the request and any written or oral response. This step is particularly important if the clinical laboratory intends to rely on that response. The laboratory should memorialize its determination as to whether reliance on any such advice is reasonable, and its efforts to develop procedures based upon such advice.

G. Responding to Detected Offenses and Developing Corrective Action Initiatives

1. Violations and Investigations

Violations of a clinical laboratory's compliance program, failures to comply with applicable Federal or State law, and other requirements of Government and private health plans, and other types of misconduct threaten a clinical laboratory's status as a reliable, honest and trustworthy provider capable of participating in Federal health care programs. Detected but uncorrected misconduct can seriously endanger the mission, reputation, and legal status of the clinical laboratory. Consequently, upon reports or reasonable indications of suspected noncompliance, it is important that the chief compliance officer or other management officials initiate prompt steps to investigate the conduct in question to determine whether a material violation of applicable law or the requirements of the compliance program has occurred, and if so, take steps to correct the problem.[24] As appropriate, such may include an immediate referral to criminal and/or civil law enforcement authorities, a corrective action plan,[25] a report to the Government,[26] and the submission of any overpayments, if applicable.

Depending upon the nature of the alleged violations, an internal investigation will probably include interviews and a review of relevant documents. Some clinical laboratories should consider engaging outside counsel, auditors, or health care experts to assist in an investigation. Records of the investigation should contain documentation of the alleged violation, a description of the investigative process, copies of interview notes and key documents, a log of the witnesses interviewed and the documents reviewed, the results of the investigation, e.g., any disciplinary action taken, and the corrective action implemented. While any action taken as the result of an investigation will necessarily vary depending upon the clinical laboratory and the situation, clinical laboratories should strive for some consistency by utilizing sound practices and disciplinary protocols. Further, after a reasonable period, the compliance officer should review the circumstances that formed the basis for the investigation to determine whether similar problems have since been uncovered.

---

[24] Instances of non-compliance must be determined on a case-by-case basis. The existence, or amount, of a monetary loss to a health care program is not solely determinative of whether or not the conduct should be investigated and reported to governmental authorities. In fact, there may be instances where there is no monetary loss at all, but corrective action and reporting are still necessary to protect the integrity of the applicable program and its beneficiaries.

[25] Advice from the clinical laboratory's in-house counsel or an outside law firm may be sought to determine the extent of the clinical laboratory's liability and to plan the appropriate course of action.

[26] The OIG currently maintains a voluntary disclosure program that encourages providers to report suspected fraud. The concept of voluntary self-disclosure is premised on a recognition that the Government alone cannot protect the integrity of the Medicare and other Federal health care programs. Health care providers must be willing to police themselves, correct underlying problems and work with the Government to resolve these matters. The OIG's voluntary self-disclosure program has four prerequisites (1) the disclosure must be on behalf of an entity and not an individual; (2) the disclosure must be truly voluntary (i.e., no pending proceeding or investigation); (3) the entity must disclose the nature of the wrongdoing and the harm to the Federal programs; and (4) the entity must not be the subject of a bankruptcy proceeding before or after the self-disclosure.

If an investigation of an alleged violation is undertaken and the compliance officer believes the integrity of the investigation may be at stake because of the presence of employees under investigation, those subjects should be removed from their current work activity until the investigation is completed (unless otherwise requested by law enforcement). In addition, the compliance officer should take appropriate steps to secure or prevent the destruction of documents or other evidence relevant to the investigation. If the clinical laboratory determines that disciplinary action is warranted, it should be prompt and imposed in accordance with the clinical laboratory's written standards of disciplinary action.

2. Reporting

If the compliance officer, compliance committee or management official discovers credible evidence of misconduct from any source and, after a reasonable inquiry, has reason to believe that the misconduct may violate criminal, civil or administrative law, then the clinical laboratory promptly should report the matter to the appropriate governmental authority [27] within a reasonable period, but not more than 60 days [28] after determining that there is credible evidence of a violation.[29] Prompt reporting will demonstrate the clinical laboratory's good faith and willingness to work with governmental authorities to correct and remedy the problem. In addition, reporting such conduct will be considered a mitigating factor by the OIG in determining administrative sanctions (e.g., penalties, assessments, and exclusion), if the reporting provider becomes the target of

---

[27] I.e., Federal and/or State law enforcement having jurisdiction over such matter. Such governmental authority would include DOJ and OIG with respect to Medicare and Medicaid violations giving rise to causes of actions under various criminal, civil andadministrative false claims statutes.

[28] To qualify for the "not less than double damages" provision of the False Claims Act, the report must be provided to the Government within thirty days after the date when the laboratory first obtained the information. 31 U.S.C. 3729(a).

[29] The OIG believes that some violations may be so serious that they warrant immediate notification to governmental authorities, prior to, or simultaneous with, commencing an internal investigation, e.g., if the conduct (1) is a clear violation of criminal law; (2) has a significant adverse effect on the quality of care provided to program beneficiaries (in addition to any other legal obligations regarding quality of care); or (3) indicates evidence of a systemic failure to comply with applicable laws, an existing corporate integrity agreement, or other standards of conduct, regardless of the financial impact on Federal health care programs.

an OIG investigation.[30]

When reporting misconduct to the Government, a clinical laboratory should provide all evidence relevant to the potential violation of applicable Federal or State law(s) and potential cost impact. The compliance officer, under advice of counsel, and with guidance from the governmental authorities, could be requested to continue to investigate the reported violation. Once the investigation is completed, the compliance officer should be required to notify the appropriate governmental authority of the outcome of the investigation, including a description of the impact of the alleged violation on the operation of the applicable health care programs or their beneficiaries. If the investigation ultimately indicates that criminal or civil violations may have occurred, the appropriate Federal and State officials[31] should be notified immediately.

As previously stated, the clinical laboratory should take appropriate corrective action, including the imposition of proper disciplinary action, and prompt identification and restitution of any overpayment to the affected payor. In cases where potential fraud or violations of the False Claims Act are involved payment should be made as part of discussions with law enforcement. Failure to repay overpayments within a reasonable period of time could be interpreted as an intentional attempt to conceal the overpayment from the Government, thereby establishing an independent basis for a criminal violation with respect to the clinical laboratory, as well as any individuals who may have been involved.[32] For this reason, clinical laboratory compliance programs should emphasize that overpayments obtained from Medicare or other Federal health care

---

[30] The OIG has published criteria setting forth those factors that the OIG takes into consideration in determining whether it is appropriate to exclude a health care provider from program participation pursuant to 42 U.S.C. 1320a-7(b)(7) for violations of various fraud and abuse laws. See 62 FR 67392 (12/24/97).

[31] Appropriate Federal and State authorities include the Criminal and Civil Divisions of the Department of Justice, the U.S. Attorney in the clinical laboratory's district, and the investigative arms for the agencies administering the affected Federal or State health care programs, such as the State Medicaid Fraud Control Unit, the Defense Criminal Investigative Service, and the Offices of Inspector General of the Department of Health and Human Services, the Department of Veterans Affairs and the Office of Personnel Management (which administers the Federal Employee Health Benefits Program).

[32] See 42 U.S.C. 1320a-7b(a)(3).

programs should be promptly returned to the payor that made the erroneous payment. Section F details the information which should be provided to the contractor when making a repayment.

Conclusion

Through this document, the OIG has attempted to provide a foundation for development of an effective and cost-efficient clinical laboratory compliance program. As previously stated, however, each program must be tailored to fit the needs and resources of an individual clinical laboratory, depending upon its particular corporate structure, mission, size and employee composition. The statutes, regulations and guidelines of the Federal and State health insurance programs, as well as the policies and procedures of the private health plans, should be integrated into every clinical laboratory's compliance program.

The OIG recognizes that the health care industry in this country, which reaches millions of beneficiaries and expends about a trillion dollars annually, is constantly evolving. As stated throughout this guidance, compliance is a dynamic process that helps to ensure that clinical laboratories and other health care providers are better able to fulfill their commitment to ethical behavior, as well as meet the changes and challenges being imposed upon them by Congress and private insurers. Ultimately, it is OIG's hope that a voluntarily created compliance program will enable clinical laboratories to meet their goals, improve the quality of services and control of claims submission, and substantially reduce fraud, waste and abuse, as well as the cost of health care to Federal, State and private health insurers.

Dated: August 14, 1998.

June Gibbs Brown,

Inspector General.

[FR Doc. 98–22559 Filed 8–21–98; 8:45 am]

BILLING CODE 4150–04-P

APPENDIX I2

OIG Notice: Publication of the OIG Compliance Program Guidance for Hospitals

Federal Register: February 23, 1998 (Volume 63, Number 35)
Pages 8987–8998.

DEPARTMENT OF HEALTH AND HUMAN SERVICES

Office of Inspector General

Publication of the OIG Compliance Program Guidance for Hospitals

AGENCY: Office of Inspector General (OIG), HHS.

ACTION: Notice.

SUMMARY: This Federal Register notice sets forth the recently issued compliance program guidance for hospitals developed by the Office of Inspector General (OIG) in cooperation with, and with input from, several provider groups and industry representatives. Many providers and provider organizations have expressed an interest in better protecting their operations from fraud and abuse through the adoption of voluntary compliance programs. The first compliance guidance, addressing clinical laboratories, was prepared by the OIG and published in the Federal Register on March 3, 1997. We believe the development of this second program guidance, for hospitals, will continue as a positive step towards promoting a higher level of ethical and lawful conduct throughout the health care industry.

FOR FURTHER INFORMATION CONTACT: Stephen Davis, Office of Counsel to the Inspector General, (202) 619–0070.

SUPPLEMENTARY INFORMATION: The creation of compliance program guidances has become a major initiative of the OIG in its efforts to engage the private health care community in combating fraud and abuse. In developing these compliance guidances, the OIG has agreed to work closely with the Health Care Financing Administration, the Department of Justice and various sectors of the health care industry. The first of these compliance guidances focused on clinical laboratories, and was intended to provide clear guidance to those segments of the health care industry that were interested in reducing fraud and abuse within their organizations. The compliance guidance was reprinted in an OIG Federal Register notice published on March 3, 1997 (62 FR 9435). This second compliance program guidance developed by the OIG continues to build upon the basic elements contained in our initial compliance guidance, and encompasses principles that are applicable to hospitals as well as a wider variety of organizations that provide health care services to beneficiaries of Medicare, Medicaid and all other Federal health care programs.

Like the previously-issued compliance program guidance for clinical laboratories and future compliance program guidances, adoption of the hospital compliance program guidance set forth below will be voluntary. Future compliance program guidances to be developed will be similarly structured and based on substantive policy recommendations, the elements of the Federal Sentencing Guidelines, and applicable statutes, regulations and Federal health care program requirements.

A reprint of the OIG compliance program guidance follows.

Compliance Program Guidance for Hospitals

I. Introduction

The Office of Inspector General (OIG) of the Department of Health and Human Services (HHS) continues in its efforts to promote voluntarily developed and implemented compliance programs for the health care industry. The following compliance program guidance is intended to assist hospitals and their agents and subproviders (referred to collectively in this document as "hospitals' ') develop effective internal controls that promote adherence to applicable Federal and State law, and the program requirements of Federal, State and private health plans. The adoption and implementation of voluntary compliance programs significantly advance the prevention of fraud, abuse and waste in these health care plans while at the same time furthering the fundamental mission of all hospitals, which is to provide quality care to patients.

Within this document, the OIG intends to provide first, its general views on the value and fundamental principles of hospital compliance programs, and, second, specific elements that each hospital should consider when developing and implementing an effective compliance program. While this document presents basic procedural and structural guidance for designing a compliance program, it is not in itself a compliance program. Rather, it is a set of guidelines for a hospital interested in implementing a compliance program to consider. The recommendations and guidelines provided in this document must be considered depending upon their applicability to each particular hospital.

Fundamentally, compliance efforts are designed to establish a culture within a hospital that promotes prevention, detection and resolution of instances of conduct that do not conform to Federal and State law, and Federal, State and private payor health care program requirements, as well as the hospital's ethical and business policies. In practice, the compliance program should effectively articulate and demonstrate the organization's commitment to the compliance process. The existence of benchmarks that demonstrate implementation and achievements are essential to any effective compliance program. Eventually, a compliance program should become part of the fabric of routine hospital operations.

Specifically, compliance programs guide a hospital's governing body (e.g., Boards of Directors or Trustees), Chief Executive Officer (CEO), managers, other employees and physicians and other health care professionals in the efficient management and operation of a hospital. They are especially critical as an internal control in the reimbursement and payment areas, where claims and billing operations are often the source of fraud and abuse and, therefore, historically have been the focus of government regulation, scrutiny and sanctions.

It is incumbent upon a hospital's corporate officers and managers to provide ethical leadership to the organization and to assure that adequate systems are in place to facilitate ethical and legal conduct. Indeed, many hospitals and hospital organizations have adopted mission statements articulating their commitment to high ethical standards. A formal compliance program, as an additional element in this process, offers a hospital a further concrete method that may improve quality of care and reduce waste. Compliance programs also provide a central coordinating mechanism for furnishing and disseminating information and guidance on applicable Federal and State statutes, regulations and other requirements.

Adopting and implementing an effective compliance program requires a substantial commitment of time, energy and resources by senior management and the hospital's governing body.[1] Programs hastily constructed and implemented without appropriate ongoing monitoring will likely be ineffective and could result in greater harm or liability to the hospital than no program at all. While it may require significant additional resources or reallocation of existing resources to implement an effective compliance program, the OIG believes that the long term benefits of implementing the program outweigh the costs.

A. Benefits of a Compliance Program

In addition to fulfilling its legal duty to ensure that it is not submitting false or inaccurate claims to government and private payors, a hospital may gain numerous additional benefits by implementing an effective compliance program. Such programs make good business sense in that they help a hospital fulfill its fundamental care-giving mission to patients and the community, and assist hospitals in identifying weaknesses in internal systems and management. Other important potential benefits include the ability to:

- Concretely demonstrate to employees and the community at large the hospital's strong commitment to honest and responsible provider and corporate conduct;
- Provide a more accurate view of employee and contractor behavior relating to fraud and abuse;
- Identify and prevent criminal and unethical conduct;
- Tailor a compliance program to a hospital's specific needs;
- Improve the quality of patient care;
- Create a centralized source for distributing information on health care statutes, regulations and other program directives related to fraud and abuse and related issues;
- Develop a methodology that encourages employees to report potential problems;
- Develop procedures that allow the prompt, thorough investigation of alleged misconduct by corporate officers, managers, employees, independent contractors, physicians, other health care professionals and consultants;

---

[1] Indeed, recent case law suggests that the failure of a corporate Director to attempt in good faith to institute a compliance program in certain situations may be a breach of a Director's fiduciary obligations. See, e.g., *In re Caremark International Inc. Derivative Litigation,* 698 A.2d 959 (Ct. Chanc. Del. 1996).

- Initiate immediate and appropriate corrective action; and
- Through early detection and reporting, minimize the loss to the Government from false claims, and thereby reduce the hospital's exposure to civil damages and penalties, criminal sanctions, and administrative remedies, such as program exclusion.[2]

Overall, the OIG believes that an effective compliance program is a sound investment on the part of a hospital.

The OIG recognizes that the implementation of a compliance program may not entirely eliminate fraud, abuse and waste from the hospital system. However, a sincere effort by hospitals to comply with applicable Federal and State standards, as well as the requirements of private health care programs, through the establishment of an effective compliance program, significantly reduces the risk of unlawful or improper conduct.

B. Application of Compliance Program Guidance

There is no single "best" hospital compliance program, given the diversity within the industry. The OIG understands the variances and complexities within the hospital industry and is sensitive to the differences among large urban medical centers, community hospitals, small, rural hospitals, specialty hospitals, and other types of hospital organizations and systems. However, elements of this guidance can be used by all hospitals, regardless of size, location or corporate structure, to establish an effective compliance program. We recognize that some hospitals may not be able to adopt certain elements to the same comprehensive degree that others with more extensive resources may achieve. This guidance represents the OIG's suggestions on how a hospital can best establish internal controls and monitoring to correct and prevent fraudulent activities. By no means should the contents of this guidance be viewed as an exclusive discussion of the advisable elements of a compliance program.

---

[2] The OIG, for example, will consider the existence of an *effective* compliance program that pre-dated any Governmental investigation when addressing the appropriateness of administrative penalties. Further, the False Claims Act, 31 U.S.C. 3729–3733, provides that a person who has violated the Act, but who voluntarily discloses the violation to the Government, in certain circumstances will be subject to not less than double, as opposed to treble, damages. See 31 U.S.C. 3729(a).

The OIG believes that input and support by representatives of the major hospital trade associations is critical to the development and success of this compliance program guidance. Therefore, in drafting this guidance, the OIG received and considered input from various hospital and medical associations, as well as professional practice organizations. Further, we took into consideration previous OIG publications, such as Special Fraud Alerts and Management Advisory Reports, the recent findings and recommendations in reports issued by OIG's Office of Audit Services and Office of Evaluation and Inspections, as well as the experience of past and recent fraud investigations related to hospitals conducted by OIG's Office of Investigations and the Department of Justice.

As appropriate, this guidance may be modified and expanded as more information and knowledge is obtained by the OIG, and as changes in the law, and in the rules, policies and procedures of the Federal, State and private health plans occur. The OIG understands that hospitals will need adequate time to react to these modifications and expansions to make any necessary changes to their voluntary compliance programs. We recognize that hospitals are already accountable for complying with an extensive set of statutory and other legal requirements, far more specific and complex than what we have referenced in this document. We also recognize that the development and implementation of compliance programs in hospitals often raise sensitive and complex legal and managerial issues.[3] However, the OIG wishes to offer what it believes is critical guidance for providers who are sincerely attempting to comply with the relevant health care statutes and regulations.

II. Compliance Program Elements

The elements proposed by these guidelines are similar to those of the clinical laboratory model compliance program published by the OIG in February 1997[4] and our corporate integrity agreements.[5]

[3] Nothing stated herein should be substituted for, or used in lieu of, competent legal advice from counsel.

[4] See 62 FR 9435, March 3, 1997.

[5] Corporate integrity agreements are executed as part of a civil settlement between the health care provider and the Government to resolve a case arising under the False Claims Act (FCA), including the *qui tam* provisions of the FCA, based on allegations of health care fraud or abuse. These OIG-imposed programs are in effect for a period of three to five years and require many of the elements included in this compliance guidance.

The elements represent a guide—a process that can be used by hospitals, large or small, urban or rural, for-profit or not for-profit. Moreover, the elements can be incorporated into the managerial structure of multi-hospital and integrated delivery systems. As we stated in our clinical laboratory plan, these suggested guidelines can be tailored to fit the needs and financial realities of a particular hospital. The OIG is cognizant that with regard to compliance programs, one model is not suitable to every hospital. Nonetheless, the OIG believes that every hospital, regardless of size or structure, can benefit from the principles espoused in this guidance.

The OIG believes that every effective compliance program must begin with a formal commitment by the hospital's governing body to include *all* of the applicable elements listed below. These elements are based on the seven steps of the Federal Sentencing Guidelines.[6] Further, we believe that every hospital can implement most of our recommended elements that expand upon the seven steps of the Federal Sentencing Guidelines.[7] We recognize that full implementation of all elements may not be immediately feasible for all hospitals. However, as a first step, a good faith and meaningful commitment on the part of the hospital administration, especially the governing body and the CEO, will substantially contribute to a program's successful implementation.

At a minimum, comprehensive compliance programs should include the following seven elements:

(1) The development and distribution of written standards of conduct, as well as written policies and procedures that promote the hospital's commitment to compliance (e.g., by including adherence to compliance as an element in evaluating managers and employees) and that address specific areas of

---

[6] See United States Sentencing Commission Guidelines, *Guidelines Manual,* 8A1.2, comment. (n.3(k)).

[7] Current HCFA reimbursement principles provide that certain of the costs associated with the creation of a voluntarily established compliance program may be allowable costs on certain types of hospitals' cost reports. These allowable costs, of course, must at a minimum be *reasonable* and related to patient care. See generally 42 U.S.C. 1395x(v)(1)(A) (definition of reasonable cost); 42 CFR 413.9(a) and (b)(2) (costs related to patient care). In contrast, however, costs specifically associated with the implementation of a corporate integrity agreement in response to a Government investigation resulting in a civil or criminal judgment or settlement are unallowable, and are also made specifically and expressly unallowable in corporate integrity agreements and civil fraud settlements.

potential fraud, such as claims development and submission processes, code gaming, and financial relationships with physicians and other health care professionals;

(2) The designation of a chief compliance officer and other appropriate bodies, e.g., a corporate compliance committee, charged with the responsibility of operating and monitoring the compliance program, and who report directly to the CEO and the governing body;

(3) The development and implementation of regular, effective education and training programs for all affected employees;

(4) The maintenance of a process, such as a hotline, to receive complaints, and the adoption of procedures to protect the anonymity of complainants and to protect whistleblowers from retaliation;

(5) The development of a system to respond to allegations of improper/illegal activities and the enforcement of appropriate disciplinary action against employees who have violated internal compliance policies, applicable statutes, regulations or Federal health care program requirements;

(6) The use of audits and/or other evaluation techniques to monitor compliance and assist in the reduction of identified problem area; and

(7) The investigation and remediation of identified systemic problems and the development of policies addressing the non-employment or retention of sanctioned individuals.

A. Written Polices and Procedures

Every compliance program should require the development and distribution of written compliance policies that identify specific areas of risk to the hospital. These policies should be developed under the direction and supervision of the chief compliance officer and compliance committee, and, at a minimum, should be provided to all individuals who are affected by the particular policy at issue, including the hospital's agents and independent contractors.

1. *Standards of Conduct.* Hospitals should develop standards of conduct for all affected employees that include a clearly delineated commitment to compliance by the hospital's senior management[8]

[8] The OIG strongly encourages high-level involvement by the hospital's governing body, chief executive officer, chief operating officer, general counsel, and chief financial officer, as well as other medical personnel, as

and its divisions, including affiliated providers operating under the hospital's control,[9] hospital-based physicians and other health care professionals (e.g., utilization review managers, nurse anesthetists, physician assistants and physical therapists). Standards should articulate the hospital's commitment to comply with all Federal and State standards, with an emphasis on preventing fraud and abuse. They should state the organization's mission, goals, and ethical requirements of compliance and reflect a carefully crafted, clear expression of expectations for all hospital governing body members, officers, managers, employees, physicians, and, where appropriate, contractors and other agents. Standards should be distributed to, and comprehensible by, all employees (e.g., translated into other languages and written at appropriate reading levels, where appropriate). Further, to assist in ensuring that employees continuously meet the expected high standards set forth in the code of conduct, any employee handbook delineating or expanding upon these standards of conduct should be regularly updated as applicable statutes, regulations and Federal health care program requirements are modified.[10]

2. *Risk Areas.* The OIG believes that a hospital's written policies and procedures should take into consideration the regulatory exposure for each function or department of the hospital. Consequently, we recommend that the individual policies and procedures be coordinated with the appropriate training and educational programs with an emphasis on areas of special concern that have been identified by the OIG through its investigative and audit functions.[11] Some of the

---

appropriate, in the development of standards of conduct. Such involvement should help communicate a strong and explicit statement of compliance goals and standards.

[9] E.g., skilled nursing facilities, home health agencies, psychiatric units, rehabilitation units, outpatient clinics, clinical laboratories, dialysis facilities.

[10] The OIG recognizes that not all standards, policies and procedures need to be communicated to all employees. However, the OIG believes that the bulk of the standards that relate to complying with fraud and abuse laws and other ethical areas should be addressed and made part of all affected employees' training. The hospital must appropriately decide which additional educational programs should be limited to the different levels of employees, based on job functions and areas of responsibility.

[11] The OIG periodically issues Special Fraud Alters setting forth activities believed to raise legal and enforcement issues. Hospital compliance programs should require that the legal staff, chief compliance officer, or other appropriate personnel, carefully consider any and all Special Fraud

special areas of OIG concern include.[12]

- Billing for items or services not actually rendered;[13]
- Providing medically unnecessary services;[14]
- Upcoding;[15]
- "DRG creep;"[16]
- Outpatient services rendered in connection with inpatient stays;[17]
- Teaching physician and resident requirements for teaching hospitals;

Alerts issued by the OIG that relate to hospitals. Moreover, the compliance programs should address the ramifications of failing to cease and correct any conduct criticized in such a Special Fraud Alert, if applicable to hospitals, or to take reasonable action to prevent such conduct from reoccurring in the future. If appropriate, a hospital should take the steps described in Section G regarding investigations, reporting and correction of identified problems.

[12] The OIG's work plan is currently available on the Internet at http://www.dhhs.gov/progorg/oig.

[13] Billing for services not actually rendered involves submitting a claim that represents that the provider performed a service all or part of which was simply not performed. This form of billing fraud occurs in many health care entities, including hospitals and nursing homes, and represents a significant part of the OIG's investigative caseload.

[14] A claim requesting payment for medically unnecessary services intentionally seeks reimbursement for a service that is not warranted by the patient's current and documented medical condition. See 42 U.S.C. 1395y(a)(1)(A) ("no payment may be made under part A or part B for any expenses incurred for items or services which . . . are not reasonable and necessary for the diagnosis or treatment of illness or injury or to improve the functioning of the malformed body member"). On every HCFA claim form, a physician must certify that the services were medically necessary for the health of the beneficiary.

[15] "Upcoding" reflects the practice of using a billing code that provides a higher payment rate than the billing code that actually reflects the service furnished to the patient. Upcoding has been a major focus of the OIG's enforcement efforts. In fact, the Health Insurance Portability and Accountability Act of 1996 added another civil monetary penalty to the OIG's sanction authorities for upcoding violations. See 42 U.S.C. 1320a-7a(a)(1)(A).

[16] Like upcoding, "DRG creep" is the practice of billing using a Diagnosis Related Group (DRG) code that provides a higher payment rate than the DRG code that accurately reflects the service furnished to the patient.

[17] Hospitals that submit claims for non-physician outpatient services that were already included in the hospital's inpatient payment under the Prospective Payment System (PPS) are in effect submitting duplicate claims.

- Duplicate billing;[18]
- False cost reports;[19]
- Unbundling;[20]
- Billing for discharge in lieu of transfer;[21]
- Patients' freedom of choice;[22]
- Credit balances — failure to refund;
- Hospital incentives that violate the anti-kickback statute or other similar Federal or State statute or regulation;[23]
- Joint ventures;[24]

---

[18] Duplicate billing occurs when the hospital submits more than one claim for the same service or the bill is submitted to more than one primary payor at the same time. Although duplicate billing can occur due to simple error, systematic or repeated double billing may be viewed as a false claim, particularly if any overpayment is not promptly refunded.

[19] As another example of health care fraud, the submission of false costs reports is usually limited to certain Part A providers, such as hospitals, skilled nursing facilities and home health agencies, which are reimbursed in part on the basis of their self-reported operating costs. An OIG audit report on the misuse of fringe benefits and general and administrative costs identified millions of dollars in unallowable costs that resulted from providers' lack of internal controls over costs included in their Medicare cost reports. In addition, the OIG is aware of practices in which hospitals inappropriately shift certain costs to cost centers that are below their reimbursement cap and shift non-Medicare related costs to Medicare cost centers.

[20] "Unbundling" is the practice of submitting bills piecemeal or in fragmented fashion to maximize the reimbursement for various tests or procedures that are required to be billed together and therefore at a reduced cost.

[21] Under the Medicare regulations, when a prospective payment system (PPS) hospital transfers a patient to another PPS hospital, only the hospital to which the patient was transferred may charge the full DRG; the transferring hospital should charge Medicare only a per diem amount.

[22] This area of concern is particularly important for hospital discharge planners referring patients to home health agencies, DME suppliers or long term care and rehabilitation providers.

[23] Excessive payment for medical directorships, free or below market rents or fees for administrative services, interest-free loans and excessive payment for intangible assets in physician practice acquisitions are examples of arrangements that may run afoul of the anti-kickback statute. See 42 U.S.C. 1320a-7b(b) and 59 FR 65372 (12/19/94).

[24] Equally troubling to the OIG is the proliferation of business arrangements that may violate the anti-kickback statute. Such arrangements are generally established between those in a position to refer business, such as physicians, and those providing items or services for which a Federal health care program pays. Sometimes established as "joint ventures," these

- Financial arrangements between hospitals and hospital-based physicians;[25]
- Stark physician self-referral law;
- Knowing failure to provide covered services or necessary care to members of a health maintenance organization; and
- Patient dumping.[26]

Additional risk areas should be assessed as well by hospitals and incorporated into the written policies and procedures and training elements developed as part of their compliance programs.

3. *Claim Development and Submission Process.* A number of the risk areas identified above, pertaining to the claim development and submission process, have been the subject of administrative proceedings, as well as investigations and prosecutions under the civil False Claims Act and criminal statutes. Settlement of these cases often has required the defendants to execute corporate integrity agreements, in addition to paying significant civil damages and/or criminal fines and penalties. These corporate integrity agreements have provided the OIG with a mechanism to advise hospitals concerning what it feels are acceptable practices to ensure compliance with applicable Federal and State statutes, regulations, and program requirements. The following recommendations include a number of provisions from various corporate integrity agreements. While these recommendations include examples of effective policies,

---

arrangements may take a variety of forms. The OIG currently has a number of investigations and audits underway that focus on such areas of concern.

[25] Another OIG concern with respect to the anti-kickback statute is hospital financial arrangements with hospital-based physicians that compensate physicians for less than the fair market value of services they provide to hospitals or require physicians to pay more than market value for services provided by the hospital. See OIG Management Advisory Report: "Financial Arrangements Between Hospitals and Hospital-Based Physicians." OEI-09–89–0030, October 1991. Examples of such arrangements that may violate the anti-kickback statute are token or no payment for Part A supervision and management services; requirements to donate equipment to hospitals; and excessive charges for billing services.

[26] The patient anti-dumping statute, 42 U.S.C. 1395dd, requires that all Medicare participating hospitals with an emergency department: (1) Provide for an appropriate medical screening examination to determine whether or not an individual requesting such examination has an emergency medical condition; and (2) if the person has such a condition, (a) stabilize that condition; or (b) appropriately transfer the patient to another hospital.

each hospital should develop its own specific policies tailored to fit its individual needs.

With respect to reimbursement claims, a hospital's written policies and procedures should reflect and reinforce current Federal and State statutes and regulations regarding the submission of claims and Medicare cost reports. The policies must create a mechanism for the billing or reimbursement staff to communicate effectively and accurately with the clinical staff. Policies and procedures should:

- Provide for proper and timely documentation of all physician and other professional services prior to billing to ensure that only accurate and properly documented services are billed;
- Emphasize that claims should be submitted only when appropriate documentation supports the claims and only when such documentation is maintained and available for audit and review. The documentation, which may include patient records, should record the length of time spent in conducting the activity leading to the record entry, and the identity of the individual providing the service. The hospital should consult with its medical staff to establish other appropriate documentation guidelines;
- State that, consistent with appropriate guidance from medical staff, physician and hospital records and medical notes used as a basis for a claim submission should be appropriately organized in a legible form so they can be audited and reviewed;
- Indicate that the diagnosis and procedures reported on the reimbursement claim should be based on the medical record and other documentation, and that the documentation necessary for accurate code assignment should be available to coding staff; and
- Provide that the compensation for billing department coders and billing consultants should not provide any financial incentive to improperly upcode claims.

The written policies and procedures concerning proper coding should reflect the current reimbursement principles set forth in applicable regulations[27] and should be developed in tandem with

---

[27] The official coding guidelines are promulgated by HCFA, the National Center for Health Statistics, the American Medical Association and the American Health Information Management Association. See International Classification of Diseases, 9th Revision, Clinical Modification (ICD9-CM); 1998 Health Care Financing Administration Common Procedure Coding System (HCPCS); and Physicians' Current Procedural Terminology (CPT).

private payor and organizational standards. Particular attention should be paid to issues of medical necessity, appropriate diagnosis codes, DRG coding, individual Medicare Part B claims (including evaluation and management coding) and the use of patient discharge codes.[28]

a. Outpatient services rendered in connection with an inpatient stay. Hospitals should implement measures designed to demonstrate their good faith efforts to comply with the Medicare billing rules for outpatient services rendered in connection with an inpatient stay. Although not a guard against intentional wrongdoing, the adoption of the following measures are advisable:

- Installing and maintaining computer software that will identify those outpatient services that may not be billed separately from an inpatient stay; or
- Implementing a periodic manual review to determine the appropriateness of billing each outpatient service claim, to be conducted by one or more appropriately trained individuals familiar with applicable billing rules; or
- With regard to each inpatient stay, scrutinizing the propriety of any potential bills for outpatient services rendered to that patient at the hospital, within the applicable time period.

In addition to the pre-submission undertakings described above, the hospital may implement a post-submission testing process, as follows:

- Implement and maintain a periodic post-submission random testing process that examines or re-examines previously submitted claims for accuracy;

---

[28] The failure of hospital staff to: (i) document items and services rendered; and (ii) properly submit them for reimbursement is a major area of potential fraud and abuse in Federal health care programs. The OIG has undertaken numerous audits, investigations, inspections and national enforcement initiatives aimed at reducing potential and actual fraud, abuse and waste. Recent OIG audit reports, which have focused on issues such as hospital patient transfers incorrectly paid as discharges, and hospitals' general and administrative costs, continue to reveal abusive, wasteful or fraudulent behavior by some hospitals. Our inspection report entitled "Financial Arrangements between Hospitals and Hospital-Based Physicians," see fn. 25, supra, and our Special Fraud Alerts on Hospital Incentives to Physicians and Joint Venture Arrangements, further illustrate how certain business practices may result in fraudulent and abusive behavior.

- Inform the fiscal intermediary and any other appropriate government fiscal agents of the hospital's testing process; and
- Advise the fiscal intermediary and any other appropriate government fiscal agents in accordance with current regulations or program instructions with respect to return of overpayments of any incorrectly submitted or paid claims and, if the claim has already been paid, promptly reimburse the fiscal intermediary and the beneficiary for the amount of the claim paid by the government payor and any applicable deductibles or copayments, as appropriate.

b. Submission of claims for laboratory services. A hospital's policies should take reasonable steps to ensure that all claims for clinical and diagnostic laboratory testing services are accurate and correctly identify the services ordered by the physician (or other authorized requestor) and performed by the laboratory. The hospital's written policies and procedures should require, at a minimum,[29] that:

- The hospital bills for laboratory services only after they are performed;
- The hospital bills only for medically necessary services;
- The hospital bills only for those tests actually ordered by a physician and provided by the hospital laboratory;
- The CPT or HCPCS code used by the billing staff accurately describes the service that was ordered by the physician and performed by the hospital laboratory;
- The coding staff: (1) Only submit diagnostic information obtained from qualified personnel; and (2) contact the appropriate personnel to obtain diagnostic information in the event that the individual who ordered the test has failed to provide such information; and
- Where diagnostic information is obtained from a physician or the physician's staff after receipt of the specimen and request for services, the receipt of such information is documented and maintained.

c. Physicians at teaching hospitals. Hospitals should ensure the following with respect to all claims submitted on behalf of teaching physicians:

---

[29] The OIG's February 1997 Model Compliance Plan for Clinical Laboratories provides more specific and detailed information than is contained in this section, and hospitals that have clinical laboratories should extract the relevant guidance from both documents.

- Only services actually provided may be billed;
- Every physician who provides or supervises the provision of services to a patient should be responsible for the correct documentation of the services that were rendered;
- The appropriate documentation must be placed in the patient record and signed by the physician who provided or supervised the provision of services to the patient;
- Every physician is responsible for assuring that in cases where that physician provides evaluation and management (E&M) services, a patient's medical record includes appropriate documentation of the applicable key components of the E&M service provided or supervised by the physician (e.g., patient history, physician examination, and medical decision making), as well as documentation to adequately reflect the procedure or portion of the service performed by the physician; and
- Every physician should document his or her presence during the key portion of any service or procedure for which payment is sought.

d. Cost reports. With regard to cost report issues, the written policies should include procedures that seek to ensure full compliance with applicable statutes, regulations and program requirements and private payor plans. Among other things, the hospital's procedures should ensure that:

- Costs are not claimed unless based on appropriate and accurate documentation;
- Allocations of costs to various cost centers are accurately made and supportable by verifiable and auditable data;
- Unallowable costs are not claimed for reimbursement;
- Accounts containing both allowable and unallowable costs are analyzed to determine the unallowable amount that should not be claimed for reimbursement;
- Costs are properly classified;
- Fiscal intermediary prior year audit adjustments are implemented and are either not claimed for reimbursement or claimed for reimbursement and clearly identified as protested amounts on the cost report;
- All related parties are identified on Form 339 submitted with the cost report and all related party charges are reduced to cost;
- Requests for exceptions to TEFRA (Tax Equity and Fiscal Responsibility Act of 1982) limits and the Routine Cost Limits

are properly documented and supported by verifiable and auditable data;
- The hospital's procedures for reporting of bad debts on the cost report are in accordance with Federal statutes, regulations, guidelines and policies;
- Allocations from a hospital chain's home office cost statement to individual hospital cost reports are accurately made and supportable by verifiable and auditable data; and
- Procedures are in place and documented for notifying promptly the Medicare fiscal intermediary (or any other applicable payor, e.g., TRICARE (formerly CHAMPUS) and Medicaid) of errors discovered after the submission of the hospital cost report, and where applicable, after the submission of a hospital chain's home office cost statement.

With regard to bad debts claimed on the Medicare cost report, see also section six, below, on Bad Debts.

4. Medical Necessity — Reasonable and Necessary Services. A hospital's compliance program should provide that claims should only be submitted for services that the hospital has reason to believe are medically necessary and that were ordered by a physician[30] or other appropriately licensed individual.

As a preliminary matter, the OIG recognizes that licensed health care professionals must be able to order any services that are appropriate for the treatment of their patients. However, Medicare and other government and private health care plans will only pay for those services that meet appropriate medical necessity standards (in the case of Medicare, i.e., "reasonable and necessary" services). Providers may not bill for services that do not meet the applicable standards. The hospital is in a unique position to deliver this information to the health care professionals on its staff. Upon request, a hospital should be able to provide documentation, such as patients' medical records and physicians' orders, to support the medical necessity of a service that the hospital has provided. The compliance officer should ensure that a clear, comprehensive summary of the "medical necessity" definitions and rules of the various government and private plans is prepared and disseminated appropriately.

---

[30] For Medicare reimbursement purposes, a physician is defined as: (1) a doctor of medicine or osteopathy; (2) a doctor of dental surgery or of dental medicine; (3) a podiatrist; (4) an optometrist; and (5) a chiropractor, all of whom must be appropriately licensed by the state. 42 U.S.C. 1395x(r).

5. Anti-Kickback and Self-Referral Concerns. The hospital should have policies and procedures in place with respect to compliance with Federal and State anti-kickback statutes, as well as the Stark physician self-referral law. [31] Such policies should provide that:

- All of the hospital's contracts and arrangements with referral sources comply with all applicable statutes and regulations;
- The hospital does not submit or cause to be submitted to the Federal health care programs claims for patients who were referred to the hospital pursuant to contracts and financial arrangements that were designed to induce such referrals in violation of the anti-kickback statute, Stark physician self-referral law or similar Federal or State statute or regulation; and
- The hospital does not enter into financial arrangements with hospital-based physicians that are designed to provide inappropriate remuneration to the hospital in return for the physician's ability to provide services to Federal health care program beneficiaries at that hospital. [32]

Further, the policies and procedures should reference the OIG's safe harbor regulations, clarifying those payment practices that would be immune from prosecution under the anti-kickback statute. See 42 CFR 1001.952.

6. Bad Debts. A hospital should develop a mechanism [33] to review, at least annually: (1) whether it is properly reporting bad debts to Medicare; and (2) all Medicare bad debt expenses claimed, to ensure that the hospital's procedures are in accordance with applicable Federal and State statutes, regulations, guidelines and policies. In addition, such a review should ensure that the hospital has appropriate and reasonable mechanisms in place regarding beneficiary deductible or copayment collection efforts and has not claimed as bad debts any routinely waived Medicare copayments and deductibles,

[31] Towards this end, the hospital's in-house counsel or compliance officer should, inter alia, obtain copies of all OIG regulations, special fraud alerts and advisory opinions concerning the anti-kickback statute, Civil Monetary Penalties Law (CMPL) and Stark physician self-referral law (the fraud alerts and anti-kickback or CMPL advisory opinions are published on HHS OIG's home page on the Internet), and ensure that the hospital's policies reflect the guidance provided by the OIG.

[32] See fn. 25, *supra.*

[33] E.g., assigning in-house counsel or contracting with an independent professional organization, such as an accounting, law or consulting firm.

which waiver also constitutes a violation of the anti-kickback statute. Further, the hospital may consult with the appropriate fiscal intermediary as to bad debt reporting requirements, if questions arise.

7. *Credit Balances.* The hospital should institute procedures to provide for the timely and accurate reporting of Medicare and other Federal health care program credit balances. For example, a hospital may redesignate segments of its information system to allow for the segregation of patient accounts reflecting credit balances. The hospital could remove these accounts from the active accounts and place them in a holding account pending the processing of a reimbursement claim to the appropriate program. A hospital's information system should have the ability to print out the individual patient accounts that reflect a credit balance in order to permit simplified tracking of credit balances.

In addition, a hospital should designate at least one person (e.g., in the Patient Accounts Department or reasonable equivalent thereof) as having the responsibility for the tracking, recording and reporting of credit balances. Further, a comptroller or an accountant in the hospital's Accounting Department (or reasonable equivalent thereof) may review reports of credit balances and reimbursements or adjustments on a monthly basis as an additional safeguard.

8. *Retention of Records.* Hospital compliance programs should provide for the implementation of a records system. This system should establish policies and procedures regarding the creation, distribution, retention, storage, retrieval and destruction of documents. The two types of documents developed under this system should include: (1) all records and documentation, e.g., clinical and medical records and claims documentation, required either by Federal or State law for participation in Federal health care programs (e.g., Medicare's conditions of participation requirement that hospital records regarding Medicare claims be retained for a minimum of five years, see 42 CFR 482.24(b)(1) and HCFA Hospital Manual section 413(C) (12–91)); and (2) all records necessary to protect the integrity of the hospital's compliance process and confirm the effectiveness of the program, e.g., documentation that employees were adequately trained; reports from the hospital's hotline, including the nature and results of any investigation that was conducted; modifications to the compliance program; self-disclosure; and the results of the hospital's

auditing and monitoring efforts.[34]

9. Compliance as an Element of a Performance Plan. Compliance programs should require that the promotion of, and adherence to, the elements of the compliance program be a factor in evaluating the performance of managers and supervisors. They, along with other employees, should be periodically trained in new compliance policies and procedures. In addition, all managers and supervisors involved in the coding, claims and cost report development and submission processes should:

- Discuss with all supervised employees the compliance policies and legal requirements applicable to their function;
- Inform all supervised personnel that strict compliance with these policies and requirements is a condition of employment; and
- Disclose to all supervised personnel that the hospital will take disciplinary action up to and including termination or revocation of privileges for violation of these policies or requirements.

In addition to making performance of these duties an element in evaluations, the compliance officer or hospital management should include in the hospital's compliance program a policy that managers and supervisors will be sanctioned for failure to instruct adequately their subordinates or for failing to detect noncompliance with applicable policies and legal requirements, where reasonable diligence on the part of the manager or supervisor would have led to the discovery of any problems or violations and given the hospital the opportunity to correct them earlier.

B. Designation of a Compliance Officer and a Compliance Committee

1. Compliance Officer. Every hospital should designate a compliance officer to serve as the focal point for compliance activities. This responsibility may be the individual's sole duty or added to other management responsibilities, depending upon the size and resources of the hospital and the complexity of the task. Designating a compliance officer with the appropriate authority is critical to the success of the program, necessitating the appointment of a

[34] The creation and retention of such documents and reports may raise a variety of legal issues, such as patient privacy and confidentiality. These issues are best discussed with legal counsel.

high-level official in the hospital with direct access to the hospital's governing body and the CEO.[35] The officer should have sufficient funding and staff to perform his or her responsibilities fully. Coordination and communication are the key functions of the compliance officer with regard to planning, implementing, and monitoring the compliance program.

The compliance officer's primary responsibilities should include:

- Overseeing and monitoring the implementation of the compliance program;[36]
- Reporting on a regular basis to the hospital's governing body, CEO and compliance committee on the progress of implementation, and assisting these components in establishing methods to improve the hospital's efficiency and quality of services, and to reduce the hospital's vulnerability to fraud, abuse and waste;
- Periodically revising the program in light of changes in the needs of the organization, and in the law and policies and procedures of government and private payor health plans;
- Developing, coordinating, and participating in a multifaceted educational and training program that focuses on the elements of the compliance program, and seeks to ensure that all appropriate employees and management are knowledgeable of, and comply with, pertinent Federal and State standards;
- Ensuring that independent contractors and agents who furnish medical services to the hospital are aware of the requirements of the hospital's compliance program with respect to coding, billing, and marketing, among other things;
- Coordinating personnel issues with the hospital's Human Resources office (or its equivalent) to ensure that the National

---

[35] The OIG believes that there is some risk to establishing an independent compliance function if that function is subordinance to the hospital's general counsel, or comptroller or similar hospital financial officer. Free standing compliance functions help to ensure independent and objective legal reviews and financial analyses of the institution's compliance efforts and activities. By separating the compliance function from the key management positions of general counsel or chief hospital financial officer (where the size and structure of the hospital make this a feasible option), a system of checks and balances is established to more effectively achieve the goals of the compliance program.

[36] For multi-hospital organizations, the OIG encourages coordination with each hospital owned by the corporation or foundation through the use of a headquarter's compliance officer, communicating with parallel positions in each facility, or regional office, as appropriate.

Practitioner Data Bank and Cumulative Sanction Report[37] have been checked with respect to all employees, medical staff and independent contractors;

- Assisting the hospital's financial management in coordinating internal compliance review and monitoring activities, including annual or periodic reviews of departments;
- Independently investigating and acting on matters related to compliance, including the flexibility to design and coordinate internal investigations (e.g., responding to reports of problems or suspected violations) and any resulting corrective action with all hospital departments, providers and sub-providers,[38] agents and, if appropriate, independent contractors; and
- Developing policies and programs that encourage managers and employees to report suspected fraud and other improprieties without fear of retaliation.

The compliance officer must have the authority to review all documents and other information that are relevant to compliance activities, including, but not limited to, patient records, billing records, and records concerning the marketing efforts of the facility and the hospital's arrangements with other parties, including employees, professionals on staff, independent contractors, suppliers, agents, and hospital-based physicians, etc. This policy enables the compliance officer to review contracts and obligations (seeking the advice of legal counsel, where appropriate) that may contain referral and payment issues that could violate the anti-kickback statute, as well as the physician self-referral prohibition and other legal or regulatory requirements.

2. Compliance Committee. The OIG recommends that a compliance committee be established to advise the compliance officer and

---

[37] The Cumulative Sanction Report is an OIG-produced report available on the Internet at http://www.dhhs.gov/progorg/oig. It is updated on a regular basis to reflect the status of health care providers who have been excluded from participation in the Medicare and Medicaid programs. In addition, the General Services Administration maintains a monthly listing of debarred contractors on the Internet at http://www.arnet.gov/epls. Also, once the data base established by the Health Care Fraud and Abuse Data Collection Act of 1996 is fully operational, the hospital should regularly request information from this data bank as part of its employee screening process.

[38] E.g., skilled nursing facilities and home health agencies.

assist in the implementation of the compliance program.[39] The committee's functions should include:

- Analyzing the organization's industry environment, the legal requirements with which it must comply, and specific risk areas;
- Assessing existing policies and procedures that address these areas for possible incorporation into the compliance program;
- Working with appropriate hospital departments to develop standards of conduct and policies and procedures to promote compliance with the institution's program;
- Recommending and monitoring, in conjunction with the relevant departments, the development of internal systems and controls to carry out the organization's standards, policies and procedures as part of its daily operations;
- Determining the appropriate strategy/approach to promote compliance with the program and detection of any potential violations, such as through hotlines and other fraud reporting mechanisms; and
- Developing a system to solicit, evaluate and respond to complaints and problems.

The committee may also address other functions as the compliance concept becomes part of the overall hospital operating structure and daily routine.

C. Conducting Effective Training and Education

The proper education and training of corporate officers, managers, employees, physicians and other health care professionals, and the continual retraining of current personnel at all levels, are significant elements of an effective compliance program. As part of their compliance programs, hospitals should require personnel to attend specific training on a periodic basis, including appropriate training in Federal and State statutes, regulations and guidelines, and the policies of private payors, and training in corporate ethics, which emphasizes the organization's commitment to compliance with these legal requirements and policies.

---

[39] The compliance committee benefits from having the perspectives of individuals with varying responsibilities in the organization, such as operations, finance, audit, human resources, utilization review, social work, discharge planning, medicine, coding and legal, as well as employees and managers of key operating units.

These training programs should include sessions highlighting the organization's compliance program, summarizing fraud and abuse laws, coding requirements, claim development and submission processes and marketing practices that reflect current legal and program standards. The organization must take steps to communicate effectively its standards and procedures to all affected employees, physicians, independent contractors and other significant agents, e.g., by requiring participation in training programs and disseminating publications that explain in a practical manner specific requirements.[40] Managers of specific departments or groups can assist in identifying areas that require training and in carrying out such training. Training instructors may come from outside or inside the organization. New employees should be targeted for training early in their employment.[41] Any formal training undertaken by the hospital as part of the compliance program should be documented by the compliance officer.

A variety of teaching methods, such as interactive training, and training in several different languages, particularly where a hospital has a culturally diverse staff, should be implemented so that all affected employees are knowledgeable of the institution's standards of conduct and procedures for alerting senior management to problems and concerns. Targeted training should be provided to corporate officers, managers and other employees whose actions affect the accuracy of the claims submitted to the Government, such as employees involved in the coding, billing, cost reporting and marketing processes. Given the complexity and interdependent relationships of many departments, proper coordination and supervision of this process by the compliance officer is important. In addition to specific training in the risk areas identified in section II.A.2, above, primary training to appropriate corporate officers, managers and other hospital staff should include such topics as:

---

[40] Some publications, such as OIG's Management Advisory Report entitled "Financial Arrangements between Hospitals and Hospital-Based Physicians," Special Fraud Alerts, audit and inspection reports, and advisory opinions, as well as the annual OIG work plan, are readily available from the OIG and could be the basis for standards, educational courses and programs for appropriate hospital employees.

[41] Certain positions, such as those involving the coding of medical services, create a greater organizational legal exposure, and therefore require specialized training. One recommendation would be for a hospital to attempt to fill such positions with individuals who have the appropriate educational background and training.

- Government and private payor reimbursement principles;
- General prohibitions on paying or receiving remuneration to induce referrals;
- Proper confirmation of diagnoses;
- Submitting a claim for physician services when rendered by a non-physician (i.e., the "incident to" rule and the physician physical presence requirement);
- Signing a form for a physician without the physician's authorization;
- Alterations to medical records;
- Prescribing medications and procedures without proper authorization;
- Proper documentation of services rendered; and
- Duty to report misconduct.

Clarifying and emphasizing these areas of concern through training and educational programs are particularly relevant to a hospital's marketing and financial personnel, in that the pressure to meet business goals may render these employees vulnerable to engaging in prohibited practices.

The OIG suggests that all relevant levels of personnel be made part of various educational and training programs of the hospital. Employees should be required to have a minimum number of educational hours per year, as appropriate, as part of their employment responsibilities.[42] For example, for certain employees involved in the billing and coding functions, periodic training in proper DRG coding and documentation of medical records should be required.[43] In hospitals with high employee turnover, periodic training updates are critical.

The OIG recommends that attendance and participation in training programs be made a condition of continued employment and that failure to comply with training requirements should result in disciplinary action, including possible termination, when such failure is

---

[42] Currently, the OIG is monitoring approximately 165 corporate integrity agreements that require many of these training elements. The OIG usually requires a minimum of one to three hours annually for basic training in compliance areas. More is required for speciality fields such as billing and coding.

[43] Accurate coding depends upon the quality and completeness of the physician's documentation. Therefore, the OIG believes that active staff physician participation in educational programs focusing on coding and documentation should be emphasized by the hospital.

serious. Adherence to the provisions of the compliance program, such as training requirements, should be a factor in the annual evaluation of each employee.[44] The hospital should retain adequate records of its training of employees, including attendance logs and material distributed at training sessions.

Finally, the OIG recommends that hospital compliance programs address the need for periodic professional education courses that may be required by statute and regulation for certain hospital personnel.

D. Developing Effective Lines of Communication

1. *Access to the Compliance Officer.* An open line of communication between the compliance officer and hospital personnel is equally important to the successful implementation of a compliance program and the reduction of any potential for fraud, abuse and waste. Written confidentiality and non-retaliation policies should be developed and distributed to all employees to encourage communication and the reporting of incidents of potential fraud.[45] The compliance committee should also develop several independent reporting paths for an employee to report fraud, waste or abuse so that such reports cannot be diverted by supervisors or other personnel.

The OIG encourages the establishment of a procedure so that hospital personnel may seek clarification from the compliance officer or members of the compliance committee in the event of any confusion or question with regard to a hospital policy or procedure. Questions and responses should be documented and dated and, if appropriate, shared with other staff so that standards, policies and procedures can be updated and improved to reflect any necessary changes or clarifications. The compliance officer may want to solicit

---

[44] In addition, where feasible, the OIG believes that a hospital's outside contractors, including physician corporations, should be afforded the opportunity to participate in, or develop their own, compliance training and educational programs, which complement the hospital's standards of conduct, compliance requirements, and other rules and regulations.

[45] The OIG believes that whistleblowers should be protected against retaliation, a concept embodied in the provisions of the False Claims Act. In many cases, employees sue their employers under the False Claims Act's *qui tam* provisions out of frustration because of the company's failure to take action when a questionable, fraudulent or abusive situation was brought to the attention of senior corporate officials.

employee input in developing these communication and reporting systems.

2. *Hotlines and Other Forms of Communication.* The OIG encourages the use of hotlines (including anonymous hotlines), e-mails, written memoranda, newsletters, and other forms of information exchange to maintain these open lines of communication. If the hospital establishes a hotline, the telephone number should be made readily available to all employees and independent contractors, possibly by conspicuously posting the telephone number in common work areas. [46] Employees should be permitted to report matters on an anonymous basis. Matters reported through the hotline or other communication sources that suggest substantial violations of compliance policies, regulations or statutes should be documented and investigated promptly to determine their veracity. A log should be maintained by the compliance officer that records such calls, including the nature of any investigation and its results. Such information should be included in reports to the governing body, the CEO and compliance committee. Further, while the hospital should always strive to maintain the confidentiality of an employee's identity, it should also explicitly communicate that there may be a point where the individual's identity may become known or may have to be revealed in certain instances when governmental authorities become involved.

The OIG recognizes that assertions of fraud and abuse by employees who may have participated in illegal conduct or committed other malfeasance raise numerous complex legal and management issues that should be examined on a case-by-case basis. The compliance officer should work closely with legal counsel, who can provide guidance regarding such issues.

E. Enforcing Standards Through Well-Publicized Disciplinary Guidelines

1. *Discipline Policy and Actions.* An effective compliance program should include guidance regarding disciplinary action for corporate officers, managers, employees, physicians and other health care professionals who have failed to comply with the hospital's standards of conduct, policies and procedures, or Federal and State laws, or those who have otherwise engaged in wrongdoing, which have the poten-

[46] Hospitals should also post in a prominent, available area the HHS OIG Hotline telephone number, 1–800-HHS-TIPS (447–8477), in addition to any company hotline number that may be posted.

tial to impair the hospital's status as a reliable, honest and trustworthy health care provider.

The OIG believes that the compliance program should include a written policy statement setting forth the degrees of disciplinary actions that may be imposed upon corporate officers, managers, employees, physicians and other health care professionals for failing to comply with the hospital's standards and policies and applicable statutes and regulations. Intentional or reckless noncompliance should subject transgressors to significant sanctions. Such sanctions could range from oral warnings to suspension, privilege revocation (subject to any applicable peer review procedures), termination or financial penalties, as appropriate. The written standards of conduct should elaborate on the procedures for handling disciplinary problems and those who will be responsible for taking appropriate action. Some disciplinary actions can be handled by department managers, while others may have to be resolved by a senior hospital administrator. Disciplinary action may be appropriate where a responsible employee's failure to detect a violation is attributable to his or her negligence or reckless conduct. Personnel should be advised by the hospital that disciplinary action will be taken on a fair and equitable basis. Managers and supervisors should be made aware that they have a responsibility to discipline employees in an appropriate and consistent manner.

It is vital to publish and disseminate the range of disciplinary standards for improper conduct and to educate officers and other hospital staff regarding these standards. The consequences of noncompliance should be consistently applied and enforced, in order for the disciplinary policy to have the required deterrent effect. All levels of employees should be subject to the same disciplinary action for the commission of similar offenses. The commitment to compliance applies to all personnel levels within a hospital. The OIG believes that corporate officers, managers, supervisors, medical staff and other health care professionals should be held accountable for failing to comply with, or for the foreseeable failure of their subordinates to adhere to, the applicable standards, laws, and procedures.

2. *New Employee Policy.* For all new employees who have discretionary authority to make decisions that may involve compliance with the law or compliance oversight, hospitals should conduct a reasonable and prudent background investigation, including a refer-

ence check, as part of every such employment application.[47] The application should specifically require the applicant to disclose any criminal conviction, as defined by 42 U.S.C. 1320a-7(i), or exclusion action. Pursuant to the compliance program, hospital policies should prohibit the employment of individuals who have been recently convicted of a criminal offense related to health care or who are listed as debarred, excluded or otherwise ineligible for participation in Federal health care programs (as defined in 42 U.S.C. 1320a-7b(f)).[48] In addition, pending the resolution of any criminal charges or proposed debarment or exclusion, the OIG recommends that such individuals should be removed from direct responsibility for or involvement in any Federal health care program.[49] With regard to current employees or independent contractors, if resolution of the matter results in conviction, debarment or exclusion, the hospital should terminate its employment or other contract arrangement with the individual or contractor.

F. Auditing and Monitoring

An ongoing evaluation process is critical to a successful compliance program. The OIG believes that an effective program should incorporate thorough monitoring of its implementation and regular reporting to senior hospital or corporate officers.[50] Compliance reports created by this ongoing monitoring, including reports of suspected noncompliance, should be maintained by the compliance officer and shared with the hospital's senior management and the compliance committee.

Although many monitoring techniques are available, one effective tool to promote and ensure compliance is the performance of regular,

---

[47] See fn. 37, *supra*.

[48] Likewise, hospital compliance programs should establish standards prohibiting the execution of contracts with companies that have been recently convicted of a criminal offense related to health care or that are listed by a Federal agency as debarred, excluded, or otherwise ineligible for participation in Federal health care programs.

[49] Prospective employees who have been officially reinstated into the Medicare and Medicaid programs by the OIG may be considered for employment upon proof of such reinstatement.

[50] Even when a hospital is owned by a larger corporate entity, the regular auditing and monitoring of the compliance activities of an individual hospital must be a key feature in any annual review. Appropriate reports on audit findings should be periodically provided and explained to a parent-organization's senior staff and officers.

periodic compliance audits by internal or external auditors who have expertise in Federal and State health care statutes, regulations and Federal health care program requirements. The audits should focus on the hospital's programs or divisions, including external relationships with third-party contractors, specifically those with substantive exposure to government enforcement actions. At a minimum, these audits should be designed to address the hospital's compliance with laws governing kickback arrangements, the physician self-referral prohibition, CPT/HCPSC ICD-9 coding, claim development and submission, reimbursement, cost reporting and marketing. In addition, the audits and reviews should inquire into the hospital's compliance with specific rules and polices that have been the focus of particular attention on the part of the Medicare fiscal intermediaries or carriers, and law enforcement, as evidenced by OIG Special Fraud Alerts, OIG audits and evaluations, and law enforcement's initiatives. See section II.A.2, *supra.* In addition, the hospital should focus on any areas of concern that have been identified by any entity, i.e., Federal, State, or internally, specific to the individual hospital.

Monitoring techniques may include sampling protocols that permit the compliance officer to identify and review variations from an established baseline.[51] Significant variations from the baseline should trigger a reasonable inquiry to determine the cause of the deviation. If the inquiry determines that the deviation occurred for legitimate, explainable reasons, the compliance officer, hospital administrator or manager may want to limit any corrective action or take no action. If it is determined that the deviation was caused by improper procedures, misunderstanding of rules, including fraud and systemic problems, the hospital should take prompt steps to correct the problem. Any overpayments discovered as a result of such deviations should be returned promptly to the affected payor, with

[51] The OIG recommends that when a compliance program is established in a hospital, the compliance officer, with the assistance of department managers, should take a "snapshot" of their operations from a compliance perspective. This assessment can be undertaken by outside consultants, law or accounting firms, or internal staff, with authoritative knowledge of health care compliance requirements. This "snapshot," often used as part of benchmarking analyses, becomes a baseline for the compliance officer and other managers to judge the hospital's progress in reducing or eliminating potential areas of vulnerability. For example, it has been suggested that a baseline level include the frequency and percentile levels of various diagnosis codes and the increased billing of complications and co-morbidities.

appropriate documentation and a thorough explanation of the reason for the refund.[52]

Monitoring techniques may also include a review of any reserves the hospital has established for payments that it may owe to Medicare, Medicaid, TRICARE or other Federal health care programs. Any reserves discovered that include funds that should have been paid to Medicare or another government program should be paid promptly, regardless of whether demand has been made for such payment.

An effective compliance program should also incorporate periodic (at least annual) reviews of whether the program's compliance elements have been satisfied, e.g., whether there has been appropriate dissemination of the program's standards, training, ongoing educational programs and disciplinary actions, among others. This process will verify actual conformance by all departments with the compliance program. Such reviews could support a determination that appropriate records have been created and maintained to document the implementation of an effective program. However, when monitoring discloses that deviations were not detected in a timely manner due to program deficiencies, appropriate modifications must be implemented. Such evaluations, when developed with the support of management, can help ensure compliance with the hospital's policies and procedures.

As part of the review process, the compliance officer or reviewers should consider techniques such as:

- On-site visits;
- Interviews with personnel involved in management, operations, coding, claim development and submission, patient care, and other related activities;
- Questionnaires developed to solicit impressions of a broad cross-section of the hospital's employees and staff;
- Reviews of medical and financial records and other source documents that support claims for reimbursement and Medicare cost reports;
- Reviews of written materials and documentation prepared by the different divisions of a hospital; and
- Trend analysis, or longitudinal studies, that seek deviations, positive or negative, in specific areas over a given period.

---

[52] In addition, when appropriate, as referenced in section G.2 reports of fraud or systemic problems should also be made to the appropriate governmental authority.

The reviewers should:

- Be independent of physicians and line management;
- Have access to existing audit and health care resources, relevant personnel and all relevant areas of operation;
- Present written evaluative reports on compliance activities to the CEO, governing body and members of the compliance committee on a regular basis, but no less than annually; and
- Specifically identify areas where corrective actions are needed.

With these reports, hospital management can take whatever steps are necessary to correct past problems and prevent them from reoccurring. In certain cases, subsequent reviews or studies would be advisable to ensure that the recommended corrective actions have been implemented successfully.

The hospital should document its efforts to comply with applicable statutes, regulations and Federal health care program requirements. For example, where a hospital, in its efforts to comply with a particular statute, regulation or program requirement, requests advice from a government agency (including a Medicare fiscal intermediary or carrier) charged with administering a Federal health care program, the hospital should document and retain a record of the request and any written or oral response. This step is extremely important if the hospital intends to rely on that response to guide it in future decisions, actions or claim reimbursement requests or appeals. Maintaining a log of oral inquiries between the hospital and third parties represents an additional basis for establishing documentation on which the organization may rely to demonstrate attempts at compliance. Records should be maintained demonstrating reasonable reliance and due diligence in developing procedures that implement such advice.

G. Responding to Detected Offenses and Developing Corrective Action Initiatives

1. *Violations and Investigations.* Violations of a hospital's compliance program, failures to comply with applicable Federal or State law, and other types of misconduct threaten a hospital's status as a reliable, honest and trustworthy provider capable of participating in Federal health care programs. Detected but uncorrected misconduct can seriously endanger the mission, reputation, and legal status of the hospital. Consequently, upon reports or reasonable indications of suspected noncompliance, it is important that the chief compliance

officer or other management officials initiate prompt steps to investigate the conduct in question to determine whether a material violation of applicable law or the requirements of the compliance program has occurred, and if so, take steps to correct the problem.[53] As appropriate, such steps may include an immediate referral to criminal and/or civil law enforcement authorities, a corrective action plan,[54] a report to the Government,[55] and the submission of any overpayments, if applicable.

Where potential fraud or False Claims Act liability is not involved, the OIG recognizes that HCFA regulations and contractor guidelines already include procedures for returning overpayments to the Government as they are discovered. However, even if the overpayment detection and return process is working and is being monitored by the hospital's audit or coding divisions, the OIG still believes that the compliance officer needs to be made aware of these overpayments, violations or deviations and look for trends or patterns that may demonstrate a systemic problem.

Depending upon the nature of the alleged violations, an internal investigation will probably include interviews and a review of relevant documents. Some hospitals should consider engaging outside counsel, auditors, or health care experts to assist in an investigation. Records of the investigation should contain documentation of the

[53] Instances of non-compliance must be determined on a case-by-case basis. The existence, or amount, of a *monetary* loss to a health care program is not solely determinative of whether or not the conduct should be investigated and reported to governmental authorities. In fact, there may be instances where there is no monetary loss at all, but corrective action and reporting are still necessary to protect the integrity of the applicable program and its beneficiaries.

[54] Advice from the hospital's in-house counsel or an outside law firm may be sought to determine the extent of the hospital's liability and to plan the appropriate course of action.

[55] The OIG currently maintains a voluntary disclosure program that encourages providers to report suspected fraud. The concept of voluntary self-disclosure is premised on a recognition that the Government alone cannot protect the integrity of the Medicare and other Federal health care programs. Health care providers must be willing to police themselves, correct underlying problems and work with the Government to resolve these matters. The OIG's voluntary self-disclosure program has four prerequisites: (1) the disclosure must be on behalf of an entity and not an individual; (2) the disclosure must be truly voluntary (i.e., no pending proceeding or investigation); (3) the entity must disclose the nature of the wrongdoing and the harm to the Federal programs; and (4) the entity must not be the subject of a bankruptcy proceeding before or after the self-disclosure.

alleged violation, a description of the investigative process, copies of interview notes and key documents, a log of the witnesses interviewed and the documents reviewed, the results of the investigation, e.g., any disciplinary action taken, and the corrective action implemented. While any action taken as the result of an investigation will necessarily vary depending upon the hospital and the situation, hospitals should strive for some consistency by utilizing sound practices and disciplinary protocols. Further, after a reasonable period, the compliance officer should review the circumstances that formed the basis for the investigation to determine whether similar problems have been uncovered.

If an investigation of an alleged violation is undertaken and the compliance officer believes the integrity of the investigation may be at stake because of the presence of employees under investigation, those subjects should be removed from their current work activity until the investigation is completed (unless an internal or Government-led undercover operation is in effect). In addition, the compliance officer should take appropriate steps to secure or prevent the destruction of documents or other evidence relevant to the investigation. If the hospital determines that disciplinary action is warranted, if should be prompt and imposed in accordance with the hospital's written standards of disciplinary action.

2. *Reporting.* If the compliance officer, compliance committee or management official discovers credible evidence of misconduct from any source and, after a reasonable inquiry, has reason to believe that the misconduct may violate criminal, civil or administrative law, then the hospital promptly should report the existence of misconduct to the appropriate governmental authority[56] within a reasonable period, but not more than sixty (60) days[57] after determining that there is credible evidence of a violation.[58] Prompt reporting will

[56] I.e., Federal and/or State law enforcement having jurisdiction over such matter. Such governmental authority would include DOJ and OIG with respect to Medicare and Medicaid violations giving rise to causes of actions under various criminal, civil and administrative false claims statutes.

[57] To qualify for the "not less than double damages'' provision of the False Claims Act, the report must be provided to the Government within thirty (30) days after the date when the hospital first obtained the information. 31 U.S.C. 3729(a).

[58] The OIG believes that some violations may be so serious that they warrant immediate notification to governmental authorities, prior to, or simultaneous with, commencing an internal investigation, e.g., if the conduct: (1) is a clear violation of criminal law; (2) has a significant adverse

demonstrate the hospital's good faith and willingness to work with governmental authorities to correct and remedy the problem. In addition, reporting such conduct will be considered a mitigating factor by the OIG in determining administrative sanctions (e.g., penalties, assessments, and exclusion), if the reporting provider becomes the target of an OIG investigation.[59]

When reporting misconduct to the Government, a hospital should provide all evidence relevant to the alleged violation of applicable Federal or State law(s) and potential cost impact. The compliance officer, under advice of counsel, and with guidance from the governmental authorities, could be requested to continue to investigate the reported violation. Once the investigation is completed, the compliance officer should be required to notify the appropriate governmental authority of the outcome of the investigation, including a description of the impact of the alleged violation on the operation of the applicable health care programs or their beneficiaries. If the investigation ultimately reveals that criminal or civil violations have occurred, the appropriate Federal and State officials[60] should be notified immediately.

As previously stated, the hospital should take appropriate corrective action, including prompt identification and restitution of any overpayment to the affected payor and the imposition of proper disciplinary action. Failure to repay overpayments within a reasonable period of time could be interpreted as an intentional attempt to conceal the overpayment from the Government, thereby establishing

---

effect on the quality of care provided to program beneficiaries (in addition to any other legal obligations regarding quality of care); or (3) indicates evidence of a systemic failure to comply with applicable laws, an existing corporate integrity agreement, or other standards of conduct, regardless of the financial impact on Federal health care programs.

[59] The OIG has published criteria setting forth those factors that the OIG takes into consideration in determining whether it is appropriate to exclude a health care provider from program participation pursuant to 42 U.S.C. 1320a-7(b)(7) for violations of various fraud and abuse laws. See 62 FR 67392, December 24, 1997.

[60] Appropriate Federal and State authorities include the Criminal and Civil Divisions of the Department of Justice, the U.S. Attorney in the hospital's district, and the investigative arms for the agencies administering the affected Federal or State health care programs, such as the State Medicaid Fraud Control Unit, the Defense Criminal Investigative Service, and the Offices of Inspector General of the Department of Health and Human Services, the Department of Veterans Affairs and the Office of Personnel Management (which administers the Federal Employee Health Benefits Program).

an independent basis for a criminal violation with respect to the hospital, as well as any individuals who may have been involved.[61] For this reason, hospital compliance programs should emphasize that overpayment obtained from Medicare or other Federal health care programs should be promptly returned to the payor that made the erroneous payment.[62]

III. Conclusion

Through this document, the OIG has attempted to provide a foundation to the process necessary to develop an effective and cost-efficient hospital compliance program. As previously stated, however, each program must be tailored to fit the needs and resources of an individual hospital, depending upon its particular corporate structure, mission, and employee composition. The statutes, regulations and guidelines of the Federal and State health insurance programs, as well as the policies and procedures of the private health plans, should be integrated into every hospital's compliance program.

The OIG recognizes that the health care industry in this country, which reaches millions of beneficiaries and expends about a trillion dollars, is constantly evolving. However, the time is right for hospitals to implement a strong voluntary compliance program concept in health care. As stated throughout this guidance, compliance is a dynamic process that helps to ensure that hospitals and other health care providers are better able to fulfill their commitment to ethical behavior, as well as meet the changes and challenges being imposed upon them by Congress and private insurers. Ultimately, it is the OIG's hope that a voluntarily created compliance program will enable hospitals to meet their goals, improve the quality of patient care, and substantially reduce fraud, waste and abuse, as well as the cost of health care to Federal, State and private health insurers.

Dated: February 11, 1998.

---

[61] See 42 U.S.C. 1320a-7b(a)(3).

[62] Normal repayment channels as described in HCFA's manuals and guidances are the appropriate vehicle for repaying identified overpayments. Hospitals should consult with its fiscal intermediary or HCFA for any further guidance regarding these repayment channels. Interest will be assessed, when appropriate. See 42 CFR 405.376.

June Gibbs Brown,

Inspector General.

[FR Doc. 98–4399 Filed 2–20–98; 8:45 am]

BILLING CODE 4150–04-M

APPENDIX I3

OIG Notice: Publication of the OIG Compliance Program Guidance for Home Health Agencies

DEPARTMENT OF HEALTH AND HUMAN SERVICES

Office of Inspector General

Publication of the OIG Compliance Program Guidance for Home Health Agencies

AGENCY: Office of Inspector General (OIG), HHS.

ACTION: Notice.

SUMMARY: This **Federal Register** notice sets forth the recently issued Compliance Program Guidance for Home Health Agencies developed by the Office of Inspector General (OIG) in cooperation with, and with input from, several provider groups and industry representatives. Many home health care providers have expressed interest in better protecting their operations from fraud and abuse through the adoption of a voluntary compliance program. The OIG has previously developed and published compliance program guidances focused on the clinical laboratory and hospital industries (62 FR 9435, March 3, 1997 and 63 FR 8987, February 23, 1998, respectively). We believe that the development of this compliance program guidance for the home health industry will continue as a positive step towards promoting a higher level of ethical and lawful conduct throughout the entire health care community.

FOR FURTHER INFORMATION CONTACT: Michael Shaw, Office of Counsel to the Inspector General, (202) 619–2078.

SUPPLEMENTARY INFORMATION: The creation of compliance program guidances has become a major initiative of the OIG in its efforts to engage the health care community in combating fraud and abuse. In formulating compliance guidances, the OIG has worked closely with the Health Care Financing Administration, the Department of Justice and various sectors of the health care industry to provide clear guidance to those segments of the industry that are interested in reducing fraud and abuse within their organizations. The first of these compliance program guidances focused on clinical laboratories and was published in the **Federal Register** on March 3, 1997 (62 FR 9435). Building on basic elements of the first issuance, the second compliance program guidance developed by the OIG focused on the hospital industry and was published in the **Federal Register** on February 23, 1998 (63 FR 8987). The development of these types of compliance program guidance is based on our belief that a health care provider can use internal controls to more efficiently monitor adherence to applicable statutes, regulations and program requirements.

The OIG has identified seven fundamental elements to an effective compliance program. They are:

- Implementing written policies, procedures and standards of conduct;
- Designating a compliance officer and compliance committee;
- Conducting effective training and education;
- Developing effective lines of communication;
- Enforcing standards through well-publicized disciplinary guidelines;
- Conducting internal monitoring and auditing; and
- Responding promptly to detected offenses and developing corrective action.

Using these seven basic elements, the OIG has identified specific areas of home health operations that, based on prior Government enforcement efforts, have proven to be vulnerable to fraud and abuse. The development of this Compliance Program Guidance for Home Health Agencies has been further enhanced by input from various home health trade associations and others with expertise in the home health industry. Regardless of a home health agency's size and structure — whether large or small, urban or rural, for-profit or non-profit — the OIG believes that every home health agency can and should strive to accomplish the objectives and principles underlying all of the compliance policies and procedures set forth in this accompanying guidance. Like the previously-issued compliance guidances for hospitals and clinical laboratories, adoption of the Compliance Program Guidance for Home Health Agencies set forth below will be voluntary.

A reprint of the OIG's Compliance Program Guidance for Home Health Agencies follows.

Office of Inspector General's Compliance Program Guidance for Home Health Agencies

I. Introduction

The Office of Inspector General (OIG) of the Department of Health and Human Services (HHS) continues in its efforts to promote voluntarily developed and implemented compliance programs for the health care industry. The following compliance program guidance is intended to assist home health agencies[1] and their agents and subproviders (referred to collectively in this document as "home health agencies") develop effective internal controls that promote adherence to applicable Federal and State law, and the program requirements of Federal, State, and private health plans.[2] The adoption and implementation of voluntary compliance programs significantly advance the prevention of fraud, abuse, and waste in these health care plans while at the same time further the fundamental mission of all home health agencies, which is to provide quality care to patients.

Within this document, the OIG first provides its general views on the value and fundamental principles of home health agency compliance programs, and then provides the specific elements that each home health agency should consider when developing and implementing an effective compliance program. While this document presents basic procedural and structural guidance for designing a compliance program, it is not in itself a compliance program. Rather, it is a set of guidelines to be considered by a home health agency interested in implementing a compliance program.

The OIG recognizes the size-differential that exists between operations of the different home health agencies and organizations that compose the home health industry. Appropriately, this guidance is pertinent for all home health agencies, whether for-profit or non-profit, large or small, urban or rural. The applicability of the recommendations and guidelines provided in this document depends on the circumstances of each particular home health agency. However, regardless of a home health agency's size and structure, the

---

[1] The term "home health agency" is applied in this document as defined in section 1861(o) of the Social Security Act, 42 U.S.C. 1395x(o).

[2] This Compliance Program Guidance for Home Health Agencies is not intended to address issues specific to suppliers of durable medical equipment, infusion therapy, and other services typically provided in the home setting.

OIG believes that every home health agency can and should strive to accomplish the objectives and principles underlying all of the compliance policies and procedures recommended within this guidance.

Fundamentally, compliance efforts are designed to establish a culture within a home health agency that promotes prevention, detection, and resolution of instances of conduct that do not conform to Federal and State law, and Federal, State, and private payor health care program requirements, as well as the home health agency's business policies. In practice, the compliance program should effectively articulate and demonstrate the organization's commitment to ethical conduct. The existence of benchmarks that demonstrate implementation and achievements are essential to any effective compliance program. Eventually, a compliance program should become part of the fabric of routine home health agency operations.

Specifically, compliance programs guide a home health agency's governing body (*e.g.,* Board of Directors or Trustees), Chief Executive Officer (CEO), managers, clinicians, billing personnel, and other employees in the efficient management and operation of a home health agency. They are especially critical as an internal control in the reimbursement and payment areas, where claims and billing operations are often the source of fraud and abuse, and therefore, historically have been the focus of Government regulation, scrutiny, and sanctions.

It is incumbent upon a home health agency's corporate officers and managers to provide ethical leadership to the organization and to assure that adequate systems are in place to facilitate ethical and legal conduct. Employees, managers, and the Government will focus on the words and actions of a home health agency's leadership as a measure of the organization's commitment to compliance. Indeed, many home health agencies have adopted mission statements articulating their commitment to high ethical standards. A formal compliance program, as an additional element in this process, offers a home health agency a further concrete method that may improve quality of care and reduce waste. Compliance programs also provide a central coordinating mechanism for furnishing and disseminating information and guidance on applicable Federal and State statutes, regulations, and other requirements.

Implementing an effective compliance program requires a substantial commitment of time, energy, and resources by senior management and the home health agency's governing body.[3] Superficial programs that simply purport to comply with the elements discussed and described in this guidance or programs that are hastily constructed and implemented without appropriate ongoing monitoring will likely be ineffective and could expose the home health agency to greater liability than no program at all. While it may require significant additional resources or reallocation of existing resources to implement an effective compliance program, the OIG believes that the long term benefits of implementing the program outweigh the costs.[4]

A. Benefits of a Compliance Program

In addition to fulfilling its legal duty to ensure that it is not submitting false or inaccurate claims to Government and private payors, a home health agency may gain numerous additional benefits by voluntarily implementing an effective compliance program. Such programs make good business sense because they help a home health agency fulfill its fundamental care-giving mission to patients and the community, and assist home health agencies in identifying weaknesses in internal systems and management. Other important potential benefits include the ability to:

- Concretely demonstrate to employees and the community at large the home health agency's strong commitment to honest and responsible provider and corporate conduct;
- Provide a more accurate view of employee and contractor behavior relating to fraud and abuse;

---

[3] Recent case law suggests that the failure of a corporate Director to attempt in good faith to institute a compliance program in certain situations may be a breach of a Director's fiduciary obligation. See, *e.g., In re Caremark International Inc. Derivative Litigation,* 698 A.2d 959 (Ct. Chanc. Del. 1996).

[4] Current Health Care Financing Administration (HCFA) reimbursement principles provide that certain of the costs associated with the creation of a voluntarily established compliance program may be allowable costs on certain types of home health agencies' cost reports. These allowable costs, of course, must at a minimum be *reasonable* and related to patient care. See generally 42 U.S.C. 1395x(v)(1)(A) (definition of reasonable cost); 42 CFR 413.9(a), (b)(2) (costs related to patent care). In contract, cost specifically associated with the implementation of a corporate integrity agreement in response to a Government investigation resulting in a civil or criminal judgment or settlement are unallowable, and are also made specifically and expressly unallowable in corporate integrity agreements and civil fraud settlements.

- Identify and prevent illegal and unethical conduct;
- Tailor a compliance program to a home health agency's specific needs;
- Improve the quality, efficiency, and consistency of patient care;
- Create a centralized source for distributing information on health care statutes, regulations, and other program directives related to fraud and abuse and related issues;
- Formulate a methodology that encourages employees to report potential problems;
- Develop procedures that allow the prompt, thorough investigation of alleged misconduct by corporate officers, managers, employees, independent contractors, consultants, nurses, and other health care professionals;
- Initiate immediate, appropriate, and decisive corrective action;
- Minimize, through early detection and reporting, the loss to the Government from false claims, and thereby reduce the home health agency's exposure to civil damages and penalties, criminal sanctions, and administrative remedies, such as program exclusion;[5] and
- Enhance the structure of home health agency operations and gain consistency between separate business units.

Overall, the OIG believes that an effective compliance program is a sound investment on the part of a home health agency.

The OIG recognizes that the implementation of a compliance program may not entirely eliminate fraud, abuse, and waste from the home health agency system. However, a sincere effort by home health agencies to comply with applicable Federal and State standards, as well as the requirements of private health care programs, through the establishment of an effective compliance program, significantly reduces the risk of unlawful or improper conduct.

---

[5] The OIG, for example, will consider the existence of an *effective* compliance program that pre-dated any governmental investigation when addressing the appropriateness of administrative sanctions. The burden is on the provider to demonstrate the operational effectiveness of a compliance program. Further, the False Claims Act, 31 U.S.C. 3729–3733, provides that a person who has violated the Act, but who voluntarily discloses the violation to the Government, in certain circumstances will be subject to not less than double, as opposed to treble, damages. See 31 U.S.C. 3729(a).

B. Application of Compliance Program Guidance

Given the diversity within the industry, there is no single "best" home health agency compliance program. The OIG understands the variances and complexities within the home health industry and is sensitive to the differences among large national and regional multi-home health agency organizations, specialty home health agencies, small independent home health agencies, and other types of home health agency organizations and systems. However, elements of this guidance can be used by all home health agencies, regardless of size, location, or corporate structure, to establish an effective compliance program. Similarly, a hospital or corporation that owns a home health agency or provides home health services may incorporate these elements into its system-wide compliance or managerial structure. We recognize that some home health agencies may not be able to adopt certain elements to the same comprehensive degree that others with more extensive resources may achieve. This guidance represents the OIG's suggestions on how a home health agency can best establish internal controls and monitoring to correct and prevent fraudulent activities. By no means should the contents of this guidance be viewed as an exclusive discussion of the advisable elements of a compliance program.

The OIG believes that input and support by representatives of the major home health trade associations is critical to the development and success of this compliance program guidance. Therefore, in drafting this guidance, the OIG received and considered input from various home health and medical associations, as well as professional practice organizations. Further, we took into consideration previous OIG publications, such as Special Fraud Alerts, the recent findings and recommendations in reports issued by OIG's Office of Audit Services and Office of Evaluation and Inspections, as well as the experience of past and recent fraud investigations related to home health agencies conducted by OIG's Office of Investigations and the Department of Justice. As appropriate, this guidance may be modified and expanded as more information and knowledge is obtained by the OIG, and as changes in the law, rules, policies, and procedures of the Federal, State, and private health plans occur. New compliance practices may eventually be incorporated into this guidance if the OIG discovers significant enhancements to better ensure an effective compliance program.

The OIG recognizes that the development and implementation of compliance programs in home health agencies often raise sensitive and complex legal and managerial issues.[6] However, the OIG wishes to offer what it believes is critical guidance for providers who are sincerely attempting to comply with the relevant health care statutes and regulations.

II. Compliance Program Elements

The elements proposed by these guidelines are similar to those of the Compliance Program Guidance for Hospitals that was published by the OIG in February 1998, the clinical laboratory compliance program guidance published by the OIG in February 1997,[7] and our corporate integrity agreements.[8] The elements represent a guide that can be tailored to fit the needs and financial realities of a particular home health agency.[9] The OIG is cognizant that, with regard to compliance programs, one model is not suitable to every home health agency. Nonetheless, the OIG believes that every home health agency, regardless of size or structure, can benefit from the principles espoused in this guidance.

The OIG believes that every effective compliance program must begin with a formal commitment by the home health agency's governing body to include all of the applicable elements listed below. These elements are based on the seven steps of the Federal Sentencing Guidelines.[10] Further, we believe that every home health agency can implement most of our recommended elements that expand

---

[6] Nothing stated within this document should be substituted for, or used in lieu of, competent legal advice from counsel.

[7] See 63 FR. 8987 (1998) for the Compliance Program Guidance for Hospitals. See 62 FR 9435 (1997) for the clinical laboratory compliance program guidance. These documents are also located on the Internet at http://www.dhhs.gov/progorg/oig.

[8] Corporate integrity agreements are executed as part of a civil settlement between the health care provider and the Government to resolve a case based on allegations of health care fraud or abuse. These OIG-imposed programs are in effect for a period of 3 to 5 years and require many of the elements included in this compliance program guidance.

[9] This is particularly true in the context of the home health industry, which includes many small independent home health agencies with limited financial resources and staff, as well as the larger multi-home health agency organizations and networks with extensive financial resources and staff.

[10] See United States Sentencing Commission Guidelines, *Guidelines Manual,* 8A1.2, Application Note 3(k). The Federal Sentencing Guidelines are detailed policies and practices for the Federal criminal justice system that prescribe the appropriate sanctions for offenders convicted of Federal crimes.

upon the seven steps of the Federal Sentencing Guidelines. We recognize that full implementation of all elements may not be immediately feasible for all home health agencies. However, as a first step, a good faith and meaningful commitment on the part of the home health agency administration, especially the governing body and the CEO, will substantially contribute to a program's successful implementation. As the compliance program is implemented, that commitment should cascade down through the management of the home health agency to every employee at all levels in the organization.

At a minimum, comprehensive compliance programs should include the following seven elements:

(1) The development and distribution of written standards of conduct, as well as written policies and procedures that promote the home health agency's commitment to compliance (*e.g.*, by including adherence to the compliance program as an element in evaluating managers and employees) and address specific areas of potential fraud, such as claims development and submission processes, cost reporting, and financial relationships with physicians and other health care professionals and entities;

(2) The designation of a compliance officer and other appropriate bodies, *e.g.*, a corporate compliance committee, charged with the responsibility for operating and monitoring the compliance program, and who reports directly to the CEO and the governing body;[11]

(3) The development and implementation of regular, effective education and training programs for all affected employees;

(4) The creation and maintenance of a process, such as a hotline or other reporting system, to receive complaints, and the adoption of procedures to protect the anonymity of complainants and to protect whistleblowers from retaliation;

(5) The development of a system to respond to allegations of improper/illegal activities and the enforcement of appropriate disciplinary action against employees who have violated internal compliance policies, applicable statutes, regulations, or Federal

---

[11] The integral functions of a compliance officer and a corporate compliance committee in implementing an effective compliance program are discussed throughout this compliance program guidance. However, the OIG recognizes that a home health agency may tailor the structure of those positions in consideration of the size and design of the home health agency, while endeavoring to address and accomplish all of the underlying objectives of a compliance officer and a corporate compliance committee.

health care program requirements;[12]

(6) The use of audits and/or other evaluation techniques to monitor compliance and assist in the reduction of identified problem areas;

(7) The investigation and remediation of identified systemic problems and the development of policies addressing the non-employment or retention of sanctioned individuals.

A. Written Policies and Procedures

Every compliance program should require the development and distribution of written compliance policies, standards, and practices that identify specific areas of risk and vulnerability to the home health agency. These policies, standards, and practices should be developed under the direction and supervision of, or subject to review by, the compliance officer and compliance committee and, at a minimum, should be provided to all individuals who are affected by the particular policy at issue, including the home health agency's agents and independent contractors.[13] In addition to these general corporate policies, it may be necessary to implement individual policies for independent components of the home health agency.

1. Standards of Conduct

Home health agencies should develop standards of conduct for all affected employees that include a clearly delineated commitment to

[12] The term "Federal health care programs" is applied in this document as defined in 42 U.S.C. 1320a-7b(f), which includes any plan or program that provides health benefits, whether directly, through insurance, or otherwise, which is funded directly, in whole or in part, by the United States Government (*i.e.,* via programs such as Medicare, Federal Employees' Compensation Act, Black Lund, or the Longshore and Harbor Worker's Compensation Act) or any State health plan (*e.g.,* Medicaid, or a program receiving funds from block grants for social services or child health services). Also, for the purposes of this document, the term "Federal health care program requirements" refers to the statutes, regulations, rules, requirements, directive, and instructions governing Medicare, Medicaid, and all other Federal health care programs.

[13] According to the Federal Sentencing Guidelines, an organization must have established compliance standards and procedures to be followed by its employees and other agents in order to receive sentencing credit for an "effective" compliance program. The Federal Sentencing Guidelines define "agent" as "any individual, including a director, an officer, an employee, or an independent contractor, authorized to act on behalf of the organization.'' See United States Sentencing Commission Guidelines, *Guidelines Manual,* 8A1.2, Application Note 3.

compliance by the home health agency's senior management [14] and its divisions, including affiliated providers operating under the home health agency's [15] control and other health care professionals (*e.g.*, physical therapists, occupational therapists, speech therapists, and medical social workers). Standards should articulate the home health agency's commitment to comply with all Federal and State standards, with an emphasis on preventing fraud and abuse. They should explicitly state the organization's mission, goals, and ethical requirements of compliance and reflect a carefully crafted, clear expression of expectations for all home health agency governing body members, officers, managers, employees, clinicians, and, where appropriate, contractors and other agents. Standards should be distributed to, and comprehensible by, all affected employees (*e.g.*, translated into other languages when necessary and written at appropriate reading levels). Standards should not only address compliance with statutes and regulations, but should also set forth broad principles that guide employees in conducting business professionally and properly. Further, to assist in ensuring that employees continuously meet the expected high standards set forth in the code of conduct, any employee handbook delineating or expanding upon these standards of conduct should be regularly updated as applicable statutes, regulations, and Federal health care program requirements are modified and/or clarified. [16]

When they first begin working for the home health agency, and each time new standards of conduct are issued, employees should be asked to sign a statement certifying that they have received, read, and understood the standards of conduct. An employee's certification

[14] The OIG strongly encourages high-level involvement by the home health agency's governing body, chief executive officer, chief operating officer, general counsel, and chief financial officer, as well as other medical or clinical personnel, as appropriate, in the development of standards of conduct. Such involvement should help communicate a strong and explicit statement of compliance goals and standards.

[15] *E.g.*, pharmacies, other home health agencies, and supplemental staffing entities.

[16] The OIG recognizes that not all standards, policies, and procedures need to be communicated to all employees. However, the OIG believes that the bulk of the standards that relate to complying with fraud and abuse laws and other ethical areas should be addressed and made part of all affected employees' training. The home health agency must decide which additional educational programs should be limited to the different levels of employees, based on job functions and areas of responsibility.

should be retained by the home health agency in the employee's personnel file, and available for review by the compliance officer.

2. Risk Areas

The OIG believes that a home health agency's written policies and procedures should take into consideration the particular statutes, rules, and program instructions that apply to each function or department of the home health agency.[17] Consequently, we recommend that the individual policies and procedures be coordinated with the appropriate training and educational programs with an emphasis on areas of special concern that have been identified by the OIG through its investigative and audit functions.[18] Some of the special areas of OIG concern include:[19]

- Billing for items or services not actually rendered;[20]

---

[17] A home health agency can conduct focus groups composed of managers from various departments to solicit their concerns and ideas about compliance risks that may be incorporated into the home health agency's policies and procedures. Such employee participation in the development of the home health agency's compliance program can enhance its credibility and foster employee acceptance of the program.

[18] The OIG periodically issues Special Fraud Alerts setting forth activities believed to raise legal and enforcement issues. Home health agency compliance programs should require that the legal staff, compliance officer, or other appropriate personnel carefully consider any and all Special Fraud Alerts issued by the OIG that relate to home health agencies. Moreover, the compliance programs should address the ramifications of failing to cease and correct any conduct criticized in such a special Fraud Alert, if applicable to home health agencies, or to take reasonable action to prevent such conduct from reoccurring in the future. If appropriate, a home health agency should take the steps described in section G.2. regarding investigations, reporting, and correction of identified problems.

[19] The OIG's work plan is currently available on the Internet at http://www.dhhs.gov/progorg/oig. The OIG Work Plan details the various projects of the Office of Audit Services, Office of Evaluation and Inspections, Office of Investigations, and Office of Counsel to the Inspector General that are planned to be addressed during each Fiscal Year.

[20] Billing for services not actually rendered involves submitting a claim that represents the provider performed a service all or part of which was simply not performed. This form of billing fraud occurs in many health care entities, including home health agencies, hospitals, laboratories, and nursing homes, and represents a significant part of the OIG's investigative caseload.

- Billing for medically unnecessary services;[21]
- Duplicate billing;[22]
- False cost reports;[23]
- Credit balances — failure to refund;[24]
- Home health agency incentives to actual or potential referral sources (*e.g.*, physicians, hospitals, patients, etc.) that may vio-

---

[21] Billing for medically unnecessary services involves knowingly seeking reimbursement for a service that is not warranted by the patient's current and documented medical condition. *See* 42 U.S.C. Sec. 1395y(a)(1)(A) ("no payment may be made under part A or part B [of Medicare] for any expenses incurred for items or services which * * * are not reasonable and necessary for the diagnosis or treatment of illness or injury or to improve the functioning of the malformed body member"). Upon submission of an HCFA claim form (whether paper or electronic), a home health agency certifies that the services provided and billed were medically necessary for the health of the beneficiary, and were rendered in accordance with orders prescribed by the beneficiary's physician. See also discussion in section II.A.3.a and accompanying notes.

[22] Duplicate billing occurs when the home health agency submits more than one claim for the same service or the bill is submitted to more than one primary payor at the same time. Although duplicate billing can occur due to simple error, knowing, duplicate billing — which is sometimes evidenced by systematic or repeated double billing — can create liability under criminal, civil, or administrative law, particularly if any overpayment is not promptly refunded.

[23] The submission of false cost reports is usually limited to certain Medicare Part A providers, such as home health agencies, hospitals, and skilled nursing facilities, which are reimbursed in part on the basis of their self-reported operating costs. The OIG is aware of practices in which home health agencies maintain records that indicate salaries are paid to employees that do not exist, lump nonpatient-related expenses with patient-related ones in an attempt to bury the non-reimbursable costs, bill Medicare for patient visits with no records to substantiate that the services were performed, inappropriately shift certain costs to cost centers that are below their reimbursement cap, shift non-Medicare related costs to Medicare cost centers, and fail to properly disclose related organizations (see 42 CFR 413.17(b)), *e.g.*, entities that provide leased space or equipment, financial management consulting, and direct patient services and supplies.

[24] A credit balance is an improper or excess payment made to a health care provider as a result of patient billing or claims processing errors. Examples of Medicare credit balances include instances where a provider is: (1) Paid twice for the same service either by Medicare or by Medicare and another insurer; or (2) paid for services planned but not performed or for non-covered services. See Home Health Agency Manual Sec. 489. Home health agencies should institute procedures to provide for the timely and accurate reporting of Medicare and other Federal health care program credit balances.

late the anti-kickback statute or other similar Federal or State statute or regulation;[25]

- Joint ventures between parties, one of whom can refer Medicare or Medicaid business to the other;[26]
- Stark physician self-referral law;[27]
- Billing for services provided to patients who are not confined to their residence (or "homebound");[28]
- Billing for visits to patients who do not require a qualifying service;[29]
- Over-utilization[30] and under-utilization;[31]
- Knowing billing for inadequate or substandard care;

---

[25] Examples of arrangements that may run afoul of the anti-kickback statute include practices in which a home health agency pays a fee to a physician for each plan of care certified, provides items or services for free or below fair market value to beneficiaries of Federal health care programs, provides nursing or administrative services for free or below fair market value to physicians, hospitals and other potential referral sources, and provides salaries to a referring physician for services either not rendered or in excess of fair market value for services rendered. See 42 U.S.C. 1320a-7b; 60 FR 40, 847 (1995). See also discussion in section II.A.4. and accompanying notes.

[26] Equally troubling to the OIG is the proliferation of business arrangements that may violate the anti-kickback statute. Such arrangements are generally established between those in a position to refer business, such as physicians, and those providing items or services for which a Federal health care program pays. Sometimes established as "joint ventures,' ' these arrangements may take a variety of forms. The OIG currently has a number of investigations and audits underway that focus on such areas of concern.

[27] Under the Stark physician self-referral law, if a physician (or an immediate family member of such physician) has a financial relationship with a home health agency, the physician may not make a referral to the home health agency for the furnishing of home health services for which payment may be made under the Federal health care programs. See 42 U.S.C. 1395nn.

[28] See discussion in section II.A.3.b. and accompanying notes.

[29] See discussion in section II.A.3.d. and accompanying notes.

[30] Physicians often rely on home health agencies to determine the need, type, and frequency of home health services provided to a beneficiary. Since Medicare does not limit the number of visits or the length of home health coverage for an individual beneficiary, home health agencies have incentives to furnish as many visits as possible, which can lead to over-utilization. Although it is a physician that determines medical necessity, a home health agency has an obligation to ensure that services it provides are medically necessary, and should consult with physicians as appropriate for the requisite assurances.

- Insufficient documentation to evidence that services were performed and to support reimbursement;
- Billing for unallowable costs of home health coordination;[32]
- Billing for services provided by unqualified or unlicensed clinical personnel;
- False dating of amendments to nursing notes;
- Falsified plans of care;[33]
- Untimely and/or forged physician certifications on plans of care;
- Forged beneficiary signatures on visit slips/logs that verify services were performed;
- Improper patient solicitation activities and high-pressure marketing of uncovered or unnecessary services;[34]
- Inadequate management and oversight of subcontracted services, which results in improper billing;
- Discriminatory admission and discharge of patients;
- Billing for unallowable costs associated with the acquisition and sale of home health agencies;
- Compensation programs that offer incentives for number of visits performed and revenue generated;[35]

---

[31] In other words, knowing denial of needed care in order to keep costs low.

[32] Home health coordination is intended to manage and facilitate the transfer of patients from a hospital or skilled nursing facility to the care of a home health agency. Although some costs of performing this service may be allowable under Medicare, the costs of services performed by home health agency personnel that constitute patient solicitation or activities duplicative of an institution's discharge planning responsibilities are not allowable. These non-reimbursable activities, as well as the allowable costs of performing home health coordination, are more specifically described in the Provider Reimbursement Manual, Part I, Sec. 2113. Further, the OIG's Home Health Fraud Alert of June 1995 specifically warned home health agencies that providing hospitals with discharge planners, home health coordinators, or home care liaisons in order to induce referrals can constitute a kickback.

[33] See discussion in section II.A.3.c. and accompanying notes.

[34] Home health agencies should not utilize prohibited or inappropriate conduct (*e.g.*, offer free gifts or services to patients) to carry out their initiatives and activities designed to maximize business growth and patient retention. Also, any marketing information offered by home health agencies should be clear, correct, non-deceptive, and fully informative.

[35] The current nature of the home health benefit (*i.e.*, no limits on reimbursable home health visits in a cost-reimbursed system) and customary business pressures create risks associated with incentives (*e.g.*, payments

- Improper influence over referrals by hospitals that own home health agencies;
- Patient abandonment in violation of applicable statutes, regulations, and Federal health care program requirements;[36]
- Knowing misuse of provider certification numbers, which results in improper billing;
- Duplication of services provided by assisted living facilities, hospitals, clinics, physicians, and other home health agencies;
- Knowing or reckless disregard of willing and able caregivers when providing home health services;[37]
- Failure to adhere to home health agency licensing requirements and Medicare conditions of participation;[38] and
- Knowing failure to return overpayments made by Federal health care programs. A home health agency's prior history of noncompliance with applicable statutes, regulations, and Federal health care program requirements may indicate additional types of risk areas where the home health agency may be vulnerable and that may require necessary policy measures to be taken to prevent avoidable recurrence.[39] Additional risk areas

---

benefits, etc.) for productivity and volume of services. Such risks include over-utilization and billing for services not provided in order to meet internal goals and budget benchmarks imposed by home health agency management.

[36] Under the Medicare conditions of participation, a home health agency has the duty to fully inform a beneficiary in advance of termination of services when further care or treatment is necessary. See generally 42 U.S.C. 395bbb. Moreover, State licensure statutes and regulations may stipulate additional requirements (*e.g.,* the minimum time period of advance notice allowed) that home health agencies must follow when terminating the services provided to a patient. The risk of abandonment may arise when a home health agency attempts to keep costs of providing services low.

[37] According to Medicare reimbursement principles, where a family member or other person is or will be providing services that adequately meet a patient's needs, it is not reasonable and necessary for a home health agency to furnish such services. Therefore, if a home health agency has first hand knowledge of an able and willing person to provide the services being rendered by the home health agency, or a patient (or patient's family) objects to a home health agency providing such services, the home health agency should neither provide nor bill for such services. See Home Health Agency Manual Sec. 203.2.

[38] See 42 U.S.C. 1395bbb for the Medicare conditions of participation that apply to home health agencies.

[39] "Recurrence of misconduct similar to that which an organization has previously committed casts doubt on whether it took all reasonable steps to

should be assessed by home health agencies as well and incorporated into the written policies and procedures and training elements developed as part of their compliance programs.

3. Claim Development and Submission Process

Of the risk areas identified above, those pertaining to the claim development and submission process have been the frequent subject of administrative recoveries, as well as investigations and prosecutions under the civil False Claims Act and criminal statutes. Settlement of these cases often has required the defendants to execute corporate integrity agreements, in addition to paying significant civil damages and/or criminal fines and penalties. These corporate integrity agreements have provided the OIG with a mechanism to specify practices that help ensure compliance with applicable Federal and State statutes, and Federal health care program requirements. The following recommendations include a number of provisions from various corporate integrity agreements. As previously discussed, each home health agency should develop its own specific policies tailored to fit its individual needs.

With respect to the reimbursement process, a home health agency's written policies and procedures should reflect and reinforce current Federal health care requirements regarding the submission of claims and Medicare cost reports. The policies must create a mechanism for the billing or reimbursement staff to communicate effectively and accurately with the clinical staff. Policies and procedures should:

- Provide for sufficient and timely documentation of all nursing and other home health services, including subcontracted services, *prior* to billing to ensure that only accurate and properly documented services are billed;
- Emphasize that a claim should be submitted only when appropriate documentation supports the claim and only when such documentation is maintained, appropriately organized in a legible form, and available for audit and review. The documentation should record the activity leading to the record entry, the identity of the individual providing the service, and any information needed to support medical necessity and other

prevent such misconduct" and is a significant factor in the assessment of whether a compliance program is effective. See United States Sentencing Commission Guidelines, *Guidelines Manual.* 8A1.2, Application Note 3(k) (iii).

applicable reimbursement coverage criteria. The home health agency should consult with its medical director(s), clinical staff, and/or governing body to establish other appropriate documentation guidelines;

- Indicate that the diagnosis and procedure codes for home health services reported on the reimbursement claim should be based on the patient's medical record and other documentation, as well as comply with all applicable official coding rules and guidelines. Any Health Care Financing Administration Common Procedure Coding System (HCPCS), International Classification of Disease (ICD), Home Health Agency's Current Procedural Terminology (CPT), or revenue code (or successor codes) used by the billing staff should accurately describe the service that was ordered by the physician and performed by the home health agency. The documentation necessary for accurate billing should be available to billing staff;
- Provide that the compensation for billing department personnel and billing consultants should not offer any financial incentive to submit claims regardless of whether they meet applicable coverage criteria for reimbursement or accurately represent the services rendered; and
- Establish and maintain a process for pre-and post-submission review of claims [40] to ensure that claims submitted for reimbursement accurately represent medically necessary services actually provided, supported by sufficient documentation, and in conformity with any applicable coverage criteria for reimbursement. [41]

The written policies and procedures concerning proper billing should reflect the current reimbursement principles set forth in applicable regulations [42] and should be developed in tandem with

---

[40] The OIG recommends that, at a minimum, a valid statistical sample of claims should be reviewed before and after billing is submitted.

[41] *E.g.,* plan of care is dated and signed by a physician, beneficiary is homebound, skilled service is required, finite and predictable endpoint exists and is documented for skilled nursing services is excess of 35 hours of per week, etc. 42 U.S.C. 1395m(x); 42 CFR 424.22; Home Health Agency Manual Sec. 204.

[42] The official reimbursement coverage guidelines for participating providers in the Medicare program are promulgated by HCFA in the Provider Reimbursement Manual and the Home Health Agency Manual. Generally, to qualify for the home health benefit covered by Medicare, individuals must

private payor and organizational standards. Particular attention should be paid to issues associated with medical necessity, homebound status of beneficiary, physician certification of plan of care, and qualifying services to establish coverage eligibility.[43]

a. Medical necessity — Reasonable and necessary services. A home health agency's compliance program should provide that claims should only be submitted for services that the home health agency has reason to believe are medically necessary and were ordered by a physician[44] or other appropriately licensed individual.

As a preliminary matter, the OIG recognizes that licensed health care professionals must be able to order any services that are appropriate for the treatment of their patients. However, Medicare and other Government and private health care plans will only pay for those services otherwise covered that meet appropriate medical necessity standards (*i.e.,* in the case of Medicare, "reasonable and necessary" services). Providers may not bill for services that do not meet the applicable standards.[45] The home health agency is in a unique position to deliver this information to the health care professionals on its staff and to the physicians who refer patients. Upon

---

be confined to their residences (be "homebound"), be under a physician's care, and need part-time or intermittent skilled nursing care and/or physical or speech therapy. See Home Health Agency Manual Sec. 204 entitled "Conditions the Patient Must Need to Qualify for Coverage of Home Health Services."

[43] The OIG undertaken numerous audits, investigations, inspections, and national enforcement initiatives aimed at reducing potential and actual fraud, abuse, and waste. For example, OIG audit reports, which have focused on issues such as home health agency billing for services not authorized by a physician, not medically necessary, not eligible for reimbursement, not rendered, and for unallowable general and administrative costs, continue to reveal abusive, wasteful or fraudulent behavior by some home health agencies. Our report on the practices of problem providers, our Operation Restore Trust Audit Report of July 1997, and our special fraud alert on home health fraud, illustrate how certain home health agency billing and business practices may result in fraudulent and abusive behavior.

[44] For Medicare reimbursement purposes, a plan for furnishing home health services must be certified by a physician who is a doctor of medicine, osteopathy, or podiatric medicine, and who does not have a significant ownership interest in, or a significant financial or contractual relationship with, the home health agency. See 42 CFR 424.22.

[45] Civil monetary penalties and administrative sanctions, as well as remedies available under criminal and civil law, including the civil False Claims Act, may be imposed against any person who submits a claim for services "that [the] person knows or should know are not medically necessary." See 42 U.S.C. 1320a-7a(a).

request, a home health agency must be able to provide documentation, such as physician orders and other patient medical records, to support the medical necessity of a service that the home health agency has provided.[46] The compliance officer should ensure that a clear, comprehensive summary of the "medical necessity" definitions and applicable rules of the various Government and private plans is prepared, disseminated, and explained to appropriate home health agency personnel.[47]

We recommend that home health agencies formulate policies and procedures that include periodic clinical reviews, both prior and subsequent to billing for services, as a means of verifying that patients are receiving only medically necessary services. As part of such reviews, home health agencies should examine the frequency and duration of the services they perform to determine, in consultation with a physician, whether patients' medical conditions justify the number of visits provided and billed. Home health agencies may choose to incorporate this clinical review function into pre-existing quality assurance mechanisms or any other quality assurance processes that may become part of the conditions of participation for home health agencies.

Additionally, home health agencies should implement policies and procedures to verify that beneficiaries have actually received the appropriate level and number of services billed. The OIG believes that a home health agency has a duty to sufficiently monitor services its employees provide to patients for confirmation that all services were provided as claimed.[48] To satisfy such an objective, home health agencies may choose to periodically contact (*i.e.,* via mail, telephone, or in person) a random sample of patients and interview the clinical staff involved.

b. Homebound beneficiaries. For a home health agency to receive reimbursement for home health services under either Medicare Part

---

[46] Medicare fiscal intermediaries and carriers have the authority to require home health agencies, which furnish items or services under the program, to submit documentation that substantiates services are actually provided and medically necessary. See Medicare Intermediary Manual Sec. 3116.1.B.

[47] As it applies to private plan requirements, this compliance function may be delegated to supervisory personnel with suitable oversight by the compliance officer.

[48] A home health agency may consider including attestations on nursing note forms to be signed by caregivers for the purpose of reinforcing the importance of accurate documentation of services performed and billed.

A or Part B, the beneficiary must be "confined to the home.''[49] Home health agencies should create oversight mechanisms to ensure that the homebound status of a Medicare beneficiary is verified and the specific factors qualifying the patient as homebound are properly documented.[50] Any determinative assessment of the homebound status of a Medicare beneficiary should be completed prior to billing Medicare for home health services provided to the beneficiary.[51] As with other conditions for Medicare coverage, a physician must certify that the beneficiary was confined to the home at the time when services were provided.[52]

One means by which home health agencies may verify the homebound status of a Medicare beneficiary is the inclusion of written prompts on nursing note forms. These prompts can direct the home health agency's clinicians (*e.g.,* registered nurse or licensed practical nurse) to adequately assess and document the homebound status of a Medicare beneficiary based upon clinical expertise, consultation with the beneficiary, and orders of the attending physician.[53] Carefully designed prompts on nursing note forms may

---

[49] Title XVIII of the Social Security Act, Sec. 1861(m), 42 U.S.C. 1395 x (m), authorizes the provision of home health services to patients who are confined to their home (or homebound). In general, a patient will be considered to be homebound if the patient has a condition due to an illness or injury that restricts the patient's ability to leave his or her place of residence except with the aid of supportive devices such as crutches, canes, wheelchairs, and walkers, or the assistance of another person or if leaving home is medically contraindicated. The condition of these patients should be such that there exists a normal inability to leave the home and, consequently, leaving home would require a considerable and taxing effort. See Home Health Agency Manual Sec. 204.1. HHS plans to submit a report to Congress by October 1, 1998, recommending criteria that should be applied, and the method of applying such criteria, in the determination of whether an individual is homebound for Medicare reimbursement purposes. See Balanced Budget Act of 1997, Pub. L. 105–33, Sec. 4614. Any new criteria developed by HHS should be incorporated into the public applicable policies and procedures of a home health agency.

[50] Recent audits, investigations, and studies of home health agencies have concluded that many home health agencies have billed Medicare for services provided to beneficiaries who are not homebound. See note 43.

[51] If a question is raised as to whether a patient is confined to the home, the home health agency will be requested to furnish its Medicare fiscal intermediary with the information necessary to establish that the patient is homebound. Home Health Agency Manual Sec. 204.1.

[52] 42 CFR 424.22(a)(1)(ii).

[53] These prompts can be in the form of directions (*e.g.,* "Consult with the patient and physician as to the patient's ability to leave the home.") or

help ensure the complete and appropriate documentation necessary to substantiate the homebound status of a Medicare beneficiary for reimbursement purposes.

Home health agencies can further ensure compliance with the homebound requirement by distributing written notices to Medicare beneficiaries, reminding them that they must satisfy the regulatory requirements for homebound status to be eligible for Medicare coverage. Since the Medicare conditions of participation require home health agencies to give all beneficiaries a written notice of their legal rights before furnishing them with home health services, providers can include reminders of homebound requirements in these notices.[54]

c. Physician certification of the plan of care. A home health agency should take all reasonable steps to ensure that claims for home health services are ordered and authorized by a physician.[55] The home health agency's written policies and procedures should require, at a minimum, that:

- Before the home health agency bills for services provided to a beneficiary, the plan of care[56] must be established, dated, and

---

questions (*e.g.*, "Does the patient ever leave the home, and if so, where does the patient go and how often? Does the patient require supportive devices to leave the home?").

[54] See 42 CFR 484.10(a)(1).

[55] As a condition for payment of home health services by Medicare, a physician must certify that a plan for furnishing the services has been established and is periodically reviewed by a physician. 42 CFR 424.22(a) and (b); Home Health Agency Manual Sec. 204.2 If employees of a home health agency believe that services ordered by a physician are excessive or otherwise inappropriate, the home health agency cannot avoid liability for filing improper claims simply because a physician has ordered the services. Medicare, through certifications that are incorporated into the claim forms (paper or electronic) and ratified by home health agencies upon submission, imposes a duty to investigate the truth, accuracy, and completeness of claims before they are submitted. To illustrate, the HCFA-1500 claim form states that the person submitting the form certifies "the services shown on the[e] form were medically necessary for the health of the patient."

[56] The Home Health Agency Manual uses the term "plan of care" to refer to the medical treatment plan established by the treating physician with the assistance of the home health care nurse. Among other things, the plan of care must contain all pertinent diagnoses, including the patient's mental status, the types of services, supplies, and equipment required, the frequency of visits to be made, prognosis, rehabilitation potential, functional limitations, activities permitted, nutritional requirements, and all medica-

signed by a qualified physician;[57]

- The plan of care must be periodically reviewed by a physician in order for the beneficiary to continue to qualify for Medicare coverage of home health benefits;[58]
- Home health services are only billed if the home health agency is acting upon a physician's certification attesting that the services provided to a patient are medically necessary and meet the requirements for home health services to be covered by Medicare;[59]
- When consulted, the home health agency assists the physician in determining the medical necessity of home health services and formulating an appropriate and certified plan of care;[60]

---

tions and treatments. See Home Health Agency Manual Sec. 204.2. The plan of care is presented in writing on the HCFA-485 form entitled "Home Health Certification and Plan of Treatment."

[57] The home health agency should employ reasonable measures to verify that the physician is appropriately licensed and no adverse actions, such as criminal conviction, debarment, or an exclusion, have been taken against the physician.

[58] The plan of care must be reviewed and signed by the physician who established the plan of care, in consultation with the home health agency professional personnel, at least every 62 days. Each review of a patient's plan of care must contain the signature of the physician and the date of review. 42 C.F.R. Sec. Sec. 424.22(a), (b); Home Health Agency Manual Sec. 204.2.F.

[59] The physician must certify that: (1) The patient is confined to the home; (2) the patient is in need of intermittent skilled nursing care, physical therapy and/or speech therapy or continues to need occupational therapy; (3) the patient is under the care of the physician while the services are or were furnished; and (4) a plan of care has been established and is periodically reviewed by the physician. See Home Health Agency Manual Sec. 204.5 and the HCFA-485 form.

[60] In practice, home health agencies often accept the responsibility of assessing a beneficiary's status and completing the HCFA-485 plan of care form for approval by a physician. In the July 1997 OIG Audit Report (A-04–96–02121) entitled, "Results of the Operation Restore Trust Audit of Medicare Home Health Services in California, Illinois, New York, and Texas" (hereinafter "OIG ORT Report"), the OIG concluded that physicians did not always review or actively participate in developing the plans of care they signed, especially for less complex cases. The report found that physicians relied heavily on home health agencies to make determinations as to homebound status, as well as the need, type, and frequency of home health services without physician participation. Since such lack of physician involvement may likely result in non-covered services, it is advisable that home health agencies undertake all reasonable efforts to procure sufficient

- The home health agency properly documents any assessment it has made of a beneficiary's home health needs, which may be used by a physician in developing and authorizing a plan of care; and
- The home health agency reminds or educates physicians, as appropriate, about the scope of their duty to certify patients for home health services to be reimbursed by Medicare.[61]

d. Lack of qualifying service. In addition to addressing the issues associated with other reimbursement coverage criteria, a home health agency's policies and procedures should ensure that all claims satisfy the requisite need of a qualifying service.[62] Since reimbursement coverage of services by other disciplines may depend on the need and the provision of the qualifying service,[63] it is critical for a home health agency to enlist measures to prevent billing for dependent services after

---

physician consultation to ensure that an appropriate plan of care is established for medically necessary services.

[61] This can be accomplished through provider education and liaison activities with physicians and physician support personnel. See Provider Reimbursement Manual Sec. 2113.4

[62] Among other criteria, to receive Medicare reimbursement for home health services, a beneficiary must have a need for skilled nursing care on an intermittent basis, physical therapy, speech-language pathology services, or a continuing need for occupational therapy. See Home Health Agency Manual Sec. 205. To qualify as skilled nursing services, the services must require the skills of a registered nurse or a licensed practical (vocational) nurse under the supervision of a registered nurse, must be reasonable and necessary to the treatment of the patient's illness or injury, and must be intermittent (as discussed in Home Health Agency Manual, Sec. 206.7). Where a service can be safely and effectively performed (or self-administered) by the average nonmedical person without the direct supervision of a licensed nurse, the service cannot be regarded as a skilled service even if a skilled nurse actually provides the service. Home Health Agency Manual Sec. 205.1 A.2.

[63] If an eligible beneficiary requires a qualifying service, Medicare also covers visits by home health aides, medical social workers, and occupational therapists, as well as medical supplies needed and used. Hands-on personal care services, such as bathing, feeding, and assistance with medications, are services customarily performed by home health aides in conjunction with a qualifying service. However, a beneficiary who needs only this type of personal or custodial care does not qualify for the home health benefit. Consequently, with no allowable skilled services, the home health aide services are also not medically necessary or reasonable. See Home Health Agency Manual Sec. 206.2.

any qualifying service has ceased.[64] Any procedures or practices that a home health agency may implement in response to this identified risk will most likely correspond with other policy measures taken by the home health agency to ensure medical necessity.

e. Cost reports. In addition to submitting claims for specific services, home health agencies submit annual cost reports to Medicare for reimbursement of administrative, overhead, and other general costs. With regard to cost report issues, the written policies should include procedures that seek to ensure full compliance with applicable statutes, regulations, and Federal health care program requirements. Among other things, the home health agency's procedures should ensure that:

- Costs are not claimed unless they are reimbursable, reasonable, and are based on appropriate and accurate documentation;
- Allocations of costs to various cost centers are accurately made and supportable by verifiable and auditable data;
- Unallowable costs are not claimed for reimbursement;[65]
- Accounts containing both allowable and unallowable costs are analyzed to determine the unallowable amount that should not be claimed for reimbursement;
- Costs are properly classified;[66]
- Medicare fiscal intermediary prior year audit adjustments are implemented and are either not claimed for reimbursement or if claimed for reimbursement, are clearly identified as protested amounts on the cost report;
- All related parties are identified on the cost report and all related party charges are reduced to the cost to the related party;

---

[64] Recent audits conducted by the OIG have revealed several instances where home health agencies have submitted substantial numbers of claims for home health aide visits to beneficiaries that did not require any skilled qualifying service. See OIG ORT Report.

[65] For administrative, overhead, and other general costs to be allowable under Medicare, regulations require that they be reasonable, necessary for the maintenance of the health care entity, and related to patient care. 42 CFR 413.9; see also Provider Reimbursement Manual, Chapter 21.

[66] *E.g.,* time must be accurately split between reimbursable home health coordination and non-reimbursable patient solicitation activities (see note 32), and between visits to Medicare beneficiaries and visits to non-Medicare beneficiaries.

- Allocations from a home health agency chain's home office cost statement to individual home health agency cost reports are accurately made and supportable by verifiable and auditable data;
- Management fees are reasonable and necessary, and do not include unallowable costs, such as certain acquisition costs associated with the purchase of a home health agency (*e.g.*, good will, non-competes);
- Any return of overpayments, including those resulting from an internal review or audit, are appropriately reflected in cost reports, *i.e.*, a repayment of an overpayment received in a prior year may necessitate changes or amendments to the cost report applicable to the prior year; and
- Procedures are in place and documented for notifying promptly the Medicare fiscal intermediary (or any other applicable payor, *e.g.*, TRICARE (formerly CHAMPUS) and Medicaid) in writing of errors discovered after the submission of the home health agency cost report, and, where applicable, after the submission of a home health agency chain's home office cost statement.

f. Services provided to patients who reside in assisted living facilities. Home health agencies should formulate effective policies and procedures to evaluate home health services provided to individuals who reside in assisted living facilities (also called residential care facilities, personal care homes, group homes, etc.) to determine whether the services are appropriate for reimbursement. [67] To avoid the submission of improper claims for services to such individuals, the adoption of the following measures is advisable upon a request to provide home health services to a resident of an assisted living facility:

---

[67] Individuals who reside in assisted living facilities may be eligible for Medicare coverage of home health services. See Home Health Agency Manual Sec. 204.1B. However, if it is determined that the services furnished by the home health agency are duplicative of services furnished by an assisted living facility, such as when provision of such care is required of the facility under State licensure requirements, claims for such services are unallowable under 42 U.S.C. 1395y(a)(1)(A) and should not be submitted. Services to people who already have access to appropriate care from a willing caregiver would not be considered reasonable and necessary to the treatment of the individual's illness or injury. See Home Health Agency Manual Sec. 203.2. See also note 37.

- Contact the appropriate State licensing authority to determine any applicable State licensure and service requirements for the specific facility involved;
- Make reasonable attempts to verify the specific license, if any, held by the facility, *e.g.*, view the license certificate hanging on the facility's wall;
- Request to view the service agreement between the facility and the resident during the initial assessment visit to determine the extent and type of the services that the facility is contractually obligated to provide to the resident; and
- Provide home health services to the resident only to the extent that they are appropriate and not duplicative of those services provided or required to be provided by the facility.[68]

The OIG strongly recommends that a home health agency contact the appropriate State licensing authority if there is reason to believe a State-licensed facility is failing to provide care that is required by its licensure, regardless of whether claims for services provided to residents of such facilities would otherwise be reimbursable by Medicare or another Federal health care program.

g. Prospective payment system. The Balanced Budget Act of 1997 provides for the establishment of a prospective payment system (PPS) for all costs of home health services. Upon the commencement of such system, all services covered and paid on a reasonable cost basis under the Medicare home health benefit, including medical supplies, will be paid for on the basis of a computed prospective payment amount.[69] Once HHS institutes the PPS, home health agencies should guard against new types of fraud, abuse, and waste that might arise in such a reimbursement system. Potential risks may include failure to report or mischaracterization of a change in patient conditions used to establish the PPS charge, denial of medically necessary care resulting in under-utilization, and duplicate

---

[68] Audits and investigations by both the OIG and Medicare fiscal intermediaries have revealed several instances where home health aids of home health agencies have provided personal care services, such as meal preparation, room cleaning, and bathing, to Medicare beneficiaries who reside in assisted living facilities required by State license to provide such services. In addition to the customary liability assumed by a home health agency for submitting claims for such duplicative and unallowable services, a home health agency may violate the anti-kickback statute for providing these services at no charge to an assisted living facility, an entity that is responsible to perform the services and is a potential source of referrals.

[69] See Balanced Budget Act of 1997, Pub. L. 105–33, Sec. 4603.

billing of charges subsumed within the PPS payment. Accordingly, home health agencies should prepare to implement policies and procedures to properly address any potential risk areas associated with the PPS.

4. Anti-Kickback and Self-Referral Concerns

The home health agency should have policies and procedures in place with respect to compliance with Federal and State anti-kickback statutes, as well as the Stark physician self-referral law.[70] Such policies should provide that:

- All of the home health agency's contracts and arrangements with actual or potential referral sources are reviewed by counsel and comply with all applicable statutes and regulations;[71]
- The home health agency does not submit or cause to be submitted to the Federal health care programs claims for patients who were referred to the home health agency pursuant to contracts or financial arrangements that were designed to induce such referrals in violation of the anti-kickback statute, Stark physician self-referral law, or similar Federal or State statute or regulation; and
- The home health agency does not offer or provide gifts, free services, or other incentives to patients, relatives of patients, physicians, hospitals, contractors, assisted living facilities, or other potential referral sources for the purpose of inducing referrals in violation of the anti-kickback statute, Stark physician self-referral law, or similar Federal or State statute or regulation.[72]

Further, the policies and procedures should specifically reference and take into account the OIG's safe harbor regulations,

[70] Towards this end, the home health agency's in-house counsel or compliance officer should, among other things, obtain copies of all relevant OIG regulations, special fraud alerts, and advisory opinions (these documents are located on the Internet at http:// www.dhhs.gov/progorg/oig), and ensure that the home health agency's policies reflect the guidance provided by the OIG.

[71] In addition to the anti-kickback statutes and the Stark physician self-referral law provisions, 42 CFR 424.22 expressly prohibits a home health agency from providing services certified or recertified by any physician who has a significant ownership interest in, or a significant financial or contractual relationship with, that home health agency.

[72] See 42 U.S.C. 1320a-7b(b); 60 FR 40847 (1995).

which clarify those payment practices that would be immune from prosecution under the anti-kickback statute.[73]

5. Retention of Records

Home health agency compliance programs should provide for the implementation of a records system. This system should establish policies and procedures regarding the creation, distribution, retention, storage, retrieval, and destruction of documents.[74] The three categories of documents developed under this system should include: (1) All records and documentation (*e.g.*, clinical and medical records, and billing and claims documentation) required either by Federal or State law for participation in Federal health care programs[75] or any other applicable Federal and State laws and regulations (*e.g.*, document retention requirements to maintain State licensure); (2) all records, documentation, and verifiable and auditable data that support the home health agency's Medicare cost report, and, where applicable, the home health agency chain's home office cost statement; and (3) all records necessary to protect the integrity of the home health agency's compliance process and confirm the effectiveness of the program. The third category includes: documentation that employees were adequately trained; reports from the home health agency's hotline, including the nature and results of any investigation that was conducted; documentation of corrective action, including disciplinary action taken and policy improvements introduced, in response to any internal investigation or audit; modifications to the compliance program; self-disclosures; and the results of the home health agency's auditing and monitoring efforts.[76]

6. Compliance as an Element of a Performance Plan

Compliance programs should require that the promotion of, and adherence to, the elements of the compliance program be a factor in

[73] See 42 CFR 1001.952.

[74] This records system should be tailored to fit the individual needs and financial resources of the home health agency.

[75] For example, as a condition of participation, Medicare requires that home health agencies retain records regarding their claims to Medicare for a minimum of 5 years after the month the cost report to which the records apply is filed with the fiscal intermediary. See 42 CFR 484.48(a).

[76] The creation and retention of such documents and reports may raise a variety of legal issues, such as patient privacy and confidentiality. These issues are best discussed with legal counsel.

evaluating the performance of all employees, who should be periodically trained in new compliance policies and procedures. In addition, all managers and supervisors involved in the claims and cost report development and submission processes should:

- Discuss with all supervised employees and relevant contractors the compliance policies and legal requirements pertinent to their function;
- Inform all supervised personnel that strict compliance with these policies and requirements is a condition of employment; and
- Disclose to all supervised personnel that the home health agency will take disciplinary action up to and including termination for violation of these policies or requirements.

In addition to making performance of these duties an element in evaluations, the compliance officer or home health agency management should include in the home health agency's compliance program a policy that managers and supervisors will be sanctioned for failing to adequately instruct their subordinates or for failing to detect noncompliance with applicable policies and legal requirements, where reasonable diligence on the part of the manager or supervisor would have led to the discovery of any problems or violations and given the home health agency the opportunity to correct them earlier.

B. Designation of a Compliance Officer and a Compliance Committee

1. Compliance Officer

Every home health agency should designate a compliance officer to serve as the focal point for compliance activities. This responsibility may be the individual's sole duty or added to other management responsibilities, depending upon the size and resources of the home health agency and the complexity of the task. Designating a compliance officer with the appropriate authority is critical to the success of the program, necessitating the appointment of a high-level official in the home health agency with direct access to the home health agency's president or CEO, governing body, all other senior management, and legal counsel. [77] The officer should have sufficient funding

[77] The OIG believes that it is not advisable for the compliance function to be subordinate to the home health agency's general counsel, or comptroller

and staff to perform his or her responsibilities fully. Coordination and communication are the key functions of the compliance officer with regard to planning, implementing, and monitoring the compliance program.

The compliance officer's primary responsibilities should include:

- Overseeing and monitoring the implementation of the compliance program;[78]
- Reporting on a regular basis to the home health agency's governing body, CEO, and compliance committee (if applicable) on the progress of implementation, and assisting these components in establishing methods to improve the home health agency's efficiency and quality of services, and to reduce the home health agency's vulnerability to fraud, abuse, and waste;
- Periodically revising the program in light of changes in the organization's needs, and in the law and policies and procedures of Government and private payor health plans;
- Reviewing employees' certifications that they have received, read, and understood the standards of conduct;
- Developing, coordinating, and participating in a multifaceted educational and training program that focuses on the elements of the compliance program, and seeks to ensure that all relevant employees and management are knowledgeable of, and comply with, pertinent Federal and State standards;
- Ensuring that independent contractors and agents who furnish nursing or other health care services to the clients of the home health agency, or billing services to the home health agency, are aware of the requirements of the home health agency's compliance program with respect to coverage, billing, and marketing, among other things;

---

or similar home health agency financial officer. Free standing compliance functions help to ensure independent and objective legal reviews and financial analyses of the institution's compliance efforts and activities. By separating the compliance function from the key management positions of general counsel or chief financial officer (where the size and structure of the home health agency make this a feasible option), a system of checks and balances is established to more effectively achieve the goals of the compliance program.

[78] For multi-home health agency organizations or hospital-owned home health agencies, the OIG encourages coordination with each home health agency owned by the corporation or hospital through the use of a headquarter's compliance officer, communicating with parallel positions in each facility, regional office, or business line, as appropriate.

- Coordinating personnel issues with the home health agency's Human Resources/Personnel office (or its equivalent) to ensure that the National Practitioner Data Bank [79] and Cumulative Sanction Report [80] have been checked with respect to all employees, medical staff, and independent contractors (as appropriate); [81]
- Assisting the home health agency's financial management in coordinating internal compliance review and monitoring activities, including annual or periodic reviews of departments;
- Independently investigating and acting on matters related to compliance, including the flexibility to design and coordinate internal investigations (*e.g.,* responding to reports of problems or suspected violations) and any resulting corrective action (*e.g.,* making necessary improvements to home health agency policies and practices, taking appropriate disciplinary action, etc.) with all home health agency departments, subcontracted providers, and health care professionals under the home health agency's control, [82] and any other agents if appropriate;
- Developing policies and programs that encourage managers and employees to report suspected fraud and other improprieties without fear of retaliation; and
- Continuing the momentum of the compliance program and the accomplishment of its objectives long after the initial years of implementation. [83]

---

[79] The National Practitioner Data Bank is a data base that contains information about medical malpractice payments, sanctions by boards of medical examiners or State licensing boards, adverse clinical privilege actions, and adverse professional society membership actions. Health care entities can have access to this data base to seek information about their own medical or clinical staff, as well as prospective employees.

[80] The Cumulative Sanction Report is an OIG-produced report available on the Internet at http://www.dhhs.gov/progorg/oig. It is updated on a regular basis to reflect the status of health care providers who have been excluded from participation in the Medicare and Medicaid programs. In addition, the General Services Administration maintains a monthly listing of debarred contractors on the Internet at http://www.arnet.gov/epls.

[81] The compliance officer may also have to ensure that the criminal backgrounds of employees have been checked depending upon State requirements or home health agency policy. See note 105.

[82] *E.g.,* physical therapists, occupational therapists, speech therapists, medical social workers, and supplemental staffing entities.

[83] Periodic on-site visits of home agency operations, bulletins with compliance updates and reminders, distribution of audiotapes or videotapes on

The compliance officer must have the authority to review all documents and other information that are relevant to compliance activities, including, but not limited to, patient records, billing records, and records concerning the marketing efforts of the facility and the home health agency's arrangements with other parties, including employees, professionals on staff, relevant independent contractors, suppliers, agents, supplemental staffing entities, and physicians. This policy enables the compliance officer to review contracts and obligations (seeking the advice of legal counsel, where appropriate) that may contain referral and payment provisions that could violate the anti-kickback statute, as well as the Stark physician self-referral prohibition and other legal or regulatory requirements.

2. Compliance Committee

The OIG recommends that a compliance committee be established to advise the compliance officer and assist in the implementation of the compliance program.[84] When developing an appropriate team of people to serve as the home health agency's compliance committee, including the compliance officer, a home health agency should consider a variety of skills and personality traits that are expected from those in such positions.[85] Once a home health agency chooses the people that will accept the responsibilities vested in members of the

---

different risk areas, lectures at management and employee meetings, circulation of recent health care article covering fraud and abuse, and innovative changes to compliance training are various examples of approaches and techniques the compliance officer can employ for the purpose of ensuring continued interest in the compliance program and the home health agency's commitment to its policies and principles.

[84] The compliance committee benefits from having the perspectives of individuals with varying responsibilities in the organization, such as operations, finance, audit, human resources, and clinical management (*e.g.*, Medical Director), as well as employees and managers of key operating units. These individuals should have the requisite seniority and comprehensive experience within their respective departments to implement any necessary changes to home health agency policies and procedures as recommended by the committee. A compliance committee for a home health agency that is part of a hospital might benefit from the participation of officials from other departments in the hospital, such as the accounting and billing departments.

[85] A health care provider should expect its compliance committee members and compliance officer to demonstrate high integrity, good judgment, assertiveness, and an approachable demeanor, while eliciting the respect and trust of employees of the home health agency and having significant

compliance committee, the home health agency needs to train these individuals on the policies and procedures of the compliance program, as well as how to discharge their duties. The committee's functions should include:

- Analyzing the organization,[86] regulatory environment, the legal requirements with which it must comply,[87] and specific risk areas;
- Assessing existing policies and procedures that address these risk areas for possible incorporation into the compliance program;
- Working with appropriate home health agency departments to develop standards of conduct and policies and procedures to promote compliance with legal and ethical requirements;
- Recommending and monitoring, in conjunction with the relevant departments, the development of internal systems and controls to carry out the organization's standards, policies, and procedures as part of its daily operations;[88]
- Determining the appropriate strategy/approach to promote compliance with the program and detection of any potential violations, such as through hotlines and other fraud reporting mechanisms;
- Developing a system to solicit, evaluate, and respond to complaints and problems; and
- Monitoring internal and external audits and investigations for the purpose of identifying troublesome issues and deficient areas experienced by the home health agency, and implementing corrective and preventive action.

---

professional experience working with billing, clinical records, documentation, and auditing principles.

[86] *E.g.,* understanding the practical implications of the fraud and abuse provisions of the Balanced Budget Act of 1997, Pub. L. 105–33, and the Health Insurance Portability and Accountability Act of 1996, Pub. L. 104–191.

[87] This includes, but is not limited to, compliance with the Medicare conditions of participation. See 42 U.S.C. 1395bbb.

[88] With respect to multi-home health agency organizations and hospital-owned home health agencies, this may include fostering coordination and communication between those employees responsible for compliance at the corporation or hospital and those responsible for compliance at the home

The committee may also address other functions as the compliance concept becomes part of the overall home health agency operating structure and daily routine.

C. Conducting Effective Training and Education

The proper education and training of corporate officers, managers, employees, nurses, and other health care professionals, and the continual retraining of current personnel at all levels, are significant elements of an effective compliance program. As part of their compliance programs, home health agencies should require personnel to attend specific training on a periodic basis, including appropriate training in Federal and State statutes, regulations, and guidelines, and the policies of private payors, and training in corporate ethics, which emphasizes the organization's commitment to compliance with these legal requirements and policies.[89]

These training programs should include sessions highlighting the organization's compliance program, summarizing fraud and abuse laws, Federal health care program requirements, claim development and submission processes, patient rights, and marketing practices that reflect current legal and program standards. The organization must take steps to communicate effectively its standards and procedures to all affected employees, physicians, independent contractors, and other significant agents, *e.g.*, by requiring participation in training programs and disseminating publications that explain specific requirements in a practical manner.[90] Managers of specific departments or groups can assist in identifying areas that require training and in carrying out such training.[91] Training instructors may come from outside or inside the organization, but must be qualified to present the subject matter involved and experienced enough in the issues presented to adequately field questions and coordinate discus-

---

[89] Specific compliance training should complement any "in-service" training sessions that a home health agency may regularly schedule to reinforce adherence to policies and practices of the particular home health agency.

[90] Some publications, such as OIG's Special Fraud Alerts, audit and inspection reports, and advisory opinions, as well as the annual OIG work plan, are readily available from the OIG and could be the basis for standards, educational courses, and programs for appropriate home health agency employees.

[91] Significant variations in the functions and responsibilities of different departments or groups may create the need for training materials that are tailored to compliance concerns associated with particular operations and duties.

sions among those being trained. New employees should be trained early in their employment.[92] Training programs and materials should be designed to take into account the skills, experience, and knowledge of the individual trainees. The compliance officer should document any formal training undertaken by the home health agency as part of the compliance program.

A variety of teaching methods, such as interactive training, and training in several different languages, particularly where a home health agency has a culturally diverse staff, should be implemented so that all affected employees are knowledgeable of the institution's standards of conduct and procedures for alerting senior management to problems and concerns.[93] Targeted training should be provided to corporate officers, managers, and other employees whose actions affect the accuracy of the claims submitted to the Government, such as employees involved in the billing, cost reporting, and marketing processes. Given the complexity and interdependent relationships of many departments, proper coordination and supervision of this process by the compliance officer is important. In addition to specific training in the risk areas identified in section II.A.2, above, primary training for appropriate corporate officers, managers, and other home health agency staff should include such topics as:

- Government and private payor reimbursement principles;
- General prohibitions on paying or receiving remuneration to induce referrals;
- Improper alterations to clinical records;
- Providing home health services with proper authorization;
- Proper documentation of services rendered, including the correct application of official ICD and CPT coding rules and guidelines;
- Patient rights and patient education;
- Compliance with Medicare conditions of participation; and
- Duty to report misconduct.

---

[92] Certain positions, such as those that involve the billing of home health services, create a greater organizational legal exposure, and therefore require specialized training. One recommendation would be for a home health agency to attempt to fill such positions with individuals who have the appropriate educational background and training.

[93] Post-training tests can be used to assess the success of training provided and employee comprehension of the home health agency's policies and procedures.

Clarifying and emphasizing these areas of concern through training and educational programs are particularly relevant to a home health agency's marketing and financial personnel, in that the pressure to meet business goals may render these employees vulnerable to engaging in prohibited practices.

The OIG suggests that all relevant levels of personnel be made part of various educational and training programs of the home health agency.[94] Employees should be required to have a minimum number of educational hours per year, as appropriate, as part of their employment responsibilities.[95] For example, for certain employees involved in the billing functions, periodic training in applicable reimbursement coverage and documentation of clinical records should be required.[96] In home health agencies with high employee turnover, periodic training updates are critical.

The OIG recommends that attendance and participation in training programs be made a condition of continued employment and that failure to comply with training requirements should result in disciplinary action, including possible termination, when such failure is serious. Adherence to the provisions of the compliance program, such as training requirements, should be a factor in the annual evaluation of each employee. The home health agency should retain adequate records of its training of employees, including attendance logs and material distributed at training sessions.

Finally, the OIG recommends that home health agency compliance programs address the need for periodic professional education

---

[94] In addition, where feasible, the OIG recommends that a home health agency afford outside contractors the opportunity to participate in the home health agency's compliance training and educational programs, or develop their own programs that complement the home health agency's standards of conduct, compliance requirements, and other rules and practices.

[95] Currently, the OIG is monitoring a significant number of corporate integrity agreements that require many of these training elements. The OIG usually requires a minimum of 1 to 3 hours annually for basic training in compliance areas. Additional training is required for specialty fields such as billing and marketing.

[96] Appropriate billing depends upon the quality and completeness of the clinical documentation. Therefore, OIG believes that active clinical staff participation in educational programs focusing on billing and documentation should be emphasized by the home health agency. Clinical staff should be reminded that thorough, precise, and timely documentation of services provided services the interests of the patient, as well as the interests of the billing department.

courses that may be required by statute and regulation for certain home health agency employees.

D. Developing Effective Lines of Communication

1. Access to the Compliance Officer

An open line of communication between the compliance officer and home health agency employees is equally important to the successful implementation of a compliance program and the reduction of any potential for fraud, abuse, and waste. Written confidentiality and non-retaliation policies should be developed and distributed to all employees to encourage communication and the reporting of incidents of potential fraud.[97] The compliance committee should also develop independent reporting paths for an employee to report fraud, waste, or abuse so that employees can feel comfortable reporting outside the normal chain of command and supervisors or other personnel cannot divert such reports.[98]

The OIG encourages the establishment of a procedure so that home health agency personnel may seek clarification from the compliance officer or members of the compliance committee in the event of any confusion or question with regard to a home health agency policy, practice, or procedure. Questions and responses should be documented and dated and, if appropriate, shared with other staff so that standards, policies, practices, and procedures can be updated and improved to reflect any necessary changes or clarifications. The compliance officer may want to solicit employee input in developing these communication and reporting systems.

---

[97] The OIG believes that whistleblowers should be protected against retaliation, a concept embodied in the provisions of the False Claims Act. See 31 U.S.C. 3730(h). In many causes, employees sue their employers under the False Claims Act's *qui tam* provisions out of frustration because of the company's failure to take action when a questionable, fraudulent, or abusive situation was brought to the attention of senior corporate officials.

[98] Home health agencies can also consider rewarding employees for appropriate use of established systems.

2. Hotlines and Other Forms of Communication

The OIG encourages the use of hotlines,[99] e-mails, written memoranda, newsletters, suggestion boxes, and other forms of information exchange to maintain these open lines of communication.[100] If the home health agency establishes a hotline, the telephone number should be made readily available to all employees and independent contractors, possibly by circulating the number on wallet cards or conspicuously posting the telephone number in common work areas.[101] Employees should be permitted to report matters on an anonymous basis. Matters reported through the hotline or other communication sources that suggest substantial violations of compliance policies, Federal health care program requirements, regulations, or statutes should be documented and investigated promptly to determine their veracity. A log should be maintained by the compliance officer that records such calls, including the nature of any investigation and its results.[102] Such information should be included in reports to the governing body, the CEO, and compliance committee.[103] Further, while the home health agency should always strive to maintain the confidentiality of an employee's identity, it should also explicitly communicate that there may be a point where the individual's identity may become known or may have to be revealed in certain instances.

---

[99] The OIG recognizes that it may not be financially feasible for a smaller home health agency to maintain a telephone hotline dedicated to receiving calls about compliance issues.

[100] In addition to methods of communication used by current employees, an effective employee exit interview program could be designed to solicit information from departing employees regarding potential misconduct and suspected violations go home health agency policy and procedures.

[101] Home health agencies should also post in a prominent, available area the HHS-OIG Hotline telephone number, 1–800–447–8477 (1–800-HHS-TIPS), in addition to any company hotline number that may be posted.

[102] To efficiently and accurately fulfill such an obligation, the home health agency should create an intake form for all compliance issues identified through reporting mechanisms. The form could include information concerning the date that the potential problem was reported, the internal investigative methods utilized, the results of the investigation, the corrective action implemented, the disciplinary measures imposed, and any identified overpayments and monies returned.

[103] Information obtained over the hotline may provide valuable insight into management practices and operations, whether reported problems are actual or perceived.

The OIG recognizes that assertions of fraud and abuse by employees who may have participated in illegal conduct or committed other malfeasance raise numerous complex legal and management issues that should be examined on a case-by-case basis. The compliance officer should work closely with legal counsel, who can provide guidance regarding such issues.

E. Enforcing Standards Through Well-Publicized Disciplinary Guidelines

1. Discipline Policy and Actions

An effective compliance program should include guidance regarding disciplinary action for corporate officers, managers, employees, and other health care professionals who have failed to comply with the home health agency's standards of conduct, policies and procedures, Federal health care program requirements, or Federal and State laws, or those who have otherwise engaged in wrongdoing, which have the potential to impair the home health agency's status as a reliable, honest, and trustworthy health care provider.

The OIG believes that the compliance program should include a written policy statement setting forth the degrees of disciplinary actions that may be imposed upon corporate officers, managers, employees, and other health care professionals for failing to comply with the home health agency's standards and policies and applicable statutes and regulations. Intentional or reckless noncompliance should subject transgressors to significant sanctions. Such sanctions could range from oral warnings to suspension, termination, or financial penalties, as appropriate. Each situation must be considered on a case-by-case basis to determine the appropriate sanction. The written standards of conduct should elaborate on the procedures for handling disciplinary problems and those who will be responsible for taking appropriate action. Some disciplinary actions can be handled by department or agency managers, while others may have to be resolved by a senior home health agency administrator. Disciplinary action may be appropriate where a responsible employee's failure to detect a violation is attributable to his or her negligence or reckless conduct. Personnel should be advised by the home health agency that disciplinary action will be taken on a fair and equitable basis. Managers and supervisors should be made aware that they have a responsibility to discipline employees in an appropriate and consistent manner.

It is vital to publish and disseminate the range of disciplinary standards for improper conduct and to educate officers and other home health agency employees regarding these standards. The consequences of noncompliance should be consistently applied and enforced, in order for the disciplinary policy to have the required deterrent effect. All levels of employees should be potentially subject to the same types of disciplinary action for the commission of similar offenses. The commitment to compliance applies to all personnel levels within a home health agency. The OIG believes that corporate officers, managers, supervisors, clinical staff, and other health care professionals should be held accountable for failing to comply with, or for the foreseeable failure of their subordinates to adhere to, the applicable standards, laws, and procedures.

2. New Employee Policy

For all new employees who have discretionary authority to make decisions that may involve compliance with the law or compliance oversight, home health agencies should conduct a reasonable and prudent background investigation, including a reference check,[104] as part of every such employment application. The application should specifically require the applicant to disclose any criminal conviction,[105] as defined by 42 U.S.C. 1320a-7(i), or exclusion action. Pursuant to the compliance program, home health agency policies should prohibit the employment of individuals who have been recently convicted of a criminal offense related to health care[106] or who are listed as debarred, excluded, or otherwise ineligible for

[104] See note 80.

[105] Slightly over a quarter of the States require, and several home health agencies voluntarily conduct, criminal background checks for prospective employees of home health agencies. Identification of a criminal background of an applicant, who may have been recently convicted of serious crimes that relate to the proposed employment duties, could be grounds for denying employment. Further, criminal background screening may deter those individuals with criminal intent from entering the field of home health. See United States General Accounting Office's September 27, 1996, *Letter Report* entitled "Long-Term Care: Some States Apply Criminal Background Checks to Home Care Workers," GAO/PEMD-96-5.

[106] Since providers of home health services have frequent, relatively unsupervised access to potentially vulnerable people and their property, a home health agency should also strictly scrutinize whether it should employ individuals who have been convicted of crimes of neglect, violence, or financial misconduct.

participation in Federal health care programs.[107] In addition, pending the resolution of any criminal charges or proposed debarment or exclusion, the OIG recommends that an individual who is the subject of such actions should be removed from direct responsibility for or involvement in any Federal health care program.[108] With regard to current employees or independent contractors, if resolution of the matter results in conviction, debarment, or exclusion, the home health agency should terminate its employment or other contract arrangement with the individual or contractor.

F. Auditing and Monitoring

An ongoing evaluation process is critical to a successful compliance program. The OIG believes that an effective program should incorporate thorough monitoring of its implementation and regular reporting to senior home health agency or corporate officers.[109] Compliance reports created by this ongoing monitoring, including reports of suspected noncompliance, should be maintained by the compliance officer and shared with the home health agency's senior management and the compliance committee. The extent and frequency of the audit function may vary depending on factors such as the size and available resources, prior history of noncompliance, and the risk factors that a particular home health agency confronts.

Although many monitoring techniques are available, one effective tool to promote and ensure compliance is the performance of regular, periodic compliance audits by internal or external auditors who have expertise in Federal and State health care statutes, regulations, and Federal health care program requirements. The audits should focus on the home health agency's programs or divisions, including exter-

---

[107] Likewise, home health agency compliance programs should establish standards prohibiting the execution of contracts with companies that have been recently convicted of a criminal offense related to health care or that are listed by a Federal agency as debarred, excluded, or otherwise ineligible for participation in Federal health care programs. See note 80.

[108] Prospective employees who have been officially reinstated into the Medicare and Medicaid programs by the OIG may be considered for employment upon proof of such reinstatement.

[109] Even when a home health agency or group of home health agencies is owned by a larger corporate entity, the regular auditing and monitoring of the compliance activities of an individual home health agency must be a key feature in any annual review. Appropriate reports on audit findings should be periodically provided and explained to a parent organization's senior staff and officers.

nal relationships with third-party contractors, specifically those with substantive exposure to Government enforcement actions. At a minimum, these audits should be designed to address the home health agency's compliance with laws governing kickback arrangements, the physician self-referral prohibition, claim development and submission, reimbursement, cost reporting, and marketing. The audits and reviews should inquire into the home health agency's compliance with the Medicare conditions of participation and the specific rules and policies that have been the focus of particular attention on the part of the Medicare fiscal intermediaries or carriers, and law enforcement, as evidenced by educational and other communications from OIG Special Fraud Alerts, OIG audits and evaluations, and law enforcement's initiatives.[110] In addition, the home health agency should focus on any areas of concern that are specific to the individual home health agency and have been identified by any entity, whether Federal, State, or internal.

Monitoring techniques may include sampling protocols that permit the compliance officer to identify and review variations from an established baseline.[111] Significant variations from the baseline should trigger a reasonable inquiry to determine the cause of the deviation. If the inquiry determines that the deviation occurred for legitimate, explainable reasons, the compliance officer and home health agency management may want to limit any corrective action or take no action. If it is determined that the deviation was caused by improper procedures, misunderstanding of rules, including fraud and systemic problems, the home health agency should take prompt steps to correct the problem. Any overpayments discovered as a result of such deviations should be returned promptly to the affected payor, with appropriate documentation and a sufficiently detailed

[110] See also section II.A.2

[111] The OIG recommends that when a compliance program is established in a home health agency, the compliance officer, with the assistance of department managers, should take a "snapshot" of their operations from a compliance perspective. This assessment can be undertaken by outside consultants, law or accounting firms, or internal staff, with authoritative knowledge of health care compliance requirements. This "snapshot,' ' often used as part of benchmarking analyses, becomes a baseline for the compliance officer and other managers to judge the home health agency's progress in reducing or eliminating potential areas of vulnerability.

explanation of the reason for the refund.[112]

Monitoring techniques may also include a review of any reserves the home health agency has established for payments that it may owe to Medicare, Medicaid, or other Federal health care programs. Any reserves discovered that include funds that should have been paid to such programs, or funds set aside for potential reimbursement of a known overpayment to the home health agency, should be paid promptly, regardless of whether demand has been made for such payment.

An effective compliance program should also incorporate periodic (at least annual) reviews of whether the program's compliance elements have been satisfied, *e.g.,* whether there has been appropriate dissemination of the program's standards, training, ongoing educational programs, and disciplinary actions, among other elements.[113] This process will verify actual conformance by all departments with the compliance program and may identify the necessity for improvements to be made to the compliance program, as well as the home health agency's operations. Such reviews could support a determination that appropriate records have been created and maintained to document the implementation of an effective program.[114] However, when monitoring discloses that deviations were not detected in a timely manner due to program deficiencies, proper modifications must be implemented. Such evaluations, when developed with the support of management, can help ensure compliance with the home health agency's policies and procedures.

As part of the review process, the compliance officer or reviewers should consider techniques such as:

- Visits and interviews of patients at their homes;
- Analysis of utilization patterns;
- Testing clinical and billing staff on their knowledge of reimbursement coverage criteria and official coding guidelines (*e.g.,*

---

[112] In addition, when appropriate, as referenced in section G.2, below, reports of fraud or systemic problems should also be made to the appropriate governmental authority.

[113] One way to assess the knowledge, awareness, and perceptions of the home health agency's employees is through the use of a validated survey instrument (*e.g.,* employee questionnaires, interviews, or focus groups).

[114] Such records should include, but not be limited to, logs of hotline calls, logs of training attendees, training agenda materials, and summaries of corrective action taken and improvements made to home health agency policies as a result of compliance activities.

present hypothetical scenarios of situations experienced in daily practice and assess responses);

- Assessment of existing relationships with physicians, hospitals, and other potential referral sources;
- Unannounced mock surveys, audits, and investigations;
- Reevaluation of deficiencies cited in past surveys for Medicare conditions of participation;
- Examination of home health agency complaint logs;
- Checking personnel records to determine whether any individuals who have been reprimanded for compliance issues in the past are among those currently engaged in improper conduct;
- Interviews with personnel involved in management, operations, claim development and submission, patient care, and other related activities;
- Questionnaires developed to solicit impressions of a broad cross-section of the home health agency's employees and staff;
- Interviews with physicians who order services provided by the home health agency;
- Reviews of clinical documentation (*e.g.,* plan of care, nursing notes, etc.), financial records, and other source documents that support claims for reimbursement and Medicare cost reports;
- Validation of qualifications of physicians who order services provided by the home health agency;
- Evaluation of written materials and documentation outlining the home health agency's policies and procedures; and
- Trend analyses, or longitudinal studies, that uncover deviations, positive or negative, in specific areas over a given period.

The reviewers should:

- Have the qualifications and experience necessary to adequately identify potential issues with the subject matter that is reviewed;
- Be objective and independent of line management to the extent reasonably possible;[115]
- Have access to existing audit and health care resources, relevant personnel, and all relevant areas of operation;

[115] The OIG recognizes that home health agencies that are small in size and have limited resources may not be able to use internal reviewers who are not part of line management or hire outsider reviewers.

- Present written evaluative reports on compliance activities to the CEO, governing body, and members of the compliance committee on a regular basis, but no less often than annually; and
- Specifically identify areas where corrective actions are needed.

With these reports, home health agency management can take whatever steps are necessary to correct past problems and prevent them from recurring. In certain cases, subsequent reviews or studies would be advisable to ensure that the recommended corrective actions have been implemented successfully.

The home health agency should document its efforts to comply with applicable statutes, regulations, and Federal health care program requirements. For example, where a home health agency, in its efforts to comply with a particular statute, regulation or program requirement, requests advice from a Government agency (including a Medicare fiscal intermediary or carrier) charged with administering a Federal health care program, the home health agency should document and retain a record of the request and any written or oral response. This step is extremely important if the home health agency intends to rely on that response to guide it in future decisions, actions, or claim reimbursement requests or appeals. A log of oral inquiries between the home health agency and third parties will help the organization document its attempts at compliance. In addition, the home health agency should maintain records relevant to the issue of whether its reliance was "reasonable" and whether it exercised due diligence in developing procedures and practices to implement the advice.

G. Responding to Detected Offenses and Developing Corrective Action Initiatives

1. Violations and Investigations

Violations of a home health agency's compliance program, failures to comply with applicable Federal or State law, and other types of misconduct threaten a home health agency's status as a reliable, honest and trustworthy provider capable of participating in Federal health care programs. Detected but uncorrected misconduct can seriously endanger the mission, reputation, and legal status of the home health agency. Consequently, upon reports or reasonable indications of suspected noncompliance, it is important that the compliance officer or other management officials immediately investigate the conduct in question to determine whether a material violation of applicable law or the requirements of the compliance program has occurred, and if so, take decisive steps to correct the problem.[116] As appropriate, such steps may include an immediate referral to criminal and/or civil law enforcement authorities, a corrective action plan,[117] a report to the Government,[118] and the return of any overpayments, if applicable.

Where potential fraud or False Claims Act liability is not involved, the OIG recommends that normal repayment channels should be used for returning overpayments to the Government as they are discovered. However, even if the overpayment detection and return process is working and is being monitored by the home health agency's audit or billing divisions, the OIG still believes that the compliance officer needs to be made aware of these overpayments, violations, or deviations that may reveal trends or patterns indicative of a systemic problem.

Depending upon the nature of the alleged violations, an internal investigation will probably include interviews and a review of relevant documents. Some home health agencies should consider engaging outside counsel, auditors, or health care experts to assist in an investigation.

---

[116] Instances of noncompliance must be determined on a case-by-case basis. The existence, or amount, of a *monetary* loss to a health care program is not solely determinative of whether or not the conduct should be investigated and reported to governmental authorities. In fact, there may be instances where there is no readily identifiable monetary loss at all, but corrective action and reporting are still necessary to protect the integrity of the applicable program and its beneficiaries, (*e.g.,* where services required by a plan of care were not provided.

[117] Advice from the home health agency's in-house counsel or an outside law firm may be sought to determine the extent of the home health agency's liability and to plan the appropriate course of action.

[118] The OIG currently maintains a voluntary disclosure program that encourages providers to report suspected fraud. The concept of voluntary self-disclosure is premised on a recognition that the Government alone cannot protect the integrity of the Medicare and other Federal health care programs. Health care providers must be willing to police themselves, correct underlying problems, and work with the Government to resolve these matters. The OIG's voluntary self-disclosure program has four prerequisites: (1) The disclosure must be on behalf of an entity and not an individual; (2) the disclosure must be truly voluntary (*i.e.,* no pending proceeding or investigation); (3) the entity must disclose the nature of the wrongdoing and the harm to the Federal health care programs; and (4) the entity must not be the subject of a bankruptcy proceeding before or after the self-disclosure.

Records of the investigation should contain documentation of the alleged violation, a description of the investigative process (including the objectivity of the investigators and methodologies utilized), copies of interview notes and key documents, a log of the witnesses interviewed and the documents reviewed, the results of the investigation, *e.g.,* any disciplinary action taken, and the corrective action implemented. While any action taken as the result of an investigation will necessarily vary depending upon the home health agency and the situation, home health agencies should strive for some consistency by utilizing sound practices and disciplinary protocols.[119] Further, after a reasonable period, the compliance officer should review the circumstances that formed the basis for the investigation to determine whether similar problems have been uncovered or modifications of the compliance program are necessary to prevent and detect other inappropriate conduct or violations.

If an investigation of an alleged violation is undertaken and the compliance officer believes the integrity of the investigation may be at stake because of the presence of employees under investigation, those subjects should be removed from their current work activity until the investigation is completed (unless an internal or Government-led undercover operation known to the home health agency is in effect). In addition, the compliance officer should take appropriate steps to secure or prevent the destruction of documents or other evidence relevant to the investigation. If the home health agency determines that disciplinary action is warranted, it should be prompt and imposed in accordance with the home health agency's written standards of disciplinary action.

2. Reporting

If the compliance officer, compliance committee, or management official discovers credible evidence of misconduct from any source and, after a reasonable inquiry, has reason to believe that the misconduct may violate criminal, civil, or administrative law, then the home health agency should promptly report the existence of miscon-

---

[119] The parameters of a claim review subject to an internal investigation will depend on the circumstances surrounding the issue(s) identified. By limiting the scope of an internal audit to current billing, a home health agency may fail to discover major problems and deficiencies in operations, as well as be subject to certain liability.

duct to the appropriate Federal and State authorities [120] within a reasonable period, but not more than sixty (60) days [121] after determining that there is credible evidence of a violation. [122] Prompt reporting will demonstrate the home health agency's good faith and willingness to work with governmental authorities to correct and remedy the problem. In addition, reporting such conduct will be considered a mitigating factor by the OIG in determining administrative sanctions (*e.g.*, penalties, assessments, and exclusion), if the reporting provider becomes the target of an OIG investigation. [123]

When reporting misconduct to the Government, a home health agency should provide all evidence relevant to the alleged violation of applicable Federal or State law(s) and potential cost impact. The compliance officer, under advice of counsel, and with guidance from the governmental authorities, could be requested to continue to investigate the reported violation. Once the investigation is completed, the compliance officer should be required to notify the appropriate governmental authority of the outcome of the investigation, including a description of the impact of the alleged violation on

---

[120] Appropriate Federal and State authorities include the Office of Inspector General of the Department of Health and Human Services, the Criminal and Civil Divisions of the Department of Justice, the U.S. Attorney in relevant districts, and the other investigative arms for the agencies administering the affected Federal or State health care programs, such as the State Medicaid Fraud Control Unit, the Defense Criminal Investigative Service, and, the Department of Veterans Affairs and the Office of Personnel Management (which administers the Federal Employee Health Benefits Program).

[121] In contrast, to qualify for the "not less than double damages" provision of the False Claims Act, the report must be provided to the government within thirty (30) days after the date when the home health agency first obtained the information. 31 U.S.C. 3729(a).

[122] The OIG believes that some violations may be so serious that they warrant immediate notification to governmental authorities, prior to, or simultaneous with, commencing an internal investigation, *e.g.*, if the conduct: (1) Is a clear violation of criminal law; (2) has a significant adverse effect on the quality of care provided to program beneficiaries (in addition to any other legal obligations regarding quality of care); or (3) indicates evidence of a systemic failure to comply with applicable laws or an existing corporate integrity agreement, regardless of the financial impact on Federal health care programs.

[123] The OIG has published criteria setting forth those factors that the OIG takes into consideration in determining whether it is appropriate to exclude a health care provider from program participation pursuant to 42 U.S.C. 1320a-7(b)(7) for violations of various fraud and abuse laws. See 62 FR 67392 (1997).

the operation of the applicable health care programs or their beneficiaries. If the investigation ultimately reveals that criminal, civil, or administrative violations have occurred, the appropriate Federal and State authorities[124] should be notified immediately.

As previously stated, the home health agency should take appropriate corrective action, including prompt identification of any overpayment to the affected payor and the imposition of proper disciplinary action. If potential fraud or violations of the False Claims Act are involved, any repayment of the overpayment should be made as part of the discussion with the Government following a report of the matter to law enforcement authorities. Otherwise, normal repayment channels should be used for repaying identified overpayments.[125] Failure to disclose overpayments within a reasonable period of time could be interpreted as an intentional attempt to conceal the overpayment from the Government, thereby establishing an independent basis for a criminal violation with respect to the home health agency, as well as any individuals who may have been involved.[126] For this reason, home health agency compliance programs should emphasize that overpayments obtained from Medicare and other Federal health care programs should be promptly disclosed and returned to the payor that made the erroneous payment.

III. Conclusion

Through this document, the OIG has attempted to provide a foundation to the process necessary to develop an effective and cost-efficient home health agency compliance program. As previously stated, however, each program must be tailored to fit the needs and resources of an individual home health agency, depending upon its particular corporate structure, mission, and employee composition. The statutes, regulations, and guidelines of the Federal and

[124] See note 120.

[125] A home health agency should consult with its Medicare fiscal intermediary or HCFA for any further guidance regarding normal repayment channels. The home health agency's Medicare fiscal intermediary or HCFA may require certain information (*e.g.,* alleged violation or issue causing overpayment, description of the internal investigative process with methodologies used to determine any overpayments, disciplinary actions taken, and corrective actions taken, etc.) To be submitted with return of any overpayments, and that such repayment information be submitted to a specific department or individual. Interest will be assessed, when appropriate. See 42 CFR 405.376.

[126] See U.S.C. 130a-7b(a)(3)

State health insurance programs, as well as the policies and procedures of the private health plans, should be integrated into every home health agency's compliance program.

The OIG recognizes that the health care industry in this country, which reaches millions of beneficiaries and expends about a trillion dollars annually, is constantly evolving. In particular, the home health industry is currently responding to recent legislative changes that have created additional program participation requirements and is gearing up for the changes underway in the areas of home health reimbursement and payment methodologies. However, the time is right for home health agencies to implement a strong voluntary compliance program concept in health care. As stated throughout this guidance, compliance is a dynamic process that helps to ensure that home health agencies and other health care providers are better able to fulfill their commitment to ethical behavior, as well as meet the changes and challenges being imposed upon them by Congress and private insurers. Ultimately, it is OIG's hope that a voluntarily created compliance program will enable home health agencies to meet their goals, improve the quality of patient care, and substantially reduce fraud, waste, and abuse, as well as the cost of health care to Federal, State, and private health insurers.

Dated: July 31, 1998.

June Gibbs Brown,

Inspector General.

[FR Doc. 98–20966 Filed 8–6-98; 8:45 am]

BILLING CODE 4150–04-P

APPENDIX I4

OIG Notice: Publication of the OIG Compliance Program Guidance for Third-Party Medical Billing Companies

DEPARTMENT OF HEALTH AND HUMAN SERVICES

Office of Inspector General

Publication of the OIG Compliance Program Guidance for Third-Party Medical Billing Companies

AGENCY: Office of Inspector General (OIG), HHS.

ACTION: Notice.

SUMMARY: This **Federal Register** notice sets forth the recently issued Compliance Program Guidance for Third-Party Medical Billing Companies developed by the Office of Inspector General (OIG) in cooperation with, and with input from, the Health Care Financing Administration, the Department of Justice and representatives of various trade associations and health care practice groups. The OIG has previously developed and published compliance program guidance focused on the clinical laboratory and hospital industries and on home health agencies. We believe that the development and issuance of this compliance program guidance for third-party medical billing companies will serve as a positive step towards promoting a higher level of ethical and lawful conduct throughout the entire health care industry.

FOR FURTHER INFORMATION CONTACT: Susan Lemanski, Office of Counsel to the Inspector General, (202) 619–2078

SUPPLEMENTARY INFORMATION:

Background

The creation of compliance program guidance remains a major effort by the OIG in its effort to engage the health care community in combating fraud and abuse. In formulating compliance guidance, the OIG has worked closely with the Health Care Financing Administration (HCFA), the Department of Justice (DOJ) and various sectors of the health care industry to provide clear guidance to those segments of the industry that are interested in reducing fraud and abuse within their organizations. The 3 previously-issued compliance program guidances were focused on the hospital industry, home health agencies clinical laboratories, and were published in the **Federal Register** on February 23, 1998 (63 FR 8987), August 7, 1998 (63 FR 42410) and August 24, 1998 (63 FR 45076) , respectively. The development of these types of compliance program guidance is based on our belief that a health care provider can use internal controls to more efficiently monitor adherence to applicable statutes, regulations and program requirements.

Elements for an Effective Compliance Program

Through experience, the OIG has identified 7 fundamental elements to an effective compliance program. They are:

- Implementing written policies, procedures and standards of conduct;
- Designating a compliance officer and compliance committee;
- Conducting effective training and education;
- Developing effective lines of communication;
- Enforcing standards through well-publicized disciplinary guidelines;
- Conducting internal monitoring and auditing; and
- Responding promptly to detected offenses and developing corrective action.

Third-Party Medical Billing Companies

Increasingly, third-party medical billing companies are providing crucial services that could greatly impact the solvency and stability of the Medicare Trust Fund. Health care providers are relying on these billing companies to a greater degree in assisting them in processing claims in accordance with applicable statutes and regulations. Additionally, health care professionals are consulting with billing companies to provide timely and accurate advice with regard to reimbursement matters, as well as overall business decision-making. As a result, the OIG considers compliance program guidance to third-party medical billing companies particularly important in efforts to combat health care fraud and abuse. Further, because individual billing companies may support a variety of providers with different specialties, we recommend that billing companies coordinate with their provider-clients in establishing compliance responsibilities. Using these 7 basic elements outlined above, the OIG has identified specific areas of third-party medical billing company operations that may prove to be vulnerable to fraud and abuse.

Like previously-issued OIG compliance guidances, adoption of the Compliance Program Guidance for Third-Party Medical Billing Companies set forth below will be strictly voluntary. A reprint of this compliance program guidance follows:

Office of Inspector General's Compliance Program Guidance for Third-Party Medical Billing Companies

I. Introduction

The Office of Inspector General (OIG) of the Department of Health and Human Services (HHS) continues in its efforts to promote voluntarily developed and implemented compliance programs for the health care industry. The following compliance program guidance is intended to assist third-party medical billing companies (hereinafter referred to as "billing companies")[1] and their agents and subcontractors in developing effective internal controls that promote adherence to applicable Federal and State law, and the program requirements of Federal, State and private health plans.

Billing companies are becoming a vital segment of the national health care industry.[2] Increasingly, health care providers[3] are rely-

---

[1] For the purposes of this compliance program guidance, "third-party medical billing companies" include clearing houses and value-added networks.

[2] Recent survey results from the Healthcare Billing and Management Association (HBMA) show that its membership processes more than 17.6 million claims per month totaling $18 billion a year.

[3] For the purposes of this compliance program guidance, "provider" shall include any individual, company, corporation or organization that submits claims for reimbursement to a Federal health care program. The term "Federal health care programs" is applied in this document as defined in 42 U.S.C. 1320a-7b(f), which includes any plan or program that provides health benefits, whether directly, through insurance, or otherwise, which is funded directly, in whole or in part by the United States Federal Government (*i.e.*, via programs such as Medicare, Federal Employees' Compensation Act, Black Lung, or Longshore and Harbor Worker's Compensation Act) or any State health plan (*e.g.*, Medicaid, or program receiving funds from block

ing on billing companies to assist them in processing claims in accordance with applicable statutes and regulations. Additionally, health care providers are consulting with billing companies to provide timely and accurate advice regarding reimbursement matters, as well as overall business decision-making. As a result, the OIG considers the compliance guidance for third-party medical billing companies particularly important in the partnership to defeat health care fraud.

At this juncture, it is important to note the tremendous variation among billing companies in terms of the type of services[4] and the manner in which these services are provided to their respective clients. For example, some billing companies code the bills for their provider clients, while others only process bills that have already been coded by the provider. Some billing companies offer a spectrum of management services, including accounts receivable management and bad debt collections, while others offer only one or none of these services. Clearly, variations in services give rise to different policies to ensure effective compliance. This guidance does not purport to provide instruction on all aspects of regulatory compliance. Rather, we have concentrated our attention on general Federal health care reimbursement principles. For those billing companies that focus their services in a particular sector of the health care industry, the billing company should also consult any compliance program guidance previously issued by the OIG for that particular sector.[5]

This guidance is pertinent for all billing companies, large or small, regardless of the type of services provided. The applicability of the recommendations and guidelines provided in this document depend on the circumstances of each particular billing company. However,

---

grants for social services or child health services). Also, for purposes of this document, the term "Federal health care program requirements" refers to the statutes, regulations, rules, requirements, directives and instructions governing Medicare, Medicaid and all other Federal health care programs.

[4] Billing companies provide services for virtually every aspect of the health care industry. Among the areas of greatest concentration for billing companies are: physicians, ambulatory surgery centers (ASCs), durable medical equipment, prosthetics, orthotics and supplies (DMEPOS) industry, home health agencies (HHAs) and hospitals.

[5] *See* 63 FR 45076 (8/24/98) for Compliance Program Guidance for Clinical Laboratories; 63 FR 42410 (8/7/98) for Compliance Program Guidance for Home Health Agencies; 63 FR 8987 (2/23/98) for Compliance Program Guidance for Hospitals. These documents are also located on the Internet at http:/ /www.dhhs.gov/progorg/oig.

regardless of the billing company's size and structure, the OIG believes every billing company can and should strive to accomplish the objectives and principles underlying all of the compliance policies and procedures recommended within this guidance.

Within this document, the OIG first provides its general views on the value and fundamental principles of billing company compliance programs, and then provides specific elements that each billing company should consider when developing and implementing an effective compliance program. Although this document presents basic procedural and structural guidance for designing a compliance program, it is not in itself a compliance program. Rather, it is a set of guidelines for consideration by a billing company interested in implementing a compliance program.

Fundamentally, compliance efforts are designed to establish a culture within a billing company that promotes prevention, detection and resolution of instances of conduct that do not conform to Federal and State law, and Federal, State and private payor health care program requirements, as well as the billing company's ethical and business policies. In practice, the compliance program should effectively articulate and demonstrate the organization's commitment to legal and ethical conduct. Eventually, a compliance program should become part of the fabric of routine billing company operations.

Specifically, compliance programs guide a billing company's governing body (*e.g.,* boards of directors or trustees), chief executive officer (CEO), managers, billing and coding personnel and other employees in the efficient management and operation of the company. They are especially critical as an internal quality assurance control in reimbursement and payment areas, where claims and billing operations are often the source of fraud and abuse and, therefore, historically have been the focus of Government regulation, scrutiny and sanctions.

It is incumbent upon a billing company's corporate officers and managers to provide ethical leadership to the organization and to assure adequate systems are in place to facilitate and promote ethical and legal conduct. Employees, managers and the Government will focus on the words and actions of a billing company's leadership as a measure of the organization's commitment to compliance. Indeed, many billing companies have adopted mission statements articulating their commitment to high ethical standards. Compliance programs also provide a central coordinating mechanism for furnishing and disseminating information and guidance on applicable Federal and State statutes, regulations and other payor requirements.

The OIG believes that open and frequent communication[6] between the billing company and the health care provider is fundamental to the success of any compliance endeavor. Billing companies are in a unique position with regard to establishing compliance programs. An individual billing company may support a variety of providers with different specialities and, consequently, different risk areas. It is with this in mind that the OIG strongly recommends the billing company coordinate with its provider clients to establish compliance responsibilities.[7] Once the responsibilities have been clearly delineated, they should be formalized in the written contract between the provider and the billing company. The OIG recommends the contract enumerate those functions that are shared responsibilities and those that are the sole responsibility of either the billing company or the provider. Implementing an effective compliance program requires a substantial commitment of time, energy and resources by senior management and the billing company's governing body. Superficial programs that simply purport to comply with the elements discussed and described in this guidance or programs hastily constructed and implemented without appropriate ongoing monitoring will likely be ineffective and could expose the billing company to greater liability than no program at all. Additionally, an ineffective compliance program may expose the billing company's provider clients to liability where those providers rely on the billing company's expertise and its assurances of an effective compliance program. Although it may require significant additional resources or reallocation of existing resources to implement an effective compliance program, the long term benefits of implementing the program significantly outweigh the costs. Undertaking a voluntary compliance program is a beneficial investment that advances both the billing company's organization and the stability and solvency of the Medicare program.

---

[6] *E.g.,* the billing company should communicate the results of audits, determinations of inappropriate claim submissions and notifications of overpayments.

[7] At a minimum, the billing company should send a copy of its compliance program to all of its provider clients. The billing company should also coordinate with its provider clients in the development of a training program, an audit plan and policies for investigating misconduct.

A. Benefits of a Compliance Program

The OIG believes an effective compliance program provides a mechanism that brings the public and private sectors together to reach mutual goals of reducing fraud and abuse, improving operational quality, improving the quality of health care and reducing the costs of health care. Attaining these goals provides positive results to business, Government and individual citizens alike. In addition to fulfilling its legal duty to ensure that it is not submitting false or inaccurate claims to Government and private payors, a billing company may gain numerous additional benefits by implementing an effective compliance program. These benefits may include:

- The formulation of effective internal controls to assure compliance with Federal regulations, private payor policies and internal guidelines;
- Improved medical record documentation;[8]
- Improved collaboration, communication and cooperation among health care providers and those processing and using health information;
- The ability to more quickly and accurately react to employees' operational compliance concerns and the capability to effectively target resources to address those concerns;
- A more efficient communications system that establishes a clear process and structure for addressing compliance concerns quickly and effectively;
- A concrete demonstration to employees and the community at large of the billing company's strong commitment to honest and responsible corporate conduct;
- The ability to obtain an accurate assessment of employee and contractor behavior relating to fraud and abuse;
- Increased likelihood of identification and prevention of criminal and unethical conduct;
- A centralized source for distributing information on health care statutes, regulations and other program directives related to fraud and abuse and related issues;
- A methodology that encourages employees to report potential problems;

[8] Billing and coding personnel can provide critical advice to physicians and other health care providers that may greatly improve the quality of medical record documentation.

- Procedures that allow the prompt, thorough investigation of possible misconduct by corporate officers, managers, employees and independent contractors, who can impact billing decisions;
- An improved relationship with the applicable Medicare contractor;
- Early detection and reporting, minimizing the loss to the Government from false claims, and thereby reducing the billing company's exposure to civil damages and penalties, criminal sanctions, and administrative remedies, such as program exclusion;[9] and
- Enhancement of the structure of the billing company's operations and the consistency between separate business units.

Overall, the OIG believes that an effective compliance program is a sound business investment on the part of a billing company.

The OIG recognizes the implementation of an effective compliance program may not entirely eliminate fraud, abuse and waste from an organization. However, a sincere effort by billing companies to comply with applicable Federal and State standards, as well as the requirements of private health care programs, through the establishment of an effective compliance program, significantly reduces the risk of unlawful or improper conduct.

B. Application of Compliance Program Guidance

Given the diversity in size and services offered by billing companies within the industry, there is no single "best" compliance program. The OIG understands the variances and complexities within the industry and is sensitive to the differences between large and small billing companies. Similarly, the OIG understands the availability of resources for any one billing company can differ vastly, given that billing companies vary greatly in the type of ser-

[9] The OIG, for example, will consider the existence of an effective compliance program that pre-dated any governmental investigation when addressing the appropriateness of administrative sanctions. However, the burden is on the billing company to demonstrate the operational effectiveness of a compliance program. Further, the False Claims Act, 31 U.S.C. 3729–3733, provides that a person who has violated the Act, but who voluntarily discloses the violation to the Government within thirty days of detection, in certain circumstances will be subject to not less than double, as opposed to treble, damages. *See* 31 U.S.C. 3729(a). Thus, the ability to react quickly when violations of the law are discovered may materially help reduce the billing company's liability.

vices offered and the manner that they are provided. Nonetheless, elements of this guidance can be used by all billing companies, regardless of size, location or corporate structure, to establish an effective compliance program. The OIG recognizes some billing companies may not be able to adopt certain elements to the same comprehensive degree that others with more extensive resources may achieve. This guidance represents the OIG's suggestions on how a billing company can best establish internal controls and monitor company conduct to correct and prevent fraudulent activities. By no means should the contents of this guidance be viewed as an exclusive discussion of the advisable elements of a compliance program. On the contrary, the OIG strongly encourages billing companies to develop and implement compliance elements that uniquely address the individual billing company's risk areas.

The OIG appreciates that the success of the compliance program guidance hinges on thoughtful and practical comments from those individuals and organizations that will utilize the tools set forth in this document. In a continuing effort to collaborate closely with the private sector, the OIG solicited input and support from representatives of the major trade associations in the development of this compliance program guidance. Further, we took into consideration previous OIG publications, such as Special Fraud Alerts,[10] the recent findings and recommendations in reports issued by OIG's Office of Audit Services, comments from the HCFA, as well as the experience of past and recent fraud investigations related to billing companies conducted by OIG's Office of Investigations and the DOJ.

As appropriate, this guidance may be modified and expanded as more information and knowledge is obtained by the OIG, and as changes in the law, and in the rules, policies and procedures of the Federal, State and private health plans occur. The OIG understands billing companies will need adequate time to react to these modifications and expansions and to make any necessary changes to their voluntary compliance programs. New compliance practices may eventually be incorporated into this guidance if the OIG discovers significant enhancements to better ensure an effective compliance program. We recognize the development and implementation of compliance programs in billing companies often raise sensitive and

[10] Special Fraud Alerts are available on the OIG website at http://www.dhhs.gov/progorg/oig.

complex legal and managerial issues.[11] However, the OIG wishes to offer what it believes is critical guidance for those who are sincerely attempting to comply with the relevant health care statutes and regulations.

II. Compliance Program Elements

The elements proposed by these guidelines are similar to those of the clinical laboratory model compliance program guidance published by the OIG in February 1997 (updated in August 1998), the hospital compliance program guidance published in February 1998, the home health compliance program guidance published in August 1998[12] and our corporate integrity agreements.[13] The elements represent a guide that can be tailored to fit the needs and financial realities of a particular billing company, large or small, regardless of the type of services offered. The OIG is cognizant that with regard to compliance programs, one model is not suitable to every organization. Nonetheless, the OIG believes every billing company, regardless of size, structure or services offered can benefit from the principles espoused in this guidance.

The OIG believes every effective compliance program must begin with a formal commitment[14] by the billing company's governing body to include all of the applicable elements listed below. These elements are based on the seven steps of the Federal Sentencing Guidelines.[15] We believe every billing company can implement all of the recommended elements, expanding upon the seven steps of the

---

[11] Nothing stated herein should be substituted for, or used in lieu of, competent legal advice from counsel.

[12] *See* note 5.

[13] Corporate integrity agreements are executed as part of a civil settlement agreement between the health care provider or entity responsible for billing for the provider and the Government to resolve a case based on allegations of health care fraud or abuse. These OIG-imposed programs are in effect for a period of three to five years and require many of the elements included in this compliance guidance.

[14] Formal commitment may include a resolution by the board of directors, where applicable. A formal commitment does include the allocation of adequate resources to ensure that each of the elements is addressed.

[15] *See* United States Sentencing Commission Guidelines, *Guidelines Manual,* **Federal Register** 8A1.2, comment. (n.3(k)). The Federal Sentencing Guidelines are detailed policies and practices for the Federal criminal justice system that prescribe appropriate sanctions for offenders convicted of Federal crimes.

Federal Sentencing Guidelines. The OIG recognizes full implementation of all elements may not be immediately feasible for all billing companies. However, as a first step, a good faith and meaningful commitment on the part of the billing company administration, especially the governing body and the CEO, will substantially contribute to the program's successful implementation. As the compliance program is implemented, that commitment should cascade down through the management to every employee in the organization. At a minimum, comprehensive compliance programs should include the following seven elements:

(1) The development and distribution of written standards of conduct, as well as written policies and procedures that promote the billing company's commitment to compliance (*e.g.,* by including adherence to the compliance program as an element in evaluating managers and employees) and that address specific areas of potential fraud, such as the claims submission process, code gaming and financial relationships with its providers;

(2) The designation of a chief compliance officer and other appropriate bodies, *e.g.,* a corporate compliance committee, charged with the responsibility of operating and monitoring the compliance program and who report directly to the CEO and the governing body;[16]

(3) The development and implementation of regular, effective education and training programs for all affected employees;[17]

(4) The creation and maintenance of a process, such as a hotline, to receive complaints and the adoption of procedures to protect the anonymity of complainants and to protect callers from retaliation;

---

[16] The integral functions of a compliance officer and a corporate compliance committee in implementing an effective compliance program are discussed throughout this compliance guidance. However, the OIG recognizes that the differences in the sizes and structures of billing companies will result in differences in the ways in which compliance programs are set up. The important thing is that the billing company structures its compliance program in such a way that the program is able to accomplish the key functions of a corporate compliance officer and a corporate compliance committee discussed within this document.

[17] Training and education programs for billing companies should be detailed and comprehensive. They should cover specific billing and coding procedures, as well as the general areas of compliance.

(5) The development of a system to respond to allegations of improper/ illegal activities and the enforcement of appropriate disciplinary action against employees who have violated internal compliance policies, applicable statutes, regulations or Federal, State or private payor health care program requirements;
(6) The use of audits and/or other risk evaluation techniques to monitor compliance and assist in the reduction of identified problem areas;[18] and
(7) The investigation and correction of identified systemic problems and the development of policies addressing the non-employment of sanctioned individuals.

A. Written Policies and Procedures

Every compliance program should require the development and distribution of written compliance policies, standards and practices that identify specific areas of risk and vulnerability to the billing company. These policies should be developed under the direction and supervision of the chief compliance officer and the compliance committee (if such a committee is practicable for the billing company) and, at a minimum, should be provided to all individuals who are affected by the particular policy at issue, including the billing company's agents and independent contractors[19] who may affect billing decisions.

1. Standards of Conduct

Billing companies should develop standards of conduct for all affected employees that include a clearly delineated commitment to

---

[18] For example, spot-checking the work of coding and billing personnel periodically should be an element of an effective compliance program. Identification of risk areas, discussed in further detail in section II.A.2, is the first step in correcting aberrant billing patterns.

[19] According to the Federal Sentencing Guidelines, an organization must have established compliance standards and procedures to be followed by its employees and other agents in order to receive sentencing credit for an "effective" compliance program. The Federal Sentencing Guidelines define "agent" as "any individual, including a director, an officer, an employee, or an independent contractor, authorized to act on behalf of the organization." *See* United States Sentencing Commission Guidelines, *Guidelines Manual,* 8A1.2, Application Note 3(d).

compliance by the billing company's senior management[20] and its divisions. The standards should function in the same fashion as a constitution, *i.e.,* as a foundational document that details the fundamental principles, values and framework for action within an organization. Standards should articulate the billing company's commitment to comply with all Federal and State standards, with an emphasis on preventing fraud and abuse. They should state the organization's mission, goals and ethical principles relating to compliance and clearly define the organization's commitment to compliance and its expectations for all billing company governing body members, officers, managers, employees, and, where appropriate, contractors and other agents. The standards should promote integrity, support objectivity and foster trust. Standards should not only address compliance with statutes and regulations, but should also set forth broad principles that guide employees in conducting business professionally and properly. Furthermore, a billing company's standards of conduct should reflect a commitment to the highest quality health data submission, as evidenced by its accuracy, reliability, timeliness and validity.

2. Written Policies for Risk Areas

As part of its commitment to compliance, billing companies should establish a comprehensive set of policies that delineate billing and coding procedures for the company. In contrast to the standards of conduct, which are designed to be a clear and concise collection of fundamental standards, the written policies should articulate specific procedures personnel should follow when submitting initial or follow-up claims to Federal health care programs.

Among the issues to be addressed in the polices are the education and training requirements for billing and coding personnel; the risk areas for fraud, waste and abuse; the integrity of the billing company's information system; the methodology for resolving ambiguities in the provider's paperwork;[21] the procedure for identi-

---

[20] The OIG strongly encourages high-level involvement by the billing company's governing body, chief executive officer, chief operating officer, general counsel and chief financial officer, in the development of standards of conduct. Such involvement should help communicate a strong and explicit organizational commitment to compliance goals and standards.

[21] Billing company personnel should maintain an open dialogue with their providers regarding documentation issues. If the documentation received from a provider is ambiguous or conflicting, the billing company should contact the provider for clarification or resolution.

fying and reporting credit balances; and the procedure to ensure duplicate bills are not submitted in an attempt to gain duplicate payment.

Billing companies that provide coding services should provide additional policies for risk areas that apply specifically to coding.[22] The policies and procedures should describe the necessary steps to take in reviewing a billing document. Specific attention should be placed on the proper steps the coder should take if unable to locate a code for a documented diagnosis or procedure or if the medical record documentation is not sufficient to determine a diagnosis or procedure.[23] Billing companies that provide additional services should consider consulting an attorney for guidance on other regulatory issues.[24]

a. Risk Assessment—All Billing Companies

The OIG believes a billing company's written policies and procedures, its educational program and its audit and investigation plans should take into consideration the particular statutes, rules and program instructions that apply to each function or department of the billing company. Consequently, we recommend coordination

---

[22] *See* section II.A.2.b.

[23] If the coding staff finds the physician's documentation to be unclear or conflicting, then they should ask the physician for clarification. This will frequently allow the coder to choose a more appropriate code. If the coder does not know how to code a particular type of bill for Medicare payment, he or she should first consult with a supervisor. If the question persists, the supervisor should contact the provider's carrier/intermediary. The billing company could also contact an authoritative coding organization. For example, the American Hospital Association maintains a central office on ICD-9-CM. All such correspondence should be maintained in a log. In the rare instance that the documentation appears to be for a new type of disease or syndrome, the supervisor can send an inquiry to the National Center for Health Statistics, 6525 Belcrest Road, Room 1100, Hyattsville, MD 20782.

[24] For example, billing companies that provide marketing services should develop policies to ensure compliance with the anti-kickback statute. 42 U.S.C. 1320a-7b(b). In addition, such policies should provide that the billing company shall not submit or cause to be submitted to health care programs claims for patients by virtue of a compensation agreement that was designed to induce such referrals in violation of the anti-kickback statute, or similar Federal or State statute or regulation. Further, the policies and procedures should reference the OIG's safe harbor regulations, clarifying those payment practices that would be immune from prosecution under the anti-kickback statute. *See* 42 CFR 1001.952.

between these functions with an emphasis on areas of special concern that have been identified by the OIG through its investigative and audit functions. [25] Furthermore, the OIG recommends that billing companies conduct a comprehensive self-administered risk analysis or contract for an independent risk analysis by experienced health care consulting professionals. This risk analysis should identify and rank the various compliance and business risks the company may experience in its daily operations.

Once completed, the risk analysis should serve as the basis for the written policies the billing company should develop. The OIG has provided the following specific list of particular risk areas that should be addressed by billing companies. It should be noted that this list is not all-encompassing and the risk analysis completed as a result of the company's audit may provide a more individualized road map. Nonetheless, this list is a compilation of several years of OIG audits, investigations and evaluations and should provide a solid starting point for a company's initial effort.

Among the risk areas the OIG has identified as particularly problematic are: [26]

- Billing for items or services not actually documented; [27]
- Unbundling; [28]

---

[25] The OIG periodically issues Special Fraud Alerts setting forth activities believed to raise legal and enforcement issues. Billing company compliance programs should require the legal staff, chief compliance officer or other appropriate personnel to carefully consider any and all Special Fraud Alerts issued by the OIG that relate to health care providers to which they offer services. Moreover, the compliance programs should address the ramifications of failing to cease and correct any conduct criticized in such a Special Fraud Alert, if applicable to billing companies, or to take reasonable action to prevent such conduct from reoccurring in the future. If appropriate, billing companies should take the steps described in Section G regarding investigations, reporting and correction of identified problems.

[26] The OIG's work plan is currently available on the Internet at http://www.dhhs.gov/progorg/oig. The OIG Work Plan details the various projects the OIG intends to address in the fiscal year. The Work Plan contains the projects of the Office of Audit Services, Office of Evaluation and Inspections, Office of Investigations and the Office of Counsel to the Inspector General.

[27] Billing for items or services not actually documented involves submitting a claim that cannot be substantiated in the documentation.

[28] Unbundling occurs when a billing entity uses separate billing codes for services that have an aggregate billing code.

- Upcoding,[29] such as, for example, DRG creep;[30]
- Inappropriate balance billing;[31]
- Inadequate resolution of overpayments;[32]
- Lack of integrity in computer systems;[33]
- Computer software programs that encourage billing personnel to enter data in fields indicating services were rendered though not actually performed or documented;
- Failure to maintain the confidentiality of information/records;[34]

---

[29] Upcoding reflects the practice of using a billing code that provides a higher reimbursement rate than the billing code that actually reflects the service furnished to the patient. Upcoding has been a major focus of the OIG's law enforcement efforts. In fact, the Health Insurance Portability and Accountability Act of 1996 added another civil monetary penalty to the OIG's sanction authorities for upcoding violations. *See* 42 U.S.C. 1320a- 7a (a)(1)(A).

[30] DRG creep is a variety of upcoding that involves the practice of billing using a Diagnosis Related Group (DRG) code that provides a higher reimbursement rate than the DRG code that accurately reflects patient's diagnosis.

[31] Inappropriate balance billing refers to the practice of billing Medicare beneficiaries for the difference between the total provider charges and the Medicare Part B allowable payment.

[32] An overpayment is an improper or excessive payment made to a health care provider as a result of patient billing or claims processing errors for which a refund is owed by the provider. Examples of Medicare overpayments include instances where a provider is: (1) Paid twice for the same service either by Medicare or by Medicare and another insurer or beneficiary; or (2) paid for services planned but not performed or for non-covered services. Billing companies should institute procedures to provide for timely and accurate reporting to both the provider and the health care program of overpayments.

[33] Because billing companies are in the business of processing health care information, it is essential they develop policies and procedures to ensure the integrity of the information they process and to ensure that records can be easily located and accessed within a well-organized filing or alternative retrieval system. All billing companies should have a back-up system (whether by disk, tape or system) to ensure the integrity of data. Policies should provide for a regular system back-up to ensure that no information is lost.

[34] All billing companies should develop, implement, audit and enforce policies and procedures to ensure the confidentiality and privacy of financial, medical, personnel and other sensitive information in their possession. These policies should address both electronic and hard copy documents.

- Knowing misuse of provider identification numbers, which results in improper billing;[35]
- Outpatient services rendered in connection with inpatient stays;[36]
- Duplicate billing in an attempt to gain duplicate payment;[37]
- Billing for discharge in lieu of transfer;[38]
- Failure to properly use modifiers;[39]
- Billing company incentives that violate the anti-kickback statute or other similar Federal or State statute or regulation;[40]

---

[35] Of particular concern, billing companies should be aware of the provisions of reassignment of benefits. These provisions govern who may receive payment due to a provider or supplier of services or a beneficiary. *See* 42 CFR §§ 424.70–424.80. *See also* Medicare Carrier Manual § 3060.10.

[36] Billing companies that submit claims for non-physician outpatient services that were already included in the hospital's inpatient payment under the Prospective Payment System (PPS) are in effect submitting duplicate claims.

[37] Duplicate billing occurs when the billing company submits more than one claim for the same service or the bill is submitted to more than one primary payor at the same time. Although duplicate billing can occur due to simple error, knowing duplicate billing-which is sometimes evidenced by systematic or repeated double billing-can create liability under criminal, civil or administrative law, particularly if any overpayment is not promptly refunded.

[38] Under the Medicare regulations, when a PPS hospital transfers a patient to another PPS hospital, only the hospital to which the patient was transferred may charge the full DRG; the transferring hospital should charge Medicare only a per diem amount. *See* 42 CFR 412.4.

[39] A modifier, as defined by the CPT-4 manual, provides the means by which the reporting position (or provider) can indicate a service or procedure that has been performed has been altered by some specific circumstance, but not changed in its definition or code. Assuming the modifier is used correctly and appropriately, this specificity provides the justification for payment for these services. For correct use of modifiers, the billing company should reference the appropriate sections of the Medicare carrier manual. For general information on the correct use of modifiers, the billing personnel should also reference the Correct Coding Initiative. *See* Medicare Carrier Manual § 4630.

[40] For billing companies that provide marketing services, percentage arrangements may implicate the anti-kickback statute. *See* 42 U.S.C. 1320a-7b(b) and 59 FR 65372 (12/19/94). Cf. OIG Ad. Op. 98- 10 (1998). The OIG has a longstanding concern that percentage billing arrangements may increase the risk of upcoding and similar abusive billing practices. *See, e.g.,* OIG Ad. Op. 98–1 (1998) and OIG Ad. Op. 98–4 (1998).

- Joint ventures;[41]
- Routine waiver of copayments and billing third-party insurance only;[42] and
- Discounts and professional courtesy.[43]

A billing company's prior history of noncompliance with applicable statutes, regulations and Federal health care program requirements may indicate additional types of risk areas where the billing company may be vulnerable and may require necessary policy measures to prevent avoidable recurrence.[44] Additional risk areas should be assessed by billing companies as well as incorporated into the written policies and procedures and training elements developed as part of their compliance programs.

Billing companies that do not code bills should implement policies that require notification to the provider who is coding to implement and follow compliance safeguards with respect to documentation of services rendered. Moreover, the OIG recommends that billing companies who do not code for their provider clients incorporate in their

---

[41] The OIG is troubled by the proliferation of business arrangements that may violate the anti-kickback statute. Such arrangements are generally established between those in a position to refer business, such as physicians, and those providing items or services for which a Federal health care program pays. Sometimes established as "joint ventures," these arrangements may take a variety of forms. The OIG currently has a number of investigations and audits underway that focus on such areas of concern. Similarly, the billing company should not confer gifts/entertainment upon the client-provider as this could also implicate the anti-kickback statute.

[42] Billing companies should encourage providers to make a good faith effort to collect copayments, deductibles and non-covered services from federally and privately-insured patients. Billing "insurance only" may violate the False Claims Act, the anti-kickback statute, the Civil Monetary Penalties Law, 42 U.S.C. 1320a-7a(a)5, as amended by Pub. L. 104–91 section 231 (h), and State laws. For additional information on this problem, the OIG has published a Special Fraud Alert on the routine waiver of copayments or deductibles under Medicare Part B. *See* 59 FR 65,373 (12/19/94).

[43] Discounts and professional courtesy may not be appropriate unless the total fee is discounted or reduced. In such situations, the payor (*e.g.*, Medicare, Medicaid or any other private payor) should receive its proportional share of the discount or reduction.

[44] "Recurrence of misconduct similar to that which an organization has previously committed casts doubt on whether it took all reasonable steps to prevent such misconduct" and is a significant factor in the assessment of whether a compliance program is effective. *See* United States Sentencing Commission Guidelines, *Guidelines Manual,* 8A1.2, Application Note 3(7) (ii).

contractual agreements the provider's acknowledgment and agreement to address the following coding compliance safeguards.[45]

b. Risk Assessment—Billing Companies That Provide Coding Services

The written policies and procedures concerning proper coding should reflect the current reimbursement principles set forth in applicable statutes, regulations[46] and Federal, State or private payor health care program requirements and should be developed in tandem with organizational standards. Furthermore, written policies and procedures should ensure that coding and billing are based on medical record documentation. Particular attention should be paid to issues of appropriate diagnosis codes, DRG coding, individual Medicare Part B claims (including documentation guidelines for evaluation and management services) and the use of patient discharge codes.[47] The billing company should also institute a policy that all rejected claims pertaining to diagnosis and procedure codes be reviewed by the coder or the coding department. This should facilitate a reduction in similar errors. Among the risk areas that billing companies who provide coding services should address are:

---

[45] The following risk areas are in no way a comprehensive list of risk areas for health care providers. They are merely a suggested list of documentation risks. They do not address the additional risk areas that apply to health care providers (*e.g.,* medical necessity issues).

[46] The official coding guidelines are promulgated by the HCFA, the National Center for Health Statistics, the American Medical Association and the American Health Information Management Association. *See* International Classification of Diseases, 9th Revision, Clinical Modification (ICD-9 CM) (and its successors); 1998 HCFA Common Procedure Coding System (HCPCS) (and its successors); and Physicians' Current Procedural Terminology (CPT) TM . In addition, there are specialized coding systems for specific segments of the health care industry. Among these are ADA (for dental procedures), DSM IV (psychiatric health benefits) and DMERCs (for durable medical equipment, prosthetics, orthotics and supplies).

[47] The failure of a provider to: (i) Document items and services rendered; and (ii) properly submit them for reimbursement is a major area of potential fraud and abuse in Federal health care programs. The OIG has undertaken numerous audits, investigations, inspections and national enforcement initiatives aimed at reducing potential and actual fraud, abuse and waste in these areas.

- Internal coding practices;[48]
- "Assumption" coding;[49]
- Alteration of the documentation;
- Coding without proper documentation[50] of all physician and other professional services;
- Billing for services provided by unqualified or unlicensed clinical personnel;
- Availability of all necessary documentation at the time of coding; and

---

[48] Internal coding practices, including software edits, should be reviewed periodically to determine consistency with all applicable Federal, State and private payor health care program requirements.

[49] This refers to the coding of a diagnosis or procedure without supporting clinical documentation. Coding personnel must be aware of the need for documented verification of services from the attending physician.

[50] While proper documentation is the responsibility of the health care provider, the coder should be aware of proper documentation requirements and should encourage providers to document their services appropriately. Depending on the circumstances, proper documentation can include:

(1) The reason for the patient encounter;
(2) An appropriate history and evaluation;
(3) Documentation of all services;
(4) Documentation of reasons for the services;
(5) An ongoing assessment of the patient's condition;
(6) Information on the patient's progress and treatment outcome;
(7) A documented treatment plan;
(8) A plan of care, including treatments, medications (including dosage and frequency), referrals and consultations, patient and family education, and follow-up care;
(9) Changes in treatment plan;
(10) Documentation of medical rationale for the services rendered;
(11) Documentation that supports the standards of medical necessity, *e.g.*, certificates of medical necessity for DMEPOS and home health services;
(12) Abnormal test results addressed in the physician's documentation;
(13) Identification of relevant health risk factors;
(14) Documentation that meets the E & M codes billed;
(15) Medical records that are dated and authenticated; and/or
(16) Prescriptions.

Billing companies should also reference the *Documentation Guidelines for Evaluation and Management (E/M) Services,* published by the HCFA. These guidelines are available on the Internet at http://www.hcfa.gov/medicare/ mcarpti.htm.

- Employment of sanctioned individuals.[51]

Billing companies that provide coding services should maintain an up-to-date, user-friendly index for coding policies and procedures to ensure that specific information can be readily located. Similarly, for billing companies that provide coding services, the billing company should assure that essential coding materials are readily accessible to all coding staff.[52]

Finally, billing companies should emphasize in their standards the importance of safeguarding the confidentiality of medical, financial and other personal information in their possession.

3. Claim Submission Process

A number of the risk areas identified above, pertaining to the claim development and submission process, have been the subject of administrative proceedings, as well as investigations and prosecutions under the civil False Claims Act and criminal statutes. Settlement of these cases often has required the defendants to execute corporate integrity agreements, in addition to paying significant civil damages and/or criminal fines and penalties. These corporate integrity agreements have provided the OIG with a mechanism to advise billing companies concerning acceptable practices to ensure compliance with applicable Federal and State statutes, regulations and program requirements. The following recommendations include a number of provisions from various corporate integrity agreements. Although these recommendations include examples of effective policies, each billing company should develop its own specific policies tailored to fit its individual needs.

With respect to claims, a billing company's written policies and procedures should reflect and reinforce current Federal and State statutes. The policies must create a mechanism for the billing or

---

[51] Billing companies should ensure that they do not employ or contract with individuals that have been sanctioned by the OIG or barred from Federal procurement programs. The Cumulative Sanction Report is available on the Internet at http:// www.dhhs.gov/progorg/oig. In addition, the General Services Administration maintains a monthly listing of debarred contractors on the Internet at http://www.arnet.gov/epls.

[52] Examples of reference resources necessary for proper coding include: a medical dictionary; an anatomy/physiology textbook; up-to-date ICD, HCPCS and CPT™ code books; Physician's Desk Reference; Merck Manual; the applicable contractor's provider manual; and subscriptions to the American Hospital Association's *Coding Clinic for ICD-9-CM* (and its successors) and the American Medical Association's *CPT Assistant*.

reimbursement staff to communicate effectively and accurately with the health care provider. Policies and procedures should:

- Ensure that proper and timely documentation of all physician and other professional services is obtained prior to billing to ensure that only accurate and properly documented services are billed;
- Emphasize that claims should be submitted only when appropriate documentation supports the claims and only when such documentation is maintained, appropriately organized in legible form and available for audit and review. The documentation, which may include patient records, should record the time spent in conducting the activity leading to the record entry and the identity of the individual providing the service;
- Indicate that the diagnosis and procedures reported on the reimbursement claim should be based on the medical record and other documentation, and that the documentation necessary for accurate code assignment should be available to coding staff at the time of coding. The HCFA Common Procedure Coding System (HCPCS), International Classification of Disease (ICD), Current Procedural Terminology (CPT TM), any other applicable code or revenue code (or successor code(s)) used by the coding staff should accurately describe the service that was ordered by the physician;
- Provide that the compensation for billing department coders and billing consultants should not provide any financial incentive to improperly upcode claims;[53]
- Establish and maintain a process for pre- and post-submission review of claims[54] to ensure claims submitted for reimbursement accurately represent services provided, are supported by sufficient documentation and are in conformity with any applicable coverage criteria for reimbursement; and
- Obtain clarification from the provider when documentation is confusing or lacking adequate justification.

Because coding for providers often involves the interpretation of medical diagnosis and other clinical data and documentation, a billing company may wish to contract with/assign a qualified physician to provide guidance to the coding staff regarding clinical issues. Procedures should be in place to access medical experts when neces-

---

[53] *See* OIG Ad. Op. 98–1 (1998) and OIG Ad. Op. 98–4 (1998). *See also* 42 CFR 424.73.

[54] The OIG recommends that, at a minimum, a valid statistical sample of claims be reviewed annually both before and after billing is submitted. This review should be done by a qualified expert in the applicable coding process.

sary. Such procedures should allow for medical personnel to be available for guidance without interrupting or interfering with the quality of patient care.

4. Credit Balances

Credit balances occur when payments, allowances or charge reversals posted to an account exceed the charges to the account. Providers and their billers should establish policies and procedures, as well as responsibility, for timely and appropriate identification and resolution of these overpayments.[55] For example, a billing company may redesignate segments of its information system to allow for the segregation of patient accounts reflecting credit balances. The billing company could remove these accounts from the active accounts and place them in a holding account pending the processing of a reimbursement claim to the appropriate payor. A billing company's information system should have the ability to print out the individual patient accounts that reflect a credit balance in order to permit simplified tracking of credit balances. The billing company should maintain a complete audit trail of all credit balances.

In addition, a billing company should designate at least one person (*e.g.,* in the patient accounts department or reasonable equivalent thereof) as having the responsibility for the tracking, recording and reporting of credit balances. Further, a comptroller or an accountant in the billing company's accounting department (or reasonable equivalent thereof) may review reports of credit balances and adjustments on a monthly basis as an additional safeguard.

5. Integrity of Data Systems

Increasingly, the health care industry is using electronic data interchange (EDI) to conduct business more quickly and efficiently. As a result, the industry is relying on the capabilities of computers. Billing companies should establish procedures for maintaining the integrity of its data collection systems. This should include procedures for regularly backing-up data (either by diskette, restricted system or tape) to ensure the accuracy of all data collected in connection with submission of claims and reporting of credit balances. At all times, the billing company should have a complete and accurate audit trail. Additionally, billing companies should develop a system

[55] The billing company should also refer to State escheat laws for the specific requirements relating to notifications, time periods and payment of any unclaimed funds.

to prevent the contamination of data by outside parties. This system should include regularly scheduled virus checks. Finally, billing companies should ensure that electronic data are protected against unauthorized access or disclosure.

6. Retention of Records

Billing company compliance programs should provide for the implementation of a records system. This system should establish policies and procedures regarding the creation, distribution, retention, storage, retrieval and destruction of documents. The three types of documents developed under this system should include: (1) All records and documentation required by either Federal or State law and the program requirements of Federal, State and private health plans (for billing companies, this should include all documents related to the billing and coding process); (2) records listing the persons responsible for implementing each part of the compliance plan; and (3) all records necessary to protect the integrity of the billing company's compliance process and confirm the effectiveness of the program. The documentation necessary to satisfy the third requirement includes: evidence of adequate employee training; reports from the billing company's hotline; results of any investigation conducted as a consequence of a hotline call; modifications to the compliance program; self-disclosure; all written notifications to providers;[56] and the results of the billing company's auditing and monitoring efforts.

7. Compliance as an Element of a Performance Plan

Compliance programs should require that the promotion of, and adherence to, the elements of the compliance program be a factor in evaluating the performance of all employees. Employees should be periodically trained in new compliance policies and procedures. In addition, all managers and supervisors involved in the coding and claims submission processes should:

- Discuss with all supervised employees and relevant contractors the compliance policies and legal requirements applicable to their function;

---

[56] This should include notifications regarding: inappropriate claims; overpayments; and termination of the contract.

- Inform all supervised personnel that strict compliance with these policies and requirements is a condition of employment; and
- Disclose to all supervised personnel that the billing company will take disciplinary action up to and including termination for violation of these policies or requirements.

In addition to making performance of these duties an element in evaluations, the compliance officer or company management should include a policy that managers and supervisors will be sanctioned for failure to instruct adequately their subordinates or for failure to detect noncompliance with applicable policies and legal requirements, where reasonable diligence on the part of the manager or supervisor should have led to the discovery of any problems or violations.

B. Designation of a Compliance Officer and a Compliance Committee

1. Compliance Officer

Every billing company should designate a compliance officer to serve as the focal point for compliance activities. This responsibility may be the individual's sole duty or added to other management responsibilities, depending upon the size and resources of the billing company and the complexity of the task. For those billing companies that have limited resources, the compliance function could be outsourced to an expert in compliance.[57]

Designating a compliance officer with the appropriate authority is critical to the success of the program, necessitating the appointment of a high-level official in the billing company with direct access to the company's governing body, the CEO, all other senior management and legal counsel.[58] The officer should have sufficient funding and

[57] If the billing company chooses to outsource the compliance function, the OIG recommends the billing company engage an individual with significant experience in the billing and coding industries. Multiple small billing and coding facilities may contract with an individual to job-share the individual's time and expertise in the area of compliance.

[58] The OIG believes that it is not advisable for the compliance function to be subordinate to the billing company's general counsel, or comptroller or similar billing company financial officer. Free standing compliance functions help to ensure independent and objective legal reviews and financial analyses of the institution's compliance efforts and activities. By separating the compliance function from the key management positions of general

staff to perform his or her responsibilities fully. Coordination and communication are the key functions of the compliance officer with regard to planning, implementing and monitoring the compliance program. With this in mind, the OIG recommends the billing company's compliance officer closely coordinate compliance functions with the provider's compliance officer.

The compliance officer's primary responsibilities should include:

- Overseeing and monitoring the implementation of the compliance program;[59]
- Reporting on a regular basis to the billing company's governing body, CEO and compliance committee (if applicable) on the progress of implementation and assisting these components in establishing methods to improve the billing company's efficiency and quality of services and to reduce the billing company's vulnerability to fraud, abuse and waste;
- Periodically revising the program in light of changes in the organization's needs and in the law and policies and procedures of Government and private payor health plans;
- Reviewing employees' certifications that they have received, read and understood the standards of conduct;
- Developing, coordinating and participating in a multifaceted educational and training program that focuses on the elements of the compliance program and seeks to ensure that all appropriate employees and management are knowledgeable of, and comply with, pertinent Federal and State standards;
- Coordinating personnel issues with the billing company's human resources/ personnel office (or its equivalent) to ensure that providers and employees do not appear in the Cumulative Sanction Report;[60]
- Assisting the billing company's financial management in coordinating internal compliance review and monitoring activities, including annual or periodic reviews of departments;
- Independently investigating and acting on matters related to compliance, including the flexibility to design and coordinate

---

counsel or chief financial officer (where the size and structure of the billing company make this a feasible option), a system of checks and balances is established to more effectively achieve the goals of the compliance program.

[59] For multi-site billing companies, the OIG encourages coordination with each billing facility owned by the billing company through the use of a corporate compliance officer.

[60] *See* note 51.

internal investigations (*e.g.,* responding to reports of problems or suspected violations) and any resulting corrective action with all billing departments, providers and sub-providers, agents and, if appropriate, independent contractors;

- Developing policies and programs that encourage managers and employees to report suspected fraud and other improprieties without fear of retaliation; and
- Continuing the momentum of the compliance program and the accomplishment of its objectives long after the initial years of implementation.[61]

The compliance officer must have the authority to review all documents and other information that are relevant to compliance activities, including, but not limited to, patient records (where appropriate), billing records and records concerning the marketing efforts of the facility and the billing company's arrangements with other parties, including employees, professionals on staff, relevant independent contractors, suppliers, agents, supplemental staffing entities and physicians. This policy enables the compliance officer to review contracts and obligations (seeking the advice of legal counsel, where appropriate) that may contain referral and payment provisions that could violate statutory or regulatory requirements.

In addition, the compliance officer should be copied on the results of all internal audit reports and work closely with key managers to identify aberrant trends in the coding and billing areas. The compliance officer should ascertain patterns that require a change in policy and forward these issues to the compliance committee to remedy the problem. A compliance officer should have full authority to stop the processing of claims that he or she believes are problematic until such time as the issue in question has been resolved.

---

[61] Periodic on-site visits of the billing company's operations, bulletins with compliance updates and reminders, distribution of audiotapes or videotapes on different risk areas, lectures at management and employee meetings, circulation of recent health care articles covering fraud and abuse and innovative changes to compliance training are various examples of approaches and techniques the compliance officer can employ for the purpose of ensuring continued interest in the compliance program and the billing company's commitment to its principles and policies.

2. Compliance Committee

The OIG recommends, where feasible,[62] that a compliance committee be established to advise the compliance officer and assist in the implementation of the compliance program.[63] When assembling a team of people to serve as the billing company's compliance committee, the company should include individuals with a variety of skills.[64] Appropriate members of the compliance committee include the director of billing and the director of coding. The OIG strongly recommends that the compliance officer manage the compliance committee. Once a billing company chooses the people that will accept the responsibilities vested in members of the compliance committee, the billing company must train these individuals on the policies and procedures of the compliance program.

The committee's responsibilities should include:

- Analyzing the organization' s regulatory environment, the legal requirements with which it must comply[65] and specific risk areas;
- Assessing existing policies and procedures that address these areas for possible incorporation into the compliance program;
- Working with appropriate departments to develop standards of conduct and policies and procedures that promote allegiance to

---

[62] The OIG recognizes that smaller billing companies may not be able to establish a compliance committee. In those situations, the compliance officer should fulfill the responsibilities of the compliance committee.

[63] The compliance committee benefits from having the perspectives of individuals with varying responsibilities in the organization, such as operations, finance, audit, human resources, utilization review, medicine, coding and legal, as well as employees and managers of key operating units. These individuals should have the requisite seniority and comprehensive experience within their respective departments to implement any necessary changes in the company's policies and procedures.

[64] A billing company should expect its compliance committee members and compliance officer to demonstrate high integrity, good judgment, assertiveness and an approachable demeanor, while eliciting the respect and trust of employees of the billing company. The compliance committee members should also have significant professional experience in working with billing, coding, clinical records and auditing principles.

[65] This includes, but is not limited to, the civil False Claims Act, 31 U.S.C. 3729–3733, the criminal false claims statutes, 18 U.S.C. 287, 1001, the fraud and abuse provisions of the Balanced Budget Act of 1997, Pub. L. 105–33 and the Health Insurance Portability and Accountability Act of 1996, Pub. L. 104–191.

the company's compliance program;[66]

- Recommending and monitoring, in conjunction with the relevant departments, the development of internal systems and controls to carry out the organization's standards, policies and procedures as part of its daily operations;
- Determining the appropriate strategy/approach to promote compliance with the program and detection of any potential violations, such as through hotlines and other fraud reporting mechanisms;
- Developing a system to solicit, evaluate and respond to complaints and problems; and
- Monitoring internal and external audits and investigations for the purpose of identifying troublesome issues and deficient areas experienced by the billing company and implementing corrective and preventive action.

The committee may also address other functions as the compliance concept becomes part of the overall operating structure and daily routine.

C. Conducting Effective Training and Education

1. Initial Training in Compliance

The proper education and training of corporate officers, managers, employees and the continual retraining of current personnel at all levels are significant elements of an effective compliance program. In order to ensure the appropriate information is being disseminated to the correct individuals, the training should be separated into two sessions, depending on the employees' involvement in the submission of claims for reimbursement. All employees should attend the general session on compliance, while employees whose job primarily focuses on submission of claims for reimbursement should be the participants in the detailed sessions. In the development of a training program, the billing company should consult with its provider clients to ensure that a consistent message is being delivered and avoid any potential conflicts in the implementation of policies and procedures.

---

[66] For billing companies, this includes developing and fostering excellent coordination and communication with its provider clients.

a. General Sessions

As part of their compliance programs, billing companies should require all affected personnel to attend training on an annual basis, including appropriate training in Federal and State statutes, regulations and guidelines, the policies of private payors and training in corporate ethics. The general training sessions should emphasize the organization's commitment to compliance with these legal requirements and policies.

These training programs should include sessions highlighting the organization's compliance program, summarizing fraud and abuse statutes and regulations, Federal, State and private payor health care program requirements, coding requirements, the claim submission process and marketing practices that reflect current legal and program standards. The organization must take steps to communicate effectively its standards and procedures to all affected employees, physicians, independent contractors and other significant agents, *e.g.*, by requiring participation in training programs and disseminating publications that explain specific requirements in a practical manner. [67] Managers of specific departments or groups can assist in identifying areas that require training and in carrying out such training. [68] Training instructors may come from outside or inside the organization. New employees should be targeted for training early in their employment. [69]

As part of the initial training, the standards of conduct should be distributed to all employees. [70] At the end of this training session, every employee, as well as contracted consultants, should be

[67] Some publications, such as Special Fraud Alerts, audit and inspection reports, and advisory opinions, as well as the annual OIG work plan, are readily available from the OIG and could be the basis for standards, educational courses and programs for appropriate billing employees.

[68] Significant variations in functions and responsibilities of different departments or groups may create the need for training materials that are tailored to the compliance concerns associated with particular operations and duties.

[69] Certain positions, such as those involving the coding of medical services, create a greater organizational legal exposure, and therefore require specialized training. Billing companies should fill such positions with individuals who have the appropriate educational background, training and credentials.

[70] Where the billing company has a culturally diverse employee base, the standards of conduct should be translated into other languages and written at appropriate reading levels.

required to sign and date a statement that reflects the employee's knowledge of and commitment to the standards of conduct.

This attestation should be retained in the employee's personnel file. For contracted consultants, the attestation should become part of the contract and remain in the file that contains such documentation. Further, to assist in ensuring employees continuously meet the expected high standards set forth in the code of conduct, any employee handbook delineating or expanding upon these standards of conduct should be regularly updated as applicable statutes, regulations and Federal health care program requirements are modified.[71] Billing companies should provide an additional attestation in the modified standards that stipulates the employee's knowledge of and commitment to the modifications.

b. Coding and Billing Training

In addition to specific training in the risk areas identified in section II.A.2, above, primary training to appropriate corporate officers, managers and other billing company staff should include such topics as:

- Specific Government and private payor reimbursement principles;[72]
- General prohibitions on paying or receiving remuneration to induce referrals;
- Proper selection and sequencing of diagnoses;
- Improper alterations to documentation;
- Submitting a claim for physician services when rendered by a non-physician (*i.e.,* the "incident to" rule and the physician physical presence requirement);
- Proper documentation of services rendered, including the correct application of official coding rules and guidelines;
- Signing a form for a physician without the physician's authorization; and
- Duty to report misconduct.

---

[71] The OIG recognizes that not all standards, policies and procedures need to be communicated to all employees. However, the OIG believes that the bulk of the standards that relate to complying with fraud and abuse laws and other ethical areas should be addressed and made part of all employees' training. The billing company should determine what additional training to provide categories of employees based upon their job responsibilities.

[72] Government, in this context, includes the appropriate Medicare carrier or intermediary.

Clarifying and emphasizing these areas of concern through training and educational programs are particularly relevant to a billing company's marketing and financial personnel, in that the pressure to meet business goals may render these employees particularly vulnerable to engaging in prohibited practices.

2. Format of the Training Program

The OIG suggests all relevant levels of personnel be made part of various educational and training programs of the billing company.[73] Employees should be required to have a minimum number of educational hours per year, as appropriate, as part of their employment responsibilities.[74] For example, as discussed above, certain employees involved in billing functions should be required to attend periodic training in applicable reimbursement coverage and documentation of records.[75] A variety of teaching methods, such as interactive training and training in several different languages, particularly where a billing company has a culturally diverse staff, should be implemented so that all affected employees are knowledgeable about the institution's standards of conduct and procedures for alerting senior management to problems and concerns.[76] Targeted training should be provided to corporate officers, managers and other employees whose actions affect the accuracy of the claims submitted to the

[73] In addition, where feasible, the OIG recommends that a billing company afford outside contractors and its provider clients the opportunity to participate in the billing company's compliance training and educational programs or develop their own programs that complement the billing company's standards of conduct, compliance requirements and other rules and practices.

[74] Currently, the OIG is monitoring a significant number of corporate integrity agreements that require many of these training elements. The OIG usually requires a minimum of one to three hours annually for basic training in compliance areas. Additional training is required for specialty fields such as billing, coding and marketing.

[75] Appropriate coding and billing depends upon the quality and completeness of documentation. Therefore, the OIG believes that the billing company must foster an environment where interactive communication is encouraged. Health care providers should be reminded that thorough, precise and timely documentation of services provided serves the interests of the patient, the interest of the provider, as well as the interests of the billing company.

[76] Post-training tests can be used to assess the success of training provided and employee comprehension of the billing company's policies and procedures.

Government, such as employees involved in the coding, billing and marketing processes. All training materials should be designed to take into account the skills, knowledge and experience of the individual trainees. Given the complexity and interdependent relationships of many departments, it is important for the compliance officer to supervise and coordinate the training program.

The OIG recommends attendance and participation at training programs be made a condition of continued employment and that failure to comply with training requirements should result in disciplinary action, including possible termination, when such failure is serious. Adherence to the provisions of the compliance program, such as training requirements, should be a factor in the annual evaluation of each employee. The billing company should retain adequate records of its training of employees, including attendance logs and material distributed at training sessions.

3. Continuing Education on Compliance Issues

It is essential that compliance issues remain at the forefront of the billing company's priorities. The OIG recommends billing company compliance programs address the need for periodic professional education courses for billing company personnel. In particular, the billing company should ensure that coding personnel receive annual professional training on the updated codes for the current year.

In order to maintain a sense of seriousness about compliance in the billing company's operations, the billing company must continue to disseminate the compliance message. One effective mechanism for maintaining a consistent presence of the compliance message is to publish a monthly newsletter to address compliance concerns. This would allow the billing company to address specific examples of problems the company encountered during its ongoing audits and risk analysis, while reinforcing the company's firm commitment to the general principles of compliance and ethical conduct. The newsletter could also include the risk areas published by the OIG in its Special Fraud Alerts. Finally, the billing company could use the newsletter as a mechanism to address areas of ambiguity in the coding and billing process. The billing company should maintain its newsletters in a central location to document the guidance offered and provide new employees with access to guidance previously provided.

D. Developing Effective Lines of Communication

1. Access to the Compliance Officer

An open line of communication between the compliance officer and the billing company personnel is equally important to the successful implementation of a compliance program and the reduction of any potential for fraud, abuse and waste. Written confidentiality and non-retaliation policies should be developed and distributed to all employees to encourage communication and the reporting of incidents of potential fraud.[77] The compliance committee should also develop several independent reporting paths for an employee to report fraud, waste or abuse so that such reports cannot be diverted by supervisors or other personnel.

The OIG encourages the establishment of procedures for personnel to seek clarification from the compliance officer or members of the compliance committee in the event of any confusion or question regarding a company policy, practice or procedure. Questions and responses should be documented and dated and, if appropriate, shared with other staff so that standards, policies, practices and procedures can be updated and improved to reflect any necessary changes or clarifications. The compliance officer may want to solicit employee input in developing these communication and reporting systems.

2. Hotlines and Other Forms of Communication

The OIG encourages the use of hotlines[78] (including anonymous hotlines), e-mails, written memoranda, newsletters and other forms of information exchange to maintain these open lines of communication.[79] If the billing company establishes a hotline, the telephone

---

[77] The OIG believes that whistle blowers should be protected against retaliation, a concept embodied in the provisions of the False Claims Act. *See* 31 U.S.C. 3730(h). In many cases, employees sue their employers under the False Claims Act's *qui tam* provisions out of frustration because of the company's failure to take action when a questionable, fraudulent or abusive situation was brought to the attention of senior corporate officials.

[78] The OIG recognizes that it may not be financially feasible for a small billing company to maintain a telephone hotline dedicated to receiving calls solely on compliance issues. These companies may explore alternative methods, *e.g.,* contracting with an independent source to provide hotline services or establishing a written method of confidential disclosure.

[79] In addition to methods of communication used by current employees, an effective employee exit interview program could be designed to solicit

number should be made readily available to all employees and independent contractors, by circulating the number on wallet cards or conspicuously posting the telephone number in common work areas.[80] Employees should be permitted to report matters on an anonymous basis. Matters reported through the hotline or other communication sources that suggest substantial violations of compliance policies, Federal, State or private payor health care program requirements, regulations or statutes should be documented and investigated promptly to determine their veracity. A log should be maintained by the compliance officer that records such calls, including the nature of any investigation and its results.[81] Such information should be included in reports to the governing body, the CEO and compliance committee.[82] Further, while the billing company should always strive to maintain the confidentiality of an employee's identity, it should also explicitly communicate that there may be a point where the individual's identity may become known or may have to be revealed.

The OIG recognizes that assertions of fraud and abuse by employees who may have participated in illegal conduct or committed other malfeasance raise numerous complex legal and management issues that should be examined on a case-by-case basis. The compliance officer should work closely with legal counsel, who can provide guidance regarding such issues.

---

information from departing employees regarding potential misconduct and suspected violations of the billing company's policy and procedures.

[80] Billing companies should also post in a prominent, available area the HHS-OIG Hotline telephone number, 1–800–447–8477 (HHS-TIPS), in addition to any company hotline number that may be posted.

[81] To efficiently and accurately fulfill such an obligation, the billing company should create an intake form for all compliance issues identified through reporting mechanisms. The form could include information concerning the date the potential problem was reported, the internal investigative methods utilized, the results of any investigation, any corrective action implemented, any disciplinary measures imposed and any overpayments and monies returned.

[82] Information obtained over the hotline may provide valuable insight into management practices and operations, whether reported problems are actual or perceived.

E. Enforcing Standards Through Well-p ublicized Disciplinary Guidelines

1. Discipline Policy and Actions

An effective compliance program should include guidance regarding disciplinary action for corporate officers, managers and employees who have failed to comply with the billing company's standards of conduct, policies and procedures, Federal, State or private payor health care program requirements, or Federal and State laws, or those who have otherwise engaged in wrongdoing, which has the potential to impair the billing company's status as a reliable, honest and trustworthy organization.

The OIG believes the compliance program should include a written policy statement setting forth the degrees of disciplinary actions that may be imposed upon corporate officers, managers and employees for failing to comply with the billing company's standards and policies and applicable statutes and regulations. Intentional or reckless noncompliance should subject transgressors to significant sanctions. Such sanctions could range from oral warnings to suspension, termination or financial penalties, as appropriate. Each situation must be considered on a case-by- case basis to determine the appropriate sanction. The written standards of conduct should elaborate on the procedures for handling disciplinary problems and identify who will be responsible for taking appropriate action. Some disciplinary actions can be handled by department managers, while others may have to be resolved by a senior manager. Disciplinary action may be appropriate where a responsible employee's failure to detect a violation is attributable to his or her negligence or reckless conduct. Personnel should be advised by the billing company that disciplinary action will be taken on a fair and equitable basis. Managers and supervisors should be made aware that they have a responsibility to discipline employees in an appropriate and consistent manner.

It is vital to publish and disseminate the range of possible disciplinary actions for improper conduct and to educate officers and other staff regarding these standards. The consequences of noncompliance should be consistently applied and enforced for the disciplinary policy to have the required deterrent effect. All levels of employees should be subject to the same disciplinary action for the commission of similar offenses. The commitment to compliance applies to all personnel levels within a billing company. The OIG believes that corporate officers, managers and supervisors should be held accountable for failing to comply with, or for the foreseeable failure of their subordinates to adhere to, the applicable standards, laws, rules, program instructions and procedures.

2. New Employee Policy

For all new employees who have discretionary authority to make decisions that may involve compliance with the law or compliance oversight, billing companies should conduct a reasonable and prudent background investigation, including a reference check, as part of every such employment application. The application should specifically require the applicant to disclose any criminal conviction, as defined by 42 U.S.C. 1320a-7(i), or exclusion action. Pursuant to the compliance program, billing company policies should prohibit the employment of individuals who have been recently convicted of a criminal offense related to health care or who are listed as debarred, excluded or otherwise ineligible for participation in Federal health care programs.[83] In addition, pending the resolution of any criminal charges or proposed debarment or exclusion, the OIG recommends that such individuals should be removed from direct responsibility for, or involvement, in any Federal health care program.[84] Similarly, with regard to current employees or independent contractors, if resolution of the matter results in conviction, debarment or exclusion, then the billing company should remove the individual from direct responsibility for or involvement with all Federal health care programs.

F. Auditing and Monitoring

An ongoing evaluation process is critical to a successful compliance program. The OIG believes an effective program should incorporate thorough monitoring of its implementation and regular

[83] *See* note 51. Likewise, billing company compliance programs should establish standards prohibiting the execution of contracts with companies that have been recently convicted of a criminal offense related to health care or that are listed by a Federal agency as debarred, excluded or otherwise ineligible for participation in Federal health care programs.

[84] Prospective employees who have been officially reinstated into the Medicare and Medicaid programs by the OIG may be considered for employment upon proof of such reinstatement.

reporting to senior company officers.[85] Compliance reports created by this ongoing monitoring, including reports of suspected noncompliance, should be maintained by the compliance officer and reviewed with the billing company's senior management and the compliance committee. The extent and frequency of the audit function may vary depending on factors such as the size of the company, the resources available to the company, the company's prior history of noncompliance and the risk factors that are prevalent in a particular billing company.

Although many monitoring techniques are available, one effective tool to promote and ensure compliance is the performance of regular, periodic compliance audits by internal or external auditors who have expertise in Federal and State health care statutes, regulations, and Federal, State and private payor health care program requirements. The audits should focus on the billing company's programs or divisions, including external relationships with third-party contractors, specifically those with substantive exposure to Government enforcement actions. At a minimum, these audits should be designed to address the billing company's compliance with laws governing kickback arrangements, coding practices, claim submission, reimbursement and marketing. In addition, the audits and reviews should examine the billing company's compliance with specific rules and policies that have been the focus of particular attention on the part of the Medicare fiscal intermediaries or carriers, and law enforcement, as evidenced by OIG Special Fraud Alerts, OIG audits and evaluations and law enforcement's initiatives.[86] In addition, the billing company should focus on any areas of specific concern identified within that billing company and those that may have been identified by any outside agency, whether Federal or State.

Monitoring techniques may include sampling protocols that permit the compliance officer to identify and review variations from an established baseline.[87] Significant variations from the baseline

---

[85] Even when a facility is owned by a larger corporate entity, the regular auditing and monitoring of the compliance activities of an individual facility must be a key feature in any annual review. Appropriate reports on audit findings should be periodically provided and explained to a parent-organization's senior staff and officers.

[86] *See* section II.A.2.

[87] The OIG recommends that when a compliance program is established in a billing company, the compliance officer, with the assistance of department managers, take a "snapshot" of the company's operations from a

should trigger a reasonable inquiry to determine the cause of the deviation. If the inquiry determines that the deviation occurred for legitimate, explainable reasons, the compliance officer or manager may want to limit any corrective action or take no action. If it is determined that the deviation was caused by improper procedures, misunderstanding of rules, including fraud and systemic problems, the billing company should take prompt steps to correct the problem.[88] Any overpayments discovered as a result of such deviations should be reported promptly to the appropriate provider, with appropriate documentation and a thorough explanation of the reason for the overpayment.[89]

An effective compliance program should also incorporate periodic (at a minimum, annual) reviews of whether the program's compliance elements have been satisfied, *e.g.,* whether there has been appropriate dissemination of the program's standards, training, ongoing educational programs and disciplinary actions, among others.[90] This process will verify actual conformance by all departments with the compliance program. Such reviews could support a determination that appropriate records have been created and maintained to document the implementation of an effective program. However, when monitoring discloses deviations were not detected in a timely manner due to program deficiencies, appropriate modifications must be implemented. Such evaluations, when developed with

---

compliance perspective. This assessment can be undertaken by outside consultants, law or accounting firms, or internal staff, with authoritative knowledge of health care compliance requirements. This "snapshot," often used as part of bench marking analysis, becomes a baseline for the compliance officer and other managers to judge the billing company's progress in reducing or eliminating potential areas of vulnerability. For example, it has been suggested that a baseline level include the frequency and percentile levels of CPT TM and HCPCS codes. Similarly, billing companies should track statistical data on claim rejection by code. This will facilitate identification of problem areas and elimination of potential areas of abusive or fraudulent conduct.

[88] Prompt steps to correct the problem include contacting the appropriate provider in situations where the provider's actions contributed to the problem.

[89] In addition, when appropriate, as referenced in section G.2, below, reports of fraud or systemic problems should also be made to the appropriate governmental authority.

[90] One way to assess the knowledge, awareness and perceptions of the billing company staff is through the use of a validated survey instrument (*e.g.,* employee questionnaires, interviews or focus groups).

the support of management, can help ensure compliance with the billing company's policies and procedures.

As part of the review process, the compliance officer or reviewers should consider techniques such as:

- On-site visits;
- Testing billing and coding staff on their knowledge of reimbursement and coverage criteria (*e.g.,* presenting hypothetical scenarios of situations experienced in daily practice and assess responses);
- Unannounced mock surveys, audits and investigations;
- Examination of the billing company's complaint logs;
- Checking personnel records to determine whether any individuals who have been reprimanded for compliance issues in the past are among those currently engaged in improper conduct;
- Interviews with personnel involved in management, operations, coding, claim development and submission and other related activities;
- Questionnaires developed to solicit impressions of a broad cross-section of the billing company's employees and staff;
- Reviews of written materials and documentation prepared by the different divisions of a billing company; and
- Trend analyses, or longitudinal studies, that seek deviations, positive or negative, in specific areas over a given period.

The reviewers should:

- Possess the qualifications and experience necessary to adequately identify potential issues with the subject matter to be reviewed;
- Be objective and independent of line management;[91]
- Have access to existing audit and health care resources, relevant personnel and all relevant areas of operation;
- Present written evaluative reports on compliance activities to the CEO, governing body members of the compliance committee and its provider clients on a regular basis, but not less than annually;[92] and

---

[91] The OIG recognizes that billing companies that are small in size and have limited resources may not be able to use internal reviewers who are not part of line management or hire outside reviewers.

[92] These evaluative reports should include a valid statistical sample of claims submitted to Federal health care programs.

- Specifically identify areas where corrective actions are needed.

With these reports, management can take whatever steps are necessary to correct past problems and prevent them from recurring. In certain cases, subsequent reviews or studies would be advisable to ensure that the recommended corrective actions have been implemented successfully.

The billing company should document its efforts to comply with applicable statutes, regulations and Federal health care program requirements. For example, where a billing company, in its efforts to comply with a particular statute, regulation or program requirement, requests advice from a Government agency (including a Medicare fiscal intermediary or carrier) charged with administering a Federal health care program, the billing company should document and retain a record of the request and any written or oral response. This step is extremely important if the billing company intends to rely on that response to guide it in future decisions, actions or claim reimbursement requests or appeals. A log of oral inquiries between the billing company and third parties will help the organization document its attempts at compliance. In addition, the billing company should maintain records relevant to the issue of whether its reliance was "reasonable," and whether it exercised due diligence in developing procedures to implement the advice.

G. Responding to Detected Offenses and Developing Corrective Action Initiatives

1. Violations and Investigations

Violations of the billing company's compliance program, failures to comply with applicable Federal or State law, rules and program instructions and other types of misconduct threaten a billing company's status as a reliable, honest and trustworthy company. Detected but uncorrected misconduct can seriously endanger the mission, reputation and legal status of the billing company. Consequently, upon reports or reasonable indications of suspected noncompliance, it is important that the chief compliance officer or other management officials promptly investigate the conduct in question to determine whether a material violation of applicable law, rule or program instruction or the requirements of the compliance program has occurred, and if so, take steps to correct the problem.[93] As appropriate, such steps may include an immediate referral to criminal and/ or civil law enforcement authorities, a corrective action plan,[94] a report to the Government,[95] and the notification to the provider of any discrepancies or overpayments, if applicable.

Even if the overpayment detection and return process is working and is being monitored by the billing company's audit or coding divisions, the OIG still believes that the compliance officer needs to be made aware of these significant overpayments, violations or deviations that may reveal trends or patterns indicative of a systemic problem.

Depending upon the nature of the alleged violations, an internal investigation will probably include interviews and a review of relevant documents. Some billing companies should consider engaging outside counsel, auditors or health care experts to assist in an investigation. Records of the investigation should contain documentation of the alleged violation, a description of the investigative process (including the objectivity of the investigators and methodologies utilized), copies of interview notes and key documents, a log of the witnesses interviewed and the documents reviewed, the results of the investigation, *e.g.,* any disciplinary action taken and any corrective action implemented. Although any action taken as the result of an investigation will necessarily vary depending upon the billing company and the situation, billing companies should strive for some

---

[93] Instances of non-compliance must be determined on a case-by-case basis. The existence, or amount, of a monetary loss to a health care program is not solely determinative of whether or not the conduct should be investigated and reported to governmental authorities. In fact, there may be instances where there is no readily identifiable monetary loss at all, but corrective action and reporting are still necessary to protect the integrity of the applicable program and its beneficiaries.

[94] Advice from the billing company's in-house counsel or an outside law firm may be sought to determine the extent of the billing company's liability and to plan the appropriate course of action.

[95] The OIG currently maintains a provider self-disclosure protocol that encourages providers to report suspected fraud. The concept of self-disclosure is premised on a recognition that the Government alone cannot protect the integrity of the Medicare and other Federal health care programs. Health care providers must be willing to police themselves, correct underlying problems and work with the Government to resolve these matters. The self-disclosure protocol can be located on the OIG's website at http://www.dhhs.gov/progorg/oig.

consistency by utilizing sound practices and disciplinary protocols.[96] Further, after a reasonable period, the compliance officer should review the circumstances that formed the basis for the investigation to determine whether similar problems have been uncovered or modifications of the compliance program are necessary to prevent and detect other inappropriate conduct or violations.

If an investigation of an alleged violation is undertaken and the compliance officer believes the integrity of the investigation may be at stake because of the presence of employees under investigation, those subjects should be removed from their current work activity until the investigation is completed (unless an internal or Government-led undercover operation known to the billing company is in effect). In addition, the compliance officer should take appropriate steps to secure or prevent the destruction of documents or other evidence relevant to the investigation. If the billing company determines disciplinary action is warranted, it should be prompt and imposed in accordance with the billing company's written standards of disciplinary action.

2. Reporting

a. Obligations Based on Billing Company Misconduct

If the compliance officer, compliance committee or a management official discovers credible evidence of misconduct by the billing company from any source and, after reasonable inquiry, has reason to believe that the misconduct may violate criminal, civil or administrative law,[97] then the billing company should report the existence

[96] The parameters of a claim review subject to an internal investigation will depend on the circumstances surrounding the issue(s) identified. By limiting the scope of the internal audit to current billing, a billing company may fail to identify major problems and deficiencies in operations, as well as be subject to certain liability.

[97] When making the determination of credible misconduct, the billing company should consider 18 U.S.C. 669 [holding an individual(s) criminally liable for knowingly and willfully embezzling, stealing or otherwise converting to the use of any person other than the rightful owner or intentionally misapplying any of the monies, funds . . . premiums, credits, property or assets of a health care benefit program] and 18 U.S.C. 2 (establishing criminal liability for an individual(s) who commits an offense against the United States or aids, abets, counsels, commands, induces or procures its commission as punishable as the principle).

of misconduct promptly to the appropriate Government authority [98] within a reasonable period, but not more than sixty (60) days after determining that there is credible evidence of a violation. Prompt reporting will demonstrate the billing company's good faith and willingness to work with governmental authorities to correct and remedy the problem. In addition, reporting such conduct will be considered a mitigating factor by the OIG in determining administrative sanctions (*e.g.,* penalties, assessments and exclusion), if the reporting company becomes the target of an OIG investigation. [99]

b. Obligations Based on Provider Misconduct

Billing companies are in a unique position to discover various types of fraud, waste, abuse and mistakes on the part of the provider for which they furnish services. This unique access to information may place the billing company in a precarious position. On the one hand, the billing company's allegiance is to the provider client. On the other, the billing company maintains a commitment to compliance with the applicable Federal and State laws, and the program requirements of Federal, State and private health plans. The OIG recognizes the importance of maintaining a positive and interactive communication between billing companies and the providers they service. It is with this understanding that the OIG has addressed the issue of obligations on the part of third-party medical billing companies with regard to provider misconduct.

---

[98] Appropriate Federal and/or State authorities include the Office of Inspector General of the Department of Health and Human Services, the Criminal and Civil Divisions of the Department of Justice, the U.S. Attorneys in the relevant districts, and the other investigative arms for agencies administering the affected Federal or State health care programs, such as the State Medicaid Fraud Control Unit, the Defense Criminal Investigative Service, the Department of Veterans Affairs, the Office of Inspector General, U.S. Department of Labor (which has primary criminal jurisdiction over FECA, Black Lung and Longshore programs) and the Office of Inspector General, U.S. Office of Personnel Management (which has primary jurisdiction over the Federal Employees Health Benefit Program).

[99] The OIG has published criteria setting forth those factors that the OIG takes into consideration in determining whether it is appropriate to exclude a health care provider from program participation pursuant to 42 U.S.C. 1320a-7(b)(7) for violations of various fraud and abuse laws. *See* 62 FR 67,392 (12/24/97).

If the billing company finds evidence of misconduct[100] (*e.g.,* inaccurate claim submission) on the part of the provider that they service, the billing company should refrain from the submission of questionable claims and notify the provider in writing within thirty (30) days of such a determination. This notification should include all claim specific information and the rationale for such a determination.

If the billing company discovers credible evidence of the provider's continued misconduct or flagrant fraudulent or abusive conduct,[101] the billing company should: (1) Refrain from submitting any false or inappropriate claims; (2) terminate the contract; and/or (3) report the misconduct to the appropriate Federal and State authorities within a reasonable time, but not more than sixty (60) days after determining that there is credible evidence of a violation.

c. Reporting Procedure

When reporting misconduct to the Government, a billing company should provide all evidence relevant to the alleged violation of applicable Federal or State law(s) and the potential cost impact. The compliance officer, with guidance from the governmental authorities, could be requested to continue to investigate the reported violation. Once the investigation is completed, the compliance officer should be required to notify the appropriate governmental authority of the outcome of the investigation, including a description of the impact of the alleged violation on the operation of the applicable health care programs or their beneficiaries. If the investigation ultimately reveals criminal, civil or administrative violations have occurred, the appropriate Federal and State officials[102] should be notified immediately.

---

[100] Misconduct does not include inadvertent errors or mistakes. Such errors should be reported through the normal channels with the applicable carrier, intermediary or other HCFA-designated payor.

[101] Such conduct may include patterns of misconduct, particularly with regard to conduct that had previously been identified by the billing company or carrier as suspect.

[102] *See* note 98.

3. Corrective Actions

Billing companies play a critical role in the restitution of overpayments to appropriate payors.[103] As previously stated, billing companies should take appropriate corrective action, including prompt identification of any overpayment to the provider and the affected payor and the imposition of proper disciplinary action, if applicable. Failure to notify authorities of an overpayment within a reasonable period of time could be interpreted as an intentional attempt to conceal the overpayment from the Government, thereby establishing an independent basis for a criminal violation with respect to the billing company, as well as any individuals who may have been involved.[104] For this reason, billing company compliance programs should ensure that overpayments are identified quickly and encourage their providers to promptly return overpayments obtained from Medicare or other Federal health care programs.[105]

III. Conclusion

Through this document, the OIG has attempted to provide a foundation to the process necessary to develop an effective and cost-efficient third-party medical billing compliance program. As previously stated, however, each program must be tailored to fit the needs and resources of an individual billing company, depending upon its particular corporate structure, mission and employee com-

[103] As a result of the limitations on reassignment, billing companies rarely engage in receiving payment on behalf of their provider clients or negotiating checks on behalf of their provider clients. Because of these provisions, the OIG recognizes that billing companies are rarely in the position to make restitution on behalf of their clients and it is generally viewed as the provider's responsibility to make restitution to the appropriate payor. *See* 42 CFR 424.73.

[104] *See* 42 U.S.C. 1320a-7b(a)(3).

[105] If a billing company needs further guidance to inform its provider clients of normal repayment channels, the company should consult with the applicable Medicare intermediary/carrier. The applicable Medicare intermediary/carrier may require certain information (*e.g.,* alleged violation or issue causing overpayment, description of overpayment, description of the internal investigative process with methodologies used to determine any overpayments, disciplinary actions taken and corrective actions taken) to be submitted with return of any overpayments, and that such repayment information be submitted to a specific department or individual in the carrier or intermediary's organization. Interest will be assessed, when appropriate. *See* 42 CFR 405.376.

position. The statutes, regulations and guidelines of the Federal and State health insurance programs, as well as the policies and procedures of the private health plans, should be integrated into every billing company's compliance program.

The OIG recognizes that the health care industry in this country, which reaches millions of beneficiaries and expends about a trillion dollars annually, is constantly evolving. In particular, the billing process has changed dramatically in recent years. As a result, the time is right for billing companies to implement strong, voluntary compliance programs. As stated throughout this guidance, compliance is a dynamic process that helps to ensure billing companies are better able to fulfill their commitment to ethical behavior and to meet the changes and challenges being imposed upon them by Congress and private insurers. Ultimately, it is OIG's hope that voluntarily created compliance programs will enable billing companies to meet their goals and substantially reduce fraud, waste and abuse, as well as the cost of health care to Federal, State and private health insurers.

Dated: December 14, 1998.

June Gibbs Brown,

Inspector General.

[FR Doc. 98–33565 Filed 12–17–98; 8:45 am]

BILLING CODE 4150–04-P

APPENDIX I5

Compliance Program Guidance for the Durable Medical Equipment, Prosthetics, Orthotics and Supply Industry; 64 FR 36368, July 16, 1999

Federal Register: July 6, 1999 (Volume 64, Number 128) [Notices]
[Page 36368–36389]

DEPARTMENT OF HEALTH AND HUMAN SERVICES

Office of Inspector General

Publication of OIG Compliance Program Guidance for the Durable Medical Equipment, Prosthetics, Orthotics and Supply Industry

AGENCY: Office of Inspector General (OIG), HHS.

ACTION: Notice.

SUMMARY: This **Federal Register** notice sets forth the recently issued Compliance Program Guidance for the Durable Medical Equipment, Prosthetics, Orthotics and Supply Industry that has been developed by the Office of Inspector General in cooperation with, and with input from, the Health Care Financing Administration (HCFA), the Department of Justice (DOJ) and representatives of various trade associations and health care practice groups. The OIG has previously developed and published compliance program guidance focusing on hospitals, clinical laboratories, home health agencies, and third-party medical billing companies. We believe that the development and issuance of this compliance guidance will serve as a positive step towards promoting a higher level of ethical and lawful conduct throughout the entire health care industry.

FOR FURTHER INFORMATION CONTACT: Christine Pullifrone, Office of Counsel to the Inspector General, (202) 619–2078.

SUPPLEMENTARY INFORMATION:

Background

The creation of compliance program guidances has been an important undertaking by the OIG in its effort to engage the health care community in combating fraud and abuse. In formulating this compliance guidance, the OIG has worked closely with HCFA, and has received input from interested parties and industry trade associations. The 4 previously-issued compliance program guidances focused on the hospital industry, home health agencies, clinical laboratories and third-party medical billing companies. The development of these types of compliance program guidances are based on our belief that a health care provider can efficiently use internal controls to monitor adherence to applicable statutes, regulations and program requirements.

Guidance for the DMEPOS Industry

On August 7, 1998, the OIG published a solicitation notice (63 FR 42409) seeking information and recommendations for developing guidance for the durable medical equipment, prosthetics, orthotics and supply (DMEPOS) industry. In response to that solicitation notice, the OIG received numerous comments from various parts of the industry and from their representatives. We carefully considered those comments, as well as consulted with DOJ, HCFA and the durable medical equipment regional carriers in developing a draft compliance program guidance for the DMEPOS industry. In an effort to ensure that all parties had a reasonable opportunity to provide input into a final product, the draft guidance for the DMEPOS industry was published in the **Federal Register** on January 28, 1999 (64 FR 4436) for further comment and recommendations.

Elements for an Effective Compliance Program

Through experience, the OIG has identified 7 fundamental elements applicable to an effective compliance program. They are:

- Implementing written policies, procedures and standards of conduct;
- Designating a compliance officer and compliance committee;
- Conducting effective training and education;
- Developing effective lines of communication;
- Enforcing standards through well-publicized disciplinary guidelines;

- Conducting internal monitoring and auditing; and
- Responding promptly to detected offenses and developing corrective action.

Using these 7 elements, the OIG has identified specific areas of DMEPOS industry operations that may prove to be vulnerable to fraud and abuse. Like previously-issued OIG compliance guidance, adoption of the Compliance Program Guidance for the Durable Medical Equipment, Prosthetics, Orthotics and Supply Industry set forth below will be strictly voluntary.

A reprint of the newly-issued compliance program guidance follows:

Office of Inspector General's Compliance Program Guidance for the Durable Medical Equipment, Prosthetics, Orthotics and Supply Industry (June 1999)

I. Introduction

The Office of Inspector General (OIG) of the Department of Health and Human Services (HHS) continues in its efforts to promote voluntarily developed and implemented compliance programs for the health care industry. The following compliance program guidance is intended to assist suppliers [1] of durable medical equipment, [2] prosthetics, [3] orthotics, [4] and supplies [5] (DMEPOS) and their agents and subcontractors (referred to collectively in this document as DMEPOS suppliers) develop effective internal controls that promote adherence to applicable Federal and State law, and the program

---

[1] The term "supplier" is defined in this document as an entity or individual, including a physician or Part A provider, that sells or rents Part B covered DMEPOS items and meets the Medicare supplier standards. *See*42 CFR 424.57(a).

[2] The term "durable medical equipment" is applied in this document as defined in 42 U.S.C. 1395x(n).

[3] The term "prosthetics" and "prosthetic devices" are applied in this document as defined in 42 U.S.C. 1395x(s)(9) and (s)(8), respectively.

[4] The term "orthotics" is applied in this document as defined in 42 U.S.C. 1395x(s)(9).

[5] The term "supplies" includes home dialysis supplies and equipment as described in 42 U.S.C. 1395x(s)(2)(f); surgical dressings and other devices as described in 42 U.S.C. 1395x(s)(5); immunosuppressive drugs as described in 42 U.S.C. 1395x(s)(2)(J); and any other items or services designated by the Health Care Financing Administration (HCFA).

requirements of Federal, State and private health plans.[6] The adoption and implementation of voluntary compliance programs significantly advance the prevention of fraud, abuse, and waste in these health care plans while at the same time further the fundamental mission of all DMEPOS suppliers, which is to provide quality items, service, and care to patients.

Within this document, the OIG first provides its general views on the value and fundamental principles of DMEPOS suppliers' compliance programs, and then provides the specific elements that each DMEPOS supplier should consider when developing and implementing an effective compliance program. While this document presents basic procedural and structural guidance for designing a compliance program, it is not in itself a compliance program. Rather, it is a set of guidelines to be considered by a DMEPOS supplier interested in implementing a compliance program.

The OIG recognizes the size-differential that exists between operations of the different DMEPOS suppliers and organizations that compose the DMEPOS industry. Appropriately, this guidance is pertinent for all DMEPOS suppliers, regardless of size (in terms of employees and gross revenue); number of locations; type of equipment provided; or corporate structure. The applicability of the recommendations and guidelines provided in this document depends on the circumstances of each individual DMEPOS supplier. However, regardless of a DMEPOS supplier's size or structure, the OIG believes that every DMEPOS supplier can and should strive to accomplish the objectives and principles underlying all of the compliance policies and procedures recommended within this guidance.

Fundamentally, compliance efforts are designed to establish a culture within a DMEPOS supplier that promotes prevention, detection, and resolution of instances of conduct that do not conform to Federal and State law, and Federal, State and private payor health care program requirements, as well as the DMEPOS supplier's ethical and business policies. In practice, the compliance program should effectively articulate and demonstrate the DMEPOS supplier's commitment to ethical conduct. Benchmarks that demonstrate implementation and achievements are essential to any effective

[6] The OIG recognizes that not every supplier provides durable medical equipment, prosthetics, orthotics and supplies. However, a compliance program incorporating the elements in this guidance can be used by all suppliers regardless of the items/services they provide.

compliance program. Eventually, a compliance program should become part of the fabric of routine DMEPOS supplier operations.

Specifically, compliance programs guide a DMEPOS supplier's owner(s), governing body (*e.g.*, board of directors or trustees), chief executive officer (CEO), president, vice president(s), managers, sales representatives, billing personnel, and other employees in the efficient management and operation of a DMEPOS supplier. They are especially critical as an internal quality assurance control in the reimbursement and payment areas, where claims and billing operations are often the source of fraud and abuse, and therefore, historically have been the focus of Government regulation, scrutiny, prosecution and sanctions.

It is incumbent upon a DMEPOS supplier's owner(s), corporate officers, and managers to provide ethical leadership to the organization and to assure that adequate systems are in place to facilitate ethical and legal conduct. Employees, managers, and the Government will focus on the words and actions of a DMEPOS supplier's leadership as a measure of the organization's commitment to compliance. Indeed, many DMEPOS suppliers have adopted mission statements articulating their commitment to high ethical standards. A formal compliance program, as an additional element in this process, offers a DMEPOS supplier a further concrete method that may improve quality of service and reduce waste. Compliance programs also provide a central coordinating mechanism for furnishing and disseminating information and guidance on applicable Federal and State statutes, regulations, and Federal, State and private health care program requirements.

Implementing an effective compliance program requires a substantial commitment of time, energy, and resources by senior management and the DMEPOS supplier's governing body.[7] Superficial programs that simply have the appearance of compliance without being wholeheartedly adopted and implemented by the DMEPOS supplier or programs that are hastily constructed and implemented without appropriate ongoing monitoring will likely be ineffective and could expose the DMEPOS supplier to greater liability than no program at all. Although it may require significant additional resources or reallocation of existing resources to imple-

---

[7] Recent case law suggests that the failure of a corporate Director to attempt in good faith to institute a compliance program in certain situations may be a breach of a Director's fiduciary obligation. *See, e.g., In re Caremark International Inc. Derivative Litigation,* 698 A.2d 959 (Ct. Chanc. Del. 1996).

ment an effective compliance program, the long term benefits of implementing the program significantly outweigh the costs. Undertaking a voluntary compliance program is a beneficial investment that advances both the DMEPOS supplier's organization and the stability and solvency of the Medicare program.

A. Benefits of a Compliance Program

The OIG believes an effective compliance program provides a mechanism that brings the public and private sectors together to reach mutual goals of reducing fraud and abuse, improving operational quality, improving the quality of health care services and reducing the cost of health care. Attaining these goals provides positive results to the DMEPOS supplier, the Government and individual citizens alike. In addition to fulfilling its legal duty to ensure that it is not submitting false or inaccurate claims to Government and private payors, a DMEPOS supplier may gain numerous additional benefits by voluntarily implementing an effective compliance program. These benefits may include:

- The formulation of effective internal controls to assure compliance
  [Page 36370]
  with Federal and State statutes, rules, and regulations, and Federal, State and private payor health care program requirements, and internal guidelines;

- A concrete demonstration to employees and the community at large of the DMEPOS supplier's strong commitment to honest and responsible corporate conduct;
- The ability to obtain an accurate assessment of employee and contractor behavior relating to fraud and abuse;
- An increased likelihood of identification and prevention of criminal and unethical conduct;
- The ability to more quickly and accurately react to employees' operational compliance concerns and the capability to effectively target resources to address those concerns;
- Improvement of the quality, efficiency, and consistency of providing services;
- Increased efficiency on the part of employees;

- A centralized source for distributing information on health care statutes, regulations, policies, and other program directives regarding fraud and abuse and related issues;
- Improved internal communication;
- A methodology that encourages employees to report potential problems;
- Procedures that allow the prompt, thorough investigation of alleged misconduct by corporate officers, managers, sales representatives, employees, independent contractors, consultants, clinicians and other health care professionals;
- Initiation of immediate, appropriate, and decisive corrective action;
- Early detection and reporting, minimizing the loss to the Government from false claims, and thereby reducing the DMEPOS supplier's exposure to civil damages and penalties, criminal sanctions, and administrative remedies, such as program exclusion;[8] and
- Enhancement of the structure of the DMEPOS supplier's operations and the consistency between: any related entities of the DMEPOS supplier; different departments within the DMEPOS supplier; the DMEPOS supplier's different locations; and the DMEPOS supplier's separate business units (*e.g.*, franchises, subsidiaries).

Overall, the OIG believes that an effective compliance program is a sound investment on the part of a DMEPOS supplier.

The OIG recognizes that the implementation of a compliance program may not entirely eliminate fraud, abuse, and waste from the DMEPOS supplier's system. However, a sincere effort by the DMEPOS supplier to comply with applicable Federal and State statutes, rules, and regulations and Federal, State and private payor health care program requirements, through the establishment of an effec-

---

[8] The OIG, for example, will consider the existence of an *effective* compliance program that pre-dated any governmental investigation when addressing the appropriateness of administrative sanctions. However, the burden is on the DMEPOS supplier to demonstrate the operational effectiveness of a compliance program. Further, the False Claims Act, 31 U.S.C. 3729–3733, provides that a person who has violated the Act, but who voluntarily discloses the violation to the Government within 30 days of detection, in certain circumstances will be subject to not less than double, as opposed to treble, damages. *See* 31 U.S.C. 3729(a). Thus, the ability to react quickly when violations of the law are discovered may materially help reduce a DMEPOS supplier's liability.

tive compliance program, significantly reduces the risk of unlawful or improper conduct.

B. Application of Compliance Program Guidance

Given the diversity within the industry, there is no single "best" DMEPOS supplier compliance program.[9] The OIG understands the variances and complexities within the DMEPOS supplier industry and is sensitive to the differences among large national and regional DMEPOS supplier organizations, and small independent DMEPOS suppliers. However, elements of this guidance can be used by all DMEPOS suppliers, regardless of size (in terms of employees and gross revenue); number of locations; type of equipment provided; or corporate structure, to establish an effective compliance program. Similarly, a DMEPOS supplier or corporation that owns a DMEPOS supplier or provides DMEPOS supplies may incorporate these elements into its system-wide compliance or managerial structure. We recognize that some DMEPOS suppliers may not be able to adopt certain elements to the same comprehensive degree that others with more extensive resources may achieve. This guidance represents the OIG's suggestions on how a DMEPOS supplier, regardless of size, can best establish internal controls and monitor its conduct to correct and prevent fraudulent activities. By no means should the contents of this guidance be viewed as an exclusive discussion of the advisable elements of a compliance program. On the contrary, the OIG strongly encourages DMEPOS suppliers to develop and implement compliance elements that uniquely address the individual DMEPOS supplier's risk areas.

The OIG believes that input and support by individuals and organizations that will utilize the tools set forth in this document is critical to the development and success of this compliance program guidance. In a continuing effort to collaborate closely with the private sector, the OIG placed a notice in the **Federal Register** soliciting recommendations and suggestions on what should be included in this Compliance Program Guidance.[10] Further, the OIG

---

[9] This is particularly true in the context of DMEPOS suppliers, which include many small independent DMEPOS suppliers with limited financial resources, staff, and product lines as well as large DMEPOS supplier chains with extensive financial resources, staff, and product lines.

[10] *See* 63 FR 42409 (August 7, 1998), Notice for Solicitation of Information and Recommendations for Developing OIG Compliance Program Guidance for the Durable Medical Equipment Industry.

published the draft Compliance Program Guidance for the DME, Prosthetics, Orthotics, and Supply Industry in the **Federal Register** for public comment.[11] In addition, we considered previous OIG publications, such as Special Fraud Alerts, Advisory Opinions,[12] the findings and recommendations in reports issued by OIG's Office of Audit Services and Office of Evaluation and Inspections, as well as the experience of past and recent fraud investigations related to DMEPOS suppliers conducted by OIG's Office of Investigations and the Department of Justice.

As appropriate, this guidance may be modified and expanded as more information and knowledge is obtained by the OIG, and as changes in the statutes, rules, regulations, policies, and procedures of Federal, State, and private health plans occur. The OIG understands DMEPOS suppliers will need adequate time to react to these modifications and expansions and to make any necessary changes to their voluntary compliance programs. New compliance practices may eventually be incorporated into this guidance if the OIG discovers significant enhancements to better ensure an effective compliance program.

The OIG recognizes that the development and implementation of compliance programs in DMEPOS suppliers often raise sensitive and complex legal and managerial issues.[13] However, the OIG wishes to offer what it believes is critical guidance for providers who are sincerely attempting to comply with the relevant health care statutes and regulations.

At the end of each section, where applicable, the OIG has included ideas to help aid the small DMEPOS supplier in implementing the principles espoused in this guidance. There is no all inclusive definition of a small DMEPOS supplier. However, as previously mentioned, each DMEPOS supplier should tailor its compliance program according to its resources.

---

[11] *See* 64 FR 4435 (January 28, 1999): Draft Compliance Program Guidance for the DME, Prosthetics, Orthotics, and Supply Industry.

[12] The OIG periodically issues Advisory Opinions responding to specific inquiries from members of the public and Special Fraud Alerts setting forth activities that raise legal and enforcement issues. Special Fraud Alerts and Advisory Opinions, as well as the regulations governing the issuance of Advisory Opinions, can be obtained on the Internet at http://www.dhhs.gov/progorg/oig, in the **Federal Register**, or by contacting the OIG's Public Information Desk at 202–619–1142.

[13] Nothing stated within this document should be substituted for, or used in lieu of, competent legal advice from counsel.

II. Compliance Program Elements

The elements proposed by these guidelines are similar to those of the other OIG Compliance Program Guidances [14] and the OIG's corporate integrity agreements. [15] The OIG believes that every DMEPOS supplier can benefit from the principles espoused in this guidance, which can be tailored to fit the needs and financial realities of a particular DMEPOS supplier.

The OIG believes that every effective compliance program must begin with a formal commitment [16] by the DMEPOS supplier's governing body to include *all* of the applicable elements listed below, which are based on the seven steps of the Federal Sentencing Guidelines. [17] The OIG recognizes full implementation of all elements may not be immediately feasible for all DMEPOS suppliers. However, as a first step, a good faith and meaningful commitment on the part of the DMEPOS supplier, especially the owner(s), governing body, president, vice president(s), CEO, and managing employees, will substantially contribute to the program's successful implementation. As the compliance program is implemented, that commitment should cascade down through the management to every employee of the DMEPOS supplier.

At a minimum, comprehensive compliance programs should include the following seven elements:

---

[14] *See* 63 FR 70138 (December 18, 1998) for the Compliance Program Guidance for Third Party Medical Billing Companies; 63 FR 42410 (August 7, 1998) for the Compliance Program Guidance for Home Health Agencies; 63 FR 45076 (August 24, 1998) for the Compliance Program Guidance for Clinical Laboratories, as revised; 63 FR 8987 (February 23, 1998) for the Compliance Program Guidance for Hospitals. These documents are also located on the Internet at http://www.dhhs.gov/progorg/oig.

[15] Corporate integrity agreements are executed as part of a civil settlement between a health care provider and the Government to resolve a case based on allegations of health care fraud or abuse. These OIG-imposed programs are in effect for a period of three to five years and require many of the elements included in this compliance program guidance.

[16] A formal commitment may include a resolution by the board of directors, owner(s) or president, where applicable. A formal commitment should include the allocation of adequate resources to ensure that each of the elements is addressed.

[17] *See* United States Sentencing Commission Guidelines, *Guidelines Manual*, 8A1.2, Application Note 3(k). The Federal Sentencing Guidelines are detailed policies and practices for the Federal criminal justice system that prescribe the appropriate sanctions for offenders convicted of Federal crimes.

(1) The development and distribution of written standards of conduct, as well as written policies and procedures that promote the DMEPOS supplier's commitment to compliance (*e.g.*, by including adherence to the compliance program as an element in evaluating managers and employees) and address specific areas of potential fraud, such as the claims development and submission process, completing certificates of medical necessity (CMNs), and financial relationships with physicians and/or other persons authorized[18] to order DMEPOS;

(2) The designation of a compliance officer and other appropriate bodies, (*e.g.*, a corporate compliance committee), charged with the responsibility for operating and monitoring the compliance program, and who report directly to the CEO and the governing body;[19]

(3) The development and implementation of regular, effective education and training for all affected employees;[20]

(4) The development of effective lines of communication between the compliance officer and all employees, including a process, such as a hotline or other reporting system, to receive complaints, and the adoption of procedures to protect the anonymity of complainants and to protect callers from retaliation;

(5) The use of audits and/or other risk evaluation techniques to monitor compliance, identify problem areas, and assist in the reduc-

---

[18] In some instances, persons other than the treating physician (*e.g.*, nurse practitioner, physician assistant, clinical nurse specialist) may be authorized to order DMEPOS for Medicare beneficiaries if permitted under State law and in accordance with HCFA policies. A DMEPOS supplier should be aware of any persons, other than the treating physician, who are authorized to order DMEPOS.

[19] The integral functions of the compliance officer and the corporate compliance committee in implementing an effective compliance program are discussed throughout this compliance program guidance. However, the OIG recognizes that the differences in the sizes and structures of DMEPOS suppliers will result in differences in the ways in which compliance programs are set up. It is important that a DMEPOS supplier structures its compliance program in such a way that the program facilitates implementation of the key functions of the corporate compliance officer and the corporate compliance committee discussed within this document. *See* section II.B and accompanying notes.

[20] Education and training programs for DMEPOS suppliers should be detailed and comprehensive. They should cover specific billing procedures, sales and marketing practices, as well as the general areas of compliance. *See* section II.C and accompanying notes.

tion of identified problem areas;[21]

(6) The development of appropriate disciplinary mechanisms to enforce standards and the development of policies addressing (i) employees who have violated internal compliance policies, applicable statutes, regulations, or Federal, State or private payor health care program requirements and (ii) the employment of sanctioned and other specified individuals;[22] and

(7) The development of policies to respond to detected offenses and to initiate corrective action to prevent similar offenses.

A. Written Policies and Procedures

Every compliance program should require the development and distribution of written compliance policies, standards, and practices that identify specific areas of risk and vulnerability to the individual DMEPOS supplier. These policies, standards, and practices should be developed under the direction and supervision of the compliance officer and the compliance committee (if such a committee is practicable for the DMEPOS supplier) and, at a minimum, should be provided to all individuals who are affected by the particular policy at issue, including the DMEPOS supplier's agents and independent contractors who may affect billing decisions.[23]

---

[21] For example, spot-checking the work of coding and billing personnel periodically and conducting periodic post-payment claim review should be elements of an effective compliance program. *See* section II.E and accompanying notes.

[22] The term "Federal health care program" is applied in this document as defined in 42 U.S.C. 1320a-7b(f), and includes any plan or program that provides health benefits, whether directly, through insurance, or otherwise, which is funded directly in whole or in part, by the United States Government (*i.e.*, via programs such as Medicare, Federal Employees' Compensation Act, Black Lung, or the Longshore and Harbor Worker's Compensation Act) or any State health plan (*e.g.*, Medicaid, or a program receiving funds from block grants for social services or child health services). Also, for the purpose of this document, the term "Federal health care program requirements" refers to the statutes, regulations, rules requirements, directives, and instructions governing Medicare, Medicare, Medicaid, and all other Federal health care programs.

[23] According to the Federal Sentencing Guidelines, an organization must have established compliance standards and procedures to be followed by its employees and other agents in order to receive sentencing credit for an "effective" compliance program. The Federal Sentencing Guidelines define "agent" as "any individual, including a director, an officer, an employee, or an independent contractor, authorized to act on behalf of the organization."

[Page 36372]

In addition to these general policies, it may be necessary to implement individual policies for the different components of the DMEPOS supplier.

1. Standards of Conduct

The OIG recommends that the DMEPOS supplier develop standards of conduct for all affected employees that include a clearly delineated commitment to compliance by the DMEPOS supplier's senior management,[24] including any related entities or affiliated providers operating under the DMEPOS supplier's control,[25] and other health care professionals (*e.g.*, nurses, licensed pharmacists, physicians, and respiratory therapists). The standards of conduct should function in the same fashion as a constitution, i.e., as a foundational document that details the fundamental principles, values, and framework for action within the DMEPOS supplier. The standards should articulate the DMEPOS supplier's commitment to comply with all Federal and State statutes, rules, regulations and Federal, State and private payor health care program requirements, with an emphasis on preventing fraud and abuse. They should explicitly state the organization's mission, goals, and ethical principles relative to compliance and clearly define the DMEPOS supplier's commitment to compliance and its expectations for all DMEPOS supplier owners, governing body members, presidents, vice presidents, corporate officers, managers, sales representatives, employees, and, where appropriate, independent contractors and other agents. These standards should promote integrity, support objectivity, and foster trust. Standards should not only address compliance with statutes and regulations, but should also set forth broad principles that guide employees in conducting business professionally and properly.

The standards should be distributed to, and comprehensible by, all affected employees (*e.g.*, translated into other languages when nec-

See United States Sentencing Commission Guidelines, *Guidelines Manual*, 8A1.2, Application Note 3(d).

[24] The OIG strongly encourages high-level involvement by a DMEPOS supplier's owner(s), governing body, CEO, president, vice president(s), as well as other personnel, as appropriate, in the development of the standards of conduct. Such involvement should help communicate a strong and explicit organizational commitment to compliance goals and standards.

[25] E.g., pharmacies, billing services, and manufacturers.

essary and written at appropriate reading levels). Further, to assist in ensuring that employees continuously meet the expected high standards set forth in the standards of conduct, any employee handbook delineating or expanding upon these standards should be regularly updated as applicable statutes, regulations, and Federal, State, and private payor health care program requirements are modified and/or clarified.[26]

When employees first begin working for the DMEPOS supplier, and each time new standards of conduct are issued, the OIG suggests employees be asked to sign a statement certifying that they have received, read, understood, and will abide by the standards of conduct. The employee's certification should be retained by the DMEPOS supplier in the employee's personnel file, and available for review by the compliance officer.

The OIG believes all DMEPOS suppliers, regardless of size, should operate professionally and ethically. The OIG recognizes that small DMEPOS suppliers may not have formal written standards of conduct. However, such unwritten standards of conduct (*e.g.*, the manner in which the DMEPOS supplier conducts its business) should be relayed to each employee. Employees should attest, in writing, that they understand and will abide by these standards.

2. Written Policies for Risk Areas

As part of its commitment to compliance, the DMEPOS supplier should establish a comprehensive set of written policies and procedures that take into consideration the particular statutes, rules, regulations, and program instructions applicable to each function of the DMEPOS supplier.[27] In contrast to the standards of conduct,

---

[26] The OIG recognizes that not all statutes, rules, regulations, standards, policies, and procedures need to be communicated to all employees. However, the OIG believes that the bulk of the standards that relate to complying with fraud and abuse laws and other ethical areas should be addressed and made part of all affected employees' training. A DMEPOS supplier must decide whether additional educational programs should be targeted to specific categories of employees based on job functions and areas of responsibility.

[27] A DMEPOS supplier can conduct focus groups, composed of managers from various departments, to solicit their concerns and ideas about compliance risks that may be incorporated into the DMEPOS supplier's policies and procedures. Such employee participation in the development of the DMEPOS supplier's compliance program can enhance its credibility and foster employee acceptance of the program.

which are designed to be a clear and concise collection of fundamental standards, the written policies should articulate specific procedures personnel should follow.

Consequently, we recommend that the individual policies and procedures be coordinated with the appropriate training and educational programs with an emphasis on areas of special concern that have been identified by the OIG.[28] Some of the special areas of OIG concern include:[29]

- Billing for items or services not provided;[30]
- Billing for services that the DMEPOS supplier believes may be denied;[31]

---

[28] A DMEPOS supplier's compliance program should require that the legal staff, compliance officer, or other appropriate personnel carefully consider any and all Special Fraud Alerts and Advisory Opinions issued by the OIG that relate to DMEPOS suppliers. *See* note 12. Moreover, the compliance program should address the ramifications of failing to cease and correct any conduct criticized in such a Special Fraud Alert or Advisory Opinion, if applicable to the DMEPOS supplier, or to take reasonable action to prevent such conduct from reoccurring in the future. If appropriate, a DMEPOS supplier should take the steps described in section II.G regarding investigations, reporting, and correction of identified problems.

[29] The OIG Work Plan details the various projects the OIG currently intends to address in the fiscal year. It should be noted that the priorities in the Work Plan are subject to modification and revision as the year progresses and does not represent a complete or final list of areas of concern to the OIG. The Work Plan is currently available on the Internet at http://www.dhhs.gov/progorg/oig.

[30] Billing for items or services not provided involves submitting a claim representing that the DMEPOS supplier provided an item or service or part of an item or service that the patient did not receive. It may also include not fulfilling a contractual agreement, for example, when the DMEPOS supplier has agreed to service the rental equipment and does not fulfill this obligation.

[31] Billing for services that may be denied involves seeking reimbursement for a service that is not covered by Medicare or does not meet the Medicare coverage criteria as documented by the patient's current medical condition. *See* 42 U.S.C. 1395y(a)(1)(A). The OIG recognizes that DMEPOS suppliers cannot make medical necessity determinations and may not be aware if an item or service will be denied in every instance. However, civil money penalties (CMPs) and administrative sanctions may be imposed against any person who submits a claim for services "that [the] person knows or should know are not medically necessary." See 42 U.S.C. 1320a-7a(a). Such conduct may also result in liability under civil and criminal laws. HCFA does allow DMEPOS suppliers to submit claims when the DMEPOS supplier believes the item or service may not be covered, provided, however, that the supplier "note[s] on the claim [its] belief that the service is noncovered and that it is

- Billing patients for denied chargs without a signed written notice;[32]
- Duplicate billing;[33]
- Billing for items or services not ordered;[34]
- Using a billing agent whose compensation arrangement violates the reassignment rule;[35]
- Upcoding;[36]

---

being submitted at the beneficiary's insistence." *See Medicare Carriers Manual*, section 3043. If the DMEPOS supplier believes the item or service may be denied for any reason (*e.g.*, not covered, not medically necessary), the DMEPOS supplier may have the beneficiary sign a written notice accepting financial responsibility if the item or service is denied (*see Medicare Carriers Manual*, section 7300.5). The DMEPOS supplier should include modifier "GA" on the claim for such item or service. This modifier indicates the beneficiary has signed a written notice. If the beneficiary signed an advance written notice, the DMEPOS supplier may directly bill the beneficiary for the denied item or service. (*See* section II.A.3.i for further discussion on written notices). *See also*discussion in section II.A.3.a and accompanying notes.

[32] This includes, but is not limited to, billing the patient for items or services denied as not medically necessary by the payor, where there has been no written notice signed by the patient, the written notice has been inappropriately obtained or the written notice was drafted inappropriately. *See* Medicare Carrier Manual, section 7300.5A, regarding the requirements for written notice.

[33] Duplicate billing occurs when more than one claim for payment is submitted for the same patient, for the same service, for the same date of service (by the same or different DMEPOS supplier), or the same claim is submitted to more than one payor as primary Although duplicate billing can occur due to simple error (which does not create civil or criminal liability), fraudulent duplicate billing is often evidenced by systematic or repeated double billing, and creates liability under criminal, civil, and administrative law, particularly if any overpayment is not promptly refunded. *See* note 72.

[34] Billing for items or services not ordered involves seeking reimbursement for items or services provided, but not ordered by the treating physician or other authorized person.

[35] If a billing agent receives payment on behalf of a DMEPOS supplier, the billing agent's compensation may not be related in any way to the dollar amounts billed or collected. *See* 42 U.S.C. 1395u(b)(6); 42 CFR 424.73; *Medicare Carriers Manual*, section 3060.

[36] Upcoding involves selecting a code to maximize reimbursement when such code is not the most appropriate descriptor of the service (*e.g.*, billing for a more expensive piece of equipment when a less expensive piece of equipment is provided).

- Unbundling items or supplies;[37]
- Billing for new equipment and providing used equipment;[38]
- Continuing to bill for rental items after they are no longer medically necessary;[39]
- Resubmission of denied claims with different information in an attempt to be improperly reimbursed;[40]
- Refusing to submit a claim to Medicare for which payment is made on a reasonable charge or fee schedule basis;[41]

---

[37] Unbundling items or supplies involves billing for individual components when a specific HCFA Common Procedure Coding System (HCPCS) code provides for the components to be billed as a unit (*e.g.*, providing a wheelchair and billing the individual parts of the wheelchair, rather than the wheeelchair as a whole).

[38] The DMEPOS supplier must indicate on the Medicare claim form, through the use of modifiers, whether the item provided is new or used. The modifier for providing new equipment is "NU." The modifies for providing used equipment is "UE." A knowing failure to correctly document the item provided would constitute falsifying information on the claim form and many constitute a violation of the False Claims Act. *See* 31 U.S.C. 3729.

[39] Once a rental item is no longer medically necessary, the DMEPOS supplier required to discontinue billing the payor for it. The OIG recognizes that DMEPOS suppliers cannot make medical necessity determinations and may not be aware that a rental item is no longer medically necessary for a particular patient. As a result, the OIG recommends that the DMEPOS supplier periodically contact the treating physician or other authorized person to ensure the rental item continues to be medically necessary. In addition, the OIG recommends that the DMEPOS supplier pick up such equipment from the patient in a timely manner. If the DMEPOS supplier bills for a rental item after it is no longer medically necessary, the DMEPOS supplier is financially responsible for that item and must remit any overpayments for that item. *See* 42 U.S.C. 1320a-7b(a)(3), which provides criminal penalties for failure to disclose an overpayment.

[40] This practice involves the DMEPOS supplier improperly changing information on a previously denied claim and continuing to resubmit the claim in an attempt to receive payment. For example, a DMEPOS supplier may submit a claim using the accurate HCPCS code for the item or service provided and the claim is subsequently denied. It is improper to change the HCPCS code to HCPCS code that the DMEPOS supplier believes is reimbursable, when such item or service was not provided.

[41] This practice involves a DMEPOS supplier not submitting a claim on behalf of the beneficiary for items or services that are Medicare benefits and are reimbursable under the Medicare program. *See* 42 U.S.C 1395w-4(g)(4).

- Inadequate management and oversight of contracted services, which results in improper billing; [42]
- Charge limitations; [43]
- Providing and/or billing for substantially excessive amounts of DMEPOS items or supplies; [44]
- Providing and/or billing for an item or service that does not meet the quality and standard of the DMEPOS item claimed; [45]

---

[42] The OIG recommends that the DMEPOS supplier create internal mechanisms to ensure that the use of contractors does not lead to improper billing practices.

[43] A DMEPOS supplier should ensure that its billing personnel are informed of the different payment rules of all the Federal, State, and private health care programs it bills. The supplier should be aware that billing for items or services furnished substantially in excess of the supplier's usual charges may result in exclusion and other sanctions. *See* 42 U.S.C. 1320a-7 (b)(6)(A). *See also* OIG Ad. Op. 98–8 (1998).

[44] This practice, which constitutes overulitization, involves providing and/or billing for substantially more items or supplies that are reasonable and necessary for the needs of each individual patient. The OIG recognizes that DMEPOS suppliers cannot make medical necessity determinations. The medical need for an item must be determined by the physician or other authorized person who is treating the patient. However, the DMEPOS supplier must ensure that the patient's condition meets coverage, payment and utilization criteria as established in the payor's medical policies. If the DMEPOS supplier is providing and/or billing for substantially excessive amounts of DMEPOS items or supplies, the DMEPOS supplier is financially responsible for remitting any overpayments relating to those items or supplies. The OIG recommends that if a DMEPOS supplier is providing and billing for a large number of items or supplies for the same patient, it may periodically want to contact the treating physician or other authorized person to confirm the medical necessity of the items or supplies. Such contact with the physician's office should be documented. The practice of billing for substantially excessive amounts of items or supplies may lead to exclusion from Federal health care programs and other sanctions. *See* 42 U.S.C. 1320a-7(b)(6)(B).

[45] This practice involves providing and./or billing for an item or service that does not meet the definition and/or requirement of the item or service ordered by the treating physician or other authorized person. Generally, such items are inferior in quality, and therefore do not meet the definition of what was ordered and/or billed. Sometimes this may mean that certin equipment was never cleared by the Food and Drug Administration, as required by law. This practice may lead to billing for items that are not reasonable and necessary. A DMEPOS supplier should ensure that the iterm or services it furnishes meet professionally recognized minimum standards of health care.

- Capped rentals;[46]
- Failure to monitor medical necessity on an on-going basis;[47]
- Delivering or billing for certain items or supplies prior to receiving a physician's order and/or appropriate CMN;[48]
- Falsifying information on the claim form, CMN, and/or accompanying documentation;[49]
  [Page 36374]
- Completing portions of CMNs reserved for completion only by the treating physician or other authorized person;[50]

---

[46] *See* discussion in section II.A.3.k and accompanying notes.

[47] In order for a patient to continue to receive items or supplies (*e.g.*, rental equipment, supplies for an on-going condition) and for the DMEPOS supplier to receive Medicare reimbursement, the patient must meet the medical necessity criteria for that specific item or supply on an on-going basis. The item or supply furnished by the DMEPOS supplier should be replaced or adjusted, in a timely manner, to reflect changes in the patient's condition. The OIG recognizes that a DMEPOS supplier cannot make medical necessity determinations and may not be aware when a patient's condition changes. However, if a DMEPOS supplier is billing for items or services that are no longer medically necessary, the supplier is financially responsible for remitting any overpayments relating to those items or services. The OIG recommends that if a DMEPOS supplier is providing the same items or supplies to a patient on a regular basis, it may periodically want to contact the treating physician or other authorized person to confirm that the items or supplies continue to be medically necessary. Such contact with the physician's office should be documented.

[48] This practice involves a DMEPOS supplier delivering to the patient, and/or billing the payor for, items or supplies that have not yet been ordered by the treating physician or other authorized person. Medicare requires written orders for certain items before delivery. *See*, e.g., 42 CFR 410.38.

[49] This practice invovles supplying false information to be included on the claim form, the CMN, or other accompanying documentation. The information reported on these documents should accurately reflect the patient's information, including medical information, and the items or services ordere by the treating physician or other authorized person and provided by the DMEPOS supplier. *See, e.g.*, 18 U.S.C. 1035, which provides criminal penalties for falsifying information on such documentation.

[50] This practice involves not completing the CMN in compliance with Medicare regulations (*i.e.*, sections B and D should never be completed by the supplier). Instructions for completing the CMN can be found on the back of the form. *See Medicare Carriers Manual*, section 3312, which provides instructions on how to complete the CMN and the CMPs that may be assessed for improper completion of the CMN. *See also* 42 U.S.C. 1395m(j)(2); section II.A.3.c and accompanying notes for further discussion on CMNs. Such conduct may also result in liability under civil and criminal laws.

- Altering medical records;[51]
- Manipulating the patient's diagnosis in an attempt to receive improper payment;[52]
- Failing to maintain medical necessity documentation;[53]
- Inappropriate use of place of service codes;[54]
- Cover letters that encourage physicians to order medically unnecessary items or services;[55]
- Improper use of the ZX modifier;[56]
- Routine waiver of deductibles and coinsurance;[57]
- Providing incentives to actual or potential referral sources (*e.g.*, physicians, hospitals, patients, skilled nursing facilities, home health agencies or others) that may violate the anti-kickback statute or other similar Federal or State statute or

---

[51] This practice involves falsifying information on a patient's medical records to justify reimbursement for an item or service.

[52] This practice involves altering the treating physician's or other authorized person's diagnosis in an attempt to receive reimbursement for a particular item or service. A DMEPOS supplier should not claim the patient has a particular medical condition in order to qualify for an item for which the patient would not otherwise qualify.

[53] This practice involves failing to ensure that the medical necessity documentation requirements for the item or service billed are properly met (*e.g.*, failing to maintain the physician orders or CMNs or failing to ensure that CMNs contain adequate and correct information). *See Medicare Carriers Manual*, section 4105.2 for evidence of medical necessity. *See also* sections II.A.3.b and II.A.3.c regarding physician orders and CMNs, respectively.

[54] This practice involves indicating on the claim form that the place of service is a location other than where the service was provided. For example, the patient resides in a skilled nursing facility (SNF) and a DMEPOS supplier submits a claim with the place of service as the patient's home. Provided that the DMEPOS items or services are ordered, provided, reasonable and necessary given the clinical condition of the patient, the items or services may be covered if the beneficiary resides at home. However, such items may not be covered if the beneficiary resides in a SNF. *See Medicare Carriers Manual*, section 2100.3 for the definition of a beneficiary's home.

[55] *See* discussion in section II.A.3.m.

[56] This practice involves the improper use of the ZX modifier, relating to maintaining medical necessity documentation. *See* discussion in section II.A.3.l.

[57] Throughout this document, the term "deductibles and coinsurance" refers to Medicare as well as to any other health insurance program requiring deductibles and coinsurance. *See* discussion in section II.A.3.j and accompanying notes.

regulation;[58]

- Compensation programs that offer incentives for items or services ordered and revenue generated;[59]
- Joint ventures between parties, one of whom can refer Medicare or Medicaid business to the other;[60]
- Billing for items or services furnished pursuant to a prohibited referral under the Stark physician self-referral law;[61]
- Improper telemarketing practices;[62]

---

[58] Examples of arrangements that may run afoul of the anti-kickback statute include practices in which a DMEPOS supplier pays a fee to a physician for each CMN the physician signs, provides free gifts to physicians for signing CMNs, provides inducements to beneficiaries, and/or provides items or services for free or below fair market value to providers or beneficiaries of Federal health care programs. *See* 42 U.S.C. 1320a-7a(a)(5); 42 U.S.C. 1320a-7b(b); 60 FR 40847 (August 10, 1995). *See also* discussion in section II.A.4 and accompanying notes.

[59] Compensation programs that offer incentives for items or services ordered or the revenue they generate may lead to the ordering of medically unnecessary items or supplies and/or the "dumping" of such items or supplies in a facility or in a beneficiary's home (*e.g.*, mail order supply companies that continue to send the patient supplies when the supplies are no longer medically necessary).

[60] Equally troubling to the OIG is the proliferation of business arrangements that may violate the anti-kickback statute or other similar Federal and State statute or regulation. Such arrangements are generally established between those in a position to refer business, such as physicians, and those providing items or services, such as DMEPOS suppliers, for which a Federal health care program pays. Sometimes established as "joint ventures," these arrangements may take a variety of forms. The OIG currently has a number of investigations and audits underway that focus on such areas of concern. The OIG has also issued a Special Fraud Alert on Joint Venture Arrangements. This Special Fraud Alert can be found at 59 FR 65372 (December 19, 1994) or on the Internet at http://www.dhhs.gov/progorg/oig.

[61] Under the Stark physician self-referral law, if a physician (or an immediate family member of such physician) has a prohibited financial relationship with a DMEPOS supplier, the physician may not make a referral to the DMEPOS supplier and the DMEPOS supplier may not bill for furnishing DMEPOS items or supplies for which payment may be made under the Federal health care programs. *See* 42 U.S.C. 1395nn.

[62] *See* 42 U.S.C. 1395m(a)(17) or Pub.L. 103–432, section 132(a) for the prohibition on telemarketing. *See also* discussion in section II.A.5 and accompanying notes.

- Improper patient solicitation activities and high-pressure marketing of noncovered or unnecessary services; [63]
- Co-location of DMEPOS items and supplies with the referral source; [64]
- Non-compliance with the Federal, State and private payor supplier standards; [65]
- Providing false information on the Medicare DMEPOS supplier enrollment form; [66]
- Not notifying the National Supplier Clearinghouse in a timely manner of changes to the information previously provided on the DMEPOS supplier enrollment form; [67]

---

[63] The DMEPOS supplier should not utilize prohibited or inappropriate conduct to carry out its initiatives and activities designed to maximize business growth and patient retention. Many cases against DMEPOS suppliers have involved the DMEPOS supplier giving the beneficiary free gifts such as angora underwear, microwaves and air conditioners in exchange for providing and billing for unnecessary items. Any marketing information offered by the DMEPOS supplier should be clear, correct, non-deceptive, and fully informative. *See* discussion in section II.A.5 and accompanying notes.

[64] In this situation, a physician allows a DMEPOS supplier to stock inventory (the storage space may or may not be rented by the DMEPOS supplier) in a physician's office. When such items and supplies are dispensed to the patient, Medicare is then billed. Although such arrangements are not prohibited per se, the OIG believes that such arrangements may potentially raise anti-kickback and self-referral issues, particularly when the DMEPOS supplier pays the physician an amount above fair market value to rent the space.

[65] A DMEPOS supplier should have appropriate personnel acknowledge they have reviewed and will abide by the Medicare supplier standards. In addition, a DMEPOS supplier should ensure it is meeting individual State and private payor supplier standards. *See* 42 CFR 424.57 for the Medicare supplier standards.

[66] Criminal penalties may be imposed against an individual who knowingly and willfully makes or causes to be made any false statements or representations of a material fact in any application for any benefit or payment under a Federal health care program. *See* 42 U.S.C. 1320a-7b(a)(1). *See also* 31 U.S.C. 3729(a) ("any person who * * * knowingly makes, uses, or causes to be made or used, a false record or statement to get a false or fraudulent claim paid or approved by the Government * * * is liable to the United States Government for a civil penalty of not less than $5,000 and not more than $10,000, plus 3 times the amount of damages which the Government sustains because of the act of that person * * *")

[67] By signing the DMEPOS supplier enrollment application, a DMEPOS supplier certifies it will notify the Medicare contractor of any changes in its enrollment information within 30 days of the effective date of the change.

- Misrepresenting a person's status as an agent or representative of Medicare;[68]
- Knowing misuse of a supplier number, which results in improper billing;[69]
- Failing to meet individual payor requirements;[70]
[Page 36375]
- Performing tests on a beneficiary to establish medical necessity;[71]
- Failing to refund overpayments to a health care program;[72]
- Failing to refund overpayments to patients;[73]
- Improper billing resulting from a lack of communication between the DMEPOS supplier, the physician, and the patient;[74]

---

[68] It is unlawful for a DMEPOS supplier to represent itself as a Medicare representative. *See* 42 U.S.C. 1320b-10.

[69] This practice may involve, but is not limited to, using another DMEPOS supplier's billing number.

[70] A DMEPOS supplier should be aware of the requirements of any payor they bill, especially in those situations where there is a primary and secondary payor.

[71] *E.g.,* Medicare does not permit DMEPOS suppliers to perform oxygen tests (*e.g.*, oximetry tests and arterial blood gas tests) to qualify patients for oxygen and oxygen supplies. *See Medicare Coverage Issues Manual,* section 60–4. *See also* discussion in section II.A.3.o.

[72] An overpayment is the amount of money received in excess of the amount due and payable under a health care program. Examples of overpayments include, but are not limited to, instances where a DMEPOS supplier is: (i) paid twice for the same service, for the same beneficiary; or (ii) paid for services that were provided but not ordered by the treating physician or other authorized person. The OIG strongly recommends that the DMEPOS supplier institute procedures to detect overpayments and to promptly remit such overpayments to the affected payor. *See* 42 U.S.C. 1320a-7b(a)(3). *See also* 18 U.S.C. 669 and 31 U.S.C. 3729(a)(7).

[73] If a patient is also due money when a DMEPOS supplier identifies an overpayment to a health care program, the DMEPOS supplier should make a prompt refund to the patient. *See* 42 U.S.C. 1395m(j)(4) on limitation of patient liability for non-assigned claims that are denied due to medical necessity. *See also* 42 U.S.C. 1395pp(h) on limitation of patient liability for assigned claims that are denied due to medical necessity.

[74] A lack of communication between the DMEPOS supplier, physician, and patient may result in the DMEPOS supplier inappropriately billing for items or supplies (*e.g.*, supplies for an on-going condition or rental equipment that are no longer medically necessary). *See* discussion in section II.A.3.n.

- Improper billing resulting from a lack of communication between different departments within the DMEPOS supplier;[75]
- Employing persons excluded from participation in Federal health care programs.[76]

A DMEPOS supplier's prior history of noncompliance with applicable statutes, regulations, and Federal, State or private health care program requirements may indicate additional types of risk areas where the DMEPOS supplier may be vulnerable and that may require policies and procedures to prevent recurrence.[77] Additional risk areas should be assessed by the DMEPOS supplier and incorporated into its written policies and procedures and training programs developed as part of its compliance program.

The OIG believes sound operating policies are essential to all DMEPOS suppliers, regardless of size. The OIG recommends that small DMEPOS suppliers focus on the risk areas most potentially problematic to its business operations. The OIG recognizes some small DMEPOS suppliers may not have the resources to independently develop a comprehensive set of written policies and procedures pertaining to such risk areas. In this case, the OIG recommends that the small DMEPOS supplier create a manual that is accessible to all employees. Such a manual should contain the specific statutes, regulations, and DMERC instructions and bulletins that address the DMEPOS supplier's identified risk areas. The goal of this manual is to provide employees direction so they can properly address any concerns/issues/questions that may arise.

---

[75] A lack of communication between the different departments of a DMEPOS supplier may result in the DMEPOS supplier filing incorrect claims and/or equipment delivery problems.

[76] This involves hiring or contracting with individuals or entities who have been excluded from participation in Federal health care programs or any other Federal procurement or non-procurement program. *See* section II.F.2.

[77] "Recurrence of misconduct similar to that which an organization has previously committed casts doubt on whether it took all reasonable steps to prevent such misconduct" and is a significant factor in the assessment of whether a compliance program is effective. *See* United States Sentencing Commission Guidelines, *Guidelines Manual*, 8A1.2, Application Note 3(k) (iii).

3. Claims Development and Submission

a. Medical Necessity

The OIG recommends that the DMEPOS supplier's compliance program communicate to physicians and other persons authorized to order items and services that claims submitted for items and services will only be paid if the item or service is ordered, provided, covered, reasonable and necessary for the patient, given his or her clinical condition. The DMEPOS suppliers should take all reasonable steps to ensure they are not submitting claims for services that are not: (i) covered; (ii) reasonable; and (iii) necessary. [78] The DMEPOS suppliers must keep the treating physician's or other authorized person's signed and dated order or CMN on file for all DMEPOS items and services. [79] Upon a payor's request, the DMEPOS supplier must be able to provide documentation, such as physician orders, completed original CMNs, [80] proof of delivery, written confirmation of verbal orders and any other documentation to support the medical necessity of an item or service the DMEPOS supplier has provided and billed to a Federal or private health care program. [81] Because the DMEPOS supplier is responsible for producing documentation upon request, the DMEPOS supplier may want to send a written notice to its clients who write orders and refer patients concerning payors' documentation requirements.

As a preliminary matter, the OIG recognizes that physicians and other authorized persons must be able to order any items or services that they believe are appropriate for the treatment of their patients. However, Medicare and other Government and private health care plans will only pay for those services that are covered and that meet the appropriate medical necessity standards (*e.g.*, ordered, provided,

[78] *See* note 31.

[79] *See Medicare Carrier Manual*, section 3312. *See alsoMedicare Carrier Manual*, section 4105.2 regarding what information must be included on the physician's order.

[80] An original CMN is that in which Section B was completed by the treating physician or other authorized person and contains the original signature of the treating physician or other authorized person.

[81] In order to ensure correct reimbursement, the payor may conduct a post-payment audit of a DMEPOS supplier's claims. Such audits may require that the DMEPOS supplier submit documentation to substantiate that the items or services were ordered by the treating physician or other authorized person, provided, covered, reasonable and necessary. *See* 42 CFR 424.5(a)(6).

reasonable, necessary, and meeting criteria established by medical review policies). "No payment may be made under Part A or Part B for any expenses incurred for items or services * * * which are not reasonable and necessary for the diagnosis or treatment of an illness or injury or to improve the functioning of a malformed body member."[82] Therefore, DMEPOS suppliers should be aware that Medicare may deny payment for an item or service that the treating physician or other authorized person believes is appropriate, but which does not meet the Medicare coverage criteria or where the documentation does not support that the item or service was reasonable and necessary for the patient. The OIG recommends that the DMEPOS supplier advise its clients that claims for items or services submitted for Federal, State or private payor reimbursement must meet program requirements[83] or the claims may be denied.

The DMEPOS supplier should take steps to ensure compliance with the applicable statutes, regulations and the requirements of Federal, State and private health plans. The OIG recognizes that DMEPOS suppliers do not and cannot treat patients or make medical necessity determinations. However, the DMEPOS supplier must take steps to ensure that the beneficiary's condition meets coverage, payment and utilization criteria established in medical policies before it submits a claim to Federal, State or private health plans. In order to help ensure compliance, the OIG recommends that DMEPOS supplier personnel understand the coverage and payment criteria of each payor they bill. To help aid supplier personnel, the DMEPOS supplier's compliance officer may want to create a clear, comprehensive summary of the "medical necessity" standards or coverage criteria and applicable rules of the various Government and private plans. This summary should be disseminated and explained to the appropriate DMEPOS supplier personnel.

We also recommend that DMEPOS suppliers formulate internal control mechanisms through their written policies and procedures to ensure the medical necessity of the items or services they provide. Such policies and procedures may include periodic claim reviews, both prior and subsequent to billing for items and services. Such a procedure will verify that patients are receiving and the DMEPOS supplier is being paid for items and/or services that are ordered, provided, covered, reasonable and necessary. The DMEPOS supplier

[82] *See* 42 U.S.C. 1395y(a)(1)(A).

[83] *See* note 31.

may choose to incorporate this claims review function into pre-existing quality assurance mechanisms.

b. Physician Orders

The DMEPOS supplier's written policies and procedures should state that the DMEPOS supplier will not bill for an item or service unless and until it has been ordered by the treating physician or other authorized person. For all Medicare reimbursed DMEPOS items or services, the DMEPOS supplier must receive a written order from the patient's treating physician or other authorized person. Such written order must be received prior to billing Medicare. When the DMEPOS supplier receives a verbal order, the DMEPOS supplier should document the verbal order and must have the treating physician or other authorized person confirm it in writing prior to billing.

The written policies and procedures should also state, for items requiring a written order prior to delivery, that the order must be received by the DMEPOS supplier before it delivers the equipment to the patient and before it bills the payor.[84]

c. Certificate of Medical Necessity[85]

For some DMEPOS items and services, the DMEPOS supplier must receive a signed CMN from the treating physician or other authorized person. Currently, CMNs are required for Medicare reimbursement for fourteen items.[86] The CMN must be retained in the DMEPOS supplier's records before it can submit a claim for payment to the Medicare program. Although faxed CMNs are per-

---

[84] *See* 42 CFR 410.38.

[85] As defined in 42 U.S.C. 1395m(j)(2)(B). *See* also OIG Special Fraud Alert regarding Physician Liability for Certifications in the Provision of Medical Equipment and Supplies and Home Health Services, 64 FR 1813 (January 12, 1999). Special Fraud Alerts are available on the OIG website.

[86] Items or services requiring CMNs are as follows: Home oxygen therapy (HCFA form 484); Hospital beds (HCFA form 841); Support surfaces (HCFA form 842); Motorized wheelchairs (HCFA form 843) (Section C continuation, HCFA form 854); Manual wheelchairs (HCFA form 844) (Section C continuation, HCFA form 854); Continuous positive airway pressure (CPAP) devices (HCFA form 845); Lymphedema pumps (pneumatic compression devices) (HCFA form 846); Osteogenesis stimulators (HCFA form 847); Transcutaneous electrical nerve stimulators (TENS) (HCFA form 848); Seat lift mechanisms (HCFA form 849); Power operated vehicles (HCFA form 850); Infusion pumps (HCFA form 851); Parenteral nutrition (HCFA form 852); and Enteral nutrition (HCFA form 853).

mitted in order to submit the claim, the DMERCs have the authority to request the original CMN from the DMEPOS supplier at any time.[87]

Each CMN has four sections: A, B, C, and D. Section A may be completed by the DMEPOS supplier. Section B may not be completed by the DMEPOS supplier.[88] Section B may only be completed by the treating physician, a non-physician clinician involved in the care of the patient or a physician employee who is knowledgeable about the patient's treatment. If section B is completed by a physician's employee, the section must be reviewed by the treating physician or other person authorized to sign section D of the CMN[89] to ensure the information's accuracy. Section C must be completed by the DMEPOS supplier prior to the CMN being furnished to the treating physician or other authorized person for signature.[90] Section D is the attestation statement and may only be signed by the treating physician or other person authorized to sign section D.[91] The DMEPOS supplier's written policies and procedures on completing CMNs should reflect these standards.

The DMEPOS supplier should take all reasonable steps to ensure that each section of the CMN is completed in accordance with the above guidelines. The OIG recommends that the DMEPOS supplier's written policies and procedures, at a minimum, provide that the DMEPOS supplier:

- Does not forward blank CMNs to the treating physician or other authorized person for signature;
- Does not complete section B (Medical Necessity) of the CMN;

---

[87] *See* HCFA Program Memorandum B-99–23 (April 1999).

[88] A supplier who knowingly and willfully completes section B of the form is, at a minimum, subject to a CMP of up to $1,000 for each form or document completed in such manner. *See* 42 U.S.C. 1395m(j)(2). That supplier may also face civil and criminal liability.

[89] *See* HCFA Program Memorandum B-98–47 (November, 1998), which discusses who is authorized to sign section D of the CMN.

[90] A supplier who knowlingly and willfully fails to include, in section C, the fee schedule amount and the supplier's charge for the equipment or supplies being furnished may be subject to a CMP up to $1,000 for each form or document so distributed. *See* 42 U.S.C. 1395m(j)(2).

[91] Physicians or persons authorized to sign section D (*see* note 89), should only sign CMNs in which sections A-C are completed and correct. Signature and date stamps are not acceptable.*See Medicare Carriers Manual*, section 3312.

- Does not alter or add any information on the CMN after receiving the completed and signed CMN from the physician or other authorized person;[92]
- Does not sign the CMN for the treating physician or other authorized person;
- Does not urge physicians or other authorized persons to order equipment or supplies that exceed what is reasonable and necessary for the patient;
- Does not deliver an item that requires a written order from the treating physician or other authorized person prior to receiving the written order;[93]
- Does not submit a claim for DMEPOS items or services prior to receiving a written order or CMN from the treating physician or other authorized person;
- Does not submit a claim for DMEPOS items or services until the CMN is properly and correctly completed by the treating physician or other authorized person;
- Maintains completed and signed CMNs in its files;
- Consults with the treating physician or other authorized person who signed the CMN when there is a question on the order;
- Properly complete sections A and C of the CMN and then forward the CMN to the treating physician or other authorized person for his/her review, information, and signature; and
- Only submit claims for services that the treating physician or other authorized person attests in section D are ordered and medically necessary for the patient.

d. Billing

The DMEPOS supplier should provide in its written policies and procedures that it will only submit to Medicare or other Federal, State or private payor health care plans claims that are properly completed, accurate, and correctly identify the item or service ordered by the treating physician or other authorized person and furnished to the patient. Also, prior to submitting the claim, the DMEPOS supplier should take all reasonable steps to ensure the item or service being claimed was provided, covered, reasonable and necessary.

---

[92] There have been many investigations centering on DMEPOS suppliers who alter information in order to affect their reimbursement (*e.g.*, altering diagnosis code, altering HCPCS code of service provided).

[93] *See* 42 U.S.C. 1395m(a)(11)(B).*See also* 42 CFR 410.38.

The written policies and procedures should also clarify that a DMEPOS supplier cannot submit bills or receive payment for drugs used in conjunction with DMEPOS, unless the DMEPOS supplier is licensed to dispense the drug. [94]

e. Selection of HCPCS Codes

The DMEPOS supplier's written policies and procedures should state that only the HCPCS code that most accurately describes the item or service ordered and provided should be billed. The OIG views knowing "upcoding" (*i.e.*, the selection of a code to maximize reimbursement when such a code is not the most appropriate descriptor of the service) as raising, among other things, false claims issues under the Civil False Claims Act. [95] To ensure code accuracy, the OIG recommends that the DMEPOS supplier include a requirement in its policies and procedures that the codes be reviewed (random sample or certain codes) by individuals with technical expertise in coding before claims containing such codes are submitted to the affected payor. If a DMEPOS supplier has questions regarding the appropriate code to be used, it should contact the Statistical Analysis Durable Medical Equipment Carrier's (SADMERC) HCPCS coding help line. [96]

f. Valid Supplier Numbers

The DMEPOS supplier should ensure that appropriate personnel are knowledgeable in (1) completing the HCFA 855S supplier application; [97] and (2) complying with the Federal requirements of 42 CFR

[94] *See* Medicare Program Memoranda B-98–6 (February, 1998) and B-98–18 (May, 1998).

[95] *See* 31 U.S.C. 3729, which provides for the imposition of penalties of $5,000 to $10,000 per false claim, plus up to three times the amount of damages suffered by the Federal Government because of the false claim.

[96] The phone number for the SADMERC's HCPCS coding help line is 803–736–6809. The hours of operation are Monday through Friday from 9:00 am to 4:00 pm, EST. Based on the information provided by the DMEPOS supplier, the SADMERC will aid the DMEPOS supplier in choosing the most accurate code for the item or service ordered and supplied. However, the DMEPOS supplier should be aware that assigning a HCPCS code to an item or service does not necessarily guarantee reimbursement.

[97] By signing the certification statement on the enrollment application, the applicant agrees that he/she has read, understood, meets and will continue to meet the supplier standards and will be disenrolled from the program if any standards are not met or violated.

424.57(e) for updating supplier number applications.

The written policies and procedures should state that the DMEPOS supplier should not bill any other Federal, State or private payor health care plan without obtaining the necessary billing numbers and that the billing numbers will be used correctly.[98]

Prior to applying for a valid supplier number, a DMEPOS supplier providing services to Medicare beneficiaries must meet the supplier standards.[99] The DMEPOS supplier should take all affirmative steps to ensure that no claims for Medicare reimbursement are submitted prior to the DMEPOS supplier being issued a valid supplier number by the National Supplier Clearinghouse. A DMEPOS supplier should not have more than one Medicare supplier number unless it is appropriate to identify subsidiary or regional entities under the supplier's ownership or control.[100]

g. Mail Order Suppliers

We recommend that any DMEPOS supplier who engages in the mail order supply business clearly articulate its protocol for this segment of its business in the company's written policies and procedures.

Mail order supplies should only be delivered in accordance with the treating physician's or other authorized person's orders. Regularly shipping supplies without such orders may lead to providing supplies substantially in excess of the patient's needs.[101] We also recommend that the supplier utilize a tracking system so it will be able to determine whether or not the patient received the supplies and will be able to track the location of an item or supply at any given time.

h. Assignment

If a DMEPOS supplier accepts Medicare assignment, its written policies and procedures should state that it will not charge Medicare beneficiaries more than the amounts allowed under the Medicare fee schedule, including coinsurance and deductibles. If the beneficiary pays the DMEPOS supplier prior to the DMEPOS supplier submit-

---

[98] E.g., if a DMEPOS supplier has more than one location, the supplier number of the location that filled the physician's or other authorized person's order will be used on the claim form.

[99] *See* 42 CFR 424.57.

[100] *See* 42 U.S.C. 1395m(j)(1)(D).

[101] *See* note 44.

ting the claim, the DMEPOS supplier should ensure it is not charging the beneficiary more than the coinsurance on the allowed amount under the fee schedule. In the event that the DMEPOS supplier collects excess payments from a Medicare beneficiary, it should have mechanisms in place to promptly refund the overpayment to the beneficiary. The DMEPOS supplier should be knowledgeable about the Medicare rules and instructions for accepting assignment and receiving direct payment from beneficiaries for items or services.

If a DMEPOS supplier chooses not to accept Medicare assignment, it is still responsible for submitting claims to Medicare on behalf of beneficiaries.[102]

If the DMEPOS supplier chooses to utilize a billing agent, the DMEPOS supplier should ensure it is complying with all of the relevant statutes and requirements governing such an arrangement.[103] The OIG strongly recommends that the DMEPOS supplier coordinate closely with the billing company to establish compliance responsibilities. Once the responsibilities have been clearly delineated, they should be formalized in the written contract between the DMEPOS supplier and the billing agent. The OIG recommends that the contract enumerate those functions that are shared responsibilities and those that are the sole responsibility of either the billing agent or the DMEPOS supplier.

i. Liability Issues

The OIG recommends that DMEPOS suppliers avoid submitting claims for items or services that the DMEPOS supplier believes are not covered by Medicare. However, HCFA does permit a DMEPOS supplier to submit a claim for an item or service that the DMEPOS supplier believes is not covered if (i) the beneficiary insists that the DMEPOS supplier submit the claim, and (ii) the DMEPOS supplier notes on the claims its belief that the service is noncovered and that it is being submitted at the beneficiary's insistence (*e.g.*, submitted for a Medicare determination of coverage and/or to obtain a denial notice in order to bill other insurers).[104]

---

[102] *See* 42 U.S.C. 1395w-4(g)(4).

[103] *See* 42 U.S.C. 1395u(b)(6); 42 CFR 424.73; *Medicare Carriers Manual*, section 3060. *See also* OIG Ad. Op. 98–1 (1998) and OIG Ad. Op. 98–4 (1998).

[104] *See Medicare Carriers Manual*, section 3043.

A DMEPOS supplier or Medicare beneficiary is not liable for payment on assigned claims where the beneficiary did not know, and could not reasonably have been expected to know, that the payment for such services would not be made.[105] However, when the DMEPOS supplier knew, or could have been expected to know, the items or services would be denied, the liability for improperly paid items or services rests with the DMEPOS supplier.[106]

In order to protect itself from financial responsibility in such situations (*i.e.*, situations in which the beneficiary is insisting that a claim be submitted to Medicare notwithstanding the DMEPOS supplier's belief that Medicare does not cover the service), the DMEPOS supplier must inform the patient prior to furnishing the item or service of the DMEPOS supplier's belief that the claim to Medicare will be denied. In this situation, the DMEPOS supplier should ask the patient to sign a written notice.[107] The written notice must be in writing, must clearly identify the particular item or service, must state that the payment for the particular item or service likely will be denied, and must give the reason(s) for the belief that payment is likely to be denied. It is the beneficiary's decision whether or not to sign the written notice. If the beneficiary does sign the written notice, the DMEPOS supplier should: (1) include the appropriate modifier on the claim form; (2) maintain the written notice in its files; and (3) be able to produce the written notice to the DMERC, upon request.

If the DMEPOS supplier improperly bills the beneficiary, Medicare will indemnify the beneficiary for any payments the beneficiary made to the DMEPOS supplier, and collect the indemnification amount from the DMEPOS supplier as an overpayment.

Routine notices to beneficiaries that do no more than state that denial of payment is possible are not considered acceptable evidence of written notice. Notices should not be given to beneficiaries unless there is some genuine doubt regarding the likelihood of payment as evidenced by the reasons stated on the written notice. Giving notice for all claims, items or services is not an acceptable practice.

The OIG recommends that the DMEPOS supplier include the foregoing liability issues in its written policies and procedures.

---

[105] *See* 42 U.S.C. 1395pp.

[106] Id.

[107] *SeeMedicare Carriers Manual*, section 7300.5.

j. Routine Waiver of Deductibles and Coinsurance

Routine waivers of deductibles and coinsurance may result in false claims, CMPs for inducements to beneficiaries, and violations of the anti-kickback statute or similar Federal or State statute or regulations.[108] In addition to the potential problems regarding kickbacks, false claims, and CMPs, the OIG has programmatic concerns when DMEPOS suppliers routinely waive deductibles and coinsurance. When DMEPOS suppliers forgive financial obligations for reasons other than genuine financial hardship of a particular patient, they may be inducing the patient to use items or services that are unnecessary, simply because they are free. Such usage may also lead to overutilization. DMEPOS suppliers are permitted to waive the Medicare coinsurance amounts for cases of financial need.[109] We recommend that the DMEPOS supplier develop and maintain written criteria documenting its policy for determining financial need and consistently apply this criteria to all cases.[110] A good faith effort must be made to collect deductibles and coinsurance.[111]

The DMEPOS supplier's written policies and procedures should state that it will not routinely waive deductibles and coinsurance for Medicare beneficiaries. The OIG recommends that such policies and procedures should include, but not be limited to, statements that DMEPOS supplier personnel are prohibited from: advertising an intent to waive deductibles or coinsurance for Medicare beneficiaries; advertising an intent to discount services for Medicare beneficiaries; or giving unsolicited advice to Medicare beneficiaries that they need not pay.

---

[108] *See* 59 FR 31157 (December 19, 1994) or the OIG website at http://www.dhhs.gov/progorg/oig for the OIG Special Fraud Alert on Medicare Deductibles and Copayments. *See also* 31 U.S.C. 3729–3733; 42 U.S.C. 1320a-7a(a)(5); 42 U.S.C. 1320a-7b.

[109] *See Medicare Carriers Manual*, section 5520.

[110] What constitutes "financial need" varies depending on the circumstances. However, the OIG believes it is important that a DMEPOS supplier make determinations of financial need on an individualized, case by case, basis in accordance with a reasonable set of income guidelines uniformly applied in all cases. The guidelines should be based on objective criteria and appropriate for the applicable locality. It is not appropriate to apply inflated income guidelines that result in waivers of copayments for persons not in genuine financial need.

[111] *See* 42 CFR 413.80; See *Provider Reimbursement Manual,* Part I, sections 308 and 310.

k. Capped Rentals

The DMEPOS supplier's written policies and procedures should address Government and private payor requirements when providing rental equipment to beneficiaries (*e.g.*, the purchase option[112] and servicing and maintenance[113]). The DMEPOS supplier must offer a purchase option to beneficiaries during the 10th continuous rental month.[114] The DMEPOS supplier should clearly, accurately, and non-deceptively discuss the pros and cons of the different options with the beneficiary. If the beneficiary does not accept the purchase option, the DMEPOS supplier must continue to provide the item. After the 15th continuous month of receiving rental payments from Medicare, providing the item or service continues to be medically necessary, the DMEPOS supplier must continue to provide the item without charge to the beneficiary or Medicare.

However, the DMEPOS supplier may submit additional claims for the maintenance and servicing fees associated with the rental item.[115] The DMEPOS supplier should ensure it is performing basic safety and operational function checks after use by each patient, and is performing routine and preventative maintenance on equipment. The DMEPOS supplier must ensure it has qualified staff or contractors to service, set up, and instruct the patient on the proper use of the equipment. The DMEPOS supplier should ensure it maintains current service manuals for all the equipment it supplies. In addition, the OIG recommends that the DMEPOS supplier's policies and procedures establish an internal control system that allows the DMEPOS supplier to track the location of each piece of equipment at any given time.

The policies and procedures should also address the guidelines for determining continuous use and criteria for a new rental period.[116] If a beneficiary dies during a rental period, the DMEPOS supplier may receive the entire monthly rental payment.[117] However, if the DMEPOS supplier continues to bill for the item because it did not receive notice of the beneficiary's death until the following month,

---

[112] *See* 42 CFR 414.229(d).

[113] *See* 42 CFR 414.229(e).

[114] DMEPOS suppliers must offer beneficiaries the option of purchasing power-driven wheelchairs at the time the DMEPOS supplier first furnishes the item *See*42 CFR 414.229(d)(1).

[115] *See* 42 CFR 414.229(e).

[116] *See* 42 CFR 414.230.

[117] *See Medicare Carriers Manual*, section 4105.3.

any payments received for rental items the month after the beneficiary dies are considered an overpayment and must promptly be refunded. The DMEPOS supplier should create internal mechanisms to ensure the correct rental month appears on the claim and the correct modifier is used.

In addition, the DMEPOS supplier should ensure it is not submitting claims for rental equipment when the beneficiary is residing in an institution. The OIG is aware that some DMEPOS suppliers bring DMEPOS items to beneficiaries residing in an institution, just prior to the beneficiary's discharge, in order to train the beneficiary on how to use the item or to fit the item for the beneficiary. Once the DMEPOS supplier has trained or fitted the beneficiary, the DMEPOS supplier should take the item and deliver it to the beneficiary's home on the date of discharge. As a result, the DMEPOS supplier should file the claim for this item with the date of delivery/date of service as the date the beneficiary is discharged from the institution. If the DMEPOS supplier delivers the item to the beneficiary in the institution prior to the beneficiary's discharge to be used by the beneficiary while in the institution, the item should be included in the institution's cost and the DMEPOS supplier should not submit the claim. The DMEPOS supplier may not submit the claim prior to the beneficiary's date of discharge.

l. ZX Modifier

The ZX modifier is used on the claim form to indicate that the DMEPOS supplier is maintaining medical necessity documentation in its files. Such documentation only needs to be submitted to the DMERC upon request.

The DMEPOS supplier should create internal mechanisms to ensure the proper use of the ZX modifier. Improper use of the modifier may result in the submission of false claims. The OIG recommends that the DMEPOS supplier's written policies and procedures address the DMEPOS supplier's protocol for using the ZX modifier.[118]

m. Cover Letters

Cover letters are commonly used by the DMEPOS supplier as a method of communication between the DMEPOS supplier and the treating physician or other authorized person. The cover letter is not

[118] *See* relevant DMERC supplier manual(s) for guidelines on proper use.

a form required or regulated by the Government. As a result, the DMERCs do not base Medicare denials solely on what may be considered inappropriate use of cover letters. However, the OIG is concerned that cover letters may influence or direct a physician's or other authorized person's answers on the CMN, particularly the questions relating to the patient's medical condition.[119] It is the treating physician's or other authorized person's responsibility to determine both the medical need for, and the utilization of, health care services. The OIG encourages the DMEPOS supplier to include language in its cover letter to remind treating physicians and other authorized persons of their responsibilities in properly completing CMNs.

n. Communication

The OIG suggests that the DMEPOS supplier create mechanisms that increase the communication among treating physicians or other authorized persons who refer business to the DMEPOS supplier, the patients, and the DMEPOS supplier. We recommend that such mechanisms be included in the DMEPOS supplier's written policies and procedures. Such mechanisms may include: (i) the DMEPOS supplier periodically calling the patient to ensure the equipment is still being used and is operating properly; or (ii) periodically calling the treating physician to ensure the provided items continue to be medically necessary for a patient.

In addition, we recommend the DMEPOS supplier create mechanisms to ensure communication between different departments (*e.g.*, sales and billing) in order to prevent the filing of incorrect claims.

o. Oxygen and Oxygen Equipment

The OIG recommends that the written policies and procedures for DMEPOS suppliers furnishing oxygen state that the DMEPOS supplier will ensure that initial claims for oxygen therapy include the written results of an arterial blood gas study or oximetry test (on the CMN) that has been ordered and evaluated by the patient's treating physician. Further, the written policies and procedures should provide for the DMEPOS supplier to maintain such test results and any

[119] Encouraging physicians or other authorized persons to order unwanted items or supplies may result in submitting claims for items or services that are not reasonable or necessary. The OIG is aware of instances where the DMEPOS supplier has copied the CMN, complieted section B of the copy, and used this completed copy as its cover letter to physicians.

other independent diagnostic treatment facility (IDTF) documents supporting the patient's medical necessity for the oxygen. The OIG recommends that the DMEPOS supplier have the IDTFs, from which it receives test results, submit, all raw test results to the treating physician for the physician's benefit, and not just a summary of the results. The written policies and procedures should provide that a DMEPOS supplier is not qualified to conduct the blood gas study or to prescribe the oxygen therapy. [120]

The OIG also recommends, for patient safety purposes, that the rental of oxygen include established maintenance safeguards and that steps are taken to ensure the equipment is properly maintained, as maintenance is included in the rental price of the equipment.

When submitting an oxygen or oxygen equipment claim for reimbursement, the DMEPOS supplier must ensure it is complying with the payment rules. [121]

4. Anti-Kickback and Self-Referral Concerns

The DMEPOS supplier should have policies and procedures in place with respect to compliance with Federal and State laws, including the anti-kickback statute, as well as the Stark physician self-referral law. [122] Such policies should provide that:

- All of the DMEPOS supplier's contracts and arrangements with actual or potential referral sources (*e.g.*, physicians) are reviewed by counsel and comply with all applicable statutes and regulations, including the anti-kickback statute and the Stark physician self-referral law; [123]

---

[120] *See Coverage Issues Manual,* section 60–4.

[121] *See* 42 CFR 414.226.

[122] Towards this end, the DMEPOS supplier should, among other things, obtain copies of all relevant OIG regulations, Special Fraud Alerts, and Advisory Opinions (these documents are located on the Internet at http://www.dhhs.gov/progorg/oig), and ensure that the DMEPOS supplier's policies reflect the guidance provided by the OIG. *See* 42 U.S.C. 1395nn(a) for the Stark physician referral laws. *See also* 42 U.S.C. 1320a-7b for prohibited activities under the anti-kickback statute.

[123] If the DMEPOS supplier questions an arrangement into which it may enter, it should consider asking the OIG for an Advisory Opionion regarding the anti-kickback statute of HCFA for an Advisory Opinion regarding Stark. *See* 62 FR 7350 (February 19, 1997) and 63 FR 38,311 (July 16, 1998) for instructions on how to submit an Advisory Opinion to the OIG. These

- The DMEPOS supplier will not submit or cause to be submitted to health care programs claims for patients who were referred to the DMEPOS supplier pursuant to contracts or financial arrangements that were designed to induce such referrals in violation of the anti-kickback statute or similar Federal or State statute or regulation or that otherwise violate the Stark physician self-referral law;
  [Page 36380]
- A DMEPOS supplier does not offer a physician or other referral source more than fair market value for space rented to store items or supplies (*i.e.*, consignment closet); and
- The DMEPOS supplier does not offer or provide gifts, free services, or other incentives or things of value to patients, relatives of patients, physicians, home health agencies, nursing homes, hospitals, contractors, assisted living facilities, or other potential referral sources for the purpose of inducing referrals in violation of the anti-kickback statute or similar Federal or State statute or regulation. [124]

Further, the OIG recommends that the written policies and procedures should specifically reference and take into account the OIG's safe harbor regulations, which describe those payment practices that are immune from criminal and administrative prosecution under the anti-kickback statute. [125]

The OIG believes all DMEPOS suppliers, regardless of size, should be concerned with potential anti-kickback and Stark violations. As a result, all DMEPOS suppliers should be knowledgeable about, and compliant with, the anti-kickback statute, the Stark physician self-referral law and other relevant Federal and State statutes or regulations.

Although all DMEPOS suppliers are responsible for ensuring compliance with these provisions, the OIG recognizes that the small DMEPOS supplier may not have the resources to implement the suggestions in this section to the same extent as a large DMEPOS supplier. Therefore, the smaller DMEPOS supplier may need to

---

instructions are also located on the Internet at http://www.dhhs.gov/progorg/oig. See 63 FR 1645 (January 9, 1998) on how to submit an Advisory Opinion to HCFA.

124 *See* 42 U.S.C. 1320a-7a(a)(5), which provides for CMPs for improper inducements to beneficiaries.

125 *See* 42 CFR 1001.952. Simply because an arrangement does not meet a safe harbor does not necessarily mean it is illegal.

employ a slightly different mechanism to ensure compliance. For example, the small DMEPOS supplier may want to choose a sample of contracts or financial arrangements to review on a periodic basis.

5. Marketing

Where marketing is permitted, the DMEPOS supplier's compliance program should require honest, straightforward, fully informative and non-deceptive marketing. It is in the best interest of patients, DMEPOS suppliers, physicians and health care programs that physicians or other persons authorized to order DMEPOS fully understand the services offered by the DMEPOS supplier, the items or services that will be provided when ordered, and the financial consequences for Medicare as well as other payors for the items or services ordered. The OIG recommends that if the DMEPOS supplier services a large number of non-English speaking patients, it should ensure that its marketing materials are available in those other languages. The DMEPOS supplier's written policies and procedures should ensure that its marketing information is clear, correct, and fully informative.

Salespeople must not offer physicians, patients or other potential referral sources incentives, in cash or in kind, for their business.[126] Similarly, they must not engage in any marketing activity that either explicitly or implicitly implies that Medicare beneficiaries are not obligated to pay their coinsurance or can receive "free" services.[127] In addition, DMEPOS suppliers must not promote items or services to patients or physicians that are not reasonable or necessary for the treatment of the individual patient. The OIG suggests that the DMEPOS supplier's written policies and procedures create internal mechanisms to avoid these situations.

With respect to marketing and sales, the OIG has a longstanding concern that percentage compensation arrangements for sales and marketing personnel may increase the risk of such persons violating the anti-kickback statute.[128] The OIG recommends that the DMEPOS supplier monitor its sales representatives on a regular basis (e.g., rotate sales staff or send a sales manager on some sales calls).

---

[126] *See* anti-kickback statute discussion in section II.A.4.

[127] *See* discussion in section II.A.3.j.

[128] *See* e.g., 42 U.S.C. 1320a-7b(B); OIG Ad. Op. 98–10 (1998); section II.A.4.

The DMEPOS suppliers are prohibited from making unsolicited telephone contacts to Medicare beneficiaries.[129] We suggest that the DMEPOS supplier's written policies and procedures reflect this prohibition.

The DMEPOS suppliers are also prohibited from using symbols, emblems, or names in reference to Social Security or Medicare in a manner that they know or should know would convey the false impression that an item is approved, endorsed, or authorized by the Social Security Administration, HCFA, or the Department of Health and Human Services or that the supplier has some connection with, or authorization from, any of these agencies.[130]

The OIG believes marketing strategies employed by all DMEPOS suppliers, regardless of size, should be clear, correct, honest, straightforward, non-deceptive and fully informative. In addition, all DMEPOS suppliers should inform their sales people of potential anti-kickback concerns, the telemarketing law, and the prohibition on inappropriately using references to Social Security and Medicare. Although the small DMEPOS supplier may not have extensive written policies and procedures, every DMEPOS supplier should ensure that its employees are clear on what is permitted and prohibited with regard to marketing.

6. Retention of Records

The DMEPOS supplier's compliance program should provide for the implementation of a records system. The DMEPOS supplier should ensure that records are maintained for the length of time required by Federal and State law and private payors, or by the DMEPOS supplier's record retention policies, whichever is longer. This system should establish policies and procedures regarding the creation, distribution, retention, storage, retrieval, and destruction of documents.[131] The three types of documents developed under this system should include: (1) all records and documentation (*e.g.*, billing and claims documentation) required either by Federal or State law and the program requirements of Federal, State, and private health plans; (2) records listing the persons responsible for implementing each part of the compliance program; and (3) all records necessary to protect the integrity of the DMEPOS supplier's compli-

---

[129] *See* 42 U.S.C. 1395m(a)(17), Pub.L. 103–432, section 132(a).

[130] *See* 42 U.S.C. 1320b-10.

[131] This records system should be tailored to fit the individual needs and financial resources of the DMEPOS supplier.

ance process and confirm the effectiveness of the program.[132] The documentation necessary to satisfy the third requirement includes, but is not limited to: evidence of adequate employee training; reports from the DMEPOS supplier's hotline; results of any investigation conducted as a consequence of a hotline call; modifications to the compliance program; self-disclosure; all written notifications to physicians and payors;[133] and the results of the DMEPOS supplier's auditing and monitoring efforts.

All DMEPOS suppliers, regardless of size, must retain documents required by the health plans in which they participate. In case of a future Government investigation, the OIG recommends that all DMEPOS suppliers retain documents relating to the implementation of their compliance programs.

7. Compliance as an Element of a Performance Plan

The DMEPOS supplier's compliance program should require that the promotion of, and adherence to, the elements of the compliance program be a factor in evaluating the performance of all employees. Employees should be periodically trained in new compliance policies and procedures. In addition, all managers and supervisors should:

- Discuss with all supervised employees and relevant contractors the compliance policies and legal requirements applicable to their function;
- Inform all supervised personnel that strict compliance with these policies and requirements is a condition of employment; and
- Disclose to all supervised personnel that the DMEPOS supplier will take disciplinary action up to and including termination for violation of these policies or requirements.

In addition to making performance of these duties an element in evaluations, the compliance officer or DMEPOS supplier management should include a policy that managers and supervisors will be sanctioned for failing to instruct adequately their subordinates or for failing to detect noncompliance with applicable policies and legal requirements, where reasonable diligence on the part of the man-

[132] The creation and retention of such documents and reports may raise a variety of legal issues, such as patient privacy and confidentiality. These issues are best discussed with legal counsel.

[133] This should include notifications regarding inappropriate claims and overpayments.

ager or supervisor would have led to the discovery of any problems or violations.

The OIG believes all DMEPOS suppliers, regardless of size, should ensure their employees understand the importance of compliance. If the small DMEPOS supplier does not have a formal performance evaluation structure, it should informally convey the employee's compliance responsibilities and the importance of these responsibilities.

B. Designation of a Compliance Officer and a Compliance Committee

1. Compliance Officer

Every DMEPOS supplier should designate a compliance officer to serve as the focal point for compliance activities. The compliance officer should be a person of high integrity. This responsibility may be the individual's sole duty or added to other management responsibilities, depending upon the size and resources of the DMEPOS supplier and the complexity of the task. When a compliance officer has other duties, the other duties should not be in conflict with the compliance goals. [134]

Designating a compliance officer with the appropriate authority is critical to the success of the program, necessitating the appointment of a high-level official in the DMEPOS supplier with direct access to the DMEPOS supplier's owner(s), president or CEO, governing body, all other senior management, and legal counsel. [135] The compliance officer should be highly enough placed in the company so that he or she can exercise independent judgment without fear of reprisal, and so that employees will know that bringing a problem to that person's attention is not a wasted exercise. The compliance officer should

---

[134] E.g., companies should not choose a sales manager who may be pressured to achieve high sales, which might result in a conflict with compliance goals.

[135] The OIG believes that it is not advisable for the compliance function to be subordinate to the DMEPOS supplier's general counsel, comptroller or similar DMEPOS supplier financial officer. Free standing compliance functions help to ensure independent and objective legal reviews and financial analyses of the institution's compliance efforts and activities. By separating the compliance function from the key management positions of general counsel or chief financial officer (where the size and structure of the DMEPOS supplier make this a feasible option), a system of checks and balances is established to more effectively achieve the goals of the compliance program.

have sufficient funding and staff to fully perform his or her responsibilities. Coordination and communication are the key functions of the compliance officer with regard to planning, implementing, and monitoring the compliance program.

The compliance officer's primary responsibilities should include:

- Overseeing and monitoring the implementation of the compliance program; [136]
- Reporting on a regular basis to the DMEPOS supplier's owner (s), governing body, CEO, president, and compliance committee (if applicable) on the progress of implementation, and assisting these components in establishing methods to improve the DMEPOS supplier's efficiency and quality of services, and to reduce the DMEPOS supplier's vulnerability to fraud, abuse, and waste;
- Periodically revising the program in light of changes in the organization's needs, and in the statutes, rules, regulations, and requirements of Federal, State, and private payor health care plans;
- Reviewing employees' certifications that they have received, read, understood, and will abide by the standards of conduct;
- Developing, coordinating, and participating in a multifaceted educational and training program that focuses on the elements of the compliance program, and seeks to ensure that all appropriate employees and managers are knowledgeable of, and comply with, pertinent Federal, State and private payor health care program requirements;
- Ensuring independent contractors and agents who provide services (*e.g.*, billing companies, delivery services and sources of referrals, i.e., physicians and others) to the DMEPOS supplier are aware of the requirements of the DMEPOS supplier's compliance program with respect to coverage, billing, marketing, and kickbacks, among other things;
- Coordinating personnel issues with the DMEPOS supplier's Human Resources/Personnel office (or its equivalent). The OIG recommends that the DMEPOS supplier check the List of

[136] For DMEPOS supplier chains, the OIG encourages coordination with each DMEPOS supplier location through the use of a headquarter's compliance officer, communicating with parallel positions in each facility or regional office, as appropriate.

Excluded Individuals/Entities,[137] and the General Services Administration's List of Parties Excluded from Federal Procurement and Nonprocurement Programs[138] to ensure employees and independent contractors have not been excluded or debarred from participating in Federal programs.[139] Depending upon State requirements or DMEPOS supplier policy, the Compliance Officer may also conduct a criminal background check of employees;

- Assisting the DMEPOS supplier's financial management in coordinating internal compliance review and monitoring activities, including annual or periodic reviews of departments;
[Page 36382]
- Independently investigating and acting on matters related to compliance, including the flexibility to design and coordinate internal investigations (*e.g.*, responding to reports of problems or suspected violations) and any resulting corrective action (e.g., making necessary improvements to DMEPOS supplier policies and practices, taking appropriate disciplinary action, etc.) with all DMEPOS supplier departments, independent contractors, and health care professionals;
- Developing policies and programs that encourage managers and employees to report suspected fraud and other improprieties without fear of retaliation; and
- Continuing the momentum of the compliance program and the accomplishment of its objectives long after the initial years of

---

[137] The List of Excluded Individuals/Entities is an OIG-produced report available on the Internet at http://www.dhhs.gov/progorg/oig. It is updated on a regular basis to reflect the status of individuals and entities who have been excluded from participation in all Federal health care programs (individuals/entities excluded before August 5, 1997 were only excluded from participation in Medicare, Medicaid, Title V and Title XX programs). The DMEPOS supplier can download the List of Excluded Individuals/Entities and the subsequent monthly exclusion and reinstatement supplements or can use the online search feature.

[138] The List of Parties Excluded from Federal Procurment and Nonprocurement programs is a GSA-produced report available on the Internet at http://www.arnet.bov/epls.

[139] The OIG recognizes that a DMEPOS supplier cannot make medical necessity determinations and may not be aware when a patient's condition changes. However, a DMEPOS supplier should be aware that if it submits a claim in which an excluded physician provided the referral, Medicare will deny payment.

implementation.[140]

The compliance officer must have the authority to review all documents and other information that are relevant to compliance activities, including, but not limited to, patient records (where appropriate), billing records, and DMEPOS supplier records concerning the marketing efforts of the DMEPOS supplier and the DMEPOS supplier's arrangements with other parties, including employees, home health agencies, skilled nursing facilities, and treating physicians or other authorized persons. This policy enables the compliance officer to review contracts and obligations (seeking the advice of legal counsel, where appropriate) that may contain referral and payment provisions that could violate the anti-kickback statute, as well as the Stark physician self-referral prohibition or other statutory or regulatory requirements.

In addition, the compliance officer should be copied on the results of all internal audit reports and work closely with key managers to identify aberrant trends in the coding and billing areas. The compliance officer should ascertain patterns that require a change in policy and forward these issues to the compliance committee to remedy the problem. The compliance officer should have full authority to stop the processing of claims that he or she believes are problematic until such time as the issue in question has been resolved.

The OIG believes all DMEPOS suppliers, regardless of size, should have a compliance officer or contact who possesses a high degree of integrity, is knowledgeable about the rules, regulations, and policies under which the DMEPOS supplier operates and has sufficient authority to exercise independent judgment. A small DMEPOS supplier may not have the need or the resources to hire/appoint a full time compliance officer. However, each DMEPOS supplier should have a person in its organization (this person may have other functional responsibilities) who can oversee the DMEPOS supplier's compliance with respect to applicable statutes, rules, regulations, and policies. The structure and comprehensiveness of

---

[140] Periodic on-site visits of DMEPOS supplier operations, bulletins with compliance updates and reminders, distribution of audiotapes or videotapes on different risk areas, lectures at management and employee meetings, circulation of recent health care articles covering fraud and abuse, and innovative changes to compliance training are various examples of approaches and techniques the compliance officer can employ for the purpose of ensuring continued interest in the compliance program and the DMEPOS supplier's commitment to its policies and principles.

the DMEPOS supplier's compliance program will help determine the responsibilities of each individual compliance officer.

2. Compliance Committee

The OIG recommends, where feasible, that a compliance committee be established to advise the compliance officer and assist in the implementation of the compliance program.[141] When assembling a team of people to serve as the DMEPOS supplier's compliance committee, the DMEPOS supplier should include individuals with a variety of skills.[142] The OIG strongly recommends that the compliance officer manage the compliance committee. Once a DMEPOS supplier chooses the people that will accept the responsibilities vested in members of the compliance committee, the DMEPOS supplier must train these individuals on the policies and procedures of the compliance program, as well as how to discharge their duties.

The committee's responsibilities should include:

- Analyzing the organization's regulatory environment, the legal requirements with which it must comply,[143] and specific risk areas;

---

[141] The compliance committee benefits from having the perspectives of individuals with varying responsibilities in the organization, such as operations, billing, coding, marketing, and human resources, as well as employees and managers of key operating units. These individuals should have the requisite seniority and comprehensive experience within their respective departments to implement any necessary changes to the DMEPOS supplier's policies and procedures as recommended by the committee. A compliance committee for a DMEPOS supplier that is part of another organization (*e.g.*, home health agency) might benefit from the participation of officials from other departments in the organization, such as the accounting and billing departments.

[142] A DMEPOS supplier should expect its compliance committee members and compliance officer to demonstrate high integrity, good judgment, assertiveness, and an approachable demeanor, while eliciting the respect and trust of employees of the DMEPOS supplier. The DMEPOS supplier's compliance committee members should also have significant professional experience working with billing, documentation, and auditing principles.

[143] This includes, but is not limited to, the civil False Claims Act, 31 U.S.C. 3729–3733; the criminal false claims statutes, 18 U.S.C. 287, 1001; the fraud and abuse provisions of the Balanced Budget Act of 1997, Pub.L. 105–33; the Health Insurance Portability and Accountability Act of 1996, Pub.L. 104–191; and compliance with the Medicare supplier standards, 42 CFR 424.57.

- Assessing existing policies and procedures that address these risk areas for possible incorporation into the compliance program;
- Working with appropriate DMEPOS supplier departments to develop standards of conduct and policies and procedures that promote allegiance to the DMEPOS supplier's compliance program;
- Recommending and monitoring, in conjunction with the relevant departments, the development of internal systems and controls to carry out the organization's standards, policies, and procedures as part of its daily operations;[144]
- Determining the appropriate strategy/approach to promote compliance with the program and detection of any potential violations, such as through hotlines and other fraud reporting mechanisms;
- Developing a system to solicit, evaluate, and respond to complaints and problems; and
- Monitoring internal and external audits and investigations for the purpose of identifying troublesome issues and deficient areas experienced by the DMEPOS supplier, and implementing corrective and preventive action.

The committee may also address other functions as the compliance concept becomes part of the overall DMEPOS supplier's operating structure and daily routine.

The compliance committee is an extension of the compliance officer and provides the organization with increased oversight. The OIG recognizes that small DMEPOS suppliers may not have the resources or the need to establish a compliance committee. However, when potential problems are identified, the OIG recommends that the small DMEPOS supplier create a "taskforce," if appropriate, to address the problem. The members of the taskforce may vary depending upon the issue.

---

[144] With respect to national DMEPOS supplier chains, this may include fostering coordination and communication between those employees responsible for compliance at headquarters and those responsible for compliance at the individual supplier branches.

C. Conducting Effective Training and Education

1. Initial Training in Compliance

The proper education and training of corporate officers, managers, employees and the continual retraining of current personnel at all levels, are significant elements of an effective compliance program. In order to ensure the appropriate information is being disseminated to the correct individuals, the training should be separated into sessions. All employees should attend the general session on compliance, and employees whose job primarily focuses on submission of claims for reimbursement, or who are involved in sales and marketing, should receive additional training on these particular subjects. In addition, the OIG recommends that the DMEPOS supplier inform physicians, independent contractors, and significant agents that it has implemented a compliance program.

a. General Sessions

The OIG recommends, as part of its compliance program, that the DMEPOS supplier require all affected personnel to attend training on an annual basis, including appropriate training in Federal and State statutes, regulations and guidelines, HCFA manual instructions, DMERC medical review policies, the policies of private payors, and training in corporate ethics. The general training session should emphasize the DMEPOS supplier's commitment to compliance with these legal requirements and policies.

These training programs should include sessions highlighting the DMEPOS supplier's compliance program, summarizing fraud and abuse statutes and regulations, Federal, State and private payor health care program requirements, claim submission procedures and marketing practices that reflect current legal and program standards. The DMEPOS supplier must take steps to communicate effectively its standards and procedures to all affected employees (*e.g.*, by requiring participation in training programs and disseminating publications that explain specific requirements in a practical manner). [145] DMEPOS suppliers may also wish to offer such training sessions to interested independent contractors and physicians. Managers of specific departments can assist in identifying areas that

[145] OIG publications such as Special Fraud Alerts, audit and inspection reports, and Advisory Opinions, as well as the annual OIG Work Plan, are readily available from the OIG and could be the basis for standards, educational courses and programs.

require training and in carrying out such training. [146] Training New employees should be targeted for training early in their employment. [147]

As part of the initial training, the standards of conduct should be distributed to all employees. [148] At the end of this training session, every employee should be required to sign and date a statement that reflects his or her knowledge of and commitment to the standards of conduct. This attestation should be retained in the employee's personnel file.

Further, to assist in ensuring that employees continuously meet the expected high standards of conduct, any employee handbook delineating or expanding upon these standards should be regularly updated as applicable statutes, regulations and Federal health care program requirements are modified. [149] The DMEPOS supplier should provide an additional attestation in the modified standards that stipulates the employee's knowledge of and commitment to the modifications.

b. Claim Development and Billing Training

In addition to specific training in the risk areas identified in section II.A.2, above, primary training to appropriate corporate officers, managers and other claim development and billing staff should include such topics as:

---

[146] Significant variations in functions and responsibilities of different departments may create the need for training materials that are tailored to the compliance concerns associated with particular operations and duties. instructors may come from outside or inside the organization.

[147] Certain positions, such as those involving developing and submitting claims, as well as sales and marketing, create a greater organizational legal exposure, and therefore require specialized training. The DMEPOS supplier should fill such positions with individuals who have the appropriate educational background, training, experience, and credentials.

[148] Where the DMEPOS supplier has a culturally diverse employee base, the standards of conduct should be translated into other languages and written at appropriate reading levels.

[149] The OIG recognizes that not all standards, policies and procedures need to be communicated to all employees. However, the OIG believes that the bulk of the standards that relate to complying with fraud and abuse laws and other ethical areas should be addressed and made part of all employees' training. A DMEPOS supplier should determine the additional training to provide categories of employees based upon their job responsibilites.

- Specific Government and private payor reimbursement principles;[150]
- Providing and billing DMEPOS items or services without proper authorization;
- Proper documentation of services rendered, including the correct application of official ICD-9 and HCPCS coding rules and guidelines;
- Improper alterations to documentation (*e.g.*, patient records, CMNs);
- Compliance with the Federal, State and private payor supplier standards; and
- Duty to report misconduct.

Clarifying and emphasizing these areas of concern through training and educational programs are particularly relevant to a DMEPOS supplier's billing and coding personnel, in that the pressure to meet business goals may render employees vulnerable to engaging in prohibited practices.

c. Sales and Marketing Training

In addition to specific training in the risk areas identified in section II.A.2, above, primary training to sales and marketing personnel should include such topics as:

- General prohibition on paying or receiving renumeration to induce referrals;
- Routine waiver of deductibles and/or coinsurance;
- Disguising referral fees as salaries;
- Offering free items or services to induce referrals;
- High pressure marketing of noncovered or unnecessary services;
- Improper patient solicitation; and
- Duty to report misconduct.

Clarifying and emphasizing these areas of concern through training and educational programs are particularly relevant to a DMEPOS supplier's sales and marketing personnel, in that the pressure to meet business goals may render employees vulnerable to engaging in prohibited practices.

[150] Government, in this context, includes the appropriate Medicare DMERC(s).

The OIG believes all DMEPOS suppliers, regardless of size, should ensure that their employees are well trained and are abiding by the applicable statutes, regulations, and policies. Each employee should know the procedures or who to consult when confronted with a particular situation.

2. Format of the Training Program

The OIG suggests that all relevant levels of personnel be made part of various educational and training programs of the DMEPOS supplier.[151] Employees should be required to have a minimum number of educational hours per year, as appropriate, as part of their employment obligations.[152] For example, as discussed above, employees involved in billing functions should be required to attend periodic training in applicable reimbursement coverage and documentation of records.[153]

A variety of teaching methods, such as interactive training and training in several different languages, particularly where a DMEPOS supplier has a culturally diverse staff, should be implemented so that all affected employees are knowledgeable about the DMEPOS supplier's standards of conduct and procedures for alerting senior management to problems and concerns.[154] Targeted training should be provided to corporate officers, managers and other employees whose actions affect the accuracy of the claims submitted to the Government, such as employees involved in the coding, billing, sales,

---

[151] In addition, where feasible, the OIG recommends that a DMEPOS supplier afford outside contractors and its physician clients the opportunity to participate in the DMEPOS supplier's compliance training and educational programs, or develop their own programs that complement the DMEPOS supplier's standards of conduct, compliance requirements and other rules and practices.

[152] Currently, the OIG is monitoring a significant number of corporate integrity agreements that require many of these training elements. The OIG usually requires a minimum of one to three hours annually for basic training in compliance areas. Additional training is required for specially fields such as billing, coding, sales and marketing.

[153] Appropriate coding and billing depends upon the quality and completeness of documentation. Therefore, the OIG believes that the DMEPOS supplier must foster an environment where interactive communication is encouraged.

[154] Post training tests can be used to assess the success of training provided and employee comprehension of the DMEPOS supplier's policies and procedures.

and marketing processes. All training materials should be designed to take into account the skills, knowledge and experience of the individual trainees. Given the complexity and interdependent relationships of many departments, it is important for the compliance officer to supervise and coordinate the training program.

The OIG recommends that attendance and participation in training programs be made a condition of continued employment and that failure to comply with training requirements should result in disciplinary action, including possible termination, when such failure is serious. Adherence to the provisions of the compliance program, such as training requirements, should be a factor in the annual evaluation of each employee. The DMEPOS supplier should retain adequate records of its training of employees, including attendance logs and material distributed at training sessions.

The OIG recognizes the format of the training program will vary depending upon the resources of the DMEPOS supplier. For example, a small DMEPOS supplier may want to create a video for each type of training session so new employees can receive training in a timely manner.

3. Continuing Education on Compliance Issues

It is essential that compliance issues remain at the forefront of the DMEPOS supplier's priorities. The OIG recommends that the DMEPOS supplier's compliance program address the need for periodic professional education courses for DMEPOS supplier personnel. In particular, the DMEPOS supplier should ensure that coding personnel receive annual professional training on the updated codes for the current year and have knowledge of the SADMERC's HCPCS coding helpline.[155]

In order to maintain a sense of seriousness about compliance in a DMEPOS supplier's operations, the DMEPOS supplier must continue to disseminate the compliance message. One effective mechanism for maintaining a consistent presence of the compliance message is to publish a monthly newsletter to address compliance concerns. This would allow the DMEPOS supplier to address specific examples of problems the company encountered during its ongoing audits and risk analyses, while reinforcing the DMEPOS supplier's firm commitment to the general principles of compliance and ethical conduct. The newsletter could also include the risk areas published by the OIG in its Special Fraud Alerts. Finally, the DMEPOS sup-

[155] *See* note 96.

plier could use the newsletter as a mechanism to address areas of ambiguity in the coding and billing process and/or its sales and marketing practices. The DMEPOS supplier should maintain its newsletters in a central location to document the guidance offered, and provide new employees with access to guidance previously provided.

The OIG believes it is important that all DMEPOS suppliers, regardless of size, maintain knowledgeable employees. The OIG recognizes that regularly sending employees to continuing education classes or publishing newsletters may not be feasible for small DMEPOS suppliers. Small DMEPOS suppliers may have their employees meet on a regular basis to discuss information in the DMERC's Medicare bulletin (*e.g.*, coding changes, procedural changes, policy changes, etc.). Such regularly held meetings will help demonstrate the DMEPOS supplier's commitment to compliance.

D. Developing Effective Lines of Communication

1. Access to the Compliance Officer

An open line of communication between the compliance officer and DMEPOS supplier employees is equally important to the successful implementation of a compliance program and the reduction of any potential for fraud, abuse, and waste. Written confidentiality and non-retaliation policies should be developed and distributed to all employees to encourage communication and the reporting of incidents of potential fraud.[156] The compliance committee should also develop several independent reporting paths for an employee to report fraud, waste, or abuse so that such reports cannot be diverted by supervisors or other personnel.

The OIG encourages the establishment of a procedure for personnel to seek clarification from the compliance officer or members of the compliance committee in the event of any confusion or question regarding a DMEPOS supplier policy, practice or procedure. Questions and responses should be documented and dated and, if appropriate, shared with other staff so that standards, policies, prac-

---

[156] The OIG believes that whistleblowers should be protected against retaliation, a concept embodied in the provisions of the False Claims Act. *See* 31 U.S.C. 3730(h). In many cases, employees sue their employers under the False Claims Act's *qui tam* provisions out of frustration because of the company's failure to take action when a questionable, fraudulent, or abusive situation was brought to the attention of senior corporate officials.

tices, and procedures can be updated and improved to reflect any necessary changes or clarifications. The compliance officer may want to solicit employee input in developing these communication and reporting systems.

2. Hotlines and Other Forms of Communication

The OIG encourages the use of hotlines,[157] e-mails, written memoranda, newsletters, suggestion boxes, and other forms of information exchange to maintain these open lines of communication.[158] If the DMEPOS supplier establishes a hotline, the telephone number should be made readily available to all employees and independent contractors, possibly by circulating the number on wallet cards or conspicuously posting the telephone number in common work areas.[159] Employees should be permitted to report matters on an anonymous basis. Matters reported through the hotline or other communication sources that suggest substantial violations of compliance policies, Federal, State or private payor health care program requirements, regulations, or statutes should be documented and investigated promptly to determine their veracity. A log should be maintained by the compliance officer that records such calls, including the nature of any investigation and its results.[160] Such information should be included in reports to the owner(s), governing

[157] The OIG recognizes that it may not be financially feasible for a small DMEPOS supplier to maintain a telephone hotline dedicated to receiving calls solely on compliance issues. These companies may want to explore alternative methods, *e.g.*, outsourcing the hotline or establishing a written method of confidential disclosure.

[158] In addition to methods of communication used by current employees, an effective employee exit interview program could be designed to solicit information from departing employees regarding potential misconduct and suspected violations of DMEPOS supplier policies and procedures.

[159] DMEPOS suppliers should also post in a prominent, available area the HHS-OIG Hotline telephone number, 1–800–447–8477 (1–800-HHS-TIPS), in addition to any company hotline number that may be posted.

[160] To efficiently and accurately fulfill such an obligation, a DMEPOS supplier should create an intake form for all compliance issues identified through reporting mechanisms. The form could include information concerning the date that the potential problem was reported, the internal investigative methods utilized, the results of the investigation, any corrective action implemented, any disciplinary measures imposed, and any overpayments returned.

body, CEO, president, and compliance committee.[161] Further, while the DMEPOS supplier should always strive to maintain the confidentiality of an employee's identity, it should also explicitly communicate that there may be a point where the individual's identity may become known or may have to be revealed.

The OIG recognizes that assertions of fraud and abuse by employees who may have participated in illegal conduct or committed other malfeasance raise numerous complex legal and management issues that should be examined on a case-by-case basis. The compliance officer should work closely with legal counsel, who can provide guidance regarding such issues.

The OIG recognizes that protecting anonymity may be infeasible for small DMEPOS suppliers. However, the OIG believes all DMEPOS supplier employees, when seeking answers to questions or reporting potential instances of fraud and abuse, should know who to consult and should be able to do so without fear of retribution.

E. Auditing and Monitoring

An ongoing evaluation process is critical to a successful compliance program. The OIG believes that an effective program should incorporate thorough monitoring of its implementation and regular reporting to the DMEPOS supplier's corporate officers.[162] Compliance reports created by this ongoing monitoring, including reports of suspected noncompliance, should be maintained by the compliance officer and shared with the DMEPOS supplier's corporate officers and the compliance committee. The extent and frequency of the audit function may vary depending on factors such as the size of the DMEPOS supplier, the resources available to the DMEPOS supplier, the DMEPOS supplier's prior history of noncompliance, and the risk factors that are prevalent in a particular DMEPOS supplier.

Although many monitoring techniques are available, one effective tool to promote and ensure compliance is the performance of regular, periodic compliance audits by internal or external auditors who have

---

[161] Information obtained over the hotline may provide valuable insight into management practices and operations, whether reported problems are actual or perceived.

[162] Even when a DMEPOS supplier is owned by a larger corporate entity, the regular auditing and monitoring of the compliance activities of an individual DMEPOS supplier location must be a key feature in any annual review. Appropriate reports on audit findings should be periodically provided and explained to a parent organization's senior staff and officers.

expertise in Federal and State health care statutes, rules, regulations, and Federal, State and private payor health care program requirements. The audits should focus on the different departments within the DMEPOS supplier, including external relationships with third-party contractors. At a minimum, these audits should be designed to address the DMEPOS supplier's compliance with laws governing kickback arrangements, the physician self-referral prohibition, pricing, contracts, claim development and submission, reimbursement, sales and marketing. In addition, the audits and reviews should examine the DMEPOS supplier's compliance with the Federal, State and private payor supplier standards and the specific rules and policies that have been the focus of particular attention on the part of the Medicare DMERCs, and law enforcement, as evidenced by educational and other communications from OIG Special Fraud Alerts, Advisory Opinions, OIG audits and evaluations, and law enforcement's initiatives.[163] In addition, the DMEPOS supplier should focus on any areas of specific concern identified within that DMEPOS supplier and those that may have been identified by any entity, whether Federal, State, private or internal.

Monitoring techniques may include sampling protocols that permit the compliance officer to identify and review variations from an established baseline.[164] Significant variations from the baseline should trigger a reasonable inquiry to determine the cause of the deviation. If the inquiry determines that the deviation occurred for legitimate, explainable reasons, the compliance officer and DMEPOS supplier management may want to limit any corrective action or take no action. If it is determined that the deviation was caused by improper procedures, misunderstanding of rules, including fraud and systemic problems, the DMEPOS supplier should take prompt

[163] *See* also section II.A.2.

[164] The OIG recommends that when a compliance program is established in a DMEPOS supplier, the compliance officer, with the assistance of department managers, should take a "snapshot" of operations from a compliance perspective. This assessment can be undertaken by outside consultants, law or accounting firms, or internal staff, with authoritative knowledge of health care compliance requirements. This "snapshot," often used as part of benchmarking analyses, becomes a baseline for the compliance officer and other managers to judge the DMEPOS supplier's progress in reducing or eliminating potential areas of vulnerability.

steps to correct the problem.[165] Any overpayments discovered as a result of such deviations should be returned promptly to the affected payor. The OIG recommends sending the payor the following information with the overpayment: (1) that the refund is being made pursuant to a voluntary compliance program; (2) a description of the complete causes and circumstances surrounding the overpayment; (3) the methodology by which the overpayment was determined; (4) the amount of the overpayment; and (5) any claim-specific information, reviewed as part of the self-audit, used to determine the overpayment (*e.g.*, beneficiary health insurance claims number, claim number, date of service, and payment date). Inclusion of such information with the overpayment will aid the payor in making the adjustment and may prevent it from requesting additional information.

An effective compliance program should also incorporate periodic (at least annual) reviews of whether the program's compliance elements have been satisfied, *e.g.*, whether there has been appropriate dissemination of the program's standards, training, ongoing educational programs, and disciplinary actions, among other elements.[166] This process will verify actual conformance by all departments with the compliance program and may identify the necessity for improvements to be made to the compliance program, as well as the DMEPOS supplier's operations. Such reviews could support a determination that appropriate records have been created and maintained to document the implementation of an effective program.[167] However, when monitoring discloses that deviations were not detected in a timely manner due to program deficiencies, appropriate modifications must be implemented. Such evaluations, when developed with the support of management, can help ensure compliance with the DMEPOS supplier's policies and procedures.

---

[165] In addition, when appropriate, as referenced in section II.G.2, below, reports of fraud or systemic problems should also be made to the appropriate governmental authority.

[166] One way to assess the knowledge, awareness, and perceptions of a DMEPOS supplier's employees is through the use of a validated survey instrument (*e.g.*, employee questionnaires, interviews, or focus groups).

[167] Such records should include, but not be limited to, logs of hotline calls, logs of training attendees, training agenda and materials, and summaries of corrective action and improvements with respect to DMEPOS supplier policies as a result of compliance activities.

As part of the review process, the compliance officer or reviewers should consider techniques such as:

- Testing billing staff on their knowledge of reimbursement coverage criteria and official coding guidelines (*e.g.*, present hypothetical scenarios of situations experienced in daily practice and assess responses);
- On-site visits to all facilities and locations;
- Ongoing risk analysis and vulnerability assessments of the DMEPOS supplier's operations;
- Assessment of existing relationships with physicians, and other potential referral sources;
- Unannounced audits, mock surveys, and investigations;
- Examination of the DMEPOS supplier's complaint logs;
- Checking personnel records to determine whether any individuals who have been reprimanded for compliance issues in the past are among those currently engaged in improper conduct;
- Interviews with personnel involved in management, operations, sales and marketing, claim development and submission, and other related activities;
- Questionnaires developed to solicit impressions of the DMEPOS supplier's employees;
- Interviews with physicians or other authorized persons who order services provided by the DMEPOS supplier;
- Interviews with independent contractors who provide services to the DMEPOS supplier;
- Reviews of medical necessity documentation (*e.g.*, physicians orders, CMNs), and other documents that support claims for reimbursement;
- Validation of qualifications of physicians or other authorized persons who order services provided by the DMEPOS supplier;
- Evaluation of written materials and documentation outlining the DMEPOS supplier's policies and procedures; and
- Utilization/trend analyses that uncover deviations, positive or negative, for specific HCPCS codes or types of items over a given period.

The reviewers should:

- Possess the qualifications and experience necessary to adequately identify potential issues with the subject matter to be reviewed;

- Be objective and independent of line management;[168]
- Have access to existing audit and health care resources, relevant personnel, and all relevant areas of operation;
- Present written evaluative reports on compliance activities to the owner(s), president, CEO, governing body, and members of the compliance committee on a regular basis, but not less than annually; and
- Specifically identify areas where corrective actions are needed.

We recommend that these audit reports be prepared and submitted to the compliance officer and senior management to ensure they are aware of the results. We suggest the reports specifically identify areas where corrective actions are needed. With these reports, DMEPOS supplier management can take whatever steps are necessary to correct past problems and prevent them from recurring. In certain cases, subsequent reviews or studies would be advisable to ensure that the recommended corrective actions have been implemented successfully.

A DMEPOS supplier should document its efforts to comply with applicable Federal and State statutes, rules, and regulations, and Federal, State and private payor health care program requirements. For example, where a DMEPOS supplier, in its efforts to comply with a particular statute, regulation or program requirement, requests advice from a Government agency (including a Medicare DMERC) charged with administering a Federal health care program, the DMEPOS supplier should document and retain a record of the request and any written or oral response, including the identity and position of the individual providing the response. The DMEPOS suppliers should take the same steps when requesting advice from private payors. This step is extremely important if the DMEPOS supplier intends to rely on that response to guide it in future decisions, actions, or claim reimbursement requests or appeals. A log of oral inquiries between the DMEPOS supplier and third parties will help the organization document its attempts at compliance. In addition, the DMEPOS supplier should maintain records relevant to the issue of whether its reliance was "reasonable" and whether it exercised due diligence in developing procedures and practices to implement the advice.

---

[168] The OIG recognizes that DMEPOS suppliers that are small in size and have limited resources may not be able to use internal reviewers who are not part of line management or hire outside reviewers.

The OIG recommends that all DMEPOS suppliers, regardless of size, conduct audits to ensure compliance with the applicable statutes, regulations and policies. The OIG recognizes that the small DMEPOS supplier may not have the resources to audit its operations to the extent suggested previously in this section. At a minimum, the OIG recommends that the small DMEPOS supplier conduct an internal audit. The DMEPOS supplier may choose to review a random sample of claims based on the risk areas it identified. We recommend that the DMEPOS supplier conduct an initial baseline audit and periodically conduct follow-up audits. If problems were identified in the baseline audit, the DMEPOS supplier may want to re-audit the same issue, at a later date, in order to measure the effectiveness of any corrective action(s) implemented as a result of the DMEPOS supplier's compliance program. The DMEPOS supplier should document the results of all audits it conducts. The DMEPOS supplier may want to use the OIG's Audit Process handbook to help design the audit.[169]

The extent of a DMEPOS supplier's audit should depend on the DMEPOS supplier's identified risk areas and resources. If the DMEPOS supplier comes under Government scrutiny in the future, the Government will assess whether or not the DMEPOS supplier developed a comprehensive audit based upon identified risk areas and resources. If the Government determines that the DMEPOS supplier failed to develop an adequate audit program, given its resources, the Government will be less likely to afford the DMEPOS supplier favorable treatment under its various enforcement authorities.

F. Enforcing Standards Through Well-Publicized Disciplinary Guidelines

1. Discipline Policy and Actions

An effective compliance program should include guidance regarding disciplinary action for corporate officers, managers, independent agents and other DMEPOS supplier employees who have failed to comply with the DMEPOS supplier's standards of conduct, policies and procedures, Federal and State statutes, rules, and regulations or Federal, State or private payor health care program requirements. It should also address disciplinary actions for those who have engaged in wrongdoing, which has the potential to impair the DME-

[169] The Audit Process handbook can be downloaded from the OIG Office of Audit Services' webpage at http://www.hhs.gov/progorg/oas.

POS supplier's status as a reliable, honest, and trustworthy health care provider.

The OIG believes that the compliance program should include a written policy statement setting forth the degrees of disciplinary actions that may be imposed upon corporate officers, managers, independent agents and other DMEPOS supplier employees for failing to comply with the DMEPOS supplier's standards, policies, and applicable statutes and regulations. Intentional or reckless noncompliance should subject transgressors to significant sanctions. Such sanctions could include oral warnings, suspension, termination, or other sanctions, as appropriate. Each situation must be considered on a case-by-case basis to determine the appropriate sanction. The written standards of conduct should elaborate on the procedures for handling disciplinary problems and specify those who will be responsible for taking appropriate action. Some disciplinary actions can be handled by managers, while others may have to be resolved by the owner(s), president or CEO. Disciplinary action may be appropriate where a responsible employee's failure to detect a violation is attributable to his or her negligence or reckless conduct. Personnel should be advised by the DMEPOS supplier that disciplinary action will be taken on a fair and equitable basis. Managers and supervisors should be made aware that they have a responsibility to discipline employees in an appropriate and consistent manner.

It is vital to publish and disseminate the range of disciplinary standards for improper conduct and to educate corporate officers, managers, and other DMEPOS supplier employees regarding these standards. The consequences of noncompliance should be consistently applied and enforced, in order for the disciplinary policy to have the required deterrent effect. All levels of employees should be subject to the same types of disciplinary action for the commission of similar offenses. The commitment to compliance applies to all personnel levels within a DMEPOS supplier. The OIG believes that corporate officers, managers, and supervisors should be held accountable for failing to comply with, or for the foreseeable failure of their subordinates to adhere to, the applicable standards, statutes, rules, regulations and procedures.

The OIG believes all DMEPOS suppliers, regardless of size, should consistently apply the consequences of non-compliance. The OIG recognizes that small DMEPOS suppliers may not have a written document detailing the disciplinary actions for non-compliance.

However, all employees should be clearly informed of such consequences.

2. New Employee Policy

For all new employees who have discretionary authority to make decisions that may involve compliance with the law or compliance oversight, DMEPOS suppliers should conduct a reasonable and prudent background investigation, including a reference check,[170] as part of every such employment application. The application should specifically require the applicant to disclose any criminal conviction, as defined by 42 U.S.C. 1320a-7(i), or exclusion action. Pursuant to the compliance program, the DMEPOS supplier's policies should prohibit the employment of individuals who have been recently convicted of a criminal offense related to health care or who are listed as debarred, excluded, or otherwise ineligible for participation in Federal health care programs (as defined in 42 U.S.C. 1320a-7b(f)).[171] In addition, pending the resolution of any criminal charges or proposed debarment or exclusion, the OIG recommends that such employees should be removed from direct responsibility for, or involvement with, the DMEPOS supplier's business operations related to any Federal health care program. In addition, we recommend that the DMEPOS supplier remove such employee from any position(s) for which the employee's salary or the items or services rendered by the employee are paid in whole or part, directly or indirectly, by Federal health care programs or otherwise with Federal funds.[172] If resolution of the matter results in conviction, debarment, or exclusion, then the DMEPOS supplier should remove the individual from direct responsibility for or involvement with all Federal health care programs. Similarly, if an independent contractor or a referring

---

[170] *See* notes 137 and 138. Since the employees of DMEPOS suppliers have access to potentially vulnerable people and their property, DMEPOS suppliers should also strictly scrutinize whether they should employ individuals who have been convicted of crimes of neglect, violence or financial misconduct.

[171] Likewise, DMEPOS supplier compliance programs should establish standards prohibiting the execution of contracts with companies that have been recently convicted of a criminal offense related to health care or that are listed by a Federal agency as debarred, excluded, or otherwise ineligible for participation in Federal health care programs. *See* notes 137 and 138.

[172] Prospective employees who have been officially reinstated into the Medicare and Medicaid programs by the OIG may be considered for employment upon proof of such reinstatement.

physician or other authorized person is debarred or excluded from participation in Federal health care programs, and the DMEPOS supplier is aware of it, the DMEPOS supplier should not involve that individual/entity in the Federal health care portion of its business.

The OIG believes all DMEPOS suppliers, regardless of size, should ensure that they do not employ or contract with anyone who has been debarred, excluded or is otherwise ineligible to participate in Federal health care programs.

G. Responding to Detected Offenses and Developing Corrective Action Initiatives

1. Violations and Investigations

Violations of a DMEPOS supplier's compliance program, failures to comply with applicable Federal or State statutes, rules, regulations or Federal, State or private payor health care program requirements, and other types of misconduct threaten a DMEPOS supplier's status as a reliable, honest and trustworthy health care provider. Detected but uncorrected misconduct can seriously endanger the mission, reputation, and legal status of the DMEPOS supplier. Consequently, upon reports or reasonable indications of suspected noncompliance, it is important that the compliance officer or other management officials immediately investigate the conduct in question to determine whether a material violation of applicable law, rules or program instructions or the requirements of the compliance program has occurred, and if so, take decisive steps to correct the problem.[173] As appropriate, such steps may include an immediate referral to criminal and/or civil law enforcement authorities, a corrective action plan,[174] a report to the Government,[175] and the

---

[173] Instances of non-compliance must be determined on a case-by-case basis. The existence, or amount, of a monetary loss to a health care program is not solely determinative of whether or not the conduct should be investigated and reported to governmental authorities. In fact, there may be instances where there is no readily identifiable*monetary* loss at all, but corrective action and reporting are still necessary to protect the integrity of the applicable program and its beneficiaries.

[174] Advice from the DMEPOS supplier's in-house counsel or an outside law firm may be sought to determine the extent of the DMEPOS supplier's liability and to plan the appropriate course of action.

[175] The OIG currently maintains a provider self-disclosure protocol that encourages providers to report suspected fraud. The concept of voluntary self-disclosure is premised on a recognition that the Government alone can-

return of any overpayments, if applicable.

Where potential fraud or False Claims Act liability is not involved, the OIG recommends that the DMEPOS supplier promptly return any overpayments to the affected payor as they are discovered. However, even if the overpayment detection and return process is working and is being monitored by the DMEPOS supplier, the OIG still believes that the compliance officer needs to be made aware of these overpayments, violations, or deviations that may reveal trends or patterns indicative of a systemic problem.

Depending upon the nature of the alleged violations, an internal investigation will probably include interviews and a review of relevant documents, such as submitted claims and CMNs. The DMEPOS supplier should consider engaging outside auditors or health care experts to assist in an investigation. Records of the investigation should contain documentation of the alleged violation, a description of the investigative process (including the objectivity of the investigators and methodologies utilized), copies of interview notes and key documents, a log of the witnesses interviewed, the documents reviewed, and the results of the investigation (*e.g.*, any disciplinary action taken and any corrective action implemented). Although any action taken as the result of an investigation will necessarily vary depending upon the DMEPOS supplier and the situation, DMEPOS suppliers should strive for some consistency by utilizing sound practices and disciplinary protocols.[176] Further, after a reasonable period, the compliance officer should review the circumstances that formed the basis for the investigation to determine whether similar problems have been uncovered or modifications of the compliance program are necessary to prevent and detect other inappropriate conduct or violations.

If an investigation of an alleged violation is undertaken and the compliance officer believes the integrity of the investigation may be at stake because of the presence of employees under investigation,

---

not protect the integrity of the Medicare and other Federal health care programs. Health care providers must be willing to police themselves, correct underlying problems, and work with the Government to resolve these matters. The self-disclosure protocol is located on the OIG's web site at http://www.dhhs.gov/progorg/oig.

[176] The parameters of a claim review subject to an internal investigation will depend on the circumstances surrounding the issue(s) identified. By limiting the scope of an internal audit to current billing, a DMEPOS supplier may fail to identify major problems and deficiencies in operations, as well as be subject to certain liability.

those subjects should be removed from their current work activity until the investigation is completed (unless an internal or Government-led undercover operation known to the DMEPOS supplier is in effect). In addition, the compliance officer should take appropriate steps to secure or prevent the destruction of documents or other evidence relevant to the investigation. If the DMEPOS supplier determines disciplinary action is warranted, it should be prompt and imposed in accordance with the DMEPOS supplier's written standards of disciplinary action.

The OIG believes all DMEPOS suppliers, regardless of size, should ensure that they are responsive to investigating allegations of potential misconduct.

2. Reporting

If the compliance officer, compliance committee or other management official discovers credible evidence of misconduct from any source and, after a reasonable inquiry, has reason to believe that the misconduct may violate criminal, civil, or administrative law, then the DMEPOS supplier should promptly report the existence of misconduct to the appropriate Federal and State authorities [177] within a reasonable period, but not more than 60 days [178] after determining that there is credible evidence of a violation. [179] Prompt reporting

[177] Appropriate Federal and State authorities include the Office of Inspector General, Department of Health and Human Services; the Criminal and Civil Divisions of the Department of Justice; the U.S. Attorney in the relevant district(s); and the other investigative arms for the agencies administering the affected Federal or State health care programs, such as: the State Medicaid Fraud Control Unit; the Defense Criminal Investigative Service; the Department of Veterans Affairs; the Office of Inspector General, U.S. Department of Labor (which has primary criminal jurisdiction over FECA, Black Lung and Longshore programs); and the Office of Inspector General, U.S. Office of Personnel Management (which has primary jurisdiction over the Federal Employee Health Benefits Program).

[178] In contrast, to qualify for the "not less than double damages" provision of the False Claims Act, the report must be provided to the Government within thirty (30) days after the date when the DMEPOS supplier first obtained the information. *See* 31 U.S.C. 3729(a).

[179] The OIG believes that some violations may be so serious that they warrant immediate notification to governmental authorities, prior to, or simultaneous with, commencing an internal investigation, *e.g.*, if the conduct: (1) is a clear violation of criminal law; (2) has a significant adverse effect on the quality of care provided to program beneficiaries (in addition to any other legal obligations regarding quality of care); or (3) indicates evi-

will demonstrate the DMEPOS supplier's good faith and willingness to work with governmental authorities to correct and remedy the problem. In addition, reporting such conduct will be considered a mitigating factor by the OIG in determining administrative sanctions (e.g., penalties, assessments, and exclusion), if the reporting provider becomes the target of an OIG investigation.[180]

When reporting misconduct to the Government, a DMEPOS supplier should provide all evidence relevant to the alleged violation of applicable Federal or State law(s) and potential cost impact. The compliance officer, with advice of counsel, and with guidance from the governmental authorities, could be requested to continue to investigate the reported violation. Once the investigation is completed, the compliance officer should be required to notify the appropriate governmental authority of the outcome of the investigation, including a description of the impact of the alleged violation on the operation of the applicable health care programs or their beneficiaries. If the investigation ultimately reveals that criminal, civil, or administrative violations have occurred, the appropriate Federal and State authorities[181] should be notified immediately.

The OIG believes all DMEPOS suppliers, regardless of size, should ensure that they are reporting the results of any overpayments or violations to the appropriate entity.

3. Corrective Actions

As previously stated, the DMEPOS supplier should take appropriate corrective action, including prompt identification of any overpayment to the affected payor and the imposition of proper disciplinary action. If potential fraud or violations of the False Claims Act are involved, any repayment of the overpayment should be made as part of the discussion with the Government following a report of the matter to law enforcement authorities. Otherwise, the overpayment should be promptly refunded to the affected payor. The OIG recommends that the overpayment refund include the information as

---

dence of a systemic failure to comply with applicable laws, rules or program instructions or an existing corporate integrity agreement, regardless of the financial impact on Federal health care programs.

[180] The OIG has published criteria setting forth those factors that the OIG takes into consideration in determining whether it is appropriate to exclude a health care provider from program participation pursuant to 42 U.S.C. 1320a-7(b)(7) for violations of various fraud and abuse laws. *See* 62 FR 67392 (December 24, 1997).

[181] *See* note 177.

outlined in section II.E. Failure to disclose overpayments within a reasonable period of time could be interpreted as an intentional or knowing attempt to conceal the overpayment from the Government, thereby establishing an independent basis for a criminal or civil violation with respect to the DMEPOS supplier, as well as any individuals who may have been involved. For this reason, DMEPOS supplier compliance programs should emphasize that overpayments obtained from Medicare or other Federal health care programs should be promptly disclosed and returned to the payor that made the erroneous payment.

The OIG believes all DMEPOS suppliers, regardless of size, should take appropriate corrective action to remedy the identified deficiency.

III. Conclusion

Through this document, the OIG has attempted to provide a foundation to the process necessary to develop an effective and cost-efficient DMEPOS supplier compliance program. As previously stated, however, each program must be tailored to fit the needs and resources of an individual DMEPOS supplier, depending upon its size; number of locations; type of equipment provided; or corporate structure. The Federal and State health care statutes, rules, and regulations and Federal, State and private payor health care program requirements, should be integrated into every DMEPOS supplier's compliance program.

The OIG recognizes that the health care industry in this country, which reaches millions of beneficiaries and expends about a trillion dollars annually, is constantly evolving. In particular, legislation has been passed that creates additional Medicare program participation requirements, such as requiring DMEPOS suppliers to purchase surety bonds and expanding the Medicare supplier standards.[182] As stated throughout this guidance, compliance is a dynamic process that helps to ensure that DMEPOS suppliers and other health care providers are better able to fulfill their commitment to ethical behavior, as well as meet the changes and challenges being imposed upon them by Congress and private insurers. Ultimately, it is OIG's hope that a voluntarily created compliance program will enable DMEPOS suppliers to meet their goals, improve the quality of service to patients, and substantially reduce fraud,

---

[182] *See* 63 FR 2926 (January 20, 1998).

waste, and abuse, as well as the cost of health care, to Federal State and private health insurers.

Dated: June 29, 1999.

June Gibbs Brown,

Inspector General.

[FR Doc. 99–16945 Filed 7–2-99; 8:45 am]

BILLING CODE 4150–04-P

APPENDIX I6

Compliance Program Guidance for Hospices; 64 FR 54031, October 5, 1999

[Federal Register: October 5, 1999 (Volume 64, Number 192)]
[Notices] [Page 54031–54049]

DEPARTMENT OF HEALTH AND HUMAN SERVICES

Office of Inspector General

Publication of the OIG Compliance Program, Guidance for Hospices

AGENCY: Office of Inspector General (OIG), HHS.
ACTION: Notice.
SUMMARY: This Federal Register notice sets forth the recently issued Compliance Program Guidance for Hospices developed by the Office of Inspector General (OIG). The OIG has previously developed and published compliance program guidance focused on several other areas and aspects of the health care industry. We believe that the development and issuance of this compliance program guidance for hospices will continue to serve as a positive step toward promoting a higher level of ethical and lawful conduct throughout the entire health care industry.
FOR FURTHER INFORMATION CONTACT: Michael Shaw, Office of Counsel to the Inspector General, (202) 619–2078.
SUPPLEMENTARY INFORMATION:
Background
The creation of compliance program guidance remains a major initiative by the OIG in its efforts to engage the health care community in combating fraud and abuse. In formulating compliance guidance, the OIG has worked closely with the Health Care Financing Administration (HCFA), the Department of Justice (DOJ) and various sectors of the health care industry to provide clear guidance to those segments of the industry that are interested in reducing fraud and abuse within their organizations. The five previ-

ously-issued compliance program guidances were focused on the hospital industry; home health agencies; clinical laboratories; third-party medical billing companies; and the durable medical equipment, prosthetics, orthotics and supply industry. The development of these types of compliance program guidance is based on our belief that a health care provider can use internal controls to more efficiently monitor adherence to applicable statutes, regulations and program requirements.

Guidance for the Hospice Industry

On January 13, 1999, the OIG published a solicitation notice (64 FR 2228) seeking information and recommendations for developing guidance for the hospice industry. In response to that solicitation notice, the OIG received numerous comments from various parts of the industry and from their representatives. After careful consideration of those initial comments, and in an effort to ensure that all parties had a reasonable opportunity to provide input into a final product, the OIG published draft guidance for the hospice industry on July 21, 1999 (64 FR 39150) for further comment and recommendations.

Elements for an Effective Compliance Program

Through experience, the OIG has identified seven fundamental elements

to an effective compliance program. They are:

- implementing written policies, procedures and standards of conduct;
- designating a compliance officer and compliance committee;
- conducting effective training and education;
- developing effective lines of communication;
- enforcing standards through well-publicized disciplinary guidelines;
- conducting internal monitoring and auditing; and
- responding promptly to detected offenses and developing corrective action.

Through application of these seven basic elements, the OIG is offering specific compliance measures that may be implemented in hospice industry operations in an effort to curtail or eliminate fraud and abuse. As with previously-issued OIG compliance guidances, adoption of the Compliance Program Guidance for Hospices set forth below will be strictly voluntary.

A reprint of this newly-issued compliance program guidance follows:

Office of Inspector General's Compliance Program Guidance for Hospices (September 1999)

I. Introduction

The Office of Inspector General (OIG) of the Department of Health and Human Services (HHS) continues to promote voluntarily developed and implemented compliance programs for the health care industry. The following compliance program guidance is intended to assist hospices[1] and their agents and subproviders (referred to collectively in this document as "hospices") develop effective internal controls that promote adherence to applicable Federal and State law, and the program requirements of Federal, State, and private health plans. The adoption and implementation of voluntary compliance programs significantly advance the prevention of fraud, abuse and waste in these health care plans while at the same time further the fundamental mission of all hospices, which is to provide palliative care[2] to patients.

Within this document, the OIG first provides its general views on the value and fundamental principles of hospice compliance programs, and then provides the specific elements that each hospice should consider when developing and implementing an effective compliance program. While this document presents basic procedural and structural guidance for designing a compliance program, it is not in itself a compliance program. Rather, it is a set of guidelines to be considered by a hospice interested in implementing a compliance program.

The OIG recognizes the size-differential that exists between operations of the different hospices and organizations that compose the hospice industry. Appropriately, this guidance is pertinent for all hospices, whether for-profit, non-profit, provider-based, indepen-

[1] The term "hospice" is applied in this document as the term "hospice program" is defined in 42 U.S.C. 1395x(dd).

[2] Palliative care is an intensive program of care that focuses on the relief of pain and suffering associated with a terminal illness. Through this emphasis on palliative rather than curative services, individuals have a choice whenever conventional approaches for medical treatment may no longer be appropriate. Hospice addresses the needs of terminally ill individuals by including the patient and family, specially trained volunteers, caregivers from the community, and representatives from medicine, nursing, social work and spiritual counseling in the caregiving team.

dent, community-based, volunteer-based, large, small, urban or rural. The applicability of the recommendations and guidelines provided in this document depends on the circumstances of each particular hospice. However, regardless of a hospice's size and structure, the OIG believes that every hospice can and should strive to accomplish the objectives and principles underlying all of the compliance policies and procedures recommended within this guidance.

Fundamentally, compliance efforts are designed to establish a culture within a hospice that promotes prevention, detection, and resolution of instances of conduct that do not conform to Federal and State law, and Federal, State and private payor health care program requirements, as well as the hospice's business policies. In practice, the compliance program should effectively articulate and demonstrate the organization's commitment to ethical conduct. Compliance programs guide a hospice's governing body (e.g., board of directors or trustees), chief executive officer (CEO), managers, physicians, clinicians, billing personnel, and other employees in the efficient management and operation of a hospice. Eventually, a compliance program should become part of the fabric of routine hospice operations.

It is incumbent upon a hospice's corporate officers and managers to provide ethical leadership to the organization and to assure that adequate systems are in place to facilitate ethical and legal conduct. Employees, managers and the Government will focus on the words and actions of a hospice's leadership as a measure of the organization's commitment to compliance. Indeed, many hospices have adopted mission statements articulating their commitment to high ethical standards. A formal compliance program, as an additional element in this process, offers a hospice a further concrete method that may improve the appropriateness and quality of care and reduce waste. Compliance programs also provide a central coordinating mechanism for furnishing and disseminating information and guidance on applicable Federal and State statutes, regulations and other requirements.

Implementing an effective compliance program requires a substantial commitment of time, energy and resources by senior management and the hospice's governing body.[3] Superficial pro-

[3] Recent case law suggests that the failure of a corporate director to attempt in good faith to institute a compliance program in certain situations may be a breach of a director's fiduciary obligation. See, e.g., In re Caremark

grams that simply purport to comply with the elements discussed and described in this guidance or programs that are hastily constructed and implemented without appropriate ongoing monitoring will likely be ineffective and could expose the hospice to greater liability than no program at all. While it may require significant additional resources or reallocation of existing resources to implement an effective compliance program, the OIG believes that the long term benefits of implementing the program outweigh the costs.[4]

A. Benefits of Compliance Plan

The OIG believes an effective compliance program provides a mechanism that brings the public and private sectors together to reach mutual goals of reducing fraud and abuse, strengthening operational quality, improving the quality of health care services and reducing the cost of health care. Attaining these goals provides positive results to hospices, the Government, and individual citizens alike. In addition to fulfilling its legal duty to ensure that it is not submitting false or inaccurate claims to Government and private payors, a hospice may gain numerous additional benefits by voluntarily implementing an effective compliance program. These benefits may include the ability to:

- formulate effective controls to assure compliance with Federal and State statutes, rules and regulations, and Federal, State and private payor health care program requirements and internal guidelines;
- concretely demonstrate to employees and the community at large the hospice's strong commitment to honest and responsible provider and corporate conduct;
- identify and prevent illegal and unethical conduct;
- improve internal communication;
- more quickly and accurately react to employees' operational compliance concerns and target resources to address those concerns;

International Inc. Derivative Litigation, 698 A.2d 959 (Ct. Chanc. Del. 1996).

[4] The conclusion of a recent report by the United States General Accounting Office (GAO) to Congress stated that "despite the investment of time and resources that compliance programs entail, many hospitals believe the benefits of these programs . . . outweigh their costs . . . and providers themselves believe that complance programs can reduce improper Mecicare payments." See GAO report GAO/HEHS-99–59 (April 1999).

- improve the quality, efficiency, and consistency of patient care;
- create a centralized source for distributing information on health care statutes, regulations, and other program directives regarding fraud, waste and abuse, and related issues;
- formulate a methodology that encourages employees to report potential problems;
- develop procedures that allow the prompt, thorough investigation of alleged misconduct by corporate officers, managers, employees, independent contractors, consultants, volunteers, physicians, nurses and other health care professionals;
- initiate immediate, appropriate, and decisive corrective action; and
- minimize, through early detection and reporting, the loss to the Government from false claims, and thereby reduce the hospice's exposure to civil damages and penalties, criminal sanctions and administrative remedies, such as program exclusion. [5]

Overall, the OIG believes that an effective compliance program is a sound investment on the part of a hospice.

The OIG recognizes that the implementation of a compliance program may not entirely eliminate fraud, abuse and waste from the hospice system. However, a sincere effort by hospices to comply with applicable Federal and State standards, as well as the requirements of private health care programs, through the establishment of an effective compliance program, significantly reduces the risk of unlawful or improper conduct.

B. Application of Compliance Program Guidance

Given the diversity within the industry, there is no single "best" hospice compliance program. The OIG understands the variances and complexities within the hospice industry and is sensitive to the differences among large national and regional multi-hospice organizations, small independent hospices and other types of hospice organizations and systems. However, elements of this guidance can

---

[5] The OIG, for example, will consider the existence of an effective compliance program that pre-dated any governmental investigation when addressing the appropriateness of administrative sanctions. See 62 FR 67392 (December 24, 1997). The burden is on the provider to demonstrate the operational effectiveness of a compliance program. Further, the False Claims Act, 31 U.S.C. 3729–3733, provides that a person who has violated the Act, but who voluntarily discloses the violation to the Government, in certain circumstances will be subject to not less than double, as opposed to treble, damages. See 31 U.S.C. 3729(a).

be used by all hospices, regardless of size, location, or corporate structure, to establish an effective compliance program. Similarly, a hospital or corporation that owns a hospice or provides hospice services may incorporate these elements into its system-wide compliance or managerial structure. We recognize that some hospices may not be able to adopt certain elements to the same comprehensive degree that others with more extensive resources may achieve. This guidance represents the OIG's suggestions on how a hospice can best establish internal controls and monitoring to correct and prevent fraudulent activities. By no means should the contents of this guidance be viewed as an exclusive discussion of the advisable elements of a compliance program. On the contrary, the OIG strongly encourages a hospice to develop and implement compliance elements that uniquely address its own particular risk areas.

The OIG believes that input and support by the individuals and organizations that will use the tools set forth in this document are critical to the development and success of this compliance program guidance. In a continuing effort to collaborate closely with the private sector, the OIG placed a notice in the Federal Register soliciting recommendations and suggestions on what should be included in this Compliance Program Guidance, and then published draft Compliance Program Guidance for Hospices in the Federal Register for public comment. [6] Further, we took into consideration previous OIG publications, such as Special Fraud Alerts, the recent findings and recommendations in reports issued by OIG's Office of Audit Services and Office of Evaluation and Inspections, as well as the experience of past and recent fraud investigations related to hospices conducted by OIG's Office of Investigations and the Department of Justice. As appropriate, this guidance may be modified and expanded as more information and knowledge is obtained by the OIG, and as changes in the law, rules, policies and procedures of the Federal, State and private health plans occur.

The OIG recognizes that the development and implementation of compliance programs in hospices often raise sensitive and complex legal and managerial issues. [7] However, the OIG wishes to offer

[6] See 64 FR 2228 (January 13, 1999), Notice for Solicitation of Information and Recommendations for Developing OIG Compliance Program Guidance for the Hospice Industry; 64 FR 39150 (July 21, 1999), Draft Compliance Program Guidance for Hospices.

[7] Nothing stated within this document should be substituted for, or used in lieu of, competent legal advice from counsel.

what it believes is critical guidance for providers who are sincerely attempting to comply with the relevant health care statutes and regulations.

II. Compliance Program Elements

The elements proposed by these guidelines are similar to those of other compliance program guidances[8] and the OIG's corporate integrity agreements.[9] The elements represent a guide that can be tailored to fit the needs and financial realities of a particular hospice. The OIG is cognizant that, with regard to compliance programs, one model is not suitable to every hospice.

The OIG believes that every effective compliance program must begin with a formal commitment[10] by the hospice's governing body to include all of the applicable elements listed below. These elements are based on the seven steps of the Federal Sentencing Guidelines.[11]

Further, we believe that every hospice can implement most of our recommended elements that expand upon these seven steps. We recognize that full implementation of all elements may not be immediately feasible for all hospices. However, as a first step, a good faith and meaningful commitment on the part of the hospice administration, especially the governing body and the CEO, will substantially contribute to a program's successful implementation. As the compliance program is implemented, that commitment should cascade

[8] See 63 FR 70138 (December 18, 1998) for the Compliance Program Guidance for Third Party Medical Billing Companies; 63 FR 42410 (August 7, 1998) for the Compliance Program Guidance for Home Health Agencies; 63 FR 45076 (August 24, 1998) for the Compliance Program Guidance for Clinical Laboratories, as revised; 63 FR 8987 (1998) for the Compliance Program Guidance for Hospitals. These documents are also located on the Internet at http://www.dhhs.gov/progorg/oig.

[9] Corporate integrity agreements are executed as part of a civil settlement between the health care provider and the Government to resolve a case based on allegations of health care fraud or abuse. These OIG-imposed programs are in effect for a period of three to five years and require many of the elements included in this compliance program guidance.

[10] E.g., a resolution by the board of directors, owner(s) or president, where applicable, and the allocation of adequate resources to ensure that each of the elements is addressed.

[11] See United States Sentencing Commission Guidelines, Guidelines Manual, 8A1.2, Application Note 3(k). The Federal Sentencing Guidelines are detailed policies and practices for the Federal criminal justice system that prescribe the appropriate sanctions for offenders convicted of Federal crimes.

down through the management of the hospice to every employee at all levels in the organization.

At a minimum, comprehensive compliance programs should include the following seven elements:

(1) The development and distribution of written standards of conduct, as well as written policies and procedures, which promote the hospice's commitment to compliance and address specific areas of potential fraud, such as assessment of Medicare eligibility, quality assurance and financial relationships with nursing facilities and other health care professionals and entities;

(2) The designation of a compliance officer and other appropriate bodies, e.g., a corporate compliance committee, charged with the responsibility for operating and monitoring the compliance program, and who report directly to the CEO and the governing body; [12]

(3) The development and implementation of regular, effective education and training programs for all affected employees;

(4) The creation and maintenance of a process, such as a hotline or other reporting system, to receive complaints and ensure effective lines of communication between the compliance officer and all employees, and the adoption of procedures to protect the anonymity of complainants and to protect whistleblowers from retaliation;

(5) The use of audits and/or other evaluation techniques to monitor compliance, identify problem areas, and assist in the reduction of identified problem areas;

(6) The development of appropriate disciplinary mechanisms to enforce standards and the development of policies to address (i) employees who have violated internal compliance policies, applicable statutes, regulations or Federal health care program requirements [13] and (ii) the employment of sanctioned and other

---

[12] The integral functions of a compliance officer and a corporate compliance committee in implementing an effective compliance program are discussed throughout this compliance program guidance. However, the OIG recognizes that a hospice may tailor the structure of those positions in consideration of the size and design of the hospice, while endeavoring to address and accomplish all of the underlying objectives of a compliance officer and a corporate compliance committee. See section II.B. and accompanying notes.

[13] The term "Federal health care programs" is applied in this document as defined in 42 U.S.C. 1320a-7b(f), which includes any plan or program that provides health benefits, whether directly, through insurance, or otherwise, which is funded directly, in whole or in part, by the United States Government (i.e., via programs such as Medicare, Federal Employees' Compensation Act, Black Lung, or the Longshore and Harbor Worker's

specified individuals; and

(7) The development of policies that direct prompt and proper responses to detected offenses, including the initiation of appropriate corrective action and preventative measures.

A. Written Policies and Procedures

Every compliance program should require the development and distribution of written compliance policies, standards, and practices that identify specific areas of risk and vulnerability to the hospice. These policies, standards and practices should be developed under the direction and supervision of, or subject to review by, the compliance officer and compliance committee and, at a minimum, should be provided to all individuals who are affected by the particular policy at issue, including the hospice's agents and independent contractors.[14]

1. Standards of Conduct

Hospices should develop standards of conduct for all affected employees that include a clearly delineated commitment to compliance by the hospice's senior management[15] and its divisions, including affiliated providers operating under the hospice's control and other health care professionals (e.g., hospice physicians,[16]

Compensation Act) or any State health plan (e.g., Medicaid, or a program receiving funds from block grants for social services or child health services). Also, for the purposes of this document, the term "Federal health care program requirements" refers to the statutes, regulations, rules, requirements, directives and instructions governing Medicare, Medicaid and all other Federal health care programs.

[14] According to the Federal Sentencing Guidelines, an organization must have established compliance standards and procedures to be followed by its employees and other agents in order to receive sentencing credit for an "effective" compliance program. The Federal Sentencing Guidelines define "agent" as "any individual, including a director, an officer, an employee or an independent contractor, authorized to act on behalf of the organization." See United States Sentencing Commission Guidelines, Guidelines Manual, 8A1.2, Application Note 3.

[15] The OIG strongly encourages high-level involvement by the hospice's governing body, CEO, chief operating officer, general counsel, and chief financial officer, as well as other medical or clinical personnel, as appropriate, in the development of standards of conduct. Such involvement should help communicate a strong and explicit statement of compliance goals and standards.

[16] When the term "hospice phyisican" is applied in this document, it refers to the hospice's medical director or the physician member of a hospice's Interdisciplinary Group. The "Interdisciplinary Group," which is composed of at least a doctor of medicine or osteopathy, registered nurse, medical

nurses, physical therapists, occupational therapists, social workers, spiritual counselors, bereavement counselors and volunteers). Standards should articulate the hospice's commitment to comply with all Federal, State and private insurer standards, with an emphasis on preventing fraud and abuse. They should explicitly state the organization's mission, goals and ethical requirements of compliance and reflect a carefully crafted, clear expression of expectations for all hospice governing body members, officers, managers, employees, physicians, clinicians and, where appropriate, volunteers, contractors and other agents. These standards should promote integrity, support objectivity, and foster trust. Standards should not only address compliance with statutes and regulations, but should also set forth broad principles that guide employees in conducting business professionally and properly.

The standards should be distributed to, and comprehensible by, all affected employees (e.g., translated into other languages when necessary and written at appropriate reading levels). Further, to assist in ensuring that employees continuously meet the expected high standards set forth in the code of conduct, any employee handbook delineating or expanding upon these standards of conduct should be regularly updated as applicable statutes, regulations and Federal health care program requirements are modified and/or clarified.[17]

When they first begin working for the hospice, and each time new standards of conduct are issued, employees should be asked to sign a statement certifying that they have received, read, and understood the standards of conduct. An employee's certification should be retained by the hospice in the employee's personnel file, and available for review by the compliance officer.2. Risk Areas

The OIG believes that a hospice's written policies and procedures should take into consideration the particular statutes, rules, and

---

social worker, and pastoral or other counselor, is responsible for: (1) participation in the establishment of the plan of care; (2) provision or supervision of hospice care and services; (3) periodic review and updating of the plan of care for each individual receiving hospice care; and (4) establishment of policies governing the day-to-day provision of hospice care and services. See 42 CFR 418.68.

[17] The OIG recognizes that not all standards, policies, and procedures need to be communicated to all employees. However, the OIG believes that the bulk of the standards that relate to complying with fraud and abuse laws and other ethical areas should be addressed and made part of all affected employees' training. The hospice must decide which additional educational programs should be limited to the different levels of employees, based on job functions and areas of responsibility.

program instructions that apply to each function or department of the hospice.[18] In contrast to the standards of conduct, which are designed to be a clear and concise collection of fundamental standards, the written policies should articulate specific procedures that hospice staff should follow.

Consequently, we recommend that these policies and procedures be coordinated with the appropriate training and educational programs, with an emphasis on areas of special concern that have been identified by the OIG through its investigative and audit functions.[19] Although the OIG concluded in a 1998 report that the Medicare hospice program seems to be working as intended,[20] compliance programs for hospices should still address areas of OIG concern that include:[21]

- Uninformed consent to elect the Medicare Hospice Benefit;[22]

---

[18] A hospice can conduct focus groups composed of managers from various departments to solicit their concerns and ideas about compliance risks that may be then addresses by the hospice's policies and procedures. Such employee participation in the development of the hospice's compliance program can promote its credibility and foster employee acceptance of the program.

[19] The OIG periodically issues Special Fraud Alerts setting forth activities believed to raise legal and enforcement issues. For example, see OIG Special Fraud Alert — "Fraud and Abuse in Nursing Home Arrangements with Hospices" (March 1998); see also OIG Medicare Advisory Bulletin on Hospice Benefits (November 1995). Hospice compliance programs should require that the legal staff, compliance officer, or other appropriate personnel carefully consider any and all Special Fraud Alerts issued by the OIG that relate to hospices. Moreover, the compliance programs should address the ramifications of failing to cease and correct any conduct criticized in a Special Fraud Alert, if applicable to hospices, or to take reasonable action to prevent such conduct from reoccurring in the future. If appropriate, a hospice should take the steps described in section II.G. regarding investigations, reporting, and correction of identified problems.

[20] See OIG report OEI-04–93–00270 — "Medicare Hospice Beneficiaries: Services and Eligibility."

[21] Hospices may also want to consult the OIG's Work Plan when conducting the risk assessment. The OIG Work Plan details the various projects the OIG intends to address in the applicable fiscal year. It should be noted that the priorities in the Work Plan are subject to modification and revision as the year progresses and it does not represent a complete or final list of areas of concern to the OIG. The Work Plan is currently available on the Internet at http://www.dhhs.gov/progorg/oig.

[22] A hospice must ensure that an individual (or authorized representative) is informed about the palliative nature of the care and services that

- Admitting patients to hospice care who are not terminally ill;[23]
- Arrangement with another health care provider who a hospice knows is submitting claims for services already covered by the Medicare Hospice Benefit;[24]

---

may be provided if the individual desires to elect the Medicare Hospice Benefit. 42 CFR 418.62. The decision to elect the Medicare Hospice Benefit has significant consequences because the patient waives the right to receive standard Medicare benefits related to the terminal illness, including all treatment for the purposes of curing the terminal illness. See 42 U.S.C. 1395d(d). A patient's hospice election statement must include the following items of information: (1) Identification of the particular hospice that will provide care to the individual; (2) the individual's or representative's acknowledgment that he or she has been given a full understanding of hospice care; (3) the individual's or representative's acknowledgment that he or she understands that certain Medicare services are waived by the election; (4) the effective date of the election; and (5) the signature of the individual or representative. See Medicare Hospice Manual Sec. 210.

[23] For a hospice patient to receive reimbursement for hospice services under Medicare, the patient must be "terminally ill." See 42 U.S.C. 1395d (a). An individual is considered to be "terminally ill" if the individual has a medical prognosis that the individual's life expectancy is six months or less if the illness runs its normal course. 42 CFR 418.3. In March 1995, Operation Restore Trust (ORT), a joint initiative, was established between the OIG, HCFA, and Administration on Aging. Among its projects, ORT assessed the medical eligibility for hospice services in the five largest States in terms of Medicare spending (New York, Florida, Illinois, Texas and California). Through ORT activities, it was discovered that many beneficiaries receiving Medicare hospice benefits did not have a terminal illness as defined by Medicare. See OIG report A-05–96–00023 — "Enhanced Controls Needed to Assure Validity of Medicare Hospice Enrollments." See also section II.A.3.a. and accompanying notes.

[24] When an individual makes an election to receive services covered by the Medicare Hospice Benefit, that individual waives the right to receive Medicare reimbursement for any treatment related to his or her terminal illness. Accordingly, a hospice should ensure it is not involved with a health care provider who the hospice knows submits claims for the following services that are unallowable for reimbursement under the Medicare Hospice Benefit: (1) Standard Medicare benefits for treatment of the terminal illness; (2) treatment by another hospice not arranged for by the patient's hospice; and (3) care from another provider that duplicates care the hospice is required to furnish. See 42 U.S.C. 1395d(d). It is expected that the hospice provider will work with other providers to coordinate care and ensure appropriate billing if these situations occur. Where a single episode of care culminates in an inpatient admission and also involves services by two different providers, the need for a clear record from both providers is critical.

- Under-utilization;[25]
- Falsified medical records or plans of care;[26]
- Untimely and/or forged physician certifications on plans of care;
- Inadequate or incomplete services rendered by the Interdisciplinary Group;[27]
- Insufficient oversight of patients, in particular, those patients receiving more than six consecutive months of hospice care;[28]

---

[25] In other words, knowing denial of needed care in order to keep costs low. A hospice is accountable for the appropriate allocation and utilization of its resources in order to provide optimal care consistent with the needs of a patient, family and/or lawful representative. When a patient is receiving hospice care, the hospice is paid a predetermined fee for each day during the length of care, no matter how much care the hospice actually provides. This means that a hospice may have a financial incentive to reduce the number of services provided to each patient, because the hospice will get paid the same amount regardless of the number of services provided. The OIG has received complaints about hospices neglecting patient needs and ignoring reasonable requests for treatment, including complaints about limited availability of durable medical equipment for patients as their medical condition decreases and failure to provide continuous care for periods of crisis due to staff shortages. The OIG has also been alerted to improper utilization of services that occurs when a hospice encourages a patient to revoke the Medicare Hospice Benefit for the purpose of obtaining expensive care under the standard Medicare benefits, only to re-elect the Medicare Hospice Benefit when expensive care is no longer necessary.

[26] OIG investigations have revealed that certain hospices have falsified patient medical records and plans of care to exaggerate the negative aspects regarding a hospice patient's condition to justify reimbursement. See section II.A.3.b. and accompanying notes.

[27] Each hospice is required to have an "Interdisciplinary Group" of personnel. See 42 U.S.C. 1395x(dd)(2)(B). See note 16. Failure of the Interdisciplinary Group to meet its responsibilities may result in standard care. In addition, inadequate review of a hospice patient may result in improper reimbursement for services provided to a patient who fails to continue to be eligible for the Medicare Hospice Benefit.

[28] Since the enactment of the Balanced Budget Act of 1997, the Medicare Hospice Benefit is divided into the following benefit periods: (1) initial 90-day; (2) subsequent 90-day; and (3) unlimited number of 60-day benefit periods as long as the patient continues to meet program eligibility requirements. See 42 U.S.C. 1395d. At the beginning of each subsequent 60-day benefit period, the hospice physician must recertify that the patient is terminally ill. See 42 U.S.C. 1395f(a)(7). If the necessary oversight is not performed during the unlimited periods of care, a hospice may receive improper reimbursement for services provided to a patient who fails to continue to be eligible for the Medicare Hospice Benefit.

- Hospice incentives to actual or potential referral sources (e.g., physicians, nursing homes, hospitals, patients, etc.) that may violate the anti-kickback statute or other similar Federal or State statute or regulation,[29] including improper arrangements with nursing homes;[30]
- Overlap in the services that a nursing home provides, which results in insufficient care provided by a hospice to a nursing home resident;[31]

---

[29] Examples of arrangements that may run afoul of the anti-kickback statute include practices in which a hospice pays a fee to a physician for each certification of terminal illness, or provides nursing, administrative, and other services for free or below fair market value to physicians, nursing homes, hospitals and other potential referral sources with the intent to influence referrals. See 42 U.S.C. 1320a-7b; 60 FR 40847 (1995). See also discussion in section II.A.4. and accompanying notes. In addition, a hospice that offers an incentive to an individual that such hospice knows or should know is likely to influence the individual to use a particular hospice may be subject to civil money penalties. See 42 U.S.C. 1320a-7a(a)(5).

[30] The OIG has observed instances of potential kickbacks between hospices and nursing homes to unlawfully influence the referral of patients. In general, payments by a hospice to a nursing home for "room and board" provided to a Medicaid hospice patient should not exceed what the nursing home otherwise would have received directly from Medicaid if the patient had not been enrolled in hospice. (If a patient receiving Medicare hospice benefits in a nursing home is also eligible for Medicaid, Medicaid will pay the hospice at least 95 percent of the State's daily nursing home rate, and the hospice is then responsible for paying the nursing home for the patient's room and board.) See Hospice Medicare Manual Sec. 204.2. See also section II.A.4. and accompanying notes.

[31] There may be some overlap in the services that the nursing homes and hospices provide, thereby providing one or the other the opportunity to reduce services and costs. Recent OIG reports found that residents of certain nursing homes receive fewer services from their hospice than patients who receive hospice services in their own homes. Upon review, it was found that many nursing home hospice patients were receiving only basic nursing and aide visits that were provided by nursing home staff as part of room and board when hospice staff were not present. Other additional treatments provided by hospice staff, such as nursing and aide visits, were often clearly within the professional skills possessed by nursing home staff. The reports found that the nature of services provided by hospice staff, while appropriate and efficacious, appeared to differ little from services a nursing home would have provided if the patient was not enrolled in hospice. See OEI report OEI-05–95–00250 — "Hospice Patients in Nursing Homes;" see also OIG report A-05–96–00023 — "Enhanced Controls Needed to Assure Validity of Medicare Hospice Enrollments." Since hospices receive a fixed daily payment regardless of the number of services provided or the location of the

- Improper relinquishment of core services and professional management responsibilities to nursing homes, volunteers and privately-paid professionals;[32]
- Providing hospice services in a nursing home before a written agreement has been finalized, if required;[33]
- Billing for a higher level of care than was necessary;[34]
- Knowingly billing for inadequate or substandard care;
- Pressure on a patient to revoke the Medicare Hospice Benefit when the patient is still eligible for and desires care, but the care has become too expensive for the hospice to deliver;[35]

---

patient, fewer services may result in higher profits per patient. See also section II.A.3.e. and accompanying notes.

[32] Certain of the hospice services (i.e.. "core services" such as nursing, medical, social, and counseling services) must be provided directly to the patient by employees of the hospice, while other non-core hospice services may be provided at fair market value in accordance with contracts with other providers. However, the hospice must retain professional management for all contracted services. See 42 CFR 418.80.

[33] A patient who resides in a skilled nursing facility or nursing facility may elect the Medicare Hospice Benefit if: (1) the residential care is paid for by (a) the beneficiary or private insurance, or (b) Medicaid (if the beneficiary is dual eligible); and (2) the hospice and facility have a written agreement under which the hospice takes full responsibility for the professional management of the individual's hospice care and the facility agrees to provide room and board. Hospice Medicare Manual Sec. 204.2

[34] Billing for unnecessary services involves knowingly seeking reimbursement for services that "are not reasonable and necessary for the palliation or management of terminal illness." See 42 U.S.C. 1395y(a)(1)(C). Because HCFA establishes different payment amounts for specific categories of covered hospice care, a hospice must ensure that it provides services to hospice patients that are reasonable and necessary. Otherwise, the hospice may be reimbursed for a higher level of care than was necessary, e.g., a hospice that provides and bills for continuous care where only routine home care is necessary. See also section II.A.3.d. and accompanying notes.

[35] Fiscal intermediaries have informed the OIG that hospices rarely offer the reasons supporting the revocation of a patient's Medicare Hospice Benefit. Although a hospice may discharge a patient if it discovers that the patient is not terminally ill, hospices should not encourage a patient to revoke the benefit merely to avoid the obligation to pay for hospice services that have become too costly. See 42 CFR 418.28; Hospice Medicare Manual Sec. 210.

- Billing for hospice care provided by unqualified or unlicensed clinical personnel;[36]
- False dating of amendments to medical records;[37]
- High-pressure marketing of hospice care to ineligible beneficiaries;[38]
- Improper patient solicitation activities, such as "patient charting;'[39]
- Inadequate management and oversight of subcontracted services, which results in improper billing;[40]

---

[36] Medicare conditions of participation require that hospices and all hospice employees must be licensed in accordance with applicable Federal, State and local laws and regulations. 42 CFR 418.72.

[37] If additions or corrections need to be made to medical records, hospices should make such entries according to standards of practice and applicable State law. For example, hospices might correct a medical record by drawing a single line through the erroneous entry, writing "error" next to the entry, initialing and dating the correction and writing the correct information near the entry or writing where the correct information could be found.

[38] Hospices should not utilize prohibited or inappropriate conduct (e.g., offer free gifts or services to patients), designed to maximize business growth and patient retention, to carry out their initiatives and activities. Also, any marketing information offered by hospices should be clear, correct, non-deceptive, and fully informative. Through ORT, it was discovered that hospice marketing materials had placed considerable emphasis on the availability of hospice benefits for long term care patients, while downplaying or ignoring the terminal illness eligibility requirement. See OIG report A-05–96–00023 — "Enhanced Controls Needed to Assure Validity of Medicare Hospice Enrollments." Hospices should not engage in marketing and sales strategies that offer incomplete or inadequate information about Medicare entitlement under the Medicare Hospice Benefit to induce beneficiaries to elect hospice and thereby waive aggressive treatment options that Medicare would otherwise cover. Marketing statements should not create the perception that the initial terminal prognosis is of limited importance and that hospice benefits may almost routinely be provided over an indefinite time period. Marketing materials should prominently feature the eligibility requirements for the Medicare Hospice Benefit.

[39] An example of an improper review of patient records is when a hospice arranges with the administration of a nursing facility to review patient records without the patent's permission, solely to determine if the patients are eligible for hospice care and to solicit hospice referrals. Hospices should not review medical records of nursing home patients in an attempt to recruit patients for hospice services based on their diagnoses. For instance, see OIG report A-05–96–00023 — "Enhanced Controls Needed to Assure Validity of Medicare Hospice Enrollments."

[40] The Balanced Budget Act of 1997, Pub.L. 105–33, amended the Social Security Act so that hospices will no longer be required to routinely provide

- Sales commissions based upon length of stay in hospice;[41]
- Deficient coordination of volunteers;[42]
- Improper indication of the location where hospice services were delivered;[43]
- Failure to comply with applicable requirements for verbal orders for hospice services;[44]

---

all physician services directly by employing a physician. See 42 U.S.C. 1395x (dd)(2). Because the OIG has received reports of limited involvement displayed by contracted physicians, as opposed to hospice-employed physicians, hospices should consider having oversight mechanisms in place to ensure that hospice physicians are thoroughly reviewing re-certification documentation.

[41] Through ORT activities, it was discovered that hospice sales staff often were paid on commission based on the length of a patient's stay in hospice. For example, commission amounts were determined by multiplying the total number of days of hospice patient care (patient days) within a sales representative's territory by a factor that reflected the level of achievement of assigned sales performance objectives. Such marketing tactics encouraged the recruitment of long-term patients, many of whom the review found ineligible for the Medicare Hospice Benefit. The OIG recommends that hospices monitor sales commissions for potential vulnerabilities associated with improper patient recruiting. See OIG report A-05-96-00023 — "Enhanced Controls Needed to Assure Validity of Medicare Hospice Enrollments."

[42] Hospices rely heavily on volunteer support. In fact, the Medicare Hospice Benefit is the only Federally funded program that mandates the provision of volunteer services. Appropriately, hospices need to recognize and attend to compliance issues associated with volunteers (i.e., screening, training, disciplining, monitoring, etc.)

[43] Medicare payments for hospice services are made on a prospective basis and adjusted by an area wage index. Hospices must submit claims based on the geographic location at which the service is furnished and not the location of the hospice. Incorrect designation of the place of service for revenue codes 651 and 652 of the hospice claim may significantly alter reimbursement and result in overpayment for services performed (e.g., hospice office in a metropolitan area may be reimbursed more than a rural home where the services were performed).

[44] Hospice staff must make an appropriate entry in the patient's medical record as soon as they receive a verbal certification of terminal illness and file written certifications in the medical record. See 42 CFR 418.22(d). State regulations may require that verbal and telephone orders from physicians should only be accepted by individuals authorized by State law to accept such orders. The OIG recommends that those authorized individuals accepting verbal and telephone orders should record, date and sign these orders and the physician(s) who ordered the service or treatment should

- Non-response to late hospice referrals by physicians;[45]
- Knowing misuse of provider certification numbers, which results in improper billing;[46]
- Failure to adhere to hospice licensing requirements and Medicare conditions of participation;[47] and
- Knowing failure to return overpayments made by Federal health care programs.[48] A hospice's prior history of noncompliance with applicable statutes, regulations and Federal health care program requirements may indicate additional types of risk areas where the hospice may be vulnerable and that may require policies and procedures to prevent recurrence.[49] Additional risk areas should be assessed by hospices as well as

---

countersign them no later than the time period required by State regulations.

[45] We have received comments expressing concern over late hospice referrals by physicians. While the onus of a timely hospice referral may be on a physician, a hospice should identify untimely referrals and provide adequate follow-up to the physicians. When hospice referrals are late, terminally ill patients may be unnecessarily denied access to the Medicare Hospice Benefit, hospices may have to admit a patient at the costliest stage of terminal illness, and quality of care may be affected because of patients being too far along to receive the optimum benefits of hospice care. Hospices need to work closely with physicians to educate and remind them as to the sensitivities and risks associated with untimely referrals. The OIG supports appropriate efforts to increase access to hospice care for eligible individuals.

[46] E.g., transfer of a patient from one hospice to another hospice owned by the same company to circumvent applicable reimbursement caps.

[47] See 42 CFR 418.50–418.100 for the Medicare conditions of participation that apply to hospices.

[48] An overpayment is the amount of money a hospice may have received in excess of the amount due and payable under a health care program. Examples of overpayments include, but are not limited to, instances where a hospice is: (1) Paid twice for the same service either by Medicare or by Medicare and another insurer; or (2) paid for care rendered to patients who are not terminally ill or are otherwise ineligible for the Medicare Hospice Benefit. For instance, see Hospice Medicare Manual Sec. 307. The OIG strongly recommends that the hospice institute procedures to detect overpayments and to promptly remit such overpayments to the affected payor. See 42 U.S.C. 2320a-7b(a)(3), which provides criminal penalties for failure to disclose an overpayment. See also 18 U.S.C. 669.

[49] "Recurrence of misconduct similar to that which an organization has previously committed casts doubt on whether it took all reasonable steps to prevent such misconduct" and is a significant factor in the assessment of whether a compliance program is effective. See United States Sentencing Commission Guidelines, Guidelines Manual, 8A1.2, Application Note 3(k) (iii).

incorporated into the written policies and procedures and training elements developed as part of their compliance programs.

3. Eligibility Requirements

Of the risk areas identified above, those pertaining to the Medicare eligibility requirements have been the frequent subject of investigations and audits. With respect to the reimbursement process, a hospice's written policies and procedures should reflect and reinforce current Federal health care requirements regarding the eligibility for Medicare reimbursement. The policies must create a mechanism for the billing or reimbursement staff to communicate effectively and accurately with the clinical staff. Policies and procedures should:

- Provide for complete and timely documentation of the specific clinical factors that qualify a patient for the Medicare Hospice Benefit;[50]
- Delineate who has authority to make entries in the patient record;
- Emphasize that patients should be admitted to hospice care only when appropriate documentation supports the applicable reimbursement eligibility criteria and only when such documentation is maintained, appropriately organized in a legible form, and available for audit and review. The documentation should record the activity leading to the record entry and the identity of the individual providing the service. Documentation should be consistent and any discrepancies discussed and reconciled. The hospice should consult with its physicians, clinical staff and/or governing body to establish other appropriate documentation guidelines;
- Indicate that the diagnosis and procedure codes for hospice services reported on the reimbursement claim should be based on the patient's clinical condition as reflected in the medical record and other documentation, and should comply with all applicable official coding rules and guidelines. Any Health Care

[50] Each patient's clinical record must contain: (1) The initial and subsequent assessments (including hospice admission history, certification, and recertification); (2) the plan of care; (3) identification data; (4) consent and authorization and election forms; (5) pertinent medical history; and (6) complete documentation of all services and events (including evaluations, treatments, progress notes, etc.) See CFR 418.74.

Financing Administration Common Procedure Coding System (HCPCS), International Classification of Disease (ICD), or revenue code (or successor codes) used by the billing staff should accurately describe the service that was ordered by the physician and performed by the hospice. The documentation necessary for accurate billing should be available to billing staff; and

- Provide that the compensation for hospice admission personnel, billing department personnel and billing consultants should not offer any financial incentive to bill for hospice care regardless of whether applicable eligibility criteria for reimbursement is met.

The written policies and procedures concerning proper billing should reflect the current reimbursement principles set forth in applicable regulations and should be developed in tandem with private payor and organizational standards. Particular attention should be paid to issues associated with patient election of the Medicare Hospice Benefit, certification of terminal illness of a patient, development and certification of a patient's interdisciplinary plan of care and reasonableness and necessity of the level of hospice care provided.[51]

a. Terminal Illness as an Eligibility Requirement. For a hospice patient to receive reimbursement for hospice services under Medicare,[52] the patient must be "terminally ill."[53] Hospices should create oversight mechanisms to ensure that the terminal illness of a Medicare beneficiary is verified[54] and the specific factors qualifying the

[51] The OIG has undertaken numerous audits, investigations, inspections, and national enforcement initiatives aimed at reducing potential and actual fraud, abuse and waste. For example, see OIG report A-05–96–00023 — "Enhanced Controls Needed to Assure Validity of Medicare Hospice Enrollments;" see also OIG Special Fraud Alert — "Fraud and Abuse in Nursing Home Arrangements with Hospices" (March 1998); OIG Medicare Advisory Bulletin on Hospice Benefits (November 1995).

[52] 42 U.S.C. 1395d(a) authorizes the reimbursement of hospice care.

[53] An individual is considered to be "terminally ill" if the individual has a medical prognosis that the individual's life expectancy is six months or less if the illness runs its normal course. 42 CFR 418.3. However, the fact that a hospice patient lives beyond this six month period, in and of itself, does not constitute grounds for a determination that the patient was never eligible for hospice care, or that the services provided to the patient were not reimbursable by Medicare.

[54] Medical reviews, audits, inspections, and investigations of hospices have concluded that hospices have billed Medicare for hospice services pro-

patient as terminally ill are properly documented.[55] Any determinative assessment of the terminal illness of a Medicare beneficiary should be completed prior to billing Medicare for hospice care. Physicians must certify that the beneficiary was terminally ill at the time when a patient was admitted for hospice services as well as at the beginning of subsequent hospice benefit periods.[56]

The hospice's written policies and procedures should require, at a minimum, that:

- Before a patient is admitted for hospice services, the hospice physician and attending physician thoroughly review and certify the admitting diagnosis and prognosis;
- A patient's medical record contain complete documentation to support the certification made by the hospice physician or attending physician;[57]
- The patient or lawful representative is informed of the determination of the patient's life limiting condition;

---

vided to patients who are not terminally ill. For instance, see OIG report OEI-04–93–00270 — "Medicare Hospice Beneficiaries: Services and Eligibility." Through Operation Restore Trust activities and the increased program integrity actions by the Regional Home Health Intermediaries (RHHIs), it was discovered that many beneficiaries receiving Medicare hospice benefits did not have a terminal illness. In the review of hospice cases between 1992 and 1996, patients did not demonstrate significant clinical symptoms of their disease nor notable functional limitations one would expect to see in a person who has a terminal illness as defined by Medicare. See OIG report A-05–96–00023 — "Enhanced Controls Needed to Assure Validity of Medicare Hospice Enrollments." Findings such as these have prompted a concern that some hospices may intentionally misrepresent a condition as terminal in order to secure Medicare reimbursement. See also note 23.

[55] See 42 CFR 418.22(d). If a question is raised as to whether a patient is terminally ill, the hospice will be requested to furnish its Medicare fiscal intermediary with the information necessary to establish that the patient is terminally ill.

[56] See 42 U.S.C. 1395f(a)(7). See also note 28.

[57] In order to verify a patient's terminal illness, Medicare fiscal intermediaries need to review physician input and rationale beyond a signature on the certification form (e.g., a recent medical history and physical if the physician does not actually examine the patient prior to admission to hospice; summary of physician review of the history and physical taken by hospice personnel; or physician documentation of his or her contribution to the Interdisciplinary Group meetings).

- The patient or lawful representative is aware that the goal of hospice is directed toward relief of symptoms, rather than the cure of the underlying disease;
- A patient's medical condition and status is sufficiently reviewed during Interdisciplinary Group meetings; and
- The clinical progression/status of a patient's disease and medical condition are properly documented.

Hospices can further ensure compliance with the terminal illness requirement through discussions with Medicare beneficiaries and their families, reminding them that they must satisfy the regulatory requirements for terminal illness status to be eligible for Medicare coverage. These discussions can take place at the beginning of hospice election and during appropriate times throughout a patient's hospice care, e.g., at time of recertification. Because the Medicare conditions of participation require hospices to give all beneficiaries an informed consent form that outlines their legal rights before furnishing them with hospice care,[58] providers can include reminders of terminal illness requirements in these forms.

The OIG recognizes that decisions to admit patients to hospices are often not based on medical factors alone. Such decisions are routinely influenced by non-medical factors that would generally be reflected in the plan of care. However, it is important to make a distinction between admitting a patient to a hospice program and certifying a patient for the Medicare Hospice Benefit. Based on an individual hospice's admission criteria, some patients may be admitted to hospice care prior to an estimated six months before death, as long as the hospice is paid fair market value for its services. Regardless, patients can be certified for the Medicare Hospice Benefit only when it is reasonable to conclude that a patient's life expectancy is six months or less if the illness runs its normal course. In other cases, alternative modes of reimbursement, often provided through community support, should be sought outside the Medicare Hospice Benefit.

b. Plan of Care. A hospice should take all reasonable steps to ensure that a written plan of care is established and maintained for each individual who receives hospice services, and that the care provided to that individual is in accordance with the plan.[59] The plan must be established by the patient's attending physician, the

[58] See 42 CFR 418.62.

[59] See 42 U.S.C. 1395f(a)(7); 42 CFR 418.58.

hospice physician, and the Interdisciplinary Group.[60] Each patient's needs should be continuously assessed and all treatment options explored and evaluated in the context of the patient's symptoms.[61] The hospice's written policies and procedures should require, at a minimum, that:

- Before the hospice bills for hospice care provided to a patient, the plan of care must be established by the hospice physician and the Interdisciplinary Group;[62]
- The plan of care includes: (i) An assessment of the hospice patient's needs and identification of services, including the management of discomfort and symptom relief, and (ii) the scope and frequency of services, in detail, needed to meet the patient's and family's needs;[63]
- The plan of care must be reviewed and updated, at intervals specified in the plan, by the attending physician, hospice physician and the Interdisciplinary Group;[64]
- See 42 U.S.C. 1395f(a)(7)(B); 42 U.S.C. 1395x(dd)(2)(B).
- The hospice properly documents any review or update of a hospice patient's plan of care by the attending physician, the hospice physician and Interdisciplinary Group; and[65]
- The hospice regularly reviews the appropriateness of Interdisciplinary Group services and level of services being provided,

[60] Id.

[61] Some ORT audits found that hospice physicians, at times, rely partly on referring, attending physicians. Although the referring physician's opinion can and should be considered as part of the decision making process, the final determination of hospice eligibility is the responsibility of the hospice physician. For instance, see OIG report A-04–95–02111. If employees of a hospice believe that services ordered by a physician are excessive or otherwise inappropriate, the hospice cannot avoid liability for filing improper claims simply because a physician has certified the need for hospice care.

[62] For Medicare reimbursement purposes, the services of the hospice medical director(s) or the physician member of the Hospice Interdisciplinary Group must be performed by a doctor of medicine or osteopathy. See 42 CFR 418.202. The hospice should employ reasonable measures to verify that physicians who establish the hospice plan are appropriately licensed and no adverse actions, such as criminal conviction, debarment or an exclusion, have been taken against them.

[63] 42 CFR 418.58(c).

[64] See 42 U.S.C. 1395f(a)(7)(B); 42 U.S.C. 1395x(dd)(2)(B).

[65] 42 CFR 418.58(b).

patient admission to hospice, patient length of stay delays and specific treatment modalities.

c. Utilization of Hospice Services. A hospice is accountable for the appropriate allocation and utilization of its resources in order to provide optimal care consistent with patient and family needs.[66] Accordingly, a hospice should monitor and evaluate its resource allocation regularly to identify and resolve problems with the utilization of services, facilities and personnel. To achieve such monitoring, a hospice should schedule Interdisciplinary Group case reviews and conferences,[67] review specific problems that may arise with services provided and use objective written criteria or treatment protocols to guide decisions about the utilization of hospice services provided. Utilization concerns may be an indication of a problem with the quality or quantity of services provided to a hospice patient or demonstrate a more fundamental concern as to the patient's eligibility for the Medicare Hospice Benefit in the first place. Therefore, a hospice should implement policies and procedures to identify, assess and rectify any problems associated with:

- Appropriateness of Interdisciplinary Group services and level of services being provided;
- Appropriateness of patient admission to hospice;
- Regular review of patient length of stay;
- Delays in admission or in the provision of Interdisciplinary Group services; and
- Specific treatment modalities.

When utilization problems are identified, a hospice should implement corrective actions and preventative measures that may include ongoing monitoring, changes in the provision of services and revisions of policies and procedures.

d. Levels of Hospice Care. A hospice's compliance program should provide that it should only seek reimbursement for services that the

---

[66] Once a Medicare beneficiary elects hospice care, the hospice is responsible for furnishing directly, or arranging for, all supplies and services that relate to the beneficary's terminal condition, except the services of an attending physician. Hospice beneficiaries have the right to receive covered medical, social and emotional support services from the hospice directly, or through arrangements made by the hospice, and should not be forced to seek or pay for such care from non-hospice providers.

[67] Interdisciplinary Group conferences are regularly scheduled periodic meetings of the Interdisciplinary Group to review the most current patient/family assessment, evaluate needs and update the plan of care.

hospice has reason to believe are reasonable and necessary[68] for the palliation or management of terminal illness and were ordered by a physician or other appropriately licensed individual. The OIG recommends the hospice's compliance program communicate to physicians authorized to certify patients for hospice care and hospice personnel authorized to admit patients for hospice care that services will only be paid if ordered, certified, covered, reasonable and necessary for the patient, given his or her clinical condition.

Although hospice services are reimbursed on a per diem basis and not per individual component of the services performed, the payment is based upon the level of care provided.[69] Because HCFA establishes different payment amounts for specific categories of covered hospice care, a hospice must ensure that it provides for services to hospice patients that are reasonable and necessary. Otherwise, the hospice may be reimbursed for a higher level of services than was necessary, e.g., a hospice that provides and bills for continuous care where only routine home care is necessary.

As a preliminary matter, the OIG recognizes that licensed health care professionals must be able to order any services that are appropriate for the care of their patients. However, Medicare and other Government and private health care plans will only pay for those services otherwise covered that meet appropriate standards (i.e., in the case of Medicare, "reasonable and necessary" services). Providers may not bill for services that do not meet the applicable standards.[70] The hospice is in a unique position to deliver this information to the health care professionals on its staff and to the

---

[68] See note 34.

[69] Payment amounts are determined within each of the following categories: (1) routine home care day; (2) continuous home care day (patient who receives hospice care that consists predominantly of nursing care on a continuous basis at home, is furnished only during brief periods of crisis and only as necessary to maintain the terminally ill patient at home); (3) inpatient respite care day (hospice patient receives care in an approved facility on a short-term basis for respite — not more than five consecutive days at a time); and (4) general inpatient care day (hospice patient receives general inpatient care in an inpatient facility for pain control or acute or chronic symptom management that cannot be managed in other settings). See 42 CFR 418.302.

[70] Administrative civil money penalties, assessments, and exclusion, as well as remedies available under criminal and civil law, including the civil False Claims Act, may be imposed against any person who submits a claim for services "that [the] person knows or should know are not medically necessary." See, e.g., 42 U.S.C. 1320a-7a(a).

physicians who certify hospice services. Upon request, a hospice must be able to provide documentation, such as physician orders and other patient medical records, to support the level of services provided to a hospice patient.[71] The compliance officer should ensure that a clear, comprehensive summary of the definitions for the different levels of hospice care[72] and applicable rules of the various Government and private plans is prepared, disseminated, and explained to appropriate hospice personnel.

We recommend that hospices formulate policies and procedures that include periodic clinical reviews, both prior and subsequent to billing for services, as a means of verifying that patients are receiving only reasonable and necessary services. As part of such reviews, hospices should examine the level, frequency, and duration of the services they perform to determine, in consultation with a physician, whether patients' medical conditions justify the level of services provided and billed. A hospice may choose to incorporate this clinical review function into pre-existing quality assurance mechanisms or any other quality assurance processes that are part of its conditions of participation.[73]

e. Services Provided to Hospice Patients in Nursing Homes. Hospice services may be appropriate and beneficial to terminally ill nursing home residents who wish to receive palliative care.[74] However, the OIG has found hospices that enroll nursing home patients in hospice care are particularly vulnerable to fraud and abuse.[75] Appropriately, a hospice should set sufficient oversight controls in place to ensure that care it provides to nursing home residents is appropriate, complete, and in accordance with applicable laws and Federal health care program requirements.

---

[71] Medicare fiscal intermediaries have the authority to require hospices that furnish items or services under the program to submit documentation that substantiates services were actually provided and medically necessary. See Medicare Intermediary Manual Sec. 3116.1.B.

[72] See note 69.

[73] See 42 CFR 418.66.

[74] See note 33.

[75] In some cases reviewed in nursing homes, OIG medical reviewers have found that while the hospice benefit may eventually have been appropriate, at the time of election, patients were stable and the electionof hospice was premature. See OEI report OEI-05-95-00250: "Hospice Patients in Nursing Homes;" see also OIG report A-05-96-00023 — "Enhanced Controls Needed to Assure Validity of Medicare Hospice Enrollments." For other examples of potential fraud and abuse in the hospice/nursing home context, see notes 30–33.

When a resident of a nursing home elects the Medicare Hospice Benefit, the hospice and the nursing home should jointly establish a coordinated plan of care that reflects the hospice philosophy, and is based on an assessment of the individual's needs and unique living situation in the nursing home. The coordinated plan should identify the care and services that the nursing home will provide to be responsive to the unique needs of the patient/resident and his or her expressed desire for hospice care.

In general, a hospice should involve nursing home personnel in assisting with the administration of a patient's prescribed therapies included in the plan of care only to the extent that the hospice would routinely utilize the services of a hospice patient's family/caregiver in implementing the plan of care.[76] To satisfy the applicable Medicare conditions of participation in the nursing home context, hospices should implement policies and procedures to ensure that:

- The hospice makes all covered services available to meet the needs of a patient and does not routinely discharge patients in need of costly inpatient care;[77]
- The hospice retains professional responsibility for services (e.g., personal care, nursing, medication for relieving pain control) furnished by nursing home staff;[78]
- All the care furnished by a nursing home related to the terminal illness or related conditions is in accordance with the hospice plan of care;[79]
- The hospice and the nursing home communicate with each other when any changes are indicated to the plan of care, and each provider is aware of the other's responsibilities in implementing the plan of care and complete those respective functions;[80]
- Evidence of the coordinated plan of care is present in the clinical records of both providers;[81]
- Hospice Certification Manual Sec. 2082.A.

---

[76] Hospice Certification Manual Sec. 2082.B.

[77] See 42 CFR 418.50.

[78] See 42 CFR 418.56.

[79] See 42 CFR 418.58.

[80] Hospice Certification Manual Sec. 2082.A.

[81] Hospice Certification Manual Sec. 2082.A.

- Substantially all the core services are routinely provided directly by hospice employees [82] and the hospice does not rely on employees of the inpatient facility to furnish needed nursing, physician, counseling, or medical social services; [83] and
- The hospice keeps its forms and documentation of services separate from the nursing home's forms and documentation. [84]

4. Anti-Kickback and Self-Referral Concerns

The hospice should have policies and procedures in place with respect to compliance with Federal and State anti-kickback statutes and other applicable laws. [85] Such policies should provide that:

- All of the hospices's contracts and arrangements with actual or potential referral sources are reviewed carefully for compliance with all applicable statutes and regulations; [86]
- The hospice does not submit or cause to be submitted to the Federal health care programs claims for patients who were referred to the hospice pursuant to contracts or financial arrangements that were designed to induce such referrals in violation of the anti-kickback statute or similar Federal or State statute or regulation; and
- The hospice does not offer or provide gifts, free services, or other incentives to patients, relatives of patients, physicians, nursing facilities, hospitals, contractors or other potential referral sources for the purpose of inducing referrals in violation of the anti-kickback statute or similar Federal or State statute or

---

[82] See 42 CFR 418.80.

[83] In limited circumstances, HFCA may approve a waiver of the requirement for core nursing services to be provided by a hospice that is located in a non-urbanized area. See 42 CFR 418.83.

[84] A Hospice may consider creating some type of payroll tracking or time study in an effort to properly differentiate services between the hospice and the nursing home.

[85] The hospice's in-house counsel or compliance officer should, among other things, obtain copies of all relevant OIG regulations, Special Fraud Alerts and advisory opinions (these documents are located on the Internet at http://www.dhhs.gov/progorg/oig), and ensure that the hospice's policies reflect the guidance provided by the OIG.

[86] Although hospices may contract with physicians, see note 40, hospices and physicians mut still tailor such agreements to avoid violation of the anti-kickback statute or similar Federal or State statute or regulation and to comply with applicable Medicare conditions of participation. See 42 CFR 418.56 and 418.86.

regulation.[87]

In particular, arrangements between nursing homes and hospices are vulnerable to fraud and abuse because nursing home operators have control over the specific hospice or hospices they will permit to provide hospice services to their residents.[88] Moreover, hospice patients residing in nursing homes may be particularly desirable from a hospice's financial standpoint.[89] Therefore, with respect to arrangements with nursing homes, a hospice should develop policies and procedures to prevent the following practices from occurring, which may constitute potential kickbacks:

- Hospice offering free or below fair market value goods to induce a nursing home to refer patients to the hospice;
- Hospice paying "room and board" payments to the nursing home in amounts in excess of what the nursing home would have received directly from Medicaid had the patient not been enrolled in hospice;[90]
- Hospice paying above fair market value for "additional" non-core services that Medicaid does not consider to be included in its "room and board" payments to the nursing home;[91]
- Hospice referring its patients to a nursing home to induce the nursing home to refer its patients to the hospice;
- Hospice providing free (or below fair market value) care to nursing home patients, for whom the nursing home is receiving Medicare payment under the Medicare Skilled Nursing Facility

---

[87] See 42 U.S.C. 1320a-7b(b); 60 FR 40847 (1995).

[88] While an exclusive or semi-exclusive arrangement with a nursing home to provide hospice services to residents can promote efficiency and safety by permitting the nursing home operator to coordinate care, screen hospice caregivers, and maintain control of the premises, such an arrangement may have substantial monetary value to a hospice. In these circumstances, some nursing home operators and/or hospices may request or offer illegal remuneration to influence a nursing home's decision to do business with a particular hospice.

[89] First, a nursing home's population represents a sizeable pool of potential hospice patients. Second, nursing home hospice patients may generate higher gross revenues per patient than patients residing in their own homes, because nursing home residents receiving hospice care have, on average, longer lengths of stay than hospice patients residing in their own homes.

[90] See note 30.

[91] See OIG Special Fraud Alert — "Fraud and Abuse in Nursing Home Arrangements with Hospices" (March 1998).

Benefit, with the expectation that after the patient exhausts the skilled nursing facility benefit, the patient will receive hospice services from that hospice; and

- Hospice providing staff at its expense to the nursing home to perform duties that otherwise would be performed by the nursing home.

Further, the policies and procedures should specifically reference and take into account the OIG's safe harbor regulations, which clarify those payment practices that would be immune from prosecution under the anti-kickback statute, as well as the OIG's civil money penalty and exclusion authorities. [92]

5. Retention of Records

Hospice compliance programs should provide for the implementation of a records system. This system should establish policies and procedures regarding the creation, distribution, retention, storage, retrieval and destruction of documents. [93] The two categories of documents developed under this system should include: (1) all records and documentation (e.g., medical records, and billing and claims documentation) required either by Federal or State law for participation in Federal health care programs [94] or any other applicable Federal and State laws and regulations (e.g., document retention requirements to maintain State licensure); and (2) all records necessary to protect the integrity of the hospice's compliance process and confirm the effectiveness of the program.

The second category includes: (1) Documentation that employees were adequately trained; (2) reports from the hospice's hotline, including the nature and results of any investigation that was conducted; (3) documentation of corrective action, including disciplinary action taken and policy improvements introduced, in response to any internal investigation or audit; (4) modifications to the compliance program; (5) self-disclosures; and (6) the results of the hospice's

[92] See 42 CFR 1001.952.

[93] This records system should be tailored to fit the individual needs and financial resources of the hospice.

[94] For example, Medicare requires that hospices must establish and maintain a clinical record for every individual receiving care and services. The record must be complete, promptly and accurately documented, readily accessible and systematically organized to facilitate retrieval. Any entries are to be made and signed by the person providing the services. See 42 CFR 418.74.

auditing and monitoring efforts.[95]

6. Compliance as an Element of a Performance Plan

Compliance programs should require that the promotion of, and adherence to, the elements of the compliance program be a factor in evaluating the performance of all employees, who should be periodically trained in new compliance policies and procedures. In addition, all managers and supervisors should:

- Discuss with all supervised employees and relevant contractors the compliance policies and legal requirements pertinent to their function;
- Inform all supervised personnel that strict compliance with these policies and requirements is a condition of employment; and
- Disclose to all supervised personnel that the hospice will take disciplinary action up to and including termination for violation of these policies or requirements.

In addition to making performance of these duties an element in evaluations, a compliance program should include a policy for sanctioning managers and supervisors who fail to adequately instruct their subordinates or fail to detect noncompliance with applicable policies and legal requirements, where reasonable diligence on the part of the manager or supervisor would have led to the discovery of any problems or violations and given the hospice the opportunity to correct them earlier.

The OIG believes all hospices should ensure that its employees understand the importance of compliance. If a small hospice does not have a formal performance evaluation structure, it should informally convey the employee's compliance responsibilities and the importance of these responsibilities in a written job description or orientation checklist. The applicable documentation should include a dated signature, with an indication that the employee has received it and will be responsible for adherence to the responsibilities expressed.

---

[95] The creation and retention of such documents and reports may raise a variety of legal issues, such as patient privacy and confidentiality. These issues are best discussed with legal counsel.

B. Designation of a Compliance Officer and a Compliance Committee

1. Compliance Officer

Every hospice should designate a compliance officer to serve as the focal point for compliance activities. This responsibility may be the individual's sole duty or added to other management responsibilities, depending upon the size and resources of the hospice and the complexity of the task. Designating a compliance officer with the appropriate authority is critical to the success of the program, necessitating the appointment of a high-level official in the hospice with direct access to the hospice's president or CEO, governing body, all other senior management, and legal counsel.[96] The officer should have sufficient funding and staff to perform his or her responsibilities fully. Coordination and communication are the key functions of the compliance officer with regard to planning, implementing and monitoring the compliance program.

The compliance officer's primary responsibilities should include:

- Overseeing and monitoring the implementation of the compliance program;[97]
- Reporting on a regular basis to the hospice's governing body, CEO and compliance committee (if applicable) on the progress of implementation, and assisting these components in establishing methods to improve the hospice's efficiency and quality of services, and to reduce the hospice's vulnerability to fraud, abuse and waste;
- Periodically revising the program in light of changes in the organization's needs, and in the law and policies and procedures of Government and private payor health plans;

---

[96] The OIG believes that it is not advisable for the compliance function to be subordinate to the hospice's general counsel, or comptroller or similar hospice financial officer. Free standing compliance functions help to ensure independent and objective legal reviews and financial analyses of the institution's compliance efforts and activities. By separating the compliance function from the key management positions of general counsel or chief financial officer (where the size and structure of the hospice make this a feasible option), a system of checks and balances is established to more effectively achieve the goals of the compliance program.

[97] For multi-hospice organizations or hospital-owned hospices, the OIG encourages coordination with each hospice owned by the corporation or hospital through the use of a headquarter's compliance officer, communicating with parallel positions in each facility, regional office or business line, as appropriate.

- Reviewing employees' certifications that they have received, read and understood the standards of conduct;
- Developing, coordinating and participating in a multifaceted educational and training program that focuses on the elements of the compliance program, and seeks to ensure that all relevant employees and management are knowledgeable of, and comply with, pertinent Federal and State standards;
- Ensuring that independent contractors and agents who furnish physician, nursing, or other health care services to the clients of the hospice, or billing services to the hospice, are aware of the requirements of the hospice's compliance program with respect to eligibility, billing and marketing, among other things;
- Coordinating personnel issues with the hospice's Human Resources/Personnel office (or its equivalent) to ensure that: (i) The National Practitioner Data Bank [98] has been checked with respect to all medical staff and independent contractors (as appropriate) and (ii) the List of Excluded Individuals/Entities [99] has been checked with respect to all employees, medical staff and independent contractors (as appropriate); [100]
- Assisting the hospice's financial management in coordinating internal compliance review and monitoring activities, including annual or periodic reviews of departments;
- Independently investigating and acting on matters related to compliance, including the flexibility to design and coordinate internal investigations (e.g., responding to reports of problems or suspected violations) and any resulting corrective action

---

[98] The National Practitioner Data Bank is a data base that contains information about medical malpractice payments, sanctions by boards of medical examiners or State licensing boards, adverse clinical privilege actions and adverse professional society membership actions. Health care entities can have access to this data base to seek information about their own medical or clinical staff, as well as prospective employees or physician contractors.

[99] The List of Excluded Individuals/Entities is an OIG-produced report available on the Internet at http://www.dhhs.gov/progorg/oig. It is updated on a regular basis to reflect the status of health care providers who have been excluded from participation in the Medicare and Medicaid programs. In addition, the General Services Administration maintains a monthly listing of debarred contractors on the Internet at http://www.arnet.gov/epls.

[100] The compliance officer may also have to ensure that the criminal backgrounds of employees have been checked depending upon State requirements or hospice policy. See note 131.

(e.g., making necessary improvements to hospice policies and practices, taking appropriate disciplinary action, etc.) with all hospice departments, subcontracted providers and health care professionals under the hospice's control, and any other agents if appropriate; and

- Continuing the momentum of the compliance program and the accomplishment of its objectives long after the initial years of implementation.[101]

The compliance officer must have the authority to review all documents and other information that are relevant to compliance activities, including, but not limited to, patient medical records, billing records, and records concerning the marketing efforts of the facility and the hospice's arrangements with other parties, including employees, physicians, professionals on staff, relevant independent contractors, suppliers, agents, and supplemental staffing entities. This policy enables the compliance officer to review contracts and obligations (seeking the advice of legal counsel, where appropriate) that may contain referral and payment provisions that could violate the anti-kickback statute and other legal or regulatory requirements.

A small hospice may not have the need or the resources to hire or appoint a full time compliance officer. However, each hospice should have a person in its organization (this person may have other functional responsibilities) who can oversee the hospice's compliance with applicable statutes, rules, regulations, and policies. The structure and comprehensiveness of the hospice's compliance program will help determine the responsibilities of each individual compliance officer.2. Compliance Committee

The OIG recommends that a compliance committee be established to advise the compliance officer and assist in the implementation of the compliance program.[102] When developing an appropriate team

---

[101] Periodic on-site visits of hospice operations, bulletins with compliance updates and reminders, distribution of audiotapes or videotapes on different risk areas, lectures at management and employee meetings, circulation of recent health care articles covering fraud and abuse, and innovative changes to compliance training are various examples of approaches and techniques the compliance officer can employ for the purpose of ensuring continued interest in the compliance program and the hospice's commitment to its policies and principles.

[102] The compliance committee benefits from having the perspectives of individuals with varying responsibilities in the organization, such as operations, finance, audit, human resources, and clinical management (e.g.,

of people to serve as the hospice's compliance committee, including the compliance officer, a hospice should consider a variety of skills and personality traits that are expected from those in such positions.[103] Once a hospice chooses the people that will accept the responsibilities vested in members of the compliance committee, the hospice needs to train these individuals on the policies and procedures of the compliance program, as well as how to discharge their duties.

The committee's functions should include:

- Analyzing the legal requirements with which it must comply, and specific risk areas;
- Assessing existing policies and procedures that address these risk areas for possible incorporation into the compliance program;
- Working with appropriate hospice departments to develop standards of conduct and policies and procedures to promote compliance with legal and ethical requirements;
- Recommending and monitoring, in conjunction with the relevant departments, the development of internal systems and controls to carry out the organization's standards, policies, and procedures as part of its daily operations;
- Determining the appropriate strategy/approach to promote compliance with the program and detection of any potential violations, such as through hotlines and other fraud reporting mechanisms;
- Developing a system to solicit, evaluate, and respond to complaints and problems; and
- Monitoring internal and external audits and investigations for the purpose of identifying troublesome issues and deficient

---

hospice physician), as well as employees and managers of key operating units. These individuals should have the requisite seniority and comprehensive experience within their respective departments to implement any necessary changes to hospice policies and procedures as recommended by the committee.

[103] A health care provider should expect its compliance committee members and compliance officer to demonstrate high integrity, good judgment, assertiveness, and an approachable demeanor, while eliciting the respect and trust of employees of the hospice and having significant professional experience working with billing, clinical records, documentation, and auditing principles.

areas experienced by the hospice, and implementing corrective and preventive action.

The committee may also address other functions as the compliance concept becomes part of the overall hospice operating structure and daily routine.

The compliance committee is an extension of the compliance officer and provides the organization with increased oversight. The OIG recognizes that small hospices may not have the resources or the need to establish a compliance committee. However, when potential problems are identified, the OIG recommends the small hospices supplier create a "taskforce," if appropriate, to address the problem. The members of the taskforce may vary depending upon the issue.

C. Conducting Effective Training and Education

The proper education and training of corporate officers, managers, employees, volunteers, nurses, physicians, and other health care professionals, and the continual retraining of current personnel at all levels, are significant elements of an effective compliance program. As part of their compliance programs, hospices should require personnel to attend specific training on a periodic basis, including appropriate training in Federal and State statutes, regulations, and guidelines, and the policies of private payors, and training in corporate ethics, which emphasizes the organization's commitment to compliance with these legal requirements and policies. [104]

These training programs should include sessions highlighting the organization's compliance program, summarizing fraud and abuse laws, Federal health care program requirements, claim development and submission processes, patient rights, and marketing practices that reflect current legal and program standards. The organization must take steps to communicate effectively its standards and procedures to all affected employees, physicians, independent contractors, and other significant agents, e.g., by requiring participation in training programs and disseminating publications that explain specific requirements in a practical manner. [105] Managers of specific departments or groups can assist in identifying areas that require training

[104] Specific compliance training should complement any "inservice" training sessions that a hospice may regularly schedule to provide an ongoing program for the training of employees as required by its conditions of participation. 42 CFR 418.64.

[105] Some publications, such as OIG's Special Fraud Alerts, audit and inspection reports, and advisory opinions, as well as the annual OIG work plan, are readily available from the OIG and could be the basis for stan-

and in carrying out such training.[106] Training instructors may come from outside or inside the organization, but must be qualified to present the subject matter involved and experienced enough in the issues presented to adequately field questions and coordinate discussions among those being trained. New employees should be trained early in their employment.[107]

Training programs and materials should be designed to take into account the skills, experience, and knowledge of the individual trainees. The compliance officer should document any formal training undertaken by the hospice as part of the compliance program.

A variety of teaching methods, such as interactive training, and training in several different languages, particularly where a hospice has a culturally diverse staff, should be implemented so that all affected employees are knowledgeable of the institution's standards of conduct and procedures for alerting senior management to problems and concerns.[108] In addition to specific training in the risk areas identified in section II.A.2, above, primary training for appropriate corporate officers, managers, and other hospice staff should include such topics as:

- Government and private payor reimbursement principles;
- General prohibitions on paying or receiving remuneration to induce referrals;
- Improper alterations to clinical records;[109]
- Providing hospice services with proper authorization;
- Patient rights and patient education;
- Compliance with Medicare conditions of participation; and

---

dards, educational courses, and programs for appropriate hospice employees.

[106] Significant variations in the functions and responsibilities of different departments or groups may create the need for training materials that are tailored to compliance concerns associated with particular operations and duties.

[107] Certain positions, such as those that involve the billing of hospice services or patient admission to hospice care, create a greater organizational legal exposure, and therefore require specialized training.

[108] Post-training tests can be used to assess the success of training provided and employee comprehension of the hospice's policies and procedures.

[109] This practice involves the hospice altering the attending physician's or other authorized physician's diagnosis in order to receive reimbursement for hospice care. A hospice should not claim the patient has a particular medical condition in order to qualify for reimbursement for which it would not otherwise qualify.

- Duty to report misconduct.

Clarifying and emphasizing these areas of concern through training and educational programs are particularly relevant to a hospice's market ing and financial personnel, in that the pressure to meet business goals may render these employees vulnerable to engaging in prohibited practices.

The OIG suggests that all relevant levels of personnel be made part of various educational and training programs of the hospice.[110] Employees should be required to have a minimum number of educational hours per year, as appropriate, as part of their employment responsibilities.[111] For example, for certain employees involved in the hospice admission functions, periodic training in applicable reimbursement coverage and eligibility requirements should be required. In hospices with high employee turnover, periodic training updates are critical.

The OIG recognizes that the format of the training program will vary depending upon the resources of the hospice. For example, a small hospice may want to create a video for each type of training session so new employees can receive training in a timely manner.[112]

The OIG recommends that attendance and participation in training programs be made a condition of continued employment and that failure to comply with training requirements should result in disciplinary action, including possible termination, when such failure is serious. Adherence to the provisions of the compliance program, such as training requirements, should be a factor in the annual evaluation of each employee. The hospice should retain adequate

[110] In addition, where feasible, the OIG recommends that a hospice afford outside contractors the opportunity to participate in the hospice's compliance training and educational programs, or develop their own programs that complement the hospice's standards of conduct, compliance requirements, and other rules and practices.

[111] Currently, the OIG is monitoring a significant number of corporate integrity agreements that require many of these training elements. The OIG usually requires a minimum of one to three hours annually for basic training in compliance areas. Additional training is required for specialty fields such as billing and marketing.

[112] If videos are utilized for compliance training, the OIG suggests that a hospice make an individual available to field questions from video trainees. In addition, those hospices that use video training should strongly consider requiring trainees to complete post training comprehension tests to ensure that trainees actively paid attention to the video.

records of its training of employees, including attendance logs and material distributed at training sessions.

D. Developing Effective Lines of Communication

1. Access to the Compliance Officer

An open line of communication between the compliance officer and hospice employees is equally important to the successful implementation of a compliance program and the reduction of any potential for fraud, abuse, and waste. Written confidentiality and non-retaliation policies should be developed and distributed to all employees to encourage communication and the reporting of incidents of potential fraud.[113] The compliance committee should also develop independent reporting paths for an employee to report fraud, waste, or abuse so that employees can feel comfortable reporting outside the normal chain of command and supervisors or other personnel cannot divert such reports.[114]

The OIG encourages the establishment of a procedure so that hospice personnel may seek clarification from the compliance officer or members of the compliance committee in the event of any confusion or question with regard to a hospice policy, practice, or procedure. Questions and responses should be documented and dated and, if appropriate, shared with other staff so that standards, policies, practices, and procedures can be updated and improved to reflect any necessary changes or clarifications. The compliance officer may want to solicit employee input in developing these communication and reporting systems.

2. Hotlines and Other Forms of Communication

The OIG encourages the use of hotlines,[115] e-mails, written memoranda, newsletters, suggestion boxes, and other forms of information

[113] The OIG believes that whistleblowers should be protected against retaliation, a concept embodied in the provisions of the False Claims Act. See 31 U.S.C. 3730(h). In many cases, employees sue their employers under the False Claims Act's qui tam provisions out of frustration because of the company's failure to take action when a questionable, fraudulent, or abusive situation was brought to the attention of senior corporate officials.

[114] Hospices can also consider rewarding employees for appropriate use of established reporting systems.

[115] The OIG recognizes that it may not be financially feasible for a smaller hospice to maintain a telephone hotline dedicated to receiving calls about compliance issues. These companies may want to explore alternative methods, e.g., outsourcing the hotline or establishing a written method of confidential disclosure.

exchange to maintain these open lines of communication.[116] If the hospice establishes a hotline, the telephone number should be made readily available to all employees and independent contractors, possibly by circulating the number on wallet cards or conspicuously posting the telephone number in common work areas.[117] Employees should be permitted to report matters on an anonymous basis. Matters reported through the hotline or other communication sources that suggest substantial violations of compliance policies, Federal health care program requirements, regulations, or statutes should be documented and investigated promptly to determine their veracity. A log should be maintained by the compliance officer that records such calls, including the nature of any investigation and its results.[118] Such information should be included in reports to the governing body, the CEO, and compliance committee.[119] Further, while the hospice should always strive to maintain the confidentiality of an employee's identity, it should also explicitly communicate that there may be a point where the individual's identity may become known or may have to be revealed in certain instances.

The OIG recognizes that assertions of fraud and abuse by employees who may have participated in illegal conduct or committed other malfeasance raise numerous complex legal and management issues that should be examined on a case-by-case basis. The compliance officer should work closely with legal counsel, who can provide guidance regarding such issues.

The OIG recognizes that protecting anonymity may be infeasible for small hospices. However, the OIG believes all hospice employees,

[116] In addition to methods of communication used by current employees, an effective employee exit interview program could be designed to solicit information from departing employees regarding potential misconduct and suspected violations of hospice policy and procedures.

[117] Hospices should also post in a prominent, available area the HHS-OIG Hotline telephone number, 1–800–447–8477 (1–800-HHS-TIPS), in addition to any company hotline number that may be posted.

[118] To efficiently and accurately fulfill such an obligation, the hospice should create an intake form for all compliance issues identified through reporting mechanisms. The form could include information concerning the date that the potential problem was reported, the internal investigative methods utilized, the results of the investigation, the corrective action implemented, the disciplinary measures imposed, and any identified overpayments and monies returned.

[119] Information obtained over the hotline may provide valuable insight into management practices and operations, whether reported problems are actual or perceived.

when seeking answers to questions or reporting potential instances of fraud and abuse, should know to whom to turn to for attention and should be able to do so without fear of retribution.

E. Auditing and Monitoring

An ongoing evaluation process is critical to a successful compliance program. The OIG believes that an effective program should incorporate thorough monitoring of its implementation and regular reporting to senior hospice or corporate officers.[120] Compliance reports created by this ongoing monitoring, including reports of suspected noncompliance, should be maintained by the compliance officer and shared with the hospice's senior management and the compliance committee. The extent and frequency of the audit function may vary depending on factors such as the size and available resources, prior history of noncompliance, and the risk factors that a particular hospice confronts.

Although many monitoring techniques are available, one effective tool to promote and ensure compliance is the performance of regular, periodic compliance audits by internal or external auditors who have expertise in Federal and State health care statutes, regulations, and Federal health care program requirements. The audits should focus on the hospice's programs or divisions, including external relationships with third-party contractors, specifically those with substantive exposure to Government enforcement actions. At a minimum, these audits should be designed to address the hospice's compliance with laws governing kickback arrangements, claim development and submission, reimbursement, eligibility, and marketing. The audits and reviews should inquire into the hospice's compliance with the Medicare conditions of participation and the specific rules and policies that have been the focus of particular attention on the part of the Medicare fiscal intermediaries or carriers, and law enforcement, as evidenced by educational and other communications from OIG Special Fraud Alerts, OIG audits and evaluations, and law enforcement's initiatives.[121] In addition, the hospice should focus on any areas of concern that are specific to the

[120] Even when a hospice or group of hospices is owned by a larger corporate entity, the regular auditing and monitoring of the compliance activities of an individual hospice must be a key feature in any annual review. Appropriate reports on audit findings should be periodically provided and explained to a parent organization's senior staff and officers.

[121] See also section II.A.2.

individual hospice and have been identified by any entity, whether Federal, State or internal.

Monitoring techniques may include sampling protocols that permit the compliance officer to identify and review variations from an established baseline.[122] Significant variations from the baseline should trigger a reasonable inquiry to determine the cause of the deviation. If the inquiry determines that the deviation occurred for legitimate, explainable reasons, the compliance officer and hospice management may want to limit any corrective action or take no action. If it is determined that the deviation was caused by improper procedures, misunderstanding of rules, including fraud and systemic problems, the hospice should take prompt steps to correct the problem. Any overpayments discovered as a result of such deviations should be returned promptly to the affected payor, with appropriate documentation and a sufficiently detailed explanation of the reason for the refund.[123]

An effective compliance program should also incorporate periodic (at least annual) reviews of whether the program's compliance elements have been satisfied, e.g., whether there has been appropriate dissemination of the program's standards, training, ongoing educational programs, and disciplinary actions, among other elements.[124] This process will verify actual conformance by all departments with the compliance program and may identify the necessity for improvements to be made to the compliance program, as well as the hospice's operations. Such reviews could support a determination that appropriate records have been created and maintained to document the

---

[122] The OIG recommends that when a compliance program is established in a hospice, the compliance officer, with the assistance of department managers, should take a "snapshot" of their operations from a compliance perspective. This assessment can be undertaken by outside consultants, law or accounting firms, or internal staff, with authoritative knowledge of health care compliance requirements. This "snapshot," often used as part of benchmarking analyses, becomes a baseline for the compliance officer and other managers to judge the hospice's progress in reducing or eliminating potential areas of vulnerability.

[123] In addition, when appropriate, as referenced in section G.2, below, reports of fraud or systemic problems should also be made to the appropriate governmental authority.

[124] One way to assess the knowledge, awareness, and perceptions of the hospice's employees is through the use of a validated survey instrument (e.g. employee questionnaires, interviews, or focus groups).

implementation of an effective program.[125] However, when monitoring discloses that deviations were not detected in a timely manner due to program deficiencies, proper modifications must be implemented. Such evaluations, when developed with the support of management, can help ensure compliance with the hospice's policies and procedures.

As part of the review process, the compliance officer or reviewers should consider techniques such as:

- Visits and interviews of patients at their residences;
- Analysis of utilization patterns;
- Testing clinical and hospice admission staff on their knowledge of reimbursement coverage criteria (e.g., present hypothetical scenarios of situations experienced in daily practice and assess responses);
- Assessment of existing relationships with physicians, nursing homes,[126] hospitals, and other potential referral sources;
- Unannounced mock audits and investigations;
- Reevaluation of deficiencies cited in past surveys for Medicare conditions of participation;
- Examination of hospice complaint logs;
- Checking personnel records to determine whether any individuals who have been reprimanded for compliance issues in the past are among those currently engaged in improper conduct;
- Questionnaires developed to solicit impressions of a broad cross-section of the hospice's employees and staff;
- Evaluation of the timeliness of physician referrals and physician signatures for hospice certifications;
- Reviews of clinical documentation (e.g., terminal illness certification, plan of care, nursing notes, etc.), financial records, and other source documents that support claims for reimbursement;
- Validation of qualifications of hospice physicians and other hospice staff, including verification of applicable state license renewals;

---

[125] Such records should include, but not be limited to, logs of horline calls, logs of training attendees, training agenda meaterials, and summaries of corrective action taken and improvments make to hospice policies as a result of compliance activities.

[126] See section II.A.3.e.

- Evaluation of written materials and documentation outlining the hospice's policies and procedures; and
- Trend analyses, or longitudinal studies, that uncover deviations, positive or negative, in specific areas over a given period.

The reviewers should:

- Have the qualifications and experience necessary to adequately identify potential issues with the subject matter that is reviewed;
- Be objective and independent of line management to the extent reasonably possible;[127]
- Have access to existing audit and health care resources, relevant personnel, and all relevant areas of operation;
- Present written evaluative reports on compliance activities to the CEO, governing body, and members of the compliance committee on a regular basis, but no less often than annually; and
- Specifically identify areas where corrective actions are needed.

Just as a hospice is required by its conditions of participation to conduct "an ongoing, comprehensive, integrated, self-assessment of the quality and appropriateness of care provided,"[128] the OIG believes that a hospice should monitor its compliance with the Federal health care program requirements in the same fashion. Furthermore, just as a hospice is required by its conditions of participation to use its quality assurance findings to correct identified problems and revise hospice policies if necessary to improve patient care,[129] the OIG believes that a hospice's management should take whatever steps are necessary to correct identified compliance problems and prevent them from recurring. In certain cases, subsequent reviews or studies would be advisable to ensure that the recommended corrective actions have been implemented successfully.

While conducting its monitoring and auditing efforts, as well as its daily operations, a hospice should document its efforts to comply with applicable statutes, regulations, and Federal health care program requirements. For example, where a hospice, in its efforts to comply with a particular statute, regulation or program require-

---

[127] The OIG recognizes that hospices that are small in size and have limited resources may not be able to use internal reviewers who are not part of line management or hire outside reviewers.

[128] 42 CFR 418.66.

[129] Id.

ment, requests advice from a Government agency (including a Medicare fiscal intermediary or carrier) charged with administering a Federal health care program, the hospice should document and retain a record of the request and any written or oral response. This step is extremely important if the hospice intends to rely on that response to guide it in future decisions, actions, or claim reimbursement requests or appeals. A log of oral inquiries between the hospice and third parties will help the organization document its attempts at compliance. In addition, the hospice agency should maintain records relevant to the issue of whether its reliance was "reasonable" and whether it exercised due diligence in developing procedures and practices to implement the advice.

The extent of a hospice's audit should depend on the hospice's identified risk areas and resources. If the hospice comes under Government scrutiny in the future, the Government will assess whether or not the hospice developed a comprehensive audit based upon identified risk areas and resources. If the Government determines the hospice failed to develop an adequate audit program, given its resources, the Government will be less likely to afford the hospice favorable treatment under the Federal Sentencing Guidelines.

F. Enforcing Standards Through Well-Publicized Disciplinary Guidelines

1. Discipline Policy and Actions

An effective compliance program should include guidance regarding disciplinary action for corporate officers, managers, employees, and other health care professionals who have failed to comply with the hospice's standards of conduct, policies and procedures, Federal health care program requirements, or Federal and State laws, or those who have otherwise engaged in wrongdoing, which have the potential to impair the hospice's status as a reliable, honest, and trustworthy health care provider.

The OIG believes that the compliance program should include a written policy statement setting forth the degrees of disciplinary actions that may be imposed upon corporate officers, managers, employees, physicians, and other health care professionals for failing to comply with the hospice's standards and policies and applicable statutes and regulations. Intentional or reckless noncompliance should subject transgressors to significant sanctions. Such sanctions could range from oral warnings to suspension, termination, or financial penalties, as appropriate. Each situation must be considered on a case-by-case basis to determine the appropriate sanction. The written standards of conduct should elaborate on the procedures for handling disciplinary problems and those who will be responsible for taking appropriate action. Some disciplinary actions can be handled by department or agency managers, while others may have to be resolved by a senior hospice administrator. Disciplinary action may be appropriate where a responsible employee's failure to detect a violation is attributable to his or her negligence or reckless conduct. Personnel should be advised by the hospice that disciplinary action will be taken on a fair and equitable basis. Managers and supervisors should be made aware that they have a responsibility to discipline employees in an appropriate and consistent manner.

It is vital to publish and disseminate the range of disciplinary standards for improper conduct and to educate officers and other hospice employees regarding these standards. The consequences of noncompliance should be consistently applied and enforced, in order for the disciplinary policy to have the required deterrent effect. All levels of employees should be potentially subject to the same types of disciplinary action for the commission of similar offenses. The commitment to compliance applies to all personnel levels within a hospice. The OIG believes that corporate officers, managers, supervisors, clinical staff, and other health care professionals should be held accountable for failing to comply with, or for the foreseeable failure of their subordinates to adhere to, the applicable standards, laws, and procedures.

2. New Employee Policy

For all new employees who have discretionary authority to make decisions that may involve compliance with the law or compliance oversight, hospices should conduct a reasonable and prudent background investigation, including a reference check,[130] as part of every such employment application. The application should specifically require the applicant to disclose any criminal conviction,[131] as

[130] See note 99.

[131] States may mandate, and many hospices voluntarily conduct, criminal background checks for prospective employees of hospices. Identification of a criminal background of an applicant, who may have been recently convicted of serious crimes that relate to the proposed employment duties, could be grounds for denying employment. Further, criminal background screening may deter those individuals with criminal intent from entering the field of hospice.

defined by 42 U.S.C. 1320a-7(i), or exclusion action. Pursuant to the compliance program, hospice policies should prohibit the employment of individuals who have been recently convicted of a criminal offense related to health care[132] or who are listed as debarred, excluded, or otherwise ineligible for participation in Federal health care programs.[133] In addition, pending the resolution of any criminal charges or proposed debarment or exclusion, the OIG recommends that an individual who is the subject of such actions should be removed from direct responsibility for or involvement in any Federal health care program. That individual's salary should not be paid in whole or part, directly or indirectly, by Federal health care programs or otherwise with Federal funds.[134] With regard to current employees or independent contractors, if resolution of the matter results in conviction, debarment or exclusion, the hospice should terminate its employment or other contract arrangement with the individual or contractor.

G. Responding to Detected Offenses and Developing Corrective Action Initiatives

1. Violations and Investigations

Violations of a hospice's compliance program, failures to comply with applicable Federal or State law, and other types of misconduct threaten a hospice's status as a reliable, honest and trustworthy provider capable of participating in Federal health care programs. Detected but uncorrected misconduct can seriously endanger the mission, reputation and legal status of the hospice. Consequently, upon reports or reasonable indications of suspected noncompliance, it is important that the compliance officer or other management officials immediately investigate the conduct in question to deter-

[132] Because providers of hospice care have frequent, relatively unsupervised access to potentially vulnerable people and their property, a hospice should also strictly scrutinize whether it should employ individuals who have been convicted of crimes of neglect, violence, theft or dishonesty, or financial misconduct.

[133] Likewise, hospice compliance programs should establish standards prohibiting the execution of contracts with companies that have been recently convicted of a criminal offense related to health care or that are listed by a Federal agency as debarred, excluded or otherwise ineligible for participation in Federal health care programs. See note 99.

[134] Prospective employees who have been officially reinstated into the Medicare and Medicaid programs by the OIG may be considered for employment upon proof of such reinstatement.

mine whether a material violation of applicable law or the requirements of the compliance program has occurred, and if so, take decisive steps to correct the problem.[135] As appropriate, such steps may include an immediate referral to criminal and/or civil law enforcement authorities, a corrective action plan,[136] a report to the Government[137] and the return of any overpayments, if applicable.

Where potential fraud or False Claims Act liability is not involved, the OIG recommends that normal repayment channels should be used for returning overpayments to the Government as they are discovered. However, even if the overpayment detection and return process is working and is being monitored by the hospice's audit or billing divisions, the OIG still believes that the compliance officer needs to be made aware of these overpayments, violations or deviations that may reveal trends or patterns indicative of a systemic problem.

Depending upon the nature of the alleged violations, an internal investigation will probably include interviews and a review of relevant documents. Some hospices should consider engaging outside counsel, auditors or health care experts to assist in an investigation. Records of the investigation should contain documentation of the alleged violation, a description of the investigative process (including the objectivity of the investigators and methodologies utilized), copies of interview notes and key documents, a log of the witnesses interviewed and the documents reviewed, the results of the investi-

---

[135] Instances of noncompliance must be determined on a case-by-case basis. The existence, or amount, of a monetary loss to a health care program is not solely determinative of whether or not the conduct should be investigated and reported to governmental authorities. In fact, there may be instances where there is no readily identifiable monetary loss at all, but corrective action and reporting are still necessary to protect the integrity of the applicable program and its beneficiaries, e.g., where services required by a plan of care were not provided.

[136] Advice from the hospice's in-house counsel or an outside law firm may be sought to determine the extent of the hospice's liability and to plan the appropriate course of action.

[137] The OIG currently maintains a provider self-disclosure protocol that encourages providers to report suspected fraud. The concept of voluntary self-disclosure is premised on a recognition that the Government alone cannot protect the integrity of the Medicare and other Federal health care programs. Health care providers must be willing to police themselves, correct underlying problems and work with the Government to resolve these matters. The self-disclosure protocol can be located on the OIG's website at http://www.dhhs.gov/progorg/oig

gation, e.g., any disciplinary action taken, and the corrective action implemented. While any action taken as the result of an investigation will necessarily vary depending upon the hospice and the situation, hospices should strive for some consistency by utilizing sound practices and disciplinary protocols.[138] Further, after a reasonable period, the compliance officer should review the circumstances that formed the basis for the investigation to determine whether similar problems have been uncovered or modifications of the compliance program are necessary to prevent and detect other inappropriate conduct or violations.

If an investigation of an alleged violation is undertaken and the compliance officer believes the integrity of the investigation may be at stake because of the presence of employees under investigation, those subjects should be removed from their current work activity until the investigation is completed (unless an internal or Government-led undercover operation known to the hospice is in effect). In addition, the compliance officer should take appropriate steps to secure or prevent the destruction of documents or other evidence relevant to the investigation. If the hospice determines that disciplinary action is warranted, it should be prompt and imposed in accordance with the hospice's written standards of disciplinary action.

2. Reporting

If the compliance officer, compliance committee, or management official discovers credible evidence of misconduct from any source and, after a reasonable inquiry, has reason to believe that the misconduct may violate criminal, civil, or administrative law, then the hospice should promptly report the existence of misconduct to the appropriate Federal and State authorities[139] within a reasonable

[138] The parameters of a claim review subject to an internal investigation will depend on the circumstances surrounding the issue(s) identified. By limiting the scope of an internal audit to current billing, a hospice may fail to discover major problems and deficiencies in operations, as well as be subject to certain liability.

[139] Appropriate Federal and State authorities include the Office of Inspector General of the Department of Health and Human Services, the Criminal and Civil Divisions of the Department of Justice, the U.S. Attorney in relevant districts, the Federal Bureau of Investigation and the other investigative arms for the agencies administering the affected Federal or State health care programs, such as the State Medicaid Fraud Control Unit, the Defense Criminal Investigative Service, the Department of Veterans

period, but not more than 60 days [140] after determining that there is credible evidence of a violation. [141] Prompt reporting will demonstrate the hospice's good faith and willingness to work with governmental authorities to correct and remedy the problem. In addition, reporting such conduct will be considered a mitigating factor by the OIG in determining administrative sanctions (e.g., penalties, assessments and exclusion), if the reporting provider becomes the target of an OIG investigation. [142]

When reporting misconduct to the Government, a hospice should provide all evidence relevant to the alleged violation of applicable Federal or State law(s) and potential cost impact. The compliance officer, under advice of counsel, and with guidance from the governmental authorities, could be requested to continue to investigate the reported violation. Once the investigation is completed, the compliance officer should be required to notify the appropriate governmental authority of the outcome of the investigation, including a description of the impact of the alleged violation on the operation of the applicable health care programs or their beneficiaries. If the investigation ultimately reveals that criminal, civil or administrative violations have occurred, the appropriate Federal and State authorities [143] should be notified immediately.

As previously stated, the hospice should take appropriate corrective action, including prompt identification of any overpayment to

Affairs and the Office of Personnel Management (which administers the Federal Employee Health Benefits Program).

[140] In contrast, to qualify for the "not less than double damages" provision of the False Claims Act, the report must be provided to the Government within 30 days after the date when the hospice first obtained the information. 31 U.S.C. 3729(a).

[141] The OIG believes that some violations may be so serious that they warrant immediate notification to governmental authorities, prior to, or simultaneous with, commencing an internal investigation, e.g., if the conduct: (1) is a clear violation of civil fraud or criminal law; (2) has a significant adverse effect on the quality of care provided to program beneficiaries (in addition to any other legal obligations regarding quality of care); or (3) indicates evidence of a systemic failure to comply with applicable laws or an existing corporate integrity agreement, regardless of the financial impact on Federal health care programs.

[142] The OIG has published criteria setting forth those factors that the OIG takes into consideration in determining whether it is appropriate to exclude a health care provider from program participation pursuant to 42 U.S.C. 1320a-7(b)(7) for violations of various fraud and abuse laws. See 62 FR 67392 (December 24, 1997).

[143] See note 139.

the affected payor and the imposition of proper disciplinary action. If potential fraud or violations of the False Claims Act are involved, any repayment of the overpayment should be made as part of the discussion with the Government following a report of the matter to law enforcement authorities. Otherwise, normal repayment channels should be used for repaying identified overpayments.[144] Failure to disclose overpayments within a reasonable period of time could be interpreted as an intentional attempt to conceal the overpayment from the Government, thereby establishing an independent basis for a criminal violation with respect to the hospice, as well as any individuals who may have been involved.[145] For this reason, hospice compliance programs should emphasize that overpayments obtained from Medicare or other Federal health care programs should be promptly disclosed and returned to the payor that made the erroneous payment.

The OIG believes all hospices, regardless of size, should ensure they are reporting the results of any overpayments or violations to the appropriate entity and taking the appropriate corrective action to remedy the identified deficiency.

III. Assessing the Effectiveness of a Compliance Program

Because the Government views the existence of a compliance program as a mitigating factor when determining culpability regarding allegations of fraud and abuse only if the compliance program is "effective," how a hospice may assess its compliance program becomes quite significant. A hospice, as well as any other type of health care provider, should consider the attributes of each individual element of its compliance program to assess the program's "effectiveness" as a whole. Examining the comprehensiveness of policies and procedures implemented to satisfy these elements is merely the first step. Evaluating how a compliance program per-

[144] A hospice should consult with its Medicare fiscal intermediary or HCFA for any further guidance regarding normal repayment channels. The hospice's Medicare fiscal intermediary or HCFA may require certain information (e.g., alleged violation or issue causing overpayment, description of the internal investigative process with methodologies used to determine any overpayments, disciplinary actions taken and corrective actions taken, etc.) to be submitted with return of any overpayments, and that such repayment information be submitted to a specific department or individual. Interest will be assessed, when appropriate. See 42 CFR 405.376.

[145] See 42 U.S.C. 1320a-7b(a)(3).

forms during a provider's day-to-day operations becomes the critical indicator.[146]

As previously stated, a compliance program should require the development and distribution of written compliance policies, standards and practices that identify specific areas of risk and vulnerability to a hospice. One way to judge whether these policies, standards and practices measure up is to observe how an organization's employees react to them. Do employees consistently experience recurring pitfalls because they lack guidance on certain issues not adequately covered in company policies? Are employees flagrantly disobeying an organization's standards of conduct because they observe no sincere buy-in from senior management? Do employees have trouble understanding policies and procedures because they are written in legalese or at difficult reading levels? Does an organization routinely experience systematic billing failures because employees are ill-instructed how to implement written policies and practices? Written compliance policies, standards and practices are only as good as an organization's commitment to apply them in practice.

Every hospice should designate a compliance officer or contact to serve as the focal point of compliance activities, and, if appropriate, a compliance committee to advise and assist the compliance officer. An organization needs to seriously consider whoever fills such integral roles and periodically monitor how the individuals chosen satisfy their responsibilities. Does a compliance officer have sufficient professional experience working with billing, clinical records, documentation, and auditing principles to perform assigned responsibilities fully? Has a compliance officer or compliance committee been negligent in ensuring an organization's compliance due to inadequate funding, staff, and authority necessary to carry out their jobs? Did adding the compliance officer function to a key management position with other significant duties compromise the goals of the compliance program (e.g., chief financial officer who discounts certain overpayments identified to improve the company's bottom line profits)? Since a compliance officer and a compliance committee can potentially have a significant impact on how effectively a compli-

[146] Evaluation may be accomplished through techniques such as employee surveys, management assessments and periodic review of benchmarks established for audits, investigations, disciplinary action, overpayments and employee feedback. All elements of an organization's compliance program can be evaluated, including policies, training, practices and compliance personnel.

ance program is implemented, those functions should not be taken for granted.

As evidenced throughout this guidance, the proper education and training of corporate officers, managers, health care professionals and other applicable employees of a provider, and the continual retraining of current personnel at all levels, are significant elements of an effective compliance program. Accordingly, such efforts should be routinely evaluated. Are employees trained frequently enough? Do employees fail post-training tests that evaluate knowledge of compliance? Do training sessions and materials adequately summarize important aspects of the organization's compliance program, such as fraud and abuse laws, Federal health care program requirements, and claim development and submission processes? Are training instructors qualified to present the subject matter and experienced enough to duly field questions? When thorough compliance training is periodically conducted, employees receive the reinforcement they need to ensure an effective compliance program.

An open line of communication between the compliance officer and a provider's employees is equally important to the success of a compliance program. In today's intensive regulatory environment, the OIG believes that a provider cannot possibly have an effective compliance program if it receives minimal or no feedback from its employees regarding compliance matters. For instance, if a compliance officer does not receive appropriate inquiries from employees: Do policies and procedures fail to adequately guide employees to whom and when they should be communicating compliance matters? Do employees fear retaliation if they report misconduct? Are employees reporting issues not related to compliance through the wrong channels? Do employees have bad-faith, ulterior motives for reporting? Regardless of the means that a provider employs, whether it be telephone hotline, email, or suggestion boxes, employees should seek clarification from compliance staff in the event of any confusion or question dealing with compliance policies, practices or procedures.

An effective compliance program should include guidance regarding disciplinary action for corporate officers, managers, health care professionals and other employees who have failed to adhere to an organization's standards of conduct, Federal health care program requirements or Federal or State laws. The number and caliber of disciplinary actions taken by an organization can be insightful. Have appropriate sanctions been applied to compliance misconduct? Are sanctions applied to all employees consistently, regardless of an employee's level in the corporate hierarchy? Have double-standards in discipline bred cynicism among employees? When disciplinary action is not taken seriously or applied haphazardly, such practices reflect poorly on senior management's commitment to foster compliance as well as the effectiveness of an organization's compliance program in general.

Another critical component of a successful compliance program is an ongoing monitoring and auditing process. The extent and frequency of the audit function may vary depending on factors such as the size and available resources, prior history of noncompliance, and risk factors of a particular hospice. The hallmark of effective monitoring and auditing efforts is how an organization determines the parameters of its reviews. Do audits focus on all pertinent departments of an organization? Does an audit cover compliance with all applicable laws and Federal health care program requirements? Are results of past audits, pre-established baselines or prior deficiencies reevaluated? Are the elements of the compliance program monitored? Are auditing techniques valid and conducted by objective reviewers? The extent and sincerity of an organization's efforts to confirm its compliance often proves to be a revealing determinant of a compliance program's effectiveness.

As was expressed in the last section of this guidance, it is essential that the compliance officer or other management officials immediately investigate reports or reasonable indications of suspected noncompliance. If a material violation of applicable law or compliance program requirements has occurred, a provider must take decisive steps to correct the problem. Providers who do not thoroughly investigate misconduct leave themselves open to undiscovered fraud, waste and abuse. When a provider learns of certain issues, does it knowingly disregard associated legal exposure? Is there a consistent and methodical approach to the correlation between compliance issues identified and the corrective action necessary to remedy? Are isolated overpayment matters properly resolved through normal repayment channels? Is credible evidence of misconduct that may violate criminal, civil or administrative law promptly reported to the appropriate Federal and State authorities? If any step in this process of responding to detected offenses is circumvented or improperly handled, such conduct would most likely demonstrate an ineffective compliance program, as well as potentially result in criminal, civil or administrative liability.

Documentation is the key to demonstrating the effectiveness of a provider's compliance program. For example, documentation of the following should be maintained: audit results; logs of hotline calls and their resolution; corrective actions plans; due diligence efforts regarding business transactions; records of employee training, including the number of training hours; disciplinary action; and modification and distribution of policies and procedures. Given that the OIG is encouraging self-disclosure of overpayments and billing irregularities, maintaining a record of disclosures and refunds to the health care programs is strongly endorsed. A documented practice of refunding of overpayments and self-disclosing incidents of non-compliance with Federal health care program requirements can serve as evidence of a meaningful compliance effort by a hospice.

Hospices, as well as all health care providers, should acknowledge that it is their responsibility to formulate policies, procedures, and practices that are tailored to their own operations, and that are comprehensive enough to ensure compliance with all applicable Federal health care program requirements. An organization is in the best position to validate the suitability of its compliance efforts based upon its own particular circumstances.

IV. Conclusion

Through this document, the OIG has attempted to provide a foundation to the process necessary to develop an effective and cost-efficient hospice compliance program. As previously stated, however, each program must be tailored to fit the needs and resources of an individual hospice, depending upon its particular corporate structure, mission and employee composition. The statutes, regulations and guidelines of the Federal and State health insurance programs, as well as the policies and procedures of the private health plans, should be integrated into every hospice's compliance program.

The OIG recognizes that the health care industry in this country, which reaches millions of beneficiaries and expends about a trillion dollars annually, is constantly evolving. The time is right for hospices to implement a strong voluntary health care compliance program. As stated throughout this guidance, compliance is a dynamic process that helps to ensure that hospices and other health care providers are better able to fulfill their commitment to ethical behavior, as well as meet the changes and challenges being imposed upon them by Congress and private insurers. Ultimately, it is OIG's hope that a voluntarily created compliance program will enable hospices to meet their goals, improve the quality of patient care, and substantially reduce fraud, waste and abuse, as well as the cost of health care to Federal, State and private health insurers.

Dated: September 29, 1999.

June Gibbs Brown,

Inspector General.

[FR Doc. 99–25787 Filed 10–4-99; 8:45 am]

BILLING CODE 4150–04-P

APPENDIX I7

Compliance Program Guidance for Medicare+Choice Organizations Offering Coordinated Care Plans; 64 FR 61893, November 15, 1999

[Federal Register: November 15, 1999 (Volume 64, Number 219)]

[Notices]

[Page 61893–61910]

DEPARTMENT OF HEALTH AND HUMAN SERVICES

Office of Inspector General

Publication of the OIG's Compliance Program Guidance for Medicare+Choice Organizations Offering Coordinated Care Plans

AGENCY: Office of Inspector General (OIG), HHS.

ACTION: Notice.

SUMMARY: This Federal Register notice sets forth the Compliance Program Guidance for Medicare+Choice Organizations Offering Coordinated Care Plans ("Medicare+Choice organizations") that was recently issued by the Office of Inspector General (OIG). The OIG has previously developed and published compliance program guidance focused on other areas of the health care industry. We believe that the development and issuance of this compliance program guidance for Medicare+Choice organizations will continue to serve as a positive step toward promoting a high level of ethical and lawful conduct throughout the entire health care industry.

FOR FURTHER INFORMATION CONTACT: Barbara Frederickson, Office of Counsel to the Inspector General, (202) 619–2078.

SUPPLEMENTARY INFORMATION:

Background

The creation of compliance program guidance continues to be a major initiative by the OIG in its effort to engage the health care community in combating fraud and abuse. In formulating compliance guidance, the OIG has worked closely with the Health Care Financing Administration (HCFA), the Department of Justice (DOJ) and various sectors of the health care industry to provide clear guidance to the industry. The previously-issued compliance program guidances addressed six areas: the hospital industry; home health agencies; clinical laboratories; third-party medical billing companies; the durable medical equipment, prosthetics, orthotics and supply industry; and hospices. The development of these compliance program guidances is based on our belief that a health care provider can use internal controls to more efficiently monitor adherence to applicable statutes, regulations and program requirements.

Guidance for Medicare+Choice Organizations

On September 22, 1998, the OIG published a solicitation notice seeking information and recommendations for developing formal guidance for Medicare+Choice organizations (63 FR 50577). In response to that solicitation notice, the OIG received five comments from the industry and their representatives. After careful consideration of those initial comments, and in an effort to ensure that all parties had a reasonable opportunity to provide input into a final product, the OIG published draft guidance for Medicare+Choice organizations on June 24, 1999 (64 FR 33869) for further comment and recommendations. A total of 16 timely-filed comments were received for consideration by the OIG in response to the publication of that draft guidance.

Elements for an Effective Compliance Program

Through experience, the OIG has identified seven fundamental elements to an effective compliance guidance program that are being reflected in this latest issuance. They are:

- Implementing written policies, procedures and standards of conduct;
- Designating a compliance officer and a compliance committee;
- Conducting effective training and education;
- Developing effective lines of communication;
- Enforcing standards through well-publicized disciplinary guidelines and developing policies addressing dealings with sanctioned individuals;
- Conducting internal monitoring and auditing; and
- Responding promptly to detected offenses, developing corrective action, and reporting to the Government.

The OIG is offering specific compliance measures that may be implemented by Medicare+Choice organizations in an effort to curtail or eliminate fraud and abuse. While HCFA regulations require Medicare+Choice organizations to implement compliance programs, adoption of the Compliance Program Guidance for Medicare+Choice Organizations Offering Coordinated Care Plans set forth below is voluntary.

A reprint of this newly-issued compliance program guidance follows:

Office of Inspector General's Compliance Program Guidance for Medicare+Choice Organizations Offering Coordinated Care Plans (November 1999)

I. Introduction

In its ongoing effort to work collaboratively with the health care industry to achieve the mutual goals of quality health care and the elimination of fraud, waste and abuse, the Office of Inspector General (OIG) of the Department of Health and Human Services (HHS) encourages voluntarily developed and implemented compliance programs for the health care industry. Fundamentally, compliance efforts are designed to establish a culture within an organization that promotes prevention, detection and resolution of instances of conduct that do not conform to Federal and State law and Federal health care program requirements, as well as the organization's ethical and business policies. In practice, the compliance program should effectively articulate and demonstrate the organization's commitment to legal and ethical conduct.

As a demonstration of the OIG's commitment to compliance, the OIG has issued recommendations, in the form of compliance program guidances, that provide suggestions regarding how specific segments of the industry can best implement compliance programs.[1] As a result of the changing nature of the health care delivery system and the growing trend toward reliance on the managed care industry in the provision of health care in the Medicare context, the OIG

[1] See 64 FR 58419 (10/29/99) for the draft compliance program guidance for nursing facilities; 64 FR 54031 (10/5/99) for the compliance program guidance for hospices; 64 FR 36368 (7/6/99) for the compliance program guidance for the durable medical equipment, prosthetics, orthotics and suppliers industry; 63 FR 70138 (12/18/98) for the compliance program guidance for third-party medical billing companies; 63 FR 45076 (8/24/98) for the compliance program guidance for clinical laboratories; 63 FR 42410 (8/7/98) for the compliance program guidance for home health agencies; and 63 FR 8987 (2/23/98) for the compliance program guidance for hospitals.

believes it is appropriate to issue a guidance focusing on Medicare+Choice organizations[2] offering coordinated care plans[3] (Medicare+Choice organizations). The OIG formulated this guidance specifically for Medicare+Choice organizations because these organizations are well-defined and are subject to a comprehensive regulatory structure.[4] In addition, Congress envisioned an important role for Medicare+Choice organizations, demonstrated by the substantial amount of Federal funds received by these organizations.

These documents are also located on the Internet at http://www.hhs.gov/oig/.

The OIG encourages Medicare+Choice organizations to read the guidance with the whole organization in mind, applying the guidance to whatever departments or divisions, including private-sector managed care areas, that are deemed appropriate by that organization. Indeed, many of the suggestions in this guidance can be used by managed care organizations that do not contract with HCFA to provide a Medicare+Choice plan. In particular, entities that participate in other public health care programs, such as Medicaid, may want to look to the general principles in this document to assist them in developing compliance programs.

While the regulations implementing the Medicare+Choice program, or Part C, require a Medicare+Choice organization to establish a compliance plan,[5] the OIG's program guidance is volun-

---

[2] A Medicare+Choice organization is defined as a public or private entity organized and licensed by a State as a risk-bearing entity (with the exception of provider-sponsored organizations receiving waivers) that is certified by the Health Care Financing Administration (HCFA) as meeting the Medicare+Choice contract requirements (42 CFR 422.2).

[3] For the purposes of this compliance program guidance, a "coordinated care plan" is a plan that includes a network of providers that are under contract or arrangement with the organization to deliver the benefit package approved by HCFA (42 U.S.C. 1395w-28(a)(1); 42 CFR 422.4).

[4] In this guidance, we have focused our attention on regulations applicable to Medicare+Choice organizations governing marketing, enrollment, disenrollment, underutilization, data collection, anti-kickback statute and emergency services, rather than providing instruction on all aspects of regulatory compliance.

[5] The regulations require that any plan contracting with HCFA implement a compliance plan that encompasses the elements detailed in the Federal Sentencing Guidelines. 42 CFR 422.501(b)(vi). HCFA will release an operational policy letter addressing the compliance requirements detailed in the regulation. In response to concerns from industry representa-

tary and simply is intended to provide assistance for Medicare+Choice organizations looking for additional direction in the development of internal controls that promote adherence to applicable Federal and State law. The OIG first provides its general views on the value and fundamental principles of Medicare+Choice organizations' compliance programs, and then provides specific elements that each Medicare+Choice organization should consider when developing and implementing an effective compliance program.

A. Benefits of a Compliance Plan

The OIG believes an effective compliance program provides a mechanism that brings the public and private sectors together to reach mutual goals of reducing fraud and abuse, improving operational quality, and ensuring the provision of high quality cost-effective care. Attaining these goals benefits business, Government, individual citizens and Medicare beneficiaries alike. In addition to fulfilling its legal duties to ensure that it is not submitting false or inaccurate information to the Government or providing substandard care to Medicare beneficiaries, a Medicare+Choice organization may gain numerous additional benefits by implementing an effective compliance program. These benefits may include:

- The formulation of effective internal controls to assure compliance with Federal regulations and internal guidelines;
- Improved communication with and satisfaction of Medicare+Choice enrollees;
- The ability to more quickly and accurately react to employees operational compliance concerns and the capability to effectively target resources to address those concerns;
- A concrete demonstration to employees and the community at large of the Medicare+Choice organization's strong commitment to honest and responsible corporate conduct;
- The ability to obtain an accurate assessment of employee and contractor behavior relating to fraud and abuse;
- Improved (clinical and non-clinical) quality of care and service;
- Improved assessment tools that could affect many or all of the Medicare+Choice organization's divisions or departments;
- Increased likelihood of identification and prevention of unlawful and unethical conduct;

---

tives on the short time frame for implementing a compliance plan, HCFA delayed the actual implementation date of the compliance plan until January 1, 2000.

- A centralized source for distributing information on health care statutes, regulations and other program directives related to fraud and abuse;
- The creation or reinforcement of an environment that encourages employees to report potential problems;
- Procedures that allow the prompt, thorough investigation of possible misconduct by corporate officers, managers, employees and independent contractors;
- An improved relationship with the Center for Health Plans and Providers (CHPP) at HCFA; and
- Early detection and reporting, minimizing the loss to the Government from false or improper claims, and thereby reducing the Medicare+Choice organization's exposure to civil damages and penalties, criminal sanctions, and administrative remedies, such as program exclusion. [6]

Overall, the OIG believes that an effective compliance program is a sound business investment that has the potential of enhancing the efficiency and effectiveness of the Medicare+Choice organization. It may also improve the Medicare+Choice organization's financial structure by addressing not only fraud and abuse concerns, but efficiency and productivity concerns in other operational areas.

The OIG recognizes the implementation of an effectivecompliance program may not entirely eliminate fraud, abuse and waste from an organization. However, a sincere effort by a Medicare+Choice organization to comply with applicable Federal and State standards, through the establishment of an effective compliance program, significantly reduces the probability of unlawful or improper conduct.

B. Application of Compliance Program Guidance

---

[6] The OIG, for example, will consider the existence of an effective compliance program that pre-dated any governmental investigation when addressing the appropriateness of administrative sanctions. However, the burden is on the Medicare+Choice organization to demonstrate the operational effectiveness of a compliance program. Further, the False Claims Act, 31 U.S.C. 3729–3733, provides that a person who has violated the Act, but who voluntarily discloses the violation to the Government within 30 days of detection, in certain circumstances will be subject to not less than double, as opposed to treble, damages. See 31 U.S.C. 3729(a). In addition, an organization will receive sentencing credit for an "effective" compliance program under the Federal Sentencing Guidelines. See United States Sentencing Commission Guidelines, Guidelines Manual, 8C2.5. Thus, the ability to react quickly when violations of the law are discovered may materially reduce the Medicare+Choice organization's liability.

Before explaining the specific elements of a compliance program, it is important to emphasize several aspects of this document: its voluntary nature, its applicability to Medicare+Choice organizations, the collaborative nature by which it was developed, and its evolving nature.

First, it should be re-emphasized that while the regulations implementing the Medicare+Choice program, or Part C, require a Medicare+Choice organization to establish a compliance plan, including specified elements,[7] this program guidance is voluntary. Although this document presents basic procedural and structural guidance for designing a compliance program, it is not in itself a compliance program. Rather, it is a set of guidelines for consideration by a Medicare+Choice organization interested in obtaining specific information on implementing a compliance program. This guidance represents the OIG's suggestions on how a Medicare+Choice organization can establish internal controls and monitor company conduct to correct and prevent fraudulent activities.

It is critical for the Medicare+Choice organization to assess its own organization and determine its needs with regard to compliance with applicable Federal and State statutes and Federal health care program requirements. By no means should the contents of this guidance be viewed as an exclusive discussion of the advisable components of a compliance program. On the contrary, the OIG strongly encourages Medicare+Choice organizations to develop and implement compliance components that uniquely address the individual organization's risk areas.

Implementing a compliance program in a Medicare+Choice organization is a complicated venture. There are significant variances and complexities among Medicare+Choice organizations in terms of the type of services and the manner in which these services are provided to the respective members. For example, some Medicare+Choice organizations cover broad service areas, while others are focused on a particular geographic region. Similarly, the range of benefits covered differ among plans, as does the size of the network and the use of a varying number of provider contracting tiers to deliver services. Clearly, these differences may give rise to different substantive policies to ensure effective compliance. Furthermore, some Medicare+Choice organizations are relatively small, while others are fully integrated and offer Medicare+Choice plans in a wide vari-

[7] See note 5.

ety of areas. Finally, the availability of resources for any one Medicare+Choice organization can differ vastly.

Notwithstanding these differences, this guidance is pertinent for all Medicare+Choice organizations, large or small, regardless of the type of services provided. The applicability of the recommendations and guidelines provided in this document may depend on the circumstances and resources of each particular Medicare+Choice organization. However, regardless of the organization's size and structure, the OIG believes every Medicare+Choice organization can and should strive to accomplish the objectives and major principles underlying all of the compliance policies and procedures recommended within this guidance.

The OIG recognizes that the success of the compliance program guidance hinges on thoughtful and practical comments from those individuals and organizations that will utilize the tools set forth in this document. In a continuing effort to collaborate closely with the private sector, the OIG solicited input and support from the public in the development of this compliance program guidance.[8] Further, we took into consideration previous OIG publications, such as Special Fraud Alerts, the recent findings and recommendations in reports issued by OIG's Office of Audit Services (OAS) and Office of Evaluation and Inspections (OEI),[9] comments from HCFA, as well as the experience of past and recent fraud investigations related to managed care organizations[10] conducted by OIG's Office of Investigations (OI) and the Department of Justice.

As appropriate, this guidance may be modified and expanded as more information and knowledge is obtained by the OIG, and as changes in the law, and in the rules, policies and procedures of the Federal and State plans occur. New compliance practices may eventually be incorporated into this guidance if the OIG discovers significant enhancements to better ensure an effective compliance

---

[8] See Solicitation of Information and Recommendations for Developing the OIG Compliance Program Guidance for Certain Medicare+Choice Organizations (63 FR 50577 (9/22/98)). We also requested public comment on the draft guidance (64 FR 33869 (6/24/99)).

[9] Special Fraud Alerts are available on the OIG website at http://www.hhs.gov/oig/. The recent findings and recommendations of OEI and OAS can be located on the Internet at http://www.hhs.gov/oei and http://www.hhs.gov/progorg/oas/cats/hcfa.html, respectively.

[10] These investigations include findings based upon Medicare risk-based Health Maintenance Organizations and competitive medical plans as defined in 42 U.S.C. 1395mm.

program. We recognize the development and implementation of compliance programs in Medicare+Choice organizations often raise sensitive and complex legal and managerial issues.[11] However, the OIG wishes to offer what it believes is critical guidance for those who are sincerely attempting to comply with the relevant health care statutes and regulations.

II. Compliance Program Elements

The elements discussed in this guidance are similar to those of the other OIG Compliance Program Guidances[12] and our corporate integrity agreements.[13] While these same elements are required by HCFA in the Medicare+Choice regulations,[14] the OIG reiterates that this guidance is not mandatory, but simply represents OIG's recommendations on how the elements can be implemented.[15]

Every effective compliance program must begin with a formal commitment[16] by the Medicare+Choice organization's governing body to include all of theapplicable elements listed below. A good faith and meaningful commitment on the part of the Medicare+Choice organization's administration, especially the governing body and the chief executive officer (CEO), will substantially contribute to the program's successful implementation. It is incumbent upon an organization's officers and managers to provide ethical leadership to the organization and to assure adequate systems and

---

[11] Nothing stated herein should be substituted for, or used in lieu of, competent legal advice from counsel.

[12] See note 1.

[13] Corporate integrity agreements are executed as part of a civil settlement agreement between the health care provider and the Government to resolve a case based on allegations of health care fraud or abuse. These OIG-imposed agreements are generally in effect for a period of 3 to 5 years and require many of the elements included in this compliance guidance.

[14] 42 CFR 422.501(b)(vi).

[15] The OIG appreciates that because Medicare+Choice organizations are subject to substantial regulations that contain extensive operational requirements as well as requirements regarding self-monitoring and monitoring or review of activities by external organizations, they may already be performing some of the activities discussed in this guidance. Each Medicare+Choice organization must determine the extent to which these activities need to be modified or supplemented to create an effective compliance program.

[16] Formal commitment may include a resolution by the board of directors, where applicable. A formal commitment does include the allocation of adequate resources to ensure that each of the elements is addressed.

resources are in place to facilitate and promote ethical and legal conduct. Employees, managers and the Government will focus on the words and actions (including decisions made on resources devoted to compliance) of an organization's leadership as a measure of the organization's commitment to compliance.

Under Medicare+Choice, an organization may, by written contract, delegate any activity required under or governed by the Medicare+Choice standards to another entity. However, an organization entering into a Medicare contract remains entirely accountable to HCFA for the performance of any delegated function.[17] It is the sole responsibility of the organization to ensure that the function is performed in accordance with applicable standards. While the activity may be delegated, the oversight responsibility remains with the Medicare+Choice organization. Each Medicare+Choice organization should keep these requirements and responsibilities in mind as it develops its compliance program.

These elements are based on the seven steps of the Federal Sentencing Guidelines.[18] As required by the HCFA regulations, every Medicare+Choice organization must implement all of the recommended elements and expand upon them, as appropriate. At a minimum, comprehensive compliance programs should include the following seven elements:

(1) The development and distribution of written standards of conduct, as well as written policies and procedures, that promote the Medicare+Choice organization's commitment to compliance and that address specific areas of potential fraud (e.g., the marketing process and utilization);

(2) The designation of a chief compliance officer and other appropriate bodies, e.g., a corporate compliance committee, charged with the responsibility and authority of operating and monitoring the compliance program and who report directly to the CEO and the governing body;

(3) The development and implementation of regular, effective education and training programs for all affected employees;

(4) The development of effective lines of communication between the compliance officer and all employees, including a process, such

---

[17] 42 CFR 422.502(i).

[18] See United States Sentencing Commission Guidelines, Guidelines Manual, 8A1.2, comment. (n.3(k)). The Federal Sentencing Guidelines are detailed policies and practices for the Federal criminal justice system that prescribe appropriate sanctions for offenders convicted of Federal crimes.

as a hotline, to receive complaints (and the adoption of procedures to protect the anonymity of complainants and to protect callers from retaliation);

(5) The use of audits or other risk evaluation techniques to monitor compliance and assist in the reduction of identified problem areas;

(6) The development of disciplinary mechanisms to consistently enforce standards and the development of policies addressing dealings with sanctioned and other specified individuals; and

(7) The development of policies to respond to detected offenses, to initiate corrective action to prevent similar offenses, and to report to Government authorities when appropriate.

A. Written Policies and Procedures

Every compliance program should require the development and distribution of written compliance policies, standards and practices that identify specific areas of risk and vulnerability to the Medicare+Choice organization. These policies should be developed by the appropriate operational officials within the Medicare+Choice organization, with appropriate review and oversight by the compliance officer and compliance committee. The OIG recommends that these policies be made available to all individuals who are affected by the particular risk or policy area at issue. Such individuals would include, for example, Medicare+Choice employees whose duties touch upon a particular risk or policy area, as well as agents and independent contractors with whom the organization has contracted to perform delegated activities, which touch upon a particular risk or policy area.[19] The OIG also recommends that Medicare+Choice organizations provide, upon request, all contractors with a summary of the standards of conduct and the number of the hotline. The distribution of these materials could be accomplished via hard copy or via electronic means.

1. Standards of Conduct

---

[19] When determining to whom to distribute various policies, the Medicare+Choice organizations should keep in mind that, according to the Federal Sentencing Guidelines, an organization must have established compliance standards to be followed by its employees and other agents in order to receive sentencing credit. The Guidelines define "agent" as "any individual, including a director, an officer, an employee, or an independent contractor, authorized to act on behalf of the organization." See United States Sentencing Commission Guidelines, Guidelines Manual, 8A1.2, Application Note 3(d).

Medicare+Choice organizations should develop standards of conduct for all affected employees that include a clearly delineated commitment to compliance by the organization's senior management and its divisions. To help communicate a strong and explicit organizational commitment to compliance goals and standards, the Medicare+Choice organization's governing body, CEO, chief operating officer (COO), general counsel, chief financial officer (CFO) and other senior officials should be directly involved in the development of standards of conduct.

The standards should function in the same fashion as a constitution, i.e., as a foundational document that details the fundamental principles, values and framework for action within an organization, as well as the organization's mission and goals. The standards should also articulate the Medicare+Choice organization's commitment to comply with all Federal and State laws and regulations, with an emphasis on preventing fraud and abuse, and include the ramifications of failure to comply with these standards. The standards should not only address compliance with statutes and regulations, but should also set forth broad principles that guide employees in conducting business professionally and properly. In short, the standards should promote integrity, support objectivity and foster trust. Furthermore, a Medicare+Choice organization's standards of conduct should reflect a commitment to high quality health care delivery, as evidenced by its conduct of on-going performance assessment, improved outcomes of care and respect for the rights of Medicare+Choice enrollees.

2. Written Policies for Risk Areas

As part of its commitment to compliance, Medicare+Choice organizations should establish a comprehensive set of written policies addressing all applicable statutes, rules and program instructions that apply to each function or department of that Medicare+Choice organization.[20] Thepolicies should address specific areas of concern, such as marketing practices and data collection and submission processes. In contrast to the standards of conduct, which are

[20] This includes, but is not limited to, the Medicare+Choice provisions and the fraud and abuse provisions of the Balanced Budget Act of 1997, Pub. L. 105–33; the Civil False Claims Act, 31 U.S.C. 3729–3733; the criminal false claims statutes, 18 U.S.C. 287, 1001; the fraud and abuse provisions of the Health Insurance Portability and Accountability Act of 1996 (HIPAA), Pub.L. 104–191; and the civil money penalties in the Social Security Act, 42 U.S.C. 1320a-7a and 42 U.S.C. 1395w-27(g). See also 42 CFR 422.1–422.312.

designed to be a clear and concise collection of fundamental standards, the written policies should articulate specific procedures personnel should follow when performing their duties. [21]

The regulations and operational policies issued by HCFA that implement the Medicare+Choice program are very comprehensive and, as required by HCFA, serve as the basis for the policies and procedures of a Medicare+Choice organization. [22] The legal, policy and contractual requirements that organizations must meet and perform as a Medicare+Choice organization are articulated in documentation promulgated by HCFA and other Federal agencies and should be considered de facto risk areas. Included among these risk areas are: (1) The election process; (2) benefits and beneficiary protections; (3) quality assessment and performance improvement; (4) cost sharing; (5) solvency, licensure and other State regulatory issues; (6) claims processing; and (7) appeals and grievance procedures.

To determine the additional policies and procedures that are needed for a given Medicare+Choice organization (and which policies may need particular attention), the OIG recommends that Medicare+Choice organizations conduct a comprehensive self-administered risk analysis or contract for an independent risk analysis by experienced health care consulting professionals. This risk analysis could include surveys and statistical analysis specifically tailored to the organization's beneficiary population, provider pool and organizational structure and should identify and rank the various compliance and business risks the company may experience

---

[21] The Medicare+Choice organization should document its efforts to formulate its policies to comply with applicable statutes, regulations and program requirements. For example, where a Medicare+Choice organization requests advice from HCFA, the Medicare+Choice organization should document and retain a record of the request and any written or oral response. This step is extremely important if the Medicare+Choice organization intends to rely on that response to guide it in future decisions, actions or appeals. In addition, the Medicare+Choice organization should maintain records relevant to the issue of whether its reliance was "reasonable," and whether it exercised due diligence in developing procedures to implement the advice.

[22] Medicare+Choice organizations should regularly access the HCFA managed care website at http://www.hcfa.gov/medicare/mgdcar1.htm for updates on regulations and operational policies. Operational Policy Letters can be located on HCFA's web site at http://www.hcfa.gov/medicare/mgd-ops.htm.

in its daily operations.[23] A Medicare+Choice organization's prior history of noncompliance with applicable statutes, regulations and Federal health care program requirements, or the failure to report such non-compliance, may indicate additional types of risk areas where the organization may be vulnerable and may require necessary policy measures to prevent avoidable recurrence.[24]

The fact that Medicare+Choice organizations may be both providers and insurers of health care increases the number and type of risk areas to which a Medicare+Choice organization must be attuned, as well as the type of auditing and monitoring procedures that must be implemented, in the development of its compliance efforts. For example, there are a variety of substantially different operational areas within the structure of a Medicare+Choice organization such as marketing, health services delivery and finances that could require different types of policies.

Given the detailed nature of the HCFA rules and regulations, we have not attempted in this document to identify each and every policy that should be established by a Medicare+Choice organization. Rather, based on a review of OIG audits, investigations and evaluations, we have identified the following areas of particular concern to OIG that the Medicare+Choice organization should include in its written policies and procedures:[25]

---

[23] Medicare+Choice organizations may also want to consult the OIG's Work Plan when conducting the risk assessment. The OIG Work Plan details the various projects the OIG currently intends to address in the fiscal year. It should be noted that the priorities in the Work Plan are subject to modification and revision as the year progresses and the Work Plan does not represent a complete or final list of areas of concern to the OIG. The Work Plan is currently available on the Internet at http://www.hhs.gov/oig/.

[24] "Recurrence of misconduct similar to that which an organization has previously committed casts doubt on whether it took all reasonable steps to prevent such misconduct" and is a significant factor in the assessment of whether a compliance program is effective. See United States Sentencing Commission Guidelines, Guidelines Manual, 8A1.2, Application Note 3(7)(ii).

[25] Although many of these areas apply specifically to Medicare+Choice organizations, many of the areas identified below have analogous issues in non-Medicare organizations. Medicare+Choice organizations that provide private managed care products should consider establishing additional policies and procedures for risk areas that apply specifically to those areas. Although the policies may be integrated, they should identify, as appropriate, where deviations may be necessary to meet Medicare+Choice requirements or State licensure requirements.

- Marketing materials and personnel;
- Selective marketing and enrollment;
- Disenrollment;
- Underutilization and quality of care;
- Data collection and submission processes;
- Anti-kickback statute and other inducements; and
- Emergency services.

The following sections provide specific guidance regarding the risk areas identified above.

a. Marketing Materials and Personnel

While each Medicare+Choice organization must comply with all of HCFA's detailed requirements relating to marketing their plans,[26] OIG is particularly concerned that organizations have policies regarding: (1) The completeness and accuracy of the marketing materials; and (2) marketing personnel.

Accurate and useful information is crucial to the success of the Medicare+Choice program. The OIG is concerned that Medicare+Choice organizations correctly and completely describe plan information in marketing materials or other materials distributed to individuals prior to and following enrollment. Medicare+Choice organizations that misrepresent or falsify information submitted to HCFA, individuals or entities are subject to civil money penalties (CMPs) or other intermediate sanctions.[27]

The submission of inaccurate or misleading information is of particular concern to OIG. Medicare+Choice organizations should be aware that the fact that materials have been approved by HCFA does not absolve them from potential liability for misrepresenting or falsifying information.[28]

HCFA considers marketing materials to include any informational materials targeted to Medicare beneficiaries. Marketing materials go beyond the public's general conception of marketing materials and include generalcirculation brochures, leaflets, news-

[26] Medicare+Choice organizations should ensure that they conform to fair marketing standards as set forth in the statute, the Medicare Managed Care National Marketing Guide (Marketing Guide) and all HCFA Operational Policy Letters affecting marketing matters.

[27] 42 U.S.C. 1395w-27(g).

[28] Medicare+Choice organizations may not distribute marketing materials or election forms unless they have submitted them to HCFA for review 45 days prior to distribution and HCFA has not disapproved their distribution (42 CFR 422.80).

papers, magazines, television, radio, billboards, yellow pages, the internet, slides and charts, and leaflets for distribution by providers. Such materials also include membership communication materials such as membership rules, subscriber agreements, or confirmation of enrollment.[29] Accordingly, Medicare+Choice organizations should carefully scrutinize all of these materials for completeness, accuracy and compliance with HCFA rules, regulations and policy letters.

In verifying that marketing materials meet all HCFA requirements, Medicare+Choice organizations should ensure that the appropriate materials contain an adequate description of enrollee rights, procedures for accessing basic benefits and services, and a clear explanation of the appeal and grievance process.[30] Of particular concern to HCFA and OIG is that the concept of "lock-in" is clearly explained in all marketing material. Many Medicare beneficiaries are unfamiliar with the notion that managed care may limit their health care provider choices. Describing the process of selecting a primary care physician and the limitations that this places on a Medicare+Choice enrollee's choice of provider will reduce the unmet expectations of Medicare beneficiaries.

Another important concept to include in the marketing materials is that the beneficiary may be terminated from enrollment in the plan due to the decision of the Medicare+Choice organization not to renew its contract with HCFA, or due to HCFA's refusal to renew the contract.[31] This termination can affect the enrollee's eligibility for supplemental insurance and other benefits.

Second, in light of the critical role that marketing personnel play in representing the plan to Medicare enrollees, the Medicare+Choice organization must take all appropriate steps to ensure that marketing personnel are presenting clear, complete and accurate information to potential enrollees. To that end, the OIG encourages Medicare+Choice organizations to employ their own marketing personnel, as opposed to contracting these responsibilities to outside entities.[32] This provides the Medicare+Choice organization the necessary control to ensure that these individuals meet all HCFA

[29] 42 CFR 422.80(b).

[30] 42 CFR 422.80(c).

[31] 42 CFR 422.80(c)(3).

[32] It should be noted that Medicare+Choice organizations have ultimate responsibility for the acts and omissions of its marketing agents (42 CFR 422.502(i)).

guidelines. Similarly, it safeguards Medicare beneficiaries from practices that could greatly affect the access to health care to which they are entitled and their ability to acquire accurate and complete information regarding their health care options.

Medicare+Choice organizations should also be aware that the OIG and HCFA strongly discourage the use of physicians as marketing agents for several reasons: (1) When a physician acts outside his or her traditional role as care provider, the physician's patients may be confused as to when the physician is acting as an agent of the plan, and when the physician is acting in his or her role as a fiduciary to act in the best interests of the patient; (2) a physician's knowledge of a patient's health status increases the potential for discriminating in favor of Medicare beneficiaries with positive health status when acting as a marketing agent; (3) physicians may not be fully aware of membership plan benefits and costs; and (4) physicians may not be the best source of membership information for their patients.[33] Therefore, the organization should develop policies to ensure that any provider promotional activities are conducted in accordance with HCFA guidelines (which allow, e.g., the distribution of health plan brochures (exclusive of applications) at a health fair or in their own offices).[34]

b. Selective marketing and Enrollment

The OIG is very concerned about the practice known as "cherry-picking," or selective marketing,[35] in which Medicare+Choice organizations discriminate in the marketing and enrollment process based upon an enrollee's degree of risk for costly or prolonged treatment.[36] Except for individuals who have been medically determined to have end-stage renal disease, a Medicare+Choice organization may not deny, limit or condition the coverage or furnishing of benefits to individuals eligible to enroll in a Medicare+Choice plan offered by the organization on the basis of any factor that is related to health status, including, but not limited to,

---

[33] Marketing Guide, Chapter IV.

[34] Id.

[35] OIG is also concerned about a similar problem, known as "gerrymandering," which is an attempt to eliminate certain high dollar risk areas from the Medicare+Choice organization's service area. Medicare+Choice organizations should have policies in place to avoid such practices.

[36] Although the Medicare+Choice program has attempted to alleviate many of the selective marketing practices through the use of risk adjustment, the phase-in period for risk-adjustment virtually assures that this will remain a troubling issue through 2004.

the following: (1) Medical condition (including mental illness); (2) claims experience; (3) receipt of health care; (4) medical history; (5) genetic information; (6) evidence of insurability; and (7) disability.[37] Engaging in practices that would reasonably be expected to have the effect of denying or discouraging enrollment by eligible individuals whose medical condition or history indicates the need for substantial future medical services subjects the Medicare+Choice organization to a CMP or other sanction, such as suspension of enrollment or suspension of payment.[38]

Certain types of practices clearly fall into the category of cherry-picking and Medicare+Choice organizations should implement policies to prohibit and prevent such practices. For example, organizations should generally prohibit employees from conducting medical screening, i.e., asking the beneficiary medical questions prior to enrollment.[39] In a 1996 survey, the OIG found that such screening for health status at application was reported by 18 percent of beneficiaries. While this represented a reduction from the 1993 level of 43 percent, it still represents a potentially serious problem.[40]

Another way in which Medicare+Choice organizations may inappropriately target healthier beneficiaries is by primarily marketing their plans in places where healthy enrollees are more likely to be present, such as at health and exercise clubs, or in areas that are difficult to access for people with disabilities (e.g., upper floors of buildings that do not have elevators).[41] Similarly, organizations may inappropriately provide inducements to potential enrollees in a way that would encourage younger, healthier beneficiaries to enroll in the plan. For example, the offering of free gym memberships or kayaking or other sporting lessons would appeal to a healthy class of enrollees and discriminate against those who would not be interested in such activities.[42] Ifa Medicare+Choice organization intends

---

[37] 42 U.S.C. 1395w-22(b)(1); 42 CFR 422.110.

[38] 42 U.S.C. 1395w-27(g)(1)(D); 42 CFR 422.750 through 422.760.

[39] Pursuant to 42 CFR 422.50(a)(2), it would be appropriate to determine whether a potential enrollee has end-stage renal disease.

[40] "Beneficiary Perspectives of Medicare Risk HMOs 1996." (OEI-06–95–00430)(March 1998).

[41] In fact, Medicare+Choice organizations are required to allocate part of their resources to marketing to the Medicare population with disabilities (42 CFR 422.80(e)(2)(i)).

[42] The statute prohibits the provision of cash or other monetary rebates as an inducement for enrollment in the plan. See 42 U.S.C. 1395w-21(h)(4)(A).

to offer such items as a Medicare+Choice benefit, the item must meet the definitional requirements of a bona fide benefit. The item must be: (1) Related to health care; and (2) costed out in the Medicare+Choice organization's Adjusted Community Rate. Any such items that do not meet these requirements are not valid Medicare+Choice benefits and must be considered "value added services" (VAS) subject to all the limitations associated with VAS.

Other examples of cherry-picking would be: (1) Attempts to give enrollment priority to newly eligible Medicare beneficiaries (who are theoretically younger and healthier), other than as set forth in the regulations;[43] (2) the tracking of costs incurred by enrollees who were enrolled in different settings (e.g., at the health fair, or at a health club), which could be used to target healthier enrollees in the future; or (3) re-enrollment campaigns targeting past plan subscribers who had low medical costs. There are many other subtle ways in which a Medicare+Choice organization may try to enroll healthy patient populations in a discriminatory manner (i.e., not making similar attempts to enroll less healthy beneficiaries) and the organization should implement policies actively to prevent such practices.

c. Disenrollment

In general, Medicare+Choice organizations are prohibited from disenrolling, or requesting or encouraging (either by action or inaction) an individual to disenroll from any plan it offers.[44] If a Medicare+Choice organization acts to expel or refuses to reenroll an individual in violation of the statute, a civil money penalty or other sanction can be imposed on the organization.[45] The OIG is particularly concerned about disenrollment in light of its recent review, which revealed that there was a problem with disenrollment of bene-

---

However, HCFA allows Medicare+Choice organizations to give Medicare beneficiaries nominal value gifts, provided that the plan offers these gifts whether or not the beneficiary enrolls in the plan. HCFA defines nominal value as an item having little or no resale value (generally, less than $10), which cannot be readily converted into cash. See Marketing Guide, Chapter II. The use of inducements is also discussed in Section II.A.2.f. — Anti-kickback and Other Inducements.

[43] 42 CFR 422.66(d).

[44] Medicare+Choice organizations are entitled to disenroll individuals under certain circumstances, e.g., failure to pay premiums or engagement in disruptive behavior. 42 CFR 422.74.

[45] 42 U.S.C. 1395w-27(g)(1)(C).

ficiaries just prior to receiving expensive inpatient services. [46]

In this review, OIG found that Medicare paid for inpatient hospital services amounting to $224 million in fee-for-service (FFS) payments within 3 months of beneficiaries' disenrollment from six risk plans during 1991 through 1996. Had these beneficiaries not disenrolled, Medicare would have paid the HMOs $20 million in monthly capitation payments. Had the beneficiaries remained in the HMOs, Medicare would have saved $204 million in expenditures. Included in the Medicare FFS payments were $41 million for beneficiaries who disenrolled, had FFS procedures performed, and then reenrolled into another or the same managed care plan.

While this study did not identify the reasons for the disenrollment as part of this review, one partial explanation of the review could be that some managed care plans or their medical personnel may be encouraging sicker beneficiaries to disenroll as a way to avert their own costs at a high cost to the Medicare system.

Each Medicare+Choice organization must implement policies to ensure that inappropriate disenrollment does not occur. [47] Such policies should include clarification of when it is appropriate for medical personnel to discuss the concept of disenrollment. Generally speaking, OIG believes it would be inappropriate for medical personnel to initiate discussion of disenrollment or to promote disenrollment (when the topic is initiated by the enrollee), except in the rare circumstance where the Medicare+Choice organization cannot or does not provide the covered medical items or services needed by the patient.

d. Underutilization and Quality of Care

Medicare+Choice organizations must ensure that all covered services are available and accessible to all enrollees. [48] The OIG views the inappropriate withholding or delay of services, known as

---

[46] Review of Inpatient Services Performed on Beneficiaries After Disenrolling from Medicare Managed Care." (A-07–98–01256) (May 1999).

[47] Such policies should be consistent with the provisions that prohibit Medicare+Choice organizations from restricting a health care professional from advising patients of the "health status of the individual or medical care or treatment for the individual's condition or disease, regardless of whether benefits for such care or treatment are provided under the plan." See 42 U.S.C. 1852(j)(3)(emphasis added).

[48] 42 U.S.C. 1395w-22. To this end, Medicare+Choice organizations must comply with the standards contained in the Quality Improvement System for Managed Care (QISMC) for Organizations Contracting with Medicare or Medicaid.

underutilization or "stinting," as a serious issue.[49] Examples of practices that can lead to underutilization and poor quality include the failure to employ or contract with sufficient institutional and individual providers to accommodate all enrollees, the failure to provide geographically reachable services to enrollees, the delay in approving or failure to approve referrals for covered services, the establishment of utilization review procedures that are so burdensome that an enrollee could not reasonably be expected to fulfill the requirements and the categorical denial of payment of claims.[50]

There are a wide variety of policies that a Medicare+Choice organization should implement to be sure it is providing all medically necessary services to its enrollees. The regulations and guidelines that implement the Medicare+Choice program contain numerous provisions that deal with this issue. While we have not attempted to develop a comprehensive list in this document, we would like to highlight three types of policies that Medicare+Choice organizations should develop that may help address underutilization and quality of care.

First, Medicare+Choice organizations should have policies that prohibit interference with health care professionals' advice to enrollees. Also known as the "gag rule," this prohibition extends to advice regarding the patient's health status, medical care, and treatment options, the risks, benefits and consequences of treatment or non-treatment, or the opportunity for the individual to refuse treatment and to express preferences about future treatment options.[51] Failure to comply with this requirement can lead to sanctions.[52]

Second, Medicare+Choice organizations should be sure, to they extent that they utilize physician incentive plans (PIPs) in their payment arrangements with individual physicians or physician groups, that they comply with all applicable regulations and that such payment arrangements are fully disclosed to HCFA as required by regulation. The PIPs raise utilization concerns because they are defined as "any compensationarrangement to pay a physician or

---

[49] Medicare+Choice organizations can be subject to sanctions for failing substantially to provide medically necessary items and services that are required to be provided, if the failure has adversely affected (or has the substantial likelihood of adversely affecting) the individual. 42 U.S.C. 1395w-27(g)(1)(A).

[50] See QISMC Standards 2.1.2, 2.2.2 and 3.1.

[51] 42 U.S.C. 1395w-22(j)(3), 42 CFR 422.206; QISMC Standard 3.3.1.7.

[52] 42 U.S.C. 1395w-27(g)(1)(F); 42 CFR 422.750 through 422.760.

physician group that may directly or indirectly have the effect of reducing or limiting services provided to any plan enrollees." [53] Any PIP operated by a Medicare+Choice organization must comply with the following requirements. First, it may make no payments to physicians (such as offerings of monetary value, including, but not limited to, stock options or waivers of debt [54]) to reduce or limit medically necessary services furnished to any particular enrollee. Second, if the PIP puts a physician or physician group at "substantial financial risk" [55] for referral services, the Medicare+Choice organization must: (1) survey current and previously enrolled members to assess access to, and satisfaction with, the quality of services; and (2) assure that there is adequate and appropriate stop-loss protection. [56] Finally, Medicare+Choice organizations must disclose to HCFA certain information regarding their PIPs. These disclosure requirements apply to direct contracting arrangements, as well as subcontracting arrangements. [57]

Finally, the OIG is aware of cases in which beneficiaries have received covered services from individuals that were not appropriately licensed. Given the serious quality of care implications of this type of practice, the OIG is particularly concerned that Medicare+Choice organizations have procedures for the selection of providers, including criteria for the credentialing of providers. This process should include an application, verification of information and a site visit, where applicable. [58] The information that must be verified includes that the individual has a valid license to practice, clinical privileges in good standing and appropriate educational qualifications.

e. Data Collection and Submission Processes

The regulations implementing the Medicare+Choice program contain numerous requirements relating to the data collection and submission process, ranging from a requirement for an effective system for receiving, controlling and processing election forms [59] to

---

[53] 42 CFR 422.208.

[54] 42 U.S.C. 1395w-22(j)(4); 42 CFR 422.208.

[55] "Substantial financial risk" threshold is set at 25 percent of potential payments for covered services, regardless of the frequency of assessment (i.e., collection) or distribution of payments. 42 CFR 422.208.

[56] 42 CFR 422.208(c).

[57] 42 CFR 422.210(a).

[58] 42 CFR 422.204.

[59] 42 CFR 422.60(e).

requirements for the timely submission of disenrollment notices.[60] These requirements cover the gamut of requirements with which a Medicare+Choice organization must comply and are too detailed to enumerate in this document. Medicare+Choice organizations should establish a policy that all required submissions to HCFA be accurate, timely and complete and that all appropriate reporting requirements are met.[61]

The OIG is particularly concerned that Medicare+Choice organizations submit accurate data when that information determines the amount of payment received from HCFA. The regulations require that when a Medicare+Choice organization requests payment under the contract, the CEO or CFO must certify the accuracy, completeness and truthfulness of relevant data, including enrollment data, encounter data and information provided as part of an adjusted community rate (ACR) proposal.[62] When a Medicare+Choice organization submits this type of data to HCFA, it is making a "claim" for capitation payment in the amount dictated by the data submitted, or in the case of the ACR submission, a "claim" to retain the portion of the capitation amount that is under the average payment rate, rather than providing additional benefits. When a Medicare+Choice organization is claiming payment (or the right to retain payment) based upon information submitted to HCFA, it must take responsibility for having taken reasonable steps to assure the accuracy of this information. The attestation forms developed by HCFA for this purpose require certification that the information submitted is true and accurate based on best knowledge, information and belief.

The requirement that the CEO or CFO certify as to the accuracy, completeness and truthfulness of data, based on best knowledge, information and belief, does not constitute an absolute guarantee of accuracy. Rather, it creates a duty on the Medicare+Choice organization to put in place an information collection and reporting system reasonably designed to yield accurate information. Further, the Medicare+Choice organization should exercise due diligence to

---

[60] 42 CFR 422.66(b)(3)(i).

[61] On a related topic, Medicare+Choice organizations should also be sure that their computer systems are Year 2000 (Y2K) compliant. An OIG report indicates that managed care organizations have made significant progress in this regard, with more than 80% indicating that they are Y2K compliant. "Y2K Readiness of Managed Care Organizations." (OEI-05–98–0591)(October 1999).

[62] 42 CFR 422.502(l) and (m). See also Contract for Year 2000, Attachments A, B and C.

ensure that these systems are working properly. The exact methods used by the Medicare+Choice organization to accomplish this can be determined by the organization, however, it should ordinarily conduct sample audits and spot checks of this system to verify whether it is yielding accurate information.

The knowing submission of false information to HCFA can lead to serious criminal or civil penalties.[63] Medicare+Choice organizations should implement policies so that the enrollment, encounter and ACR data submitted to HCFA are accurate, complete and truthful. While information from a variety of sources can affect this data, Medicare+Choice organizations should take note of two reports issued by the OIG that have identified concerns in two aspects of this data.

First, the OIG recommends that Medicare+Choice organizations have policies and procedures in place that ensure that the administrative component of the ACR is calculated accurately.[64] As part of this process, Medicare+Choice organizations should have clearly defined criteria for claiming reimbursement for their administrative costs. These costs should not include any costs that are directly associated with furnishing patient care. All such costs should be allocated to the applicable operating component. The OIG has articulated serious concerns about the methodology used by managed care organizations in computing their administrative rate on the ACR proposal.[65] For example, computing an administrative rate based on the use of a medical utilization factor could generate a payment that is almost three times what would be charged on the commercial side.

Second, the OIG recommends that Medicare+Choice organizations have adequate internal controls in place to ensure that the

---

[63] Falsification of documentation in any application for any benefit or payment under a Federal health care program is a Federal offense punishable by not more than $25,000 or imprisonment for 5 years, or both. See 42 U.S.C. 1320a-7b. In addition, a CMP can be imposed for the misrepresentation or falsification of information submitted to HCFA under Medicare+Choice. See 42 U.S.C. 1395w-27(g)(1)(E).

[64] The administrative component of the ACR covers any management, financial or other costs that are incurred by or allocated to a business unit for the management or administration of the business unit as a whole.

[65] See, e.g.,"Administrative Costs Submitted by Risk-Based Health Maintenance Organizations on the Adjusted Community Rate Proposals are Highly Inflated." (A-14–97–00202) (July 1998).

institutional status ofbeneficiaries is reported accurately.[66] A recent report issued by the OIG estimated that risk-based HMOs received Medicare overpayments of $22.2 million for beneficiaries incorrectly classified as institutionalized.[67] The incorrect classification was largely due to deficiencies in the HMOs internal controls in two areas: (1) Verification of beneficiaries' institutional status; and (2) reporting of institutional beneficiaries to HCFA. The results were based on audits of eight randomly selected HMOs.

f. Anti-Kickback Statute and Other Inducements

The anti-kickback statute provides criminal penalties for individuals or entities that knowingly and willfully offer, pay, solicit or receive remuneration to induce the referral of business reimbursable under a Federal health care program (including Medicare and Medicaid).[68] The OIG has promulgated safe harbor regulations that define practices that are not subject to the anti-kickback statute because such practices would be unlikely to result in fraud or abuse.[69]

The anti-kickback statute potentially applies to many managed care arrangements because a common strategy of these arrangements is to offer physicians, hospitals and other providers increased patient volume in return for substantial fee discounts. Because discounts to managed care organizations can constitute "remuneration" within the meaning of the anti-kickback statute, a number of health care providers have expressed concern that many relatively innocu-

---

[66] This will remain a concern until risk adjustment is fully implemented.

[67] "Review of Medicare Managed Care Payments for Beneficiaries with Institutional Status." (A-05–98–00046)(April 1999).

[68] 42 U.S.C. 1320a-7b(b). If it is determined that a party has violated the anti-kickback statute, the individual or entity can be excluded from participation in the Medicare and other Federal health care programs (as defined in 42 U.S.C. 1320a-7b(f)). 42 U.S.C. 1320a-7(b)(7). In addition, there is an administrative CMP provision for violating the anti-kickback statute (42 U.S.C. 1320a-7a(a)(7)).

[69] 42 CFR 1001.952. The safe harbors set forth specific conditions that, if met, assure entities involved of not being prosecuted or sanctioned for the arrangement qualifying for the safe harbor. However, safe harbor protection is afforded only to those arrangements that precisely meet all of the conditions set forth in the safe harbor. The failure of an arrangement to fit inside a safe harbor or statutory exception does not mean that the arrangement is illegal. It is incorrect to assume that arrangements outside of a safe harbor are suspect due to that fact alone. That an arrangement does not meet a safe harbor only means that the arrangement does not have guaranteed protection and must be evaluated on a case-by-case basis.

ous, or even beneficial, commercial managed care arrangements implicate the statute and may subject them to criminal prosecution and administrative sanctions.

The OIG recognizes that when managed care organizations are paid a capitated amount for all of the services they provide regardless of the dates, frequency or type of services, there is no incentive for them to overutilize. In any event, even if overutilization occurs, the Federal health care programs are not at risk for these increased costs. Accordingly, OIG will be issuing a safe harbor from the anti-kickback statute that will provide protection for certain financial arrangements between managed care organizations (including Medicare+Choice organizations) and individuals or entities with whom they contract for the provision of health care items or services, where a Federal health care program pays such organizations on a capitated basis.[70]

In general, the safe harbor protects payments between capitated managed care organizations (including Medicare+Choice organizations offering coordinated care plans) and individuals or entities with which it has direct contracts to provide or arrange for the provision of items or services.[71] While this is a broad exception, there are three important limitations.

The first significant limitation is that there is no protection if the financial arrangements under the managed care agreement are implicitly or explicitly part of a broader agreement to steer fee-for-service Federal health care program business to the entity giving the discount to induce the referral of managed care business. Specifically, we understand that most managed care organizations have multiple relationships with their contractors and subcontrac-

---

[70] This safe harbor was developed in accordance with section 216 of HIPAA and section 14 of the Medicare and Medicaid Patient and Program Protection Act of 1987 (Pub. L. 100–93) through a negotiated rulemaking process that began in the spring of 1997. For a more detailed description of the negotiated rulemaking, see the Committee Statement of the Negotiated Rulemaking Committee on the Shared Risk Exception (January 22, 1998), which can be found on the Internet at http://www.hhs.gov/oig/.

[71] In addition, arrangements between direct contractors and all subcontractors or successive tiers of subcontractors are protected, as long as the arrangement is for the provision of health care items or services that are covered by the arrangement between the direct contractor and the managed care organization and the arrangement meets the requirements applicable to arrangements between the direct contractor and the managed care organization.

tors for the provision of services for various product lines, including non-federal HMOs, preferred provider organizations (PPOs) and point of service networks. Consequently, although neither a managed care organization receiving a capitated payment from a Federal health care program nor its contractors or subcontractors has an incentive to overutilize items or services or pass additional costs back to the Federal health care programs under the capitated arrangement, we are concerned that a managed care organization or contractor may offer (or be offered) a reduced rate for its items or services in the Federal capitated arrangement in order to have the opportunity to participate in other product lines that do not have stringent payment or utilization constraints. This practice is a form of a practice known as "swapping;" in the case of managed care arrangements, low capitation rates could be traded for access to additional fee-for-service lines of business. We are concerned when these discounts are in exchange for access to fee-for-service lines of business, where there is an incentive to overutilize services provided to Federal health care program beneficiaries.

For example, we would have concerns where an HMO with a Medicare risk contract under Medicare Part C also has an employer-sponsored PPO that includes retirees and requires participating providers to accept a low capitation rate for the Medicare HMO risk patients in exchange for access to the Medicare fee-for-service patients in the PPO. Although in such circumstances the cost to the Medicare program for the risk-based HMO beneficiaries will not be increased, there may be increased expenditures for Medicare beneficiaries in the PPO arrangement, because the providers may have an incentive to increase services to the Medicare enrollees in the PPO to offset the discounted rates to the Medicare HMO. Accordingly, such arrangements could violate the anti-kickback statute and should not be protected.

A second limitation on the regulatory safe harbor protection is that it only applies to remuneration for health care items and services and those items or services reasonably related to the provision of health care items and services. It does not cover marketing services or any services provided prior to a beneficiary's enrollment in a health plan.

Finally, the broad protection is limited to risk-based managed care plans that do not claim any payment from a Federal health care program other than the capitated amount set forth in the managed care organization's agreement with the Federal health careprogram.

Where the managed care plan, its contractors or its subcontractors are permitted to seek additional payments from any of the Federal health care programs, the regulatory safe harbor protection is significantly more limited. For example, protection is not extended to arrangements with subcontractors when the contract under section 1876 of the Social Security Act is cost-based or where the prime contract is protected solely because the contracting entity is a Federally-qualified HMO.[72] In the first instance, reimbursement from the Federal health care program is based on costs, and in the latter case, services for Medicare enrollees are reimbursed on a fee-for-services basis. In both instances, reimbursement will increase with utilization, thus providing the same incentive to overutilize as any fee-for-service payment methodology.

While the new safe harbor will provide protection from the anti-kickback statute for most arrangements between Medicare+Choice organizations and their contractors, Medicare+Choice organizations should also have policies in place that ensure that any incentives that the Medicare+Choice organization offers directly or indirectly to beneficiaries and potential beneficiaries do not run afoul of the anti-kickback statute or the new civil money penalty relating to incentives to beneficiaries.[73] The CMP was enacted in section 231(h) of HIPAA (42 U.S.C. 1320a-7a(a)(5)) and imposes sanctions against individuals or entities that offer remuneration to a program beneficiary that they know, or should know, will influence the beneficiary's decision to order or receive items or services from a particular provider, practitioner or supplier reimbursable by Medicare or the State health care programs.

Pending the publication of the final rule implementing this CMP, we can provide the following guidance. It is our view that organizations that provide incentives to Federal health care program beneficiaries to enroll in a plan are not offering remuneration to induce the enrollees to use a particular provider, practitioner or supplier. Accordingly, we anticipate that organizations that provide incentives to enroll in a plan will not be subject to sanctions under this provision. However, incentives provided by organizations to

---

[72] The arrangements may qualify for other safe harbors, such as the discount or personal services safe harbors.

[73] Our concerns regarding the use of inducements in a manner that leads to enrollment of only healthy beneficiaries, such as offering memberships to exercise clubs for purposes of patient screening, is discussed above in Section II.A.2.b. — Selective Marketing and Enrollment.

induce a beneficiary to use a particular provider, practitioner or supplier once the beneficiary has enrolled in a plan are within the purview of this CMP and are prohibited if they do not meet an exception. For example, incentives given to beneficiaries by a particular physician group within the physician panel of a Medicare+Choice organization to encourage the beneficiary to use that physician group over another physician in the panel would be prohibited.

g. Emergency Services

The OIG and HCFA believe that there may be special concerns regarding the provision of emergency services to enrollees of Medicare+Choice plans. The anti-dumping statute[74] imposes specific obligations on Medicare-participating hospitals that offer emergency services to individuals presenting themselves at the hospital seeking possible emergency treatment. While the obligations under the anti-dumping statute prohibit a hospital from inquiring into the patient's method of payment or insurance status when it results in the delay of a medical screening examination and/or stabilizing treatment, it has come to our attention that some hospitals routinely seek prior authorization from the patient's primary care physician or from the managed care plan when a managed care patient requests emergency services. Investigations of allegations of the anti-dumping statute across the country have persuaded the OIG that managed care patients may be at risk of being discharged or transferred without receiving a medical screening examination, largely because of the problems inherent in seeking "prior authorization."

To ensure appropriate access to emergency services for Medicare+Choice enrollees, Medicare+Choice organizations should comply with several key provisions. First, Medicare+Choice organizations are prohibited from requiring prior authorization for emergency services and must provide coverage for such services without regard to the emergency care provider's contractual relationship with the Medicare+Choice organization.[75] Second, payment must be provided for emergency services based on a "prudent layperson standard," which means that the need for emergency services should be determined from a reasonable patient's perspec-

---

[74] 42 U.S.C. 1395dd.

[75] 42 U.S.C. 1395w-22(d)(1)(E). Medicare+Choice organizations should not offer, or enter into, contracts with hospitals that are inconsistent with the anti-dumping statute.

tive at the time of presentation of the symptoms[76] Finally, Medicare+Choice organizations must comply with all guidelines relating to the efficient and timely coordination of appropriate maintenance and post-stabilization of an enrollee after the enrollee has been stabilized under the anti-dumping statute.[77]

Medicare+Choice organizations should be particularly careful of the requirements of the anti-dumping statute in the event that they participate in the so-called "dual staffing" of emergency departments. Dual staffing occurs when hospitals enter into arrangements allowing a managed care organization to station its own physicians in the hospital's emergency department for the purpose of screening and treating managed care enrollees. Implementation of dual staffing raises some concerns under the anti-dumping statute, particularly where different procedures and protocols have been established for each staff.

In addition, Medicare+Choice organizations should be particularly careful in operating "urgent care" services and in instructing enrollees to contact such services when enrollees need care. The organizations should ensure that such operations and instructions do not delay or otherwise compromise enrollees' access to services that should be provided in a hospital emergency room.3. Retention of Records and Information Systems

Medicare+Choice organizations' compliance programs should provide for the implementation of a records retention system. This system should establish policies and procedures regarding the creation, distribution, retention, storage, retrieval and destruction of documents. The three types of documents developed under this system should include: (1) All records and documentation required by either Federal or State law and the program requirements of Federal and State health plans;[78] (2) records listing the persons responsible for implementing each part of the compliance plan; and (3) all records necessary to protect the integrity of the Medicare+Choice organization's compliance process and confirm the effectiveness of the program. The documentation necessary to satisfy the third category includes, but is notlimited to the following: evidence of adequate employee training; reports from the Medicare+Choice organization's

---

[76] 42 U.S.C. 1395w-22(d)(3).

[77] 42 U.S.C. 1395w-22(d)(2).

[78] These documents should be maintained for the periods required by the HCFA Medicare+Choice regulations.

hotline; results of any investigation conducted as a consequence of a hotline call; modifications to the compliance program; all written notifications to providers regarding compliance activities;[79] and the results of the Medicare+Choice organization's auditing and monitoring efforts.

In light of the increasing reliance on electronic data interchange by the health care industry, Medicare+Choice organizations should take particular care in establishing procedures for maintaining the integrity of its data collection systems. This should include procedures for regularly backing-up data (either by diskette, restricted system or tape) collected in connection with all aspects of the Medicare+Choice program requirements.

In addition, all Medicare+Choice organizations should develop and implement policies and procedures to ensure the confidentiality and privacy of financial, medical, personnel and other sensitive information in their possession.[80] These policies should address both electronic and hard copy documents.

4. Compliance as an Element of a Performance Plan

Compliance programs should require that the promotion of, and adherence to, the elements of the compliance program be a factor in evaluating the performance of all relevant employees. Such employees should be periodically trained in new compliance policies and procedures.

Policies should require that managers:

- Discuss with all relevant employees the compliance policies and legal requirements applicable to their function;
- inform all relevant personnel that strict compliance with these policies and requirements is a condition of employment; and
- Disclose to all relevant personnel that the Medicare+Choice organization will take disciplinary action up to and including termination for violation of these policies or requirements.

In addition to making performance of these duties an element in evaluations, the compliance officer or company management should include a policy that managers and supervisors will be sanctioned for failure to instruct adequately their subordinates or for failure to detect noncompliance with applicable policies and legal requirements, where reasonable diligence on the part of the manager or

[79] This should include notifications regarding: quality of care issues; confusing or inaccurate encounter data; and termination of the contract.

[80] 42 U.S.C. 1395w-22(h); 42 CFR 422.118.

supervisor should have led to the discovery of any problems or violations.

B. Designation of a Compliance Officer and a Compliance Committee

1. Compliance Officer

Every Medicare+Choice organization should designate a compliance officer to serve as the focal point for compliance activities. This responsibility may be the individual's sole duty or added to other management responsibilities, depending upon the size and resources of the Medicare+Choice organization and the complexity of the task.

Designating a compliance officer with the appropriate authority is critical to the success of the program, necessitating the appointment of a high-level official in the Medicare+Choice organization with direct access to the company's governing body, the CEO and all other senior management and legal counsel. [81] While it is important that the compliance officer have appropriate authority, we are not suggesting that the compliance officer should have operational responsibility for the various aspects of the Medicare+Choice program. For example, the compliance officer should have full authority to stop the submission of data that he or she believes is problematic until such time as the issue in question has been resolved. In addition, the compliance officer should be copied on the results of all internal audit reports and work closely with key managers to identify aberrant trends in the areas that require certification. The compliance officer must have the authority to review all documents and other information that are relevant to compliance activities, including, but not limited to, enrollee records (where appropriate) and records concerning the marketing efforts of the organization and the Medicare+Choice organization arrangements with other parties, including employees, professionals on staff, relevant independent

---

[81] The OIG believes that it is not advisable for the compliance function to be subordinate to the Medicare+Choice organization's general counsel, comptroller or similar company financial officer. Free-standing compliance functions help to ensure independent legal reviews and financial analyses of the institution's compliance activities. By separating the compliance function from the key management positions of general counsel or CFO (where the size and structure of the organization make this a feasible option), a system of checks and balances is established to more effectively achieve the compliance program's goals.

contractors, suppliers, agents and physicians. This policy enables the compliance officer to review contracts and obligations (seeking the advice of legal counsel, where appropriate) that may contain referral and payment provisions that could violate statutory or regulatory requirements.

Coordination and communication are the key functions of the compliance officer with regard to planning, implementing and monitoring the compliance program. With this in mind, the OIG recommends that the Medicare+Choice organization's compliance officer closely coordinate compliance functions with providers' compliance officers.

The compliance officer should have sufficient funding and staff to fully perform his or her responsibilities. These duties should include:

- Overseeing and monitoring the implementation of the compliance program; [82]
- Reporting on a regular basis to the Medicare+Choice organization's governing body, CEO and compliance committee on the progress of implementation;
- Periodically revising the program in light of changes in the organization's needs and in the law and policies and procedures of Government and private payor health plans;
- Reviewing employees' certifications stating that they have received, read and understood the standards of conduct;
- Developing, coordinating and participating in a multifaceted educational and training program that focuses on the elements of the compliance program and seeks to ensure that all appropriate employees and management are knowledgeable of, and comply with, pertinent Federal and State standards;
- Coordinating personnel issues with the Medicare+Choice organization's human resources/personnel office (or its equivalent) to ensure that providers and employees do not appear in the List of Excluded Individuals/Entities and the General Services Administration (GSA) list of debarred contractors; [83]
- Assisting the Medicare+Choice organization's management in coordinating internal compliance review and monitoring activities, including annual or periodic reviews of departments;

---

[82] For multi-site Medicare+Choice organizations, the OIG encourages coordination with each facility owned by the Medicare+Choice organization through the use of compliance liaisons at each site.

[83] See note 101.

- Independently investigating and acting on matters related to compliance, including the flexibility to design andcoordinate internal investigations (e.g., responding to reports of problems or suspected violations) and any resulting corrective action with all departments, providers, agents, and, if appropriate, independent contractors;
- Developing policies and programs that encourage managers and employees to report suspected fraud and other improprieties without fear of retaliation; and
- Continuing the momentum of the compliance program and the accomplishment of its objectives long after the initial years of implementation.2. Compliance Committee

The OIG recommends that a compliance committee be established to advise the compliance officer and assist in the implementation of the compliance program.[84] When assembling a team of people to serve as the Medicare+Choice organization's compliance committee, the company should include individuals with a variety of skills.[85] The OIG strongly recommends that the compliance officer manage the compliance committee. Once a managed care organization chooses the people that will accept the responsibilities vested in members of the compliance committee, the organization must train these individuals on the policies and procedures of the compliance program.

The committee's responsibilities should include:

---

[84] The compliance committee benefits from having the perspectives of individuals with varying responsibilities in the organization, such as operations, finance, audit, human resources, utilization review, medicine, claims processing, information systems, legal, marketing, enrollment and disenrollment as well as employees and managers of key operating units. These individuals should have the requisite seniority and comprehensive experience within their respective departments to implement any necessary changes in the company's policies and procedures. Some organizations have found it helpful to include an outside director on its compliance committee to provide a different perspective.

[85] A Medicare+Choice organization should expect its compliance committee members and compliance officer to demonstrate high integrity, good judgment, assertiveness and an approachable demeanor, while eliciting the respect and trust of employees of the organization. The compliance committee members should also have significant professional experience in working with quality assurance, enrollment, marketing, clinical records and auditing principles.

- Analyzing the organization's regulatory environment, the legal requirements with which it must comply and specific risk areas;
- Assessing existing policies and procedures that address these areas for possible incorporation into the compliance program;
- Working with appropriate departments, as well as affiliated providers, to develop standards of conduct and policies and procedures that promote allegiance to the organization's compliance program;
- Recommending and monitoring, in conjunction with the relevant departments, the development of internal systems and controls to carry out the organization's standards, policies and procedures as part of its daily operations;
- Determining the appropriate strategy/approach to promote compliance with the program and detection of any potential violations, such as through hotlines and other fraud reporting mechanisms;
- Developing a system to solicit, evaluate and respond to complaints and problems; and
- Monitoring internal and external audits and investigations for the purpose of identifying troublesome issues and deficient areas experienced by the Medicare+Choice organization and implementing corrective and preventive action.

The committee may also address other functions as the compliance concept becomes part of the overall operating structure and daily routine.

C. Conducting Effective Training and Education

The proper education and training of corporate officers, managers, employees and the continual retraining of current personnel at all levels are significant elements of an effective compliance program. Where appropriate, the Medicare+Choice organization may afford its contractors the opportunity to participate in the organization's compliance training and educational programs.[86] The contractors should be encouraged to develop their own compliance programs that complement the Medicare+Choice organization's compliance program.

---

[86] While some Medicare+Choice organizations may encourage providers to participate in education programs designed for its own employees, other organizations may prefer to develop provider-specific education programs about compliance.

1. Formal Training Programs

To ensure the appropriate information is being disseminated to the correct individuals, the Medicare+Choice organization training program should include both a general session and specialized sessions on specific risk areas. All employees should attend the general session on compliance. Employees whose job responsibilities implicate specific risk areas (e.g., marketing or data collection and submission) should attend the specialized sessions.

The OIG recommends that attendance and participation at training programs be made a condition of continued employment and that failure to comply with training requirements should result in disciplinary action, including possible termination, when such failure is serious. The Medicare+Choice organization should retain adequate records of its training of employees, including attendance logs and material distributed at training sessions. New employees should be targeted for training early in their employment, and to the extent that they perform complicated tasks with greater organizational legal exposure, should be monitored closely until all training is completed.

a. General Sessions

As part of their compliance programs, Medicare+Choice organizations should require all employees to attend annual training that emphasizes the organization's commitment to compliance with all Federal and State statutes and requirements, and the policies of private payors. While the OIG recognizes that not all standards, policies and procedures need to be communicated to all employees, it believes that the general message about the importance of complying with fraud and abuse laws and other ethical areas should be addressed and made part of the general training.

As part of the initial training, the standards of conduct should be distributed to all employees. Every employee should be required to sign and date a statement that reflects the employee's knowledge of, and commitment to the standards of conduct. This attestation should be retained in the employee's personnel file. The standards of conduct should be updated and revised as appropriate.

b. Specialized Training

Because Medicare+Choice organizations are responsible for compliance in all of the risk areas mentioned in section II.A. above, the OIG recommends Medicare+Choice organizations require individuals who are involved in the risk areas to receive specialized training. For example, marketing employees should receive training on the marketing, enrollment, disenrollment and anti-kickback policies. All employees who work with beneficiaries or providers regarding medical services should receive appropriate training on the risks associated with underutilization. Those employees who are involved in developing enrollment, encounter and ACR data should receive training onHCFA policies in these areas. Clarifying and emphasizing these areas of concern through training and educational programs are particularly relevant to a Medicare+Choice organization's marketing and financial personnel, in that the pressure to meet business goals may render these employees particularly vulnerable to engaging in prohibited practices.

The OIG recommends Medicare+Choice organizations' compliance programs address the need for periodic professional education courses for relevant personnel. Such courses would be in addition to the internal training sessions provided by the organization.

c. Format of the Training Program

The OIG suggests all relevant levels of personnel be made part of various educational and training programs of the Medicare+Choice organization. Employees should be required to have a minimum number of educational hours per year, as appropriate, as part of their employment responsibilities. A variety of teaching methods, such as interactive training and training in several different languages (including the translation of standards of conducts and other materials), particularly where a Medicare+Choice organization has a culturally diverse staff, should be implemented so that all affected employees are knowledgeable about the institution's standards of conduct and procedures for alerting senior management to problems and concerns. In addition, the materials should be written at appropriate reading levels for targeted employees. All training materials should be designed to take into account the skills, knowledge and experience of the individual trainees. Post-training tests can be used to assess the success of training provided and employee comprehension of the Medicare+Choice organization's policies and procedures.

2. Informal and Ongoing Compliance Training

It is essential that compliance issues remain at the forefront of the Medicare+Choice organization's priorities. The organization must demonstrate its commitment by continuing to disseminate the compliance message. One effective mechanism to achieve this goal is to publish a monthly compliance newsletter, or devote a section to compliance in a general weekly or monthly existing newsletter. This would allow the Medicare+Choice organization to address specific examples of problems the company encountered during its ongoing audits and risk analysis, while reinforcing the company's firm commitment to the general principles of compliance and ethical conduct. The newsletter could also include the risk areas identified in current OIG publications or investigations. Finally, the Medicare+Choice organization could use the newsletter as a mechanism to notify employees of significant legal or regulatory developments. The Medicare+Choice organization should maintain its newsletters in a central location to document the guidance offered and provide new employees with access to guidance previously provided. Other written materials, such as posters, fliers or articles in other company publications, could also be used to disseminate the compliance message.

Another effective method of maintaining the presence of the compliance message is to maintain a website devoted to compliance issues. This could be linked to the homepage of the organization. Many organizations have chosen to maintain these sites internally on the Intranet to alleviate any confidentiality concerns. The Intranet (or Internet) also facilitates the use of hypertext links that allow the organization to maintain a centralized source on statutory, regulatory and other program guidance disseminated by HCFA, the OIG, the Department of Justice and the Congress. These links, along with any other webpages that the Medicare+Choice organization deems pertinent and useful can be assembled on a single site that can, by hypertext link, provide access to all of these useful resources.

D. Developing Effective Lines of Communication

An open line of communication between the compliance officer and Medicare+Choice organization personnel, as well as among the organization, health care providers and enrollees, is critical to the successful implementation of a compliance program and the reduction of any potential for fraud, abuse and waste. Each organization should have in place both a mechanism for the reporting of improper conduct, as well a mechanism for more routine types of communication among the compliance officer and relevant groups.

1. Hotline or Other System for Reports of Potential Misconduct

Each Medicare+Choice organization should have in place a hotline or other mechanism [87] through which employees, enrollees or other

[87] The OIG recognizes that it may not be financially feasible for a small Medicare+Choice organization to maintain a telephone hotline dedicated to

parties can report potential violations of the organization's compliance policies or of Federal or State health care program requirements. In any event, several independent reporting paths should be created for an employee to report fraud, waste or abuse so that such reports cannot be diverted by supervisors or other personnel. If the organization establishes a hotline, the telephone number should be made readily available to all employees, enrollees and independent contractors, by circulating the number on wallet cards or conspicuously posting the telephone number in common work areas.[88]

Matters reported through the hotline or other communication sources that suggest violations of compliance policies, Federal and State health care program requirements, regulations or statutes should be documented and investigated promptly to determine their veracity and significance. A log should be maintained by the compliance officer or authorized designee that records such calls, including the nature of any investigation and its results.[89] Such information should be included in reports to the governing body, the CEO and compliance committee.

Employees, enrollees and providers should be permitted to report matters on a confidential basis. To encourage such reporting, written confidentiality and non-retaliation policies should be developed. Employees, enrollees, providers and other contractors should be made aware of these policies to encourage communication and the reporting of incidents of potential fraud.[90] While the Medi-

---

receiving calls solely on compliance issues. These companies may explore alternative methods, e.g., contracting with an independent source to provide hotline services or establishing a written method of confidential disclosure.

[88] Medicare+Choice organizations should also post in a prominent, available area the HHS-OIG Hotline telephone number, 1–800–447–8477 (1–800-HHS-TIPS), in addition to any organization's hotline number that may be posted.

[89] To efficiently and accurately fulfill such an obligation, the Medicare+Choice organization should create an intake form for all issues identified through reporting mechanisms. The form could include information concerning the date the potential problem was reported, the internal investigative methods utilized, the results of any investigation, any corrective action implemented, any disciplinary measures imposed and any overpayments and monies returned.

[90] The OIG believes that whistleblowers should be protected against retaliation, a concept embodied in the provisions of the False Claims Act. See 31 U.S.C. 3730(h). In many cases, employees sue their employers under the False Claims Act's qui tam provisions out of frustration because of the

care+Choiceorganization should always strive to maintain the confidentiality of the reporter's identity, the policies should explicitly communicate that there may be a point where the individual's identity may become known or may have to be revealed.

The OIG recognizes that assertions of fraud and abuse by those who may have participated in illegal conduct or committed other malfeasance raise numerous complex legal and management issues that should be examined on a case-by-case basis. The compliance officer may wish to work closely with legal counsel to obtain guidance on these issues.

2. Routine Communication/Access to the Compliance Officer

While it is crucial that Medicare+Choice organizations have effective systems in place for the reporting of suspected misconduct, it is equally important that the compliance officer foster more routine communication both among its employees and among its health care providers and enrollees.

With respect to its own employees, the OIG encourages the establishment of procedures for personnel to seek clarification from the compliance officer or members of the compliance committee in the event of any confusion or question regarding a company policy, practice or procedure. Questions and responses should be documented and dated and, if appropriate, shared with other staff so that standards, policies, practices and procedures can be updated and improved to reflect any necessary changes or clarifications. The compliance officer may want to solicit employee input in developing these communication and reporting systems. The methods discussed above relating to ongoing training and education are an integral part of this communication. [91]

The communication and coordination function of the compliance program serves an even more critical role in the context of the managed care environment because the managed care entity serves as an intermediary between the health care provider and the enrollee. In fact, the raison d'etre of a managed care organization is to coordinate the care of its enrollees. As with providers, communications with

---

company's failure to take action when a questionable, fraudulent or abusive situation was brought to the attention of senior corporate officials.

[91] In addition to methods of communication used by current employees, an effective employee exit interview program could be designed to solicit information from departing employees regarding potential misconduct and suspected violations of the Medicare+Choice organization's policy and procedures.

beneficiaries and communications with HCFA (and its designees) must demonstrate the highest level of integrity, honesty and judgment. The Medicare+Choice organization should implement methods to encourage communication among its enrollees and providers. For example, as appropriate, a Medicare+Choice organization should communicate the results of audits, disenrollment surveys, utilization data and quality of care determinations to its contracting suppliers and providers in order to facilitate open discussion regarding appropriate health care delivery.

E. Auditing and Monitoring

An ongoing evaluation process is critical to a successful compliance program.[92] The OIG believes an effective program should incorporate thorough monitoring of its implementation and regular reporting to senior company officers. Compliance reports created by this ongoing monitoring, including reports of suspected noncompliance, should be maintained by the compliance officer and reviewed with the Medicare+Choice organization's senior management and the compliance committee. The extent and frequency of the audit function may vary depending on factors such as the size of the company, the resources available to the company, the company's prior history of noncompliance and the risk factors that are prevalent in a particular organization. However, all Medicare+Choice organizations have an obligation to establish an adequate audit function and meet all of HCFA's requirements.

Although many monitoring techniques are available, one effective tool to promote and ensure compliance is the performance of regular, periodic compliance audits by internal or external auditors who have expertise in Federal and State health care statutes, regulations and Federal health care program requirements. The audits should focus on the Medicare+Choice organization's programs or divisions, including external relationships with third-party contractors, specifically those with substantive exposure to Government enforcement actions. The audits should cover the range of programmatic requirements of the Medicare+Choice program and comply with generally accepted protocols governing such audits. In particular, the audits

[92] The OIG recognizes that Medicare+Choice organizations have a variety of ongoing monitoring processes and would most likely incorporate these existing processes, as appropriate, into their compliance program. We do not anticipate that the compliance monitoring function would exist entirely independently of the operational program.

should focus on the risk areas identified earlier in this document, especially the data and information that affect payments by Medicare. Finally, the Medicare+Choice organization should focus on any areas of specific concern identified within that organization and those that may have been identified by any outside agency, whether Federal or State.

Monitoring techniques may include sampling protocols that permit the compliance officer to identify and review variations from an established baseline.[93] Significant variations from the baseline should trigger a reasonable inquiry to determine the cause of the deviation. If the inquiry determines that the deviation occurred for legitimate, explainable reasons, the compliance officer or manager may want to limit any corrective action or take no action. If it is determined that the deviation was caused by improper procedures, misunderstanding of rules, including fraud and systemic problems, the Medicare+Choice organization should take prompt steps to correct the problem.[94] Any overpayments discovered as a result of such deviations should be reported promptly to HCFA (or its designees), with appropriate documentation and a thorough explanation of the reason for the overpayment.[95]

An effective compliance program should also incorporate periodic (at a minimum, annual) reviews of whether the program's compliance elements have been satisfied, e.g., whether there has been appropriate dissemination of the program's standards, training,

---

[93] The OIG recommends that when a compliance program is established in a Medicare+Choice organization, the compliance officer, with the assistance of department managers, take a "snapshot" of the organization's operations from a compliance perspective. This assessment can be undertaken by outside consultants, law or accounting firms, or internal staff, with authoritative knowledge of health care compliance requirements. This "snapshot," often used as part of bench marking analysis, becomes a baseline for the compliance officer and other managers to judge the Medicare+Choice organization's progress in reducing or eliminating potential areas of vulnerability. Medicare+Choice organizations should track statistical data on utilization review and quality data based on customer satisfaction and renewal data. This will facilitate identification of problem areas and elimination of potential areas of abusive or fraudulent conduct.

[94] Prompt steps to correct the problem include contacting the appropriate provider in situations where the provider's actions contributed to the problem.

[95] In addition, when appropriate, as referenced in section G, below, reports of fraud or systemic problems should also be made to the appropriate Government authority.

ongoing educational programs anddisciplinary actions.[96] This process will verify actual conformance by all departments with the compliance program. Such reviews may support a determination that appropriate records have been created and maintained to document the implementation of an effective program.

The reviewers involved in any audits should:

- Possess the qualifications and experience necessary to adequately identify potential issues with the subject matter to be reviewed;
- Be independent of the specific functional area examined;
- Have access to existing audit resources, relevant personnel and all relevant areas of operation;
- Present written evaluative reports on compliance activities to the CEO, governing body members of the compliance committee on a regular basis, but not less than annually; and
- Specifically identify areas where corrective actions are needed.

In the Medicare+Choice context, a variety of different methods will be necessary to adequately monitor and evaluate the ongoing operations of the Medicare+Choice organization. In general, the OIG recommends the use of techniques such as on-site visits, questionnaires (for providers, enrollees and employees), and trend analyses, to name just several.[97] Because the auditing and monitoring function is very different and much more complex in the managed care context than in any other segment of the health care industry, we have provided additional guidance on the methods to be used in evaluating selected risk areas.

1. Marketing/Enrollment/Diseenrollment

Developing a system for evaluating the compliance of the marketing, enrollment and disenrollment functions of a Medicare+Choice organization requires innovative techniques. Each Medicare+Choice organization will have to develop an individualized method as to how to obtain this data. Some of the methods that the OIG suggests

---

[96] One way to assess the knowledge, awareness and perceptions of the Medicare+Choice organization's staff is through the use of a validated survey instrument (e.g., employee questionnaires, interviews or focus groups).

[97] Medicare+Choice organizations may want to consult HCFA's Contractor Performance Monitoring System Manual to get additional ideas for monitoring methods. In addition, organizations may want to consult the OAS website for information on conducting audits, including information on statistical sampling (RAT-STATS). See note 10.

include: using secret shoppers; surveying[98] current enrollees;[99] and conducting exit interviews with former enrollees (particularly those that disenrolled just prior to obtaining an expensive service) on their experience with the Medicare+Choice marketing and enrollment process. Once this data is collected, it must be maintained in a format that can be accessed readily.

In an effort to integrate the monitoring function with its training function, a Medicare+Choice organization may wish to test its marketing staff on their knowledge of the company's policies and procedures, as well as the Federal and State statutes that govern the marketing process. This assessment can be developed using many formats. Many companies have customized interactive software to test employees' knowledge of relevant policies and procedures. It may also be formulated in the traditional written version.

Methods used to monitor marketing agents include the analysis of disenrollment data to identify marketing agents with high and low percentages of member disenrollments within a set number of days (e.g., 90 days). In addition, Medicare+Choice organizations may want to establish enrollment verification systems requiring that a different individual from the sales agent meet with beneficiaries who have applied for enrollment to ensure that they understand restrictions of the plan, such as the lock-in provision.

Finally, it is essential for all marketing materials to be reviewed by an independent and competent reviewer, such as an individual in the general counsel's office, to ensure that they do not mislead, confuse or misrepresent any aspect of the plan. Similarly, a Medicare+Choice organization may want to consider having the materials examined by individuals familiar with the claims processing department and utilization review office for consistency with the policies, procedures and practices of these departments.

2. Underutilization and Quality of Care

Procedures for tracking and reporting utilization review data are vital to the success of any compliance endeavor. Medicare+Choice

[98] Medicare+Choice organizations may be able to use response data from already existing surveys, such as from the Health of Seniors survey (HEDIS) and for certain organizations, the mandatory disenrollment surveys required under PIP.

[99] It should be noted, while this method may be less expensive, it may not provide unbiased data, particularly in the area of selective marketing. In fact, in the selective marketing area, the data may be skewed significantly in favor of the Medicare+Choice organization.

organizations should periodically review the service areas that are part of the Medicare+Choice organization to ensure that enrollees are receiving adequate access to care. In reviewing service areas, Medicare+Choice organizations should collect data on a variety of topics, including the number of primary care physicians in the service area, the number and type of specialists in the service area, the waiting time for appointments, the telephone access to the Medicare+Choice organization, rates of denial of emergency services claims and the problems associated with the coordination of care. All of this data should be maintained in a database in a format that can be used to generate statistical data and analysis.

Medicare+Choice organizations should ensure that there are adequate systems in place to monitor underutilization and inappropriate denials. Such procedures include collecting data on utilization patterns and detecting aberrant patterns. This data should be checked against utilization rates in the industry. This function could be performed by a medical affairs department that is responsible for regular review of claims, the payment system, encounter data and medical record review to assess the degree to which care is under (or over) utilized.

Similarly, the Medicare+Choice organization should survey its enrollees on utilization patterns and whether they felt they were subjected to inadequate health care services, inappropriate denials, type of practitioner providing treatment and whether a beneficiary's request for another provider was denied or approved. Such survey results should be reviewed and investigated, when appropriate. Generally, these may be skewed in favor of the Medicare+Choice organization if the enrollees are current members. Presumably, if an enrollee was truly dissatisfied with the Medicare+Choice organization's attitude toward enrollee rights, the enrollee would have disenrolled from the plan. As a result, a Medicare+Choice organization should evaluate both current enrollee satisfaction surveys and exit interview surveys of former enrollees.

Medicare+Choice organizations have a good source of information regarding utilization issues, simply by tracking the type of appeals and grievances they receive from beneficiaries. This information should be tracked in a database that can be easily accessed by type of grievance or appeal and results.

3. Data Collection and Submission Processes

Given the importance of the enrollment, encounter and ACR data, the Medicare+Choice organization should develop ways to audit this information to assure its accuracy, completeness and truthfulness, on best knowledge, information and belief. As indicated earlier, such methods would ordinarily include sample audits and spot checks of the system. These activities should be facilitated by the fact that HCFA requires Medicare+Choice organizations to detail in their contractual relationships with providers the access that they will need to the provider's medical record documentation.4. Anti-Kickback and Other Inducements

Medicare+Choice organizations should periodically review their contractual documents and discussions with providers to ensure that "swapping" is not occurring. In addition, contracts with marketing personnel should be reviewed by legal counsel to be sure they do not violate the anti-kickback statute and other applicable statutes and regulations.

F. Enforcing Standards Through Well-Publicized Disciplinary Guidelines and Policies Regarding Dealings With Ineligible Persons

The OIG recommends that all Medicare +Choice organizations' compliance programs include several key policies in the area of personnel/human resources. The first deals with the establishment, and consistent application of, appropriate disciplinary policies to deal with improper conduct and the second deals with the employment of certain ineligible individuals.

1. Consistent Enforcement of Disciplinary Policies

An effective compliance program should include guidance regarding disciplinary action for all employees who have failed to comply with the Medicare+Choice organization's standards of conduct, policies and procedures, Federal health care program requirements, or Federal and State laws, or those who have otherwise engaged in wrongdoing. It is vital to publish and disseminate the range of possible disciplinary actions for improper conduct and to educate officers and other staff regarding these standards. Employees should be advised that disciplinary action may be appropriate where a responsible employee's failure to detect a violation is attributable to his or her negligence or reckless conduct. The sanctions could range from oral warnings to suspension, termination or other sanctions, as appropriate. While each situation must be considered on a case-by-case basis to determine the appropriate sanction, intentional or reckless noncompliance should subject transgressors to significant sanctions.

The written standards of conduct should elaborate on the procedures for handling disciplinary problems and identify who will be responsible for taking appropriate action. For example, while disciplinary actions can be handled by department managers, others may have to be resolved by a more senior official of the organization. Personnel should be advised by the organization that disciplinary action will be taken on a fair and equitable basis, that is, all levels of employees should be subject to similar disciplinary action for the commission of similar offenses. Managers and supervisors should be held accountable to implement the disciplinary policy consistently so that the policy will have the required deterrent effect.

2. Employment of, and Contracting With, Ineligible Persons

All Medicare+Choice organizations should use care when delegating substantial discretionary authority to make decisions that may involve compliance with the law or compliance oversight. In particular, the organization should ensure that it does not delegate such responsibilities to individuals or entities that it knows, or should have known, have a propensity to engage in inappropriate or improper conduct. Pursuant to the compliance program, a Medicare+Choice organization's policies should prohibit the hiring of, or entering into, contracts with individuals or entities who have been recently convicted of a criminal offense related to health care or who are listed as debarred, excluded or otherwise ineligible for participation in Federal health care programs.[100] The policies should require the Medicare+Choice organization to utilize Government resources to determine whether such individuals or entities are debarred or excluded. These resources should be used for both potential employees (as part of the employment application process, which should also include a reasonable and prudent background investigation), and should be used to periodically check existing employees and contractors.

Lists of debarred and excluded individuals and entities are currently maintained by both the OIG and the General Services

---

[100] Prospective employees who have been officially reinstated into the Medicare and Medicaid programs by the OIG may be considered for employment upon proof of such reinstatement.

Administration.[101] By approximately January 2000, the Healthcare Integrity Protection Data Bank (HIPDB) will be available to Medicare+Choice organizations (for a nominal fee) to use in conducting these checks on employees and contractors.[102] The HIPDB is an electronic data collection program that will collect, store and disseminate reports on practitioners, providers and suppliers that have been the subject of health care related final adverse actions in criminal, civil and administrative proceedings. The final adverse actions to be reported to the HIPDB include criminal convictions or civil judgments related to the delivery of health care, actions by Federal or State agencies responsible for licensing or certification of health care providers, suppliers and practitioners, exclusions from Federal or State health care programs, and certain final adverse actions taken by health plans.[103] Pending the resolution of any known criminal charges or proposed debarment or exclusion, the OIG recommends that such individuals should be removed from direct responsibility for, or involvement in, any Federal health care program. If labor agreements make such removal legally impermissible, the OIG recommends that the individual be closely supervised in all aspects of his or her duties that relate to Federal health care programs. If the resolution of the matter results in conviction, debarment or exclusion of a current employee or contractor, then the Medicare+Choice organization must not continue to employ or contract with such individual for the provision of health care, utilization review, medical social work or administrative services.[104]

G. Responding to Detected Offenses, Developing Corrective Action Initiatives, and Reporting to Government Authorities

Violations of the Medicare+Choice organization's compliance program, failures to comply with applicableFederal or State law, rules and program instructions and other types of misconduct may

---

[101] OIG's List of Excluded Individuals/Entities is available on the Internet at http://www.hhs.gov/oig/ and the GSA list of debarred contractors is available on the Internet at http://www.arnet.gov/epls.

[102] 42 U.S.C. 1320a-7e.

[103] Note that agencies and health plans are required by HIPAA to report to the HIPDB. Failure by a health plan to make the mandated reports to the HIPDB may result in CMPs being assessed against the health plan, pursuant to 42 U.S.C. 1320a-7e(b)(6).

[104] 42 CFR 422.752(a)(8).

threaten a Medicare+Choice organization's status as a reliable, honest and trustworthy company. Detected but uncorrected misconduct can seriously endanger the mission, reputation and legal status of the organization. Consequently, it is important that the chief compliance officer or other management officials promptly investigate and take appropriate action with respect to any reports or reasonable indications of suspected noncompliance.[105]

Pending issuance of final HCFA regulations[106] regarding the obligations of a Medicare+Choice organizations to report misconduct, the OIG recommends that the following procedures be followed when a Medicare+Choice organization discovers from any source evidence of misconduct related to payment or delivery of health care items or services under the Medicare+Choice contract. First, the Medicare+Choice organization should conduct a timely, reasonable inquiry into the misconduct. Second, if after reasonable inquiry, the organization has determined that the misconduct may violate criminal, civil or administrative law, it should report the existence of the misconduct promptly to the appropriate Government authority[107] within a reasonable period, but not more than 60 days[108] after a determination that a violation may have occurred.[109] When report-

---

[105] Instances of non-compliance must be determined on a case-by-case basis. The existence, or amount, of a monetary loss to a health care program is not solely determinative of whether or not the conduct should be investigated and reported to governmental authorities. In fact, there may be instances where there is no readily identifiable monetary loss at all, but corrective action and reporting are still necessary to protect the integrity of the applicable program and its beneficiaries.

[106] 42 CFR 422.501(b)(vi).

[107] For example, if the potential violation relates to federal criminal law, the Civil False Claims Act, the civil money penalty authorities (primarily under sections 1128A and 1857 of the Social Security Act) and related statutes administered by the HHS/OIG, the report must be made to that office.

[108] While the OIG recommends reporting in 60 days, the organization must report within 30 days in order to attempt to obtain favorable treatment under the Civil False Claims Act. See note 6. In addition, reporting such conduct may be considered a mitigating factor by the OIG in determining administrative sanctions (e.g., penalties, assessments and exclusion), if the reporting company becomes the subject of an OIG investigation. See 62 FR 67392 (12/24/97).

[109] The OIG believes that some potential violations may be so serious that they warrant immediate notification to Government authorities, prior to, or simultaneous with, commencing an internal inquiry. Examples of such situations include instances when the misconduct: (1) Is a clear violation of civil

ing potential violations to the Government, a Medicare+Choice organization should provide all evidence relevant to the potential violation, including the impact of the potential violation on beneficiaries and any potential cost impact. Finally, the Medicare+Choice organization should initiate and implement appropriate corrective actions, e.g., repayment of overpayments, disciplinary actions and modifications of procedures to ensure the problem does not recur.

Failure to notify HCFA of an overpayment within a reasonable period of time could be interpreted as an intentional attempt to conceal the overpayment from the Government, thereby establishing an independent basis for a criminal violation with respect to the Medicare+Choice organization, as well as any individuals who may have been involved.[110] For this reason, Medicare+Choice compliance programs should ensure that overpayments are identified quickly and promptly return overpayments obtained from Medicare or other Federal health care programs.

The OIG recommends that Medicare+Choice organizations consider the following guidance as they structure internal inquiries. Depending upon the nature of the alleged violations, an internal inquiry will probably include interviews and a review of relevant documents. Medicare+Choice organizations should consider engaging outside counsel, auditors or health care experts to assist in an inquiry. Records of the inquiry should contain documentation of the alleged violation, a description of the process (including the objectivity of the investigators and methodologies utilized), copies of interview notes and key documents, a log of the witnesses interviewed and the documents reviewed, and the results of the investigation, e.g., any disciplinary action taken and any corrective action implemented. Although any action taken as the result of an inquiry will necessarily vary depending upon the Medicare+Choice organization and the situation, Medicare+Choice organizations should strive for some consistency by utilizing sound practices and disciplinary protocols. Further, after a reasonable period, the compliance officer should review the circumstances that formed the basis for the inquiry to determine whether similar problems have

fraud or criminal law; (2) has a significant adverse effect on the quality of care provided to program beneficiaries (in addition to any other legal obligations regarding quality of care); or (3) indicates evidence of a systemic failure to comply with applicable laws or an existing corporate integrity agreement, regardless of the financial impact on Federal health care programs.

110 42 U.S.C. 1320a-7b(a)(3).

been uncovered or modifications of the compliance program are necessary to prevent and detect other inappropriate conduct or violations.

If an inquiry of an alleged violation is undertaken and the compliance officer believes the integrity of the inquiry may be at stake because of the presence of employees under investigation, those subjects should be removed from their current work activity until the inquiry is completed (unless an internal or Government-led undercover operation known to the Medicare+Choice organization is in effect). In addition, the compliance officer should take appropriate steps to secure or prevent the destruction of documents or other evidence relevant to the inquiry. If the Medicare+Choice organization determines disciplinary action is warranted, it should be prompt and imposed in accordance with the organization's written standards of disciplinary action.

III. Conclusion

Through this document, the OIG has attempted to provide a foundation for the development of effective and comprehensive Medicare+Choice compliance programs. These principles can also be used by entities to develop compliance programs applicable to other Federal and health care programs, as well as for their private lines of business. As previously stated, however, each program must be tailored to fit the needs and resources of an individual organization, depending upon its particular corporate structure, mission and employee composition. The statutes, regulations and guidelines of the Federal and State health insurance programs, as well as the policies and procedures of the private health plans, should be integrated into every Medicare+Choice organization's compliance program.

The OIG recognizes that the health care industry, which reaches millions of beneficiaries and expends about a trillion dollars annually, is constantly evolving. In no area of the industry is this more evident than in the growing area of managed care, particularly Medicare managed care. As a result, the time is right for Medicare+Choice organizations to implement strong, voluntary compliance programs. Compliance is a dynamic process that helps to ensure Medicare+Choice organizations are better able to fulfill their commitment to ethical behavior and to meet the changes and challenges being imposed upon them by the Congress and private insurers. It isOIG's hope that voluntarily created compliance programs will enable Medicare+Choice organizations to meet their goal of providing efficient and quality health care and, at the same time, substantially reducing fraud, waste and abuse.

Dated: November 5, 1999.

June Gibbs Brown,

Inspector General.

[FR Doc. 99–29632 Filed 11–12–99; 8:45 am]

BILLING CODE 4150–04-P

APPENDIX I8

Compliance Program Guidance for Nursing Facilities; 65 FR 14289, March 16, 2000

[Federal Register: March 16, 2000 (Volume 65, Number 52)]
[Notices] [Page 14289–14306]

DEPARTMENT OF HEALTH AND HUMAN SERVICES

Office of Inspector General

Publication of the OIG Compliance Program Guidance for Nursing Facilities

AGENCY: Office of Inspector General (OIG), HHS.

ACTION: Notice.

SUMMARY: This **Federal Register** notice sets forth the recently issued Compliance Program Guidance for Nursing Facilities developed by the Office of Inspector General (OIG). The OIG has previously developed and published compliance program guidance focused on several other areas and aspects of the health care industry. We believe that the development and issuance of this compliance program guidance for nursing facilities will continue to serve as a positive step toward promoting a higher level of ethical and lawful conduct throughout the entire health care industry.

FOR FURTHER INFORMATION CONTACT: Nicole C. Hall, Office of Counsel to the Inspector General, (202) 619–2078.

SUPPLEMENTARY INFORMATION:

Background

The creation of compliance program guidances is a major initiative of the OIG in its effort to engage the private health care community in combating fraud and abuse. In the last several years, the OIG has developed and issued compliance program guidances directed at the following segments of the health care industry: the hospital industry; home health agencies; clinical laboratories; third-party medical billing companies; the durable medical equipment, prosthetics, orthotics and supply industry; hospices; and Medicare+Choice organizations offering coordinated care plans. The development of these types of compliance program guidances is based on our belief that a health care provider can use internal controls to more efficiently monitor adherence to applicable statutes, regulations and program requirements.

Copies of these compliance program guidances can be found on the OIG web site at http://www.hhs.gov/oig.

Developing Compliance Program Guidance for Nursing Facilities

On December 18, 1998, the OIG published a solicitation notice seeking information and recommendations for developing formal guidance for nursing facilities (63 FR 70137). In response to that solicitation notice, the OIG received 16 comments from various outside sources. We carefully considered those comments, as well as previous OIG publications, such as other compliance program guidances and Special Fraud Alerts, in developing a compliance program guidance for nursing facilities. In addition, we have taken into account past and recent fraud investigations conducted by the OIG's Office of Investigations and the Department of Justice, and have consulted with the Health Care Financing Administration. In an effort to ensure that all parties had a reasonable opportunity to provide input into a final product, the draft guidance for nursing facilities was published in the **Federal Register** on October 29, 1999 (64 FR 58419) for further comments and recommendations.

Elements for an Effective Compliance Program

This compliance guidance for nursing facilities contains seven elements that the OIG has determined to be fundamental to an effective compliance program:

- implementing written policies, procedures and standards of conduct;
- designating a compliance officer and compliance committee;
- conducting effective training and education;
- developing effective lines of communication;
- enforcing standards through well-publicized disciplinary guidelines;
- conducting internal monitoring and auditing; and

- responding promptly to detected offenses and developing corrective action.

These elements are contained in previous guidances issued by the OIG. As with previously-issued guidances, this compliance program guidance represents the OIG's suggestions on how nursing facilities can best establish internal controls and prevent fraudulent activities. The contents of this guidance should not be viewed as mandatory or as an exclusive discussion of the advisable elements of a compliance program; the document is intended to present voluntary guidance to the industry and not represent binding standards for nursing facilities.

Office of Inspector General's Compliance Program Guidance for Nursing Facilities

I. Introduction

The Office of Inspector General (OIG) of the Department of Health and Human Services (DHHS) continues in its efforts to promote voluntarily implemented compliance programs for the health care industry.[1] This compliance guidance is intended to assist nursing facilities[2] develop and implement internal controls and procedures that promote adherence to applicable statutes and regulations of the Federal health care programs[3] and private insurance

---

[1] The OIG1 has issued compliance program guidances for the following seven industry sectors: hospitals, clinical laboratories, home health agencies, durable medical equipment suppliers, third-party medical billing companies, hospices, and Medicare+Choice organizations offering coordinated care plans. Over the next year, the OIG plans to issue compliance guidances for ambulance companies and individual and small group physician practices.

[2] For the purpose of this guidance, the term "nursing facility" includes a skilled nursing facility (SNF) and a nursing facility (NF) that meet the requirements of sections 1819 and 1919 of the Social Security Act (Act), respectively, 42 U.S.C. 1395i-3 and 42 U.S.C. 1396r. Where appropriate, we distinguish between SNFs and other nursing facilities.

[3] The term "Federal health care programs" includes any plan or program that provides health benefits, whether directly, through insurance, or otherwise, which is funded directly, in whole or in part, by the United States Government (i.e., via programs such as Medicare, Federal Employees Health Benefits Act, Federal Employees'Compensation Act, Black Lung, or the Longshore and Harbor Worker's Compensation Act) or any State health plan (e.g., Medicaid, or a program receiving funds from block grants for social services or child health services). *See* 42 U.S.C. 1320a-7b(f). In this

[Page 14290]

program requirements. Compliance programs strengthen Government efforts to prevent and reduce fraud and abuse, as well as further the mission of all nursing facilities to provide quality care to their residents.

Through this document, the OIG provides its views on the fundamental elements of nursing facility compliance programs, as well as the principles that each nursing facility should consider when developing and implementing an effective compliance program. While this document presents basic procedural and structural guidance for designing a compliance program, it is not in and of itself a compliance program. Rather, it is a set of guidelines that nursing facilities should consider when developing and implementing a compliance program. For those nursing facilities that have an existing program or are already in the process of implementing a compliance program, these guidelines may serve as a benchmark against which to measure their ongoing efforts.

Implementing an effective compliance program in a nursing facility may require a significant commitment of time and resources by all parts of the organization. However, superficial efforts or programs that are hastily constructed and implemented without a long term commitment to a culture of compliance likely will be ineffective and may expose the nursing facility to greater liability than if it had no program at all.[4] Although an effective compliance program may require a reallocation of existing resources, the long term benefits of establishing a compliance program significantly outweigh the initial costs. In short, compliance measures are an investment that advance the goals of the nursing facility, the solvency of the Federal health care programs, and the quality of care provided to the nursing home resident.

In a continuing effort to collaborate closely with health care providers and the private sector, the OIG placed a notice in the **Federal Register** soliciting comments and recommendations on what should

---

document, the term "Federal health care program requirements" refers to the statutes, regulations and other written directives governing Medicare, Medicaid, and all other Federal health care programs.

[4] Recent case law suggests that the failure of a corporate director to attempt in good faith to institute a compliance program in certain situations may be a breach of a director's fiduciary obligation. *See, e.g., In re Caremark Int'l Inc. Derivative Litig.,* 698 A.2d 959, 970 (Ct. Chanc. Del. 1996).

be included in this compliance program guidance.[5] In addition to considering these comments in drafting this guidance, we reviewed previous OIG publications, including OIG Special Fraud Alerts and OIG Medicare Advisory Bulletins, as well as reports issued by OIG's Office of Audit Services (OAS) and Office of Evaluation and Inspections (OEI) affecting the nursing home industry.[6] In addition, we relied on the experience gained from fraud investigations of nursing home operators conducted by OIG's Office of Investigations, the Department of Justice, and the Medicaid Fraud Control Units.

A. Benefits of a Compliance Program

The OIG believes a comprehensive compliance program provides a mechanism that brings the public and private sectors together to reach mutual goals of reducing fraud and abuse, enhancing operational functions, improving the quality of health care services, and decreasing the cost of health care. Attaining these goals provides positive results to the nursing facility, the Government, and individual citizens alike. In addition to fulfilling its legal duty to ensure that it is not submitting false or inaccurate claims to Government and private payors, a nursing facility may gain numerous other benefits by voluntarily implementing a compliance program. The benefits may include:

- the formulation of effective internal controls to ensure compliance with statutes, regulations and rules;
- a concrete demonstration to employees and the community at large of the nursing facility's commitment to responsible corporate conduct;
- the ability to obtain an accurate assessment of employee and contractor behavior;

[5] *See* 63 FR 70137 (December 12, 1998), Notice for Solicitation of Information and Recommendations for Developing OIG Compliance Program Guidance for the Nursing Home Industry.

[6] The OIG periodically issues advisory opinions responding to specific inquires concerning the application of the OIG's authorities and Special Fraud Alerts, setting forth activities that raise legal and enforcement issues. These documents, as well as reports from OAS and OEI can be obtained on the Internet at: http://www.hhs.gov/oig. We also recommend that nursing home providers regularly review the Health Care Financing Administration (HCFA) website on the Internet at: http://www.hcfa.gov, for up-to-date regulations, manuals, and program memoranda related to the Medicare and Medicaid programs.

- an increased likelihood of identifying and preventing unlawful and unethical behavior;
- the ability to quickly react to employees' operational compliance concerns and effectively target resources to address those concerns;
- an improvement in the quality, efficiency, and consistency of providing services;
- a mechanism to encourage employees to report potential problems and allow for appropriate internal inquiry and corrective action;
- a centralized source for distributing information on health care statutes, regulations and other program directives;[7]
- a mechanism to improve internal communications;
- procedures that allow prompt and thorough investigation of alleged misconduct; and
- through early detection and reporting, minimizing loss to the Government from false claims, and thereby reducing the nursing facility's exposure to civil damages and penalties, criminal sanctions, and administrative remedies.[8]

The OIG recognizes that the implementation of a compliance program may not entirely eliminate fraud and abuse from the operations of a nursing facility. However, a sincere effort by the nursing facility to comply with applicable statutes and regulations as well as Government and private payer health care program requirements, through the establishment of a compliance program, significantly reduces the risk of unlawful or improper conduct.

---

[7] Counsel to the nursing facility should be consulted as appropriate regarding interpretation and legal analysis of laws related to the Federal health care programs and laws related to fraud, abuse and other legal requirements.

[8] For example, the OIG will consider the existence of an effective compliance program that pre-dated any governmental investigation when addressing the appropriateness of administrative sanctions. However, the burden is on the nursing facility to demonstrate the operational effectiveness of the compliance program. Further, the False Claims Act, 31 U.S.C. 3729–3733, provides that a person who has violated the Act, but who voluntarily discloses the violation to the Government within 30 days of detection, in certain circumstances will be subject to not less than double, as opposed to treble, damages. *See* 31 U.S.C. 3729(a). In addition, criminal sanctions may be mitigated by an effective compliance program that was in place at the time of the criminal offense. *See* note 11.

B. Application of Compliance Program Guidance

Given the diversity within the long term care industry, there is no single "best" nursing facility compliance program. The OIG recognizes the complexities of this industry and is sensitive to the differences among large national chains, regional multi-facility operators, and small independent homes. However, the elements of this guidance can be used by all nursing facilities to establish a compliance program, regardless of size (in terms of employees and gross revenues), number of locations, or corporate structure.

[Page 14291]

Similarly, a corporation that provides long term care as part of an integrated health care delivery system may incorporate these elements into its structure. [9]

We recognize that some nursing facilities may not be able to adopt certain elements to the same degree as others with more extensive resources. At the end of several sections of this document, the OIG has offered suggestions to assist these smaller nursing facility providers in implementing the principles expressed in this guidance. Regardless of size, structure or available resources, the OIG recommends that every nursing facility should strive to accomplish the objectives and principles underlying all of the compliance polices and procedures in this guidance.

By no means should the contents of this guidance be viewed as an exclusive or complete discussion of the advisable elements of a compliance program. On the contrary, the OIG strongly encourages nursing facilities to develop and implement compliance elements that uniquely address the areas of potential problems, common concerns, or high risk areas that apply to their own facilities. Furthermore, this guidance may be modified and expanded as more information and knowledge is obtained by the OIG, and as changes occur in the statutes, regulations and rules of the Federal health care programs and private health plans. New compliance practices also may be incorporated into this guidance if the OIG discovers enhancements that promote effective compliance.

---

[9] For example, this would include providers that own hospitals, skilled nursing facilities, long term care facilities and hospices.

II. Compliance Program Elements

A. The Seven Basic Compliance Elements

The OIG believes that every effective compliance program must begin with a formal commitment[10] by the nursing facility's governing body to address all of the applicable elements listed below, which are based on the seven steps of the Federal Sentencing Guidelines.[11] The OIG recognizes that full implementation of all elements may not be immediately feasible for all nursing facilities. However, as a first step, a good faith and meaningful commitment on the part of nursing facility management will substantially contribute to the program's successful implementation. As the compliance program is effectuated, that commitment should cascade down through management to every employee and contractor of the nursing facility.

At a minimum, a comprehensive compliance program should include the following seven elements:

1. The development and distribution of written standards of conduct, as well as written policies, procedures and protocols that promote the nursing facility's commitment to compliance (e.g., including adherence to the compliance program as an element in evaluating managers and employees) and address specific areas of potential fraud and abuse, such as claims development and submission processes, quality of care issues, and financial arrangements with physicians and outside contractors;
2. The designation of a compliance officer and other appropriate bodies (e.g., a corporate compliance committee) charged with the responsibility for developing, operating and monitoring

[10] A formal commitment may include a resolution by the board of directors, owner(s), or president, where applicable. Evidence of that commitment should include the allocation of adequate resources, a timetable, and the identification of an individual to serve as a compliance officer or coordinator to ensure that each of the recommended and adopted elements is addressed. Once a commitment has been established, a compliance officer should immediately be chosen to oversee the implementation and ongoing operation of the compliance program.

[11] *See* United States Sentencing Commission Guidelines, *Guidelines Manual,* 8A1.2, Application Note 3(k). The Federal Sentencing Guidelines are detailed policies and practices for the Federal criminal justice system that prescribe the appropriate sanctions for offenders convicted of Federal crimes.

the compliance program, and who reports directly to the owner(s), governing body and/or CEO;[12]

3. The development and implementation of regular, effective education and training programs for all affected employees;[13]
4. The creation and maintenance of an effective line of communication between the compliance officer and all employees, including a process, such as a hotline or other reporting system, to receive complaints, and the adoption of procedures to protect the anonymity of complainants and to protect whistle blowers from retaliation;
5. The use of audits and/or other risk evaluation techniques to monitor compliance, identify problem areas, and assist in the reduction of identified problems;[14]
6. The development of policies and procedures addressing the non-employment or retention of excluded individuals or entities and the enforcement of appropriate disciplinary action against employees or contractors who have violated corporate or compliance policies and procedures, applicable statutes, regulations, or Federal, State, or private payor health care program requirements; and
7. The development of policies and procedures with respect to the investigation of identified systemic problems, which include direction regarding the prompt and proper response to detected offenses, such as the initiation of appropriate corrective action, repayments, and preventive measures.

---

[12] The roles of the compliance officer and the corporate compliance committee in implementing an effective compliance program are discussed throughout this guidance. However, the OIG recognizes that differences in the sizes and structures of nursing facilities may result in differences in the ways in which compliance programs function.

[13] Training and educational programs for nursing facilities should be detailed, comprehensive and at the same time targeted to address the needs of specific employees based on their responsibilities within the facility. Existing in-service training programs can be expanded to address general compliance issues, as well as the risk areas identified in that part of nursing home operations.

[14] For example, periodically spot-checking the work of coding and billing personnel should be part of a compliance program. In addition, procedures to regularly monitor the care provided to nursing facility residents and to ensure that deficiencies identified by surveyors are corrected should be incorporated into the compliance program's evaluation and monitoring functions.

B. Written Policies and Procedures

Every compliance program should develop and distribute written compliance standards, procedures, and practices that guide the nursing facility and the conduct of its employees throughout day-to-day operations. These policies and procedures should be developed under the direction and supervision of the compliance officer, the compliance committee, and operational managers. At a minimum, they should be provided to all employees who are affected by these policies, as well as physicians, suppliers, nursing facility agents, and contractors, as applicable to those entities. [15] In addition to general corporate policies and procedures, an effective compliance program should include specific policies and procedures for the different clinical, financial, and administrative functions of a nursing facility.

[Page 14292]

1. Code of Conduct

While a clear statement of policies and procedures is at the core of a compliance program, the OIG recommends that nursing facilities start the process with the development of a corporate statement of principles that will guide the operations of the provider. One common expression of this statement of principles is the code of conduct. [16] The code should function in the same fashion as a constitution, *i.e.,* as a foundational document that details the fundamental principles, values, and framework for action within an organization. The code of conduct for a nursing facility should articulate the organ-

---

[15] According to the Federal Sentencing Guidelines, an organization must have established compliance standards and procedures to be followed by its employees and other agents in order to receive sentencing credit for an "effective" compliance program. The Federal Sentencing Guidelines define "agent" as "any individual, including a director, an officer, an employee, or an independent contractor, authorized to act on behalf of the organization." See United States Sentencing Commission Guidelines, *Guidelines Manual,* 8A1.2, Application Note 3(d).

[16] The OIG strongly encourages the participation and involvement of the nursing facility's owner(s), governing board, CEO, as well as other personnel from various levels of the organizational structure in the development of all aspects of the compliance program, especially the standards of conduct. Management and employee involvement in this process communicates a strong and explicit commitment to all employees of the need to comply with the organization's standards of conduct.

ization's expectations of employees, as well as summarize the basic legal principles under which the organization must operate. Unlike the more detailed policies and procedures, the code of conduct should be brief, easily readable and cover general principles applicable to all employees.

The code of conduct should be distributed to, and comprehensible by, all affected employees. [17] Depending on the facility's work force, this may mean that the code should be translated into other languages when necessary and written at appropriate reading levels. Further, any employee handbook delineating the standards of conduct should be regularly updated to reflect developments in applicable Government and private health care program requirements. Finally, the OIG recommends that current employees, as well as those newly hired, should certify that they have received, read, and will abide by the organization's code of conduct. These certifications, updated any time the code is revised or amended by the organization, should be retained in the employee's personnel file and made available for review. [18]

The OIG believes that *all* nursing facilities should operate under the guidance of a code of conduct. While the OIG recognizes that some nursing facilities may not have the resources to establish a comprehensive compliance program, we believe that every nursing facility can design a program that addresses the seven elements set out in this guidance, albeit at different levels of sophistication and complexity. In its most fundamental form, a facility's code of conduct is a basic set of standards that articulate the organization's philosophy, summarize basic legal principles, and teach employees how to respond to practices that may violate the code of conduct. These standards should be posted and distributed to every employee. Further, even a small nursing facility should obtain written attestation from its employees to confirm their understanding and commitment to the nursing facility's code of conduct.

---

[17] The code also should be distributed, or at least available, to the residents and their families, as well as the physicians and contractors associated with the facility.

[18] Documentation of employee training and other compliance efforts is important in conducting internal assessments of the compliance program, as well as during any third-party evaluation of the facility's efforts to comply with Federal health care program requirements. *See* section II.F.

2. Specific Risk Areas

As part of their commitment to a compliance program, nursing facilities should prepare a comprehensive set of written policies and procedures that are in place to prevent fraud and abuse in facility operations and to ensure the appropriate care of their residents. These policies and procedures should educate and alert all affected managers and employees of the Federal health care program and private payor requirements, the consequences of noncompliance, and the specific procedures that nursing facility employees should follow to report problems, to ensure compliance, and to rectify any prior noncompliance.

The OIG recognizes that many States require nursing facilities to have a policies and procedures manual and that most facilities have in place procedures to prevent fraud and abuse in their institutions. These providers may not need to develop a new, comprehensive set of policies as part of their compliance program if existing policies effectively encompass the provider's operations and relevant rules. However, the nursing home industry is subject to numerous Federal and State statutes, rules, regulations and manual instructions.[19] Because these program requirements are frequently modified, the OIG recommends that all nursing facilities evaluate their current compliance policies and procedures by conducting a baseline assessment of risk areas, as well as subsequent reevaluations.[20] The OIG also recommends that these internal compliance reviews be undertaken on a regular basis to ensure compliance with current program requirements.

To assist nursing facilities in performing this internal assessment, the OIG has developed a list of potential risk areas affecting nursing facility providers. These risk areas include quality of care and residents' rights, employee screening, vendor relationships, billing and cost reporting, and record keeping and documentation. This list of risk areas is not exhaustive, nor all encompassing. Rather, it should be viewed as a starting point for an internal review of poten-

---

[19] *See* http://www.hcfa.gov for information on obtaining a set of all Medicare and Medicaid manuals.

[20] In addition, all providers should be aware of the enforcement priorities of Federal and State regulators and law enforcement agencies. OIG periodically issues Special Fraud Alerts and Special Advisory Bulletins that identify activities believed to raise enforcement concerns. These documents and other materials that provide insight into the nursing home enforcement priorities of the OIG are referenced throughout this guidance.

tial vulnerabilities within the nursing facility.[21] The objective of this assessment should be to ensure that the employees, managers and directors are aware of these risk areas and that steps are taken to minimize, to the extent possible, the types of problems identified. While there are many ways to accomplish this objective, comprehensive written policies and procedures that are communicated to all appropriate employees and contractors are the first step in an effective compliance program.

The OIG believes that sound operating compliance policies are essential to all nursing facilities, regardless of size and capability. If a lack of resources to develop such policies is genuinely an issue, the OIG recommends that those nursing facilities focus first on those risk areas most likely to arise in their business operations. At a minimum, resources should be directed to analyze the results of annual surveys,[22] and to verify that the facility has effectively addressed any deficiencies cited by the surveyors. An effective and low-cost means to accomplish this is through the use of the facility's Quality Assessment and Assurance Committee. The committee should consist of facility staff members, including the Director of

[Page 14293]

Nursing and the medical director. Inclusion and participation of direct care staff (e.g., nurses and nurses' aides who provide direct resident care) should be encouraged. This committee is best suited to establish measurable, outcome-based criteria that focus on vulnerabilities that adversely affect the care of residents. On a periodic basis, the committee should meet to identify issues affecting the quality of care provided to the residents and to develop and implement appropriate corrective actions. The time commitment required for this collaborative effort will vary according to the magnitude of the facility's quality assessment and assurance issues.

---

[21] The OIG recommends that, in addition to the list set forth below, the provider review the OIG's Work Plan to identify vulnerabilities and risk areas on which the OIG will focus during the following year. In addition, it is recommended that the nursing facility routinely review the OIG's semiannual reports, which identify program vulnerabilities and risk areas that the OIG has targeted during the preceding six months. All of these documents are available on the OIG's webpage at http://www.hhs.gov/oig.

[22] State and local agegncies enter into agreements with DHHS under which they survey and make recommendations regarding whether providers meet the Medicare participation requirements or other requirements for SNFs and NFs. *See* 42 CFR 488.10, 488.12.

Creating a resource manual from publicly available information may be a cost-effective approach for developing policies and procedures to improve the quality of each resident's life. For example, a simple binder that contains a facility's written policies and procedures, the most recent survey findings and plan of correction, relevant HCFA instructions and bulletins, and summaries of key OIG documents (e.g., Special Fraud Alerts, Advisory Bulletins, inspection and audit reports) can be regularly updated and made accessible to all employees. Particularly in the case of more technical materials, it may be advisable to provide summaries in the handbook and make the source documents available upon request. If individualized copies of this handbook are not made available to all employees, then a reference copy should be available in a readily accessible location, as well as from the designated compliance officer.

a. Quality of Care

The OIG believes that a nursing facility's compliance policies should start with a statement that affirms the facility's commitment to providing the care and services necessary to attain or maintain the resident's "highest practicable physical, mental and psychosocial well-being."[23] To achieve the goal of providing quality care, nursing facilities should continually measure their performance against comprehensive standards that, at a minimum, must include Medicare requirements.[24] In addition to these regulations, a facility should develop its own quality of care protocols and implement mechanisms for evaluating compliance with those protocols. As part of its ongoing commitment to quality care, the facility should implement a system that reviews each resident's outcomes and improves on those outcomes through analysis and modification of the delivery of care. After the care delivery protocols have been modified, the facility should re-analyze the residents' outcomes to assure that the

[23] 42 CFR 483.25. *See* OIG report OEI-02-98-00060 "Quality of Care in Nursing Homes: An Overview," in which the OIG found that, although the overall number of deficiencies identified through the survey and certification process was decreasing, the number of "quality of care" and other serious deficiencies was increasing.

[24] *See* 42 CFR part 483, which establishes requirements for long term care facilities. HCFA's regulations establish requirements that must be met for a nursing facility to qualify to participate in the Medicare and Medicaid programs. State licensure laws may impose additional requirements for the establishment and certification of a nursing facility.

modification had the desired result and has actually improved care. Although resident care protocols are a useful tool for maintaining or improving the quality of care, facilities should ensure that measurable resident outcomes are used to determine the adequacy of the care actually rendered.

As noted above, current and past surveys are a good place to begin to identify specific risk areas and regulatory vulnerabilities at the individual facility. Any deficiencies discovered by an annual State agency survey, Federal validation survey or complaint survey reflect noncompliance with the program requirements for nursing homes and can be the basis for enforcement actions.[25] Those deficiencies identified by the State agency survey instrument must be addressed and, where appropriate, the corrective action should be incorporated into the facility's policies and procedures as well as reflected in its training and educational programs. In addition to responding promptly to deficiencies identified through the survey and certification process, nursing facilities should take proactive measures to identify, anticipate, and respond to quality of care risk areas identified by the nursing home ombudsman or other sources.

As noted throughout this guidance, each provider must assess its vulnerability to particular abusive practices in light of its unique circumstances. However, the OIG, HCFA, the Department of Justice, and State enforcement agencies have substantial experience in identifying quality of care risk areas. Some of the special areas of concern include:

- absence of a comprehensive, accurate assessment of each resident's functional capacity and a comprehensive care plan that includes measurable objectives and timetables to meet the resident's medical, nursing, and mental and psychosocial needs;[26]

---

[25] *See* 42 CFR part 488, subparts A, B, C, E, and F. The survey instrument is used to identify deficiencies, such as: failure to notify residents of their rights; improper use of restraints for discipline purposes; lack of a clean and safe environment; failure to provide care for basic living activities, including failing to prevent and/or treat pressure ulcers, urinary incontinence and hydration; and failing to properly feed residents.

[26] As stated above, each resident must receive the necessary care and services to attain or maintain the highest practicable physical, mental, and psychosocial well-being, in accordance with the resident's assessment and plan of care. *See* 42 CFR 483.25. The OIG recognizes that this standard does not always lend itself to easy, objective evaluation. The matter is further complicated by the right of the resident, or his or her legal representative, to decide on a course of treatment that may be contraindicated. The Patient

- inappropriate or insufficient treatment and services to address residents' clinical conditions, including pressure ulcers, dehydration, malnutrition, incontinence of the bladder, and mental or psychosocial problems;[27]
- failure to accommodate individual resident needs and preferences;[28]
- failure to properly prescribe, administer and monitor prescription drug usage;[29]
- inadequate staffing levels or insufficiently trained or supervised staff to provide medical, nursing, and related services;[30]

Self-Determination Act (Omnibus Budget Reconciliation Act of 1990, Pub. L. 101–508, sec. 4206 and 4751) requires health care institutions to educate patients about advance directives and to document their decision on life-sustaining treatments.

[27] HCFA has created a repository of best practice guidelines for the care of residents at risk of pressure ulcers, dehydration, malnutrition, and other clinical conditions. See http://www.hcfa.gov/medicaid/siq/siqhmpg.htm.

[28] 42 CFR 483.15(e)(1).

[29] The OIG has conducted a series of reviews that focused on prescription drug use in nursing homes. See OIG reports OEI-06-96-00080, OEI-06–96–00081, OEI-06–96–00082 — "Prescription Drug Use in Nursing Homes — Reports 1, 2 and 3." The OIG found that patients experienced adverse reactions to various drugs as a result of inappropriate prescribing and inadequate monitoring of medication usage. The reviews revealed serious concerns, including residents receiving drugs for which their medical records lacked evidence of a prescription and the prescription of drugs judged inappropriate for use by elderly persons. The studies also found that medication records were often incomplete and not readily accessible, making it difficult for a pharmacist to identify or confirm drug regimens or problems.

[30] For example, Federal regulations require that the medical care of each resident be supervised by a physician, who must see the resident at least once every 30 days for the first 90 days after admission and at least once every 60 days thereafter. See 42 CFR 483.40(c). The facility also must retain the services of a registered nurse for at least 8 consecutive hours a day, 7 days a week (42 CFR 483.30), as well as a qualified dietitian (42 CFR 483.35). In addition to these basic Federal requirements, the OIG strongly believes that the facility should conform to State-mandated staffing levels where they exist and, in addition, adopt its own minimum "hours per patient" (or acuity) staffing standards. A facility should ensure that it has a sufficient number of staff, including registered nurses (RNs), Licensed Practical Nurses (LPNs,) Certified Nurses Assistants (CNAs) and Nursing Assistants (collectively "Nursing Staff") and other health care professionals to fully meet the needs of all of its residents. Sufficient staff should be provided to ensure that residents receive nursing and other health care services on a 24-hour basis that allows each resident to attain or maintain

[Page 14294]

- failure to provide appropriate therapy services;[31]
- failure to provide appropriate services to assist residents with activities of daily living (e.g., feeding, dressing, bathing, etc.);
- failure to provide an ongoing activities program to meet the individual needs of all residents; and
- failure to report incidents of mistreatment, neglect, or abuse to the administrator of the facility and other officials as required by law.[32]

As noted previously, a nursing facility that has a history of serious deficiencies should use those survey results as a starting point for implementing a comprehensive plan to improve its quality of care. The quality of life for nursing home residents can be improved most directly by effectively addressing these risk areas with written policies and procedures, which are then implemented through effective training programs and supervision.

---

the highest practicable physical, mental and psychosocial well-being as determined by individual resident assessments and plans of care. A facility should establish staffing standards on a facility-specific (or, often more appropriately, a unit-specific) basis that reflect the acuity level and needs of the residents. The use of an acuity level/staffing ratio model gives the facility the ability to adjust staffing levels as resident needs fluctuate, as well as a basis for conducting compliance audits. On an ongoing basis, the compliance officer should monitor the facility's compliance with the staffing ratios established by the quality assurance committee, to ensure that the facility maintains staffing levels sufficient to serve resident needs. At the heart of many quality of care deficiencies is a lack of adequate staff needed to provide basic nursing services.

[31] *See* OIG report OEI-09–97–00120 "Medical Necessity of Physical and Occupational Therapy in Skilled Nursing Facilities," which found a high rate of medically unnecessary therapies in a number of nursing facilities; such unnecessary services may lead to inappropriate care. *See also* OAS Report A-06–99–00058 "Infusion Therapy Services Provided in Skilled Nursing Facilities," which found similar problems with unnecessary infusion therapy services.With the introduction of the prospective payment system, nursing facilities should ensure that financial pressures do not create incentives to *underutilize* medically necessary therapeutic services.

[32] In addition to providing the facility's management important information about the state of care in the facility, the self-reporting of resident abuse, including injuries of unknown sources, is a condition of participation. *See* 42 CFR 483.13(c)(2). Although State surveyors conduct complaint surveys when they receive a complaint, these surveys can only occur if the surveyors are aware of the problem.

b. Residents' Rights

The Budget Reconciliation Act (OBRA) of 1987, Public Law 100–203, established a number of requirements to protect and promote the rights of each resident.[33] In addition, many States have adopted specific lists of residents' rights.[34] The nursing facility's policies should address the residents' right to a dignified existence that promotes freedom of choice, self-determination, and reasonable accommodation of individual needs. To protect the rights of each resident, the OIG recommends that a provider address the following risk areas as part of its compliance policies:

- discriminatory admission or improper denial of access to care;[35]
- verbal, mental or physical abuse, corporal punishment and involuntary seclusion;[36]

---

[33] *See generally,* 42 U.S.C. 1395i-3 and 42 CFR part 483.

[34] In OIG report OEI-02–98–00350 "Long Term Ombudsman Program: Complaint Trends," the OIG points out that complaints about resident care and resident rights have been increasing. Resident care concerns included complaints about personal care, such as pressure ulcers and hygiene, lack of rehabilitation, the inappropriate use of restraints, abuse and neglect, problems with admissions and eviction, and the exercise of personal rights. Some ombudsmen observed that the increasing number of complaints could be due to a greater presence of ombudsmen staff in nursing homes. However, a comparison of each State's staffing ratio and visitation rate to their complaint ratio found that States with more staff and more frequent visits did not necessarily have more complaints.

[35] Nursing facilities must offer care to all residents who are eligible in accordance with Federal and State laws governing admissions. See 42 CFR 483.12(d). The provider also must maintain identical policies regarding "transfer, discharge, and provision of services under the State plan" for all residents, regardless of payment source. See 42 CFR 483.12(c). See also OIG report OEI-02–99-00401 "Early Effects of the Prospective Payment System on Access to Skilled Nursing Facilities." It also is inappropriate to condition admission on a prospective resident's agreement to hold the facility harmless for injuries or poor care provided to the individual.

[36] *See California Nursing Homes: Care Problems Persist Despite Federal and State Oversight,* GAO/HEHS-98–202 (July 1998). As noted previously, the facility must establish a process by which the facility administrator and other officials in accordance with State law (including the State survey and certification agency) are informed of incidents of abuse and an investigation is conducted within 5 days of the incident. *See* 42 CFR 483.13(c)(4).

- inappropriate use of physical or chemical restraints;[37]
- failure to ensure that residents have personal privacy and access to their personal records upon request and that the privacy and confidentiality of those records are protected;[38]
- denial of a resident's right to participate in care and treatment decisions;[39] and
- failure to safeguard residents' financial affairs.[40]

c. Billing and Cost Reporting

Abusive and fraudulent billing practices in the Federal health care programs drain the public fisc of the funds needed to provide program beneficiaries medically necessary items and services. These types of abusive practices also have had an adverse financial impact on private health insurance plans and their subscribers. Over the last twenty years, the OIG has identified patterns of improper and fraudulent activities that cover the spectrum of health care services and have cost taxpayers billions of dollars.[41] These fraudulent bill-

[37] *See* OIG report OEI-01–91–00840 "Minimizing Restraints in Nursing Homes: A Guide to Action."

[38] It is a violation of the Medicare participation requirements to make unauthorized disclosures from the resident's medical records. *See* 42 CFR 483.10(e). The facility also must establish policies that respect each resident's right to privacy in personal communications, including the right to receive mail that is unopened and to the use of a telephone where calls can be made in privacy. *See* 42 CFR 483.10(i) and (k).

[39] The right of self-determination includes the resident's right to choose a personal physician, to be fully informed of his or her health status, and participate in advance in treatment decisions, including the right to refuse treatment, unless adjudged incompetent or incapacitated. *See* 42 CFR 483.10(d).

[40] This includes preserving the resident's right to manage his or her financial affairs or permit the facility to hold and manage personal funds. The resident must receive a full and complete accounting of personal funds held by the facility. *See* 42 CFR 483.10(c). If misappropriation of a resident's property is uncovered, the facility administrator and other officials, in accordance with State law, must be notified immediately and an investigation conducted. Finally, the provider must take measures to ensure that personal funds have not been used to pay for items or services paid for by Medicare or Medicaid. *Id.*

[41] *See* OIG report A-17–99–00099 "Improper Fiscal Year 1998 Fee-for-Service Payments," in which the OIG estimated that improper Medicare benefit payments made during fiscal year 1998 totaled $12.6 billion in processed fee-for-service payments. SNF payment errors were a result of claims for services lacking medical necessity and represented 7 percent of the total estimated improper payments. The OIG could not and

ing practices, as well as abuses in other risk areas that are described in this compliance program guidance, have resulted in criminal, civil and administrative enforcement actions. Because the consequences of these enforcement actions can have a profound adverse impact on a provider, the identification of risk areas associated with billing and cost reporting should be a major component of a nursing facility's compliance program.

[Page 14295]

The introduction of a prospective payments system (PPS) for Medicare SNFs, consolidated billing of all services furnished to a resident in a covered Part A stay and the forthcoming implementation of consolidated billing for SNF residents in a Part B stay create additional issues to be addressed when designing billing and cost reporting compliance policies and procedures.[42] In the following discussion of billing risk areas, the OIG has attempted to identify issues that pose concerns under the current systems of reimbursement and the transition period to consolidated billing, as well as anticipate potential compliance issues stemming from these program changes. As is the case with all aspects of compliance, the nursing facility must continually reassess its billing procedures and policies to

---

did not quantify what percentage of the improper payments was the result of fraud. Significantly, it was only through a review of medical records that the majority of these billing errors were detected, since when the claims were submitted to the Medicare contractor, they contained no visible errors.

[42] The Balanced Budget Act of 1997 (BBA) (Pub. L. 105–33), established PPS for SNFs. Under PPS, all costs (routine, ancillary, and capital) related to services furnished to beneficiaries covered under Part A, including certain Part B services, are paid a predetermined per diem amount. This amount is based on the medical condition and needs of the resident, as reflected in the Resource Utilization Group (RUG) code assigned to that resident. The BBA also required consolidated billing for SNFs. Under consolidated billing, all services provided by the SNF, including those furnished under arrangements with an outside supplier, for a resident of a SNF in a covered Part A stay are included in the SNF's Part A bill. If a resident is not in a covered Part A stay, under consolidated billing, the SNF still bills for all services furnished to the resident (except for those services specifically excluded from consolidated billing). However, the implementation of consolidated billing with respect to services furnished to residents in a Part B stay has been delayed indefinitely, and various ancillary services continue to be reimbursed separately to outside suppliers until further notice. *See* HCFA Program Memorandum (PM) Transmittal No. AB-98–35 (July 1998); PM Transmittal No. AB-98–45 (August 1998); and PM Transmittal No. AB-99–90 (Dec. 1999).

ensure that unanticipated problems are promptly identified and corrected. Listed below are some of the reimbursement risk areas a nursing facility should consider addressing as part of its written compliance policies and procedures:

- billing for items or services not rendered or provided as claimed;[43]
- submitting claims for equipment, medical supplies and services that are medically unnecessary;[44]
- submitting claims to Medicare Part A for residents who are not eligible for Part A coverage;[45]

---

[43] For example, the OIG has investigated suppliers of ancillary services that improperly bill for an hour of therapy when only a few minutes were provided. Similarly, vendors that knowingly submit a claim for an expensive prosthetic device when the resident only received non-covered adult diapers have been the subject of enforcement actions. When consolidated billing is implemented, vendors will not submit bills directly to Medicare for such services. As the entity submitting the claim, the nursing facility will need to have any certifications or orders necessary to provide the service, as well as any required supporting documentation, to receive payment.

[44] Billing for medically unnecessary services, supplies and equipment involves seeking reimbursement for a service that is not warranted by a resident's documented medical condition. *See* 42 U.S.C. 1395y(a)(1)(A) ("no payment may be made under part A or part B [of Medicare] for any expenses incurred for items or services which * * * are not reasonable and necessary for the diagnosis or treatment of illness or injury or to improve the functioning of the malformed body member"). At the same time, nursing facilities are required to provide the services necessary to attain or maintain the highest practicable physical, mental and psychosocial well-being of each resident. *See* 42 U.S.C. 1395i-3(b)(2) and 1396r(b)(2). In order to meet these obligations, nursing homes should formulate policies and procedures that include periodic clinical reviews, both prior and subsequent to billing for services, as a means of verifying that patients receive appropriate services.

In the Special Fraud Alert "Fraud and Abuse in the Provision of Services in Nursing Facilities" (June 1996), the OIG identified several types of fraudulent arrangements through which health care providers inappropriately billed Medicare and Medicaid for unnecessary or non-rendered items and services. Under PPS, the provision of unnecessary services may take a different form. As discussed below, manipulation of the Minimum Data Set (MDS) to fit a resident into a higher RUG can result in the provision of medically unnecessary services. In addition, a nursing facility may not enter into arrangements with providers of ancillary services through which the facility overutilizes services reimbursed under Part B in return for an offset in the cost of items or services covered under Part A.

[45] In order for a SNF stay to be covered by Medicare, the beneficiary must have a preceding three-day inpatient hospital stay. Observational stays and emergency room care do not qualify towards the 3-day hospital stay require-

- duplicate billing;[46]
- failing to identify and refund credit balances;[47]
- submitting claims for items or services not ordered;[48]
- knowingly billing for inadequate or substandard care;[49]

---

ment. In addition, Medicare Part A benefits in skilled nursing facilities are limited to beneficiaries who require skilled services rendered by technical or professional personnel in a skilled nursing setting. *See* 42 CFR 409.31. Knowingly misrepresenting the nature or level of services provided to a Medicare beneficiary to circumvent the program's limitation is fraudulent.

[46] Duplicate billing occurs when the nursing facility bills for the same item or service more than once or when a vendor bills the Federal health care program for an item or service also billed by the facility. Although duplicate billing can occur due to simple error, the knowing submission of duplicate claims — which is sometimes evidenced by systematic or repeated double billing — can create liability under criminal, civil, or administrative law. A recent OIG survey of SNF PPS claims found a significant number of erroneous payments made by the Medicare carrier for services for which payments were already included in the SNF's PPS payment. As Medicare continues the implementation of consolidated billing, facilities should modify all agreements with vendors to require that the vendor bill the facility for those services covered under consolidated billing requirements and not submit bills directly to Medicare for such services. Communication mechanisms also should be established to ensure duplicative billings do not occur. For example, a facility may wish to flag a referral to an outpatient provider as a "PPS resident" and inform the provider that the nursing home will be responsible for billing Medicare for the ancillary services.

[47] A credit balance is an excess payment made to a health care provider as a result of patient billing or claims processing error. Nursing facilities should institute procedures to provide for the timely identification, accurate reporting and repayment of credit balances. In addition, the provider should promptly repay if a resident is also entitled to a credit. See OIG reports OEI-07–09-00910 "Medicare Credit Balances in Skilled Nursing Facility Patient Accounts" and OEI-07–09–00911 "Medicaid Credit Balances in Skilled Nursing Facility Patient Accounts," in which the OIG found that skilled nursing facilities were not accurately or completely adjusting and reporting credit balance amounts due to the Medicare and Medicaid programs. Significantly, the intentional concealment of a known overpayment may expose a provider to criminal sanctions (see 42 U.S.C. 1320a-7b(a)(3)), and civil liability under the False Claims Act.

[48] Billing for services or items not ordered involves seeking reimbursement for services provided but not ordered by the treating physician or other authorized person.

[49] See discussion on quality of care standards in nursing facilities in section II.B.2.a above and the accompanying notes. Although the OIG is not suggesting that each and every survey citation or failure to meet the applicable standard of care is a *per se* violation of the False Claims Act (or a criminal, other civil, or administrative violation), knowingly billing for non-

- providing misleading information about a resident's medical condition on the MDS or otherwise providing inaccurate information used to determine the RUG assigned to the resident;
- upcoding the level of service provided;[50]
- billing for individual items or services when they either are included in the facility's per diem rate or are of the type of item or service that must be billed as a unit and may not be unbundled;[51]
- billing residents for items or services that are included in the per diem rate or otherwise covered by the third-party payor;
- altering documentation or forging a physician signature on documents used to verify that services were ordered and/or provided;[52]
- failing to maintain sufficient documentation to support the diagnosis, justify treatment, document the course of treatment and results, and promote continuity of care; and

[Page 14296]

- false cost reports.[53]

---

existent or substandard care, items, or services may give rise to criminal, civil, and/or administrative liability.

[50] Upcoding involves the selection of a billing code that is not the most appropriate descriptor of the service or condition, in order to maximize reimbursement. Under PPS, upcoding may take the form of "RUG creep." RUG creep occurs when a provider falsely or fraudulently completes the MDS, which results in assigning a resident to a higher RUG category.

[51] A related risk area involves bill splitting schemes. This billing abuse usually takes the form of manipulating the billing for procedures to create the appearance that the services were rendered over a period of days when, in fact, all treatment occurred during one visit.

[52] The OIG has investigated a number of cases where signatures were forged, either to fabricate evidence that a physician ordered equipment or services or to create a paper trail in support of items or services that were never provided.

[53] Nursing homes are required to submit various reports to Federal and State agencies in connection with facility operations and to receive reimbursement for the care provided to program beneficiaries. Because program payments are in part based on self-reported operating costs, providers must implement procedures to ensure that these reports are prepared as accurately as possible. This should include measures to ensure that adequate documentation exists to support information provided in the report, non-allowable costs are appropriately identified and removed, and related party transactions are treated consistent with program requirements. *See* 42 CFR part 413. If the provider intends to claim costs in non-conformity

The OIG recommends that a nursing facility, through its policies and procedures, take all reasonable steps to ensure compliance with the Federal health care programs when submitting information that affects reimbursement decisions. A key component of ensuring accurate information is the proper and ongoing training and evaluation of the staff responsible for coding diagnoses and regular internal audits of coding policies and procedures. With the arrival of consolidated billing and the next edition of the coding manuals, it will be even more critical that knowledgeable individuals are performing these coding tasks.

The risk areas associated with billing and cost reporting have been among the most frequent subjects of investigations and audits by the OIG. In addition to facing criminal sanctions and significant monetary penalties, providers that have failed to adequately ensure the accuracy of their claims and cost report submissions can have their Medicare payments suspended (42 CFR 405.371), be excluded from program participation (42 U.S.C. 1320a-7(b)), or, in lieu of exclusion, be required by the OIG to execute a corporate integrity agreement (CIA).[54]

d. Employee Screening

Nursing facilities are required by Federal, and in some cases State, law to investigate the background of certain employees.[55] Nursing facilities should conduct a reasonable and prudent background investigation and reference check before hiring those employees who have access to patients or their possessions, or who have discretionary authority to make decisions that may involve compliance with the law. The employment application should specif-

---

with program rules, those items should be flagged in a letter accompanying the cost report.

Prior enforcement actions involving nursing home cost reports have focused on nursing facilities that claimed salary expenses for employees who did not exist, inflated the number of residents served, included non-reimbursable costs with nursing home-related expenses, inappropriately shifted costs to cost centers that were below the reimbursement cap, and shifted non-Medicare related costs to Medicare cost centers.

[54] The CIA imposes reporting requirements, independent audits, and other procedures on providers who have demonstrated an inability or unwillingness to independently adopt these measures. It is clearly in a provider's best interest to avoid the implementation of a CIA by instituting its own prevention, detection, and disclosure mechanisms.

[55] 42 CFR 483.13(c)(1).

ically require the applicant to disclose any criminal conviction, as defined by 42 U.S.C. 1320a-7(i); or exclusion from participation in the Federal health care programs. Because many of the services provided in nursing facilities are furnished under arrangement with non-employee personnel, including registry and personnel agency staff, the nursing facility also should require these individuals to be subject to the same scrutiny by their agency prior to placement in the facility.

This pre-employment screening is critical to ensuring the integrity of the facility's work force and safeguarding the welfare of its residents. Because providers of nursing care have frequent, relatively unsupervised access to vulnerable people and their property, a nursing facility also should seriously consider whether to employ individuals who have been convicted of crimes of neglect, violence, theft or dishonesty, financial misconduct, or other offenses related to the particular job.[56]

Nursing facility policies should prohibit the continued employment of individuals who have been convicted of a criminal offense related to health care or who are debarred, excluded, or otherwise become ineligible for participation in Federal health care programs.[57] In addition, if the facility has notice that an employee or contractor is currently charged with a criminal offense related to the delivery of health care services or is proposed for exclusion during his or her employment or contract, the facility should take all appropriate actions to ensure that the responsibilities of that employee or

---

[56] In OIG report A-12–97–0003 "Safeguarding Long Term Care Residents," it was noted that, although no Federal requirement exists for criminal background checks on nursing home staff, 33 States currently require that such checks occur. However, there appears to be great diversity in the way States identify, investigate, and report suspected abuse of nursing home residents.

[57] The effect of an OIG exclusion from Federal health care programs is that no Federal health care program payment may be made for any items or services: (1) furnished by an excluded individual or entity; or (2) directed or prescribed by an excluded physician. See 42 CFR 1001.1901. An excluded individual or entity that submits a claim for reimbursement to a Federal health care program, or causes such a claim to be submitted, may be subject to a civil money penalty of $10,000 for each item or service furnished during the period that the person or entity was excluded. See 42 U.S.C. 1320a-7a(a)(1)(D). The individual or entity also may be subject to treble damages for the amount claimed for each item or service. See 42 U.S.C. 1320a-7a(a). See also OIG Special Advisory Bulletin "The Effect of Exclusion From Participation in Federal Health Care Programs" (September 1999).

contractor do not adversely affect the quality of care rendered to any patient or resident, or the accuracy of any claims submitted to any Federal health care program.[58] If resolution of the matter results in conviction, debarment, or exclusion, the nursing facility should terminate its employment or contract arrangement with the individual.

In order to ensure that nursing facilities undertake background checks of all employees to the extent required by law, the OIG recommends that the following measures be incorporated into the compliance program's policies and procedures:

- investigate the background of employees by checking with all applicable licensing and certification authorities to verify that requisite licenses and certifications are in order;[59]
- require all potential employees to certify (e.g., on the employment application) that they have not been convicted of an offense that would preclude employment in a nursing facility and that they are not excluded from participation in the Federal health care programs;
- require temporary employment agencies to ensure that temporary staff assigned to the facility have undergone background checks that verify that they have not been convicted of an offense

[Page 14297]

that would preclude employment in the facility;

---

[58] Likewise, the facility should establish standards prohibiting the execution of contracts with companies that recently have been convicted of a criminal offense related to health care or that are listed by a Federal agency as debarred, excluded, or otherwise ineligible for participation in Federal health care programs. Prospective employees or contractors that have been officially reinstated into the Medicare and Medicaid programs by the OIG may be considered for employment upon proof of such reinstatement.

[59] Among the sources of information on prospective employees are the State registry of nurses' aides, which provides a list of nurse aides that have successfully completed training and competency evaluations and the National Practitioner Data Bank (NPDB). The NPDB is a database that contains information about physicians subject to medical malpractice payments, sanctions by boards of medical examiners or State licensing boards, adverse clinical privilege actions, and adverse professional society membership actions. Health care entities can have access to this database to seek information about their own medical or clinical staff, as well as prospective employees or physician contractors.

- check the OIG's List of Excluded Individuals/Entities and the GSA's list of debarred contractors to verify that employees are not excluded from participating in the Federal health care programs;[60]
- require current employees to report to the nursing facility if, subsequent to their employment, they are convicted of an offense that would preclude employment in a nursing facility or are excluded from participation in any Federal health care program; and
- periodically check the OIG and GSA web sites to verify the participation/exclusion status of independent contractors and retain on file the results of that query.[61]

Regardless of the size or resources of the nursing facility, employee screening is critical. Nursing facilities, like all corporations, must act through their employees and are held accountable for their actions. One of the best ways to ensure that the organization will act in conformance with the law is to hire employees and contractors who can be trusted to embrace a culture of compliance. While the resources required to check the OIG List of Excluded Individuals/Entities are minimal, the absence of an accessible centralized

---

[60] The OIG "List of Excluded Individuals/Entities" provides information to health care providers, patients, and others regarding individuals and entities that are excluded from participation in Medicare, Medicaid, and other Federal health care programs. This report, in both an on-line searchable and downloadable database, can be located on the Internet at http://www.hhs.gov/oig. In addition, the General Services Administration maintains a monthly listing of debarred contractors, "List of Parties Excluded From Federal Procurement and Nonprocurement Programs," at http://epls.arnet.gov.

The OIG sanction information is readily available to users in two formats on over 15,000 individuals and entities currently excluded from program participation through action taken by the OIG. The on-line searchable database allows users to obtain information regarding excluded individuals and entities sorted by: (1) the legal bases for exclusions; (2) the types of individuals and entities excluded by the OIG; and (3) the States where excluded individuals reside or entities do business.

[61] The introduction of PPS and consolidated billing for Medicare Part B services means that vendors and their subcontractors no longer submit bills directly to Medicare for their services. Instead, the nursing facility will be submitting consolidated bills for certain services provided to residents. Because of the new responsibilities that are imposed on nursing facilities under these reimbursement schemes, the facility may be held responsible if it claims reimbursement for items or services provided by a contractor that has been excluded.

site for criminal background checks may result in inefficiencies and expense. While large providers may elect to outsource the screening process, this may not be a realistic option for smaller nursing facilities. Nevertheless, the OIG recommends that all nursing facilities implement a policy to undertake background checks of all employees.

e. Kickbacks, Inducements and Self-Referrals

A nursing facility should have policies and procedures to ensure compliance with the anti-kickback statute,[62] the Stark physician self-referral law[63] and other relevant Federal and State laws by providing guidance in situations that could lead to a violation of these laws.[64] In particular, arrangements with hospitals, hospices, physicians and vendors are vulnerable to abuse. For example, in the case of hospitals, physicians and hospital staff exert influence over the patient and can influence the choice of a nursing facility. In addition, in his or her roles as medical director and/or attending physician, a physician frequently can influence the utilization of ancillary services.[65] Moreover, by contrast, a nursing facility operator can influence the selection of which hospices will provide hospice services and which vendors will deliver equipment and services to the facility's residents. In addition to developing policies to address arrangements with other health care providers and suppliers, nursing facilities also should implement measures to avoid offering

[62] The anti-kickback statute provides criminal penalties for individuals and entities that knowingly offer, pay, solicit or receive bribes, kickbacks, or other remuneration in order to induce business reimbursable by Federal health care programs. *See* 42 U.S.C. 1320a-7b(b). Civil penalties and exclusion from participation in the Federal health care programs may also result from a violation of the prohibition. *See* 42 U.S.C. 1320a-7a(a)(5) and 1320a-7 (b)(7).

[63] The Stark physician self-referral law prohibits a physician from making a referral to an entity with which the physician or any member of the physician's immediate family has a financial relationship, if the referral is for the furnishing of designated health services. See 42 U.S.C. 1395nn.

[64] The OIG has issued several advisory opinions applying the anti-kickback statute to arrangements that affect nursing facilities. The opinions are available on the Internet at http://www.hhs.gov/oig.

[65] Contracts between the facility and any entity in which the facility's medical director has a financial interest may be subject to the Stark law and should be reviewed and approved by legal counsel.

inappropriate inducements to residents. Possible risk areas that should be addressed in the policies and procedures include:

- routinely waiving coinsurance or deductible amounts without a good faith determination that the resident is in financial need, or absent reasonable efforts to collect the cost-sharing amount;[66]
- agreements between the facility and a hospital, home health agency, or hospice that involve the referral or transfer of any resident to or by the nursing home;[67]
- soliciting, accepting or offering any gift or gratuity of more than nominal value to or from residents, potential referral sources, and other individuals and entities with which the nursing facility has a business relationship;[68]

---

[66] In the OIG Special Fraud Alert "Routine Waiver of Part B Co-payments/Deductibles" (May 1991), the OIG describes several reasons why routine waivers of these cost-sharing amounts pose abuse concerns. The Alert sets forth the circumstances under which it may be appropriate to waive these amounts.

[67] In the Special Fraud Alert "Fraud and Abuse in Nursing Home Arrangements with Hospices" (March 1998), the OIG sets out the vulnerabilities in nursing home arrangements with hospices. The Alert provides several examples of questionable arrangements between hospices and nursing homes that could inappropriately influence the referral of patients. Examples include the offering of free goods or goods at below fair market value to induce a nursing home to refer patients to the hospice. Other examples demonstrating vulnerability to fraud and abuse include: (1) a hospice paying for room and board in excess of the amounts the nursing home would normally charge or receive from Medicaid; (2) a hospice paying for additional services that should be already included in the room and board payment; and (3) a hospice referring patients to the nursing home in return for the nursing home's referral to the hospice. While the Special Fraud Alert focused on arrangements with hospices, nursing facilities should adopt policies that prohibit similar questionable arrangements with all health care providers.

[68] Providers should establish clear policies governing gift-giving, because such exchanges may be viewed as inducements to influence business decisions. Offering or providing any gift of more than nominal value to any beneficiary may be done with the intent to inappropriately influence health care decisions of the beneficiary or his or her family. Similarly, accepting gifts, hospitality, or entertainment from a source that is in a position to benefit from the referral of business, raises concerns that the gift may influence the employee's independent judgment. If the provider decides to allow employees to accept gifts or other gratuities below a certain nominal value or in an aggregate amount below an established amount per year, the provider should consider requiring employees to report those gifts.

- conditioning admission or continued stay at a facility on a third-party guarantee of payment, or soliciting payment for services covered by Medicaid, in addition to any amount required to be paid under the State Medicaid plan; [69]
- arrangements between a nursing facility and a hospital under which the facility will only accept a Medicare beneficiary on the condition that the hospital pays the facility an amount over and above what the facility would receive through PPS; [70]

[Page 14298]

- financial arrangements with physicians, including the facility's medical director; [71]
- arrangements with vendors that result in the nursing facility receiving non-covered items (such as disposable adult diapers) at below market prices or no charge, provided the facility orders Medicare-reimbursed products; [72]

---

[69] See 42 U.S.C. 1320a-7b(d)(2), which prescribes criminal penalties for knowingly and willfully charging for services provided to a Medicaid patient in excess of the rates established by the State. See also 42 CFR 483.12(d).

[70] Under PPS, the payment rates represent payment in full, subject to applicable coinsurance. This includes payment for all costs associated with furnishing covered SNF services to Medicare beneficiaries. It is impermissible for a hospital to pay for SNF services if it were to do so only for those residents who are Medicare beneficiaries discharged from that hospital. However, it would be permissible for a hospital to provide or pay for items or services that are furnished to SNF residents generally, if such payments are made without regard to the payment source for the individual resident. In addition, a hospital and a SNF can enter into a permissible bed reservation agreement. *See Provider Reimbursement Manual,* Part I, section 2105.3.

[71] All physician contracts and agreements should be reviewed to avoid violation of the anti-kickback, self-referral, and other relevant Federal and State laws. The OIG has published safe harbors that define practices not subject to the anti-kickback statute, because such arrangements would be unlikely to result in fraud or abuse. Failure to comply with a safe harbor provision does not make an arrangement per se illegal. Rather, the safe harbors set forth specific conditions that, if fully met, would assure the entities involved of not being prosecuted or sanctioned for the arrangement qualifying for the safe harbor. One such safe harbor applies to personal services contracts. *See* 42 CFR 1001.952(d).

[72] *See* OIG Special Fraud Alert "Fraud and Abuse in the Provision of Medical Supplies to Nursing Facilities" (August 1995). As well as violating the anti-kickback statute, both the supplier and the nursing facility may be liable for false claims if the medically unnecessary items are billed to Fed-

- soliciting or receiving items of value in exchange for providing the supplier access to residents' medical records and other information needed to bill Medicare;[73]
- joint ventures with entities supplying goods or services;[74] and
- swapping.[75]

In order to keep current with this area of the law, a nursing facility should obtain copies of all relevant OIG and HCFA regulations, Special Fraud Alerts, and Advisory Opinions that address the application of the anti-kickback and Stark self-referral laws to ensure that the policies reflect current positions and opinions. Most of these documents are readily available on the Internet. Further, nursing facility policies should provide that all nursing facility contracts and arrangements with actual or potential sources of referrals are reviewed by counsel and comply with applicable statutes and requirements.

3. Creation and Retention of Records

When implementing a compliance program, nursing facilities should provide for the development and implementation of a records system that ensures complete and accurate medical record documentation. This system should establish policies and procedures regarding the creation, distribution, retention, and destruction of documents. Policies should provide for the complete, accurate, and timely documentation of all nursing and therapy services, including subcontracted services, as well as MDS information. In designing a records systems, privacy concerns and regulatory requirements also should be taken into consideration.

---

eral health care programs. *See also* OIG Advisory Opinion 99–2 (February 1999).

[73] In addition to raising concerns related to the anti-kickback statute, the unauthorized disclosure of confidential records violates the resident's rights. *See* 42 CFR 483.10(e).

[74] *See* OIG Special Fraud Alert "Joint Venture Arrangements" (August 1989); OIG Special Fraud Alert "Fraud and Abuse in the Provision of Services in Nursing Facilities" (May 1996).

[75] "Swapping" occurs when a supplier gives a nursing facility discounts on Medicare Part A items and services in return for the referrals of Medicare Part B business. With swapping, there is a risk that suppliers may offer a SNF an excessively low price for items or services reimbursed under PPS in return for the ability to service and bill nursing facility residents with Part B coverage. See OIG Advisory Opinion 99–2 (February 1999).

In addition to maintaining appropriate and thorough medical records on each resident, the OIG recommends that the system should include the following types of documents:

• all records and documentation (e.g., billing and claims documentation) required for participation in Federal, State, and private health care programs, including the resident assessment instrument, the comprehensive plan of care and all corrective actions taken in response to surveys;[76]

• all records, documentation, and audit data that support and explain cost reports and other financial activity, including any internal or external compliance monitoring activities; and

• all records necessary to demonstrate the integrity of the nursing facility compliance process and to confirm the effectiveness of the program.[77]

While conducting its compliance activities, as well as its daily operations, a nursing facility should document its efforts to comply with applicable statutes, regulations, and Federal health care program requirements. For example, where a nursing facility requests advice from a Government agency (including a Medicare fiscal intermediary or carrier) charged with administering a Federal health care program, the nursing facility should document and retain a record of the request and any written or oral response. This step is extremely important if the nursing facility intends to rely on that response to guide it in future decisions, actions, or claim reimbursement requests or appeals. A log of oral inquiries between the nursing facility and third parties will help the organization document its attempts at compliance. In addition, these records may become relevant in a subsequent investigation to the issue of whether the facility's reliance was "reasonable" and whether it exercised due diligence in developing procedures and practices to implement the advice.

---

[76] Medical record documentation should support the medical necessity of the services provided as well as the level of service billed.

[77] Among the materials useful in documenting the compliance program are employee certifications relating to training and other compliance initiatives, copies of compliance training materials, and hotline logs and any corresponding reports of investigation, outcomes, and employee disciplinary actions. In addition, the facility should keep all relevant correspondence with carriers, fiscal intermediaries, private health insurers, HCFA, and State survey and certification agencies.

In short, all nursing facilities, regardless of size, must retain appropriate documentation. Further, the OIG recommends that the nursing facility:

- secure this information in a safe place;
- maintain hard copies of all electronic or database documentation;
- limit access to such documentation to avoid accidental or intentional fabrication or destruction of records;[78] and
- conform document retention and destruction policies to applicable laws.

As the Government increases its reliance on electronic data interchange to conduct business and gather information more quickly and efficiently, it is important that the nursing facility work toward the goal of developing the capacity to ensure that all informational systems maintained by the facility are in working order, secured, and capable of accessing Federal and State databases.

4. Compliance as an Element of Employee Performance

Compliance programs should require the promotion of, and adherence to, the elements of the compliance program to be a factor in evaluating the performance of all employees. Employees should be periodically trained in new compliance policies and procedures. In addition, policies should require that managers, especially those

[Page 14299]

involved in the direct care of residents and in claims development and submission:

- discuss with all supervised employees and relevant contractors the compliance policies and legal requirements applicable to their function;
- inform all supervised personnel that strict compliance with these policies and procedures is a condition of employment; and
- disclose to all supervised personnel that the nursing facility will take disciplinary action, up to and including termination, for violation of these policies or requirements.

---

[78] In addition to prohibiting the falsification and backdating of records, the provider should have clear guidelines, consistent with applicable professional and legal standards, that set out those individuals with authority to make entries in the medical record and the circumstances when late entries may be made in a record.

Managers and supervisors should be disciplined for failing to adequately instruct their subordinates or for failing to detect noncompliance with applicable policies and legal requirements, where reasonable diligence would have led to the discovery of any problems or violations and given the nursing facility the opportunity to correct them earlier. Conversely, those supervisors who have demonstrated leadership in the advancement of the company's code of conduct and compliance objectives should be singled out for recognition.

The OIG believes that all nursing facilities, regardless of resources or size, should ensure that its employees understand the importance of compliance with program requirements and the value the company places on its compliance program. If the small nursing facility does not have a formal employee evaluation system, it should informally convey to employees their compliance responsibilities whenever the opportunity arises. Positive reenforcement is generally more effective than sanctions in conditioning behavior and managers should be given mechanisms to reward employees who promote compliance.

C. Designation of a Compliance Officer and a Compliance Committee

1. Compliance Officer

Every nursing home provider should designate a compliance officer to serve as the focal point for compliance activities.[79] This responsibility may be the individual's sole duty or added to other management responsibilities, depending upon the size and resources of the nursing facility and the complexity of the task. Designating a compliance officer with the appropriate authority is critical to the success of the program, necessitating the appointment of a high-level official with direct access to the nursing facility's president or CEO, governing body, all other senior management, and legal counsel.[80] The officer should have sufficient funding and staff

---

[79] For multi-facility organizations, the OIG encourages coordination with each facility owned by the corporation through the use of a headquarter's compliance officer, communicating with parallel positions or compliance liaison in each facility or regional office, as appropriate.

[80] The OIG believes it is not advisable for the compliance function to be subordinate to the nursing facility's general counsel, or comptroller or similar financial officer. Free-standing compliance functions help to ensure

to perform his or her responsibilities fully.

Coordination and communication are the key functions of the compliance officer with regard to planning, implementing, and monitoring the compliance program. Particularly in a small facility, the compliance officer may need to rely on the expertise of several professionals within the facility to carry out all of his or her responsibilities. For example, the compliance officer may need the payment specialist to help with billing issues, the director of nursing to address quality of care issues, etc. At the same time, the compliance officer must retain the integrity and objectivity not to compromise the program in deference to one or more disciplines or departments.

The compliance officer's primary responsibilities should include:

- overseeing and monitoring implementation of the compliance program;
- reporting on a regular basis to the nursing facility's governing body, CEO, and compliance committee (if applicable) on the progress of implementation, and assisting these components in establishing methods to improve the nursing facility's efficiency and quality of services, and to reduce the facility's vulnerability to fraud, abuse, and waste;
- periodically revising the program in light of changes in the organization's needs, and in the law and policies of Government and private payor health plans;
- developing, coordinating, and participating in a multifaceted educational and training program that focuses on the elements of the compliance program, and seeking to ensure that all relevant employees and management understand and comply with pertinent Federal and State standards;
- ensuring that independent contractors and agents who furnish physician, nursing, or other health care services to the residents of the nursing facility are aware of the residents' rights as well as requirements of the nursing facility's compliance program applicable to the services they provide;
- coordinating personnel issues with the nursing facility's Human Resources/Personnel office (or its equivalent) to ensure

---

independent and objective legal reviews and financial analysis of the institution's compliance efforts and activities. By separating the compliance function from the key management positions of general counsel or chief financial officer (where the size and structure of the nursing facility make this a feasible option), a system of checks and balances is established to more effectively achieve the goals of the compliance program.

that (i) the National Practitioner Data Bank[81] has been checked with respect to all medical staff and independent contractors (as appropriate) and (ii) the OIG's List of Excluded Individuals/Entities[82] has been checked with respect to all employees, medical staff, and independent contractors;[83]

- assisting the nursing facility's financial management in coordinating internal compliance review and monitoring activities, including annual or periodic reviews of departments;
- independently investigating and acting on matters related to compliance, including the flexibility to design and coordinate internal investigations (e.g., responding to reports of problems or suspected violations) and any resulting corrective action (e.g., making necessary improvements to nursing facility policies and practices, taking appropriate disciplinary action, etc.) with all nursing facility departments, subcontracted providers, and health care professionals under the nursing facility's control;
- participating with facility's counsel in the appropriate reporting of self-discovered violations of program requirements; and
- continuing the momentum of the compliance program after the initial years of implementation.[84]

The compliance officer must have the authority to review all documents and other information that are relevant to compliance activities, including, but not limited to, medical and billing records, and documents concerning the marketing efforts of the nursing facility and its arrangements with other health

[81] See note 59.

[82] See note 60.

[83] The compliance officer may also have to ensure that the criminal backgrounds of employees have been checked depending upon State requirements or nursing facility policy.

[84] There are many approaches the compliance officer may enlist to maintain the vitality of the compliance program. Periodic on-site visits of nursing facility operations, bulletins with compliance updates and reminders, distribution of audiotapes or videotapes on different risk areas, lectures at management and employee meetings, and circulation of recent health care articles covering fraud and abuse are some examples of approaches the compliance officer can employ.

[Page 14300]

care providers, including physicians and independent contractors. This review authority enables the compliance officer to examine contracts and obligations (seeking the advice of legal counsel, where appropriate) that may contain referral and payment provisions that could violate the anti-kickback statute or regulatory requirements.

A small nursing facility may not have the resources to hire or appoint a full time compliance officer. Multi-facility providers also may consider appointing one compliance officer at the corporate level and designating compliance liaisons at each facility. In any event, each facility should have a person in its organization (this person may have other functional responsibilities) who can oversee the nursing facility's compliance with applicable statutes, rules, regulations, and policies. The structure and comprehensiveness of the facility's compliance program will help determine the responsibilities of each individual compliance officer.

2. Compliance Committee

The OIG recommends that a compliance committee be established to advise the compliance officer and assist in the implementation of the compliance program.[85] When developing an appropriate team of people to serve as the nursing facility's compliance committee, a facility should consider a variety of skills and personality traits that are expected from those in such positions.[86] Once a nursing facility chooses the people that will accept the responsibilities vested in members of the compliance committee, the nursing facility needs to

[85] The compliance committee benefits from having the perspectives of individuals with varying responsibilities in the organization, such as operations, finance, audit, human resources, and clinical management (*e.g.*, the medical director), as well as employees and managers of key operating units. The compliance officer should be an integral member of the committee as well. All committee members should have the requisite seniority and comprehensive experience within their respective departments to implement any necessary changes to policies and procedures as recommended by the committee.

[86] A health care provider should expect its compliance committee members and compliance officer to demonstrate high integrity, good judgment, assertiveness, and an approachable demeanor, while eliciting the respect and trust of employees of the nursing facility. These interpersonal skills are as important as the professional experience of each member of the compliance committee.

train these individuals on the policies and procedures of the compliance program, as well as how to discharge their duties.

The committee's functions may include:

- analyzing the legal requirements with which the nursing facility must comply, and specific risk areas;
- assessing existing policies and procedures that address these risk areas for possible incorporation into the compliance program;
- working with appropriate departments to develop standards of conduct and policies and procedures to promote compliance with legal and ethical requirements;
- recommending and monitoring, in conjunction with the relevant departments, the development of internal systems and controls to carry out the organization's policies;
- determining the appropriate strategies and approaches to promote compliance with program requirements and detection of any potential violations, such as through hotlines and other fraud reporting mechanisms;
- developing a system to solicit, evaluate, and respond to complaints and problems; and
- monitoring internal and external audits and investigations for the purpose of identifying deficiencies, and implementing corrective action.

The committee also may undertake other functions as the compliance concept becomes part of the overall nursing facility operating structure and daily routine. The compliance committee is an extension of the compliance officer and provides the organization with increased oversight. The OIG recognizes that some nursing facilities may not have the resources or the need to establish a compliance committee. However, when potential problems are identified, the OIG recommends these nursing facilities create a "task force" to address the particular problem. The members of the task force may vary depending upon the issue.

D. Conducting Effective Training and Education

The proper education and training of corporate officers, managers, and health care professionals, and the continual retraining of current personnel at all levels, are critical elements of an effective compliance program. These training programs should include sessions summarizing the organization's compliance program, fraud and abuse laws, and Federal health care program and private payor requirements. More specific training on issues such as claims development and submission processes, residents' rights, and marketing practices should be targeted at those employees and contractors whose job requirements make the information relevant.[87]

The organization must take steps to communicate effectively its standards and procedures to all affected employees, physicians, independent contractors, and other significant agents by requiring participation in such training programs or by other means, such as disseminating publications that explain specific requirements in a practical manner.[88]

Managers of specific departments or groups can assist in identifying areas that require training and in carrying out such training.[89] Training instructors may come from outside or inside the organization, but must be qualified to present the subject matter involved and sufficiently experienced in the issues presented to adequately field questions and coordinate discussions among those being trained.

The nursing facility should train new employees soon after they have started working.[90] Appropriate training for temporary employees should be provided by the facility before they are assigned responsibility for resident care. Training programs and materials should be designed to take into account the skills, experience, and knowledge of the individual trainees. The compliance officer should document any formal training undertaken by the nursing facility as part of the compliance program.

---

[87] Specific compliance training should complement any "in-service" training sessions that a nursing facility may regularly schedule to provide an ongoing program for the training of employees as required by the Medicare program.

[88] Some publications, such as OIG's special Fraud Alerts, audit and inspection reports, and advisory opinions are readily available from the OIG and can provide a basis for educational courses and programs for appropriate nursing facility employees.

[89] Significant variations in the functions and responsibilities of different departments or groups may create the need for training materials that are tailored to compliance concerns associated with particular operations and duties.

[90] Certain positions, such as those that involve billing, coding and the submission of reimbursement data, create greater organizational legal exposure, and therefore require specialized training. Those hired to treat residents should undergo specialized training in residents' rights.

A variety of teaching methods, such as interactive training and, where a nursing facility has a culturally diverse staff, training in different languages, should be implemented so that all affected employees (including temporary employees) understand the institution's standards of conduct and procedures for alerting senior management to problems and concerns.[91]

[Page 14301]

In addition to specific training in the risk areas identified in section II.B.2, primary training for appropriate corporate officers, managers, and facility staff should include such topics as:

- compliance with Medicare participation requirements relevant to their respective duties and responsibilities;
- appropriate and sufficient documentation;
- prohibitions on paying or receiving remuneration to induce referrals;
- proper documentation in clinical or financial records;
- residents' rights; and
- the duty to report misconduct.

The OIG suggests that all relevant personnel participate in the various educational and training programs of the nursing facility.[92] Employees should be required to have a minimum number of educational hours per year, as appropriate, as part of their employment responsibilities.[93] For example, for certain employees involved in the nursing facility admission functions, periodic training in applicable reimbursement coverage and eligibility requirements should be

[91] Post-training tests can be used to assess the success of training provided and employee comprehension of the nursing facility's policies and procedures.

[92] In addition, where feasible, the OIG recommends that a nursing facility give vendors and outside contractors the opportunity to participate in the nursing facility's compliance training and educational programs. Such training is particularly important for facilities that rely on agencies to provide temporary direct care staff. The introduction of consolidated billing gives added importance to educating vendors about the facility's compliance policies and procedures.

[93] Currently, the OIG is monitoring a significant number of corporate integrity agreements that require many of these training elements. The OIG usually requires a minimum of one to three hours annually for basic training in compliance areas. Additional training is required for specialty fields such as claims development and billing.

required. In nursing facilities with high employee turnover, periodic training updates are critical.

The OIG recognizes that the format of the training program will vary depending upon the resources of the nursing facility. For example, a nursing facility with limited resources may want to create a videotape for each type of training session so new employees can receive training in a timely manner. If videos are used for compliance training, the OIG suggests that a nursing facility make a knowledgeable individual available to field questions from video trainees.

The OIG recommends that participation in training programs be made a condition of continued employment and that failure to comply with training requirements should result in disciplinary action, when such failure is serious. Adherence to the training requirements as well as other provisions of the compliance program should be a factor in the annual evaluation of each employee. The nursing facility should retain adequate records of its training of employees, including attendance logs and material distributed at training sessions.

E. Developing Effective Lines of Communication

1. Access to the Compliance Officer

In order for a compliance program to work, employees must be able to ask questions and report problems. The first line supervisors play a key role in responding to employee concerns and it is appropriate that they serve as a first line of communications. In order to encourage communications, confidentiality and non-retaliation policies should be developed and distributed to all employees.[94]

Open lines of communication between the compliance officer and nursing facility employees is equally important to the successful implementation of a compliance program and the reduction of any potential for fraud and abuse. In addition to serving as a contact point for reporting problems, the compliance officer should be viewed as someone to whom personnel can go to get clarification on the facility's policies. Questions and responses should be documented

[94] In some cases, employees sue their employers under the False Claims Act's qui tam provisions out of frustration because of the company?s failure to take action when the employee brought a questionable, fraudulent, or abusive situation to the attention of senior corporate officials. Whistle blowers must be protected against retaliation, a concept embodied in the provisions of the False Claims Act. See 31 U.S.C. 3730(h).

and dated and, if appropriate, shared with other staff so that standards can be updated and improved to reflect any necessary changes or clarifications.[95]

2. Hotlines and Other Forms of Communication

The OIG encourages the use of hotlines,[96] e-mails, newsletters, suggestion boxes, and other forms of information exchange to maintain open lines of communication.[97] If the nursing facility establishes a hotline, the telephone number should be made readily available to all employees, independent contractors, residents, and family members by circulating the number on wallet cards or conspicuously posting the telephone number in common work areas. Nursing facilities also are required to post the names, addresses and telephone numbers of all pertinent State client advocacy groups such as the State survey and certification agency, State licensure office, State ombudsman program, the protection and advocacy network, and the State Medicaid Fraud Control Unit.[98]

Employees should be permitted to report matters on an anonymous basis. Matters reported through the hotline or other communication sources that suggest substantial violations of compliance policies or Federal health care program statutes and regulations should be documented and investigated promptly to determine their veracity. The compliance officer should maintain a log that records such calls, including the nature of any investigation

---

[95] Nursing facilities also may wish to consider rewarding employees for appropriate use of established reporting systems. After all, the employee who identifies and helps stop an abusive practice can benefit the corporation as much as one who identifies cost-savings measures or increases corporate revenues.

[96] The OIG recognizes that it may not be financially feasible for a smaller nursing facility to maintain a telephone hotline dedicated to receiving calls about compliance issues. These companies may want to explore alternative methods, e.g., outsourcing the hotline or establishing a written method of confidential disclosure.

[97] In addition, an effective employee exit interview program could be designed to solicit information from departing employees regarding potential misconduct and suspected violations of nursing facility policy and procedures.

[98] 42 CFR 483.10(b)(7)(iii). Nursing facilities also should post in a prominent area the HHS-OIG Hotline telephone number, 1-800–447–8477 (1–800-HHS-TIPS).

and its results.[99] Such information, redacted of individual identifiers, should be included in reports to the governing body, the CEO, and compliance committee.[100] While the nursing facility should always strive to maintain the confidentiality of an employee's identity, it also should make clear that there may be a point where the individual's identity may become known or may have to be revealed in certain instances. The OIG recognizes that protecting anonymity may be infeasible for small nursing facilities. However, the OIG believes all facility employees, when seeking answers to questions or reporting potential instances of fraud and abuse, should know to whom to turn for attention and

[Page 14302]

should be able to do so without fear of retribution.

F. Auditing and Monitoring

The OIG believes that an effective program should incorporate thorough monitoring of its implementation and an ongoing evaluation process. The compliance officer should document this ongoing monitoring, including reports of suspected noncompliance, and share these assessments with the nursing facility's senior management and the compliance committee. The extent and frequency of the compliance audits may vary depending on variables such as the nursing facility's available resources, prior history of noncompliance, and the risk factors particular to the facility.[101]

Although many assessment techniques are available, one effective tool is the performance of regular, periodic compliance audits by

---

[99] To efficiently and accurately fulfill such an obligation, the nursing facility should create an intake form for all compliance issues identified through reporting mechanisms. The form could include information concerning the date that the potential problem was reported, the results of the internal investigation, and, as appropriate, the corrective action implemented, the disciplinary measures imposed, and any identified overpayments returned.

[100] Information obtained over the hotline may provide valuable insight into management practices and operations, whether reported problems are actual or perceived.

[101] Even when a nursing facility or group of facilities is owned by a larger corporate entity, the regular auditing and monitoring of the compliance activities of an individual facility must be a key feature in any annual review. Appropriate reports on audit findings should be periodically provided and explained to a parent organization's senior staff and officers.

internal or external evaluators who have expertise in Federal and State health care statutes, regulations, and program requirements, as well as private payor rules. These assessments should focus both on the nursing facility's day-to-day operations, as well as its adherence to the rules governing claims development, billing and cost reports, and relationships with third parties. The reviews also should address the nursing facility's compliance with Medicare requirements and the specific rules and policies that have been the focus of particular attention by the Medicare fiscal intermediaries or carriers, survey agencies, and law enforcement.[102]

Monitoring techniques may include sampling protocols that permit the compliance officer to identify and review variations from an established performance baseline.[103] This performance baseline should include measurable patient outcomes, such as resident weight maintenance and pressure ulcers, established by the facility's Quality Assessment and Assurance Committee. Significant variations from the baseline should trigger an inquiry to determine the cause of the deviation. If the inquiry determines that the deviation occurred for legitimate reasons, the compliance officer and nursing facility management may want to take no action. If it is determined that the deviation was caused by a departure from or misunderstanding of the facility's policies, the nursing facility should take prompt steps to correct the problem. Any overpayments discovered as a result of such deviations should be returned promptly to the affected payor,[104] with appropriate documentation and a sufficiently detailed explanation of the reason for the refund.[105]

---

[102] See also section II.B.2.

[103] The OIG recommends that when a compliance program is established in a nursing facility, the compliance officer, with the assistance of department managers, should take a "snapshot" of their operations from a compliance perspective. This assessment can be undertaken by outside consultants or internal staff, provided they have knowledge of health care program requirements. This "snapshot" can serve as a baseline for the compliance officer and other managers to judge the nursing facility's progress in reducing potential areas of vulnerability.

[104] See Provider Reimbursement Manual Part I, section 2836(D)(3), which sets out the MDS correction policy.

[105] In addition, when appropriate, as referenced in section II.H.2, below, reports of fraud or systemic problems also should be made to the appropriate governmental authority.

In addition to evaluating the facility's conformance with program rules, an effective compliance program also should incorporate periodic (at least annual) reviews of whether the program's compliance elements have been satisfied, e.g., whether there has been appropriate dissemination of the program's standards, ongoing educational programs, and internal investigations of alleged non-compliance. This process will assess actual conformance by all departments with the compliance program and may identify areas for improvements in the program, as well as the nursing facility's general operations.

The OIG requires a provider operating under a CIA to conduct an annual assessment of its compliance with the elements of the CIA. A compliance officer may want to review several CIAs in designing the facility's self-audit protocol.[106]

As part of the review process, the compliance officer or reviewers should consider techniques such as:

- on-site visits to all facilities owned and/or operated by the nursing home owner;
- testing the billing and claims reimbursement staff on its knowledge of applicable program requirements and claims and billing criteria;
- unannounced mock surveys and audits;
- examination of the organization's complaint logs and investigative files;
- legal assessment of all contractual relationships with contractors, consultants and potential referral sources;
- reevaluation of deficiencies cited in past surveys for State requirements and Medicare participation requirements;
- checking personnel records to determine whether individuals who previously have been reprimanded for compliance issues are now conforming to facility policies;
- questionnaires developed to solicit impressions of a broad cross-section of the nursing facility's employees and staff con-

[106] Examples of CIA audit protocols can be obtained from the OIG by submitting a request pursuant to the Freedom of Information Act. The OIG recently has entered into CIAs with a number of nursing home providers that may be of particular relevance. In addition, the American Institute of Certified Public Accountants (AICPA) has issued a detailed guide for conducting an independent assessment of a health care provider's conformance to a CIA. See AICPA Statement of Position 99–1, "Guidance to Practitioners in Conducting and Reporting on an Agreed-Upon Procedures Engagement to Assist in Evaluating Compliance with a Corporate Integrity Agreement" (May 1999).

cerning adherence to the code of conduct and policies and procedures, as well as their work loads and ability to address the residents' activities of daily living;

- validation of qualifications of nursing facility physicians and other staff, including verification of applicable State license renewals;
- trend analysis, or longitudinal studies, that uncover deviations in specific areas over a given period; and
- analyzing past survey reports for patterns of deficiencies to determine if the proposed corrective plan of action identified and corrected the underlying problem.

The reviewers should:

- have the qualifications and experience necessary to adequately identify potential issues with the subject matter that is reviewed;
- be objective and independent of line management to the extent reasonably possible; [107]
- have access to existing audit and health care resources, relevant personnel, and all relevant areas of operation;
- present written evaluative reports on compliance activities to the CEO, governing body, and members of the compliance committee on a regular basis, but no less often than annually; and
- specifically identify areas where corrective actions are needed.

The extent and scope of a nursing facility's compliance self-audits will depend on the facility's identified risk areas, past history of deficiencies and

[Page 14303]

enforcement actions, and resources. If the facility comes under Government scrutiny in the future, the Government will assess whether the facility developed a reasonable audit plan based upon identified risk areas and resources. If the Government determines that the nursing facility failed to develop an adequate audit program, the Government will be less likely to afford the nursing facility favorable treatment under the Federal Sentencing Guidelines.

---

[107] The OIG recognizes that nursing facilities that have limited resources may not be able to use internal reviewers who are not part of line management or hire outside reviewers.

G. Enforcing Standards Through Well-Publicized Disciplinary Guidelines

1. Disciplinary Policy and Enforcement

An effective compliance program should include disciplinary policies that set out the consequences of violating the nursing facility's standards of conduct, policies, and procedures. Intentional noncompliance should subject transgressors to significant sanctions. Such sanctions could range from oral warnings to suspension, termination, or financial penalties, as appropriate. Disciplinary action may be appropriate where a responsible employee's failure to detect a violation is attributable to his or her negligence or reckless conduct. Each situation must be considered on a case-by-case basis to determine the appropriate response.

The written standards of conduct should elaborate on the procedures for handling disciplinary problems and those who will be responsible for taking appropriate action. Some disciplinary actions can be handled by department or agency managers, while others may have to be resolved by a senior administrator. The nursing facility should advise personnel that disciplinary action will be taken on a fair and equitable basis. Managers and supervisors should be made aware that they have a responsibility to discipline employees in an appropriate and consistent manner.

It is vital to publish and disseminate the range of disciplinary standards for improper conduct and to educate employees regarding these standards. The consequences of noncompliance should be consistently applied and enforced, in order for the disciplinary policy to have the required deterrent effect. All levels of employees should be potentially subject to the same types of disciplinary action for the commission of similar offenses, because the commitment to compliance applies to all personnel within a nursing facility. This means that corporate officers, managers, and supervisors should be held accountable for failing to comply with, or for the foreseeable failure of their subordinates to adhere to, the applicable standards, laws, and procedures.

H. Responding to Detected Offenses and Developing Corrective Action Initiatives

Violations of a nursing facility's compliance program, failures to comply with applicable Federal or State law, and other types of misconduct threaten a facility's status as a reliable, honest and trustworthy provider of health care. Detected but uncorrected deficiencies can seriously endanger the reputation and legal status of the nursing facility. Consequently, upon receipt of reports or reasonable indications of suspected noncompliance, it is important that the compliance officer or other management officials immediately investigate the allegations to determine whether a material violation of applicable law or the requirements of the compliance program has occurred and, if so, take decisive steps to correct the problem.[108] As appropriate, such steps may include a corrective action plan,[109] the return of any overpayments, a report to the Government,[110] and/or a referral to criminal and/or civil law enforcement authorities.

Where potential fraud is not involved, the OIG recommends that the nursing facility use normal repayment channels to return overpayments as they are discovered. However, even if the nursing facility's billing department is effectively using the overpayment detection and return process, the OIG believes that the facility needs to alert the compliance officer to those overpayments that may reveal trends or patterns indicative of a systemic problem.

---

[108] Instances of noncompliance must be determined on a case-by-case basis. The existence or amount of a *monetary* loss to a health care program is not solely determinative of whether the conduct should be investigated and reported to governmental authorities. In fact, there may be instances where there is no readily identifiable monetary loss, but corrective actions are still necessary to protect the integrity of the applicable program and its beneficiaries, *e.g.*, where failure to comply with the facility's policies and procedures results in inadequate or inappropriate care being furnished to a facility resident.

[109] The nursing facility may seek advice from its in-house counsel or an outside law firm to determine the extent of the facility's liability and to plan the appropriate course of action.

[110] Nursing facilities are required to immediately report all alleged incidents of mistreatment, neglect, abuse (including injuries of unknown source), and misappropriation of resident property to both the facility administrator and other officials in accordance with State law. See 42 CFR 483.13(c)(2). This is the appropriate channel for reporting quality of care issues. The OIG also has established a provider self-disclosure protocol that encourages providers voluntarily to report suspected fraud. The concept of voluntary self-disclosure is premised on a recognition that the Government alone cannot protect the integrity of Medicare and other Federal health care programs. Health care providers must be willing to police themselves, correct underlying problems, and work with the Government to resolve these matters. The self-disclosure protocol can be located on the OIG's web site at: http://www.hhs.gov/oig.

Where there are indications of potential fraud, an internal investigation may be warranted and will probably include interviews and a review of relevant documents. Under some circumstances, the facility may need to consider engaging outside counsel, auditors, or health care experts to assist in an investigation. The investigative file should contain documentation of the alleged violation, a description of the investigative process (including the objectivity of the investigators and methodologies utilized), copies of interview notes and key documents, a log of the witnesses interviewed and the documents reviewed, the results of the investigation, e.g., any disciplinary action taken, and the corrective action implemented. While any action taken as the result of an investigation will necessarily vary depending upon the situation, nursing facilities should strive for some consistency by using sound practices and disciplinary protocols.[111] Further, the compliance officer should review the circumstances that formed the basis for the investigation to determine whether similar problems have been uncovered or modifications of the compliance program are necessary to prevent and detect other inappropriate conduct or violations.

If the nursing facility undertakes an investigation of an alleged violation and the compliance officer believes the integrity of the investigation may be at stake because of the presence of employees under investigation, the facility should remove those individuals from their current responsibilities until the investigation is completed (unless there is an ongoing internal or Government-led undercover operation known to the nursing facility). In addition, the compliance officer should take appropriate steps to secure or prevent the destruction of documents or other evidence relevant to the investigation. If the nursing facility determines that disciplinary action is warranted, it should be promptly imposed in accordance with the facility's written standards of disciplinary action.

---

[111] The parameters of a claims review subject to an internal investigation will depend on the circumstances surrounding the issues identified. By limiting the scope of an internal audit to current billing, a nursing facility may fail to discover major problems and deficiencies in operations, and may subject itself to liability.

[Page 14304]

1. Reporting

Where the compliance officer, compliance committee, or a management official discovers credible evidence of misconduct from any source and, after a reasonable inquiry, has reason to believe that the misconduct may violate criminal, civil or administrative law, the facility should promptly report the existence of misconduct to the appropriate Federal and State authorities [112] within a reasonable period, but not more than 60 days [113] after determining that there is credible evidence of a violation. [114] Prompt voluntary reporting will demonstrate the nursing facility's good faith and willingness to work with governmental authorities to correct and remedy the problem. In addition, reporting such conduct will be considered a mitigating factor by the OIG in determining administrative sanctions (e.g., penalties, assessments, and exclusion), if the reporting provider becomes the target of an OIG investigation. [115]

---

[112] Appropriate Federal and State authorities include the OIG, the Criminal and Civil Divisions of the Department of Justice, the U.S. Attorney in relevant districts, the Federal Bureau of Investigation, and the other investigative arms for the agencies administering the affected Federal or State health care programs, such as the State Survey Agency, the State Medicaid Fraud Control Unit, the Defense Criminal Investigative Service, the Department of Veterans Affairs, and the Office of Personnel Management (which administers the Federal Employee Health Benefits Program). State law may further specify types of misconduct and to whom a facility must report its findings. See note 110.

[113] In contrast, to qualify for the "not less than double damages" provision of the False Claims Act, the provider must provide the report to the Government within 30 days after the date when the provider first obtained the information. See 31 U.S.C. 3729(a).

[114] Some violations may be so serious that they warrant immediate notification to governmental authorities prior to, or simultaneous with, commencing an internal investigation. By way of example, the OIG believes a provider should report misconduct that: (1) is a clear violation of OIG administrative authorities, or civil or criminal fraud laws; (2) has a significant adverse effect on the quality of care provided to residents (in addition to any other legal obligations regarding quality of care); or (3) indicates evidence of a systemic failure to comply with applicable laws or an existing corporate integrity agreement, regardless of the financial impact on Federal health care programs.

[115] The OIG has published criteria setting forth those factors that the OIG takes into consideration in determining whether it is appropriate to exclude a health care provider from program participation pursuant to 42 U.S.C.

When reporting to the Government, a nursing facility should provide all evidence relevant to the alleged violation of applicable Federal or State law(s) and potential cost impact. The compliance officer, under advice of counsel and with guidance from the governmental authorities, could be requested to continue to investigate the reported violation. Once the investigation is completed, the compliance officer should notify the appropriate governmental authority of the outcome of the investigation, including a description of the impact of the alleged violation on the operation of the applicable health care programs or their beneficiaries. If the investigation ultimately reveals that criminal, civil or administrative violations have occurred, the nursing facility should immediately notify appropriate Federal and State authorities.

As previously stated, the nursing facility should take appropriate corrective action, including prompt identification and return of any overpayment to the affected payor. If potential fraud is involved, the nursing facility should return any overpayment during the course of its disclosure to the Government. Otherwise, the nursing facility should use normal repayment channels for reimbursing identified overpayments.[116] A knowing and willful failure to disclose overpayments within a reasonable period of time could be interpreted as an attempt to conceal the overpayment from the Government, thereby establishing an independent basis for a criminal violation with respect to the nursing facility, as well as any individual who may have been involved.[117] For this reason, nursing facility compliance programs should emphasize that overpayments should be promptly disclosed and returned to the entity that made the erroneous payment.

1320a-7(b)(7) for violations of various fraud and abuse laws. See 62 FR 67392 (December 24, 1997).

[116] A nursing facility should consult with its Medicare fiscal intermediary (FI) and the appropriate sections of the Provider Reimbursement Manual for additional guidance regarding refunds under Medicare Part A. See note 104. The FI may require certain information (e.g., alleged violation or issue causing overpayment, description of the internal investigative process with methodologies used to determine any overpayments, and corrective actions taken, etc.) to be submitted with the return of any overpayments, and that such repayment information be submitted to a specific department or individual. When appropriate, interest may be assessed on the overpayment. See 42 CFR 405.378.

[117] See 42 U.S.C. 1320a-7b(a)(3) and 18 U.S.C. 669.

III. Assessing the Effectiveness of a Compliance Program

Considering the financial and human resources needed to establish an effective compliance program, sound business principles dictate that the nursing home's management evaluate the return on that investment. In addition, a compliance program must be "effective" for the Government to view its existence as a mitigating factor when assessing culpability. How a nursing facility assesses its compliance program performance is therefore integral to its success. The attributes of each individual element of a compliance program must be evaluated in order to assess the program's "effectiveness" as a whole. Examining the comprehensiveness of policies and procedures implemented to satisfy these elements is merely the first step. Evaluating how a compliance program performs during the provider's day-to-day operations becomes the critical indicator.[118]

As previously stated, a compliance program should require the development and distribution of written compliance policies, standards, and practices that identify specific areas of risk and vulnerability. One way to judge whether these policies, standards, and practices measure up is to observe how an organization's employees react to them. Do employees experience recurring pitfalls because the guidance on certain issues is not adequately covered in company policies? Do employees flagrantly disobey an organization's standards of conduct because they observe no sincere buy-in from senior management? Do employees have trouble understanding policies and procedures because they are written in legalese or at difficult reading levels? Does an organization routinely experience systematic billing failures because of poor instructions to employees on how to implement written policies and practices? Written compliance policies, standards, and practices are only as good as an organization's commitment to apply them in practice.

Every nursing facility needs to seriously consider whoever fills the integral roles of compliance officer and compliance committee members, and periodically monitor how the individuals chosen satisfy their responsibilities. Does a compliance officer have sufficient professional experience working with billing, clinical records,

---

[118] Evaluation may be accomplished through techniques such as employee surveys, management assessments, and periodic review of benchmarks established for audits, investigations, disciplinary action, overpayments, and employee feedback. The nursing facility should evaluate all elements of its compliance program, including policies, training, practices, and compliance personnel.

documentation, and auditing principles to perform assigned responsibilities fully? Has a compliance officer or compliance committee been unsuccessful in fulfilling their duties because of inadequate funding, staff, and authority necessary to carry out their jobs? Did the addition of the compliance officer function to a key management position with other significant duties compromise the goals of the compliance program (e.g., chief financial officer who discounts certain overpayments identified to improve the company's bottom line profits)? Since a

[Page 14305]

compliance officer and a compliance committee can have a significant impact on how effectively a compliance program is implemented, those functions should not be taken for granted.

As evidenced throughout this guidance, the proper education and training of corporate officers, managers, health care professionals, and other applicable employees of a provider, and the continual retraining of current personnel at all levels, are significant elements of an effective compliance program. Accordingly, such efforts should be routinely evaluated. How frequently are employees trained? Are employees tested after training? Do the training sessions and materials adequately summarize the important aspects of the organization's compliance program? Are training instructors qualified to present the subject matter and field questions? When thorough compliance training is periodically conducted, employees receive the reinforcement they need to ensure an effective compliance program.

An open line of communication between the compliance officer and a provider's employees is equally important to the success of a compliance program. In today's intensive regulatory environment, the OIG believes that a provider cannot possibly have an effective compliance program if it does not receive feedback from its employees regarding compliance matters. For instance, if a compliance officer does not receive appropriate inquiries from employees: Do policies and procedures adequately guide employees to whom and when they should be communicating compliance matters? Are employees confident that they can report compliance matters to management without fear of retaliation? Are employees reporting issues through the proper channels? Do employees have the proper motives for reporting compliance matters? Regardless of the means that a provider uses, whether it is telephone hotline, email, or suggestion boxes, employees should seek clarification from compliance staff in the event of any confusion or question dealing with compliance policies, practices, or procedures.

An effective compliance program should include guidance regarding disciplinary action for corporate officers, managers, health care professionals, and other employees who have failed to adhere to an organization's standards of conduct, Federal health care program requirements, or Federal or State laws. The number and caliber of disciplinary actions taken by an organization can be insightful. Have appropriate sanctions been applied to compliance misconduct? Are sanctions applied to all employees consistently, regardless of an employee's level in the corporate hierarchy? Have double-standards in discipline bred cynicism among employees? When disciplinary action is not taken seriously or applied haphazardly, such practices reflect poorly on senior management's commitment to foster compliance as well as the effectiveness of an organization's compliance program in general.

Another critical component of a successful compliance program is an ongoing monitoring and auditing process. The extent and frequency of the audit function may vary depending on factors such as the size and available resources, prior history of noncompliance, and risk factors of a particular nursing facility. The hallmark of effective monitoring and auditing efforts is how an organization determines the parameters of its reviews. Do audits focus on all pertinent departments of an organization? Does an audit cover compliance with all applicable laws, as well as Federal and private payor requirements? Are results of past audits, pre-established baselines, or prior deficiencies reevaluated? Are the elements of the compliance program monitored? Are auditing techniques valid and conducted by objective reviewers? The extent and sincerity of an organization's efforts to confirm its compliance often proves to be a revealing determinant of a compliance program's effectiveness.

It is essential that the compliance officer or other management officials immediately investigate reports or reasonable indications of suspected noncompliance. If a material violation of applicable law or compliance program requirements has occurred, a provider must take decisive steps to correct the problem. Nursing facilities that do not thoroughly investigate misconduct leave themselves open to undiscovered problems. When a provider learns of certain issues, it should evaluate how it assesses its legal exposure. What is the correlation between the deficiency identified and the corrective action necessary to remedy? Are isolated overpayment matters properly resolved through normal repayment channels? Is credible evidence of misconduct that may violate criminal, civil or administrative law promptly reported to the appropriate Federal and State authorities? If the process of responding to detected offenses is circumvented, such conduct would indicate an ineffective compliance program.

Documentation is the key to demonstrating the effectiveness of a nursing facility's compliance program. For example, documentation of the following should be maintained: audit results; logs of hotline calls and their resolution; corrective action plans; due diligence efforts regarding business transactions; records of employee training, including the number of training hours; disciplinary action; and modification and distribution of policies and procedures. Because the OIG encourages self-disclosure of overpayments and billing irregularities, maintaining a record of disclosures and refunds to the Federal health care programs and private insurers is strongly endorsed. A documented practice of refunding of overpayments and self-disclosing incidents of non-compliance with Federal and private payor health care program requirements is powerful evidence of a meaningful compliance effort.

IV. Conclusion

Through this document, the OIG has attempted to provide a foundation for the process necessary to develop an effective and cost-efficient nursing facility compliance program. However, each program must be tailored to fit the needs and resources of a particular facility, depending upon its unique corporate structure, mission, and employee composition. The statutes, regulations, and guidelines of the Federal health care programs, as well as the policies and procedures of private health plans, should be integrated into every nursing facility's compliance program.

The OIG recognizes that the health care industry in this country, which reaches millions of beneficiaries and expends about a trillion dollars annually, is constantly evolving. The time is right for nursing facilities to implement a strong voluntary health care compliance program. Compliance is a dynamic process that helps to ensure that nursing facilities and other health care providers are better able to fulfill their commitment to ethical behavior, as well as meet the changes and challenges being placed upon them by Congress and private insurers. Ultimately, it is the OIG's hope that a voluntarily created compliance program will enable nursing facilities to meet their goals, improve the quality of resident care, and substantially reduce fraud, waste, and abuse, as well as the cost of health care to Federal, State, and private health insurers.

[Page 14306]

Dated: March 9, 2000.

June Gibbs Brown,

Inspector General.

[FR Doc. 00–6423 Filed 3–15–00; 8:45 am]

BILLING CODE 4150–04-P

APPENDIX I9

Compliance Program Guidance for Individual and Small Group Physician Practices; 65 FR 59434, October 5, 2000

[Federal Register: October 5, 2000 (Volume 65, Number 194)]
[Notices] [Page 59434–59452]

DEPARTMENT OF HEALTH AND HUMAN SERVICES

Office of Inspector General

AGENCY: Office of Inspector General (OIG), HHS.

ACTION: Notice.

SUMMARY: This Federal Register notice sets forth the recently issued Compliance Program Guidance for Individual and Small Group Physician Practices developed by the Office of Inspector General (OIG). The OIG has previously developed and published voluntary compliance program guidance focused on several other areas and aspects of the health care industry. We believe that the development and issuance of this voluntary compliance program guidance for individual and small group physician practices will serve as a positive step towards assisting providers in preventing the submission of erroneous claims or engaging in unlawful conduct involving the Federal health care programs.

FOR FURTHER INFORMATION CONTACT: Kimberly Brandt, Office of Counsel to the Inspector General, (202) 619–2078.

SUPPLEMENTARY INFORMATION:

Background

The creation of compliance program guidances is a major initiative of the OIG in its effort to engage the private health care community in preventing the submission of erroneous claims and in combating fraudulent conduct. In the past several years, the OIG has developed and issued compliance program guidances directed at a variety of segments in the health care industry. The development of these types of compliance program guidances is based on our belief that a health care provider can use internal controls to more efficiently monitor adherence to applicable statutes, regulations and program requirements.

Copies of these compliance program guidances can be found on the OIG web site at http://www.hhs.gov/oig.

Developing the Compliance Program Guidance for Individual and Small Group Physician Practices

On September 8, 1999, the OIG published a solicitation notice seeking information and recommendations for developing formal guidance for individual and small group physician practices (64 FR 48846). In response to that solicitation notice, the OIG received 83 comments from various outside sources. We carefully considered those comments, as well as previous OIG publications, such as other compliance program guidance and Special Fraud Alerts, in developing a guidance for individual and small group physician practices. In addition, we have consulted with the Health Care Financing Administration and the Department of Justice. In an effort to ensure that all parties had a reasonable opportunity to provide input into a final product, draft guidance for individual and small group physician practices was published in the Federal Register on June 12, 2000 (65 FR 36818) for further comments and recommendations.

Components of an Effective Compliance Program

This compliance program guidance for individual and small group physician practices contains seven components that provide a solid basis upon which a physician practice can create a voluntary compliance program:

- Conducting internal monitoring and auditing;
- Implementing compliance and practice standards;
- Designating a compliance officer or contact;
- Conducting appropriate training and education;
- Responding appropriately to detected offenses and developing corrective action;
- Developing open lines of communication; and
- Enforcing disciplinary standards through well-publicized guidelines.

Similar components have been contained in previous guidances issued by the OIG. However, unlike other guidances issued by OIG, this guidance for physicians does not suggest that physician practices implement all seven components of a full scale compliance program. Instead, the guidance emphasizes a step by step approach to follow in developing and implementing a voluntary compliance program. This change is in recognition of the financial and staffing resource constraints faced by physician practices. The guidance should not be viewed as mandatory or as an all-inclusive discussion of the advisable components of a compliance program. Rather, the document is intended to present guidance to assist physician practices that voluntarily choose to develop a compliance program.

Office of Inspector General's Compliance Program Guidance for Individual and Small Group Physician Practices

I. Introduction

This compliance program guidance is intended to assist individual and small group physician practices ("physician practices")[1] in developing a voluntary compliance program that promotes adherence to statutes and regulations applicable to the Federal health care programs ("Federal health care program requirements"). The goal of voluntary compliance programs is to provide a tool to strengthen the efforts of health care providers to prevent and reduce improper conduct. These programs can also benefit physician practices[2] by helping to streamline business operations.

Many physicians have expressed an interest in better protecting their practices from the potential for erroneous or fraudulent conduct through the implementation of voluntary compliance programs. The Office of Inspector General (OIG) believes that the great majority of physicians are honest and share our goal of protecting the integrity of Medicare and other Federal health care programs. To that end, all health care providers have a duty to ensure that the claims submitted to Federal health care programs are true and accu-

[1] For the purpose of this guidance, the term "physician" is defined as: (1) a doctor of medicine or osteopathy; (2) a doctor of dental surgery or of dental medicine; (3) a podiatrist; (4) an optometrist; or (5) a chiropractor, all of whom must be appropriately licensed by the State. 42 U.S.C. 1395x(r).

[2] Much of this guidance can also apply to other independent practitioners, such as psychologists, physical therapists, speech language pathologists, and occupational therapists.

rate. The development of voluntary compliance programs and the active application of compliance principles in physician practices will go a long way toward achieving this goal.

Through this document, the OIG provides its views on the fundamental components of physician practice compliance programs, as well as the principles that a physician practice might consider when developing and implementing a voluntary compliance program. While this document presents basic procedural and structural guidance for designing a voluntary compliance program, it is not in and of itself a compliance program. Indeed, as recognized by the OIG and the health care industry, there is no "one size fits all" compliance program, especially for physician practices. Rather, it is a set of guidelines that physician practices can consider if they choose to develop and implement a compliance program.

As with the OIG's previous guidance,[3] these guidelines are not mandatory. Nor do they represent an all-inclusive document containing all components of a compliance program. Other OIG outreach efforts, as well as other Federal agency efforts to promote compliance,[4] can also be used in developing a compliance program. However, as explained later, if a physician practice adopts a voluntary and active compliance program, it may well lead to benefits for the physician practice.

---

[3] Currently, the OIG has issued compliance program guidance for the following eight industry sectors: hospitals, clinical laboratories, home health agencies, durable medical equipment suppliers, third-party medical billing companies, hospices, Medicare+Choice organizations offering coordinated care plans, and nursing facilities. The guidance listed here and referenced in this document is available on the OIG web site at http://www.hhs.gov/oig in the Electronic Reading Room or by calling the OIG Public Affairs office at (202) 619–1343.

[4] The OIG has issued Advisory Opinions responding to specific inquiries concerning the application of the OIG's authorities, in particular, the anti-kickback statute, and Special Fraud Alerts setting forth activities that raise legal and enforcement issues. These documents, as well as reports from the OIG's Office of Audit Services and Office of Evaluation and Inspections can be obtained via the Internet address or phone number provided in Footnote 3. Physician practices can also review the Health Care Financing Administration (HCFA) web site on the Internet at http:// www.hcfa.gov, for up-to-date regulations, manuals, and program memoranda related to the Medicare and Medicaid programs.

A. Scope of the Voluntary Compliance Program Guidance

This guidance focuses on voluntary compliance measures related to claims submitted to the Federal health care programs. Issues related to private payor claims may also be covered by a compliance plan if the physician practice so desires.

The guidance is also limited in scope by focusing on the development of voluntary compliance programs for individual and small group physician practices. The difference between a small practice and a large practice cannot be determined by stating a particular number of physicians. Instead, our intent in narrowing the guidance to the small practices subset was to provide guidance to those physician practices whose financial or staffing resources would not allow them to implement a full scale, institutionally structured compliance program as set forth in the Third Party Medical Billing Guidance or other previously released OIG guidance. A compliance program can be an important tool for physician practices of all sizes and does not have to be costly, resource-intensive or time-intensive.

B. Benefits of a Voluntary Compliance Program

The OIG acknowledges that patient care is, and should be, the first priority of a physician practice. However, a practice's focus on patient care can be enhanced by the adoption of a voluntary compliance program. For example, the increased accuracy of documentation that may result from a compliance program will actually assist in enhancing patient care. The OIG believes that physician practices can realize numerous other benefits by implementing a compliance program. A well-designed compliance program can:

- Speed and optimize proper payment of claims;
- Minimize billing mistakes;
- Reduce the chances that an audit will be conducted by HCFA or the OIG; and
- Avoid conflicts with the self-referral and anti-kickback statutes.

The incorporation of compliance measures into a physician practice should not be at the expense of patient care, but instead should augment the ability of the physician practice to provide quality patient care.

Voluntary compliance programs also provide benefits by not only helping to prevent erroneous or fraudulent claims, but also by showing that the physician practice is making additional good faith efforts to submit claims appropriately. Physicians should view compliance programs as analogous to practicing preventive medicine for their practice. Practices that embrace the active application of compliance principles in their practice culture and put efforts towards compliance on a continued basis can help to prevent problems from occurring in the future.

A compliance program also sends an important message to a physician practice's employees that while the practice recognizes that mistakes will occur, employees have an affirmative, ethical duty to come forward and report erroneous or fraudulent conduct, so that it may be corrected.

C. Application of Voluntary Compliance Program Guidance

The applicability of these recommendations will depend on the circumstances and resources of the particular physician practice.

Each physician practice can undertake reasonable steps to implement compliance measures, depending on the size and resources of that practice. Physician practices can rely, at least in part, upon standard protocols and current practice procedures to develop an appropriate compliance program for that practice. In fact, many physician practices already have established the framework of a compliance program without referring to it as such.

D. The Difference Between "Erroneous" and "Fraudulent" Claims To Federal Health Programs

There appear to be significant misunderstandings within the physician community regarding the critical differences between what the Government views as innocent "erroneous" claims on the one hand and "fraudulent" (intentionally or recklessly false) health care claims on the other. Some physicians feel that Federal law enforcement agencies have maligned medical professionals, in part, by a perceived focus on innocent billing errors. These physicians are under the impression that innocent billing errors can subject them to civil penalties, or even jail. These impressions are mistaken.

To address these concerns, the OIG would like to emphasize the following points. First, the OIG does not disparage physicians, other medical professionals or medical enterprises. In our view, the great majority of physicians are working ethically to render high quality medical care and to submit proper claims.

Second, under the law, physicians are not subject to criminal, civil or administrative penalties for innocent errors, or even negligence. The Government's primary enforcement tool, the civil False Claims Act, covers only offenses that are committed with actual knowledge of the falsity of the claim, reckless disregard, or deliberate ignorance of the falsity of the claim. [5] The False Claims Act does not encompass mistakes, errors, or negligence. The Civil Monetary Penalties Law, an administrative remedy, similar in scope and effect to the False Claims Act, has exactly the same standard of proof. [6] The OIG is very mindful of the difference between innocent errors ("erroneous claims") on one hand, and reckless or intentional conduct ("fraudulent claims") on the other. For criminal penalties, the standard is even higher — criminal intent to defraud must be proved beyond a reasonable doubt.

Third, even ethical physicians (and their staffs) make billing mistakes and errors through inadvertence or negligence. When physicians discover that their billing errors, honest mistakes, or negligence result in erroneous claims, the physician practice should return the funds erroneously claimed, but without penalties. In other words, absent a violation of a civil, criminal or administrative law, erroneous claims result only in the return of funds claimed in error.

Fourth, innocent billing errors are a significant drain on the Federal health care programs. All parties (physicians, providers, carriers, fiscal intermediaries, Government agencies, and beneficiaries) need to work cooperatively to reduce the overall error rate.

Finally, it is reasonable for physicians (and other providers) to ask: what duty do they owe the Federal health care programs? The answer is that all health care providers have a duty to reasonably ensure that the claims submitted to Medicare and other Federal health care programs are true and accurate. The OIG continues to engage the provider community in an extensive, good faith effort to work cooperatively on voluntary compliance to minimize errors and to prevent potential penalties for improper billings before they occur. We encourage all physicians and other providers to join in this effort.

---

[5] 31 U.S.C. 3729.

[6] 42 U.S.C. 1320a-7a.

II. Developing a Voluntary Compliance Program

A. The Seven Basic Components of a Voluntary Compliance Program

The OIG believes that a basic framework for any voluntary compliance program begins with a review of the seven basic components of an effective compliance program. A review of these components provides physician practices with an overview of the scope of a fully developed and implemented compliance program. The following list of components, as set forth in previous OIG compliance program guidances, can form the basis of a voluntary compliance program for a physician practice:

- Conducting internal monitoring and auditing through the performance of periodic audits;
- Implementing compliance and practice standards through the development of written standards and procedures;
- Designating a compliance officer or contact(s) to monitor compliance efforts and enforce practice standards;
- Conducting appropriate training and education on practice standards and procedures;
- Responding appropriately to detected violations through the investigation of allegations and the disclosure of incidents to appropriate Government entities;
- Developing open lines of communication, such as (1) discussions at staff meetings regarding how to avoid erroneous or fraudulent conduct and (2) community bulletin boards, to keep practice employees updated regarding compliance activities; and
- Enforcing disciplinary standards through well-publicized guidelines.

These seven components provide a solid basis upon which a physician practice can create a compliance program. The OIG acknowledges that full implementation of all components may not be feasible for all physician practices. Some physician practices may never fully implement all of the components. However, as a first step, physician practices can begin by adopting only those components which, based on a practice's specific history with billing problems and other compliance issues, are most likely to provide an identifiable benefit.

The extent of implementation will depend on the size and resources of the practice. Smaller physician practices may incorporate each of the components in a manner that best suits the practice. By contrast, larger physician practices often have the means to incorporate the components in a more systematic manner. For example, larger physician practices can use both this guidance and the Third-Party Medical Billing Compliance Program Guidance, which provides a more detailed compliance program structure, to create a compliance program unique to the practice.

The OIG recognizes that physician practices need to find the best way to achieve compliance for their given circumstances. Specifically, the OIG encourages physician practices to participate in other provider's compliance programs, such as the compliance programs of the hospitals or other settings in which the physicians practice. Physician Practice Management companies also may serve as a source of compliance program guidance. A physician practice's participation in such compliance programs could be a way, at least partly, to augment the practice's own compliance efforts.

The opportunities for collaborative compliance efforts could include participating in training and education programs or using another entity's policies and procedures as a template from which the physician practice creates its own version. The OIG encourages this type of collaborative effort, where the content is appropriate to the setting involved (i.e., the training is relevant to physician practices as well as the sponsoring provider), because it provides a means to promote the desired objective without imposing excessive burdens on the practice or requiring physicians to undertake duplicative action. However, to prevent possible anti-kickback or self-referral issues, the OIG recommends that physicians consider limiting their participation in a sponsoring provider's compliance program to the areas of training and education or policies and procedures.

The key to avoiding possible conflicts is to ensure that the entity providing compliance services to a physician practice (its referral source) is not perceived as nor is it operating the practice compliance program at no charge. For example, if the sponsoring entity conducted claims review for the physician practice as part of a compliance program or provided compliance oversight without charging the practice fair market value for those services, the anti-kickback and Stark self-referral laws would be implicated. The payment of fair market value by referral sources for compliance services will generally address these concerns.

B. Steps for Implementing a Voluntary Compliance Program

As previously discussed, implementing a voluntary compliance program can be a multi-tiered process. Initial development of the compliance program can be focused on practice risk areas that have been problematic for the practice such as coding and billing. Within this area, the practice should examine its claims denial history or claims that have resulted in repeated overpayments, and identify and correct the most frequent sources of those denials or overpayments. A review of claim denials will help the practice scrutinize a significant risk area and improve its cash flow by submitting correct claims that will be paid the first time they are submitted. As this example illustrates, a compliance program for a physician practice often makes sound business sense.

The following is a suggested order of the steps a practice could take to begin the development of a compliance program. The steps outlined below articulate all seven components of a compliance program and there are numerous suggestions for implementation within each component. Physician practices should keep in mind, as stated earlier, that it is up to the practice to determine the manner in which and the extent to which the practice chooses to implement these voluntary measures.

Step One: Auditing and Monitoring

An ongoing evaluation process is important to a successful compliance program. This ongoing evaluation includes not only whether the physician practice's standards and procedures are in fact current and accurate, but also whether the compliance program is working, i.e., whether individuals are properly carrying out their responsibilities and claims are submitted appropriately. Therefore, an audit is an excellent way for a physician practice to ascertain what, if any, problem areas exist and focus on the risk areas that are associated with those problems. There are two types of reviews that can be performed as part of this evaluation: (1) A standards and procedures review; and (2) a claims submission audit.

1. Standards and Procedures

It is recommended that an individual(s) in the physician practice be charged with the responsibility of periodically reviewing the practice's standards and procedures to determine if they are current and complete. If the standards and procedures are found to be ineffective or outdated, they should be updated to reflect changes in Government regulations or compendiums generally relied upon by physicians and insurers (i.e., changes in Current Procedural Terminology (CPT) and ICD-9-CM codes).

2. Claims Submission Audit

In addition to the standards and procedures themselves, it is advisable that bills and medical records be reviewed for compliance with applicable coding, billing and documentation requirements. The individuals from the physician practice involved in these self-audits would ideally include the person in charge of billing (if the practice has such a person) and a medically trained person (e.g., registered nurse or preferably a physician (physicians can rotate in this position)). Each physician practice needs to decide for itself whether to review claims retrospectively or concurrently with the claims submission. In the Third-Party Medical Billing Compliance Program Guidance, the OIG recommended that a baseline, or "snapshot," be used to enable a practice to judge over time its progress in reducing or eliminating potential areas of vulnerability. This practice, known as "benchmarking," allows a practice to chart its compliance efforts by showing a reduction or increase in the number of claims paid and denied.

The practice's self-audits can be used to determine whether:

- Bills are accurately coded and accurately reflect the services provided (as documented in the medical records);
- Documentation is being completed correctly;
- Services or items provided are reasonable and necessary; and
- Any incentives for unnecessary services exist.

A baseline audit examines the claim development and submission process, from patient intake through claim submission and payment, and identifies elements within this process that may contribute to non-compliance or that may need to be the focus for improving execution. [7] This audit will establish a consistent methodology for selecting and examining records, and this methodology will then serve as a basis for future audits.

There are many ways to conduct a baseline audit. The OIG recommends that claims/services that were submitted and paid during the initial three months after implementation of the education and

[7] See Appendix D.II. referencing the Provider Self-Disclosure Protocol for information on how to conduct a baseline audit.

training program be examined, so as to give the physician practice a benchmark against which to measure future compliance effectiveness.

Following the baseline audit, a general recommendation is that periodic audits be conducted at least once each year to ensure that the compliance program is being followed. Optimally, a randomly selected number of medical records could be reviewed to ensure that the coding was performed accurately. Although there is no set formula to how many medical records should be reviewed, a basic guide is five or more medical records per Federal payor (i.e., Medicare, Medicaid), or five to ten medical records per physician. The OIG realizes that physician practices receive reimbursement from a number of different payors, and we would encourage a physician practice's auditing/monitoring process to consist of a review of claims from all Federal payors from which the practice receives reimbursement. Of course, the larger the sample size, the larger the comfort level the physician practice will have about the results. However, the OIG is aware that this may be burdensome for some physician practices, so, at a minimum, we would encourage the physician practice to conduct a review of claims that have been reimbursed by Federal health care programs.

If problems are identified, the physician practice will need to determine whether a focused review should be conducted on a more frequent basis. When audit results reveal areas needing additional information or education of employees and physicians, the physician practice will need to analyze whether these areas should be incorporated into the training and educational system.

There are many ways to identify the claims/services from which to draw the random sample of claims to be audited. One methodology is to choose a random sample of claims/services from either all of the claims/services a physician has received reimbursement for or all claims/services from a particular payor. Another method is to identify risk areas or potential billing vulnerabilities. The codes associated with these risk areas may become the universe of claims/services from which to select the sample. The OIG recommends that the physician practice evaluate claims/services selected to determine if the codes billed and reimbursed were accurately ordered, performed, and reasonable and necessary for the treatment of the patient.

One of the most important components of a successful compliance audit protocol is an appropriate response when the physician practice identifies a problem. This action should be taken as soon as possible after the date the problem is identified. The specific action a physician practice takes should depend on the circumstances of the situation. In some cases, the response can be as straight forward as generating a repayment with appropriate explanation to Medicare or the appropriate payor from which the overpayment was received. In others, the physician practice may want to consult with a coding/billing expert to determine the next best course of action. There is no boilerplate solution to how to handle problems that are identified.

It is a good business practice to create a system to address how physician practices will respond to and report potential problems. In addition, preserving information relating to identification of the problem is as important as preserving information that tracks the physician practice's reaction to, and solution for, the issue.

Step Two: Establish Practice Standards and Procedures

After the internal audit identifies the practice's risk areas, the next step is to develop a method for dealing with those risk areas through the practice's standards and procedures. Written standards and procedures are a central component of any compliance program. Those standards and procedures help to reduce the prospect of erroneous claims and fraudulent activity by identifying risk areas for the practice and establishing tighter internal controls to counter those risks, while also helping to identify any aberrant billing practices. Many physician practices already have something similar to this called "practice standards" that include practice policy statements regarding patient care, personnel matters and practice standards and procedures on complying with Federal and State law.

The OIG believes that written standards and procedures can be helpful to all physician practices, regardless of size and capability. If a lack of resources to develop such standards and procedures is genuinely an issue, the OIG recommends that a physician practice focus first on those risk areas most likely to arise in its particular practice.[8] Additionally, if the physician practice works with a physician practice management company (PPMC), independent practice association (IPA), physician-hospital organization, management services organization (MSO) or third-party billing company, the

[8] Physician practices with laboratories or arrangements with third-party billing companies can also check the risk areas included in the OIG compliance program guidance for those industries.

practice can incorporate the compliance standards and procedures of those entities, if appropriate, into its own standards and procedures. Many physician practices have found that the adoption of a third party's compliance standards and procedures, as appropriate, has many benefits and the result is a consistent set of standards and procedures for a community of physicians as well as having just one entity that can then monitor and refine the process as needed. This sharing of compliance responsibilities assists physician practices in rural areas that do not have the staff to perform these functions, but do belong to a group that does have the resources. Physician practices using another entity's compliance materials will need to tailor those materials to the physician practice where they will be applied.

Physician practices that do not have standards or procedures in place can develop them by: (1) Developing a written standards and procedures manual; and (2) updating clinical forms periodically to make sure they facilitate and encourage clear and complete documentation of patient care. A practice's standards could also identify the clinical protocol(s), pathway(s), and other treatment guidelines followed by the practice.

Creating a resource manual from publicly available information may be a cost-effective approach for developing additional standards and procedures. For example, the practice can develop a "binder" that contains the practice's written standards and procedures, relevant HCFA directives and carrier bulletins, and summaries of informative OIG documents (e.g., Special Fraud Alerts, Advisory Opinions, inspection and audit reports).[9] If the practice chooses to adopt this idea, the binder should be updated as appropriate and located in a readily accessible location.

If updates to the standards and procedures are necessary, those updates should be communicated to employees to keep them informed regarding the practice's operations. New employees can be made aware of the standards and procedures when hired and can be trained on their contents as part of their orientation to the practice. The OIG recommends that the communication of updates and train-

---

[9] The OIG and HCFA are working to compile a list of basic documents issued by both entities that could be included in such a binder. We expect to complete this list later this fall, and will post it on the OIG and HCFA web sites, as well as publicize this list to physician organizations and representatives (information on how to contact the OIG is contained in Footnote 3; HCFA information can be obtained at www.hcfa.gov/medlearn or by calling 1–800-MEDICARE).

ing of new employees occur as soon as possible after either the issuance of a new update or the hiring of a new employee.

1. Specific Risk Areas

The OIG recognizes that many physician practices may not have in place standards and procedures to prevent erroneous or fraudulent conduct in their practices. In order to develop standards and procedures, the physician practice may consider what types of fraud and abuse related topics need to be addressed based on its specific needs. One of the most important things in making that determination is a listing of risk areas where the practice may be vulnerable.

To assist physician practices in performing this initial assessment, the OIG has developed a list of four potential risk areas affecting physician practices. These risk areas include: (a) Coding and billing; (b) reasonable and necessary services; (c) documentation; and (d) improper inducements, kickbacks and self-referrals. This list of risk areas is not exhaustive, or all-encompassing. Rather, it should be viewed as a starting point for an internal review of potential vulnerabilities within the physician practice.[10] The objective of such an assessment is to ensure that key personnel in the physician practice are aware of these major risk areas and that steps are taken to minimize, to the extent possible, the types of problems identified. While there are many ways to accomplish this objective, clear written standards and procedures that are communicated to all employees are important to ensure the effectiveness of a compliance program. Specifically, the following are discussions of risk areas for physician practices:[11]

a. Coding and Billing. A major part of any physician practice's compliance program is the identification of risk areas associated with coding and billing. The following risk areas associated with billing have been among the most frequent subjects of investigations and audits by the OIG:

---

[10] Physician practices seeking additional guidance on potential risk areas can review the OIG's Work Plan to identify vulnerabilities and risk areas on which the OIG will focus in the future. In addition, physician practices can also review the OIG's semiannual reports, which identify program vulnerabilities and risk areas that the OIG has targeted during the preceding six months. All of these documents are available on the OIG's webpage at http://www.hhs.gov/oig.

[11] Appendix A of this document lists additional risk areas that a physician practice may want to review and incorporate into their practice standards and procedures.

- Billing for items or services not rendered or not provided as claimed; [12]
- Submitting claims for equipment, medical supplies and services that are not reasonable and necessary; [13]
- Double billing resulting in duplicate payment; [14]
- Billing for non-covered services as if covered; [15]
- Knowing misuse of provider identification numbers, which results in improper billing; [16]
- Unbundling (billing for each component of the service instead of billing or using an all-inclusive code); [17]

---

[12] For example, Dr. X, an ophthalmologist, billed for laser surgery he did not perform. As one element of proof, he did not even have laser equipment or access to such equipment at the place of service designated on the claim form where he performed the surgery.

[13] Billing for services, supplies and equipment that are not reasonable and necessary involves seeking reimbursement for a service that is not warranted by a patient's documented medical condition. See 42 U.S.C. 1395i (a)(1)(A) ("no payment may be made under part A or part B [of Medicare] for any expenses incurred for items or services which * * * are not reasonable and necessary for the diagnosis or treatment of illness or injury or to improve the functioning of the malformed body member"). See also Appendix A for further discussion on this topic.

[14] Double billing occurs when a physician bills for the same item or service more than once or another party billed the Federal health care program for an item or service also billed by the physician. Although duplicate billing can occur due to simple error, the knowing submission of duplicate claims — which is sometimes evidenced by systematic or repeated double billing — can create liability under criminal, civil, and/or administrative law.

[15] For example, Dr. Y bills Medicare using a covered office visit code when the actual service was a non-covered annual physical. Physician practices should remember that "necessary" does not always constitute "covered" and that this example is a misrepresentation of services to the Federal health care programs.

[16] An example of this is when the practice bills for a service performed by Dr. B, who has not yet been issued a Medicare provider number, using Dr. A's Medicare provider number. Physician practices need to bill using the correct Medicare provider number, even if that means delaying billing until the physician receives his/her provider number.

[17] Unbundling is the practice of a physician billing for multiple components of a service that must be included in a single fee. For example, if dressings and instruments are included in a fee for a minor procedure, the provider may not also bill separately for the dressings and instruments.

- Failure to properly use coding modifiers;[18]
- Clustering;[19] and
- Upcoding the level of service provided.[20]

The physician practice written standards and procedures concerning proper coding reflect the current reimbursement principles set forth in applicable statutes, regulations[21] and Federal, State or private payor health care program requirements and should be developed in tandem with coding and billing standards used in the physician practice. Furthermore, written standards and procedures should ensure that coding and billing are based on medical record documentation. Particular attention should be paid to issues of appropriate diagnosis codes and individual Medicare Part B claims (including documentation guidelines for evaluation and manage-

[18] A modifier, as defined by the CPT-4 manual, provides the means by which a physician practice can indicate a service or procedure that has been performed has been altered by some specific circumstance, but not changed in its definition or code. Assuming the modifier is used correctly and appropriately, this specificity provides the justification for payment for those services. For correct use of modifiers, the physician practice should reference the appropriate sections of the Medicare Provider Manual. See *Medicare Carrier Manual* Section 4630. For general information on the correct use of modifiers, a physician practice can consult the National Correct Coding Initiative (NCCI). See Appendix F for information on how to download the NCCI edits. The NCCI coding edits are updated on a quarterly basis and are used to process claims and determine payments to physicians.

[19] This is the practice of coding/charging one or two middle levels of service codes exclusively, under the philosophy that some will be higher, some lower, and the charges will average out over an extended period (in reality, this overcharges some patients while undercharging others).

[20] Upcoding is billing for a more expensive service than the one actually performed. For example, Dr. X intentionally bills at a higher evaluation and management (E&M) code than what he actually renders to the patient.

[21] The official coding guidelines are promulgated by HCFA, the National Center for Health Statistics, the American Hospital Association, the American Medical Association and the American Health Information Management Association. See International Classification of Diseases, 9th Revision, Clinical Modification (ICD-9 CM)(and its successors); 1998 Health Care Financing Administration Common Procedure Coding System (HCPCS) (and its successors); and Physicians' CPT. In addition, there are specialized coding systems for specific segments of the health care industry. Among these are ADA (for dental procedures), DSM IV (psychiatric health benefits) and DMERCs (for durable medical equipment, prosthetics, orthotics and supplies).

ment services).[22] A physician practice can also institute a policy that the coder and/or physician review all rejected claims pertaining to diagnosis and procedure codes. This step can facilitate a reduction in similar errors.

b. Reasonable and Necessary Services. A practice's compliance program may provide guidance that claims are to be submitted only for services that the physician practice finds to be reasonable and necessary in the particular case. The OIG recognizes that physicians should be able to order any tests, including screening tests, they believe are appropriate for the treatment of their patients. However, a physician practice should be aware that Medicare will only pay for services that meet the Medicare definition of reasonable and necessary.[23]

Medicare (and many insurance plans) may deny payment for a service that is not reasonable and necessary according to the Medicare reimbursement rules. Thus, when a physician provides services to a Medicare beneficiary, he or she should only bill those services that meet the Medicare standard of being reasonable and necessary for the diagnosis and treatment of a patient. A physician practice can bill in order to receive a denial for services, but only if the denial is needed for reimbursement from the secondary payor. Upon request, the physician practice should be able to provide documentation, such as a patient's medical records and physician's orders, to support the appropriateness of a service that the physician has provided.

c. Documentation. Timely, accurate and complete documentation is important to clinical patient care. This same documentation serves as a second function when a bill is submitted for payment, namely, as verification that the bill is accurate as submitted. Therefore, one of the most important physician practice compliance issues is the appropriate documentation of diagnosis and treatment. Physician documentation is necessary to determine the appropriate medical treatment for the patient and is the basis for coding and billing determinations. Thorough and accurate documentation also

---

[22] The failure of a physician practice to: (i) document items and services rendered; and (ii) properly submit the corresponding claims for reimbursement is a major area of potential erroneous or fraudulent conduct involving Federal health care programs. The OIG has undertaken numerous audits, investigations, inspections and national enforcement initiatives in these areas.

[23] "* * * for the diagnosis or treatment of illness or injury or to improve the functioning of a malformed body member." 42 U.S.C. 1395y(a)(1)(A).

helps to ensure accurate recording and timely transmission of information.

i. Medical Record Documentation. In addition to facilitating high quality patient care, a properly documented medical record verifies and documents precisely what services were actually provided. The medical record may be used to validate: (a) The site of the service; (b) the appropriateness of the services provided; (c) the accuracy of the billing; and (d) the identity of the care giver (service provider). Examples of internal documentation guidelines a practice might use to ensure accurate medical record documentation include the following: [24]

- The medical record is complete and legible;
- The documentation of each patient encounter includes the reason for the encounter; any relevant history; physical examination findings; prior diagnostic test results; assessment, clinical impression, or diagnosis; plan of care; and date and legible identity of the observer;
- If not documented, the rationale for ordering diagnostic and other ancillary services can be easily inferred by an independent reviewer or third party who has appropriate medical training;
- CPT and ICD-9-CM codes used for claims submission are supported by documentation and the medical record; and
- Appropriate health risk factors are identified. The patient's progress, his or her response to, and any changes in, treatment, and any revision in diagnosis is documented.

The CPT and ICD-9-CM codes reported on the health insurance claims form should be supported by documentation in the medical record and the medical chart should contain all necessary information. Additionally, HCFA and the local carriers should be able to determine the person who provided the services. These issues can be the root of investigations of inappropriate or erroneous conduct, and have been identified by HCFA and the OIG as a leading cause of improper payments.

---

[24] For additional information on proper documentation, physician practices should also reference the *Documentation Guidelines for Evaluation and Management Services*, published by HCFA. Currently, physicians may document based on the 1995 or 1997 E&M Guidelines, whichever is most advantageous to the physician. A new set of draft guidelines were announced in June 2000, and are undergoing pilot testing and revision, but are not in current use.

One method for improving quality in documentation is for a physician practice to compare the practice's claim denial rate to the rates of other practices in the same specialty to the extent that the practice can obtain that information from the carrier. Physician coding and diagnosis distribution can be compared for each physician within the same specialty to identify variances.

ii. HCFA 1500 Form. Another documentation area for physician practices to monitor closely is the proper completion of the HCFA 1500 form. The following practices will help ensure that the form has been properly completed:

- Link the diagnosis code with the reason for the visit or service;
- Use modifiers appropriately; and
- Provide Medicare with all information about a beneficiary's other insurance coverage under the Medicare Secondary Payor (MSP) policy, if the practice is aware of a beneficiary's additional coverage.

d. Improper Inducements, Kickbacks and Self-Referrals. A physician practice would be well advised to have standards and procedures that encourage compliance with the anti-kickback statute[25] and the physician self-referral law.[26] Remuneration for referrals is illegal because it can distort medical decision-making, cause overutilization of services or supplies, increase costs to Federal health care programs, and result in unfair competition by shutting out competitors who are unwilling to pay for referrals. Remuneration for referrals can also affect the quality of patient care by encouraging physicians to order services or supplies based on

[25] The anti-kickback statute provides criminal penalties for individuals and entities that knowingly offer, pay, solicit, or receive bribes or kickbacks or other remuneration in order to induce business reimbursable by Federal health care programs. See 42 U.S.C. 1320a-7b(b). Civil penalties, exclusion from participation in the Federal health care programs, and civil False Claims Act liability may also result from a violation of the prohibition. See 42 U.S.C. 1320a-7a(a)(5), 42 U.S.C. 1320a-7(b)(7), and 31 U.S.C. 3729–3733.

[26] The physician self-referral law, 42 U.S.C. 1395nn (also known as the "Stark law"), prohibits a physician from making a referral to an entity with which the physician or any member of the physician's immediate family has a financial relationship if the referral is for the furnishing of designated health services, unless the financial relationship fits into an exception set forth in the statute or implementing regulations.

profit rather than the patients' best medical interests.[27]

In particular, arrangements with hospitals, hospices, nursing facilities, home health agencies, durable medical equipment suppliers, pharmaceutical manufacturers and vendors are areas of potential concern. In general the anti-kickback statute prohibits knowingly and willfully giving or receiving anything of value to induce referrals of Federal health care program business. It is generally recommended that all business arrangements wherein physician practices refer business to, or order services or items from, an outside entity should be on a fair market value basis.[28] Whenever a physician practice intends to enter into a business arrangement that involves making referrals, the arrangement should be reviewed by legal counsel familiar with the anti-kickback statute and physician self-referral statute.

In addition to developing standards and procedures to address arrangements with other health care providers and suppliers, physician practices should also consider implementing measures to avoid offering inappropriate inducements to patients.[29] Examples of such inducements include routinely waiving coinsurance or deductible amounts without a good faith determination that the patient is in financial need or failing to make reasonable efforts to collect the cost-sharing amount.[30]

Possible risk factors relating to this risk area that could be addressed in the practice's standards and procedures include:

- Financial arrangements with outside entities to whom the practice may refer Federal health care program business;[31]

---

27 See Appendix B for additional information on the anti-kickback statute.

28 The OIG's definition of "fair market value" excludes any value attributable to referrals of Federal program business or the ability to influence the flow of such business. See 42 U.S.C. 1395nn(h)(3). Adhering to the rule of keeping business arrangements at fair market value is not a guarantee of legality, but is a highly useful general rule.

29 See 42 U.S.C. 1320a-7a(a)(5).

30 In the OIG Special Fraud Alert "Routine Waiver of Part B Co-payments/Deductibles" (May 1991), the OIG describes several reasons why routine waivers of these cost-sharing amounts pose concerns. The Alert sets forth the circumstances under which it may be appropriate to waive these amounts. See also 42 U.S.C. 1320a-7a(a)(5).

31 All physician contracts and agreements with parties in a position to influence Federal health care program business or to whom the doctor is in such a position to influence should be reviewed to avoid violation of the

- Joint ventures with entities supplying goods or services to the physician practice or its patients;[32]
- Consulting contracts or medical directorships;
- Office and equipment leases with entities to which the physician refers; and
- Soliciting, accepting or offering any gift or gratuity of more than nominal value to or from those who may benefit from a physician practice's referral of Federal health care program business.[33]

In order to keep current with this area of the law, a physician practice may obtain copies, available on the OIG web site or in hard copy from the OIG, of all relevant OIG Special Fraud Alerts and Advisory Opinions that address the application of the anti-kickback and physician self-referral laws to ensure that the standards and procedures reflect current positions and opinions.

2. Retention of Records

In light of the documentation requirements faced by physician practices, it would be to the practice's benefit if its standards and procedures contained a section on the retention of compliance, business and medical records. These records primarily include documents relating to patient care and the practice's business activities. A physician practice's designated compliance contact could keep an updated binder or record of these documents, including information relating to compliance activities. The primary compliance documents that a practice would want to retain are those that relate to educational activities, internal investigations and internal audit

---

anti-kickback, self-referral, and other relevant Federal and State laws. The OIG has published safe harbors that define practices not subject to the anti-kickback statute, because such arrangements would be unlikely to result in fraud or abuse. Failure to comply with a safe harbor provision does not make an arrangement per se illegal. Rather, the safe harbors set forth specific conditions that, if fully met, would assure the entities involved of not being prosecuted or sanctioned for the arrangement qualifying for the safe harbor. One such safe harbor applies to personal services contracts. See 42 CFR 1001.952(d).

[32] See OIG Special Fraud Alert "Joint Venture Arrangements" (August 1989) available on the OIG web site at http://www.hhs.gov/ oig. See also OIG Advisory Opinion 97–5.

[33] Physician practices should establish clear standards and procedures governing gift-giving because such exchanges may be viewed as inducements to influence business decisions.

results. We suggest that particular attention should be paid to documenting investigations of potential violations uncovered by the compliance program and the resulting remedial action. Although there is no requirement that the practice retain its compliance records, having all the relevant documentation relating to the practice's compliance efforts or handling of a particular problem can benefit the practice should it ever be questioned regarding those activities.

Physician practices that implement a compliance program might also want to provide for the development and implementation of a records retention system. This system would establish standards and procedures regarding the creation, distribution, retention, and destruction of documents. If the practice decides to design a record system, privacy concerns and Federal or State regulatory requirements should be taken into consideration. [34]

While conducting its compliance activities, as well as its daily operations, a physician practice would be well advised, to the extent it is possible, to document its efforts to comply with applicable Federal health care program requirements. For example, if a physician practice requests advice from a Government agency (including a Medicare carrier) charged with administering a Federal health care program, it is to the benefit of the practice to document and retain a record of the request and any written or oral response (or nonresponse). This step is extremely important if the practice intends to rely on that response to guide it in future decisions, actions, or claim reimbursement requests or appeals.

In short, it is in the best interest of all physician practices, regardless of size, to have procedures to create and retain appropriate documentation. The following record retention guidelines are suggested:

The length of time that a practice's records are to be retained can be specified in the physician practice's standards and procedures (Federal and State statutes should be consulted for specific time frames, if applicable);

---

[34] There are various Federal regulations governing the privacy of patient records and the retention of certain types of patient records. Many states also have record retention statutes. Practices should check with their state medical society and/or affiliated professional association for assistance in ascertaining these requirements for their particular specialty and location.

Medical records (if in the possession of the physician practice) need to be secured against loss, destruction, unauthorized access, unauthorized reproduction, corruption, or damage; and

Standards and procedures can stipulate the disposition of medical records in the event the practice is sold or closed.

Step Three: Designation of a Compliance Officer/Contact(s)

After the audits have been completed and the risk areas identified, ideally one member of the physician practice staff needs to accept the responsibility of developing a corrective action plan, if necessary, and oversee the practice's adherence to that plan. This person can either be in charge of all compliance activities for the practice or play a limited role merely to resolve the current issue. In a formalized institutional compliance program there is a compliance officer who is responsible for overseeing the implementation and day-to-day operations of the compliance program. However, the resource constraints of physician practices make it so that it is often impossible to designate one person to be in charge of compliance functions.

It is acceptable for a physician practice to designate more than one employee with compliance monitoring responsibility. In lieu of having a designated compliance officer, the physician practice could instead describe in its standards and procedures the compliance functions for which designated employees, known as "compliance contacts," would be responsible. For example, one employee could be responsible for preparing written standards and procedures, while another could be responsible for conducting or arranging for periodic audits and ensuring that billing questions are answered. Therefore, the compliance-related responsibilities of the designated person or persons may be only a portion of his or her duties.

Another possibility is that one individual could serve as compliance officer for more than one entity. In situations where staffing limitations mandate that the practice cannot afford to designate a person(s) to oversee compliance activities, the practice could outsource all or part of the functions of a compliance officer to a third party, such as a consultant, PPMC, MSO, IPA or third-party billing company. However, if this role is outsourced, it is beneficial for the compliance officer to have sufficient interaction with the physician practice to be able to effectively understand the inner workings of the practice. For example, consultants that are not in close geographic proximity to a practice may not be effective compliance officers for the practice.

One suggestion for how to maintain continual interaction is for the practice to designate someone to serve as a liaison with the outsourced compliance officer. This would help ensure a strong tie between the compliance officer and the practice's daily operations. Outsourced compliance officers, who spend most of their time offsite, have certain limitations that a physician practice should consider before making such a critical decision. These limitations can include lack of understanding as to the inner workings of the practice, accessibility and possible conflicts of interest when one compliance officer is serving several practices.

If the physician practice decides to designate a particular person (s) to oversee all compliance activities, not just those in conjunction with the audit-related issue, the following is a list of suggested duties that the practice may want to assign to that person(s):

- Overseeing and monitoring the implementation of the compliance program;
- Establishing methods, such as periodic audits, to improve the practice's efficiency and quality of services, and to reduce the practice's vulnerability to fraud and abuse;
- Periodically revising the compliance program in light of changes in the needs of the practice or changes in the law and in the standards and procedures of Government and private payor health plans;
- Developing, coordinating and participating in a training program that focuses on the components of the compliance program, and seeks to ensure that training materials are appropriate;
- Ensuring that the HHS-OIG's List of Excluded Individuals and Entities, and the General Services Administration's (GSA's) List of Parties Debarred from Federal Programs have been checked with respect to all employees, medical staff and independent contractors;[35] and

---

[35] The HHS-OIG "List of Excluded Individuals/Entities" provides information to health care providers, patients, and others regarding individuals and entities that are excluded from participation in Federal health care programs. This report, in both an on-line searchable and downloadable database, can be located on the Internet at http://www.hhs.gov/oig. The OIG sanction information is readily available to users in two formats on over 15,000 individuals and entities currently excluded from program participa-

- Investigating any report or allegation concerning possible unethical or improper business practices, and monitoring subsequent corrective action and/or compliance.

Each physician practice needs to assess its own practice situation and determine what best suits that practice in terms of compliance oversight.

Step Four: Conducting Appropriate Training and Education

Education is an important part of any compliance program and is the logical next step after problems have been identified and the practice has designated a person to oversee educational training. Ideally, education programs will be tailored to the physician practice's needs, specialty and size and will include both compliance and specific training.

There are three basic steps for setting up educational objectives:

- Determining who needs training (both in coding and billing and in compliance);
- Determining the type of training that best suits the practice's needs (e.g., seminars, in-service training, self-study or other programs); and
- Determining when and how often education is needed and how much each person should receive.

Training may be accomplished through a variety of means, including in-person training sessions (i.e., either on site or at outside seminars), distribution of newsletters,[36] or even a readily accessible office bulletin board. Regardless of the training modality used, a physician practice should ensure that the necessary education is communicated effectively and that the practice's employees come away from the training with a better understanding of the issues covered.

---

tion through action taken by the OIG. The on-line searchable database allows users to obtain information regarding excluded individuals and entities sorted by: (1) The legal bases for exclusions; (2) the types of individuals and entities excluded by the OIG; and (3) the States where excluded individuals reside or entities do business. In addition, the General Services Administration maintains a monthly listing of debarred contractors, "List of Parties Debarred from Federal Programs," at http:// www.arnet.gov/epls.

[36] HCFA also offers free online training for general fraud and abuse issues at http://www.hcfa.gov/medlearn. See Appendix F for additional information.

1. Compliance Training

Under the direction of the designated compliance officer/contact, both initial and recurrent training in compliance is advisable, both with respect to the compliance program itself and applicable statutes and regulations. Suggestions for items to include in compliance training are: The operation and importance of the compliance program; the consequences of violating the standards and procedures set forth in the program; and the role of each employee in the operation of the compliance program.

There are two goals a practice should strive for when conducting compliance training: (1) All employees will receive training on how to perform their jobs in compliance with the standards of the practice and any applicable regulations; and (2) each employee will understand that compliance is a condition of continued employment. Compliance training focuses on explaining why the practice is developing and establishing a compliance program. The training should emphasize that following the standards and procedures will not get a practice employee in trouble, but violating the standards and procedures may subject the employee to disciplinary measures. It is advisable that new employees be trained on the compliance program as soon as possible after their start date and employees should receive refresher training on an annual basis or as appropriate.

2. Coding and Billing Training

Coding and billing training on the Federal health care program requirements may be necessary for certain members of the physician practice staff depending on their respective responsibilities. The OIG understands that most physician practices do not employ a professional coder and that the physician is often primarily responsible for all coding and billing. However, it is in the practice's best interest to ensure that individuals who are directly involved with billing, coding or other aspects of the Federal health care programs receive extensive education specific to that individual's responsibilities. Some examples of items that could be covered in coding and billing training include:

- Coding requirements;
- Claim development and submission processes;
- Signing a form for a physician without the physician's authorization;
- Proper documentation of services rendered;

- Proper billing standards and procedures and submission of accurate bills for services or items rendered to Federal health care program beneficiaries; and
- The legal sanctions for submitting deliberately false or reckless billings.

3. Format of the Training Program

Training may be conducted either in-house or by an outside source.[37] Training at outside seminars, instead of internal programs and in-service sessions, may be an effective way to achieve the practice's training goals. In fact, many community colleges offer certificate or associate degree programs in billing and coding, and professional associations provide various kinds of continuing education and certification programs. Many carriers also offer billing training.

The physician practice may work with its third-party billing company, if one is used, to ensure that documentation is of a level that is adequate for the billing company to submit accurate claims on behalf of the physician practice. If it is not, these problem areas should also be covered in the training. In addition to the billing training, it is advisable for physician practices to maintain updated ICD-9, HCPCS and CPT manuals (in addition to the carrier bulletins construing those sources) and make them available to all employees involved in the billing process. Physician practices can also provide a source of continuous updates on current billing standards and procedures by making publications or Government documents that describe current billing policies available to its employees.[38]

Physician practices do not have to provide separate education and training programs for the compliance and coding and billing training. All in-service training and continuing education can integrate

[37] As noted earlier in this guidance, another way for physician practices to receive training is for the physicians and/or the employees of the practice to attend training programs offered by outside entities, such as a hospital, a local medical society or a carrier. This sort of collaborative effort is an excellent way for the practice to meet the desired training objective without having to expend the resources to develop and implement in-house training.

[38] Some publications, such as OIG's Special Fraud Alerts, audit and inspection reports, and Advisory Opinions are readily available from the OIG and can provide a basis for educational courses and programs for physician practice employees. See Appendix F for a partial listing of these documents. See Footnote 3 for information on how to obtain copies of these documents.

compliance issues, as well as other core values adopted by the practice, such as quality improvement and improved patient service, into their curriculum.

4. Continuing Education on Compliance Issues

There is no set formula for determining how often training sessions should occur. The OIG recommends that there be at least an annual training program for all individuals involved in the coding and billing aspects of the practice.[39] Ideally, new billing and coding employees will be trained as soon as possible after assuming their duties and will work under an experienced employee until their training has been completed.

Step Five: Responding To Detected Offenses and Developing Corrective Action Initiatives

When a practice determines it has detected a possible violation, the next step is to develop a corrective action plan and determine how to respond to the problem. Violations of a physician practice's compliance program, significant failures to comply with applicable Federal or State law, and other types of misconduct threaten a practice's status as a reliable, honest, and trustworthy provider of health care. Consequently, upon receipt of reports or reasonable indications of suspected noncompliance, it is important that the compliance contact or other practice employee look into the allegations to determine whether a significant violation of applicable law or the requirements of the compliance program has indeed occurred, and, if so, take decisive steps to correct the problem.[40] As appropriate, such

---

[39] Currently, the OIG is monitoring a significant number of corporate integrity agreements that require many of these training elements. The OIG usually requires a minimum of one hour annually for basic training in compliance areas. Additional training may be necessary for specialty fields such as claims development and billing.

[40] Instances of noncompliance must be determined on a case-by-case basis. The existence or amount of a monetary loss to a health care program is not solely determinative of whether the conduct should be investigated and reported to governmental authorities. In fact, there may be instances where there is no readily identifiable monetary loss to a health care provider, but corrective actions are still necessary to protect the integrity of the applicable program and its beneficiaries, e.g., where services required by a plan of care are not provided.

steps may involve a corrective action plan,[41] the return of any overpayments, a report to the Government,[42] and/or a referral to law enforcement authorities.

One suggestion is that the practice, in developing its compliance program, develop its own set of monitors and warning indicators. These might include: Significant changes in the number and/or types of claim rejections and/or reductions; correspondence from the carriers and insurers challenging the medical necessity or validity of claims; illogical patterns or unusual changes in the pattern of CPT-4, HCPCS or ICD-9 code utilization; and high volumes of unusual charge or payment adjustment transactions. If any of these warning indicators become apparent, then it is recommended that the practice follow up on the issues. Subsequently, as appropriate, the compliance procedures of the practice may need to be changed to prevent the problem from recurring.

For potential criminal violations, a physician practice would be well advised in its compliance program procedures to include steps for prompt referral or disclosure to an appropriate Government authority or law enforcement agency. In regard to overpayment issues, it is advised that the physician practice take appropriate corrective action, including prompt identification and repayment of any overpayment to the affected payor.

It is also recommended that the compliance program provide for a full internal assessment of all reports of detected violations. If the physician practice ignores reports of possible fraudulent activity, it is undermining the very purpose it hoped to achieve by implementing a compliance program.

It is advised that the compliance program standards and procedures include provisions to ensure that a violation is not compounded once discovered. In instances involving individual mis-

---

[41] The physician practice may seek advice from its legal counsel to determine the extent of the practice's liability and to plan the appropriate course of action.

[42] The OIG has established a Provider Self-Disclosure Protocol that encourages providers to voluntarily report suspected fraud. The concept of voluntary self-disclosure is premised on a recognition that the Government alone cannot protect the integrity of the Medicare and other Federal health care programs. Health care providers must be willing to police themselves, correct underlying problems, and work with the Government to resolve these matters. The Provider Self-Disclosure Protocol can be located on the OIG's web site at: www.hhs.gov/oig. See Appendix D for further information on the Provider Self-Disclosure Protocol.

conduct, the standards and procedures might also advise as to whether the individuals involved in the violation either be retrained, disciplined, or, if appropriate, terminated. The physician practice may also prevent the compounding of the violation by conducting a review of all confirmed violations, and, if appropriate, self-reporting the violations to the applicable authority.

The physician practice may consider the fact that if a violation occurred and was not detected, its compliance program may require modification. Physician practices that detect violations could analyze the situation to determine whether a flaw in their compliance program failed to anticipate the detected problem, or whether the compliance program's procedures failed to prevent the violation. In any event, it is prudent, even absent the detection of any violations, for physician practices to periodically review and modify their compliance programs.

Step Six: Developing Open Lines of Communication

In order to prevent problems from occurring and to have a frank discussion of why the problem happened in the first place, physician practices need to have open lines of communication. Especially in a smaller practice, an open line of communication is an integral part of implementing a compliance program. Guidance previously issued by the OIG has encouraged the use of several forms of communication between the compliance officer/committee and provider personnel, many of which focus on formal processes and are more costly to implement (e.g., hotlines and e-mail). However, the OIG recognizes that the nature of some physician practices is not as conducive to implementing these types of measures. The nature of a small physician practice dictates that such communication and information exchanges need to be conducted through a less formalized process than that which has been envisioned by prior OIG guidance.

In the small physician practice setting, the communication element may be met by implementing a clear "open door" policy between the physicians and compliance personnel and practice employees. This policy can be implemented in conjunction with less formal communication techniques, such as conspicuous notices posted in common areas and/or the development and placement of a compliance bulletin board where everyone in the practice can receive up-to-date compliance information.[43]

A compliance program's system for meaningful and open communication can include the following:

- The requirement that employees report conduct that a reasonable person would, in good faith, believe to be erroneous or fraudulent;
- The creation of a user-friendly process (such as an anonymous drop box for larger practices) for effectively reporting erroneous or fraudulent conduct;
- Provisions in the standards and procedures that state that a failure to report erroneous or fraudulent conduct is a violation of the compliance program;
- The development of a simple and readily accessible procedure to process reports of erroneous or fraudulent conduct;
- If a billing company is used, communication to and from the billing company's compliance officer/contact and other responsible staff to coordinate billing and compliance activities of the practice and the billing company, respectively. Communication can include, as appropriate, lists of reported or identified concerns, initiation and the results of internal assessments, training needs, regulatory changes, and other operational and compliance matters;
- The utilization of a process that maintains the anonymity of the persons involved in the reported possible erroneous or fraudulent conduct and the person reporting the concern; and
- Provisions in the standards and procedures that there will be no retribution for reporting conduct that a reasonable person acting in good faith would have believed to be erroneous or fraudulent.

The OIG recognizes that protecting anonymity may not be feasible for small physician practices. However, the OIG believes all practice employees, when seeking answers to questions or reporting potential instances of erroneous or fraudulent conduct, should know to whom to turn for assistance in these matters and should be able to do so without fear of retribution. While the physician practice may strive to maintain the anonymity of an employee's identity, it also needs to make clear that there may be a point at which the individual's

[43] In addition to whatever other method of communication is being utilized, the OIG recommends that physician practices post the HHS-OIG Hotline telephone number (1–800-HHS-TIPS) in a prominent area.

identity may become known or may have to be revealed in certain instances.

Step Seven: Enforcing Disciplinary Standards Through Well-Publicized Guidelines

Finally, the last step that a physician practice may wish to take is to incorporate measures into its practice to ensure that practice employees understand the consequences if they behave in a non-compliant manner. An effective physician practice compliance program includes procedures for enforcing and disciplining individuals who violate the practice's compliance or other practice standards. Enforcement and disciplinary provisions are necessary to add credibility and integrity to a compliance program.

The OIG recommends that a physician practice's enforcement and disciplinary mechanisms ensure that violations of the practice's compliance policies will result in consistent and appropriate sanctions, including the possibility of termination, against the offending individual. At the same time, it is advisable that the practice's enforcement and disciplinary procedures be flexible enough to account for mitigating or aggravating circumstances. The procedures might also stipulate that individuals who fail to detect or report violations of the compliance program may also be subject to discipline. Disciplinary actions could include: Warnings (oral); reprimands (written); probation; demotion; temporary suspension; termination; restitution of damages; and referral for criminal prosecution. Inclusion of disciplinary guidelines in in-house training and procedure manuals is sufficient to meet the "well publicized" standard of this element.

It is suggested that any communication resulting in the finding of non-compliant conduct be documented in the compliance files by including the date of incident, name of the reporting party, name of the person responsible for taking action, and the follow-up action taken. Another suggestion is for physician practices to conduct checks to make sure all current and potential practice employees are not listed on the OIG or GSA lists of individuals excluded from participation in Federal health care or Government procurement programs.[44]

[44] See Footnote 35 for information on how to access these lists.

C. Assessing A Voluntary Compliance Program

A practice's commitment to compliance can best be assessed by the active application of compliance principles in the day-to-day operations of the practice. Compliance programs are not just written standards and procedures that sit on a shelf in the main office of a practice, but are an everyday part of the practice operations. It is by integrating the compliance program into the practice culture that the practice can best achieve maximum benefit from its compliance program.

III. Conclusion

Just as immunizations are given to patients to prevent them from becoming ill, physician practices may view the implementation of a voluntary compliance program as comparable to a form of preventive medicine for the practice. This voluntary compliance program guidance is intended to assist physician practices in developing and implementing internal controls and procedures that promote adherence to Federal health care program requirements.

As stated earlier, physician compliance programs do not need to be time or resource intensive and can be developed in a manner that best reflects the nature of each individual practice. Many of the recommendations set forth in this document are ones that many physician practices already have in place and are simply good business practices that can be adhered to with a reasonable amount of effort. By implementing an effective compliance program, appropriate for its size and resources, and making compliance principles an active part of the practice culture, a physician practice can help prevent and reduce erroneous or fraudulent conduct in its practice. These efforts can also streamline and improve the business operations within the practice and therefore innoculate itself against future problems.

Dated: September 27, 2000.
June Gibbs Brown,
Inspector General.

Appendix A: Additional Risk Areas

Appendix A describes additional risk areas that a physician practice may wish to address during the development of its compliance program. If any of the following risk areas are applicable to the practice, the practice may want to consider addressing the risk areas by incorporating them into the practice's written standards and procedures manual and addressing them in its training program.

I. Reasonable and Necessary Services

A. Local Medical Review Policy

An area of concern for physicians relating to determinations of reasonable and necessary services is the variation in local medical review policies (LMRPs) among carriers. Physicians are supposed to bill the Federal health care programs only for items and services that are reasonable and necessary. However, in order to determine whether an item or service is reasonable and necessary under Medicare guidelines, the physician must apply the appropriate LMRP.[1]

With the exception of claims that are properly coded and submitted to Medicare solely for the purpose of obtaining a written denial, physician practices are to bill the Federal health programs only for items and services that are covered. In order to determine if an item or service is covered for Medicare, a physician practice must be knowledgeable of the LMRPs applicable to its practice's jurisdiction. The practice may contact its carrier to request a copy of the pertinent LMRPs, and once the practice receives the copies, they can be incorporated into the practice's written standards and procedures manual. When the LMRP indicates that an item or service may not be covered by Medicare, the physician practice is responsible to convey this information to the patient so that the patient can make an informed decision concerning the health care services he/she may want to receive. Physician practices convey this information through Advance Beneficiary Notices (ABNs).

B. Advance Beneficiary Notices

Physicians are required to provide ABNs before they provide services that they know or believe Medicare does not consider reasonable and necessary. (The one exception to this requirement is for services that are performed pursuant to EMTALA requirements as described in section II.A). A properly executed ABN acknowledges that coverage is uncertain or yet to be determined, and stipulates that the patient promises to pay the bill if Medicare does not. Patients who are not notified before they receive such services are

[1] HCFA has recently developed a web site which, when completed by the end of the year 2000, will contain the LMRPs for each of the contractors across the country. The web site can be accessed at http://www.lmrp.net.

not responsible for payment. The ABN must be sufficient to put the patient on notice of the reasons why the physician believes that the payment may be denied. The objective is to give the patient sufficient information to allow an informed choice as to whether to pay for the service.

Accordingly, each ABN should:

I. Be in writing;

II. Identify the specific service that may be denied (procedure name and CPT/HCPC code is recommended);

III. State the specific reason why the physician believes that service may be denied; and

IV. Be signed by the patient acknowledging that the required information was provided and that the patient assumes responsibility to pay for the service.

The *Medicare Carrier's Manual* [2] provides that an ABN will not be acceptable if: (1) The patient is asked to sign a blank ABN form; or (2) the ABN is used routinely without regard to a particularized need. The routine use of ABNs is generally prohibited because the ABN must state the specific reason the physician anticipates that the specific service will not be covered.

A common risk area associated with ABNs is in regard to diagnostic tests or services. There are three steps that a physician practice can take to help ensure it is in compliance with the regulations concerning ABNs for diagnostic tests or services:

1. Determine which tests are not covered under national coverage rules;

2. Determine which tests are not covered under local coverage rules such as LMRPs (contact the practice's carrier to see if a listing has been assembled); and

3. Determine which tests are only covered for certain diagnoses.

The OIG is aware that the use of ABNs is an area where physician practices experience numerous difficulties. Practices can help to reduce problems in this area by educating their physicians and office staff on the correct use of ABNs, obtaining guidance from the carrier regarding their interpretation of whether an ABN is necessary where the service is not covered, developing a standard form for all

---

[2] The relevant manual provisions are located at *MCM*, Part III, Secs. 7300 and 7320. This section of the manual also includes the carrier's recommended form of an ABN.

diagnostic tests (most carriers have a developed model), and developing a process for handling patients who refuse to sign ABNs.

C. Physician Liability for Certifications in the Provision of Medical Equipment and Supplies and Home Health Services

In January 1999, the OIG issued a Special Fraud Alert on this topic, which is available on the OIG web site at www.hhs.gov/oig/frdalrt/index.htm. The following is a summary of the Special Fraud Alert.

The OIG issued the Special Fraud Alert to reiterate to physicians the legal and programmatic significance of physician certifications made in connection with the ordering of certain items and services for Medicare patients. In light of information obtained through OIG provider audits, the OIG deemed it necessary to remind physicians that they may be subject to criminal, civil and administrative penalties for signing a certification when they know that the information is false or for signing a certification with reckless disregard as to the truth of the information. (See Appendix B and Appendix C for more detailed information on the applicable statutes).

Medicare has conditioned payment for many items and services on a certification signed by a physician attesting that the physician has reviewed the patient's condition and has determined that an item or service is reasonable and necessary. Because Medicare primarily relies on the professional judgment of the treating physician to determine the reasonable and necessary nature of a given service or supply, it is important that physicians provide complete and accurate information on any certifications they sign. Physician certification is obtained through a variety of forms, including prescriptions, orders, and Certificates of Medical Necessity (CMNs). Two areas where physician certification as to whether an item or service is reasonable and necessary is essential and which are vulnerable to abuse are: (1) Home health services; and (2) durable medical equipment.

By signing a CMN, the physician represents that:

1. he or she is the patient's treating physician and that the information regarding the physician's address and unique physician identification number (UPIN) is correct;

2. the entire CMN, including the sections filled out by the supplier, was completed prior to the physician's signature; and

3. the information in section B relating to whether the item or service is reasonable and necessary is true, accurate, and complete to the best of the physician's knowledge.

Activities such as signing blank CMNs, signing a CMN without seeing the patient to verify the item or service is reasonable and necessary, and signing a CMN for a service that the physician knows is not reasonable and necessary are activities that can lead to criminal, civil and administrative penalties.

Ultimately, it is advised that physicians carefully review any form of certification (order, prescription or CMN) before signing it to verify that the information contained in the certification is both complete and accurate.

D. Billing for Non-covered Services as if Covered

In some instances, we are aware that physician practices submit claims for services in order to receive a denial from the carrier, thereby enabling the patient to submit the denied claim for payment to a secondary payer.

A common question relating to this risk area is: If the medical services provided are not covered under Medicare, but the secondary or supplemental insurer requires a Medicare rejection in order to cover the services, then would the original submission of the claim to Medicare be considered fraudulent? Under the applicable regulations, the OIG would not consider such submissions to be fraudulent. For example, the denial may be necessary to establish patient liability protections as stated in section 1879 of the Social Security Act (the Act) (codified at 42 U.S.C. 1395pp). As stated, Medicare denials may also be required so that the patient can seek payment from a secondary insurer. In instances where a claim is being submitted to Medicare for this purpose, the physician should indicate on the claim submission that the claim is being submitted for the purpose of receiving a denial, in order to bill a secondary insurance carrier. This step should assist carriers and prevent inadvertent payments to which the physician is not entitled.

In some instances, however, the carrier pays the claim even though the service is non-covered, and even though the physician did not intend for payment to be made. When this occurs, the physician has a responsibility to refund the amount paid and indicate that the service is not covered.

II. Physician Relationships with Hospitals

A. The Physician Role in EMTALA

The Emergency Medical Treatment and Active Labor Act (EMTALA), 42 U.S.C. 1395dd, is an area that has been receiving increasing scrutiny. The statute is intended to ensure that all patients who come to the emergency department of a hospital receive care, regardless of their insurance or ability to pay. Both hospitals and physicians need to work together to ensure compliance with the provisions of this law.

The statute imposes three fundamental requirements upon hospitals that participate in the Medicare program with regard to patients requesting emergency care. First, the hospital must conduct an appropriate medical screening examination to determine if an emergency medical condition exists.[3] Second, if the hospital determines that an emergency medical condition exists, it must either provide the treatment necessary to stabilize the emergency medical condition or comply with the statute's requirements to effect a proper transfer of a patient whose condition has not been stabilized.[4] A hospital is considered to have met this second requirement if an individual refuses the hospital's offer of additional examination or treatment, or refuses to consent to a transfer, after having been informed of the risks and benefits.[5]

If an individual's emergency medical condition has not been stabilized, the statute's third requirement is activated. A hospital may not transfer an individual with an unstable emergency medical condition unless: (1) The individual or his or her representative makes a written request for transfer to another medical facility after being informed of the risk of transfer and the transferring hospital's obligation under the statute to provide additional examination or treatment; (2) a physician has signed a certification summarizing the medical risks and benefits of a transfer and certifying that, based upon the information available at the time of transfer, the medical benefits reasonably expected from the transfer outweigh the increased risks; or (3) if a physician is not physically present when the transfer decision is made, a qualified medical person signs the certification after the physician, in consultation with the qualified medical person, has made the determination that the benefits of

---

[3] See 42 U.S.C. 1395dd(a).

[4] See 42 U.S.C. 1395dd(b)(1).

[5] See 42 U.S.C. 1395dd(b)(2) and (3).

transfer outweigh the increased risks. The physician must later countersign the certification.[6]

Physician and/or hospital misconduct may result in violations of the statute.[7] One area of particular concern is physician on-call responsibilities. Physician practices whose members serve as on-call emergency room physicians with hospitals are advised to familiarize themselves with the hospital's policies regarding on-call physicians. This can be done by reviewing the medical staff bylaws or policies and procedures of the hospital that must define the responsibility of on-call physicians to respond to, examine, and treat patients with emergency medical conditions. Physicians should also be aware of the requirement that, when medically indicated, on-call physicians must generally come to the hospital to examine the patient. The exception to this requirement is that a patient may be sent to see the on-call physician at a hospital-owned contiguous or on-campus facility to conduct or complete the medical screening examination as long as:

1. all persons with the same medical condition are moved to this location;
2. there is a bona fide medical reason to move the patient; and
3. qualified medical personnel accompany the patient.

B. Teaching Physicians

Special regulations apply to teaching physicians' billings. Regulations provide that services provided by teaching physicians in teaching settings are generally payable under the physician fee schedule only if the services are personally furnished by a physician who is not a resident or the services are furnished by a resident in the presence of a teaching physician.[8]

Unless a service falls under a specified exception, such as the Primary Care Exception,[9] the teaching physician must be present during the key portion of any service or procedure for which payment

---

[6] See 42 U.S.C. 1395dd(c)(1)(A).

[7] Hospitals and physicians, including on-call physicians, who violate the statute may face penalties that include civil fines of up to $50,000 (or not more than $25,000 in the case of a hospital with less than 100 beds) per violation, and physicians may be excluded from participation in the Federal health care programs.

[8] 42 CFR 415.150 through 415.190.

[9] 42 CFR 415.174.

is sought.[10] Physicians should ensure the following with respect to services provided in the teaching physician setting:[11]

Only services actually provided are billed;

Every physician who provides or supervises the provision of services to a patient is responsible for the correct documentation of the services that were rendered;

Every physician is responsible for assuring that in cases where the physician provides evaluation and management (E&M) services, a patient's medical record includes appropriate documentation of the applicable key components of the E&M services provided or supervised by the physician (e.g., patient history, physician examination, and medical decision making), as well as documentation to adequately reflect the procedure or portion of the services provided by the physician; and

Unless specifically excepted by regulation, every physician must document his or her presence during the key portion of any service or procedure for which payment is sought.

C. Gainsharing Arrangements and Civil Monetary Penalties for Hospital Payments to Physicians to Reduce or Limit Services to Beneficiaries

In July 1999, the OIG issued a Special Fraud Alert on this topic, which is available on the OIG web site at www.hhs.gov/oig/frdalrt/index.htm. The following is a summary of the Special Fraud Alert.

The term "gainsharing" typically refers to an arrangement in which a hospital gives a physician a percentage share of any reduction in the hospital's costs for patient care attributable in part to the physician's efforts. The civil monetary penalty (CMP) that applies to gainsharing arrangements is set forth in 42 U.S.C. 1320a-7a(b)(1). This section prohibits any hospital or critical access hospital from knowingly making a payment directly or indirectly to a physician as an inducement to reduce or limit services to Medicare or Medicaid beneficiaries under a physician's care.

It is the OIG's position that the Civil Monetary Penalties Law clearly prohibits any gainsharing arrangements that involve pay-

[10] Id.

[11] This section is not intended to be and is not a complete reference for teaching physicians. It is strongly recommended that those physicians who practice in a teaching setting consult their respective hospitals for more guidance.

ments by, or on behalf of, a hospital to physicians with clinical care responsibilities to induce a reduction or limitation of services to Medicare or Medicaid beneficiaries. However, hospitals and physicians are not prohibited from working together to reduce unnecessary hospital costs through other arrangements. For example, hospitals and physicians may enter into personal services contracts where hospitals pay physicians based on a fixed fee at fair market value for services rendered to reduce costs rather than a fee based on a share of cost savings.

D. Physician Incentive Arrangements

The OIG has identified potentially illegal practices involving the offering of incentives by entities in an effort to recruit and retain physicians. The OIG is concerned that the intent behind offering incentives to physicians may not be to recruit physicians, but instead the offer is intended as a kickback to obtain and increase patient referrals from physicians. These recruitment incentive arrangements are implicated by the Anti-Kickback Statute because they can constitute remuneration offered to induce, or in return for, the referral of business paid for by Medicare or Medicaid.

Some examples of questionable incentive arrangements are:

- Provision of free or significantly discounted billing, nursing, or other staff services.
- Payment of the cost of a physician's travel and expenses for conferences.
- Payment for a physician's services that require few, if any, substantive duties by the physician.
- Guarantees that if the physician's income fails to reach a predetermined level, the entity will supplement the remainder up to a certain amount.

III. Physician Billing Practices

A. Third-Party Billing Services

Physicians should remember that they remain responsible to the Medicare program for bills sent in the physician's name or containing the physician's signature, even if the physician had no actual knowledge of a billing impropriety. The attestation on the HCFA 1500 form, i.e., the physician's signature line, states that the physician's services were billed properly. In other words, it is no defense for the physician if the physician's billing service improperly bills Medicare.

One of the most common risk areas involving billing services deals with physician practices contracting with billing services on a percentage basis. Although percentage based billing arrangements are not illegal per se, the Office of Inspector General has a longstanding concern that such arrangements may increase the risk of intentional upcoding and similar abusive billing practices.[12]

A physician may contract with a billing service on a percentage basis. However, the billing service cannot directly receive the payment of Medicare funds into a bank account that it solely controls. Under 42 U.S.C. 1395u(b)(6), Medicare payments can only be made to either the beneficiary or a party (such as a physician) that furnished the services and accepted assignment of the beneficiary's claim. A billing service that contracts on a percentage basis does not qualify as a party that furnished services to a beneficiary, thus a billing service cannot directly receive payment of Medicare funds. According to the Medicare Carriers Manual Section 3060(A), a payment is considered to be made directly to the billing service if the service can convert the payment to its own use and control without the payment first passing through the control of the physician. For example, the billing service should not bill the claims under its own name or tax identification number. The billing service should bill claims under the physician's name and tax identification number. Nor should a billing service receive the payment of Medicare funds directly into a bank account over which the billing service maintains sole control. The Medicare payments should instead be deposited into a bank account over which the provider has signature control.

Physician practices should review the third-party medical billing guidance for additional information on third-party billing companies and the compliance risk areas associated with billing companies.

B. Billing Practices by Non-Participating Physicians

Even though nonparticipating physicians do not accept payment directly from the Medicare program, there are a number of laws that apply to the billing of Medicare beneficiaries by non-participating physicians.

---

[12] This concern is noted in Advisory Opinion No. 98–4 and also the Office of Inspector General Compliance Program Guidance for Third-Party Medical Billing Companies. Both are available on the OIG web site at http://www.hhs.gov/oig.

Limiting Charges

42 U.S.C. 1395w-4(g) prohibits a nonparticipating physician from knowingly and willfully billing or collecting on a repeated basis an actual charge for a service that is in excess of the Medicare limiting charge. For example, a nonparticipating physician may not bill a Medicare beneficiary $50 for an office visit when the Medicare limiting charge for the visit is $25. Additionally, there are numerous provisions that prohibit nonparticipating physicians from knowingly and willfully charging patients in excess of the statutory charge limitations for certain specified procedures, such as cataract surgery, mammography screening and coronary artery bypass surgery. Failure to comply with these sections can result in a fine of up to $10,000 per violation or exclusion from participation in Federal health care programs for up to 5 years.

Refund of Excess Charges

42 U.S.C. 1395w-4(g) mandates that if a nonparticipating physician collects an actual charge for a service that is in excess of the limiting charge, the physician must refund the amount collected above the limiting charge to the individual within 30 days notice of the violation. For example, if a physician collected $50 from a Medicare beneficiary for an office visit, but the limiting charge for the visit was $25, the physician must refund $25 to the beneficiary, which is the difference between the amount collected ($50) and the limiting charge ($25). Failure to comply with this requirement may result in a fine of up to $10,000 per violation or exclusion from participation in Federal health care programs for up to 5 years.

Specifically, 42 U.S.C. 1395u(l)(A)(iii) mandates that a nonparticipating physician must refund payments received from a Medicare beneficiary if it is later determined by a Peer Review Organization or a Medicare carrier that the services were not reasonable and necessary. Failure to comply with this requirement may result in a fine of up to $10,000 per violation or exclusion from participation in Federal health care programs for up to 5 years.

C. Professional Courtesy

The term "professional courtesy" is used to describe a number of analytically different practices. The traditional definition is the practice by a physician of waiving all or a part of the fee for services provided to the physician's office staff, other physicians, and/or their families. In recent times, "professional courtesy" has also come to mean the waiver of coinsurance obligations or other out-of-pocket expenses for physicians or their families (i.e., "insurance only" billing), and similar payment arrangements by hospitals or other institutions for services provided to their medical staffs or employees. While only the first of these practices is truly "professional courtesy," in the interests of clarity and completeness, we will address all three.

In general, whether a professional courtesy arrangement runs afoul of the fraud and abuse laws is determined by two factors: (i) How the recipients of the professional courtesy are selected; and (ii) how the professional courtesy is extended. If recipients are selected in a manner that directly or indirectly takes into account their ability to affect past or future referrals, the anti-kickback statute — which prohibits giving anything of value to generate Federal health care program business — may be implicated. If the professional courtesy is extended through a waiver of copayment obligations (i.e., "insurance only" billing), other statutes may be implicated, including the prohibition of inducements to beneficiaries, section 1128A(a)(5) of the Act (codified at 42 U.S.C. 1320a-7a (a)(5)). Claims submitted as a result of either practice may also implicate the civil False Claims Act.

The following are general observations about professional courtesy arrangements for physician practices to consider:

A physician's regular and consistent practice of extending professional courtesy by waiving the entire fee for services rendered to a group of persons (including employees, physicians, and/or their family members) may not implicate any of the OIG's fraud and abuse authorities so long as membership in the group receiving the courtesy is determined in a manner that does not take into account directly or indirectly any group member's ability to refer to, or otherwise generate Federal health care program business for, the physician.

A physician's regular and consistent practice of extending professional courtesy by waiving otherwise applicable copayments for services rendered to a group of persons (including employees, physicians, and/or their family members), would not implicate the anti-kickback statute so long as membership in the group is determined in a manner that does not take into account directly or indirectly any group member's ability to refer to, or otherwise generate Federal health care program business for, the physician.

Any waiver of copayment practice, including that described in the preceding bullet, does implicate section 1128A(a)(5) of the Act if the patient for whom the copayment is waived is a Federal health care program beneficiary who is not financially needy.

The legality of particular professional courtesy arrangements will turn on the specific facts presented, and, with respect to the anti-kickback statute, on the specific intent of the parties. A physician practice may wish to consult with an attorney if it is uncertain about its professional courtesy arrangements.

IV. Other Risk Areas

A. Rental of Space in Physician Offices by Persons or Entities to Which Physicians Refer

In February 2000, the OIG issued a Special Fraud Alert on this topic, which is available on the OIG web site at www.hhs.gov/oig/frdalrt/index.htm. The following is a summary of the Special Fraud Alert.

Among various relationships between physicians and labs, hospitals, home health agencies, etc., the OIG has identified potentially illegal practices involving the rental of space in a physician's office by suppliers that provide items or services to patients who are referred or sent to the supplier by the physician-landlord. An example of a suspect arrangement is the rental of physician office space by a durable medical equipment (DME) supplier in a position to benefit from referrals of the physician's patients. The OIG is concerned that in such arrangements the rental payments may be disguised kickbacks to the physician-landlord to induce referrals.

Space Rental Safe Harbor to the Anti-Kickback Statute

To avoid potentially violating the anti-kickback statute, the OIG recommends that rental agreements comply with all of the following criteria for the space rental safe harbor:

- The agreement is set out in writing and signed by the parties.
- The agreement covers all of the space rented by the parties for the term of the agreement and specifies the space covered by the agreement.
- If the agreement is intended to provide the lessee with access to the space for periodic intervals of time rather than on a full-time basis for the term of the rental agreement, the rental

agreement specifies exactly the schedule of such intervals, the precise length of each interval, and the exact rent for each interval.

- The term of the rental agreement is for not less than one year.
- The aggregate rental charge is set in advance, is consistent with fair market value, and is not determined in a manner that takes into account the volume or value of any referrals or business otherwise generated between the parties for which payment may be made in whole or in part under Medicare or a State health care program.
- The aggregate space rented does not exceed that which is reasonably necessary to accomplish the commercially reasonable business purpose of the rental.

B. Unlawful Advertising

42 U.S.C. 1320b-10 makes it unlawful for any person to advertise using the names, abbreviations, symbols, or emblems of the Social Security Administration, Health Care Financing Administration, Department of Health and Human Services, Medicare, Medicaid or any combination or variation of such words, abbreviations, symbols or emblems in a manner that such person knows or should know would convey the false impression that the advertised item is endorsed by the named entities. For instance, a physician may not place an ad in the newspaper that reads "Dr. X is a cardiologist approved by both the Medicare and Medicaid programs." A violation of this section may result in a penalty of up to $5,000 ($25,000 in the case of a broadcast or telecast) for each violation.

Appendix B: Criminal Statutes

This Appendix contains a description of criminal statutes related to fraud and abuse in the context of health care. The Appendix is not intended to be a compilation of all Federal statutes related to health care fraud and abuse. It is merely a summary of some of the more frequently cited Federal statutes.

I. Health Care Fraud (18 U.S.C. 1347)

Description of Unlawful Conduct

It is a crime to knowingly and willfully execute (or attempt to execute) a scheme to defraud any health care benefit program, or to obtain money or property from a health care benefit program through false representations. Note that this law applies not only to Federal health care programs, but to most other types of health care benefit programs as well.

Penalty for Unlawful Conduct

The penalty may include the imposition of fines, imprisonment of up to 10 years, or both. If the violation results in serious bodily injury, the prison term may be increased to a maximum of 20 years. If the violation results in death, the prison term may be expanded to include any number of years, or life imprisonment.

Examples

1. Dr. X, a chiropractor, intentionally billed Medicare for physical therapy and chiropractic treatments that he never actually rendered for the purpose of fraudulently obtaining Medicare payments.

2. Dr. X, a psychiatrist, billed Medicare, Medicaid, TRICARE, and private insurers for psychiatric services that were provided by his nurses rather than himself.

II. Theft or Embezzlement in Connection with Health Care (18 U.S.C. 669)

Description of Unlawful Conduct

It is a crime to knowingly and willfully embezzle, steal or intentionally misapply any of the assets of a health care benefit program. Note that this law applies not only to Federal health care programs, but to most other types of health care benefit programs as well.

Penalty for Unlawful Conduct

The penalty may include the imposition of a fine, imprisonment of up to 10 years, or both. If the value of the asset is $100 or less, the penalty is a fine, imprisonment of up to a year, or both.

Example

An office manager for Dr. X knowingly embezzles money from the bank account for Dr. X's practice. The bank account includes reimbursement received from the Medicare program; thus, intentional embezzlement of funds from this account is a violation of the law.

III. False Statements Relating to Health Care Matters (18 U.S.C. 1035)

Description of Unlawful Conduct

It is a crime to knowingly and willfully falsify or conceal a material fact, or make any materially false statement or use any materially false writing or document in connection with the delivery of or payment for health care benefits, items or services. Note that this law applies not only to Federal health care programs, but to most other types of health care benefit programs as well.

Penalty for Unlawful Conduct

The penalty may include the imposition of a fine, imprisonment of up to 5 years, or both.

Example

Dr. X certified on a claim form that he performed laser surgery on a Medicare beneficiary when he knew that the surgery was not actually performed on the patient.

IV. Obstruction of Criminal Investigations of Health Care Offenses (18 U.S.C. 1518)

Description of Unlawful Conduct

It is a crime to willfully prevent, obstruct, mislead, delay or attempt to prevent, obstruct, mislead, or delay the communication of records relating to a Federal health care offense to a criminal investigator. Note that this law applies not only to Federal health care programs, but to most other types of health care benefit programs as well.

Penalty for Unlawful Conduct

The penalty may include the imposition of a fine, imprisonment of up to 5 years, or both.

Examples

1. Dr. X instructs his employees to tell OIG investigators that Dr. X personally performs all treatments when, in fact, medical technicians do the majority of the treatment and Dr. X is rarely present in the office.

2. Dr. X was under investigation by the FBI for reported fraudulent billings. Dr. X altered patient records in an attempt to cover up the improprieties.

V. Mail and Wire Fraud (18 U.S.C. 1341 and 1343)

Description of Unlawful Conduct

It is a crime to use the mail, private courier, or wire service to conduct a scheme to defraud another of money or property. The term "wire services" includes the use of a telephone, fax machine or computer. Each use of a mail or wire service to further fraudulent activities is considered a separate crime. For instance, each fraudulent claim that is submitted electronically to a carrier would be considered a separate violation of the law.

Penalty for Unlawful Conduct

The penalty may include the imposition of a fine, imprisonment of up to 5 years, or both.

Examples

1. Dr. X knowingly and repeatedly submits electronic claims to the Medicare carrier for office visits that he did not actually provide to Medicare beneficiaries with the intent to obtain payments from Medicare for services he never performed.

2. Dr. X, a neurologist, knowingly submitted claims for tests that were not reasonable and necessary and intentionally upcoded office visits and electromyograms to Medicare.

VI. Criminal Penalties for Acts Involving Federal Health Care Programs (42 U.S.C. 1320a-7b)

Description of Unlawful Conduct

False Statement and Representations

It is a crime to knowingly and willfully:

(1) make, or cause to be made, false statements or representations in applying for benefits or payments under all Federal health care programs;

(2) make, or cause to be made, any false statement or representation for use in determining rights to such benefit or payment;

(3) conceal any event affecting an individual's initial or continued right to receive a benefit or payment with the intent to fraudulently receive the benefit or payment either in an amount or quantity greater than that which is due or authorized;

(4) convert a benefit or payment to a use other than for the use and benefit of the person for whom it was intended;

(5) present, or cause to be presented, a claim for a physician's service when the service was not furnished by a licensed physician;

(6) for a fee, counsel an individual to dispose of assets in order to become eligible for medical assistance under a State health program, if disposing of the assets results in the imposition of an ineligibility period for the individual.

Anti-Kickback Statute

It is a crime to knowingly and willfully solicit, receive, offer, or pay remuneration of any kind (e.g., money, goods, services):

for the referral of an individual to another for the purpose of supplying items or services that are covered by a Federal health care program; or

for purchasing, leasing, ordering, or arranging for any good, facility, service, or item that is covered by a Federal health care program.

There are a number of limited exceptions to the law, also known as "safe harbors," which provide immunity from criminal prosecution and which are described in greater detail in the statute and related regulations (found at 42 CFR 1001.952 and www.hhs.gov/ oig/ak). Current safe harbors include:

- investment interests;
- space rental;
- equipment rental;
- personal services and management contracts;
- sale of practice;
- referral services;
- warranties;
- discounts;
- employment relationships;
- waiver of Part A co-insurance and deductible amounts;
- group purchasing organizations;
- increased coverage or reduced cost sharing under a risk-basis or prepaid plan; and
- charge reduction agreements with health plans.

Penalty for Unlawful Conduct

The penalty may include the imposition of a fine of up to $25,000, imprisonment of up to 5 years, or both. In addition, the provider can be excluded from participation in Federal health care programs. The regulations defining the aggravating and mitigating circumstances that must be reviewed by the OIG in making an exclusion determination are set forth in 42 CFR part 1001.

Examples

1. Dr. X accepted payments to sign Certificates of Medical Necessity for durable medical equipment for patients she never examined.
2. Home Health Agency disguises referral fees as salaries by paying referring physician Dr. X for services Dr. X never rendered to the Medicare beneficiaries or by paying Dr. X a sum in excess of fair market value for the services he rendered to the Medicare beneficiaries.

Appendix C: Civil and Administrative Statutes

This Appendix contains a description of civil and administrative statutes related to fraud and abuse in the context of health care. The Appendix is not intended to be a compilation of all federal statutes related to health care fraud and abuse. It is merely a summary of some of the more frequently cited Federal statutes.

I. The False Claims Act (31 U.S.C. 3729–3733)

Description of Unlawful Conduct

This is the law most often used to bring a case against a health care provider for the submission of false claims to a Federal health care program. The False Claims Act prohibits knowingly presenting (or causing to be presented) to the Federal Government a false or fraudulent claim for payment or approval. Additionally, it prohibits knowingly making or using (or causing to be made or used) a false record or statement to get a false or fraudulent claim paid or approved by the Federal Government or its agents, like a carrier, other claims processor, or State Medicaid program.

Definitions

False Claim — A "false claim" is a claim for payment for services or supplies that were not provided specifically as presented or for which the provider is otherwise not entitled to payment. Examples of false claims for services or supplies that were not provided specifically as presented include, but are not limited to:

- A claim for a service or supply that was never provided.
- A claim indicating the service was provided for some diagnosis code other than the true diagnosis code in order to obtain reimbursement for the service (which would not be covered if the true diagnosis code were submitted).
- A claim indicating a higher level of service than was actually provided.
- A claim for a service that the provider knows is not reasonable and necessary.
- A claim for services provided by an unlicensed individual.

Knowingly — To "knowingly" present a false or fraudulent claim means that the provider: (1) Has actual knowledge that the information on the claim is false; (2) acts in deliberate ignorance of the truth or falsity of the information on the claim; or (3) acts in reckless disregard of the truth or falsity of the information on the claim. It is important to note the provider does not have to deliberately intend to defraud the Federal Government in order to be found liable under this Act. The provider need only "knowingly" present a false or fraudulent claim in the manner described above.

Deliberate Ignorance — To act in "deliberate ignorance" means that the provider has deliberately chosen to ignore the truth or falsity of the information on a claim submitted for payment, even though the provider knows, or has notice, that information may be false. An example of a provider who submits a false claim with deliberate ignorance would be a physician who ignores provider update bulletins and thus does not inform his/her staff of changes in the Medicare billing guidelines or update his/her billing system in accordance with changes to the Medicare billing practices. When claims for non-reimbursable services are submitted as a result, the False Claims Act has been violated.

Reckless Disregard — To act in "reckless disregard" means that the provider pays no regard to whether the information on a claim submitted for payment is true or false. An example of a provider who submits a false claim with reckless disregard would be a physician who assigns the billing function to an untrained office person without inquiring whether the employee has the requisite knowledge and training to accurately file such claims.

Penalty for Unlawful Conduct

The penalty for violating the False Claims Act is a minimum of $5,500 up to a maximum of $11,000 for each false claim submitted. In addition to the penalty, a provider could be found liable for damages of up to three times the amount unlawfully claimed.

Examples

1. A physician submitted claims to Medicare and Medicaid representing that he had personally performed certain services when, in reality, the services were performed by a nonphysician and they were not reimbursable under the Federal health care programs.

2. Dr. X intentionally upcoded office visits and angioplasty consultations that were submitted for payment to Medicare.

3. Dr. X, a podiatrist, knowingly submitted claims to the Medicare and Medicaid programs for non-routine surgical procedures when he actually performed routine, non-covered services such as the cutting and trimming of toenails and the removal of corns and calluses.

II. Civil Monetary Penalties Law (42 U.S.C. 1320a-7a)

Description of Unlawful Conduct

The Civil Monetary Penalties Law (CMPL) is a comprehensive statute that covers an array of fraudulent and abusive activities and is very similar to the False Claims Act. For instance, the CMPL prohibits a health care provider from presenting, or causing to be presented, claims for services that the provider "knows or should know" were:

- not provided as indicated by the coding on the claim;
- not medically necessary;
- furnished by a person who is not licensed as a physician (or who was not properly supervised by a licensed physician);
- furnished by a licensed physician who obtained his or her license through misrepresentation of a material fact (such as cheating on a licensing exam);
- furnished by a physician who was not certified in the medical specialty that he or she claimed to be certified in; or
- furnished by a physician who was excluded from participation in the Federal health care program to which the claim was submitted.

Additionally, the CMPL contains various other prohibitions, including:

- offering remuneration to a Medicare or Medicaid beneficiary that the person knows or should know is likely to influence the beneficiary to obtain items or services billed to Medicare or Medicaid from a particular provider;
- employing or contracting with an individual or entity that the person knows or should know is excluded from participation in a Federal health care program.

The term "should know" means that a provider: (1) Acted in deliberate ignorance of the truth or falsity of the information; or (2) acted in reckless disregard of the truth or falsity of the information. The Federal Government does not have to show that a provider specifically intended to defraud a Federal health care program in order to prove a provider violated the statute.

Penalty for Unlawful Conduct

Violation of the CMPL may result in a penalty of up to $10,000 per item or service and up to three times the amount unlawfully claimed. In addition, the provider may be excluded from participation in Federal health care programs. The regulations defining the aggravating and mitigating circumstances that must be reviewed by the OIG in making an exclusion determination are set forth in 42 CFR part 1001.

Examples

1. Dr. X paid Medicare and Medicaid beneficiaries $20 each time they visited him to receive services and have tests performed that were not preventive care services and tests.
2. Dr. X hired Physician Assistant P to provide services to Medicare and Medicaid beneficiaries without conducting a background check on P. Had Dr. X performed a background check by reviewing the HHS-OIG List of Excluded Individuals/Entities, Dr. X would have discovered that he should not hire P because P is excluded from participation in Federal health care programs for a period of 5 years.
3. Dr. X and his oximetry company billed Medicare for pulse oximetry that they knew they did not perform and services that had been intentionally upcoded.

III. Limitations on Certain Physician Referrals ("Stark Laws") (42 U.S.C. 1395nn)

Description of Unlawful Conduct

Physicians (and immediate family members) who have an ownership, investment or compensation relationship with an entity providing "designated health services" are prohibited from referring patients for these services where payment may be made by a Federal health care program unless a statutory or regulatory exception applies. An entity providing a designated health service is prohibited from billing for the provision of a service that was provided based on a prohibited referral. Designated health services include: clinical laboratory services; physical therapy services; occupational therapy services; radiology services, including magnetic resonance imaging, axial tomography scans, and ultrasound services; radiation therapy services and supplies; durable medical equipment and supplies; parenteral and enteral nutrients, equipment and supplies; prosthetics, orthotics, prosthetic devices and supplies; home health services; outpatient prescription drugs; and inpatient and outpatient hospital services.

New regulations clarifying the exceptions to the Stark Laws are expected to be issued by HCFA shortly. Current exceptions articulated within the Stark Laws include the following, provided all conditions of each exception as set forth in the statute and regulations are satisfied.

Exceptions for Ownership or Compensation Arrangements

- Physician's services;
- In-office ancillary services; and
- Prepaid plans.

Exceptions for Ownership or Investment in Publicly Traded Securities and Mutual Funds

- Ownership of investment securities which may be purchased on terms generally available to the public;
- Ownership of shares in a regulated investment company as defined by Federal law, if such company had, at the end of the company's most recent fiscal year, or on average, during the previous 3 fiscal years, total assets exceeding $75,000,000;
- Hospital in Puerto Rico;

- Rural provider; and
- Hospital ownership (whole hospital exception).

Exceptions Relating to Other Compensation Arrangements

- Rental of office space and rental of equipment;
- Bona fide employment relationship;
- Personal service arrangement;
- Remuneration unrelated to the provision of designated health services;
- Physician recruitment;
- Isolated transactions;
- Certain group practice arrangements with a hospital (pre-1989); and
- Payments by a physician for items and services.

Penalty for Unlawful Conduct

Violations of the statute subject the billing entity to denial of payment for the designated health services, refund of amounts collected from improperly submitted claims, and a civil monetary penalty of up to $15,000 for each improper claim submitted. Physicians who violate the statute may also be subject to additional fines per prohibited referral. In addition, providers that enter into an arrangement that they know or should know circumvents the referral restriction law may be subject to a civil monetary penalty of up to $100,000 per arrangement.

Examples

1. Dr. A worked in a medical clinic located in a major city. She also owned a free standing laboratory located in a major city. Dr. A referred all orders for laboratory tests on her patients to the laboratory she owned.

2. Dr. X agreed to serve as the Medical Director of Home Health Agency, HHA, for which he was paid a sum substantially above the fair market value for his services. In return, Dr. X routinely referred his Medicare and Medicaid patients to HHA for home health services.

3. Dr. Y received a monthly stipend of $500 from a local hospital to assist him in meeting practice expenses. Dr. Y performed no specific service for the stipend and had no obligation to repay the hospital. Dr. Y referred patients to the hospital for in-patient surgery.

IV. Exclusion of Certain Individuals and Entities From Participation in Medicare and other Federal Health Care Programs (42 U.S.C. 1320a-7)

Mandatory Exclusion

Individuals or entities convicted of the following conduct must be excluded from participation in Medicare and Medicaid for a minimum of 5 years:

(1) a criminal offense related to the delivery of an item or service under Medicare or Medicaid;

(2) a conviction under Federal or State law of a criminal offense relating to the neglect or abuse of a patient;

(3) a conviction under Federal or State law of a felony relating to fraud, theft, embezzlement, breach of fiduciary responsibility or other financial misconduct against a health care program financed by any Federal, State, or local government agency;

(4) a conviction under Federal or State law of a felony relating to the unlawful manufacture, distribution, prescription, or dispensing of a controlled substance.

If there is one prior conviction, the exclusion will be for 10 years. If there are two prior convictions, the exclusion will be permanent.

Permissive Exclusion

Individuals or entities convicted of the following offenses, may be excluded from participation in Federal health care programs for a minimum of 3 years:

(1) a criminal offense related to the delivery of an item or service under Medicare or Medicaid;

(2) a misdemeanor related to fraud, theft, embezzlement, breach of fiduciary responsibility or other financial misconduct against a health care program financed by any Federal, State, or local government agency;

(3) interference with, or obstruction of, any investigation into certain criminal offenses;

(4) a misdemeanor related to the unlawful manufacture, distribution, prescription or dispensing of a controlled substance;

(5) exclusion or suspension under a Federal or State health care program;

(6) submission of claims for excessive charges, unnecessary services or services that were of a quality that fails to meet professionally recognized standards of health care;

(7) violating the Civil Monetary Penalties Law or the statute entitled "Criminal Penalties for Acts Involving Federal Health Care Programs;"

(8) ownership or control of an entity by a sanctioned individual or immediate family member (spouse, natural or adoptive parent, child, sibling, stepparent, stepchild, stepbrother or stepsister, in-laws, grandparent and grandchild);

(9) failure to disclose information required by law;

(10) failure to supply claims payment information; and

(11) defaulting on health education loan or scholarship obligations.

The above list of offenses is not all inclusive. Additional grounds for permissive exclusion are detailed in the statute.

Examples

1. Nurse R was excluded based on a conviction involving obtaining dangerous drugs by forgery. She also altered prescriptions that were given for her own health problems before she presented them to the pharmacist to be filled.

2. Practice T was excluded due to its affiliation with its excluded owner. The practice owner, excluded from participation in the Federal health care programs for soliciting and receiving illegal kickbacks, was still participating in the day-to-day operations of the practice after his exclusion was effective.

Appendix D: OIG-HHS Contact Information

I. OIG Hotline Number

One method for providers to report potential fraud, waste, and abuse problems is to contact the OIG Hotline number. All HHS and contractor employees have a responsibility to assist in combating fraud, waste and abuse in all departmental programs. As such, providers are encouraged to report matters involving fraud, waste and mismanagement in any departmental program to the OIG. The OIG maintains a hotline that offers a confidential means for reporting these matters.

Contacting the OIG Hotline

By Phone: 1–800-HHS-TIPS (1–800–447–8477)

By E-Mail: HTips@os.dhhs.gov

By Mail: Office of Inspector General, Department of Health and Human Services, Attn: HOTLINE, 330 Independence Ave., SW., Washington, DC 20201

When contacting the Hotline, please provide the following information to the best of your ability:

- **Type of Complaint:**

Medicare Part A
Medicare Part B
Indian Health Service
TRICARE
Other (please specify)

- **HHS Department or program being affected by your allegation of fraud, waste, abuse/mismanagement:**

Health Care Financing Administration (HCFA)
Indian Health Service
Other (please specify)

Please provide the following information. (However, if you would like your referral to be submitted anonymously, please indicate such in your correspondence or phone call.)

Your Name
Your Street Address
Your City/County
Your State
Your Zip Code
Your email Address

- **Subject/Person/Business/Department that allegation is against.**

Name of Subject
Title of Subject
Subject's Street Address
Subject's City/County
Subject's State
Subject's Zip Code

Please provide a brief summary of your allegation and the relevant facts.

II. Provider Self-Disclosure Protocol

The recommended method for a provider to contact the OIG regarding potential fraud or abuse issues that may exist in the provider's own organization is through the use of the Provider Self-Disclosure Protocol. This program encourages providers to voluntarily disclose irregularities in their dealings with Federal health care programs. While voluntary disclosure under the protocol does not guarantee a provider protection from civil, criminal, or administrative actions, the fact that a provider voluntarily disclosed possible wrongdoing is a mitigating factor in OIG's recommendations to prosecuting agencies. Although other agencies may not have formal policies offering immunity or mitigation for self-disclosure, they typically view self-disclosure favorably for the self-disclosing entity. Self-reporting offers providers the opportunity to minimize the potential cost and disruption of a full-scale audit and investigation, to negotiate a fair monetary settlement, and to avoid an OIG permissive exclusion preventing the provider from doing business with Federal health care programs. In addition, if the provider is obligated to enter into an Integrity Agreement (IA) as part of the resolution of a voluntary disclosure, there are three benefits the provider might receive as a result of self-reporting:

If the provider has an effective compliance program and agrees to maintain its compliance program as part of the False Claims Act settlement, the OIG may not even require an IA;

In cases where the provider's own audits detected the disclosed problem, the OIG may consider alternatives to the IA's auditing provisions. The provider may be able to perform some or all of its billing audits through internal auditing methods rather than be required to retain an independent review organization to perform the billing review; and

Self-disclosing can help to demonstrate a provider's trustworthiness to the OIG and may result in the OIG determining that it can sufficiently safeguard the Federal health care programs through an IA without the exclusion remedy for a material breach, which is typically included in an IA.

Specific instructions on how a physician practice can submit a voluntary disclosure under the Provider Self-Disclosure Protocol can be found on the OIG's internet site at www.hhs.gov/oig or in the

Federal Register at 63 FR 58399 (1998). A physician practice may, however, wish to consult with an attorney prior to submitting a disclosure to the OIG.

The Provider Self-Disclosure Protocol can also be a useful tool for baseline audits. The protocol details the OIG's views on the appropriate elements of an effective investigative and audit plan for providers. Physician practices can use the self-disclosure protocol as a model for conducting audits and self-assessments.

In relying on the protocol for audit design and sample selection, a physician practice should pay close attention to the sections on self-assessment and sample selection. These two sections provide valuable guidance regarding how these two functions should be performed.

The self-assessment section of the protocol contains information that can be applied to audit design. Self-assessment is an internal financial assessment to determine the monetary impact of the matter. The approach of a review can include reviewing either all claims affected or a statistically valid sample of the claims.

Sample selection must include several elements. These elements are drawn from the Government sampling program known as RAT-STATS.[1] All of these elements are set forth in more detail in the Provider Self-Disclosure Protocol, but the elements are (1) Sampling unit, (2) sampling frame, (3) probe, (4) sample size, (5) random numbers, (6) sample design and (7) missing sample items. All of these sampling items should be clearly documented by the physician practice and compiled in the format set forth in the Provider Self-Disclosure Protocol. Use of the format set forth in the Provider Self-Disclosure Protocol will help physician practices to ensure that the elements of their internal audits are in conformance with OIG standards.

Appendix E: Carrier Contact Information

Medicare

A complete list of contact information (address, phone number, email address) for Medicare Part A Fiscal Intermediaries, Medicare Part B Carriers, Regional Home Health Intermediaries, and Dura-

[1] Available through the OIG web site at http://www.hhs.gov/oas/ratstat.html.

ble Medical Equipment Regional Carriers can be found on the HCFA web site at www.hcfa.gov/medicare/incardir.htm.

Medicaid

Contact information (address, phone number, email address) for each State Medicaid carrier can be found on the HCFA web site at www.hcfa.gov/medicaid/mcontact.htm. In addition to a list of Medicaid carriers, the web site includes contact information for each State survey agency and the HCFA Regional Offices.

Contact information for each State Medicaid Fraud Control Unit can be found on the OIG web site at www.hhs.gov/oig/oi/mfcu/index.htm.

Appendix F: Internet Resources

Office of Inspector General — U.S. Department of Health and Human Services

www.hhs.gov/oig

This web site includes a variety of information relating to Federal health care programs, including the following:

Advisory Opinions
Anti-kickback Information
Compliance Program Guidance
Corporate Integrity Agreements
Fraud Alerts
Links to web pages for the:
Office of Audit Services (OAS)
Office of Evaluation and Inspections (OEI)
Office of Investigations (OI)
OIG List of Excluded Individuals/Entities
OIG News
OIG Regulations
OIG Semi-Annual Report
OIG Workplan

Health Care Financing Administration

www.hcfa.gov

This web site includes information on a wide array of topics, including the following:

Medicare

National Correct Coding Initiative
Intermediary-Carrier Directory
Payment
Program Manuals
Program Transmittals & Memorandum
Provider Billing/HCFA Forms
Statistics and Data

Medicaid

HCFA Regional Offices
Letters to State Medicaid Directors
Medicaid Hotline Numbers
Policy & Program Information
State Medicaid Contacts
State Medicaid Manual
State Survey Agencies
Statistics and Data

HCFA Medicare Training

www.hcfa.gov/medlearn

This site provides computer-based training on the following topics:
HCFA 1500 Form
Fraud & Abuse
ICD-9-CM Diagnosis Coding
Adult Immunization
Medicare Secondary Payer (MSP)
Women's Health
Front Office Management
Introduction to the World of Medicare
Home Health Agency
HCFA 1450 (UB92)

Government Printing Office

www.access.gpo.gov

This site provides access to Federal statutes and regulations pertaining to Federal health care programs.

The U.S. House of Representatives Internet Library

uscode.house.gov/usc.htm

This site provides access to the United States Code, which contains laws pertaining to Federal health care programs. [FR Doc. 00–25500 Filed 10–4-00; 8:45 am] BILLING CODE 4152–01-P

APPENDIX I10

Solicitation of Information and Recommendations for Developing a Compliance Risk Guidance for the Ambulance Industry

[Federal Register: August 17, 2000 (Volume 65, Number 160)] [Notices]

DEPARTMENT OF HEALTH AND HUMAN SERVICES

Office of Inspector General

AGENCY: Office of Inspector General (OIG), HHS.

ACTION: Notice.

SUMMARY: This Federal Register notice seeks the input and recommendations of interested parties as the OIG develops a Compliance Risk Guidance (CRG) for ambulance service providers, especially those serving Medicare, Medicaid and other Federal health care program beneficiaries. The ambulance industry has experienced a number of instances of ambulance provider and supplier fraud and abuse and has expressed interest in increasing the awareness of the industry to assist in protecting against such conduct. In response to the industry's concerns, the OIG has, to date, written seven Advisory Opinions on a variety of ambulance-related issues[1] and has published a proposed rule concerning a safe harbor for ambulance restocking.[2]

In an effort to provide further guidance, the OIG is soliciting comments, recommendations and other suggestions from concerned parties and organizations on how best to develop an ambulance CRG to reduce the potential for fraud and abuse. The OIG expects that the CRG will outline the most common and prevalent fraud and abuse risk areas for the ambulance industry. In addition, the CRG will provide guidance on how to: (1) Address these risk areas; (2) prevent

[1] See Advisory Opinions Nos. 97–6, 98–3, 98–7, 98–13, 99–1, 99–2 and 99–5. The Advisory Opinions can be found on the OIG web site at http://www.hhs.gov/oig.

[2] See 65 FR 32060; May 22, 2000.

the occurrence of instances of fraud and abuse; and (3) develop corrective actions when those risks or instances of fraud and abuse are identified.

The OIG expects that the risk areas identified in the CRG will not be all-inclusive. Ambulance providers and suppliers will remain responsible for identifying those risk areas particular to their specific operations.

DATES: To assure consideration, comments must be delivered to the address provided below by no later than 5 p.m. on October 16, 2000.

ADDRESSES: Please mail or deliver your written comments, recommendations and suggestions to the following address: Department of Health and Human Services, Office of Inspector General, Attention: OIG-1-CRG, Room 5527 A, Cohen Building, 330 Independence Avenue, S.W., Washington, D.C. 20201.

We do not accept comments by facsimile (FAX) transmission. In commenting, please refer to the file code OIG-1-CRG. Comments received timely will be available for public inspection as they are received, generally beginning approximately 3 weeks after publication of a document, in Room 5541 of the Office of Inspector General at 330 Independence Avenue, S.W., Washington, D.C. 20201 on Monday through Friday of each week from 8 A.M. to 4:30 P.M.

FOR FURTHER INFORMATION CONTACT: Sonya Castro, Office of Counsel to the Inspector General, (202) 619–2078.

SUPPLEMENTARY INFORMATION: The contents of this CRG will differ from the previous OIG compliance program guidances.[3] Although the CRG will refer to the seven elements of establishing an effective compliance program, set forth in the previous compliance program guidances,[4] the CRG will concentrate on

---

[3] The OIG has issued compliance program guidance for the following eight industry sectors: hospitals, clinical laboratories, home health agencies, durable medical equipment suppliers, third- party medical billing companies, hospices, Medicare+Choice organizations offering coordinated care plans and nursing facilities. Additionally, the Individual and Small Group Physician Practice Compliance Program Guidance has been issued in draft form (June 12, 2000; 65 FR 36818). The Compliance Program Guidances can be found on the OIG web site at http://www.hhs.gov/oig in the Electronic Reading Room, or by calling the OIG Public Affairs office at (202) 619–1343.

[4] The seven elements of an effective compliance program include: (1) The development of written policies and procedures; (2) the designation of a compliance officer and other appropriate bodies; (3) the development and implementation of effective training and education programs; (4) the devel-

specific identified risk areas and related compliance program best practices.

The CRG will include an additional section relating to risk areas associated with the Medical Assistance or Medicaid program requirements. The OIG intends to broadly address the Medicaid risks in light of the fact that the coverage and reimbursement rules differ among the various Medicaid programs. In order for the OIG to adequately incorporate the most prevalent Medicaid risk areas, we are requesting comments and suggestions from the various State agencies providing Medicaid services and from those ambulance providers and suppliers that furnish a significant level of services to Medicaid beneficiaries.

The OIG would also appreciate specific comments related to compliance regarding the proposed Medicare ambulance fee schedule. [5] As appropriate, we ask that commenters please provide detailed justifications and empirical data supporting such comments.

Dated: August 11, 2000.

Michael F. Mangano,

Principal Deputy Inspector General.

[FR Doc. 00–20856 Filed 8–16–00; 8:45 am]

BILLING CODE 4152–01-P

---

opment and maintenance of effective lines of communication; (5) the enforcement of standards through well-publicized disciplinary guidelines; (6) the use of audits and other evaluation techniques to monitor compliance; and (7) the development of procedures to respond to detected offenses and to initiate corrective action.

[5] The Health Care Financing Administration's proposed Medicare ambulance fee schedule is expected to be published in the Federal Register shortly.

APPENDIX J

RECENT REGULATORY PROVISIONS APPLICABLE TO CIVIL MONEY PENALTIES, EXCLUSIONS AND OTHER REMEDIES

APPENDIX J1

Revised OIG Exclusion Authorities Resulting From Public Law 104–191, the Health Insurance Portability and Accountability Act (HIPPA) of 1996

Federal Register: September 8, 1997 (Volume 62, Number 173)
Proposed Rules
Page 47182–47195

DEPARTMENT OF HEALTH AND HUMAN SERVICES

Office of Inspector General

42 CFR Parts 1000, 1001, 1002 and 1005

RIN 0991-AA87

Health Care Programs: Fraud and Abuse; Revised OIG Exclusion Authorities Resulting From Public Law 104–191

AGENCY: Office of Inspector General (OIG), HHS.

ACTION: Notice of proposed rulemaking.

SUMMARY: This rulemaking addresses proposed revisions to the OIG's sanction authorities in conjunction with sections 211, 212 and 213 of the Health Insurance Portability and Accountability Act of 1996, along with other technical and conforming changes to the OIG exclusion authorities set forth in 42 CFR parts 1000, 1001, 1002 and 1005. These proposed revisions are specifically designed to expand the protection of certain basic fraud authorities, and revise and strengthen the current legal authorities pertaining to exclusions from the Medicare and State health care programs.

DATES: To assure consideration, public comments must be delivered to the address provided below by no later than 5 p.m. on November 7, 1997.

ADDRESSES: Please mail or deliver your written comments to the following address: Office of Inspector General, Department of Health and Human Services, Attention: OIG-20-P, Room 5246, Cohen Building, 330 Independence Avenue, S.W., Washington, D.C. 20201. Because of staffing and resource limitations, we cannot accept comments by facsimile (FAX) transmission. In commenting, please refer to file code OIG-20-P.

FOR FURTHER INFORMATION CONTACT: Joel Schaer, (202) 619–0089, OIG Regulations Officer.

SUPPLEMENTARY INFORMATION: Comments will be available for public inspection September 22, 1997 in Room 5550 of the Office of Inspector General at 330 Independence Avenue, S.W., Washington, D.C., on Monday through Friday of each week from 8:00 a.m. to 4:30 p.m., (202) 619–0089.

I. Background

A. Overview of OIG Exclusion Authorities

All exclusions imposed by the Office of Inspector General (OIG) are based on the authorities set forth in sections 1128, 1156 and 1892 of the Social Security Act (Act). In imposing these exclusions, the Secretary's primary objective and obligation is to protect the health and safety of patients receiving care under the Medicare and State health care programs, and to safeguard the integrity of these programs. The authorities contained in these sections of the Act were designed to protect the programs and their beneficiaries from unfit health care providers, individuals and businesses whose behavior has demonstrated that they pose a risk to program beneficiaries or to the integrity of the Medicare and State health care programs.

In 1987, the OIG's civil administrative sanction authorities were significantly revised and expanded by the Medicare and Medicaid Patient and Program Protection Act (MMPPPA), Public Law 100–93. Congress enacted MMPPPA "to improve the ability of the [Department] to protect the Medicare and Medicaid programs for fraud and abuse, and to protect the beneficiaries of these programs from incompetent practioners and from inappropriate and inadequate care.' ' MMPPPA authorized both mandatory and discretionary program exclusions intended to protect the integrity of the Medicare and State health care programs, as well as beneficiaries.

Manadatory exclusions. Section 1128(a) of the Act specifically sets forth the exclusion authorities with mandated enforcement provisions. This section of the Act requires the OIG to exclude from program participation any individuals or entities convicted of a program-related crime or patient abuse or neglect. These mandatory exclusions must be imposed for a minimum 5-year period.

Permissive exclusions. In addition, section 1128(b) sets forth a variety of sanction authorities all of which are permissive authorities that do not necessarily mandate an action by the Department. Prior to recent statutory changes discussed below, a conviction relating to the delivery of a health care item or service that was not program-related, whether a felony or a misdemeanor, served as grounds for a permissive exclusion only. A number of these authorities are "derivative" exclusions, based on actions previously taken by a court, or other law enforcement or regulatory agencies. For example, these exclusions have been based on convictions for fraud, theft, financial misconduct and controlled substance violations, as well as license suspensions and revocations, and sanctions by other health agencies. Other permissive exclusions are "non-derivative" exclusions, that is, they are based on OIG-initiated determinations of misconduct that relate to such matters as quality of care and access of information. There were no specified minimum periods of exclusion under these permissive exclusion authorities, with the exception of the exclusion for failure to grant "immediate access" under section 1128(b)(12) of the Act.

These authorities have provided for the imposition of an exclusion from the Medicare (title 18), Medicaid (title 19), Maternal and Child Health Service Block Grant (title 5) and Block Grants to States for Social Services (title 20) programs, and are codified in 42 CFR parts 1001 and 1002 of the OIG regulations.

B. The Health Insurance Portability and Accountability Act of 1996

In the first significant amendments to the OIG's exclusion authorities since MMPPA, the Health Insurance Portability and Accountability Act (HIPAA) of 1996, Public Law 104–191, contains many important improvements to the laws that are intended as major steps towards the elimination of health care fraud and abuse. Among other things, HIPAA revises and strengthens the OIG's current sanction authorities pertaining to exclusions from Medicare and the State health care programs. Specifically, HIPAA broadens the OIG's mandatory exclusion; and establishes a new permissive exclusion applicable to individuals with ownership or control interest in sanctioned entities.

The revisions to the OIG's sanction authorities regarding our mandatory exclusion authority and the permissive exclusion authorities related to fraud under section 1128(b)(1) of the Act are effective upon enactment; the amendments regarding the minimum exclusion period and the permissive exclusion of individuals with ownership or control interest are effective on January 1, 1997. The provisions do allow, however, the Department some policy discretion in their implementation. As a result, we are developing this proposed rulemaking to address these new statutory provisions, along with other technical revisions to the OIG's exclusion authorities codified in 42 CFR parts 1000, 1001, 1002 and 1005.

II. Provisions of the Proposed Rule

A. Mandatory OIG Exclusion From Participation in the Medicare and State Health Care Programs

Section 211 of HIPAA has expanded the minimum 5-year mandatory exclusion authority of the OIG to cover any felony conviction under Federal, State or local law relating to health care fraud, even if governmental programs were not involved. Felony convictions relating to controlled substances are also the basis for a mandatory exclusion. The expanded mandatory exclusion provisions serve to recognize the seriousness of such felony convictions and ensure that beneficiaries of the Medicare and State health care programs are well protected from dealing with such individuals and entities. Section 211 still provides the Secretary with discretionary authority to exclude those individuals and entities from Medicare and State health care programs who have been convicted of a misdemeanor criminal health care fraud offense or who have been convicted of a criminal offense relating to fraud, theft, embezzlement, breach of fiduciary responsibility or other financial misconduct in programs (other than health care programs) funded by any Federal, State or local agency.

In accordance with section 211 of HIPAA, we would revise Sec. 1001.101 of our regulations by adding new paragraphs (c) and (d) to address the mandatory provisions set forth in sections 1128a(3) and 1128a(4) of the Act. In terms of the scope of this provision, in order to appropriately restrict the imposition of these mandatory exclusions to only individuals and entities who might reasonably be expected to have future contact with Medicare, the State health care programs or other health care programs or systems, we are also proposing in Secs. 1001.101(d) and 1001.401(a) to limit the applicability of this provision to any individual or entity that: (1) Is or has ever been a health care practitioner, provider or supplier; (2) holds or has held a direct or indirect ownership or control interest, as defined in section

1124(a)(3) of the Act, in an entity that is a health care provider or supplier; or (3) is or has ever been an officer, director, agent or managing employee, as defined in section 1126(b) of the Act, of such an entity, or is or has ever been employed in any capacity in the health care industry. A conforming change to our regulations at Sec. 1001.102(b)(1), consistent with the sections 1128(a)(3) 1128(a)(4) of the statute, would also be made to reference any fraudulent acts — including theft, breach of fiduciary responsibility or other financial misconduct — committee in other governmental programs as a basis for an exclusion by the OIG from Medicare and the State health care programs.

The section heading for Sec. 1001.201 would be revised to read as "Conviction relating to fraud" to indicate that this authority is not just relating to program and health care fraud. The section heading for Sec. 1001.401 would be revised to read as "Misdemeanor conviction relating to controlled substances."

B. Establishment of Minimum Periods of Exclusion for Certain Permissive Exclusions

The absence of a statutorily required minimum exclusion period for permissive exclusions has resulted in an exceptional amount of administrative litigation over the issue of the length of exclusion in these cases. Since the reasonableness of the length of exclusions imposed is the single most litigated issue, this has required significant agency resources in each instance to defend the exclusion period imposed by the OIG. Section 212 has established minimum periods of exclusion from 1 to 3 years for permissive exclusions from the Medicare and State health care programs.

For (1) convictions of misdemeanor criminal health care fraud offenses, (2) criminal offenses relating to fraud in non-health care Federal or State programs, (3) convictions relating to obstruction of an investigation of health care fraud and (4) convictions of misdemeanor offenses relating to controlled substances, section 212 of HIPAA has established a minimum period of exclusion of 3 years, unless the Secretary determines that a longer or shorter period is appropriate due to aggravating or mitigating circumstances.

For permissive exclusions from Medicare and the State health care programs as a result of revocation, surrender or suspension of an individual's or entity's health care license, section 212 establishes a minimum exclusion period that would be not less than the period during which the individual's or entity's license was revoked or suspended. Likewise, for permissive exclusions due to a suspension or exclusion from other Federal health care programs (such as CHAMPUS or the Veterans' Administration) or other State health care programs for reasons bearing on an individual's or entity's professional competence, professional performance or financial integrity, section 212 of HIPAA also establishes a minimum period of exclusion of not less than the period the individual or entity is excluded or suspended from that Federal or State health care program. As indicated above, this statutory provision is effective for any exclusion imposed or proposed by the OIG on or after January 1, 1997.

In addition, section 212 establishes a minimum of a 1-year period of exclusion for (1) individuals or entities who are found to have submitted (or caused to be submitted) claims for excessive charges, or who furnished (or caused to be furnished) unnecessary items or services; or (2) health maintenance organizations (as defined by section 1903(m) of the Act), or entity under a waiver established by section 1915(b)(1) of the Act, that are found to have failed to provide medically necessary items and services. The establishment of these minimum exclusion periods will aid to conserve governmental resources by reducing the amount of litigation and will foster more consistency.

Consistent with these statutory amendments, we would revise Secs. 1001.701(d)(1) and 1001.801(c)(1) to add that with regard to the length of exclusion under these authorities, in no case may the period be shorter than one year. Furthermore, we would also revise Sec. Sec. 1001.501 and 1001.601 to state that the length of exclusion under this authority will never be for a period of time less than the period during which the individual or entity is excluded from that Federal or State health care program.

C. Permissive Exclusions of Individuals With Ownership or Control Interest in Sanctioned Entities

Prior to HIPAA, section 1128(b)(8) of the Act permitted the Secretary to exclude an entity when a convicted individual had an ownership, control or agency relationship with such entity. However, if an entity, rather than an individual, was convicted of Medicare or State health care program fraud, the OIG did not have the authority to exclude the individuals(s) who owned or controlled the entity and who may, in fact, have been responsible for the fraud. This created an obvious loophole whereby an individual who was indicted for fraud along with a business entity owned or controlled by that individual could avoid program exclusion by agreeing to have the business entity plead guilty and pay the fines. Having avoided conviction, the individual was then free to form a new corporation and continue to participate in the health care programs.

Section 213 of HIPAA has now expanded the statute by adding a new permissive exclusion authority (section 1128(b)(15) of the Act) applicable to individuals who have an ownership interest in, or have significant control over the operations of, an entity that has been convicted of a program-related offense. Specifically, under this provision, an individual who has a direct or indirect ownership or control interest in a sanctioned entity and who knows, or should know, of the action constituting the basis for the conviction or exclusion, may also be excluded from participation in Medicare and the State health care programs if the entity has been convicted of an offense under sections 1128(a) or 1128 (b)(1) through (b)(3) of the Act, or otherwise excluded from program participation. Under this authority, the culpable individual is also subject to program exclusion even if not initially convicted or excluded.

Accordingly, we would add a new Sec. 1001.1051, Exclusion of individuals with ownership or control interest in sanctioned entities, to reflect the new statutory authority. Consistent with the statute, under this regulatory authority the OIG would need to demonstrate that, in the case of an investor, the individual acted in deliberate ignorance of the offense constituting the sanctionable action. In the case of an officer or managing employee of the business entity, the OIG will not need to demonstrate such knowledge. Under proposed Sec. 1001.1051, when the entity has been excluded, the length of the individual's exclusion would be for the same period as that of the sanctioned entity with which the individual has had the prohibited relationship. Consistent with statutory intent, we are defining the term "sanctioned entity" under this section to mean an entity that has been convicted of any offense under Secs. 1001.101 through 1001.104 of these regulations, or that has been terminated or excluded from participation in Medicare or a State health care program. Thus, under this authority, when an entity is no longer reimbursed under Medicare or the State health care programs as a result of a termination or exclusion by the Department, the owners of the entity will be subject to an exclusion as well.

In a conforming change, we also propose to revise Sec. 1001.3002 by adding a new paragraph to clarify that if the specified criteria of this section are met, an individual excluded in accordance with the new proposed Sec. 1001.1051 would be reinstated only upon an OIG determination that the excluded entity upon which the individual's exclusion was based has been reinstated in accordance with Secs. 1001.3002(a) or 1001.3005.

D. Technical and Conforming Regulatory Revisions

In addition to the changes to the OIG regulations at 42 CFR parts 1001 and 1002 to comply with the revised sanction provisions set forth in HIPAA, we are proposing a number of technical and conforming regulatory changes in accordance with the HIPAA. Specifically, under the new statute, the OIG has been delegated authority for 3 new authorities referenced in Public Law 104–191 — sections 1128 (a)(3) and (a)(4) and 1128 (b)(15) of the Act. As a result, technical and conforming changes to the OIG regulations are necessary. In addition, several minor conforming changes are also being proposed to correct omissions from previous regulatory issuances, and to clarify and expand the applicability of the existing regulations. A limited number of policy decisions are being proposed that relate to the clarification of (1) The definition of the term "furnished;" (2) the OIG's exclusion authority under section 1128(a)(2) of the Act concerning patient neglect and abuse convictions; (3) time limits on payments to suppliers for services by excluded providers; (4) when a reinstatement request will be received in accordance with an OIG exclusion taken under section 1128(b)(5) of the Act; and (5) terms "incarceration" and "patient."

Section 1000.10, General definitions: We would clarify the current definition of the term "furnished" to indicate that exclusions will apply to any individual or entity that provides or supplies items or services, directly or indirectly. When an individual or entity is excluded from Medicare and the State health care programs, the effect of the exclusion is that the programs may not pay for items and services furnished by that excluded individual or entity. The OIG has the authority — and sometimes the obligation when a mandatory exclusion is appropriate — to impose an exclusion on individuals or entities when the statutory requirements of section 1128 of the Act are met, regardless of whether (1) The individual or entity is paid by the programs directly or (2) the items or services provided by the individual or entity are reimbursed by the programs indirectly through the submission of claims by a third party who is a direct provider, supplier or practitioner. In the past, we have elected not to exercise this authority in the case of manufacturers or distributors that do not submit claims for the items they provide because of concern that it would be difficult to administer exclusions against such entities are not reimbursed directly by the Department. At this time, the OIG is proposing to change this approach by exercising the authority given to us and clarifying the existing definition for "furnished."

Notwithstanding the difficulty in monitoring and administering exclusion against so-called "indirect" providers — such as manufacturers and distributors of drugs, medical devices and other items of durable medical equipment reimbursable under Medicare and the State health care programs — the OIG has determined that an exception for indirect providers and suppliers is not appropriate as a matter of policy. As a result, in clarifying the definition for the term "furnished," we would make clear that exclusions of indirect providers will be imposed when appropriate, and that the effect of such exclusions will be that no payment may be made to any direct provider, practitioner or supplier for items or services manufactured, distributed or otherwise provided by any excluded individual or entity.

Section 1001.2, Definitions: Throughout part 1001, the current regulations list various aggravating factors to be considered as a basis for lengthening a period of exclusion. One aggravating factor in all instances when the exclusion is based on a conviction is whether the sentence imposed by the court included incarceration. Because many white collar criminals are not actually placed in jails, there has been some uncertainty over what incarceration entails. Consistent with Federal sentencing guidelines, we are proposing to add a definition in Sec. 1002 for the term "incarceration" to include imprisonment or any type of confinement with or without supervised release. This would include, but would not be limited to, a correctional facility or other community confinement (such as a work release center), as well as house arrest and home detention.

We are proposing a new definition for the term "patient" to include any individual who is receiving health care items or services, including any item or service provided to meet his or her physical, mental or emotional needs, whether or not the item or service is reimbursed under Medicare or a State health care program and regardless of the location in which it is provided. We are concerned that the term "patient" has been narrowly defined in some instances to restrict its meaning to only an individual in a traditional medical care setting or within a traditional physician/patient relationship. We believe that the statute intended to prohibit neglect and abuse of all individuals receiving health care items and services regardless of the caretaker or the location within which the items or services are provided.

We are also proposing two changes to the existing definition of the term "exclusion." To conform to the statutory language set forth in MMPPPA, Public Law 100–93, we are adding the words "ordered or prescribed" to indicate that items and services will not be reimbursed under Medicare and the State health care programs when furnished, ordered or prescribed by a specified individual or entity (underlining added). Under this definition, we are also codifying current OIG policy to indicate that even after an exclusion has expired, the individual or entity will not be eligible for program reimbursement until they are formally reinstated by the OIG.

A revision to the term "sole source of essential specialized services in the community" is also being proposed to indicate that it is a health professional shortage area (formally known as a health man power shortage area); and that this designation is now made by the Health Resources Services Administration, and not the Public Health Service. A proposed change under the term "professionally recognized standards of health care" would remove the specific references to the "Food and Drug Administration," the "Health Care Financing Administration" (HCFA) and the "Public Health Service," and substitute "the Department" as the entity in general who may declare a particular treatment modality as not being safe and effective.

Section 1001.101, Basis for liability: We are proposing to revise paragraph (b) to clarify the scope of the term "neglect or patient abuse" to indicate that it covers both the individual's custodial as well as medical treatment. In recent years, we have been seeing more cases arise from abuse and neglect in residential settings where the abused or neglected individual is not referred to as a "patient." Further, the individual may not be receiving strictly medical care treatment, but rather may be provided with custodial care, such as ensuring that medicines are taken and meals are prepared. In implementing the OIG's exclusion authorities, administrative law judges (ALJs) have varied in their interpretation of the statute and have not developed a consistent standard for defining a patient and patient abuse. In order to provide consistent protection for all individuals similarly situated, notwithstanding the variations of State law, we are proposing to revise the regulations to indicate that the delivery of a health care service includes the provision of any items or services to an individual designed to meet their physical, mental or emotional needs or well-being, whether or not reimbursed under Medicare or a State health care program.

Section 1001.102, Length of exclusion: We are proposing to add a new factor that may be considered aggravating and therefore a basis for lengthening the exclusion period. In order to help distinguish between more egregious and less egregious cases involving patient abuse, we propose to include a new Sec. 1001.102(b)(4) to provide that in the case of any conviction involving patient abuse or neglect, we will consider whether the action that resulted in the conviction (1) was premeditated, (2) was part of a continuing pattern of behavior, or (3) consisted of non-consensual sexual acts.

In addition, we are proposing an additional aggravating factor for consideration in Sec. 1001.102 and elsewhere throughout part 1001 (see Secs. 1001.201(b)(2)(vi), 1001.301(b)(2)(vi), 1001.401(c)(2)(v), 1001.501(b)(2)(iv), 1001.601(b)(2)(iii), 1001.701(d)(2)(v), 1001.801(c)(2)(v), 1001.901(b)(4), and 1001.951(b)(1)(iv). The proposed factor specifically relates to any other adverse action taken by any other Federal, State or local government agency or board based on the same set of circumstances that is serving as the basis for imposition of the exclusion. This additional factor is consistent with ALJ decisions regarding aggravating factors and the length of exclusion.

Further, Sec. 1001.102(b) and the other sections referenced above, as currently written, do not allow the OIG to increase the length of exclusion if an individual or entity was convicted of other offenses at the same time as he or she was convicted of the offense that served as the basis for the exclusion. For example, this aggravating factor permits the OIG to increase the length of exclusion when the individual convicted of Medicare fraud has a prior drug conviction or income tax evasion conviction. However, if the individual is simultaneously convicted of Medicare fraud and any other offense, such as drug distribution or income tax evasion, there is currently no aggravating factor that permits the OIG to consider the additional conviction or convictions. We believe it is not sensible to factor in conduct or wrongdoing that occurred in the past to demonstrate that an individual or entity lacks trustworthiness, but not to give as much weight to more recent conduct. To address this problem and allow greater flexibility to the OIG, we are proposed to amend Sec. 1001.102(b) to indicate that in determining the length of exclusion, the OIG will consider whether the individual or entity (1) was convicted of other offenses besides those which formed the basis for the exclusion, or (2) has a documented history of criminal, civil or administrative wrongdoing. This would permit the OIG to consider any conviction prior to, concurrent with or subsequent to the conviction upon which the exclusion is based. (Parallel changes would be made, as applicable, throughout part 1001 in Secs. 1001.201(b)(2), 1001.301(b)(2), 1001.401(c)(2), 1001.501(b)(2), 1001.601(b)(2), 1001.701(d)(2), 1001.801(c)(2), 1001.901(b), 1001.951(b)(1), 1001.1101(b), 1001.1201.(b), 1001.1301(b)(2), 1001.1401(b), 1001.1601(b)(1) and 1001,1701(c)(1).)

In addition to these aggravating factors, we are also proposing to include in Sec. 1001.102(c)(3) (as well as in Secs. 1001.201(b)(3)(iii), 1001.301.(b)(3)(ii), 101.401(c)(3)(i), 1001.501(b)(3)(i) and 1001.601(b)(3)(ii)) a new mitigating factor that would take into account whether the cooperation of an individual or entity resulted in additional cases being investigated, or reports being issued, by the appropriate law enforcement agency identifying program vulnerabilities or weaknesses. This new mitigating factor would only be taken into consideration in those situations where the law enforcement agency validated the person's information by opening up a case or by writing a report where, for example, a system vulnerability to HCFA or other program agency is identified and a solution recommended. We believe that the inclusion of this additional mitigating factor would (1) encourage greater cooperation by individuals and entities, and (2) afford the OIG greater flexibility in identifying and addressing issues related to program waste, fraud and abuse.

Section 1001.501, License revocation or suspension: Consistent with and to conform to the new statutory authority, we would delete paragraph (c) of Sec. 1001.501, currently setting forth exceptions related to the length of exclusion for license revocation or suspension.

Section 1001.601, Exclusion or suspension under a Federal or State health care program: Prior to HIPAA, Sec. 1001.601 set forth both mitigating and aggravating factors that are to be considered in determining the length of exclusion under this authority. To conform with the statute, we would revise paragraph (b)(3) of this section to indicate that with the establishment of a base exclusion period under this authority, mitigating factors may only be considered if aggravating factors exist that would justify a longer exclusion beyond the base period.

We are also proposing to clarify OIG policy and correct an inadvertent inconsistency that exists in the language set forth in Sec.

1001.601(b)(4). The current paragraph states that "[t]he OIG will normally not consider a request for reinstatement * * * until the period of exclusion imposed by the OIG expires." This language has created a problem for these OIG exclusions which are based entirely on State-imposed exclusions, and which must continue until the State exclusion ends. Since the law requires the Medicaid program to exclude for the same period as Medicare, this has resulted in a loop that makes it technically impossible for either the OIG of the State to end the exclusion except by an arrangement to do so simultaneously. Specifically, in many instances, a State is prepared to reinstate an individual or entity but is unable to do so because of the existing Medicare exclusion that the OIG has imposed in as a result of the original State Action. To solve this problem, we are proposing to revise paragraph (b)(4) of this section to state that if an individual or entity is eligible to apply for reinstatement, and the sole reason that the State has denied reinstatement is that the existing exclusion under Medicare imposed by the OIG is still in effect, the OIG will consider a request for reinstatement.

Section 1001.701, Excessive claims or furnishing of unnecessary or substandard items or services: In an effort to more clearly define the scope of an action under section 1128(b)(6) of the act, we are proposing to revise paragraph (a)(1) of this section to further clarify to whom an individual's or entity's excess charges or costs apply. The revised language would indicate that the OIG may exclude an individual or entity that has submitted, or caused to be submitted, bills or requests for Medicare or State health care program payments that contain charges or costs that are substantially in excess of their usual charges or costs for items or services furnished to any of their customers, clients or patients. We specifically welcome comments on this OIG policy clarification.

Section 1001.953, OIG report on compliance with investment interest safe harbor: We would delete this section since the time frame being reflected in this section is no longer operative. The current language stipulates that an OIG report to the Secretary be prepared within 180 days of the effective date addressing the investment interest safe harbor provisions. Those provisions were published as part of a final rulemaking (56 FR 35952, July 29, 1991) became effective upon the date of its publication. The report was not prepared for several reasons. The overriding reason for not issuing this report within the stipulated time frame was that it was not practical to effectively study this subject area until health care businesses had the opportunity to alter their practices to take advantage of this safe harbor. By the time a study might appropriately have been undertaken, this subject was superseded to a large degree by the enactment of section 1877 of the Act.

Section 1001.1001; Exclusion of entities owned or controlled by a sanctioned person: Questions have been raised regarding the legitimacy of the transfer of health care entities from excluded individuals to their spouses, and the circumstances under which such a transfer should constitute divestment of ownership and control of the entity by the excluded individual, and should thus preclude exclusion of the entity under Sec. 1001.1001. In an effort to reiterate and emphasize existing OIG policy on this matter, we are proposing to revise the definition set forth in Sec. 1001.1001(a)(2) for the term "agent." This policy was clearly enunciated in the preamble of the final regulations implementing amendments to the OIG's exclusion authorities resulting from Public Law 100–93 (57 FR 3309, January 29, 1992), and we are now proposing to codify it in regulations.

Section 1001.1901, Scope and effect of exclusion: Some individuals and entities have mistakenly believed that merely obtaining a program provider number would automatically result in their reinstatement back into the programs. This has never been the case; an individual or entity must formally be reinstated by the OIG in order to again participate in the Medicare and State health care programs. We would revise paragraph (b)(1) of this section, regarding the effect of an exclusion on excluded individuals and entities, to specifically clarify existing OIG policy that an excluded individual or entity continues to be excluded until officially reinstated by the OIG, regardless of whether he, she or it has obtained a program number — either as an individual or as a member of a group — prior to their being reinstated for program participation. (A similar clarification would be made in Secs. 1001.3001(a)(1) and 1001.3002(a) to indicate that the obtaining of a program provider number does not in and of itself reinstate eligibility for an entity or an individual, either as a single person or as a member of a group.) The word "person" appearing in the first sentence of paragraph (b)(1) would be revised to read as "individual or entity."

In addition, we would revise paragraph (b)(3) of this section to clearly indicate that submitting claims, or causing claims to be submitted or payment to be made by the programs for items or services that were furnished, ordered or prescribed by the excluded individual or entity — including any administrative and management services or salaries — may serve as the basis for denying the individual's or entity's reinstatement back into the programs. The addition of this language would serve to more clearly define what an excluded individual or entity can do, and would codify and re-enforce existing OIG policy that is currently contained in the exclusion notice letters sent to individuals and entities.

We are also proposing to add a new Sec. 1001.1901(c)(4) that serves to codify the current HCFA policy with regard to payment to suppliers for claims after notice of an excluded provider's exclusion. Specifically, we would reiterate that HCFA will not pay for any claims submitted by, or for items or services ordered or prescribed by, an excluded provider for dates of service 5 days or more after the date that notice of the provider's exclusion was mailed by the contractor to the supplier.

Section 1001.2001, Notice of intent to exclude: We propose to delete existing paragraph (b) of Sec. 1001.2001. The language currently states that if the OIG proposes to exclude an individual or entity in accordance with Sec. 1001.701 or 1001.801, the individual or entity may submit a written request to present evidence or argument orally to the OIG. In eliminating the in-person hearing on these cases, the individual or entity would still have the opportunity to submit additional material for review to the OIG. The vast majority of cases for proposed exclusion are medical in nature, and while the OIG contracts for the review of medical records and related material, we do not retain an in-house medical review officer that would be readily accessible to hear and review such submitted material. We believe this existing provision does not represent an effective use of time and current OIG resources, and are therefore proposing to delete this language. This change would not diminish due process since the individual or entity retains the ability to challenge the OIG's proposed exclusion.

Section 1001.2002, Notice of exclusion: We are proposing to amend this section by adding a new paragraph (e) indicating, consistent with existing OIG policy, that the notice letter to the affected individual or entity could be amended should any additional information come to our attention or wrongdoing occur subsequent to the issuance of the initial notice letter. We are also proposing to make a similar clarifying change in Sec. 1005.15 by revising paragraph (f) to explicitly state that, with certain exceptions, additional items or information — including any aggravating and mitigating circumstances that arose or became known subsequent to the issue of the notice letter — may be introduced by either party.

Section 1001.2003, Notice of proposal to exclude: A discrepancy currently existing between the language in Sec. 1001.2003(a) — indicating that an exclusion is effective 60 days after the date of notice, unless an individual or entity files a written request for a hearing — and the language set forth in Sec. 1005.2(c) — that a request for a hearing is to be filed 60 days after the notice letter is received by the respondent, which is presumed to be 5 days after the date of the notice unless there is a reasonable showing to the contrary. To be consistent in our language and intent, we would revised Sec. 1001.2003(a) to reference the language and procedure set forth in Sec. 1005.(c). i.e., that a request for a hearing be made 60 days after service of the notice letter.

Section 1001.2005, Notice to State licensing agencies: We propose deleting paragraph (b) of this section. While the regulations would still indicate that the Department will notify the appropriate State or local agencies or authorities responsible for licensing or certification of the circumstances leading to an individual's or entity's exclusion, we do not want to be locked into a specific notification process if alternative methods can be considered for notifying provider licensing and certification boards.

Section 1001.2006, Notice to others regarding exclusion: Section 221 of HIPAA established a new national health care fraud and abuse data collection program for the reporting of final adverse actions against health care providers, suppliers and practitioners. As a result, we would revise Sec. 1001.2006(a) to indicate that, in addition to the general public and program beneficiaries, the Department will not also provide notice of the exclusion and its effective date to the new Adverse Action Data Bank.

Section 1001.3001, Timing and method of request for reinstatement: Because there has been some misunderstanding as to when an exclusion period ends, in addition to clarifying that the act of obtaining a provider number does not reinstate program eligibility (see discussion of Sec. 1001.1901 above), we would also revise paragraphs (1) (a) and (b) to indicate that an excluded individual or entity (other than those excluded in accordance with Secs. 1001.1001, 1001.1051 and 1001.1101) may submit a request for reinstatement to the OIG only after the minimum period of exclusion specified in the notice of exclusion has expired. A conforming change would also be made in Sec. 1001.3002(a)(1).

Section 1001.3002, Basis for reinstatement: Section 214(b) of HIPAA has amended the statute by indicating that in making a determination on whether to sanction a practitioner or other person — based on a recommendation from a Peer Review Organization (PRO) — for failing to comply with statutory obligations relating to quality and medical necessity of health care services, the Department will no longer to be required to prove that the practitioner or other person was either unwilling or unable to comply with such obligations. While this statutory change is being addressed through separate rulemaking addressing the PRO sanctions process and changes to part 1004 of our regulations, we would make a conforming change to paragraph (b) of Sec. 1001.3002 to delete the "unwillingness and inability" factor as a basis for consideration by the OIG in making a reinstatement determination.

Section 1002.3, Disclosure by providers; information on persons convicted of crimes: Under part 1002, which addresses State-initiated exclusions from the Medicaid program, we would revise Sec. 1002.3(b) to codify in regulations as new paragraph (b)(3) concerning Medicaid State agency requirements for notification to the OIG. Specifically, the new paragraph would clearly state that the Medicaid agency is required to promptly notify the OIG of any and all actions it takes to limit the individual's or entity's ability to participate in its program. Th is would include, but would not be limited to: (1) Suspension actions, (2) settlement agreements and (3) situations where the individual or entity may have voluntarily agreed to withdraw from the program in order to avoid a formal sanction action.

III. Regulatory Impact Statement

Executive Order 12866 and Regulatory Flexibility Act

The Office of Management and Budget (OMB) has reviewed this proposed rule in accordance with the provisions of Executive Order 12866 and the Regulatory Flexibility Act (5 U.S.C. 601–612), and has determined that it does not meet the criteria for a significant regulatory action. Executive Order 12866 directs agencies to assess all costs and benefits of available regulatory alternatives and, when rulemaking is necessary, to select regulatory approaches that maximize net benefits (including potential economic, environmental, public health, safety distributive and equity effects). In addition, under the Regulatory Flexibility Act, if a rule has a significant economic effect on a number of small businesses the Secretary must specifically consider the economic effect of a rule on small business entities and analyze regulatory options that could lessen the impact of the rule.

The provisions set forth in this proposed rulemaking, for the most part, implement statutory requirements, and are designed to lengthen and broaden the scope of the OIG's authority to include individuals and entities from the Medicare and the State health care programs. As indicated above, these provisions would implement the new statutory requirements regarding the period of exclusion for some individuals and entities by: (1) Broadening the minimum 5-year mandatory exclusion authority to cover felony convictions under Federal, State or local law relating to health care fraud, and (2) establishing minimum periods of exclusion for certain permissive exclusions. We believe that the number of individuals and entities effected by this lengthening of exclusions would be minimal.

Further, while the provisions in this rule serve to clarify the OIG's sanction authorities by (1) Establishing a new permissive exclusion applicable to individuals having majoring ownership interest in (or significant control over the operations of) an entity convicted of a program-related offenses; (2) clarifying what would constitute patient abuse or neglect for purposes of exclusion; and (3) setting forth a definition for "furnished" that would apply to individuals and entities that provide or supply items or services directly or indirectly, we likewise believe the increase in the number of exclusion cases will be small. Specifically, while the statutory requirement to impose exclusions in cases of certain types of convictions has been broadened in sections 1128 (a)(3) and (a)(4) of the Act, the process for excluding individuals and entities who are convicted in accordance with the new requirements remains essentially the same. Cases to be processed under the new mandatory provisions set forth in sections 1128 (a)(3) and (a)(4) for the minimum mandatory 5-year exclusion were previously processed under the permissive authority provisions in sections 1128 (b)(1) and (b)(3) of the Act, with a benchmark of 3 years. As a result, while there may be minor increases in the number of mandatory exclusions imposed, we see no significant increase or decrease in the number of these cases. Similarly, the clarification of what constitutes patient neglect or abuse should not result in a significant increase in the number of cases under section 1128(a)(2) of the Act, but merely support prior findings of abuse and neglect while delivering health care services.

In addition, we do not anticipate a significant workload resulting from the implementation of section 1128(b)(15) of the Act, and proposed Sec. 1001.1051 of these regulations, as the requirements for effectuating this authority are rather stringent at the present time, and will limit the number of exclusions to be implemented under this authority.

Since the vast majority of individuals, organizations and entities addressed by these regulations do not engage in such prohibited activities and practices, we believe that any aggregate economic effect of these revised exclusion regulations will be minimal, affecting only those limited few who engage in prohibited behavior in violation of the statute. As such, this proposed rule should have no significant economic impact. Similarly, while some sanctions may have an impact on small entities, it is the nature of the violation and not the size of the entity that will result in an action by the OIG. We believe that the aggregate economic impact of this rulemaking should be minimal, affecting only those limited few who have chosen to engage in prohibited arrangements, schemes or practices in violation of statutory intent. Therefore, we have concluded, and the Secretary certifies, that this proposed rule would not have a significant economic impact on a number of small business entities, and that a regulatory flexibility analysis is not required for this rulemaking.

Paperwork Reduction Act

Section 1002.3 of this rulemaking contains information collection requirements that require approval by OMB. We are required to solicit public comments under section 3506(c)(2)(A) of the Paperwork Reduction Act of 1995. Specifically, we are inviting comments on (1) whether the collection of information is necessary for the proper performance of the functions of the agency, including whether the information will have practical utility; (2) the accuracy of the estimate of the burden of the collection of information; (3) ways to enhance the quality, utility and clarity of the information collected; and (4) ways to minimize the burden of the collection of information on practitioners and other persons, including through the use of automated collection techniques or other forms of information technology.

Title: Information on persons convicted of crimes.

Summary of the collection of information: In order to effectuate the requirements of section 1128(b)(5) of the Social Security Act, authorizing the OIG to exclude individuals and entities that are sanctioned by a Federal or State agency (including State Medicaid agencies), a State Medicaid agency must promptly notify the OIG of any action it takes to limit an individual's or entity's participation in Medicaid. To implement this statutory authority, we are clarifying in Sec. 1002.3 of the regulations the scope of conduct constituting a basis for State Medicaid notice of denials of participation or imposition of a sanction. Specifically, under section 1902(a) (39) and (41) of the Social Security Act, State agencies are required to notify the Secretary when a provider has been denied participation status in Medicaid, or has been terminated, suspended or "otherwise sanctioned" under the Medicaid program. We are clarifying what actions fall within the ambit of these provisions. The reporting obligation set forth in Sec. 1002.3 is consistent with the requirements of the statute.

Respondents: The "respondents" for the collection of information described in Sec. 1002.3 are the individual State Medicaid agencies.

Estimated number of respondents: The OIG annually receives approximately 500 notifications from State Medicaid agencies regarding actions taken against an individual or entity. While we are specifically clarifying that these actions are to include any suspension actions, settlement agreements and situations where an individual or entity voluntarily withdraws from the program to avoid a formal sanction, we believe that the number of actions reported by the State agencies to the Secretary will remain low.

Estimated number of responses per respondent: 1.

Estimated total annual burden on respondents: We believe that the burden on the State Medicaid agencies in preparing the notification to the OIG will be minimal. We estimate that the average burden for each submitted notification to the OIG will be less than one-half hour. The total burden for this information collection activity is estimated not to exceed 250 hours annually.

Comments on these information collection activities should be sent to both:

Cynthia Agens Bauer, OS Reports Clearance Officer, ASMB Budget Office, Room 503-H, Humphrey Building, 200 Independence Avenue, S.W., Washington, D.C. 20201, FAX: (202) 690–6352Allison Herron Eydt, OIG Desk Officer, Office of Management and Budget, Room 10235, New Executive Office Building, 715 17th Street, N.W., Washington, D.C. 20053, FAX: (202) 395–6974

Comments on these paperwork reduction requirements should be submitted to the above individuals within 60 days following the Federal Register publication of this proposed rule.

List of Subjects

42 CFR Part 1001

Administrative practice and procedure, Fraud, Health facilities, Health professions, Medicaid, Medicare.

42 CFR Part 1002

Fraud, Grant programs — health, Health facilities, Health professions, Medicaid, Reporting and recordkeeping.

42 CFR Part 1005

Administrative practice and procedure, Fraud, Penalties.

Accordingly, 42 CFR Parts 1000, 1001, 1002 and 1005 would be amended as set forth below:

A. Part 1000 would be amended as follows:

PART 1000 — [AMENDED]

1. The authority citation for part 1000 would continue to read as follows:

Authority: 42 U.S.C. 1320 and 1395hh.

2. Section 1000.10 would be amended by republishing the introductory paragraph and by revising the definition for the term *Furnished* to read as follows:

Sec. 1000.10 General definitions.

In this chapter, unless the context indicates otherwise — * * * * *

Furnished refers to items or services provided or supplied, directly or indirectly, by any individual or entity. This includes items and services manufactured, distributed or otherwise provided by individuals or entities that do not directly submit claims to Medicare or State health care programs, but that supply items or services to providers, practitioners or suppliers who submit claims to these programs for such items or services.* * * * *

B. Part 1001 would be amended as follows:

PART 1001 — [AMENDED]

1. The authority citation for part 1001 would be revised to read as follows:

Authority: 42 U.S.C. 1302, 1320a-7, 1320a-7b, 1395u(j), 1359u(k), 1395y(d), 1395y(e), 1395cc(b)(2) (D), (E) and (F), and 1395hh; and sec. 2455, Pub. L. 103–355, 108 Stat. 3327 (31 U.S.C. 6101 note).

(2) Section 1001.2 would be amended by revising the definitions for the terms *Exclusion, Professionally recognized standards of health care,* and *Sole source of essential specialized services in the community;* and by adding definitions for the terms *Incarceration* and *Patient* to read as follows:

Sec. 1001.2 Definitions.

* * * * *

Exclusion means that items and services furnished, ordered or prescribed by a specified individual or entity will not be reimbursed under Medicare or the State health care programs until the individual or entity is reinstated by the OIG.* * * * *

Incarceration means imprisonment or any type of confinement with or without supervised release, including, but not limited to, community confinement, house arrest and home detention.* * * * *

Patient means any individual who is receiving health care items or services, including any item or service provided to meet his or her physical, mental or emotional needs or well-being, whether or not reimbursed under Medicare or a State health care program and regardless of the location in which such item or service is provided. * * * * *

Professionally recognized standards of health care are Statewide or national standards of care, whether in writing or not, that professional peers of the individual or entity whose provision of care is an issue, recognized as applying to those peers practicing or providing care within a State. When the Department has declared a treatment modality not to be safe and effective, practitioners who employ such a treatment modality will be deemed not to meet professionally recognized standards of health care. This definition shall not be construed to mean that all other treatments meet professionally recognized standards.* * * * *

Sole source of essential specialized services in the community means that an individual or entity —

(a) Is the only practitioner, supplier or provider furnishing specialized services in an area designated by the Health Resources Services Administration as a health professional shortage area for that medical specialty, as listed in 42 CFR part 5, appendices B-F;

(b) Is a sole community hospital, as defined in Sec. 412.92 of this title; or

(c) Is the only source of specialized services in a reasonably defined service area where services by a non-specialist could not be substituted for the source without jeopardizing the health or safety of beneficiaries.* * * * *

3. Section 1001.101 would be revised to read as follows:

Sec. 1001.101 Basis for liability.

The OIG will exclude any individual or entity that —

(a) Has been convicted of a criminal offense related to the delivery of an item or service under Medicare or a State health care program, including the performance of management or administrative services relating to the delivery of items or services under any such program;

(b) Has been convicted, under Federal or State law, of a criminal offense related to the neglect or abuse of a patient, in connection with the delivery of a health care item or service, including any offense that the OIG concludes entailed, or resulted in, neglect or abuse of patients (the delivery of a health care item or service includes the provision of any item or service to an individual to meet his or her physical, mental or emotional needs or well-being, whether or not reimbursed under Medicare or a State health care program);

(c) Has been convicted, under Federal or State law, of a felony that occurred after August 21, 1996 relating to fraud, theft, embezzlement, breach of fiduciary responsibility, or other misconduct —

(1) In connection with the delivery of a health care item or service, including the performance of management or administrative services relating to the delivery of such items or services, or

(2) With respect to any act or omission in a health care program (other than Medicare or the State health care programs) operated by, or financed in whole or in part, by any Federal, State or local government agency; or

(d) Has been convicted, under Federal or State law, of a felony that occurred after August 21, 1996 relating to the unlawful manufacture, distribution, prescription or dispensing of a controlled substance, as defined under Federal or State law. This applies to any individual or entity that —

(1) Is, or has ever been, a health care practitioner, provider or supplier;

(2) Holds, or has held, a direct or indirect ownership or control interest (as defined in section 1124(a)(3) of the Act) in an entity that is a health care provider or supplier, or is, or has ever been, an officer, director, agent or managing employee (as defined in section 1126(b) of the Act) of such an entity; or

(3) Is, or has ever been, employed in any capacity in the health care industry.

4. Section 1001.102 would be amended by revising paragraph (b); republishing the introductory text of paragraph (c); and revising paragraph (c)(3) to read as follows:

Sec. 1001.102 Length of exclusion.

* * * * *

(b) Any of the following factors may be considered to be aggravating and a basis for lengthening the period of exclusion —

(1) The acts resulting in the conviction, or similar acts, resulted in financial loss to a government program or to one or more entities of $1,500 or more. (The entire amount of financial loss to such programs or entities, including any amounts resulting from similar acts not adjudicated, will be considered regardless of whether full or partial restitution has been made);

(2) The acts that resulted from in the conviction, or similar acts, were committed over a period of one year or more;

(3) The acts that resulted in the conviction, or similar acts, had a significant adverse physical, mental or financial impact on one or more program beneficiaries or other individuals;

(4) In convictions involving patient abuse or neglect, the action that resulted in the conviction was premeditated, was part of a continuing pattern or behavior, or consisted of non-consensual sexual acts;

(5) The sentence imposed by the court included incarceration;

(6) Whether the individual or entity has a documented history of criminal, civil or administrative wrongdoing;

(7) The individual or entity has at any time been overpaid a total of $1,500 or more by Medicare or State health care programs, or other third-party payers, as a result of improper billings; or

(8) Whether the individual or entity was convicted of other offenses besides those which formed the basis for the exclusion, or has been the subject of any other adverse action by any Federal, State or local government agency or board, even if the adverse action is based on the same set of circumstances that serves as the basis for imposition of the exclusion.

(c) Only if any of the aggravating factors set forth in paragraph (b) of this section justifies an exclusion longer than 5 years, may mitigating factors be considered as the basis for reducing the period of exclusion to no less than 5 years. Only the following factors may be considered mitigating — * * * * *

(3) The individual's or entity's cooperation with Federal or State officials resulted in —

(i) Others being convicted or excluded from Medicare or any of the State health care programs,

(ii) Additional cases being investigated or reports being issued by the appropriate law enforcement agency identifying program vulnerabilities or weaknesses, or

(iii) The imposition against anyone of a civil money penalty or assessment under part 1003 of this chapter.

5. Section 1001.201 would be amended by revising the section heading; revising paragraph (a); republishing the introductory text of paragraph (b)(2), revising paragraphs (b)(2) (iv) and (v), and adding a new paragraph (b)(2)(vi); and by republishing the introductory text of paragraph (b)(3) and revising paragraphs (b)(3)(i) and (b)(3)(iii) to read as follows:

Sec. 1001.201 Conviction relating to fraud.

(a) Circumstance for exclusion. The OIG may exclude an individual or entity convicted under Federal or State law of—

(1) A misdemeanor relating to fraud, theft, embezzlement, breach of fiduciary responsibility, or other financial misconduct —

(i) In connection with the delivery of any health care item or service, including the performance of management or administrative services relating to the delivery of such items or services, or

(ii) With respect to any act or omission in a health care program, other than Medicare or a State health care program, operated by, or financed in whole or in part by, any Federal, State or local government agency; or

(2) Fraud, theft, embezzlement, breach or fiduciary responsibility, or other financial misconduct with respect to any act or omission in a program, other than a health care program, operated by or financed in whole or in part by any Federal, State or local government agency.

(b) Length of exclusion. * * *

(2) Any of the following factors may be considered to be aggravating and a basis for lengthening the period of exclusion — * * * * *

(iv) The sentence imposed by the court included incarceration;

(v) Whether the individual or entity has a documented history of criminal, civil or administrative wrongdoing; or

(vi) Whether the individual or entity was convicted of other offenses besides those which formed the basis for the exclusion, or has been the subject of any other adverse action by any Federal, State or local government agency or board, even if the adverse action is based on the same set of circumstances that serves as the basis for the imposition of the exclusion.

(3) Only the following factors may be considered as mitigating and a basis for reducing the period of exclusion —

(i) The individual or entity was convicted of 3 or fewer offenses, and the entire amount of financial loss to a government program or to other individuals or entities due to the acts that resulted in the conviction and similar acts is less than $1,500;* * * * *

(iii) The individual's or entity's cooperation with Federal or State officials resulted in —

(A) Others being convicted or excluded from Medicare or any of the State health care programs,

(B) Additional cases being investigated or reports being used by the appropriate law enforcement agency identifying program vulnerabilities or weaknesses, or

(C) The imposition of a civil money penalty against others; or* * * * *

6. Section 1001.301 would be amended by republishing the introductory text of paragraph (b)(2); revising paragraphs (b)(2) (iv) and (v); by adding a new paragraph (b)(2)(vi); by republishing the introductory text of paragraph (b)(3); and by revising paragraph (b)(3)(ii) to read as follows:

Sec. 1001.301 Conviction relating to obstruction of an investigation.

* * * * *

(b) Length of exclusion. * * *

(2) Any of the following factors may be considered to be aggravating and a basis for lengthening the period of exclusion — * * * * *

(iv) The sentence imposed by the court included incarceration;

(v) Whether the individual or entity has a documented history of criminal, civil or administrative wrongdoing; or

(vi) Whether the individual or entity was convicted of other offenses besides those which formed the basis for the exclusion, or has been the subject of any other adverse action by any Federal, State or local government agency or board, even if the adverse action is based on the same set of circumstances that serves as the basis for the imposition of the exclusion.

(3) Only the following factors may be considered as mitigating and a basis for reducing the period of exclusion — * * * * *

(ii) The individual's or entity's cooperation with Federal or State officials resulted in —

(A) Others being convicted or excluded from Medicare or any of the State health care programs,

(B) Additional cases being investigated or reports being issued by the appropriate law enforcement agency identifying program vulnerabilities or weaknesses, or

(C) The imposition of a civil money penalty against others; or* * * * *

7. Section 1001.401 would be amended by revising the section heading; revising paragraph (a); by republishing the introductory text of paragraph (c)(2); by revising paragraphs (c)(2) (iii) and (iv); by adding a new paragraph (c)(2)(v); by republishing introductory paragraph (c)(3); and by revising paragraph (c)(3)(i) to read as follows:

Sec. 1001.401 Misdemeanor conviction relating to controlled substances.

(a) Circumstance for exclusion. The OIG may exclude an individual or entity convicted under Federal or State law of a misdemeanor relating to the unlawful manufacture, distribution, prescription or dispensing of a controlled substance, as defined under Federal or State law. This section applies to any individual or entity that —

(1) Is, or has ever been, a health care practitioner, provider or supplier;

(2) Holds or has held a direct or indirect ownership or control interest, as defined in section 1124(a)(3) of the Act, in an entity that is a health care provider or supplier, or is or has been an officer, director, agent or managing employee, as defined in section 1126(b) of the Act, of such an entity; or

(3) Is, or has ever been, employed in any capacity in the health care industry.* * * * *

(c) Length of exclusion. * * *

(2) Any of the following factors may be considered to be aggravating and a basis for lengthening the period of exclusion — * * * * *

(iii) The sentence imposed by the court included incarceration;

(iv) Whether the individual or entity has a documented history of criminal, civil or administrative wrongdoing; or

(v) Whether the individual or entity was convicted of other offenses besides those which formed the basis for the exclusion, or has been the subject of any other adverse action by any other Federal, State or local government agency or board, even if the adverse action is based on the same set of circumstances that serves as the basis for the imposition of the exclusion.

(3) Only the following factors may be considered as mitigating and a basis for shortening the period of exclusion —

(i) The individual's or entity's cooperation with Federal or State officials resulted in —

(A) Others being convicted or excluded from Medicare or any of the State health care programs,

(B) Additional cases being investigated or reports being issued by the appropriate law enforcement agency identifying program vulnerabilities or weaknesses, or

(C) The imposition of a civil money penalty against others; or* * * * *

8. Section 1001.501 would be amended by revising paragraph (b)(1); republishing the introductory text of paragraph (b)(2), revising paragraphs (b)(2) (ii) and (iii), and adding a new paragraph (b)(2)(iv); by republishing the introductory text of paragraph (b)(3) and revising paragraph (b)(3)(i); and by deleting paragraph (c) to read as follows:

Sec. 1001.501 License revocation or suspension.

* * * * *

(b) Length of exclusion. (1) An exclusion imposed in accordance with this section will not be for a period of time less than the period during which an individual's or entity's license is revoked, suspended or otherwise not in effect as a result of, or in connection with, a State licensing agency action.

(2) Any of the following factors may be considered aggravating and a basis for lengthening the period for exclusion — * * * * *

(ii) Whether the individual or entity has a documented history of criminal, civil or administrative wrongdoing;

(iii) The acts, or similar acts, had or could have had a significant adverse impact on the financial integrity of the programs; or

(iv) The individual or entity has been the subject of any other adverse action by any other Federal, State or local government agency or board, even if the adverse action is based on the same set of circumstances that serves as the basis for the imposition of the exclusion.

(3) Only if any of the aggravating factors listed in paragraph (b)(2) of this section justifies a longer exclusion may mitigating factors be considered as a basis for reducing the period of exclusion to a period not less than that set forth in paragraph (b)(1) of this section. Only the following factors may be considered mitigating —

(i) The individual's or entity's cooperation with a State licensing authority resulted in —

(A) The sanctioning of other individuals or entities, or

(B) Additional cases being investigated or reports being issued by the appropriate law enforcement agency identifying program vulnerabilities or weaknesses; or* * * * *

9. Section 1001.601 would be amended by revising paragraph (b) to read as follows:

Sec. 1001.601 Exclusion or suspension under a Federal or State health care program.

* * * * *

(b) Length of exclusion. (1) An exclusion imposed in accordance with this section will not be for a period of time less than the period during which the individual or entity license is excluded or suspended from a Federal or State health care program.

(2) Any of the following factors may be considered aggravating and a basis for lengthening the period of exclusion —

(i) The acts that resulted in the exclusion, suspension or other sanction under the Federal or State healthy care program had, or could have had, a significant adverse impact on Federal or State health care programs or the beneficiaries of those programs or other individuals;

(ii) Whether the individual or entity has a documented history of criminal, civil or administrative wrongdoing; or

(iii) The individual or entity has been the subject of any other adverse action by any Federal, State or local government agency or board, even if the adverse action is based on the same set of circumstances that serves as the basis for the imposition of the exclusion.

(3) Only if any of the aggravating factors set forth in paragraph (b)(2) of this section justifies a longer exclusion may mitigating factors be considered as a basis for reducing the period of exclusion to a period not less than that set forth in paragraph (b)(1) of this section. Only the following factors may be considered mitigating —

(i) The individual or entity's cooperation with Federal or State officials resulted in —

(A) The sanctioning of other individuals or entities, or

(B) Additional cases being investigated or reports being issued by the appropriate law enforcement agency identifying program vulnerabilities or weaknesses; or

(ii) Alternative sources of the types of health care items or services furnished by the individual or entity are not available.

(4) If the individual or entity is eligible to apply for reinstatement in accordance with Sec. 1001.3001 of this part, and the sole reason for the State denying reinstatement is the existing Medicare exclusion imposed by the OIG as a result of the original State action, the OIG will consider a request for reinstatement.

10. Section 1001.701 would be amended by republishing introductory paragraph (a) and revising paragraph (a)(1); revising paragraph (d)(1); and by republishing introductory paragraph (d)(2), revising paragraphs (d)(2) (iii) and (iv), and adding paragraph (d)(2)(v) to read as follows:

Sec. 1001.701 Excessive claims or furnishing of unnecessary or substandard items or services.

(a) Circumstance for exclusion. The OIG may exclude an individual or entity that has —

(1) Submitted, or caused to be submitted, bills or requests for payments under Medicare or any of the State health care programs containing charges or costs for items or services furnished that are substantially in excess of such individual's or entity's usual charges or costs for such items or services to any of their customers, clients or patients; or* * * * *

(d) Length of exclusion. (1) An exclusion imposed in accordance with this section will be for a period of 3 years, unless aggravating or mitigating factors set forth in paragraphs (d)(2) and (d)(3) of this section form a basis for lengthening or shortening the period. In no case may the period be shorter than 1 year.

(2) Any of the following factors may be considered aggravating and a basis for lengthening the period of exclusion — * * * * *

(iii) Whether the individual or entity has a documented history of criminal, civil or administrative wrongdoing;

(iv) The violation resulted in financial loss to Medicare or the State health care programs of $1,500 or more; or

(iv) The individual or entity has been the subject of any other adverse action by any Federal, State or local government agency or board, even if the adverse action is based on the same set of circumstances that serves as the basis for the imposition of the exclusion.* * * * *

11. Section 1001.801 would be amended by revising paragraph (c)(1); and by republishing introductory paragraph (c)(2), revising paragraphs (c)(2) (iii) and (iv), and adding a new paragraph (c)(2)(v) to read as follows:

Sec. 1001.801 Failure of HMOs and CMPs to furnish medically necessary items and services.

* * * * *

(c) Length of exclusion. (1) An exclusion imposed in accordance with this section will be for a period of 3 years, unless aggravating or mitigating factors set forth in paragraphs (c)(2) and (c)(3) of this section form a basis of lengthening or shortening the period. In no case may the period be shorter than 1 year.

(2) Any of the following factors may be considered aggravating and a basis for lengthening the period of exclusion — * * * * *

(iii) The entity's failure to provide a necessary item or service that had or could have had a serious adverse effect;

(iv) Whether the individual or entity has a documented history of criminal, civil or administrative wrongdoing; or

(v) The individual or entity has been the subject of any other adverse action by any Federal, State or local government agency or board, even if the adverse action is based on the same set of circumstances that serves as the basis for the imposition of the exclusion.* * * * *

12. Section 1001.901 would be amended by republishing introductory paragraph (b), revising paragraph (b)(3), redesignating existing paragraph (b)(4) as (b)(5), and adding a new paragraph (b)(4) to read as follows:

Sec. 1001.901 False or improper claims.

* * * * *

(b) Length of exclusion. In determining the length of exclusion imposed in accordance with this section, the OIG will consider the following factors — * * * * *

(3) Whether the individual or entity has a documented history of criminal, civil or administrative wrongdoing (The lack of any prior is to be considered neutral);

(4) The individual or entity has been the subject of any other adverse action by any Federal, State or local government agency or board, even if the adverse action is based on the same set of circumstances that serves as the basis for the imposition of the exclusion; or

(5) Other matters as justice may require.

13. Section 1001.951 would be amended by republishing introductory paragraph (b)(1), revising paragraph (b)(1)(iii), redesignating existing paragraph (b)(1)(iv) as (b)(1)(v), and adding a new paragraph (b)(1)(iv) to read as follows:

Sec. 1001.951 Fraud and kickbacks and other prohibited activities.

* * * * *

(b) Length of exclusion. (1) The following factors will be considered in determining the length of exclusion in accordance with this section — * * * * *

(iii) Whether the individual or entity has a documented history of criminal, civil or administrative wrongdoing (The lack of any prior record is to be considered neutral);

(iv) The individual or entity has been the subject of any other adverse action by any Federal, State or local government agency or board, even if the adverse action is based on the same set of circumstances that serves as the basis for the imposition of the exclusion; or* * * * *

Sec. 1001.953 [Removed]

14. Section 1001.953 would be removed.

15. Section 1001.1001 would be amended by republishing the heading for paragraph (a) and introductory paragraph (a)(2); and by revising the definition for the term *agent* set forth in paragraph (a)(2) to read as follows:

Sec. 1001.1001 Exclusion of entities owned or controlled by a sanctioned person.

(a) Circumstances for exclusion. * * *

(2) For purposes of this section, the term:

Agent means any person who has express or implied authority to obligate or act on behalf of an entity. The excluded individual may be considered an agent even if he or she has transferred ownership or control interest to his or her spouse or children. For example, if the excluded individual transfers control of an entity to his or her spouse, but still acts on behalf of the entity or exercises some control over the entity, the excluded individual would be an agent since he or she would have the implied authority to act on behalf of that entity.* * * * *

16. A new Sec. 1001.1051 would be added to read as follows:

Sec. 1001.1051 Exclusion of individuals with ownership or control interest in sanctioned entities.

(a) Circumstance for exclusion. The OIG may exclude any individual who —

(1) Has a direct or indirect ownership or control interest in a sanctioned entity, and who knows or should know (as defined in section 1128A(i)(6) of the Act) of the action constituting the basis for the conviction or exclusion set forth in paragraph (b) of this section; or

(2) Is an officer or managing employee (as defined in section 1126(b) of the Act) of such an entity.

(b) For purposes of paragraph (a) of this section, the term sanctioned entity means an entity that —

(1) Has been convicted of any offense described in Secs. 1001.101 through 1001.401 of this part; or

(2) Has been terminated or excluded from participation in Medicare or a State health care program.

(c) Length of exclusion. (1) If the entity has been excluded, the length of the individual's exclusion will be for the same period as that of the sanctioned entity with which the individual has the prohibited relationship.

(2) If the entity was not excluded, the length of the individual's exclusion will be determined by considering the factors that would have been considered if the entity had been excluded.

(3) An individual excluded under this section may apply for reinstatement at any time in accordance with the procedures set forth in Sec. 1001.3001.

17. Section 1001.1101 would be amended by revising paragraph (b)(3) to read as follows:

Sec. 1001.1101 Failed to disclose certain information.

* * * * *

(b) Length of exclusion. The following factors will be considered in determining the length of an exclusion under this section — * * * * *

(3) Whether the individual or entity has a documented history of criminal, civil or administrative wrongdoing (The lack of any prior record is to be considered neutral);* * * * *

18. Section 1001.1201 would be amended by revising paragraph (b)(4) to read as follows:

Sec. 1001.1201 Failure to provide payment information.

* * * * *

(b) * * *

(4) Whether the individual or entity has a documented history of criminal, civil or administrative wrongdoing (The lack of any prior record is to be considered neutral); and* * * * *

19. Section 1001.1301 would be amended by revising paragraph (b)(2)(iv) to read as follows:

Sec. 1001.1301 Failure to grant immediate access.

* * * * *

(b) * * *

(2) * * ** * * * *

(iv) Whether the entity has a documented history of criminal, civil or administrative wrongdoing (The lack of any prior record is to be considered neutral).* * * * *

20. Section 1001.1401 would be amended by revising paragraph (b)(5) to read as follows:

Sec. 1001.1401 Violations of PPS corrective action.

* * * * *

(b) Length of exclusion. * * ** * * * *

(5) Whether the individual or entity has a documented history of criminal, civil or administrative wrongdoing (The lack of any prior record is to be considered neutral).

21. Section 1001.1601 would be amended by revising paragraph (b)(1)(iv) to read as follows:

Sec. 1001.1601 Violations of the limitations on physician charges.

* * * * *

(b) Length of exclusion. (1) * * *

(iv) Whether the physicians has a documented history of criminal, civil or administrative wrongdoing (The lack of any prior record is to be considered neutral); and* * * * *

22. Section 1001.1701 would be amended by revising paragraph (c)(1)(v) to read as follows:

Sec. 1001.1701 Billing for services of assistant at surgery during cataract operations.

* * * * *

(c) Length of exclusion. * * *

(v) Whether the physician has a documented history of criminal, civil or administrative wrongdoing (The lack of any prior record is to be considered neutral); and

23. Section 1001.1901 would be amended by revising paragraphs (b)(1) and (b)(3); revising existing paragraph (c)(4) and redesignating is as (c)(5); and by adding a new paragraph (c)(4) to read as follows:

Sec. 1001.1901 Scope and effect of exclusion.

* * * * *

(b) Effect of exclusion on excluded individuals and entities. (1) Unless and until an individual or entity is reinstated into the Medicare program in accordance with subpart F of this part, no payment will be made by Medicare or any of the State health care programs for any item or service furnished, on or after the effective date specified in the notice period, by an excluded individual or entity, or at the medical direction or on the prescription of a physician or other authorized individual who is excluded when the individual or entity furnishing such item or service knew, or had reason to know, of the exclusion. This section applies regardless of whether an individual or entity has obtained a program provider number, either as an individual or as a member of a group, prior to being reinstated.* * * * *

(3) An excluded individual or entity that submits, or causes to be submitted, claims for items or services furnished during the exclusion period is subject to civil money penalty liability under section 1128A(a)(1)(D) of the Act, and criminal liability under section 1128B(a)(3) of the Act and other provisions. In addition, submitting claims, or causing claims to be submitted or payments to be made for items or services furnished, ordered or prescribed, including administrative and management services or salary, may serve as the basis for denying reinstatement to the programs.

(c) Exceptions to paragraph (b)(1) of this section.* * * * *

(4) HCFA will not pay any claims submitted by, or for items or services ordered or prescribed by, an excluded provider for dates of service 5 days or more after that notice of the provider's exclusion was mailed by the contractor to the supplier.

(5) * * *

(ii) Notwithstanding paragraph (c)(5)(i) of this section, no claim for emergency items or services will be payable if such items or services were provided by an excluded individual who, through an employment, contractual or any other arrangement, routinely provides emergency health care items or services.

24. Section 1001.2001 would be revised to read as follows:

Sec. 1001.2001 Notice of intent to exclude.

(a) Except as provided in paragraph (b) of this section, if the OIG proposes to exclude an individual or entity in accordance with subpart C of this part, or in accordance with subpart B of this part where the exclusion is for a period exceeding 5 years, it will send written notice of its intent, the basis for the proposed exclusion the potential effect of an exclusion. Within 30 days of receipt of notice, which will be deemed to be 5 days after the date on the notice, the individual or entity may submit documentary evidence and written argument concerning whether the exclusion is warranted and any related issues.

(b) Exception. If the OIG proposes to exclude an individual or entity under the provisions of Secs. 1001.1301, 1001.1401 or 1001.1501 of this part, paragraph (a) of this section will not apply.

(c) If an entity has a provider agreement under section 1866 of the Act, and the OIG proposes to terminate that agreement in accordance with section 1866(b)(2)(C) of the Act, the notice provided for in paragraph (a) of this section will so state.

25. Section 1001.2002 would be amended by adding a new paragraph (e) to read as follows:

Sec. 1001.2002 Notice of exclusion.

* * * * *

(e) No later than 15 days prior to the final exhibit exchanges required under Sec. 1005.8 of this chapter, the OIG may amend its notice letter if information comes to light that justifies the imposition of a different period of exclusion other than the one proposed in the original notice letter.

26. Section 1001.2003 would be amended by revising introductory paragraph (a) to read as follows:

Sec. 1001.2003 Notice of proposal to exclude.

(a) Except as provided in paragraph (c) of this section, if the OIG proposes to exclude an individual or entity in accordance with Secs. 1001.901, 1001.951, 1001.1601 or 1001.1701, it will send written notice of this decision to the affected individual or entity. The written notice will provide the same information set forth in Sec. 1001.2002(c). If an entity has a provider agreement under section 1866 of the Act, and the OIG also proposes to terminate that agreement in accordance with section 1866(b)(2)(C) of the Act, the notice will so indicate. The exclusion will be effective 60 days after the receipt of the notice (as defined in Sec. 1005.2 of this chapter) unless, within that period, the individual or entity files a written request for a hearing in accordance with part 1005 of this chapter. Such request must set forth — * * * * *

27. Section 1001.2005 would be revised to read as follows:

Sec. 1001.2005 Notice to state licensing agencies.

HHS will promptly notify the appropriate State(s) or local agencies or authorities having responsibility for the licensing or certification of an individual or entity excluded (or directed to be excluded) from participation of the facts and circumstances of the exclusion.

28. Section 1001.2006 would be amended by republishing introductory paragraph (a); revising paragraphs (a)(1) and (a)(7); redesignating existing paragraph (a)(8) as (a)(9); and by adding a new paragraph (a)(8) to read as follows:

Sec. 1001.2006 Notice to others regarding exclusion.

(a) HHS will give notice of the exclusion and the effective date to the public, to beneficiaries (in accordance with Sec. 1001.1901(c)), and, as appropriate, to —

(1) Any entity in which the excluded individual is known to be serving as an employee, administrator, operator, or in which the individual is serving in any other capacity and is receiving payment for providing services (The lack of this notice will not affect HCFA's ability to deny payment for services);* * * * *

(7) The State and Area Agencies on Aging established under title III of the Older Americans Act;

(8) The Adverse Action Data Bank; and* * * * *

29. Section 1001.3001 would be amended by revising paragraphs (a)(1) and (a)(2) to read as follows:

Sec. 1001.3001 Timing and method of request for reinstatement.

(a)(1) Except as provided in paragraphs (a)(2) and (a)(3) of this section or in Sec. 1001.501(b)(4) of this part, an excluded individual or entity (other than those excluded in accordance with Secs. 1001.1001, 1001.1051 and 1001.1501) may submit a written request for reinstatement to the OIG only after the minimum period of exclusion specified in the notice of exclusion has expired. Obtaining a program provider number does not reinstate eligibility.

(2) An entity excluded under Sec. 1001.1001 of this part may apply for reinstatement prior to the minimum period of exclusion specified in the notice of exclusion by submitting a written request for reinstatement that includes documentation demonstrating that the standards set forth in Sec. 1001.3002(c) have been met.* * * * *

30. Section 1001.3002 would be amended by revising paragraph (a); republishing introductory paragraph (b), revising paragraphs (b)(3) and (4) and removing paragraph (b)(5); revising introductory paragraph (c); revising existing paragraph (d) and redesignating paragraphs (d), (e), and (f) as paragraphs (e), (f) and (g) respectively; and by adding a new paragraph (d) to read as follows:

Sec. 1001.3002 Basis for reinstatement.

(a)(1) The OIG will authorize reinstatement if it determines that—

(i) The minimum period of exclusion has expired;

(ii) There are reasonable assurances that the types of actions that formed the basis for the original exclusion have not recurred and will not recur; and

(iii) There is no additional basis under sections 1128 (a) or (b) or 1128A of the Act for continuation of the exclusion.

(2) Submitting claims or causing claims to be submitted or payments to be made by the programs for items or services furnished, ordered or prescribed, including administrative and management

services or salary, may serve as the basis for denying reinstatement. This section applies regardless of whether an individual or entity has obtained a program provider number, either as an individual or as a member of a group, prior to being reinstated.

(b) In making the reinstatement determination, the OIG will consider — * * * * *

(3) Whether all fines, and all debts due and owing (including overpayments) to any Federal, State or local government that relate to Medicare or any of the State health care programs, have been paid or satisfactory arrangements have been made to fulfill these obligations; and

(4) Whether HCFA has determined that the individual or entity complies with, or has made satisfactory arrangements to fulfill, all of the applicable conditions of participation or supplier conditions for coverage under the statutes and regulations.

(c) If the OIG determines that the criteria in paragraphs (a)(1) (ii) and (iii) of this section have been met, an entity excluded in accordance with Sec. 1001.1001 will be reinstated upon a determination by the OIG that the individual whose conviction, exclusion or civil money penalty was the basis for the entity's exclusion — * * * * *

(d) If the OIG determines that the criteria in paragraphs (a)(1) (ii) and (iii) of this section have been met, an individual excluded in accordance with Sec. 1001.1051 will be reinstated upon a determination with paragraph (a) of this section of Sec. 1001.3005.

(e) Reinstatement will not be effective until the OIG grants the request and provides notice under Sec. 1001.3003(a) of this part. Reinstatement will be effective as provided in the notice.

(f) A determination with respect to reinstatement is not appealable or reviewable except as provided in Sec. 1001.3004.

(g) An ALJ may not require reinstatement of an individual or entity in accordance with this chapter.

C. Part 1002 would be amended as follows:

PART 1002 — [AMENDED]

1. The authority citation for part 1002 would continue to read as follows:

Authority: 42 U.S.C. 1302, 1320a-3, 1320a-5, 1320a-7, 1396(a)(4)(A), 1396(p)(1), 1396a(30), 1396a(39) 1396b(a)(6), 1396b(b)(3), 1396b(i)(2) and 1396b(q).

2. Section 1002.3 would be amended by revising paragraph (b)(2) and by adding a new paragraph (b)(3) to read as follows:

Sec. 1002.3 Disclosure by providers; information on persons convicted of crimes.

* * * * *

(b) Notification to Inspector General. * * *

(2) The agency must promptly notify the Inspector General of any action it takes on the provider's application for participation in the program.

(3) The agency must also promptly notify the Inspector General of any action it takes to limit the ability of an individual or entity to participate in its program, regardless of what such an action is called. This includes, but is not limited to, suspension actions, settlement agreements and situations where an individual or entity voluntarily withdraws from the program to avoid a formal sanction.* * * * *

3. Section 1002.203 would be amended by revising paragraph (a) to read as follows:

Sec. 1002.203 Mandatory exclusion.

(a) The State agency, in order to receive Federal financial participation (FFP), must provide that it will exclude from participation any HMO, or entity furnishing services under a waiver approved under section 1915(b)(1) of the Act, if such organization or entity —

(1) Could be excluded under Secs. 1001.1001 or 1001.1051 of this chapter, or

(2) Has, directly or indirectly, a substantial contractual relationship with an individual or entity that could be excluded under Secs. 1001.1001 or 1001.1051 of this chapter.* * * * *

4. Section 1002.211 would be amended by revising paragraph (a) to read as follows:

Sec. 1002.211 Effect of exclusion.

(a) Denial of payment. Except as provided for in Sec. 1001.1901 (c)(3), (c)(4) and (c)(5)(i) of this chapter, no payment may be made by the State agency for any item or service furnished on or after the effective date specified in the notice by an excluded individual or entity, or at the medical direction or on the prescription of a physician who is excluded when a person furnishing such item or service knew, or had reason to know, of the exclusion.

PART 1005 — [AMENDED]

D. Part 1005 would be amended as follows:

1. The authority citation for part 1005 would continue to read as follows:

Authority: 42 U.S.C. 405(a), 405(b), 1302, 1320a-7, 1320a-7a and 1320c-5.

2. Section 1005.15 would be amended by revising introductory paragraph (f)(1) to read as follows:

Sec. 1005.15 The hearing and burden of proof.

* * * * *

(f)(1) A hearing under this part is not limited to specific items and information set forth in the notice letter to the petitioner or respondent. Subject to the 15-day requirement under Sec. 1005.8, additional items and information, including aggravating or mitigating circumstances that arose or became known subsequent to the issuance of the notice letter, may be introduced by either party during its case-in-chief unless such information or items are — * * * * *

Dated: March 13, 1997.

June Gibbs Brown,

Inspector General, Department of Health and Human Services.

Approved: June 18, 1997.

Donna E. Shalala,

Secretary.

[FR Doc. 97–23379 Filed 9–5-97; 8:45 am]

BILLING CODE 4150–04-M

APPENDIX J2

Civil Money Penalties, Assessments, Exclusions, and Related Appeals — Final Rule With Comment Period; 63 FR 68687, December 14, 1998

Federal Register: December 14, 1998 (Volume 63, Number 239)
Rules and Regulations Page 68687–68697

DEPARTMENT OF HEALTH AND HUMAN SERVICES

Health Care Financing Administration

42 CFR Parts 400, and 402

[HCFA-6135-FC]

Medicare and Medicaid Program; Civil Money Penalties, Assessments, Exclusions, and Related Appeals Procedures

AGENCY: Health Care Financing Administration (HCFA), HHS.

ACTION: Final rule with comment period.

SUMMARY: This rule establishes procedures for imposing civil money penalties, assessments, and exclusions for certain violations of the Medicare and Medicaid programs. The regulations also provide for hearings and appeals when those penalties, assessments, and exclusions are imposed. These procedures are based on the procedures that the Office of the Inspector General has promulgated for the civil money penalties, assessments, and exclusions. These regulations are designed to protect program beneficiaries from unfit health care practitioners and to otherwise improve antifraud provisions under the Medicare and Medicaid Acts.

DATES: These regulations are effective on January 13, 1999. Comments must be received by February 12, 1999.

FOR FURTHER INFORMATION CONTACT: Joel Cohen, (410) 786–3349

ADDRESSES: Mail written comments (1 original and 3 copies) to the following address: Health Care Financing Administration, Department of Health and Human Services, Attention: HCFA-6135-FC, PO Box 26676, Baltimore, MD 21207–0519.

If you prefer, you may deliver your written comments (1 original and 3 copies) to one of the following addresses: Room 309-G, Hubert H. Humphrey Building, 200 Independence Avenue, SW., Washington, DC 20201, or Room C5–09–26, 7500 Security Boulevard, Baltimore, MD 21244–1850

Comments may also be submitted electronically to the following e-mail address: HCFA6135FC@hcfa.gov. For e-mail comment procedures, see the beginning of **SUPPLEMENTARY INFORMATION.** For further information on ordering copies of the **Federal Register** containing this document and on electronic access, see the beginning of **SUPPLEMENTARY INFORMATION.** Electronically submitted comments will be available for public inspection at the Independence Avenue address below.

SUPPLEMENTARY INFORMATION:

E-Mail, Comments, Procedures, Availability of Copies, and Electronic Access

E-mail comments must include the full name and address of the sender and must be submitted to the referenced address to be considered. All comments must be incorporated in the e-mail message because we may not be able to access attachments.

Because of staffing and resource limitations, we cannot accept comments by facsimile (FAX) transmission. In commenting, please refer to file code HCFA-0047-P and the specific section or sections of the proposed rule. Both electronic and written comments received by the time and date indicated above will be available for public inspection as they are received, generally beginning approximately 3 weeks after publication of a document, in Room 309-G of the Department's offices at 200 Independence Avenue, SW., Washington, DC, on Monday through Friday of each week from 8:30 a.m. to 5 p.m. (phone: (202) 690–7890). Electronic and legible written comments will also be posted, along with this proposed rule, at the following web site: http://aspe.os.dhhs.gov/ admnsimp/

Copies: To order copies of the **Federal Register** containing this document, send your request to: New Orders, Superintendent of Documents, P.O. Box 371954, Pittsburgh, PA 15250–7954. Specify the date of the issue requested and enclose a check or money order payable to the Superintendent of Documents, or enclose your Visa or Master Card number and expiration date. Credit card orders can also be placed by calling the order desk at (202) 512–1800 or by faxing to (202) 512- 2250. The cost for each copy is $8. As an alternative, you can view and photocopy the **Federal Register** document at most libraries designated as Federal Depository Libraries and at many other public and academic libraries throughout the country that receive the **Federal Register.**

This **Federal Register** document is also available from the Federal Register online database through GPO Access, a service of the U.S. Government Printing Office. Free public access is available on a Wide Area Information Server (WAIS) through the Internet and via asynchronous dial-in. Internet users can access the database by using the World Wide Web, http://www.access.gpo.gov/nara/, by using local WAIS client software, or by telnet to swais.access.gpo.gov, then login as guest (no password required). Dial-in users should use communications software and modem to call (202) 512–1661; type swais, then login as guest (no password required).

I. Background

In 1981, the Congress added section 1128A to the Social Security Act (the Act) (section 2105 of Pub.L. 97–35) to authorize the Secretary of Health and Human Services to impose civil money penalties and assessments on certain health care facilities, health care practitioners, and other suppliers under the Medicare and Medicaid programs. Civil money penalties and assessments provide an alternative enforcement tool for agencies to establish compliance with legal and program standards and are in addition to potential criminal proceedings.

Since 1981, the Congress has significantly increased both the number and the types of circumstances under which the Secretary may impose civil money penalties. Some of the civil money penalty authorities address fraud, misrepresentation, or falsification while others address noncompliance with programmatic or regulations requirements. The Secretary has delegated the authority for these provisions to either the Office of Inspector General (OIG) or HCFA (58 FR 52967, October 20, 1994). Under this delegation of authority, the OIG has the authority to impose civil money penalties and prosecute cases involving civil money penalties and assessments that were delegated to HCFA if HCFA and the OIG jointly determine it to be

[Page 68688]

in the interest of economy, efficiency, or effective coordination of activities.

On October 31, 1994, the Social Security Amendments of 1994 (Pub. L. 103–432) were enacted. This law repealed several statutory provisions providing for civil money penalties and established additional civil money penalty provisions. On August 21, 1996, the Health Insurance Portability and Accountability Act of 1996 (Pub. L. 104–191) was enacted. This law provides for higher maximum civil money penalties ($10,000 instead of $2,000) for certain of the violations and also increased the assessments that can be imposed for those violations.

Most of the specific statutory provisions authorizing civil money penalties also permit the Secretary of Health and Human Services (or his or her designee) to impose an assessment in addition to the civil money penalty. An assessment is an additional monetary payment in lieu of damages sustained by HHS or a State agency. The maximum amount of the assessment varies according to the civil money penalty (from $1,000 to $25,000) and is not more than three times the amount claimed for each service upon which the civil money penalty was based. Also, for many statutory violations, the Secretary of Health and Human Services or his or her designee may exclude the individual or entity violating the statute from participating in a Federal health care program for certain specific periods of time. A Federal health care program is defined in section 1128B of the Act (42 U.S.C. 1320(a)-7b) as "any plan or program that provides health benefits, whether directly, through insurance, or otherwise, which is funded directly, in whole or in part, by the United States Government (other than the health insurance program under chapter 89 of title 5, United States Code); or * * * any State health care program as defined in section 1128(h) of the Social Security Act."

The regulations currently governing civil money penalties, assessments, and civil money penalty-related exclusions are contained in 42 CFR part 1003. Procedures for hearings and appeals of civil money penalties, assessments, and exclusions are in 42 CFR part 1005.

II. Regulations Revisions

This final rule with comment period duplicates in substance 42 CFR part 1003 for most of the civil money penalties and related assessments that have been delegated to HCFA. Other rules concerning civil money penalties and assessment authorities that have been delegated to HCFA, such as those imposed for violations by long term care facilities and clinical laboratories, have already been codified in the Code of Federal Regulations. Civil money penalties and assessments that were added by the Balanced Budget Act of 1997 (BBA), Pub. L. 105–33 (August 5, 1997) and that are delegated to HCFA in the future will be added to the Code of Federal Regulations through another **Federal Register** document, as will the specific rules concerning the exclusions that HCFA is authorized to impose.

Although we are not addressing the civil money penalties and assessments added by the BBA in this regulation, it is important to recognize the impact of the BBA on certain provisions of this regulation. Section 4507 of the BBA permits a physician or practitioner to enter into private contracts with Medicare beneficiaries for services furnished on or after January 1, 1998. If a physician or practitioner enters into a private contract, he or she has "opted out" of the Medicare program for two years for all covered items or services furnished to Medicare beneficiaries. A beneficiary who enters into a private contract agrees to waive the right to Medicare payment for services rendered by the physician or practitioner and to pay the physician or practitioner without regard to any limits that would otherwise apply to what the physician or practitioner could charge. We are clarifying here that physicians and practitioners who enter into valid private contracts will not be subject to civil money penalties and assessments under this regulation unless they knowingly and willfully violate the terms of the private agreement. In particular, physicians and practitioners will not be subject to penalties and assessments pursuant to section 1834(c)(4) of the Social Security Act, which provides for sanctions against physicians who charge in excess of the limiting charge, or section 1848(g)(4) of the Act, which imposes sanctions on physicians and practitioners who violate the mandatory submission of claims requirement of the statute.

The civil money penalties to which this rule pertains include those that apply to Medicare payments or billings as "assignment" violations; violations involving the failure to provide information or improperly providing information; violations of charge or service limits; and violations of Medigap and Medicare Select requirements.

This rule adds a new part to chapter IV of title 42 of the Code of Federal Regulations. This new part is part 402 and is entitled Civil Money Penalties, Assessments and Exclusions. We are dividing the part into three subparts for the present: Subpart A-General Requirements; Subpart B-Civil Money Penalties and Assessments; and Subpart C- Exclusions (which is reserved for future use).

Subpart A contains the statutory authorities for most of the civil money penalties, assessments, and exclusions that the Secretary has delegated to HCFA. The remainder of the subpart contains the general requirements and procedures that are common to the imposition of civil money penalties, assessments, and exclusions. These procedures are based on the OIG regulations in 42 CFR part 1003.

Under the Secretary's delegation, some authorities will be enforced by the Office of Inspector General, even though similar penalties, applicable under other statutes, are delegated to HCFA. For instance, two of the statutory citations that subject violators to potential sanctions (section 1842(p)(3)(A) and 1848(g)(1)(B)) authorize HCFA to impose various penalties for abusive practices involving bills or requests for payment that are not made on an assignment-related basis. We note that the OIG has the comparable authority under section 1128A of the Act to impose civil money penalties for those abusive practices in cases where payment is requested on an assignment-related basis. Although the OIG penalties are not listed in this section, we want to make clear that individuals involved in abusive billing practices are subject to penalties, whether or not the claim is submitted on an assignment-related basis.

Subpart B includes procedures specific to the imposition of civil money penalties and assessments. These rules are also based on those the OIG uses in 42 CFR part 1003.

Our regulations are based on those in part 1003 but are organized somewhat differently in order to be able to, in the future, include all our rules regarding exclusions in more detail. The organization will also make the regulations easier to understand and to find. The organizational changes are not substantive; they change neither the procedures nor the extent of the regulations' applicability.

Although the OIG regulations generally refer to the OIG as the government entity implementing a given function, our new regulations will refer to "HCFA or OIG" as the government agent.

Another purely technical departure from the OIG regulations is our inclusion of a description of all the statutory citations. HCFA is revising its rules to include a description of all pertinent statutory citations in a

[Page 68689]

particular section, rather than using a long list of citations (by number only) in the "Authority" paragraph that currently appears in each part or subpart in title 42 of the Code of Federal Regulations. The descriptions, of course, also include the new authorities that are not in the existing OIG rules. We also make several editorial changes and clarifying changes designed to make the language clearer to the public.

The regulations provisions in this rule do not revise any procedures or rights currently available to any person on whom we may impose a civil money penalty, assessment, or exclusion. The procedures we will follow also remain the same.

III. Impact Analysis

Consistent with the Regulatory Flexibility Act (RFA) (5 U.S.C. 601 through 612), we prepare a regulatory flexibility analysis unless we certify that a rule will not have a significant economic impact on a substantial number of small entities. For purposes of the RFA, all health care providers and suppliers of services (except some individual physicians) are considered to be small entities. Individuals and States are not included in the definition of a small entity.

In addition, section 1102(b) of the Act requires us to prepare a regulatory impact analysis if a rule may have a significant impact on the operations of a substantial number of small rural hospitals. Such an analysis must conform to the provisions of section 604 of the RFA. For purposes of section 1102(b) of the Act, we define a small rural hospital as a hospital that is located outside of a Metropolitan Statistical Area and has fewer than 50 beds.

As indicated above, the provisions in this final rule with comment period provide HCFA (and the OIG) with regulations to implement the statutory authorities to levy civil money penalties and assessments against providers and physicians and other suppliers of services. The civil money penalties to which this rule pertains include those that apply to Medicare payments or billings as "assignment" violations; violations involving the failure to provide information or the improper provision of information; violations of charge or service limits; and violations of Medigap and Medicare Select requirements. Most of these authorities rested solely with the

OIG until October 1994; there are also a few new authorities, which are included in the new part 402. These new authorities do not materially expand or increase the overall impact of civil money penalty oversight activities. This final rule basically transfers the existing civil money penalty functional responsibility (along with the new authorities) for assuring compliance with programatic and/or regulations violations (versus fraud, misrepresentation, and falsification types of violations, which remain with the OIG) from the OIG to HCFA. It is expected that no significant economic impact will be imposed on a substantial number of small business entities as a result of this action.

For this reason, any new economic effect of these regulations should be minimal, affecting only those that have engaged in prohibited behavior contained in the authorities put in place on or after October 31, 1994; the economic effect of the already existing authorities is not new and is also minimal because of the relatively few violators involved. We believe the majority of the persons and entities subject to these regulations do not commit the violations discussed in these regulations. Those providers, physicians, and suppliers that are not currently in compliance with existing and new authorities will be subject to more vigorous enforcement of these provisions of the CMP oversight activity and may experience a significant economic impact as a result of such violations. However, the population subject to such actions is reasonably believed to be a very minor portion of the total population of providers, physicians and other suppliers. Moreover, small rural hospitals are not expected to be appreciably affected by this final rule. In addition, there are minimal costs and savings to the government.

For these reasons, we are not preparing analyses for either the RFA or section 1102(b) of the Act because we have determined, and we certify, that this rule will not have a significant economic impact on a substantial number of small entities or a significant impact on the operations of a substantial number of small rural hospitals.

In accordance with the provisions of Executive Order 12866, this regulation was reviewed by the Office of Management and Budget.

IV. Response to Comments

Because of the large number of items of correspondence we normally receive on **Federal Register** documents published for comment, we are not able to acknowledge or respond to them individually. We will consider all comments we receive by the date and time specified in the "DATES" section of this preamble and will respond to the comments in the preamble to any subsequent **Federal Register** document.

V. Waiver of Proposed Rulemaking

We ordinarily publish a notice of proposed rulemaking in the **Federal Register** and invite prior public comment on proposed rules. The notice of proposed rulemaking includes a reference to the legal authority under which the rule is proposed and the terms and substances of the proposed rule or a description of the subjects and issues involved. This procedure can be waived, however, if an agency finds good cause that a notice-and-comment procedure is impracticable, unnecessary, or contrary to the public interest and incorporates a statement of the finding and its reasons in the rule issued.

It would be contrary to the public interest to delay the publication of these rules pending completion of the usual notice and comment procedures. The delay would be contrary to the public interest because HCFA would not be able to utilize fully civil money penalties and assessments as tools to encourage compliance with certain provisions of the Medicare Act as the Congress intended. These provisions are designed to discourage entities from engaging in fraudulent and abusive behavior. According to the General Accounting Office's report, *Vulnerable Payers Lose Billions to Fraud and Abuse* (GAO/HRD-92–69), costs of health care fraud and abuse are estimated to be ten percent of our total health care spending. The Medicare trust funds and the public are significantly harmed by these abusive practices, and we find that further delaying the use of these sanctions pending the end of a public comment period would be contrary to the public's interest.

We also believe it is unnecessary to delay publication of these final rules pending completion of a notice and comment period. We are adopting the OIG's procedures and policies as our own and are not revising the rights of persons to whom the provisions pertain. Over the years, the Department of Health and Human Services has published the substance of the OIG's regulations in proposed rules that solicited comment and responded to those comments in final rules (55 FR 12205, April 2, 1990; 57 FR 3298, January 29, 1992). The procedures in this rule do not differ significantly from the OIG rules and we believe it is redundant to, in effect, propose rules that are already contained in the Code of Federal Regulations.

Finally, a delay of publication of the final rule is unnecessary because all of

[Page 68690]

the specific civil money penalties are required by the current statute. Thus, the one significant addition to the OIG rules, the addition of the new authorities, is not discretionary and we would not be able to change these authorities in the regulations in response to public comment.

Accordingly, we find good cause for waiving the prior notice-and-comment procedure as unnecessary and contrary to the public interest.

List of Subjects in 42 CFR Part 402

Administrative practice and procedure, Health facilities, Health professions, Medicaid, Medicare, Penalties.

42 CFR chapter IV is amended as set forth below:

PART 400 — [AMENDED]

42 CFR chapter IV is amended as set forth below:

A. Part 400 is amended as follows:

1. The authority citation continues to read as follows:

Authority: §§ 1102 and 1871 of the Social Security Act (42 U.S.C. 1302 and 1395hh) and 44 U.S.C. Chapter 35.

2. Section 400.200 is amended by adding, in alphabetical order, a definition for "DAB" to read as follows:

§ 400.200 General definitions.

* * * * *

DAB stands for Departmental Appeals Board.

* * * * *

B. A new part 402 is added to read as follows:

PART 402 — CIVIL MONEY PENALTIES, ASSESSMENTS, AND EXCLUSIONS

Subpart A — General Provisions

Secs.

Subpart B — Penalties and Assessments

Secs.

Subpart C — Exclusions [Reserved]

Authority: §§ 1102 and 1871 of the Social Security Act (42 U.S.C. 1302 and 1395hh).

Subpart A — General Provisions

§ 402.1 Basis and scope.

(a) *Basis.* This part is based on the sections of the Act that are specified in paragraph (c) of this section.

(b) *Scope.* This part —

(1) Provides for the imposition of civil money penalties, assessments, and exclusions against persons that violate the provisions of the Act specified in paragraph (c), (d), or (e) of this section; and

(2) Sets forth the appeal rights of persons subject to penalties, assessments, or exclusion and the procedures for reinstatement following exclusion.

(c) *Civil money penalties.* HCFA or OIG may impose civil money penalties against any person or other entity specified in paragraphs (c)(1) through (c)(30) of this section under the identified section of the

Act. The authorities that also permit imposition of an assessment or exclusion are noted in the applicable paragraphs.

(1) Sections 1833(h)(5)(D) and 1842(j)(2)—Any person that knowingly and willfully, and on a repeated basis, bills for a clinical diagnostic laboratory test, other than on an assignment-related basis. This provision includes tests performed in a physician's office but excludes tests performed in a rural health clinic. (This violation may also include an assessment and cause exclusion.)

(2) Section 1833(i)(6)—Any person that knowingly and willfully presents, or causes to be presented, a bill or request for payment for an intraocular lens inserted during or after cataract surgery for which the Medicare payment rate includes the cost of acquiring the class of lens involved.

(3) Section 1833(q)(2)(B)—Any entity that knowingly and willfully fails to provide information about a referring physician, including the physician's name and unique physician identification number for the referring physician, when seeking payment on an unassigned basis. (This violation, if it occurs in repeated cases, may also cause an exclusion.)

(4) Sections 1834(a)(11)(A) and 1842(j)(2)—Any durable medical equipment supplier that knowingly and willfully charges for a covered service that is furnished on a rental basis after the rental payments may no longer be made (except for maintenance and servicing) as provided in section 1834(a)(7)(A). (This violation may also include an assessment and cause exclusion.)

(5) Sections 1834(a)(18)(B) and 1842(j)(2)—Any nonparticipating durable medical equipment supplier that knowingly and willfully, in violation of section 1834(a)(18)(A), fails to make a refund to Medicare beneficiaries for a covered service for which payment is precluded due to an unsolicited telephone contact from the supplier. (This violation may also include an assessment and cause exclusion.)

(6) Sections 1834(b)(5)(C) and 1842(j)(2)—Any nonparticipating physician or supplier that knowingly and willfully charges a Medicare beneficiary more than the limiting charge, as specified in section 1834(b)(5)(B), for radiologist services. (This violation may also include an assessment and cause exclusion.)

(7) Sections 1834(c)(4)(C) and 1842(j)(2)—Any nonparticipating physician or supplier that knowingly and willfully charges a Medicare beneficiary more than the limiting charge, as specified in section 1834(c)(4)(B), for mammography screening. (This violation may also include an assessment and cause exclusion.)

(8) Sections 1834(h)(3) and 1842(j)(2)—Any supplier of prosthetic devices, orthotics, and prosthetics that knowingly and willfully charges for a covered prosthetic device, orthotic, or prosthetic that is furnished on a rental basis after the rental payment may no longer be made (except for maintenance and servicing). (This violation may also include an assessment and cause exclusion.)

(9) Section 1834(j)(2)(A)(iii)—Any supplier of durable medical equipment, including a supplier of prosthetic devices, prosthetics, orthotics, or supplies, that knowingly and willfully distributes a certificate of medical necessity in violation of section 1834(j)(2)(A)(i) or fails to provide the information required under section 1834(j)(2)(A)(ii).

(10) Sections 1834(j)(4) and 1842(j)(2)—

(i) Any supplier of durable medical equipment, including a supplier of prosthetic devices, prosthetics, orthotics, or supplies, that knowingly and willfully fails to make refunds in a timely manner to Medicare beneficiaries for services billed other than on an assignment- related basis if—

(A) The supplier does not possess a Medicare supplier number;

[Page 68691]

(B) The service is denied in advance under section 1834(a)(15); or

(C) The service is determined not to be medically necessary or reasonable.

(ii) These violations may also include an assessment and cause exclusion.

(11) Sections 1842(b)(18)(B) and 1842(j)(2)—Any practitioner specified in section 1842(b)(18)(C) (physician assistants, nurse practitioners, clinical nurse specialists, certified registered nurse anesthetists, certified nurse-midwives, clinical social workers, and clinical psychologists) or other person that knowingly and willfully bills or collects for any services by the practitioners on other than an assignment-related basis. (This violation may also include an assessment and cause exclusion.)

(12) Sections 1842(k) and 1842(j)(2)—Any physician who knowingly and willfully presents, or causes to be presented, a claim or bill for an assistant at cataract surgery performed on or after March 1, 1987 for which payment may not be made because of section 1862(a)(15). (This violation may also include an assessment and cause exclusion.)

(13) Sections 1842(l)(3) and 1842(j)(2)—Any nonparticipating physician who does not accept payment on an assignment-related

basis and who knowingly and willfully fails to refund on a timely basis any amounts collected for services that are not reasonable or medically necessary or are of poor quality, in accordance with section 1842(l)(1)(A). (This violation may also include an assessment and cause exclusion.)

(14) Sections 1842(m)(3) and 1842(j)(2) — (i) Any nonparticipating physician, who does not accept payment for an elective surgical procedure on an assignment-related basis and whose charge is at least $500, who knowingly and willfully fails to —

(A) Disclose the information required by section 1842(m)(1) concerning charges and coinsurance amounts; and

(B) Refund on a timely basis any amount collected for the procedure in excess of the charges recognized and approved by the Medicare program.

(ii) This violation may also include an assessment and cause exclusion.

(15) Sections 1842(n)(3) and 1842(j)(2) — Any physician who knowingly and willfully, in repeated cases, bills one or more beneficiaries, for purchased diagnostic tests, any amount other than the payment amount specified in section 1842(n)(1)(A) or section 1842(n)(1)(B). (This violation may also include an assessment and cause exclusion.)

(16) Section 1842(p)(3)(A) — Any physician who knowingly and willfully fails promptly to provide the appropriate diagnosis code or codes upon request by HCFA or a carrier on any request for payment or bill not submitted on an assignment-related basis for any service furnished by the physician. (This violation, if it occurs in repeated cases, may also cause exclusion.)

(17) Sections 1848(g)(1)(B) and 1842(j)(2) —

(i) Any nonparticipating physician, supplier, or other person that furnishes physicians' services and does not accept payment on an assignment-related basis, that —

(A) Knowingly and willfully bills or collects in excess of the limiting charge (as defined in section 1848(g)(2)) on a repeated basis; or

(B) Fails to make an adjustment or refund on a timely basis as required by section 1848(g)(1)(A)(iii) or (iv).

(ii) These violations may also include an assessment and cause exclusion.

(18) Section 1848(g)(3)(B) and 1842(j)(2) — Any person that knowingly and willfully bills for State plan approved physicians' services, as defined in section 1848(j)(3), on other than an assignment-related

basis for a Medicare beneficiary who is also eligible for Medicaid (these individuals include qualified Medicare beneficiaries). This provision applies to services furnished on or after April 1, 1990. (This violation may also include an assessment and cause exclusion.)

(19) Section 1848(g)(4)(B)(ii), 1842(p)(3), and 1842(j)(2)(A)—

(i) Any physician, supplier, or other person (except any person that has been excluded from the Medicare program) that, for services furnished after September 1, 1990, knowingly and willfully—

(A) Fails to submit a claim on a standard claim form for services provided for which payment is made under Part B on a reasonable charge or fee schedule basis; or

(B) Imposes a charge for completing and submitting the standard claims form.

(ii) These violations, if they occur in repeated cases, may also cause exclusion.

(20) Section 1862(b)(5)(C)—Any employer (other than a Federal or other governmental agency) that, before October 1, 1998, willfully or repeatedly fails to provide timely and accurate information requested relating to an employee's group health insurance coverage.

(21) Section 1862(b)(6)(B)—Any entity that knowingly, willfully, and repeatedly—

(i) Fails to complete a claim form relating to the availability of other health benefit plans in accordance with section 1862(b)(6)(A); or

(ii) Provides inaccurate information relating to the availability of other health benefit plans on the claim form.

(22) Section 1877(g)(5)—Any person that fails to report information required by HHS under section 1877(f) concerning ownership, investment, and compensation arrangements. (This violation may also include an assessment and cause exclusion.)

(23) Sections 1879(h), 1834(a)(18), and 1842(j)(2)—

(i) Any durable medical equipment supplier, including a supplier of prosthetic devices, prosthetics, orthotics, or supplies, that knowingly and willfully fails to make refunds in a timely manner to Medicare beneficiaries for services billed on an assignment-related basis if—

(A) The supplier did not possess a Medicare supplier number;

(B) The service is denied in advance under section 1834(a)(15) of the Act; or

(C) The service is determined not to be payable under section 1834(a)(17)(b) because of unsolicited telephone contacts.

(ii) These violations may also include an assessment and cause exclusion.

(24) Section 1882(a)(2) — Any person that issues a Medicare supplemental policy that has not been approved by the State regulatory program or does not meet Federal standards on and after the effective date in section 1882(p)(1)(C). (This violation may also include an assessment and cause exclusion.)

(25) Section 1882(p)(8) — Any person that sells or issues Medicare supplemental policies, on or after July 30, 1992, that fail to conform to the NAIC or Federal standards established under section 1882(p). (This violation may also include an assessment and cause exclusion.)

(26) Section 1882(p)(9)(C) —

(i) Any person that sells a Medicare supplemental policy and —

(A) Fails to make available for sale the core group of basic benefits when selling other Medicare supplemental policies with additional benefits; or

(B) Fails to provide the individual, before the sale of the policy, an outline of coverage describing the benefits provided by the policy.

(ii) These violations may also include an assessment and cause exclusion.

(27) Section 1882(q)(5)(C) —

(i) Any person that fails to —

(A) Suspend a Medicare supplemental policy at the policyholder's request, if

[Page 68692]

the policyholder applies for and is determined eligible for medical assistance, and the policyholder provides notice within 90 days of the eligibility determination; or

(B) Automatically reinstate the policy as of the date of termination of medical assistance if the policyholder loses eligibility for medical assistance and the policyholder provides notice within 90 days of loss of eligibility.

(ii) These violations may also include an assessment and cause exclusion.

(28) Section 1882(r)(6)(A) — Any person that fails to provide refunds or credits as required by section 1882(r)(1)(B). (This violation may also include an assessment and cause exclusion.)

(29) Section 1882(s)(3) —

(i) Any issuer of a Medicare supplemental policy that—

(A) Does not waive any time periods applicable to preexisting conditions, waiting periods, elimination periods, or probationary periods if the time periods were already satisfied under a preceding Medicare supplemental policy; or

(B) Denies a policy, conditions the issuance or effectiveness of the policy, or discriminates in the pricing of the policy based on health status or other criteria as specified in section 1882(s)(2)(A).

(ii) These violations may also include an assessment and cause exclusion.

(30) Section 1882(t)(2)—

(i) Any issuer of a Medicare supplemental policy that—

(A) Fails substantially to provide medically necessary services to enrollees seeking the services through the issuer's network of entities;

(B) Imposes premiums on enrollees in excess of the premiums approved by the State;

(C) Acts to expel an enrollee for reasons other than nonpayment of premiums; or

(D) Does not provide each enrollee at the time of enrollment with the specific information provided in section 1882(t)(1)(E)(i) or fails to obtain a written acknowledgment from the enrollee of receipt of the information (as required by section 1882(t)(1)(E)(ii)).

(ii) These violations may also include an assessment and cause exclusion.

(d) *Assessments.* HCFA or OIG may impose assessments in addition to civil money penalties for violations of the following statutory sections:

(1) Section 1833: Paragraph (h)(5)(D).

(2) Section 1834: Paragraphs (a)(11)(A), (a)(18)(B), (b)(5)(C), (c)(4)(C), (h)(3), and (j)(4).

(3) Section 1842: Paragraphs (k), (l)(3), (m)(3), and (n)(3).

(4) Section 1848: Paragraph (g)(1)(B).

(5) Section 1877: Paragraph (g)(5).

(6) Section 1879: Paragraph (h).

(7) Section 1882: Paragraphs (a)(2), (p)(8), (p)(9)(C), (q)(5)(C), (r)(6)(A), (s)(3), and (t)(2).

(e) *Exclusions.* (1) HCFA or OIG may exclude any person from participation in the Medicare program on the basis of any of the following violations of the statute:

(i) Section 1833: Paragraphs (h)(5)(D) and, in repeated cases, (q)(2)(B).

(ii) Section 1834: Paragraphs (a)(11)(A), (a)(18)(B), (b)(5)(C), (c)(4)(C), (h)(3), and (j)(4).

(iii) Section 1842: Paragraphs (b)(18)(B), (k), (l)(3), (m)(3), (n)(3), and, in repeated cases, (p)(3)(B).

(iv) Section 1848: Paragraphs (g)(1)(B), (g)(3)(B), and, in repeated cases, (g)(4)(B)(ii).

(v) Section 1877: Paragraph (g)(5).

(vi) Section 1879: Paragraph (h).

(vii) Section 1882: Paragraphs (a)(2), (p)(8), (p)(9)(C), (q)(5)(C), (r)(6)(A), (s)(3), and (t)(2).

(2) HCFA or OIG must exclude from participation in the Medicare program any of the following, under the identified section of the Act:

(i) Section 1834(a)(17)(C)—Any supplier of durable medical equipment and supplies that are covered under section 1834(a)(13) that knowingly contacts Medicare beneficiaries by telephone regarding the furnishing of covered services in violation of section 1834(a)(17)(A) and whose conduct establishes a pattern of prohibited contacts as described under section 1834(a)(17)(A).

(ii) Section 1834(h)(3)—Any supplier of prosthetic devices, orthotics, and prosthetics that knowingly contacts Medicare beneficiaries by telephone regarding the furnishing of prosthetic devices, orthotics, or prosthetics in the same manner as in the violation under section 1834(a)(17)(A) and whose conduct establishes a pattern of prohibited contacts in the same manner as described in section 1834(a)(17)(C).

(f) *Responsible persons.* (1) If HCFA or OIG determines that more than one person is responsible for any of the violations described in paragraph (c) or paragraph (d) of this section, it may impose a civil money penalty or a civil money penalty and assessment against any one of those persons or jointly and severally against two or more of those persons. However, the aggregate amount of the assessments collected may not exceed the amount that could be assessed if only one person were responsible.

(2) A principal is liable for penalties and assessments for the actions of his or her agent acting within the scope of the agency.

(g) *Time limits.* Neither HCFA nor OIG initiates an action to impose a civil money penalty, assessment, or proceeding to exclude a person from participation in the Medicare program unless it begins the action within 6 years from the date on which the claim was presented, the request for payment was made, or the incident occurred.

§ 402.3 Definitions.

For purposes of this part:

Assessment means the amount described in § 402.107 and includes the plural of that term.

Assignment-related basis means that the claim submitted by a physician, supplier or other person is paid on the basis of an assignment, whereby the physician, supplier or other person agrees to accept the Medicare payment as payment in full for the services furnished to the beneficiary and is precluded from charging the beneficiary more than the deductible and coinsurance based upon the approved Medicare fee amount. Additional obligations, including obligations to make refunds in certain circumstances, are established at section 1842(b)(3) of the Act.

Claim means an application for payment for a service for which the Medicare or Medicaid program may pay.

Covered means that a service is described as reasonable and necessary for the diagnosis or treatment of illness or injury or to improve the functioning of a malformed body member. A service is not covered if it is specifically identified as excluded from Medicare Part B coverage or is not a defined Medicare Part B benefit.

Exclusion means the temporary or permanent barring of a person or other entity from participation in the Medicare or State health care program and that services furnished or ordered by that person are not paid for under either program.

General Counsel means the General Counsel of HHS or his or her designees.

Knowingly or *knowingly and willfully* means that a person, with respect to information —

(1) Has actual knowledge of the information;

(2) Acts in deliberate ignorance of the truth or falsity of the information; or

(3) Acts in reckless disregard of the truth or falsity of the information; and

(4) No proof of specific intent is required.

Medicare supplemental policy means a policy guaranteeing that a health plan will pay a policyholder's coinsurance and deductible and will cover other

[Page 68693]

limitations on payment imposed under title XVIII of the Act and will provide additional health plan or non-Medicare coverage for services up to a predefined benefit limit.

NAIC stands for the National Association of Insurance Commissioners.

Nonparticipating describes a physician, supplier, or other person (excluding any provider of services) that, at the time of furnishing the services to Medicare Part B beneficiaries, is not a participating physician or supplier.

Participating describes a physician or supplier (excluding any provider of services) that, before the beginning of any given year, enters into an agreement with HHS that provides that the physician or supplier will accept payment under the Medicare program on an assignment-related basis for all services furnished to Medicare Part B beneficiaries.

Penalty means the amount described in § 402.105 and includes the plural of that term.

Person means an individual, trust or estate, partnership, corporation, professional association or corporation, or other entity, public or private.

Physicians' services means the following Medicare covered professional services:

(1) Surgery, consultation, home, office and institutional calls, and other professional services performed by physicians.

(2) Services and supplies furnished "incident to" a physician's professional services.

(3) Outpatient physical and occupational therapy services.

(4) Diagnostic x-ray tests and other diagnostic tests (excluding clinical diagnostic laboratory tests).

(5) X-ray, radium, and radioactive isotope therapy, including materials and services of technicians.

(6) Antigens prepared by a physician.

Radiologist service means radiology services performed only by, or under the direction of, a physician who is certified, or eligible to be certified, by the American Board of Radiology or for whom radiology services account for at least 50 percent of the total amount of charges made under part B of title XVIII of the Act.

Request for payment means an application submitted by a person to any person for payment for a service.

Respondent means the person upon which HCFA or OIG has imposed, or proposes to impose, a civil money penalty, assessment, or exclusion.

Service includes —

(1) Any item, device, medical supply, or service claimed to have been furnished to a patient and listed in an itemized claim for program payment; or

(2) In the case of a claim based on costs, any entry or omission in a cost report, books of account or other documents supporting the claim.

State includes the District of Columbia, Puerto Rico, the Virgin Islands, Guam, American Samoa, the Northern Mariana Islands, and the Trust Territory of the Pacific Islands.

Timely basis means that the adjustment to a bill or a refund is considered "on a timely basis" if the physician, supplier, or other person makes the adjustment or refund to the appropriate party no later than 30 days after the date the physician, supplier, or other person is notified by the Medicare Part B contractor of the violation and the requirement to refund any excess collections.

§ 402.5 Right to a hearing before the final determination.

HCFA or OIG does not make a determination adverse to any person under this part until the person has been given a written notice and opportunity for the determination to be made on the record after a hearing at which the person is entitled to be represented by counsel, to present witnesses, and to cross-examine witnesses against the person.

(a) If HCFA or OIG proposes a penalty and, as applicable, an assessment, or proposes to exclude a respondent from participation in Medicare in accordance with this part, it sends the respondent written notice of its intent by certified mail, return receipt requested. The notice includes the following information:

(1) Reference to the statutory basis or bases for the penalty, assessment, exclusion, or any combination, as applicable.

(2)(i) A description of the claims, requests for payment, or incidents with respect to which the penalty, assessment, and exclusion are proposed; or

(ii) If HCFA or OIG is relying upon statistical sampling to project the number and types of claims or requests for payment and the dollar amount, a description of the claims and requests for payment comprising the sample and a brief description of the statistical sampling technique HCFA or OIG used.

(3) The reason why the claims, requests for payment, or incidents are subject to a penalty and assessment.

(4) The amount of the proposed penalty and of any proposed assessment.

(5) Any mitigating or aggravating circumstances that HCFA or OIG considered when it determined the amount of the proposed penalty and any applicable assessment.

(6) Information concerning response to the notice, including—

(i) A specific statement of the respondent's right to a hearing; and

(ii) A statement that failure to request a hearing within 60 days renders the proposed determination final and permits the imposition of the proposed penalty and any assessment.

(iii) A statement that the debt may be collected through an administrative offset.

(7) In the case of a respondent that has an agreement under section 1866 of the Act, notice that imposition of an exclusion may result in termination of the provider's agreement in accordance with section 1866(b)(2)(C) of the Act.

§ 402.9 Failure to request a hearing.

(a) If the respondent does not request a hearing within 60 days of receipt of the notice of proposed determination specified in § 402.7, any civil money penalty, assessment, or exclusion becomes final and HCFA or OIG may impose the proposed penalty, assessment, or exclusion, or any less severe penalty, assessment, or suspension.

(b) HCFA or OIG notifies the respondent by certified mail, return receipt requested, of any penalty, assessment, or exclusion that has been imposed and of the means by which the respondent may satisfy the judgment.

(c) The respondent has no right to appeal a penalty, assessment, or exclusion for which he or she has not requested a hearing.

§ 402.11 Notice to other agencies and other entities.

(a) Whenever a penalty, assessment, or exclusion becomes final, HCFA or OIG notifies the following organizations and entities about the action and the reasons for it:

(1) The appropriate State or local medical or professional association.

(2) The appropriate peer review organization.

(3) As appropriate, the State agency responsible for the administration of each State health care program (Medicaid, the Maternal and Child Health Services Block Grant Program, and the Social Services Block Grant Program).

(4) The appropriate Medicare carrier or fiscal intermediary.

(5) The appropriate State or local licensing agency or organization (including the Medicare and Medicaid State survey agencies).

[Page 68694]

(6) The long-term care ombudsman.

(b) For exclusions, HCFA or OIG also notifies the public and specifies the effective date.

§ 402.13 Penalty, assessment, and exclusion not exclusive.

Penalties, assessments, and exclusions imposed under this part are in addition to any other penalties prescribed by law.

§ 402.15 Collateral estoppel.

(a) When a final determination that the respondent presented or caused to be presented a claim or request for payment falling within the scope of § 402.1 has been rendered in any proceeding in which the respondent was a party and had an opportunity to be heard, the respondent is bound by that determination in any proceeding under this part.

(b) A person who has been convicted (whether upon a verdict after trial or upon a plea of guilty or nolo contendere) of a Federal crime charging fraud or false statements is barred from denying the essential elements of the criminal offense if the proceedings under this part involve the same transactions.

§ 402.17 Settlement.

HCFA or OIG has exclusive authority to settle any issues or case, without the consent of the ALJ or the Secretary, at any time before a final decision by the Secretary. Thereafter, the General Counsel has the exclusive authority.

§ 402.19 Hearings and appeals.

The hearings and appeals procedures set forth in part 1005 of chapter V of this title are available to any person that receives an adverse determination under this part. For an appeal of a civil money penalty, assessment, or exclusion imposed under this part, either HCFA or OIG may represent the government in the hearing and appeals process.

§ 402.21 Judicial review.

After exhausting all available administrative remedies, a respondent may seek judicial review of a penalty, assessment, or exclusion that has become final. The respondent may seek review only with respect to a penalty, assessment, or exclusion with respect to which the respondent filed an exception under § 1005.21(c) of this title unless the court excuses the failure or neglect to urge the exception in accordance with section 1128A(e) of the Act because of extraordinary circumstances.

Subpart B — Civil Money Penalties and Assessments

§ 402.105 Amount of penalty.

(a) *$2,000.* Except as provided in paragraphs (b) through (f) of this section, HCFA or OIG may impose a penalty of not more than $2,000 for each service, bill, or refusal to issue a timely refund that is subject to a determination under this part and for each incident involving the knowing, willful, and repeated failure of an entity furnishing a service to submit a properly completed claim form or to include on the claim form accurate information regarding the availability of other health insurance benefit plans (§ 402.1(c)(21)).

(b) *$1,000.* HCFA or OIG may impose a penalty of not more than $1,000 for the following:

(1) Per certificate of medical necessity knowingly and willfully distributed to physicians on or after December 31, 1994 that —

(i) Contains information concerning the medical condition of the patient; or

(ii) Fails to include cost information.

(2) Per individual about whom information is requested, for willful or repeated failure of an employer to respond to an intermediary or carrier about coverage of an employee or spouse under the employer's group health plan (§ 402.1(c)(20)).

(c) *$5,000.* HCFA or OIG may impose a penalty of not more than $5,000 for each violation resulting from the following:

(1) The failure of a Medicare supplemental policy issuer, on a replacement policy, to waive any time periods applicable to preexisting conditions, waiting periods, elimination periods, or proba-

tionary periods that were satisfied under a preceding policy (§ 402.1(c)(29)); and

(2) Any issuer of any Medicare supplemental policy denying a policy, conditioning the issuance or effectiveness of the policy, or discriminating in the pricing of the policy based on health status or other criteria as specified in section 1882(s)(2)(A). (§ 402.1(c)(29)).

(d) *$10,000.* (1) HCFA or OIG may impose a penalty of not more than $10,000 for each day that reporting entity ownership arrangements is late (§ 402.1(c)(22)).

(2) HCFA or OIG may impose a penalty of not more than $10,000 for the following violations that occur on or after January 1, 1997:

(i) Knowingly and willfully, and on a repeated basis, billing for a clinical diagnostic laboratory test, other than on an assignment-related basis (§ 402.1(c)(1)).

(ii) By any durable medical equipment supplier, knowingly and willfully charging for a covered service that is furnished on a rental basis after the rental payments may no longer be made (except for maintenance and servicing) as provided in section 1834(a)(7)(A) (§ 402.1(c)(4)).

(iii) By any durable medical equipment supplier, knowingly and willfully, in violation of section 1834(a)(18)(A), failing to make a refund to Medicare beneficiaries for a covered service for which payment is precluded due to an unsolicited telephone contact from the supplier (§ 402.1(c)(5)).

(iv) By any nonparticipating physician or supplier, knowingly and willfully charging a Medicare beneficiary more than the limiting charge, as specified in section 1834(b)(5)(B), for radiologist services (§ 402.1(c)(6)).

(v) By any nonparticipating physician or supplier, knowingly and willfully charging a Medicare beneficiary more than the limiting charge, as specified in section 1834(c)(3), for mammography screening (§ 402.1(c)(7)).

(vi) By any supplier of prosthetic devices, orthotics, and prosthetics, knowingly and willfully charging for a covered prosthetic device, orthotic, or prosthetic that is furnished on a rental basis after the rental payment may no longer be made (except for maintenance and servicing) (§ 401.2(c)(8)).

(vii) By any supplier of durable medical equipment, including a supplier of prosthetic devices, prosthetics, orthotics, or supplies, knowingly and willfully failing to make refunds in a timely manner to Medicare beneficiaries for services billed other than on an assigned- related basis if—

(A) The supplier does not possess a Medicare supplier number;

(B) The service is denied in advance; or

(C) The service is determined not to be medically necessary or reasonable (§ 402.1(c)(10)).

(viii) Knowingly and willfully billing or collecting for any services on other than an assignment-related basis for practitioners specified in section 1842(b)(18)(B) (§ 402.1(c)(11)).

(xix) By any physician, knowingly and willfully presenting, or causing to be presented, a claim or bill for an assistant at cataract surgery performed on or after March 1, 1987 for which payment may not be made because of section 1862(a)(15) (§ 402.1(c)(12)).

(x) By any nonparticipating physician who does not accept payment on an

[Page 68695]

assignment-related basis, knowingly and willfully failing to refund on a timely basis any amounts collected for services that are not reasonable or medically necessary or are of poor quality, in accordance with section 1842(l)(1)(A) (§ 402.1(c)(13)).

(xi) By any nonparticipating physician, who does not accept payment for an elective surgical procedure on an assignment-related basis and whose charge is at least $500, knowingly and willfully failing to—

(A) Disclose the information required by section 1842(m)(1) concerning charges and coinsurance amounts; and

(B) Refund on a timely basis any amount collected for the procedure in excess of the charges recognized and approved by the Medicare program (§ 402.1(c)(14)).

(xii) By any physician, in repeated cases, knowingly and willfully billing one or more beneficiaries, for purchased diagnostic tests, any amount other than the payment amount specified in section 1842(n)(1)(A) or section 1842(n)(1)(B) (§ 402.1(c)(15)).

(xiii) By any nonparticipating physician, supplier, or other person that furnishes physicians' services and does not accept payment on an assignment-related basis—

(A) Knowingly and willfully billing or collecting in excess of the limiting charge (as defined in section 1843(g)(2)) on a repeated basis; or

(B) Failing to make an adjustment or refund on a timely basis as required by section 1848(g)(1)(A)(iii) or (iv) (§ 402.1(c)(17)).

(xiv) Knowingly and willfully billing for State plan approved physicians' services on other than an assignment-related basis for a Medicare beneficiary who is also eligible for Medicaid (§ 402.1(c)(18)).

(xv) By any supplier of durable medical equipment, including a supplier of prosthetic devices, prosthetics, orthotics, or supplies, knowingly and willfully failing to make refunds in a timely manner to Medicare beneficiaries for services billed on an assignment-related basis if—

(A) The supplier did not possess a Medicare supplier number;

(B) The service is denied in advance; or

(C) The service is determined not to be medically necessary or reasonable (§ 402.1(c)(23)).

(e) *$15,000.* HCFA or OIG may impose a penalty of not more than $15,000 if the seller of a Medicare supplemental policy is not the issuer, for each violation described in paragraphs (f)(2) and (f)(3) of this section (§ 402.1 (c)(25) and (c)(26)).

(f) *$25,000.* HCFA or OIG may impose a penalty of not more than $25,000 for each of the following violations:

(1) Issuance of a Medicare supplemental policy that has not been approved by an approved State regulatory program or does not meet Federal standards on and after the effective date in section 1882(p)(1)(C) of the Act (§ 402.1(c)(23)).

(2) Sale or issuance after July 30, 1992, of a Medicare supplemental policy that fails to conform with the NAIC or Federal standards established under section 1882(p) of the Act (§ 402.1(c)(25)).

(3) Failure to make the core group of basic benefits available for sale when selling other Medicare supplemental plans with additional benefits (§ 402.1(c)(26)).

(4) Failure to provide, before sale of a Medicare supplemental policy, an outline of coverage describing the benefits provided by the policy (§ 402.1(c)(26)).

(5) Failure of an issuer of a policy to suspend or reinstate a policy, based on the policy holder's request, during entitlement to or upon loss of eligibility for medical assistance (§ 402.1(c)(27)).

(6) Failure to provide refunds or credits for Medicare supplemental policies as required by section 1882(r)(1)(B) (§ 402.1(c)(28)).

(7) By an issuer of a Medicare supplemental policy—

(i) Substantial failure to provide medically necessary services to enrollees seeking the services through the issuer's network of entities;

(ii) Imposition of premiums on enrollees in excess of the premiums approved by the State;

(iii) Action to expel an enrollee for reasons other than nonpayment of premiums; or

(iv) Failure to provide each enrollee, at the time of enrollment, with the specific information provided in section 1882(t)(1)(E)(i) or failure to obtain a written acknowledgment from the enrollee of receipt of the information (as required by section 1882(t)(1)(E)(ii)) (section 1882(t)(2)).

§ 402.107 Amount of assessment.

A person subject to civil money penalties specified in § 402.1(c) may be subject, in addition, to an assessment. An assessment is a monetary payment in lieu of damages sustained by HHS or a State agency.

(a) The assessment may not be more than twice the amount claimed for each service that was a basis for the civil money penalty, except for the violations specified in paragraph (b) of this section that occur before January 1, 1997.

(b) For the violations specified in this paragraph occurring after January 1, 1997, the assessment may not be more than three times the amount claimed for each service that was the basis for a civil money penalty. The violations are the following:

(1) Knowingly and willfully billing, and on a repeated basis, for a clinical diagnostic laboratory test, other than on an assignment-related basis (§ 402.1(c)(1)).

(2) By any durable medical equipment supplier, knowingly and willfully charging for a covered service that is furnished on a rental basis after the rental payments may no longer be made (except for maintenance and servicing) as provided in section 1834(a)(7)(A) (§ 402.1(c)(4)).

(3) By any durable medical equipment supplier, knowingly and willfully failing, in violation of section 1834(a)(18)(A), to make a refund to Medicare beneficiaries for a covered service for which payment is precluded due to an unsolicited telephone contact from the supplier (§ 402.1(c)(5)).

(4) By any nonparticipating physician or supplier, knowingly and willfully charging a Medicare beneficiary more than the limiting charge, as specified in section 1834(b)(5)(B), for radiologist services (§ 402.1(c)(6)).

(5) By any nonparticipating physician or supplier, knowingly and willfully charging a Medicare beneficiary more than the limiting charge as specified in section 1834(c)(3), for mammography screening (§ 402.1(c)(7)).

(6) By any supplier of prosthetic devices, orthotics, and prosthetics, knowingly and willfully charging for a covered prosthetic device, orthotic, or prosthetic that is furnished on a rental basis after the rental payment may no longer be made (except for maintenance and servicing) (§ 401.2(c)(8)).

(7) By any supplier of durable medical equipment, including a supplier of prosthetic devices, prosthetics, orthotics, or supplies, knowingly and willfully failing to make refunds in a timely manner to Medicare beneficiaries for services billed other than on an assignment- related basis if—

(i) The supplier does not possess a Medicare supplier number;

(ii) The service is denied in advance; or

(iii) The service is determined not to be medically necessary or reasonable (§ 402.1(c)(10)).

[Page 68696]

(8) Knowingly and willfully billing or collecting for any services on other than an assignment-related basis for practitioners specified in section 1842(b)(18)(B) (§ 402.1(c)(11)).

(9) By any physician, knowingly and willfully presenting, or causing to be presented, a claim or bill for an assistant at cataract surgery performed on or after March 1, 1987 for which payment may not be made because of section 1862(a)(15) (§ 402.1(c)(12)).

(10) By any nonparticipating physician who does not accept payment on an assignment-related basis, knowingly and willfully failing to refund on a timely basis any amounts collected for services that are not reasonable or medically necessary or are of poor quality, in accordance with section 1842(l)(1)(A) (§ 402.1(c)(13)).

(11) By any nonparticipating physician, who does not accept payment for an elective surgical procedure on an assignment-related basis and whose charge is at least $500, knowingly and willfully failing to—

(i) Disclose the information required by section 1842(m)(1) concerning charges and coinsurance amounts; and

(ii) Refund on a timely basis any amount collected for the procedure in excess of the charges recognized and approved by the Medicare program (§ 402.1(c)(14)).

(12) By any physician, in repeated cases, knowingly and willfully billing one or more beneficiaries, for purchased diagnostic tests, any amount other than the payment amount specified in section 1842(n)(1)(A) or section 1842(n)(1)(B) (§ 402.1(c)(15)).

(13) By any nonparticipating physician, supplier, or other person that furnishes physicians' services and does not accept payment on an assignment-related basis —

(i) Knowingly and willfully billing or collecting in excess of the limiting charge (as defined in section 1843(g)(2)) on a repeated basis; or

(ii) Failing to make an adjustment or refund on a timely basis as required by section 1848(g)(1)(A) (iii) or (iv) (§ 402.1(c)(17)).

(14) Knowingly and willfully billing for State plan approved physicians' services on other than an assignment-related basis for a Medicare beneficiary who is also eligible for Medicaid (§ 402.1(c)(18)).

(15) By any supplier of durable medical equipment, including suppliers of prosthetic devices, prosthetics, orthotics, or supplies, knowingly and willfully failing to make refunds in a timely manner to Medicare beneficiaries for services billed on an assignment-related basis if—

(i) The supplier did not possess a Medicare supplier number;

(ii) The service is denied in advance; or

(iii) The service is determined not to be medically necessary or reasonable (§ 402.1(c)(23)).

§ 402.109 Statistical sampling.

(a) *Purpose.* HCFA or OIG may introduce the results of a statistical sampling study to show the number and amount of claims subject to sanction under this part that the respondent presented or caused to be presented.

(b) *Prima facie evidence.* The results of the statistical sampling study, if based upon an appropriate sampling and computed by valid statistical methods, constitute prima facie evidence of the number and amount of claims or requests for payment subject to sanction under § 402.1.

(c) *Burden of proof.* Once HCFA or OIG has made a prima facie case, the burden is on the respondent to produce evidence reasonably calculated to rebut the findings of the statistical sampling study. HCFA or OIG then has the opportunity to rebut this evidence.

§ 402.111 Factors considered in determinations regarding the amount of penalties and assessments.

(a) *Basic factors.* In determining the amount of any penalty or assessment, HCFA or OIG takes into account the following:

(1) The nature of the claim, request for payment, or information given and the circumstances under which it was presented or given.

(2) The degree of culpability, history of prior offenses, and financial condition of the person submitting the claim or request for payment or giving the information.

(3) The resources available to the person submitting the claim or request for payment or giving the information.

(4) Such other matters as justice may require.

(b) *Criteria to be considered.* As guidelines for taking into account the factors listed in paragraph (a) of this section, HCFA or OIG considers the following circumstances:

(1) *Aggravating circumstances of the incident.* An aggravating circumstance is any of the following:

(i) The services or incidents were of several types, occurring over a lengthy period of time.

(ii) There were many of these services or incidents or the nature and circumstances indicate a pattern of claims or requests for payment for these services or a pattern of incidents.

(iii) The amount claimed or requested for these services was substantial.

(iv) Before the incident or presentation of any claim or request for payment subject to imposition of a civil money penalty, the respondent was held liable for criminal, civil, or administrative sanctions in connection with a program covered by this part or any other public or private program of payment for medical services.

(v) There is proof that a respondent engaged in wrongful conduct, other than the specific conduct upon which liability is based, relating to government programs or in connection with the delivery of a health care service. (The statute of limitations governing civil money penalty proceedings does not apply to proof of other wrongful conduct as an aggravating circumstance.)

(2) *Mitigating circumstances.* The following circumstances are mitigating circumstances:

(i) All the services or incidents subject to a civil money penalty were few in number and of the same type, occurred within a short period of time, and the total amount claimed or requested for the services was less than $1,000.

(ii) The claim or request for payment for the service was the result of an unintentional and unrecognized error in the process of presenting claims or requesting payment and the respondent took corrective steps promptly after discovering the error.

(iii) Imposition of the penalty or assessment without reduction would jeopardize the ability of the respondent to continue as a health care provider.

(3) *Other matters as justice may require.* Other circumstances of an aggravating or mitigating nature are taken into account if, in the interests of justice, they require either a reduction of the penalty or assessment or an increase in order to ensure the achievement of the purposes of this part.

(c) *Effect of aggravating or mitigating circumstances.* In determining the amount of the penalty and assessment to be imposed for every service or incident subject to a determination under § 402.1(c) —

(1) If there are substantial or several mitigating circumstances, the aggregate amount of the penalty and assessment is set at an amount sufficiently below the maximum permitted by §§ 402.105(a) and 402.107 to reflect that fact.

(2) If there are substantial or several aggravating circumstances, the aggregate

[Page 68697]

amount of the penalty and assessment is set at an amount at or sufficiently close to the maximum permitted by §§ 402.105(a) and 402.107 to reflect that fact.

(d)(1) The standards set forth in this section are binding, except to the extent that their application would result in imposition of an amount that would exceed limits imposed by the United States Constitution.

(2) The amount imposed is not less than the approximate amount required to fully compensate the United States, or any State, for its damages and costs, tangible and intangible, including but not lim-

ited to the costs attributable to the investigation, prosecution, and administrative review of the case.

(3) Nothing in this section limits the authority of HCFA or OIG to settle any issue or case as provided by § 402.19 or to compromise any penalty and assessment as provided by § 402.115.

§ 402.113 When a penalty and assessment are collectible.

A civil money penalty and assessment become collectible after the earliest of the following:

(a) Sixty days after the respondent receives HCFA's or OIG's notice of proposed determination under § 402.7, if the respondent has not requested a hearing before an ALJ.

(b) Immediately after the respondent abandons or waives his or her appeal right at any administrative level.

(c) Thirty days after the respondent receives the ALJ's decision imposing a civil money penalty or assessment under § 1005.20(d) of this title, if the respondent has not requested a review before the DAB.

(d) If the DAB grants an extension of the period for requesting the DAB's review, the day after the extension expires if the respondent has not requested the review.

(e) Immediately after the ALJ's decision denying a request for a stay of the effective date under § 1005.22(b) of this title.

(f) If the ALJ grants a stay under § 1005.22(b) of this title, immediately after the judicial ruling is completed.

(g) Sixty days after the respondent receives the DAB's decision imposing a civil money penalty if the respondent has not requested a stay of the decision under § 1005.22(b) of this title.

§ 402.115 Collection of penalty or assessment.

(a) Once a determination by HHS has become final, HCFA is responsible for the collection of any penalty or assessment.

(b) The General Counsel may compromise a penalty or assessment imposed under this part, after consultation with HCFA or OIG, and the Federal government may recover the penalty or assessment in a civil action brought in the United States district court for the district where the claim was presented or where the respondent resides.

(c) The United States or a State agency may deduct the amount of a penalty and assessment when finally determined, or the amount agreed upon in compromise, from any sum then or later owing to the respondent.

(d) Matters that were raised or that could have been raised in a hearing before an ALJ or in an appeal under section 1128A(e) of the Act may not be raised as a defense in a civil action by the United States to collect a penalty under this part.

Subpart C — Exclusions [Reserved]

(Catalog of Federal Domestic Assistance Program No. 93.773, Medicare — Hospital Insurance; Program No. 93.774, Medicare — Supplementary Medical Insurance Program; and Program No. 93.778, Medical Assistance Program)

Dated: July 7, 1998.

Nancy-Ann Min De Parle,

Administrator, Health Care Financing Administration.

[FR Doc. 98–33010 Filed 12–11–98; 8:45 am]

BILLING CODE 4120–01-P

APPENDIX J3

Civil Money Penalties for Nursing Homes (SNF/NF), Change in Notice Requirements, and Expansion of Discretionary Remedy Delegation — Final Rule with Comment Period; 64 FR 13354, March 18, 1999

Federal Register: March 18, 1999 (Volume 64, Number 52) Rules and Regulations Page 13354–13362

DEPARTMENT OF HEALTH AND HUMAN SERVICES

Health Care Financing Administration

42 CFR Part 488

[HCFA-2035-FC]

RIN 0938-AJ35

Medicare and Medicaid Programs; Civil Money Penalties for Nursing Homes (SNF/NF), Change in Notice Requirements, and Expansion of Discretionary Remedy Delegation

AGENCY: Health Care Financing Administration (HCFA), HHS.

ACTION: Final rule with comment period.

SUMMARY: This final rule with comment period expands current Medicare and Medicaid regulations regarding the imposition of civil money penalties imposed on nursing homes that are not in compliance with program requirements. The existing regulations provide for the imposition of a civil money penalty in a specific amount for each day of noncompliance and provide further that the civil money penalty stays in place until the facility comes into substantial compliance with all participation requirements or the facility is terminated from participation in the program. This new rule adds the ability for HCFA or the State to impose a single civil money penalty amount for an instance of a nursing home's noncompliance. We are also deleting language to remove the requirement of a maximum notification period for imposition of a remedy.

DATES: *Effective date:* These regulations are effective on May 17, 1999.

Comment date: Comments will be considered if we receive them at the appropriate address, as provided below, no later than 5 p.m. on May 17, 1999.

ADDRESSES: Mail an original and 3 copies of written comments to the following address: Health Care Financing Administration, Department of Health and Human Services, Attention: HCFA-2035-FC, P.O. Box 26585, Baltimore, MD 21207–0385.

If you prefer, you may deliver an original and 3 copies of your written comments to one of the following addresses: Room 309-G, Hubert H. Humphrey Building, 200 Independence Avenue, SW., Washington, D.C. 20201, or Room C5–09–26, 7500 Security Boulevard, Baltimore, Maryland 21244–1850.

Comments may also be submitted electronically to the following e-mail address: HCFA2035FC@hcfa.gov. For e-mail comment procedures, see the beginning of **SUPPLEMENTARY INFORMATION**. For further information on ordering copies of the **Federal Register** contained in this document, see the beginning of **SUPPLEMENTARY INFORMATION**.

FOR FURTHER INFORMATION CONTACT: Cynthia Graunke, 410–786–6782

SUPPLEMENTARY INFORMATION:

E-mail, Comments, Procedures, and Availability of Copies

E-mail comments must include the full name and address of the sender, and must be submitted to the referenced address in order to be considered. All comments must be incorporated in the e-mail message because we may not be able to access attachments. Electronically submitted comments will be available for public inspection at the Independence Avenue address, below. Because of staffing and resource limitations, we cannot accept comments by facsimile (FAX) transmission. In commenting, please refer to file code HCFA-2035-FC. Comments received timely will be available for public inspection as they are received, generally beginning approximately 3 weeks after publication of a document, in Room 309-G of the Department's offices at 200 Independence Avenue, SW., Washington, D.C., on Monday through Friday of each week from 8:30 a.m. to 5 p.m. (phone: (202) 690–7890).

Copies: To order copies of the **Federal Register** containing this document, send your request to: New Orders, Superintendent of Documents, P.O. Box 371954, Pittsburgh, PA 15250–7954. Specify the date of the issue requested and enclose a check or money order payable to the Superintendent of Documents, or enclose your Visa or Master Card number and expiration date. Credit card orders can also be placed by calling the order desk at (202) 512–1800 or by faxing to (202) 512-2250. The cost for each copy is $8. As an alternative, you can view and photocopy the **Federal Register** document at most libraries designated as Federal Depository Libraries and at many other public and academic libraries throughout the country that receive the **Federal Register**.

This **Federal Register** document is also available from the Federal Register online database through GPO Access, a service of the U.S. Government Printing Office. Free public access is available on a Wide Area Information Server (WAIS) through the Internet and via asynchronous dial-in. Internet users can access the database by using the World Wide Web; the Superintendent of Documents home page address is http://www.access.gpo.gov/nara/, by using local WAIS client software, or by telnet to swais.access.gpo.gov, then login as guest (no password required). Dial-in users should use communications software and modem to call (202) 512–1661; type swais, then login as guest (no password required).

I. Background

To participate in the Medicare and or Medicaid programs, long-term care facilities must be certified as meeting Federal participation requirements. Long-term care facilities include skilled nursing facilities for Medicare and nursing facilities for Medicaid. The Federal participation requirements for these facilities are specified in the statute at sections 1819 and 1919 of the Social Security Act (the Act) and in implementing regulations at 42 CFR Part 483, Subpart B.

Section 1864(a) of the Act authorizes the Secretary to enter into agreements with State survey agencies to determine whether skilled nursing facilities meet the Federal participation requirements for Medicare. Section 1902(a)(33)(B) of the Act provides for State survey agencies to perform the same survey tasks for facilities participating or seeking to participate in the Medicaid program. The results of these Medicare and Medicaid surveys are used by HCFA and the State Medicaid agency, respectively, as the basis for a decision

[Page 13355]

to enter into, deny, or terminate a provider agreement with the facility. They are also used to determine whether one or more remedies should be imposed where noncompliance is identified.

To assess compliance with Federal participation requirements, surveyors conduct onsite inspections (surveys) of facilities. In the survey process, surveyors directly observe the actual provision of care and services to residents and the effect or possible effects of that care to assess whether the care provided meets the assessed needs of individual residents.

Among the remedies available to the Secretary and the States under the statute to address facility noncompliance is a civil money penalty. Authorized by sections 1819(h) and 1919(h) of the Act, civil money penalties may be imposed to remedy noncompliance at amounts not to exceed $10,000 per day. The statute additionally permits the Secretary and the States to impose a civil money penalty for past instances of noncompliance even if a facility is in compliance at the time of a current survey. The Secretary is obliged to follow the procedures set out at section 1128A of the Act in processing these remedies.

The implementing regulations that govern the imposition of civil money penalties, as well as the other remedies authorized by the statute, were published on November 10, 1994 (59 FR 56116). The enforcement rules are set forth at 42 CFR Part 488, Subpart F, and the provisions directly affecting civil money penalties are set forth at 42 CFR 488.430 to 488.444. The final enforcement rule was indicative of more fundamental changes in the principles upon which the enforcement system is based. We implemented the Congress' mandate, as originally embodied in the Omnibus Budget Reconciliation Act of 1987, to abandon our hierarchical system of requirements and to develop instead a system capable of detecting and responding to noncompliance with any requirement. The new system is built on the assumption that all requirements must be met and enforced and that requirements take on greater or lesser significance as a function of the circumstances and resident outcomes in the facility at the time of the survey. Thus, in the case of civil money penalties, facilities can expect to receive increased penalties as the nature and extent of their noncompliance increases. Current procedures allow for penalties to be assessed for $3,050 per day up to $10,000 per day for noncompliance that constitutes immediate jeopardy to patient health and safety, while penalties of $50 to $3,000 per day may be imposed where immediate jeopardy does not exist.

In addition, the regulations currently require multiple notices prior to imposition of remedies. One of the notification requirements contained at 42 CFR 488.402(f)(5) establishes a maximum number of days that may pass before a remedy must be imposed.

II. Provisions of the Final Rule with Comment

A. Latest date of enforcement action.

Regulations at 42 CFR 488.402(f)(5) establish a maximum time frame of 20 calendar days for HCFA or the State, as appropriate, to both notify a provider that remedies will be imposed and actually impose the remedy(ies). Establishment of a maximum time frame to accomplish both notice and imposition of remedies has proven to be problematic as well as unnecessarily restrictive for HCFA and the State. Briefly stated, this regulation requires that remedies must be imposed within 20 days of their notice to the provider and when they are not, HCFA or the State, as appropriate, must issue another notice. The purpose of providing notice is to assure an entity that it will be reasonably informed in advance of an adverse action of the factual and legal basis for that action. Such due process concerns have been satisfied for many years by providing nursing homes with at least 2 days' notice in immediate jeopardy cases and 15 days in all other cases. Since a provider is initially notified of the remedies to be imposed following the survey, establishing a maximum time of twenty days for a remedy to be imposed unnecessarily requires an additional notice.

By eliminating the maximum notice period, providers will receive no less prior notice than has traditionally been the case and, as importantly, would receive no less information than were the maximum notice period requirement to stay in effect. Thus, the only impact of the current rule has been to artificially delay enforcement actions when providers have already been well apprised of the grounds for the action in previous correspondence from either HCFA or the State, but HCFA or the State is unable to administratively impose the remedy (ies) within 20 days of that notice. That is not a sufficient reason to retain the requirement.

Therefore, § 488.402(f)(5) will merely state that the 2-and 15- day notice periods begin when the facility receives the initial notice that a remedy is being imposed.

B. Per instance civil money penalties

When the civil money penalty provisions of the enforcement regulations were published four years ago, they reflected an interpretation of the statute that required HCFA and the States to make a determination of not only the beginning date of identified deficiencies, but an ending date as well. Where the beginning date of a deficiency could be determined, that date would signify the beginning of the provider's liability even if that date preceded the time of the survey that first surfaced the issue. When the beginning date of the deficiency could not be determined, the liability, for purposes of a civil money penalty, would be the date of the survey. Determining the ending date of the noncompliance, however, has at times proved to be more troublesome because it has required, most often, a revisit to the facility to document that the noncompliance has, in fact, been corrected. It has been an issue of some consequence between the provider industry and HCFA and States that survey teams have not returned to facilities as quickly as facilities might like in order to establish that noncompliance no longer exists. It has also been an issue to providers that civil money penalty liability has continued in many cases even where the originally identified deficiencies have been corrected, but new ones have arisen. This has occurred because providers must establish substantial compliance with all requirements to avoid civil money penalty liability, not just compliance with the deficiencies that triggered the decision to impose the penalty in the first place. At the same time, current utilization of our civil money penalty authority has been an issue with the consumer community because of what it perceives to be a less than fully effective enforcement tool. As relevant here, some consumers have expressed their belief that whatever the features are to the regulatory scheme that arguably slow the pace of enforcement, these features should be revised quickly to maximize the benefits conferred by the enforcement provisions of the statute.

Beyond this, under the enforcement scheme that HCFA and the States have followed, it has largely been the case that, except where immediate jeopardy has been involved or the provider has been found to be a poor performing facility, civil money penalties have not been imposed where facilities have been able to correct deficiencies before a predetermined date for the completion of corrections. As a result, we believe that many facilities have avoided the

[Page 13356]

imposition of penalties although subsequent to achieving compliance these same facilities have failed to maintain substantial compliance. This phenomenon has, to some degree, perpetuated the problem posed by the so-called "yo-yo" facilities that were of concern to the Congress when it enacted nursing home reform as well as to the Institute of Medicine whose recommendations formed the basis for many of the changes now appearing in the statute. When the per instance civil money penalty is selected we do not envision a period to correct prior to imposition. As we have noted previously, many facilities have avoided the imposition of penalties because a period to correct has been provided and they have initially come into compliance but failed to maintain substantial compliance. Since the per instance civil money penalty will be used when noncompliance is documented, and the penalty does not accrue until substantial compliance is achieved, permitting a period to correct before imposing the penalty defeats the purpose of this remedy.

While we believe that the basic approach we have taken to the imposition of civil money penalties is still merited since we believe it has provided both a sentinel effect in discouraging facility noncompliance and has provided an effective response to facility noncompliance where it has been identified, we have concluded that the statute offers greater flexibility than we have exercised up to now. Specifically, we believe the statute permits the Secretary and the States to focus on individual instances of noncompliance without having to track the duration of time that the facility remains out of compliance with those requirements (or with other program requirements). Thus, where sections 1819(h)(2)(B)(ii) and 1919(h)(2) of the Act provide that a civil money penalty may be imposed for up to $10,000 for each day of noncompliance, it is entirely consistent with the statute that HCFA or a State impose a penalty for the noncompliance it identifies without regard to additional days of noncompliance that might yet be identified. Indeed, there is nothing in the statute that compels either us or the States to await a determination of the total number of days of noncompliance before having the authority to react to the noncompliance that has been identified. By statute, HCFA or the State may increase a civil money penalty to reflect additional days of noncompliance beyond those identified during the survey. However, this neither reflects an exclusive route to a civil money penalty liability nor establishes a necessary precondition to the triggering of this particular remedy. Not only do we derive this interpretation directly from the civil money penalty provisions of the statute, but we find support as well in the statute's broader mandate (at sections 1819(h)(2)(A) and 1919(h)(1) of the Act) that nothing in the enforcement provisions "shall be construed as restricting the remedies available to the Secretary [or the State] to remedy a skilled nursing facility's [or nursing facility's] deficiencies."

Thus, should a survey team identify a particular instance of noncompliance during a survey, such as the presence of an avoidable pressure sore in a facility resident, we believe the statute authorizes us or a State to impose an immediate civil money penalty for that one instance of noncompliance. The only limitation that the statute would provide is that the civil money penalty liability for that instance of noncompliance could not be more than $10,000 for the day during which the noncompliance was identified.

On the other hand, HCFA or a State could identify several instances of noncompliance, perhaps relating to different aspects of facility obligations (as, for example, could be the case when deficiencies have been identified in areas of hydration, diet, resident assessment, and resident rights) and find itself imposing several different civil money penalties for each instance of noncompliance as long as the total facility liability did not exceed $10,000 per day.

What we mean by an "instance" in this regulation is a single deficiency identified by the tag number used as a reference on the statement of deficiencies. While we consider an instance as a singular event of noncompliance, there can be more than one instance of noncompliance identified during a survey. For example, during the course of a survey, HCFA or a State may identify several instances of noncompliance, each in distinct regulatory areas such as resident rights (42 CFR 483.10) and quality of care (§ 483.25). If the noncompliance in the former area involves a violation of a resident's right to privacy, that instance of noncompliance might trigger a civil money penalty of $1,000. If noncompliance with the latter requirement relates to an avoidable pressure sore, that instance of noncompliance might trigger a civil money penalty of $4,000. The sum of these penalties, $5,000, would be within the statutory limitation of

$10,000 specified by the statute for a facility's liability for any given day of noncompliance.

When considering whether a civil money penalty will be used as a remedy, the survey agency must also decide whether to establish the penalty on the basis of per day or per instance. This regulation does not authorize the use of both. When compliance with Federal requirements is evaluated by the survey agency and a decision is reached to impose a civil money penalty, a concomitant decision must be made whether the civil money penalty will be based on a determination of per instance or per day.

Accordingly, we are adopting in this regulation the option of permitting the imposition of civil money penalties for each instance of noncompliance in addition to the option already set out in existing regulations to assess a civil money penalty for each day of noncompliance as long as the facility fails to achieve substantial compliance with all requirements.

Therefore, we are revising § 488.408, Selection of remedies; § 488.430, Civil money penalties: Basis for imposing penalty; § 488.432, Civil money penalties: When penalty is collected; § 488.434, Civil money penalties: Notice of penalty; § 488.438, Civil money penalties: Amount of penalty; § 488.440, Civil money penalties: Effective date and duration of penalty; § 488.442, Civil money penalties: Due date for payment of penalty; and § 488.454, Duration of remedies, to incorporate per instance civil money penalties to our procedures.

Since a per instance civil money penalty is not cumulative, we believe that a different calculus needs to be applied to better formulate amounts that may be imposed as penalties under this regulation. First, we are establishing a minimum of $1,000 for a per instance civil money penalty. Because this penalty will not lap over to a second or successive days of noncompliance, we believe it is important that this penalty have a significant impact on noncompliant providers to encourage their compliance at the earliest possible date and to discourage similar conduct in the future. Were we to impose penalties in lower amounts, we do not believe the necessary incentive would be present. Additionally, we are not limiting penalty amounts (as we did in the already existing rule) depending on whether immediate jeopardy is present. First, the statute does not distinguish between these two types of noncompliance in terms of determining an appropriate penalty amount. Second, because here, too, a per instance penalty would be a response to a specifically identified example of noncompliance

[Page 13357]

that would provide for no penalty aggregation beyond the first day, we believe there needs to be an ability for HCFA and States to respond to egregious instances of noncompliance in a way that is commensurate with the seriousness that this type of violation represents.

Determination of the actual amount per instance will be governed by the following:

- Use of scope and severity (as that matrix has been applied under the existing enforcement rule) to assist in determining the magnitude of the noncompliance, including whether actual harm has occurred.
- The facility's degree of culpability.
- The facility's history of prior offenses, including repeat deficiencies.

These criteria are the same as those applied to determining penalty amounts under the current regulation.

The seriousness of the infraction should be apparent in the decision; e.g., an unnecessary death of a resident as a result of no active supervision presents a far different problem than does the infraction of finding that a confused person has been inappropriately attired or that a resident has not been given the proper privacy while receiving personal care from a caregiver. A determination of the scope and severity of the infraction should occur before any determination of the amount of the per instance civil money penalty is made. Ultimately, the amount of money assigned to a per instance issue of noncompliance when compared to the problem, and whether the civil money penalty proves sufficient to provide a long term remedy, will have to withstand the test of reasonableness.

We do not expect these penalty determinations to be made with mathematical precision. As we have learned from our experience over the past few years, the determination of deficiencies (and decisions concerning an appropriate enforcement response) involve some degree of judgment. This is not only inevitable but desirable because patient care failings, for the most part, do not represent arithmetic deviations from a norm. Rather, they represent varying degrees of the many forms of harm that facility residents may experience. Our expectation is that, as a whole, what we will see in the implementation of this regulation is a pattern that generally associates more severe penalties as deficiencies pose greater harm or risks to residents' well-being. We expect to provide additional guidance and training to surveyors and others who will be asked to apply this regulation, and this guidance and training will reflect the approach taken in this regulation.

The Department is considering as well another CMP methodology on which we seek public comment. If comment is favorable, we would implement this option when we finalize this interim regulation.

Under this additional option, a survey agency could recommend a per day penalty of not more than $3,000 for non-immediate jeopardy violations (or not more than $10,000 in cases of immediate jeopardy) for any documented period of noncompliance without having an obligation to determine the entire period of time that the noncompliance may be present. For example, a survey team enters a facility on June 1 and observes that a facility is not in substantial compliance. The team returns July 1 and determines that the noncompliance it initially identified has continued unabated. The survey agency could at that time recommend a penalty of up to $3,000 per day (or $10,000 in the case of immediate jeopardy) for each of the 30 days of noncompliance between June 1 and July 1. This would be the case even if the noncompliance might yet extend for additional days or weeks. Thus, the CMP in such a case would be based on the number of days of noncompliance actually identified without an affirmative obligation on HCFA's or the State's part to ascertain when, in fact, the noncompliance ceases to exist in order to calculate the penalty amount. Or, in another hypothetical situation, a survey team that enters a facility on June 1 may determine from facility records or other evidence that the facility has been out of compliance since May 15. The survey agency could then determine that there have been 15 days of noncompliance for this past period and recommend a penalty up to the regulatory maximum amounts for each of those days of noncompliance without regard to how much longer after June 1 the noncompliance may be present.

The new option would be intended to complement, not supplant, the current CMP authority and the new per instance CMP described above. Our goal in considering the adoption of this third option is to improve nursing home compliance in a way that does not require multiple revisits to impose but which also could have significant financial impact. The potential advantage of this new option over the current CMP authority is that a penalty can be imposed for documented violations without the requirement of multiple revisits by the survey team, in order to determine the amount of the CMP. Under current CMP authority, no penalty may be collected until an ending date for the noncompliance is determined. We believe this policy would serve to motivate a facility to provide care to its residents in a fully compliant manner that would enable it to avoid these potentially significant CMP's in the first place. If a facility were not to undertake its responsibilities in this fashion, it would know in advance that there would be swift action taken to remedy noncompliant behavior.

The Department is especially interested in hearing from states, consumer groups, and providers as to whether they regard this additional type of penalty authority to be useful, and likely to enhance the objective of seeing nursing homes achieve substantial compliance on a sustained basis. We would also want to receive comments on whether this proposal would be administratively practical. Lastly, we encourage comments on whether there should be a maximum daily penalty amount established for this option other than what the statute already provides.

III. State Authorization to Initiate Notice-Notice of Policy Change

Regulations at § 488.402(f)(1) currently permit States, as authorized by HCFA, to send notice of adverse actions to facilities which would otherwise be notified directly by HCFA. In the preamble of the **Federal Register** document that set forth this specific regulation (60 FR 50115, September 28, 1995), we discussed our intent to permit States to give notice of remedies, on behalf of HCFA, only in cases of minimal noncompliance. Limiting the State notification to situations of minimal noncompliance was based on our belief at the time that HCFA should be more directly involved in providing notice of remedies in cases of serious noncompliance.

Our experience has shown us that the current interpretation impedes our ability to respond as quickly as we would like to in instances of facility noncompliance because of the extra time that HCFA's direct involvement requires. Just as we retain responsibility for making decisions about the imposition of remedies for lesser degrees of noncompliance, so too we want to provide the same review, and retain the same responsibility, of cases that pose more serious examples of noncompliance before authorizing a State to impose remedies on our behalf. Thus, under the interpretation we are adopting here for § 488.402(f)(1), States are authorized to impose any remedy which we have the authority to impose, but only as directed by HCFA. We

[Page 13358]

expect that this adjustment to our process will result in the imposition of remedies in a more expeditious and efficient manner than has previously been the case.

IV. Response to Comments

Because of the large number of items of correspondence we normally receive on **Federal Register** documents published for comment, we are not able to acknowledge or respond to them individually. We will consider all comments we receive by the date and time specified in the **DATES** section of this preamble, and, when we proceed with a subsequent document, we will respond to the major comments in the preamble to that document.

V. Waiver of Proposed Rulemaking

We ordinarily publish a notice of proposed rulemaking in the **Federal Register** and invite public comment on the proposed rule. The notice of proposed rulemaking includes a reference to the legal authority under which the rule is proposed, and the terms and substances of the proposed rule or a description of the subjects and issues involved. This procedure can be waived, however, if an agency finds good cause that a notice-and-comment procedure is impracticable, unnecessary, or contrary to the public interest and incorporates a statement of the finding and its reasons in the rule issued. We believe that dispensing with proposed rulemaking is in the public interest and, accordingly, are proceeding here directly with a final rule.

Residents of the nation's nursing homes are among the most vulnerable members of our society. Their well-being is entrusted completely to the care givers with whom they come into contact at these facilities, and, in no small measure, they rely significantly on the machinery of Federal and State government to protect their interests through the enforcement mechanisms authorized by the Medicare and Medicaid statutes. We believe that the more diligent we are in our enforcement efforts, the greater the likelihood that facilities will be encouraged to comply with our requirements, and the greater the likelihood that facility residents will receive the kind of quality care that the statute envisions.

While we believe that we have made material progress in advancing the well-being of facility residents since the advent of nursing home reform, we know that there are opportunities to improve on our record. A report recently issued by the United States General Accounting Office (GAO), in which there was a focus on nursing home conditions, spoke of the continuing presence of unacceptable care in many facilities. Citing continuing problems with meeting some of the most basic needs of residents, such as hydration, nutrition, weight maintenance, and the avoidance of pressure sores, the GAO concluded that there was still important work to be done to make the enforcement scheme of the nursing home reform legislation as effective as it might be. The GAO made strong recommendations for HCFA to bolster its enforcement scheme in an effort to minimize, if not eliminate, the kinds of care problems it identified.

We are most troubled by these reports of poor care. We recognize the importance of making whatever adjustments we have the authority to make as swiftly as we reasonably can if we are to best protect resident well-being. Were we to subject these rules on the imposition of civil money penalties to the full course of proposed rulemaking before finalizing them, we believe we would lose valuable opportunities to respond to cases of noncompliance where the more rapid imposition of penalties would likely reduce the exposure of larger numbers of the nation's nursing home residents to substandard, and sometimes dangerous, levels of care. Because these rules would focus on specific instances of noncompliance, and would permit HCFA and the States to thereby focus swiftly on pinpointed unacceptable care practices, we believe it is in the public interest to make these rules effective at the earliest possible time. We believe additionally that where this rule is so reflective of what it is that the statute is aimed at, there is particular urgency to make these rules available quickly.

For similar reasons, we believe we have good cause to eliminate the requirement establishing a maximum time frame of 20 days to notify a provider of the imposition of remedies contained at § 488.402(f)(5). Elimination of this maximum time frame does not eliminate the providers' right to notice in advance of an adverse action. Such due process continues to be satisfied with at least 2 days' notice in immediate jeopardy cases and 15 days in all other cases. The only impact of the current rule is to artificially delay enforcement actions when providers have already been well apprised of the grounds for the action in previous correspondence from either HCFA or the State. Again, we believe it is in the public interest to make this rule change effective at the earliest possible time and dispense with the full course of proposed rulemaking.

In the case of the change to our interpretation of 42 CFR 488.402(f)(1), in addition to the reasons already cited, we believe that engaging in proposed rulemaking would be unnecessary. In the case of this modification of our enforcement process, no change in the regulation text is needed since it is only an interpretation of the current rule that is being affected. Beyond this, providers will receive no less notice of impending adverse actions than they have in the past. The only difference will be that the letter they receive will arrive under the signature of a State official rather than one from a HCFA regional office. We believe this change will permit HCFA and the States to focus more swiftly on specific instances of noncompliance and, therefore, it is in the public interest for this change to be accomplished as quickly as possible.

Therefore, we find good cause to waive the notice of proposed rulemaking and to issue this rule as a final rule with comment. We are, however, providing a 60-day comment period and will respond to comments we receive in any subsequent **Federal Register** document.

VI. Collection of Information Requirements

Sections 4204(b) and 4214(d) of the Omnibus Budget Reconciliation Act of 1987 (Public Law 100–203) provide a waiver of Office of Management and Budget review of information collection requirements for the purpose of implementing the nursing home reform amendments and these enforcement provisions as referred to in section 4203 of that act.

VII. Regulatory Impact Statement

We have examined the impacts of this final rule with comment as required by Executive Order 12866 and the Regulatory Flexibility Act (RFA) (Public Law 96–354). Executive Order 12866 directs agencies to assess all costs and benefits of available regulatory alternatives and, when regulation is necessary, to select regulatory approaches that maximize net benefits (including potential economic, environmental, public health and safety effects, distributive impacts, and equity). The RFA requires agencies to analyze options for regulatory relief of small businesses. For purposes of the RFA, small entities include small businesses, non-profit organizations and government agencies. For purposes of the RFA, most long term care facilities are considered to be small entities.

Section 1102(b) of the Social Security Act requires us to prepare a regulatory impact analysis if a rule may have a

[Page 13359]

significant impact on the operations of a substantial number of small rural hospitals. Such an analysis must conform to the provisions of section 604 of the RFA.

The intent of the "per instance" penalty in this final rule and the "limited per day" option discussed earlier in this preamble is to offer greater administrative ease to the survey agency in applying penalties and offer a more flexible approach to ensuring compliance. The current per day penalty is administratively difficult to apply, consuming increased surveyor time. The "per instance" and "limited per day" would allow the imposition of financial penalties that on a per case basis may be less onerous. In developing these two options HCFA is recognizing the range of severity of violations and providing survey agencies increased enforcement flexibility, in the form of additional civil money penalty options.

We view the anticipated results of this rule as beneficial to nursing home residents. Specifically, we believe that a per instance civil money penalty will allow us to more specifically tailor the response to facility noncompliance in a way that assures that appropriate resident care occurs. Nevertheless, we recognize that this rule could be controversial and may be responded to unfavorably by some interested parties. We also recognize that not all of the potential effects of this rule can be definitely anticipated, especially in view of their interaction with other Federal, State, and local activities regarding health and safety assurance. In particular, considering the effects of our simultaneous efforts to improve the survey and enforcement activities, through both new and existing instruments and the nursing home provider's responsibility to maintain continuous compliance with the participation requirements, it is impossible to quantify meaningfully the future effect of this rule on facilities' compliance activities or costs. We also are unable to project the frequency with, or increase or decrease in, which facilities will be found to be out of compliance and subject to the imposition of a civil money penalty. While it is not possible to anticipate frequency HCFA must consider the facility's financial condition in determining the amount of penalty if a civil money penalty is selected.

Affected Entities

As of August 24, 1998, there are a total of 17,346 nursing homes participating in the Medicare and Medicaid programs; there are 1,488 skilled nursing facilities certified for Medicare, 2,343 nursing facilities certified for Medicaid, and 13,515 dually participating facilities certified for both Medicare and Medicaid. The majority (65 percent) of these facilities are proprietary. Approximately 28 percent are not-for-profit and 7 percent are government operated.

In order to determine what is a small entity, we use $5 million as a threshold. In estimating the number of nursing facilities with annual revenues in excess of $5 million, bed size was used as a proxy. We assumed facilities with 120 beds or more would have annual gross revenues of $5 million or more. Information on average revenue per day was obtained from the HCFA Office of the Actuary, National Health Statistics Group. In determining the facility bed size, the national 1997 average facility occupancy was considered. The occupancy rate was taken from a January 1999 report "Nursing Facilities, Staffing, Residents, and Facility Deficiencies, 1991 Through 1997." The Online Survey Certification and Report (OSCAR) was used in preparing the report as well as our using the data to gather information regarding facility size. Approximately 61 percent of the proprietary facilities have 119 beds or fewer. Government-owned facilities are not considered small entities because they are not independently owned and operated even though they are not-for-profit.

There should be no additional cost to the provider. This is based upon the fact the regulations and operating directions against which compliance is evaluated have been readily available and widely distributed to the provider community for a number of years and the requirements have not changed. The requirements against which compliance is evaluated are known and the provider has both the ability and expectation to maintain compliance. The provider should be in compliance. This would mean no civil money penalty would be imposed. However, should the provider be determined out of compliance and a decision reached to impose a per instance civil money penalty, it is difficult to project the number of times that may occur.

While it may not be fully instructive to evaluate the impact of the current process for imposing a civil money penalty, the only experience the HCFA has to draw upon is our experience since the regulation became effective in July 1995. Historical information spanning the three fiscal years since July 1995 indicates the average number of facilities per year that have had civil money penalties imposed is between one and 1.5 and 3 percent. The yearly average amount of the civil money penalty per facility has been $15,672 to $21,280. The facility's management has the ability to control operation of the business. The facility's management also has the ability and legal responsibility to maintain compliance with requirements. Since the majority of the businesses have annual operating budgets in excess of $1 million dollars, the impact of the per instance civil money penalty, when compliance is not maintained, does not appear particularly onerous.

We do not know the impact of this rule on nursing homes. As has previously been stated, if the facility is in substantial compliance with Federal regulations, there is no basis to utilize any enforcement remedy. However, should a remedy be indicated, a number of alternative remedies may be considered in addition to a civil money penalty. It would not be accurate to assume that a civil money penalty would be the remedy of choice or the one most frequently used. Selection of enforcement remedies appropriate to the noncompliance requires careful consideration on the part of the regulatory agency and does not automatically imply a civil money penalty will be imposed. While it may be argued the per instance civil money penalty will be more heavily utilized than the per day civil money penalty, we have no data to support that perspective.

We have also considered the potential impact of the "limited per day" methodology of imposing a civil money penalty on nursing homes. The same difficulty is present in attempting to assess the impact of this approach as is present with the per instance provision. It is not possible to project the frequency of noncompliance or increases or decreases in the number of facilities that will be found to be out of compliance and subject to imposition of a civil money penalty. This is especially true when considering that selection of a civil money penalty is not a requirement and but one of an array of remedies that may be selected.

A nursing home certified to participate in the Medicare and Medicaid programs is expected to be in compliance with Federal requirements as a condition of receiving payment for services provided to beneficiaries. If the provider is in compliance, no action to impose a remedy, which could include a civil money penalty, would be justified. However, should the provider be determined out of compliance and a decision reached to impose a civil money penalty, it is difficult to project the number of times that may occur. As we have indicated, if a civil money

[Page 13360]

penalty is selected as an enforcement option, the facility's financial condition must be considered in determining the amount of the penalty.

There are currently a number of activities occurring that we believe will sharpen public and provider awareness of problems in nursing homes. These activities include the President's "Initiatives to Improve the Quality of care In Nursing Homes" and activities of the Senate Committee on Aging. We believe that the increased awareness of nursing homes problems may influence greater facility compliance and mitigate against increased use of remedies to achieve compliance with Federal requirements.

Because this rule affects no rural hospitals, we are not preparing an analysis for section 1102(b) of the Act because we have determined, and we certify, that this rule will not have a significant impact on the operations of a substantial number of small rural hospitals.

This rule has been reviewed in accordance with the Unfunded Mandates Reform Act of 1995 (2 U.S.C. 1501 *et seq.*), which requires that agencies assess anticipated costs and benefits before issuing any rule that may result in an annual expenditure by State, local, or tribal governments, in the aggregate, or by the private sector, of $100 million. Although this interim final rule will affect nursing facilities, we anticipate this effect to be less than $100 million in the aggregate.

In accordance with the provisions of Executive Order 12866, this regulation was reviewed by the Office of Management and Budget.

List of Subjects in 42 CFR Part 488

Health facilities, Medicare, Reporting and recordkeeping requirements.

For the reasons set forth in the preamble, 42 CFR part 488, subpart F, is amended as set forth below:

PART 488 — SURVEY, CERTIFICATION, AND ENFORCEMENT PROCEDURES

1. The authority citation for Part 488 continues to read as follows:
Authority: §§ 1102 and 1871 of the Social Security Act (42 U.S.C. 1302 and 1395hh).

Subpart F — Enforcement of Compliance for Long-Term Care Facilities with Deficiencies

2. In § 488.402, paragraph (f)(5) is revised to read as follows:

§ 488.402 General provisions.

* * * * *

(f) Notification requirements — * * *
(5) Date of enforcement action. The 2-and 15-day notice periods begin when the facility receives the notice.

* * * * *

3. In § 488.408, the introductory text of paragraphs (d)(1), (e)(1), and (e)(2) are republished, paragraphs (d)(1)(iv) and (e)(1)(iv) are added, and paragraph (e)(2)(ii) is revised to read as follows:

§ 488.408 Selection of remedies.

* * * * *

(d) Category 2. (1) Category 2 remedies include the following:

* * * * *

(iv) Civil money penalty of $1,000-$10,000 per instance of noncompliance.

* * * * *

(e) Category 3. (1) Category 3 remedies include the following:

* * * * *

(iv) Civil money penalty of $1,000-$10,000 per instance of noncompliance.
(2) When there are one or more deficiencies that constitute immediate jeopardy to resident health or safety —

* * * * *

(ii) HCFA and the State may impose a civil money penalty of $3,050- $10,000 per day or $1,000-$10,000 per instance of noncompliance, in addition to imposing the remedies specified in paragraph (e)(2)(i) of this section.

* * * * *

4. Section 488.430(a) is revised to read as follows:

§ 488.430 Civil money penalties: Basis for imposing penalty.

(a) HCFA or the State may impose a civil money penalty for either the number of days a facility is not in substantial compliance with one or more participation requirements or for each instance that a facility is not in substantial compliance, regardless of whether or not the deficiencies constitute immediate jeopardy.

* * * * *

5. In § 488.432, the section heading and paragraphs (a)(2), (b), and (c) are revised to read as follows:

§ 488.432 Civil money penalties: When a penalty is collected.

(a) When a facility requests a hearing. * * *

(2) (i) If a facility requests a hearing within the time specified in paragraph (a)(1) of this section, for a civil money penalty imposed per day, HCFA or the State initiates collection of the penalty when there is a final administrative decision that upholds HCFA's or the State's determination of noncompliance after the facility achieves substantial compliance or is terminated.

(ii) If a facility requests a hearing for a civil money penalty imposed per instance of noncompliance within the time specified in paragraph (a)(1) of this section, HCFA or the State initiates collection of the penalty when there is a final administrative decision that upholds HCFA's or the State's determination of noncompliance.

(b) When a facility does not request a hearing for a civil money penalty imposed per day. (1) If a facility does not request a hearing in accordance with paragraph (a) of this section, HCFA or the State initiates collection of the penalty when the facility—

(i)Achieves substantial compliance; or

(ii) Is terminated.

(2) When a facility does not request a hearing for a civil money penalty imposed per instance of noncompliance. If a facility does not request a hearing in accordance with paragraph (a) of this section, HCFA or the State initiates collection of the penalty when the time frame for requesting a hearing expires.

(c) When a facility waives a hearing. (1) If a facility waives, in writing, its right to a hearing as specified in § 488.436, for a civil money penalty imposed per day, HCFA or the State initiates collection of the penalty when the facility —

(i) Achieves substantial compliance; or (ii) Is terminated.

(2) If a facility waives, in writing, its right to a hearing as specified in § 488.436, for a civil money penalty imposed per instance of noncompliance, HCFA or the State initiates collection of the penalty upon receipt of the facility's notification.

* * * * *

6. In § 488.434, the introductory text of paragraph (a)(2) is republished and paragraphs (a)(2)(iii), (a)(2)(v), and (a)(2)(vi) are revised to read as follows:

§ 488.434 Civil money penalties: Notice of penalty.

(a) HCFA notice of penalty. * * *

(2) Content of notice. The notice that HCFA sends includes —

* * * * *

(iii) The amount of penalty per day of noncompliance or the amount of the penalty per instance of noncompliance;

* * * * *

(v) The date of the instance of noncompliance or the date on which the penalty begins to accrue;

(vi) When the penalty stops accruing, if applicable;

* * * * *

7. In § 488.438, the introductory text of paragraph (a) is redesignated as (a)(1) and republished; paragraphs (a)(1) and (a)(2) are redesignated as paragraphs (a)(1)(i) and (a)(1)(ii), respectively; a new paragraph (a)(2) is added; and

[Page 13361]

paragraphs (c) and (d) are revised to read as follows:

§ 488.438 Civil money penalties: Amount of penalty.

(a) *Amount of penalty* — (1) Per day penalties. The per day penalties are within the following ranges, set at $50 increments:

(i) Upper range. * * *

(ii) Lower range. * * *

(2) Per instance penalty. When penalties are imposed for an instance of noncompliance, the penalties will be in the range of $1,000-$10,000 per instance.

* * * * *

(c) Decreased penalty amounts. Except as specified in paragraph (d)(2) of this section, if immediate jeopardy is removed, but the noncompliance continues, HCFA or the State will shift the penalty amount imposed per day to the lower range.

(d) Increased penalty amounts. (1) Before a hearing requested in accordance with § 488.432(a), HCFA or the State may propose to increase the per day penalty amount for facility noncompliance which, after imposition of a lower level penalty amount, becomes sufficiently serious to pose immediate jeopardy.

(2) HCFA does and the State must increase the per day penalty amount for any repeated deficiencies for which a lower level penalty amount was previously imposed, regardless of whether the increased penalty amount would exceed the range otherwise reserved for nonimmediate jeopardy deficiencies.

* * * * *

8. In § 488.440, paragraphs (a), (c), (d), (g), and (h); the introductory text of paragraphs (b) and (e); and paragraph (f)(1) are revised to read as follows:

§ 488.440 Civil money penalties: Effective date and duration of penalty.

(a)(1) The per day civil money penalty may start accruing as early as the date that the facility was first out of compliance, as determined by HCFA or the State.

(2) A civil money penalty for each instance of noncompliance is imposed in a specific amount for that particular deficiency.

(b) The per day civil money penalty is computed and collectible, as specified in § § 488.432 and 488.442, for the number of days of noncompliance until the date the facility achieves substantial compliance, or, if applicable, the date of termination when—

* * * * *

(c) The entire penalty, whether imposed on a per day or per instance basis, is due and collectible as specified in the notice sent to the provider under paragraphs (d) and (e) of this section.

(d) (1) When a civil money penalty is imposed on a per day basis and the facility achieves substantial compliance, HCFA does or the State must send a separate notice to the facility containing the following information:

(i) The amount of penalty per day.

(ii) The number of days involved.

(iii) The total amount due.

(iv) The due date of the penalty.

(v) The rate of interest assessed on the unpaid balance beginning on the due date, as provided in § 488.442.

(2) When a civil money penalty is imposed for an instance of noncompliance, HCFA does or the State must send a separate notice to the facility containing the following information:

(i) The amount of the penalty.

(ii) The total amount due.

(iii) The due date of the penalty.

(iv) The rate of interest assessed on the unpaid balance beginning on the due date, as provided in § 488.442.

(e) In the case of a facility for which the provider agreement has been terminated and on which a civil money penalty was imposed on a per day basis, HCFA does or the State must send this penalty information after the—

* * * * *

(f)(1) In the case of noncompliance that does not pose immediate jeopardy, the daily accrual of per day civil money penalties is imposed for the days of noncompliance prior to the notice specified in § 488.434 and an additional period of no longer than 6 months following the last day of the survey.

* * * * *

(g)(1) In a case when per day civil money penalties are imposed, when a facility has deficiencies that pose immediate jeopardy, HCFA does or the State must terminate the provider agreement within 23 calendar days after the last day of the survey if the immediate jeopardy remains.

(2) The accrual of the civil money penalty imposed on a per day basis stops on the day the provider agreement is terminated.

(h)(1) If an on-site revisit is necessary to confirm substantial compliance and the provider can supply documentation acceptable to HCFA or the State agency that substantial compliance was achieved on a date preceding the revisit, penalties imposed on a per day basis only accrue until that date of correction for which there is written credible evidence.

(2) If an on-site revisit is not necessary to confirm substantial compliance, penalties imposed on a per day basis only accrue until the date of correction for which HCFA or the State receives and accepts written credible evidence.

9. In § 488.442, the heading of paragraph (a) is revised, paragraphs (b) through (f) are redesignated as paragraphs (c) through (g), respectively, and new paragraph (b) is added to read as follows:

§ 488.442 Civil money penalties: Due date for payment of penalty.

(a) When payments are due for a civil money penalty imposed on a per day basis —

* * * * *

(b) When payments are due for a civil money penalty imposed for an instance of noncompliance. Payment of a civil money penalty is due 15 days after one of the following dates:

(1) The final administrative decision is made;

(2) The time for requesting a hearing has expired and the facility did not request a hearing; or

(3) The facility waived its right to a hearing.

* * * * *

10. In § 488.454, the introductory text of paragraph (a) is revised, paragraph (d) is redesignated as paragraph (e) and revised, and new paragraph (d) is added to read as follows:

§ 488.454 Duration of remedies.

(a) Except as specified in paragraphs (b) and (d) of this section, alternative remedies continue until —

* * * * *

(d) In the case of a civil money penalty imposed for an instance of noncompliance, the remedy is the specific amount of the civil money penalty imposed for the particular deficiency.

(e) If the facility can supply documentation acceptable to HCFA or the State survey agency that it was in substantial compliance and was capable of remaining in substantial compliance, if necessary, on a date preceding that of the revisit, the remedies terminate on the date that HCFA or the State can verify as the date that substantial compliance was achieved and the facility demonstrated that it could maintain substantial compliance, if necessary.

(Catalog of Federal Domestic Assistance Program No. 93.778, Medical Assistance Program; Program No. 93.773, Medicare — Hospital Insurance; and Program No. 93.774, Medicare — Supplementary Medical Insurance Program)

[Page 13362]

Dated: February 12, 1999.

Nancy-Ann Min DeParle,

Administrator, Health Care Financing Administration.

Dated: March 3, 1999.

Donna E. Shalala,

Secretary.

[FR Doc. 99–6618 Filed 3–16–99; 9:20 am]

BILLING CODE 4120–01-P

APPENDIX J4

Revised OIG Sanction Authorities Resulting From P.L. 105–33, the Balanced Budget Act of 1997 — Final Rule; 64 FR 39420, July 22, 1999

Federal Register: July 22, 1999 (Volume 64, Number 140) Rules and Regulations Page 39420–39429

DEPARTMENT OF HEALTH AND HUMAN SERVICES

Office of Inspector General

42 CFR Parts 1001, 1002 and 1003

RIN 0991-AA95

Health Care Programs: Fraud and Abuse; Revised OIG Sanction Authorities Resulting From Public Law 105–33

AGENCY: Office of Inspector General (OIG), HHS.

ACTION: Final rule.

SUMMARY: This rulemaking revises the OIG's exclusion and civil money penalty authorities set forth in 42 CFR parts 1001, 1002 and 1003, as a result of the Balanced Budget Act of 1997, Public Law 105–33. These revisions are intended to protect Medicare and other Federal health care programs by enhancing the OIG's administrative sanction authority through new or revised exclusion and civil money penalty provisions.

EFFECTIVE DATE: This rule is effective on July 22, 1999.

FOR FURTHER INFORMATION CONTACT: Joel Schaer, (202) 619–0089, OIG Regulations Officer.

SUPPLEMENTARY INFORMATION:

I. Background

A. The Health Insurance Portability and Accountability Act

The Health Insurance Portability and Accountability Act (HIPAA) of 1996, Public Law 104–191, was enacted on August 21, 1996, and set forth a number of significant amendments to the OIG's exclusion and civil money penalty (CMP) authorities. Among the various provisions related to the program exclusion authority, HIPAA: (1) Expanded the OIG's minimum 5-year mandatory exclusion authority to cover any felony conviction under Federal, State or local law relating to health care fraud, even if governmental programs were not involved; (2) established minimum periods of exclusion from 1 to 3 years for certain permissive exclusions; and (3) established a new permissive exclusion authority applicable to individuals who have a

[Page 39421]

majority ownership in, or have significant control over the operations of an entity that has been convicted of a program-related offense. Proposed regulations addressing these revised or expanded OIG exclusion authorities were published in the **Federal Register** on September 8, 1997 (62 FR 47182) and final regulations were issued on September 2, 1998 (63 FR 46676).

In addition, HIPAA revised and strengthened the OIG's existing CMP authorities, and extended the application of the CMP provisions beyond those programs funded by the Department to include all Federal health care programs. Separate OIG proposed rulemaking addressing the revised or expanded CMP provisions resulting from HIPAA were published in the **Federal Register** on March 25, 1998 (63 FR 14393).

B. The Balanced Budget Act of 1997

In conjunction with many of the HIPAA fraud and abuse authorities, the Balanced Budget Act (BBA) of 1997, enacted on August 5, 1997, contained a number of provisions designed to further protect the integrity of Medicare, Medicaid and all other Federal health care programs for current and future beneficiaries, and combat fraudulent and abusive program activities. Specifically, the fraud and abuse provisions of BBA serve to strengthen the OIG's exclusion and CMP authorities with respect to Federal health care programs.

While the new exclusion and CMP authorities under BBA were effective for violations occurring on or after August 5, 1997, since the statutory provisions allowed the Department some policy discretion in their implementation, the OIG developed and issued a proposed rulemaking on September 2, 1998, that solicited public comments on proposed exclusion and CMP regulatory revisions resulting from BBA (63 FR 46736).

II. Summary of the Proposed Rule

In accordance with the Department's expanded and revised exclusion and CMP authorities resulting from BBA, the proposed regulations were designed to codify in 42 CFR parts 1001, 1002 and 1003 as follows:

A. Revised Exclusion Authorities Resulting From BBA

1. OIG authority to direct exclusions from State health care programs, and to extend application of OIG exclusions to all Federal health care programs —Prior to BBA, the OIG was authorized under section 1128 of the Act to impose exclusions from participation in Medicare under its own authority, but could not impose other health care program exclusions directly. Instead, the OIG directed State health care programs (such as Medicaid) to impose parallel exclusions, but had no authority with respect to the exclusion from State health care programs, as listed in section 1128(i) of the Act. Section 4331(c) of BBA specifically amended sections 1128(a) and (b) of the Act to extend the scope of an OIG exclusion beyond the Medicare and State health care programs to all Federal health care programs (as defined in section 1128B(f) of the Act), and to enable the OIG to impose exclusions from all Federal health care programs directly. We proposed amending various sections of 42 CFR part 1001 to reflect this expanded authority.

The proposed regulations also addressed the effect of this expanded exclusion authority on the employment of excluded individuals, and program reimbursement for items and services they may provide to other Federal health care programs. Prior to BBA, with limited exceptions, no payment could be made under Medicare and the State health care programs for any health care item or service furnished, ordered or prescribed by an excluded individual. However, an individual excluded from Medicare and the State health care programs could still be employed or receive payment from other Federal health care programs, such as Tricare or the

Department of Veterans Affairs. With the expanded scope of the exclusion authority, the proposed rule stated that Federal health care agencies may neither reimburse for items and services which excluded individuals provide, order or prescribe, nor pay the salaries or expenses of such persons using Federal funds. As indicated in the proposed rule, in accordance with the BBA provision, with limited exceptions, an exclusion would effectively preclude the employment of an excluded individual in any capacity by a Federal or State agency, or other entity, where payment is made by any Federal health care program.

2. *Permanent exclusions for individuals convicted of 3 or more health care-related crimes, and 10 year exclusions for individuals convicted of 2 health care-related crimes* — Most excluded health care providers become eligible for reinstatement in the Federal and State health care programs after a specified exclusion period. Section 4301 of BBA established a mandatory exclusion period of not less than 10 years for individuals who have been twice convicted of mandatory exclusion offenses under section 1128(a) of the Act. In addition, a permanent program exclusion must be imposed against those individuals who have been convicted on 3 or more occasions of such mandatory exclusion offenses. Accordingly, we proposed to amend § 1001.102 to reflect these new mandatory exclusion periods.

3. *Exclusion of entities controlled by family or household members of sanctioned individuals* — The OIG is authorized to exclude entities owned or controlled by an individual who has been convicted of a health care related offense, or who has been sanctioned by the OIG. However, some excluded individuals have been able to circumvent the impact of an exclusion and retain silent control of operating health care entities by engaging in paper transfers of their ownership and control interests to family or household members. To address the problem of excluded individuals retaining "silent" control of participating entities, section 4303 of BBA allowed for the exclusion of entities owned or controlled by the family or household members of excluded individuals when the transfer of ownership or control interest in the entity was made in anticipation of, or following, a conviction, CMP or exclusion. We proposed to amend § 1001.1001(a) to reflect this new authority.

B. Revised CMP Authorities Resulting From BBA

1. CMPs against institutional health care providers that employ or enter into contracts for medical services with excluded individuals —In some instances, individuals who have been excluded from Medicare or the State health care programs have been able to obtain (or retain) employment, staff privileges or other affiliations with various health care entities that then bill the programs for their services. CMP authority has existed for health maintenance organizations that submit claims for items or services furnished by excluded employees or other excluded individuals with whom they contract, but no parallel sanction authority existed with respect to a group medical practice, hospital, nursing home, home health agency, hospice or other provider that failed to check the credentials of individuals whose services they utilize and bill to Medicare or State health care programs. In accordance with new authority set forth in section 4304(a) of BBA, we proposed amending Secs. 1003.102(a) and 1003.103(a) to allow the OIG to impose a CMP of up to $10,000 against any entity that submits, or causes to be submitted, claims for items or services rendered by employees or other individuals with whom they

[Page 39422]

contract, and whom they know, or should know, have been excluded from participation in the Federal health care programs.

2. CMP for failure to report information to the Healthcare Integrity and Protection Data Bank —Section 221 of HIPAA established a national health care fraud and abuse data collection program, the Healthcare Integrity and Protection Data Bank (HIPDB), for the reporting of final adverse actions (such as convictions, exclusions and licensing restrictions) against health care providers, suppliers and practitioners.[1] While this authority mandated that private health plans, as well as certain State and Federal entities, report adverse actions to the HIPDB, no penalty provision was included to address failure by a health care plan to comply with the reporting requirements. In accordance with section 4331(d) of BBA, § 1003.102 (b) of the proposed regulations set forth a new CMP of not more than $25,000 against any health plan that fails to report a final adverse action to HIPDB as required by the statute and regulations.

[1] Proposed regulations setting forth the policies and procedures for implementing the new HIPDB were published in the **Federal Register** on October 29, 1998 (63 FR 58341).

3. CMPs for health care providers who violate the anti-kickback statute —Prior to BBA, criminal penalties or program exclusions were the only remedies available against those who offered or received remuneration in return for the referral of business paid for by Federal health care programs, in violation of the anti-kickback statute. Since both remedies are potentially quite severe, section 4304 of BBA set forth an alternative remedy, i.e., a new CMP for violations of the anti-kickback statute. In accordance with this new statutory provision, we proposed to amend Secs. 1003.102(b), 1003.103(h) and 1003.104 to implement a CMP of not more than $50,000 for each kickback violation, and an assessment of up to 3 times the total amount of remuneration offered, paid, solicited or received without regard to whether a portion of such remuneration was offered, paid, solicited or received for a lawful purpose.

C. Additional Technical and Other Revisions to 42 CFR Parts 1001 and 1003

1. Technical revisions — A number of proposed technical revisions consistent with the policy provisions resulting from BBA and the proposed regulatory amendments were also indicated in the notice of proposed rulemaking. Specifically, we proposed to amend the authority citation cites for parts 1001 and 1003, §§ 1001.302 (Basis for reinstatement), 1003.100 (Basis and purpose), and 1003.114 (Collateral estoppel) to reflect the revisions being proposed in accordance with the revised BBA exclusion and CMP authorities. In addition, we proposed a revision to § 1003.109(a)(3), to delete the phrase "the amount of the proposed penalty, assessment and the period of proposed exclusion (where applicable)." This language appears in paragraph (a)(4) of this section, and appears inadvertently in paragraph (a)(3).

2. Proposed revision to OIG reinstatement considerations —We also proposed to add two new elements to § 1001.3002(b), pertaining to the OIG's review of an individual's or entity's request for reinstatement in the Federal health care programs after the individual's or entity's exclusion period. The first new proposed element was designed to address the OIG's expectation that excluded parties adequately and promptly inform all their clients or patients of the exclusion so that the clients or patients will have a clear understanding that items and services provided, directed or ordered by that individual or entity will not be paid for under any Federal health care program. Under § 1001.1901(b) of the proposed regulations, Medicare reimbursement is authorized to a beneficiary for the first claim submitted for an item or service provided by the excluded party, at which time the beneficiary is notified that future claims will be denied due to the provider's excluded status. (We did not believe that notification only after the submission of a claim provides adequate protection for program beneficiaries.) By stating in the proposed regulations that the OIG, in making its reinstatement decisions, would consider whether a provider has adequately and promptly informed clients or patients of an exclusion, we hoped to offer an incentive for providers to give the earliest possible notification to beneficiaries of their exclusion.

A second proposed reinstatement element was designed to codify existing OIG policy which, in making reinstatement decisions, considers whether the individual or entity has, during the period of exclusion, submitted claims or caused claims to be submitted, or payments to be made by any Federal health care program for items or services the excluded party furnished, ordered or prescribed, including health care administrative services during the period of exclusion. By setting forth this regulatory clarification, we hoped to make clear that the submission of claims for payment to any Federal health care program during a provider's period of exclusion will jeopardize the provider's reinstatement into the programs.

III. Responses to Comments and Summary of Revisions

In response to the notice of proposed rulemaking, the OIG received a total of five timely-filed public comments from various health care associations and other interested parties. Set forth below is a synopsis of the various comments and recommendations received, our response to those concerns, and a summary of the specific revisions and clarifications being made to the regulations.

Section 1001.102 Factors in Length of Exclusion

Comment: Two commenters raised concern over the language in proposed § 1001.102(b)(6), one of the possible aggravating factors which would provide a basis for lengthening the period of exclusion. The provision would consider whether the "individual or entity has at any time been overpaid a total of $1,500 or more by Medicare, Medicaid or any Federal health care program as a result of improper billings." The commenters indicated that this language was too general and gives no clear indication of what constitutes "improper billings." The commenters stated that any overpayments of $1,500 or more, whether part of the same circumstance that led to the exclusion in the first place, or ones that are billing error mistakes or simple negligence, could be deemed an aggravating circumstance. The commenters indicated that aggravating factors should serve as valid predictors of future violations of Medicare and other Federal program statutes and regulations and, therefore, urged that the OIG delete the $1,500 threshold.

Response: It is not our intention to consider overpayment of $1,500 or more based on inadvertent billing errors as an aggravating circumstance. We agree with the commenters that the $1,500 threshold for overpayments needs to be related to improper conduct, such as the submission of false, fraudulent or otherwise improper claims for payment. This criterion with respect to determining aggravating circumstances has been included in the OIG's regulations since 1992 and has not been identified as a problem by either providers or the OIG. Therefore, this provision, which was not proposed for

[Page 39423]

any revision in our proposed rule, will not be revised at this time.

Section 1001.3002(b)(5) Basis for Reinstatement

Comment: Two commenters raised concern over the proposed language in § 1001.3002(b)(5) that would add a new factor in determining whether an individual or entity can be reinstated to participate in Federally-funded health care programs. Specifically, we indicated that the OIG would consider "whether the individual or entity, during the period of exclusion, has adequately and promptly informed its clients or patients that any items or services provided will not be reimbursable under any Federal health care program." One commenter requested that the OIG clarify both the terms "adequate" and "prompt" so that an excluded individual can be aware of whether they have met the criteria for reinstatement. The commenter also asked for additional clarification what is meant by a physician's or entity's "clients and patients."

A second commenter recommended that the language in this paragraph be deleted entirely, stating that an excluded party's unwillingness to notify those affected should not have a bearing on his or her fitness to be readmitted to the health care programs.

Response: We have considered the comments regarding this proposed factor for reviewing reinstatement requests, and agree that this factor may impose an additional burden on excluded individuals and entities with respect to notification of patients and clients and that this notification obligation is not mandated by law. In addition, we are persuaded by the fact that beneficiaries are adequately protected, since the current procedures provide for payment of the first claim submitted by or on behalf of a beneficiary for services furnished, ordered or prescribed by an excluded provider or practitioner, and simultaneous notification regarding the exclusion. Moreover, we believe that it would be very difficult to monitor such notifications by excluded individuals and entities in order to assess their trustworthiness for purposes of future participation in Federal health care programs. Based on these reasons, we are deleting this proposed factor from those to be evaluated in assessing a reinstatement request.

Section 1003.102(a) CMP for Relationships With Excluded Individuals

Comment: A commenter was concerned that the OIG misinterpreted the statute (42 U.S.C. 1320a-7a(a)(6)) and congressional intent with regard to the basis for CMPs arising from relationships with excluded individuals. They indicated that the proposed regulations imply the existence of an affirmative duty on providers to monitor, on an ongoing basis, the eligibility of employees and others with whom they enter into contracts to participate in the Federal health care programs. The commenter believed that the conditional phrase "or should have known" in proposed § 1003.102(a)(2) would effectively impose a duty upon contracting providers to monitor the list of excluded individuals and entities on a regular basis or risk imposition of a CMP. The commenter raised questions regarding (1) how often should they check on employees and contracting parties, e.g., when employees are hired and when contracting parties enter into a contract, or rechecked at regular intervals), and (2) which persons should be checked, e.g., ongoing contracts, subcontractors or employees of a corporation with whom they are contracting. The commenter believed the appropriate burden should be on the OIG or the excluded individual or entity to notify contracting providers with whom they have employment or other contractual relationships of their exclusion from the Federal health care programs.

Response: Providers and contracting parties have a duty to check the sanction report on the OIG web site prior to entering into employment or contractual arrangements with new hires or run the risk of CMP liability if they fail to do so. All exclusion information is maintained on the OIG web site (www.dhhs.gov/progorg/oig) and updated on a regular basis. While it is not possible for the OIG to be aware of every employment arrangement being entered into by providers and excluded individuals or entities, the OIG does notify and inform employers of excluded individuals and entities when such pending employment arrangements are specifically known to the OIG. In addition, hospitals are under an affirmative obligation to query the National Practitioner Data Bank (NPDB) when they grant privileges, and subsequently at 2-year intervals, to determine whether any actions have been taken against physicians that they employ. Information on exclusions is contained in the NPDB.

Comment: Another commenter contended that use of the OIG's Sanction Report posted on the Internet is confusing and inadequate. The commenter stated that the current information contained on the OIG web site is not easily accessible, requiring providers to create their own "cumulative list" and to manually input data which could leave providers open to fraud and abuse claims because of simple mistakes or errors. In light of the new CMP authority under BBA for providers contracting with or employing an individual or entity that is excluded from the Federal health care programs, the commenter requested that the OIG reevaluate the current Sanction Report to create a "cumulative list" of excluded individuals and entities that providers can easily access and use.

Response: We believe that the current OIG web site containing the Cumulative Sanction Report is accessible, with large numbers of users of this web site having no problems in obtaining the information needed. However, we have also been aware that some users want to be able to do an on-line search for a single individual or entity, and agree that the sanction report on the web site needs to be modified to be more user-friendly in order to permit parties to look for one name at a time. Early in 1999, the OIG web site was modified so that parties can search by either name or location in order to ascertain an individual's or entity's exclusion status, as well as being able to download the entire file.

It should also be pointed out that the OIG's web site is not the sole source of information regarding sanctioned individuals and entities. The NPDB, which hospitals are required to query, contains information on our sanctioned providers. In addition, the exclusion information is also available on the GSA list of "Parties Excluded from Federal Procurement and Nonprocurement Programs" and is on-line searchable.[2] Furthermore, the new HIPDB will contain the OIG exclusion information. With the various avenues of information on excluded individuals and entities available, we believe parties will be able to readily obtain the necessary information on current Federal health care program exclusions.

Comment: The preamble discussion of the proposed rule stated the OIG's concern that "individuals who have been excluded from Medicare or State health care program participation have, nonetheless, been able to obtain (or retain) employment, staff privileges or other affiliation with various health care entities * * *." A commenter emphasized that it is both possible and common for a physician to have medical staff privileges at a hospital without having either an employment or a contractual relationship with the

[Page 39424]

hospital, particularly in States that prohibit the corporate practice of medicine. The commenter further stated that a physician's medical staff privileges at a hospital and his or her provision of items and services covered by Medicare mean that the hospital and the physician are "arranging" for the provision of such services.

Response: We agree with the commenter's point regarding the reference to staff privileges. A medical staff relationship, in the absence of any employment or contractual relationship or arrangement, in and of itself, remains outside the scope of these regulations. However, when claims are generated by physicians having privileges in the hospital for services they furnish, order or prescribe, the hospital must be held accountable if the items or services are provided by excluded physicians. Clearly, an excluded physician cannot have any Federal or State health care program payments made for items and services that they furnish, order or prescribe; not to hold a hospital or other organization accountable for allowing such a person to generate bills to the programs would be inappropriate.

Section 1003.102(b) CMP for Failure To Report Information to the HIPDB

Comment: One commenter believed that the OIG should not proceed with regulations relating to the new CMP for failure to report information to the HIPDB until the implementing regulations for the new data bank have been finalized.

---

[2] See http://anet.gov/epls/.

Response: The OIG published proposed regulations in the **Federal Register** on October 30, 1998 (63 FR 58341) addressing policies and procedures for implementing the new HIPDB. Those proposed regulations are designed to address, among other things, how and when specific information is to be reported to the data bank; the requirements for the disclosure and confidentiality of information received by the HIPDB; applicable fees when requesting data bank information; and the process for disputing the accuracy of HIPDB information. The HIPDB is not expected to be operational until final regulations are in place some time later this year. The OIG will take no CMP action for failure to report information to the HIPDB until the issuance of final implementing regulations regarding reporting to he HIPDB.

Section 1003.103 Amount of Penalty

Comment: One commenter indicated that the proposed regulatory language in § 1003.103(h)(1), that indicates that the OIG may impose "a penalty of $50,000" against persons who commit an act in violation of the anti-kickback statute, is not consistent with the statutory language set forth in BBA. The statutory language (42 U.S.C. 1320a-7a(a)) indicates that a person may be subject to a civil money penalty of not more than * * * $50,000 for each such act." The commenter recommended that the rule be modified to comport with the statutory language.

Response: We agree that the proposed language was inconsistent, and are amending paragraph (h)(1) of this section to indicate that the OIG may not impose "a penalty of not more than $50,000" (emphasis added).

Section 1003.106 Factors in Calculating CMPs

Comment: One commenter cited an ambiguity in the preamble and proposed regulations text at § 1003.106(a)(1)(vii) with regard to determinations on the amount of a penalty. The commenter states that the preamble discussion indicates one of the criteria for determining the appropriate amount of penalty would be "whether the contracting provider knew or should have known of the exclusion." Also, the commenter indicates that the proposed language in § 1003.106(a)(1)(vii) describes this factor as "whether the contracting provider knew of the exclusion when employing or otherwise contracting with an excluded individual or entity." The commenter recommended adding the word "actually" before the word "knew" in this paragraph.

The commenter also believed a number of additional factors relating to the overall culpability of a contracting party should be considered. They included (i) the volume or value of items or services provided by an excluded individual or entity with which the contracting provider has an employment or contractual relationship; (ii) whether the contracting provider has in place an effective compliance program; and (iii) the length of time between when the provider knew or should have known of the exclusion, and when the provider terminated the employment or other contractual relationship with the excluded individual or entity.

Response: In making any determinations regarding the amount of penalty, the OIG intends to draw clear distinctions between cases where there was actual versus constructive knowledge. As a result, we are amending the language in § 1003.106(a)(1)(vii) to indicate that in determining the amount of any penalty in accordance with this provision, we will take into account whether "the contracting provider actually knew of the exclusion when employing or otherwise contracting with an excluded individual or entity * * *" (emphasis added).

Comment: Two commenters raised objection to the existing factor, being redesignated as paragraph (a)(1)(ix) in this section, which allows the OIG to assess penalties in accordance with "[S]uch other matters as justice may require." The commenters believe that this language is unacceptably vague wide-ranging.

Response: The language in § 1003.106(a)(1)(ix), among other places in part 1003, is not new, and is intended to encompass other mitigating and aggravating factors that may arise on a case-by-case basis. It was included in the CMP statutory authority when initially enacted in 1981. This phrase allows for the consideration of individual factors, both aggravating and mitigating, that may be meaningful to one distinct case. For example, the additional factors cited by a commenter and referenced above, relating to the overall culpability of a contracting party, may be considered under this factor.

IV. Provisions of the Final Rule

For the most part, this final rule incorporates the provisions of the September 2, 1998 proposed rule. A brief description of the provisions of this final rule follow.

• In § 1001.2, we are adding a definition for the term "Federal health care program," and are making conforming changes to include the term "and other Federal health care programs" in Secs. 1001.1(a), 1001.201(b)(3)(iii)(A), 1001.301(b)(2)(ii), 1001.401(c)((2)(ii), 1001.1301(b)(2)(iii), 1001.1401.(b)(1) and (b)(4), 1001.1501(a)(3), 1001.1901(b)(1), 1001.3003, 1001.303 and 1002.2(a). Similar proposed revisions to Secs. 1001.301(b)(3)(ii)(A) and 1001.401(c)(3)(i)(A) have already been addressed in the OIG final regulations published on September 2, 1998 (63 FR 46676) addressing revised OIG exclusion authorities resulting from Public Law 104–191.

• In the proposed rule, we set forth in § 1001.2, Definitions, a revised definition for the term "exclusion." A revised definition of the term was promulgated in the OIG final regulations published on September 2, 1998 (63 FR 46676) addressing revised OIG exclusion authorities resulting from Public Law 104–191. We are retaining that definition of the term "exclusion," set forth in the September 2, 1998 final

[Page 39425]

rule, in these final regulations as well. We are also adding a definition in § 1001.2 for the term "Federal health care program."

• The proposed rule indicated our intention to amend § 1001.102 (b) by revising paragraphs (b)(5) and (b)(6), and by adding a new paragraph (b)(7). However, in the proposed rule, we inadvertently deleted existing paragraph (b)(5). In addition, final OIG regulations published on September 2, 1998 (63 FR 46676) added a new paragraph (b)(8). As a result, in these final regulations we are revising current paragraphs (b)(6) and (b)(7) (and not (b)(5) and (b)(6) as the proposed rule indicated); redesignating the recently-added paragraph (b)(8) as new paragraph (b)(9); and adding a new paragraph (b)(8) (designated as new (b)(7) in the proposed rule). We are also adding a new § 1001.102(d) to reflect the new mandatory lengths of exclusion.

• We are amending § 1001.1001(a) to reflect the statutory authority that allows for the exclusion of entities controlled by family or household members of sanctioned individuals. In § 1001.1001(a)(2), we are also adding definitions for the terms "immediate family member" and "member of household," consistent with the statute.

• To reflect the revised scope of exclusions under title XI of the Act, that allows the Secretary, through the OIG, to direct the imposition of exclusions from all Federal health care programs and to directly impose exclusions from all Federal health care programs, we are revising § 1001.1901(a), (b)(1), introductory paragraph (c)(3) and (c)(5)(i). While the proposed rule indicated our intention of revising paragraph (c)(4)(i) (and not (c)(5)(i)) of this section, the OIG final regulations published on September 2, 1998 (63 FR 46676) amended paragraph (b)(1), and redesignated paragraph (c)(4) as (c)(5) and added a new paragraph (c)(4) in its place. The changes being made in § 1001.1901 in this rule reflect the revisions and redesignation made in the September 2, 1998 final rule.

• With respect to considerations in the OIG's review of an individual's or entity's request for reinstatement in the Federal health care programs after the individual's or entity's exclusion period, we are not including the language proposed for a new § 1001.3002(b)(5) as indicated in the proposed rule. However, we are adopting the language proposed for new paragraph (b)(6) of this section, and are now designating this as new paragraph (b)(5). Technical revisions to § 1001.3002(b)(3) and (b)(4) are also being made.

• Sections 1003.102(a)(2) and 1003.103(a) are being revised to reflect the new CMP authority against entities that submit, or cause to be submitted, claims for health care services rendered by employees or other individuals under contract whom they know, or should know, have been excluded from participation in the Federal health care programs. We are also revising § 1003.106(a)(1) to set forth five criteria to be considered in determining the penalty amount.

• We are amending § 1003.102(b)(5) to address CMPs imposed against any health plan that fails to report information on an adverse action required to be reported to the new HIPDB. Section 1003.103(g) is being added to set forth the penalty amount for such violations.

• A new § 1003.102(b)(11) — to codify the CMP authority for health care providers who violate the anti-kickback statute, and a new § 1003.103(h), as revised in accordance with the discussion above, to address the maximum penalty amount — are being added. Section 1003.104 is also being revised to address assessments of not more than three times the amount of remuneration offered, paid, solicited or received with regard to this violation.

• Technical amendments are also being made in Secs. 1001.302, 1003.100 and 1003.114 to reflect the regulatory changes set forth in the OIG's revised exclusion and CMP authorities revisions in accordance with BBA.

V. Regulatory Impact Statement

Executive Order 12866 and Regulatory Flexibility Act

The Office of Management and Budget (OMB) has reviewed this final rule in accordance with the provisions of Executive Order 12866 and the Regulatory Flexibility Act (5 U.S.C. 601–612), and has determined that it does not meet the criteria for a significant regulatory action. Executive Order 12866 directs agencies to assess all costs and benefits of available regulatory alternatives and, when rulemaking is necessary, to select regulatory approaches that maximize net benefits (including potential economic, environmental, public health, safety distributive and equity effects). In addition, under the Regulatory Flexibility Act, if a rule has a significant economic effect on a substantial number of small entities the Secretary must specifically consider the economic effect of a rule on small entities and analyze regulatory options that could lessen the impact of the rule.

The provisions set forth in this final rulemaking implement new or revised OIG statutory requirements set forth in Public Law 105–33. These provisions are designed both to broaden the scope of the OIG's authority to exclude individuals and entities from Medicare, Medicaid and all other Federal health care programs, and strengthen current legal authorities pertaining to the imposition of CMPs against individuals and entities engaged in prohibited actions and activities. These regulations implement the new statutory requirements by (1) expanding the application of the OIG's exclusions to all Federal health care programs; (2) implementing permanent exclusions for individuals convicted of three or more offenses for which an exclusion can be imposed under section 1128(a) of the Act, and 10 year exclusions for individuals convicted of two or more such offenses; (3) allowing for the exclusion of entities controlled by family or household members of sanctioned individuals; and (4) establishing new CMPs in three specific areas.

With regard to the OIG's new exclusion authorities, the process for excluding individuals and entities who are convicted in accordance with these new provisions remains essentially the same, even though the types of convictions requiring mandatory exclusions have been broadened. While there may be a resulting increase in the number of mandatory and permissive exclusions imposed as a result of the expanded scope of the OIG's exclusion authority, we do not believe these increases will be significant. The clarification of exclusion authority in § 1001.1001 regarding a sanctioned individual's transfer of ownership or control interest to a family or household member, for example, should not result in a significant increase in exclusion actions in accordance with section 1128(b)(8) of the Act since the provision is likely to act as an effective deterrent against the occurrence of such transfer arrangements. In addition, we do not foresee significant increases resulting from the implementation of section 4301 of BBA and § 1001.102, regarding the permanent exclusion of individuals convicted of three or more health care related crimes. The authority for promulgating this exclusion is clear cut, and should limit the total number of repeat exclusions effectuated by the OIG against such fraudulent providers.

The final regulations addressing the new OIG CMPs also remain consistent with the congressional intent of BBA and with the OIG's existing CMP authority which allows for imposition of

[Page 39426]

civil money penalties against individuals and entities who commit fraud. These CMPs are targeted to a limited group of individuals and entities; that is, those institutional health care providers that employ or enter into medical service contracts with excluded individuals, health care plans that fail to report information to the HIPDB, and health care providers who violate the anti-kickback statute.

As indicated, these final regulations are narrow in scope and effect, comport with congressional and statutory intent, and strengthen the Department's legal authorities against those who defraud or otherwise act improperly against the Federal and State health care programs. Since the vast majority of individuals, organizations and entities involved in delivering health care do not engage in the prohibited activities and practices described in this rulemaking, we believe that the aggregate economic impact of these regulations will not be economically significant. Since there is minimal economic effect on the industry as a whole, there would be little likelihood of effect on Federal or State expenditures to implement these regulations.

With regard to the effect of these regulations on a substantial number of small entities, the provisions are targeted specifically to those individuals and entities who would defraud or abuse the health care programs, rather than to the health care industry as a whole. While some of the perpetrators of fraud effected by this rule may be small entities, it is the nature of the violation and not the size of the entity that will induce action on the part of the OIG.

In summary, we have concluded, and the Secretary certifies, that since this final rule will not have a significant economic impact on Federal, State or local economies and expenditures, nor have a significant economic impact on a substantial number of small entities, a regulatory flexibility analysis is not required.

Paperwork Reduction Act

The provisions of these final regulations impose no new reporting or recordkeeping requirements necessitating clearance by OMB.

List of Subjects

42 CFR Part 1001

Administrative practice and procedure, Fraud, Health facilities, Health professions, Medicaid, Medicare.

42 CFR Part 1002

Fraud, Grant programs — health, Health facilities, Health professions, Medicaid, Reporting and recordkeeping.

42 CFR Part 1003

Administrative practice and procedure, Fraud, Grant programs — health, Health facilities, Health professions, Maternal and child health, Medicaid, Medicare, Penalties.

Accordingly, 42 Parts 1001, 1002 and 1003 is amended as set forth below:

PART 1001 — [AMENDED]

1. The authority citation for part 1001 continues to read as follows:

Authority: 42 U.S.C. 1302, 1320a-7, 1320a-7b, 1395u(h), 1395u(j), 1395u(k), 1395y(d), 1395y(e), 1395cc(b)(2)(D), (E) and (F), and 1395hh; and § 2455, Pub.L. 103–355, 108 Stat. 3327 (31 U.S.C. 6101 note).

2. Section 1001.1 is amended by revising paragraph (a) to read as follows:

§ 1001.1 Scope and purpose.

(a) The regulations in this part specify certain bases upon which individuals and entities may, or in some cases must, be excluded from participation in Medicare, Medicaid and all other Federal health care programs. They also state the effect of exclusion, the factors that will be considered in determining the length of any exclusion, the provisions governing notices of exclusions, and the process by which an excluded individual or entity may seek reinstatement into the programs.

* * * * *

3. Section 1001.2 is amended by adding a definition for the term Federal health care program to read as follows:

§ 1001.2 Definitions.

* * * * *

Federal health care program means any plan or program providing health care benefits, whether directly through insurance or otherwise, that is funded directly, in whole or part, by the United States Government (other than the Federal Employees Health Benefits Program), or any State health care program as defined in this section.

* * * * *

4. Section 1001.102 is amended by revising paragraphs (b)(6) and (b)(7); redesignating existing paragraph (b)(8) as (b)(9); and by adding new paragraphs (b)(8) and (9) to read as follows:

§ 1001.102 Length of exclusion.

* * * * *

(b) * * *

(6) The convicted individual or entity has a prior criminal, civil or administrative sanction record;

(7) The individual or entity has at any time been overpaid a total of $1,500 or more by Medicare, Medicaid or any other Federal health care programs as a result of *intentional* improper billings;

(8) The individual or entity has previously been convicted of a criminal offense involving the same or similar circumstances; or

(9) * * *

* * * * *

(d) In the case of an exclusion under this subpart, based on a conviction occurring on or after August 5, 1997, an exclusion will be—

(1) For not less than 10 years if the individual has been convicted on one other occasion of one or more offenses for which an exclusion may be effected under section 1128(a) of the Act (The aggravating and mitigating factors in paragraphs (b) and (c) of this section can be used to impose a period of time in excess of the 10-year mandatory exclusion); or

(2) Permanent if the individual has been convicted on two or more other occasions of one or more offenses for which an exclusion may be effected under section 1128(a) of the Act.

5. Section 1001.201 is amended by revising the heading and paragraph (b)(3)(iii)(A) to read as follows:

§ 1001.201 Conviction relating to program or health care fraud.

* * * * *

(b) Length of exclusion. * * *

(3) * * *

(iii) * * *

(A) Others being convicted or excluded from Medicare, Medicaid or any of the other Federal health care programs, or

* * * * *

6. Section 1001.301 is amended by revising paragraphs (b)(2)(ii) to read as follows:

§ 1001.301 Conviction relating to obstruction of an investigation.

* * * * *

(b) * * *

(2) * * *

(ii) The interference or obstruction had a significant adverse mental, physical or financial impact on program beneficiaries or other individuals or on the Medicare, Medicaid or other Federal health care programs;

* * * * *

7. Section 1001.401 is amended by revising the heading and paragraph (c)(2)(ii) to read as follows:

§ 1001.401 Conviction relating to controlled substances.

* * * * *

(c) * * *

[Page 39427]
(2) * * *
(ii) The acts that resulted in the conviction or similar acts had a significant adverse mental, physical or financial impact on program beneficiaries or other individuals or the Medicare, Medicaid or other Federal health care programs;

* * * * *

8. Section 1001.1001 is amended by revising paragraph (a)(1)(ii); and by amending paragraph (a)(2) by adding definitions for the terms *Immediate family member* and *Member of household* to read as follows:

§ 1001.1001 Exclusion of entities owned or controlled by a sanctioned person.

(a) * * *
(1) * * *
(ii) Such a person —
(A)(*1*) Has a direct or indirect ownership interest (or any combination thereof) of 5 percent or more in the entity;
(*2*) Is the owner of a whole or part interest in any mortgage, deed of trust, note or other obligation secured (in whole or in part) by the entity or any of the property assets thereof, in which whole or part interest is equal to or exceeds 5 percent of the total property and assets of the entity;
(*3*) Is an officer or director of the entity, if the entity is organized as a corporation;
(*4*) Is partner in the entity, if the entity is organized as a partnership;
(*5*) Is an agent of the entity; or
(*6*) Is a managing employee, that is, an individual (including a general manager, business manager, administrator or director) who

exercises operational or managerial control over the entity or part thereof, or directly or indirectly conducts the day-to-day operations of the entity or part thereof, or

(B) Was formerly described in paragraph (a)(1)(ii)(A) of this section, but is no longer so described because of a transfer of ownership or control interest to an immediate family member or a member of the person's household as defined in paragraph (a)(2) of this section, in anticipation of or following a conviction, assessment of a CMP, or imposition of an exclusion.

(2) * * *

Immediate family member means, a person's husband or wife; natural or adoptive parent; child or sibling; stepparent, stepchild, stepbrother or stepsister; father-, mother-, daughter-, son-, brother- or sister-in-law; grandparent or grandchild; or spouse of a grandparent or grandchild. * * *

Member of household means, with respect to a person, any individual with whom they are sharing a common abode as part of a single family unit, including domestic employees and others who live together as a family unit. A roomer or boarder is not considered a member of household.

* * * * *

9. Section 1001.1301 is amended by revising paragraph (b)(2)(iii) to read as follows:

§ 1001.1301 Failure to grant immediate access.

* * * * *

(b) * * *

(2) * * *

(iii) The impact of the exclusion on Medicare, Medicaid or any of the other Federal health care programs, beneficiaries or the public; and

* * * * *

10. Section 1001.1401 is amended by revising paragraphs (b)(1) and (b)(4) to read as follows:

§ 1001.1401 Violations of PPS corrective action.

* * * * *

(b) * * *

(1) The impact of the hospital's failure to comply on Medicare, Medicaid or any of the other Federal health care programs, program beneficiaries or other individuals;

* * * * *

(4) The impact of the exclusion on Medicare, Medicaid or any of the other Federal health care programs, beneficiaries or the public; and

* * * * *

11. Section 1001.1501 is amended by revising paragraph (a)(3) to read as follows:

§ 1001.1501 Default of health education loan or scholarship obligations.

(a) * * *

(3) The OIG will take into account access of beneficiaries to physicians' services for which payment may be made under Medicare, Medicaid or other Federal health care programs in determining whether to impose an exclusion.

* * * * *

12. Section 1001.1901 is amended by revising paragraphs (a), (b)(1), (c)(3) introductory text and (c)(5)(i) to read as follows:

§ 1001.1901 Scope and effect of exclusion.

(a) *Scope of exclusion.* Exclusions of individuals and entities under this title will be from Medicare, Medicaid and any of the other Federal health care programs, as defined in § 1001.2.

(b) *Effect of exclusion on excluded individuals and entities.* (1) Unless and until an individual or entity is reinstated into the Medicare, Medicaid and other Federal health care programs in accordance with subpart F of this part, no payment will be made by Medicare, Medicaid or any of the other Federal health care programs for any item or service furnished, on or after the effective date specified in the notice period, by an excluded individual or entity, or at the medical direction or on the prescription of a physician or other authorized individual who is excluded when the person furnishing such item or service knew or had reason to know of the exclusion. This section applies regardless of whether an individual or entity has obtained a program provider number or equivalent, either as an individual or as a member of a group, prior to being reinstated.

* * * * *

(c) * * *

(3) Unless the Secretary determines that the health and safety of beneficiaries receiving services under Medicare, Medicaid or any of the other Federal health care programs warrants the exclusion taking effect earlier, payment may be made under such program for up to 30 days after the effective date of the exclusion for—

* * * * *

(5)(i) Notwithstanding the other provisions of this section, payment may be made under Medicare, Medicaid or other Federal health care programs for certain emergency items or services furnished by an excluded individual or entity, or at the medical direction or on the prescription of an excluded physician or other authorized individual during the period of exclusion. To be payable, a claim for such emergency items or services must be accompanied by a sworn statement of the person furnishing the items or services specifying the nature of the emergency and why the items or services could not have been furnished by an individual or entity eligible to furnish or order such items or services.

* * * * *

13. Section 1001.3002 is amended by republishing introductory paragraph (b) introductory text, revising paragraphs (b)3) and (b)(4); adding new paragraph (b)(6); and by revising paragraph (c)(1) to read as follows:

§ 1001.3002 Basis for reinstatement.

* * * * *

(b) In making the reinstatement determination, the OIG will consider—

* * * * *

(3) Whether all fines, and all debts due and owing (including overpayments) to any Federal, State or local government that relate to

[Page 39428]

Medicare, Medicaid and all other Federal health care programs, have been paid or satisfactory arrangements have been made to fulfill obligations;

(4) Whether HCFA has determined that the individual or entity complies with, or has made satisfactory arrangements to fulfill, all of the applicable conditions of participation or supplier conditions for coverage under the statutes and regulations; and

* * * * *

(6) Whether the individual or entity has, during the period of exclusion, submitted claims, or caused claims to be submitted or payment to be made by any Federal health care program, for items or services the excluded party furnished, ordered or prescribed, including health care administrative services.

(c) * * *

(1) Has properly reduced his or her ownership or control interest in the entity below 5 percent;

* * * * *

14. Section 1001.3003 is revised to read as follows:

§ 1001.3003 Approval of request for reinstatement.

(a) If the OIG grants a request for reinstatement, the OIG will—

(1) Give written notice to the excluded individual or entity specifying the date of reinstatement;

(2) Notify HCFA of the date of the individual's or entity's reinstatement;

(3) Notify appropriate Federal and State agencies that administer health care programs that the individual or entity has been reinstated into all Federal health care programs; and

(4) To the extent applicable, give notice to others that were originally notified of the exclusion.

(b) A determination by the OIG to reinstate an individual or entity has no effect if a Federal health care program has imposed a longer period of exclusion under its own authorities.

15. Section 1001.3005 is amended by revising paragraphs (a) introductory text, (b) and (d) to read as follows:

§ 1001.3005 Reversed or vacated decisions.

(a) An individual or entity will be reinstated into Medicare, Medicaid and other Federal health care programs retroactive to the effective date of the exclusion when such exclusion is based on—

* * * * *

(b) If an individual or entity is reinstated in accordance with paragraph (a) of this section, HCFA and other Federal health care programs will make payment for services covered under such program that were furnished or performed during the period of exclusion.

* * * * *

(d) An action taken by the OIG under this section will not require any other Federal health care program to reinstate the individual or entity if such program has imposed an exclusion under its own authority.

PART 1002—[AMENDED]

1. The authority citation for part 1002 continues to read as follows:

Authority: 42 U.S.C. 1302, 1320a-3, 1320a-5, 1320a-7, 1396(a)(4)(A), 1396(p)(1), 1396a(30), 1396a(39), 1396b(a)(6), 1396b(b)(3), 1396b(i)(2) and 1396b(q).

2. Section 1002.2 is amended by revising paragraph (a) to read as follows:

§ 1002.2 General authority.

(a) In addition to any other authority it may have, a State may exclude an individual or entity from participation in the Medicaid program for any reason for which the Secretary could exclude that individual or entity from participation in the Medicare, Medicaid and other Federal health care programs under sections 1128, 1128A or 1866(b)(2) of the Social Security Act.

* * * * *

PART 1003 — [AMENDED]

1. The authority citation for part 1003 is revised to read as follows:
Authority: 42 U.S.C. 1302, 1320–7, 1320a-7a, 1320a-7e, 1320b-10, 1395dd(d)(1), 1395mm, 1395nn(g), 1395ss(d), 1396b(m), 11131(c) and 11137(b)(2).

2. Section 1003.100 is amended by revising paragraphs (a) and (b)(1)(iv), (viii), (x) and (xi) and adding paragraph (b)(1)(xii) to read as follows:

§ 1003.100 Basis and purpose.

(a) *Basis.* This part implements sections 1128(c), 1128A, 1128E, 1140, 1876(i)(6), 1877(g), 1882(d) and 1903(m)(5) of the Social Security Act, and sections 421(c) and 427(b)(2) of Public Law 99–660 (42 U.S.C. 1320a-7, 1320a-7a, 1320a-7e, 1320a-7(c), 1320b(10), 1395mm, 1395ss(d), 1396(m), 11131(c) and 11137(b)(2)).

(b) * * *

(1) * * *

(iv)(A) Fail to report information concerning medical malpractice payments or who improperly disclose, use or permit access to information reported under part B of title IV of Public Law 99–660, and regulations specified in 45 CFR part 60, or

(B) Are health plans and fail to report information concerning sanctions or other adverse actions imposed on providers as required to be reported to the Healthcare Integrity and Protection Data Bank (HIPDB) in accordance with section 1128E of the Act;

* * * * *

(viii) Have submitted, or caused to be submitted, certain prohibited claims, including claims for services rendered by excluded individuals employed by or otherwise under contract with such person, under one or more Federal health care programs;

* * * * *

(x) Have collected amounts that they know or should know were billed in violation of § 411.353 of this title and have not refunded the amounts collected on a timely basis;

(xi) Are physicians or entities that enter into an arrangement or scheme that they know or should know has as a principal purpose the assuring of referrals by the physician to a particular entity which, if made directly, would violate the provisions of § 411.353 of this title; or

(xii) Violate the Federal health care programs' anti-kickback statute as set forth in section 1128B of the Act.

* * * * *

3. Section 1003.102 is amended by revising paragraphs (a)(2) and (b)(5); and by adding a new paragraph (b)(11) to read as follows:

§ 1003.102 Basis for civil money penalties and assessments.

(a) * * *

(2) An item or service for which the person knew, or should have known, that the claim was false or fraudulent, including a claim for any item or service furnished by an excluded individual employed by or otherwise under contract with that person;

* * * * *

(b) * * *

(5) Fails to report information concerning—

(i) A payment made under an insurance policy, self-insurance or otherwise, for the benefit of a physician, dentist or other health care practitioner in settlement of, or in satisfaction in whole or in part of, a medical malpractice claim or action or a judgment against such a physician, dentist or other practitioner in accordance with section 421 of Public Law 99–660 (42 U.S.C. 11131) and as required by regulations at 45 CFR part 60; or

(ii) An adverse action required to be reported to the Healthcare Integrity and Protection Data Bank as established by section 221 of Public Law 104–191 and set forth in section 1128E of the Act.

* * * * *

[Page 39429]

(11) Has violated section 1128B of the Act by unlawfully offering, paying, soliciting or receiving remuneration in return for the referral of business paid for by Medicare, Medicaid or other Federal health care programs.

* * * * *

4. Section 1003.103 is amended by revising paragraph (a); and by adding new paragraphs (g) and (h) to read as follows:

§ 1003.103 Amount of penalty.

(a) Except as provided in paragraphs (b) and (d) through (h) of this section, the OIG may impose a penalty of not more than $10,000 for each item or service that is subject to a determination under § 1003.102.

* * * * *

(g) The OIG may impose a penalty of not more than $25,000 against a health plan for failing to report information on an adverse action required to be reported to the Healthcare Integrity and Protection Data Bank in accordance with section 1128E of the Act and § 1003.102(b)(5)(ii).

(h) For each violation of § 1003.102(b)(11), the OIG may impose—

(1) A penalty of not more than $50,000, and

(2) An assessment of up to three times the total amount of remuneration offered, paid, solicited or received, as specified in § 1003.104(b).

5. Section 1003.104 is revised to read as follows:

§ 1003.104 Amount of assessment.

(a) The OIG may impose an assessment, where authorized, in accordance with § 1003.102 (except for § 1003.102(b)(11)), of not more than three times the amount claimed for each item or service which was a basis for the penalty. The assessment is in lieu of damages sustained by the Department or a State because of that claim.

(b) In accordance with § 1003.102(b)(11), the OIG may impose an assessment of not more than three times the total amount of remuneration offered, paid, solicited or received, without regard to whether a portion of such remuneration was offered, paid, solicited or received for a lawful purpose.

6. Section 1003.105 is amended by revising the section heading, paragraph (a)(1) introductory text and paragraph (b)(1) to read as follows:

§ 1003.105 Exclusion from participation in Medicare, Medicaid and other Federal health care programs.

(a)(1) Except as set forth in paragraph (b) of this section, in lieu of or in addition to any penalty or assessment, the OIG may exclude from participation in Medicare, Medicaid and other Federal health care programs the following persons for a period of time determined under § 1003.107 —

* * * * *

(b)(1)(i) With respect to determinations under § 1003.102(b)(2) or (b)(3), a physician may not be excluded if the OIG determines that he or she is the sole community physician or the sole source of essential specialized services in a community.

(ii) With respect to determinations under § 1003.102(b)(5)(ii), no exclusion shall be imposed.

* * * * *

7. Section 1003.106 is amended by redesignating paragraph (a)(1)(vii) as paragraph (a)(1)(ix); by adding new paragraphs (a)(1)(vii) and (a)(1)(viii); and by revising paragraphs (a)(1)(ii), (a)(1)(iii), (a)(1)(vi), (a)(2)(i), (a)(2)(ii) and (a)(2)(iii) to read as follows:

§ 1003.106 Determinations regarding the amount of the penalty and assessment.

(a) * * *

(1) * * *

(ii) The degree of culpability of the contracting provider, or the person submitting the claim or request for payment, or giving the information;

(iii) The history of prior offenses of the contracting provider (or principals of the contracting provider), or the person submitting the claim or request for payment, or giving the information;

* * * * *

(vi) The amount of financial interest involved with respect to § 1003.102(b)(10);

(vii) Whether the contracting provider actually knew of the exclusion when employing or otherwise contracting with an excluded individual or entity in accordance with § 1003.102(a)(2);

(viii) The harm to patients or any Federal or State health care program which resulted or could have resulted from the provision of care by a person or entity with which the contracting provider is expressly prohibited from contracting under section 1128A(a)(6) of the Act; and

(ix) * * *

(2) * * *

(i) The nature and circumstances of the failure to properly report information, or the improper disclosure of information, as required;

(ii) The degree of culpability of the person in failing to provide timely and complete data or in improperly disclosing, using or permitting access to information, as appropriate;

(iii) The materiality, or significance of omission, of the information to be reported, or the materiality of the improper disclosure of, or use of, or access to information, as appropriate;

* * * * *

8. Section 1003.109 is amended by revising paragraph (a) introductory text and paragraph (a)(3) to read as follows:

§ 1003.109 Notice of proposed determination.

(a) If the Inspector General proposes a penalty and, when applicable, an assessment, or proposes to exclude a respondent from participation in Medicare, Medicaid and any other Federal health care program, as applicable, in accordance with this part, he or she must deliver or send by certified mail, return receipt requested, to the respondent, written notice of his or her intent to impose a penalty, assessment and exclusion, as applicable. The notice includes —

* * * * *

(3) The reason why such claims, requests for payments or incidents subject the respondent to a penalty, assessment and exclusion;

* * * * *

9. Section 1003.114 is amended by revising paragraph (a) to read as follows:

§ 1003.114 Collateral estoppel.

(a) Where a final determination pertaining to the respondent's liability under § 1003.102 has been rendered in any proceeding in which the respondent was a party and had an opportunity to be heard, the respondent shall be bound by such determination in any proceeding under this part.

* * * * *

Dated: February 4, 1999.

June Gibbs Brown,

Inspector General.

Approved: April 8, 1999.

Donna E. Shalala,

Secretary.

[FR Doc. 99–18515 Filed 7–21–99; 8:45 am]

BILLING CODE 4150–04-P

APPENDIX K

OIG ADVISORY OPINIONS UNDER THE STARK BILL — § 1877 OF THE SOCIAL SECURITY ACT

APPENDIX K1

Advisory Opinion No. HCFA-AO-98–001, October 1998

Concerning whether a physician's referrals for certain services are prohibited under section 1877 of the Social Security Act

[Names and addresses of Requestors have been redacted]

Re: Proposed Ambulatory Surgical Treatment Center for [Material redacted] HealthCare, LLC.

Advisory Opinion No. HCFA-AO-98–001.

Dear Dr. [Material redacted]:

We are writing in response to your recent request for an advisory opinion ("AO") concerning whether a physician's referrals for certain services are prohibited under section 1877 of the Social Security Act (the "Act"). In your request, you posed the following questions:

1. Would the investment in and ownership of an Ambulatory Surgical Treatment Center ("ASTC") by physicians, who will refer patients to the ASTC and who will perform surgeries at that ASTC, violate the prohibition in section 1877 of the Act against certain physician referrals?
2. Is the proposed location of the ASTC a rural area under the rural provider exception in section 1877(d)(2) of the Act (referencing the rural definition in section 1886(d)(2)(D) of the Act)?
3. Would the rural exception in section 1877(d)(2) of the Act apply to the proposed ASTC arrangement?
4. Under section 1877 of the Act, can non-surgeon physician investors in the ASTC refer patients there without violating the Federal prohibition against referring patients to an entity with which a physician has a financial relationship?

You have certified that all of the information you have provided in your request, including all supplementary materials and letters, is true and correct and constitutes a complete description of the parties, relationships and facts regarding the proposed arrangement (the "Arrangement").

In issuing this opinion, we have relied solely upon the information that you have presented to us. We have not undertaken an independent investigation of this information. If material facts have not been disclosed, or have changed since we accepted your request, those differences would nullify the validity of this AO.

Based upon the information provided, we conclude that the Arrangement would qualify for the rural provider exception to the prohibition against physician referrals, provided that the designated health services for which Medicare patients are referred to the ASTC by the owner physicians are actually furnished in a rural area and that substantially all of the designated health services furnished by the ASTC are furnished to individuals residing in a rural area.

FACTUAL BACKGROUND

[Material redacted] HealthCare, LLC ("[Material redacted]"), a newly formed limited liability company in [Material redacted], is proposing to build and operate the ASTC. [Material redacted] indicates that the ASTC will provide outpatient ambulatory surgery as well as ancillary services such as clinical laboratory services, radiology services, ultrasound, parenteral nutrients, and outpatient prescription drugs. We expect that physician investors will refer some patients for services furnished by the ambulatory surgical center located within the ASTC. These ambulatory surgical services will be furnished by the part of the facility that meets the ambulatory surgical center conditions and requirements in section 42 CFR part 416. In addition, physician investors will also refer patients for other services to parts of the facility that are not included within the ambulatory surgical center.

The ASTC will be located in [Material redacted], [Material redacted], which is in [Material redacted] County. [Material redacted] expects that substantially all of the designated health services provided by the ASTC will be furnished to individuals residing in a rural area. [Material redacted] indicates that, upon completion, the ASTC will be the first such center located in [Material redacted] County.

In order to finance the construction and operation of the ASTC, [Material redacted] will sell shares of the company to investors. The investors will be physicians who will refer patients to the ASTC. Further, some of these physicians will perform medical and surgical procedures at the ASTC. [Material redacted] expects that physician investors will refer Medicare beneficiaries to the ASTC.

LEGAL ANALYSIS

A. The Referral Prohibition

Section 1877 of the Social Security Act prohibits a physician from referring a Medicare patient to an entity for certain designated health services if the physician has a financial relationship with the entity, unless an exception applies. Specifically, Section 1877(a)(1) of the Act states that:

> [I]f a physician (or an immediate family member of such physician) has a financial relationship with an entity . . ., then (A) the physician may not make a referral to the entity for the furnishing of designated health services for which payment otherwise may be made under this title, and (B) the entity may not present or cause to be presented a claim under this title or bill to any individual, third party payor, or other entity for designated health services furnished pursuant to a referral prohibited under subparagraph (A).

Under section 1877(g) of the Act, the statutory sanctions for violating this prohibition can include denial of payment to an entity furnishing services under a prohibited referral, refunds of billed amounts to any individual who has paid for a service furnished under a prohibited referral, assessment of civil money penalties, or exclusion from the Medicare program.

B. Financial Relationship

The statute specifies two categories of financial relationship: (1) an ownership or investment interest in an entity and (2) a compensation arrangement between a physician and an entity. An ownership or investment interest can be through debt, equity, or other means. [Material redacted]'s Proposed Private Offering Memorandum (the "POM") indicates that, in exchange for capital contributions to the limited liability company, [Material redacted] proposes to offer investor physicians up to 49 percent of the company's interest in profits, losses and cash flow. Units are being offered to individual physicians licensed to practice medicine in [Material redacted] and who are residents of [Material redacted]. Also the physician investors are expected to maintain medical staff privileges at the ASTC.

The remaining 51 percent of the equity of [Material redacted] will be owned and controlled by Dr. [Material redacted]. We conclude that the Arrangement as described to us between [Material redacted] and the investors fits within the definition of an ownership or investment interest under section 1877(a)(2) of the Act. [Material redacted] has not presented any issues regarding compensation relationships between the physicians and [Material redacted]. Therefore, this AO applies to just the ownership or investment interest.

The POM indicates that the investment offer is being made to "individual physicians licensed to practice medicine in [Material redacted] and who are residents of [Material redacted]." [Material redacted] indicates that the investors will include physicians who practice in the same vicinity as the ASTC. [Material redacted] plans that during the course of their respective practices local physician investors will refer some of their patients to the ASTC for services. Section 1877(h)(5) of the Act defines a referral to include: (1) the request by a physician for an item or service for which payment may be made under Medicare part B, including the request by a physician for a consultation with another physician and (2) the request or establishment of a plan of care by a physician which includes the provision of a designated health service.

The Act prohibits referrals for designated health services. Designated health services include: clinical laboratory services, radiology services (including magnetic resonance imaging, computerized axial tomography scans and ultrasound services), radiation therapy services and supplies, durable medical equipment and supplies, prosthetics, orthotics, and prosthetic devices and supplies, physical and occupational therapy services, home health services, parenteral and enteral nutrients, equipment and supplies, inpatient and outpatient hospital services and outpatient prescription drugs. [Material redacted] indicates that it anticipates providing some of these designated health services. Unless an exception applies, a physician investor in [Material redacted] who refers Medicare patients for a designated health service to the ASTC would be making a prohibited referral.

Some of the exceptions to the physician referral prohibition apply both to ownership and compensation relationships while others apply only to ownership or only to compensation arrangements. The rural provider exception, discussed below, is available to parties that are involved in an ownership arrangement.

C. Rural Provider Exception

The rural provider exception is potentially appropriate for designated health services furnished by the ASTC. The rural provider exception in section 1877(d)(2) of the Act applies ". . .[i]n the case of designated health services furnished in a rural area (as defined in section 1886(d)(2)(D)) by an entity, if substantially all of the designated health services furnished by such entity are furnished to individuals residing in such a rural area." In essence, a rural area is defined in section 1886(d)(2)(D) of the Act as what an urban area is not:

> the term "urban area" means an area within a Metropolitan Statistical Area (as defined by the Office of Management and Budget) or within such similar area as the Secretary has recognized . . . by regulation . . . and the term "rural area" means any area outside such area or such similar area.

We refer you to Table 4A of the FY 1999 PPS Hospital Update Final Rule, (63 FR 41052; July 31, 1998 (copy enclosed)) for the list of urban areas and their constituent counties. Since [Material redacted] County, [Material redacted] is not listed as an urban area or a constituent county of an urban area, it is considered to be a rural area. If the designated health services referred by the owner physicians are actually furnished in [Material redacted] County, the first part of the rural provider test will be met.

The rural provider exception involves a two part test, however. In addition to the requirement that designated health services be furnished in a rural area, substantially all designated health services furnished by the provider must be furnished to individuals residing in a rural area. By regulation regarding referrals involving clinical laboratory services, we have interpreted "substantially all" to mean at least 75 percent in 42 CFR 411.356(c)(1). In terms of referrals for the other designated health services, we have proposed to apply this same definition in a proposed rule published in the Federal Register on January 9, 1998 at 63 FR 1659. Although the 75 percent standard is not included in a final regulation governing referrals for the other designated health services, it reflects our current interpretation of the "substantially all" standard. At this time we do not anticipate changing this standard.

Because [Material redacted] has not begun to operate the ASTC, it is not possible to make a final determination whether substantially all of the ASTC's designated health services are provided to the residents of rural areas. However, [Material redacted] has certified that essentially all of the patients who will be utilizing the [Material redacted] HealthCare LLC facility reside in the [Material redacted] area and [Material redacted] County, [Material redacted] and that more than 99 percent of the population who will be utilizing the facility reside in the non-Metropolitan Service area of [Material redacted] County. If, as [Material redacted] certifies, substantially all of the designated health services furnished by the ASTC are furnished to individuals residing in a rural area, the ASTC will meet the second element of the rural provider exception. We caution, however, that the "substantially all" test is an ongoing requirement. Therefore, to remain within the rural provider exception on an ongoing basis, it is necessary that substantially all of the designated health services be furnished to patients who reside in a rural area.

D. Physician Specialty and Referral Prohibition

You have also raised the question of whether the non-surgeon physician investors in the ASTC can refer patients to the ASTC without violating the referral prohibition. The referral prohibition in section 1877(a) of the Act applies to any individual who meets the definition of a "physician" under section 1861(r) of the Act and who has an unexcepted financial relationship with an entity, regardless of the physician's specialty. However, section 1877(h)(5)(C) excepts from the term "referral" a pathologist's request for clinical diagnostic laboratory tests and pathological examination services, a radiologist's request for diagnostic radiology services, and a radiation oncologist's request for radiation therapy. The provision applies if two conditions are met: (1) the request results from a consultation initiated by another physician and (2) the tests or services are furnished by, or under the supervision of, the pathologist, radiologist, or radiation oncologist. Since it appears that the ASTC will meet the rural provider exception, however, we see no reason at this time to consider the application of section 1877(h)(5)(C).

LIMITATIONS OF THIS OPINION

The limitations that apply to this AO include the following:

- This AO and the validity of the conclusions reached in it are based entirely upon the accuracy of facts and information that you have presented to us.

- This AO is only relevant to the specific questions posed at the beginning of this opinion. This AO is limited in scope to the specific Arrangement described in this letter and has no application to other arrangements, even those which appear to be similar in nature or scope.
- This AO does not apply to nor can it be relied upon by any individual or entity other than the requester. This AO may not be introduced in any matter involving an entity or individual that is not a requester to this opinion.
- This AO applies only to the statutory provisions specifically noted above. No opinion is herein expressed or implied with respect to the application of any other Federal, State, or local statute, rule, regulation, ordinance or other law that may apply to the Arrangement.
- This AO will not bind or obligate any agency other than the U.S. Department of Health and Human Services. Under 42 CFR 411.382, HCFA reserves the right to reconsider the issues posed in this AO and where public interest requires, rescind or revoke this opinion.
- This AO is also subject to any additional limitations set forth at 42 CFR 411.370 et seq.

Very truly yours,
/S/
Robert A. Berenson, M.D.
Director
Center for Health Plans and Providers
Enclosure
cc [Material redacted]

APPENDIX K2

Advisory Opinion No. HCFA-AO-98–002, November 1998

Whether the partners and physician employees of a proposed partnership may, under the "in-office ancillary services" exception defined in section 1877(b)(2) of the Social Security Act, refer Medicare and/or Medicaid patients to the partnership for eyeglass prescriptions filled subsequent to cataract surgery with the insertion of an intraocular lens.

[Names and addresses of Requestors have been redacted]

Re: Advisory Opinion No. HCFA-AO-98–002

Dear [Redacted]:

We are writing in response to your request for an advisory opinion (AO), in which you pose the following question: Whether the partners and physician employees of a proposed partnership may, under the "in-office ancillary services" exception defined in section 1877(b)(2) of the Social Security Act (the Act), refer Medicare and/or Medicaid patients to the partnership for eyeglass prescriptions filled subsequent to cataract surgery with the insertion of an intraocular lens.

You have certified that all of the information you have provided in your request, including all supplementary materials and letters, is true and correct, and constitutes a complete description of the parties, relationships and facts regarding the proposed arrangement. In issuing this opinion we have relied solely on the facts and information you have presented to us. We have not undertaken an independent investigation of this information. If material facts have not been disclosed or have changed since we accepted your request, these differences could nullify the validity of this AO.

Based on the information provided, we conclude that the partners and employees of the proposed partnership would qualify for the in-office ancillary services exception.

FACTUAL BACKGROUND

The two Requestors propose to form a partnership, "Partnership," for the purpose of providing ophthalmology services for patients, and eyeglasses and contact lenses for patients and non-patients. We are using the term non-patient to mean a person who gets a prescription for eyeglasses or contact lenses from someplace other than the partnership, but comes to Partnership to have that prescription filled.

Each Requestor has one ophthalmologist shareholder and several physician employees; each Requestor currently leases its own office space, and proposes an additional site for the partnership, so Partnership would operate at three locations. Requestors have proposed to assign all leases and employment contracts to Partnership, for those employees who have agreed to work for the partnership.[1] Each Requestor will contribute 50 percent of the assets of the partnership and will receive 50 percent of the revenues left after expenses are met and each employee has been paid. Each physician owner and physician employee is paid a salary that is unrelated to referrals.

LEGAL ANALYSIS

A. The Referral Prohibition

Section 1877 of the Act prohibits a physician from referring a Medicare patient to an entity for certain designated health services if the physician has a financial relationship with the entity, unless an exception applies. A financial relationship exists if the physician has an ownership or investment interest in the furnishing entity, or a compensation arrangement with the entity. In the proposed arrangement, it appears that the physician partners will have an ownership interest in an entity that will furnish eyeglasses and contact lenses to patients following cataract surgery with the insertion of an intraocular lens. The partners will also have a compensation arrangement with the entity in the form of salary payments, as will other physician employees who will be paid a salary.

The list of designated health services that appears in section 1877 (h)(6) of the Act includes "prosthetic devices," which are defined in

[1] One of the employees of one of the Requestors has refused to assign his contract to the partnership. Requestors have since submitted that this physician has not renewed his contract, and will no longer be a factor in the proposed arrangement.

the Medicare statute in section 1861 (s)(8) as including one pair of conventional eyeglasses or contact lenses furnished subsequent to each cataract surgery with insertion of an intraocular lens. (This is the only circumstance under which Medicare covers prescription eyeglasses or contact lenses.) We have stated in a proposed rule covering a physician's referrals for designated health services that we are proposing to define the term "prosthetic devices" for the purposes of the referral prohibition in the same manner as it is defined in the Medicare statute. (See 63 FR 1678 (January 9, 1998.)) Although the proposed rule has not been promulgated in final form, it reflects our current interpretation of the law.

Section 1903(s) of the Act applies some of the referral rules to the Medicaid program.

In the Medicaid context, eyeglasses are generally covered under a category separate from prosthetic devices under the authority of section 1905 (a)(12) of the Act. As we have explained in the proposed rule mentioned above, when the definition of a designated health service differs under a State's Medicaid plan (which lists the services a State covers) from the definition under Medicare, we propose to assume that the services included under the State's plan take precedence. (See 63 FR 1673–74.) In Requestors' state, eyeglasses are not considered to be a prosthetic device. As long as a State does not classify eyeglasses as a prosthetic device or otherwise as a designated health service, there are no physician referral implications for any Medicaid referrals for them.

Since it appears that the proposed arrangement would be a financial relationship for purposes of Medicare referrals under section 1877, the physicians involved can only refer to Partnership if an exception applies. The Requestors have specifically asked whether the in-office ancillary services exception would make the referrals of the partners and physician employees acceptable.

B. Group Practice

Requestors have stated that they wish their partnership to be considered a group practice, and that they want this group practice to qualify for the in-office ancillary services exception.

To qualify for the in-office ancillary services exception, Requestors must first meet the definition of a group practice as set forth in section 1877(h)(4)(A)of the Act: "The term 'group practice' means a group of 2 or more physicians legally organized as a partnership . . . or similar association — (i) in which each physician who is a member of the group provides substantially the full range of services which the physician routinely provides . . . through the joint use of shared office space, facilities, equipment and personnel, (ii) for which substantially all of the services of the physicians who are members of the group are provided through the group and are billed under a billing number assigned to the group and amounts so received are treated as receipts of the group, (iii) in which the overhead expenses of and the income from the practice are distributed in accordance with methods previously determined, (iv) except as provided in subparagraph (B)(i) [which relates to profits and productivity bonuses], in which no physician who is a member of the group directly or indirectly receives compensation based on the volume or value of referrals by the physician, and (v) in which members of the group personally conduct no less than 75 percent of the physician-patient encounters of the group practice, . . . "

1. Substantially the full range of services

Section 1877(h)(4)(A)(i) requires that each member of the group provide "substantially the full range of services which the physician routinely provides . . . through the joint use of shared office space, facilities, equipment and personnel." Requestors have certified that each physician who is a member of Partnership will practice the same range of ophthalmology services as the physician currently does. Further, since all leases have been assigned to the partnership, it appears that all facilities and office space will be shared, as well as the personnel who will be employed by the partnership.

2. Substantially all of the members' services are provided through the group and are billed by the group

Section 1877(h)(4)(A)(ii) requires that "substantially all of the services of the physicians who are members of the group are provided through the group and are billed under a billing number assigned to the group and amounts so received are treated as receipts of the group, . . . " In our final regulation governing referrals for clinical laboratory services in 42 CFR 411.351, we defined a group practice by stating that at least 75 percent of the total patient care services of the group practice members must be furnished through the group and be billed in the name of the group. We measured "patient care services" by the total patient care time each member spends on these services. In our proposed rule covering referrals for other designated health services, we proposed to clarify certain aspects of the "substantially all" test. In the discussion at 63 FR 1688, we stated that we expect a group to look at a physician's total patient care time during a week, furnished both inside and outside of the group practice, to determine what percent of this time is furnished through the one group. Requestors have indicated to us that member physicians will be performing 100 percent of their patient care services through Partnership. Provided that this is accurate, we conclude that they will meet this part of the test. Requestors have certified in a letter to HCFA that billing will be done under one billing number assigned to the partnership, all receipts from billing done on behalf of the partners and the employees of the partnership will be treated as receipts of the group, and expenses will be paid as expenses of the group. We therefore believe that this part of the test will be satisfied.

3. Overhead expenses and income from the practice shall be distributed in accordance with previously determined methods

HCFA believes that this provision is ambiguous and has proposed to interpret it to mean that a group must have in place methods for distribution prior to the time period the group has earned the income or incurred the costs. (See 63 FR 1690).

The Partnership Agreement details that expenses of the practice such as rent, utilities, and salaries will be paid out of the income to the practice before any profits are distributed, and the employment contracts detail the precise amounts of each member's annual salary. Profits over and above salaries and expenses will be distributed on a 50 percent basis between the partners, as detailed in the Partnership Agreement. We therefore believe that the arrangement satisfies our interpretation of this part of the test.

4. No physician member will be compensated, directly or indirectly, based on the volume or value of referrals

Under section 1877(h)(4)(A)(iv), no physician member of the group may receive compensation based on the volume or value of that physician's own referrals. However, section 1877(h)(4)(B)(I) qualifies this statement by allowing that "a physician in a group practice may be paid a share of overall profits of the group, or a productivity bonus based on services personally performed or services incident to such personally performed services, so long as the share or bonus is not determined in any manner which is directly related to the volume or value of referrals by such physician."

Partnership's employment contracts indicate that physician employees will be compensated on a straight salary basis. These salaries are based on the number of hours worked, multiplied by a pre-determined amount that varies slightly among the employees. This variance reflects differences in education and experience among the members, and is not based on the volume or value of past or projected future referrals. In addition to salary, employees also receive a health benefit package. While there is no fair market value test for the compensation that a group practice can pay a physician member under section 1877(h) (4) (A), if a physician appears to be paid an inordinatly high salary for his or her work, we would assume that the group is compensating the physician for referrals by including the payments as part of a set salary. Because we are not in a position to determine whether the wages and benefits under the arrangement are fair, we condition this advisory opinion on the requirement that the salaries and benefits are in line with what similarly situated ophthalmologists in the geographical area receive for comparable work, without the value of any referrals included in the development of the salary package.

The Partnership Agreement states that physician owners will each be paid both an annual salary and a 50 percent share of the profits, which will be based solely on the percentage of the ownership interest of each owner. The employees are to be paid on a pre-determined hourly salary, without receiving a bonus related to the volume or value of referrals for designated health services. Partnership has not proposed any other forms of compensation or incentives for owners or employees. It therefore appears that this part of the test will be satisfied.

5. Members of the group provide at least 75 percent of the physician-patient encounters

HCFA has proposed to interpret "member of the group" to include physician owners and employees of the group. (See 63 FR 1687.) Since Partnership has indicated in correspondence with HCFA that all physician-patient encounters will be performed by members of the group, Partnership's proposal will meet this part of the test.

B. In-office Ancillary Services Exception

In order to qualify for the in-office ancillary services exception, Partnership must not only meet the definition of a group practice but also demonstrate that it meets the criteria set forth in section 1877 (b)(2)(A) of the Act, which exempts services that are furnished "(i) personally by the referring physician, personally by a physician who is a member of the same group practice as the referring physician, or personally by individuals who are directly supervised by the physician or another physician in the group practice, and (ii)(I) in a building in which the referring physician (or another physician who is a member of the same group practice) furnishes physicians' services unrelated to the furnishing of designated health services, or (II) in the case of a referring physician who is a member of a group practice, in another building which is used by the group practice for the centralized provision of the group's designated health services (other than clinical laboratory services), . . . " In addition, under (b)(2)(B), the services must be billed by the physician performing or supervising the services or the group practice of which such physician is a member under a billing number assigned to the group practice, or by an entity that is wholly owned by the physician or the group practice.

1. Services furnished or supervised by the referring physician or by a member of the same group practice

Requestors would meet this part of the test if a member of the group personally furnishes or directly supervises a non-member in the furnishing of the designated health service. By regulation in 42 CFR 411.351, in terms of referrals involving only clinical laboratory services, we have interpreted "direct supervision" to mean "supervision by a physician who is present in the office suite and immediately available to provide assistance and direction throughout the time services are being performed." The January 9, 1998 proposed rule further defines "present in the office suite" as meaning that the physician must be present in the suite in which the services are being furnished, at the time they are being furnished, except that the definition does allow certain unexpected absences and certain routine absences of short duration. (See 63 FR 1684.)

Requestors can meet this requirement by assuring that at least one of the four physician members of the group is present at each of the three locations at any given time. Requestors have not specifically addressed this management issue in their communication with us, but have stated verbally that they intend to comply with HCFA's opinion on how to meet each prong of each test. The direct supervision requirement applies only to Medicare covered designated health services. Thus, as long as at least one physician member is in the office suite performing or directly supervising a non-member employee in the furnishing of eyeglasses or contact lenses that qualify as designated health services that are covered under Medicare, this part of the test will be met.

2. Services furnished in an appropriate location

Except as described below, designated health services must be furnished in a building in which the referring physician or another physician member of the group practice is furnishing physicians' services unrelated to the furnishing of designated health services. We have proposed to interpret "unrelated to designated health services" as any services that are not listed as designated health services in section 1877 (h) (6), even if these services lead to a physician requesting a designated health service (see 63 FR 1695). Since the partnership proposes to offer a broader range of ophthalmology services than those considered to be designated health services at each of its locations, we believe that this requirement will be met.

Alternatively, a group practice can meet the location test if the designated health services are furnished in another building that is used by the group for the centralized provision of designated health services. Partnership could arrange its locations such that no additional physicians' services are furnished where the eyeglasses are furnished, provided that a physician is on the premises to either furnish the eyeglasses or to directly supervise non-member employees who are furnishing the eyeglasses.

3. Services billed under the billing number assigned to the group practice

Requestors have certified that partners and physician employees of Partnership would bill under a common billing number assigned to the partnership. Provided that they obtain and use a billing number assigned to the group practice, this provision will be met.

CONCLUSION

We find that the proposed partnership arrangement is a group practice and that the designated health services performed or supervised by members of the group will meet the in-office ancillary services exception, provided that all of the above-mentioned criteria are met.

LIMITATIONS OF THIS OPINION

The limitations that apply to this Advisory Opinion include the following:

- This AO and the validity of conclusions reached in it are based entirely on the accuracy of the information that you have presented to us.
- This AO is relevant only to the specific question(s) posed at the beginning of this opinion. This AO is limited in scope to the specific arrangement described in this letter and has no application to other arrangements, even those which appear to be similar in nature or scope.
- This AO does not apply to, nor can it be relied upon, by any individual or entity other than the Requestor. This AO may not be introduced in any matter involving an entity or individual that is not a Requestor to this opinion.
- Our Advisory Opinion authority originates from Section 1877 of the Social Security Act, which specifically contains a prohibition against certain physician referrals. This AO may not be construed as permission to avoid compliance with any other Federal, State or local laws which may apply to the arrangement.
- This AO will not bind or obligate any agency other than the U.S. Department of Health and Human Services. Under 42 CFR 411.382, HCFA reserves the right to reconsider the issues posed in this AO and, where public interest requires, rescind or revoke this opinion.
- This opinion is also subject to any additional limitations set forth at 42 CFR 411.370 et seq.

Sincerely,
/S/
Robert A. Berenson, M.D.
Director
Center for Health Plans and Providers

Guide 9

EXCLUSION AUTHORITIES

The following chapters set forth bases for excluding persons and entities from participation in Medicare, Medicaid, and other Federally-funded State health care programs.

PART II, CHAPTER 2: SANCTIONS IN THE MEDICARE STATUTE

§ 2:5

Improper billing for clinical diagnostic laboratory tests: Section 1833(h)(5)(D) [42 U.S.C.A. 1395l(h)(5)(D)]
Affects: "Any person who"
Period of exclusion: Not to exceed 5 years
Cross references to sections 1842(j)(2) and 1128

§ 2:8

Overcharging by physicians for services of a certified registered nurse anesthetist: Section 1833(l)(6) [42 U.S.C.A. 1395l(l)(6)]
Affects: Physicians
Period of exclusion: Not to exceed 5 years
Cross references to sections 1842(j)(1)(D), 1842(j)(2), and 1128

§ 2:10

Failure to include information about referring physicians on requests for payments or bills: Section 1833(q) [42 U.S.C.A. 1395l(q)]
Affects: Any entity that submits a bill or request for payment for an item or service covered under Medicare Part B, that does not take Medicare assignment, and that knowingly and willfully and in repeated cases fails to provide required information after being notified by the Secretary of Health and Human Services of the obligation to do so
Period of exclusion: Not to exceed 5 years
Cross reference to section 1128

§ 2:12

Improper billing for rental items such as durable medical equipment, prosthetic devices, orthotics, and prosthetics: Section 1834(a)(11)(A) [42 U.S.C.A. 1395m(a)(11)(A)]

Affects: Suppliers

Period of exclusion: Not to exceed 5 years

Cross references to sections 1842(j)(2) and 1128

§ 2:13.1

Violation of prohibition against unsolicited telephone contacts by suppliers: Section 1834(a)(17) [42 U.S.C.A. 1395m(a)(17)]

Affects: Suppliers

Period of exclusion: Not specified

Cross reference to section 1128

§ 2:13.2

Failure by suppliers to make required refunds: Section 1834(a)(18) [42 U.S.C.A. 1395m(a)(18)]

Affects: Suppliers

Period of exclusion: Not specified

Cross reference to sections 1842(j)(2) and 1128

§ 2:14

Improper billing by physicians or suppliers for radiologist services: Section 1834(b)(5)(C) [42 U.S.C.A. 1395m(b)(5)(C)]

Affects: Physicians and suppliers

Period of exclusion: Not to exceed 5 years

Cross references to sections 1842(j)(2) and 1128

§ 2:15.1

Failure by practitioners to bill on an assignment-related basis: Section 1842(b)(18) and Sections 1834(k) and (l) [42 U.S.C.A. 1395u(b)(18) and 42 U.S.C.A. 1395m(k) and (l)]

Affects: Physicians assistants, nurse practitioners, clinical nurse specialists, certified registered nurse anesthetists, certified nurse-midwives, clinical social workers, clinical psychologists, outpatient rehabilitation suppliers, ambulance suppliers

CMP: Same as for civil monetary penalty under section 1128A(a), 42 U.S.C.A. 1320a-7a(a)

Assessment: Same as under Section 1128A, with provision for compensation from proceeds to overcharged patients
Period of exclusion: Not to exceed 5 years
Cross reference to 1128, 42 U.S.C.A. 1320

§ 2:16

Violating the freeze on physician fees: Section 1842(j)(1) [42 U.S.C.A. 1395u(j)(1)]
Affects: Physicians
Period of exclusion: Not to exceed 5 years
Cross references to sections 1842(j)(2) and 1128

§ 2:17

Improper billing for services of assistants at cataract surgery: Sections 1842(k)(1) and (2) [42 U.S.C.A. 1395u(k)(1) and (2)]
Affects: Physicians
Period of exclusion: Not to exceed 5 years
Cross references to sections 1842(j)(2) and 1128

§ 2:18

Wrongful charges by nonparticipating physicians: Section 1842(l) [42 U.S.C.A. 1395u(l)]
Affects: Physicians
Period of exclusion: Not to exceed 5 years
Cross references to sections 1842(j)(2) and 1128

§ 2:19

Wrongful charges by nonparticipating physicians for certain elective surgical procedures: Section 1842(m) [42 U.S.C.A. 1395u(m)]
Affects: Physicians
Period of exclusion: Not to exceed 5 years
Cross references to sections 1842(j)(2) and 1128

§ 2:20

Physician failure to eliminate the mark-up for certain purchased diagnostic tests: Section 1842(n) [42 U.S.C.A. 1395u(n)]
Affects: Physicians
Period of exclusion: Not to exceed 5 years
Cross references to sections 1842(j)(2) and 1128

§ 2:21

Physician failure to provide appropriate diagnosis codes on bills: Section 1842(p) [42 U.S.C.A. 1395u(p)]
Affects: Physicians
Period of exclusion: Not to exceed 5 years
Cross references to sections 1842(j)(2) and 1128

§ 2:23

Wrongful charges for interpreting electrocardiograms: Section 1848(b)(3) [42 U.S.C.A. 1395w-4(b)(3)]

◆ [NOTE: Repealed for services after January 1, 1994, by section 13514(a) of the Omnibus Budget Reconciliation Act of 1993, P.L. 103-66]

Affects: Physicians
Period of exclusion: Not to exceed 5 years
Cross references to sections 1842(j)(2) and 1128

§ 2:24

Violating limitations on physician charges by nonparticipating physicians, suppliers, or other persons after 1990: Section 1848(g)(1) [42 U.S.C.A. 1395w-4(g)(1)]
Affects: Physicians
Period of exclusion: Not to exceed 5 years
Cross references to sections 1842(j)(2) and 1128

§ 2:25

Failure to bill on an assignment-related basis for services to persons enrolled under Medicare Part B and eligible for Medicaid: Section 1848(g)(3) [42 U.S.C.A. 1395w-4(g)(3)]
Affects: "Any person"
Period of exclusion: Not to exceed 5 years
Cross references to sections 1842(j)(2) and 1128

§ 2:26

Failure by physicians, suppliers, and others, including their employers and related facilities, to submit claims on specified claim forms: Section 1848(g)(4) [42 U.S.C.A. 1395w-(g)(4)]
Affects: Physicians, suppliers, or other persons, including, in certain cases, employers and facilities

Period of exclusion: Not to exceed 5 years
Cross references to sections 1842(p), 1842(j)(2), and 1128

§ 2:35

Failure by hospitals and certain physicians to examine and treat persons for emergency medical conditions and women in labor: Section 1867 [42 U.S.C.A. 1395(dd)]
Affects: Physicians
Period of exclusion: Not specified; pre-OBRA 90 applies to physicians for knowing and willful or negligent false certification about benefits and risks of an individual's transfer and to misrepresentation of an individual's condition or other information, including a hospital's obligation under section 1867; post-OBRA 90, effective May 1991, applies to any physician responsible for examination, treatment, or transfer of an individual in a participating hospital, including a physician on-call for the care of such an individual who negligently violates a requirement under section 1867, if the violation is gross and flagrant or is repeated

§ 2:42

Violating limitations on physician referrals and related reporting requirements: Section 1877 [42 U.S.C.A. 1395nn]
Affects: Physicians and providers of the following designated health services: clinical laboratory services; physical therapy services; occupational therapy services; radiology or other diagnostic services; radiation therapy services; durable medical equipment; parenteral and enteral nutrients, equipment, and supplies; prosthetics, orthotics, and prosthetic devices, home health services, outpatient prescription drugs, and inpatient and outpatient hospital services, including health maintenance organizations, competitive medical plans and prepaid health care plans; "any person that presents or causes to be presented"
Period of exclusion: Not specified
Cross reference to section 1128A, which authorizes exclusion along with imposition of civil money penalties

§ 2:58

Unnecessary hospital admissions and other inappropriate practices by hospitals to circumvent reimbursement requirements: Section 1886(f) [42 U.S.C.A. 1395ww(f)]
Affects: Hospitals

Period of exclusion: Not specified
Cross reference to section 1128(b)(13)

PART II, CHAPTER 3: SANCTIONS IN THE MEDICAID STATUTE

§ 3:2

Additional penalties for persons or entities sanctioned by exclusion under section 1128 or under section 1128A: Section 1902(a)(39) [42 U.S.C.A. 1396a(a)(39)]

Affects: Any person or entity excluded under Medicare pursuant to section 1128 or section 1128A; mandatory for States

Period of exclusion: At least as long as the period of exclusion imposed under Medicare

Cross references to sections 1128 and 1128A

§ 3:5.1

Overcharging Medicaid eligibles who are qualified Medicare beneficiaries: Section 1902(n)(3) [42 U.S.C.A. 1396a(n)(3)]

◆ NOTE: Any sanction that may be imposed upon a provider or Medicaid managed care organization for excess charges under Medicaid or Medicare applies.

§ 3:6

Providing Medicaid exclusions for the same grounds as Medicare exclusions: Section 1902(p)(1) [42 U.S.C.A. 1396a(p)(1)]

Affects: Any person or entity excluded under Medicare pursuant to section 1128, section 1128A, or 1866(b)(2)

Period of exclusion: Permissive with States

Cross references to sections 1128, 1128A, and 1866(b)(2)

§ 3:7

Excluding health maintenance organizations and other entities authorized to implement primary care case management or specialty physician services: Section 1902(p)(2) [42 U.S.C.A. 1396a(p)(2)]

Affects: Health maintenance organizations

Period of exclusion: Not specified

Cross reference to section 1128(b)(8), which permits exclusion for improper business relationships with or employment of individuals convicted of certain crimes or sanctioned under Medicare; additional cross reference to section 1128A, which permits exclusion in conjunction with imposition of a civil money penalty

PART II, CHAPTER 4: SANCTIONS IN TITLE XI OF THE SOCIAL SECURITY ACT

§ 4:6

Exclusion from Federal and Federally-funded State healthcare programs: Section 1128 [42 U.S.C.A. 1320a-6]

Affects: Almost any individual or entity participating in Federal or Federally-funded State health care programs

Period of exclusion: For mandatory exclusions, not less than 5 years, but if a person has been convicted of an offense for which exclusion is authorized on or after August 5, 1997, not less than 10 years; and if there were two such prior convictions, permanent exclusion

Applies to any individual or entity convicted of a crime related to delivery of an item or service under Medicare or Federally funded State health care programs, or convicted under Federal or State law for neglect or abuse of a patient in connection with delivery of a health care item or service

Period of exclusion: For permissive exclusions, not specified

Applies for any criminal conviction under Federal or State law for fraud, theft, embezzlement, breach of fiduciary responsibility, or other financial misconduct related to delivery of a health care item or service under Federal, State, or local government health care programs; for any criminal conviction under Federal or State law related to interference with or obstruction of any investigation of any such criminal offenses or of a criminal offense related to neglect or abuse of a patient in connection with delivery of a health care item or service; for criminal conviction under Federal or State law relating to unlawful manufacture, distribution, prescription, or dispensing of a controlled substance; for any individual or entity that has had a license to provide health care revoked or suspended by a State licensure authority or that has lost such a license, or the right to apply for or renew such a license, for reasons bearing on professional competence, professional performance, or financial integrity, or that has surrendered such a license while a formal disciplinary proceeding was pending for such reasons; for any individual or entity suspended or excluded from participation, or otherwise sanctioned, under any Federal program, including those of the Defense Department and the Veterans Administration, involving provision of health care, or under any State health care program, for reasons bearing on professional competence, professional performance, or financial integrity; for making a claim for payment for an item or service furnished that is substantially in excess of an individual or entity's usual cost or charge; for furnishing or causing to be furnished a health care item or service substantially in excess of a patient's need or of a quality that fails to meet professionally recognized standards of health care; for a substantial failure by a health maintenance organization or other entity furnishing items or services under a case-management or specialty physician services arrangement under Medicaid to provide required medically necessary items and services; for substantial failure by risk-sharing organizations under Medicare to provide required medically necessary items or services; for any individual or entity that has committed an act subject to a civil money penalty under section 1128A or that has committed a criminal act punishable under section 1128B; for any entity controlled by an individual convicted of program-related crimes specified above, of sanctioned by civil money penalty under section 1128A, or excluded from Medicare or Federally funded State health care programs; for any entity which fails to disclose ownership and control information required by section 1124 or section 1126 or, post-OBRA 90, section 1124A; for any entity failing to disclose business relationships with subcontractors required by section 1124; for any individual or entity that fails to provide required information or to permit access to documents and records to determine the appropriateness of payment under Medicare or Federally funded State health care programs; for a hospital that fails to make required corrective action regarding unnecessary hospital admissions designed to circumvent DRG reimbursement; for any individual that fails to repay scholarship obligations or loans obtained in connection with health professions education and made or secured by the Secretary

Period of exclusion: For the permissive exclusion applicable to any individual or entity that fails to grant immediate access to the Secretary of Health and Human Services or to State survey agencies, as required by section 1864 and sections 1902(a)(26), 1902(a)(31), and 1902(a)(33), to determine compliance with Medicare and Medicaid requirements, or to the Inspector General of the Department of Health and Human Services, or to a State Medicaid fraud control unit, not less than the period during which access was denied plus an additional period not to exceed 90 days

§ 4:8

Civil money penalties: Section 1128A [42 U.S.C.A. 1320a-7a]

Affects: Almost any individual or entity participating in Medicare or Federally funded State health care programs

Period of exclusion: Not specified; the statute permits exclusions to be imposed in conjunction with any proceeding to impose a civil money penalty (See Guide to Civil Money Penalties)

§ 4:19

Sanctions recommended by peer review organizations: Section 1156 [42 U.S.C.A. 1320c-5]

Affects: Any health care practitioner and any other person, including a hospital or other health care facility, organization, or agency, that provides health care services for which payment may be made in whole or in part under the Social Security Act

Period of exclusion: Not specified, but may be permanent

Cross reference to section 1128

Guide 8

CIVIL MONEY PENALTIES

The following chapters set forth bases for imposing civil money penalties.

PART II, CHAPTER 2: SANCTIONS IN THE MEDICARE STATUTE

§ 2:1

Falsifying assessments of residents of skilled nursing facilities: Section 1819(b)(3)(B)(ii) [42 U.S.C.A. 1395i-3(b)(3)(B)(ii)]

Affects: "Any individual who"

CMP: $1,000 for each false certification; $5,000 for each offense for causing others to falsely certify: cross reference to section 1128A

Amount of assessment: None

§ 2:2.1

Failure by physicians, providers, suppliers, and others to furnish an itemized statement of items and services provided to Medicare beneficiaries: Section 1806 [42 U.S.C.A. 1395b-7]

Affects: Physicians, providers, suppliers, and any other person (including an organization, agency, or other entity)

CMP: $100.00 for each failure to furnish an itemized statement

Assessment: None

Cross-reference to section 1128A, 42 U.S.C.A. 1320a-7a

§ 2:3

Giving a skilled nursing facility advance notice of a State or Federal survey: Section 1819(g)(2) [42 U.S.C.A. 1395i-3(g)(2)]

Affects: "Any individual who"

CMP: $2,000 for each offense: cross reference to section 1128A

Amount of assessment: None

§ 2:4

Failing a skilled nursing facility survey: Sections 1819(g) and (h) [42 U.S.C.A. 1395i-3(g) and (h)]

Affects: Nursing facilities

CMP: $10,000 for each day of noncompliance: cross reference to section 1128A

Amount of assessment: None

§ 2:5

Improper billing for clinical diagnostic laboratory tests: Section 1833(h)(5)(D) [42 U.S.C.A. 1395l(h)(5)(D)]

Affects: "A person"

CMP: Pursuant to section 1128A: $2,000 for each offense: cross reference to section 1842(j)(2) and (3)

Amount of assessment: Double the amount claimed in lieu of damages

§ 2:6

Improper billing for intraocular lenses: Section 1833(i)(6) [42 U.S.C.A. 1395l(i)(6)]

Affects: "Any person, including a facility," that accepts assignment

CMP: $2,000 for each improper bill or request for payment: cross reference to section 1128A

Amount of assessment: None

§ 2:7

Improper billing for services of a certified registered nurse anesthetist: Section 1833(l)(5)(B) [42 U.S.C.A. 1395l(l)(5)(B)]

Affects: "Any person who"

CMP: $2,000 per improper bill or request for payment: cross reference to section 1128A

Amount of assessment: Double the amount claimed in lieu of damages

§ 2:8

Overcharging by physicians for services of a certified registered nurse anesthetist: Section 1833(l)(6) [42 U.S.C.A. 1395l(l)(6)]

Affects: Physicians

CMP: Pursuant to section 1128A: $2,000 per offense: cross reference to sections 1842(j)(1)(D) and 1842(j)(2)

Amount of assessment: Double the amount claimed in lieu of damages

§ 2:9

Improper billing for certified nurse-midwife services and services of qualified psychologists and clinical social workers: Section 1833(p) [42 U.S.C.A. 1395l(p)]

◆ [NOTE: Repealed effective January 1, 1995, by section 123(b)(2)(A)(ii) of the Social Security Act Amendments of 1994, P.L. 103-432]

Affects: "Whoever" presents or causes to be presented
CMP: $2,000 per offense: cross reference to section 1128A
Amount of assessment: None

§ 2:10

Failure to include information about referring physicians on requests for payments or bills: Section 1833(q) [42 U.S.C.A. 1395l(q)]
Affects: Any entity that submits a bill or request for payment under Medicare Part B
CMP: $2,000 per offense; cross reference to section 1128A
Amount of assessment: None

§ 2:11

Failure to bill on an assignment -related basis for covered services of a nurse practitioner or clinical specialist: Section 1833(r)(3)(B) [42 U.S.C.A. 1395(r)(3)(B)]

◆ [NOTE: Repealed effective January 1, 1995, by section 123(b)(2)(B)(iii) of the Social Security Act Amendments of 1994, P.L. 103-432]

Affects: "Anyone who"
CMP: $2,000 per offense: cross reference to section 1128A
Amount of assessment: None

§ 2:12

Improper billing for rental items such as durable medical equipment, prosthetic devices, orthotics, and prosthetics: Section 1834(a)(11)(A) [42 U.S.C.A. 1395m(a)(11)(A)]
Affects: Suppliers

CMP: Pursuant to section 1128A: $2,000 per offense: cross reference to section 1842(j)(2)

Amount of assessment: Double the amount claimed for each item in lieu of damages

§ 2:13

Improper distribution by suppliers of forms documenting medical necessity: Section 1834(a)(16) [42 U.S.C.A. 1395m(a)(16)]

◆ [NOTE: Repealed effective after December 30, 1994, by section 131(a)(2) of the Social Security Act Amendments of 1994, P.L. 103-432]

Affects: Suppliers

CMP: $1,000 for each form or document improperly distributed: cross reference to section 1128A

Amount of assessment: None

§ 2:13.2

Failure by suppliers to make required refunds: Section 1834(a)(18) [42 U.S.C.A. 1395m(a)(18)]

Afffects: Suppliers

CMP: Not specified: cross reference to section 1128A

Amount of assessment: Not specified: cross reference to section 1128A

§ 2:14

Improper billing by physicians or suppliers for radiologist services: Section 1834(b)(5)(C) [42 U.S.C.A. 1395m(b)(5)(C)]

Affects: Physicians and suppliers

CMP: Pursuant to section 1128A: $2,000 per offense: cross reference to section 1842(j)(2)

Amount of assessment: Double the amount claimed for each item in lieu of damages

§ 2:15

Overcharging for services of a physician assistant or nurse practitioner: Section 1842(b)(12)(C) [42 U.S.C.A. 1395u(b)(12)(C)]

◆ [NOTE: Repealed effective October 31, 1995, by section 123(b)(2)(B) of the Social Security Act Amendments of 1994, P.L. 103-432]

Affects: "Any person who"
CMP: $2,000 per offense: cross reference to section 1128A
Amount of assessment: None

§ 2:15.1

Failure by practitioners to bill on an assignment-related basis: Section 1842(b)(18) and Sections 1834(k) and (l) [42 U.S.C.A. 1395u(b)(18) and 42 U.S.C.A. 1395m(k) and (l)]

Affects: Physicians assistants, nurse practitioners, clinical nurse specialists, certified registered nurse anesthetists, certified nurse-midwives, clinical social workers, clinical psychologists, outpatient rehabilitation suppliers, ambulance suppliers

CMP: Same as for civil monetary penalty under section 1128A(a), 42 U.S.C.A. 1320a-7a(a)

Assessment: Same as under Section 1128A, with provision for compensation from proceeds to overcharged patients

§ 2:16

Violating the freeze on physician fees: Section 1842(j)(1) [42 U.S.C.A. 1395u(j)(1)]

Affects: Physicians

CMP: Pursuant to section 1128A: $2,000 per offense: cross reference to sections 1842(j)(1)(D)(iv) and (2)

Amount of assessment: Double the amount claimed for each service in lieu of damages

§ 2:17

Improper billing for services of assistants at cataract surgery: Sections 1842(k)(1) and (2) [42 U.S.C.A. 1395u-(k)(1) and (2)]

Affects: Physicians

CMP: Pursuant to section 1128A: $2,000 per offense: cross reference to sections 1842(j)(2)

Amount of assessment: Double the amount claimed for each service in lieu of damages

§ 2:18

Wrongful charges by nonparticipating physicians: Section 1842(l) [42 U.S.C.A. 1395u(l)]

Affects: Physicians

CMP: Pursuant to section 1128A: $2,000 per offense: cross reference to sections 1842(j)(2)

Amount of assessment: Double the amount claimed for each offense in lieu of damages

§ 2:19

Wrongful charges by nonparticipating physicians for certain elective surgical procedures: Section 1842(m) [42 U.S.C.A. 1395u(m)]

Affects: Physicians

CMP: Pursuant to section 1128A: $2,000 per offense: cross reference to sections 1842(j)(2)

Amount of assessment: Double the amount claimed for each offense in lieu of damages

§ 2:20

Physician failure to eliminate the mark-up for certain purchased diagnostic tests: Section 1842(n) [42 U.S.C.A. 1395u(n)]

Affects: Physicians

CMP: Pursuant to section 1128A: $2,000 per offense: cross reference to sections 1842(j)(2)

Amount of assessment: Double the amount claimed for each offense in lieu of damages

§ 2:21

Physician failure to provide appropriate diagnosis codes on bills: Section 1842(p) [42 U.S.C.A. 1395u(p)]

Affects: Physicians

CMP: Pursuant to section 1128A: $2,000 per offense: cross reference to sections 1842(j)(2)

Amount of assessment: Double the amount claimed for each offense in lieu of damages

§ 2:22

Intermediate sanctions for providers or suppliers of clinical diagnostic laboratory tests: Section 1846 [42 U.S.C.A. 1395w-2]

Affects: Any provider or clinical laboratory

CMP: $10,000 for each day of substantial noncompliance with Medicare conditions for coverage: cross reference to section 1128A

Amount of assessment: None

§ 2:23

Wrongful charges for interpreting electrocardiograms: Section 1848(b)(3) [42 U.S.C.A. 395w-4(b)(3)]

◆ [NOTE: Repealed for services after January 1, 1994, by section 13514(a) of the Omnibus Budget Reconciliation Act of 1993, P.L. 103-66]

Affects: Physicians
CMP: Pursuant to section 1128A: $2,000 per offense: cross reference to sections 1842(j)(2)
Amount of assessment: Double the amount claimed for each offense in lieu of damages

§ 2:24

Violating limitations on physician charges by nonparticipating physicians, suppliers, or other persons after 1990: Section 1848(g)(1) [42 U.S.C.A. 1395w-4(g)(1)]
Affects: Physicians
CMP: Pursuant to section 1128A: $2,000 for each offense: cross-reference to section 1842(j)(2)
Amount of assessment: Double the amount claimed for each offense in lieu of damages

§ 2:25

Failure to bill on an assignment-related basis for services to persons enrolled under Medicare Part B and eligible for Medicaid: Section 1848(g)(3) [42 U.S.C.A. 1395w-4(g)(3)]
Affects: Physicians
CMP: Pursuant to section 1842(j)(2): $2,000 for each offense: cross-reference to section 1128A
Amount of assessment: Double the amount claimed for each offense in lieu of damages

§ 2:26

Failure by physicians, suppliers, and others, including their employers and related facilities, to submit claims on specified claim forms: Section 1848(g)(4) [42 U.S.C.A. 1395w-(g)(4)]
Affects: Physicians, suppliers, and others, including their employers and related facilities

CMP: Pursuant to section 1842(p): $2,000 for each offense: cross reference to section 1128A

Amount of assessment: None

§ 2:26.2

Failure by Medicare+Choice organization to comply with requirements for beneficiary protections and protections against fraud: Section 1857(d)

Affects: Medicare+Choice organizations

CMP: For substantial failure to provide medically necessary items or services; imposition of excessive premiums; illegal expulsion or failure to re-enroll an individual; practices which deny or discourage enrollment by individuals likely to need substantial future medical services; misrepresentation or submission of false information to the Secretary of Health and Human Services or any other individual or entity; interference with advice from healthcare professionals to enrollees; failure to establish procedures to enforce balance billing limits for contract providers in fee-for-service plans; employment of or contracts with individuals or entities excluded from Medicare: not more than $25,000 for each determination

Also:

- For denying or discouraging enrollment and for making a misrepresentation or providing false information to the Secretary: not more than $100,000 for each determination
- For illegally denying or discouraging enrollment: $15,000 for each individual not enrolled
- For excessive premiums: double the excess charged
- For contract deficiencies (in conjunction with a contract termination proceeding) that adversely affected (or likely would have adversely affected) an enrollee: not more than $25,000 for each determination
- For contract deficiencies (in conjunction with a contract termination proceeding): $10,000 for each week a deficiency exists

Cross-reference to section 1128A, 42 U.S.C.A. 1320a-7a

§ 2:27

Failure by Primary Payers to Comply with Medicare Secondary Payer Requirements: Section 1862(b) [42 U.S.C.A. 1395y(b)]

Affects: Any employer or other entity

CMP: To prohibit certain incentives not to enroll or to terminate enrollment in certain group health plans: $5,000 for each violation: cross reference to section 1128A

Amount of assessment: None

§ 2:28

Failure by employers to comply with Medicare secondary payer requirements: Section 1862(b)(5)(C)(ii) [42 U.S.C.A. 1395y(b)(5)(C)(ii)]

Affects: Employers, not including Federal or other governmental entities, having certain group health plans

CMP: $1,000 for each individual with respect to whom an inquiry is made regarding coverage under a group health plan by an intermediary or carrier: cross reference to section 1128A

Amount of assessment: None

§ 2:28.1

Violation of Medicare secondary payor screening requirements by providers and suppliers: Section 1862(b)(6) [42 U.S.C.A. 1395y(b)(6)]

Affects: Any entity

CMP: Not to exceed $2,000 for each incident: cross reference to section 1128A

Amount of assessment: None

§ 2:34

Failure by hospitals to have arrangements which preclude certain practitioners and suppliers from seeking further payment from beneficiaries: Section 1866(g) [42 U.S.C.A. 1395cc(g)]

Affects: Hospitals; "any person who"

CMP: $2,000 for each offense: cross reference to section 1128A

Amount of assessment: None

§ 2:35

Failure by hospitals and certain physicians to examine and treat persons for emergency medical conditions and women in labor: Section 1867 [42 U.S.C.A. 1395(dd)]

Affects: Hospitals and physicians

CMP: $50,000 for each violation by a participating hospital, unless the hospital has fewer than 100 beds, then $25,000; $50,000 for each violation by a physician: cross reference to section 1128A

Amount of assessment: None (but see statute prior to amendment by OBRA '89 regarding physicians when there was cross reference to section 1842(j)(2))

§ 2:41

Failure by risk-sharing organizations (such as health maintenance organizations and competitive medical plans) to comply with requirements for provision of services, premiums, treatment of applicants and members, truthfulness, prompt payment, and avoiding business relationships with excluded individuals and entities: Section 1876(i)(6) [42 U.S.C.A. 1395mm(i)(6)]

Affects: Health maintenance organizations and competitive medical plans

CMP: For failure to provide required services, for charging excessive premiums, for wrongfully expelling or refusing to re-enroll individual, for practices that would reasonably be expected to deny or discourage enrollment improperly, for misrepresentation or falsified information, for failure to meet prompt payment requirements, for employing or contracting with individuals or entities excluded under section 1128 or 1128A: $25,000 for each violation; for discouraging potential high users of medical services from enrolling: $100,000 for each violation, plus $15,000 for each individual not enrolled as a result of the violation; for misrepresentation of false information to the Secretary of Health and Human Services: $100,000 for each violation: cross reference to section 1128A

Amount of assessment: For overcharging premiums, double the amount of the excessive charge

§ 2:42

Violating limitations on physician referrals and related reporting requirements: Section 1877 [42 U.S.C.A. 1395nn]

Affects: Physicians and providers of the following designated health services: clinical laboratory services; physical therapy services; occupational therapy services; radiology or other diagnostic services; radiation therapy services; durable medical equipment; parenteral and enteral nutrients, equipment, and supplies; prosthetics, orthotics, and prosthetic devices, home health services, outpatient prescription drugs, and inpatient and outpatient hospital services, including health maintenance organizations, competitive medical plans and prepaid health care plans; "any person that presents or causes to be presented"

CMP: $15,000 for each improper claim or bill for a service; $100,000 for each improper circumvention scheme; $10,000 per day for each day of failure to report required ownership and investment interests, and covered items and services provided by affected entities: cross reference to section 1128A

Amount of assessment: None

§ 2:45

Issuing Medicare supplemental health insurance policies in violation of State or Federal standards: Section 1882(a)(2) [42 U.S.C.A. 1395ss(a)(2)]

Affects: Any person who issues a policy

CMP: $25,000 for each violation: cross reference to section 1128A

Amount of assessment: None

§ 2:46

Misrepresentation and fraud in obtaining and using Secretarial certification of Medicare supplemental health insurance policies: Section 1882(d)(1) [42 U.S.C.A. 1395ss(d)(1)]

Affects: "Whoever"

CMP: $5,000 for each violation: cross reference to section 1128A

Amount of assessment: None

§ 2:47

Misrepresentation by sellers of Medicare supplemental health insurance policies that they act by authority of or in association with Medicare or any Federal agency: Section 1882(d)(2) [42 U.S.C.A. 1395ss(d)(2)]

Affects: "Whoever"

CMP: $5,000 for each violation: cross reference to section 1128A

Amount of assessment: None

§ 2:48

Selling Medicare beneficiaries supplemental health insurance policies that duplicate Medicare benefits/Not obtaining a valid buyer's statement/Not preparing a seller's acknowledgement: Section 1882(d)(3) [42 U.S.C.A. 1395ss(d)(3)]

Affects: "Whoever"

CMP: $5,000 for each violation: cross reference to section 1128A

Amount of assessment: None

§ 2:49

Using the mail to market Medicare supplemental health insurance policies which have not been Stateapproved: Section 1882(d)(4) [42 U.S.C.A. 1395ss(d)(4)]

Affects: "Whoever"

CMP: $5,000 for each violation: cross reference to section 1128A

Amount of assessment: None

§ 2:50

Issuing or selling Medicare supplemental health insurance policies that do not comply with form and content requirements: Section 1882(p)(8) [42 U.S.C.A. 1395ss(p)(8)]

Affects: "Any person who"

CMP: $25,000, or in the case of a seller who is not the issuer of a policy, $15,000 for each violation: cross reference to section 1128A

Amount of assessment: None

§ 2:51

Failure to offer a Medicare supplemental health insurance policy that provides only the core group of basic benefits: Section 1882(p)(9)(C) [42 U.S.C.A. 1395ss(p)(9)(C)]

Affects: "Anyone who sells"

CMP: $25,000, or in the case of a seller who is not the issuer of a policy, $15,000: cross reference to section 1128A

Amount of assessment: None

§ 2:52

Failure to provide reinstatement rights to purchasers of Medicare supplemental health insurance policies who become eligible for Medicaid: Section 1882(q)(5) [42 U.S.C.A. 1395ss(q)(5)]

Affects: "Any person who issues"

CMP: $25,000 for each violation: cross reference to section 1128A

Amount of assessment: None

§ 2:53

Failure by issuers of Medicare supplemental health insurance policies to meet requirements for preexisting conditions, waiting periods, elimination periods, probationary periods, and price and coverage nondiscrimination: Section 1882(s)(3) [42 U.S.C.A. 1395ss(s)(3)]

Affects: Any issuer

CMP: $5,000 for each failure: cross reference to section 1128A

Amount of assessment: None

§ 2:54

Special obligations for issuers of Medicare supplemental health insurance policies in selected States who provide benefits through contracts with networks of providers: Section 1882(t)(2) [42 U.S.C.A. 1395ss(t)(2)]

Affects: Any issuer

CMP: $25,000 for each violation: cross reference to section 1128A

Amount of assessment: None

§ 2:59

Giving a home health agency advance notice of a standard survey: Section 1891(c)(1) [42 U.S.C.A. 1395bbb(c)(1)]

Affects: "Any individual who"

CMP: $2,000 for each offense: cross reference to section 1128A

Amount of assessment: None

§ 2:60

Failure by a home health agency to comply with medicare conditions of participation: Sections 1891(e) and (f) [42 U.S.C.A. 1395bbb(e) and (f)]

Affects: Home health agencies

CMP: $10,000 for each day of noncompliance: cross reference to section 1128A

Amount of assessment: None

§ 2:62

Termination of PACE provider agreements: Section 1894 [42 U.S.C.A. 1395eee]

Affects: PACE providers

CMP: For substantial failure to provide medically necessary items and services; imposition of excessive premiums; illegally expelling or refusing to re-enroll an individual; practices that deny or discourage enrollment by individuals who may need substantial future medical services; misrepresenting or falsifying information to the Secretary of Health and Human Services, or to any other individual or entity;

interference with medical advice by healthcare practitioners to enrollees; failure to enforce balance billing limits by physicians, providers, and suppliers in fee-for-service plans; employment of or contracting with individuals or entities excluded from Medicare: not more than $25,000 for each violation

Also:

- For each finding of illegally denying or refusing to enroll individuals: not more than $100,000 and $15,000 for each individual illegally denied or refused enrollment
- For misrepresentation to or providing false information to the Secretary: not more than $100,000
- For excessive premiums: double the excess charge

◆ NOTE: See text for variations applicable to acts prior to January 1, 1999.

PART II, CHAPTER 3: SANCTIONS IN THE MEDICAID STATUTE

§ 3:5.1

Overcharging Medicaid eligibles who are qualified Medicare beneficiaries: Section 1902(n)(3) [42 U.S.C.A. 1396a(n)(3)]

◆ NOTE: Any sanction that may be imposed upon a provider or Medicaid managed care organization for excess charges under Medicaid or Medicare applies.

§ 3:9

Failure by health maintenance organizations to comply with Medicaid requirements: Section 1903(m)(5) [42 U.S.C.A. 1396b(m)(5)]

Affects: Health maintenance organizations

CMP: For failure to provide required items or services, for imposing excessive premiums, for discriminating among individuals on the basis of their health status or need for health care services, or for misrepresenting or falsifying information to the Secretary of Health and Human Services or to an individual or any other entity: $25,000 for each violation; for discrimination among eligible persons and misrepresentation and false information to the Secretary or to the State: $100,000 for each violation, plus $15,000 for each individual not enrolled as a result of prohibited discrimination: cross reference to section 1128A

Amount of assessment: For overcharging premiums, double the amount of the excessive charge

§ 3:14

Failure by nursing facilities to comply with Medicaid requirements for resident assessments: Section 1919(b) [42 U.S.C.A. 1396r(b)]

Affects: "Any individual who"

CMP: $1,000 for each certification of a material and false statement in a resident assessment; $5,000 for each offense for causing another individual to certify a material and false statement in a resident assessment: cross reference to section 1128A

Amount of assessment: None

§ 3:16

Giving nursing facilities advance notice of a survey: Section 1919(g)(2)(A)(i) [42 U.S.C.A. 1396r(g)(2)(A)(i)]

Affects: "Any individual who"

CMP: $2,000 for each offense: cross reference to section 1128A

Amount of assessment: None

§ 3:17

Failing a nursing facility survey: Section 1919(g)(5), 1919(h), and 1919(i) [42 U.S.C.A. 1396r(g)(5), 1396r(h), and 1396r(i)]

Affects: Nursing facilities

CMP: Authorizes States to impose civil money penalties plus interest (see State plan); $10,000 for each day of noncompliance as determined by the Secretary of Health and Human Services: cross reference to section 1128A

Amount of assessment: None

§ 3:19

Failure by drug manufacturers and wholesalers to comply with Medicaid drug rebate requirements: Section 1927 [42 U.S.C.A. 1396s]

Affects: Wholesalers and manufacturers and direct sellers

CMP: For refusing a request by the Secretary for information about covered outpatient drugs: $100,000; for providing false information in response to surveys of drug prices by the Secretary:

$100,000 for each item of false information; for failure to provide timely information on prices: $10,000 for each day's delay: cross reference to section 1128A

Amount of assessment: None

§ 3:20

Giving advance notice of a survey to a community care setting for functionally disabled elderly individuals: Section 1929(i)(3))A) [42 U.S.C.A. 1396u(i)(3)(A)]

Affects: "Any individual who"

CMP: $2,000: cross reference to section 1128A

Amount of assessment: None

§ 3:23

Failure by home and community care settings for functionally disabled elderly individuals to comply with Medicaid requirements: Section 1929(j) [42 U.S.C.A. 1396u(j)]

Affects: Providers

CMP: Obligates States to establish civil money penalties to be imposed with interest for each day of noncompliance; permits the Secretary to impose $2,000 for each day of noncompliance: cross reference to section 1128A

Amount of assessment: None

§ 3:24

Failure by providers of community supported living arrangements services to comply with statutory requirements: Section 1930(h)(2) [42 U.S.C.A. 1396v(h)(2)]

Affects: Providers

CMP: $10,000 for each day of noncompliance: cross reference to section 1128A

Amount of assessment: None

§ 3:25

Failure by Medicaid managed care organizations to comply with fraud and abuse protection requirements: Sections 1932(d) and (e) [42 U.S.C.A. 1396u-2(e)]

Affects: Managed care entities

CMP: For discrimination based on health status or requirement for healthcare services: not more than $100,000, plus $15,000 for each individual affected by the discrimination

- For imposing an illegal premium: double the excess amount charged
- For any other violation: not more than $25,000

§ 3:28

Intermediate sanctions for Medicaid PACE providers: Section 1934(e)(6)(B) [42 U.S.C.A. 1396u-4(e)(6)(B)]

Affects: Medicaid PACE providers

CMP: For substantial failure to provide medically necessary items and services; imposition of excessive premiums; illegally expelling or refusing to re-enroll an individual; practices that deny or discourage enrollment by individuals who may need substantial future medical services; misrepresentation to or providing false information to the Secretary of Health and Human Services, or to any other individual or entity; interference with medical advice to enrollees by healthcare practitioners; failure to impose balance billing limits by physicians, providers, and suppliers in fee-for-services plans; employment of or contracting with individuals or entities excluded from Medicare: not more than $25,000 for each violation

Also: For each finding of illegal denial of enrollment or refusal to re-enroll an individual: not more than $100,000, plus $15,000 for each individual not enrolled as a result of the illegal action

- For misrepresentation or providing false information to the Secretary: not more than $100,000
- For excessive premiums: double the excess amount

◆ NOTE: See text for variations applicable to acts prior to January 1, 1999.

PART II, CHAPTER 4: SANCTIONS IN TITLE XI OF THE SOCIAL SECURITY ACT

§ 4:8

Civil money penalties: Section 1128A [42 U.S.C.A. 1320a-7a]

Affects: Almost any individual or entity participating in Federal or Federally-funded State healthcare programs

CMP: For presenting or causing to be presented claims for items or services not provided as claimed, for false or fraudulent claims, for claims for a physician's service when the individual was not a physician, or when the physician obtained his license through misrepresentation of material fact or cheating, or when the physician falsely represented to the patient that he was certified in a specialty, or when the item or service was furnished during a period when the person furnishing the item or service was excluded from Federal or Federally-funded State healthcare programs, or when the claim is in violation of a Medicare assignment, or of a Medicaid agreement or Medicaid requirement, or of an agreement to be a participating physician or supplier or pharmacy, or of a provider agreement for contracting or employing excluded persons or entities: $10,000 for each violation; for false or misleading information which could reasonably be expected to influence a decision to discharge someone from a hospital prematurely: $15,000 for each individual with respect to whom false or misleading information was given; for health maintenance organizations and competitive medical plans, hospitals, and critical access hospitals that knowingly make direct or indirect payments to a physician to induce him to reduce or limit services to a patient entitled to Medicare or Medicaid or enrolled in the organization: $2,000 for each individual with respect to whom such a payment is made (not applicable to HMO's and CMP's on or after November 5, 1990); for a physician who receives such a payment: $2,000 for each individual with respect to whom such payment is received; for retaining ownership or management in a healthcare entity after exclusion: $10,000 for each day the relationship exists

Amount of assessment: Triple the amount claimed in lieu of damages for illegal remuneration for referrals: $50,000 for each act; for a physician who falsely certifies that an individual meets requirements for home health services: $5,000 or three times the amount of home healthcare payment made pursuant to the certification, whichever is greater

§ 4:13.1

Failure to report information about final adverse actions against healthcare providers, suppliers, and practitioners to the National Health Care Fraud and Abuse Data Collection Program: Section 1128E(b)(6) [42 U.S.C.A. 1320a-7e(b)(6)]

Affects: Any plan or program that provides health benefits, including a policy of health insurance, a contract of a service benefit organization, and a membership agreement with a health maintenance organization or other prepaid health plan

CMP: For each failure to report an adverse action: not more than $25,000

§ 4:14

Misuse of Federal government names, symbols, and emblems: Section 1140 [42 U.S.C.A. 1320b-10]

Affects: "Any person"

CMP: $5,000 for each violation, unless it is by broadcast or telecast, in which event, $25,000 for each violation, but in no case more than $100,000: cross references to sections 1140(c) and 1128A

Amount of assessment: None

§ 4:16

Violating reporting and disclosure obligations regarding the Medicare and Medicaid Coverage Data Bank: Section 1144 [42 U.S.C.A. 1320b-14]

Affects: Certain employers and third parties, such as a group health plan, obligated to pay for health care goods and services furnished to Medicare beneficiaries and Medicaid recipients, that have reporting obligations related to Medicare secondary payer requirements under section 1862(b), 42 U.S.C.A. 1395y(b); anyone who wrongfully discloses or who solicits a wrongful disclosure of information or who illegally prints or publishes wrongfully disclosed information

CMP: $50 for each failure to report not to exceed $100,000 in a calendar year for all such failures; also a wrongful disclosure or a solicitation for a wrongful disclosure or willfully printing or publishing information wrongfully disclosed is a felony subject to a fine not exceeding $5,000 or imprisonment up to 5 years, or both, plus costs of prosecution, and in the case of certain government officials or employees, loss of position or employment; cross references to various provisions of the Internal Revenue Code of 1986, including chapter 68, 26 U.S.C.A. 6721-6724

Amount of assessment: None

PART II, CHAPTER 5: SANCTIONS IN THE HEALTH CARE QUALITY IMPROVEMENT ACT OF 1986

§ 5:2

Failure to report medical malpractice payments: Section 421 [42 U.S.C.A. 11131]

Affects: Entities, including insurance companies, that make medical malpractice payments, whether via insurance, self-insurance, or in settlement or partial settlement or satisfaction of a judgment

CMP: $10,000 for each payment not reported: cross reference to section 1128A

Amount of assessment: Arguably none

§ 5:5

Unlawful disclosure of information collected pursuant to the Health Care Quality Improvement Act: Section 427 [42 U.S.C.A. 11137]

Affects: "Any person who"

CMP: $10,000 for each unlawful disclosure: cross reference to section 1128A

Amount of assessment: Arguably none

Guide 7

CHAPTERS FOR INSURANCE COMPANIES

The following chapters set forth bases for imposing sanctions which are relevant to insurance companies.

PART II, CHAPTER 2: SANCTIONS IN THE MEDICARE STATUTE

§ 2:27

Failure by primary payers to comply with Medicare secondary payer requirements: Section 1862(b) [42 U.S.C.S. 1395y(b)]

§ 2:28

Failure by employers to comply with Medicare secondary payer requirements: Section 1862(b)(5)(C)(ii) [42 U.S.C.S. 1395y(b)(5)(C)(ii)]

§ 2:28.1

Violation of Medicare secondary payor screening requirements by providers and suppliers: Section 1862(b)(6) [42 U.S.C.S. 1394y(b)(6)]

§ 2:45

Issuing Medicare supplemental health insurance policies in violation of State or Federal Standards: Section 1882(A)(2) [42 U.S.C.S. 1395ss(a)(2)]

§ 2:46

Misrepresentation and fraud in obtaining and using Secretarial certification of Medicare supplemental health insurance policies: Section 1882(d)(1) [42 U.S.C.S. 1395ss(d)(1)]

§ 2:47

Misrepresentation by sellers of Medicare supplemental health insurance policies that they act by authority of or in association with Medicare or any Federal agency: Section 1882(d)(2) [42 U.S.C.S. 1395ss(d)(2)]

§ 2:48

Selling Medicare beneficiaries supplemental health insurance policies that substantially duplicate Medicare benefits: Section 1882(d)(3) [42 U.S.C.S. 1395ss(d)(3)]

§ 2:49

Using the mail to market Medicare supplemental insurance policies which have not been State-approved: Section 1882(d)(4) [42 U.S.C.S. 1395ss(d)(4)]

§ 2:50

Issuing or selling Medicare supplemental policies that do not comply with form and content requirements: Section 1882(p)(8) [42 U.S.C.S. 1395ss(p)(8)]

§ 2:51

Failure to offer a Medicare supplemental health insurance policy that provides only the core group of basic benefits: Section 1882(p)(9)(C) [42 U.S.C.S. 1395ss(p)(9)(C)]

§ 2:52

Failure to provide reinstatement rights to purchasers of Medicare supplemental health insurance policies who become eligible for Medicaid: Section 1882(q)(5) [42 U.S.C.S. 1395ss(q)(5)]

§ 2:53

Failure by issuers of Medicare supplemental health insurance policies to meet requirements for preexisting conditions, waiting periods, elimination periods, probationary periods, and price and coverage nondiscrimination: Section 1882(s)(3) [42 U.S.C.S. 1395ss(s)(3)]

§ 2:54

Special obligations for issuers of Medicare supplemental health insurance policies in selected States who provide benefits through contracts with networks of providers: Section 1882(t)(2) [42 U.S.C.S. 1395ss(t)(2)]

PART II, CHAPTER 3: SANCTIONS IN THE MEDICAID STATUTE

§ 3:4

Billing Medicaid eligibles or financially responsible relatives or representatives for medical expenses when third parties are liable to pay: Sections 1902(g) and 1902(a)(25) [42 U.S.C.S. 1396a(g) and 1396a(a)(25)]

PART II, CHAPTER 4: SANCTIONS IN TITLE XI OF THE SOCIAL SECURITY ACT

§ 4:1

Disclosure of information in the possession of the Secretary of Health and Human Services: Section 1106 [42 U.S.C.S. 1306]

§ 4:2

False representations about requirements of the Social Security Act: Section 1107(a) [42 U.S.C.S. 1307]

§ 4:3

False representations to elicit information from the Secretary of Health and Human Services: Section 1107(b) [42 U.S.C.S. 1307(b)]

§ 4:5

Failure to comply with subpoenas issued by the Comptroller General: Section 1125(b) [42 U.S.C.S. 1320a-4(b)]

§ 4:6

Exclusion from Medicare and State health care programs: Section 1128 [42 U.S.C.S. 1320a-6]

§ 4:7

Disclosure by institutions, organizations, and agencies of owners and other individuals sanctioned or convicted and of certain business relationships: Sections 1128(b)(9) and (b)(10), 1124, and 1126 [42 U.S.C.S. 1320a-7(b)(9) and (b)(10), 1320a-3, and 1320a-5]

§ 4:8

Civil money penalties: Section 1128A [42 U.S.C.S. 1320a-7a]

§ 4:9

Criminal penalties: false statements, false representations, concealment, failure to disclose, and conversion with respect to benefits and payments: Section 1128B(a) [42 U.S.C.S. 1320a-7b(a)]

§ 4:10

Criminal penalties: kickbacks, bribes, and rebates: Section 1128B(b) [42 U.S.C.S. 1320a-7b(b)]

§ 4:14

Misuse of Federal government names, symbols, and emblems: Section 1140 [42 U.S.C.S. 1320b-10]

§ 4:16

Violating reporting and disclosure obligations regarding the Medicare and Medicaid Coverage Data Bank: Section 1144 [42 U.S.C.S. 1320b-14]

PART II, CHAPTER 5: SANCTIONS IN THE HEALTH CARE QUALITY IMPROVEMENT ACT OF 1986

§ 5:2

Failure to report medical malpractice payments: Section 421 [42 U.S.C.S. 11131]

§ 5:5

Unlawful disclosure of information collected pursuant to the Health Care Quality Improvement Act: Section 427 [42 U.S.C.S. 11137]

Guide 5

CHAPTERS FOR PEER REVIEW ORGANIZATIONS

The following chapters set forth bases for imposing sanctions which are relevant to peer review organizations.

PART II, CHAPTER 2: SANCTIONS IN THE MEDICARE STATUTE

§ 2:17

Improper billing for services of assistants at cataract surgery: Sections 1842(k)(1) and (2) [42 U.S.C.A. 1395u-(k)(1) and (2)]

§ 2:18

Wrongful charges by nonparticipating physicians: Section 1842(l) [42 U.S.C.A. 1395u(l)]

§ 2:29

Prohibition against payment to individuals and entities sanctioned under the Social Security Act: Section 1862(e) [42 U.S.C.A. 1395y(e)]

§ 2:32

Terminating provider agreements: Section 1866(b) [42 U.S.C.A. 1395cc]

§ 2:58

Unnecessary hospital admissions and other inappropriate practices by hospitals to circumvent reimbursement requirements: Section 1886(f) [42 U.S.C.A. 1395ww(f)]

PART II, CHAPTER 3: SANCTIONS IN THE MEDICAID STATUTE

§ 3:2

Additional penalties for persons or entities sanctioned by exclusion under section 1128 or under section 1128A: Section 1902(a)(39) [42 U.S.C.A. 1396a(a)(39)]

§ 3:3

Disclosing information about sanctions against health care practitioners and providers: Section 1902(a)(49) and Section 1921 [42 U.S.C.A. 1396a(a)(49) and 42 U.S.C.A. 1396r-2]

§ 3:6

Providing Medicaid exclusions for the same grounds as Medicare exclusions: Section 1902(p)(1) [42 U.S.C.A. 1396a(p)(1)]

PART II, CHAPTER 4: SANCTIONS IN TITLE XI OF THE SOCIAL SECURITY ACT

§ 4:1

Disclosure of information in the possession of the Secretary of Health and Human Services: Section 1106 [42 U.S.C.A. 1306]

§ 4:5

Failure to comply with subpoenas issued by the Comptroller General: Section 1125(b) [42 U.S.C.A. 1320a-4(b)]

§ 4:6

Exclusion from Medicare and State health care programs: Section 1128 [42 U.S.C.A. 1320a-6]

§ 4:8

Civil money penalties: Section 1128A [42 U.S.C.A. 1320a-7a]

§ 4:13

Criminal penalties: violating a physician or supplier participation agreement or a Medicare assignment of benefits agreement: Section 1128B(e) [42 U.S.C.A. 1320a-7b(e)]

§ 4:13.1

Failure to report information about final adverse actions against healthcare providers, suppliers, and practitioners to the National Health Care Fraud and Abuse Data Collection Program: Section 1128E(b)(6) [42 U.S.C.A. 1320a-7e(b)(6)]

Affects: Any plan or program that provides health benefits, including a policy of health insurance, a contract of a service benefit organization, and a membership agreement with a health maintenance organization or other prepaid health plan

CMP: For each failure to report an adverse action: not more than $25,000

§ 4:17

Terminating contracts with peer review organizations: Section 1153 [42 U.S.C.A. 1320c-2]

§ 4:18

Disallowance of Medicare claims by peer review organizations: Section 1154 [42 U.S.C.A. 1320c-3]

§ 4:19

Sanctions recommended by peer review organizations: Section 1156 [42 U.S.C.A. 1320c-5]

§ 4:20

Unlawful disclosure of information obtained by peer review organizations: Section 1160 [42 U.S.C.A. 1320c-9]

§ 4:21

Disqualification of physicians from giving second opinions about surgery: Section 1164(b)(4)(D) [42 U.S.C.A. 1320c-13(b)(4)(D)]

◆ [NOTE: Repealed effective October 31, 1994, by section 146(a)(1) of the Social Security Act of 1994, P.L. 103-432]

Guide 6

CHAPTERS FOR RISK-SHARING ORGANIZATIONS: MANAGED CARE ENTITIES, HMOs, COMPETITIVE MEDICAL PLANS, MEDICARE+CHOICE AND PACE PROVIDERS

The following chapters set forth bases for imposing sanctions which are relevant to risk-sharing organizations, such as health maintenance organizations and competitive medical plans.

PART II, CHAPTER 2: SANCTIONS IN THE MEDICARE STATUTE

§ 2:10

Failure to include information about referring physicians on requests for payments or bills: Section 1833(q) [42 U.S.C.S. 1395l(q)]

§ 2:26.1

Termination of Medicare+Choice contracts: Section 1857(c)(2)

§ 2:26.2

Failure by Medicare+Choice organizations to comply with requirements for beneficiary protections and protections against fraud: Section 1857(d)

Affects: Medicare+Choice organizations

CMP: For substantial failure to provide medically necessary items or services; imposition of excessive premiums; illegal expulsion or failure to re-enroll an individual; practices which deny or discourage enrollment by individuals likely to need substantial future medical services; misrepresentation or submission of false information to the Secretary of Health and Human Services or any other individual or entity; interference with advice from healthcare professionals to enrollees; failure to establish procedures to enforce balance billing limits for contract providers in fee-for-service plans; employment of or contracts with individuals or entities excluded from Medicare: not more than $25,000 for each determination.

Also:

- For denying or discouraging enrollment and for making a misrepresentation or providing false information to the Secretary: not more than $100,000 for each determination
- For illegally denying or discouraging enrollment: $15,000 for each individual not enrolled
- For excessive premiums: double the excess charged
- For contract deficiencies (in conjunction with a contract termination proceeding) that adversely affected (or likely would have adversely affected) an enrollee: not more than $25,000 for each determination
- For contract deficiencies (in conjunction with a contract termination proceeding): $10,000 for each week a deficiency exists

Cross-reference to section 1128A, 42 U.S.C.A. 1320a-7a

§ 2:29

Prohibition against payment to individuals and entities sanctioned under the Social Security Act: Section 1862(e) [42 U.S.C.S. 1395y(e)]

§ 2:36

Failure by organizations with risk-sharing contracts under Medicare (such as health maintenance organizations and competitive medical plans) to provide required information about their services: Section 1876(c)(3)(C) [42 U.S.C.S. 1395mm(c)(3)(C)]

§ 2:37

Failure by organizations with risk-sharing contracts under Medicare (such as health maintenance organizations and competitive medical plans) to have at least one-half of their enrolled members be persons not eligible for Medicare or Medicaid: Section 1876(f) [42 U.S.C.S. 1395mm(f)]

§ 2:38

Failure by organizations with risk-sharing contracts (such as health maintenance organizations and competitive medical plans) to make prompt payment of claims: Section 1876(g) [42 U.S.C.S. 1395mm(g)]

§ 2:39

Limiting cost reimbursement to risk-sharing organizations (such as health maintenance organizations and competitive medical plans) not eligible to participate in Medicare: Section 1876(h) [42 U.S.C.S. 1395mm(h)]

§ 2:40

Terminating contracts of risk-sharing organizations (such as health maintenance organizations and competitive medical plans): Section 1876(i)(1) [42 U.S.C.S. 1395mm(i)(1)]

§ 2:41

Failure by risk-sharing organizations (such as health maintenance organizations and competitive medical plans) to comply with requirements for provision of services, premiums, treatment of applicants and members, truthfulness, prompt payment, and avoiding business relationships with excluded individuals and entities: Section 1876(i)(6) [42 U.S.C.S. 1395mm(i)(6)]

§ 2:42

Violating limitations on physician referrals and related reporting requirements: Section 1877 [42 U.S.C.S. 1395nn]

§ 2:62

Termination of PACE provider agreements: Section 1894 [42 U.S.C.A. 1395eee]

Affects: PACE providers

CMP: For substantial failure to provide medicaly necessary items and services; imposition of excessive premiums; illegally expelling or refusing to re-enroll an individual; practices that deny or discourage enrollment by individuals who may need substantial future medical services; misrepresenting or falsifying information to the Secretary of Health and Human Services, or to any other individual or entity; interference with medical advice by healthcare practitioners to enrollees; failure to enforce balance billing limits by physicians, providers, and suppliers in fee-for-service plans; employment of or contracting with individuals or entities excluded from Medicare: not more than $25,000 for each violation

Also:

- For each finding of illegally denying or refusing to enroll individuals: not more than $100,000 and $15,000 for each individual illegally denied or refused enrollment
- For misrepresentation to or providing false information to the Secretary: not more than $100,000
- For excessive premiums: double the excess charge

◆ NOTE: See text for variations applicable to acts prior to January 1, 1999

PART II, CHAPTER 3: SANCTIONS IN THE MEDICAID STATUTE

§ 3:2

Additional penalties for persons or entities sanctioned by exclusion under section 1128 or under section 1128A: Section 1902(a)(39) [42 U.S.C.A. 1396a(a)(39)]

§ 3:3

Disclosing information about sanctions against health care practitioners and providers: Section 1902(a)(49) and Section 1921 [42 U.S.C.S. 1396a(a)(49) and 42 U.S.C.S. 1396r-2]

§ 3:4

Billing Medicaid eligibles or financially responsible relatives or representatives for medical expenses when third parties are liable to pay: Sections 1902(g) and 1902(a)(25) [42 U.S.C.S. 1396a(g) and 1396a(a)(25)]

§ 3:6

Providing Medicaid exclusions for the same grounds as Medicare exclusions: Section 1902(p)(1) [42 U.S.C.S. 1396a(p)(1)]

§ 3:7

Excluding health maintenance organizations and other entities authorized to implement primary care case management or specialty physician services: Section 1902(p)(2) [42 U.S.C.S. 1396a(p)(2)]

§ 3:9

Failure by health maintenance organizations to comply with Medicaid requirements: Section 1903(m)(5) [42 U.S.C.S. 1396b(m)(5)]

§ 3:25

Failure by Medicaid managed care organizations to comply with fraud and abuse protection requirements: Sections 1932(d) and (e) [42 U.S.C.A. 1396u-2(e)]

Affects: Managed care entities

CMP: For discrimination based on health status or requirement for healthcare services: not more than $100,000, plus $15,000 for each individual affected by the discrimination

- For imposing an illegal premium: double the excess amount charged
- For any other violation: not more than $25,000

§ 3:26

Termination of Medicaid contracts with managed care entities: Section 1932(e)(4) [42 U.S.C.A. 1396u-2(e)(4)]

§ 3:27

Termination of Medicaid PACE provider agreements: Section 1934(e)(5) [42 U.S.C.A. 1396u-4(e)(5)]

§ 3:28

Intermediate sanctions for Medicaid PACE providers: Section 1934(e)(6)(B) [42 U.S.C.A. 1396u-4(e)(6)(B)]

Affects: Medicaid PACE providers

CMP: For substantial failure to provide medically necessary items and services; imposition of excessive premiums; illegally expelling or refusing to re-enroll an individual; practices that deny or discourage enrollment by individuals who may need substantial future medical services; misrepresentation to or providing false information to the Secretary of Health and Human Services, or to any other individual or entity; interference with medical advice to enrollees by healthcare practitioners; failure to impose balance billing limits by physicians, providers, and suppliers in fee-for-services plans; employment of or contracting with individuals or entities excluded from Medicare: not more than $25,000 for each violation

Also: For each finding of illegal denial of enrollment or refusal to re-enroll an individual: not more than $100,000, plus $15,000 for each individual not enrolled as a result of the illegal action

- For misrepresentation or providing false information to the Secretary: not more than $100,000
- For excessive premiums: double the excess amount

◆ NOTE: See text for variations applicable to acts prior to January 1, 1999.

PART II, CHAPTER 4: SANCTIONS IN TITLE XI OF THE SOCIAL SECURITY ACT

§ 4:2

False representations about requirements of the Social Security Act: Section 1107(a) [42 U.S.C.S. 1307]

§ 4:4

Failure to comply with State health planning requirements: Section 1122 [42 U.S.C.S. 1320a-1]

§ 4:5

Failure to comply with subpoenas issued by the Comptroller General: Section 1125(b) [42 U.S.C.S. 1320a]

§ 4:6

Exclusion from Medicare and State health care programs: Section 1128 [42 U.S.C.S. 1320a-6]

§ 4:7

Disclosure by institutions, organizations, and agencies of owners and other individuals sanctioned or convicted and of certain business relationships: Sections 1128(b)(9) and (b)(10), 1124, and 1126 [42 U.S.C.S. 1320a-7(b)(9) and (b)(10), 1320a-3, and 1320a-5]

§ 4:8

Civil money penalties: Section 1128A [42 U.S.C.S. 1320a-7a]

§ 4:9

Criminal penalties: false statements, false representations, concealment, failure to disclose, and conversion with respect to benefits and payments: Section 1128B(a) [42 U.S.C.S. 1320a-7b(a)]

§ 4:10

Criminal penalties: kickbacks, bribes, and rebates: Section 1128B(b) [42 U.S.C.S. 1320a-7b(b)]

§ 4:13.1

Failure to report information about final adverse actions against healthcare providers, suppliers, and practitioners to the National Health Care Fraud and Abuse Data Collection Program: Section 1128E(b)(6) [42 U.S.C.A. 1320a-7e(b)(6)]

Affects: Any plan or program that provides health benefits, including a policy of health insurance, a contract of a service benefit organization, and a membership agreement with a health maintenance organization or other prepaid health plan

CMP: For each failure to report an adverse action: not more than $25,000

§ 4:14

Misuse of Federal government names, symbols, and emblems: Section 1140 [42 U.S.C.S. 1320b-10]

§ 4:18

Disallowance of Medicare claims by peer review organizations: Section 1154 [42 U.S.C.S. 1320c-3]

§ 4:19

Sanctions recommended by peer review organizations: Section 1156 [42 U.S.C.S. 1320c-5]

§ 4:20

Unlawful disclosure of information obtained by peer review organizations: Section 1160 [42 U.S.C.S. 1320c-9]

§ 4:21

Disqualification of physicians from giving second opinions about surgery: Section 1164(b)(4)(D) [42 U.S.C.S. 1320c-13(b)(4)(D)]

◆ [NOTE: Repealed effective October 31, 1994, by section 146(a)(1) of the Social Security Act of 1994, P.L. 103-432]

PART II, CHAPTER 5: SANCTIONS IN THE HEALTH CARE QUALITY IMPROVEMENT ACT OF 1986

§ 5:1

Failure by health care entities to report adverse actions against physicians: Section 411(b) and Section 423(c)(1) [42 U.S.C.S. 11111(b) and 11133(c)(1)]

§ 5:2

Failure to report medical malpractice payments: Section 421 [42 U.S.C.S. 11131]

§ 5:3

Failure by medical examiner boards to report information about adverse actions taken by health care entities against physicians and about health care entities that fail to make such reports: Sections 422 and 423(c)(2) [42 U.S.C.S. 11132 and 11133(c)(2)]

§ 5:4

Failure by hospitals to obtain adverse information about physicians from the Secretary of Health and Human Services and from State medical examiner boards: Section 425 [42 U.S.C.S. 11135]

§ 5:5

Unlawful disclosure of information collected pursuant to the Health Care Quality Improvement Act: Section 427 [42 U.S.C.S. 11137]

Guide 4

CHAPTERS FOR PHYSICIANS

The following chapters set forth bases for imposing sanctions which are relevant to physicians.

PART II, CHAPTER 2: SANCTIONS IN THE MEDICARE STATUTE

§ 2:1

Falsifying assessments of residents of skilled nursing facilities: Section 1819(b)(3)(B)(ii) [42 U.S.C.A. 1395i-3(b)(3)(B)(ii)]

§ 2:1.1

Violation of requirements for private contracts with Medicare beneficiaries by physicians and other practitioners: Section 1802(b) [42 U.S.C.A. 1395a(b)]

§ 2:2

Abuse or neglect of skilled nursing facility residents or misappropriation of their property: Section 1819(g)(1)-(C) [42 U.S.C.A. 1395i-3(g)(1)(C)]

§ 2:2.1

Failure by physicians, providers, suppliers, and others to furnish an itemized statement of items and services provided to Medicare beneficiaries: Section 1806 [42 U.S.C.A. 1395b-7]

Affects: Physicians, providers, suppliers, and any other person (including an organization, agency, or other entity)

CMP: $100.00 for each failure to furnish an itemized statement

Assessment: None

Cross-reference to section 1128A, 42 U.S.C.A. 1320a-7a

§ 2:5

Improper billing for clinical diagnostic laboratory tests: Section 1833(h)(5)(D) [42 U.S.C.A. 1395l(h)(5)(D)]

§ 2:6

Improper billing for intraocular lenses: Section 1833(i)(6) [42 U.S.C.A. 1395l(i)(6)]

§ 2:7

Improper billing for services of a certified registered nurse anesthetist: Section 1833(l)(5)(B) [42 U.S.C.A. 1395l(l)(5)(B)]

§ 2:8

Overcharging by physicians for services of a certified registered nurse anesthetist: Section 1833(l)(6) [42 U.S.C.A. 1395l(l)(6)]

§ 2:10

Failure to include information about referring physicians on requests for payments or bills: Section 1833(q) [42 U.S.C.A. 1395l(q)]

§ 2:11

Failure to bill on an assignment related basis for covered services of a nurse practitioner or clinical nurse specialist: Section 1833(r)(3)(B) [42 U.S.C.A. 1395(r)(3)(B)]

◆ [NOTE: Repealed effected January 1, 1995, by section 123(b)(2)(B)(iii) of the Social Security Act Amendments of 1994, P.L. 103-432]

§ 2:13

Improper distribution by suppliers of forms documenting medical necessity: Secton 1834(a)(16) [42 U.S.C.A. 1395m(a)(16)]

◆ [NOTE: Repealed effective after December 30, 1994, by section 131(a)(2) of the Social Security Act Amendments of 1994, P.L. 103-432]

§ 2:14

Improper billing by physicians or suppliers for radiologist services: Section 1834(b)(5)(C) [42 U.S.C.A. 1395m(b)(5)(C)]

§ 2:15

Overcharging for services of a physician assistant or nurse practitioner: Section 1842(b)(12)(C) [42 U.S.C.A. 1395u(b)(12)(C)]

◆ [NOTE: Repealed effective October 31, 1994, by section 123(b)(2)(B) of the Social Security Act Amendments of 1994, P.L. 103-432]

§ 2:15.1

Failure by practitioners to bill on an assignment-related basis: Section 1842(b)(18) and Sections 1834(k) and (l) [42 U.S.C.A. 1395u(b)(18) and 42 U.S.C.A. 1395m(k) and (l)]

Affects: Physicians assistants, nurse practitioners, clinical nurse specialists, certified registered nurse anesthetists, certified nurse-midwives, clinical social workers, clinical psychologists, outpatient rehabilitation suppliers, ambulance suppliers

CMP: Same as for civil monetary penalty under section 1128A(a), 42 U.S.C.A. 1320a-7a(a)

Assessment: Same as under Section 1128A, with provision for compensation from proceeds to overcharged patients

§ 2:15.2

Denial, termination, and nonrenewal of physician and supplier participation agreements: Section 1842(h) [42 U.S.C.A. 1395u(h)]

§ 2:16

Violating the freeze on physician fees: Section 1842(j)(1) [42 U.S.C.A. 1395u(j)(1)]

§ 2:17

Improper billing for services of assistants at cataract surgery: Sections 1842(k)(1) and (2) [42 U.S.C.A. 1395u-(k)(1) and (2)]

§ 2:18

Wrongful charges by nonparticipating physicians: Section 1842(l) [42 U.S.C.A. 1395u(l)]

§ 2:19

Wrongful charges by nonparticipating physicians for certain elective surgical procedures: Section 1842(m) [42 U.S.C.A. 1395u(m)]

§ 2:20

Physician failure to eliminate the mark-up for certain purchased diagnostic tests: Section 1842(n) [42 U.S.C.A. 1395u(n)]

§ 2:21

Physician failure to provide appropriate diagnosis codes on bills: Section 1842(p) [42 U.S.C.A. 1395u(p)]

§ 2:22

Intermediate sanctions for providers of clinical diagnostic laboratory tests: Section 1846 [42 U.S.C.A. 1395w-2]

§ 2:23

Wrongful charges for interpreting electrocardiograms: Section 1848(b)(3) [42 U.S.C.A. 1395w-4(b)(3)]

◆ [NOTE: Repealed for services after January 1, 1994, section 13514(a) of the Omnibus Budget Reconciliation Act of 1993, P.L. 103-66]

§ 2:24

Violating limitations on physician charges by nonparticipating physicians, suppliers, or other persons after 1990: Section 1848(g)(1) [42 U.S.C.A. 1395w-4(g)(1)]

§ 2:25

Failure to bill on an assignment-related basis for services to persons enrolled under Medicare Part B and eligible for Medicaid: Section 1848(g)(3) [42 U.S.C.A. 1395w-4(g)(3)]

§ 2:26

Failure by physicians, suppliers, and others, including their employers and related facilities, to submit claims on specified claim forms: Section 1848(g)(4) [42 U.S.C.A. 1395w-(g)(4)]

§ 2:29

Prohibition against payment to individuals and entities sanctioned under the Social Security Act: Section 1862(e) [42 U.S.C.A. 1395y(e)]

§ 2:30

Special obligations regarding pacemakers: Section 1862(h) [42 U.S.C.A. 1395y(h)]

§ 2:31

Failure by hospitals to make timely review of long-stay cases: Section 1866(d) [42 U.S.C.A. 1395cc(d)]

§ 2:33

Failure by hospitals and skilled nursing facilities to make timely review of long-stay cases: Section 1866(d) [42 U.S.C.A. 1395cc(d)]

§ 2:35

Failure by hospitals and certain physicians to examine and treat persons for emergency medical conditions and women in labor: Section 1867 [42 U.S.C.A. 1395(dd)]

§ 2:42

Violating limitations on physician referrals and related reporting requirements: Section 1877 [42 U.S.C.A. 1395nn]

§ 2:56

Withholding Medicare payments from overpaid Medicaid providers: Section 1885 [42 U.S.C.A. 1395vv]

§ 2:61

Offsetting Medicare payments to individuals to collect past-due obligations arising from breach of scholarship and loan contracts: Section 1892 [42 U.S.C.A. 1395ccc]

PART II, CHAPTER 3: SANCTIONS IN THE MEDICAID STATUTE

§ 3:2

Additional penalties for persons or entities sanctioned by exclusion under section 1128 or under section 1128A: Section 1902(a)(39) [42 U.S.C.A. 1396a(a)(39)]

§ 3:3

Disclosing information about sanctions against health care practitioners and providers: Section 1902(a)(49) and Section 1921 [42 U.S.C.A. 1396a(a)(49) and 42 U.S.C.A. 1396r-2]

§ 3:4

Billing Medicaid eligibles or financially responsible relatives or representatives for medical expenses when third parties are liable to pay: Sections 1902(g) and 1902(a)(25) [42 U.S.C.A. 1396a(g) and 1396a(a)(25)]

§ 3:5.1

Overcharging Medicaid eligibles who are qualified Medicare beneficiaries: Section 1902(n)(3) [42 U.S.C.A. 1396a(n)(3)]

◆ NOTE: Any sanction that may be imposed upon a provider or Medicaid managed care organization for excess charges under Medicaid or Medicare applies.

§ 3:6

Providing Medicaid exclusions for the same grounds as Medicare exclusions: Section 1902(p)(1) [42 U.S.C.A. 1396a(p)(1)]

§ 3:7

Excluding health maintenance organizations and other entities authorized to implement primary care case management or specialty physician services: Section 1902(p)(2) [42 U.S.C.A. 1396a(p)(2)]

§ 3:13

Requiring States to withhold Medicaid underpayments to offset Medicare overpayments: Section 1914 [42 U.S.C.A. 1396m]

§ 3:14

Failure by nursing facilities to comply with Medicaid requirements for resident assessments: Section 1919(b) [42 U.S.C.A. 1396r(b)]

§ 3:15

Abuse or neglect of nursing facility residents or misappropriation of their property: Section 1919(g)(1)(C) [42 U.S.C.A. 1396r(g)(1)(C)]

PART II, CHAPTER 4: SANCTIONS IN TITLE XI OF THE SOCIAL SECURITY ACT

§ 4:5

Failure to comply with subpoenas issued by the Comptroller General: Section 1125(b) [42 U.S.C.A. 1320a-4(b)]

§ 4:6

Exclusion from Medicare and State health care programs: Section 1128 [42 U.S.C.A. 1320a-6]

§ 4:7

Disclosure by institutions, organizations, and agencies of owners and other individuals sanctioned or convicted and of certain business relationships: Sections 1128(b)(9) and (b)(10), 1124, and 1126 [42 U.S.C.A. 1320a-7(b)(9) and (b)(10), 1320a-3, and 1320a-5]

§ 4:8

Civil money penalties: Section 1128A [42 U.S.C.A. 1320a-7a]

§ 4:9

Criminal penalties: false statements, false representations, concealment, failure to disclose, and conversion with respect to benefits and payments: Section 1128B(a) [42 U.S.C.A. 1320a-7b(a)]

§ 4:10

Criminal penalties: kickbacks, bribes, and rebates: Section 1128B(b) [42 U.S.C.A. 1320a-7b(b)]

§ 4:13

Criminal penalties: violating a physician or supplier participation agreement or a Medicare assignment of benefits agreement: Section 1128B(e) [42 U.S.C.A. 1320a-7b(e)]

§ 4:13.1

Failure to report information about final adverse actions against healthcare providers, suppliers, and practitioners to the National Health Care Fraud and Abuse Data Collection Program: Section 1128E(b)(6) [42 U.S.C.A. 1320a-7e(b)(6)]

Affects: Any plan or program that provides health benefits, including a policy of health insurance, a contract of a service benefit organization, and a membership agreement with a health maintenance organization or other prepaid health plan

CMP: For each failure to report an adverse action: not more than $25,000

§ 4:14

Misuse of Federal government names, symbols, and emblems: Section 1140 [42 U.S.C.A. 1320b-10]

§ 4:18

Disallowance of Medicare claims by peer review organizations: Section 1154 [42 U.S.C.A. 1320c-3]

§ 4:19

Sanctions recommended by peer review organizations: Section 1156 [42 U.S.C.A. 1320c-5]

§ 4:20

Unlawful disclosure of information obtained by peer review organizations: Section 1160 [42 U.S.C.A. 1320c-9]

§ 4:21

Disqualification of physicians from giving second opinions about surgery: Section 1164(b)(4)(D) [42 U.S.C.A. 1320c-13(b)(4)(D)]

◆ [NOTE: Repealed effective October 31, 1994, by section 146(a)(1) of the Social Security Act of 1994, P.L. 103-432]

PART II, CHAPTER 5: SANCTIONS IN THE HEALTH CARE QUALITY IMPROVEMENT ACT OF 1986

§ 5:1

Failure by health care entities to report adverse actions against physicians: Section 411(b) and Section 423(c)(1) [42 U.S.C.A. 11111(b) and 11133(c)(1)]

§ 5:2

Failure to report medical malpractice payments: Section 421 [42 U.S.C.A. 11131]

§ 5:3

Failure by medical examiner boards to report information about adverse actions taken by health care entities against physicians and about health care entities that fail to make such reports: Sections 422 and 423(c)(2) [42 U.S.C.A. 11132 and 11133(c)(2)]

§ 5:4

Failure by hospitals to obtain adverse information about physicians from the Secretary of Health and Human Services and from State medical examiner boards: Section 425 [42 U.S.C.A. 11135]

§ 5:5

Unlawful disclosure of information collected pursuant to the Health Care Quality Improvement Act: Section 427 [42 U.S.C.A. 11137]

Guide 3

CHAPTERS FOR NURSING HOMES

The following chapters set forth bases for imposing sanctions which are relevant to nursing homes.

PART II, CHAPTER 2: SANCTIONS IN THE MEDICARE STATUTE

§ 2:1

Falsifying assessments of residents of skilled nursing facilities: Section 1819(b)(3)(B)(ii) [42 U.S.C.A. 1395i-3(b)(3)(B)(ii)]

§ 2:2

Abuse or neglect of skilled nursing facility residents or misappropriation of their property: Section 1819(g)(1)-(C) [42 U.S.C.A. 1395i-3(g)(1)(C)]

§ 2:2.1

Failure by physicians, providers, suppliers, and others to furnish an itemized statement of items and services provided to Medicare beneficiaries: Section 1806 [42 U.S.C.A. 1395b-7]

Affects: Physicians, providers, suppliers, and any other person (including an organization, agency, or other entity)

CMP: $100.00 for each failure to furnish an itemized statement

Assessment: None

Cross-reference to section 1128A, 42 U.S.C.A. 1320a-7a

§ 2:3

Giving a skilled nursing facility advance notice of a State or Federal survey: Section 1819(g)(2) [42 U.S.C.A. 1395i-3(g)(2)]

§ 2:4

Failing a skilled nursing facility survey: Sections 1819(g) and (h) [42 U.S.C.A. 1395i-3(g) and (h)]

§ 2:10

Failure to include information about referring physicians on requests for payments or bills: Section 1833(q) [42 U.S.C.A. 1395l(q)]

§ 2:11

Failure to bill on an assignment related basis for covered services of a nurse practitioner or clinical nurse specialist: Section 1833(r)(3)(B) [42 U.S.C.A. 1395(r)(3)(B)]

◆ [NOTE: Repealed effective January 1, 1995, by section 123(b)(2)(B)(iii) of the Social Security Act Amendments of 1994, P.L. 103-432]

§ 2:29

Prohibition against payment to individuals and entities sanctioned under the Social Security Act: Section 1862(e) [42 U.S.C.A. 1395y(e)]

§ 2:31

Publicizing provider survey results: Section 1864 [42 U.S.C.A. 1395aa]

§ 2:32

Terminating provider agreements: Section 1866(b) [42 U.S.C.A. 1395cc]

§ 2:33

Failure by hospitals and skilled nursing facilities to make timely review of long-stay cases: Section 1866(d) [42 U.S.C.A. 1395cc(d)]

§ 2:35

Failure by hospitals to make timely review of long-stay cases: Section 1866(d) [42 U.S.C.A. 1395cc(d)]

§ 2:42

Violating limitations on physician referrals and related reporting requirements: Section 1877 [42 U.S.C.A. 1395nn]

§ 2:55

Terminating provider agreements of hospital providers of extended care services: Section 1883 [42 U.S.C.A. 1395tt]

§ 2:56

Withholding Medicare payments from overpaid Medicaid providers: Section 1885 [42 U.S.C.A. 1395vv]

PART II, CHAPTER 3: SANCTIONS IN THE MEDICAID STATUTE

§ 3:1

Publicizing findings of State surveys of health care facilities: Section 1902(a)(36) [42 U.S.C.A. 1396a(a)(36)]

§ 3:2

Additional penalties for persons or entities sanctioned by exclusion under section 1128 or under section 1128A: Section 1902(a)(39) [42 U.S.C.A. 1396a(a)(39)]

§ 3:3

Disclosing information about sanctions against health care practitioners and providers: Section 1902(a)(49) and Section 1921 [42 U.S.C.A. 1396a(a)(49) and 42 U.S.C.A. 1396r-2]

§ 3:4

Billing Medicaid eligibles or financially responsible relatives or representatives for medical expenses when third parties are liable to pay: Sections 1902(g) and 1902(a)(25) [42 U.S.C.A. 1396a(g) and 1396a(a)(25)]

§ 3:5

Failure by an intermediate care facility for the mentally retarded to comply with Medicaid conditions for participation: Section 1902(i) [42 U.S.C.A. 1396a(i)]

§ 3:5.1

Overcharging Medicaid eligibles who are qualified Medicare beneficiaries: Section 1902(n)(3) [42 U.S.C.A. 1396a(n)(3)]

◆ NOTE: Any sanction that may be imposed upon a provider or Medicaid managed care organization for excess charges under Medicaid or Medicare applies.

§ 3:6

Providing Medicaid exclusions for the same grounds as Medicare exclusions: Section 1902(p)(1) [42 U.S.C.A. 1396a(p)(1)]

§ 3:11

Canceling certification and approval of skilled nursing facilities, intermediate care facilities, and intermediate care facilities for the mentally retarded: Section 1910 [42 U.S.C.A. 1396i]

§ 3:13

Requiring States to withhold Medicaid underpayments to offset Medicare overpayments: Section 1914 [42 U.S.C.A. 1396m]

§ 3:14

Failure by nursing facilities to comply with Medicaid requirements for resident assessments: Section 1919(b) [42 U.S.C.A. 1396r(b)]

§ 3:15

Abuse or neglect of nursing facility residents or misappropriation of their property: Section 1919(g)(1)(C) [42 U.S.C.A. 1396r(g)(1)(C)]

§ 3:16

Giving nursing facilities advance notice of a survey: Section 1919(g)(2)(A)(i) [42 U.S.C.A. 1396r(g)(2)(A)(i)]

§ 3:17

Failing a nursing facility survey: Section 1919(g)(5), 1919(h), and 1919(i) [42 U.S.C.A. 1396r(g)(5), 1396r(h), and 1396r(i)]

§ 3:18

Failure by intermediate care facilities for the mentally retarded to meet Federal standards: Section 1922 [42 U.S.C.A. 1396r-3]

PART II, CHAPTER 4: SANCTIONS IN TITLE XI OF THE SOCIAL SECURITY ACT

§ 4:1

Disclosure of information in the possession of the Secretary of Health and Human Services: Section 1106 [42 U.S.C.A. 1306]

§ 4:2

False representations about requirements of the Social Security Act: Section 1107(a) [42 U.S.C.A. 1307]

§ 4:3

False representations to elicit information from the Secretary of Health and Human Services: Section 1107(b) [42 U.S.C.A. 1307(b)]

§ 4:4

Failure to comply with State health planning requirements: Section 1122 [42 U.S.C.A. 1320a-1]

§ 4:5

Failure to comply with subpoenas issued by the Comptroller General: Section 1125(b) [42 U.S.C.A. 1320a-4(b)]

§ 4:6

Exclusion from Medicare and State health care programs: Section 1128 [42 U.S.C.A. 1320a-6]

§ 4:7

Disclosure by institutions, organizations, and agencies of owners and other individuals sanctioned or convicted and of certain business relationships: Sections 1128(b)(9) and (b)(10), 1124, and 1126 [42 U.S.C.A. 1320a-7(b)(9) and (b)(10), 1320a-3, and 1320a-5]

§ 4:8

Civil money penalties: Section 1128A [42 U.S.C.A. 1320a-7a]

§ 4:9

Criminal penalties: false statements, false representations, concealment, failure to disclose, and conversion with respect to benefits and payments: Section 1128B(a) [42 U.S.C.A. 1320a-7b(a)]

§ 4:10

Criminal penalties: kickbacks, bribes, and rebates: Section 1128B(b) [42 U.S.C.A. 1320a-7b(b)]

§ 4:11

Criminal penalties: false statements and false representations to qualify for provider status: Section 1128B(c) [42 U.S.C.A. 1320a-7b(c)]

§ 4:12

Criminal penalties: excessive Medicaid charges and unlawful financial preconditions for care in hospitals and nursing facilities: Section 1128B(d) [42 U.S.C.A. 1320a-7b(d)]

§ 4:13.1

Failure to report information about final adverse actions against healthcare providers, suppliers, and practitioners to the National Health Care Fraud and Abuse Data Collection Program: Section 1128E(b)(6) [42 U.S.C.A. 1320a-7e(b)(6)]

Affects: Any plan or program that provides health benefits, including a policy of health insurance, a contract of a service benefit organization, and a membership agreement with a health maintenance organization or other prepaid health plan

CMP: For each failure to report an adverse action: not more than $25,000

§ 4:14

Misuse of Federal government names, symbols, and emblems: Section 1140 [42 U.S.C.A. 1320b-10]

§ 4:18

Disallowance of Medicare claims by peer review organizations: Section 1154 [42 U.S.C.A. 1320c-3]

§ 4:19

Sanctions recommended by peer review organizations: Section 1156 [42 U.S.C.A. 1320c-5]

§ 4:20

Unlawful disclosure of information obtained by peer review organizations: Section 1160 [42 U.S.C.A. 1320c-9]

PART II, CHAPTER 5: SANCTIONS IN THE HEALTH CARE QUALITY IMPROVEMENT ACT OF 1986

§ 5:1

Failure by health care entities to report adverse actions against physicians: Section 411(b) and Section 423(c)(1) [42 U.S.C.A. 11111(b) and 11133(c)(1)]

§ 5:2

Failure to report medical malpractice payments: Section 421 [42 U.S.C.A. 11131]

§ 5:3

Failure by medical examiner boards to report information about adverse actions taken by health care entities against physicians and about health care entities that fail to make such reports: Sections 422 and 423(c)(2) [42 U.S.C.A. 11132 and 11133(c)(2)]

§ 5:4

Failure by hospitals to obtain adverse information about physicians from the Secretary of Health and Human Services and from State medical examiner boards: Section 425 [42 U.S.C.A. 11135]

§ 5:5

Unlawful disclosure of information collected pursuant to the Health Care Quality Improvement Act: Section 427 [42 U.S.C.A. 11137]

Guide 1

CHAPTERS OF GENERAL APPLICABILITY

The following chapters set forth bases for imposing sanctions on almost any person or entity participating in Medicare and Federally funded State health care programs, including medical practitioners, providers, and suppliers.

PART II, CHAPTER 2: SANCTIONS IN THE MEDICARE STATUTE

§ 2:1.1

Violation of requirements for private contracts with Medicare beneficiaries by physicians and other practitioners: Section 1802(b) [42 U.S.C.A. 1395a(b)]

§ 2:2.1

Failure by physicians, providers, suppliers, and others to furnish an itemized statement of items and services provided to Medicare beneficiaries: Section 1806 [42 U.S.C.A. 1395b-7]

Affects: Physicians, providers, suppliers, and any other person (including an organization, agency, or other entity)

CMP: $100.00 for each failure to furnish an itemized statement

Assessment: None

Cross-reference to section 1128A, 42 U.S.C.A. 1320a-7a

§ 2:7

Improper billing for services of a certified registered nurse anesthetist: Section 1833(l)(5)(B) [42 U.S.C.A. 1395l(l)(5)(B)]

◆ [NOTE: This sanction was repealed affective January 1, 1995, by section 123(b)(2)(A)(i) of the Social Security Act Amendments of 1994, P.L. 100-432.

§ 2:10

Failure to include information about referring physicians on requests for payments or bills: Section 1833(q) [42 U.S.C.A. 1395l(q)]

§ 2:11

Failure to bill on an assignment related basis for covered services of a nurse practitioner or clinical nurse specialist: Section 1833(r)(3)(B) [42 U.S.C.A. 1395(r)(3)(B)]

◆ [NOTE: Repealed effective January 1, 1995, by section 123(b)(2)(B)(iii) of the Social Security Act Amendments of 1994, P.L. 103-432.]

§ 2:13

Improper distribution by suppliers of forms documenting medical necessity: Section 1834(a)(16) [42 U.S.C.A. 1395m(a)(16)]

◆ [NOTE: Repealed effective after December 30, 1994, by section 131(a)(2) of the Social Security Act Amendments of 1994, P.L. 103-432.]

§ 2:15.1

Failure by practitioners to bill on an assignment-related basis: Section 1842(b)(18) and Sections 1834(k) and (l) [42 U.S.C.A. 1395u(b)(18) and 42 U.S.C.A. 1395m(k) and (l)]

Affects: Physicians assistants, nurse practitioners, clinical nurse specialists, certified registered nurse anesthetists, certified nurse-midwives, clinical social workers, clinical psychologists, outpatient rehabilitation suppliers, ambulance suppliers

CMP: Same as for civil monetary penalty under section 1128A(a), 42 U.S.C.A. 1320a-7a(a)

Assessment: Same as under Section 1128A, with provision for compensation from proceeds to overcharged patients

§ 2:15.2

Denial, termination, and nonrenewal of physician and supplier participation agreements: Section 1842(h) [42 U.S.C.A. 1395u(h)]

§ 2:21

Failure by physicians and other practitioners to provide appropriate diagnosis codes on bills: Section 1842(p) [42 U.S.C.A. 1395u(p)]

§ 2:25

Failure to bill on an assignment-related basis for services to persons enrolled under Medicare Part B and eligible for Medicaid: Section 1848(g)(3) [42 U.S.C.A. 1395w-4(g)(3)]

§ 2:26

Failure by physicians, suppliers, and others, including their employers and related facilities, to submit claims on specified claim forms: Section 1848(g)(4) [42 U.S.C.A. 1395w-(g)(4)]

§ 2:26.1

Termination of Medicare+Choice contracts: Section 1857(c)(2)

§ 2:26.2

Failure by Medicare+Choice organization to comply with requirements for beneficiary protections and protections against fraud: Section 1857(d)

Affects: Medicare+Choice organizations

CMP: For substantial failure to provide medically necessary items or services; imposition of excessive premiums; illegal expulsion or failure to re-enroll an individual; practices which deny or discourage enrollment by individuals likely to need substantial future medical services; misrepresentation or submission of false information to the Secretary of Health and Human Services or any other individual or entity; interference with advice from health care professionals to enrollees; failure to establish procedures to enforce balance billing limits for contract providers in fee-for-service plans; employment of or contracts with individuals or entities excluded from Medicare: not more than $25,000 for each determination.

Also:

- For denying or discouraging enrollment and for making a misrepresentation or providing false information to the Secretary: not more than $100,000 for each determination
- For illegally denying or discouraging enrollment: $15,000 for each individual not enrolled
- For excessive premiums: double the excess charged

- For contract deficiencies (in conjunction with a contract termination proceeding) that adversely affected (or likely would have adversely affected) an enrollee: not more than $25,000 for each determination
- For contract deficiencies (in conjunction with a contract termination proceeding): $10,000 for each week a deficiency exists

Cross-reference to section 1128A, 42 U.S.C.A. 1320a-7a

§ 2:29

Prohibition against payment to individuals and entities sanctioned under the Social Security Act: Section 1862(e) [42 U.S.C.A. 1395y(e)]

§ 2:31

Publicizing provider survey results: Section 1864 [42 U.S.C.A. 1395aa]

§ 2:32

Terminating provider agreements: Section 1866(b) [42 U.S.C.A. 1395cc]

§ 2:41

Violating limitations on physician referrals and related reporting requirements: Section 1877 [42 U.S.C.A. 1395nn]

§ 2:56

Withholding Medicare payments from overpaid Medicaid providers: Section 1885 [42 U.S.C.A. 1395vv]

§ 2:61

Offsetting Medicare payments to individuals to collect past-due obligations arising from breach of scholarship and loan contracts: Section 1892 [42 U.S.C.A. 1395ccc]

§ 2:62

Termination o PACE provider agreements: Section 1894 [42 U.S.C.A. 1395eee]

Affects: PACE providers

CMP: For substantial failure to provide medically necessary items and services; imposition of excessive premiums; illegally expelling or refusing to re-enroll an individual; practices that deny or discourage enrollment by individuals who may need substantial future medical services; misrepresenting or falsifying information to the Secretary of Health and Human Services, or to any other individual or entity; interference with medical advice by healthcare practitioners to enrollees; failure to enforce balance billing limits by physicians, providers, and suppliers in fee-for-service plans; employment of or contracting with individuals or entities excluded from Medicare: not more than $25,000 for each violation

Also:

- For each finding of illegally denying or refusing to enroll individuals: not more than $100,000 and $15,000 for each individual illegally denied or refused enrollment
- For misrepresentation to or providing false information to the Secretary: not more than $100,000
- For excessive premiums: double the excess charge

◆ NOTE: See text for variations applicable to acts prior to January 1, 1999.

PART II, CHAPTER 3: SANCTIONS IN THE MEDICAID STATUTE

§ 3:1

Publicizing findings of State surveys of health care facilities: Section 1902(a)(36) [42 U.S.C.A. 1396a(a)(36)]

§ 3:2

Additional penalties for persons or entities sanctioned by exclusion under section 1128 or under section 1128A: Section 1902(a)(39) [42 U.S.C.A. 1396a(a)(39)]

§ 3:3

Disclosing information about sanctions against health care practitioners and providers: Section 1902(a)(49) and Section 1921 [42 U.S.C.A. 1396a(a)(49) and 42 U.S.C.A. 1396r-2]

§ 3:5.1

Overcharging Medicaid eligibles who are qualified Medicare beneficiaries: Section 1902(n)(3) [42 U.S.C.A. 1396a(n)(3)]

◆ NOTE: Any sanction that may be imposed upon a provider or Medicaid managed care organization for excess charges nuder Medicaid or Medicare applies.

§ 3:6

Providing Medicaid exclusions for the same grounds as Medicare exclusions: Section 1902(p)(1) [42 U.S.C.A. 1396a(p)(1)]

§ 3:25

Failure by Medicaid managed care organizations to comply with fraud and abuse protection requirements: Sections 1932(d) and (e) [42 U.S.C.A. 1396u-2(e)]

Affects: Managed care entities

CMP: For discrimination based on health status or requirement for healthcare services; not more than $100,000, plus $15,000 for each individual affected by the discrimination

- For imposing an illegal premium: double the excess amount charged
- For any other violation: not more than $25,000

§ 3:26

Termination of Medicaid contracts with managed care entities: Section 1932(e)(4) [42 U.S.C.A. 1396u-2(e)(4)]

§ 3:27

Termination of Medicaid PACE provider agreements: Section 1934(e)(5) [42 U.S.C.A. 1396u-4(e)(5)]

§ 3:28

Intermediate sanctions for Medicaid PACE providers: Section 1934(e)(6)(B) [42 U.S.C.A. 1396u-4(e)(6)(B)]

Affects: Medicaid PACE providers

CMP: For substantial failure to provide medically necessary items and services; imposition of excessive premiums; illegally expelling or refusing to re-enroll an individual; practices that deny or discourage enrollment by individuals who may need substantial future medical services; misrepresentation to or providing false information to the Secretary of Health and Human Services, or to any other individual or entity; interference with medical advice to enrollees by healthcare practitioners; failure to impose balance billing limits by physicians, providers, and suppliers in fee-for-services plans; employment of or contracting with individuals or entities excluded from Medicare: not more than $25,000 for each violation

Also: For each finding of illegal denial of enrollment or refusal to re-enroll an individual: not more than $100,000, plus $15,000 for each individual not enrolled as a result of the illegal action

- For misrepresentation or providing false information to the Secretary: not mare than $100,000
- For excessive premiums: double the excess amount

◆ NOTE: See text for variations applicable to acts prior to January 1, 1999.

§ 3:31

Requiring States to withhold Medicaid underpayments to offset Medicare overpayments: Section 1914 [42 U.S.C.A. 1396m]

PART II, CHAPTER 4: SANCTIONS IN TITLE XI OF THE SOCIAL SECURITY ACT

§ 4:1

Disclosure of information in the possession of the Secretary of Health and Human Services: Section 1106 [42 U.S.C.A. 1306]

§ 4:2

False representations about requirements of the Social Security Act: Section 1107(a) [42 U.S.C.A. 1307]

§ 4:3

False representations to elicit information from the Secretary of Health and Human Services: Section 1107(b) [42 U.S.C.A. 1307(b)]

§ 4:4

Failure to comply with State health planning requirements: Section 1122 [42 U.S.C.A. 1320a-1]

§ 4:5

Failure to comply with subpoenas issued by the Comptroller General: Section 1125(b) [42 U.S.C.A. 1320a-4(b)]

§ 4:6

Exclusion from Medicare and State health care programs: Section 1128 [42 U.S.C.A. 1320a-6]

§ 4:7

Disclosure by institutions, organizations, and agencies of owners and other individuals sanctioned or convicted and of certain business relationships: Sections 1128(b)(9) and (b)(10), 1124, and 1126 [42 U.S.C.A. 1320a-7(b)(9) and (b)(10), 1320a-3, and 1320a-5]

§ 4:8

Civil money penalties: Section 1128A [42 U.S.C.A. 1320a-7a]

§ 4:9

Criminal penalties: false statements, false representations, concealment, failure to disclose, and conversion with respect to benefits and payments: Section 1128B(a) [42 U.S.C.A. 1320a-7b(a)]

§ 4:10

Criminal penalties: kickbacks, bribes, and rebates: Section 1128B(b) [42 U.S.C.A. 1320a-7b(b)]

§ 4:11

Criminal penalties: false statements and false representations to qualify for provider status: Section 1128B(c) [42 U.S.C.A. 1320a-7b(c)]

§ 4:12

Criminal penalties: excessive Medicaid charges and unlawful financial preconditions for care in hospitals and nursing facilities: Section 1128B(d) [42 U.S.C.A. 1320a-7b(d)]

§ 4:13

Criminal penalties: violating a physician or supplier participation agreement or a Medicare assignment of benefits agreement: Section 1128B(e) [42 U.S.C.A. 1320a-7b(e)]

§ 4:13.1

Failure to report information about final adverse actions against healthcare providers, suppliers, and practitioners to the National Health Care Fraud and Abuse Data Collection Program: Section 1128E(b)(6) [42 U.S.C.A. 1320a-7e(b)(6)]

Affects: Any plan or program that provides health benefits, including a policy of health insurance, a contract of a service benefit organization, and a membership agreement with a health maintenance organization or other prepaid health plan

CMP: For each failure to report an adverse action: not more than $25,000

§ 4:14

Misuse of Federal government names, symbols, and emblems: Section 1140 [42 U.S.C.A. 1320b-10]

§ 4:16.1

Public access to information about hospital financial interests in entities to which referrals of patients are made: Sections 1146 and 1866(a)(1)(S) [42 U.S.C.A. 1320b-16and 1395cc(a)(1)(S)]

§ 4:18

Disallowance of Medicare claims by peer review organizations: Section 1154 [42 U.S.C.A. 1320c-3]

§ 4:19

Sanctions recommended by peer review organizations: Section 1156 [42 U.S.C.A. 1320c-5]

PART II, CHAPTER 5: SANCTIONS IN THE HEALTH CARE QUALITY IMPROVEMENT ACT OF 1986

§ 5:2

Failure to report medical malpractice payments: Section 421 [42 U.S.C.A. 11131]

PART I
GUIDES

Guide 2

CHAPTERS FOR HOSPITALS

The following chapters set forth bases for imposing sanctions which are relevant to hospitals.

PART II, CHAPTER 2: SANCTIONS IN THE MEDICARE STATUTE

§ 2:2.1

Failure by physicians, providers, suppliers, and others to furnish an itemized statement of items and services provided to Medicare beneficiaries: Section 1806 [42 U.S.C.A. 1395b-7]

Affects: Physicians, providers, suppliers, and any other person (including an organization, agency, or other entity)

CMP: $100.00 for each failure to furnish an itemized statement

Assessment: None

Cross-reference to section 1128A, 42 U.S.C.A. 1320a-7a

§ 2:5

Improper billing for clinical diagnostic laboratory tests: Section 1833(h)(5)(D) [42 U.S.C.A. 1395l(h)(5)(D)]

§ 2:6

Improper billing for intraocular lenses: Section 1833(i)(6) [42 U.S.C.A. 1395l(i)(6)]

§ 2:7

Improper billing for services of a certified registered nurse anesthetist: Section 1833(l)(5)(B) [42 U.S.C.A. 1395l(l)(5)(B)]

§ 2:10

Failure to include information about referring physicians on requests for payments or bills: Section 1833(q) [42 U.S.C.A. 1395l(q)]

§ 2:11

Failure to bill on an assignment related basis for covered services of a nurse practitioner or clinical nurse specialist: Section 1833(r)(3)(B) [42 U.S.C.A. 1395(r)(3)(B)]

◆ [NOTE: Repealed effective January 1, 1995, by section 123(b)(2)(B)(iii) of the Social Security Act Amendments of 1994, P.L. 103-432]

§ 2:29

Prohibition against payment to individuals and entities sanctioned under the Social Security Act: Section 1862(e) [42 U.S.C.A. 1395y(e)]

§ 2:30

Special obligations regarding pacemakers: Section 1862(h) [42 U.S.C.A. 1395y(h)]

§ 2:31

Publicizing provider survey results: Section 1864 [42 U.S.C.A. 1395aa]

§ 2:32

Terminating provider agreements: Section 1866(b) [42 U.S.C.A. 1395cc]

§ 2:33

Failure by hospitals to make timely review of long-stay cases: Section 1866(d) [42 U.S.C.A. 1395cc(d)]

§ 2:34

Failure by hospitals to have arrangements which preclude certain practitioners and suppliers from seeking further payment from beneficiaries: Section 1866(g) [42 U.S.C.A. 1395cc(g)]

§ 2:35

Failure by hospitals and certain physicians to examine and treat persons for emergency medical conditions and women in labor: Section 1867 [42 U.S.C.A. 1395(dd)]

§ 2:42

Violating limitations on physician referrals and related reporting requirements: Section 1877 [42 U.S.C.A. 1395nn]

§ 2:44

Failure by end stage renal disease facilities and providers of end stage renal disease care to cooperate with end stage renal disease network plans and goals and failure to follow end stage renal disease medical review board recommendations: Section 1881(c)(3) and (g) [42 U.S.C.A. 1395rr(c)(3) and (g)]

§ 2:55

Terminating provider agreements of hospital providers of extended care services: Section 1883 [42 U.S.C.A. 1395tt]

§ 2:56

Withholding Medicare payments from overpaid Medicaid providers: Section 1885 [42 U.S.C.A. 1395vv]

§ 2:57

Discontinuing and reducing payments to hospitals for inpatient hospital services in States which have alternative (non-Federal DRG) hospital reimbursement systems: Section 1886(c) [42 U.S.C.A. 1395ww(c)]

§ 2:58

Unnecessary hospital admissions and other inappropriate practices by hospitals to circumvent reimbursement requirements: Section 1886(f) [42 U.S.C.A. 1395ww(f)]

PART II, CHAPTER 3: SANCTIONS IN THE MEDICAID STATUTE

§ 3:1

Publicizing findings of State surveys of health care facilities: Section 1902(a)(36) [42 U.S.C.A. 1396a(a)(36)]

§ 3:2

Additional penalties for persons or entities sanctioned by exclusion under section 1128 or under section 1128A: Section 1902(a)(39) [42 U.S.C.A. 1396a(a)(39)]

§ 3:3

Disclosing information about sanctions against health care practitioners and providers: Section 1902(a)(49) and Section 1921 [42 U.S.C.A. 1396a(a)(49) and 42 U.S.C.A. 1396r-2]

§ 3:4

Billing Medicaid eligibles or financially responsible relatives or representatives for medical expenses when third parties are liable to pay: Sections 1902(g) and 1902(a)(25) [42 U.S.C.A. 1396a(g) and 1396a(a)(25)]

§ 3:5.1

Overcharging Medicaid eligibles who are qualified Medicare beneficiaries: Section 1902(n)(3) [42 U.S.C.A. 1396a(n)(3)]

◆ NOTE: Any sanction that may be imposed upon a provider or Medicaid managed care organization for excess charges under Medicaid or Medicare applies.

§ 3:6

Providing Medicaid exclusions for the same grounds as Medicare exclusions: Section 1902(p)(1) [42 U.S.C.A. 1396a(p)(1)]

§ 3:8

Termination of Medicaid certification of and intermediate sanctions for psychiatric hospitals: Section 1902(y) [42 U.S.C.A. 1396a(y)]

§ 3:8

Requiring States to withhold Medicaid underpayments to offset Medicare overpayments: Section 1914 [42 U.S.C.A. 1396m]

PART II, CHAPTER 4: SANCTIONS IN TITLE XI OF THE SOCIAL SECURITY ACT

§ 4:1

Disclosure of information in the possession of the Secretary of Health and Human Services: Section 1106 [42 U.S.C.A. 1306]

§ 4:3

False representations to elicit information from the Secretary of Health and Human Services: Section 1107(b) [42 U.S.C.A. 1307(b)]

§ 4:4

Failure to comply with State health planning requirements: Section 1122 [42 U.S.C.A. 1320a-1]

§ 4:5

Failure to comply with subpoenas issued by the Comptroller General: Section 1125(b) [42 U.S.C.A. 1320a-4(b)]

§ 4:6

Exclusion from Medicare and State health care programs: Section 1128 [42 U.S.C.A. 1320a-6]

§ 4:7

Disclosure by institutions, organizations, and agencies of owners and other individuals sanctioned or convicted and of certain business relationships: Sections 1128(b)(9) and (b)(10), 1124, and 1126 [42 U.S.C.A. 1320a-7(b)(9) and (b)(10), 1320a-3, and 1320a-5]

§ 4:8

Civil money penalties: Section 1128A [42 U.S.C.A. 1320a-7a]

I§ 4:9

Criminal penalties: false statements, false representations, concealment, failure to disclose, and conversion with respect to benefits and payments: Section 1128B(a) [42 U.S.C.A. 1320a-7b(a)]

§ 4:10

Criminal penalties: kickbacks, bribes, and rebates: Section 1128B(b) [42 U.S.C.A. 1320a-7b(b)]

§ 4:11

Criminal penalties: false statements and false representations to qualify for provider status: Section 1128B(c) [42 U.S.C.A. 1320a-7b(c)]

§ 4:12

Criminal penalties: excessive Medicaid charges and unlawful financial preconditions for care in hospitals and nursing facilities: Section 1128B(d) [42 U.S.C.A. 1320a-7b(d)]

§ 4:13.1

Failure to report information about final adverse actions against healthcare providers, suppliers, and practitioners to the National Health Care Fraud and Abuse Data Collection Program: Section 1128E(b)(6) [42 U.S.C.A. 1320a-7e(b)(6)]

Affects: Any plan or program that provides health benefits, including a policy of health insurance, a contract of a service benefit organization, and a membership agreement with a health maintenance organization or other prepaid health plan

CMP: For each failure to report an adverse action: not more than $25,000

§ 4:14

Misuse of Federal government names, symbols, and emblems: Section 1140 [42 U.S.C.A. 1320b-10]

§ 4:16.1

Public access to information about hospital financial interests in entities to which referrals of patients are made: Sections 1146 and 1866(a)(1)(S) [42 U.S.C.A. 1320b-16 and 1395cc(a)(1)(S)]

§ 4:18

Disallowance of Medicare claims by peer review organizations: Section 1154 [42 U.S.C.A. 1320c-3]

§ 4:19

Sanctions recommended by peer review organizations: Section 1156 [42 U.S.C.A. 1320c-5]

§ 4:20

Unlawful disclosure of information obtained by peer review organizations: Section 1160 [42 U.S.C.A. 1320c-9]

PART II, CHAPTER 5: SANCTIONS IN THE HEALTH CARE QUALITY IMPROVEMENT ACT OF 1986

§ 5:1

Failure by health care entities to report adverse actions against physicians: Section 411(b) and Section 423(c)(1) [42 U.S.C.A. 11111(b) and 11133(c)(1)]

§ 5:2

Failure to report medical malpractice payments: Section 421 [42 U.S.C.A. 11131]

§ 5:3

Failure by medical examiner boards to report information about adverse actions taken by health care entities against physicians and about health care entities that fail to make such reports: Sections 422 and 423(c)(2) [42 U.S.C.A. 11132 and 11133(c)(2)]

§ 5:4

Failure by hospitals to obtain adverse information about physicians from the Secretary of Health and Human Services and from State medical examiner boards: Section 425 [42 U.S.C.A. 11135]

§ 5:5

Unlawful disclosure of information collected pursuant to the Health Care Quality Improvement Act: Section 427 [42 U.S.C.A. 11137]